THE CROSSWORD ANSWER BOOK

COMPILED BY
STANLEY NEWMAN
AND
DANIEL STARK

TIMES BOOKS

 Published in the United States by Times Books, a division of Random House, Inc., New York, and simultaneously in Canada by Random House of Canada Limited, Toronto.

ISBN 0-8129-2729-0

Text design and typography by Daniel Stark
Manufactured in the United States of America
2 4 6 8 9 7 5 3

INTRODUCTION

Welcome to *The Crossword Answer Book*. Our objective in compiling it has been to fill what we know is an important need for crossword fans – a comprehensive one-volume source for finding troublesome puzzle answers.

If you've used crossword dictionaries, like we have, you've probably discovered that, while these books pack a lot of information, all too often the answer you're looking for just isn't there. The reason why: These books, as good as they are, have been compiled from standard reference sources (dictionaries, thesauruses, and atlases) and bear no direct relationship to the words that actually appear in crosswords.

This gap – between the true "crossword lexicon" and the information available in crossword dictionaries – has been apparent to us for a long time. So, we decided to do something about it. This is the first in what we hope will be a series of "populist" crossword references, designed to be more useful to puzzlers than the books that are currently available.

The first thing you'll notice when you open this book is that it's not organized like crossword dictionaries, where the answers are alphabetized by keywords in the clue. *The Crossword Answer Book* has no clues, only *answers*. It is this emphasis on answers and, more importantly, how we've compiled these answers, that makes this book unique.

So you can see what we mean, let's describe the process by which we selected the words for this book. First, the many thousands of crosswords we've created or edited were examined and their answers compiled. Thus, the majority of the words and phrases included here come from *actual* crosswords. This initial word list was supplemented by the latest editions of standard reference sources, *plus* "popular culture" reference books – covering such things as television, movies, literature, music and the business world. This use of "non-traditional" reference books is crucial in the quest for comprehensiveness. Today's crosswords, as exemplified by the *New York Times*, are filled with contemporary phrases, names and titles that can't be found in dictionaries and atlases.

Once all of these words were compiled, our next job was to decide which words to keep. Space considerations led us to include words up to seven letters long (adding even eight-letter words would have doubled the size of this book). This is not as limiting as you might think, because over 90% of the answers appearing in crosswords are seven letters long or less. Next, we deleted those words that, due to propriety or obscurity, are unlikely to appear in crosswords. Other categories of words that were excluded were: plurals of personal names (like HARRYS or DAVISES), multi-word partial phrases (like A HAT and IS MY), and uncommon forms of common words (such as HELIUMS and BEWARED).

Once we were finished deleting, we started adding again. In addition to ourselves, three other puzzle professionals examined our word list for completeness and consistency, and suggested words to be added. (Special thanks to Henry Hook, Trip Payne, and Rebecca Kornbluh.) Finally, we added words that are too new to be in any book, such as: JUMANJI (a recent Robin Williams film), WEB SITE, and OLESTRA (a fat substitute in the news). As a result of this word-selection process, we can say with complete confidence that no other reference of *any* kind contains all the words found here.

For their help in the preparation of this book, we'd like to thank the following Times Books folks: Eli Hausknecht, Kerry McCormack, and, for the "authoritative" cover design, Gabrielle Bordwin and Robbin Schiff.

Your comments on any aspect of this book are most welcome. In particular, we'd like to know how useful you find this book, as well as your suggestions for words to include in future editions. You may write to us at: Times Books Puzzles and Games, 201 East 50th Street, New York, New York 10022. We will thank the first sender of any new word we include in future editions by including his or her name in the introduction.

May all your puzzles be completely solved – with or without our help.

Stanley Newman
Daniel Stark

HOW TO USE THIS BOOK

The Crossword Answer Book is arranged first by word length, then alphabetically by the position of two given letters. So, once you have two letters of an answer filled in, you can quickly find a list of words and phrases that have those two letters in those two positions.

For example, six-letter answers whose third letter is S and sixth letter is A include: BOSNIA, CESSNA, DESICA, RUSSIA and URSULA. The context of the clue, as well as any additional letters you fill in, will help you determine which of the listed choices is the correct one.

We recognize that, unlike traditional crossword dictionaries, this book does not give additional information about words you're not familiar with. For this reason, we recommend that you do what many crossword fans do: use new words as a "springboard" to learn more about a particular subject.

3

AA•
AAA
AAH
AAR
AAU

A•A
AAA
ABA
ACA
ADA
AEA
AGA
AHA
AIA
AKA
ALA
AMA
ANA
APA
ARA
ASA
ATA
AVA

•AA
AAA
BAA
CAA
FAA
MAA

AB•
ABA
ABB
ABC
ABD
ABE
ABM
ABN
ABO
ABP
ABR
ABS
ABT
ABU
ABY

A•B
ABB
AFB
ALB
AMB
APB
ARB

•AB
BAB
CAB
DAB
FAB
GAB
HAB
JAB
LAB
MAB
NAB
SAB
TAB

AC•
ACA
ACC
ACE
ACH
ACK
ACP
ACR
ACS
ACT
ACU
ACV
ACY

A•C
ABC
ACC
ADC
AEC
AFC
AKC
ALC
AMC
ANC
APC
ARC
ASC
AUC
AVC

•AC
BAC
FAC
LAC
MAC
PAC
SAC
TAC
VAC
WAC

AD•
ADA
ADC
ADD
ADE
ADH
ADJ
ADL
ADM
ADO
ADP
ADS
ADV
ADZ

A•D
ABD
ADD
AID
ALD
AND
ARD
AUD

•AD
BAD
CAD
DAD
FAD
GAD
HAD
LAD
MAD
NAD
PAD
RAD
SAD
TAD
WAD

AE•
AEA
AEC
AEE
AEF
AER
AES
AET

A•E
ABE
ACE
ADE
AEE
AGE
ALE
AME
ANE
APE
ARE
ASE
ATE
AVE
AWE
AXE
AYE

•AE
BAE
HAE
LAE
MAE
NAE
RAE
SAE
TAE
UAE

AF•
AFB
AFC
AFF
AFL
AFM
AFP
AFR
AFS
AFT

A•F
AEF
AFF
AHF
ALF
AMF
ARF
AUF

•AF
KAF
OAF
RAF
WAF

AG•
AGA
AGE
AGO
AGR
AGS
AGT

A•G
ALG
ANG
ARG
AUG
AVG

•AG
BAG
DAG
GAG
HAG
JAG
LAG
MAG
NAG
PAG
RAG
SAG
TAG
WAG
YAG
ZAG

AH•
AHA
AHF
AHS
AHU

A•H
AAH
ACH
ADH
AOH
ASH
AYH

•AH
AAH
BAH
DAH
HAH
LAH
MAH
NAH
PAH
RAH
WAH
YAH

AI•
AIA
AID
AIL
AIM
AIN
AIR
AIS
AIT
AIX

A•I
ALI
AMI
ANI
API
ARI
ASI
AVI

•AI
CAI
DAI
GAI
HAI
JAI
KAI
LAI
MAI
RAI
TAI

A•J
ADJ

•AJ
HAJ
MAJ
RAJ
TAJ

AK•
AKA
AKC
AKU

A•K
ACK
ALK
AOK
ARK
ASK
AUK

•AK
DAK
OAK
PAK
YAK

AL•
ALA
ALB
ALC
ALD
ALE
ALF
ALG
ALI
ALK
ALL
ALP
ALS
ALT
ALY

A•L
ADL
AFL
AIL
ALL
AOL
APL
ASL
ATL
AWL
AXL

•AL
BAL
CAL
DAL
GAL
HAL
IAL
JAL
MAL
PAL
SAL
TAL
VAL

AM•
AMA
AMB
AMC
AME
AMF
AMI
AMN
AMO
AMP
AMS
AMT
AMU
AMY

A•M
ABM
ADM
AFM
AIM
ARM
ATM
AUM

•AM
BAM
CAM
DAM
EAM
FAM
GAM
HAM
IAM
JAM
LAM
NAM
PAM
RAM
SAM
TAM
YAM

AN•
ANA
ANC
AND
ANE
ANG
ANI
ANN
ANS
ANT
ANU
ANY

A•N
ABN
AIN
AMN
ANN
ARN
ASN
AVN
AWN
AYN

•AN
BAN
CAN
DAN
FAN
HAN
IAN
JAN
KAN
LAN
MAN
NAN
PAN
RAN
SAN
TAN
VAN
WAN

AO•
AOH
AOK
AOL
AOR

A•O
ABO
ADO
AGO
AMO
APO
ARO
ASO
AVO
AZO

•AO
BAO
FAO
GAO
HAO
LAO
MAO
PAO
SAO
TAO
YAO

AP•
APA
APB
APC
APE
API
APL
APO
APP
APR
APS
APT

A•P
ABP
ACP
ADP
AFP
ALP
AMP
APP
ARP
ASP
ATP

•AP
BAP
CAP
DAP
EAP
GAP
HAP
LAP
MAP
NAP
PAP
RAP
SAP
TAP
YAP
ZAP

AR•
ARA
ARB
ARC
ARD
ARE
ARF
ARG
ARI
ARK
ARM
ARN
ARO
ARP
ARR
ARS
ART
ARU
ARY

A•R
AAR
ABR
ACR
AER
AFR
AGR
AIR
AOR
APR
ARR
ASR
AYR

•AR
AAR
BAR
CAR
DAR
EAR
FAR
GAR
HAR
JAR
LAR
MAR
OAR
PAR
SAR
TAR
UAR
VAR
WAR
YAR

AS•
ASA
ASC
ASE
ASH
ASI
ASK
ASL
ASN
ASO
ASP
ASR
ASS
AST
ASU
ASV

A•S
ABS
ACS
ADS
AES
AFS
AGS
AHS
AIS
ALS
AMS
ANS
APS
ARS
ASS
AUS
AVS

•AS
BAS
CAS
DAS
FAS
GAS
HAS
JAS
KAS
LAS
MAS
NAS
OAS
PAS
RAS
SAS
TAS
VAS
WAS

AT•
ATA
ATE
ATL
ATM
ATP
ATT
ATV

A•T
ABT
ACT
AET
AFT
AGT
AIT
ALT
AMT
ANT
APT
ART
AST
ATT
AUT

•AT
BAT
CAT
DAT
EAT
FAT
GAT
HAT
JAT
KAT
LAT
MAT
NAT
OAT
PAT
RAT
SAT
TAT
VAT
WAT
YAT

AU•
AUC
AUD
AUF
AUG
AUK
AUM
AUS
AUT
AUX

A•U
AAU
ABU
ACU
AHU
AKU
AMU
ANU
ARU
ASU

•AU
AAU
DAU
EAU
PAU
RAU
TAU

AV•
AVA
AVC
AVE
AVG
AVI
AVN
AVO
AVS

A•V
ACV
ADV
ASV
ATV

•AV
CAV
DAV
JAV
LAV
NAV
TAV
VAV

AW•
AWE
AWL
AWN

•AW
CAW
DAW
GAW
HAW
JAW
KAW
LAW
MAW
NAW
PAW
RAW
SAW
TAW
UAW
WAW
YAW

AX•
AXE
AXL

A•X
AIX
AUX

•AX
BAX
FAX
LAX
MAX
PAX
SAX
TAX
WAX
ZAX

AY•
AYE
AYH
AYN
AYR

A•Y
ABY
ACY
ALY
AMY
ANY
ARY

•AY
BAY
CAY
DAY
FAY
GAY
HAY
JAY
KAY
LAY
MAY
NAY
PAY
RAY
SAY
TAY
WAY
YAY

AZ•
AZO

A•Z
ADZ

•AZ
PAZ
YAZ

BA•
BAA
BAB
BAC
BAD
BAE
BAG
BAH
BAL
BAM
BAN
BAO
BAP
BAR
BAS
BAT
BAX
BAY

B•A
BAA
BBA
BEA
BFA
BHA
BIA
BLA
BOA
BRA
BSA

•BA
ABA
BBA
CBA
DBA
MBA
NBA
OBA
PBA
SBA
TBA
WBA

BB•
BBA
BBB
BBC
BBL
BBQ
BBS

B•B BAB BBB BIB BOB BUB

•BB ABB BBB EBB

BC• BCE BCG

B•C BAC BBC BHC BIC BSC BUC

•BC ABC BBC CBC NBC RBC WBC

BD• BDL BDS

B•D BAD BED BHD BID BOD BPD BUD BVD

•BD ABD MBD

BE• BEA BED BEE BEF BEG BEI BEL BEM BEN BES BET BEV BEY

B•E BAE BCE BEE BLE BME BPE BRE BYE

•BE ABE GBE MBE NBE OBE SBE

BF• BFA

B•F BEF

BG• BGH BGS

B•G BAG BCG BEG BIG BKG BOG BUG

BH• BHA BHC BHD BHP BHT

B•H BAH BGH BPH BSH BTH

BI• BIA BIB BIC BID BIG BIL BIN BIO BIP BIS BIT BIV BIX BIZ

B•I BEI BMI BPI BWI

•BI FBI OBI RBI UBI

•BJ LBJ OBJ

BK• BKG BKS BKT

B•K BLK BOK

BL• BLA BLE BLK BLS BLT BLU BLY

B•L BAL BBL BDL BEL BIL BOL BPL BTL BUL

•BL BBL DBL OBL

BM• BME BMI BMR BMS BMW BMX

B•M BAM BEM BUM BVM

•BM ABM IBM

B•N BAN BEN BIN BON BUN

•BN ABN EBN IBN WBN

BO• BOA BOB BOD BOG BOK BOL BON BOO BOP BOR BOS BOT BOW BOX BOY BOZ

B•O BAO BIO BOO BRO

•BO ABO EBO HBO IBO LBO

BP• BPD BPE BPH BPI BPL BPS

B•P BAP BHP BIP BOP

•BP ABP

B•Q BBQ

•BQ BBQ

BR• BRA BRE BRO BRR BRS

B•R BAR BMR BOR BRR BUR

•BR ABR

BS• BSA BSC BSH

B•S BAS BBS BDS BES BGS BIS BKS BLS BMS BOS BPS BRS BTS BUS

•BS ABS BBS CBS DBS EBS FBS GBS LBS NBS OBS PBS QBS TBS VBS WBS YBS

BT• BTH BTL BTS BTU

B•T BAT BET BHT BIT BKT BLT BOT BUT BVT

•BT ABT

BU• BUB BUC BUD BUG BUL BUM BUN BUR BUS BUT BUY

B•U BLU BTU BYU

•BU ABU

BV• BVD BVM BVT

B•V BEV BIV

•BV OBV

BW• BWI

B•W BMW BOW

•BW NBW SBW

B•X BAX BIX BMX BOX

•BX PBX

BY• BYE BYU

B•Y BAY BEY BLY BOY BUY

•BY ABY

B•Z BIZ BOZ

CA• CAA CAB CAD CAI CAL CAM CAN CAP CAR CAS CAT CAV CAW CAY

C•A CAA CBA CEA CFA CHA CIA CMA COA CPA CSA

•CA ACA FCA GCA ICA MCA OCA RCA

CB• CBA CBC CBS

C•B CAB COB CUB

•CB PCB

CC• CCC CCD CCI CCL CCS CCU CCV CCW CCX

C•C CBC CCC CDC CIC CSC CXC

•CC ACC CCC DCC FCC ICC MCC NCC

CD• CDC CDI CDL CDR CDS CDT CDV CDX

C•D CAD CCD CID CLD CMD COD CPD CUD CYD

•CD CCD GCD JCD LCD MCD RCD SCD

CE• CEA CEE CEL CEN CEO CEP CES CET CEY

C•E CEE CHE CIE CLE COE CUE

•CE ACE BCE ICE

CF• CFA CFI CFL CFO CFS

C•F CIF CTF

•CF GCF HCF MCF

CG• CGM CGS

C•G CHG COG

•CG BCG ECG MCG

CH• CHA CHE CHG CHI CHM

•CH ACH HCH ICH OCH SCH

CI• CIA CIC CID CIE CIF CII CIM CIO CIR CIS CIT CIV CIX

C•I CAI CCI CDI CFI CHI CII CLI CMI CPI CRI CUI CVI CXI

•CI CCI DCI ICI MCI SCI XCI

C•K CLK CSK

•CK ACK ECK ICK OCK

CL• CLD CLE CLI CLK CLR CLS CLU CLV CLX

C•L CAL CCL CDL CEL CFL CML COL CPL CUL CXL CYL

•CL CCL DCL JCL KCL MCL

CM• CMA CMD CMI CML CMS CMV CMX

C•M CAM CGM CHM CIM COM CPM CUM CWM

•CM DCM ECM LCM MCM

CN• CNN CNO CNS

C•N CAN CEN CNN CON CTN

•CN RCN

CO• COA COB COD COE COG COL COM CON COO COP COQ COR COS COT COW COX COY COZ

C•O CEO CFO CIO CNO COO CPO CRO CTO CWO CYO

•CO ECO NCO

CP• CPA CPD CPI CPL CPM CPO CPR CPS CPT CPU

C•P CAP CEP COP CUP CWP

•CP ACP FCP MCP RCP

C•Q COQ

•CQ MCQ

CR• CRI CRO CRS CRT CRU CRY

C•R CAR CDR CIR CLR COR CPR CTR CUR CYR

•CR ACR NCR OCR VCR

CS• CSA CSC CSK CST

C•S CAS CBS CCS CDS CES CFS CGS CIS CLS CMS CNS COS CPS CRS CTS CVS

•CS ACS CCS FCS ICS JCS LCS MCS OCS PCS RCS WCS

CT• CTF CTN CTO CTR CTS

C•T CAT CDT CET CIT COT CPT CRT CST CUT CWT

•CT ACT ECT JCT LCT OCT PCT RCT

CU• CUB CUD CUE CUI CUL CUM CUP CUR CUT

C•U CCU CLU CPU CRU

•CU ACU CCU ECU ICU TCU

CV• CVI CVS

C•V CAV CCV CDV CIV CLV CMV CXV

•CV ACV CCV DCV MCV XCV

CW• CWM CWO CWP CWT

C•W CAW CCW COW

•CW CCW

CX• CXC CXI CXL CXV CXX

C•X CCX CDX CIX CLX CMX COX CXX

•CX CCX DCX MCX

CY• CYD CYL CYO CYR

C•Y CAY CEY COY CRY

•CY ACY FCY ICY

C•Z COZ

DA• DAB DAD DAG DAH DAI DAK DAL DAM DAN DAP DAR DAS DAT DAU DAV DAW DAY

D•A DBA DEA DFA DHA DIA DMA DNA DOA

•DA ADA EDA FDA IDA ODA RDA

DB• DBA DBL DBS

D•B DAB DEB DIB DOB DUB

•DB EDB PDB

DC• DCC DCI DCL DCM DCV DCX

D•C DCC DEC DFC DOC DSC DUC DXC

•DC ADC CDC MDC UDC

DD• DDE DDR DDS DDT

D•D DAD DED DID DMD DOD DUD

•DD ADD EDD ODD PDD TDD

DE• DEA DEB DEC DED DEE DEF DEG DEI DEK DEL DEM DEN DEO DEP DER DES DET DEV DEW DEX DEY

D•E DDE DEE DIE DOE DUE DYE

•DE ADE DDE EDE IDE ODE

DF• DFA DFC DFM

D•F DEF DIF

•DF RDF

D•G DAG DEG DIG DKG DOG DUG

•DG LDG

DH• DHA DHL DHS DHU

D•H DAH DOH DPH DUH

•DH ADH EDH

DI• DIA DIB DID DIE DIF DIG DII DIK DIL DIM DIN DIO DIP DIR DIS DIT DIU DIV DIX

D•I DAI DCI DEI DII DLI DOI DPI DVI DXI

•DI CDI IDI MDI SDI

DJ• DJS

D•J DRJ

•DJ ADJ

DK• DKG DKL DKM

D•K DAK DEK DIK DRK

DL• DLI DLO DLR DLS DLV DLX

D•L DAL DBL DCL DEL DHL DIL DKL DML DOL DPL DXL

•DL ADL BDL CDL HDL LDL MDL

DM• DMA DMD DML DMS DMV DMZ

D•M DAM DCM DEM DFM DIM DKM DOM DSM DUM DVM

•DM ADM EDM PDM

DN• DNA DNR

D•N DAN DEN DIN DON DUN DYN

DO• DOA DOB DOC DOD DOE DOG DOH DOI DOL DOM DON DOO DOP DOR DOS DOT DOU DOW DOZ

D•O DEO DIO DLO DOO DSO DUO

•DO ADO EDO IDO UDO

DP• DPH DPI DPL DPS DPT DPW

D•P DAP DEP DIP DOP DUP

•DP ADP EDP IDP

•DQ PDQ

DR• DRJ DRK DRS DRU DRY

D•R DAR DDR DER DIR DLR DNR DOR

•DR CDR DDR FDR GDR LDR MDR

DS• DSC DSM DSO DST

D•S DAS DBS DDS DES DHS DIS DJS DLS DMS DOS DPS DRS DTS DYS

•DS ADS BDS CDS DDS EDS FDS GDS HDS IDS LDS MDS ODS RDS SDS TDS WDS YDS

DT• DTS

D•T DAT DDT DET DIT DOT DPT DST DWT

•DT CDT DDT EDT MDT PDT VDT

DU• DUB DUC DUD DUE DUG DUH DUM DUN DUO DUP DUX DUZ

D•U DAU DHU DIU DOU DRU

DV• DVI DVM

D•V DAV DCV DEV DIV DLV DMV DXV

•DV
ADV
CDV
MDV

DW•
DWT

D•W
DAW
DEW
DOW
DPW

•DW
HDW

DX•
DXC
DXI
DXL
DXV
DXX

D•X
DCX
DEX
DIX
DLX
DUX
DXX

•DX
CDX
MDX

DY•
DYE
DYN
DYS

D•Y
DAY
DEY
DRY

D•Z
DMZ
DOZ
DUZ

•DZ
ADZ

EA•
EAM
EAP
EAR
EAT
EAU

E•A
EDA
EKA
ELA
ENA
EPA
ERA
ESA
ETA
EVA

•EA
AEA
BEA
CEA
DEA
KEA
LEA
MEA
NEA
PEA
REA
SEA
TEA
YEA

EB•
EBB
EBN
EBO
EBS

E•B
EBB
EDB
EMB

•EB
DEB
FEB
HEB
JEB
LEB
NEB
REB
WEB

EC•
ECG
ECK
ECM
ECO
ECT
ECU

E•C
EEC
ENC
ESC
ETC
EXC

•EC
AEC
DEC
EEC
FEC
JEC
NEC
PEC
REC
SEC
TEC

ED•
EDA
EDB
EDD
EDE
EDH
EDM
EDO
EDP
EDS
EDT

E•D
EDD
ELD
END
ESD
ETD

•ED
BED
DED
FED
GED
HED
JED
LED
MED
NED
OED
PED
QED
RED
TED
WED
XED
ZED

EE•
EEC
EEE
EEG
EEK
EEL
EEN
EEO
EER
EES

E•E
EDE
EEE
EKE
EME
ENE
EOE
ERE
ESE
ETE
EVE
EWE
EXE
EYE

•EE
AEE
BEE
CEE
DEE
EEE
FEE
GEE
HEE
LEE
NEE
REE
SEE
TEE
VEE
WEE
ZEE

EF•
EFF
EFT

E•F
EFF
EHF
ELF
EMF
EOF

•EF
AEF
BEF
DEF
HEF
KEF
NEF
QEF
REF

EG•
EGG
EGO
EGR

E•G
ECG
EEG
EGG
EKG
EMG
ENG
ERG
EVG

•EG
BEG
DEG
EEG
KEG
LEG
MEG
NEG
PEG
REG
TEG
VEG

EH•
EHF
EHV

E•H
EDH
EPH
ETH

•EH
HEH
NEH
PEH
VEH

EI•
EIN
EIS

E•I
ELI
EMI
EPI
ERI

•EI
BEI
DEI
LEI
PEI
REI
SEI
WEI

EK•
EKA
EKE
EKG

E•K
ECK
EEK
ELK
ESK

•EK
DEK
EEK
LEK

EL•
ELA
ELD
ELF
ELI
ELK
ELL
ELM
ELO
ELS
ELY

E•L
EEL
ELL
ENL
ESL

•EL
BEL
CEL
DEL
EEL
GEL
HEL
KEL
MEL
REL
SEL
TEL
VEL

EM•
EMB
EME
EMF
EMG
EMI
EMO
EMP
EMS
EMT
EMU

E•M
EAM
ECM
EDM
ELM
EOM

•EM
BEM
DEM
FEM
GEM
HEM
LEM
MEM
REM
SEM
TEM

EN•
ENA
ENC
END
ENE
ENG
ENL
ENO
ENS
ENT
ENV

E•N
EBN
EEN
EIN
EON
ERN

•EN
BEN
CEN
DEN
EEN
FEN
GEN
HEN
KEN
LEN
MEN
OEN
PEN
REN
SEN
TEN
VEN
WEN
XEN
YEN
ZEN

EO•
EOE
EOF
EOM
EON
EOS

E•O
EBO
ECO
EDO
EEO
EGO
ELO
EMO
ENO
ESO
ETO
EXO

•EO
CEO
DEO
EEO
GEO
LEO
MEO
NEO
OEO
REO
YEO

EP•
EPA
EPH
EPI
EPS

E•P
EAP
EDP
EMP
ESP
EXP

•EP
CEP
DEP
HEP
NEP
PEP
REP
SEP
YEP

E•Q
ESQ

•EQ
REQ
SEQ

ER•
ERA
ERE
ERG
ERI
ERN
ERR
ERS
ERY
ERZ

E•R
EAR
EER
EGR
ERR
EUR
EXR
EZR

•ER
AER
DER
EER
FER
GER
HER
IER
JER
KER
LER
MER
NER
OER
PER
SER
TER
VER
XER
YER

ES•
ESA
ESC
ESD
ESE
ESK
ESL
ESO
ESP
ESQ
ESS
EST
ESU

E•S
EBS
EDS
EES
EIS
ELS
EMS
ENS
EOS
EPS
ERS
ESS
ETS
EVS

•ES
AES
BES
CES
DES
EES
HES
LES
MES
NES
PES
RES
SES
WES
XES
YES

ET•
ETA
ETC
ETD
ETE
ETH
ETO
ETS
ETV

E•T
EAT
ECT
EDT
EFT
EMT
ENT
EST
EXT

•ET
AET
BET
CET
DET
FET
GET
HET
JET
KET
LET
MET
NET
PET
RET
SET
TET
VET
WET
YET

EU•
EUR

E•U
EAU
ECU
EMU
ESU

•EU
FEU
JEU
LEU
NEU
PEU

EV•
EVA
EVE
EVG
EVS

E•V
EHV
ENV
ETV

•EV
BEV
DEV
GEV
KEV
LEV
MEV
NEV
REV

EW•
EWE

•EW
DEW
FEW
HEW
JEW
KEW
LEW
MEW
NEW
PEW
SEW
YEW

EX•
EXC
EXE
EXO
EXP
EXR
EXT

•EX
DEX
HEX
LEX
MEX
REX
SEX
TEX
VEX

EY•
EYE

E•Y
ELY
ERY

•EY
BEY
CEY
DEY
FEY
GEY
HEY
KEY
LEY
NEY
REY
TEY

EZ•
EZR

E•Z
ERZ

•EZ
FEZ
NEZ
PEZ

FA•
FAA
FAB
FAC
FAD
FAM
FAN
FAO
FAR
FAS
FAT
FAX
FAY

F•A
FAA
FCA
FDA
FFA
FHA
FLA
FPA
FRA

•FA
BFA
CFA
DFA
FFA
MFA
UFA

FB•
FBI
FBS

F•B
FAB
FEB
FIB
FMB
FOB
FRB

•FB
AFB
LFB
RFB

FC•
FCA
FCC
FCP
FCS
FCY

F•C
FAC
FCC
FEC
FIC
FMC
FPC
FTC

•FC
AFC
DFC
KFC
NFC
PFC
SFC

FD•
FDA
FDR
FDS

F•D
FAD
FED
FID
FLD
FTD
FWD

•FD
MFD
NFD
PFD
RFD
VFD

FE•
FEB
FEC
FED
FEE
FEM
FEN
FER
FET
FEU
FEW
FEY
FEZ

F•E
FEE
FIE
FOE

•FE
IFE

FF•
FFA
FFF
FFV

F•F
FFF

•FF
AFF
EFF
FFF
IFF
OFF

F•G
FIG
FOG
FRG
FUG

•FG
MFG
PFG

FH•
FHA

F•H
FTH

FI•
FIB
FIC
FID
FIE
FIG
FIN
FIR
FIT
FIX

F•I
FBI
FRI
FYI

•FI
CFI

•FK
JFK
RFK

FL•
FLA
FLD
FLO
FLU
FLY

F•L
FOL
FPL
FRL
FUL

•FL
AFL
CFL
NFL

FM•
FMB
FMC
FMS

F•M
FAM
FEM
FPM

•FM
AFM
DFM

FN•
FNS

F•N
FAN
FEN
FIN
FON
FUN
FYN

FO•
FOB
FOE
FOG
FOL
FON
FOO
FOP
FOR
FOU
FOX
FOY

F•O
FAO
FLO
FOO
FPO
FRO

•FO
CFO
SFO
UFO

FP•
FPA
FPC
FPL
FPM
FPO
FPS

F•P
FCP
FOP

•FP
AFP

FR•
FRA
FRB
FRG
FRI
FRL
FRO
FRS
FRT
FRY

F•R
FAR
FDR
FER
FIR
FOR
FUR

•FR
AFR
MFR
TFR

FS•
FSU

F•S
FAS
FBS
FCS
FDS
FMS
FNS
FPS
FRS

•FS
AFS
CFS
IFS
LFS

FT•
FTC
FTD
FTH

F•T
FAT
FET
FIT
FRT
FUT

•FT
AFT
EFT
OFT
UFT

FU•
FUG
FUL
FUN
FUR
FUT

F•U
FEU
FLU
FOU
FSU

F•V
FFV

•FV
FFV

FW•
FWD

F•W
FEW

•FW
UFW
VFW

F•X
FAX
FIX
FOX

FY•
FYI
FYN

F•Y
FAY
FCY
FEY
FLY
FOY
FRY

•FY
IFY

F•Z
FEZ

•FZ
SFZ

GA•
GAB
GAD
GAG
GAI
GAL
GAM
GAO
GAP
GAR
GAS
GAT
GAW
GAY

G•A
GCA
GIA
GOA
GPA
GSA

•GA
AGA
IGA
PGA

GB•
GBE
GBS

G•B
GAB
GIB
GOB

•GB
KGB
RGB

GC•
GCA
GCD
GCF

G•C
GMC

GD•
GDR
GDS

G•D
GAD
GCD
GED
GLD
GOD
GPD
GTD

•GD
MGD
SGD

GE•
GED
GEE
GEL
GEM
GEN
GEO
GER
GET
GEV
GEY

G•E
GBE
GEE
GIE
GRE
GTE

•GE
AGE
LGE

G•F
GCF
GRF

•GF
KGF
NGF

G•G
GAG
GIG
GOG

•GG
EGG
IGG

GH•
GHQ
GHZ

•GH
BGH
HGH
UGH

GI•
GIA
GIB
GIE
GIG
GIL
GIN
GIP
GIS
GIT

G•I
GAI
GUI

GL•
GLD
GLO

G•L
GAL
GEL
GIL

GM•
GMC
GMP
GMS
GMT
GMW

G•M
GAM
GEM
GPM
GUM
GYM

•GM
CGM
KGM
MGM

GN•
GNP
GNU

G•N
GEN
GIN
GON
GUN
GYN

•GN
IGN

GO•
GOA
GOB
GOD
GOG
GON
GOO
GOP
GOT
GOV

G•O
GAO
GEO
GLO
GOO
GPO
GRO
GTO

•GO
AGO
EGO
UGO

GP•
GPA
GPD
GPM
GPO
GPS

G•P
GAP
GIP
GMP
GNP
GOP
GTP
GYP

G•Q
GHQ

GR•
GRE
GRF
GRO
GRR

G•R
GAR
GDR
GER
GRR
GUR

•GR
AGR
EGR
MGR

GS•
GSA
GST

G•S
GAS
GBS
GDS
GIS
GMS
GPS
GUS

•GS
AGS
BGS
CGS
JGS
LGS
MGS
PGS
RGS

GT•
GTD
GTE
GTO
GTP
GTT

G•T
GAT
GET
GIT
GMT
GOT
GST
GTT
GUT

•GT
AGT
HGT
MGT
RGT
SGT

GU•
GUI
GUM
GUN
GUR
GUS
GUT
GUV
GUY

G•U
GNU

GV•
GVW

G•V
GEV
GOV
GUV

G•W
GAW
GMW
GVW

•GW
HGW

GY•
GYM
GYN
GYP

G•Y
GAY
GEY
GUY

G•Z
GHZ

HA•
HAB
HAD
HAE
HAG
HAH
HAI
HAJ
HAL
HAM
HAN
HAO
HAP
HAR
HAS
HAT
HAW
HAY

H•A
HUA

•HA
AHA
BHA
CHA
DHA
FHA
KHA
SHA

HB•
HBO

H•B
HAB
HEB
HOB
HUB

•HB
LHB
PHB
THB

HC•
HCF
HCH

H•C
HIC
HOC

•HC
BHC
MHC

HD•
HDL
HDS
HDW

H•D
HAD
HED
HHD
HID
HOD
HUD
HYD

•HD
BHD
HHD
LHD
PHD
THD

HE•
HEB
HED
HEE
HEF
HEH
HEL
HEM
HEN
HEP
HER
HES
HET
HEW
HEX
HEY

H•E
HAE
HEE
HIE
HOE
HRE
HUE

•HE
CHE
SHE
THE

H•F
HCF
HEF
HMF
HOF

•HF
AHF
EHF
SHF
UHF
VHF
WHF

HG•
HGH
HGT
HGW

H•G
HAG
HOG
HUG

•HG
CHG

HH•
HHD
HHH
HHS

H•H
HAH
HCH
HEH
HGH
HHH
HIH
HRH
HSH
HUH

•HH
HHH
SHH
WHH

HI•
HIC
HID
HIE
HIH
HIM
HIN
HIP
HIS
HIT

H•I
HAI
HOI
HSI
HUI

•HI
CHI
PHI
THI

H•J
HAJ

H•L
HAL
HDL
HEL
HOL

•HL
DHL
NHL

HM•
HMF
HMM
HMO
HMS

H•M
HAM
HEM
HIM
HMM
HOM
HUM
HWM

•HM
CHM
OHM
PHM
THM

H•N
HAN
HEN
HIN
HON
HUN

HO•
HOB
HOC
HOD
HOE
HOF
HOG
HOI
HOL
HOM
HON
HOO
HOP
HOR
HOS
HOT
HOW
HOY

H•O
HAO
HBO
HMO
HOO

•HO
MHO
OHO
RHO
SHO
THO
WHO

H•P
HAP
HEP
HIP
HOP
HUP
HYP

•HP
BHP

HQ•
HQS

•HQ
GHQ

HR•
HRE
HRH
HRS

H•R
HAR
HER
HOR
HUR

•HR
IHR
PHR
SHR
WHR

HS•
HSH
HSI
HST

H•S
HAS
HDS
HES
HHS
HIS
HMS
HOS
HQS
HRS
HTS
HUS

•HS
AHS
DHS
HHS
IHS
JHS
LHS
OHS
VHS
WHS

HT•
HTS

H•T
HAT
HET
HGT
HIT
HOT
HST
HUT

•HT
BHT
SHT

HU•
HUA
HUB
HUD
HUE
HUG
HUH
HUI
HUM
HUN
HUP
HUR
HUS
HUT

•HU
AHU
DHU
PHU
SHU
THU

HV•
HVY

•HV
EHV

HW•
HWM
HWY

H•W
HAW
HDW
HEW
HGW
HOW

•HW
MHW

H•X
HEX

•HX
THX

HY•
HYD
HYP

H•Y
HAY
HEY
HOY
HVY
HWY

•HY
SHY
THY
WHY

•HZ
GHZ
KHZ
MHZ

IA•
IAL
IAM
IAN

I•A
ICA
IDA
IGA
ILA
INA
IPA
IRA
ISA
IVA

•IA
AIA
BIA
CIA
DIA
GIA
LIA
MIA
NIA
PIA
RIA
TIA
VIA
XIA
ZIA

IB•
IBM
IBN
IBO

•IB
BIB
DIB
FIB
GIB
JIB
LIB
MIB
NIB
RIB
SIB

IC•
ICA
ICC
ICE
ICH
ICI
ICK
ICS
ICU
ICY

I•C
ICC
INC
IOC

•IC
BIC
CIC
FIC
HIC
LIC
MIC
PIC
RIC
SIC
TIC
VIC

ID•
IDA
IDE
IDI
IDO
IDP
IDS

I•D
IND
IOD
ITD

•ID
AID
BID
CID
DID
FID
HID
KID
LID
MID
OID
QID
RID
SID
TID

IE•
IER

I•E
ICE
IDE
IFE
IKE
ILE
INE
IRE
ISE
ITE
IVE
IZE

•IE
CIE
DIE
FIE
GIE
HIE
LIE
NIE
PIE
SIE
TIE
VIE
WIE

IF•
IFE
IFF
IFS
IFY

I•F
IFF
IMF
INF

•IF
CIF
DIF
JIF
KIF
RIF

IG•
IGA
IGG
IGN

I•G
IGG
ING

•IG
BIG
DIG
FIG
GIG
JIG
MIG
NIG
PIG
RIG
SIG
WIG
ZIG

IH•
IHR
IHS

I•H
ICH
ISH

•IH
HIH
NIH

II•
III

I•I
ICI
IDI
III

•II
CII
DII
III
LII
MII
VII
XII

IK•
IKE

I•K
ICK
ILK
INK
IRK

•IK
DIK
NIK

IL•
ILA
ILE
ILK
ILL
ILO
ILS

I•L
IAL
ILL
ISL

•IL
AIL
BIL
DIL
GIL
KIL
LIL
MIL
NIL
OIL
SIL
TIL
VIL
WIL

IM•
IMF
IMP

I•M
IAM
IBM
IPM
ISM
IUM

•IM
AIM
CIM
DIM
HIM
JIM
KIM
LIM
MIM
NIM
PIM
RIM
SIM
TIM
VIM
WIM

IN•
INA
INC
IND
INE
INF
ING
INK
INN
INO
INQ
INS
INT
INV

I•N
IAN
IBN
IGN
INN
ION

•IN
AIN
BIN
DIN
EIN
FIN
GIN
HIN
JIN
KIN
LIN
MIN
NIN
PIN
QIN
RIN
SIN
TIN
VIN
WIN
YIN

IO•
IOC
IOD
ION
IOR
IOU

I•O
IBO
IDO
ILO
INO
IRO
ISO
ITO
IVO
IWO

•IO
BIO
CIO
DIO
MIO
RIO
TIO

IP•
IPA
IPM
IPS

I•P
IDP
IMP

•IP
BIP
DIP
GIP
HIP
KIP
LIP
NIP
PIP
RIP
SIP
TIP
VIP
YIP
ZIP

IQ•
IQS

I•Q
INQ

•IQ
LIQ

IR•
IRA
IRE
IRK
IRO
IRR
IRS
IRT
IRV

I•R
IER
IHR
IOR
IRR
ISR

•IR
AIR
CIR
DIR
FIR
KIR
MIR
SIR
VIR

IS•
ISA
ISE
ISH
ISL
ISM
ISO
ISR
ISS
IST

I•S
ICS
IDS
IFS
IHS
ILS
INS
IPS
IQS
IRS
ISS
ITS
IVS

•IS
AIS
BIS
CIS
DIS
EIS
GIS
HIS
LIS
MIS
NIS
PIS
SIS
TIS
VIS
WIS
XIS

IT•
ITD
ITE
ITO
ITS
ITT
ITY

I•T
INT
IRT
IST
ITT

•IT
AIT
BIT
CIT
DIT
FIT
GIT
HIT
KIT
LIT
MIT
NIT
PIT
RIT
SIT
UIT
WIT

IU•
IUM

I•U
ICU
IOU

•IU
DIU
LIU
NIU
PIU
TIU

IV•
IVA
IVE
IVO
IVS
IVY

I•V
INV
IRV

•IV
BIV
CIV
DIV
LIV
MIV
RIV
VIV
XIV

IW•
IWO
IWW

I•W
IWW

•IX
AIX
BIX
CIX
DIX
FIX
KIX
LIX
MIX
NIX
PIX
SIX
XIX

I•Y
ICY
IFY
ITY
IVY

IZ•
IZE

•IZ
BIZ
LIZ
VIZ
WIZ

JA•
JAB
JAG
JAI
JAL
JAM
JAN
JAR
JAS
JAT
JAV
JAW
JAY

J•B
JAB
JEB
JIB
JOB

JC•
JCD
JCL
JCS
JCT

J•C
JEC
JRC
JSC

J•D
JCD
JED
JSD
JUD

•JD
SJD

JE•
JEB
JEC
JED
JER
JET
JEU
JEW

J•E
JOE

JF•
JFK

J•F
JIF

JG•
JGS

J•G
JAG
JIG
JOG
JUG

JH•
JHS

JI•
JIB
JIF
JIG
JIM
JIN

J•I
JAI
JOI

JK•
JKP

J•K
JFK

J•L
JAL
JCL
JUL

J•M
JAM
JIM

•JM
WJM

JN•
JNT

J•N
JAN
JIN
JON
JPN
JUN

JO•
JOB
JOE
JOG
JOI
JON
JOS
JOT
JOY

•JO
OJO

JP•
JPN
JPS

J•P
JKP

JR•
JRC
JRS

J•R
JAR
JER

JS•
JSC
JSD

J•S
JAS
JCS
JGS
JHS
JOS
JPS
JRS
JUS

•JS
DJS
PJS
VJS

J•T
JAT
JCT
JET
JNT
JOT
JUT

JU•
JUD
JUG
JUL
JUN
JUS
JUT
JUV

J•U
JEU

J•V
JAV
JUV

•JV
KJV

J•W
JAW
JEW

J•Y
JAY
JOY

KA•
KAF
KAI
KAN
KAS
KAT
KAW
KAY

K•A
KEA
KHA
KOA
KRA
KWA

•KA
AKA
EKA
OKA
SKA

K•B
KGB
KOB

KC•
KCL

K•C
KFC

•KC
AKC

K•D
KID
KOD
KYD

•KD
OKD

KE•
KEA
KEF
KEG
KEL
KEN
KER
KET
KEV
KEW
KEY

K•E
KUE

•KE
EKE
IKE
OKE
UKE
XKE

KF•
KFC

K•F
KAF
KEF
KGF
KIF

KG•
KGB
KGF
KGM

K•G
KEG

•KG
BKG
DKG
EKG
PKG

KH•
KHA
KHZ

K•H
KPH
KWH

KI•
KID
KIF
KIL
KIM
KIN
KIP
KIR
KIT
KIX

K•I
KAI
KOI

•KI
OKI
SKI

KJ•
KJV

KK•
KKT

KL•
KLM

K•L
KCL
KEL
KIL
KOL
KUL

•KL
DKL

K•M
KGM
KIM
KLM
KUM

•KM
DKM

KN•
KNT

K•N
KAN
KEN
KIN
KON
KUN

KO•
KOA
KOB
KOD
KOI
KOL
KON
KOO
KOP
KOR
KOS

K•O
KOO

•KO
RKO
TKO

KP•
KPH
KPS

K•P
KIP
KOP

•KP
JKP

KR•
KRA

K•R
KER
KIR
KOR

K•S
KAS
KOS
KPS
KTS

•KS
BKS
MKS
OKS
PKS
WKS

KT•
KTS

K•T
KAT
KET
KIT
KKT
KNT

•KT
BKT
KKT
MKT
PKT
QKT
SKT
TKT

KU•
KUE
KUL
KUM
KUN

•KU
AKU
PKU

K•V
KEV
KJV

KW•
KWA
KWH

K•W
KAW
KEW

K•X
KIX

KY•
KYD

K•Y
KAY
KEY

•KY
SKY

K•Z
KHZ

LA•
LAB
LAC
LAD
LAE
LAG
LAH
LAI
LAM
LAN
LAO
LAP
LAR
LAS
LAT
LAV
LAW
LAX
LAY

L•A
LEA
LIA
LOA

•LA
ALA
BLA
ELA
FLA
ILA
MLA
OLA
SLA

LB•
LBJ
LBO
LBS

L•B
LAB
LEB
LFB
LHB
LIB
LLB
LOB
LUB

•LB
ALB
LLB

LC•
LCD
LCM
LCS
LCT

L•C
LAC
LIC
LOC
LTC
LUC

•LC
ALC
TLC

LD•
LDG
LDL

LDR LDS

L•D LAD LCD LED LHD LID LLD LSD LTD

•LD ALD CLD ELD FLD GLD LLD OLD SLD YLD

LE• LEA LEB LED LEE LEG LEI LEK LEM LEN LEO LER LES LET LEU LEV LEW LEX LEY

L•E LAE LEE LGE LIE LYE

•LE ALE BLE CLE ILE OLE ULE

LF• LFB LFS

•LF ALF ELF NLF PLF ULF VLF

LG• LGE LGS

L•G LAG LDG LEG LNG LOG LPG LUG

•LG ALG

LH• LHB LHD LHS

L•H LAH

LI• LIA LIB LIC LID LIE LII LIL LIM LIN LIP LIQ LIS LIT LIU LIV LIX LIZ

L•I LAI LEI LII LOI LSI LUI LVI LXI

•LI ALI CLI DLI ELI MLI XLI

L•J LBJ

L•K LEK

•LK ALK BLK CLK ELK

ILK MLK

LL• LLB LLD LLM

L•L LDL LIL

•LL ALL ELL ILL

L•M LAM LCM LEM LIM LLM LOM LPM LUM

•LM ELM KLM LLM ULM

LN• LNG

L•N LAN LEN LIN LON LPN LYN

LO• LOA LOB LOC LOG LOI LOM LON LOO LOP LOQ LOS LOT LOU LOW LOX LOY

L•O LAO LBO LEO LOO LYO

•LO DLO ELO

FLO GLO ILO PLO SLO

LP• LPG LPM LPN LPS

L•P LAP LIP LOP

•LP ALP

L•Q LIQ LOQ

LR• LRS

L•R LAR LDR LER LTR

•LR CLR DLR SLR

LS• LSD LSI LST LSU

L•S LAS LBS LCS LDS LES LFS LGS LHS LIS LOS LPS LRS LTS LYS

•LS ALS BLS CLS DLS ELS ILS MLS PLS RLS XLS

LT• LTC LTD LTR LTS

L•T LAT LCT LET LIT LOT LST

•LT ALT BLT ULT

LU• LUB LUC LUG LUI LUM LUV LUX LUZ

L•U LEU LIU LOU LSU

•LU BLU CLU FLU PLU ULU

LV• LVI

L•V LAV LEV LIV LUV LXV

•LV CLV DLV MLV XLV

L•W LAW LEW LOW

•LW MLW

LX• LXI LXV LXX

L•X LAX LEX LIX LOX LUX LXX

•LX CLX DLX MLX

LY• LYE LYN LYO LYS

L•Y LAY LEY LOY

•LY ALY BLY ELY FLY PLY SLY

L•Z LIZ LUZ

MA• MAA MAB MAC MAD MAE MAG MAH MAI MAJ MAL MAN MAO MAP MAR MAS MAT MAW MAX MAY

M•A MAA MBA MCA MEA MFA MIA MLA MOA MPA

•MA AMA CMA DMA

SMA UMA YMA

MB• MBA MBD MBE MIB MOB

•MB AMB EMB FMB OMB

MC• MCA MCC MCD MCF MCG MCI MCL MCM MCP MCQ MCS MCV MCX

M•C MAC MCC MDC MHC MIC MMC MOC MSC MVC MXC MYC

•MC AMC FMC GMC MMC QMC

MD• MDC MDI MDL MDR MDS MDT MDV MDX

M•D MAD MBD MCD MED MFD MGD

MID MMD MOD MUD MXD

•MD CMD DMD MMD VMD

ME• MEA MED MEG MEL MEM MEN MEO MER MES MET MEV MEW MEX

M•E MAE MBE MME MOE MPE MRE

•ME AME BME EME MME UME

MF• MFA MFD MFG MFR

M•F MCF MMF

•MF AMF EMF HMF IMF MMF

MG• MGD MGM MGR MGS MGT

M•G MAG MCG MEG MFG MIG

MPG MSG MTG MUG

•MG EMG PMG QMG

MH• MHC MHO MHW MHZ

M•H MAH MPH

MI• MIA MIB MIC MID MIG MII MIL MIM MIN MIO MIR MIS MIT MIV MIX

M•I MAI MCI MDI MII MLI MMI MOI MRI MVI MXI

•MI AMI BMI CMI EMI MMI NMI VMI

M•J MAJ

•MJ TMJ

MK• MKS MKT

M•K MLK

•MK PMK WMK

ML• MLA MLI MLK MLS MLV MLW MLX

M•L MAL MCL MDL MEL MIL MML MOL MSL MXL

•ML CML DML MML

MM• MMC MMD MME MMF MMI MML MMM MMV MMX

M•M MCM MEM MGM MIM MMM MOM MTM MUM

•MM HMM MMM

M•N MAN MEN MIN MON MSN MTN

•MN AMN RMN

MO• MOA MOB MOC MOD MOE

MOI MOL MOM MON MOO MOP MOR MOS MOT MOW

M•O MAO MEO MHO MIO MOO MYO

•MO AMO EMO HMO

MP• MPA MPE MPG MPH MPS

M•P MAP MCP MOP MVP

•MP AMP EMP GMP IMP UMP

M•Q MCQ

MR• MRE MRI MRS MRT

M•R MAR MDR MER MFR MGR MIR MOR

•MR BMR NMR

MS• MSC MSG MSL MSN MSS

MST MSU MSW

M•S MAS MCS MDS MES MGS MIS MKS MLS MOS MPS MRS MSS MTS MUS

•MS AMS BMS CMS DMS EMS FMS GMS HMS OMS RMS TMS

MT• MTG MTM MTN MTS MTV

M•T MAT MDT MET MGT MIT MKT MOT MRT MST MUT

•MT AMT EMT GMT PMT

MU• MUD MUG MUM MUS MUT MUX MUY

M•U MSU

•MU AMU

EMU NMU SMU

MV• MVC MVI MVP

M•V MCV MDV MEV MIV MLV MMV MTV MXV

•MV CMV DMV MMV

M•W MAW MEW MHW MLW MOW MSW

•MW BMW GMW

MX• MXC MXD MXI MXL MXV MXX

M•X MAX MCX MDX MEX MIX MLX MMX MUX MXX MYX

•MX BMX CMX MMX

MY• MYC MYO MYX

M•Y MAY MUY

•MY AMY

M•Z MHZ

•MZ DMZ

NA• NAB NAD NAE NAG NAH NAM NAN NAP NAS NAT NAV NAW NAY

N•A NBA NEA NIA NRA NSA

•NA ANA DNA ENA INA ONA RNA UNA

NB• NBA NBC NBE NBS NBW

N•B NAB NEB NIB NOB NUB

NC• NCC NCO NCR

N•C NBC NCC NEC NFC NRC NSC NYC

•NC ANC ENC INC

N•D NAD

NED NFD NOD

•ND AND END IND RND UND

NE• NEA NEB NEC NED NEE NEF NEG NEH NEO NEP NER NES NET NEU NEV NEW NEY NEZ

N•E NAE NBE NEE NIE NNE NYE

•NE ANE ENE INE NNE ONE UNE

NF• NFC NFD NFL

N•F NEF NGF NLF NSF

•NF INF

NG• NGF

N•G NAG NEG NIG NOG

•NG ANG

ENG ING LNG SNG

NH• NHL

N•H NAH NEH NIH NOH NTH

•NH UNH

NI• NIA NIB NIE NIG NIH NIK NIL NIM NIN NIP NIS NIT NIU NIX

N•I NMI NUI

•NI ANI ONI UNI

N•K NIK

•NK INK

NL• NLF

N•L NFL NHL NIL NOL NUL

•NL ENL SNL

NM• NMI NMR NMU

N•M NAM NIM NOM

NUM

NN• NNE NNW

N•N NAN NIN NON NUN

•NN ANN CNN INN TNN

NO• NOB NOD NOG NOH NOL NOM NON NOR NOS NOT NOV NOW NOX

N•O NCO NEO

•NO CNO ENO INO ONO SNO UNO

NP• NPR NPS

N•P NAP NEP NIP

•NP GNP RNP UNP

•NQ INQ UNQ

NR• NRA NRC

N•R NCR NER NMR NOR

NPR

•NR DNR

NS• NSA NSC NSF NSW

N•S NAS NBS NES NIS NOS NPS NUS

•NS ANS CNS ENS FNS INS ONS PNS RNS TNS UNS

NT• NTH

N•T NAT NET NIT NOT NUT NWT

•NT ANT ENT INT JNT KNT ONT TNT

NU• NUB NUI NUL NUM NUN NUS NUT

N•U NEU NIU NMU NWU NYU

•NU ANU GNU UNU

N•V NAV NEV NOV

•NV ENV INV

NW• NWT NWU

N•W NAW NBW NEW NNW NOW NSW

•NW NNW WNW

N•X NIX NOX NYX

NY• NYC NYE NYU NYX

N•Y NAY NEY

•NY ANY SNY

N•Z NEZ

OA• OAF OAK OAR OAS OAT

O•A OBA OCA ODA OKA OLA ONA OPA ORA OSA OTA OVA

•OA BOA COA DOA GOA

KOA LOA MOA VOA ZOA

OB• OBA OBE OBI OBJ OBL OBS OBV

O•B OMB ORB OSB OTB

•OB BOB COB DOB FOB GOB HOB JOB KOB LOB MOB NOB POB ROB SOB TOB YOB

OC• OCA OCH OCK OCR OCS OCT

O•C ORC OTC

•OC DOC HOC IOC LOC MOC POC ROC SOC VOC

OD• ODA ODD ODE ODS

O•D ODD OED OID

OKD OLD OOD ORD OUD
•OD BOD COD DOD GOD HOD IOD KOD MOD NOD OOD POD ROD SOD TOD YOD ZOD
OE• OED OEN OEO OER
O•E OBE ODE OKE OLE ONE OPE ORE OSE OTE OWE
•OE COE DOE EOE FOE HOE JOE MOE POE ROE TOE WOE ZOE
OF• OFF OFT
O•F OAF OFF OOF OSF
•OF EOF HOF OOF SOF
O•G ORG
•OG BOG COG DOG FOG GOG HOG JOG LOG NOG SOG TOG ZOG
OH• OHM OHO OHS
O•H OCH OOH OSH
•OH AOH DOH NOH OOH
OI• OID OIL
O•I OBI OKI ONI OUI OVI OWI
•OI DOI HOI JOI KOI LOI MOI POI ROI SOI TOI
OJ• OJO
O•J OBJ
OK• OKA OKD OKE OKI OKS
O•K OAK OCK ORK
•OK AOK BOK ROK WOK
OL• OLA OLD OLE
O•L OBL OIL OWL OYL
•OL AOL BOL COL DOL FOL HOL KOL MOL NOL POL SOL VOL
OM• OMB OMS
O•M OHM
•OM COM DOM EOM HOM LOM MOM NOM POM QOM ROM TOM YOM
ON• ONA ONE ONI ONO ONS ONT
O•N OEN OON OWN
•ON BON CON DON EON FON GON HON ION JON KON LON MON NON OON RON SON TON VON WON YON
OO• OOD OOF OOH OON OOO OOP OOX
O•O OEO OHO OJO ONO OOO ORO OSO OTO OVO OXO
•OO BOO COO DOO FOO GOO HOO KOO LOO MOO OOO ROO SOO TOO WOO XOO YOO ZOO
OP• OPA OPE OPP OPR OPS OPT
O•P OOP OPP
•OP BOP COP DOP FOP GOP HOP KOP LOP MOP OOP POP SOP TOP
•OQ COQ LOQ
OR• ORA ORB ORC ORD ORE ORG ORK ORO ORR ORS ORT ORV ORY
O•R OAR OCR OER OPR ORR OUR
•OR AOR BOR COR DOR FOR HOR IOR KOR MOR NOR POR SOR TOR XOR
OS• OSA OSB OSE OSF OSH OSO OSS OST OSU
O•S OAS OBS OCS ODS OHS OKS OMS ONS OPS ORS OSS OTS OUS
•OS BOS COS DOS EOS HOS JOS KOS LOS MOS NOS POS SOS
OT• OTA OTB OTC OTE OTO OTS OTT
O•T OAT OCT OFT ONT OPT ORT OST OTT OUT OZT
•OT BOT COT DOT GOT HOT JOT LOT MOT NOT POT ROT SOT TOT WOT
OU• OUD OUI OUR OUS OUT
O•U OSU
•OU DOU FOU IOU LOU SOU VOU YOU
OV• OVA OVI OVO
O•V OBV ORV
•OV GOV NOV POV SOV TOV
OW• OWE OWI OWL OWN
•OW BOW COW DOW HOW LOW MOW NOW POW ROW SOW TOW VOW WOW YOW
OX• OXO OXX OXY
O•X OOX OXX
•OX BOX COX FOX LOX NOX OOX POX SOX TOX VOX XOX
OY• OYL
O•Y ORY OXY
•OY BOY COY FOY HOY JOY LOY ROY SOY TOY
OZ• OZT
•OZ BOZ COZ DOZ ROZ
PA• PAC PAD PAG PAH PAK PAL PAM PAN PAO PAP PAR PAS PAT PAU PAW PAX PAY PAZ
P•A PBA PEA PGA PIA PTA PWA PYA
•PA APA CPA EPA FPA GPA IPA MPA OPA SPA TPA WPA
PB• PBA PBS PBX
P•B PCB PDB PHB POB PPB PUB
•PB APB PPB
PC• PCB PCS PCT
P•C PAC PEC PFC PIC POC PRC PTC PUC PVC
•PC APC FPC UPC
PD• PDB PDD PDM PDQ PDT
P•D PAD PDD PED PFD PHD POD PPD
•PD BPD CPD GPD PPD
PE• PEA PEC PED PEG PEH PEI PEN PEP PER PES PET PEU PEW PEZ
P•E PIE POE PRE PYE
•PE APE BPE MPE OPE
PF• PFC PFD PFG
P•F PLF PRF PSF
•PF SPF
PG• PGA PGS
P•G PAG PEG PFG PIG PKG PMG PTG PUG
•PG LPG MPG RPG ZPG
PH• PHB PHD PHI PHM PHR PHU
P•H PAH PEH PPH PTH
•PH BPH DPH EPH KPH MPH PPH
PI• PIA PIC PIE PIG PIM PIN PIP PIS PIT PIU PIX
P•I PEI PHI POI PSI
•PI API BPI CPI DPI EPI UPI
PJ• PJS
PK• PKG PKS PKT PKU
P•K PAK PMK
•PK TPK
PL• PLF PLO PLS PLU PLY
P•L PAL POL PUL
•PL APL BPL CPL DPL FPL
PM• PMG PMK PMT
P•M PAM PDM PHM PIM POM PPM PYM
•PM CPM FPM GPM IPM LPM PPM RPM WPM
PN• PNS
P•N PAN PEN PIN PRN PUN
•PN JPN LPN WPN
PO• POB POC POD POE POI POL POM POP POR POS POT POV POW POX
P•O PAO PLO PPO PRO PTO
•PO APO CPO FPO GPO PPO
PP• PPB PPD PPH PPM PPO PPP PPS PPT PPV
P•P PAP PEP PIP POP PPP PRP PUP
•PP APP OPP PPP SPP
P•Q PDQ
PR• PRC PRE PRF PRN PRO PRP PRS PRY
P•R PAR PER PHR POR PUR PWR PYR
•PR APR CPR NPR OPR SPR
PS• PSF PSI PSS PST
P•S PAS PBS PCS PES PGS PIS PJS PKS PLS PNS POS PPS PRS PSS PTS
•PS APS BPS CPS DPS EPS FPS GPS IPS JPS KPS LPS MPS NPS OPS PPS QPS RPS SPS TPS UPS VPS
PT• PTA PTC PTG PTH PTO PTS PTV
P•T PAT PCT PDT PET PIT PKT PMT POT PPT PST PUT PVT PWT PXT
•PT APT CPT DPT OPT PPT RPT SPT
PU• PUB PUC PUG PUL PUN PUP PUR PUT
P•U PAU PEU PHU PIU PKU PLU
•PU CPU
PV• PVC PVT
P•V POV PPV PTV
•PV PPV
PW• PWA PWR PWT
P•W PAW PEW POW
•PW DPW
PX• PXT
P•X PAX PBX PIX POX PYX
PY• PYA PYE PYM PYR PYX
P•Y PAY PLY PRY
•PY SPY
P•Z PAZ PEZ
Q•A QUA
QB• QBS
Q•C QMC QVC
Q•D QED QID
QE• QED QEF
Q•E QUE
Q•F QEF
Q•G QMG
QI• QID QIN
Q•I QUI
QK• QKT
QM• QMC QMG
Q•M QOM QUM
Q•N QIN
QO• QOM
Q•O QTO QUO
QP• QPS
QQ• QQV
Q•R QTR
Q•S QBS QPS QTS
•QS HQS IQS
QT• QTO QTR QTS QTY
Q•T QKT
QU• QUA QUE QUI QUM QUO
QV• QVC
Q•V QQV
•QV QQV
Q•Y QTY
RA• RAD RAE RAF RAG RAH RAI RAJ RAM RAN RAP RAS RAT RAU RAW RAY
R•A RCA RDA REA RIA RNA RSA RYA
•RA ARA BRA ERA FRA IRA KRA NRA ORA SRA TRA
RB• RBC RBI
R•B REB RFB RGB RIB ROB RUB
•RB ARB FRB ORB URB
RC• RCA RCD RCN RCP RCS RCT
R•C RBC REC RIC ROC
•RC ARC JRC NRC ORC PRC
RD• RDA RDF RDS
R•D RAD RCD RED RFD RID RND ROD RUD
•RD ARD ORD URD
RE• REA REB REC RED REE REF REG REI REL REM REN REO REP REQ RES RET REV REX REY
R•E RAE REE ROE RTE RUE RYE
•RE ARE BRE ERE GRE HRE IRE MRE ORE PRE TRE URE
RF• RFB RFD RFK
R•F RAF RDF REF RIF
•RF ARF GRF PRF
RG• RGB RGS RGT
R•G RAG REG RIG RPG RUG
•RG ARG ERG FRG ORG
RH• RHO
R•H RAH
•RH HRH
RI• RIA RIB RIC RID RIF RIG RIM RIN RIO RIP RIT RIV
R•I RAI RBI REI ROI
•RI ARI CRI ERI FRI MRI SRI TRI URI
R•J RAJ
•RJ DRJ
RK• RKO
R•K RFK ROK
•RK ARK DRK IRK ORK
RL• RLS
R•L REL
•RL FRL
RM• RMN RMS
R•M RAM REM RIM ROM RPM RUM
•RM ARM VRM
RN• RNA RND RNP RNS
R•N RAN RCN REN RIN RMN RON RUN
•RN ARN ERN PRN URN
RO• ROB ROC

ROD
ROE
ROI
ROK
ROM
RON
ROO
ROT
ROW
ROY
ROZ

R•O
REO
RHO
RIO
RKO
ROO

•RO
ARO
BRO
CRO
FRO
GRO
IRO
ORO
PRO
SRO
URO

RP•
RPG
RPM
RPS
RPT

R•P
RAP
RCP
REP
RIP
RNP

•RP
ARP
PRP
TRP

R•Q
REQ

RR•
RRR
RRS

R•R
RRR
RUR

•RR
ARR
BRR
ERR
GRR
IRR
ORR
RRR

RS•
RSA
RSV

R•S
RAS
RCS
RDS
RES
RGS
RLS
RMS
RNS
RPS
RRS
RTS
RUS
RVS

•RS
ARS
BRS
CRS
DRS
ERS
FRS
HRS
IRS
JRS
LRS
MRS
ORS
PRS
RRS
SRS
TRS
YRS

RT•
RTE
RTS
RTW

R•T
RAT
RCT
RET
RGT
RIT
ROT
RPT
RUT

•RT
ART
CRT
FRT
IRT
MRT
ORT

RU•
RUB
RUD
RUE
RUG
RUM
RUN
RUR
RUS
RUT

R•U
RAU

•RU
ARU
CRU
DRU
TRU
URU

RV•
RVS

R•V
REV
RIV
RSV

•RV
IRV
ORV

RW•
RWY

R•W
RAW
ROW
RTW

R•X
REX

RY•
RYA
RYE

R•Y
RAY
REY
ROY
RWY

•RY
ARY
CRY
DRY
ERY
FRY
ORY
PRY
TRY
WRY

R•Z
ROZ

•RZ
ERZ

SA•
SAB
SAC
SAD
SAE
SAG
SAL
SAM
SAN
SAO
SAP
SAR
SAS
SAT
SAW
SAX
SAY

S•A
SBA
SEA
SHA
SKA
SLA
SMA
SPA
SRA
SSA
STA
SWA

•SA
ASA
BSA
CSA
ESA
GSA
ISA
NSA
OSA
RSA
SSA
USA

SB•
SBA
SBE
SBW

S•B
SAB
SIB
SOB
STB
SUB

•SB
OSB

SC•
SCD
SCH
SCI

S•C
SAC
SEC
SFC
SIC
SOC
SVC

•SC
ASC
BSC
CSC
DSC
ESC
JSC
MSC
NSC
USC

SD•
SDI
SDS

S•D
SAD
SCD
SGD
SID
SJD
SLD
SOD
STD
SUD
SYD

•SD
ESD
JSD
LSD

SE•
SEA
SEC
SEE
SEI
SEL
SEM
SEN
SEP
SEQ
SER
SES
SET
SEW
SEX

S•E
SAE
SBE
SEE
SHE
SIE
SSE
STE
SUE

•SE
ASE
ESE
ISE
OSE
SSE
TSE
USE

SF•
SFC
SFO
SFZ

S•F
SHF
SOF
SPF
SUF

•SF
NSF
OSF
PSF

SG•
SGD
SGT

S•G
SAG
SIG
SNG
SOG
STG
SUG

•SG
MSG

SH•
SHA
SHE
SHF
SHH
SHO
SHR
SHT
SHU
SHY

S•H
SCH
SHH

•SH
ASH
BSH
HSH
ISH
OSH
USH

SI•
SIB
SIC
SID
SIE
SIG
SIL
SIM
SIN
SIP
SIR
SIS
SIT
SIX

S•I
SCI
SDI
SEI
SKI
SOI
SRI
SUI

•SI
ASI
HSI
LSI
PSI

SJ•
SJD

SK•
SKA
SKI
SKT
SKY

S•K
STK
SUK

•SK
ASK
CSK
ESK
TSK

SL•
SLA
SLD
SLO
SLR
SLY

S•L
SAL
SEL
SIL
SNL
SOL
STL
SYL

•SL
ASL
ESL
ISL
MSL
YSL

SM•
SMA
SMU

S•M
SAM
SEM
SIM
STM
SUM
SYM

•SM
DSM
ISM
USM

SN•
SNG
SNL
SNO
SNY

S•N
SAN
SEN
SIN
SON
SSN
STN
SUN
SYN

•SN
ASN
MSN
SSN
USN

SO•
SOB
SOC
SOD
SOF
SOG
SOI
SOL
SON
SOO
SOP
SOR
SOS
SOT
SOU
SOV
SOW
SOX
SOY

S•O
SAO
SFO
SHO
SLO
SNO
SOO
SRO

•SO
ASO
DSO
ESO
ISO
OSO
USO

SP•
SPA
SPF
SPP
SPR
SPS
SPT
SPY

S•P
SAP
SEP
SIP
SOP
SPP
STP
SUP

•SP
ASP
ESP
TSP
USP

S•Q
SEQ
SUQ

•SQ
ESQ

SR•
SRA
SRI
SRO
SRS

S•R
SAR
SER
SHR
SIR
SLR
SOR
SPR
SSR
STR
SUR
SYR

•SR
ASR
ISR
SSR

SS•
SSA
SSE
SSN
SSR
SSS
SST
SSW

S•S
SAS
SDS
SES
SIS
SOS
SPS
SRS
SSS
STS
SUS
SYS

•SS
ASS
ESS
ISS
MSS
OSS
PSS
SSS
USS
VSS

ST•
STA
STB
STD
STE
STG
STK
STL
STM
STN
STP
STR
STS
STU
STY

S•T
SAT
SET
SGT
SHT
SIT
SKT
SOT
SPT
SST

•ST
AST
CST
DST
EST
GST
HST
IST
LST
MST
OST
PST
SST

SU•
SUB
SUD
SUE
SUF
SUG
SUI
SUK
SUM
SUN
SUP
SUQ
SUR
SUS

S•U
SHU
SMU
SOU
STU

•SU
ASU
ESU
FSU
LSU
MSU
OSU
TSU
USU

SV•
SVC

S•V
SOV

•SV
ASV
RSV

SW•
SWA

S•W
SAW
SBW
SEW
SOW
SSW

•SW
MSW
NSW
SSW
WSW

S•X
SAX
SEX
SIX
SOX

SY•
SYD
SYL
SYM
SYN
SYR
SYS

S•Y
SAY
SHY
SKY
SLY
SNY
SOY
SPY
STY

S•Z
SFZ

TA•
TAB
TAC
TAD
TAE
TAG
TAI
TAJ
TAL
TAM
TAN
TAO
TAP
TAR
TAS
TAT
TAU
TAV
TAW
TAX
TAY

T•A
TBA
TEA
TIA
TPA
TRA
TVA
TWA

•TA
ATA
ETA
OTA
PTA
STA
UTA

TB•
TBA
TBS

T•B
TAB
THB
TOB
TUB

•TB
OTB
STB

TC•
TCU

T•C
TAC
TEC
TIC
TLC

•TC
ETC
FTC
LTC
OTC
PTC

TD•
TDD
TDS

T•D
TAD
TDD
TED
THD
TID
TOD

•TD
ETD
FTD
GTD
ITD
LTD
STD
YTD

TE•
TEA
TEC
TED
TEE
TEG
TEL
TEM
TEN
TER
TET
TEX
TEY

T•E
TAE
TEE
THE
TIE
TOE
TRE
TSE
TUE
TYE

•TE
ATE
ETE
GTE
ITE
OTE
RTE
STE
UTE

TF•
TFR

•TF
CTF

T•G
TAG
TEG
TOG
TUG

•TG
MTG
PTG
STG

TH•
THB
THD
THE
THI
THM
THO
THU
THX
THY

•TH
BTH
ETH
FTH
NTH
PTH

TI•
TIA
TIC
TID
TIE
TIL
TIM
TIN
TIO
TIP
TIS
TIU

T•I
TAI
THI
TOI
TRI
TUI
TWI

T•J
TAJ
TMJ

TK•
TKO
TKT

T•K
TPK
TSK

•TK
STK

TL•
TLC

T•L
TAL
TEL
TIL

•TL
ATL
BTL
STL

TM•
TMJ
TMS

T•M
TAM
TEM
THM
TIM
TOM

•TM
ATM
MTM
STM

TN•
TNN
TNS
TNT

T•N
TAN
TEN
TIN
TNN
TON
TUN

•TN
CTN
MTN
STN

TO•
TOB
TOD
TOE
TOG
TOI
TOM
TON
TOO
TOP
TOR
TOT
TOV
TOW
TOX
TOY

T•O
TAO
THO
TIO
TKO
TOO
TWO

•TO
CTO
ETO
GTO
ITO
OTO
PTO
QTO

TP•
TPA
TPK
TPS

T•P
TAP
TIP
TOP
TRP
TSP
TUP
TWP
TYP

•TP
ATP
GTP
STP

TR•
TRA
TRE
TRI
TRP
TRS
TRU
TRY

T•R
TAR
TER
TFR
TOR
TYR

•TR
CTR
LTR
QTR
STR
VTR

TS•
TSE
TSK
TSP
TSU

T•S
TAS
TBS
TDS
TIS
TMS
TNS
TPS
TRS
TVS

•TS
BTS
CTS
DTS
ETS
HTS
ITS
KTS
LTS
MTS
OTS
PTS
QTS
RTS
STS
WTS

TT•
TTY

T•T
TAT
TET
TKT
TNT
TOT
TUT

•TT
ATT
GTT
ITT
OTT

TU•
TUB
TUE
TUG
TUI
TUN
TUP
TUT
TUX

T•U
TAU
TCU
THU
TIU
TRU
TSU
TZU

•TU
BTU
STU
UTU

TV•
TVA
TVS

T•V
TAV
TOV

•TV
ATV
ETV
MTV
PTV

TW•
TWA
TWI
TWO
TWP
TWX

T•W
TAW
TOW

•TW
RTW

T•X
TAX
TEX
THX
TOX
TUX
TWX

TY•
TYE
TYP
TYR

T•Y
TAY
TEY
THY
TOY
TRY
TTY

•TY
ITY
QTY
STY
TTY

TZ•
TZU

UA•
UAE
UAR
UAW

U•A
UFA
UMA
UNA
USA
UTA
UVA

•UA
HUA
QUA

UB•
UBI

U•B
URB

•UB
BUB
CUB
DUB
HUB
LUB
NUB
PUB
RUB
SUB
TUB

U•C
UDC
UPC
USC

•UC
AUC
BUC
DUC
LUC
PUC

UD•
UDC
UDO

U•D
UND
URD

•UD
AUD
BUD
CUD
DUD
HUD
JUD
MUD
OUD
RUD
SUD

U•E
UAE
UKE
ULE
UME
UNE
URE
USE
UTE

•UE
CUE
DUE
HUE
KUE
QUE
RUE
SUE
TUE

UF•
UFA
UFO
UFT
UFW

U•F
UHF
ULF

•UF
AUF
SUF

UG•
UGH
UGO

•UG
AUG
BUG
DUG
FUG
HUG
JUG
LUG
MUG
PUG
RUG
SUG
TUG
VUG
ZUG

UH•
UHF

U•H
UGH
UNH
USH

•UH
DUH
HUH

UI•
UIT

U•I
UBI
UNI
UPI
URI
UZI

•UI
CUI
GUI
HUI
LUI
NUI
OUI
QUI
SUI
TUI

UK•
UKE

•UK
AUK
SUK
YUK

UL•
ULE
ULF
ULM
ULT
ULU

•UL
BUL
CUL
FUL
JUL
KUL
NUL
PUL
VUL
YUL

UM•
UMA
UME
UMP

U•M
ULM
USM

•UM
AUM
BUM
CUM
DUM
GUM
HUM
IUM
KUM
LUM
MUM
NUM
QUM
RUM
SUM
YUM

UN•
UNA
UND
UNE
UNH
UNI
UNO
UNP
UNQ
UNS
UNU

U•N
URN
USN

•UN
BUN
DUN
FUN
GUN
HUN
JUN
KUN
NUN
PUN
RUN
SUN

TUN

U•O
UDO
UFO
UGO
UNO
URO
USO

•UO
DUO
QUO

UP•
UPC
UPI
UPS

U•P
UMP
UNP
USP

•UP
CUP
DUP
HUP
PUP
SUP
TUP
YUP

U•Q
UNQ

•UQ
SUQ

UR•
URB
URD
URE
URI
URN
URO
URU

U•R
UAR

•UR
BUR
CUR
EUR
FUR
GUR
HUR
OUR
PUR
RUR
SUR

US•
USA
USC
USE
USH
USM
USN
USO
USP
USS
USU

U•S
UNS
UPS
USS

•US
AUS
BUS
GUS
HUS
JUS
MUS
NUS
OUS
RUS
SUS

UT•
UTA
UTE
UTU

U•T
UFT
UIT
ULT

•UT
AUT
BUT
CUT
FUT
GUT
HUT
JUT
MUT
NUT
OUT
PUT
RUT
TUT

U•U
ULU
UNU
URU
USU
UTU

UV•
UVA

•UV
GUV
JUV
LUV

U•W
UAW
UFW

•UX
AUX
DUX
LUX
MUX
TUX

•UY
BUY
GUY
MUY

UZ•
UZI

•UZ
DUZ
LUZ

VA•
VAC
VAL
VAN
VAR
VAS
VAT
VAV

V•A
VIA
VOA

•VA
AVA
EVA
IVA
OVA
TVA
UVA
WVA

VB•
VBS

VC•
VCR

V•C
VAC
VIC
VOC

•VC
AVC
MVC
PVC
QVC
SVC

VD•
VDT

V•D
VFD
VMD

•VD
BVD

VE•
VEE
VEG
VEH
VEL
VEN
VER
VET
VEX

V•E
VEE
VIE

•VE
AVE
EVE
IVE

VF•
VFD
VFW

V•F
VHF
VLF

V•G
VEG
VUG

•VG
AVG
EVG

VH•
VHF
VHS

V•H
VEH

VI•
VIA
VIC
VIE
VII
VIL
VIM
VIN
VIP
VIR
VIS
VIV
VIZ

V•I
VII
VMI

•VI
AVI
CVI
DVI
LVI
MVI
OVI
XVI

VJ•
VJS

VL•
VLF

V•L
VAL
VEL
VIL
VOL
VUL

VM•
VMD
VMI

V•M
VIM
VRM

•VM
BVM
DVM

V•N
VAN
VEN
VIN
VON

•VN
AVN

VO•
VOA
VOC
VOL
VON
VOU
VOW
VOX

•VO
AVO
IVO
OVO

VP•
VPS

V•P
VIP

•VP
MVP

VR•
VRM

V•R
VAR
VCR
VER
VIR
VTR

VS•
VSS

V•S
VAS
VBS
VHS
VIS
VJS
VPS
VSS
VWS

•VS
AVS
CVS
EVS
IVS
RVS
TVS

VT•
VTR

V•T
VAT
VDT
VET

•VT
BVT
PVT

VU•
VUG
VUL

V•U
VOU

V•V
VAV
VIV

VW•
VWS

V•W
VFW
VOW

•VW
GVW

V•X
VEX
VOX

•VY
HVY
IVY

V•Z
VIZ

WA•
WAC
WAD
WAF
WAG
WAH
WAN
WAR
WAS
WAT
WAW
WAX
WAY

W•A
WBA
WPA
WVA

•WA
KWA
PWA
SWA
TWA

WB•
WBA
WBC
WBN
WBS

W•B
WEB

WC•
WCS

W•C
WAC
WBC

WD•
WDS

W•D
WAD
WED

•WD
FWD

WE•
WEB
WED
WEE
WEI
WEN
WES
WET

W•E
WEE
WIE
WOE
WYE

•WE
AWE
EWE
OWE

W•F
WAF
WHF
WWF

•WF
WWF

W•G
WAG
WIG

WH•
WHF
WHH
WHO
WHR
WHS
WHY

W•H
WAH
WHH

•WH
KWH

WI•
WIE
WIG
WIL
WIM
WIN
WIS
WIT
WIZ

W•I
WEI
WWI

•WI
BWI
OWI
TWI
WWI

WJ•
WJM

WK•
WKS

W•K
WMK
WOK

W•L
WIL

•WL
AWL
OWL

WM•
WMK

W•M
WIM
WJM
WPM

•WM
CWM
HWM

WN•
WNW

W•N
WAN
WBN
WEN
WIN
WON
WPN

•WN
AWN
OWN

WO•
WOE
WOK
WON
WOO
WOT
WOW

W•O
WHO
WOO
WYO

•WO
CWO
IWO
TWO

WP•
WPA
WPM
WPN

•WP
CWP
TWP

WR•
WRY

W•R
WAR
WHR

•WR
PWR

WS•
WSW

W•S
WAS
WBS
WCS
WDS
WES
WHS
WIS
WKS
WTS

•WS
VWS

WT•
WTS

W•T
WAT
WET
WIT
WOT

•WT
CWT
DWT
NWT
PWT

•WU
NWU

WV•
WVA

WW•
WWF
WWI
WWW

W•W
WAW
WNW
WOW
WSW
WWW

•WW
IWW
WWW

W•X
WAX

•WX
TWX

WY•
WYE
WYO

W•Y
WAY
WHY
WRY

•WY
HWY
RWY

W•Z
WIZ

X•A
XIA

XC•
XCI
XCV

•XC
CXC
DXC
EXC
MXC

X•D
XED

•XD
MXD

XE•
XED
XEN
XER
XES

X•E
XKE

•XE
AXE
EXE

XI•
XIA
XII
XIS
XIV
XIX

X•I
XCI
XII
XLI
XVI
XXI

•XI
CXI
DXI
LXI
MXI
XXI

XK•
XKE

XL•
XLI
XLS
XLV

X•L
XYL

•XL
AXL
CXL
DXL
MXL

X•N
XEN

XO•
XOO
XOR
XOX

X•O
XOO
XXO

•XO
EXO
OXO
XXO

•XP
EXP

X•R
XER
XOR

•XR
EXR

X•S
XES
XIS
XLS

•XT
EXT
PXT

XV•
XVI

X•V
XCV
XIV
XLV
XXV

•XV
CXV
DXV
LXV
MXV
XXV

XX•
XXI
XXO
XXV
XXX

X•X
XIX
XOX
XXX

•XX
CXX
DXX
LXX
MXX
OXX
XXX

XY•
XYL

•XY
OXY

YA•
YAG
YAH
YAK
YAM
YAO
YAP
YAR
YAT
YAW
YAY
YAZ

Y•A
YEA
YMA

•YA
PYA
RYA

YB•
YBS

Y•B
YOB

•YC
MYC
NYC

YD•
YDS

Y•D
YLD
YOD
YTD

•YD
CYD
HYD
KYD
SYD

YE•
YEA
YEN
YEO
YEP
YER
YES
YET
YEW

•YE
AYE
BYE
DYE
EYE
LYE
NYE
PYE
RYE
TYE
WYE

Y•G
YAG

•YG
ZYG

Y•H
YAH

•YH
AYH

YI•
YIN
YIP

•YI
FYI

Y•K
YAK
YUK

YL•
YLD

Y•L
YSL
YUL

•YL
CYL
OYL
SYL
XYL

YM•
YMA

Y•M
YAM
YOM
YUM

•YM
GYM
PYM
SYM
ZYM

Y•N
YEN
YIN
YON

•YN
AYN
DYN
FYN
GYN
LYN
SYN

YO•
YOB
YOD
YOM
YON
YOO
YOU
YOW

Y•O
YAO
YEO
YOO

•YO
CYO
LYO
MYO
WYO

Y•P
YAP
YEP
YIP
YUP

•YP
GYP
HYP
TYP

YR•
YRS

Y•R
YAR
YER

•YR
AYR
CYR
PYR
SYR
TYR

YS•
YSL

Y•S
YBS
YDS
YES
YRS

•YS
DYS
LYS
SYS

YT•
YTD

Y•T
YAT
YET

YU•
YUK
YUL
YUM
YUP

Y•U
YOU

•YU
BYU
NYU

Y•W
YAW
YEW
YOW

•YX
MYX
NYX
PYX

Y•Y
YAY

Y•Z
YAZ

ZA•
ZAG
ZAP
ZAX

Z•A
ZIA
ZOA

Z•D
ZED
ZOD

ZE•
ZED
ZEE
ZEN

Z•E
ZEE
ZOE

•ZE
IZE

Z•G
ZAG
ZIG
ZOG
ZPG
ZUG
ZYG

ZI•
ZIA
ZIG
ZIP

•ZI
UZI

Z•M
ZYM

Z•N
ZEN

ZO•
ZOA
ZOD
ZOE
ZOG
ZOO

Z•O
ZOO

•ZO
AZO

ZP•
ZPG

Z•P
ZAP
ZIP

•ZR
EZR

•ZT
OZT

ZU•
ZUG

•ZU
TZU

Z•X
ZAX

ZY•
ZYG
ZYM

ZZ•
ZZZ

Z•Z
ZZZ

•ZZ
ZZZ

4

AA••
AAHS AARE AARP

A•A•
ABAS ACAD ADAH ADAK ADAM ADAR AFAR AGAR AGAS AHAB AHAZ AJAR AJAX AKAN ALAE ALAI ALAN ALAR ALAS AMAH AMAS AMAT ANAS ANAT ARAB ARAD ARAK ARAL ARAM ARAN ARAS ASAP AVAL AVAR AWAY AYAH AZAN

A••A
ABBA ACEA ACTA AFTA AGFA AGHA AGRA AGUA AIDA AIEA AIWA ALBA ALDA ALFA ALGA ALIA ALLA ALMA ALTA ALVA AMIA ANKA ANNA ANOA ANSA ANTA ANYA ANZA APIA AQUA AREA ARIA ARMA ARPA ARRA ASEA ASIA ASTA ATKA ATRA ATTA AULA AURA AVIA AYLA

•AA•
BAAL BAAS CAAN HAAG MAAM MAAR MAAS MAAT PAAR SAAB SAAR TAAL VAAL WAAC WAAF WAAL

•A•A
BABA BAJA BAMA BARA BAYA CAMA CANA CAPA CARA CASA CATA CAVA DADA DAMA DANA DATA FALA FATA FAVA GABA GAEA GAGA GAIA GALA GAMA GAPA GAYA GAZA HAHA HAMA HANA IANA JADA JAVA KAKA KAMA KANA KARA KAVA LALA LAMA LANA LARA LAVA MAIA MAJA MALA MAMA MANA MARA MATA MAYA NADA NAHA NANA NAPA NARA NASA PABA PACA PAPA PARA PASA RAGA RAJA RAMA RANA RAPA RARA RASA RATA SABA SADA SAGA SALA SANA SARA SAVA TADA TAKA TALA TAMA TANA TAPA TARA TATA TAXA VACA VARA VAYA WAKA WAWA YAMA YANA ZAMA

••AA
MPAA NCAA NOAA

AB••
ABAS ABBA ABBE ABBR ABBS ABBY ABCS ABED ABEL ABER ABET ABIB ABIE ABLE ABLY ABMS ABOU ABRI ABUT

A•B•
ABBA ABBE ABBR ABBS ABBY ALBA ALBI ALBS AMBI AMBO AMBS APBS ARBS AUBE

A••B
ABIB AHAB ARAB

•AB•
BABA BABE BABS BABU BABY CABS DABO DABS GABA GABE GABO GABS GABY HABE JABS LABS NABS PABA RABE RABI SABA SABE SABU TABI TABS TABU

•A•B
BARB CARB DAUB GARB IAMB JAMB KALB LAMB SAAB

••AB
AHAB ARAB BLAB CRAB DRAB FLAB GRAB JOAB MOAB SAAB SCAB SLAB STAB SWAB

AC••
ACAD ACCS ACCT ACDC ACEA ACED ACER ACES ACET ACEY ACHE ACHT ACHY ACID ACIS ACLU ACME ACNE ACRE ACRO ACTA ACTE ACTG ACTH ACTI ACTS ACTV ACYL

A•C•
ABCS ACCS ACCT ADCS AGCY ANCE ANCY ARCH ARCO ARCS ASCH ASCI ASCO

A••C
ACDC ALEC AMIC APOC AVEC

•AC•
BACH BACK BACS BACT CACO DACE EACH FACE FACP FACS FACT HACK JACK LACE LACK LACS LACT LACY MACE MACH MACK MACS MACY NACL PACA PACE PACK PACS PACT RACE RACK RACY SACK SACS TACH TACK TACO TACT VACA VACS WACE WACK WACO WACS ZACK

•A•C
BANC BASC CALC CANC LAIC MARC MASC NARC PARC TALC WAAC

••AC
BOAC BRAC GMAC HUAC WAAC WRAC

AD••
ADAH ADAK ADAM ADAR ADCS ADDN ADDS ADDY ADEN ADES ADIN ADIT ADJS ADJT ADMS ADUE ADVT ADZE

A•D•
ACDC ADDN ADDS ADDY AIDA AIDE AIDS ALDA ALDO ANDS ANDY AUDE AUDI AVDP

A••D
ABED ACAD ACED ACID AGED AMID APED ARAD ARID AULD AVID AWED AXED

•AD•
BADE CADE CADI CADS DADA DADE DADO DADS EADS FADE FADO FADS GADS HADE HADJ JADA JADE LADD LADE LADS LADY MADD MADE NADA NADH NADP PADS QADI RADM RADS SADA SADD SADE SADR TADA TADS VADE VADM WADE WADI WADS

•A•D
BALD BAND BARD BAUD CARD DARD DASD FAHD FARD GAUD HAND HARD LADD LAID LAND LAPD LARD LAUD MADD MAID MAUD NARD NASD PAID PARD PATD QAID RAID RAND SADD SAID SAND SARD SAUD VAUD WALD WAND WARD YARD YAZD

••AD
ACAD ARAD BEAD BRAD CHAD CLAD DEAD DUAD DYAD EGAD FUAD GLAD GOAD GRAD HEAD JOAD LEAD LOAD MEAD OBAD ORAD QUAD READ ROAD SCAD SHAD SPAD TOAD WOAD

AE••
AERO AERY

A•E•
ABED ABEL ABER ABET ACEA ACED ACER ACES ACET ACEY ADEN ADES AGED AGEE AGER AGES AHEM AIEA AKEE ALEC ALEE ALEF ALEP ALES ALEX AMEN AMER AMES AMEX ANEW APED APER APES APEX AREA AREO ARES ASEA ATEN AUEL AUER AVEC AVER AVES AWED AWES AXED AXEL AXES AYER AYES

A••E
AARE ABBE ABIE ABLE ACHE ACME ACNE ACRE ACTE ADUE ADZE AGEE AGUE AIDE AIME AIRE AKEE ALAE ALEE ALLE ALOE ALTE AMIE ANCE ANGE ANNE ANTE AONE APSE ARME ARNE ARTE ASHE AUBE AUDE AUGE AUNE AXLE AYME

•AE•
BAER BAEZ CAEN GAEA GAEL JAEL JAEN KAEL TAEL

•A•E
AARE BABE BADE BAKE BALE BANE BARE BASE BATE CADE CAFE CAGE CAKE CALE CAME CANE CAPE CARE CASE CATE CAVE DACE DADE DALE DAME DANE DARE DATE DAVE DAZE EASE EAVE FACE FADE FAKE FAME FANE FARE FATE FAVE FAYE FAZE GABE GAGE GALE GAME GAPE GARE GATE GAVE GAYE GAZE HABE HADE HAKE HALE HAME HARE HATE HAVE HAZE JADE JAKE JANE JAPE JAYE KALE KAME KANE KATE KAYE LACE LADE LAKE LAME LANE LASE LATE LAUE LAVE LAZE MACE MADE MAGE MAKE MALE MAME MANE MARE MATE MAZE NAME NAPE NATE NAVE PACE PAGE PALE PANE PARE PASE PATE PAVE RABE RACE RAGE RAKE RARE RATE RAVE RAYE RAZE SABE SADE SAFE SAGE SAKE SALE SAME SANE SASE SATE SAVE SAXE TAKE TALE TAME TANE TAPE TARE TATE

VADE VALE VANE VASE WACE WADE WAGE WAKE WALE WANE WARE WAVE YALE YARE ZANE

••AE
ALAE BRAE FRAE IDAE IRAE

AF••
AFAR AFRO AFTA AFTS

A•F•
AGFA ALFA AMFM

A••F
ALEF ALIF ASIF ASOF

•AF•
BAFF CAFE DAFF DAFT GAFF HAFT OAFS RAFT SAFE SAFR TAFT WAFS WAFT

•A•F
BAFF CALF DAFF GAFF HALF NAIF WAAF WAIF ZARF

••AF
DEAF GRAF LEAF LOAF OLAF PIAF RCAF USAF WAAF WRAF

AG••
AGAR AGAS AGCY AGED AGEE AGER AGES AGFA AGHA AGIN AGIO AGNI AGOG AGON AGRA AGRI AGRO AGTS AGUA AGUE

A•G•
ALGA ALGO ALGY ANGE ANGL ARGO ARGY AUGE AVGS

A••G
ACTG AGOG

•AG•
BAGS CAGE CAGY DAGS GAGA GAGE GAGS HAGI HAGS IAGO JAGS LAGO LAGS MAGE MAGI MAGS NAGS NAGY PAGE PAGO RAGA RAGE RAGG RAGS RAGU SAGA SAGE SAGO SAGS TAGS WAGE WAGS YAGI ZAGS

•A•G
BANG DANG FANG GANG HAAG HAIG HANG LANG MARG NANG PANG RAGG RANG SANG TANG VANG WANG YANG

••AG
BRAG CRAG DIAG DRAG FLAG HAAG PEAG QUAG SHAG SLAG SNAG STAG SWAG

AH••
AHAB AHAZ AHEM AHOY AHSO

A•H•
AAHS ACHE ACHT ACHY AGHA ASHE ASHY

A••H
ACTH ADAH ALPH AMAH ANKH ANTH ARCH ASCH AUTH AYAH

•AH•
AAHS BAHR BAHS BAHT CAHN DAHL DAHS FAHD FAHR HAHA HAHN HAHS JAHR KAHN LAHR NAHA OAHU PAHO PAHS SAHL TAHR WAHL ZAHN

•A•H
BACH BASH BATH CASH CATH DASH EACH FATH GASH GATH HASH HATH KAPH LASH LATH MACH MASH MATH NADH NAOH NASH OATH PASH PATH RASH SASH TACH TANH WASH

••AH
ADAH AMAH AYAH BLAH ETAH EVAH LEAH NOAH OPAH PTAH SHAH UTAH YEAH

AI••
AIDA AIDE AIDS AIEA AILS AIME AIMS AINT AINU AIRE AIRS AIRT AIRY AITS AIWA

A•I•
ABIB ABIE ACID ACIS ADIN ADIT AGIN AGIO AKIM AKIN ALIA ALIF ALII ALIT AMIA AMIC AMID AMIE AMIN AMIR AMIS ANIL ANIM ANIS APIA APIS ARIA ARID ARIL ARIZ ASIA ASIF ASIR ASIS ATIT AVIA AVID AVIS AVIV AXIL AXIS AYIN AZIZ

A••I
ABRI ACTI AGNI AGRI ALAI ALBI ALII ALTI ALUI AMBI AMOI ANSI ANTI AQUI ASCI ASTI ATLI ATOI ATRI AUDI AURI

•AI•
BAIL BAIN BAIO BAIT CAIN DAIN DAIS FAIL FAIN FAIR FAIT GAIA GAIL GAIN GAIT HAIG HAIK HAIL HAIM HAIR JAIL JAIN KAIN LAIC LAID LAIN LAIR LAIT MAIA MAID MAIL MAIN MAIS NAIF NAIL PAID PAIL PAIN PAIR PAIX QAID RAID RAIL RAIN SAID SAIL SAIS TAIL TAIN TAIT TAIZ VAIL VAIN VAIR WAIF WAIL WAIN WAIT

•A•I
BALI BANI BARI CADI CALI CAMI DALI DARI HAGI HAJI HAPI HARI IASI KAKI KALI KAMI LARI MAGI MALI MARI MAUI MAXI MAYI NAOI PALI PARI QADI RABI RAKI RAMI RANI RAVI SAKI SARI TABI TALI TATI TAVI TAXI WADI YAGI

••AI
ALAI BNAI ESAI KWAI OJAI QUAI THAI VRAI

AJ••
AJAR AJAX

A•J•
ADJS ADJT

•AJ•
BAJA HAJI HAJJ MAJA RAJA TAJS

•A•J
HADJ HAJJ

AK••
AKAN AKEE AKIM AKIN

A•K•
ANKA ANKH ARKS ASKS ATKA AUKS

A••K
ADAK AMOK ARAK

•AK•
BAKE BAKR BAKU CAKE CAKY FAKE HAKE JAKE KAKA KAKI LAKE MAKE MAKO OAKS RAKE RAKI RAKU SAKE SAKI SAKS TAKA TAKE WAKA WAKE YAKS

•A•K
BACK BALK BANK BARK BASK CALK CARK CASK DANK DARK FALK GAWK HACK HAIK HANK HARK HAWK JACK LACK LANK LARK MACK MARK MASK NARK PACK PARK RACK RANK RASK SACK SALK SANK SARK SASK SAUK TACK TALK TANK TASK WACK WALK YANK ZACK

••AK
ADAK ARAK BEAK BIAK DOAK DYAK FLAK ISAK LEAK NDAK PEAK SDAK SOAK SWAK TEAK WEAK

AL••
ALAE ALAI ALAN ALAR ALAS ALBA ALBI ALBS ALDA ALDO ALEC ALEE ALEF ALEP ALES ALEX ALFA ALGA ALGO ALGY ALIA ALIF ALII ALIT ALLA ALLE ALLO ALLS ALLY ALMA ALMS ALOE ALOU ALPH ALPO ALPS ALSO ALTA ALTE ALTI ALTO ALTS ALUI ALUM ALVA

A•L•
ABLE ABLY ACLU AILS ALLA ALLE ALLO ALLS ALLY ARLO ATLI AULA AULD AWLS AXLE AYLA

A••L
ABEL ACYL AMYL ANGL ANIL APPL ARAL ARIL ARYL AUEL AVAL AWOL AXEL AXIL AZUL

•AL•
BALD BALE BALI BALK BALL BALM BALT CALC CALE CALF CALI CALK CALL CALM CALS CALX DALE DALI DALY FALA FALK FALL FALX GALA GALE GALL GALS GALV HALE HALF HALL HALM HALO HALS HALT KALB KALE KALI KALT LALA LALO MALA MALE MALI MALL MALM MALO MALT PALE PALI PALL PALM PALO PALP PALS PALY RALL SALA SALE SALK SALP SALS SALT TALA TALC TALE TALI TALK TALL VALE WALD WALE WALK WALL WALT YALE YALL YALU

•A•L
BAAL BAIL BALL BAWL CALL CARL CAUL DAHL DANL EARL FAIL FALL GAEL GAIL GALL GAOL GAUL HAIL HALL HAUL JAEL JAIL JARL KAEL KARL MAIL MALL MARL MAUL NACL NAIL NASL NATL PAIL PALL PARL PAUL PAWL RAIL RALL RAUL SAHL SAIL SAML SAUL TAAL TAEL TAIL TALL VAAL VAIL WAAL WAHL WAIL WALL YALL YAWL

••AL
ARAL AVAL BAAL BEAL COAL DEAL DHAL DIAL DUAL EGAL ELAL ETAL FOAL GOAL HEAL ICAL ITAL KCAL LEAL MEAL NEAL OPAL ORAL OVAL PEAL REAL RIAL RYAL SEAL SIAL TAAL TEAL URAL VAAL VEAL VIAL WAAL WEAL ZEAL

AM••
AMAH AMAS AMAT AMBI AMBO AMBS AMEN AMER AMES AMEX AMFM AMIA AMIC AMID AMIE AMIN AMIR AMIS AMMO AMOI AMOK AMON AMOR AMOS AMOY AMPS AMTS AMUR AMYL

A•M•
ABMS ACME ADMS AIME AIMS ALMA ALMS AMMO ARMA ARME ARMS ARMY ATMO ATMS AYME

A••M
ADAM AHEM AKIM ALUM AMFM ANIM ARAM ARUM ATOM ATUM AXUM

•AM•
BAMA BAMS CAMA CAME CAMI CAMO CAMP CAMS DAMA DAME DAMN DAMP DAMS FAME GAMA GAME GAMO GAMP GAMS GAMY HAMA HAME HAMM HAMS IAMB JAMB JAMS KAMA KAME KAMI LAMA LAMB LAME LAMP LAMS LAMY MAMA MAME NAME RAMA RAMI RAMP RAMS SAME SAML SAMO SAMP TAMA TAME TAMM TAMO TAMP TAMS VAMP YAMA YAMS ZAMA

•A•M
BALM BARM BAUM CALM FARM GAUM HAIM HALM HAMM HARM MAAM MALM PALM RADM TAMM VADM WARM

••AM
ADAM ARAM BEAM BRAM CHAM CLAM CRAM DIAM DRAM EDAM ELAM EXAM FLAM FOAM FRAM GLAM GRAM GUAM IMAM LIAM LOAM MAAM NOAM PRAM REAM ROAM SCAM SEAM SHAM SIAM SLAM SPAM SWAM TEAM TRAM WHAM

AN••
ANAS ANAT ANCE ANCY ANDS ANDY ANEW ANGE ANGL ANIL ANIM ANIS ANKA ANKH ANNA ANNE ANNO ANOA ANON ANSA ANSI ANTA ANTE ANTH ANTI ANTS ANYA ANZA

A•N•
ACNE AGNI AINT AINU ANNA ANNE ANNO AONE ARNE ARNO ATNO AUNE AUNT AWNS

A••N
ADDN ADEN ADIN AGIN AGON AKAN AKIN ALAN AMEN AMIN AMON ANON ARAN ARON ASSN ATEN ATON ATTN AVON AXON AYIN AZAN

•AN•
BANC BAND BANE BANG BANI BANK BANS CANA CANC CANE CANS CANT DANA DANE DANG DANK DANL DANO DANU FANE FANG FANS GANG GANN HANA HAND HANG HANK HANS IANA JANE KANA KANE KANO KANS KANT LANA LAND LANE LANG LANK MANA MANE MANN MANO MANS MANU MANX MANY NANA NANG NANO PANE PANG PANS PANT RANA RAND RANG RANI RANK RANT SANA SAND SANE SANG SANK SANS TANA TANE TANG TANH TANK TANS VANE VANG VANS WAND WANE WANG WANT WANY YANA YANG YANK ZANE ZANY

•A•N
BAIN BARN CAAN CAEN CAHN CAIN CAPN DAIN DAMN DARN DAWN EARN FAIN FAUN FAWN GAIN GANN GARN HAHN HAWN JAEN JAIN KAHN KAIN KAON LAIN LAWN MAIN MANN PAIN PAWN RAIN SAWN TAIN TARN VAIN WAIN WARN YARN YAWN ZAHN

••AN
AKAN ALAN ARAN AZAN BEAN BRAN CAAN CHAN CLAN CYAN DEAN DIAN DYAN EBAN EGAN ELAN EVAN FLAN FRAN GMAN GRAN GUAN IBAN IMAN IRAN IVAN JEAN JOAN JUAN KEAN KHAN KOAN KWAN LEAN LOAN MEAN MOAN OLAN OMAN ORAN PLAN ROAN RYAN SCAN SEAN SHAN SPAN STAN SWAN THAN TMAN TUAN ULAN WEAN XIAN YEAN YUAN

AO••
AONE AOUT

A•O•
ABOU AGOG AGON AHOY ALOE ALOU AMOI AMOK AMON AMOR AMOS AMOY ANOA ANON APOC APOS ARON AROO ASOF ASOR ATOI ATOM ATON ATOP ATOR AVON AVOS AVOW AWOL AXON AZOV

A••O
ACRO AERO AFRO AGIO AGRO AHSO ALDO ALGO ALLO ALPO ALSO ALTO AMBO AMMO ANNO APSO ARCO

AREO
ARGO
ARLO
ARNO
AROO
ASCO
ASTO
ATMO
ATNO
ATTO
AUTO

•AO•
GAOL
KAON
LAOS
NAOH
NAOI
NAOS
TAOS

•A•O
BAIO
BARO
CACO
CAMO
CAPO
CARO
CATO
DABO
DADO
DANO
DAYO
FADO
FARO
FASO
GABO
GAMO
GATO
HALO
IAGO
JATO
KANO
KARO
KATO
KAYO
LAGO
LALO
MAKO
MALO
MANO
MAYO
MAZO
NANO
NASO
NATO
PAGO
PAHO
PALO
PASO
PAVO
SAGO
SAMO
SATO
TACO
TAMO
TARO
TAXO
WACO

••AO
CIAO
JIAO

AP••
APBS
APED
APER
APES
APEX
APIA
APIS
APOC
APOS
APPL
APPS
APPT
APRS
APSE
APSO
APTS

A•P•
ALPH
ALPO
ALPS
AMPS
APPL
APPS
APPT
ARPA
ASPS

A••P
AARP
ALEP
ASAP
ATOP
AVDP

•AP•
BAPS
BAPT
CAPA
CAPE
CAPN
CAPO
CAPP
CAPS
CAPT
DAPS
GAPA
GAPE
GAPS
HAPI
HAPS
JAPE
KAPH
LAPD
LAPP
LAPS
MAPS
NAPA
NAPE
NAPS
PAPA
PAPP
RAPA
RAPP
RAPS
RAPT
SAPS
TAPA
TAPE
TAPS
YAPP
YAPS
ZAPS

•A•P
AARP
CAMP
CAPP
CARP
DAMP
EARP
FACP
GAMP
GARP
GASP
GAWP
HARP
HASP
LAMP
LAPP
NADP
PALP
PAPP
RAMP
RAPP
RASP
SALP
SAMP
TAMP
TARP
VAMP
WARP
WASP
YAPP
YAWP

••AP
ASAP
CHAP
CLAP
EVAP
FLAP
FRAP
HEAP
KNAP
LEAP
NEAP
REAP
SLAP
SNAP
SOAP
SWAP
TRAP
WRAP

AQ••
AQUA
AQUI

••AQ
IRAQ
SHAQ

AR••
ARAB
ARAD
ARAK
ARAL
ARAM
ARAN
ARAS
ARBS
ARCH
ARCO
ARCS
AREA
AREO
ARES
ARGO
ARGY
ARIA
ARID
ARIL
ARIZ
ARKS
ARLO
ARMA
ARME
ARMS
ARMY
ARNE
ARNO
ARON
AROO
ARPA
ARRA
ARRS
ARTE
ARTS
ARTY
ARUM
ARYL

A•R•
AARE
AARP
ABRI
ACRE
ACRO
AERO
AERY
AFRO
AGRA
AGRI
AGRO
AIRE
AIRS
AIRT
AIRY
APRS
ARRA
ARRS
ATRA
ATRI
AURA
AURI
AWRY

A••R
ABBR
ABER
ACER
ADAR
AFAR
AGAR
AGER
AJAR
ALAR
AMER
AMIR
AMOR
AMUR
APER
ASIR
ASOR
ASTR
ATOR
AUER
AVAR
AVER
AYER
AZUR

•AR•
AARE
AARP
BARA
BARB
BARD
BARE
BARI
BARK
BARM
BARN
BARO
BARR
BARS
BART
CARA
CARB
CARD
CARE
CARK
CARL
CARO
CARP
CARR
CARS
CART
CARY
DARD
DARE
DARI
DARK
DARN
DART
EARL
EARN
EARP
EARS
FARD
FARE
FARM
FARO
FARR
FARS
GARB
GARE
GARN
GARP
GARR
GARS
GARY
HARD
HARE
HARI
HARK
HARM
HARP
HART
HARZ
JARL
JARS
KARA
KARL
KARO
KART
LARA
LARD
LARI
LARK
LARS
MARA
MARC
MARE
MARG
MARI
MARK
MARL
MARS
MART
MARU
MARV
MARX
MARY
NARA
NARC
NARD
NARK
NARY
NARZ
OARS
PARA
PARC
PARD
PARE
PARI
PARK
PARL
PARR
PARS
PART
RARA
RARE
SARA
SARD
SARI
SARK
TARA
TARE
TARN
TARO
TARP
TARS
TART
VARA
VARY
WARD
WARE
WARM
WARN
WARP
WARS
WART
WARY
YARD
YARE
YARN
ZARF

•A•R
BAER
BAHR
BAKR
BARR
CARR
FAHR
FAIR
FARR
GARR
GAUR
HAIR
JAHR
LAHR
LAIR
MAAR
MAWR
PAAR
PAIR
PARR
SAAR
SADR
SAFR
SAUR
TAHR
VAIR

••AR
ADAR
AFAR
AGAR
AJAR
ALAR
AVAR
BEAR
BOAR
CHAR
CLAR
CZAR
DEAR
FEAR
GEAR
GNAR
GUAR
HEAR
HOAR
IBAR
ISAR
IYAR
IZAR
JBAR
KNAR
LBAR
LEAR
LIAR
MAAR
NEAR
OMAR
OSAR
PAAR
PEAR
PHAR
QUAR
REAR
ROAR
SAAR
SCAR
SEAR
SOAR
SPAR
STAR
TBAR
TEAR
THAR
TSAR
TZAR
USAR
WEAR
YEAR
ZBAR
ZOAR

AS••
ASAP
ASCH
ASCI
ASCO
ASEA
ASHE
ASHY
ASIA
ASIF
ASIR
ASIS
ASKS
ASOF
ASOR
ASPS
ASSN
ASST
ASTA
ASTI
ASTO
ASTR

A•S•
AHSO
ALSO
ANSA
ANSI
APSE
APSO
ASSN
ASST
AUST

A••S
AAHS
ABAS
ABBS
ABCS
ABMS
ACCS
ACES
ACIS
ACTS
ADCS
ADDS
ADES
ADJS
ADMS
AFTS
AGAS
AGES
AGTS
AIDS
AILS
AIMS
AIRS
AITS
ALAS
ALBS
ALES
ALLS
ALMS
ALPS
ALTS
AMAS
AMBS
AMES
AMIS
AMOS
AMPS
AMTS
ANAS
ANDS
ANIS
ANTS
APBS
APES
APIS
APOS
APPS
APRS
APTS
ARAS
ARBS
ARCS
ARES
ARKS
ARMS
ARRS
ARTS
ASIS
ASKS
ASPS
ATMS
ATTS
ATVS
AUKS
AVES
AVGS
AVIS
AVOS
AWES
AWLS
AWNS
AXES
AXIS
AYES

•AS•
BASC
BASE
BASH
BASK
BASS
BAST
CASA
CASE
CASH
CASK
CASS
CAST
DASD
DASH
EASE
EAST
EASY
FASO
FAST
GASH
GASP
GAST
HASH
HASP
HAST
IASI
LASE
LASH
LASS
LAST
MASC
MASH
MASK
MASS
MAST
NASA
NASD
NASH
NASL
NASO
NAST
OAST
PASA
PASE
PASH
PASO
PASS
PAST
RASA
RASH
RASK
RASP
SASE
SASH
SASK
SASS
TASK
TASS
VASE
VAST
WASH
WASP
WAST
ZASU

•A•S
AAHS
BAAS
BABS
BACS
BAGS
BAHS
BAMS
BANS
BAPS
BARS
BASS
BATS
BAYS
CABS
CADS
CALS
CAMS
CANS
CAPS
CARS
CASS
CATS
CAUS
CAVS
CAWS
CAYS
DABS
DADS
DAGS
DAHS
DAIS
DAMS
DAPS
DATS
DAWS
DAYS
EADS
EARS
EATS
FACS
FADS
FANS
FARS
FATS
GABS
GADS
GAGS
GALS
GAMS
GAPS
GARS
GATS
HAGS
HAHS
HALS
HAMS
HANS
HAPS
HATS
HAUS
HAWS
HAYS
JABS
JAGS
JAMS
JARS
JAWS
JAYS
KANS
LABS
LACS
LADS
LAGS
LAMS
LAOS
LAPS
LARS
LASS
LATS
LAVS
LAWS
LAYS
MAAS
MACS
MAGS
MAIS
MANS
MAPS
MARS
MASS
MATS
MAVS
MAWS
MAYS
NABS
NAGS
NAOS
NAPS
NAYS
OAFS
OAKS
OARS
OATS
PACS
PADS
PAHS
PALS
PANS
PARS
PASS
PATS
PAWS
PAYS
RADS
RAGS
RAMS
RAPS
RATS
RAYS
SACS
SAGS
SAIS
SAKS
SALS
SANS
SAPS
SASS
SAWS
SAYS
TABS
TADS
TAGS
TAJS
TAMS
TANS
TAOS
TAPS
TARS
TASS
TATS
TAUS
TAWS
VACS
VANS
VATS
VAVS
WACS
WADS
WAFS
WAGS
WARS
WATS
WAYS
YAKS
YAMS
YAPS
YAWS
ZAGS
ZAPS

••AS
ABAS
AGAS
ALAS
AMAS
ANAS
ARAS
BAAS
BEAS
BIAS
BLAS
BOAS
BRAS
CHAS
CPAS
DIAS
ERAS
ESAS
ETAS
EYAS
GRAS
IRAS
KEAS
LEAS
MAAS
MBAS
MEAS
MFAS
MOAS
OCAS
ODAS
PEAS
RDAS
RIAS
RYAS
SEAS
SPAS
SRAS
STAS
TEAS
TWAS
UPAS
XMAS
YEAS

AT••
ATEN
ATIT
ATKA
ATLI
ATMO
ATMS
ATNO
ATOI
ATOM
ATON
ATOP
ATOR
ATRA
ATRI
ATTA
ATTN
ATTO
ATTS
ATTU
ATTY
ATUM
ATVS
ATWT

A•T•
ACTA
ACTE
ACTG
ACTH
ACTI
ACTS
ACTV
AFTA
AFTS
AGTS
AITS
ALTA
ALTE
ALTI
ALTO
ALTS
AMTS
ANTA
ANTE
ANTH
ANTI
ANTS
APTS
ARTE
ARTS
ARTY
ASTA
ASTI
ASTO
ASTR
ATTA
ATTN
ATTO
ATTS
ATTU
ATTY
AUTH
AUTO

A••T
ABET
ABUT
ACCT
ACET
ACHT
ADIT
ADJT
ADVT
AINT
AIRT
ALIT
AMAT
ANAT
AOUT
APPT
ASST
ATIT
ATWT
AUNT
AUST

•AT•
BATE
BATH
BATS
BATT
CATA
CATE
CATH
CATO
CATS
CATT
CATV
DATA
DATE
DATS
EATS
FATA
FATE
FATH
FATS
GATE
GATH
GATO
GATS
GATT
HATE
HATH
HATS
JATO
KATE
KATO
KATY
KATZ
LATE
LATH
LATS
MATA
MATE
MATH
MATS
MATT
NATE
NATL
NATO
OATH
OATS
OATY
PATD
PATE
PATH
PATS
RATA
RATE
RATS
RATT
SATE
SATO
TATA
TATE
TATI
TATS
VATS
VATU
WATS
WATT

•A•T
BACT
BAHT
BAIT
BALT
BAPT
BART
BAST
BATT
CANT
CAPT
CART
CAST
CATT
DAFT
DART
EAST
FACT
FAIT
FAST
FAUT
GAIT
GAST
GATT
HAFT
HALT
HART
HAST
HAUT
KALT
KANT
KART
LACT
LAIT
LAST
MAAT
MALT
MART
MAST
MATT
NAST
NAUT
OAST
PACT
PANT
PART
PAST
PAYT
RAFT
RANT
RAPT
RATT
SALT
TACT
TAFT
TAIT
TART
TAUT
VAST
WAFT
WAIT
WALT
WANT
WART
WAST
WATT

••AT
AMAT
ANAT
BEAT
BLAT
BOAT
BRAT
CHAT
COAT
CRAT
DRAT
ERAT
ETAT
FEAT
FIAT
FLAT
FRAT
GHAT
GMAT
GNAT
GOAT
HEAT
KHAT
KYAT
LSAT
MAAT
MCAT
MEAT
MOAT
NEAT
NLAT
PEAT
PLAT
PSAT
SCAT
SEAT
SKAT
SLAT
SPAT
STAT
SWAT
THAT
TOAT
WHAT

AU••
AUBE
AUDE
AUDI
AUEL
AUER
AUGE
AUKS
AULA
AULD
AUNE
AUNT
AURA
AURI
AUST
AUTH
AUTO

A•U•
ABUT
ADUE
AGUA
AGUE
ALUI
ALUM
AMUR
AOUT
AQUA
AQUI
ARUM
ATUM
AXUM
AZUL
AZUR

A••U
ABOU
ACLU
AINU
ALOU
ATTU

•AU•
BAUD
BAUM
CAUL
CAUS
DAUB
EAUX
FAUN
FAUT
FAUX
GAUD
GAUL
GAUM
GAUR
HAUL
HAUS
HAUT
LAUD
LAUE
MAUD
MAUI
MAUL
NAUT
PAUL
RAUL
SAUD
SAUK
SAUL
SAUR
TAUS
TAUT
VAUD
VAUX

•A•U
BABU
BAKU
DANU
MANU
MARU
OAHU
RAGU
RAKU
SABU
TABU
VATU
YALU
ZASU

••AU
BEAU
BLAU
ESAU
FRAU
GRAU
LUAU
PEAU
UNAU
VEAU

AV••
AVAL
AVAR
AVDP
AVEC
AVER
AVES
AVGS
AVIA
AVID
AVIS
AVIV
AVON
AVOS
AVOW

A•V•
ADVT
ALVA
ATVS

A••V
ACTV
AVIV
AZOV

•AV•
CAVA
CAVE
CAVS
CAVY
DAVE
DAVY
EAVE
FAVA
FAVE
GAVE
HAVE
JAVA
KAVA
LAVA
LAVE
LAVS
MAVS
NAVE
NAVY
PAVE
PAVO
RAVE
RAVI
SAVA
SAVE
TAVI
VAVS
WAVE
WAVY

•A•V
CATV
GALV
MARV

••AV
FLAV
OLAV
OZAV
SLAV

AW••
AWAY
AWED
AWES
AWLS
AWNS
AWOL
AWRY

A•W•
AIWA
ATWT

A••W
ANEW
AVOW

•AW•
BAWL
CAWS
DAWN
DAWS
FAWN
GAWK
GAWP
HAWK
HAWN
HAWS
JAWS
LAWN
LAWS
MAWR
MAWS
PAWL
PAWN
PAWS
SAWN
SAWS
TAWS
WAWA
YAWL
YAWN
YAWP
YAWS

••AW
BRAW
CHAW
CLAW
CRAW
DRAW
FLAW
GNAW
SHAW
SKAW
SLAW
THAW

AX••
AXED
AXEL
AXES
AXIL
AXIS
AXLE
AXON
AXUM

A••X
AJAX
ALEX
AMEX
APEX

•AX•
MAXI
SAXE
TAXA
TAXI
TAXO
WAXY

•A•X
CALX
EAUX
FALX
FAUX
MANX
MARX
PAIX
VAUX

••AX
AJAX
COAX
FLAX
HOAX
PLAX
SFAX
TRAX

AY••
AYAH
AYER
AYES
AYIN
AYLA
AYME

A•Y•
ACYL
AMYL
ANYA
ARYL

A••Y
ABBY
ABLY
ACEY
ACHY
ADDY
AERY
AGCY
AHOY
AIRY
ALGY
ALLY
AMOY
ANCY
ANDY
ARGY
ARMY
ARTY
ASHY
ATTY
AWAY
AWRY

•AY•
BAYA
BAYS
CAYS
DAYO
DAYS
FAYE
GAYA
GAYE
HAYS
JAYE
JAYS
KAYE
KAYO
LAYS
MAYA
MAYI
MAYO
MAYS
NAYS
PAYS
PAYT
RAYE
RAYS
SAYS
VAYA
WAYS

•A•Y
BABY
CAGY
CAKY
CARY
CAVY
DALY
DAVY
EASY
GABY
GAMY
GARY
HAZY
KATY
LACY
LADY
LAMY
LAZY
MACY
MANY
MARY
MAZY
NAGY
NARY
NAVY
OATY
PALY
RACY
VARY
WANY
WARY
WAVY
WAXY
ZANY

••AY
AWAY
BRAY
CLAY
CRAY
DDAY
DRAY
FLAY
FRAY
GRAY
ISAY
ODAY
OKAY
PLAY
PRAY
QUAY
SHAY
SLAY
SPAY
STAY
SWAY
TRAY
VDAY
WRAY
XRAY

AZ••
AZAN
AZIZ
AZOV
AZUL
AZUR

A•Z•
ADZE
ANZA

A••Z
AHAZ
ARIZ
AZIZ

•AZ•
DAZE
FAZE
GAZA
GAZE
HAZE
HAZY
JAZZ
LAZE
LAZY
MAZE
MAZO
MAZY
RAZE
RAZZ
YAZD

•A•Z
BAEZ
HARZ
JAZZ
KATZ
NARZ
RAZZ
TAIZ

••AZ
AHAZ
BOAZ
BRAZ
CHAZ
DIAZ
GRAZ

BA••
BAAL
BAAS
BABA
BABE
BABS
BABU
BABY
BACH
BACK
BACS
BACT
BADE
BAER
BAEZ
BAFF
BAGS
BAHR
BAHS
BAHT
BAIL
BAIN
BAIO
BAIT
BAJA
BAKE
BAKR
BAKU
BALD
BALE
BALI
BALK
BALL
BALM
BALT
BAMA
BAMS
BANC
BAND
BANE
BANG
BANI
BANK
BANS
BAPS
BAPT
BARA
BARB
BARD
BARE
BARI
BARK
BARM
BARN
BARO
BARR
BARS
BART
BASC
BASE
BASH
BASK
BASS
BAST
BATE
BATH
BATS
BATT
BAUD
BAUM
BAWL
BAYA
BAYS

B•A•
BAAL
BAAS
BEAD
BEAK
BEAL
BEAM
BEAN
BEAR
BEAS
BEAT
BEAU
BIAK
BIAS
BLAB
BLAH
BLAS
BLAT
BLAU
BNAI
BOAC
BOAR
BOAS
BOAT
BOAZ
BRAC
BRAD
BRAE
BRAG
BRAM
BRAN
BRAS
BRAT
BRAW
BRAY
BRAZ

B••A
BABA
BAJA
BAMA
BARA
BAYA
BELA
BEMA
BETA
BIWA
BOCA
BOLA
BOMA
BONA
BORA
BOTA
BOVA
BREA
BUNA

•BA•
ABAS
EBAN
IBAN
IBAR
JBAR
LBAR
MBAS
OBAD
TBAR
ZBAR

•B•A
ABBA
EBLA

••BA
ABBA
ALBA
BABA
CUBA
ELBA
GABA
ISBA
IZBA
JUBA
PABA
REBA
SABA
TUBA
YUBA

BB••
BBLS
BBOY
BBQS

B•B•
BABA
BABE
BABS
BABU
BABY
BEBE
BIBB
BIBI
BIBL
BIBS
BOBS

B••B
BARB
BEEB
BIBB
BLAB
BLEB
BLOB
BOMB
BOOB
BULB
BURB
BYOB

•BB•
ABBA
ABBE
ABBR
ABBS
ABBY
EBBS

•B•B
ABIB
DBIB

••BB
BIBB
COBB
GIBB
ROBB
TUBB
WEBB

B•C•
BACH
BACK
BACS
BACT
BECK
BICE
BICS
BOCA
BOCK
BUCK
BUCO
BUCS

B••C
BANC
BASC
BLOC
BMOC
BOAC
BOSC
BRAC
BRIC
BSEC

•BC•
ABCS

BD••
BDRM

B•D•
BADE
BEDE
BEDS
BIDE
BIDS
BLDG
BLDR
BODE
BODO
BODS
BODY
BUDD
BUDS
BVDS

B••D
BALD
BAND
BARD
BAUD
BEAD
BEND
BIGD
BIND
BIRD
BLED
BLVD
BOLD
BOND
BOYD
BRAD
BRED
BSED
BUDD
BUND
BYRD

•B•D
ABED
IBID
OBAD

••BD
STBD

BE••
BEAD
BEAK
BEAL
BEAM
BEAN
BEAR
BEAS
BEAT
BEAU
BEBE
BECK
BEDE
BEDS
BEEB
BEEF
BEEN
BEEP
BEER
BEES
BEET
BEGS
BEIN
BELA
BELG
BELL
BELO
BELS
BELT
BELY
BEMA
BEMS
BEND
BENE
BENG
BENI
BENT
BENU
BENZ
BERG
BERM
BERN
BERT
BESO
BESS
BEST
BETA
BETE
BETH
BETS
BETZ
BEVY
BEYS

B•E•
BAER
BAEZ
BEEB
BEEF
BEEN
BEEP
BEER
BEES
BEET
BIEL
BIEN
BLEB
BLED
BLEU
BLEW
BOER
BREA
BRED
BREL
BREN
BRER
BRET
BREV
BREW
BSEC
BSED
BYES

B••E
BABE
BADE
BAKE
BALE
BANE
BARE
BASE
BATE
BEBE
BEDE
BENE
BETE
BICE
BIDE
BIKE
BILE
BINE
BISE
BITE
BLUE
BODE
BOLE
BONE
BORE
BOSE
BOWE
BPOE
BRAE
BRIE
BUTE
BYRE
BYTE

•BE•
ABED
ABEL
ABER
ABET
CBER
IBET
IBEX
MBES
OBEY
UBER

•B•E
ABBE
ABIE
ABLE
IBLE
OBIE
OBOE

••BE
ABBE
AUBE
BABE
BEBE
CUBE
ELBE
GABE
GIBE
HABE
HEBE
JIBE
KOBE
LOBE
LUBE
NEBE
RABE
ROBE
RUBE
SABE
SEBE
TUBE
VIBE

B•F•
BAFF
BIFF
BOFF
BUFF

B••F
BAFF
BEEF
BIFF
BOFF
BUFF

B•G•
BAGS
BEGS
BIGD
BOGS
BOGY
BUGS

B••G
BANG
BELG
BENG
BERG
BING
BIOG
BONG
BORG
BRAG
BRIG
BULG
BUNG
BURG
BYNG

B•H•
BAHR
BAHS
BAHT
BOHM
BOHR
BUHL
BUHR

B••H
BACH
BASH
BATH
BETH
BLAH
BOSH
BOTH
BUSH

••BH
COBH

BI••
BIAK
BIAS
BIBB
BIBI
BIBL
BIBS
BICE
BICS
BIDE
BIDS
BIEL
BIEN
BIFF
BIGD
BIKE
BIKO
BILE
BILK
BILL
BIND
BINE
BING
BINS
BIOG
BIOL
BION
BIOS
BIRD
BIRK
BIRL
BIRR
BISE
BITE
BITS
BITT
BIWA

B•I•
BAIL
BAIN
BAIO
BAIT
BEIN
BLIN
BLIP
BLIT
BOIL
BOIS
BRIC
BRIE
BRIG
BRIM
BRIO
BRIT
BRIX

B••I
BALI
BANI
BARI
BENI
BIBI
BNAI
BONI
BURI

•BI•
ABIB
ABIE
DBIB
IBID
IBIS
OBIE
OBIS
OBIT
RBIS

•B•I
ABRI

••BI
ALBI
AMBI
BIBI
DEBI
GOBI
RABI
TABI

B•J•
BAJA

••BJ
SUBJ

B•K•
BAKE
BAKR
BAKU
BIKE
BIKO

B••K
BACK
BALK
BANK
BARK
BASK
BEAK
BECK
BIAK
BILK
BIRK
BOCK
BONK
BOOK
BORK
BOSK
BUCK
BULK
BUNK
BUSK

••BK
HDBK

BL••
BLAB
BLAH
BLAS
BLAT
BLAU
BLDG
BLDR
BLEB
BLED
BLEU
BLEW
BLIN
BLIP
BLIT
BLOB
BLOC
BLOT
BLOW
BLTS
BLUE
BLUM
BLUR
BLVD

B•L•
BALD
BALE
BALI
BALK
BALL
BALM
BALT
BBLS
BELA
BELG
BELL
BELO
BELS
BELT
BELY
BILE
BILK
BILL
BOLA
BOLD
BOLE
BOLL
BOLO
BOLT
BULB
BULG
BULK
BULL

B••L
BAAL
BAIL
BALL
BAWL
BEAL
BELL
BIBL
BIEL
BILL
BIOL
BIRL
BOIL
BOLL
BOWL
BREL
BUHL
BULL
BURL

•BL•
ABLE
ABLY
BBLS
EBLA
IBLE

•B•L
ABEL
OBOL

••BL
BIBL
PUBL

BM••
BMOC
BMUS
BMWS

B•M•
BAMA
BAMS
BEMA
BEMS
BOMA
BOMB
BOMP
BOMU
BSMT
BUMP
BUMS

B••M
BALM
BARM
BAUM
BDRM
BEAM
BERM
BLUM
BOHM
BOOM
BRAM
BRIM
BROM

•BM•
ABMS

••BM
ICBM
IRBM
SLBM

BN••
BNAI

B•N•
BANC
BAND
BANE
BANG
BANI
BANK
BANS
BEND
BENE
BENG
BENI
BENT
BENU
BENZ
BIND
BINE
BING
BINS
BONA
BOND
BONE
BONG
BONI
BONK
BONN
BONO
BONY
BRNO
BUNA
BUND
BUNG
BUNK
BUNS
BUNT
BYNG

B••N
BAIN
BARN
BEAN
BEEN
BEIN
BERN
BIEN
BION
BLIN
BONN
BOON
BORN
BOSN
BRAN
BREN
BRYN
BURN

•B•N
EBAN
EBON
IBAN

••BN
ISBN
NEBN
NWBN

BO••
BOAC
BOAR
BOAS
BOAT
BOAZ
BOBS
BOCA
BOCK
BODE
BODO
BODS
BODY
BOER
BOFF
BOGS
BOGY
BOHM
BOHR
BOIL
BOIS
BOLA
BOLD
BOLE
BOLL
BOLO
BOLT
BOMA
BOMB
BOMP
BOMU
BONA
BOND
BONE
BONG
BONI
BONK
BONN
BONO
BONY
BOOB
BOOK
BOOM
BOON
BOOP
BOOR
BOOS
BOOT
BOPP
BOPS
BORA
BORE
BORG
BORK
BORN
BORO
BORS
BORT
BOSC
BOSE
BOSH
BOSK
BOSN
BOSS
BOTA
BOTH
BOTS
BOTT
BOUT
BOVA
BOWE
BOWL
BOWS
BOXY
BOYD
BOYS
BOYZ
BOZO

B•O•
BBOY
BIOG
BIOL
BION
BIOS
BLOB
BLOC
BLOT
BLOW
BMOC
BOOB
BOOK
BOOM
BOON
BOOP
BOOR
BOOS
BOOT
BPOE
BROM
BROS
BROW
BROZ
BUOY
BYOB

B••O
BAIO
BARO
BELO
BESO
BIKO
BODO
BOLO
BONO
BORO
BOZO
BRIO
BRNO
BRYO
BUCO

•BO•
ABOU
BBOY
EBON
IBOS
MBOY
OBOE
OBOL

•B•O
EBRO

••BO
AMBO
DABO
GABO
GOBO
HOBO
IGBO
KOBO
LOBO
NEBO
ROBO
UMBO

BP••
BPOE

B•P•
BAPS
BAPT
BOPP
BOPS

B••P
BEEP
BLIP
BOMP
BOOP
BOPP
BUMP
BURP

•B•P
TBSP

B•Q•
BBQS

•BQ•
BBQS

BR••
BRAC
BRAD
BRAE
BRAG
BRAM
BRAN
BRAS
BRAT
BRAW
BRAY
BRAZ
BREA
BRED
BREL
BREN
BRER
BRET
BREV
BREW
BRIC
BRIE
BRIG
BRIM
BRIO
BRIT
BRIX
BRNO
BROM
BROS
BROW
BROZ
BRUT
BRYN
BRYO

B•R•
BARA
BARB
BARD
BARE
BARI
BARK
BARM
BARN
BARO
BARR
BARS
BART
BDRM
BERG
BERM
BERN
BERT
BIRD
BIRK
BIRL
BIRR
BORA
BORE
BORG
BORK
BORN
BORO
BORS
BORT
BURB
BURG
BURI
BURL
BURN
BURP
BURR
BURS
BURT
BURY
BYRD
BYRE

B••R
BAER
BAHR
BAKR
BARR
BEAR
BEER
BIRR
BLDR
BLUR
BOAR
BOER
BOHR
BOOR
BRER
BUHR
BURR

•BR•
ABRI
EBRO

•B•R
ABBR
ABER
CBER
IBAR
JBAR
LBAR
TBAR
UBER
ZBAR

••BR
ABBR
GRBR
GTBR
HEBR
NEBR

BS••
BSEC
BSED
BSMT

B•S•
BASC BASE BASH BASK BASS BAST BESO BESS BEST BISE BOSC BOSE BOSH BOSK BOSN BOSS BUSH BUSK BUSS BUST BUSY

B••S
BAAS BABS BACS BAGS BAHS BAMS BANS BAPS BARS BASS BATS BAYS BBLS BBQS BEAS BEDS BEES BEGS BELS BEMS BESS BETS BEYS BIAS BIBS BICS BIDS BINS BIOS BITS BLAS BLTS BMUS BMWS BOAS BOBS BODS BOGS BOIS BOOS BOPS BORS BOSS BOTS BOWS BOYS BRAS BROS BTUS BUCS BUDS BUGS BUMS BUNS BURS BUSS BUTS BUYS BVDS BYES

•BS•
TBSP

•B•S
ABAS ABBS ABCS ABMS BBLS BBQS EBBS IBIS IBOS MBAS MBES OBIS RBIS

••BS
ABBS ALBS AMBS APBS ARBS BABS BIBS BOBS CABS COBS CUBS DABS DEBS DIBS DUBS EBBS FIBS FOBS GABS GIBS GOBS HOBS HUBS JABS JIBS JOBS KOBS LABS LIBS LLBS LOBS MIBS MOBS NABS NEBS NIBS NOBS NUBS ORBS PCBS PUBS REBS RHBS RIBS ROBS RUBS SEBS SIBS SOBS SUBS SWBS TABS TUBS URBS WEBS YOBS

BT••
BTUS

B•T•
BATE BATH BATS BATT BETA BETE BETH BETS BETZ BITE BITS BITT BLTS BOTA BOTH BOTS BOTT BUTE BUTS BUTT BYTE

B••T
BACT BAHT BAIT BALT BAPT BART BAST BATT BEAT BEET BELT BENT BERT BEST BITT BLAT BLIT BLOT BOAT BOLT BOOT BORT BOTT BOUT BRAT BRET BRIT BRUT BSMT BUNT BURT BUST BUTT

•B•T
ABET ABUT IBET OBIT

••BT
DEBT

BU••
BUCK BUCO BUCS BUDD BUDS BUFF BUGS BUHL BUHR BULB BULG BULK BULL BUMP BUMS BUNA BUND BUNG BUNK BUNS BUNT BUOY BURB BURG BURI BURL BURN BURP BURR BURS BURT BURY BUSH BUSK BUSS BUST BUSY BUTE BUTS BUTT BUYS BUZZ

B•U•
BAUD BAUM BLUE BLUM BLUR BMUS BOUT BRUT BTUS

B••U
BABU BAKU BEAU BENU BLAU BLEU BOMU

•BU•
ABUT

•B•U
ABOU

••BU
BABU CEBU SABU TABU ZEBU

BV••
BVDS

B•V•
BEVY BLVD BOVA

B••V
BREV

B•W•
BAWL BIWA BMWS BOWE BOWL BOWS

B••W
BLEW BLOW BRAW BREW BROW

••BW
NWBW SWBW

B•X•
BOXY

B••X
BRIX

•B•X
IBEX

BY••
BYES BYNG BYOB BYRD BYRE BYTE

B•Y•
BAYA BAYS BEYS BOYD BOYS BOYZ BRYN BRYO BUYS

B••Y
BABY BBOY BELY BEVY BODY BOGY BONY BOXY BRAY BUOY BURY BUSY

•B•Y
ABBY ABLY BBOY MBOY OBEY

••BY
ABBY BABY GABY GOBY MOBY RUBY TCBY TOBY

B•Z•
BOZO BUZZ

B••Z
BAEZ BENZ BETZ BOAZ BOYZ BRAZ BROZ BUZZ

CA••
CAAN CABS CACO CADE CADI CADS CAEN CAFE CAGE CAGY CAHN CAIN CAKE CAKY CALC CALE CALF CALI CALK CALL CALM CALS CALX CAMA CAME CAMI CAMO CAMP CAMS CANA CANC CANE CANS CANT CAPA CAPE CAPN CAPO CAPP CAPS CAPT CARA CARB CARD CARE CARK CARL CARO CARP CARR CARS CART CARY CASA CASE CASH CASK CASS CAST CATA CATE CATH CATO CATS CATT CATV CAUL CAUS CAVA CAVE CAVS CAVY CAWS CAYS

C•A•
CAAN CHAD CHAM CHAN CHAP CHAR CHAS CHAT CHAW CHAZ CIAO CLAD CLAM CLAN CLAP CLAR CLAW CLAY COAL COAT COAX CPAS CRAB CRAG CRAM CRAT CRAW CRAY CYAN CZAR

C••A
CAMA CANA CAPA CARA CASA CATA CAVA CELA CENA CERA CETA CHIA COCA CODA COLA COMA CORA COSA COXA CUBA CUNA CYMA

•CA•
ACAD ICAL KCAL MCAT NCAA OCAS RCAF SCAB SCAD SCAM SCAN SCAR SCAT

•C•A
ACEA ACTA ECUA NCAA OCTA UCLA

••CA
BOCA COCA DECA FICA INCA MICA ORCA PACA PICA RICA ROCA SOCA SPCA VACA YMCA YWCA

CB••
CBER

C•B•
CABS CEBU COBB COBH COBS CUBA CUBE CUBS

C••B
CARB CHUB CLUB COBB COMB CRAB CRIB CURB

•CB•
ICBM PCBS TCBY

•C•B
SCAB

CC••
CCCI CCCL CCCP CCCV CCCX CCII CCIV CCIX CCLI CCLV CCLX CCTV CCVI CCXC CCXI CCXL CCXV CCXX

C•C•
CACO CCCI CCCL CCCP CCCV CCCX COCA COCK COCO CXCI CXCV CYCL

C••C
CALC CANC CCXC CDXC CHIC CHOC CINC CIRC CMXC COFC CONC CROC

•CC•
ACCS ACCT CCCI CCCL CCCP CCCV CCCX DCCC DCCI DCCL DCCV DCCX ECCE ECCL MCCC MCCI MCCL MCCV MCCX

•C•C
ACDC CCXC DCCC DCXC MCCC MCXC

••CC
DCCC MCCC MDCC MLCC MMCC SNCC SPCC

CD••
CDII CDIV CDIX CDLI CDLV CDLX CDRS CDVI CDXC CDXI CDXL CDXV CDXX

C•D•
CADE CADI CADS CEDE CEDI CIDE CMDG CMDR CODA CODE CODS CODY CUDS

C••D
CARD CHAD CHID CLAD CLOD COED COLD COMD COND CORD CRUD CUED CURD

•CD•
ACDC LCDS MCDI MCDL MCDV MCDX

•C•D
ACAD ACED ACID ICED SCAD SCUD

••CD
MMCD RECD

CE••
CEBU CEDE CEDI CEES CEIL CELA CELL CELS CELT CENA CENO CENS CENT CEOS CEPE CEPS CERA CERE CERF CERN CERO CERT CESS CEST CETA CETE

C•E•
CAEN CBER CEES CHEE CHEF CHEM CHEN CHER CHET CHEW CHEX CHEZ CIEL CLEF CLEM CLEO CLEW COED COEL COEN CREE CREW CUED CUER CUES

C••E
CADE CAFE CAGE CAKE CALE CAME CANE CAPE CARE CASE CATE CAVE CEDE CEPE CERE CETE CHEE CIDE CINE CIRE CITE CLUE CODE COKE COLE COME CONE COPE CORE COTE COUE COVE CREE CRUE CTGE CUBE CUKE CULE CURE CUTE CYME CYTE

•CE•
ACEA ACED ACER ACES ACET ACEY ICED ICEL ICER ICES ICET

•C•E
ACHE ACME ACNE ACRE ACTE ECCE

••CE
ANCE BICE DACE DICE DUCE DYCE ECCE ENCE ESCE FACE FICE LACE LICE LUCE MACE MICE NICE ONCE PACE PUCE RACE RICE SYCE VICE VOCE WACE

C•F•
CAFE COFC COFS CUFF CUFT

C••F
CALF CERF CHEF CLEF COIF CONF CORF CUFF

•C•F
RCAF

C•G•
CAGE CAGY CHGS CIGS COGS CTGE

C••G
CHUG CLOG CMDG CONG CRAG

•C•G
ACTG

••CG
USCG

CH••
CHAD CHAM CHAN CHAP CHAR CHAS CHAT CHAW CHAZ CHEE CHEF CHEM CHEN CHER CHET CHEW CHEX CHEZ CHGS CHIA CHIC CHID CHIN CHIP CHIS CHIT CHMN CHOC CHOL CHON CHOP CHOU CHOW CHOY CHUB CHUG CHUM CHUR

C•H•
CAHN COHN COHO

C••H
CASH CATH COBH COSH CUSH

•CH•
ACHE ACHT ACHY ECHO ECHT OCHO OCHS TCHR

•C•H
ACTH

••CH
ARCH ASCH BACH DICH EACH ETCH EXCH FOCH HOCH INCH ITCH KOCH LECH LOCH MACH MECH MICH MUCH ORCH OUCH RICH SECH SUCH TACH TECH WYCH YECH ZECH

CI••
CIAO CIDE CIEL CIGS CIII CINC CINE CINQ CION CIRC CIRE CIST CITE CITS CITY

C•I•
CAIN CCII CCIV CCIX CDII CDIV CDIX CEIL CHIA CHIC CHID CHIN CHIP CHIS CHIT CIII CLII CLIN CLIO CLIP CLIV CLIX CMII CMIV CMIX COIF COIL COIN COIR CRIB CRIM CRIN CRIT CUIN CVII CXII CXIV CXIX

C••I
CADI CALI CAMI CCCI CCII CCLI CCVI CCXI CDII CDLI CDVI CDXI CEDI CIII CLII CLVI CLXI CMII CMLI CMVI CMXI CORI CVII CXCI CXII CXLI CXVI CXXI

•CI•
ACID ACIS CCII CCIV CCIX DCII DCIV DCIX MCII MCIV MCIX SCIL XCII XCIV XCIX

•C•I
ACTI CCCI CCII CCLI CCVI CCXI DCCI DCII DCLI DCVI DCXI MCCI MCDI MCII MCLI MCMI MCVI MCXI SCSI XCII XCVI

••CI
ASCI CCCI CXCI DCCI DECI DXCI FOCI LOCI MCCI MDCI MMCI MXCI UNCI VICI

C•J•
CUJO

C••J
CONJ

C•K•
CAKE CAKY COKE COKY CUKE

C••K
CALK CARK CASK COCK CONK COOK CORK CUSK

•CK•
ICKY

••CK
BACK BECK BOCK BUCK COCK DECK DICK DOCK DUCK EYCK GUCK HACK HECK HICK HOCK HUCK JACK JOCK KICK LACK LICK LOCK LUCK MACK MICK MOCK MUCK NECK NICK NOCK PACK PECK PICK PUCK RACK RICK ROCK RUCK SACK SICK SOCK SUCK TACK TICK TOCK TUCK WACK WICK YUCK ZACK

CL••
CLAD CLAM CLAN CLAP CLAR CLAW CLAY CLEF CLEM CLEO CLEW CLII CLIN CLIO CLIP CLIV CLIX CLOD CLOG CLOP CLOT CLOY CLUB CLUE CLVI CLXI CLXV CLXX

C•L•
CALC CALE CALF CALI CALK CALL CALM CALS CALX CCLI CCLV CCLX CDLI CDLV CDLX CELA CELL CELS CELT CMLI CMLV CMLX COLA COLD COLE COLL COLO COLS COLT COLY CPLS CULE CULL CULM CULP CULS CULT CXLI CXLV

C••L
CALL CARL CAUL CCCL CCXL CDXL CEIL CELL CHOL CIEL CMXL COAL COEL COIL COLL COML COOL COWL CULL CURL CYCL

•CL•
ACLU CCLI CCLV CCLX

DCLI DCLV DCLX MCLI MCLV MCLX UCLA

•C•L
ACYL CCCL CCXL DCCL DCXL ECCL ECOL ICAL ICEL KCAL MCCL MCDL MCML MCXL SCIL

••CL
CCCL CYCL DCCL DECL ECCL ENCL EXCL INCL MCCL MDCL MMCL NACL

CM••
CMDG CMDR CMII CMIV CMIX CMLI CMLV CMLX CMON CMOS CMVI CMXC CMXI CMXL CMXV CMXX

C•M•
CAMA CAME CAMI CAMO CAMP CAMS CHMN COMA COMB COMD COME COML COMM COMO COMP COMR CWMS CYMA CYME

C••M
CALM CHAM CHEM CHUM CLAM CLEM COMM CORM COSM CRAM CRIM CULM

•CM•
ACME MCMI MCML MCMV MCMX RCMP

•C•M
ICBM SCAM SCUM

••CM
MMCM

CN••
CNUT

C•N•
CANA CANC CANE CANS CANT CENA CENO CENS CENT CINC CINE CINQ CONC COND CONE CONF CONG CONJ CONK CONN CONS CONT CONV CONY CTNS CUNA CUNY

C••N
CAAN CAEN CAHN CAIN CAPN CERN CHAN CHEN CHIN CHMN CHON CION CLAN CLIN CMON COEN COHN COIN CONN COON CORN CRIN CUIN CYAN

•CN•
ACNE

•C•N
DCON ECON ICON SCAN

CO••
COAL COAT COAX COBB COBH COBS COCA COCK COCO CODA CODE CODS CODY COED COEL COEN COFC COFS COGS COHN COHO COIF COIL COIN COIR COKE COKY COLA COLD COLE COLL COLO COLS COLT COLY COMA COMB COMD COME COML COMM COMO COMP COMR CONC COND CONE CONF CONG CONJ CONK CONN CONS CONT CONV CONY COOK COOL COON COOP COOS COOT COPE COPS COPT COPY CORA CORD CORE CORF CORI CORK CORM CORN CORO CORP CORR CORY COSA COSH COSM COST COSY COTE COTS COTY COUE COUP COVE COWL COWS COXA COZY

C•O•
CEOS CHOC CHOL CHON CHOP CHOU CHOW CHOY CION CLOD CLOG CLOP CLOT CLOY CMON CMOS COOK COOL COON COOP COOS COOT CPOS CROC CROP CROW CWOS

C••O
CACO CAMO CAPO CARO CATO CENO CERO CIAO CLEO CLIO COCO COHO COLO COMO CORO CRYO CUJO CYTO

•CO•
DCON ECOL ECON ICON ICOS NCOS SCOP SCOT SCOW

•C•O
ACRO ECHO ECTO OCHO OCTO

••CO
ARCO ASCO BUCO CACO COCO DECO EKCO LOCO MECO MYCO PICO POCO RICO TACO TICO WACO

CP••
CPAS CPLS CPOS

C•P•
CAPA CAPE CAPN CAPO CAPP CAPS CAPT CEPE CEPS COPE COPS COPT COPY CUPR CUPS

C••P
CAMP CAPP CARP CCCP CHAP CHIP CHCP CLAP CLIP CLOP COMP COOP CORP COUP CROP CULP CUSP

•CP•
RCPT

•C•P
CCCP RCMP SCOP SCUP

••CP
CCCP FACP FRCP

C••Q
CINQ

CR••
CRAB CRAG CRAM CRAT CRAW CRAY CREE CREW CRIB CRIM CRIN CRIT CROC CROP CROW CRTS CRUD CRUE CRUS CRUX CRUZ CRYO

C•R•
CARA CARB CARD CARE CARK CARL CARO CARP CARR CARS CART CARY CDRS CERA CERE CERF CERN CERO CERT CIRC CIRE CORA CORD CORE CORF CORI CORK CORM CORN CORO CORP CORR CORY CURB CURD CURE CURL CURR CURS CURT

C••R
CARR CBER CHAR CHER CHUR CLAR CMDR COIR COMR CORR CUER CUPR CURR CZAR

•CR•
ACRE ACRO ECRU SCRY VCRS

•C•R
ACER ICER SCAR TCHR

••CR
INCR MICR

C•S•
CASA CASE CASH CASK CASS CAST CESS CEST CIST COSA COSH COSM COST COSY CUSH CUSK CUSP CUSS

C••S
CABS CADS CALS CAMS CANS CAPS CARS CASS CATS CAUS CAVS CAWS CAYS CDRS CEES CELS CENS CEOS CEPS CESS CHAS CHGS CHIS CIGS CITS CMOS COBS CODS COFS COGS COLS CONS COOS COPS COTS COWS CPAS CPLS CPOS CRTS CRUS CTNS CUBS CUDS CUES CULS CUPS CURS CUSS CUTS CWMS CWOS

•CS•
SCSI

•C•S
ACCS ACES ACIS ACTS ECUS ICES ICOS ICUS LCDS NCOS OCAS OCHS PCBS RCTS VCRS

••CS
ABCS ACCS ADCS ARCS BACS BICS BUCS DOCS DSCS ENCS FACS FRCS LACS MACS MICS MOCS ORCS PACS PECS PFCS PICS RECS ROCS SACS SECS SICS TECS TICS VACS WACS

CT••
CTGE CTNS

C•T•
CATA CATE CATH CATO CATS CATT CATV CCTV CETA CETE CITE CITS CITY COTE COTS COTY CRTS CUTE CUTS CYTE CYTO

C••T
CANT CAPT CART CAST CATT CELT CENT CERT CEST CHAT CHET CHIT CIST CLOT CNUT COAT COLT CONT COOT COPT COST CRAT CRIT CUFT CULT CURT

•CT•
ACTA ACTE ACTG ACTH ACTI ACTS ACTV CCTV ECTO OCTA OCTO RCTS WCTU

•C•T
ACCT ACET ACHT ECHT ICET MCAT RCPT SCAT SCOT SCUT

••CT
ACCT BACT DICT DUCT FACT FICT HECT LACT LECT PACT PICT RECT SECT TACT

CU••
CUBA CUBE CUBS CUDS CUED CUER CUES CUFF CUFT CUIN CUJO CUKE CULE CULL CULM CULP CULS CULT CUNA CUNY CUPR CUPS CURB CURD CURE CURL CURR CURS CURT CUSH CUSK CUSP CUSS CUTE CUTS

C•U•
CAUL CAUS CHUB CHUG CHUM CHUR CLUB CLUE CNUT COUE COUP CRUD CRUE CRUS CRUX CRUZ

C••U
CEBU CHOU

•CU•
ECUA ECUS ICUS SCUD SCUM SCUP SCUT

•C•U
ACLU ECRU WCTU

CV••
CVII

C•V•
CAVA CAVE CAVS CAVY CCVI CDVI CLVI CMVI COVE CXVI

C••V
CATV CCCV CCIV CCLV CCTV CCXV CDIV CDLV CDXV CLIV CLXV CMIV CMLV CMXV CONV CXCV CXIV CXLV CXXV

•CV•
CCVI DCVI MCVI XCVI

•C•V
ACTV CCCV CCIV CCLV CCTV CCXV DCCV DCIV DCLV DCXV MCCV MCDV MCIV MCLV MCMV MCXV XCIV

••CV
CCCV CXCV DCCV DXCV MCCV MDCV MMCV MXCV

CW••
CWMS CWOS

C•W•
CAWS COWL COWS

C••W
CHAW CHEW CHOW CLAW CLEW CRAW CREW CROW

•C•W
SCOW

CX••
CXCI CXCV CXII CXIV CXIX CXLI CXLV CXVI CXXI CXXV CXXX

C•X•
CCXC CCXI CCXL CCXV CCXX CDXC CDXI CDXL CDXV CDXX CLXI CLXV CLXX CMXC CMXI CMXL CMXV CMXX COXA CXXI CXXV CXXX

C••X
CALX CCCX CCIX CCLX CCXX CDIX CDLX CDXX CHEX CLIX CLXX CMIX CMLX CMXX COAX CRUX CXIX CXXX

•CX•
CCXC CCXI CCXL CCXV CCXX DCXC DCXI DCXL DCXV DCXX MCXC MCXI MCXL MCXV MCXX

•C•X
CCCX CCIX CCLX CCXX DCCX DCIX DCLX DCXX MCCX MCDX MCIX MCLX MCMX MCXX XCIX

••CX
CCCX DCCX MCCX MDCX MMCX

CY••
CYAN CYCL CYMA CYME CYTE CYTO

C•Y•
CAYS CRYO

C••Y
CAGY CAKY CARY CAVY CHOY CITY CLAY CLOY CODY COKY COLY CONY COPY CORY COSY COTY COZY CRAY CUNY

•CY•
ACYL

•C•Y
ACEY ACHY ICKY SCRY TCBY

••CY
AGCY ANCY ENCY LACY LUCY MACY RACY SECY

CZ••
CZAR

C•Z•
COZY

C••Z
CHAZ CHEZ CRUZ

DA••
DABO DABS DACE DADA DADE DADO DADS DAFF DAFT DAGS DAHL DAHS DAIN DAIS DALE DALI DALY DAMA DAME DAMN DAMP DAMS DANA DANE DANG DANK DANL DANO DANU DAPS DARD DARE DARI DARK DARN DART DASD DASH DATA DATE DATS DAUB DAVE DAVY DAWN DAWS DAYO DAYS DAZE

D•A•
DDAY DEAD DEAF DEAL DEAN DEAR DHAL DIAG DIAL DIAM DIAN DIAS DIAZ DOAK DRAB DRAG DRAM DRAT DRAW DRAY DUAD DUAL DYAD DYAK DYAN

D••A
DADA DAMA DANA DATA DECA DEJA DEKA DINA DIVA DOHA DONA DOPA DORA DUMA DUNA DURA DYNA

•DA•
ADAH ADAK ADAM ADAR DDAY EDAM IDAE NDAK ODAS ODAY RDAS SDAK VDAY

•D•A
EDDA EDNA EDTA IDEA ODEA

••DA
AIDA ALDA CODA DADA EDDA ERDA JADA LEDA NADA PODA SADA SODA TADA USDA VEDA VIDA YODA

DB••
DBIB

D•B•
DABO DABS DEBI DEBS DEBT DIBS DUBS

D••B
DAUB DBIB DRAB DRIB DRUB DUMB

•DB•
HDBK

DC••
DCCC DCCI DCCL DCCV DCCX DCII DCIV DCIX DCLI DCLV DCLX DCON DCVI DCXC DCXI DCXL DCXV DCXX

D•C•
DACE DCCC DCCI DCCL DCCV DCCX DECA DECI DECK DECL DECO DICE DICH DICK DICT DOCK DOCS DSCS DUCE DUCK DUCT DXCI DXCV DYCE

D••C
DCCC DCXC DESC DISC

•DC•
ADCS MDCC MDCI MDCL MDCV MDCX

•D•C
CDXC EDUC FDIC MDCC MDXC ODIC

••DC
ACDC MMDC

DD••
DDAY

D•D•
DADA DADE DADO DADS DIDO DMDS DODD DODO DUDE DUDS

D••D
DARD DASD DEAD DEED DIED DODD DOWD DRED DUAD DYAD DYED

•DD•
ADDN ADDS ADDY EDDA EDDO EDDS EDDY ODDS

••DD
BUDD DODD FUDD JUDD KIDD LADD MADD MUDD REDD RIDD RUDD SADD SUDD TODD

DE••
DEAD DEAF DEAL DEAN DEAR DEBI DEBS DEBT DECA DECI DECK DECL DECO DEED DEEM DEEP DEER

DEET
DEFS
DEFT
DEFY
DEGS
DEIL
DEJA
DEKA
DEKE
DELE
DELI
DELL
DELS
DELY
DEME
DEMI
DEMO
DEMS
DEMY
DENE
DENG
DENS
DENT
DENY
DEPP
DEPT
DERM
DERN
DESC
DESI
DESK
DETS
DEUM
DEUS
DEUT
DEUX
DEVI
DEVO
DEWS
DEWY
DEYS

D•E•
DEED
DEEM
DEEP
DEER
DEET
DIED
DIEM
DIEN
DIES
DIET
DIEU
DOER
DOES
DRED
DREE
DREG
DREI
DREW
DUEL
DUES
DUET
DYED
DYER
DYES

D••E
DACE
DADE
DALE
DAME
DANE
DARE
DATE
DAVE
DAZE
DEKE
DELE
DEME
DENE
DICE
DIKE
DIME
DINE
DIRE
DIVE
DOGE
DOLE
DOME
DONE
DOPE
DORE
DOSE
DOTE
DOVE
DOZE
DREE
DUCE
DUDE
DUKE
DUNE
DUPE
DUSE
DUVE
DYCE
DYNE

•DE•
ADEN
ADES
EDEN
EDER
IDEA
IDEE
IDEM
IDEO
IDES
ODEA
ODER
ODES

•D•E
ADUE
ADZE
EDGE
EDIE
HDWE
IDAE
IDEE
IDLE
MDSE
ODIE

••DE
AIDE
AUDE
BADE
BEDE
BIDE
BODE
CADE
CEDE
CIDE
CODE
DADE
DUDE
ENDE
ERDE
FADE
FIDE
GIDE
HADE
HIDE
HYDE
JADE
JUDE
LADE
LODE
MADE
MEDE
MODE
NIDE
NODE
NUDE
OLDE
PODE
RIDE
RODE
RUDE
SADE
SIDE
TIDE
VADE
VIDE
WADE
WIDE

D•F•
DAFF
DAFT
DEFS
DEFT
DEFY
DIFF
DOFF
DUFF
DUFY

D••F
DAFF
DEAF
DIFF
DOFF
DOLF
DUFF

D•G•
DAGS
DEGS
DIGS
DOGE
DOGG
DOGS
DOGY

D••G
DANG
DENG
DIAG
DING
DOGG
DONG
DOUG
DRAG
DREG
DRUG

•DG•
EDGE
EDGY

••DG
BLDG
CMDG
JUDG

DH••
DHAL
DHOW

D•H•
DAHL
DAHS
DOHA

D••H
DASH
DICH
DISH
DOTH

•DH•
EDHS

•D•H
ADAH

••DH
NADH
SIDH
YODH

DI••
DIAG
DIAL
DIAM
DIAN
DIAS
DIAZ
DIBS
DICE
DICH
DICK
DICT
DIDO
DIED
DIEM
DIEN
DIES
DIET
DIEU
DIFF
DIGS
DIII
DIKE
DILL
DIME
DIMS
DINA
DINE
DING
DINK
DINO
DINS
DINT
DION
DIOR
DIOS
DIPL
DIPS
DIRE
DIRK
DIRS
DIRT
DISC
DISH
DISK
DISS
DIST
DITS
DITZ
DIVA
DIVE
DIVS

D•I•
DAIN
DAIS
DBIB
DCII
DCIV
DCIX
DEIL
DIII
DLII
DLIT
DLIV
DLIX
DOIL
DOIN
DOIT
DRIB
DRIP
DRIQ
DVII
DXII
DXIV
DXIX

D••I
DALI
DARI
DCCI
DCII
DCLI
DCVI
DCXI
DEBI
DECI
DELI
DEMI
DESI
DEVI
DIII
DLII
DLVI
DLXI
DREI
DVII
DXCI
DXII
DXLI
DXVI
DXXI

•DI•
ADIN
ADIT
CDII
CDIV
CDIX
EDIE
EDIT
FDIC
IDIO
MDII
MDIV
MDIX
ODIC
ODIE
ODIN
XDIV

•D•I
CDII
CDLI
CDVI
CDXI
MDCI
MDII
MDLI
MDVI
MDXI

••DI
AUDI
CADI
CEDI
JEDI
LODI
MCDI
MIDI
MMDI
NIDI
NODI
NUDI
PEDI
QADI
REDI
RUDI
VIDI
WADI

D•J•
DEJA
DOJO

•DJ•
ADJS
ADJT

••DJ
HADJ

DK••
DKNY

D•K•
DEKA
DEKE
DIKE
DUKE

D••K
DANK
DARK
DECK
DESK
DICK
DINK
DIRK
DISK
DOAK
DOCK
DUCK
DUNK
DUSK
DYAK

•D•K
ADAK
HDBK
NDAK
SDAK

DL••
DLII
DLIT
DLIV
DLIX
DLVI
DLXI
DLXV
DLXX

D•L•
DALE
DALI
DALY
DCLI
DCLV
DCLX
DELE
DELI
DELL
DELS
DELY
DILL
DOLE
DOLF
DOLL
DOLT
DULL
DULY
DXLI
DXLV

D••L
DAHL
DANL
DCCL
DCXL
DEAL
DECL
DEIL
DELL
DHAL
DIAL
DILL
DIPL
DOIL
DOLL
DUAL
DUEL
DULL

•DL•
CDLI
CDLV
CDLX
IDLE
IDLY
MDLI
MDLV
MDLX

•D•L
CDXL
IDOL
IDYL
MDCL
MDXL

••DL
MCDL
MMDL

DM••
DMDS
DMSO

D•M•
DAMA
DAME
DAMN
DAMP
DAMS
DEME
DEMI
DEMO
DEMS
DEMY
DIME
DIMS
DOME
DOMO
DOMS
DPMS
DSMS
DUMA
DUMB
DUMP
DVMS

D••M
DEEM
DERM
DEUM
DIAM
DIEM
DOOM
DORM
DRAM
DRUM

•DM•
ADMS

•D•M
ADAM
BDRM
EDAM
EDOM
IDEM

••DM
RADM
VADM

D•N•
DANA
DANE
DANG
DANK
DANL
DANO
DANU
DENE
DENG
DENS
DENT
DENY
DINA
DINE
DING
DINK
DINO
DINS
DINT
DKNY
DONA
DONE
DONG
DONS
DONT
DRNO
DUNA
DUNE
DUNK
DUNN
DUNS
DYNA
DYNE

D••N
DAIN
DAMN
DARN
DAWN
DCON
DEAN
DERN
DIAN
DIEN
DION
DOIN
DOON
DORN
DOWN
DUNN
DURN
DYAN

•DN•
EDNA

•D•N
ADDN
ADEN
ADIN
EDEN
IDUN
ODIN

••DN
ADDN
MIDN

DO••
DOAK
DOCK
DOCS
DODD
DODO
DOER
DOES
DOFF
DOGE
DOGG
DOGS
DOGY
DOHA
DOIL
DOIN
DOIT
DOJO
DOLE
DOLF
DOLL
DOLT
DOME
DOMO
DOMS
DONA
DONE
DONG
DONS
DONT
DOOM
DOON
DOOR
DOPA
DOPE
DOPY
DORA
DORE
DORM
DORN
DORP
DORR
DORS
DORT
DORY
DOSE
DOSS
DOST
DOTE
DOTH
DOTS
DOUG
DOUP
DOUR
DOUX
DOVE
DOWD
DOWN
DOZE
DOZY

D•O•
DCON
DHOW
DION
DIOR
DIOS
DOOM
DOON
DOOR
DROP
DSOS
DUOS

D••O
DABO
DADO
DANO
DAYO
DECO
DEMO
DEVO
DIDO
DINO
DMSO
DODO
DOJO
DOMO
DRNO
DURO

•DO•
EDOM
IDOL
ODOR
UDOS

•D•O
EDDO
IDEO
IDIO

••DO
ALDO
BODO
DADO
DIDO
DODO
EDDO
ENDO
FADO
FIDO
INDO
IODO
JUDO
LIDO
ORDO
PEDO
REDO
TODO
UNDO
UPDO

DP••
DPMS

D•P•
DAPS
DEPP
DEPT
DIPL
DIPS
DOPA
DOPE
DOPY
DUPE

D••P
DAMP
DEEP
DEPP
DORP
DOUP
DRIP
DROP
DUMP

••DP
AVDP
NADP

D••Q
DRIQ

DR••
DRAB
DRAG
DRAM
DRAT
DRAW
DRAY
DRED
DREE
DREG
DREI
DREW
DRIB
DRIP
DRIQ
DRNO
DROP
DRUB
DRUG
DRUM
DRYS

D•R•
DARD
DARE
DARI
DARK
DARN
DART
DERM
DERN
DIRE
DIRK
DIRS
DIRT
DORA
DORE
DORM
DORN
DORP
DORR
DORS
DORT
DORY
DURA
DURN
DURO

D••R
DEAR
DEER
DIOR
DOER
DOOR
DORR
DOUR
DYER

•DR•
BDRM
CDRS
LDRS

•D•R
ADAR
EDER
ODER
ODOR

••DR
BLDR
CMDR
HYDR
RMDR
SADR

DS••
DSCS
DSMS
DSOS

D•S•
DASD
DASH
DESC
DESI
DESK
DISC
DISH
DISK
DISS
DIST
DMSO
DOSE
DOSS
DOST
DUSE
DUSK
DUST

D••S
DABS
DADS
DAGS
DAHS
DAIS
DAMS
DAPS
DATS
DAWS
DAYS
DEBS
DEFS
DEGS
DELS
DEMS
DENS
DETS
DEUS
DEWS
DEYS
DIAS
DIBS
DIES
DIGS
DIMS
DINS
DIOS
DIPS
DIRS
DISS
DITS
DIVS
DMDS
DOCS
DOES
DOGS
DOMS
DONS
DORS
DOSS
DOTS
DPMS
DRYS
DSCS
DSMS
DSOS
DUBS
DUDS
DUES
DUNS
DUOS
DVMS
DYES

•DS•
MDSE

•D•S
ADCS
ADDS
ADES
ADJS
ADMS
CDRS
EDDS
EDHS
IDES
LDRS
ODAS
ODDS
ODES
RDAS
UDOS
VDTS

••DS
ADDS
AIDS
ANDS
BEDS
BIDS
BODS
BUDS
BVDS
CADS
CODS
CUDS
DADS
DMDS
DUDS
EADS
EDDS
ENDS
ETDS
FADS
FEDS
GADS
GODS
HODS
INDS
KIDS
LADS
LCDS
LEDS
LIDS
LLDS
MEDS
MODS
MUDS
NODS
ODDS
OLDS
OUDS
PADS
PEDS
PHDS
PODS
RADS
REDS
RFDS
RIDS
RNDS
RODS
SODS
STDS
SUDS
TADS
TEDS
TODS
WADS
WEDS
ZEDS

D•T•
DATA
DATE
DATS
DETS
DITS
DITZ
DOTE
DOTH
DOTS
DUTY

D••T
DAFT
DART
DEBT
DEET
DEFT
DENT
DEPT
DEUT
DICT
DIET
DINT
DIRT
DIST
DLIT
DOIT
DOLT
DONT
DORT
DOST
DRAT
DUCT
DUET
DUST

•DT•
EDTA
HDTV
VDTS

•D•T
ADIT
ADJT
ADVT
EDIT

DU••
DUAD
DUAL
DUBS
DUCE
DUCK
DUCT
DUDE
DUDS
DUEL
DUES
DUET
DUFF
DUFY
DUKE
DULL
DULY
DUMA
DUMB
DUMP
DUNA
DUNE
DUNK
DUNN
DUNS
DUOS
DUPE
DURA
DURN
DURO
DUSE
DUSK
DUST
DUTY
DUVE

D•U•
DAUB
DEUM
DEUS
DEUT
DEUX
DOUG
DOUP
DOUR
DOUX
DRUB
DRUG
DRUM

D••U
DANU
DIEU

•DU•
ADUE
EDUC
IDUN

••DU
KUDU
PUDU
URDU

DV••
DVII
DVMS

D•V•
DAVE
DAVY
DCVI
DEVI
DEVO
DIVA
DIVE
DIVS
DLVI
DOVE
DUVE
DXVI

D••V
DCCV
DCIV
DCLV
DCXV
DLIV
DLXV
DXCV
DXIV
DXLV
DXXV

•DV•
ADVT
CDVI
MDVI

•D•V
CDIV
CDLV
CDXV
HDTV
MDCV
MDIV
MDLV
MDXV
XDIV

••DV
MCDV
MMDV

D•W•
DAWN
DAWS
DEWS
DEWY
DOWD
DOWN

D••W
DHOW
DRAW
DREW

•DW•
HDWE

DX••
DXCI
DXCV
DXII
DXIV
DXIX
DXLI
DXLV
DXVI
DXXI
DXXV
DXXX

D•X•
DCXC
DCXI
DCXL
DCXV
DCXX
DLXI
DLXV
DLXX
DXXI
DXXV
DXXX

D••X
DCCX
DCIX
DCLX
DCXX
DEUX
DLIX
DLXX
DOUX
DXIX
DXXX

•DX•
CDXC
CDXI
CDXL
CDXV
CDXX
MDXC
MDXI
MDXL
MDXV
MDXX

•D•X
CDIX
CDLX
CDXX
MDCX
MDIX
MDLX
MDXX

••DX
MCDX
MMDX

DY••
DYAD
DYAK
DYAN
DYCE
DYED
DYER
DYES
DYNA
DYNE

D•Y•
DAYO
DAYS
DEYS
DRYS

D••Y
DALY
DAVY
DDAY
DEFY
DELY
DEMY
DENY
DEWY
DKNY
DOGY
DOPY
DORY
DOZY
DRAY
DUFY
DULY
DUTY

•DY•
IDYL

•D•Y
ADDY
DDAY
EDDY
EDGY
IDLY
ODAY
VDAY

••DY
ADDY
ANDY
BODY
CODY
EDDY
HEDY
INDY
JODY
JUDY
LADY
RUDY
TIDY
TODY

D•Z•
DAZE
DOZE
DOZY

D••Z
DIAZ
DITZ

•DZ•
ADZE

••DZ
LODZ

EA••
EACH
EADS
EARL
EARN
EARP
EARS
EASE
EAST
EASY
EATS
EAUX
EAVE

E•A•
EBAN
EDAM
EGAD
EGAL
EGAN

ELAL
ELAM
ELAN
ERAS
ERAT
ESAI
ESAS
ESAU
ETAH
ETAL
ETAS
ETAT
EVAH
EVAN
EVAP
EXAM
EYAS

E••A
EBLA
ECUA
EDDA
EDNA
EDTA
ELBA
ELEA
ELIA
ELLA
ELSA
EMIA
EMMA
ENNA
ENYA
EPHA
ERDA
ERMA
ESSA
ESTA
ETNA
ETTA
EYRA
EZRA

•EA•
BEAD
BEAK
BEAL
BEAM
BEAN
BEAR
BEAS
BEAT
BEAU
DEAD
DEAF
DEAL
DEAN
DEAR
FEAR
FEAT
GEAR
HEAD
HEAL
HEAP
HEAR
HEAT
JEAN
KEAN
KEAS
LEAD
LEAF
LEAH
LEAK
LEAL
LEAN
LEAP
LEAR
LEAS
MEAD
MEAL
MEAN
MEAS
MEAT
NEAL
NEAP
NEAR
NEAT
PEAG
PEAK
PEAL
PEAR
PEAS
PEAT
PEAU
READ
REAL
REAM
REAP
REAR
SEAL
SEAM
SEAN
SEAR
SEAS
SEAT
TEAK
TEAL
TEAM
TEAR
TEAS
VEAL
VEAU
WEAK
WEAL
WEAN
WEAR
YEAH
YEAN
YEAR
YEAS
ZEAL

•E•A
BELA
BEMA
BETA
CELA
CENA
CERA
CETA
DECA
DEJA
DEKA
FEMA
FETA
GENA
GERA
GETA
HEMA
HERA
HEXA
JENA
LEDA
LEIA
LENA
MEGA
MESA
META
NEVA
PENA
PEPA
REBA
REZA
SEGA
SELA
SERA
SETA
TERA
TEWA
VEDA
VEGA
VELA
VENA
VERA
WEKA
ZETA

••EA
ACEA
AIEA
AREA
ASEA
BREA
ELEA
FLEA
GAEA
IDEA
ITEA
ODEA
ONEA
PLEA
RHEA
SHEA
TOEA
UMEA
UVEA
ZOEA

EB••
EBAN
EBBS
EBLA
EBON
EBRO

E•B•
EBBS
ELBA
ELBE

•EB•
BEBE
CEBU
DEBI
DEBS
DEBT
HEBE
HEBR
NEBE
NEBN
NEBO
NEBR
NEBS
REBA
REBS
SEBE
SEBS
WEBB
WEBS
ZEBU

•E•B
BEEB
HERB
KERB
SERB
VERB
WEBB
WEEB

••EB
BEEB
BLEB
LIEB
LOEB
PLEB
SHEB
WEEB

EC••
ECCE
ECCL
ECHO
ECHT
ECOL
ECON
ECRU
ECTO
ECUA
ECUS

E•C•
EACH
ECCE
ECCL
EKCO
ENCE
ENCL
ENCS
ENCY
ESCE
ETCH
EXCH
EXCL
EYCK

E••C
EDUC
EEOC
ELEC
EPIC
ERIC
ETIC
EXEC

•EC•
BECK
DECA
DECI
DECK
DECL
DECO
HECK
HECT
LECH
LECT
MECH
MECO
NECK
PECK
PECS
RECD
RECS
RECT
SECH
SECS
SECT
SECY
TECH
TECS
YECH
ZECH

•E•C
DESC
EEOC

••EC
ALEC
AVEC
BSEC
ELEC
EXEC
MSEC
OPEC
PREC
PSEC
SPEC

ED••
EDAM
EDDA
EDDO
EDDS
EDDY
EDEN
EDER
EDGE
EDGY
EDHS
EDIE
EDIT
EDNA
EDOM
EDTA
EDUC

E•D•
EADS
EDDA
EDDO
EDDS
EDDY
ENDE
ENDO
ENDS
ERDA
ERDE
ETDS

E••D
EGAD
EKED
ENID
EXOD
EYED

•ED•
BEDE
BEDS
CEDE
CEDI
FEDS
HEDY
JEDI
LEDA
LEDS
MEDE
MEDS
PEDI
PEDO
PEDS
REDD
REDI
REDO
REDS
TEDS
VEDA
WEDS
ZEDS

•E•D
BEAD
BEND
DEAD
DEED
FEED
FEND
FEUD
GEED
HEAD
HEED
HELD
HERD
LEAD
LEND
LEWD
MEAD
MELD
MEND
NEED
NEJD
NERD
PEND
READ
RECD
REDD
REED
REGD
REID
REND
RETD
SEED
SEND
TEED
TEND
VELD
VEND
VERD
WEED
WELD
WEND
ZEND

••ED
ABED
ACED
AGED
APED
AWED
AXED
BLED
BRED
BSED
COED
CUED
DEED
DIED
DRED
DYED
EKED
EYED
FEED
FLED
FRED
GEED
HEED
HIED
HOED
HUED
ICED
IRED
LIED
MRED
NEED
OHED
OPED
OWED
PIED
PLED
PRED
REED
RUED
SEED
SHED
SKED
SLED
SPED
SUED
SWED
TEED
TIED
TOED
USED
VIED
WEED

EE••
EEGS
EEKS
EELS
EELY
EEOC
EERO
EERY

E•E•
EDEN
EDER
EGER
EKED
EKES
ELEA
ELEC
ELEM
ELEV
EPEE
ESEL
ETES
EVEL
EVEN
EVER
EVES
EWER
EWES
EXEC
EXES
EYED
EYES
EZEK

E••E
EASE
EAVE
ECCE
EDGE
EDIE
EINE
EIRE
ELBE
ELIE
ELKE
ELLE
ELSE
ENCE
ENDE
ENNE
EPEE
ERDE
ERIE
ERLE
ERNE
ERSE
ERTE
ESCE
ESME
ESNE
ESSE
ESTE
ETRE
ETTE
EVOE
EYRE

•EE•
BEEB
BEEF
BEEN
BEEP
BEER
BEES
BEET
CEES
DEED
DEEM
DEEP
DEER
DEET
FEED
FEEL
FEES
FEET
GEED
GEEK
GEER
GEES
GEEZ
HEED
HEEL
HEEP
HEER
HEET
JEEP
JEER
JEEZ
KEEL
KEEN
KEEP
KEET
LEEK
LEER
LEES
LEET
MEEK
MEER
MEET
NEED
NEEL
NEEM
NEER
PEEK
PEEL
PEEN
PEEP
PEER
REED
REEF
REEK
REEL
REES
SEED
SEEK
SEEL
SEEM
SEEN
SEEP
SEER
SEES
TEED
TEEM
TEEN
TEES
VEEP
VEER
VEES
WEEB
WEED
WEEK
WEEN
WEEP
ZEES

•E•E
BEBE
BEDE
BENE
BETE
CEDE
CEPE
CERE
CETE
DEKE
DELE
DEME
DENE
FEME
FERE
FETE
GENE
GERE
HEBE
HEME
HERE
JEFE
JETE
LESE
MEDE
MEME
MERE
METE
NEBE
NENE
NEVE
PEKE
PELE
PEPE
PERE
PETE
RENE
RETE
REVE
SEBE
SEME
SENE
SERE
SEVE
TELE
TENE
TETE
UELE
VERE
WERE
WEVE
ZEKE

••EE
AGEE
AKEE
ALEE
CHEE
CREE
DREE
EPEE
FLEE
FREE
GHEE
GLEE
GREE
IDEE
INEE
ISEE
KLEE
KNEE
OGEE
RHEE
SKEE
SMEE
SNEE
SPEE
THEE
TREE
TWEE
WHEE

EF••
EFFS
EFIK
EFTS

E•F•
EFFS

E••F
ENUF

•EF•
DEFS
DEFT
DEFY
HEFT
JEFE
JEFF
LEFT
NEFF
REFL
REFS
REFT
TEFF
WEFT

•E•F
BEEF
CERF
DEAF
JEFF
KERF
LEAF
LEIF
NEFF
NERF
NEUF
NEWF
OEUF
PELF
PERF
REEF
SELF
SERF
TEFF

••EF
ALEF
BEEF
CHEF
CLEF
FIEF
LIEF
PREF
REEF
TREF

EG••
EGAD
EGAL
EGAN
EGER
EGGO
EGGS
EGGY
EGIS
EGON
EGOS

E•G•
EDGE
EDGY
EEGS
EGGO
EGGS
EGGY
ENGR
ENGS
ERGO
ERGS

•EG•
BEGS
DEGS
EEGS
KEGS
LEGO
LEGS
MEGA
NEGS
PEGS
REGD
REGS
REGT
SEGA
SEGO
TEGS
VEGA
YEGG

•E•G
BELG
BENG
BERG
DENG
GEOG
PEAG
WENG
YEGG

••EG
DREG
GLEG
GREG
OLEG
OREG
SKEG

E•H•
ECHO
ECHT
EDHS
ELHI
EPHA
ETHS

E••H
EACH
ESTH
ETAH
ETCH
EVAH
EXCH

•EH•
JEHU
LEHR
NEHI
SEHR

•E•H
BETH
HETH
IEOH
LEAH
LECH
MECH
MESH
METH
NETH
PENH
RESH
SECH
SETH
TECH
TESH
TETH
YEAH
YECH
ZECH
ZEPH

EI••
EINE
EINS
EIRE

E•I•
EDIE
EDIT
EFIK
EGIS
ELIA
ELIE
ELIS
ELIZ
EMIA
EMIL
EMIR
EMIT
ENID
EPIC
EPIS
ERIC
ERIE
ERIK
ERIN
ERIS
ETIC
EVIL
EXIT
EZIO

E••I
ELHI
ELOI
EQUI
ESAI
ETUI

•EI•
BEIN
CEIL
DEIL
FEIN
GEIN
HEIN
HEIR
LEIA
LEIF
LEIS
MEIN
MEIR
NEIL
NEIN
OEIL
QEII
REID
REIN
REIT
SEIN
SEIS
VEII
VEIL
VEIN
WEIL
WEIR
ZEIN

•E•I
BENI
CEDI
DEBI
DECI
DELI
DEMI
DESI
DEVI
HELI
HEMI
JEDI
KEPI
LENI
LEVI
NEHI
NERI
PEDI
PERI
QEII
REDI
RENI
SEMI
SETI
TERI
VEII
VENI
YETI

••EI
DREI
FREI
ZWEI

•EJ•
DEJA
NEJD
SEJM

EK••
EKCO
EKED
EKES

E•K•
EEKS
ELKE
ELKO
ELKS

E••K
EFIK
ERIK
EWOK
EYCK
EZEK

•EK•
DEKA
DEKE
EEKS
LEKS
PEKE
WEKA
ZEKE

•E•K
BEAK
BECK
DECK
DESK
GEEK
HECK
JERK
LEAK
LEEK
LEUK
MEEK
NECK
PEAK
PECK
PEEK
PERK
REEK
SEEK
TEAK
WEAK
WEEK
WELK

••EK
EZEK
GEEK
LEEK
MEEK
PEEK
REEK
SEEK
TREK
WEEK

EL••
ELAL
ELAM
ELAN
ELBA
ELBE
ELEA
ELEC
ELEM
ELEV
ELHI
ELIA
ELIE
ELIS
ELIZ
ELKE
ELKO
ELKS
ELLA
ELLE
ELLS
ELLY
ELMO
ELMS
ELOI
ELON
ELSA
ELSE
ELUL

E•L•
EBLA
EELS
EELY
ELLA
ELLE
ELLS
ELLY
EMLY
ERLE

E••L
EARL
ECCL
ECOL
EGAL
ELAL
ELUL
EMIL
ENCL
ENOL
ESEL
ETAL
EVEL
EVIL
EXCL

•EL•
BELA
BELG
BELL
BELO
BELS
BELT
BELY
CELA
CELL
CELS
CELT
DELE
DELI
DELL
DELS
DELY
EELS
EELY
FELL
FELT
GELL
GELS
GELT
HELD
HELI
HELL
HELM
HELO
HELP
JELL
KELP
LELY
MELD
MELL
MELT
NELL
PELE
PELF
PELL
PELT
RELS
RELY
SELA
SELF
SELL
TELE
TELL
TELO
UELE
VELA
VELD
WELD
WELK
WELL
WELT
YELL
YELP

•E•L
BEAL
BELL
CEIL
CELL
DEAL
DECL
DEIL
DELL
FEEL
FELL
GELL
GENL
GEOL
HEAL
HEEL
HELL
HERL
JELL
KEEL
LEAL
MEAL
MELL
MEWL
NEAL
NEEL
NEIL
NELL
OEIL
PEAL
PEEL
PELL
REAL
REEL
REFL
REPL
SEAL
SEEL
SELL
SEUL
TEAL
TELL
VEAL
VEIL
WEAL
WEIL
WELL
YELL
ZEAL

••EL
ABEL
AUEL
AXEL
BIEL
BREL
CIEL
COEL
DUEL
ESEL
EVEL
FEEL
FUEL
GAEL
HEEL
ICEL
JAEL
JOEL
KAEL
KEEL
KIEL
NEEL
NOEL
OPEL
OREL
PEEL
QUEL
REEL
RIEL
SEEL
SHEL
TAEL

EM••
EMIA
EMIL
EMIR
EMIT
EMLY
EMMA
EMMY
EMPS
EMTS
EMUS

E•M•
ELMO
ELMS
EMMA
EMMY
ERMA
ESME

E••M
EDAM
EDOM
ELAM
ELEM
ETYM
EXAM

•EM•
BEMA
BEMS
DEME
DEMI
DEMO
DEMS
DEMY
FEMA
FEME
GEMS
HEMA
HEME
HEMI
HEMO
HEMP
HEMS
KEMO
KEMP
LEMS
MEME
MEMO
MEMS
NEMO
REMO
REMS
SEME
SEMI
SEMS
TEMP

•E•M
BEAM
BERM
DEEM
DERM
DEUM
GEOM
GERM
GEUM
HELM
HERM
NEEM
PERM
REAM
SEAM
SEEM
SEJM
TEAM
TEEM
TERM

••EM
AHEM
CHEM
CLEM
DEEM
DIEM
ELEM
FLEM
IDEM
ITEM
NEEM
OREM
POEM
PREM
SEEM
SHEM
STEM
TEEM
THEM
YLEM

EN••
ENCE
ENCL
ENCS
ENCY
ENDE
ENDO
ENDS
ENGR
ENGS
ENID
ENNA
ENNE
ENOL
ENOS
ENOW
ENTO
ENUF
ENVS
ENVY
ENYA
ENYO
ENZO

E•N•
EDNA
EINE
EINS
ENNA
ENNE
EONS
ERNE
ERNO
ERNS

ESNE ETNA

E••N

EARN EBAN EBON ECON EDEN EGAN EGON ELAN ELON ERIN ESPN ETON EVAN EVEN EXON

•EN•

BEND BENE BENG BENI BENT BENU BENZ CENA CENO CENS CENT DENE DENG DENS DENT DENY FEND FENN FENS GENA GENE GENL GENS GENT GENU HENS HENT JENA JENS KENO KENS KENT LENA LEND LENI LENO LENS LENT LENZ MEND MENS MENT MENU NENE OENO PENA PEND PENH PENN PENS PENT REND RENE RENI RENO RENT SEND SENE SENS SENT TEND TENE TENN TENO TENS TENT VENA VEND VENI VENN VENT WEND WENG WENS WENT XENO YENS ZEND ZENO

•E•N

BEAN BEEN BEIN BERN CERN DEAN DERN FEIN FENN FERN GEIN HEIN HERN HEWN JEAN KEAN KEEN KERN LEAN LEON MEAN MEIN NEBN NEIN NEON NEUN PEEN PENN PEON REIN SEAN SEEN SEIN SEWN TEEN TENN TERN VEIN VENN VERN WEAN WEEN YEAN ZEIN

••EN

ADEN AMEN ATEN BEEN BIEN BREN CAEN CHEN COEN DIEN EDEN EVEN GLEN GMEN GWEN JAEN KEEN LIEN MIEN OMEN OPEN OVEN OWEN OXEN PEEN RIEN SEEN STEN SVEN TEEN THEN TMEN WEEN WHEN WIEN WREN XMEN

EO••

EONS EOUS

E•O•

EBON ECOL ECON EDOM EEOC EGON EGOS ELOI ELON ENOL ENOS ENOW EPOS EROO EROS ESOP ESOS ETON EVOE EWOK EXOD EXON

E••O

EBRO ECHO ECTO EDDO EERO EGGO EKCO ELKO ELMO ENDO ENTO ENYO ENZO ERGO ERNO EROO ESSO ESTO EURO EXPO EZIO

•EO•

CEOS EEOC GEOG GEOL GEOM IEOH KEOS LEON LEOS MEOW NEON PEON REOS

•E•O

AERO BELO BESO CENO CERO DECO DEMO DEVO EERO HELO HEMO HERO KEMO KENO KETO LEGO LENO LETO LEVO MECO MEMO MERO MESO NEBO NEMO NERO OENO PEDO PEPO PESO PETO REDO REMO RENO REPO SEGO SERO TELO TENO VERO VETO XENO XERO ZENO ZERO

••EO

AREO CLEO IDEO OLEO OREO PLEO RHEO THEO

EP••

EPEE EPHA EPIC EPIS EPOS

E•P•

EMPS ESPN ESPY EXPO EXPT

E••P

EARP ESOP EVAP

•EP•

CEPE CEPS DEPP DEPT HEPT KEPI KEPT PEPA PEPE PEPO PEPS REPL REPO REPP REPS REPT SEPT TEPP WEPT ZEPH

•E•P

BEEP DEEP DEPP HEAP HEEP HELP HEMP JEEP KEEP KELP KEMP LEAP NEAP PEEP PERP REAP REPP RESP REUP SEEP TEMP TEPP TERP VEEP WEEP YELP

••EP

ALEP BEEP DEEP HEEP JEEP KEEP PEEP PREP SEEP SHEP SKEP STEP UTEP VEEP WEEP

EQ••

EQUI

E•Q•

ESQS

•EQ•

SEQQ

•E•Q

SEQQ

••EQ

FREQ

ER••

ERAS ERAT ERDA ERDE ERGO ERGS ERIC ERIE ERIK ERIN ERIS ERLE ERMA ERNE ERNO ERNS EROO EROS ERRS ERSE ERST ERTE

E•R•

EARL EARN EARP EARS EBRO ECRU EERO EERY EIRE ERRS ETRE EURO EURY EYRA EYRE EZRA

E••R

EDER EGER EMIR ENGR EVER EWER

•ER•

AERO AERY BERG BERM BERN BERT CERA CERE CERF CERN CERO CERT DERM DERN EERO EERY FERE FERN GERA GERE GERM HERA HERB HERD HERE HERL HERM HERN HERO HERR HERS JERK KERB KERF KERN KERR KERT MERE MERO MERV NERD NERF NERI NERO PERE PERF PERI PERK PERM PERP PERS PERT PERU SERA SERB SERE SERF SERO SERS SERT SERV TERA TERI TERM TERN TERP TERR VERA VERB VERD VERE VERN VERO VERS VERT VERY WERE WERT XERO ZERO

•E•R

BEAR BEER DEAR DEER FEAR GEAR GEER HEAR HEBR HEER HEIR HERR JEER KERR LEAR LEER LEHR MEER MEIR NEAR NEBR NEER PEAR PEER REAR SEAR SEER SEHR TEAR TERR VEER WEAR WEIR YEAR

••ER

ABER ACER AGER AMER APER AUER AVER AYER BAER BEER BOER BRER CBER CHER CUER DEER DOER DYER EDER EGER EVER EWER GEER GOER HEER HIER HOER ICER ITER JEER LEER MEER NEER NLER ODER OMER ONER OPER OVER OYER PEER PIER PUER SEER STER SUER TIER UBER USER VEER VIER YSER

ES••

ESAI ESAS ESAU ESCE ESEL ESME ESNE ESOP ESOS ESPN ESPY ESQS ESSA ESSE ESSO ESTA ESTE ESTH ESTO ESUS

E•S•

EASE EAST EASY ELSA ELSE ERSE ERST ESSA ESSE ESSO

E••S

EADS EARS EATS EBBS ECUS EDDS EDHS EEGS EEKS EELS EFFS EFTS EGGS EGIS EGOS EINS EKES ELIS ELKS ELLS ELMS EMPS EMTS EMUS ENCS ENDS ENGS ENOS ENVS EONS EOUS EPIS EPOS ERAS ERGS ERIS ERNS EROS ERRS ESAS ESOS ESQS ESUS ETAS ETDS ETES ETHS EVES EWES EXES EXTS EYAS EYES

•ES•

BESO BESS BEST CESS CEST DESC DESI DESK FESS FEST GEST HESS HEST JESS JEST JESU LESE LESS LEST MESA MESH MESO MESS NESS NEST PESO PEST RESH RESP REST SESS TESH TESS TEST VEST WEST ZEST

•E•S

BEAS BEDS BEES BEGS BELS BEMS BESS BETS BEYS CEES CELS CENS CEOS CEPS CESS DEBS DEFS DEGS DELS DEMS DENS DETS DEUS DEWS DEYS EEGS EEKS EELS FEDS FEES FENS FESS GEES GELS GEMS GENS GETS HEMS HENS HERS HESS HEWS JENS JESS JETS JEWS KEAS KEGS KENS KEOS KEYS LEAS LEDS LEES LEGS LEIS LEKS LEMS LENS LEOS LESS LETS MEAS MEDS MEMS MENS MESS METS MEWS NEBS NEGS NESS NETS NEWS PEAS PECS PEDS PEGS PENS PEPS PERS PETS PEWS REBS RECS REDS REES REFS REGS RELS REMS REOS REPS RETS REVS SEAS SEBS SECS SEES SEIS SEMS SENS SERS SESS SETS SEWS TEAS TECS TEDS TEES TEGS TENS TESS TETS VEES VERS VETS WEBS WEDS WENS WETS YEAS YENS YEWS ZEDS ZEES ZEUS

••ES

ACES ADES AGES ALES AMES APES ARES AVES AWES AXES AYES BEES BYES CEES CUES DIES DOES DUES DYES EKES ETES EVES EWES EXES EYES FEES FOES GEES GOES HIES HOES HRES HUES ICES IDES ILES IRES IVES LEES LIES LYES MBES MIES MMES NOES ODES OLES ONES OPES ORES OWES PIES PRES QUES REES ROES RTES RUES RYES SEES SHES STES SUES TEES TIES TOES TRES TUES UKES USES UTES VEES VIES WOES WYES YVES ZEES

ET••

ETAH ETAL ETAS ETAT ETCH ETDS ETES ETHS ETIC ETNA ETON ETRE ETTA ETTE ETUI ETYM

E•T•

EATS ECTO EDTA EFTS EMTS ENTO ERTE ESTA ESTE ESTH ESTO ETTA ETTE EXTS

E••T

EAST ECHT EDIT EMIT ERAT ERST ETAT EXIT EXPT

•ET•

BETA BETE BETH BETS BETZ CETA CETE DETS FETA FETE GETA GETS GETZ HETH JETE JETS JETT KETO KETT LETO LETS LETT META METE METH METS METZ NETH NETS PETE PETO PETS RETD RETE RETS SETA SETH SETI SETS SETT TETE TETH TETS VETO VETS WETS YETI ZETA

•E•T

BEAT BEET BELT BENT BERT BEST CELT CENT CERT CEST DEBT DEET DEFT DENT DEPT DEUT FEAT FEET FELT FEST GELT GENT GEST HEAT HECT HEET HEFT HENT HEPT HEST JEST JETT KEET KENT KEPT KERT KETT LECT LEET LEFT LENT LEST LETT MEAT MEET MELT MENT NEAT NEST NEUT NEWT NEXT PEAT PELT PENT PERT PEST RECT REFT REGT REIT RENT REPT REST SEAT SECT SENT SEPT SERT SETT SEXT TENT TEST TEUT TEXT VENT VERT VEST WEFT WELT WENT WEPT WERT WEST ZEST

••ET

ABET ACET BEET BRET CHET DEET DIET DUET FEET FRET HEET IBET ICET KEET LEET MEET NYET PIET POET PRET RHET SPET STET SUET TRET VIET WHET

EU••

EURO EURY

E•U•

EAUX ECUA ECUS EDUC ELUL EMUS ENUF EOUS EQUI ESUS ETUI

E••U

ECRU ESAU

•EU•

DEUM DEUS DEUT DEUX FEUD GEUM JEUX LEUK NEUF NEUN NEUT OEUF REUP SEUL TEUT YEUX ZEUS

•E•U

BEAU BENU CEBU GENU JEHU JESU MENU PEAU PERU VEAU ZEBU

••EU

BLEU DIEU LIEU

EV••

EVAH EVAN EVAP EVEL EVEN EVER EVES EVIL EVOE

E•V•

EAVE ENVS ENVY

E••V

ELEV

•EV•

BEVY DEVI DEVO LEVI LEVO LEVY NEVA NEVE REVE REVS SEVE WEVE

•E•V

MERV SERV

••EV

BREV ELEV KIEV PREV

EW••

EWER EWES EWOK

E••W

ENOW

•EW•

DEWS DEWY HEWN HEWS JEWS LEWD MEWL MEWS NEWF NEWS NEWT PEWS SEWN SEWS TEWA YEWS

•E•W

MEOW

••EW

ANEW BLEW BREW CHEW CLEW CREW DREW FLEW GREW KNEW LOEW PHEW SKEW SLEW SMEW SPEW STEW THEW VIEW WHEW

EX••

EXAM EXCH EXCL EXEC EXES EXIT EXOD EXON EXPO EXPT EXTS

E••X

EAUX

•EX•

HEXA NEXT SEXT TEXT

•E•X

DEUX JEUX YEUX

••EX

ALEX AMEX APEX CHEX FLEX GREX IBEX ILEX NMEX PLEX

TREX

EY••
EYAS EYCK EYED EYES EYRA EYRE

E•Y•
ENYA ENYO ETYM

E••Y
EASY EDDY EDGY EELY EERY EGGY ELLY EMLY EMMY ENCY ENVY ESPY EURY

•EY•
BEYS DEYS KEYS

•E•Y
AERY BELY BEVY DEFY DELY DEMY DENY DEWY EELY EERY HEDY LELY LEVY RELY SECY VERY

••EY
ACEY FLEY FREY GLEY GREY HUEY IVEY JOEY OBEY OKEY PREY SUEY THEY TREY UREY WHEY

EZ••
EZEK EZIO EZRA

E•Z•
ENZO

E••Z
ELIZ

•EZ•
REZA

•E•Z
BENZ BETZ GEEZ GETZ JEEZ LENZ METZ

••EZ
BAEZ CHEZ GEEZ INEZ JEEZ OYEZ PREZ SUEZ

FA••
FACE FACP FACS FACT FADE FADO FADS FAHD FAHR FAIL FAIN FAIR FAIT FAKE FALA FALK FALL FALX FAME FANE FANG FANS FARD FARE FARM FARO FARR FARS FASO FAST FATA FATE FATH FATS FAUN FAUT FAUX FAVA FAVE FAWN FAYE FAZE

F•A•
FEAR FEAT FIAT FLAB FLAG FLAK FLAM FLAN FLAP FLAT FLAV FLAW FLAX FLAY FOAL FOAM FRAE FRAM FRAN FRAP FRAT FRAU FRAY FUAD

F••A
FALA FATA FAVA FEMA FETA FICA FILA FINA FLEA FNMA FORA FRIA FULA

•FA•
AFAR MFAS SFAX

•F•A
AFTA

••FA
AGFA ALFA SOFA TUFA URFA

F•B•
FIBS FOBS

F••B
FLAB FLUB FORB

F•C•
FACE FACP FACS FACT FICA FICE FICT FOCH FOCI FRCP FRCS

F••C
FDIC FISC FLIC FLOC

•FC•
PFCS

••FC
COFC KOFC

FD••
FDIC

F•D•
FADE FADO FADS FEDS FIDE FIDO FUDD

F••D
FAHD FARD FEED FEND FEUD FIND FLED FOLD FOND FOOD FORD FRED FUAD FUDD FUND

•FD•
RFDS

•F•D
NFLD SFPD

FE••
FEAR FEAT FEDS FEED FEEL FEES FEET FEIN FELL FELT FEMA FEME FEND FENN FENS FERE FERN FESS FEST FETA FETE FEUD

F•E•
FEED FEEL FEES FEET FIEF FLEA FLED FLEE FLEM FLEW FLEX FLEY FOES FRED FREE FREI FREQ FRET FREY FUEL

F••E
FACE FADE FAKE FAME FANE FARE FATE FAVE FAYE FAZE FEME FERE FETE FICE FIDE FIFE FILE FINE FIRE FIVE FIXE FLEE FLOE FLUE FOIE FORE FOXE FRAE FREE FROE FRYE FUME FUSE FUZE FYKE

••FE
CAFE FIFE JEFE LIFE RIFE SAFE WIFE

F•F•
FIFE FIFI FIFO

F••F
FIEF FUNF

•FF•
EFFS IFFY OFFS PFFT

••FF
BAFF BIFF BOFF BUFF CUFF DAFF DIFF DOFF DUFF GAFF GUFF HOFF HUFF JEFF JIFF LUFF MIFF MUFF NEFF ORFF PUFF RIFF RUFF SUFF TEFF TIFF TOFF TUFF

F•G•
FIGS FOGG FOGS FOGY FUGU

F••G
FANG FLAG FLOG FOGG FROG FRUG

F•H•
FAHD FAHR FOHN

F••H
FATH FISH FOCH

FI••
FIAT FIBS FICA FICE FICT FIDE FIDO FIEF FIFE FIFI FIFO FIGS FIJI FILA FILE FILL FILM FILS FINA FIND FINE FINI FINK FINN FINO FINS FIRE FIRM FIRN FIRS FISC FISH FISK FIST FITS FITZ FIVE FIXE FIZZ

F•I•
FAIL FAIN FAIR FAIT FDIC FEIN FLIC FLIM FLIP FLIT FLIX FOIE FOIL FOIN FOIS FRIA FRIO FRIS FRIT FRIZ

F••I
FIFI FIJI FINI FOCI FREI FUJI

•FI•
EFIK

•F•I
IFNI PFUI

••FI
FIFI HIFI SUFI

F•J•
FIJI FUJI

F•K•
FAKE FYKE

F••K
FALK FINK FISK FLAK FOLK FORK FUNK

•F•K
EFIK

FL••
FLAB FLAG FLAK FLAM FLAN FLAP FLAT FLAV FLAW FLAX FLAY FLEA FLED FLEE FLEM FLEW FLEX FLEY FLIC FLIM FLIP FLIT FLIX FLOC FLOE FLOG FLOP FLOR FLOW FLOZ FLUB FLUE FLUS FLUX

F•L•
FALA FALK FALL FALX FELL FELT FILA FILE FILL FILM FILS FOLD FOLK FULA FULL

F••L
FAIL FALL FEEL FELL FILL FOAL FOIL FOOL FOUL FOWL FUEL FULL FURL

•FL•
NFLD

••FL
INFL REFL

F•M•
FAME FEMA FEME FNMA FUME FUMY

F••M
FARM FILM FIRM FLAM FLEM FLIM FOAM FORM FRAM FROM

••FM
AMFM

FN••
FNMA

F•N•
FANE FANG FANS FEND FENN FENS FINA FIND FINE FINI FINK FINN FINO FINS FOND FONS FONT FONZ FUND FUNF FUNK FUNT

F••N
FAIN FAUN FAWN FEIN FENN FERN FINN FIRN FLAN FOHN FOIN FRAN

•FN•
IFNI

FO••
FOAL FOAM FOBS FOCH FOCI FOES FOGG FOGS FOGY FOHN FOIE FOIL FOIN FOIS FOLD FOLK FOND FONS FONT FONZ FOOD FOOL FOOT FOPS FORA FORB FORD FORE FORK FORM FORT FOSS FOUL FOUR FOWL FOXE FOXX FOXY FOYS FOYT

F•O•
FLOC FLOE FLOG FLOP FLOR FLOW FLOZ FOOD FOOL FOOT FROE FROG FROM FROW

F••O
FADO FARO FASO FIDO FIFO FINO FRIO FURO

•FO•
UFOS

•F•O
AFRO IFSO

••FO
FIFO INFO LIFO

F•P•
FOPS

F••P
FACP FLAP FLIP FLOP FRAP FRCP

•FP•
SFPD

••FP
KOFP

F••Q
FREQ

FR••
FRAE FRAM FRAN FRAP FRAT FRAU FRAY FRCP FRCS FRED FREE FREI FREQ FRET FREY FRIA FRIO FRIS FRIT FRIZ FROE FROG FROM FROW FRUG FRYE

F•R•
FARD FARE FARM FARO FARR FARS FERE FERN FIRE FIRM FIRN FIRS FORA FORB FORD FORE FORK FORM FORT FURL FURO FURS FURY

F••R
FAHR FAIR FARR FEAR FLOR FOUR

•FR•
AFRO MFRS

•F•R
AFAR

••FR
SAFR

F•S•
FASO FAST FESS FEST FISC FISH FISK FIST FOSS FUSE FUSS FUST

F••S
FACS FADS FANS FARS FATS FEDS FEES FENS FESS FIBS FIGS FILS FINS FIRS FITS FLUS FOBS FOES FOGS FOIS FONS FOPS FOSS FOYS FRCS FRIS FURS FUSS

•FS•
IFSO

•F•S
AFTS EFFS EFTS MFAS MFRS OFFS PFCS RFDS UFOS

••FS
COFS DEFS EFFS INFS OAFS OFFS REFS RIFS WAFS

F•T•
FATA FATE FATH FATS FETA FETE FITS FITZ FUTZ

F••T
FACT FAIT FAST FAUT FEAT FEET FELT FEST FIAT FICT FIST FLAT FLIT FONT FOOT FORT FOYT FRAT FRET FRIT FUNT FUST

•FT•
AFTA AFTS EFTS

•F•T
PFFT

••FT
CUFT DAFT DEFT GIFT HAFT HEFT LEFT LIFT LOFT LUFT PFFT RAFT REFT RIFT SIFT SOFT SQFT TAFT TOFT TUFT WAFT WEFT

FU••
FUAD FUDD FUEL FUGU FUJI FULA FULL FUME FUMY FUND FUNF FUNK FUNT FURL FURO FURS FURY FUSE FUSS FUST FUTZ FUZE FUZZ

F•U•
FAUN FAUT FAUX FEUD FLUB FLUE FLUS FLUX FOUL FOUR FRUG

F••U
FRAU FUGU

•FU•
PFUI

••FU
GIFU TOFU TUFU

F•V•
FAVA FAVE FIVE

F••V
FLAV

F•W•
FAWN FOWL

F••W
FLAW FLEW FLOW FROW

F•X•
FIXE FOXE FOXX FOXY

F••X
FALX FAUX FLAX FLEX FLIX FLUX FOXX

•F•X
SFAX

FY••
FYKE

F•Y•
FAYE FOYS FOYT FRYE

F••Y
FLAY FLEY FOGY FOXY FRAY FREY FUMY FURY

•F•Y
IFFY

••FY
DEFY DUFY IFFY

F•Z•
FAZE FIZZ FUZE FUZZ

F••Z
FITZ FIZZ FLOZ FONZ FRIZ FUTZ FUZZ

GA••
GABA GABE GABO GABS GABY GADS GAEA GAEL GAFF GAGA GAGE GAGS GAIA GAIL GAIN GAIT GALA GALE GALL GALS GALV GAMA GAME GAMO GAMP GAMS GAMY GANG GANN GAOL GAPA GAPE GAPS GARB GARE GARN GARP GARR GARS GARY GASH GASP GAST GATE GATH GATO GATS GATT GAUD GAUL GAUM GAUR GAVE GAWK GAWP GAYA GAYE GAZA GAZE

G•A•
GEAR GHAT GLAD GLAM GMAC GMAN GMAT GNAR GNAT GNAW GOAD GOAL GOAT GRAB GRAD GRAF GRAM GRAN GRAS GRAU GRAY GRAZ GUAM GUAN GUAR

G••A
GABA GAEA GAGA GAIA GALA GAMA GAPA GAYA GAZA GENA GERA GETA GHIA GIGA GILA GINA GITA GIZA GLIA GNMA GOYA

•GA•
AGAR AGAS EGAD EGAL EGAN

•G•A
AGFA AGHA AGRA AGUA

••GA
ALGA GAGA GIGA INGA JUGA LPGA MEGA OLGA RAGA RIGA RUGA SAGA SEGA TOGA URGA USGA VEGA VIGA YOGA YUGA

G•B•
GABA GABE GABO GABS GABY GIBB GIBE GIBS GOBI GOBO GOBS GOBY GRBR GTBR

G••B
GARB GIBB GLIB GLOB GRAB GRUB

•GB•
IGBO

G•C•
GUCK

G••C
GLUC GLYC GMAC

•GC•
AGCY

G•D•
GADS GIDE GODS

G••D
GAUD GEED GILD GIRD GLAD GOAD GOLD GOND GOOD GRAD GRID

•G•D
AGED EGAD

••GD
BIGD REGD

GE••
GEAR GEED GEEK GEER GEES GEEZ GEIN GELL GELS GELT GEMS GENA GENE GENL GENS GENT GENU GEOG GEOL GEOM GERA GERE GERM GEST GETA GETS GETZ GEUM

G•E•
GAEA GAEL GEED GEEK GEER GEES GEEZ

GHEE GLEE GLEG GLEN GLEY GMEN GOER GOES GREE GREG GREW GREX GREY GWEN

G••E GABE GAGE GALE GAME GAPE GARE GATE GAVE GAYE GAZE GENE GERE GHEE GIBE GIDE GIVE GLEE GLUE GONE GORE GREE GYRE GYVE

•GE• AGED AGEE AGER AGES EGER OGEE

•G•E AGEE AGUE OGEE OGLE OGRE

••GE ANGE AUGE CAGE CTGE DOGE EDGE GAGE HUGE INGE LOGE LUGE MAGE MTGE PAGE RAGE SAGE STGE TIGE URGE WAGE

G•F• GAFF GIFT GIFU GUFF

G••F GAFF GOLF GOOF GRAF GUFF GULF

•GF• AGFA

•G•F TGIF

G•G• GAGA GAGE GAGS GIGA GIGI GIGO GIGS GOGH GOGI GOGO

G••G GANG GEOG GLEG GLUG GONG GREG GRIG GROG GUNG

•GG• EGGO EGGS EGGY IGGY OGGI

•G•G AGOG

••GG DOGG FOGG HOGG RAGG RIGG YEGG

GH•• GHAT GHEE GHIA

G••H GASH GATH GISH GNRH GOGH GOSH GOTH GUSH

•GH• AGHA UGHS

•G•H LGTH

••GH GOGH HIGH HUGH NIGH PUGH SIGH YOGH

GI•• GIBB GIBE GIBS GIDE GIFT GIFU GIGA GIGI GIGO GIGS GILA GILD GILL GILT GIMP GINA GINO GINS GIPS GIRD GIRL GIRN GIRO GIRT GISH GIST GITA GITS GIVE GIZA

G•I• GAIA GAIL GAIN GAIT GEIN GHIA GLIA GLIB GLIM GOIN GRID GRIG GRIM GRIN GRIP GRIS GRIT GUIN

G••I GIGI GOBI GOGI GYRI

•GI• AGIN AGIO EGIS TGIF

•G•I AGNI AGRI OGGI UGLI

••GI GIGI GOGI HAGI MAGI OGGI RIGI YAGI YOGI ZOGI

G••K GAWK GEEK GOOK GOWK GROK GUCK GUNK

GL•• GLAD GLAM GLEE GLEG GLEN GLEY GLIA GLIB GLIM GLOB GLOM GLOP GLOT GLOW GLUC GLUE GLUG GLUM GLUT GLYC GLYN

G•L• GALA GALE GALL GALS GALV GELL GELS GELT GILA GILD GILL GILT GOLD GOLF GULF GULL GULP

G••L GAEL GAIL GALL GAOL GAUL GELL GENL GEOL GILL GIRL GOAL GULL

•GL• IGLU OGLE UGLI UGLY

•G•L EGAL

••GL ANGL

GM•• GMAC GMAN GMAT GMEN

G•M• GAMA GAME GAMO GAMP GAMS GAMY GEMS GIMP GNMA GUMM GUMP GUMS GYMS

G••M GAUM GEOM GERM GEUM GLAM GLIM GLOM GLUM GRAM GRIM GUAM GUMM

•GM• MGMT

GN•• GNAR GNAT GNAW GNMA GNRH GNUS

G•N• GANG GANN GENA GENE GENL GENS GENT GENU GINA GINO GINS GOND GONE GONG GONY GUNG GUNK GUNN GUNS GYNT

G••N GAIN GANN GARN GEIN GIRN GLEN GLYN GMAN GMEN GOIN GOON GOWN GRAN GRIN GUAN GUIN GUNN GWEN GWYN

•GN• AGNI

•G•N AGIN AGON EGAN EGON

••GN SIGN

GO•• GOAD GOAL GOAT GOBI GOBO GOBS GOBY GODS GOER GOES GOGH GOGI GOGO GOIN GOLD GOLF GOND GONE GONG GONY GOOD GOOF GOOK GOON GOOP GOOS GORE GORP GORY GOSH GOTH GOUP GOUT GOVT GOWK GOWN GOYA

G•O• GAOL GEOG GEOL GEOM GLOB GLOM GLOP GLOT GLOW GOOD GOOF GOOK GOON GOOP GOOS GPOS GROG GROK GROS GROT GROW GYOR

G••O GABO GAMO GATO GIGO GINO GIRO GOBO GOGO GYRO

•GO• AGOG AGON EGON EGOS IGOR

•G•O AGIO AGRO EGGO IGBO

••GO ALGO ARGO EGGO ERGO GIGO GOGO HUGO IAGO LAGO LEGO LOGO NOGO PAGO POGO SAGO SEGO TOGO VIGO YUGO ZYGO

GP•• GPOS

G•P• GAPA GAPE GAPS GIPS GYPS

G••P GAMP GARP GASP GAWP GIMP GLOP GOOP GORP GOUP GRIP GULP GUMP

GR•• GRAB GRAD GRAF GRAM GRAN GRAS GRAU GRAY GRAZ GRBR GREE GREG GREW GREX GREY GRID GRIG GRIM GRIN GRIP GRIS GRIT GROG GROK GROS GROT GROW GRUB GRUS GRWT

G•R• GARB GARE GARN GARP GARR GARS GARY GERA GERE GERM GIRD GIRL GIRN GIRO GIRT GNRH GORE GORP GORY GURU GYRE GYRI GYRO

G••R GARR GAUR GEAR GEER GNAR GOER GRBR GTBR GUAR GYOR

•GR• AGRA AGRI AGRO

•G•R AGAR AGER EGER IGOR

••GR ENGR MNGR MSGR SPGR

G•S• GASH GASP GAST GEST GISH GIST GOSH GUSH GUST

G••S GABS GADS GAGS GALS GAMS GAPS GARS GATS GEES GELS GEMS GENS GETS GIBS GIGS GINS GIPS GITS GNUS GOBS GODS GOES GOOS GPOS GRAS GRIS GROS GRUS GUMS GUNS GUTS GUYS GYMS GYPS

•G•S AGAS AGES AGTS EGGS EGIS EGOS MGRS RGTS SGTS UGHS

••GS AVGS BAGS BEGS BOGS BUGS CHGS CIGS COGS DAGS DEGS DIGS DOGS EEGS EGGS ENGS ERGS FIGS FOGS GAGS GIGS HAGS HOGS HUGS JAGS JIGS JOGS JUGS KEGS LAGS LEGS LOGS LUGS MAGS MIGS MSGS MTGS MUGS NAGS NEGS NOGS ORGS PEGS PIGS POGS PUGS RAGS REGS RIGS RUGS SAGS SVGS TAGS TEGS TOGS TUGS VUGS WAGS WIGS ZAGS ZIGS

GT•• GTBR

G•T• GATE GATH GATO GATS GATT GETA GETS GETZ GITA GITS GOTH GUTS GWTW

G••T GAIT GAST GATT GELT GENT GEST GHAT GIFT GILT GIRT GIST GLOT GLUT GMAT GNAT GOAT GOUT GOVT GRIT GROT GRWT GUST GYNT

•GT• AGTS LGTH RGTS SGTS

•G•T MGMT

••GT MSGT REGT SSGT TSGT

GU•• GUAM GUAN GUAR GUCK GUFF GUIN GULF GULL GULP GUMM GUMP GUMS GUNG GUNK GUNN GUNS GURU GUSH GUST GUTS GUYS

G•U• GAUD GAUL GAUM GAUR GEUM GLUC GLUE GLUG GLUM GLUT GNUS GOUP GOUT GRUB GRUS

G••U GENU GIFU GRAU GURU

•GU• AGUA AGUE

•G•U IGLU

••GU FUGU RAGU

G•V• GAVE GIVE GOVT GYVE

G••V GALV

GW•• GWEN GWTW GWYN

G•W• GAWK GAWP GOWK GOWN GRWT

G••W GLOW GNAW GREW GROW GWTW

•GW• HGWY

G••X GREX

GY•• GYMS GYNT GYOR GYPS GYRE GYRI GYRO GYVE

G•Y• GAYA GAYE GLYC GLYN GOYA GUYS GWYN

G••Y GABY GAMY GARY GLEY GOBY GONY GORY GRAY GREY

•G•Y AGCY EGGY HGWY IGGY UGLY

••GY ALGY ARGY BOGY CAGY DOGY EDGY EGGY FOGY IGGY LOGY NAGY ORGY POGY

G•Z• GAZA GAZE GIZA

G••Z GEEZ GETZ GRAZ

HA•• HAAG HABE HACK HADE HADJ HAFT HAGI HAGS HAHA HAHN HAHS HAIG HAIK HAIL HAIM HAIR HAJI HAJJ HAKE HALE HALF HALL HALM HALO HALS HALT HAMA HAME HAMM HAMS HANA HAND HANG HANK HANS HAPI HAPS HARD HARE HARI HARK HARM HARP HART HARZ HASH HASP HAST HATE HATH HATS HAUL HAUS HAUT HAVE HAWK HAWN HAWS HAYS HAZE HAZY

H•A• HAAG HEAD HEAL HEAP HEAR HEAT HOAR HOAX HUAC

H••A HAHA HAMA HANA HEMA HERA HEXA HIJA HILA HOLA HORA HOYA HSIA HULA HUPA HYLA

•HA• AHAB AHAZ CHAD CHAM CHAN CHAP CHAR CHAS CHAT CHAW CHAZ DHAL GHAT KHAN KHAT PHAR SHAD SHAG SHAH SHAM SHAN SHAQ SHAW SHAY THAI THAN THAR THAT THAW WHAM WHAT

•H•A CHIA GHIA RHEA SHEA WHOA

••HA AGHA DOHA EPHA HAHA NAHA OSHA

H•B• HABE HDBK HEBE HEBR HOBO HOBS HUBS

H••B HERB

•HB• RHBS

•H•B AHAB CHUB SHEB

H•C• HACK HECK HECT HICK HOCH HOCK HUCK

H••C HUAC

•H•C CHIC CHOC

HD•• HDBK HDTV HDWE

H•D• HADE HADJ HEDY HIDE HODS HYDE HYDR

H••D HAND HARD HEAD HEED HELD HERD HIED HIND HOED HOLD HOND HOOD HUED HUND

•HD• PHDS

•H•D CHAD CHID OHED SHAD SHED SHOD THUD WHOD

••HD FAHD

HE•• HEAD HEAL HEAP HEAR HEAT HEBE HEBR HECK HECT HEDY HEED HEEL HEEP HEER HEET HEFT HEIN HEIR HELD HELI HELL HELM HELO HELP HEMA HEME HEMI HEMO HEMP HEMS HENS HENT HEPT HERA HERB HERD HERE HERL HERM HERN HERO HERR HERS HESS HEST HETH HEWN HEWS HEXA

H•E• HEED HEEL HEEP HEER HEET HIED HIER HIES HOED HOER HOES HRES HUED HUES HUEY

H••E HABE HADE HAKE HALE HAME HARE HATE HAVE HAZE HDWE HEBE HEME HERE HIDE HIKE HIRE HITE HIVE HOKE HOLE HOME HONE HOPE HOSE HOTE HOVE HOWE HUGE HUME HYDE HYPE

•HE• AHEM CHEE CHEF CHEM CHEN CHER CHET CHEW CHEX CHEZ GHEE OHED PHEW RHEA RHEE RHEO RHET SHEA SHEB SHED SHEL SHEM SHEP SHES THEE THEM THEN THEO THEW THEY WHEE WHEN WHET WHEW WHEY

•H•E CHEE GHEE IHRE OHNE RHEE RHUE SHOE SHUE THEE WHEE WHSE

••HE ACHE ASHE

H•F• HAFT HEFT HIFI HOFF HUFF

H••F HALF HOFF HOOF HUFF

•H•F CHEF

HG•• HGWY

H•G• HAGI HAGS HIGH HOGG HOGS HUGE HUGH HUGO HUGS

H••G HAAG HAIG HANG HOGG HONG HUNG

•HG• CHGS

•H•G CHUG SHAG THUG WHIG

H•H• HAHA HAHN HAHS HOHO

H••H HASH HATH HETH HIGH HOCH HUGH HUSH

•H•H OHOH SHAH SHIH UHOH UHUH

HI•• HICK HIDE HIED HIER HIES HIFI HIGH HIJA HIJO HIKE HILA HILL HILO HILT HIND HINT HIPS HIRE HIRT HISS HIST HITE HITS HIVE HIYO

H•I• HAIG HAIK HAIL HAIM HAIR HEIN HEIR HSIA

H••I HAGI HAJI HAPI HARI HELI HEMI HIFI HONI HOPI

•HI• CHIA CHIC CHID CHIN CHIP CHIS CHIT GHIA OHIO PHIL PHIS PHIZ SHIH SHIM SHIN SHIP SHIV THIN THIO THIS WHIG WHIM WHIP WHIR WHIT WHIZ

•H•I THAI

••HI ELHI NEHI

H•J• HAJI HAJJ HIJA HIJO HOJO

H••J HADJ HAJJ

H•K• HAKE HIKE HOKE

H••K HACK HAIK HANK HARK HAWK HDBK HECK HICK HOCK HONK HOOK HUCK HULK HUNK HUSK

H•L• HALE HALF HALL HALM HALO HALS HALT HELD HELI HELL HELM HELO HELP HILA HILL HILO HILT HOLA HOLD HOLE HOLM HOLO HOLP HOLT HOLY HULA HULK HULL HYLA

H••L HAIL HALL HAUL HEAL HEEL HELL HERL HILL HOWL HULL HURL

•H•L CHOL DHAL PHIL SHEL SHUL

••HL BUHL DAHL KOHL POHL SAHL WAHL WOHL

HM•• HMOS

H•M• HAMA HAME HAMM HAMS HEMA HEME HEMI HEMO HEMP HEMS HOME HOMO HOMS HOMY HUME HUMP HUMS HYMN

H••M HAIM HALM HAMM HARM HELM HERM HOLM

•HM• CHMN OHMS OHMY

•H•M AHEM CHAM CHEM CHUM RHUM SHAM SHEM SHIM THEM THOM WHAM WHIM WHOM

••HM BOHM

H•N• HANA HAND HANG HANK HANS HENS HENT HIND HINT HOND HONE HONG HONI HONK HUND HUNG HUNK HUNS HUNT

H••N HAHN HAWN HEIN HERN HEWN HORN HUON HYMN HYPN

•HN• OHNE OHNO

•H•N CHAN CHEN CHIN CHMN CHON KHAN PHON SHAN SHIN SHUN THAN THEN THIN WHEN

••HN CAHN COHN FOHN HAHN JOHN KAHN KUHN SOHN ZAHN

HO•• HOAR HOAX HOBO HOBS HOCH HOCK HODS HOED HOER HOES HOFF HOGG HOGS HOHO HOJO HOKE HOLA HOLD HOLE HOLM HOLO HOLP HOLT HOLY HOME HOMO HOMS HOMY HOND HONE HONG HONI HONK HOOD HOOF HOOK HOOP HOOT HOPE HOPI HOPS HORA HORN HORS HORT HOSE HOSP HOSS HOST HOTE HOUR HOVE HOWE HOWL HOWS HOYA HOYS HOYT

H•O• HMOS HOOD HOOF HOOK HOOP HOOT HUON

H••O HALO HELO HEMO HERO HIJO HILO HIYO HOBO HOHO HOJO HOLO HOMO HUGO HYPO

•HO• AHOY CHOC CHOL CHON CHOP CHOU CHOW CHOY DHOW IHOP MHOS OHOH PHON PHOT RHOS SHOD SHOE SHOO SHOP SHOT SHOW THOM THOR THOU UHOH WHOA WHOD WHOM WHOP WHOS ZHOU

•H•O AHSO OHIO OHNO RHEO SHOO THEO THIO

••HO COHO ECHO HOHO MOHO OCHO OTHO PAHO SOHO TOHO YOHO

H•P• HAPI HAPS HEPT HIPS HOPE HOPI HOPS HUPA HYPE HYPN HYPO HYPS

H••P HARP HASP HEAP HEEP HELP HEMP HOLP HOOP HOSP HUMP

•HP• SHPT

•H•P CHAP CHIP CHOP IHOP SHEP SHIP SHOP WHIP WHOP WHUP

•H•Q SHAQ

HR•• HRES

H•R• HARD HARE HARI HARK HARM HARP HART HARZ HERA HERB HERD HERE HERL HERM HERN HERO HERR HERS HIRE HIRT HORA HORN HORS HORT HURL HURT

H••R HAIR HEAR HEBR HEER HEIR HERR HIER HOAR HOER HOUR HYDR

•HR• IHRE THRU

•H•R CHAR CHER CHUR PHAR THAR THOR THUR WHIR

••HR BAHR BOHR BUHR FAHR JAHR KWHR LAHR LEHR RUHR SEHR TAHR TCHR

HS•• HSIA

H•S• HASH HASP HAST HESS HEST HISS HIST HOSE HOSP HOSS HOST HUSH HUSK HUSS

H••S HAGS HAHS HALS HAMS HANS HAPS HATS HAUS HAWS HAYS HEMS HENS HERS HESS HEWS HIES HIPS HISS HITS HMOS HOBS HODS HOES HOGS HOMS HOPS HORS HOSS HOWS HOYS HRES HUBS HUES HUGS HUMS HUNS HUSS HUTS HWYS HYPS

•HS• AHSO WHSE

•H•S CHAS CHGS CHIS MHOS OHMS PHDS PHIS PHYS RHBS RHOS SHES THIS THUS WHOS WHYS

••HS AAHS BAHS DAHS EDHS ETHS HAHS MOHS OCHS OOHS PAHS UGHS

H•T• HATE HATH HATS HDTV HETH HITE HITS HOTE HUTS HUTT

H••T HAFT HALT HART HAST HAUT HEAT HECT HEET HEFT HENT HEPT HEST HILT HINT HIRT HIST HOLT HOOT HORT HOST HOYT HUNT HURT HUTT

•H•T CHAT CHET CHIT GHAT KHAT PHOT RHET SHOT SHPT SHUT THAT WHAT WHET WHIT

••HT ACHT BAHT ECHT SPHT

HU•• HUAC HUBS HUCK HUED HUES HUEY HUFF HUGE HUGH HUGO HUGS HULA HULK HULL HUME HUMP HUMS HUND HUNG HUNK HUNS HUNT HUON HUPA HURL HURT HUSH HUSK HUSS HUTS HUTT

H•U• HAUL HAUS HAUT HOUR

•HU• CHUB CHUG CHUM CHUR RHUE RHUM SHUE SHUL SHUN SHUT THUD THUG THUR THUS UHUH WHUP

•H•U CHOU THOU THRU ZHOU

••HU JEHU OAHU

H•V• HAVE HIVE HOVE

H••V HDTV

•H•V SHIV

HW•• HWYS

H•W• HAWK HAWN HAWS HDWE HEWN HEWS HGWY HOWE HOWL HOWS

•H•W CHAW CHEW CHOW DHOW PHEW SHAW SHOW THAW THEW WHEW

H•X• HEXA

H••X HOAX

•H•X CHEX

HY•• HYDE HYDR HYLA HYMN HYPE HYPN HYPO HYPS

H•Y• HAYS HIYO HOYA HOYS HOYT HWYS

H••Y HAZY HEDY HGWY HOLY HOMY HUEY

•HY• PHYS WHYS

•H•Y AHOY CHOY OHMY SHAY THEY WHEY

••HY ACHY ASHY

H•Z• HAZE HAZY

H••Z HARZ

•H•Z AHAZ CHAZ CHEZ PHIZ WHIZ

IA•• IAGO IAMB IANA IASI

I•A• IBAN IBAR ICAL IDAE IMAM IMAN IRAE IRAN IRAQ IRAS ISAK ISAR ISAY ITAL IVAN IYAR IZAR

I••A IANA IDEA ILIA ILKA ILSA INCA INGA INKA IOLA IONA IOTA IOWA IRMA ISBA ISLA ITEA ITZA IXIA IZBA

•IA• BIAK BIAS CIAO DIAG DIAL DIAM DIAN DIAS DIAZ FIAT JIAO LIAM LIAR PIAF RIAL RIAS SIAL SIAM VIAL XIAN

•I•A AIDA AIEA AIWA BIWA DINA DIVA FICA FILA FINA GIGA GILA GINA GITA GIZA HIJA HILA JIMA KINA KIVA LILA LIMA LINA LIRA LISA LIZA MICA MINA MIRA MITA NINA NIPA NITA PICA PIKA PIMA PINA PISA PITA RICA RIGA RIMA RITA SIMA TINA TIWA VIDA VIGA VILA VINA VISA VITA VIVA YIMA

••IA ALIA AMIA APIA ARIA ASIA AVIA CHIA ELIA EMIA FRIA GAIA GHIA GLIA HSIA ILIA IXIA LEIA MAIA OPIA USIA

IB•• IBAN IBAR IBET IBEX IBID IBIS IBLE IBOS

I•B• ICBM IGBO IRBM ISBA ISBN IZBA

I••B IAMB

•IB• BIBB BIBI BIBL BIBS DIBS FIBS GIBB GIBE GIBS JIBE JIBS LIBS MIBS NIBS RIBS SIBS VIBE

•I•B BIBB GIBB LIEB LIMB LITB

••IB ABIB CRIB DBIB DRIB GLIB TRIB

IC•• ICAL ICBM ICED ICEL ICER ICES ICET ICKY ICON ICOS ICUS

I•C• INCA INCH INCL INCR ITCH

•IC• BICE BICS DICE DICH DICK DICT FICA FICE FICT HICK KICK LICE LICK MICA MICE MICH MICK MICR MICS NICE NICK PICA PICK PICO PICS PICT RICA RICE RICH RICK RICO SICK SICS TICK TICO TICS VICE VICI WICK

•I•C CINC CIRC DISC FISC MISC WISC ZINC

••IC AMIC BRIC CHIC EPIC ERIC ETIC FDIC FLIC LAIC ODIC OTIC ZOIC

ID•• IDAE IDEA IDEE IDEM IDEO IDES IDIO IDLE IDLY IDOL IDUN IDYL

I•D• INDO INDS INDY IODO

I••D IBID ICED IRED IRID IZOD

•ID• AIDA AIDE AIDS BIDE BIDS CIDE DIDO FIDE FIDO GIDE HIDE KIDD KIDS LIDO LIDS MIDI MIDN NIDE NIDI RIDD RIDE RIDS SIDE SIDH TIDE TIDY VIDA VIDE VIDI WIDE

•I•D BIGD BIND BIRD DIED FIND GILD GIRD HIED HIND KIDD KIND LIED LIND LITD MILD MIND PIED RIDD RIND SILD SIND TIED VIED WILD WIND

••ID ACID AMID ARID AVID CHID ENID GRID IBID IRID LAID LOID MAID OLID OOID OVID PAID QAID QUID RAID REID SAID SKID SLID VOID

IE•• IEOH

I•E• IBET IBEX ICED ICEL ICER ICES ICET IDEA IDEE IDEM IDEO IDES ILES ILEX INEE INEZ IRED IRES ISEE ITEA ITEM ITER IVES IVEY

I••E IBLE IDAE IDEE IDLE IHRE ILIE ILLE

INEE
INGE
INRE
IOLE
IONE
IPSE
IRAE
ISEE
ISLE

•IE•
AIEA
BIEL
BIEN
CIEL
DIED
DIEM
DIEN
DIES
DIET
DIEU
FIEF
HIED
HIER
HIES
KIEL
KIEV
LIEB
LIED
LIEF
LIEN
LIES
LIEU
MIEN
MIES
PIED
PIER
PIES
PIET
RIEL
RIEN
TIED
TIER
TIES
VIED
VIER
VIES
VIET
VIEW
WIEN

•I•E
AIDE
AIME
AIRE
BICE
BIDE
BIKE
BILE
BINE
BISE
BITE
CIDE
CINE
CIRE
CITE
DICE
DIKE
DIME
DINE
DIRE
DIVE
EINE
EIRE
FICE
FIDE
FIFE
FILE
FINE
FIRE
FIVE
FIXE
GIBE
GIDE
GIVE
HIDE
HIKE
HIRE
HITE
HIVE
JIBE
JIVE
KINE
KITE
LICE
LIFE
LIKE
LIME
LINE
LIRE
LISE
LITE
LIVE
MICE
MIKE
MILE
MIME
MINE
MIRE
MISE
MITE
NICE
NIDE
NIKE
NILE
NINE
NITE
NIUE
OISE
PIKE
PILE
PINE
PIPE
PIRE
RICE
RIDE
RIFE
RILE
RIME
RIPE
RIRE
RISE
RITE
RIVE
SIDE
SINE
SIRE
SITE
SIZE
TIDE
TIGE
TIKE
TILE
TIME
TINE
TIRE
VIBE
VICE
VIDE
VILE
VINE
VISE
VITE
VIVE
WIDE
WIFE
WILE
WINE
WIPE
WIRE
WISE
WITE
XIPE
YIPE
ZINE

••IE
ABIE
AMIE
BRIE
EDIE
ELIE
ERIE
FOIE
ILIE
JOIE
OBIE
ODIE
OKIE
OPIE
PLIE
PRIE
SOIE

IF••
IFFY
IFNI
IFSO

I•F•
IFFY
INFL
INFO
INFS

I••F
IOOF

•IF•
BIFF
DIFF
FIFE
FIFI
FIFO
GIFT
GIFU
HIFI
JIFF
LIFE
LIFO
LIFT
MIFF
RIFE
RIFF
RIFS
RIFT
SIFT
TIFF
WIFE

•I•F
BIFF
DIFF
FIEF
JIFF
LIEF
MIFF
PIAF
RIFF
TIFF

••IF
ALIF
ASIF
COIF
LEIF
NAIF
TGIF
WAIF

IG••
IGBO
IGGY
IGLU
IGOR

I•G•
IAGO
IGGY
INGA
INGE

•IG•
BIGD
CIGS
DIGS
FIGS
GIGA
GIGI
GIGO
GIGS
HIGH
JIGS
MIGS
NIGH
PIGS
RIGA
RIGG
RIGI
RIGS
SIGH
SIGN
TIGE
VIGA
VIGO
WIGS
ZIGS

•I•G
BING
BIOG
DIAG
DING
KING
LING
MING
PING
RIGG
RING
SING
TING
WING
XING
ZING

••IG
BRIG
GRIG
HAIG
ORIG
PRIG
SWIG
TRIG
TWIG
WHIG

IH••
IHOP
IHRE

I••H
IEOH
INCH
IPOH
ISTH
ITCH

•I•H
DICH
DISH
FISH
GISH
HIGH
KISH
KITH
LITH
MICH
MINH
NIGH
PISH
PITH
RICH
SIDH
SIGH
SIKH
SINH
TISH
WISH
WITH

••IH
SHIH

II••
IIII
IIWI

I•I•
IBID
IBIS
IDIO
IIII
ILIA
ILIE
ILIO
IMIT
INIT
IRID
IRIS
ISIS
ITIS
IWIS
IXIA

I••I
IASI
IFNI
IIII
IIWI
IMPI
INRI

•II•
CIII
DIII
IIII
LIII
MIII
RIIS
VIII
XIII

•I•I
BIBI
CIII
DIII
FIFI
FIJI
FINI
GIGI
HIFI
IIII
IIWI
JIMI
KIKI
KIWI
LIII
LILI
MIDI
MIII
MIMI
MINI
NIDI
NISI
PILI
RIGI
SIMI
SISI
TIKI
TITI
VICI
VIDI
VIII
VINI
VITI
XIII
ZITI

••II
ALII
CCII
CDII
CIII
CLII
CMII
CVII
CXII
DCII
DIII
DLII
DVII
DXII
IIII
LIII
LVII
LXII
MCII
MDII
MIII
MLII
MMII
MVII
MXII
QEII
VEII
VIII
WWII
XCII
XIII
XLII
XVII
XXII

•IJ•
FIJI
HIJA
HIJO
RIJN

I•K•
ICKY
ILKA
ILKS
INKA
INKS
INKY
IRKS

I••K
ISAK

•IK•
BIKE
BIKO
DIKE
HIKE
KIKI
LIKE
MIKE
NIKE
PIKA
PIKE
SIKH
TIKE
TIKI

•I•K
BIAK
BILK
BIRK
DICK
DINK
DIRK
DISK
FINK
FISK
HICK
JINK
KICK
KINK
KIRK
LICK
LINK
MICK
MILK
MINK
NICK
OINK
PICK
PINK
RICK
RINK
RISK
SICK
SILK
SINK
TICK
WICK
WINK
WISK

••IK
EFIK
ERIK
HAIK

IL••
ILES
ILEX
ILIA
ILIE
ILIO
ILKA
ILKS
ILLE
ILLS
ILLY
ILSA

I•L•
IBLE
IDLE
IDLY
IGLU
ILLE
ILLS
ILLY
INLY
IOLA
IOLE
ISLA
ISLE
ISLS
ITLL

I••L
ICAL
ICEL
IDOL
IDYL
INCL
INFL
INTL
ITAL
ITLL
ITOL

•IL•
AILS
BILE
BILK
BILL
DILL
FILA
FILE
FILL
FILM
FILS
GILA
GILD
GILL
GILT
HILA
HILL
HILO
HILT
JILL
JILT
KILL
KILN
KILO
KILT
LILA
LILI
LILT
LILY
MILD
MILE
MILK
MILL
MILO
MILS
MILT
NILE
NILS
OILS
OILY
PILE
PILI
PILL
RILE
RILL
SILD
SILK
SILL
SILO
SILT
TILE
TILL
TILS
TILT
VILA
VILE
WILD
WILE
WILL
WILT
WILY
ZILL

•I•L
BIBL
BIEL
BILL
BIOL
BIRL
CIEL
DIAL
DILL
DIPL
FILL
GILL
GIRL
HILL
JILL
KIEL
KILL
MILL
PILL
RIAL
RIEL
RILL
SIAL
SILL
TILL
VIAL
VIOL
WILL
ZILL

••IL
ANIL
ARIL
AXIL
BAIL
BOIL
CEIL
COIL
DEIL
DOIL
EMIL
EVIL
FAIL
FOIL
GAIL
HAIL
JAIL
MAIL
MOIL
NAIL
NEIL
NOIL
OEIL
PAIL
PHIL
POIL
RAIL
ROIL
SAIL
SCIL
SKIL
SOIL
TAIL
TOIL
UTIL
VAIL
VEIL
WAIL
WEIL

IM••
IMAM
IMAN
IMIT
IMPI
IMPS

I•M•
IAMB
IRMA
ISMS

I••M
ICBM
IDEM
IMAM
IRBM
ITEM

•IM•
AIME
AIMS
DIME
DIMS
GIMP
JIMA
JIMI
LIMA
LIMB
LIME
LIMN
LIMO
LIMP
LIMY
MIME
MIMI
PIMA
RIMA
RIME
RIMS
RIMY
SIMA
SIMI
SIMP
SIMS
TIME
WIMP
YIMA

•I•M
DIAM
DIEM
FILM
FIRM
LIAM
SIAM

••IM
AKIM
ANIM
BRIM
CRIM
FLIM
GLIM
GRIM
HAIM
PRIM
SHIM
SKIM
SLIM
SWIM
TRIM
URIM
WHIM

IN••
INCA
INCH
INCL
INCR
INDO
INDS
INDY
INEE
INEZ
INFL
INFO
INFS
INGA
INGE
INIT
INKA
INKS
INKY
INLY
INNS
INON
INRE
INRI
INRO
INSP
INST
INTL
INTO
INTR
INTS
INXS

I•N•
IANA
IFNI
INNS
IONA
IONE
IONS
ISNT

I••N
IBAN
ICON
IDUN
IMAN
INON
IRAN
IRON
ISBN
ISSN
IVAN

•IN•
AINT
AINU
BIND
BINE
BING
BINS
CINC
CINE
CINQ
DINA
DINE
DING
DINK
DINO
DINS
DINT
EINE
EINS
FINA
FIND
FINE
FINI
FINK
FINN
FINO
FINS
GINA
GINO
GINS
HIND
HINT
JINK
JINN
JINX
KINA
KIND
KINE
KING
KINK
KINO
LINA
LIND
LINE
LING
LINK
LINT
LINY
LINZ
MINA
MIND
MINE
MING
MINH
MINI
MINK
MINN
MINS
MINT
MINX
NINA
NINE
NINO
OINK
PINA
PINE
PING
PINK
PINS
PINT
PINX
PINY
RIND
RING
RINK
SIND
SINE
SING
SINH
SINK
SINO
SINS
TINA
TINE
TING
TINS
TINT
TINY
VINA
VINE
VINI
VINO
VINS
VINY
WIND
WINE
WING
WINK
WINS
XING
ZINC
ZINE
ZING

•I•N
BIEN
BION
CION
DIAN
DIEN
DION
FINN
FIRN
GIRN
JINN
KILN
LIEN
LIMN
LION
MIDN
MIEN
MINN
PION
RIEN
RIJN
SIGN
TION
WIEN
XIAN
ZION

••IN
ADIN
AGIN
AKIN
AMIN
AYIN
BAIN
BEIN
BLIN
CAIN
CHIN
CLIN
COIN
CRIN
CUIN
DAIN
DOIN
ERIN
FAIN
FEIN
FOIN
GAIN
GEIN
GOIN
GRIN
GUIN
HEIN
JAIN
JOIN
KAIN
LAIN
LOIN
MAIN
MEIN
NEIN
ODIN
OLIN
PAIN
PNIN
PRIN
RAIN
REIN
RUIN
SEIN
SHIN
SKIN
SPIN
SQIN
TAIN
THIN
TWIN
VAIN
VEIN
WAIN
ZEIN

IO••
IODO
IOLA
IOLE
IONA
IONE
IONS
IOOF
IOTA
IOUS
IOWA

I•O•
IBOS
ICON
ICOS
IDOL
IEOH
IGOR
IHOP
INON
IOOF
IPOH
IRON
ITOL
IVOR
IZOD

I••O
IAGO
IDEO
IDIO
IFSO
IGBO
ILIO
INDO
INFO
INRO
INTO
IODO
IPSO

•IO•
BIOG
BIOL
BION
BIOS
CION
DION
DIOR
DIOS
LION
PION
RIOS
RIOT
TION
VIOL
ZION

•I•O
BIKO
CIAO
DIDO
DINO
FIDO
FIFO
FINO
GIGO
GINO
GIRO
HIJO
HILO
HIYO
JIAO
KILO
KINO
LIDO
LIFO
LIMO
LIPO
MILO
MIRO
MISO
NINO
PICO
RICO
SILO
SINO
TICO
TITO
VIGO
VINO
VITO

••IO
AGIO
BAIO
BRIO
CLIO
EZIO
FRIO
IDIO
ILIO
KRIO
OHIO
OLIO
THIO
TRIO

IP••
IPOH
IPSE
IPSO

I•P•
IMPI
IMPS
ISPY

I••P
IHOP
INSP

•IP•
DIPL
DIPS
GIPS
HIPS
KIPS
LIPO
LIPS
MIPS
NIPA
NIPS
PIPE
PIPS
RIPE
RIPS
SIPS
TIPS
VIPS
WIPE
XIPE
YIPE
YIPS
ZIPS

•I•P
GIMP
LIMP
LISP
SIMP
WIMP
WISP

••IP
BLIP
CHIP
CLIP
DRIP
FLIP
GRIP
QTIP
QUIP
SHIP
SKIP
SLIP
SNIP
TRIP
WHIP

I••Q
IRAQ

•I•Q
CINQ

••IQ
DRIQ

IR••
IRAE
IRAN
IRAQ
IRAS
IRBM
IRED
IRES
IRID
IRIS
IRKS
IRMA
IRON

I•R•
IHRE
INRE
INRI
INRO

I••R
IBAR
ICER
IGOR
INCR
INTR
ISAR
ITER
IVOR
IYAR
IZAR

•IR•
AIRE
AIRS
AIRT
AIRY
BIRD
BIRK
BIRL
BIRR
CIRC
CIRE
DIRE
DIRK
DIRS
DIRT
EIRE
FIRE
FIRM
FIRN
FIRS
GIRD
GIRL
GIRN
GIRO
GIRT
HIRE
HIRT
KIRK
KIRS
LIRA
LIRE
MIRA
MIRE
MIRO
MIRS
MIRV
MIRY
PIRE
RIRE
SIRE
SIRS
TIRE
WIRE
WIRY

•I•R
BIRR
DIOR
HIER
LIAR
MICR
PIER
TIER
VIER

••IR
AMIR
ASIR
COIR
EMIR
FAIR
HAIR
HEIR
LAIR
MEIR
MUIR
NOIR
PAIR
SOIR
STIR
VAIR
VOIR
WEIR
WHIR
YMIR

IS••
ISAK
ISAR
ISAY
ISBA
ISBN
ISEE
ISIS
ISLA
ISLE
ISLS
ISMS
ISNT
ISPY
ISSN
ISTH

I•S•
IASI
IFSO
ILSA
INSP
INST
IPSE
IPSO
ISSN
ITSY

I••S
IBIS
IBOS
ICES
ICOS
ICUS
IDES
ILES
ILKS
ILLS
IMPS
INDS
INFS
INKS
INNS
INTS
INXS
IONS
IOUS
IRAS
IRES
IRIS
IRKS
ISIS
ISLS
ISMS
ITIS
IVES
IWIS

•IS•
BISE
CIST
DISC
DISH

DISK
DISS
DIST
FISC
FISH
FISK
FIST
GISH
GIST
HISS
HIST
KISH
KISS
LISA
LISE
LISP
LIST
MISC
MISE
MISO
MISS
MIST
NISI
OISE
PISA
PISH
RISE
RISK
SISI
TISH
VISA
VISE
WISC
WISE
WISH
WISK
WISP

•I•S
AIDS
AILS
AIMS
AIRS
AITS
BIAS
BIBS
BICS
BIDS
BINS
BIOS
BITS
CIGS
CITS
DIAS
DIBS
DIES
DIGS
DIMS
DINS
DIOS
DIPS
DIRS
DISS
DITS
DIVS
EINS
FIBS
FIGS
FILS
FINS
FIRS
FITS
GIBS
GIGS
GINS
GIPS
GITS
HIES
HIPS
HISS
HITS
JIBS
JIGS
KIDS
KIPS
KIRS
KISS
KITS
LIBS
LIDS
LIES
LIPS
MIBS
MICS
MIES
MIGS
MILS
MINS
MIPS
MIRS
MISS
NIBS
NILS
NIPS
NITS
OILS
PICS
PIES
PIGS
PINS
PIPS
PITS
PIUS
RIAS
RIBS
RIDS
RIFS
RIGS
RIIS
RIMS
RIOS
RIPS
SIBS
SICS
SIMS
SINS
SIPS
SIRS
SITS
TICS
TIES
TILS
TINS
TIPS
VIES
VINS
VIPS
WIGS
WINS
WITS
YIPS
ZIGS
ZIPS

••IS
ACIS
AMIS
ANIS
APIS
ASIS
AVIS
AXIS
BOIS
CHIS
DAIS
EGIS
ELIS
EPIS
ERIS
FOIS
FRIS
GRIS
IBIS
IRIS
ISIS
ITIS
IWIS
KOIS
KRIS
LEIS
LOIS
LUIS
MAIS
OBIS
OSIS
OTIS
OVIS
PHIS
POIS
PSIS
RBIS
RIIS
SAIS
SEIS
SKIS
THIS
TRIS
TUIS
URIS
UZIS

IT••
ITAL
ITCH
ITEA
ITEM
ITER
ITIS
ITLL
ITOL
ITSY
ITTY
ITZA

I•T•
INTL
INTO
INTR
INTS
IOTA
ISTH
ITTY

I••T
IBET
ICET
IMIT
INIT
INST
ISNT

•IT•
AITS
BITE
BITS
BITT
CITE
CITS
CITY
DITS
DITZ
FITS
FITZ
GITA
GITS
HITE
HITS
KITE
KITH
KITS
KITT
LITB
LITD
LITE
LITH
MITA
MITE
MITT
NITA
NITE
NITS
PITA
PITH
PITS
PITT
PITY
RITA
RITE
RITT
RITZ
SITE
SITS
SITU
TITI
TITO
VITA
VITE
VITI
VITO
WITE
WITH
WITS
WITT
ZITI

•I•T
AINT
AIRT
BITT
CIST
DICT
DIET
DINT
DIRT
DIST
FIAT
FICT
FIST
GIFT
GILT
GIRT
GIST
HILT
HINT
HIRT
HIST
JILT
KILT
KITT
LIFT
LILT
LINT
LIST
MILT
MINT
MIST
MITT
MIXT
PICT
PIET
PINT
PITT
RIFT
RIOT
RITT
SIFT
SILT
TILT
TINT
VIET
WILT
WITT

••IT
ADIT
ALIT
ATIT
BAIT
BLIT
BRIT
CHIT
CRIT
DLIT
DOIT
EDIT
EMIT
EXIT
FAIT
FLIT
FRIT
GAIT
GRIT
IMIT
INIT
KNIT
LAIT
NUIT
OBIT
OMIT
QUIT
REIT
SKIT
SLIT
SMIT
SNIT
SPIT
SUIT
SWIT
TAIT
TWIT
UNIT
WAIT
WHIT
WRIT

I•U•
ICUS
IDUN
IOUS

I••U
IGLU

•IU•
NIUE
PIUS

•I•U
AINU
DIEU
GIFU
KIVU
LIEU
SITU

IV••
IVAN
IVES
IVEY
IVOR

•IV•
DIVA
DIVE
DIVS
FIVE
GIVE
HIVE
JIVE
JIVY
KIVA
KIVU
LIVE
LIVY
RIVE
VIVA
VIVE

••IV
AVIV
CCIV
CDIV
CLIV
CMIV
CXIV
DCIV
DLIV
DXIV
LXIV
MCIV
MDIV
MLIV
MMIV
MXIV
PRIV
SHIV
SPIV
UNIV
XCIV
XDIV
XLIV
XXIV

IW••
IWIS

I•W•
IIWI

I••W
IOWA

•IW•
AIWA
BIWA
IIWI
KIWI
TIWA

•I•W
VIEW

IX••
IXIA

I•X•
INXS

I••X
IBEX
ILEX

•IX•
FIXE
MIXT
PIXY

•I•X
JINX
MINX
PINX

••IX
BRIX
CCIX
CDIX
CLIX
CMIX
CXIX
DCIX
DLIX
DXIX
FLIX
LXIX
MCIX
MDIX
MLIX
MMIX
MXIX
PAIX
PRIX
TRIX
TWIX
UNIX
VOIX
VSIX
XCIX
XLIX
XXIX

IY••
IYAR

I•Y•
IDYL

I••Y
ICKY
IDLY
IFFY
IGGY
ILLY
INDY
INKY
INLY
ISAY
ISPY
ITSY
ITTY
IVEY
IZZY

•IY•
HIYO

•I•Y
AIRY
CITY
JIVY
LILY
LIMY
LINY
LIVY
MIRY
OILY
PINY
PITY
PIXY
RIMY
TIDY
TINY
VINY
WILY
WIRY

IZ••
IZAR
IZBA
IZOD
IZZY

I•Z•
ITZA
IZZY

I••Z
INEZ

•IZ•
FIZZ
GIZA
LIZA
PIZZ
SIZE

•I•Z
DIAZ
DITZ
FITZ
FIZZ
LINZ
PIZZ
RITZ

••IZ
ARIZ
AZIZ
ELIZ
FRIZ
PHIZ
QUIZ
TAIZ
WHIZ

JA••
JABS
JACK
JADA
JADE
JAEL
JAEN
JAGS
JAHR
JAIL
JAIN
JAKE
JAMB
JAMS
JANE
JAPE
JARL
JARS
JATO
JAVA
JAWS
JAYE
JAYS
JAZZ

J•A•
JBAR
JEAN
JIAO
JOAB
JOAD
JOAN
JUAN

J••A
JADA
JAVA
JENA
JIMA
JUBA
JUGA
JURA

•JA•
AJAR
AJAX
OJAI

••JA
BAJA
DEJA
HIJA
MAJA
RAJA

JB••
JBAR

J•B•
JABS
JIBE
JIBS
JOBS
JUBA

J••B
JAMB
JOAB

J•C•
JACK
JOCK

J••C
JUNC

J•D•
JADA
JADE
JEDI
JODY
JUDD
JUDE
JUDG
JUDO
JUDY

J••D
JOAD
JUDD

••JD
NEJD

JE••
JEAN
JEDI
JEEP
JEER
JEEZ
JEFE
JEFF
JEHU
JELL
JENA
JENS
JERK
JESS
JEST
JESU
JETE
JETS
JETT
JEUX
JEWS

J•E•
JAEL
JAEN
JEEP
JEER
JEEZ
JOEL
JOEY

J••E
JADE
JAKE
JANE
JAPE
JAYE
JEFE
JETE
JIBE
JIVE
JOIE
JOKE
JOSE
JOVE
JUDE
JUKE
JULE
JUNE
JURE
JUTE

J•F•
JEFE
JEFF
JIFF

J••F
JEFF
JIFF

J•G•
JAGS
JIGS
JOGS
JUGA
JUGS

J••G
JONG
JUDG
JUNG

••JG
LTJG

J•H•
JAHR
JEHU
JOHN

J••H
JOSH

JI••
JIAO
JIBE
JIBS
JIFF
JIGS
JILL
JILT
JIMA
JIMI
JINK
JINN
JINX
JIVE
JIVY

J•I•
JAIL
JAIN
JOIE
JOIN

J••I
JEDI
JIMI
JOLI
JONI

•J•I
OJAI

••JI
FIJI
FUJI
HAJI
KOJI

J•J•
JUJU

••JJ
HAJJ

J•K•
JAKE
JOKE
JUKE

J••K
JACK
JERK
JINK
JOCK
JUNK

J•L•
JELL
JILL
JILT
JOLI
JOLO
JOLT
JULE
JULY

J••L
JAEL
JAIL
JARL
JELL
JILL
JOEL
JOWL

J•M•
JAMB
JAMS
JIMA
JIMI
JUMP

••JM
SEJM

J•N•
JANE
JENA
JENS
JINK
JINN
JINX
JONG
JONI
JUNC
JUNE
JUNG
JUNK
JUNO

J••N
JAEN
JAIN
JEAN
JINN
JOAN
JOHN
JOIN
JUAN

••JN
RIJN

JO••
JOAB
JOAD
JOAN
JOBS
JOCK
JODY
JOEL
JOEY
JOGS
JOHN
JOIE
JOIN
JOKE
JOLI
JOLO
JOLT
JONG
JONI
JOSE
JOSH
JOSS
JOTS
JOUR
JOVE
JOWL
JOYS

J••O
JATO
JIAO
JOLO
JUDO
JUNO

••JO
CUJO
DOJO
HIJO
HOJO
MOJO
ROJO
TOJO

J•P•
JAPE

J••P
JEEP
JUMP

J•R•
JARL
JARS
JERK
JURA
JURE
JURY

J••R
JAHR
JBAR
JEER
JOUR

•J•R
AJAR

J•S•
JESS
JEST
JESU
JOSE
JOSH
JOSS
JUST

J••S
JABS
JAGS
JAMS
JARS
JAWS
JAYS
JENS
JESS
JETS
JEWS
JIBS
JIGS
JOBS
JOGS
JOSS
JOTS
JOYS
JUGS
JUTS

••JS
ADJS
TAJS

J•T•
JATO
JETE
JETS
JETT
JOTS
JUTE
JUTS

J••T
JEST
JETT
JILT
JOLT
JUST

••JT
ADJT

JU••
JUAN
JUBA
JUDD
JUDE
JUDG
JUDO
JUDY
JUGA
JUGS
JUJU
JUKE
JULE
JULY
JUMP
JUNC
JUNE
JUNG
JUNK
JUNO
JURA
JURE
JURY
JUST
JUTE
JUTS

J•U•
JEUX
JOUR

J••U
JEHU
JESU
JUJU

••JU
JUJU

J•V•
JAVA
JIVE
JIVY
JOVE

J•W•
JAWS
JEWS
JOWL

J••X
JEUX
JINX

•J•X
AJAX

J•Y•
JAYE
JAYS
JOYS

J••Y
JIVY
JODY
JOEY
JUDY
JULY
JURY

J•Z•
JAZZ

J••Z
JAZZ
JEEZ

KA••
KAEL
KAHN
KAIN
KAKA
KAKI
KALB
KALE
KALI
KALT
KAMA
KAME
KAMI
KANA
KANE
KANO
KANS
KANT
KAON
KAPH
KARA
KARL
KARO
KART
KATE
KATO
KATY
KATZ
KAVA
KAYE
KAYO

K•A•
KCAL
KEAN
KEAS
KHAN
KHAT
KNAP
KNAR
KOAN
KWAI
KWAN
KYAT

K••A
KAKA
KAMA
KANA
KARA
KAVA
KINA
KIVA
KOLA
KONA
KYRA

•KA•
AKAN
OKAY
SKAT
SKAW

•K•A
MKSA
OKLA
OKRA
SKUA

••KA
ANKA
ATKA
DEKA
ILKA
INKA
KAKA
PIKA
PUKA
TAKA
WAKA
WEKA

K•B•
KOBE
KOBO
KOBS

K••B
KALB
KERB
KNOB

KC••
KCAL

K•C•
KICK
KOCH

K••C
KOFC
KROC

•KC•
EKCO

K•D•
KIDD
KIDS
KUDU

K••D
KIDD
KIND
KNUD
KURD

•K•D
EKED
NKVD
SKED
SKID

KE••
KEAN
KEAS
KEEL
KEEN
KEEP
KEET
KEGS
KELP
KEMO
KEMP
KENO
KENS
KENT
KEOS
KEPI
KEPT
KERB
KERF
KERN
KERR
KERT
KETO
KETT
KEYS

K•E•
KAEL
KEEL
KEEN
KEEP
KEET
KIEL
KIEV
KLEE
KNEE
KNEW

K••E
KALE
KAME
KANE
KATE
KAYE
KINE
KITE
KLEE
KNEE
KOBE
KORE
KYLE

•KE•
AKEE
EKED
EKES
OKEY
SKED
SKEE
SKEG
SKEP
SKEW
UKES

•K•E
AKEE
OKIE
SKEE
SKYE

••KE
BAKE
BIKE
CAKE
COKE
CUKE
DEKE
DIKE
DUKE
ELKE
FAKE
FYKE
HAKE
HIKE
HOKE
JAKE
JOKE
JUKE
LAKE
LIKE
LUKE
MAKE
MIKE
NIKE
NUKE
PEKE
PIKE
POKE
RAKE
SAKE
SOKE
TAKE
TIKE
TOKE
TYKE
WAKE
WOKE
YOKE
ZEKE

K•F•
KOFC
KOFP

K••F
KERF
KOPF

K•G•
KEGS

K••G
KING
KONG
KUNG

•K•G
MKTG
SKEG

KH••
KHAN
KHAT

K•H•
KAHN
KOHL
KUHN
KWHR

K••H
KAPH
KISH
KITH
KOCH
KOPH
KUSH

••KH
ANKH
SIKH

KI••
KICK
KIDD
KIDS
KIEL
KIEV
KIKI
KILL
KILN
KILO
KILT
KINA
KIND
KINE
KING
KINK
KINO
KIPS

KIRK
KIRS
KISH
KISS
KITE
KITH
KITS
KITT
KIVA
KIVU
KIWI

K•I•
KAIN
KNIT
KOIS
KRIO
KRIS

K••I
KAKI
KALI
KAMI
KEPI
KIKI
KIWI
KOJI
KOMI
KWAI

•KI•
AKIM
AKIN
OKIE
SKID
SKIL
SKIM
SKIN
SKIP
SKIS
SKIT

••KI
KAKI
KIKI
LOKI
RAKI
SAKI
TIKI

K•J•
KOJI

K•K•
KAKA
KAKI
KIKI
KOKO

K••K
KICK
KINK
KIRK
KOOK
KRUK

KL••
KLEE

K•L•
KALB
KALE
KALI
KALT
KELP
KILL
KILN
KILO
KILT
KOLA
KOLN
KOLO
KYLE

K••L
KAEL
KARL
KCAL
KEEL
KIEL
KILL
KOHL
KOOL

•KL•
OKLA
WKLY

•K•L
SKIL
SKOL

K•M•
KAMA
KAME
KAMI
KEMO
KEMP
KOMI

•K•M
AKIM
SKIM

KN••
KNAP
KNAR
KNEE
KNEW
KNIT
KNOB
KNOP
KNOT
KNOW
KNOX
KNUD
KNUR
KNUT

K•N•
KANA
KANE
KANO
KANS
KANT
KENO
KENS
KENT
KINA
KIND
KINE
KING
KINK
KINO
KONA
KONG
KUNG

K••N
KAHN
KAIN
KAON
KEAN
KEEN
KERN
KHAN
KILN
KOAN
KOLN
KUHN
KWAN
KWON

•KN•
DKNY

•K•N
AKAN
AKIN
SKIN

KO••
KOAN
KOBE
KOBO
KOBS
KOCH
KOFC
KOFP
KOHL
KOIS
KOJI
KOKO
KOLA
KOLN
KOLO
KOMI
KONA
KONG
KOOK
KOOL
KOOP
KOPF
KOPH
KOPS
KORE
KOTO

K•O•
KAON
KEOS
KNOB
KNOP
KNOT
KNOW
KNOX
KOOK
KOOL
KOOP
KROC
KWON

K••O
KANO
KARO
KATO
KAYO
KEMO
KENO
KETO
KILO
KINO
KOBO
KOKO
KOLO
KOTO
KRIO

•KO•
SKOL
TKOS

•K•O
EKCO

••KO
BIKO
ELKO
KOKO
MAKO
YOKO

K•P•
KAPH
KEPI
KEPT
KIPS
KOPF
KOPH
KOPS

K••P
KEEP
KELP
KEMP
KNAP
KNOP
KOFP
KOOP

•K•P
SKEP
SKIP
WKRP

KR••
KRIO
KRIS
KROC
KRUK

K•R•
KARA
KARL
KARO
KART
KERB
KERF
KERN
KERR
KERT
KIRK
KIRS
KORE
KURD
KURT
KYRA

K••R
KERR
KNAR
KNUR
KWHR

•KR•
OKRA
WKRP

••KR
BAKR

K•S•
KISH
KISS
KUSH

K••S
KANS
KEAS
KEGS
KENS
KEOS
KEYS
KIDS
KIPS
KIRS
KISS
KITS
KOBS
KOIS
KOPS
KRIS

•KS•
MKSA

•K•S
EKES
SKIS
SKYS
TKOS
TKTS
UKES

••KS
ARKS
ASKS
AUKS
EEKS
ELKS
ILKS
INKS
IRKS
LEKS
LUKS
OAKS
SAKS
SUKS
TPKS
TSKS
WOKS
YAKS
YUKS

K•T•
KATE
KATO
KATY
KATZ
KETO
KETT
KITE
KITH
KITS
KITT
KOTO

K••T
KALT
KANT
KART
KEET
KENT
KEPT
KERT
KETT
KHAT
KILT
KITT
KNIT
KNOT
KNUT
KURT
KYAT

•KT•
MKTG
TKTS

•K•T
SKAT
SKIT

KU••
KUDU
KUHN
KUNG
KURD
KURT
KUSH

K•U•
KNUD
KNUR
KNUT
KRUK

K••U
KIVU
KUDU

•KU•
SKUA

••KU
BAKU
PUKU
RAKU

K•V•
KAVA
KIVA
KIVU

K••V
KIEV

•KV•
NKVD

KW••
KWAI
KWAN
KWHR
KWON

K•W•
KIWI

K••W
KNEW
KNOW

•KW•
PKWY

•K•W
SKAW
SKEW

K••X
KNOX

KY••
KYAT
KYLE
KYRA

K•Y•
KAYE
KAYO
KEYS

K••Y
KATY

•KY•
SKYE
SKYS

•K•Y
DKNY
OKAY
OKEY
PKWY
WKLY

••KY
CAKY
COKY
ICKY
INKY
POKY

K••Z
KATZ

LA••
LABS
LACE
LACK
LACS
LACT
LACY
LADD
LADE
LADS
LADY
LAGO
LAGS
LAHR
LAIC
LAID
LAIN
LAIR
LAIT
LAKE
LALA
LALO
LAMA
LAMB
LAME
LAMP
LAMS
LAMY
LANA
LAND
LANE
LANG
LANK
LAOS
LAPD
LAPP
LAPS
LARA
LARD
LARI
LARK
LARS
LASE
LASH
LASS
LAST
LATE
LATH
LATS
LAUD
LAUE
LAVA
LAVE
LAVS
LAWN
LAWS
LAYS
LAZE
LAZY

L•A•
LBAR
LEAD
LEAF
LEAH
LEAK
LEAL
LEAN
LEAP
LEAR
LEAS
LIAM
LIAR
LOAD
LOAF
LOAM
LOAN
LSAT
LUAU

L••A
LALA
LAMA
LANA
LARA
LAVA
LEDA
LEIA
LENA
LILA
LIMA
LINA
LIRA
LISA
LIZA
LOLA
LOMA
LPGA
LUNA
LYRA

•LA•
ALAE
ALAI
ALAN
ALAR
ALAS
BLAB
BLAH
BLAS
BLAT
BLAU
CLAD
CLAM
CLAN
CLAP
CLAR
CLAW
CLAY
ELAL
ELAM
ELAN
FLAB
FLAG
FLAK
FLAM
FLAN
FLAP
FLAT
FLAV
FLAW
FLAX
FLAY
GLAD
GLAM
NLAT
OLAF
OLAN
OLAV
PLAN
PLAT
PLAX
PLAY
SLAB
SLAG
SLAM
SLAP
SLAT
SLAV
SLAW
SLAY
ULAN

•L•A
ALBA
ALDA
ALFA
ALGA
ALIA
ALLA
ALMA
ALTA
ALVA
ELBA
ELEA
ELIA
ELLA
ELSA
FLEA
GLIA
ILIA
ILKA
ILSA
OLGA
OLLA
PLEA
ULNA

••LA
ALLA
AULA
AYLA
BELA
BOLA
CELA
COLA
EBLA
ELLA
FALA
FILA
FULA
GALA
GILA
HILA
HOLA
HULA
HYLA
IOLA
ISLA
KOLA
LALA
LILA
LOLA
MALA
MOLA
NOLA
OKLA
OLLA
POLA
PULA
SALA
SELA
SOLA
TALA
TOLA
TULA
UCLA
VELA
VILA
ZOLA

LB••
LBAR

L•B•
LABS
LIBS
LLBS
LOBE
LOBO
LOBS
LUBE

L••B
LAMB
LIEB
LIMB
LITB
LOEB

•LB•
ALBA
ALBI
ALBS
ELBA
ELBE
LLBS
SLBM

•L•B
BLAB
BLEB
BLOB
CLUB
FLAB
FLUB
GLIB
GLOB
NLRB
PLEB
SLAB
SLOB
SLUB

••LB
BULB
KALB

LC••
LCDS

L•C•
LACE
LACK
LACS
LACT
LACY
LECH
LECT
LICE
LICK
LOCH
LOCI
LOCK
LOCO
LUCE
LUCK
LUCY

L••C
LAIC

•LC•
MLCC

•L•C
ALEC
BLOC
ELEC
FLIC
FLOC
GLUC
GLYC
MLCC

••LC
CALC
TALC

LD••
LDRS

L•D•
LADD
LADE
LADS
LADY
LCDS
LEDA
LEDS
LIDO
LIDS
LLDS
LODE
LODI
LODZ

L••D
LADD
LAID
LAND
LAPD
LARD
LAUD
LEAD
LEND
LEWD
LIED
LIND
LITD
LOAD
LOID
LORD
LOUD

•LD•
ALDA
ALDO
BLDG
BLDR
LLDS
OLDE
OLDS

•L•D
BLED
BLVD
CLAD
CLOD
FLED
GLAD
OLID
PLED
PLOD
SLED
SLID

••LD
AULD
BALD
BOLD
COLD
FOLD
GILD
GOLD
HELD
HOLD
MELD
MILD
MOLD
NFLD
SILD
SOLD
TOLD
VELD
WALD
WELD
WILD
WOLD

LE••
LEAD
LEAF
LEAH
LEAK
LEAL
LEAN
LEAP
LEAR
LEAS
LECH
LECT
LEDA
LEDS
LEEK
LEER
LEES
LEET
LEFT
LEGO
LEGS
LEHR
LEIA
LEIF
LEIS
LEKS
LELY
LEMS
LENA
LEND
LENI
LENO
LENS
LENT
LENZ
LEON
LEOS
LESE
LESS
LEST
LETO
LETS
LETT
LEUK
LEVI
LEVO
LEVY
LEWD

L•E•
LEEK
LEER
LEES
LEET
LIEB
LIED
LIEF
LIEN
LIES
LIEU
LOEB
LOEW
LYES

L••E
LACE
LADE
LAKE
LAME
LANE
LASE
LATE
LAUE
LAVE
LAZE
LESE
LICE
LIFE
LIKE
LIME
LINE
LIRE
LISE
LITE
LIVE
LOBE
LODE
LOGE
LOME
LONE
LOPE
LORE
LOSE
LOVE
LOWE
LUBE
LUCE
LUGE
LUKE
LUNE
LUPE
LURE
LUTE
LUXE
LYLE
LYNE
LYRE

•LE•
ALEC
ALEE
ALEF
ALEP
ALES
ALEX
BLEB
BLED
BLEU
BLEW
CLEF
CLEM
CLEO
CLEW
ELEA
ELEC
ELEM
ELEV
FLEA
FLED
FLEE
FLEM
FLEW
FLEX
FLEY
GLEE
GLEG
GLEN
GLEY
ILES
ILEX
KLEE
NLER
OLEG
OLEO
OLES
PLEA
PLEB
PLED
PLEO
PLEX
SLED
SLEW
YLEM

•L•E
ALAE
ALEE
ALLE
ALOE
ALTE
BLUE
CLUE
ELBE
ELIE
ELKE
ELLE
ELSE
FLEE
FLOE
FLUE
GLEE
GLUE
ILIE
ILLE
KLEE
MLLE
OLDE
PLIE
SLOE
SLUE
SLYE

••LE
ABLE
ALLE
AXLE
BALE
BILE
BOLE
CALE
COLE
CULE
DALE
DELE
DOLE
ELLE
ERLE
FILE
GALE
HALE
HOLE
IBLE
IDLE
ILLE
IOLE
ISLE
JULE
KALE
KYLE
LYLE
MALE
MILE
MLLE
MOLE
MULE
NILE
OGLE
ORLE
PALE
PELE
PILE
POLE
PULE
PYLE
RILE
ROLE
RULE
RYLE
SALE
SOLE
TALE
TELE
TILE
TOLE
TULE
UELE
VALE
VILE
VOLE
WALE
WILE
YALE
YULE

L•F•
LEFT
LIFE
LIFO
LIFT
LOFT
LUFF
LUFT

L••F
LEAF
LEIF
LIEF
LOAF
LUFF

•LF•
ALFA

•L•F
ALEF
ALIF
CLEF
OLAF

••LF
CALF
DOLF
GOLF
GULF
HALF
PELF
ROLF
SELF
SULF
WOLF

LG••
LGTH

L•G•
LAGO
LAGS
LEGO
LEGS
LOGE
LOGO
LOGS
LOGY
LPGA
LUGE
LUGS

L••G
LANG
LING
LONG
LTJG
LUNG

•LG•
ALGA
ALGO
ALGY
OLGA

•L•G
BLDG
CLOG
FLAG
FLOG
GLEG
GLUG
OLEG
PLUG
SLAG
SLOG
SLUG

••LG
BELG
BULG
VULG

L•H•
LAHR
LEHR

L••H
LASH
LATH
LEAH
LECH
LGTH
LITH
LOCH
LUSH
LUTH

•LH•
ELHI

•L•H
ALPH
BLAH

LI••
LIAM
LIAR
LIBS
LICE
LICK
LIDO
LIDS
LIEB
LIED
LIEF
LIEN
LIES
LIEU
LIFE
LIFO
LIFT
LIII
LIKE
LILA
LILI
LILT
LILY
LIMA
LIMB
LIME
LIMN
LIMO
LIMP
LIMY
LINA
LIND
LINE
LING
LINK
LINT
LINY
LINZ
LION
LIPO
LIPS
LIRA
LIRE
LISA
LISE
LISP
LIST
LITB
LITD
LITE
LITH
LIVE
LIVY
LIZA

L•I•
LAIC
LAID
LAIN
LAIR
LAIT
LEIA
LEIF
LEIS
LIII
LOID
LOIN
LOIS
LUIS
LVII
LXII
LXIV
LXIX

L••I
LARI
LENI
LEVI
LIII
LILI
LOCI
LODI
LOKI
LONI
LORI
LOTI
LVII
LXII
LXVI
LXXI

•LI•
ALIA
ALIF
ALII
ALIT
BLIN
BLIP
BLIT
CLII
CLIN
CLIO
CLIP
CLIV
CLIX
DLII
DLIT
DLIV
DLIX
ELIA
ELIE
ELIS
ELIZ
FLIC
FLIM
FLIP
FLIT
FLIX
GLIA
GLIB
GLIM
ILIA
ILIE
ILIO
MLII
MLIV
MLIX
OLID
OLIN
OLIO
PLIE
SLID
SLIM
SLIP
SLIT
XLII
XLIV
XLIX

•L•I
ALAI
ALBI
ALII
ALTI
ALUI
CLII
CLVI
CLXI
DLII
DLVI
DLXI
ELHI
ELOI
MLII
MLVI
MLXI
XLII
XLVI

••LI
ATLI
BALI
CALI
CCLI
CDLI
CMLI
CXLI
DALI
DCLI
DELI
DXLI
HELI
JOLI
KALI
LILI
MALI
MCLI
MDLI
MMLI
MXLI
NOLI
PALI
PILI
PULI
SOLI
TALI
UGLI

L•J•
LTJG

L•K•
LAKE
LEKS
LIKE
LOKI
LUKE
LUKS

L••K
LACK
LANK
LARK
LEAK
LEEK
LEUK
LICK
LINK
LOCK
LOOK
LUCK
LURK

•LK•
ELKE
ELKO
ELKS
ILKA
ILKS

•L•K
FLAK

••LK
BALK
BILK
BULK
CALK
FALK
FOLK
HULK
MILK
POLK
SALK
SILK
SULK
TALK
WALK
WELK
YOLK

LL••
LLBS
LLDS
LLMS

L•L•
LALA
LALO
LELY
LILA
LILI
LILT
LILY
LOLA
LOLL
LULL
LULU
LYLE
LYLY

L••L
LEAL
LOLL
LULL

•LL•
ALLA
ALLE
ALLO
ALLS
ALLY
ELLA
ELLE
ELLS
ELLY
ILLE
ILLS
ILLY
MLLE
OLLA

•L•L
ELAL
ELUL

••LL
BALL
BELL
BILL
BOLL
BULL
CALL
CELL
COLL
CULL
DELL
DILL
DOLL
DULL
FALL
FELL
FILL
FULL
GALL
GELL
GILL
GULL
HALL
HELL
HILL
HULL
ITLL
JELL
JILL
KILL
LOLL
LULL
MALL
MELL
MILL
MOLL
MULL
NELL
NOLL
NULL
PALL
PELL
PILL
POLL
PULL
RALL
RILL
ROLL
SELL
SILL
SYLL
TALL
TELL
TILL
TOLL
TULL
WALL
WELL
WILL
YALL
YELL
ZILL

L•M•
LAMA
LAMB
LAME
LAMP
LAMS
LAMY
LEMS
LIMA
LIMB
LIME
LIMN
LIMO
LIMP
LIMY
LLMS
LOMA
LOME
LUMP

L••M
LIAM
LOAM
LOOM

•LM•
ALMA
ALMS
ELMO
ELMS
LLMS

•L•M
ALUM
BLUM
CLAM
CLEM
ELAM
ELEM
FLAM
FLEM
FLIM
GLAM
GLIM
GLOM
GLUM
PLUM
SLAM
SLBM
SLIM
SLUM
YLEM

••LM
BALM
CALM
CULM
FILM
HALM
HELM
HOLM
MALM
PALM

L•N•
LANA
LAND
LANE
LANG
LANK
LENA
LEND
LENI
LENO
LENS
LENT
LENZ
LINA
LIND
LINE
LING
LINK
LINT
LINY
LINZ
LONE
LONG
LONI
LUNA
LUNE
LUNG
LUNN
LUNT
LYNE
LYNN
LYNX

L••N
LAIN
LAWN
LEAN
LEON
LIEN
LIMN
LION
LOAN
LOIN
LOON
LORN
LRON
LUNN
LYNN
LYON

•LN•
ULNA

•L•N
ALAN
BLIN
CLAN
CLIN
ELAN
ELON
FLAN
GLEN
GLYN
OLAN
OLIN
PLAN
ULAN

••LN
KILN
KOLN
SOLN

LO••
LOAD
LOAF
LOAM
LOAN
LOBE
LOBO
LOBS
LOCH
LOCI
LOCK
LOCO
LODE
LODI
LODZ
LOEB
LOEW
LOFT
LOGE
LOGO
LOGS
LOGY
LOID
LOIN
LOIS
LOKI
LOLA
LOLL
LOMA
LOME
LONE
LONG
LONI
LOOK
LOOM
LOON
LOOP
LOOS
LOOT
LOPE
LOPS
LORD
LORE
LORI
LORN
LORY
LOSE
LOSS
LOST
LOTI
LOTS
LOTT
LOUD
LOUP
LOUT
LOVE
LOWE
LOWS

L•O•
LAOS
LEON
LEOS
LION
LOOK
LOOM
LOON
LOOP
LOOS
LOOT
LRON
LVOV
LYON

L••O
LAGO
LALO
LEGO
LENO
LETO
LEVO
LIDO
LIFO
LIMO
LIPO
LOBO
LOCO
LOGO

•LO•
ALOE
ALOU
BLOB
BLOC
BLOT
BLOW
CLOD
CLOG
CLOP
CLOT
CLOY
ELOI
ELON
FLOC
FLOE
FLOG
FLOP
FLOR
FLOW
FLOZ
GLOB
GLOM
GLOP
GLOT
GLOW
PLOD
PLOP
PLOT
PLOW
PLOY
SLOB
SLOE
SLOG
SLOP
SLOT
SLOW

•L•O
ALDO
ALGO
ALLO
ALPO
ALSO
ALTO
CLEO
CLIO
ELKO
ELMO
ILIO
OLEO
OLIO
PLEO

••LO
ALLO
ARLO
BELO
BOLO
COLO
HALO
HELO
HILO
HOLO
JOLO
KILO
KOLO
LALO
MALO
MILO
NOLO
OSLO
PALO
POLO
SILO
SOLO
STLO
TELO
XYLO

LP••
LPGA

L•P•
LAPD
LAPP
LAPS
LIPO
LIPS
LOPE
LOPS
LUPE

L••P
LAMP
LAPP
LEAP
LIMP
LISP
LOOP
LOUP
LUMP

•LP•
ALPH
ALPO
ALPS

•L•P
ALEP
BLIP
CLAP
CLIP
CLOP
FLAP
FLIP
FLOP
GLOP
PLOP
SLAP
SLIP
SLOP

••LP
CULP
GULP
HELP
HOLP
KELP
PALP
PULP
SALP
YELP

LR••
LRON

L•R•
LARA
LARD
LARI
LARK
LARS
LDRS
LIRA
LIRE
LORD
LORE
LORI
LORN
LORY
LURE
LURK
LYRA
LYRE

L••R
LAHR
LAIR
LBAR
LEAR
LEER
LEHR
LIAR

•LR•
NLRB
SLRS

•L•R
ALAR
BLDR
BLUR
CLAR
FLOR
NLER
PLUR
SLUR

LS••
LSAT
LSTS

L•S•
LASE
LASH
LASS
LAST
LESE
LESS
LEST
LISA
LISE
LISP
LIST
LOSE
LOSS
LOST
LUSH
LUST

L••S
LABS
LACS
LADS
LAGS
LAMS
LAOS
LAPS
LARS
LASS
LATS
LAVS
LAWS
LAYS
LCDS
LDRS
LEAS
LEDS
LEES
LEGS
LEIS
LEKS
LEMS
LENS
LEOS
LESS
LETS
LIBS
LIDS
LIES
LIPS
LLBS
LLDS
LLMS
LOBS
LOGS
LOIS
LOOS
LOPS
LOSS
LOTS
LOWS
LSTS
LUGS
LUIS
LUKS
LUVS
LYES

•LS•
ALSO
ELSA
ELSE
ILSA

•L•S
ALAS
ALBS
ALES
ALLS
ALMS
ALPS
ALTS
BLAS
BLTS
ELIS
ELKS
ELLS
ELMS
FLUS
ILES
ILKS
ILLS
LLBS
LLDS
LLMS
OLDS
OLES
PLUS
SLRS
ULUS

••LS
AILS
ALLS
AWLS
BBLS
BELS
CALS
CELS
COLS
CPLS
CULS
DELS
EELS
ELLS
FILS
GALS
GELS
HALS
ILLS
ISLS
MILS
NILS
OILS
OWLS
PALS
POLS
RELS
SALS
SOLS
SYLS
TILS
VOLS

LT••
LTJG

L•T•
LATE
LATH
LATS
LETO
LETS
LETT
LGTH
LITB
LITD
LITE
LITH
LOTI
LOTS
LOTT
LSTS
LUTE
LUTH
LUTZ

L••T
LACT
LAIT
LAST
LECT
LEET
LEFT
LENT
LEST
LETT
LIFT
LILT
LINT
LIST
LOFT
LOOT
LOST
LOTT
LOUT
LSAT
LUFT
LUNT
LUST

•LT•
ALTA
ALTE
ALTI
ALTO
ALTS
BLTS

•L•T
ALIT
BLAT
BLIT
BLOT
CLOT
DLIT
FLAT
FLIT
GLOT
GLUT
NLAT
PLAT
PLOT
SLAT
SLIT
SLOT

••LT
BALT
BELT
BOLT
CELT
COLT
CULT
DOLT
FELT
GELT
GILT
HALT
HILT
HOLT
JILT
JOLT
KALT
KILT
LILT
MALT
MELT
MILT
MOLT
PELT
SALT
SILT
TILT
VOLT
WALT
WELT
WILT

LU••
LUAU
LUBE
LUCE
LUCK
LUCY
LUFF
LUFT
LUGE
LUGS
LUIS
LUKE
LUKS
LULL
LULU
LUMP
LUNA
LUNE
LUNG
LUNN
LUNT
LUPE
LURE
LURK
LUSH
LUST
LUTE
LUTH
LUTZ
LUVS
LUXE

L•U•
LAUD
LAUE
LEUK
LOUD
LOUP
LOUT

L••U
LIEU
LUAU
LULU

•LU•
ALUI
ALUM
BLUE
BLUM
BLUR
CLUB
CLUE
ELUL
FLUB
FLUE
FLUS
FLUX
GLUC
GLUE
GLUG
GLUM
GLUT
PLUG
PLUM
PLUR
PLUS
SLUB
SLUE
SLUG
SLUM
SLUR
ULUS

•L•U
ALOU
BLAU
BLEU

••LU
ACLU
IGLU
LULU
SULU
TOLU
YALU
ZULU

LV••
LVII
LVOV

L•V•
LAVA
LAVE
LAVS
LEVI
LEVO
LEVY
LIVE
LIVY
LOVE
LUVS
LXVI

L••V
LVOV
LXIV
LXXV

•LV•
ALVA
BLVD
CLVI
DLVI
MLVI
XLVI

•L•V
CLIV
CLXV
DLIV
DLXV
ELEV
FLAV
MLIV
MLXV
OLAV
SLAV
XLIV

••LV
CCLV
CDLV
CMLV
CXLV
DCLV
DXLV
GALV
MCLV
MDLV
MMLV
MXLV
UNLV

L•W•
LAWN
LAWS
LEWD
LOWE
LOWS

L••W
LOEW

•L•W
BLEW
BLOW
CLAW
CLEW
FLAW
FLEW
FLOW
GLOW
PLOW
SLAW
SLEW
SLOW

LX••
LXII
LXIV
LXIX
LXVI
LXXI
LXXV
LXXX

L•X•
LUXE
LXXI
LXXV
LXXX

L••X
LXIX
LXXX
LYNX

•LX•
CLXI
CLXV
CLXX
DLXI
DLXV
DLXX
MLXI
MLXV
MLXX

•L•X
ALEX
CLIX
CLXX
DLIX
DLXX
FLAX
FLEX
FLIX
FLUX
ILEX
MLIX
MLXX
PLAX
PLEX
XLIX

••LX
CALX
CCLX
CDLX
CMLX
DCLX
FALX
MCLX
MDLX
MMLX

LY••
LYES
LYLE
LYLY
LYNE
LYNN
LYNX
LYON
LYRA
LYRE

L•Y•
LAYS

L••Y
LACY
LADY
LAMY
LAZY
LELY
LEVY
LILY
LIMY
LINY
LIVY
LOGY
LORY
LUCY
LYLY

•LY•
GLYC
GLYN
SLYE

•L•Y
ALGY
ALLY
CLAY
CLOY
ELLY
FLAY
FLEY
GLEY
ILLY
PLAY
PLOY
SLAY

••LY
ABLY
ALLY
BELY
COLY
DALY
DELY
DULY
EELY
ELLY
EMLY
HOLY
IDLY
ILLY
INLY
JULY
LELY
LILY
LYLY
MOLY
OILY
ONLY
ORLY
PALY
POLY
RELY
ROLY
UGLY
WILY
WKLY

L•Z•
LAZE
LAZY
LIZA

L••Z
LENZ
LINZ
LODZ
LUTZ

•L•Z
ELIZ
FLOZ

MA••
MAAM
MAAR
MAAS
MAAT
MACE
MACH
MACK
MACS
MACY
MADD
MADE
MAGE
MAGI
MAGS
MAIA
MAID
MAIL
MAIN
MAIS
MAJA
MAKE
MAKO
MALA
MALE
MALI
MALL
MALM
MALO
MALT
MAMA
MAME
MANA
MANE
MANN
MANO
MANS
MANU
MANX
MANY
MAPS
MARA
MARC
MARE
MARG
MARI
MARK
MARL
MARS
MART
MARU
MARV
MARX
MARY
MASC
MASH
MASK
MASS
MAST
MATA
MATE
MATH
MATS
MATT
MAUD
MAUI
MAUL
MAVS
MAWR
MAWS
MAXI
MAYA
MAYI
MAYO
MAYS
MAZE
MAZO
MAZY

M•A•
MAAM
MAAR
MAAS
MAAT
MBAS
MCAT
MEAD
MEAL
MEAN
MEAS
MEAT
MFAS
MOAB
MOAN
MOAS
MOAT
MPAA

M••A
MAIA
MAJA
MALA
MAMA
MANA
MARA
MATA
MAYA
MEGA
MESA
META
MICA
MINA
MIRA
MITA
MKSA
MOLA
MOMA
MONA
MORA
MOTA
MPAA
MRNA
MYNA
MYRA

•MA•
AMAH
AMAS
AMAT
GMAC
GMAN
GMAT
IMAM
IMAN
OMAN
OMAR
TMAN
XMAS

•M•A
AMIA
EMIA
EMMA
SMSA
UMEA
YMCA

••MA
ALMA
ARMA
BAMA
BEMA
BOMA
CAMA
COMA
CYMA
DAMA
DUMA
EMMA
ERMA
FEMA
FNMA
GAMA
GNMA
HAMA
HEMA
IRMA
JIMA
KAMA
LAMA
LIMA
LOMA
MAMA
MOMA
PIMA
PUMA
RAMA
RIMA
ROMA
SIMA
SOMA
TAMA
USMA
YAMA
YIMA
YUMA
ZAMA

MB••
MBAS MBES MBOY

M•B•
MIBS MOBS MOBY

M••B
MOAB MUSB MYOB

•MB•
AMBI AMBO AMBS UMBO

••MB
BOMB COMB DUMB IAMB JAMB LAMB LIMB NUMB TOMB

MC••
MCAT MCCC MCCI MCCL MCCV MCCX MCDI MCDL MCDV MCDX MCII MCIV MCIX MCLI MCLV MCLX MCMI MCML MCMV MCMX MCVI MCXC MCXI MCXL MCXV MCXX

M•C•
MACE MACH MACK MACS MACY MCCC MCCI MCCL MCCV MCCX MDCC MDCI MDCL MDCV MDCX MECH MECO MICA MICE MICH MICK MICR MICS MLCC MMCC MMCD MMCI MMCL MMCM MMCV MMCX MOCK MOCS MUCH MUCK MXCI MXCV MYCO

M••C
MARC MASC MCCC MCXC MDCC MDXC MISC MLCC MMCC MMDC MMMC MMXC MSEC

•MC•
MMCC MMCD MMCI MMCL MMCM MMCV MMCX YMCA

•M•C
AMIC BMOC CMXC GMAC MMCC MMDC MMMC MMXC

••MC
MMMC USMC

MD••
MDCC MDCI MDCL MDCV MDCX MDII MDIV MDIX MDLI MDLV MDLX MDSE MDVI MDXC MDXI MDXL MDXV MDXX

M•D•
MADD MADE MCDI MCDL MCDV MCDX MEDE MEDS MIDI MIDN MMDC MMDI MMDL MMDV MMDX MODE MODS MUDD MUDS

M••D
MADD MAID MAUD MEAD MELD MEND MILD MIND MMCD MMMD MOLD MOOD MRED MUDD

•MD•
CMDG CMDR DMDS MMDC MMDI MMDL MMDV MMDX RMDR

•M•D
AMID MMCD MMMD

••MD
COMD MMMD

ME••
MEAD MEAL MEAN MEAS MEAT MECH MECO MEDE MEDS MEEK MEER MEET MEGA MEIN MEIR MELD MELL MELT MEME MEMO MEMS MEND MENS MENT MENU MEOW MERE MERO MERV MESA MESH MESO MESS META METE METH METS METZ MEWL MEWS

M•E•
MBES MEEK MEER MEET MIEN MIES MMES MRED MSEC

M••E
MACE MADE MAGE MAKE MALE MAME MANE MARE MATE MAZE MDSE MEDE MEME MERE METE MICE MIKE MILE MIME MINE MIRE MISE MITE MLLE MODE MOLE MOME MOPE MORE MOSE MOTE MOUE MOVE MTGE MULE MUSE MUTE

•ME•
AMEN AMER AMES AMEX GMEN MMES NMEX OMEN OMER SMEE SMEW TMEN UMEA XMEN

•M•E
AMIE SMEE

••ME
ACME AIME ARME AYME CAME COME CYME DAME DEME DIME DOME ESME FAME FEME FUME GAME HAME HEME HOME HUME KAME LAME LIME LOME MAME MEME MIME MOME NAME NOME POME RIME ROME SAME SEME SOME TAME TIME TOME

MF••
MFAS MFRS

M•F•
MIFF MUFF

M••F
MIFF MUFF

•MF•
AMFM

MG••
MGMT MGRS

M•G•
MAGE MAGI MAGS MEGA MIGS MNGR MSGR MSGS MSGT MTGE MTGS MUGS

M••G
MARG MING MKTG MOOG MUNG

•M•G
CMDG SMOG SMUG

MH••
MHOS

M•H•
MOHO MOHS

M••H
MACH MASH MATH MECH MESH METH MICH MINH MOTH MUCH MUSH MYTH

•M•H
AMAH UMPH

MI••
MIBS MICA MICE MICH MICK MICR MICS MIDI MIDN MIEN MIES MIFF MIGS MIII MIKE MILD MILE MILK MILL MILO MILS MILT MIME MIMI MINA MIND MINE MING MINH MINI MINK MINN MINS MINT MINX MIPS MIRA MIRE MIRO MIRS MIRV MIRY MISC MISE MISO MISS MIST MITA MITE MITT MIXT

M•I•
MAIA MAID MAIL MAIN MAIS MCII MCIV MCIX MDII MDIV MDIX MEIN MEIR MIII MLII MLIV MLIX MMII MMIV MMIX MOIL MUIR MVII MXII MXIV MXIX

M••I
MAGI MALI MARI MAUI MAXI MAYI MCCI MCDI MCII MCLI MCMI MCVI MCXI MDCI MDII MDLI MDVI MDXI MIDI MIII MIMI MINI MLII MLVI MLXI MMCI MMDI MMII MMLI MMMI MMVI MMXI MUNI MVII MXCI MXII MXLI MXVI MXXI

•MI•
AMIA AMIC AMID AMIE AMIN AMIR AMIS CMII CMIV CMIX EMIA EMIL EMIR EMIT IMIT MMII MMIV MMIX OMIT SMIT YMIR

•M•I
AMBI AMOI CMII CMLI CMVI CMXI IMPI MMCI MMDI MMII MMLI MMMI MMVI MMXI OMNI OMRI

••MI
CAMI DEMI HEMI JIMI KAMI KOMI MCMI MIMI MMMI RAMI SEMI SIMI SQMI

M•J•
MAJA MOJO

MK••
MKSA MKTG

M•K•
MAKE MAKO MIKE

M••K
MACK MARK MASK MEEK MICK MILK MINK MOCK MONK MORK MUCK MURK MUSK

•M•K
AMOK OMSK

ML••
MLCC MLII MLIV MLIX MLLE MLVI MLXI MLXV MLXX

M•L•
MALA MALE MALI MALL MALM MALO MALT MCLI MCLV MCLX MDLI MDLV MDLX MELD MELL MELT MILD MILE MILK MILL MILO MILS MILT MLLE MMLI MMLV MMLX MOLA MOLD MOLE MOLL MOLT MOLY MULE MULL MXLI MXLV

M••L
MAIL MALL MARL MAUL MCCL MCDL MCML MCXL MDCL MDXL MEAL MELL MEWL MILL MMCL MMDL MMML MMXL MOIL MOLL MULL

•ML•
CMLI CMLV CMLX EMLY MMLI MMLV MMLX

•M•L
AMYL CMXL EMIL MMCL MMDL MMML MMXL

••ML
COML MCML MMML SAML

MM••
MMCC MMCD MMCI MMCL MMCM MMCV MMCX MMDC MMDI MMDL MMDV MMDX MMES MMII MMIV MMIX MMLI MMLV MMLX MMMC MMMD MMMI MMML MMMM MMMV MMMX MMVI MMXC MMXI MMXL MMXV MMXX

M•M•
MAMA MAME MCMI MCML MCMV MCMX MEME MEMO MEMS MGMT MIME MIMI MMMC MMMD MMMI MMML MMMM MMMV MMMX MOMA MOME MOMS MUMS MYMY

M••M
MAAM MALM MMCM MMMM MUSM

•MM•
AMMO EMMA EMMY MMMC MMMD MMMI MMML MMMM MMMV MMMX

•M•M
AMFM IMAM MMCM MMMM

••MM
COMM GUMM HAMM MMMM TAMM

MN••
MNGR

M•N•
MANA MANE MANN MANO MANS MANU MANX MANY MEND MENS MENT MENU MINA MIND MINE MING MINH MINI MINK MINN MINS MINT MINX MONA MONK MONO MONS MONT MONY MRNA MTNS MUNG MUNI MYNA

M••N
MAIN MANN MEAN MEIN MIDN MIEN MINN MOAN MOON MORN MOWN MUON

•MN•
OMNI

•M•N
AMEN AMIN AMON CMON GMAN GMEN IMAN OMAN OMEN TMAN TMEN XMEN

••MN
CHMN DAMN HYMN LIMN

MO••
MOAB MOAN MOAS MOAT MOBS MOBY MOCK MOCS MODE MODS MOHO MOHS MOIL MOJO MOLA MOLD MOLE MOLL MOLT MOLY MOMA MOME MOMS MONA MONK MONO MONS MONT MONY MOOD MOOG MOON MOOR MOOS MOOT MOPE MOPS MORA MORE MORK MORN MORO MORT MOSE MOSS MOST MOTA MOTE MOTH MOTO MOTS MOTT MOUE MOVE MOWN MOWS

M•O•
MBOY MEOW MHOS MOOD MOOG MOON MOOR MOOS MOOT MUON MYOB

M••O
MAKO MALO MANO MAYO MAZO MECO MEMO MERO MESO MILO MIRO MISO MOHO MOJO MONO MORO MOTO MYCO MYXO

•MO•
AMOI AMOK AMON AMOR AMOS AMOY BMOC CMON CMOS HMOS OMOO SMOG

•M•O
AMBO AMMO DMSO OMOO UMBO

••MO
AMMO ATMO CAMO COMO DEMO DOMO ELMO GAMO HEMO HOMO KEMO LIMO MEMO NEMO POMO REMO SAMO SUMO TAMO ZYMO

MP••
MPAA

M•P•
MAPS MIPS MOPE MOPS

•MP•
AMPS EMPS IMPI IMPS UMPH UMPS

••MP
BOMP BUMP CAMP COMP DAMP DUMP GAMP GIMP GUMP HEMP HUMP JUMP KEMP LAMP LIMP LUMP POMP PUMP RAMP RCMP ROMP RUMP SAMP SIMP SUMP TAMP TEMP TYMP VAMP WIMP

MR••
MRED MRNA

M•R•
MARA MARC MARE MARG MARI MARK MARL MARS MART MARU MARV MARX MARY MERE MERO MERV MFRS MGRS MIRA MIRE MIRO MIRS MIRV MIRY MORA MORE MORK MORN MORO MORT MURK MYRA

M••R
MAAR MAWR MEER MEIR MICR MNGR MOOR MSGR MUIR

•MR•
OMRI

•M•R
AMER AMIR AMOR AMUR CMDR EMIR OMAR OMER RMDR YMIR

••MR
COMR

MS••
MSEC MSGR MSGS MSGT

M•S•
MASC MASH MASK MASS MAST MDSE MESA MESH MESO MESS MISC MISE MISO MISS MIST MKSA MOSE MOSS MOST MUSB MUSE MUSH MUSK MUSM MUSS MUST MYST

M••S
MAAS MACS MAGS MAIS MANS MAPS MARS MASS MATS MAVS MAWS MAYS MBAS MBES MEAS MEDS MEMS MENS MESS METS MEWS MFAS MFRS MGRS MHOS MIBS MICS MIES MIGS MILS MINS MIPS MIRS MISS MMES MOAS MOBS MOCS MODS MOHS MOMS MONS MOOS MOPS MOSS MOTS MOWS MSGS MTGS MTNS MUDS MUGS MUMS MUSS

•MS•
DMSO OMSK SMSA

•M•S
AMAS AMBS AMES AMIS AMOS AMPS AMTS BMUS BMWS CMOS DMDS EMPS EMTS EMUS HMOS IMPS MMES PMTS UMPS XMAS

••MS
ABMS ADMS AIMS ALMS ARMS ATMS BAMS BEMS BUMS CAMS CWMS DAMS DEMS DIMS DOMS DPMS DSMS DVMS ELMS GAMS GEMS GUMS GYMS HAMS HEMS HOMS HUMS ISMS JAMS LAMS LEMS LLMS MEMS MOMS MUMS NOMS OHMS POMS RAMS REMS RIMS ROMS RPMS RUMS SEMS SIMS SUMS TAMS TOMS TUMS YAMS

MT••
MTGE MTGS MTNS

M•T•
MATA MATE MATH MATS MATT META METE METH METS METZ MITA MITE MITT MKTG MOTA MOTE MOTH MOTO MOTS MOTT MUTE MUTT MYTH

M••T
MAAT MALT MART

MAST MATT MCAT MEAT MEET MELT MENT MGMT MILT MINT MIST MITT MIXT MOAT MOLT MONT MOOT MORT MOST MOTT MSGT MUST MUTT MYST

•MT•
AMTS EMTS PMTS

•M•T
AMAT EMIT GMAT IMIT OMIT SMIT SMUT

••MT
BSMT MGMT STMT

MU••
MUCH MUCK MUDD MUDS MUFF MUGS MUIR MULE MULL MUMS MUNG MUNI MUON MURK MUSB MUSE MUSH MUSK MUSM MUSS MUST MUTE MUTT

M•U•
MAUD MAUI MAUL MOUE

M••U
MANU MARU MENU

•MU•
AMUR BMUS EMUS SMUG SMUT

••MU
BOMU

MV••
MVII

M•V•
MAVS MCVI MDVI MLVI MMVI MOVE MXVI

M••V
MARV MCCV MCDV MCIV MCLV MCMV MCXV MDCV MDIV MDLV MDXV MERV MIRV MLIV MLXV MMCV MMDV MMIV MMLV MMMV MMXV MXCV MXIV MXLV MXXV

•MV•
CMVI MMVI

•M•V
CMIV CMLV CMXV MMCV MMDV MMIV MMLV MMMV MMXV

••MV
MCMV MMMV

M•W•
MAWR MAWS MEWL MEWS MOWN MOWS

M••W
MEOW

•MW•
BMWS

•M•W
SMEW

MX••
MXCI MXCV MXII MXIV MXIX MXLI MXLV MXVI MXXI MXXV MXXX

M•X•
MAXI MCXC MCXI MCXL MCXV MCXX MDXC MDXI MDXL MDXV MDXX MIXT MLXI MLXV MLXX MMXC MMXI MMXL MMXV MMXX MXXI MXXV MYXO

M••X
MANX MARX MCCX MCDX MCIX MCLX MCMX MCXX MDCX MDIX MDLX MDXX MINX MLIX MLXX MMCX MMDX MMIX MMLX MMMX MMXX MXIX MXXX

•MX•
CMXC CMXI CMXL CMXV CMXX MMXC MMXI MMXL MMXV MMXX

•M•X
AMEX CMIX CMLX CMXX MMCX MMDX MMIX MMLX MMMX MMXX NMEX

••MX
MCMX MMMX

MY••
MYCO MYMY MYNA MYOB MYRA MYST MYTH MYXO

M•Y•
MAYA MAYI MAYO MAYS

M••Y
MACY MANY MARY MAZY MBOY MIRY MOBY MOLY MONY MYMY

•MY•
AMYL

•M•Y
AMOY EMLY EMMY

••MY
ARMY DEMY EMMY FUMY GAMY HOMY LAMY LIMY MYMY OHMY RIMY ROMY

M•Z•
MAZE MAZO MAZY

M••Z
METZ

NA••
NABS NACL NADA NADH NADP NAGS NAGY NAHA NAIF NAIL NAME NANA NANG NANO NAOH NAOI NAOS NAPA NAPE NAPS NARA NARC NARD NARK NARY NARZ NASA NASD NASH NASL NASO NAST NATE NATL NATO NAUT NAVE NAVY NAYS

N•A•
NCAA NDAK NEAL NEAP NEAR NEAT NLAT NOAA NOAH NOAM

N••A
NADA NAHA NANA NAPA NARA NASA NCAA NEVA NINA NIPA NITA NOAA NOLA NONA NORA NOTA NOVA

•NA•
ANAS ANAT BNAI GNAR GNAT GNAW KNAP KNAR SNAG SNAP UNAU

•N•A
ANKA ANNA ANOA ANSA ANTA ANYA ANZA ENNA ENYA FNMA GNMA INCA INGA INKA ONEA

••NA
ANNA BONA BUNA CANA CENA CUNA DANA DINA DONA DUNA DYNA EDNA ENNA ETNA FINA GENA GINA HANA IANA IONA JENA KANA KINA KONA LANA LENA LINA LUNA MANA MINA MONA MRNA MYNA NANA NINA NONA OONA PENA PINA PUNA RANA RONA RRNA SANA TANA TINA TRNA TUNA ULNA USNA VENA VINA YANA ZONA

N•B•
NABS NEBE NEBN NEBO NEBR NEBS NIBS NOBS NUBS NWBN NWBW

N••B
NLRB NTSB NUMB

•N•B
KNOB SNOB SNUB

NC••
NCAA NCOS

N•C•
NACL NECK NICE NICK NOCK

N••C
NARC NUNC

•NC•
ANCE ANCY ENCE ENCL ENCS ENCY INCA INCH INCL INCR ONCE SNCC UNCI

•N•C
SNCC

••NC
BANC CANC CINC CONC JUNC NUNC SYNC ZINC

ND••
NDAK

N•D•
NADA NADH NADP NIDE NIDI NODE NODI NODS NUDE NUDI

N••D
NARD NASD NEED NEJD NERD NFLD NKVD NORD

•ND•
ANDS ANDY ENDE ENDO ENDS INDO INDS INDY RNDS UNDO

•N•D
ENID KNUD

••ND
BAND BEND BIND BOND BUND COND FEND FIND FOND FUND GOND HAND HIND HOND HUND KIND LAND LEND LIND MEND MIND PEND POND RAND REND RIND SAND SEND SIND SYND TEND VEND WAND WEND WIND YOND ZEND

NE••
NEAL NEAP NEAR NEAT NEBE NEBN NEBO NEBR NEBS NECK NEED NEEL NEEM NEER NEFF NEGS NEHI NEIL NEIN NEJD NELL NEMO NENE NEON NERD NERF NERI NERO NESS NEST NETH NETS NEUF NEUN NEUT NEVA NEVE NEWF NEWS NEWT NEXT

N•E•
NEED NEEL NEEM NEER NLER NMEX NOEL NOES NYET

N••E
NAME NAPE NATE NAVE NEBE NENE NEVE NICE NIDE NIKE NILE NINE NITE NIUE NODE NOME NONE NOPE NOSE NOTE NUDE NUKE NYSE

•NE•
ANEW INEE INEZ KNEE KNEW ONEA ONER ONES SNEE

•N•E
ANCE ANGE ANNE ANTE ENCE ENDE ENNE INEE INGE INRE KNEE ONCE SNEE

••NE
ACNE ANNE AONE ARNE AUNE BANE BENE BINE BONE CANE CINE CONE DANE DENE DINE DONE DUNE DYNE EINE ENNE ERNE ESNE FANE FINE GENE GONE HONE IONE JANE JUNE KANE KINE LANE LINE LONE LUNE LYNE MANE MINE NENE NINE NONE OHNE ORNE PANE PINE PONE RENE RUNE RYNE SANE SENE SINE SONE SYNE TANE TENE TINE TONE TUNE TYNE UTNE VANE VINE WANE WINE ZANE ZINE ZONE

NF••
NFLD

N•F•
NEFF

N••F
NAIF NEFF NERF NEUF NEWF

•NF•
INFL INFO INFS

•N•F
ENUF

••NF
CONF FUNF

N•G•
NAGS NAGY NEGS NIGH NOGO NOGS

N••G
NANG

•NG•
ANGE ANGL ENGR ENGS INGA INGE MNGR

•N•G
SNAG SNUG

••NG
BANG BENG BING BONG BUNG BYNG CONG DANG DENG DING DONG FANG GANG GONG GUNG HANG HONG HUNG JONG JUNG KING KONG KUNG LANG LING LONG LUNG MING MUNG NANG PANG PING PONG PUNG RANG RING RUNG SANG SING SONG SUNG TANG TING TONG TUNG VANG WANG WENG WING WONG XING YANG ZING

N•H•
NAHA NEHI

N••H
NADH NAOH NASH NETH NIGH NOAH NOSH

•N•H
ANKH ANTH GNRH INCH

••NH
MINH PENH SINH TANH

NI••
NIBS NICE NICK NIDE NIDI NIGH NIKE NILE NILS NINA NINE NINO NIPA NIPS NISI NITA NITE NITS NIUE

N•I•
NAIF NAIL NEIL NEIN NOIL NOIR NUIT

N••I
NAOI NEHI NERI NIDI NISI NODI NOLI NORI NOTI NUDI

•NI•
ANIL ANIM ANIS ENID INIT KNIT PNIN SNIP SNIT UNIT UNIV UNIX

•N•I
ANSI ANTI BNAI INRI UNCI

••NI
AGNI BANI BENI BONI FINI HONI IFNI JONI LENI LONI MINI MUNI OMNI RANI RENI TONI VENI VINI ZUNI

N•J•
NEJD

••NJ
CONJ

NK••
NKVD

N•K•
NIKE NUKE

N••K
NARK NDAK NECK NICK NOCK NOOK

•NK•
ANKA ANKH INKA INKS INKY

•N•K
TNPK

••NK
BANK BONK BUNK CONK DANK DINK DUNK FINK FUNK GUNK HANK HONK HUNK JINK JUNK KINK LANK LINK MINK MONK OINK PINK PUNK RANK RINK SANK SINK SUNK TANK TONK WINK WONK YANK ZONK

NL••
NLAT NLER NLRB

N•L•
NELL NFLD NILE NILS NOLA NOLI NOLL NOLO NULL

N••L
NACL NAIL NASL NATL NEAL NEEL NEIL NELL NOEL NOIL NOLL NULL

•NL•
INLY ONLY UNLV

•N•L
ANGL ANIL ENCL ENOL INCL INFL INTL

••NL
DANL GENL

NM••
NMEX

N•M•
NAME NEMO NOME NOMS NUMB

N••M
NEEM NOAM NORM

•NM•
FNMA GNMA

•N•M
ANIM ONYM UNUM

N•N•
NANA NANG NANO NENE NINA NINE NINO NONA NONE NONO NUNC NUNN NUNS

N••N
NEBN NEIN NEON NEUN NOON NORN NOUN NUNN NWBN

•NN•
ANNA ANNE ANNO ENNA ENNE INNS

•N•N
ANON INON PNIN

••NN
BONN CONN DUNN FENN FINN GANN GUNN JINN LUNN LYNN MANN MINN NUNN PENN SUNN TENN VENN WYNN

NO••
NOAA NOAH NOAM NOBS NOCK NODE NODI NODS NOEL NOES NOGO NOGS NOIL NOIR NOLA NOLI NOLL NOLO NOME NOMS NONA NONE NONO NOOK NOON NOOR NOPE NORA NORD NORI NORM NORN NOSE NOSH NOSY NOTA NOTE NOTI NOTS NOUN NOUS NOVA NOVO

N•O•
NAOH NAOI NAOS NCOS NEON NOOK NOON NOOR

N••O
NANO NASO NATO NEBO NEMO NERO NINO NOGO NOLO NONO NOVO NYRO

•NO•
ANOA ANON ENOL ENOS ENOW INON KNOB KNOP KNOT KNOW KNOX SNOB SNOW

•N•O
ANNO ENDO ENTO ENYO ENZO INDO INFO INRO INTO ONTO UNDO UNTO

••NO
ANNO ARNO ATNO BONO BRNO CENO DANO DINO DRNO ERNO FINO GINO JUNO KANO KENO KINO LENO MANO MONO NANO NINO NONO OENO OHNO RENO SINO TENO VINO XENO ZENO

N•P•
NAPA NAPE NAPS NIPA NIPS NOPE

N••P
NADP NEAP

•NP•
TNPK

•N•P
INSP KNAP KNOP SNAP SNIP

••NQ
CINQ

N•R•
NARA NARC NARD NARK NARY NARZ

NERD NERF NERI NERO NLRB NORA NORD NORI NORM NORN NYRO

N • • R
NEAR NEBR NEER NLER NOIR NOOR

• NR •
GNRH INRE INRI INRO

• N • R
ENGR GNAR INCR INTR KNAR KNUR MNGR ONER

• • NR
USNR

N • S •
NASA NASD NASH NASL NASO NAST NESS NEST NISI NOSE NOSH NOSY NTSB NYSE

N • • S
NABS NAGS NAOS NAPS NAYS NCOS NEBS NEGS NESS NETS NEWS NIBS NILS NIPS NITS NOBS NODS NOES NOGS NOMS NOTS NOUS NUBS NUNS NUTS NUYS

• NS •
ANSA ANSI INSP INST

• N • S
ANAS ANDS ANIS ANTS ENCS ENDS ENGS ENOS ENVS GNUS INDS INFS INKS INNS INTS INXS ONES ONUS RNDS

• • NS
AWNS BANS BINS BUNS CANS CENS CONS CTNS DENS DINS DONS DUNS EINS EONS ERNS FANS FENS FINS FONS GENS GINS GUNS HANS HENS HUNS INNS IONS JENS KANS KENS LENS MANS MENS MINS MONS MTNS NUNS OWNS PANS PENS PINS PONS PUNS RUNS SANS SENS SINS SONS SSNS STNS SUNS SYNS TANS TENS TINS TONS TUNS URNS VANS VINS WENS WINS WONS YENS

NT • •
NTSB NTWT

N • T •
NATE NATL NATO NETH NETS NITA NITE NITS NOTA NOTE NOTI NOTS NUTS NUTT

N • • T
NAST NAUT NEAT NEST NEUT NEWT NEXT NLAT NTWT NUIT NUTT NYET

• NT •
ANTA ANTE ANTH ANTI ANTS ENTO INTL INTO INTR INTS ONTO UNTO

• N • T
ANAT CNUT GNAT INIT INST KNIT KNOT KNUT SNIT TNUT UNIT

• • NT
AINT AUNT BENT BUNT CANT CENT CONT DENT DINT DONT FONT FUNT GENT GYNT HENT HINT HUNT ISNT KANT KENT LENT LINT LUNT MENT MINT MONT PANT PENT PINT PONT PUNT RANT RENT RUNT SENT TENT TINT VENT WANT WENT WONT

NU • •
NUBS NUDE NUDI NUIT NUKE NULL NUMB NUNC NUNN NUNS NUTS NUTT NUYS

N • U •
NAUT NEUF NEUN NEUT NIUE NOUN NOUS

• NU •
CNUT ENUF GNUS KNUD KNUR KNUT ONUS SNUB SNUG TNUT UNUM

• N • U
UNAU

• • NU
AINU BENU DANU GENU MANU MENU

N • V •
NAVE NAVY NEVA NEVE NKVD NOVA NOVO

• NV •
ENVS ENVY

• N • V
UNIV UNLV

• • NV
CONV

NW • •
NWBN NWBW

N • W •
NEWF NEWS NEWT NTWT

N • • W
NWBW

• N • W
ANEW ENOW GNAW KNEW KNOW SNOW

N • X •
NEXT

N • • X
NMEX

• NX •
INXS

• N • X
KNOX ONYX UNIX

• • NX
JINX LYNX MANX MINX PINX

NY • •
NYET NYRO NYSE

N • Y •
NAYS NUYS

N • • Y
NAGY NARY NAVY NOSY

• NY •
ANYA ENYA ENYO ONYM ONYX

• N • Y
ANCY ANDY ENCY ENVY INDY INKY INLY ONLY

• • NY
BONY CONY CUNY DENY DKNY GONY LINY MANY MONY PINY PONY PUNY SONY SUNY TINY TONY VINY WANY ZANY

N • • Z
NARZ

• NZ •
ANZA ENZO

• N • Z
INEZ

• • NZ
BENZ FONZ LENZ LINZ

OA • •
OAFS OAHU OAKS OARS OAST OATH OATS OATY

O • A •
OBAD OCAS ODAS ODAY OJAI OKAY OLAF OLAN OLAV OMAN OMAR OPAH OPAL ORAD ORAL ORAN OSAR OVAL OZAV

O • • A
OCTA ODEA OKLA OKRA OLGA OLLA ONEA OONA OPIA ORCA OSHA OSSA OTRA

• OA •
BOAC BOAR BOAS BOAT BOAZ COAL COAT COAX DOAK FOAL FOAM GOAD GOAL GOAT HOAR HOAX JOAB JOAD JOAN KOAN LOAD LOAF LOAM LOAN MOAB MOAN MOAS MOAT NOAA NOAH NOAM ROAD ROAM ROAN ROAR SOAK SOAP SOAR TOAD TOAT WOAD ZOAR

• O • A
BOCA BOLA BOMA BONA BORA BOTA BOVA COCA CODA COLA COMA CORA COSA COXA DOHA DONA DOPA DORA FORA GOYA HOLA HORA HOYA IOLA IONA IOTA IOWA KOLA KONA LOLA LOMA MOLA MOMA MONA MORA MOTA NOAA NOLA NONA NORA NOTA NOVA OONA PODA POLA ROCA ROMA RONA ROSA ROTA SOCA SODA SOFA SOLA SOMA SORA SOYA TOEA TOGA TOLA YODA YOGA ZOEA ZOLA ZONA

• • OA
ANOA PROA STOA WHOA

OB • •
OBAD OBEY OBIE OBIS OBIT OBOE OBOL

O • B •
ORBS

• OB •
BOBS COBB COBH COBS FOBS GOBI GOBO GOBS GOBY HOBO HOBS JOBS KOBE KOBO KOBS LOBE LOBO LOBS MOBS MOBY NOBS ROBB ROBE ROBO ROBS SOBS TOBY YOBS

• O • B
BOMB BOOB COBB COMB FORB JOAB LOEB MOAB ROBB SORB TOMB

• • OB
BLOB BOOB BYOB GLOB KNOB MYOB PROB SLOB SNOB SWOB

OC • •
OCAS OCHO OCHS OCTA OCTO

O • C •
ONCE ORCA ORCH ORCS OUCH

O • • C
ODIC OPEC OTIC

• OC •
BOCA BOCK COCA COCK COCO DOCK DOCS FOCH FOCI HOCH HOCK JOCK KOCH LOCH LOCI LOCK LOCO MOCK MOCS NOCK POCO ROCA ROCK ROCS SOCA SOCK TOCK VOCE

• O • C
BOAC BOSC COFC CONC KOFC ROTC ZOIC

• • OC
APOC BLOC BMOC CHOC CROC EEOC FLOC KROC PROC

OD • •
ODAS ODAY ODDS ODEA ODER ODES ODIC ODIE ODIN ODOR

O • D •
ODDS OLDE OLDS ORDO OUDS

O • • D
OBAD OHED OLID OOID OPED ORAD OVID OWED

• OD •
BODE BODO BODS BODY CODA CODE CODS CODY DODD DODO GODS HODS IODO JODY LODE LODI LODZ MODE MODS NODE NODI NODS PODA PODE PODS RODE RODS SODA SODS TODD TODO TODS TODY YODA YODH

• O • D
BOLD BOND BOYD COED COLD COMD COND CORD DODD DOWD FOLD FOND FOOD FORD GOAD GOLD GOND GOOD HOED HOLD HOND HOOD JOAD LOAD LOID LORD LOUD MOLD MOOD NORD OOID POND POOD ROAD ROOD SOLD TOAD TODD TOED TOLD VOID WOAD WOLD WOOD WORD YOND YOUD

• • OD
CLOD EXOD FOOD GOOD HOOD IZOD MOOD PLOD POOD PROD QUOD ROOD SHOD TROD TWOD WHOD WOOD

OE • •
OEIL OENO OEUF

O • E •
OBEY ODEA ODER ODES OGEE OHED OKEY OLEG OLEO OLES OMEN OMER ONEA ONER ONES OPEC OPED OPEL OPEN OPER OPES OREG OREL OREM OREO ORES OVEN OVER OWED OWEN OWES OXEN OYER OYEZ

O • • E
OBIE OBOE ODIE OGEE OGLE OGRE OHNE OISE OKIE OLDE ONCE OOZE OPIE ORLE ORNE OSTE OTOE OUSE

• OE •
BOER COED COEL COEN DOER DOES FOES GOER GOES HOED HOER HOES JOEL JOEY LOEB LOEW NOEL NOES POEM POET ROES TOEA TOED TOES WOES ZOEA

• O • E
AONE BODE BOLE BONE BORE BOSE BOWE CODE COKE COLE COME CONE COPE CORE COTE COUE COVE DOGE DOLE DOME DONE DOPE DORE DOSE DOTE DOVE DOZE FOIE FORE FOXE GONE GORE HOKE HOLE HOME HONE HOPE HOSE HOTE HOVE HOWE IOLE IONE JOIE JOKE JOSE JOVE KOBE KORE LOBE LODE LOGE LOME LONE LOPE LORE LOSE LOVE LOWE MODE MOLE MOME MOPE MORE MOSE MOTE MOUE MOVE NODE NOME NONE NOPE NOSE NOTE OOZE PODE POKE POLE POME PONE POPE PORE POSE ROBE RODE ROLE ROME ROPE ROSE ROTE ROUE ROVE ROWE SOIE SOKE SOLE SOME SONE SORE TOKE TOLE TOME TONE TOPE TORE TOTE VOCE VOLE VOTE WOKE WORE WOVE YOKE YORE ZONE

• • OE
ALOE BPOE EVOE FLOE FROE OBOE OTOE SHOE SLOE

OF • •
OFFS

O • F •
OAFS OFFS ORFF

O • • F
OEUF OLAF ORFF

• OF •
BOFF COFC COFS DOFF HOFF KOFC KOFP LOFT SOFA SOFT TOFF TOFT TOFU

• O • F
BOFF COIF CONF CORF DOFF DOLF GOLF GOOF HOFF HOOF IOOF KOPF LOAF POOF POUF ROLF ROOF TOFF WOLF WOOF

• • OF
ASOF GOOF HOOF IOOF POOF PROF ROOF WOOF

OG • •
OGEE OGGI OGLE OGRE

O • G •
OGGI OLGA ORGS ORGY

O • • G
OLEG OREG ORIG

• OG •
BOGS BOGY COGS DOGE DOGG DOGS DOGY FOGG FOGS FOGY GOGH GOGI GOGO HOGG HOGS JOGS LOGE LOGO LOGS LOGY NOGO NOGS POGO POGS POGY TOGA TOGO TOGS YOGA YOGH YOGI ZOGI

• O • G
BONG BORG CONG DOGG DONG DOUG FOGG GONG HOGG HONG JONG KONG LONG MOOG PONG SONG TONG WONG

• • OG
AGOG BIOG CLOG FLOG FROG GEOG GROG MOOG PROG SLOG SMOG

OH • •
OHED OHIO OHMS OHMY OHNE OHNO OHOH

O • H •
OAHU OCHO OCHS OOHS OSHA OTHO

O • • H
OATH OHOH OPAH ORCH ORTH OUCH

• OH •
BOHM BOHR COHN COHO DOHA FOHN HOHO JOHN KOHL MOHO MOHS OOHS POHL SOHN SOHO TOHO WOHL YOHO

• O • H
BOSH BOTH COBH COSH DOTH FOCH GOGH GOSH GOTH HOCH JOSH KOCH KOPH LOCH MOTH NOAH NOSH POOH POSH QOPH ROSH ROTH SOPH TOSH YODH YOGH

• • OH
IEOH IPOH NAOH OHOH POOH UHOH

OI • •
OILS OILY OINK OISE

O • I •
OBIE OBIS OBIT ODIC ODIE ODIN OEIL OHIO OKIE OLID OLIN OLIO OMIT OOID OPIA OPIE ORIG OSIS OTIC OTIS OVID OVIS

O • • I
OGGI OJAI OMNI OMRI

•OI•
BOIL
BOIS
COIF
COIL
COIN
COIR
DOIL
DOIN
DOIT
FOIE
FOIL
FOIN
FOIS
GOIN
JOIE
JOIN
KOIS
LOID
LOIN
LOIS
MOIL
NOIL
NOIR
OOID
POIL
POIS
ROIL
SOIE
SOIL
SOIR
TOIL
VOID
VOIR
VOIX
ZOIC

•O•I
BONI
CORI
FOCI
GOBI
GOGI
HONI
HOPI
JOLI
JONI
KOJI
KOMI
LOCI
LODI
LOKI
LONI
LORI
LOTI
NODI
NOLI
NORI
NOTI
ROTI
SOLI
SORI
TONI
TOPI
TORI
YOGI
ZOGI
ZORI

••OI
AMOI
ATOI
ELOI
NAOI
QUOI
TROI

OJ••
OJAI

•OJ•
DOJO
HOJO
KOJI
MOJO
ROJO
TOJO

•O•J
CONJ

OK••
OKAY
OKEY
OKIE
OKLA
OKRA

O•K•
OAKS

O••K
OINK
OMSK
ORSK

•OK•
COKE
COKY
HOKE
JOKE
KOKO
LOKI
POKE
POKY
SOKE
TOKE
WOKE
WOKS
YOKE
YOKO

•O•K
BOCK
BONK
BOOK
BORK
BOSK
COCK
CONK
COOK
CORK
DOAK
DOCK
FOLK
FORK
GOOK
GOWK
HOCK
HONK
HOOK
JOCK
KOOK
LOCK
LOOK
MOCK
MONK
MORK
NOCK
NOOK
POLK
PORK
ROCK
ROOK
SOAK
SOCK
SOUK
TOCK
TONK
TOOK
TORK
WONK
WORK
WOUK
YOLK
YORK
ZONK
ZOUK

••OK
AMOK
BOOK
COOK
EWOK
GOOK
GROK
HOOK
KOOK
LOOK
NOOK
ROOK
TOOK

OL••
OLAF
OLAN
OLAV
OLDE
OLDS
OLEG
OLEO
OLES
OLGA
OLID
OLIN
OLIO
OLLA

O•L•
OGLE
OILS
OILY
OKLA
OLLA
ONLY
ORLE
ORLY
OSLO
OWLS

O••L
OBOL
OEIL
OPAL
OPEL
ORAL
OREL
OVAL

•OL•
BOLA
BOLD
BOLE
BOLL
BOLO
BOLT
COLA
COLD
COLE
COLL
COLO
COLS
COLT
COLY
DOLE
DOLF
DOLL
DOLT
FOLD
FOLK
GOLD
GOLF
HOLA
HOLD
HOLE
HOLM
HOLO
HOLP
HOLT
HOLY
IOLA
IOLE
JOLI
JOLO
JOLT
KOLA
KOLN
KOLO
LOLA
LOLL
MOLA
MOLD
MOLE
MOLL
MOLT
MOLY
NOLA
NOLI
NOLL
NOLO
POLA
POLE
POLK
POLL
POLO
POLS
POLY
ROLE
ROLF
ROLL
ROLY
SOLA
SOLD
SOLE
SOLI
SOLN
SOLO
SOLS
TOLA
TOLD
TOLE
TOLL
TOLU
VOLE
VOLS
VOLT
WOLD
WOLF
YOLK
ZOLA

•O•L
BOIL
BOLL
BOWL
COAL
COEL
COIL
COLL
COML
COOL
COWL
DOIL
DOLL
FOAL
FOIL
FOOL
FOUL
FOWL
GOAL
HOWL
JOEL
JOWL
KOHL
KOOL
LOLL
MOIL
MOLL
NOEL
NOIL
NOLL
POHL
POIL
POLL
POOL
ROIL
ROLL
ROTL
SOIL
SOUL
TOIL
TOLL
TOOL
WOHL
WOOL
YOWL
ZOOL

••OL
AWOL
BIOL
CHOL
COOL
ECOL
ENOL
FOOL
GAOL
GEOL
IDOL
ITOL
KOOL
OBOL
POOL
SKOL
STOL
TOOL
VIOL
VTOL
WOOL
ZOOL

OM••
OMAN
OMAR
OMEN
OMER
OMIT
OMNI
OMOO
OMRI
OMSK

O•M•
OHMS
OHMY

O••M
ONYM
OREM
OVUM

•OM•
BOMA
BOMB
BOMP
BOMU
COMA
COMB
COMD
COME
COML
COMM
COMO
COMP
COMR
DOME
DOMO
DOMS
HOME
HOMO
HOMS
HOMY
KOMI
LOMA
LOME
MOMA
MOME
MOMS
NOME
NOMS
POME
POMO
POMP
POMS
ROMA
ROME
ROMP
ROMS
ROMY
SOMA
SOME
TOMB
TOME
TOMS

•O•M
BOHM
BOOM
COMM
CORM
COSM
DOOM
DORM
FOAM
FORM
HOLM
LOAM
LOOM
NOAM
NORM
POEM
ROAM
ROOM
VOOM
WORM
ZOOM

••OM
ATOM
BOOM
BROM
DOOM
EDOM
FROM
GEOM
GLOM
LOOM
PROM
ROOM
THOM
VOOM
WHOM
ZOOM

ON••
ONCE
ONEA
ONER
ONES
ONLY
ONTO
ONUS
ONYM
ONYX

O•N•
OENO
OHNE
OHNO
OINK
OMNI
OONA
ORNE
OWNS

O••N
ODIN
OLAN
OLIN
OMAN
OMEN
OPEN
ORAN
OVEN
OWEN
OXEN
OXON

•ON•
AONE
BONA
BOND
BONE
BONG
BONI
BONK
BONN
BONO
BONY
CONC
COND
CONE
CONF
CONG
CONJ
CONK
CONN
CONS
CONT
CONV
CONY
DONA
DONE
DONG
DONS
DONT
EONS
FOND
FONS
FONT
FONZ
GOND
GONE
GONG
GONY
HOND
HONE
HONG
HONI
HONK
IONA
IONE
IONS
JONG
JONI
KONA
KONG
LONE
LONG
LONI
MONA
MONK
MONO
MONS
MONT
MONY
NONA
NONE
NONO
OONA
POND
PONE
PONG
PONS
PONT
PONY
RONA
SONE
SONG
SONS
SONY
TONE
TONG
TONI
TONK
TONS
TONY
WONG
WONK
WONS
WONT
YOND
ZONA
ZONE
ZONK

•O•N
BONN
BOON
BORN
BOSN
COEN
COHN
COIN
CONN
COON
CORN
DOIN
DOON
DORN
DOWN
FOHN
FOIN
GOIN
GOON
GOWN
HORN
JOAN
JOHN
JOIN
KOAN
KOLN
LOAN
LOIN
LOON
LORN
MOAN
MOON
MORN
MOWN
NOON
NORN
NOUN
POON
ROAN
SOHN
SOLN
SOON
SOWN
TOON
TORN
TOWN
WORN
ZOON
ZORN

••ON
AGON
AMON
ANON
ARON
ATON
AVON
AXON
BION
BOON
CHON
CION
CMON
COON
DCON
DION
DOON
EBON
ECON
EGON
ELON
ETON
EXON
GOON
HUON
ICON
INON
IRON
KAON
KWON
LEON
LION
LOON
LRON
LYON
MOON
MUON
NEON
NOON
OXON
PEON
PHON
PION
POON
PRON
SOON
TION
TOON
TRON
UPON
ZION
ZOON

OO••
OOHS
OOID
OONA
OOPS
OORT
OOZE
OOZY

O•O•
OBOE
OBOL
ODOR
OHOH
OMOO
OTOE
OTOS
OXON

O••O
OCHO
OCTO
OENO
OHIO
OHNO
OLEO
OLIO
OMOO
ONTO
OPTO
ORDO
OREO
ORZO
OSLO
OSSO
OTHO
OTRO
OTTO
OUZO

•OO•
BOOB
BOOK
BOOM
BOON
BOOP
BOOR
BOOS
BOOT
COOK
COOL
COON
COOP
COOS
COOT
DOOM
DOON
DOOR
FOOD
FOOL
FOOT
GOOD
GOOF
GOOK
GOON
GOOP
GOOS
HOOD
HOOF
HOOK
HOOP
HOOT
IOOF
KOOK
KOOL
KOOP
LOOK
LOOM
LOON
LOOP
LOOS
LOOT
MOOD
MOOG
MOON
MOOR
MOOS
MOOT
NOOK
NOON
NOOR
POOD
POOF
POOH
POOL
POON
POOP
POOR
ROOD
ROOF
ROOK
ROOM
ROOS
ROOT
SOON
SOOT
TOOK
TOOL
TOON
TOOT
VOOM
WOOD
WOOF
WOOL
WOOS
ZOOL
ZOOM
ZOON
ZOOS
ZOOT

•O•O
BODO
BOLO
BONO
BORO
BOZO
COCO
COHO
COLO
COMO
CORO
DODO
DOJO
DOMO
GOBO
GOGO
HOBO
HOHO
HOJO
HOLO
HOMO
IODO
JOLO
KOBO
KOKO
KOLO
KOTO
LOBO
LOCO
LOGO
MOHO
MOJO
MONO
MORO
MOTO
NOGO
NOLO
NONO
NOVO
POCO
POGO
POLO
POMO
ROBO
ROJO
ROTO
SOHO
SOLO
SOSO
TODO
TOGO
TOHO
TOJO
TOPO
TORO
TOTO
YOHO
YOKO
YOYO

••OO
AROO
EROO
OMOO
SHOO

OP••
OPAH
OPAL
OPEC
OPED
OPEL
OPEN
OPER
OPES
OPIA
OPIE
OPRY
OPTO
OPTS
OPUS

O•P•
OOPS

•OP•
BOPP
BOPS
COPE
COPS
COPT
COPY
DOPA
DOPE
DOPY
FOPS
HOPE
HOPI
HOPS
KOPF
KOPH
KOPS
LOPE
LOPS
MOPE
MOPS
NOPE
OOPS
POPE
POPS
QOPH
ROPE
ROPY
SOPH
SOPS
TOPE
TOPI
TOPO
TOPS

•O•P
BOMP
BOOP
BOPP
COMP
COOP
CORP
COUP
DORP
DOUP
GOOP
GORP
GOUP
HOLP
HOOP
HOSP
KOFP
KOOP
LOOP
LOUP
POMP
POOP
ROMP
ROUP
SOAP
SOUP

••OP
ATOP
BOOP
CHOP
CLOP
COOP
CROP
DROP
ESOP
FLOP
GLOP
GOOP
HOOP
IHOP
KNOP
KOOP
LOOP
PLOP
POOP
PROP
SCOP
SHOP
SLOP
STOP
SWOP
TROP
VSOP
WHOP

OR••
ORAD
ORAL
ORAN
ORBS
ORCA
ORCH
ORCS
ORDO
OREG
OREL
OREM
OREO
ORES
ORFF
ORGS
ORGY
ORIG
ORLE
ORLY
ORNE
ORSK
ORTH
ORTS
ORYX
ORZO

O•R•
OARS
OGRE
OKRA
OMRI
OORT
OPRY
OTRA
OTRO
OURS

O••R
ODER
ODOR
OMAR
OMER
ONER
OPER
OSAR
OVER
OYER

•OR•
BORA
BORE
BORG
BORK
BORN
BORO
BORS
BORT
CORA
CORD
CORE
CORF
CORI
CORK
CORM
CORN
CORO
CORP
CORR
CORY
DORA
DORE
DORM
DORN
DORP
DORR
DORS
DORT
DORY
FORA
FORB
FORD
FORE
FORK
FORM
FORT
GORE
GORP
GORY
HORA
HORN
HORS
HORT
KORE
LORD
LORE
LORI
LORN
LORY
MORA
MORE
MORK
MORN
MORO
MORT
NORA
NORD
NORI
NORM
NORN
OORT
PORE
PORK
PORT
RORY
SORA
SORB
SORE
SORI
SORT
TORE
TORI
TORK
TORN
TORO
TORR
TORS
TORT
TORY
WORD
WORE
WORK
WORM
WORN
WORT
YORE
YORK
ZORI
ZORN

•O•R
BOAR
BOER
BOHR
BOOR
COIR
COMR
CORR
DOER
DOOR
DORR
DOUR
FOUR
GOER
HOAR
HOER
HOUR
JOUR
MOOR
NOIR
NOOR
POOR
POUR
ROAR
SOAR
SOIR
SOUR
TORR
TOUR
VOIR
YOUR
ZOAR

••OR
AMOR
ASOR
ATOR
BOOR
DIOR
DOOR
FLOR
GYOR
IGOR
IVOR
MOOR
NOOR
ODOR
POOR
THOR
UXOR

OS••
OSAR
OSHA
OSIS
OSLO
OSSA
OSSO
OSTE

O•S•
OAST
OISE
OMSK
ORSK
OSSA
OSSO
OUSE
OUST

O••S
OAFS
OAKS
OARS
OATS
OBIS
OCAS
OCHS
ODAS
ODDS
ODES
OFFS
OHMS
OILS
OLDS
OLES
ONES
ONUS
OOHS
OOPS
OPES
OPTS
OPUS
ORBS
ORCS
ORES
ORGS
ORTS
OSIS
OTIS
OTOS
OUDS
OURS
OUTS
OVIS
OWES
OWLS
OWNS
OXUS

•OS•
BOSC
BOSE
BOSH
BOSK
BOSN
BOSS
COSA
COSH
COSM
COST
COSY
DOSE
DOSS
DOST
FOSS
GOSH
HOSE
HOSP
HOSS
HOST
JOSE
JOSH
JOSS
LOSE
LOSS
LOST
MOSE
MOSS
MOST
NOSE
NOSH
NOSY
POSE
POSH
POSS
POST
POSY
ROSA
ROSE
ROSH
ROSS
ROSY
SOSO
TOSH
TOSS

•O•S
BOAS
BOBS
BODS
BOGS
BOIS
BOOS
BOPS
BORS
BOSS
BOTS
BOWS
BOYS
COBS
CODS
COFS
COGS
COLS
CONS
COOS
COPS
COTS
COWS
DOCS
DOES
DOGS
DOMS
DONS
DORS
DOSS
DOTS
EONS
EOUS
FOBS
FOES
FOGS
FOIS
FONS
FOPS
FOSS
FOYS
GOBS
GODS
GOES
GOOS
HOBS
HODS
HOES
HOGS
HOMS
HOPS
HORS
HOSS
HOWS
HOYS
IONS
IOUS
JOBS
JOGS
JOSS
JOTS
JOYS
KOBS
KOIS
KOPS
LOBS
LOGS
LOIS
LOOS
LOPS
LOSS
LOTS
LOWS
MOAS
MOBS

MOCS MODS MOHS MOMS MONS MOOS MOPS MOSS MOTS MOWS NOBS NODS NOES NOGS NOMS NOTS NOUS OOHS OOPS PODS POGS POIS POLS POMS PONS POPS POSS POTS POWS ROBS ROCS RODS ROES ROMS ROOS ROSS ROTS ROUS ROWS SOBS SODS SOLS SONS SOPS SOTS SOUS SOWS SOYS TODS TOES TOGS TOMS TONS TOPS TORS TOSS TOTS TOWS TOYS VOLS VOUS VOWS WOES WOKS WONS WOOS WOWS YOBS ZOOS

••OS AMOS APOS AVOS BIOS BOOS BROS CEOS CMOS COOS CPOS CWOS DIOS DSOS DUOS EGOS ENOS EPOS EROS ESOS GOOS GPOS GROS HMOS IBOS ICOS KEOS LAOS LEOS LOOS MHOS MOOS NAOS NCOS OTOS PROS REOS RHOS RIOS ROOS TAOS TKOS TWOS UDOS UFOS WHOS WOOS ZOOS

OT•• OTHO OTIC OTIS OTOE OTOS OTRA OTRO OTTO

O•T• OATH OATS OATY OCTA OCTO ONTO OPTO OPTS ORTH ORTS OSTE OTTO OUTS

O••T OAST OBIT OMIT OORT OUST

•OT• BOTA BOTH BOTS BOTT COTE COTS COTY DOTE DOTH DOTS GOTH HOTE IOTA JOTS KOTO LOTI LOTS LOTT MOTA MOTE MOTH MOTO MOTS MOTT NOTA NOTE NOTI NOTS POTS ROTA ROTC ROTE ROTH ROTI ROTL ROTO ROTS SOTS TOTE TOTO TOTS VOTE ZOTZ

•O•T AOUT BOAT BOLT BOOT BORT BOTT BOUT COAT COLT CONT COOT COPT COST DOIT DOLT DONT DORT DOST FONT FOOT FORT FOYT GOAT GOUT GOVT HOLT HOOT HORT HOST HOYT JOLT LOFT LOOT LOST LOTT LOUT MOAT MOLT MONT MOOT MORT MOST MOTT OORT POET PONT PORT POST POUT ROOT ROUT SOFT SOOT SORT TOAT TOFT TOOT TORT TOUT VOLT WONT WORT XOUT ZOOT

••OT BLOT BOOT CLOT COOT FOOT GLOT GROT HOOT KNOT LOOT MOOT PHOT PLOT PROT QUOT RIOT ROOT RYOT SCOT SHOT SLOT SOOT SPOT STOT TOOT TROT ZOOT

OU•• OUCH OUDS OURS OUSE OUST OUTS OUZO

O•U• OEUF ONUS OPUS OVUM OXUS

O••U OAHU

•OU• AOUT BOUT COUE COUP DOUG DOUP DOUR DOUX EOUS FOUL FOUR GOUP GOUT HOUR IOUS JOUR LOUD LOUP LOUT MOUE NOUN NOUS POUF POUR POUT ROUE ROUP ROUS ROUT ROUX SOUK SOUL SOUP SOUR SOUS TOUR TOUT VOUS WOUK XOUT YOUD YOUR ZOUK

•O•U BOMU TOFU TOLU

••OU ABOU ALOU CHOU THOU ZHOU

OV•• OVAL OVEN OVER OVID OVIS OVUM

O••V OLAV OZAV

•OV• BOVA COVE DOVE GOVT HOVE JOVE LOVE MOVE NOVA NOVO ROVE WOVE

•O•V CONV

••OV AZOV LVOV PROV

OW•• OWED OWEN OWES OWLS OWNS

•OW• BOWE BOWL BOWS COWL COWS DOWD DOWN FOWL GOWK GOWN HOWE HOWL HOWS IOWA JOWL LOWE LOWS MOWN MOWS POWS ROWE ROWS SOWN SOWS TOWN TOWS VOWS WOWS YOWL

•O•W LOEW

••OW AVOW BLOW BROW CHOW CROW DHOW ENOW FLOW FROW GLOW GROW KNOW MEOW PLOW PROW SCOW SHOW SLOW SNOW STOW

OX•• OXEN OXON OXUS

O••X ONYX ORYX

•OX• BOXY COXA FOXE FOXX FOXY

•O•X COAX DOUX FOXX HOAX ROUX VOIX

••OX KNOX PROX

OY•• OYER OYEZ

O•Y• ONYM ONYX ORYX

O••Y OATY OBEY ODAY OHMY OILY OKAY OKEY ONLY OOZY OPRY ORGY ORLY OZZY

•OY• BOYD BOYS BOYZ FOYS FOYT GOYA HOYA HOYS HOYT JOYS SOYA SOYS TOYS YOYO

•O•Y BODY BOGY BONY BOXY CODY COKY COLY CONY COPY CORY COSY COTY COZY DOGY DOPY DORY DOZY FOGY FOXY GOBY GONY GORY HOLY HOMY JODY JOEY LOGY LORY MOBY MOLY MONY NOSY OOZY POGY POKY POLY PONY POSY ROLY ROMY ROPY RORY ROSY SONY TOBY TODY TONY TORY

••OY AHOY AMOY BBOY BUOY CHOY CLOY MBOY PLOY TROY

OZ•• OZAV OZZY

O•Z• OOZE OOZY ORZO OUZO OZZY

O••Z OYEZ

•OZ• BOZO COZY DOZE DOZY OOZE OOZY

•O•Z BOAZ BOYZ FONZ LODZ ZOTZ

••OZ BROZ FLOZ

PA•• PAAR PABA PACA PACE PACK PACS PACT PADS PAGE PAGO PAHO PAHS PAID PAIL PAIN PAIR PAIX PALE PALI PALL PALM PALO PALP PALS PALY PANE PANG PANS PANT PAPA PAPP PARA PARC PARD PARE PARI PARK PARL PARR PARS PART PASA PASE PASH PASO PASS PAST PATD PATE PATH PATS PAUL PAVE PAVO PAWL PAWN PAWS PAYS PAYT

P•A• PAAR PEAG PEAK PEAL PEAR PEAS PEAT PEAU PHAR PIAF PLAN PLAT PLAX PLAY PRAM PRAY PSAT PTAH

P••A PABA PACA PAPA PARA PASA PENA PEPA PICA PIKA PIMA PINA PISA PITA PLEA PODA POLA PROA PUKA PULA PUMA PUNA PUPA

•PA• CPAS MPAA OPAH OPAL SPAD SPAM SPAN SPAR SPAS SPAT SPAY UPAS

•P•A APIA EPHA LPGA MPAA OPIA SPCA

••PA ARPA CAPA DOPA GAPA HUPA NAPA NIPA PAPA PEPA PUPA RAPA TAPA

P•B• PABA PCBS PUBL PUBS

P••B PLEB PROB

•PB• APBS

PC•• PCBS

P•C• PACA PACE PACK PACS PACT PECK PECS PFCS PICA PICK PICO PICS PICT POCO PUCE PUCK

P••C PARC PREC PROC PSEC

•PC• SPCA SPCC

•P•C APOC EPIC OPEC SPCC SPEC

P•D• PADS PEDI PEDO PEDS PHDS PODA PODE PODS PUDU

P••D PAID PARD PATD PEND PIED PLED PLOD POND POOD PRED PROD

•PD• UPDO

•P•D APED OPED SPAD SPED SPUD

••PD LAPD SFPD

PE•• PEAG PEAK PEAL PEAR PEAS PEAT PEAU PECK PECS PEDI PEDO PEDS PEEK PEEL PEEN PEEP PEER PEGS PEKE PELE PELF PELL PELT PENA PEND PENH PENN PENS PENT PEON PEPA PEPE PEPO PEPS PERE PERF PERI PERK PERM PERP PERS PERT PERU PESO PEST PETE PETO PETS PEWS

P•E• PEEK PEEL PEEN PEEP PEER PHEW PIED PIER PIES PIET PLEA PLEB PLED PLEO PLEX POEM POET PREC PRED PREF PREM PREP PRES PRET PREV PREY PREZ PSEC PUER

P••E PACE PAGE PALE PANE PARE PASE PATE PAVE PEKE PELE PEPE PERE PETE PIKE PILE PINE PIPE PIRE PLIE PODE POKE POLE POME PONE POPE PORE POSE PRIE PUCE PULE PURE PYLE PYRE

•PE• APED APER APES APEX EPEE OPEC OPED OPEL OPEN OPER OPES SPEC SPED SPEE SPET SPEW

•P•E APSE BPOE EPEE IPSE OPIE SPEE

••PE CAPE CEPE COPE DOPE DUPE GAPE HOPE HYPE JAPE LOPE LUPE MOPE NAPE NOPE PEPE PIPE POPE RIPE ROPE SUPE TAPE TOPE TYPE WIPE XIPE YIPE

PF•• PFCS PFFT PFUI

P•F• PFFT PUFF

P••F PELF PERF PIAF POOF POUF PREF PROF PUFF

••PF KOPF

P•G• PAGE PAGO PEGS PIGS POGO POGS POGY PUGH PUGS

P••G PANG PEAG PING PLUG PONG PRIG PROG PUNG

•PG• LPGA SPGR

PH•• PHAR PHDS PHEW PHIL PHIS PHIZ PHON PHOT PHYS

P•H• PAHO PAHS POHL

P••H PASH PATH PENH PISH PITH POOH POSH PTAH PUGH PUSH

•PH• EPHA SPHT

•P•H IPOH OPAH

••PH ALPH KAPH KOPH QOPH SOPH UMPH ZEPH

PI•• PIAF PICA PICK PICO PICS PICT PIED PIER PIES PIET PIGS PIKA PIKE PILE PILI PILL PIMA PINA PINE PING PINK PINS PINT PINX PINY PION PIPE PIPS PIRE PISA PISH PITA PITH PITS PITT PITY PIUS PIXY PIZZ

P•I• PAID PAIL PAIN PAIR PAIX PHIL PHIS PHIZ PLIE PNIN POIL POIS PRIE PRIG PRIM PRIN PRIV PRIX PSIS

P••I PALI PARI PEDI PERI PFUI PILI PULI PUYI

•PI• APIA APIS EPIC EPIS OPIA OPIE SPIN SPIT SPIV

••PI HAPI HOPI IMPI KEPI TOPI TUPI

PK•• PKWY

P•K• PEKE PIKA PIKE POKE POKY PUKA PUKU

P••K PACK PARK PEAK PECK PEEK PERK PICK PINK POLK PORK PUCK PUNK

•PK• TPKS

••PK TNPK

PL•• PLAN PLAT PLAX PLAY PLEA PLEB PLED PLEO PLEX PLIE PLOD PLOP PLOT PLOW PLOY PLUG PLUM PLUR PLUS

P•L• PALE PALI PALL PALM PALO PALP PALS PALY PELE PELF PELL PELT PILE PILI PILL POLA POLE POLK POLL POLO POLS POLY PULA PULE PULI PULL PULP PYLE

P••L PAIL PALL PARL PAUL PAWL PEAL PEEL PELL PHIL PILL POHL POIL POLL POOL PUBL PULL PURL

•PL• CPLS

•P•L APPL OPAL OPEL

••PL APPL DIPL REPL

PM•• PMTS

P•M• PIMA POME POMO POMP POMS PUMA PUMP

P••M PALM PERM PLUM POEM PRAM PREM PRIM PROM

•PM• DPMS RPMS

•P•M SPAM

PN•• PNIN

P•N• PANE PANG PANS PANT PENA PEND PENH PENN PENS PENT

PINA
PINE
PING
PINK
PINS
PINT
PINX
PINY
POND
PONE
PONG
PONS
PONT
PONY
PUNA
PUNG
PUNK
PUNS
PUNT
PUNY

P••N
PAIN
PAWN
PEEN
PENN
PEON
PHON
PION
PLAN
PNIN
POON
PRIN
PRON

•P•N
OPEN
SPAN
SPIN
SPUN
UPON

••PN
CAPN
ESPN
HYPN

PO••
POCO
PODA
PODE
PODS
POEM
POET
POGO
POGS
POGY
POHL
POIL
POIS
POKE
POKY
POLA
POLE
POLK
POLL
POLO
POLS
POLY
POME
POMO
POMP
POMS
POND
PONE
PONG
PONS
PONT
PONY
POOD
POOF
POOH
POOL
POON
POOP
POOR
POPE
POPS
PORE
PORK
PORT
POSE
POSH
POSS
POST
POSY
POTS
POUF
POUR
POUT
POWS

P•O•
PEON
PHON
PHOT
PION
PLOD
PLOP
PLOT
PLOW
PLOY
POOD
POOF
POOH
POOL
POON
POOP
POOR
PROA
PROB
PROC
PROD
PROF
PROG
PROM
PRON
PROP
PROS
PROT
PROV
PROW
PROX

P••O
PAGO
PAHO
PALO
PASO
PAVO
PEDO
PEPO
PESO
PETO
PICO
PLEO
POCO
POGO
POLO
POMO
PUZO
PYRO

•PO•
APOC
APOS
BPOE
CPOS
EPOS
GPOS
IPOH
SPOT
UPON

•P•O
APSO
IPSO
OPTO
UPDO
UPTO

••PO
ALPO
CAPO
EXPO
HYPO
LIPO
PEPO
REPO
TOPO
TYPO
USPO

P•P•
PAPA
PAPP
PEPA
PEPE
PEPO
PEPS
PIPE
PIPS
POPE
POPS
PUPA
PUPS

P••P
PALP
PAPP
PEEP
PERP
PLOP
POMP
POOP
PREP
PROP
PULP
PUMP

•PP•
APPL
APPS
APPT

••PP
BOPP
CAPP
DEPP
LAPP
PAPP
RAPP
REPP
RUPP
SUPP
TEPP
YAPP

•PQ•
SPQR

PR••
PRAM
PRAY
PREC
PRED
PREF
PREM
PREP
PRES
PRET
PREV
PREY
PREZ
PRIE
PRIG
PRIM
PRIN
PRIV
PRIX
PROA
PROB
PROC
PROD
PROF
PROG
PROM
PRON
PROP
PROS
PROT
PROV
PROW
PROX
PRUT

P•R•
PARA
PARC
PARD
PARE
PARI
PARK
PARL
PARR
PARS
PART
PERE
PERF
PERI
PERK
PERM
PERP
PERS
PERT
PERU
PIRE
PORE
PORK
PORT
PURE
PURL
PURR
PYRE
PYRO

P••R
PAAR
PAIR
PARR
PEAR
PEER
PHAR
PIER
PLUR
POOR
POUR
PUER
PURR

•PR•
APRS
OPRY
SPRY

•P•R
APER
OPER
SPAR
SPGR
SPQR
SPUR

••PR
CUPR
SUPR

PS••
PSAT
PSEC
PSIS
PSST

P•S•
PASA
PASE
PASH
PASO
PASS
PAST
PESO
PEST
PISA
PISH
POSE
POSH
POSS
POST
POSY
PSST
PUSH
PUSS

P••S
PACS
PADS
PAHS
PALS
PANS
PARS
PASS
PATS
PAWS
PAYS
PCBS
PEAS
PECS
PEDS
PEGS
PENS
PEPS
PERS
PETS
PEWS
PFCS
PHDS
PHIS
PHYS
PICS
PIES
PIGS
PINS
PIPS
PITS
PIUS
PLUS
PMTS
PODS
POGS
POIS
POLS
POMS
PONS
POPS
POSS
POTS
POWS
PRES
PROS
PSIS
PUBS
PUGS
PUNS
PUPS
PUSS
PUTS
PVTS

•PS•
APSE
APSO
IPSE
IPSO

•P•S
APBS
APES
APIS
APOS
APPS
APRS
APTS
CPAS
CPLS
CPOS
DPMS
EPIS
EPOS
GPOS
OPES
OPTS
OPUS
RPMS
RPTS
SPAS
TPKS
UPAS

••PS
ALPS
AMPS
APPS
ASPS
BAPS
BOPS
CAPS
CEPS
COPS
CUPS
DAPS
DIPS
EMPS
FOPS
GAPS
GIPS
GYPS
HAPS
HIPS
HOPS
HYPS
IMPS
KIPS
KOPS
LAPS
LIPS
LOPS
MAPS
MIPS
MOPS
NAPS
NIPS
OOPS
PEPS
PIPS
POPS
PUPS
RAPS
REPS
RIPS
SAPS
SIPS
SOPS
SUPS
TAPS
TIPS
TOPS
TSPS
TWPS
UMPS
USPS
VIPS
YAPS
YIPS
ZAPS
ZIPS

PT••
PTAH

P•T•
PATD
PATE
PATH
PATS
PETE
PETO
PETS
PITA
PITH
PITS
PITT
PITY
PMTS
POTS
PUTS
PUTT
PVTS

P••T
PACT
PANT
PART
PAST
PAYT
PEAT
PELT
PENT
PERT
PEST
PFFT
PHOT
PICT
PIET
PINT
PITT
PLAT
PLOT
POET
PONT
PORT
POST
POUT
PRET
PROT
PRUT
PSAT
PSST
PUNT
PUTT

•PT•
APTS
OPTO
OPTS
RPTS
UPTO

•P•T
APPT
SPAT
SPET
SPHT
SPIT
SPOT

••PT
APPT
BAPT
CAPT
COPT
DEPT
EXPT
HEPT
KEPT
RAPT
RCPT
REPT
SEPT
SHPT
SUPT
WEPT

PU••
PUBL
PUBS
PUCE
PUCK
PUDU
PUER
PUFF
PUGH
PUGS
PUKA
PUKU
PULA
PULE
PULI
PULL
PULP
PUMA
PUMP
PUNA
PUNG
PUNK
PUNS
PUNT
PUNY
PUPA
PUPS
PURE
PURL
PURR
PUSH
PUSS
PUTS
PUTT
PUYI
PUZO

P•U•
PAUL
PFUI
PIUS
PLUG
PLUM
PLUR
PLUS
POUF
POUR
POUT
PRUT

P••U
PEAU
PERU
PUDU
PUKU

•PU•
OPUS
SPUD
SPUN
SPUR

PV••
PVTS

P•V•
PAVE
PAVO

P••V
PREV
PRIV
PROV

•P•V
SPIV

P•W•
PAWL
PAWN
PAWS
PEWS
PKWY
POWS

P••W
PHEW
PLOW
PROW

•P•W
SPEW

P•X•
PIXY

P••X
PAIX
PINX
PLAX
PLEX
PRIX
PROX

•P•X
APEX

PY••
PYLE
PYRE
PYRO

P•Y•
PAYS
PAYT
PHYS
PUYI

P••Y
PALY
PINY
PITY
PIXY
PKWY
PLAY
PLOY
POGY
POKY
POLY
PONY
POSY
PRAY
PREY
PUNY

•P•Y
OPRY
SPAY
SPRY

••PY
COPY
DOPY
ESPY
ISPY
ROPY
TYPY

P•Z•
PIZZ
PUZO

P••Z
PHIZ
PIZZ
PREZ

QA••
QADI
QAID

Q•A•
QUAD
QUAG
QUAI
QUAR
QUAY

•Q•A
AQUA

Q•D•
QADI

Q••D
QAID
QUAD
QUID
QUOD

•Q•D
SQYD

QE••
QEII

Q•E•
QUEL
QUES

•QF•
SQFT

Q••G
QUAG

Q••H
QOPH

Q•I•
QAID
QEII
QTIP
QUID
QUIP
QUIT
QUIZ

Q••I
QADI
QEII
QUAI
QUOI

•QI•
SQIN

•Q•I
AQUI
EQUI
SQMI

Q••L
QUEL

•QM•
SQMI

•Q•N
SQIN

QO••
QOPH

Q•O•
QUOD
QUOI
QUOT

Q•P•
QOPH

Q••P
QTIP
QUIP

••QQ
SEQQ

Q•R•
QTRS

Q••R
QUAR

••QR
SPQR

Q••S
QTRS
QUES

••QS
BBQS
ESQS

QT••
QTIP
QTRS

Q••T
QUIT
QUOT

•Q•T
SQFT

QU••
QUAD
QUAG
QUAI
QUAR
QUAY
QUEL
QUES
QUID
QUIP
QUIT
QUIZ
QUOD
QUOI
QUOT

•QU•
AQUA
AQUI
EQUI

Q••Y
QUAY

•QY•
SQYD

Q••Z
QUIZ

RA••
RABE
RABI
RACE
RACK
RACY
RADM
RADS
RAFT
RAGA
RAGE
RAGG
RAGS
RAGU
RAID
RAIL
RAIN
RAJA
RAKE
RAKI
RAKU
RALL
RAMA
RAMI
RAMP
RAMS
RANA
RAND
RANG
RANI
RANK
RANT
RAPA
RAPP
RAPS
RAPT
RARA
RARE
RASA
RASH
RASK
RASP
RATA
RATE
RATS
RATT
RAUL
RAVE
RAVI
RAYE
RAYS
RAZE
RAZZ

R•A•
RCAF
RDAS
READ
REAL
REAM
REAP
REAR
RIAL
RIAS
ROAD
ROAM
ROAN
ROAR
RYAL
RYAN
RYAS

R••A
RAGA
RAJA
RAMA
RANA
RAPA
RARA
RASA
RATA
REBA
REZA
RHEA
RICA
RIGA
RIMA
RITA
ROCA
ROMA
RONA
ROSA
ROTA
RRNA
RUGA

•RA•
ARAB
ARAD
ARAK
ARAL
ARAM
ARAN
ARAS
BRAC
BRAD
BRAE
BRAG
BRAM
BRAN
BRAS
BRAT
BRAW
BRAY
BRAZ
CRAB
CRAG
CRAM
CRAT
CRAW
CRAY
DRAB
DRAG
DRAM
DRAT
DRAW
DRAY
ERAS
ERAT
FRAE
FRAM
FRAN
FRAP
FRAT
FRAU
FRAY
GRAB
GRAD
GRAF
GRAM
GRAN
GRAS
GRAU
GRAY
GRAZ
IRAE
IRAN
IRAQ
IRAS
ORAD
ORAL
ORAN
PRAM
PRAY
SRAS
TRAM
TRAP
TRAX
TRAY
URAL
VRAI
WRAC
WRAF
WRAP
WRAY
XRAY

•R•A
AREA
ARIA
ARMA
ARPA
ARRA
BREA
ERDA
ERMA
FRIA
IRMA
MRNA
ORCA
PROA
RRNA
SRTA
TRNA
URFA
URGA
URSA

••RA
AGRA
ARRA
ATRA
AURA
BARA
BORA
CARA
CERA
CORA
DORA
DURA
EYRA
EZRA
FORA
GERA
HERA
HORA
JURA
KARA
KYRA
LARA
LIRA
LYRA
MARA
MIRA
MORA
MYRA
NARA
NORA
OKRA
OTRA
PARA
RARA
SARA
SERA
SORA
SURA
TARA
TERA
VARA
VERA

RB••
RBIS

R•B•
RABE
RABI
REBA
REBS
RHBS
RIBS
ROBB
ROBE
ROBO
ROBS
RUBE
RUBS
RUBY

R••B
ROBB

•RB•
ARBS
GRBR
IRBM
ORBS
URBS

•R•B
ARAB
CRAB
CRIB
DRAB
DRIB
DRUB
GRAB
GRUB
PROB
TRIB

••RB
BARB
BURB
CARB
CURB
FORB
GARB
HERB
KERB
NLRB
SERB
SORB
VERB

RC••
RCAF
RCMP
RCPT
RCTS

R•C•
RACE
RACK
RACY
RECD
RECS
RECT
RICA
RICE
RICH
RICK
RICO
ROCA
ROCK
ROCS
RUCK

R••C
ROTC

•RC•
ARCH
ARCO
ARCS
FRCP
FRCS
ORCA
ORCH
ORCS

•R•C
BRAC
BRIC
CROC
ERIC
KROC
PREC
PROC
WRAC

••RC
CIRC
MARC
NARC
PARC

RD••
RDAS

R•D•
RADM
RADS
REDD
REDI
REDO
REDS
RFDS
RIDD
RIDE
RIDS
RMDR
RNDS
RODE
RODS
RUDD
RUDE
RUDI
RUDY

R••D
RAID
RAND
READ
RECD
REDD
REED
REGD
REID
REND
RETD
RIDD
RIND
ROAD
ROOD
RUDD
RUED

•RD•
ERDA
ERDE
ORDO
URDU

•R•D
ARAD
ARID
BRAD
BRED
CRUD
DRED
FRED
GRAD
GRID
IRED
IRID
MRED
ORAD
PRED
PROD
TROD

••RD
BARD
BIRD
BYRD
CARD
CORD
CURD
DARD
FARD
FORD
GIRD
HARD
HERD
KURD
LARD
LORD
NARD
NERD
NORD
PARD
SARD
SURD
VERD
WARD
WORD
YARD

RE••
READ
REAL
REAM
REAP
REAR
REBA
REBS
RECD
RECS
RECT
REDD
REDI
REDO
REDS
REED
REEF
REEK
REEL
REES
REFL
REFS
REFT
REGD
REGS
REGT
REID
REIN
REIT
RELS
RELY
REMO
REMS
REND
RENE
RENI
RENO
RENT
REOS
REPL
REPO
REPP
REPS
REPT
RESH

RESP
REST
RETD
RETE
RETS
REUP
REVE
REVS
REZA

R•E•
REED
REEF
REEK
REEL
REES
RHEA
RHEE
RHEO
RHET
RIEL
RIEN
ROES
RTES
RUED
RUES
RYES

R••E
RABE
RACE
RAGE
RAKE
RARE
RATE
RAVE
RAYE
RAZE
RENE
RETE
REVE
RHEE
RHUE
RICE
RIDE
RIFE
RILE
RIME
RIPE
RIRE
RISE
RITE
RIVE
ROBE
RODE
ROLE
ROME
ROPE
ROSE
ROTE
ROUE
ROVE
ROWE
RUBE
RUDE
RULE
RUNE
RUSE
RYLE
RYNE

•RE•
AREA
AREO
ARES
BREA
BRED
BREL
BREN
BRER
BRET
BREV
BREW
CREE
CREW
DRED
DREE
DREG
DREI
DREW
FRED
FREE
FREI
FREQ
FRET
FREY
GREE
GREG
GREW
GREX
GREY
HRES
IRED
IRES
MRED
OREG
OREL
OREM
OREO
ORES
PREC
PRED
PREF
PREM
PREP
PRES
PRET
PREV
PREY
PREZ
TREE
TREF
TREK
TRES
TRET
TREX
TREY
UREY
WREN

•R•E
ARME
ARNE
ARTE
BRAE
BRIE
CREE
CRUE
DREE
ERDE
ERIE
ERLE
ERNE
ERSE
ERTE
FRAE
FREE
FROE
FRYE
GREE
IRAE
ORLE
ORNE
PRIE
TREE
TRUE
URGE

••RE
AARE
ACRE
AIRE
BARE
BORE
BYRE
CARE
CERE
CIRE
CORE
CURE
DARE
DIRE
DORE
EIRE
ETRE
EYRE
FARE
FERE
FIRE
FORE
GARE
GERE
GORE
GYRE
HARE
HERE
HIRE
IHRE
INRE
JURE
KORE
LIRE
LORE
LURE
LYRE
MARE
MERE
MIRE
MORE
OGRE
PARE
PERE
PIRE
PORE
PURE
PYRE
RARE
RIRE
SERE
SIRE
SORE
SURE
TARE
TIRE
TORE
TYRE
VERE
WARE
WERE
WIRE
WORE
YARE
YORE

RF••
RFDS

R•F•
RAFT
REFL
REFS
REFT
RIFE
RIFF
RIFS
RIFT
RUFF

R••F
RCAF
REEF
RIFF
ROLF
ROOF
RUFF

•RF•
ORFF
URFA

•R•F
GRAF
ORFF
PREF
PROF
TREF
WRAF

••RF
CERF
CORF
KERF
NERF
PERF
SERF
SURF
TURF
ZARF

RG••
RGTS

R•G•
RAGA
RAGE
RAGG
RAGS
RAGU
REGD
REGS
REGT
RIGA
RIGG
RIGI
RIGS
RUGA
RUGS

R••G
RAGG
RANG
RIGG
RING
RUNG

•RG•
ARGO
ARGY
ERGO
ERGS
ORGS
ORGY
URGA
URGE

•R•G
BRAG
BRIG
CRAG
DRAG
DREG
DRUG
FROG
FRUG
GREG
GRIG
GROG
OREG
ORIG
PRIG
PROG
TRIG

••RG
BERG
BORG
BURG
MARG
SURG

RH••
RHBS
RHEA
RHEE
RHEO
RHET
RHOS
RHUE
RHUM

R•H•
RUHR

R••H
RASH
RESH
RICH
ROSH
ROTH
RUSH
RUTH

•R•H
ARCH
ORCH
ORTH

••RH
GNRH

RI••
RIAL
RIAS
RIBS
RICA
RICE
RICH
RICK
RICO
RIDD
RIDE
RIDS
RIEL
RIEN
RIFE
RIFF
RIFS
RIFT
RIGA
RIGG
RIGI
RIGS
RIIS
RIJN
RILE
RILL
RIMA
RIME
RIMS
RIMY
RIND
RING
RINK
RIOS
RIOT
RIPE
RIPS
RIRE
RISE
RISK
RITA
RITE
RITT
RITZ
RIVE

R•I•
RAID
RAIL
RAIN
RBIS
REID
REIN
REIT
RIIS
ROIL
RUIN

R••I
RABI
RAKI
RAMI
RANI
RAVI
REDI
RENI
RIGI
ROTI
RUDI

•RI•
ARIA
ARID
ARIL
ARIZ
BRIC
BRIE
BRIG
BRIM
BRIO
BRIT
BRIX
CRIB
CRIM
CRIN
CRIT
DRIB
DRIP
DRIQ
ERIC
ERIE
ERIK
ERIN
ERIS
FRIA
FRIO
FRIS
FRIT
FRIZ
GRID
GRIG
GRIM
GRIN
GRIP
GRIS
GRIT
IRID
IRIS
KRIO
KRIS
ORIG
PRIE
PRIG
PRIM
PRIN
PRIV
PRIX
TRIB
TRIG
TRIM
TRIO
TRIP
TRIS
TRIX
URIM
URIS
WRIT

•R•I
DREI
FREI
TROI
VRAI

••RI
ABRI
AGRI
ATRI
AURI
BARI
BURI
CORI
DARI
GYRI
HARI
INRI
LARI
LORI
MARI
NERI
NORI
OMRI
PARI
PERI
SARI
SORI
TERI
TORI
YURI
ZORI

R•J•
RAJA
RIJN
ROJO

R•K•
RAKE
RAKI
RAKU

R••K
RACK
RANK
RASK
REEK
RICK
RINK
RISK
ROCK
ROOK
RUCK
RUSK

•RK•
ARKS
IRKS

•R•K
ARAK
ERIK
GROK
KRUK
ORSK
TREK
TRUK
URUK

••RK
BARK
BIRK
BORK
CARK
CORK
DARK
DIRK
FORK
HARK
JERK
KIRK
LARK
LURK
MARK
MORK
MURK
NARK
PARK
PERK
PORK
SARK
TORK
TURK
WORK
YORK

R•L•
RALL
RELS
RELY
RILE
RILL
ROLE
ROLF
ROLL
ROLY
RULE
RYLE

R••L
RAIL
RALL
RAUL
REAL
REEL
REFL
REPL
RIAL
RIEL
RILL
ROIL
ROLL
ROTL
RYAL

•RL•
ARLO
ERLE
ORLE
ORLY

•R•L
ARAL
ARIL
ARYL
BREL
ORAL
OREL
URAL

••RL
BIRL
BURL
CARL
CURL
EARL
FURL
GIRL
HERL
HURL
JARL
KARL
MARL
PARL
PURL

RM••
RMDR

R•M•
RAMA
RAMI
RAMP
RAMS
RCMP
REMO
REMS
RIMA
RIME
RIMS
RIMY
ROMA
ROME
ROMP
ROMS
ROMY
RPMS
RUMP
RUMS

R••M
RADM
REAM
RHUM
ROAM
ROOM

•RM•
ARMA
ARME
ARMS
ARMY
ERMA
IRMA

•R•M
ARAM
ARUM
BRAM
BRIM
BROM
CRAM
CRIM
DRAM
DRUM
FRAM
FROM
GRAM
GRIM
IRBM
OREM
PRAM
PREM
PRIM
PROM
TRAM
TRIM
URIM

••RM
BARM
BDRM
BERM
CORM
DERM
DORM
FARM
FIRM
FORM
GERM
HARM
HERM
NORM
PERM
TERM
WARM
WORM

RN••
RNDS

R•N•
RANA
RAND
RANG
RANI
RANK
RANT
REND
RENE
RENI
RENO
RENT
RIND
RING
RINK
RONA
RRNA
RUNE
RUNG
RUNS
RUNT
RYNE

R••N
RAIN
REIN
RIEN
RIJN
ROAN
RUIN
RYAN
RYUN

•RN•
ARNE
ARNO
BRNO
DRNO
ERNE
ERNO
ERNS
MRNA
ORNE
RRNA
TRNA
URNS

•R•N
ARAN
ARON
BRAN
BREN
BRYN
CRIN
ERIN
FRAN
GRAN
GRIN
IRAN
IRON
LRON
ORAN
PRIN
PRON
TRON
WREN

••RN
BARN
BERN
BORN
BURN
CERN
CORN
DARN
DERN
DORN
DURN
EARN
FERN
FIRN
GARN
GIRN
HERN
HORN
KERN
LORN
MORN
NORN
TARN
TERN
TORN
TURN
VERN
WARN
WORN
YARN
ZORN

RO••
ROAD
ROAM
ROAN
ROAR
ROBB
ROBE
ROBO
ROBS
ROCA
ROCK
ROCS
RODE
RODS
ROES
ROIL
ROJO
ROLE
ROLF
ROLL
ROLY
ROMA
ROME
ROMP
ROMS
ROMY
RONA
ROOD
ROOF
ROOK
ROOM
ROOS
ROOT
ROPE
ROPY
RORY
ROSA
ROSE
ROSH
ROSS
ROSY
ROTA
ROTC
ROTE
ROTH
ROTI
ROTL
ROTO
ROTS
ROUE
ROUP
ROUS
ROUT
ROUX
ROVE
ROWE
ROWS

R•O•
REOS
RHOS
RIOS
RIOT
ROOD
ROOF
ROOK
ROOM
ROOS
ROOT
RYOT

R••O
REDO
REMO
RENO
REPO
RHEO
RICO
ROBO
ROJO
ROTO

•RO•
ARON
AROO
BROM
BROS
BROW
BROZ
CROC
CROP
CROW
DROP
EROO
EROS
FROE
FROG
FROM
FROW
GROG
GROK
GROS
GROT
GROW
IRON
KROC
LRON
PROA
PROB
PROC
PROD
PROF
PROG
PROM
PRON
PROP
PROS
PROT
PROV
PROW
PROX
TROD
TROI
TRON
TROP
TROT
TROY

•R•O
ARCO
AREO
ARGO
ARLO
ARNO
AROO
BRIO
BRNO
BRYO
CRYO
DRNO
ERGO
ERNO
EROO
FRIO
KRIO
ORDO
OREO
ORZO
TRIO

••RO
ACRO
AERO
AFRO
AGRO
BARO
BORO
CARO
CERO
CORO
DURO
EBRO
EERO
EURO
FARO
FURO
GIRO
GYRO
HERO
INRO
KARO
MERO
MIRO
MORO
NERO
NYRO
OTRO
PYRO
SERO
TARO
TORO
TYRO
VERO
XERO
ZERO

RP••
RPMS
RPTS

R•P•
RAPA
RAPP
RAPS
RAPT
RCPT
REPL
REPO
REPP
REPS
REPT
RIPE
RIPS
ROPE
ROPY
RUPP

R••P
RAMP
RAPP
RASP
RCMP
REAP
REPP
RESP
REUP
ROMP
ROUP
RSVP
RUMP
RUPP

•RP•
ARPA

•R•P
CROP
DRIP
DROP
FRAP
FRCP
GRIP
PREP
PROP
TRAP
TRIP
TROP
WRAP

••RP
AARP
BURP
CARP
CORP
DORP
EARP
GARP
GORP
HARP
PERP
TARP
TERP
WARP
WKRP

•R•Q
DRIQ
FREQ
IRAQ

RR••
RRNA

R•R•
RARA
RARE
RIRE
RORY

R••R
REAR
RMDR
ROAR
RUHR

•RR•
ARRA
ARRS
ERRS

•R•R
BRER
GRBR

••RR
BARR
BIRR
BURR
CARR
CORR
CURR
DORR
FARR
GARR
HERR
KERR
PARR
PURR
TERR
TORR

RS••
RSVP

R•S•
RASA
RASH
RASK
RASP
RESH
RESP
REST
RISE
RISK
ROSA
ROSE
ROSH
ROSS
ROSY
RUSE
RUSH
RUSK
RUSS
RUST

R••S
RADS
RAGS
RAMS
RAPS
RATS
RAYS
RBIS
RCTS
RDAS
REBS
RECS
REDS
REES
REFS
REGS
RELS
REMS
REOS
REPS
RETS
REVS
RFDS
RGTS
RHBS
RHOS
RIAS
RIBS
RIDS
RIFS
RIGS
RIIS
RIMS
RIOS
RIPS
RNDS
ROBS
ROCS
RODS
ROES
ROMS
ROOS
ROSS
ROTS
ROUS
ROWS
RPMS
RPTS
RTES
RUBS
RUES
RUGS
RUMS
RUNS
RUSS
RUTS
RYAS
RYES

•RS•
ERSE
ERST
ORSK
URSA

•R•S
ARAS
ARBS
ARCS
ARES
ARKS
ARMS
ARRS
ARTS
BRAS
BROS
CRTS
CRUS
DRYS
ERAS
ERGS
ERIS
ERNS
EROS
ERRS
FRCS
FRIS
GRAS
GRIS
GROS
GRUS
HRES
IRAS
IRES
IRIS
IRKS
KRIS
ORBS
ORCS
ORES
ORGS
ORTS
PRES
PROS
SRAS
TRES
TRIS
URBS
URIS
URNS
URUS

••RS
AIRS
APRS
ARRS
BARS
BORS
BURS
CARS
CDRS
CURS
DIRS
DORS
EARS
ERRS
FARS
FIRS
FURS
GARS
HERS
HORS
JARS
KIRS
LARS
LDRS
MARS
MFRS
MGRS
MIRS
OARS
OURS
PARS
PERS
QTRS
SERS
SIRS
SLRS
SSRS
STRS
TARS
TORS
VCRS
VERS
WARS

RT••
RTES

R•T•
RATA
RATE
RATS
RATT
RCTS
RETD
RETE
RETS
RGTS
RITA
RITE
RITT
RITZ
ROTA
ROTC
ROTE
ROTH
ROTI
ROTL
ROTO
ROTS
RPTS
RUTH
RUTS

R••T
RAFT
RANT
RAPT
RATT
RCPT
RECT
REFT
REGT
REIT
RENT
REPT
REST
RHET
RIFT
RIOT
RITT
ROOT
ROUT
RUNT
RUST
RYOT

•RT•
ARTE
ARTS
ARTY
CRTS
ERTE

ORTH ORTS SRTA

•R•T
BRAT BRET BRIT BRUT CRAT CRIT DRAT ERAT ERST FRAT FRET FRIT GRIT GROT GRWT PRET PROT PRUT TRET TROT WRIT

••RT
AIRT BART BERT BORT BURT CART CERT CURT DART DIRT DORT FORT GIRT HART HIRT HORT HURT KART KERT KURT MART MORT OORT PART PERT PORT SERT SORT TART TORT VERT WART WERT WORT YURT

RU••
RUBE RUBS RUBY RUCK RUDD RUDE RUDI RUDY RUED RUES RUFF RUGA RUGS RUHR RUIN RULE RUMP RUMS RUNE RUNG RUNS RUNT RUPP RUSE RUSH RUSK RUSS RUST RUTH RUTS

R•U•
RAUL REUP RHUE RHUM ROUE ROUP ROUS ROUT ROUX RYUN

R••U
RAGU RAKU

•RU•
ARUM BRUT CRUD CRUE CRUS CRUX CRUZ DRUB DRUG DRUM FRUG GRUB GRUS KRUK PRUT TRUE TRUK URUK URUS

•R•U
FRAU GRAU URDU

••RU
ECRU GURU MARU PERU THRU

R•V•
RAVE RAVI REVE REVS RIVE ROVE RSVP

•R•V
BREV PREV PRIV PROV

••RV
MARV MERV MIRV SERV

R•W•
ROWE ROWS

•RW•
GRWT

•R•W
BRAW BREW BROW CRAW CREW CROW DRAW DREW FROW GREW GROW PROW

R••X
ROUX

•R•X
BRIX CRUX GREX ORYX PRIX PROX TRAX TREX TRIX

••RX
MARX

RY••
RYAL RYAN RYAS RYES RYLE RYNE RYOT RYUN

R•Y•
RAYE RAYS

R••Y
RACY RELY RIMY ROLY ROMY ROPY RORY ROSY RUBY RUDY

•RY•
ARYL BRYN BRYO CRYO DRYS FRYE ORYX

•R•Y
ARGY ARMY ARTY BRAY CRAY DRAY FRAY FREY GRAY GREY ORGY ORLY PRAY PREY TRAY TREY TROY UREY WRAY XRAY

••RY
AERY AIRY AWRY BURY CARY CORY DORY EERY EURY FURY GARY GORY JURY LORY MARY MIRY NARY OPRY RORY SCRY SPRY TORY VARY VERY WARY WIRY

R•Z•
RAZE RAZZ REZA

R••Z
RAZZ RITZ

•RZ•
ORZO

•R•Z
ARIZ BRAZ BROZ CRUZ FRIZ GRAZ PREZ

••RZ
HARZ NARZ

SA••
SAAB SAAR SABA SABE SABU SACK SACS SADA SADD SADE SADR SAFE SAFR SAGA SAGE SAGO SAGS SAHL SAID SAIL SAIS SAKE SAKI SAKS SALA SALE SALK SALP SALS SALT SAME SAML SAMO SAMP SANA SAND SANE SANG SANK SANS SAPS SARA SARD SARI SARK SASE SASH SASK SASS SATE SATO SAUD SAUK SAUL SAUR SAVA SAVE SAWN SAWS SAXE SAYS

S•A•
SAAB SAAR SCAB SCAD SCAM SCAN SCAR SCAT SDAK SEAL SEAM SEAN SEAR SEAS SEAT SFAX SHAD SHAG SHAH SHAM SHAN SHAQ SHAW SHAY SIAL SIAM SKAT SKAW SLAB SLAG SLAM SLAP SLAT SLAV SLAW SLAY SNAG SNAP SOAK SOAP SOAR SPAD SPAM SPAN SPAR SPAS SPAT SPAY SRAS STAB STAG STAN STAR STAS STAT STAY SWAB SWAG SWAK SWAM SWAN SWAP SWAT SWAY

S••A
SABA SADA SAGA SALA SANA SARA SAVA SEGA SELA SERA SETA SHEA SIMA SKUA SMSA SOCA SODA SOFA SOLA SOMA SORA SOYA SPCA SRTA STOA SURA SUSA SUVA

•SA•
ASAP ESAI ESAS ESAU ISAK ISAR ISAY LSAT OSAR PSAT TSAR USAF USAR

•S•A
ASEA ASIA ASTA ESSA ESTA HSIA ISBA ISLA OSHA OSSA USDA USGA USIA USMA USNA USTA

••SA
ANSA CASA COSA ELSA ESSA ILSA LISA MESA MKSA NASA OSSA PASA PISA RASA ROSA SMSA SUSA URSA VISA WUSA

S•B•
SABA SABE SABU SEBE SEBS SIBS SLBM SOBS STBD SUBJ SUBS SWBS SWBW

S••B
SAAB SCAB SERB SHEB SLAB SLOB SLUB SNOB SNUB SORB STAB STUB SWAB SWOB

•SB•
ISBA ISBN

••SB
MUSB NTSB

SC••
SCAB SCAD SCAM SCAN SCAR SCAT SCIL SCOP SCOT SCOW SCRY SCSI SCUD SCUM SCUP SCUT

S•C•
SACK SACS SECH SECS SECT SECY SICK SICS SNCC SOCA SOCK SPCA SPCC SUCH SUCK SYCE

S••C
SNCC SPCC SPEC SYNC

•SC•
ASCH ASCI ASCO DSCS ESCE USCG

•S•C
BSEC MSEC PSEC USMC

••SC
BASC BOSC DESC DISC FISC MASC MISC WISC

SD••
SDAK

S•D•
SADA SADD SADE SADR SIDE SIDH SODA SODS STDS SUDD SUDS

S••D
SADD SAID SAND SARD SAUD SCAD SCUD SEED SEND SFPD SHAD SHED SHOD SILD SIND SKED SKID SLED SLID SOLD SPAD SPED SPUD SQYD STBD STUD SUDD SUED SURD SWED SYND

•SD•
USDA

•S•D
BSED USED

••SD
DASD NASD

SE••
SEAL SEAM SEAN SEAR SEAS SEAT SEBE SEBS SECH SECS SECT SECY SEED SEEK SEEL SEEM SEEN SEEP SEER SEES SEGA SEGO SEHR SEIN SEIS SEJM SELA SELF SELL SEME SEMI SEMS SEND SENE SENS SENT SEPT SEQQ SERA SERB SERE SERF SERO SERS SERT SERV SESS SETA SETH SETI SETS SETT SEUL SEVE SEWN SEWS SEXT

S•E•
SEED SEEK SEEL SEEM SEEN SEEP SEER SEES SHEA SHEB SHED SHEL SHEM SHEP SHES SKED SKEE SKEG SKEP SKEW SLED SLEW SMEE SMEW SNEE SPEC SPED SPEE SPET SPEW STEM STEN STEP STER STES STET STEW SUED SUER SUES SUET SUEY SUEZ SVEN SWED

S••E
SABE SADE SAFE SAGE SAKE SALE SAME SANE SASE SATE SAVE SAXE SEBE SEME SENE SERE SEVE SHOE SHUE SIDE SINE SIRE SITE SIZE SKEE SKYE SLOE SLUE SLYE SMEE SNEE SOIE SOKE SOLE SOME SONE SORE SPEE STGE SUPE SURE SYCE SYNE

•SE•
ASEA BSEC BSED ESEL ISEE MSEC PSEC USED USER USES YSER

•S•E
ASHE ESCE ESME ESNE ESSE ESTE ISEE ISLE OSTE

••SE
APSE BASE BISE BOSE CASE DOSE DUSE EASE ELSE ERSE ESSE FUSE HOSE IPSE JOSE LASE LESE LISE LOSE MDSE MISE MOSE MUSE NOSE NYSE OISE OUSE PASE POSE RISE ROSE RUSE SASE VASE VISE WHSE WISE

SF••
SFAX SFPD

S•F•
SAFE SAFR SIFT SOFA SOFT SQFT SUFF SUFI

S••F
SELF SERF SUFF SULF SURF

•S•F
ASIF ASOF USAF

SG••
SGTS

S•G•
SAGA SAGE SAGO SAGS SEGA SEGO SIGH SIGN SPGR SSGT STGE SVGS

S••G
SANG SHAG SING SKEG SLAG SLOG SLUG SMOG SMUG SNAG SNUG SONG STAG SUNG SURG SWAG SWIG

•SG•
MSGR MSGS MSGT SSGT TSGT USGA

•S•G
USCG

SH••
SHAD SHAG SHAH SHAM SHAN SHAQ SHAW SHAY SHEA SHEB SHED SHEL SHEM SHEP SHES SHIH SHIM SHIN SHIP SHIV SHOD SHOE SHOO SHOP SHOT SHOW SHPT SHUE SHUL SHUN SHUT

S•H•
SAHL SEHR SOHN SOHO SPHT

S••H
SASH SECH SETH SHAH SHIH SIDH SIGH SIKH SINH SOPH SUCH

•SH•
ASHE ASHY OSHA

•S•H
ASCH ESTH ISTH

••SH
BASH BOSH BUSH CASH COSH CUSH DASH DISH FISH GASH GISH GOSH GUSH HASH HUSH JOSH KISH KUSH LASH LUSH MASH MESH MUSH NASH NOSH PASH PISH POSH PUSH RASH RESH ROSH RUSH SASH TESH TISH TOSH TUSH WASH WISH

SI••
SIAL SIAM SIBS SICK SICS SIDE SIDH SIFT SIGH SIGN SIKH SILD SILK SILL SILO SILT SIMA SIMI SIMP SIMS SIND SINE SING SINH SINK SINO SINS SIPS SIRE SIRS SISI SITE SITS SITU SIZE

S•I•
SAID SAIL SAIS SCIL SEIN SEIS SHIH SHIM SHIN SHIP SHIV SKID SKIL SKIM SKIN SKIP SKIS SKIT SLID SLIM SLIP SLIT SMIT SNIP SNIT SOIE SOIL SOIR SPIN SPIT SPIV SQIN STIR SUIT SWIG SWIM SWIT

S••I
SAKI SARI SCSI SEMI SETI SIMI SISI SOLI SORI SQMI SUFI SUZI

•SI•
ASIA ASIF ASIR ASIS HSIA ISIS OSIS PSIS USIA VSIX

•S•I
ASCI ASTI ESAI

••SI
ANSI DESI IASI NISI SCSI SISI

S•J•
SEJM

S••J
SUBJ

SK••
SKAT SKAW SKED SKEE SKEG SKEP SKEW SKID SKIL SKIM SKIN SKIP SKIS SKIT SKOL SKUA SKYE SKYS

S•K•
SAKE SAKI SAKS SIKH SOKE SUKS

S••K
SACK SALK SANK SARK SASK SAUK SDAK SEEK SICK SILK SINK SOAK SOCK SOUK SUCK SULK SUNK SWAK

•SK•
ASKS TSKS

•S•K
ISAK

••SK
BASK BOSK BUSK CASK CUSK DESK DISK DUSK FISK HUSK MASK MUSK OMSK ORSK RASK RISK RUSK SASK TASK TUSK WISK

SL••
SLAB SLAG SLAM SLAP SLAT SLAV SLAW SLAY SLBM SLED SLEW SLID SLIM SLIP SLIT SLOB SLOE SLOG SLOP SLOT SLOW SLRS SLUB SLUE SLUG SLUM SLUR SLYE

S•L•
SALA SALE SALK SALP SALS SALT SELA SELF SELL SILD SILK SILL SILO SILT SOLA SOLD SOLE SOLI SOLN SOLO SOLS STLO SULF SULK SULU SYLL SYLS

S••L
SAHL SAIL SAML SAUL SCIL SEAL SEEL SELL SEUL SHEL SHUL SIAL SILL SKIL SKOL SOIL SOUL STOL SYLL

•SL•
ISLA ISLE ISLS

OSLO

•S•L
ESEL

••SL
NASL

SM••
SMEE
SMEW
SMIT
SMOG
SMSA
SMUG
SMUT

S•M•
SAME
SAML
SAMO
SAMP
SEME
SEMI
SEMS
SIMA
SIMI
SIMP
SIMS
SOMA
SOME
SQMI
STMT
SUMO
SUMP
SUMS

S••M
SCAM
SCUM
SEAM
SEEM
SEJM
SHAM
SHEM
SHIM
SIAM
SKIM
SLAM
SLBM
SLIM
SLUM
SPAM
STEM
STUM
SWAM
SWIM
SWUM

•SM•
BSMT
DSMS
ESME
ISMS
USMA
USMC

••SM
COSM
MUSM

SN••
SNAG
SNAP
SNCC
SNEE
SNIP
SNIT
SNOB
SNOW
SNUB
SNUG

S•N•
SANA
SAND
SANE
SANG
SANK
SANS
SEND
SENE
SENS
SENT
SIND
SINE
SING
SINH
SINK
SINO
SINS
SONE
SONG
SONS
SONY
SSNS
STNS
SUNG
SUNK
SUNN
SUNS
SUNY
SYNC
SYND
SYNE
SYNS

S••N
SAWN
SCAN
SEAN
SEEN
SEIN
SEWN
SHAN
SHIN
SHUN
SIGN
SKIN
SOHN
SOLN
SOON
SOWN
SPAN
SPIN
SPUN
SQIN
STAN
STEN
STUN
SUNN
SVEN
SWAN

•SN•
ESNE
ISNT
SSNS
USNA
USNR

•S•N
ASSN
ESPN
ISBN
ISSN

••SN
ASSN
BOSN
ISSN

SO••
SOAK
SOAP
SOAR
SOBS
SOCA
SOCK
SODA
SODS
SOFA
SOFT
SOHN
SOHO
SOIE
SOIL
SOIR
SOKE
SOLA
SOLD
SOLE
SOLI
SOLN
SOLO
SOLS
SOMA
SOME
SONE
SONG
SONS
SONY
SOON
SOOT
SOPH
SOPS
SORA
SORB
SORE
SORI
SORT
SOSO
SOTS
SOUK
SOUL
SOUP
SOUR
SOUS
SOWN
SOWS
SOYA
SOYS

S•O•
SCOP
SCOT
SCOW
SHOD
SHOE
SHOO
SHOP
SHOT
SHOW
SKOL
SLOB
SLOE
SLOG
SLOP
SLOT
SLOW
SMOG
SNOB
SNOW
SOON
SOOT
SPOT
STOA
STOL
STOP
STOT
STOW
SWOB
SWOP

S••O
SAGO
SAMO
SATO
SEGO
SERO
SHOO
SILO
SINO
SOHO
SOLO
SOSO
STLO
SUMO

•SO•
ASOF
ASOR
DSOS
ESOP
ESOS
VSOP

•S•O
ASCO
ASTO
ESSO
ESTO
OSLO
OSSO
USPO

••SO
AHSO
ALSO
APSO
BESO
DMSO
ESSO
FASO
IFSO
IPSO
MESO
MISO
NASO
OSSO
PASO
PESO
SOSO

SP••
SPAD
SPAM
SPAN
SPAR
SPAS
SPAT
SPAY
SPCA
SPCC
SPEC
SPED
SPEE
SPET
SPEW
SPGR
SPHT
SPIN
SPIT
SPIV
SPOT
SPQR
SPRY
SPUD
SPUN
SPUR

S•P•
SAPS
SEPT
SFPD
SHPT
SIPS
SOPH
SOPS
SUPE
SUPP
SUPR
SUPS
SUPT

S••P
SALP
SAMP
SCOP
SCUP
SEEP
SHEP
SHIP
SHOP
SIMP
SKEP
SKIP
SLAP
SLIP
SLOP
SNAP
SNIP
SOAP
SOUP
STEP
STOP
SUMP
SUPP
SWAP
SWOP

•SP•
ASPS
ESPN
ESPY
ISPY
TSPS
USPO
USPS

•S•P
ASAP
ESOP
RSVP
VSOP

••SP
CUSP
GASP
HASP
HOSP
INSP
LISP
RASP
RESP
TBSP
WASP
WISP

SQ••
SQFT
SQIN
SQMI
SQYD

S•Q•
SEQQ
SPQR

S••Q
SEQQ
SHAQ

•SQ•
ESQS

SR••
SRAS
SRTA

S•R•
SARA
SARD
SARI
SARK
SCRY
SERA
SERB
SERE
SERF
SERO
SERS
SERT
SERV
SIRE
SIRS
SLRS
SORA
SORB
SORE
SORI
SORT
SPRY
SSRS
STRS
SURA
SURD
SURE
SURF
SURG

S••R
SAAR
SADR
SAFR
SAUR
SCAR
SEAR
SEER
SEHR
SLUR
SOAR
SOIR
SOUR
SPAR
SPGR
SPQR
SPUR
STAR
STER
STIR
SUER
SUPR

•SR•
SSRS

•S•R
ASIR
ASOR
ASTR
ISAR
MSGR
OSAR
TSAR
USAR
USER
USNR
USSR
YSER

••SR
USSR

SS••
SSGT
SSNS
SSRS
SSTS

S•S•
SASE
SASH
SASK
SASS
SCSI
SESS
SISI
SMSA
SOSO
SUSA
SYST

S••S
SACS
SAGS
SAIS
SAKS
SALS
SANS
SAPS
SASS
SAWS
SAYS
SEAS
SEBS
SECS
SEES
SEIS
SEMS
SENS
SERS
SESS
SETS
SEWS
SGTS
SHES
SIBS
SICS
SIMS
SINS
SIPS
SIRS
SITS
SKIS
SKYS
SLRS
SOBS
SODS
SOLS
SONS
SOPS
SOTS
SOUS
SOWS
SOYS
SPAS
SRAS
SSNS
SSRS
SSTS
STAS
STDS
STES
STNS
STRS
SUBS
SUDS
SUES
SUKS
SUMS
SUNS
SUPS
SVGS
SWBS
SYLS
SYNS

•SS•
ASSN
ASST
ESSA
ESSE
ESSO
ISSN
OSSA
OSSO
PSST
USSR

•S•S
ASIS
ASKS
ASPS
DSCS
DSMS
DSOS
ESAS
ESOS
ESQS
ESUS
ISIS
ISLS
ISMS
LSTS
MSGS
OSIS
PSIS
SSNS
SSRS
SSTS
TSKS
TSPS
USES
USPS

••SS
BASS
BESS
BOSS
BUSS
CASS
CESS
CUSS
DISS
DOSS
FESS
FOSS
FUSS
HESS
HISS
HOSS
HUSS
JESS
JOSS
KISS
LASS
LESS
LOSS
MASS
MESS
MISS
MOSS
MUSS
NESS
PASS
POSS
PUSS
ROSS
RUSS
SASS
SESS
TASS
TESS
TOSS
WYSS

ST••
STAB
STAG
STAN
STAR
STAS
STAT
STAY
STBD
STDS
STEM
STEN
STEP
STER
STES
STET
STEW
STGE
STIR
STLO
STMT
STNS
STOA
STOL
STOP
STOT
STOW
STRS
STUB
STUD
STUM
STUN
STYX

S•T•
SATE
SATO
SETA
SETH
SETI
SETS
SETT
SGTS
SITE
SITS
SITU
SOTS
SRTA
SSTS

S••T
SALT
SCAT
SCOT
SCUT
SEAT
SECT
SENT
SEPT
SERT
SETT
SEXT
SHOT
SHPT
SHUT
SIFT
SILT
SKAT
SKIT
SLAT
SLIT
SLOT
SMIT
SMUT
SNIT
SOFT
SOOT
SORT
SPAT
SPET
SPHT
SPIT
SPOT
SQFT
SSGT
STAT
STET
STMT
STOT
SUET
SUIT
SUPT
SWAT
SWIT
SYST

•ST•
ASTA
ASTI
ASTO
ASTR
ESTA
ESTE
ESTH
ESTO
ISTH
LSTS
OSTE
SSTS
USTA

•S•T
ASST
BSMT
ISNT
LSAT
MSGT
PSAT
PSST
SSGT
TSGT

••ST
ASST
AUST
BAST
BEST
BUST
CAST
CEST
CIST
COST
DIST
DOST
DUST
EAST
ERST
FAST
FEST
FIST
FUST
GAST
GEST
GIST
GUST
HAST
HEST
HIST
HOST
INST
JEST
JUST
LAST
LEST
LIST
LOST
LUST
MAST
MIST
MOST
MUST
MYST
NAST
NEST
OAST
OUST
PAST
PEST
POST
PSST
REST
RUST
SYST
TEST
VAST
VEST
WAST
WEST
ZEST

SU••
SUBJ
SUBS
SUCH
SUCK
SUDD
SUDS
SUED
SUER
SUES
SUET
SUEY
SUEZ
SUFF
SUFI
SUIT
SUKS
SULF
SULK
SULU
SUMO
SUMP
SUMS
SUNG
SUNK
SUNN
SUNS
SUNY
SUPE
SUPP
SUPR
SUPS
SUPT
SURA
SURD
SURE
SURF
SURG
SUSA
SUVA
SUZI
SUZY

S•U•
SAUD
SAUK
SAUL
SAUR
SCUD
SCUM
SCUP
SCUT
SEUL
SHUE
SHUL
SHUN
SHUT
SKUA
SLUB
SLUE
SLUG
SLUM
SLUR
SMUG
SMUT
SNUB
SNUG
SOUK
SOUL
SOUP
SOUR
SOUS
SPUD
SPUN
SPUR
STUB
STUD
STUM
STUN
SWUM

S••U
SABU
SITU
SULU

•SU•
ESUS

•S•U
ESAU

••SU
JESU
ZASU

SV••
SVEN
SVGS

S•V•
SAVA
SAVE
SEVE
SUVA

S••V
SERV
SHIV
SLAV
SPIV

•SV•
RSVP

SW••
SWAB
SWAG
SWAK
SWAM
SWAN
SWAP
SWAT
SWAY
SWBS
SWBW
SWED
SWIG
SWIM
SWIT
SWOB
SWOP
SWUM

S•W•
SAWN
SAWS
SEWN
SEWS
SOWN
SOWS

S••W
SCOW
SHAW
SHOW
SKAW
SKEW
SLAW
SLEW
SLOW
SMEW
SNOW
SPEW
STEW
STOW
SWBW

S•X•
SAXE
SEXT

S••X
SFAX
STYX

•S•X
VSIX

SY••
SYCE
SYLL
SYLS
SYNC
SYND
SYNE
SYNS
SYST

S•Y•
SAYS
SKYE
SKYS
SLYE
SOYA
SOYS
SQYD
STYX

S••Y
SCRY
SECY
SHAY
SLAY
SONY
SPAY
SPRY
STAY
SUEY
SUNY
SUZY
SWAY

•S•Y
ASHY
ESPY
ISAY
ISPY

••SY
BUSY
COSY
EASY
ITSY
NOSY
POSY
ROSY

S•Z•
SIZE
SUZI
SUZY

S••Z
SUEZ

TA••
TAAL
TABI
TABS
TABU
TACH
TACK
TACO
TACT
TADA
TADS
TAEL
TAFT
TAGS
TAHR
TAIL
TAIN
TAIT
TAIZ
TAJS
TAKA
TAKE
TALA
TALC
TALE
TALI
TALK
TALL
TAMA
TAME
TAMM
TAMO
TAMP
TAMS
TANA
TANE
TANG
TANH
TANK
TANS
TAOS
TAPA
TAPE
TAPS
TARA
TARE
TARN
TARO
TARP
TARS
TART
TASK
TASS
TATA
TATE
TATI
TATS
TAUS
TAUT
TAVI
TAWS
TAXA
TAXI
TAXO

T•A•
TAAL
TBAR
TEAK
TEAL
TEAM
TEAR
TEAS
THAI
THAN
THAR
THAT
THAW
TMAN
TOAD
TOAT
TRAM
TRAP
TRAX
TRAY
TSAR
TUAN
TWAS
TZAR

T••A
TADA
TAKA
TALA
TAMA
TANA
TAPA
TARA
TATA
TAXA
TERA
TEWA
TINA
TIWA
TOEA
TOGA
TOLA
TRNA
TUBA
TUFA
TULA
TUNA

•TA•
ETAH
ETAL
ETAS
ETAT
ITAL
PTAH
STAB
STAG
STAN
STAR
STAS
STAT
STAY
UTAH

•T•A
ATKA
ATRA
ATTA
ETNA
ETTA
ITEA
ITZA
OTRA
STOA

••TA
ACTA
AFTA
ALTA
ANTA
ASTA
ATTA
BETA
BOTA
CATA
CETA
DATA
EDTA
ESTA
ETTA
FATA
FETA
GETA
GITA
IOTA
MATA
META
MITA
MOTA
NITA
NOTA
OCTA
PITA
RATA
RITA
ROTA
SETA
SRTA
TATA
USTA
VITA
ZETA

TB••
TBAR
TBSP

T•B•
TABI
TABS
TABU
TCBY
TOBY
TUBA
TUBB
TUBE
TUBS

T••B
TOMB
TRIB
TUBB

•TB•
GTBR
STBD

•T•B
NTSB
STAB
STUB

••TB
LITB

TC••
TCBY
TCHR

T•C•
TACH
TACK
TACO
TACT
TECH
TECS
TICK
TICO
TICS
TOCK
TUCK

T••C
TALC

•TC•
ETCH
ITCH

•T•C
ETIC
OTIC

••TC
ROTC

T•D•
TADA
TADS
TEDS
TIDE
TIDY
TODD
TODO
TODS
TODY

T••D
TEED
TEND
THUD
TIED
TOAD
TODD
TOED
TOLD
TROD
TWOD

•TD•
ETDS
STDS

•T•D
STBD
STUD

••TD
LITD
PATD
RETD

TE••
TEAK
TEAL
TEAM
TEAR
TEAS
TECH
TECS
TEDS
TEED
TEEM
TEEN
TEES
TEFF
TEGS
TELE
TELL
TELO
TEMP
TEND
TENE
TENN
TENO
TENS
TENT
TEPP
TERA
TERI
TERM
TERN
TERP
TERR
TESH
TESS
TEST
TETE
TETH
TETS
TEUT

TEWA
TEXT

T•E•
TAEL
TEED
TEEM
TEEN
TEES
THEE
THEM
THEN
THEO
THEW
THEY
TIED
TIER
TIES
TMEN
TOEA
TOED
TOES
TREE
TREF
TREK
TRES
TRET
TREX
TREY
TUES
TWEE

T••E
TAKE
TALE
TAME
TANE
TAPE
TARE
TATE
TELE
TENE
TETE
THEE
TIDE
TIGE
TIKE
TILE
TIME
TINE
TIRE
TOKE
TOLE
TOME
TONE
TOPE
TORE
TOTE
TREE
TRUE
TUBE
TULE
TUNE
TWEE
TYKE
TYNE
TYPE
TYRE

•TE•
ATEN
ETES
ITEA
ITEM
ITER
RTES
STEM
STEN
STEP
STER
STES
STET
STEW
UTEP
UTES

•T•E
CTGE
ETRE
ETTE
MTGE
OTOE
STGE
UTNE

••TE
ACTE
ALTE
ANTE
ARTE
BATE
BETE
BITE
BUTE
BYTE
CATE
CETE
CITE
COTE
CUTE
CYTE
DATE
DOTE
ERTE
ESTE
ETTE
FATE
FETE
GATE
HATE
HITE
HOTE
JETE
JUTE
KATE
KITE
LATE
LITE
LUTE
MATE
METE
MITE
MOTE
MUTE
NATE
NITE
NOTE
OSTE
PATE
PETE
RATE
RETE
RITE
ROTE
SATE
SITE
TATE
TETE
TOTE
VITE
VOTE
WITE

T•F•
TAFT
TEFF
TIFF
TOFF
TOFT
TOFU
TUFA
TUFF
TUFT
TUFU

T••F
TEFF
TGIF
TIFF
TOFF
TREF
TUFF
TURF

TG••
TGIF

T•G•
TAGS
TEGS
TIGE
TOGA
TOGO
TOGS
TSGT
TUGS

T••G
TANG
THUG
TING
TONG
TRIG
TUNG
TWIG

•TG•
CTGE
MTGE
MTGS
STGE

•T•G
LTJG
STAG

••TG
ACTG
MKTG

TH••
THAI
THAN
THAR
THAT
THAW
THEE
THEM
THEN
THEO
THEW
THEY
THIN
THIO
THIS
THOM
THOR
THOU
THRU
THUD
THUG
THUR
THUS

T•H•
TAHR
TCHR
TOHO

T••H
TACH
TANH
TECH
TESH
TETH
TISH
TOSH
TUSH

•TH•
ETHS
OTHO

•T•H
ETAH
ETCH
ITCH
PTAH
UTAH

••TH
ACTH
ANTH
AUTH
BATH
BETH
BOTH
CATH
DOTH
ESTH
FATH
GATH
GOTH
HATH
HETH
ISTH
KITH
LATH
LGTH
LITH
LUTH
MATH
METH
MOTH
MYTH
NETH
OATH
ORTH
PATH
PITH
ROTH
RUTH
SETH
TETH
WITH

TI••
TICK
TICO
TICS
TIDE
TIDY
TIED
TIER
TIES
TIFF
TIGE
TIKE
TIKI
TILE
TILL
TILS
TILT
TIME
TINA
TINE
TING
TINS
TINT
TINY
TION
TIPS
TIRE
TISH
TITI
TITO
TIWA

T•I•
TAIL
TAIN
TAIT
TAIZ
TGIF
THIN
THIO
THIS
TOIL
TRIB
TRIG
TRIM
TRIO
TRIP
TRIS
TRIX
TUIS
TWIG
TWIN
TWIT
TWIX

T••I
TABI
TALI
TATI
TAVI
TAXI
TERI
THAI
TIKI
TITI
TONI
TOPI
TORI
TROI
TUPI

•TI•
ATIT
ETIC
ITIS
OTIC
OTIS
QTIP
STIR
UTIL

•T•I
ATLI
ATOI
ATRI
ETUI

••TI
ACTI
ALTI
ANTI
ASTI
LOTI
NOTI
ROTI
SETI
TATI
TITI
VITI
YETI
ZITI

T•J•
TAJS
TOJO

•TJ•
LTJG

TK••
TKOS
TKTS

T•K•
TAKA
TAKE
TIKE
TIKI
TOKE
TPKS
TSKS
TYKE

T••K
TACK
TALK
TANK
TASK
TEAK
TICK
TNPK
TOCK
TONK
TOOK
TORK
TREK
TRUK
TUCK
TURK
TUSK

•TK•
ATKA

T•L•
TALA
TALC
TALE
TALI
TALK
TALL
TELE
TELL
TELO
TILE
TILL
TILS
TILT
TOLA
TOLD
TOLE
TOLL
TOLU
TULA
TULE
TULL

T••L
TAAL
TAEL
TAIL
TALL
TEAL
TELL
TILL
TOIL
TOLL
TOOL
TULL

•TL•
ATLI
ITLL
STLO

•T•L
ETAL
ITAL
ITLL
ITOL
STOL
UTIL
VTOL

••TL
INTL
NATL
ROTL

TM••
TMAN
TMEN

T•M•
TAMA
TAME
TAMM
TAMO
TAMP
TAMS
TEMP
TIME
TOMB
TOME
TOMS
TUMS
TYMP

T••M
TAMM
TEAM
TEEM
TERM
THEM
THOM
TRAM
TRIM

•TM•
ATMO
ATMS
STMT

•T•M
ATOM
ATUM
ETYM
ITEM
STEM
STUM

TN••
TNPK
TNUT

T•N•
TANA
TANE
TANG
TANH
TANK
TANS
TEND
TENE
TENN
TENO
TENS
TENT
TINA
TINE
TING
TINS
TINT
TINY
TONE
TONG
TONI
TONK
TONS
TONY
TRNA
TUNA
TUNE
TUNG
TUNS
TYNE

T••N
TAIN
TARN
TEEN
TENN
TERN
THAN
THEN
THIN
TION
TMAN
TMEN
TOON
TORN
TOWN
TRON
TUAN
TURN
TWIN

•TN•
ATNO
CTNS
ETNA
MTNS
STNS
UTNE

•T•N
ATEN
ATON
ATTN
ETON
STAN
STEN
STUN

••TN
ATTN

TO••
TOAD
TOAT
TOBY
TOCK
TODD
TODO
TODS
TODY
TOEA
TOED
TOES
TOFF
TOFT
TOFU
TOGA
TOGO
TOGS
TOHO
TOIL
TOJO
TOKE
TOLA
TOLD
TOLE
TOLL
TOLU
TOMB
TOME
TOMS
TONE
TONG
TONI
TONK
TONS
TONY
TOOK
TOOL
TOON
TOOT
TOPE
TOPI
TOPO
TOPS
TORE
TORI
TORK
TORN
TORO
TORR
TORS
TORT
TORY
TOSH
TOSS
TOTE
TOTO
TOTS
TOUR
TOUT
TOWN
TOWS
TOYS

T•O•
TAOS
THOM
THOR
THOU
TION
TKOS
TOOK
TOOL
TOON
TOOT
TROD
TROI
TRON
TROP
TROT
TROY
TWOD
TWOS

T••O
TACO
TAMO
TARO
TAXO
TELO
TENO
THEO
THIO
TICO
TITO
TODO
TOGO
TOHO
TOJO
TOPO
TORO
TOTO
TRIO
TYPO
TYRO

•TO•
ATOI
ATOM
ATON
ATOP
ATOR
ETON
ITOL
OTOE
OTOS
STOA
STOL
STOP
STOT
STOW
VTOL

•T•O
ATMO
ATNO
ATTO
OTHO
OTRO
OTTO
STLO

••TO
ALTO
ASTO
ATTO
AUTO
CATO
CYTO
ECTO
ENTO
ESTO
GATO
INTO
JATO
KATO
KETO
KOTO
LETO
MOTO
NATO
OCTO
ONTO
OPTO
OTTO
PETO
ROTO
SATO
TITO
TOTO
UNTO
UPTO
VETO
VITO

TP••
TPKS

T•P•
TAPA
TAPE
TAPS
TEPP
TIPS
TNPK
TOPE
TOPI
TOPO
TOPS
TSPS
TUPI
TWPS
TYPE
TYPO
TYPY

T••P
TAMP
TARP
TBSP
TEMP
TEPP
TERP
TRAP
TRIP
TROP
TYMP

•T•P
ATOP
QTIP
STEP
STOP
UTEP

TR••
TRAM
TRAP
TRAX
TRAY
TREE
TREF
TREK
TRES
TRET
TREX
TREY
TRIB
TRIG
TRIM
TRIO
TRIP
TRIS
TRIX
TRNA
TROD
TROI
TRON
TROP
TROT
TROY
TRUE
TRUK

T•R•
TARA
TARE
TARN
TARO
TARP
TARS
TART
TERA
TERI
TERM
TERN
TERP
TERR
THRU
TIRE
TORE
TORI
TORK
TORN
TORO
TORR
TORS
TORT
TORY
TURF
TURK
TURN
TYRE
TYRO

T••R
TAHR
TBAR
TCHR
TEAR
TERR
THAR
THOR
THUR
TIER
TORR
TOUR
TSAR
TZAR

•TR•
ATRA
ATRI
ETRE
OTRA
OTRO
QTRS
STRS

•T•R
ATOR
GTBR
ITER
STAR
STER
STIR

••TR
ASTR
INTR

TS••
TSAR
TSGT
TSKS
TSPS

T•S•
TASK
TASS
TBSP
TESH
TESS
TEST
TISH
TOSH
TOSS
TUSH
TUSK

T••S
TABS
TADS
TAGS
TAJS
TAMS
TANS
TAOS
TAPS
TARS
TASS
TATS
TAUS
TAWS
TEAS
TECS
TEDS
TEES
TEGS
TENS
TESS
TETS
THIS
THUS
TICS
TIES
TILS
TINS
TIPS
TKOS
TKTS
TODS
TOES
TOGS
TOMS
TONS
TOPS
TORS
TOSS
TOTS
TOWS
TOYS
TPKS
TRES
TRIS
TSKS
TSPS
TUBS
TUES
TUGS
TUIS
TUMS
TUNS
TUTS
TWAS
TWOS
TWPS

•TS•
ITSY
NTSB

•T•S
ATMS
ATTS
ATVS
BTUS
CTNS
ETAS
ETDS
ETES
ETHS
ITIS
MTGS
MTNS
OTIS
OTOS
QTRS
RTES
STAS
STDS
STES
STNS
STRS
UTES

••TS
ACTS
AFTS
AGTS
AITS
ALTS
AMTS
ANTS
APTS
ARTS
ATTS
BATS
BETS
BITS
BLTS
BOTS
BUTS
CATS
CITS
COTS
CRTS
CUTS
DATS
DETS
DITS
DOTS
EATS
EFTS
EMTS
EXTS
FATS
FITS
GATS
GETS
GITS
GUTS
HATS
HITS
HUTS
INTS
JETS
JOTS
JUTS
KITS
LATS
LETS
LOTS
LSTS
MATS
METS
MOTS
NETS
NITS
NOTS
NUTS
OATS
OPTS
ORTS
OUTS
PATS
PETS
PITS
PMTS
POTS
PUTS
PVTS
RATS
RCTS
RETS
RGTS
ROTS
RPTS
RUTS
SETS
SGTS
SITS
SOTS
SSTS
TATS
TETS
TKTS
TOTS
TUTS
VATS
VDTS
VETS
WATS
WETS
WITS

T•T•
TATA
TATE
TATI
TATS
TETE
TETH
TETS
TITI
TITO
TKTS
TOTE
TOTO
TOTS
TUTS
TUTU

T••T
TACT
TAFT
TAIT
TART
TAUT
TENT
TEST
TEUT
TEXT
THAT
TILT
TINT
TNUT
TOAT
TOFT
TOOT
TORT
TOUT
TRET
TROT
TSGT
TUFT
TWIT

•TT•
ATTA
ATTN
ATTO
ATTS
ATTU
ATTY
ETTA
ETTE
ITTY
OTTO

•T•T
ATIT
ATWT
ETAT
NTWT
STAT
STET
STMT
STOT

••TT
BATT
BITT
BOTT
BUTT
CATT
GATT
HUTT
JETT
KETT
KITT
LETT
LOTT
MATT
MITT
MOTT
MUTT
NUTT
PITT
PUTT
RATT
RITT
SETT
WATT
WITT

TU••
TUAN
TUBA
TUBB
TUBE
TUBS
TUCK
TUES
TUFA
TUFF
TUFT
TUFU
TUGS
TUIS
TULA
TULE
TULL
TUMS
TUNA
TUNE
TUNG
TUNS
TUPI
TURF
TURK
TURN
TUSH
TUSK
TUTS
TUTU

T•U•
TAUS
TAUT
TEUT
THUD
THUG
THUR
THUS
TNUT
TOUR
TOUT
TRUE
TRUK

T••U
TABU
THOU
THRU
TOFU
TOLU
TUFU
TUTU

•TU•
ATUM
BTUS
ETUI
STUB
STUD
STUM
STUN

•T•U
ATTU

••TU
ATTU
SITU
TUTU
VATU
WCTU

T•V•
TAVI

•TV•
ATVS

••TV
ACTV
CATV
CCTV
HDTV

TW••
TWAS
TWEE
TWIG
TWIN
TWIT
TWIX
TWOD
TWOS
TWPS

T•W•
TAWS
TEWA
TIWA
TOWN
TOWS

T••W
THAW
THEW

•TW•
ATWT
NTWT

•T•W
STEW
STOW

••TW
GWTW

T•X•
TAXA
TAXI
TAXO
TEXT

T••X
TRAX
TREX
TRIX
TWIX

•T•X
STYX

TY••
TYKE
TYMP
TYNE
TYPE
TYPO
TYPY
TYRE
TYRO

T•Y•
TOYS

T••Y
TCBY
THEY
TIDY
TINY
TOBY
TODY
TONY
TORY
TRAY
TREY
TROY
TYPY

•TY•
ETYM
STYX

•T•Y
ATTY
ITSY
ITTY

STAY

••TY
ARTY
ATTY
CITY
COTY
DUTY
ITTY
KATY
OATY
PITY

TZ••
TZAR

T••Z
TAIZ

•TZ•
ITZA

••TZ
BETZ
DITZ
FITZ
FUTZ
GETZ
KATZ
LUTZ
METZ
RITZ
ZOTZ

U•A•
ULAN
UNAU
UPAS
URAL
USAF
USAR
UTAH

U••A
UCLA
ULNA
UMEA
URFA
URGA
URSA
USDA
USGA
USIA
USMA
USNA
USTA
UVEA

•UA•
DUAD
DUAL
FUAD
GUAM
GUAN
GUAR
HUAC
JUAN
LUAU
QUAD
QUAG
QUAI
QUAR
QUAY
TUAN
YUAN

•U•A
AULA
AURA
BUNA
CUBA
CUNA
DUMA
DUNA
DURA
FULA
HULA
HUPA
JUBA
JUGA
JURA
LUNA
PUKA
PULA
PUMA
PUNA
PUPA
RUGA
SURA
SUSA
SUVA
TUBA
TUFA
TULA
TUNA
WUSA
YUBA
YUGA
YUMA

••UA
AGUA
AQUA
ECUA
SKUA

UB••
UBER

U•B•
UMBO
URBS

•UB•
AUBE
CUBA
CUBE
CUBS
DUBS
HUBS
JUBA
LUBE
NUBS
PUBL
PUBS
RUBE
RUBS
RUBY
SUBJ
SUBS
TUBA
TUBB
TUBE
TUBS
YUBA

•U•B
BULB
BURB
CURB
DUMB
MUSB
NUMB
TUBB

••UB
CHUB
CLUB
DAUB
DRUB
FLUB
GRUB
SLUB
SNUB
STUB

UC••
UCLA

U•C•
UNCI
USCG

U••C
USMC

•UC•
BUCK
BUCO
BUCS
DUCE
DUCK
DUCT
GUCK
HUCK
LUCE
LUCK
LUCY
MUCH
MUCK
OUCH
PUCE
PUCK
RUCK
SUCH
SUCK
TUCK
YUCK

•U•C
HUAC
JUNC
NUNC

••UC
EDUC
GLUC

UD••
UDOS

U•D•
UNDO
UPDO
URDU
USDA

U••D
USED

•UD•
AUDE
AUDI
BUDD
BUDS
CUDS
DUDE
DUDS
FUDD
JUDD
JUDE
JUDG
JUDO
JUDY
KUDU
MUDD
MUDS
NUDE
NUDI
OUDS
PUDU
RUDD
RUDE
RUDI
RUDY
SUDD
SUDS

•U•D
AULD
BUDD
BUND
CUED
CURD
DUAD
FUAD
FUDD
FUND
HUED
HUND
JUDD
KURD
MUDD
QUAD
QUID
QUOD
RUDD
RUED
SUDD
SUED
SURD

••UD
BAUD
CRUD
FEUD
GAUD
KNUD
LAUD
LOUD
MAUD
SAUD
SCUD
SPUD
STUD
THUD
VAUD
YOUD

UE••
UELE

U•E•
UBER
UKES
UMEA
UREY
USED
USER
USES
UTEP
UTES
UVEA

U••E
UELE
URGE
UTNE

•UE•
AUEL
AUER
CUED
CUER
CUES
DUEL
DUES
DUET
FUEL
HUED
HUES
HUEY
PUER
QUEL
QUES
RUED
RUES
SUED
SUER
SUES
SUET
SUEY
SUEZ
TUES

•U•E
AUBE
AUDE
AUGE
AUNE
BUTE
CUBE
CUKE
CULE
CURE
CUTE
DUCE
DUDE
DUKE
DUNE
DUPE
DUSE
DUVE
FUME
FUSE
FUZE
HUGE
HUME
JUDE
JUKE
JULE
JUNE
JURE
JUTE
LUBE
LUCE
LUGE
LUKE
LUNE
LUPE
LURE
LUTE
LUXE
MULE
MUSE
MUTE
NUDE
NUKE
OUSE
PUCE
PULE
PURE
RUBE
RUDE
RULE
RUNE
RUSE
SUPE
SURE
TUBE
TULE
TUNE
YULE

••UE
ADUE
AGUE
BLUE
CLUE
COUE
CRUE
FLUE
GLUE
LAUE
MOUE
NIUE
RHUE
ROUE
SHUE
SLUE
TRUE

UF••
UFOS

U•F•
URFA

U••F
USAF

•UF•
BUFF
CUFF
CUFT
DUFF
DUFY
GUFF
HUFF
LUFF
LUFT
MUFF
PUFF
RUFF
SUFF
SUFI
TUFA
TUFF
TUFT
TUFU

•U•F
BUFF
CUFF
DUFF
FUNF
GUFF
GULF
HUFF
LUFF
MUFF
PUFF
RUFF
SUFF
SULF
SURF
TUFF
TURF

••UF
ENUF
NEUF
OEUF
POUF

UG••
UGHS
UGLI
UGLY

U•G•
URGA
URGE
USGA

U••G
USCG

•UG•
AUGE
BUGS
FUGU
HUGE
HUGH
HUGO
HUGS
JUGA
JUGS
LUGE
LUGS
MUGS
PUGH
PUGS
RUGA
RUGS
TUGS
VUGS
YUGA
YUGO

•U•G
BULG
BUNG
BURG
GUNG
HUNG
JUDG
JUNG
KUNG
LUNG
MUNG
PUNG
QUAG
RUNG
SUNG
SURG
TUNG
VULG

••UG
CHUG
DOUG
DRUG
FRUG
GLUG
PLUG
SLUG
SMUG
SNUG
THUG

UH••
UHOH
UHUH

U•H•
UGHS

U••H
UHOH
UHUH
UMPH
UTAH

•UH•
BUHL
BUHR
KUHN
RUHR

•U•H
AUTH
BUSH
CUSH
GUSH
HUGH
HUSH
KUSH
LUSH
LUTH
MUCH
MUSH
OUCH
PUGH
PUSH
RUSH
RUTH
SUCH
TUSH

••UH
UHUH

U•I•
UNIT
UNIV
UNIX
URIM
URIS
USIA
UTIL
UZIS

U••I
UGLI
UNCI

•UI•
CUIN
GUIN
LUIS
MUIR
NUIT
QUID
QUIP
QUIT
QUIZ
RUIN
SUIT
TUIS

•U•I
AUDI
AURI
BURI
FUJI
MUNI
NUDI
PULI
PUYI
QUAI
QUOI
RUDI
SUFI
SUZI
TUPI
WUXI
YURI
ZUNI

••UI
ALUI
AQUI
EQUI
ETUI
MAUI
PFUI

•UJ•
CUJO
FUJI
JUJU

•U•J
SUBJ

UK••
UKES

U••K
URUK

•UK•
AUKS
CUKE
DUKE
JUKE
LUKE
LUKS
NUKE
PUKA
PUKU
SUKS
YUKS

•U•K
BUCK
BULK
BUNK
BUSK
CUSK
DUCK
DUNK
DUSK
FUNK
GUCK
GUNK
HUCK
HULK
HUNK
HUSK
JUNK
LUCK
LURK
MUCK
MURK
MUSK
PUCK
PUNK
RUCK
RUSK
SUCK
SULK
SUNK
TUCK
TURK
TUSK
YUCK

••UK
KRUK
LEUK
SAUK
SOUK
TRUK
URUK
WOUK
ZOUK

UL••
ULAN
ULNA
ULUS

U•L•
UCLA
UELE
UGLI
UGLY
UNLV

U••L
URAL
UTIL

•UL•
AULA
AULD
BULB
BULG
BULK
BULL
CULE
CULL
CULM
CULP
CULS
CULT
DULL
DULY
FULA
FULL
GULF
GULL
GULP
HULA
HULK
HULL
JULE
JULY
LULL
LULU
MULE
MULL
NULL
PULA
PULE
PULI
PULL
PULP
RULE
SULF
SULK
SULU
TULA
TULE
TULL
VULG
YULE
ZULU

•U•L
AUEL
BUHL
BULL
BURL
CULL
CURL
DUAL
DUEL
DULL
FUEL
FULL
FURL
GULL
HULL
HURL
LULL
MULL
NULL
PUBL
PULL
PURL
QUEL
TULL

••UL
AZUL
CAUL
ELUL
FOUL
GAUL
HAUL
MAUL
PAUL
RAUL
SAUL
SEUL
SHUL
SOUL

UM••
UMBO
UMEA
UMPH
UMPS

U•M•
USMA
USMC

U••M
UNUM
URIM

•UM•
BUMP
BUMS
DUMA
DUMB
DUMP
FUME
FUMY
GUMM
GUMP
GUMS
HUME
HUMP
HUMS
JUMP
LUMP
MUMS
NUMB
PUMA
PUMP
RUMP
RUMS
SUMO
SUMP
SUMS
TUMS
YUMA

•U•M
CULM
GUAM
GUMM
MUSM

••UM
ALUM
ARUM
ATUM
AXUM
BAUM
BLUM
CHUM
DEUM
DRUM
GAUM
GEUM
GLUM
OVUM
PLUM
RHUM
SCUM
SLUM
STUM
SWUM
UNUM

UN••
UNAU
UNCI
UNDO
UNIT
UNIV
UNIX
UNLV
UNTO
UNUM

U•N•
ULNA
URNS
USNA
USNR
UTNE

U••N
ULAN
UPON

•UN•
AUNE
AUNT
BUNA
BUND
BUNG
BUNK
BUNS
BUNT
CUNA
CUNY
DUNA
DUNE
DUNK
DUNN
DUNS
FUND
FUNF
FUNK
FUNT
GUNG
GUNK
GUNN
GUNS
HUND
HUNG
HUNK
HUNS
HUNT
JUNC
JUNE
JUNG
JUNK
JUNO
KUNG
LUNA
LUNE
LUNG
LUNN
LUNT
MUNG
MUNI
NUNC
NUNN
NUNS
PUNA
PUNG
PUNK
PUNS
PUNT
PUNY
RUNE
RUNG
RUNS
RUNT
SUNG
SUNK
SUNN
SUNS
SUNY
TUNA
TUNE
TUNG
TUNS
ZUNI

•U•N
BURN
CUIN
DUNN
DURN
GUAN
GUIN
GUNN
HUON
JUAN
KUHN
LUNN
MUON
NUNN
RUIN
SUNN
TUAN
TURN
YUAN

••UN
FAUN
IDUN
NEUN
NOUN
RYUN
SHUN
SPUN
STUN

U•O•
UDOS
UFOS
UHOH
UPON
UXOR

U••O
UMBO
UNDO
UNTO
UPDO
UPTO
USPO

•UO•
BUOY
DUOS
HUON
MUON
QUOD
QUOI
QUOT

•U•O
AUTO
BUCO
CUJO
DURO
EURO
FURO
HUGO
JUDO
JUNO
OUZO
PUZO
SUMO
YUGO

UP••
UPAS
UPDO
UPON
UPTO

U•P•
UMPH
UMPS
USPO
USPS

U••P
UTEP

•UP•
CUPR
CUPS
DUPE
HUPA
LUPE
PUPA
PUPS
RUPP
SUPE
SUPP
SUPR
SUPS
SUPT
TUPI

•U•P
BUMP
BURP
CULP
CUSP
DUMP
GULP
GUMP
HUMP
JUMP
LUMP
PULP
PUMP
QUIP
RUMP
RUPP
SUMP
SUPP

••UP
COUP
DOUP
GOUP
LOUP
REUP
ROUP
SCUP
SOUP
WHUP

UR••
URAL
URBS
URDU
UREY
URFA
URGA
URGE
URIM
URIS
URNS
URSA
URUK
URUS

U••R
UBER
USAR
USER
USNR
USSR
UXOR

•UR•
AURA
AURI
BURB
BURG
BURI
BURL
BURN
BURP
BURR
BURS
BURT
BURY
CURB
CURD
CURE
CURL
CURR
CURS
CURT
DURA
DURN
DURO
EURO
EURY
FURL
FURO
FURS
FURY
GURU
HURL
HURT
JURA
JURE
JURY
KURD
KURT
LURE
LURK
MURK
OURS
PURE
PURL
PURR
SURA
SURD
SURE
SURF
SURG
TURF
TURK
TURN
YURI
YURT

•U•R
AUER
BUHR
BURR
CUER
CUPR
CURR
GUAR
MUIR
PUER
PURR
QUAR
RUHR
SUER
SUPR

••UR
AMUR
AZUR
BLUR
CHUR
DOUR
FOUR
GAUR
HOUR
JOUR
KNUR
PLUR
POUR
SAUR
SLUR
SOUR
SPUR
THUR
TOUR
YOUR

US••
USAF
USAR
USCG
USDA
USED
USER
USES
USGA
USIA
USMA
USMC
USNA
USNR
USPO
USPS
USSR
USTA

U•S•
URSA
USSR

U••S
UDOS
UFOS
UGHS
UKES
ULUS
UMPS
UPAS
URBS
URIS
URNS
URUS
USES
USPS
UTES
UZIS

•US•
AUST
BUSH
BUSK
BUSS
BUST
BUSY
CUSH
CUSK
CUSP
CUSS
DUSE
DUSK
DUST
FUSE
FUSS
FUST
GUSH
GUST
HUSH
HUSK
HUSS
JUST
KUSH
LUSH
LUST
MUSB
MUSE
MUSH
MUSK
MUSM
MUSS
MUST
OUSE
OUST
PUSH
PUSS
RUSE
RUSH
RUSK
RUSS
RUST
SUSA
TUSH
TUSK
WUSA

•U•S
AUKS
BUCS
BUDS
BUGS
BUMS
BUNS
BURS
BUSS
BUTS
BUYS
CUBS
CUDS
CUES
CULS
CUPS
CURS
CUSS
CUTS
DUBS
DUDS
DUES
DUNS
DUOS
FURS
FUSS
GUMS
GUNS
GUTS
GUYS
HUBS
HUES
HUGS
HUMS
HUNS
HUSS
HUTS
JUGS
JUTS
LUGS
LUIS
LUKS
LUVS
MUDS
MUGS
MUMS
MUSS
NUBS
NUNS
NUTS
NUYS
OUDS
OURS
OUTS
PUBS
PUGS
PUNS
PUPS
PUSS
PUTS
QUES
RUBS
RUES
RUGS
RUMS
RUNS
RUSS
RUTS
SUBS
SUDS
SUES
SUKS
SUMS
SUNS
SUPS
TUBS
TUES
TUGS

TUIS
TUMS
TUNS
TUTS
VUGS
YUKS

••US
BMUS
BTUS
CAUS
CRUS
DEUS
ECUS
EMUS
EOUS
ESUS
FLUS
GNUS
GRUS
HAUS
ICUS
IOUS
NOUS
ONUS
OPUS
OXUS
PIUS
PLUS
ROUS
SOUS
TAUS
THUS
ULUS
URUS
VOUS
ZEUS

UT••
UTAH
UTEP
UTES
UTIL
UTNE

U•T•
UNTO
UPTO
USTA

U••T
UNIT

•UT•
AUTH
AUTO
BUTE
BUTS
BUTT
CUTE
CUTS
DUTY
FUTZ
GUTS
HUTS
HUTT
JUTE
JUTS
LUTE
LUTH
LUTZ
MUTE
MUTT
NUTS
NUTT
OUTS
PUTS
PUTT
RUTH
RUTS
TUTS
TUTU

•U•T
AUNT
AUST
BUNT
BURT
BUST
BUTT
CUFT
CULT
CURT
DUCT
DUET
DUST
FUNT
FUST
GUST
HUNT
HURT
HUTT
JUST
KURT
LUFT
LUNT
LUST
MUST
MUTT
NUIT
NUTT
OUST
PUNT
PUTT
QUIT
QUOT
RUNT
RUST
SUET
SUIT
SUPT
TUFT
YURT

••UT
ABUT
AOUT
BOUT
BRUT
CNUT
DEUT
FAUT
GLUT
GOUT
HAUT
KNUT
LOUT
NAUT
NEUT
POUT
PRUT
ROUT
SCUT
SHUT
SMUT
TAUT
TEUT
TNUT
TOUT
XOUT

U•U•
UHUH
ULUS
UNUM
URUK
URUS

U••U
UNAU
URDU

•U•U
FUGU
GURU
JUJU
KUDU
LUAU
LULU
PUDU
PUKU
SULU
TUFU
TUTU
ZULU

UV••
UVEA

U••V
UNIV
UNLV

•UV•
DUVE
LUVS
SUVA

UX••
UXOR

U••X
UNIX

•UX•
LUXE
WUXI

••UX
CRUX
DEUX
DOUX
EAUX
FAUX
FLUX
JEUX
ROUX
VAUX
YEUX

U••Y
UGLY
UREY

•UY•
BUYS
GUYS
NUYS
PUYI

•U•Y
BUOY
BURY
BUSY
CUNY
DUFY
DULY
DUTY
EURY
FUMY
FURY
HUEY
JUDY
JULY
JURY
LUCY
PUNY
QUAY
RUBY
RUDY
SUEY
SUNY
SUZY

UZ••
UZIS

•UZ•
BUZZ
FUZE
FUZZ
OUZO
PUZO
SUZI
SUZY

•U•Z
BUZZ
FUTZ
FUZZ
LUTZ
QUIZ
SUEZ

••UZ
CRUZ

VA••
VAAL
VACA
VACS
VADE
VADM
VAIL
VAIN
VAIR
VALE
VAMP
VANE
VANG
VANS
VARA
VARY
VASE
VAST
VATS
VATU
VAUD
VAUX
VAVS
VAYA

V•A•
VAAL
VDAY
VEAL
VEAU
VIAL
VRAI

V••A
VACA
VARA
VAYA
VEDA
VEGA
VELA
VENA
VERA
VIDA
VIGA
VILA
VINA
VISA
VITA
VIVA

•VA•
AVAL
AVAR
EVAH
EVAN
EVAP
IVAN
OVAL

•V•A
AVIA
UVEA

••VA
ALVA
BOVA
CAVA
DIVA
FAVA
JAVA
KAVA
KIVA
LAVA
NEVA
NOVA
SAVA
SUVA
VIVA

V•B•
VIBE

V••B
VERB

VC••
VCRS

V•C•
VACA
VACS
VICE
VICI
VOCE

•V•C
AVEC

VD••
VDAY
VDTS

V•D•
VADE
VADM
VEDA
VIDA
VIDE
VIDI

V••D
VAUD
VELD
VEND
VERD
VIED
VOID

•VD•
AVDP
BVDS

•V•D
AVID
OVID

••VD
BLVD
NKVD

VE••
VEAL
VEAU
VEDA
VEEP
VEER
VEES
VEGA
VEII
VEIL
VEIN
VELA
VELD
VENA
VEND
VENI
VENN
VENT
VERA
VERB
VERD
VERE
VERN
VERO
VERS
VERT
VERY
VEST
VETO
VETS

V•E•
VEEP
VEER
VEES
VIED
VIER
VIES
VIET
VIEW

V••E
VADE
VALE
VANE
VASE
VERE
VIBE
VICE
VIDE
VILE
VINE
VISE
VITE
VIVE
VOCE
VOLE
VOTE

•VE•
AVEC
AVER
AVES
EVEL
EVEN
EVER
EVES
IVES
IVEY
OVEN
OVER
SVEN
UVEA
YVES

•V•E
EVOE

••VE
CAVE
COVE
DAVE
DIVE
DOVE
DUVE
EAVE
FAVE
FIVE
GAVE
GIVE
GYVE
HAVE
HIVE
HOVE
JIVE
JOVE
LAVE
LIVE
LOVE
MOVE
NAVE
NEVE
PAVE
RAVE
REVE
RIVE
ROVE
SAVE
SEVE
VIVE
WAVE
WEVE
WOVE

V•G•
VEGA
VIGA
VIGO
VUGS

V••G
VANG
VULG

•VG•
AVGS
SVGS

•V•H
EVAH

VI••
VIAL
VIBE
VICE
VICI
VIDA
VIDE
VIDI
VIED
VIER
VIES
VIET
VIEW
VIGA
VIGO
VIII
VILA
VILE
VINA
VINE
VINI
VINO
VINS
VINY
VIOL
VIPS
VISA
VISE
VITA
VITE
VITI
VITO
VIVA
VIVE

V•I•
VAIL
VAIN
VAIR
VEII
VEIL
VEIN
VIII
VOID
VOIR
VOIX
VSIX

V••I
VEII
VENI
VICI
VIDI
VIII
VINI
VITI
VRAI

•VI•
AVIA
AVID
AVIS
AVIV
CVII
DVII
EVIL
LVII
MVII
OVID
OVIS
XVII

•V•I
CVII
DVII
LVII
MVII
XVII

••VI
CCVI
CDVI
CLVI
CMVI
CXVI
DCVI
DEVI
DLVI
DXVI
LEVI
LXVI
MCVI
MDVI
MLVI
MMVI
MXVI
RAVI
TAVI
XCVI
XLVI
XXVI

V•L•
VALE
VELA
VELD
VILA
VILE
VOLE
VOLS
VOLT
VULG

V••L
VAAL
VAIL
VEAL
VEIL
VIAL
VIOL
VTOL

•V•L
AVAL
EVEL
EVIL
OVAL

V•M•
VAMP

V••M
VADM
VOOM

•VM•
DVMS

•V•M
OVUM

V•N•
VANE
VANG
VANS
VENA
VEND
VENI
VENN
VENT
VINA
VINE
VINI
VINO
VINS
VINY

V••N
VAIN
VEIN
VENN
VERN

•V•N
AVON
EVAN
EVEN
IVAN
OVEN
SVEN

VO••
VOCE
VOID
VOIR
VOIX
VOLE
VOLS
VOLT
VOOM
VOTE
VOUS
VOWS

V•O•
VIOL
VOOM
VSOP
VTOL

V••O
VERO
VETO
VIGO
VINO
VITO

•VO•
AVON
AVOS
AVOW
EVOE
IVOR
LVOV

••VO
DEVO
LEVO
NOVO
PAVO

V•P•
VIPS

V••P
VAMP
VEEP
VSOP

•V•P
AVDP
EVAP

••VP
RSVP

VR••
VRAI

V•R•
VARA
VARY
VCRS
VERA
VERB
VERD
VERE
VERN
VERO
VERS
VERT
VERY

V••R
VAIR
VEER
VIER
VOIR

•V•R
AVAR
AVER
EVER
IVOR
OVER

VS••
VSIX
VSOP

V•S•
VASE
VAST
VEST
VISA
VISE

V••S
VACS
VANS
VATS
VAVS
VCRS
VDTS
VEES
VERS
VETS
VIES
VINS
VIPS
VOLS
VOUS
VOWS
VUGS

•V•S
AVES
AVGS
AVIS
AVOS
BVDS
DVMS
EVES
IVES
OVIS
PVTS
SVGS
YVES

••VS
ATVS
CAVS
DIVS
ENVS
LAVS
LUVS
MAVS
REVS
VAVS

VT••
VTOL

V•T•
VATS
VATU
VDTS
VETO
VETS
VITA
VITE
VITI
VITO
VOTE

V••T
VAST
VENT
VERT
VEST
VIET
VOLT

•VT•
PVTS

••VT
ADVT
GOVT

VU••
VUGS
VULG

V•U•
VAUD
VAUX
VOUS

V••U
VATU
VEAU

•VU•
OVUM

••VU
KIVU

V•V•
VAVS
VIVA
VIVE

•V•V
AVIV
LVOV

V•W•
VOWS

V••W
VIEW

•V•W
AVOW

V••X
VAUX
VOIX
VSIX

V•Y•
VAYA

V••Y
VARY
VDAY
VERY
VINY

•V•Y
IVEY

••VY
BEVY
CAVY
DAVY
ENVY
JIVY
LEVY
LIVY
NAVY
WAVY

WA••
WAAC
WAAF
WAAL
WACE
WACK
WACO
WACS
WADE
WADI
WADS
WAFS
WAFT
WAGE
WAGS
WAHL
WAIF
WAIL
WAIN
WAIT
WAKA
WAKE
WALD
WALE
WALK
WALL
WALT
WAND
WANE
WANG
WANT
WANY
WARD
WARE
WARM
WARN
WARP
WARS
WART
WARY
WASH
WASP
WAST
WATS
WATT
WAVE
WAVY
WAWA
WAXY
WAYS

W•A•
WAAC
WAAF
WAAL
WEAK
WEAL
WEAN
WEAR
WHAM
WHAT
WOAD
WRAC
WRAF
WRAP
WRAY

W••A
WAKA
WAWA
WEKA
WHOA
WUSA

•WA•
AWAY
KWAI
KWAN
SWAB
SWAG
SWAK
SWAM
SWAN
SWAP
SWAT
SWAY
TWAS

•W•A
YWCA

••WA
AIWA
BIWA
IOWA
TEWA
TIWA
WAWA

W•B•
WEBB
WEBS

W••B
WEBB
WEEB

•WB•
NWBN
NWBW
SWBS
SWBW

•W•B
SWAB
SWOB

WC••
WCTU

W•C•
WACE
WACK
WACO
WACS
WICK
WYCH

W••C
WAAC
WISC
WRAC

•WC•
YWCA

W•D•
WADE
WADI
WADS
WEDS
WIDE

W••D
WALD
WAND
WARD
WEED
WELD
WEND
WHOD
WILD
WIND
WOAD
WOLD
WOOD
WORD

•W•D
AWED
OWED
SWED
TWOD

••WD
DOWD
LEWD

WE••
WEAK
WEAL
WEAN
WEAR
WEBB
WEBS
WEDS
WEEB
WEED
WEEK
WEEN
WEEP
WEFT
WEIL
WEIR
WEKA
WELD
WELK
WELL
WELT
WEND
WENG
WENS
WENT
WEPT
WERE
WERT
WEST
WETS
WEVE

W•E•
WEEB
WEED
WEEK
WEEN
WEEP
WHEE
WHEN
WHET
WHEW
WHEY
WIEN
WOES
WREN
WYES

W••E
WACE
WADE
WAGE
WAKE
WALE
WANE
WARE
WAVE
WERE
WEVE
WHEE
WHSE
WIDE
WIFE
WILE
WINE
WIPE
WIRE
WISE
WITE
WOKE
WORE
WOVE

•WE•
AWED
AWES
EWER
EWES
GWEN
OWED
OWEN
OWES
SWED
TWEE
ZWEI

•W•E
TWEE

••WE
BOWE
HDWE
HOWE
LOWE
ROWE

W•F•
WAFS
WAFT
WEFT
WIFE

W••F
WAAF
WAIF
WOLF
WOOF
WRAF

••WF
NEWF

W•G•
WAGE
WAGS
WIGS

W••G
WANG
WENG
WHIG
WING
WONG

•W•G
SWAG
SWIG
TWIG

WH••
WHAM
WHAT
WHEE
WHEN
WHET
WHEW
WHEY
WHIG
WHIM
WHIP
WHIR
WHIT
WHIZ
WHOA
WHOD
WHOM
WHOP
WHOS
WHSE
WHUP
WHYS

W•H•
WAHL
WOHL

W••H
WASH
WISH
WITH
WYCH

•WH•
KWHR

WI••
WICK
WIDE
WIEN
WIFE
WIGS
WILD
WILE
WILL
WILT
WILY
WIMP
WIND
WINE
WING
WINK
WINS
WIPE
WIRE
WIRY
WISC
WISE
WISH
WISK
WISP
WITE
WITH
WITS
WITT

W•I•
WAIF
WAIL
WAIN
WAIT
WEIL
WEIR
WHIG
WHIM
WHIP
WHIR
WHIT
WHIZ
WRIT
WWII

W••I
WADI
WUXI
WWII

•WI•
IWIS
SWIG
SWIM
SWIT
TWIG
TWIN
TWIT
TWIX
WWII

•W•I
KWAI
WWII
ZWEI

••WI
IIWI
KIWI

WK••
WKLY
WKRP

W•K•
WAKA
WAKE
WEKA
WOKE
WOKS

W••K
WACK
WALK
WEAK
WEEK
WELK
WICK
WINK
WISK
WONK
WORK
WOUK

•W•K
EWOK
SWAK

••WK
GAWK
GOWK

HAWK

W•L•
WALD
WALE
WALK
WALL
WALT
WELD
WELK
WELL
WELT
WILD
WILE
WILL
WILT
WILY
WKLY
WOLD
WOLF

W••L
WAAL
WAHL
WAIL
WALL
WEAL
WEIL
WELL
WILL
WOHL
WOOL

•WL•
AWLS
OWLS

•W•L
AWOL

••WL
BAWL
BOWL
COWL
FOWL
HOWL
JOWL
MEWL
PAWL
YAWL
YOWL

W•M•
WIMP

W••M
WARM
WHAM
WHIM
WHOM
WORM

•WM•
CWMS

•W•M
SWAM
SWIM
SWUM

W•N•
WAND
WANE
WANG
WANT
WANY
WEND
WENG
WENS
WENT
WIND
WINE
WING
WINK
WINS
WONG
WONK
WONS
WONT
WYNN

W••N
WAIN
WARN
WEAN
WEEN
WHEN
WIEN
WORN
WREN
WYNN

•WN•
AWNS
OWNS

•W•N
GWEN
GWYN
KWAN
KWON
NWBN
OWEN
SWAN
TWIN

••WN
DAWN
DOWN
FAWN
GOWN
HAWN
HEWN
LAWN
MOWN
PAWN
SAWN
SEWN
SOWN
TOWN
YAWN

WO••
WOAD
WOES
WOHL
WOKE
WOKS
WOLD
WOLF
WONG
WONK
WONS
WONT
WOOD
WOOF
WOOL
WOOS
WORD
WORE
WORK
WORM
WORN
WORT
WOUK
WOVE
WOWS

W•O•
WHOA
WHOD
WHOM
WHOP
WHOS
WOOD
WOOF
WOOL
WOOS

W••O
WACO

•WO•
AWOL
CWOS
EWOK
KWON
SWOB
SWOP
TWOD
TWOS

W•P•
WEPT
WIPE

W••P
WARP
WASP
WEEP
WHIP
WHOP
WHUP
WIMP
WISP
WKRP
WRAP

•WP•
TWPS

•W•P
SWAP
SWOP

••WP
GAWP
YAWP

WR••
WRAC
WRAF
WRAP
WRAY
WREN
WRIT

W•R•
WARD
WARE
WARM
WARN
WARP
WARS
WART
WARY
WERE
WERT
WIRE
WIRY
WKRP
WORD
WORE
WORK
WORM
WORN
WORT

W••R
WEAR
WEIR
WHIR

•WR•
AWRY

•W•R
EWER
KWHR

••WR
MAWR

W•S•
WASH
WASP
WAST
WEST
WHSE
WISC
WISE
WISH
WISK
WISP
WUSA
WYSS

W••S
WACS
WADS
WAFS
WAGS
WARS
WATS
WAYS
WEBS
WEDS
WENS
WETS
WHOS
WHYS
WIGS
WINS
WITS
WOES
WOKS
WONS
WOOS
WOWS
WYES
WYSS

•W•S
AWES
AWLS
AWNS
CWMS
CWOS
EWES
HWYS
IWIS
OWES
OWLS
OWNS
SWBS
TWAS
TWOS
TWPS

••WS
BMWS
BOWS
CAWS
COWS
DAWS
DEWS
HAWS
HEWS
HOWS
JAWS
JEWS
LAWS
LOWS
MAWS
MEWS
MOWS
NEWS
PAWS
PEWS
POWS
ROWS
SAWS
SEWS
SOWS
TAWS
TOWS
VOWS
WOWS
YAWS
YEWS

W•T•
WATS
WATT
WCTU
WETS
WITE
WITH
WITS
WITT

W••T
WAFT
WAIT
WALT
WANT
WART
WAST
WATT
WEFT
WELT
WENT
WEPT
WERT
WEST
WHAT
WHET
WHIT
WILT
WITT
WONT
WORT
WRIT

•WT•
GWTW

•W•T
SWAT
SWIT
TWIT

••WT
ATWT
GRWT
NEWT
NTWT

WU••
WUSA
WUXI

W•U•
WHUP
WOUK

W••U
WCTU

•WU•
SWUM

W•V•
WAVE
WAVY
WEVE
WOVE

WW••
WWII

W•W•
WAWA
WOWS

W••W
WHEW

•W•W
GWTW
NWBW
SWBW

W•X•
WAXY
WUXI

•W•X
TWIX

WY••
WYCH
WYES
WYNN
WYSS

W•Y•
WAYS
WHYS

W••Y
WANY
WARY
WAVY
WAXY
WHEY
WILY
WIRY
WKLY
WRAY

•WY•
GWYN
HWYS

•W•Y
AWAY
AWRY
SWAY

••WY
DEWY
HGWY
PKWY

W••Z
WHIZ

X•A•
XIAN
XMAS
XRAY

•XA•
EXAM

•X•A
IXIA

••XA
COXA
HEXA
TAXA

XC••
XCII
XCIV
XCIX
XCVI

•XC•
CXCI
CXCV
DXCI
DXCV
EXCH
EXCL
MXCI
MXCV

•X•C
EXEC

••XC
CCXC
CDXC
CMXC
DCXC
MCXC
MDXC
MMXC

XD••
XDIV

•X•D
AXED
EXOD

XE••
XENO
XERO

X•E•
XMEN

X••E
XIPE

•XE•
AXED
AXEL
AXES
EXEC
EXES
OXEN

•X•E
AXLE

••XE
FIXE
FOXE
LUXE
SAXE

X••G
XING

•X•H
EXCH

XI••
XIAN
XIII
XING
XIPE

X•I•
XCII
XCIV
XCIX
XDIV
XIII
XLII
XLIV
XLIX
XVII
XXII
XXIV
XXIX

X••I
XCII
XCVI
XIII
XLII
XLVI
XVII
XXII
XXVI
XXXI

•XI•
AXIL
AXIS
CXII
CXIV
CXIX
DXII
DXIV
DXIX
EXIT
IXIA
LXII
LXIV
LXIX
MXII
MXIV
MXIX
XXII
XXIV
XXIX

•X•I
CXCI
CXII
CXLI
CXVI
CXXI
DXCI
DXII
DXLI
DXVI
DXXI
LXII
LXVI
LXXI
MXCI
MXII
MXLI
MXVI
MXXI
XXII
XXVI
XXXI

••XI
CCXI
CDXI
CLXI
CMXI
CXXI
DCXI
DLXI
DXXI
LXXI
MAXI
MCXI
MDXI
MLXI
MMXI
MXXI
TAXI
WUXI
XXXI

XL••
XLII
XLIV
XLIX
XLVI

X•L•
XYLO

•XL•
AXLE
CXLI
CXLV
DXLI
DXLV
MXLI
MXLV

•X•L
AXEL
AXIL
EXCL

••XL
CCXL
CDXL
CMXL
DCXL
MCXL
MDXL
MMXL

XM••
XMAS
XMEN

•X•M
AXUM
EXAM

X•N•
XENO
XING

X••N
XIAN
XMEN

•X•N
AXON
EXON
OXEN
OXON

XO••
XOUT

X••O
XENO
XERO
XYLO

•XO•
AXON
EXOD
EXON
OXON
UXOR

•X•O
EXPO

••XO
MYXO
TAXO

X•P•
XIPE

•XP•
EXPO
EXPT

XR••
XRAY

X•R•
XERO

•X•R
UXOR

X••S
XMAS

•X•S
AXES
AXIS
EXES
EXTS
OXUS

••XS
INXS

X••T
XOUT

•XT•
EXTS

•X•T
EXIT
EXPT

••XT
MIXT
NEXT
SEXT
TEXT

X•U•
XOUT

•XU•
AXUM
OXUS

XV••
XVII

X•V•
XCVI
XLVI
XXVI

X••V
XCIV
XDIV
XLIV
XXIV
XXXV

•XV•
CXVI
DXVI
LXVI
MXVI
XXVI

•X•V
CXCV
CXIV
CXLV
CXXV
DXCV
DXIV
DXLV
DXXV
LXIV
LXXV
MXCV
MXIV
MXLV
MXXV
XXIV
XXXV

••XV
CCXV
CDXV
CLXV
CMXV
CXXV
DCXV
DLXV
DXXV
LXXV
MCXV
MDXV
MLXV
MMXV
MXXV
XXXV

XX••
XXII
XXIV
XXIX
XXVI
XXXI
XXXV

X•X•
XXXI
XXXV

X••X
XCIX
XL!X
XXIX

•XX•
CXXI
CXXV
CXXX
DXXI
DXXV
DXXX
LXXI
LXXV
LXXX
MXXI
MXXV
MXXX
XXXI
XXXV

•X•X
CXIX
CXXX
DXIX
DXXX
LXIX
LXXX
MXIX
MXXX
XXIX

••XX
CCXX
CDXX
CLXX
CMXX
CXXX
DCXX
DLXX
DXXX
FOXX
LXXX
MCXX
MDXX
MLXX
MMXX
MXXX

XY••
XYLO

X••Y
XRAY

••XY
BOXY
FOXY
PIXY
WAXY

YA••
YAGI
YAKS
YALE
YALL
YALU
YAMA
YAMS
YANA
YANG
YANK
YAPP
YAPS
YARD
YARE
YARN
YAWL
YAWN
YAWP
YAWS
YAZD

Y•A•
YEAH
YEAN
YEAR
YEAS
YUAN

Y••A
YAMA
YANA
YIMA
YMCA
YODA
YOGA
YUBA
YUGA
YUMA
YWCA

•YA•
AYAH
CYAN
DYAD
DYAK
DYAN
EYAS
IYAR
KYAT
RYAL
RYAN
RYAS

•Y•A
AYLA
CYMA
DYNA
EYRA
HYLA
KYRA
LYRA
MYNA
MYRA

••YA
ANYA
BAYA
ENYA
GAYA
GOYA
HOYA
MAYA
SOYA
VAYA

Y•B•
YOBS
YUBA

•Y•B
BYOB
MYOB

Y•C•
YECH
YMCA
YUCK
YWCA

•YC•
CYCL
DYCE
EYCK
MYCO
SYCE
WYCH

•Y•C
SYNC

••YC
GLYC

Y•D•
YODA
YODH

Y••D
YARD
YAZD
YOND
YOUD

•YD•
HYDE
HYDR

•Y•D
BYRD
DYAD
DYED
EYED
SYND

••YD
BOYD
SQYD

YE••
YEAH
YEAN
YEAR
YEAS
YECH
YEGG
YELL
YELP
YENS
YETI
YEUX
YEWS

Y•E•
YLEM
YSER
YVES

Y••E
YALE
YARE
YIPE
YOKE
YORE
YULE

•YE•
AYER
AYES
BYES
DYED
DYER
DYES
EYED
EYES
LYES
NYET
OYER
OYEZ
RYES
WYES

•Y•E
AYME
BYRE
BYTE
CYME
CYTE
DYCE
DYNE
EYRE
FYKE
GYRE
GYVE
HYDE
HYPE
KYLE
LYLE
LYNE
LYRE
NYSE
PYLE
PYRE
RYLE
RYNE
SYCE
SYNE
TYKE
TYNE
TYPE
TYRE

••YE
FAYE
FRYE
GAYE
JAYE
KAYE
RAYE
SKYE
SLYE

Y•G•
YAGI
YEGG
YOGA
YOGH
YOGI
YUGA
YUGO

Y••G
YANG
YEGG

•YG•
ZYGO

•Y•G
BYNG

Y•H•
YOHO

Y••H
YEAH
YECH
YODH
YOGH

•Y•H
AYAH
MYTH
WYCH

YI••
YIMA
YIPE
YIPS

Y•I•
YMIR

Y••I
YAGI
YETI
YOGI
YURI

•YI•
AYIN

•Y•I
GYRI

••YI
MAYI
PUYI

Y•K•
YAKS
YOKE
YOKO
YUKS

Y••K
YANK
YOLK
YORK
YUCK

•YK•
FYKE
TYKE

•Y•K
DYAK
EYCK

YL••
YLEM

Y•L•
YALE
YALL
YALU
YELL
YELP
YOLK
YULE

Y••L
YALL
YAWL
YELL
YOWL

•YL•
AYLA
HYLA
KYLE
LYLE
LYLY
PYLE
RYLE
SYLL
SYLS
XYLO

•Y•L
CYCL
RYAL
SYLL

••YL
ACYL
AMYL
ARYL
IDYL

YM••
YMCA
YMIR

Y•M•
YAMA
YAMS
YIMA
YUMA

Y••M
YLEM

•YM•
AYME
CYMA
CYME
GYMS
HYMN
MYMY
TYMP
ZYMO

••YM
ETYM
ONYM

Y•N•
YANA
YANG
YANK
YENS
YOND

Y••N
YARN
YAWN
YEAN
YUAN

•YN•
BYNG
DYNA
DYNE
GYNT
LYNE
LYNN
LYNX
MYNA
RYNE
SYNC
SYND
SYNE
SYNS
TYNE
WYNN

•Y•N
AYIN
CYAN
DYAN
HYMN
HYPN
LYNN
LYON
RYAN
RYUN
WYNN

••YN
BRYN
GLYN
GWYN

YO••
YOBS
YODA
YODH
YOGA
YOGH
YOGI
YOHO
YOKE
YOKO
YOLK
YOND
YORE
YORK
YOUD
YOUR
YOWL
YOYO

Y••O
YOHO
YOKO
YOYO
YUGO

•YO•
BYOB
GYOR
LYON
MYOB
RYOT

•Y•O
CYTO
GYRO
HYPO
MYCO
MYXO
NYRO
PYRO
TYPO
TYRO
XYLO
ZYGO
ZYMO

••YO
BRYO
CRYO
DAYO
ENYO
HIYO
KAYO
MAYO
YOYO

Y•P•
YAPP
YAPS

YIPE
YIPS

Y••P
YAPP
YAWP
YELP

•YP•
GYPS
HYPE
HYPN
HYPO
HYPS
TYPE
TYPO
TYPY

•Y•P
TYMP

Y•R•
YARD
YARE
YARN
YORE
YORK
YURI
YURT

Y••R
YEAR
YMIR
YOUR
YSER

•YR•
BYRD
BYRE
EYRA
EYRE
GYRE
GYRI
GYRO
KYRA
LYRA
LYRE
MYRA
NYRO
PYRE
PYRO
TYRE
TYRO

•Y•R
AYER
DYER
GYOR
HYDR
IYAR
OYER

YS••
YSER

Y••S
YAKS
YAMS
YAPS
YAWS
YEAS
YENS
YEWS
YIPS
YOBS
YUKS
YVES

•YS•
MYST
NYSE
SYST
WYSS

•Y•S
AYES
BYES
DYES
EYAS
EYES
GYMS
GYPS
HYPS
LYES
RYAS
RYES
SYLS
SYNS
WYES
WYSS

••YS
BAYS
BEYS
BOYS
BUYS
CAYS
DAYS
DEYS
DRYS
FOYS
GUYS
HAYS
HOYS
HWYS
JAYS
JOYS
KEYS
LAYS
MAYS
NAYS
NUYS
PAYS
PHYS
RAYS
SAYS
SKYS
SOYS
TOYS
WAYS
WHYS

Y•T•
YETI

Y••T
YURT

•YT•
BYTE
CYTE
CYTO
MYTH

•Y•T
GYNT
KYAT
MYST
NYET
RYOT
SYST

••YT
FOYT
HOYT
PAYT

YU••
YUAN
YUBA
YUCK
YUGA
YUGO
YUKS
YULE
YUMA
YURI
YURT

Y•U•
YEUX
YOUD
YOUR

Y••U
YALU

•YU•
RYUN

YV••
YVES

•YV•
GYVE

YW••
YWCA

Y•W•
YAWL
YAWN
YAWP
YAWS
YEWS
YOWL

Y••X
YEUX

•YX•
MYXO

•Y•X
LYNX

••YX
ONYX
ORYX
STYX

Y•Y•
YOYO

•Y•Y
LYLY
MYMY
TYPY

Y•Z•
YAZD

•Y•Z
OYEZ

••YZ
BOYZ

ZA••
ZACK
ZAGS
ZAHN
ZAMA
ZANE
ZANY
ZAPS
ZARF
ZASU

Z•A•
ZBAR
ZEAL
ZOAR

Z••A
ZAMA
ZETA
ZOEA
ZOLA
ZONA

•ZA•
AZAN
CZAR
IZAR
OZAV
TZAR

•Z•A
EZRA
IZBA

••ZA
ANZA
GAZA
GIZA
ITZA
LIZA
REZA

ZB••
ZBAR

Z•B•
ZEBU

•ZB•
IZBA

Z•C•
ZACK
ZECH

Z••C
ZINC
ZOIC

Z•D•
ZEDS

Z••D
ZEND

•Z•D
IZOD

••ZD
YAZD

ZE••
ZEAL
ZEBU
ZECH
ZEDS
ZEES
ZEIN
ZEKE
ZEND
ZENO
ZEPH
ZERO
ZEST
ZETA
ZEUS

Z•E•
ZEES
ZOEA
ZWEI

Z••E
ZANE
ZEKE
ZINE
ZONE

•ZE•
EZEK

••ZE
ADZE
DAZE
DOZE
FAZE
FUZE
GAZE
HAZE
LAZE
MAZE
OOZE
RAZE
SIZE

Z••F
ZARF

Z•G•
ZAGS
ZIGS
ZOGI
ZYGO

Z••G
ZING

ZH••
ZHOU

Z•H•
ZAHN

Z••H
ZECH
ZEPH

ZI••
ZIGS
ZILL
ZINC
ZINE
ZING
ZION
ZIPS
ZITI

Z•I•
ZEIN
ZOIC

Z••I
ZITI
ZOGI
ZORI
ZUNI
ZWEI

•ZI•
AZIZ
EZIO
UZIS

••ZI
SUZI

Z•K•
ZEKE

Z••K
ZACK
ZONK
ZOUK

•Z•K
EZEK

Z•L•
ZILL
ZOLA
ZULU

Z••L
ZEAL
ZILL
ZOOL

•Z•L
AZUL

Z•M•
ZAMA
ZYMO

Z••M
ZOOM

Z•N•
ZANE
ZANY
ZEND
ZENO
ZINC
ZINE
ZING
ZONA
ZONE
ZONK
ZUNI

Z••N
ZAHN
ZEIN
ZION
ZOON
ZORN

•Z•N
AZAN

ZO••
ZOAR
ZOEA
ZOGI
ZOIC
ZOLA
ZONA
ZONE
ZONK
ZOOL
ZOOM
ZOON
ZOOS
ZOOT
ZORI
ZORN
ZOTZ
ZOUK

Z•O•
ZHOU
ZION
ZOOL
ZOOM
ZOON
ZOOS
ZOOT

Z••O
ZENO
ZERO
ZYGO
ZYMO

•ZO•
AZOV
IZOD

•Z•O
EZIO

••ZO
BOZO
ENZO
MAZO
ORZO
OUZO
PUZO

Z•P•
ZAPS
ZEPH
ZIPS

Z•R•
ZARF
ZERO
ZORI
ZORN

Z••R
ZBAR
ZOAR

•ZR•
EZRA

•Z•R
AZUR
CZAR
IZAR
TZAR

Z•S•
ZASU
ZEST

Z••S
ZAGS
ZAPS
ZEDS
ZEES
ZEUS
ZIGS
ZIPS
ZOOS

•Z•S
UZIS

Z•T•
ZETA
ZITI
ZOTZ

Z••T
ZEST
ZOOT

ZU••
ZULU
ZUNI

Z•U•
ZEUS
ZOUK

Z••U
ZASU
ZEBU
ZHOU
ZULU

•ZU•
AZUL
AZUR

•Z•V
AZOV
OZAV

ZW••
ZWEI

ZY••
ZYGO
ZYMO

Z••Y
ZANY

•Z•Y
IZZY
OZZY

••ZY
COZY
DOZY
HAZY
IZZY
LAZY
MAZY
OOZY
OZZY
SUZY

Z••Z
ZOTZ

•ZZ•
IZZY
OZZY

•Z•Z
AZIZ

••ZZ
BUZZ
FIZZ
FUZZ
JAZZ
PIZZ
RAZZ

5

AA•••
AAHED
AALTO
AAMES
AANDM
AARON

A•A••
ABABA
ABACA
ABACI
ABACK
ABACO
ABAFT
ABASE
ABASH
ABATE
ABAYA
ACADS
ACARI
ADAGE
ADAIR
ADAMS
ADANA
ADANO
ADAPT
AEAEA
AFARS
AGAIN
AGALS
AGAMA
AGANA
AGAPE
AGARS
AGASP
AGATE
AGAVE
AGAZE
ALACK
ALAIN
ALAMO
ALARM
ALATE
ALAVA
AMADO
AMAHL
AMAHS
AMAIN
AMANA
AMARA
AMASS
AMATI
AMATO
AMAZE
ANAIS
APACE
APART
AQABA
ARABS
ARABY
ARAME
ASAMA
ASANA
ATALL
ATARI
AVAIL
AVANT
AVARS
AVAST
AWACS
AWAIT
AWAKE
AWARD
AWARE
AWASH
AYAHS
AZANS

A••A•
ABBAS
ABEAM
ABRAM
ADDAX
ADLAI
ADMAN
AETAT
AFLAT
AGHAS
AHEAD
AHMAD
AIDAN
AIMAT
AKBAR
AKKAD
ALBAN
ALCAN
ALDAN
ALGAE
ALGAL
ALIAS
ALLAH
ALLAN
ALLAY
ALMAY
ALTAI
ALTAR
ALVAR
AMMAN
AMPAS
AMWAY
ANEAR
ANNAL
ANNAM
ANOAS
ANSAE
ANTAE
ANTAL
ANTAS
ANWAR
ANZAC
AODAI
APEAK
APIAN
APPAL
AQUAE
AQUAS
AREAL
AREAR
AREAS
ARHAT
ARIAN
ARIAS
ARNAZ
AROAR
ARPAD
ARRAN
ARRAS
ARRAU
ARRAY
ARTAL
ARYAN
ASCAP
ASIAN
ASSAD
ASSAI
ASSAM
ASSAY
ASWAN
ATBAT
ATBAY
ATEAM
ATLAS
ATMAN
ATPAR
ATTAR
ATWAR
AURAE
AURAL
AURAR
AURAS
AVGAS
AVIAN
AXIAL

A•••A
ABABA
ABACA
ABAYA
ABUJA
ACCRA
ACOMA
ACURA
ADANA
ADELA
ADUWA
ADYTA
AEAEA
AECIA
AETNA
AFTRA
AGAMA
AGANA
AGENA
AGITA
AGORA
AHORA
AISHA
AKELA
AKIRA
AKITA
ALAVA
ALCOA
ALETA
ALIDA
ALOHA
ALPHA
ALULA
AMANA
AMARA
AMEBA
AMIGA
ANIMA
ANITA
ANTRA
AORTA
APNEA
AQABA
ARECA
ARENA
ARICA
AROMA
ARUBA
ASAMA
ASANA
ASOKA
ASPCA
ASTRA
ASYLA
ATRIA
ATSEA
AUDRA
AVENA
AVILA
AZUSA

•AA••
BAAED
BAALS
KAABA
NAACP
PAAVO
SAABS
WAALS

•A•A•
BABAR
BABAS
BAHAI
BALAS
BANAL
BASAL
BATAK
BAYAR
CABAL
CACAO
CAMAY
CANAL
CARAT
CAVAE
DAKAR
DALAI
DAMAN
DAMAR
DANAE
DAVAO
DAYAK
DAYAN
EATAT
FARAD
FARAH
FATAL
GALAS
GALAX
GAMAL
GAYAL
HADAR
HADAT
HAGAR
HAHAS
HALAS
HAMAL
HAMAN
HARAR
HASAT
JAMAL
JAPAN
JAVAS
KADAR
KAKAS
KARAN
KARAT
KAUAI
KAVAS
KAYAK
KAZAN
LABAN
LAGAN
LALAW
LAMAR
LAMAS
LANAI
LAPAZ
LARAM
LARAS
LAVAL
LAVAS
LAZAR
MACAO
MACAW
MADAM
MAHAL
MAHAN
MALAN
MALAR
MALAY
MAMAS
MARAS
MARAT
MASAI
MAYAN
MAYAS
NAIAD
NANAS
NARAS
NASAL
NATAL
NAVAL
NAWAB
PACAS
PAEAN
PAGAN
PALAE
PALAU
PANAM
PANAY
PAPAL
PAPAS
PAPAW
PAWAT
QATAR
RABAT
RADAR
RAGAS
RAHAB
RAJAH
RAJAS
RAMAN
RAMAR
RANAT
SABAH
SADAT
SAGAL
SAGAN
SAGAS
SAJAK
SALAD
SALAL
SALAM
SAMAR
SANAA
SARAH
SARAN
SATAN
TAPAS
TATAR
VARAS

•A••A
BABKA
BAHIA
BAIZA
BALSA
BANDA
BARCA
BASRA
CALLA
CANEA
CANNA
CAPRA
CARIA
CARLA
CARTA
CASCA
DACCA
DACHA
DACIA
DAIWA
DANZA
DARLA
DARYA
FANTA
FATHA
FAUNA
GALBA
GALEA
GAMBA
GAMMA
GARDA
HABLA
HAEMA
HAIFA
HANNA
HANSA
HASTA
HAUSA
JABBA
JAFFA
KAABA
KAFKA
KANGA
KANSA
KAPPA
KARLA
KARMA
KASHA
LAIKA
LAMIA
LANKA
LANZA
LARVA
LAURA
LAYLA
MAGDA
MAGMA
MAGNA
MAKUA
MALTA
MAMBA
MAMMA
MANIA
MANNA
MANTA
MARIA
MARLA
MARTA
MAUNA
MAZDA
NADIA
NAFTA
NAHUA
NAIRA
NAMPA
NANNA
PADUA
PALEA
PALMA
PAMPA
PANDA
PANGA
PANZA
PAPUA
PARCA
PARKA
PARMA
PASHA
PASTA
PATNA
PAULA
PAVIA
QANDA
RAISA
RASTA
SABRA
SACHA
SACRA
SAIGA
SALPA
SALSA
SALTA
SAMBA
SAMOA
SANAA
SANKA
SANTA
SASHA
SAUNA
TABLA
TAIGA
TALIA
TAMPA
TANKA
TANYA
TATRA
TAYRA
TAZZA
VACUA
VANNA
VANYA
VARIA
VARNA
WANDA
WANNA
YABBA
YALTA
YAMPA
ZAMIA
ZAPPA

••AA•
ISAAC
IZAAK
KRAAL
SPAAK

••A•A
ABABA
ABACA
ABAYA
ADANA
AEAEA
AGAMA
AGANA
ALAVA
AMANA
AMARA
AQABA
ASAMA
ASANA
BRAGA
BRAVA
BWANA
CHAKA
CLARA
DIANA
DRAMA
GHANA
GRAMA
GRATA
GUAVA
IPANA
IVANA
KAABA
KOALA
KUALA
LHASA
LIANA
LLAMA
MEARA
NYALA
NYASA
OCALA
OHARA
OMAHA
OMASA
OSAKA
OZAWA
PLATA
PLAYA
PLAZA
REATA
RIATA
RUANA
SCALA
SCAPA
SHANA
TIARA
TRALA

•••AA
SANAA

AB•••
ABABA
ABACA
ABACI
ABACK
ABACO
ABAFT
ABASE
ABASH
ABATE
ABAYA
ABBAS
ABBES
ABBEY
ABBIE
ABBOT
ABBRS
ABDUL
ABEAM
ABELE
ABEND
ABETS
ABHOR
ABIDE
ABLER
ABNER
ABODE
ABOHM
ABOIL
ABOMB
ABORT
ABOUT
ABOVE
ABOVO
ABRAM
ABRIS
ABUJA
ABUSE
ABUTS
ABUZZ
ABYSM
ABYSS
ABZUG

A•B••
ABBAS
ABBES
ABBEY
ABBIE
ABBOT
ABBRS
AKBAR
ALBAN
ALBEE
ALBEN
ALBUM
AMBER
AMBIT
AMBLE
AMBOS
AMBRY
ARBER
ARBOR
ARBRE
ATBAT
ATBAY
AUBER

A••B•
ABABA
ADOBE
ALIBI
AMEBA
AQABA
ARABS
ARABY
ARUBA
ASHBY

A•••B
ABOMB
ACERB
ADLIB

•AB••
BABAR
BABAS
BABEL
BABER
BABES
BABKA
BABUL
BABYS
CABAL
CABBY
CABER
CABIN
CABLE
CABOT
FABER
FABIO
FABLE
GABBY
GABLE
GABON
GABOR
HABER
HABIT
HABLA
JABBA
JABOT
KABOB
KABUL
LABAN
LABEL
LABIO
LABOR
MABEL
NABES
NABOB
PABLO
PABST
RABAT
RABBI
RABID
RABIN
SABAH
SABER
SABIN
SABLE
SABOT
SABRA
SABRE
TABBY
TABIS
TABLA
TABLE
TABOO
TABOR
YABBA

•A•B•
BAMBI
BARBQ
BARBS
CABBY
CANBY
CARBO
CARBS
DARBY
DAUBS
GABBY
GALBA
GAMBA
GARBO
GARBS
IAMBI
IAMBS
JABBA
JAMBS
KAABA
LAMBS
LAYBY
MAMBA
MAMBO
MAYBE
NAMBY
NASBY
PAMBY
RABBI
RAMBO
SAABS
SAMBA
SATBY
TABBY
TAMBO
YABBA

•A••B
BANDB
CALEB
CARIB
CAROB
JACOB
KABOB
NABOB
NAMIB
NAWAB
RAHAB
RANDB
SAHIB

••AB•
ABABA
AQABA
ARABS
ARABY
BLABS
CRABS
DHABI
DRABS
GRABS
KAABA
PEABO
SAABS
SCABS
SLABS
STABS
SWABS

••A•B
PLANB

•••AB
DCCAB
ESTAB
KEBAB
NAWAB
RAHAB
REHAB
SQUAB

AC•••
ACADS
ACARI
ACCEL
ACCRA
ACCTS
ACERB
ACETO

ACHED
ACHES
ACHOO
ACIDS
ACIDY
ACING
ACMES
ACOMA
ACORN
ACRED
ACRES
ACRID
ACTED
ACTER
ACTII
ACTIN
ACTIV
ACTON
ACTOR
ACTUP
ACUFF
ACURA
ACUTE

A•C••
ACCEL
ACCRA
ACCTS
AECIA
ALCAN
ALCOA
ALCOR
ANCON
ARCED
ARCHI
ARCHY
ASCAP
ASCII
ASCOT
ASCUS

A••C•
ABACA
ABACI
ABACK
ABACO
AITCH
ALACK
ALECK
ALICE
ALYCE
AMICE
AMOCO
AMUCK
APACE
ARECA
ARICA
ASPCA
AWACS

A•••C
ADHOC
ADLOC
AGRIC
ANTIC
ANZAC
ASDIC
ASPIC
ASSOC
ATTIC
AURIC
AZOIC
AZTEC

•AC••
BACKS
BACON
CACAO
CACHE
CACTI
DACCA
DACES
DACHA
DACHE
DACIA
FACED
FACER
FACES
FACET
FACIE
FACTO
FACTS
HACEK
HACKS
JACKS
JACOB
LACED
LACER
LACES
LACEY
LACKS
LACTI
LACTO
MACAO
MACAW
MACED
MACES
MACHE
MACHO
MACHU
MACLE
MACON
MACRO
MACYS
NACHO
NACHT
NACRE
PACAS
PACED
PACER
PACES
PACKS
PACTS
RACED
RACER
RACES
RACKS
RACON
SACCO
SACHA
SACHS
SACKS
SACRA
SACRE
SACRO
TACET
TACIT
TACKS
TACKY
TACOS
VACUA
WACKO
WACKY
XACTO
YACHT

•A•C•
BALCH
BANCO
BANCS
BARCA
BATCH
CALCI
CASCA
CASCO
CATCH
CAYCE
DACCA
DANCE
DANCY
FANCY
FARCE
FARCI
HATCH
LAICS
LANCE
LARCH
LATCH
MARCH
MARCO
MARCY
MATCH
NAACP
NANCY
NARCO
NARCS
NATCH
PARCA
PARCH
PASCH
PASCO
PATCH
RANCH
RATCH
SACCO
SAUCE
SAUCY
TAXCO
VANCE
VASCO
WATCH

•A••C
BARIC
BASIC
HAVOC
MAGIC
MALIC
PANIC
SALIC
VATIC

••AC•
ABACA
ABACI
ABACK
ABACO
ALACK
APACE
AWACS
BEACH
BLACK
BRACE
BRACT
CHACO
CLACK
COACH
COACT
CRACK
DRACO
ENACT
EPACT
EXACT
FLACK
GLACE
GRACE
GUACO
KEACH
KNACK
KYACK
LEACH
LOACH
NAACP
NYACK
ORACH
ORACY
PEACE
PEACH
PLACE
POACH
QUACK
REACH
REACT
ROACH
SHACK
SLACK
SMACK
SNACK
SPACE
STACK
STACY
TEACH
TRACE
TRACK
TRACT
TRACY
WHACK
WRACK

••A•C
BLANC
FRANC
ISAAC

•••AC
ANZAC
DIRAC
ENIAC
ILIAC
ISAAC
LILAC
SERAC
SUMAC

AD•••
ADAGE
ADAIR
ADAMS
ADANA
ADANO
ADAPT
ADDAX
ADDED
ADDER
ADDIE
ADDIN
ADDIS
ADDLE
ADDNL
ADDON
ADDTO
ADDUP
ADEEM
ADELA
ADELE
ADENO
ADEPT
ADEUX
ADHEM
ADHOC
ADIEU
ADIGE
ADINT
ADIOS
ADITS
ADLAI
ADLER
ADLIB
ADLOC
ADMAN
ADMEN
ADMIN
ADMIT
ADMIX
ADOBE
ADOLF
ADOPT
ADORE
ADORN
ADOUT
ADREM
ADULT
ADUST
ADUWA
ADVIL
ADYTA
ADZES

A•D••
ABDUL
ADDAX
ADDED
ADDER
ADDIE
ADDIN
ADDIS
ADDLE
ADDNL
ADDON
ADDTO
ADDUP
AEDES
AIDAN
AIDED
AIDES
ALDAN
ALDEN
ALDER
ALDOL
ALDUS
ANDES
ANDIE
ANDOR
ANDRE
ANDRO
AODAI
ARDEN
ARDOR
ASDIC
AUDEN
AUDIE
AUDIO
AUDIS
AUDIT
AUDRA

A••D•
AANDM
ABIDE
ABODE
ACADS
ACIDS
ACIDY
ALIDA
AMADO
AMIDE
ANODE
ASIDE
AZIDE

A•••D
AAHED
ABEND
ACHED
ACRED
ACRID
ACTED
ADDED
AHEAD
AHMAD
AHMED
AIDED
AILED
AIMED
AIRED
AKKAD
ALGID
ALKYD
ALOUD
AMEND
AMPED
ANTED
APHID
APIED
APPTD
APTED
ARCED
ARMED
AROID
ARPAD
ASKED
ASSAD
ASSTD
AVOID
AWARD
AWNED

•AD••
BADEN
BADGE
BADLY
CADDO
CADDY
CADET
CADGE
CADIS
CADIZ
CADRE
DADDY
DADOS
FADED
FADES
FADOS
GADID
HADAR
HADAT
HADES
HADJI
HADNT
HADON
HADST
HADTO
JADED
JADES
KADAR
LADED
LADEN
LADER
LADES
LADLE
LADYS
MADAM
MADGE
MADLY
MADRE
NADER
NADIA
NADIR
PADDY
PADRE
PADUA
RADAR
RADII
RADIO
RADIX
RADON
SADAT
SADHE
SADHU
SADIE
SADLY
VADER
VADIM
VADIS
VADUZ
WADED
WADER
WADES
WADIS
WADUP

•A•D•
AANDM
BALDS
BANDA
BANDB
BANDO
BANDS
BANDY
BARDS
BAWDY
CADDO
CADDY
CANDO
CANDW
CANDY
CARDI
CARDS
DADDY
DANDY
FALDO
GANDY
GARDA
GARDE
GAUDS
GAUDY
HANDS
HANDY
HARDY
HAYDN
LANDO
LANDS
LARDS
LARDY
LAUDE
LAUDS
MAGDA
MAHDI
MAIDS
MANDY
MARDI
MAUDE
MAZDA
NALDI
NARDS
PADDY
PANDA
PANDL
PARDI
PARDO
PARDS
QANDA
RAIDS
RANDB
RANDD
RANDI
RANDR
RANDS
RANDY
SANDH
SANDL
SANDS
SANDY
SARDS
SAUDI
TANDY
TARDE
TARDY
WALDO
WANDA
WANDS
WARDS
YARDS

•A••D
AAHED
BAAED
BAIRD
BAKED
BALED
BARED
BASED
BATED
BAYED
CAGED
CAKED
CANED
CANID
CAPED
CARED
CASED
CAVED
CAWED
DARED
DATED
DAVID
DAZED
EARED
EASED
EAVED
FACED
FADED
FAKED
FAMED
FARAD
FARED
FATED
FAXED
FAZED
GADID
GAMED
GAPED
GATED
GAZED
HALED
HARED
HASID
HATED
HAWED
HAYED
HAZED
JADED
JAPED
JAWED
LACED
LADED
LAIRD
LAMED
LASED
LAVED
LAZED
MACED
MANED
MATED
MAUND
MAXED
NAIAD
NAKED
NAMED
OARED
PACED
PAGED
PALED
PANED
PARED
PATED
PAVED
PAVID
PAWED
PAYED
RABID
RACED
RAGED
RAKED
RANDD
RANID
RAPID
RASED
RATED
RAVED
RAYED
RAZED
SALAD
SALUD
SAPID
SAROD
SATED
SAVED
SAWED
TAMED
TAPED
TAXED
VALID
VAPID
WADED
WAGED
WAKED
WALED
WANED
WAVED
WAXED
YAWED

••AD•
ACADS
AMADO
BEADS
BEADY
BLADE
BRADS
BRADY
DUADS
DYADS
EGADI
EGADS
EVADE
GLADE
GLADS
GOADS
GRADE
GRADS
GRADY
HEADS
HEADY
IRADE
LEADS
LOADS
MEADE
MEADS
PRADO
QUADR
QUADS
READE
READS
READY
ROADS
SCADS
SHADE
SHADS
SHADY
SLADE
SPADE
SPADS
STADT
TOADS
TOADY
TRADE
TSADE
WOADS

••A•D
AWARD
BAAED
BEARD
BLAND
BOARD
BRAID
BRAND
CHARD
CHAUD
ELAND
FRAUD
GLAND
GRAND
GUARD
HEARD
HOARD
IZARD
LIARD
OLAND
PLAID
QUAID
QUAND
ROALD
SCALD
SCAND
SHARD
SKALD
STAID
STAND
SWARD
VIAND
WHATD

•••AD
AHEAD
AHMAD
AKKAD
ARPAD
ASSAD
BREAD
BROAD
CYCAD
DREAD
DRYAD
FARAD
GOBAD
HEXAD
HODAD
ILIAD
INBAD
JIHAD
KNEAD
MONAD
NAIAD
NICAD
NOMAD
NORAD
OCTAD
OREAD
PLEAD
SALAD
SNEAD
SQUAD
STEAD
STRAD
TREAD
TRIAD

AE•••
AEAEA
AECIA
AEDES
AEGIR
AEGIS
AEONS
AERIE
AESIR
AESOP
AETAT
AETNA

A•E••
ABEAM
ABELE
ABEND
ABETS
ACERB
ACETO
ADEEM
ADELA
ADELE
ADENO
ADEPT
ADEUX
AGENA
AGENT
AGERS
AHEAD
AKEEM
AKEES
AKELA
ALECK
ALEFS
ALENE
ALEPH
ALERT
ALETA
ALEUT
AMEBA
AMEER
AMEND
AMENS
AMENT
ANEAR
ANEMO
ANENT
APEAK
APERS
APERY
AREAL
AREAR
AREAS
ARECA
ARENA
ARENS
ARENT
ARETE
ATEAM
ATEIN
ATEUP
AVENA
AVENS
AVERS
AVERT
AVERY
AXELS
AYERS

A••E•
AAHED
AAMES
ABBES
ABBEY
ABLER
ABNER
ACCEL
ACHED
ACHES
ACMES
ACRED
ACRES
ACTED
ACTER
ADDED
ADDER
ADEEM
ADHEM
ADIEU
ADLER
ADMEN
ADREM
ADZES
AEAEA
AEDES
AFTER
AGLET
AGLEY
AGNES
AGNEW
AGREE
AGUES
AHMED
AIDED
AIDES
AIKEN
AILED
AILER
AILEY
AIMED
AIMEE
AIMER
AIRED
AIRES
AKEEM
AKEES
ALBEE
ALBEN
ALDEN
ALDER
ALGER
ALIEN
ALLEE
ALLEN
ALLER
ALLES
ALLEY
ALLEZ
ALOES
ALTER
AMBER
AMEER
AMIES
AMPED
AMVET
ANDES
ANGEL
ANGER
ANGES
ANNEE
ANNES
ANNEX
ANSEL
ANSER
ANTED
ANTES
APFEL
APIED
APLEY
APNEA
APPEL
APRES
APSES
APTED
APTER
ARBER
ARCED
ARDEN
ARIEL
ARIES
ARLEN
ARLES
ARMED
ARMEE
ARMET
ARNEL
ARPEL
ARRET
ARTEL
ARTES
ASHEN
ASHER
ASHES
ASKED
ASKER
ASKEW
ASNER
ASPEN
ASSES
ASSET
ASSEZ
ASTER
ASYET
ATSEA
AUBER
AUDEN
AUGER
AUREI
AWNED
AXLES
AYRES
AZTEC

A•••E
ABASE
ABATE
ABBIE
ABELE
ABIDE
ABODE
ABOVE
ABUSE
ACUTE
ADAGE
ADDIE
ADDLE
ADELE
ADIGE
ADOBE
ADORE
AERIE
AFIRE
AFORE
AGAPE
AGATE
AGAVE
AGAZE
AGGIE
AGILE
AGREE
AIMEE
AINGE
AISLE
AISNE
ALATE
ALBEE
ALENE
ALFIE
ALFRE
ALGAE
ALICE
ALIKE
ALINE
ALIVE
ALLEE
ALLIE
ALONE
ALYCE
AMAZE
AMBLE
AMICE
AMIDE
AMINE
AMOLE
AMORE
AMPLE
AMUSE
ANDIE
ANDRE
ANGIE
ANGLE
ANIME
ANISE
ANKLE
ANNEE
ANNIE
ANODE
ANOLE
ANSAE
ANTAE
ANTRE
APACE
APPLE
AQUAE
ARAME
ARBRE
ARETE
ARGUE
ARISE
ARMEE
ARNIE
AROSE
ARTIE
ASIDE
ASONE
ASTRE
ATIVE
ATONE
AUDIE
AURAE
AUTRE
AWAKE
AWARE
AWOKE
AZIDE
AZINE
AZOTE
AZURE

•AE••
GAELS
HAEMA
HAEMO
PAEAN
PAEON
SAENS
TAEGU
TAELS

•A•E•
AAHED
AAMES
BAAED
BABEL
BABER
BABES
BADEN
BAGEL
BAKED
BAKER
BAKES
BALED
BALER
BALES
BANES
BARED
BARER
BARES
BASED
BASEL
BASER
BASES
BATED
BATES
BAUER
BAYED
BAYER
CABER
CADET
CAFES
CAGED
CAGER
CAGES
CAGEY
CAKED
CAKES
CAKEY
CALEB
CAMEL
CAMEO
CANEA
CANED
CANER
CANES
CAPED
CAPEK
CAPER
CAPES
CAPET
CARED
CARER
CARES
CARET
CAREW
CAREY
CASED
CASES
CASEY
CATER
CATES
CAVED
CAVER
CAVES
CAWED
DACES
DALES
DALEY
DAMES
DANES
DARED
DARER
DARES
DATED
DATER
DATES
DAWES
DAZED
DAZES
EAGER
EAMES
EARED
EASED
EASEL
EASES
EATEN
EATER
EAVED
EAVES
FABER
FACED
FACER
FACES
FACET
FADED
FADES
FAKED
FAKER
FAKES
FAMED
FAMES
FANES
FARED
FARER
FARES
FATED
FATES
FAVES
FAXED
FAXES
FAZED
FAZES
GAGES
GALEA
GALEN
GALES
GAMED
GAMER
GAMES
GANEF
GAPED
GAPER
GAPES
GASES
GATED
GATES
GAVEL
GAYER
GAZED
GAZER
GAZES
HABER
HACEK
HADES
HAGEN
HAKES
HALED
HALER
HALES
HALEY
HAMEL
HAMES
HANES
HARED
HAREM
HARES
HATED
HATER
HATES
HAUER
HAVEL
HAVEN
HAVER
HAVES
HAWED
HAYED
HAYEK
HAYES
HAZED
HAZEL
HAZER
HAZES
JADED
JADES
JAKES
JAMES
JANET
JAPED
JAPES
JAWED
KALEL
KALES
KAREL
KAREN
KASEM
LABEL
LACED
LACER
LACES

LACEY
LADED
LADEN
LADER
LADES
LAGER
LAKER
LAKES
LAMED
LAMER
LAMES
LANES
LAPEL
LARES
LASED
LASER
LASES
LATEN
LATER
LATEX
LAVED
LAVER
LAVES
LAWES
LAXER
LAYER
LAZED
LAZES
MABEL
MACED
MACES
MAGES
MAKER
MAKES
MALES
MAMET
MANED
MANES
MANET
MARES
MASER
MATED
MATEO
MATER
MATES
MATEY
MAVEN
MAXED
MAXES
MAYER
MAZEL
MAZER
MAZES
NABES
NADER
NAGEL
NAKED
NAMED
NAMER
NAMES
NAPES
NARES
NAREW
NAVEL
NAVES
OAKEN
OAKES
OARED
OASES
OATEN
OATER
OATES
PACED
PACER
PACES
PAGED
PAGER
PAGES
PAGET
PALEA
PALED
PALEO
PALER
PALES
PALEY
PANED
PANEL
PANES
PAPER
PARED
PAREE
PAREN
PARER
PARES
PAREU
PASEO
PASES
PATED
PATEK
PATEN
PATER
PATES
PAVED
PAVER
PAVES
PAWED
PAWER
PAYED
PAYEE
PAYER
RACED
RACER
RACES
RAFER
RAGED
RAGES
RAKED
RAKER
RAKES
RAMEE
RAMEN
RAMET
RANEE
RAPEE
RAREE
RARER
RARES
RASED
RASES
RATED
RATEL
RATER
RATES
RAVED
RAVEL
RAVEN
RAVER
RAVES
RAWER
RAYED
RAZED
RAZES
SABER
SAFER
SAFES
SAGER
SAGES
SAGET
SAHEL
SAKER
SAKES
SALEM
SALEP
SALES
SANER
SASES
SATED
SATES
SAVED
SAVER
SAVES
SAWED
SAXES
SAYER
TACET
TAKEI
TAKEN
TAKER
TAKES
TALER
TALES
TAMED
TAMER
TAMES
TANEY
TAPED
TAPER
TAPES
TARES
TASER
TATER
TAXED
TAXER
TAXES
VADER
VALES
VALET
VANES
VASES
VATER
WADED
WADER
WADES
WAFER
WAGED
WAGER
WAGES
WAKED
WAKEN
WAKES
WALED
WALER
WALES
WANED
WANER
WANES
WARES
WATER
WAVED
WAVER
WAVES
WAXED
WAXEN
WAXER
WAXES
XAXES
YATES
YAWED
YAXES
ZAXES
ZAZEN

•A••E
BADGE
BAIZE
BARGE
BARRE
BASIE
BASTE
BATHE
BAUME
BAYLE
CABLE
CACHE
CADGE
CADRE
CAINE
CALPE
CALVE
CANOE
CARLE
CARNE
CARPE
CARRE
CARTE
CARVE
CASTE
CAUSE
CAVAE
CAYCE
DACHE
DAFOE
DANAE
DANCE
DANKE
DANSE
DANTE
DAVIE
DAYNE
EAGLE
EAGRE
EARLE
FABLE
FACIE
FAIRE
FALSE
FARCE
FAROE
FAURE
FAUVE
GABLE
GAFFE
GARDE
GASPE
GAUGE
GAUZE
GAYLE
HAGUE
HAILE
HALLE
HALVE
HAOLE
HARTE
HASTE
HAUTE
HAVRE
HAWKE
HAWSE
JAFFE
JAHRE
JAIME
JAMIE
JANIE
JARRE
JAUNE
JAYNE
KATIE
LADLE
LAINE
LAKME
LANCE
LANGE
LAPSE
LARGE
LARUE
LATHE
LATKE
LATTE
LAUDE
LAYNE
MACHE
MACLE
MADGE
MADRE
MAHRE
MAINE
MAIZE
MALLE
MAMIE
MANSE
MAPLE
MARGE
MARIE
MARNE
MASSE
MATTE
MAUDE
MAUVE
MAXIE
MAYBE
NACRE
NAIVE
NAPPE
NASHE
OAKIE
PADRE
PAIGE
PAINE
PALAE
PALME
PANNE
PAREE
PARLE
PARSE
PARTE
PASSE
PASTE
PATHE
PAUSE
PAYEE
PAYNE
RAISE
RAMEE
RAMIE
RANEE
RANGE
RANKE
RAPEE
RAPHE
RAREE
SABLE
SABRE
SACRE
SADHE
SADIE
SALLE
SALVE
SANTE
SAONE
SARGE
SATIE
SAUCE
SAUTE
TABLE
TAHOE
TAINE
TANTE
TARDE
TARGE
TASSE
TASTE
TAUPE
VAGUE
VALLE
VALSE
VALUE
VALVE
VANCE
WAITE
WAIVE
WASTE
WAYNE
YALIE
ZAIRE
ZANTE

••AE•
AEAEA
BAAED
BRAES
SHAEF
STAEL

••A•E
ABASE
ABATE
ADAGE
AGAPE
AGATE
AGAVE
AGAZE
ALATE
AMAZE
APACE
ARAME
AWAKE
AWARE
BLADE
BLAKE
BLAME
BLARE
BLASE
BLAZE
BRACE
BRAHE
BRAKE
BRAVE
BRAZE
CEASE
CHAFE
CHASE
CLARE
CLAVE
CRAKE
CRANE
CRAPE
CRATE
CRAVE
CRAZE
DEANE
DIANE
DNASE
DRAKE
DRAPE
DUANE
ELATE
ENATE
ERASE
ETAGE
ETAPE
EVADE
FLAKE
FLAME
FLARE
FRAME
GLACE
GLADE
GLARE
GLAZE
GOAPE
GRACE
GRADE
GRAPE
GRATE
GRAVE
GRAZE
HEAVE
IMAGE
INANE
INAWE
IRADE
IRATE
JEANE
KEANE
KNAVE
LEASE
LEAVE
LIANE
MEADE
NEALE
OFAGE
OHARE
ONATE
ORALE
ORATE
OSAGE
OVATE
PEACE
PEALE
PEASE
PHAGE
PHASE
PLACE
PLAGE
PLANE
PLATE
PRASE
PRATE
QUAKE
QUALE
READE
RNASE
SCALE
SCAPE
SCARE
SEALE
SHADE
SHAKE
SHALE
SHAME
SHANE
SHAPE
SHARE
SHAVE
SKATE
SLADE
SLAKE
SLATE
SLAVE
SMAZE
SNAKE
SNARE
SOAVE
SPACE
SPADE
SPAKE
SPARE
SPATE
STAGE
STAKE
STALE
STARE
STATE
STAVE
SUAVE
SWAGE
SWALE
TEASE
THANE
TRACE
TRADE
TRAVE
TSADE
UKASE
USAGE
WEAVE
WHALE

•••AE
ALGAE
ANSAE
ANTAE
AQUAE
AURAE
CAVAE
COMAE
COXAE
CUMAE
CYMAE
DANAE
HORAE
MCRAE
NOVAE
PALAE
PUPAE
RUGAE
SETAE
STOAE
ULNAE
VENAE
VITAE

AF•••
AFARS
AFFIX
AFIRE
AFLAT
AFOFL
AFOOT
AFORE
AFOUL
AFRIT
AFROS
AFTER
AFTON
AFTRA

A•F••
AFFIX
ALFIE
ALFRE
APFEL
AWFUL

A••F•
ABAFT
ACUFF
AFOFL
ALEFS
ALIFS
ALOFT

A•••F
ACUFF
ADOLF
ALOOF

•AF••
CAFES
DAFFY
DAFOE
GAFFE
GAFFS
HAFIZ
HAFTS
HAFUN
JAFFA
JAFFE
KAFIR
KAFKA
NAFTA
RAFER
RAFFI
RAFTS
SAFER
SAFES
TAFFY
WAFER
WAFTS

•A•F•
BANFF
DAFFY
GAFFE
GAFFS
HAIFA
JAFFA
JAFFE
RAFFI
TAFFY
WAIFS
ZARFS

•A••F
BANFF
CALIF
GANEF

••AF•
ABAFT
CHAFE
CHAFF
CRAFT
DRAFT
GRAFT
KRAFT
LEAFS
LEAFY
LOAFS
QUAFF
SHAFT
SNAFU
STAFF

••A•F
CHAFF
DWARF
QUAFF
SCARF
SHAEF
STAFF
SWARF
WHARF

•••AF
DECAF
PILAF
SHEAF

AG•••
AGAIN
AGALS
AGAMA
AGANA
AGAPE
AGARS
AGASP
AGATE
AGAVE
AGAZE
AGENA
AGENT
AGERS
AGGIE
AGGRO
AGHAS
AGILE
AGING
AGIOS
AGITA
AGLET
AGLEY
AGLOW
AGNES
AGNEW
AGNON
AGNUS
AGOGO
AGONY
AGORA
AGREE
AGRIC
AGRON
AGUES

A•G••
AEGIR
AEGIS
AGGIE
AGGRO
ALGAE
ALGAL
ALGER
ALGID
ALGIN
ALGOL
ANGEL
ANGER
ANGES
ANGIE
ANGLE
ANGLO
ANGRY
ANGST
ANGUS
ARGIL
ARGOL
ARGON
ARGOS
ARGOT
ARGUE
ARGUS
AUGER
AUGHT
AUGUR
AVGAS

A••G•
ADAGE
ADIGE
AGOGO
AINGE
ALIGN
AMIGA
AMIGO

A•••G
ABZUG
ACING
AGING
ALONG
AMONG
APING
AWING
AXING

•AG••
BAGEL
BAGGY
BAGIT
CAGED
CAGER
CAGES
CAGEY
DAGON
EAGER
EAGLE
EAGRE
FAGIN
FAGOT
GAGES
HAGAR
HAGEN
HAGIO
HAGUE
JAGGY
LAGAN
LAGER
LAGOS
MAGDA
MAGES
MAGIC
MAGMA
MAGNA
MAGOG
MAGOO
MAGOT
MAGUS
NAGEL
NAGGY
PAGAN
PAGED
PAGER
PAGES
PAGET
RAGAS
RAGED
RAGES
SAGAL
SAGAN
SAGAS
SAGER
SAGES
SAGET
SAGGY
SAGOS
TAGUP
TAGUS
VAGUE
VAGUS
WAGED
WAGER
WAGES
WAGON

•A•G•
BADGE
BAGGY
BANGS
BARGE
BAUGH
CADGE
CARGO
DANGS
FANGS
FARGO
GANGS
GAUGE
HANGS
JAGGY
KANGA
LANGE
LARGE
LARGO
LAUGH
MADGE
MANGO
MARGE
MARGO
NAGGY
PAIGE
PANGA
PANGS
RANGE
RANGY
SAGGY
SAIGA
SARGE
SARGO
TAEGU
TAIGA
TANGO
TANGS
TANGY
TARGE
WAUGH

•A••G
LAING
MAGOG
NAVIG
VARIG

••AG•
ADAGE
BRAGA
BRAGG
BRAGS
CRAGS
DRAGS
ETAGE
FLAGG
FLAGS
HOAGY
IMAGE
IMAGO
OFAGE
OSAGE
PHAGE
PHAGO
PLAGE
QUAGS
SHAGS
SLAGS
SNAGS
STAGE
STAGG
STAGS
STAGY
SWAGE
SWAGS
USAGE

••A•G
BRAGG
CHANG
CLANG
CRAIG
DRANG
FLAGG
GRAIG
KIANG
LIANG
ORANG
SLANG
SPANG
STAGG
STANG
TWANG
WHANG

•••AG
GULAG
REBAG
RETAG
SCRAG
SPRAG

AH•••
AHEAD
AHMAD
AHMED
AHORA
AHOYS
AHSIN

A•H••
AAHED
ABHOR
ACHED
ACHES
ACHOO
ADHEM
ADHOC
AGHAS
ANHUI
APHID
APHIS
ARHAT
ARHUS
ASHBY
ASHEN
ASHER
ASHES
ASHUR
ATHOL
ATHON
ATHOS

A••H•
ABOHM
AISHA
ALOHA
ALPHA
ALTHO
AMAHL
AMAHS
AMPHI
AMPHR
ANKHS
ANTHO
ARCHI
ARCHY
ARTHR
AUGHT
AYAHS

A•••H
ABASH
AITCH
ALEPH
ALLAH
AMISH
APISH
ARITH
AWASH
AZOTH

•AH••
AAHED
BAHAI
BAHIA
BAHTS
HAHAS
JAHRE
KAHLO
LAHTI
MAHAL
MAHAN
MAHDI
MAHRE
NAHUA
NAHUM
RAHAB
SAHEL
SAHIB
TAHOE
TAHRS
WAHOO
YAHOO

•A•H•
BASHO
BATHE
BATHO
BATHS
BATHY
CACHE
CATHY
DACHA
DACHE
DASHI
FATHA
KASHA
KATHY
LATHE
LATHS
MACHE
MACHO
MACHU
MASHY
MATHS
NACHO
NACHT
NASHE
OATHS
PASHA
PATHE
PATHO
PATHS
RAPHE
RASHT
RATHS
SACHA
SACHS
SADHE
SADHU
SASHA
WASHY
YACHT

•A••H
BALCH
BALKH
BARTH
BATCH
BAUGH
CATCH
DARTH
EARTH
FAITH
FARAH
GARTH
HARSH
HATCH
KARSH
LARCH
LATCH
LAUGH
MARCH
MARSH
MATCH
NAISH
NATCH
PARCH
PASCH
PATCH
RAJAH
RALPH
RANCH
RATCH
SABAH
SANDH
SARAH
WALSH
WATCH
WAUGH

••AH•
AMAHL
AMAHS
AYAHS
BLAHS
BRAHE
ICAHN
IDAHO
LEAHY
NOAHS
OMAHA
OPAHS
SHAHN
SHAHS
SPAHI
SPAHN
STAHL
UTAHN

••A•H
ABASH
AWASH
BEACH
BRASH
CLASH
COACH
CRASH
FLASH
GNASH
GRAPH
HEATH
KEACH
LEACH
LEASH
LOACH
LOATH
NEATH
ORACH
PEACH
PLASH
PLATH
POACH
QUASH
REACH
ROACH
SLASH
SMASH
SNATH
STASH
SWASH
SWATH
TEACH
TRASH
WRATH

•••AH
ALLAH
BORAH
DINAH
EPHAH
FARAH
GERAH
JONAH
JUDAH
MICAH
MYNAH
NORAH
OBEAH
OPRAH
RAJAH
SABAH
SARAH
SELAH
SHOAH
SURAH
TORAH
URIAH

AI•••
AIDAN
AIDED
AIDES
AIKEN
AILED
AILER
AILEY
AIMAT
AIMED
AIMEE
AIMER
AIMTO
AINGE
AINUS
AIOLI
AIRED
AIRES
AISHA
AISLE
AISNE
AITCH

A•I••
ABIDE
ACIDS
ACIDY
ACING
ADIEU
ADIGE
ADINT
ADIOS
ADITS
AFIRE
AGILE
AGING
AGIOS
AGITA
AKINS
AKIRA
AKITA
ALIAS
ALIBI
ALICE
ALIDA
ALIEN
ALIFS
ALIGN
ALIKE
ALINE
ALIST
ALIVE
AMICE
AMIDE
AMIES
AMIGA
AMIGO
AMINE
AMINO
AMIRS
AMISH
AMISS
AMITY
ANILS
ANIMA
ANIME
ANION
ANISE
ANITA
APIAN
APIED
APING
APISH
ARIAN
ARIAS
ARICA
ARIEL
ARIES
ARILS
ARION
ARISE
ARITH
ARIUM
ARIUS
ASIAN
ASIDE
ATILT
ATION
ATIVE
AVIAN
AVILA
AVION

AVISO AWING AXIAL AXILS AXING AXIOM AXION AZIDE AZINE ATEIN ATRIA ATRIP ATTIC AUDIE AUDIO AUDIS AUDIT AULIS AURIC AUXIL AUXIN AVAIL AVOID AVOIR AVRIL AWAIT AZOIC

A••I•

ABBIE ABOIL ABRIS ACRID ACTII ACTIN ACTIV ADAIR ADDIE ADDIN ADDIS ADLIB ADMIN ADMIT ADMIX ADVIL AECIA AEGIR AEGIS AERIE AESIR AFFIX AFRIT AGAIN AGGIE AGRIC AHSIN ALAIN ALFIE ALGID ALGIN ALLIE ALLIN ALVIN AMAIN AMBIT ANAIS ANDIE ANGIE ANNIE ANNIV ANTIC ANTIQ ANTIS ANVIL ANZIO APHID APHIS APRIL APSIS ARGIL ARKIN ARNIE AROID ARRIS ARSIS ARTIE ARTIS ASCII ASDIC ASPIC ASTIN ASTIR ATEIN ATRIA ATRIP ATTIC AUDIE AUDIO AUDIS AUDIT AULIS AURIC AUXIL AUXIN AVAIL AVOID AVOIR AVRIL AWAIT AZOIC

A•••I

ABACI ACARI ACTII ADLAI AIOLI ALIBI ALTAI AMATI AMPHI ANHUI AODAI ARCHI ASCII ASSAI ATARI AUREI AUSSI

•AI••

BAILS BAIRD BAIRN BAITS BAIZA BAIZE CAINE CAIRN CAIRO DAILY DAIRY DAISY DAIWA FAILS FAINT FAIRE FAIRS FAIRY FAITH GAINS GAITS GAIUS HAIFA HAIKS HAIKU HAILE HAILS HAIRS HAIRY HAITI JAILS JAIME JAINS LAICS LAIKA LAINE LAING LAIRD LAIRS LAITY LAIUS MAIDS MAILS MAINE MAINS MAINZ MAIZE NAIAD NAILS NAIRA NAIRN NAISH NAIVE PAIGE PAILS PAINE PAINS PAINT PAIRS RAIDS RAILS RAINS RAINY RAISA RAISE RAITT SAIGA SAILS SAINT TAIGA TAILS TAINE TAINT WAIFS WAILS WAINS WAIST WAITE WAITS WAITZ WAIVE ZAIRE

•A•I•

BAGIT BAHIA BALIN BARIC BARIT BASIC BASIE BASIL BASIN BASIS BATIK CABIN CADIS CADIZ CALIF CALIX CANID CANIS CANIT CARIA CARIB CASIO CAVIL DACIA DANIO DARIN DARIO DAVID DAVIE DAVIS DAVIT EATIN EATIT FABIO FACIE FAGIN FAKIR GADID GAMIN GAVIN HABIT HAFIZ HAGIO HAJIS HAKIM HASID JAMIE JAMIN JANIE JANIS KAFIR KAKIS KANIN KATIE LABIO LAMIA LAPIN LAPIS LATIN LAVIN LAYIN MAGIC MALIC MAMIE MANIA MARIA MARIE MARIN MARIO MARIS MATIN MAVIS MAXIE MAXIM MAXIS NADIA NADIR NAMIB NARIS NAVIG OAKIE OASIS PAMIR PANIC PARIS PATIO PAVIA PAVID PAVIS PAYIN RABID RABIN RADII RADIO RADIX RAJIV RAKIS RAMIE RAMIS RANID RANIN RANIS RAPID RATIO RAVIN SABIN SADIE SAHIB SALIC SAPID SAPIR SARIS SATIE SATIN SAWIN TABIS TACIT TAKIN TALIA TAMIL TAPIN TAPIR TAXIS VADIM VADIS VALID VANIR VAPID VARIA VARIG VARIX VATIC WADIS XAXIS YALIE YASIR YAXIS ZAMIA ZAXIS ZAYIN

•A••I

BAHAI BAMBI BASSI CACTI CALCI CALLI CAPRI CARDI CARPI DALAI DASHI FARCI FARSI GALLI GARNI HADJI HAITI HAJJI HANOI IAMBI KANJI KAUAI KAURI LACTI LAHTI LANAI MAHDI MAORI MAQUI MARDI MARTI MASAI MATRI NALDI NAOMI PALPI PAOLI PAPPI PARDI PARTI PATRI PATTI RABBI RADII RAFFI RANDI SALMI SAUDI TAKEI TARSI VALLI YANNI YAQUI

••AI•

ADAIR AGAIN ALAIN AMAIN ANAIS AVAIL AWAIT BLAIR BRAID BRAIL BRAIN CHAIM CHAIN CHAIR CLAIM CLAIR CRAIG CRAIN DRAIL DRAIN EMAIL FLAIL FLAIR FRAIL FRAIS GLAIR GRAIG GRAIL GRAIN KRAIT NGAIO OHAIR ONAIR PLAID PLAIN PLAIT QUAID QUAIL REAIM REAIR SLAIN SNAIL SPAIN STAID STAIN STAIR SWAIN THAIS TRAIL TRAIN TRAIT TWAIN USAIR

••A•I

ABACI ACARI AMATI ATARI COATI DHABI EGADI GHAZI GRANI INARI IRANI IRAQI KHAKI MIAMI NGAMI OKAPI OMANI PLANI QUASI SHARI SPAHI SWAMI SWAZI

•••AI

ADLAI ALTAI AODAI ASSAI BAHAI BOHAI DALAI DOUAI DUBAI ENLAI KAUAI KENAI LANAI MASAI POHAI SERAI SINAI

A•J••

ANJOU AUJUS

A••J•

ABUJA

•AJ••

CAJUN HAJIS HAJJI MAJOR RAJAH RAJAS RAJIV SAJAK

•A•J•

BANJO HADJI HAJJI KANJI

AK•••

AKBAR AKEEM AKEES AKELA AKINS AKIRA AKITA AKKAD AKRON AKSUM

A•K••

AIKEN AKKAD ALKYD ALKYL ANKHS ANKLE ARKIN ASKED ASKER ASKEW

A••K•

ALIKE ASOKA AWAKE AWOKE

A•••K

ABACK ALACK ALECK AMUCK ANOUK APEAK

•AK••

BAKED BAKER BAKES BAKST CAKED CAKES CAKEY DAKAR FAKED FAKER FAKES FAKIR HAKES HAKIM JAKES KAKAS KAKIS LAKER LAKES LAKME MAKER MAKES MAKOS MAKUA NAKED OAKEN OAKES OAKIE OAKUM RAKED RAKER RAKES RAKIS SAKER SAKES TAKEI TAKEN TAKER TAKES TAKIN WAKED WAKEN WAKES YAKOV YAKUT

•A•K•

BABKA BACKS BALKH BALKS BALKY BANKS BANKY BARKS BASKS CALKS CARKS CASKS DANKE DARKS GAWKS GAWKY HACKS HAIKS HAIKU HANKS HANKY HARKS HAWKE HAWKS JACKS KAFKA LACKS LAIKA LANKA LANKY LARKS LATKE MARKS MASKS NARKS PACKS PANKY PARKA PARKS RACKS RANKE RANKS SACKS SANKA SAUKS TACKS TACKY TALKS TALKY TANKA TANKS TASKS WACKO WACKY WALKS YANKS

•A••K

BATAK BATIK CAPEK CAULK DAYAK HACEK HAYEK KAPOK KAYAK PATEK SAJAK TAROK YAPOK

••AK•

AWAKE BEAKS BLAKE BRAKE CHAKA CRAKE DRAKE FLAKE FLAKY KHAKI LEAKS LEAKY OSAKA PEAKS QUAKE QUAKY SHAKE SHAKO SHAKY SLAKE SNAKE SNAKY SOAKS SPAKE STAKE TEAKS

••A•K

ABACK ALACK BLACK BLANK CHALK CLACK CLANK CLARK CRACK CRANK DRANK FLACK FLANK FLASK FRANK IZAAK KNACK KYACK NYACK OZARK PLANK PRANK QUACK QUARK RUARK SHACK SHANK SHARK SLACK SMACK SNACK SNARK SPAAK SPANK SPARK STACK STALK STANK STARK SWANK THANK TRACK WHACK WRACK

•••AK

APEAK BATAK BLEAK BREAK CLOAK CREAK CROAK DAYAK FREAK IZAAK KAYAK KODAK KOJAK KULAK MUZAK NOVAK SAJAK SNEAK SPAAK SPEAK STEAK TWEAK UMIAK WREAK

AL•••

ALACK ALAIN ALAMO ALARM ALATE ALAVA ALBAN ALBEE ALBEN ALBUM ALCAN ALCOA ALCOR ALDAN ALDEN ALDER ALDOL ALDUS ALECK ALEFS ALENE ALEPH ALERT ALETA ALEUT ALFIE ALFRE ALGAE ALGAL ALGER ALGID ALGIN ALGOL ALIAS ALIBI ALICE ALIDA ALIEN ALIFS ALIGN ALIKE ALINE ALIST ALIVE ALKYD ALKYL ALLAH ALLAN ALLAY ALLEE ALLEN ALLER ALLES ALLEY ALLEZ ALLIE ALLIN ALLOT ALLOW ALLOY ALLYL ALMAY ALOES ALOFT ALOHA ALONE ALONG ALOOF ALORS ALOUD ALPHA ALSOP ALTAI ALTAR ALTER ALTHO ALTON ALTOS ALTUS ALULA ALUMS ALVAR ALVIN ALYCE

A•L••

AALTO ABLER ADLAI ADLER ADLIB ADLOC AFLAT AGLET AGLEY AGLOW AILED AILER AILEY ALLAH ALLAN ALLAY ALLEE ALLEN ALLER ALLES ALLEY ALLEZ ALLIE ALLIN ALLOT ALLOW ALLOY ALLYL APLEY APLUS ARLEN ARLES ATLAS AULIS AXLES

A••L•

ABELE ADDLE ADELA ADELE ADOLF ADULT AGALS AGILE AIOLI AISLE AKELA ALULA AMBLE AMOLE AMPLE AMPLY AMYLO AMYLS ANGLE ANGLO ANILS ANKLE ANOLE APPLE APPLY APTLY ARILS ASYLA ATALL ATILT ATOLL AVILA AWOLS AXELS AXILS

A•••L

ABDUL ABOIL ACCEL ADDNL ADVIL AFOFL AFOUL ALDOL ALGAL ALGOL ALKYL ALLYL AMAHL ANGEL ANNAL ANNUL ANSEL ANTAL ANVIL APFEL APPAL APPEL APRIL AREAL ARGIL ARGOL ARIEL ARNEL ARPEL ARTAL ARTEL ATALL ATHOL ATOLL AURAL AUXIL AVAIL AVRIL AWFUL AXIAL

•AL••

AALTO BALAS BALCH BALDS BALED BALER BALES BALIN BALKH BALKS BALKY BALLS BALLY BALMS BALMY BALSA BALTS CALCI CALEB CALIF CALIX CALKS CALLA CALLI CALLS CALMS CALPE CALVE CALYX DALAI DALES DALEY DALLY FALDO FALLS FALSE GALAS GALAX GALBA GALEA GALEN GALES GALLI GALLO GALLS GALOP HALAS HALED HALER HALES HALEY HALLE HALLO HALLS HALON HALOS HALTS HALVE KALEL KALES LALAW MALAN MALAR MALAY MALES MALIC MALLE MALLS MALMO MALTA MALTS MALTY NALDI PALAE PALAU PALEA PALED PALEO PALER PALES PALEY PALLS PALLY PALMA PALME PALMS PALMY PALOS PALPI PALPS PALSY RALLY RALPH SALAD SALAL SALAM SALEM SALEP SALES SALIC SALLE SALLY SALMI SALON SALPA SALPS SALSA SALTA SALTS SALTY SALUD SALUT SALVE SALVO TALER TALES TALIA TALKS TALKY TALLY TALON TALUS VALES VALET VALID VALLE VALLI VALOR VALSE VALUE VALVE WALDO WALED WALER WALES WALKS WALLS WALLY WALSH WALSY WALTZ YALIE YALOW YALTA

•A•L•

BAALS BADLY BAILS BALLS BALLY BAWLS BAYLE CABLE CALLA CALLI CALLS CARLA CARLE CARLO CARLY CAULK CAULS DAILY DALLY DARLA EAGLE EARLE EARLS EARLY FABLE FAILS FALLS FATLY FAULT GABLE GAELS GALLI GALLO GALLS GAOLS GAULS GAYLE GAYLY HABLA HAILE HAILS HALLE HALLO HALLS HAOLE HAPLY HATLO HAULM HAULS JAILS JARLS KAHLO KARLA LADLE LAXLY LAYLA MACLE MADLY MAILS MALLE MALLS MANLY MAPLE MARLA MARLO MARLS MARLY MAULS NAILS PABLO PAILS PALLS PALLY PAOLI PAOLO PARLE PATLY PAULA PAWLS RAILS RALLY RAWLS RAWLY SABLE SADLY SAILS SALLE SALLY SAULT TABLA TABLE TAELS TAILS TALLY VALLE VALLI VAULT WAALS WAILS WALLS WALLY WANLY YAWLS

•A••L

BABEL BABUL BAGEL BANAL BASAL BASEL BASIL CABAL CAMEL CANAL CAROL CAVIL DARYL EASEL FATAL GAMAL GAVEL GAYAL HAMAL HAMEL HAVEL HAZEL JAMAL KABUL KALEL KAREL KAROL LABEL LAPEL LAVAL MABEL

MAHAL
MAZEL
NAGEL
NASAL
NATAL
NAVAL
NAVEL
PANDL
PANEL
PAPAL
PAROL
RAOUL
RATEL
RAVEL
SAGAL
SAHEL
SALAL
SANDL
TAMIL

••AL•
AGALS
ATALL
BAALS
BBALL
BEALL
BEALS
BIALY
CHALK
COALS
DEALS
DEALT
DIALS
EXALT
FOALS
GOALS
HEALS
HEALY
INALL
ITALO
ITALS
ITALY
KOALA
KUALA
MEALS
MEALY
NEALE
NYALA
OCALA
OPALS
ORALE
ORALS
OVALS
PEALE
PEALS
PSALM
QUALE
QUALM
REALM
REALS
RIALS
ROALD
SCALA
SCALD
SCALE
SCALP
SCALY
SEALE
SEALS
SEALY
SHALE
SHALL
SHALT
SIALS
SKALD
SMALL
SMALT
SPALL
STALE
STALK
STALL
SWALE
TEALS
TRALA
UDALL
URALS
VIALS
WAALS
WEALS
WHALE
ZEALS

••A•L
AMAHL
ATALL
AVAIL
BBALL
BEALL
BRAIL
BRAWL
CRAWL
DRAIL
DRAWL
EMAIL
FLAIL
FRAIL
GNARL
GRAIL
INALL
KRAAL
PEARL
QUAIL
SHALL
SHAWL
SMALL
SNAIL
SNARL
SPALL
STAEL
STAHL
STALL
TRAIL
TRAWL
UDALL
UHAUL

•••AL
ALGAL
ANNAL
ANTAL
APPAL
AREAL
ARTAL
AURAL
AXIAL
BANAL
BASAL
BINAL
CABAL
CANAL
COPAL
CORAL
COXAL
DECAL
DORAL
DOTAL
DUCAL
EQUAL
FATAL
FERAL
FETAL
FINAL
FOCAL
FUGAL
GAMAL
GAYAL
GORAL
HAMAL
HORAL
IDEAL
JAMAL
JOUAL
JUBAL
JUGAL
JURAL
KEMAL
KRAAL
LAVAL
LEGAL
LOCAL
LOYAL
MAHAL
MEDAL
METAL
MODAL
MORAL
MURAL
NASAL
NATAL
NAVAL
NEPAL
NIVAL
NOCAL
NODAL
NOPAL
OCTAL
OFFAL
ONEAL
PAPAL
PEDAL
PENAL
PETAL
PHIAL
PIPAL
PUPAL
REGAL
RENAL
RIVAL
RIYAL
ROYAL
RURAL
SAGAL
SALAL
SEGAL
SEPAL
SHOAL
SISAL
SKOAL
STEAL
SURAL
TEPAL
TIDAL
TIKAL
TONAL
TOTAL
TRIAL
URIAL
USUAL
UXMAL
VENAL
VIDAL
VIRAL
VITAL
VOCAL
WHEAL
ZONAL

AM•••
AMADO
AMAHL
AMAHS
AMAIN
AMANA
AMARA
AMASS
AMATI
AMATO
AMAZE
AMBER
AMBIT
AMBLE
AMBOS
AMBRY
AMEBA
AMEER
AMEND
AMENS
AMENT
AMICE
AMIDE
AMIES
AMIGA
AMIGO
AMINE
AMINO
AMIRS
AMISH
AMISS
AMITY
AMMAN
AMMON
AMOCO
AMOLE
AMONG
AMORE
AMORT
AMORY
AMOUR
AMPAS
AMPED
AMPHI
AMPHR
AMPLE
AMPLY
AMUCK
AMUSE
AMVET
AMWAY
AMYLO
AMYLS

A•M••
AAMES
ACMES
ADMAN
ADMEN
ADMIN
ADMIT
ADMIX
AHMAD
AHMED
AIMAT
AIMED
AIMEE
AIMER
AIMTO
ALMAY
AMMAN
AMMON
ARMED
ARMEE
ARMET
ARMOR
ATMAN
ATMOS

A••M•
ABOMB
ACOMA
ADAMS
AGAMA
ALAMO
ALUMS
ANEMO
ANIMA
ANIME
ANOMY
ARAME
AROMA
ARUMS
ASAMA
ATOMS
ATOMY

A•••M
AANDM
ABEAM
ABOHM
ABRAM
ABYSM
ADEEM
ADHEM
ADREM
AKEEM
AKSUM
ALARM
ALBUM
ANNAM
ANNUM
ARIUM
ASSAM
ATEAM
AURUM
AXIOM

•AM••
AAMES
BAMBI
CAMAY
CAMEL
CAMEO
CAMPO
CAMPS
CAMPY
CAMRY
CAMUS
DAMAN
DAMAR
DAMES
DAMNS
DAMON
DAMPS
DAMUP
EAMES
EAMON
FAMED
FAMES
GAMAL
GAMBA
GAMED
GAMER
GAMES
GAMIN
GAMMA
GAMOW
GAMPS
GAMUT
HAMAL
HAMAN
HAMEL
HAMES
HAMMY
IAMBI
IAMBS
JAMAL
JAMBS
JAMES
JAMIE
JAMIN
JAMUP
LAMAR
LAMAS
LAMBS
LAMED
LAMER
LAMES
LAMIA
LAMPS
MAMAS
MAMBA
MAMBO
MAMET
MAM!E
MAMMA
MAMMY
NAMBY
NAMED
NAMER
NAMES
NAMIB
NAMPA
NAMUR
PAMBY
PAMIR
PAMPA
RAMAN
RAMAR
RAMBO
RAMEE
RAMEN
RAMET
RAMIE
RAMIS
RAMON
RAMOS
RAMPS
SAMAR
SAMBA
SAMMS
SAMMY
SAMOA
SAMOS
SAMPS
TAMBO
TAMED
TAMER
TAMES
TAMIL
TAMMY
TAMPA
TAMPS
VAMOS
VAMPS
YAMPA
ZAMIA

•A•M•
BALMS
BALMY
BARMS
BARMY
BAUME
CALMS
FARMS
GAMMA
HAEMA
HAEMO
HAMMY
HARMS
JAIME
KARMA
LAKME
MAGMA
MALMO
MAMMA
MAMMY
NAOMI
PALMA
PALME
PALMS
PALMY
PARMA
SALMI
SAMMS
SAMMY
TAMMY
WARMS

•A••M
AANDM
CAROM
DATUM
HAKIM
HAREM
HARUM
HAULM
KASEM
LARAM
MADAM
MAXIM
NAHUM
OAKUM
PANAM
SALAM
SALEM
TATUM
VADIM

••AM•
ADAMS
AGAMA
ALAMO
ARAME
ASAMA
BEAMS
BEAMY
BLAME
CHAMP
CLAMP
CLAMS
CRAMP
CRAMS
DRAMA
DRAMS
EDAMS
EXAMS
FLAME
FLAMS
FLAMY
FOAMS
FOAMY
FRAME
GRAMA
GRAMM
GRAMP
GRAMS
IMAMS
ISAMU
LLAMA
LOAMS
LOAMY
MIAMI
NGAMI
PRAMS
REAMS
ROAMS
SCAMP
SCAMS
SEAMS
SEAMY
SHAME
SHAMS
SHAMU
SLAMS
STAMP
SWAMI
SWAMP
TEAMS
TRAMP
TRAMS
WHAMO
WHAMS

••A•M
ALARM
CHAIM
CHARM
CHASM
CLAIM
GRAMM
PHARM
PLASM
PSALM
QUALM
REAIM
REALM
REARM
SHAWM
SPASM
SWARM
UNARM

•••AM
ABEAM
ABRAM
ANNAM
ASSAM
ATEAM
BREAM
CERAM
CREAM
DREAM
GLEAM
GLOAM
HIRAM
IBEAM
ISLAM
LARAM
MADAM
NIZAM
OCCAM
OGHAM
PANAM
PRIAM
PROAM
SALAM
SCRAM
STEAM
UNJAM

AN•••
ANAIS
ANCON
ANDES
ANDIE
ANDOR
ANDRE
ANDRO
ANEAR
ANEMO
ANENT
ANGEL
ANGER
ANGES
ANGIE
ANGLE
ANGLO
ANGRY
ANGST
ANGUS
ANHUI
ANILS
ANIMA
ANIME
ANION
ANISE
ANITA
ANJOU
ANKHS
ANKLE
ANNAL
ANNAM
ANNEE
ANNES
ANNEX
ANNIE
ANNIV
ANNOY
ANNUL
ANNUM
ANNUS
ANOAS
ANODE
ANOLE
ANOMY
ANOUK
ANSAE
ANSEL
ANSER
ANSON
ANTAE
ANTAL
ANTAS
ANTED
ANTES
ANTHO
ANTIC
ANTIQ
ANTIS
ANTON
ANTRA
ANTRE
ANTSY
ANVIL
ANWAR
ANZAC
ANZIO

A•N••
AANDM
ABNER
AGNES
AGNEW
AGNON
AGNUS
AINGE
AINUS
ANNAL
ANNAM
ANNEE
ANNES
ANNEX
ANNIE
ANNIV
ANNOY
ANNUL
ANNUM
ANNUS
APNEA
ARNAZ
ARNEL
ARNIE
ASNER
ATNOS
AUNTS
AUNTY
AWNED

A••N•
ABEND
ACING
ADANA
ADANO
ADDNL
ADENO
ADINT
AEONS
AETNA
AGANA
AGENA
AGENT
AGING
AGONY
AISNE
AKINS
ALENE
ALINE
ALONE
ALONG
AMANA
AMEND
AMENS
AMENT
AMINE
AMINO
AMONG
ANENT
APING
ARENA
ARENS
ARENT
ASANA
ASONE
ASSNS
ATONE
AVANT
AVENA
AVENS
AWING
AXING
AXONS
AZANS
AZINE

A•••N
AARON
ACORN
ACTIN
ACTON
ADDIN
ADDON
ADMAN
ADMEN
ADMIN
ADORN
AFTON
AGAIN
AGNON
AGRON
AHSIN
AIDAN
AIKEN
AKRON
ALAIN
ALBAN
ALBEN
ALCAN
ALDAN
ALDEN
ALGIN
ALIEN
ALIGN
ALLAN
ALLEN
ALLIN
ALTON
ALVIN
AMAIN
AMMAN
AMMON
ANCON
ANION
ANSON
ANTON
APIAN
APRON
ARDEN
ARGON
ARIAN
ARION
ARKIN
ARLEN
ARRAN
ARSON
ARYAN
ASHEN
ASIAN
ASPEN
ASTIN
ASTON
ASWAN
ATEIN
ATHON
ATION
ATMAN
AUDEN
AUXIN
AVIAN
AVION
AXION

•AN••
AANDM
BANAL
BANCO
BANCS
BANDA
BANDB
BANDO
BANDS
BANDY
BANES
BANFF
BANGS
BANJO
BANKS
BANKY
BANNS
BANTU
CANAL
CANBY
CANDO
CANDW
CANDY
CANEA
CANED
CANER
CANES
CANID
CANIS
CANIT
CANNA
CANNY
CANOE
CANON
CANSO
CANST
CANTO
CANTS
DANAE
DANCE
DANCY
DANDY
DANES
DANGS
DANIO
DANKE
DANNY
DANSE
DANTE
DANZA
FANCY
FANES
FANGS
FANNY
FANON
FANTA
GANDY
GANEF
GANGS
HANDS
HANDY
HANES
HANGS
HANKS
HANKY
HANNA
HANNO
HANOI
HANSA
JANET
JANIE
JANIS
JANUS
KANGA
KANIN
KANJI
KANSA
KANZU
LANAI
LANCE
LANDO
LANDS
LANES
LANGE
LANKA
LANKY
LANTZ
LANZA
MANDY
MANED
MANES
MANET
MANGO
MANIA
MANLY
MANNA
MANNY
MANON
MANOR
MANOS
MANSE
MANTA
NANAS
NANCY
NANNA
NANNY
PANAM
PANAY
PANDA
PANDL
PANED
PANEL
PANES
PANGA
PANGS
PANIC
PANKY
PANNE
PANSY
PANTO
PANTS
PANTY
PANZA
QANDA
RANAT
RANCH
RANDB
RANDD
RANDI
RANDR
RANDS
RANDY
RANEE
RANGE
RANGY
RANID
RANIN
RANIS
RANKE
RANKS
RANON
RANTO
RANTS
RANUP
SANAA
SANDH
SANDL
SANDS
SANDY
SANER
SANKA
SANTA
SANTE
SANTO
SANYO
TANDY
TANEY
TANGO
TANGS
TANGY
TANKA
TANKS
TANSY
TANTE
TANYA
VANCE
VANES
VANIR
VANNA
VANYA
WANDA
WANDS
WANED
WANER
WANES
WANLY
WANNA
WANTS
YANKS
YANNI
ZANTE

•A•N•
BANNS
BARNS
CAINE
CANNA
CANNY
CARNE
CARNY
DAMNS
DANNY
DARNS
DAUNT
DAWNS
DAYNE
EARNS
FAINT
FANNY
FAUNA
FAUNS
FAWNS
GAINS
GARNI
GAUNT
HADNT
HANNA
HANNO
HASNT
HAUNT
JAINS
JAUNE
JAUNT
JAYNE
LAINE
LAING
LAWNS
LAYNE
MAGNA
MAINE
MAINS
MAINZ
MANNA
MANNY
MARNE
MAUNA
MAUND
NANNA
NANNY
PAINE
PAINS
PAINT
PANNE
PATNA
PAWNS
PAYNE
RAINS
RAINY
SAENS
SAINT
SAONE
SAUNA
TAINE
TAINT
TARNS
TAUNT
TAWNY
VANNA
VARNA
VAUNT
WAINS
WANNA
WARNS
WASNT
WAYNE
YANNI
YARNS
YAWNS

•A••N
AARON
BACON
BADEN
BAIRN
BALIN
BARON
BASIN
BATON
CABIN
CAIRN
CAJUN
CANON
CAPON
CARON
DAGON
DAMAN
DAMON
DARIN
DAYAN
EAMON
EATEN
EATIN
EATON
FAGIN
FANON
FARON
GABON
GALEN
GAMIN
GATUN
GAVIN
HADON
HAFUN
HAGEN
HALON
HAMAN
HASON
HAVEN
HAYDN
JAMIN
JAPAN
JASON
KANIN
KARAN
KAREN
KAZAN
LABAN
LADEN
LAGAN
LAPIN
LATEN
LATIN
LAVIN
LAYIN
LAYON
MACON
MAHAN
MALAN
MANON
MARIN
MASON
MATIN
MAVEN
MAYAN
MAYON
NAIRN
OAKEN
OATEN
PAEAN
PAEON
PAGAN
PAREN
PATEN
PATON
PAYIN
RABIN
RACON
RADON
RAMAN
RAMEN
RAMON
RANIN
RANON
RATON
RAVEN
RAVIN
RAYON
SABIN
SAGAN
SALON
SARAN
SATAN
SATIN
SATON
SAWIN
SAXON
TAKEN
TAKIN
TALON
TAPIN
TAUON
TAXON
WAGON
WAKEN
WAXEN
ZAYIN
ZAZEN

••AN•
ADANA
ADANO
AGANA
AMANA
ASANA
AVANT
AZANS
BEANO
BEANS
BEANY
BLANC
BLAND
BLANK
BRAND
BRANS
BRANT
BWANA
CHANG
CHANT
CLANG
CLANK
CLANS
CRANE
CRANK
CYANO
DEANE
DEANS
DIANA
DIANE
DRANG
DRANK
DRANO
DUANE
ELAND
EVANS
FLANK
FLANS
FRANC
FRANK
FRANS
FRANZ
GHANA
GIANT
GLAND
GRAND
GRANI
GRANT
INANE
IPANA
IRANI
IVANA
JEANE
JEANS
KEANE
KEANU
KHANS
KIANG
KOANS
LEANS
LEANT
LIANA
LIANE
LIANG
LLANO
LOANS
MEANS
MEANT
MEANY
MOANS
OLAND
OMANI
ORANG
ORANT
PIANO
PLANB
PLANE
PLANI
PLANK

PLANO
PLANS
PLANT
PRANK
QUAND
QUANT
RIANT
ROANS
RUANA
SCAND
SCANS
SCANT
SHANA
SHANE
SHANK
SHANS
SHANT
SLANG
SLANT
SPANG
SPANK
SPANS
STAND
STANG
STANK
SWANK
SWANN
SWANS
THANE
THANK
THANT
TIANT
TRANS
TWANG
VIAND
WEANS
WHANG
YEANS
YUANS

••A•N

AGAIN
ALAIN
AMAIN
BRAIN
BRAUN
BRAWN
CHAIN
CRAIN
DRAIN
DRAWN
GRAIN
HEARN
ICAHN
LEARN
PLAIN
PRAWN
SHAHN
SHAUN
SHAWN
SLAIN
SPAHN
SPAIN
SPAWN
STAIN
SWAIN
SWANN
TRAIN
TWAIN
UTAHN
YEARN

•••AN

ADMAN
AIDAN
ALBAN
ALCAN
ALDAN
ALLAN
AMMAN
APIAN
ARIAN
ARRAN
ARYAN
ASIAN
ASWAN
ATMAN
AVIAN
BEGAN
BEHAN
BRIAN
BRYAN
CLEAN
COHAN
CONAN
COPAN
CUBAN
DAMAN
DAYAN
DEWAN
DIVAN
DORAN
DUGAN
DURAN
DYLAN
ELMAN
ETHAN
EVIAN
FURAN
GLEAN
GOLAN
GROAN
HAMAN
HEMAN
HENAN
HOBAN
HOGAN
HONAN
HUMAN
HUNAN
HYMAN
INCAN
IOWAN
JAPAN
KARAN
KAZAN
KORAN
LABAN
LAGAN
LEXAN
LOGAN
LOMAN
LORAN
LUCAN
LYMAN
MAHAN
MALAN
MAYAN
MEGAN
MELAN
MIKAN
MILAN
MORAN
NEMAN
NISAN
NOLAN
OCEAN
OLEAN
ORGAN
OSCAN
OSMAN
PAEAN
PAGAN
PECAN
PERAN
PISAN
PUSAN
RAMAN
REDAN
REGAN
REHAN
REMAN
RENAN
RERAN
RODAN
ROMAN
ROWAN
SAGAN
SARAN
SATAN
SEDAN
SHEAN
SIVAN
SKEAN
SLOAN
SOLAN
SUDAN
SUSAN
TEXAN
TIRAN
TITAN
TYNAN
UHLAN
UNMAN
URBAN
VEGAN
WIGAN
WOMAN
WOTAN
WUHAN
WYMAN
YUMAN

AO•••

AODAI
AORTA

A•O••

ABODE
ABOHM
ABOIL
ABOMB
ABORT
ABOUT
ABOVE
ABOVO
ACOMA
ACORN
ADOBE
ADOLF
ADOPT
ADORE
ADORN
ADOUT
AEONS
AFOFL
AFOOT
AFORE
AFOUL
AGOGO
AGONY
AGORA
AHORA
AHOYS
AIOLI
ALOES
ALOFT
ALOHA
ALONE
ALONG
ALOOF
ALORS
ALOUD
AMOCO
AMOLE
AMONG
AMORE
AMORT
AMORY
AMOUR
ANOAS
ANODE
ANOLE
ANOMY
ANOUK
APORT
AROAR
AROID
AROMA
AROSE
ASOKA
ASONE
ATOLL
ATOMS
ATOMY
ATONE
AVOID
AVOIR
AVOWS
AWOKE
AWOLS
AXONS
AZOIC
AZOTE
AZOTH

A••O•

AARON
ABBOT
ABHOR
ACHOO
ACTON
ACTOR
ADDON
ADHOC
ADIOS
ADLOC
AESOP
AFOOT
AFROS
AFTON
AGIOS
AGLOW
AGNON
AGRON
AKRON
ALCOA
ALCOR
ALDOL
ALGOL
ALLOT
ALLOW
ALLOY
ALOOF
ALSOP
ALTON
ALTOS
AMBOS
AMMON
ANCON
ANDOR
ANION
ANJOU
ANNOY
ANSON
ANTON
APRON
APSOS
ARBOR
ARDOR
ARGOL
ARGON
ARGOS
ARGOT
ARION
ARMOR
ARROW
ARROZ
ARSON
ARTOO
ASCOT
ASSOC
ASTON
ASTOR
ATHOL
ATHON
ATHOS
ATION
ATMOS
ATNOS
AUTOS
AVION
AXIOM
AXION

A•••O

AALTO
ABACO
ABOVO
ACETO
ACHOO
ADANO
ADDTO
ADENO
AGGRO
AGOGO
AIMTO
ALAMO
ALTHO
AMADO
AMATO
AMIGO
AMINO
AMOCO
AMYLO
ANDRO
ANEMO
ANGLO
ANTHO
ANZIO
ARTOO
ASTRO
AUDIO
AVISO

•AO••

GAOLS
HAOLE
MAORI
NAOMI
PAOLI
PAOLO
RAOUL
SAONE

•A•O•

AARON
BACON
BARON
BASOV
BATON
BATOR
BAYOU
CABOT
CANOE
CANON
CAPON
CAPOS
CAROB
CAROL
CAROM
CARON
DADOS
DAFOE
DAGON
DAMON
DAVOS
EAMON
EATON
FADOS
FAGOT
FANON
FAROE
FARON
FAROS
FAVOR
GABON
GABOR
GALOP
GAMOW
GAROU
GATOR
GATOS
GAVOT
HADON
HALON
HALOS
HANOI
HASON
HAVOC
JABOT
JACOB
JASON
JATOS
KABOB
KAPOK
KAROL
KAYOS
KAZOO
LABOR
LAGOS
LAYON
MACON
MAGOG
MAGOO
MAGOT
MAJOR
MAKOS
MANON
MANOR
MANOS
MASON
MAYON
MAYOR
NABOB
NAXOS
PAEON
PALOS
PAROL
PAROS
PATON
RACON
RADON
RAMON
RAMOS
RANON
RATON
RAYON
RAZOR
SABOT
SAGOS
SALON
SAMOA
SAMOS
SAPOR
SAROD
SAROS
SATON
SAVOR
SAVOY
SAXON
TABOO
TABOR
TACOS
TAHOE
TALON
TAROK
TAROT
TAUON
TAXON
VALOR
VAMOS
VAPOR
WAGON
WAHOO
YAHOO
YAKOV
YALOW
YAPOK
YAZOO

•A••O

AALTO
BANCO
BANDO
BANJO
BASHO
BASSO
BATHO
CACAO
CADDO
CAIRO
CAMEO
CAMPO
CANDO
CANSO
CANTO
CARBO
CARGO
CARLO
CASCO
CASIO
DANIO
DARIO
DAVAO
FABIO
FACTO
FALDO
FARGO
GALLO
GARBO
HADTO
HAEMO
HAGIO
HALLO
HANNO
HARPO
HASSO
HASTO
HATLO
IATRO
KAHLO
KAZOO
LABIO
LACTO
LANDO
LARGO
LASSO
LAYTO
MACAO
MACHO
MACRO
MAGOO
MALMO
MAMBO
MANGO
MARCO
MARGO
MARIO
MARLO
MATEO
MATRO
MATZO
MAYPO
NACHO
NARCO
PAAVO
PABLO
PALEO
PANTO
PAOLO
PARDO
PASCO
PASEO
PASTO
PATHO
PATIO
RADIO
RAMBO
RANTO
RATIO
RATSO
SACCO
SACRO
SALVO
SANTO
SANYO
SARGO
SARTO
SAWTO
SAYSO
TABOO
TAMBO
TANGO
TASSO
TAXCO
VASCO
WACKO
WAHOO
WALDO
XACTO
YAHOO
YAZOO

••AO•

CHAOS
MIAOW

••A•O

ABACO
ADANO
ALAMO
AMADO
AMATO
BEANO
BRAVO
CHACO
CHARO
CLARO
CYANO
DIAZO
DRACO
DRANO
ERATO
GLAXO
GUACO
IDAHO
IMAGO
ITALO
LLANO
NEATO
NGAIO
PAAVO
PEABO
PHAGO
PIANO
PLANO
PLATO
PRADO
PRATO
SEATO
SHAKO
WHAMO

•••AO

CACAO
DAVAO
DRLAO
MACAO

AP•••

APACE
APART
APEAK
APERS
APERY
APFEL
APHID
APHIS
APIAN
APIED
APING
APISH
APLEY
APLUS
APNEA
APORT
APPAL
APPEL
APPLE
APPLY
APPTD
APPTS
APRES
APRIL
APRON
APSES
APSIS
APSOS
APTED
APTER
APTLY

A•P••

ALPHA
AMPAS
AMPED
AMPHI
AMPHR
AMPLE
AMPLY
APPAL
APPEL
APPLE
APPLY
APPTD
APPTS
ARPAD
ARPEL
ASPCA
ASPEN
ASPIC
ATPAR

A••P•

ADAPT
ADEPT
ADOPT
AGAPE
ALEPH

A•••P

ACTUP
ADDUP
AESOP
AGASP
ALSOP
ASCAP
ATEUP
ATRIP

•AP••

CAPED
CAPEK
CAPER
CAPES
CAPET
CAPON
CAPOS
CAPRA
CAPRI
CAPTS
GAPED
GAPER
GAPES
HAPLY
HAPPY
JAPAN
JAPED
JAPES
KAPOK
KAPPA
KAPUT
LAPAZ
LAPEL
LAPIN
LAPIS
LAPPS
LAPSE
LAPUP
MAPLE
NAPES
NAPPE
NAPPY
PAPAL
PAPAS
PAPAW
PAPER
PAPPI
PAPPY
PAPUA
RAPEE
RAPHE
RAPID
SAPID
SAPIR
SAPOR
SAPPY
TAPAS
TAPED
TAPER
TAPES
TAPIN
TAPIR
VAPID
VAPOR
YAPOK
ZAPPA
ZAPPY

•A•P•

CALPE
CAMPO
CAMPS
CAMPY
CARPE
CARPI
CARPS
DAMPS
GAMPS
GASPE
GASPS
HAPPY
HARPO
HARPS
HARPY
HASPS
KAPPA
LAMPS
LAPPS
MAYPO
NAMPA
NAPPE
NAPPY
PALPI
PALPS
PAMPA
PAPPI
PAPPY
RALPH
RAMPS
RASPS
RASPY
SALPA
SALPS
SAMPS
SAPPY
TAMPA
TAMPS
TARPS
TAUPE
VAMPS
WARPS
WASPS
YAMPA
YAWPS
ZAPPA
ZAPPY

•A••P

DAMUP
EATUP
GALOP
GASUP
JAMUP
LAPUP
LAYUP
NAACP
PAYUP
RANUP
SALEP
SATUP
TAGUP
WADUP

••AP•

ADAPT
AGAPE
CHAPS
CLAPS
COAPT
CRAPE
CRAPS
DRAPE
ETAPE
FLAPS
FRAPS
GOAPE
GRAPE
GRAPH
GRAPY
HEAPS
INAPT
KNAPS
LEAPS
LEAPT
NEAPS
OKAPI
REAPS
SCAPA
SCAPE
SHAPE
SLAPS
SNAPS
SOAPS
SOAPY
SWAPS
TRAPP
TRAPS
UNAPT
WRAPS
WRAPT

••A•P

AGASP
CHAMP
CLAMP
CLASP
CRAMP
GRAMP
GRASP
NAACP
SCALP
SCAMP
SCARP
SCAUP
SHARP
STAMP
SWAMP
THARP
TRAMP
TRAPP

•••AP

ASCAP
CHEAP
ONTAP
PTRAP
RECAP
REMAP
RETAP
SCRAP
STRAP
UNCAP

AQ•••

AQABA
AQUAE
AQUAS

A•••Q

ANTIQ

•AQ••

MAQUI
YAQUI

•A••Q

BARBQ

••AQ•

IRAQI

AR•••

ARABS
ARABY
ARAME
ARBER
ARBOR
ARBRE
ARCED
ARCHI
ARCHY
ARDEN
ARDOR
AREAL
AREAR
AREAS
ARECA
ARENA
ARENS
ARENT
ARETE
ARGIL
ARGOL
ARGON
ARGOS
ARGOT
ARGUE
ARGUS
ARHAT
ARHUS
ARIAN
ARIAS
ARICA
ARIEL
ARIES
ARILS
ARION
ARISE
ARITH
ARIUM
ARIUS
ARKIN
ARLEN
ARLES
ARMED
ARMEE
ARMET
ARMOR
ARNAZ
ARNEL
ARNIE
AROAR
AROID
AROMA
AROSE
ARPAD
ARPEL
ARRAN
ARRAS
ARRAU
ARRAY
ARRET
ARRIS
ARROW
ARROZ
ARSIS
ARSON
ARTAL
ARTEL
ARTES
ARTHR
ARTIE
ARTIS
ARTOO
ARTSY
ARTUR
ARUBA
ARUMS
ARYAN

A•R••

AARON
ABRAM
ABRIS
ACRED
ACRES
ACRID
ADREM
AERIE
AFRIT
AFROS
AGREE
AGRIC
AGRON
AIRED
AIRES
AKRON
AORTA
APRES
APRIL
APRON
ARRAN
ARRAS
ARRAU
ARRAY
ARRET
ARRIS
ARROW
ARROZ
ATRIA
ATRIP
AURAE
AURAL
AURAR
AURAS
AUREI
AURIC
AURUM
AVRIL
AYRES

A••R•

ABBRS
ABORT
ACARI
ACCRA
ACERB
ACORN
ACURA
ADORE
ADORN
AFARS
AFIRE
AFORE
AFTRA
AGARS
AGERS
AGGRO
AGORA
AHORA
AKIRA
ALARM
ALERT
ALFRE
ALORS
AMARA
AMBRY
AMIRS
AMORE
AMORT
AMORY
ANDRE
ANDRO
ANGRY
ANTRA
ANTRE
APART
APERS
APERY
APORT
ARBRE
ASTRA
ASTRE
ASTRO
ATARI
AUDRA
AUTRE
AUTRY
AVARS
AVERS
AVERT
AVERY
AWARD
AWARE
AYERS
AZURE

A•••R

ABHOR
ABLER
ABNER
ACTER
ACTOR
ADAIR
ADDER
ADLER
AEGIR
AESIR
AFTER
AILER
AIMER
AKBAR
ALCOR
ALDER
ALGER
ALLER
ALTAR
ALTER
ALVAR
AMBER
AMEER
AMOUR
AMPHR
ANDOR
ANEAR
ANGER
ANSER
ANWAR
APTER
ARBER
ARBOR
ARDOR
AREAR
ARMOR
AROAR
ARTHR
ARTUR
ASHER
ASHUR
ASKER
ASNER
ASSUR
ASSYR
ASTER
ASTIR
ASTOR
ATPAR
ATTAR
ATWAR
AUBER
AUGER
AUGUR
AURAR
AUSTR
AVOIR

•AR••

AARON
BARBQ
BARBS
BARCA
BARDS
BARED
BARER
BARES
BARGE
BARIC
BARIT
BARKS
BARMS
BARMY
BARNS
BARON
BARRE
BARRY
BARTH
BARTS
BARTY
CARAT
CARBO
CARBS
CARDI
CARDS
CARED
CARER
CARES
CARET
CAREW
CAREY
CARGO
CARIA
CARIB
CARKS
CARLA
CARLE
CARLO
CARLY
CARNE
CARNY
CAROB
CAROL
CAROM
CARON
CARPE
CARPI
CARPS
CARRE
CARRY
CARTA
CARTE
CARTS
CARVE
DARBY
DARED
DARER
DARES
DARIN
DARIO
DARKS
DARLA
DARNS
DARTH
DARTS
DARYA
DARYL
EARED
EARLE
EARLS
EARLY
EARNS
EARTH
FARAD
FARAH
FARCE
FARCI
FARED
FARER
FARES
FARGO
FARMS
FAROE
FARON
FAROS
FARSI
GARBO
GARBS
GARDA
GARDE
GARNI
GAROU
GARRY
GARTH
HARAR
HARDY
HARED
HAREM

HARES
HARKS
HARMS
HARPO
HARPS
HARPY
HARRY
HARSH
HARTE
HARTS
HARUM
JARLS
JARRE
KARAN
KARAT
KAREL
KAREN
KARLA
KARMA
KAROL
KARSH
LARAM
LARAS
LARCH
LARDS
LARDY
LARES
LARGE
LARGO
LARKS
LARRY
LARUE
LARVA
MARAS
MARAT
MARCH
MARCO
MARCY
MARDI
MARES
MARGE
MARGO
MARIA
MARIE
MARIN
MARIO
MARIS
MARKS
MARLA
MARLO
MARLS
MARLY
MARNE
MARRY
MARSH
MARTA
MARTI
MARTS
MARTY
MARVY
MARYS
NARAS
NARCO
NARCS
NARDS
NARES
NAREW
NARIS
NARKS
OARED
PARCA
PARCH
PARDI
PARDO
PARDS
PARED
PAREE
PAREN
PARER
PARES
PAREU
PARIS
PARKA
PARKS
PARLE
PARMA
PAROL
PAROS
PARRY
PARSE
PARTE
PARTI
PARTS
PARTY
RAREE
RARER
RARES
SARAH
SARAN
SARDS
SARGE
SARGO
SARIS
SAROD
SAROS
SARTO
TARDE
TARDY
TARES
TARGE
TARNS
TAROK
TAROT
TARPS
TARRY
TARSI
TARTS
VARAS
VARIA
VARIG
VARIX
VARNA
WARDS
WARES
WARMS
WARNS
WARPS
WARTS
WARTY
YARDS
YARNS
ZARFS

•A•R•

BAIRD
BAIRN
BARRE
BARRY
BASRA
CADRE
CAIRN
CAIRO
CAMRY
CAPRA
CAPRI
CARRE
CARRY
DAIRY
EAGRE
FAIRE
FAIRS
FAIRY
FAURE
GARRY
GAURS
HAIRS
HAIRY
HARRY
HAVRE
IATRO
IATRY
JAHRE
JARRE
KAURI
LAIRD
LAIRS
LARRY
LAURA
MACRO
MADRE
MAHRE
MAORI
MARRY
MATRI
MATRO
MAURY
NACRE
NAIRA
NAIRN
NAURU
PADRE
PAIRS
PARRY
PATRI
SABRA
SABRE
SACRA
SACRE
SACRO
TAHRS
TARRY
TATRA
TAYRA
ZAIRE

•A••R

BABAR
BABER
BAKER
BALER
BARER
BASER
BATOR
BAUER
BAYAR
BAYER
CABER
CAGER
CANER
CAPER
CARER
CATER
CAVER
DAKAR
DAMAR
DARER
DATER
EAGER
EATER
FABER
FACER
FAKER
FAKIR
FARER
FAVOR
GABOR
GAMER
GAPER
GASTR
GATOR
GAYER
GAZER
HABER
HADAR
HAGAR
HALER
HARAR
HATER
HAUER
HAVER
HAZER
KADAR
KAFIR
LABOR
LACER
LADER
LAGER
LAKER
LAMAR
LAMER
LASER
LATER
LAVER
LAXER
LAYER
LAZAR
MAJOR
MAKER
MALAR
MANOR
MASER
MASUR
MATER
MAYER
MAYOR
MAZER
NADER
NADIR
NAMER
NAMUR
OATER
PACER
PAGER
PALER
PAMIR
PAPER
PARER
PATER
PAVER
PAWER
PAYER
QATAR
RACER
RADAR
RAFER
RAKER
RAMAR
RANDR
RARER
RATER
RAVER
RAWER
RAZOR
SABER
SAFER
SAGER
SAKER
SAMAR
SANER
SAPIR
SAPOR
SATYR
SAVER
SAVOR
SAYER
TABOR
TAKER
TALER
TAMER
TAPER
TAPIR
TASER
TATAR
TATER
TAXER
VADER
VALOR
VANIR
VAPOR
VATER
WADER
WAFER
WAGER
WALER
WANER
WATER
WAVER
WAXER
YASIR

••AR•

ACARI
AFARS
AGARS
ALARM
AMARA
APART
ATARI
AVARS
AWARD
AWARE
BEARD
BEARS
BLARE
BOARD
BOARS
CHARD
CHARM
CHARO
CHARS
CHART
CHARY
CLARA
CLARE
CLARK
CLARO
CZARS
DEARS
DEARY
DIARY
DWARF
FEARS
FLARE
GEARS
GEARY
GLARE
GLARY
GNARL
GNARS
GUARD
GUARS
HEARD
HEARN
HEARS
HEART
HOARD
HOARS
HOARY
IBARS
INARI
IZARD
IZARS
JBARS
KMART
KNARS
LEARN
LEARY
LIARD
LIARS
MEARA
NEARS
OHARA
OHARE
OMARR
OPART
OTARU
OTARY
OZARK
PEARL
PEARS
PEARY
PHARM
QUARK
QUART
REARM
REARS
ROARS
RUARK
SCARE
SCARF
SCARP
SCARS
SCARY
SEARS
SHARD
SHARE
SHARI
SHARK
SHARP
SMART
SNARE
SNARK
SNARL
SOARS
SPARE
SPARK
SPARS
STARE
STARK
STARR
STARS
START
SWARD
SWARF
SWARM
SWART
TBARS
TEARS
TEARY
THARP
TIARA
TSARS
UNARM
WEARS
WEARY
WHARF
YEARN
YEARS
ZBARS

••A•R

ADAIR
BLAIR
CHAIR
CLAIR
FLAIR
GLAIR
OHAIR
OMARR
ONAIR
QUADR
REAIR
STAIR
STARR
USAIR

•••AR

AKBAR
ALTAR
ALVAR
ANEAR
ANWAR
AREAR
AROAR
ATPAR
ATTAR
ATWAR
AURAR
BABAR
BAYAR
BIHAR
BLEAR
BOYAR
BRIAR
BYFAR
CEDAR
CESAR
CIGAR
CLEAR
DAKAR
DAMAR
DEBAR
DEWAR
DINAR
DREAR
EDGAR
EGGAR
ELGAR
EMBAR
FILAR
FRIAR
GOFAR
GULAR
HADAR
HAGAR
HARAR
KADAR
LAMAR
LAZAR
LEHAR
LEVAR
LUNAR
MALAR
MIZAR
MOLAR
MYLAR
NOPAR
OSCAR
OSKAR
PILAR
POLAR
QATAR
RADAR
RAMAR
REBAR
RETAR
SAMAR
SEGAR
SHEAR
SITAR
SMEAR
SOFAR
SOLAR
SONAR
SPEAR
SUGAR
SWEAR
TATAR
UNBAR
VELAR
VICAR
VOLAR
ZOHAR

AS•••

ASAMA
ASANA
ASCAP
ASCII
ASCOT
ASCUS
ASDIC
ASHBY
ASHEN
ASHER
ASHES
ASHUR
ASIAN
ASIDE
ASKED
ASKER
ASKEW
ASNER
ASOKA
ASONE
ASPCA
ASPEN
ASPIC
ASSAD
ASSAI
ASSAM
ASSAY
ASSES
ASSET
ASSEZ
ASSNS
ASSOC
ASSTD
ASSTS
ASSUR
ASSYR
ASTER
ASTIN
ASTIR
ASTON
ASTOR
ASTRA
ASTRE
ASTRO
ASWAN
ASYET
ASYLA

A•S••

AESIR
AESOP
AHSIN
AISHA
AISLE
AISNE
AKSUM
ALSOP
ANSAE
ANSEL
ANSER
ANSON
APSES
APSIS
APSOS
ARSIS
ARSON
ASSAD
ASSAI
ASSAM
ASSAY
ASSES
ASSET
ASSEZ
ASSNS
ASSOC
ASSTD
ASSTS
ASSUR
ASSYR
ATSEA
AUSSI
AUSTR

A••S•

ABASE
ABASH
ABUSE
ABYSM
ABYSS
ADUST
AGASP
ALIST
AMASS
AMISH
AMISS
AMUSE
ANGST
ANISE
ANTSY
APISH
ARISE
AROSE
ARTSY
AUSSI
AVAST
AVISO
AWASH
AZUSA

A•••S

AAMES
ABBAS
ABBES
ABBRS
ABETS
ABRIS
ABUTS
ABYSS
ACADS
ACCTS
ACHES
ACIDS
ACMES
ACRES
ADAMS
ADDIS
ADIOS
ADITS
ADZES
AEDES
AEGIS
AEONS
AFARS
AFROS
AGALS
AGARS
AGERS
AGHAS
AGIOS
AGNES
AGNUS
AGUES
AHOYS
AIDES
AINUS
AIRES
AKEES
AKINS
ALDUS
ALEFS
ALIAS
ALIFS
ALLES
ALOES
ALORS
ALTOS
ALTUS
ALUMS
AMAHS
AMASS
AMBOS
AMENS
AMIES
AMIRS
AMISS
AMPAS
AMYLS
ANAIS
ANDES
ANGES
ANGUS
ANILS
ANKHS
ANNES
ANNUS
ANOAS
ANTAS
ANTES
ANTIS
APERS
APHIS
APLUS
APPTS
APRES
APSES
APSIS
APSOS
AQUAS
ARABS
AREAS
ARENS
ARGOS
ARGUS
ARHUS
ARIAS
ARIES
ARILS
ARIUS
ARLES
ARRAS
ARRIS
ARSIS
ARTES
ARTIS
ARUMS
ASCUS
ASHES
ASSES
ASSNS
ASSTS
ATHOS
ATLAS
ATMOS
ATNOS
ATOMS
ATTYS
AUDIS
AUJUS
AULIS
AUNTS
AURAS
AUTOS
AVARS
AVENS
AVERS
AVGAS
AVOWS
AWACS
AWOLS
AXELS
AXILS
AXLES
AXONS
AYAHS
AYERS
AYRES
AZANS

•AS••

BASAL
BASED
BASEL
BASER
BASES
BASHO
BASIC
BASIE
BASIL
BASIN
BASIS
BASKS
BASOV
BASRA
BASSI
BASSO
BASTE
CASCA
CASCO
CASED
CASES
CASEY
CASIO
CASKS
CASTE
CASTS
CASUS
DASHI
EASED
EASEL
EASES
EASTS
FASTS
GASES
GASPE
GASPS
GASSY
GASTR
GASUP
HASAT
HASID
HASNT
HASON
HASPS
HASSO
HASTA
HASTE
HASTO
HASTY
JASON
KASEM
KASHA
LASED
LASER
LASES
LASSO
LASTS
MASAI
MASER
MASHY
MASKS
MASON
MASSE
MASSY
MASTS
MASUR
NASAL
NASBY
NASHE
NASTY
OASES
OASIS
OASTS
PASCH
PASCO
PASEO
PASES
PASHA
PASSE
PASSU
PASSY
PASTA
PASTE
PASTO
PASTS
PASTY
RASED
RASES
RASHT
RASPS
RASPY
RASTA
SASES
SASHA
SASSY
TASER
TASKS
TASSE
TASSO
TASTE
TASTY
VASCO
VASES
WASHY
WASNT
WASPS
WASTE
YASIR

•A•S•

BAKST
BALSA
BASSI
BASSO
CANSO
CANST
CAUSE
DAISY
DANSE
FALSE
FARSI
FAUST
GASSY
GAUSS
HADST
HANSA
HARSH
HASSO
HAUSA
HAWSE
KANSA
KARSH
LAPSE
LASSO
MANSE
MARSH
MASSE
MASSY
MATSU
MAYST
NAISH
PABST
PALSY
PANSY
PARSE
PASSE
PASSU
PASSY
PATSY
PAUSE
RAISA
RAISE
RATSO
SALSA
SASSY
SAYSO
TANSY
TARSI
TASSE
TASSO
VALSE
WAIST
WALSH
WALSY

•A••S

AAMES
BAALS
BABAS
BABES
BABYS
BACKS
BAHTS
BAILS
BAITS
BAKES
BALAS
BALDS
BALES
BALKS
BALLS
BALMS
BALTS
BANCS
BANDS
BANES
BANGS
BANKS
BANNS
BARBS
BARDS
BARES
BARKS
BARMS
BARNS
BARTS
BASES
BASIS
BASKS
BATES
BATHS
BATTS
BAWLS
CADIS
CAFES
CAGES
CAKES
CALKS
CALLS
CALMS
CAMPS
CAMUS
CANES
CANIS
CANTS
CAPES
CAPOS
CAPTS
CARBS
CARDS
CARES
CARKS
CARPS
CARTS
CASES
CASKS
CASTS
CASUS
CATES
CAULS
CAVES
DACES
DADOS
DALES
DAMES
DAMNS
DAMPS
DANES
DANGS
DARES
DARKS
DARNS
DARTS
DATES
DAUBS
DAVIS
DAVOS
DAVYS
DAWES
DAWNS
DAZES
EAMES
EARLS
EARNS
EASES
EASTS
EAVES
FACES
FACTS
FADES
FADOS
FAILS
FAIRS
FAKES
FALLS
FAMES
FANES
FANGS
FARES
FARMS
FAROS
FASTS
FATES
FAUNS
FAVES
FAWNS
FAXES
FAZES
GAELS
GAFFS
GAGES
GAINS
GAITS
GAIUS
GALAS
GALES
GALLS
GAMES
GAMPS
GANGS
GAOLS
GAPES
GARBS
GASES
GASPS
GATES
GATOS
GAUDS
GAULS
GAURS
GAUSS
GAWKS
GAZES
HACKS
HADES
HAFTS
HAHAS
HAIKS
HAILS
HAIRS
HAJIS
HAKES
HALAS
HALES
HALLS
HALOS
HALTS
HAMES
HANDS
HANES
HANGS
HANKS
HARES
HARKS
HARMS
HARPS
HARTS
HASPS
HATES
HAULS
HAVES
HAWKS
HAYES
HAZES
IAMBS
JACKS
JADES
JAILS
JAINS
JAKES
JAMBS
JAMES
JANIS
JANUS
JAPES
JARLS
JATOS
JAVAS
KAKAS
KAKIS
KALES
KAVAS
KAYOS
LACES
LACKS
LADES
LADYS
LAGOS
LAICS
LAIRS
LAIUS
LAKES
LAMAS
LAMBS
LAMES
LAMPS
LANDS
LANES
LAPIS
LAPPS
LARAS
LARDS
LARES
LARKS
LASES
LASTS
LATHS
LAUDS
LAVAS
LAVES
LAWES
LAWNS
LAZES
MACES
MACYS
MAGES
MAGUS
MAIDS
MAILS
MAINS
MAKES
MAKOS
MALES
MALLS
MALTS
MAMAS
MANES
MANOS
MARAS
MARES
MARIS
MARKS
MARLS
MARTS
MARYS
MASKS
MASTS
MATES
MATHS
MAULS
MAVIS
MAXES
MAXIS
MAYAS
MAZES
NABES
NAILS
NAMES
NANAS
NAPES
NARAS
NARCS
NARDS
NARES
NARIS
NARKS
NAVES
NAXOS
OAKES
OASES
OASIS
OASTS
OATES
OATHS
PACAS
PACES
PACKS
PACTS
PAGES
PAILS
PAINS
PAIRS
PALES
PALLS
PALMS
PALOS
PALPS
PANES
PANGS
PANTS
PAPAS
PARDS
PARES
PARIS
PARKS
PAROS
PARTS
PASES
PASTS
PATES
PATHS
PAVES
PAVIS
PAWLS
PAWNS
RACES
RACKS
RAFTS
RAGAS
RAGES
RAIDS
RAILS
RAINS
RAJAS
RAKES

RAKIS RAMIS RAMOS RAMPS RANDS RANIS RANKS RANTS RARES RASES RASPS RATES RATHS RAVES RAWLS RAZES SAABS SACHS SACKS SAENS SAFES SAGAS SAGES SAGOS SAILS SAKES SALES SALPS SALTS SAMMS SAMOS SAMPS SANDS SARDS SARIS SAROS SASES SATES SAUKS SAVES SAXES TABIS TACKS TACOS TAELS TAGUS TAHRS TAILS TAKES TALES TALKS TALUS TAMES TAMPS TANGS TANKS TAPAS TAPES TARES TARNS TARPS TARTS TASKS TAXES TAXIS VADIS VAGUS VALES VAMOS VAMPS VANES VARAS VASES WAALS

WADES WADIS WAFTS WAGES WAIFS WAILS WAINS WAITS WAKES WALES WALKS WALLS WANDS WANES WANTS WARDS WARES WARMS WARNS WARPS WARTS WASPS WATTS WAVES WAXES XAXES XAXIS YANKS YARDS YARNS YATES YAWLS YAWNS YAWPS YAXES YAXIS ZARFS ZAXES ZAXIS

••AS•

ABASE ABASH AGASP AMASS AVAST AWASH BEAST BLASE BLASS BLAST BOAST BRASH BRASS CEASE CHASE CHASM CLASH CLASP CLASS COAST CRASH CRASS DNASE ERASE FEAST FLASH FLASK GLASS GNASH GRASP GRASS IPASS KVASS

LEASE LEASH LEAST LHASA NYASA OMASA PEASE PHASE PLASH PLASM PRASE QUASH QUASI RNASE ROAST SLASH SMASH SPASM STASH SWASH TEASE TOAST TRASH UKASE YEAST

••A•S

ACADS ADAMS AFARS AGALS AGARS AMAHS AMASS ANAIS ARABS AVARS AWACS AYAHS AZANS BAALS BEADS BEAKS BEALS BEAMS BEANS BEARS BEATS BEAUS BLABS BLAHS BLASS BLATS BOARS BOATS BRADS BRAES BRAGS BRANS BRASS BRATS BRAYS CHAOS CHAPS CHARS CHATS CHAWS CLAMS CLANS CLAPS CLASS CLAUS CLAWS CLAYS

COALS COATS CRABS CRAGS CRAMS CRAPS CRASS CRAWS CZARS DEALS DEANS DEARS DIALS DRABS DRAGS DRAMS DRATS DRAWS DRAYS DUADS DYADS EDAMS EGADS EVANS EXAMS FEARS FEATS FIATS FLAGS FLAMS FLANS FLAPS FLATS FLAWS FLAYS FOALS FOAMS FRAIS FRANS FRAPS FRATS FRAYS GEARS GHATS GLADS GLASS GNARS GNATS GNAWS GOADS GOALS GOATS GRABS GRADS GRAMS GRASS GRAYS GUARS HEADS HEALS HEAPS HEARS HEATS HOARS IBARS IMAMS IPASS ITALS IZARS JBARS JEANS KEATS KHANS KLAUS

KNAPS KNARS KOANS KRAUS KVASS KYATS LEADS LEAFS LEAKS LEANS LEAPS LIARS LOADS LOAFS LOAMS LOANS LUAUS MEADS MEALS MEANS MEATS MOANS MOATS NEAPS NEARS NEATS NOAHS OKAYS OPAHS OPALS ORALS OVALS PEAKS PEALS PEARS PEATS PLANS PLATS PLAYS PRAMS PRAUS PRAYS PSATS QUADS QUAGS QUAYS READS REALS REAMS REAPS REARS RIALS ROADS ROAMS ROANS ROARS SAABS SCABS SCADS SCAMS SCANS SCARS SCATS SEALS SEAMS SEARS SEATS SHADS SHAGS SHAHS SHAMS SHANS SHAYS SIALS

SLABS SLAGS SLAMS SLAPS SLATS SLAVS SLAWS SLAYS SNAGS SNAPS SOAKS SOAPS SOARS SPADS SPANS SPARS SPATS SPAYS STABS STAGS STARS STATS STAYS SWABS SWAGS SWANS SWAPS SWATS SWAYS TBARS TEAKS TEALS TEAMS TEARS THAIS THATS THAWS TOADS TRAMS TRANS TRAPS TRAYS TSARS UNAUS URALS VIALS WAALS WEALS WEANS WEARS WHAMS WHATS WOADS WRAPS XRAYS YEANS YEARS YEATS YUANS ZBARS ZEALS

•••AS

ABBAS AGHAS ALIAS AMPAS ANOAS ANTAS AQUAS AREAS ARIAS ARRAS ATLAS

AURAS AVGAS BABAS BALAS BEMAS BETAS BOLAS BORAS CHIAS CODAS COLAS COMAS CUNAS CYMAS DEGAS DIVAS DONAS DUKAS DUMAS EDDAS ELIAS EPHAS ETNAS EYRAS FETAS FLEAS GALAS GETAS HAHAS HALAS HORAS HOYAS HULAS HYLAS IDEAS INCAS IOTAS IZBAS JAVAS JONAS JOTAS JUDAS KAKAS KAVAS KIVAS KOLAS LAMAS LARAS LAVAS LIMAS LIRAS LOTAS LUBAS LUCAS LUKAS MAMAS MARAS MAYAS MESAS MICAS MIDAS MIMAS MINAS MOLAS MYNAS NANAS NARAS NINAS NIPAS NOVAS OCCAS OKRAS OLLAS ORCAS

PACAS PAPAS PICAS PIKAS PIMAS PITAS PLEAS PROAS PSOAS PULAS PUMAS PUNAS PUPAS RAGAS RAJAS RHEAS ROTAS SAGAS SILAS SKUAS SODAS SOFAS SOMAS SORAS SOYAS SRTAS STOAS SURAS TAPAS TEXAS TOGAS TUBAS TUNAS ULNAS UNCAS VARAS VEDAS VEGAS VILAS VINAS VISAS VITAS YMCAS YUMAS YWCAS ZETAS

AT•••

ATALL ATARI ATBAT ATBAY ATEAM ATEIN ATEUP ATHOL ATHON ATHOS ATILT ATION ATIVE ATLAS ATMAN ATMOS ATNOS ATOLL ATOMS ATOMY ATONE ATPAR ATRIA ATRIP ATSEA ATTAR

ATTIC ATTYS ATWAR

A•T••

ACTED ACTER ACTII ACTIN ACTIV ACTON ACTOR ACTUP AETAT AETNA AFTER AFTON AFTRA AITCH ALTAI ALTAR ALTER ALTHO ALTON ALTOS ALTUS ANTAE ANTAL ANTAS ANTED ANTES ANTHO ANTIC ANTIQ ANTIS ANTON ANTRA ANTRE ANTSY APTED APTER APTLY ARTAL ARTEL ARTES ARTHR ARTIE ARTIS ARTOO ARTSY ARTUR ASTER ASTIN ASTIR ASTON ASTOR ASTRA ASTRE ASTRO ATTAR ATTIC ATTYS AUTOS AUTRE AUTRY AZTEC

A••T•

AALTO ABATE ABETS ABUTS ACCTS ACETO

ACUTE ADDTO ADITS ADYTA AGATE AGITA AIMTO AKITA ALATE ALETA AMATI AMATO AMITY ANITA AORTA APPTD APPTS ARETE ARITH ASSTD ASSTS AUNTS AUNTY AUSTR AZOTE AZOTH

A•••T

ABAFT ABBOT ABORT ABOUT ADAPT ADEPT ADINT ADMIT ADOPT ADOUT ADULT ADUST AETAT AFLAT AFOOT AFRIT AGENT AGLET AIMAT ALERT ALEUT ALIST ALLOT ALOFT AMBIT AMENT AMORT AMVET ANENT ANGST APART APORT ARENT ARGOT ARHAT ARMET ARRET ASCOT ASSET ASYET ATBAT ATILT AUDIT AUGHT AVANT AVAST

AVERT AWAIT

•AT••

BATAK BATCH BATED BATES BATHE BATHO BATHS BATHY BATIK BATON BATOR BATTS BATTY CATCH CATER CATES CATHY CATTY DATED DATER DATES DATUM EATAT EATEN EATER EATIN EATIT EATON EATUP FATAL FATED FATES FATHA FATLY FATTY GATED GATES GATOR GATOS GATUN HATCH HATED HATER HATES HATLO IATRO IATRY JATOS KATHY KATIE LATCH LATEN LATER LATEX LATHE LATHS LATIN LATKE LATTE MATCH MATED MATEO MATER MATES MATEY MATHS MATIN MATRI MATRO MATSU

MATTE MATZO NATAL NATCH NATTY OATEN OATER OATES OATHS PATCH PATED PATEK PATEN PATER PATES PATHE PATHO PATHS PATIO PATLY PATNA PATON PATRI PATSY PATTI PATTY QATAR RATCH RATED RATEL RATER RATES RATHS RATIO RATON RATSO RATTY SATAN SATBY SATED SATES SATIE SATIN SATON SATUP SATYR TATAR TATER TATRA TATTY TATUM VATER VATIC WATCH WATER WATTS YATES

•A•T•

AALTO BAHTS BAITS BALTS BANTU BARTH BARTS BARTY BASTE BATTS BATTY CACTI CANTO CANTS CAPTS

CARTA CARTE CARTS CASTE CASTS CATTY DANTE DARTH DARTS EARTH EASTS FACTO FACTS FAITH FANTA FASTS FATTY GAITS GARTH GASTR HADTO HAFTS HAITI HALTS HARTE HARTS HASTA HASTE HASTO HASTY HAUTE LACTI LACTO LAHTI LAITY LANTZ LASTS LATTE LAYTO MALTA MALTS MALTY MANTA MARTA MARTI MARTS MARTY MASTS MATTE NAFTA NASTY NATTY OASTS PACTS PANTO PANTS PANTY PARTE PARTI PARTS PARTY PASTA PASTE PASTO PASTS PASTY PATTI PATTY PAYTV RAFTS RAITT RANTO RANTS RASTA

RATTY SALTA SALTS SALTY SANTA SANTE SANTO SARTO SAUTE SAWTO TANTE TARTS TASTE TASTY TATTY WAFTS WAITE WAITS WAITZ WALTZ WANTS WARTS WARTY WASTE WATTS XACTO YALTA ZANTE

•A••T

BAGIT BAKST BARIT CABOT CADET CANIT CANST CAPET CARAT CARET DAUNT DAVIT EATAT EATIT FACET FAGOT FAINT FAULT FAUST GAMUT GAUNT GAVOT HABIT HADAT HADNT HADST HASAT HASNT HAUNT JABOT JANET JAUNT KAPUT KARAT MAGOT MAMET MANET MARAT MAYST NACHT PABST PAGET PAINT PAWAT

RABAT RAITT RAMET RANAT RASHT SABOT SADAT SAGET SAINT SALUT SAULT TACET TACIT TAINT TAROT TAUNT VALET VAULT VAUNT WAIST WASNT YACHT YAKUT

••AT•

ABATE AGATE ALATE AMATI AMATO BEATS BLATS BOATS BRATS CHATS COATI COATS CRATE DRATS ELATE ENATE ERATO FEATS FIATS FLATS FLATT FRATS GHATS GNATS GOATS GRATA GRATE HEATH HEATS HYATT IRATE KEATS KYATS LOATH MEATS MEATY MOATS NEATH NEATO NEATS ONATE ORATE OVATE PEATS PEATY PLATA PLATE PLATH PLATO

PLATS PLATT PLATY PRATE PRATO PRATT PSATS REATA RIATA SCATS SEATO SEATS SKATE SLATE SLATS SLATY SNATH SPATE SPATS STATE STATS SWATH SWATS THATS WHATD WHATS WRATH WYATT YEATS

••A•T

ABAFT ADAPT APART AVANT AVAST AWAIT BEAST BEAUT BLAST BOAST BRACT BRANT CHANT CHART COACT COAPT COAST CRAFT DEALT DRAFT ENACT EPACT EXACT EXALT FEAST FLATT GIANT GRAFT GRANT HEART HYATT INAPT KMART KRAFT KRAIT KRAUT LEANT LEAPT LEAST MEANT OPART ORANT PLAIT

PLANT PLATT PRATT QUANT QUART REACT RIANT ROAST SCANT SHAFT SHALT SHANT SLANT SMALT SMART STADT START SWART THANT TIANT TOAST TRACT TRAIT UNAPT WRAPT WYATT YEAST

•••AT

AETAT AFLAT AIMAT ARHAT ATBAT BEGAT BFLAT BLEAT BLOAT CARAT CERAT CFLAT CHEAT CLEAT CROAT CUGAT DEFAT DERAT DETAT DFLAT DONAT DUCAT EATAT ECLAT EFLAT ESBAT FFLAT FLOAT FLYAT GETAT GFLAT GLOAT GOTAT GREAT GROAT HADAT HASAT HERAT JURAT KARAT KERAT LETAT LOFAT LOPAT MARAT

MURAT NEMAT NIPAT NOFAT PAWAT PLEAT RABAT RANAT SADAT SETAT SHOAT SKEAT SPLAT SPRAT SQUAT STOAT SURAT SWEAT TREAT UBOAT WHEAT

AU•••
AUBER AUDEN AUDIE AUDIO AUDIS AUDIT AUDRA AUGER AUGHT AUGUR AUJUS AULIS AUNTS AUNTY AURAE AURAL AURAR AURAS AUREI AURIC AURUM AUSSI AUSTR AUTOS AUTRE AUTRY AUXIL AUXIN

A•U••
ABUJA ABUSE ABUTS ABUZZ ACUFF ACURA ACUTE ADULT ADUST ADUWA AGUES ALULA ALUMS AMUCK AMUSE AQUAE AQUAS ARUBA ARUMS AZURE AZUSA

A••U•
ABDUL ABOUT ABZUG ACTUP ADDUP ADEUX ADOUT AFOUL AGNUS AINUS AKSUM ALBUM ALDUS ALEUT ALOUD ALTUS AMOUR ANGUS ANHUI ANNUL ANNUM ANNUS ANOUK APLUS ARGUE ARGUS ARHUS ARIUM ARIUS ARTUR ASCUS ASHUR ASSUR ATEUP AUGUR AUJUS AURUM AWFUL

A•••U
ADIEU ANJOU ARRAU

•AU••
BAUER BAUGH BAUME CAULK CAULS CAUSE DAUBS DAUNT FAULT FAUNA FAUNS FAURE FAUST FAUVE GAUDS GAUDY GAUGE GAULS GAUNT GAURS GAUSS GAUZE GAUZY HAUER HAULM HAULS HAUNT HAUSA HAUTE JAUNE JAUNT KAUAI KAURI LAUDE LAUDS LAUGH LAURA MAUDE MAULS MAUNA MAUND MAURY MAUVE NAURU PAULA PAUSE SAUCE SAUCY SAUDI SAUKS SAULT SAUNA SAUTE TAUNT TAUON TAUPE VAULT VAUNT WAUGH

•A•U•
BABUL CAJUN CAMUS CASUS DAMUP DATUM EATUP GAIUS GAMUT GASUP GATUN HAFUN HAGUE HARUM JAMUP JANUS KABUL KAPUT LAIUS LAPUP LARUE LAYUP MAGUS MAKUA MAQUI MASUR NAHUA NAHUM NAMUR OAKUM PADUA PAPUA PAYUP RANUP RAOUL SALUD SALUT SATUP TAGUP TAGUS TALUS TATUM VACUA VADUZ VAGUE VAGUS VALUE WADUP YAKUT YAQUI

•A••U
BANTU BAYOU GAROU HAIKU KANZU MACHU MATSU NAURU PALAU PAREU PASSU SADHU TAEGU

••AU•
BEAUS BEAUT BEAUX BRAUN CHAUD CLAUS FRAUD KLAUS KRAUS KRAUT LUAUS PRAUS SCAUP SHAUN UHAUL UNAUS

••A•U
ISAMU KEANU OTARU SHAMU SNAFU

•••AU
ARRAU DONAU PALAU

AV•••
AVAIL AVANT AVARS AVAST AVENA AVENS AVERS AVERT AVERY AVGAS AVIAN AVILA AVION AVISO AVOID AVOIR AVOWS AVRIL

A•V••
ADVIL ALVAR ALVIN AMVET ANVIL

A••V•
ABOVE ABOVO AGAVE ALAVA ALIVE ATIVE

A•••V
ACTIV ANNIV

•AV••
CAVAE CAVED CAVER CAVES CAVIL DAVAO DAVID DAVIE DAVIS DAVIT DAVOS DAVYS EAVED EAVES FAVES FAVOR GAVEL GAVIN GAVOT HAVEL HAVEN HAVER HAVES HAVOC HAVRE JAVAS KAVAS LAVAL LAVAS LAVED LAVER LAVES LAVIN MAVEN MAVIS NAVAL NAVEL NAVES NAVIG NAVVY PAVED PAVER PAVES PAVIA PAVID PAVIS RAVED RAVEL RAVEN RAVER RAVES RAVIN SAVED SAVER SAVES SAVOR SAVOY SAVVY WAVED WAVER WAVES

•A•V•
CALVE CARVE FAUVE HALVE LARVA MARVY MAUVE NAIVE NAVVY PAAVO SALVE SALVO SAVVY VALVE WAIVE

•A••V
BASOV PAYTV RAJIV YAKOV

••AV•
AGAVE ALAVA BRAVA BRAVE BRAVO CLAVE CRAVE GRAVE GRAVY GUAVA HEAVE HEAVY KNAVE LEAVE PAAVO PEAVY SHAVE SLAVE SLAVS SOAVE STAVE SUAVE TRAVE WEAVE

•••AV
SCHAV

AW•••
AWACS AWAIT AWAKE AWARD AWARE AWASH AWFUL AWING AWNED AWOKE AWOLS

A•W••
AMWAY ANWAR ASWAN ATWAR

A••W•
ADUWA AVOWS

A•••W
AGLOW AGNEW ALLOW ARROW ASKEW

•AW••
BAWDY BAWLS CAWED DAWES DAWNS FAWNS GAWKS GAWKY HAWED HAWKE HAWKS HAWSE JAWED LAWES LAWNS NAWAB PAWAT PAWED PAWER PAWLS PAWNS RAWER RAWLS RAWLY SAWED SAWIN SAWTO TAWNY YAWED YAWLS YAWNS YAWPS

•A•W•
DAIWA

•A••W
CANDW CAREW GAMOW LALAW MACAW NAREW PAPAW YALOW

••AW•
BRAWL BRAWN CHAWS CLAWS CRAWL CRAWS DRAWL DRAWN DRAWS FLAWS GNAWS INAWE OZAWA PRAWN SHAWL SHAWM SHAWN SLAWS SPAWN THAWS TRAWL

••A•W
MIAOW

•••AW
BYLAW INLAW LALAW MACAW PAPAW PSHAW STRAW

AX•••
AXELS AXIAL AXILS AXING AXIOM AXION AXLES AXONS

A•X••
AUXIL AUXIN

A•••X
ADDAX ADEUX ADMIX AFFIX ANNEX

•AX••
FAXED FAXES LAXER LAXLY MAXED MAXES MAXIE MAXIM MAXIS NAXOS SAXES SAXON TAXCO TAXED TAXER TAXES TAXIS TAXON WAXED WAXEN WAXER WAXES XAXES XAXIS YAXES YAXIS ZAXES ZAXIS

•A••X
CALIX CALYX GALAX LATEX RADIX VARIX

••AX•
FLAXY GLAXO

••A•X
BEAUX

•••AX
ADDAX BORAX GALAX HYRAX ICEAX LOMAX LORAX RELAX RETAX REWAX

AY•••
AYAHS AYERS AYRES

A•Y••
ABYSM ABYSS ADYTA ALYCE AMYLO AMYLS ARYAN ASYET ASYLA

A••Y•
ABAYA AHOYS ALKYD ALKYL ALLYL ASSYR ATTYS

A•••Y
ABBEY ACIDY AGLEY AGONY AILEY ALLAY ALLEY ALLOY ALMAY AMBRY AMITY AMORY AMPLY AMWAY ANGRY ANNOY ANOMY ANTSY APERY APLEY APPLY APTLY ARABY ARCHY ARRAY ARTSY ASHBY ASSAY ATBAY ATOMY AUNTY AUTRY AVERY

•AY••
BAYAR BAYED BAYER BAYLE BAYOU CAYCE DAYAK DAYAN DAYNE GAYAL GAYER GAYLE GAYLY HAYDN HAYED HAYEK HAYES JAYNE KAYAK KAYOS LAYBY LAYER LAYIN LAYLA LAYNE LAYON LAYTO LAYUP MAYAN MAYAS MAYBE MAYER MAYON MAYOR MAYPO MAYST PAYED PAYEE PAYER PAYIN PAYNE PAYTV PAYUP RAYED RAYON SAYER SAYSO TAYRA WAYNE ZAYIN

•A•Y•
BABYS CALYX DARYA DARYL DAVYS LADYS MACYS MARYS SANYO SATYR TANYA VANYA

•A••Y
BADLY BAGGY BALKY BALLY BALMY BANDY BANKY BARMY BARRY BARTY BATHY BATTY BAWDY CABBY CADDY CAGEY CAKEY CAMAY CAMPY CAMRY CANBY CANDY CANNY CAREY CARLY CARNY CARRY CASEY CATHY CATTY DADDY DAFFY DAILY DAIRY DAISY DALEY DALLY DANCY DANDY DANNY DARBY EARLY FAIRY FANCY FANNY FATLY FATTY GABBY GANDY GARRY GASSY GAUDY GAUZY GAWKY GAYLY HAIRY HALEY HAMMY HANDY HANKY HAPLY HAPPY HARDY HARPY HARRY HASTY IATRY JAGGY JAZZY KATHY LACEY LAITY LANKY LARDY LARRY LAXLY LAYBY MADLY MALAY MALTY MAMMY MANDY MANLY MANNY MARCY MARLY MARRY MARTY MARVY MASHY MASSY MATEY MAURY NAGGY NAMBY NANCY NANNY NAPPY NASBY NASTY NATTY NAVVY PADDY PALEY PALLY PALMY PALSY PAMBY PANAY PANKY PANSY PANTY PAPPY PARRY PARTY PASSY PASTY PATLY PATSY PATTY RAINY RALLY RANDY RANGY RASPY RATTY RAWLY SADLY SAGGY SALLY SALTY SAMMY SANDY SAPPY SASSY SATBY SAUCY SAVOY SAVVY TABBY TACKY TAFFY TALKY TALLY TAMMY TANDY TANEY TANGY TANSY TARDY TARRY TASTY TATTY TAWNY WACKY WALLY WALSY WANLY WARTY WASHY ZAPPY

••AY•
ABAYA BRAYS CLAYS DRAYS FLAYS FRAYS GRAYS OKAYS PLAYA PLAYS PRAYS QUAYS SHAYS SLAYS SPAYS STAYS SWAYS TRAYS XRAYS

••A•Y
ARABY BEADY BEAMY BEANY BIALY BRADY CHARY CRAZY DEARY DIARY FLAKY FLAMY FLAXY FOAMY GEARY GLARY GRADY GRAPY GRAVY HEADY HEALY HEAVY HOAGY HOARY ITALY LEAFY LEAHY LEAKY LEARY LOAMY MEALY MEANY MEATY ORACY OTARY PEARY PEATY PEAVY PLATY QUAKY READY SCALY SCARY SEALY SEAMY SHADY SHAKY SLATY SNAKY SOAPY STACY STAGY TEARY TOADY TRACY WEARY

•••AY
ALLAY ALMAY AMWAY ARRAY ASSAY ATBAY BELAY BYWAY CAMAY COPAY DECAY DELAY DOUAY DUFAY ELWAY EMBAY ESSAY FORAY INLAY IXNAY LEFAY LEMAY LURAY MALAY MCKAY MORAY MYWAY NOWAY ONLAY OTWAY PANAY POWAY RELAY REPAY SPLAY SPRAY STRAY TODAY TOKAY UNSAY VEDAY VJDAY

AZ•••
AZANS AZIDE AZINE AZOIC AZOTE AZOTH AZTEC AZURE AZUSA

A•Z••
ABZUG ADZES ANZAC ANZIO

A••Z•
ABUZZ AGAZE AMAZE

A•••Z
ABUZZ ALLEZ ARNAZ ARROZ ASSEZ

•AZ••
DAZED DAZES FAZED FAZES GAZED GAZER GAZES HAZED HAZEL HAZER HAZES JAZZY KAZAN KAZOO LAZAR LAZED LAZES MAZDA MAZEL MAZER MAZES RAZED RAZES RAZOR TAZZA YAZOO ZAZEN

•A•Z•
BAIZA BAIZE BAIZE DANZA GAUZE GAUZY JAZZY KANZU LANZA MAIZE MATZO PANZA TAZZA

•A••Z
CADIZ HAFIZ LANTZ LAPAZ MAINZ VADUZ WAITZ WALTZ

••AZ•
AGAZE AMAZE BLAZE BRAZE CRAZE CRAZY DIAZO GHAZI GLAZE GRAZE PLAZA SMAZE SWAZI

••A•Z
FRANZ

•••AZ
ARNAZ HEJAZ LAPAZ TOPAZ

BA•••
BAAED BAALS BABAR BABAS BABEL BABER BABES BABKA BABUL BABYS BACKS BACON BADEN BADGE BADLY BAGEL BAGGY BAGIT BAHAI BAHIA BAHTS BAILS BAIRD BAIRN BAITS BAIZA BAIZE BAKED BAKER BAKES BAKST BALAS BALCH BALDS BALED BALER BALES BALIN BALKH BALKS BALKY BALLS BALLY BALMS BALMY BALSA BALTS BAMBI BANAL BANCO BANCS BANDA BANDB BANDO BANDS BANDY BANES BANFF BANGS BANJO BANKS BANKY BANNS BANTU BARBQ BARBS BARCA BARDS BARED BARER BARES BARGE BARIC BARIT BARKS BARMS BARMY BARNS BARON BARRE BARRY BARTH BARTS BARTY BASAL BASED BASEL BASER BASES BASHO BASIC BASIE BASIL BASIN BASIS BASKS BASOV BASRA BASSI BASSO BASTE BATAK BATCH BATED BATES BATHE BATHO BATHS BATHY BATIK BATON BATOR BATTS BATTY BAUER BAUGH BAUME BAWDY

BAWLS BAYAR BAYED BAYER BAYLE BAYOU

B•A••

BAAED BAALS BBALL BEACH BEADS BEADY BEAKS BEALL BEALS BEAMS BEAMY BEANO BEANS BEANY BEARD BEARS BEAST BEATS BEAUS BEAUT BEAUX BIALY BLABS BLACK BLADE BLAHS BLAIR BLAKE BLAME BLANC BLAND BLANK BLARE BLASE BLASS BLAST BLATS BLAZE BOARD BOARS BOAST BOATS BRACE BRACT BRADS BRADY BRAES BRAGA BRAGG BRAGS BRAHE BRAID BRAIL BRAIN BRAKE BRAND BRANS BRANT BRASH BRASS BRATS BRAUN BRAVA BRAVE BRAVO BRAWL BRAWN BRAYS BRAZE BWANA

B••A•

BABAR BABAS BAHAI BALAS BANAL BASAL BATAK BAYAR BEGAN BEGAT BEHAN BELAY BEMAS BETAS BFLAT BIHAR BINAL BLEAK BLEAR BLEAT BLOAT BOHAI BOLAS BORAH BORAS BORAX BOYAR BREAD BREAK BREAM BRIAN BRIAR BROAD BRYAN BYFAR BYLAW BYWAY

B•••A

BABKA BAHIA BAIZA BALSA BANDA BARCA BASRA BELLA BELVA BEREA BERRA BETTA BIOTA BOHEA BOOLA BOSSA BOTHA BRAGA BRAVA BREDA BROCA BUBBA BUENA BUFFA BULBA BULLA BURMA BURSA BWANA

•BA••

ABABA ABACA ABACI ABACK ABACO ABAFT ABASE ABASH ABATE ABAYA BBALL IBARS JBARS TBARS ZBARS

•B•A•

ABBAS ABEAM ABRAM IBEAM OBEAH UBOAT

•B••A

ABABA ABACA ABAYA ABUJA IBIZA MBIRA

••BA•

ABBAS AKBAR ALBAN ATBAT ATBAY BABAR BABAS CABAL CUBAN DEBAR DUBAI EMBAR EMBAY ESBAT GOBAD HOBAN INBAD IZBAS JUBAL KEBAB LABAN LUBAS RABAT REBAG REBAR SABAH TUBAS UNBAR URBAN

••B•A

BABKA BUBBA COBIA COBRA DEBRA DOBLA DOBRA HABLA HUBBA JABBA LIBRA LIBYA NUBIA SABRA TABLA TIBIA UMBRA YABBA ZEBRA

•••BA

ABABA AMEBA AQABA ARUBA BUBBA BULBA CEIBA CHIBA GALBA GAMBA HUBBA JABBA KAABA MAMBA MELBA PEMBA RUMBA SAMBA SCUBA SHEBA SIMBA SUMBA YABBA YERBA YORBA ZORBA

BB•••

BBALL BBGUN

B•B••

BABAR BABAS BABEL BABER BABES BABKA BABUL BABYS BEBOP BIBBS BIBLE BOBBY BOBUP BUBBA BUBER

B••B•

BAMBI BARBQ BARBS BEEBE BIBBS BILBO BIXBY BLABS BLEBS BLOBS BOBBY BOMBE BOMBS BOOBS BOOBY BRIBE BUBBA BULBA BULBS BURBS BUSBY

B•••B

BANDB BLURB

•BB••

ABBAS ABBES ABBEY ABBIE ABBOT ABBRS EBBED

•B•B•

ABABA

•B••B

ABOMB HBOMB

••BB•

BIBBS BOBBY BUBBA CABBY CUBBY DEBBY GABBY GIBBS HOBBS HOBBY HUBBA HUBBY JABBA LIBBY LOBBY NOBBY NUBBY RABBI REBBE RIBBY ROBBY TABBY TIBBS TUBBY YABBA

••B•B

CUBEB KABOB KEBAB NABOB

BC•••

BCELL

B•C••

BACKS BACON BECHE BECKS BECKY BOCCE BOCCI BUCKO BUCKS BUCKY

B••C•

BALCH BANCO BANCS BARCA BATCH BEACH BEECH BELCH BENCH BIRCH BLACK BLOCH BLOCK BLOCS BOCCE BOCCI BOSCH BOSCO BOSCS BOTCH BRACE BRACT BRECK BRICE BRICK BROCA BROCK BRUCE BRUCH BRYCE BUICK BUNCH BUSCH BUTCH

B•••C

BARIC BASIC BLANC BORIC BRONC

•BC••

NBCTV

•B•C•

ABACA ABACI ABACK ABACO

••B•C

CUBIC REBEC SUBIC XEBEC

B•D••

BADEN BADGE BADLY BEDEW BEDIM BIDDY BIDED BIDEN BIDES BIDON BIDUP BLDGS BODED BODES BUDDY BUDGE

B••D•

BALDS BANDA BANDB BANDO BANDS BANDY BARDS BAWDY BEADS BEADY BENDS BIDDY BINDS BIRDS BIRDY BLADE BLVDS BONDI BONDS BRADS BRADY BREDA BRIDE BRODY BSIDE BUDDY BUNDS BUNDT BUNDY BYRDS

B•••D

BAAED BAIRD BAKED BALED BARED BASED BATED BAYED BEARD BIDED BIFID BIKED BIPED BIPOD BLAND BLEED BLEND BLIND BLOND BLOOD BLUED BOARD BODED BONED BOOED BORED BOUND BOVID BOWED BOXED BRAID BRAND BREAD BREED BROAD BROOD BUILD BUSED

•BD••

ABDUL

•B•D•

ABIDE ABODE

•B••D

ABEND EBBED TBIRD TBOND

••B•D

CUBED EBBED EMBED GIBED GOBAD INBAD INBED JIBED LOBED LUBED RABID REBID ROBED TUBED UNBID

BE•••

BEACH BEADS BEADY BEAKS BEALL BEALS BEAMS BEAMY BEANO BEANS BEANY BEARD BEARS BEAST BEATS BEAUS BEAUT BEAUX BEBOP BECHE BECKS BECKY BEDEW BEDIM BEEBE BEECH BEEFS BEEFY BEENE BEEPS BEERS BEERY BEETS BEFIT BEFOG BEGAN BEGAT BEGET BEGIN BEGOT BEGUM BEGUN BEHAN BEIGE BEING BELAY BELCH BELEM BELIE BELLA BELLE BELLI BELLS BELLY BELOW BELTS BELVA BEMAS BENCH BENDS BENES BENET BENIN BENJI BENNY BENTS BENUE BENZO BEREA BERET BERGH BERGS BERLE BERME BERMS BERNE BERRA BERRY BERTH BERYL BESET BESOM BESOT BESTS BETAS BETEL BETON BETSY BETTA BETTE BETTY BEVEL BEVIN BEYLE BEZEL

B•E••

BCELL BEEBE BEECH BEEFS BEEFY BEENE BEEPS BEERS BEERY BEETS BLEAK BLEAR BLEAT BLEBS BLEED BLEEP BLEND BLENT BLESS BLEST BOEHM BOERS BOEUF BREAD BREAK BREAM BRECK BREDA BREED BREEN BRENT BRERS BREST BRETT BREVE BREWS BUELL BUENA BUENO

B••E•

BAAED BABEL BABER BABES BADEN BAGEL BAKED BAKER BAKES BALED BALER BALES BANES BARED BARER BARES BASED BASEL BASER BASES BATED BATES BAUER BAYED BAYER BEDEW BEGET BELEM BENES BENET BEREA BERET BESET BETEL BEVEL BEZEL BIDED BIDEN BIDES BIKED BIKEL BIKER BIKES BINES BINET BIPED BISES BITER BITES BIZET BLEED BLEEP BLUED BLUER BLUES BLUET BLUEY BODED BODES BOGEY BOHEA BOLES BONED BONER BONES BONET BOOED BOOER BORED BORER BORES BOWED BOWEN BOWER BOWES BOXED BOXER BOXES BOYER BRAES BREED BREEN BRIEF BRIER BRIES BUBER BUSED BUSES BUSEY BUTEO BUYER BYNER BYTES

B•••E

BADGE BAIZE BARGE BARRE BASIE BASTE BATHE BAUME BAYLE BECHE BEEBE BEENE BEIGE BELIE BELLE BENUE BERLE BERME BERNE BETTE BEYLE BIBLE BILGE BINGE BIOME BITTE BLADE BLAKE BLAME BLARE BLASE BLAZE BLOKE BLUME BOCCE BOGIE BOGLE BOHME BOISE BOITE BOMBE BONNE BONZE BOOLE BOONE BOOZE BORGE BORNE BOTHE BOULE BOUSE BOWIE BOYLE BOYNE BRACE BRAHE BRAKE BRAVE BRAZE BREVE BRIBE BRICE BRIDE BRINE BRITE BROKE BROME BRUCE BRULE BRUME BRUTE BRYCE BSIDE BUDGE BUGLE BULGE BURKE BURSE BUTTE BYRNE

•BE••

ABEAM ABELE ABEND ABETS CBERS EBERT IBEAM IBERT OBEAH OBELI OBESE OBEYS

•B•E•

ABBES ABBEY ABLER ABNER EBBED EBSEN IBSEN OBIES OBJET OBOES

•B••E

ABASE ABATE ABBIE ABELE ABIDE ABODE ABOVE ABUSE OBESE TBONE

••BE•

ABBES ABBEY ALBEE ALBEN AMBER ARBER AUBER BABEL BABER BABES BUBER CABER CUBEB CUBED CUBES EBBED EMBED EMBER FABER FIBER GIBED GIBER GIBES GOBEL HABER INBED JIBED JIBES LABEL LIBEL LOBED LOBES LUBED LUBES MABEL NABES NOBEL OMBER REBEC REBEL ROBED ROBES RUBEN RUBES SABER SOBER TIBER TIBET TOBEY TUBED TUBER TUBES UMBEL UMBER UZBEK VIBES WEBER XEBEC ZIBET

••B•E

ABBIE ALBEE AMBLE ARBRE BIBLE CABLE DOBIE DOBLE EUBIE FABLE FIBRE GABLE IMBUE LIBRE NOBLE OMBRE REBBE ROBLE RUBLE SABLE SABRE TABLE

•••BE

ADOBE BEEBE BOMBE BRIBE FROBE GLEBE GLOBE GREBE LETBE MAYBE NIOBE PHOBE PLEBE PROBE REBBE THEBE TRIBE

BF•••

BFLAT

B•F••

BEFIT BEFOG BIFFS BIFFY BIFID BOFFO BOFFS BUFFA BUFFI BUFFO BUFFS BUFFY BYFAR

B••F•

BANFF BEEFS BEEFY BIFFS BIFFY BLUFF BOFFO BOFFS BUFFA BUFFI BUFFO BUFFS BUFFY

B•••F

BANFF BLUFF BOEUF BRIEF

•B•F•

ABAFT

BG•••

BGIRL

B•G••

BAGEL BAGGY BAGIT BBGUN BEGAN BEGAT BEGET BEGIN BEGOT BEGUM BEGUN BIGHT BIGON BIGOS BIGOT BOGEY BOGGS BOGGY BOGIE BOGLE BOGUS BUGGY BUGLE BUGSY BYGUM

B••G•

BADGE BAGGY BANGS BARGE BAUGH BEIGE BERGH BERGS BILGE BILGY BINGE BINGO BINGS BLDGS BLIGH BOGGS BOGGY BONGO BONGS BORGE BOUGH BRAGA BRAGG BRAGS BRIGS BUDGE BUGGY BULGE BULGY BUNGS BURGS

B•••G

BEFOG BEING BOING BOURG BRAGG BRING BRUNG

•BG••

BBGUN

•B••G

ABZUG

••B•G

DEBUG INBIG MRBIG REBAG SOBIG

B•H••

BAHAI BAHIA BAHTS BEHAN BIHAR BOHAI BOHEA BOHME BUHLS

B••H•

BASHO BATHE BATHO BATHS BATHY BECHE BIGHT BLAHS BOEHM BOTHA BOTHE BRAHE BRUHN BUSHY

B•••H

BALCH BALKH BARTH BATCH BAUGH BEACH BEECH BELCH BENCH BERGH BERTH BIRCH BIRTH BLIGH BLOCH BLUSH BLUTH BLYTH BOOTH BORAH BOSCH BOTCH BOUGH BRASH BRITH BROTH BRUCH BRUSH BUNCH BUSCH BUTCH

•BH••

ABHOR

•B•H•

ABOHM

•B••H

ABASH OBEAH

••B•H

SABAH

BI•••

BIALY BIBBS BIBLE BIDDY BIDED BIDEN BIDES BIDON BIDUP BIFFS BIFFY BIFID BIGHT BIGON BIGOS BIGOT BIHAR BIJOU BIKED BIKEL BIKER BIKES BILBO BILGE BILGY BILKO BILKS BILLS BILLY BINAL BINDS BINES BINET BINGE BINGO BINGS BIOME BIOTA BIPED BIPOD BIRCH BIRDS BIRDY BIRLS BIRRS BIRTH BISES BISON BITER

BITES
BITSY
BITTE
BITTS
BITTY
BIXBY
BIZET

B•I••
BAILS
BAIRD
BAIRN
BAITS
BAIZA
BAIZE
BEIGE
BEING
BGIRL
BLIGH
BLIMP
BLIND
BLINI
BLINK
BLIPS
BLISS
BLITT
BLITZ
BOILS
BOING
BOISE
BOITE
BOITO
BRIAN
BRIAR
BRIBE
BRICE
BRICK
BRIDE
BRIEF
BRIER
BRIES
BRIGS
BRILL
BRIMS
BRINE
BRING
BRINK
BRINY
BRISK
BRITE
BRITH
BRITS
BRITT
BSIDE
BUICK
BUILD
BUILT

B••I•
BAGIT
BAHIA
BALIN
BARIC
BARIT
BASIC
BASIE
BASIL
BASIN
BASIS
BATIK
BEDIM
BEFIT
BEGIN
BELIE
BENIN
BEVIN
BIFID
BLAIR
BLOIS
BOGIE
BORIC
BORIS
BOVID
BOWIE
BOXIN
BRAID
BRAIL
BRAIN
BROIL
BRUIN
BRUIT
BUNIN
BURIN

B•••I
BAHAI
BAMBI
BASSI
BELLI
BENJI
BLINI
BOCCI
BOHAI
BONDI
BUFFI
BUZZI

•BI••
ABIDE
IBIZA
MBIRA
OBIES
TBILL
TBIRD

•B•I•
ABBIE
ABOIL
ABRIS
QBVII

•B••I
ABACI
EBOLI
OBELI
OBOLI
QBVII

••BI•
ABBIE
AMBIT
CABIN
COBIA
CUBIC
CUBIT
DEBIT
DOBIE
DUBIN
EUBIE
FABIO
HABIT
INBIG
LABIO
MOBIL
MRBIG
NUBIA
ORBIT
RABID
RABIN
REBID
ROBIN
RUBIK
RUBIN
SABIN
SOBIG
SUBIC
SYBIL
TABIS
TIBIA
TOBIT
UNBID
ZUBIN

••B•I
DUBAI
RABBI

•••BI
ALIBI
BAMBI
DHABI
IAMBI
LIMBI
NIMBI
ORIBI
RABBI

BJ•••
BJORN

B•J••
BIJOU

B••J•
BANJO
BENJI

•BJ••
OBJET

•B•J•
ABUJA

B•K••
BAKED
BAKER
BAKES
BAKST
BIKED
BIKEL
BIKER
BIKES

B••K•
BABKA
BACKS
BALKH
BALKS
BALKY
BANKS
BANKY
BARKS
BASKS
BEAKS
BECKS
BECKY
BILKO
BILKS
BLAKE
BLOKE
BONKS
BOOKS
BOSKS
BOSKY
BRAKE
BROKE
BUCKO
BUCKS
BUCKY
BULKS
BULKY
BUNKO
BUNKS
BURKE

B•••K
BATAK
BATIK
BLACK
BLANK
BLEAK
BLINK
BLOCK
BREAK
BRECK
BRICK
BRINK
BRISK
BROCK
BROOK
BUICK

•B••K
ABACK

••BK•
BABKA

••B•K
RUBIK
UZBEK

BL•••
BLABS
BLACK
BLADE
BLAHS
BLAIR
BLAKE
BLAME
BLANC
BLAND
BLANK
BLARE
BLASE
BLASS
BLAST
BLATS
BLAZE
BLDGS
BLEAK
BLEAR
BLEAT
BLEBS
BLEED
BLEEP
BLEND
BLENT
BLESS
BLEST
BLIGH
BLIMP
BLIND
BLINI
BLINK
BLIPS
BLISS
BLITT
BLITZ
BLOAT
BLOBS
BLOCH
BLOCK
BLOCS
BLOIS
BLOKE
BLOND
BLOOD
BLOOM
BLOOP
BLOTS
BLOWN
BLOWS
BLOWY
BLUED
BLUER
BLUES
BLUET
BLUEY
BLUFF
BLUME
BLUNT
BLURB
BLURS
BLURT
BLUSH
BLUTH
BLUTO
BLVDS
BLYTH

B•L••
BALAS
BALCH
BALDS
BALED
BALER
BALES
BALIN
BALKH
BALKS
BALKY
BALLS
BALLY
BALMS
BALMY
BALSA
BALTS
BELAY
BELCH
BELEM
BELIE
BELLA
BELLE
BELLI
BELLS
BELLY
BELOW
BELTS
BELVA
BFLAT
BILBO
BILGE
BILGY
BILKO
BILKS
BILLS
BILLY
BOLAS
BOLES
BOLLS
BOLOS
BOLTS
BOLUS
BPLUS
BULBA
BULBS
BULGE
BULGY
BULKS
BULKY
BULLA
BULLS
BULLY
BULOW
BYLAW

B••L•
BAALS
BADLY
BAILS
BALLS
BALLY
BAWLS
BAYLE
BBALL
BCELL
BEALL
BEALS
BELLA
BELLE
BELLI
BELLS
BELLY
BERLE
BEYLE
BIALY
BIBLE
BILLS
BILLY
BIRLS
BOGLE
BOILS
BOLLS
BOOLA
BOOLE
BOULE
BOULT
BOWLS
BOYLE
BRILL
BRULE
BUELL
BUGLE
BUHLS
BUILD
BUILT
BULLA
BULLS
BULLY
BURLS
BURLY

B•••L
BABEL
BABUL
BAGEL
BANAL
BASAL
BASEL
BASIL
BBALL
BCELL
BEALL
BERYL
BETEL
BEVEL
BEZEL
BGIRL
BIKEL
BINAL
BRAIL
BRAWL
BRILL
BROIL
BUELL
BUTYL

•BL••
ABLER

•B•L•
ABELE
BBALL
EBOLI
OBELI
OBOLI
OBOLS
TBILL
UBOLT

•B••L
ABDUL
ABOIL
BBALL
TBILL

••BL•
AMBLE
BIBLE
CABLE
DOBLA
DOBLE
FABLE
GABLE
HABLA
NOBLE
NOBLY
PABLO
ROBLE
RUBLE
SABLE
TABLA
TABLE

••B•L
BABEL
BABUL
CABAL
COBOL
GOBEL
JUBAL
KABUL
LABEL
LIBEL
MABEL
MOBIL
NOBEL
REBEL
SIBYL
SYBIL
UMBEL

B•M••
BAMBI
BEMAS
BOMBE
BOMBS
BUMPS
BUMPY

B••M•
BALMS
BALMY
BARMS
BARMY
BAUME
BEAMS
BEAMY
BERME
BERMS
BIOME
BLAME
BLIMP
BLUME
BOHME
BOOMS
BOOMY
BRIMS
BROME
BROMO
BRUME
BURMA

B•••M
BEDIM
BEGUM
BELEM
BESOM
BLOOM
BOEHM
BOSOM
BREAM
BROOM
BYGUM

•B•M•
ABOMB
HBOMB

•B••M
ABEAM
ABOHM
ABRAM
ABYSM
IBEAM

••B•M
ALBUM
SEBUM

B•N••
BANAL
BANCO
BANCS
BANDA
BANDB
BANDO
BANDS
BANDY
BANES
BANFF
BANGS
BANJO
BANKS
BANKY
BANNS
BANTU
BENCH
BENDS
BENES
BENET
BENIN
BENJI
BENNY
BENTS
BENUE
BENZO
BINAL
BINDS
BINES
BINET
BINGE
BINGO
BINGS
BONDI
BONDS
BONED
BONER
BONES
BONET
BONGO
BONGS
BONKS
BONNE
BONNY
BONUS
BONZE
BONZO
BUNCH
BUNDS
BUNDT
BUNDY
BUNGS
BUNIN
BUNKO
BUNKS
BUNNY
BUNTS
BYNER
BYNOW

B••N•
BANNS
BARNS
BEANO
BEANS
BEANY
BEENE
BEING
BENNY
BERNE
BLANC
BLAND
BLANK
BLEND
BLENT
BLIND
BLINI
BLINK
BLOND
BLUNT
BOING
BONNE
BONNY
BOONE
BOONS
BORNE
BOSNS
BOUND
BOYNE
BRAND
BRANS
BRANT
BRENT
BRINE
BRING
BRINK
BRINY
BRONC
BRONX
BRUNG
BRUNO
BRUNT
BUENA
BUENO
BUNNY
BUONO
BURNS
BURNT
BWANA
BYRNE

B•••N
BACON
BADEN
BAIRN
BALIN
BARON
BASIN
BATON
BBGUN
BEGAN
BEGIN
BEGUN
BEHAN
BENIN
BETON
BEVIN
BIDEN
BIDON
BIGON
BISON
BJORN
BLOWN
BORON
BOURN
BOWEN
BOXIN
BRAIN
BRAUN
BRAWN
BREEN
BRIAN
BROUN
BROWN
BRUHN
BRUIN
BRYAN
BUNIN
BURIN
BYRON

•BN••
ABNER

•B•N•
ABEND
EBONY
TBOND
TBONE

•B••N
BBGUN
EBSEN
IBSEN

••B•N
ALBAN
ALBEN
CABIN
CUBAN
DUBIN
GABON
HOBAN
LABAN
RABIN
ROBIN
RUBEN
RUBIN
SABIN
URBAN
ZUBIN

BO•••
BOARD
BOARS
BOAST
BOATS
BOBBY
BOBUP
BOCCE
BOCCI
BODED
BODES
BOEHM
BOERS
BOEUF
BOFFO
BOFFS
BOGEY
BOGGS
BOGGY
BOGIE
BOGLE
BOGUS
BOHAI
BOHEA
BOHME
BOILS
BOING
BOISE
BOITE
BOITO
BOLAS
BOLES
BOLLS
BOLOS
BOLTS
BOLUS
BOMBE
BOMBS
BONDI
BONDS
BONED
BONER
BONES
BONET
BONGO
BONGS
BONKS
BONNE
BONNY
BONUS
BONZE
BONZO
BOOBS
BOOBY
BOOED
BOOER
BOOKS
BOOLA
BOOLE
BOOMS
BOOMY
BOONE
BOONS
BOORS
BOOST
BOOTH
BOOTS
BOOTY
BOOZE
BORAH
BORAS
BORAX
BORED
BORER
BORES
BORGE
BORIC
BORIS
BORNE
BORON
BOSCH
BOSCO
BOSCS
BOSKS
BOSKY
BOSNS
BOSOM
BOSOX
BOSSA
BOSSY
BOTCH
BOTHA
BOTHE
BOUGH
BOULE
BOULT
BOUND
BOURG
BOURN
BOUSE
BOUTS
BOVID
BOWED
BOWEN
BOWER
BOWES
BOWIE
BOWLS
BOXED
BOXER
BOXES
BOXIN
BOXUP
BOYAR
BOYER
BOYLE
BOYNE
BOZOS

B•O••
BIOME
BIOTA
BJORN
BLOAT
BLOBS
BLOCH
BLOCK
BLOCS
BLOIS
BLOKE
BLOND
BLOOD
BLOOM
BLOOP
BLOTS
BLOWN
BLOWS
BLOWY
BOOBS
BOOBY
BOOED
BOOER
BOOKS
BOOLA
BOOLE
BOOMS
BOOMY
BOONE
BOONS
BOORS
BOOST
BOOTH
BOOTS
BOOTY
BOOZE
BROAD
BROCA
BROCK
BRODY
BROIL
BROKE
BROME
BROMO
BRONC
BRONX
BROOD
BROOK
BROOM
BROTH
BROUN
BROWN
BROWS
BUONO
BUOYS

B••O•
BACON
BARON
BASOV
BATON
BATOR
BAYOU
BEBOP
BEFOG
BEGOT
BELOW
BESOM
BESOT
BETON
BIDON
BIGON
BIGOS
BIGOT
BIJOU
BIPOD
BISON
BLOOD
BLOOM
BLOOP
BOLOS
BORON
BOSOM
BOSOX
BOZOS
BROOD
BROOK
BROOM
BULOW
BYNOW
BYRON

B•••O
BANCO
BANDO
BANJO
BASHO
BASSO
BATHO
BEANO
BENZO
BILBO
BILKO
BINGO
BLUTO
BOFFO
BOITO
BONGO
BONZO
BOSCO
BRAVO
BROMO
BRUNO
BUCKO
BUENO
BUFFO
BUNKO
BUONO
BURRO
BUTEO

•BO••
ABODE
ABOHM
ABOIL
ABOMB
ABORT
ABOUT
ABOVE
ABOVO
EBOLI
EBONY
HBOMB
OBOES
OBOLI
OBOLS
TBOND
TBONE
UBOAT
UBOLT

•B•O•
ABBOT
ABHOR

•B••O
ABACO
ABOVO

••BO•
ABBOT
AMBOS
ARBOR
BEBOP
CABOT
COBOL
DUBOS
ELBOW
GABON
GABOR
HOBOS
JABOT
KABOB
KOBOS
LABOR
LOBOS
NABOB
OHBOY
OXBOW
POBOX
POBOY
ROBOT
SABOT
TABOO
TABOR
UMBOS
UNBOX
UPBOW

••B•O
DOBRO
FABIO
FIBRO
LABIO
PABLO
TABOO

•••BO
BILBO
CARBO
COMBO
DUMBO
GARBO
GUMBO
JUMBO
LIMBO
MAMBO
MUMBO
PEABO
RAMBO
TAMBO
TURBO

BP•••
BPLUS

B•P••
BIPED
BIPOD

B••P•
BEEPS
BLIPS
BUMPS
BUMPY
BURPS

B•••P
BEBOP
BIDUP
BLEEP
BLIMP
BLOOP
BOBUP
BOXUP
BUYUP

••B•P
BEBOP
BOBUP

B•••Q
BARBQ

•••BQ
BARBQ

BR•••
BRACE
BRACT
BRADS
BRADY
BRAES
BRAGA
BRAGG
BRAGS
BRAHE
BRAID
BRAIL
BRAIN
BRAKE
BRAND
BRANS
BRANT
BRASH
BRASS
BRATS
BRAUN
BRAVA
BRAVE
BRAVO
BRAWL
BRAWN
BRAYS
BRAZE
BREAD
BREAK
BREAM
BRECK
BREDA
BREED
BREEN
BRENT
BRERS
BREST
BRETT
BREVE
BREWS
BRIAN
BRIAR
BRIBE
BRICE
BRICK
BRIDE
BRIEF
BRIER
BRIES
BRIGS
BRILL
BRIMS
BRINE
BRING
BRINK
BRINY
BRISK
BRITE
BRITH
BRITS
BRITT
BROAD
BROCA
BROCK
BRODY
BROIL
BROKE
BROME
BROMO
BRONC
BRONX
BROOD
BROOK
BROOM
BROTH
BROUN
BROWN
BROWS
BRUCE
BRUCH
BRUHN
BRUIN
BRUIT
BRULE
BRUME
BRUNG
BRUNO
BRUNT
BRUSH
BRUTE
BRUTS
BRYAN
BRYCE

B•R••
BARBQ
BARBS
BARCA
BARDS
BARED
BARER
BARES
BARGE
BARIC
BARIT
BARKS
BARMS
BARMY
BARNS
BARON
BARRE
BARRY
BARTH
BARTS
BARTY
BEREA
BERET
BERGH
BERGS
BERLE
BERME
BERMS
BERNE
BERRA
BERRY
BERTH
BERYL
BIRCH
BIRDS
BIRDY
BIRLS
BIRRS
BIRTH
BORAH
BORAS
BORAX
BORED
BORER
BORES
BORGE
BORIC
BORIS
BORNE
BORON
BURBS
BURGS
BURIN

BURKE BURLS BURLY BURMA BURNS BURNT BURPS BURRO BURRS BURRY BURSA BURSE BURST BYRDS BYRNE BYRON

B••R•

BAIRD BAIRN BARRE BARRY BASRA BEARD BEARS BEERS BEERY BERRA BERRY BGIRL BIRRS BJORN BLARE BLURB BLURS BLURT BOARD BOARS BOERS BOORS BOURG BOURN BRERS BURRO BURRS BURRY

B•••R

BABAR BABER BAKER BALER BARER BASER BATOR BAUER BAYAR BAYER BIHAR BIKER BITER BLAIR BLEAR BLUER BONER BOOER BORER BOWER BOXER BOYAR BOYER BRIAR BRIER BUBER BUYER BYFAR BYNER

•BR••

ABRAM ABRIS

•B•R•

ABBRS ABORT CBERS EBERT IBARS IBERT JBARS MBIRA TBARS TBIRD ZBARS

•B••R

ABHOR ABLER ABNER

••BR•

ABBRS AMBRY ARBRE COBRA DEBRA DOBRA DOBRO FIBRE FIBRO LIBRA LIBRE OMBRE SABRA SABRE UMBRA ZEBRA

••B•R

AKBAR AMBER ARBER ARBOR AUBER BABAR BABER BUBER CABER DEBAR EMBAR EMBER FABER FIBER GABOR GIBER HABER LABOR OMBER REBAR SABER SOBER TABOR TIBER TUBER UMBER UNBAR WEBER

BS•••

BSIDE

B•S••

BASAL BASED BASEL BASER BASES BASHO BASIC BASIE BASIL BASIN BASIS BASKS BASOV BASRA BASSI BASSO BASTE BESET BESOM BESOT BESTS BISES BISON BOSCH BOSCO BOSCS BOSKS BOSKY BOSNS BOSOM BOSOX BOSSA BOSSY BUSBY BUSCH BUSED BUSES BUSEY BUSHY BUSTS

B••S•

BAKST BALSA BASSI BASSO BEAST BETSY BITSY BLASE BLASS BLAST BLESS BLEST BLISS BLUSH BOAST BOISE BOOST BOSSA BOSSY BOUSE BRASH BRASS BREST BRISK BRUSH BUGSY BURSA BURSE BURST

B•••S

BAALS BABAS BABES BABYS BACKS BAHTS BAILS BAITS BAKES BALAS BALDS BALES BALKS BALLS BALMS BALTS BANCS BANDS BANES BANGS BANKS BANNS BARBS BARDS BARES BARKS BARMS BARNS BARTS BASES BASIS BASKS BATES BATHS BATTS BAWLS BEADS BEAKS BEALS BEAMS BEANS BEARS BEATS BEAUS BECKS BEEFS BEEPS BEERS BEETS BELLS BELTS BEMAS BENDS BENES BENTS BERGS BERMS BESTS BETAS BIBBS BIDES BIFFS BIGOS BIKES BILKS BILLS BINDS BINES BINGS BIRDS BIRLS BIRRS BISES BITES BITTS BLABS BLAHS BLASS BLATS BLDGS BLEBS BLESS BLIPS BLISS BLOBS BLOCS BLOIS BLOTS BLOWS BLUES BLURS BLVDS BOARS BOATS BODES BOERS BOFFS BOGGS BOGUS BOILS BOLAS BOLES BOLLS BOLOS BOLTS BOLUS BOMBS BONDS BONES BONGS BONKS BONUS BOOBS BOOKS BOOMS BOONS BOORS BOOTS BORAS BORES BORIS BOSCS BOSKS BOSNS BOUTS BOWES BOWLS BOXES BOZOS BPLUS BRADS BRAES BRAGS BRANS BRASS BRATS BRAYS BRERS BREWS BRIES BRIGS BRIMS BRITS BROWS BRUTS BUCKS BUFFS BUHLS BULBS BULKS BULLS BUMPS BUNDS BUNGS BUNKS BUNTS BUOYS BURBS BURGS BURLS BURNS BURPS BURRS BUSES BUSTS BUTTS BYRDS BYTES

•BS••

CBSTV EBSEN IBSEN

•B•S•

ABASE ABASH ABUSE ABYSM ABYSS OBESE

•B••S

ABBAS ABBES ABBRS ABETS ABRIS ABUTS ABYSS CBERS IBARS JBARS OBEYS OBIES OBOES OBOLS TBARS ZBARS

••BS•

FUBSY PABST

••B•S

ABBAS ABBES ABBRS AMBOS BABAS BABES BABYS BIBBS CUBES DEBTS DUBOS GIBBS GIBES HOBBS HOBOS IZBAS JIBES KOBOS LOBES LOBOS LUBAS LUBES NABES REBUS ROBES RUBES TABIS TIBBS TUBAS TUBES UMBOS VIBES ZEBUS

•••BS

ARABS BARBS BIBBS BLABS BLEBS BLOBS BOMBS BOOBS BULBS BURBS CARBS CHUBS CLUBS COMBS CRABS CRIBS CURBS DAUBS DRABS DRIBS DRUBS DUMBS FLUBS FORBS GARBS GIBBS GLOBS GRABS GRUBS HERBS HOBBS IAMBS JAMBS KERBS KNOBS KREBS LAMBS LIMBS NUMBS PLEBS SAABS SCABS SERBS SLABS SLOBS SNOBS SNUBS SORBS STABS STUBS SWABS TIBBS VERBS

B•T••

BATAK BATCH BATED BATES BATHE BATHO BATHS BATHY BATIK BATON BATOR BATTS BATTY BETAS BETEL BETON BETSY BETTA BETTE BETTY BITER BITES BITSY BITTE BITTS BITTY BOTCH BOTHA BOTHE BUTCH BUTEO BUTTE BUTTS BUTYL BYTES

B••T•

BAHTS BAITS BALTS BANTU BARTH BARTS BARTY BASTE BATTS BATTY BEATS BEETS BELTS BENTS BERTH BESTS BETTA BETTE BETTY BIOTA BIRTH BITTE BITTS BITTY BLATS BLITT BLITZ BLOTS BLUTH BLUTO BLYTH BOATS BOITE BOITO BOLTS BOOTH BOOTS BOOTY BOUTS BRATS BRETT BRITE BRITH BRITS BRITT BROTH BRUTE BRUTS BUNTS BUSTS BUTTE BUTTS

B•••T

BAGIT BAKST BARIT BEAST BEAUT BEFIT BEGAT BEGET BEGOT BENET BERET BESET BESOT BFLAT BIGHT BIGOT BINET BIZET BLAST BLEAT BLENT BLEST BLITT BLOAT BLUET BLUNT BLURT BOAST BONET BOOST BOULT BRACT BRANT BRENT BREST BRETT BRITT BRUIT BRUNT BUILT BUNDT BURNT BURST

•B•T•

ABATE ABETS ABUTS CBSTV NBCTV

•B••T

ABAFT ABBOT ABORT ABOUT EBERT IBERT OBJET UBOAT UBOLT

••BT•

DEBTS

••B•T

ABBOT AMBIT ATBAT CABOT CUBIT DEBIT DEBUT ESBAT HABIT JABOT ORBIT PABST RABAT REBUT ROBOT SABOT TIBET TOBIT ZIBET

•••BT

DOUBT

BU•••

BUBBA BUBER BUCKO BUCKS BUCKY BUDDY BUDGE BUELL BUENA BUENO BUFFA BUFFI BUFFO BUFFS BUFFY BUGGY BUGLE BUGSY BUHLS BUICK BUILD BUILT BULBA BULBS BULGE BULGY BULKS BULKY BULLA BULLS BULLY BULOW BUMPS BUMPY BUNCH BUNDS BUNDT BUNDY BUNGS BUNIN BUNKO BUNKS BUNNY BUNTS BUONO BUOYS BURBS BURGS BURIN BURKE BURLS BURLY BURMA BURNS BURNT BURPS BURRO BURRS BURRY BURSA BURSE BURST BUSBY BUSCH BUSED BUSES BUSEY BUSHY BUSTS BUTCH BUTEO BUTTE BUTTS BUTYL BUYER BUYUP BUZZI

B•U••

BAUER BAUGH BAUME BLUED BLUER BLUES BLUET BLUEY BLUFF BLUME BLUNT BLURB BLURS BLURT BLUSH BLUTH BLUTO BOUGH BOULE BOULT BOUND BOURG BOURN BOUSE BOUTS BRUCE BRUCH BRUHN BRUIN BRUIT BRULE BRUME BRUNG BRUNO BRUNT BRUSH BRUTE BRUTS

B••U•

BABUL BBGUN BEAUS BEAUT BEAUX BEGUM BEGUN BENUE BIDUP BOBUP BOEUF BOGUS BOLUS BONUS BOXUP BPLUS BRAUN BROUN BUYUP BYGUM

B•••U

BANTU BAYOU BIJOU

•BU••

ABUJA ABUSE ABUTS ABUZZ

•B•U•

ABDUL ABOUT ABZUG BBGUN

••BU•

ALBUM BABUL BOBUP DEBUG DEBUT IMBUE KABUL REBUS REBUT SEBUM ZEBUS

B•V••

BEVEL BEVIN BLVDS BOVID

B••V•

BELVA BRAVA BRAVE BRAVO BREVE

B•••V

BASOV

•BV••

QBVII

•B•V•

ABOVE ABOVO

•B••V

CBSTV NBCTV

BW•••

BWANA

B•W••

BAWDY BAWLS BOWED BOWEN BOWER BOWES BOWIE BOWLS BYWAY

B••W•

BLOWN BLOWS BLOWY BRAWL BRAWN BREWS BROWN BROWS

B•••W

BEDEW BELOW BULOW BYLAW BYNOW

••B•W

ELBOW OXBOW UPBOW

B•X••

BIXBY BOXED BOXER BOXES BOXIN BOXUP

B•••X

BEAUX BORAX BOSOX BRONX

••B•X

POBOX UNBOX

BY•••

BYFAR BYGUM BYLAW BYNER BYNOW BYRDS BYRNE BYRON BYTES BYWAY

B•Y••

BAYAR BAYED BAYER BAYLE BAYOU BEYLE BLYTH BOYAR BOYER BOYLE BOYNE BRYAN BRYCE BUYER BUYUP

B••Y•

BABYS BERYL BRAYS BUOYS BUTYL

B•••Y

BADLY BAGGY BALKY BALLY BALMY BANDY BANKY BARMY BARRY BARTY BATHY BATTY BAWDY BEADY BEAMY BEANY BECKY BEEFY BEERY BELAY BELLY BENNY BERRY BETSY BETTY BIALY BIDDY BIFFY BILGY BILLY BIRDY BITSY BITTY BIXBY BLOWY BLUEY BOBBY BOGEY BOGGY BONNY BOOBY BOOMY BOOTY BOSKY BOSSY BRADY BRINY BRODY BUCKY BUDDY BUFFY BUGGY BUGSY BULGY BULKY BULLY BUMPY BUNDY BUNNY BURLY BURRY BUSBY BUSEY BUSHY BYWAY

•BY••

ABYSM ABYSS

•B•Y•

ABAYA OBEYS

•B••Y

ABBEY EBONY

••BY•

BABYS LIBYA SIBYL

••B•Y

ABBEY AMBRY ATBAY BOBBY CABBY CUBBY DEBBY EMBAY FUBSY GABBY HOBBY HUBBY LIBBY LOBBY NOBBY NOBLY NUBBY OHBOY POBOY RIBBY ROBBY TABBY TOBEY TUBBY

•••BY

ARABY ASHBY BIXBY BOBBY BOOBY BUSBY CABBY CANBY COLBY CORBY COSBY CUBBY DARBY DEBBY DERBY DIGBY DOLBY FLYBY GABBY GETBY GOTBY HERBY HOBBY HUBBY KIRBY LAYBY LIBBY LOBBY MOSBY NAMBY NASBY NIMBY NOBBY NUBBY PAMBY PUTBY RIBBY RIGBY ROBBY RUGBY SATBY SETBY SITBY TABBY TUBBY WELBY

B•Z••

BEZEL BIZET BOZOS BUZZI

B••Z•

BAIZA BAIZE BENZO BLAZE BONZE BONZO BOOZE BRAZE BUZZI

B•••Z

BLITZ

•BZ••

ABZUG

•B•Z•

ABUZZ IBIZA

•B••Z

ABUZZ

CA•••

CABAL CABBY CABER CABIN CABLE CABOT CACAO CACHE CACTI CADDO CADDY CADET CADGE CADIS CADIZ CADRE CAFES CAGED CAGER CAGES CAGEY CAINE CAIRN CAIRO CAJUN CAKED CAKES CAKEY CALCI CALEB CALIF CALIX CALKS CALLA CALLI CALLS CALMS CALPE CALVE CALYX CAMAY CAMEL CAMEO CAMPO CAMPS CAMPY CAMRY CAMUS CANAL CANBY CANDO CANDW CANDY CANEA CANED CANER CANES CANID CANIS CANIT CANNA CANNY CANOE CANON CANSO CANST CANTO CANTS CAPED CAPEK CAPER CAPES CAPET CAPON CAPOS CAPRA CAPRI CAPTS CARAT CARBO CARBS CARDI CARDS

CARED
CARER
CARES
CARET
CAREW
CAREY
CARGO
CARIA
CARIB
CARKS
CARLA
CARLE
CARLO
CARLY
CARNE
CARNY
CAROB
CAROL
CAROM
CARON
CARPE
CARPI
CARPS
CARRE
CARRY
CARTA
CARTE
CARTS
CARVE
CASCA
CASCO
CASED
CASES
CASEY
CASIO
CASKS
CASTE
CASTS
CASUS
CATCH
CATER
CATES
CATHY
CATTY
CAULK
CAULS
CAUSE
CAVAE
CAVED
CAVER
CAVES
CAVIL
CAWED
CAYCE

C•A••

CEASE
CHACO
CHAFE
CHAFF
CHAIM
CHAIN
CHAIR
CHAKA
CHALK
CHAMP
CHANG
CHANT
CHAOS
CHAPS
CHARD
CHARM
CHARO
CHARS
CHART
CHARY
CHASE
CHASM
CHATS
CHAUD
CHAWS
CLACK
CLAIM
CLAIR
CLAMP
CLAMS
CLANG
CLANK
CLANS
CLAPS
CLARA
CLARE
CLARK
CLARO
CLASH
CLASP
CLASS
CLAUS
CLAVE
CLAWS
CLAYS
COACH
COACT
COALS
COAPT
COAST
COATI
COATS
CRABS
CRACK
CRAFT
CRAGS
CRAIG
CRAIN
CRAKE
CRAMP
CRAMS
CRANE
CRANK
CRAPE
CRAPS
CRASH
CRASS
CRATE
CRAVE
CRAWL
CRAWS
CRAZE
CRAZY
CYANO
CZARS

C••A•

CABAL
CACAO
CAMAY
CANAL
CARAT
CAVAE
CEDAR
CERAM
CERAT
CESAR
CFLAT
CHEAP
CHEAT
CHIAS
CIGAR
CLEAN
CLEAR
CLEAT
CLOAK
CODAS
COHAN
COLAS
COMAE
COMAS
CONAN
COPAL
COPAN
COPAY
CORAL
COXAE
COXAL
CREAK
CREAM
CROAK
CROAT
CUBAN
CUGAT
CUMAE
CUNAS
CYCAD
CYMAE
CYMAS

C•••A

CALLA
CANEA
CANNA
CAPRA
CARIA
CARLA
CARTA
CASCA
CEIBA
CELIA
CELLA
CERIA
CESTA
CEUTA
CHAKA
CHEKA
CHELA
CHIBA
CHINA
CHITA
CHULA
CIERA
CILIA
CILLA
CIRCA
CLARA
CNIDA
COBIA
COBRA
COCOA
COMMA
CONGA
COOSA
COPRA
COREA
COSTA
COTTA
CRURA
CULPA
CUPPA
CURIA

•CA••

ACADS
ACARI
ICAHN
OCALA
SCABS
SCADS
SCALA
SCALD
SCALE
SCALP
SCALY
SCAMP
SCAMS
SCAND
SCANS
SCANT
SCAPA
SCAPE
SCARE
SCARF
SCARP
SCARS
SCARY
SCATS
SCAUP

•C•A•

DCCAB
ECLAT
ICEAX
MCKAY
MCRAE
OCCAM
OCCAS
OCEAN
OCTAD
OCTAL
SCHAV
SCRAG
SCRAM
SCRAP

•C••A

ACCRA
ACOMA
ACURA
ICOSA
OCALA
OCHOA
OCREA
SCALA
SCAPA
SCENA
SCHWA
SCUBA
SCUTA

••CA•

ALCAN
ASCAP
CACAO
CYCAD
DCCAB
DECAF
DECAL
DECAY
DUCAL
DUCAT
FOCAL
INCAN
INCAS
LOCAL
LUCAN
LUCAS
MACAO
MACAW
MICAH
MICAS
NICAD
NOCAL
OCCAM
OCCAS
ORCAS
OSCAN
OSCAR
PACAS
PECAN
PICAS
RECAP
UNCAP
UNCAS
VICAR
VOCAL
YMCAS
YWCAS

••C•A

ACCRA
AECIA
ALCOA
COCOA
DACCA
DACHA
DACIA
DECCA
DICTA
LICIA
LUCCA
LUCIA
LYCRA
MECCA
MICRA
MOCHA
NUCHA
SACHA
SACRA
USCGA
VACUA
WICCA
YUCCA

•••CA

ABACA
ARECA
ARICA
ASPCA
BARCA
BROCA
CASCA
CIRCA
DACCA
DECCA
ERICA
FINCA
LEICA
LORCA
LUCCA
MECCA
MUSCA
PARCA
PONCA
SPICA
THECA
TOSCA
UTICA
WICCA
YUCCA

CB•••

CBERS
CBSTV

C•B••

CABAL
CABBY
CABER
CABIN
CABLE
CABOT
COBIA
COBOL
COBRA
CUBAN
CUBBY
CUBEB
CUBED
CUBES
CUBIC
CUBIT

C••B•

CABBY
CANBY
CARBO
CARBS
CEIBA
CHIBA
CHUBS
CLUBS
COLBY
COMBO
COMBS
CORBY
COSBY
CRABS
CRIBS
CUBBY
CURBS

C•••B

CALEB
CARIB
CAROB
CELEB
CLIMB
CRUMB
CUBEB

•C•B•

SCABS
SCUBA

•C••B

ACERB
DCCAB
SCRUB

••C•B

DCCAB
JACOB

CC•••

CCCII
CCCIV
CCCIX
CCCLI
CCCLV
CCCLX
CCCVI
CCCXC
CCCXI
CCCXL
CCCXV
CCCXX
CCIII
CCLEF
CCLII
CCLIV
CCLIX
CCLVI
CCLXI
CCLXV
CCLXX
CCVII
CCXCI
CCXCV
CCXII
CCXIV
CCXIX
CCXLI
CCXLV
CCXVI
CCXXI
CCXXV
CCXXX

C•C••

CACAO
CACHE
CACTI
CCCII
CCCIV
CCCIX
CCCLI
CCCLV
CCCLX
CCCVI
CCCXC
CCCXI
CCCXL
CCCXV
CCCXX
CECIL
COCKS
COCKY
COCOA
CXCII
CXCIV
CXCIX
CXCVI
CYCAD
CYCLE
CYCLO

C••C•

CALCI
CASCA
CASCO
CATCH
CAYCE
CCXCI
CCXCV
CDXCI
CDXCV
CENCI
CHACO
CHECK
CHICK
CHICO
CHOCK
CHUCK
CINCH
CINCO
CIRCA
CIRCE
CIRCS
CISCO
CLACK
CLICK
CLOCK
CLUCK
CMXCI
CMXCV
COACH
COACT
CONCH
COUCH
CRACK
CRECY
CRICK
CROCE
CROCI
CROCK
CROCS
CULCH
CURCI
CUZCO
CZECH

C•••C

CCCXC
CIVIC
COMIC
CONIC
COSEC
CRESC
CUBIC
CYNIC

•CC••

ACCEL
ACCRA
ACCTS
CCCII
CCCIV
CCCIX
CCCLI
CCCLV
CCCLX
CCCVI
CCCXC
CCCXI
CCCXL
CCCXV
CCCXX
DCCAB
DCCCI
DCCCL
DCCCV
DCCCX
DCCII
DCCIV
DCCIX
DCCLI
DCCLV
DCCLX
DCCVI
DCCXC
DCCXI
DCCXL
DCCXV
DCCXX
MCCCI
MCCCL
MCCCV
MCCCX
MCCII
MCCIV
MCCIX
MCCLI
MCCLV
MCCLX
MCCOO
MCCOY
MCCVI
MCCXC
MCCXI
MCCXL
MCCXV
MCCXX
OCCAM
OCCAS
OCCUR

•C•C•

CCXCI
CCXCV
DCCCI
DCCCL
DCCCV
DCCCX
DCXCI
DCXCV
MCCCI
MCCCL
MCCCV
MCCCX
MCXCI
MCXCV

•C••C

CCCXC
DCCXC
MCCXC
MCDXC
MCMXC

••CC•

BOCCE
BOCCI
DACCA
DCCCI
DCCCL
DCCCV
DCCCX
DECCA
GUCCI
LUCCA
LUCCI
MCCCI
MCCCL
MCCCV
MCCCX
MDCCC
MDCCI
MDCCL
MDCCV
MDCCX
MECCA
MMCCC
MMCCI
MMCCL
MMCCV
MMCCX
PUCCI
RECCE
RICCI
ROCCO
SACCO
SECCO
WICCA
YECCH
YUCCA

••C•C

CCCXC
DCCXC
ENCYC
MCCXC
MDCCC
MDCXC
MMCCC
MMCXC

•••CC

MDCCC
MMCCC
MMDCC
MMMCC

CD•••

CDIII
CDLII
CDLIV
CDLIX
CDLVI
CDLXI
CDLXV
CDLXX
CDROM
CDVII
CDXCI
CDXCV
CDXII
CDXIV
CDXIX
CDXLI
CDXLV
CDXVI
CDXXI
CDXXV
CDXXX

C•D••

CADDO
CADDY
CADET
CADGE
CADIS
CADIZ
CADRE
CEDAR
CEDED
CEDES
CIDER
CMDRS
CODAS
CODED
CODER
CODES
CODEX
CUDDY
CYDER

C••D•

CADDO
CADDY
CANDO
CANDW
CANDY
CARDI
CARDS
CHIDE
CINDY
CLODS
CLYDE
CNIDA
COEDS
COLDS
CONDE
CONDO
CORDS
CREDO
CRUDE
CUDDY
CURDS
CURDY
CYNDI

C•••D

CAGED
CAKED
CANED
CANID
CAPED
CARED
CASED
CAVED
CAWED
CEDED
CERED
CHARD
CHAUD
CHILD
CHORD
CITED
CLOUD
CLUED
CODED
COKED
CONTD
COOED
COPED
CORED
COULD
COWED
COXED
CREED
CRIED
CROWD
CUBED
CUPID
CURED
CYCAD

•CD••

MCDII
MCDIV
MCDIX
MCDLI
MCDLV
MCDLX
MCDVI
MCDXC
MCDXI
MCDXL
MCDXV
MCDXX

•C•D•

ACADS
ACIDS
ACIDY
SCADS
SCUDI
SCUDO
SCUDS

•C••D

ACHED
ACRED
ACRID
ACTED
OCTAD
SCALD
SCAND
SCEND
SCHED
SCOLD
SCROD

••CD•

MMCDI
MMCDL
MMCDV
MMCDX

••C•D

ARCED
CYCAD
DICED
ELCID
FACED
LACED
LUCID
MACED
NICAD
PACED
RACED
RICED

•••CD

MMMCD

CE•••

CEASE
CECIL
CEDAR
CEDED
CEDES
CEIBA
CEILS
CELEB
CELIA
CELIE
CELLA
CELLI
CELLO
CELLS
CELTS
CENCI
CENSE
CENTI
CENTO
CENTS
CEORL
CEPES
CERAM
CERAT
CERED
CERES
CERIA
CEROS
CERRO
CERTS
CESAR
CESTA
CESTI
CETUS
CEUTA

C•E••

CBERS
CHEAP
CHEAT
CHECK
CHEEK
CHEEP
CHEER
CHEFS
CHEKA
CHELA
CHERE
CHERI
CHERT
CHESS
CHEST
CHEVY
CHEWS
CHEWY
CIERA
CLEAN
CLEAR
CLEAT
CLEEK
CLEFS
CLEFT
CLEON
CLERK
CLEWS
COEDS
COEUR
CREAK
CREAM
CRECY
CREDO
CREED
CREEK
CREEL
CREEP
CREES
CREME
CREON
CREPE
CREPT
CRESC
CRESS
CREST
CRETE
CREWS
CUEIN
CZECH

C••E•

CABER
CADET
CAFES
CAGED
CAGER
CAGES
CAGEY
CAKED
CAKES
CAKEY
CALEB
CAMEL
CAMEO
CANEA
CANED
CANER
CANES
CAPED
CAPEK
CAPER
CAPES
CAPET
CARED
CARER
CARES
CARET
CAREW
CAREY
CASED
CASES
CASEY
CATER
CATES
CAVED
CAVER
CAVES
CAWED
CCLEF
CEDED
CEDES
CELEB
CEPES
CERED
CERES
CHEEK
CHEEP
CHEER
CHIEF
CHIEN
CIDER
CINES
CIRES
CITED
CITER
CITES
CIVET
CLEEK
CLUED
CLUES
CODED
CODER
CODES
CODEX
COHEN
COKED
COKES
COLES
COLET
COMER
COMES
COMET
COMEX
CONES
CONEY
COOED
COOEE
COOER
COPED
COPES
COREA
CORED
CORER
CORES
COREY
COSEC
COTES
COVEN
COVER
COVES
COVET
COVEY
COWED
COWER
COWES
COXED
COXES
COXEY
COYER
COZEN
COZES
CREED
CREEK
CREEL
CREEP
CREES
CRIED
CRIER
CRIES
CRUEL
CRUET
CUBEB
CUBED
CUBES
CUKES
CULET
CULEX
CUNEO
CUPEL
CURED
CURER
CURES
CUTER
CUTEX
CUVEE
CYDER
CYMES

C•••E

CABLE
CACHE
CADGE
CADRE
CAINE
CALPE
CALVE
CANOE
CARLE
CARNE
CARPE
CARRE
CARTE
CARVE
CASTE
CAUSE
CAVAE
CAYCE
CEASE
CELIE
CENSE
CHAFE
CHASE
CHERE
CHIDE
CHILE
CHIME
CHINE
CHIVE
CHLOE
CHOKE
CHORE
CHOSE
CHUTE
CIRCE
CLARE
CLAVE
CLIME
CLINE
CLIVE
CLONE
CLOSE
CLOVE
CLYDE
CNOTE
COMAE
COMME
COMTE
CONDE
CONGE
CONTE
COOEE
COOKE
COPSE
COUPE
COXAE
CRAKE
CRANE
CRAPE
CRATE
CRAVE
CRAZE
CREME
CREPE
CRETE
CRIME
CROCE
CRONE
CROZE
CRUDE
CRUSE
CUMAE
CURIE
CURSE
CURVE
CUTIE
CUVEE
CYCLE
CYMAE

•CE••

ACERB
ACETO
BCELL
ICEAX
ICEIN
ICENI
ICERS
ICEUP
OCEAN
SCENA
SCEND
SCENE
SCENT

•C•E•

ACCEL
ACHED
ACHES
ACMES
ACRED
ACRES
ACTED
ACTER
CCLEF
FCLEF
GCLEF
ICIER
ICKES
MCGEE
OCHER
OCREA
OCTET
SCHED
SCREE
SCREW

•C••E

ACUTE
ECOLE
MCGEE
MCRAE
MCVIE
OCHRE
SCALE
SCAPE
SCARE
SCENE
SCONE
SCOPE
SCORE
SCREE
SCUTE

••CE•

ACCEL
ARCED
DACES
DICED
DICER
DICES
DICEY
DUCES
EMCEE
EXCEL
FACED
FACER
FACES
FACET
HACEK
LACED
LACER
LACES
LACEY
LYCEE
MACED
MACES
NICER
PACED
PACER
PACES
RACED
RACER
RACES
RICED
RICER
RICES
SYCEE
SYCES
TACET
ULCER
VICES

••C•E

BECHE
BOCCE
CACHE
CYCLE
DACHE
EMCEE
FACIE
FICHE
LOCKE
LUCIE
LUCRE
LYCEE
MACHE
MACLE
NACRE
NICHE
ONCLE
ONCUE
RECCE
RICHE
ROCHE
RUCHE

SACRE SOCLE SUCRE SYCEE TYCHE UNCLE

•••CE
ALICE ALYCE AMICE APACE BOCCE BRACE BRICE BRUCE BRYCE CAYCE CIRCE CROCE DANCE DEICE DEUCE DOLCE DUNCE EDUCE FARCE FENCE FORCE GLACE GRACE HENCE HULCE JOYCE JUICE LANCE MERCE MINCE NIECE NONCE ONICE OUNCE PEACE PENCE PERCE PIECE PINCE PLACE PONCE PRICE RECCE ROYCE SAUCE SINCE SLICE SPACE SPICE TRACE TRICE TRUCE TWICE VANCE VINCE VOICE WINCE

CF•••
CFLAT

C•F••
CAFES CUFFS

C••F•
CHAFE CHAFF CHEFS CHUFF CLEFS CLEFT CLIFF CLIFT COIFS COMFY CORFU CRAFT CROFT CUFFS

C•••F
CALIF CCLEF CHAFF CHIEF CHUFF CLIFF

•C•F•
ACUFF SCIFI SCOFF SCUFF

•C••F
ACUFF CCLEF FCLEF GCLEF SCARF SCOFF SCUFF SCURF

••C•F
DECAF

C•G••
CAGED CAGER CAGES CAGEY CIGAR CUGAT

C••G•
CADGE CARGO CHUGS CLOGS CONGA CONGE CONGO CORGI COUGH CRAGS

C•••G
CHANG CHING CHONG CHUNG CLANG CLING CLUNG CRAIG CUING

•CG••
MCGEE

•C••G
ACING ICING SCRAG

••CG•
USCGA

••C•G
INCOG

CH•••
CHACO CHAFE CHAFF CHAIM CHAIN CHAIR CHAKA CHALK CHAMP CHANG CHANT CHAOS CHAPS CHARD CHARM CHARO CHARS CHART CHARY CHASE CHASM CHATS CHAUD CHAWS CHEAP CHEAT CHECK CHEEK CHEEP CHEER CHEFS CHEKA CHELA CHERE CHERI CHERT CHESS CHEST CHEVY CHEWS CHEWY CHIAS CHIBA CHICK CHICO CHIDE CHIEF CHIEN CHILD CHILE CHILI CHILL CHIME CHIMP CHINA CHINE CHING CHINK CHINO CHINS CHIOS CHIPS CHIRO CHIRP CHIRR CHITA CHITS CHIVE CHIVY CHLOE CHLOR CHOCK CHOIR CHOKE CHOKY CHOMP CHONG CHOPS CHORD CHORE CHOSE CHOWS CHRIS CHROM CHRON CHRYS CHUBS CHUCK CHUFF CHUGS CHULA CHUMP CHUMS CHUNG CHUNK CHURL CHURN CHUTE

C•H••
COHAN COHEN COHOS

C••H•
CACHE CATHY CUSHY

C•••H
CATCH CINCH CLASH CLOTH COACH CONCH COUCH COUGH COUTH CRASH CRUSH CULCH CZECH

•CH••
ACHED ACHES ACHOO ECHIN ICHOR ICHTH OCHER OCHOA OCHRE SCHAV SCHED SCHMO SCHON SCHWA

•C•H•
ICAHN

•C••H
ICHTH

••CH•
ARCHI ARCHY BECHE CACHE DACHA DACHE DICHO DUCHY FICHE FICHU FUCHS HECHT ITCHY KOCHI LOCHS MACHE MACHO MACHU MOCHA NACHO NACHT NICHE NUCHA ORCHS RICHE ROCHE RUCHE SACHA SACHS SOCHI TECHS TYCHE TYCHO VICHY YACHT

••C•H
MICAH RICOH YECCH

•••CH
AITCH BALCH BATCH BEACH BEECH BELCH BENCH BIRCH BLOCH BOSCH BOTCH BRUCH BUNCH BUSCH BUTCH CATCH CINCH COACH CONCH COUCH CULCH CZECH DITCH DUTCH ENOCH EPOCH ERICH FETCH FILCH FINCH FITCH GULCH HATCH HENCH HITCH HOOCH HUNCH HUTCH KEACH KENCH KETCH KOTCH LARCH LATCH LEACH LEECH LOACH LUNCH LURCH LYNCH MARCH MATCH MILCH MITCH MOOCH MULCH MUNCH NATCH NOTCH ORACH PARCH PASCH PATCH PEACH PERCH PINCH PITCH POACH PONCH POOCH PORCH POUCH PSYCH PUNCH RANCH RATCH REACH REICH ROACH STICH TEACH TENCH TORCH TOUCH URICH VETCH VOUCH WATCH WELCH WENCH WHICH WINCH WITCH YECCH ZILCH

CI•••
CIDER CIERA CIGAR CILIA CILLA CINCH CINCO CINDY CINES CIRCA CIRCE CIRCS CIRES CIRRI CIRRO CISCO CISSY CITED CITER CITES CIVET CIVIC CIVIL

C•I••
CAINE CAIRN CAIRO CCIII CDIII CEIBA CEILS CHIAS CHIBA CHICK CHICO CHIDE CHIEF CHIEN CHILD CHILE CHILI CHILL CHIME CHIMP CHINA CHINE CHING CHINK CHINO CHINS CHIOS CHIPS CHIRO CHIRP CHIRR CHITA CHITS CHIVE CHIVY CLICK CLIFF CLIFT CLIII CLIMB CLIME CLINE CLING CLINK CLINT CLIOS CLIPS CLIVE CMIII CNIDA COIFS COILS COINS COIRS CRIBS CRICK CRIED CRIER CRIES CRIME CRIMP CRISP CRISS CRIST CUING CVIII CXIII

C••I•
CABIN CADIS CADIZ CALIF CALIX CANID CANIS CANIT CARIA CARIB CASIO CAVIL CCCII CCCIV CCCIX CCIII CCLII CCLIV CCLIX CCVII CCXII CCXIV CCXIX CDIII CDLII CDLIV CDLIX CDVII CDXII CDXIV CDXIX CECIL CELIA CELIE CERIA CHAIM CHAIN CHAIR CHOIR CHRIS CILIA CIVIC CIVIL CLAIM CLAIR CLIII CLVII CLXII CLXIV CLXIX CMIII CMLII CMLIV CMLIX CMVII CMXII CMXIV CMXIX COBIA COLIN COMIC COMIX CONIC CRAIG CRAIN CROIX CUBIC CUBIT CUEIN CUMIN CUPID CURIA CURIE CURIO CUTIE CUTIN CUTIS CVIII CXCII CXCIV CXCIX CXIII CXLII CXLIV CXLIX CXVII CXXII CXXIV CXXIX CYNIC CYRIL

C•••I
CACTI CALCI CALLI CAPRI CARDI CARPI CCCII CCCLI CCCVI CCCXI CCIII CCLII CCLVI CCLXI CCVII CCXCI CCXII CCXLI CCXVI CCXXI CDIII CDLII CDLVI CDLXI CDVII CDXCI CDXII CDXLI CDXVI CDXXI CELLI CENCI CENTI CESTI CHERI CHILI CIRRI CLIII CLVII CLXII CLXVI CLXXI CMIII CMLII CMLVI CMLXI CMVII CMXCI CMXII CMXLI CMXVI CMXXI COATI CONTI CORGI CROCI CUPRI CURCI CVIII CXCII CXCVI CXIII CXLII CXLVI CXVII CXXII CXXVI CXXXI CYNDI

•CI••
ACIDS ACIDY ACING CCIII DCIII ICIER ICILY ICING MCIII SCIFI SCION XCIII

•C•I•
ACRID ACTII ACTIN ACTIV CCCII CCCIV CCCIX CCIII CCLII CCLIV CCLIX CCVII CCXII CCXIV CCXIX DCCII DCCIV DCCIX DCIII DCLII DCLIV DCLIX DCVII DCXII DCXIV DCXIX ECHIN ICEIN MCCII MCCIV MCCIX MCDII MCDIV MCDIX MCIII MCLII MCLIV MCLIX MCMII MCMIV MCMIX MCVIE MCVII MCXII MCXIV MCXIX SCRIM SCRIP XCIII XCVII

•C••I
ACARI ACTII CCCII CCCLI CCCVI CCCXI CCIII CCLII CCLVI CCLXI CCVII CCXCI CCXII CCXLI CCXVI CCXXI DCCCI DCCII DCCLI DCCVI DCCXI DCIII DCLII DCLVI DCLXI DCVII DCXCI DCXII DCXLI DCXVI DCXXI ICENI ICOSI MCCCI MCCII MCCLI MCCVI MCCXI MCDII MCDLI MCDVI MCDXI MCIII MCLII MCLVI MCLXI MCMII MCMLI MCMVI MCMXI MCVII MCXCI MCXII MCXLI MCXVI MCXXI SCIFI SCUDI XCIII XCVII

••CI•
AECIA ASCII CCCII CCCIV CCCIX CECIL CXCII CXCIV CXCIX DACIA DCCII DCCIV DCCIX DXCII DXCIV DXCIX ELCID FACIE LICIA LICIT LUCIA LUCID LUCIE MCCII MCCIV MCCIX MDCII MDCIV MDCIX MMCII MMCIV MMCIX MUCIN MXCII MXCIV MXCIX OPCIT RECIP SOCIO TACIT

••C•I
ARCHI ASCII BOCCI CACTI CCCII CCCLI CCCVI CCCXI CXCII CXCVI DCCCI DCCII DCCLI DCCVI DCCXI DXCII DXCVI GUCCI KOCHI LACTI LUCCI MCCCI MCCII MCCLI MCCVI MCCXI MDCCI MDCII MDCLI MDCVI MDCXI MMCCI MMCDI MMCII MMCLI MMCMI MMCVI MMCXI MXCII MXCVI NOCTI PUCCI RECTI RICCI RICKI SOCHI VICKI

•••CI
ABACI BOCCI CALCI CCXCI CDXCI CENCI CMXCI CROCI CURCI DCCCI DCXCI FARCI GUCCI LUCCI MCCCI MCXCI MDCCI MDXCI MERCI MMCCI MMDCI MMMCI MMXCI PESCI PISCI PUCCI RICCI SULCI VINCI VOICI

C•J••
CAJUN

C•K••
CAKED CAKES CAKEY COKED COKES CUKES CUKOR

C••K•
CALKS CARKS CASKS CHAKA CHEKA CHOKE CHOKY COCKS COCKY CONKS COOKE COOKS CORKS CORKY CRAKE CUSKS

C•••K
CAPEK CAULK CHALK CHECK CHEEK CHICK CHINK CHOCK CHUCK CHUNK CLACK CLANK CLARK CLEEK CLERK CLICK CLINK CLOAK CLOCK CLONK CLUCK CLUNK CRACK CRANK CREAK CREEK CRICK CROAK CROCK CROOK

•CK••
ICKES MCKAY

••CK•
BACKS BECKS BECKY BUCKO BUCKS BUCKY COCKS COCKY DECKS DICKS DICKY DOCKS DUCKS DUCKY GECKO HACKS HECKS HICKS HOCKS JACKS JOCKO JOCKS KICKS KICKY LACKS LICKS LOCKE LOCKS LUCKS LUCKY MOCKS MUCKS MUCKY NECKS NICKS NOCKS PACKS PECKS PICKS PICKY PUCKS RACKS RICKI RICKS RICKY ROCKS ROCKY RUCKS SACKS SOCKO SOCKS SUCKS TACKS TACKY TICKS TICKY TUCKS VICKI VICKS WACKO WACKY WICKS YUCKY

••C•K
HACEK

•••CK
ABACK ALACK ALECK AMUCK BLACK BLOCK BRECK BRICK BROCK BUICK CHECK CHICK CHOCK CHUCK CLACK CLICK CLOCK CLUCK CRACK CRICK CROCK FLACK FLECK FLICK FLOCK FRICK FROCK GLUCK KNACK KNICK KNOCK KYACK MONCK NYACK PLUCK PRICK QUACK QUICK SHACK SHOCK SHUCK SLACK SLICK SMACK SMOCK SNACK SNICK SNUCK SPECK SPOCK STACK STICK STOCK STUCK THICK TRACK TRICK TRUCK VNECK WHACK WRACK WRECK

CL•••
CLACK CLAIM CLAIR CLAMP CLAMS CLANG CLANK CLANS CLAPS CLARA CLARE CLARK CLARO CLASH CLASP CLASS CLAUS CLAVE CLAWS CLAYS CLEAN CLEAR CLEAT CLEEK CLEFS CLEFT CLEON CLERK CLEWS CLICK CLIFF CLIFT CLIII CLIMB CLIME CLINE CLING CLINK CLINT CLIOS CLIPS CLIVE CLOAK CLOCK CLODS CLOGS CLOMP CLONE CLONK CLOPS CLOSE CLOTH CLOTS CLOUD CLOUT CLOVE CLOWN CLOYS CLUBS CLUCK CLUED CLUES CLUMP CLUNG CLUNK CLUNY CLVII CLXII CLXIV CLXIX CLXVI CLXXI CLXXV CLXXX CLYDE

C•L••
CALCI CALEB CALIF CALIX CALKS CALLA CALLI CALLS CALMS CALPE CALVE CALYX CCLEF CCLII CCLIV CCLIX CCLVI CCLXI CCLXV CCLXX CDLII CDLIV CDLIX CDLVI CDLXI

CDLXV
CDLXX
CELEB
CELIA
CELIE
CELLA
CELLI
CELLO
CELLS
CELTS
CFLAT
CHLOE
CHLOR
CILIA
CILLA
CMLII
CMLIV
CMLIX
CMLVI
CMLXI
CMLXV
CMLXX
COLAS
COLBY
COLDS
COLES
COLET
COLIN
COLON
COLOR
COLTS
COLUM
CPLUS
CULCH
CULET
CULEX
CULLS
CULMS
CULPA
CULTS
CXLII
CXLIV
CXLIX
CXLVI

C••L•

CABLE
CALLA
CALLI
CALLS
CARLA
CARLE
CARLO
CARLY
CAULK
CAULS
CCCLI
CCCLV
CCCLX
CCXLI
CCXLV
CDXLI
CDXLV
CEILS
CELLA
CELLI
CELLO
CELLS
CHALK
CHELA
CHILD
CHILE
CHILI
CHILL
CHULA
CILLA
CMXLI
CMXLV
COALS
COILS
COOLS
COULD
COWLS
COYLY
CROLY
CULLS
CURLS
CURLY
CYCLE
CYCLO

C•••L

CABAL
CAMEL
CANAL
CAROL
CAVIL
CCCXL
CECIL
CEORL
CHILL
CHURL
CIVIL
COBOL
COPAL
CORAL
COXAL
CRAWL
CREEL
CRUEL
CUMUL
CUPEL
CYRIL

•CL••

CCLEF
CCLII
CCLIV
CCLIX
CCLVI
CCLXI
CCLXV
CCLXX
DCLII
DCLIV
DCLIX
DCLVI
DCLXI
DCLXV
DCLXX
ECLAT
FCLEF
GCLEF
MCLII
MCLIV
MCLIX
MCLVI
MCLXI
MCLXV
MCLXX

•C•L•

BCELL
CCCLI
CCCLV
CCCLX
CCXLI
CCXLV
DCCLI
DCCLV
DCCLX
DCXLI
DCXLV
ECOLE
ICILY
MCCLI
MCCLV
MCCLX
MCDLI
MCDLV
MCDLX
MCMLI
MCMLV
MCMLX
MCXLI
MCXLV
OCALA
OCULO
SCALA
SCALD
SCALE
SCALP
SCALY
SCOLD
SCULL

•C••L

ACCEL
BCELL
CCCXL
DCCCL
DCCXL
MCCCL
MCCXL
MCDXL
MCMXL
OCTAL
SCOWL
SCULL

••CL•

CCCLI
CCCLV
CCCLX
CYCLE
CYCLO
DCCLI
DCCLV
DCCLX
MACLE
MCCLI
MCCLV
MCCLX
MDCLI
MDCLV
MDCLX
MMCLI
MMCLV
MMCLX
ONCLE
SOCLE
UNCLE

••C•L

ACCEL
CCCXL
CECIL
DCCCL
DCCXL
DECAL
DUCAL
EXCEL
FOCAL
LOCAL
LTCOL
MCCCL
MCCXL
MDCCL
MDCXL
MMCCL
MMCDL
MMCML
MMCXL
NICOL
NOCAL
PICUL
VOCAL

•••CL

DCCCL
MCCCL
MDCCL
MMCCL
MMDCL
MMMCL

CM•••

CMDRS
CMIII
CMLII
CMLIV
CMLIX
CMLVI
CMLXI
CMLXV
CMLXX
CMVII
CMXCI
CMXCV
CMXII
CMXIV
CMXIX
CMXLI
CMXLV
CMXVI
CMXXI
CMXXV
CMXXX

C•M••

CAMAY
CAMEL
CAMEO
CAMPO
CAMPS
CAMPY
CAMRY
CAMUS
COMAE
COMAS
COMBO
COMBS
COMER
COMES
COMET
COMEX
COMFY
COMIC
COMIX
COMMA
COMME
COMPO
COMPS
COMPT
COMTE
COMUS
CUMAE
CUMIN
CUMUL
CYMAE
CYMAS
CYMES
CYMRY

C••M•

CALMS
CHAMP
CHIME
CHIMP
CHOMP
CHUMP
CHUMS
CLAMP
CLAMS
CLIMB
CLIME
CLOMP
CLUMP
COMMA
COMME
CORMS
COSMO
CRAMP
CRAMS
CREME
CRIME
CRIMP
CRUMB
CRUMP
CULMS
CUOMO

C•••M

CAROM
CDROM
CERAM
CHAIM
CHARM
CHASM
CHROM
CLAIM
COLUM
CREAM

•CM••

ACMES
MCMII
MCMIV
MCMIX
MCMLI
MCMLV
MCMLX
MCMVI
MCMXC
MCMXI
MCMXL
MCMXV
MCMXX

•C•M•

ACOMA
SCAMP
SCAMS
SCHMO
SCUMS

•C••M

OCCAM
SCRAM
SCRIM
SCRUM

••CM•

MMCMI
MMCML
MMCMV
MMCMX

••C•M

MECUM
OCCAM

CN•••

CNIDA
CNOTE

C•N••

CANAL
CANBY
CANDO
CANDW
CANDY
CANEA
CANED
CANER
CANES
CANID
CANIS
CANIT
CANNA
CANNY
CANOE
CANON
CANSO
CANST
CANTO
CANTS
CENCI
CENSE
CENTI
CENTO
CENTS
CINCH
CINCO
CINDY
CINES
CONAN
CONCH
CONDE
CONDO
CONES
CONEY
CONGA
CONGE
CONGO
CONIC
CONKS
CONTD
CONTE
CONTI
CONTR
CUNAS
CUNEO
CYNDI
CYNIC

C••N•

CAINE
CANNA
CANNY
CARNE
CARNY
CHANG
CHANT
CHINA
CHINE
CHING
CHINK
CHINO
CHINS
CHONG
CHUNG
CHUNK
CLANG
CLANK
CLANS
CLINE
CLING
CLINK
CLINT
CLONE
CLONK
CLUNG
CLUNK
CLUNY
COINS
COONS
CORNO
CORNS
CORNU
CORNY
COUNT
CRANE
CRANK
CRONE
CRONY
CUING
CYANO

C•••N

CABIN
CAIRN
CAJUN
CANON
CAPON
CARON
CHAIN
CHIEN
CHRON
CHURN
CLEAN
CLEON
CLOWN
COHAN
COHEN
COLIN
COLON
CONAN
COPAN
COVEN
COZEN
CRAIN
CREON
CROON
CROWN
CUBAN
CUEIN
CUMIN
CUTIN

•C•N•

ACING
ICENI
ICING
ICONO
ICONS
SCAND
SCANS
SCANT
SCENA
SCEND
SCENE
SCENT
SCONE

•C••N

ACORN
ACTIN
ACTON
ECHIN
ICAHN
ICEIN
OCEAN
SCHON
SCION
SCORN

••C•N

ALCAN
ANCON
BACON
INCAN
LUCAN
MACON
MUCIN
OSCAN
PECAN
RACON
RECON

CO•••

COACH
COACT
COALS
COAPT
COAST
COATI
COATS
COBIA
COBOL
COBRA
COCKS
COCKY
COCOA
CODAS
CODED
CODER
CODES
CODEX
COEDS
COEUR
COHAN
COHEN
COHOS
COIFS
COILS
COINS
COIRS
COKED
COKES
COLAS
COLBY
COLDS
COLES
COLET
COLIN
COLON
COLOR
COLTS
COLUM
COMAE
COMAS
COMBO
COMBS
COMER
COMES
COMET
COMEX
COMFY
COMIC
COMIX
COMMA
COMME
COMPO
COMPS
COMPT
COMTE
COMUS
CONAN
CONCH
CONDE
CONDO
CONES
CONEY
CONGA
CONGE
CONGO
CONIC
CONKS
CONTD
CONTE
CONTI
CONTR
COOED
COOEE
COOER
COOKE
COOKS
COOLS
COONS
COOPS
COOPT
COORS
COOSA
COOTS
COPAL
COPAN
COPAY
COPED
COPES
COPRA
COPSE
COPTS
CORAL
CORBY
CORDS
COREA
CORED
CORER
CORES
COREY
CORFU
CORGI
CORKS
CORKY
CORMS
CORNO
CORNS
CORNU
CORNY
COROT
CORPS
COSBY
COSEC
COSMO
COSTA
COSTS
COTES
COTTA
COUCH
COUGH
COULD
COUNT
COUPE
COUPS
COURT
COUSY
COUTH
COVEN
COVER
COVES
COVET
COVEY
COWED
COWER
COWES
COWLS
COXAE
COXAL
COXED
COXES
COXEY
COYER
COYLY
COYPU
COZEN
COZES

C•O••

CEORL
CHOCK
CHOIR
CHOKE
CHOKY
CHOMP
CHONG
CHOPS
CHORD
CHORE
CHOSE
CHOWS
CLOAK
CLOCK
CLODS
CLOGS
CLOMP
CLONE
CLONK
CLOPS
CLOSE
CLOTH
CLOTS
CLOUD
CLOUT
CLOVE
CLOWN
CLOYS
CNOTE
COOED
COOEE
COOER
COOKE
COOKS
COOLS
COONS
COOPS
COOPT
COORS
COOSA
COOTS
CROAK
CROAT
CROCE
CROCI
CROCK
CROCS
CROFT
CROIX
CROLY
CRONE
CRONY
CROOK
CROON
CROPS
CROSS
CROUP
CROWD
CROWN
CROWS
CROZE
CUOMO

C••O•

CABOT
CANOE
CANON
CAPON
CAPOS
CAROB
CAROL
CAROM
CARON
CDROM
CEROS
CHAOS
CHIOS
CHLOE
CHLOR
CHROM
CHRON
CLEON
CLIOS
COBOL
COCOA
COHOS
COLON
COLOR
COROT
CREON
CROOK
CROON
CUKOR

C•••O

CACAO
CADDO
CAIRO
CAMEO
CAMPO
CANDO
CANSO
CANTO
CARBO
CARGO
CARLO
CASCO
CASIO
CELLO
CENTO
CERRO
CHACO
CHARO
CHICO
CHINO
CHIRO
CINCO
CIRRO
CISCO
CLARO
COMBO
COMPO
CONDO
CONGO
CORNO
COSMO
CREDO
CUNEO
CUOMO
CUPRO
CURIO
CUZCO
CYANO
CYCLO

•CO••

ACOMA
ACORN
ECOLE
ICONO
ICONS
ICOSA
ICOSI
SCOFF
SCOLD
SCONE
SCOOP
SCOOT
SCOPE
SCOPS
SCORE
SCORN
SCOTS
SCOTT
SCOUR
SCOUT
SCOWL
SCOWS

•C•O•

ACHOO
ACTON
ACTOR
ICHOR
MCCOO
MCCOY
OCHOA
SCHON
SCION
SCOOP
SCOOT
SCROD

•C••O

ACETO
ACHOO
ICONO
MCCOO
OCULO
SCHMO
SCUDO

••CO•

ALCOA
ALCOR
ANCON
ASCOT
BACON
COCOA
DECOR
DECOY
DICOT
EPCOT
INCOG
JACOB
LOCOS
LTCOL
MACON
MCCOO
MCCOY
NICOL
PECOS
PICOT
RACON
RECON
RICOH
TACOS

••C•O

BUCKO
CACAO
CYCLO
DICHO
FACTO
GECKO
HECTO
JOCKO
LACTO
MACAO
MACHO
MACRO
MCCOO
MICRO
NACHO
PICRO
RECTO
ROCCO
SACCO
SACRO
SECCO
SOCIO
SOCKO
TYCHO
WACKO
XACTO

•••CO

ABACO
AMOCO
BANCO
BOSCO
CASCO
CHACO
CHICO
CINCO
CISCO
CUZCO
DELCO
DISCO
DRACO
GLUCO
GLYCO
GRECO
GUACO
JUNCO
MARCO
NARCO
PASCO
PHYCO
PISCO
ROCCO
SACCO
SECCO
TAXCO
VASCO
WILCO

CP•••

CPLUS

C•P••

CAPED
CAPEK
CAPER
CAPES
CAPET
CAPON
CAPOS
CAPRA
CAPRI
CAPTS
CEPES
COPAL
COPAN
COPAY
COPED
COPES
COPRA
COPSE
COPTS
CUPEL
CUPID
CUPPA
CUPRI
CUPRO

C••P•

CALPE
CAMPO
CAMPS
CAMPY
CARPE
CARPI
CARPS
CHAPS
CHIPS
CHOPS
CLAPS
CLIPS
CLOPS
COAPT
COMPO
COMPS
COMPT
COOPS
COOPT
CORPS
COUPE
COUPS
COYPU
CRAPE
CRAPS
CREPE
CREPT
CROPS
CRYPT
CULPA
CUPPA
CUSPS

C•••P

CHAMP
CHEAP
CHEEP
CHIMP
CHIRP
CHOMP
CHUMP
CLAMP
CLASP
CLOMP
CLUMP
CRAMP
CREEP
CRIMP
CRISP
CROUP
CRUMP
CUTUP

•C•P•

SCAPA
SCAPE
SCOPE
SCOPS
SCUPS

•C••P

ACTUP
ICEUP
SCALP
SCAMP
SCARP
SCAUP
SCOOP
SCRAP
SCRIP

••C•P

ASCAP
RECAP
RECIP
UNCAP

•••CP

NAACP

CR•••

CRABS
CRACK
CRAFT
CRAGS
CRAIG
CRAIN
CRAKE
CRAMP
CRAMS
CRANE
CRANK
CRAPE
CRAPS
CRASH
CRASS
CRATE
CRAVE
CRAWL
CRAWS
CRAZE
CRAZY
CREAK
CREAM
CRECY
CREDO
CREED
CREEK
CREEL
CREEP
CREES
CREME
CREON
CREPE
CREPT
CRESC
CRESS
CREST
CRETE
CREWS
CRIBS
CRICK
CRIED
CRIER
CRIES
CRIME
CRIMP
CRISP
CRISS
CRIST
CROAK
CROAT
CROCE
CROCI
CROCK
CROCS
CROFT
CROIX
CROLY
CRONE
CRONY
CROOK
CROON
CROPS
CROSS
CROUP
CROWD
CROWN
CROWS
CROZE
CRUDE
CRUEL
CRUET
CRUMB
CRUMP
CRURA
CRUSE
CRUSH
CRUST
CRYPT

C•R••

CARAT
CARBO
CARBS
CARDI
CARDS
CARED
CARER
CARES
CARET
CAREW
CAREY
CARGO
CARIA
CARIB
CARKS
CARLA
CARLE
CARLO
CARLY
CARNE
CARNY
CAROB
CAROL
CAROM
CARON
CARPE
CARPI
CARPS
CARRE
CARRY
CARTA
CARTE
CARTS
CARVE
CDROM
CERAM
CERAT
CERED
CERES
CERIA
CEROS
CERRO
CERTS
CHRIS
CHROM
CHRON
CHRYS
CIRCA
CIRCE
CIRCS
CIRES
CIRRI
CIRRO
CORAL
CORBY
CORDS
COREA
CORED
CORER
CORES
COREY
CORFU
CORGI
CORKS
CORKY
CORMS
CORNO
CORNS
CORNU
CORNY
COROT
CORPS
CURBS
CURCI
CURDS
CURDY
CURED
CURER
CURES
CURIA
CURIE
CURIO
CURLS
CURLY
CURRY
CURSE
CURST
CURVE
CURVY
CYRIL
CYRUS

C••R•

CADRE
CAIRN
CAIRO
CAMRY
CAPRA
CAPRI
CARRE

CARRY CBERS CEORL CERRO CHARD CHARM CHARO CHARS CHART CHARY CHERE CHERI CHERT CHIRO CHIRP CHIRR CHORD CHORE CHURL CHURN CIERA CIRRI CIRRO CLARA CLARE CLARK CLARO CLERK CMDRS COBRA COIRS COORS COPRA COURT CRURA CUPRI CUPRO CURRY CYMRY CZARS

C•••R

CABER CAGER CANER CAPER CARER CATER CAVER CEDAR CESAR CHAIR CHEER CHIRR CHLOR CHOIR CIDER CIGAR CITER CLAIR CLEAR CODER COEUR COLOR COMER CONTR COOER CORER COVER COWER COYER CRIER CUKOR CURER CUTER CYDER

•CR••

ACRED ACRES ACRID ECRUS MCRAE OCREA SCRAG SCRAM SCRAP SCREE SCREW SCRIM SCRIP SCROD SCRUB SCRUM

•C•R•

ACARI ACCRA ACERB ACORN ACURA ICERS OCHRE SCARE SCARF SCARP SCARS SCARY SCORE SCORN SCURF

•C••R

ACTER ACTOR ICHOR ICIER OCCUR OCHER SCOUR

••CR•

ACCRA DECRY LUCRE LYCRA MACRO MICRA MICRO NACRE PICRO SACRA SACRE SACRO SUCRE

••C•R

ALCOR DECOR DICER FACER INCUR LACER NICER OCCUR OSCAR PACER RACER RECUR RICER ULCER VICAR

C•S••

CASCA CASCO CASED CASES CASEY CASIO CASKS CASTE CASTS CASUS CBSTV CESAR CESTA CESTI CISCO CISSY COSBY COSEC COSMO COSTA COSTS CUSHY CUSKS CUSPS

C••S•

CANSO CANST CAUSE CEASE CENSE CHASE CHASM CHESS CHEST CHOSE CISSY CLASH CLASP CLASS CLOSE COAST COOSA COPSE COUSY CRASH CRASS CRESC CRESS CREST CRISP CRISS CRIST CROSS CRUSE CRUSH CRUST CURSE CURST

C•••S

CADIS CAFES CAGES CAKES CALKS CALLS CALMS CAMPS CAMUS CANES CANIS CANTS CAPES CAPOS CAPTS CARBS CARDS CARES CARKS CARPS CARTS CASES CASKS CASTS CASUS CATES CAULS CAVES CBERS CEDES CEILS CELLS CELTS CENTS CEPES CERES CEROS CERTS CETUS CHAOS CHAPS CHARS CHATS CHAWS CHEFS CHESS CHEWS CHIAS CHINS CHIOS CHIPS CHITS CHOPS CHOWS CHRIS CHRYS CHUBS CHUGS CHUMS CINES CIRCS CIRES CITES CLAMS CLANS CLAPS CLASS CLAUS CLAWS CLAYS CLEFS CLEWS CLIOS CLIPS CLODS CLOGS CLOPS CLOTS CLOYS CLUBS CLUES CMDRS COALS COATS COCKS CODAS CODES COEDS COHOS COIFS COILS COINS COIRS COKES COLAS COLDS COLES COLTS COMAS COMBS COMES COMPS COMUS CONES CONKS COOKS COOLS COONS COOPS COORS COOTS COPES COPTS CORDS CORES CORKS CORMS CORNS CORPS COSTS COTES COUPS COVES COWES COWLS COXES COZES CPLUS CRABS CRAGS CRAMS CRAPS CRASS CRAWS CREES CRESS CREWS CRIBS CRIES CRISS CROCS CROPS CROSS CROWS CUBES CUFFS CUKES CULLS CULMS CULTS CUNAS CURBS CURDS CURES CURLS CUSKS CUSPS CUTIS CYMAS CYMES CYRUS CZARS

•C•S•

ICOSA ICOSI

•C••S

ACADS ACCTS ACHES ACIDS ACMES ACRES ECRUS ICERS ICKES ICONS ICTUS OCCAS SCABS SCADS SCAMS SCANS SCARS SCATS SCOPS SCOTS SCOWS SCUDS SCUMS SCUPS SCUTS

••C•S

ACCTS ASCUS BACKS BECKS BUCKS COCKS DACES DECKS DICES DICKS DICTS DOCKS DUCES DUCKS DUCTS FACES FACTS FICUS FOCUS FUCHS HACKS HECKS HICKS HOCKS HOCUS INCAS INCUS JACKS JOCKS KICKS LACES LACKS LICKS LOCHS LOCKS LOCOS LOCUS LUCAS LUCKS MACES MACYS MICAS MOCKS MUCKS NECKS NICKS NOCKS OCCAS ORCAS ORCHS ORCUS PACAS PACES PACKS PACTS PECKS PECOS PICAS PICKS PICTS POCUS PUCKS RACES RACKS RICES RICKS ROCKS RUCKS SACHS SACKS SECTS SOCKS SUCKS SYCES TACKS TACOS TECHS TICKS TUCKS UNCAS VICES VICKS WICKS YMCAS YWCAS

•••CS

AWACS BANCS BLOCS BOSCS CIRCS CROCS DISCS EPICS EXECS FISCS LAICS NARCS SPECS SYNCS ZINCS

C•T••

CATCH CATER CATES CATHY CATTY CETUS CITED CITER CITES COTES COTTA CUTER CUTEX CUTIE CUTIN CUTIS CUTUP

C••T•

CACTI CANTO CANTS CAPTS CARTA CARTE CARTS CASTE CASTS CATTY CBSTV CELTS CENTI CENTO CENTS CERTS CESTA CESTI CEUTA CHATS CHITA CHITS CHUTE CLOTH CLOTS CNOTE COATI COATS COLTS COMTE CONTD CONTE CONTI CONTR COOTS COPTS COSTA COSTS COTTA COUTH CRATE CRETE CULTS

C•••T

CABOT CADET CANIT CANST CAPET CARAT CARET CERAT CFLAT CHANT CHART CHEAT CHERT CHEST CIVET CLEAT CLEFT CLIFT CLINT CLOUT COACT COAPT COAST COLET COMET COMPT COOPT COROT COUNT COURT COVET CRAFT CREPT CREST CRIST CROAT CROFT CRUET CRUST CRYPT CUBIT CUGAT CULET CURST

•CT••

ACTED ACTER ACTII ACTIN ACTIV ACTON ACTOR ACTUP ICTUS OCTAD OCTAL OCTET

•C•T•

ACCTS ACETO ACUTE ICHTH SCATS SCOTS SCOTT SCUTA SCUTE SCUTS

•C••T

ECLAT OCTET SCANT SCENT SCOOT SCOTT SCOUT

••CT•

ACCTS CACTI DICTA DICTS DICTU DUCTS FACTO FACTS HECTO LACTI LACTO NBCTV NOCTI PACTS PICTS RECTI RECTO SECTS XACTO

••C•T

ASCOT DICOT DUCAT EPCOT FACET HECHT LICIT NACHT OPCIT PICOT TACET TACIT UNCUT YACHT

•••CT

BRACT COACT EDICT EDUCT EJECT ELECT ENACT EPACT ERECT ERUCT EVICT EXACT MULCT REACT TINCT TRACT

CU•••

CUBAN CUBBY CUBEB CUBED CUBES CUBIC CUBIT CUDDY CUEIN CUFFS CUGAT CUING CUKES CUKOR CULCH CULET CULEX CULLS CULMS CULPA CULTS CUMAE CUMIN CUMUL CUNAS CUNEO CUOMO CUPEL CUPID CUPPA CUPRI CUPRO CURBS CURCI CURDS CURDY CURED CURER CURES CURIA CURIE CURIO CURLS CURLY CURRY CURSE CURST CURVE CURVY CUSHY CUSKS CUSPS CUTER CUTEX CUTIE CUTIN CUTIS CUTUP CUVEE CUZCO

C•U••

CAULK CAULS CAUSE CEUTA CHUBS CHUCK CHUFF CHUGS CHULA CHUMP CHUMS CHUNG CHUNK CHURL CHURN CHUTE CLUBS CLUCK CLUED CLUES CLUMP CLUNG CLUNK CLUNY COUCH COUGH COULD COUNT COUPE COUPS COURT COUSY COUTH CRUDE CRUEL CRUET CRUMB CRUMP CRURA CRUSE CRUSH CRUST

C••U•

CAJUN CAMUS CASUS CETUS CHAUD CLAUS CLOUD CLOUT COEUR COLUM COMUS CPLUS CROUP CUMUL CUTUP CYRUS

C•••U

CORFU CORNU COYPU

•CU••

ACUFF ACURA ACUTE OCULO SCUBA SCUDI SCUDO SCUDS SCUFF SCULL SCUMS SCUPS SCURF SCUTA SCUTE SCUTS

•C•U•

ACTUP ECRUS ICEUP ICTUS OCCUR SCAUP SCOUR SCOUT SCRUB SCRUM

••CU•

ASCUS FICUS FOCUS HOCUS INCUR INCUS LOCUS MECUM OCCUR ONCUE ORCUS PICUL POCUS RECUR UNCUT VACUA

••C•U

DICTU FICHU MACHU

CV•••

CVIII

C•V••

CAVAE CAVED CAVER CAVES CAVIL CCVII CDVII CIVET CIVIC CIVIL CLVII CMVII COVEN COVER COVES COVET COVEY CUVEE CXVII

C••V•

CALVE CARVE CCCVI CCLVI CCXVI CDLVI CDXVI CHEVY CHIVE CHIVY CLAVE CLIVE CLOVE CLXVI CMLVI CMXVI CRAVE CURVE CURVY CXCVI CXLVI CXXVI

C•••V

CBSTV CCCIV CCCLV CCCXV CCLIV CCLXV CCXCV CCXIV CCXLV CCXXV CDLIV CDLXV CDXCV CDXIV CDXLV CDXXV CLXIV CLXXV CMLIV CMLXV CMXCV CMXIV CMXLV CMXXV CXCIV CXLIV CXXIV CXXXV

•CV••

CCVII DCVII MCVIE MCVII XCVII

•C•V•

CCCVI CCLVI CCXVI DCCVI DCLVI DCXVI MCCVI MCDVI MCLVI MCMVI MCXVI

•C••V

ACTIV CCCIV CCCLV CCCXV CCLIV CCLXV CCXCV CCXIV CCXLV CCXXV DCCCV DCCIV DCCLV DCCXV DCLIV DCLXV DCXCV DCXIV DCXLV DCXXV MCCCV MCCIV MCCLV MCCXV MCDIV MCDLV MCDXV MCLIV MCLXV MCMIV MCMLV MCMXV MCXCV MCXIV MCXLV MCXXV SCHAV

••CV•

CCCVI CXCVI DCCVI DXCVI MCCVI MDCVI MMCVI MXCVI

••C•V

CCCIV CCCLV CCCXV CXCIV DCCCV DCCIV DCCLV DCCXV DXCIV MCCCV MCCIV MCCLV MCCXV MDCCV MDCIV MDCLV MDCXV MMCGV MMCDV MMCIV MMCLV MMCMV MMCXV MXCIV NBCTV

•••CV

CCXCV CDXCV CMXCV DCCCV DCXCV MCCCV MCXCV MDCCV MDXCV MMCCV MMDCV MMMCV MMXCV

C•W••

CAWED COWED COWER COWES COWLS

C••W•

CHAWS CHEWS CHEWY CHOWS CLAWS CLEWS CLOWN CRAWL CRAWS CREWS CROWD CROWN CROWS

C•••W

CANDW CAREW

•C•W•

SCHWA SCOWL SCOWS

•C••W

SCREW

••C•W

MACAW

CX•••

CXCII CXCIV CXCIX CXCVI CXIII CXLII CXLIV CXLIX CXLVI CXVII CXXII CXXIV CXXIX CXXVI CXXXI CXXXV

C•X••

CCXCI CCXCV CCXII CCXIV CCXIX CCXLI CCXLV CCXVI CCXXI CCXXV CCXXX CDXCI CDXCV CDXII CDXIV CDXIX CDXLI CDXLV CDXVI CDXXI CDXXV CDXXX CLXII CLXIV CLXIX CLXVI CLXXI CLXXV CLXXX CMXCI CMXCV CMXII CMXIV CMXIX CMXLI CMXLV CMXVI CMXXI CMXXV CMXXX COXAE COXAL COXED COXES COXEY CXXII CXXIV CXXIX CXXVI CXXXI CXXXV

C••X•

CCCXC CCCXI CCCXL CCCXV CCCXX CCLXI CCLXV CCLXX CCXXI CCXXV CCXXX CDLXI CDLXV CDLXX CDXXI CDXXV CDXXX CLXXI CLXXV CLXXX CMLXI CMLXV CMLXX CMXXI CMXXV CMXXX CXXXI CXXXV

C•••X

CALIX CALYX CCCIX CCCLX CCCXX CCLIX CCLXX CCXIX CCXXX CDLIX CDLXX CDXIX CDXXX CLXIX CLXXX CMLIX CMLXX CMXIX CMXXX CODEX COMEX COMIX CROIX CULEX CUTEX CXCIX CXLIX CXXIX

•CX••

CCXCI CCXCV CCXII CCXIV CCXIX

CCXLI
CCXLV
CCXVI
CCXXI
CCXXV
CCXXX
DCXCI
DCXCV
DCXII
DCXIV
DCXIX
DCXLI
DCXLV
DCXVI
DCXXI
DCXXV
DCXXX
MCXCI
MCXCV
MCXII
MCXIV
MCXIX
MCXLI
MCXLV
MCXVI
MCXXI
MCXXV
MCXXX

•C•X•
CCCXC
CCCXI
CCCXL
CCCXV
CCCXX
CCLXI
CCLXV
CCLXX
CCXXI
CCXXV
CCXXX
DCCXC
DCCXI
DCCXL
DCCXV
DCCXX
DCLXI
DCLXV
DCLXX
DCXXI
DCXXV
DCXXX
MCCXC
MCCXI
MCCXL
MCCXV
MCCXX
MCDXC
MCDXI
MCDXL
MCDXV
MCDXX
MCLXI
MCLXV
MCLXX
MCMXC
MCMXI
MCMXL
MCMXV
MCMXX
MCXXI
MCXXV
MCXXX

•C••X
CCCIX
CCCLX
CCCXX
CCLIX
CCLXX
CCXIX
CCXXX
DCCCX
DCCIX
DCCLX
DCCXX
DCLIX
DCLXX
DCXIX
DCXXX
ICEAX
MCCCX
MCCIX
MCCLX
MCCXX
MCDIX
MCDLX
MCDXX
MCLIX
MCLXX
MCMIX
MCMLX
MCMXX
MCXIX
MCXXX

••CX•
CCCXC
CCCXI
CCCXL
CCCXV
CCCXX
DCCXC
DCCXI
DCCXL
DCCXV
DCCXX
MCCXC
MCCXI
MCCXL
MCCXV
MCCXX
MDCXC
MDCXI
MDCXL
MDCXV
MDCXX
MMCXC
MMCXI
MMCXL
MMCXV
MMCXX

••C•X
CCCIX
CCCLX
CCCXX
CXCIX
DCCCX
DCCIX
DCCLX
DCCXX
DXCIX
MCCCX
MCCIX
MCCLX
MCCXX
MDCCX
MDCIX
MDCLX
MDCXX
MMCCX
MMCDX
MMCIX
MMCLX
MMCMX
MMCXX
MXCIX

•••CX
DCCCX
MCCCX
MDCCX
MMCCX
MMDCX
MMMCX

CY•••
CYANO
CYCAD
CYCLE
CYCLO
CYDER
CYMAE
CYMAS
CYMES
CYMRY
CYNDI
CYNIC
CYRIL
CYRUS

C•Y••
CAYCE
CLYDE
COYER
COYLY
COYPU
CRYPT

C••Y•
CALYX
CHRYS
CLAYS
CLOYS

C•••Y
CABBY
CADDY
CAGEY
CAKEY
CAMAY
CAMPY
CAMRY
CANBY
CANDY
CANNY
CAREY
CARLY
CARNY
CARRY
CASEY
CATHY
CATTY
CHARY
CHEVY
CHEWY
CHIVY
CHOKY
CINDY
CISSY
CLUNY
COCKY
COLBY
COMFY
CONEY
COPAY
CORBY
COREY
CORKY
CORNY
COSBY
COUSY
COVEY
COXEY
COYLY
CRAZY
CRECY
CROLY
CRONY
CUBBY
CUDDY
CURDY
CURLY
CURRY
CURVY
CUSHY
CYMRY

•C••Y
ACIDY
ICILY
MCCOY
MCKAY
SCALY
SCARY

••CY•
ENCYC
MACYS

••C•Y
ARCHY
BECKY
BUCKY
COCKY
DECAY
DECOY
DECRY
DICEY
DICKY
DUCHY
DUCKY
ITCHY
KICKY
LACEY
LUCKY
MCCOY
MUCKY
ORCZY
PICKY
RICKY
ROCKY
TACKY
TICKY
VICHY
WACKY
YUCKY

•••CY
CRECY
DANCY
DEUCY
FANCY
JUICY
MARCY
MERCY
NANCY
ORACY
PERCY
PRICY
SAUCY
SPICY
STACY
TRACY

CZ•••
CZARS
CZECH

C•Z••
COZEN
COZES
CUZCO

C••Z•
CRAZE
CRAZY
CROZE

C•••Z
CADIZ

••CZ•
ORCZY

DA•••
DACCA
DACES
DACHA
DACHE
DACIA
DADDY
DADOS
DAFFY
DAFOE
DAGON
DAILY
DAIRY
DAISY
DAIWA
DAKAR
DALAI
DALES
DALEY
DALLY
DAMAN
DAMAR
DAMES
DAMNS
DAMON
DAMPS
DAMUP
DANAE
DANCE
DANCY
DANDY
DANES
DANGS
DANIO
DANKE
DANNY
DANSE
DANTE
DANZA
DARBY
DARED
DARER
DARES
DARIN
DARIO
DARKS
DARLA
DARNS
DARTH
DARTS
DARYA
DARYL
DASHI
DATED
DATER
DATES
DATUM
DAUBS
DAUNT
DAVAO
DAVID
DAVIE
DAVIS
DAVIT
DAVOS
DAVYS
DAWES
DAWNS
DAYAK
DAYAN
DAYNE
DAZED
DAZES

D•A••
DEALS
DEALT
DEANE
DEANS
DEARS
DEARY
DHABI
DIALS
DIANA
DIANE
DIARY
DIAZO
DNASE
DRABS
DRACO
DRAFT
DRAGS
DRAIL
DRAIN
DRAKE
DRAMA
DRAMS
DRANG
DRANK
DRANO
DRAPE
DRATS
DRAWL
DRAWN
DRAWS
DRAYS
DUADS
DUANE
DWARF
DYADS

D••A•
DAKAR
DALAI
DAMAN
DAMAR
DANAE
DAVAO
DAYAK
DAYAN
DCCAB
DEBAR
DECAF
DECAL
DECAY
DEFAT
DEGAS
DELAY
DERAT
DETAT
DEWAN
DEWAR
DFLAT
DINAH
DINAR
DIRAC
DIVAN
DIVAS
DONAS
DONAT
DONAU
DORAL
DORAN
DOTAL
DOUAI
DOUAY
DREAD
DREAM
DREAR
DRLAO
DRYAD
DUBAI
DUCAL
DUCAT
DUFAY
DUGAN
DUKAS
DUMAS
DURAN
DYLAN

D•••A
DACCA
DACHA
DACIA
DAIWA
DANZA
DARLA
DARYA
DEBRA
DECCA
DELLA
DELTA
DERMA
DESNA
DIANA
DICTA
DITKA
DOBLA
DOBRA
DOGMA
DOLMA
DONNA
DORSA
DRAMA
DRINA
DURRA
DVINA

•DA••
ADAGE
ADAIR
ADAMS
ADANA
ADANO
ADAPT
EDAMS
IDAHO
UDALL

•D•A•
ADDAX
ADLAI
ADMAN
EDDAS
EDGAR
IDEAL
IDEAS

•D••A
ADANA
ADELA
ADUWA
ADYTA
EDEMA
EDINA
NDOLA

••DA•
ADDAX
AIDAN
ALDAN
AODAI
CEDAR
CODAS
EDDAS
HADAR
HADAT
HODAD
JUDAH
JUDAS
KADAR
KODAK
MADAM
MEDAL
MIDAS
MODAL
NODAL
PEDAL
RADAR
REDAN
RODAN
SADAT
SEDAN
SODAS
SUDAN
TIDAL
TODAY
VEDAS
VEDAY
VIDAL
VJDAY

••D•A
AUDRA
HEDDA
HYDRA
INDIA
INDRA
JIDDA
JUDEA
LYDIA
MEDEA
MEDIA
MUDRA
NADIA
PADUA
PODIA
SIDEA
SIDRA
SUDRA
VEDDA
VODKA

•••DA
ALIDA
BANDA
BREDA
CNIDA
FONDA
FREDA
FULDA
GARDA
GILDA
GOLDA
GOUDA
HEDDA
HILDA
HONDA
JIDDA
KINDA
KORDA
LINDA
LYNDA
MAGDA
MAZDA
OUIDA
PANDA
QANDA
RHODA
SKODA
SUNDA
THEDA
VEDDA
VENDA
WANDA
ZELDA
ZENDA

D•B••
DEBAR
DEBBY
DEBIT
DEBRA
DEBTS
DEBUG
DEBUT
DOBIE
DOBLA
DOBLE
DOBRA
DOBRO
DUBAI
DUBIN
DUBOS

D••B•
DARBY
DAUBS
DEBBY
DERBY
DHABI
DIGBY
DOLBY
DOUBT
DRABS
DRIBS
DRUBS
DUMBO
DUMBS

D•••B
DCCAB
DEMOB
DENEB
DWEEB

•D•B•
ADOBE

•D••B
ADLIB

••D•B
REDUB
SIDEB

•••DB
BANDB
RANDB

DC•••
DCCAB
DCCCI
DCCCL
DCCCV
DCCCX
DCCII
DCCIV
DCCIX
DCCLI
DCCLV
DCCLX
DCCVI
DCCXC
DCCXI
DCCXL
DCCXV
DCCXX
DCIII
DCLII
DCLIV
DCLIX
DCLVI
DCLXI
DCLXV
DCLXX
DCVII
DCXCI
DCXCV
DCXII
DCXIV
DCXIX
DCXLI
DCXLV
DCXVI
DCXXI
DCXXV
DCXXX

D•C••
DACCA
DACES
DACHA
DACHE
DACIA
DCCAB
DCCCI
DCCCL
DCCCV
DCCCX
DCCII
DCCIV
DCCIX
DCCLI
DCCLV
DCCLX
DCCVI
DCCXC
DCCXI
DCCXL
DCCXV
DCCXX
DECAF
DECAL
DECAY
DECCA
DECKS
DECOR
DECOY
DECRY
DICED
DICER
DICES
DICEY
DICHO
DICKS
DICKY
DICOT
DICTA
DICTS
DICTU
DOCKS
DUCAL
DUCAT
DUCES
DUCHY
DUCKS
DUCKY
DUCTS
DXCII
DXCIV
DXCIX
DXCVI

D••C•
DACCA
DANCE
DANCY
DCCCI
DCCCL
DCCCV
DCCCX
DCXCI
DCXCV
DECCA
DEICE
DELCO
DEUCE
DEUCY
DISCO
DISCS
DITCH
DOLCE
DRACO
DUNCE
DUTCH

D•••C
DCCXC
DIRAC
DORIC
DUROC

•DC••
MDCCC
MDCCI
MDCCL
MDCCV
MDCCX
MDCII
MDCIV
MDCIX
MDCLI
MDCLV
MDCLX
MDCVI
MDCXC
MDCXI
MDCXL
MDCXV
MDCXX

•D•C•
CDXCI
CDXCV
EDICT
EDUCE
EDUCT
MDCCC
MDCCI
MDCCL
MDCCV
MDCCX
MDXCI
MDXCV

•D••C
ADHOC
ADLOC
EDDIC
MDCCC
MDCXC

••DC•
MMDCC
MMDCI
MMDCL
MMDCV
MMDCX

••D•C
ASDIC
EDDIC
INDIC
IODIC
LUDIC
MCDXC
MEDIC
MEDOC
MMDCC
MMDXC
MODOC
VEDIC

•••DC
MMMDC

D•D••
DADDY
DADOS
DIDIN
DIDNT
DIDOS
DIDST
DIDUP
DODGE
DODGY
DODOS
DUDDY
DUDES

D••D•
DADDY
DANDY
DEEDS
DENDR
DIODE
DONDI
DOODY
DOWDY
DUADS
DUDDY
DYADS

D•••D
DARED
DATED
DAVID
DAZED
DEKED
DELED
DEWED
DICED
DIKED
DIMED
DINED
DIVED
DOLED
DOMED
DOSED
DOTED
DOZED
DREAD
DRIED
DROID
DROOD
DRUID
DRYAD
DUKED
DUPED

•DD••
ADDAX
ADDED
ADDER
ADDIE
ADDIN
ADDIS
ADDLE
ADDNL
ADDON
ADDTO
ADDUP
EDDAS
EDDIC
EDDIE
ODDER
ODDLY
UDDER

•D••D
ADDED
EDGED
IDLED

••DD•
BIDDY
BUDDY
CADDO
CADDY
CUDDY
DADDY
DUDDY
FUDDY
GIDDY
HEDDA
JIDDA
KIDDO
LIDDY
MIDDY
MUDDY
NEDDY
NODDY
PADDY
REDDY
RODDY
RUDDS
RUDDY
SODDY
SUDDS
TEDDY
TODDY
VEDDA

••D•D
ADDED
AIDED
BIDED
BODED
CEDED
CODED
ENDED
FADED
GADID
HODAD
JADED
LADED
REDID
SIDED
TIDED
UNDID
WADED

•••DD
RANDD

DE•••
DEALS
DEALT
DEANE
DEANS
DEARS
DEARY
DEBAR
DEBBY
DEBIT
DEBRA
DEBTS
DEBUG
DEBUT
DECAF
DECAL
DECAY
DECCA
DECKS
DECOR
DECOY
DECRY
DEEDS
DEEMS
DEEPS
DEERE
DEERS
DEFAT
DEFER
DEFOE
DEFOG
DEGAS
DEICE
DEIFY
DEIGN
DEISM
DEIST
DEITY
DEKED
DEKES
DELAY
DELCO
DELED
DELES
DELFT
DELHI
DELIS
DELLA
DELLS
DELON
DELOS
DELTA
DELTS
DELVE
DEMES
DEMIT
DEMME
DEMOB
DEMON
DEMOS
DEMUR
DENDR
DENEB
DENES
DENIM
DENIS
DENNY
DENOM
DENSE
DENTE
DENTI
DENTS
DENYS
DEOXY
DEPEW
DEPOT
DEPTH
DEPTS
DERAT
DERBY
DEREK
DERIV
DERMA
DERMO
DERRY
DESKS
DESNA
DETAT
DETER
DETOO
DETRE
DEUCE
DEUCY
DEUTO
DEVIL
DEVON
DEVRY
DEWAN
DEWAR
DEWED
DEWEY
DEXTR

D•E••
DEEDS
DEEMS
DEEPS
DEERE
DEERS
DIEGO
DIEMS
DIENE
DIETS
DOERS
DOEST
DOETH
DREAD
DREAM
DREAR
DREGS
DRESS
DUELS
DUETS
DWEEB
DWELL
DWELT
DYERS

D••E•
DACES
DALES
DALEY
DAMES
DANES
DARED
DARER
DARES
DATED
DATER
DATES
DAWES
DAZED
DAZES
DEFER
DEKED
DEKES
DELED
DELES
DEMES
DENEB
DENES
DEPEW
DEREK
DETER
DEWED
DEWEY
DICED
DICER
DICES
DICEY
DIKED
DIKES
DIMED
DIMES
DINED
DINER
DINES
DIRER
DIVED
DIVER
DIVES
DIZEN
DOGES
DOLED
DOLES
DOMED
DOMES
DONEE
DOPES
DOPEY
DOREN
DOSED
DOSER
DOSES
DOTED
DOTER
DOTES
DOVER
DOVES
DOVEY
DOWEL
DOWER
DOYEN
DOZED
DOZEN
DOZER
DOZES
DRIED
DRIER
DRIES
DRYER
DUCES
DUDES
DUKED
DUKES
DUNES
DUPED
DUPES
DURER
DUVET
DWEEB
DYNEL
DYNES

D•••E
DACHE
DAFOE
DANAE
DANCE
DANKE
DANSE
DANTE
DAVIE
DAYNE
DEANE
DEERE
DEFOE
DEICE
DELVE
DEMME
DENSE
DENTE
DETRE
DEUCE
DHOLE
DHOTE
DIANE
DIENE
DINGE
DIODE
DIONE
DIRGE
DISME
DIXIE
DNASE
DOBIE
DOBLE
DODGE
DOGIE
DOLCE
DONEE
DONNE
DOONE
DOUSE

DOWSE
DOYLE
DRAKE
DRAPE
DRIVE
DROME
DRONE
DROVE
DRUPE
DRUSE
DRUZE
DUANE
DULSE
DUNCE
DUNNE
DUPLE
DUPRE

•DE••
ADEEM
ADELA
ADELE
ADENO
ADEPT
ADEUX
EDEMA
EDENS
IDEAL
IDEAS
IDEST
ODELL
ODETS
ODEUM

•D•E•
ADDED
ADDER
ADEEM
ADHEM
ADIEU
ADLER
ADMEN
ADREM
ADZES
EDGED
EDGER
EDGES
EDSEL
IDLED
IDLER
IDLES
ODDER
UDDER

•D••E
ADAGE
ADDIE
ADDLE
ADELE
ADIGE
ADOBE
ADORE
EDDIE
EDILE
EDUCE
ODILE

••DE•
ADDED
ADDER
AEDES
AIDED
AIDES
ALDEN
ALDER
ANDES
ARDEN
AUDEN
BADEN
BEDEW
BIDED
BIDEN
BIDES
BODED
BODES
CADET
CEDED
CEDES
CIDER
CODED
CODER
CODES
CODEX
CYDER
DUDES
EIDER
ELDER
EMDEN
ENDED
ENDER
FADED
FADES
FIDEL
GODEL
GODET
GODEY
HADES
HIDER
HIDES
INDEF
INDEX
JADED
JADES
JUDEA
LADED
LADEN
LADER
LADES
LODEN
LODES
MEDEA
MEDES
MODEL
MODEM
MODES
NADER
NIDES
NODES
NUDER
NUDES
ODDER
OGDEN
OLDEN
OLDER
ORDER
RIDER
RIDES
RODEO
RUDER
RYDER
SEDER
SIDEA
SIDEB
SIDED
SIDER
SIDES
TIDED
TIDES
UDDER
UNDER
VADER
VIDEO
WADED
WADER
WADES
WEDEL
WIDEN
WIDER
WODEN
YODEL

••D•E
ADDIE
ADDLE
ANDIE
ANDRE
AUDIE
BADGE
BUDGE
CADGE
CADRE
DODGE
EDDIE
ENDUE
EYDIE
FUDGE
HEDGE
INDIE
JODIE
JUDGE
KEDGE
LADLE
LEDGE
LODGE
MADGE
MADRE
MIDGE
NIDRE
NUDGE
OLDIE
PADRE
REDYE
RIDGE
RUDGE
SADHE
SADIE
SEDGE
SIDHE
SIDLE
UNDUE
WEDGE

•••DE
ABIDE
ABODE
AMIDE
ANODE
ASIDE
AZIDE
BLADE
BRIDE
BSIDE
CHIDE
CLYDE
CONDE
CRUDE
DIODE
ELIDE
ELUDE
EPODE
ERODE
ETUDE
EVADE
EXUDE
FERDE
GARDE
GEODE
GLADE
GLEDE
GLIDE
GOLDE
GRADE
GUIDE
HORDE
IMIDE
IRADE
LAUDE
LYNDE
MAUDE
MEADE
MONDE
OXIDE
PRIDE
PRUDE
READE
RHODE
SHADE
SLADE
SLIDE
SNIDE
SONDE
SPADE
SPODE
SUEDE
SWEDE
TARDE
TEIDE
TILDE
TRADE
TSADE
VERDE
WILDE

DF•••
DFLAT

D•F••
DAFFY
DAFOE
DEFAT
DEFER
DEFOE
DEFOG
DOFFS
DUFAY
DUFFS
DUFFY

D••F•
DAFFY
DEIFY
DELFT
DOFFS
DRAFT
DRIFT
DUFFS
DUFFY

D•••F
DECAF
DWARF

•D•F•
EDIFY

•D••F
ADOLF

••D•F
INDEF
RIDOF

D•G••
DAGON
DEGAS
DIGBY
DIGIN
DIGIT
DIGUP
DOGES
DOGGO
DOGGY
DOGIE
DOGIT
DOGMA
DOGON
DUGAN
DUGIN
DUGUP

D••G•
DANGS
DEIGN
DIEGO
DINGE
DINGO
DINGS
DINGY
DIRGE
DODGE
DODGY
DOGGO
DOGGY
DONGS
DOUGH
DRAGS
DREGS
DRUGS

D•••G
DEBUG
DEFOG
DOING
DRANG
DYING

•DG••
EDGAR
EDGED
EDGER
EDGES

•D•G•
ADAGE
ADIGE

••DG•
BADGE
BLDGS
BUDGE
CADGE
DODGE
DODGY
FUDGE
HEDGE
HEDGY
JUDGE
KEDGE
LEDGE
LODGE
MADGE
MIDGE
NUDGE
PODGY
PUDGY
RIDGE
RIDGY
RUDGE
SEDGE
WEDGE
WEDGY

DH•••
DHABI
DHOLE
DHOTE
DHOTI
DHOWS

D••H•
DACHA
DACHE
DASHI
DELHI
DICHO
DONHO
DUCHY

D•••H
DARTH
DEPTH
DINAH
DITCH
DOETH
DOLPH
DOUGH
DUTCH

•DH••
ADHEM
ADHOC

•D•H•
IDAHO

•D••H
EDITH

••DH•
SADHE
SADHU
SIDHE

••D•H
JUDAH
WIDTH

•••DH
SANDH

DI•••
DIALS
DIANA
DIANE
DIARY
DIAZO
DICED
DICER
DICES
DICEY
DICHO
DICKS
DICKY
DICOT
DICTA
DICTS
DICTU
DIDIN
DIDNT
DIDOS
DIDST
DIDUP
DIEGO
DIEMS
DIENE
DIETS
DIGBY
DIGIN
DIGIT
DIGUP
DIJON
DIKED
DIKES
DILLS
DILLY
DIMED
DIMES
DIMLY
DINAH
DINAR
DINED
DINER
DINES
DINGE
DINGO
DINGS
DINGY
DINKS
DINKY
DINTS
DIODE
DIONE
DIPLO
DIPPY
DIRAC
DIRER
DIRGE
DIRKS
DIRTY
DISCO
DISCS
DISKS
DISME
DISTR
DITCH
DITKA
DITSY
DITTO
DITTY
DITZY
DIVAN
DIVAS
DIVED
DIVER
DIVES
DIVOT
DIVVY
DIXIE
DIXIT
DIXON
DIZEN
DIZZY

D•I••
DAILY
DAIRY
DAISY
DAIWA
DCIII
DEICE
DEIFY
DEIGN
DEISM
DEIST
DEITY
DJINN
DLIII
DOILY
DOING
DOITS
DRIBS
DRIED
DRIER
DRIES
DRIFT
DRILL
DRINA
DRINK
DRIPS
DRIVE
DVIII
DVINA
DXIII
DYING

D••I•
DACIA
DANIO
DARIN
DARIO
DAVID
DAVIE
DAVIS
DAVIT
DCCII
DCCIV
DCCIX
DCIII
DCLII
DCLIV
DCLIX
DCVII
DCXII
DCXIV
DCXIX
DEBIT
DELIS
DEMIT
DENIM
DENIS
DERIV
DEVIL
DIDIN
DIGIN
DIGIT
DIXIE
DIXIT
DLIII
DLVII
DLXII
DLXIV
DLXIX
DOBIE
DOGIE
DOGIT
DORIC
DORIS
DRAIL
DRAIN
DROID
DROIT
DRUID
DUBIN
DUGIN
DVIII
DXCII
DXCIV
DXCIX
DXIII
DXLII
DXLIV
DXLIX
DXVII
DXXII
DXXIV
DXXIX

D•••I
DALAI
DASHI
DCCCI
DCCII
DCCLI
DCCVI
DCCXI
DCIII
DCLII
DCLVI
DCLXI
DCVII
DCXCI
DCXII
DCXLI
DCXVI
DCXXI
DELHI
DENTI
DHABI
DHOTI
DLIII
DLVII
DLXII
DLXVI
DLXXI
DONDI
DORSI
DOUAI
DUBAI
DVIII
DXCII
DXCVI
DXIII
DXLII
DXLVI
DXVII
DXXII
DXXVI
DXXXI

•DI••
ADIEU
ADIGE
ADINT
ADIOS
ADITS
CDIII
EDICT
EDIFY
EDILE
EDINA
EDITH
EDITS
IDIOM
IDIOT
MDIII
ODILE
ODIST
ODIUM

•D•I•
ADAIR
ADDIE
ADDIN
ADDIS
ADLIB
ADMIN
ADMIT
ADMIX
ADVIL
CDIII
CDLII
CDLIV
CDLIX
CDVII
CDXII
CDXIV
CDXIX
EDDIC
EDDIE
EDWIN
MDCII
MDCIV
MDCIX
MDIII
MDLII
MDLIV
MDLIX
MDVII
MDXII
MDXIV
MDXIX

•D••I
ADLAI
CDIII
CDLII
CDLVI
CDLXI
CDVII
CDXCI
CDXII
CDXLI
CDXVI
CDXXI
MDCCI
MDCII
MDCLI
MDCVI
MDCXI
MDIII
MDLII
MDLVI
MDLXI
MDVII
MDXCI
MDXII
MDXLI
MDXVI
MDXXI

••DI•
ADDIE
ADDIN
ADDIS
ANDIE
ASDIC
AUDIE
AUDIO
AUDIS
AUDIT
BEDIM
CADIS
CADIZ
DIDIN
EDDIC
EDDIE
EYDIE
GADID
HEDIN
INDIA
INDIC
INDIE
INDIO
INDIV
IODIC
JODIE
LEDIN
LUDIC
LYDIA
MCDII
MCDIV
MCDIX
MEDIA
MEDIC
MEDIT
MIDIS
MMDII
MMDIV
MMDIX
NADIA
NADIR
OLDIE
ONDIT
PODIA
RADII
RADIO
RADIX
REDID
RODIN
SADIE
UNDID
VADIM
VADIS
VEDIC
WADIS

••D•I
AODAI
HADJI
INDRI
MCDII
MCDLI
MCDVI
MCDXI
MMDCI
MMDII
MMDLI
MMDVI
MMDXI
RADII

•••DI
BONDI
CARDI
CYNDI
DONDI
EGADI
GONDI
HEIDI
HINDI
JEUDI
LUNDI
MAHDI
MARDI
MMCDI
MMMDI
NALDI
PARDI
RANDI
SAUDI
SCUDI
SOLDI
TONDI
VERDI

DJ•••
DJINN

D•J••
DIJON
DOJOS

••DJ•
HADJI

D•K••
DAKAR
DEKED
DEKES
DIKED
DIKES
DUKAS
DUKED
DUKES

D••K•
DANKE
DARKS
DECKS
DESKS
DICKS
DICKY
DINKS
DINKY
DIRKS
DISKS
DITKA
DOCKS
DRAKE
DUCKS
DUCKY
DUNKS
DUSKS
DUSKY

D•••K
DAYAK
DEREK
DRANK
DRINK
DRUNK

••DK•
VODKA

••D•K
KODAK

DL•••
DLIII
DLVII
DLXII
DLXIV
DLXIX
DLXVI
DLXXI
DLXXV
DLXXX

D•L••
DALAI
DALES
DALEY
DALLY
DCLII
DCLIV
DCLIX
DCLVI
DCLXI
DCLXV
DCLXX
DELAY
DELCO
DELED
DELES
DELFT
DELHI
DELIS
DELLA
DELLS
DELON
DELOS
DELTA
DELTS
DELVE
DFLAT
DILLS
DILLY
DOLBY
DOLCE
DOLED
DOLES
DOLLS
DOLLY
DOLMA
DOLOR
DOLPH
DOLTS
DPLUS
DRLAO
DULLS
DULLY
DULSE
DXLII
DXLIV
DXLIX
DXLVI
DYLAN

D••L•
DAILY
DALLY
DARLA
DCCLI
DCCLV
DCCLX
DCXLI
DCXLV
DEALS
DEALT
DELLA
DELLS
DHOLE
DIALS
DILLS
DILLY
DIMLY
DIPLO
DOBLA
DOBLE
DOILY
DOLLS
DOLLY
DOYLE
DRILL
DROLL
DRYLY
DUELS
DULLS
DULLY
DUPLE
DWELL
DWELT

D•••L
DARYL
DCCCL
DCCXL
DECAL
DEVIL
DORAL
DOTAL
DOWEL
DRAIL
DRAWL
DRILL
DROLL
DROOL
DUCAL
DWELL
DYNEL

•DL••
ADLAI
ADLER
ADLIB
ADLOC
CDLII
CDLIV
CDLIX
CDLVI
CDLXI
CDLXV
CDLXX
IDLED
IDLER
IDLES
MDLII
MDLIV
MDLIX
MDLVI
MDLXI
MDLXV
MDLXX

•D•L•
ADDLE
ADELA
ADELE
ADOLF
ADULT
CDXLI
CDXLV
EDILE
IDOLS
IDYLL
IDYLS
MDCLI
MDCLV
MDCLX
MDXLI
MDXLV
NDOLA
ODDLY
ODELL
ODILE
UDALL

•D••L
ADDNL
ADVIL
EDSEL
IDEAL
IDYLL
MDCCL
MDCXL
ODELL
UDALL

••DL•
ADDLE
BADLY
GODLY
LADLE
MADLY
MCDLI
MCDLV
MCDLX
MMDLI
MMDLV
MMDLX
ODDLY
SADLY
SIDLE

••D•L
ABDUL
ADDNL
ALDOL
FIDEL
GODEL
MCDXL
MEDAL
MMDCL
MMDXL
MODAL
MODEL
NODAL
PEDAL
TIDAL
VIDAL
WEDEL
YODEL

•••DL
LENDL
MMCDL
MMMDL
PANDL
SANDL

D•M••
DAMAN
DAMAR
DAMES
DAMNS
DAMON
DAMPS
DAMUP
DEMES
DEMIT
DEMME
DEMOB
DEMON
DEMOS
DEMUR
DIMED
DIMES
DIMLY
DOMED
DOMES
DUMAS
DUMBO
DUMBS
DUMMY
DUMPS
DUMPY

D••M•
DEEMS
DEMME
DERMA
DERMO
DIEMS
DISME
DOGMA
DOLMA
DOOMS
DORMS
DRAMA
DRAMS
DROME
DRUMS
DUMMY
DUOMO

D•••M
DATUM
DEISM
DENIM
DENOM
DREAM
DURUM

•DM••
ADMAN
ADMEN
ADMIN
ADMIT
ADMIX

•D•M•
ADAMS
EDAMS
EDEMA

•D••M
ADEEM
ADHEM
ADREM
CDROM
IDIOM
ODEUM
ODIUM

••D•M
BEDIM
MADAM
MODEM
SEDUM
SODOM
VADIM

•••DM
AANDM

DN•••
DNASE

D•N••
DANAE
DANCE
DANCY
DANDY
DANES
DANGS
DANIO
DANKE
DANNY
DANSE
DANTE
DANZA
DENDR
DENEB
DENES
DENIM
DENIS
DENNY
DENOM
DENSE
DENTE
DENTI
DENTS
DENYS
DINAH
DINAR
DINED
DINER
DINES
DINGE
DINGO
DINGS
DINGY
DINKS
DINKY
DINTS
DONAS
DONAT
DONAU
DONDI
DONEE
DONGS
DONHO
DONNA
DONNE
DONNY
DONOR
DONUT
DUNCE
DUNES
DUNKS
DUNNE
DUNNO
DYNEL
DYNES

D••N•
DAMNS
DANNY
DARNS
DAUNT
DAWNS
DAYNE
DEANE
DEANS
DENNY
DESNA
DIANA
DIANE
DIDNT
DIENE
DIONE
DJINN
DOING
DONNA
DONNE
DONNY

DOONE DOWNS DOWNY DRANG DRANK DRANO DRINA DRINK DRONE DRUNK DUANE DUNNE DUNNO DVINA DYING

D•••N
DAGON DAMAN DAMON DARIN DAYAN DEIGN DELON DEMON DEVON DEWAN DIDIN DIGIN DIJON DIVAN DIXON DIZEN DJINN DOGON DORAN DOREN DOYEN DOZEN DRAIN DRAWN DROWN DUBIN DUGAN DUGIN DURAN DYLAN

•D•N•
ADANA ADANO ADDNL ADENO ADINT EDENS EDINA ODONT

•D••N
ADDIN ADDON ADMAN ADMEN ADMIN ADORN EDWIN

••DN•
ADDNL DIDNT HADNT

••D•N
ADDIN ADDON AIDAN ALDAN ALDEN ARDEN AUDEN BADEN BIDEN BIDON DIDIN EMDEN FEDON HADON HEDIN LADEN LEDIN LEDON LODEN OGDEN OLDEN RADON REDAN REDON RODAN RODIN SEDAN SIDON SUDAN WIDEN WODEN

•••DN
HAYDN

DO•••
DOBIE DOBLA DOBLE DOBRA DOBRO DOCKS DODGE DODGY DODOS DOERS DOEST DOETH DOFFS DOGES DOGGO DOGGY DOGIE DOGIT DOGMA DOGON DOILY DOING DOITS DOJOS DOLBY DOLCE DOLED DOLES DOLLS DOLLY DOLMA DOLOR DOLPH DOLTS DOMED DOMES DONAS DONAT DONAU DONDI DONEE DONGS DONHO DONNA DONNE DONNY DONOR DONUT DOODY DOOMS DOONE DOORS DOOZY DOPES DOPEY DORAL DORAN DOREN DORIC DORIS DORMS DORPS DORSA DORSI DORSO DOSED DOSER DOSES DOTAL DOTED DOTER DOTES DOTTO DOTTY DOUAI DOUAY DOUBT DOUGH DOURO DOUSE DOVER DOVES DOVEY DOWDY DOWEL DOWER DOWNS DOWNY DOWRY DOWSE DOYEN DOYLE DOZED DOZEN DOZER DOZES

D•O••
DEOXY DHOLE DHOTE DHOTI DHOWS DIODE DIONE DOODY DOOMS DOONE DOORS DOOZY DROID DROIT DROLL DROME DRONE DROOD DROOL DROOP DROPS DROSS DROVE DROWN DUOMO

D••O•
DADOS DAFOE DAGON DAMON DAVOS DECOR DECOY DEFOE DEFOG DELON DELOS DEMOB DEMON DEMOS DENOM DEPOT DETOO DEVON DICOT DIDOS DIJON DIVOT DIXON DODOS DOGON DOJOS DOLOR DONOR DROOD DROOL DROOP DUBOS DUROC DUROS

D•••O
DANIO DARIO DAVAO DELCO DERMO DETOO DEUTO DIAZO DICHO DIEGO DINGO DIPLO DISCO DITTO DOBRO DOGGO DONHO DORSO DOTTO DOURO DRACO DRANO DRLAO DUMBO DUNNO DUOMO

•DO••
ADOBE ADOLF ADOPT ADORE ADORN ADOUT IDOLS NDOLA ODONT ODORS ODOUR

•D•O•
ADDON ADHOC ADIOS ADLOC CDROM IDIOM IDIOT

•D••O
ADANO ADDTO ADENO IDAHO

••DO•
ADDON ALDOL ANDOR ARDOR BIDON DADOS DIDOS DODOS ENDOR ENDOW FADOS FEDON FODOR GODOT HADON KUDOS LEDON LIDOS MEDOC MODOC MSDOS NODOZ ORDOS RADON REDON REDOX RIDOF SIDON SODOM SYDOW TODOS TUDOR UPDOS VIDOR WIDOW

••D•O
ADDTO ANDRO AUDIO CADDO HADTO HYDRO INDIO KIDDO LEDTO PEDRO RADIO RODEO VIDEO

•••DO
AMADO BANDO CADDO CANDO CONDO CREDO FALDO FORDO FRODO GORDO GUIDO HONDO IMIDO IRIDO KENDO KIDDO LANDO MISDO MONDO OUTDO PARDO PRADO RHODO RONDO SCUDO SOLDO TONDO WALDO ZENDO

DP•••
DPLUS

D•P••
DEPEW DEPOT DEPTH DEPTS DIPLO DIPPY DOPES DOPEY DUPED DUPES DUPLE DUPRE

D••P•
DAMPS DEEPS DIPPY DOLPH DORPS DRAPE DRIPS DROPS DRUPE DUMPS DUMPY

D•••P
DAMUP DIDUP DIGUP DROOP DRYUP DUGUP

•D•P•
ADAPT ADEPT ADOPT

•D••P
ADDUP

••D•P
ADDUP BIDUP DIDUP ENDUP FEDUP WADUP

DR•••
DRABS DRACO DRAFT DRAGS DRAIL DRAIN DRAKE DRAMA DRAMS DRANG DRANK DRANO DRAPE DRATS DRAWL DRAWN DRAWS DRAYS DREAD DREAM DREAR DREGS DRESS DRIBS DRIED DRIER DRIES DRIFT DRILL DRINA DRINK DRIPS DRIVE DRLAO DROID DROIT DROLL DROME DRONE DROOD DROOL DROOP DROPS DROSS DROVE DROWN DRUBS DRUGS DRUID DRUMS DRUNK DRUPE DRURY DRUSE DRUZE DRYAD DRYER DRYLY DRYUP

D•R••
DARBY DARED DARER DARES DARIN DARIO DARKS DARLA DARNS DARTH DARTS DARYA DARYL DERAT DERBY DEREK DERIV DERMA DERMO DERRY DIRAC DIRER DIRGE DIRKS DIRTY DORAL DORAN DOREN DORIC DORIS DORMS DORPS DORSA DORSI DORSO DURAN DURER DUROC DUROS DURRA DURST DURUM

D••R•
DAIRY DEARS DEARY DEBRA DECRY DEERE DEERS DERRY DETRE DEVRY DIARY DOBRA DOBRO DOERS DOORS DOURO DOWRY DRURY DUPRE DURRA DWARF DYERS

D•••R
DAKAR DAMAR DARER DATER DEBAR DECOR DEFER DEMUR DENDR DETER DEWAR DEXTR DICER DINAR DINER DIRER DISTR DIVER DOLOR DONOR DOSER DOTER DOVER DOWER DOZER DREAR DRIER DRYER DURER

•DR••
ADREM CDROM

•D•R•
ADORE ADORN ODORS

•D••R
ADAIR ADDER ADLER EDGAR EDGER IDLER ODDER ODOUR UDDER

••DR•
ANDRE ANDRO AUDRA CADRE CMDRS HYDRA HYDRO INDRA INDRI MADRE MUDRA NIDRE PADRE PEDRO SIDRA SUDRA

••D•R
ADDER ALDER ANDOR ARDOR CEDAR CIDER CODER CYDER EIDER ELDER ENDER ENDOR FODOR HADAR HIDER KADAR LADER NADER NADIR NUDER ODDER OLDER ORDER RADAR RIDER RUDER RYDER SEDER SIDER TUDOR UDDER UNDER VADER VIDOR WADER WIDER

•••DR
DENDR QUADR RANDR

D•S••
DASHI DESKS DESNA DISCO DISCS DISKS DISME DISTR DOSED DOSER DOSES DUSKS DUSKY DUSTS DUSTY

D••S•
DAISY DANSE DEISM DEIST DENSE DIDST DITSY DNASE DOEST DORSA DORSI DORSO DOUSE DOWSE DRESS DROSS DRUSE DULSE DURST

D•••S
DACES DADOS DALES DAMES DAMNS DAMPS DANES DANGS DARES DARKS DARNS DARTS DATES DAUBS DAVIS DAVOS DAVYS DAWES DAWNS DAZES DEALS DEANS DEARS DEBTS DECKS DEEDS DEEMS DEEPS DEERS DEGAS DEKES DELES DELIS DELLS DELOS DELTS DEMES DEMOS DENES DENIS DENTS DENYS DEPTS DESKS DHOWS DIALS DICES DICKS DICTS DIDOS DIEMS DIETS DIKES DILLS DIMES DINES DINGS DINKS DINTS DIRKS DISCS DISKS DIVAS DIVES DOCKS DODOS DOERS DOFFS DOGES DOITS DOJOS DOLES DOLLS DOLTS DOMES DONAS DONGS DOOMS DOORS DOPES DORIS DORMS DORPS DOSES DOTES DOVES DOWNS DOZES DPLUS DRABS DRAGS DRAMS DRATS DRAWS DRAYS DREGS DRESS DRIBS DRIES DRIPS DROPS DROSS DRUBS DRUGS DRUMS DUADS DUBOS DUCES DUCKS DUCTS DUDES DUELS DUETS DUFFS DUKAS DUKES DULLS DUMAS DUMBS DUMPS DUNES DUNKS DUPES DUROS DUSKS DUSTS DYADS DYERS DYNES

•DS••
EDSEL

•D•S•
ADUST IDEST ODIST

•D••S
ADAMS ADDIS ADIOS ADITS ADZES EDAMS EDDAS EDENS EDGES EDITS IDEAS IDLES IDOLS IDYLS ODETS ODORS

••DS•
DIDST HADST MIDST SUDSY

••D•S
ADDIS AEDES AIDES ALDUS ANDES AUDIS BIDES BLDGS BODES CADIS CEDES CMDRS CODAS CODES DADOS DIDOS DODOS DUDES EDDAS FADES FADOS HADES HIDES INDUS JADES JUDAS KUDOS KUDUS LADES LADYS LIDOS LODES MEDES MIDAS MIDIS MODES MODUS MSDOS NIDES NIDUS NODES NODUS NUDES ORDOS PUDUS RIDES RUDDS SIDES SODAS SUDDS TIDES TODOS UPDOS VADIS VEDAS WADES WADIS

•••DS
ACADS ACIDS BALDS BANDS BARDS BEADS BENDS BINDS BIRDS BLVDS BONDS BRADS BUNDS BYRDS CARDS CLODS COEDS COLDS CORDS CURDS DEEDS DUADS DYADS EGADS FEEDS FENDS FEUDS FINDS FOLDS FONDS FOODS FORDS FUNDS GAUDS GILDS GIRDS GLADS GOADS GOLDS GONDS GOODS GRADS GRIDS HANDS HEADS HEEDS HERDS HINDS HOLDS HOODS KINDS KURDS LANDS LARDS LAUDS LEADS LEEDS LENDS LOADS LORDS MAIDS MEADS MEEDS MELDS MENDS MINDS MOLDS MOODS NARDS NEEDS NERDS OPEDS PARDS PENDS PIEDS PLODS PONDS POODS PRODS QUADS QUIDS QUODS RAIDS RANDS READS REEDS RENDS RINDS ROADS ROODS RUDDS SANDS SARDS SCADS SCUDS SEEDS SENDS SHADS SHEDS SKIDS SLEDS SPADS SPUDS STUDS SUDDS SURDS TENDS THUDS TOADS VELDS VENDS VOIDS WANDS WARDS WEEDS WELDS WENDS WILDS WINDS WOADS WOLDS WOODS WORDS YARDS

D•T••
DATED DATER DATES DATUM DETAT DETER DETOO DETRE DITCH DITKA DITSY DITTO DITTY DITZY DOTAL DOTED DOTER DOTES DOTTO DOTTY DUTCH

D••T•
DANTE DARTH DARTS DEBTS DEITY DELTA DELTS DENTE DENTI DENTS DEPTH DEPTS DEUTO DEXTR DHOTE DHOTI DICTA DICTS DICTU DIETS DINTS DIRTY DISTR DITTO DITTY DOETH DOITS DOLTS DOTTO DOTTY DRATS DUCTS DUETS DUSTS DUSTY

D•••T
DAUNT DAVIT DEALT DEBIT DEBUT DEFAT DEIST DELFT DEMIT DEPOT DERAT DETAT DFLAT DICOT DIDNT DIDST DIGIT DIVOT DIXIT DOEST DOGIT DONAT DONUT DOUBT DRAFT DRIFT DROIT DUCAT DURST DUVET DWELT

•D•T•
ADDTO ADITS ADYTA EDITH EDITS ODETS

•D••T
ADAPT ADEPT ADINT ADMIT ADOPT ADOUT ADULT ADUST EDICT EDUCT IDEST IDIOT ODIST ODONT

••DT•
ADDTO HADTO LEDTO WIDTH

••D•T
AUDIT CADET DIDNT DIDST GODET GODOT HADAT HADNT HADST MEDIT MIDST ONDIT SADAT

•••DT
BUNDT HEIDT STADT VEIDT VELDT WENDT

DU•••
DUADS DUANE DUBAI DUBIN DUBOS DUCAL DUCAT DUCES DUCHY DUCKS DUCKY DUCTS DUDDY DUDES DUELS DUETS DUFAY DUFFS DUFFY DUGAN DUGIN DUGUP DUKAS DUKED

DUKES DULLS DULLY DULSE DUMAS DUMBO DUMBS DUMMY DUMPS DUMPY DUNCE DUNES DUNKS DUNNE DUNNO DUOMO DUPED DUPES DUPLE DUPRE DURAN DURER DUROC DUROS DURRA DURST DURUM DUSKS DUSKY DUSTS DUSTY DUTCH DUVET

D•U••
DAUBS DAUNT DEUCE DEUCY DEUTO DOUAI DOUAY DOUBT DOUGH DOURO DOUSE DRUBS DRUGS DRUID DRUMS DRUNK DRUPE DRURY DRUSE DRUZE

D••U•
DAMUP DATUM DEBUG DEBUT DEMUR DIDUP DIGUP DONUT DPLUS DRYUP DUGUP DURUM

D•••U
DICTU DONAU

•DU••
ADULT ADUST ADUWA EDUCE EDUCT

•D•U•
ADDUP ADEUX ADOUT ODEUM ODIUM ODOUR

•D••U
ADIEU

••DU•
ABDUL ADDUP ALDUS BIDUP DIDUP ENDUE ENDUP FEDUP INDUS KUDUS MODUS NIDUS NODUS PADUA PUDUS REDUB REDUX SEDUM UNDUE VADUZ WADUP

••D•U
KUDZU SADHU

•••DU
FONDU HINDU PERDU

DV•••
DVIII DVINA

D•V••
DAVAO DAVID DAVIE DAVIS DAVIT DAVOS DAVYS DCVII DEVIL DEVON DEVRY DIVAN DIVAS DIVED DIVER DIVES DIVOT DIVVY DLVII DOVER DOVES DOVEY DUVET DXVII

D••V•
DCCVI DCLVI DCXVI DELVE DIVVY DLXVI DRIVE DROVE DXCVI DXLVI DXXVI

D•••V
DCCCV DCCIV DCCLV DCCXV DCLIV DCLXV DCXCV DCXIV DCXLV DCXXV DERIV DLXIV DLXXV DXCIV DXLIV DXXIV DXXXV

•DV••
ADVIL CDVII MDVII

•D•V•
CDLVI CDXVI MDCVI MDLVI MDXVI

•D••V
CDLIV CDLXV CDXCV CDXIV CDXLV CDXXV MDCCV MDCIV MDCLV MDCXV MDLIV MDLXV MDXCV MDXIV MDXLV MDXXV

••DV•
MCDVI MMDVI

••D•V
INDIV MCDIV MCDLV MCDXV MMDCV MMDIV MMDLV MMDXV

•••DV
MMCDV MMMDV

DW•••
DWARF DWEEB DWELL DWELT

D•W••
DAWES DAWNS DEWAN DEWAR DEWED DEWEY DOWDY DOWEL DOWER DOWNS DOWNY DOWRY DOWSE

D••W•
DAIWA DHOWS DRAWL DRAWN DRAWS DROWN

D•••W
DEPEW

•DW••
EDWIN

•D•W•
ADUWA

••D•W
BEDEW ENDOW SYDOW WIDOW

•••DW
CANDW

DX•••
DXCII DXCIV DXCIX DXCVI DXIII DXLII DXLIV DXLIX DXLVI DXVII DXXII DXXIV DXXIX DXXVI DXXXI DXXXV

D•X••
DCXCI DCXCV DCXII DCXIV DCXIX DCXLI DCXLV DCXVI DCXXI DCXXV DCXXX DEXTR DIXIE DIXIT DIXON DLXII DLXIV DLXIX DLXVI DLXXI DLXXV DLXXX DXXII DXXIV DXXIX DXXVI DXXXI DXXXV

D••X•
DCCXC DCCXI DCCXL DCCXV DCCXX DCLXI DCLXV DCLXX DCXXI DCXXV DCXXX DEOXY DLXXI DLXXV DLXXX DXXXI DXXXV

D•••X
DCCCX DCCIX DCCLX DCCXX DCLIX DCLXX DCXIX DCXXX DLXIX DLXXX DXCIX DXLIX DXXIX

•DX••
CDXCI CDXCV CDXII CDXIV CDXIX CDXLI CDXLV CDXVI CDXXI CDXXV CDXXX MDXCI MDXCV MDXII MDXIV MDXIX MDXLI MDXLV MDXVI MDXXI MDXXV MDXXX

•D•X•
CDLXI CDLXV CDLXX CDXXI CDXXV CDXXX MDCXC MDCXI MDCXL MDCXV MDCXX MDLXI MDLXV MDLXX MDXXI MDXXV MDXXX

•D••X
ADDAX ADEUX ADMIX CDLIX CDLXX CDXIX CDXXX MDCCX MDCIX MDCLX MDCXX MDLIX MDLXX MDXIX MDXXX

••DX•
MCDXC MCDXI MCDXL MCDXV MCDXX MMDXC MMDXI MMDXL MMDXV MMDXX

••D•X
ADDAX CODEX INDEX MCDIX MCDLX MCDXX MMDCX MMDIX MMDLX MMDXX RADIX REDOX REDUX

•••DX
MMCDX MMMDX

DY•••
DYADS DYERS DYING DYLAN DYNEL DYNES

D•Y••
DAYAK DAYAN DAYNE DOYEN DOYLE DRYAD DRYER DRYLY DRYUP

D••Y•
DARYA DARYL DAVYS DENYS DRAYS

D•••Y
DADDY DAFFY DAILY DAIRY DAISY DALEY DALLY DANCY DANDY DANNY DARBY DEARY DEBBY DECAY DECOY DECRY DEIFY DEITY DELAY DENNY DEOXY DERBY DERRY DEUCY DEVRY DEWEY DIARY DICEY DICKY DIGBY DILLY DIMLY DINGY DINKY DIPPY DIRTY DITSY DITTY DITZY DIVVY DIZZY DODGY DOGGY DOILY DOLBY DOLLY DONNY DOODY DOOZY DOPEY DOTTY DOUAY DOVEY DOWDY DOWNY DOWRY DRURY DRYLY DUCHY DUCKY DUDDY DUFAY DUFFY DULLY DUMMY DUMPY DUSKY DUSTY

•DY••
ADYTA IDYLL IDYLS

•D••Y
EDIFY ODDLY

••DY•
LADYS REDYE

••D•Y
BADLY BIDDY BUDDY CADDY CUDDY DADDY DODGY DUDDY FUDDY GIDDY GODEY GODLY HEDGY KIDDY LIDDY MADLY MIDDY MUDDY NEDDY NODDY ODDLY PADDY PODGY PUDGY REDDY RIDGY RODDY RUDDY SADLY SODDY SUDSY TEDDY TODAY TODDY VEDAY VJDAY WEDGY

•••DY
ACIDY BANDY BAWDY BEADY BIDDY BIRDY BRADY BRODY BUDDY BUNDY CADDY CANDY CINDY CUDDY CURDY DADDY DANDY DOODY DOWDY DUDDY FUDDY FUNDY GANDY GAUDY GIDDY GOODY GORDY GOUDY GOWDY GRADY GRODY GURDY HANDY HARDY HEADY HOWDY HURDY KIDDY LARDY LIDDY LINDY LUNDY MANDY MIDDY MINDY MOLDY MOODY MUDDY NEDDY NEEDY NERDY NODDY PADDY RANDY READY REDDY REEDY RODDY ROWDY RUDDY SANDY SEEDY SHADY SODDY STUDY TANDY TARDY TEDDY TOADY TODDY WEEDY WENDY WINDY WOODY WORDY

D•Z••
DAZED DAZES DIZEN DIZZY DOZED DOZEN DOZER DOZES

D••Z•
DANZA DIAZO DITZY DIZZY DOOZY DRUZE

•DZ••
ADZES

••DZ•
KUDZU

••D•Z
CADIZ NODOZ VADUZ

EA•••
EAGER EAGLE EAGRE EAMES EAMON EARED EARLE EARLS EARLY EARNS EARTH EASED EASEL EASES EASTS EATAT EATEN EATER EATIN EATIT EATON EATUP EAVED EAVES

E•A••
EDAMS EGADI EGADS ELAND ELATE EMAIL ENACT ENATE EPACT ERASE ERATO ETAGE ETAPE EVADE EVANS EXACT EXALT EXAMS

E••A•
EATAT ECLAT EDDAS EDGAR EFLAT EGGAR ELGAR ELIAS ELMAN ELWAY EMBAR EMBAY ENIAC ENLAI EPHAH EPHAS EQUAL ESBAT ESSAY ESTAB ETHAN ETNAS EVIAN EYRAS

E•••A
EDEMA EDINA ELENA ELIZA ENNEA ENTIA ERICA ERIKA ERISA ETYMA EVITA EVORA EXTRA

•EA••
AEAEA BEACH BEADS BEADY BEAKS BEALL BEALS BEAMS BEAMY BEANO BEANS BEANY BEARD BEARS BEAST BEATS BEAUS BEAUT BEAUX CEASE DEALS DEALT DEANE DEANS DEARS DEARY FEARS FEAST FEATS GEARS GEARY HEADS HEADY HEALS HEALY HEAPS HEARD HEARN HEARS HEART HEATH HEATS HEAVE HEAVY JEANE JEANS KEACH KEANE KEANU KEATS LEACH LEADS LEAFS LEAFY LEAHY LEAKS LEAKY LEANS LEANT LEAPS LEAPT LEARN LEARY LEASE LEASH LEAST LEAVE MEADE MEADS MEALS MEALY MEANS MEANT MEANY MEARA MEATS MEATY NEALE NEAPS NEARS NEATH NEATO NEATS PEABO PEACE PEACH PEAKS PEALE PEALS PEARL PEARS PEARY PEASE PEATS PEATY PEAVY REACH REACT READE READS READY REAIM REAIR REALM REALS REAMS REAPS REARM REARS REATA SEALE SEALS SEALY SEAMS SEAMY SEARS SEATO SEATS TEACH TEAKS TEALS TEAMS TEARS TEARY TEASE WEALS WEANS WEARS WEARY WEAVE YEANS YEARN YEARS YEAST YEATS ZEALS

•E•A•
AETAT BEGAN BEGAT BEHAN BELAY BEMAS BETAS CEDAR CERAM CERAT CESAR DEBAR DECAF DECAL DECAY DEFAT DEGAS DELAY DERAT DETAT DEWAN DEWAR FERAL FETAL FETAS GERAH GETAS GETAT HEJAZ HEMAN HENAN HERAT HEXAD KEBAB KEMAL KENAI KERAT LEFAY LEGAL LEHAR LEMAY LETAT LEVAR LEXAN MEDAL MEGAN MELAN MESAS METAL NEMAN NEMAT NEPAL PECAN PEDAL PENAL PERAN PETAL REBAG REBAR RECAP REDAN REGAL REGAN REHAB REHAN RELAX RELAY REMAN REMAP RENAL RENAN REPAY RERAN RETAG RETAP RETAR RETAX REWAX SEDAN SEGAL SEGAR SELAH SEPAL SERAC SERAI SETAE SETAT TEPAL TEXAN TEXAS VEDAS VEDAY VEGAN VEGAS VELAR VENAE VENAL ZETAS

•E••A
AEAEA AECIA AETNA BELLA BELVA BEREA BERRA BETTA CEIBA CELIA CELLA CERIA CESTA CEUTA DEBRA DECCA DELLA DELTA DERMA DESNA FELLA FERIA FESTA GEENA GEMMA GENOA HEDDA HEKLA HELGA HENNA HEPTA KENYA LEEZA LEHUA LEICA LEILA LEMMA LENYA LEONA LEORA LEPTA MEARA MECCA MEDEA MEDIA MEHTA MELBA MENSA MESTA NEMEA PELLA PEMBA PENNA PENTA PENZA PEPLA PETRA REATA REGIA RENTA RETIA SEEYA SEHNA SELMA SELVA SENNA SEPIA SEPTA SERRA SERTA TEENA TERRA TERZA TESLA TESTA TETRA VEDDA VENDA VERSA VESTA XENIA YENTA YERBA ZEBRA ZELDA ZENDA

••EA•
ABEAM AHEAD ANEAR APEAK AREAL AREAR AREAS ATEAM BLEAK BLEAR BLEAT BREAD BREAK BREAM CHEAP CHEAT CLEAN CLEAR CLEAT CREAK CREAM DREAD DREAM DREAR FLEAS FREAK GLEAM GLEAN GREAT IBEAM ICEAX IDEAL IDEAS KNEAD OBEAH OCEAN OLEAN ONEAL OREAD PAEAN PLEAD PLEAS PLEAT RHEAS SHEAF SHEAN SHEAR SKEAN SKEAT SMEAR SNEAD SNEAK SPEAK SPEAR STEAD STEAK STEAL STEAM SWEAR SWEAT TREAD TREAT TWEAK WHEAL WHEAT WREAK

••E•A
ADELA AGENA AKELA ALETA AMEBA ARECA ARENA AVENA BREDA BUENA CHEKA CHELA CIERA EDEMA ELENA FREDA FRENA FREYA GEENA GRETA HAEMA HYENA LEEZA OMEGA ONEGA OPERA OVETA PIETA PLENA SCENA SEEYA SHEBA SIENA SNEVA STELA TEENA THECA THEDA THEMA THERA THETA

•••EA
AEAEA APNEA ATSEA BEREA BOHEA CANEA COREA ENNEA FOVEA GALEA HOSEA JUDEA KOREA LULEA MEDEA NEMEA OCREA OSHEA PALEA PILEA SIDEA TYPEA

EB•••
EBBED

EBERT
EBOLI
EBONY
EBSEN

E•B••
EBBED
ELBOW
EMBAR
EMBAY
EMBED
EMBER
ESBAT
EUBIE

E•••B
ESTAB
EXURB

•EB••
BEBOP
DEBAR
DEBBY
DEBIT
DEBRA
DEBTS
DEBUG
DEBUT
KEBAB
REBAG
REBAR
REBBE
REBEC
REBEL
REBID
REBUS
REBUT
SEBUM
WEBER
XEBEC
ZEBRA
ZEBUS

•E•B•
BEEBE
CEIBA
DEBBY
DERBY
GETBY
HERBS
HERBY
KERBS
LETBE
MELBA
PEABO
PEMBA
REBBE
SERBS
SETBY
VERBS
WELBY
YERBA

•E••B
CELEB
DEMOB
DENEB
KEBAB
REDUB
REHAB

••EB•
AMEBA
BEEBE
BLEBS
GLEBE
GREBE
KREBS
PLEBE
PLEBS
SHEBA
THEBE

••E•B
ACERB
DWEEB

•••EB
CALEB
CELEB
CUBEB
DENEB
DWEEB
HOREB
SIDEB
TYPEB

EC•••
ECHIN
ECLAT
ECOLE
ECRUS

E•C••
ELCID
EMCEE
ENCYC
EPCOT
EXCEL

E••C•
EDICT
EDUCE
EDUCT
EJECT
ELECT
ENACT
ENOCH
EPACT
EPICS
EPOCH
ERECT
ERICA
ERICH
ERUCT
EVICT
EXACT
EXECS

E•••C
EDDIC
ENCYC
ENIAC
EPISC
ETHIC

•EC••
AECIA
BECHE
BECKS
BECKY
CECIL
DECAF
DECAL
DECAY
DECCA
DECKS
DECOR
DECOY
DECRY
GECKO
HECHT
HECKS
HECTO
MECCA
MECUM
NECKS
PECAN
PECKS
PECOS
RECAP
RECCE
RECIP
RECON
RECTI
RECTO
RECUR
SECCO
SECTS
TECHS
YECCH

•E•C•
BEACH
BEECH
BELCH
BENCH
CENCI
DECCA
DEICE
DELCO
DEUCE
DEUCY
FENCE
FETCH
HENCE
HENCH
KEACH
KENCH
KETCH
LEACH
LEECH
LEICA
MECCA
MERCE
MERCI
MERCY
PEACE
PEACH
PENCE
PERCE
PERCH
PERCY
PESCI
REACH
REACT
RECCE
REICH
SECCO
TEACH
TENCH
VETCH
WELCH
WENCH
YECCH

•E••C
GENIC
HELIC
MEDIC
MEDOC
MELIC
MESIC
REBEC
RELIC
SERAC
TELIC
VEDIC
XEBEC
XERIC

••EC•
ALECK
ARECA
BEECH
BRECK
CHECK
CRECY
CZECH
EJECT
ELECT
ERECT
EXECS
FLECK
GRECO
LEECH
NIECE
PIECE
SPECK
SPECS
THECA
VNECK
WRECK

••E•C
CRESC
OLEIC

•••EC
AZTEC
COSEC
OLMEC
REBEC
XEBEC

ED•••
EDAMS
EDDAS
EDDIC
EDDIE
EDEMA
EDENS
EDGAR
EDGED
EDGER
EDGES
EDICT
EDIFY
EDILE
EDINA
EDITH
EDITS
EDSEL
EDUCE
EDUCT
EDWIN

E•D••
EDDAS
EDDIC
EDDIE
EIDER
ELDER
EMDEN
ENDED
ENDER
ENDOR
ENDOW
ENDUE
ENDUP
EYDIE

E••D•
EGADI
EGADS
ELIDE
ELUDE
EPODE
ERODE
ETUDE
EVADE
EXUDE

E•••D
EARED
EASED
EAVED
EBBED
EDGED
EELED
EGGED
ELAND
ELCID
EMBED
EMEND
ENDED
EPHOD
ERRED

•ED••
AEDES
BEDEW
BEDIM
CEDAR
CEDED
CEDES
FEDON
FEDUP
HEDDA
HEDGE
HEDGY
HEDIN
KEDGE
LEDGE
LEDIN
LEDON
LEDTO
MEDAL
MEDEA
MEDES
MEDIA
MEDIC
MEDIT
MEDOC
NEDDY
PEDAL
PEDRO
REDAN
REDDY
REDID
REDON
REDOX
REDUB
REDUX
REDYE
SEDAN
SEDER
SEDGE
SEDUM
TEDDY
VEDAS
VEDAY
VEDDA
VEDIC
WEDEL
WEDGE
WEDGY

•E•D•
BEADS
BEADY
BENDS
DEEDS
DENDR
FEEDS
FENDS
FERDE
FEUDS
GEODE
HEADS
HEADY
HEDDA
HEEDS
HEIDI
HEIDT
HERDS
JEUDI
KENDO
LEADS
LEEDS
LENDL
LENDS
MEADE
MEADS
MEEDS
MELDS
MENDS
NEDDY
NEEDS
NEEDY
NERDS
NERDY
PENDS
PERDU
READE
READS
READY
REDDY
REEDS
REEDY
RENDS
SEEDS
SEEDY
SENDS
TEDDY
TEIDE
TENDS
VEDDA
VEIDT
VELDS
VELDT
VENDA
VENDS
VERDE
VERDI
WEEDS
WEEDY
WELDS
WENDS
WENDT
WENDY
ZELDA
ZENDA
ZENDO

•E••D
BEARD
CEDED
CERED
DEKED
DELED
DEWED
EELED
FELID
FETED
FETID
GELID
GEOID
HEARD
HEROD
HEWED
HEXAD
HEXED
KEYED
METED
MEWED
NEFUD
REBID
REDID
RESOD
REWED
SEWED
TEPID
VEXED
WEIRD

••ED•
BREDA
COEDS
CREDO
DEEDS
FEEDS
FREDA
GLEDE
HEEDS
LEEDS
MEEDS
NEEDS
NEEDY
OPEDS
PIEDS
REEDS
REEDY
SEEDS
SEEDY
SHEDS
SLEDS
SUEDE
SWEDE
THEDA
WEEDS
WEEDY

••E•D
ABEND
AHEAD
AMEND
BLEED
BLEND
BREAD
BREED
CREED
DREAD
EMEND
FIELD
FIEND
FJELD
FREED
FREUD
GREED
KNEAD
KNEED
NOEND
ONEND
OREAD
PLEAD
PSEUD
SCEND
SHEED
SNEAD
SNEED
SNERD
SPEED
SPEND
STEAD
STEED
THEYD
TREAD
TREED
TREND
TWEED
UPEND
WIELD
YIELD

•••ED
AAHED
ACHED
ACRED
ACTED
ADDED
AHMED
AIDED
AILED
AIMED
AIRED
AMPED
ANTED
APIED
APTED
ARCED
ARMED
ASKED
AWNED
BAAED
BAKED
BALED
BARED
BASED
BATED
BAYED
BIDED
BIKED
BIPED
BLEED
BLUED
BODED
BONED
BOOED
BORED
BOWED
BOXED
BREED
BUSED
CAGED
CAKED
CANED
CAPED
CARED
CASED
CAVED
CAWED
CEDED
CERED
CITED
CLUED
CODED
COKED
COOED
COPED
CORED
COWED
COXED
CREED
CRIED
CUBED
CURED
DARED
DATED
DAZED
DEKED
DELED
DEWED
DICED
DIKED
DIMED
DINED
DIVED
DOLED
DOMED
DOSED
DOTED
DOZED
DRIED
DUKED
DUPED
EARED
EASED
EAVED
EBBED
EDGED
EELED
EGGED
EMBED
ENDED
ERRED
FACED
FADED
FAKED
FAMED
FARED
FATED
FAXED
FAZED
FETED
FIFED
FILED
FINED
FIRED
FIXED
FLIED
FOXED
FREED
FRIED
FUMED
FUSED
GAMED
GAPED
GATED
GAZED
GIBED
GLUED
GORED
GREED
GUYED
GYVED
HALED
HARED
HATED
HAWED
HAYED
HAZED
HEWED
HEXED
HIKED
HIRED
HIVED
HOKED
HOLED
HOMED
HONED
HOPED
HOSED
HYPED
IDLED
INBED
INKED
IRKED
IVIED
JADED
JAPED
JAWED
JIBED
JIVED
JOKED
JUKED
KEYED
KITED
KNEED
LACED
LADED
LAMED
LASED
LAVED
LAZED
LIKED
LIMED
LINED
LIVED
LOBED
LOPED
LOVED
LOWED
LUBED
LURED
MACED
MANED
MATED
MAXED
METED
MEWED
MIKED
MIMED
MINED
MIRED
MIXED
MOOED
MOPED
MOVED
MOWED
MUSED
MUTED
NAKED
NAMED
NIXED
NOSED
NOTED
NUKED
OARED
OGLED
OILED
OOHED
OOZED
OPTED
OUTED
OWNED
PACED
PAGED
PALED
PANED
PARED
PATED
PAVED
PAWED
PAYED
PIKED
PILED
PINED
PIPED
PLIED
POKED
POLED
PORED
POSED
PRIED
PULED
RACED
RAGED
RAKED
RASED
RATED
RAVED
RAYED
RAZED
REWED
RICED
RILED
RIMED
RIVED
ROBED
ROPED
ROVED
ROWED
RULED
SATED
SAVED
SAWED
SCHED
SEWED
SHEED
SHIED
SHOED
SHRED
SIDED
SIRED
SITED
SIXED
SIZED
SKIED
SLUED
SNEED
SOLED
SOWED
SPEED
SPIED
STEED
TAMED
TAPED
TAXED
TIDED
TILED
TIMED
TINED
TIRED
TONED
TOPED
TOTED
TOWED
TOYED
TREED
TRIED
TRUED
TUBED
TUNED
TWEED
TYPED
UMPED
UNFED
UNWED
UPPED
URGED
USHED
USTED
VEXED
VINED
VOTED
VOWED
WADED
WAGED
WAKED
WALED
WANED
WAVED
WAXED
WILED
WINED
WIPED
WIRED
WIVED
WOOED
WOWED
YAWED
YOKED
ZONED

EE•••
EELED
EELER
EERIE

E•E••
EBERT
EDEMA
EDENS
EGEST
EIEIO
EJECT
ELECT
ELEGY
ELEMI
ELENA
ELENI
ELEVE
EMEER
EMEND
EMERY
ENEMY
ENERO
EPEES
ERECT
EVENS
EVENT
EVERS
EVERT
EVERY
EWELL
EWERS
EXECS
EXERT
EYERS

E••E•
EAGER
EAMES
EARED
EASED
EASEL
EASES
EATEN
EATER
EAVED
EAVES
EBBED
EBSEN
EDGED
EDGER
EDGES
EDSEL
EELED
EELER
EFREM
EGGED
EGRET
EIDER
EIGEN
ELDER
ELIEL
ELLEN
ELLER
ELLES
ELMER
ELVER
ELVES
EMBED
EMBER
EMCEE
EMDEN
EMEER
EMMER
EMMET
ENDED
ENDER
ENGEL
ENNEA
ENTER
EPEES
ERIES
ERNES
ERRED
ESKER
ESNES
ESSEN
ESSES
ESSEX
ESTEE
ESTER
ESTES
ETHEL
ETHER
ETSEQ
ETZEL
EULER
EXCEL
EXPEL
EYRES

E•••E
EAGLE
EAGRE
EARLE
ECOLE
EDDIE
EDILE
EDUCE
EERIE
EFFIE
ELATE
ELEVE
ELIDE
ELISE
ELITE
ELLIE
ELOPE
ELSIE
ELUDE
ELUTE
ELYSE
EMCEE
EMILE
EMOTE
ENATE
ENDUE
ENSUE
ENTRE
ENURE
EPODE
ERASE
ERNIE
ERODE
EROSE
ESQUE
ESTEE
ETAGE
ETAPE
ETUDE
EUBIE
EVADE
EVOKE
EXILE
EXUDE
EYDIE
EYRIE

•EE••
BEEBE
BEECH
BEEFS
BEEFY
BEENE
BEEPS
BEERS
BEERY
BEETS
DEEDS
DEEMS
DEEPS
DEERE
DEERS
FEEDS
FEELS
GEEKS
GEEKY
GEENA
GEESE
HEEDS
HEELS
JEEPS
JEERS
KEELS
KEENE
KEENS
KEEPS
LEECH
LEEDS
LEEKS
LEERS
LEERY
LEETS
LEEZA
MEEDS
MEESE
MEETS
NEEDS
NEEDY
PEEKS
PEELE
PEELS
PEENS
PEEPS
PEERS
PEETE
PEEVE
REEDS
REEDY
REEFS
REEKS
REELS
REESE
REEVE
SEEDS
SEEDY
SEEIN
SEEKS
SEELS
SEEMS
SEEPS
SEEPY
SEERS
SEETO
SEEYA
TEEMS
TEENA
TEENS
TEENY
TEETH
TEEUP
VEEPS
VEERS
VEERY
WEEDS
WEEDY
WEEKS
WEEMS
WEENY
WEEPS
WEEPY
WEEST

•E•E•
AEAEA
AEDES
BEDEW
BEGET
BELEM
BENES
BENET
BEREA
BERET
BESET
BETEL
BEVEL
BEZEL
CEDED
CEDES
CELEB
CEPES
CERED
CERES
DEFER
DEKED
DEKES
DELED
DELES
DEMES
DENEB
DENES
DEPEW
DEREK
DETER
DEWED
DEWEY
EELED
EELER
FETED
FETES
FEVER
FEWER
GELEE
GENES
GENET
HEGEL
HELEN
HEMEN
HEMET
HERES
HEWED
HEWER
HEXED
HEXER
HEXES
JEREZ
JETER
JETES
JEWEL
KESEY
KEYED
KEYES
LEGER
LEVEE
LEVEL
LEVER
LEWES
MEDEA
MEDES
MELEE
MEMEL
MERES
METED
METER
METES
MEWED
MEYER
NEGEV
NEMEA
NENES
NEVER
NEVES
NEWEL
NEWER
PEKES
PELEE
PELEG
PERES
PEREZ
PETER
PEWEE
REBEC
REBEL
REFER
REHEM
REKEY
RELEE
RELET
REMET
REMEX
RENEE
RENEW
REPEG
REPEL
RESEE
RESET
RESEW
REVEL
REVET
REWED
REXES
REYES
SEDER
SEGER
SELES
SERES
SEVEN
SEVER
SEWED
SEWER
SEXES
TEHEE
TELEO
TELEX
TENET
TEPEE
TEVET
VELEZ
VENEZ
VESEY
VEXED
VEXER
VEXES
WEBER
WEDEL
WESER
XEBEC
YEMEN
YESES

•E••E
AERIE
BECHE
BEEBE
BEENE
BEIGE
BELIE
BELLE
BENUE
BERLE
BERME
BERNE
BETTE
BEYLE
CEASE
CELIE
CENSE
DEANE
DEERE
DEFOE
DEICE
DELVE
DEMME
DENSE
DENTE
DETRE
DEUCE
EERIE
FEMME
FENCE
FERDE
GEESE
GELEE
GENIE

GENRE
GEODE
GESTE
GETME
HEAVE
HEDGE
HEINE
HELVE
HENCE
HENGE
HENIE
HERNE
HERVE
HESSE
HEURE
HEUTE
HEYSE
JEANE
JESSE
JEUNE
KEANE
KEDGE
KEENE
LEASE
LEAVE
LEDGE
LEONE
LETBE
LETHE
LEVEE
LEYTE
MEADE
MEESE
MELEE
MERCE
MERGE
MERLE
MEROE
MESNE
METRE
MEUSE
NEALE
NEIGE
NERVE
NEUME
PEACE
PEALE
PEASE
PEELE
PEETE
PEEVE
PEKOE
PELEE
PENCE
PENNE
PENTE
PERCE
PERLE
PERSE
PEWEE
READE
REBBE
RECCE
REDYE
REESE
REEVE
RELEE
RENEE
RESEE
RETIE
REUNE
REUSE
REVUE
SEALE
SEDGE
SEGUE
SEINE
SEIZE
SENSE
SERGE
SERVE
SETAE
SEULE
TEASE
TEHEE
TEIDE
TEMPE
TENSE
TEPEE
TERNE
TERRE
TERSE
TEVYE
VENAE
VENUE
VERDE
VERGE
VERNE
VERRE
VERSE
VERTE
VERVE
WEAVE
WEDGE
YENTE

••EE•

ADEEM
AKEEM
AKEES
AMEER
BLEED
BLEEP
BREED
BREEN
CHEEK
CHEEP
CHEER
CLEEK
CREED
CREEK
CREEL
CREEP
CREES
DWEEB
EMEER
EPEES
FLEER
FLEES
FLEET
FREED
FREER
FREES
GHEES
GLEES
GREED
GREEK
GREEN
GREER
GREET
KNEED
KNEEL
KNEES
OGEES
PREEN
QUEEG
QUEEN
QUEER
SHEED
SHEEN
SHEEP
SHEER
SHEET
SKEET
SLEEK
SLEEP
SLEET
SNEED
SNEER
SPEED
STEED
STEEL
STEEN
STEEP
STEER
SWEEP
SWEET
TREED
TREEN
TREES
TWEED
TWEEN
TWEET
WHEEL
WHEEN

••E•E

ABELE
ADELE
ALENE
ARETE
BEEBE
BEENE
BREVE
CHERE
CREME
CREPE
CRETE
DEERE
DIENE
ELEVE
FRERE
GEESE
GLEBE
GLEDE
GREBE
GRETE
ILENE
IRENE
ISERE
KEENE
LIEGE
LOEWE
MEESE
MNEME
MYEYE
NIECE
OBESE
OXEYE
PEELE
PEETE
PEEVE
PIECE
PLEBE
POEME
POETE
QUEUE
REESE
REEVE
SCENE
SHERE
SIEGE
SIETE
SIEVE
SKETE
SPEKE
STELE
STERE
STEVE
SUEDE
SUEME
SWEDE
THEBE
THEME
THERE
THESE
TWERE
WHERE

•••EE

AGREE
AIMEE
ALBEE
ALLEE
ANNEE
ARMEE
COOEE
CUVEE
DONEE
EMCEE
ESTEE
FUSEE
GELEE
GOSEE
LEVEE
LYCEE
MCGEE
MELEE
PAREE
PAYEE
PELEE
PEWEE
PUREE
RAMEE
RANEE
RAPEE
RAREE
RELEE
RENEE
RESEE
RONEE
RUPEE
SCREE
SPREE
SYCEE
TEHEE
TEPEE
THREE
TUTEE
TYPEE

EF•••

EFFIE
EFIKS
EFLAT
EFREM

E•F••

EFFIE
ELFIN
ENFIN

E••F•

EDIFY

•EF••

BEFIT
BEFOG
DEFAT
DEFER
DEFOE
DEFOG
HEFTS
HEFTY
KEFIR
LEFAY
LEFTS
LEFTY
NEFUD
REFER
REFIT
REFRY
WEFTS

•E•F•

BEEFS
BEEFY
DEIFY
DELFT
FEOFF
LEAFS
LEAFY
REEFS
REIFY
SERFS

•E••F

DECAF
FEOFF
SERIF

••EF•

ALEFS
BEEFS
BEEFY
CHEFS
CLEFS
CLEFT
FIEFS
REEFS
THEFT

••E•F

BOEUF
SHEAF
SHELF

•••EF

BRIEF
CCLEF
CHIEF
FCLEF
GANEF
GCLEF
GRIEF
INDEF
JOSEF
SHAEF
THIEF

E•G••

EAGER
EAGLE
EAGRE
EDGAR
EDGED
EDGER
EDGES
EGGAR
EGGED
EGGON
EIGEN
EIGHT
ELGAR
ELGIN
ENGEL
ENGRS
ERGOT

E••G•

ELEGY
ETAGE

E•••G

EKING
EWING

•EG••

AEGIR
AEGIS
BEGAN
BEGAT
BEGET
BEGIN
BEGOT
BEGUM
BEGUN
DEGAS
HEGEL
LEGAL
LEGER
LEGGS
LEGGY
LEGIS
LEGIT
LEGOS
LEGUP
MEGAN
NEGEV
NEGRI
NEGUS
PEGGY
REGAL
REGAN
REGIA
REGIS
SEGAL
SEGAR
SEGER
SEGNI
SEGNO
SEGOS
SEGUE
VEGAN
VEGAS
YEGGS

•E•G•

BEIGE
BERGH
BERGS
DEIGN
FEIGN
GETGO
HEDGE
HEDGY
HEIGH
HELGA
HENGE
KEDGE
KEOGH
LEDGE
LEGGS
LEGGY
LEIGH
LETGO
MERGE
NEIGE
NEIGH
PEGGY
PENGO
REIGN
SEDGE
SERGE
VERGE
WEDGE
WEDGY
WEIGH
YEGGS

•E••G

BEFOG
BEING
DEBUG
DEFOG
GEORG
PELEG
REBAG
RELIG
REPEG
RETAG
ZELIG

••EG•

DIEGO
DREGS
ELEGY
FUEGO
GREGG
LIEGE
LUEGO
OMEGA
ONEGA
PREGO
SIEGE
SKEGS
TAEGU
TIEGS

••E•G

GREGG
QUEEG
ZWEIG

•••EG

GRIEG
IRREG
KLIEG
PELEG
QUEEG
REPEG
UNPEG

E•H••

ECHIN
EPHAH
EPHAS
EPHOD
EPHOR
ETHAN
ETHEL
ETHER
ETHIC
ETHNO
ETHOS
ETHYL

E••H•

EIGHT
ELIHU

E•••H

EARTH
EDITH
ENOCH
EPHAH
EPOCH
ERICH

•EH••

BEHAN
LEHAR
LEHUA
MEHTA
NEHRU
REHAB
REHAN
REHEM
SEHNA
TEHEE

•E•H•

BECHE
DELHI
HECHT
LEAHY
LETHE
MESHY
TECHS
TETHS

•E••H

BEACH
BEECH
BELCH
BENCH
BERGH
BERTH
DEPTH
FETCH
GERAH
HEATH
HEIGH
HENCH
KEACH
KEITH
KENCH
KEOGH
KETCH
LEACH
LEASH
LEECH
LEIGH
LEITH
NEATH
NEIGH
PEACH
PERCH
PERTH
REACH
REICH
SELAH
TEACH
TEETH
TENCH
TENTH
VETCH
WEIGH
WELCH
WELSH
WENCH
YECCH

••EH•

BOEHM
FOEHN
RUEHL

••E•H

ALEPH
BEECH
CZECH
DOETH
FLESH
FRESH
LEECH
OBEAH
TEETH
WYETH

EI•••

EIDER
EIEIO
EIGEN
EIGHT

E•I••

EDICT
EDIFY
EDILE
EDINA
EDITH
EDITS
EFIKS
EKING
ELIAS
ELIDE
ELIEL
ELIHU
ELION
ELIOT
ELISE
ELITE
ELIZA
EMILE
EMILY
EMIRS
EMITS
ENIAC
EPICS
EPISC
ERICA
ERICH
ERIES
ERIKA
ERISA
EVIAN
EVICT
EVILS
EVITA
EWING
EXILE
EXIST
EXITS

E••I•

EATIN
EATIT
ECHIN
EDDIC
EDDIE
EDWIN
EERIE
EFFIE
EIEIO
ELCID
ELFIN
ELGIN
ELLIE
ELLIS
ELSIE
ELVIN
ELVIS
EMAIL
ENFIN
ENNIO
ENNIS
ENTIA
EOSIN
EQUIP
EQUIV
ERNIE
ERVIL
ERVIN
ERWIN
ETHIC
ETUIS
EUBIE
EYDIE
EYRIE
EYRIR

E•••I

EBOLI
EGADI
ELEMI
ELENI
ENLAI
ENNUI
ENVOI

•EI••

BEIGE
BEING
CEIBA
CEILS
DEICE
DEIFY
DEIGN
DEISM
DEIST
DEITY
FEIGN
FEINT
FEIST
HEIDI
HEIDT
HEIGH
HEINE
HEINZ
HEIRS
HEISS
HEIST
KEITH
LEICA
LEIGH
LEILA
LEITH
MEIJI
NEIGE
NEIGH
NEILL
REICH
REIFY
REIGN
REIMS
REINK
REINS
SEIKO
SEINE
SEISM
SEIZE
TEIDE
VEIDT
VEILS
VEINS
WEIGH
WEILL
WEIRD
WEIRS
WEISS
ZEISS
ZEIST

•E•I•

AECIA
AEGIR
AEGIS
AERIE
AESIR
BEDIM
BEFIT
BEGIN
BELIE
BENIN
BEVIN
CECIL
CELIA
CELIE
CERIA
DEBIT
DELIS
DEMIT
DENIM
DENIS
DERIV
DEVIL
EERIE
FELID
FELIS
FELIX
FELIZ
FERIA
FETID
GELID
GENIC
GENIE
GENII
GEOID
GETIN
GETIT
HEDIN
HELIC
HELIO
HELIX
HEMIN
HENIE
KEFIR
KEPIS
KEVIN
KEYIN
LEDIN
LEGIS
LEGIT
LENIN
LENIS
LETIN
LEVIN
LEVIS
LEWIS
LEXIS
MEDIA
MEDIC
MEDIT
MELIC
MERIT
MESIC
METIS
NEVIL
NEVIN
NEVIS
PEKIN
PEPIN
PERIL
PERIS
PETIT
PEWIT
REAIM
REAIR
REBID
RECIP
REDID
REFIT
REGIA
REGIS
RELIC
RELIG
RELIT
REMIT
REMIX
RENIN
REOIL
REPIN
RESIN
RETIA
RETIE
REWIN
SEEIN
SEMIS
SEPIA
SERIF
SERIN
SETIN
TELIC
TEPID
VEDIC
VENIN
XENIA
XERIC
YETIS
ZELIG

•E••I

BELLI
BENJI
CELLI
CENCI
CENTI
CESTI
DELHI
DENTI
FERMI
FERRI
GENII
HEIDI
HENRI
JEUDI
KENAI
LEROI
MEIJI
MERCI
NEGRI
PENNI
PEPSI
PESCI
PETRI
PETTI
RECTI
SEGNI
SERAI
TEMPI
TERRI
VERDI
VERMI

••EI•

ATEIN
CUEIN
EIEIO
ICEIN
KLEIN
LIEIN
OLEIC
OLEIN
ONEIL
PLEIO
SEEIN
SHEIK
SKEIN
STEIN
THEIR
TIEIN
TOEIN
ZWEIG

••E•I

CHERI
ELEMI
ELENI
FLEXI
ICENI
OBELI
SIEPI
TREVI
UMEKI

•••EI

AUREI
IMPEI
ISSEI
NISEI
PILEI
TAKEI
TOMEI

EJ•••

EJECT

E•J••

ENJOY

•EJ••

HEJAZ

•E•J•

BENJI
MEIJI

••EJ•

VIEJO

EK•••

EKING

E•K••

ESKER

E••K•

EFIKS
ENSKY
ERIKA
EVOKE
EWOKS

•EK••

DEKED
DEKES
HEKLA
PEKES
PEKIN
PEKOE
REKEY

•E•K•

BEAKS
BECKS
BECKY
DECKS
DESKS
GECKO
GEEKS
GEEKY
HECKS
HERKY
JERKS
JERKY
LEAKS
LEAKY
LEEKS
NECKS
PEAKS
PECKS
PEEKS
PERKS
PERKY
PESKY
REEKS
SEEKS
SEIKO
TEAKS
WEEKS

•E••K

DEREK
REINK

••EK•

CHEKA
GEEKS
GEEKY
LEEKS
PEEKS
REEKS
SEEKS
SPEKE
TREKS
UMEKI
WEEKS

••E•K

ALECK
APEAK
BLEAK
BREAK
BRECK
CHECK
CHEEK
CLEEK
CLERK
CREAK
CREEK
FLECK
FREAK
GREEK
SHEIK
SLEEK
SNEAK
SPEAK
SPECK
STEAK
TWEAK
VNECK
WHELK
WREAK
WRECK

•••EK

CAPEK
CHEEK
CLEEK
CREEK
DEREK
GREEK
HACEK
HAYEK
KOPEK
PATEK
SLEEK
UZBEK

EL•••

ELAND
ELATE
ELBOW
ELCID
ELDER
ELECT
ELEGY
ELEMI
ELENA
ELENI
ELEVE
ELFIN
ELGAR
ELGIN
ELIAS
ELIDE
ELIEL
ELIHU
ELION
ELIOT
ELISE
ELITE
ELIZA
ELLEN
ELLER
ELLES
ELLIE
ELLIS
ELMAN
ELMER
ELMOS
ELOPE
ELROY
ELSIE
ELTON
ELUDE
ELUTE
ELVER
ELVES
ELVIN
ELVIS
ELWAY
ELYSE

E•L••

ECLAT
EELED
EELER
EFLAT
ELLEN
ELLER
ELLES
ELLIE
ELLIS
EMLYN
ENLAI
EOLUS
EULER

E••L•

EAGLE
EARLE
EARLS
EARLY
EBOLI
ECOLE
EDILE
EMILE
EMILY
ENOLS
EVILS
EWELL
EXALT
EXILE
EXULT

E•••L

EASEL
EDSEL
ELIEL
EMAIL
ENGEL
ENROL
EQUAL
ERROL
ERVIL
ETHEL
ETHYL
ETZEL
EWELL
EXCEL
EXPEL
EXTOL

•EL••

BELAY
BELCH
BELEM
BELIE
BELLA
BELLE
BELLI
BELLS
BELLY
BELOW
BELTS
BELVA
CELEB
CELIA
CELIE
CELLA
CELLI
CELLO
CELLS
CELTS
DELAY
DELCO
DELED
DELES
DELFT
DELHI
DELIS
DELLA
DELLS
DELON
DELOS
DELTA
DELTS
DELVE
EELED
EELER
FELID
FELIS
FELIX
FELIZ
FELLA
FELLS
FELLY
FELON
FELTS
GELEE
GELID
HELEN
HELGA
HELIC
HELIO
HELIX
HELLO
HELMS
HELOS
HELOT
HELPS
HELVE
JELLO
JELLS
JELLY
KELLY
KELPS
KELPY
KELSO
MELAN
MELBA
MELDS
MELEE
MELIC
MELON
MELOS
MELTS
MELTY
NELLY
PELEE
PELEG
PELLA
PELTS
RELAX
RELAY
RELEE
RELET
RELIC
RELIG
RELIT
SELAH
SELES
SELLS
SELMA
SELVA

TELEO
TELEX
TELIC
TELLS
TELLY
TELOS
VELAR
VELDS
VELDT
VELEZ
VELUM
WELBY
WELCH
WELDS
WELLS
WELSH
WELTS
WELTY
YELLS
YELPS
ZELDA
ZELIG

•E•L•
BEALL
BEALS
BELLA
BELLE
BELLI
BELLS
BELLY
BERLE
BEYLE
CEILS
CELLA
CELLI
CELLO
CELLS
DEALS
DEALT
DELLA
DELLS
FEELS
FELLA
FELLS
FELLY
FEYLY
HEALS
HEALY
HEELS
HEKLA
HELLO
HERLS
JELLO
JELLS
JELLY
KEELS
KELLY
LEILA
MEALS
MEALY
MENLO
MERLE
MERLS
MEWLS
NEALE
NEILL
NELLY
NEWLY
PEALE
PEALS
PEELE
PEELS
PELLA

PEPLA
PERLE
REALM
REALS
REELS
REPLY
SEALE
SEALS
SEALY
SEELS
SELLS
SEULE
TEALS
TELLS
TELLY
TESLA
VEILS
WEALS
WEILL
WELLS
WETLY
YELLS
ZEALS

•E••L
BEALL
BERYL
BETEL
BEVEL
BEZEL
CECIL
CEORL
DECAL
DEVIL
FERAL
FETAL
HEGEL
HERZL
HEXYL
JEWEL
KEMAL
LEGAL
LENDL
LEVEL
MEDAL
MEMEL
MERYL
METAL
NEILL
NEPAL
NEROL
NEVIL
NEWEL
PEARL
PEDAL
PENAL
PERIL
PETAL
REBEL
REGAL
RENAL
REOIL
REPEL
REVEL
SEGAL
SEOUL
SEPAL
TEPAL
VENAL
WEDEL
WEILL
YENTL

••EL•
ABELE
ADELA
ADELE
AKELA
AXELS
BCELL
BUELL
CHELA
DUELS
DWELL
DWELT
EWELL
FEELS
FIELD
FJELD
FUELS
GAELS
HEELS
KEELS
KNELL
KNELT
KVELL
LYELL
MYELO
NIELS
NOELS
OBELI
ODELL
OPELS
PEELE
PEELS
PRELL
QUELL
REELS
RIELS
SEELS
SHELF
SHELL
SMELL
SMELT
SNELL
SPELL
SPELT
STELA
STELE
SWELL
SZELL
TAELS
WHELK
WHELM
WHELP
WIELD
YIELD

••E•L
AREAL
BCELL
BUELL
CREEL
DWELL
EWELL
IDEAL
KNEEL
KNELL
KVELL
LYELL
ODELL
ONEAL
ONEIL
PRELL
QUELL
RUEHL
SHELL

SMELL
SNELL
SPELL
STEAL
STEEL
SWELL
SZELL
THEOL
WHEAL
WHEEL

•••EL
ACCEL
ANGEL
ANSEL
APFEL
APPEL
ARIEL
ARNEL
ARPEL
ARTEL
BABEL
BAGEL
BASEL
BETEL
BEVEL
BEZEL
BIKEL
CAMEL
CREEL
CRUEL
CUPEL
DOWEL
DYNEL
EASEL
EDSEL
ELIEL
ENGEL
ETHEL
ETZEL
EXCEL
EXPEL
FIDEL
GAVEL
GIMEL
GOBEL
GODEL
GRUEL
HAMEL
HAVEL
HAZEL
HEGEL
HOSEL
HOTEL
HOVEL
IMPEL
INTEL
JEWEL
JOREL
KALEL
KAREL
KNEEL
KUGEL
LABEL
LAPEL
LEVEL
LIBEL
MABEL
MAZEL
MEMEL
MODEL
MONEL
MOREL
MOTEL

NAGEL
NAVEL
NEWEL
NIGEL
NOBEL
NOVEL
ORIEL
OUSEL
OUZEL
PANEL
PIXEL
RATEL
RAVEL
REBEL
REPEL
REVEL
RIGEL
ROWEL
SAHEL
SOREL
SPIEL
STAEL
STEEL
TOWEL
UMBEL
URIEL
VOWEL
WEDEL
WHEEL
YODEL
YOKEL

EM•••
EMAIL
EMBAR
EMBAY
EMBED
EMBER
EMCEE
EMDEN
EMEER
EMEND
EMERY
EMILE
EMILY
EMIRS
EMITS
EMLYN
EMMER
EMMET
EMMYS
EMORY
EMOTE
EMPTY

E•M••
EAMES
EAMON
ELMAN
ELMER
ELMOS
EMMER
EMMET
EMMYS

E••M•
EDAMS
EDEMA
ELEMI
ENEMY
ETYMA
EXAMS

E•••M
EFREM
ENORM
ENTOM
EPSOM

•EM••
BEMAS
DEMES
DEMIT
DEMME
DEMOB
DEMON
DEMOS
DEMUR
FEMME
FEMTO
FEMUR
GEMMA
GEMMY
GEMOT
HEMAN
HEMEN
HEMET
HEMIN
HEMPS
JEMMY
KEMAL
KEMPT
LEMAY
LEMMA
LEMON
LEMUR
MEMEL
MEMOS
NEMAN
NEMAT
NEMEA
PEMBA
REMAN
REMAP
REMET
REMEX
REMIT
REMIX
REMOP
REMOW
REMUS
SEMIS
TEMPE
TEMPI
TEMPO
TEMPS
TEMPT
YEMEN

•E•M•
BEAMS
BEAMY
BERME
BERMS
DEEMS
DEMME
DERMA
DERMO
FEMME
FERMI
GEMMA
GEMMY
GERMS
GERMY
GETME
HELMS
HERMS

JEMMY
LEMMA
NEUME
PERMS
REAMS
REIMS
SEAMS
SEAMY
SEEMS
SELMA
TEAMS
TEEMS
TERMS
VERMI
WEEMS

•E••M
BEDIM
BEGUM
BELEM
BESOM
CERAM
DEISM
DENIM
DENOM
MECUM
REAIM
REALM
REARM
REHEM
SEBUM
SEDUM
SEISM
SERUM
VELUM
VENOM

••EM•
ANEMO
CREME
DEEMS
DIEMS
EDEMA
ELEMI
ENEMY
HAEMA
HAEMO
ITEMS
MNEME
POEME
POEMS
SEEMS
SHEMP
STEMS
SUEME
TEEMS
THEMA
THEME
THEMS
WEEMS

••E•M
ABEAM
ADEEM
AKEEM
ATEAM
BOEHM
BREAM
CREAM
DREAM
GLEAM
IBEAM
ODEUM
OLEUM

RHEUM
STEAM
THERM
WHELM

•••EM
ADEEM
ADHEM
ADREM
AKEEM
BELEM
EFREM
GOLEM
HAREM
INREM
KASEM
MODEM
PROEM
REHEM
ROREM
SALEM
TOTEM
XYLEM

EN•••
ENACT
ENATE
ENCYC
ENDED
ENDER
ENDOR
ENDOW
ENDUE
ENDUP
ENEMY
ENERO
ENFIN
ENGEL
ENGRS
ENIAC
ENJOY
ENLAI
ENNEA
ENNIO
ENNIS
ENNUI
ENOCH
ENOLS
ENORM
ENROL
ENSKY
ENSOR
ENSUE
ENTER
ENTIA
ENTOM
ENTRE
ENTRY
ENURE
ENVOI
ENVOY

E•N••
ENNEA
ENNIO
ENNIS
ENNUI
ERNES
ERNIE
ERNST
ESNES
ETNAS

E••N•
EARNS
EBONY
EDENS
EDINA
EKING
ELAND
ELENA
ELENI
EMEND
ETHNO
ETONS
EVANS
EVENS
EVENT
EWING
EXONS

E•••N
EAMON
EATEN
EATIN
EATON
EBSEN
ECHIN
EDWIN
EGGON
EIGEN
ELFIN
ELGIN
ELION
ELLEN
ELMAN
ELTON
ELVIN
EMDEN
EMLYN
ENFIN
EOSIN
EPSON
ERVIN
ERWIN
ESSEN
ETHAN
EVIAN
EXXON

•EN••
BENCH
BENDS
BENES
BENET
BENIN
BENJI
BENNY
BENTS
BENUE
BENZO
CENCI
CENSE
CENTI
CENTO
CENTS
DENDR
DENEB
DENES
DENIM
DENIS
DENNY
DENOM
DENSE
DENTE
DENTI
DENTS

DENYS
FENCE
FENDS
FENNY
GENES
GENET
GENIC
GENIE
GENII
GENOA
GENRE
GENRO
GENTS
GENUS
HENAN
HENCE
HENCH
HENGE
HENIE
HENNA
HENNY
HENRI
HENRY
JENNY
KENAI
KENCH
KENDO
KENNY
KENOS
KENYA
LENDL
LENDS
LENIN
LENIS
LENNY
LENOS
LENOX
LENTO
LENTS
LENYA
MENDS
MENLO
MENSA
MENUS
NENES
PENAL
PENCE
PENDS
PENGO
PENNA
PENNE
PENNI
PENNY
PENTA
PENTE
PENZA
RENAL
RENAN
RENDS
RENEE
RENEW
RENIN
RENTA
RENTS
SENDS
SENNA
SENOR
SENSE
TENCH
TENDS
TENET
TENON
TENOR
TENSE

TENTH
TENTS
VENAE
VENAL
VENDA
VENDS
VENEZ
VENIN
VENOM
VENTS
VENUE
VENUS
WENCH
WENDS
WENDT
WENDY
XENIA
XENON
YENTA
YENTE
YENTL
ZENDA
ZENDO

•E•N•
AEONS
AETNA
BEANO
BEANS
BEANY
BEENE
BEING
BENNY
BERNE
DEANE
DEANS
DENNY
DESNA
FEINT
FENNY
FERNS
FERNY
GEENA
HEINE
HEINZ
HENNA
HENNY
HERNE
JEANE
JEANS
JENNY
JEUNE
KEANE
KEANU
KEENE
KEENS
KENNY
KERNS
LEANS
LEANT
LENNY
LEONA
LEONE
MEANS
MEANT
MEANY
MESNE
NEONS
PEENS
PENNA
PENNE
PENNI
PENNY
PEONS

PEONY
REINK
REINS
REUNE
SEGNI
SEGNO
SEHNA
SEINE
SENNA
TEENA
TEENS
TEENY
TERNE
TERNS
VEINS
VERNE
WEANS
WEENY
YEANS

•E••N
BEGAN
BEGIN
BEGUN
BEHAN
BENIN
BETON
BEVIN
DEIGN
DELON
DEMON
DEVON
DEWAN
FEDON
FEIGN
FELON
GETIN
GETON
HEARN
HEDIN
HELEN
HEMAN
HEMEN
HEMIN
HENAN
HERON
KEVIN
KEYIN
LEARN
LEDIN
LEDON
LEMON
LENIN
LETIN
LETON
LEVIN
LEVON
LEXAN
MEGAN
MELAN
MELON
MESON
NEMAN
NEVIN
PECAN
PEKIN
PEPIN
PERAN
PERON
RECON
REDAN
REDON
REGAN
REHAN

REIGN
REMAN
RENAN
RENIN
REPIN
RERAN
RERUN
RESIN
REWIN
REWON
SEDAN
SEEIN
SERIN
SETIN
SETON
SEVEN
SEWON
TENON
TETON
TEXAN
VEGAN
VENIN
XENON
YEARN
YEMEN
ZEVON

••EN•
ABEND
ADENO
AGENA
AGENT
ALENE
AMEND
AMENS
AMENT
ANENT
ARENA
ARENS
ARENT
AVENA
AVENS
BEENE
BLEND
BLENT
BRENT
BUENA
BUENO
DIENE
EDENS
ELENA
ELENI
EMEND
EVENS
EVENT
FIEND
FRENA
GEENA
GHENT
GLENN
GLENS
GWENN
HYENA
ICENI
ILENE
IRENE
KEENE
KEENS
LIENS
MIENS
NOEND
OMENS
ONEND
OPENS

OVENS
OWENS
PEENS
PHENO
PLENA
SAENS
SCENA
SCEND
SCENE
SCENT
SIENA
SPEND
SPENT
STENO
STENS
TEENA
TEENS
TEENY
TREND
TRENT
UPEND
WEENY
WRENS

••E•N
ATEIN
BREEN
CLEAN
CLEON
CREON
CUEIN
FOEHN
FREON
GLEAN
GLENN
GREEN
GWENN
ICEIN
KLEIN
LIEIN
OCEAN
OLEAN
OLEIN
PAEAN
PAEON
PLEON
PREEN
QUEEN
QUERN
SEEIN
SHEAN
SHEEN
SKEAN
SKEIN
STEEN
STEIN
STERN
TIEIN
TOEIN
TREEN
TWEEN
WHEEN

•••EN
ADMEN
AIKEN
ALBEN
ALDEN
ALIEN
ALLEN
ARDEN
ARLEN
ASHEN
ASPEN

AUDEN
BADEN
BIDEN
BOWEN
BREEN
CHIEN
COHEN
COVEN
COZEN
DIZEN
DOREN
DOYEN
DOZEN
EATEN
EBSEN
EIGEN
ELLEN
EMDEN
ESSEN
GALEN
GIVEN
GOREN
GREEN
GUTEN
HAGEN
HAVEN
HELEN
HEMEN
IBSEN
KAREN
LADEN
LATEN
LIKEN
LIMEN
LINEN
LIVEN
LODEN
LOREN
LTGEN
LUMEN
MAVEN
NIVEN
NOMEN
NUMEN
NUYEN
OAKEN
OATEN
OFTEN
OGDEN
OLDEN
OLSEN
PAREN
PATEN
PHREN
PREEN
QUEEN
QUIEN
RAMEN
RAVEN
RIPEN
RISEN
RIVEN
ROSEN
ROUEN
ROWEN
RUBEN
RUMEN
SEVEN
SHEEN
SIREN
SOREN
STEEN
TAKEN
TOKEN

TREEN
TWEEN
UNPEN
VIXEN
WAKEN
WAXEN
WHEEN
WIDEN
WIZEN
WODEN
WOKEN
WOMEN
WOVEN
YEMEN
ZAZEN

EO•••
EOLUS
EOSIN

E•O••
EBOLI
EBONY
ECOLE
ELOPE
EMORY
EMOTE
ENOCH
ENOLS
ENORM
EPOCH
EPODE
EPOXY
ERODE
EROSE
ETONS
EVOKE
EVORA
EWOKS
EXONS

E••O•
EAMON
EATON
EGGON
ELBOW
ELION
ELIOT
ELMOS
ELROY
ELTON
ENDOR
ENDOW
ENJOY
ENROL
ENSOR
ENTOM
ENVOI
ENVOY
EPCOT
EPHOD
EPHOR
EPSOM
EPSON
ERGOT
ERROL
ERROR
ESPOO
ESTOP
ETHOS
EUROS
EXPOS
EXTOL
EXXON

E•••O
EIEIO
ENERO
ENNIO
ERATO
ESPOO
ETHNO
EXTRO

•EO••
AEONS
CEORL
DEOXY
FEOFF
GEODE
GEOID
GEORG
KEOGH
LEONA
LEONE
LEORA
MEOWS
NEONS
PEONS
PEONY
REOIL
SEOUL

•E•O•
AESOP
BEBOP
BEFOG
BEGOT
BELOW
BESOM
BESOT
BETON
CEROS
DECOR
DECOY
DEFOE
DEFOG
DELON
DELOS
DEMOB
DEMON
DEMOS
DENOM
DEPOT
DETOO
DEVON
FEDON
FELON
FETOR
GEMOT
GENOA
GETON
HELOS
HELOT
HEROD
HERON
HEROS
KENOS
LEDON
LEGOS
LEMON
LENOS
LENOX
LEROI
LEROY
LETON
LEVON
MEDOC
MELON

MELOS
MEMOS
MEROE
MESON
METOO
NEPOS
NEROL
PECOS
PEKOE
PEPOS
PERON
PEROT
PESOS
RECON
REDON
REDOX
REMOP
REMOW
REPOS
REPOT
RESOD
RETOP
RETOW
REWON
SEGOS
SENOR
SEPOY
SEROW
SETON
SEWON
TELOS
TENON
TENOR
TETON
VENOM
XENON
XEROX
ZEROS
ZEVON

•E••O

BEANO
BENZO
CELLO
CENTO
CERRO
DELCO
DERMO
DETOO
DEUTO
FEMTO
FERRO
GECKO
GENRO
GESSO
GETGO
GETTO
HECTO
HELIO
HELLO
JELLO
KELSO
KENDO
LEDTO
LENTO
LEPTO
LETGO
MENLO
METOO
METRO
MEZZO
NEATO
NEURO
PEABO
PEDRO
PENGO
PESTO
PETRO
RECTO
REPRO
RETRO
SEATO
SECCO
SEETO
SEGNO
SEIKO
SERVO
SETTO
TELEO
TEMPO
VERSO
ZENDO
ZEPPO

••EO•

CLEON
CREON
FREON
OLEOS
OREOS
PAEON
PLEON
THEOL

••E•O

ACETO
ADENO
ANEMO
BUENO
CREDO
DIEGO
EIEIO
ENERO
FUEGO
GRECO
HAEMO
HIERO
LIETO
LUEGO
MYELO
PHENO
PLEIO
PREGO
PTERO
SEETO
STENO
VIEJO

•••EO

BUTEO
CAMEO
CUNEO
HOMEO
MATEO
MIMEO
MINEO
ORFEO
OSSEO
OSTEO
PALEO
PASEO
RODEO
ROLEO
ROMEO
TELEO
VIDEO
VIREO

EP•••

EPACT
EPCOT
EPEES
EPHAH
EPHAS
EPHOD
EPHOR
EPICS
EPISC
EPOCH
EPODE
EPOXY
EPSOM
EPSON

E•P••

EMPTY
ESPOO
EXPEL
EXPOS

E••P•

EGYPT
ELOPE
ERUPT
ETAPE

E•••P

EATUP
ENDUP
EQUIP
ESTOP

•EP••

CEPES
DEPEW
DEPOT
DEPTH
DEPTS
HEPTA
KEPIS
LEPTA
LEPTO
LEPUS
NEPAL
NEPOS
PEPIN
PEPLA
PEPOS
PEPPY
PEPSI
PEPUP
PEPYS
REPAY
REPEG
REPEL
REPIN
REPLY
REPOS
REPOT
REPPS
REPRO
SEPAL
SEPIA
SEPOY
SEPTA
TEPAL
TEPEE
TEPID
ZEPPO

•E•P•

BEEPS
DEEPS
HEAPS
HELPS
HEMPS
JEEPS
KEEPS
KELPS
KELPY
KEMPT
LEAPS
LEAPT
NEAPS
PEEPS
PEPPY
PERPS
REAPS
REPPS
REUPS
SEEPS
SEEPY
TEMPE
TEMPI
TEMPO
TEMPS
TEMPT
VEEPS
WEEPS
WEEPY
YELPS
ZEPPO

•E••P

AESOP
BEBOP
FEDUP
GETUP
HETUP
KEYUP
LEGUP
LETUP
PEPUP
RECAP
RECIP
REMAP
REMOP
RETAP
RETOP
SETUP
SEWUP
TEEUP

••EP•

ADEPT
ALEPH
BEEPS
CREPE
CREPT
DEEPS
INEPT
JEEPS
KEEPS
PEEPS
PREPS
SEEPS
SEEPY
SIEPI
SKEPS
SLEPT
STEPS
SWEPT
VEEPS
WEEPS
WEEPY

••E•P

ATEUP
BLEEP
CHEAP
CHEEP
CREEP
ICEUP
ONEUP
SHEEP
SHEMP
SLEEP
STEEP
SWEEP
TEEUP
TIEUP
TWERP
USEUP
WHELP

•••EP

BLEEP
CHEEP
CREEP
JULEP
SALEP
SHEEP
SLEEP
STEEP
SWEEP

EQ•••

EQUAL
EQUIP
EQUIV
EQUUS

E•Q••

ESQUE

E•••Q

ETSEQ

•••EQ

ETSEQ

ER•••

ERASE
ERATO
ERECT
ERGOT
ERICA
ERICH
ERIES
ERIKA
ERISA
ERNES
ERNIE
ERNST
ERODE
EROSE
ERRED
ERROL
ERROR
ERUCT
ERUPT
ERVIL
ERVIN
ERWIN

E•R••

EARED
EARLE
EARLS
EARLY
EARNS
EARTH
ECRUS
EERIE
EFREM
EGRET
ELROY
ENROL
ERRED
ERROL
ERROR
EUROS
EURUS
EYRAS
EYRES
EYRIE
EYRIR

E••R•

EAGRE
EBERT
EMERY
EMIRS
EMORY
ENERO
ENGRS
ENORM
ENTRE
ENTRY
ENURE
EVERS
EVERT
EVERY
EVORA
EWERS
EXERT
EXTRA
EXTRO
EXURB
EYERS

E•••R

EAGER
EATER
EDGAR
EDGER
EELER
EGGAR
EIDER
ELDER
ELGAR
ELLER
ELMER
ELVER
EMBAR
EMBER
EMEER
EMMER
ENDER
ENDOR
ENSOR
ENTER
EPHOR
ERROR
ESKER
ESTER
ETHER
EULER
EYRIR

•ER••

AERIE
BEREA
BERET
BERGH
BERGS
BERLE
BERME
BERMS
BERNE
BERRA
BERRY
BERTH
BERYL
CERAM
CERAT
CERED
CERES
CERIA
CEROS
CERRO
CERTS
DERAT
DERBY
DEREK
DERIV
DERMA
DERMO
DERRY
EERIE
FERAL
FERDE
FERIA
FERMI
FERNS
FERNY
FERRI
FERRO
FERRY
GERAH
GERMS
GERMY
GERRY
HERAT
HERBS
HERBY
HERDS
HERES
HERKY
HERLS
HERMS
HERNE
HEROD
HERON
HEROS
HERTZ
HERVE
HERZL
JEREZ
JERKS
JERKY
JERRY
JERZY
KERAT
KERBS
KERNS
KERRY
LEROI
LEROY
MERCE
MERCI
MERCY
MERES
MERGE
MERIT
MERLE
MERLS
MEROE
MERRY
MERTZ
MERYL
NERDS
NERDY
NEROL
NERTS
NERTZ
NERVE
NERVY
PERAN
PERCE
PERCH
PERCY
PERDU
PERES
PEREZ
PERIL
PERIS
PERKS
PERKY
PERLE
PERMS
PERON
PEROT
PERPS
PERRY
PERSE
PERTH
RERAN
RERUN
SERAC
SERAI
SERBS
SERES
SERFS
SERGE
SERIF
SERIN
SEROW
SERRA
SERTA
SERUM
SERVE
SERVO
TERMS
TERNE
TERNS
TERRA
TERRE
TERRI
TERRY
TERSE
TERZA
VERBS
VERDE
VERDI
VERGE
VERMI
VERNE
VERRE
VERSA
VERSE
VERSO
VERST
VERTE
VERTS
VERVE
XERIC
XEROX
XERUS
YERBA
ZEROS

•E•R•

BEARD
BEARS
BEERS
BEERY
BERRA
BERRY
CEORL
CERRO
DEARS
DEARY
DEBRA
DECRY
DEERE
DEERS
DERRY
DETRE
DEVRY
FEARS
FERRI
FERRO
FERRY
GEARS
GEARY
GENRE
GENRO
GEORG
GERRY
HEARD
HEARN
HEARS
HEART
HEIRS
HENRI
HENRY
HEURE
JEERS
JERRY
KERRY
LEARN
LEARY
LEERS
LEERY
LEORA
MEARA
MERRY
METRE
METRO
NEARS
NEGRI
NEHRU
NEURO
PEARL
PEARS
PEARY
PEDRO
PEERS
PERRY
PETRA
PETRI
PETRO
REARM
REARS
REFRY
REPRO
RETRO
RETRY
SEARS
SEERS
SERRA
TEARS
TEARY
TERRA
TERRE
TERRI
TERRY
TETRA
VEERS
VEERY
VERRE
WEARS
WEARY
WEIRD
WEIRS
YEARN
YEARS
ZEBRA

•E••R

AEGIR
AESIR
CEDAR
CESAR
DEBAR
DECOR
DEFER
DEMUR
DENDR
DETER
DEWAR
DEXTR
EELER
FEMUR
FETOR
FEVER
FEWER
HEWER
HEXER
JETER
KEFIR
LEGER
LEHAR
LEMUR
LEVAR
LEVER
METER
MEYER
NEVER
NEWER
PETER
REAIR
REBAR
RECUR
REFER
RETAR
SEDER
SEGAR
SEGER
SENOR
SEVER
SEWER
TENOR
VELAR
VEXER
WEBER
WESER

••ER•

ACERB
AGERS
ALERT
APERS
APERY
AVERS
AVERT
AVERY
AYERS
BEERS
BEERY
BOERS
BRERS
CBERS
CHERE
CHERI
CHERT
CIERA
CLERK
DEERE
DEERS
DOERS
DYERS
EBERT
EMERY
ENERO
EVERS
EVERT
EVERY
EWERS
EXERT
EYERS
FIERY
FRERE
GOERS
HIERO
HOERS
IBERT
ICERS
INERT
ISERE
JEERS
LEERS
LEERY
MYERS
NLERS
OMERS
ONERS
OPERA
OVERS
OVERT
OWERS
PEERS
PIERS
PTERO
QUERN
QUERY
SEERS
SHERE
SNERD
SNERT
STERE
STERN
SUERS
THERA
THERE
THERM
TIERS
TWERE
TWERP
USERS
VEERS
VEERY
VIERS
WHERE

••E•R

AMEER
ANEAR
AREAR
BLEAR
CHEER
CLEAR
COEUR
DREAR
EMEER
FLEER
FLEUR
FREER
GREER
QUEER
SHEAR
SHEER
SIEUR
SMEAR
SNEER
SOEUR
SPEAR
STEER
SWEAR
THEIR

•••ER

ABLER
ABNER
ACTER
ADDER
ADLER
AFTER
AILER
AIMER
ALDER
ALGER
ALLER
ALTER
AMBER
AMEER
ANGER
ANSER
APTER
ARBER
ASHER
ASKER
ASNER
ASTER
AUBER
AUGER
BABER
BAKER
BALER
BARER
BASER
BAUER
BAYER
BIKER
BITER
BLUER
BONER
BOOER
BORER
BOWER
BOXER
BOYER
BRIER
BUBER
BUYER
BYNER
CABER
CAGER
CANER
CAPER
CARER
CATER
CAVER
CHEER
CIDER
CITER
CODER
COMER
COOER
CORER
COVER
COWER
COYER
CRIER
CURER
CUTER
CYDER
DARER
DATER
DEFER
DETER
DICER
DINER
DIRER
DIVER
DOSER
DOTER
DOVER
DOWER
DOZER
DRIER
DRYER
DURER
EAGER
EATER
EDGER
EELER
EIDER
ELDER
ELLER
ELMER
ELVER
EMBER
EMEER
EMMER
ENDER
ENTER
ESKER
ESTER
ETHER
EULER
FABER
FACER
FAKER
FARER
FEVER
FEWER
FIBER
FIFER
FILER
FINER
FIRER
FIVER
FIXER
FLEER
FLIER
FLYER
FOYER
FREER
FRIER
FRYER
GAMER
GAPER
GAYER
GAZER
GIBER
GIVER
GLUER
GOFER
GOMER
GONER
GOWER
GREER
GRIER
HABER
HALER
HATER
HAUER
HAVER
HAZER
HEWER
HEXER
HIDER
HIKER
HIRER
HOMER
HOPER
HOVER
HUGER
HYPER
ICIER
IDLER
ILLER
INFER
INGER
INKER
INNER
INTER
JETER
JIVER
JOKER
KHMER
KINER
KITER
KYSER
LACER
LADER
LAGER
LAKER
LAMER
LASER
LATER
LAVER
LAXER
LAYER
LEGER
LEVER
LIGER
LINER
LITER
LIVER
LONER
LOPER
LOSER
LOVER
LOWER
LUGER
MAKER
MASER
MATER
MAYER
MAZER
METER
MEYER
MILER
MIMER
MINER
MISER
MITER
MIXER
MOPER
MOVER
MOWER
MUSER
MUTER
NADER
NAMER
NEVER
NEWER
NFLER
NHLER
NICER
NIGER
NINER
NITER
NIZER
NOTER
NUDER
OATER
OCHER
ODDER
OFFER
OGLER
OILER
OLDER
OMBER
ORDER
ORSER
OSIER
OSLER
OTHER
OTTER
OUTER
OWNER
PACER
PAGER
PALER
PAPER
PARER
PATER
PAVER
PAWER
PAYER
PETER
PIKER
PIPER
POKER
POLER
POSER
POWER
PRIER
PURER
QUEER
RACER
RAFER
RAKER
RARER
RATER
RAVER
RAWER
REFER
RICER
RIDER
RIFER
RIKER
RIPER
RISER
RIVER
ROGER
ROMER
ROPER
ROVER
ROWER
RUDER
RULER
RYDER
SABER
SAFER
SAGER
SAKER
SANER
SAVER
SAYER
SEDER
SEGER
SEVER
SEWER
SHEER
SHIER
SHOER
SHYER
SIDER
SIZER
SKIER
SLIER
SLYER
SNEER
SOBER
SOLER
SORER
SOWER
SOXER
STEER
SUMER
SUPER
SURER
TAKER
TALER
TAMER
TAPER
TASER
TATER
TAXER
TIBER
TIGER
TILER
TIMER
TITER
TOLER
TONER
TOPER
TOTER
TOWER
TRIER
TRUER
TUBER
TUNER
TYLER
TYPER
UDDER
ULCER
UMBER
UNDER
UNGER
UNSER
UNTER
UPPER
URGER
USHER
UTHER
UTTER
VADER
VATER
VEXER
VILER
VIPER
VOTER
VOWER
WADER
WAFER
WAGER
WALER
WANER
WATER
WAVER
WAXER
WEBER
WESER
WIDER
WIPER
WIRER
WISER
WOOER
WRIER
WRYER
WYLER

ES•••

ESBAT
ESKER
ESNES
ESPOO
ESQUE
ESSAY
ESSEN
ESSES
ESSEX
ESTAB
ESTEE
ESTER
ESTES
ESTOP

E•S••

EASED
EASEL
EASES
EASTS
EBSEN
EDSEL
ELSIE
ENSKY
ENSOR
ENSUE
EOSIN
EPSOM
EPSON
ESSAY
ESSEN
ESSES
ESSEX
ETSEQ

E••S•

EGEST
ELISE
ELYSE
EPISC
ERASE
ERISA
ERNST
EROSE
EXIST

E•••S

EAMES
EARLS
EARNS
EASES
EASTS
EAVES
ECRUS
EDAMS
EDDAS
EDENS
EDGES
EDITS

EFIKS
EGADS
ELIAS
ELLES
ELLIS
ELMOS
ELVES
ELVIS
EMIRS
EMITS
EMMYS
ENGRS
ENNIS
ENOLS
EOLUS
EPEES
EPHAS
EPICS
EQUUS
ERIES
ERNES
ESNES
ESSES
ESTES
ETHOS
ETNAS
ETONS
ETUIS
EUROS
EURUS
EVANS
EVENS
EVERS
EVILS
EWERS
EWOKS
EXAMS
EXECS
EXITS
EXONS
EXPOS
EYERS
EYRAS
EYRES

•ES••

AESIR
AESOP
BESET
BESOM
BESOT
BESTS
CESAR
CESTA
CESTI
DESKS
DESNA
FESTA
FESTS
GESSO
GESTE
GESTS
HESSE
HESTS
JESSE
JESTS
KESEY
MESAS
MESHY
MESIC
MESNE
MESON
MESSY
MESTA
NESTS
PESCI
PESKY
PESOS
PESTO
PESTS
RESEE
RESET
RESEW
RESIN
RESOD
RESTS
TESLA
TESTA
TESTS
TESTY
VESEY
VESTA
VESTS
WESER
YESES
ZESTS
ZESTY

•E•S•

BEAST
BETSY
CEASE
CENSE
DEISM
DEIST
DENSE
FEAST
FEIST
GEESE
GESSO
HEISS
HEIST
HESSE
HEYSE
JESSE
KELSO
LEASE
LEASH
LEAST
MEESE
MENSA
MESSY
MEUSE
NEWSY
PEASE
PEPSI
PERSE
REESE
REUSE
SEISM
SENSE
SEUSS
TEASE
TENSE
TERSE
VERSA
VERSE
VERSO
VERST
WEEST
WEISS
WELSH
YEAST
ZEISS
ZEIST

•E••S

AEDES
AEGIS
AEONS
BEADS
BEAKS
BEALS
BEAMS
BEANS
BEARS
BEATS
BEAUS
BECKS
BEEFS
BEEPS
BEERS
BEETS
BELLS
BELTS
BEMAS
BENDS
BENES
BENTS
BERGS
BERMS
BESTS
BETAS
CEDES
CEILS
CELLS
CELTS
CENTS
CEPES
CERES
CEROS
CERTS
CETUS
DEALS
DEANS
DEARS
DEBTS
DECKS
DEEDS
DEEMS
DEEPS
DEERS
DEGAS
DEKES
DELES
DELIS
DELLS
DELOS
DELTS
DEMES
DEMOS
DENES
DENIS
DENTS
DENYS
DEPTS
DESKS
FEARS
FEATS
FEEDS
FEELS
FELIS
FELLS
FELTS
FENDS
FERNS
FESTS
FETAS
FETES
FEUDS
GEARS
GEEKS
GENES
GENTS
GENUS
GERMS
GESTS
GETAS
HEADS
HEALS
HEAPS
HEARS
HEATS
HECKS
HEEDS
HEELS
HEFTS
HEIRS
HEISS
HELMS
HELOS
HELPS
HEMPS
HERBS
HERDS
HERES
HERLS
HERMS
HEROS
HESTS
HEXES
JEANS
JEEPS
JEERS
JELLS
JERKS
JESTS
JETES
KEATS
KEELS
KEENS
KEEPS
KELPS
KENOS
KEPIS
KERBS
KERNS
KEYES
LEADS
LEAFS
LEAKS
LEANS
LEAPS
LEEDS
LEEKS
LEERS
LEETS
LEFTS
LEGGS
LEGIS
LEGOS
LENDS
LENIS
LENOS
LENTS
LEPUS
LETTS
LEVIS
LEWES
LEWIS
LEXIS
LEXUS
MEADS
MEALS
MEANS
MEATS
MEDES
MEEDS
MEETS
MELDS
MELOS
MELTS
MEMOS
MENDS
MENUS
MEOWS
MERES
MERLS
MESAS
METES
METIS
MEWLS
NEAPS
NEARS
NEATS
NECKS
NEEDS
NEGUS
NENES
NEONS
NEPOS
NERDS
NERTS
NESTS
NEVES
NEVIS
NEVUS
NEWTS
NEXUS
PEAKS
PEALS
PEARS
PEATS
PECKS
PECOS
PEEKS
PEELS
PEENS
PEEPS
PEERS
PEKES
PELTS
PENDS
PEONS
PEPOS
PEPYS
PERES
PERIS
PERKS
PERMS
PERPS
PESOS
PESTS
READS
REALS
REAMS
REAPS
REARS
REBUS
REEDS
REEFS
REEKS
REELS
REGIS
REIMS
REINS
REMUS
RENDS
RENTS
REPOS
REPPS
RESTS
REUPS
REXES
REYES
SEALS
SEAMS
SEARS
SEATS
SECTS
SEEDS
SEEKS
SEELS
SEEMS
SEEPS
SEERS
SEGOS
SELES
SELLS
SEMIS
SENDS
SERBS
SERES
SERFS
SEUSS
SEXES
SEXTS
TEAKS
TEALS
TEAMS
TEARS
TECHS
TEEMS
TEENS
TELLS
TELOS
TEMPS
TENDS
TENTS
TERMS
TERNS
TESTS
TETHS
TEXAS
TEXTS
VEDAS
VEEPS
VEERS
VEGAS
VEILS
VEINS
VELDS
VENDS
VENTS
VENUS
VERBS
VERTS
VESTS
VEXES
WEALS
WEANS
WEARS
WEEDS
WEEKS
WEEMS
WEEPS
WEFTS
WEIRS
WEISS
WELDS
WELLS
WELTS
WENDS
XERUS
YEANS
YEARS
YEATS
YEGGS
YELLS
YELPS
YESES
YETIS
ZEALS
ZEBUS
ZEISS
ZEROS
ZESTS
ZETAS

••ES•

BLESS
BLEST
BREST
CHESS
CHEST
CRESC
CRESS
CREST
DOEST
DRESS
EGEST
FLESH
FRESH
GEESE
GLESS
GOEST
GUESS
GUEST
IDEST
LOESS
MEESE
OBESE
POESY
PRESS
QUEST
REESE
THESE
TRESS
WEEST
WIEST
WREST

••E•S

ABETS
AGERS
AKEES
ALEFS
AMENS
APERS
AREAS
ARENS
AVENS
AVERS
AXELS
AYERS
BEEFS
BEEPS
BEERS
BEETS
BLEBS
BLESS
BOERS
BRERS
BREWS
CBERS
CHEFS
CHESS
CHEWS
CLEFS
CLEWS
COEDS
CREES
CRESS
CREWS
DEEDS
DEEMS
DEEPS
DEERS
DIEMS
DIETS
DOERS
DREGS
DRESS
DUELS
DUETS
DYERS
EDENS
EPEES
EVENS
EVERS
EWERS
EXECS
EYERS
FEEDS
FEELS
FIEFS
FLEAS
FLEES
FLEWS
FREES
FRETS
FUELS
GAELS
GEEKS
GHEES
GLEES
GLENS
GLESS
GOERS
GREYS
GUESS
HEEDS
HEELS
HOERS
ICERS
IDEAS
ITEMS
JEEPS
JEERS
JOEYS
KEELS
KEENS
KEEPS
KNEES
KREBS
LEEDS
LEEKS
LEERS
LEETS
LIENS
LIEUS
LOESS
MEEDS
MEETS
MIENS
MYERS
NEEDS
NIELS
NLERS
NOELS
OBEYS
ODETS
OGEES
OLEOS
OMENS
OMERS
ONERS
OPEDS
OPELS
OPENS
OREOS
OVENS
OVERS
OWENS
OWERS
PEEKS
PEELS
PEENS
PEEPS
PEERS
PIEDS
PIERS
PLEAS
PLEBS
POEMS
POETS
PREPS
PRESS
PREYS
REEDS
REEFS
REEKS
REELS
RHEAS
RIELS
SAENS
SEEDS
SEEKS
SEELS
SEEMS
SEEPS
SEERS
SHEDS
SKEGS
SKEPS
SKEWS
SLEDS
SLEWS
SMEWS
SPECS
SPETS
SPEWS
STEMS
STENS
STEPS
STETS
STEWS
SUERS
SUETS
TAELS
TEEMS
TEENS
THEMS
THEWS
TIEGS
TIERS
TREES
TREKS
TRESS
TREWS
TREYS
USERS
VEEPS
VEERS
VIERS
VIEWS
WEEDS
WEEKS
WEEMS
WEEPS
WHETS
WHEYS
WRENS

•••ES

AAMES
ABBES
ACHES
ACMES
ACRES
ADZES
AEDES
AGNES
AGUES
AIDES
AIRES
AKEES
ALLES
ALOES
AMIES
ANDES
ANGES
ANNES
ANTES
APRES
APSES
ARIES
ARLES
ARTES
ASHES
ASSES
AXLES
AYRES
BABES
BAKES
BALES
BANES
BARES
BASES
BATES
BENES
BIDES
BIKES
BINES
BISES
BITES
BLUES
BODES
BOLES
BONES
BORES
BOWES
BOXES
BRAES
BRIES
BUSES
BYTES
CAFES
CAGES
CAKES
CANES
CAPES
CARES
CASES
CATES
CAVES
CEDES
CEPES
CERES
CINES
CIRES
CITES
CLUES
CODES
COKES
COLES
COMES
CONES
COPES
CORES
COTES
COVES
COWES
COXES
COZES
CREES
CRIES
CUBES
CUKES
CURES
CYMES
DACES
DALES
DAMES
DANES
DARES
DATES
DAWES
DAZES
DEKES
DELES
DEMES
DENES
DICES
DIKES
DIMES
DINES
DIVES
DOGES
DOLES
DOMES
DOPES
DOSES
DOTES
DOVES
DOZES
DRIES
DUCES
DUDES
DUKES
DUNES
DUPES
DYNES
EAMES
EASES
EAVES
EDGES
ELLES
ELVES
EPEES
ERIES
ERNES
ESNES
ESSES
ESTES
EYRES
FACES
FADES
FAKES
FAMES
FANES
FARES
FATES
FAVES
FAXES
FAZES
FETES
FIFES
FILES
FINES
FIRES
FIVES
FIXES
FLEES
FLIES
FLOES
FLUES
FORES
FOXES
FREES
FRIES
FROES
FUMES
FUSES
FYKES
GAGES
GALES
GAMES
GAPES
GASES
GATES
GAZES
GENES
GHEES
GIBES
GILES
GIVES
GLEES
GLUES
GORES
GULES
GYRES
GYVES
HADES
HAKES
HALES
HAMES
HANES
HARES
HATES
HAVES
HAYES
HAZES
HERES
HEXES
HIDES
HIKES
HINES
HIRES
HIVES
HOKES
HOLES
HOMES
HONES
HOPES
HOSES
HYPES
ICKES
IDLES
IGNES
ISLES
IVIES
JADES
JAKES
JAMES
JAPES
JETES
JIBES
JIVES
JOKES
JONES
JUKES
JULES
JUTES
KALES
KEYES
KITES
KNEES
LACES
LADES
LAKES
LAMES
LANES
LARES
LASES
LAVES
LAWES
LAZES
LEWES
LIKES
LIMES
LINES
LITES
LIVES
LOBES
LODES
LOGES
LOPES
LORES
LOSES
LOVES
LOXES
LUBES
LUGES
LUNES
LURES
LUTES
LYRES
MACES
MAGES
MAKES
MALES
MANES
MARES
MATES
MAXES
MAZES
MEDES
MERES
METES
MIKES
MILES
MIMES
MINES
MIRES
MITES
MIXES
MLLES
MODES
MOLES
MOPES
MORES
MOSES
MOTES
MOUES
MOVES
MULES
MUSES
MUTES
MYLES
NABES
NAMES
NAPES
NARES
NAVES
NENES
NEVES
NIDES
NIKES
NILES
NIMES
NINES
NITES
NIXES
NODES
NONES
NOSES
NOTES
NOYES
NUDES
NUKES
OAKES
OASES
OATES
OBIES
OBOES
OGEES
OGLES
OGRES
OKIES
OOZES
ORLES
OTOES
PACES
PAGES
PALES
PANES
PARES
PASES
PATES
PAVES
PEKES
PERES
PIKES
PILES
PINES
PIPES
PLIES
POKES
POLES
POMES
PONES
POPES
PORES
POSES
PRIES
PULES
PYRES
RACES
RAGES
RAKES
RARES
RASES
RATES
RAVES
RAZES
REXES
REYES
RICES
RIDES
RILES
RIMES
RISES
RITES
RIVES
ROBES
ROLES
ROPES
ROSES
ROTES
ROUES
ROVES
RUBES
RULES
RUNES
RUSES
SAFES
SAGES
SAKES
SALES
SASES
SATES
SAVES
SAXES
SELES
SERES
SEXES
SHIES
SHOES
SIDES
SIKES
SINES
SIRES
SITES
SIXES
SIZES
SKIES
SLOES
SLUES
SOLES
SONES
SORES
SPIES
STIES
SYCES
TAKES
TALES
TAMES
TAPES
TARES
TAXES
TIDES
TILES
TIMES
TINES
TIRES
TOMES
TONES
TOPES
TOTES
TOVES
TREES
TRIES
TRUES
TUBES
TULES
TUNES
TUXES
TYKES
TYNES
TYPES
TYRES
URGES
VALES
VANES
VASES
VEXES
VIBES
VICES
VINES
VISES
VOLES
VOTES
WADES
WAGES
WAKES
WALES
WANES
WARES
WAVES
WAXES
WILES
WINES
WIPES
WIRES
WIVES
XAXES
YATES
YAXES
YESES
YIKES
YIPES
YOKES
YPRES
ZAXES
ZONES

ET•••

ETAGE
ETAPE
ETHAN
ETHEL
ETHER
ETHIC
ETHNO
ETHOS
ETHYL
ETNAS
ETONS
ETSEQ
ETUDE
ETUIS
ETYMA
ETZEL

E•T••

EATAT
EATEN
EATER
EATIN
EATIT
EATON
EATUP
ELTON
ENTER
ENTIA
ENTOM
ENTRE
ENTRY
ESTAB
ESTEE
ESTER
ESTES
ESTOP
EXTOL
EXTRA
EXTRO

E••T•

EARTH
EASTS
EDITH
EDITS
ELATE
ELITE
ELUTE
EMITS
EMOTE
EMPTY
ENATE
ERATO
EVITA
EXITS

E•••T

EATAT
EATIT
EBERT
ECLAT
EDICT
EDUCT
EFLAT
EGEST
EGRET
EGYPT
EIGHT
EJECT
ELECT
ELIOT
EMMET
ENACT
EPACT
EPCOT
ERECT
ERGOT
ERNST
ERUCT
ERUPT
ESBAT
EVENT
EVERT
EVICT
EXACT
EXALT
EXERT
EXIST
EXULT

•ET••

AETAT
AETNA
BETAS
BETEL
BETON
BETSY
BETTA
BETTE
BETTY
CETUS
DETAT
DETER
DETOO
DETRE
FETAL
FETAS
FETCH
FETED
FETES
FETID
FETOR
GETAS
GETAT
GETBY
GETGO
GETIN
GETIT
GETME
GETON

GETTO
GETTY
GETUP
HETTY
HETUP
JETER
JETES
JETTY
KETCH
LETAT
LETBE
LETGO
LETHE
LETIN
LETON
LETTS
LETUP
METAL
METED
METER
METES
METIS
METOO
METRE
METRO
PETAL
PETER
PETIT
PETRA
PETRI
PETRO
PETTI
PETTY
RETAG
RETAP
RETAR
RETAX
RETIA
RETIE
RETOP
RETOW
RETRO
RETRY
SETAE
SETAT
SETBY
SETIN
SETON
SETTO
SETUP
TETHS
TETON
TETRA
VETCH
WETLY
YETIS
ZETAS

•E•T•

BEATS
BEETS
BELTS
BENTS
BERTH
BESTS
BETTA
BETTE
BETTY
CELTS
CENTI
CENTO
CENTS
CERTS
CESTA
CESTI
CEUTA
DEBTS
DEITY
DELTA
DELTS
DENTE
DENTI
DENTS
DEPTH
DEPTS
DEUTO
DEXTR
FEATS
FELTS
FEMTO
FESTA
FESTS
GENTS
GESTE
GESTS
GETTO
GETTY
HEATH
HEATS
HECTO
HEFTS
HEFTY
HEPTA
HERTZ
HESTS
HETTY
HEUTE
JESTS
JETTY
KEATS
KEITH
LEDTO
LEETS
LEFTS
LEFTY
LEITH
LENTO
LENTS
LEPTA
LEPTO
LETTS
LEYTE
MEATS
MEATY
MEETS
MEHTA
MELTS
MELTY
MERTZ
MESTA
NEATH
NEATO
NEATS
NERTS
NERTZ
NESTS
NEWTS
PEATS
PEATY
PEETE
PELTS
PENTA
PENTE
PERTH
PESTO
PESTS
PETTI
PETTY
REATA
RECTI
RECTO
RENTA
RENTS
RESTS
SEATO
SEATS
SECTS
SEETO
SEPTA
SERTA
SETTO
SEXTS
TEETH
TENTH
TENTS
TESTA
TESTS
TESTY
TEXTS
VENTS
VERTE
VERTS
VESTA
VESTS
WEFTS
WELTS
WELTY
YEATS
YENTA
YENTE
YENTL
ZESTS
ZESTY

•E••T

AETAT
BEAST
BEAUT
BEFIT
BEGAT
BEGET
BEGOT
BENET
BERET
BESET
BESOT
CERAT
DEALT
DEBIT
DEBUT
DEFAT
DEIST
DELFT
DEMIT
DEPOT
DERAT
DETAT
FEAST
FEINT
FEIST
GEMOT
GENET
GETAT
GETIT
HEART
HECHT
HEIDT
HEIST
HELOT
HEMET
HERAT
KEMPT
KERAT
LEANT
LEAPT
LEAST
LEGIT
LETAT
MEANT
MEDIT
MERIT
NEMAT
PEROT
PETIT
PEWIT
REACT
REBUT
REFIT
RELET
RELIT
REMET
REMIT
REPOT
RESET
REVET
SETAT
TEMPT
TENET
TEVET
VEIDT
VELDT
VERST
WEEST
WENDT
YEAST
ZEIST

••ET•

ABETS
ACETO
ALETA
ARETE
BEETS
BRETT
CRETE
DIETS
DOETH
DUETS
FRETS
GRETA
GRETE
LEETS
LIETO
MEETS
ODETS
OVETA
OVETT
PEETE
PIETA
PIETY
POETE
POETS
RHETT
SEETO
SIETE
SKETE
SPETS
STETS
SUETS
TEETH
THETA
WHETS
WYETH

••E•T

ADEPT
AGENT
ALERT
ALEUT
AMENT
ANENT
ARENT
AVERT
BLEAT
BLENT
BLEST
BRENT
BREST
BRETT
CHEAT
CHERT
CHEST
CLEAT
CLEFT
CREPT
CREST
DOEST
DWELT
EBERT
EGEST
EJECT
ELECT
ERECT
EVENT
EVERT
EXERT
FLEET
GHENT
GOEST
GREAT
GREET
GUEST
IBERT
IDEST
INEPT
INERT
KNELT
LIEUT
OVERT
OVETT
PLEAT
QUEST
RHETT
SCENT
SHEET
SKEAT
SKEET
SLEET
SLEPT
SMELT
SNERT
SPELT
SPENT
SWEAT
SWEET
SWEPT
THEFT
TREAT
TRENT
TWEET
WEEST
WHEAT
WIEST
WREST

•••ET

AGLET
AMVET
ARMET
ARRET
ASSET
ASYET
BEGET
BENET
BERET
BESET
BINET
BIZET
BLUET
BONET
CADET
CAPET
CARET
CIVET
COLET
COMET
COVET
CRUET
CULET
DUVET
EGRET
EMMET
FACET
FILET
FLEET
GENET
GODET
GREET
HEMET
INLET
INSET
ISLET
JANET
LUMET
MAMET
MANET
MONET
MOTET
NONET
NYMET
OBJET
OCTET
ONSET
OWLET
PAGET
PUGET
QUIET
RAMET
RELET
REMET
RESET
REVET
RIVET
ROGET
SAGET
SHEET
SKEET
SLEET
SWEET
TACET
TENET
TEVET
TIBET
TOLET
TVSET
TWEET
UNMET
UNSET
UPSET
VALET
ZIBET

EU•••

EUBIE
EULER
EUROS
EURUS

E•U••

EDUCE
EDUCT
ELUDE
ELUTE
ENURE
EQUAL
EQUIP
EQUIV
EQUUS
ERUCT
ERUPT
ETUDE
ETUIS
EXUDE
EXULT
EXURB

E••U•

EATUP
ECRUS
ENDUE
ENDUP
ENNUI
ENSUE
EOLUS
EQUUS
ESQUE
EURUS

E•••U

ELIHU

•EU••

CEUTA
DEUCE
DEUCY
DEUTO
FEUDS
HEURE
HEUTE
JEUDI
JEUNE
MEUSE
NEUME
NEURO
REUNE
REUPS
REUSE
SEULE
SEUSS

•E•U•

BEAUS
BEAUT
BEAUX
BEGUM
BEGUN
BENUE
CETUS
DEBUG
DEBUT
DEMUR
FEDUP
FEMUR
GENUS
GETUP
HETUP
KEYUP
LEGUP
LEHUA
LEMUR
LEPUS
LETUP
LEXUS
MECUM
MENUS
NEFUD
NEGUS
NEVUS
NEXUS
PEPUP
REBUS
REBUT
RECUR
REDUB
REDUX
REMUS
RERUN
REVUE
SEBUM
SEDUM
SEGUE
SEOUL
SERUM
SETUP
SEWUP
TEEUP
VELUM
VENUE
VENUS
XERUS
ZEBUS

•E••U

KEANU
NEHRU
PERDU

••EU•

ADEUX
ALEUT
ATEUP
BOEUF
COEUR
FLEUR
FREUD
ICEUP
LIEUS
LIEUT
ODEUM
OLEUM
ONEUP
PSEUD
QUEUE
RHEUM
SIEUR
SOEUR
TEEUP
TIEUP
USEUP

••E•U

TAEGU

•••EU

ADIEU
PAREU

EV•••

EVADE
EVANS
EVENS
EVENT
EVERS
EVERT
EVERY
EVIAN
EVICT
EVILS
EVITA
EVOKE
EVORA

E•V••

EAVED
EAVES
ELVER
ELVES
ELVIN
ELVIS
ENVOI
ENVOY
ERVIL
ERVIN

E••V•

ELEVE

E•••V

EQUIV

•EV••

BEVEL
BEVIN
DEVIL
DEVON
DEVRY
FEVER
KEVIN
LEVAR
LEVEE
LEVEL
LEVER
LEVIN
LEVIS
LEVON
NEVER
NEVES
NEVIL
NEVIN
NEVIS
NEVUS
REVEL
REVET
REVUE
SEVEN
SEVER
TEVET
TEVYE
ZEVON

•E•V•

BELVA
DELVE
HEAVE
HEAVY
HELVE
HERVE
LEAVE
NERVE
NERVY
PEAVY
PEEVE
REEVE
SELVA
SERVE
SERVO
VERVE
WEAVE

•E••V

DERIV
NEGEV

••EV•

BREVE
CHEVY
ELEVE
PEEVE
REEVE
SIEVE
SNEVA
STEVE
TREVI

•••EV

NEGEV

EW•••

EWELL
EWERS
EWING
EWOKS

E•W••

EDWIN
ELWAY
ERWIN

E•••W

ELBOW
ENDOW

•EW••

DEWAN
DEWAR
DEWED
DEWEY
FEWER
HEWED
HEWER
JEWEL
LEWES
LEWIS
MEWED
MEWLS
NEWEL
NEWER
NEWLY
NEWSY
NEWTS
PEWEE
PEWIT
REWAX
REWED
REWIN
REWON
SEWED
SEWER
SEWON
SEWUP

•E•W•

MEOWS

•E••W

BEDEW
BELOW
DEPEW
REMOW
RENEW
RESEW
RETOW
SEROW

••EW•

BREWS
CHEWS
CHEWY
CLEWS
CREWS
FLEWS
LOEWE
LOEWY
SKEWS
SLEWS
SMEWS
SPEWS
STEWS
THEWS
TREWS
VIEWS

•••EW

AGNEW
ASKEW
BEDEW
CAREW
DEPEW
NAREW
RENEW
RESEW
SCREW
SHREW
SINEW
STREW
THREW

EX•••

EXACT
EXALT
EXAMS
EXCEL
EXECS
EXERT
EXILE
EXIST
EXITS
EXONS
EXPEL
EXPOS
EXTOL
EXTRA
EXTRO
EXUDE
EXULT
EXURB
EXXON

E•X••

EXXON

E••X•

EPOXY

E•••X

ESSEX

•EX••

DEXTR
HEXAD
HEXED
HEXER
HEXES
HEXYL
LEXAN
LEXIS
LEXUS
NEXUS
REXES
SEXES
SEXTS
TEXAN
TEXAS
TEXTS
VEXED
VEXER
VEXES

•E•X•

DEOXY

•E••X

BEAUX
FELIX
HELIX
LENOX
REDOX
REDUX
RELAX
REMEX
REMIX
RETAX
REWAX
TELEX
XEROX

••EX•

FLEXI
PREXY

••E•X

ADEUX
ICEAX

•••EX

ANNEX
CODEX
COMEX
CULEX
CUTEX
ESSEX
INDEX
LATEX
LUREX
MUREX
NYNEX
PUREX
PYREX
REMEX
ROLEX
SILEX
TELEX
TIMEX
TRUEX

EY•••

EYDIE
EYERS
EYRAS
EYRES
EYRIE
EYRIR

E•Y••

EGYPT
ELYSE
ETYMA

E••Y•

EMLYN
EMMYS
ENCYC
ETHYL

E•••Y

EARLY
EBONY
EDIFY
ELEGY
ELROY
ELWAY
EMBAY
EMERY
EMILY
EMORY
EMPTY
ENEMY
ENJOY
ENSKY
ENTRY
ENVOY
EPOXY
ESSAY
EVERY

•EY••

BEYLE
FEYLY
HEYSE
KEYED
KEYES
KEYIN
KEYUP
LEYTE
MEYER
REYES

•E•Y•

BERYL
DENYS
HEXYL
KENYA
LENYA
MERYL
PEPYS
REDYE
SEEYA
TEVYE

•E••Y

BEADY
BEAMY
BEANY
BECKY
BEEFY
BEERY
BELAY
BELLY
BENNY
BERRY
BETSY
BETTY
DEARY
DEBBY
DECAY
DECOY
DECRY
DEIFY
DEITY
DELAY
DENNY
DEOXY
DERBY
DERRY
DEUCY
DEVRY
DEWEY
FELLY
FENNY
FERNY
FERRY
FEYLY
GEARY
GEEKY
GEMMY
GERMY
GERRY
GETBY
GETTY
HEADY
HEALY
HEAVY
HEDGY
HEFTY
HENNY
HENRY
HERBY
HERKY
HETTY
JELLY
JEMMY
JENNY
JERKY
JERRY
JERZY
JETTY
KELLY
KELPY
KENNY
KERRY
KESEY
LEAFY
LEAHY
LEAKY
LEARY
LEERY
LEFAY
LEFTY
LEGGY
LEMAY
LENNY
LEROY
MEALY
MEANY
MEATY
MELTY
MERCY
MERRY
MESHY
MESSY
NEDDY
NEEDY
NELLY
NERDY
NERVY
NEWLY
NEWSY
PEARY
PEATY
PEAVY
PEGGY
PENNY
PEONY
PEPPY
PERCY
PERKY
PERRY
PESKY
PETTY
READY
REDDY
REEDY
REFRY
REIFY
REKEY
RELAY
REPAY
REPLY
RETRY
SEALY
SEAMY
SEEDY
SEEPY
SEPOY
SETBY
TEARY
TEDDY
TEENY
TELLY
TERRY
TESTY
VEDAY
VEERY
VESEY
WEARY
WEDGY
WEEDY
WEENY
WEEPY
WELBY
WELTY
WENDY
WETLY
ZESTY

••EY•

FREYA
GREYS
JOEYS
MYEYE
OBEYS
OXEYE
PREYS
SEEYA
THEYD
TREYS
WHEYS

••E•Y

APERY
AVERY
BEEFY
BEERY
CHEVY
CHEWY
CRECY
ELEGY
EMERY
ENEMY
EVERY
FIERY
GEEKY
LEERY
LOEWY
NEEDY
PIETY
POESY
PREXY
QUERY
REEDY
SEEDY
SEEPY
TEENY
VEERY
WEEDY
WEENY
WEEPY

•••EY

ABBEY
AGLEY
AILEY
ALLEY
APLEY
BLUEY
BOGEY
BUSEY
CAGEY
CAKEY
CAREY
CASEY
CONEY
COREY
COVEY
COXEY
DALEY
DEWEY
DICEY
DOPEY
DOVEY
FOGEY
FOLEY
GLUEY
GODEY
GOOEY
HALEY
HOKEY
HOLEY
HOMEY
HONEY
HOOEY
HOVEY
ISLEY
JIVEY
KESEY
KILEY
LACEY
LOVEY
MATEY
MONEY
MOPEY
MOREY
MOSEY
MULEY
ONKEY
PALEY
PINEY
POKEY
PUSEY
REKEY
RILEY
ROPEY
ROSEY
SOOEY
TANEY
TOBEY
UTLEY
VESEY
WILEY
ZOOEY

E•Z••

ETZEL

E••Z•

ELIZA

•EZ••

BEZEL
MEZZO

•E•Z•

BENZO
HERZL
JERZY
LEEZA
MEZZO
PENZA
SEIZE
TERZA

•E••Z

FELIZ
HEINZ
HEJAZ
HERTZ
JEREZ
MERTZ
NERTZ
PEREZ
VELEZ
VENEZ

••EZ•

LEEZA

•••EZ

ALLEZ
ASSEZ
GOMEZ
JEREZ
LOPEZ
PEREZ
VELEZ
VENEZ

FA•••

FABER
FABIO
FABLE
FACED
FACER
FACES
FACET
FACIE
FACTO
FACTS
FADED
FADES
FADOS
FAGIN
FAGOT
FAILS
FAINT
FAIRE
FAIRS
FAIRY
FAITH
FAKED
FAKER
FAKES
FAKIR
FALDO
FALLS
FALSE
FAMED
FAMES
FANCY

FANES
FANGS
FANNY
FANON
FANTA
FARAD
FARAH
FARCE
FARCI
FARED
FARER
FARES
FARGO
FARMS
FAROE
FARON
FAROS
FARSI
FASTS
FATAL
FATED
FATES
FATHA
FATLY
FATTY
FAULT
FAUNA
FAUNS
FAURE
FAUST
FAUVE
FAVES
FAVOR
FAWNS
FAXED
FAXES
FAZED
FAZES

F•A••
FEARS
FEAST
FEATS
FIATS
FLACK
FLAGG
FLAGS
FLAIL
FLAIR
FLAKE
FLAKY
FLAME
FLAMS
FLAMY
FLANK
FLANS
FLAPS
FLARE
FLASH
FLASK
FLATS
FLATT
FLAWS
FLAXY
FLAYS
FOALS
FOAMS
FOAMY
FRAIL
FRAIS
FRAME
FRANC
FRANK
FRANS
FRANZ
FRAPS
FRATS
FRAUD
FRAYS

F••A•
FARAD
FARAH
FATAL
FERAL
FETAL
FETAS
FFLAT
FILAR
FINAL
FLEAS
FLOAT
FLYAT
FOCAL
FORAY
FREAK
FRIAR
FUGAL
FURAN

F•••A
FANTA
FATHA
FAUNA
FELLA
FERIA
FESTA
FINCA
FIONA
FIRMA
FLORA
FOLIA
FONDA
FORMA
FOSSA
FOVEA
FREDA
FRENA
FREYA
FULDA

•FA••
AFARS
OFAGE

•F•A•
AFLAT
BFLAT
CFLAT
DFLAT
EFLAT
FFLAT
GFLAT
OFFAL

•F••A
AFTRA

••FA•
BYFAR
DEFAT
DUFAY
GOFAR
LEFAY
LOFAT
NOFAT
OFFAL
SOFAR
SOFAS

••F•A
BUFFA
HOFFA
INFRA
JAFFA
KAFKA
NAFTA
SOFIA

•••FA
BUFFA
HAIFA
HOFFA
JAFFA
SOLFA
SULFA

F•B••
FABER
FABIO
FABLE
FIBER
FIBRE
FIBRO
FUBSY

F••B•
FLUBS
FLYBY
FORBS
FROBE

FC•••
FCLEF

F•C••
FACED
FACER
FACES
FACET
FACIE
FACTO
FACTS
FICHE
FICHU
FICUS
FOCAL
FOCUS
FUCHS

F••C•
FANCY
FARCE
FARCI
FENCE
FETCH
FILCH
FINCA
FINCH
FISCS
FITCH
FLACK
FLECK
FLICK
FLOCK
FORCE
FRICK
FROCK

F•••C
FOLIC
FRANC
FSLIC

F•D••
FADED
FADES
FADOS
FEDON
FEDUP
FIDEL
FODOR
FUDDY
FUDGE

F••D•
FALDO
FEEDS
FENDS
FERDE
FEUDS
FINDS
FOLDS
FONDA
FONDS
FONDU
FOODS
FORDO
FORDS
FREDA
FRODO
FUDDY
FULDA
FUNDS
FUNDY

F•••D
FACED
FADED
FAKED
FAMED
FARAD
FARED
FATED
FAXED
FAZED
FELID
FETED
FETID
FIELD
FIEND
FIFED
FILED
FINED
FIORD
FIRED
FIXED
FJELD
FJORD
FLIED
FLOOD
FLOYD
FLUID
FOUND
FOXED
FRAUD
FREED
FREUD
FRIED
FROID
FROND
FUMED
FUSED

••F•D
BIFID
FIFED
NEFUD
UNFED

FE•••
FEARS
FEAST
FEATS
FEDON
FEDUP
FEEDS
FEELS
FEIGN
FEINT
FEIST
FELID
FELIS
FELIX
FELIZ
FELLA
FELLS
FELLY
FELON
FELTS
FEMME
FEMTO
FEMUR
FENCE
FENDS
FENNY
FEOFF
FERAL
FERDE
FERIA
FERMI
FERNS
FERNY
FERRI
FERRO
FERRY
FESTA
FESTS
FETAL
FETAS
FETCH
FETED
FETES
FETID
FETOR
FEUDS
FEVER
FEWER
FEYLY

F•E••
FEEDS
FEELS
FIEFS
FIELD
FIEND
FIERY
FJELD
FLEAS
FLECK
FLEER
FLEES
FLEET
FLESH
FLEUR
FLEWS
FLEXI
FOEHN
FREAK
FREDA
FREED
FREER
FREES
FRENA
FREON
FRERE
FRESH
FRETS
FREUD
FREYA
FUEGO
FUELS

F••E•
FABER
FACED
FACER
FACES
FACET
FADED
FADES
FAKED
FAKER
FAKES
FAMED
FAMES
FANES
FARED
FARER
FARES
FATED
FATES
FAVES
FAXED
FAXES
FAZED
FAZES
FCLEF
FETED
FETES
FEVER
FEWER
FIBER
FIDEL
FIFED
FIFER
FIFES
FILED
FILER
FILES
FILET
FINED
FINER
FINES
FIRED
FIRER
FIRES
FIVER
FIVES
FIXED
FIXER
FIXES
FLEER
FLEES
FLEET
FLIED
FLIER
FLIES
FLOES
FLUES
FLYER
FOGEY
FOLEY
FORES
FOVEA
FOXED
FOXES
FOYER
FREED
FREER
FREES
FRIED
FRIER
FRIES
FROES
FRYER
FUMED
FUMES
FUSED
FUSEE
FUSES
FYKES

F•••E
FABLE
FACIE
FAIRE
FALSE
FARCE
FAROE
FAURE
FAUVE
FEMME
FENCE
FERDE
FIBRE
FICHE
FILLE
FISKE
FLAKE
FLAME
FLARE
FLUKE
FLUME
FLUTE
FOOTE
FORCE
FORGE
FORTE
FOSSE
FOYLE
FRAME
FRERE
FROBE
FROME
FROZE
FUDGE
FUGUE
FURZE
FUSEE

•F•E•
AFTER
EFREM
NFLER
OFFER
OFTEN

•F••E
AFIRE
AFORE
EFFIE
OFAGE
OFUSE

••FE•
APFEL
CAFES
DEFER
FIFED
FIFER
FIFES
GOFER
INFER
OFFER
ORFEO
RAFER
REFER
RIFER
SAFER
SAFES
UNFED
WAFER

••F•E
ALFIE
ALFRE
DAFOE
DEFOE
EFFIE
GAFFE
JAFFE
RIFLE

•••FE
CHAFE
GAFFE
GROFE
JAFFE
KNIFE
PHYFE
ROLFE
WOLFE

FF•••
FFLAT

F•F••
FIFED
FIFER
FIFES
FIFTH
FIFTY

F••F•
FEOFF
FIEFS
FLUFF

F•••F
FCLEF
FEOFF
FLUFF

•FF••
AFFIX
EFFIE
OFFAL
OFFER

•F•F•
AFOFL

••FF•
BIFFS
BIFFY
BOFFO
BOFFS
BUFFA
BUFFI
BUFFO
BUFFS
BUFFY
CUFFS
DAFFY
DOFFS
DUFFS
DUFFY
GAFFE
GAFFS
HOFFA
HUFFS
HUFFY
JAFFA
JAFFE
JIFFY
LUFFS
MIFFS
MIFFY
MOFFO
MUFFS
PUFFS
PUFFY
RAFFI
RIFFI
RIFFS
RUFFS
TAFFY
TIFFS
TOFFS

•••FF
ACUFF
BANFF
BLUFF
CHAFF
CHUFF
CLIFF
FEOFF
FLUFF
GOOFF
GRUFF
ONOFF
QUAFF
SCOFF
SCUFF
SKIFF
SNIFF
SNUFF
SPIFF
STAFF
STIFF
STUFF
WHIFF
WOLFF

F•G••
FAGIN
FAGOT
FIGHT
FOGEY
FOGGY
FOGIN
FUGAL
FUGIT
FUGUE

F••G•
FANGS
FARGO
FEIGN
FLAGG
FLAGS
FLOGS
FOGGY
FORGE
FORGO
FRIGG
FROGS
FUDGE
FUEGO
FUNGI
FUNGO

F•••G
FLAGG
FLING
FLUNG
FRIGG

•F•G•
OFAGE

••F•G
BEFOG
DEFOG

F•H••
FATHA
FICHE
FICHU
FIGHT
FISHY
FOEHN
FUCHS

F•••H
FAITH
FARAH
FETCH
FIFTH
FILCH
FILTH
FINCH
FIRTH
FITCH
FLASH
FLESH
FLUSH
FORTH
FOURH
FRESH
FROSH
FROTH
FURTH

••F•H
FIFTH

FI•••
FIATS
FIBER
FIBRE
FIBRO
FICHE
FICHU
FICUS
FIDEL
FIEFS
FIELD
FIEND
FIERY
FIFED
FIFER
FIFES
FIFTH
FIFTY
FIGHT
FILAR
FILCH
FILED
FILER
FILES
FILET
FILLE
FILLS
FILLY
FILMS
FILMY
FILTH
FILUM
FINAL
FINCA
FINCH
FINDS
FINED
FINER
FINES
FINIS
FINKS
FINNO
FINNS
FINNY
FIONA
FIORD
FIRED
FIRER
FIRES
FIRMA
FIRMS
FIRNS
FIRPO
FIRRY
FIRST
FIRTH
FISCS
FISHY
FISKE
FISTS
FITCH
FITIN
FITLY
FIVER
FIVES
FIXED
FIXER
FIXES
FIXIT
FIXUP
FIZZY

F•I••
FAILS
FAINT
FAIRE
FAIRS
FAIRY
FAITH
FEIGN
FEINT
FEIST
FLICK
FLIED
FLIER
FLIES
FLING
FLINT
FLIPS
FLIRT
FLITS
FOILS
FOIST
FRIAR
FRICK
FRIED
FRIER
FRIES
FRIGG
FRILL
FRIML
FRISK
FRITO
FRITS
FRITZ
FRIZZ

F••I•
FABIO
FACIE
FAGIN
FAKIR
FELID
FELIS
FELIX
FELIZ
FERIA
FETID
FINIS
FITIN
FIXIT
FLAIL
FLAIR
FLUID
FLYIN
FOGIN
FOLIA
FOLIC
FOLIO
FRAIL
FRAIS
FROID
FRUIT
FSLIC
FUGIT
FUSIL

F•••I
FARCI
FARSI
FERMI
FERRI
FLEXI
FUNGI

•FI••
AFIRE
EFIKS

•F•I•
AFFIX
AFRIT
EFFIE

••FI•
AFFIX
ALFIE
BEFIT
BIFID
EFFIE
ELFIN
ENFIN
HAFIZ
HIFIS
INFIN
INFIX
KAFIR
KEFIR
REFIT
SOFIA
SUFIS
UNFIT
UNFIX

••F•I
BUFFI
MUFTI
RAFFI
RIFFI

•••FI
BUFFI
RAFFI
RIFFI
SCIFI

FJ•••
FJELD
FJORD

F•K••
FAKED
FAKER
FAKES
FAKIR
FYKES

F••K•
FINKS
FISKE
FLAKE
FLAKY
FLUKE
FLUKY
FOLKS
FOLKY
FORKS
FORKY
FUNKS
FUNKY

F•••K
FLACK
FLANK
FLASK
FLECK
FLICK
FLOCK
FLUNK
FRANK
FREAK
FRICK
FRISK
FROCK

•F•K•
EFIKS

••FK•
KAFKA

FL•••
FLACK
FLAGG
FLAGS
FLAIL
FLAIR
FLAKE
FLAKY
FLAME
FLAMS
FLAMY
FLANK
FLANS
FLAPS
FLARE
FLASH
FLASK
FLATS
FLATT
FLAWS
FLAXY
FLAYS
FLEAS
FLECK
FLEER
FLEES
FLEET
FLESH
FLEUR
FLEWS
FLEXI
FLICK
FLIED
FLIER
FLIES
FLING
FLINT
FLIPS
FLIRT
FLITS
FLOAT
FLOCK
FLOES
FLOGS
FLOOD
FLOOR
FLOPS
FLORA
FLOSS
FLOUR
FLOUT
FLOWN
FLOWS
FLOYD
FLUBS
FLUES
FLUFF
FLUID
FLUKE
FLUKY
FLUME
FLUNG
FLUNK
FLUOR
FLUSH
FLUTE
FLUTY
FLYAT
FLYBY
FLYER
FLYIN
FLYNN

F•L••
FALDO
FALLS
FALSE
FCLEF
FELID
FELIS
FELIX
FELIZ
FELLA
FELLS
FELLY
FELON
FELTS
FFLAT
FILAR
FILCH
FILED
FILER
FILES
FILET
FILLE
FILLS
FILLY
FILMS
FILMY
FILTH
FILUM
FOLDS
FOLEY
FOLIA
FOLIC
FOLIO
FOLKS
FOLKY
FOLLY
FSLIC
FULDA
FULLY

F••L•
FABLE
FAILS
FALLS
FATLY
FAULT
FEELS
FELLA
FELLS
FELLY
FEYLY
FIELD
FILLE
FILLS
FILLY
FITLY
FJELD
FOALS
FOILS
FOLLY
FOOLS
FOULS
FOWLS
FOYLE
FRILL
FUELS
FULLY
FURLS

F•••L
FATAL
FERAL
FETAL
FIDEL
FINAL
FLAIL
FOCAL
FRAIL
FRILL
FRIML
FUGAL
FUSIL

•FL••
AFLAT
BFLAT
CFLAT
DFLAT
EFLAT
FFLAT
GFLAT
NFLER

•F••L
AFOFL
AFOUL
OFFAL

••FL•
RIFLE

••F•L
APFEL
AWFUL
OFFAL

•••FL
AFOFL

F•M••
FAMED
FAMES
FEMME
FEMTO
FEMUR
FUMED
FUMES

F••M•
FARMS
FEMME
FERMI
FILMS
FILMY
FIRMA
FIRMS
FLAME
FLAMS
FLAMY
FLUME
FOAMS
FOAMY
FORMA
FORMS
FRAME
FRIML
FROME
FROMM
FRUMP

F•••M
FILUM
FORUM
FROMM

•F••M
EFREM

F•N••
FANCY
FANES
FANGS
FANNY
FANON
FANTA
FENCE
FENDS
FENNY
FINAL
FINCA
FINCH
FINDS
FINED
FINER
FINES
FINIS
FINKS
FINNO
FINNS
FINNY
FONDA
FONDS
FONDU
FONTS
FUNDS
FUNDY
FUNGI
FUNGO
FUNKS
FUNKY
FUNNY

F••N•
FAINT
FANNY
FAUNA
FAUNS
FAWNS
FEINT
FENNY
FERNS
FERNY
FIEND
FINNO
FINNS
FINNY
FIONA
FIRNS
FLANK
FLANS
FLING
FLINT
FLUNG
FLUNK
FLYNN
FOUND
FOUNT
FRANC
FRANK
FRANS
FRANZ
FRENA
FROND
FRONT
FUNNY

F•••N
FAGIN
FANON
FARON
FEDON
FEIGN
FELON
FITIN
FLOWN
FLYIN
FLYNN
FOEHN
FOGIN
FREON
FROWN
FURAN
FUTON

•FN••
IFNOT

•F••N
AFTON
OFTEN

••F•N
ELFIN
ENFIN
HAFUN
INFIN
INFUN

FO•••
FOALS
FOAMS
FOAMY
FOCAL
FOCUS
FODOR
FOEHN
FOGEY
FOGGY
FOGIN
FOILS
FOIST
FOLDS
FOLEY
FOLIA
FOLIC
FOLIO
FOLKS
FOLKY
FOLLY
FONDA
FONDS
FONDU
FONTS
FOODS
FOOLS
FOOTE
FOOTS
FORAY
FORBS
FORCE
FORDO
FORDS
FORES
FORGE
FORGO
FORKS
FORKY
FORMA
FORMS
FORTE
FORTH
FORTS
FORTY
FORUM
FOSSA
FOSSE
FOULS
FOUND
FOUNT
FOURH
FOURS
FOUTS
FOVEA
FOWLS
FOXED
FOXES
FOYER
FOYLE

F•O••
FEOFF
FIONA
FIORD
FJORD
FLOAT
FLOCK
FLOES
FLOGS
FLOOD
FLOOR
FLOPS
FLORA
FLOSS
FLOUR
FLOUT
FLOWN
FLOWS
FLOYD
FOODS
FOOLS
FOOTE
FOOTS
FROBE
FROCK
FRODO
FROES
FROGS
FROID
FROME
FROMM
FROND
FRONT
FROSH
FROST
FROTH
FROWN
FROWS
FROZE

F••O•
FADOS
FAGOT
FANON
FAROE
FARON
FAROS
FAVOR
FEDON
FELON
FETOR
FLOOD
FLOOR
FLUOR
FODOR
FREON
FSTOP
FUROR
FUTON

F•••O
FABIO
FACTO
FALDO
FARGO
FEMTO
FERRO
FIBRO
FINNO
FIRPO
FOLIO
FORDO
FORGO
FRITO
FRODO
FUEGO
FUNGO

•FO••
AFOFL
AFOOT
AFORE
AFOUL

•F•O•
AFOOT
AFROS
AFTON
IFNOT

••FO•
BEFOG
DAFOE
DEFOE
DEFOG
GOFOR

••F•O
BOFFO
BUFFO
MOFFO
ORFEO

•••FO
BOFFO
BUFFO
MOFFO

F••P•
FIRPO
FLAPS
FLIPS
FLOPS
FRAPS

F•••P
FEDUP
FIXUP
FRUMP
FSTOP

FR•••
FRAIL
FRAIS
FRAME
FRANC
FRANK
FRANS
FRANZ
FRAPS
FRATS
FRAUD
FRAYS
FREAK
FREDA
FREED
FREER
FREES
FRENA
FREON
FRERE
FRESH
FRETS
FREUD
FREYA
FRIAR
FRICK
FRIED
FRIER
FRIES
FRIGG
FRILL
FRIML
FRISK
FRITO
FRITS
FRITZ
FRIZZ
FROBE
FROCK
FRODO
FROES
FROGS
FROID
FROME
FROMM
FROND
FRONT
FROSH
FROST
FROTH
FROWN
FROWS
FROZE
FRUIT
FRUMP
FRYER

F•R••
FARAD
FARAH
FARCE
FARCI
FARED
FARER
FARES
FARGO
FARMS
FAROE
FARON
FAROS
FARSI
FERAL
FERDE
FERIA
FERMI
FERNS
FERNY
FERRI
FERRO
FERRY
FIRED
FIRER
FIRES
FIRMA
FIRMS
FIRNS
FIRPO
FIRRY
FIRST
FIRTH
FORAY
FORBS
FORCE
FORDO
FORDS
FORES
FORGE
FORGO
FORKS
FORKY
FORMA
FORMS
FORTE
FORTH
FORTS
FORTY
FORUM
FURAN
FURLS
FUROR
FURRY
FURTH
FURZE

F••R•
FAIRE
FAIRS
FAIRY
FAURE
FEARS
FERRI
FERRO
FERRY
FIBRE
FIBRO
FIERY
FIORD
FIRRY
FJORD
FLARE
FLIRT
FLORA
FOURH
FOURS
FRERE
FURRY

F•••R
FABER
FACER
FAKER
FAKIR
FARER
FAVOR
FEMUR
FETOR
FEVER
FEWER
FIBER
FIFER
FILAR
FILER
FINER
FIRER
FIVER
FIXER
FLAIR
FLEER
FLEUR
FLIER
FLOOR
FLOUR
FLUOR
FLYER
FODOR
FOYER
FREER
FRIAR
FRIER
FRYER
FUROR

•FR••
AFRIT
AFROS
EFREM

•F•R•
AFARS
AFIRE
AFORE
AFTRA

•F••R
AFTER
NFLER
OFFER

••FR•
ALFRE
INFRA
REFRY

••F•R
BYFAR
DEFER
FIFER
GOFAR
GOFER
GOFOR
INFER
KAFIR
KEFIR
OFFER
RAFER
REFER
RIFER
SAFER
SOFAR
WAFER

FS•••
FSLIC
FSTOP

F•S••
FASTS
FESTA
FESTS
FISCS
FISHY
FISKE
FISTS
FOSSA
FOSSE
FUSED
FUSEE
FUSES
FUSIL
FUSSY
FUSTY

F••S•
FALSE
FARSI
FAUST
FEAST
FEIST
FIRST
FLASH
FLASK
FLESH
FLOSS
FLUSH
FOIST
FOSSA
FOSSE
FRESH
FRISK
FROSH
FROST
FUBSY
FUSSY

F•••S
FACES
FACTS
FADES
FADOS
FAILS
FAIRS
FAKES
FALLS
FAMES
FANES
FANGS
FARES
FARMS
FAROS
FASTS
FATES
FAUNS
FAVES
FAWNS
FAXES
FAZES
FEARS
FEATS
FEEDS
FEELS
FELIS
FELLS
FELTS
FENDS
FERNS
FESTS
FETAS
FETES
FEUDS
FIATS
FICUS
FIEFS
FIFES
FILES
FILLS
FILMS
FINDS
FINES
FINIS
FINKS
FINNS
FIRES
FIRMS
FIRNS
FISCS
FISTS
FIVES
FIXES
FLAGS
FLAMS
FLANS
FLAPS
FLATS
FLAWS
FLAYS
FLEAS
FLEES
FLEWS
FLIES
FLIPS
FLITS
FLOES
FLOGS
FLOPS
FLOSS
FLOWS
FLUBS
FLUES
FOALS
FOAMS
FOCUS
FOILS
FOLDS
FOLKS
FONDS
FONTS
FOODS
FOOLS
FOOTS
FORBS
FORDS
FORES
FORKS
FORMS
FORTS
FOULS
FOURS
FOUTS
FOWLS
FOXES
FRAIS
FRANS
FRAPS
FRATS
FRAYS
FREES
FRETS
FRIES
FRITS
FROES
FROGS
FROWS
FUCHS
FUELS
FUMES
FUNDS
FUNKS
FURLS
FUSES
FYKES

•F•S•
OFUSE

•F••S
AFARS
AFROS
EFIKS

••F•S
BIFFS
BOFFS
BUFFS
CAFES
CUFFS
DOFFS
DUFFS
FIFES
GAFFS
GIFTS
HAFTS
HEFTS
HIFIS
HUFFS
LEFTS
LIFTS
LOFTS
LUFFS
MIFFS
MUFFS
PUFFS
RAFTS
RIFFS
RIFTS
RUFFS
RUFUS
SAFES
SIFTS
SOFAS
SUFIS
TIFFS
TOFFS
TUFTS
WAFTS
WEFTS

•••FS
ALEFS
ALIFS
BEEFS
BIFFS
BOFFS
BUFFS
CHEFS
CLEFS
COIFS
CUFFS
DOFFS
DUFFS
FIEFS
GAFFS
GOLFS
GOOFS
GULFS
HOOFS
HUFFS
LEAFS
LOAFS
LUFFS
MIFFS
MUFFS
POUFS
PROFS
PUFFS
REEFS
RIFFS
ROOFS
RUFFS
SERFS
SURFS
TIFFS
TOFFS
TURFS
WAIFS
WOOFS
ZARFS

F•T••
FATAL
FATED
FATES
FATHA
FATLY
FATTY
FETAL
FETAS
FETCH
FETED
FETES
FETID
FETOR
FITCH
FITIN
FITLY
FSTOP
FUTON

F••T•
FACTO
FACTS
FAITH
FANTA
FASTS
FATTY
FEATS
FELTS
FEMTO
FESTA
FESTS
FIATS
FIFTH
FIFTY
FILTH
FIRTH
FISTS
FLATS
FLATT
FLITS
FLUTE
FLUTY
FONTS
FOOTE
FOOTS
FORTE
FORTH
FORTS
FORTY
FOUTS
FRATS
FRETS
FRITO
FRITS
FRITZ
FROTH
FURTH
FUSTY

F•••T
FACET
FAGOT
FAINT
FAULT
FAUST
FEAST
FEINT
FEIST
FFLAT
FIGHT
FILET
FIRST
FIXIT
FLATT
FLEET
FLINT
FLIRT
FLOAT
FLOUT
FLYAT
FOIST
FOUNT
FRONT
FROST
FRUIT
FUGIT

•FT••
AFTER
AFTON
AFTRA
OFTEN

•F••T
AFLAT
AFOOT
AFRIT
BFLAT
CFLAT
DFLAT
EFLAT
FFLAT
GFLAT
IFNOT

••FT•
FIFTH
FIFTY
GIFTS
HAFTS
HEFTS
HEFTY
LEFTS
LEFTY
LIFTS
LOFTS
LOFTY
MUFTI
NAFTA
NIFTY
RAFTS
RIFTS
SIFTS
SOFTY
TUFTS
WAFTS
WEFTS

••F•T
BEFIT
DEFAT
LOFAT
NOFAT
REFIT
UNFIT

•••FT
ABAFT
ALOFT
CLEFT
CLIFT
CRAFT
CROFT
DELFT
DRAFT
DRIFT
GRAFT
GRIFT
KRAFT
SHAFT
SHIFT
SWIFT
THEFT

FU•••
FUBSY
FUCHS
FUDDY
FUDGE
FUEGO
FUELS
FUGAL
FUGIT
FUGUE
FULDA
FULLY
FUMED
FUMES
FUNDS
FUNDY
FUNGI
FUNGO
FUNKS
FUNKY
FUNNY
FURAN
FURLS
FUROR
FURRY
FURTH
FURZE
FUSED
FUSEE
FUSES
FUSIL
FUSSY
FUSTY
FUTON
FUZZY

F•U••
FAULT
FAUNA
FAUNS
FAURE
FAUST
FAUVE
FEUDS
FLUBS
FLUES
FLUFF
FLUID
FLUKE
FLUKY
FLUME
FLUNG
FLUNK
FLUOR
FLUSH
FLUTE
FLUTY
FOULS
FOUND
FOUNT
FOURH
FOURS
FOUTS
FRUIT
FRUMP

F••U•
FEDUP
FEMUR
FICUS
FILUM
FIXUP
FLEUR
FLOUR
FLOUT
FOCUS
FORUM
FRAUD
FREUD
FUGUE

F•••U
FICHU
FONDU

•FU••
OFUSE

•F•U•
AFOUL

••FU•
AWFUL
HAFUN
INFUN
NEFUD
RUFUS

•••FU
CORFU
KHUFU
SNAFU

F•V••
FAVES
FAVOR
FEVER
FIVER
FIVES
FOVEA

F••V•
FAUVE

F•W••
FAWNS
FEWER
FOWLS

F••W•
FLAWS
FLEWS
FLOWN
FLOWS
FROWN
FROWS

F•X••
FAXED
FAXES
FIXED
FIXER
FIXES
FIXIT
FIXUP
FOXED
FOXES

F••X•
FLAXY
FLEXI

F•••X
FELIX

•F••X
AFFIX

••F•X
AFFIX
INFIX
UNFIX

FY•••
FYKES

F•Y••
FEYLY
FLYAT
FLYBY
FLYER
FLYIN
FLYNN
FOYER
FOYLE
FRYER

F••Y•
FLAYS
FLOYD
FRAYS
FREYA

F•••Y
FAIRY
FANCY
FANNY
FATLY
FATTY
FELLY
FENNY
FERNY
FERRY
FEYLY
FIERY
FIFTY
FILLY
FILMY
FINNY
FIRRY
FISHY
FITLY
FIZZY
FLAKY
FLAMY
FLAXY
FLUKY
FLUTY
FLYBY
FOAMY
FOGEY
FOGGY
FOLEY
FOLKY
FOLLY
FORAY
FORKY
FORTY
FUBSY
FUDDY
FULLY
FUNDY
FUNKY
FUNNY
FURRY
FUSSY
FUSTY
FUZZY

••F•Y
BIFFY
BUFFY
DAFFY
DUFAY
DUFFY
FIFTY
HEFTY
HUFFY
JIFFY
LEFAY
LEFTY
LOFTY
MIFFY
NIFTY
PUFFY
REFRY
SOFTY
TAFFY

•••FY
BEEFY
BIFFY
BUFFY
COMFY
DAFFY
DEIFY
DUFFY
EDIFY
GOOFY
HUFFY
JIFFY
LEAFY
MIFFY
PUFFY
REIFY
SURFY
TAFFY
UNIFY

F•Z••
FAZED
FAZES
FIZZY
FUZZY

F••Z•
FIZZY
FRIZZ
FROZE
FURZE
FUZZY

F•••Z
FELIZ
FRANZ
FRITZ
FRIZZ

••F•Z
HAFIZ

GA•••
GABBY
GABLE
GABON
GABOR
GADID
GAELS
GAFFE
GAFFS
GAGES
GAINS
GAITS
GAIUS
GALAS
GALAX
GALBA
GALEA
GALEN
GALES
GALLI
GALLO
GALLS
GALOP
GAMAL
GAMBA
GAMED
GAMER
GAMES
GAMIN
GAMMA
GAMOW
GAMPS
GAMUT
GANDY
GANEF
GANGS
GAOLS
GAPED
GAPER
GAPES
GARBO
GARBS
GARDA
GARDE
GARNI
GAROU
GARRY
GARTH
GASES
GASPE
GASPS
GASSY
GASTR
GASUP
GATED
GATES
GATOR
GATOS
GATUN
GAUDS
GAUDY
GAUGE
GAULS
GAUNT
GAURS
GAUSS
GAUZE
GAUZY
GAVEL
GAVIN
GAVOT
GAWKS
GAWKY
GAYAL
GAYER
GAYLE
GAYLY
GAZED
GAZER
GAZES

G•A••
GEARS
GEARY
GHANA
GHATS
GHAZI
GIANT
GLACE
GLADE
GLADS
GLAIR
GLAND
GLARE
GLARY
GLASS
GLAXO
GLAZE
GNARL
GNARS
GNASH
GNATS
GNAWS
GOADS
GOALS
GOAPE
GOATS
GRABS
GRACE
GRADE
GRADS
GRADY
GRAFT
GRAIG
GRAIL
GRAIN
GRAMA
GRAMM
GRAMP
GRAMS
GRAND
GRANI
GRANT
GRAPE
GRAPH
GRAPY
GRASP
GRASS
GRATA
GRATE
GRAVE
GRAVY
GRAYS
GRAZE
GUACO
GUARD
GUARS
GUAVA

G••A•
GALAS
GALAX
GAMAL
GAYAL
GERAH
GETAS
GETAT
GFLAT
GLEAM
GLEAN
GLOAM
GLOAT
GOBAD
GOFAR
GOLAN
GORAL
GOTAT
GREAT
GROAN
GROAT
GULAG
GULAR

G•••A
GALBA
GALEA
GAMBA
GAMMA
GARDA
GEENA
GEMMA

GENOA GHANA GILDA GINZA GOLDA GONNA GOTHA GOTTA GOUDA GRAMA GRATA GRETA GROZA GUAVA GUNGA GUTTA

•GA••
AGAIN AGALS AGAMA AGANA AGAPE AGARS AGASP AGATE AGAVE AGAZE EGADI EGADS NGAIO NGAMI

•G•A•
AGHAS EGGAR OGHAM

•G••A
AGAMA AGANA AGENA AGITA AGORA

••GA•
ALGAE ALGAL AVGAS BEGAN BEGAT CIGAR CUGAT DEGAS DUGAN EDGAR EGGAR ELGAR FUGAL HAGAR HOGAN JUGAL LAGAN LEGAL LOGAN MEGAN ORGAN PAGAN RAGAS REGAL REGAN RUGAE SAGAL SAGAN SAGAS SEGAL SEGAR SUGAR TOGAS VEGAN VEGAS WIGAN

••G•A
DOGMA LOGIA MAGDA MAGMA MAGNA REGIA SIGMA

•••GA
AMIGA BRAGA CONGA GUNGA HELGA KANGA KIOGA KYOGA LONGA OMEGA ONEGA PANGA SAIGA TAIGA TONGA USCGA VIRGA VOLGA

G•B••
GABBY GABLE GABON GABOR GIBBS GIBED GIBER GIBES GOBAD GOBEL

G••B•
GABBY GALBA GAMBA GARBO GARBS GETBY GIBBS GLEBE GLOBE GLOBS GOTBY GRABS GREBE GRUBS GUMBO

••GB•
DIGBY RIGBY RUGBY

GC•••
GCLEF

G•C••
GECKO GUCCI

G••C•
GLACE GLUCK GLUCO GLYCO GRACE GRECO GUACO GUCCI GULCH

G•••C
GENIC

•G••C
AGRIC UGRIC

••G•C
HIGHC LOGIC MAGIC

G•D••
GADID GIDDY GODEL GODET GODEY GODLY GODOT

G••D•
GANDY GARDA GARDE GAUDS GAUDY GEODE GIDDY GILDA GILDS GIRDS GLADE GLADS GLEDE GLIDE GOADS GOLDA GOLDE GOLDS GONDI GONDS GOODS GOODY GORDO GORDY GOUDA GOUDY GOWDY GRADE GRADS GRADY GRIDS GRODY GUIDE GUIDO GURDY

G•••D
GADID GAMED GAPED GATED GAZED GELID GEOID GIBED GLAND GLUED GOBAD GORED GOULD GOURD GRAND GREED GRIND GUARD GUILD GUYED GYVED

•GD••
OGDEN

•G•D•
EGADI EGADS

•G••D
EGGED OGLED

••GD•
MAGDA

••G•D
ALGID CAGED EDGED EGGED OHGOD PAGED RAGED RIGID URGED WAGED

GE•••
GEARS GEARY GECKO GEEKS GEEKY GEENA GEESE GELEE GELID GEMMA GEMMY GEMOT GENES GENET GENIC GENIE GENII GENOA GENRE GENRO GENTS GENUS GEODE GEOID GEORG GERAH GERMS GERMY GERRY GESSO GESTE GESTS GETAS GETAT GETBY GETGO GETIN GETIT GETME GETON GETTO GETTY GETUP

G•E••
GAELS GEEKS GEEKY GEENA GEESE GHEES GHENT GLEAM GLEAN GLEBE GLEDE GLEES GLENN GLENS GLESS GOERS GOEST GREAT GREBE GRECO GREED GREEK GREEN GREER GREET GREGG GRETA GRETE GREYS GUESS GUEST GWENN

G••E•
GAGES GALEA GALEN GALES GAMED GAMER GAMES GANEF GAPED GAPER GAPES GASES GATED GATES GAVEL GAYER GAZED GAZER GAZES GCLEF GELEE GENES GENET GHEES GIBED GIBER GIBES GILES GIMEL GIVEN GIVER GIVES GLEES GLUED GLUER GLUES GLUEY GOBEL GODEL GODET GODEY GOFER GOLEM GOMER GOMEZ GONER GOOEY GORED GOREN GORES GOSEE GOWER GREED GREEK GREEN GREER GREET GRIEF GRIEG GRIER GRUEL GULES GUTEN GUYED GYRES GYVED GYVES

G•••E
GABLE GAFFE GARDE GASPE GAUGE GAUZE GAYLE GEESE GELEE GENIE GENRE GEODE GESTE GETME GIGUE GIJOE GIMME GLACE GLADE GLARE GLAZE GLEBE GLEDE GLIDE GLOBE GLOVE GLOZE GNOME GOAPE GOLDE GOOSE GORGE GORME GORSE GOSEE GOSSE GOUGE GRACE GRADE GRAPE GRATE GRAVE GRAZE GREBE GRETE GRIME GRIPE GROFE GROPE GROVE GUIDE GUILE GUISE

•GE••
AGENA AGENT AGERS EGEST OGEES

•G•E•
AGLET AGLEY AGNES AGNEW AGREE AGUES EGGED EGRET IGNES OGDEN OGEES OGLED OGLER OGLES OGRES

•G••E
AGAPE AGATE AGAVE AGAZE AGGIE AGILE AGREE OGIVE

••GE•
ALGER ANGEL ANGER ANGES AUGER BAGEL BEGET BOGEY CAGED CAGER CAGES CAGEY DOGES EAGER EDGED EDGER EDGES EGGED EIGEN ENGEL FOGEY GAGES HAGEN HEGEL HUGER INGER KUGEL LAGER LEGER LIGER LOGES LTGEN LUGER LUGES MAGES MCGEE NAGEL NEGEV NIGEL NIGER PAGED PAGER PAGES PAGET PUGET RAGED RAGES RIGEL ROGER ROGET SAGER SAGES SAGET SEGER TIGER UNGER URGED URGER URGES WAGED WAGER WAGES

••G•E
AGGIE ALGAE ANGIE ANGLE ARGUE BOGIE BOGLE BUGLE DOGIE EAGLE EAGRE FUGUE GIGUE HAGUE INGLE LOGUE MCGEE ROGUE RUGAE SEGUE SIGNE VAGUE VOGUE

•••GE
ADAGE ADIGE AINGE BADGE BARGE BEIGE BILGE BINGE BORGE BUDGE BULGE CADGE CONGE DINGE DIRGE DODGE ETAGE FORGE FUDGE GAUGE GORGE GOUGE HEDGE HENGE HINGE IMAGE JORGE JUDGE KEDGE KLUGE LANGE LARGE LEDGE LIEGE LODGE LUNGE MADGE MARGE MERGE MIDGE NEIGE NORGE NUDGE OFAGE OSAGE PAIGE PHAGE PLAGE PURGE RANGE RIDGE ROUGE RUDGE SARGE SEDGE SERGE SIEGE SINGE STAGE SURGE SWAGE SYNGE TARGE TINGE USAGE VERGE WEDGE

GF•••
GFLAT

G•F••
GAFFE GAFFS GIFTS GOFAR GOFER GOFOR

G••F•
GAFFE GAFFS GOLFS GOOFF GOOFS GOOFY GRAFT GRIFT GROFE GRUFF GULFS

G•••F
GANEF GCLEF GOOFF GRIEF GRUFF

G•G••
GAGES GIGOT GIGUE GOGOL GOGOS

G••G•
GANGS GAUGE GETGO GLOGG GOLGI GONGS GORGE GOUGE GREGG GRIGS GROGS GUNGA

G•••G
GEORG GLOGG GOING GRAIG GREGG GRIEG GULAG

•GG••
AGGIE AGGRO EGGAR EGGED EGGON

•G•G•
AGOGO

•G••G
AGING

••GG•
BAGGY BOGGS BOGGY BUGGY DOGGO DOGGY FOGGY HOGGS JAGGY LEGGS LEGGY MUGGY NAGGY PEGGY PIGGY RIGGS SAGGY SOGGY WIGGY YEGGS ZIGGY

••G•G
MAGOG

•••GG
BRAGG FLAGG FRIGG GLOGG GREGG STAGG

GH•••
GHANA GHATS GHAZI GHEES GHENT GHOST GHOUL

G••H•
GOTHA GOTHS GUSHY

G•••H
GARTH GERAH GIRTH GLYPH GNASH GRAPH GULCH

•GH••
AGHAS OGHAM

••GH•
AUGHT BIGHT EIGHT FIGHT HIGHC HIGHS LIGHT MIGHT NIGHT OUGHT RIGHT SIGHS SIGHT TIGHT WIGHT YOGHS

•••GH
BAUGH BERGH BLIGH BOUGH COUGH DOUGH HEIGH HOUGH KEOGH KROGH LAUGH LEIGH LOUGH NEIGH ROUGH SOUGH THIGH TOUGH WAUGH WEIGH

GI•••
GIANT GIBBS GIBED GIBER GIBES GIDDY GIFTS GIGOT GIGUE GIJOE GILDA GILDS GILES GILLS GILTS GIMEL GIMME GIMPS GIMPY GINNY GINZA GIPSY GIRDS GIRLS GIRLY GIRNS GIROS GIRTH GIRTS GISTS GIVEN GIVER GIVES GIZMO

G•I••
GAINS GAITS GAIUS GLIDE GLIMS GLINT GLITZ GOING GRIDS GRIEF GRIEG GRIER GRIFT GRIGS GRILL GRIME GRIMM GRIMY GRIND GRINS GRIOT GRIPE GRIPS GRIST GRITS GUIDE GUIDO GUILD GUILE GUILT GUISE

G••I•
GADID GAMIN GAVIN GELID GENIC GENIE GENII GEOID GETIN GETIT GLAIR GOTIN GRAIG GRAIL GRAIN GROIN GSUIT

G•••I
GALLI GARNI GENII GHAZI GOLGI GONDI GORKI GRANI GUCCI

•GI••
AGILE AGING AGIOS AGITA BGIRL OGIVE

•G•I•
AGAIN AGGIE AGRIC NGAIO UGRIC

•G••I
EGADI NGAMI

••GI•
AEGIR AEGIS AGGIE ALGID ALGIN ANGIE ARGIL BAGIT BEGIN BOGIE DIGIN DIGIT DOGIE DOGIT DUGIN ELGIN FAGIN FOGIN FUGIT HAGIO LEGIS LEGIT LOGIA LOGIC LOGIN MAGIC REGIA REGIS RIGID SIGIL VIGIL YOGIS

••G•I
LIGNI NEGRI SEGNI

•••GI
CORGI FUNGI GOLGI LONGI LUIGI SHOGI

G•J••
GIJOE

G••K•
GAWKS GAWKY GECKO GEEKS GEEKY GORKI GORKY GROKS GUNKY

G•••K
GLUCK GREEK

GL•••
GLACE GLADE GLADS GLAIR GLAND GLARE GLARY GLASS GLAXO GLAZE GLEAM GLEAN GLEBE GLEDE GLEES GLENN GLENS GLESS GLIDE GLIMS GLINT GLITZ GLOAM GLOAT GLOBE GLOBS GLOGG GLOMS GLOOM GLOPS GLORY GLOSS GLOVE GLOWS GLOZE GLUCK GLUCO GLUED GLUER GLUES GLUEY GLUON GLUTS GLYCO GLYPH

G•L••
GALAS GALAX GALBA GALEA GALEN GALES GALLI GALLO GALLS GALOP GCLEF GELEE GELID GFLAT GILDA GILDS GILES GILLS GILTS GOLAN GOLDA GOLDE GOLDS GOLEM GOLFS GOLGI GOLLY GULAG GULAR GULCH GULES GULFS GULLS GULLY GULPS

G••L•
GABLE GAELS GALLI GALLO GALLS GAOLS GAULS GAYLE GAYLY GILLS GIRLS GIRLY GOALS GODLY GOLLY GOULD GRILL GUILD GUILE GUILT GULLS GULLY

G•••L
GAMAL GAVEL GAYAL GHOUL GIMEL GNARL GOBEL GODEL GOGOL GORAL GRAIL GRILL GROWL GRUEL

•GL••
AGLET AGLEY AGLOW IGLOO IGLUS OGLED OGLER OGLES

•G•L•
AGALS AGILE

•G••L
BGIRL

••GL•
ANGLE ANGLO BOGLE BUGLE EAGLE INGLE

••G•L
ALGAL ALGOL ANGEL ARGIL ARGOL BAGEL ENGEL FUGAL GOGOL HEGEL JUGAL KUGEL LEGAL MOGUL NAGEL NIGEL REGAL RIGEL SAGAL SEGAL SIGIL VIGIL

G•M••
GAMAL GAMBA GAMED GAMER GAMES GAMIN GAMMA GAMOW GAMPS GAMUT GEMMA GEMMY GEMOT GIMEL GIMME GIMPS GIMPY GOMER GOMEZ GUMBO GUMMO GUMMY GUMUP

G••M•
GAMMA GEMMA GEMMY GERMS GERMY GETME GIMME GIZMO GLIMS GLOMS GNOME GORME GRAMA GRAMM GRAMP GRAMS GRIME GRIMM GRIMY GRUMP GUMMO GUMMY

G•••M
GLEAM GLOAM GLOOM GOLEM GRAMM GRIMM GROOM

•G•M•
AGAMA NGAMI

•G••M
OGHAM

••GM•
DOGMA
MAGMA
PYGMY
SIGMA

••G•M
BEGUM
BYGUM
JUGUM

GN•••
GNARL
GNARS
GNASH
GNATS
GNAWS
GNOME

G•N••
GANDY
GANEF
GANGS
GENES
GENET
GENIC
GENIE
GENII
GENOA
GENRE
GENRO
GENTS
GENUS
GINNY
GINZA
GONDI
GONDS
GONER
GONGS
GONNA
GONZO
GUNGA
GUNKY
GUNNY

G••N•
GAINS
GARNI
GAUNT
GEENA
GHANA
GHENT
GIANT
GINNY
GIRNS
GLAND
GLENN
GLENS
GLINT
GOING
GONNA
GOONS
GOONY
GOWNS
GRAND
GRANI
GRANT
GRIND
GRINS
GRUNT
GUNNY
GWENN
GWYNN

G•••N
GABON
GALEN
GAMIN
GATUN
GAVIN
GETIN
GETON
GIVEN
GLEAN
GLENN
GLUON
GOLAN
GOREN
GOTIN
GOTON
GRAIN
GREEN
GROAN
GROIN
GROWN
GUTEN
GWENN
GWYNN
GYRON

•GN••
AGNES
AGNEW
AGNON
AGNUS
IGNES

•G•N•
AGANA
AGENA
AGENT
AGING
AGONY

•G••N
AGAIN
AGNON
AGRON
EGGON
OGDEN

••GN•
LIGNI
LIGNO
MAGNA
SEGNI
SEGNO
SIGNE
SIGNO
SIGNS

••G•N
ALGIN
ARGON
BBGUN
BEGAN
BEGIN
BEGUN
BIGON
DAGON
DIGIN
DOGON
DUGAN
DUGIN
EGGON
EIGEN
ELGIN
FAGIN
FOGIN
HAGEN
HOGAN
LAGAN
LOGAN
LOGIN
LOGON
LTGEN
MEGAN
ORGAN
PAGAN
REGAN
SAGAN
VEGAN
WAGON
WIGAN

•••GN
ALIGN
DEIGN
FEIGN
REIGN
VSIGN

GO•••
GOADS
GOALS
GOAPE
GOATS
GOBAD
GOBEL
GODEL
GODET
GODEY
GODLY
GODOT
GOERS
GOEST
GOFAR
GOFER
GOFOR
GOGOL
GOGOS
GOING
GOLAN
GOLDA
GOLDE
GOLDS
GOLEM
GOLFS
GOLGI
GOLLY
GOMER
GOMEZ
GONDI
GONDS
GONER
GONGS
GONNA
GONZO
GOODS
GOODY
GOOEY
GOOFF
GOOFS
GOOFY
GOONS
GOONY
GOOPS
GOOPY
GOOSE
GOOSY
GOOUT
GORAL
GORDO
GORDY
GORED
GOREN
GORES
GORGE
GORKI
GORKY
GORME
GORPS
GORSE
GOSEE
GOSSE
GOTAT
GOTBY
GOTHA
GOTHS
GOTIN
GOTON
GOTTA
GOTTO
GOTUP
GOUDA
GOUDY
GOUGE
GOULD
GOURD
GOUTY
GOWDY
GOWER
GOWNS

G•O••
GAOLS
GEODE
GEOID
GEORG
GHOST
GHOUL
GLOAM
GLOAT
GLOBE
GLOBS
GLOGG
GLOMS
GLOOM
GLOPS
GLORY
GLOSS
GLOVE
GLOWS
GLOZE
GNOME
GOODS
GOODY
GOOEY
GOOFF
GOOFS
GOOFY
GOONS
GOONY
GOOPS
GOOPY
GOOSE
GOOSY
GOOUT
GROAN
GROAT
GRODY
GROFE
GROGS
GROIN
GROKS
GROOM
GROPE
GROSS
GROSZ
GROTS
GROUP
GROUT
GROVE
GROWL
GROWN
GROWS
GROZA

G••O•
GABON
GABOR
GALOP
GAMOW
GAROU
GATOR
GATOS
GAVOT
GEMOT
GENOA
GETON
GIGOT
GIJOE
GIROS
GLOOM
GLUON
GODOT
GOFOR
GOGOL
GOGOS
GOTON
GRIOT
GROOM
GUYOT
GYRON
GYROS

G•••O
GALLO
GARBO
GECKO
GENRO
GESSO
GETGO
GETTO
GIZMO
GLAXO
GLUCO
GLYCO
GONZO
GORDO
GOTTO
GRECO
GUACO
GUIDO
GUMBO
GUMMO
GUSTO

•GO••
AGOGO
AGONY
AGORA

•G•O•
AGIOS
AGLOW
AGNON
AGRON
EGGON
IGLOO

•G••O
AGGRO
AGOGO
IGLOO
NGAIO

••GO•
ALGOL
ARGOL
ARGON
ARGOS
ARGOT
BEGOT
BIGON
BIGOS
BIGOT
DAGON
DOGON
EGGON
ERGOT
FAGOT
GIGOT
GOGOL
GOGOS
INGOT
LAGOS
LEGOS
LOGON
LOGOS
LTGOV
MAGOG
MAGOO
MAGOT
NOGOS
OHGOD
RIGOR
SAGOS
SEGOS
VIGOR
WAGON
YUGOS

••G•O
AGGRO
ANGLO
DOGGO
HAGIO
HYGRO
LIGNO
MAGOO
SEGNO
SIGNO

•••GO
AGOGO
AMIGO
BINGO
BONGO
CARGO
CONGO
DIEGO
DINGO
DOGGO
FARGO
FORGO
FUEGO
FUNGO
GETGO
IMAGO
INIGO
JINGO
LARGO
LETGO
LINGO
LUEGO
MANGO
MARGO
MONGO
MUNGO
OINGO
OLIGO
OUTGO
PENGO
PHAGO
PINGO
PREGO
RINGO
SARGO
SLIGO
SORGO
TANGO
VIRGO

G•P••
GAPED
GAPER
GAPES
GIPSY
GUPPY
GYPSY

G••P•
GAMPS
GASPE
GASPS
GIMPS
GIMPY
GLOPS
GLYPH
GOAPE
GOOPS
GOOPY
GORPS
GRAPE
GRAPH
GRAPY
GRIPE
GRIPS
GROPE
GULPS
GUPPY

G•••P
GALOP
GASUP
GETUP
GOTUP
GRAMP
GRASP
GROUP
GRUMP
GUMUP

•G•P•
AGAPE
EGYPT

•G••P
AGASP

••G•P
DIGUP
DUGUP
LEGUP
RIGUP
TAGUP

GR•••
GRABS
GRACE
GRADE
GRADS
GRADY
GRAFT
GRAIG
GRAIL
GRAIN
GRAMA
GRAMM
GRAMP
GRAMS
GRAND
GRANI
GRANT
GRAPE
GRAPH
GRAPY
GRASP
GRASS
GRATA
GRATE
GRAVE
GRAVY
GRAYS
GRAZE
GREAT
GREBE
GRECO
GREED
GREEK
GREEN
GREER
GREET
GREGG
GRETA
GRETE
GREYS
GRIDS
GRIEF
GRIEG
GRIER
GRIFT
GRIGS
GRILL
GRIME
GRIMM
GRIMY
GRIND
GRINS
GRIOT
GRIPE
GRIPS
GRIST
GRITS
GROAN
GROAT
GRODY
GROFE
GROGS
GROIN
GROKS
GROOM
GROPE
GROSS
GROSZ
GROTS
GROUP
GROUT
GROVE
GROWL
GROWN
GROWS
GROZA
GRUBS
GRUEL
GRUFF
GRUMP
GRUNT

G•R••
GARBO
GARBS
GARDA
GARDE
GARNI
GAROU
GARRY
GARTH
GERAH
GERMS
GERMY
GERRY
GIRDS
GIRLS
GIRLY
GIRNS
GIROS
GIRTH
GIRTS
GORAL
GORDO
GORDY
GORED
GOREN
GORES
GORGE
GORKI
GORKY
GORME
GORPS
GORSE
GURDY
GURUS
GYRES
GYRON
GYROS
GYRUS

G••R•
GARRY
GAURS
GEARS
GEARY
GENRE
GENRO
GEORG
GERRY
GLARE
GLARY
GLORY
GNARL
GNARS
GOERS
GOURD
GUARD
GUARS

G•••R
GABOR
GAMER
GAPER
GASTR
GATOR
GAYER
GAZER
GIBER
GIVER
GLAIR
GLUER
GOFAR
GOFER
GOFOR
GOMER
GONER
GOWER
GREER
GRIER
GULAR

•GR••
AGREE
AGRIC
AGRON
EGRET
OGRES
UGRIC

•G•R•
AGARS
AGERS
AGGRO
AGORA
BGIRL

•G••R
EGGAR
OGLER

••GR•
AGGRO
ANGRY
EAGRE
ENGRS
HYGRO
NEGRI

••G•R
AEGIR
ALGER
ANGER
AUGER
AUGUR
CAGER
CIGAR
EAGER
EDGAR
EDGER
EGGAR
ELGAR
HAGAR
HUGER
INGER
LAGER
LEGER
LIGER
LUGER
NIGER
PAGER
RIGOR
ROGER
SAGER
SEGAR
SEGER
SUGAR
TIGER
UIGUR
UNGER
URGER
VIGOR
WAGER

GS•••
GSUIT

G•S••
GASES
GASPE
GASPS
GASSY
GASTR
GASUP
GESSO
GESTE
GESTS
GISTS
GOSEE
GOSSE
GUSHY
GUSSY
GUSTO
GUSTS
GUSTY

G••S•
GASSY
GAUSS
GEESE
GESSO
GHOST
GIPSY
GLASS
GLESS
GLOSS
GNASH
GOEST
GOOSE
GOOSY
GORSE
GOSSE
GRASP
GRASS
GRIST
GROSS
GROSZ
GUESS
GUEST
GUISE
GUSSY
GUTSY
GYPSY

G•••S
GAELS
GAFFS
GAGES
GAINS
GAITS
GAIUS
GALAS
GALES
GALLS
GAMES
GAMPS
GANGS
GAOLS
GAPES
GARBS
GASES
GASPS
GATES
GATOS
GAUDS
GAULS
GAURS
GAUSS
GAWKS
GAZES
GEARS
GEEKS
GENES
GENTS
GENUS
GERMS
GESTS
GETAS
GHATS
GHEES
GIBBS
GIBES
GIFTS
GILDS
GILES
GILLS
GILTS
GIMPS
GIRDS
GIRLS
GIRNS
GIROS
GIRTS
GISTS
GIVES
GLADS
GLASS
GLEES
GLENS
GLESS
GLIMS
GLOBS
GLOMS
GLOPS
GLOSS
GLOWS
GLUES
GLUTS
GNARS
GNATS
GNAWS
GOADS
GOALS
GOATS
GOERS
GOGOS
GOLDS
GOLFS
GONDS
GONGS
GOODS
GOOFS
GOONS
GOOPS
GORES
GORPS
GOTHS
GOWNS
GRABS
GRADS
GRAMS
GRASS
GRAYS
GREYS
GRIDS
GRIGS
GRINS
GRIPS
GRITS
GROGS
GROKS
GROSS
GROTS
GROWS
GRUBS
GUARS
GUESS
GULES
GULFS
GULLS
GULPS
GURUS
GUSTS
GYRES
GYROS
GYRUS
GYVES

•G•S•
AGASP
EGEST

•G••S
AGALS
AGARS
AGERS
AGHAS
AGIOS
AGNES
AGNUS
AGUES
EGADS
IGLUS
IGNES
OGEES
OGLES
OGRES

••GS•
ANGST
BUGSY

••G•S
AEGIS
ANGES
ANGUS
ARGOS
ARGUS
AVGAS
BIGOS
BOGGS
BOGUS
CAGES
DEGAS
DOGES
EDGES
ENGRS
GAGES
GOGOS
HIGHS
HOGGS
LAGOS
LEGGS
LEGIS
LEGOS
LOGES
LOGOS
LUGES
MAGES
MAGUS
MSGTS
NEGUS
NOGOS
PAGES
RAGAS
RAGES
REGIS
RIGGS
SAGAS
SAGES
SAGOS
SEGOS
SIGHS
SIGNS
SSGTS
TAGUS
TOGAS
TSGTS
URGES
VAGUS
VEGAS
WAGES
YEGGS
YOGHS
YOGIS
YUGOS

•••GS
BANGS
BERGS
BINGS
BLDGS
BOGGS
BONGS
BRAGS
BRIGS
BUNGS
BURGS
CHUGS
CLOGS
CRAGS
DANGS
DINGS
DONGS
DRAGS
DREGS
DRUGS
FANGS
FLAGS
FLOGS
FROGS
GANGS
GONGS
GRIGS
GROGS
HANGS
HOGGS
HONGS
KINGS
LEGGS
LONGS
LUNGS
MINGS
MOOGS
PANGS
PINGS
PLUGS
PRIGS
PUNGS
QUAGS
RIGGS
RINGS
RUNGS
SHAGS
SINGS
SKEGS
SLAGS
SLOGS
SLUGS
SMOGS
SNAGS
SNUGS
SONGS
STAGS
SWAGS
SWIGS
TANGS
THUGS
TIEGS
TINGS
TONGS
TRIGS
TWIGS
WHIGS
WINGS
YEGGS
ZINGS

G•T••
GATED
GATES
GATOR
GATOS
GATUN
GETAS
GETAT
GETBY
GETGO
GETIN
GETIT
GETME
GETON
GETTO
GETTY
GETUP
GOTAT
GOTBY
GOTHA
GOTHS
GOTIN
GOTON
GOTTA
GOTTO
GOTUP
GUTEN
GUTSY
GUTTA
GUTTY

G••T•
GAITS
GARTH
GASTR
GENTS
GESTE
GESTS
GETTO
GETTY
GHATS
GIFTS
GILTS
GIRTH
GIRTS
GISTS
GLITZ
GLUTS
GNATS
GOATS
GOTTA
GOTTO
GOUTY
GRATA
GRATE
GRETA
GRETE
GRITS
GROTS
GUSTO
GUSTS
GUSTY
GUTTA
GUTTY

G•••T
GAMUT
GAUNT
GAVOT
GEMOT
GENET
GETAT
GETIT
GFLAT
GHENT
GHOST
GIANT
GIGOT
GLINT
GLOAT
GODET
GODOT
GOEST
GOOUT
GOTAT
GRAFT
GRANT
GREAT
GREET
GRIFT
GRIOT
GRIST
GROAT
GROUT
GRUNT
GSUIT
GUEST
GUILT
GUYOT

•G•T•
AGATE
AGITA

•G••T
AGENT
AGLET
EGEST
EGRET
EGYPT

••GT•
MSGTS
SSGTS
TSGTS

••G•T
ANGST
ARGOT
AUGHT
BAGIT
BEGAT
BEGET
BEGOT
BIGHT
BIGOT
CUGAT
DIGIT
DOGIT
EIGHT
ERGOT
FAGOT
FIGHT
FUGIT
GIGOT
INGOT
LEGIT
LIGHT
MAGOT
MIGHT
NIGHT
OUGHT
PAGET
PUGET
RIGHT
ROGET
SAGET
SIGHT
TIGHT
WIGHT

•••GT
VINGT

GU•••
GUACO
GUARD
GUARS
GUAVA
GUCCI
GUESS
GUEST
GUIDE
GUIDO
GUILD
GUILE
GUILT
GUISE
GULAG
GULAR
GULCH
GULES
GULFS
GULLS
GULLY
GULPS
GUMBO
GUMMO
GUMMY
GUMUP
GUNGA
GUNKY
GUNNY
GUPPY
GURDY
GURUS
GUSHY
GUSSY
GUSTO
GUSTS
GUSTY
GUTEN
GUTSY
GUTTA
GUTTY
GUYED
GUYOT

G•U••
GAUDS GAUDY GAUGE GAULS GAUNT GAURS GAUSS GAUZE GAUZY GLUCK GLUCO GLUED GLUER GLUES GLUEY GLUON GLUTS GOUDA GOUDY GOUGE GOULD GOURD GOUTY GRUBS GRUEL GRUFF GRUMP GRUNT GSUIT

G••U•
GAIUS GAMUT GASUP GATUN GENUS GETUP GHOUL GIGUE GOOUT GOTUP GROUP GROUT GUMUP GURUS GYRUS

G•••U
GAROU

•GU••
AGUES

•G•U•
AGNUS IGLUS

••GU•
ANGUS ARGUE ARGUS AUGUR BBGUN BEGUM BEGUN BOGUS BYGUM DIGUP DUGUP FUGUE GIGUE HAGUE JUGUM LEGUP LOGUE MAGUS MOGUL MYGUY NEGUS RIGUP ROGUE SEGUE TAGUP TAGUS UIGUR VAGUE VAGUS VOGUE

••G•U
ILGWU

•••GU
TAEGU XINGU

G•V••
GAVEL GAVIN GAVOT GIVEN GIVER GIVES GYVED GYVES

G••V•
GLOVE GRAVE GRAVY GROVE GUAVA

•G•V•
AGAVE OGIVE

••G•V
LTGOV NEGEV

GW•••
GWENN GWYNN

G•W••
GAWKS GAWKY GOWDY GOWER GOWNS

G••W•
GLOWS GNAWS GROWL GROWN GROWS

G•••W
GAMOW

•G••W
AGLOW AGNEW

••GW•
ILGWU

G••X•
GLAXO

G•••X
GALAX

GY•••
GYPSY GYRES GYRON GYROS GYRUS GYVED GYVES

G•Y••
GAYAL GAYER GAYLE GAYLY GLYCO GLYPH GUYED GUYOT GWYNN

G••Y•
GRAYS GREYS

G•••Y
GABBY GANDY GARRY GASSY GAUDY GAUZY GAWKY GAYLY GEARY GEEKY GEMMY GERMY GERRY GETBY GETTY GIDDY GIMPY GINNY GIPSY GIRLY GLARY GLORY GLUEY GODEY GODLY GOLLY GOODY GOOEY GOOFY GOONY GOOPY GOOSY GORDY GORKY GOTBY GOUDY GOUTY GOWDY GRADY GRAPY GRAVY GRIMY GRODY GULLY GUMMY GUNKY GUNNY GUPPY GURDY GUSHY GUSSY GUSTY GUTSY GUTTY GYPSY

•GY••
EGYPT

•G••Y
AGLEY AGONY

••G•Y
ANGRY BAGGY BOGEY BOGGY BUGGY BUGSY CAGEY DIGBY DOGGY FOGEY FOGGY JAGGY LEGGY MUGGY MYGUY NAGGY PEGGY PIGGY PYGMY RIGBY RUGBY SAGGY SOGGY WIGGY ZIGGY

•••GY
BAGGY BILGY BOGGY BUGGY BULGY DINGY DODGY DOGGY ELEGY FOGGY HEDGY JAGGY LEGGY MUGGY NAGGY OLOGY PEGGY PIGGY PODGY PORGY PUDGY RANGY RIDGY SAGGY SOGGY STAGY STOGY TANGY WEDGY WIGGY ZIGGY ZINGY

G•Z••
GAZED GAZER GAZES GIZMO

G••Z•
GAUZE GAUZY GHAZI GINZA GLAZE GLOZE GONZO GRAZE GROZA

G•••Z
GLITZ GOMEZ GROSZ

•G•Z•
AGAZE

HA•••
HABER HABIT HABLA HACEK HACKS HADAR HADAT HADES HADJI HADNT HADON HADST HADTO HAEMA HAEMO HAFIZ HAFTS HAFUN HAGAR HAGEN HAGIO HAGUE HAHAS HAIFA HAIKS HAIKU HAILE HAILS HAIRS HAIRY HAITI HAJIS HAJJI HAKES HAKIM HALAS HALED HALER HALES HALEY HALLE HALLO HALLS HALON HALOS HALTS HALVE HAMAL HAMAN HAMEL HAMES HAMMY HANDS HANDY HANES HANGS HANKS HANKY HANNA HANNO HANOI HANSA HAOLE HAPLY HAPPY HARAR HARDY HARED HAREM HARES HARKS HARMS HARPO HARPS HARPY HARRY HARSH HARTE HARTS HARUM HASAT HASID HASNT HASON HASPS HASSO HASTA HASTE HASTO HASTY HATCH HATED HATER HATES HATLO HAUER HAULM HAULS HAUNT HAUSA HAUTE HAVEL HAVEN HAVER HAVES HAVOC HAVRE HAWED HAWKE HAWKS HAWSE HAYDN HAYED HAYEK HAYES HAZED HAZEL HAZER HAZES

H•A••
HEADS HEADY HEALS HEALY HEAPS HEARD HEARN HEARS HEART HEATH HEATS HEAVE HEAVY HOAGY HOARD HOARS HOARY HYATT

H••A•
HADAR HADAT HAGAR HAHAS HALAS HAMAL HAMAN HARAR HASAT HEJAZ HEMAN HENAN HERAT HEXAD HIRAM HOBAN HODAD HOGAN HONAN HORAE HORAL HORAS HOYAS HULAS HUMAN HUNAN HYLAS HYMAN HYRAX

H•••A
HABLA HAEMA HAIFA HANNA HANSA HASTA HAUSA HEDDA HEKLA HELGA HENNA HEPTA HILDA HOFFA HONDA HOOHA HOSEA HOSTA HOUMA HUBBA HYDRA HYENA HYPHA

•HA••
CHACO CHAFE CHAFF CHAIM CHAIN CHAIR CHAKA CHALK CHAMP CHANG CHANT CHAOS CHAPS CHARD CHARM CHARO CHARS CHART CHARY CHASE CHASM CHATS CHAUD CHAWS DHABI GHANA GHATS GHAZI KHAKI KHANS LHASA OHAIR OHARA OHARE PHAGE PHAGO PHARM PHASE SHACK SHADE SHADS SHADY SHAEF SHAFT SHAGS SHAHN SHAHS SHAKE SHAKO SHAKY SHALE SHALL SHALT SHAME SHAMS SHAMU SHANA SHANE SHANK SHANS SHANT SHAPE SHARD SHARE SHARI SHARK SHARP SHAUN SHAVE SHAWL SHAWM SHAWN SHAYS THAIS THANE THANK THANT THARP THATS THAWS UHAUL WHACK WHALE WHAMO WHAMS WHANG WHARF WHATD WHATS

•H•A•
AHEAD AHMAD CHEAP CHEAT CHIAS PHIAL RHEAS SHEAF SHEAN SHEAR SHOAH SHOAL SHOAT UHLAN WHEAL WHEAT

•H••A
AHORA CHAKA CHEKA CHELA CHIBA CHINA CHITA CHULA GHANA LHASA OHARA PHYLA RHODA SHANA SHEBA SHIVA SHULA THECA THEDA THEMA THERA THETA THUJA UHURA XHOSA

••HA•
AGHAS ARHAT BAHAI BEHAN BIHAR BOHAI COHAN EPHAH EPHAS ETHAN HAHAS JIHAD LEHAR MAHAL MAHAN OGHAM POHAI PSHAW RAHAB REHAB REHAN SCHAV WUHAN ZOHAR

••H•A
BAHIA BOHEA LEHUA MEHTA NAHUA OCHOA OSHEA SCHWA SEHNA

•••HA
AISHA ALOHA ALPHA BOTHA DACHA FATHA GOTHA HOOHA HYPHA KASHA MISHA MOCHA NUCHA OMAHA PASHA SACHA SASHA

HB•••
HBOMB

H•B••
HABER HABIT HABLA HOBAN HOBBS HOBBY HOBOS HUBBA HUBBY

H••B•
HERBS HERBY HOBBS HOBBY HUBBA HUBBY

H•••B
HBOMB HOREB

•HB••
OHBOY

•H•B•
CHIBA CHUBS DHABI PHOBE SHEBA THEBE

•H••B
RHOMB RHUMB SHRUB THROB THUMB

••HB•
ASHBY

••H•B
RAHAB REHAB SAHIB

H•C••
HACEK HACKS HECHT HECKS HECTO HICKS HOCKS HOCUS

H••C•
HATCH HENCE HENCH HITCH HOOCH HULCE HUNCH HUTCH

H•••C
HAVOC HELIC HIGHC

•H•C•
CHACO CHECK CHICK CHICO CHOCK CHUCK PHYCO SHACK SHOCK SHUCK THECA THICK WHACK WHICH

••H•C
ADHOC ETHIC

•••HC
HIGHC

H•D••
HADAR HADAT HADES HADJI HADNT HADON HADST HADTO HEDDA HEDGE HEDGY HEDIN HIDER HIDES HODAD HYDRA HYDRO

H••D•
HANDS HANDY HARDY HAYDN HEADS HEADY HEDDA HEEDS HEIDI HEIDT HERDS HILDA HINDI HINDS HINDU HOLDS HONDA HONDO HOODS HORDE HOWDY HURDY

H•••D
HALED HARED HASID HATED HAWED HAYED HAZED HEARD HEROD HEWED HEXAD HEXED HIKED HIRED HIVED HOARD HODAD HOKED HOLED HOMED HONED HOPED HOSED HOUND HUMID HYOID HYPED

•H•D•
CHIDE RHODA RHODE RHODO SHADE SHADS SHADY SHEDS THEDA THUDS

•H••D
AHEAD AHMAD AHMED CHARD CHAUD CHILD CHORD OHGOD SHARD SHEED SHIED SHOED SHRED THEYD THIRD WHATD

••HD•
MAHDI

••H•D
AAHED ACHED APHID EPHOD JIHAD OOHED SCHED USHED

HE•••
HEADS HEADY HEALS HEALY HEAPS HEARD HEARN HEARS HEART HEATH HEATS HEAVE HEAVY HECHT HECKS HECTO HEDDA HEDGE HEDGY HEDIN HEEDS HEELS HEFTS HEFTY HEGEL HEIDI HEIDT HEIGH HEINE HEINZ HEIRS HEISS HEIST HEJAZ HEKLA HELEN HELGA HELIC HELIO HELIX HELLO HELMS HELOS HELOT HELPS HELVE HEMAN HEMEN HEMET HEMIN HEMPS HENAN HENCE HENCH HENGE HENIE HENNA HENNY HENRI HENRY HEPTA HERAT HERBS HERBY HERDS HERES HERKY HERLS HERMS HERNE HEROD HERON HEROS HERTZ HERVE HERZL HESSE HESTS HETTY HETUP HEURE HEUTE HEWED HEWER HEXAD HEXED HEXER HEXES HEXYL HEYSE

H•E••
HAEMA HAEMO HEEDS HEELS HIERO HOERS HYENA

H••E•
HABER HACEK HADES HAGEN HAKES HALED HALER HALES HALEY HAMEL HAMES HANES HARED HAREM HARES HATED HATER HATES HAUER HAVEL HAVEN HAVER HAVES HAWED HAYED HAYEK HAYES HAZED HAZEL HAZER HAZES HEGEL HELEN HEMEN HEMET HERES HEWED HEWER HEXED HEXER HEXES HIDER HIDES HIKED HIKER HIKES HINES HIRED HIRER HIRES HIVED HIVES HOKED HOKES HOKEY HOLED HOLES HOLEY HOMED HOMEO HOMER HOMES HOMEY HONED HONES HONEY HOOEY HOPED HOPER HOPES HOREB HOSEA HOSED HOSEL HOSES HOTEL HOVEL HOVER HOVEY HUGER HYPED HYPER HYPES

H•••E
HAGUE HAILE HALLE HALVE HAOLE HARTE HASTE HAUTE HAVRE HAWKE HAWSE HEAVE HEDGE HEINE HELVE HENCE HENGE HENIE HERNE HERVE HESSE HEURE HEUTE HEYSE HINGE HITME HOMME HOOKE HOPPE HORAE HORDE HORNE HORSE HOUSE HOWIE HOXIE HOYLE HULCE

•HE••
AHEAD CHEAP CHEAT CHECK CHEEK CHEEP CHEER CHEFS CHEKA CHELA CHERE CHERI CHERT CHESS CHEST CHEVY CHEWS CHEWY GHEES GHENT PHENO RHEAS RHETT RHEUM SHEAF SHEAN SHEAR SHEBA SHEDS SHEED SHEEN SHEEP SHEER SHEET SHEIK SHELF SHELL SHEMP SHERE THEBE THECA THEDA THEFT THEIR THEMA THEME THEMS THEOL THERA THERE THERM THESE THETA THEWS THEYD WHEAL WHEAT WHEEL WHEEN WHELK WHELM WHELP WHERE WHETS WHEYS

•H•E•
AHMED CHEEK CHEEP CHEER CHIEF CHIEN GHEES KHMER NHLER PHREN SHAEF SHEED SHEEN SHEEP SHEER SHEET SHIED SHIER SHIES SHOED SHOER SHOES SHRED SHREW SHYER THIEF THREE THREW WHEEL

WHEEN

•H••E
CHAFE
CHASE
CHERE
CHIDE
CHILE
CHIME
CHINE
CHIVE
CHLOE
CHOKE
CHORE
CHOSE
CHUTE
DHOLE
DHOTE
OHARE
PHAGE
PHASE
PHILE
PHOBE
PHONE
PHYFE
PHYLE
RHINE
RHODE
RHONE
RHYME
SHADE
SHAKE
SHALE
SHAME
SHANE
SHAPE
SHARE
SHAVE
SHERE
SHINE
SHIRE
SHONE
SHORE
SHOVE
SHUTE
THANE
THEBE
THEME
THERE
THESE
THINE
THOLE
THOSE
THREE
THROE
THULE
THYME
WHALE
WHERE
WHILE
WHINE
WHITE
WHOLE
WHOSE
WHYME

••HE•
AAHED
ACHED
ACHES
ADHEM
ASHEN
ASHER
ASHES
BOHEA
COHEN
ETHEL
ETHER
OCHER
OOHED
OSHEA
OTHER
REHEM
SAHEL
SCHED
TEHEE
USHED
USHER
UTHER

••H•E
BOHME
JAHRE
MAHRE
OCHRE
TAHOE
TEHEE

•••HE
BATHE
BECHE
BOTHE
BRAHE
CACHE
DACHE
FICHE
LATHE
LETHE
LITHE
MACHE
MOSHE
NASHE
NICHE
PATHE
RAPHE
RICHE
ROCHE
RUCHE
SADHE
SIDHE
TITHE
TYCHE
WITHE
WYTHE

H•F••
HAFIZ
HAFTS
HAFUN
HEFTS
HEFTY
HIFIS
HOFFA
HUFFS
HUFFY

H••F•
HAIFA
HOFFA
HOOFS
HUFFS
HUFFY

•H•F•
CHAFE
CHAFF
CHEFS
CHUFF
KHUFU
PHYFE
SHAFT
SHIFT
THEFT
WHIFF

•H••F
CHAFF
CHIEF
CHUFF
SHAEF
SHEAF
SHELF
THIEF
WHARF
WHIFF
WHOOF

H•G••
HAGAR
HAGEN
HAGIO
HAGUE
HEGEL
HIGHC
HIGHS
HOGAN
HOGGS
HUGER
HYGRO

H••G•
HANGS
HEDGE
HEDGY
HEIGH
HELGA
HENGE
HINGE
HOAGY
HOGGS
HONGS
HOUGH

H•••G
HMONG

•HG••
OHGOD

•H•G•
CHUGS
PHAGE
PHAGO
SHAGS
SHOGI
THIGH
THUGS
WHIGS

•H••G
CHANG
CHING
CHONG
CHUNG
SHRUG
THING
THONG
WHANG

HH•••
HHOUR

H•H••
HAHAS
HOHOS
HOHUM

H••H•
HECHT
HIGHC
HIGHS
HOOHA
HYPHA

H•••H
HARSH
HATCH
HEATH
HEIGH
HENCH
HITCH
HOOCH
HOUGH
HUMPH
HUNCH
HUTCH

•HH••
UHHUH

•H•H•
SHAHN
SHAHS

•H••H
SHISH
SHOAH
SHUSH
THIGH
THOTH
UHHUH
WHICH

••H•H
EPHAH
ICHTH
UHHUH

HI•••
HICKS
HIDER
HIDES
HIERO
HIFIS
HIGHC
HIGHS
HIKED
HIKER
HIKES
HILDA
HILLS
HILLY
HILTS
HILUM
HINDI
HINDS
HINDU
HINES
HINGE
HINNY
HINTS
HIPPO
HIPPY
HIPTO
HIRAM
HIRED
HIRER
HIRES
HISSY
HITCH
HITIT
HITME
HITON
HITUP
HIVED
HIVES

H•I••
HAIFA
HAIKS
HAIKU
HAILE
HAILS
HAIRS
HAIRY
HAITI
HEIDI
HEIDT
HEIGH
HEINE
HEINZ
HEIRS
HEISS
HEIST
HOIST
HOITY

H••I•
HABIT
HAFIZ
HAGIO
HAJIS
HAKIM
HASID
HEDIN
HELIC
HELIO
HELIX
HEMIN
HENIE
HIFIS
HITIT
HOPIS
HOWIE
HOXIE
HUMID
HYOID

H•••I
HADJI
HAITI
HAJJI
HANOI
HEIDI
HENRI
HINDI
HOSNI
HOURI

•HI••
CHIAS
CHIBA
CHICK
CHICO
CHIDE
CHIEF
CHIEN
CHILD
CHILE
CHILI
CHILL
CHIME
CHIMP
CHINA
CHINE
CHING
CHINK
CHINO
CHINS
CHIOS
CHIPS
CHIRO
CHIRP
CHIRR
CHITA
CHITS
CHIVE
CHIVY
PHIAL
PHILE
PHILO
RHINE
RHINO
RHIZO
SHIED
SHIER
SHIES
SHIFT
SHILL
SHIMS
SHINE
SHINS
SHINY
SHIPS
SHIRE
SHIRK
SHIRR
SHIRT
SHISH
SHIVA
SHIVS
THICK
THIEF
THIGH
THILL
THINE
THING
THINK
THINS
THIRD
WHICH
WHIFF
WHIGS
WHILE
WHIMS
WHINE
WHINY
WHIPS
WHIRL
WHIRR
WHIRS
WHISK
WHIST
WHITE
WHITS

•H•I•
AHSIN
CHAIM
CHAIN
CHAIR
CHOIR
CHRIS
OHAIR
SHEIK
THAIS
THEIR

•H••I
CHERI
CHILI
DHABI
DHOTI
GHAZI
KHAKI
PHYSI
SHARI
SHOGI
SHOJI

••HI•
APHID
APHIS
BAHIA
ECHIN
ETHIC
NIHIL
NOHIT
OPHIR
SAHIB
SOHIO
UNHIP

••H•I
ANHUI
BAHAI
BOHAI
LAHTI
MAHDI
POHAI

•••HI
AMPHI
ARCHI
DASHI
DELHI
KOCHI
RISHI
SOCHI
SPAHI
SUSHI

H•J••
HAJIS
HAJJI
HEJAZ

H••J•
HADJI
HADJI
HAJJI

•H•J•
SHOJI
THUJA

H•K••
HAKES
HAKIM
HEKLA
HIKED
HIKER
HIKES
HOKED
HOKES
HOKEY
HOKUM

H••K•
HACKS
HAIKS
HAIKU
HANKS
HANKY
HARKS
HAWKE
HAWKS
HECKS
HERKY
HICKS
HOCKS
HONKS
HOOKE
HOOKS
HOOKY
HULKS
HUNKS
HUSKS
HUSKY

H•••K
HACEK
HAYEK
HUROK

•H•K•
CHAKA
CHEKA
CHOKE
CHOKY
KHAKI
SHAKE
SHAKO
SHAKY

•H••K
CHALK
CHECK
CHEEK
CHICK
CHINK
CHOCK
CHUCK
CHUNK
SHACK
SHANK
SHARK
SHEIK
SHIRK
SHOCK
SHOOK
SHUCK
THANK
THICK
THINK
THUNK
WHACK
WHELK
WHISK

H•L••
HALAS
HALED
HALER
HALES
HALEY
HALLE
HALLO
HALLS
HALON
HALOS
HALTS
HALVE
HELEN
HELGA
HELIC
HELIO
HELIX
HELLO
HELMS
HELOS
HELOT
HELPS
HELVE
HILDA
HILLS
HILLY
HILTS
HILUM
HOLDS
HOLED
HOLES
HOLEY
HOLLY
HOLMS
HOLST
HOLTZ
HULAS
HULCE
HULKS
HULLO
HULLS
HYLAS

H••L•
HABLA
HAILE
HAILS
HALLE
HALLO
HALLS
HAOLE
HAPLY
HATLO
HAULM
HAULS
HEALS
HEALY
HEELS
HEKLA
HELLO
HERLS
HILLS
HILLY
HOLLY
HOTLY
HOWLS
HOYLE
HULLO
HULLS
HURLS
HURLY

H•••L
HAMAL
HAMEL
HAVEL
HAZEL
HEGEL
HERZL
HEXYL
HORAL
HOROL
HOSEL
HOTEL
HOVEL

•HL••
CHLOE
CHLOR
NHLER
PHLOX
UHLAN

•H•L•
CHALK
CHELA
CHILD
CHILE
CHILI
CHILL
CHULA
DHOLE
PHILE
PHILO
PHYLA
PHYLE
PHYLL
SHALE
SHALL
SHALT
SHELF
SHELL
SHILL
SHULA
SHULS
SHYLY
THILL
THOLE
THULE
WHALE
WHELK
WHELM
WHELP
WHILE
WHOLE
WHOLL

•H••L
CHILL
CHURL
GHOUL
PHIAL
PHYLL
SHALL
SHAWL
SHELL
SHILL
SHOAL
THEOL
THILL
UHAUL
WHEAL
WHEEL
WHIRL
WHOLL
WHORL

••HL•
BUHLS
KAHLO

••H•L
ATHOL
ETHEL
ETHYL
MAHAL
NIHIL
SAHEL

•••HL
AMAHL
RUEHL
STAHL

HM•••
HMONG

H•M••
HAMAL
HAMAN
HAMEL
HAMES
HAMMY
HEMAN
HEMEN
HEMET
HEMIN
HEMPS
HOMED
HOMEO
HOMER
HOMES
HOMEY
HOMME
HUMAN
HUMID
HUMOR
HUMPH
HUMPS
HUMPY
HUMUS
HYMAN
HYMNS

H••M•
HAEMA
HAEMO
HAMMY
HARMS
HBOMB
HELMS
HERMS
HITME
HOLMS
HOMME
HOUMA

H•••M
HAKIM
HAREM
HARUM
HAULM
HILUM
HIRAM
HOHUM
HOKUM

•HM••
AHMAD
AHMED
KHMER

•H•M•
CHAMP
CHIME
CHIMP
CHOMP
CHUMP
CHUMS
RHOMB
RHUMB
RHYME
SHAME
SHAMS
SHAMU
SHEMP
SHIMS
THEMA
THEME
THEMS
THUMB
THUMP
THYME
WHAMO
WHAMS
WHIMS
WHOMP
WHYME

•H••M
CHAIM
CHARM
CHASM
CHROM
PHARM
PHNOM
RHEUM
SHAWM
THERM
THRUM
WHELM

••HM•
BOHME
SCHMO

••H•M
ADHEM
HOHUM
NAHUM
OGHAM
REHEM

•••HM
ABOHM
BOEHM

H•N••
HANDS
HANDY
HANES
HANGS
HANKS
HANKY
HANNA
HANNO
HANOI
HANSA
HENAN
HENCE
HENCH
HENGE
HENIE
HENNA
HENNY
HENRI
HENRY
HINDI
HINDS
HINDU
HINES
HINGE
HINNY
HINTS
HONAN
HONDA
HONDO
HONED
HONES
HONEY
HONGS
HONKS
HONOR
HONUS
HUNAN
HUNCH
HUNKS
HUNTS

H••N•
HADNT
HANNA
HANNO
HASNT
HAUNT
HEINE
HEINZ
HENNA
HENNY
HERNE
HINNY
HMONG
HORNE
HORNS
HOSNI
HOUND
HYENA
HYMNS
HYPNO

H•••N
HADON
HAFUN
HAGEN
HALON
HAMAN
HASON
HAVEN
HAYDN
HEARN
HEDIN
HELEN
HEMAN
HEMEN
HEMIN
HENAN
HERON
HITON
HOBAN
HOGAN
HONAN
HUMAN
HUNAN
HURON
HYMAN
HYSON

•HN••
PHNOM

•H•N•
CHANG
CHANT
CHINA
CHINE
CHING
CHINK
CHINO
CHINS
CHONG
CHUNG
CHUNK
GHANA
GHENT
KHANS
PHENO
PHONE
PHONO
PHONS
PHONY
RHINE
RHINO
RHONE
SHANA
SHANE
SHANK
SHANS
SHANT
SHINE
SHINS
SHINY
SHONE
SHUNS
SHUNT
THANE
THANK
THANT
THINE
THING
THINK
THINS
THONG
THUNK
WHANG
WHINE
WHINY

•H••N
AHSIN
CHAIN
CHIEN
CHRON
CHURN
PHREN
SHAHN
SHAUN
SHAWN
SHEAN
SHEEN
SHORN
SHOWN
THORN
UHLAN
WHEEN

••HN•
ETHNO
JOHNS
SEHNA

••H•N
ASHEN
ATHON
BEHAN
COHAN
COHEN
ECHIN
ETHAN
MAHAN
REHAN
SCHON
WUHAN

•••HN
BRUHN
FOEHN
ICAHN
SHAHN
SPAHN
UTAHN

HO•••
HOAGY
HOARD
HOARS
HOARY
HOBAN
HOBBS
HOBBY
HOBOS
HOCKS
HOCUS
HODAD
HOERS
HOFFA
HOGAN
HOGGS
HOHOS
HOHUM
HOIST
HOITY
HOKED
HOKES
HOKEY
HOKUM
HOLDS
HOLED
HOLES
HOLEY
HOLLY
HOLMS
HOLST
HOLTZ
HOMED
HOMEO
HOMER
HOMES
HOMEY
HOMME
HONAN
HONDA
HONDO
HONED
HONES
HONEY
HONGS
HONKS
HONOR
HONUS
HOOCH
HOODS
HOOEY
HOOFS
HOOHA
HOOKE
HOOKS
HOOKY
HOOPS
HOOTS
HOPED
HOPER
HOPES
HOPIS
HOPPE
HOPUP
HORAE
HORAL
HORAS
HORDE
HOREB
HORNE
HORNS
HOROL
HORSE
HORST
HORSY
HORUS
HOSEA
HOSED
HOSEL
HOSES
HOSNI
HOSTA
HOSTS
HOTEL
HOTLY
HOUGH
HOUMA
HOUND
HOURI
HOURS
HOUSE
HOVEL
HOVER
HOVEY
HOWDY
HOWIE
HOWLS
HOWSO
HOWTO
HOXIE
HOYAS
HOYLE

H•O••
HAOLE
HBOMB
HHOUR
HMONG
HOOCH
HOODS
HOOEY
HOOFS
HOOHA
HOOKE
HOOKS
HOOKY
HOOPS
HOOTS
HYOID

H••O•
HADON
HALON
HALOS
HANOI
HASON
HAVOC
HELOS
HELOT
HEROD
HERON
HEROS
HITON
HOBOS
HOHOS
HONOR
HOROL
HUMOR
HUROK
HURON
HYPOS
HYSON

H•••O
HADTO
HAEMO
HAGIO
HALLO
HANNO
HARPO
HASSO
HASTO
HATLO
HECTO
HELIO
HELLO
HIERO
HIPPO
HIPTO
HOMEO
HONDO
HOWSO
HOWTO
HULLO
HYDRO
HYGRO
HYPNO
HYPSO

•HO••
AHORA
AHOYS
CHOCK
CHOIR
CHOKE
CHOKY
CHOMP
CHONG
CHOPS
CHORD
CHORE
CHOSE
CHOWS
DHOLE
DHOTE
DHOTI
DHOWS
GHOST
GHOUL
HHOUR
PHOBE
PHONE
PHONO
PHONS
PHONY
PHOTO
PHOTS
RHODA
RHODE
RHODO
RHOMB
RHONE
SHOAH
SHOAL
SHOAT
SHOCK
SHOED
SHOER
SHOES
SHOGI
SHOJI
SHONE
SHOOK
SHOOS
SHOOT
SHOPS
SHORE

SHORN
SHORT
SHOTS
SHOUT
SHOVE
SHOWN
SHOWS
SHOWY
THOLE
THONG
THORN
THORP
THOSE
THOTH
THOUS
WHOLE
WHOLL
WHOMP
WHOOF
WHOOP
WHOPS
WHORL
WHOSE
WHOSO
XHOSA

•H•O•
CHAOS
CHIOS
CHLOE
CHLOR
CHROM
CHRON
OHBOY
OHGOD
PHLOX
PHNOM
SHOOK
SHOOS
SHOOT
THEOL
THROB
THROE
THROW
WHOOF
WHOOP

•H••O
CHACO
CHARO
CHICO
CHINO
CHIRO
PHAGO
PHENO
PHILO
PHONO
PHOTO
PHYCO
PHYTO
RHINO
RHIZO
RHODO
SHAKO
WHAMO
WHOSO

••HO•
ABHOR
ACHOO
ADHOC
ATHOL
ATHON
ATHOS
COHOS
EPHOD
EPHOR
ETHOS
HOHOS
ICHOR
NOHOW
OCHOA
SCHON
TAHOE
WAHOO
YAHOO

••H•O
ACHOO
ETHNO
KAHLO
SCHMO
SOHIO
WAHOO
YAHOO

•••HO
ALTHO
ANTHO
BASHO
BATHO
DICHO
DONHO
IDAHO
LITHO
MACHO
MINHO
NACHO
ORTHO
PATHO
SOTHO
TYCHO

H•P••
HAPLY
HAPPY
HEPTA
HIPPO
HIPPY
HIPTO
HOPED
HOPER
HOPES
HOPIS
HOPPE
HOPUP
HYPED
HYPER
HYPES
HYPHA
HYPNO
HYPOS
HYPSO

H••P•
HAPPY
HARPO
HARPS
HARPY
HASPS
HEAPS
HELPS
HEMPS
HIPPO
HIPPY
HOOPS
HOPPE
HUMPH
HUMPS
HUMPY

H•••P
HETUP
HITUP
HOPUP

•H•P•
CHAPS
CHIPS
CHOPS
SHAPE
SHIPS
SHOPS
WHIPS
WHOPS
WHUPS

•H••P
CHAMP
CHEAP
CHEEP
CHIMP
CHIRP
CHOMP
CHUMP
SHARP
SHEEP
SHEMP
THARP
THORP
THUMP
WHELP
WHOMP
WHOOP

••H•P
UNHIP

H•R••
HARAR
HARDY
HARED
HAREM
HARES
HARKS
HARMS
HARPO
HARPS
HARPY
HARRY
HARSH
HARTE
HARTS
HARUM
HERAT
HERBS
HERBY
HERDS
HERES
HERKY
HERLS
HERMS
HERNE
HEROD
HERON
HEROS
HERTZ
HERVE
HERZL
HIRAM
HIRED
HIRER
HIRES
HORAE
HORAL
HORAS
HORDE
HOREB
HORNE
HORNS
HOROL
HORSE
HORST
HORSY
HORUS
HURDY
HURLS
HURLY
HUROK
HURON
HURRY
HURST
HURTS
HYRAX

H••R•
HAIRS
HAIRY
HARRY
HAVRE
HEARD
HEARN
HEARS
HEART
HEIRS
HENRI
HENRY
HEURE
HIERO
HOARD
HOARS
HOARY
HOERS
HOURI
HOURS
HURRY
HYDRA
HYDRO
HYGRO

H•••R
HABER
HADAR
HAGAR
HALER
HARAR
HATER
HAUER
HAVER
HAZER
HEWER
HEXER
HHOUR
HIDER
HIKER
HIRER
HOMER
HONOR
HOPER
HOVER
HUGER
HUMOR
HYPER

•HR••
CHRIS
CHROM
CHRON
CHRYS
PHREN
SHRED
SHREW
SHRUB
SHRUG
THREE
THREW
THROB
THROE
THROW
THRUM

•H•R•
AHORA
CHARD
CHARM
CHARO
CHARS
CHART
CHARY
CHERE
CHERI
CHERT
CHIRO
CHIRP
CHIRR
CHORD
CHORE
CHURL
CHURN
OHARA
OHARE
PHARM
SHARD
SHARE
SHARI
SHARK
SHARP
SHERE
SHIRE
SHIRK
SHIRR
SHIRT
SHORE
SHORN
SHORT
THARP
THERA
THERE
THERM
THIRD
THORN
THORP
THURS
UHURA
UHURU
WHARF
WHERE
WHIRL
WHIRR
WHIRS
WHORL

•H••R
CHAIR
CHEER
CHIRR
CHLOR
CHOIR
HHOUR
KHMER
NHLER
OHAIR
SHEAR
SHEER
SHIER
SHIRR
SHOER
SHYER
THEIR
WHIRR

••HR•
JAHRE
MAHRE
NEHRU
OCHRE
TAHRS

••H•R
ABHOR
ASHER
ASHUR
BIHAR
EPHOR
ETHER
ICHOR
LEHAR
MOHUR
OCHER
OPHIR
OTHER
USHER
UTHER
ZOHAR

•••HR
AMPHR
ARTHR

H•S••
HASAT
HASID
HASNT
HASON
HASPS
HASSO
HASTA
HASTE
HASTO
HASTY
HESSE
HESTS
HISSY
HOSEA
HOSED
HOSEL
HOSES
HOSNI
HOSTA
HOSTS
HUSKS
HUSKY
HUSSY
HYSON

H••S•
HADST
HANSA
HARSH
HASSO
HAUSA
HAWSE
HEISS
HEIST
HESSE
HEYSE
HISSY
HOIST
HOLST
HORSE
HORST
HORSY
HOUSE
HOWSO
HURST
HUSSY
HYPSO

H•••S
HACKS
HADES
HAFTS
HAHAS
HAIKS
HAILS
HAIRS
HAJIS
HAKES
HALAS
HALES
HALLS
HALOS
HALTS
HAMES
HANDS
HANES
HANGS
HANKS
HARES
HARKS
HARMS
HARPS
HARTS
HASPS
HATES
HAULS
HAVES
HAWKS
HAYES
HAZES
HEADS
HEALS
HEAPS
HEARS
HEATS
HECKS
HEEDS
HEELS
HEFTS
HEIRS
HEISS
HELMS
HELOS
HELPS
HEMPS
HERBS
HERDS
HERES
HERLS
HERMS
HEROS
HESTS
HEXES
HICKS
HIDES
HIFIS
HIGHS
HIKES
HILLS
HILTS
HINDS
HINES
HINTS
HIRES
HIVES
HOARS
HOBBS
HOBOS
HOCKS
HOCUS
HOERS
HOGGS
HOHOS
HOKES
HOLDS
HOLES
HOLMS
HOMES
HONES
HONGS
HONKS
HONUS
HOODS
HOOFS
HOOKS
HOOPS
HOOTS
HOPES
HOPIS
HORAS
HORNS
HORUS
HOSES
HOSTS
HOURS
HOWLS
HOYAS
HUFFS
HULAS
HULKS
HULLS
HUMPS
HUMUS
HUNKS
HUNTS
HURLS
HURTS
HUSKS
HYLAS
HYMNS
HYPES
HYPOS

•HS••
AHSIN

•H•S•
CHASE
CHASM
CHESS
CHEST
CHOSE
GHOST
LHASA
PHASE
PHYSI
SHISH
SHUSH
THESE
THOSE
WHISK
WHIST
WHOSE
WHOSO
XHOSA

•H••S
AHOYS
CHAOS
CHAPS
CHARS
CHATS
CHAWS
CHEFS
CHESS
CHEWS
CHIAS
CHINS
CHIOS
CHIPS
CHITS
CHOPS
CHOWS
CHRIS
CHRYS
CHUBS
CHUGS
CHUMS
DHOWS
GHATS
GHEES
KHANS
PHONS
PHOTS
RHEAS
SHADS
SHAGS
SHAHS
SHAMS
SHANS
SHAYS
SHEDS
SHIES
SHIMS
SHINS
SHIPS
SHIVS
SHOES
SHOOS
SHOPS
SHOTS
SHOWS
SHULS
SHUNS
SHUTS
THAIS
THATS
THAWS
THEMS
THEWS
THINS
THOUS
THUDS
THUGS
THURS
WHAMS
WHATS
WHETS
WHEYS
WHIGS
WHIMS
WHIPS
WHIRS
WHITS
WHOPS
WHUPS

••H•S
ACHES
AGHAS
APHIS
ARHUS
ASHES
ATHOS
BAHTS
BUHLS
COHOS
EPHAS
ETHOS
HAHAS
HOHOS
JOHNS
TAHRS

•••HS
AMAHS
ANKHS
AYAHS
BATHS
BLAHS
FUCHS
GOTHS
HIGHS
LATHS
LOCHS
MATHS
MOTHS
MYTHS
NOAHS
OATHS
OPAHS
ORCHS
PATHS
PITHS
POOHS
RATHS
SACHS
SHAHS
SIGHS
SIKHS
SOPHS
TECHS
TETHS
YOGHS

H•T••
HATCH
HATED
HATER
HATES
HATLO
HETTY
HETUP
HITCH
HITIT
HITME
HITON
HITUP
HOTEL
HOTLY
HUTCH

H••T•
HADTO
HAFTS
HAITI
HALTS
HARTE
HARTS
HASTA
HASTE
HASTO
HASTY
HAUTE
HEATH
HEATS
HECTO
HEFTS
HEFTY
HEPTA
HERTZ
HESTS
HETTY
HEUTE
HILTS
HINTS
HIPTO
HOITY
HOLTZ
HOOTS
HOSTA
HOSTS
HOWTO
HUNTS
HURTS
HYATT

H•••T
HABIT
HADAT
HADNT
HADST
HASAT
HASNT
HAUNT
HEART
HECHT
HEIDT
HEIST
HELOT
HEMET
HERAT
HITIT
HOIST
HOLST
HORST
HURST
HYATT

•H•T•
CHATS
CHITA
CHITS
CHUTE
DHOTE
DHOTI
GHATS
PHOTO
PHOTS
PHYTO
RHETT
SHOTS
SHUTE
SHUTS
THATS
THETA
THOTH
WHATD
WHATS
WHETS
WHITE
WHITS

•H••T
CHANT
CHART
CHEAT
CHERT
CHEST
GHENT
GHOST
RHETT
SHAFT
SHALT
SHANT
SHEET
SHIFT
SHIRT
SHOAT
SHOOT
SHORT
SHOUT
SHUNT
THANT
THEFT
WHEAT
WHIST

••HT•
BAHTS
ICHTH
LAHTI
MEHTA

••H•T
ARHAT
NOHIT

•••HT
AUGHT
BIGHT
EIGHT
FIGHT
HECHT
LIGHT
MIGHT
NACHT
NIGHT
OUGHT
RASHT
RIGHT
SIGHT
TIGHT
WIGHT
YACHT

HU•••
HUBBA
HUBBY
HUFFS
HUFFY
HUGER
HULAS
HULCE
HULKS
HULLO
HULLS
HUMAN
HUMID
HUMOR
HUMPH
HUMPS
HUMPY
HUMUS
HUNAN
HUNCH
HUNKS
HUNTS
HURDY
HURLS
HURLY
HUROK
HURON
HURRY
HURST
HURTS
HUSKS
HUSKY
HUSSY
HUTCH

H•U••
HAUER
HAULM
HAULS
HAUNT
HAUSA
HAUTE
HEURE
HEUTE
HOUGH
HOUMA
HOUND
HOURI
HOURS
HOUSE

H••U•
HAFUN
HAGUE
HARUM
HETUP
HHOUR
HILUM
HITUP
HOCUS
HOHUM
HOKUM
HONUS
HOPUP
HORUS
HUMUS

H•••U
HAIKU
HINDU

•HU••
CHUBS
CHUCK
CHUFF
CHUGS
CHULA
CHUMP
CHUMS
CHUNG
CHUNK
CHURL
CHURN
CHUTE
KHUFU
RHUMB
SHUCK
SHULA
SHULS
SHUNS
SHUNT
SHUSH
SHUTE
SHUTS
THUDS
THUGS
THUJA
THULE
THUMB
THUMP
THUNK
THURS
UHURA
UHURU
WHUPS

•H•U•
CHAUD
GHOUL
HHOUR
RHEUM
SHAUN
SHOUT
SHRUB
SHRUG
THOUS
THRUM
UHAUL
UHHUH

•H••U
KHUFU
SHAMU
UHURU

••HU•
ANHUI
ARHUS
ASHUR
HOHUM
LEHUA
MOHUR
NAHUA
NAHUM
UHHUH

••H•U
NEHRU

•••HU
ELIHU
FICHU
MACHU
SADHU
WUSHU

H•V••
HAVEL
HAVEN
HAVER
HAVES
HAVOC
HAVRE
HIVED
HIVES
HOVEL
HOVER
HOVEY

H••V•
HALVE
HEAVE
HEAVY
HELVE
HERVE

•H•V•
CHEVY
CHIVE
CHIVY
SHAVE
SHIVA
SHIVS
SHOVE

••H•V
SCHAV

H•W••
HAWED
HAWKE
HAWKS
HAWSE
HEWED
HEWER
HOWDY
HOWIE
HOWLS
HOWSO
HOWTO

•H•W•
CHAWS
CHEWS
CHEWY
CHOWS
DHOWS
SHAWL
SHAWM
SHAWN
SHOWN
SHOWS
SHOWY
THAWS
THEWS

•H••W
SHREW
THREW
THROW

••HW•
SCHWA

••H•W
NOHOW
PSHAW

H•X••
HEXAD
HEXED
HEXER
HEXES
HEXYL
HOXIE

H•••X
HELIX
HYRAX

•H••X
PHLOX

HY•••
HYATT
HYDRA
HYDRO
HYENA
HYGRO
HYLAS
HYMAN
HYMNS
HYOID
HYPED
HYPER
HYPES
HYPHA
HYPNO
HYPOS
HYPSO
HYRAX
HYSON

H•Y••
HAYDN
HAYED
HAYEK
HAYES
HEYSE
HOYAS
HOYLE

H••Y•
HEXYL

H•••Y
HAIRY
HALEY
HAMMY
HANDY
HANKY
HAPLY
HAPPY
HARDY
HARPY
HARRY
HASTY
HEADY
HEALY
HEAVY
HEDGY
HEFTY
HENNY
HENRY
HERBY
HERKY
HETTY
HILLY
HINNY
HIPPY
HISSY
HOAGY
HOARY
HOBBY
HOITY
HOKEY
HOLEY
HOLLY
HOMEY
HONEY
HOOEY
HOOKY
HORSY
HOTLY
HOVEY
HOWDY
HUBBY
HUFFY
HUMPY
HURDY
HURLY
HURRY
HUSKY
HUSSY

•HY••
PHYCO
PHYFE
PHYLA
PHYLE
PHYLL
PHYSI
PHYTO
RHYME
SHYER
SHYLY
THYME
WHYME

•H•Y•
AHOYS
CHRYS
SHAYS
THEYD
WHEYS

•H••Y
CHARY
CHEVY
CHEWY
CHIVY
CHOKY
OHBOY
PHONY
SHADY
SHAKY
SHINY
SHOWY
SHYLY
WHINY

••HY•
ETHYL

••H•Y
ASHBY

•••HY
ARCHY
BATHY
BUSHY
CATHY
CUSHY
DUCHY
FISHY
GUSHY
ITCHY
KATHY
LEAHY
MASHY
MESHY
MOTHY
MUSHY
PITHY
PUSHY
RUSHY
SOPHY
VICHY
WASHY
WISHY

H•Z••
HAZED
HAZEL
HAZER
HAZES

H••Z•
HERZL

H•••Z
HAFIZ
HEINZ

HEJAZ
HERTZ
HOLTZ

•H•Z•
GHAZI
RHIZO

IA•••
IAMBI
IAMBS
IATRO
IATRY

I•A••
IBARS
ICAHN
IDAHO
IMAGE
IMAGO
IMAMS
INALL
INANE
INAPT
INARI
INAWE
IPANA
IPASS
IRADE
IRANI
IRAQI
IRATE
ISAAC
ISAMU
ITALO
ITALS
ITALY
IVANA
IZAAK
IZARD
IZARS

I••A•
IBEAM
ICEAX
IDEAL
IDEAS
ILIAC
ILIAD
INBAD
INCAN
INCAS
INLAW
INLAY
IOTAS
IOWAN
ISAAC
ISLAM
IXNAY
IZAAK
IZBAS

I•••A
IBIZA
ICOSA
ILONA
INDIA
INDRA
INFRA
INTRA
IONIA
IPANA
IRINA
IVANA

•IA••
BIALY
DIALS
DIANA
DIANE
DIARY
DIAZO
FIATS
GIANT
KIANG
LIANA
LIANE
LIANG
LIARD
LIARS
MIAMI
MIAOW
PIANO
RIALS
RIANT
RIATA
SIALS
TIANT
TIARA
VIALS
VIAND

•I•A•
AIDAN
AIMAT
BIHAR
BINAL
CIGAR
DINAH
DINAR
DIRAC
DIVAN
DIVAS
FILAR
FINAL
HIRAM
JIHAD
KIVAS
LILAC
LIMAS
LIRAS
MICAH
MICAS
MIDAS
MIKAN
MILAN
MIMAS
MINAS
MIZAR
NICAD
NINAS
NIPAS
NIPAT
NISAN
NIVAL
NIZAM
PICAS
PIKAS
PILAF
PILAR
PIMAS
PIPAL
PISAN
PITAS
RIVAL
RIYAL
SILAS
SINAI
SISAL
SITAR
SIVAN
TIDAL
TIKAL
TIRAN
TITAN
VICAR
VIDAL
VILAS
VINAS
VIRAL
VISAS
VITAE
VITAL
VITAS
WIGAN

•I••A
AISHA
BIOTA
CIERA
CILIA
CILLA
CIRCA
DIANA
DICTA
DITKA
FINCA
FIONA
FIRMA
GILDA
GINZA
HILDA
JIDDA
KINDA
KIOGA
KIOWA
KISKA
LIANA
LIBRA
LIBYA
LICIA
LINDA
LIVIA
MICRA
MISHA
MISSA
NINJA
PIETA
PILEA
PINNA
PINTA
PINZA
PIPPA
PITTA
PIURA
PIZZA
RIATA
RIOJA
SIDEA
SIDRA
SIENA
SIGMA
SILVA
SIMBA
SITKA
TIARA
TIBIA
UINTA
VILLA
VILMA
VIOLA
VIRGA
VIRNA
VISTA
WICCA
WILLA
WILMA
WIRRA
ZIZKA

••IA•
ALIAS
APIAN
ARIAN
ARIAS
ASIAN
AVIAN
AXIAL
BRIAN
BRIAR
CHIAS
ELIAS
ENIAC
EVIAN
FRIAR
ILIAC
ILIAD
NAIAD
PHIAL
PRIAM
TRIAD
TRIAL
UMIAK
URIAH
URIAL

••I•A
AGITA
AKIRA
AKITA
ALIDA
AMIGA
ANIMA
ANITA
ARICA
AVILA
BAIZA
CEIBA
CHIBA
CHINA
CHITA
CNIDA
DAIWA
DRINA
DVINA
EDINA
ELIZA
ERICA
ERIKA
ERISA
EVITA
HAIFA
IBIZA
IRINA
LAIKA
LEICA
LEILA
LUISA
MBIRA
MOIRA
NAIRA
ORIYA
OUIDA
OUIJA
PRIMA
RAISA
SAIGA
SHIVA
SLIWA
SPICA
TAIGA
UTICA
VOILA

•••IA
AECIA
ATRIA
BAHIA
CARIA
CELIA
CERIA
CILIA
COBIA
CURIA
DACIA
ENTIA
FERIA
FOLIA
INDIA
IONIA
JULIA
LAMIA
LICIA
LIVIA
LOGIA
LUCIA
LURIA
LYDIA
MANIA
MARIA
MEDIA
NADIA
NORIA
NUBIA
OMNIA
OSSIA
OSTIA
PAVIA
PODIA
REGIA
RETIA
SEPIA
SOFIA
SONIA
STRIA
SYRIA
TALIA
TIBIA
VARIA
XENIA
ZAMIA

IB•••
IBARS
IBEAM
IBERT
IBIZA
IBSEN

I•B••
IMBUE
INBAD
INBED
INBIG
IZBAS

I••B•
IAMBI
IAMBS

•IB••
BIBBS
BIBLE
FIBER
FIBRE
FIBRO
GIBBS
GIBED
GIBER
GIBES
JIBED
JIBES
LIBBY
LIBEL
LIBRA
LIBRE
LIBYA
RIBBY
SIBYL
TIBBS
TIBER
TIBET
TIBIA
VIBES
ZIBET

•I•B•
BIBBS
BILBO
BIXBY
DIGBY
GIBBS
KIRBY
LIBBY
LIMBI
LIMBO
LIMBS
NIMBI
NIMBY
NIOBE
RIBBY
RIGBY
SIMBA
SITBY
TIBBS

•I••B
SIDEB

••IB•
ALIBI
BRIBE
CEIBA
CHIBA
CRIBS
DRIBS
ORIBI
TRIBE

••I•B
CLIMB

•••IB
ADLIB
CARIB
NAMIB
SAHIB
SQUIB

IC•••
ICAHN
ICEAX
ICEIN
ICENI
ICERS
ICEUP
ICHOR
ICHTH
ICIER
ICILY
ICING
ICKES
ICONO
ICONS
ICOSA
ICOSI
ICTUS

I•C••
INCAN
INCAS
INCOG
INCUR
INCUS
ITCHY

I•••C
ILIAC
INDIC
IODIC
IONIC
ISAAC
ISTIC

•IC••
DICED
DICER
DICES
DICEY
DICHO
DICKS
DICKY
DICOT
DICTA
DICTS
DICTU
FICHE
FICHU
FICUS
HICKS
KICKS
KICKY
LICIA
LICIT
LICKS
MICAH
MICAS
MICRA
MICRO
NICAD
NICER
NICHE
NICKS
NICOL
PICAS
PICKS
PICKY
PICOT
PICRO
PICTS
PICUL
RICCI
RICED
RICER
RICES
RICHE
RICKI
RICKS
RICKY
RICOH
TICKS
TICKY
VICAR
VICES
VICHY
VICKI
VICKS
WICCA
WICKS

•I•C•
AITCH
BIRCH
CINCH
CINCO
CIRCA
CIRCE
CIRCS
CISCO
DISCO
DISCS
DITCH
FILCH
FINCA
FINCH
FISCS
FITCH
HITCH
MILCH
MINCE
MITCH
NIECE
PIECE
PINCE
PINCH
PISCI
PISCO
PITCH
RICCI
SINCE
TINCT
VINCE
VINCI
WICCA
WILCO
WINCE
WINCH
WITCH
ZILCH
ZINCS

•I••C
CIVIC
DIRAC
HIGHC
LILAC
MIMIC

••IC•
ALICE
AMICE
ARICA
BRICE
BRICK
BUICK
CHICK
CHICO
CLICK
CRICK
DEICE
EDICT
EPICS
ERICA
ERICH
EVICT
FLICK
FRICK
JUICE
JUICY
KNICK
LAICS
LEICA
ONICE
PRICE
PRICK
PRICY
QUICK
REICH
SLICE
SLICK
SNICK
SPICA
SPICE
SPICY
STICH
STICK
THICK
TRICE
TRICK
TWICE
URICH
UTICA
VOICE
VOICI
WHICH

••I•C
ENIAC
EPISC
ILIAC

•••IC
AGRIC
ANTIC
ASDIC
ASPIC
ATTIC
AURIC
AZOIC
BARIC
BASIC
BORIC
CIVIC
COMIC
CONIC
CUBIC
CYNIC
DORIC
EDDIC
ETHIC
FOLIC
FSLIC
GENIC
HELIC
INDIC
IODIC
IONIC
ISTIC
LOGIC
LUDIC
LYRIC
MAGIC
MALIC
MEDIC
MELIC
MESIC
MIMIC
MUSIC
OLEIC
OPTIC
OSMIC
OSRIC
PANIC
PUNIC
PYRIC
RELIC
RUNIC
SALIC
SONIC
STOIC
SUBIC
TELIC
TONIC
TOPIC
TORIC
TOXIC
TUNIC
UGRIC
VATIC
VEDIC
XERIC

ID•••
IDAHO
IDEAL
IDEAS
IDEST
IDIOM
IDIOT
IDLED
IDLER
IDLES
IDOLS
IDYLL
IDYLS

I•D••
INDEF
INDEX
INDIA
INDIC
INDIE
INDIO
INDIV
INDRA
INDRI
INDUS
IODIC

I••D•
IMIDE
IMIDO
IRADE
IRIDO

I•••D
IDLED
ILIAD
INBAD
INBED
INKED
IRKED
IVIED
IZARD

•ID••
AIDAN
AIDED
AIDES
BIDDY
BIDED
BIDEN
BIDES
BIDON
BIDUP
CIDER
DIDIN
DIDNT
DIDOS
DIDST
DIDUP
EIDER
FIDEL
GIDDY
HIDER
HIDES
JIDDA
KIDDO
KIDDY
LIDDY
LIDOS
MIDAS
MIDDY
MIDGE
MIDIS
MIDST
NIDES
NIDRE
NIDUS
RIDER
RIDES
RIDGE
RIDGY
RIDOF
SIDEA
SIDEB
SIDED
SIDER
SIDES
SIDHE
SIDLE
SIDON
SIDRA
TIDAL
TIDED
TIDES
VIDAL
VIDEO
VIDOR
WIDEN
WIDER
WIDOW
WIDTH

•I•D•
BIDDY
BINDS
BIRDS
BIRDY
CINDY
DIODE
FINDS
GIDDY
GILDA
GILDS
GIRDS
HILDA
HINDI
HINDS
HINDU
JIDDA
KIDDO
KIDDY
KINDA
KINDS
LIDDY
LINDA
LINDY
MIDDY
MINDS
MINDY
MISDO
PIEDS
RINDS
TILDE
WILDE
WILDS
WINDS
WINDY

•I••D
AIDED
AILED
AIMED
AIRED
BIDED
BIFID
BIKED
BIPED
BIPOD
CITED
DICED
DIKED
DIMED
DINED
DIVED
FIELD
FIEND
FIFED
FILED
FINED
FIORD
FIRED
FIXED
GIBED
HIKED
HIRED
HIVED
JIBED
JIHAD
JIVED
KITED
LIARD
LIKED
LIKUD
LIMED
LINED
LIPID
LIVED
LIVID
MIKED
MIMED
MINED
MIRED
MIXED
NICAD
NIXED
OILED
PIKED
PILED
PINED
PIPED
RICED
RIGID
RILED
RIMED
RIVED
SIDED
SIRED
SITED
SIXED
SIZED
TIDED
TILED
TIMED
TIMID
TINED
TIRED
VIAND
VINED
VIRID
VIVID
WIELD
WILED
WINED
WIPED
WIRED
WIVED
YIELD

••ID•
ABIDE
ACIDS
ACIDY
ALIDA
AMIDE
ASIDE
AZIDE
BRIDE
BSIDE
CHIDE
CNIDA
ELIDE
GLIDE
GRIDS
GUIDE
GUIDO
HEIDI
HEIDT
IMIDE
IMIDO
IRIDO
MAIDS
OUIDA
OXIDE
PRIDE
QUIDS
RAIDS
SKIDS
SLIDE
SNIDE
TEIDE
VEIDT
VOIDS

••I•D
APIED
BAIRD
BLIND
BUILD
CHILD
CRIED
DRIED
FLIED
FRIED
GRIND
GUILD
ILIAD
IVIED
LAIRD
NAIAD
PLIED
PRIED
SHIED
SKIED
SPIED
TBIRD
THIRD
TRIAD
TRIED
WEIRD

•••ID
ACRID
ALGID
APHID
AROID
AVOID
BIFID
BOVID
BRAID
CANID
CUPID
DAVID
DROID
DRUID
ELCID
FELID
FETID
FLUID
FROID
GADID
GELID
GEOID
HASID
HUMID
HYOID
LIPID
LIVID
LUCID
LURID
OOTID
OVOID
PAVID
PLAID
QUAID
RABID
RANID
RAPID
REBID
REDID
RIGID
SAPID
SOLID
SQUID
STAID
TEPID
TIMID
TUMID
UNBID
UNDID
URSID
VALID
VAPID
VIRID
VIVID
ZOOID

I•E••
IBEAM
IBERT
ICEAX
ICEIN
ICENI
ICERS
ICEUP
IDEAL
IDEAS
IDEST
ILENE
INEPT
INERT
IRENE
ISERE
ITEMS

I••E•
IBSEN
ICIER
ICKES
IDLED
IDLER
IDLES
IGNES
ILLER
IMPEI
IMPEL
INBED
INDEF
INDEX
INFER
INGER
INKED
INKER
INLET
INNER
INREM
INSET
INTEL
INTER
IRKED
IRREG
ISLES
ISLET
ISLEY
ISSEI
IVIED
IVIES

I•••E
ILENE
IMAGE
IMBUE
IMIDE
IMINE
INANE
INAWE
INDIE
INGLE
INKLE
INURE
INUSE
IRADE
IRATE
IRENE
ISERE
ISSUE
ISTLE
ITSME

•IE••
CIERA
DIEGO
DIEMS
DIENE
DIETS
EIEIO
FIEFS
FIELD
FIEND
FIERY
HIERO
LIEGE
LIEIN
LIENS
LIETO
LIEUS
LIEUT
MIENS
NIECE
NIELS
PIECE
PIEDS
PIERS
PIETA
PIETY
RIELS
SIEGE
SIENA
SIEPI
SIETE
SIEUR
SIEVE
TIEGS
TIEIN
TIERS
TIEUP
VIEJO
VIERS
VIEWS
WIELD
WIEST
YIELD

•I•E•
AIDED
AIDES
AIKEN
AILED
AILER
AILEY
AIMED
AIMEE
AIMER
AIRED
AIRES
BIDED
BIDEN
BIDES
BIKED
BIKEL
BIKER
BIKES
BINES
BINET
BIPED
BISES
BITER
BITES
BIZET
CIDER
CINES
CIRES
CITED
CITER
CITES
CIVET
DICED
DICER
DICES
DICEY
DIKED
DIKES
DIMED
DIMES
DINED
DINER
DINES
DIRER
DIVED
DIVER
DIVES
DIZEN
EIDER
EIGEN
FIBER
FIDEL
FIFED
FIFER
FIFES
FILED
FILER
FILES
FILET
FINED
FINER
FINES
FIRED
FIRER
FIRES
FIVER
FIVES
FIXED
FIXER
FIXES
GIBED
GIBER
GIBES
GILES
GIMEL
GIVEN
GIVER
GIVES
HIDER
HIDES
HIKED
HIKER
HIKES
HINES
HIRED
HIRER
HIRES
HIVED
HIVES
JIBED
JIBES
JIVED
JIVER
JIVES
JIVEY
KILEY
KINER
KITED
KITER
KITES
LIBEL
LIGER
LIKED
LIKEN
LIKES
LIMED
LIMEN
LIMES
LINED
LINEN
LINER
LINES
LITER

LITES LIVED LIVEN LIVER LIVES MIKED MIKES MILER MILES MIMED MIMEO MIMER MIMES MINED MINEO MINER MINES MIRED MIRES MISER MITER MITES MIXED MIXER MIXES NICER NIDES NIGEL NIGER NIKES NILES NIMES NINER NINES NISEI NITER NITES NIVEN NIXED NIXES NIZER OILED OILER PIKED PIKER PIKES PILEA PILED PILEI PILES PINED PINES PINEY PIPED PIPER PIPES PIXEL RICED RICER RICES RIDER RIDES RIFER RIGEL RIKER RILED RILES RILEY RIMED RIMES RIPEN RIPER RISEN RISER

RISES RITES RIVED RIVEN RIVER RIVES RIVET SIDEA SIDEB SIDED SIDER SIDES SIKES SILEX SINES SINEW SIRED SIREN SIRES SITED SITES SIXED SIXES SIZED SIZER SIZES TIBER TIBET TIDED TIDES TIGER TILED TILER TILES TIMED TIMER TIMES TIMEX TINED TINES TIRED TIRES TITER VIBES VICES VIDEO VILER VINED VINES VIPER VIREO VISES VIXEN WIDEN WIDER WILED WILES WILEY WINED WINES WIPED WIPER WIPES WIRED WIRER WIRES WISER WIVED WIVES WIZEN YIKES YIPES ZIBET

•I••E

AIMEE AINGE AISLE AISNE BIBLE BILGE BINGE BIOME BITTE CIRCE DIANE DIENE DINGE DIODE DIONE DIRGE DISME DIXIE FIBRE FICHE FILLE FISKE GIGUE GIJOE GIMME HINGE HITME KINTE LIANE LIBRE LIEGE LILLE LISLE LISSE LITHE LITRE LIVRE MIDGE MILLE MILNE MINCE MITRE NICHE NIDRE NIECE NIOBE NITRE NIXIE PIECE PINCE PIQUE PISTE PIXIE RICHE RIDGE RIFLE RILKE RILLE RINSE SIDHE SIDLE SIEGE SIETE SIEVE SIGNE SINCE SINGE TILDE TINGE TITHE TITLE VILLE VINCE VITAE VIVRE WILDE WINCE WINZE WITHE WITTE

••IE•

ADIEU ALIEN AMIES APIED ARIEL ARIES BRIEF BRIER BRIES CHIEF CHIEN CRIED CRIER CRIES DRIED DRIER DRIES ELIEL ERIES FLIED FLIER FLIES FRIED FRIER FRIES GRIEF GRIEG GRIER ICIER IVIED IVIES KLIEG OBIES OKIES ORIEL OSIER PLIED PLIES PRIED PRIER PRIES QUIEN QUIET SHIED SHIER SHIES SKIED SKIER SKIES SLIER SPIED SPIEL SPIES STIES THIEF TRIED TRIER TRIES URIEL WRIER

••I•E

ABIDE ADIGE AFIRE AGILE ALICE ALIKE ALINE ALIVE AMICE AMIDE AMINE ANIME ANISE ARISE ASIDE ATIVE AZIDE AZINE BAIZE BEIGE BOISE BOITE BRIBE BRICE BRIDE BRINE BRITE BSIDE CAINE CHIDE CHILE CHIME CHINE CHIVE CLIME CLINE CLIVE CRIME DEICE DRIVE EDILE ELIDE ELISE ELITE EMILE EXILE FAIRE GLIDE GRIME GRIPE GUIDE GUILE GUISE HAILE HEINE IMIDE IMINE JAIME JUICE KLINE KNIFE KOINE LAINE LOIRE LUISE MAINE MAIZE MOIRE NAIVE NEIGE NOIRE NOISE ODILE OGIVE OLIVE ONICE OPINE OVINE OXIDE PAIGE PAINE PHILE POISE PRICE PRIDE PRIME PRIZE QUIRE QUITE RAISE RHINE SEINE SEIZE SHINE SHIRE SKIVE SLICE SLIDE SLIME SMILE SMITE SNIDE SNIPE SPICE SPIKE SPILE SPINE SPIRE SPITE STILE STIPE SUITE SWINE SWIPE TAINE TEIDE THINE TOILE TRIBE TRICE TRIKE TRINE TRIPE TRITE TWICE TWINE UNITE UTILE VOICE VOILE WAITE WAIVE WHILE WHINE WHITE WRITE ZAIRE

•••IE

ABBIE ADDIE AERIE AGGIE ALFIE ALLIE ANDIE ANGIE ANNIE ARNIE ARTIE AUDIE BASIE BELIE BOGIE BOWIE CELIE CURIE CUTIE DAVIE DIXIE DOBIE DOGIE EDDIE EERIE EFFIE ELLIE ELSIE ERNIE EUBIE EYDIE EYRIE FACIE GENIE HENIE HOWIE HOXIE INDIE JAMIE JANIE JODIE JOLIE JULIE KATIE KYRIE LOUIE LUCIE LURIE MAMIE MARIE MAXIE MCVIE MOVIE MOXIE NIXIE OAKIE OLDIE OLLIE OSSIE OZZIE PIXIE PYXIE RAMIE RETIE ROSIE ROXIE SADIE SATIE SUSIE TOTIE UNTIE WYLIE YALIE ZOWIE

IF•••

IFNOT

I•F••

INFER INFIN INFIX INFRA INFUN

I•••F

INDEF

•IF••

BIFFS BIFFY BIFID FIFED FIFER FIFES FIFTH FIFTY GIFTS HIFIS JIFFY LIFTS MIFFS MIFFY NIFTY RIFER RIFFI RIFFS RIFLE RIFTS SIFTS TIFFS

•I•F•

BIFFS BIFFY FIEFS JIFFY MIFFS MIFFY RIFFI RIFFS TIFFS

•I••F

PILAF RIDOF

••IF•

ALIFS CLIFF CLIFT COIFS DEIFY DRIFT EDIFY GRIFT HAIFA KNIFE REIFY SCIFI SHIFT SKIFF SNIFF SPIFF STIFF SWIFT UNIFY WAIFS WHIFF

••I•F

BRIEF CHIEF CLIFF GRIEF SKIFF SNIFF SPIFF STIFF THIEF WHIFF

•••IF

CALIF MOTIF SERIF

IG•••

IGLOO IGLUS IGNES

I•G••

ILGWU INGER INGLE INGOT

I••G•

IMAGE IMAGO INIGO

I•••G

ICING INBIG INCOG IRREG

•IG••

BIGHT BIGON BIGOS BIGOT CIGAR DIGBY DIGIN DIGIT DIGUP EIGEN EIGHT FIGHT GIGOT GIGUE HIGHC HIGHS LIGER LIGHT LIGNI LIGNO MIGHT NIGEL NIGER NIGHT PIGGY RIGBY RIGEL RIGGS RIGHT RIGID RIGOR RIGUP SIGHS SIGHT SIGIL SIGMA SIGNE SIGNO SIGNS TIGER TIGHT UIGUR VIGIL VIGOR WIGAN WIGGY WIGHT ZIGGY

•I•G•

AINGE BILGE BILGY BINGE BINGO BINGS DIEGO DINGE DINGO DINGS DINGY DIRGE HINGE JINGO KINGS KIOGA LIEGE LINGO MIDGE MINGS OINGO PIGGY PINGO PINGS RIDGE RIDGY RIGGS RINGO RINGS SIEGE SINGE SINGS TIEGS TINGE TINGS VINGT VIRGA VIRGO WIGGY WINGS XINGU ZIGGY ZINGS ZINGY

•I••G

KIANG LIANG

••IG•

ADIGE ALIGN AMIGA AMIGO BEIGE BLIGH BRIGS DEIGN FEIGN FRIGG GRIGS HEIGH INIGO LEIGH LUIGI NEIGE NEIGH OLIGO PAIGE PRIGS REIGN SAIGA SLIGO SWIGS TAIGA THIGH TRIGS TWIGS VSIGN WEIGH WHIGS

••I•G

ACING AGING APING AWING AXING BEING BOING BRING CHING CLING CUING DOING DYING EKING EWING FLING FRIGG GOING GRIEG ICING KLIEG LAING LYING ORING OWING RUING SLING STING SUING SWING THING TYING USING VYING WRING

•••IG

CRAIG GRAIG INBIG MRBIG NAVIG RELIG SOBIG SPRIG UNRIG VARIG ZELIG ZWEIG

I•H••

ICHOR ICHTH

I••H•

ICAHN IDAHO ITCHY

I•••H

ICHTH IRISH

•IH••

BIHAR JIHAD NIHIL

•I•H•

AISHA BIGHT DICHO EIGHT FICHE FICHU FIGHT FISHY HIGHC HIGHS LIGHT LITHE LITHO MIGHT MINHO MISHA NICHE NIGHT PITHS PITHY RICHE RIGHT RISHI SIDHE SIGHS SIGHT SIKHS TIGHT TITHE VICHY WIGHT WISHY WITHE

•I••H

AITCH BIRCH BIRTH CINCH DINAH DITCH FIFTH FILCH FILTH FINCH FIRTH FITCH GIRTH HITCH MICAH MILCH MIRTH MITCH NINTH PINCH PITCH RICOH SIXTH TILTH WIDTH WINCH WITCH ZILCH

••IH•

ELIHU

••I•H

AMISH APISH ARITH BLIGH BRITH EDITH ERICH FAITH HEIGH IRISH KEITH KNISH LEIGH LEITH NAISH NEIGH REICH SHISH SMITH STICH SWISH THIGH TRISH URIAH URICH WEIGH WHICH

I•I••

IBIZA ICIER ICILY ICING IDIOM IDIOT ILIAC ILIAD ILION ILIUM IMIDE IMIDO IMINE IMINO INIGO INION INITS IRIDO IRINA IRISH IVIED IVIES IVINS IXION

I••I•

ICEIN IMMIX INBIG INDIA INDIC INDIE INDIO INDIV INFIN INFIX INUIT IODIC IONIA IONIC IQUIT IRVIN IRWIN ISTIC IZMIR IZMIT

I•••I

IAMBI ICENI ICOSI IMPEI INARI INDRI IRANI IRAQI ISSEI

•I•I•

BIFID CILIA CIVIC CIVIL DIDIN DIGIN DIGIT DIXIE DIXIT EIEIO FINIS FITIN FIXIT HIFIS HITIT KILIM KIRIN KIWIS LICIA LICIT LIEIN LIMIT LIPID LIVIA LIVID MIDIS MIMIC MINIM MINIS NIHIL NIXIE PIPIT PIXIE RIGID SIGIL SITIN TIBIA TIEIN TIKIS TIMID TIPIN TITIS VIGIL VIRID VISIT VIVID ZITIS

•I••I

AIOLI CIRRI HINDI JINNI LIGNI LIMBI LIPPI MIAMI MILLI MISTI MITZI NIKKI NIMBI NISEI NITTI PILEI PIPPI PISCI RICCI RICKI RIFFI RIKKI RISHI SIEPI SINAI TIKKI TIPPI VICKI VIKKI VILLI VINCI

••II•

CCIII CDIII CLIII CMIII CVIII CXIII DCIII DLIII DVIII DXIII LVIII LXIII MCIII MDIII MLIII MMIII MVIII MXIII XCIII XLIII XVIII XXIII

••I•I

ALIBI BLINI CCIII CDIII CHILI CLIII CMIII CVIII CXIII DCIII DLIII DVIII DXIII HAITI HEIDI LUIGI LVIII LXIII MCIII MDIII MEIJI MLIII MMIII MVIII MXIII ORIBI SCIFI TRINI VOICI XCIII XLIII XVIII XXIII

•••II

ACTII ASCII CCCII CCIII CCLII CCVII CCXII CDIII CDLII CDVII CDXII CLIII CLVII CLXII CMIII CMLII CMVII CMXII CVIII CXCII CXIII CXLII CXVII CXXII DCCII DCIII DCLII DCVII DCXII DLIII DLVII DLXII DVIII DXCII DXIII DXLII DXVII DXXII GENII LVIII LXIII LXVII LXXII MCCII MCDII MCIII MCLII MCMII MCVII MCXII MDCII MDIII MDLII MDVII MDXII MLIII MLVII MLXII MMCII MMDII MMIII MMLII MMMII MMVII MMXII MVIII MXCII MXIII MXLII MXMII MXVII MXXII QBVII RADII TORII XCIII XCVII XLIII XLVII XVIII XXIII XXVII XXXII

•IJ••

BIJOU DIJON GIJOE

•I•J•

NINJA RIOJA VIEJO

••IJ•

MEIJI OUIJA

I•K••

ICKES INKED INKER INKLE IRKED

I•••K

IZAAK

•IK••

AIKEN BIKED BIKEL BIKER BIKES DIKED DIKES HIKED HIKER HIKES LIKED LIKEN LIKES LIKUD MIKAN MIKED MIKES NIKES NIKKI NIKKO NIKON PIKAS PIKED PIKER PIKES RIKER RIKKI SIKES

SIKHS
TIKAL
TIKIS
TIKKI
VIKKI
YIKES

•I•K•
BILKO
BILKS
DICKS
DICKY
DINKS
DINKY
DIRKS
DISKS
DITKA
FINKS
FISKE
HICKS
JINKS
KICKS
KICKY
KINKS
KINKY
KIRKS
KISKA
LICKS
LINKS
MILKS
MILKY
MINKS
NICKS
NIKKI
NIKKO
OINKS
PICKS
PICKY
PINKS
PINKY
RICKI
RICKS
RICKY
RIKKI
RILKE
RINKS
RINKY
RISKS
RISKY
SILKS
SILKY
SINKS
SITKA
TICKS
TICKY
TIKKI
VICKI
VICKS
VIKKI
WICKS
WINKS
ZIZKA

•I••K
KIOSK
MINSK
PINSK

••IK•
ALIKE
EFIKS
ERIKA
HAIKS
HAIKU
LAIKA
SEIKO
SPIKE
SPIKY
TRIKE

••I•K
BLINK
BRICK
BRINK
BRISK
BUICK
CHICK
CHINK
CLICK
CLINK
CRICK
DRINK
FLICK
FRICK
FRISK
KNICK
PLINK
PRICK
PRINK
QUICK
QUIRK
REINK
SHIRK
SKINK
SLICK
SLINK
SMIRK
SNICK
STICK
STINK
THICK
THINK
TRICK
UMIAK
WHISK

•••IK
BATIK
LUNIK
RUBIK
RURIK
SHEIK
YUPIK

IL•••
ILENE
ILGWU
ILIAC
ILIAD
ILION
ILIUM
ILLER
ILLUS
ILONA

I•L••
IDLED
IDLER
IDLES
IGLOO
IGLUS
ILLER
ILLUS
INLAW
INLAY
INLET
ISLAM
ISLES
ISLET
ISLEY

I••L•
ICILY
IDOLS
IDYLL
IDYLS
IMPLY
INALL
INGLE
INKLE
ISTLE
ITALO
ITALS
ITALY

I•••L
IDEAL
IDYLL
IMPEL
INALL
INTEL

•IL••
AILED
AILER
AILEY
BILBO
BILGE
BILGY
BILKO
BILKS
BILLS
BILLY
CILIA
CILLA
DILLS
DILLY
FILAR
FILCH
FILED
FILER
FILES
FILET
FILLE
FILLS
FILLY
FILMS
FILMY
FILTH
FILUM
GILDA
GILDS
GILES
GILLS
GILTS
HILDA
HILLS
HILLY
HILTS
HILUM
JILTS
KILEY
KILIM
KILLS
KILLY
KILNS
KILOS
KILTS
LILAC
LILLE
LILTS
MILAN
MILCH
MILER
MILES
MILKS
MILKY
MILLE
MILLI
MILLS
MILNE
MILOS
MILTS
MILTY
NILES
NILLY
NILOT
OILED
OILER
PILAF
PILAR
PILEA
PILED
PILEI
PILES
PILLS
PILOT
PILUM
PILUS
RILED
RILES
RILEY
RILKE
RILLE
RILLS
SILAS
SILEX
SILKS
SILKY
SILLS
SILLY
SILOS
SILTS
SILTY
SILVA
TILDE
TILED
TILER
TILES
TILLS
TILLY
TILTH
TILTS
VILAS
VILER
VILLA
VILLE
VILLI
VILMA
WILCO
WILDE
WILDS
WILED
WILES
WILEY
WILLA
WILLS
WILLY
WILMA
WILTS
ZILCH
ZILLS

•I•L•
AIOLI
AISLE
BIALY
BIBLE
BILLS
BILLY
BIRLS
CILLA
DIALS
DILLS
DILLY
DIMLY
DIPLO
FIELD
FILLE
FILLS
FILLY
FITLY
GILLS
GIRLS
GIRLY
HILLS
HILLY
KILLS
KILLY
LILLE
LISLE
MILLE
MILLI
MILLS
NIELS
NILLY
PILLS
RIALS
RIELS
RIFLE
RILLE
RILLS
SIALS
SIDLE
SILLS
SILLY
TILLS
TILLY
TITLE
VIALS
VILLA
VILLE
VILLI
VIOLA
VIOLS
WIELD
WILLA
WILLS
WILLY
YIELD
ZILLS

•I••L
BIKEL
BINAL
CIVIL
FIDEL
FINAL
GIMEL
LIBEL
NICOL
NIGEL
NIHIL
NIVAL
PICUL
PIPAL
PIXEL
RIGEL
RIVAL
RIYAL
SIBYL
SIGIL
SISAL
TIDAL
TIKAL
VIDAL
VIGIL
VINYL
VIRAL
VITAL

••IL•
AGILE
ANILS
ARILS
ATILT
AVILA
AXILS
BAILS
BOILS
BRILL
BUILD
BUILT
CEILS
CHILD
CHILE
CHILI
CHILL
COILS
DAILY
DOILY
DRILL
EDILE
EMILE
EMILY
EVILS
EXILE
FAILS
FOILS
FRILL
GRILL
GUILD
GUILE
GUILT
HAILE
HAILS
ICILY
JAILS
KRILL
LEILA
MAILS
MOILS
NAILS
NEILL
NOILS
ODILE
PAILS
PHILE
PHILO
POILS
POILU
QUILL
QUILP
QUILT
RAILS
ROILS
ROILY
SAILS
SHILL
SKILL
SMILE
SOILS
SPILE
SPILL
SPILT
STILE
STILL
STILT
SWILL
TAILS
TBILL
THILL
TOILE
TOILS
TRILL
TWILL
UTILE
VEILS
VOILA
VOILE
WAILS
WEILL
WHILE

••I•L
ARIEL
AXIAL
BGIRL
BRILL
CHILL
DRILL
ELIEL
FRILL
FRIML
GRILL
KRILL
NEILL
ORIEL
PHIAL
QUILL
SHILL
SKILL
SKIRL
SPIEL
SPILL
STILL
SWILL
SWIRL
TBILL
THILL
TRIAL
TRILL
TWILL
TWIRL
URIAL
URIEL
WEILL
WHIRL

•••IL
ABOIL
ADVIL
ANVIL
APRIL
ARGIL
AUXIL
AVAIL
AVRIL
BASIL
BRAIL
BROIL
CAVIL
CECIL
CIVIL
CYRIL
DEVIL
DRAIL
EMAIL
ERVIL
FLAIL
FRAIL
FUSIL
GRAIL
MOBIL
NEVIL
NIHIL
ONEIL
PERIL
PUPIL
QUAIL
REOIL
SIGIL
SNAIL
SPOIL
SYBIL
TAMIL
TRAIL
UNTIL
VIGIL
ZORIL

IM•••
IMAGE
IMAGO
IMAMS
IMBUE
IMIDE
IMIDO
IMINE
IMINO
IMMIX
IMPEI
IMPEL
IMPLY

I•M••
IAMBI
IAMBS
IMMIX
IZMIR
IZMIT

I••M•
IMAMS
ISAMU
ITEMS
ITSME

I•••M
IBEAM
IDIOM
ILIUM
INREM
ISLAM

•IM••
AIMAT
AIMED
AIMEE
AIMER
AIMTO
DIMED
DIMES
DIMLY
GIMEL
GIMME
GIMPS
GIMPY
JIMMY
LIMAS
LIMBI
LIMBO
LIMBS
LIMED
LIMEN
LIMES
LIMIT
LIMNS
LIMON
LIMOS
LIMPS
MIMAS
MIMED
MIMEO
MIMER
MIMES
MIMIC
MIMSY
NIMBI
NIMBY
NIMES
NIMOY
PIMAS
RIMED
RIMES
SIMBA
SIMMS
SIMON
SIMPS
TIMED
TIMER
TIMES
TIMEX
TIMID
TIMMY
TIMON
TIMOR
WIMPS
WIMPY

•I•M•
BIOME
DIEMS
DISME
FILMS
FILMY
FIRMA
FIRMS
GIMME
GIZMO
HITME
JIMMY
MIAMI
PISMO
SIGMA
SIMMS
SIXMO
TIMMY
VILMA
WILMA

•I••M
FILUM
HILUM
HIRAM
KILIM
MINIM
NIZAM
PILUM

••IM•
ANIMA
ANIME
BLIMP
BRIMS
CHIME
CHIMP
CLIMB
CLIME
CRIME
CRIMP
FRIML
GLIMS
GRIME
GRIMM
GRIMY
JAIME
KLIMT
PRIMA
PRIME
PRIMO
PRIMP
PRIMS
REIMS
SHIMS
SKIMP
SKIMS
SLIME
SLIMS
SLIMY
SWIMS
TRIMS
WHIMS

••I•M
ARIUM
AXIOM
DEISM
GRIMM
IDIOM
ILIUM
ODIUM
OPIUM
PRIAM
PRISM
SEISM

•••IM
BEDIM
CHAIM
CLAIM
DENIM
HAKIM
KILIM
MAXIM
MINIM
PURIM
REAIM
SCRIM
VADIM

IN•••
INALL
INANE
INAPT
INARI
INAWE
INBAD
INBED
INBIG
INCAN
INCAS
INCOG
INCUR
INCUS
INDEF
INDEX
INDIA
INDIC
INDIE
INDIO
INDIV
INDRA
INDRI
INDUS
INEPT
INERT
INFER
INFIN
INFIX
INFRA
INFUN
INGER
INGLE
INGOT
INIGO
INION
INITS
INKED
INKER
INKLE
INLAW
INLAY
INLET
INNER
INONU
INPUT
INREM
INSET
INSTR
INSTS
INTEL
INTER
INTOW
INTRA
INTRO
INTWO
INUIT
INURE
INUSE

I•N••
IFNOT
IGNES
INNER
IONIA
IONIC
IXNAY

I••N•
ICENI
ICING
ICONO
ICONS
ILENE
ILONA
IMINE
IMINO
INANE
INONU
IPANA
IRANI
IRENE
IRINA
IRONS
IRONY
IVANA
IVINS

I•••N
IBSEN
ICAHN
ICEIN
ILION
INCAN
INFIN
INFUN
INION
IOWAN
IRVIN
IRWIN
IXION

•IN••
AINGE
AINUS
BINAL
BINDS
BINES
BINET
BINGE
BINGO
BINGS
CINCH
CINCO
CINDY
CINES
DINAH
DINAR
DINED
DINER
DINES
DINGE
DINGO
DINGS
DINGY
DINKS
DINKY
DINTS
FINAL
FINCA
FINCH
FINDS
FINED
FINER
FINES
FINIS
FINKS
FINNO
FINNS
FINNY
GINNY
GINZA
HINDI
HINDS
HINDU
HINES
HINGE
HINNY
HINTS
JINGO
JINKS
JINNI
JINNS
KINDA
KINDS
KINER
KINGS
KINKS
KINKY
KINTE
LINDA
LINDY
LINED
LINEN
LINER
LINES
LINGO
LINKS
LINTS
LINTY
LINUS
MINAS
MINCE
MINDS
MINDY
MINED
MINEO
MINER
MINES
MINGS
MINHO
MINIM
MINIS
MINKS
MINOR
MINOS
MINOT
MINSK
MINTS
MINTY
MINUS
NINAS
NINER
NINES
NINJA
NINNY
NINON
NINOS
NINTH
OINGO
OINKS
PINCE
PINCH
PINED
PINES
PINEY
PINGO
PINGS
PINKS
PINKY
PINNA
PINON
PINOT
PINSK
PINTA
PINTO
PINTS
PINUP
PINZA
RINDS
RINGO
RINGS
RINKS
RINKY
RINSE
RINSO
SINAI
SINCE
SINES
SINEW
SINGE
SINGS
SINKS
SINUS
TINCT
TINED
TINES
TINGE
TINGS
TINNY
TINTS
UINTA
VINAS
VINCE
VINCI
VINED
VINES
VINGT
VINNY
VINYL
WINCE
WINCH
WINDS
WINDY
WINED
WINES
WINGS
WINKS
WINZE
XINGU
ZINCS
ZINGS
ZINGY

•I•N•
AISNE
DIANA
DIANE
DIDNT
DIENE
DIONE
FIEND
FINNO
FINNS
FINNY
FIONA
FIRNS
GIANT
GINNY
GIRNS
HINNY
JINNI
JINNS
KIANG
KILNS
LIANA
LIANE
LIANG
LIENS
LIGNI
LIGNO
LIMNS
LIONS
MIENS
MILNE
NINNY
PIANO
PINNA
PIONS
RIANT
SIENA
SIGNE
SIGNO
SIGNS
TIANT
TINNY
VIAND
VINNY
VIRNA

•I••N
AIDAN
AIKEN
BIDEN
BIDON
BIGON
BISON
DIDIN
DIGIN
DIJON
DIVAN
DIXON
DIZEN
EIGEN
FITIN
GIVEN
HITON
KIRIN
LIEIN
LIKEN
LIMEN
LIMON
LINEN
LITON
LIVEN
MIKAN
MILAN
NIKON
NINON
NISAN
NIVEN
NIXON
PINON
PISAN
PITON
RIPEN
RISEN
RIVEN
SIDON
SIMON
SIREN
SITIN
SITON
SIVAN
TIEIN
TIMON
TIPIN
TIRAN
TITAN
VIXEN
WIDEN
WIGAN
WIZEN

••IN•
ACING
ADINT
AGING
AKINS
ALINE
AMINE
AMINO
APING
AWING
AXING
AZINE
BEING
BLIND
BLINI
BLINK
BOING
BRINE
BRING
BRINK
BRINY
CAINE
CHINA
CHINE
CHING
CHINK
CHINO
CHINS
CLINE
CLING
CLINK
CLINT
COINS
CUING
DJINN
DOING
DRINA
DRINK
DVINA
DYING
EDINA
EKING
EWING
FAINT
FEINT
FLING
FLINT
GAINS
GLINT
GOING
GRIND
GRINS
HEINE
HEINZ
ICING
IMINE
IMINO
IRINA
IVINS
JAINS
JOINS
JOINT
KLINE
KOINE
LAINE
LAING
LOINS
LYING
MAINE
MAINS
MAINZ
OPINE
ORING
OVINE
OWING
PAINE
PAINS
PAINT
PLINK
PLINY
POINT
PRINK
PRINT
QUINN
QUINO
QUINT
RAINS
RAINY
REINK
REINS
RHINE
RHINO
RUING
RUINS
SAINT
SEINE
SHINE
SHINS
SHINY
SKINK
SKINS
SKINT
SLING
SLINK
SPINE
SPINS
SPINY
STING
STINK
STINT
SUING
SUINT
SWINE
SWING
TAINE
TAINT
THINE
THING
THINK
THINS
TRINE
TRINI
TWINE
TWINS
TYING
USING
VEINS
VYING
WAINS
WHINE
WHINY
WRING

••I•N
ALIEN
ALIGN
ANION
APIAN
ARIAN
ARION
ASIAN
ATION
AVIAN
AVION
AXION
BAIRN
BRIAN
CAIRN
CHIEN
DEIGN
DJINN
ELION
EVIAN
FEIGN
ILION
INION
IXION
NAIRN
ONION
ORION
QUIEN
QUINN
REIGN
SCION
UNION
VSIGN

•••IN
ACTIN
ADDIN
ADMIN
AGAIN
AHSIN

ALAIN ALGIN ALLIN ALVIN AMAIN ARKIN ASTIN ATEIN AUXIN BALIN BASIN BEGIN BENIN BEVIN BOXIN BRAIN BRUIN BUNIN BURIN CABIN CHAIN COLIN CRAIN CUEIN CUMIN CUTIN DARIN DIDIN DIGIN DRAIN DUBIN DUGIN EATIN ECHIN EDWIN ELFIN ELGIN ELVIN ENFIN EOSIN ERVIN ERWIN FAGIN FITIN FLYIN FOGIN GAMIN GAVIN GETIN GOTIN GRAIN GROIN HEDIN HEMIN ICEIN INFIN IRVIN IRWIN JAMIN KANIN KEVIN KEYIN KIRIN KLEIN LAPIN LATIN LAVIN LAYIN LEDIN LENIN LETIN LEVIN LIEIN LOGIN LUPIN LYSIN MARIN MATIN MUCIN MYSIN NEVIN NOTIN OLEIN OPSIN ORRIN OSLIN PAYIN PEKIN PEPIN PLAIN POPIN PUPIN PUTIN QUOIN RABIN RANIN RAVIN RENIN REPIN RESIN REWIN ROBIN RODIN ROSIN RUBIN RUNIN RUTIN SABIN SATIN SAWIN SEEIN SERIN SETIN SITIN SKEIN SLAIN SPAIN STAIN STEIN SWAIN TAKIN TAPIN TIEIN TIPIN TOEIN TOXIN TRAIN TURIN TWAIN UNPIN VENIN ZAYIN ZUBIN

IO•••

IODIC IONIA IONIC IOTAS IOWAN

I•O••

ICONO ICONS ICOSA ICOSI IDOLS ILONA INONU IRONS IRONY IVORY

I••O•

ICHOR IDIOM IDIOT IFNOT IGLOO ILION INCOG INGOT INION INTOW IXION

I•••O

IATRO ICONO IDAHO IGLOO IMAGO IMIDO IMINO INDIO INIGO INTRO INTWO IRIDO ITALO

•IO••

AIOLI BIOME BIOTA DIODE DIONE FIONA FIORD KIOGA KIOSK KIOWA LIONS NIOBE PIONS PIOUS RIOJA RIOTS SIOUX VIOLA VIOLS

•I•O•

BIDON BIGON BIGOS BIGOT BIJOU BIPOD BISON DICOT DIDOS DIJON DIVOT DIXON GIGOT GIJOE GIROS HITON KILOS KIROV LIDOS LIMON LIMOS LITON MIAOW MILOS MINOR MINOS MINOT MISOS NICOL NIKON NILOT NIMOY NINON NINOS NIXON PICOT PILOT PINON PINOT PITON PITOT PIVOT RICOH RIDOF RIGOR SIDON SILOS SIMON SITON TIMON TIMOR VIDOR VIGOR VISOR WIDOW

•I••O

AIMTO BILBO BILKO BINGO CINCO CIRRO CISCO DIAZO DICHO DIEGO DINGO DIPLO DISCO DITTO EIEIO FIBRO FINNO FIRPO GIZMO HIERO HIPPO HIPTO JINGO KIDDO LIETO LIGNO LIMBO LINGO LIPPO LITHO MICRO MIMEO MINEO MINHO MIRRO MISDO NIKKO NITRO OINGO PIANO PICRO PINGO PINTO PISCO PISMO RINGO RINSO RIZZO SIGNO SIXMO VIDEO VIEJO VIREO VIRGO WILCO

••IO•

ADIOS AGIOS ANION ARION ATION AVION AXIOM AXION CHIOS CLIOS ELION ELIOT GRIOT IDIOM IDIOT ILION INION IXION OLIOS ONION ORION PRIOR SCION TRIOS UNION

••I•O

AMIGO AMINO AVISO BOITO CAIRO CHICO CHINO CHIRO FRITO GUIDO IMIDO IMINO INIGO IRIDO OLIGO PHILO PRIMO QUINO QUITO RHINO RHIZO SEIKO SLIGO SPIRO

•••IO

ANZIO AUDIO CASIO CURIO DANIO DARIO EIEIO ENNIO FABIO FOLIO HAGIO HELIO INDIO JULIO LABIO MARIO NGAIO PATIO PLEIO RADIO RATIO SOCIO SOHIO TONIO

IP•••

IPANA IPASS

I•P••

IMPEI IMPEL IMPLY INPUT

I••P•

INAPT INEPT

I•••P

ICEUP

•IP••

BIPED BIPOD DIPLO DIPPY GIPSY HIPPO HIPPY HIPTO LIPID LIPPI LIPPO LIPPY NIPAS NIPAT NIPPY NIPUP PIPAL PIPED PIPER PIPES PIPIT PIPPA PIPPI RIPEN RIPER RIPUP TIPIN TIPPI TIPPY TIPSY TIPUP VIPER WIPED WIPER WIPES YIPES ZIPPY ZIPUP

•I•P•

DIPPY FIRPO GIMPS GIMPY HIPPO HIPPY LIMPS LIPPI LIPPO LIPPY LISPS NIPPY PIPPA PIPPI SIEPI SIMPS TIPPI TIPPY WIMPS WIMPY WISPS WISPY ZIPPY

•I••P

BIDUP DIDUP DIGUP FIXUP HITUP LITUP MIXUP NIPUP PINUP RIGUP RIPUP SITUP TIEUP TIPUP ZIPUP

••IP•

BLIPS CHIPS CLIPS DRIPS FLIPS GRIPE GRIPS QTIPS QUIPS QUIPU SHIPS SKIPS SLIPS SNIPE SNIPS STIPE SWIPE TRIPE TRIPS WHIPS

••I•P

BLIMP CHIMP CHIRP CRIMP CRISP PRIMP QUILP SKIMP

•••IP

ATRIP EQUIP JOSIP OXLIP RECIP SCRIP STRIP TULIP UNHIP UNZIP

IQ•••

IQUIT

I••Q•

IRAQI

•IQ••

PIQUE

•••IQ

ANTIQ

IR•••

IRADE IRANI IRAQI IRATE IRENE IRIDO IRINA IRISH IRKED IRONS IRONY IRREG IRVIN IRWIN

I•R••

INREM IRREG

I••R•

IATRO IATRY IBARS IBERT ICERS INARI INDRA INDRI INERT INFRA INTRA INTRO INURE ISERE IVORY IZARD IZARS

I•••R

ICHOR ICIER IDLER ILLER INCUR INFER INGER INKER INNER INSTR INTER IZMIR

•IR••

AIRED AIRES BIRCH BIRDS BIRDY BIRLS BIRRS BIRTH CIRCA CIRCE CIRCS CIRES CIRRI CIRRO DIRAC DIRER DIRGE DIRKS DIRTY FIRED FIRER FIRES FIRMA FIRMS FIRNS FIRPO FIRRY FIRST FIRTH GIRDS GIRLS GIRLY GIRNS GIROS GIRTH GIRTS HIRAM HIRED HIRER HIRES KIRBY KIRIN KIRKS KIROV LIRAS MIRED MIRES MIRRO MIRTH MIRVS SIRED SIREN SIRES TIRAN TIRED TIRES VIRAL VIREO VIRGA VIRGO VIRID VIRNA VIRTU VIRUS WIRED WIRER WIRES WIRRA

•I•R•

BIRRS CIERA CIRRI CIRRO DIARY FIBRE FIBRO FIERY FIORD FIRRY HIERO LIARD LIARS LIBRA LIBRE LITRE LIVRE MICRA MICRO MIRRO MITRE NIDRE NITRE NITRO PICRO PIERS PIURA SIDRA TIARA TIERS VIERS VIVRE WIRRA

•I••R

AILER AIMER BIHAR BIKER BITER CIDER CIGAR CITER DICER DINAR DINER DIRER DISTR DIVER EIDER FIBER FIFER FILAR FILER FINER FIRER FIVER FIXER GIBER GIVER HIDER HIKER HIRER JIVER KINER KITER LIGER LINER LITER LIVER MILER MIMER MINER MINOR MISER MITER MIXER MIZAR NICER NIGER NINER NITER NIZER OILER PIKER PILAR PIPER RICER RIDER RIFER RIGOR RIKER RIPER RISER RIVER SIDER SIEUR SITAR SIZER TIBER TIGER TILER TIMER TIMOR TITER UIGUR VICAR VIDOR VIGOR VILER VIPER VISOR WIDER WIPER WIRER WISER

••IR•

AFIRE AKIRA AMIRS BAIRD BAIRN BGIRL CAIRN CAIRO CHIRO CHIRP CHIRR COIRS DAIRY EMIRS FAIRE FAIRS FAIRY FLIRT HAIRS HAIRY HEIRS LAIRD LAIRS LOIRE MBIRA MOIRA MOIRE NAIRA NAIRN NOIRE PAIRS QUIRE QUIRK QUIRT SHIRE SHIRK SHIRR SHIRT SKIRL SKIRR SKIRT SMIRK SPIRE SPIRO STIRS SWIRL TBIRD THIRD TWIRL WEIRD WEIRS WHIRL WHIRR WHIRS ZAIRE

••I•R

BRIAR BRIER CHIRR CRIER DRIER FLIER FRIAR FRIER GRIER ICIER OSIER PRIER PRIOR SHIER SHIRR SKIER SKIRR SLIER TRIER WHIRR WRIER

•••IR

ADAIR AEGIR AESIR ASTIR AVOIR BLAIR CHAIR CHOIR CLAIR EYRIR FAKIR FLAIR GLAIR IZMIR KAFIR KEFIR NADIR NOSIR OHAIR ONAIR OPHIR PAMIR REAIR SAPIR STAIR TAPIR THEIR USAIR VANIR YASIR

IS•••

ISAAC ISAMU ISERE ISLAM ISLES ISLET ISLEY ISSEI ISSUE ISSUS ISTIC ISTLE ISUZU

I•S••

IBSEN INSET INSTR INSTS ISSEI ISSUE ISSUS ITSME

I••S•

ICOSA ICOSI IDEST INUSE IPASS IRISH

I•••S

IAMBS IBARS ICERS ICKES ICONS ICTUS IDEAS IDLES IDOLS IDYLS IGLUS IGNES ILLUS IMAMS INCAS INCUS INDUS INITS INSTS IOTAS IPASS IRONS ISLES ISSUS ITALS ITEMS IVIES IVINS IZARS IZBAS

•IS••

AISHA AISLE AISNE BISES BISON CISCO CISSY DISCO DISCS DISKS DISME DISTR FISCS FISHY FISKE FISTS GISTS HISSY KISKA LISLE LISPS LISSE LISTS LISZT MISDO MISER MISHA MISOS MISSA MISSY MISTI MISTS MISTY NISAN NISEI NISUS PISAN PISCI PISCO PISMO PISTE RISEN RISER RISES RISHI RISKS RISKY SISAL SISSY VISAS VISES VISIT VISOR VISTA WISER WISHY WISPS WISPY

•I•S•

BITSY CISSY DIDST DITSY FIRST GIPSY HISSY KIOSK LISSE MIDST MIMSY MINSK MISSA MISSY PINSK RINSE RINSO SISSY TIPSY WIEST

•I••S

AIDES AINUS AIRES BIBBS BIDES BIFFS BIGOS BIKES BILKS BILLS BINDS BINES BINGS BIRDS BIRLS BIRRS BISES BITES BITTS CINES CIRCS CIRES CITES DIALS DICES DICKS DICTS DIDOS DIEMS DIETS DIKES DILLS DIMES DINES DINGS DINKS DINTS DIRKS DISCS DISKS DIVAS DIVES FIATS FICUS FIEFS FIFES FILES FILLS FILMS FINDS FINES FINIS FINKS FINNS FIRES FIRMS FIRNS FISCS FISTS FIVES FIXES GIBBS GIBES GIFTS GILDS GILES GILLS GILTS GIMPS GIRDS GIRLS GIRNS GIROS GIRTS GISTS GIVES HICKS HIDES HIFIS HIGHS HIKES HILLS HILTS HINDS HINES HINTS HIRES HIVES JIBES JILTS JINKS JINNS JIVES KICKS KILLS KILNS KILOS KILTS KINDS KINGS KINKS KIRKS KITES KITTS KIVAS KIWIS LIARS LICKS LIDOS LIENS LIEUS LIFTS LIKES LILTS LIMAS LIMBS LIMES LIMNS LIMOS LIMPS LINES LINKS LINTS LINUS LIONS LIRAS LISPS LISTS LITES LIVES MICAS MIDAS MIDIS MIENS MIFFS MIKES MILES MILKS MILLS MILOS MILTS MIMAS MIMES MINAS MINDS MINES MINGS MINIS MINKS MINOS MINTS MINUS MIRES MIRVS MISOS MISTS MITES MITTS MIXES NICKS NIDES NIDUS NIELS NIKES NILES NIMES NINAS NINES NINOS NIPAS NISUS NITES NIXES OINKS PICAS PICKS PICTS PIEDS PIERS PIKAS PIKES PILES PILLS PILUS PIMAS PINES PINGS PINKS PINTS PIONS PIOUS PIPES PITAS PITHS PITTS RIALS RICES RICKS RIDES RIELS RIFFS RIFTS RIGGS RILES

RILLS
RIMES
RINDS
RINGS
RINKS
RIOTS
RISES
RISKS
RITES
RIVES
SIALS
SIDES
SIFTS
SIGHS
SIGNS
SIKES
SIKHS
SILAS
SILKS
SILLS
SILOS
SILTS
SIMMS
SIMPS
SINES
SINGS
SINKS
SINUS
SIRES
SITES
SITUS
SIXES
SIZES
TIBBS
TICKS
TIDES
TIEGS
TIERS
TIFFS
TIKIS
TILES
TILLS
TILTS
TIMES
TINES
TINGS
TINTS
TIRES
TITIS
TITUS
VIALS
VIBES
VICES
VICKS
VIERS
VIEWS
VILAS
VINAS
VINES
VIOLS
VIRUS
VISAS
VISES
VITAS
VITUS
WICKS
WILDS
WILES
WILLS
WILTS
WIMPS
WINDS
WINES
WINGS
WINKS
WIPES
WIRES
WISPS
WIVES
YIKES
YIPES
ZILLS
ZINCS
ZINGS
ZITIS

••IS•
ALIST
AMISH
AMISS
ANISE
APISH
ARISE
AVISO
BLISS
BOISE
BRISK
CRISP
CRISS
CRIST
DAISY
DEISM
DEIST
ELISE
EPISC
ERISA
EXIST
FEIST
FOIST
FRISK
GRIST
GUISE
HEISS
HEIST
HOIST
IRISH
JOIST
KNISH
KRISS
LUISA
LUISE
MOIST
NAISH
NOISE
NOISY
ODIST
POISE
PRISM
RAISA
RAISE
SEISM
SHISH
SWISH
SWISS
TRISH
TWIST
WAIST
WEISS
WHISK
WHIST
WRIST
ZEISS
ZEIST

••I•S
ACIDS
ADIOS
ADITS
AGIOS
AKINS
ALIAS
ALIFS
AMIES
AMIRS
AMISS
ANILS
ARIAS
ARIES
ARILS
ARIUS
AXILS
BAILS
BAITS
BLIPS
BLISS
BOILS
BRIES
BRIGS
BRIMS
BRITS
CEILS
CHIAS
CHINS
CHIOS
CHIPS
CHITS
CLIOS
CLIPS
COIFS
COILS
COINS
COIRS
CRIBS
CRIES
CRISS
DOITS
DRIBS
DRIES
DRIPS
EDITS
EFIKS
ELIAS
EMIRS
EMITS
EPICS
ERIES
EVILS
EXITS
FAILS
FAIRS
FLIES
FLIPS
FLITS
FOILS
FRIES
FRITS
GAINS
GAITS
GAIUS
GLIMS
GRIDS
GRIGS
GRINS
GRIPS
GRITS
HAIKS
HAILS
HAIRS
HEIRS
HEISS
INITS
IVIES
IVINS
JAILS
JAINS
JOINS
KNITS
KRISS
LAICS
LAIRS
LAIUS
LOINS
MAIDS
MAILS
MAINS
MOILS
NAILS
NOILS
OBIES
OKIES
OLIOS
OMITS
PAILS
PAINS
PAIRS
PLIES
POILS
PRIES
PRIGS
PRIMS
QTIPS
QUIDS
QUIPS
QUITS
RAIDS
RAILS
RAINS
REIMS
REINS
ROILS
RUINS
SAILS
SHIES
SHIMS
SHINS
SHIPS
SHIVS
SKIDS
SKIES
SKIMS
SKINS
SKIPS
SKITS
SLIMS
SLIPS
SLITS
SMITS
SNIPS
SNITS
SOILS
SPIES
SPINS
SPITS
SPIVS
STIES
STIRS
SUITS
SWIGS
SWIMS
SWISS
TAILS
THINS
TOILS
TRIES
TRIGS
TRIMS
TRIOS
TRIPS
TWIGS
TWINS
TWITS
UNITS
UNIVS
VEILS
VEINS
VOIDS
WAIFS
WAILS
WAINS
WAITS
WEIRS
WEISS
WHIGS
WHIMS
WHIPS
WHIRS
WHITS
WRITS
ZEISS

•••IS
ABRIS
ADDIS
AEGIS
ANAIS
ANTIS
APHIS
APSIS
ARRIS
ARSIS
ARTIS
AUDIS
AULIS
BASIS
BLOIS
BORIS
CADIS
CANIS
CHRIS
CUTIS
DAVIS
DELIS
DENIS
DORIS
ELLIS
ELVIS
ENNIS
ETUIS
FELIS
FINIS
FRAIS
HAJIS
HIFIS
HOPIS
JANIS
KAKIS
KEPIS
KIWIS
LAPIS
LEGIS
LENIS
LEVIS
LEWIS
LEXIS
LORIS
LOUIS
MARIS
MAVIS
MAXIS
METIS
MIDIS
MINIS
MUNIS
NARIS
NEVIS
NUMIS
OASIS
OPSIS
ORNIS
ORRIS
PARIS
PAVIS
PERIS
POLIS
PULIS
PYXIS
RAKIS
RAMIS
RANIS
REGIS
SARIS
SEMIS
SUFIS
TABIS
TAXIS
THAIS
TIKIS
TITIS
TOPIS
TROIS
TUNIS
VADIS
WADIS
XAXIS
YAXIS
YETIS
YOGIS
ZAXIS
ZITIS
ZORIS
ZUNIS

IT•••
ITALO
ITALS
ITALY
ITCHY
ITEMS
ITSME

I•T••
IATRO
IATRY
ICTUS
INTEL
INTER
INTOW
INTRA
INTRO
INTWO
IOTAS
ISTIC
ISTLE

I••T•
ICHTH
INITS
INSTR
INSTS
IRATE

I•••T
IBERT
IDEST
IDIOT
IFNOT
INAPT
INEPT
INERT
INGOT
INLET
INPUT
INSET
INUIT
IQUIT
ISLET
IZMIT

•IT••
AITCH
BITER
BITES
BITSY
BITTE
BITTS
BITTY
CITED
CITER
CITES
DITCH
DITKA
DITSY
DITTO
DITTY
DITZY
FITCH
FITIN
FITLY
HITCH
HITIT
HITME
HITON
HITUP
KITED
KITER
KITES
KITTS
KITTY
LITER
LITES
LITHE
LITHO
LITON
LITRE
LITUP
MITCH
MITER
MITES
MITRE
MITTS
MITTY
MITZI
NITER
NITES
NITRE
NITRO
NITTI
NITTY
PITAS
PITCH
PITHS
PITHY
PITON
PITOT
PITTA
PITTS
RITES
RITZY
SITAR
SITBY
SITED
SITES
SITIN
SITKA
SITON
SITUP
SITUS
TITAN
TITER
TITHE
TITIS
TITLE
TITUS
VITAE
VITAL
VITAS
VITUS
WITCH
WITHE
WITTE
WITTY
ZITIS

•I•T•
AIMTO
BIOTA
BIRTH
BITTE
BITTS
BITTY
DICTA
DICTS
DICTU
DIETS
DINTS
DIRTY
DISTR
DITTO
DITTY
FIATS
FIFTH
FIFTY
FILTH
FIRTH
FISTS
GIFTS
GILTS
GIRTH
GIRTS
GISTS
HILTS
HINTS
HIPTO
JILTS
KILTS
KINTE
KITTS
KITTY
LIETO
LIFTS
LILTS
LINTS
LINTY
LISTS
MILTS
MILTY
MINTS
MINTY
MIRTH
MISTI
MISTS
MISTY
MITTS
MITTY
NIFTY
NINTH
NITTI
NITTY
PICTS
PIETA
PIETY
PINTA
PINTO
PINTS
PISTE
PITTA
PITTS
RIATA
RIFTS
RIOTS
SIETE
SIFTS
SILTS
SILTY
SIXTH
SIXTY
TILTH
TILTS
TINTS
UINTA
VIRTU
VISTA
WIDTH
WILTS
WITTE
WITTY

•I••T
AIMAT
BIGHT
BIGOT
BINET
BIZET
CIVET
DICOT
DIDNT
DIDST
DIGIT
DIVOT
DIXIT
EIGHT
FIGHT
FILET
FIRST
FIXIT
GIANT
GIGOT
HITIT
LICIT
LIEUT
LIGHT
LIMIT
LISZT
MIDST
MIGHT
MINOT
NIGHT
NILOT
NIPAT
PICOT
PILOT
PINOT
PIPIT
PITOT
PIVOT
RIANT
RIGHT
RIVET
SIGHT
TIANT
TIBET
TIGHT
TINCT
VINGT
VISIT
WIEST
WIGHT
ZIBET

••IT•
ADITS
AGITA
AKITA
AMITY
ANITA
ARITH
BAITS
BLITT
BLITZ
BOITE
BOITO
BRITE
BRITH
BRITS
BRITT
CHITA
CHITS
DEITY
DOITS
EDITH
EDITS
ELITE
EMITS
EVITA
EXITS
FAITH
FLITS
FRITO
FRITS
FRITZ
GAITS
GLITZ
GRITS
HAITI
HOITY
INITS
KEITH
KNITS
LAITY
LEITH
OMITS
QUITE
QUITO
QUITS
RAITT
SKITS
SLITS
SMITE
SMITH
SMITS
SNITS
SPITE
SPITS
SPITZ
SUITE
SUITS
SWITZ
TOITY
TRITE
TRITT
TWITS
UNITE
UNITS
UNITY
WAITE
WAITS
WAITZ
WHITE
WHITS
WRITE
WRITS

••I•T
ADINT
ALIST
ATILT
BLITT
BRITT
BUILT
CLIFT
CLINT
CRIST
DEIST
DRIFT
EDICT
ELIOT
EVICT
EXIST
FAINT
FEINT
FEIST
FLINT
FLIRT
FOIST
GLINT
GRIFT
GRIOT
GRIST
GUILT
HEIDT
HEIST
HOIST
IDIOT
JOINT
JOIST
KLIMT
MOIST
ODIST
PAINT
POINT
PRINT
QUIET
QUILT
QUINT
QUIRT
RAITT
SAINT
SHIFT
SHIRT
SKINT
SKIRT
SPILT
STILT
STINT
SUINT
SWIFT
TAINT
TRITT
TWIST
TWIXT
VEIDT
WAIST
WHIST
WRIST
ZEIST

•••IT
ADMIT
AFRIT
AMBIT
AUDIT
AWAIT
BAGIT
BARIT
BEFIT
BRUIT
CANIT
CUBIT
DAVIT
DEBIT
DEMIT
DIGIT
DIXIT
DOGIT
DROIT
EATIT
FIXIT
FRUIT
FUGIT
GETIT
GSUIT
HABIT
HITIT
INUIT
IQUIT
IZMIT
KRAIT
LEGIT
LICIT
LIMIT
MEDIT
MERIT
NOHIT
ONDIT
OPCIT
ORBIT
PETIT
PEWIT
PIPIT
PLAIT
POLIT
POSIT
QUOIT
REFIT
RELIT
REMIT
SPLIT
SPRIT
TACIT
TOBIT
TOWIT
TRAIT
UNFIT
UNLIT
VISIT

I•U••
INUIT
INURE
INUSE
IQUIT
ISUZU

I••U•
ICEUP
ICTUS
IGLUS
ILIUM
ILLUS
IMBUE
INCUR
INCUS
INDUS
INFUN
INPUT
ISSUE
ISSUS

I•••U
ILGWU
INONU
ISAMU
ISUZU

•IU••
PIURA

•I•U•
AINUS
BIDUP
DIDUP
DIGUP
FICUS
FILUM
FIXUP
GIGUE
HILUM
HITUP
LIEUS
LIEUT
LIKUD
LINUS
LITUP
MINUS
MIXUP
NIDUS
NIPUP
NISUS
PICUL
PILUM
PILUS
PINUP
PIOUS
PIQUE
RIGUP
RIPUP
SIEUR
SINUS
SIOUX
SITUP
SITUS
TIEUP
TIPUP
TITUS
UIGUR
VIRUS
VITUS
ZIPUP

•I••U
BIJOU
DICTU
FICHU
HINDU
VIRTU
XINGU

••IU•
ARIUM
ARIUS
GAIUS
ILIUM
LAIUS
ODIUM
OPIUM

••I•U
ADIEU
ELIHU
HAIKU
POILU
QUIPU

IV•••
IVANA
IVIED
IVIES
IVINS
IVORY

I•V••
IRVIN

I•••V
INDIV

•IV••
CIVET
CIVIC
CIVIL
DIVAN
DIVAS
DIVED
DIVER
DIVES
DIVOT
DIVVY
FIVER
FIVES
GIVEN
GIVER
GIVES
HIVED
HIVES
JIVED
JIVER
JIVES
JIVEY
KIVAS
LIVED
LIVEN
LIVER
LIVES
LIVIA
LIVID
LIVRE
NIVAL
NIVEN
PIVOT
RIVAL
RIVED
RIVEN
RIVER
RIVES
RIVET
SIVAN
VIVID
VIVRE
WIVED
WIVES

•I•V•
DIVVY
MIRVS
SIEVE
SILVA

•I••V
KIROV

••IV•
ALIVE
ATIVE
CHIVE
CHIVY
CLIVE
DRIVE
NAIVE
OGIVE
OLIVE
PRIVY
SHIVA
SHIVS
SKIVE
SPIVS
UNIVS
WAIVE

•••IV
ACTIV
ANNIV
CCCIV
CCLIV
CCXIV
CDLIV
CDXIV
CLXIV
CMLIV
CMXIV
CXCIV
CXLIV
CXXIV
DCCIV
DCLIV
DCXIV
DERIV
DLXIV
DXCIV
DXLIV
DXXIV
EQUIV
INDIV
LXXIV
MCCIV
MCDIV
MCLIV
MCMIV
MCXIV
MDCIV
MDLIV
MDXIV
MLXIV
MMCIV
MMDIV
MMLIV
MMMIV
MMXIV
MXCIV
MXLIV
MXMIV
MXXIV
RAJIV
XXXIV

I•W••
IOWAN
IRWIN

I••W•
ILGWU
INAWE
INTWO

I•••W
INLAW
INTOW

•IW••
KIWIS

•I•W•
KIOWA
VIEWS

•I••W
MIAOW
SINEW
WIDOW

••IW•
DAIWA
SLIWA

IX•••
IXION
IXNAY

I•••X
ICEAX
IMMIX
INDEX
INFIX

•IX••
BIXBY
DIXIE
DIXIT
DIXON
FIXED
FIXER
FIXES
FIXIT
FIXUP
MIXED
MIXER
MIXES
MIXUP
NIXED
NIXES
NIXIE
NIXON
PIXEL
PIXIE
SIXED
SIXES
SIXMO
SIXTH
SIXTY
VIXEN

•I••X
SILEX
SIOUX
TIMEX

••IX•
TWIXT

•••IX
ADMIX
AFFIX
CALIX
CCCIX
CCLIX
CCXIX
CDLIX
CDXIX
CLXIX
CMLIX
CMXIX
COMIX
CROIX
CXCIX
CXLIX
CXXIX
DCCIX
DCLIX
DCXIX
DLXIX
DXCIX
DXLIX
DXXIX
FELIX
HELIX
IMMIX
INFIX
KYLIX
LXXIX
MCCIX
MCDIX
MCLIX
MCMIX
MCXIX
MDCIX
MDLIX
MDXIX
MLXIX
MMCIX
MMDIX
MMLIX
MMMIX
MMXIX
MXCIX
MXLIX
MXXIX
RADIX
REMIX
UNFIX
VARIX
XXXIX

I•Y••
IDYLL
IDYLS

I•••Y
IATRY
ICILY
IMPLY
INLAY
IRONY
ISLEY
ITALY
ITCHY
IVORY
IXNAY

•IY••
RIYAL

•I•Y•
LIBYA
SIBYL
VINYL

•I••Y
AILEY
BIALY
BIDDY

BIFFY
BILGY
BILLY
BIRDY
BITSY
BITTY
BIXBY
CINDY
CISSY
DIARY
DICEY
DICKY
DIGBY
DILLY
DIMLY
DINGY
DINKY
DIPPY
DIRTY
DITSY
DITTY
DITZY
DIVVY
DIZZY
FIERY
FIFTY
FILLY
FILMY
FINNY
FIRRY
FISHY
FITLY
FIZZY
GIDDY
GIMPY
GINNY
GIPSY
GIRLY
HILLY
HINNY
HIPPY
HISSY
JIFFY
JIMMY
JIVEY
KICKY
KIDDY
KILEY
KILLY
KINKY
KIRBY
KITTY
LIBBY
LIDDY
LINDY
LINTY
LIPPY
MIDDY
MIFFY
MILKY
MILTY
MIMSY
MINDY
MINTY
MISSY
MISTY
MITTY
NIFTY
NILLY
NIMBY
NIMOY
NINNY
NIPPY
NITTY
PICKY
PIETY
PIGGY
PINEY
PINKY
PITHY
RIBBY
RICKY
RIDGY
RIGBY
RILEY
RINKY
RISKY
RITZY
SILKY
SILLY
SILTY
SISSY
SITBY
SIXTY
TICKY
TILLY
TIMMY
TINNY
TIPPY
TIPSY
TIZZY
VICHY
VINNY
WIGGY
WILEY
WILLY
WIMPY
WINDY
WISHY
WISPY
WITTY
ZIGGY
ZINGY
ZIPPY

••IY•
ORIYA

••I•Y
ACIDY
AMITY
BRINY
CHIVY
DAILY
DAIRY
DAISY
DEIFY
DEITY
DOILY
EDIFY
EMILY
FAIRY
GRIMY
HAIRY
HOITY
ICILY
JUICY
LAITY
NOISY
PLINY
PRICY
PRIVY
RAINY
REIFY
ROILY
SHINY
SLIMY
SPICY
SPIKY
SPINY
TOITY
UNIFY
UNITY
WHINY

IZ•••
IZAAK
IZARD
IZARS
IZBAS
IZMIR
IZMIT

I••Z•
IBIZA
ISUZU

•IZ••
BIZET
DIZEN
DIZZY
FIZZY
GIZMO
MIZAR
NIZAM
NIZER
PIZZA
RIZZO
SIZED
SIZER
SIZES
TIZZY
WIZEN
ZIZKA

•I•Z•
DIAZO
DITZY
DIZZY
FIZZY
GINZA
LISZT
MITZI
PINZA
PIZZA
RITZY
RIZZO
TIZZY
WINZE

••IZ•
BAIZA
BAIZE
ELIZA
FRIZZ
IBIZA
MAIZE
PRIZE
RHIZO
SEIZE

••I•Z
BLITZ
FRITZ
FRIZZ
GLITZ
HEINZ
MAINZ
SPITZ
SWITZ
WAITZ

•••IZ
CADIZ
FELIZ
HAFIZ

JA•••
JABBA
JABOT
JACKS
JACOB
JADED
JADES
JAFFA
JAFFE
JAGGY
JAHRE
JAILS
JAIME
JAINS
JAKES
JAMAL
JAMBS
JAMES
JAMIE
JAMIN
JAMUP
JANET
JANIE
JANIS
JANUS
JAPAN
JAPED
JAPES
JARLS
JARRE
JASON
JATOS
JAUNE
JAUNT
JAVAS
JAWED
JAYNE
JAZZY

J•A••
JBARS
JEANE
JEANS

J••A•
JAMAL
JAPAN
JAVAS
JIHAD
JONAH
JONAS
JOTAS
JOUAL
JUBAL
JUDAH
JUDAS
JUGAL
JURAL
JURAT

J•••A
JABBA
JAFFA
JIDDA
JOLLA
JUDEA
JULIA
JUMNA
JUNTA

•J•A•
VJDAY

••JA•
HEJAZ
KOJAK
RAJAH
RAJAS
SAJAK
UNJAM

•••JA
ABUJA
NINJA
OUIJA
RIOJA
SONJA
THUJA

JB•••
JBARS

J•B••
JABBA
JABOT
JIBED
JIBES
JUBAL

J••B•
JABBA
JAMBS
JUMBO

J•••B
JACOB

J•C••
JACKS
JACOB
JOCKO
JOCKS

J••C•
JOYCE
JUICE
JUICY
JUNCO

•J•C•
EJECT

J•D••
JADED
JADES
JIDDA
JODIE
JUDAH
JUDAS
JUDEA
JUDGE

J••D•
JEUDI
JIDDA

J•••D
JADED
JAPED
JAWED
JIBED
JIVED
JOKED
JUKED

•JD••
VJDAY

•J••D
FJELD
FJORD

JE•••
JEANE
JEANS
JEEPS
JEERS
JELLO
JELLS
JELLY
JEMMY
JENNY
JEREZ
JERKS
JERKY
JERRY
JERZY
JESSE
JESTS
JETER
JETES
JETTY
JEUDI
JEUNE
JEWEL

J•E••
JEEPS
JEERS
JOEYS

J••E•
JADED
JADES
JAKES
JAMES
JANET
JAPED
JAPES
JAWED
JEREZ
JETER
JETES
JEWEL
JIBED
JIBES
JIVED
JIVER
JIVES
JIVEY
JOKED
JOKER
JOKES
JONES
JOREL
JOSEF
JUDEA
JUKED
JUKES
JULEP
JULES
JUTES
JAIME
JAMIE
JANIE
JARRE
JAUNE
JAYNE
JEANE
JESSE
JEUNE
JODIE
JOLIE
JORGE
JOULE
JOYCE
JUDGE
JUICE
JULIE
JUSTE

•JE••
EJECT
FJELD

••JE•
OBJET

••J•E
GIJOE

•••JE
KOPJE

J•F••
JAFFA
JAFFE
JIFFY

J••F•
JAFFA
JAFFE
JIFFY

J•••F
JOSEF

J•G••
JAGGY
JUGAL
JUGUM

J••G•
JAGGY
JINGO
JORGE
JUDGE

J•H••
JAHRE
JIHAD
JOHNS

J•••H
JONAH
JUDAH

••J•H
RAJAH

JI•••
JIBED
JIBES
JIDDA
JIFFY
JIHAD
JILTS
JIMMY
JINGO
JINKS
JINNI
JINNS
JIVED
JIVER
JIVES
JIVEY

J•I••
JAILS
JAIME
JAINS
JOINS
JOINT
JOIST
JUICE
JUICY

J••I•
JAMIE
JAMIN
JANIE
JANIS
JODIE
JOLIE
JOSIP
JULIA
JULIE
JULIO

J•••I
JEUDI
JINNI

•JI••
DJINN

••JI•
HAJIS
RAJIV

••J•I
HAJJI

•••JI
BENJI
HADJI
HAJJI
KANJI
MEIJI
SHOJI

J•J••
JUJUS

••JJ•
HAJJI

J•K••
JAKES
JOKED
JOKER
JOKES
JUKED
JUKES

J••K•
JACKS
JERKS
JERKY
JINKS
JOCKO
JOCKS
JUNKS
JUNKY

••J•K
KOJAK
SAJAK

J•L••
JELLO
JELLS
JELLY
JILTS
JOLIE
JOLLA
JOLLY
JOLTS
JOLTY
JULEP
JULES
JULIA
JULIE
JULIO

J••L•
JAILS
JARLS
JELLO
JELLS
JELLY
JOLLA
JOLLY
JOULE
JOWLS
JOWLY

J•••L
JAMAL
JEWEL
JOREL
JOUAL
JUBAL
JUGAL
JURAL

•J•L•
FJELD

J•M••
JAMAL
JAMBS
JAMES
JAMIE
JAMIN
JAMUP
JEMMY
JIMMY
JUMBO
JUMNA
JUMPS
JUMPY

J••M•
JAIME
JEMMY
JIMMY

J•••M
JORUM
JUGUM

••J•M
UNJAM

J•N••
JANET
JANIE
JANIS
JANUS
JENNY
JINGO
JINKS
JINNI
JINNS
JONAH
JONAS
JONES
JUNCO
JUNKS
JUNKY
JUNTA
JUNTO

J••N•
JAINS
JAUNE
JAUNT
JAYNE
JEANE
JEANS
JENNY
JEUNE
JINNI
JINNS
JOHNS
JOINS
JOINT
JUMNA

J•••N
JAMIN
JAPAN
JASON

•J•N•
DJINN

•J••N
BJORN
DJINN

••J•N
CAJUN
DIJON

JO•••
JOCKO
JOCKS
JODIE
JOEYS
JOHNS
JOINS
JOINT
JOIST
JOKED
JOKER
JOKES
JOLIE
JOLLA
JOLLY
JOLTS
JOLTY
JONAH
JONAS
JONES
JOREL
JORGE
JORUM
JOSEF
JOSIP
JOTAS
JOUAL
JOULE
JOUST
JOWLS
JOWLY
JOYCE

J••O•
JABOT
JACOB
JASON
JATOS
JUROR

J•••O
JELLO
JINGO
JOCKO
JULIO
JUMBO
JUNCO
JUNTO

•JO••
BJORN
FJORD

••JO•
ANJOU
BIJOU
DIJON
DOJOS
ENJOY
GIJOE
MAJOR
MOJOS

•••JO
BANJO
VIEJO

J•P••
JAPAN
JAPED
JAPES

J••P•
JEEPS
JUMPS
JUMPY

J•••P
JAMUP
JOSIP
JULEP

J•R••
JARLS
JARRE
JEREZ
JERKS
JERKY
JERRY
JERZY
JOREL
JORGE
JORUM
JURAL
JURAT
JUROR

J••R•
JAHRE
JARRE
JBARS
JEERS
JERRY

J•••R
JETER
JIVER
JOKER
JUROR

•J•R•
BJORN
FJORD

••J•R
MAJOR

J•S••
JASON
JESSE
JESTS
JOSEF
JOSIP
JUSTE

J••S•
JESSE
JOIST
JOUST

J•••S
JACKS
JADES
JAILS
JAINS
JAKES
JAMBS
JAMES
JANIS
JANUS
JAPES
JARLS
JATOS
JAVAS
JBARS
JEANS
JEEPS
JEERS
JELLS
JERKS
JESTS
JETES
JIBES
JILTS
JINKS
JINNS
JIVES
JOCKS
JOEYS
JOHNS
JOINS
JOKES
JOLTS
JONAS
JONES
JOTAS
JOWLS
JUDAS
JUJUS
JUKES
JULES
JUMPS
JUNKS
JUTES

••J•S
AUJUS
DOJOS
HAJIS
JUJUS
MOJOS
RAJAS

J•T••
JATOS
JETER
JETES
JETTY
JOTAS
JUTES

J••T•
JESTS
JETTY
JILTS
JOLTS
JOLTY
JUNTA
JUNTO
JUSTE

J•••T
JABOT
JANET
JAUNT
JOINT
JOIST
JOUST
JURAT

•J••T
EJECT

••J•T
OBJET

JU•••
JUBAL
JUDAH
JUDAS
JUDEA
JUDGE
JUGAL
JUGUM
JUICE
JUICY
JUJUS
JUKED
JUKES
JULEP
JULES
JULIA
JULIE
JULIO
JUMBO
JUMNA
JUMPS
JUMPY
JUNCO
JUNKS
JUNKY
JUNTA
JUNTO
JURAL
JURAT
JUROR
JUSTE
JUTES

J•U••
JAUNE
JAUNT
JEUDI
JEUNE
JOUAL
JOULE
JOUST

J••U•
JAMUP
JANUS
JORUM
JUGUM
JUJUS

••JU•
AUJUS
CAJUN
JUJUS

••J•U
ANJOU
BIJOU

J•V••
JAVAS
JIVED
JIVER
JIVES
JIVEY

••J•V
RAJIV

J•W••
JAWED
JEWEL
JOWLS
JOWLY

J•Y••
JAYNE
JOYCE

J••Y•
JOEYS

J•••Y
JAGGY
JAZZY
JELLY
JEMMY
JENNY
JERKY
JERRY
JERZY
JETTY
JIFFY
JIMMY
JIVEY
JOLLY
JOLTY
JOWLY
JUICY
JUMPY
JUNKY

•J••Y
VJDAY

••J•Y
ENJOY

J•Z••
JAZZY

J••Z•
JAZZY
JERZY

J•••Z
JEREZ

••J•Z
HEJAZ

KA•••
KAABA
KABOB
KABUL
KADAR
KAFIR
KAFKA
KAHLO
KAKAS
KAKIS
KALEL
KALES
KANGA
KANIN
KANJI
KANSA
KANZU
KAPOK
KAPPA
KAPUT
KARAN
KARAT
KAREL
KAREN
KARLA
KARMA
KAROL
KARSH
KASEM
KASHA
KATHY
KATIE
KAUAI
KAURI
KAVAS
KAYAK
KAYOS
KAZAN
KAZOO

K•A••
KAABA
KEACH
KEANE
KEANU
KEATS
KHAKI
KHANS
KIANG
KLAUS
KMART
KNACK
KNAPS
KNARS
KNAVE
KOALA
KOANS
KRAAL
KRAFT
KRAIT
KRAUS
KRAUT
KUALA
KVASS
KYACK
KYATS

K••A•
KADAR
KAKAS
KARAN
KARAT
KAUAI
KAVAS
KAYAK
KAZAN
KEBAB
KEMAL
KENAI
KERAT
KIVAS
KNEAD
KODAK
KOJAK
KOLAS
KORAN
KRAAL
KULAK

K•••A
KAABA
KAFKA
KANGA
KANSA
KAPPA
KARLA
KARMA
KASHA
KENYA
KINDA
KIOGA
KIOWA
KISKA
KOALA
KORDA
KOREA
KRONA
KRUPA
KUALA
KUKLA
KYOGA

•KA••
OKAPI
OKAYS
SKALD
SKATE
UKASE

•K•A•
AKBAR
AKKAD
OKRAS
SKEAN
SKEAT
SKOAL
SKUAS

•K••A
AKELA
AKIRA
AKITA
SKODA

••KA•
AKKAD
DAKAR
DUKAS
KAKAS
LUKAS
MCKAY
MIKAN
OSKAR
PIKAS
TIKAL
TOKAY

••K•A
HEKLA
KUKLA
MAKUA
PUKKA

•••KA
ASOKA
BABKA
CHAKA
CHEKA
DITKA
ERIKA
KAFKA
KISKA
LAIKA
LANKA
OSAKA
PARKA
POLKA
PUKKA
SANKA
SITKA
STUKA
TANKA
TONKA
VODKA
ZIZKA

K•B••
KABOB
KABUL
KEBAB
KOBOS

K••B•
KAABA
KERBS
KIRBY
KNOBS
KREBS

K•••B
KABOB
KEBAB

•KB••
AKBAR

K•C••
KICKS
KICKY
KOCHI

K••C•
KEACH
KENCH
KETCH
KNACK

KNICK KNOCK KOTCH KYACK

K•D••
KADAR KEDGE KIDDO KIDDY KODAK KUDOS KUDUS KUDZU

K••D•
KENDO KIDDO KIDDY KINDA KINDS KORDA KURDS

K•••D
KEYED KITED KNEAD KNEED

•K•D•
SKIDS SKODA

•K••D
AKKAD SKALD SKIED

••K•D
AKKAD ALKYD ASKED BAKED BIKED CAKED COKED DEKED DIKED DUKED FAKED HIKED HOKED INKED IRKED JOKED JUKED LIKED LIKUD MIKED NAKED NUKED PIKED POKED RAKED WAKED YOKED

KE•••
KEACH KEANE KEANU KEATS KEBAB KEDGE KEELS KEENE KEENS KEEPS KEFIR KEITH KELLY KELPS KELPY KELSO KEMAL KEMPT KENAI KENCH KENDO KENNY KENOS KENYA KEOGH KEPIS KERAT KERBS KERNS KERRY KESEY KETCH KEVIN KEYED KEYES KEYIN KEYUP

K•E••
KEELS KEENE KEENS KEEPS KLEIN KNEAD KNEED KNEEL KNEES KNELL KNELT KREBS KVELL

K••E•
KALEL KALES KAREL KAREN KASEM KESEY KEYED KEYES KHMER KILEY KINER KITED KITER KITES KLIEG KNEED KNEEL KNEES KOPEK KOREA KUGEL KYSER

K•••E
KATIE KEANE KEDGE KEENE KINTE KLINE KLUGE KLUTE KNAVE KNIFE KNUTE KOINE KOPJE KRONE KYRIE

•KE••
AKEEM AKEES AKELA SKEAN SKEAT SKEET SKEGS SKEIN SKEPS SKETE SKEWS

•K•E•
AKEEM AKEES OKIES SKEET SKIED SKIER SKIES

•K••E
SKATE SKETE SKIVE UKASE

••KE•
AIKEN ASKED ASKER ASKEW BAKED BAKER BAKES BIKED BIKEL BIKER BIKES CAKED CAKES CAKEY COKED COKES CUKES DEKED DEKES DIKED DIKES DUKED DUKES ESKER FAKED FAKER FAKES FYKES HAKES HIKED HIKER HIKES HOKED HOKES HOKEY ICKES INKED INKER IRKED JAKES JOKED JOKER JOKES JUKED JUKES LAKER LAKES LIKED LIKEN LIKES MAKER MAKES MIKED MIKES NAKED NIKES NUKED NUKES OAKEN OAKES ONKEY PEKES PIKED PIKER PIKES POKED POKER POKES POKEY RAKED RAKER RAKES REKEY RIKER SAKER SAKES SIKES TAKEI TAKEN TAKER TAKES TOKEN TYKES WAKED WAKEN WAKES WOKEN YIKES YOKED YOKEL YOKES

••K•E
ANKLE INKLE LAKME OAKIE PEKOE

•••KE
ALIKE AWAKE AWOKE BLAKE BLOKE BRAKE BROKE BURKE CHOKE COOKE CRAKE DANKE DRAKE EVOKE FISKE FLAKE FLUKE HAWKE HOOKE LATKE LOCKE QUAKE RANKE RILKE SHAKE SLAKE SMOKE SNAKE SPAKE SPEKE SPIKE SPOKE STAKE STOKE TRIKE

K•F••
KAFIR KAFKA KEFIR

K••F•
KHUFU KNIFE KRAFT

K•••F
KNOPF

•K•F•
SKIFF

•K••F
SKIFF

K•G••
KUGEL

K••G•
KANGA KEDGE KEOGH KINGS KIOGA KLUGE KROGH KYOGA

K•••G
KIANG KLIEG

•K•G•
SKEGS

•K••G
EKING

KH•••
KHAKI KHANS KHMER KHUFU

K•H••
KAHLO

K••H•
KASHA KATHY KOCHI

K•••H
KARSH KEACH KEITH KENCH KEOGH KETCH KNISH KOTCH KROGH

•K••H
SKOSH

••KH•
ANKHS SIKHS

•••KH
BALKH

KI•••
KIANG KICKS KICKY KIDDO KIDDY KILEY KILIM KILLS KILLY KILNS KILOS KILTS KINDA KINDS KINER KINGS KINKS KINKY KINTE KIOGA KIOSK KIOWA KIRBY KIRIN KIRKS KIROV KISKA KITED KITER KITES KITTS KITTY KIVAS KIWIS

K•I••
KEITH KLIEG KLIMT KLINE KNICK KNIFE KNISH KNITS KOINE KRILL KRISS

K••I•
KAFIR KAKIS KANIN KATIE KEFIR KEPIS KEVIN KEYIN KILIM KIRIN KIWIS KLEIN KRAIT KYLIX KYRIE

K•••I
KANJI KAUAI KAURI KENAI KHAKI KOCHI

•KI••
AKINS AKIRA AKITA EKING OKIES SKIDS SKIED SKIER SKIES SKIFF SKILL SKIMP SKIMS SKINK SKINS SKINT SKIPS SKIRL SKIRR SKIRT SKITS SKIVE

•K•I•
SKEIN

•K••I
OKAPI

••KI•
ARKIN FAKIR HAKIM KAKIS OAKIE PEKIN RAKIS TAKIN TIKIS

••K•I
NIKKI RIKKI TAKEI TIKKI VIKKI

•••KI
GORKI KHAKI NIKKI RICKI RIKKI TIKKI UMEKI VICKI VIKKI

K•J••
KOJAK

K••J•
KANJI KOPJE

K•K••
KAKAS KAKIS KUKLA

K••K•
KAFKA KHAKI KICKS KICKY KINKS KINKY KIRKS KISKA KOOKS KOOKY

K•••K
KAPOK KAYAK KIOSK KNACK KNICK KNOCK KODAK KOJAK KOPEK KULAK KURSK KYACK

•KK••
AKKAD

•K••K
SKINK SKULK SKUNK

••KK•
NIKKI NIKKO PUKKA RIKKI TIKKI VIKKI

KL•••
KLAUS KLEIN KLIEG KLIMT KLINE KLUGE KLUTE KLUTZ

K•L••
KALEL KALES KELLY KELPS KELPY KELSO KILEY KILIM KILLS KILLY KILNS KILOS KILTS KOLAS KULAK KYLIX

K••L•
KAHLO KARLA KEELS KELLY KILLS KILLY KNELL KNELT KNOLL KOALA KRILL KRULL KUALA KUKLA KVELL

K•••L
KABUL KALEL KAREL KAROL KEMAL KNEEL KNELL KNOLL KNURL KRAAL KRILL KRULL KUGEL KVELL KYZYL

•K•L•
AKELA SKALD SKILL SKULK SKULL

•K••L
SKILL SKIRL SKOAL SKULL

••KL•
ANKLE HEKLA INKLE KUKLA

••K•L
ALKYL BIKEL TIKAL YOKEL

KM•••
KMART

K•M••
KEMAL KEMPT KHMER

K••M•
KARMA KLIMT

K•••M
KASEM KILIM

•K•M•
SKIMP SKIMS

•K••M
AKEEM AKSUM

••KM•
LAKME

••K•M
HAKIM HOKUM OAKUM YOKUM

KN•••
KNACK KNAPS KNARS KNAVE KNEAD KNEED KNEEL KNEES KNELL KNELT KNICK KNIFE KNISH KNITS KNOBS KNOCK KNOLL KNOPF KNORR KNOTS KNOUT KNOWN KNOWS KNURL KNURS KNUTE

K•N••
KANGA KANIN KANJI KANSA KANZU KENAI KENCH KENDO KENNY KENOS KENYA KINDA KINDS KINER KINGS KINKS KINKY KINTE

K••N•
KEANE KEANU KEENE KEENS KENNY KERNS KHANS KIANG KILNS KLINE KOANS KOINE KRONA KRONE

K•••N
KANIN KARAN KAREN KAZAN KEVIN KEYIN KIRIN KLEIN KNOWN KORAN

•K•N•
AKINS EKING SKINK SKINS SKINT SKUNK

•K••N
AKRON SKEAN SKEIN

••K•N
AIKEN ARKIN LIKEN MIKAN NIKON OAKEN PEKIN TAKEN TAKIN TOKEN WAKEN WOKEN YUKON

KO•••
KOALA KOANS KOBOS KOCHI KODAK KOINE KOJAK KOLAS KOOKS KOOKY KOPEK KOPJE KORAN KORDA KOREA KOTCH KOTOS

K•O••
KEOGH KIOGA KIOSK KIOWA KNOBS KNOCK KNOLL KNOPF KNORR KNOTS KNOUT KNOWN KNOWS KOOKS KOOKY KROGH KRONA KRONE KYOGA KYOTO

K••O•
KABOB KAPOK KAROL KAYOS KAZOO KENOS KILOS KIROV KOBOS KOTOS KUDOS

K•••O
KAHLO KAZOO KELSO KENDO KIDDO KYOTO

•KO••
SKOAL SKODA SKOSH

•K•O•
AKRON

••KO•
CUKOR MAKOS NIKON PEKOE YAKOV YUKON ZUKOR

••K•O
NIKKO

•••KO
BILKO BUCKO BUNKO GECKO JOCKO NIKKO ROYKO SEIKO SHAKO SOCKO WACKO

K•P••
KAPOK KAPPA KAPUT KEPIS KOPEK KOPJE

K••P•
KAPPA KEEPS KELPS KELPY KEMPT KNAPS KNOPF KRUPA KRUPP

K•••P
KEYUP KRUPP

•K•P•
OKAPI SKEPS SKIPS

•K••P
SKIMP

KR•••
KRAAL KRAFT KRAIT KRAUS KRAUT KREBS KRILL KRISS KROGH KRONA KRONE KRULL KRUPA KRUPP

K•R••
KARAN KARAT KAREL KAREN KARLA KARMA KAROL KARSH KERAT KERBS KERNS KERRY KIRBY KIRIN KIRKS KIROV KORAN KORDA KOREA KURDS KURSK KURTZ KYRIE

K••R•
KAURI KERRY KMART KNARS KNORR KNURL KNURS

K•••R
KADAR KAFIR KEFIR KHMER KINER KITER KNORR KYSER

•KR••
AKRON OKRAS

•K•R•
AKIRA SKIRL SKIRR SKIRT

•K••R
AKBAR SKIER SKIRR

••K•R
ASKER BAKER BIKER CUKOR DAKAR ESKER FAKER FAKIR HIKER INKER JOKER LAKER MAKER OSKAR PIKER POKER RAKER RIKER SAKER TAKER ZUKOR

K•S••
KASEM KASHA KESEY KISKA KYSER

K••S•
KANSA KARSH KELSO KIOSK KNISH KRISS KURSK KVASS

K•••S
KAKAS KAKIS KALES KAVAS KAYOS KEATS KEELS KEENS KEEPS KELPS KENOS KEPIS KERBS KERNS KEYES KHANS KICKS KILLS KILNS KILOS KILTS KINDS KINGS KINKS KIRKS KITES KITTS KIVAS KIWIS KLAUS KNAPS KNARS KNEES KNITS KNOBS KNOTS KNOWS KNURS KOANS KOBOS KOLAS KOOKS KOTOS KRAUS KREBS KRISS KUDOS KUDUS KURDS KVASS KYATS

•KS••
AKSUM

•K•S•
SKOSH UKASE

•K••S
AKEES AKINS OKAYS OKIES OKRAS SKEGS SKEPS SKEWS SKIDS SKIES SKIMS SKINS SKIPS SKITS SKUAS

••KS•
BAKST

••K•S
ANKHS BAKES BIKES CAKES COKES CUKES DEKES DIKES DUKAS DUKES FAKES FYKES HAKES HIKES HOKES ICKES JAKES JOKES JUKES KAKAS KAKIS LAKES LIKES LUKAS MAKES MAKOS MIKES NIKES NUKES OAKES PEKES PIKAS PIKES POKES RAKES RAKIS SAKES SIKES SIKHS TAKES TIKIS TYKES WAKES YIKES YOKES

•••KS
BACKS BALKS BANKS BARKS BASKS BEAKS BECKS BILKS BONKS BOOKS BOSKS BUCKS BULKS BUNKS CALKS CARKS CASKS COCKS CONKS COOKS CORKS CUSKS DARKS DECKS DESKS DICKS DINKS DIRKS DISKS DOCKS DUCKS DUNKS DUSKS EFIKS EWOKS FINKS FOLKS FORKS FUNKS GAWKS GEEKS GROKS HACKS HAIKS HANKS HARKS HAWKS HECKS HICKS HOCKS HONKS HOOKS HULKS HUNKS HUSKS JACKS JERKS JINKS JOCKS JUNKS KICKS KINKS KIRKS KOOKS LACKS LARKS LEAKS LEEKS LICKS LINKS LOCKS LOOKS LUCKS

LURKS
MARKS
MASKS
MILKS
MINKS
MOCKS
MONKS
MUCKS
MUSKS
NARKS
NECKS
NICKS
NOCKS
NOOKS
OINKS
PACKS
PARKS
PEAKS
PECKS
PEEKS
PERKS
PICKS
PINKS
PORKS
PUCKS
PUNKS
RACKS
RANKS
REEKS
RICKS
RINKS
RISKS
ROCKS
ROOKS
RUCKS
RUSKS
SACKS
SAUKS
SEEKS
SILKS
SINKS
SOAKS
SOCKS
SUCKS
SULKS
TACKS
TALKS
TANKS
TASKS
TEAKS
TICKS
TREKS
TUCKS
TURKS
TUSKS
VICKS
WALKS
WEEKS
WICKS
WINKS
WONKS
WORKS
YANKS
YOLKS
ZONKS

K•T••
KATHY
KATIE
KETCH
KITED
KITER
KITES
KITTS
KITTY
KOTCH
KOTOS

K••T•
KEATS
KEITH
KILTS
KINTE
KITTS
KITTY
KLUTE
KLUTZ
KNITS
KNOTS
KNUTE
KURTZ
KYATS
KYOTO

K•••T
KAPUT
KARAT
KEMPT
KERAT
KLIMT
KMART
KNELT
KNOUT
KRAFT
KRAIT
KRAUT

•K•T•
AKITA
SKATE
SKETE
SKITS

•K••T
SKEAT
SKEET
SKINT
SKIRT

••K•T
BAKST
YAKUT

KU•••
KUALA
KUDOS
KUDUS
KUDZU
KUGEL
KUKLA
KULAK
KURDS
KURSK
KURTZ

K•U••
KAUAI
KAURI
KHUFU
KLUGE
KLUTE
KLUTZ
KNURL
KNURS
KNUTE
KRULL
KRUPA
KRUPP

K••U•
KABUL
KAPUT
KEYUP
KLAUS
KNOUT
KRAUS
KRAUT
KUDUS

K•••U
KANZU
KEANU
KHUFU
KUDZU

•KU••
SKUAS
SKULK
SKULL
SKUNK

•K•U•
AKSUM

••KU•
HOKUM
LIKUD
MAKUA
OAKUM
YAKUT
YOKUM

•••KU
HAIKU
TURKU

KV•••
KVASS
KVELL

K•V••
KAVAS
KEVIN
KIVAS

K••V•
KNAVE

K•••V
KIROV

•K•V•
SKIVE

••K•V
YAKOV

K•W••
KIWIS

K••W•
KIOWA
KNOWN
KNOWS

•K•W•
SKEWS

••K•W
ASKEW

K•••X
KYLIX

KY•••
KYACK
KYATS
KYLIX
KYOGA
KYOTO
KYRIE
KYSER
KYZYL

K•Y••
KAYAK
KAYOS
KEYED
KEYES
KEYIN
KEYUP

K••Y•
KENYA
KYZYL

K•••Y
KATHY
KELLY
KELPY
KENNY
KERRY
KESEY
KICKY
KIDDY
KILEY
KILLY
KINKY
KIRBY
KITTY
KOOKY

•K•Y•
OKAYS

••KY•
ALKYD
ALKYL
TOKYO

••K•Y
CAKEY
HOKEY
MCKAY
ONKEY
POKEY
REKEY
TOKAY

•••KY
BALKY
BANKY
BECKY
BOSKY
BUCKY
BULKY
CHOKY
COCKY
CORKY
DICKY
DINKY
DUCKY
DUSKY
ENSKY
FLAKY
FLUKY
FOLKY
FORKY
FUNKY
GAWKY
GEEKY
GORKY
GUNKY
HANKY
HERKY
HOOKY
HUSKY
JERKY
JUNKY
KICKY
KINKY
KOOKY
LANKY
LEAKY
LUCKY
MILKY
MUCKY
MURKY
MUSKY
PANKY
PERKY
PESKY
PICKY
PINKY
PORKY
PUNKY
QUAKY
RICKY
RINKY
RISKY
ROCKY
ROOKY
SHAKY
SILKY
SMOKY
SNAKY
SPIKY
SULKY
TACKY
TALKY
TICKY
WACKY
WONKY
YUCKY

K•Z••
KAZAN
KAZOO
KYZYL

K••Z•
KANZU
KUDZU

K•••Z
KLUTZ
KURTZ

LA•••
LABAN
LABEL
LABIO
LABOR
LACED
LACER
LACES
LACEY
LACKS
LACTI
LACTO
LADED
LADEN
LADER
LADES
LADLE
LADYS
LAGAN
LAGER
LAGOS
LAHTI
LAICS
LAIKA
LAINE
LAING
LAIRD
LAIRS
LAITY
LAIUS
LAKER
LAKES
LAKME
LALAW
LAMAR
LAMAS
LAMBS
LAMED
LAMER
LAMES
LAMIA
LAMPS
LANAI
LANCE
LANDO
LANDS
LANES
LANGE
LANKA
LANKY
LANTZ
LANZA
LAPAZ
LAPEL
LAPIN
LAPIS
LAPPS
LAPSE
LAPUP
LARAM
LARAS
LARCH
LARDS
LARDY
LARES
LARGE
LARGO
LARKS
LARRY
LARUE
LARVA
LASED
LASER
LASES
LASSO
LASTS
LATCH
LATEN
LATER
LATEX
LATHE
LATHS
LATIN
LATKE
LATTE
LAUDE
LAUDS
LAUGH
LAURA
LAVAL
LAVAS
LAVED
LAVER
LAVES
LAVIN
LAWES
LAWNS
LAXER
LAXLY
LAYBY
LAYER
LAYIN
LAYLA
LAYNE
LAYON
LAYTO
LAYUP
LAZAR
LAZED
LAZES

L•A••
LEACH
LEADS
LEAFS
LEAFY
LEAHY
LEAKS
LEAKY
LEANS
LEANT
LEAPS
LEAPT
LEARN
LEARY
LEASE
LEASH
LEAST
LEAVE
LHASA
LIANA
LIANE
LIANG
LIARD
LIARS
LLAMA
LLANO
LOACH
LOADS
LOAFS
LOAMS
LOAMY
LOANS
LOATH
LUAUS

L••A•
LABAN
LAGAN
LALAW
LAMAR
LAMAS
LANAI
LAPAZ
LARAM
LARAS
LAVAL
LAVAS
LAZAR
LEFAY
LEGAL
LEHAR
LEMAY
LETAT
LEVAR
LEXAN
LILAC
LIMAS
LIRAS
LOCAL
LOFAT
LOGAN
LOMAN
LOMAX
LOPAT
LORAN
LORAX
LOTAS
LOYAL
LUBAS
LUCAN
LUCAS
LUKAS
LUNAR
LURAY
LYMAN

L•••A
LAIKA
LAMIA
LANKA
LANZA
LARVA
LAURA
LAYLA
LEEZA
LEHUA
LEICA
LEILA
LEMMA
LENYA
LEONA
LEORA
LEPTA
LHASA
LIANA
LIBRA
LIBYA
LICIA
LINDA
LIVIA
LLAMA
LOGIA
LONGA
LORCA
LORNA
LOTTA
LUCCA
LUCIA
LUISA
LULEA
LURIA
LYCRA
LYDIA
LYNDA
LYTTA

•LA••
ALACK
ALAIN
ALAMO
ALARM
ALATE
ALAVA
BLABS
BLACK
BLADE
BLAHS
BLAIR
BLAKE
BLAME
BLANC
BLAND
BLANK
BLARE
BLASE
BLASS
BLAST
BLATS
BLAZE
CLACK
CLAIM
CLAIR
CLAMP
CLAMS
CLANG
CLANK
CLANS
CLAPS
CLARA
CLARE
CLARK
CLARO
CLASH
CLASP
CLASS
CLAUS
CLAVE
CLAWS
CLAYS
ELAND
ELATE
FLACK
FLAGG
FLAGS
FLAIL
FLAIR
FLAKE
FLAKY
FLAME
FLAMS
FLAMY
FLANK
FLANS
FLAPS
FLARE
FLASH
FLASK
FLATS
FLATT
FLAWS
FLAXY
FLAYS
GLACE
GLADE
GLADS
GLAIR
GLAND
GLARE
GLARY
GLASS
GLAXO
GLAZE
KLAUS
LLAMA
LLANO
OLAND
PLACE
PLAGE
PLAID
PLAIN
PLAIT
PLANB
PLANE
PLANI
PLANK
PLANO
PLANS
PLANT
PLASH
PLASM
PLATA
PLATE
PLATH
PLATO
PLATS
PLATT
PLATY
PLAYA
PLAYS
PLAZA
SLABS
SLACK
SLADE
SLAGS
SLAIN
SLAKE
SLAMS
SLANG
SLANT
SLAPS
SLASH
SLATE
SLATS
SLATY
SLAVE
SLAVS
SLAWS
SLAYS

•L•A•
ALBAN
ALCAN
ALDAN
ALGAE
ALGAL
ALIAS
ALLAH
ALLAN
ALLAY
ALMAY
ALTAI
ALTAR
ALVAR
BLEAK
BLEAR
BLEAT
BLOAT
CLEAN
CLEAR
CLEAT
CLOAK
ELGAR
ELIAS
ELMAN
ELWAY
FLEAS
FLOAT
FLYAT
GLEAM
GLEAN
GLOAM
GLOAT
ILIAC
ILIAD
OLEAN
OLLAS
PLEAD
PLEAS
PLEAT
SLOAN
ULNAE
ULNAS

•L••A
ALAVA
ALCOA
ALETA
ALIDA
ALOHA
ALPHA
ALULA
CLARA
ELENA
ELIZA
FLORA
ILONA
LLAMA
PLATA
PLAYA
PLAZA
PLENA
SLIWA
ULTRA

••LA•
ADLAI
AFLAT
ALLAH
ALLAN
ALLAY
ATLAS
BALAS
BELAY
BFLAT
BOLAS
BYLAW
CFLAT
COLAS
DALAI
DELAY
DFLAT
DRLAO
DYLAN
ECLAT
EFLAT
ENLAI
FFLAT
FILAR
GALAS
GALAX
GFLAT
GOLAN
GULAG
GULAR
HALAS
HULAS
HYLAS
INLAW
INLAY
ISLAM
KOLAS
KULAK
LALAW
LILAC
MALAN
MALAR
MALAY
MELAN
MILAN
MOLAR
MOLAS
MYLAR
NOLAN
OLLAS
ONLAY
PALAE
PALAU
PILAF
PILAR
POLAR
PULAS
RELAX
RELAY
SALAD
SALAL
SALAM
SELAH
SILAS
SOLAN
SOLAR
SPLAT
SPLAY
UHLAN
VELAR
VILAS
VOLAR

••L•A
BALSA
BELLA
BELVA
BULBA
BULLA
CALLA
CELIA
CELLA
CILIA
CILLA
CULPA
DELLA
DELTA
DOLMA
FELLA
FOLIA
FULDA
GALBA
GALEA
GILDA
GOLDA
HELGA
HILDA
JOLLA
JULIA
LULEA
MALTA
MELBA
PALEA
PALMA
PELLA
PILEA
POLKA
SALPA
SALSA
SALTA
SELMA
SELVA
SILVA
SOLFA
SULFA
SULLA
TALIA
TULSA
USLTA
VILLA
VILMA
VOLGA
VOLTA
WILLA
WILMA
YALTA
ZELDA

•••LA
ADELA
AKELA
ALULA
ASYLA
AVILA
BELLA
BOOLA
BULLA
CALLA
CARLA
CELLA
CHELA
CHULA
CILLA
DARLA
DELLA
DOBLA
FELLA
HABLA
HEKLA
JOLLA
KARLA
KOALA
KUALA
KUKLA
LAYLA
LEILA
MARLA
MOOLA
NDOLA
NYALA
OCALA
OOOLA
PAULA
PELLA
PEPLA
PHYLA
SCALA
SHULA
STELA
STOLA
SULLA
TABLA
TESLA
TRALA
TWYLA
UVULA
VILLA
VIOLA
VOILA
WILLA

L•B••
LABAN
LABEL
LABIO
LABOR
LIBBY
LIBEL
LIBRA
LIBRE
LIBYA
LOBBY
LOBED
LOBES
LOBOS
LUBAS
LUBED
LUBES

L••B•
LAMBS
LAYBY
LETBE
LIBBY
LIMBI
LIMBO
LIMBS
LOBBY

•LB••
ALBAN
ALBEE
ALBEN
ALBUM
ELBOW

•L•B•
ALIBI
BLABS
BLEBS
BLOBS
CLUBS
FLUBS
FLYBY
GLEBE
GLOBE
GLOBS
PLEBE
PLEBS
SLABS
SLOBS

•L••B
BLURB
CLIMB
PLANB
PLUMB

••LB•
BILBO
BULBA
BULBS
COLBY
DOLBY
GALBA
MELBA
WELBY

••L•B
ADLIB
CALEB
CELEB

L•C••
LACED
LACER
LACES
LACEY
LACKS
LACTI
LACTO
LICIA
LICIT
LICKS
LOCAL
LOCHS
LOCKE
LOCKS
LOCOS
LOCUS
LTCOL
LUCAN
LUCAS
LUCCA
LUCCI
LUCIA
LUCID
LUCIE
LUCKS
LUCKY
LUCRE
LYCEE
LYCRA

L••C•
LAICS
LANCE
LARCH
LATCH
LEACH
LEECH
LEICA
LOACH
LORCA
LUCCA
LUCCI
LUNCH
LURCH
LYNCH

L•••C
LILAC
LOGIC
LUDIC
LYRIC

•LC••
ALCAN
ALCOA
ALCOR
ELCID
ULCER

•L•C•
ALACK
ALECK
ALICE
ALYCE
BLACK
BLOCH
BLOCK
BLOCS
CLACK
CLICK
CLOCK
CLUCK
ELECT
FLACK
FLECK
FLICK
FLOCK
GLACE
GLUCK
GLUCO
GLYCO
PLACE
PLUCK
SLACK
SLICE
SLICK

•L••C
BLANC
ILIAC
OLEIC
OLMEC

••LC•
BALCH
BELCH
CALCI
CULCH
DELCO
DOLCE
FILCH
GULCH
HULCE
MILCH
MULCH
MULCT
SULCI
WELCH
WILCO
ZILCH

••L•C
ADLOC
FOLIC
FSLIC
HELIC
LILAC
MALIC
MELIC
RELIC
SALIC
TELIC

L•D••
LADED
LADEN
LADER
LADES
LADLE
LADYS
LEDGE
LEDIN
LEDON
LEDTO
LIDDY
LIDOS
LODEN
LODES
LODGE
LUDIC
LYDIA

L••D•
LANDO
LANDS
LARDS
LARDY
LAUDE
LAUDS
LEADS
LEEDS
LENDL
LENDS
LIDDY
LINDA
LINDY
LOADS
LORDS
LUNDI
LUNDY
LYNDA
LYNDE

L•••D
LACED
LADED
LAIRD
LAMED
LASED
LAVED
LAZED
LIARD
LIKED
LIKUD
LIMED
LINED
LIPID
LIVED
LIVID
LLOYD
LOBED
LOPED
LOVED
LOWED
LUBED
LUCID
LURED
LURID

•LD••
ALDAN
ALDEN
ALDER
ALDOL
ALDUS
BLDGS
ELDER
OLDEN
OLDER
OLDIE

•L•D•
ALIDA
BLADE
BLVDS
CLODS
CLYDE
ELIDE
ELUDE
GLADE
GLADS
GLEDE
GLIDE
PLODS
SLADE
SLEDS
SLIDE

•L••D
ALGID
ALKYD
ALOUD
BLAND
BLEED
BLEND
BLIND
BLOND
BLOOD
BLUED
CLOUD
CLUED
ELAND
ELCID

FLIED FLOOD FLOYD FLUID GLAND GLUED ILIAD LLOYD OLAND PLAID PLEAD PLIED SLOYD SLUED

••LD•

BALDS COLDS FALDO FOLDS FULDA GILDA GILDS GOLDA GOLDE GOLDS HILDA HOLDS MELDS MOLDS MOLDY NALDI SOLDI SOLDO TILDE VELDS VELDT WALDO WELDS WILDE WILDS WOLDS ZELDA

••L•D

AILED BALED DELED DOLED EELED FELID FILED GELID HALED HOLED IDLED OGLED OILED PALED PILED POLED PULED RILED RULED SALAD SALUD SOLED SOLID TILED VALID WALED WILED

•••LD

BUILD CHILD COULD FIELD FJELD GOULD GUILD MOULD ROALD SCALD SCOLD SKALD SZOLD WIELD WORLD WOULD YIELD

LE•••

LEACH LEADS LEAFS LEAFY LEAHY LEAKS LEAKY LEANS LEANT LEAPS LEAPT LEARN LEARY LEASE LEASH LEAST LEAVE LEDGE LEDIN LEDON LEDTO LEECH LEEDS LEEKS LEERS LEERY LEETS LEEZA LEFAY LEFTS LEFTY LEGAL LEGER LEGGS LEGGY LEGIS LEGIT LEGOS LEGUP LEHAR LEHUA LEICA LEIGH LEILA LEITH LEMAY LEMMA LEMON LEMUR LENDL LENDS LENIN LENIS LENNY LENOS LENOX LENTO LENTS LENYA LEONA LEONE LEORA LEPTA LEPTO LEPUS LEROI LEROY LETAT LETBE LETGO LETHE LETIN LETON LETTS LETUP LEVAR LEVEE LEVEL LEVER LEVIN LEVIS LEVON LEWES LEWIS LEXAN LEXIS LEXUS LEYTE

L•E••

LEECH LEEDS LEEKS LEERS LEERY LEETS LEEZA LIEGE LIEIN LIENS LIETO LIEUS LIEUT LOESS LOEWE LOEWY LUEGO LYELL

L••E•

LABEL LACED LACER LACES LACEY LADED LADEN LADER LADES LAGER LAKER LAKES LAMED LAMER LAMES LANES LAPEL LARES LASED LASER LASES LATEN LATER LATEX LAVED LAVER LAVES LAWES LAXER LAYER LAZED LAZES LEGER LEVEE LEVEL LEVER LEWES LIBEL LIGER LIKED LIKEN LIKES LIMED LIMEN LIMES LINED LINEN LINER LINES LITER LITES LIVED LIVEN LIVER LIVES LOBED LOBES LODEN LODES LOGES LONER LOPED LOPER LOPES LOPEZ LOREN LORES LOSER LOSES LOVED LOVER LOVES LOVEY LOWED LOWER LOXES LTGEN LUBED LUBES LUGER LUGES LULEA LUMEN LUMET LUNES LURED LURES LUREX LUTES LYCEE LYRES

L•••E

LADLE LAINE LAKME LANCE LANGE LAPSE LARGE LARUE LATHE LATKE LATTE LAUDE LAYNE LEASE LEAVE LEDGE LEONE LETBE LETHE LEVEE LEYTE LIANE LIBRE LIEGE LILLE LISLE LISSE LITHE LITRE LIVRE LOCKE LODGE LOEWE LOGUE LOIRE LOOSE LORNE LORRE LOTTE LOUIE LOUPE LOUSE LUCIE LUCRE LUISE LUNGE LURIE LYCEE LYNDE LYNNE

•LE••

ALECK ALEFS ALENE ALEPH ALERT ALETA ALEUT BLEAK BLEAR BLEAT BLEBS BLEED BLEEP BLEND BLENT BLESS BLEST CLEAN CLEAR CLEAT CLEEK CLEFS CLEFT CLEON CLERK CLEWS ELECT ELEGY ELEMI ELENA ELENI ELEVE FLEAS FLECK FLEER FLEES FLEET FLESH FLEUR FLEWS FLEXI GLEAM GLEAN GLEBE GLEDE GLEES GLENN GLENS GLESS ILENE KLEIN NLERS OLEAN OLEIC OLEIN OLEOS OLEUM PLEAD PLEAS PLEAT PLEBE PLEBS PLEIO PLENA PLEON SLEDS SLEEK SLEEP SLEET SLEPT SLEWS

•L•E•

ALBEE ALBEN ALDEN ALDER ALGER ALIEN ALLEE ALLEN ALLER ALLES ALLEY ALLEZ ALOES ALTER BLEED BLEEP BLUED BLUER BLUES BLUET BLUEY CLEEK CLUED CLUES ELDER ELIEL ELLEN ELLER ELLES ELMER ELVER ELVES FLEER FLEES FLEET FLIED FLIER FLIES FLOES FLUES FLYER GLEES GLUED GLUER GLUES GLUEY ILLER KLIEG MLLES OLDEN OLDER OLMEC OLSEN PLIED PLIES SLEEK SLEEP SLEET SLIER SLOES SLUED SLUES SLYER ULCER

•L••E

ALATE ALBEE ALENE ALFIE ALFRE ALGAE ALICE ALIKE ALINE ALIVE ALLEE ALLIE ALONE ALYCE BLADE BLAKE BLAME BLARE BLASE BLAZE BLOKE BLUME CLARE CLAVE CLIME CLINE CLIVE CLONE CLOSE CLOVE CLYDE ELATE ELEVE ELIDE ELISE ELITE ELLIE ELOPE ELSIE ELUDE ELUTE ELYSE FLAKE FLAME FLARE FLUKE FLUME FLUTE GLACE GLADE GLARE GLAZE GLEBE GLEDE GLIDE GLOBE GLOVE GLOZE ILENE KLINE KLUGE KLUTE OLDIE OLIVE OLLIE PLACE PLAGE PLANE PLATE PLEBE PLUME SLADE SLAKE SLATE SLAVE SLICE SLIDE SLIME SLOPE SLYPE ULNAE

••LE•

ABLER ADLER AGLET AGLEY AILED AILER AILEY ALLEE ALLEN ALLER ALLES ALLEY ALLEZ APLEY ARLEN ARLES AXLES BALED BALER BALES BELEM BOLES CALEB CCLEF CELEB COLES COLET CULET CULEX DALES DALEY DELED DELES DOLED DOLES EELED EELER ELLEN ELLER ELLES EULER FCLEF FILED FILER FILES FILET FOLEY GALEA GALEN GALES GCLEF GELEE GILES GOLEM GULES HALED HALER HALES HALEY HELEN HOLED HOLES HOLEY IDLED IDLER IDLES ILLER INLET ISLES ISLET ISLEY JULEP JULES KALEL KALES KILEY LULEA MALES MELEE MILER MILES MLLES MOLES MULES MULEY MYLES NFLER NHLER NILES OGLED OGLER OGLES OILED OILER ORLES OSLER OWLET PALEA PALED PALEO PALER PALES PALEY PELEE PELEG PILEA PILED PILEI PILES POLED POLER POLES PULED PULES RELEE RELET RILED RILES RILEY ROLEO ROLES ROLEX RULED RULER RULES SALEM SALEP SALES SELES SILEX SOLED SOLER SOLES TALER TALES TELEO TELEX TILED TILER TILES TOLER TOLET TULES TYLER UTLEY VALES VALET VELEZ VILER VOLES WALED WALER WALES WILED WILES WILEY WYLER XYLEM

••L•E

ALLEE ALLIE BELIE BELLE BILGE BULGE CALPE CALVE CELIE CHLOE DELVE DOLCE DULSE ELLIE FALSE FILLE GELEE GOLDE HALLE HALVE HELVE HULCE JOLIE JULIE LILLE MALLE MELEE MILLE MILNE NOLLE NOLTE OLLIE PALAE PALME PELEE PULSE RELEE RILKE RILLE ROLFE ROLLE SALLE SALVE SOLVE TILDE TULLE VALLE VALSE VALUE VALVE VILLE VOLTE WILDE WOLFE WYLIE YALIE

•••LE

ABELE ADDLE ADELE AGILE AISLE AMBLE AMOLE AMPLE ANGLE ANKLE ANOLE APPLE BAYLE BELLE BERLE BEYLE BIBLE BOGLE BOOLE BOULE BOYLE BRULE BUGLE CABLE CARLE CHILE CYCLE DHOLE DOBLE DOYLE DUPLE EAGLE EARLE ECOLE EDILE EMILE EXILE FABLE FILLE FOYLE GABLE GAYLE GUILE HAILE HALLE HAOLE HOYLE INGLE INKLE ISTLE JOULE LADLE LILLE LISLE MACLE MALLE MAPLE MERLE MILLE NEALE NOBLE NOLLE ODILE ONCLE ORALE OVULE PARLE PEALE PEELE PERLE PHILE PHYLE POOLE PROLE QUALE RIFLE RILLE ROBLE ROLLE RUBLE SABLE SALLE SCALE SEALE SEULE SHALE SIDLE SMILE SOCLE SPILE STALE STELE STILE STOLE STYLE SWALE TABLE THOLE THULE TITLE TOILE TULLE UNCLE UTILE VALLE VILLE VOILE WHALE WHILE WHOLE

L•F••

LEFAY LEFTS LEFTY LIFTS LOFAT LOFTS LOFTY LUFFS

L••F•

LEAFS LEAFY LOAFS LUFFS

•LF••

ALFIE ALFRE ELFIN

•L•F•

ALEFS ALIFS ALOFT BLUFF CLEFS CLEFT CLIFF CLIFT FLUFF

•L••F

ALOOF BLUFF CLIFF FLUFF

••LF•

DELFT GOLFS GULFS ROLFE SOLFA SULFA WOLFE WOLFF

••L•F

CALIF CCLEF FCLEF GCLEF PILAF WOLFF

•••LF

ADOLF SHELF WOOLF

L•G••

LAGAN LAGER LAGOS LEGAL LEGER LEGGS LEGGY LEGIS LEGIT LEGOS LEGUP LIGER LIGHT LIGNI LIGNO LOGAN LOGES LOGIA LOGIC LOGIN LOGON LOGOS LOGUE LTGEN LTGOV LUGER LUGES

L••G•

LANGE LARGE LARGO LAUGH LEDGE LEGGS LEGGY LEIGH LETGO LIEGE LINGO LODGE LONGA LONGI LONGS LOUGH LUEGO LUIGI LUNGE LUNGS

L•••G

LAING LIANG LYING

•LG••

ALGAE ALGAL ALGER ALGID ALGIN ALGOL ELGAR ELGIN ILGWU

•L•G•

ALIGN BLDGS BLIGH CLOGS ELEGY FLAGG FLAGS FLOGS GLOGG KLUGE OLIGO OLOGY PLAGE PLUGS SLAGS SLIGO SLOGS SLUGS

•L••G

ALONG CLANG CLING CLUNG FLAGG FLING FLUNG GLOGG KLIEG SLANG SLING SLUNG

••LG•

BILGE BILGY BULGE BULGY GOLGI HELGA VOLGA

••L•G

GULAG PELEG RELIG ZELIG

LH•••

LHASA

L•H••

LAHTI LEHAR LEHUA

L••H•

LATHE LATHS LEAHY LETHE LIGHT LITHE LITHO LOCHS

L•••H

LARCH LATCH LAUGH LEACH LEASH LEECH LEIGH LEITH LOACH LOATH LOUGH LUNCH LURCH LYMPH LYNCH

•L•H•

ALOHA ALPHA ALTHO BLAHS ELIHU

•L••H

ALEPH ALLAH BLIGH BLOCH BLUSH BLUTH BLYTH CLASH CLOTH FLASH FLESH FLUSH GLYPH PLASH PLATH PLUSH SLASH SLOSH SLOTH SLUSH

••LH•

DELHI

••L•H

ALLAH BALCH BALKH BELCH CULCH DOLPH FILCH FILTH GULCH MILCH MULCH RALPH SELAH SYLPH TILTH WALSH WELCH WELSH ZILCH

LI•••

LIANA LIANE LIANG LIARD LIARS LIBBY LIBEL LIBRA LIBRE LIBYA LICIA LICIT LICKS LIDDY LIDOS LIEGE LIEIN LIENS LIETO LIEUS LIEUT LIFTS LIGER LIGHT LIGNI LIGNO LIKED LIKEN LIKES LIKUD LILAC LILLE LILTS LIMAS LIMBI LIMBO LIMBS LIMED LIMEN LIMES LIMIT LIMNS LIMON LIMOS LIMPS LINDA LINDY LINED LINEN LINER LINES LINGO LINKS LINTS LINTY LINUS LIONS LIPID LIPPI LIPPO LIPPY LIRAS LISLE LISPS LISSE LISTS LISZT LITER LITES LITHE LITHO LITON LITRE LITUP LIVED LIVEN LIVER LIVES LIVIA LIVID LIVRE

L•I••

LAICS LAIKA LAINE LAING LAIRD LAIRS LAITY LAIUS

LEICA
LEIGH
LEILA
LEITH
LOINS
LOIRE
LUIGI
LUISA
LUISE
LVIII
LXIII
LYING

L••I•
LABIO
LAMIA
LAPIN
LAPIS
LATIN
LAVIN
LAYIN
LEDIN
LEGIS
LEGIT
LENIN
LENIS
LETIN
LEVIN
LEVIS
LEWIS
LEXIS
LICIA
LICIT
LIEIN
LIMIT
LIPID
LIVIA
LIVID
LOGIA
LOGIC
LOGIN
LORIS
LOUIE
LOUIS
LUCIA
LUCID
LUCIE
LUDIC
LUNIK
LUPIN
LURIA
LURID
LURIE
LVIII
LXIII
LXVII
LXXII
LXXIV
LXXIX
LYDIA
LYRIC
LYSIN

L•••I
LACTI
LAHTI
LANAI
LEROI
LIGNI
LIMBI
LIPPI
LONGI
LUCCI
LUIGI
LUNDI
LVIII
LXIII
LXVII
LXXII
LXXVI
LXXXI

•LI••
ALIAS
ALIBI
ALICE
ALIDA
ALIEN
ALIFS
ALIGN
ALIKE
ALINE
ALIST
ALIVE
BLIGH
BLIMP
BLIND
BLINI
BLINK
BLIPS
BLISS
BLITT
BLITZ
CLICK
CLIFF
CLIFT
CLIII
CLIMB
CLIME
CLINE
CLING
CLINK
CLINT
CLIOS
CLIPS
CLIVE
DLIII
ELIAS
ELIDE
ELIEL
ELIHU
ELION
ELIOT
ELISE
ELITE
ELIZA
FLICK
FLIED
FLIER
FLIES
FLING
FLINT
FLIPS
FLIRT
FLITS
GLIDE
GLIMS
GLINT
GLITZ
ILIAC
ILIAD
ILION
ILIUM
KLIEG
KLIMT
KLINE
MLIII
OLIGO
OLIOS
OLIVE
PLIED
PLIES
PLINK
PLINY
SLICE
SLICK
SLIDE
SLIER
SLIGO
SLIME
SLIMS
SLIMY
SLING
SLINK
SLIPS
SLITS
SLIWA
XLIII

•L•I•
ALAIN
ALFIE
ALGID
ALGIN
ALLIE
ALLIN
ALVIN
BLAIR
BLOIS
CLAIM
CLAIR
CLIII
CLVII
CLXII
CLXIV
CLXIX
DLIII
DLVII
DLXII
DLXIV
DLXIX
ELCID
ELFIN
ELGIN
ELLIE
ELLIS
ELSIE
ELVIN
ELVIS
FLAIL
FLAIR
FLUID
FLYIN
GLAIR
KLEIN
MLIII
MLVII
MLXII
MLXIV
MLXIX
OLDIE
OLEIC
OLEIN
OLLIE
PLAID
PLAIN
PLAIT
PLEIO
SLAIN
XLIII
XLVII

•L••I
ALIBI
ALTAI
BLINI
CLIII
CLVII
CLXII
CLXVI
CLXXI
DLIII
DLVII
DLXII
DLXVI
DLXXI
ELEMI
ELENI
FLEXI
MLIII
MLVII
MLXII
MLXVI
MLXXI
PLANI
XLIII
XLVII

••LI•
ADLIB
ALLIE
ALLIN
AULIS
BALIN
BELIE
CALIF
CALIX
CCLII
CCLIV
CCLIX
CDLII
CDLIV
CDLIX
CELIA
CELIE
CILIA
CMLII
CMLIV
CMLIX
COLIN
CXLII
CXLIV
CXLIX
DCLII
DCLIV
DCLIX
DELIS
DXLII
DXLIV
DXLIX
ELLIE
ELLIS
FELID
FELIS
FELIX
FELIZ
FOLIA
FOLIC
FOLIO
FSLIC
GELID
HELIC
HELIO
HELIX
JOLIE
JULIA
JULIE
JULIO
KILIM
KYLIX
MALIC
MCLII
MCLIV
MCLIX
MDLII
MDLIV
MDLIX
MELIC
MMLII
MMLIV
MMLIX
MXLII
MXLIV
MXLIX
OLLIE
OSLIN
OXLIP
POLIS
POLIT
PULIS
RELIC
RELIG
RELIT
SALIC
SOLID
SPLIT
TALIA
TELIC
TULIP
UNLIT
VALID
WYLIE
YALIE
ZELIG

••L•I
ADLAI
BELLI
CALCI
CALLI
CCLII
CCLVI
CCLXI
CDLII
CDLVI
CDLXI
CELLI
CMLII
CMLVI
CMLXI
CXLII
CXLVI
DALAI
DCLII
DCLVI
DCLXI
DELHI
DXLII
DXLVI
ENLAI
GALLI
GOLGI
MCLII
MCLVI
MCLXI
MDLII
MDLVI
MDLXI
MILLI
MMLII
MMLVI
MMLXI
MULTI
MXLII
MXLVI
NALDI
PALPI
PILEI
SALMI
SOLDI
SOLTI
SULCI
VALLI
VILLI

•••LI
AIOLI
BELLI
CALLI
CCCLI
CCXLI
CDXLI
CELLI
CHILI
CMXLI
DCCLI
DCXLI
EBOLI
GALLI
MCCLI
MCDLI
MCMLI
MCXLI
MDCLI
MDXLI
MILLI
MMCLI
MMDLI
MMMLI
MMXLI
OBELI
OBOLI
OVOLI
PAOLI
STYLI
VALLI
VILLI

L•K••
LAKER
LAKES
LAKME
LIKED
LIKEN
LIKES
LIKUD
LUKAS

L••K•
LACKS
LAIKA
LANKA
LANKY
LARKS
LATKE
LEAKS
LEAKY
LEEKS
LICKS
LINKS
LOCKE
LOCKS
LOOKS
LUCKS
LUCKY
LURKS

L•••K
LUNIK

•LK••
ALKYD
ALKYL

•L•K•
ALIKE
BLAKE
BLOKE
FLAKE
FLAKY
FLUKE
FLUKY
SLAKE

•L••K
ALACK
ALECK
BLACK
BLANK
BLEAK
BLINK
BLOCK
CLACK
CLANK
CLARK
CLEEK
CLERK
CLICK
CLINK
CLOAK
CLOCK
CLONK
CLUCK
CLUNK
FLACK
FLANK
FLASK
FLECK
FLICK
FLOCK
FLUNK
GLUCK
PLANK
PLINK
PLONK
PLUCK
PLUNK
SLACK
SLEEK
SLICK
SLINK
SLUNK

••LK•
BALKH
BALKS
BALKY
BILKO
BILKS
BULKS
BULKY
CALKS
FOLKS
FOLKY
HULKS
MILKS
MILKY
POLKA
RILKE
SILKS
SILKY
SULKS
SULKY
TALKS
TALKY
WALKS
YOLKS

••L•K
KULAK

•••LK
CAULK
CHALK
SKULK
STALK
WHELK

LL•••
LLAMA
LLANO
LLOYD

L•L••
LALAW
LILAC
LILLE
LILTS
LOLLS
LOLLY
LULEA
LULLS
LULLY
LULUS

L••L•
LADLE
LAXLY
LAYLA
LEILA
LILLE
LISLE
LOLLS
LOLLY
LOWLY
LULLS
LULLY
LYELL

L•••L
LABEL
LAPEL
LAVAL
LEGAL
LENDL
LEVEL
LIBEL
LOCAL
LOYAL
LTCOL
LYELL
LYSOL

•LL••
ALLAH
ALLAN
ALLAY
ALLEE
ALLEN
ALLER
ALLES
ALLEY
ALLEZ
ALLIE
ALLIN
ALLOT
ALLOW
ALLOY
ALLYL
ELLEN
ELLER
ELLES
ELLIE
ELLIS
ILLER
ILLUS
MLLES
OLLAS
OLLIE

•L•L•
ALULA
SLYLY

•L••L
ALDOL
ALGAL
ALGOL
ALKYL
ALLYL
ELIEL
FLAIL

••LL•
BALLS
BALLY
BELLA
BELLE
BELLI
BELLS
BELLY
BILLS
BILLY
BOLLS
BULLA
BULLS
BULLY
CALLA
CALLI
CALLS
CELLA
CELLI
CELLO
CELLS
CILLA
CULLS
DALLY
DELLA
DELLS
DILLS
DILLY
DOLLS
DOLLY
DULLS
DULLY
FALLS
FELLA
FELLS
FELLY
FILLE
FILLS
FILLY
FOLLY
FULLY
GALLI
GALLO
GALLS
GILLS
GOLLY
GULLS
GULLY
HALLE
HALLO
HALLS
HELLO
HILLS
HILLY
HOLLY
HULLO
HULLS
JELLO
JELLS
JELLY
JOLLA
JOLLY
KELLY
KILLS
KILLY
LILLE
LOLLS
LOLLY
LULLS
LULLY
MALLE
MALLS
MILLE
MILLI
MILLS
MOLLS
MOLLY
MULLS
NELLY
NILLY
NOLLE
NULLS
PALLS
PALLY
PELLA
PILLS
POLLO
POLLS
POLLY
PULLS
RALLY
RILLE
RILLS
ROLLE
ROLLO
ROLLS
SALLE
SALLY
SELLS
SILLS
SILLY
SULLA
SULLY
TALLY
TELLS
TELLY
TILLS
TILLY
TOLLS
TULLE
TULLY
VALLE
VALLI
VILLA
VILLE
VILLI
WALLS
WALLY
WELLS
WILLA
WILLS
WILLY
YELLS
ZILLS

••L•L
ALLYL
KALEL
SALAL

•••LL
ATALL
ATOLL
BBALL
BCELL
BEALL
BRILL
BUELL
CHILL
DRILL
DROLL
DWELL
EWELL
FRILL
GRILL
IDYLL
INALL
KNELL
KNOLL
KRILL
KRULL
KVELL
LYELL
NEILL
ODELL
PHYLL
PRELL
QUELL
QUILL
SCULL
SHALL
SHELL
SHILL
SKILL
SKULL
SMALL
SMELL
SNELL
SPALL
SPELL
SPILL
STALL
STILL
STULL
SWELL
SWILL
SZELL
TBILL
THILL
TRILL
TROLL
TWILL
UDALL
WEILL
WHOLL
YOULL

L•M••
LAMAR
LAMAS
LAMBS
LAMED
LAMER
LAMES
LAMIA
LAMPS
LEMAY
LEMMA
LEMON
LEMUR
LIMAS
LIMBI
LIMBO
LIMBS
LIMED
LIMEN
LIMES
LIMIT
LIMNS
LIMON
LIMOS
LIMPS
LOMAN
LOMAX
LUMEN
LUMET
LUMPS
LUMPY
LYMAN
LYMON
LYMPH

L••M•
LAKME
LEMMA
LLAMA
LOAMS
LOAMY
LOOMS

L•••M
LARAM

•LM••
ALMAY
ELMAN
ELMER
ELMOS
OLMEC
OLMOS

•L•M•
ALAMO
ALUMS
BLAME
BLIMP
BLUME
CLAMP
CLAMS
CLIMB
CLIME
CLOMP
CLUMP
ELEMI
FLAME
FLAMS
FLAMY
FLUME
GLIMS
GLOMS
KLIMT
LLAMA
PLUMB
PLUME
PLUMP
PLUMS
PLUMY
SLAMS
SLIME
SLIMS
SLIMY
SLOMO
SLUMP
SLUMS

•L••M
ALARM
ALBUM
BLOOM
CLAIM
GLEAM
GLOAM
GLOOM
ILIUM
OLEUM
PLASM

••LM•
BALMS
BALMY
CALMS
CULMS
DOLMA
FILMS
FILMY
HELMS
HOLMS
MALMO
PALMA
PALME
PALMS
PALMY
SALMI
SELMA
VILMA
WILMA

••L•M
BELEM
COLUM
FILUM
GOLEM
HILUM
ISLAM
KILIM
PILUM
SALAM
SALEM
SOLUM
VELUM
XYLEM

•••LM
HAULM
PSALM
QUALM
REALM
WHELM

L•N••
LANAI
LANCE
LANDO
LANDS
LANES
LANGE
LANKA
LANKY
LANTZ
LANZA
LENDL
LENDS
LENIN
LENIS
LENNY
LENOS
LENOX
LENTO
LENTS
LENYA
LINDA
LINDY
LINED
LINEN
LINER
LINES
LINGO
LINKS
LINTS
LINTY
LINUS
LONER
LONGA
LONGI
LONGS
LUNAR
LUNCH
LUNDI
LUNDY
LUNES
LUNGE
LUNGS
LUNIK
LYNCH
LYNDA
LYNDE
LYNNE

L••N•
LAINE
LAING
LAWNS
LAYNE
LEANS
LEANT
LENNY
LEONA
LEONE
LIANA
LIANE
LIANG
LIENS
LIGNI
LIGNO
LIMNS
LIONS
LLANO
LOANS
LOINS
LOONS
LOONY
LORNA
LORNE
LYING
LYNNE
LYONS

L•••N
LABAN
LADEN
LAGAN
LAPIN
LATEN
LATIN
LAVIN
LAYIN
LAYON
LEARN
LEDIN
LEDON
LEMON
LENIN
LETIN
LETON
LEVIN
LEVON
LEXAN
LIEIN
LIKEN
LIMEN
LIMON
LINEN
LITON
LIVEN
LODEN
LOGAN
LOGIN
LOGON
LOMAN
LORAN
LOREN
LTGEN
LUCAN
LUMEN
LUPIN
LUZON
LYMAN
LYMON
LYSIN

•LN••
ULNAE
ULNAS

•L•N•
ALENE
ALINE
ALONE
ALONG
BLANC
BLAND
BLANK
BLEND
BLENT
BLIND
BLINI
BLINK
BLOND
BLUNT
CLANG
CLANK
CLANS
CLINE
CLING
CLINK
CLINT
CLONE
CLONK
CLUNG
CLUNK
CLUNY
ELAND
ELENA
ELENI
FLANK
FLANS
FLING
FLINT
FLUNG
FLUNK
FLYNN
GLAND
GLENN
GLENS
GLINT
ILENE
ILONA
KLINE
LLANO
OLAND
PLANB
PLANE
PLANI
PLANK
PLANO
PLANS
PLANT
PLENA
PLINK
PLINY
PLONK
PLUNK
SLANG
SLANT
SLING
SLINK
SLUNG
SLUNK

•L••N
ALAIN
ALBAN
ALBEN
ALCAN
ALDAN
ALDEN
ALGIN
ALIEN
ALIGN
ALLAN
ALLEN
ALLIN
ALTON
ALVIN
BLOWN
CLEAN
CLEON
CLOWN
ELFIN
ELGIN
ELION
ELLEN
ELMAN
ELTON
ELVIN
FLOWN
FLYIN
FLYNN
GLEAN
GLENN
GLUON
ILION
KLEIN
OLDEN
OLEAN
OLEIN
OLSEN
OLSON
PLAIN
PLEON
SLAIN
SLOAN

••LN•
KILNS
MILNE

••L•N
ALLAN
ALLEN
ALLIN
ARLEN
BALIN
COLIN
COLON
DELON
DYLAN
ELLEN
EMLYN
FELON
GALEN
GOLAN
HALON
HELEN
MALAN
MELAN
MELON
MILAN
NOLAN
NYLON
ORLON
OSLIN
PYLON
SALON
SOLAN
SOLON
TALON
UHLAN

LO•••
LOACH
LOADS
LOAFS
LOAMS
LOAMY
LOANS
LOATH
LOBBY
LOBED
LOBES
LOBOS
LOCAL
LOCHS
LOCKE
LOCKS
LOCOS
LOCUS
LODEN
LODES
LODGE
LOESS
LOEWE
LOEWY
LOFAT
LOFTS
LOFTY
LOGAN
LOGES
LOGIA
LOGIC
LOGIN
LOGON
LOGOS
LOGUE
LOINS

LOIRE LOLLS LOLLY LOMAN LOMAX LONER LONGA LONGI LONGS LOOKS LOOMS LOONS LOONY LOOPS LOOPY LOOSE LOOTS LOPAT LOPED LOPER LOPES LOPEZ LOPPY LORAN LORAX LORCA LORDS LOREN LORES LORIS LORNA LORNE LORRE LORRY LOSER LOSES LOTAS LOTTA LOTTE LOTTO LOTUS LOUGH LOUIE LOUIS LOUPE LOUSE LOUSY LOUTS LOVED LOVER LOVES LOVEY LOWED LOWER LOWLY LOWRY LOXES LOYAL

L•O••
LEONA LEONE LEORA LIONS LLOYD LOOKS LOOMS LOONS LOONY LOOPS LOOPY LOOSE LOOTS LYONS

L••O•
LABOR LAGOS LAYON LEDON LEGOS LEMON LENOS LENOX LEROI LEROY LETON LEVON LIDOS LIMON LIMOS LITON LOBOS LOCOS LOGON LOGOS LTCOL LTGOV LUXOR LUZON LYMON LYSOL

L•••O
LABIO LACTO LANDO LARGO LASSO LAYTO LEDTO LENTO LEPTO LETGO LIETO LIGNO LIMBO LINGO LIPPO LITHO LLANO LOTTO LUEGO

•LO••
ALOES ALOFT ALOHA ALONE ALONG ALOOF ALORS ALOUD BLOAT BLOBS BLOCH BLOCK BLOCS BLOIS BLOKE BLOND BLOOD BLOOM BLOOP BLOTS BLOWN BLOWS BLOWY CLOAK CLOCK CLODS CLOGS CLOMP CLONE CLONK CLOPS CLOSE CLOTH CLOTS CLOUD CLOUT CLOVE CLOWN CLOYS ELOPE FLOAT FLOCK FLOES FLOGS FLOOD FLOOR FLOPS FLORA FLOSS FLOUR FLOUT FLOWN FLOWS FLOYD GLOAM GLOAT GLOBE GLOBS GLOGG GLOMS GLOOM GLOPS GLORY GLOSS GLOVE GLOWS GLOZE ILONA LLOYD OLOGY PLODS PLONK PLOPS PLOTS PLOWS PLOYS SLOAN SLOBS SLOES SLOGS SLOMO SLOOP SLOPE SLOPS SLOSH SLOTH SLOTS SLOWS SLOYD ZLOTY

•L•O•
ALCOA ALCOR ALDOL ALGOL ALLOT ALLOW ALLOY ALOOF ALSOP ALTON ALTOS BLOOD BLOOM BLOOP CLEON CLIOS ELBOW ELION ELIOT ELMOS ELROY ELTON FLOOD FLOOR FLUOR GLOOM GLUON ILION OLEOS OLIOS OLMOS OLSON PLEON SLOOP

•L••O
ALAMO ALTHO BLUTO CLARO GLAXO GLUCO GLYCO LLANO OLIGO PLANO PLATO PLEIO PLUTO SLIGO SLOMO

••LO•
ADLOC AGLOW ALLOT ALLOW ALLOY BELOW BOLOS BULOW CHLOE CHLOR COLON COLOR DELON DELOS DOLOR FELON GALOP HALON HALOS HELOS HELOT IGLOO KILOS MELON MELOS MILOS NILOT NYLON ONLOW ORLON ORLOP PALOS PHLOX PILOT POLOS PYLON SALON SILOS SOLON SOLOS TALON TELOS VALOR YALOW

••L•O
AALTO BILBO BILKO CELLO DELCO DRLAO FALDO FOLIO GALLO HALLO HELIO HELLO HULLO IGLOO JELLO JULIO KELSO MALMO MOLTO PALEO POLLO ROLEO ROLLO SALVO SOLDO TELEO VOLVO WALDO WILCO

•••LO
AMYLO ANGLO CARLO CELLO CYCLO DIPLO GALLO HALLO HATLO HELLO HULLO ITALO JELLO KAHLO MARLO MENLO MYELO OCULO OVOLO PABLO PAOLO PHILO POLLO ROLLO STYLO

L•P••
LAPAZ LAPEL LAPIN LAPIS LAPPS LAPSE LAPUP LEPTA LEPTO LEPUS LIPID LIPPI LIPPO LIPPY LOPAT LOPED LOPER LOPES LOPEZ LOPPY LUPIN

L••P•
LAMPS LAPPS LEAPS LEAPT LIMPS LIPPI LIPPO LIPPY LISPS LOOPS LOOPY LOPPY LOUPE LUMPS LUMPY LYMPH

L•••P
LAPUP LAYUP LEGUP LETUP LITUP

•LP••
ALPHA

•L•P•
ALEPH BLIPS CLAPS CLIPS CLOPS ELOPE FLAPS FLIPS FLOPS GLOPS GLYPH PLOPS SLAPS SLEPT SLIPS SLOPE SLOPS SLYPE

•L••P
ALSOP BLEEP BLIMP BLOOP CLAMP CLASP CLOMP CLUMP PLUMP SLEEP SLOOP SLUMP SLURP

••LP•
CALPE CULPA DOLPH GULPS HELPS KELPS KELPY PALPI PALPS PULPS PULPY RALPH SALPA SALPS SYLPH YELPS

••L•P
GALOP JULEP ORLOP OXLIP POLYP SALEP TULIP

•••LP
QUILP SCALP WHELP

L•R••
LARAM LARAS LARCH LARDS LARDY LARES LARGE LARGO LARKS LARRY LARUE LARVA LEROI LEROY LIRAS LORAN LORAX LORCA LORDS LOREN LORES LORIS LORNA LORNE LORRE LORRY LURAY LURCH LURED LURES LUREX LURIA LURID LURIE LURKS LYRES LYRIC

L••R•
LAIRD LAIRS LARRY LAURA LEARN LEARY LEERS LEERY LEORA LIARD LIARS LIBRA LIBRE LITRE LIVRE LOIRE LORRE LORRY LOWRY LUCRE LYCRA

L•••R
LABOR LACER LADER LAGER LAKER LAMAR LAMER LASER LATER LAVER LAXER LAYER LAZAR LEGER LEHAR LEMUR LEVAR LEVER LIGER LINER LITER LIVER LONER LOPER LOSER LOVER LOWER LUGER LUNAR LUXOR

•LR••
ELROY

•L•R•
ALARM ALERT ALFRE ALORS BLARE BLURB BLURS BLURT CLARA CLARE CLARK CLARO CLERK FLARE FLIRT FLORA GLARE GLARY GLORY NLERS SLURP SLURS ULTRA

•L••R
ALCOR ALDER ALGER ALLER ALTAR ALTER ALVAR BLAIR BLEAR BLUER CLAIR CLEAR ELDER ELGAR ELLER ELMER ELVER FLAIR FLEER FLEUR FLIER FLOOR FLOUR FLUOR FLYER GLAIR GLUER ILLER OLDER SLIER SLYER ULCER

••L•R
ABLER ADLER AILER ALLER BALER CHLOR COLOR DOLOR EELER ELLER EULER FILAR FILER GULAR HALER IDLER ILLER MALAR MILER MOLAR MYLAR NFLER NHLER OGLER OILER OSLER PALER PILAR POLAR POLER RULER SOLAR SOLER TALER TILER TOLER TYLER VALOR VELAR VILER VOLAR WALER WYLER

L•S••
LASED LASER LASES LASSO LASTS LISLE LISPS LISSE LISTS LISZT LOSER LOSES LUSTS LUSTY LYSIN LYSOL

L••S•
LAPSE LASSO LEASE LEASH LEAST LHASA LISSE LOESS LOOSE LOUSE LOUSY LUISA LUISE

L•••S
LACES LACKS LADES LADYS LAGOS LAICS LAIRS LAIUS LAKES LAMAS LAMBS LAMES LAMPS LANDS LANES LAPIS LAPPS LARAS LARDS LARES LARKS LASES LASTS LATHS LAUDS LAVAS LAVES LAWES LAWNS LAZES LEADS LEAFS LEAKS LEANS LEAPS LEEDS LEEKS LEERS LEETS LEFTS LEGGS LEGIS LEGOS LENDS LENIS LENOS LENTS LEPUS LETTS LEVIS LEWES LEWIS LEXIS LEXUS LIARS LICKS LIDOS LIENS LIEUS LIFTS LIKES LILTS LIMAS LIMBS LIMES LIMNS LIMOS LIMPS LINES LINKS LINTS LINUS LIONS LIRAS LISPS LISTS LITES LIVES LOADS LOAFS LOAMS LOANS LOBES LOBOS LOCHS LOCKS LOCOS LOCUS LODES LOESS LOFTS LOGES LOGOS LOINS LOLLS LONGS LOOKS LOOMS LOONS LOOPS LOOTS LOPES LORDS LORES LORIS LOSES LOTAS LOTUS LOUIS LOUTS LOVES LOXES LUAUS LUBAS LUBES LUCAS LUCKS LUFFS LUGES LUKAS LULLS LULUS LUMPS LUNES LUNGS LURES LURKS LUSTS LUTES LYONS LYRES

•LS••
ALSOP ELSIE OLSEN OLSON

•L•S•
ALIST BLASE BLASS BLAST BLESS BLEST BLISS BLUSH CLASH CLASP CLASS CLOSE ELISE ELYSE FLASH FLASK FLESH FLOSS FLUSH GLASS GLESS GLOSS PLASH PLASM PLUSH SLASH SLOSH SLUSH

•L••S
ALDUS ALEFS ALIAS ALIFS ALLES ALOES ALORS ALTOS ALTUS ALUMS BLABS BLAHS BLASS BLATS BLDGS BLEBS BLESS BLIPS BLISS BLOBS BLOCS BLOIS BLOTS BLOWS BLUES BLURS BLVDS CLAMS CLANS CLAPS CLASS CLAUS CLAWS CLAYS CLEFS CLEWS CLIOS CLIPS CLODS CLOGS CLOPS CLOTS CLOYS CLUBS CLUES ELIAS ELLES ELLIS ELMOS ELVES ELVIS FLAGS FLAMS FLANS FLAPS FLATS FLAWS FLAYS FLEAS FLEES FLEWS FLIES FLIPS FLITS FLOES FLOGS FLOPS FLOSS FLOWS FLUBS FLUES GLADS GLASS GLEES GLENS GLESS GLIMS GLOBS GLOMS GLOPS GLOSS GLOWS GLUES GLUTS ILLUS KLAUS MLLES NLERS OLEOS OLIOS OLLAS OLMOS PLANS PLATS PLAYS PLEAS PLEBS PLIES PLODS PLOPS PLOTS PLOWS PLOYS PLUGS PLUMS SLABS SLAGS SLAMS SLAPS SLATS SLAVS SLAWS SLAYS SLEDS SLEWS SLIMS SLIPS SLITS SLOBS SLOES SLOGS SLOPS SLOTS SLOWS SLUES SLUGS SLUMS SLURS ULNAS

••LS•
BALSA DULSE FALSE HOLST KELSO PALSY PULSE SALSA TULSA VALSE WALSH WALSY WELSH

••L•S
ALLES APLUS ARLES ATLAS AULIS AXLES BALAS BALDS BALES BALKS BALLS BALMS BALTS BELLS BELTS BILKS BILLS BOLAS BOLES BOLLS BOLOS BOLTS BOLUS BPLUS BULBS BULKS BULLS CALKS CALLS CALMS CELLS CELTS COLAS COLDS COLES COLTS CPLUS CULLS CULMS CULTS DALES DELES DELIS DELLS DELOS DELTS DILLS DOLES DOLLS DOLTS DPLUS DULLS ELLES ELLIS EOLUS FALLS FELIS FELLS FELTS FILES FILLS FILMS FOLDS FOLKS GALAS GALES GALLS GILDS GILES GILLS GILTS GOLDS GOLFS GULES GULFS GULLS GULPS HALAS HALES HALLS HALOS HALTS HELMS HELOS HELPS HILLS HILTS HOLDS HOLES HOLMS HULAS HULKS HULLS HYLAS IDLES IGLUS ILLUS ISLES JELLS JILTS JOLTS JULES KALES KELPS KILLS KILNS KILOS KILTS KOLAS LILTS LOLLS LULLS LULUS MALES MALLS MALTS MELDS MELOS MELTS MILES MILKS MILLS MILOS MILTS MLLES MOLAS MOLDS MOLES MOLLS MOLTS MULES MULLS MYLES NILES NULLS OGLES OLLAS ORLES PALES PALLS PALMS PALOS PALPS PELTS PILES PILLS PILUS POLES POLIS POLLS POLOS PULAS PULES PULIS PULLS PULPS RILES RILLS ROLES ROLLS RULES SALES SALPS SALTS SELES SELLS SILAS SILKS SILLS SILOS SILTS SOLES SOLOS SOLUS SULKS TALES TALKS TALUS TELLS TELOS TILES TILLS TILTS TOLLS TULES VALES VELDS VILAS VOLES VOLTS WALES WALKS WALLS WELDS WELLS WELTS WILDS WILES WILLS WILTS WOLDS YELLS YELPS YOLKS ZILLS ZULUS

•••LS
AGALS AMYLS ANILS ARILS AWOLS AXELS AXILS BAALS BAILS

BALLS
BAWLS
BEALS
BELLS
BILLS
BIRLS
BOILS
BOLLS
BOWLS
BUHLS
BULLS
BURLS
CALLS
CAULS
CEILS
CELLS
COALS
COILS
COOLS
COWLS
CULLS
CURLS
DEALS
DELLS
DIALS
DILLS
DOLLS
DUELS
DULLS
EARLS
ENOLS
EVILS
FAILS
FALLS
FEELS
FELLS
FILLS
FOALS
FOILS
FOOLS
FOULS
FOWLS
FUELS
FURLS
GAELS
GALLS
GAOLS
GAULS
GILLS
GIRLS
GOALS
GULLS
HAILS
HALLS
HAULS
HEALS
HEELS
HERLS
HILLS
HOWLS
HULLS
HURLS
IDOLS
IDYLS
ITALS
JAILS
JARLS
JELLS
JOWLS
KEELS
KILLS
LOLLS
LULLS
MAILS
MALLS
MARLS
MAULS
MEALS
MERLS
MEWLS
MILLS
MOILS
MOLLS
MULLS
NAILS
NIELS
NOELS
NOILS
NULLS
OBOLS
OPALS
OPELS
ORALS
OVALS
PAILS
PALLS
PAWLS
PEALS
PEELS
PILLS
POILS
POLLS
POOLS
PULLS
PURLS
RAILS
RAWLS
REALS
REELS
RIALS
RIELS
RILLS
ROILS
ROLLS
ROTLS
SAILS
SEALS
SEELS
SELLS
SHULS
SIALS
SILLS
SOILS
SOULS
STOLS
TAELS
TAILS
TEALS
TELLS
TILLS
TOILS
TOLLS
TOOLS
URALS
VEILS
VIALS
VIOLS
VTOLS
WAALS
WAILS
WALLS
WEALS
WELLS
WILLS
WOOLS
YAWLS
YELLS
YOWLS
ZEALS
ZILLS

LT•••
LTCOL
LTGEN
LTGOV

L•T••
LATCH
LATEN
LATER
LATEX
LATHE
LATHS
LATIN
LATKE
LATTE
LETAT
LETBE
LETGO
LETHE
LETIN
LETON
LETTS
LETUP
LITER
LITES
LITHE
LITHO
LITON
LITRE
LITUP
LOTAS
LOTTA
LOTTE
LOTTO
LOTUS
LUTES
LYTTA

L••T•
LACTI
LACTO
LAHTI
LAITY
LANTZ
LASTS
LATTE
LAYTO
LEDTO
LEETS
LEFTS
LEFTY
LEITH
LENTO
LENTS
LEPTA
LEPTO
LETTS
LEYTE
LIETO
LIFTS
LILTS
LINTS
LINTY
LISTS
LOATH
LOFTS
LOFTY
LOOTS
LOTTA
LOTTE
LOTTO
LOUTS
LUSTS
LUSTY
LYTTA

L•••T
LEANT
LEAPT
LEAST
LEGIT
LETAT
LICIT
LIEUT
LIGHT
LIMIT
LISZT
LOFAT
LOPAT
LUMET

•LT••
ALTAI
ALTAR
ALTER
ALTHO
ALTON
ALTOS
ALTUS
ELTON
ULTRA

•L•T•
ALATE
ALETA
BLATS
BLITT
BLITZ
BLOTS
BLUTH
BLUTO
BLYTH
CLOTH
CLOTS
ELATE
ELITE
ELUTE
FLATS
FLATT
FLITS
FLUTE
FLUTY
GLITZ
GLUTS
KLUTE
KLUTZ
PLATA
PLATE
PLATH
PLATO
PLATS
PLATT
PLATY
PLOTS
PLUTO
SLATE
SLATS
SLATY
SLITS
SLOTH
SLOTS
ZLOTY

•L••T
ALERT
ALEUT
ALIST
ALLOT
ALOFT
BLAST
BLEAT
BLENT
BLEST
BLITT
BLOAT
BLUET
BLUNT
BLURT
CLEAT
CLEFT
CLIFT
CLINT
CLOUT
ELECT
ELIOT
FLATT
FLEET
FLINT
FLIRT
FLOAT
FLOUT
FLYAT
GLINT
GLOAT
KLIMT
PLAIT
PLANT
PLATT
PLEAT
SLANT
SLEET
SLEPT

••LT•
AALTO
BALTS
BELTS
BOLTS
CELTS
COLTS
CULTS
DELTA
DELTS
DOLTS
FELTS
FILTH
GILTS
HALTS
HILTS
HOLTZ
JILTS
JOLTS
JOLTY
KILTS
LILTS
MALTA
MALTS
MALTY
MELTS
MELTY
MILTS
MILTY
MOLTO
MOLTS
MULTI
NOLTE
PELTS
SALTA
SALTS
SALTY
SILTS
SILTY
SOLTI
TILTH
TILTS
USLTA
VOLTA
VOLTE
VOLTS
WALTZ
WELTS
WELTY
WILTS
YALTA

••L•T
AFLAT
AGLET
ALLOT
BFLAT
CFLAT
COLET
CULET
DELFT
DFLAT
ECLAT
EFLAT
FFLAT
FILET
GFLAT
HELOT
HOLST
INLET
ISLET
MULCT
NILOT
OWLET
PILOT
POLIT
RELET
RELIT
SALUT
SPLAT
SPLIT
TOLET
UNLIT
VALET
VELDT

•••LT
ADULT
ATILT
BOULT
BUILT
DEALT
DWELT
EXALT
EXULT
FAULT
GUILT
KNELT
MOULT
POULT
QUILT
SAULT
SHALT
SMALT
SMELT
SMOLT
SOULT
SPELT
SPILT
STILT
UBOLT
VAULT

LU•••
LUAUS
LUBAS
LUBED
LUBES
LUCAN
LUCAS
LUCCA
LUCCI
LUCIA
LUCID
LUCIE
LUCKS
LUCKY
LUCRE
LUDIC
LUEGO
LUFFS
LUGER
LUGES
LUIGI
LUISA
LUISE
LUKAS
LULEA
LULLS
LULLY
LULUS
LUMEN
LUMET
LUMPS
LUMPY
LUNAR
LUNCH
LUNDI
LUNDY
LUNES
LUNGE
LUNGS
LUNIK
LUPIN
LURAY
LURCH
LURED
LURES
LUREX
LURIA
LURID
LURIE
LURKS
LUSTS
LUSTY
LUTES
LUXOR
LUZON

L•U••
LAUDE
LAUDS
LAUGH
LAURA
LOUGH
LOUIE
LOUIS
LOUPE
LOUSE
LOUSY
LOUTS

L••U•
LAIUS
LAPUP
LARUE
LAYUP
LEGUP
LEHUA
LEMUR
LEPUS
LETUP
LEXUS
LIEUS
LIEUT
LIKUD
LINUS
LITUP
LOCUS
LOGUE
LOTUS
LUAUS
LULUS

•LU••
ALULA
ALUMS
BLUED
BLUER
BLUES
BLUET
BLUEY
BLUFF
BLUME
BLUNT
BLURB
BLURS
BLURT
BLUSH
BLUTH
BLUTO
CLUBS
CLUCK
CLUED
CLUES
CLUMP
CLUNG
CLUNK
CLUNY
ELUDE
ELUTE
FLUBS
FLUES
FLUFF
FLUID
FLUKE
FLUKY
FLUME
FLUNG
FLUNK
FLUOR
FLUSH
FLUTE
FLUTY
GLUCK
GLUCO
GLUED
GLUER
GLUES
GLUEY
GLUON
GLUTS
KLUGE
KLUTE
KLUTZ
PLUCK
PLUGS
PLUMB
PLUME
PLUMP
PLUMS
PLUMY
PLUNK
PLUSH
PLUTO
SLUED
SLUES
SLUGS
SLUMP
SLUMS
SLUNG
SLUNK
SLURP
SLURS
SLUSH

•L•U•
ALBUM
ALDUS
ALEUT
ALOUD
ALTUS
CLAUS
CLOUD
CLOUT
FLEUR
FLOUR
FLOUT
ILIUM
ILLUS
KLAUS
OLEUM

•L••U
ELIHU
ILGWU

••LU•
APLUS
BOLUS
BPLUS
COLUM
CPLUS
DPLUS
EOLUS
FILUM
HILUM
IGLUS
ILLUS
LULUS
PILUM
PILUS
SALUD
SALUT
SOLUM
SOLUS
TALUS
VALUE
VELUM
ZULUS

••L•U
PALAU

•••LU
POILU
UPOLU

LV•••
LVIII

L•V••
LAVAL
LAVAS
LAVED
LAVER
LAVES
LAVIN
LEVAR
LEVEE
LEVEL
LEVER
LEVIN
LEVIS
LEVON
LIVED
LIVEN
LIVER
LIVES
LIVIA
LIVID
LIVRE
LOVED
LOVER
LOVES
LOVEY
LXVII

L••V•
LARVA
LEAVE
LXXVI

L•••V
LTGOV
LXXIV
LXXXV

•LV••
ALVAR
ALVIN
BLVDS
CLVII
DLVII
ELVER
ELVES
ELVIN
ELVIS
MLVII
XLVII

•L•V•
ALAVA
ALIVE
CLAVE
CLIVE
CLOVE
CLXVI
DLXVI
ELEVE
GLOVE
MLXVI
OLIVE
SLAVE
SLAVS

•L••V
CLXIV
CLXXV
DLXIV
DLXXV
MLXIV
MLXXV

••LV•
BELVA
CALVE
CCLVI
CDLVI
CMLVI
CXLVI
DCLVI
DELVE
DXLVI
HALVE
HELVE
MCLVI
MDLVI
MMLVI
MXLVI
SALVE
SALVO
SELVA
SILVA
SOLVE
VALVE
VOLVO

••L•V
CCLIV
CCLXV
CDLIV
CDLXV
CMLIV
CMLXV
CXLIV
DCLIV
DCLXV
DXLIV
MCLIV
MCLXV
MDLIV
MDLXV
MMLIV
MMLXV
MXLIV

•••LV
CCCLV
CCXLV
CDXLV
CMXLV
DCCLV
DCXLV
MCCLV
MCDLV
MCMLV
MCXLV
MDCLV
MDXLV
MMCLV
MMDLV
MMMLV
MMXLV

L•W••
LAWES
LAWNS
LEWES
LEWIS
LOWED
LOWER
LOWLY
LOWRY

L••W•
LOEWE
LOEWY

L•••W
LALAW

•LW••
ELWAY

•L•W•
BLOWN
BLOWS
BLOWY
CLAWS
CLEWS
CLOWN
FLAWS
FLEWS
FLOWN
FLOWS
GLOWS
ILGWU
PLOWS
SLAWS
SLEWS
SLIWA
SLOWS

•L••W
ALLOW
ELBOW

••L•W
AGLOW
ALLOW
BELOW
BULOW
BYLAW
INLAW
LALAW
ONLOW
YALOW

LX•••
LXIII
LXVII
LXXII
LXXIV
LXXIX
LXXVI
LXXXI
LXXXV

L•X••
LAXER
LAXLY
LEXAN
LEXIS
LEXUS
LOXES
LUXOR
LXXII
LXXIV
LXXIX
LXXVI
LXXXI
LXXXV

L••X•
LXXXI
LXXXV

L•••X
LATEX
LENOX
LOMAX
LORAX
LUREX
LXXIX

•LX••
CLXII
CLXIV
CLXIX
CLXVI
CLXXI
CLXXV
CLXXX
DLXII
DLXIV
DLXIX
DLXVI
DLXXI
DLXXV
DLXXX
MLXII
MLXIV
MLXIX
MLXVI
MLXXI
MLXXV
MLXXX

•L•X•
CLXXI
CLXXV
CLXXX
DLXXI
DLXXV
DLXXX
FLAXY
FLEXI
GLAXO
MLXXI
MLXXV
MLXXX

•L••X
CLXIX
CLXXX
DLXIX
DLXXX
MLXIX
MLXXX

••LX•
CCLXI
CCLXV
CCLXX
CDLXI
CDLXV
CDLXX
CMLXI
CMLXV
CMLXX
DCLXI
DCLXV
DCLXX
MCLXI
MCLXV
MCLXX
MDLXI
MDLXV
MDLXX
MMLXI
MMLXV
MMLXX

••L•X
CALIX
CALYX
CCLIX
CCLXX
CDLIX
CDLXX
CMLIX
CMLXX
CULEX
CXLIX
DCLIX
DCLXX
DXLIX
FELIX
GALAX
HELIX
KYLIX
MCLIX
MCLXX
MDLIX
MDLXX
MMLIX
MMLXX
MXLIX
PHLOX
RELAX
ROLEX
SILEX
TELEX

•••LX
CCCLX
DCCLX
MCCLX
MCDLX
MCMLX
MDCLX
MMCLX
MMDLX
MMMLX

LY•••
LYCEE
LYCRA
LYDIA
LYELL
LYING
LYMAN
LYMON
LYMPH
LYNCH
LYNDA
LYNDE
LYNNE
LYONS
LYRES
LYRIC
LYSIN
LYSOL
LYTTA

L•Y••
LAYBY
LAYER
LAYIN
LAYLA
LAYNE
LAYON
LAYTO
LAYUP
LEYTE
LOYAL

L••Y•
LADYS
LENYA
LIBYA
LLOYD

L•••Y
LACEY
LAITY
LANKY
LARDY
LARRY
LAXLY
LAYBY
LEAFY
LEAHY
LEAKY
LEARY
LEERY
LEFAY
LEFTY
LEGGY
LEMAY
LENNY
LEROY
LIBBY
LIDDY
LINDY
LINTY
LIPPY
LOAMY
LOBBY
LOEWY
LOFTY
LOLLY
LOONY
LOOPY
LOPPY
LORRY
LOUSY
LOVEY
LOWLY
LOWRY
LUCKY
LULLY
LUMPY
LUNDY
LURAY
LUSTY

•LY••
ALYCE
BLYTH
CLYDE
ELYSE
FLYAT
FLYBY
FLYER
FLYIN
FLYNN
GLYCO
GLYPH
SLYER
SLYLY
SLYPE

•L•Y•
ALKYD
ALKYL
ALLYL
CLAYS
CLOYS
FLAYS
FLOYD
LLOYD
PLAYA
PLAYS
PLOYS
SLAYS
SLOYD

•L••Y
ALLAY
ALLEY
ALLOY
ALMAY
BLOWY
BLUEY
CLUNY
ELEGY
ELROY
ELWAY
FLAKY
FLAMY
FLAXY
FLUKY
FLUTY
FLYBY
GLARY
GLORY
GLUEY
OLOGY
PLATY
PLINY
PLUMY
SLATY
SLIMY
SLYLY
ZLOTY

••LY•
ALLYL
CALYX
EMLYN
POLYP

••L•Y
AGLEY
AILEY
ALLAY
ALLEY
ALLOY
APLEY
BALKY
BALLY
BALMY
BELAY
BELLY
BILGY
BILLY
BULGY
BULKY
BULLY
COLBY
DALEY
DALLY
DELAY
DILLY
DOLBY
DOLLY
DULLY
FELLY
FILLY
FILMY
FOLEY
FOLKY
FOLLY
FULLY
GOLLY
GULLY
HALEY
HILLY
HOLEY
HOLLY
INLAY
ISLEY
JELLY
JOLLY
JOLTY
KELLY
KELPY
KILEY
KILLY
LOLLY
LULLY
MALAY
MALTY
MELTY
MILKY
MILTY
MOLDY
MOLLY
MULEY
NELLY
NILLY
ONLAY
PALEY
PALLY
PALMY
PALSY
POLLY
PULPY
RALLY
RELAY
RILEY
SALLY
SALTY
SILKY
SILLY
SILTY
SPLAY
SULKY
SULLY
TALKY
TALLY
TELLY
TILLY
TULLY
UTLEY
WALLY
WALSY
WELBY
WELTY
WILEY
WILLY

•••LY
AMPLY
APPLY
APTLY
BADLY
BALLY
BELLY
BIALY
BILLY
BULLY
BURLY
CARLY
COYLY
CROLY
CURLY
DAILY
DALLY
DILLY
DIMLY

DOILY
DOLLY
DRYLY
DULLY
EARLY
EMILY
FATLY
FELLY
FEYLY
FILLY
FITLY
FOLLY
FULLY
GAYLY
GIRLY
GODLY
GOLLY
GULLY
HAPLY
HEALY
HILLY
HOLLY
HOTLY
HURLY
ICILY
IMPLY
ITALY
JELLY
JOLLY
JOWLY
KELLY
KILLY
LAXLY
LOLLY
LOWLY
LULLY
MADLY
MANLY
MARLY
MEALY
MOLLY
NELLY
NEWLY
NILLY
NOBLY
ODDLY
PALLY
PATLY
POLLY
RALLY
RAWLY
REPLY
ROILY
SADLY
SALLY
SCALY
SEALY
SHYLY
SILLY
SLYLY
SULLY
SURLY
TALLY
TELLY
TILLY
TRULY
TULLY
WALLY
WANLY
WETLY
WILLY
WRYLY

L•Z••
LAZAR
LAZED
LAZES
LUZON

L••Z•
LANZA
LEEZA
LISZT

L•••Z
LANTZ
LAPAZ
LOPEZ

•L•Z•
BLAZE
ELIZA
GLAZE
GLOZE
PLAZA

•L••Z
ALLEZ
BLITZ
GLITZ
KLUTZ

••L•Z
ALLEZ
FELIZ
HOLTZ
VELEZ
WALTZ

MA•••
MABEL
MACAO
MACAW
MACED
MACES
MACHE
MACHO
MACHU
MACLE
MACON
MACRO
MACYS
MADAM
MADGE
MADLY
MADRE
MAGDA
MAGES
MAGIC
MAGMA
MAGNA
MAGOG
MAGOO
MAGOT
MAGUS
MAHAL
MAHAN
MAHDI
MAHRE
MAIDS
MAILS
MAINE
MAINS
MAINZ
MAIZE
MAJOR
MAKER
MAKES
MAKOS
MAKUA
MALAN
MALAR
MALAY
MALES
MALIC
MALLE
MALLS
MALMO
MALTA
MALTS
MALTY
MAMAS
MAMBA
MAMBO
MAMET
MAMIE
MAMMA
MAMMY
MANDY
MANED
MANES
MANET
MANGO
MANIA
MANLY
MANNA
MANNY
MANON
MANOR
MANOS
MANSE
MANTA
MAORI
MAPLE
MAQUI
MARAS
MARAT
MARCH
MARCO
MARCY
MARDI
MARES
MARGE
MARGO
MARIA
MARIE
MARIN
MARIO
MARIS
MARKS
MARLA
MARLO
MARLS
MARLY
MARNE
MARRY
MARSH
MARTA
MARTI
MARTS
MARTY
MARVY
MARYS
MASAI
MASER
MASHY
MASKS
MASON
MASSE
MASSY
MASTS
MASUR
MATCH
MATED
MATEO
MATER
MATES
MATEY
MATHS
MATIN
MATRI
MATRO
MATSU
MATTE
MATZO
MAUDE
MAULS
MAUNA
MAUND
MAURY
MAUVE
MAVEN
MAVIS
MAXED
MAXES
MAXIE
MAXIM
MAXIS
MAYAN
MAYAS
MAYBE
MAYER
MAYON
MAYOR
MAYPO
MAYST
MAZDA
MAZEL
MAZER
MAZES

M•A••
MEADE
MEADS
MEALS
MEALY
MEANS
MEANT
MEANY
MEARA
MEATS
MEATY
MIAMI
MIAOW
MOANS
MOATS

M••A•
MACAO
MACAW
MADAM
MAHAL
MAHAN
MALAN
MALAR
MALAY
MAMAS
MARAS
MARAT
MASAI
MAYAN
MAYAS
MCKAY
MCRAE
MEDAL
MEGAN
MELAN
MESAS
METAL
MICAH
MICAS
MIDAS
MIKAN
MILAN
MIMAS
MINAS
MIZAR
MODAL
MOLAR
MOLAS
MONAD
MORAL
MORAN
MORAY
MURAL
MURAT
MUZAK
MYLAR
MYNAH
MYNAS
MYWAY

M•••A
MAGDA
MAGMA
MAGNA
MAKUA
MALTA
MAMBA
MAMMA
MANIA
MANNA
MANTA
MARIA
MARLA
MARTA
MAUNA
MAZDA
MBIRA
MEARA
MECCA
MEDEA
MEDIA
MEHTA
MELBA
MENSA
MESTA
MICRA
MISHA
MISSA
MOCHA
MOIRA
MOMMA
MONZA
MOOLA
MOTTA
MUDRA
MURRA
MUSCA
MYRNA

•MA••
AMADO
AMAHL
AMAHS
AMAIN
AMANA
AMARA
AMASS
AMATI
AMATO
AMAZE
EMAIL
IMAGE
IMAGO
IMAMS
KMART
OMAHA
OMANI
OMARR
OMASA
SMACK
SMALL
SMALT
SMART
SMASH
SMAZE

•M•A•
AMMAN
AMPAS
AMWAY
EMBAR
EMBAY
SMEAR
UMIAK
YMCAS

•M••A
AMANA
AMARA
AMEBA
AMIGA
OMAHA
OMASA
OMEGA
OMNIA
UMBRA

••MA•
ADMAN
AHMAD
AIMAT
ALMAY
AMMAN
ATMAN
BEMAS
CAMAY
COMAE
COMAS
CUMAE
CYMAE
CYMAS
DAMAN
DAMAR
DUMAS
ELMAN
GAMAL
HAMAL
HAMAN
HEMAN
HUMAN
HYMAN
JAMAL
KEMAL
LAMAR
LAMAS
LEMAY
LIMAS
LOMAN
LOMAX
LYMAN
MAMAS
MIMAS
NEMAN
NEMAT
NOMAD
OSMAN
PIMAS
PUMAS
RAMAN
RAMAR
REMAN
REMAP
ROMAN
SAMAR
SOMAS
SUMAC
UNMAN
UXMAL
WOMAN
WYMAN
YUMAN
YUMAS

••M•A
COMMA
GAMBA
GAMMA
GEMMA
JUMNA
LAMIA
LEMMA
MAMBA
MAMMA
MOMMA
NAMPA
NEMEA
OMAHA
OMASA
PAMPA
PEMBA
RUMBA
SAMBA
SAMOA
SIMBA
SUMBA
SUMMA
TAMPA
YAMPA
ZAMIA

•••MA
ACOMA
AGAMA
ANIMA
AROMA
ASAMA
BURMA
COMMA
DERMA
DOGMA
DOLMA
DRAMA
EDEMA
ETYMA
FIRMA
FORMA
GAMMA
GEMMA
GRAMA
HAEMA
HOUMA
KARMA
LEMMA
LLAMA
MAGMA
MAMMA
MOMMA
NORMA
PALMA
PARMA
PRIMA
SELMA
SIGMA
STOMA
SUMMA
THEMA
VILMA
WILMA

MB•••
MBIRA

M•B••
MABEL
MOBIL
MRBIG

M••B•
MAMBA
MAMBO
MAYBE
MELBA
MOSBY
MUMBO

•MB••
AMBER
AMBIT
AMBLE
AMBOS
AMBRY
EMBAR
EMBAY
EMBED
EMBER
IMBUE
OMBER
OMBRE
UMBEL
UMBER
UMBOS
UMBRA

•M•B•
AMEBA

••MB•
BAMBI
BOMBE
BOMBS
COMBO
COMBS
DUMBO
DUMBS
GAMBA
GUMBO
IAMBI
IAMBS
JAMBS
JUMBO
LAMBS
LIMBI
LIMBO
LIMBS
MAMBA
MAMBO
MUMBO
NAMBY
NIMBI
NIMBY
NUMBS
PAMBY
PEMBA
RAMBO
RUMBA
SAMBA
SIMBA
SUMBA
TAMBO

••M•B
DEMOB
NAMIB

•••MB
ABOMB
CLIMB
CRUMB
HBOMB
PLUMB
RHOMB
RHUMB
THUMB

MC•••
MCCCI
MCCCL
MCCCV
MCCCX
MCCII
MCCIV
MCCIX
MCCLI
MCCLV
MCCLX
MCCOO
MCCOY
MCCVI
MCCXC
MCCXI
MCCXL
MCCXV
MCCXX
MCDII
MCDIV
MCDIX
MCDLI
MCDLV
MCDLX
MCDVI
MCDXC
MCDXI
MCDXL
MCDXV
MCDXX
MCGEE
MCIII
MCKAY
MCLII
MCLIV
MCLIX
MCLVI
MCLXI
MCLXV
MCLXX
MCMII
MCMIV
MCMIX
MCMLI
MCMLV
MCMLX
MCMVI
MCMXC
MCMXI
MCMXL
MCMXV
MCMXX
MCRAE
MCVIE
MCVII
MCXCI
MCXCV
MCXII
MCXIV
MCXIX
MCXLI
MCXLV
MCXVI
MCXXI
MCXXV
MCXXX

M•C••
MACAO
MACAW
MACED
MACES
MACHE
MACHO
MACHU
MACLE
MACON
MACRO
MACYS
MCCCI
MCCCL
MCCCV
MCCCX
MCCII
MCCIV
MCCIX
MCCLI
MCCLV
MCCLX
MCCOO
MCCOY
MCCVI
MCCXC
MCCXI
MCCXL
MCCXV
MCCXX
MDCCC
MDCCI
MDCCL
MDCCV
MDCCX
MDCII
MDCIV
MDCIX
MDCLI
MDCLV
MDCLX
MDCVI
MDCXC
MDCXI
MDCXL
MDCXV
MDCXX
MECCA
MECUM
MICAH
MICAS
MICRA
MICRO
MMCCC
MMCCI
MMCCL
MMCCV
MMCCX
MMCDI
MMCDL
MMCDV
MMCDX
MMCII
MMCIV
MMCIX
MMCLI
MMCLV
MMCLX
MMCMI
MMCML
MMCMV
MMCMX
MMCVI
MMCXC
MMCXI
MMCXL
MMCXV
MMCXX
MOCHA
MOCKS
MUCIN
MUCKS
MUCKY
MXCII
MXCIV
MXCIX
MXCVI

M••C•
MARCH
MARCO
MARCY
MATCH
MCCCI
MCCCL
MCCCV
MCCCX
MCXCI
MCXCV
MDCCC
MDCCI
MDCCL
MDCCV
MDCCX
MDXCI
MDXCV
MECCA
MERCE
MERCI
MERCY
MILCH
MINCE
MITCH
MMCCC
MMCCI
MMCCL
MMCCV
MMCCX
MMDCC
MMDCI
MMDCL
MMDCV
MMDCX
MMMCC
MMMCD
MMMCI
MMMCL
MMMCV
MMMCX
MMXCI
MMXCV
MONCK
MOOCH
MULCH
MULCT
MUNCH
MUSCA

M•••C
MAGIC
MALIC
MCCXC
MCDXC
MCMXC
MDCCC
MDCXC
MEDIC
MEDOC
MELIC
MESIC
MIMIC
MMCCC
MMCXC
MMDCC
MMDXC
MMMCC
MMMDC
MMMXC
MODOC
MUSIC

•MC••
EMCEE
MMCCC
MMCCI
MMCCL
MMCCV
MMCCX
MMCDI
MMCDL
MMCDV
MMCDX
MMCII
MMCIV
MMCIX
MMCLI
MMCLV
MMCLX
MMCMI
MMCML
MMCMV
MMCMX
MMCVI
MMCXC
MMCXI
MMCXL
MMCXV
MMCXX
YMCAS

•M•C•
AMICE
AMOCO
AMUCK
CMXCI
CMXCV
MMCCC
MMCCI
MMCCL
MMCCV
MMCCX
MMDCC
MMDCI
MMDCL
MMDCV
MMDCX
MMMCC
MMMCD
MMMCI
MMMCL
MMMCV
MMMCX
MMXCI
MMXCV
SMACK
SMOCK

•M••C
MMCCC
MMCXC
MMDCC
MMDXC
MMMCC
MMMDC
MMMXC

••MC•
MMMCC
MMMCD
MMMCI
MMMCL
MMMCV
MMMCX

••M•C
COMIC
MCMXC
MIMIC
MMMCC
OLMEC
OSMIC
SUMAC

MD•••
MDCCC
MDCCI
MDCCL
MDCCV
MDCCX
MDCII
MDCIV
MDCIX
MDCLI
MDCLV
MDCLX
MDCVI
MDCXC
MDCXI
MDCXL
MDCXV
MDCXX
MDIII
MDLII
MDLIV
MDLIX
MDLVI
MDLXI
MDLXV
MDLXX
MDVII
MDXCI
MDXCV
MDXII
MDXIV
MDXIX
MDXLI
MDXLV
MDXVI
MDXXI
MDXXV
MDXXX

M•D••
MADAM
MADGE
MADLY
MADRE
MCDII
MCDIV
MCDIX
MCDLI
MCDLV
MCDLX
MCDVI
MCDXC
MCDXI
MCDXL
MCDXV
MCDXX
MEDAL
MEDEA
MEDES
MEDIA
MEDIC
MEDIT
MEDOC
MIDAS
MIDDY
MIDGE
MIDIS
MIDST
MMDCI
MMDCL
MMDCV
MMDCX
MMDII
MMDIV
MMDIX
MMDLI
MMDLV
MMDLX
MMDVI
MMDXC
MMDXI
MMDXL
MMDXV
MMDXX
MODAL
MODEL
MODEM
MODES
MODOC
MODUS
MSDOS
MUDDY
MUDRA

M••D•
MAGDA
MAHDI
MAIDS
MANDY
MARDI
MAUDE
MAZDA
MEADE
MEADS
MEEDS
MELDS
MENDS
MIDDY
MINDS
MINDY
MISDO
MMCDI
MMCDL
MMCDV
MMCDX
MMMDC
MMMDI
MMMDL
MMMDV
MMMDX
MOLDS
MOLDY
MONDE
MONDO
MOODS
MOODY
MUDDY

M•••D
MACED
MANED
MATED
MAUND
MAXED
METED
MEWED
MIKED
MIMED
MINED
MIRED
MIXED
MMMCD
MONAD
MONOD
MOOED
MOPED
MOULD
MOUND
MOVED
MOWED
MUSED
MUTED

•MD••
CMDRS
EMDEN
MMDCC
MMDCI
MMDCL
MMDCV
MMDCX
MMDII
MMDIV
MMDIX
MMDLI
MMDLV
MMDLX
MMDVI
MMDXC
MMDXI
MMDXL
MMDXV
MMDXX

•M•D•
AMADO
AMIDE
IMIDE
IMIDO
MMCDI
MMCDL
MMCDV
MMCDX
MMMDC
MMMDI
MMMDL
MMMDV
MMMDX

•M••D
AMEND
AMPED
EMBED
EMEND
MMMCD
UMPED

••MD•
MMMDC
MMMDI
MMMDL
MMMDV
MMMDX

••M•D
AHMAD
AHMED
AIMED
ARMED
DIMED
DOMED
FAMED
FUMED
GAMED
HOMED
HUMID
LAMED
LIMED
MIMED
MMMCD
NAMED
NOMAD
RIMED
TAMED
TIMED
TIMID
TUMID

ME•••
MEADE
MEADS
MEALS
MEALY
MEANS
MEANT
MEANY
MEARA
MEATS
MEATY
MECCA
MECUM
MEDAL
MEDEA
MEDES
MEDIA
MEDIC
MEDIT
MEDOC
MEEDS
MEESE
MEETS
MEGAN
MEHTA
MEIJI
MELAN
MELBA
MELDS
MELEE
MELIC
MELON
MELOS
MELTS
MELTY
MEMEL
MEMOS
MENDS
MENLO
MENSA
MENUS
MEOWS
MERCE
MERCI
MERCY
MERES
MERGE
MERIT
MERLE
MERLS
MEROE
MERRY
MERTZ
MERYL
MESAS
MESHY
MESIC
MESNE
MESON
MESSY
MESTA
METAL
METED
METER
METES
METIS
METOO
METRE
METRO
MEUSE
MEWED
MEWLS
MEYER
MEZZO

M•E••
MEEDS
MEESE
MEETS
MIENS
MNEME
MYELO
MYERS
MYEYE

M••E•
MABEL
MACED
MACES
MAGES
MAKER
MAKES
MALES
MAMET
MANED
MANES
MANET
MARES
MASER
MATED
MATEO

MATER MATES MATEY MAVEN MAXED MAXES MAYER MAZEL MAZER MAZES MCGEE MEDEA MEDES MELEE MEMEL MERES METED METER METES MEWED MEYER MIKED MIKES MILER MILES MIMED MIMEO MIMER MIMES MINED MINEO MINER MINES MIRED MIRES MISER MITER MITES MIXED MIXER MIXES MLLES MODEL MODEM MODES MOLES MONEL MONET MONEY MOOED MOPED MOPER MOPES MOPEY MOREL MORES MOREY MOSES MOSEY MOTEL MOTES MOTET MOUES MOVED MOVER MOVES MOWED MOWER MULES MULEY MUREX MUSED MUSER MUSES MUTED MUTER MUTES MYLES

M•••E

MACHE MACLE MADGE MADRE MAHRE MAINE MAIZE MALLE MAMIE MANSE MAPLE MARGE MARIE MARNE MASSE MATTE MAUDE MAUVE MAXIE MAYBE MCGEE MCRAE MCVIE MEADE MEESE MELEE MERCE MERGE MERLE MEROE MESNE METRE MEUSE MIDGE MILLE MILNE MINCE MITRE MNEME MOIRE MONDE MONTE MOORE MOOSE MORSE MOSHE MOUSE MOVIE MOXIE MURRE MYEYE MYOPE

•ME••

AMEBA AMEER AMEND AMENS AMENT EMEER EMEND EMERY OMEGA OMENS OMERS SMEAR SMELL SMELT SMEWS UMEKI

•M•E•

AMBER AMEER AMIES AMPED AMVET EMBED EMBER EMCEE EMDEN EMEER EMMER EMMET IMPEI IMPEL OMBER UMBEL UMBER UMPED

•M••E

AMAZE AMBLE AMICE AMIDE AMINE AMOLE AMORE AMPLE AMUSE EMCEE EMILE EMOTE IMAGE IMBUE IMIDE IMINE OMBRE SMAZE SMILE SMITE SMOKE SMOTE

••ME•

AAMES ACMES ADMEN AHMED AIMED AIMEE AIMER ARMED ARMEE ARMET CAMEL CAMEO COMER COMES COMET COMEX CYMES DAMES DEMES DIMED DIMES DOMED DOMES EAMES ELMER EMMER EMMET FAMED FAMES FUMED FUMES GAMED GAMER GAMES GIMEL GOMER GOMEZ HAMEL HAMES HEMEN HEMET HOMED HOMEO HOMER HOMES HOMEY JAMES KHMER LAMED LAMER LAMES LIMED LIMEN LIMES LUMEN LUMET MAMET MEMEL MIMED MIMEO MIMER MIMES NAMED NAMER NAMES NEMEA NIMES NOMEN NUMEN NYMET OLMEC POMES RAMEE RAMEN RAMET REMET REMEX RIMED RIMES ROMEO ROMER RUMEN SUMER TAMED TAMER TAMES TIMED TIMER TIMES TIMEX TOMEI TOMES UNMET WOMEN YEMEN

••M•E

AIMEE ARMEE BOMBE COMAE COMME COMTE CUMAE CYMAE DEMME FEMME GIMME HOMME JAMIE MAMIE POMME RAMEE RAMIE SOMME TEMPE

•••ME

ANIME ARAME BAUME BERME BIOME BLAME BLUME BOHME BROME BRUME CHIME CLIME COMME CREME CRIME DEMME DISME DROME FEMME FLAME FLUME FRAME FROME GETME GIMME GNOME GORME GRIME HITME HOMME ITSME JAIME LAKME MNEME NEUME NOTME PALME PLUME POEME POMME PRIME RHYME SHAME SLIME SOMME SPUME SUEME THEME THYME TORME TRYME WHYME

M•F••

MIFFS MIFFY MOFFO MUFFS MUFTI

M••F•

MIFFS MIFFY MOFFO MUFFS

M•••F

MOTIF

•M••F

SMURF

••MF•

COMFY

M•G••

MAGDA MAGES MAGIC MAGMA MAGNA MAGOG MAGOO MAGOT MAGUS MCGEE MEGAN MIGHT MOGUL MSGTS MUGGY MYGUY

M••G•

MADGE MANGO MARGE MARGO MERGE MIDGE MINGS MONGO MOOGS MUGGY MUNGO

M•••G

MAGOG MRBIG

•M•G•

AMIGA AMIGO IMAGE IMAGO OMEGA SMOGS

•M••G

AMONG HMONG

M•H••

MAHAL MAHAN MAHDI MAHRE MEHTA MOHUR

M••H•

MACHE MACHO MACHU MASHY MATHS MESHY MIGHT MINHO MISHA MOCHA MOSHE MOTHS MOTHY MUSHY MYTHS

M•••H

MARCH MARSH MATCH MICAH MILCH MIRTH MITCH MONTH MOOCH MORPH MOUTH MULCH MUNCH MYNAH MYRRH

•M•H•

AMAHL AMAHS AMPHI AMPHR OMAHA

•M••H

AMISH SMASH SMITH SMYTH

••M•H

HUMPH LYMPH NYMPH OOMPH

MI•••

MIAMI MIAOW MICAH MICAS MICRA MICRO MIDAS MIDDY MIDGE MIDIS MIDST MIENS MIFFS MIFFY MIGHT MIKAN MIKED MIKES MILAN MILCH MILER MILES MILKS MILKY MILLE MILLI MILLS MILNE MILOS MILTS MILTY MIMAS MIMED MIMEO MIMER MIMES MIMIC MIMSY MINAS MINCE MINDS MINDY MINED MINEO MINER MINES MINGS MINHO MINIM MINIS MINKS MINOR MINOS MINOT MINSK MINTS MINTY MINUS MIRED MIRES MIRRO MIRTH MIRVS MISDO MISER MISHA MISOS MISSA MISSY MISTI MISTS MISTY MITCH MITER MITES MITRE MITTS MITTY MITZI MIXED MIXER MIXES MIXUP MIZAR

M•I••

MAIDS MAILS MAINE MAINS MAINZ MAIZE MBIRA MCIII MDIII MEIJI MLIII MMIII MOILS MOIRA MOIRE MOIST MVIII MXIII

M••I•

MAGIC MALIC MAMIE MANIA MARIA MARIE MARIN MARIO MARIS MATIN MAVIS MAXIE MAXIM MAXIS MCCII MCCIV MCCIX MCDII MCDIV MCDIX MCIII MCLII MCLIV MCLIX MCMII MCMIV MCMIX MCVIE MCVII MCXII MCXIV MCXIX MDCII MDCIV MDCIX MDIII MDLII MDLIV MDLIX MDVII MDXII MDXIV MDXIX MEDIA MEDIC MEDIT MELIC MERIT MESIC METIS MIDIS MIMIC MINIM MINIS MLIII MLVII MLXII MLXIV MLXIX MMCII MMCIV MMCIX MMDII MMDIV MMDIX MMIII MMLII MMLIV MMLIX MMMII MMMIV MMMIX MMVII MMXII MMXIV MMXIX MOBIL MOTIF MOVIE MOXIE MRBIG MUCIN MUNIS MUSIC MVIII MXCII MXCIV MXCIX MXIII MXLII MXLIV MXLIX MXMII MXMIV MXVII MXXII MXXIV MXXIX MYSIN

M•••I

MAHDI MAORI MAQUI MARDI MARTI MASAI MATRI MCCCI MCCII MCCLI MCCVI MCCXI MCDII MCDLI MCDVI MCDXI MCIII MCLII MCLVI MCLXI MCMII MCMLI MCMVI MCMXI MCVII MCXCI MCXII MCXLI MCXVI MCXXI MDCCI MDCII MDCLI MDCVI MDCXI MDIII MDLII MDLVI MDLXI MDVII MDXCI MDXII MDXLI MDXVI MDXXI MEIJI MERCI MIAMI MILLI MISTI MITZI MLIII MLVII MLXII MLXVI MLXXI MMCCI MMCDI MMCII MMCLI MMCMI MMCVI MMCXI MMDCI MMDII MMDLI MMDVI MMDXI MMIII MMLII MMLVI MMLXI MMMCI MMMDI MMMII MMMLI MMMVI MMMXI MMVII MMXCI MMXII MMXLI MMXVI MMXXI MUFTI MULTI MVIII MXCII MXCVI MXIII MXLII MXLVI MXMII MXVII MXXII MXXVI MXXXI

•MI••

AMICE AMIDE AMIES AMIGA AMIGO AMINE AMINO AMIRS AMISH AMISS AMITY CMIII EMILE EMILY EMIRS EMITS IMIDE IMIDO IMINE IMINO MMIII OMITS SMILE SMIRK SMITE SMITH SMITS UMIAK

•M•I•

AMAIN AMBIT CMIII CMLII CMLIV CMLIX CMVII CMXII CMXIV CMXIX DEMIT EMAIL IMMIX MMCII MMCIV MMCIX MMDII MMDIV MMDIX MMIII MMLII MMLIV MMLIX MMMII MMMIV MMMIX MMVII MMXIV MMXIX OMNIA

•M••I

AMATI AMPHI CMIII CMLII CMLVI CMLXI CMVII CMXCI CMXII CMXLI CMXVI CMXXI IMPEI MMCCI MMCDI MMCII MMCLI MMCMI MMCVI MMCXI MMDCI MMDII MMDLI MMDVI MMDXI MMIII MMLII MMLVI MMLXI MMMCI MMMDI MMMII MMMLI MMMVI MMMXI MMVII MMXCI MMXII MMXLI MMXVI MMXXI OMANI UMEKI

••MI•

ADMIN ADMIT ADMIX COMIC COMIX CUMIN DEMIT GAMIN HEMIN HUMID IMMIX IZMIR IZMIT JAMIE JAMIN LAMIA LIMIT MAMIE MCMII MCMIV MCMIX MIMIC MMMII MMMIV MMMIX MXMII MXMIV NAMIB NUMIS OSMIC PAMIR RAMIE RAMIS REMIT REMIX SEMIS TAMIL TIMID TUMID ZAMIA

••M•I

BAMBI IAMBI LIMBI MCMII MCMLI MCMVI MCMXI MMMCI MMMDI MMMII MMMLI MMMVI MMMXI MXMII NIMBI SOMNI TEMPI TOMEI

•••MI

ELEMI FERMI MIAMI MMCMI NAOMI NGAMI NURMI OTOMI SALMI SUOMI SWAMI VERMI

M•J••

MAJOR MOJOS

M••J•

MEIJI

M•K••

MAKER MAKES MAKOS MAKUA MCKAY MIKAN MIKED MIKES

M••K•

MARKS MASKS MILKS MILKY MINKS MOCKS MONKS MUCKS MUCKY MURKY MUSKS MUSKY

M•••K

MINSK MONCK MUZAK

•M•K•

SMOKE SMOKY UMEKI

•M••K

AMUCK SMACK SMIRK SMOCK UMIAK

ML•••

MLIII MLLES MLVII MLXII MLXIV MLXIX MLXVI MLXXI MLXXV MLXXX

M•L••

MALAN MALAR MALAY MALES MALIC MALLE MALLS MALMO MALTA MALTS MALTY MCLII MCLIV MCLIX MCLVI MCLXI MCLXV MCLXX MDLII MDLIV MDLIX MDLVI MDLXI MDLXV MDLXX MELAN MELBA MELDS MELEE MELIC MELON MELOS MELTS MELTY MILAN MILCH MILER MILES MILKS MILKY MILLE MILLI MILLS MILNE MILOS MILTS MILTY MLLES MMLII MMLIV MMLIX MMLVI MMLXI MMLXV MMLXX MOLAR MOLAS MOLDS MOLDY MOLES MOLLS MOLLY MOLTO MOLTS MULCH MULCT MULES MULEY MULLS MULTI MXLII MXLIV MXLIX MXLVI MYLAR MYLES

M••L•

MACLE MADLY MAILS MALLE MALLS MANLY MAPLE MARLA MARLO MARLS MARLY MAULS MCCLI MCCLV MCCLX MCDLI MCDLV MCDLX MCMLI MCMLV MCMLX MCXLI MCXLV MDCLI MDCLV MDCLX MDXLI MDXLV MEALS MEALY MENLO MERLE MERLS MEWLS MILLE MILLI MILLS MMCLI MMCLV MMCLX MMDLI MMDLV MMDLX MMMLI MMMLV MMMLX MMXLI MMXLV MOILS MOLLS MOLLY MOOLA MOULD MOULT MULLS MYELO

M•••L

MABEL MAHAL MAZEL MCCCL MCCXL MCDXL MCMXL MDCCL MDCXL MEDAL MEMEL MERYL METAL MMCCL MMCDL MMCML MMCXL MMDCL MMDXL MMMCL MMMDL MMMXL MOBIL MODAL MODEL MOGUL MONEL MORAL MOREL MOSUL MOTEL MURAL

•ML••

CMLII CMLIV CMLIX CMLVI CMLXI CMLXV CMLXX EMLYN MMLII MMLIV MMLIX MMLVI MMLXI MMLXV MMLXX

•M•L•

AMBLE AMOLE AMPLE AMPLY AMYLO AMYLS CMXLI CMXLV EMILE EMILY IMPLY MMCLI MMCLV MMCLX MMDLI MMDLV MMDLX MMMLI MMMLV MMMLX MMXLI MMXLV SMALL SMALT

SMELL
SMELT
SMILE
SMOLT

•M••L
AMAHL
EMAIL
IMPEL
MMCCL
MMCDL
MMCML
MMCXL
MMDCL
MMDXL
MMMCL
MMMDL
MMMXL
SMALL
SMELL
UMBEL

••ML•
DIMLY
MCMLI
MCMLV
MCMLX
MMMLI
MMMLV
MMMLX

••M•L
CAMEL
CUMUL
GAMAL
GIMEL
HAMAL
HAMEL
JAMAL
KEMAL
MCMXL
MEMEL
MMMCL
MMMDL
MMMXL
TAMIL
UXMAL

•••ML
FRIML
MMCML

MM•••
MMCCC
MMCCI
MMCCL
MMCCV
MMCCX
MMCDI
MMCDL
MMCDV
MMCDX
MMCII
MMCIV
MMCIX
MMCLI
MMCLV
MMCLX
MMCMI
MMCML
MMCMV
MMCMX
MMCVI
MMCXC
MMCXI
MMCXL
MMCXV
MMCXX
MMDCC
MMDCI
MMDCL
MMDCV
MMDCX
MMDII
MMDIV
MMDIX
MMDLI
MMDLV
MMDLX
MMDVI
MMDXC
MMDXI
MMDXL
MMDXV
MMDXX
MMIII
MMLII
MMLIV
MMLIX
MMLVI
MMLXI
MMLXV
MMLXX
MMMCC
MMMCD
MMMCI
MMMCL
MMMCV
MMMCX
MMMDC
MMMDI
MMMDL
MMMDV
MMMDX
MMMII
MMMIV
MMMIX
MMMLI
MMMLV
MMMLX
MMMVI
MMMXC
MMMXI
MMMXL
MMMXV
MMMXX
MMVII
MMXCI
MMXCV
MMXII
MMXIV
MMXIX
MMXLI
MMXLV
MMXVI
MMXXI
MMXXV
MMXXX

M•M••
MAMAS
MAMBA
MAMBO
MAMET
MAMIE
MAMMA
MAMMY
MCMII
MCMIV
MCMIX
MCMLI
MCMLV
MCMLX
MCMVI
MCMXC
MCMXI
MCMXL
MCMXV
MCMXX
MEMEL
MEMOS
MIMAS
MIMED
MIMEO
MIMER
MIMES
MIMIC
MIMSY
MMMCC
MMMCD
MMMCI
MMMCL
MMMCV
MMMCX
MMMDC
MMMDI
MMMDL
MMMDV
MMMDX
MMMII
MMMIV
MMMIX
MMMLI
MMMLV
MMMLX
MMMVI
MMMXC
MMMXI
MMMXL
MMMXV
MMMXX
MOMMA
MOMMY
MOMUS
MRMOM
MUMBO
MUMMY
MUMPS
MXMII
MXMIV

M••M•
MAGMA
MALMO
MAMMA
MAMMY
MIAMI
MMCMI
MMCML
MMCMV
MMCMX
MNEME
MOMMA
MOMMY
MUMMY

M•••M
MADAM
MAXIM
MECUM
MINIM
MODEM
MRMOM
MRMOM

•MM••
AMMAN
AMMON
EMMER
EMMET
EMMYS
IMMIX
MMMCC
MMMCD
MMMCI
MMMCL
MMMCV
MMMCX
MMMDC
MMMDI
MMMDL
MMMDV
MMMDX
MMMII
MMMIV
MMMIX
MMMLI
MMMLV
MMMLX
MMMVI
MMMXC
MMMXI
MMMXL
MMMXV
MMMXX

•M•M•
IMAMS
MMCMI
MMCML
MMCMV
MMCMX

••MM•
COMMA
COMME
DEMME
DUMMY
FEMME
GAMMA
GEMMA
GEMMY
GIMME
GUMMO
GUMMY
HAMMY
HOMME
JEMMY
JIMMY
LEMMA
MAMMA
MAMMY
MOMMA
MOMMY
MUMMY
POMME
RUMMY
SAMMS
SAMMY
SIMMS
SOMME
SUMMA
TAMMY
TIMMY
TOMMY
TUMMY
YUMMY

••M•M
MRMOM

•••MM
FROMM
GRAMM
GRIMM

MN•••
MNEME

M•N••
MANDY
MANED
MANES
MANET
MANGO
MANIA
MANLY
MANNA
MANNY
MANON
MANOR
MANOS
MANSE
MANTA
MENDS
MENLO
MENSA
MENUS
MINAS
MINCE
MINDS
MINDY
MINED
MINEO
MINER
MINES
MINGS
MINHO
MINIM
MINIS
MINKS
MINOR
MINOS
MINOT
MINSK
MINTS
MINTY
MINUS
MONAD
MONCK
MONDE
MONDO
MONEL
MONET
MONEY
MONGO
MONKS
MONOD
MONTE
MONTH
MONTY
MONZA
MUNCH
MUNGO
MUNIS
MUNRO
MYNAH
MYNAS

M••N•
MAGNA
MAINE
MAINS
MAINZ
MANNA
MANNY
MARNE
MAUNA
MAUND
MEANS
MEANT
MEANY
MESNE
MIENS
MILNE
MOANS
MOONS
MOONY
MORNS
MOUND
MOUNT
MUONS
MYRNA

M•••N
MACON
MAHAN
MALAN
MANON
MARIN
MASON
MATIN
MAVEN
MAYAN
MAYON
MEGAN
MELAN
MELON
MESON
MIKAN
MILAN
MORAN
MORON
MUCIN
MYRON
MYSIN

•MN••
OMNIA

•M•N•
AMANA
AMEND
AMENS
AMENT
AMINE
AMINO
AMONG
EMEND
HMONG
IMINE
IMINO
OMANI
OMENS

•M••N
AMAIN
AMMAN
AMMON
EMDEN
EMLYN

••MN•
DAMNS
HYMNS
JUMNA
LIMNS
SOMNI

••M•N
ADMAN
ADMEN
ADMIN
AMMAN
AMMON
ATMAN
CUMIN
DAMAN
DAMON
DEMON
EAMON
ELMAN
GAMIN
HAMAN
HEMAN
HEMEN
HEMIN
HUMAN
HYMAN
JAMIN
LEMON
LIMEN
LIMON
LOMAN
LUMEN
LYMAN
LYMON
NEMAN
NOMEN
NUMEN
OSMAN
RAMAN
RAMEN
RAMON
REMAN
ROMAN
RUMEN
SIMON
TIMON
UNMAN
WOMAN
WOMEN
WYMAN
YEMEN
YUMAN

MO•••
MOANS
MOATS
MOBIL
MOCHA
MOCKS
MODAL
MODEL
MODEM
MODES
MODOC
MODUS
MOFFO
MOGUL
MOHUR
MOILS
MOIRA
MOIRE
MOIST
MOJOS
MOLAR
MOLAS
MOLDS
MOLDY
MOLES
MOLLS
MOLLY
MOLTO
MOLTS
MOMMA
MOMMY
MOMUS
MONAD
MONCK
MONDE
MONDO
MONEL
MONET
MONEY
MONGO
MONKS
MONOD
MONTE
MONTH
MONTY
MONZA
MOOCH
MOODS
MOODY
MOOED
MOOGS
MOOLA
MOONS
MOONY
MOORE
MOORS
MOOSE
MOOTS
MOPED
MOPER
MOPES
MOPEY
MOPSY
MOPUP
MORAL
MORAN
MORAY
MOREL
MORES
MOREY
MORNS
MORON
MOROS
MORPH
MORRO
MORSE
MORTS
MOSBY
MOSES
MOSEY
MOSHE
MOSSO
MOSSY
MOSUL
MOTEL
MOTES
MOTET
MOTHS
MOTHY
MOTIF
MOTOR
MOTTA
MOTTO
MOTTS
MOUES
MOULD
MOULT
MOUND
MOUNT
MOUSE
MOUSY
MOUTH
MOVED
MOVER
MOVES
MOVIE
MOWED
MOWER
MOXIE

M•O••
MAORI
MEOWS
MOOCH
MOODS
MOODY
MOOED
MOOGS
MOOLA
MOONS
MOONY
MOORE
MOORS
MOOSE
MOOTS
MUONS
MYOPE

M••O•
MACON
MAGOG
MAGOO
MAGOT
MAJOR
MAKOS
MANON
MANOR
MANOS
MASON
MAYON
MAYOR
MCCOO
MCCOY
MEDOC
MELON
MELOS
MEMOS
MEROE
MESON
METOO
MIAOW
MILOS
MINOR
MINOS
MINOT
MISOS
MODOC
MOJOS
MONOD
MORON
MOROS
MOTOR
MRMOM
MSDOS
MYRON

M•••O
MACAO
MACHO
MACRO
MAGOO
MALMO
MAMBO
MANGO
MARCO
MARGO
MARIO
MARLO
MATEO
MATRO
MATZO
MAYPO
MCCOO
MENLO
METOO
METRO
MEZZO
MICRO
MIMEO
MINEO
MINHO
MIRRO
MISDO
MOFFO
MOLTO
MONDO
MONGO
MORRO
MOSSO
MOTTO
MUMBO
MUNGO
MUNRO
MYELO

•MO••
AMOCO
AMOLE
AMONG
AMORE
AMORT
AMORY
AMOUR
EMORY
EMOTE
HMONG
SMOCK
SMOGS
SMOKE
SMOKY
SMOLT
SMOOT
SMOTE

•M•O•
AMBOS
AMMON
SMOOT
UMBOS

•M••O
AMADO
AMATO
AMIGO
AMINO
AMOCO
AMYLO
IMAGO
IMIDO
IMINO

••MO•
AMMON
ARMOR
ATMOS
DAMON
DEMOB
DEMON
DEMOS
EAMON
ELMOS
GAMOW
GEMOT
HUMOR
LEMON
LIMON
LIMOS
LYMON
MEMOS
MRMOM
NIMOY
OLMOS
POMOS
RAMON
RAMOS
REMOP
REMOW
RUMOR
SAMOA
SAMOS
SIMON
TIMON
TIMOR
VAMOS

••M•O
AIMTO
CAMEO
CAMPO
COMBO
COMPO
DUMBO
FEMTO
GUMBO
GUMMO
HOMEO
JUMBO
LIMBO
MAMBO
MIMEO
MUMBO
RAMBO
ROMEO
TAMBO
TEMPO

•••MO
ALAMO
ANEMO
BROMO
COSMO
CUOMO
DERMO
DUOMO
GIZMO
GUMMO
HAEMO
MALMO
PISMO
PRIMO
PROMO
SCHMO
SIXMO
SLOMO
WHAMO

M•P••
MAPLE
MOPED
MOPER
MOPES
MOPEY
MOPSY
MOPUP

M••P•
MAYPO
MORPH
MUMPS
MYOPE

M•••P
MIXUP
MOPUP

•MP••
AMPAS
AMPED
AMPHI
AMPHR
AMPLE
AMPLY
EMPTY
IMPEI
IMPEL
IMPLY
UMPED

••MP•
BUMPS
BUMPY
CAMPO
CAMPS
CAMPY
COMPO
COMPS
COMPT
DAMPS
DUMPS
DUMPY
GAMPS
GIMPS
GIMPY
HEMPS
HUMPH
HUMPS
HUMPY
JUMPS
JUMPY
KEMPT
LAMPS
LIMPS
LUMPS
LUMPY
LYMPH
MUMPS
NAMPA
NYMPH
OOMPH
PAMPA
PUMPS
RAMPS
ROMPS
RUMPS
SAMPS
SIMPS
SUMPS
TAMPA
TAMPS
TEMPE
TEMPI
TEMPO
TEMPS
TEMPT
VAMPS
WIMPS
WIMPY
YAMPA

••M•P
DAMUP
GUMUP
JAMUP
REMAP
REMOP
SUMUP

•••MP
BLIMP
CHAMP
CHIMP
CHOMP
CHUMP
CLAMP
CLOMP
CLUMP
CRAMP
CRIMP
CRUMP
FRUMP
GRAMP
GRUMP
PLUMP
PRIMP
SCAMP
SHEMP
SKIMP
SLUMP
STAMP
STOMP
STUMP
SWAMP
THUMP
TRAMP
TROMP
TRUMP
WHOMP

M•Q••
MAQUI

MR•••
MRBIG
MRMOM

M•R••
MARAS
MARAT
MARCH
MARCO
MARCY
MARDI
MARES
MARGE
MARGO
MARIA
MARIE
MARIN
MARIO
MARIS
MARKS
MARLA
MARLO
MARLS
MARLY
MARNE
MARRY
MARSH
MARTA
MARTI
MARTS
MARTY
MARVY
MARYS
MCRAE
MERCE
MERCI
MERCY
MERES
MERGE
MERIT
MERLE
MERLS
MEROE
MERRY
MERTZ
MERYL
MIRED
MIRES
MIRRO
MIRTH
MIRVS
MORAL
MORAN
MORAY
MOREL
MORES
MOREY
MORNS
MORON
MOROS
MORPH
MORRO
MORSE
MORTS
MURAL
MURAT
MUREX
MURKY
MURRA
MURRE
MYRNA
MYRON
MYRRH

M••R•
MACRO
MADRE
MAHRE
MAORI
MATRI
MATRO
MAURY
MBIRA
MEARA
MERRY
METRE
METRO
MICRA
MICRO
MIRRO
MITRE
MOIRA
MOIRE
MOORE
MOORS
MORRO
MUDRA
MUNRO
MURRA
MURRE
MYERS
MYRRH

M•••R
MAJOR
MAKER
MALAR
MANOR
MASER
MASUR
MATER
MAYER
MAYOR
MAZER
METER
MEYER
MILER
MIMER
MINER
MINOR
MISER
MITER
MIXER
MIZAR
MOHUR
MOLAR
MOPER
MOTOR
MOVER
MOWER
MUSER
MUTER
MYLAR

•M•R•
AMARA
AMBRY
AMIRS
AMORE
AMORT
AMORY
CMDRS
EMERY
EMIRS
EMORY
KMART
OMARR
OMBRE
OMERS
SMART
SMIRK
SMURF
UMBRA

•M••R
AMBER
AMEER
AMOUR
AMPHR
EMBAR
EMBER
EMEER
EMMER
OMARR
OMBER
SMEAR
UMBER

••MR•
CAMRY
CYMRY

••M•R
AIMER
ARMOR
COMER
DAMAR
DEMUR
ELMER
EMMER
FEMUR
GAMER
GOMER
HOMER
HUMOR
IZMIR
KHMER
LAMAR
LAMER
LEMUR
MIMER
NAMER
NAMUR
PAMIR
RAMAR
ROMER
RUMOR
SAMAR
SUMER
TAMER
TIMER
TIMOR

MS•••
MSDOS
MSGTS

M•S••
MASAI
MASER
MASHY
MASKS
MASON
MASSE
MASSY
MASTS
MASUR
MESAS
MESHY
MESIC
MESNE
MESON
MESSY
MESTA
MISDO
MISER
MISHA
MISOS
MISSA
MISSY
MISTI
MISTS
MISTY
MOSBY
MOSES
MOSEY
MOSHE
MOSSO
MOSSY
MOSUL
MUSCA
MUSED
MUSER
MUSES
MUSHY
MUSIC
MUSKS
MUSKY
MUSSY
MUSTS
MUSTY
MYSIN

M••S•
MANSE
MARSH
MASSE
MASSY
MATSU
MAYST
MEESE
MENSA
MESSY
MEUSE
MIDST
MIMSY
MINSK
MISSA
MISSY
MOIST
MOOSE
MOPSY
MORSE
MOSSO
MOSSY
MOUSE
MOUSY
MUSSY

M•••S
MACES
MACYS
MAGES
MAGUS
MAIDS
MAILS
MAINS
MAKES
MAKOS
MALES
MALLS
MALTS
MAMAS
MANES
MANOS
MARAS
MARES
MARIS
MARKS
MARLS
MARTS
MARYS
MASKS
MASTS
MATES
MATHS
MAULS
MAVIS
MAXES
MAXIS
MAYAS
MAZES
MEADS
MEALS
MEANS
MEATS
MEDES
MEEDS
MEETS
MELDS
MELOS
MELTS

MEMOS
MENDS
MENUS
MEOWS
MERES
MERLS
MESAS
METES
METIS
MEWLS
MICAS
MIDAS
MIDIS
MIENS
MIFFS
MIKES
MILES
MILKS
MILLS
MILOS
MILTS
MIMAS
MIMES
MINAS
MINDS
MINES
MINGS
MINIS
MINKS
MINOS
MINTS
MINUS
MIRES
MIRVS
MISOS
MISTS
MITES
MITTS
MIXES
MLLES
MOANS
MOATS
MOCKS
MODES
MODUS
MOILS
MOJOS
MOLAS
MOLDS
MOLES
MOLLS
MOLTS
MOMUS
MONKS
MOODS
MOOGS
MOONS
MOORS
MOOTS
MOPES
MORES
MORNS
MOROS
MORTS
MOSES
MOTES
MOTHS
MOTTS
MOUES
MOVES
MSDOS
MSGTS
MUCKS
MUFFS
MULES
MULLS
MUMPS
MUNIS
MUONS
MUSES
MUSKS
MUSTS
MUTES
MUTTS
MYERS
MYLES
MYNAS
MYTHS

•M•S•
AMASS
AMISH
AMISS
AMUSE
OMASA
SMASH

•M••S
AMAHS
AMASS
AMBOS
AMENS
AMIES
AMIRS
AMISS
AMPAS
AMYLS
CMDRS
EMIRS
EMITS
EMMYS
IMAMS
OMENS
OMERS
OMITS
SMEWS
SMITS
SMOGS
SMUTS
UMBOS
YMCAS

••MS•
MIMSY

••M•S
AAMES
ACMES
ATMOS
BEMAS
BOMBS
BUMPS
CAMPS
CAMUS
COMAS
COMBS
COMES
COMPS
COMUS
CYMAS
CYMES
DAMES
DAMNS
DAMPS
DEMES
DEMOS
DIMES
DOMES
DUMAS
DUMBS
DUMPS
EAMES
ELMOS
EMMYS
FAMES
FUMES
GAMES
GAMPS
GIMPS
HAMES
HEMPS
HOMES
HUMPS
HUMUS
HYMNS
IAMBS
JAMBS
JAMES
JUMPS
LAMAS
LAMBS
LAMES
LAMPS
LIMAS
LIMBS
LIMES
LIMNS
LIMOS
LIMPS
LUMPS
MAMAS
MEMOS
MIMAS
MIMES
MOMUS
MUMPS
NAMES
NIMES
NUMBS
NUMIS
OLMOS
PIMAS
POMES
POMOS
PUMAS
PUMPS
RAMIS
RAMOS
RAMPS
REMUS
RIMES
ROMPS
RUMPS
SAMMS
SAMOS
SAMPS
SEMIS
SIMMS
SIMPS
SOMAS
SUMPS
TAMES
TAMPS
TEMPS
TIMES
TOMES
VAMOS
VAMPS
WIMPS
YUMAS

•••MS
ADAMS
ALUMS
ARUMS
ATOMS
BALMS
BARMS
BEAMS
BERMS
BOOMS
BRIMS
CALMS
CHUMS
CLAMS
CORMS
CRAMS
CULMS
DEEMS
DIEMS
DOOMS
DORMS
DRAMS
DRUMS
EDAMS
EXAMS
FARMS
FILMS
FIRMS
FLAMS
FOAMS
FORMS
GERMS
GLIMS
GLOMS
GRAMS
HARMS
HELMS
HERMS
HOLMS
IMAMS
ITEMS
LOAMS
LOOMS
NORMS
PALMS
PERMS
PLUMS
POEMS
PRAMS
PRIMS
PROMS
REAMS
REIMS
ROAMS
ROOMS
SAMMS
SCAMS
SCUMS
SEAMS
SEEMS
SHAMS
SHIMS
SIMMS
SKIMS
SLAMS
SLIMS
SLUMS
STEMS
STUMS
SWIMS
TEAMS
TEEMS
TERMS
THEMS
TRAMS
TRIMS
WARMS
WEEMS
WHAMS
WHIMS
WORMS
ZOOMS

M•T••
MATCH
MATED
MATEO
MATER
MATES
MATEY
MATHS
MATIN
MATRI
MATRO
MATSU
MATTE
MATZO
METAL
METED
METER
METES
METIS
METOO
METRE
METRO
MITCH
MITER
MITES
MITRE
MITTS
MITTY
MITZI
MOTEL
MOTES
MOTET
MOTHS
MOTHY
MOTIF
MOTOR
MOTTA
MOTTO
MOTTS
MUTED
MUTER
MUTES
MUTTS
MYTHS

M••T•
MALTA
MALTS
MALTY
MANTA
MARTA
MARTI
MARTS
MARTY
MASTS
MATTE
MEATS
MEATY
MEETS
MEHTA
MELTS
MELTY
MERTZ
MESTA
MILTS
MILTY
MINTS
MINTY
MIRTH
MISTI
MISTS
MISTY
MITTS
MITTY
MOATS
MOLTO
MOLTS
MONTE
MONTH
MONTY
MOOTS
MORTS
MOTTA
MOTTO
MOTTS
MOUTH
MSGTS
MUFTI
MULTI
MUSTS
MUSTY
MUTTS

M•••T
MAGOT
MAMET
MANET
MARAT
MAYST
MEANT
MEDIT
MERIT
MIDST
MIGHT
MINOT
MOIST
MONET
MOTET
MOULT
MOUNT
MULCT
MURAT

•M•T•
AMATI
AMATO
AMITY
EMITS
EMOTE
EMPTY
OMITS
SMITE
SMITH
SMITS
SMOTE
SMUTS
SMYTH

•M••T
AMBIT
AMENT
AMORT
AMVET
EMMET
KMART
SMALT
SMART
SMELT
SMOLT
SMOOT

••MT•
AIMTO
COMTE
FEMTO

••M•T
ADMIT
AIMAT
ARMET
COMET
COMPT
DEMIT
EMMET
GAMUT
GEMOT
HEMET
IZMIT
KEMPT
LIMIT
LUMET
MAMET
NEMAT
NYMET
RAMET
REMET
REMIT
TEMPT
UNMET

•••MT
KLIMT

MU•••
MUCIN
MUCKS
MUCKY
MUDDY
MUDRA
MUFFS
MUFTI
MUGGY
MULCH
MULCT
MULES
MULEY
MULLS
MULTI
MUMBO
MUMMY
MUMPS
MUNCH
MUNGO
MUNIS
MUNRO
MUONS
MURAL
MURAT
MUREX
MURKY
MURRA
MURRE
MUSCA
MUSED
MUSER
MUSES
MUSHY
MUSIC
MUSKS
MUSKY
MUSSY
MUSTS
MUSTY
MUTED
MUTER
MUTES
MUTTS
MUZAK
MUZZY

M•U••
MAUDE
MAULS
MAUNA
MAUND
MAURY
MAUVE
MEUSE
MOUES
MOULD
MOULT
MOUND
MOUNT
MOUSE
MOUSY
MOUTH

M••U•
MAGUS
MAKUA
MAQUI
MASUR
MECUM
MENUS
MINUS
MIXUP
MODUS
MOGUL
MOHUR
MOMUS
MOPUP
MOSUL
MYGUY

M•••U
MACHU
MATSU

•MU••
AMUCK
AMUSE
SMURF
SMUTS

•M•U•
AMOUR
IMBUE

••MU•
CAMUS
COMUS
CUMUL
DAMUP
DEMUR
FEMUR
GAMUT
GUMUP
HUMUS
JAMUP
LEMUR
MOMUS
NAMUR
REMUS
SUMUP

•••MU
ISAMU
SHAMU

MV•••
MVIII

M•V••
MAVEN
MAVIS
MCVIE
MCVII
MDVII
MLVII
MMVII
MOVED
MOVER
MOVES
MOVIE
MXVII

M••V•
MARVY
MAUVE
MCCVI
MCDVI
MCLVI
MCMVI
MCXVI
MDCVI
MDLVI
MDXVI
MIRVS
MLXVI
MMCVI
MMDVI
MMLVI
MMMVI
MMXVI
MXCVI
MXLVI
MXXVI

M•••V
MCCCV
MCCIV
MCCLV
MCCXV
MCDIV
MCDLV
MCDXV
MCLIV
MCLXV
MCMIV
MCMLV
MCMXV
MCXCV
MCXIV
MCXLV
MCXXV
MDCCV
MDCIV
MDCLV
MDCXV
MDLIV
MDLXV
MDXCV
MDXIV
MDXLV
MDXXV
MLXIV
MLXXV
MMCCV
MMCDV
MMCIV
MMCLV
MMCMV
MMCXV
MMDCV
MMDIV
MMDLV
MMDXV
MMLIV
MMLXV
MMMCV
MMMDV
MMMIV
MMMLV
MMMXV
MMXCV
MMXIV
MMXLV
MMXXV
MXCIV
MXLIV
MXMIV
MXXIV
MXXXV

•MV••
AMVET
CMVII
MMVII

•M•V•
CMLVI
CMXVI
MMCVI
MMDVI
MMLVI
MMMVI
MMXVI

•M••V
CMLIV
CMLXV
CMXCV
CMXIV
CMXLV
CMXXV
MMCCV
MMCDV
MMCIV
MMCLV
MMCMV
MMCXV
MMDCV
MMDIV
MMDLV
MMDXV
MMLIV
MMLXV
MMMCV
MMMDV
MMMIV
MMMLV
MMMXV
MMXCV
MMXIV
MMXLV
MMXXV

••MV•
MCMVI
MMMVI

••M•V
MCMIV
MCMLV
MCMXV
MMMCV
MMMDV
MMMIV
MMMLV
MMMXV
MXMIV

•••MV
MMCMV

M•W••
MEWED
MEWLS
MOWED
MOWER
MYWAY

M••W•
MEOWS

M•••W
MACAW
MIAOW

•MW••
AMWAY

•M•W•
SMEWS

••M•W
GAMOW
REMOW

MX•••
MXCII
MXCIV
MXCIX
MXCVI
MXIII
MXLII
MXLIV
MXLIX
MXLVI
MXMII
MXMIV
MXVII
MXXII
MXXIV
MXXIX
MXXVI
MXXXI
MXXXV

M•X••
MAXED
MAXES
MAXIE
MAXIM
MAXIS
MCXCI
MCXCV
MCXII
MCXIV
MCXIX
MCXLI
MCXLV
MCXVI
MCXXI
MCXXV
MCXXX
MDXCI
MDXCV
MDXII
MDXIV
MDXIX
MDXLI
MDXLV
MDXVI
MDXXI
MDXXV
MDXXX
MIXED
MIXER
MIXES
MIXUP
MLXII
MLXIV
MLXIX
MLXVI
MLXXI
MLXXV
MLXXX
MMXCI
MMXCV
MMXII
MMXIV
MMXIX
MMXLI
MMXLV
MMXVI
MMXXI
MMXXV
MMXXX
MOXIE
MXXII
MXXIV
MXXIX
MXXVI
MXXXI
MXXXV

M••X•
MCCXC
MCCXI
MCCXL
MCCXV
MCCXX
MCDXC
MCDXI
MCDXL
MCDXV
MCDXX
MCLXI
MCLXV
MCLXX
MCMXC
MCMXI
MCMXL
MCMXV
MCMXX
MCXXI
MCXXV
MCXXX
MDCXC
MDCXI
MDCXL
MDCXV
MDCXX
MDLXI
MDLXV
MDLXX
MDXXI
MDXXV
MDXXX
MLXXI
MLXXV
MLXXX
MMCXC
MMCXI
MMCXL
MMCXV
MMCXX
MMDXC
MMDXI
MMDXL
MMDXV
MMDXX
MMLXI
MMLXV
MMLXX
MMMXC
MMMXI
MMMXL
MMMXV
MMMXX
MMXXI
MMXXV
MMXXX
MXXXI
MXXXV

M•••X
MCCCX
MCCIX
MCCLX
MCCXX
MCDIX
MCDLX
MCDXX
MCLIX
MCLXX
MCMIX
MCMLX
MCMXX
MCXIX
MCXXX
MDCCX
MDCIX
MDCLX
MDCXX
MDLIX
MDLXX
MDXIX
MDXXX
MLXIX
MLXXX
MMCCX
MMCDX
MMCIX
MMCLX
MMCMX
MMCXX
MMDCX
MMDIX
MMDLX
MMDXX
MMLIX
MMLXX
MMMCX
MMMDX
MMMIX
MMMLX
MMMXX
MMXIX
MMXXX
MUREX
MXCIX
MXLIX
MXXIX

•MX••
CMXCI
CMXCV
CMXII
CMXIV
CMXIX
CMXLI
CMXLV
CMXVI
CMXXI
CMXXV
CMXXX
MMXCI
MMXCV
MMXII
MMXIV
MMXIX
MMXLI
MMXLV
MMXVI
MMXXI
MMXXV
MMXXX

•M•X•
CMLXI
CMLXV
CMLXX
CMXXI
CMXXV
CMXXX
MMCXC
MMCXI
MMCXL
MMCXV
MMCXX
MMDXC
MMDXI
MMDXL
MMDXV
MMDXX
MMLXI
MMLXV
MMLXX
MMMXC
MMMXI
MMMXL
MMMXV
MMMXX
MMXXI
MMXXV
MMXXX

•M••X
CMLIX
CMLXX
CMXIX
CMXXX
IMMIX
MMCCX
MMCDX
MMCIX
MMCLX
MMCMX
MMCXX
MMDCX
MMDIX
MMDLX
MMDXX
MMLIX
MMLXX
MMMCX
MMMDX
MMMIX
MMMLX
MMMXX
MMXIX
MMXXX

••MX•
MCMXC
MCMXI
MCMXL
MCMXV
MCMXX
MMMXC
MMMXI
MMMXL
MMMXV
MMMXX

••M•X
ADMIX
COMEX
COMIX
IMMIX
LOMAX
MCMIX
MCMLX
MCMXX
MMMCX
MMMDX
MMMIX
MMMLX
MMMXX
REMEX
REMIX
TIMEX

•••MX
MMCMX

MY•••
MYELO
MYERS
MYEYE
MYGUY
MYLAR
MYLES
MYNAH
MYNAS
MYOPE
MYRNA
MYRON
MYRRH
MYSIN
MYTHS
MYWAY

M•Y••
MAYAN
MAYAS
MAYBE
MAYER
MAYON
MAYOR
MAYPO
MAYST
MEYER

M••Y•
MACYS
MARYS
MERYL
MYEYE

M•••Y
MADLY
MALAY
MALTY
MAMMY
MANDY
MANLY
MANNY
MARCY
MARLY
MARRY
MARTY
MARVY
MASHY
MASSY
MATEY
MAURY
MCCOY
MCKAY
MEALY
MEANY
MEATY
MELTY
MERCY
MERRY
MESHY
MESSY
MIDDY
MIFFY
MILKY
MILTY
MIMSY
MINDY
MINTY
MISSY
MISTY
MITTY
MOLDY
MOLLY
MOMMY
MONEY
MONTY
MOODY
MOONY
MOPEY
MOPSY
MORAY
MOREY
MOSBY
MOSEY
MOSSY
MOTHY
MOUSY
MUCKY
MUDDY
MUGGY
MULEY
MUMMY
MURKY
MUSHY
MUSKY
MUSSY
MUSTY
MUZZY
MYGUY
MYWAY

•MY••
AMYLO
AMYLS
SMYTH

•M•Y•
EMLYN
EMMYS

•M••Y
AMBRY
AMITY
AMORY
AMPLY
AMWAY
EMBAY
EMERY
EMILY
EMORY
EMPTY
IMPLY
SMOKY

••MY•
EMMYS

••M•Y
ALMAY
BUMPY
CAMAY
CAMPY
CAMRY
COMFY
CYMRY
DIMLY
DUMMY
DUMPY
GEMMY
GIMPY
GUMMY
HAMMY
HOMEY
HUMPY
JEMMY
JIMMY
JUMPY
LEMAY
LUMPY
MAMMY
MIMSY
MOMMY
MUMMY
NAMBY
NIMBY
NIMOY
PAMBY
RUMMY
SAMMY
TAMMY
TIMMY
TOMMY
TUMMY
WIMPY
YUMMY

•••MY
ANOMY
ATOMY
BALMY
BARMY
BEAMY
BOOMY
DUMMY
ENEMY
FILMY
FLAMY
FOAMY
GEMMY
GERMY
GRIMY
GUMMY
HAMMY
JEMMY

JIMMY LOAMY MAMMY MOMMY MUMMY PALMY PLUMY PYGMY ROOMY RUMMY SAMMY SEAMY SLIMY SPUMY TAMMY TIMMY TOMMY TUMMY WORMY YUMMY

M•Z••

MAZDA MAZEL MAZER MAZES MEZZO MIZAR MUZAK MUZZY

M••Z•

MAIZE MATZO MEZZO MITZI MONZA MUZZY

M•••Z

MAINZ MERTZ

•M•Z•

AMAZE SMAZE

••M•Z

GOMEZ

NA•••

NAACP NABES NABOB NACHO NACHT NACRE NADER NADIA NADIR NAFTA NAGEL NAGGY NAHUA NAHUM NAIAD NAILS NAIRA NAIRN NAISH NAIVE NAKED NALDI NAMBY NAMED NAMER NAMES NAMIB NAMPA NAMUR NANAS NANCY NANNA NANNY NAOMI NAPES NAPPE NAPPY NARAS NARCO NARCS NARDS NARES NAREW NARIS NARKS NASAL NASBY NASHE NASTY NATAL NATCH NATTY NAURU NAVAL NAVEL NAVES NAVIG NAVVY NAWAB NAXOS

N•A••

NAACP NEALE NEAPS NEARS NEATH NEATO NEATS NGAIO NGAMI NOAHS NYACK NYALA NYASA

N••A•

NAIAD NANAS NARAS NASAL NATAL NAVAL NAWAB NEMAN NEMAT NEPAL NICAD NINAS NIPAS NIPAT NISAN NIVAL NIZAM NOCAL NODAL NOFAT NOLAN NOMAD NOPAL NOPAR NORAD NORAH NOVAE NOVAK NOVAS NOWAY

N•••A

NADIA NAFTA NAHUA NAIRA NAMPA NANNA NDOLA NEMEA NINJA NORIA NORMA NUBIA NUCHA NYALA NYASA

•NA••

ANAIS DNASE ENACT ENATE GNARL GNARS GNASH GNATS GNAWS INALL INANE INAPT INARI INAWE KNACK KNAPS KNARS KNAVE ONAIR ONATE RNASE SNACK SNAFU SNAGS SNAIL SNAKE SNAKY SNAPS SNARE SNARK SNARL SNATH UNAPT UNARM UNAUS

•N•A•

ANEAR ANNAL ANNAM ANOAS ANSAE ANTAE ANTAL ANTAS ANWAR ANZAC ENIAC ENLAI INBAD INCAN INCAS INLAW INLAY KNEAD ONEAL ONLAY ONTAP SNEAD SNEAK UNBAR UNCAP UNCAS UNJAM UNMAN UNSAY

•N••A

ANIMA ANITA ANTRA CNIDA ENNEA ENTIA INDIA INDRA INFRA INTRA ONEGA SNEVA

••NA•

ANNAL ANNAM ARNAZ BANAL BINAL CANAL CONAN CUNAS DANAE DINAH DINAR DONAS DONAT DONAU ETNAS FINAL HENAN HONAN HUNAN IXNAY JONAH JONAS KENAI LANAI LUNAR MINAS MONAD MYNAH MYNAS NANAS NINAS PANAM PANAY PENAL PUNAS RANAT RENAL RENAN SANAA SINAI SONAR TONAL TUNAS TYNAN ULNAE ULNAS VENAE VENAL VINAS ZONAL

••N•A

APNEA BANDA CANEA CANNA CONGA DANZA DONNA ENNEA FANTA FINCA FONDA GENOA GINZA GONNA GUNGA HANNA HANSA HENNA HONDA IONIA JUNTA KANGA KANSA KENYA KINDA LANKA LANZA LENYA LINDA LONGA LYNDA MANIA MANNA MANTA MENSA MONZA NANNA NINJA OMNIA PANDA PANGA PANZA PENNA PENTA PENZA PINNA PINTA PINZA PONCA PUNTA QANDA RENTA SANAA SANKA SANTA SENNA SONIA SONJA SONYA SUNDA SUNNA TANKA TANYA TONGA TONKA TONYA UINTA VANNA VANYA VENDA WANDA WANNA XENIA YENTA ZENDA

•••NA

ADANA AETNA AGANA AGENA AMANA ARENA ASANA AVENA BUENA BWANA CANNA CHINA DESNA DIANA DONNA DRINA DVINA EDINA ELENA FAUNA FIONA FRENA GEENA GHANA GONNA HANNA HENNA HYENA ILONA IPANA IRINA IVANA JUMNA KRONA LEONA LIANA LORNA MAGNA MANNA MAUNA MYRNA NANNA PATNA PENNA PINNA PLENA POONA RUANA SAUNA SCENA SEHNA SENNA SHANA SIENA SUNNA TEENA VANNA VARNA VIRNA WANNA

NB•••

NBCTV

N•B••

NABES NABOB NOBBY NOBEL NOBLE NOBLY NUBBY NUBIA

N••B•

NAMBY NASBY NIMBI NIMBY NIOBE NOBBY NUBBY NUMBS

N•••B

NABOB NAMIB NAWAB

•NB••

INBAD INBED INBIG UNBAR UNBID UNBOX

•N•B•

KNOBS SNOBS SNUBS

••NB•

CANBY

••N•B

BANDB DENEB RANDB

•••NB

PLANB

N•C••

NACHO NACHT NACRE NBCTV NECKS NICAD NICER NICHE NICKS NICOL NOCAL NOCKS NOCTI NUCHA

N••C•

NAACP NANCY NARCO NARCS NATCH NIECE NONCE NOTCH NYACK

•NC••

ANCON ENCYC INCAN INCAS INCOG INCUR INCUS ONCLE ONCUE UNCAP UNCAS UNCLE UNCUT

•N•C•

ENACT ENOCH KNACK KNICK KNOCK ONICE SNACK SNICK SNUCK VNECK

•N••C

ANTIC ANZAC ENCYC ENIAC INDIC

••NC•

BANCO BANCS BENCH BUNCH CENCI CINCH CINCO CONCH DANCE DANCY DUNCE FANCY FENCE FINCA FINCH HENCE HENCH HUNCH JUNCO KENCH LANCE LUNCH LYNCH MINCE MONCK MUNCH NANCY NONCE OUNCE PENCE PINCE PINCH PONCA PONCE PONCH PUNCH RANCH SINCE SYNCS TENCH TINCT VANCE VINCE VINCI WENCH WINCE WINCH ZINCS

••N•C

CONIC CYNIC GENIC IONIC PANIC PUNIC RUNIC SONIC TONIC TUNIC

•••NC

BLANC BRONC FRANC

ND•••

NDOLA

N•D••

NADER NADIA NADIR NEDDY NIDES NIDRE NIDUS NODAL NODDY NODES NODOZ NODUS NUDER NUDES NUDGE

N••D•

NALDI NARDS NEDDY NEEDS NEEDY NERDS NERDY NODDY

N•••D

NAIAD NAKED NAMED NEFUD NICAD NIXED NOEND NOMAD NORAD NOSED NOTED NUKED

•ND••

ANDES ANDIE ANDOR ANDRE ANDRO ENDED ENDER ENDOR ENDOW ENDUE ENDUP INDEF INDEX INDIA INDIC INDIE INDIO INDIV INDRA INDRI INDUS ONDIT UNDER UNDID UNDUE

•N•D•

ANODE CNIDA SNIDE

•N••D

ANTED ENDED INBAD INBED INKED KNEAD KNEED ONEND SNEAD SNEED SNERD SNOOD UNBID UNDID UNFED UNWED

••ND•

AANDM BANDA BANDB BANDO BANDS BANDY BENDS BINDS BONDI BONDS BUNDS BUNDT BUNDY CANDO CANDW CANDY CINDY CONDE CONDO CYNDI DANDY DENDR DONDI FENDS FINDS FONDA FONDS FONDU FUNDS FUNDY GANDY GONDI GONDS HANDS HANDY HINDI HINDS HINDU HONDA HONDO KENDO KINDA KINDS LANDO LANDS LENDL LENDS LINDA LINDY LUNDI LUNDY LYNDA LYNDE MANDY MENDS MINDS MINDY MONDE MONDO PANDA PANDL PENDS PONDS QANDA RANDB RANDD RANDI RANDR RANDS RANDY RENDS RINDS RONDO SANDH SANDL SANDS SANDY SENDS SONDE SUNDA TANDY TENDS TONDI TONDO VENDA VENDS WANDA WANDS WENDS WENDT WENDY WINDS WINDY ZENDA ZENDO

••N•D

AWNED BONED CANED CANID CONTD DINED FINED HONED LINED MANED MINED MONAD MONOD OWNED PANED PINED RANDD RANID SYNOD TINED TONED TUNED VINED WANED WINED ZONED

•••ND

ABEND AMEND BLAND BLEND BLIND BLOND BOUND BRAND ELAND EMEND FIEND FOUND FROND GLAND GRAND GRIND HOUND MAUND MOUND NOEND OLAND ONEND POUND QUAND ROUND SCAND SCEND SOUND SPEND STAND TBOND TREND UPEND VIAND WOUND

NE•••

NEALE NEAPS NEARS NEATH NEATO NEATS NECKS NEDDY NEEDS NEEDY NEFUD NEGEV NEGRI NEGUS NEHRU NEIGE NEIGH NEILL NELLY NEMAN NEMAT NEMEA NENES NEONS NEPAL NEPOS NERDS NERDY NEROL NERTS NERTZ NERVE NERVY NESTS NEUME NEURO NEVER NEVES NEVIL NEVIN NEVIS NEVUS NEWEL NEWER NEWLY NEWSY NEWTS NEXUS

N•E••

NEEDS NEEDY NIECE NIELS NLERS NOELS NOEND

N••E•

NABES NADER NAGEL NAKED NAMED NAMER NAMES NAPES NARES NAREW NAVEL NAVES NEGEV NEMEA NENES NEVER NEVES NEWEL NEWER NFLER NHLER NICER NIDES NIGEL NIGER NIKES NILES NIMES NINER NINES NISEI NITER NITES NIVEN NIXED NIXES NIZER NOBEL NODES NOMEN NONES NONET NOSED NOSES NOTED NOTER NOTES NOVEL NOYES NUDER NUDES NUKED NUKES NUMEN NUYEN NYMET NYNEX

N•••E

NACRE NAIVE NAPPE NASHE NEALE NEIGE NERVE NEUME NICHE NIDRE NIECE NIOBE NITRE NIXIE NOBLE NOIRE NOISE NOLLE NOLTE NONCE NOONE NOOSE NORGE NORSE NORTE NOTME NOTRE NOVAE NUDGE NURSE

•NE••

ANEAR ANEMO ANENT ENEMY ENERO INEPT INERT KNEAD KNEED KNEEL KNEES KNELL KNELT MNEME ONEAL ONEGA ONEIL ONEND ONERS ONEUP SNEAD SNEAK SNEED SNEER SNELL SNERD SNERT SNEVA VNECK

•N•E•

ANDES ANGEL ANGER ANGES ANNEE ANNES ANNEX ANSEL ANSER ANTED ANTES ENDED ENDER ENGEL ENNEA ENTER INBED INDEF INDEX INFER INGER INKED INKER INLET INNER INREM INSET INTEL INTER KNEED KNEEL KNEES ONKEY ONSET SNEED SNEER UNDER UNFED UNGER UNMET UNPEG UNPEN UNSER UNSET UNTER UNWED

•N••E

ANDIE ANDRE ANGIE ANGLE ANIME ANISE ANKLE ANNEE ANNIE ANODE ANOLE ANSAE ANTAE ANTRE CNOTE DNASE ENATE ENDUE ENSUE ENTRE ENURE GNOME INANE INAWE INDIE INGLE INKLE INURE INUSE KNAVE KNIFE KNUTE MNEME ONATE ONCLE ONCUE ONICE RNASE SNAKE SNARE SNIDE SNIPE SNORE TNOTE UNCLE UNDUE UNITE UNTIE

••NE•

ABNER AGNES AGNEW ANNEE ANNES ANNEX APNEA ARNEL ASNER AWNED BANES BENES BENET BINES BINET BONED BONER BONES BONET BYNER CANEA CANED CANER CANES CINES CONES CONEY CUNEO DANES DENEB DENES DINED DINER DINES DONEE DUNES DYNEL DYNES ENNEA ERNES ESNES FANES FINED FINER FINES GANEF GENES GENET GONER HANES HINES HONED HONES HONEY IGNES INNER JANET JONES KINER LANES LINED LINEN LINER LINES LONER LUNES MANED MANES MANET MINED MINEO MINER MINES MONEL MONET MONEY NENES NINER NINES NONES NONET NYNEX OWNED OWNER PANED PANEL PANES PINED PINES PINEY PONES RANEE

RENEE
RENEW
RONEE
RUNES
SANER
SINES
SINEW
SONES
TANEY
TENET
TINED
TINES
TONED
TONER
TONES
TUNED
TUNER
TUNES
TYNES
VANES
VENEZ
VINED
VINES
WANED
WANER
WANES
WINED
WINES
ZONED
ZONES

••N•E
AINGE
ANNEE
ANNIE
ARNIE
BENUE
BINGE
BONNE
BONZE
CANOE
CENSE
CONDE
CONGE
CONTE
DANAE
DANCE
DANKE
DANSE
DANTE
DENSE
DENTE
DINGE
DONEE
DONNE
DUNCE
DUNNE
ERNIE
FENCE
GENIE
GENRE
HENCE
HENGE
HENIE
HINGE
JANIE
KINTE
LANCE
LANGE
LUNGE
LYNDE
LYNNE
MANSE
MINCE
MONDE
MONTE
NONCE
OUNCE
PANNE
PENCE
PENNE
PENTE
PINCE
PONCE
PONTE
RANEE
RANGE
RANKE
RENEE
RINSE
RONEE
SANTE
SENSE
SINCE
SINGE
SONDE
SYNGE
TANTE
TENSE
TINGE
TONNE
ULNAE
VANCE
VENAE
VENUE
VINCE
WINCE
WINZE
YENTE
ZANTE

•••NE
AISNE
ALENE
ALINE
ALONE
AMINE
ASONE
ATONE
AZINE
BEENE
BERNE
BONNE
BOONE
BORNE
BOYNE
BRINE
BYRNE
CAINE
CARNE
CHINE
CLINE
CLONE
CRANE
CRONE
DAYNE
DEANE
DIANE
DIENE
DIONE
DONNE
DOONE
DRONE
DUANE
DUNNE
HEINE
HERNE
HORNE
ILENE
IMINE
INANE
IRENE
JAUNE
JAYNE
JEANE
JEUNE
KEANE
KEENE
KLINE
KOINE
KRONE
LAINE
LAYNE
LEONE
LIANE
LORNE
LYNNE
MAINE
MARNE
MESNE
MILNE
NOONE
OPINE
OVINE
OZONE
PAINE
PANNE
PAYNE
PENNE
PHONE
PLANE
PRONE
PRUNE
REUNE
RHINE
RHONE
ROONE
SAONE
SCENE
SCONE
SEINE
SHANE
SHINE
SHONE
SIGNE
SPINE
STONE
STYNE
SWINE
TAINE
TBONE
TERNE
THANE
THINE
TONNE
TOWNE
TRINE
TWINE
VERNE
WAYNE
WHINE

NF•••
NFLER

N•F••
NAFTA
NEFUD
NIFTY
NOFAT

•NF••
ENFIN
INFER
INFIN
INFIX
INFRA
INFUN
UNFED
UNFIT
UNFIX

•N•F•
KNIFE
ONOFF
SNAFU
SNIFF
SNUFF
UNIFY

•N••F
INDEF
KNOPF
ONOFF
SNIFF
SNUFF

••NF•
BANFF

••N•F
BANFF
GANEF

NG•••
NGAIO
NGAMI

N•G••
NAGEL
NAGGY
NEGEV
NEGRI
NEGUS
NIGEL
NIGER
NIGHT
NOGOS

N••G•
NAGGY
NEIGE
NEIGH
NORGE
NUDGE

N•••G
NAVIG

•NG••
ANGEL
ANGER
ANGES
ANGIE
ANGLE
ANGLO
ANGRY
ANGST
ANGUS
ENGEL
ENGRS
INGER
INGLE
INGOT
UNGER

•N•G•
INIGO
ONEGA
SNAGS
SNUGS

•N••G
INBIG
INCOG
UNPEG
UNRIG

••NG•
AINGE
BANGS
BINGE
BINGO
BINGS
BONGO
BONGS
BUNGS
CONGA
CONGE
CONGO
DANGS
DINGE
DINGO
DINGS
DINGY
DONGS
FANGS
FUNGI
FUNGO
GANGS
GONGS
GUNGA
HANGS
HENGE
HINGE
HONGS
JINGO
KANGA
KINGS
LANGE
LINGO
LONGA
LONGI
LONGS
LUNGE
LUNGS
MANGO
MINGS
MONGO
MUNGO
OINGO
PANGA
PANGS
PENGO
PINGO
PINGS
PUNGS
RANGE
RANGY
RINGO
RINGS
RUNGS
SINGE
SINGS
SONGS
SYNGE
TANGO
TANGS
TANGY
TINGE
TINGS
TONGA
TONGS
VINGT
WINGS
XINGU
ZINGS
ZINGY

•••NG
ACING
AGING
ALONG
AMONG
APING
AWING
AXING
BEING
BOING
BRING
BRUNG
CHANG
CHING
CHONG
CHUNG
CLANG
CLING
CLUNG
CUING
DOING
DRANG
DYING
EKING
EWING
FLING
FLUNG
GOING
HMONG
ICING
KIANG
LAING
LIANG
LYING
ORANG
ORING
OWING
PRONG
RUING
SLANG
SLING
SLUNG
SOONG
SPANG
STANG
STING
STUNG
SUING
SWING
SWUNG
THING
THONG
TWANG
TYING
USING
VYING
WHANG
WRING
WRONG
WRUNG
YOUNG

NH•••
NHLER

N•H••
NAHUA
NAHUM
NEHRU
NIHIL
NOHIT
NOHOW

N••H•
NACHO
NACHT
NASHE
NICHE
NIGHT
NOAHS
NUCHA

N•••H
NAISH
NATCH
NEATH
NEIGH
NINTH
NORAH
NORTH
NOTCH
NYMPH

•NH••
ANHUI
UNHIP

•N•H•
ANKHS
ANTHO

•N••H
ENOCH
GNASH
KNISH
SNATH

••NH•
DONHO
MINHO

••N•H
BENCH
BUNCH
CINCH
CONCH
DINAH
FINCH
HENCH
HUNCH
JONAH
KENCH
LUNCH
LYNCH
MONTH
MUNCH
MYNAH
NINTH
PINCH
PONCH
PUNCH
RANCH
SANDH
TENCH
TENTH
WENCH
WINCH

NI•••
NICAD
NICER
NICHE
NICKS
NICOL
NIDES
NIDRE
NIDUS
NIECE
NIELS
NIFTY
NIGEL
NIGER
NIGHT
NIHIL
NIKES
NIKKI
NIKKO
NIKON
NILES
NILLY
NILOT
NIMBI
NIMBY
NIMES
NIMOY
NINAS
NINER
NINES
NINJA
NINNY
NINON
NINOS
NINTH
NIOBE
NIPAS
NIPAT
NIPPY
NIPUP
NISAN
NISEI
NISUS
NITER
NITES
NITRE
NITRO
NITTI
NITTY
NIVAL
NIVEN
NIXED
NIXES
NIXIE
NIXON
NIZAM
NIZER

N•I••
NAIAD
NAILS
NAIRA
NAIRN
NAISH
NAIVE
NEIGE
NEIGH
NEILL
NOILS
NOIRE
NOISE
NOISY

N••I•
NADIA
NADIR
NAMIB
NARIS
NAVIG
NEVIL
NEVIN
NEVIS
NGAIO
NIHIL
NIXIE
NOHIT
NORIA
NOSIR
NOTIN
NUBIA
NUMIS

N•••I
NALDI
NAOMI
NEGRI
NGAMI
NIKKI
NIMBI
NISEI
NITTI
NOCTI
NURMI

•NI••
ANILS
ANIMA
ANIME
ANION
ANISE
ANITA
CNIDA
ENIAC
INIGO
INION
INITS
KNICK
KNIFE
KNISH
KNITS
ONICE
ONION
SNICK
SNIDE
SNIFF
SNIPE
SNIPS
SNITS
UNIFY
UNION
UNITE
UNITS
UNITY
UNIVS

•N•I•
ANAIS
ANDIE
ANGIE
ANNIE
ANNIV
ANTIC
ANTIQ
ANTIS
ANVIL
ANZIO
ENFIN
ENNIO
ENNIS
ENTIA
INBIG
INDIA
INDIC
INDIE
INDIO
INDIV
INFIN
INFIX
INUIT
ONAIR
ONDIT
ONEIL
SNAIL
UNBID
UNDID
UNFIT
UNFIX
UNHIP
UNLIT
UNPIN
UNRIG
UNTIE
UNTIL
UNZIP

•N••I
ANHUI
ENLAI
ENNUI
ENVOI
INARI
INDRI

••NI•
ANNIE
ANNIV
ARNIE
BENIN
BUNIN
CANID
CANIS
CANIT
CONIC
CYNIC
DANIO
DENIM
DENIS
ENNIO
ENNIS
ERNIE
FINIS
GENIC
GENIE
GENII
HENIE
IONIA
IONIC
JANIE
JANIS
KANIN
LENIN
LENIS
LUNIK
MANIA
MINIM
MINIS
MUNIS
OMNIA
ORNIS
PANIC
PUNIC
RANID
RANIN
RANIS
RENIN
RUNIC
RUNIN
SONIA
SONIC
TONIC
TONIO
TUNIC
TUNIS
VANIR
VENIN
XENIA
ZUNIS

••N•I
BENJI
BONDI
CENCI
CENTI
CONTI
CYNDI
DENTI
DONDI
ENNUI
FUNGI
GENII
GONDI
HANOI
HENRI
HINDI
JINNI
KANJI
KENAI
LANAI
LONGI
LUNDI
PENNI
PONTI
PONZI
RANDI
SINAI
SUNNI
TONDI
VINCI
YANNI

•••NI
BLINI
ELENI
GARNI
GRANI
HOSNI
ICENI
IRANI
JINNI
LIGNI
OMANI
PENNI
PLANI
SEGNI
SOMNI
SUNNI
TRINI
YANNI

N••J•
NINJA

•NJ••
ANJOU
ENJOY
UNJAM

••NJ•
BANJO
BENJI
KANJI
NINJA
SONJA

N•K••
NAKED
NIKES
NIKKI
NIKKO
NIKON
NUKED
NUKES

N••K•
NARKS
NECKS
NICKS
NIKKI
NIKKO
NOCKS
NOOKS

N•••K
NOVAK
NYACK

•NK••
ANKHS
ANKLE
INKED
INKER
INKLE
ONKEY

•N•K•
ENSKY
SNAKE
SNAKY

•N••K
ANOUK
KNACK
KNICK
KNOCK
SNACK
SNARK
SNEAK
SNICK
SNOOK
SNUCK
VNECK

••NK•
BANKS
BANKY
BONKS
BUNKO
BUNKS
CONKS
DANKE
DINKS
DINKY
DUNKS
FINKS
FUNKS
FUNKY
GUNKY
HANKS
HANKY
HONKS
HUNKS
JINKS
JUNKS
JUNKY
KINKS
KINKY
LANKA
LANKY
LINKS
MINKS
MONKS
OINKS
PANKY
PINKS
PINKY
PUNKS
PUNKY
RANKE
RANKS
RINKS
RINKY
SANKA
SINKS
TANKA
TANKS
TONKA
WINKS
WONKS
WONKY
YANKS
ZONKS

••N•K
LUNIK
MINSK
MONCK
PINSK

•••NK
BLANK
BLINK
BRINK
CHINK
CHUNK
CLANK
CLINK
CLONK
CLUNK
CRANK
DRANK
DRINK
DRUNK
FLANK
FLUNK
FRANK
PLANK
PLINK
PLONK
PLUNK
PRANK
PRINK
REINK
SHANK
SKINK
SKUNK
SLINK
SLUNK
SPANK
SPUNK
STANK
STINK
STUNK
SWANK
THANK
THINK
THUNK
TRUNK

NL•••
NLERS

N•L••
NALDI
NELLY
NFLER
NHLER
NILES
NILLY
NILOT
NOLAN
NOLLE
NOLTE
NULLS
NYLON

N••L•
NAILS
NDOLA
NEALE
NEILL
NELLY
NEWLY
NIELS
NILLY
NOBLE
NOBLY
NOELS
NOILS
NOLLE
NULLS
NYALA

N•••L
NAGEL
NASAL
NATAL
NAVAL
NAVEL
NEILL
NEPAL
NEROL
NEVIL
NEWEL
NICOL
NIGEL
NIHIL
NIVAL
NOBEL
NOCAL
NODAL
NOPAL
NOVEL

•NL••
ENLAI
INLAW
INLAY
INLET
ONLAY
ONLOW
UNLIT

•N•L•
ANGLE
ANGLO
ANILS
ANKLE
ANOLE
ENOLS
INALL
INGLE
INKLE
KNELL
KNELT
KNOLL
ONCLE
SNELL
UNCLE

•N••L
ANGEL
ANNAL
ANNUL
ANSEL
ANTAL
ANVIL
ENGEL
ENROL
GNARL
INALL
INTEL
KNEEL
KNELL
KNOLL
KNURL
ONEAL
ONEIL
SNAIL
SNARL
SNELL
UNTIL

••NL•
MANLY
MENLO
WANLY

••N•L
ANNAL
ANNUL
ARNEL
BANAL
BINAL
CANAL
DYNEL
FINAL
LENDL
MONEL
PANDL
PANEL
PENAL
RENAL
SANDL
TONAL
VENAL
VINYL
YENTL
ZONAL

•••NL
ADDNL

N•M••
NAMBY
NAMED
NAMER
NAMES
NAMIB
NAMPA
NAMUR
NEMAN
NEMAT
NEMEA
NIMBI
NIMBY
NIMES
NIMOY
NOMAD
NOMEN
NUMBS
NUMEN
NUMIS
NYMET
NYMPH

N••M•
NAOMI
NEUME
NGAMI
NORMA
NORMS
NOTME
NURMI

N•••M
NAHUM
NIZAM

•NM••
UNMAN
UNMET

•N•M•
ANEMO
ANIMA
ANIME
ANOMY
ENEMY
GNOME
MNEME

•N••M
ANNAM
ANNUM
ENORM
ENTOM
INREM
UNARM
UNJAM

••N•M
AANDM
ANNAM
ANNUM
DENIM
DENOM
MINIM
PANAM
PHNOM
VENOM

N•N••
NANAS
NANCY
NANNA
NANNY
NENES
NINAS
NINER
NINES
NINJA
NINNY
NINON
NINOS
NINTH
NONCE
NONES
NONET
NONOS
NYNEX

N••N•
NANNA
NANNY
NEONS
NINNY
NOEND
NOONE
NOONS
NORNS
NOUNS

N•••N
NAIRN
NEMAN
NEVIN
NIKON
NINON
NISAN
NIVEN
NIXON
NOLAN
NOMEN
NOTIN
NUMEN
NUYEN
NYLON

•NN••
ANNAL
ANNAM
ANNEE
ANNES
ANNEX
ANNIE
ANNIV
ANNOY
ANNUL
ANNUM
ANNUS
ENNEA
ENNIO
ENNIS
ENNUI
INNER

•N•N•
ANENT
INANE
INONU
ONEND

•N••N
ANCON
ANION
ANSON
ANTON
ENFIN
INCAN
INFIN
INFUN
INION
KNOWN
ONION
UNION
UNMAN
UNPEN
UNPIN

••NN•
BANNS
BENNY
BONNE
BONNY
BUNNY
CANNA
CANNY
DANNY
DENNY
DONNA
DONNE
DONNY
DUNNE
DUNNO
FANNY
FENNY
FINNO
FINNS
FINNY
FUNNY
GINNY
GONNA
GUNNY
HANNA
HANNO
HENNA
HENNY
HINNY
JENNY
JINNI
JINNS
KENNY
LENNY
LYNNE
MANNA
MANNY
NANNA
NANNY
NINNY
PANNE
PENNA
PENNE
PENNI
PENNY
PINNA
PUNNY
RONNY
RUNNY
SENNA
SONNY
SUNNA
SUNNI
SUNNY
TINNY
TONNE
TUNNY
VANNA
VINNY
WANNA
YANNI

••N•N
AGNON
BENIN
BUNIN
CANON
CONAN
FANON
HENAN
HONAN
HUNAN
KANIN
LENIN
LINEN
MANON
NINON
PINON
RANIN
RANON
RENAN
RENIN
RUNIN
RUNON
TENON
TYNAN
VENIN
XENON

•••NN
DJINN
FLYNN
GLENN
GWENN
GWYNN
QUINN
SWANN

NO•••
NOAHS
NOBBY
NOBEL
NOBLE
NOBLY
NOCAL
NOCKS
NOCTI
NODAL
NODDY
NODES
NODOZ
NODUS
NOELS
NOEND
NOFAT
NOGOS
NOHIT
NOHOW
NOILS
NOIRE
NOISE
NOISY
NOLAN
NOLLE
NOLTE
NOMAD
NOMEN
NONCE
NONES
NONET
NONOS
NOOKS
NOONE
NOONS
NOOSE
NOPAL
NOPAR
NORAD
NORAH
NORGE
NORIA
NORMA
NORMS
NORNS
NORSE
NORTE
NORTH
NORVO
NOSED
NOSES
NOSIR
NOTCH
NOTED
NOTER
NOTES
NOTIN
NOTME
NOTRE
NOTSO
NOTUP
NOUNS
NOVAE
NOVAK
NOVAS
NOVEL
NOWAY
NOYES

N•O••
NAOMI
NDOLA
NEONS
NIOBE
NOOKS
NOONE
NOONS
NOOSE

N••O•
NABOB
NAXOS
NEPOS
NEROL
NICOL
NIKON
NILOT
NIMOY
NINON
NINOS
NIXON
NODOZ
NOGOS
NOHOW
NONOS
NYLON

N•••O
NACHO
NARCO
NEATO
NEURO
NGAIO
NIKKO
NITRO
NORVO
NOTSO

•NO••
ANOAS
ANODE
ANOLE
ANOMY
ANOUK
CNOTE
ENOCH
ENOLS
ENORM
GNOME
INONU
KNOBS
KNOCK
KNOLL
KNOPF
KNORR
KNOTS
KNOUT
KNOWN
KNOWS
ONOFF
SNOBS
SNOOD
SNOOK
SNOOP
SNOOT
SNORE
SNORT
SNOUT
SNOWS
SNOWY
TNOTE

•N•O•
ANCON
ANDOR
ANION
ANJOU
ANNOY
ANSON
ANTON
ENDOR
ENDOW
ENJOY
ENROL
ENSOR
ENTOM
ENVOI
ENVOY
INCOG
INGOT
INION
INTOW
ONION
ONLOW
ONTOP
SNOOD
SNOOK
SNOOP
SNOOT
UNBOX
UNION

•N••O
ANDRO
ANEMO
ANGLO
ANTHO
ANZIO
ENERO
ENNIO
INDIO
INIGO
INTRO
INTWO

••NO•
AGNON
ANNOY
ATNOS
BYNOW
CANOE
CANON
DENOM
DONOR
FANON
GENOA
HANOI
HONOR
IFNOT
KENOS
LENOS
LENOX
MANON
MANOR
MANOS
MINOR
MINOS
MINOT
MONOD
NINON
NINOS
NONOS
PHNOM
PINON
PINOT
RANON
RUNON
SENOR
SYNOD
TENON
TENOR
VENOM
XENON

••N•O
BANCO
BANDO
BANJO
BENZO
BINGO
BONGO
BONZO
BUNKO
CANDO
CANSO
CANTO
CENTO
CINCO
CONDO
CONGO
CUNEO
DANIO
DINGO
DONHO
DUNNO
ENNIO
FINNO
FUNGO
GENRO
GONZO
HANNO
HONDO
JINGO
JUNCO
JUNTO
KENDO
LANDO
LENTO
LINGO
MANGO
MENLO
MINEO
MINHO
MONDO
MONGO
MUNGO
MUNRO
OINGO
PANTO
PENGO
PINGO
PINTO
RANTO
RINGO
RINSO
RONDO
RUNTO
SANTO
SANYO
TANGO
TONDO
TONIO
TONTO
ZENDO

•••NO
ADANO
ADENO
AMINO
BEANO
BRUNO
BUENO
BUONO
CHINO
CORNO
CYANO
DRANO
DUNNO
ETHNO
FINNO
HANNO
HYPNO
ICONO
IMINO
LIGNO
LLANO
ORONO
PHENO
PHONO
PIANO
PLANO
QUINO
RHINO
SEGNO
SIGNO
STENO

N•P••
NAPES
NAPPE
NAPPY
NEPAL
NEPOS
NIPAS
NIPAT
NIPPY
NIPUP
NOPAL
NOPAR

N••P•
NAMPA
NAPPE
NAPPY
NEAPS
NIPPY
NYMPH

N•••P
NAACP
NIPUP
NOTUP

•NP••
INPUT
UNPEG
UNPEN
UNPIN

•N•P•
INAPT
INEPT
KNAPS
KNOPF
SNAPS
SNIPE
SNIPS
UNAPT

•N••P
ENDUP
ONEUP
ONTAP
ONTOP
SNOOP
UNCAP
UNHIP
UNZIP

••N•P
OWNUP
PINUP
RANUP
RUNUP
SUNUP

•N••Q
ANTIQ

N•R••
NARAS
NARCO
NARCS
NARDS
NARES
NAREW
NARIS
NARKS
NERDS
NERDY
NEROL
NERTS
NERTZ
NERVE
NERVY
NORAD
NORAH
NORGE
NORIA
NORMA
NORMS
NORNS
NORSE
NORTE
NORTH
NORVO
NURMI
NURSE

N••R•
NACRE
NAIRA
NAIRN
NAURU
NEARS
NEGRI
NEHRU
NEURO
NIDRE
NITRE
NITRO
NLERS
NOIRE
NOTRE

N•••R
NADER
NADIR
NAMER
NAMUR
NEVER
NEWER
NFLER
NHLER
NICER
NIGER
NINER
NITER
NIZER
NOPAR
NOSIR
NOTER
NUDER

•NR••
ENROL
INREM
UNRIG

•N•R•
ANDRE
ANDRO
ANGRY
ANTRA
ANTRE
ENERO
ENGRS
ENORM
ENTRE
ENTRY
ENURE
GNARL
GNARS
INARI
INDRA
INDRI
INERT
INFRA
INTRA
INTRO
INURE
KNARS
KNORR
KNURL
KNURS
ONERS
SNARE
SNARK
SNARL
SNERD
SNERT
SNORE
SNORT
UNARM

•N••R
ANDOR
ANEAR
ANGER
ANSER
ANWAR
ENDER
ENDOR
ENSOR
ENTER
INCUR
INFER
INGER
INKER
INNER
INSTR
INTER
KNORR
ONAIR
SNEER
UNBAR
UNDER
UNGER
UNSER
UNTER

••NR•
GENRE
GENRO
HENRI
HENRY
MUNRO

••N•R
ABNER
ASNER
BONER
BYNER
CANER
CONTR
DENDR
DINAR
DINER
DONOR
FINER
GONER
HONOR
INNER
KINER
LINER
LONER
LUNAR
MANOR
MINER
MINOR
NINER
OWNER
RANDR
SANER
SENOR
SONAR
TENOR
TONER
TUNER
VANIR
WANER

N•S••
NASAL
NASBY
NASHE
NASTY
NESTS
NISAN
NISEI
NISUS
NOSED
NOSES
NOSIR

N••S•
NAISH
NEWSY
NOISE
NOISY
NOOSE
NORSE
NOTSO
NURSE
NYASA

N•••S
NABES
NAILS
NAMES
NANAS
NAPES
NARAS
NARCS
NARDS
NARES
NARIS
NARKS
NAVES
NAXOS
NEAPS
NEARS
NEATS
NECKS
NEEDS
NEGUS
NENES
NEONS
NEPOS
NERDS
NERTS
NESTS
NEVES
NEVIS
NEVUS
NEWTS
NEXUS
NICKS
NIDES
NIDUS
NIELS
NIKES
NILES
NIMES
NINAS
NINES
NINOS
NIPAS
NISUS
NITES
NIXES
NLERS
NOAHS
NOCKS
NODES
NODUS
NOELS
NOGOS
NOILS
NONES
NONOS
NOOKS
NOONS
NORMS
NORNS
NOSES
NOTES
NOUNS
NOVAS
NOYES
NUDES
NUKES
NULLS
NUMBS
NUMIS

•NS••
ANSAE
ANSEL
ANSER
ANSON
ENSKY
ENSOR
ENSUE
INSET
INSTR
INSTS
ONSET
UNSAY
UNSER
UNSET

•N•S•
ANGST
ANISE
ANTSY
DNASE
GNASH
INUSE
KNISH
RNASE

•N••S
ANAIS
ANDES
ANGES
ANGUS
ANILS
ANKHS
ANNES
ANNUS
ANOAS
ANTAS
ANTES
ANTIS
ENGRS
ENNIS
ENOLS
GNARS
GNATS
GNAWS
INCAS
INCUS
INDUS
INITS
INSTS
KNAPS
KNARS
KNEES
KNITS
KNOBS
KNOTS
KNOWS
KNURS
ONERS
SNAGS
SNAPS
SNIPS
SNITS
SNOBS
SNOWS
SNUBS
SNUGS
TNUTS
UNAUS
UNCAS
UNITS
UNIVS

••NS•
CANSO
CANST
CENSE
DANSE
DENSE
ERNST
HANSA
KANSA
MANSE
MENSA
MINSK
PANSY
PINSK
RINSE
RINSO
SENSE
TANSY
TENSE

••N•S
AGNES
AGNUS
AINUS
ANNES
ANNUS
ATNOS
AUNTS
BANCS
BANDS
BANES
BANGS
BANKS
BANNS
BENDS
BENES
BENTS
BINDS
BINES
BINGS
BONDS
BONES
BONGS
BONKS
BONUS
BUNDS
BUNGS
BUNKS
BUNTS
CANES
CANIS
CANTS
CENTS
CINES
CONES
CONKS
CUNAS
DANES
DANGS
DENES
DENIS
DENTS
DENYS
DINES
DINGS
DINKS
DINTS
DONAS
DONGS
DUNES
DUNKS
DYNES
ENNIS
ERNES
ESNES
ETNAS
FANES
FANGS
FENDS
FINDS
FINES
FINIS
FINKS
FINNS
FONDS
FONTS
FUNDS
FUNKS
GANGS
GENES
GENTS
GENUS
GONDS
GONGS
HANDS
HANES
HANGS
HANKS
HINDS
HINES
HINTS
HONES
HONGS
HONKS
HONUS
HUNKS
HUNTS
IGNES
JANIS
JANUS
JINKS
JINNS
JONAS
JONES
JUNKS
KENOS
KINDS
KINGS
KINKS
LANDS
LANES
LENDS
LENIS
LENOS
LENTS
LINES
LINKS
LINTS
LINUS
LONGS
LUNES
LUNGS
MANES
MANOS
MENDS
MENUS
MINAS
MINDS
MINES
MINGS
MINIS
MINKS
MINOS
MINTS
MINUS
MONKS
MUNIS
MYNAS
NANAS
NENES
NINAS
NINES
NINOS
NONES
NONOS
OINKS
ORNIS
PANES
PANGS
PANTS
PENDS
PINES
PINGS
PINKS
PINTS
PONDS
PONES
PUNAS
PUNGS
PUNKS
PUNTS
RANDS
RANIS
RANKS
RANTS
RENDS
RENTS
RINDS
RINGS
RINKS
RUNES
RUNGS
RUNTS
SANDS
SENDS
SINES
SINGS
SINKS
SINUS
SONES
SONGS
SYNCS
TANGS
TANKS
TENDS
TENTS
TINES
TINGS
TINTS
TONES
TONGS
TONUS
TONYS
TUNAS
TUNES
TUNIS
TYNES
ULNAS
VANES
VENDS
VENTS
VENUS
VINAS
VINES
WANDS
WANES
WANTS
WENDS
WINDS
WINES
WINGS
WINKS
WONKS
WONTS
YANKS
ZINCS
ZINGS
ZONES
ZONKS
ZUNIS

•••NS
AEONS
AKINS
AMENS
ARENS
ASSNS
AVENS
AXONS
AZANS
BANNS
BARNS
BEANS
BOONS
BOSNS
BRANS
BURNS
CHINS
CLANS
COINS
COONS
CORNS
DAMNS
DARNS
DAWNS
DEANS
DOWNS
EARNS
EDENS
ETONS
EVANS
EVENS
EXONS
FAUNS
FAWNS
FERNS
FINNS
FIRNS
FLANS
FRANS
GAINS
GIRNS
GLENS
GOONS
GOWNS
GRINS
HORNS
HYMNS
ICONS
IRONS
IVINS
JAINS
JEANS
JINNS
JOHNS
JOINS
KEENS
KERNS
KHANS
KILNS
KOANS
LAWNS
LEANS
LIENS
LIMNS
LIONS
LOANS
LOINS
LOONS
LYONS
MAINS
MEANS
MIENS
MOANS
MOONS
MORNS
MUONS
NEONS
NOONS
NORNS
NOUNS
OMENS
OPENS
OVENS
OWENS
PAINS
PAWNS
PEENS
PEONS
PHONS
PIONS
PLANS
POONS
RAINS
REINS
ROANS
RUINS
SAENS
SCANS
SHANS
SHINS
SHUNS
SIGNS
SKINS
SPANS
SPINS
STENS
STUNS
SWANS
TARNS
TEENS
TERNS
THINS
TOONS
TOWNS
TRANS
TURNS
TWINS
VEINS
WAINS
WARNS
WEANS
WRENS
YARNS
YAWNS
YEANS
YUANS

N•T••
NATAL
NATCH
NATTY
NITER
NITES
NITRE
NITRO
NITTI
NITTY
NOTCH
NOTED
NOTER
NOTES
NOTIN
NOTME
NOTRE
NOTSO
NOTUP
NUTTY

N••T•
NAFTA
NASTY
NATTY
NBCTV
NEATH
NEATO
NEATS
NERTS
NERTZ
NESTS
NEWTS
NIFTY
NINTH
NITTI
NITTY
NOCTI
NOLTE
NORTE
NORTH
NUTTY

N•••T
NACHT
NEMAT
NIGHT
NILOT
NIPAT
NOFAT
NOHIT
NONET
NYMET

•NT••
ANTAE
ANTAL
ANTAS
ANTED
ANTES
ANTHO
ANTIC
ANTIQ
ANTIS
ANTON
ANTRA
ANTRE
ANTSY
ENTER
ENTIA
ENTOM
ENTRE
ENTRY
INTEL
INTER
INTOW
INTRA
INTRO
INTWO
ONTAP
ONTOP
UNTER

UNTIE
UNTIL

•N•T•
ANITA
CNOTE
ENATE
GNATS
INITS
INSTR
INSTS
KNITS
KNOTS
KNUTE
ONATE
SNATH
SNITS
TNOTE
TNUTS
UNITE
UNITS
UNITY

•N••T
ANENT
ANGST
ENACT
INAPT
INEPT
INERT
INGOT
INLET
INPUT
INSET
INUIT
KNELT
KNOUT
ONDIT
ONSET
SNERT
SNOOT
SNORT
SNOUT
UNAPT
UNCUT
UNFIT
UNLIT
UNMET
UNSET

••NT•
AUNTS
AUNTY
BANTU
BENTS
BUNTS
CANTO
CANTS
CENTI
CENTO
CENTS
CONTD
CONTE
CONTI
CONTR
DANTE
DENTE
DENTI
DENTS
DINTS
FANTA
FONTS
GENTS
HINTS
HUNTS
JUNTA
JUNTO
KINTE
LANTZ
LENTO
LENTS
LINTS
LINTY
MANTA
MINTS
MINTY
MONTE
MONTH
MONTY
NINTH
PANTO
PANTS
PANTY
PENTA
PENTE
PINTA
PINTO
PINTS
PONTE
PONTI
PUNTA
PUNTS
PUNTY
RANTO
RANTS
RENTA
RENTS
RUNTO
RUNTS
RUNTY
SANTA
SANTE
SANTO
TANTE
TENTH
TENTS
TINTS
TONTO
UINTA
VENTS
WANTS
WONTS
YENTA
YENTE
YENTL
ZANTE

••N•T
BENET
BINET
BONET
BUNDT
CANIT
CANST
DONAT
DONUT
ERNST
GENET
IFNOT
JANET
MANET
MINOT
MONET
NONET
PINOT
RANAT
TENET
TINCT
VINGT
WENDT

•••NT
ADINT
AGENT
AMENT
ANENT
ARENT
AVANT
BLENT
BLUNT
BRANT
BRENT
BRUNT
BURNT
CHANT
CLINT
COUNT
DAUNT
DIDNT
EVENT
FAINT
FEINT
FLINT
FOUNT
FRONT
GAUNT
GHENT
GIANT
GLINT
GRANT
GRUNT
HADNT
HASNT
HAUNT
JAUNT
JOINT
LEANT
MEANT
MOUNT
ODONT
ORANT
PAINT
PLANT
POINT
PRINT
QUANT
QUINT
RIANT
SAINT
SCANT
SCENT
SHANT
SHUNT
SKINT
SLANT
SPENT
STINT
STUNT
SUINT
TAINT
TAUNT
THANT
TIANT
TRENT
VAUNT
WASNT
YOUNT

NU•••
NUBBY
NUBIA
NUCHA
NUDER
NUDES
NUDGE
NUKED
NUKES
NULLS
NUMBS
NUMEN
NUMIS
NURMI
NURSE
NUTTY
NUYEN

N•U••
NAURU
NEUME
NEURO
NOUNS

N••U•
NAHUA
NAHUM
NAMUR
NEFUD
NEGUS
NEVUS
NEXUS
NIDUS
NIPUP
NISUS
NODUS
NOTUP

N•••U
NAURU
NEHRU

•NU••
ENURE
INUIT
INURE
INUSE
KNURL
KNURS
KNUTE
SNUBS
SNUCK
SNUFF
SNUGS
TNUTS

•N•U•
ANGUS
ANHUI
ANNUL
ANNUM
ANNUS
ANOUK
ENDUE
ENDUP
ENNUI
ENSUE
INCUR
INCUS
INDUS
INFUN
INPUT
KNOUT
ONCUE
ONEUP
SNOUT
UNAUS
UNCUT
UNDUE

•N••U
ANJOU
INONU
SNAFU

••NU•
AGNUS
AINUS
ANNUL
ANNUM
ANNUS
BENUE
BONUS
DONUT
ENNUI
GENUS
HONUS
JANUS
LINUS
MENUS
MINUS
OWNUP
PINUP
RANUP
RUNUP
SINUS
SUNUP
TONUS
VENUE
VENUS

••N•U
BANTU
DONAU
FONDU
HINDU
KANZU
XINGU

•••NU
CORNU
INONU
KEANU

N•V••
NAVAL
NAVEL
NAVES
NAVIG
NAVVY
NEVER
NEVES
NEVIL
NEVIN
NEVIS
NEVUS
NIVAL
NIVEN
NOVAE
NOVAK
NOVAS
NOVEL

N••V•
NAIVE
NAVVY
NERVE
NERVY
NORVO

N•••V
NBCTV
NEGEV

•NV••
ANVIL
ENVOI
ENVOY

•N•V•
KNAVE
SNEVA
UNIVS

•N••V
ANNIV
INDIV

••N•V
ANNIV

N•W••
NAWAB
NEWEL
NEWER
NEWLY
NEWSY
NEWTS
NOWAY

N•••W
NAREW
NOHOW

•NW••
ANWAR
UNWED

•N•W•
GNAWS
INAWE
INTWO
KNOWN
KNOWS
SNOWS
SNOWY

•N••W
ENDOW
INLAW
INTOW
ONLOW

••N•W
AGNEW
BYNOW
CANDW
RENEW
SINEW

N•X••
NAXOS
NEXUS
NIXED
NIXES
NIXIE
NIXON

N•••X
NYNEX

•N••X
ANNEX
INDEX
INFIX
UNBOX
UNFIX

••N•X
ANNEX
LENOX
NYNEX

•••NX
BRONX

NY•••
NYACK
NYALA
NYASA
NYLON
NYMET
NYMPH
NYNEX

N•Y••
NOYES
NUYEN

N•••Y
NAGGY
NAMBY
NANCY
NANNY
NAPPY
NASBY
NASTY
NATTY
NAVVY
NEDDY
NEEDY
NELLY
NERDY
NERVY
NEWLY
NEWSY
NIFTY
NILLY
NIMBY
NIMOY
NINNY
NIPPY
NITTY
NOBBY
NOBLY
NODDY
NOISY
NOWAY
NUBBY
NUTTY

•N•Y•
ENCYC

•N••Y
ANGRY
ANNOY
ANOMY
ANTSY
ENEMY
ENJOY
ENSKY
ENTRY
ENVOY
INLAY
ONKEY
ONLAY
SNAKY
SNOWY
UNIFY
UNITY
UNSAY

••NY•
DENYS
KENYA
LENYA
SANYO
SONYA
TANYA
TONYA
TONYS
VANYA
VINYL

••N•Y
ANNOY
AUNTY
BANDY
BANKY
BENNY
BONNY
BUNDY
BUNNY
CANBY
CANDY
CANNY
CINDY
CONEY
DANCY
DANDY
DANNY
DENNY
DINGY
DINKY
DONNY
FANCY
FANNY
FENNY
FINNY
FUNDY
FUNKY
FUNNY
GANDY
GINNY
GUNKY
GUNNY
HANDY
HANKY
HENNY
HENRY
HINNY
HONEY
IXNAY
JENNY
JUNKY
KENNY
KINKY
LANKY
LENNY
LINDY
LINTY
LUNDY
MANDY
MANLY
MANNY
MINDY
MINTY
MONEY
MONTY
NANCY
NANNY
NINNY
PANAY
PANKY
PANSY
PANTY
PENNY
PINEY
PINKY
PUNKY
PUNNY
PUNTY
RANDY
RANGY
RINKY
RONNY
RUNNY
RUNTY
SANDY
SONNY
SUNNY
TANDY
TANEY
TANGY
TANSY
TINNY
TUNNY
VINNY
WANLY
WENDY
WINDY
WONKY
ZINGY

•••NY
AGONY
BEANY
BENNY
BONNY
BRINY
BUNNY
CANNY
CARNY
CLUNY
CORNY
CRONY
DANNY
DENNY
DONNY
DOWNY
EBONY
FANNY
FENNY
FERNY
FINNY
FUNNY
GINNY
GOONY
GUNNY
HENNY
HINNY
IRONY
JENNY
KENNY
LENNY
LOONY
MANNY
MEANY
MOONY
NANNY
NINNY
PENNY
PEONY
PHONY
PLINY
PUNNY
RAINY
RONNY
RUNNY
SHINY
SONNY
SPINY
STONY
SUNNY
TAWNY
TEENY
TINNY
TUNNY
VINNY
WEENY
WHINY

N•Z••
NIZAM
NIZER

N•••Z
NERTZ
NODOZ

•NZ••
ANZAC
ANZIO
UNZIP

••NZ•
BENZO
BONZE
BONZO
DANZA
GINZA
GONZO
KANZU
LANZA
MONZA
PANZA
PENZA
PINZA
PONZI
WINZE

••N•Z
ARNAZ
LANTZ
VENEZ

•••NZ
FRANZ
HEINZ
MAINZ

OA•••
OAKEN
OAKES
OAKIE
OAKUM
OARED
OASES
OASIS
OASTS
OATEN
OATER
OATES
OATHS

O•A••
OCALA
OFAGE
OHAIR
OHARA
OHARE
OKAPI
OKAYS
OLAND
OMAHA
OMANI
OMARR
OMASA
ONAIR
ONATE
OPAHS
OPALS
OPART
ORACH
ORACY
ORALE
ORALS
ORANG
ORANT
ORATE
OSAGE
OSAKA
OTARU
OTARY
OVALS
OVATE
OZARK
OZAWA

O••A•
OBEAH
OCCAM
OCCAS
OCEAN
OCTAD
OCTAL
OFFAL
OGHAM
OKRAS
OLEAN
OLLAS
ONEAL
ONLAY
ONTAP
OPRAH
ORCAS
OREAD
ORGAN
OSCAN
OSCAR
OSKAR
OSMAN
OTWAY

O•••A
OCALA
OCHOA
OCREA
OHARA
OMAHA
OMASA
OMEGA
OMNIA
ONEGA
OOOLA
OPERA
ORIYA
OSAKA
OSHEA
OSSIA
OSTIA
OUIDA
OUIJA
OVETA
OZAWA

•OA••
BOARD
BOARS
BOAST
BOATS
COACH
COACT
COALS
COAPT
COAST
COATI
COATS
FOALS
FOAMS
FOAMY
GOADS
GOALS
GOAPE
GOATS
HOAGY
HOARD
HOARS
HOARY
KOALA
KOANS
LOACH
LOADS
LOAFS
LOAMS
LOAMY
LOANS
LOATH
MOANS
MOATS
NOAHS
POACH
ROACH
ROADS
ROALD
ROAMS
ROANS
ROARS
ROAST
SOAKS
SOAPS
SOAPY
SOARS
SOAVE
TOADS
TOADY
TOAST
WOADS

•O•A•
AODAI
BOHAI
BOLAS
BORAH
BORAS
BORAX
BOYAR
CODAS
COHAN
COLAS
COMAE
COMAS
CONAN
COPAL
COPAN
COPAY
CORAL
COXAE
COXAL
DONAS
DONAT
DONAU
DORAL
DORAN
DOTAL
DOUAI
DOUAY
FOCAL
FORAY
GOBAD
GOFAR
GOLAN
GORAL
GOTAT
HOBAN
HODAD
HOGAN
HONAN
HORAE
HORAL
HORAS
HOYAS
IOTAS
IOWAN
JONAH
JONAS
JOTAS
JOUAL
KODAK
KOJAK
KOLAS
KORAN
LOCAL
LOFAT
LOGAN
LOMAN
LOMAX
LOPAT
LORAN
LORAX
LOTAS
LOYAL
MODAL
MOLAR
MOLAS
MONAD
MORAL
MORAN
MORAY
NOCAL
NODAL
NOFAT
NOLAN
NOMAD
NOPAL
NOPAR
NORAD
NORAH
NOVAE
NOVAK
NOVAS
NOWAY
POHAI
POLAR
POWAY
RODAN
ROMAN
ROTAS
ROWAN
ROYAL
SODAS
SOFAR
SOFAS
SOLAN
SOLAR
SOMAS
SONAR
SORAS
SOYAS
TODAY
TOGAS
TOKAY
TONAL
TOPAZ
TORAH
TOTAL
VOCAL
VOLAR
WOMAN
WOTAN
ZOHAR
ZONAL

•O••A
AORTA
BOHEA
BOOLA
BOSSA
BOTHA
COBIA
COBRA
COCOA
COMMA
CONGA
COOSA
COPRA
COREA
COSTA
COTTA
DOBLA
DOBRA
DOGMA
DOLMA
DONNA
DORSA
FOLIA
FONDA
FORMA
FOSSA
FOVEA
GOLDA
GONNA
GOTHA
GOTTA
GOUDA
HOFFA
HONDA
HOOHA
HOSEA
HOSTA
HOUMA
IONIA
JOLLA
KOALA
KORDA
KOREA
LOGIA
LONGA
LORCA
LORNA
LOTTA
MOCHA
MOIRA
MOMMA
MONZA
MOOLA
MOTTA
NORIA
NORMA
OOOLA
PODIA
POLKA
PONCA
POONA
POPPA
SOFIA
SOLFA
SONIA
SONJA
SONYA
SORTA
SOUSA
TONGA
TONKA
TONYA
TOSCA
VODKA
VOILA
VOLGA
VOLTA
YORBA
ZORBA

••OA•
ANOAS
AROAR
BLOAT
BROAD
CLOAK
CROAK
CROAT
FLOAT
GLOAM
GLOAT
GROAN
GROAT
PROAM
PROAS
PSOAS
SHOAH
SHOAL
SHOAT
SKOAL
SLOAN
STOAE
STOAS
STOAT
UBOAT

••O•A
ACOMA
AGORA
AHORA
ALOHA
AROMA
ASOKA
BIOTA
BOOLA
BROCA
COOSA
EVORA
FIONA
FLORA
GROZA
HOOHA
ICOSA
ILONA
KIOGA
KIOWA
KRONA
KYOGA
LEONA
LEORA
MOOLA
NDOLA
OOOLA
POONA
QUOTA
RHODA
RIOJA
SKODA
STOLA
STOMA
VIOLA
XHOSA

•••OA
ALCOA
COCOA
GENOA
OCHOA
SAMOA

OB•••
OBEAH
OBELI
OBESE
OBEYS
OBIES
OBJET
OBOES
OBOLI
OBOLS

O•B••
OHBOY
OMBER
OMBRE
ORBIT
OXBOW

O••B•
ORIBI

•OB••
BOBBY
BOBUP
COBIA
COBOL
COBRA
DOBIE
DOBLA
DOBLE
DOBRA
DOBRO
GOBAD
GOBEL
HOBAN
HOBBS
HOBBY
HOBOS
KOBOS
LOBBY
LOBED
LOBES
LOBOS
MOBIL
NOBBY
NOBEL
NOBLE
NOBLY
POBOX
POBOY
ROBBY
ROBED
ROBES
ROBIN
ROBLE
ROBOT
SOBER
SOBIG
TOBEY
TOBIT

•O•B•
BOBBY
BOMBE
BOMBS
BOOBS
BOOBY
COLBY
COMBO
COMBS
CORBY
COSBY
DOLBY
DOUBT
FORBS
GOTBY
HOBBS
HOBBY
LOBBY
MOSBY
NOBBY
ROBBY
SORBS
YORBA
ZORBA

•O••B
HOREB

••OB•
ADOBE
BLOBS
BOOBS
BOOBY
FROBE
GLOBE
GLOBS
KNOBS
NIOBE
PHOBE
PROBE
SLOBS
SNOBS

••O•B
ABOMB
HBOMB
RHOMB

•••OB
CAROB
DEMOB
JACOB
KABOB
NABOB
THROB

OC•••
OCALA
OCCAM
OCCAS
OCCUR
OCEAN
OCHER
OCHOA
OCHRE
OCREA

OCTAD
OCTAL
OCTET
OCULO

O•C••

OCCAM
OCCAS
OCCUR
ONCLE
ONCUE
OPCIT
ORCAS
ORCHS
ORCUS
ORCZY
OSCAN
OSCAR

O••C•

ONICE
ORACH
ORACY
OUNCE

O•••C

OLEIC
OLMEC
OPTIC
OSMIC
OSRIC

•OC••

BOCCE
BOCCI
COCKS
COCKY
COCOA
DOCKS
FOCAL
FOCUS
HOCKS
HOCUS
JOCKO
JOCKS
KOCHI
LOCAL
LOCHS
LOCKE
LOCKS
LOCOS
LOCUS
MOCHA
MOCKS
NOCAL
NOCKS
NOCTI
POCUS
ROCCO
ROCHE
ROCKS
ROCKY
SOCHI
SOCIO
SOCKO
SOCKS
SOCLE
VOCAL

•O•C•

BOCCE
BOCCI
BOSCH
BOSCO
BOSCS
BOTCH
COACH
COACT
CONCH
COUCH
DOLCE
FORCE
HOOCH
JOYCE
KOTCH
LOACH
LORCA
MONCK
MOOCH
NONCE
NOTCH
POACH
PONCA
PONCE
PONCH
POOCH
PORCH
POUCH
ROACH
ROCCO
ROYCE
TORCH
TOSCA
TOUCH
VOICE
VOICI
VOUCH

•O••C

BORIC
COMIC
CONIC
COSEC
DORIC
FOLIC
IODIC
IONIC
LOGIC
MODOC
SONIC
TONIC
TOPIC
TORIC
TOXIC

••OC•

AMOCO
BLOCH
BLOCK
BLOCS
BROCA
BROCK
CHOCK
CLOCK
CROCE
CROCI
CROCK
CROCS
ENOCH
EPOCH
FLOCK
FROCK
HOOCH
KNOCK
MOOCH
POOCH
SHOCK
SMOCK
SPOCK
STOCK

••O•C

AZOIC
BRONC
STOIC

•••OC

ADHOC
ADLOC
ASSOC
DUROC
HAVOC
MEDOC
MODOC

OD•••

ODDER
ODDLY
ODELL
ODETS
ODEUM
ODILE
ODIST
ODIUM
ODONT
ODORS
ODOUR

O•D••

ODDER
ODDLY
OGDEN
OLDEN
OLDER
OLDIE
ONDIT
ORDER
ORDOS

O••D•

OPEDS
OUIDA
OUTDO
OXIDE

O•••D

OARED
OCTAD
OGLED
OHGOD
OILED
OLAND
ONEND
OOHED
OOTID
OOZED
OPTED
OREAD
OUTED
OVOID
OWNED

•OD••

AODAI
BODED
BODES
CODAS
CODED
CODER
CODES
CODEX
DODGE
DODGY
DODOS
FODOR
GODEL
GODET
GODEY
GODLY
GODOT
HODAD
IODIC
JODIE
KODAK
LODEN
LODES
LODGE
MODAL
MODEL
MODEM
MODES
MODOC
MODUS
NODAL
NODDY
NODES
NODOZ
NODUS
PODGY
PODIA
RODAN
RODDY
RODEO
RODIN
SODAS
SODDY
SODOM
TODAY
TODDY
TODOS
VODKA
WODEN
YODEL

•O•D•

BONDI
BONDS
COEDS
COLDS
CONDE
CONDO
CORDS
DONDI
DOODY
DOWDY
FOLDS
FONDA
FONDS
FONDU
FOODS
FORDO
FORDS
GOADS
GOLDA
GOLDE
GOLDS
GONDI
GONDS
GOODS
GOODY
GORDO
GORDY
GOUDA
GOUDY
GOWDY
HOLDS
HONDA
HONDO
HOODS
HORDE
HOWDY
KORDA
LOADS
LORDS
MOLDS
MOLDY
MONDE
MONDO
MOODS
MOODY
NODDY
PONDS
POODS
ROADS
RODDY
RONDO
ROODS
ROWDY
SODDY
SOLDI
SOLDO
SONDE
TOADS
TOADY
TODDY
TONDI
TONDO
VOIDS
WOADS
WOLDS
WOODS
WOODY
WORDS
WORDY

•O••D

BOARD
BODED
BONED
BOOED
BORED
BOUND
BOVID
BOWED
BOXED
CODED
COKED
CONTD
COOED
COPED
CORED
COULD
COWED
COXED
DOLED
DOMED
DOSED
DOTED
DOZED
FOUND
FOXED
GOBAD
GORED
GOULD
GOURD
HOARD
HODAD
HOKED
HOLED
HOMED
HONED
HOPED
HOSED
HOUND
JOKED
LOBED
LOPED
LOVED
LOWED
MONAD
MONOD
MOOED
MOPED
MOULD
MOUND
MOVED
MOWED
NOEND
NOMAD
NORAD
NOSED
NOTED
OOHED
OOTID
OOZED
POKED
POLED
PORED
POSED
POUND
ROALD
ROBED
ROPED
ROUND
ROVED
ROWED
SOLED
SOLID
SOUND
SOWED
TONED
TOPED
TOTED
TOWED
TOYED
VOTED
VOWED
WOOED
WORLD
WOULD
WOUND
WOWED
YOKED
ZONED
ZOOID

••OD•

ABODE
ANODE
BRODY
CLODS
DIODE
DOODY
EPODE
ERODE
FOODS
FRODO
GEODE
GOODS
GOODY
GRODY
HOODS
MOODS
MOODY
PLODS
POODS
PRODS
QUODS
RHODA
RHODE
RHODO
ROODS
SKODA
SPODE
WOODS
WOODY

••O•D

ALOUD
AROID
AVOID
BLOND
BLOOD
BOOED
BROAD
BROOD
CHORD
CLOUD
COOED
CROWD
DROID
DROOD
FIORD
FJORD
FLOOD
FLOYD
FROID
FROND
GEOID
HYOID
LLOYD
MOOED
OVOID
PROUD
SCOLD
SHOED
SLOYD
SNOOD
STOOD
SWORD
SZOLD
TBOND
WOOED
ZOOID

•••OD

BIPOD
BLOOD
BROOD
DROOD
EPHOD
FLOOD
HEROD
MONOD
OHGOD
RESOD
SAROD
SCROD
SNOOD
STOOD
SYNOD

O•E••

OBEAH
OBELI
OBESE
OBEYS
OCEAN
ODELL
ODETS
ODEUM
OGEES
OLEAN
OLEIC
OLEIN
OLEOS
OLEUM
OMEGA
OMENS
OMERS
ONEAL
ONEGA
ONEIL
ONEND
ONERS
ONEUP
OPEDS
OPELS
OPENS
OPERA
OREAD
OREOS
OVENS
OVERS
OVERT
OVETA
OVETT
OWENS
OWERS
OXEYE

O••E•

OAKEN
OAKES
OARED
OASES
OATEN
OATER
OATES
OBIES
OBJET
OBOES
OCHER
OCREA
OCTET
ODDER
OFFER
OFTEN
OGDEN
OGEES
OGLED
OGLER
OGLES
OGRES
OILED
OILER
OKIES
OLDEN
OLDER
OLMEC
OLSEN
OMBER
ONKEY
ONSET
OOHED
OOZED
OOZES
OPTED
ORDER
ORFEO
ORIEL
ORLES
ORSER
OSHEA
OSIER
OSLER
OSSEO
OSTEO
OTHER
OTOES
OTTER
OUSEL
OUTED
OUTER
OUZEL
OWLET
OWNED
OWNER

O•••E

OAKIE
OBESE
OCHRE
ODILE
OFAGE
OFUSE
OGIVE
OHARE
OLDIE
OLIVE
OLLIE
OMBRE
ONATE
ONCLE
ONCUE
ONICE
OPINE
ORALE
ORATE
OSAGE
OSSIE
OUNCE
OUTRE
OVATE
OVINE
OVULE
OXEYE
OXIDE
OZONE
OZZIE

•OE••

BOEHM
BOERS
BOEUF
COEDS
COEUR
DOERS
DOEST
DOETH
FOEHN
GOERS
GOEST
HOERS
JOEYS
LOESS
LOEWE
LOEWY
NOELS
NOEND
POEME
POEMS
POESY
POETE
POETS
SOEUR
TOEIN

•O•E•

BODED
BODES
BOGEY
BOHEA
BOLES
BONED
BONER
BONES
BONET
BOOED
BOOER
BORED
BORER
BORES
BOWED
BOWEN
BOWER
BOWES
BOXED
BOXER
BOXES
BOYER
CODED
CODER
CODES
CODEX
COHEN
COKED
COKES
COLES
COLET
COMER
COMES
COMET
COMEX
CONES
CONEY
COOED
COOEE
COOER
COPED
COPES
COREA
CORED
CORER
CORES
COREY
COSEC
COTES
COVEN
COVER
COVES
COVET
COVEY
COWED
COWER
COWES
COXED
COXES
COXEY
COYER
COZEN
COZES
DOGES
DOLED
DOLES
DOMED
DOMES
DONEE
DOPES
DOPEY
DOREN
DOSED
DOSER
DOSES
DOTED
DOTER
DOTES
DOVER
DOVES
DOVEY
DOWEL
DOWER
DOYEN
DOZED
DOZEN
DOZER
DOZES
FOGEY
FOLEY
FORES
FOVEA
FOXED
FOXES
FOYER
GOBEL
GODEL
GODET
GODEY
GOFER
GOLEM
GOMER
GOMEZ
GONER
GOOEY
GORED
GOREN
GORES
GOSEE
GOWER
HOKED
HOKES
HOKEY
HOLED
HOLES
HOLEY
HOMED
HOMEO
HOMER
HOMES
HOMEY
HONED
HONES
HONEY
HOOEY
HOPED
HOPER
HOPES
HOREB
HOSEA
HOSED
HOSEL
HOSES
HOTEL
HOVEL
HOVER
HOVEY
JOKED
JOKER
JOKES
JONES
JOREL
JOSEF
KOPEK
KOREA
LOBED
LOBES
LODEN
LODES
LOGES
LONER
LOPED
LOPER
LOPES
LOPEZ
LOREN
LORES
LOSER
LOSES
LOVED
LOVER
LOVES
LOVEY
LOWED
LOWER
LOXES
MODEL
MODEM
MODES
MOLES
MONEL
MONET
MONEY
MOOED
MOPED
MOPER
MOPES
MOPEY
MOREL
MORES
MOREY
MOSES
MOSEY
MOTEL
MOTES
MOTET
MOUES
MOVED
MOVER
MOVES
MOWED
MOWER
NOBEL
NODES
NOMEN
NONES
NONET
NOSED
NOSES
NOTED
NOTER
NOTES
NOVEL
NOYES
OOHED
OOZED
OOZES
POKED
POKER
POKES
POKEY
POLED
POLER
POLES
POMES
PONES
POPES
PORED
PORES
POSED
POSER
POSES
POWER
ROBED
ROBES
RODEO
ROGER
ROGET
ROLEO
ROLES
ROLEX
ROMEO
ROMER
RONEE
ROPED
ROPER
ROPES
ROPEY
ROREM
ROSEN
ROSES
ROSEY
ROTES
ROUEN
ROUES
ROVED
ROVER
ROVES
ROWED
ROWEL
ROWEN
ROWER
SOBER
SOLED
SOLER
SOLES
SONES
SOOEY
SOREL
SOREN
SORER
SORES
SOWED
SOWER
SOXER
TOBEY
TOKEN
TOLER
TOLET
TOMEI
TOMES
TONED
TONER
TONES
TOPED
TOPER
TOPES
TOTED
TOTEM
TOTER
TOTES
TOVES
TOWED
TOWEL
TOWER
TOYED
VOLES
VOTED
VOTER
VOTES
VOWED
VOWEL
VOWER
WODEN
WOKEN
WOMEN
WOOED
WOOER
WOVEN
WOWED
YODEL
YOKED
YOKEL
YOKES
ZONED
ZONES
ZOOEY

•O••E

BOCCE
BOGIE
BOGLE
BOHME
BOISE
BOITE
BOMBE
BONNE
BONZE
BOOLE
BOONE
BOOZE
BORGE
BORNE
BOTHE
BOULE
BOUSE
BOWIE
BOYLE
BOYNE
COMAE
COMME
COMTE
CONDE
CONGE
CONTE
COOEE
COOKE
COPSE
COUPE
COXAE
DOBIE
DOBLE
DODGE
DOGIE
DOLCE
DONEE
DONNE
DOONE
DOUSE
DOWSE
DOYLE
FOOTE
FORCE
FORGE
FORTE
FOSSE
FOYLE
GOAPE
GOLDE
GOOSE
GORGE
GORME
GORSE
GOSEE
GOSSE
GOUGE
HOMME
HOOKE
HOPPE
HORAE
HORDE
HORNE
HORSE
HOUSE
HOWIE
HOXIE
HOYLE
JODIE
JOLIE
JORGE
JOULE
JOYCE
KOINE
KOPJE
LOCKE
LODGE
LOEWE
LOGUE
LOIRE
LOOSE
LORNE
LORRE
LOTTE
LOUIE
LOUPE
LOUSE
MOIRE
MONDE
MONTE
MOORE
MOOSE
MORSE
MOSHE
MOUSE
MOVIE
MOXIE
NOBLE
NOIRE
NOISE
NOLLE
NOLTE
NONCE
NOONE
NOOSE
NORGE
NORSE
NORTE
NOTME
NOTRE
NOVAE
POEME
POETE
POISE
POMME
PONCE
PONTE
POOLE
PORTE
POSSE
POSTE
ROBLE
ROCHE
ROGUE
ROLFE
ROLLE
RONEE
ROONE
ROQUE
ROSIE
ROUGE
ROUSE
ROUTE
ROXIE
ROYCE
SOAVE
SOCLE
SOLVE
SOMME
SONDE
SOUSE
TOILE
TONNE
TOQUE
TORME
TORRE
TORTE
TOTIE
TOUTE
TOWNE
VOGUE
VOICE
VOILE
VOLTE
VOTRE
WOLFE
WORSE
YOURE
YOUVE
ZOWIE

••OE•

ALOES
BOOED
BOOER
COOED
COOEE
COOER
FLOES
FROES
GOOEY
HOOEY
MOOED
OBOES
OTOES
PROEM
SHOED
SHOER
SHOES
SLOES
SOOEY
WOOED
WOOER
ZOOEY

••O•E

ABODE
ABOVE
ADOBE
ADORE
AFORE
ALONE
AMOLE
AMORE
ANODE
ANOLE
AROSE
ASONE
ATONE
AWOKE
AZOTE
BIOME
BLOKE
BOOLE
BOONE
BOOZE
BROKE
BROME
CHOKE
CHORE
CHOSE
CLONE
CLOSE
CLOVE
CNOTE
COOEE
COOKE
CROCE
CRONE
CROZE
DHOLE
DHOTE
DIODE
DIONE
DOONE
DROME
DRONE
DROVE
ECOLE
ELOPE
EMOTE
EPODE
ERODE
EROSE
EVOKE
FOOTE
FROBE
FROME
FROZE
GEODE
GLOBE
GLOVE
GLOZE
GNOME
GOOSE
GROFE
GROPE
GROVE
HAOLE
HOOKE
KRONE
LEONE
LOOSE
MOORE
MOOSE
MYOPE
NIOBE
NOONE
NOOSE
OZONE
PHOBE
PHONE
POOLE
PROBE
PROLE
PRONE
PROSE
PROVE
QUOTE
RHODE
RHONE
ROONE
SAONE
SCONE
SCOPE
SCORE
SHONE
SHORE
SHOVE
SLOPE

SMOKE
SMOTE
SNORE
SPODE
SPOKE
SPORE
STOAE
STOKE
STOLE
STONE
STOPE
STORE
STOVE
STOWE
SWOPE
SWORE
TBONE
THOLE
THOSE
TNOTE
TROPE
TROVE
WHOLE
WHOSE
WROTE

•••OE
CANOE
CHLOE
DAFOE
DEFOE
FAROE
GIJOE
MEROE
PEKOE
TAHOE
THROE

OF•••
OFAGE
OFFAL
OFFER
OFTEN
OFUSE

O•F••
OFFAL
OFFER
ORFEO

O••F•
ONOFF

O•••F
ONOFF

•OF••
BOFFO
BOFFS
DOFFS
GOFAR
GOFER
GOFOR
HOFFA
LOFAT
LOFTS
LOFTY
MOFFO
NOFAT
SOFAR
SOFAS
SOFIA
SOFTY
TOFFS

•O•F•
BOFFO
BOFFS
COIFS
COMFY
CORFU
DOFFS
GOLFS
GOOFF
GOOFS
GOOFY
HOFFA
HOOFS
LOAFS
MOFFO
POUFS
ROLFE
ROOFS
SOLFA
TOFFS
WOLFE
WOLFF
WOOFS

•O••F
BOEUF
GOOFF
JOSEF
MOTIF
WOLFF
WOOLF

••OF•
AFOFL
ALOFT
CROFT
FEOFF
GOOFF
GOOFS
GOOFY
GROFE
HOOFS
ONOFF
PROFS
ROOFS
SCOFF
WOOFS

••O•F
ADOLF
ALOOF
FEOFF
GOOFF
KNOPF
ONOFF
PROOF
SCOFF
SPOOF
WHOOF
WOOLF

•••OF
ALOOF
PROOF
RIDOF
SPOOF
WHOOF

OG•••
OGDEN
OGEES
OGHAM
OGIVE
OGLED
OGLER
OGLES
OGRES

O•G••
OHGOD
ORGAN
OUGHT

O••G•
OFAGE
OINGO
OLIGO
OLOGY
OMEGA
ONEGA
OSAGE
OUTGO

O•••G
ORANG
ORING
OWING

•OG••
BOGEY
BOGGS
BOGGY
BOGIE
BOGLE
BOGUS
DOGES
DOGGO
DOGGY
DOGIE
DOGIT
DOGMA
DOGON
FOGEY
FOGGY
FOGIN
GOGOL
GOGOS
HOGAN
HOGGS
LOGAN
LOGES
LOGIA
LOGIC
LOGIN
LOGON
LOGOS
LOGUE
MOGUL
NOGOS
ROGER
ROGET
ROGUE
SOGGY
TOGAS
VOGUE
YOGHS
YOGIS

•O•G•
BOGGS
BOGGY
BONGO
BONGS
BORGE
BOUGH
CONGA
CONGE
CONGO
CORGI
COUGH
DODGE
DODGY
DOGGO
DOGGY
DONGS
DOUGH
FOGGY
FORGE
FORGO
GOLGI
GONGS
GORGE
GOUGE
HOAGY
HOGGS
HONGS
HOUGH
JORGE
LODGE
LONGA
LONGI
LONGS
LOUGH
MONGO
MOOGS
NORGE
PODGY
PORGY
ROUGE
ROUGH
SOGGY
SONGS
SORGO
SOUGH
TONGA
TONGS
TOUGH
VOLGA

•O••G
BOING
BOURG
DOING
GOING
SOBIG
SOONG
YOUNG

••OG•
AGOGO
CLOGS
FLOGS
FROGS
GLOGG
GROGS
KEOGH
KIOGA
KROGH
KYOGA
MOOGS
OLOGY
SHOGI
SLOGS
SMOGS
STOGY

••O•G
ALONG
AMONG
CHONG
GEORG
GLOGG
HMONG
PRONG
SOONG
THONG
WRONG

•••OG
BEFOG
DEFOG
INCOG
MAGOG

OH•••
OHAIR
OHARA
OHARE
OHBOY
OHGOD

O•H••
OCHER
OCHOA
OCHRE
OGHAM
OOHED
OPHIR
OSHEA
OTHER

O••H•
OATHS
OMAHA
OPAHS
ORCHS
ORTHO
OUGHT

O•••H
OBEAH
OOMPH
OPRAH
ORACH

•OH••
BOHAI
BOHEA
BOHME
COHAN
COHEN
COHOS
HOHOS
HOHUM
JOHNS
MOHUR
NOHIT
NOHOW
OOHED
POHAI
SOHIO
ZOHAR

•O•H•
BOEHM
BOTHA
BOTHE
DONHO
FOEHN
GOTHA
GOTHS
HOOHA
KOCHI
LOCHS
MOCHA
MOSHE
MOTHS
MOTHY
NOAHS
POOHS
ROCHE
SOCHI
SOPHS
SOPHY
SOTHO
YOGHS

•O••H
BOOTH
BORAH
BOSCH
BOTCH
BOUGH
COACH
CONCH
COUCH
COUGH
COUTH
DOETH
DOLPH
DOUGH
FORTH
FOURH
HOOCH
HOUGH
JONAH
KOTCH
LOACH
LOATH
LOUGH
MONTH
MOOCH
MORPH
MOUTH
NORAH
NORTH
NOTCH
OOMPH
POACH
PONCH
POOCH
PORCH
POUCH
ROACH
ROUGH
SOOTH
SOUGH
SOUTH
TOOTH
TORAH
TORCH
TOUCH
TOUGH
VOUCH
WORTH
YOUTH

••OH•
ABOHM
ALOHA
HOOHA
POOHS

••O•H
AZOTH
BLOCH
BOOTH
BROTH
CLOTH
ENOCH
EPOCH
FROSH
FROTH
HOOCH
KEOGH
KROGH
MOOCH
POOCH
QUOTH
SHOAH
SKOSH
SLOSH
SLOTH
SOOTH
THOTH
TOOTH
TROTH
WROTH

•••OH
RICOH

OI•••
OILED
OILER
OINGO
OINKS

O•I••
OBIES
ODILE
ODIST
ODIUM
OGIVE
OKIES
OLIGO
OLIOS
OLIVE
OMITS
ONICE
ONION
OPINE
OPIUM
ORIBI
ORIEL
ORING
ORION
ORIYA
OSIER
OUIDA
OUIJA
OVINE
OWING
OXIDE

O••I•
OAKIE
OASIS
OHAIR
OLDIE
OLEIC
OLEIN
OLLIE
OMNIA
ONAIR
ONDIT
ONEIL
OOTID
OPCIT
OPHIR
OPSIN
OPSIS
OPTIC
ORBIT
ORNIS
ORRIN
ORRIS
OSLIN
OSMIC
OSRIC
OSSIA
OSSIE
OSTIA
OVOID
OXLIP
OZZIE

O•••I
OBELI
OBOLI
OKAPI
OMANI
ORIBI
OTOMI
OVOLI

•OI••
BOILS
BOING
BOISE
BOITE
BOITO
COIFS
COILS
COINS
COIRS
DOILY
DOING
DOITS
FOILS
FOIST
GOING
HOIST
HOITY
JOINS
JOINT
JOIST
KOINE
LOINS
LOIRE
MOILS
MOIRA
MOIRE
MOIST
NOILS
NOIRE
NOISE
NOISY
POILS
POILU
POINT
POISE
ROILS
ROILY
SOILS
TOILE
TOILS
TOITY
VOICE
VOICI
VOIDS
VOILA
VOILE

•O•I•
BOGIE
BORIC
BORIS
BOVID
BOWIE
BOXIN
COBIA
COLIN
COMIC
COMIX
CONIC
DOBIE
DOGIE
DOGIT
DORIC
DORIS
EOSIN
FOGIN
FOLIA
FOLIC
FOLIO
GOTIN
HOPIS
HOWIE
HOXIE
IODIC
IONIA
IONIC
JODIE
JOLIE
JOSIP
LOGIA
LOGIC
LOGIN
LORIS
LOUIE
LOUIS
MOBIL
MOTIF
MOVIE
MOXIE
NOHIT
NORIA
NOSIR
NOTIN
OOTID
PODIA
POLIS
POLIT
POPIN
POSIT
ROBIN
RODIN
ROSIE
ROSIN
ROXIE
SOBIG
SOCIO
SOFIA
SOHIO
SOLID
SONIA
SONIC
TOBIT
TOEIN
TONIC
TONIO
TOPIC
TOPIS
TORIC
TORII
TOTIE
TOWIT
TOXIC
TOXIN
YOGIS
ZOOID
ZORIL
ZORIS
ZOWIE

•O••I
AODAI
BOCCI
BOHAI
BONDI
COATI
CONTI
CORGI
DONDI
DORSI
DOUAI
GOLGI
GONDI
GORKI
HOSNI
HOURI
KOCHI
LONGI
NOCTI
POHAI
PONTI
PONZI
ROSSI
SOCHI
SOLDI
SOLTI
SOMNI
TOMEI
TONDI
TOPOI
TORII
TORSI
VOICI

••OI•
ABOIL
AROID
AVOID
AVOIR
AZOIC
BLOIS
BROIL
CHOIR
CROIX
DROID
DROIT
FROID
GEOID
GROIN
HYOID
OVOID
QUOIN
QUOIT
REOIL
SPOIL
STOIC
TROIS
ZOOID

••O•I
AIOLI
CROCI
DHOTI
EBOLI
ICOSI
MAORI
NAOMI
OBOLI
OTOMI
OVOLI
PAOLI
SHOGI
SHOJI
SUOMI

•••OI
ENVOI
HANOI
LEROI
TOPOI

O•J••
OBJET

O••J•
OUIJA

•OJ••
DOJOS
KOJAK
MOJOS

•O•J•
KOPJE
SONJA

••OJ•
RIOJA
SHOJI

OK•••
OKAPI
OKAYS
OKIES
OKRAS

O•K••
OAKEN
OAKES
OAKIE
OAKUM
ONKEY
OSKAR

O••K•
OINKS
OSAKA

O•••K
OZARK

•OK••
COKED
COKES
HOKED
HOKES
HOKEY
HOKUM
JOKED
JOKER
JOKES
POKED
POKER
POKES
POKEY
TOKAY
TOKEN
TOKYO
WOKEN
YOKED
YOKEL
YOKES
YOKUM

•O•K•
BONKS
BOOKS
BOSKS
BOSKY
COCKS
COCKY
CONKS
COOKE
COOKS
CORKS
CORKY
DOCKS
FOLKS
FOLKY
FORKS
FORKY
GORKI
GORKY
HOCKS
HONKS
HOOKE
HOOKS
HOOKY
JOCKO
JOCKS
KOOKS
KOOKY
LOCKE
LOCKS
LOOKS
MOCKS
MONKS
NOCKS
NOOKS
POLKA
PORKS
PORKY
ROCKS
ROCKY
ROOKS
ROOKY
ROYKO
SOAKS
SOCKO
SOCKS
TONKA
VODKA
WONKS
WONKY
WORKS
YOLKS
ZONKS

•O••K
KODAK
KOJAK
KOPEK
MONCK
NOVAK
POTOK

••OK•
ASOKA
AWOKE
BLOKE
BOOKS
BROKE
CHOKE
CHOKY
COOKE
COOKS
EVOKE
EWOKS
GROKS
HOOKE
HOOKS
HOOKY
KOOKS
KOOKY
LOOKS
NOOKS
ROOKS
ROOKY
SMOKE
SMOKY
SPOKE
STOKE

••O•K
ANOUK
BLOCK
BROCK
BROOK
CHOCK
CLOAK
CLOCK
CLONK
CROAK
CROCK
CROOK
FLOCK
FROCK
KIOSK
KNOCK
PLONK
SHOCK
SHOOK
SMOCK
SNOOK
SPOCK
SPOOK
SPORK
STOCK
STORK

•••OK
BROOK
CROOK
HUROK
KAPOK
POTOK
SHOOK
SNOOK
SPOOK
TAROK
YAPOK

OL•••
OLAND
OLDEN
OLDER
OLDIE
OLEAN
OLEIC
OLEIN
OLEOS
OLEUM
OLIGO
OLIOS
OLIVE
OLLAS
OLLIE
OLMEC
OLMOS
OLOGY
OLSEN
OLSON

O•L••
OGLED
OGLER
OGLES
OILED
OILER
OLLAS
OLLIE
ONLAY
ONLOW
ORLES
ORLON
ORLOP
OSLER
OSLIN
OWLET
OXLIP

O••L•
OBELI
OBOLI
OBOLS
OCALA
OCULO
ODDLY
ODELL
ODILE
ONCLE
OOOLA
OPALS
OPELS
ORALE
ORALS
OVALS
OVOLI
OVOLO
OVULE

O•••L
OCTAL
ODELL
OFFAL
ONEAL
ONEIL
ORIEL
OUSEL
OUZEL

•OL••
BOLAS
BOLES
BOLLS
BOLOS
BOLTS
BOLUS
COLAS
COLBY
COLDS
COLES
COLET
COLIN
COLON
COLOR
COLTS
COLUM
DOLBY
DOLCE
DOLED
DOLES
DOLLS
DOLLY
DOLMA
DOLOR
DOLPH
DOLTS
EOLUS
FOLDS
FOLEY
FOLIA
FOLIC
FOLIO
FOLKS
FOLKY
FOLLY
GOLAN
GOLDA
GOLDE
GOLDS
GOLEM
GOLFS
GOLGI
GOLLY
HOLDS
HOLED
HOLES
HOLEY
HOLLY
HOLMS
HOLST
HOLTZ
JOLIE
JOLLA
JOLLY
JOLTS
JOLTY
KOLAS
LOLLS
LOLLY
MOLAR
MOLAS
MOLDS
MOLDY
MOLES
MOLLS
MOLLY
MOLTO
MOLTS
NOLAN
NOLLE
NOLTE
POLAR
POLED
POLER
POLES
POLIS
POLIT
POLKA
POLLO
POLLS
POLLY
POLOS
POLYP
ROLEO
ROLES
ROLEX
ROLFE
ROLLE
ROLLO
ROLLS
SOLAN
SOLAR
SOLDI
SOLDO
SOLED
SOLER
SOLES
SOLFA
SOLID
SOLON
SOLOS
SOLTI
SOLUM
SOLUS
SOLVE
TOLER
TOLET
TOLLS
VOLAR
VOLES
VOLGA
VOLTA
VOLTE
VOLTS
VOLVO
WOLDS
WOLFE
WOLFF
YOLKS

•O•L•
BOGLE
BOILS
BOLLS
BOOLA
BOOLE
BOULE
BOULT
BOWLS
BOYLE
COALS
COILS
COOLS
COULD
COWLS
COYLY
DOBLA
DOBLE
DOILY
DOLLS
DOLLY
DOYLE
FOALS
FOILS
FOLLY
FOOLS
FOULS
FOWLS
FOYLE
GOALS
GODLY
GOLLY
GOULD
HOLLY
HOTLY
HOWLS
HOYLE
JOLLA
JOLLY
JOULE
JOWLS
JOWLY
KOALA
LOLLS
LOLLY
LOWLY
MOILS
MOLLS
MOLLY
MOOLA
MOULD
MOULT
NOBLE
NOBLY
NOELS
NOILS
NOLLE
OOOLA
POILS
POILU
POLLO
POLLS
POLLY
POOLE
POOLS
POULT
ROALD
ROBLE
ROILS
ROILY
ROLLE
ROLLO
ROLLS
ROTLS
SOCLE
SOILS
SOULS
SOULT
TOILE
TOILS
TOLLS
TOOLS
VOILA
VOILE
WOOLF
WOOLS
WORLD
WOULD
YOULL
YOWLS

•O••L
COBOL
COPAL
CORAL
COXAL
DORAL
DOTAL
DOWEL
FOCAL
GOBEL
GODEL
GOGOL
GORAL
HORAL
HOROL
HOSEL
HOTEL
HOVEL
JOREL
JOUAL
LOCAL
LOYAL
MOBIL
MODAL
MODEL
MOGUL
MONEL
MORAL
MOREL
MOSUL
MOTEL
NOBEL
NOCAL
NODAL
NOPAL
NOVEL

ROWEL
ROYAL
SOREL
SOTOL
TONAL
TOPOL
TOTAL
TOWEL
VOCAL
VOWEL
YODEL
YOKEL
YOULL
ZONAL
ZORIL

••OL•

ADOLF
AIOLI
AMOLE
ANOLE
ATOLL
AWOLS
BOOLA
BOOLE
COOLS
CROLY
DHOLE
DROLL
EBOLI
ECOLE
ENOLS
FOOLS
GAOLS
HAOLE
IDOLS
KNOLL
MOOLA
NDOLA
OBOLI
OBOLS
OOOLA
OVOLI
OVOLO
PAOLI
PAOLO
POOLE
POOLS
PROLE
SCOLD
SMOLT
STOLA
STOLE
STOLS
SZOLD
THOLE
TOOLS
TROLL
UBOLT
UPOLU
VIOLA
VIOLS
VTOLS
WHOLE
WHOLL
WOOLF
WOOLS

••O•L

ABOIL
AFOFL
AFOUL
ATOLL
BROIL
CEORL
DROLL
DROOL
GHOUL
GROWL
KNOLL
PROWL
RAOUL
REOIL
SCOWL
SEOUL
SHOAL
SKOAL
SPOIL
SPOOL
STOOL
TROLL
WHOLL
WHORL

•••OL

ALDOL
ALGOL
ARGOL
ATHOL
CAROL
COBOL
DROOL
ENROL
ERROL
EXTOL
GOGOL
HOROL
KAROL
LTCOL
LYSOL
NEROL
NICOL
PAROL
SOTOL
SPOOL
STOOL
THEOL
TOPOL
TYROL

OM•••

OMAHA
OMANI
OMARR
OMASA
OMBER
OMBRE
OMEGA
OMENS
OMERS
OMITS
OMNIA

O•M••

OLMEC
OLMOS
OOMPH
OSMAN
OSMIC

O••M•

OTOMI

O•••M

OAKUM
OCCAM
ODEUM
ODIUM
OGHAM
OLEUM
OPIUM

•OM••

BOMBE
BOMBS
COMAE
COMAS
COMBO
COMBS
COMER
COMES
COMET
COMEX
COMFY
COMIC
COMIX
COMMA
COMME
COMPO
COMPS
COMPT
COMTE
COMUS
DOMED
DOMES
GOMER
GOMEZ
HOMED
HOMEO
HOMER
HOMES
HOMEY
HOMME
LOMAN
LOMAX
MOMMA
MOMMY
MOMUS
NOMAD
NOMEN
OOMPH
POMES
POMME
POMOS
ROMAN
ROMEO
ROMER
ROMPS
SOMAS
SOMME
SOMNI
TOMEI
TOMES
TOMMY
WOMAN
WOMEN

•O•M•

BOHME
BOOMS
BOOMY
COMMA
COMME
CORMS
COSMO
DOGMA
DOLMA
DOOMS
DORMS
FOAMS
FOAMY
FORMA
FORMS
GORME
HOLMS
HOMME
HOUMA
LOAMS
LOAMY
LOOMS
MOMMA
MOMMY
NORMA
NORMS
NOTME
POEME
POEMS
POMME
ROAMS
ROOMS
ROOMY
SOMME
TOMMY
TORME
WORMS
WORMY
ZOOMS

•O••M

BOEHM
BOSOM
COLUM
FORUM
GOLEM
HOHUM
HOKUM
JORUM
MODEM
ROREM
SODOM
SOLUM
TOTEM
YOKUM

••OM•

ABOMB
ACOMA
ANOMY
AROMA
ATOMS
ATOMY
BIOME
BOOMS
BOOMY
BROME
BROMO
CHOMP
CLOMP
CUOMO
DOOMS
DROME
DUOMO
FROME
FROMM
GLOMS
GNOME
HBOMB
LOOMS
NAOMI
OTOMI
PROMO
PROMS
RHOMB
ROOMS
ROOMY
SLOMO
STOMA
STOMP
SUOMI
TROMP
WHOMP
ZOOMS

••O•M

ABOHM
BLOOM
BROOM
ENORM
FROMM
GLOAM
GLOOM
GROOM
PROAM
PROEM
STORM
VROOM

•••OM

AXIOM
BESOM
BLOOM
BOSOM
BROOM
CAROM
CDROM
CHROM
DENOM
ENTOM
EPSOM
GLOOM
GROOM
IDIOM
MRMOM
PHNOM
SODOM
STROM
VENOM
VROOM

ON•••

ONAIR
ONATE
ONCLE
ONCUE
ONDIT
ONEAL
ONEGA
ONEIL
ONEND
ONERS
ONEUP
ONICE
ONION
ONKEY
ONLAY
ONLOW
ONOFF
ONSET
ONTAP
ONTOP

O•N••

OINGO
OINKS
OMNIA
ORNIS
OUNCE
OWNED
OWNER
OWNUP

O••N•

ODONT
OLAND
OMANI
OMENS
ONEND
OPENS
OPINE
ORANG
ORANT
ORING
ORONO
OVENS
OVINE
OWENS
OWING
OZONE

O•••N

OAKEN
OATEN
OCEAN
OFTEN
OGDEN
OLDEN
OLEAN
OLEIN
OLSEN
OLSON
ONION
OPSIN
ORGAN
ORION
ORLON
ORRIN
ORSON
ORTON
OSCAN
OSLIN
OSMAN

•ON••

BONDI
BONDS
BONED
BONER
BONES
BONET
BONGO
BONGS
BONKS
BONNE
BONNY
BONUS
BONZE
BONZO
CONAN
CONCH
CONDE
CONDO
CONES
CONEY
CONGA
CONGE
CONGO
CONIC
CONKS
CONTD
CONTE
CONTI
CONTR
DONAS
DONAT
DONAU
DONDI
DONEE
DONGS
DONHO
DONNA
DONNE
DONNY
DONOR
DONUT
FONDA
FONDS
FONDU
FONTS
GONDI
GONDS
GONER
GONGS
GONNA
GONZO
HONAN
HONDA
HONDO
HONED
HONES
HONEY
HONGS
HONKS
HONOR
HONUS
IONIA
IONIC
JONAH
JONAS
JONES
LONER
LONGA
LONGI
LONGS
MONAD
MONCK
MONDE
MONDO
MONEL
MONET
MONEY
MONGO
MONKS
MONOD
MONTE
MONTH
MONTY
MONZA
NONCE
NONES
NONET
NONOS
PONCA
PONCE
PONCH
PONDS
PONES
PONTE
PONTI
PONZI
RONDO
RONEE
RONNY
SONAR
SONDE
SONES
SONGS
SONIA
SONIC
SONJA
SONNY
SONYA
TONAL
TONDI
TONDO
TONED
TONER
TONES
TONGA
TONGS
TONIC
TONIO
TONKA
TONNE
TONTO
TONUS
TONYA
TONYS
WONKS
WONKY
WONTS
ZONAL
ZONED
ZONES
ZONKS

•O•N•

BOING
BONNE
BONNY
BOONE
BOONS
BORNE
BOSNS
BOUND
BOYNE
COINS
COONS
CORNO
CORNS
CORNU
CORNY
COUNT
DOING
DONNA
DONNE
DONNY
DOONE
DOWNS
DOWNY
FOUND
FOUNT
GOING
GONNA
GOONS
GOONY
GOWNS
HORNE
HORNS
HOSNI
HOUND
JOHNS
JOINS
JOINT
KOANS
KOINE
LOANS
LOINS
LOONS
LOONY
LORNA
LORNE
MOANS
MOONS
MOONY
MORNS
MOUND
MOUNT
NOEND
NOONE
NOONS
NORNS
NOUNS
POINT
POONA
POONS
POUND
ROANS
RONNY
ROONE
ROUND
SOMNI
SONNY
SOONG
SOUND
TONNE
TOONS
TOWNE
TOWNS
WOUND
YOUNG
YOUNT

•O••N

BORON
BOURN
BOWEN
BOXIN
COHAN
COHEN
COLIN
COLON
CONAN
COPAN
COVEN
COZEN
DOGON
DORAN
DOREN
DOYEN
DOZEN
EOSIN
FOEHN
FOGIN
GOLAN
GOREN
GOTIN
GOTON
HOBAN
HOGAN
HONAN
IOWAN
KORAN
LODEN
LOGAN
LOGIN
LOGON
LOMAN
LORAN
LOREN
MORAN
MORON
NOLAN
NOMEN
NOTIN
POPIN
ROBIN
RODAN
RODIN
ROMAN
ROSEN
ROSIN
ROUEN
ROWAN
ROWEN
SOLAN
SOLON
SOREN
TOEIN
TOKEN
TOXIN
TOYON
WODEN
WOKEN
WOMAN
WOMEN
WOTAN
WOVEN

••ON•

AEONS
AGONY
ALONE
ALONG
AMONG
ASONE
ATONE
AXONS
BLOND
BOONE
BOONS
BRONC
BRONX
BUONO
CHONG
CLONE
CLONK
COONS
CRONE
CRONY
DIONE
DOONE
DRONE
EBONY
ETONS
EXONS
FIONA
FROND
FRONT
GOONS
GOONY
HMONG
ICONO
ICONS
ILONA
INONU
IRONS
IRONY
KRONA
KRONE
LEONA
LEONE
LIONS
LOONS
LOONY
LYONS
MOONS
MOONY
MUONS
NEONS
NOONE
NOONS
ODONT
ORONO
OZONE
PEONS
PEONY
PHONE
PHONO
PHONS
PHONY
PIONS
PLONK
POONA
POONS
PRONE
PRONG
RHONE
ROONE
SAONE
SCONE
SHONE
SOONG
STONE
STONY
TBOND
TBONE
THONG
TOONS
WRONG

••O•N

ACORN
ADORN
BJORN
BLOWN
BROUN
BROWN
CLOWN
CROON
CROWN
DROWN
FLOWN
FROWN
GROAN
GROIN
GROWN
KNOWN
QUOIN
SCORN
SHORN
SHOWN
SLOAN
SPOON
SWOON
SWORN
THORN

•••ON

AARON
ACTON
ADDON
AFTON
AGNON
AGRON
AKRON
ALTON
AMMON
ANCON
ANION
ANSON
ANTON
APRON
ARGON
ARION
ARSON
ASTON
ATHON
ATION
AVION
AXION
BACON
BARON
BATON
BETON
BIDON
BIGON
BISON
BORON
BYRON
CANON
CAPON
CARON
CHRON
CLEON
COLON
CREON
CROON
DAGON
DAMON
DELON
DEMON
DEVON
DIJON
DIXON
DOGON
EAMON
EATON
EGGON
ELION
ELTON
EPSON
EXXON
FANON
FARON
FEDON
FELON
FREON
FUTON
GABON
GETON
GLUON
GOTON
GYRON
HADON
HALON
HASON
HERON
HITON
HURON
HYSON
ILION
INION
IXION
JASON
LAYON
LEDON
LEMON
LETON
LEVON
LIMON
LITON
LOGON
LUZON
LYMON
MACON
MANON
MASON
MAYON
MELON
MESON
MORON
MYRON
NIKON
NINON
NIXON
NYLON
OLSON
ONION
ORION
ORLON
ORSON
ORTON
PAEON
PATON
PERON
PINON
PITON
PLEON
PUTON
PYLON
RACON
RADON
RAMON
RANON
RATON
RAYON
RECON
REDON
REWON
RUNON
SALON
SATON
SAXON
SCHON
SCION
SETON
SEWON
SIDON
SIMON
SITON
SOLON
SPOON
SPYON
SWOON
TALON
TAUON
TAXON
TENON
TETON
TIMON
TOYON
TRYON
TYSON
UNION
UPTON
WAGON
XENON
YUKON
ZEVON

OO•••

OOHED
OOMPH
OOOLA
OOTID
OOZED
OOZES

O•O••

OBOES
OBOLI
OBOLS
ODONT
ODORS
ODOUR
OLOGY
ONOFF
OOOLA
ORONO
OTOES
OTOMI
OVOID
OVOLI
OVOLO
OZONE

O••O•

OCHOA
OHBOY
OHGOD
OLEOS
OLIOS
OLMOS
OLSON
ONION
ONLOW
ONTOP
ORDOS
OREOS
ORION
ORLON
ORLOP
ORSON
ORTON
ORZOS
OUZOS
OXBOW

O•••O

OCULO
OINGO
OLIGO
ORFEO
ORONO
ORTHO
ORURO
OSSEO
OSTEO
OUTDO
OUTGO
OVOLO

•OO••

BOOBS
BOOBY
BOOED
BOOER
BOOKS
BOOLA
BOOLE
BOOMS
BOOMY
BOONE
BOONS
BOORS
BOOST
BOOTH
BOOTS
BOOTY
BOOZE
COOED
COOEE
COOER
COOKE
COOKS
COOLS
COONS
COOPS
COOPT
COORS
COOSA
COOTS
DOODY
DOOMS
DOONE
DOORS
DOOZY
FOODS
FOOLS
FOOTE
FOOTS
GOODS
GOODY
GOOEY
GOOFF
GOOFS
GOOFY
GOONS
GOONY
GOOPS
GOOPY
GOOSE
GOOSY
GOOUT
HOOCH
HOODS
HOOEY
HOOFS
HOOHA
HOOKE
HOOKS
HOOKY
HOOPS
HOOTS
KOOKS
KOOKY
LOOKS
LOOMS
LOONS
LOONY
LOOPS
LOOPY
LOOSE
LOOTS
MOOCH
MOODS
MOODY
MOOED
MOOGS
MOOLA
MOONS
MOONY
MOORE
MOORS
MOOSE
MOOTS
NOOKS
NOONE
NOONS
NOOSE
OOOLA
POOCH
POODS
POOHS
POOLE
POOLS
POONA
POONS
POOPS
ROODS
ROOFS
ROOKS
ROOKY
ROOMS
ROOMY
ROONE
ROOST
ROOTS
SOOEY
SOONG
SOOTH
SOOTS
SOOTY
TOOLS
TOONS
TOOTH
TOOTS
WOODS
WOODY
WOOED
WOOER
WOOFS
WOOLF
WOOLS
WOOZY
ZOOEY
ZOOID
ZOOMS

•O•O•

BOLOS
BORON
BOSOM
BOSOX
BOZOS
COBOL
COCOA
COHOS
COLON
COLOR
COROT
DODOS
DOGON
DOJOS
DOLOR
DONOR
FODOR
GODOT
GOFOR
GOGOL
GOGOS
GOTON
HOBOS
HOHOS
HONOR
HOROL
KOBOS
KOTOS
LOBOS
LOCOS
LOGON
LOGOS
MODOC
MOJOS
MONOD
MORON
MOROS
MOTOR
NODOZ
NOGOS
NOHOW
NONOS
POBOX
POBOY
POLOS
POMOS
POPOV
POTOK
ROBOT
ROTOR
ROTOS
SODOM
SOLON
SOLOS
SOPOR
SOTOL
TODOS
TOPOI
TOPOL
TOPOS
TOROS
TOYON
YOYOS

•O••O

BOFFO
BOITO
BONGO
BONZO
BOSCO
COMBO
COMPO
CONDO
CONGO
CORNO
COSMO
DOBRO
DOGGO
DONHO
DORSO
DOTTO
DOURO
FOLIO
FORDO
FORGO
GONZO
GORDO
GOTTO
HOMEO
HONDO
HOWSO
HOWTO
JOCKO
LOTTO
MOFFO
MOLTO
MONDO
MONGO
MORRO
MOSSO
MOTTO
NORVO
NOTSO
POLLO
PORTO
POTTO
ROCCO
RODEO
ROLEO
ROLLO
ROMEO
RONDO
ROYKO
SOCIO
SOCKO
SOHIO
SOLDO
SORGO
SOTHO

SOTTO
TOKYO
TONDO
TONIO
TONTO
TORSO
VOLVO
ZORRO

••OO•
AFOOT
ALOOF
BLOOD
BLOOM
BLOOP
BROOD
BROOK
BROOM
CROOK
CROON
DROOD
DROOL
DROOP
FLOOD
FLOOR
GLOOM
GROOM
PROOF
SCOOP
SCOOT
SHOOK
SHOOS
SHOOT
SLOOP
SMOOT
SNOOD
SNOOK
SNOOP
SNOOT
SPOOF
SPOOK
SPOOL
SPOON
SPOOR
STOOD
STOOL
STOOP
SWOON
SWOOP
TROOP
VROOM
WHOOF
WHOOP

••O•O
ABOVO
AGOGO
AMOCO
BROMO
BUONO
CUOMO
DUOMO
FRODO
ICONO
KYOTO
ORONO
OVOLO
PAOLO
PHONO
PHOTO
PROMO
PROTO
PROVO
RHODO
SLOMO
TROPO
WHOSO

•••OO
ACHOO
ARTOO
DETOO
ESPOO
IGLOO
KAZOO
MAGOO
MCCOO
METOO
TABOO
WAHOO
YAHOO
YAZOO

OP•••
OPAHS
OPALS
OPART
OPCIT
OPEDS
OPELS
OPENS
OPERA
OPHIR
OPINE
OPIUM
OPRAH
OPSIN
OPSIS
OPTED
OPTIC

O••P•
OKAPI
OOMPH

O•••P
ONEUP
ONTAP
ONTOP
ORLOP
OWNUP
OXLIP

•OP••
COPAL
COPAN
COPAY
COPED
COPES
COPRA
COPSE
COPTS
DOPES
DOPEY
HOPED
HOPER
HOPES
HOPIS
HOPPE
HOPUP
KOPEK
KOPJE
LOPAT
LOPED
LOPER
LOPES
LOPEZ
LOPPY
MOPED
MOPER
MOPES
MOPEY
MOPSY
MOPUP
NOPAL
NOPAR
POPES
POPIN
POPOV
POPPA
POPPY
POPUP
ROPED
ROPER
ROPES
ROPEY
SOPHS
SOPHY
SOPOR
SOPPY
SOPUP
TOPAZ
TOPED
TOPER
TOPES
TOPIC
TOPIS
TOPOI
TOPOL
TOPOS
TOPPS
TOPSY

•O•P•
COAPT
COMPO
COMPS
COMPT
COOPS
COOPT
CORPS
COUPE
COUPS
COYPU
DOLPH
DORPS
GOAPE
GOOPS
GOOPY
GORPS
HOOPS
HOPPE
LOOPS
LOOPY
LOPPY
LOUPE
MORPH
OOMPH
POOPS
POPPA
POPPY
ROMPS
SOAPS
SOAPY
SOPPY
SOUPS
SOUPY
TOPPS

•O••P
BOBUP
BOXUP
GOTUP
HOPUP
JOSIP
MOPUP
NOTUP
POLYP
POPUP
SOPUP
TOTUP

••OP•
ADOPT
CHOPS
CLOPS
COOPS
COOPT
CROPS
DROPS
ELOPE
FLOPS
GLOPS
GOOPS
GOOPY
GROPE
HOOPS
KNOPF
LOOPS
LOOPY
MYOPE
PLOPS
POOPS
PROPS
SCOPE
SCOPS
SHOPS
SLOPE
SLOPS
STOPE
STOPS
SWOPE
TROPE
TROPO
WHOPS

••O•P
BLOOP
CHOMP
CLOMP
CROUP
DROOP
GROUP
SCOOP
SLOOP
SNOOP
STOMP
STOOP
STOUP
SWOOP
THORP
TROMP
TROOP
WHOMP
WHOOP

•••OP
AESOP
ALSOP
BEBOP
BLOOP
DROOP
ESTOP
FSTOP
GALOP
ONTOP
ORLOP
REMOP
RETOP
SCOOP
SLOOP
SNOOP
STOOP
STROP
SWOOP
SYSOP
TROOP
WHOOP
ZZTOP

•OQ••
ROQUE
TOQUE

OR•••
ORACH
ORACY
ORALE
ORALS
ORANG
ORANT
ORATE
ORBIT
ORCAS
ORCHS
ORCUS
ORCZY
ORDER
ORDOS
OREAD
OREOS
ORFEO
ORGAN
ORIBI
ORIEL
ORING
ORION
ORIYA
ORLES
ORLON
ORLOP
ORNIS
ORONO
ORRIN
ORRIS
ORSER
ORSON
ORTHO
ORTON
ORURO
ORZOS

O•R••
OARED
OCREA
OGRES
OKRAS
OPRAH
ORRIN
ORRIS
OSRIC

O••R•
OCHRE
ODORS
OHARA
OHARE
OMARR
OMBRE
OMERS
ONERS
OPART
OPERA
ORURO
OTARU
OTARY
OUTRE
OVERS
OVERT
OWERS
OZARK

O•••R
OATER
OCCUR
OCHER
ODDER
ODOUR
OFFER
OGLER
OHAIR
OILER
OLDER
OMARR
OMBER
ONAIR
OPHIR
ORDER
ORSER
OSCAR
OSIER
OSKAR
OSLER
OTHER
OTTER
OUTER
OWNER

•OR••
AORTA
BORAH
BORAS
BORAX
BORED
BORER
BORES
BORGE
BORIC
BORIS
BORNE
BORON
CORAL
CORBY
CORDS
COREA
CORED
CORER
CORES
COREY
CORFU
CORGI
CORKS
CORKY
CORMS
CORNO
CORNS
CORNU
CORNY
COROT
CORPS
DORAL
DORAN
DOREN
DORIC
DORIS
DORMS
DORPS
DORSA
DORSI
DORSO
FORAY
FORBS
FORCE
FORDO
FORDS
FORES
FORGE
FORGO
FORKS
FORKY
FORMA
FORMS
FORTE
FORTH
FORTS
FORTY
FORUM
GORAL
GORDO
GORDY
GORED
GOREN
GORES
GORGE
GORKI
GORKY
GORME
GORPS
GORSE
HORAE
HORAL
HORAS
HORDE
HOREB
HORNE
HORNS
HOROL
HORSE
HORST
HORSY
HORUS
JOREL
JORGE
JORUM
KORAN
KORDA
KOREA
LORAN
LORAX
LORCA
LORDS
LOREN
LORES
LORIS
LORNA
LORNE
LORRE
LORRY
MORAL
MORAN
MORAY
MOREL
MORES
MOREY
MORNS
MORON
MOROS
MORPH
MORRO
MORSE
MORTS
NORAD
NORAH
NORGE
NORIA
NORMA
NORMS
NORNS
NORSE
NORTE
NORTH
NORVO
PORCH
PORED
PORES
PORGY
PORKS
PORKY
PORTE
PORTO
PORTS
ROREM
SORAS
SORBS
SOREL
SOREN
SORER
SORES
SORGO
SORRY
SORTA
SORTS
SORUS
TORAH
TORCH
TORIC
TORII
TORME
TOROS
TORRE
TORRS
TORSI
TORSO
TORTE
TORTS
TORUS
WORDS
WORDY
WORKS
WORLD
WORMS
WORMY
WORRY
WORSE
WORST
WORTH
WORTS
YORBA
ZORBA
ZORIL
ZORIS
ZORRO

•O•R•
BOARD
BOARS
BOERS
BOORS
BOURG
BOURN
COBRA
COIRS
COORS
COPRA
COURT
DOBRA
DOBRO
DOERS
DOORS
DOURO
DOWRY
FOURH
FOURS
GOERS
GOURD
HOARD
HOARS
HOARY
HOERS
HOURI
HOURS
LOIRE
LORRE
LORRY
LOWRY
MOIRA
MOIRE
MOORE
MOORS
MORRO
NOIRE
NOTRE
POURS
ROARS
SOARS
SORRY
SOURS
TORRE
TORRS
TOURS
VOTRE
WORRY
YOURE
YOURS
ZORRO

•O••R
BONER
BOOER
BORER
BOWER
BOXER
BOYAR
BOYER
CODER
COEUR
COLOR
COMER
CONTR
COOER
CORER
COVER
COWER
COYER
DOLOR
DONOR
DOSER
DOTER
DOVER
DOWER
DOZER
FODOR
FOYER
GOFAR
GOFER
GOFOR
GOMER
GONER
GOWER
HOMER
HONOR
HOPER
HOVER
JOKER
LONER
LOPER
LOSER
LOVER
LOWER
MOHUR
MOLAR
MOPER
MOTOR
MOVER
MOWER
NOPAR
NOSIR
NOTER
POKER
POLAR
POLER
POSER
POWER
ROGER
ROMER
ROPER
ROTOR
ROVER
ROWER
SOBER
SOEUR
SOFAR
SOLAR
SOLER
SONAR
SOPOR
SORER
SOWER
SOXER
TOLER
TONER
TOPER
TOTER
TOWER
VOLAR
VOTER
VOWER
WOOER
ZOHAR

••OR•
ABORT
ACORN
ADORE
ADORN
AFORE
AGORA
AHORA
ALORS
AMORE
AMORT
AMORY
APORT
BJORN
BOORS
CEORL
CHORD
CHORE
COORS
DOORS
EMORY
ENORM
EVORA
FIORD
FJORD
FLORA
GEORG
GLORY
IVORY
KNORR
LEORA
MAORI
MOORE
MOORS
ODORS
SCORE
SCORN
SHORE
SHORN
SHORT
SNORE
SNORT
SPORE
SPORK
SPORT
STORE
STORK
STORM
STORY
SWORD
SWORE
SWORN
THORN
THORP
WHORL

••O•R
AMOUR
AROAR
AVOIR
BOOER
CHOIR
COOER
FLOOR
FLOUR
HHOUR
KNORR
ODOUR
SCOUR
SHOER
SPOOR
WOOER

•••OR
ABHOR
ACTOR
ALCOR
ANDOR
ARBOR
ARDOR
ARMOR
ASTOR
BATOR
CHLOR
COLOR
CUKOR
DECOR
DOLOR
DONOR
ENDOR
ENSOR
EPHOR
ERROR
FAVOR
FETOR
FLOOR
FLUOR
FODOR
FUROR
GABOR
GATOR
GOFOR
HONOR
HUMOR
ICHOR
JUROR
LABOR
LUXOR
MAJOR
MANOR
MAYOR
MINOR
MOTOR
PRIOR
PRYOR
RAZOR
RIGOR
ROTOR
RUMOR
SAPOR
SAVOR
SENOR
SOPOR
SPOOR
TABOR
TENOR
TIMOR
TUDOR
TUTOR
VALOR
VAPOR
VIDOR
VIGOR
VISOR
ZUKOR

OS•••
OSAGE
OSAKA
OSCAN
OSCAR
OSHEA
OSIER
OSKAR
OSLER
OSLIN
OSMAN
OSMIC
OSRIC
OSSEO
OSSIA
OSSIE
OSTEO
OSTIA

O•S••
OASES
OASIS
OASTS
OLSEN
OLSON
ONSET
OPSIN
OPSIS
ORSER
ORSON
OSSEO
OSSIA
OSSIE
OUSEL
OUSTS

O••S•
OBESE
ODIST
OFUSE
OMASA

O•••S
OAKES
OASES
OASIS
OASTS
OATES
OATHS
OBEYS
OBIES
OBOES
OBOLS
OCCAS
ODETS
ODORS
OGEES
OGLES
OGRES
OINKS
OKAYS
OKIES
OKRAS
OLEOS
OLIOS
OLLAS
OLMOS
OMENS
OMERS
OMITS
ONERS
OOZES
OPAHS
OPALS
OPEDS
OPELS
OPENS
OPSIS
ORALS
ORCAS
ORCHS
ORCUS
ORDOS
OREOS
ORLES
ORNIS
ORRIS
ORZOS
OTOES
OUSTS
OUZOS
OVALS
OVENS
OVERS
OWENS
OWERS

•OS••
BOSCH
BOSCO
BOSCS
BOSKS
BOSKY
BOSNS
BOSOM
BOSOX
BOSSA
BOSSY
COSBY
COSEC
COSMO
COSTA
COSTS
DOSED
DOSER
DOSES
EOSIN
FOSSA
FOSSE
GOSEE
GOSSE
HOSEA
HOSED
HOSEL
HOSES
HOSNI
HOSTA
HOSTS
JOSEF
JOSIP
LOSER
LOSES
MOSBY
MOSES
MOSEY
MOSHE
MOSSO
MOSSY
MOSUL
NOSED
NOSES
NOSIR
POSED
POSER
POSES
POSIT
POSSE
POSTE
POSTS
ROSEN
ROSES
ROSEY
ROSIE
ROSIN
ROSSI
TOSCA

•O•S•
BOAST
BOISE
BOOST
BOSSA
BOSSY
BOUSE
COAST
COOSA
COPSE
COUSY
DOEST
DORSA
DORSI
DORSO
DOUSE
DOWSE
FOIST
FOSSA
FOSSE
GOEST
GOOSE
GOOSY
GORSE
GOSSE
HOIST
HOLST
HORSE
HORST
HORSY
HOUSE
HOWSO
JOIST
JOUST
LOESS
LOOSE
LOUSE
LOUSY
MOIST
MOOSE
MOPSY
MORSE
MOSSO
MOSSY
MOUSE
MOUSY
NOISE
NOISY
NOOSE
NORSE
NOTSO
POESY
POISE
POSSE
POTSY
ROAST
ROOST
ROSSI
ROUSE
ROUST
SOUSA
SOUSE
TOAST
TOPSY
TORSI
TORSO
WORSE
WORST

•O••S
BOARS
BOATS
BODES
BOERS
BOFFS
BOGGS
BOGUS
BOILS
BOLAS
BOLES
BOLLS
BOLOS
BOLTS
BOLUS
BOMBS
BONDS
BONES
BONGS
BONKS
BONUS
BOOBS
BOOKS
BOOMS
BOONS
BOORS
BOOTS
BORAS
BORES
BORIS
BOSCS
BOSKS
BOSNS
BOUTS
BOWES
BOWLS
BOXES
BOZOS
COALS
COATS
COCKS
CODAS
CODES
COEDS
COHOS
COIFS
COILS
COINS
COIRS
COKES
COLAS
COLDS
COLES
COLTS
COMAS
COMBS
COMES
COMPS
COMUS
CONES
CONKS
COOKS
COOLS
COONS
COOPS
COORS
COOTS
COPES
COPTS
CORDS
CORES
CORKS
CORMS
CORNS
CORPS
COSTS
COTES
COUPS
COVES
COWES
COWLS
COXES
COZES
DOCKS
DODOS
DOERS
DOFFS
DOGES
DOITS
DOJOS
DOLES
DOLLS
DOLTS
DOMES
DONAS
DONGS
DOOMS
DOORS
DOPES
DORIS
DORMS
DORPS
DOSES
DOTES
DOVES
DOWNS
DOZES
EOLUS
FOALS
FOAMS
FOCUS
FOILS
FOLDS
FOLKS
FONDS
FONTS
FOODS
FOOLS
FOOTS
FORBS
FORDS
FORES
FORKS
FORMS
FORTS
FOULS
FOURS
FOUTS
FOWLS
FOXES
GOADS
GOALS
GOATS
GOERS
GOGOS
GOLDS
GOLFS
GONDS
GONGS
GOODS
GOOFS
GOONS
GOOPS
GORES
GORPS
GOTHS
GOWNS
HOARS
HOBBS
HOBOS
HOCKS
HOCUS
HOERS
HOGGS
HOHOS
HOKES
HOLDS
HOLES
HOLMS
HOMES
HONES
HONGS
HONKS
HONUS
HOODS
HOOFS
HOOKS
HOOPS
HOOTS
HOPES
HOPIS
HORAS
HORNS
HORUS
HOSES
HOSTS

HOURS
HOWLS
HOYAS
IOTAS
JOCKS
JOEYS
JOHNS
JOINS
JOKES
JOLTS
JONAS
JONES
JOTAS
JOWLS
KOANS
KOBOS
KOLAS
KOOKS
KOTOS
LOADS
LOAFS
LOAMS
LOANS
LOBES
LOBOS
LOCHS
LOCKS
LOCOS
LOCUS
LODES
LOESS
LOFTS
LOGES
LOGOS
LOINS
LOLLS
LONGS
LOOKS
LOOMS
LOONS
LOOPS
LOOTS
LOPES
LORDS
LORES
LORIS
LOSES
LOTAS
LOTUS
LOUIS
LOUTS
LOVES
LOXES
MOANS
MOATS
MOCKS
MODES
MODUS
MOILS
MOJOS
MOLAS
MOLDS
MOLES
MOLLS
MOLTS
MOMUS
MONKS
MOODS
MOOGS
MOONS
MOORS
MOOTS
MOPES
MORES
MORNS
MOROS
MORTS
MOSES
MOTES
MOTHS
MOTTS
MOUES
MOVES
NOAHS
NOCKS
NODES
NODUS
NOELS
NOGOS
NOILS
NONES
NONOS
NOOKS
NOONS
NORMS
NORNS
NOSES
NOTES
NOUNS
NOVAS
NOYES
OOZES
POCUS
POEMS
POETS
POILS
POKES
POLES
POLIS
POLLS
POLOS
POMES
POMOS
PONDS
PONES
POODS
POOHS
POOLS
POONS
POOPS
POPES
PORES
PORKS
PORTS
POSES
POSTS
POTTS
POUFS
POURS
POUTS
POWYS
ROADS
ROAMS
ROANS
ROARS
ROBES
ROCKS
ROILS
ROLES
ROLLS
ROMPS
ROODS
ROOFS
ROOKS
ROOMS
ROOTS
ROPES
ROSES
ROTAS
ROTES
ROTLS
ROTOS
ROUES
ROUTS
ROVES
SOAKS
SOAPS
SOARS
SOCKS
SODAS
SOFAS
SOILS
SOLES
SOLOS
SOLUS
SOMAS
SONES
SONGS
SOOTS
SOPHS
SORAS
SORBS
SORES
SORTS
SORUS
SOULS
SOUPS
SOURS
SOYAS
TOADS
TODOS
TOFFS
TOGAS
TOILS
TOLLS
TOMES
TONES
TONGS
TONUS
TONYS
TOOLS
TOONS
TOOTS
TOPES
TOPIS
TOPOS
TOPPS
TOROS
TORRS
TORTS
TORUS
TOTES
TOURS
TOUTS
TOVES
TOWNS
VOIDS
VOLES
VOLTS
VOTES
WOADS
WOLDS
WONKS
WONTS
WOODS
WOOFS
WOOLS
WORDS
WORKS
WORMS
WORTS
YOGHS
YOGIS
YOKES
YOLKS
YOURS
YOWLS
YOYOS
ZONES
ZONKS
ZOOMS
ZORIS

••OS•

AROSE
BOOST
CHOSE
CLOSE
COOSA
CROSS
DROSS
EROSE
FLOSS
FROSH
FROST
GHOST
GLOSS
GOOSE
GOOSY
GROSS
GROSZ
ICOSA
ICOSI
KIOSK
LOOSE
MOOSE
NOOSE
PROSE
PROST
PROSY
ROOST
SKOSH
SLOSH
STOSS
THOSE
WHOSE
WHOSO
XHOSA

••O•S

AEONS
AHOYS
ALOES
ALORS
ANOAS
ATOMS
AVOWS
AWOLS
AXONS
BLOBS
BLOCS
BLOIS
BLOTS
BLOWS
BOOBS
BOOKS
BOOMS
BOONS
BOORS
BOOTS
BROWS
BUOYS
CHOPS
CHOWS
CLODS
CLOGS
CLOPS
CLOTS
CLOYS
COOKS
COOLS
COONS
COOPS
COORS
COOTS
CROCS
CROPS
CROSS
CROWS
DHOWS
DOOMS
DOORS
DROPS
DROSS
ENOLS
ETONS
EWOKS
EXONS
FLOES
FLOGS
FLOPS
FLOSS
FLOWS
FOODS
FOOLS
FOOTS
FROES
FROGS
FROWS
GAOLS
GLOBS
GLOMS
GLOPS
GLOSS
GLOWS
GOODS
GOOFS
GOONS
GOOPS
GROGS
GROKS
GROSS
GROTS
GROWS
HOODS
HOOFS
HOOKS
HOOPS
HOOTS
ICONS
IDOLS
IRONS
KNOBS
KNOTS
KNOWS
KOOKS
LIONS
LOOKS
LOOMS
LOONS
LOOPS
LOOTS
LYONS
MEOWS
MOODS
MOOGS
MOONS
MOORS
MOOTS
MUONS
NEONS
NOOKS
NOONS
OBOES
OBOLS
ODORS
OTOES
PEONS
PHONS
PHOTS
PIONS
PIOUS
PLODS
PLOPS
PLOTS
PLOWS
PLOYS
POODS
POOHS
POOLS
POONS
POOPS
PROAS
PRODS
PROFS
PROMS
PROPS
PROTS
PROWS
PSOAS
QUODS
RIOTS
ROODS
ROOFS
ROOKS
ROOMS
ROOTS
RYOTS
SCOPS
SCOTS
SCOWS
SHOES
SHOOS
SHOPS
SHOTS
SHOWS
SLOBS
SLOES
SLOGS
SLOPS
SLOTS
SLOWS
SMOGS
SNOBS
SNOWS
SOOTS
SPOTS
STOAS
STOLS
STOPS
STOSS
STOTS
STOWS
THOUS
TOOLS
TOONS
TOOTS
TROIS
TROTS
VIOLS
VTOLS
WHOPS
WOODS
WOOFS
WOOLS
ZOOMS

•••OS

ADIOS
AFROS
AGIOS
ALTOS
AMBOS
APSOS
ARGOS
ATHOS
ATMOS
ATNOS
AUTOS
BIGOS
BOLOS
BOZOS
CAPOS
CEROS
CHAOS
CHIOS
CLIOS
COHOS
DADOS
DAVOS
DELOS
DEMOS
DIDOS
DODOS
DOJOS
DUBOS
DUROS
ELMOS
ETHOS
EUROS
EXPOS
FADOS
FAROS
GATOS
GIROS
GOGOS
GYROS
HALOS
HELOS
HEROS
HOBOS
HOHOS
HYPOS
JATOS
KAYOS
KENOS
KILOS
KOBOS
KOTOS
KUDOS
LAGOS
LEGOS
LENOS
LIDOS
LIMOS
LOBOS
LOCOS
LOGOS
MAKOS
MANOS
MELOS
MEMOS
MILOS
MINOS
MISOS
MOJOS
MOROS
MSDOS
NAXOS
NEPOS
NINOS
NOGOS
NONOS
OLEOS
OLIOS
OLMOS
ORDOS
OREOS
ORZOS
OUZOS
PALOS
PAROS
PECOS
PEPOS
PESOS
POLOS
POMOS
RAMOS
REPOS
ROTOS
SAGOS
SAMOS
SAROS
SEGOS
SHOOS
SILOS
SOLOS
TACOS
TELOS
TODOS
TOPOS
TOROS
TRIOS
TYPOS
TYROS
UMBOS
UPDOS
VAMOS
YOYOS
YUGOS
ZEROS

OT•••

OTARU
OTARY
OTHER
OTOES
OTOMI
OTTER
OTWAY

O•T••

OATEN
OATER
OATES
OATHS
OCTAD
OCTAL
OCTET
OFTEN
ONTAP
ONTOP
OOTID
OPTED
OPTIC
ORTHO
ORTON
OSTEO
OSTIA
OTTER
OUTDO
OUTED
OUTER
OUTGO
OUTRE

O••T•

OASTS
ODETS
OMITS
ONATE
ORATE
OUSTS
OVATE
OVETA
OVETT

O•••T

OBJET
OCTET
ODIST
ODONT
ONDIT
ONSET
OPART
OPCIT
ORANT
ORBIT
OUGHT
OVERT
OVETT
OWLET

•OT••

BOTCH
BOTHA
BOTHE
COTES
COTTA
DOTAL
DOTED
DOTER
DOTES
DOTTO
DOTTY
GOTAT
GOTBY
GOTHA
GOTHS
GOTIN
GOTON
GOTTA
GOTTO
GOTUP
HOTEL
HOTLY
IOTAS
JOTAS
KOTCH
KOTOS
LOTAS
LOTTA
LOTTE
LOTTO
LOTUS
MOTEL
MOTES
MOTET
MOTHS
MOTHY
MOTIF
MOTOR
MOTTA
MOTTO
MOTTS
NOTCH
NOTED
NOTER
NOTES
NOTIN
NOTME
NOTRE
NOTSO
NOTUP
OOTID
POTOK
POTSY
POTTO
POTTS
POTTY
ROTAS
ROTES
ROTLS
ROTOR
ROTOS
SOTHO
SOTOL
SOTTO
TOTAL
TOTED
TOTEM
TOTER
TOTES
TOTIE
TOTUP
VOTED
VOTER
VOTES
VOTRE
WOTAN

•O•T•

AORTA
BOATS
BOITE
BOITO
BOLTS
BOOTH
BOOTS
BOOTY
BOUTS
COATI
COATS
COLTS
COMTE
CONTD
CONTE
CONTI
CONTR
COOTS
COPTS
COSTA
COSTS
COTTA
COUTH
DOETH
DOITS
DOLTS
DOTTO
DOTTY
FONTS
FOOTE
FOOTS
FORTE
FORTH
FORTS
FORTY
FOUTS
GOATS
GOTTA
GOTTO
GOUTY
HOITY
HOLTZ
HOOTS
HOSTA
HOSTS
HOWTO
JOLTS
JOLTY
LOATH
LOFTS
LOFTY
LOOTS
LOTTA
LOTTE
LOTTO
LOUTS
MOATS
MOLTO
MOLTS
MONTE
MONTH
MONTY
MOOTS
MORTS
MOTTA
MOTTO
MOTTS
MOUTH
NOCTI
NOLTE
NORTE
NORTH
POETE
POETS
PONTE
PONTI
PORTE
PORTO
PORTS
POSTE
POSTS
POTTO
POTTS
POTTY
POUTS
POUTY
ROOTS
ROUTE
ROUTS
SOFTY
SOLTI
SOOTH
SOOTS
SOOTY
SORTA
SORTS
SOTTO
SOUTH
TOITY
TONTO
TOOTH
TOOTS
TORTE
TORTS
TOUTE
TOUTS
VOLTA
VOLTE
VOLTS
WONTS
WORTH
WORTS
YOUTH

•O••T

BOAST
BONET
BOOST
BOULT
COACT
COAPT
COAST
COLET
COMET
COMPT
COOPT
COROT
COUNT
COURT
COVET
DOEST
DOGIT
DONAT
DONUT
DOUBT
FOIST
FOUNT
GODET
GODOT
GOEST
GOOUT
GOTAT
HOIST
HOLST
HORST
JOINT
JOIST
JOUST
LOFAT
LOPAT
MOIST
MONET
MOTET
MOULT
MOUNT
NOFAT
NOHIT
NONET
POINT
POLIT
POSIT
POULT
ROAST
ROBOT
ROGET
ROOST
ROUST
SOULT
TOAST
TOBIT
TOLET
TOWIT
WORST
YOUNT

••OT•

AZOTE
AZOTH
BIOTA
BLOTS
BOOTH
BOOTS
BOOTY
BROTH
CLOTH
CLOTS
CNOTE
COOTS
DHOTE
DHOTI
EMOTE
FOOTE
FOOTS
FROTH
GROTS
HOOTS
KNOTS
KYOTO
LOOTS
MOOTS
PHOTO
PHOTS
PLOTS
PROTO
PROTS
QUOTA
QUOTE
QUOTH
RIOTS
ROOTS
RYOTS
SCOTS
SCOTT
SHOTS
SLOTH
SLOTS
SMOTE
SOOTH
SOOTS
SOOTY
SPOTS
STOTS
THOTH
TNOTE
TOOTH
TOOTS
TROTH
TROTS
WROTE
WROTH
ZLOTY

••O•T

ABORT
ABOUT
ADOPT
ADOUT
AFOOT
ALOFT
AMORT
APORT
BLOAT
BOOST
CLOUT
COOPT
CROAT
CROFT
DROIT
FLOAT
FLOUT
FRONT
FROST
GHOST
GLOAT
GOOUT
GROAT
GROUT
KNOUT
ODONT
PROST
QUOIT
ROOST
SCOOT
SCOTT
SCOUT
SHOAT
SHOOT
SHORT
SHOUT
SMOLT
SMOOT
SNOOT
SNORT
SNOUT
SPORT
SPOUT
STOAT
STOUT
TROUT
UBOAT
UBOLT
XSOUT

•••OT

ABBOT
AFOOT
ALLOT
ARGOT
ASCOT
BEGOT
BESOT
BIGOT
CABOT
COROT
DEPOT
DICOT
DIVOT
ELIOT
EPCOT
ERGOT
FAGOT
GAVOT
GEMOT
GIGOT
GODOT
GRIOT
GUYOT
HELOT
IDIOT
IFNOT
INGOT
JABOT
MAGOT
MINOT
NILOT
PEROT
PICOT
PILOT
PINOT
PITOT
PIVOT
REPOT
ROBOT
SABOT
SCOOT
SHOOT
SMOOT
SNOOT
TAROT

OU•••

OUGHT
OUIDA
OUIJA
OUNCE
OUSEL
OUSTS
OUTDO
OUTED
OUTER
OUTGO
OUTRE
OUZEL
OUZOS

O•U••

OCULO
OFUSE
ORURO
OVULE

O••U•

OAKUM
OCCUR
ODEUM
ODIUM
ODOUR
OLEUM
ONCUE
ONEUP
OPIUM
ORCUS
OWNUP

O•••U

OTARU

•OU••

BOUGH
BOULE
BOULT
BOUND
BOURG
BOURN
BOUSE
BOUTS
COUCH
COUGH
COULD
COUNT
COUPE
COUPS
COURT
COUSY
COUTH
DOUAI
DOUAY
DOUBT
DOUGH
DOURO
DOUSE
FOULS
FOUND
FOUNT
FOURH
FOURS
FOUTS
GOUDA
GOUDY
GOUGE
GOULD
GOURD
GOUTY
HOUGH
HOUMA
HOUND
HOURI
HOURS
HOUSE
JOUAL
JOULE
JOUST
LOUGH
LOUIE
LOUIS
LOUPE
LOUSE
LOUSY
LOUTS
MOUES
MOULD
MOULT
MOUND
MOUNT
MOUSE
MOUSY
MOUTH
NOUNS
POUCH
POUFS
POULT
POUND
POURS
POUTS
POUTY
ROUEN
ROUES
ROUGE
ROUGH
ROUND
ROUSE
ROUST
ROUTE
ROUTS
SOUGH
SOULS
SOULT
SOUND
SOUPS
SOUPY
SOURS
SOUSA
SOUSE
SOUTH
TOUCH
TOUGH
TOURS
TOUTE
TOUTS
VOUCH
WOULD
WOUND
YOULL
YOUNG
YOUNT
YOURE
YOURS
YOUTH
YOUVE

•O•U•

BOBUP
BOEUF
BOGUS
BOLUS
BONUS
BOXUP
COEUR
COLUM
COMUS
DONUT
EOLUS
FOCUS
FORUM
GOOUT
GOTUP
HOCUS
HOHUM
HOKUM
HONUS
HOPUP
HORUS
JORUM
LOCUS
LOGUE
LOTUS
MODUS
MOGUL
MOHUR
MOMUS
MOPUP
MOSUL
NODUS
NOTUP
POCUS
POPUP
ROGUE
ROQUE
SOEUR
SOLUM
SOLUS
SOPUP
SORUS
SOYUZ
TONUS
TOQUE
TORUS
TOTUP
VOGUE
YOKUM

•O••U

CORFU
CORNU
COYPU
DONAU
FONDU
POILU

••OU•

ABOUT
ADOUT
AFOUL
ALOUD
AMOUR
ANOUK
BROUN
CLOUD
CLOUT
CROUP
FLOUR
FLOUT
GHOUL
GOOUT
GROUP
GROUT
HHOUR
KNOUT
ODOUR
PIOUS
PROUD
RAOUL
SCOUR
SCOUT
SEOUL
SHOUT

SIOUX SNOUT SPOUT STOUP STOUT THOUS TROUT XSOUT

••O•U
INONU UPOLU

•••OU
ANJOU BAYOU BIJOU GAROU

OV•••
OVALS OVATE OVENS OVERS OVERT OVETA OVETT OVINE OVOID OVOLI OVOLO OVULE

O••V•
OGIVE OLIVE

•OV••
BOVID COVEN COVER COVES COVET COVEY DOVER DOVES DOVEY FOVEA HOVEL HOVER HOVEY LOVED LOVER LOVES LOVEY MOVED MOVER MOVES MOVIE NOVAE NOVAK NOVAS NOVEL ROVED ROVER ROVES TOVES WOVEN

•O•V•
NORVO SOAVE SOLVE VOLVO YOUVE

•O••V
POPOV

••OV•
ABOVE ABOVO CLOVE DROVE GLOVE GROVE PROVE PROVO SHOVE STOVE TROVE

•••OV
BASOV KIROV LTGOV POPOV YAKOV

OW•••
OWENS OWERS OWING OWLET OWNED OWNER OWNUP

O•W••
OTWAY

O••W•
OZAWA

O•••W
ONLOW OXBOW

•OW••
BOWED BOWEN BOWER BOWES BOWIE BOWLS COWED COWER COWES COWLS DOWDY DOWEL DOWER DOWNS DOWNY DOWRY DOWSE FOWLS GOWDY GOWER GOWNS HOWDY HOWIE HOWLS HOWSO HOWTO IOWAN JOWLS JOWLY LOWED LOWER LOWLY LOWRY MOWED MOWER NOWAY POWAY POWER POWYS ROWAN ROWDY ROWED ROWEL ROWEN ROWER SOWED SOWER TOWED TOWEL TOWER TOWIT TOWNE TOWNS VOWED VOWEL VOWER WOWED YOWLS ZOWIE

•O•W•
LOEWE LOEWY

•O••W
NOHOW

••OW•
AVOWS BLOWN BLOWS BLOWY BROWN BROWS CHOWS CLOWN CROWD CROWN CROWS DHOWS DROWN FLOWN FLOWS FROWN FROWS GLOWS GROWL GROWN GROWS KIOWA KNOWN KNOWS MEOWS PLOWS PROWL PROWS SCOWL SCOWS SHOWN SHOWS SHOWY SLOWS SNOWS SNOWY STOWE STOWS

•••OW
AGLOW ALLOW ARROW BELOW BULOW BYNOW ELBOW ENDOW GAMOW INTOW MIAOW NOHOW ONLOW OXBOW REMOW RETOW SEROW SYDOW THROW TUROW UPBOW WIDOW YALOW

OX•••
OXBOW OXEYE OXIDE OXLIP

•OX••
BOXED BOXER BOXES BOXIN BOXUP COXAE COXAL COXED COXES COXEY FOXED FOXES HOXIE LOXES MOXIE ROXIE SOXER TOXIC TOXIN

•O••X
BORAX BOSOX CODEX COMEX COMIX LOMAX LORAX POBOX ROLEX

••OX•
DEOXY EPOXY PROXY

••O•X
BRONX CROIX SIOUX

•••OX
BOSOX LENOX PHLOX POBOX REDOX UNBOX XEROX

O••Y•
OBEYS OKAYS ORIYA OXEYE

O•••Y
ODDLY OHBOY OLOGY ONKEY ONLAY ORACY ORCZY OTARY OTWAY

•OY••
BOYAR BOYER BOYLE BOYNE COYER COYLY COYPU DOYEN DOYLE FOYER FOYLE HOYAS HOYLE JOYCE LOYAL NOYES ROYAL ROYCE ROYKO SOYAS SOYUZ TOYED TOYON YOYOS

•O•Y•
JOEYS POLYP POWYS SONYA TOKYO TONYA TONYS

•O••Y
BOBBY BOGEY BOGGY BONNY BOOBY BOOMY BOOTY BOSKY BOSSY COCKY COLBY COMFY CONEY COPAY CORBY COREY CORKY CORNY COSBY COUSY COVEY COXEY COYLY DODGY DOGGY DOILY DOLBY DOLLY DONNY DOODY DOOZY DOPEY DOTTY DOUAY DOVEY DOWDY DOWNY DOWRY FOAMY FOGEY FOGGY FOLEY FOLKY FOLLY FORAY FORKY FORTY GODEY GODLY GOLLY GOODY GOOEY GOOFY GOONY GOOPY GOOSY GORDY GORKY GOTBY GOUDY GOUTY GOWDY HOAGY HOARY HOBBY HOITY HOKEY HOLEY HOLLY HOMEY HONEY HOOEY HOOKY HORSY HOTLY HOVEY HOWDY JOLLY JOLTY JOWLY KOOKY LOAMY LOBBY LOEWY LOFTY LOLLY LOONY LOOPY LOPPY LORRY LOUSY LOVEY LOWLY LOWRY MOLDY MOLLY MOMMY MONEY MONTY MOODY MOONY MOPEY MOPSY MORAY MOREY MOSBY MOSEY MOSSY MOTHY MOUSY NOBBY NOBLY NODDY NOISY NOWAY POBOY PODGY POESY POKEY POLLY POPPY PORGY PORKY POTSY POTTY POUTY POWAY ROBBY ROCKY RODDY ROILY RONNY ROOKY ROOMY ROPEY ROSEY ROWDY SOAPY SODDY SOFTY SOGGY SONNY SOOEY SOOTY SOPHY SOPPY SORRY SOUPY TOADY TOBEY TODAY TODDY TOITY TOKAY TOMMY TOPSY WONKY WOODY WOOZY WORDY WORMY WORRY ZOOEY

••OY•
AHOYS BUOYS CLOYS FLOYD LLOYD PLOYS SLOYD

••O•Y
AGONY AMORY ANOMY ATOMY BLOWY BOOBY BOOMY BOOTY BRODY CHOKY CROLY CRONY DEOXY DOODY DOOZY EBONY EMORY EPOXY GLORY GOODY GOOEY GOOFY GOONY GOOPY GOOSY GRODY HOOEY HOOKY IRONY IVORY KOOKY LOONY LOOPY MOODY MOONY OLOGY PEONY PHONY PROSY PROXY ROOKY ROOMY SHOWY SMOKY SNOWY SOOEY SOOTY STOGY STONY STORY WOODY WOOZY ZLOTY ZOOEY

•••OY
ALLOY ANNOY DECOY ELROY ENJOY ENVOY LEROY MCCOY NIMOY OHBOY POBOY SAVOY SEPOY

OZ•••
OZARK OZAWA OZONE OZZIE

O•Z••
OOZED OOZES ORZOS OUZEL OUZOS OZZIE

O••Z•
ORCZY

•OZ••
BOZOS COZEN COZES DOZED DOZEN DOZER DOZES OOZED OOZES

•O•Z•
BONZE BONZO BOOZE DOOZY GONZO MONZA PONZI WOOZY

•O••Z
GOMEZ HOLTZ LOPEZ NODOZ SOYUZ TOPAZ

••OZ•
BOOZE CROZE DOOZY FROZE GLOZE GROZA WOOZY

••O•Z
GROSZ

•••OZ
ARROZ NODOZ

PA•••
PAAVO PABLO PABST PACAS PACED PACER PACES PACKS PACTS PADDY PADRE PADUA PAEAN PAEON PAGAN PAGED PAGER PAGES PAGET PAIGE PAILS PAINE PAINS PAINT PAIRS PALAE PALAU PALEA PALED PALEO PALER PALES PALEY PALLS PALLY PALMA PALME PALMS PALMY PALOS PALPI PALPS PALSY PAMBY PAMIR PAMPA PANAM PANAY PANDA PANDL PANED PANEL PANES PANGA PANGS PANIC PANKY PANNE PANSY PANTO PANTS PANTY PANZA PAOLI PAOLO PAPAL PAPAS PAPAW PAPER PAPPI PAPPY PAPUA PARCA PARCH PARDI PARDO PARDS PARED PAREE PAREN PARER PARES PAREU PARIS PARKA PARKS PARLE PARMA PAROL PAROS PARRY PARSE PARTE PARTI PARTS PARTY PASCH PASCO PASEO PASES PASHA PASSE PASSU PASSY PASTA PASTE PASTO PASTS PASTY PATCH PATED PATEK PATEN PATER PATES PATHE PATHO PATHS PATIO PATLY PATNA PATON PATRI PATSY PATTI PATTY PAULA PAUSE PAVED PAVER PAVES PAVIA PAVID PAVIS PAWAT PAWED PAWER PAWLS PAWNS PAYED PAYEE PAYER PAYIN PAYNE PAYTV PAYUP

P•A••
PAAVO PEABO PEACE PEACH PEAKS PEALE PEALS PEARL PEARS PEARY PEASE PEATS PEATY PEAVY PHAGE PHAGO PHARM PHASE PIANO PLACE PLAGE PLAID PLAIN PLAIT PLANB PLANE PLANI PLANK PLANO PLANS PLANT PLASH PLASM PLATA PLATE PLATH PLATO PLATS PLATT PLATY PLAYA PLAYS PLAZA POACH PRADO PRAMS PRANK PRASE PRATE PRATO PRATT PRAUS PRAWN PRAYS PSALM PSATS

P••A•
PACAS PAEAN PAGAN PALAE PALAU PANAM PANAY PAPAL PAPAS PAPAW PAWAT PECAN PEDAL PENAL PERAN PETAL PHIAL PICAS PIKAS PILAF PILAR PIMAS PIPAL PISAN PITAS PLEAD PLEAS PLEAT POHAI POLAR POWAY PRIAM PROAM PROAS PSHAW PSOAS PTRAP PULAS PUMAS PUNAS PUPAE PUPAL PUPAS PUSAN

P•••A
PADUA PALEA PALMA PAMPA PANDA PANGA PANZA PAPUA PARCA PARKA PARMA PASHA PASTA PATNA PAULA PAVIA PELLA PEMBA PENNA PENTA PENZA PEPLA PETRA PHYLA PIETA PILEA PINNA PINTA PINZA PIPPA PITTA PIURA PIZZA PLATA PLAYA PLAZA PLENA PODIA POLKA PONCA POONA POPPA PRIMA PUKKA PUNTA

•PA••
APACE APART EPACT IPANA IPASS OPAHS OPALS OPART SPAAK SPACE SPADE SPADS SPAHI SPAHN SPAIN SPAKE SPALL SPANG SPANK SPANS SPARE SPARK SPARS SPASM SPATE SPATS SPAWN SPAYS

•P•A•
APEAK APIAN APPAL EPHAH EPHAS OPRAH SPAAK SPEAK SPEAR SPLAT SPLAY SPRAG SPRAT SPRAY

•P••A
APNEA IPANA OPERA SPICA

••PA•
AMPAS APPAL ARPAD ATPAR COPAL COPAN COPAY JAPAN LAPAZ LOPAT NEPAL NIPAS NIPAT NOPAL NOPAR PAPAL PAPAS PAPAW PIPAL PUPAE PUPAL PUPAS REPAY SEPAL TAPAS TEPAL TOPAZ

••P•A
ALPHA ASPCA CAPRA COPRA CUPPA HEPTA HYPHA KAPPA LEPTA PAPUA PEPLA PIPPA POPPA SEPIA SEPTA SUPRA TYPEA ZAPPA

•••PA
CULPA CUPPA KAPPA KRUPA NAMPA PAMPA PIPPA POPPA SALPA SCAPA STUPA TAMPA YAMPA ZAPPA

P•B••
PABLO PABST POBOX POBOY

P••B•
PAMBY PEABO PEMBA PHOBE PLEBE PLEBS PROBE PUTBY

P•••B
PLANB PLUMB

•PB••
UPBOW

••P•B
TYPEB

P•C••
PACAS PACED PACER PACES PACKS PACTS PECAN PECKS PECOS PICAS PICKS PICKY PICOT PICRO PICTS PICUL POCUS PUCCI PUCKS

P••C•
PARCA PARCH PASCH PASCO PATCH PEACE PEACH PENCE PERCE PERCH PERCY PESCI PHYCO PIECE PINCE PINCH PISCI PISCO PITCH PLACE PLUCK POACH PONCA PONCE PONCH POOCH PORCH POUCH PRICE PRICK PRICY PSYCH PUCCI PUNCH

P•••C
PANIC PUNIC PYRIC

•PC••
EPCOT OPCIT

•P•C•
APACE EPACT EPICS EPOCH SPACE SPECK SPECS SPICA SPICE SPICY SPOCK

•P••C
EPISC OPTIC

••PC•
ASPCA

••P•C
ASPIC TOPIC

P•D••
PADDY PADRE PADUA PEDAL PEDRO PODGY PODIA PUDGY PUDUS

P••D•
PADDY PANDA PANDL PARDI PARDO PARDS PENDS PERDU PIEDS PLODS PONDS POODS PRADO PRIDE PRODS PRUDE

P•••D
PACED PAGED PALED PANED PARED PATED PAVED PAVID PAWED PAYED PIKED PILED PINED PIPED PLAID PLEAD PLIED POKED POLED PORED POSED POUND PRIED PROUD PSEUD PULED

•PD••
UPDOS

•P•D•
EPODE
OPEDS
SPADE
SPADS
SPODE
SPUDS

•P••D
APHID
APIED
APPTD
APTED
EPHOD
OPTED
SPEED
SPEND
SPIED
UPEND
UPPED

••P•D
AMPED
APPTD
ARPAD
BIPED
BIPOD
CAPED
COPED
CUPID
DUPED
GAPED
HOPED
HYPED
JAPED
LIPID
LOPED
MOPED
PIPED
RAPID
ROPED
SAPID
TAPED
TEPID
TOPED
TYPED
UMPED
UPPED
VAPID
WIPED

PE•••
PEABO
PEACE
PEACH
PEAKS
PEALE
PEALS
PEARL
PEARS
PEARY
PEASE
PEATS
PEATY
PEAVY
PECAN
PECKS
PECOS
PEDAL
PEDRO
PEEKS
PEELE
PEELS
PEENS
PEEPS
PEERS
PEETE
PEEVE
PEGGY
PEKES
PEKIN
PEKOE
PELEE
PELEG
PELLA
PELTS
PEMBA
PENAL
PENCE
PENDS
PENGO
PENNA
PENNE
PENNI
PENNY
PENTA
PENTE
PENZA
PEONS
PEONY
PEPIN
PEPLA
PEPOS
PEPPY
PEPSI
PEPUP
PEPYS
PERAN
PERCE
PERCH
PERCY
PERDU
PERES
PEREZ
PERIL
PERIS
PERKS
PERKY
PERLE
PERMS
PERON
PEROT
PERPS
PERRY
PERSE
PERTH
PESCI
PESKY
PESOS
PESTO
PESTS
PETAL
PETER
PETIT
PETRA
PETRI
PETRO
PETTI
PETTY
PEWEE
PEWIT

P•E••
PAEAN
PAEON
PEEKS
PEELE
PEELS
PEENS
PEEPS
PEERS
PEETE
PEEVE
PHENO
PIECE
PIEDS
PIERS
PIETA
PIETY
PLEAD
PLEAS
PLEAT
PLEBE
PLEBS
PLEIO
PLENA
PLEON
POEME
POEMS
POESY
POETE
POETS
PREEN
PREGO
PRELL
PREPS
PRESS
PREXY
PREYS
PSEUD
PTERO

P••E•
PACED
PACER
PACES
PAGED
PAGER
PAGES
PAGET
PALEA
PALED
PALEO
PALER
PALES
PALEY
PANED
PANEL
PANES
PAPER
PARED
PAREE
PAREN
PARER
PARES
PAREU
PASEO
PASES
PATED
PATEK
PATEN
PATER
PATES
PAVED
PAVER
PAVES
PAWED
PAWER
PAYED
PAYEE
PAYER
PEKES
PELEE
PELEG
PERES
PEREZ
PETER
PEWEE
PHREN
PIKED
PIKER
PIKES
PILEA
PILED
PILEI
PILES
PINED
PINES
PINEY
PIPED
PIPER
PIPES
PIXEL
PLIED
PLIES
POKED
POKER
POKES
POKEY
POLED
POLER
POLES
POMES
PONES
POPES
PORED
PORES
POSED
POSER
POSES
POWER
PREEN
PRIED
PRIER
PRIES
PROEM
PUGET
PULED
PULES
PUREE
PURER
PUREX
PUSEY
PYRES
PYREX

P•••E
PADRE
PAIGE
PAINE
PALAE
PALME
PANNE
PAREE
PARLE
PARSE
PARTE
PASSE
PASTE
PATHE
PAUSE
PAYEE
PAYNE
PEACE
PEALE
PEASE
PEELE
PEETE
PEEVE
PEKOE
PELEE
PENCE
PENNE
PENTE
PERCE
PERLE
PERSE
PEWEE
PHAGE
PHASE
PHILE
PHOBE
PHONE
PHYFE
PHYLE
PIECE
PINCE
PIQUE
PISTE
PIXIE
PLACE
PLAGE
PLANE
PLATE
PLEBE
PLUME
POEME
POETE
POISE
POMME
PONCE
PONTE
POOLE
PORTE
POSSE
POSTE
PRASE
PRATE
PRICE
PRIDE
PRIME
PRIZE
PROBE
PROLE
PRONE
PROSE
PROVE
PRUDE
PRUNE
PULSE
PUPAE
PUREE
PURGE
PURSE
PYXIE

•PE••
APEAK
APERS
APERY
EPEES
OPEDS
OPELS
OPENS
OPERA
SPEAK
SPEAR
SPECK
SPECS
SPEED
SPEKE
SPELL
SPELT
SPEND
SPENT
SPETS
SPEWS
UPEND

•P•E•
APFEL
APIED
APLEY
APNEA
APPEL
APRES
APSES
APTED
APTER
EPEES
OPTED
SPEED
SPIED
SPIEL
SPIES
SPREE
UPPED
UPPER
UPSET
YPRES

•P••E
APACE
APPLE
EPODE
OPINE
SPACE
SPADE
SPAKE
SPARE
SPATE
SPEKE
SPICE
SPIKE
SPILE
SPINE
SPIRE
SPITE
SPODE
SPOKE
SPORE
SPREE
SPRUE
SPUME

••PE•
AMPED
APPEL
ARPEL
ASPEN
BIPED
CAPED
CAPEK
CAPER
CAPES
CAPET
CEPES
COPED
COPES
CUPEL
DEPEW
DOPES
DOPEY
DUPED
DUPES
EXPEL
GAPED
GAPER
GAPES
HOPED
HOPER
HOPES
HYPED
HYPER
HYPES
IMPEI
IMPEL
JAPED
JAPES
KOPEK
LAPEL
LOPED
LOPER
LOPES
LOPEZ
MOPED
MOPER
MOPES
MOPEY
NAPES
PAPER
PIPED
PIPER
PIPES
POPES
RAPEE
REPEG
REPEL
RIPEN
RIPER
ROPED
ROPER
ROPES
ROPEY
RUPEE
SUPER
TAPED
TAPER
TAPES
TEPEE
TOPED
TOPER
TOPES
TYPEA
TYPEB
TYPED
TYPEE
TYPER
TYPES
UMPED
UNPEG
UNPEN
UPPED
UPPER
VIPER
WIPED
WIPER
WIPES
YIPES

••P•E
AMPLE
APPLE
COPSE
DUPLE
DUPRE
HOPPE
KOPJE
LAPSE
MAPLE
NAPPE
PUPAE
RAPEE
RAPHE
RUPEE
TEPEE
TYPEE

•••PE
AGAPE
CALPE
CARPE
COUPE
CRAPE
CREPE
DRAPE
DRUPE
ELOPE
ETAPE
GASPE
GOAPE
GRAPE
GRIPE
GROPE
HOPPE
LOUPE
MYOPE
NAPPE
SCAPE
SCOPE
SHAPE
SLOPE
SLYPE
SNIPE
STIPE
STOPE
SWIPE
SWOPE
TAUPE
TEMPE
TRIPE
TROPE

P•F••
PUFFS
PUFFY

P••F•
PHYFE
POUFS
PROFS
PUFFS
PUFFY

P•••F
PILAF
PROOF

•PF••
APFEL

•P•F•
SPIFF

•P••F
SPIFF
SPOOF

•••PF
KNOPF

P•G••
PAGAN
PAGED
PAGER
PAGES
PAGET
PEGGY
PIGGY
PUGET
PYGMY

P••G•
PAIGE
PANGA
PANGS
PEGGY
PENGO
PHAGE
PHAGO
PIGGY
PINGO
PINGS
PLAGE
PLUGS
PODGY
PORGY
PREGO
PRIGS
PUDGY
PUNGS
PURGE

P•••G
PELEG
PRONG

•P••G
APING
SPANG
SPRAG
SPRIG

••P•G
REPEG
UNPEG

PH•••
PHAGE
PHAGO
PHARM
PHASE
PHENO
PHIAL
PHILE
PHILO
PHLOX
PHNOM
PHOBE
PHONE
PHONO
PHONS
PHONY
PHOTO
PHOTS
PHREN
PHYCO
PHYFE
PHYLA
PHYLE
PHYLL
PHYSI
PHYTO

P•H••
POHAI
PSHAW

P••H•
PASHA
PATHE
PATHO
PATHS
PITHS
PITHY
POOHS
PUSHY

P•••H
PARCH
PASCH
PATCH
PEACH
PERCH
PERTH
PINCH
PITCH
PLASH
PLATH
PLUSH
POACH
PONCH
POOCH
PORCH
POUCH
PSYCH
PUNCH

•PH••
APHID
APHIS
EPHAH
EPHAS
EPHOD
EPHOR
OPHIR

•P•H•
OPAHS
SPAHI
SPAHN

•P••H
APISH
EPHAH
EPOCH
OPRAH

••PH•
ALPHA
AMPHI
AMPHR
HYPHA
RAPHE
SOPHS
SOPHY

••P•H
DEPTH

•••PH
ALEPH
DOLPH
GLYPH
GRAPH
HUMPH
LYMPH
MORPH
NYMPH
OOMPH
RALPH
SYLPH

PI•••
PIANO
PICAS
PICKS
PICKY
PICOT
PICRO
PICTS
PICUL
PIECE
PIEDS
PIERS
PIETA
PIETY
PIGGY
PIKAS
PIKED
PIKER
PIKES
PILAF
PILAR
PILEA
PILED
PILEI
PILES
PILLS
PILOT
PILUM
PILUS
PIMAS
PINCE
PINCH
PINED
PINES
PINEY
PINGO
PINGS
PINKS
PINKY
PINNA
PINON
PINOT
PINSK
PINTA
PINTO
PINTS
PINUP
PINZA
PIONS
PIOUS
PIPAL
PIPED
PIPER
PIPES
PIPIT
PIPPA
PIPPI
PIQUE
PISAN
PISCI
PISCO
PISMO
PISTE
PITAS
PITCH
PITHS
PITHY
PITON
PITOT
PITTA
PITTS
PIURA
PIVOT
PIXEL
PIXIE
PIZZA

P•I••
PAIGE
PAILS
PAINE
PAINS
PAINT
PAIRS
PHIAL
PHILE
PHILO
PLIED
PLIES
PLINK
PLINY
POILS
POILU
POINT
POISE
PRIAM
PRICE
PRICK
PRICY
PRIDE
PRIED
PRIER
PRIES
PRIGS
PRIMA
PRIME
PRIMO
PRIMP
PRIMS
PRINK
PRINT
PRIOR
PRISM
PRIVY
PRIZE

P••I•
PAMIR
PANIC
PARIS
PATIO
PAVIA
PAVID
PAVIS
PAYIN
PEKIN
PEPIN
PERIL
PERIS
PETIT
PEWIT
PIPIT
PIXIE
PLAID
PLAIN
PLAIT
PLEIO
PODIA
POLIS
POLIT
POPIN
POSIT
PULIS
PUNIC
PUPIL
PUPIN
PURIM
PUTIN
PYRIC
PYXIE
PYXIS

P•••I
PALPI
PAOLI
PAPPI
PARDI
PARTI
PATRI
PATTI
PENNI
PEPSI
PESCI
PETRI
PETTI
PHYSI
PILEI
PIPPI
PISCI
PLANI
POHAI
PONTI
PONZI
PUCCI
PUTTI

•PI••
APIAN
APIED
APING
APISH
EPICS
EPISC
OPINE
OPIUM
SPICA
SPICE
SPICY
SPIED
SPIEL
SPIES
SPIFF
SPIKE
SPIKY
SPILE
SPILL
SPILT
SPINE
SPINS
SPINY
SPIRE
SPIRO
SPITE
SPITS
SPITZ
SPIVS

•P•I•
APHID
APHIS
APRIL
APSIS
OPCIT
OPHIR
OPSIN
OPSIS
OPTIC
SPAIN
SPLIT
SPOIL
SPRIG
SPRIT

•P••I
SPAHI
SPYRI

••PI•
ASPIC
CUPID
HOPIS
KEPIS
LAPIN
LAPIS
LIPID
LUPIN
PEPIN
PIPIT
POPIN
PUPIL
PUPIN
RAPID
REPIN
SAPID
SAPIR
SEPIA
TAPIN
TAPIR
TEPID
TIPIN
TOPIC
TOPIS
UNPIN
VAPID
YUPIK

••P•I
AMPHI
CAPRI
CUPRI
IMPEI
LIPPI
PAPPI
PEPSI
PIPPI
TIPPI
TOPOI

•••PI
CARPI
LIPPI
OKAPI
PALPI
PAPPI
PIPPI
SIEPI
TEMPI
TIPPI

••PJ•
KOPJE

P•K••
PEKES
PEKIN
PEKOE
PIKAS
PIKED
PIKER
PIKES
POKED
POKER
POKES
POKEY
PUKKA

P••K•
PACKS
PANKY
PARKA
PARKS
PEAKS
PECKS
PEEKS
PERKS
PERKY
PESKY
PICKS
PICKY
PINKS
PINKY
POLKA
PORKS
PORKY
PUCKS
PUKKA
PUNKS
PUNKY

P•••K
PATEK
PINSK
PLANK
PLINK
PLONK
PLUCK
PLUNK
POTOK
PRANK
PRICK
PRINK

•P•K•
SPAKE
SPEKE
SPIKE
SPIKY
SPOKE

•P••K
APEAK
SPAAK
SPANK
SPARK
SPEAK
SPECK
SPOCK
SPOOK
SPORK
SPUNK

••P•K
CAPEK
KAPOK
KOPEK
YAPOK
YUPIK

PL•••
PLACE
PLAGE
PLAID
PLAIN
PLAIT
PLANB
PLANE
PLANI
PLANK
PLANO
PLANS
PLANT
PLASH
PLASM
PLATA
PLATE
PLATH
PLATO
PLATS
PLATT
PLATY
PLAYA
PLAYS
PLAZA
PLEAD
PLEAS
PLEAT
PLEBE
PLEBS
PLEIO
PLENA
PLEON
PLIED
PLIES
PLINK
PLINY
PLODS
PLONK
PLOPS
PLOTS
PLOWS
PLOYS
PLUCK
PLUGS
PLUMB
PLUME
PLUMP
PLUMS
PLUMY
PLUNK
PLUSH
PLUTO

P•L••
PALAE
PALAU
PALEA
PALED
PALEO
PALER
PALES
PALEY
PALLS
PALLY
PALMA
PALME
PALMS
PALMY
PALOS
PALPI
PALPS
PALSY
PELEE
PELEG
PELLA
PELTS
PHLOX
PILAF
PILAR
PILEA
PILED
PILEI
PILES
PILLS
PILOT
PILUM
PILUS
POLAR
POLED
POLER
POLES
POLIS
POLIT
POLKA
POLLO
POLLS
POLLY
POLOS
POLYP
PULAS
PULED
PULES
PULIS
PULLS
PULPS
PULPY
PULSE
PYLON

P••L•
PABLO
PAILS
PALLS
PALLY
PAOLI
PAOLO
PARLE
PATLY
PAULA
PAWLS
PEALE
PEALS
PEELE
PEELS
PELLA
PEPLA
PERLE
PHILE
PHILO
PHYLA
PHYLE
PHYLL
PILLS
POILS
POILU
POLLO
POLLS
POLLY
POOLE
POOLS
POULT
PRELL
PROLE
PSALM
PULLS
PURLS

P•••L
PANDL
PANEL
PAPAL
PAROL
PEARL
PEDAL

PENAL
PERIL
PETAL
PHIAL
PHYLL
PICUL
PIPAL
PIXEL
PRELL
PROWL
PUPAL
PUPIL

•PL••
APLEY
APLUS
BPLUS
CPLUS
DPLUS
SPLAT
SPLAY
SPLIT

•P•L•
APPLE
APPLY
APTLY
OPALS
OPELS
SPALL
SPELL
SPELT
SPILE
SPILL
SPILT
UPOLU

•P••L
APFEL
APPAL
APPEL
APRIL
SPALL
SPELL
SPIEL
SPILL
SPOIL
SPOOL

••PL•
AMPLE
AMPLY
APPLE
APPLY
DIPLO
DUPLE
HAPLY
IMPLY
MAPLE
PEPLA
REPLY

••P•L
APPAL
APPEL
ARPEL
COPAL
CUPEL
EXPEL
IMPEL
LAPEL
NEPAL
NOPAL
PAPAL
PIPAL
PUPAL
PUPIL
REPEL
SEPAL
TEPAL
TOPOL

P•M••
PAMBY
PAMIR
PAMPA
PEMBA
PIMAS
POMES
POMME
POMOS
PUMAS
PUMPS

P••M•
PALMA
PALME
PALMS
PALMY
PARMA
PERMS
PISMO
PLUMB
PLUME
PLUMP
PLUMS
PLUMY
POEME
POEMS
POMME
PRAMS
PRIMA
PRIME
PRIMO
PRIMP
PRIMS
PROMO
PROMS
PYGMY

P•••M
PANAM
PHARM
PHNOM
PILUM
PLASM
PRIAM
PRISM
PROAM
PROEM
PSALM
PURIM

•P•M•
SPUME
SPUMY

•P••M
EPSOM
OPIUM
SPASM

P•N••
PANAM
PANAY
PANDA
PANDL
PANED
PANEL
PANES
PANGA
PANGS
PANIC
PANKY
PANNE
PANSY
PANTO
PANTS
PANTY
PANZA
PENAL
PENCE
PENDS
PENGO
PENNA
PENNE
PENNI
PENNY
PENTA
PENTE
PENZA
PHNOM
PINCE
PINCH
PINED
PINES
PINEY
PINGO
PINGS
PINKS
PINKY
PINNA
PINON
PINOT
PINSK
PINTA
PINTO
PINTS
PINUP
PINZA
PONCA
PONCE
PONCH
PONDS
PONES
PONTE
PONTI
PONZI
PUNAS
PUNCH
PUNGS
PUNIC
PUNKS
PUNKY
PUNNY
PUNTA
PUNTS
PUNTY

P••N•
PAINE
PAINS
PAINT
PANNE
PATNA
PAWNS
PAYNE
PEENS
PENNA
PENNE
PENNI
PENNY
PEONS
PEONY
PHENO
PHONE
PHONO
PHONS
PHONY
PIANO
PINNA
PIONS
PLANB
PLANE
PLANI
PLANK
PLANO
PLANS
PLANT
PLENA
PLINK
PLINY
PLONK
PLUNK
POINT
POONA
POONS
POUND
PRANK
PRINK
PRINT
PRONE
PRONG
PRUNE
PUNNY

P•••N
PAEAN
PAEON
PAGAN
PAREN
PATEN
PATON
PAYIN
PECAN
PEKIN
PEPIN
PERAN
PERON
PHREN
PINON
PISAN
PITON
PLAIN
PLEON
POPIN
PRAWN
PREEN
PUPIN
PUSAN
PUTIN
PUTON
PYLON

•PN••
APNEA

•P•N•
APING
IPANA
OPENS
OPINE
SPANG
SPANK
SPANS
SPEND
SPENT
SPINE
SPINS
SPINY
SPUNK
UPEND

•P••N
APIAN
APRON
EPSON
OPSIN
SPAHN
SPAIN
SPAWN
SPOON
SPURN
SPYON
UPTON

••PN•
HYPNO

••P•N
ASPEN
CAPON
COPAN
JAPAN
LAPIN
LUPIN
PEPIN
POPIN
PUPIN
REPIN
RIPEN
TAPIN
TIPIN
UNPEN
UNPIN

PO•••
POACH
POBOX
POBOY
POCUS
PODGY
PODIA
POEME
POEMS
POESY
POETE
POETS
POHAI
POILS
POILU
POINT
POISE
POKED
POKER
POKES
POKEY
POLAR
POLED
POLER
POLES
POLIS
POLIT
POLKA
POLLO
POLLS
POLLY
POLOS
POLYP
POMES
POMME
POMOS
PONCA
PONCE
PONCH
PONDS
PONES
PONTE
PONTI
PONZI
POOCH
POODS
POOHS
POOLE
POOLS
POONA
POONS
POOPS
POPES
POPIN
POPOV
POPPA
POPPY
POPUP
PORCH
PORED
PORES
PORGY
PORKS
PORKY
PORTE
PORTO
PORTS
POSED
POSER
POSES
POSIT
POSSE
POSTE
POSTS
POTOK
POTSY
POTTO
POTTS
POTTY
POUCH
POUFS
POULT
POUND
POURS
POUTS
POUTY
POWAY
POWER
POWYS

P•O••
PAOLI
PAOLO
PEONS
PEONY
PHOBE
PHONE
PHONO
PHONS
PHONY
PHOTO
PHOTS
PIONS
PIOUS
PLODS
PLONK
PLOPS
PLOTS
PLOWS
PLOYS
POOCH
POODS
POOHS
POOLE
POOLS
POONA
POONS
POOPS
PROAM
PROAS
PROBE
PRODS
PROEM
PROFS
PROLE
PROMO
PROMS
PRONE
PRONG
PROOF
PROPS
PROSE
PROST
PROSY
PROTO
PROTS
PROUD
PROVE
PROVO
PROWL
PROWS
PROXY
PSOAS

P••O•
PAEON
PALOS
PAROL
PAROS
PATON
PECOS
PEKOE
PEPOS
PERON
PEROT
PESOS
PHLOX
PHNOM
PICOT
PILOT
PINON
PINOT
PITON
PITOT
PIVOT
PLEON
POBOX
POBOY
POLOS
POMOS
POPOV
POTOK
PRIOR
PROOF
PRYOR
PUTON
PYLON

P•••O
PAAVO
PABLO
PALEO
PANTO
PAOLO
PARDO
PASCO
PASEO
PASTO
PATHO
PATIO
PEABO
PEDRO
PENGO
PESTO
PETRO
PHAGO
PHENO
PHILO
PHONO
PHOTO
PHYCO
PHYTO
PIANO
PICRO
PINGO
PINTO
PISCO
PISMO
PLANO
PLATO
PLEIO
PLUTO
POLLO
PORTO
POTTO
PRADO
PRATO
PREGO
PRIMO
PROMO
PROTO
PROVO
PTERO
PUTTO

•PO••
APORT
EPOCH
EPODE
EPOXY
SPOCK
SPODE
SPOIL
SPOKE
SPOOF
SPOOK
SPOOL
SPOON
SPOOR
SPORE
SPORK
SPORT
SPOTS
SPOUT
UPOLU

•P•O•
APRON
APSOS
EPCOT
EPHOD
EPHOR
EPSOM
EPSON
SPOOF
SPOOK
SPOOL
SPOON
SPOOR
SPYON
UPBOW
UPDOS
UPTON

•P••O
SPIRO

••PO•
BIPOD
CAPON
CAPOS
DEPOT
ESPOO
EXPOS
HYPOS
KAPOK
NEPOS
PEPOS
POPOV
REPOS
REPOT
SAPOR
SEPOY
SOPOR
TOPOI
TOPOL
TOPOS
TYPOS
VAPOR
YAPOK

••P•O
CUPRO
DIPLO
ESPOO
HIPPO
HIPTO
HYPNO
HYPSO
LEPTO
LIPPO
REPRO
ZEPPO

•••PO
CAMPO
COMPO
FIRPO
HARPO
HIPPO
LIPPO
MAYPO
TEMPO
TROPO
ZEPPO

P•P••
PAPAL
PAPAS
PAPAW
PAPER
PAPPI
PAPPY
PAPUA
PEPIN
PEPLA
PEPOS
PEPPY
PEPSI
PEPUP
PEPYS
PIPAL
PIPED
PIPER
PIPES
PIPIT
PIPPA
PIPPI
POPES
POPIN
POPOV
POPPA
POPPY
POPUP
PUPAE
PUPAL
PUPAS
PUPIL
PUPIN
PUPPY

P••P•
PALPI
PALPS
PAMPA
PAPPI
PAPPY
PEEPS
PEPPY
PERPS
PIPPA
PIPPI
PLOPS
POOPS
POPPA
POPPY
PREPS
PROPS
PULPS
PULPY
PUMPS
PUPPY

P•••P
PAYUP
PEPUP
PINUP
PLUMP
POLYP
POPUP
PRIMP
PTRAP
PUTUP

•PP••
APPAL
APPEL
APPLE
APPLY
APPTD
APPTS
UPPED
UPPER

••PP•
CUPPA
DIPPY
GUPPY
HAPPY
HIPPO
HIPPY
HOPPE
KAPPA
LAPPS
LIPPI
LIPPO
LIPPY
LOPPY
NAPPE
NAPPY
NIPPY
PAPPI
PAPPY
PEPPY
PIPPA
PIPPI
POPPA
POPPY
PUPPY
REPPS
SAPPY
SOPPY
TIPPI
TIPPY
TOPPS
ZAPPA
ZAPPY
ZEPPO
ZIPPY

••P•P
HOPUP
LAPUP
MOPUP
NIPUP
PEPUP
POPUP
RIPUP
SOPUP
TIPUP
ZIPUP

•••PP
KRUPP
TRAPP

P•Q••
PIQUE

PR•••
PRADO
PRAMS
PRANK
PRASE
PRATE
PRATO
PRATT
PRAUS
PRAWN
PRAYS
PREEN
PREGO
PRELL
PREPS
PRESS
PREXY
PREYS
PRIAM
PRICE
PRICK
PRICY
PRIDE
PRIED
PRIER
PRIES
PRIGS
PRIMA
PRIME
PRIMO
PRIMP
PRIMS
PRINK
PRINT
PRIOR
PRISM
PRIVY
PRIZE
PROAM
PROAS
PROBE
PRODS
PROEM
PROFS
PROLE
PROMO
PROMS
PRONE
PRONG
PROOF
PROPS
PROSE
PROST
PROSY
PROTO
PROTS
PROUD
PROVE
PROVO
PROWL
PROWS
PROXY
PRUDE
PRUNE
PRYOR

P•R••
PARCA
PARCH
PARDI
PARDO
PARDS
PARED
PAREE
PAREN
PARER
PARES
PAREU
PARIS
PARKA
PARKS
PARLE
PARMA
PAROL
PAROS
PARRY
PARSE
PARTE
PARTI
PARTS
PARTY
PERAN
PERCE
PERCH
PERCY
PERDU
PERES
PEREZ
PERIL
PERIS
PERKS
PERKY
PERLE
PERMS
PERON
PEROT
PERPS
PERRY
PERSE
PERTH
PHREN
PORCH
PORED
PORES
PORGY
PORKS
PORKY
PORTE
PORTO
PORTS
PTRAP
PUREE
PURER
PUREX
PURGE
PURIM
PURLS
PURRS
PURSE
PURSY
PURUS
PYRES
PYREX
PYRIC

P••R•
PADRE
PAIRS
PARRY
PATRI
PEARL
PEARS
PEARY
PEDRO
PEERS
PERRY
PETRA
PETRI
PETRO
PHARM
PICRO
PIERS
PIURA
POURS
PTERO
PURRS

P•••R
PACER
PAGER
PALER
PAMIR
PAPER
PARER
PATER
PAVER
PAWER
PAYER
PETER
PIKER
PILAR
PIPER
POKER
POLAR
POLER
POSER
POWER
PRIER
PRIOR
PRYOR
PURER

•PR••
APRES
APRIL
APRON
OPRAH
SPRAG
SPRAT
SPRAY
SPREE
SPRIG
SPRIT
SPRUE
YPRES

•P•R•
APART
APERS
APERY
APORT
OPART
OPERA
SPARE
SPARK
SPARS
SPIRE
SPIRO
SPORE
SPORK
SPORT
SPURN
SPURS
SPURT
SPYRI

•P••R
APTER
EPHOR
OPHIR
SPEAR
SPOOR
UPPER

••PR•
CAPRA
CAPRI
COPRA
CUPRI
CUPRO
DUPRE
REPRO
SUPRA

••P•R
AMPHR
ATPAR
CAPER
GAPER
HOPER
HYPER
LOPER
MOPER
NOPAR
PAPER
PIPER
RIPER
ROPER
SAPIR
SAPOR
SOPOR
SUPER
SUPVR
TAPER
TAPIR
TOPER
TYPER
UPPER
VAPOR
VIPER
WIPER

PS•••
PSALM
PSATS
PSEUD
PSHAW
PSOAS
PSYCH

P•S••
PASCH
PASCO
PASEO
PASES
PASHA
PASSE
PASSU
PASSY
PASTA
PASTE
PASTO
PASTS
PASTY
PESCI
PESKY
PESOS
PESTO
PESTS
PISAN
PISCI
PISCO
PISMO
PISTE
POSED
POSER
POSES
POSIT
POSSE
POSTE
POSTS
PUSAN
PUSEY
PUSHY
PUSSY

P••S•
PABST
PALSY
PANSY
PARSE
PASSE
PASSU
PASSY
PATSY
PAUSE
PEASE
PEPSI
PERSE
PHASE
PHYSI
PINSK
PLASH
PLASM
PLUSH
POESY
POISE
POSSE
POTSY
PRASE
PRESS
PRISM
PROSE
PROST
PROSY
PULSE
PURSE
PURSY
PUSSY

P•••S
PACAS
PACES
PACKS
PACTS
PAGES
PAILS
PAINS
PAIRS
PALES
PALLS
PALMS
PALOS
PALPS
PANES
PANGS
PANTS
PAPAS
PARDS
PARES
PARIS
PARKS
PAROS
PARTS
PASES
PASTS
PATES
PATHS
PAVES
PAVIS
PAWLS
PAWNS
PEAKS
PEALS
PEARS
PEATS
PECKS
PECOS
PEEKS
PEELS
PEENS
PEEPS
PEERS
PEKES
PELTS
PENDS
PEONS
PEPOS
PEPYS
PERES
PERIS
PERKS
PERMS
PERPS
PESOS
PESTS
PHONS
PHOTS
PICAS
PICKS
PICTS
PIEDS
PIERS
PIKAS
PIKES
PILES
PILLS
PILUS
PIMAS
PINES
PINGS
PINKS
PINTS
PIONS
PIOUS
PIPES
PITAS
PITHS
PITTS
PLANS
PLATS
PLAYS
PLEAS
PLEBS
PLIES
PLODS
PLOPS
PLOTS
PLOWS
PLOYS
PLUGS
PLUMS
POCUS
POEMS
POETS
POILS
POKES
POLES
POLIS
POLLS
POLOS
POMES
POMOS
PONDS
PONES
POODS
POOHS
POOLS
POONS
POOPS
POPES
PORES
PORKS
PORTS
POSES
POSTS
POTTS
POUFS
POURS
POUTS
POWYS
PRAMS
PRAUS
PRAYS
PREPS
PRESS
PREYS
PRIES
PRIGS
PRIMS
PROAS
PRODS
PROFS

PROMS PROPS PROTS PROWS PSATS PSOAS PUCKS PUDUS PUFFS PULAS PULES PULIS PULLS PULPS PUMAS PUMPS PUNAS PUNGS PUNKS PUNTS PUPAS PURLS PURRS PURUS PUTTS PYRES PYXIS

•PS••
APSES APSIS APSOS EPSOM EPSON OPSIN OPSIS UPSET

•P•S•
APISH EPISC IPASS SPASM

•P••S
APERS APHIS APLUS APPTS APRES APSES APSIS APSOS BPLUS CPLUS DPLUS EPEES EPHAS EPICS IPASS OPAHS OPALS OPEDS OPELS OPENS OPSIS SPADS SPANS SPARS SPATS SPAYS SPECS SPETS SPEWS SPIES SPINS SPITS SPIVS SPOTS SPUDS SPURS UPDOS YPRES

••PS•
COPSE GIPSY GYPSY HYPSO LAPSE MOPSY PEPSI TIPSY TOPSY

••P•S
AMPAS APPTS CAPES CAPOS CAPTS CEPES COPES COPTS DEPTS DOPES DUPES EXPOS GAPES HOPES HOPIS HYPES HYPOS JAPES KEPIS LAPIS LAPPS LEPUS LOPES MOPES NAPES NEPOS NIPAS PAPAS PEPOS PEPYS PIPES POPES PUPAS REPOS REPPS ROPES SOPHS SUPTS TAPAS TAPES TOPES TOPIS TOPOS TOPPS TYPES TYPOS WIPES YIPES

•••PS
BEEPS BLIPS BUMPS BURPS CAMPS CARPS CHAPS CHIPS CHOPS CLAPS CLIPS CLOPS COMPS COOPS CORPS COUPS CRAPS CROPS CUSPS DAMPS DEEPS DORPS DRIPS DROPS DUMPS FLAPS FLIPS FLOPS FRAPS GAMPS GASPS GIMPS GLOPS GOOPS GORPS GRIPS GULPS HARPS HASPS HEAPS HELPS HEMPS HOOPS HUMPS JEEPS JUMPS KEEPS KELPS KNAPS LAMPS LAPPS LEAPS LIMPS LISPS LOOPS LUMPS MUMPS NEAPS PALPS PEEPS PERPS PLOPS POOPS PREPS PROPS PULPS PUMPS QTIPS QUIPS RAMPS RASPS REAPS REPPS REUPS ROMPS RSVPS RUMPS SALPS SAMPS SCOPS SCUPS SEEPS SHIPS SHOPS SIMPS SKEPS SKIPS SLAPS SLIPS SLOPS SNAPS SNIPS SOAPS SOUPS STEPS STOPS SUMPS SWAPS TAMPS TARPS TEMPS TOPPS TRAPS TRIPS VAMPS VEEPS WARPS WASPS WEEPS WHIPS WHOPS WHUPS WIMPS WISPS WRAPS YAWPS YELPS

PT•••
PTERO PTRAP

P•T••
PATCH PATED PATEK PATEN PATER PATES PATHE PATHO PATHS PATIO PATLY PATNA PATON PATRI PATSY PATTI PATTY PETAL PETER PETIT PETRA PETRI PETRO PETTI PETTY PITAS PITCH PITHS PITHY PITON PITOT PITTA PITTS POTOK POTSY POTTO POTTS POTTY PUTBY PUTIN PUTON PUTTI PUTTO PUTTS PUTTY PUTUP

P••T•
PACTS PANTO PANTS PANTY PARTE PARTI PARTS PARTY PASTA PASTE PASTO PASTS PASTY PATTI PATTY PAYTV PEATS PEATY PEETE PELTS PENTA PENTE PERTH PESTO PESTS PETTI PETTY PHOTO PHOTS PHYTO PICTS PIETA PIETY PINTA PINTO PINTS PISTE PITTA PITTS PLATA PLATE PLATH PLATO PLATS PLATT PLATY PLOTS PLUTO POETE POETS PONTE PONTI PORTE PORTO PORTS POSTE POSTS POTTO POTTS POTTY POUTS POUTY PRATE PRATO PRATT PROTO PROTS PSATS PUNTA PUNTS PUNTY PUTTI PUTTO PUTTS PUTTY

P•••T
PABST PAGET PAINT PAWAT PEROT PETIT PEWIT PICOT PILOT PINOT PIPIT PITOT PIVOT PLAIT PLANT PLATT PLEAT POINT POLIT POSIT POULT PRATT PRINT PROST PUGET

•PT••
APTED APTER APTLY OPTED OPTIC UPTON

•P•T•
APPTD APPTS SPATE SPATS SPETS SPITE SPITS SPITZ SPOTS

•P••T
APART APORT EPACT EPCOT OPART OPCIT SPELT SPENT SPILT SPLAT SPLIT SPORT SPOUT SPRAT SPRIT SPURT UPSET

••PT•
APPTD APPTS CAPTS COPTS DEPTH DEPTS EMPTY HEPTA HIPTO LEPTA LEPTO SEPTA SUPTS

••P•T
CAPET DEPOT INPUT KAPUT LOPAT NIPAT PIPIT REPOT

•••PT
ADAPT ADEPT ADOPT COAPT COMPT COOPT CREPT CRYPT EGYPT ERUPT INAPT INEPT KEMPT LEAPT SLEPT SWEPT TEMPT UNAPT WRAPT

PU•••
PUCCI PUCKS PUDGY PUDUS PUFFS PUFFY PUGET PUKKA PULAS PULED PULES PULIS PULLS PULPS PULPY PULSE PUMAS PUMPS PUNAS PUNCH PUNGS PUNIC PUNKS PUNKY PUNNY PUNTA PUNTS PUNTY PUPAE PUPAL PUPAS PUPIL PUPIN PUPPY PUREE PURER PUREX PURGE PURIM PURLS PURRS PURSE PURSY PURUS PUSAN PUSEY PUSHY PUSSY PUTBY PUTIN PUTON PUTTI PUTTO PUTTS PUTTY PUTUP

P•U••
PAULA PAUSE PIURA PLUCK PLUGS PLUMB PLUME PLUMP PLUMS PLUMY PLUNK PLUSH PLUTO POUCH POUFS POULT POUND POURS POUTS POUTY PRUDE PRUNE

P••U•
PADUA PAPUA PAYUP PEPUP PICUL PILUM PILUS PINUP PIOUS PIQUE POCUS POPUP PRAUS PROUD PSEUD PUDUS PURUS PUTUP

P•••U
PALAU PAREU PASSU PERDU POILU

•PU••
SPUDS SPUME SPUMY SPUNK SPURN SPURS SPURT

•P•U•
APLUS BPLUS CPLUS DPLUS OPIUM SPOUT SPRUE

•P••U
UPOLU

••PU•
HOPUP INPUT KAPUT LAPUP LEPUS MOPUP NIPUP PAPUA PEPUP POPUP RIPUP SOPUP TIPUP ZIPUP

•••PU
COYPU QUIPU

P•V••
PAVED PAVER PAVES PAVIA PAVID PAVIS PIVOT

P••V•
PAAVO PEAVY PEEVE PRIVY PROVE PROVO

P•••V
PAYTV POPOV

•P•V•
SPIVS

••PV•
SUPVR

••P•V
POPOV

P•W••
PAWAT PAWED PAWER PAWLS PAWNS PEWEE PEWIT POWAY POWER POWYS

P••W•
PLOWS PRAWN PROWL PROWS

P•••W
PAPAW PSHAW

•P•W•
SPAWN SPEWS

•P••W
UPBOW

••P•W
DEPEW PAPAW

P•X••
PIXEL PIXIE PYXIE PYXIS

P••X•
PREXY PROXY

P•••X
PHLOX POBOX PUREX PYREX

•P•X•
EPOXY

PY•••
PYGMY PYLON PYRES PYREX PYRIC PYXIE PYXIS

P•Y••
PAYED PAYEE PAYER PAYIN PAYNE PAYTV PAYUP PHYCO PHYFE PHYLA PHYLE PHYLL PHYSI PHYTO PRYOR PSYCH

P••Y•
PEPYS PLAYA PLAYS PLOYS POLYP POWYS PRAYS PREYS

P•••Y
PADDY PALEY PALLY PALMY PALSY PAMBY PANAY PANKY PANSY PANTY PAPPY PARRY PARTY PASSY PASTY PATLY PATSY PATTY PEARY PEATY PEAVY PEGGY PENNY PEONY PEPPY PERCY PERKY PERRY PESKY PETTY PHONY PICKY PIETY PIGGY PINEY PINKY PITHY PLATY PLINY PLUMY POBOY PODGY POESY POKEY POLLY POPPY PORGY PORKY POTSY POTTY POUTY POWAY PREXY PRICY PRIVY PROSY PROXY PUDGY PUFFY PULPY PUNKY PUNNY PUNTY PUPPY PURSY PUSEY PUSHY PUSSY PUTBY PUTTY PYGMY

•PY••
SPYON SPYRI

•P•Y•
SPAYS

•P••Y
APERY APLEY APPLY APTLY EPOXY SPICY SPIKY SPINY SPLAY SPRAY SPUMY

••PY•
PEPYS

••P•Y
AMPLY APPLY COPAY DIPPY DOPEY EMPTY GIPSY GUPPY GYPSY HAPLY HAPPY HIPPY IMPLY LIPPY LOPPY MOPEY MOPSY NAPPY NIPPY PAPPY PEPPY POPPY PUPPY REPAY REPLY ROPEY SAPPY SEPOY SOPHY SOPPY TIPPY TIPSY TOPSY ZAPPY ZIPPY

•••PY
BUMPY CAMPY DIPPY DUMPY GIMPY GOOPY GRAPY GUPPY HAPPY HARPY HIPPY HUMPY JUMPY KELPY LIPPY LOOPY LOPPY LUMPY NAPPY NIPPY PAPPY PEPPY POPPY PULPY PUPPY RASPY SAPPY SEEPY SOAPY SOPPY SOUPY TIPPY WEEPY WIMPY WISPY ZAPPY ZIPPY

P•Z••
PIZZA

P••Z•
PANZA PENZA PINZA PIZZA PLAZA PONZI PRIZE

P•••Z
PEREZ

•P••Z
SPITZ

••P•Z
LAPAZ LOPEZ TOPAZ

QA•••
QANDA QATAR

Q•A••
QUACK QUADR QUADS QUAFF QUAGS QUAID QUAIL QUAKE QUAKY QUALE QUALM QUAND QUANT QUARK QUART QUASH QUASI QUAYS

Q••A•
QATAR

Q•••A
QANDA QUOTA

•QA••
AQABA

•Q•A•
AQUAE AQUAS EQUAL SQUAB SQUAD SQUAT

•Q••A
AQABA

QB•••
QBVII

•Q•B•
AQABA

•Q••B
SQUAB SQUIB

Q••C•
QUACK QUICK

Q••D•
QANDA QUADR QUADS QUIDS QUODS

Q•••D
QUAID QUAND

•Q••D
SQUAD SQUID

Q•E••
QUEEG QUEEN QUEER QUELL QUERN QUERY QUEST QUEUE

Q••E•
QUEEG QUEEN QUEER QUIEN QUIET

Q•••E
QUAKE QUALE QUEUE QUIRE QUITE QUOTE

•Q••E
AQUAE

••Q•E
ESQUE PIQUE ROQUE TOQUE TUQUE

Q••F•
QUAFF

Q•••F
QUAFF

Q••G•
QUAGS

Q•••G
QUEEG

Q•••H
QUASH QUOTH

Q•I••
QTIPS QUICK QUIDS QUIEN QUIET QUILL QUILP QUILT QUINN QUINO QUINT QUIPS QUIPU QUIRE QUIRK QUIRT QUITE QUITO QUITS

Q••I•
QBVII QUAID QUAIL QUOIN QUOIT

Q•••I
QBVII QUASI

•Q•I•
EQUIP EQUIV IQUIT SQUIB SQUID

••Q•I
MAQUI YAQUI

•••QI
IRAQI

Q••K•
QUAKE QUAKY

Q•••K
QUACK QUARK QUICK QUIRK

Q••L•
QUALE QUALM QUELL QUILL QUILP QUILT

Q•••L
QUAIL QUELL QUILL

•Q••L
EQUAL

Q•••M
QUALM

Q•N••
QANDA QUAND QUANT QUINN QUINO QUINT

Q•••N
QUEEN QUERN QUIEN QUINN QUOIN

Q•O••
QUODS QUOIN QUOIT QUOTA QUOTE QUOTH

Q•••O
QUINO QUITO

Q••P•
QTIPS QUIPS QUIPU

Q•••P
QUILP

•Q••P
EQUIP

Q••R•
QUARK QUART QUERN QUERY QUIRE QUIRK QUIRT

Q•••R
QATAR QUADR QUEER

Q••S•
QUASH QUASI QUEST

Q•••S
QTIPS QUADS QUAGS QUAYS QUIDS QUIPS QUITS QUODS

•Q••S
AQUAS EQUUS

QT•••
QTIPS

Q•T••
QATAR

Q••T•
QUITE QUITO QUITS

Q•••T
QUANT QUART QUEST

QUIET
QUILT
QUINT
QUIRT
QUOIT

•Q••T
IQUIT
SQUAT

QU•••
QUACK
QUADR
QUADS
QUAFF
QUAGS
QUAID
QUAIL
QUAKE
QUAKY
QUALE
QUALM
QUAND
QUANT
QUARK
QUART
QUASH
QUASI
QUAYS
QUEEG
QUEEN
QUEER
QUELL
QUERN
QUERY
QUEST
QUEUE
QUICK
QUIDS
QUIEN
QUIET
QUILL
QUILP
QUILT
QUINN
QUINO
QUINT
QUIPS
QUIPU
QUIRE
QUIRK
QUIRT
QUITE
QUITO
QUITS
QUODS
QUOIN
QUOIT
QUOTA
QUOTE
QUOTH

Q••U•
QUEUE

Q•••U
QUIPU

•QU••
AQUAE
AQUAS
EQUAL
EQUIP
EQUIV
EQUUS
IQUIT
SQUAB
SQUAD
SQUAT
SQUIB
SQUID

•Q•U•
EQUUS

••QU•
ESQUE
MAQUI
PIQUE
ROQUE
TOQUE
TUQUE
YAQUI

Q•V••
QBVII

•Q••V
EQUIV

Q••Y•
QUAYS

Q•••Y
QUAKY
QUERY

RA•••
RABAT
RABBI
RABID
RABIN
RACED
RACER
RACES
RACKS
RACON
RADAR
RADII
RADIO
RADIX
RADON
RAFER
RAFFI
RAFTS
RAGAS
RAGED
RAGES
RAHAB
RAIDS
RAILS
RAINS
RAINY
RAISA
RAISE
RAITT
RAJAH
RAJAS
RAJIV
RAKED
RAKER
RAKES
RAKIS
RALLY
RALPH
RAMAN
RAMAR
RAMBO
RAMEE
RAMEN
RAMET
RAMIE
RAMIS
RAMON
RAMOS
RAMPS
RANAT
RANCH
RANDB
RANDD
RANDI
RANDR
RANDS
RANDY
RANEE
RANGE
RANGY
RANID
RANIN
RANIS
RANKE
RANKS
RANON
RANTO
RANTS
RANUP
RAOUL
RAPEE
RAPHE
RAPID
RAREE
RARER
RARES
RASED
RASES
RASHT
RASPS
RASPY
RASTA
RATCH
RATED
RATEL
RATER
RATES
RATHS
RATIO
RATON
RATSO
RATTY
RAVED
RAVEL
RAVEN
RAVER
RAVES
RAVIN
RAWER
RAWLS
RAWLY
RAYED
RAYON
RAZED
RAZES
RAZOR

R•A••
REACH
REACT
READE
READS
READY
REAIM
REAIR
REALM
REALS
REAMS
REAPS
REARM
REARS
REATA
RIALS
RIANT
RIATA
RNASE
ROACH
ROADS
ROALD
ROAMS
ROANS
ROARS
ROAST
RUANA
RUARK

R••A•
RABAT
RADAR
RAGAS
RAHAB
RAJAH
RAJAS
RAMAN
RAMAR
RANAT
REBAG
REBAR
RECAP
REDAN
REGAL
REGAN
REHAB
REHAN
RELAX
RELAY
REMAN
REMAP
RENAL
RENAN
REPAY
RERAN
RETAG
RETAP
RETAR
RETAX
REWAX
RHEAS
RIVAL
RIYAL
RODAN
ROMAN
ROTAS
ROWAN
ROYAL
RUGAE
RURAL

R•••A
RAISA
RASTA
REATA
REGIA
RENTA
RETIA
RHODA
RIATA
RIOJA
RUANA
RUMBA

•RA••
ARABS
ARABY
ARAME
BRACE
BRACT
BRADS
BRADY
BRAES
BRAGA
BRAGG
BRAGS
BRAHE
BRAID
BRAIL
BRAIN
BRAKE
BRAND
BRANS
BRANT
BRASH
BRASS
BRATS
BRAUN
BRAVA
BRAVE
BRAVO
BRAWL
BRAWN
BRAYS
BRAZE
CRABS
CRACK
CRAFT
CRAGS
CRAIG
CRAIN
CRAKE
CRAMP
CRAMS
CRANE
CRANK
CRAPE
CRAPS
CRASH
CRASS
CRATE
CRAVE
CRAWL
CRAWS
CRAZE
CRAZY
DRABS
DRACO
DRAFT
DRAGS
DRAIL
DRAIN
DRAKE
DRAMA
DRAMS
DRANG
DRANK
DRANO
DRAPE
DRATS
DRAWL
DRAWN
DRAWS
DRAYS
ERASE
ERATO
FRAIL
FRAIS
FRAME
FRANC
FRANK
FRANS
FRANZ
FRAPS
FRATS
FRAUD
FRAYS
GRABS
GRACE
GRADE
GRADS
GRADY
GRAFT
GRAIG
GRAIL
GRAIN
GRAMA
GRAMM
GRAMP
GRAMS
GRAND
GRANI
GRANT
GRAPE
GRAPH
GRAPY
GRASP
GRASS
GRATA
GRATE
GRAVE
GRAVY
GRAYS
GRAZE
IRADE
IRANI
IRAQI
IRATE
KRAAL
KRAFT
KRAIT
KRAUS
KRAUT
ORACH
ORACY
ORALE
ORALS
ORANG
ORANT
ORATE
PRADO
PRAMS
PRANK
PRASE
PRATE
PRATO
PRATT
PRAUS
PRAWN
PRAYS
TRACE
TRACK
TRACT
TRACY
TRADE
TRAIL
TRAIN
TRAIT
TRALA
TRAMP
TRAMS
TRANS
TRAPP
TRAPS
TRASH
TRAVE
TRAWL
TRAYS
URALS
WRACK
WRAPS
WRAPT
WRATH
XRAYS

•R•A•
AREAL
AREAR
AREAS
ARHAT
ARIAN
ARIAS
ARNAZ
AROAR
ARPAD
ARRAN
ARRAS
ARRAU
ARRAY
ARTAL
ARYAN
BREAD
BREAK
BREAM
BRIAN
BRIAR
BROAD
BRYAN
CREAK
CREAM
CROAK
CROAT
DREAD
DREAM
DREAR
DRLAO
DRYAD
FREAK
FRIAR
GREAT
GROAN
GROAT
KRAAL
ORCAS
OREAD
ORGAN
PRIAM
PROAM
PROAS
SRTAS
TREAD
TREAT
TRIAD
TRIAL
URBAN
URIAH
URIAL
WREAK

•R••A
ARECA
ARENA
ARICA
AROMA
ARUBA
BRAGA
BRAVA
BREDA
BROCA
CRURA
DRAMA
DRINA
ERICA
ERIKA
ERISA
FREDA
FRENA
FREYA
GRAMA
GRATA
GRETA
GROZA
IRINA
KRONA
KRUPA
ORIYA
PRIMA
TRALA

••RA•
ABRAM
ARRAN
ARRAS
ARRAU
ARRAY
AURAE
AURAL
AURAR
AURAS
BORAH
BORAS
BORAX
CARAT
CERAM
CERAT
CORAL
DERAT
DIRAC
DORAL
DORAN
DURAN
EYRAS
FARAD
FARAH
FERAL
FORAY
FURAN
GERAH
GORAL
HARAR
HERAT
HIRAM
HORAE
HORAL
HORAS
HYRAX
JURAL
JURAT
KARAN
KARAT
KERAT
KORAN
LARAM
LARAS
LIRAS
LORAN
LORAX
LURAY
MARAS
MARAT
MCRAE
MORAL
MORAN
MORAY
MURAL
MURAT
NARAS
NORAD
NORAH
OKRAS
OPRAH
PERAN
PTRAP
RERAN
RURAL
SARAH
SARAN
SCRAG
SCRAM
SCRAP
SERAC
SERAI
SORAS
SPRAG
SPRAT
SPRAY
STRAD
STRAP
STRAW
STRAY
SURAH
SURAL
SURAS
SURAT
TIRAN
TORAH
VARAS
VIRAL

••R•A
AORTA
ATRIA
BARCA
BEREA
BERRA
BURMA
BURSA
CARIA
CARLA
CARTA
CERIA
CIRCA
COREA
CURIA
DARLA
DARYA
DERMA
DORSA
DURRA
FERIA
FIRMA
FORMA
GARDA
KARLA
KARMA
KORDA
KOREA
LARVA
LORCA
LORNA
LURIA
MARIA
MARLA
MARTA
MURRA
MYRNA
NORIA
NORMA
OCREA
PARCA
PARKA
PARMA
SERRA
SERTA
SORTA
STRIA
SYRIA
TERRA
TERZA
VARIA
VARNA
VERSA
VIRGA
VIRNA
WIRRA
YERBA
YORBA
ZORBA

•••RA
ACCRA
ACURA
AFTRA
AGORA
AHORA
AKIRA
AMARA
ANTRA
ASTRA
AUDRA
BASRA
BERRA
CAPRA
CIERA
CLARA
COBRA
COPRA
CRURA
DEBRA
DOBRA
DURRA
EVORA
EXTRA
FLORA
HYDRA
INDRA
INFRA
INTRA
LAURA
LEORA
LIBRA
LYCRA
MBIRA
MEARA
MICRA
MOIRA
MUDRA
MURRA
NAIRA
OHARA
OPERA
PETRA
PIURA
SABRA
SACRA
SERRA
SIDRA
SUDRA
SUPRA
SUTRA
TATRA
TAYRA
TERRA
TETRA
THERA
TIARA
UHURA
ULTRA
UMBRA
WIRRA
ZEBRA

R•B••
RABAT
RABBI
RABID
RABIN
REBAG
REBAR
REBBE
REBEC
REBEL
REBID
REBUS
REBUT
RIBBY
ROBBY
ROBED
ROBES
ROBIN
ROBLE
ROBOT
RUBEN
RUBES
RUBIK
RUBIN
RUBLE

R••B•
RABBI
RAMBO
REBBE
RIBBY
RIGBY
ROBBY
RUGBY
RUMBA

R•••B
RAHAB
RANDB
REDUB
REHAB
RHOMB
RHUMB

•RB••
ARBER
ARBOR
ARBRE
MRBIG
ORBIT
URBAN

•R•B•
ARABS
ARABY
ARUBA
BRIBE
CRABS
CRIBS
DRABS
DRIBS
DRUBS
FROBE
GRABS
GREBE
GRUBS
KREBS
ORIBI
PROBE
TRIBE

•R••B
CRUMB

••RB•
BARBQ
BARBS
BURBS
CARBO
CARBS
CORBY
CURBS
DARBY
DERBY
FORBS
GARBO
GARBS
HERBS
HERBY
KERBS
KIRBY
SERBS
SORBS
TURBO
VERBS
YERBA
YORBA
ZORBA

••R•B
CARIB
CAROB
HOREB
SCRUB
SHRUB
THROB

•••RB
ACERB
BLURB
EXURB

R•C••
RACED
RACER
RACES
RACKS
RACON
RECAP
RECCE
RECIP
RECON
RECTI
RECTO
RECUR
RICCI
RICED
RICER
RICES
RICHE
RICKI
RICKS
RICKY
RICOH
ROCCO
ROCHE
ROCKS
ROCKY
RUCHE
RUCKS

R••C•
RANCH
RATCH
REACH
REACT
RECCE
REICH
RICCI
ROACH
ROCCO
ROYCE

R•••C
REBEC
RELIC
RUNIC

•RC••
ARCED
ARCHI
ARCHY
ORCAS
ORCHS
ORCUS
ORCZY

•R•C•
ARECA
ARICA
BRACE
BRACT
BRECK
BRICE
BRICK
BROCA
BROCK
BRUCE
BRUCH
BRYCE
CRACK
CRECY
CRICK
CROCE
CROCI
CROCK
CROCS
DRACO
ERECT
ERICA
ERICH
ERUCT
FRICK
FROCK
GRACE
GRECO
ORACH
ORACY
PRICE
PRICK
PRICY
TRACE
TRACK
TRACT
TRACY
TRICE
TRICK
TRUCE
TRUCK
URICH
WRACK
WRECK

•R••C
BRONC
CRESC
FRANC

••RC•
BARCA
BIRCH
CIRCA
CIRCE
CIRCS
CURCI
FARCE
FARCI
FORCE
LARCH
LORCA
LURCH
MARCH
MARCO
MARCY
MERCE
MERCI
MERCY
NARCO
NARCS
PARCA
PARCH
PERCE
PERCH
PERCY
PORCH
TORCH

••R•C
AGRIC
AURIC
BARIC
BORIC
DIRAC
DORIC
DUROC
LYRIC
OSRIC
PYRIC
SERAC
TORIC
UGRIC
XERIC

R•D••
RADAR
RADII
RADIO
RADIX
RADON
REDAN
REDDY
REDID
REDON
REDOX
REDUB
REDUX
REDYE
RIDER
RIDES
RIDGE
RIDGY
RIDOF
RODAN
RODDY
RODEO
RODIN
RUDDS
RUDDY
RUDER
RUDGE
RYDER

R••D•
RAIDS
RANDB
RANDD
RANDI
RANDR
RANDS
RANDY
READE
READS
READY
REDDY
REEDS
REEDY
RENDS
RHODA
RHODE
RHODO
RINDS
ROADS
RODDY
RONDO
ROODS
ROWDY
RUDDS
RUDDY

R•••D
RABID
RACED
RAGED
RAKED
RANDD
RANID
RAPID
RASED
RATED
RAVED
RAYED
RAZED
REBID
REDID
RESOD
REWED
RICED
RIGID
RILED
RIMED
RIVED
ROALD
ROBED
ROPED
ROUND
ROVED
ROWED
RULED

•RD••
ARDEN
ARDOR
ORDER
ORDOS

•R•D•
BRADS
BRADY
BREDA
BRIDE
BRODY
CREDO
CRUDE
ERODE
FREDA
FRODO
GRADE
GRADS
GRADY
GRIDS
GRODY
IRADE
IRIDO
PRADO
PRIDE
PRODS
PRUDE
TRADE

•R••D
ARCED
ARMED
AROID
ARPAD
BRAID
BRAND
BREAD
BREED
BROAD
BROOD
CREED
CRIED
CROWD
DREAD
DRIED
DROID
DROOD
DRUID
DRYAD
ERRED
FRAUD
FREED
FREUD
FRIED
FROID
FROND
GRAND
GREED
GRIND
IRKED
OREAD
PRIED
PROUD
TREAD
TREED
TREND
TRIAD
TRIED
TRUED
URGED
URSID

••RD•
BARDS
BIRDS
BIRDY
BYRDS
CARDI
CARDS
CORDS
CURDS
CURDY
FERDE
FORDO
FORDS
GARDA
GARDE
GIRDS
GORDO
GORDY
GURDY
HARDY
HERDS
HORDE
HURDY
KORDA
KURDS
LARDS
LARDY
LORDS
MARDI
NARDS
NERDS
NERDY
PARDI
PARDO
PARDS
PERDU
SARDS
SURDS
TARDE
TARDY
VERDE
VERDI
WARDS
WORDS
WORDY
YARDS

••R•D
ACRED
ACRID
AIRED
BARED
BORED
CARED
CERED
CORED
CURED
DARED
EARED
ERRED
FARAD
FARED
FIRED
GORED
HARED
HEROD
HIRED
LURED
LURID
MIRED
NORAD
OARED
PARED
PORED
SAROD
SCROD
SHRED
SIRED
STRAD
TIRED
VIRID

WIRED
WORLD

•••RD
AWARD
BAIRD
BEARD
BOARD
CHARD
CHORD
FIORD
FJORD
GOURD
GUARD
HEARD
HOARD
IZARD
LAIRD
LIARD
SHARD
SNERD
SWARD
SWORD
TBIRD
THIRD
WEIRD

RE•••
REACH
REACT
READE
READS
READY
REAIM
REAIR
REALM
REALS
REAMS
REAPS
REARM
REARS
REATA
REBAG
REBAR
REBBE
REBEC
REBEL
REBID
REBUS
REBUT
RECAP
RECCE
RECIP
RECON
RECTI
RECTO
RECUR
REDAN
REDDY
REDID
REDON
REDOX
REDUB
REDUX
REDYE
REEDS
REEDY
REEFS
REEKS
REELS
REESE
REEVE
REFER
REFIT
REFRY
REGAL
REGAN
REGIA
REGIS
REHAB
REHAN
REHEM
REICH
REIFY
REIGN
REIMS
REINK
REINS
REKEY
RELAX
RELAY
RELEE
RELET
RELIC
RELIG
RELIT
REMAN
REMAP
REMET
REMEX
REMIT
REMIX
REMOP
REMOW
REMUS
RENAL
RENAN
RENDS
RENEE
RENEW
RENIN
RENTA
RENTS
REOIL
REPAY
REPEG
REPEL
REPIN
REPLY
REPOS
REPOT
REPPS
REPRO
RERAN
RERUN
RESEE
RESET
RESEW
RESIN
RESOD
RESTS
RETAG
RETAP
RETAR
RETAX
RETIA
RETIE
RETOP
RETOW
RETRO
RETRY
REUNE
REUPS
REUSE
REVEL
REVET
REVUE
REWAX
REWED
REWIN
REWON
REXES
REYES

R•E••
REEDS
REEDY
REEFS
REEKS
REELS
REESE
REEVE
RHEAS
RHETT
RHEUM
RIELS
RUEHL

R••E•
RACED
RACER
RACES
RAFER
RAGED
RAGES
RAKED
RAKER
RAKES
RAMEE
RAMEN
RAMET
RANEE
RAPEE
RAREE
RARER
RARES
RASED
RASES
RATED
RATEL
RATER
RATES
RAVED
RAVEL
RAVEN
RAVER
RAVES
RAWER
RAYED
RAZED
RAZES
REBEC
REBEL
REFER
REHEM
REKEY
RELEE
RELET
REMET
REMEX
RENEE
RENEW
REPEG
REPEL
RESEE
RESET
RESEW
REVEL
REVET
REWED
REXES
REYES
RICED
RICER
RICES
RIDER
RIDES
RIFER
RIGEL
RIKER
RILED
RILES
RILEY
RIMED
RIMES
RIPEN
RIPER
RISEN
RISER
RISES
RITES
RIVED
RIVEN
RIVER
RIVES
RIVET
ROBED
ROBES
RODEO
ROGER
ROGET
ROLEO
ROLES
ROLEX
ROMEO
ROMER
RONEE
ROPED
ROPER
ROPES
ROPEY
ROREM
ROSEN
ROSES
ROSEY
ROTES
ROUEN
ROUES
ROVED
ROVER
ROVES
ROWED
ROWEL
ROWEN
ROWER
RUBEN
RUBES
RUDER
RULED
RULER
RULES
RUMEN
RUNES
RUPEE
RUSES
RYDER

R•••E
RAISE
RAMEE
RAMIE
RANEE
RANGE
RANKE
RAPEE
RAPHE
RAREE
READE
REBBE
RECCE
REDYE
REESE
REEVE
RELEE
RENEE
RESEE
RETIE
REUNE
REUSE
REVUE
RHINE
RHODE
RHONE
RHYME
RICHE
RIDGE
RIFLE
RILKE
RILLE
RINSE
RNASE
ROBLE
ROCHE
ROGUE
ROLFE
ROLLE
RONEE
ROONE
ROQUE
ROSIE
ROUGE
ROUSE
ROUTE
ROXIE
ROYCE
RUBLE
RUCHE
RUDGE
RUGAE
RUPEE
RUSSE

•RE••
AREAL
AREAR
AREAS
ARECA
ARENA
ARENS
ARENT
ARETE
BREAD
BREAK
BREAM
BRECK
BREDA
BREED
BREEN
BRENT
BRERS
BREST
BRETT
BREVE
BREWS
CREAK
CREAM
CRECY
CREDO
CREED
CREEK
CREEL
CREEP
CREES
CREME
CREON
CREPE
CREPT
CRESC
CRESS
CREST
CRETE
CREWS
DREAD
DREAM
DREAR
DREGS
DRESS
ERECT
FREAK
FREDA
FREED
FREER
FREES
FRENA
FREON
FRERE
FRESH
FRETS
FREUD
FREYA
GREAT
GREBE
GRECO
GREED
GREEK
GREEN
GREER
GREET
GREGG
GRETA
GRETE
GREYS
IRENE
KREBS
OREAD
OREOS
PREEN
PREGO
PRELL
PREPS
PRESS
PREXY
PREYS
TREAD
TREAT
TREED
TREEN
TREES
TREKS
TREND
TRENT
TRESS
TREVI
TREWS
TREYS
WREAK
WRECK
WRENS
WREST

•R•E•
ARBER
ARCED
ARDEN
ARIEL
ARIES
ARLEN
ARLES
ARMED
ARMEE
ARMET
ARNEL
ARPEL
ARRET
ARTEL
ARTES
BRAES
BREED
BREEN
BRIEF
BRIER
BRIES
CREED
CREEK
CREEL
CREEP
CREES
CRIED
CRIER
CRIES
CRUEL
CRUET
DRIED
DRIER
DRIES
DRYER
ERIES
ERNES
ERRED
FREED
FREER
FREES
FRIED
FRIER
FRIES
FROES
FRYER
GREED
GREEK
GREEN
GREER
GREET
GRIEF
GRIEG
GRIER
GRUEL
IRKED
IRREG
ORDER
ORFEO
ORIEL
ORLES
ORSER
PREEN
PRIED
PRIER
PRIES
PROEM
TREED
TREEN
TREES
TRIED
TRIER
TRIES
TRUED
TRUER
TRUES
TRUEX
URGED
URGER
URGES
URIEL
WRIER
WRYER

•R••E
ARAME
ARBRE
ARETE
ARGUE
ARISE
ARMEE
ARNIE
AROSE
ARTIE
BRACE
BRAHE
BRAKE
BRAVE
BRAZE
BREVE
BRIBE
BRICE
BRIDE
BRINE
BRITE
BROKE
BROME
BRUCE
BRULE
BRUME
BRUTE
BRYCE
CRAKE
CRANE
CRAPE
CRATE
CRAVE
CRAZE
CREME
CREPE
CRETE
CRIME
CROCE
CRONE
CROZE
CRUDE
CRUSE
DRAKE
DRAPE
DRIVE
DROME
DRONE
DROVE
DRUPE
DRUSE
DRUZE
ERASE
ERNIE
ERODE
EROSE
FRAME
FRERE
FROBE
FROME
FROZE
GRACE
GRADE
GRAPE
GRATE
GRAVE
GRAZE
GREBE
GRETE
GRIME
GRIPE
GROFE
GROPE
GROVE
IRADE
IRATE
IRENE
KRONE
ORALE
ORATE
PRASE
PRATE
PRICE
PRIDE
PRIME
PRIZE
PROBE
PROLE
PRONE
PROSE
PROVE
PRUDE
PRUNE
TRACE
TRADE
TRAVE
TRIBE
TRICE
TRIKE
TRINE
TRIPE
TRITE
TROPE
TROVE
TRUCE
TRYME
WRITE
WROTE

••RE•
ACRED
ACRES
ADREM
AGREE
AIRED
AIRES
APRES
ARRET
AUREI
AYRES
BARED
BARER
BARES
BEREA
BERET
BORED
BORER
BORES
CARED
CARER
CARES
CARET
CAREW
CAREY
CERED
CERES
CIRES
COREA
CORED
CORER
CORES
COREY
CURED
CURER
CURES
DARED
DARER
DARES
DEREK
DIRER
DOREN
DURER
EARED
EFREM
EGRET
ERRED
EYRES
FARED
FARER
FARES
FIRED
FIRER
FIRES
FORES
GORED
GOREN
GORES
GYRES
HARED
HAREM
HARES
HERES
HIRED
HIRER
HIRES
HOREB
INREM
IRREG
JEREZ
JOREL
KAREL
KAREN
KOREA
LARES
LOREN
LORES
LURED
LURES
LUREX
LYRES
MARES
MERES
MIRED
MIRES
MOREL
MORES
MOREY
MUREX
NARES
NAREW
OARED
OCREA
OGRES
PARED
PAREE
PAREN
PARER
PARES
PAREU
PERES
PEREZ
PHREN
PORED
PORES
PUREE
PURER
PUREX
PYRES
PYREX
RAREE
RARER
RARES
ROREM
SCREE
SCREW
SERES
SHRED
SHREW
SIRED
SIREN
SIRES
SOREL
SOREN
SORER
SORES
SPREE
STREW
SURER
TARES
THREE
THREW
TIRED
TIRES
TYRES
VIREO
WARES
WIRED
WIRER
WIRES
YPRES

••R•E
AERIE
AGREE
AURAE
BARGE
BARRE
BERLE
BERME
BERNE
BORGE
BORNE
BURKE
BURSE
BYRNE
CARLE
CARNE
CARPE
CARRE
CARTE
CARVE
CIRCE
CURIE
CURSE
CURVE
DIRGE
EARLE
EERIE
EYRIE
FARCE
FAROE
FERDE
FORCE
FORGE
FORTE
FURZE
GARDE
GORGE
GORME
GORSE
HARTE
HERNE
HERVE
HORAE
HORDE
HORNE
HORSE
JARRE
JORGE
KYRIE
LARGE
LARUE
LORNE
LORRE
LURIE
MARGE
MARIE
MARNE
MCRAE
MERCE
MERGE
MERLE
MEROE
MORSE
MURRE
NERVE
NORGE
NORSE
NORTE
NURSE
PAREE
PARLE
PARSE
PARTE
PERCE
PERLE
PERSE
PORTE
PUREE
PURGE
PURSE
RAREE
SARGE
SCREE
SERGE
SERVE
SPREE
SPRUE
SURGE
TARDE
TARGE
TERNE
TERRE
TERSE
THREE
THROE
TORME
TORRE
TORTE
VERDE
VERGE
VERNE
VERRE
VERSE
VERTE
VERVE
WORSE

•••RE
ADORE
AFIRE
AFORE
ALFRE
AMORE
ANDRE
ANTRE
ARBRE
ASTRE
AUTRE
AWARE
AZURE
BARRE
BLARE
CADRE
CARRE
CHERE
CHORE
CLARE
DEERE
DETRE
DUPRE
EAGRE
ENTRE
ENURE
FAIRE
FAURE
FIBRE
FLARE
FRERE
GENRE
GLARE
HAVRE
HEURE
INURE
ISERE
JAHRE
JARRE
LIBRE
LITRE
LIVRE
LOIRE
LORRE
LUCRE
MADRE
MAHRE
METRE
MITRE
MOIRE
MOORE
MURRE
NACRE
NIDRE
NITRE
NOIRE
NOTRE
OCHRE
OHARE
OMBRE
OUTRE
PADRE
QUIRE
SABRE
SACRE
SCARE
SCORE
SHARE
SHERE
SHIRE
SHORE
SNARE
SNORE
SPARE
SPIRE
SPORE
STARE
STERE
STORE
SUCRE
SWORE
TERRE
THERE
TORRE
TWERE
VERRE
VIVRE
VOTRE
WHERE
YOURE
ZAIRE

R•F••
RAFER
RAFFI
RAFTS
REFER
REFIT
REFRY
RIFER
RIFFI
RIFFS
RIFLE
RIFTS
RUFFS
RUFUS

R••F•
RAFFI
REEFS
REIFY
RIFFI
RIFFS
ROLFE
ROOFS
RUFFS

R•••F
RIDOF

•RF••
ORFEO

•R•F•
CRAFT
CROFT
DRAFT
DRIFT
GRAFT
GRIFT
GROFE
GRUFF
KRAFT
PROFS

•R••F
BRIEF
GRIEF
GRUFF
PROOF

••RF•
CORFU
SERFS
SURFS
SURFY
TURFS
ZARFS

••R•F
SERIF

•••RF
DWARF
SCARF
SCURF
SMURF
SWARF
WHARF

R•G••
RAGAS
RAGED
RAGES
REGAL
REGAN
REGIA
REGIS
RIGBY
RIGEL
RIGGS
RIGHT
RIGID
RIGOR
RIGUP
ROGER
ROGET
ROGUE
RUGAE
RUGBY

R••G•
RANGE
RANGY
REIGN
RIDGE
RIDGY
RIGGS
RINGO
RINGS
ROUGE
ROUGH
RUDGE
RUNGS

R•••G
REBAG
RELIG
REPEG
RETAG
RUING

•RG••
ARGIL
ARGOL
ARGON
ARGOS
ARGOT
ARGUE
ARGUS
ERGOT
ORGAN
URGED
URGER
URGES

•R•G•
BRAGA
BRAGG
BRAGS
BRIGS
CRAGS
DRAGS
DREGS
DRUGS
FRIGG
FROGS
GREGG
GRIGS
GROGS
KROGH
PREGO
PRIGS
TRIGS

•R••G
BRAGG
BRING
BRUNG
CRAIG
DRANG
FRIGG
GRAIG
GREGG
GRIEG
IRREG
MRBIG
ORANG
ORING
PRONG
WRING
WRONG
WRUNG

••RG•
BARGE
BERGH
BERGS
BORGE
BURGS
CARGO
CORGI
DIRGE
FARGO
FORGE
FORGO
GORGE
JORGE
LARGE
LARGO
MARGE
MARGO
MERGE
NORGE
PORGY
PURGE
SARGE
SARGO
SERGE
SORGO
SURGE
TARGE
VERGE
VIRGA
VIRGO

••R•G
IRREG
SCRAG
SHRUG
SPRAG
SPRIG
UNRIG
VARIG

•••RG
BOURG
GEORG

RH•••
RHEAS
RHETT
RHEUM
RHINE
RHINO
RHIZO
RHODA
RHODE
RHODO
RHOMB
RHONE
RHUMB
RHYME

R•H••
RAHAB
REHAB
REHAN
REHEM

R••H•
RAPHE
RASHT
RATHS
RICHE
RIGHT
RISHI
ROCHE
RUCHE
RUEHL
RUSHY

R•••H
RAJAH
RALPH
RANCH
RATCH
REACH
REICH
RICOH
ROACH
ROUGH

•RH••
ARHAT
ARHUS

•R•H•
ARCHI
ARCHY
ARTHR
BRAHE
BRUHN
ORCHS
ORTHO

•R••H
ARITH
BRASH
BRITH
BROTH
BRUCH
BRUSH
CRASH
CRUSH
ERICH
FRESH
FROSH
FROTH
GRAPH
IRISH
KROGH
ORACH

TRASH TRISH TROTH TRUTH URIAH URICH WRATH WROTH

••R•H

BARTH BERGH BERTH BIRCH BIRTH BORAH DARTH EARTH FARAH FIRTH FORTH FURTH GARTH GERAH GIRTH HARSH KARSH LARCH LURCH MARCH MARSH MIRTH MORPH MYRRH NORAH NORTH OPRAH PARCH PERCH PERTH PORCH SARAH SURAH TORAH TORCH WORTH

•••RH

FOURH MYRRH

RI•••

RIALS RIANT RIATA RIBBY RICCI RICED RICER RICES RICHE RICKI RICKS RICKY RICOH RIDER RIDES RIDGE RIDGY RIDOF RIELS RIFER RIFFI RIFFS RIFLE RIFTS RIGBY RIGEL RIGGS RIGHT RIGID RIGOR RIGUP RIKER RIKKI RILED RILES RILEY RILKE RILLE RILLS RIMED RIMES RINDS RINGO RINGS RINKS RINKY RINSE RINSO RIOJA RIOTS RIPEN RIPER RIPUP RISEN RISER RISES RISHI RISKS RISKY RITES RITZY RIVAL RIVED RIVEN RIVER RIVES RIVET RIYAL RIZZO

R•I••

RAIDS RAILS RAINS RAINY RAISA RAISE RAITT REICH REIFY REIGN REIMS REINK REINS RHINE RHINO RHIZO ROILS ROILY RUING RUINS

R••I•

RABID RABIN RADII RADIO RADIX RAJIV RAKIS RAMIE RAMIS RANID RANIN RANIS RAPID RATIO RAVIN REAIM REAIR REBID RECIP REDID REFIT REGIA REGIS RELIC RELIG RELIT REMIT REMIX RENIN REOIL REPIN RESIN RETIA RETIE REWIN RIGID ROBIN RODIN ROSIE ROSIN ROXIE RUBIK RUBIN RUNIC RUNIN RURIK RUTIN

R•••I

RABBI RADII RAFFI RANDI RECTI RICCI RICKI RIFFI RIKKI RISHI ROSSI

•RI••

ARIAN ARIAS ARICA ARIEL ARIES ARILS ARION ARISE ARITH ARIUM ARIUS BRIAN BRIAR BRIBE BRICE BRICK BRIDE BRIEF BRIER BRIES BRIGS BRILL BRIMS BRINE BRING BRINK BRINY BRISK BRITE BRITH BRITS BRITT CRIBS CRICK CRIED CRIER CRIES CRIME CRIMP CRISP CRISS CRIST DRIBS DRIED DRIER DRIES DRIFT DRILL DRINA DRINK DRIPS DRIVE ERICA ERICH ERIES ERIKA ERISA FRIAR FRICK FRIED FRIER FRIES FRIGG FRILL FRIML FRISK FRITO FRITS FRITZ FRIZZ GRIDS GRIEF GRIEG GRIER GRIFT GRIGS GRILL GRIME GRIMM GRIMY GRIND GRINS GRIOT GRIPE GRIPS GRIST GRITS IRIDO IRINA IRISH KRILL KRISS ORIBI ORIEL ORING ORION ORIYA PRIAM PRICE PRICK PRICY PRIDE PRIED PRIER PRIES PRIGS PRIMA PRIME PRIMO PRIMP PRIMS PRINK PRINT PRIOR PRISM PRIVY PRIZE TRIAD TRIAL TRIBE TRICE TRICK TRIED TRIER TRIES TRIGS TRIKE TRILL TRIMS TRINE TRINI TRIOS TRIPE TRIPS TRISH TRITE TRITT URIAH URIAL URICH URIEL WRIER WRING WRIST WRITE WRITS

•R•I•

ARGIL ARKIN ARNIE AROID ARRIS ARSIS ARTIE ARTIS BRAID BRAIL BRAIN BROIL BRUIN BRUIT CRAIG CRAIN CROIX DRAIL DRAIN DROID DROIT DRUID ERNIE ERVIL ERVIN ERWIN FRAIL FRAIS FROID FRUIT GRAIG GRAIL GRAIN GROIN IRVIN IRWIN KRAIT MRBIG ORBIT ORNIS ORRIN ORRIS TRAIL TRAIN TRAIT TROIS URSID

•R••I

ARCHI CROCI GRANI IRANI IRAQI ORIBI TREVI TRINI

••RI•

ABRIS ACRID AERIE AFRIT AGRIC APRIL ARRIS ATRIA ATRIP AURIC AVRIL BARIC BARIT BORIC BORIS BURIN CARIA CARIB CERIA CHRIS CURIA CURIE CURIO CYRIL DARIN DARIO DERIV DORIC DORIS EERIE EYRIE EYRIR FERIA KIRIN KYRIE LORIS LURIA LURID LURIE LYRIC MARIA MARIE MARIN MARIO MARIS MERIT NARIS NORIA ORRIN ORRIS OSRIC PARIS PERIL PERIS PURIM PYRIC RURIK SARIS SCRIM SCRIP SERIF SERIN SPRIG SPRIT STRIA STRIP SYRIA TORIC TORII TURIN UGRIC UNRIG VARIA VARIG VARIX VIRID XERIC ZORIL ZORIS

••R•I

AUREI CARDI CARPI CIRRI CORGI CURCI DORSI FARCI FARSI FERMI FERRI GARNI GORKI LEROI MARDI MARTI MERCI NURMI PARDI PARTI SERAI TARSI TERRI TORII TORSI VERDI VERMI

•••RI

ACARI ATARI CAPRI CHERI CIRRI CUPRI FERRI HENRI HOURI INARI INDRI KAURI MAORI MATRI NEGRI PATRI PETRI SHARI SPYRI TERRI

R•J••

RAJAH RAJAS RAJIV

R••J•

RIOJA

R•K••

RAKED RAKER RAKES RAKIS REKEY RIKER RIKKI

R••K•

RACKS RANKE RANKS REEKS RICKI RICKS RICKY RIKKI RILKE RINKS RINKY RISKS RISKY ROCKS ROCKY ROOKS ROOKY ROYKO RUCKS RUSKS

R•••K

REINK RUARK RUBIK RURIK

•RK••

ARKIN IRKED

•R•K•

BRAKE BROKE CRAKE DRAKE ERIKA GROKS TREKS TRIKE

•R••K

BREAK BRECK BRICK BRINK BRISK BROCK BROOK CRACK CRANK CREAK CREEK CRICK CROAK CROCK CROOK DRANK DRINK DRUNK FRANK FREAK FRICK FRISK FROCK GREEK PRANK PRICK PRINK TRACK TRICK TRUCK TRUNK WRACK WREAK WRECK

••RK•

BARKS BURKE CARKS CORKS CORKY DARKS DIRKS FORKS FORKY GORKI GORKY HARKS HERKY JERKS JERKY KIRKS LARKS LURKS MARKS MURKY NARKS PARKA PARKS PERKS PERKY PORKS PORKY TURKS TURKU WORKS

••R•K

DEREK HUROK KURSK RURIK TAROK

•••RK

CLARK CLERK OZARK QUARK QUIRK RUARK SHARK SHIRK SMIRK SNARK SPARK SPORK STARK STORK

R•L••

RALLY RALPH RELAX RELAY RELEE RELET RELIC RELIG RELIT RILED RILES RILEY RILKE RILLE RILLS ROLEO ROLES ROLEX ROLFE ROLLE ROLLO ROLLS RULED RULER RULES

R••L•

RAILS RALLY RAWLS RAWLY REALM REALS REELS REPLY RIALS RIELS RIFLE RILLE RILLS ROALD ROBLE ROILS ROILY ROLLE ROLLO ROLLS ROTLS RUBLE

R•••L

RAOUL RATEL RAVEL REBEL REGAL RENAL REOIL REPEL REVEL RIGEL RIVAL RIYAL ROWEL ROYAL RUEHL RURAL

•RL••

ARLEN ARLES DRLAO ORLES ORLON ORLOP

•R•L•

ARILS BRILL BRULE CROLY DRILL DROLL DRYLY FRILL GRILL KRILL KRULL ORALE ORALS PRELL PROLE TRALA TRILL TROLL TRULY URALS WRYLY

•R••L

AREAL ARGIL ARGOL ARIEL ARNEL ARPEL ARTAL ARTEL BRAIL BRAWL BRILL BROIL CRAWL CREEL CRUEL DRAIL DRAWL DRILL DROLL DROOL ERROL ERVIL FRAIL FRILL FRIML GRAIL GRILL GROWL GRUEL KRAAL KRILL KRULL ORIEL PRELL PROWL TRAIL TRAWL TRIAL TRILL TROLL URIAL URIEL

••RL•

BERLE BIRLS BURLS BURLY CARLA CARLE CARLO CARLY CURLS CURLY DARLA EARLE EARLS EARLY FURLS GIRLS GIRLY HERLS HURLS HURLY JARLS KARLA MARLA MARLO MARLS MARLY MERLE MERLS PARLE PERLE PURLS SURLY WORLD

••R•L

APRIL AURAL AVRIL BERYL CAROL CORAL CYRIL DARYL DORAL ENROL ERROL FERAL GORAL HERZL HORAL HOROL JOREL JURAL KAREL KAROL MERYL MORAL MOREL MURAL NEROL PAROL PERIL RURAL SOREL SURAL TYROL VIRAL ZORIL

•••RL

BGIRL CEORL CHURL GNARL KNURL PEARL SKIRL SNARL SWIRL TWIRL WHIRL WHORL

R•M••

RAMAN RAMAR RAMBO RAMEE RAMEN RAMET RAMIE RAMIS RAMON RAMOS RAMPS REMAN REMAP REMET REMEX REMIT REMIX REMOP REMOW REMUS RIMED RIMES ROMAN ROMEO ROMER ROMPS RUMBA RUMEN RUMMY RUMOR RUMPS

R••M•

REAMS REIMS RHOMB RHUMB RHYME ROAMS ROOMS ROOMY RUMMY

R•••M

REAIM REALM REARM REHEM RHEUM ROREM

•RM••

ARMED ARMEE ARMET ARMOR MRMOM

•R•M•

ARAME AROMA ARUMS BRIMS BROME BROMO BRUME CRAMP CRAMS CREME CRIME CRIMP CRUMB CRUMP DRAMA DRAMS DROME DRUMS FRAME FRIML FROME FROMM FRUMP GRAMA GRAMM GRAMP GRAMS GRIME GRIMM GRIMY GRUMP PRAMS PRIMA PRIME PRIMO PRIMP PRIMS PROMO PROMS TRAMP TRAMS TRIMS TROMP TRUMP TRYME

•R••M

ARIUM BREAM BROOM CREAM DREAM FROMM GRAMM GRIMM GROOM MRMOM PRIAM PRISM PROAM PROEM VROOM

••RM•

BARMS BARMY BERME BERMS BURMA CORMS DERMA DERMO DORMS FARMS FERMI FIRMA FIRMS FORMA FORMS GERMS GERMY GORME HARMS HERMS KARMA NORMA NORMS NURMI PARMA PERMS TERMS TORME VERMI WARMS WORMS WORMY

••R•M

ABRAM ADREM AURUM CAROM CDROM CERAM CHROM DURUM EFREM FORUM HAREM HARUM HIRAM INREM JORUM LARAM PURIM ROREM SCRAM SCRIM SCRUM SERUM STROM STRUM THRUM

•••RM

ALARM CHARM ENORM PHARM REARM STORM STURM SWARM THERM UNARM

RN•••

RNASE

R•N••

RANAT RANCH RANDB RANDD RANDI RANDR RANDS RANDY RANEE RANGE RANGY RANID RANIN RANIS RANKE RANKS RANON RANTO RANTS RANUP RENAL RENAN RENDS RENEE RENEW RENIN RENTA RENTS RINDS RINGO RINGS RINKS RINKY RINSE RINSO RONDO RONEE RONNY RUNES RUNGS RUNIC RUNIN RUNNY RUNON RUNTO RUNTS RUNTY RUNUP

R••N•

RAINS RAINY REINK REINS REUNE RHINE RHINO RHONE RIANT ROANS RONNY ROONE ROUND RUANA RUING RUINS RUNNY

R•••N

RABIN RACON RADON RAMAN RAMEN RAMON RANIN RANON RATON RAVEN RAVIN RAYON RECON REDAN REDON REGAN REHAN REIGN REMAN RENAN RENIN REPIN RERAN RERUN RESIN REWIN REWON RIPEN RISEN RIVEN ROBIN RODAN RODIN ROMAN ROSEN ROSIN ROUEN ROWAN ROWEN RUBEN RUBIN RUMEN RUNIN RUNON RUTIN

•RN••

ARNAZ ARNEL ARNIE ERNES ERNIE ERNST ORNIS

•R•N•

ARENA ARENS ARENT BRAND BRANS BRANT BRENT BRINE BRING BRINK

BRINY
BRONC
BRONX
BRUNG
BRUNO
BRUNT
CRANE
CRANK
CRONE
CRONY
DRANG
DRANK
DRANO
DRINA
DRINK
DRONE
DRUNK
FRANC
FRANK
FRANS
FRANZ
FRENA
FROND
FRONT
GRAND
GRANI
GRANT
GRIND
GRINS
GRUNT
IRANI
IRENE
IRINA
IRONS
IRONY
KRONA
KRONE
ORANG
ORANT
ORING
ORONO
PRANK
PRINK
PRINT
PRONE
PRONG
PRUNE
TRANS
TREND
TRENT
TRINE
TRINI
TRUNK
WRENS
WRING
WRONG
WRUNG

•R••N

ARDEN
ARGON
ARIAN
ARION
ARKIN
ARLEN
ARRAN
ARSON
ARYAN
BRAIN
BRAUN
BRAWN
BREEN
BRIAN
BROUN
BROWN
BRUHN
BRUIN
BRYAN
CRAIN
CREON
CROON
CROWN
DRAIN
DRAWN
DROWN
ERVIN
ERWIN
FREON
FROWN
GRAIN
GREEN
GROAN
GROIN
GROWN
IRVIN
IRWIN
ORGAN
ORION
ORLON
ORRIN
ORSON
ORTON
PRAWN
PREEN
TRAIN
TREEN
TRYON
URBAN

••RN•

BARNS
BERNE
BORNE
BURNS
BURNT
BYRNE
CARNE
CARNY
CORNO
CORNS
CORNU
CORNY
DARNS
EARNS
FERNS
FERNY
FIRNS
GARNI
GIRNS
HERNE
HORNE
HORNS
KERNS
LORNA
LORNE
MARNE
MORNS
MYRNA
NORNS
TARNS
TERNE
TERNS
TURNS
VARNA
VERNE
VIRNA
WARNS
YARNS

••R•N

AARON
AGRON
AKRON
APRON
ARRAN
BARON
BORON
BURIN
BYRON
CARON
CHRON
DARIN
DORAN
DOREN
DURAN
FARON
FURAN
GOREN
GYRON
HERON
HURON
KARAN
KAREN
KIRIN
KORAN
LORAN
LOREN
MARIN
MORAN
MORON
MYRON
ORRIN
PAREN
PERAN
PERON
PHREN
RERAN
RERUN
SARAN
SERIN
SIREN
SOREN
TIRAN
TURIN

•••RN

ACORN
ADORN
BAIRN
BJORN
BOURN
CAIRN
CHURN
HEARN
LEARN
NAIRN
QUERN
SCORN
SHORN
SPURN
STERN
SWORN
THORN
UTURN
YEARN

RO•••

ROACH
ROADS
ROALD
ROAMS
ROANS
ROARS
ROAST
ROBBY
ROBED
ROBES
ROBIN
ROBLE
ROBOT
ROCCO
ROCHE
ROCKS
ROCKY
RODAN
RODDY
RODEO
RODIN
ROGER
ROGET
ROGUE
ROILS
ROILY
ROLEO
ROLES
ROLEX
ROLFE
ROLLE
ROLLO
ROLLS
ROMAN
ROMEO
ROMER
ROMPS
RONDO
RONEE
RONNY
ROODS
ROOFS
ROOKS
ROOKY
ROOMS
ROOMY
ROONE
ROOST
ROOTS
ROPED
ROPER
ROPES
ROPEY
ROQUE
ROREM
ROSEN
ROSES
ROSEY
ROSIE
ROSIN
ROSSI
ROTAS
ROTES
ROTLS
ROTOR
ROTOS
ROUEN
ROUES
ROUGE
ROUGH
ROUND
ROUSE
ROUST
ROUTE
ROUTS
ROVED
ROVER
ROVES
ROWAN
ROWDY
ROWED
ROWEL
ROWEN
ROWER
ROXIE
ROYAL
ROYCE
ROYKO

R•O••

RAOUL
REOIL
RHODA
RHODE
RHODO
RHOMB
RHONE
RIOJA
RIOTS
ROODS
ROOFS
ROOKS
ROOKY
ROOMS
ROOMY
ROONE
ROOST
ROOTS
RYOTS

R••O•

RACON
RADON
RAMON
RAMOS
RANON
RATON
RAYON
RAZOR
RECON
REDON
REDOX
REMOP
REMOW
REPOS
REPOT
RESOD
RETOP
RETOW
REWON
RICOH
RIDOF
RIGOR
ROBOT
ROTOR
ROTOS
RUMOR
RUNON

R•••O

RADIO
RAMBO
RANTO
RATIO
RATSO
RECTO
REPRO
RETRO
RHINO
RHIZO
RHODO
RINGO
RINSO
RIZZO
ROCCO
RODEO
ROLEO
ROLLO
ROMEO
RONDO
ROYKO
RUNTO
RUSSO

•RO••

AROAR
AROID
AROMA
AROSE
BROAD
BROCA
BROCK
BRODY
BROIL
BROKE
BROME
BROMO
BRONC
BRONX
BROOD
BROOK
BROOM
BROTH
BROUN
BROWN
BROWS
CROAK
CROAT
CROCE
CROCI
CROCK
CROCS
CROFT
CROIX
CROLY
CRONE
CRONY
CROOK
CROON
CROPS
CROSS
CROUP
CROWD
CROWN
CROWS
CROZE
DROID
DROIT
DROLL
DROME
DRONE
DROOD
DROOL
DROOP
DROPS
DROSS
DROVE
DROWN
ERODE
EROSE
FROBE
FROCK
FRODO
FROES
FROGS
FROID
FROME
FROMM
FROND
FRONT
FROSH
FROST
FROTH
FROWN
FROWS
FROZE
GROAN
GROAT
GRODY
GROFE
GROGS
GROIN
GROKS
GROOM
GROPE
GROSS
GROSZ
GROTS
GROUP
GROUT
GROVE
GROWL
GROWN
GROWS
GROZA
IRONS
IRONY
KROGH
KRONA
KRONE
ORONO
PROAM
PROAS
PROBE
PRODS
PROEM
PROFS
PROLE
PROMO
PROMS
PRONE
PRONG
PROOF
PROPS
PROSE
PROST
PROSY
PROTO
PROTS
PROUD
PROVE
PROVO
PROWL
PROWS
PROXY
TROIS
TROLL
TROMP
TROOP
TROPE
TROPO
TROTH
TROTS
TROUT
TROVE
VROOM
WRONG
WROTE
WROTH

•R•O•

ARBOR
ARDOR
ARGOL
ARGON
ARGOS
ARGOT
ARION
ARMOR
ARROW
ARROZ
ARSON
ARTOO
BROOD
BROOK
BROOM
CREON
CROOK
CROON
DROOD
DROOL
DROOP
ERGOT
ERROL
ERROR
FREON
GRIOT
GROOM
MRMOM
ORDOS
OREOS
ORION
ORLON
ORLOP
ORONO
ORSON
ORTON
ORZOS
PRIOR
PROOF
PRYOR
TRIOS
TROOP
TRYON
VROOM

•R••O

ARTOO
BRAVO
BROMO
BRUNO
CREDO
DRACO
DRANO
DRLAO
ERATO
FRITO
FRODO
GRECO
IRIDO
ORFEO
ORONO
ORTHO
ORURO
PRADO
PRATO
PREGO
PRIMO
PROMO
PROTO
PROVO
TROPO
TRURO

••RO•

AARON
AFROS
AGRON
AKRON
APRON
ARROW
ARROZ
BARON
BORON
BYRON
CAROB
CAROL
CAROM
CARON
CDROM
CEROS
CHROM
CHRON
COROT
DUROC
DUROS
ELROY
ENROL
ERROL
ERROR
EUROS
FAROE
FARON
FAROS
FUROR
GAROU
GIROS
GYRON
GYROS
HEROD
HERON
HEROS
HOROL
HUROK
HURON
JUROR
KAROL
KIROV
LEROI
LEROY
MEROE
MORON
MOROS
MYRON
NEROL
PAROL
PAROS
PERON
PEROT
SAROD
SAROS
SCROD
SEROW
STROM
STROP
TAROK
TAROT
THROB
THROE
THROW
TOROS
TUROW
TYROL
TYROS
XEROX
ZEROS

••R•O

BURRO
CARBO
CARGO
CARLO
CERRO
CIRRO
CORNO
CURIO
DARIO
DERMO
DORSO
FARGO
FERRO
FIRPO
FORDO
FORGO
GARBO
GORDO
HARPO
LARGO
MARCO
MARGO
MARIO
MARLO
MIRRO
MORRO
NARCO
NORVO
PARDO
PORTO
SARGO
SARTO
SERVO
SORGO
TORSO
TURBO
VERSO
VIREO
VIRGO
ZORRO

•••RO

AGGRO
ANDRO
ASTRO
BURRO
CAIRO
CERRO
CHARO
CHIRO
CIRRO
CLARO
CUPRO
DOBRO
DOURO
ENERO
EXTRO
FERRO
FIBRO
GENRO
HIERO
HYDRO
HYGRO
IATRO
INTRO
MACRO
MATRO
METRO
MICRO
MIRRO
MORRO
MUNRO
NEURO
NITRO
ORURO
PEDRO
PETRO
PICRO
PTERO
REPRO
RETRO
SACRO
SPIRO
TRURO
ZORRO

R•P••

RAPEE
RAPHE
RAPID
REPAY
REPEG
REPEL
REPIN
REPLY
REPOS
REPOT
REPPS
REPRO
RIPEN
RIPER
RIPUP
ROPED
ROPER
ROPES
ROPEY
RUPEE

R••P•

RALPH
RAMPS
RASPS
RASPY
REAPS
REPPS
REUPS
ROMPS
RSVPS
RUMPS

R•••P

RANUP
RECAP
RECIP
REMAP
REMOP
RETAP
RETOP
RIGUP
RIPUP
RUNUP

•RP••

ARPAD
ARPEL

•R•P•

CRAPE
CRAPS
CREPE
CREPT
CROPS
CRYPT
DRAPE
DRIPS
DROPS
DRUPE
ERUPT
FRAPS
GRAPE
GRAPH
GRAPY
GRIPE
GRIPS
GROPE
KRUPA
KRUPP
PREPS
PROPS
TRAPP
TRAPS
TRIPE
TRIPS
TROPE
TROPO
WRAPS
WRAPT

•R••P

CRAMP
CREEP
CRIMP
CRISP
CROUP
CRUMP
DROOP
DRYUP
FRUMP
GRAMP
GRASP
GROUP
GRUMP
KRUPP
ORLOP
PRIMP
TRAMP
TRAPP
TROMP
TROOP
TRUMP

••RP•

BURPS
CARPE
CARPI
CARPS
CORPS
DORPS
FIRPO
GORPS
HARPO
HARPS
HARPY
MORPH
PERPS
TARPS
WARPS

••R•P

ATRIP
PTRAP
SCRAP
SCRIP
STRAP
STRIP
STROP
SYRUP

•••RP

CHIRP
SCARP
SHARP
SLURP
THARP
THORP
TWERP
USURP

R•Q••

ROQUE

•R•Q•

IRAQI

••R•Q

BARBQ

R•R••

RAREE
RARER
RARES
RERAN
RERUN
ROREM
RURAL
RURIK

R••R•

REARM
REARS
REFRY
REPRO
RETRO
RETRY
ROARS
RUARK

R•••R

RACER
RADAR
RAFER
RAKER
RAMAR
RANDR
RARER
RATER
RAVER
RAWER
RAZOR
REAIR
REBAR
RECUR
REFER
RETAR
RICER
RIDER
RIFER
RIGOR
RIKER
RIPER
RISER
RIVER
ROGER
ROMER
ROPER
ROTOR
ROVER
ROWER
RUDER
RULER
RUMOR
RYDER

•RR••

ARRAN
ARRAS
ARRAU
ARRAY
ARRET
ARRIS
ARROW
ARROZ
ERRED
ERROL
ERROR
IRREG
ORRIN
ORRIS

•R•R•

ARBRE
BRERS
CRURA
DRURY
FRERE
ORURO
TRURO

•R••R

ARBER
ARBOR
ARDOR
AREAR
ARMOR
AROAR
ARTHR
ARTUR
BRIAR
BRIER
CRIER
DREAR
DRIER
DRYER
ERROR
FREER
FRIAR
FRIER
FRYER
GREER
GRIER
ORDER
ORSER
PRIER
PRIOR
PRYOR
TRIER
TRUER
URGER
WRIER
WRYER

••RR•

BARRE
BARRY
BERRA
BERRY
BIRRS
BURRO
BURRS
BURRY
CARRE
CARRY
CERRO
CIRRI
CIRRO
CURRY
DERRY
DURRA
FERRI
FERRO
FERRY
FIRRY
FURRY
GARRY
GERRY
HARRY
HURRY
JARRE
JERRY
KERRY
LARRY
LORRE
LORRY
MARRY
MERRY
MIRRO
MORRO
MURRA
MURRE
MYRRH
PARRY
PERRY
PURRS
SERRA
SORRY
TARRY
TERRA
TERRE
TERRI
TERRY
TORRE
TORRS
VERRE
WIRRA
WORRY
ZORRO

••R•R

AURAR
BARER
BORER
CARER
CORER
CURER
DARER
DIRER
DURER
ERROR
EYRIR
FARER
FIRER
FUROR
HARAR
HIRER
JUROR
PARER
PURER
RARER
SORER
SURER
WIRER

•••RR

CHIRR
KNORR
OMARR
SHIRR
SKIRR
STARR
WHIRR

RS•••

RSVPS

R•S••

RASED
RASES
RASHT
RASPS
RASPY
RASTA
RESEE
RESET
RESEW
RESIN
RESOD
RESTS
RISEN
RISER
RISES
RISHI
RISKS
RISKY
ROSEN
ROSES
ROSEY
ROSIE
ROSIN
ROSSI
RUSES
RUSHY
RUSKS
RUSSE
RUSSO
RUSTS
RUSTY

R••S•

RAISA
RAISE
RATSO
REESE
REUSÉ
RINSE
RINSO
RNASE
ROAST
ROOST
ROSSI
ROUSE
ROUST
RUSSE
RUSSO

R•••S

RACES
RACKS
RAFTS
RAGAS
RAGES
RAIDS
RAILS
RAINS
RAJAS
RAKES
RAKIS
RAMIS
RAMOS
RAMPS
RANDS
RANIS
RANKS
RANTS
RARES
RASES
RASPS
RATES
RATHS
RAVES
RAWLS
RAZES
READS
REALS
REAMS
REAPS
REARS
REBUS
REEDS
REEFS
REEKS
REELS
REGIS
REIMS
REINS
REMUS
RENDS
RENTS
REPOS
REPPS
RESTS
REUPS
REXES
REYES
RHEAS
RIALS
RICES
RICKS
RIDES
RIELS
RIFFS
RIFTS
RIGGS
RILES
RILLS
RIMES
RINDS
RINGS
RINKS
RIOTS
RISES
RISKS
RITES
RIVES
ROADS
ROAMS
ROANS
ROARS
ROBES
ROCKS
ROILS
ROLES
ROLLS
ROMPS
ROODS
ROOFS
ROOKS
ROOMS
ROOTS
ROPES
ROSES
ROTAS
ROTES
ROTLS
ROTOS
ROUES
ROUTS
ROVES
RSVPS
RUBES
RUCKS
RUDDS
RUFFS
RUFUS
RUINS
RULES

RUMPS RUNES RUNGS RUNTS RUSES RUSKS RUSTS RYOTS

•RS••

ARSIS ARSON ORSER ORSON URSID

•R•S•

ARISE AROSE ARTSY BRASH BRASS BREST BRISK BRUSH CRASH CRASS CRESC CRESS CREST CRISP CRISS CRIST CROSS CRUSE CRUSH CRUST DRESS DROSS DRUSE ERASE ERISA ERNST EROSE FRESH FRISK FROSH FROST GRASP GRASS GRIST GROSS GROSZ IRISH KRISS PRASE PRESS PRISM PROSE PROST PROSY TRASH TRESS TRISH TRUSS TRUST TRYST WREST WRIST

•R••S

ARABS AREAS ARENS ARGOS ARGUS ARHUS ARIAS ARIES ARILS ARIUS ARLES ARRAS ARRIS ARSIS ARTES ARTIS ARUMS BRADS BRAES BRAGS BRANS BRASS BRATS BRAYS BRERS BREWS BRIES BRIGS BRIMS BRITS BROWS BRUTS CRABS CRAGS CRAMS CRAPS CRASS CRAWS CREES CRESS CREWS CRIBS CRIES CRISS CROCS CROPS CROSS CROWS DRABS DRAGS DRAMS DRATS DRAWS DRAYS DREGS DRESS DRIBS DRIES DRIPS DROPS DROSS DRUBS DRUGS DRUMS ERIES ERNES FRAIS FRANS FRAPS FRATS FRAYS FREES FRETS FRIES FRITS FROES FROGS FROWS GRABS GRADS GRAMS GRASS GRAYS GREYS GRIDS GRIGS GRINS GRIPS GRITS GROGS GROKS GROSS GROTS GROWS GRUBS IRONS KRAUS KREBS KRISS ORALS ORCAS ORCHS ORCUS ORDOS OREOS ORLES ORNIS ORRIS ORZOS PRAMS PRAUS PRAYS PREPS PRESS PREYS PRIES PRIGS PRIMS PROAS PRODS PROFS PROMS PROPS PROTS PROWS SRTAS TRAMS TRANS TRAPS TRAYS TREES TREKS TRESS TREWS TREYS TRIES TRIGS TRIMS TRIOS TRIPS TROIS TROTS TRUES TRUSS URALS URGES WRAPS WRENS WRITS XRAYS

••RS•

BURSA BURSE BURST CURSE CURST DORSA DORSI DORSO DURST FARSI FIRST GORSE HARSH HORSE HORST HORSY HURST KARSH KURSK MARSH MORSE NORSE NURSE PARSE PERSE PURSE PURSY TARSI TERSE TORSI TORSO VERSA VERSE VERSO VERST WORSE WORST WURST

••R•S

ABRIS ACRES AFROS AIRES APRES ARRAS ARRIS AURAS AYRES BARBS BARDS BARES BARKS BARMS BARNS BARTS BERGS BERMS BIRDS BIRLS BIRRS BORAS BORES BORIS BURBS BURGS BURLS BURNS BURPS BURRS BYRDS CARBS CARDS CARES CARKS CARPS CARTS CERES CEROS CERTS CHRIS CHRYS CIRCS CIRES CORDS CORES CORKS CORMS CORNS CORPS CURBS CURDS CURES CURLS CYRUS DARES DARKS DARNS DARTS DIRKS DORIS DORMS DORPS DUROS EARLS EARNS ECRUS EUROS EURUS EYRAS EYRES FARES FARMS FAROS FERNS FIRES FIRMS FIRNS FORBS FORDS FORES FORKS FORMS FORTS FURLS GARBS GERMS GIRDS GIRLS GIRNS GIROS GIRTS GORES GORPS GURUS GYRES GYROS GYRUS HARES HARKS HARMS HARPS HARTS HERBS HERDS HERES HERLS HERMS HEROS HIRES HORAS HORNS HORUS HURLS HURTS JARLS JERKS KERBS KERNS KIRKS KURDS LARAS LARDS LARES LARKS LIRAS LORDS LORES LORIS LURES LURKS LYRES MARAS MARES MARIS MARKS MARLS MARTS MARYS MERES MERLS MIRES MIRVS MORES MORNS MOROS MORTS NARAS NARCS NARDS NARES NARIS NARKS NERDS NERTS NORMS NORNS OGRES OKRAS ORRIS PARDS PARES PARIS PARKS PAROS PARTS PERES PERIS PERKS PERMS PERPS PORES PORKS PORTS PURLS PURRS PURUS PYRES RARES SARDS SARIS SAROS SERBS SERES SERFS SIRES SORAS SORBS SORES SORTS SORUS SURAS SURDS SURFS TARES TARNS TARPS TARTS TERMS TERNS TIRES TOROS TORRS TORTS TORUS TURFS TURKS TURNS TYRES TYROS VARAS VERBS VERTS VIRUS WARDS WARES WARMS WARNS WARPS WARTS WIRES WORDS WORKS WORMS WORTS XERUS YARDS YARNS YPRES YURTS ZARFS ZEROS ZORIS

•••RS

ABBRS AFARS AGARS AGERS ALORS AMIRS APERS AVARS AVERS AYERS BEARS BEERS BIRRS BLURS BOARS BOERS BOORS BRERS BURRS CBERS CHARS CMDRS COIRS COORS CZARS DEARS DEERS DOERS DOORS DYERS EMIRS ENGRS EVERS EWERS EYERS FAIRS FEARS FOURS GAURS GEARS GNARS GOERS GUARS HAIRS HEARS HEIRS HOARS HOERS HOURS IBARS ICERS IZARS JBARS JEERS KNARS KNURS LAIRS LEERS LIARS MOORS MYERS NEARS NLERS ODORS OMERS ONERS OVERS OWERS PAIRS PEARS PEERS PIERS POURS PURRS REARS ROARS SCARS SEARS SEERS SLURS SOARS SOURS SPARS SPURS STARS STIRS SUERS TAHRS TBARS TEARS THURS TIERS TORRS TOURS TSARS USERS VEERS VIERS WEARS WEIRS WHIRS YEARS YOURS ZBARS

R•T••

RATCH RATED RATEL RATER RATES RATHS RATIO RATON RATSO RATTY RETAG RETAP RETAR RETAX RETIA RETIE RETOP RETOW RETRO RETRY RITES RITZY ROTAS ROTES ROTLS ROTOR ROTOS RUTIN RUTTY

R••T•

RAFTS RAITT RANTO RANTS RASTA RATTY REATA RECTI RECTO RENTA RENTS RESTS RHETT RIATA RIFTS RIOTS ROOTS ROUTE ROUTS RUNTO RUNTS RUNTY RUSTS RUSTY RUTTY RYOTS

R•••T

RABAT RAITT RAMET RANAT RASHT REACT REBUT REFIT RELET RELIT REMET REMIT REPOT RESET REVET RHETT RIANT RIGHT RIVET ROAST ROBOT ROGET ROOST ROUST

•RT••

ARTAL ARTEL ARTES ARTHR ARTIE ARTIS ARTOO ARTSY ARTUR ORTHO ORTON SRTAS

•R•T•

ARETE ARITH BRATS BRETT BRITE BRITH BRITS BRITT BROTH BRUTE BRUTS CRATE CRETE DRATS ERATO FRATS FRETS FRITO FRITS FRITZ FROTH GRATA GRATE GRETA GRETE GRITS GROTS IRATE ORATE PRATE PRATO PRATT PROTO PROTS TRITE TRITT TROTH TROTS TRUTH WRATH WRITE WRITS WROTE WROTH

•R••T

ARENT ARGOT ARHAT ARMET ARRET BRACT BRANT BRENT BREST BRETT BRITT BRUIT BRUNT CRAFT CREPT CREST CRIST CROAT CROFT CRUET CRUST CRYPT DRAFT DRIFT DROIT ERECT ERGOT ERNST ERUCT ERUPT FRONT FROST FRUIT GRAFT GRANT GREAT GREET GRIFT GRIOT GRIST GROAT GROUT GRUNT KRAFT KRAIT KRAUT ORANT ORBIT PRATT PRINT PROST TRACT TRAIT TREAT TRENT TRITT TROUT TRUST TRYST WRAPT WREST WRIST

••RT•

AORTA BARTH BARTS BARTY BERTH BIRTH CARTA CARTE CARTS CERTS DARTH DARTS DIRTY EARTH FIRTH FORTE FORTH FORTS FORTY FURTH GARTH GIRTH GIRTS HARTE HARTS HERTZ HURTS KURTZ MARTA MARTI MARTS MARTY MERTZ MIRTH MORTS NERTS NERTZ NORTE NORTH PARTE PARTI PARTS PARTY PERTH PORTE PORTO PORTS SARTO SERTA SORTA SORTS TARTS TORTE TORTS VERTE VERTS VIRTU WARTS WARTY WORTH WORTS YURTS

••R•T

AFRIT ARRET BARIT BERET BURNT BURST CARAT CARET CERAT COROT CURST DERAT DURST EGRET FIRST HERAT HORST HURST JURAT KARAT KERAT MARAT MERIT MURAT PEROT SPRAT SPRIT STRUT SURAT TAROT VERST WORST WURST

•••RT

ABORT ALERT AMORT APART APORT AVERT BLURT CHART CHERT COURT EBERT EVERT EXERT FLIRT HEART IBERT INERT KMART OPART OVERT QUART QUIRT SHIRT SHORT SKIRT SMART SNERT SNORT SPORT SPURT START SWART

RU•••

RUANA RUARK RUBEN RUBES RUBIK RUBIN RUBLE RUCHE RUCKS RUDDS RUDDY RUDER RUDGE RUEHL RUFFS RUFUS RUGAE RUGBY RUING RUINS RULED RULER RULES RUMBA RUMEN RUMMY RUMOR RUMPS RUNES RUNGS RUNIC RUNIN RUNNY RUNON RUNTO RUNTS RUNTY RUNUP RUPEE RURAL RURIK RUSES RUSHY RUSKS RUSSE RUSSO RUSTS RUSTY RUTIN RUTTY

R•U••

REUNE REUPS REUSE RHUMB ROUEN ROUES ROUGE ROUGH ROUND ROUSE ROUST ROUTE ROUTS

R••U•

RANUP RAOUL REBUS REBUT RECUR REDUB REDUX REMUS RERUN REVUE RHEUM RIGUP RIPUP ROGUE ROQUE RUFUS RUNUP

•RU••

ARUBA ARUMS BRUCE BRUCH BRUHN BRUIN BRUIT BRULE BRUME BRUNG BRUNO BRUNT BRUSH BRUTE BRUTS CRUDE CRUEL CRUET CRUMB CRUMP CRURA CRUSE CRUSH CRUST DRUBS DRUGS DRUID DRUMS DRUNK DRUPE DRURY DRUSE DRUZE ERUCT ERUPT FRUIT FRUMP GRUBS GRUEL GRUFF GRUMP GRUNT KRULL KRUPA KRUPP ORURO PRUDE PRUNE TRUCE TRUCK TRUED TRUER TRUES TRUEX TRULY TRUMP TRUNK TRURO TRUSS TRUST TRUTH WRUNG

•R•U•

ARGUE ARGUS ARHUS ARIUM ARIUS ARTUR BRAUN BROUN CROUP DRYUP FRAUD FREUD GROUP GROUT KRAUS KRAUT ORCUS PRAUS PROUD TROUT

•R••U

ARRAU

••RU•

AURUM CYRUS DURUM ECRUS EURUS FORUM GURUS GYRUS HARUM HORUS JORUM LARUE PURUS RERUN SCRUB SCRUM SERUM SHRUB SHRUG SORUS SPRUE STRUM STRUT SYRUP THRUM TORUS VIRUS XERUS

••R•U

ARRAU CORFU CORNU GAROU PAREU PERDU TURKU VIRTU

•••RU

NAURU NEHRU OTARU UHURU

R•V••

RAVED RAVEL RAVEN RAVER RAVES RAVIN REVEL REVET REVUE RIVAL RIVED RIVEN RIVER RIVES RIVET ROVED ROVER ROVES RSVPS

R••V•

REEVE

R•••V

RAJIV

•RV••

ERVIL ERVIN IRVIN

•R•V•

BRAVA BRAVE BRAVO BREVE CRAVE DRIVE DROVE GRAVE GRAVY GROVE PRIVY PROVE PROVO TRAVE TREVI TROVE

••RV•

CARVE CURVE CURVY HERVE LARVA MARVY MIRVS NERVE NERVY NORVO SERVE SERVO TURVY VERVE

••R•V

DERIV KIROV

R•W••

RAWER RAWLS RAWLY REWAX REWED REWIN REWON ROWAN ROWDY ROWED ROWEL ROWEN ROWER

R•••W

REMOW RENEW RESEW RETOW

•RW••
ERWIN
IRWIN

•R•W•
BRAWL
BRAWN
BREWS
BROWN
BROWS
CRAWL
CRAWS
CREWS
CROWD
CROWN
CROWS
DRAWL
DRAWN
DRAWS
DROWN
FROWN
FROWS
GROWL
GROWN
GROWS
PRAWN
PROWL
PROWS
TRAWL
TREWS

•R••W
ARROW

••R•W
ARROW
CAREW
NAREW
SCREW
SEROW
SHREW
STRAW
STREW
THREW
THROW
TUROW

R•X••
REXES
ROXIE

R•••X
RADIX
REDOX
REDUX
RELAX
REMEX
REMIX
RETAX
REWAX
ROLEX

•R•X•
PREXY
PROXY

•R••X
BRONX
CROIX
TRUEX

••R•X
BORAX
HYRAX
LORAX
LUREX
MUREX
PUREX
PYREX
VARIX
XEROX

RY•••
RYDER
RYOTS

R•Y••
RAYED
RAYON
REYES
RHYME
RIYAL
ROYAL
ROYCE
ROYKO

R••Y•
REDYE

R•••Y
RAINY
RALLY
RANDY
RANGY
RASPY
RATTY
RAWLY
READY
REDDY
REEDY
REFRY
REIFY
REKEY
RELAY
REPAY
REPLY
RETRY
RIBBY
RICKY
RIDGY
RIGBY
RILEY
RINKY
RISKY
RITZY
ROBBY
ROCKY
RODDY
ROILY
RONNY
ROOKY
ROOMY
ROPEY
ROSEY
ROWDY
RUDDY
RUGBY
RUMMY
RUNNY
RUNTY
RUSHY
RUSTY
RUTTY

•RY••
ARYAN
BRYAN
BRYCE
CRYPT
DRYAD
DRYER
DRYLY
DRYUP
FRYER
PRYOR
TRYME
TRYON
TRYST
WRYER
WRYLY

•R•Y•
BRAYS
DRAYS
FRAYS
FREYA
GRAYS
GREYS
ORIYA
PRAYS
PREYS
TRAYS
TREYS
XRAYS

•R••Y
ARABY
ARCHY
ARRAY
ARTSY
BRADY
BRINY
BRODY
CRAZY
CRECY
CROLY
CRONY
DRURY
DRYLY
GRADY
GRAPY
GRAVY
GRIMY
GRODY
IRONY
ORACY
ORCZY
PREXY
PRICY
PRIVY
PROSY
PROXY
TRACY
TRULY
WRYLY

••RY•
BERYL
CHRYS
DARYA
DARYL
MARYS
MERYL

••R•Y
ARRAY
BARMY
BARRY
BARTY
BERRY
BIRDY
BURLY
BURRY
CAREY
CARLY
CARNY
CARRY
CORBY
COREY
CORKY
CORNY
CURDY
CURLY
CURRY
CURVY
DARBY
DERBY
DERRY
DIRTY
EARLY
ELROY
FERNY
FERRY
FIRRY
FORAY
FORKY
FORTY
FURRY
GARRY
GERMY
GERRY
GIRLY
GORDY
GORKY
GURDY
HARDY
HARPY
HARRY
HERBY
HERKY
HORSY
HURDY
HURLY
HURRY
JERKY
JERRY
JERZY
KERRY
KIRBY
LARDY
LARRY
LEROY
LORRY
LURAY
MARCY
MARLY
MARRY
MARTY
MARVY
MERCY
MERRY
MORAY
MOREY
MURKY
NERDY
NERVY
PARRY
PARTY
PERCY
PERKY
PERRY
PORGY
PORKY
PURSY
SORRY
SPRAY
STRAY
SURFY
SURLY
TARDY
TARRY
TERRY
TURVY
WARTY
WORDY
WORMY
WORRY

•••RY
AMBRY
AMORY
ANGRY
APERY
AUTRY
AVERY
BARRY
BEERY
BERRY
BURRY
CAMRY
CARRY
CHARY
CURRY
CYMRY
DAIRY
DEARY
DECRY
DERRY
DEVRY
DIARY
DOWRY
DRURY
EMERY
EMORY
ENTRY
EVERY
FAIRY
FERRY
FIERY
FIRRY
FURRY
GARRY
GEARY
GERRY
GLARY
GLORY
HAIRY
HARRY
HENRY
HOARY
HURRY
IATRY
IVORY
JERRY
KERRY
LARRY
LEARY
LEERY
LORRY
LOWRY
MARRY
MAURY
MERRY
OTARY
PARRY
PEARY
PERRY
QUERY
REFRY
RETRY
SCARY
SORRY
STORY
TARRY
TEARY
TERRY
USURY
VEERY
WEARY
WORRY

R•Z••
RAZED
RAZES
RAZOR
RIZZO

R••Z•
RHIZO
RITZY
RIZZO

•RZ••
ORZOS

•R•Z•
BRAZE
CRAZE
CRAZY
CROZE
DRUZE
FRIZZ
FROZE
GRAZE
GROZA
ORCZY
PRIZE

•R••Z
ARNAZ
ARROZ
FRANZ
FRITZ
FRIZZ
GROSZ

••RZ•
FURZE
HERZL
JERZY
TERZA

••R•Z
ARROZ
HERTZ
JEREZ
KURTZ
MERTZ
NERTZ
PEREZ

SA•••
SAABS
SABAH
SABER
SABIN
SABLE
SABOT
SABRA
SABRE
SACCO
SACHA
SACHS
SACKS
SACRA
SACRE
SACRO
SADAT
SADHE
SADHU
SADIE
SADLY
SAENS
SAFER
SAFES
SAGAL
SAGAN
SAGAS
SAGER
SAGES
SAGET
SAGGY
SAGOS
SAHEL
SAHIB
SAIGA
SAILS
SAINT
SAJAK
SAKER
SAKES
SALAD
SALAL
SALAM
SALEM
SALEP
SALES
SALIC
SALLE
SALLY
SALMI
SALON
SALPA
SALPS
SALSA
SALTA
SALTS
SALTY
SALUD
SALUT
SALVE
SALVO
SAMAR
SAMBA
SAMMS
SAMMY
SAMOA
SAMOS
SAMPS
SANAA
SANDH
SANDL
SANDS
SANDY
SANER
SANKA
SANTA
SANTE
SANTO
SANYO
SAONE
SAPID
SAPIR
SAPOR
SAPPY
SARAH
SARAN
SARDS
SARGE
SARGO
SARIS
SAROD
SAROS
SARTO
SASES
SASHA
SASSY
SATAN
SATBY
SATED
SATES
SATIE
SATIN
SATON
SATUP
SATYR
SAUCE
SAUCY
SAUDI
SAUKS
SAULT
SAUNA
SAUTE
SAVED
SAVER
SAVES
SAVOR
SAVOY
SAVVY
SAWED
SAWIN
SAWTO
SAXES
SAXON
SAYER
SAYSO

S•A••
SAABS
SCABS
SCADS
SCALA
SCALD
SCALE
SCALP
SCALY
SCAMP
SCAMS
SCAND
SCANS
SCANT
SCAPA
SCAPE
SCARE
SCARF
SCARP
SCARS
SCARY
SCATS
SCAUP
SEALE
SEALS
SEALY
SEAMS
SEAMY
SEARS
SEATO
SEATS
SHACK
SHADE
SHADS
SHADY
SHAEF
SHAFT
SHAGS
SHAHN
SHAHS
SHAKE
SHAKO
SHAKY
SHALE
SHALL
SHALT
SHAME
SHAMS
SHAMU
SHANA
SHANE
SHANK
SHANS
SHANT
SHAPE
SHARD
SHARE
SHARI
SHARK
SHARP
SHAUN
SHAVE
SHAWL
SHAWM
SHAWN
SHAYS
SIALS
SKALD
SKATE
SLABS
SLACK
SLADE
SLAGS
SLAIN
SLAKE
SLAMS
SLANG
SLANT
SLAPS
SLASH
SLATE
SLATS
SLATY
SLAVE
SLAVS
SLAWS
SLAYS
SMACK
SMALL
SMALT
SMART
SMASH
SMAZE
SNACK
SNAFU
SNAGS
SNAIL
SNAKE
SNAKY
SNAPS
SNARE
SNARK
SNARL
SNATH
SOAKS
SOAPS
SOAPY
SOARS
SOAVE
SPAAK
SPACE
SPADE
SPADS
SPAHI
SPAHN
SPAIN
SPAKE
SPALL
SPANG
SPANK
SPANS
SPARE
SPARK
SPARS
SPASM
SPATE
SPATS
SPAWN
SPAYS
STABS
STACK
STACY
STADT
STAEL
STAFF
STAGE
STAGG
STAGS
STAGY
STAHL
STAID
STAIN
STAIR
STAKE
STALE
STALK
STALL
STAMP
STAND
STANG
STANK
STARE
STARK
STARR
STARS
START
STASH
STATE
STATS
STAVE
STAYS
SUAVE
SWABS
SWAGE
SWAGS
SWAIN
SWALE
SWAMI
SWAMP
SWANK
SWANN
SWANS
SWAPS
SWARD
SWARF
SWARM
SWART
SWASH
SWATH
SWATS
SWAYS
SWAZI

S••A•
SABAH
SADAT
SAGAL
SAGAN
SAGAS
SAJAK
SALAD
SALAL
SALAM
SAMAR
SANAA
SARAH
SARAN
SATAN
SCHAV
SCRAG
SCRAM
SCRAP
SEDAN
SEGAL
SEGAR
SELAH
SEPAL
SERAC
SERAI
SETAE
SETAT
SHEAF
SHEAN
SHEAR
SHOAH
SHOAL
SHOAT
SILAS
SINAI
SISAL
SITAR
SIVAN
SKEAN
SKEAT
SKOAL
SKUAS
SLOAN
SMEAR
SNEAD
SNEAK
SODAS
SOFAR
SOFAS
SOLAN
SOLAR
SOMAS
SONAR
SORAS
SOYAS
SPAAK
SPEAK
SPEAR
SPLAT
SPLAY
SPRAG
SPRAT
SPRAY
SQUAB
SQUAD
SQUAT
SRTAS
STEAD
STEAK
STEAL
STEAM
STOAE
STOAS
STOAT
STRAD
STRAP
STRAW
STRAY
SUDAN
SUGAR
SUMAC
SURAH
SURAL
SURAS
SURAT
SUSAN
SWEAR
SWEAT

S•••A
SABRA
SACHA
SACRA
SAIGA
SALPA
SALSA
SALTA
SAMBA
SAMOA
SANAA
SANKA
SANTA
SASHA
SAUNA
SCALA
SCAPA
SCENA
SCHWA
SCUBA
SCUTA
SEEYA
SEHNA
SELMA
SELVA
SENNA
SEPIA
SEPTA
SERRA
SERTA
SHANA
SHEBA
SHIVA
SHULA
SIDEA
SIDRA
SIENA
SIGMA
SILVA
SIMBA
SITKA
SKODA
SLIWA
SNEVA
SOFIA
SOLFA
SONIA
SONJA
SONYA
SORTA
SOUSA
SPICA
STELA
STOLA
STOMA
STRIA
STUKA
STUPA
SUDRA
SULFA
SULLA
SUMBA
SUMMA
SUNDA
SUNNA
SUPRA
SUTRA
SYRIA

•SA••
ASAMA
ASANA
ISAAC
ISAMU
OSAGE
OSAKA
PSALM
PSATS
TSADE
TSARS
USAGE
USAIR

•S•A•
ASCAP
ASIAN
ASSAD
ASSAI
ASSAM
ASSAY
ASWAN
ESBAT
ESSAY
ESTAB
ISAAC
ISLAM
OSCAN
OSCAR
OSKAR
OSMAN
PSHAW
PSOAS
USUAL

•S••A
ASAMA
ASANA
ASOKA
ASPCA
ASTRA
ASYLA
OSAKA
OSHEA
OSSIA
OSTIA
USCGA
USLTA

••SA•
ANSAE
ASSAD
ASSAI
ASSAM
ASSAY
BASAL
CESAR
ESSAY
HASAT
MASAI
MESAS
NASAL
NISAN
PISAN
PUSAN
SISAL
SUSAN
UNSAY
VISAS

••S•A
AISHA
ATSEA
BASRA
BOSSA
CASCA
CESTA
COSTA
DESNA
FESTA
FOSSA
HASTA
HOSEA
HOSTA
KASHA
KISKA
MESTA
MISHA
MISSA
MUSCA
OSSIA
PASHA
PASTA
RASTA
SASHA
TESLA
TESTA
TOSCA
VESTA
VISTA

•••SA
AZUSA
BALSA
BOSSA
BURSA
COOSA
DORSA
ERISA
FOSSA
HANSA
HAUSA
ICOSA
KANSA
LHASA
LUISA
MENSA
MISSA
NYASA
OMASA
RAISA
SALSA
SOUSA
TULSA
VERSA
XHOSA

S•B••
SABAH
SABER
SABIN
SABLE
SABOT
SABRA
SABRE
SEBUM
SIBYL
SOBER
SOBIG
SUBIC
SYBIL

S••B•
SAABS
SAMBA
SATBY
SCABS
SCUBA
SERBS
SETBY
SHEBA
SIMBA
SITBY
SLABS
SLOBS
SNOBS
SNUBS
SORBS
STABS
STUBS
SUMBA
SWABS

S•••B
SAHIB
SCRUB
SHRUB
SIDEB
SQUAB
SQUIB

•SB••
ESBAT

•S•B•
ASHBY

•S••B
ESTAB

••SB•
BUSBY
COSBY
MOSBY
NASBY

SC•••
SCABS
SCADS
SCALA
SCALD
SCALE
SCALP
SCALY
SCAMP
SCAMS
SCAND
SCANS
SCANT
SCAPA
SCAPE
SCARE
SCARF
SCARP
SCARS
SCARY
SCATS
SCAUP
SCENA
SCEND
SCENE
SCENT
SCHAV
SCHED
SCHMO
SCHON
SCHWA
SCIFI
SCION
SCOFF
SCOLD
SCONE
SCOOP
SCOOT
SCOPE
SCOPS
SCORE
SCORN
SCOTS
SCOTT
SCOUR
SCOUT
SCOWL
SCOWS
SCRAG
SCRAM
SCRAP
SCREE
SCREW
SCRIM
SCRIP
SCROD
SCRUB
SCRUM
SCUBA
SCUDI
SCUDO
SCUDS
SCUFF
SCULL
SCUMS
SCUPS
SCURF
SCUTA
SCUTE
SCUTS

S•C••
SACCO
SACHA
SACHS
SACKS
SACRA
SACRE
SACRO
SECCO
SECTS
SOCHI
SOCIO
SOCKO
SOCKS
SOCLE
SUCKS
SUCRE
SYCEE
SYCES

S••C•
SACCO
SAUCE
SAUCY
SECCO
SHACK
SHOCK
SHUCK
SINCE
SLACK
SLICE
SLICK
SMACK
SMOCK
SNACK
SNICK
SNUCK
SPACE
SPECK
SPECS
SPICA
SPICE
SPICY
SPOCK
STACK
STACY
STICH
STICK
STOCK
STUCK
SULCI
SYNCS

S•••C
SALIC
SERAC
SONIC
STOIC
SUBIC
SUMAC

•SC••
ASCAP
ASCII
ASCOT
ASCUS
OSCAN
OSCAR
USCGA

•S•C•
ASPCA
PSYCH

•S••C
ASDIC
ASPIC
ASSOC
FSLIC
ISAAC
ISTIC
OSMIC
OSRIC

••SC•
BOSCH
BOSCO
BOSCS
BUSCH
CASCA
CASCO
CISCO
DISCO
DISCS
FISCS
MUSCA
PASCH
PASCO
PESCI
PISCI
PISCO
TOSCA

VASCO STUDS STUDY SUDDS SUEDE SUNDA SURDS SWEDE

••S•C
ASSOC BASIC COSEC MESIC MUSIC

•••SC
CRESC EPISC

S•D••
SADAT SADHE SADHU SADIE SADLY SEDAN SEDER SEDGE SEDUM SIDEA SIDEB SIDED SIDER SIDES SIDHE SIDLE SIDON SIDRA SODAS SODDY SODOM SUDAN SUDDS SUDRA SUDSY SYDOW

S••D•
SANDH SANDL SANDS SANDY SARDS SAUDI SCADS SCUDI SCUDO SCUDS SEEDS SEEDY SENDS SHADE SHADS SHADY SHEDS SKIDS SKODA SLADE SLEDS SLIDE SNIDE SODDY SOLDI SOLDO SONDE SPADE SPADS SPODE SPUDS STADT

S•••D
SALAD SALUD SAPID SAROD SATED SAVED SAWED SCALD SCAND SCEND SCHED SCOLD SCROD SEWED SHARD SHEED SHIED SHOED SHRED SIDED SIRED SITED SIXED SIZED SKALD SKIED SLOYD SLUED SNEAD SNEED SNERD SNOOD SOLED SOLID SOUND SOWED SPEED SPEND SPIED SQUAD SQUID STAID STAND STEAD STEED STOOD STRAD SWARD SWORD SYNOD SZOLD

•SD••
ASDIC MSDOS

•S•D•
ASIDE BSIDE TSADE

•S••D
ASKED ASSAD ASSTD PSEUD USHED USTED

••SD•
MISDO

••S•D
ASSAD ASSTD BASED BUSED CASED DOSED EASED FUSED HASID HOSED LASED MUSED NOSED POSED RASED RESOD URSID

SE•••
SEALE SEALS SEALY SEAMS SEAMY SEARS SEATO SEATS SEBUM SECCO SECTS SEDAN SEDER SEDGE SEDUM SEEDS SEEDY SEEIN SEEKS SEELS SEEMS SEEPS SEEPY SEERS SEETO SEEYA SEGAL SEGAR SEGER SEGNI SEGNO SEGOS SEGUE SEHNA SEIKO SEINE SEISM SEIZE SELAH SELES SELLS SELMA SELVA SEMIS SENDS SENNA SENOR SENSE SEOUL SEPAL SEPIA SEPOY SEPTA SERAC SERAI SERBS SERES SERFS SERGE SERIF SERIN SEROW SERRA SERTA SERUM SERVE SERVO SETAE SETAT SETBY SETIN SETON SETTO SETUP SEULE SEUSS SEVEN SEVER SEWED SEWER SEWON SEWUP SEXES SEXTS

S•E••
SAENS SCENA SCEND SCENE SCENT SEEDS SEEDY SEEIN SEEKS SEELS SEEMS SEEPS SEEPY SEERS SEETO SEEYA SHEAF SHEAN SHEAR SHEBA SHEDS SHEED SHEEN SHEEP SHEER SHEET SHEIK SHELF SHELL SHEMP SHERE SIEGE SIENA SIEPI SIETE SIEUR SIEVE SKEAN SKEAT SKEET SKEGS SKEIN SKEPS SKETE SKEWS SLEDS SLEEK SLEEP SLEET SLEPT SLEWS SMEAR SMELL SMELT SMEWS SNEAD SNEAK SNEED SNEER SNELL SNERD SNERT SNEVA SOEUR SPEAK SPEAR SPECK SPECS SPEED SPEKE SPELL SPELT SPEND SPENT SPETS SPEWS STEAD STEAK STEAL STEAM STEED STEEL STEEN STEEP STEER STEIN STELA STELE STEMS STENO STENS STEPS STERE STERN STETS STEVE STEWS SUEDE SUEME SUERS SUETS SWEAR SWEAT SWEDE SWEEP SWEET SWELL SWEPT SZELL

S••E•
SABER SAFER SAFES SAGER SAGES SAGET SAHEL SAKER SAKES SALEM SALEP SALES SANER SASES SATED SATES SAVED SAVER SAVES SAWED SAXES SAYER SCHED SCREE SCREW SEDER SEGER SELES SERES SEVEN SEVER SEWED SEWER SEXES SHAEF SHEED SHEEN SHEEP SHEER SHEET SHIED SHIER SHIES SHOED SHOER SHOES SHRED SHREW SHYER SIDEA SIDEB SIDED SIDER SIDES SIKES SILEX SINES SINEW SIRED SIREN SIRES SITED SITES SIXED SIXES SIZED SIZER SIZES SKEET SKIED SKIER SKIES SLEEK SLEEP SLEET SLIER SLOES SLUED SLUES SLYER SNEED SNEER SOBER SOLED SOLER SOLES SONES SOOEY SOREL SOREN SORER SORES SOWED SOWER SOXER SPEED SPIED SPIEL SPIES SPREE STAEL STEED STEEL STEEN STEEP STEER STIES STREW SUMER SUPER SURER SWEEP SWEET SYCEE SYCES

S•••E
SABLE SABRE SACRE SADHE SADIE SALLE SALVE SANTE SAONE SARGE SATIE SAUCE SAUTE SCALE SCAPE SCARE SCENE SCONE SCOPE SCORE SCREE SCUTE SEALE SEDGE SEGUE SEINE SEIZE SENSE SERGE SERVE SETAE SEULE SHADE SHAKE SHALE SHAME SHANE SHAPE SHARE SHAVE SHERE SHINE SHIRE SHONE SHORE SHOVE SHUTE SIDHE SIDLE SIEGE SIETE SIEVE SIGNE SINCE SINGE SKATE SKETE SKIVE SLADE SLAKE SLATE SLAVE SLICE SLIDE SLIME SLOPE SLYPE SMAZE SMILE SMITE SMOKE SMOTE SNAKE SNARE SNIDE SNIPE SNORE SOAVE SOCLE SOLVE SOMME SONDE SOUSE SPACE SPADE SPAKE SPARE SPATE SPEKE SPICE SPIKE SPILE SPINE SPIRE SPITE SPODE SPOKE SPORE SPREE SPRUE SPUME STAGE STAKE STALE STARE STATE STAVE STELE STERE STEVE STILE STIPE STOAE STOKE STOLE STONE STOPE STORE STOVE STOWE STYLE STYNE SUAVE SUCRE SUEDE SUEME SUITE SURGE SUSIE SWAGE SWALE SWEDE SWINE SWIPE SWOPE SWORE SYCEE SYNGE

•SE••
ISERE PSEUD USERS USEUP

•S•E•
ASHEN ASHER ASHES ASKED ASKER ASKEW ASNER ASPEN ASSES ASSET ASSEZ ASTER ASYET ESKER ESNES ESSEN ESSES ESSEX ESTEE ESTER ESTES ISLES ISLET ISLEY ISSEI OSHEA OSIER OSLER OSSEO OSTEO USHED USHER USTED

•S••E
ASIDE ASONE ASTRE BSIDE ESQUE ESTEE ISERE ISSUE ISTLE OSAGE OSSIE TSADE USAGE

••SE•
ANSEL ANSER APSES ASSES ASSET ASSEZ ATSEA BASED BASEL BASER BASES BESET BISES BUSED BUSES BUSEY CASED CASES CASEY COSEC DOSED DOSER DOSES EASED EASEL EASES EBSEN EDSEL ESSEN ESSES ESSEX ETSEQ FUSED FUSEE FUSES GASES GOSEE HOSEA HOSED HOSEL HOSES IBSEN INSET ISSEI JOSEF KASEM KESEY KYSER LASED LASER LASES LOSER LOSES MASER MISER MOSES MOSEY MUSED MUSER MUSES NISEI NOSED NOSES OASES OLSEN ONSET ORSER OSSEO OUSEL PASEO PASES POSED POSER POSES PUSEY RASED RASES RESEE RESET RESEW RISEN RISER RISES ROSEN ROSES ROSEY RUSES SASES TASER TVSET UNSER UNSET UPSET VASES VESEY VISES WESER WISER YESES

••S•E
AISLE AISNE ANSAE BASIE BASTE CASTE DISME ELSIE ENSUE FISKE FOSSE FUSEE GASPE GESTE GOSEE GOSSE HASTE HESSE ISSUE ITSME JESSE JUSTE LISLE LISSE MASSE MESNE MOSHE NASHE OSSIE PASSE PASTE PISTE POSSE POSTE RESEE ROSIE RUSSE SUSIE TASSE TASTE WASTE

•••SE
ABASE ABUSE AMUSE ANISE ARISE AROSE BLASE BOISE BOUSE BURSE CAUSE CEASE CENSE CHASE CHOSE CLOSE COPSE CRUSE CURSE DANSE DENSE DNASE DOUSE DOWSE DRUSE DULSE ELISE ELYSE ERASE EROSE FALSE FOSSE GEESE GOOSE GORSE GOSSE GUISE HAWSE HESSE HEYSE HORSE HOUSE INUSE JESSE LAPSE LEASE LISSE LOOSE LOUSE LUISE MANSE MASSE MEESE MEUSE MOOSE MORSE MOUSE NOISE NOOSE NORSE NURSE OBESE OFUSE PARSE PASSE PAUSE PEASE PERSE PHASE POISE POSSE PRASE PROSE PULSE PURSE RAISE REESE REUSE RINSE RNASE ROUSE RUSSE SENSE SOUSE TASSE TEASE TENSE TERSE THESE THOSE UKASE VALSE VERSE WHOSE WORSE

S•F••
SAFER SAFES SIFTS SOFAR SOFAS SOFIA SOFTY SUFIS

S••F•
SCIFI SCOFF SCUFF SERFS SHAFT SHIFT SKIFF SNAFU SNIFF SNUFF SOLFA SPIFF STAFF STIFF STUFF SULFA SURFS SURFY SWIFT

S•••F
SCARF SCOFF SCUFF SCURF SERIF SHAEF SHEAF SHELF SKIFF SMURF SNIFF SNUFF SPIFF SPOOF STAFF STIFF STUFF SWARF

••S•F
JOSEF

S•G••
SAGAL SAGAN SAGAS SAGER SAGES SAGET SAGGY SAGOS SEGAL SEGAR SEGER SEGNI SEGNO SEGOS SEGUE SIGHS SIGHT SIGIL SIGMA SIGNE SIGNO SIGNS SOGGY SSGTS SUGAR

S••G•
SAGGY SAIGA SARGE SARGO SEDGE SERGE SHAGS SHOGI SIEGE SINGE SINGS SKEGS SLAGS SLIGO SLOGS SLUGS SMOGS SNAGS SNUGS SOGGY SONGS SORGO SOUGH STAGE STAGG STAGS STAGY STOGY SURGE SWAGE SWAGS SWIGS SYNGE

S•••G
SCRAG SHRUG SLANG SLING SLUNG SOBIG SOONG SPANG SPRAG SPRIG STAGG STANG STING STUNG SUING SWING SWUNG

•SG••
MSGTS SSGTS TSGTS

•S•G•
OSAGE USAGE USCGA VSIGN

•S••G
USING

SH•••
SHACK SHADE SHADS SHADY SHAEF SHAFT SHAGS SHAHN SHAHS SHAKE SHAKO SHAKY SHALE SHALL SHALT SHAME SHAMS SHAMU SHANA SHANE SHANK SHANS SHANT SHAPE SHARD SHARE SHARI SHARK SHARP SHAUN SHAVE SHAWL SHAWM SHAWN SHAYS SHEAF SHEAN SHEAR SHEBA SHEDS SHEED SHEEN SHEEP SHEER SHEET SHEIK SHELF SHELL SHEMP SHERE SHIED SHIER SHIES SHIFT SHILL SHIMS SHINE SHINS SHINY SHIPS SHIRE SHIRK SHIRR SHIRT SHISH SHIVA SHIVS SHOAH SHOAL SHOAT SHOCK SHOED SHOER SHOES SHOGI SHOJI SHONE SHOOK SHOOS SHOOT SHOPS SHORE SHORN SHORT SHOTS SHOUT SHOVE SHOWN SHOWS SHOWY SHRED SHREW SHRUB SHRUG SHUCK SHULA SHULS SHUNS SHUNT SHUSH SHUTE SHUTS SHYER SHYLY

S•H••
SAHEL SAHIB SCHAV SCHED SCHMO SCHON SCHWA SEHNA SOHIO

S••H•
SACHA SACHS SADHE SADHU SASHA SHAHN SHAHS SIDHE SIGHS SIGHT SIKHS SOCHI SOPHS SOPHY SOTHO SPAHI SPAHN STAHL SUSHI

S•••H
SABAH SANDH SARAH SELAH SHISH SHOAH SHUSH SIXTH SKOSH SLASH SLOSH SLOTH SLUSH SMASH SMITH SMYTH SNATH SOOTH SOUGH SOUTH STASH STICH SURAH SWASH SWATH SWISH SYLPH

•SH••
ASHBY ASHEN ASHER ASHES ASHUR OSHEA PSHAW USHED USHER

•S••H
PSYCH

••SH•
AISHA BASHO BUSHY

CUSHY DASHI FISHY GUSHY KASHA MASHY MESHY MISHA MOSHE MUSHY NASHE PASHA PUSHY RASHT RISHI RUSHY SASHA SUSHI WASHY WISHY WUSHU

••S•H

BOSCH BUSCH PASCH

•••SH

ABASH AMISH APISH AWASH BLUSH BRASH BRUSH CLASH CRASH CRUSH FLASH FLESH FLUSH FRESH FROSH GNASH HARSH IRISH KARSH KNISH LEASH MARSH NAISH PLASH PLUSH QUASH SHISH SHUSH SKOSH SLASH SLOSH SLUSH SMASH STASH SWASH SWISH TRASH TRISH WALSH WELSH

SI•••

SIALS SIBYL SIDEA SIDEB SIDED SIDER SIDES SIDHE SIDLE SIDON SIDRA SIEGE SIENA SIEPI SIETE SIEUR SIEVE SIFTS SIGHS SIGHT SIGIL SIGMA SIGNE SIGNO SIGNS SIKES SIKHS SILAS SILEX SILKS SILKY SILLS SILLY SILOS SILTS SILTY SILVA SIMBA SIMMS SIMON SIMPS SINAI SINCE SINES SINEW SINGE SINGS SINKS SINUS SIOUX SIRED SIREN SIRES SISAL SISSY SITAR SITBY SITED SITES SITIN SITKA SITON SITUP SITUS SIVAN SIXED SIXES SIXMO SIXTH SIXTY SIZED SIZER SIZES

S•I••

SAIGA SAILS SAINT SCIFI SCION SEIKO SEINE SEISM SEIZE SHIED SHIER SHIES SHIFT SHILL SHIMS SHINE SHINS SHINY SHIPS SHIRE SHIRK SHIRR SHIRT SHISH SHIVA SHIVS SKIDS SKIED SKIER SKIES SKIFF SKILL SKIMP SKIMS SKINK SKINS SKINT SKIPS SKIRL SKIRR SKIRT SKITS SKIVE SLICE SLICK SLIDE SLIER SLIGO SLIME SLIMS SLIMY SLING SLINK SLIPS SLITS SLIWA SMILE SMIRK SMITE SMITH SMITS SNICK SNIDE SNIFF SNIPE SNIPS SNITS SOILS SPICA SPICE SPICY SPIED SPIEL SPIES SPIFF SPIKE SPIKY SPILE SPILL SPILT SPINE SPINS SPINY SPIRE SPIRO SPITE SPITS SPITZ SPIVS STICH STICK STIES STIFF STILE STILL STILT STING STINK STINT STIPE STIRS SUING SUINT SUITE SUITS SWIFT SWIGS SWILL SWIMS SWINE SWING SWIPE SWIRL SWISH SWISS SWITZ

S••I•

SABIN SADIE SAHIB SALIC SAPID SAPIR SARIS SATIE SATIN SAWIN SCRIM SCRIP SEEIN SEMIS SEPIA SERIF SERIN SETIN SHEIK SIGIL SITIN SKEIN SLAIN SNAIL SOBIG SOCIO SOFIA SOHIO SOLID SONIA SONIC SPAIN SPLIT SPOIL SPRIG SPRIT SQUIB SQUID STAID STAIN STAIR STEIN STOIC STRIA STRIP SUBIC SUFIS SUSIE SWAIN SYBIL SYRIA

S•••I

SALMI SAUDI SCIFI SCUDI SEGNI SERAI SHARI SHOGI SHOJI SIEPI SINAI SOCHI SOLDI SOLTI SOMNI SPAHI SPYRI STYLI SULCI SUNNI SUOMI SUSHI SWAMI SWAZI

•SI••

ASIAN ASIDE BSIDE OSIER USING VSIGN

•S•I•

ASCII ASDIC ASPIC ASTIN ASTIR FSLIC GSUIT ISTIC OSLIN OSMIC OSRIC OSSIA OSSIE OSTIA USAIR

•S••I

ASCII ASSAI ISSEI

••SI•

AESIR AHSIN APSIS ARSIS BASIC BASIE BASIL BASIN BASIS CASIO ELSIE EOSIN FUSIL HASID JOSIP LYSIN MESIC MUSIC MYSIN NOSIR OASIS OPSIN OPSIS OSSIA OSSIE POSIT RESIN ROSIE ROSIN SUSIE URSID VISIT YASIR

••S•I

ASSAI AUSSI BASSI CESTI DASHI HOSNI ISSEI MASAI MISTI NISEI PESCI PISCI RISHI ROSSI SUSHI

•••SI

AUSSI BASSI DORSI FARSI ICOSI PEPSI PHYSI QUASI ROSSI TARSI TORSI

S•J••

SAJAK

S••J•

SHOJI SONJA

SK•••

SKALD SKATE SKEAN SKEAT SKEET SKEGS SKEIN SKEPS SKETE SKEWS SKIDS SKIED SKIER SKIES SKIFF SKILL SKIMP SKIMS SKINK SKINS SKINT SKIPS SKIRL SKIRR SKIRT SKITS SKIVE SKOAL SKODA SKOSH SKUAS SKULK SKULL SKUNK

S•K••

SAKER SAKES SIKES SIKHS

S••K•

SACKS SANKA SAUKS SEEKS SEIKO SHAKE SHAKO SHAKY SILKS SILKY SINKS SITKA SLAKE SMOKE SMOKY SNAKE SNAKY SOAKS SOCKO SOCKS SPAKE SPEKE SPIKE SPIKY SPOKE STAKE STOKE STUKA SUCKS SULKS SULKY

S•••K

SAJAK SHACK SHANK SHARK SHEIK SHIRK SHOCK SHOOK SHUCK SKINK SKULK SKUNK SLACK SLEEK SLICK SLINK SLUNK SMACK SMIRK SMOCK SNACK SNARK SNEAK SNICK SNOOK SNUCK SPAAK SPANK SPARK SPEAK SPECK SPOCK SPOOK SPORK SPUNK STACK STALK STANK STARK STEAK STICK STINK STOCK STORK STUCK STUNK SWANK

•SK••

ASKED ASKER ASKEW ESKER OSKAR

•S•K•

ASOKA OSAKA

••SK•

BASKS BOSKS BOSKY CASKS CUSKS DESKS DISKS DUSKS DUSKY ENSKY FISKE HUSKS HUSKY KISKA MASKS MUSKS MUSKY PESKY RISKS RISKY RUSKS TASKS TUSKS

•••SK

BRISK FLASK FRISK KIOSK KURSK MINSK PINSK WHISK

SL•••

SLABS SLACK SLADE SLAGS SLAIN SLAKE SLAMS SLANG SLANT SLAPS SLASH SLATE SLATS SLATY SLAVE SLAVS SLAWS SLAYS SLEDS SLEEK SLEEP SLEET SLEPT SLEWS SLICE SLICK SLIDE SLIER SLIGO SLIME SLIMS SLIMY SLING SLINK SLIPS SLITS SLIWA SLOAN SLOBS SLOES SLOGS SLOMO SLOOP SLOPE SLOPS SLOSH SLOTH SLOTS SLOWS SLOYD SLUED SLUES SLUGS SLUMP SLUMS SLUNG SLUNK SLURP SLURS SLUSH SLYER SLYLY SLYPE

S•L••

SALAD SALAL SALAM SALEM SALEP SALES SALIC SALLE SALLY SALMI SALON SALPA SALPS SALSA SALTA SALTS SALTY SALUD SALUT SALVE SALVO SELAH SELES SELLS SELMA SELVA SILAS SILEX SILKS SILKY SILLS SILLY SILOS SILTS SILTY SILVA SOLAN SOLAR SOLDI SOLDO SOLED SOLER SOLES SOLFA SOLID SOLON SOLOS SOLTI SOLUM SOLUS SOLVE SPLAT SPLAY SPLIT SULCI SULFA SULKS SULKY SULLA SULLY SYLPH

S••L•

SABLE SADLY SAILS SALLE SALLY SAULT SCALA SCALD SCALE SCALP SCALY SCOLD SCULL SEALE SEALS SEALY SEELS SELLS SEULE SHALE SHALL SHALT SHELF SHELL SHILL SHULA SHULS SHYLY SIALS SIDLE SILLS SILLY SKALD SKILL SKULK SKULL SLYLY SMALL SMALT SMELL SMELT SMILE SMOLT SNELL SOCLE SOILS SOULS SOULT SPALL SPELL SPELT SPILE SPILL SPILT STALE STALK STALL STELA STELE STILE STILL STILT STOLA STOLE STOLS STULL STYLE STYLI STYLO SULLA SULLY SURLY SWALE SWELL SWILL SZELL SZOLD

S•••L

SAGAL SAHEL SALAL SANDL SCOWL SCULL SEGAL SEOUL SEPAL SHALL SHAWL SHELL SHILL SHOAL SIBYL SIGIL SISAL SKILL SKIRL SKOAL SKULL SMALL SMELL SNAIL SNARL SNELL SOREL SOTOL SPALL SPELL SPIEL SPILL SPOIL SPOOL STAEL STAHL STALL STEAL STEEL STILL STOOL STULL SURAL SWELL SWILL SWIRL SYBIL SZELL

•SL••

FSLIC ISLAM ISLES ISLET ISLEY OSLER OSLIN USLTA

•S•L•

ASYLA ISTLE PSALM

•S••L

USUAL

••SL•

AISLE LISLE TESLA

••S•L

ANSEL BASAL BASEL BASIL EASEL EDSEL FUSIL HOSEL LYSOL MOSUL NASAL OUSEL SISAL

SM•••

SMACK SMALL SMALT SMART SMASH SMAZE SMEAR SMELL SMELT SMEWS SMILE SMIRK SMITE SMITH SMITS SMOCK SMOGS SMOKE SMOKY SMOLT SMOOT SMOTE SMURF SMUTS SMYTH

S•M••

SAMAR SAMBA SAMMS SAMMY SAMOA SAMOS SAMPS SEMIS SIMBA SIMMS SIMON SIMPS SOMAS SOMME SOMNI SUMAC SUMBA SUMER SUMMA SUMPS SUMUP

S••M•

SALMI SAMMS SAMMY SCAMP SCAMS SCHMO SCUMS SEAMS SEAMY SEEMS SELMA SHAME SHAMS SHAMU SHEMP SHIMS SIGMA SIMMS SIXMO SKIMP SKIMS SLAMS SLIME SLIMS SLIMY SLOMO SLUMP SLUMS SOMME SPUME SPUMY STAMP STEMS STOMA STOMP STUMP STUMS SUEME SUMMA SUOMI SWAMI SWAMP SWIMS

S•••M

SALAM SALEM SCRAM SCRIM SCRUM SEBUM SEDUM SEISM SERUM SHAWM SODOM SOLUM SPASM STEAM STORM STROM STRUM STURM SWARM

•SM••

OSMAN OSMIC

•S•M•

ASAMA ISAMU

•S••M

ASSAM ISLAM PSALM

••SM•

COSMO DISME ITSME PISMO

••S•M

AKSUM ASSAM BESOM BOSOM EPSOM KASEM

•••SM

ABYSM CHASM DEISM PLASM PRISM SEISM SPASM

SN•••

SNACK SNAFU SNAGS SNAIL SNAKE SNAKY SNAPS SNARE SNARK SNARL SNATH SNEAD SNEAK SNEED SNEER SNELL SNERD SNERT SNEVA SNICK SNIDE SNIFF SNIPE SNIPS SNITS SNOBS SNOOD SNOOK SNOOP SNOOT SNORE SNORT SNOUT SNOWS SNOWY SNUBS SNUCK SNUFF SNUGS

S•N••

SANAA SANDH SANDL SANDS SANDY SANER SANKA SANTA SANTE SANTO SANYO SENDS SENNA SENOR SENSE SINAI SINCE SINES SINEW SINGE SINGS SINKS SINUS SONAR SONDE SONES SONGS SONIA SONIC SONJA SONNY SONYA SUNDA SUNNA SUNNI SUNNY SUNUP SYNCS SYNGE SYNOD

S••N•

SAENS SAINT SAONE SAUNA SCAND SCANS SCANT SCENA SCEND SCENE SCENT SCONE SEGNI SEGNO SEHNA SEINE SENNA SHANA SHANE SHANK SHANS SHANT SHINE SHINS SHINY SHONE SHUNS SHUNT SIENA SIGNE SIGNO SIGNS SKINK SKINS SKINT SKUNK SLANG SLANT SLING SLINK SLUNG SLUNK SOMNI SONNY SOONG SOUND SPANG SPANK SPANS SPEND SPENT SPINE SPINS SPINY SPUNK STAND STANG STANK STENO STENS STING STINK STINT STONE STONY STUNG STUNK STUNS STUNT STYNE SUING SUINT SUNNA SUNNI SUNNY SWANK SWANN SWANS SWINE SWING SWUNG

S•••N

SABIN SAGAN SALON SARAN SATAN SATIN SATON SAWIN SAXON SCHON SCION SCORN SEDAN SEEIN SERIN SETIN SETON SEVEN SEWON SHAHN SHAUN SHAWN SHEAN SHEEN SHORN SHOWN SIDON SIMON SIREN SITIN SITON SIVAN

SKEAN SKEIN SLAIN SLOAN SOLAN SOLON SOREN SPAHN SPAIN SPAWN SPOON SPURN SPYON STAIN STEEN STEIN STERN SUDAN SUSAN SWAIN SWANN SWOON SWORN

•SN••
ASNER ESNES

•S•N•
ASANA ASONE ASSNS USING

•S••N
ASHEN ASIAN ASPEN ASTIN ASTON ASWAN ESSEN OSCAN OSLIN OSMAN VSIGN

••SN•
AISNE ASSNS BOSNS DESNA HASNT HOSNI MESNE WASNT

••S•N
AHSIN ANSON ARSON BASIN BISON EBSEN EOSIN EPSON ESSEN HASON HYSON IBSEN JASON LYSIN MASON MESON MYSIN NISAN OLSEN OLSON OPSIN ORSON PISAN PUSAN RESIN RISEN ROSEN ROSIN SUSAN TYSON

SO•••
SOAKS SOAPS SOAPY SOARS SOAVE SOBER SOBIG SOCHI SOCIO SOCKO SOCKS SOCLE SODAS SODDY SODOM SOEUR SOFAR SOFAS SOFIA SOFTY SOGGY SOHIO SOILS SOLAN SOLAR SOLDI SOLDO SOLED SOLER SOLES SOLFA SOLID SOLON SOLOS SOLTI SOLUM SOLUS SOLVE SOMAS SOMME SOMNI SONAR SONDE SONES SONGS SONIA SONIC SONJA SONNY SONYA SOOEY SOONG SOOTH SOOTS SOOTY SOPHS SOPHY SOPOR SOPPY SOPUP SORAS SORBS SOREL SOREN SORER SORES SORGO SORRY SORTA SORTS SORUS SOTHO SOTOL SOTTO SOUGH SOULS SOULT SOUND SOUPS SOUPY SOURS SOUSA SOUSE SOUTH SOWED SOWER SOXER SOYAS SOYUZ

S•O••
SAONE SCOFF SCOLD SCONE SCOOP SCOOT SCOPE SCOPS SCORE SCORN SCOTS SCOTT SCOUR SCOUT SCOWL SCOWS SEOUL SHOAH SHOAL SHOAT SHOCK SHOED SHOER SHOES SHOGI SHOJI SHONE SHOOK SHOOS SHOOT SHOPS SHORE SHORN SHORT SHOTS SHOUT SHOVE SHOWN SHOWS SHOWY SIOUX SKOAL SKODA SKOSH SLOAN SLOBS SLOES SLOGS SLOMO SLOOP SLOPE SLOPS SLOSH SLOTH SLOTS SLOWS SLOYD SMOCK SMOGS SMOKE SMOKY SMOLT SMOOT SMOTE SNOBS SNOOD SNOOK SNOOP SNOOT SNORE SNORT SNOUT SNOWS SNOWY SOOEY SOONG SOOTH SOOTS SOOTY SPOCK SPODE SPOIL SPOKE SPOOF SPOOK SPOOL SPOON SPOOR SPORE SPORK SPORT SPOTS SPOUT STOAE STOAS STOAT STOCK STOGY STOIC STOKE STOLA STOLE STOLS STOMA STOMP STONE STONY STOOD STOOL STOOP STOPE STOPS STORE STORK STORM STORY STOSS STOTS STOUP STOUT STOVE STOWE STOWS SUOMI SWOON SWOOP SWOPE SWORD SWORE SWORN SZOLD

S••O•
SABOT SAGOS SALON SAMOA SAMOS SAPOR SAROD SAROS SATON SAVOR SAVOY SAXON SCHON SCION SCOOP SCOOT SCROD SEGOS SENOR SEPOY SEROW SETON SEWON SHOOK SHOOS SHOOT SIDON SILOS SIMON SITON SLOOP SMOOT SNOOD SNOOK SNOOP SNOOT SODOM SOLON SOLOS SOPOR SOTOL SPOOF SPOOK SPOOL SPOON SPOOR SPYON STOOD STOOL STOOP STROM STROP SWOON SWOOP SYDOW SYNOD SYSOP

S•••O
SACCO SACRO SALVO SANTO SANYO SARGO SARTO SAWTO SAYSO SCHMO SCUDO SEATO SECCO SEETO SEGNO SEIKO SERVO SETTO SHAKO SIGNO SIXMO SLIGO SLOMO SOCIO SOCKO SOHIO SOLDO SORGO SOTHO SOTTO SPIRO STENO STYLO

•SO••
ASOKA ASONE PSOAS XSOUT

•S•O•
ASCOT ASSOC ASTON ASTOR ESPOO ESTOP FSTOP MSDOS

•S••O
ASTRO ESPOO OSSEO OSTEO

••SO•
AESOP ALSOP ANSON APSOS ARSON ASSOC BASOV BESOM BESOT BISON BOSOM BOSOX ENSOR EPSOM EPSON HASON HYSON JASON LYSOL MASON MESON MISOS OLSON ORSON PESOS RESOD SYSOP TYSON VISOR

••S•O
BASHO BASSO BOSCO CASCO CASIO CISCO COSMO DISCO GESSO GUSTO HASSO HASTO LASSO MISDO MOSSO OSSEO PASCO PASEO PASTO PESTO PISCO PISMO RUSSO TASSO VASCO

•••SO
AVISO BASSO CANSO DORSO GESSO HASSO HOWSO HYPSO KELSO LASSO MOSSO NOTSO RATSO RINSO RUSSO SAYSO TASSO TORSO VERSO WHOSO

SP•••
SPAAK SPACE SPADE SPADS SPAHI SPAHN SPAIN SPAKE SPALL SPANG SPANK SPANS SPARE SPARK SPARS SPASM SPATE SPATS SPAWN SPAYS SPEAK SPEAR SPECK SPECS SPEED SPEKE SPELL SPELT SPEND SPENT SPETS SPEWS SPICA SPICE SPICY SPIED SPIEL SPIES SPIFF SPIKE SPIKY SPILE SPILL SPILT SPINE SPINS SPINY SPIRE SPIRO SPITE SPITS SPITZ SPIVS SPLAT SPLAY SPLIT SPOCK SPODE SPOIL SPOKE SPOOF SPOOK SPOOL SPOON SPOOR SPORE SPORK SPORT SPOTS SPOUT SPRAG SPRAT SPRAY SPREE SPRIG SPRIT SPRUE SPUDS SPUME SPUMY SPUNK SPURN SPURS SPURT SPYON SPYRI

S•P••
SAPID SAPIR SAPOR SAPPY SEPAL SEPIA SEPOY SEPTA SOPHS SOPHY SOPOR SOPPY SOPUP SUPER SUPRA SUPTS SUPVR

S••P•
SALPA SALPS SAMPS SAPPY SCAPA SCAPE SCOPE SCOPS SCUPS SEEPS SEEPY SHAPE SHIPS SHOPS SIEPI SIMPS SKEPS SKIPS SLAPS SLEPT SLIPS SLOPE SLOPS SLYPE SNAPS SNIPE SNIPS SOAPS SOAPY SOPPY SOUPS SOUPY STEPS STIPE STOPE STOPS STUPA SUMPS SWAPS SWEPT SWIPE SWOPE SYLPH

S•••P
SALEP SATUP SCALP SCAMP SCARP SCAUP SCOOP SCRAP SCRIP SETUP SEWUP SHARP SHEEP SHEMP SITUP SKIMP SLEEP SLOOP SLUMP SLURP SNOOP SOPUP STAMP STEEP STOMP STOOP STOUP STRAP STRIP STROP STUMP SUMUP SUNUP SWAMP SWEEP SWOOP SYRUP SYSOP

•SP••
ASPCA ASPEN ASPIC ESPOO

•S•P•
RSVPS

•S••P
ASCAP ESTOP FSTOP USEUP USURP

••SP•
CUSPS GASPE GASPS HASPS LISPS RASPS RASPY WASPS WISPS WISPY

••S•P
AESOP ALSOP GASUP JOSIP SYSOP

•••SP
AGASP CLASP CRISP GRASP

SQ•••
SQUAB SQUAD SQUAT SQUIB SQUID

•SQ••
ESQUE

••S•Q
ETSEQ

SR•••
SRTAS

S•R••
SARAH SARAN SARDS SARGE SARGO SARIS SAROD SAROS SARTO SCRAG SCRAM SCRAP SCREE SCREW SCRIM SCRIP SCROD SCRUB SCRUM SERAC SERAI SERBS SERES SERFS SERGE SERIF SERIN SEROW SERRA SERTA SERUM SERVE SERVO SHRED SHREW SHRUB SHRUG SIRED SIREN SIRES SORAS SORBS SOREL SOREN SORER SORES SORGO SORRY SORTA SORTS SORUS SPRAG SPRAT SPRAY SPREE SPRIG SPRIT SPRUE STRAD STRAP STRAW STRAY STREW STRIA STRIP STROM STROP STRUM STRUT SURAH SURAL SURAS SURAT SURDS SURER SURFS SURFY SURGE SURLY SYRIA SYRUP

S••R•
SABRA SABRE SACRA SACRE SACRO SCARE SCARF SCARP SCARS SCARY SCORE SCORN SCURF SEARS SEERS SERRA SHARD SHARE SHARI SHARK SHARP SHERE SHIRE SHIRK SHIRR SHIRT SHORE SHORN SHORT SIDRA SKIRL SKIRR SKIRT SLURP SLURS SMART SMIRK SMURF SNARE SNARK SNARL SNERD SNERT SNORE SNORT SOARS SORRY SOURS SPARE SPARK SPARS SPIRE SPIRO SPORE SPORK SPORT SPURN SPURS SPURT SPYRI STARE STARK STARR STARS START STERE STERN STIRS STORE STORK STORM STORY STURM SUCRE SUDRA SUERS SUPRA SUTRA SWARD SWARF SWARM SWART SWIRL SWORD SWORE SWORN

S•••R
SABER SAFER SAGER SAKER SAMAR SANER SAPIR SAPOR SATYR SAVER SAVOR SAYER SCOUR SEDER SEGAR SEGER SENOR SEVER SEWER SHEAR SHEER SHIER SHIRR SHOER SHYER SIDER SIEUR SITAR SIZER SKIER SKIRR SLIER SLYER SMEAR SNEER SOBER SOEUR SOFAR SOLAR SOLER SONAR SOPOR SORER SOWER SOXER SPEAR SPOOR STAIR STARR STEER SUGAR SUMER SUPER SUPVR SURER SWEAR

•SR••
OSRIC

•S•R•
ASTRA ASTRE ASTRO ISERE TSARS USERS USURP USURY

•S••R
ASHER ASHUR ASKER ASNER ASSUR ASSYR ASTER ASTIR ASTOR ESKER ESTER OSCAR OSIER OSKAR OSLER USAIR USHER

••SR•
BASRA

••S•R
AESIR ANSER ASSUR ASSYR AUSTR BASER CESAR DISTR DOSER ENSOR GASTR INSTR KYSER LASER LOSER MASER MASUR MISER MUSER NOSIR ORSER POSER RISER TASER UNSER VISOR WESER WISER YASIR

SS•••
SSGTS

S•S••
SASES SASHA SASSY SISAL SISSY SUSAN SUSHI SUSIE SUSUS SYSOP

S••S•
SALSA SASSY SAYSO SEISM SENSE SEUSS SHISH SHUSH SISSY SKOSH SLASH SLOSH SLUSH SMASH SOUSA SOUSE SPASM STASH STOSS SUDSY SWASH SWISH SWISS

S•••S
SAABS SACHS SACKS SAENS SAFES SAGAS SAGES SAGOS SAILS SAKES SALES SALPS SALTS SAMMS SAMOS SAMPS SANDS SARDS SARIS SAROS SASES SATES SAUKS SAVES SAXES SCABS SCADS SCAMS SCANS SCARS SCATS SCOPS SCOTS SCOWS SCUDS SCUMS SCUPS SCUTS SEALS SEAMS SEARS SEATS SECTS SEEDS SEEKS SEELS SEEMS SEEPS SEERS SEGOS SELES SELLS SEMIS SENDS SERBS SERES SERFS SEUSS SEXES SEXTS SHADS SHAGS SHAHS SHAMS SHANS SHAYS SHEDS SHIES SHIMS SHINS SHIPS SHIVS SHOES SHOOS SHOPS SHOTS SHOWS SHULS SHUNS SHUTS SIALS SIDES SIFTS SIGHS SIGNS SIKES SIKHS SILAS SILKS SILLS SILOS SILTS SIMMS SIMPS SINES SINGS SINKS SINUS SIRES SITES SITUS SIXES SIZES SKEGS SKEPS SKEWS SKIDS SKIES SKIMS SKINS SKIPS SKITS SKUAS SLABS SLAGS SLAMS SLAPS SLATS SLAVS SLAWS SLAYS SLEDS SLEWS SLIMS SLIPS SLITS SLOBS SLOES SLOGS SLOPS SLOTS SLOWS SLUES SLUGS SLUMS SLURS SMEWS SMITS SMOGS SMUTS SNAGS SNAPS SNIPS SNITS SNOBS SNOWS SNUBS SNUGS SOAKS SOAPS SOARS SOCKS SODAS SOFAS SOILS SOLES SOLOS SOLUS SOMAS SONES SONGS SOOTS SOPHS SORAS

SORBS SORES SORTS SORUS SOULS SOUPS SOURS SOYAS SPADS SPANS SPARS SPATS SPAYS SPECS SPETS SPEWS SPIES SPINS SPITS SPIVS SPOTS SPUDS SPURS SRTAS SSGTS STABS STAGS STARS STATS STAYS STEMS STENS STEPS STETS STEWS STIES STIRS STOAS STOLS STOPS STOSS STOTS STOWS STUBS STUDS STUMS STUNS SUCKS SUDDS SUERS SUETS SUFIS SUITS SULKS SUMPS SUPTS SURAS SURDS SURFS SUSUS SWABS SWAGS SWANS SWAPS SWATS SWAYS SWIGS SWIMS SWISS SYCES SYNCS

•SS••

ASSAD ASSAI ASSAM ASSAY ASSES ASSET ASSEZ ASSNS ASSOC ASSTD ASSTS ASSUR ASSYR ESSAY ESSEN ESSES ESSEX ISSEI ISSUE ISSUS OSSEO OSSIA OSSIE

•S••S

ASCUS ASHES ASSES ASSNS ASSTS ESNES ESSES ESTES ISLES ISSUS MSDOS MSGTS PSATS PSOAS RSVPS SSGTS TSARS TSGTS USERS

••SS•

AUSSI BASSI BASSO BOSSA BOSSY CISSY FOSSA FOSSE FUSSY GASSY GESSO GOSSE GUSSY HASSO HESSE HISSY HUSSY JESSE LASSO LISSE MASSE MASSY MESSY MISSA MISSY MOSSO MOSSY MUSSY PASSE PASSU PASSY POSSE PUSSY ROSSI RUSSE RUSSO SASSY SISSY TASSE TASSO

••S•S

APSES APSIS APSOS ARSIS ASSES ASSNS ASSTS BASES BASIS BASKS BESTS BISES BOSCS BOSKS BOSNS BUSES BUSTS CASES CASKS CASTS CASUS COSTS CUSKS CUSPS DESKS DISCS DISKS DOSES DUSKS DUSTS EASES EASTS ESSES FASTS FESTS FISCS FISTS FUSES GASES GASPS GESTS GISTS GUSTS HASPS HESTS HOSES HOSTS HUSKS INSTS ISSUS JESTS LASES LASTS LISPS LISTS LOSES LUSTS MASKS MASTS MESAS MISOS MISTS MOSES MUSES MUSKS MUSTS NESTS NISUS NOSES OASES OASIS OASTS OPSIS OUSTS PASES PASTS PESOS PESTS POSES POSTS RASES RASPS RESTS RISES RISKS ROSES RUSES RUSKS RUSTS SASES SUSUS TASKS TESTS TUSKS VASES VESTS VISAS VISES WASPS WISPS YESES ZESTS

•••SS

ABYSS AMASS AMISS BLASS BLESS BLISS BRASS CHESS CLASS CRASS CRESS CRISS CROSS DRESS DROSS FLOSS GAUSS GLASS GLESS GLOSS GRASS GROSS GUESS HEISS IPASS KRISS KVASS LOESS PRESS SEUSS STOSS SWISS TRESS TRUSS WEISS ZEISS

ST•••

STABS STACK STACY STADT STAEL STAFF STAGE STAGG STAGS STAGY STAHL STAID STAIN STAIR STAKE STALE STALK STALL STAMP STAND STANG STANK STARE STARK STARR STARS START STASH STATE STATS STAVE STAYS STEAD STEAK STEAL STEAM STEED STEEL STEEN STEEP STEER STEIN STELA STELE STEMS STENO STENS STEPS STERE STERN STETS STEVE STEWS STICH STICK STIES STIFF STILE STILL STILT STING STINK STINT STIPE STIRS STOAE STOAS STOAT STOCK STOGY STOIC STOKE STOLA STOLE STOLS STOMA STOMP STONE STONY STOOD STOOL STOOP STOPE STOPS STORE STORK STORM STORY STOSS STOTS STOUP STOUT STOVE STOWE STOWS STRAD STRAP STRAW STRAY STREW STRIA STRIP STROM STROP STRUM STRUT STUBS STUCK STUDS STUDY STUFF STUKA STULL STUMP STUMS STUNG STUNK STUNS STUNT STUPA STURM STUTZ STYLE STYLI STYLO STYNE

S•T••

SATAN SATBY SATED SATES SATIE SATIN SATON SATUP SATYR SETAE SETAT SETBY SETIN SETON SETTO SETUP SITAR SITBY SITED SITES SITIN SITKA SITON SITUP SITUS SOTHO SOTOL SOTTO SRTAS SUTRA

S••T•

SALTA SALTS SALTY SANTA SANTE SANTO SARTO SAUTE SAWTO SCATS SCOTS SCOTT SCUTA SCUTE SCUTS SEATO SEATS SECTS SEETO SEPTA SERTA SETTO SEXTS SHOTS SHUTE SHUTS SIETE SIFTS SILTS SILTY SIXTH SIXTY SKATE SKETE SKITS SLATE SLATS SLATY SLITS SLOTH SLOTS SMITE SMITH SMITS SMOTE SMUTS SMYTH SNATH SNITS SOFTY SOLTI SOOTH SOOTS SOOTY SORTA SORTS SOTTO SOUTH SPATE SPATS SPETS SPITE SPITS SPITZ SPOTS SSGTS STATE STATS STETS STOTS STUTZ SUETS SUITE SUITS SUPTS SWATH SWATS SWITZ

S•••T

SABOT SADAT SAGET SAINT SALUT SAULT SCANT SCENT SCOOT SCOTT SCOUT SETAT SHAFT SHALT SHANT SHEET SHIFT SHIRT SHOAT SHOOT SHORT SHOUT SHUNT SIGHT SKEAT SKEET SKINT SKIRT SLANT SLEET SLEPT SMALT SMART SMELT SMOLT SMOOT SNERT SNOOT SNORT SNOUT SOULT SPELT SPENT SPILT SPLAT SPLIT SPORT SPOUT SPRAT SPRIT SPURT SQUAT STADT START STILT STINT STOAT STOUT STRUT STUNT SUINT SURAT SWART SWEAT SWEET SWEPT SWIFT

•ST••

ASTER ASTIN ASTIR ASTON ASTOR ASTRA ASTRE ASTRO ESTAB ESTEE ESTER ESTES ESTOP FSTOP ISTIC ISTLE OSTEO OSTIA USTED

•S•T•

ASSTD ASSTS MSGTS PSATS SSGTS TSGTS USLTA

•S••T

ASCOT ASSET ASYET ESBAT GSUIT ISLET XSOUT

••ST•

ASSTD ASSTS AUSTR BASTE BESTS BUSTS CASTE CASTS CBSTV CESTA CESTI COSTA COSTS DISTR DUSTS DUSTY EASTS FASTS FESTA FESTS FISTS FUSTY GASTR GESTE GESTS GISTS GUSTO GUSTS GUSTY HASTA HASTE HASTO HASTY HESTS HOSTA HOSTS INSTR INSTS JESTS JUSTE LASTS LISTS LUSTS LUSTY MASTS MESTA MISTI MISTS MISTY MUSTS MUSTY NASTY NESTS OASTS OUSTS PASTA PASTE PASTO PASTS PASTY PESTO PESTS PISTE POSTE POSTS RASTA RESTS RUSTS RUSTY TASTE TASTY TESTA TESTS TESTY VESTA VESTS VISTA WASTE ZESTS ZESTY

••S•T

ASSET BESET BESOT HASAT HASNT INSET LISZT ONSET POSIT RASHT RESET TVSET UNSET UPSET VISIT WASNT

•••ST

ADUST ALIST ANGST AVAST BAKST BEAST BLAST BLEST BOAST BOOST BREST BURST CANST CHEST COAST CREST CRIST CRUST CURST DEIST DIDST DOEST DURST EGEST ERNST EXIST FAUST FEAST FEIST FIRST FOIST FROST GHOST GOEST GRIST GUEST HADST HEIST HOIST HOLST HORST HURST IDEST JOIST JOUST LEAST MAYST MIDST MOIST ODIST PABST PROST QUEST ROAST ROOST ROUST TOAST TRUST TRYST TWIST VERST WAIST WEEST WHIST WIEST WORST WREST WRIST WURST YEAST ZEIST

SU•••

SUAVE SUBIC SUCKS SUCRE SUDAN SUDDS SUDRA SUDSY SUEDE SUEME SUERS SUETS SUFIS SUGAR SUING SUINT SUITE SUITS SULCI SULFA SULKS SULKY SULLA SULLY SUMAC SUMBA SUMER SUMMA SUMPS SUMUP SUNDA SUNNA SUNNI SUNNY SUNUP SUOMI SUPER SUPRA SUPTS SUPVR SURAH SURAL SURAS SURAT SURDS SURER SURFS SURFY SURGE SURLY SUSAN SUSHI SUSIE SUSUS SUTRA

S•U••

SAUCE SAUCY SAUDI SAUKS SAULT SAUNA SAUTE SCUBA SCUDI SCUDO SCUDS SCUFF SCULL SCUMS SCUPS SCURF SCUTA SCUTE SCUTS SEULE SEUSS SHUCK SHULA SHULS SHUNS SHUNT SHUSH SHUTE SHUTS SKUAS SKULK SKULL SKUNK SLUED SLUES SLUGS SLUMP SLUMS SLUNG SLUNK SLURP SLURS SLUSH SMURF SMUTS SNUBS SNUCK SNUFF SNUGS SOUGH SOULS SOULT SOUND SOUPS SOUPY SOURS SOUSA SOUSE SOUTH SPUDS SPUME SPUMY SPUNK SPURN SPURS SPURT SQUAB SQUAD SQUAT SQUIB SQUID STUBS STUCK STUDS STUDY STUFF STUKA STULL STUMP STUMS STUNG STUNK STUNS STUNT STUPA STURM STUTZ SWUNG

S••U•

SALUD SALUT SATUP SCAUP SCOUR SCOUT SCRUB SCRUM SEBUM SEDUM SEGUE SEOUL SERUM SETUP SEWUP SHAUN SHOUT SHRUB SHRUG SIEUR SINUS SIOUX SITUP SITUS SNOUT SOEUR SOLUM SOLUS SOPUP SORUS SOYUZ SPOUT SPRUE STOUP STOUT STRUM STRUT SUMUP SUNUP SUSUS SYRUP

S•••U

SADHU SHAMU SNAFU

•SU••

GSUIT ISUZU USUAL USURP USURY

•S•U•

ASCUS ASHUR ASSUR ESQUE ISSUE ISSUS PSEUD USEUP XSOUT

•S••U

ISAMU ISUZU

••SU•

AKSUM ASSUR CASUS ENSUE GASUP ISSUE ISSUS MASUR MOSUL NISUS SUSUS

••S•U

PASSU WUSHU

•••SU

MATSU PASSU

S•V••

SAVED SAVER SAVES SAVOR SAVOY SAVVY SEVEN SEVER SIVAN

S••V•

SALVE SALVO SAVVY SELVA SERVE SERVO SHAVE SHIVA SHIVS SHOVE SIEVE SILVA SKIVE SLAVE SLAVS SNEVA SOAVE SOLVE SPIVS STAVE STEVE STOVE SUAVE SUPVR

S•••V

SCHAV

•SV••

RSVPS

••S•V

BASOV CBSTV

SW•••

SWABS SWAGE SWAGS SWAIN SWALE SWAMI SWAMP SWANK SWANN SWANS SWAPS SWARD SWARF SWARM SWART SWASH SWATH SWATS SWAYS SWAZI SWEAR SWEAT SWEDE SWEEP SWEET SWELL SWEPT SWIFT SWIGS SWILL SWIMS SWINE SWING SWIPE SWIRL SWISH SWISS SWITZ SWOON SWOOP SWOPE SWORD SWORE SWORN SWUNG

S•W••

SAWED SAWIN SAWTO SEWED SEWER SEWON SEWUP SOWED SOWER

S••W•

SCHWA SCOWL SCOWS SHAWL SHAWM SHAWN SHOWN SHOWS SHOWY SKEWS SLAWS SLEWS SLIWA SLOWS SMEWS SNOWS SNOWY SPAWN SPEWS STEWS STOWE STOWS

S•••W

SCREW SEROW SHREW SINEW STRAW STREW SYDOW

•SW••

ASWAN

•S••W

ASKEW PSHAW

••S•W

RESEW

S•X••

SAXES SAXON SEXES SEXTS SIXED SIXES SIXMO SIXTH SIXTY SOXER

S•••X

SILEX SIOUX

•S••X

ESSEX

••S•X

BOSOX ESSEX

SY•••

SYBIL SYCEE SYCES SYDOW SYLPH SYNCS SYNGE SYNOD SYRIA SYRUP SYSOP

S•Y••

SAYER SAYSO SHYER SHYLY SLYER SLYLY SLYPE SMYTH SOYAS SOYUZ SPYON SPYRI

STYLE
STYLI
STYLO
STYNE

S••Y•
SANYO
SATYR
SEEYA
SHAYS
SIBYL
SLAYS
SLOYD
SONYA
SPAYS
STAYS
SWAYS

S•••Y
SADLY
SAGGY
SALLY
SALTY
SAMMY
SANDY
SAPPY
SASSY
SATBY
SAUCY
SAVOY
SAVVY
SCALY
SCARY
SEALY
SEAMY
SEEDY
SEEPY
SEPOY
SETBY
SHADY
SHAKY
SHINY
SHOWY
SHYLY
SILKY
SILLY
SILTY
SISSY
SITBY
SIXTY
SLATY
SLIMY
SLYLY
SMOKY
SNAKY
SNOWY
SOAPY
SODDY
SOFTY
SOGGY
SONNY
SOOEY
SOOTY
SOPHY
SOPPY
SORRY
SOUPY
SPICY
SPIKY
SPINY
SPLAY
SPRAY
SPUMY
STACY
STAGY
STOGY
STONY
STORY
STRAY
STUDY
SUDSY
SULKY
SULLY
SUNNY
SURFY
SURLY

•SY••
ASYET
ASYLA
PSYCH

•S•Y•
ASSYR

•S••Y
ASHBY
ASSAY
ESSAY
ISLEY
USURY

••SY•
ASSYR

••S•Y
ASSAY
BOSKY
BOSSY
BUSBY
BUSEY
BUSHY
CASEY
CISSY
COSBY
CUSHY
DUSKY
DUSTY
ENSKY
ESSAY
FISHY
FUSSY
FUSTY
GASSY
GUSHY
GUSSY
GUSTY
HASTY
HISSY
HUSKY
HUSSY
KESEY
LUSTY
MASHY
MASSY
MESHY
MESSY
MISSY
MISTY
MOSBY
MOSEY
MOSSY
MUSHY
MUSKY
MUSSY
MUSTY
NASBY
NASTY
PASSY
PASTY
PESKY
PUSEY
PUSHY
PUSSY
RASPY
RISKY
ROSEY
RUSHY
RUSTY
SASSY
SISSY
TASTY
TESTY
UNSAY
VESEY
WASHY
WISHY
WISPY
ZESTY

•••SY
ANTSY
ARTSY
BETSY
BITSY
BOSSY
BUGSY
CISSY
COUSY
DAISY
DITSY
FUBSY
FUSSY
GASSY
GIPSY
GOOSY
GUSSY
GUTSY
GYPSY
HISSY
HORSY
HUSSY
LOUSY
MASSY
MESSY
MIMSY
MISSY
MOPSY
MOSSY
MOUSY
MUSSY
NEWSY
NOISY
PALSY
PANSY
PASSY
PATSY
POESY
POTSY
PROSY
PURSY
PUSSY
SASSY
SISSY
SUDSY
TANSY
TIPSY
TOPSY
WALSY

SZ•••
SZELL
SZOLD

S•Z••
SIZED
SIZER
SIZES

S••Z•
SEIZE
SMAZE
SWAZI

S•••Z
SOYUZ
SPITZ
STUTZ
SWITZ

•S•Z•
ISUZU

•S••Z
ASSEZ

••SZ•
LISZT

••S•Z
ASSEZ

•••SZ
GROSZ

TA•••
TABBY
TABIS
TABLA
TABLE
TABOO
TABOR
TACET
TACIT
TACKS
TACKY
TACOS
TAEGU
TAELS
TAFFY
TAGUP
TAGUS
TAHOE
TAHRS
TAIGA
TAILS
TAINE
TAINT
TAKEI
TAKEN
TAKER
TAKES
TAKIN
TALER
TALES
TALIA
TALKS
TALKY
TALLY
TALON
TALUS
TAMBO
TAMED
TAMER
TAMES
TAMIL
TAMMY
TAMPA
TAMPS
TANDY
TANEY
TANGO
TANGS
TANGY
TANKA
TANKS
TANSY
TANTE
TANYA
TAPAS
TAPED
TAPER
TAPES
TAPIN
TAPIR
TARDE
TARDY
TARES
TARGE
TARNS
TAROK
TAROT
TARPS
TARRY
TARSI
TARTS
TASER
TASKS
TASSE
TASSO
TASTE
TASTY
TATAR
TATER
TATRA
TATTY
TATUM
TAUNT
TAUON
TAUPE
TAWNY
TAXCO
TAXED
TAXER
TAXES
TAXIS
TAXON
TAYRA
TAZZA

T•A••
TBARS
TEACH
TEAKS
TEALS
TEAMS
TEARS
TEARY
TEASE
THAIS
THANE
THANK
THANT
THARP
THATS
THAWS
TIANT
TIARA
TOADS
TOADY
TOAST
TRACE
TRACK
TRACT
TRACY
TRADE
TRAIL
TRAIN
TRAIT
TRALA
TRAMP
TRAMS
TRANS
TRAPP
TRAPS
TRASH
TRAVE
TRAWL
TRAYS
TSADE
TSARS
TWAIN
TWANG

T••A•
TAPAS
TATAR
TEPAL
TEXAN
TEXAS
TIDAL
TIKAL
TIRAN
TITAN
TODAY
TOGAS
TOKAY
TONAL
TOPAZ
TORAH
TOTAL
TREAD
TREAT
TRIAD
TRIAL
TUBAS
TUNAS
TWEAK
TYNAN

T•••A
TABLA
TAIGA
TALIA
TAMPA
TANKA
TANYA
TATRA
TAYRA
TAZZA
TEENA
TERRA
TERZA
TESLA
TESTA
TETRA
THECA
THEDA
THEMA
THERA
THETA
THUJA
TIARA
TIBIA
TONGA
TONKA
TONYA
TOSCA
TRALA
TULSA
TWYLA
TYPEA

•TA••
ATALL
ATARI
ETAGE
ETAPE
ITALO
ITALS
ITALY
OTARU
OTARY
STABS
STACK
STACY
STADT
STAEL
STAFF
STAGE
STAGG
STAGS
STAGY
STAHL
STAID
STAIN
STAIR
STAKE
STALE
STALK
STALL
STAMP
STAND
STANG
STANK
STARE
STARK
STARR
STARS
START
STASH
STATE
STATS
STAVE
STAYS
UTAHN

•T•A•
ATBAT
ATBAY
ATEAM
ATLAS
ATMAN
ATPAR
ATTAR
ATWAR
ETHAN
ETNAS
OTWAY
PTRAP
STEAD
STEAK
STEAL
STEAM
STOAE
STOAS
STOAT
STRAD
STRAP
STRAW
STRAY

•T••A
ATRIA
ATSEA
ETYMA
STELA
STOLA
STOMA
STRIA
STUKA
STUPA
UTICA

••TA•
AETAT
ALTAI
ALTAR
ANTAE
ANTAL
ANTAS
ARTAL
ATTAR
BATAK
BETAS
DETAT
DOTAL
EATAT
ESTAB
FATAL
FETAL
FETAS
GETAS
GETAT
GOTAT
IOTAS
JOTAS
LETAT
LOTAS
METAL
NATAL
OCTAD
OCTAL
ONTAP
PETAL
PITAS
QATAR
RETAG
RETAP
RETAR
RETAX
ROTAS
SATAN
SETAE
SETAT
SITAR
SRTAS
TATAR
TITAN
TOTAL
VITAE
VITAL
VITAS
WOTAN
ZETAS

••T•A
AETNA
AFTRA
ANTRA
ASTRA
BETTA
BOTHA
COTTA
DITKA
ENTIA
EXTRA
FATHA
GOTHA
GOTTA
GUTTA
INTRA
LOTTA
LYTTA
MOTTA
OSTIA
PATNA
PETRA
PITTA
RETIA
SITKA
SUTRA
TATRA
TETRA
ULTRA

•••TA
ADYTA
AGITA
AKITA
ALETA
ANITA
AORTA
BETTA
BIOTA
CARTA
CESTA
CEUTA
CHITA
COSTA
COTTA
DELTA
DICTA
EVITA
FANTA
FESTA
GOTTA
GRATA
GRETA
GUTTA
HASTA
HEPTA
HOSTA
JUNTA
LEPTA
LOTTA
LYTTA
MALTA
MANTA
MARTA
MEHTA
MESTA
MOTTA
NAFTA
OVETA
PASTA
PENTA
PIETA
PINTA
PITTA
PLATA
PUNTA
QUOTA
RASTA
REATA
RENTA
RIATA
SALTA
SANTA
SCUTA
SEPTA
SERTA
SORTA
TESTA
THETA
UINTA
USLTA
VESTA
VISTA
VOLTA
YALTA
YENTA

TB•••
TBARS
TBILL
TBIRD
TBOND
TBONE

T•B••
TABBY
TABIS
TABLA
TABLE
TABOO
TABOR
TIBBS
TIBER
TIBET
TIBIA
TOBEY
TOBIT
TUBAS
TUBBY
TUBED
TUBER
TUBES

T••B•
TABBY
TAMBO
THEBE
TIBBS
TRIBE
TUBBY
TURBO

T•••B
THROB
THUMB
TYPEB

•TB••
ATBAT
ATBAY

•T•B•
STABS
STUBS

••TB•
GETBY
GOTBY
LETBE
PUTBY
SATBY
SETBY
SITBY

••T•B
ESTAB

T•C••
TACET
TACIT
TACKS
TACKY
TACOS
TECHS
TICKS
TICKY
TUCKS
TYCHE
TYCHO

T••C•
TAXCO
TEACH
TENCH
THECA
THICK
TINCT
TORCH
TOSCA
TOUCH
TRACE
TRACK
TRACT
TRACY
TRICE
TRICK
TRUCE
TRUCK
TWICE

T•••C
TELIC
TONIC
TOPIC
TORIC
TOXIC
TUNIC

•TC••
ITCHY
LTCOL

•T•C•
STACK
STACY
STICH
STICK
STOCK
STUCK
UTICA

•T••C
ATTIC
ETHIC
STOIC

••TC•
AITCH
BATCH
BOTCH
BUTCH
CATCH
DITCH
DUTCH
FETCH
FITCH
HATCH
HITCH
HUTCH
KETCH
KOTCH
LATCH
MATCH
MITCH
NATCH
NOTCH
PATCH
PITCH
RATCH
VETCH
WATCH
WITCH

••T•C
ANTIC
ATTIC
AZTEC
ISTIC
OPTIC
VATIC

T•D••
TEDDY
TIDAL
TIDED
TIDES
TODAY
TODDY
TODOS
TUDOR

T••D•
TANDY
TARDE
TARDY
TEDDY
TEIDE
TENDS
THEDA
THUDS
TILDE
TOADS
TOADY
TODDY
TONDI
TONDO
TRADE
TSADE

T•••D
TAMED
TAPED
TAXED
TBIRD
TBOND
TEPID
THEYD
THIRD
TIDED
TILED
TIMED
TIMID
TINED
TIRED
TONED
TOPED
TOTED
TOWED
TOYED
TREAD
TREED
TREND
TRIAD
TRIED
TRUED
TUBED
TUMID
TUNED
TWEED
TYPED

•T•D•
ETUDE
STADT
STUDS
STUDY

•T••D
STAID
STAND
STEAD
STEED
STOOD
STRAD

••TD•
OUTDO

••T•D
ACTED
ANTED
APTED
BATED
CITED
DATED
DOTED
FATED
FETED
FETID
GATED
HATED
KITED
MATED
METED
MUTED
NOTED
OCTAD
OOTID
OPTED
OUTED
PATED
RATED
SATED
SITED
TOTED
USTED
VOTED

•••TD
APPTD
ASSTD
CONTD
WHATD

TE•••
TEACH
TEAKS
TEALS
TEAMS
TEARS
TEARY
TEASE
TECHS
TEDDY
TEEMS
TEENA
TEENS
TEENY
TEETH
TEEUP
TEHEE
TEIDE
TELEO
TELEX
TELIC
TELLS
TELLY
TELOS
TEMPE
TEMPI
TEMPO
TEMPS
TEMPT
TENCH
TENDS
TENET
TENON
TENOR
TENSE
TENTH
TENTS
TEPAL
TEPEE
TEPID
TERMS
TERNE
TERNS
TERRA
TERRE
TERRI
TERRY
TERSE
TERZA
TESLA
TESTA
TESTS
TESTY
TETHS
TETON
TETRA
TEVET
TEVYE
TEXAN
TEXAS
TEXTS

T•E••
TAEGU
TAELS
TEEMS
TEENA
TEENS
TEENY
TEETH
TEEUP
THEBE
THECA
THEDA
THEFT
THEIR
THEMA
THEME
THEMS
THEOL
THERA
THERE
THERM
THESE
THETA
THEWS
THEYD
TIEGS
TIEIN
TIERS
TIEUP
TOEIN
TREAD
TREAT
TREED
TREEN
TREES
TREKS
TREND
TRENT
TRESS
TREVI
TREWS
TREYS
TWEAK
TWEED
TWEEN
TWEET
TWERE
TWERP

T••E•
TACET
TAKEI
TAKEN
TAKER
TAKES
TALER
TALES
TAMED
TAMER
TAMES
TANEY
TAPED
TAPER
TAPES
TARES
TASER
TATER
TAXED
TAXER
TAXES
TEHEE
TELEO
TELEX
TENET
TEPEE
TEVET
THIEF
THREE
THREW
TIBER
TIBET
TIDED
TIDES
TIGER
TILED
TILER
TILES
TIMED
TIMER
TIMES
TIMEX
TINED
TINES
TIRED
TIRES
TITER
TOBEY
TOKEN
TOLER
TOLET
TOMEI
TOMES
TONED
TONER
TONES
TOPED
TOPER
TOPES
TOTED
TOTEM
TOTER
TOTES
TOVES
TOWED
TOWEL
TOWER
TOYED
TREED
TREEN
TREES
TRIED
TRIER
TRIES
TRUED
TRUER
TRUES
TRUEX
TUBED
TUBER
TUBES
TULES
TUNED
TUNER
TUNES
TUTEE
TUXES
TVSET
TWEED
TWEEN
TWEET
TYKES
TYLER
TYNES
TYPEA
TYPEB
TYPED
TYPEE
TYPER
TYPES
TYRES

T•••E
TABLE
TAHOE
TAINE
TANTE
TARDE
TARGE
TASSE
TASTE
TAUPE
TBONE
TEASE
TEHEE
TEIDE
TEMPE
TENSE
TEPEE
TERNE
TERRE
TERSE
TEVYE
THANE
THEBE
THEME
THERE
THESE
THINE
THOLE
THOSE
THREE
THROE
THULE
THYME
TILDE
TINGE
TITHE
TITLE
TNOTE
TOILE
TONNE
TOQUE
TORME
TORRE
TORTE
TOTIE
TOUTE
TOWNE
TRACE
TRADE
TRAVE
TRIBE
TRICE
TRIKE
TRINE
TRIPE
TRITE
TROPE
TROVE
TRUCE
TRYME
TSADE
TULLE
TUQUE
TUTEE
TWERE
TWICE
TWINE
TYCHE
TYPEE

•TE••
ATEAM
ATEIN
ATEUP
ITEMS
PTERO
STEAD
STEAK
STEAL
STEAM
STEED
STEEL
STEEN
STEEP
STEER
STEIN
STELA
STELE
STEMS
STENO
STENS
STEPS
STERE
STERN
STETS

STEVE
STEWS

•T•E•
ATSEA
ETHEL
ETHER
ETSEQ
ETZEL
LTGEN
OTHER
OTOES
OTTER
STAEL
STEED
STEEL
STEEN
STEEP
STEER
STIES
STREW
UTHER
UTLEY
UTTER

•T••E
ATIVE
ATONE
ETAGE
ETAPE
ETUDE
ITSME
STAGE
STAKE
STALE
STARE
STATE
STAVE
STELE
STERE
STEVE
STILE
STIPE
STOAE
STOKE
STOLE
STONE
STOPE
STORE
STOVE
STOWE
STYLE
STYNE
UTILE

••TE•
ACTED
ACTER
AFTER
ALTER
ANTED
ANTES
APTED
APTER
ARTEL
ARTES
ASTER
AZTEC
BATED
BATES
BETEL
BITER
BITES
BUTEO
BYTES
CATER
CATES
CITED
CITER
CITES
COTES
CUTER
CUTEX
DATED
DATER
DATES
DETER
DOTED
DOTER
DOTES
EATEN
EATER
ENTER
ESTEE
ESTER
ESTES
FATED
FATES
FETED
FETES
GATED
GATES
GUTEN
HATED
HATER
HATES
HOTEL
INTEL
INTER
JETER
JETES
JUTES
KITED
KITER
KITES
LATEN
LATER
LATEX
LITER
LITES
LUTES
MATED
MATEO
MATER
MATES
MATEY
METED
METER
METES
MITER
MITES
MOTEL
MOTES
MOTET
MUTED
MUTER
MUTES
NITER
NITES
NOTED
NOTER
NOTES
OATEN
OATER
OATES
OCTET
OFTEN
OPTED
OSTEO
OTTER
OUTED
OUTER
PATED
PATEK
PATEN
PATER
PATES
PETER
RATED
RATEL
RATER
RATES
RITES
ROTES
SATED
SATES
SITED
SITES
TATER
TITER
TOTED
TOTEM
TOTER
TOTES
TUTEE
UNTER
USTED
UTTER
VATER
VOTED
VOTER
VOTES
WATER
YATES

••T•E
ANTAE
ANTRE
ARTIE
ASTRE
AUTRE
BATHE
BETTE
BITTE
BOTHE
BUTTE
CUTIE
DETRE
ENTRE
ESTEE
GETME
HITME
ISTLE
KATIE
LATHE
LATKE
LATTE
LETBE
LETHE
LITHE
LITRE
LOTTE
MATTE
METRE
MITRE
NITRE
NOTME
NOTRE
OUTRE
PATHE
RETIE
SATIE
SETAE
TITHE
TITLE
TOTIE
TUTEE
UNTIE
VITAE
VOTRE
WITHE
WITTE
WYTHE

•••TE
ABATE
ACUTE
AGATE
ALATE
ARETE
AZOTE
BASTE
BETTE
BITTE
BOITE
BRITE
BRUTE
BUTTE
CARTE
CASTE
CHUTE
CNOTE
COMTE
CONTE
CRATE
CRETE
DANTE
DENTE
DHOTE
ELATE
ELITE
ELUTE
EMOTE
ENATE
FLUTE
FOOTE
FORTE
GESTE
GRATE
GRETE
HARTE
HASTE
HAUTE
HEUTE
IRATE
JUSTE
KINTE
KLUTE
KNUTE
LATTE
LEYTE
LOTTE
MATTE
MONTE
NOLTE
NORTE
ONATE
ORATE
OVATE
PARTE
PASTE
PEETE
PENTE
PISTE
PLATE
POETE
PONTE
PORTE
POSTE
PRATE
QUITE
QUOTE
ROUTE
SANTE
SAUTE
SCUTE
SHUTE
SIETE
SKATE
SKETE
SLATE
SMITE
SMOTE
SPATE
SPITE
STATE
SUITE
TANTE
TASTE
TNOTE
TORTE
TOUTE
TRITE
UNITE
VERTE
VOLTE
WAITE
WASTE
WHITE
WITTE
WRITE
WROTE
YENTE
ZANTE

T•F••
TAFFY
TIFFS
TOFFS
TUFTS

T••F•
TAFFY
THEFT
TIFFS
TOFFS
TURFS

T•••F
THIEF

•T•F•
STAFF
STIFF
STUFF

•T••F
STAFF
STIFF
STUFF

••T•F
MOTIF

T•G••
TAGUP
TAGUS
TIGER
TIGHT
TOGAS
TSGTS

T••G•
TAEGU
TAIGA
TANGO
TANGS
TANGY
TARGE
THIGH
THUGS
TIEGS
TINGE
TINGS
TONGA
TONGS
TOUGH
TRIGS
TWIGS

T•••G
THING
THONG
TWANG
TYING

•TG••
LTGEN
LTGOV

•T•G•
ETAGE
STAGE
STAGG
STAGS
STAGY
STOGY

•T••G
STAGG
STANG
STING
STUNG

••TG•
GETGO
LETGO
OUTGO

••T•G
RETAG

TH•••
THAIS
THANE
THANK
THANT
THARP
THATS
THAWS
THEBE
THECA
THEDA
THEFT
THEIR
THEMA
THEME
THEMS
THEOL
THERA
THERE
THERM
THESE
THETA
THEWS
THEYD
THICK
THIEF
THIGH
THILL
THINE
THING
THINK
THINS
THIRD
THOLE
THONG
THORN
THORP
THOSE
THOTH
THOUS
THREE
THREW
THROB
THROE
THROW
THRUM
THUDS
THUGS
THUJA
THULE
THUMB
THUMP
THUNK
THURS
THYME

T•H••
TAHOE
TAHRS
TEHEE

T••H•
TECHS
TETHS
TIGHT
TITHE
TYCHE
TYCHO

T•••H
TEACH
TEETH
TENCH
TENTH
THIGH
THOTH
TILTH
TOOTH
TORAH
TORCH
TOUCH
TOUGH
TRASH
TRISH
TROTH
TRUTH

•TH••
ATHOL
ATHON
ATHOS
ETHAN
ETHEL
ETHER
ETHIC
ETHNO
ETHOS
ETHYL
OTHER
UTHER

•T•H•
ITCHY
STAHL
UTAHN

•T••H
STASH
STICH

••TH•
ALTHO
ANTHO
ARTHR
BATHE
BATHO
BATHS
BATHY
BOTHA
BOTHE
CATHY
FATHA
GOTHA
GOTHS
KATHY
LATHE
LATHS
LETHE
LITHE
LITHO
MATHS
MOTHS
MOTHY
MYTHS
OATHS
ORTHO
PATHE
PATHO
PATHS
PITHS
PITHY
RATHS
SOTHO
TETHS
TITHE
WITHE
WYTHE

••T•H
AITCH
BATCH
BOTCH
BUTCH
CATCH
DITCH
DUTCH
FETCH
FITCH
HATCH
HITCH
HUTCH
KETCH
KOTCH
LATCH
MATCH
MITCH
NATCH
NOTCH
PATCH
PITCH
RATCH
VETCH
WATCH
WITCH

•••TH
ARITH
AZOTH
BARTH
BERTH
BIRTH
BLUTH
BLYTH
BOOTH
BRITH
BROTH
CLOTH
COUTH
DARTH
DEPTH
DOETH
EARTH
EDITH
FAITH
FIFTH
FILTH
FIRTH
FORTH
FROTH
FURTH
GARTH
GIRTH
HEATH
ICHTH
KEITH
LEITH
LOATH
MIRTH
MONTH
MOUTH
NEATH
NINTH
NORTH
PERTH
PLATH
QUOTH
SIXTH
SLOTH
SMITH
SMYTH
SNATH
SOOTH
SOUTH
SWATH
TEETH
TENTH
THOTH
TILTH
TOOTH
TROTH
TRUTH
WIDTH
WORTH
WRATH
WROTH
WYETH
YOUTH

TI•••
TIANT
TIARA
TIBBS
TIBER
TIBET
TIBIA
TICKS
TICKY
TIDAL
TIDED
TIDES
TIEGS
TIEIN
TIERS
TIEUP
TIFFS
TIGER
TIGHT
TIKAL
TIKIS
TIKKI
TILDE
TILED
TILER
TILES
TILLS
TILLY
TILTH
TILTS
TIMED
TIMER
TIMES
TIMEX
TIMID
TIMMY
TIMON
TIMOR
TINCT
TINED
TINES
TINGE
TINGS
TINNY
TINTS
TIPIN
TIPPI
TIPPY
TIPSY
TIPUP
TIRAN
TIRED
TIRES
TITAN
TITER
TITHE
TITIS
TITLE
TITUS
TIZZY

T•I••
TAIGA
TAILS
TAINE
TAINT
TBILL
TBIRD
TEIDE
THICK
THIEF
THIGH
THILL
THINE
THING
THINK
THINS
THIRD
TOILE
TOILS
TOITY
TRIAD
TRIAL
TRIBE
TRICE
TRICK
TRIED
TRIER
TRIES
TRIGS
TRIKE
TRILL
TRIMS
TRINE
TRINI
TRIOS
TRIPE
TRIPS
TRISH
TRITE
TRITT
TWICE
TWIGS
TWILL
TWINE
TWINS
TWIRL
TWIST
TWITS
TWIXT
TYING

T••I•
TABIS
TACIT
TAKIN
TALIA
TAMIL
TAPIN
TAPIR
TAXIS
TELIC
TEPID
THAIS
THEIR
TIBIA
TIEIN
TIKIS
TIMID
TIPIN
TITIS
TOBIT
TOEIN
TONIC
TONIO
TOPIC
TOPIS
TORIC
TORII
TOTIE
TOWIT
TOXIC
TOXIN
TRAIL
TRAIN
TRAIT
TROIS
TULIP
TUMID
TUNIC
TUNIS
TURIN
TWAIN

T•••I
TAKEI
TARSI
TEMPI
TERRI
TIKKI
TIPPI
TOMEI
TONDI
TOPOI
TORII
TORSI
TREVI
TRINI
TUTTI

•TI••
ATILT
ATION
ATIVE
QTIPS
STICH
STICK
STIES
STIFF
STILE
STILL
STILT
STING
STINK
STINT
STIPE
STIRS
UTICA
UTILE

•T•I•
ATEIN
ATRIA
ATRIP
ATTIC
ETHIC
ETUIS
STAID
STAIN
STAIR
STEIN
STOIC
STRIA
STRIP

•T••I
ATARI
OTOMI
STYLI

••TI•
ACTII
ACTIN
ACTIV
ANTIC
ANTIQ
ANTIS
ARTIE
ARTIS
ASTIN
ASTIR
ATTIC
BATIK
CUTIE
CUTIN
CUTIS
EATIN
EATIT
ENTIA
FETID
FITIN
GETIN
GETIT
GOTIN
HITIT
ISTIC
KATIE
LATIN
LETIN
MATIN
METIS
MOTIF
NOTIN
OOTID
OPTIC
OSTIA
PATIO
PETIT
PUTIN
RATIO
RETIA
RETIE
RUTIN
SATIE
SATIN
SETIN
SITIN
TITIS
TOTIE
UNTIE
UNTIL
VATIC
YETIS
ZITIS

••T•I
ACTII
ALTAI
MATRI
MITZI
NITTI
PATRI
PATTI
PETRI
PETTI
PUTTI
TUTTI

•••TI
AMATI
CACTI
CENTI
CESTI
COATI
CONTI
DENTI
DHOTI
HAITI
LACTI
LAHTI
MARTI
MISTI
MUFTI
MULTI
NITTI
NOCTI
PARTI
PATTI
PETTI
PONTI
PUTTI
RECTI
SOLTI
TUTTI

T••J•
THUJA

T•K••
TAKEI
TAKEN
TAKER
TAKES
TAKIN
TIKAL
TIKIS
TIKKI
TOKAY
TOKEN
TOKYO
TYKES

T••K•
TACKS
TACKY
TALKS
TALKY
TANKA
TANKS
TASKS
TEAKS
TICKS
TICKY
TIKKI
TONKA
TREKS
TRIKE
TUCKS
TURKS
TURKU
TUSKS

T•••K
TAROK
THANK
THICK
THINK
THUNK
TRACK
TRICK
TRUCK
TRUNK
TWEAK

•T•K•
STAKE
STOKE
STUKA

•T••K
STACK
STALK
STANK
STARK
STEAK
STICK
STINK
STOCK
STORK
STUCK
STUNK

••TK•
DITKA
LATKE
SITKA

••T•K
BATAK
BATIK
PATEK
POTOK

T•L••
TALER
TALES
TALIA
TALKS
TALKY
TALLY
TALON
TALUS
TELEO
TELEX
TELIC
TELLS
TELLY
TELOS
TILDE
TILED
TILER
TILES
TILLS
TILLY
TILTH
TILTS
TOLER
TOLET
TOLLS
TULES
TULIP
TULLE
TULLY
TULSA
TYLER

T••L•
TABLA
TABLE
TAELS
TAILS
TALLY
TBILL
TEALS
TELLS
TELLY
TESLA
THILL
THOLE
THULE
TILLS
TILLY
TITLE
TOILE
TOILS
TOLLS
TOOLS
TRALA
TRILL
TROLL
TRULY
TULLE
TULLY
TWILL
TWYLA

T•••L
TAMIL
TBILL
TEPAL
THEOL
THILL
TIDAL
TIKAL
TONAL
TOPOL
TOTAL
TOWEL
TRAIL
TRAWL
TRIAL
TRILL
TROLL
TWILL
TWIRL
TYROL

•TL••
ATLAS
UTLEY

•T•L•
ATALL
ATILT
ATOLL
ITALO
ITALS
ITALY
STALE
STALK
STALL
STELA
STELE
STILE
STILL
STILT
STOLA
STOLE
STOLS
STULL
STYLE
STYLI
STYLO
UTILE
VTOLS

•T••L
ATALL
ATHOL
ATOLL
ETHEL
ETHYL
ETZEL
LTCOL
STAEL
STAHL
STALL
STEAL
STEEL
STILL
STOOL
STULL

••TL•
APTLY
FATLY
FITLY
HATLO
HOTLY
ISTLE
PATLY
ROTLS
TITLE
WETLY

••T•L
ANTAL
ARTAL
ARTEL
BETEL
BUTYL
DOTAL
EXTOL
FATAL
FETAL
HOTEL
INTEL
METAL
MOTEL
NATAL
OCTAL
PETAL
RATEL
SOTOL
TOTAL
UNTIL
VITAL

•••TL
YENTL

T•M••
TAMBO
TAMED
TAMER
TAMES
TAMIL
TAMMY
TAMPA
TAMPS
TEMPE
TEMPI
TEMPO
TEMPS
TEMPT
TIMED
TIMER
TIMES
TIMEX
TIMID
TIMMY
TIMON
TIMOR
TOMEI
TOMES
TOMMY
TUMID
TUMMY

T••M•
TAMMY
TEAMS
TEEMS
TERMS
THEMA
THEME
THEMS
THUMB
THUMP
THYME
TIMMY
TOMMY
TORME
TRAMP
TRAMS
TRIMS
TROMP
TRUMP
TRYME

TUMMY

T•••M
TATUM
THERM
THRUM
TOTEM

•TM••
ATMAN
ATMOS

•T•M•
ATOMS
ATOMY
ETYMA
ITEMS
ITSME
OTOMI
STAMP
STEMS
STOMA
STOMP
STUMP
STUMS

•T••M
ATEAM
STEAM
STORM
STROM
STRUM
STURM

••TM•
GETME
HITME
NOTME

••T•M
DATUM
ENTOM
TATUM
TOTEM

TN•••
TNOTE
TNUTS

T•N••
TANDY
TANEY
TANGO
TANGS
TANGY
TANKA
TANKS
TANSY
TANTE
TANYA
TENCH
TENDS
TENET
TENON
TENOR
TENSE
TENTH
TENTS
TINCT
TINED
TINES
TINGE
TINGS
TINNY
TINTS
TONAL
TONDI
TONDO
TONED
TONER
TONES
TONGA
TONGS
TONIC
TONIO
TONKA
TONNE
TONTO
TONUS
TONYA
TONYS
TUNAS
TUNED
TUNER
TUNES
TUNIC
TUNIS
TUNNY
TYNAN
TYNES

T••N•
TAINE
TAINT
TARNS
TAUNT
TAWNY
TBOND
TBONE
TEENA
TEENS
TEENY
TERNE
TERNS
THANE
THANK
THANT
THINE
THING
THINK
THINS
THONG
THUNK
TIANT
TINNY
TONNE
TOONS
TOWNE
TOWNS
TRANS
TREND
TRENT
TRINE
TRINI
TRUNK
TUNNY
TURNS
TWANG
TWINE
TWINS
TYING

T•••N
TAKEN
TAKIN
TALON
TAPIN
TAUON
TAXON
TENON
TETON
TEXAN
THORN
TIEIN
TIMON
TIPIN
TIRAN
TITAN
TOEIN
TOKEN
TOXIN
TOYON
TRAIN
TREEN
TRYON
TURIN
TWAIN
TWEEN
TYNAN
TYSON

•TN••
ATNOS
ETNAS

•T•N•
ATONE
ETHNO
ETONS
STAND
STANG
STANK
STENO
STENS
STING
STINK
STINT
STONE
STONY
STUNG
STUNK
STUNS
STUNT
STYNE

•T••N
ATEIN
ATHON
ATION
ATMAN
ETHAN
LTGEN
STAIN
STEEN
STEIN
STERN
UTAHN
UTURN

••TN•
AETNA
PATNA

••T•N
ACTIN
ACTON
AFTON
ALTON
ANTON
ASTIN
ASTON
BATON
BETON
CUTIN
EATEN
EATIN
EATON
ELTON
FITIN
FUTON
GATUN
GETIN
GETON
GOTIN
GOTON
GUTEN
HITON
LATEN
LATIN
LETIN
LETON
LITON
MATIN
NOTIN
OATEN
OFTEN
ORTON
PATEN
PATON
PITON
PUTIN
PUTON
RATON
RUTIN
SATAN
SATIN
SATON
SETIN
SETON
SITIN
SITON
TETON
TITAN
UPTON
WOTAN

TO•••
TOADS
TOADY
TOAST
TOBEY
TOBIT
TODAY
TODDY
TODOS
TOEIN
TOFFS
TOGAS
TOILE
TOILS
TOITY
TOKAY
TOKEN
TOKYO
TOLER
TOLET
TOLLS
TOMEI
TOMES
TOMMY
TONAL
TONDI
TONDO
TONED
TONER
TONES
TONGA
TONGS
TONIC
TONIO
TONKA
TONNE
TONTO
TONUS
TONYA
TONYS
TOOLS
TOONS
TOOTH
TOOTS
TOPAZ
TOPED
TOPER
TOPES
TOPIC
TOPIS
TOPOI
TOPOL
TOPOS
TOPPS
TOPSY
TOQUE
TORAH
TORCH
TORIC
TORII
TORME
TOROS
TORRE
TORRS
TORSI
TORSO
TORTE
TORTS
TORUS
TOSCA
TOTAL
TOTED
TOTEM
TOTER
TOTES
TOTIE
TOTUP
TOUCH
TOUGH
TOURS
TOUTE
TOUTS
TOVES
TOWED
TOWEL
TOWER
TOWIT
TOWNE
TOWNS
TOXIC
TOXIN
TOYED
TOYON

T•O••
TBOND
TBONE
THOLE
THONG
THORN
THORP
THOSE
THOTH
THOUS
TNOTE
TOOLS
TOONS
TOOTH
TOOTS
TROIS
TROLL
TROMP
TROOP
TROPE
TROPO
TROTH
TROTS
TROUT
TROVE

T••O•
TABOO
TABOR
TACOS
TAHOE
TALON
TAROK
TAROT
TAUON
TAXON
TELOS
TENON
TENOR
TETON
THEOL
THROB
THROE
THROW
TIMON
TIMOR
TODOS
TOPOI
TOPOL
TOPOS
TOROS
TOYON
TRIOS
TROOP
TRYON
TUDOR
TUROW
TUTOR
TYPOS
TYROL
TYROS
TYSON

T•••O
TABOO
TAMBO
TANGO
TASSO
TAXCO
TELEO
TEMPO
TOKYO
TONDO
TONIO
TONTO
TORSO
TROPO
TRURO
TURBO
TYCHO

•TO••
ATOLL
ATOMS
ATOMY
ATONE
ETONS
OTOES
OTOMI
STOAE
STOAS
STOAT
STOCK
STOGY
STOIC
STOKE
STOLA
STOLE
STOLS
STOMA
STOMP
STONE
STONY
STOOD
STOOL
STOOP
STOPE
STOPS
STORE
STORK
STORM
STORY
STOSS
STOTS
STOUP
STOUT
STOVE
STOWE
STOWS
VTOLS

•T•O•
ATHOL
ATHON
ATHOS
ATION
ATMOS
ATNOS
ETHOS
LTCOL
LTGOV
STOOD
STOOL
STOOP
STROM
STROP

•T••O
ETHNO
ITALO
PTERO
STENO
STYLO

••TO•
ACTON
ACTOR
AFTON
ALTON
ALTOS
ANTON
ARTOO
ASTON
ASTOR
AUTOS
BATON
BATOR
BETON
DETOO
EATON
ELTON
ENTOM
ESTOP
EXTOL
FETOR
FSTOP
FUTON
GATOR
GATOS
GETON
GOTON
HITON
INTOW
JATOS
KOTOS
LETON
LITON
METOO
MOTOR
ONTOP
ORTON
PATON
PITON
PITOT
POTOK
PUTON
RATON
RETOP
RETOW
ROTOR
ROTOS
SATON
SETON
SITON
SOTOL
TETON
TUTOR
UPTON
ZZTOP

••T•O
ALTHO
ANTHO
ARTOO
ASTRO
BATHO
BUTEO
DETOO
DITTO
DOTTO
EXTRO
GETGO
GETTO
GOTTO
HATLO
IATRO
INTRO
INTWO
LETGO
LITHO
LOTTO
MATEO
MATRO
MATZO
METOO
METRO
MOTTO
NITRO
NOTSO
ORTHO
OSTEO
OUTDO
OUTGO
PATHO
PATIO
PETRO
POTTO
PUTTO
RATIO
RATSO
RETRO
SETTO
SOTHO
SOTTO

•••TO
AALTO
ACETO
ADDTO
AIMTO
AMATO
BLUTO
BOITO
CANTO
CENTO
DEUTO
DITTO
DOTTO
ERATO
FACTO
FEMTO
FRITO
GETTO
GOTTO
GUSTO
HADTO
HASTO
HECTO
HIPTO
HOWTO
JUNTO
KYOTO
LACTO
LAYTO
LEDTO
LENTO
LEPTO
LIETO
LOTTO
MOLTO
MOTTO
NEATO
PANTO
PASTO
PESTO
PHOTO
PHYTO
PINTO
PLATO
PLUTO
PORTO
POTTO
PRATO
PROTO
PUTTO
QUITO
RANTO
RECTO
RUNTO
SANTO
SARTO
SAWTO
SEATO
SEETO
SETTO
SOTTO
TONTO
XACTO

T•P••
TAPAS
TAPED
TAPER
TAPES
TAPIN
TAPIR
TEPAL
TEPEE
TEPID
TIPIN
TIPPI
TIPPY
TIPSY
TIPUP
TOPAZ
TOPED
TOPER
TOPES
TOPIC
TOPIS
TOPOI
TOPOL
TOPOS
TOPPS
TOPSY
TYPEA
TYPEB
TYPED
TYPEE
TYPER
TYPES
TYPOS

T••P•
TAMPA
TAMPS
TARPS
TAUPE
TEMPE
TEMPI
TEMPO
TEMPS
TEMPT
TIPPI
TIPPY
TOPPS
TRAPP
TRAPS
TRIPE
TRIPS
TROPE
TROPO

T•••P
TAGUP
TEEUP
THARP
THORP
THUMP
TIEUP
TIPUP
TOTUP
TRAMP
TRAPP
TROMP
TROOP
TRUMP
TULIP
TWERP

•TP••
ATPAR

•T•P•
ETAPE
QTIPS
STEPS
STIPE
STOPE
STOPS
STUPA

•T••P
ATEUP
ATRIP
PTRAP
STAMP
STEEP
STOMP
STOOP
STOUP
STRAP
STRIP
STROP
STUMP

••T•P
ACTUP
CUTUP
EATUP
ESTOP
FSTOP
GETUP
GOTUP
HETUP
HITUP
LETUP
LITUP
NOTUP
ONTAP
ONTOP
PUTUP
RETAP
RETOP
SATUP
SETUP
SITUP
TOTUP
ZZTOP

T•Q••
TOQUE
TUQUE

•T••Q
ETSEQ

••T•Q
ANTIQ

TR•••
TRACE
TRACK
TRACT
TRACY
TRADE
TRAIL
TRAIN
TRAIT
TRALA
TRAMP
TRAMS
TRANS
TRAPP
TRAPS
TRASH
TRAVE
TRAWL
TRAYS
TREAD
TREAT
TREED
TREEN
TREES
TREKS
TREND
TRENT
TRESS
TREVI
TREWS
TREYS
TRIAD
TRIAL
TRIBE
TRICE
TRICK
TRIED
TRIER
TRIES
TRIGS
TRIKE
TRILL
TRIMS
TRINE
TRINI
TRIOS
TRIPE
TRIPS
TRISH
TRITE
TRITT
TROIS
TROLL
TROMP
TROOP
TROPE
TROPO
TROTH
TROTS
TROUT
TROVE
TRUCE
TRUCK
TRUED
TRUER
TRUES
TRUEX
TRULY
TRUMP
TRUNK
TRURO
TRUSS
TRUST
TRUTH
TRYME
TRYON
TRYST

T•R••
TARDE
TARDY
TARES
TARGE
TARNS
TAROK
TAROT
TARPS
TARRY
TARSI
TARTS
TERMS
TERNE
TERNS
TERRA
TERRE
TERRI
TERRY
TERSE
TERZA
THREE
THREW
THROB
THROE
THROW
THRUM
TIRAN
TIRED
TIRES
TORAH
TORCH
TORIC
TORII
TORME
TOROS
TORRE
TORRS
TORSI
TORSO
TORTE
TORTS
TORUS
TURBO
TURFS
TURIN
TURKS
TURKU
TURNS
TUROW
TURVY
TYRES
TYROL
TYROS

T••R•
TAHRS
TARRY
TATRA
TAYRA
TBARS
TBIRD
TEARS
TEARY
TERRA
TERRE
TERRI
TERRY
TETRA
THARP
THERA
THERE
THERM
THIRD
THORN
THORP
THURS
TIARA
TIERS
TORRE
TORRS
TOURS
TRURO
TSARS
TWERE
TWERP
TWIRL

T•••R
TABOR
TAKER
TALER
TAMER
TAPER
TAPIR
TASER
TATAR
TATER
TAXER
TENOR
THEIR
TIBER
TIGER
TILER
TIMER
TIMOR
TITER
TOLER
TONER
TOPER
TOTER
TOWER
TRIER
TRUER
TUBER
TUDOR
TUNER
TUTOR
TYLER
TYPER

•TR••
ATRIA
ATRIP
PTRAP
STRAD
STRAP
STRAW
STRAY
STREW
STRIA
STRIP
STROM
STROP
STRUM
STRUT

•T•R•
ATARI
OTARU
OTARY
PTERO
STARE
STARK
STARR
STARS
START
STERE
STERN
STIRS
STORE
STORK
STORM
STORY
STURM
UTURN

•T••R
ATPAR
ATTAR
ATWAR
ETHER
OTHER
OTTER
STAIR
STARR
STEER
UTHER
UTTER

••TR•
AFTRA
ANTRA
ANTRE
ASTRA
ASTRE
ASTRO
AUTRE
AUTRY
DETRE
ENTRE
ENTRY
EXTRA
EXTRO
IATRO
IATRY
INTRA
INTRO
LITRE
MATRI
MATRO
METRE
METRO
MITRE
NITRE
NITRO
NOTRE
OUTRE
PATRI
PETRA
PETRI
PETRO
RETRO
RETRY
SUTRA
TATRA
TETRA
ULTRA
VOTRE

••T•R
ACTER
ACTOR
AFTER
ALTAR
ALTER
APTER
ARTHR
ARTUR
ASTER
ASTIR
ASTOR
ATTAR
BATOR
BITER
CATER
CITER
CUTER
DATER
DETER
DOTER
EATER
ENTER
ESTER
FETOR
GATOR
HATER
INTER
JETER
KITER
LATER
LITER
MATER
METER
MITER
MOTOR
MUTER
NITER
NOTER
OATER
OTTER
OUTER
PATER
PETER
QATAR
RATER
RETAR
ROTOR
SATYR
SITAR
TATAR
TATER
TITER
TOTER
TUTOR
UNTER
UTTER
VATER
VOTER
WATER

•••TR
AUSTR
CONTR
DEXTR
DISTR
GASTR
INSTR

TS•••
TSADE
TSARS
TSGTS

T•S••
TASER
TASKS
TASSE
TASSO
TASTE
TASTY
TESLA
TESTA
TESTS
TESTY
TOSCA
TUSKS
TVSET
TYSON

T••S•
TANSY
TARSI
TASSE
TASSO
TEASE
TENSE
TERSE
THESE
THOSE
TIPSY
TOAST
TOPSY
TORSI
TORSO
TRASH
TRESS
TRISH
TRUSS
TRUST
TRYST
TULSA
TWIST

T•••S
TABIS
TACKS
TACOS
TAELS
TAGUS
TAHRS
TAILS
TAKES
TALES
TALKS
TALUS
TAMES
TAMPS
TANGS
TANKS
TAPAS
TAPES
TARES
TARNS
TARPS
TARTS
TASKS
TAXES
TAXIS
TBARS
TEAKS
TEALS
TEAMS
TEARS
TECHS
TEEMS
TEENS
TELLS
TELOS
TEMPS
TENDS
TENTS
TERMS
TERNS
TESTS
TETHS
TEXAS
TEXTS
THAIS
THATS
THAWS
THEMS
THEWS
THINS
THOUS
THUDS
THUGS
THURS
TIBBS

TICKS
TIDES
TIEGS
TIERS
TIFFS
TIKIS
TILES
TILLS
TILTS
TIMES
TINES
TINGS
TINTS
TIRES
TITIS
TITUS
TNUTS
TOADS
TODOS
TOFFS
TOGAS
TOILS
TOLLS
TOMES
TONES
TONGS
TONUS
TONYS
TOOLS
TOONS
TOOTS
TOPES
TOPIS
TOPOS
TOPPS
TOROS
TORRS
TORTS
TORUS
TOTES
TOURS
TOUTS
TOVES
TOWNS
TRAMS
TRANS
TRAPS
TRAYS
TREES
TREKS
TRESS
TREWS
TREYS
TRIES
TRIGS
TRIMS
TRIOS
TRIPS
TROIS
TROTS
TRUES
TRUSS
TSARS
TSGTS
TUBAS
TUBES
TUCKS
TUFTS
TULES
TUNAS
TUNES
TUNIS
TURFS
TURKS
TURNS
TUSKS
TUTUS
TUXES
TWIGS
TWINS
TWITS
TYKES
TYNES
TYPES
TYPOS
TYRES
TYROS

•TS••
ATSEA
ETSEQ
ITSME

•T•S•
STASH
STOSS

•T••S
ATHOS
ATLAS
ATMOS
ATNOS
ATOMS
ATTYS
ETHOS
ETNAS
ETONS
ETUIS
ITALS
ITEMS
OTOES
QTIPS
STABS
STAGS
STARS
STATS
STAYS
STEMS
STENS
STEPS
STETS
STEWS
STIES
STIRS
STOAS
STOLS
STOPS
STOSS
STOTS
STOWS
STUBS
STUDS
STUMS
STUNS
VTOLS

••TS•
ANTSY
ARTSY
BETSY
BITSY
DITSY
GUTSY
MATSU
NOTSO
PATSY
POTSY
RATSO

••T•S
ALTOS
ALTUS
ANTAS
ANTES
ANTIS
ARTES
ARTIS
ATTYS
AUTOS
BATES
BATHS
BATTS
BETAS
BITES
BITTS
BUTTS
BYTES
CATES
CETUS
CITES
COTES
CUTIS
DATES
DOTES
ESTES
FATES
FETAS
FETES
GATES
GATOS
GETAS
GOTHS
HATES
ICTUS
IOTAS
JATOS
JETES
JOTAS
JUTES
KITES
KITTS
KOTOS
LATHS
LETTS
LITES
LOTAS
LOTUS
LUTES
MATES
MATHS
METES
METIS
MITES
MITTS
MOTES
MOTHS
MOTTS
MUTES
MUTTS
MYTHS
NITES
NOTES
OATES
OATHS
PATES
PATHS
PITAS
PITHS
PITTS
POTTS
PUTTS
RATES
RATHS
RITES
ROTAS
ROTES
ROTLS
ROTOS
SATES
SITES
SITUS
SRTAS
TETHS
TITIS
TITUS
TOTES
TUTUS
VITAS
VITUS
VOTES
WATTS
YATES
YETIS
ZETAS
ZITIS

•••TS
ABETS
ABUTS
ACCTS
ADITS
APPTS
ASSTS
AUNTS
BAHTS
BAITS
BALTS
BARTS
BATTS
BEATS
BEETS
BELTS
BENTS
BESTS
BITTS
BLATS
BLOTS
BOATS
BOLTS
BOOTS
BOUTS
BRATS
BRITS
BRUTS
BUNTS
BUSTS
BUTTS
CANTS
CAPTS
CARTS
CASTS
CELTS
CENTS
CERTS
CHATS
CHITS
CLOTS
COATS
COLTS
COOTS
COPTS
COSTS
CULTS
DARTS
DEBTS
DELTS
DENTS
DEPTS
DICTS
DIETS
DINTS
DOITS
DOLTS
DRATS
DUCTS
DUETS
DUSTS
EASTS
EDITS
EMITS
EXITS
FACTS
FASTS
FEATS
FELTS
FESTS
FIATS
FISTS
FLATS
FLITS
FONTS
FOOTS
FORTS
FOUTS
FRATS
FRETS
FRITS
GAITS
GENTS
GESTS
GHATS
GIFTS
GILTS
GIRTS
GISTS
GLUTS
GNATS
GOATS
GRITS
GROTS
GUSTS
HAFTS
HALTS
HARTS
HEATS
HEFTS
HESTS
HILTS
HINTS
HOOTS
HOSTS
HUNTS
HURTS
INITS
INSTS
JESTS
JILTS
JOLTS
KEATS
KILTS
KITTS
KNITS
KNOTS
KYATS
LASTS
LEETS
LEFTS
LENTS
LETTS
LIFTS
LILTS
LINTS
LISTS
LOFTS
LOOTS
LOUTS
LUSTS
MALTS
MARTS
MASTS
MEATS
MEETS
MELTS
MILTS
MINTS
MISTS
MITTS
MOATS
MOLTS
MOOTS
MORTS
MOTTS
MSGTS
MUSTS
MUTTS
NEATS
NERTS
NESTS
NEWTS
OASTS
ODETS
OMITS
OUSTS
PACTS
PANTS
PARTS
PASTS
PEATS
PELTS
PESTS
PHOTS
PICTS
PINTS
PITTS
PLATS
PLOTS
POETS
PORTS
POSTS
POTTS
POUTS
PROTS
PSATS
PUNTS
PUTTS
QUITS
RAFTS
RANTS
RENTS
RESTS
RIFTS
RIOTS
ROOTS
ROUTS
RUNTS
RUSTS
RYOTS
SALTS
SCATS
SCOTS
SCUTS
SEATS
SECTS
SEXTS
SHOTS
SHUTS
SIFTS
SILTS
SKITS
SLATS
SLITS
SLOTS
SMITS
SMUTS
SNITS
SOOTS
SORTS
SPATS
SPETS
SPITS
SPOTS
SSGTS
STATS
STETS
STOTS
SUETS
SUITS
SUPTS
SWATS
TARTS
TENTS
TESTS
TEXTS
THATS
TILTS
TINTS
TNUTS
TOOTS
TORTS
TOUTS
TROTS
TSGTS
TUFTS
TWITS
UNITS
VENTS
VERTS
VESTS
VOLTS
WAFTS
WAITS
WANTS
WARTS
WATTS
WEFTS
WELTS
WHATS
WHETS
WHITS
WILTS
WONTS
WORTS
WRITS
YEATS
YURTS
ZESTS

T•T••
TATAR
TATER
TATRA
TATTY
TATUM
TETHS
TETON
TETRA
TITAN
TITER
TITHE
TITIS
TITLE
TITUS
TOTAL
TOTED
TOTEM
TOTER
TOTES
TOTIE
TOTUP
TUTEE
TUTOR
TUTTI
TUTUS

T••T•
TANTE
TARTS
TASTE
TASTY
TATTY
TEETH
TENTH
TENTS
TESTA
TESTS
TESTY
TEXTS
THATS
THETA
THOTH
TILTH
TILTS
TINTS
TNOTE
TNUTS
TOITY
TONTO
TOOTH
TOOTS
TORTE
TORTS
TOUTE
TOUTS
TRITE
TRITT
TROTH
TROTS
TRUTH
TSGTS
TUFTS
TUTTI
TWITS

T•••T
TACET
TACIT
TAINT
TAROT
TAUNT
TEMPT
TENET
TEVET
THANT
THEFT
TIANT
TIBET
TIGHT
TINCT
TOAST
TOBIT
TOLET
TOWIT
TRACT
TRAIT
TREAT
TRENT
TRITT
TROUT
TRUST
TRYST
TVSET
TWEET
TWIST
TWIXT

•TT••
ATTAR
ATTIC
ATTYS
OTTER
UTTER

•T•T•
STATE
STATS
STETS
STOTS
STUTZ

•T••T
ATBAT
ATILT
STADT
START
STILT
STINT
STOAT
STOUT
STRUT
STUNT

••TT•
BATTS
BATTY
BETTA
BETTE
BETTY
BITTE
BITTS
BITTY
BUTTE
BUTTS
CATTY
COTTA
DITTO
DITTY
DOTTO
DOTTY
FATTY
GETTO
GETTY
GOTTA
GOTTO
GUTTA
GUTTY
HETTY
JETTY
KITTS
KITTY
LATTE
LETTS
LOTTA
LOTTE
LOTTO
LYTTA
MATTE
MITTS
MITTY
MOTTA
MOTTO
MOTTS
MUTTS
NATTY
NITTI
NITTY
NUTTY
PATTI
PATTY
PETTI
PETTY
PITTA
PITTS
POTTO
POTTS
POTTY
PUTTI
PUTTO
PUTTS
PUTTY
RATTY
RUTTY
SETTO
SOTTO
TATTY
TUTTI
WATTS
WITTE
WITTY

••T•T
AETAT
DETAT
EATAT
EATIT
GETAT
GETIT
GOTAT
HITIT
LETAT
MOTET
OCTET
PETIT
PITOT
SETAT

•••TT
BLITT
BRETT
BRITT
FLATT
HYATT
OVETT
PLATT
PRATT
RAITT
RHETT
SCOTT
TRITT
WYATT

TU•••
TUBAS
TUBBY
TUBED
TUBER
TUBES
TUCKS
TUDOR
TUFTS
TULES
TULIP
TULLE
TULLY
TULSA
TUMID
TUMMY
TUNAS
TUNED
TUNER
TUNES
TUNIC
TUNIS
TUNNY
TUQUE
TURBO
TURFS
TURIN
TURKS
TURKU
TURNS
TUROW
TURVY
TUSKS
TUTEE
TUTOR
TUTTI
TUTUS
TUXES

T•U••
TAUNT
TAUON
TAUPE
THUDS
THUGS
THUJA
THULE
THUMB
THUMP
THUNK
THURS
TNUTS
TOUCH
TOUGH
TOURS
TOUTE
TOUTS
TRUCE
TRUCK
TRUED
TRUER
TRUES
TRUEX
TRULY
TRUMP
TRUNK
TRURO
TRUSS
TRUST
TRUTH

T••U•
TAGUP
TAGUS
TALUS
TATUM
TEEUP
THOUS
THRUM
TIEUP
TIPUP
TITUS
TONUS
TOQUE
TORUS
TOTUP
TROUT
TUQUE
TUTUS

T•••U
TAEGU
TURKU

•TU••
ETUDE
ETUIS
STUBS
STUCK
STUDS
STUDY
STUFF
STUKA
STULL
STUMP
STUMS
STUNG
STUNK
STUNS
STUNT
STUPA
STURM
STUTZ
UTURN

•T•U•
ATEUP
STOUP
STOUT
STRUM
STRUT

•T••U
OTARU

••TU•
ACTUP
ALTUS
ARTUR
CETUS
CUTUP
DATUM
EATUP
GATUN
GETUP
GOTUP
HETUP
HITUP
ICTUS
LETUP
LITUP
LOTUS
NOTUP
PUTUP
SATUP
SETUP
SITUP
SITUS
TATUM
TITUS
TOTUP
TUTUS
VITUS

••T•U
MATSU

•••TU
BANTU
DICTU
VIRTU

TV•••
TVSET

T•V••
TEVET
TEVYE
TOVES

T••V•
TRAVE
TREVI
TROVE
TURVY

•T•V•
ATIVE
STAVE
STEVE
STOVE

•T••V
LTGOV

••T•V
ACTIV

•••TV
CBSTV
NBCTV
PAYTV

TW•••
TWAIN
TWANG
TWEAK
TWEED
TWEEN
TWEET
TWERE
TWERP
TWICE
TWIGS
TWILL
TWINE
TWINS
TWIRL
TWIST
TWITS
TWIXT
TWYLA

T•W••
TAWNY
TOWED
TOWEL
TOWER
TOWIT
TOWNE
TOWNS

T••W•
THAWS
THEWS
TRAWL
TREWS

T•••W
THREW
THROW
TUROW

•TW••
ATWAR
OTWAY

•T•W•
STEWS
STOWE
STOWS

•T••W
STRAW
STREW

••TW•
INTWO

••T•W
INTOW
RETOW

T•X••
TAXCO
TAXED
TAXER
TAXES
TAXIS
TAXON
TEXAN
TEXAS
TEXTS
TOXIC
TOXIN
TUXES

T••X•
TWIXT

T•••X
TELEX
TIMEX
TRUEX

••T•X
CUTEX
LATEX
RETAX

TY•••
TYCHE
TYCHO
TYING
TYKES
TYLER
TYNAN
TYNES
TYPEA
TYPEB
TYPED
TYPEE
TYPER
TYPES
TYPOS
TYRES
TYROL
TYROS
TYSON

T•Y••
TAYRA
THYME
TOYED
TOYON
TRYME
TRYON
TRYST
TWYLA

T••Y•
TANYA
TEVYE
THEYD
TOKYO
TONYA
TONYS
TRAYS
TREYS

T•••Y
TABBY
TACKY
TAFFY
TALKY
TALLY
TAMMY
TANDY
TANEY
TANGY
TANSY
TARDY
TARRY
TASTY
TATTY
TAWNY
TEARY
TEDDY
TEENY
TELLY
TERRY
TESTY
TICKY
TILLY
TIMMY
TINNY
TIPPY
TIPSY
TIZZY
TOADY
TOBEY
TODAY
TODDY
TOITY
TOKAY
TOMMY
TOPSY
TRACY
TRULY
TUBBY
TULLY
TUMMY
TUNNY
TURVY

•TY••
ETYMA
STYLE
STYLI
STYLO
STYNE

•T•Y•
ATTYS
ETHYL
STAYS

•T••Y
ATBAY
ATOMY
ITALY
ITCHY
OTARY
OTWAY
STACY
STAGY
STOGY
STONY
STORY
STRAY
STUDY
UTLEY

••TY•
ATTYS
BUTYL
SATYR

••T•Y
ANTSY
APTLY
ARTSY
AUTRY
BATHY
BATTY
BETSY
BETTY
BITSY
BITTY
CATHY
CATTY
DITSY
DITTY
DITZY
DOTTY
ENTRY
FATLY
FATTY
FITLY
GETBY
GETTY
GOTBY
GUTSY
GUTTY
HETTY
HOTLY
IATRY
JETTY
KATHY
KITTY
MATEY
MITTY
MOTHY
NATTY
NITTY
NUTTY
PATLY
PATSY
PATTY
PETTY
PITHY
POTSY
POTTY
PUTBY
PUTTY
RATTY
RETRY
RITZY
RUTTY
SATBY
SETBY
SITBY
TATTY
WETLY
WITTY

•••TY
AMITY
AUNTY
BARTY
BATTY
BETTY
BITTY
BOOTY
CATTY
DEITY
DIRTY
DITTY
DOTTY
DUSTY
EMPTY
FATTY
FIFTY
FLUTY
FORTY
FUSTY
GETTY
GOUTY
GUSTY
GUTTY
HASTY
HEFTY
HETTY
HOITY
JETTY
JOLTY
KITTY
LAITY
LEFTY
LINTY
LOFTY
LUSTY
MALTY
MARTY
MEATY
MELTY
MILTY
MINTY
MISTY
MITTY
MONTY
MUSTY
NASTY
NATTY
NIFTY
NITTY
NUTTY
PANTY
PARTY
PASTY
PATTY
PEATY
PETTY
PIETY
PLATY
POTTY
POUTY
PUNTY
PUTTY
RATTY
RUNTY
RUSTY
RUTTY
SALTY
SILTY
SIXTY
SLATY
SOFTY
SOOTY
TASTY

TATTY
TESTY
TOITY
UNITY
WARTY
WELTY
WITTY
ZESTY
ZLOTY

T•Z••
TAZZA
TIZZY

T••Z•
TAZZA
TERZA
TIZZY

T•••Z
TOPAZ

•TZ••
ETZEL

•T••Z
STUTZ

••TZ•
DITZY
MATZO
MITZI
RITZY

•••TZ
BLITZ
FRITZ
GLITZ
HERTZ
HOLTZ
KLUTZ
KURTZ
LANTZ
MERTZ
NERTZ
SPITZ
STUTZ
SWITZ
WAITZ
WALTZ

U•A••
UDALL
UHAUL
UKASE
UNAPT
UNARM
UNAUS
URALS
USAGE
USAIR
UTAHN

U••A•
UBOAT
UHLAN
ULNAE
ULNAS
UMIAK
UNBAR
UNCAP
UNCAS
UNJAM
UNMAN
UNSAY
URBAN
URIAH
URIAL
USUAL
UXMAL

U•••A
UHURA
UINTA
ULTRA
UMBRA
USCGA
USLTA
UTICA
UVULA

•UA••
DUADS
DUANE
GUACO
GUARD
GUARS
GUAVA
KUALA
LUAUS
QUACK
QUADR
QUADS
QUAFF
QUAGS
QUAID
QUAIL
QUAKE
QUAKY
QUALE
QUALM
QUAND
QUANT
QUARK
QUART
QUASH
QUASI
QUAYS
RUANA
RUARK
SUAVE
YUANS

•U•A•
AURAE
AURAL
AURAR
AURAS
CUBAN
CUGAT
CUMAE
CUNAS
DUBAI
DUCAL
DUCAT
DUFAY
DUGAN
DUKAS
DUMAS
DURAN
FUGAL
FURAN
GULAG
GULAR
HULAS
HUMAN
HUNAN
JUBAL
JUDAH
JUDAS
JUGAL
JURAL
JURAT
KULAK
LUBAS
LUCAN
LUCAS
LUKAS
LUNAR
LURAY
MURAL
MURAT
MUZAK
PULAS
PUMAS
PUNAS
PUPAE
PUPAL
PUPAS
PUSAN
RUGAE
RURAL
SUDAN
SUGAR
SUMAC
SURAH
SURAL
SURAS
SURAT
SUSAN
TUBAS
TUNAS
WUHAN
YUMAN
YUMAS

•U••A
AUDRA
BUBBA
BUENA
BUFFA
BULBA
BULLA
BURMA
BURSA
CULPA
CUPPA
CURIA
DURRA
FULDA
GUAVA
GUNGA
GUTTA
HUBBA
JUDEA
JULIA
JUMNA
JUNTA
KUALA
KUKLA
LUCCA
LUCIA
LUISA
LULEA
LURIA
MUDRA
MURRA
MUSCA
NUBIA
NUCHA
OUIDA
OUIJA
PUKKA
PUNTA
QUOTA
RUANA
RUMBA
SUDRA
SULFA
SULLA
SUMBA
SUMMA
SUNDA
SUNNA
SUPRA
SUTRA
TULSA
YUCCA

••UA•
AQUAE
AQUAS
DOUAI
DOUAY
EQUAL
JOUAL
KAUAI
SKUAS
SQUAB
SQUAD
SQUAT
USUAL

••U•A
ABUJA
ACURA
ADUWA
ALULA
ARUBA
AZUSA
CEUTA
CHULA
CRURA
FAUNA
GOUDA
HAUSA
HOUMA
KRUPA
LAURA
MAUNA
PAULA
PIURA
SAUNA
SCUBA
SCUTA
SHULA
SOUSA
STUKA
STUPA
THUJA
UHURA
UVULA

•••UA
LEHUA
MAKUA
NAHUA
PADUA
PAPUA
VACUA

UB•••
UBOAT
UBOLT

U•B••
UMBEL
UMBER
UMBOS
UMBRA
UNBAR
UNBID
UNBOX
UPBOW
URBAN
UZBEK

•UB••
AUBER
BUBBA
BUBER
CUBAN
CUBBY
CUBEB
CUBED
CUBES
CUBIC
CUBIT
DUBAI
DUBIN
DUBOS
EUBIE
FUBSY
HUBBA
HUBBY
JUBAL
LUBAS
LUBED
LUBES
NUBBY
NUBIA
RUBEN
RUBES
RUBIK
RUBIN
RUBLE
SUBIC
TUBAS
TUBBY
TUBED
TUBER
TUBES
ZUBIN

•U•B•
BUBBA
BULBA
BULBS
BURBS
BUSBY
CUBBY
CURBS
DUMBO
DUMBS
GUMBO
HUBBA
HUBBY
JUMBO
MUMBO
NUBBY
NUMBS
PUTBY
RUGBY
RUMBA
SUMBA
TUBBY
TURBO

•U••B
CUBEB

••UB•
ARUBA
CHUBS
CLUBS
DAUBS
DOUBT
DRUBS
FLUBS
GRUBS
SCUBA
SNUBS
STUBS

••U•B
BLURB
CRUMB
EXURB
PLUMB
RHUMB
SQUAB
SQUIB
THUMB

•••UB
REDUB
SCRUB
SHRUB

U•C••
ULCER
UNCAP
UNCAS
UNCLE
UNCUT
USCGA

U••C•
URICH
UTICA

U•••C
UGRIC

•UC••
BUCKO
BUCKS
BUCKY
DUCAL
DUCAT
DUCES
DUCHY
DUCKS
DUCKY
DUCTS
FUCHS
GUCCI
LUCAN
LUCAS
LUCCA
LUCCI
LUCIA
LUCID
LUCIE
LUCKS
LUCKY
LUCRE
MUCIN
MUCKS
MUCKY
NUCHA
PUCCI
PUCKS
RUCHE
RUCKS
SUCKS
SUCRE
TUCKS
YUCCA
YUCKY

•U•C•
BUICK
BUNCH
BUSCH
BUTCH
CULCH
CURCI
CUZCO
DUNCE
DUTCH
GUACO
GUCCI
GULCH
HULCE
HUNCH
HUTCH
JUICE
JUICY
JUNCO
LUCCA
LUCCI
LUNCH
LURCH
MULCH
MULCT
MUNCH
MUSCA
OUNCE
PUCCI
PUNCH
QUACK
QUICK
SULCI
YUCCA

•U••C
AURIC
CUBIC
DUROC
LUDIC
MUSIC
PUNIC
RUNIC
SUBIC
SUMAC
TUNIC

••UC•
AMUCK
BRUCE
BRUCH
CHUCK
CLUCK
COUCH
DEUCE
DEUCY
EDUCE
EDUCT
ERUCT
GLUCK
GLUCO
PLUCK
POUCH
SAUCE
SAUCY
SHUCK
SNUCK
STUCK
TOUCH
TRUCE
TRUCK
VOUCH

UD•••
UDALL
UDDER

U•D••
UDDER
UNDER
UNDID
UNDUE
UPDOS

U•••D
UMPED
UNBID
UNDID
UNFED
UNWED
UPEND
UPPED
URGED
URSID
USHED
USTED

•UD••
AUDEN
AUDIE
AUDIO
AUDIS
AUDIT
AUDRA
BUDDY
BUDGE
CUDDY
DUDDY
DUDES
FUDDY
FUDGE
JUDAH
JUDAS
JUDEA
JUDGE
KUDOS
KUDUS
KUDZU
LUDIC
MUDDY
MUDRA
NUDER
NUDES
NUDGE
PUDGY
PUDUS
RUDDS
RUDDY
RUDER
RUDGE
SUDAN
SUDDS
SUDRA
SUDSY
TUDOR

•U•D•
BUDDY
BUNDS
BUNDT
BUNDY
CUDDY
CURDS
CURDY
DUADS
DUDDY
FUDDY
FULDA
FUNDS
FUNDY
GUIDE
GUIDO
GURDY
HURDY
KURDS
LUNDI
LUNDY
MUDDY
OUIDA
OUTDO
QUADR
QUADS
QUIDS
QUODS
RUDDS
RUDDY
SUDDS
SUEDE
SUNDA
SURDS

•U••D
BUILD
BUSED
CUBED
CUPID
CURED
DUKED
DUPED
FUMED
FUSED
GUARD
GUILD
GUYED
HUMID
JUKED
LUBED
LUCID
LURED
LURID
MUSED
MUTED
NUKED
OUTED
PULED
QUAID
QUAND
RULED
TUBED
TUMID
TUNED

••UD•
CRUDE
ELUDE
ETUDE
EXUDE
FEUDS
GAUDS
GAUDY
GOUDA
GOUDY
JEUDI
LAUDE
LAUDS
MAUDE
PRUDE
SAUDI
SCUDI
SCUDO
SCUDS
SPUDS
STUDS
STUDY
THUDS

••U•D
BLUED
BOUND
CLUED
COULD
DRUID
FLUID
FOUND
GLUED
GOULD
GOURD
HOUND
MAUND
MOULD
MOUND
POUND
ROUND
SLUED
SOUND
SQUAD
SQUID
TRUED
WOULD
WOUND

•••UD
ALOUD
CHAUD
CLOUD
FRAUD
FREUD
LIKUD
NEFUD
PROUD
PSEUD
SALUD

U•E••
UMEKI
UPEND
USERS
USEUP

U••E•
UDDER
ULCER
UMBEL
UMBER
UMPED
UNDER
UNFED
UNGER
UNMET
UNPEG
UNPEN
UNSER
UNSET
UNTER
UNWED
UPPED
UPPER
UPSET
URGED
URGER
URGES
URIEL
USHED
USHER
USTED
UTHER
UTLEY
UTTER
UZBEK

U•••E
UKASE
ULNAE
UNCLE
UNDUE
UNITE
UNTIE
USAGE
UTILE

•UE••
BUELL
BUENA
BUENO
CUEIN
DUELS
DUETS
FUEGO
FUELS
GUESS
GUEST
LUEGO
QUEEG
QUEEN
QUEER
QUELL
QUERN
QUERY
QUEST
QUEUE
RUEHL
SUEDE
SUEME
SUERS
SUETS

•U•E•
AUBER
AUDEN
AUGER
AUREI
BUBER
BUSED
BUSES
BUSEY
BUTEO
BUYER
CUBEB
CUBED
CUBES
CUKES
CULET
CULEX
CUNEO
CUPEL
CURED
CURER
CURES
CUTER
CUTEX
CUVEE
DUCES
DUDES
DUKED
DUKES
DUNES
DUPED
DUPES
DURER
DUVET
EULER
FUMED
FUMES
FUSED
FUSEE
FUSES
GULES
GUTEN
GUYED
HUGER
JUDEA
JUKED
JUKES
JULEP
JULES
JUTES
KUGEL
LUBED
LUBES
LUGER
LUGES
LULEA
LUMEN
LUMET
LUNES
LURED
LURES
LUREX
LUTES
MULES
MULEY
MUREX
MUSED
MUSER
MUSES
MUTED
MUTER
MUTES
NUDER
NUDES
NUKED
NUKES
NUMEN
NUYEN
OUSEL
OUTED
OUTER
OUZEL
PUGET
PULED
PULES
PUREE
PURER
PUREX
PUSEY
QUEEG
QUEEN
QUEER
QUIEN
QUIET
RUBEN
RUBES
RUDER
RULED
RULER
RULES
RUMEN
RUNES
RUPEE
RUSES
SUMER
SUPER
SURER
TUBED
TUBER
TUBES
TULES
TUNED
TUNER
TUNES
TUTEE
TUXES

•U••E
AUDIE
AURAE
AUTRE
BUDGE
BUGLE
BULGE
BURKE
BURSE
BUTTE
CUMAE
CURIE
CURSE
CURVE
CUTIE
CUVEE
DUANE
DULSE
DUNCE
DUNNE
DUPLE
DUPRE
EUBIE
FUDGE
FUGUE
FURZE
FUSEE
GUIDE
GUILE
GUISE
HULCE
JUDGE
JUICE
JULIE
JUSTE
LUCIE
LUCRE
LUISE
LUNGE
LURIE
MURRE
NUDGE
NURSE
OUNCE
OUTRE
PULSE
PUPAE
PUREE
PURGE
PURSE
QUAKE
QUALE
QUEUE
QUIRE
QUITE
QUOTE
RUBLE
RUCHE
RUDGE
RUGAE
RUPEE
RUSSE
SUAVE
SUCRE
SUEDE
SUEME
SUITE
SURGE
SUSIE
TULLE
TUQUE
TUTEE

••UE•
AGUES
BAUER
BLUED
BLUER
BLUES
BLUET
BLUEY
CLUED
CLUES
CRUEL
CRUET
FLUES
GLUED
GLUER
GLUES
GLUEY
GRUEL
HAUER
MOUES
ROUEN
ROUES
SLUED
SLUES
TRUED
TRUER
TRUES
TRUEX

••U•E
ABUSE
ACUTE
AMUSE
AQUAE
AZURE
BAUME
BLUME
BOULE
BOUSE
BRUCE
BRULE
BRUME
BRUTE
CAUSE
CHUTE
COUPE
CRUDE
CRUSE
DEUCE
DOUSE
DRUPE
DRUSE
DRUZE
EDUCE
ELUDE
ELUTE
ENURE
ETUDE
EXUDE
FAURE
FAUVE
FLUKE
FLUME
FLUTE
GAUGE
GAUZE
GOUGE
HAUTE
HEURE
HEUTE
HOUSE
INURE
INUSE
JAUNE
JEUNE
JOULE
KLUGE
KLUTE
KNUTE
LAUDE
LOUIE
LOUPE
LOUSE
MAUDE
MAUVE
MEUSE
MOUSE
NEUME
OFUSE
OVULE
PAUSE
PLUME
PRUDE
PRUNE
REUNE
REUSE
ROUGE
ROUSE
ROUTE
SAUCE
SAUTE
SCUTE
SEULE
SHUTE
SOUSE
SPUME
TAUPE
THULE
TOUTE
TRUCE
YOURE
YOUVE

•••UE
ARGUE
BENUE
ENDUE
ENSUE
ESQUE
FUGUE
GIGUE
HAGUE
IMBUE
ISSUE
LARUE
LOGUE
ONCUE
PIQUE
QUEUE
REVUE
ROGUE
ROQUE
SEGUE
SPRUE
TOQUE
TUQUE
UNDUE
VAGUE
VALUE
VENUE
VOGUE

U•F••
UNFED
UNFIT
UNFIX

U••F•
UNIFY

•UF••
BUFFA
BUFFI
BUFFO
BUFFS
BUFFY
CUFFS
DUFAY
DUFFS
DUFFY
HUFFS
HUFFY
LUFFS
MUFFS
MUFTI
PUFFS
PUFFY
RUFFS
RUFUS
SUFIS
TUFTS

•U•F•
BUFFA
BUFFI
BUFFO
BUFFS
BUFFY
CUFFS
DUFFS
DUFFY
GULFS
HUFFS
HUFFY
LUFFS
MUFFS
PUFFS
PUFFY
QUAFF
RUFFS
SULFA
SURFS
SURFY
TURFS

•U••F
QUAFF

••UF•
ACUFF
BLUFF
CHUFF
FLUFF
GRUFF
KHUFU
POUFS
SCUFF
SNUFF
STUFF

••U•F
ACUFF
BLUFF
CHUFF
FLUFF
GRUFF
SCUFF
SCURF
SMURF
SNUFF
STUFF

•••UF
BOEUF

UG•••
UGRIC

U•G••
UIGUR
UNGER
URGED
URGER
URGES

U••G•
USAGE
USCGA

U•••G
UNPEG
UNRIG
USING

•UG••
AUGER
AUGHT
AUGUR
BUGGY
BUGLE
BUGSY
CUGAT
DUGAN
DUGIN
DUGUP
FUGAL
FUGIT
FUGUE
HUGER
JUGAL
JUGUM
KUGEL
LUGER
LUGES
MUGGY
OUGHT
PUGET
RUGAE
RUGBY
SUGAR
YUGOS

•U•G•
BUDGE
BUGGY
BULGE
BULGY
BUNGS
BURGS

FUDGE
FUEGO
FUNGI
FUNGO
GUNGA
JUDGE
LUEGO
LUIGI
LUNGE
LUNGS
MUGGY
MUNGO
NUDGE
OUTGO
PUDGY
PUNGS
PURGE
QUAGS
RUDGE
RUNGS
SURGE

•U••G
CUING
GULAG
QUEEG
RUING
SUING

••UG•
BAUGH
BOUGH
CHUGS
COUGH
DOUGH
DRUGS
GAUGE
GOUGE
HOUGH
KLUGE
LAUGH
LOUGH
PLUGS
ROUGE
ROUGH
SLUGS
SNUGS
SOUGH
THUGS
TOUGH
WAUGH

••U•G
BOURG
BRUNG
CHUNG
CLUNG
FLUNG
SLUNG
STUNG
SWUNG
WRUNG
YOUNG

•••UG
ABZUG
DEBUG
SHRUG

UH•••
UHAUL
UHHUH
UHLAN
UHURA
UHURU

U•H••
UHHUH
UNHIP
USHED
USHER
UTHER

U••H•
UTAHN

U•••H
UHHUH
URIAH
URICH

•UH••
BUHLS
WUHAN

•U•H•
AUGHT
BUSHY
CUSHY
DUCHY
FUCHS
GUSHY
MUSHY
NUCHA
OUGHT
PUSHY
RUCHE
RUEHL
RUSHY
SUSHI
WUSHU

•U••H
BUNCH
BUSCH
BUTCH
CULCH
DUTCH
FURTH
GULCH
HUMPH
HUNCH
HUTCH
JUDAH
LUNCH
LURCH
MULCH
MUNCH
PUNCH
QUASH
QUOTH
SURAH

••UH•
BRUHN

••U•H
BAUGH
BLUSH
BLUTH
BOUGH
BRUCH
BRUSH
COUCH
COUGH
COUTH
CRUSH
DOUGH
FLUSH
FOURH
HOUGH
LAUGH
LOUGH
MOUTH
PLUSH
POUCH
ROUGH
SHUSH
SLUSH
SOUGH
SOUTH
TOUCH
TOUGH
TRUTH
VOUCH
WAUGH
YOUTH

•••UH
UHHUH

UI•••
UIGUR
UINTA

U•I••
UMIAK
UNIFY
UNION
UNITE
UNITS
UNITY
UNIVS
URIAH
URIAL
URICH
URIEL
USING
UTICA
UTILE

U••I•
UGRIC
UNBID
UNDID
UNFIT
UNFIX
UNHIP
UNLIT
UNPIN
UNRIG
UNTIE
UNTIL
UNZIP
URSID
USAIR

U•••I
UMEKI

•UI••
BUICK
BUILD
BUILT
CUING
GUIDE
GUIDO
GUILD
GUILE
GUILT
GUISE
JUICE
JUICY
LUIGI
LUISA
LUISE
OUIDA
OUIJA
QUICK
QUIDS
QUIEN
QUIET
QUILL
QUILP
QUILT
QUINN
QUINO
QUINT
QUIPS
QUIPU
QUIRE
QUIRK
QUIRT
QUITE
QUITO
QUITS
RUING
RUINS
SUING
SUINT
SUITE
SUITS

•U•I•
AUDIE
AUDIO
AUDIS
AUDIT
AULIS
AURIC
AUXIL
AUXIN
BUNIN
BURIN
CUBIC
CUBIT
CUEIN
CUMIN
CUPID
CURIA
CURIE
CURIO
CUTIE
CUTIN
CUTIS
DUBIN
DUGIN
EUBIE
FUGIT
FUSIL
HUMID
JULIA
JULIE
JULIO
LUCIA
LUCID
LUCIE
LUDIC
LUNIK
LUPIN
LURIA
LURID
LURIE
MUCIN
MUNIS
MUSIC
NUBIA
NUMIS
PULIS
PUNIC
PUPIL
PUPIN
PURIM
PUTIN
QUAID
QUAIL
QUOIN
QUOIT
RUBIK
RUBIN
RUNIC
RUNIN
RURIK
RUTIN
SUBIC
SUFIS
SUSIE
TULIP
TUMID
TUNIC
TUNIS
TURIN
YUPIK
ZUBIN
ZUNIS

•U••I
AUREI
AUSSI
BUFFI
BUZZI
CUPRI
CURCI
DUBAI
FUNGI
GUCCI
LUCCI
LUIGI
LUNDI
MUFTI
MULTI
NURMI
PUCCI
PUTTI
QUASI
SULCI
SUNNI
SUOMI
SUSHI
TUTTI

••UI•
BRUIN
BRUIT
DRUID
EQUIP
EQUIV
ETUIS
FLUID
FRUIT
GSUIT
INUIT
IQUIT
LOUIE
LOUIS
SQUIB
SQUID

••U•I
DOUAI
HOURI
JEUDI
KAUAI
KAURI
SAUDI
SCUDI

•••UI
ANHUI
ENNUI
MAQUI
YAQUI

U•J••
UNJAM

•UJ••
AUJUS
JUJUS

•U•J•
OUIJA

••UJ•
ABUJA
THUJA

UK•••
UKASE

U••K•
UMEKI

U•••K
UMIAK
UZBEK

•UK••
CUKES
CUKOR
DUKAS
DUKED
DUKES
JUKED
JUKES
KUKLA
LUKAS
NUKED
NUKES
PUKKA
YUKON
ZUKOR

•U•K•
BUCKO
BUCKS
BUCKY
BULKS
BULKY
BUNKO
BUNKS
BURKE
CUSKS
DUCKS
DUCKY
DUNKS
DUSKS
DUSKY
FUNKS
FUNKY
GUNKY
HULKS
HUNKS
HUSKS
HUSKY
JUNKS
JUNKY
LUCKS
LUCKY
LURKS
MUCKS
MUCKY
MURKY
MUSKS
MUSKY
PUCKS
PUKKA
PUNKS
PUNKY
QUAKE
QUAKY
RUCKS
RUSKS
SUCKS
SULKS
SULKY
TUCKS
TURKS
TURKU
TUSKS
YUCKY

•U••K
BUICK
HUROK
KULAK
KURSK
LUNIK
MUZAK
QUACK
QUARK
QUICK
QUIRK
RUARK
RUBIK
RURIK
YUPIK

••UK•
FLUKE
FLUKY
SAUKS
STUKA

••U•K
AMUCK
CAULK
CHUCK
CHUNK
CLUCK
CLUNK
DRUNK
FLUNK
GLUCK
PLUCK
PLUNK
SHUCK
SKULK
SKUNK
SLUNK
SNUCK
SPUNK
STUCK
STUNK
THUNK
TRUCK
TRUNK

•••UK
ANOUK

UL•••
ULCER
ULNAE
ULNAS
ULTRA

U•L••
UHLAN
UNLIT
USLTA
UTLEY

U••L•
UBOLT
UDALL
UNCLE
UPOLU
URALS
UTILE
UVULA

U•••L
UDALL
UHAUL
UMBEL
UNTIL
URIAL
URIEL
USUAL
UXMAL

•UL••
AULIS
BULBA
BULBS
BULGE
BULGY
BULKS
BULKY
BULLA
BULLS
BULLY
BULOW
CULCH
CULET
CULEX
CULLS
CULMS
CULPA
CULTS
DULLS
DULLY
DULSE
EULER
FULDA
FULLY
GULAG
GULAR
GULCH
GULES
GULFS
GULLS
GULLY
GULPS
HULAS
HULCE
HULKS
HULLO
HULLS
JULEP
JULES
JULIA
JULIE
JULIO
KULAK
LULEA
LULLS
LULLY
LULUS
MULCH
MULCT
MULES
MULEY
MULLS
MULTI
NULLS
PULAS
PULED
PULES
PULIS
PULLS
PULPS
PULPY
PULSE
RULED
RULER
RULES
SULCI
SULFA
SULKS
SULKY
SULLA
SULLY
TULES
TULIP
TULLE
TULLY
TULSA
ZULUS

•U•L•
BUELL
BUGLE
BUHLS
BUILD
BUILT
BULLA
BULLS
BULLY
BURLS
BURLY
CULLS
CURLS
CURLY
DUELS
DULLS
DULLY
DUPLE
FUELS
FULLY
FURLS
GUILD
GUILE
GUILT
GULLS
GULLY
HULLO
HULLS
HURLS
HURLY
KUALA
KUKLA
LULLS
LULLY
MULLS
NULLS
PULLS
PURLS
QUALE
QUALM
QUELL
QUILL
QUILP
QUILT
RUBLE
SULLA
SULLY
SURLY
TULLE
TULLY

•U••L
AURAL
AUXIL
BUELL
BUTYL
CUMUL
CUPEL
DUCAL
FUGAL
FUSIL
JUBAL
JUGAL
JURAL
KUGEL
MURAL
OUSEL
OUZEL
PUPAL
PUPIL
QUAIL
QUELL
QUILL
RUEHL
RURAL
SURAL

••UL•
ADULT
ALULA
BOULE
BOULT
BRULE
CAULK
CAULS
CHULA
COULD
EXULT
FAULT
FOULS
GAULS
GOULD
HAULM
HAULS
JOULE
KRULL
MAULS
MOULD
MOULT
OCULO
OVULE
PAULA
POULT
SAULT
SCULL
SEULE
SHULA
SHULS
SKULK
SKULL
SOULS
SOULT
STULL
THULE
TRULY
UVULA
VAULT
WOULD
YOULL

••U•L
CHURL
CRUEL
EQUAL
GRUEL
JOUAL
KNURL
KRULL
SCULL
SKULL
STULL
USUAL
YOULL

•••UL
ABDUL
AFOUL
ANNUL
AWFUL
BABUL
CUMUL
GHOUL
KABUL
MOGUL
MOSUL
PICUL
RAOUL
SEOUL
UHAUL

UM•••
UMBEL
UMBER
UMBOS
UMBRA
UMEKI
UMIAK
UMPED

U•M••
UNMAN
UNMET
UXMAL

U•••M
UNARM
UNJAM

•UM••
BUMPS
BUMPY
CUMAE
CUMIN
CUMUL
DUMAS
DUMBO
DUMBS
DUMMY
DUMPS
DUMPY
FUMED
FUMES
GUMBO
GUMMO
GUMMY
GUMUP
HUMAN
HUMID
HUMOR
HUMPH
HUMPS
HUMPY
HUMUS
JUMBO
JUMNA
JUMPS
JUMPY
LUMEN
LUMET
LUMPS
LUMPY
MUMBO
MUMMY
MUMPS
NUMBS
NUMEN
NUMIS
PUMAS
PUMPS
RUMBA
RUMEN
RUMMY
RUMOR
RUMPS
SUMAC
SUMBA
SUMER
SUMMA
SUMPS
SUMUP
TUMID
TUMMY
YUMAN
YUMAS
YUMMY

•U•M•
BURMA
CULMS
CUOMO
DUMMY
DUOMO
GUMMO
GUMMY
MUMMY
NURMI
RUMMY
SUEME
SUMMA
SUOMI
TUMMY
YUMMY

•U••M
AURUM
DURUM
JUGUM
PURIM
QUALM

••UM•
ALUMS
ARUMS
BAUME
BLUME
BRUME
CHUMP
CHUMS
CLUMP
CRUMB
CRUMP
DRUMS
FLUME
FRUMP
GRUMP
HOUMA
NEUME
PLUMB
PLUME
PLUMP
PLUMS
PLUMY
RHUMB
SCUMS
SLUMP
SLUMS
SPUME
SPUMY
STUMP
STUMS
THUMB
THUMP
TRUMP

••U•M
HAULM
STURM

•••UM
AKSUM
ALBUM
ANNUM
ARIUM
AURUM
BEGUM
BYGUM
COLUM
DATUM
DURUM
FILUM
FORUM
HARUM
HILUM
HOHUM
HOKUM
ILIUM
JORUM
JUGUM
MECUM
NAHUM
OAKUM
ODEUM
ODIUM
OLEUM
OPIUM
PILUM
RHEUM
SCRUM
SEBUM
SEDUM
SERUM
SOLUM
STRUM
TATUM
THRUM
VELUM
YOKUM

UN•••
UNAPT
UNARM
UNAUS
UNBAR
UNBID
UNBOX
UNCAP
UNCAS
UNCLE
UNCUT
UNDER
UNDID
UNDUE
UNFED
UNFIT
UNFIX
UNGER
UNHIP
UNIFY
UNION
UNITE
UNITS
UNITY
UNIVS
UNJAM
UNLIT
UNMAN
UNMET
UNPEG
UNPEN
UNPIN
UNRIG
UNSAY
UNSER
UNSET
UNTER
UNTIE
UNTIL
UNWED
UNZIP

U•N••
UINTA
ULNAE
ULNAS

U••N•
UPEND
USING

U•••N
UHLAN
UNION
UNMAN
UNPEN
UNPIN
UPTON
URBAN
UTAHN
UTURN

•UN••
AUNTS
AUNTY
BUNCH
BUNDS
BUNDT
BUNDY
BUNGS
BUNIN
BUNKO
BUNKS
BUNNY
BUNTS
CUNAS
CUNEO
DUNCE
DUNES
DUNKS
DUNNE
DUNNO
FUNDS
FUNDY
FUNGI
FUNGO
FUNKS
FUNKY
FUNNY
GUNGA
GUNKY
GUNNY
HUNAN
HUNCH
HUNKS
HUNTS
JUNCO
JUNKS
JUNKY
JUNTA
JUNTO
LUNAR
LUNCH
LUNDI
LUNDY
LUNES
LUNGE
LUNGS
LUNIK
MUNCH
MUNGO
MUNIS
MUNRO
OUNCE
PUNAS
PUNCH
PUNGS
PUNIC
PUNKS
PUNKY
PUNNY
PUNTA
PUNTS
PUNTY
RUNES
RUNGS
RUNIC
RUNIN
RUNNY
RUNON
RUNTO
RUNTS
RUNTY
RUNUP
SUNDA
SUNNA
SUNNI
SUNNY
SUNUP
TUNAS
TUNED
TUNER
TUNES
TUNIC
TUNIS
TUNNY
ZUNIS

•U•N•
BUENA
BUENO
BUNNY
BUONO
BURNS
BURNT
CUING
DUANE
DUNNE
DUNNO
FUNNY
GUNNY
JUMNA
MUONS
PUNNY
QUAND
QUANT
QUINN
QUINO
QUINT
RUANA
RUING
RUINS
RUNNY
SUING
SUINT
SUNNA
SUNNI
SUNNY
TUNNY
TURNS
YUANS

•U••N
AUDEN
AUXIN
BUNIN
BURIN
CUBAN
CUEIN
CUMIN
CUTIN
DUBIN
DUGAN
DUGIN
DURAN
FURAN
FUTON
GUTEN
HUMAN
HUNAN
HURON
LUCAN
LUMEN
LUPIN
LUZON
MUCIN
NUMEN
NUYEN
PUPIN
PUSAN
PUTIN
PUTON
QUEEN
QUERN
QUIEN
QUINN
QUOIN
RUBEN
RUBIN
RUMEN
RUNIN
RUNON
RUTIN
SUDAN
SUSAN
TURIN
WUHAN
YUKON
YUMAN
ZUBIN

••UN•
BLUNT
BOUND
BRUNG
BRUNO
BRUNT
CHUNG
CHUNK
CLUNG
CLUNK
CLUNY
COUNT
DAUNT
DRUNK
FAUNA
FAUNS
FLUNG
FLUNK
FOUND
FOUNT
GAUNT
GRUNT
HAUNT
HOUND
JAUNE
JAUNT
JEUNE
MAUNA
MAUND
MOUND
MOUNT
NOUNS
PLUNK
POUND
PRUNE
REUNE
ROUND
SAUNA
SHUNS
SHUNT
SKUNK
SLUNG
SLUNK
SOUND
SPUNK
STUNG
STUNK
STUNS
STUNT
SWUNG
TAUNT
THUNK
TRUNK
VAUNT
WOUND
WRUNG
YOUNG
YOUNT

••U•N
BOURN
BRUHN
BRUIN
CHURN
GLUON
ROUEN
SPURN
TAUON

UTURN

•••UN
BBGUN
BEGUN
BRAUN
BROUN
CAJUN
GATUN
HAFUN
INFUN
RERUN
SHAUN

U•O••
UBOAT
UBOLT
UPOLU

U••O•
UMBOS
UNBOX
UNION
UPBOW
UPDOS
UPTON

•UO••
BUONO
BUOYS
CUOMO
DUOMO
MUONS
QUODS
QUOIN
QUOIT
QUOTA
QUOTE
QUOTH
SUOMI

•U•O•
AUTOS
BULOW
CUKOR
DUBOS
DUROC
DUROS
EUROS
FUROR
FUTON
GUYOT
HUMOR
HUROK
HURON
JUROR
KUDOS
LUXOR
LUZON
OUZOS
PUTON
RUMOR
RUNON
TUDOR
TUROW
TUTOR
YUGOS
YUKON
ZUKOR

•U••O
AUDIO
BUCKO
BUENO
BUFFO
BUNKO
BUONO
BURRO
BUTEO
CUNEO
CUOMO
CUPRO
CURIO
CUZCO
DUMBO
DUNNO
DUOMO
FUEGO
FUNGO
GUACO
GUIDO
GUMBO
GUMMO
GUSTO
HULLO
JULIO
JUMBO
JUNCO
JUNTO
LUEGO
MUMBO
MUNGO
MUNRO
OUTDO
OUTGO
PUTTO
QUINO
QUITO
RUNTO
RUSSO
TURBO

••UO•
FLUOR
GLUON
TAUON

••U•O
BLUTO
BRUNO
DEUTO
DOURO
GLUCO
NEURO
OCULO
ORURO
PLUTO
SCUDO
TRURO

UP•••
UPBOW
UPDOS
UPEND
UPOLU
UPPED
UPPER
UPSET
UPTON

U•P••
UMPED
UNPEG
UNPEN
UNPIN
UPPED
UPPER

U••P•
UNAPT

U•••P
UNCAP
UNHIP
UNZIP
USEUP
USURP

•UP••
CUPEL
CUPID
CUPPA
CUPRI
CUPRO
DUPED
DUPES
DUPLE
DUPRE
GUPPY
LUPIN
PUPAE
PUPAL
PUPAS
PUPIL
PUPIN
PUPPY
RUPEE
SUPER
SUPRA
SUPTS
SUPVR
YUPIK

•U•P•
BUMPS
BUMPY
BURPS
CULPA
CUPPA
CUSPS
DUMPS
DUMPY
GULPS
GUPPY
HUMPH
HUMPS
HUMPY
JUMPS
JUMPY
LUMPS
LUMPY
MUMPS
PULPS
PULPY
PUMPS
PUPPY
QUIPS
QUIPU
RUMPS
SUMPS

•U••P
BUYUP
CUTUP
DUGUP
GUMUP
JULEP
PUTUP
QUILP
RUNUP
SUMUP
SUNUP
TULIP

••UP•
COUPE
COUPS
DRUPE
ERUPT
KRUPA
KRUPP
LOUPE
REUPS
SCUPS
SOUPS
SOUPY
STUPA
TAUPE
WHUPS

••U•P
CHUMP
CLUMP
CRUMP
EQUIP
FRUMP
GRUMP
KRUPP
PLUMP
SLUMP
SLURP
STUMP
THUMP
TRUMP
USURP

•••UP
ACTUP
ADDUP
ATEUP
BIDUP
BOBUP
BOXUP
BUYUP
CROUP
CUTUP
DAMUP
DIDUP
DIGUP
DRYUP
DUGUP
EATUP
ENDUP
FEDUP
FIXUP
GASUP
GETUP
GOTUP
GROUP
GUMUP
HETUP
HITUP
HOPUP
ICEUP
JAMUP
KEYUP
LAPUP
LAYUP
LEGUP
LETUP
LITUP
MIXUP
MOPUP
NIPUP
NOTUP
ONEUP
OWNUP
PAYUP
PEPUP
PINUP
POPUP
PUTUP
RANUP
RIGUP
RIPUP
RUNUP
SATUP
SCAUP
SETUP
SEWUP
SITUP
SOPUP
STOUP
SUMUP
SUNUP
SYRUP
TAGUP
TEEUP
TIEUP
TIPUP
TOTUP
USEUP
WADUP
ZIPUP

•UQ••
TUQUE

UR•••
URALS
URBAN
URGED
URGER
URGES
URIAH
URIAL
URICH
URIEL
URSID

U•R••
UGRIC
UNRIG

U••R•
UHURA
UHURU
ULTRA
UMBRA
UNARM
USERS
USURP
USURY
UTURN

U•••R
UDDER
UIGUR
ULCER
UMBER
UNBAR
UNDER
UNGER
UNSER
UNTER
UPPER
URGER
USAIR
USHER
UTHER
UTTER

•UR••
AURAE
AURAL
AURAR
AURAS
AUREI
AURIC
AURUM
BURBS
BURGS
BURIN
BURKE
BURLS
BURLY
BURMA
BURNS
BURNT
BURPS
BURRO
BURRS
BURRY
BURSA
BURSE
BURST
CURBS
CURCI
CURDS
CURDY
CURED
CURER
CURES
CURIA
CURIE
CURIO
CURLS
CURLY
CURRY
CURSE
CURST
CURVE
CURVY
DURAN
DURER
DUROC
DUROS
DURRA
DURST
DURUM
EUROS
EURUS
FURAN
FURLS
FUROR
FURRY
FURTH
FURZE
GURDY
GURUS
HURDY
HURLS
HURLY
HUROK
HURON
HURRY
HURST
HURTS
JURAL
JURAT
JUROR
KURDS
KURSK
KURTZ
LURAY
LURCH
LURED
LURES
LUREX
LURIA
LURID
LURIE
LURKS
MURAL
MURAT
MUREX
MURKY
MURRA
MURRE
NURMI
NURSE
PUREE
PURER
PUREX
PURGE
PURIM
PURLS
PURRS
PURSE
PURSY
PURUS
RURAL
RURIK
SURAH
SURAL
SURAS
SURAT
SURDS
SURER
SURFS
SURFY
SURGE
SURLY
TURBO
TURFS
TURIN
TURKS
TURKU
TURNS
TUROW
TURVY
WURST
YURTS

•U•R•
AUDRA
AUTRE
AUTRY
BURRO
BURRS
BURRY
CUPRI
CUPRO
CURRY
DUPRE
DURRA
FURRY
GUARD
GUARS
HURRY
LUCRE
MUDRA
MUNRO
MURRA
MURRE
OUTRE
PURRS
QUARK
QUART
QUERN
QUERY
QUIRE
QUIRK
QUIRT
RUARK
SUCRE
SUDRA
SUERS
SUPRA
SUTRA

•U••R
AUBER
AUGER
AUGUR
AURAR
AUSTR
BUBER
BUYER
CUKOR
CURER
CUTER
DURER
EULER
FUROR
GULAR
HUGER
HUMOR
JUROR
LUGER
LUNAR
LUXOR
MUSER
MUTER
NUDER
OUTER
PURER
QUADR
QUEER
RUDER
RULER
RUMOR
SUGAR
SUMER
SUPER
SUPVR
SURER
TUBER
TUDOR
TUNER
TUTOR
ZUKOR

••UR•
ACURA
AZURE
BLURB
BLURS
BLURT
BOURG
BOURN
CHURL
CHURN
COURT
CRURA
DOURO
DRURY
ENURE
EXURB
FAURE
FOURH
FOURS
GAURS
GOURD
HEURE
HOURI
HOURS
INURE
KAURI
KNURL
KNURS
LAURA
MAURY
NAURU
NEURO
ORURO
PIURA
POURS
SCURF
SLURP
SLURS
SMURF
SOURS
SPURN
SPURS
SPURT
STURM
THURS
TOURS
TRURO
UHURA
UHURU
USURP
USURY
UTURN
YOURE
YOURS

••U•R
BAUER
BLUER
FLUOR
GLUER
HAUER
TRUER

•••UR
AMOUR
ARTUR
ASHUR
ASSUR
AUGUR
COEUR
DEMUR
FEMUR
FLEUR
FLOUR
HHOUR
INCUR
LEMUR
MASUR
MOHUR
NAMUR
OCCUR
ODOUR
RECUR
SCOUR
SIEUR
SOEUR
UIGUR

US•••
USAGE
USAIR
USCGA
USERS
USEUP
USHED
USHER
USING
USLTA
USTED
USUAL
USURP
USURY

U•S••
UNSAY
UNSER
UNSET
UPSET
URSID

U••S•
UKASE

U•••S
ULNAS
UMBOS
UNAUS
UNCAS
UNITS
UNIVS
UPDOS
URALS
URGES
USERS

•US••
AUSSI
AUSTR
BUSBY
BUSCH
BUSED
BUSES
BUSEY
BUSHY
BUSTS
CUSHY
CUSKS
CUSPS
DUSKS
DUSKY
DUSTS
DUSTY
FUSED
FUSEE
FUSES
FUSIL
FUSSY
FUSTY
GUSHY
GUSSY
GUSTO
GUSTS
GUSTY
HUSKS
HUSKY
HUSSY
JUSTE
LUSTS
LUSTY
MUSCA
MUSED
MUSER
MUSES
MUSHY
MUSIC
MUSKS
MUSKY
MUSSY
MUSTS
MUSTY
OUSEL
OUSTS
PUSAN
PUSEY
PUSHY
PUSSY
RUSES
RUSHY
RUSKS
RUSSE
RUSSO
RUSTS
RUSTY
SUSAN
SUSHI
SUSIE
SUSUS
TUSKS
WUSHU

•U•S•
AUSSI
BUGSY
BURSA
BURSE
BURST
CURSE
CURST
DULSE
DURST
FUBSY
FUSSY
GUESS
GUEST
GUISE
GUSSY
GUTSY
HURST
HUSSY
KURSK
LUISA
LUISE
MUSSY
NURSE
PULSE
PURSE
PURSY
PUSSY
QUASH
QUASI
QUEST
RUSSE
RUSSO
SUDSY
TULSA
WURST

•U••S
AUDIS
AUJUS
AULIS
AUNTS
AURAS
AUTOS
BUCKS
BUFFS
BUHLS
BULBS
BULKS
BULLS
BUMPS
BUNDS
BUNGS
BUNKS
BUNTS
BUOYS
BURBS
BURGS
BURLS
BURNS
BURPS
BURRS
BUSES
BUSTS
BUTTS
CUBES
CUFFS
CUKES
CULLS
CULMS
CULTS
CUNAS
CURBS
CURDS
CURES
CURLS
CUSKS
CUSPS
CUTIS
DUADS
DUBOS
DUCES
DUCKS
DUCTS
DUDES
DUELS
DUETS
DUFFS
DUKAS
DUKES
DULLS
DUMAS
DUMBS
DUMPS
DUNES
DUNKS
DUPES
DUROS
DUSKS
DUSTS
EUROS
EURUS
FUCHS
FUELS
FUMES
FUNDS
FUNKS
FURLS
FUSES
GUARS
GUESS
GULES
GULFS
GULLS
GULPS
GURUS
GUSTS
HUFFS
HULAS
HULKS
HULLS
HUMPS
HUMUS
HUNKS
HUNTS
HURLS
HURTS
HUSKS
JUDAS
JUJUS
JUKES
JULES
JUMPS
JUNKS
JUTES
KUDOS
KUDUS
KURDS
LUAUS
LUBAS
LUBES
LUCAS
LUCKS
LUFFS
LUGES
LUKAS
LULLS
LULUS
LUMPS
LUNES
LUNGS
LURES
LURKS
LUSTS
LUTES
MUCKS
MUFFS
MULES
MULLS
MUMPS
MUNIS
MUONS
MUSES
MUSKS
MUSTS
MUTES
MUTTS
NUDES
NUKES
NULLS
NUMBS
NUMIS
OUSTS
OUZOS
PUCKS
PUDUS
PUFFS
PULAS
PULES
PULIS
PULLS
PULPS
PUMAS
PUMPS
PUNAS
PUNGS
PUNKS
PUNTS
PUPAS
PURLS
PURRS
PURUS
PUTTS
QUADS
QUAGS
QUAYS
QUIDS
QUIPS
QUITS
QUODS
RUBES
RUCKS
RUDDS
RUFFS
RUFUS
RUINS
RULES
RUMPS
RUNES
RUNGS
RUNTS
RUSES
RUSKS
RUSTS
SUCKS
SUDDS
SUERS
SUETS
SUFIS
SUITS
SULKS
SUMPS
SUPTS
SURAS
SURDS
SURFS
SUSUS
TUBAS
TUBES
TUCKS
TUFTS
TULES
TUNAS
TUNES
TUNIS
TURFS
TURKS
TURNS
TUSKS
TUTUS
TUXES
YUANS
YUGOS
YUMAS
YURTS
ZULUS
ZUNIS

••US•
ABUSE
ADUST
AMUSE
AZUSA
BLUSH
BOUSE
BRUSH
CAUSE
COUSY
CRUSE
CRUSH
CRUST
DOUSE
DRUSE
FAUST
FLUSH
GAUSS
HAUSA
HOUSE
INUSE
JOUST
LOUSE
LOUSY
MEUSE
MOUSE
MOUSY
OFUSE
PAUSE
PLUSH
REUSE
ROUSE
ROUST
SEUSS
SHUSH
SLUSH
SOUSA
SOUSE
TRUSS
TRUST

••U•S
ABUTS
AGUES
ALUMS
AQUAS
ARUMS
BLUES
BLURS
BOUTS
BRUTS
CAULS
CHUBS
CHUGS
CHUMS
CLUBS
CLUES
COUPS
DAUBS
DRUBS
DRUGS
DRUMS
EQUUS
ETUIS
FAUNS
FEUDS
FLUBS
FLUES
FOULS
FOURS
FOUTS
GAUDS
GAULS
GAURS
GAUSS
GLUES
GLUTS
GRUBS
HAULS
HOURS
KNURS
LAUDS
LOUIS
LOUTS
MAULS
MOUES
NOUNS
PLUGS
PLUMS
POUFS
POURS
POUTS
REUPS
ROUES
ROUTS
SAUKS
SCUDS
SCUMS
SCUPS
SCUTS
SEUSS
SHULS
SHUNS
SHUTS
SKUAS
SLUES
SLUGS
SLUMS
SLURS
SMUTS
SNUBS
SNUGS
SOULS
SOUPS
SOURS
SPUDS
SPURS
STUBS
STUDS
STUMS
STUNS
THUDS
THUGS
THURS
TNUTS
TOURS
TOUTS
TRUES
TRUSS
WHUPS
YOURS

•••US
AGNUS
AINUS
ALDUS
ALTUS
ANGUS
ANNUS
APLUS
ARGUS
ARHUS
ARIUS
ASCUS
AUJUS
BEAUS
BOGUS
BOLUS
BONUS
BPLUS
CAMUS
CASUS
CETUS
CLAUS
COMUS
CPLUS
CYRUS
DPLUS
ECRUS
EOLUS
EQUUS
EURUS
FICUS
FOCUS
GAIUS
GENUS
GURUS
GYRUS
HOCUS
HONUS
HORUS
HUMUS
ICTUS
IGLUS
ILLUS
INCUS
INDUS
ISSUS
JANUS
JUJUS
KLAUS
KRAUS
KUDUS
LAIUS
LEPUS
LEXUS
LIEUS
LINUS
LOCUS
LOTUS
LUAUS
LULUS
MAGUS
MENUS
MINUS
MODUS
MOMUS
NEGUS
NEVUS
NEXUS
NIDUS
NISUS
NODUS
ORCUS
PILUS
PIOUS
POCUS
PRAUS
PUDUS
PURUS
REBUS
REMUS
RUFUS
SINUS
SITUS
SOLUS
SORUS
SUSUS
TAGUS
TALUS
THOUS
TITUS
TONUS
TORUS
TUTUS
UNAUS
VAGUS
VENUS
VIRUS
VITUS
XERUS
ZEBUS
ZULUS

UT•••
UTAHN
UTHER
UTICA
UTILE
UTLEY
UTTER
UTURN

U•T••
ULTRA
UNTER
UNTIE

UNTIL
UPTON
USTED
UTTER

U••T•
UINTA
UNITE
UNITS
UNITY
USLTA

U•••T
UBOAT
UBOLT
UNAPT
UNCUT
UNFIT
UNLIT
UNMET
UNSET
UPSET

•UT••
AUTOS
AUTRE
AUTRY
BUTCH
BUTEO
BUTTE
BUTTS
BUTYL
CUTER
CUTEX
CUTIE
CUTIN
CUTIS
CUTUP
DUTCH
FUTON
GUTEN
GUTSY
GUTTA
GUTTY
HUTCH
JUTES
LUTES
MUTED
MUTER
MUTES
MUTTS
NUTTY
OUTDO
OUTED
OUTER
OUTGO
OUTRE
PUTBY
PUTIN
PUTON
PUTTI
PUTTO
PUTTS
PUTTY
PUTUP
RUTIN
RUTTY
SUTRA
TUTEE
TUTOR
TUTTI
TUTUS

•U•T•
AUNTS
AUNTY
AUSTR
BUNTS
BUSTS
BUTTE
BUTTS
CULTS
DUCTS
DUETS
DUSTS
DUSTY
FURTH
FUSTY
GUSTO
GUSTS
GUSTY
GUTTA
GUTTY
HUNTS
HURTS
JUNTA
JUNTO
JUSTE
KURTZ
LUSTS
LUSTY
MUFTI
MULTI
MUSTS
MUSTY
MUTTS
NUTTY
OUSTS
PUNTA
PUNTS
PUNTY
PUTTI
PUTTO
PUTTS
PUTTY
QUITE
QUITO
QUITS
QUOTA
QUOTE
QUOTH
RUNTO
RUNTS
RUNTY
RUSTS
RUSTY
RUTTY
SUETS
SUITE
SUITS
SUPTS
TUFTS
TUTTI
YURTS

•U••T
AUDIT
AUGHT
BUILT
BUNDT
BURNT
BURST
CUBIT
CUGAT
CULET
CURST
DUCAT
DURST
DUVET
FUGIT
GUEST
GUILT
GUYOT
HURST
JURAT
LUMET
MULCT
MURAT
OUGHT
PUGET
QUANT
QUART
QUEST
QUIET
QUILT
QUINT
QUIRT
QUOIT
SUINT
SURAT
WURST

••UT•
ABUTS
ACUTE
BLUTH
BLUTO
BOUTS
BRUTE
BRUTS
CEUTA
CHUTE
COUTH
DEUTO
ELUTE
FLUTE
FLUTY
FOUTS
GLUTS
GOUTY
HAUTE
HEUTE
KLUTE
KLUTZ
KNUTE
LOUTS
MOUTH
PLUTO
POUTS
POUTY
ROUTE
ROUTS
SAUTE
SCUTA
SCUTE
SCUTS
SHUTE
SHUTS
SMUTS
SOUTH
STUTZ
TNUTS
TOUTE
TOUTS
TRUTH
YOUTH

••U•T
ADULT
ADUST
BLUET
BLUNT
BLURT
BOULT
BRUIT
BRUNT
COUNT
COURT
CRUET
CRUST
DAUNT
DOUBT
EDUCT
ERUCT
ERUPT
EXULT
FAULT
FAUST
FOUNT
FRUIT
GAUNT
GRUNT
GSUIT
HAUNT
INUIT
IQUIT
JAUNT
JOUST
MOULT
MOUNT
POULT
ROUST
SAULT
SHUNT
SOULT
SPURT
SQUAT
STUNT
TAUNT
TRUST
VAULT
VAUNT
YOUNT

•••UT
ABOUT
ADOUT
ALEUT
BEAUT
CLOUT
DEBUT
DONUT
FLOUT
GAMUT
GOOUT
GROUT
INPUT
KAPUT
KNOUT
KRAUT
LIEUT
REBUT
SALUT
SCOUT
SHOUT
SNOUT
SPOUT
STOUT
STRUT
TROUT
UNCUT
XSOUT
YAKUT

U•U••
UHURA
UHURU
USUAL
USURP
USURY
UTURN
UVULA

U••U•
UHAUL
UHHUH
UIGUR
UNAUS
UNCUT
UNDUE
USEUP

U•••U
UHURU
UPOLU

•U•U•
AUGUR
AUJUS
AURUM
BUYUP
CUMUL
CUTUP
DUGUP
DURUM
EURUS
FUGUE
GUMUP
GURUS
HUMUS
JUGUM
JUJUS
KUDUS
LUAUS
LULUS
PUDUS
PURUS
PUTUP
QUEUE
RUFUS
RUNUP
SUMUP
SUNUP
SUSUS
TUQUE
TUTUS
ZULUS

•U••U
KUDZU
QUIPU
TURKU
WUSHU

••UU•
EQUUS

••U•U
ISUZU
KHUFU
NAURU
UHURU

UV•••
UVULA

U••V•
UNIVS

•UV••
CUVEE
DUVET

•U•V•
CURVE
CURVY
GUAVA
SUAVE
SUPVR
TURVY

••UV•
FAUVE
MAUVE
YOUVE

••U•V
EQUIV

U•W••
UNWED

U•••W
UPBOW

•U••W
BULOW
TUROW

••UW•
ADUWA

UX•••
UXMAL

U•••X
UNBOX
UNFIX

•UX••
AUXIL
AUXIN
LUXOR
TUXES

•U••X
CULEX
CUTEX
LUREX
MUREX
PUREX

••U•X
TRUEX

•••UX
ADEUX
BEAUX
REDUX
SIOUX

U•••Y
UNIFY
UNITY
UNSAY
USURY
UTLEY

•UY••
BUYER
BUYUP
GUYED
GUYOT
NUYEN

•U•Y•
BUOYS
BUTYL
QUAYS

•U••Y
AUNTY
AUTRY
BUCKY
BUDDY
BUFFY
BUGGY
BUGSY
BULGY
BULKY
BULLY
BUMPY
BUNDY
BUNNY
BURLY
BURRY
BUSBY
BUSEY
BUSHY
CUBBY
CUDDY
CURDY
CURLY
CURRY
CURVY
CUSHY
DUCHY
DUCKY
DUDDY
DUFAY
DUFFY
DULLY
DUMMY
DUMPY
DUSKY
DUSTY
FUBSY
FUDDY
FULLY
FUNDY
FUNKY
FUNNY
FURRY
FUSSY
FUSTY
FUZZY
GULLY
GUMMY
GUNKY
GUNNY
GUPPY
GURDY
GUSHY
GUSSY
GUSTY
GUTSY
GUTTY
HUBBY
HUFFY
HUMPY
HURDY
HURLY
HURRY
HUSKY
HUSSY
JUICY
JUMPY
JUNKY
LUCKY
LULLY
LUMPY
LUNDY
LURAY
LUSTY
MUCKY
MUDDY
MUGGY
MULEY
MUMMY
MURKY
MUSHY
MUSKY
MUSSY
MUSTY
MUZZY
NUBBY
NUTTY
PUDGY
PUFFY
PULPY
PUNKY
PUNNY
PUNTY
PUPPY
PURSY
PUSEY
PUSHY
PUSSY
PUTBY
PUTTY
QUAKY
QUERY
RUDDY
RUGBY
RUMMY
RUNNY
RUNTY
RUSHY
RUSTY
RUTTY
SUDSY
SULKY
SULLY
SUNNY
SURFY
SURLY
TUBBY
TULLY
TUMMY
TUNNY
TURVY
YUCKY
YUMMY

••U•Y
BLUEY
CLUNY
COUSY
DEUCY
DOUAY
DRURY
FLUKY
FLUTY
GAUDY
GAUZY
GLUEY
GOUDY
GOUTY
LOUSY
MAURY
MOUSY
PLUMY
POUTY
SAUCY
SOUPY
SPUMY
STUDY
TRULY
USURY

•••UY
MYGUY

UZ•••
UZBEK

U•Z••
UNZIP

•UZ••
BUZZI
CUZCO
FUZZY
LUZON
MUZAK
MUZZY
OUZEL
OUZOS

•U•Z•
BUZZI
FURZE
FUZZY
KUDZU
MUZZY

•U••Z
KURTZ

••UZ•
ABUZZ
DRUZE
GAUZE
GAUZY
ISUZU

••U•Z
ABUZZ
KLUTZ
STUTZ

•••UZ
SOYUZ
VADUZ

VA•••
VACUA
VADER
VADIM
VADIS
VADUZ
VAGUE
VAGUS
VALES
VALET
VALID
VALLE
VALLI
VALOR
VALSE
VALUE
VALVE
VAMOS
VAMPS
VANCE
VANES
VANIR
VANNA
VANYA
VAPID
VAPOR
VARAS
VARIA
VARIG
VARIX
VARNA
VASCO
VASES
VATER
VATIC
VAULT
VAUNT

V•A••
VIALS
VIAND

V••A•
VARAS
VEDAS
VEDAY
VEGAN
VEGAS
VELAR
VENAE
VENAL
VICAR
VIDAL
VILAS
VINAS
VIRAL
VISAS
VITAE
VITAL
VITAS
VJDAY
VOCAL
VOLAR

V•••A
VACUA
VANNA
VANYA
VARIA
VARNA
VEDDA
VENDA
VERSA
VESTA
VILLA
VILMA
VIOLA
VIRGA
VIRNA
VISTA
VODKA
VOILA
VOLGA
VOLTA

•VA••
AVAIL
AVANT
AVARS
AVAST
EVADE
EVANS
IVANA
KVASS
OVALS
OVATE

•V•A•
AVGAS
AVIAN
EVIAN

•V••A
AVENA
AVILA
DVINA
EVITA
EVORA
IVANA
OVETA
UVULA

••VA•
ALVAR
CAVAE
DAVAO
DIVAN
DIVAS
JAVAS
KAVAS
KIVAS
LAVAL
LAVAS
LEVAR
NAVAL
NIVAL
NOVAE
NOVAK
NOVAS
RIVAL
SIVAN

••V•A
FOVEA
LIVIA
PAVIA

•••VA
ALAVA
BELVA
BRAVA
GUAVA
LARVA
SELVA
SHIVA
SILVA
SNEVA

V•B••
VIBES

V••B•
VERBS

V•C••
VACUA
VICAR
VICES
VICHY
VICKI
VICKS
VOCAL

V••C•
VANCE
VASCO
VETCH
VINCE
VINCI
VNECK
VOICE
VOICI
VOUCH

V•••C
VATIC
VEDIC

•V•C•
EVICT

••V•C
CIVIC
HAVOC

V•D••
VADER
VADIM
VADIS
VADUZ
VEDAS
VEDAY
VEDDA
VEDIC
VIDAL
VIDEO
VIDOR
VJDAY
VODKA

V••D•
VEDDA
VEIDT
VELDS
VELDT
VENDA
VENDS
VERDE
VERDI
VOIDS

V•••D
VALID
VAPID
VEXED
VIAND
VINED
VIRID
VIVID
VOTED
VOWED

•V•D•
EVADE

•V••D
AVOID
IVIED
OVOID

••VD•
BLVDS

••V•D
BOVID
CAVED
DAVID
DIVED
EAVED
GYVED
HIVED
JIVED
LAVED
LIVED
LIVID
LOVED
MOVED
PAVED
PAVID
RAVED
RIVED
ROVED
SAVED
VIVID
WAVED
WIVED

VE•••
VEDAS
VEDAY
VEDDA
VEDIC
VEEPS
VEERS
VEERY
VEGAN
VEGAS
VEIDT
VEILS
VEINS
VELAR
VELDS
VELDT
VELEZ
VELUM
VENAE
VENAL
VENDA
VENDS
VENEZ
VENIN
VENOM
VENTS
VENUE
VENUS
VERBS
VERDE
VERDI
VERGE
VERMI
VERNE
VERRE
VERSA
VERSE
VERSO
VERST
VERTE
VERTS
VERVE
VESEY
VESTA
VESTS
VETCH
VEXED
VEXER
VEXES

V•E••
VEEPS
VEERS
VEERY
VIEJO
VIERS
VIEWS
VNECK

V••E•
VADER
VALES
VALET
VANES
VASES
VATER
VELEZ
VENEZ
VESEY
VEXED
VEXER
VEXES
VIBES
VICES
VIDEO
VILER
VINED
VINES
VIPER
VIREO
VISES
VIXEN
VOLES
VOTED
VOTER
VOTES
VOWED
VOWEL
VOWER

V•••E
VAGUE
VALLE
VALSE
VALUE
VALVE
VANCE
VENAE
VENUE
VERDE
VERGE
VERNE
VERRE
VERSE
VERTE
VERVE
VILLE
VINCE
VITAE
VIVRE
VOGUE
VOICE
VOILE
VOLTE
VOTRE

•VE••
AVENA
AVENS
AVERS
AVERT
AVERY
EVENS
EVENT
EVERS
EVERT
EVERY
KVELL
OVENS
OVERS
OVERT
OVETA
OVETT

•V•E•
IVIED
IVIES
TVSET

•V••E
EVADE
EVOKE
OVATE
OVINE
OVULE

••VE•
AMVET
BEVEL
CAVED
CAVER
CAVES
CIVET
COVEN
COVER
COVES
COVET
COVEY
CUVEE
DIVED
DIVER
DIVES
DOVER
DOVES
DOVEY
DUVET
EAVED
EAVES
ELVER
ELVES
FAVES
FEVER
FIVER
FIVES
FOVEA
GAVEL
GIVEN
GIVER
GIVES
GYVED
GYVES
HAVEL
HAVEN
HAVER
HAVES
HIVED
HIVES
HOVEL
HOVER
HOVEY
JIVED
JIVER
JIVES
JIVEY
LAVED
LAVER
LAVES
LEVEE
LEVEL
LEVER
LIVED
LIVEN
LIVER
LIVES
LOVED
LOVER
LOVES
LOVEY
MAVEN
MOVED
MOVER
MOVES
NAVEL
NAVES
NEVER
NEVES
NIVEN
NOVEL
PAVED
PAVER
PAVES
RAVED
RAVEL
RAVEN
RAVER
RAVES
REVEL
REVET
RIVED
RIVEN
RIVER
RIVES
RIVET
ROVED
ROVER
ROVES
SAVED
SAVER
SAVES
SEVEN
SEVER
TEVET
TOVES
WAVED
WAVER
WAVES
WIVED
WIVES
WOVEN

••V•E
CAVAE
CUVEE
DAVIE
HAVRE
LEVEE
LIVRE
MCVIE
MOVIE
NOVAE
REVUE
TEVYE
VIVRE

•••VE
ABOVE
AGAVE
ALIVE
ATIVE
BRAVE
BREVE
CALVE
CARVE
CHIVE
CLAVE
CLIVE
CLOVE
CRAVE
CURVE
DELVE
DRIVE
DROVE
ELEVE
FAUVE
GLOVE
GRAVE
GROVE
HALVE
HEAVE
HELVE
HERVE
KNAVE
LEAVE
MAUVE
NAIVE
NERVE
OGIVE
OLIVE
PEEVE
PROVE
REEVE
SALVE
SERVE
SHAVE
SHOVE
SIEVE
SKIVE
SLAVE
SOAVE
SOLVE
STAVE
STEVE
STOVE
SUAVE
TRAVE
TROVE
VALVE
VERVE
WAIVE
WEAVE
YOUVE

V•G••
VAGUE
VAGUS
VEGAN
VEGAS
VIGIL
VIGOR
VOGUE

V••G•
VERGE
VINGT
VIRGA
VIRGO
VOLGA
VSIGN

V•••G
VARIG
VYING

•VG••
AVGAS

••V•G
NAVIG

V••H•
VICHY

V•••H
VETCH
VOUCH

VI•••
VIALS VIAND VIBES VICAR VICES VICHY VICKI VICKS VIDAL VIDEO VIDOR VIEJO VIERS VIEWS VIGIL VIGOR VIKKI VILAS VILER VILLA VILLE VILLI VILMA VINAS VINCE VINCI VINED VINES VINGT VINNY VINYL VIOLA VIOLS VIPER VIRAL VIREO VIRGA VIRGO VIRID VIRNA VIRTU VIRUS VISAS VISES VISIT VISOR VISTA VITAE VITAL VITAS VITUS VIVID VIVRE VIXEN

V•I••
VEIDT VEILS VEINS VOICE VOICI VOIDS VOILA VOILE VSIGN VYING

V••I•
VADIM VADIS VALID VANIR VAPID VARIA VARIG VARIX VATIC VEDIC VENIN VIGIL VIRID VISIT VIVID

V•••I
VALLI VERDI VERMI VICKI VIKKI VILLI VINCI VOICI

•VI••
AVIAN AVILA AVION AVISO CVIII DVIII DVINA EVIAN EVICT EVILS EVITA IVIED IVIES IVINS LVIII MVIII OVINE XVIII

•V•I•
AVAIL AVOID AVOIR AVRIL CVIII DVIII LVIII MVIII OVOID XVIII

•V••I
CVIII DVIII LVIII MVIII OVOLI XVIII

••VI•
ADVIL ALVIN ANVIL BEVIN BOVID CAVIL CCVII CDVII CIVIC CIVIL CLVII CMVII CXVII DAVID DAVIE DAVIS DAVIT DCVII DEVIL DLVII DXVII ELVIN ELVIS ERVIL ERVIN GAVIN IRVIN KEVIN LAVIN LEVIN LEVIS LIVIA LIVID LXVII MAVIS MCVIE MCVII MDVII MLVII MMVII MOVIE MXVII NAVIG NEVIL NEVIN NEVIS PAVIA PAVID PAVIS QBVII RAVIN VIVID XCVII XLVII XXVII

••V•I
CCVII CDVII CLVII CMVII CXVII DCVII DLVII DXVII ENVOI LXVII MCVII MDVII MLVII MMVII MXVII QBVII XCVII XLVII XXVII

•••VI
CCCVI CCLVI CCXVI CDLVI CDXVI CLXVI CMLVI CMXVI CXCVI CXLVI CXXVI DCCVI DCLVI DCXVI DLXVI DXCVI DXLVI DXXVI LXXVI MCCVI MCDVI MCLVI MCMVI MCXVI MDCVI MDLVI MDXVI MLXVI MMCVI MMDVI MMLVI MMMVI MMXVI MXCVI MXLVI MXXVI TREVI XXXVI

VJ•••
VJDAY

V••J•
VIEJO

V•K••
VIKKI

V••K•
VICKI VICKS VIKKI VODKA

V•••K
VNECK

•V•K•
EVOKE

••V•K
NOVAK

V•L••
VALES VALET VALID VALLE VALLI VALOR VALSE VALUE VALVE VELAR VELDS VELDT VELEZ VELUM VILAS VILER VILLA VILLE VILLI VILMA VOLAR VOLES VOLGA VOLTA VOLTE VOLTS VOLVO

V••L•
VALLE VALLI VAULT VEILS VIALS VILLA VILLE VILLI VIOLA VIOLS VOILA VOILE VTOLS

V•••L
VENAL VIDAL VIGIL VINYL VIRAL VITAL VOCAL VOWEL

•V•L•
AVILA EVILS KVELL OVALS OVOLI OVOLO OVULE UVULA

•V••L
AVAIL AVRIL KVELL

••V•L
ADVIL ANVIL BEVEL CAVIL CIVIL DEVIL ERVIL GAVEL HAVEL HOVEL LAVAL LEVEL NAVAL NAVEL NEVIL NIVAL NOVEL RAVEL REVEL RIVAL

V•M••
VAMOS VAMPS

V••M•
VERMI VILMA

V•••M
VADIM VELUM VENOM VROOM

VN•••
VNECK

V•N••
VANCE VANES VANIR VANNA VANYA VENAE VENAL VENDA VENDS VENEZ VENIN VENOM VENTS VENUE VENUS VINAS VINCE VINCI VINED VINES VINGT VINNY VINYL

V••N•
VANNA VARNA VAUNT VEINS VERNE VIAND VINNY VIRNA VYING

V•••N
VEGAN VENIN VIXEN VSIGN

•V•N•
AVANT AVENA AVENS DVINA EVANS EVENS EVENT IVANA IVINS OVENS OVINE

•V••N
AVIAN AVION EVIAN

••V•N
ALVIN BEVIN COVEN DEVON DIVAN ELVIN ERVIN GAVIN GIVEN HAVEN IRVIN KEVIN LAVIN LEVIN LEVON LIVEN MAVEN NEVIN NIVEN RAVEN RAVIN RIVEN SEVEN SIVAN WOVEN ZEVON

VO•••
VOCAL VODKA VOGUE VOICE VOICI VOIDS VOILA VOILE VOLAR VOLES VOLGA VOLTA VOLTE VOLTS VOLVO VOTED VOTER VOTES VOTRE VOUCH VOWED VOWEL VOWER

V•O••
VIOLA VIOLS VROOM VTOLS

V••O•
VALOR VAMOS VAPOR VENOM VIDOR VIGOR VISOR VROOM

V•••O
VASCO VERSO VIDEO VIEJO VIREO VIRGO VOLVO

•VO••
AVOID AVOIR AVOWS EVOKE EVORA IVORY OVOID OVOLI OVOLO

•V•O•
AVION

•V••O
AVISO OVOLO

••VO•
DAVOS DEVON DIVOT ENVOI ENVOY FAVOR GAVOT HAVOC LEVON PIVOT SAVOR SAVOY ZEVON

••V•O
DAVAO

•••VO
ABOVO BRAVO NORVO PAAVO PROVO SALVO SERVO VOLVO

V•P••
VAPID VAPOR VIPER

V••P•
VAMPS VEEPS

••VP•
RSVPS

VR•••
VROOM

V•R••
VARAS VARIA VARIG VARIX VARNA VERBS VERDE VERDI VERGE VERMI VERNE VERRE VERSA VERSE VERSO VERST VERTE VERTS VERVE VIRAL VIREO VIRGA VIRGO VIRID VIRNA VIRTU VIRUS

V••R•
VEERS VEERY VERRE VIERS VIVRE VOTRE

V•••R
VADER VALOR VANIR VAPOR VATER VELAR VEXER VICAR VIDOR VIGOR VILER VIPER VISOR VOLAR VOTER VOWER

•VR••
AVRIL

•V•R•
AVARS AVERS AVERT AVERY EVERS EVERT EVERY EVORA IVORY OVERS OVERT

•V••R
AVOIR

••VR•
DEVRY HAVRE LIVRE VIVRE

••V•R
ALVAR CAVER COVER DIVER DOVER ELVER FAVOR FEVER FIVER GIVER HAVER HOVER JIVER LAVER LEVAR LEVER LIVER LOVER MOVER NEVER PAVER RAVER RIVER ROVER SAVER SAVOR SEVER WAVER

•••VR
SUPVR

VS•••
VSIGN

V•S••
VASCO VASES VESEY VESTA VESTS VISAS VISES VISIT VISOR VISTA

V••S•
VALSE VERSA VERSE VERSO VERST

V•••S
VADIS VAGUS VALES VAMOS VAMPS VANES VARAS VASES VEDAS VEEPS VEERS VEGAS VEILS VEINS VELDS VENDS VENTS VENUS VERBS VERTS VESTS VEXES VIALS VIBES VICES VICKS VIERS VIEWS VILAS VINAS VINES VIOLS VIRUS VISAS VISES VITAS VITUS VOIDS VOLES VOLTS VOTES VTOLS

•VS••
TVSET

•V•S•
AVAST AVISO KVASS

•V••S
AVARS AVENS AVERS AVGAS AVOWS EVANS EVENS EVERS EVILS IVIES IVINS KVASS OVALS OVENS OVERS

••V•S
BLVDS CAVES COVES DAVIS DAVOS DAVYS DIVAS DIVES DOVES EAVES ELVES ELVIS FAVES FIVES GIVES GYVES HAVES HIVES JAVAS JIVES KAVAS KIVAS LAVAS LAVES LEVIS LIVES LOVES MAVIS MOVES NAVES NEVES NEVIS NEVUS NOVAS PAVES PAVIS RAVES RIVES ROVES RSVPS SAVES TOVES WAVES WIVES

•••VS
MIRVS SHIVS SLAVS SPIVS UNIVS

VT•••
VTOLS

V•T••
VATER VATIC VETCH VITAE VITAL VITAS VITUS VOTED VOTER VOTES VOTRE

V••T•
VENTS VERTE VERTS VESTA VESTS VIRTU VISTA VOLTA VOLTE VOLTS

V•••T
VALET VAULT VAUNT VEIDT VELDT VERST VINGT VISIT

•V•T•
EVITA OVATE OVETA OVETT

•V••T
AVANT AVAST AVERT EVENT EVERT EVICT OVERT OVETT TVSET

••V•T
AMVET CIVET COVET DAVIT DIVOT DUVET GAVOT PIVOT REVET RIVET TEVET

V•U••
VAULT VAUNT VOUCH

V••U•
VACUA VADUZ VAGUE VAGUS VALUE VELUM VENUE VENUS VIRUS VITUS VOGUE

V•••U
VIRTU

•VU••
OVULE UVULA

••VU•
NEVUS REVUE

V•V••
VIVID VIVRE

V••V•
VALVE VERVE VOLVO

••VV•
DIVVY NAVVY SAVVY

V•W••
VOWED VOWEL VOWER

V••W•
VIEWS

•V•W•
AVOWS

V•X••
VEXED VEXER VEXES VIXEN

V•••X
VARIX

VY•••
VYING

V••Y•
VANYA VINYL

V•••Y
VEDAY VEERY VESEY VICHY VINNY VJDAY

•V••Y
AVERY EVERY IVORY

••VY•
DAVYS TEVYE

••V•Y
COVEY DEVRY DIVVY DOVEY ENVOY HOVEY JIVEY LOVEY NAVVY SAVOY SAVVY

•••VY
CHEVY CHIVY CURVY DIVVY GRAVY HEAVY MARVY NAVVY NERVY PEAVY PRIVY SAVVY TURVY

V•••Z
VADUZ VELEZ VENEZ

WA•••
WAALS WACKO WACKY WADED WADER WADES WADIS WADUP WAFER WAFTS WAGED WAGER WAGES WAGON WAHOO WAIFS WAILS WAINS WAIST WAITE WAITS WAITZ WAIVE WAKED WAKEN WAKES WALDO WALED WALER WALES WALKS WALLS WALLY WALSH WALSY WALTZ WANDA WANDS WANED WANER WANES WANLY WANNA WANTS WARDS WARES WARMS WARNS WARPS WARTS WARTY WASHY WASNT WASPS WASTE WATCH WATER WATTS WAUGH WAVED WAVER WAVES WAXED WAXEN WAXER WAXES WAYNE

W•A••
WAALS WEALS WEANS WEARS WEARY WEAVE WHACK WHALE WHAMO WHAMS WHANG WHARF WHATD WHATS WOADS WRACK WRAPS WRAPT WRATH WYATT

W••A•
WHEAL WHEAT WIGAN WOMAN WOTAN WREAK WUHAN WYMAN

W•••A
WANDA WANNA WICCA WILLA WILMA WIRRA

•WA••
AWACS AWAIT AWAKE AWARD AWARE AWASH BWANA DWARF SWABS SWAGE SWAGS SWAIN SWALE SWAMI SWAMP SWANK SWANN SWANS SWAPS SWARD SWARF SWARM SWART SWASH SWATH SWATS SWAYS SWAZI TWAIN TWANG

•W•A•
SWEAR SWEAT TWEAK YWCAS

•W••A
BWANA TWYLA

••WA•
AMWAY ANWAR ASWAN ATWAR BYWAY DEWAN DEWAR ELWAY IOWAN MYWAY NAWAB NOWAY OTWAY PAWAT POWAY REWAX ROWAN

•••WA
ADUWA DAIWA KIOWA OZAWA SCHWA SLIWA

W•B••
WEBER

W••B•
WELBY

•W•B•
SWABS

•W••B
DWEEB

••W•B
NAWAB

W•C••
WACKO WACKY WICCA WICKS

W••C•
WATCH WELCH WENCH WHACK WHICH WICCA WILCO WINCE WINCH WITCH WRACK WRECK

•WC••
YWCAS

•W•C•
AWACS TWICE

W•D••
WADED WADER WADES WADIS WADUP WEDEL WEDGE WEDGY WIDEN

WIDER WIDOW WIDTH WODEN

W••D•
WALDO WANDA WANDS WARDS WEEDS WEEDY WELDS WENDS WENDT WENDY WILDE WILDS WINDS WINDY WOADS WOLDS WOODS WOODY WORDS WORDY

W•••D
WADED WAGED WAKED WALED WANED WAVED WAXED WEIRD WHATD WIELD WILED WINED WIPED WIRED WIVED WOOED WORLD WOULD WOUND WOWED

•W•D•
SWEDE

•W••D
AWARD AWNED OWNED SWARD SWORD TWEED

••WD•
BAWDY DOWDY GOWDY HOWDY ROWDY

••W•D
BOWED CAWED COWED DEWED HAWED HEWED JAWED LOWED MEWED MOWED PAWED REWED ROWED SAWED SEWED SOWED TOWED UNWED VOWED WOWED YAWED

•••WD
CROWD

WE•••
WEALS WEANS WEARS WEARY WEAVE WEBER WEDEL WEDGE WEDGY WEEDS WEEDY WEEKS WEEMS WEENY WEEPS WEEPY WEEST WEFTS WEIGH WEILL WEIRD WEIRS WEISS WELBY WELCH WELDS WELLS WELSH WELTS WELTY WENCH WENDS WENDT WENDY WESER WETLY

W•E••
WEEDS WEEDY WEEKS WEEMS WEENY WEEPS WEEPY WEEST WHEAL WHEAT WHEEL WHEEN WHELK WHELM WHELP WHERE WHETS WHEYS WIELD WIEST WREAK WRECK WRENS WREST WYETH

W••E•
WADED WADER WADES WAFER WAGED WAGER WAGES WAKED WAKEN WAKES WALED WALER WALES WANED WANER WANES WARES WATER WAVED WAVER WAVES WAXED WAXEN WAXER WAXES WEBER WEDEL WESER WHEEL WHEEN WIDEN WIDER WILED WILES WILEY WINED WINES WIPED WIPER WIPES WIRED WIRER WIRES WISER WIVED WIVES WIZEN WODEN WOKEN WOMEN WOOED WOOER WOVEN WOWED WRIER WRYER WYLER

W•••E
WAITE WAIVE WASTE WAYNE WEAVE WEDGE WHALE WHERE WHILE WHINE WHITE WHOLE WHOSE WHYME WILDE WINCE WINZE WITHE WITTE WOLFE WORSE WRITE WROTE WYLIE WYTHE

•WE••
DWEEB DWELL DWELT EWELL EWERS GWENN OWENS OWERS SWEAR SWEAT SWEDE SWEEP SWEET SWELL SWEPT TWEAK TWEED TWEEN TWEET TWERE TWERP ZWEIG

•W•E•
AWNED DWEEB OWLET OWNED OWNER SWEEP SWEET TWEED TWEEN TWEET

•W••E
AWAKE AWARE AWOKE SWAGE SWALE SWEDE SWINE SWIPE SWOPE SWORE TWERE TWICE TWINE

••WE•
BOWED BOWEN BOWER BOWES CAWED COWED COWER COWES DAWES DEWED DEWEY DOWEL DOWER FEWER GOWER HAWED HEWED HEWER JAWED JEWEL LAWES LEWES LOWED LOWER MEWED MOWED MOWER NEWEL NEWER PAWED PAWER PEWEE POWER RAWER REWED ROWED ROWEL ROWEN ROWER SAWED SEWED SEWER SOWED SOWER TOWED TOWEL TOWER UNWED VOWED VOWEL VOWER WOWED YAWED

••W•E
BOWIE DOWSE HAWKE HAWSE HOWIE PEWEE TOWNE ZOWIE

•••WE
INAWE LOEWE STOWE

W•F••
WAFER WAFTS WEFTS

W••F•
WAIFS WHIFF WOLFE WOLFF WOOFS

W•••F
WHARF WHIFF WHOOF WOLFF WOOLF

•WF••
AWFUL

•W•F•
SWIFT

•W••F
DWARF SWARF

W•G••
WAGED WAGER WAGES WAGON WIGAN WIGGY WIGHT

W••G•
WAUGH WEDGE WEDGY WEIGH WHIGS WIGGY WINGS

W•••G
WHANG WRING WRONG WRUNG

•W•G•
SWAGE SWAGS SWIGS TWIGS

•W••G
AWING EWING OWING SWING SWUNG TWANG ZWEIG

WH•••
WHACK WHALE WHAMO WHAMS WHANG WHARF WHATD WHATS WHEAL WHEAT WHEEL WHEEN WHELK WHELM WHELP WHERE WHETS WHEYS WHICH WHIFF WHIGS WHILE WHIMS WHINE WHINY WHIPS WHIRL WHIRR WHIRS WHISK WHIST WHITE WHITS WHOLE WHOLL WHOMP WHOOF WHOOP WHOPS WHORL WHOSE WHOSO WHUPS WHYME

W•H••
WAHOO WUHAN

W••H•
WASHY WIGHT WISHY WITHE WUSHU WYTHE

W•••H
WALSH WATCH WAUGH WEIGH WELCH WELSH WENCH WHICH WIDTH WINCH WITCH WORTH WRATH WROTH WYETH

•W••H
AWASH SWASH SWATH SWISH

WI•••
WICCA WICKS WIDEN WIDER WIDOW WIDTH WIELD WIEST WIGAN WIGGY WIGHT WILCO WILDE WILDS WILED WILES WILEY WILLA WILLS WILLY WILMA WILTS WIMPS WIMPY WINCE WINCH WINDS WINDY WINED WINES WINGS WINKS WINZE WIPED WIPER WIPES WIRED WIRER WIRES WIRRA WISER WISHY WISPS WISPY WITCH WITHE WITTE WITTY WIVED WIVES WIZEN

W•I••
WAIFS WAILS WAINS WAIST WAITE WAITS WAITZ WAIVE WEIGH WEILL WEIRD WEIRS WEISS WHICH WHIFF WHIGS WHILE WHIMS WHINE WHINY WHIPS WHIRL WHIRR WHIRS WHISK WHIST WHITE WHITS WRIER WRING WRIST WRITE WRITS

W••I•
WADIS WYLIE

•WI••
AWING EWING OWING SWIFT SWIGS SWILL SWIMS SWINE SWING SWIPE SWIRL SWISH SWISS SWITZ TWICE TWIGS TWILL TWINE TWINS TWIRL TWIST TWITS TWIXT

•W•I•
AWAIT SWAIN TWAIN ZWEIG

•W••I
SWAMI SWAZI

••WI•
BOWIE EDWIN ERWIN HOWIE IRWIN KIWIS LEWIS PEWIT REWIN SAWIN TOWIT ZOWIE

W•K••
WAKED WAKEN WAKES WOKEN

W••K•
WACKO WACKY WALKS WEEKS WICKS WINKS WONKS WONKY WORKS

W•••K
WHACK WHELK WHISK WRACK WREAK WRECK

•W•K•
AWAKE AWOKE EWOKS

•W••K
SWANK TWEAK

••WK•
GAWKS GAWKY HAWKE HAWKS

W•L••
WALDO WALED WALER WALES WALKS WALLS WALLY WALSH WALSY WALTZ WELBY WELCH WELDS WELLS WELSH WELTS WELTY WILCO WILDE WILDS WILED WILES WILEY WILLA WILLS WILLY WILMA WILTS WOLDS WOLFE WOLFF WYLER WYLIE

W••L•
WAALS WAILS WALLS WALLY WANLY WEALS WEILL WELLS WETLY WHALE WHELK WHELM WHELP WHILE WHOLE WHOLL WIELD WILLA WILLS WILLY WOOLF WOOLS WORLD WOULD WRYLY

W•••L
WEDEL WEILL WHEAL WHEEL WHIRL WHOLL WHORL

•WL••
OWLET

•W•L•
AWOLS DWELL DWELT EWELL SWALE SWELL SWILL TWILL TWYLA

•W••L
AWFUL DWELL EWELL SWELL SWILL SWIRL TWILL TWIRL

••WL•
BAWLS BOWLS COWLS FOWLS HOWLS JOWLS JOWLY LOWLY MEWLS NEWLY PAWLS RAWLS RAWLY YAWLS YOWLS

••W•L
DOWEL JEWEL NEWEL ROWEL TOWEL VOWEL

•••WL
BRAWL CRAWL DRAWL GROWL PROWL SCOWL SHAWL TRAWL

W•M••
WIMPS WIMPY WOMAN WOMEN WYMAN

W••M•
WARMS WEEMS WHAMO WHAMS WHIMS WHOMP WHYME WILMA WORMS WORMY

W•••M
WHELM

•W•M•
SWAMI SWAMP SWIMS

•W••M
SWARM

•••WM
SHAWM

W•N••
WANDA WANDS WANED WANER WANES WANLY WANNA WANTS WENCH WENDS WENDT WENDY WINCE WINCH WINDS WINDY WINED WINES WINGS WINKS WINZE WONKS WONKY WONTS

W••N•
WAINS WANNA WARNS WASNT WAYNE WEANS WEENY WHANG WHINE WHINY WOUND WRENS WRING WRONG WRUNG

W•••N
WAGON WAKEN WAXEN WHEEN WIDEN WIGAN WIZEN WODEN WOKEN WOMAN WOMEN WOTAN WOVEN WUHAN WYMAN

•WN••
AWNED OWNED OWNER OWNUP

•W•N•
AWING BWANA EWING GWENN GWYNN OWENS OWING SWANK SWANN SWANS SWINE SWING SWUNG TWANG TWINE TWINS

•W••N
GWENN GWYNN SWAIN SWANN SWOON SWORN TWAIN TWEEN

••WN•
DAWNS DOWNS DOWNY FAWNS GOWNS LAWNS PAWNS TAWNY TOWNE TOWNS YAWNS

••W•N
ASWAN BOWEN DEWAN EDWIN ERWIN IOWAN IRWIN REWIN REWON ROWAN ROWEN SAWIN SEWON

•••WN
BLOWN BRAWN BROWN CLOWN CROWN DRAWN DROWN FLOWN FROWN GROWN KNOWN PRAWN SHAWN SHOWN SPAWN

WO•••
WOADS WODEN WOKEN WOLDS WOLFE WOLFF WOMAN WOMEN WONKS WONKY WONTS WOODS WOODY WOOED WOOER WOOFS WOOLF WOOLS WOOZY WORDS WORDY WORKS WORLD WORMS WORMY WORRY WORSE WORST WORTH WORTS WOTAN WOULD WOUND WOVEN WOWED

W•O••
WHOLE WHOLL WHOMP WHOOF WHOOP WHOPS WHORL WHOSE WHOSO WOODS WOODY WOOED WOOER WOOFS WOOLF WOOLS WOOZY WRONG WROTE WROTH

W••O•
WAGON WAHOO WHAMO WHOOF WHOOP WIDOW

W•••O
WACKO WAHOO WALDO WHAMO WHOSO WILCO

•WO••
AWOKE AWOLS EWOKS SWOON SWOOP SWOPE SWORD SWORE SWORN

•W•O•
SWOON SWOOP

••WO•
REWON SEWON

••W•O
HOWSO HOWTO SAWTO

•••WO
INTWO

W•P••
WIPED WIPER WIPES

W••P•
WARPS WASPS WEEPS WEEPY WHIPS WHOPS WHUPS WIMPS WIMPY WISPS WISPY WRAPS WRAPT

W•••P
WADUP WHELP WHOMP WHOOP

•W•P•
SWAPS SWEPT SWIPE SWOPE

•W••P
OWNUP SWAMP SWEEP SWOOP TWERP

••WP•
YAWPS

••W•P
SEWUP

WR•••
WRACK WRAPS WRAPT WRATH WREAK WRECK WRENS WREST WRIER WRING WRIST WRITE WRITS WRONG WROTE WROTH WRUNG WRYER WRYLY

W•R••
WARDS WARES WARMS WARNS WARPS WARTS WARTY WIRED WIRER WIRES WIRRA WORDS WORDY WORKS WORLD WORMS WORMY WORRY WORSE WORST WORTH WORTS WURST

W••R•
WEARS WEARY WEIRD WEIRS WHARF WHERE WHIRL WHIRR WHIRS WHORL WIRRA WORRY

W•••R
WADER WAFER WAGER WALER WANER WATER WAVER WAXER WEBER WESER WHIRR WIDER WIPER WIRER WISER WOOER WRIER WRYER WYLER

•W•R•
AWARD AWARE DWARF EWERS OWERS SWARD SWARF SWARM SWART SWIRL SWORD SWORE SWORN TWERE TWERP TWIRL

•W••R
OWNER SWEAR

••WR•
DOWRY LOWRY

••W•R
ANWAR ATWAR BOWER COWER DEWAR DOWER FEWER

GOWER
HEWER
LOWER
MOWER
NEWER
PAWER
POWER
RAWER
ROWER
SEWER
SOWER
TOWER
VOWER

W•S••
WASHY
WASNT
WASPS
WASTE
WESER
WISER
WISHY
WISPS
WISPY
WUSHU

W••S•
WAIST
WALSH
WALSY
WEEST
WEISS
WELSH
WHISK
WHIST
WHOSE
WHOSO
WIEST
WORSE
WORST
WREST
WRIST
WURST

W•••S
WAALS
WADES
WADIS
WAFTS
WAGES
WAIFS
WAILS
WAINS
WAITS
WAKES
WALES
WALKS
WALLS
WANDS
WANES
WANTS
WARDS
WARES
WARMS
WARNS
WARPS
WARTS
WASPS
WATTS
WAVES
WAXES
WEALS
WEANS
WEARS
WEEDS
WEEKS
WEEMS
WEEPS
WEFTS
WEIRS
WEISS
WELDS
WELLS
WELTS
WENDS
WHAMS
WHATS
WHETS
WHEYS
WHIGS
WHIMS
WHIPS
WHIRS
WHITS
WHOPS
WHUPS
WICKS
WILDS
WILES
WILLS
WILTS
WIMPS
WINDS
WINES
WINGS
WINKS
WIPES
WIRES
WISPS
WIVES
WOADS
WOLDS
WONKS
WONTS
WOODS
WOOFS
WOOLS
WORDS
WORKS
WORMS
WORTS
WRAPS
WRENS
WRITS

•W•S•
AWASH
SWASH
SWISH
SWISS
TWIST

•W••S
AWACS
AWOLS
EWERS
EWOKS
OWENS
OWERS
SWABS
SWAGS
SWANS
SWAPS
SWATS
SWAYS
SWIGS
SWIMS
SWISS
TWIGS
TWINS
TWITS
YWCAS

••WS•
DOWSE
HAWSE
HOWSO
NEWSY

••W•S
BAWLS
BOWES
BOWLS
COWES
COWLS
DAWES
DAWNS
DOWNS
FAWNS
FOWLS
GAWKS
GOWNS
HAWKS
HOWLS
JOWLS
KIWIS
LAWES
LAWNS
LEWES
LEWIS
MEWLS
NEWTS
PAWLS
PAWNS
POWYS
RAWLS
TOWNS
YAWLS
YAWNS
YAWPS
YOWLS

•••WS
AVOWS
BLOWS
BREWS
BROWS
CHAWS
CHEWS
CHOWS
CLAWS
CLEWS
CRAWS
CREWS
CROWS
DHOWS
DRAWS
FLAWS
FLEWS
FLOWS
FROWS
GLOWS
GNAWS
GROWS
KNOWS
MEOWS
PLOWS
PROWS
SCOWS
SHOWS
SKEWS
SLAWS
SLEWS
SLOWS
SMEWS
SNOWS
SPEWS
STEWS
STOWS
THAWS
THEWS
TREWS
VIEWS

W•T••
WATCH
WATER
WATTS
WETLY
WITCH
WITHE
WITTE
WITTY
WOTAN
WYTHE

W••T•
WAFTS
WAITE
WAITS
WAITZ
WALTZ
WANTS
WARTS
WARTY
WASTE
WATTS
WEFTS
WELTS
WELTY
WHATD
WHATS
WHETS
WHITE
WHITS
WIDTH
WILTS
WITTE
WITTY
WONTS
WORTH
WORTS
WRATH
WRITE
WRITS
WROTE
WROTH
WYATT
WYETH

W•••T
WAIST
WASNT
WEEST
WENDT
WHEAT
WHIST
WIEST
WIGHT
WORST
WRAPT
WREST
WRIST
WURST
WYATT

•W•T•
SWATH
SWATS
SWITZ
TWITS

•W••T
AWAIT
DWELT
OWLET
SWART
SWEAT
SWEET
SWEPT
SWIFT
TWEET
TWIST
TWIXT

••WT•
HOWTO
NEWTS
SAWTO

••W•T
PAWAT
PEWIT
TOWIT

WU•••
WUHAN
WURST
WUSHU

W•U••
WAUGH
WHUPS
WOULD
WOUND
WRUNG

W••U•
WADUP

W•••U
WUSHU

•WU••
SWUNG

•W•U•
AWFUL
OWNUP

••WU•
SEWUP

•••WU
ILGWU

W•V••
WAVED
WAVER
WAVES
WIVED
WIVES
WOVEN

W••V•
WAIVE
WEAVE

W•W••
WOWED

W•••W
WIDOW

W•X••
WAXED
WAXEN
WAXER
WAXES

•W•X•
TWIXT

••W•X
REWAX

WY•••
WYATT
WYETH
WYLER
WYLIE
WYMAN
WYTHE

W•Y••
WAYNE
WHYME
WRYER
WRYLY

W••Y•
WHEYS

W•••Y
WACKY
WALLY
WALSY
WANLY
WARTY
WASHY
WEARY
WEDGY
WEEDY
WEENY
WEEPY
WELBY
WELTY
WENDY
WETLY
WHINY
WIGGY
WILEY
WILLY
WIMPY
WINDY
WISHY
WISPY
WITTY
WONKY
WOODY
WOOZY
WORDY
WORMY
WORRY
WRYLY

•WY••
GWYNN
TWYLA

•W•Y•
SWAYS

••WY•
POWYS

••W•Y
AMWAY
BAWDY
BYWAY
DEWEY
DOWDY
DOWNY
DOWRY
ELWAY
GAWKY
GOWDY
HOWDY
JOWLY
LOWLY
LOWRY
MYWAY
NEWLY
NEWSY
NOWAY
OTWAY
POWAY
RAWLY
ROWDY
TAWNY

•••WY
BLOWY
CHEWY
LOEWY
SHOWY
SNOWY

W•Z••
WIZEN

W••Z•
WINZE
WOOZY

W•••Z
WAITZ
WALTZ

•W•Z•
SWAZI

•W••Z
SWITZ

XA•••
XACTO
XAXES
XAXIS

X•A••
XRAYS

X•••A
XENIA
XHOSA

•XA••
EXACT
EXALT
EXAMS

•X•A•
AXIAL
IXNAY
UXMAL

•X••A
EXTRA

••XA•
COXAE
COXAL
HEXAD
LEXAN
TEXAN
TEXAS

X•B••
XEBEC

•XB••
OXBOW

•X••B
EXURB

••XB•
BIXBY

XC•••
XCIII
XCVII

X•C••
XACTO

X•••C
XEBEC
XERIC

•XC••
CXCII
CXCIV
CXCIX
CXCVI
DXCII
DXCIV
DXCIX
DXCVI
EXCEL
MXCII
MXCIV
MXCIX
MXCVI

•X•C•
EXACT
EXECS

••XC•
CCXCI
CCXCV
CDXCI
CDXCV
CMXCI
CMXCV
DCXCI
DCXCV
MCXCI
MCXCV
MDXCI
MDXCV
MMXCI
MMXCV
TAXCO

••X•C
TOXIC

•••XC
CCCXC
DCCXC
MCCXC
MCDXC
MCMXC
MDCXC
MMCXC
MMDXC
MMMXC

•X•D•
EXUDE
OXIDE

••X•D
BOXED
COXED
FAXED
FIXED
FOXED
HEXAD
HEXED
MAXED
MIXED
NIXED
SIXED
TAXED
VEXED
WAXED

XE•••
XEBEC
XENIA
XENON
XERIC
XEROX
XERUS

X••E•
XAXES
XEBEC
XYLEM

•XE••
AXELS
EXECS
EXERT
OXEYE

•X•E•
AXLES
EXCEL
EXPEL

•X••E
EXILE
EXUDE
OXEYE
OXIDE

••XE•
BOXED
BOXER
BOXES
COXED
COXES
COXEY
FAXED
FAXES
FIXED
FIXER
FIXES
FOXED
FOXES
HEXED
HEXER
HEXES
LAXER
LOXES
MAXED
MAXES
MIXED
MIXER
MIXES
NIXED
NIXES
PIXEL
REXES
SAXES
SEXES
SIXED
SIXES
SOXER
TAXED
TAXER
TAXES
TUXES
VEXED
VEXER
VEXES
VIXEN
WAXED
WAXEN
WAXER
WAXES
XAXES
YAXES
ZAXES

••X•E
COXAE
DIXIE
HOXIE
MAXIE
MOXIE
NIXIE
PIXIE
PYXIE
ROXIE

X••G•
XINGU

•X••G
AXING

XH•••
XHOSA

••X•H
SIXTH

XI•••
XINGU

X•I••
XCIII
XLIII
XVIII
XXIII

X••I•
XAXIS
XCIII
XCVII
XENIA
XERIC
XLIII
XLVII
XVIII
XXIII
XXVII
XXXII
XXXIV
XXXIX

X•••I
XCIII
XCVII
XLIII
XLVII
XVIII
XXIII
XXVII
XXXII
XXXVI

•XI••
AXIAL
AXILS
AXING
AXIOM
AXION
CXIII
DXIII
EXILE
EXIST
EXITS
IXION
LXIII
MXIII
OXIDE
XXIII

•X•I•
CXCII
CXCIV
CXCIX
CXIII
CXLII
CXLIV
CXLIX
CXVII
CXXII
CXXIV
CXXIX
DXCII
DXCIV
DXCIX
DXIII
DXLII
DXLIV
DXLIX
DXVII
DXXII
DXXIV
DXXIX
LXIII
LXVII
LXXII
LXXIV
LXXIX
MXCII
MXCIV
MXCIX
MXIII
MXLII
MXLIV
MXLIX
MXMII
MXMIV
MXVII
MXXII
MXXIV
MXXIX
OXLIP
XXIII
XXVII
XXXII
XXXIV
XXXIX

•X••I
CXCII
CXCVI
CXIII
CXLII
CXLVI
CXVII
CXXII
CXXVI
CXXXI
DXCII
DXCVI
DXIII
DXLII
DXLVI
DXVII
DXXII
DXXVI
DXXXI
LXIII
LXVII
LXXII
LXXVI
LXXXI
MXCII
MXCVI
MXIII
MXLII
MXLVI
MXMII
MXVII
MXXII
MXXVI
MXXXI
XXIII
XXVII
XXXII
XXXVI

••XI•
AUXIL
AUXIN
BOXIN
CCXII
CCXIV
CCXIX
CDXII
CDXIV
CDXIX
CLXII
CLXIV
CLXIX
CMXII
CMXIV
CMXIX
CXXII
CXXIV
CXXIX
DCXII
DCXIV
DCXIX
DIXIE
DIXIT
DLXII
DLXIV
DLXIX
DXXII
DXXIV
DXXIX
FIXIT
HOXIE
LEXIS
LXXII
LXXIV
LXXIX
MAXIE
MAXIM
MAXIS
MCXII
MCXIV
MCXIX
MDXII
MDXIV
MDXIX
MLXII
MLXIV
MLXIX
MMXII
MMXIV
MMXIX
MOXIE
MXXII
MXXIV
MXXIX
NIXIE
PIXIE
PYXIE
PYXIS
ROXIE
TAXIS
TOXIC
TOXIN
XAXIS
XXXII
XXXIV
XXXIX
YAXIS
ZAXIS

••X•I
CCXCI
CCXII
CCXLI
CCXVI
CCXXI
CDXCI
CDXII
CDXLI
CDXVI
CDXXI
CLXII
CLXVI
CLXXI
CMXCI
CMXII
CMXLI
CMXVI
CMXXI
CXXII
CXXVI
CXXXI
DCXCI
DCXII
DCXLI
DCXVI
DCXXI
DLXII
DLXVI
DLXXI
DXXII
DXXVI
DXXXI
LXXII
LXXVI
LXXXI
MCXCI
MCXII
MCXLI
MCXVI
MCXXI
MDXCI
MDXII
MDXLI
MDXVI
MDXXI
MLXII
MLXVI
MLXXI
MMXCI
MMXII
MMXLI
MMXVI
MMXXI
MXXII
MXXVI
MXXXI
XXXII
XXXVI

•••XI
CCCXI
CCLXI
CCXXI
CDLXI
CDXXI
CLXXI
CMLXI
CMXXI
CXXXI
DCCXI
DCLXI
DCXXI
DLXXI
DXXXI
FLEXI
LXXXI
MCCXI
MCDXI
MCLXI
MCMXI
MCXXI
MDCXI
MDLXI
MDXXI
MLXXI
MMCXI
MMDXI
MMLXI
MMMXI
MMXXI
MXXXI

XL•••
XLIII
XLVII

X•L••
XYLEM

•XL••
AXLES
CXLII
CXLIV
CXLIX
CXLVI
DXLII
DXLIV
DXLIX
DXLVI
MXLII
MXLIV
MXLIX
MXLVI
OXLIP

•X•L•
AXELS
AXILS
EXALT
EXILE
EXULT

•X••L
AXIAL
EXCEL
EXPEL
EXTOL
UXMAL

••XL•
CCXLI
CCXLV
CDXLI
CDXLV
CMXLI
CMXLV
DCXLI
DCXLV
LAXLY
MCXLI
MCXLV
MDXLI
MDXLV
MMXLI
MMXLV

••X•L
AUXIL
COXAL
HEXYL
PIXEL

•••XL
CCCXL
DCCXL
MCCXL
MCDXL
MCMXL
MDCXL
MMCXL
MMDXL
MMMXL

X•••M
XYLEM

•XM••
MXMII
MXMIV
UXMAL

•X•M•
EXAMS

•X••M
AXIOM

••XM•
SIXMO

••X•M
MAXIM

X•N••
XENIA
XENON
XINGU

X•••N
XENON

•XN••
IXNAY

•X•N•
AXING
AXONS
EXONS

•X••N
AXION
EXXON
IXION

••X•N
AUXIN
BOXIN
DIXON
EXXON
LEXAN
NIXON
SAXON
TAXON
TEXAN
TOXIN
VIXEN
WAXEN

X•O••
XHOSA
XSOUT

X••O•
XENON
XEROX

X•••O
XACTO

•XO••
AXONS
EXONS

•X•O•
AXIOM
AXION
EXPOS
EXTOL
EXXON
IXION
OXBOW

•X••O
EXTRO

••XO•
DIXON
EXXON
LUXOR
NAXOS
NIXON
SAXON
TAXON

••X•O
SIXMO
TAXCO

•••XO
GLAXO

•XP••
EXPEL
EXPOS

•X••P
OXLIP

••X•P
BOXUP
FIXUP
MIXUP

XR•••
XRAYS

X•R••
XERIC
XEROX
XERUS

•X•R•
EXERT
EXTRA
EXTRO
EXURB

••X•R
BOXER
DEXTR
FIXER
HEXER
LAXER
LUXOR
MIXER
SOXER
TAXER
VEXER
WAXER

XS•••
XSOUT

X••S•
XHOSA

X•••S
XAXES
XAXIS
XERUS
XRAYS

•X•S•
EXIST

•X••S
AXELS
AXILS
AXLES
AXONS
EXAMS
EXECS
EXITS
EXONS
EXPOS

••X•S
BOXES

COXES FAXES FIXES FOXES HEXES LEXIS LEXUS LOXES MAXES MAXIS MIXES NAXOS NEXUS NIXES PYXIS REXES SAXES SEXES SEXTS SIXES TAXES TAXIS TEXAS TEXTS TUXES VEXES WAXES XAXES XAXIS YAXES YAXIS ZAXES ZAXIS

X••T•
XACTO

X•••T
XSOUT

•XT••
EXTOL EXTRA EXTRO

•X•T•
EXITS

•X••T
EXACT EXALT EXERT EXIST EXULT

••XT•
DEXTR SEXTS SIXTH SIXTY TEXTS

••X•T
DIXIT FIXIT

•••XT
TWIXT

X••U•
XERUS XSOUT

X•••U
XINGU

•XU••
EXUDE EXULT EXURB

••XU•
BOXUP FIXUP LEXUS MIXUP NEXUS

XV•••
XVIII

X•V••
XCVII XLVII XXVII

X••V•
XXXVI

X•••V
XXXIV

•XV••
CXVII DXVII LXVII MXVII XXVII

•X•V•
CXCVI CXLVI CXXVI DXCVI DXLVI DXXVI LXXVI MXCVI MXLVI MXXVI XXXVI

•X••V
CXCIV CXLIV CXXIV CXXXV DXCIV DXLIV DXXIV DXXXV LXXIV LXXXV MXCIV MXLIV MXMIV MXXIV MXXXV XXXIV

••XV•
CCXVI CDXVI CLXVI CMXVI CXXVI DCXVI DLXVI DXXVI LXXVI MCXVI MDXVI MLXVI MMXVI MXXVI XXXVI

••X•V
CCXCV CCXIV CCXLV CCXXV CDXCV CDXIV CDXLV CDXXV CLXIV CLXXV CMXCV CMXIV CMXLV CMXXV CXXIV CXXXV DCXCV DCXIV DCXLV DCXXV DLXIV DLXXV DXXIV DXXXV LXXIV LXXXV MCXCV MCXIV MCXLV MCXXV MDXCV MDXIV MDXLV MDXXV MLXIV MLXXV MMXCV MMXIV MMXLV MMXXV MXXIV MXXXV XXXIV

•••XV
CCCXV CCLXV CCXXV CDLXV CDXXV CLXXV CMLXV CMXXV CXXXV DCCXV DCLXV DCXXV DLXXV DXXXV LXXXV MCCXV MCDXV MCLXV MCMXV MCXXV MDCXV MDLXV MDXXV MLXXV MMCXV MMDXV MMLXV MMMXV MMXXV MXXXV

•X••W
OXBOW

XX•••
XXIII XXVII XXXII XXXIV XXXIX XXXVI

X•X••
XAXES XAXIS XXXII XXXIV XXXIX XXXVI

X•••X
XEROX XXXIX

•XX••
CXXII CXXIV CXXIX CXXVI CXXXI CXXXV DXXII DXXIV DXXIX DXXVI DXXXI DXXXV EXXON LXXII LXXIV LXXIX LXXVI LXXXI LXXXV MXXII MXXIV MXXIX MXXVI MXXXI MXXXV XXXII XXXIV XXXIX XXXVI

•X•X•
CXXXI CXXXV DXXXI DXXXV LXXXI LXXXV MXXXI MXXXV

•X••X
CXCIX CXLIX CXXIX DXCIX DXLIX DXXIX LXXIX MXCIX MXLIX MXXIX XXXIX

••XX•
CCXXI CCXXV CCXXX CDXXI CDXXV CDXXX CLXXI CLXXV CLXXX CMXXI CMXXV CMXXX CXXXI CXXXV DCXXI DCXXV DCXXX DLXXI DLXXV DLXXX DXXXI DXXXV LXXXI LXXXV MCXXI MCXXV MCXXX MDXXI MDXXV MDXXX MLXXI MLXXV MLXXX MMXXI MMXXV MMXXX MXXXI MXXXV

••X•X
CCXIX CCXXX CDXIX CDXXX CLXIX CLXXX CMXIX CMXXX CXXIX DCXIX DCXXX DLXIX DLXXX DXXIX LXXIX MCXIX MCXXX MDXIX MDXXX MLXIX MLXXX MMXIX MMXXX MXXIX XXXIX

•••XX
CCCXX CCLXX CCXXX CDLXX CDXXX CLXXX CMLXX CMXXX DCCXX DCLXX DCXXX DLXXX MCCXX MCDXX MCLXX MCMXX MCXXX MDCXX MDLXX MDXXX MLXXX MMCXX MMDXX MMLXX MMMXX MMXXX

XY•••
XYLEM

X••Y•
XRAYS

•X•Y•
OXEYE

•X••Y
IXNAY

••XY•
HEXYL

••X•Y
BIXBY COXEY LAXLY SIXTY

•••XY
DEOXY EPOXY FLAXY PREXY PROXY

YA•••
YABBA YACHT YAHOO YAKOV YAKUT YALIE YALOW YALTA YAMPA YANKS YANNI YAPOK YAQUI YARDS YARNS YASIR YATES YAWED YAWLS YAWNS YAWPS YAXES YAXIS YAZOO

Y•A••
YEANS YEARN YEARS YEAST YEATS YUANS

Y••A•
YMCAS YUMAN YUMAS YWCAS

Y•••A
YABBA YALTA YAMPA YENTA YERBA YORBA YUCCA

•YA••
AYAHS CYANO DYADS HYATT KYACK KYATS NYACK NYALA NYASA WYATT

•Y•A•
BYFAR BYLAW BYWAY CYCAD CYMAE CYMAS DYLAN EYRAS HYLAS HYMAN HYRAX LYMAN MYLAR MYNAH MYNAS MYWAY TYNAN WYMAN

•Y••A
HYDRA HYENA HYPHA KYOGA LYCRA LYDIA LYNDA LYTTA MYRNA NYALA NYASA SYRIA TYPEA

••YA•
ARYAN BAYAR BOYAR BRYAN DAYAK DAYAN DRYAD FLYAT GAYAL HOYAS KAYAK LOYAL MAYAN MAYAS RIYAL ROYAL SOYAS

••Y•A
ADYTA ASYLA ETYMA LAYLA PHYLA TAYRA TWYLA

•••YA
ABAYA DARYA FREYA KENYA LENYA LIBYA ORIYA PLAYA SEEYA SONYA TANYA TONYA VANYA

Y•B••
YABBA

Y••B•
YABBA YERBA YORBA

•YB••
SYBIL

•Y••B
TYPEB

••YB•
FLYBY LAYBY MAYBE

Y•C••
YACHT YECCH YMCAS YUCCA YUCKY YWCAS

Y••C•
YECCH YUCCA

•YC••
CYCAD CYCLE CYCLO LYCEE LYCRA SYCEE SYCES TYCHE TYCHO

•Y•C•
KYACK LYNCH NYACK SYNCS

•Y••C
CYNIC LYRIC PYRIC

••YC•
ALYCE BRYCE CAYCE GLYCO JOYCE PHYCO PSYCH ROYCE

•••YC
ENCYC

Y•D••
YODEL

Y••D•
YARDS

Y•••D
YAWED YIELD YOKED

•YD••
CYDER EYDIE HYDRA HYDRO LYDIA RYDER SYDOW

•Y•D•
BYRDS CYNDI DYADS LYNDA LYNDE

•Y••D
CYCAD GYVED HYOID HYPED SYNOD TYPED

••YD•
CLYDE HAYDN

••Y•D
BAYED DRYAD GUYED HAYED KEYED PAYED RAYED TOYED

•••YD
ALKYD FLOYD LLOYD SLOYD THEYD

YE•••
YEANS YEARN YEARS YEAST YEATS YECCH YEGGS YELLS YELPS YEMEN YENTA YENTE YENTL YERBA YESES YETIS

Y•E••
YIELD

Y••E•
YATES YAWED YAXES YEMEN YESES YIKES YIPES YODEL YOKED YOKEL YOKES YPRES

Y•••E
YALIE YENTE YOURE YOUVE

•YE••
AYERS DYERS EYERS HYENA LYELL MYELO MYERS MYEYE WYETH

•Y•E•
AYRES BYNER BYTES CYDER CYMES DYNEL DYNES EYRES FYKES GYRES GYVED GYVES HYPED HYPER HYPES KYSER LYCEE LYRES MYLES NYMET NYNEX PYRES PYREX RYDER SYCEE SYCES TYKES TYLER TYNES TYPEA TYPEB TYPED TYPEE TYPER TYPES TYRES WYLER XYLEM

•Y••E
BYRNE CYCLE CYMAE EYDIE EYRIE KYRIE LYCEE LYNDE LYNNE MYEYE MYOPE PYXIE SYCEE SYNGE TYCHE TYPEE WYLIE WYTHE

••YE•
ASYET BAYED BAYER BOYER BUYER COYER DOYEN DRYER FLYER FOYER FRYER GAYER GUYED HAYED HAYEK HAYES KEYED KEYES LAYER MAYER MEYER NOYES NUYEN PAYED PAYEE PAYER RAYED REYES SAYER SHYER SLYER TOYED WRYER

••Y•E
ALYCE BAYLE BEYLE BOYLE BOYNE BRYCE CAYCE CLYDE DAYNE DOYLE ELYSE FOYLE GAYLE HEYSE HOYLE JAYNE JOYCE LAYNE LEYTE MAYBE PAYEE PAYNE PHYFE PHYLE RHYME ROYCE SLYPE STYLE STYNE THYME TRYME WAYNE WHYME

•••YE
MYEYE OXEYE REDYE TEVYE

•YF••
BYFAR

••YF•
PHYFE

Y•G••
YEGGS YOGHS YOGIS YUGOS

Y••G•
YEGGS

Y•••G
YOUNG

•YG••
BYGUM HYGRO MYGUY PYGMY

•Y•G•
KYOGA SYNGE

•Y••G
DYING LYING TYING VYING

Y•H••
YAHOO

Y••H•
YACHT YOGHS

Y•••H
YECCH YOUTH

•Y•H•
AYAHS HYPHA MYTHS TYCHE TYCHO WYTHE

•Y••H
LYMPH LYNCH MYNAH MYRRH NYMPH SYLPH WYETH

••Y•H
BLYTH GLYPH PSYCH SMYTH

YI•••
YIELD YIKES YIPES

Y••I•
YALIE YASIR YAXIS YETIS YOGIS YUPIK

Y•••I
YANNI YAQUI

•YI••
DYING LYING TYING VYING

•Y•I•
CYNIC CYRIL EYDIE EYRIE EYRIR HYOID KYLIX KYRIE LYDIA LYRIC LYSIN MYSIN PYRIC PYXIE PYXIS SYBIL SYRIA WYLIE

•Y••I
CYNDI

••YI•
FLYIN KEYIN LAYIN PAYIN ZAYIN

••Y•I
PHYSI SPYRI STYLI

Y•K••
YAKOV YAKUT YIKES YOKED YOKEL YOKES YOKUM YUKON

Y••K•
YANKS YOLKS YUCKY

Y•••K
YAPOK YUPIK

•YK••
FYKES TYKES

•Y••K
KYACK NYACK

••YK•
ROYKO

••Y•K
DAYAK HAYEK KAYAK

Y•L••
YALIE YALOW YALTA YELLS YELPS YOLKS

Y••L•
YAWLS YELLS YIELD YOULL YOWLS

Y•••L
YENTL YODEL YOKEL YOULL

•YL••
BYLAW DYLAN HYLAS KYLIX MYLAR MYLES NYLON PYLON SYLPH TYLER WYLER WYLIE XYLEM

•Y•L•
CYCLE CYCLO LYELL MYELO NYALA

•Y••L
CYRIL DYNEL KYZYL LYELL LYSOL SYBIL TYROL

••YL•
AMYLO AMYLS ASYLA BAYLE BEYLE BOYLE COYLY DOYLE DRYLY FEYLY FOYLE GAYLE GAYLY HOYLE IDYLL IDYLS LAYLA PHYLA PHYLE PHYLL SHYLY SLYLY STYLE STYLI STYLO TWYLA WRYLY

••Y•L
GAYAL IDYLL LOYAL PHYLL RIYAL ROYAL

•••YL
ALKYL ALLYL BERYL BUTYL DARYL ETHYL HEXYL KYZYL MERYL SIBYL VINYL

YM•••
YMCAS

Y•M••
YAMPA YEMEN YUMAN YUMAS YUMMY

Y••M•
YUMMY

Y•••M
YOKUM

•YM••
CYMAE CYMAS CYMES CYMRY HYMAN HYMNS LYMAN LYMON LYMPH NYMET NYMPH WYMAN

•Y•M•
PYGMY

•Y••M
BYGUM XYLEM

••YM•
ETYMA RHYME THYME TRYME WHYME

••Y•M
ABYSM

Y•N••
YANKS YANNI YENTA YENTE YENTL

Y••N•
YANNI YARNS YAWNS YEANS YOUNG YOUNT YUANS

Y•••N
YEARN YEMEN YUKON YUMAN

•YN••
BYNER BYNOW CYNDI CYNIC DYNEL DYNES LYNCH LYNDA LYNDE LYNNE MYNAH MYNAS NYNEX SYNCS SYNGE SYNOD TYNAN TYNES

•Y•N•
BYRNE CYANO DYING HYENA HYMNS HYPNO LYING LYNNE LYONS MYRNA TYING VYING

•Y••N
BYRON DYLAN GYRON HYMAN HYSON LYMAN LYMON LYSIN MYRON MYSIN NYLON

PYLON TYNAN TYSON WYMAN

••YN• BOYNE DAYNE FLYNN GWYNN JAYNE LAYNE PAYNE STYNE WAYNE

••Y•N ARYAN BRYAN DAYAN DOYEN FLYIN FLYNN GWYNN HAYDN KEYIN LAYIN LAYON MAYAN MAYON NUYEN PAYIN RAYON SPYON TOYON TRYON ZAYIN

•••YN EMLYN

YO••• YODEL YOGHS YOGIS YOKED YOKEL YOKES YOKUM YOLKS YORBA YOULL YOUNG YOUNT YOURE YOURS YOUTH YOUVE YOWLS YOYOS

Y••O• YAHOO YAKOV YALOW YAPOK YAZOO YOYOS YUGOS YUKON

Y•••O YAHOO YAZOO

•YO•• HYOID KYOGA KYOTO LYONS MYOPE RYOTS

•Y•O• BYNOW BYRON GYRON GYROS HYPOS HYSON LYMON LYSOL MYRON NYLON PYLON SYDOW SYNOD SYSOP TYPOS TYROL TYROS TYSON

•Y••O CYANO CYCLO HYDRO HYGRO HYPNO HYPSO KYOTO MYELO TYCHO

••YO• BAYOU GUYOT KAYOS LAYON MAYON MAYOR PRYOR RAYON SPYON TOYON TRYON YOYOS

••Y•O AMYLO GLYCO LAYTO MAYPO PHYCO PHYTO ROYKO SAYSO STYLO

•••YO SANYO TOKYO

YP••• YPRES

Y•P•• YAPOK YIPES

YUPIK

Y••P• YAMPA YAWPS YELPS

•YP•• GYPSY HYPED HYPER HYPES HYPHA HYPNO HYPOS HYPSO TYPEA TYPEB TYPED TYPEE TYPER TYPES TYPOS

•Y•P• LYMPH MYOPE NYMPH SYLPH

•Y••P SYRUP SYSOP

••YP• COYPU CRYPT EGYPT GLYPH MAYPO SLYPE

••Y•P BUYUP DRYUP KEYUP LAYUP PAYUP

•••YP POLYP

Y•Q•• YAQUI

Y•R•• YARDS YARNS YERBA YORBA YPRES YURTS

Y••R• YEARN YEARS YOURE YOURS

Y•••R YASIR

•YR•• AYRES BYRDS BYRNE BYRON CYRIL CYRUS EYRAS EYRES EYRIE EYRIR GYRES GYRON GYROS GYRUS HYRAX KYRIE LYRES LYRIC MYRNA MYRON MYRRH PYRES PYREX PYRIC SYRIA SYRUP TYRES TYROL TYROS

•Y•R• AYERS CYMRY DYERS EYERS HYDRA HYDRO HYGRO LYCRA MYERS MYRRH

•Y••R BYFAR BYNER CYDER EYRIR HYPER KYSER MYLAR RYDER TYLER TYPER WYLER

••YR• SPYRI TAYRA

••Y•R BAYAR BAYER BOYAR BOYER BUYER COYER DRYER FLYER FOYER FRYER GAYER LAYER MAYER MAYOR MEYER PAYER PRYOR SAYER SHYER SLYER WRYER

•••YR ASSYR SATYR

Y•S•• YASIR YESES

Y••S• YEAST

Y•••S YANKS YARDS YARNS YATES YAWLS YAWNS YAWPS YAXES YAXIS YEANS YEARS YEATS YEGGS YELLS YELPS YESES YETIS YIKES YIPES YMCAS YOGHS YOGIS YOKES YOLKS YOURS YOWLS YOYOS YPRES YUANS YUGOS YUMAS YURTS YWCAS

•YS•• HYSON KYSER LYSIN LYSOL MYSIN SYSOP TYSON

•Y•S• GYPSY HYPSO NYASA

•Y••S AYAHS AYERS AYRES BYRDS BYTES CYMAS CYMES CYRUS DYADS DYERS DYNES EYERS EYRAS EYRES FYKES GYRES GYROS GYRUS GYVES HYLAS HYMNS HYPES HYPOS KYATS LYONS LYRES MYERS MYLES MYNAS MYTHS PYRES PYXIS RYOTS SYCES SYNCS TYKES TYNES TYPES TYPOS TYRES TYROS

••YS• ABYSM ABYSS ELYSE HEYSE MAYST PHYSI SAYSO TRYST

••Y•S ABYSS AMYLS HAYES HOYAS IDYLS KAYOS KEYES MAYAS NOYES REYES SOYAS YOYOS

•••YS AHOYS ATTYS BABYS BRAYS BUOYS CHRYS CLAYS CLOYS DAVYS DENYS DRAYS EMMYS FLAYS FRAYS GRAYS GREYS JOEYS LADYS MACYS MARYS OBEYS OKAYS PEPYS PLAYS PLOYS POWYS PRAYS PREYS QUAYS SHAYS SLAYS SPAYS STAYS SWAYS TONYS TRAYS TREYS WHEYS XRAYS

Y•T•• YATES YETIS

Y••T• YALTA YEATS YENTA YENTE YENTL YOUTH YURTS

Y•••T YACHT YAKUT YEAST YOUNT

•YT•• BYTES LYTTA MYTHS WYTHE

•Y•T• HYATT KYATS KYOTO LYTTA RYOTS WYATT WYETH

•Y••T HYATT NYMET WYATT

••YT• ADYTA BLYTH LAYTO LEYTE PAYTV PHYTO SMYTH

••Y•T ASYET CRYPT EGYPT FLYAT GUYOT MAYST TRYST

YU••• YUANS YUCCA YUCKY YUGOS YUKON YUMAN YUMAS YUMMY YUPIK YURTS

Y•U•• YOULL YOUNG YOUNT YOURE YOURS YOUTH YOUVE

Y••U• YAKUT YAQUI YOKUM

•Y•U• BYGUM CYRUS GYRUS MYGUY SYRUP

••YU• BUYUP DRYUP KEYUP LAYUP PAYUP SOYUZ

••Y•U BAYOU COYPU

Y••V• YOUVE

Y•••V YAKOV

•YV•• GYVED GYVES

••Y•V PAYTV

YW••• YWCAS

Y•W•• YAWED YAWLS YAWNS YAWPS YOWLS

Y•••W YALOW

•YW•• BYWAY MYWAY

•Y••W BYLAW BYNOW SYDOW

Y•X•• YAXES YAXIS

•YX•• PYXIE PYXIS

•Y••X HYRAX KYLIX NYNEX PYREX

•••YX CALYX

Y•Y•• YOYOS

Y•••Y YUCKY YUMMY

•Y•Y• KYZYL MYEYE

•Y••Y BYWAY CYMRY GYPSY MYGUY MYWAY PYGMY

••Y•Y COYLY DRYLY FEYLY FLYBY GAYLY LAYBY SHYLY SLYLY WRYLY

Y•Z•• YAZOO

•YZ•• KYZYL

••Y•Z SOYUZ

ZA••• ZAIRE ZAMIA ZANTE ZAPPA ZAPPY ZARFS ZAXES ZAXIS ZAYIN ZAZEN

Z•A•• ZBARS ZEALS

Z••A• ZETAS ZOHAR ZONAL

Z•••A ZAMIA ZAPPA ZEBRA ZELDA ZENDA ZIZKA ZORBA

•ZA•• AZANS CZARS IZAAK IZARD IZARS OZARK OZAWA

•Z•A• IZAAK IZBAS

•Z••A AZUSA OZAWA

••ZA• ANZAC KAZAN LAZAR MIZAR MUZAK NIZAM

••Z•A MAZDA PIZZA TAZZA ZIZKA

•••ZA BAIZA DANZA ELIZA GINZA GROZA IBIZA LANZA LEEZA MONZA PANZA PENZA PINZA PIZZA PLAZA TAZZA TERZA

ZB••• ZBARS

Z•B•• ZEBRA ZEBUS ZIBET ZUBIN

Z••B• ZORBA

•ZB•• IZBAS UZBEK

Z••C• ZILCH ZINCS

•Z•C• CZECH

•Z••C AZOIC AZTEC

••ZC• CUZCO

••Z•C ANZAC

Z••D• ZELDA ZENDA ZENDO

Z•••D ZONED ZOOID

•Z•D• AZIDE

•Z••D IZARD SZOLD

••ZD• MAZDA

••Z•D DAZED DOZED FAZED GAZED HAZED LAZED OOZED RAZED SIZED

ZE••• ZEALS ZEBRA ZEBUS ZEISS ZEIST ZELDA ZELIG ZENDA ZENDO ZEPPO ZEROS ZESTS ZESTY ZETAS ZEVON

Z•E•• ZWEIG

Z••E• ZAXES ZAZEN ZIBET ZONED ZONES ZOOEY

Z•••E ZAIRE ZANTE ZOWIE

•ZE•• CZECH SZELL

•Z•E• AZTEC UZBEK

•Z••E AZIDE AZINE AZOTE AZURE OZONE OZZIE

••ZE• ADZES BEZEL BIZET COZEN COZES DAZED DAZES DIZEN DOZED DOZEN DOZER DOZES ETZEL FAZED FAZES GAZED GAZER GAZES HAZED HAZEL HAZER HAZES LAZED LAZES MAZEL MAZER MAZES NIZER OCZED OOZES OUZEL RAZED RAZES SIZED SIZER SIZES WIZEN ZAZEN

••Z•E OZZIE

•••ZE AGAZE AMAZE BAIZE BLAZE BONZE BOOZE BRAZE CRAZE CROZE DRUZE FROZE FURZE GAUZE GLAZE GLOZE GRAZE MAIZE PRIZE SEIZE SMAZE WINZE

Z••F• ZARFS

Z•G•• ZIGGY

Z••G• ZIGGY ZINGS ZINGY

Z•••G ZELIG ZWEIG

••Z•G ABZUG

Z•H•• ZOHAR

Z•••H ZILCH

•Z••H AZOTH CZECH

ZI••• ZIBET ZIGGY ZILCH ZILLS ZINCS ZINGS ZINGY ZIPPY ZIPUP ZITIS ZIZKA

Z•I•• ZAIRE ZEISS ZEIST

Z••I• ZAMIA ZAXIS ZAYIN ZELIG ZITIS ZOOID ZORIL ZORIS ZOWIE ZUBIN ZUNIS ZWEIG

•ZI•• AZIDE AZINE

•Z•I• AZOIC IZMIR IZMIT OZZIE

••ZI• ANZIO OZZIE UNZIP

••Z•I BUZZI

•••ZI BUZZI GHAZI MITZI PONZI SWAZI

Z•K•• ZUKOR

Z••K• ZIZKA ZONKS

•Z••K IZAAK OZARK UZBEK

••ZK• ZIZKA

••Z•K MUZAK

ZL••• ZLOTY

Z•L•• ZELDA ZELIG ZILCH ZILLS ZULUS

Z••L• ZEALS ZILLS

Z•••L ZONAL ZORIL

•Z•L• SZELL SZOLD

•Z••L SZELL

••Z•L BEZEL ETZEL HAZEL KYZYL MAZEL OUZEL

•••ZL HERZL

Z•M•• ZAMIA

Z••M• ZOOMS

•ZM•• IZMIR IZMIT

••ZM• GIZMO

••Z•M NIZAM

Z•N•• ZANTE ZENDA ZENDO ZINCS ZINGS ZINGY ZONAL ZONED ZONES ZONKS ZUNIS

Z•••N ZAYIN ZAZEN ZEVON ZUBIN

•Z•N• AZANS AZINE OZONE

••Z•N COZEN DIZEN DOZEN KAZAN LUZON WIZEN ZAZEN

ZO••• ZOHAR ZONAL ZONED ZONES ZONKS ZOOEY ZOOID ZOOMS ZORBA ZORIL ZORIS ZORRO ZOWIE

Z•O•• ZLOTY ZOOEY ZOOID ZOOMS

Z••O• ZEROS ZEVON ZUKOR ZZTOP

Z•••O ZENDO ZEPPO ZORRO

•ZO•• AZOIC AZOTE AZOTH OZONE SZOLD

•Z•O• ZZTOP

••ZO• BOZOS KAZOO LUZON ORZOS OUZOS RAZOR YAZOO

••Z•O ANZIO CUZCO GIZMO KAZOO MEZZO RIZZO YAZOO

•••ZO BENZO BONZO DIAZO GONZO MATZO MEZZO RHIZO RIZZO

Z•P•• ZAPPA ZAPPY ZEPPO ZIPPY ZIPUP

Z••P• ZAPPA ZAPPY ZEPPO ZIPPY

Z•••P ZIPUP ZZTOP

•Z••P ZZTOP

••Z•P UNZIP

Z•R•• ZARFS ZEROS ZORBA ZORIL ZORIS ZORRO

Z••R• ZAIRE ZBARS ZEBRA ZORRO

Z•••R ZOHAR ZUKOR

•Z•R• AZURE CZARS IZARD IZARS OZARK

•Z••R IZMIR

••Z•R DOZER GAZER HAZER LAZAR MAZER MIZAR NIZER RAZOR SIZER

Z•S•• ZESTS ZESTY

Z••S• ZEISS ZEIST

Z•••S ZARFS ZAXES ZAXIS ZBARS ZEALS ZEBUS ZEISS

ZEROS
ZESTS
ZETAS
ZILLS
ZINCS
ZINGS
ZITIS
ZONES
ZONKS
ZOOMS
ZORIS
ZULUS
ZUNIS

•Z•S•
AZUSA

•Z••S
AZANS
CZARS
IZARS
IZBAS

••Z•S
ADZES
BOZOS
COZES
DAZES
DOZES
FAZES
GAZES
HAZES
LAZES
MAZES
OOZES
ORZOS
OUZOS
RAZES
SIZES

Z•T••
ZETAS
ZITIS
ZZTOP

Z••T•
ZANTE
ZESTS
ZESTY
ZLOTY

Z•••T
ZEIST
ZIBET

•ZT••
AZTEC
ZZTOP

•Z•T•
AZOTE
AZOTH

•Z••T
IZMIT

••Z•T
BIZET

•••ZT
LISZT

ZU•••
ZUBIN
ZUKOR
ZULUS
ZUNIS

Z••U•
ZEBUS
ZIPUP
ZULUS

•ZU••
AZURE
AZUSA

••ZU•
ABZUG

•••ZU
ISUZU
KANZU
KUDZU

Z•V••
ZEVON

ZW•••
ZWEIG

Z•W••
ZOWIE

•Z•W•
OZAWA

Z•X••
ZAXES
ZAXIS

Z•Y••
ZAYIN

Z•••Y
ZAPPY
ZESTY
ZIGGY
ZINGY
ZIPPY
ZLOTY
ZOOEY

••ZY•
KYZYL

••Z•Y
DIZZY
FIZZY
FUZZY
JAZZY
MUZZY
TIZZY

•••ZY
CRAZY
DITZY
DIZZY
DOOZY
FIZZY
FUZZY
GAUZY
JAZZY
JERZY
MUZZY
ORCZY
RITZY
TIZZY
WOOZY

ZZ•••
ZZTOP

Z•Z••
ZAZEN
ZIZKA

•ZZ••
OZZIE

••ZZ•
BUZZI
DIZZY
FIZZY
FUZZY
JAZZY
MEZZO
MUZZY
PIZZA
RIZZO
TAZZA
TIZZY

6

AA••••
AACHEN
AAFAIR
AAHING

A•A•••
ABACAS
ABACUS
ABASED
ABASES
ABATED
ABATES
ABATIS
ACACIA
ACADIA
ACAJOU
ACARID
ACARUS
ADAGES
ADAGIO
ADAPTS
AGADIR
AGAMAS
AGARIC
AGASSI
AGATES
AGATHA
AGAVES
AJANTA
ALAMOS
ALANON
ALARIC
ALARMS
ALARUM
ALASKA
ALATAU
AMADIS
AMADOU
AMAJOR
AMALFI
AMALIE
AMANDA
AMATIS
AMATOL
AMAZED
AMAZES
AMAZON
ANACIN
ANADEM
ANALOG
ANANDA
ANATTO
APACHE
APATHY
ARABIA
ARABIC
ARABLE
ARAFAT
ARAGON
ARALIA
ARALLU
ARAMIS
ARARAT
ARAWAK
ASANAS
ATAMAN
AVAILS
AVALON
AVANTI
AVATAR
AVAUNT
AWAITS
AWAKED
AWAKEN
AWAKES
AWARDS
AZALEA

A••A••
AAFAIR
ABBACY
ABLATE
ABLAUT
ABLAZE
ABOARD
ABRADE
ABRAMS
ACHAEA
ACKACK
ACUATE
ADDAMS
ADNATE
AERATE
AFFAIR
AFLAME
AFLATS
AFRAID
AFRAME
AGHAST
AGLAIA
AGLARE
AGNATE
AIRARM
AKUAKU
ALBANO
ALBANY
ALCAPP
ALEAST
ALKALI
ALLAYS
ALPACA
ALSACE
ALTAIC
ALTAIR
ALTARS
ALWAYS
AMHARA
ANKARA
ANNABA
ANNALS
ANSATE
AODAIS
APIARY
APPALL
APPALS
AQUATE
ARCADE
ARCANA
ARCANE
ARCARO
ARGALI
ARMADA
ARMAGH
ARMAND
ARMANI
ARRACK
ARRANT
ARRAYS
ARVADA
ARYANS
ASGARD
ASHARP
ASIANS
ASKARI
ASLANT
ASMARA
ASSAIL
ASSAYS
ATBATS
ATEAMS
ATEASE
ATHAND
ATLAST
ATLATL
ATTACH
ATTACK
ATTAIN
ATTARS
AUBADE
AUFAIT
AUPAIR
AVIANS
AVIARY
AVIATE
AWEARY
AYEAYE
AYMARA

A•••A•
ABACAS
ABORAL
ABROAD
ACETAL
ACTUAL
ADIDAS
ADONAI
ADRIAN
AEGEAN
AENEAS
AERIAL
AFFRAY
AFGHAN
AFLOAT
AGAMAS
AGENAS
AGLEAM
AGORAE
AGORAS
AIMSAT
AIRBAG
AIRDAM
AIRMAN
AIRSAC
AIRWAY
AKELAS
AKITAS
ALATAU
ALEGAR
ALEMAN
ALLDAY
ALLMAN
ALOHAS
ALOMAR
ALPHAS
ALTMAN
ALULAE
ALULAR
AMEBAE
AMEBAS
AMORAL
AMTRAC
AMTRAK
AMYTAN
ANDEAN
ANIMAL
ANIMAS
ANNEAL
ANNUAL
ANORAK
ANSGAR
ANURAN
ANYWAY
AORTAE
AORTAL
AORTAS
AOUDAD
APEMAN
APICAL
APODAL
APPEAL
APPEAR
APPIAN
ARAFAT
ARARAT
ARAWAK
ARECAS
ARENAS
AROMAS
ARUBAN
ASANAS
ASCHAM
ASHCAN
ASHLAR
ASHRAM
ASOSAN
ASTRAL
ASTRAY
ATAMAN
ATONAL
ATRIAL
ATTHAT
AUDIAL
AUGEAN
AVATAR
AVOWAL
AXONAL

A••••A
ABOLLA
ACACIA
ACADIA
ACEDIA
ACHAEA
AEOLIA
AFRICA
AGATHA
AGENDA
AGLAIA
AHIMSA
AJANTA
ALASKA
ALEXIA
ALICIA
ALPACA
ALTHEA
ALUMNA
ALYSSA
AMANDA
AMELIA
AMENRA
AMHARA
AMOEBA
ANANDA
ANCONA
ANDREA
ANEMIA
ANGELA
ANGLIA
ANGOLA
ANGORA
ANITRA
ANKARA
ANNABA
APULIA
AQUILA
ARABIA
ARALIA
ARBELA
ARCANA
AREOLA
ARETHA
ARISTA
ARJUNA
ARMADA
ARNICA
ARRIBA
ARROBA
ARVADA
ASMARA
ASPERA
ATHENA
ATTICA
ATTILA
AURIGA
AURORA
AVESTA
AXILLA
AYESHA
AYMARA
AZALEA

•AA•••
BAAING
LAAGER
PAANGA

•A•A••
AAFAIR
BACALL
BAHAMA
BALAAM
BALATA
BAMAKO
BANANA
BASALT
BATAAN
BAYARD
BAZAAR
CABALA
CABALS
CABANA
CACAOS
CALAIS
CALASH
CANAAN
CANADA
CANALS
CANAPE
CANARD
CANARY
CARAFE
CARATS
CASABA
CASALS
CASAVA
DACAPO
DAGAMA
DALASI
DAMAGE
DAMASK
DAMATO
DANANG
DANAUS
DATARY
FACADE
FALANA
FARADS
FATALE
GALATA
GALAXY
GAMAYS
GARAGE
GAWAIN
GAYALS
HABANA
HAMALS
HARARE
HARASS
HATARI
HAVANA
HAVASU
HAWAII
HAZANS
HAZARD
JACALS
JACANA
JALAPA
JAMAAL
JAPANS
JAVARI
KAKAPO
KALAKH
KAMALA
KANAKA
KARATE
KARATS
KAYAKS
KAZAKH
KAZAKS
LAGASH
LALALA
LAMARR
LAMAZE
LANAIS
LANATE
LARAMS
LAVABO
LAVAGE
MACACO
MACAWS
MADAME
MADAMS
MAKALU
MALABO
MALADY
MALAGA
MALATE
MALAWI
MALAYA
MALAYS
MANAGE
MANAMA
MANANA
MANAUS
MARACA
MARAUD
MASADA
MASAIS
MAYANS
NAGANO
NAIADS
NAMATH
NASALS
NATANT
NAVAHO
NAVAJO
NAWABS
OAXACA
PADANG
PAEANS
PAGANS
PAHANG
PAHARI
PAJAMA
PALACE
PALAEO
PALATE
PANADA
PANAMA
PAPACY
PAPAGO
PAPAIN
PAPAWS
PAPAYA
PARADE
PARANA
PARANG
PARAPH
PATACA
PAVANE
QATARI
RABATO
RAFAEL
RAJAHS
RAMADA
RAMATE
RAVAGE
SABATO
SAFARI
SAHARA
SALAAM
SALADS
SALALS
SALAMI
SALARY
SAMARA
SARANS
SATANG
SAVAGE
SAVAII
SAVANT
SAVATE
TABARD
TAMALE
TAMARA
TAMAYO
TANAKA
TARAWA
TATAMI
TATARS
UAKARI
VACANT
VACATE
VAGARY
WABASH
WASABI
XANADU
YAMAHA
ZAPATA

•A••A•
BABKAS
BAGDAD
BAHIAN
BAIKAL
BALAAM
BALKAN
BALLAD
BALSAM
BALZAC
BANTAM
BANYAN
BANZAI
BAOBAB
BARMAN
BARTAB
BATAAN
BATEAU
BATMAN
BAZAAR
CAESAR
CAFTAN
CAGUAS
CAIMAN
CALLAO
CALLAS
CALPAC
CAMEAT
CANAAN
CANCAN
CANNAE
CANTAB
CANVAS
CAPIAS
CAPTAN
CARMAN
CARNAL
CARPAL
CASBAH
CASPAR
CASUAL
CATHAY
CATNAP
CAUDAL
CAUSAL
CAVEAT
CAVIAR
CAYMAN
DACHAS
DAEDAL
DALLAS
DAMMAR
DANNAY
DARNAY
EARLAP
EARWAX
EATSAT
FABIAN
FABRAY
FACIAL
FAISAL
FANTAN
FARRAH
FARRAR
FATCAT
FAUNAE
FAUNAL
FAUNAS
GAGLAW
GAGMAN
GALEAE
GALWAY
GALYAK
GAMMAS
GASBAG
GASCAP
GASMAN
GASPAR
GATEAU
GAVIAL
HABEAS
HAEMAT
HAGMAN
HAIDAS
HAINAN
HALVAH
HANGAR
HANNAH
HARLAN
HASSAM
HASSAN
HAUSAS
HAVEAT
HAWHAW
JABBAR
JACKAL
JAGUAR
JAMAAL
JARRAH
KALKAN
KALMAR
KANSAN
KANSAS
KAPLAN
KAPPAS
KARNAK
KARRAS
KASBAH
KATMAI
KAUNAS
LABIAL
LAMIAS
LAMMAS
LANDAU
LAPHAM
LARIAT
LARVAE
LARVAL
LARVAS
LASCAR
LAWMAN
LAYMAN
MACRAE
MADCAP
MADMAN
MADMAX
MADRAS
MAENAD
MAGMAS
MAGYAR
MAITAI
MAMBAS
MAMMAL
MAMMAS
MANDAN
MANDAY
MANIAC
MANIAS
MANRAY
MANTAS
MANUAL
MAOTAI
MARGAY
MARIAH
MARIAN
MAUMAU
MAYDAY
MAYHAP
MAYTAG
NAIRAS
NARIAL
NARWAL
NASCAR
NASDAQ
NASSAU
NATHAN
NAYSAY
PACMAN
PADUAN
PALEAE
PALLAS
PALMAS
PAMPAS
PANDAS
PAPPAS
PAPUAN
PARCAE
PARIAH
PARKAS
PARKAY
PARLAY
PASCAL
PASHAS
PASTAS
PATHAN
PAWPAW
PAWSAT
PAYDAY
QANTAS
RACIAL
RADIAL
RADIAN
RAGBAG
RAGLAN
RAGMAN
RAGTAG
RAHRAH
RAILAT
RAMEAU

RAMSAY
RASCAL
RASHAD
RATTAN
SABRAS
SACRAL
SADDAM
SAIGAS
SAIPAN
SALAAM
SALMAN
SALSAS
SAMBAL
SAMBAR
SAMBAS
SAMIAM
SAMOAN
SAMPAN
SANDAL
SASHAY
SATRAP
SAUNAS
TABLAS
TAGDAY
TAIGAS
TAINAN
TAIPAN
TAIWAN
TALKAT
TAMTAM
TANKAS
TANOAK
TANOAN
TAPPAN
TARMAC
TARPAN
TARSAL
TARTAN
TARTAR
TARZAN
TASMAN
TAXMAN
TAYRAS
TAZZAS
VACLAV
VANDAL
VARNAS
VASLAV
VASSAL
VASSAR
WAHWAH
WANTAD
WARSAW
WAUSAU
WAYLAY

•A•••A
BAHAMA
BALATA
BALBOA
BANANA
BANGKA
BARBRA
BAROJA
CABALA
CABANA
CAMERA
CANADA
CANOLA
CANOVA
CAPITA
CARINA
CASABA
CASAVA
CASSIA
CATENA
CAYUGA
DAGAMA
DAHLIA
DAKOTA
DAMITA
DATURA
EARTHA
FACULA
FAENZA
FAJITA
FALANA
FARINA
FASCIA
FATIMA
GALATA
GALENA
GALLIA
GAMBIA
GARCIA
HABANA
HAVANA
JACANA
JALAPA
JASCHA
KAGERA
KAHLUA
KAHUNA
KAILUA
KAMALA
KANAKA
KARIBA
KAUNDA
LABREA
LACUNA
LADIDA
LADOGA
LAGUNA
LAKOTA
LALALA
LAMBDA
LAMESA
LAMINA
LAPUTA
LAROSA
LATINA
LATONA
LATOYA
LATVIA
MACULA
MADURA
MAKUTA
MALAGA
MALAYA
MANAMA
MANANA
MANCHA
MANILA
MANTRA
MANTUA
MARACA
MARCIA
MARINA
MARISA
MARKKA
MARSHA
MARTHA
MASADA
MATTEA
MAURYA
MAXIMA
MAZOLA
MAZUMA
NAGOYA
NARNIA
NASHUA
NAUSEA
OAXACA
PAANGA
PAELLA
PAGODA
PAJAMA
PALLIA
PALOMA
PAMELA
PANADA
PANAMA
PAPAYA
PARANA
PARULA
PATACA
PATINA
PAYOLA
RADULA
RAFFIA
RAMADA
RAMBLA
RAMONA
SABENA
SAHARA
SALINA
SALIVA
SALVIA
SAMARA
SAMOSA
SANCTA
SANDIA
SANDRA
TABULA
TACOMA
TAMARA
TANAKA
TANTRA
TARAWA
VAISYA
VARUNA
WALESA
YAKIMA
YAMAHA
ZADORA
ZAMBIA
ZAPATA
ZAREBA

••AA••
KRAALS

••A•A•
ABACAS
AGAMAS
ALATAU
ARAFAT
ARARAT
ARAWAK
ASANAS
ATAMAN
AVATAR
BRAVAS
BWANAS
CRAVAT
DRAMAS
FRACAS
GOAWAY
GRABAT
GRAHAM
GRAMAS
GUAVAS
HIATAL
IBADAN
INAJAM
INAWAY
ISAIAH
IZABAL
KOALAS
LIANAS
LLAMAS
MCADAM
NYALAS
OMAHAN
OMAHAS
PLAGAL
PLANAR
PLAYAS
PLAYAT
PLAZAS
QUASAR
REAGAN
REATAS
RIATAS
RUANAS
RYAZAN
SCALAR
SCARAB
SEABAG
SEAFAN
SEAGAL
SEALAB
SEAMAN
SEAWAY
SHABAN
SHAMAN
SHAZAM
SNAPAT
STABAT
STALAG
SWARAJ
TEABAG
TEARAT
TIARAS
TOAMAN
TRAJAN
UTAHAN

••A••A
ACACIA
ACADIA
AGATHA
AJANTA
ALASKA
AMANDA
ANANDA
ARABIA
ARALIA
AZALEA
BIAFRA
BIANCA
BLANCA
BLANDA
BRAHMA
BRAZZA
CHACHA
CHACMA
CRANIA
DEANNA
DHARMA
ETALIA
EXACTA
FLAVIA
FRANCA
GOANNA
GRADEA
GRAPPA
GRATIA
ICARIA
ITALIA
ITASCA
JOANNA
KWACHA
KWANZA
LUANDA
MIASMA
NYASSA
PAANGA
PIAZZA
PLASMA
PRAJNA
PRAVDA
QUAGGA
QUANTA
REALIA
RUANDA
RWANDA
SCALIA
SHARIA
SHASTA
SPARTA
STADIA
STANZA
THALIA
TRAUMA
UGANDA
URANIA
ZSAZSA

•••AA•
BALAAM
BATAAN
BAZAAR
CANAAN
GSTAAD
JAMAAL
SALAAM

•••A•A
ACHAEA
AGLAIA
ALPACA
AMHARA
ANKARA
ANNABA
ARCANA
ARMADA
ARVADA
ASMARA
AYMARA
BAHAMA
BALATA
BANANA
CABALA
CABANA
CANADA
CASABA
CASAVA
CICADA
CLOACA
COLADA
CUIABA
CUNAXA
DAGAMA
ERRATA
ESPANA
FALANA
GALATA
GELADA
GEMARA
GUIANA
GUYANA
HABANA
HAVANA
HIVAOA
IGUANA
ILEANA
IMPALA
INDABA
ITHACA
JACANA
JALAPA
JICAMA
JUDAEA
JUMADA
KAMALA
KANAKA
KERALA
LALALA
LUSAKA
MALAGA
MALAYA
MANAMA
MANANA
MARACA
MASADA
MEDAKA
MEGARA
MORAVA
MUFASA
NEVADA
NICAEA
OAXACA
OGLALA
OOLALA
ORGANA
ORIANA
OSHAWA
OTTAVA
OTTAWA
PAJAMA
PANADA
PANAMA
PAPAYA
PARANA
PATACA
PICARA
PINATA
PIRANA
POSADA
PYJAMA
RAMADA
RENATA
ROXANA
SAHARA
SAMARA
SEDAKA
SOMATA
SONATA
STRATA
TAMARA
TANAKA
TARAWA
TIRANA
TUCANA
UMTATA
URBANA
YAMAHA
YUKATA
YUKAWA
ZAPATA
ZENANA

AB••••
ABACAS
ABACUS
ABASED
ABASES
ABATED
ABATES
ABATIS
ABBACY
ABBESS
ABBEYS
ABBOTS
ABBOTT
ABDUCT
ABELES
ABHORS
ABIDED
ABIDES
ABJECT
ABJURE
ABLATE
ABLAUT
ABLAZE
ABLEST
ABLOOM
ABLUSH
ABOARD
ABODES
ABOHMS
ABOLLA
ABOMBS
ABORAL
ABORTS
ABOUND
ABRADE
ABRAMS
ABROAD
ABRUPT
ABSENT
ABSORB
ABSURD
ABUKIR
ABUSED
ABUSER
ABUSES
ABYDOS
ABYSMS

A•B•••
ABBACY
ABBESS
ABBEYS
ABBOTS
ABBOTT
ALBANO
ALBANY
ALBEDO
ALBEIT
ALBERT
ALBINO
ALBION
ALBOIN
ALBORG
ALBUMS
AMBERS
AMBITS
AMBLED
AMBLER
AMBLES
AMBLIN
AMBUSH
ARBELA
ARBORS
ARBOUR
ASBURY
ATBATS
ATBEST
AUBADE
AUBREY
AUBURN

A••B••
ADOBES
AIRBAG
AIRBUS
ALIBIS
ALIBLE
ALLBUT
AMEBAE
AMEBAS
AMEBIC
ANUBIS
ARABIA
ARABIC
ARABLE
ARUBAN

A•••B•
ABOMBS
ACHEBE
ADLIBS
AEROBE
AKIMBO
AMOEBA
ANNABA
ARDEBS
ARRIBA
ARROBA

A••••B
ABSORB
ADSORB
ADVERB
APLOMB

•AB•••
BABBLE
BABIED
BABIES
BABKAS
BABOON
BABSON
BABULS
CABALA
CABALS
CABANA
CABBED
CABBIE
CABERS
CABINS
CABLED
CABLER
CABLES
DABBED
DABBLE
DABNEY
FABIAN
FABLED
FABLER
FABLES
FABRAY
FABRIC
GABBED
GABBER
GABBLE
GABBRO
GABION
GABLED
GABLES
HABANA
HABEAS
HABILE
HABITS
JABBAR
JABBED
JABBER
JABIRU
JABOTS
KABOBS
KABOOM
KABUKI
LABELS
LABIAL
LABILE
LABORS
LABOUR
LABREA
LABRET
LABRUM
MABELL
NABBED
NABBER
NABOBS
NABORS
PABLUM
RABATO
RABBET
RABBIS
RABBIT
RABBLE
RABIES
SABATO
SABENA
SABERS
SABINE
SABINS
SABLES
SABOTS
SABRAS
SABRES
TABARD
TABBED
TABLAS
TABLED
TABLES
TABLET
TABOOS
TABORS
TABRIZ
TABULA
WABASH

•A•B••
BABBLE
BALBOA
BAMBOO
BAOBAB
BARBED
BARBEL
BARBER
BARBET
BARBIE
BARBRA
BATBOY
BAUBLE
CABBED
CABBIE
CAMBER
CARBON
CARBOY
CASBAH
DABBED
DABBLE
DAUBED
DAUBER
DAUBES
DAYBED
GABBED
GABBER
GABBLE
GABBRO
GAMBIA
GAMBIT
GAMBLE
GAMBOL
GARBED
GARBLE
GASBAG
HARBIN
HARBOR
HASBRO
HATBOX
IAMBIC
JABBAR
JABBED
JABBER
KASBAH
LAMBDA
LAMBED
LAYBYS
LAZBOY
MAMBAS
MAMBOS
MARBLE
MARBLY
MAYBES
NABBED
NABBER
RABBET
RABBIS
RABBIT
RABBLE
RAGBAG
RAMBLA
RAMBLE
SAMBAL
SAMBAR
SAMBAS
TABBED
TALBOT
WAMBLE
WAMBLY
WARBLE
ZAMBIA

•A••B•
CAMEBY
CARIBE
CARIBS
CAROBS
CASABA
DANUBE
GATSBY
GAZEBO
JACOBI
KABOBS
KARIBA
LAIDBY
LAVABO
LAYSBY
MALABO
MALIBU
NABOBS
NASEBY
NAWABS
PASSBY
SAHIBS
SASEBO
WASABI
ZAREBA

•A•••B
BAOBAB
BARTAB
CANTAB
ZAGREB

••AB••
ARABIA
ARABIC
ARABLE
BLABBY
CRABBE
CRABBY
DIABLO
DOABLE
DRABEK
DRABLY
ENABLE
FLABBY
GRABAT
GRABBY
GRABEN
GRABLE
ISABEL
IZABAL
LIABLE
SCABBY
SEABAG
SEABED
SEABEE
SHABAN
SHABBY
STABAT
STABLE
STABLY
SWABBY
TEABAG
UNABLE
USABLE
USABLY
VIABLE
VIABLY

••A•B•
BLABBY
CRABBE
CRABBY
CRAMBO
FLABBY
FLAMBE
GRABBY
NEARBY
SCABBY
SHABBY
SWABBY

••A••B
SCARAB
SEALAB

•••AB•
ANNABA
CASABA
CUIABA
INDABA
KEBABS
LAVABO
MALABO
MCCABE
MESABI
MUGABE
NAWABS
PICABO
SQUABS
STRABO
WASABI

•••A•B
BEDAUB
BICARB
DEKALB

••••AB
BAOBAB
BARTAB
CANTAB
CONFAB
MIHRAB
PREFAB
PUNJAB
SCARAB
SEALAB
SKYLAB

AC••••
ACACIA
ACADIA
ACAJOU
ACARID
ACARUS
ACCEDE
ACCENT
ACCEPT
ACCESS
ACCORD
ACCOST
ACCRUE
ACCUSE
ACEDIA
ACEOUS
ACEOUT
ACESUP
ACETAL
ACETIC
ACETYL
ACHAEA
ACHEBE
ACHENE
ACHIER
ACHING
ACIDIC
ACIDLY
ACINUS
ACKACK
ACORNS
ACQUIT
ACROSS
ACTIII
ACTING
ACTINO
ACTION
ACTIUM
ACTIVE
ACTONE
ACTORS
ACTOUT
ACTSON
ACTSUP
ACTTWO
ACTUAL
ACUATE
ACUITY
ACUMEN

A•C•••
AACHEN
ACCEDE
ACCENT
ACCEPT
ACCESS
ACCORD
ACCOST
ACCRUE
ACCUSE
AHCHOO
ALCAPP
ALCOTT
ALCOVE
ALCUIN
ANCHOR
ANCIEN
ANCONA
ARCADE
ARCANA
ARCANE
ARCARO
ARCHED
ARCHER
ARCHES
ARCHIE
ARCHLY
ARCHON
ARCING
ARCTIC
ASCEND
ASCENT
ASCHAM
ASCOTS
ATCOST

A••C••
ABACAS
ABACUS
ACACIA
AFLCIO
ALECKY
ALECTO
ALICIA
AMECHE
AMICES
AMICUS
ANACIN
ANTCOW
APACHE
APICAL
APICES
ARECAS
ASHCAN
AVOCET

A•••C•
ABBACY
ABDUCT
ABJECT
ACKACK
ADDUCE
ADDUCT
ADVICE
AFFECT
AFRICA
AGENCY
ALNICO
ALPACA
ALSACE
AMERCE
ANTICS
APERCU
APIECE
ARNICA
ARRACK
ASPECT
ASPICS
ATONCE
ATTACH
ATTACK
ATTICA
ATTICS
AVOUCH
AZTECS

A••••C
ACETIC
ACIDIC
AEOLIC
AGARIC
AIRSAC
ALARIC
ALTAIC
AMEBIC
AMTRAC
ANEMIC
ANODIC
AORTIC
ARABIC
ARCTIC
ATOMIC
ATONIC

•AC•••
AACHEN
BACALL
BACKED
BACKER
BACKIN
BACKUP
BACKUS
CACAOS
CACHED
CACHES
CACHET
CACHOU
CACKLE
CACTUS
DACAPO
DACHAS
DACOIT
DACRON
DACTYL
FACADE
FACETS
FACEUP
FACIAL
FACIES
FACILE
FACING
FACTOR
FACULA
HACEKS
HACKED
HACKER
HACKIE
HACKLE
JACALS
JACANA
JACKAL
JACKED
JACKET
JACKIE
JACKUP
JACLYN
JACOBI
LACERS
LACEUP
LACHES
LACIER
LACING
LACKED
LACKEY
LACTIC
LACUNA
MACACO
MACAWS
MACHES
MACHOS
MACRAE
MACRON
MACROS
MACULA
NACHOS
PACERS
PACIFY
PACING
PACINO
PACKED
PACKER
PACKET
PACKUP
PACMAN
RACEME
RACERS
RACHEL
RACHIS
RACIAL
RACIER
RACILY
RACINE
RACING
RACKED
RACKET
RACKUP
RACONS
SACHEM
SACHET
SACKED
SACKER
SACQUE
SACRAL
SACRED
SACRUM
TACKED
TACKER
TACKLE
TACKON
TACOMA
TACTIC
VACANT
VACATE
VACHEL
VACLAV
VACUUM
YACHTS

•A•C••
BAUCIS
CAICOS
CALCES
CANCAN
CANCEL
CANCUN
CATCHY
CAUCHO
CAUCUS
DANCED
DANCER
DANCES
FALCON

FARCED
FARCES
FARCRY
FASCES
FASCIA
FATCAT
FAUCES
FAUCET
GARCIA
GARCON
GASCAP
GASCON
GAUCHE
GAUCHO
JASCHA
JAYCEE
LANCED
LANCER
LANCES
LANCET
LASCAR
MADCAP
MANCHA
MANCHU
MARCEL
MARCHE
MARCIA
MARCIE
MARCOS
MARCUS
MASCOT
NASCAR
PANCHO
PARCAE
PARCEL
PASCAL
PATCHY
RANCHO
RANCID
RANCOR
RASCAL
SANCHO
SANCTA
SAUCED
SAUCER
SAUCES
TAICHI
TALCED
TALCUM
WARCRY

•A••C•
BARUCH
BASICS
CALICO
HAUNCH
HAVOCS
JANICE
LAMECH
LAUNCH
MACACO
MALICE
MARACA
NATICK
NAUTCH
OAXACA
PALACE
PANICS
PAPACY
PATACA
PAUNCH
ZANUCK

•A•••C
BALTIC
BALZAC
BARDIC
CADMIC
CALPAC
FABRIC
GAELIC
GALLIC
GARLIC
IAMBIC
IATRIC
KARMIC
LACTIC
MANIAC
MANIOC
MANTIC
MASTIC
PARSEC
TACTIC
TANNIC
TARMAC

••AC••
ABACAS
ABACUS
ACACIA
ANACIN
APACHE
BEACON
BLACKS
BRACED
BRACER
BRACES
BRACTS
CHACHA
CHACMA
CLACKS
CRACKS
DEACON
ENACTS
EXACTA
EXACTO
EXACTS
FIACRE
FLACKS
FLACON
FRACAS
GLACES
GLACIS
GRACED
GRACES
GRACIE
GUACOS
KNACKS
KWACHA
KYACKS
NIACIN
ORACLE
PEACHY
PLACED
PLACER
PLACES
PLACID
POACHY
QUACKS
REACTS
SEACOW
SHACKS
SLACKS
SMACKS
SNACKS
SPACED
SPACEK
SPACER
SPACES
SPACEY
STACKS
STACTE
TEACUP
TRACED
TRACER
TRACES
TRACEY
TRACKS
TRACTS
URACIL
VIACOM
WHACKS
WHACKY
WRACKS

••A•C•
BIANCA
BLANCA
BLANCH
BRANCH
CHALCO
CHANCE
CHANCY
CLANCY
EPARCH
EXARCH
FIANCE
FIASCO
FRANCA
FRANCE
FRANCK
FRANCO
FRANCS
GLANCE
GRAECO
INARCH
ITASCA
KLATCH
NUANCE
PLAICE
PLANCK
PRANCE
SCARCE
SEANCE
SEARCH
SNATCH
STANCE
STANCH
STARCH
SWATCH
THATCH
TRANCE
USANCE

••A••C
AGARIC
ALARIC
ARABIC
CYANIC
DYADIC
ITALIC
PHATIC
SLAVIC
STATIC
TLALOC
TRAGIC
URALIC
URANIC

•••AC•
ABBACY
ACKACK
ALPACA
ALSACE
ARRACK
ATTACH
ATTACK
BLEACH
BREACH
BROACH
CLOACA
CURACY
DEFACE
DETACH
DIDACT
EFFACE
ENLACE
GOBACK
HIJACK
HORACE
IGNACE
IGUACU
IMPACT
INFACT
INTACT
ITHACA
KOVACS
LEGACY
LILACS
LUNACY
MACACO
MARACA
MENACE
MONACO
OAXACA
ORBACH
OUTACT
PALACE
PAPACY
PATACA
PESACH
PIRACY
PLEACH
POMACE
PREACH
PURACE
REDACT
REFACE
RELACE
SERACS
SOLACE
SUMACS
TENACE
TEXACO
THRACE
THWACK
UNLACE
UNPACK
UNTACK
VIVACE

•••A•C
ALTAIC
JUDAIC
MOSAIC
ROMAIC

••••AC
AIRSAC
AMTRAC
BALZAC
BIGMAC
CALPAC
COGNAC
CONTAC
IPECAC
MANIAC
MELMAC
MICMAC
OVISAC
SENLAC
TARMAC
TICTAC
TOMBAC
UNIVAC
ZODIAC

AD••••
ADAGES
ADAGIO
ADAPTS
ADDAMS
ADDEND
ADDERS
ADDING
ADDLED
ADDLES
ADDONS
ADDSIN
ADDSON
ADDSTO
ADDSUP
ADDUCE
ADDUCT
ADEEMS
ADELIE
ADELLE
ADEPTS
ADESTE
ADHERE
ADIDAS
ADIEUS
ADIEUX
ADJOIN
ADJURE
ADJUST
ADLIBS
ADMIRE
ADMITS
ADNATE
ADOBES
ADOLPH
ADONAI
ADONIS
ADOPTS
ADORED
ADOREE
ADORER
ADORES
ADORNS
ADRENO
ADRIAN
ADRIEN
ADRIFT
ADROIT
ADSORB
ADULTS
ADVENT
ADVERB
ADVERT
ADVICE
ADVISE
ADWEEK
ADYTUM
ADZUKI

A•D•••
ABDUCT
ADDAMS
ADDEND
ADDERS
ADDING
ADDLED
ADDLES
ADDONS
ADDSIN
ADDSON
ADDSTO
ADDSUP
ADDUCE
ADDUCT
AEDILE
AIDING
ALDERS
ALDINE
ALDOSE
ALDOUS
ALDRIN
ANDEAN
ANDHOW
ANDREA
ANDREI
ANDRES
ANDREW
ANDREY
ANDROS
AODAIS
ARDEBS
ARDENT
ARDORS
ARDOUR
AUDENS
AUDIAL
AUDIOS
AUDITS
AUDREY

A••D••
ABIDED
ABIDES
ABODES
ABYDOS
ACADIA
ACEDIA
ACIDIC
ACIDLY
AGADIR
AIRDAM
AIRDRY
ALLDAY
AMADIS
AMADOU
AMEDEO
AMIDES
AMIDOL
AMIDST
ANADEM
ANODES
ANODIC
AOUDAD
APODAL
ARIDLY
ASIDES
ATODDS
AVEDON
AVIDLY
AZODYE

A•••D•
ABRADE
ACCEDE
AGENDA
AIKIDO
ALBEDO
ALKYDS
ALLUDE
AMANDA
AMENDS
ANANDA
ANHYDR
APHIDS
ARCADE
ARENDT
ARMADA
AROIDS
ARVADA
ATODDS
AUBADE
AVOIDS
AWARDS

A••••D
ABASED
ABATED
ABIDED
ABOARD
ABOUND
ABROAD
ABSURD
ABUSED
ACARID
ACCORD
ADDEND
ADDLED
ADORED
AENEID
AFFORD
AFIELD
AFRAID
AGEOLD
AGREED
ALFRED
ALLIED
ALMOND
AMAZED
AMBLED
AMPHID
AMUSED
ANGLED
ANKLED
ANTEED
AOUDAD
APPEND
ARCHED
ARGUED
ARMAND
ARNOLD
AROUND
ASCEND
ASGARD
ASTRID
ATHAND
ATONED
ATSTUD
ATTEND
ATWOOD
AUFOND
AUGEND
AVOWED
AWAKED
AXSEED

•AD•••
BADDIE
BADEGG
BADGER
BADGES
BADGUY
BADLOT
CADDIE
CADDIS
CADENT
CADETS
CADGED
CADGER
CADGES
CADMIC
CADMUS
CADRES
DADDYO
DADOED
DADOES
FADEIN
FADING
GADDED
GADDER
GADFLY
GADGET
HADDIE
HADJES
HADJIS
HADRON
JADING
LADDER
LADDIE
LADERS
LADIDA
LADIES
LADING
LADINO
LADLED
LADLER
LADLES
LADOGA
MADAME
MADAMS
MADCAP
MADDEN
MADDER
MADDIE
MADEDO
MADEIT
MADERO
MADEUP
MADMAN
MADMAX
MADMEN
MADRAS
MADRES
MADRID
MADTOM
MADURA
MADURO
NADINE
NADIRS
PADANG
PADDED
PADDER
PADDLE
PADRES
PADUAN
RADDLE
RADIAL
RADIAN
RADIOS
RADISH
RADIUM
RADIUS
RADNER
RADOME
RADULA
SADDAM
SADDEN
SADDER
SADDLE
VADOSE
WADDED
WADDLE
WADDLY
WADEIN
WADERS
WADING
WADSUP
ZADDIK
ZADORA

•A•D••
BADDIE
BAGDAD
BALDER
BALDLY
BANDED
BANDIT
BANDOG
BARDIC
BARDOT
CADDIE
CADDIS
CALDER
CAMDEN
CANDID
CANDLE
CANDOR
CARDED
CARDER
CARDIN
CARDIO
CAUDAL
CAUDEX
CAUDLE
CAWDOR
DADDYO
DAEDAL
DANDER
DANDIE
DANDLE
DAWDLE
FANDOM
GADDED
GADDER
GANDER
GANDHI
GARDEN
HADDIE
HAIDAS
HANDED
HANDEL
HANDIN
HANDLE
HANDON
HARDEN
HARDER
HARDLY
HARDUP
HAYDEN
KANDER
LADDER
LADDIE
LAIDBY
LAIDIN
LAIDON
LAIDTO
LAIDUP
LANDAU
LANDED
LANDER
LANDHO
LANDIS
LANDON
LANDRY
LAPDOG
LARDED
LARDER
LARDON
LAUDED
LAUDER
MADDEN
MADDER
MADDIE
MAHDIS
MAIDEN
MAIDUS
MALDEN
MANDAN
MANDAY
MARDUK
MAYDAY
NASDAQ
PADDED
PADDER
PADDLE
PAIDIN
PAIDUP
PANDAS
PANDER
PANDIT
PARDON
PAYDAY
RADDLE
RAIDED
RAIDER
RANDOM
RANDRY
SADDAM
SADDEN
SADDER
SADDLE
SANDAL
SANDED
SANDER
SANDIA
SANDRA
SARDIS
SAUDIS
TAGDAY
TANDEM
TAWDRY
VALDEZ
VANDAL
VARDEN
WADDED
WADDLE
WADDLY
WALDEN
WANDER
WARDED
WARDEN
WARDER
YARDED
ZADDIK
ZANDER

•A••D•
CANADA
CANIDS
FACADE
FARADS
HAIRDO
HALIDE
KAUNDA
LADIDA
LAIRDS
LAMBDA
LAMEDH
LAMEDS
LAREDO
MADEDO
MAKEDO
MALADY
MASADA
MAUNDY
NAIADS
PAGODA
PANADA
PARADE
PARODY
RAMADA
RANIDS
RAPIDS
RATEDG
RATEDR
RATEDX
SALADS
SARODS
XANADU

•A•••D
BABIED
BACKED
BAGDAD
BAGGED
BAILED
BAITED
BALKED
BALLAD
BANDED
BANGED
BANKED
BANNED
BARBED
BARGED
BARKED
BARRED
BASHED
BASKED
BASTED
BATHED
BATTED
BAWLED
BAYARD
CABBED
CABLED
CACHED
CADGED
CALKED
CALLED
CALMED
CALVED
CAMPED
CANARD
CANDID
CANNED
CANOED
CANTED
CAPPED
CAPSID
CARDED
CARPED
CARTED
CARVED
CASHED
CATTED
CAUSED
DABBED
DADOED
DAMMED
DAMNED
DAMPED
DANCED
DAPPED
DARNED
DARTED
DASHED
DAUBED
DAWNED
DAYBED
EAGLED
EARNED
FABLED
FAGEND
FAGGED
FAILED
FAIRED
FANGED
FANNED
FARCED
FARMED
FASTED
FATTED
FAWNED
GABBED
GABLED
GADDED
GAFFED
GAGGED
GAINED
GAITED
GALLED
GANGED
GAPPED
GARBED
GASHED
GASPED
GASSED
GAUGED
GAUZED
GAWKED
HACKED
HAFTED
HAILED
HAIRED
HALOED
HALOID
HALTED
HALVED
HAMMED
HANDED
HANGED
HARKED
HARMED
HAROLD
HARPED
HASHED
HASPED
HATRED
HATTED
HAULED
HAWKED
HAZARD
JABBED
JACKED
JAGGED
JAILED
JAMMED
JARRED
JAZZED
KAYOED
LACKED
LADLED
LAGGED
LAMBED
LAMMED
LANCED
LANDED
LAPPED
LAPSED
LARDED
LARKED
LASHED
LASTED
LATHED
LAUDED
MADRID
MAENAD
MAILED
MALTED
MANNED
MAPPED
MARAUD
MARKED
MARLED
MARRED
MASHED
MASKED
MASSED
MATTED
MAULED
NABBED
NAGGED
NAILED
NAPPED
PACKED
PADDED
PAINED
PAIRED
PALLED
PALLID
PALMED
PANNED
PANTED
PARKED
PARRED
PARSED
PARTED
PASSED
PASTED
PATTED
PAUSED
PAWNED
RACKED
RAFTED
RAGGED
RAIDED
RAILED
RAINED
RAISED
RAMMED
RAMPED
RAMROD
RANCID
RANGED
RANKED
RANTED
RAPPED
RASHAD
RASHID
RASPED
RATTED
RAZZED
SACKED
SACRED
SAGGED
SAILED
SALTED
SALVED
SANDED
SAPPED
SASHED
SASSED
SAUCED
SAWRED
SAYYID
TABARD
TABBED
TABLED
TACKED
TAGEND
TAGGED
TAILED
TALCED
TALKED
TALMUD
TAMPED
TANGED
TANKED
TANNED
TAPPED
TARRED
TASKED
TASTED
TATTED
TAXIED
VALUED
VALVED
VAMPED
VANNED
VARIED
WADDED
WAFTED
WAGGED
WAILED
WAITED
WAIVED
WALKED
WALLED
WANNED
WANTAD
WANTED
WARDED
WARGOD
WARMED
WARNED
WARPED
WARRED
WASHED
WASTED
YAKKED
YANKED
YAPPED
YARDED
YARNED
YAWNED
YAWPED
ZAGGED
ZAPPED

••AD••
ACADIA
AGADIR
AMADIS
AMADOU
ANADEM
BEADED
BEADLE
BEADUP
BLADED
BLADES
CHADOR
CRADLE
DEADEN
DEADER
DEADLY
DEADON
DIADEM
DYADIC
EVADED
EVADER
EVADES
GLADES
GLADLY
GLADYS
GOADED
GRADEA
GRADED
GRADER
GRADES
GRADIN
GRADUS
HEADED
HEADER
HEADIN
HEADON
HEADUP
HYADES
IBADAN
ISADOR
LEADED
LEADEN
LEADER
LEADIN
LEADON
LEADTO
LEADUP
LOADED
LOADER
MCADAM
MCADOO
MEADOW
QUADRI
READER
READIN
ROADIE
SEADOG
SHADED
SHADES
SHADOW
SPADED
SPADER
SPADES
SPADIX
STADIA
TRADED
TRADER
TRADES

••A•D•
AMANDA
ANANDA
AWARDS
BEARDS
BLANDA
BOARDS
BRAIDS
BRANDO
BRANDS
BRANDT
BRANDX
BRANDY

CIARDI
CLAUDE
ELANDS
FRAUDS
GLANDS
GRANDE
GRANDS
GUARDS
HOARDS
LUANDA
PLAIDS
PRAVDA
RUANDA
RWANDA
SCALDS
SHANDY
SHARDS
SKALDS
STANDS
SWARDS
UGANDA
VIANDS

••A••D
ABASED
ABATED
ACARID
AMAZED
AWAKED
BEADED
BEAKED
BEAMED
BEANED
BIASED
BLADED
BLAMED
BLARED
BLAZED
BOATED
BRACED
BRAKED
BRAVED
BRAYED
BRAZED
CEASED
CHAFED
CHASED
CLAWED
COATED
COAXED
CRANED
CRATED
CRAVED
CRAZED
DIALED
DRAPED
DRAYED
ELAPID
ELATED
ERASED
EVADED
FEARED
FLAKED
FLAMED
FLARED
FLAWED
FLAYED
FOALED
FOAMED
FRAMED
FRAYED
GEARED
GLARED
GLAZED
GNAWED
GOADED
GRACED
GRADED
GRATED
GRAVED
GRAVID
GRAYED
GRAZED
HEADED
HEALED
HEAPED
HEATED
HEAVED
HOAXED
IMAGED
KHALID
LEADED
LEAFED
LEAKED
LEANED
LEAPED
LEASED
LEAVED
LOADED
LOAFED
LOAMED
LOANED
MOANED
MOATED
NEARED
OKAYED
ORATED
PEAKED
PEALED
PEAPOD
PHASED
PLACED
PLACID
PLANED
PLATED
PLAYED
PRATED
PRAYED
QUAKED
REAMED
REAPED
REARED
ROAMED
ROARED
RRATED
SCALED
SCARED
SEABED
SEALED
SEAMED
SEARED
SEATED
SHADED
SHAMED
SHAPED
SHARED
SHAVED
SKATED
SLAKED
SLATED
SLAVED
SLAYED
SNAKED
SNARED
SOAKED
SOAPED
SOARED
SPACED
SPADED
SPARED
SPAYED
STAGED
STAKED
STALED
STARED
STATED
STAVED
STAYED
SWAGED
SWAYED
TEAMED
TEARED
TEASED
THAWED
TRACED
TRADED
UNAGED
UNAWED
WEANED
WEAVED
XRATED
XRAYED

•••AD•
ABRADE
ARCADE
ARMADA
ARVADA
AUBADE
BREADS
BROADS
CANADA
CICADA
COLADA
CYCADS
DECADE
DORADO
DREADS
DRYADS
FACADE
FARADS
GELADA
HEXADS
HODADS
INVADE
JIHADS
JUMADA
JURADO
KNEADS
MALADY
MASADA
MIKADO
MILADY
MONADS
NAIADS
NEVADA
NOMADS
OCTADS
OREADS
PANADA
PARADE
PLEADS
POMADE
POSADA
RAMADA
REMADE
RIYADH
SALADS
SQUADS
STEADS
STEADY
STRADS
TIRADE
TREADS
TRIADS
UNLADE
UNMADE
XANADU

•••A•D
ABOARD
AFRAID
ARMAND
ASGARD
ATHAND
BAYARD
BRIAND
BRIARD
BYHAND
CANARD
COWARD
CUNARD
DEMAND
DONALD
DOTARD
EDGARD
EDUARD
EDVARD
EDWARD
ERHARD
ERRAND
EXPAND
FUGARD
GERALD
GERARD
GIRARD
GODARD
GSTAAD
HAZARD
HERALD
HOWARD
IDCARD
INHAND
INLAID
INLAND
INWARD
ISLAND
IZZARD
LELAND
LIZARD
MARAUD
ONHAND
ONLAND
ONWARD
OSWALD
OXNARD
PETARD
PICARD
POLAND
REGARD
RELAID
REMAND
REPAID
REPAND
RESAND
RETARD
REWARD
RIBALD
RIBAND
RITARD
ROLAND
RONALD
SEWARD
STRAND
TABARD
TOGAED
TOWARD
UNHAND
UNLAID
UNPAID
UNSAID
UPLAND
UPWARD
VISAED
WIZARD

••••AD
ABROAD
AOUDAD
BAGDAD
BALLAD
BYROAD
CIUDAD
CONRAD
DOODAD
EMQUAD
ENNEAD
ENQUAD
FORBAD
GILEAD
GOTMAD
GSTAAD
HEPTAD
INROAD
KEYPAD
KONRAD
MAENAD
MYRIAD
NOLEAD
NOLOAD
NOTBAD
OGDOAD
PENTAD
PLEIAD
RASHAD
RELOAD
REREAD
SINBAD
SINEAD
SPREAD
TETRAD
THREAD
TOOBAD
UNCLAD
UNLEAD
UNLOAD
UNREAD
UPLOAD
WANTAD

AE••••
AEDILE
AEETES
AEGEAN
AENEAS
AENEID
AEOLIA
AEOLIC
AEOLUS
AERATE
AERIAL
AERIES
AEROBE
AETHER

A•E•••
ABELES
ACEDIA
ACEOUS
ACEOUT
ACESUP
ACETAL
ACETIC
ACETYL
ADEEMS
ADELIE
ADELLE
ADEPTS
ADESTE
AEETES
AGEING
AGEISM
AGEIST
AGENAS
AGENCY
AGENDA
AGENTS
AGEOLD
AHERNE
AIELLO
AKELAS
AKENES
ALEAST
ALECKY
ALECTO
ALEGAR
ALEGRE
ALEMAN
ALEPHS
ALEPPO
ALERTS
ALEUTS
ALEXEI
ALEXIA
ALEXIS
AMEBAE
AMEBAS
AMEBIC
AMECHE
AMEDEO
AMEERS
AMELIA
AMENDS
AMENRA
AMENTS
AMERCE
ANEMIA
ANEMIC
APEMAN
APEMEN
APERCU
APEXES
ARECAS
ARENAS
ARENDT
AREOLA
ARETES
ARETHA
AREZZO
ATEAMS
ATEASE
ATEMPO
ATERGO
ATESTS
AVEDON
AVENGE
AVENUE
AVERNO
AVERSE
AVERTS
AVESTA
AWEARY
AWEIGH
AYEAYE
AYESHA

A••E••
ABBESS
ABBEYS
ABJECT
ABLEST
ABSENT
ACCEDE
ACCENT
ACCEPT
ACCESS
ACHEBE
ACHENE
ADDEND
ADDERS
ADEEMS
ADHERE
ADIEUS
ADIEUX
ADRENO
ADVENT
ADVERB
ADVERT
ADWEEK
AEGEAN
AENEAS
AENEID
AFFECT
AFIELD
AFREET
AFRESH
AGLEAM
AGLETS
AGREED
AGREES
AILEEN
AILERS
ALBEDO
ALBEIT
ALBERT
ALDERS
ALIENS
ALKENE
ALLEES
ALLEGE
ALLELE
ALLEYS
ALPERT
ALTERS
ALWEST
AMBERS
AMEERS
AMIENS
AMOEBA
AMPERE
AMVETS
ANDEAN
ANGELA
ANGELI
ANGELL
ANGELO
ANGELS
ANGERS
ANNEAL
ANNEXE
ANSELM
ANTEED
ANTERO
ANTEUP
APIECE
APPEAL
APPEAR
APPEND
APTEST
ARBELA
ARDEBS
ARDENT
ARGENT
ARLENE
ARMETS
ARNESS
ARNETT
ARPENT
ARREST
ARSENE
ARTELS
ARTERY
ASCEND
ASCENT
ASKERS
ASLEEP
ASPECT
ASPENS
ASPERA
ASSENT
ASSERT
ASSESS
ASSETS
ASTERN
ASTERS
ASWELL
ATBEST
ATHENA
ATHENE
ATHENS
ATREST
ATREUS
ATTEND
ATTEST
AUDENS
AUGEAN
AUGEND
AUGERS
AUREUS
AUTEUR
AXSEED
AZTECS

A•••E•
AACHEN
ABASED
ABASES
ABATED
ABATES
ABELES
ABIDED
ABIDES
ABODES
ABUSED
ABUSER
ABUSES
ACHAEA
ACHIER
ACUMEN
ADAGES
ADDLED
ADDLES
ADOBES
ADORED
ADOREE
ADORER
ADORES
ADRIEN
ADWEEK
AEETES
AERIES
AETHER
AFREET
AGATES
AGAVES
AGGIES
AGREED
AGREES
AIGRET
AILEEN
AIRIER
AIRMEN
AISLES
AKENES
ALEXEI
ALFRED
ALFVEN
ALINES
ALLEES
ALLIED
ALLIES
ALLSET
ALLWET
ALTHEA
AMAZED
AMAZES
AMBLED
AMBLER
AMBLES
AMEDEO
AMICES
AMIDES
AMINES
AMOLES
AMPLER
AMSTEL
AMULET
AMUSED
AMUSES
ANADEM
ANCIEN
ANDREA
ANDREI
ANDRES
ANDREW
ANDREY
ANGLED
ANGLER
ANGLES
ANIMES
ANKLED
ANKLES
ANKLET
ANNLEE
ANODES
ANOLES
ANSWER
ANTEED
ANTHEM
ANTHER
ANTLER
ANTRES
APEMEN
APEXES
APICES
APOGEE
APPLES
ARCHED
ARCHER
ARCHES
ARETES
ARGUED
ARGUER
ARGUES
ARISEN
ARISES
ARMIES
ARMLET
ARNHEM
ARTIER
ASHIER
ASHLEY
ASIDES
ASLEEP
ATONED
ATONES
ATTLEE
AUBREY
AUDREY
AUKLET
AUSPEX
AUSTEN
AVOCET
AVOWED
AVOWER
AWAKED
AWAKEN
AWAKES
AWOKEN
AXSEED
AZALEA
AZORES

A••••E
ABJURE
ABLATE
ABLAZE
ABRADE
ACCEDE
ACCRUE
ACCUSE
ACHEBE
ACHENE
ACTIVE
ACTONE
ACUATE
ADDUCE
ADELIE
ADELLE
ADESTE
ADHERE
ADJURE
ADMIRE
ADNATE
ADOREE
ADVICE
ADVISE
AEDILE
AERATE
AEROBE
AFFINE
AFLAME
AFRAME
AGLARE
AGNATE
AGORAE
AHERNE
ALCOVE
ALDINE
ALDOSE
ALEGRE
ALFINE
ALGORE
ALIBLE
ALKENE
ALLEGE
ALLELE
ALLUDE
ALLURE
ALPINE
ALSACE
ALULAE
AMALIE
AMEBAE
AMECHE
AMERCE
AMPERE
AMPULE
ANNEXE
ANNLEE
ANOMIE
ANSATE
ANYONE
AORTAE
APACHE
APIECE
APLITE
APOGEE
APPOSE
AQUATE
ARABLE
ARCADE
ARCANE
ARCHIE
ARGIVE
ARGYLE
ARIOSE
ARLENE
ARMURE
AROUSE
ARRIVE
ARSENE
ASHORE
ASLOPE
ASPIRE
ASSIZE
ASSUME
ASSURE
ASTUTE
ATEASE
ATHENE
ATHOME
ATONCE
ATTIRE
ATTLEE
ATTUNE
AUBADE
AUNTIE
AUSSIE
AVENGE
AVENUE
AVERSE
AVIATE
AVULSE
AWHILE
AYEAYE
AZODYE

•AE•••
CAESAR
DAEDAL
FAENZA
FAERIE
FAEROE
GAELIC
HAEMAT
HAEMON
JAEGER
MAENAD
PAEANS
PAELLA
PAEONS

•A•E••
BADEGG
BAGELS
BAKERS
BAKERY
BALEEN
BALERS
BAREGE
BARELY
BAREST
BASELY
BASEST
BATEAU
BAYEUX
CABERS
CADENT
CADETS
CAGERS
CAMEAT
CAMEBY
CAMEIN
CAMELS
CAMEON
CAMEOS
CAMERA
CAMETO
CAMEUP
CANERS
CAPERS
CAREEN
CAREER
CARESS
CARETO
CARETS
CASERN
CATENA
CATERS
CAVEAT
CAVEIN
CAVELL
CAVERN
CAVERS
CAVETT
DALETH
DARETO
DATERS
EASEIN
EASELS
EASEUP
EATERS
EATERY
FACETS
FACEUP
FADEIN
FAGEND
FAKERS
FAKERY
FARERS
GAIETY
GALEAE
GALENA
GAMELY
GAMEST
GAMETE
GAPERS
GARETH
GATEAU
GATERS
GAVEIN
GAVELS
GAVEUP
GAYEST
GAZEBO
HABEAS
HACEKS
HALERS
HALERU
HALEST
HALEVY
HAREMS
HATERS
HAVEAT
HAVENS
HAVENT
HAVEON
HAZELS
HAZERS
JAPERS
JAPERY
KAGERA
KAREEM
LABELS
LACERS
LACEUP
LADERS
LAGERS
LAKERS
LAMECH
LAMEDH
LAMEDS
LAMELY
LAMENT
LAMESA
LAMEST
LAPELS
LAREDO
LASERS
LATEEN
LATELY
LATENE
LATENS
LATENT
LATEST
LAVERS
LAXEST
LAYERS
MABELL
MADEDO
MADEIT
MADERO
MADEUP
MAKEDO
MAKEIT
MAKERS
MAKEUP
MANEGE
MASERS
MASERU
MATERS
MATEYS
MAVENS
MAZERS
NAMELY
NAMERS
NAPERY
NASEBY
NAVELS
OATERS
PACERS
PAGERS
PALEAE
PALELY
PALEST
PAMELA
PANELS
PAPERS
PAPERY
PARENS
PARENT
PARERS
PARETO
PAREVE
PASEOS
PATENS
PATENT
PAVERS
PAWERS
PAYEES
PAYERS
RACEME
RACERS
RAKEIN
RAKERS
RAKEUP
RAMEAU
RANEES
RAREFY
RARELY
RAREST
RATEDG
RATEDR
RATEDX
RATELS
RATERS
RAVELS
RAVENS
RAVERS
RAWEGG
RAWEST
SABENA
SABERS
SAFELY
SAFEST
SAFETY
SAGELY
SAGEST
SAKERS
SAMEKH
SANELY
SANEST
SASEBO
SATEEN
SAVERS
SAVEUP
SAYERS
TAGEND
TAKEIN
TAKEON
TAKERS
TAKETH
TAKETO
TAKEUP
TALENT
TALESE
TAMELY
TAMERS
TAMEST
TAPERS
TATERS
TAVERN
TAXERS
VALENS
VALENT
VALERY
VALETS
VARESE
WADEIN
WADERS
WAFERS
WAGERS
WAKENS
WAKEUP
WALERS
WALESA
WANERS
WATERS
WATERY
WAVEIN
WAVERS
WAVERY
WAXERS
YARELY
ZAREBA

•A••E•
AACHEN
BABIED
BABIES
BACKED
BACKER
BADGER
BADGES
BAGGED
BAGGER
BAILED
BAILEE
BAILER
BAILEY
BAINES
BAITED
BALDER
BALEEN
BALKED
BALLET
BANDED
BANGED
BANGER
BANKED
BANKER
BANNED
BANNER
BANTER
BARBED
BARBEL
BARBER
BARBET
BARGED
BARGES
BARKED
BARKER
BARLEY
BARMEN
BARNES
BARNEY
BARRED
BARREL
BARREN
BARRES
BARTER
BASHED
BASHES
BASKED
BASKET
BASSES
BASSET
BASTED
BASTER
BASTES
BATHED
BATHER
BATHES
BATMEN
BATTED
BATTEN
BATTER
BAWLED

BAWLER
BAXTER
CABBED
CABLED
CABLER
CABLES
CACHED
CACHES
CACHET
CADGED
CADGER
CADGES
CADRES
CAGIER
CAGNEY
CAHIER
CALCES
CALDER
CALKED
CALLED
CALLER
CALLES
CALMED
CALMER
CALVED
CALVES
CALXES
CAMBER
CAMDEN
CAMLET
CAMPED
CAMPER
CANCEL
CANKER
CANNED
CANNEL
CANNER
CANNES
CANOED
CANOES
CANTED
CANTER
CAPLET
CAPPED
CAPPER
CARDED
CARDER
CAREEN
CAREER
CARIES
CARMEL
CARMEN
CARNES
CARNET
CARNEY
CARPED
CARPEL
CARPER
CARPET
CARREL
CARREY
CARTED
CARTEL
CARTER
CARTES
CARVED
CARVER
CARVES
CARVEY
CASHED
CASHES
CASHEW
CASPER
CASTER

CASTES
CATHER
CATTED
CAUDEX
CAUSED
CAUSES
DABBED
DABNEY
DADOED
DADOES
DAFTER
DAGGER
DAILEY
DAIREN
DAISES
DALLES
DAMIEN
DAMMED
DAMNED
DAMPED
DAMPEN
DAMPER
DAMSEL
DANCED
DANCER
DANCES
DANDER
DANGER
DANIEL
DANKER
DANNER
DANTES
DAPPED
DAPPER
DARIEN
DARKEN
DARKER
DARNED
DARNEL
DARNER
DARREN
DARTED
DARTER
DASHED
DASHER
DASHES
DAUBED
DAUBER
DAUBES
DAVIES
DAWNED
DAYBED
EAGLED
EAGLES
EAGLET
EAGRES
EARNED
EARNER
EASIER
EASTER
FABLED
FABLER
FABLES
FACIES
FAGGED
FAILED
FAIRED
FAIRER
FALLEN
FALSER
FALTER
FANGED
FANJET
FANNED

FARCED
FARCES
FARLEY
FARMED
FARMER
FASCES
FASTED
FASTEN
FASTER
FATHER
FATTED
FATTEN
FATTER
FAUCES
FAUCET
FAWKES
FAWNED
FAWNER
GABBED
GABBER
GABLED
GABLES
GADDED
GADDER
GADGET
GAFFED
GAFFER
GAFFES
GAGGED
GAGMEN
GAINED
GAINER
GAITED
GAITER
GALLED
GALLEY
GAMIER
GANDER
GANGED
GANGES
GANNET
GAPPED
GARBED
GARDEN
GARNER
GARNET
GARRET
GARTER
GARVEY
GASHED
GASHES
GASJET
GASKET
GASMEN
GASPED
GASSED
GASSER
GASSES
GATHER
GAUGED
GAUGER
GAUGES
GAUZED
GAUZES
GAWKED
GAWKER
HACKED
HACKER
HADJES
HAFTED
HAILED
HAILEY
HAINES
HAIRED

HAJJES
HALLEL
HALLEY
HALOED
HALOES
HALSEY
HALTED
HALTER
HALVED
HALVES
HAMLET
HAMMED
HAMMER
HAMPER
HANDED
HANDEL
HANGED
HANGER
HANKER
HANSEL
HAPPEN
HARDEN
HARDER
HARKED
HARKEN
HARKER
HARLEM
HARLEY
HARMED
HARPED
HARPER
HARVEY
HASHED
HASHES
HASPED
HASTEN
HASTES
HATRED
HATTED
HATTER
HAULED
HAULER
HAWKED
HAWKER
HAWSER
HAWSES
HAYDEN
HAYLEY
HAZIER
JABBED
JABBER
JACKED
JACKET
JAEGER
JAGGED
JAGGER
JAILED
JAILER
JAMMED
JAMMER
JANSEN
JARRED
JASPER
JAURES
JAVIER
JAYCEE
JAYVEE
JAZZED
JAZZES
KAISER
KANDER
KAREEM
KAYOED
LAAGER

LABREA
LABRET
LACHES
LACIER
LACKED
LACKEY
LADDER
LADIES
LADLED
LADLER
LADLES
LAFFER
LAGGED
LAGGER
LAMBED
LAMMED
LANCED
LANCER
LANCES
LANCET
LANDED
LANDER
LANIER
LANKER
LAPPED
LAPPET
LAPSED
LAPSES
LAPTEV
LARDED
LARDER
LARGER
LARKED
LARSEN
LASHED
LASHER
LASHES
LASSEN
LASSER
LASSES
LASTED
LASTEX
LATEEN
LATHED
LATHER
LATHES
LATKES
LATTEN
LATTER
LAUDED
LAUDER
LAUPER
LAUREL
LAUREN
LAWMEN
LAWYER
LAYMEN
LAZIER
MACHES
MADDEN
MADDER
MADMEN
MADRES
MAGNET
MAGUEY
MAHLER
MAIDEN
MAILED
MAILER
MAILES
MAIZES
MAJGEN
MALDEN
MALLEE

MALLEI
MALLET
MALTED
MANGER
MANNED
MANNER
MANSES
MANTEL
MANUEL
MAPLES
MAPPED
MAPPER
MARCEL
MARIEL
MARKED
MARKER
MARKET
MARLED
MARLEE
MARLEY
MARMEE
MARNER
MARRED
MARTEL
MARTEN
MARVEL
MASHED
MASHER
MASHES
MASKED
MASKER
MASSED
MASSES
MASSEY
MASTER
MATHER
MATTEA
MATTED
MATTEL
MATTER
MATTES
MAULED
MAULER
MAUMEE
MAUSER
MAUVES
MAYBES
MAYHEM
NABBED
NABBER
NAGGED
NAGGER
NAILED
NAILER
NANSEN
NANTES
NAPIER
NAPLES
NAPPED
NAPPER
NAPPES
NASSER
NATTER
NAUSEA
NAVIES
OAKLEY
OATIER
PACKED
PACKER
PACKET
PADDED
PADDER
PADRES
PAINED

PAIRED
PALAEO
PALLED
PALLET
PALMED
PALMER
PALTER
PAMPER
PANDER
PANNED
PANNER
PANNES
PANTED
PANZER
PAPIER
PARCEL
PARGET
PARKED
PARKER
PARLEY
PARRED
PARREL
PARSEC
PARSED
PARSEE
PARSER
PARSES
PARTED
PASSED
PASSEL
PASSER
PASSES
PASTED
PASTEL
PASTES
PATTED
PATTEN
PATTER
PAULEY
PAUPER
PAUSED
PAUSES
PAWNED
PAWNEE
PAWNER
PAYEES
RABBET
RABIES
RACHEL
RACIER
RACKED
RACKET
RADNER
RAFAEL
RAFTED
RAFTER
RAGGED
RAGMEN
RAIDED
RAIDER
RAILED
RAILER
RAINED
RAINER
RAINES
RAISED
RAISER
RAISES
RAMIES
RAMJET
RAMMED
RAMPED
RAMSES
RAMSEY

RANEES
RANGED
RANGER
RANGES
RANKED
RANKER
RANTED
RANTER
RAPIER
RAPPED
RAPPEE
RAPPEL
RAPPER
RAQUEL
RASHER
RASHES
RASPED
RASPER
RASTER
RATHER
RATTED
RATTER
RAZZED
RAZZES
SABLES
SABRES
SACHEM
SACHET
SACKED
SACKER
SACRED
SADDEN
SADDER
SAGGED
SAILED
SALLET
SALTED
SALTEN
SALTER
SALVED
SALVER
SALVES
SAMUEL
SANDED
SANDER
SANGER
SANSEI
SANTEE
SAPPED
SAPPER
SARGES
SASHED
SASHES
SASSED
SASSER
SASSES
SATEEN
SAUCED
SAUCER
SAUCES
SAUGER
SAUREL
SAUTES
SAWRED
SAWYER
SAYYES
TABBED
TABLED
TABLES
TABLET
TACKED
TACKER
TAGGED
TAILED

TAIPEI
TALCED
TALKED
TALKER
TALLER
TAMPED
TAMPER
TANDEM
TANGED
TANKED
TANKER
TANNED
TANNER
TAPPED
TAPPER
TAPPET
TARGES
TARGET
TARRED
TARTER
TASKED
TASSEL
TASSES
TASTED
TASTER
TASTES
TATTED
TATTER
TAUPES
TAUTEN
TAUTER
TAXIED
TAXIES
TAXMEN
VACHEL
VAGUER
VAINER
VALDEZ
VALLEE
VALLEY
VALUED
VALUES
VALVED
VALVES
VAMPED
VAMPER
VANIER
VANNED
VARDEN
VARIED
VARIES
VARLET
VARNEY
VASTER
WADDED
WAFTED
WAGGED
WAGNER
WAILED
WAILER
WAITED
WAITER
WAIVED
WAIVER
WAIVES
WALDEN
WALKED
WALKER
WALLED
WALLER
WALLET
WALTER
WANDER
WANNED

WANNER
WANTED
WAPNER
WARDED
WARDEN
WARDER
WARIER
WARMED
WARMER
WARNED
WARNER
WARPED
WARRED
WARREN
WASHED
WASHER
WASHES
WASTED
WASTER
WASTES
WATNEY
WAVIER
WAXIER
XAVIER
YAHWEH
YAKKED
YAKKER
YALIES
YAMMER
YANKED
YANKEE
YAPPED
YARDED
YARNED
YASSER
YAWNED
YAWNER
YAWPED
YAWPER
ZAFFER
ZAGGED
ZAGREB
ZANDER
ZANIER
ZANIES
ZAPPED
ZAPPER

•A•••E

BABBLE
BADDIE
BAFFLE
BAGGIE
BAILEE
BANGLE
BARBIE
BAREGE
BARITE
BARQUE
BARRIE
BASQUE
BATTLE
BATTUE
BAUBLE
CABBIE
CACKLE
CADDIE
CAIQUE
CAJOLE
CALQUE
CAMISE
CANAPE
CANDLE
CANINE

CANNAE
CANTLE
CANUTE
CAPONE
CAPOTE
CARAFE
CARIBE
CAROLE
CARRIE
CASQUE
CASTLE
CATTLE
CAUDLE
CAYUSE
DABBLE
DAMAGE
DAMONE
DAMORE
DANDIE
DANDLE
DANGLE
DANGME
DANUBE
DAPHNE
DAPPLE
DARKLE
DATIVE
DAWDLE
DAYONE
DAZZLE
FACADE
FACILE
FAERIE
FAEROE
FAILLE
FALINE
FAMINE
FANNIE
FATALE
FAUNAE
GABBLE
GAGGLE
GALEAE
GALORE
GAMBLE
GAMETE
GAMINE
GANGLE
GANGUE
GARAGE
GARBLE
GARGLE
GAUCHE
HABILE
HACKIE
HACKLE
HADDIE
HAGGLE
HALIDE
HALITE
HAMITE
HANDLE
HANKIE
HARARE
HASSLE
HATTIE
JACKIE
JAMOKE
JANGLE
JANICE
JANINE
JAYCEE
JAYVEE
KALINE

KARATE
KATHIE
LABILE
LADDIE
LAHORE
LAINIE
LAMAZE
LANATE
LANOSE
LAOTSE
LARVAE
LASSIE
LATENE
LAURIE
LAVAGE
MACRAE
MADAME
MADDIE
MAGGIE
MAGPIE
MAISIE
MAITRE
MALATE
MALICE
MALLEE
MALONE
MANAGE
MANEGE
MANGLE
MANQUE
MANTLE
MARBLE
MARCHE
MARCIE
MARGIE
MARINE
MARLEE
MARMEE
MARNIE
MARPLE
MARQUE
MASHIE
MASQUE
MATTIE
MATURE
MAUMEE
MAXINE
MAXIXE
NADINE
NATIVE
NATURE
PADDLE
PAIUTE
PALACE
PALATE
PALEAE
PARADE
PARCAE
PAREVE
PAROLE
PARSEE
PARURE
PATINE
PAVANE
PAWNEE
RABBLE
RACEME
RACINE
RADDLE
RADOME
RAFFLE
RAMATE
RAMBLE
RAMONE

RAMOSE
RANKLE
RAPINE
RAPPEE
RASSLE
RATINE
RATITE
RATTLE
RAVAGE
RAVINE
RAZZLE
SABINE
SACQUE
SADDLE
SAFIRE
SAINTE
SALINE
SALOME
SALUTE
SAMITE
SAMMIE
SAMPLE
SANTEE
SARTRE
SATIRE
SAVAGE
SAVATE
SAVOIE
TACKLE
TAGORE
TAILLE
TALESE
TALKIE
TAMALE
TANGLE
TATTLE
VACATE
VADOSE
VALISE
VALLEE
VARESE
WADDLE
WAFFLE
WAGGLE
WAHINE
WALKIE
WAMBLE
WANGLE
WARBLE
WASHOE
WATTLE
YANKEE

••AE••

GRAECO
URAEUS

••A•E•

ABASED
ABASES
ABATED
ABATES
ADAGES
AGATES
AGAVES
AMAZED
AMAZES
ANADEM
AWAKED
AWAKEN
AWAKES
AZALEA
BEADED
BEAKED

BEAKER
BEAMED
BEANED
BEARER
BEATEN
BEATER
BEAVER
BIASED
BIASES
BLADED
BLADES
BLAMED
BLAMES
BLARED
BLARES
BLAZED
BLAZER
BLAZES
BOATED
BOATER
BRACED
BRACER
BRACES
BRAKED
BRAKES
BRAVED
BRAVER
BRAVES
BRAYED
BRAYER
BRAZED
BRAZEN
BRAZER
BRAZES
CEASED
CEASES
CHAFED
CHAFES
CHALET
CHANEL
CHANEY
CHAPEL
CHASED
CHASER
CHASES
CHAVEZ
CLARET
CLAWED
CLAWER
CLAYEY
COALER
COATED
COAXED
COAXER
COAXES
CRAKES
CRANED
CRANES
CRAPES
CRATED
CRATER
CRATES
CRAVED
CRAVEN
CRAVER
CRAVES
CRAZED
CRAZES
DEADEN
DEADER
DEAFEN
DEAFER
DEALER
DEARER

DIADEM
DIALED
DIALER
DIAPER
DLAYER
DRABEK
DRAGEE
DRAKES
DRAPED
DRAPER
DRAPES
DRAWER
DRAYED
EDAMES
ELATED
ELATER
ELATES
ELAYER
ENAMEL
ENATES
ERASED
ERASER
ERASES
EVADED
EVADER
EVADES
FEARED
FEARER
FLAKED
FLAKER
FLAKES
FLAMED
FLAMES
FLARED
FLARES
FLAWED
FLAXEN
FLAXES
FLAYED
FLAYER
FOALED
FOAMED
FRAMED
FRAMES
FRASER
FRAYED
FRAZER
GEARED
GLACES
GLADES
GLARED
GLARES
GLASER
GLAZED
GLAZER
GLAZES
GNAWED
GNAWER
GOADED
GOATEE
GRABEN
GRACED
GRACES
GRADEA
GRADED
GRADER
GRADES
GRAPES
GRATED
GRATER
GRATES
GRAVED
GRAVEL
GRAVEN

GRAVER
GRAVES
GRAYED
GRAYER
GRAZED
GRAZER
GRAZES
HEADED
HEADER
HEALED
HEALER
HEAPED
HEARER
HEATED
HEATER
HEAVED
HEAVEN
HEAVER
HEAVES
HOAXED
HOAXER
HOAXES
HYADES
IMAGED
IMAGER
IMAGES
IMARET
INANER
INAPET
IRATER
ISABEL
JUAREZ
KNAVES
KRAKEN
KRAMER
KRATER
LAAGER
LEADED
LEADEN
LEADER
LEAFED
LEAKED
LEAKER
LEAKEY
LEANED
LEANER
LEAPED
LEAPER
LEASED
LEASER
LEASES
LEAVED
LEAVEN
LEAVES
LOADED
LOADER
LOAFED
LOAFER
LOAMED
LOANED
LOANER
LOAVES
MEAGER
MEANER
MOANED
MOANER
MOATED
NEARED
NEARER
NEATEN
NEATER
NIAMEY
OCASEK
OCASEY
OKAYED
ONAGER
ORALES
ORATED
ORATES
OSAGES
PEAHEN
PEAKED
PEALED
PEAVEY
PHAGES
PHASED
PHASER
PHASES
PIAGET
PLACED
PLACER
PLACES
PLAGES
PLANED
PLANER
PLANES
PLANET
PLATED
PLATEN
PLATER
PLATES
PLAYED
PLAYER
PRATED
PRATER
PRATES
PRAXES
PRAYED
PRAYER
QUAKED
QUAKER
QUAKES
QUAVER
READER
REALER
REALES
REAMED
REAMER
REAPED
REAPER
REARED
REARER
ROAMED
ROAMER
ROARED
ROARER
RRATED
SCALED
SCALER
SCALES
SCAPES
SCARED
SCARER
SCARES
SEABED
SEABEE
SEALED
SEALER
SEAMED
SEAMEN
SEARED
SEATED
SEATER
SHADED
SHADES
SHAKEN
SHAKER
SHAKES
SHALES
SHALEY
SHAMED
SHAMES
SHAPED
SHAPER
SHAPES
SHARED
SHARER
SHARES
SHAVED
SHAVEN
SHAVER
SHAVES
SKATED
SKATER
SKATES
SLAKED
SLAKES
SLATED
SLATER
SLATES
SLAVED
SLAVER
SLAVES
SLAYED
SLAYER
SNAKED
SNAKES
SNARED
SNARES
SOAKED
SOAKER
SOAPED
SOAPER
SOARED
SOARER
SOARES
SOAVES
SPACED
SPACEK
SPACER
SPACES
SPACEY
SPADED
SPADER
SPADES
SPARED
SPARER
SPARES
SPATES
SPAYED
STAGED
STAGER
STAGES
STAKED
STAKES
STALED
STALER
STALES
STAMEN
STAPES
STARED
STARER
STARES
STASES
STATED
STATER
STATES
STAVED
STAVES
STAYED
SUAVER
SWAGED
SWAGES
SWALES
SWANEE
SWAYED
SWAYER
TEAMED
TEARED
TEASED
TEASEL
TEASER
TEASES
TEASET
THALER
THALES
THAMES
THANES
THAWED
THAYER
TOATEE
TRACED
TRACER
TRACES
TRACEY
TRADED
TRADER
TRADES
TRALEE
TRAVEL
TUAREG
UKASES
UNAGED
UNAWED
USAGES
WEAKEN
WEAKER
WEANED
WEARER
WEASEL
WEAVED
WEAVER
WEAVES
WHALER
WHALES
XIAMEN
XRATED
XRAYED
YEAGER

••A••E

AMALIE
APACHE
ARABLE
BEADLE
BEAGLE
BEANIE
BEATLE
BLAINE
BLAISE
BRAISE
BRAQUE
CHAINE
CHAISE
CHANCE
CHANGE
CHARGE
CHASSE
CHASTE
CLAIRE
CLAQUE
CLARKE
CLAUDE
CLAUSE
COARSE
CRABBE
CRADLE
DEARIE
DEARME
DOABLE
DRAGEE
DUARTE
DWAYNE
ECARTE
ELAINE
ELAPSE
ELAYNE
ENABLE
FIACRE
FIANCE
FLAMBE
FLANGE
FRAISE
FRANCE
FRAPPE
GLANCE
GOALIE
GOATEE
GRABLE
GRACIE
GRAMME
GRANDE
GRANGE
HEARYE
HOAGIE
HOARSE
JEANNE
JOANIE
JOANNE
KHAFRE
LEAGUE
LIABLE
LIAISE
LOATHE
MEAGRE
MEALIE
MEANIE
NUANCE
OPAQUE
ORACLE
ORANGE
PIAFFE
PLAGUE
PLAICE
PLANTE
PLAQUE
PLATTE
PRAGUE
PRAISE
PRANCE
QUAYLE
ROADIE
RVALUE
SCARCE
SCARNE
SCATHE
SEABEE
SEANCE
SEARLE
SHAYNE
SNATHE
SPARGE
SPARSE
SPATHE
STABLE
STACTE
STANCE
STAPLE
STARVE
STATUE
SWANEE
SWATHE
SWAYZE
TOATEE
TRALEE
TRANCE
UNABLE
USABLE
USANCE
UVALUE
VIABLE
WRASSE

•••AE•

ACHAEA
ISRAEL
JUDAEA
NICAEA
PALAEO
RAFAEL
TOGAED
VISAED

•••A•E

ABLATE
ABLAZE
ABRADE
ACUATE
ADNATE
AERATE
AFLAME
AFRAME
AGLARE
AGNATE
ALSACE
ANSATE
AQUATE
ARCADE
ARCANE
ATEASE
AUBADE
AVIATE
AYEAYE
BECAME
BEDAZE
BEHAVE
BERATE
BETAKE
BEWARE
BINATE
BORAGE
BORATE
BUTANE
BYNAME
CANAPE
CARAFE
CERATE
CESARE
CETANE
CHOATE
CLEAVE
COMATE
CREASE
CREATE
CUBAGE
CURARE
CURATE
DAMAGE
DEBASE
DEBATE
DECADE
DEFACE
DEFAME
DEGAGE
DELATE
DILATE
DONATE
DOSAGE
DOTAGE
EFFACE
ENCAGE
ENCASE
ENGAGE
ENLACE
ENRAGE
EQUATE
ERGATE
ESCAPE
ESTATE
ETHANE
EXHALE
FACADE
FATALE
FEMALE
FINALE
FIXATE
FORAGE
GARAGE
GREASE
GREAVE
GYRATE
HARARE
HECATE
HOMAGE
HORACE
HUMANE
ICEAGE
IDEATE
IGNACE
IMPALE
INCASE
INHALE
INMATE
INNAGE
INNATE
INSANE
INTAKE
INVADE
IODATE
KARATE
LAMAZE
LANATE
LAVAGE
LEGATE
LENAPE
LESAGE
LIGATE
LINAGE
LIPASE
LOBATE
LOCALE
LOCATE
LOVAGE
LUNATE
LUXATE
MADAME
MALATE
MANAGE
MCCABE
MCHALE
MENACE
MENAGE
METATE
MIRAGE
MOHAVE
MOJAVE
MORALE
MUGABE
MUTATE
NEGATE
NEWAGE
NONAGE
NONAME
NOSALE
NOTATE
NUTATE
OBLATE
OCTANE
OCTAVE
OFLATE
OLEATE
ONSALE
ONTAPE
OPIATE
ORGATE
ORNATE
OUTAGE
OUTATE
PALACE
PALATE
PARADE
PAVANE
PEDATE
PELAGE
PHRASE
PIKAKE
PILATE
PIRATE
PLEASE
POMACE
POMADE
POTAGE
PURACE
RAMATE
RAVAGE
REBATE
RECANE
REDATE
REFACE
REGALE
RELACE
RELATE
REMADE
REMAKE
RENAME
REPAVE
RERATE
RESALE
RETAKE
RETAPE
ROTATE
ROXANE
ROYALE
RUGATE
SAVAGE
SAVATE
SCRAPE
SEDATE
SENATE
SERAPE
SESAME
SEWAGE
SHEAVE
SILAGE
SLEAVE
SLEAZE
SLOANE
SOCAGE
SOLACE
SQUARE
STRAFE
STRAKE
TAMALE
TENACE
THRACE
THRALE
TIRADE
TIRANE
TISANE
TODATE
TOWAGE
TRIAGE
TUBATE
TULANE
TULARE
ULLAGE
UNCAGE
UNCASE
UNEASE
UNIATE
UNLACE
UNLADE
UNMADE
UNMAKE
UNSAFE
UPDATE
UPTAKE
URBANE
VACATE
VISAGE
VIVACE
VOLARE
VOYAGE
ZONATE
ZOUAVE
ZYMASE

••••AE

AGORAE
ALULAE
AMEBAE
AORTAE
BULLAE
BURSAE
CANNAE
CELLAE
CHELAE
COSTAE
CURIAE
FAUNAE
FLORAE
FOSSAE
FOVEAE
GALEAE
GEMMAE
GUTTAE
HYDRAE
LARVAE
MACRAE
MENSAE
NUCHAE
OCREAE
PALEAE
PARCAE
PENNAE
PHILAE
PHYLAE
PINNAE
PLICAE
REGGAE
STELAE
STRIAE
SUMMAE
SUNDAE
TESTAE
THECAE
TIBIAE
UMBRAE
UVULAE

AF••••

AFFAIR
AFFECT
AFFINE
AFFIRM
AFFORD
AFFRAY
AFGHAN
AFIELD
AFLAME
AFLATS
AFLCIO
AFLOAT
AFRAID
AFRAME
AFREET
AFRESH
AFRICA

A•F•••

AAFAIR
AFFAIR
AFFECT
AFFINE
AFFIRM
AFFORD
AFFRAY
AJFOYT
ALFINE
ALFRED
ALFVEN
AUFAIT
AUFOND

A••F••

ARAFAT
ARMFUL
ARTFUL
ASKFOR

A•••F•

ADRIFT
AMALFI

•AF•••

AAFAIR
BAFFIN
BAFFLE
CAFTAN
DAFTER
FAFNIR
GAFFED
GAFFER
GAFFES
HAFTED
KAFFIR
LAFFER
OAFISH
RAFAEL
RAFFIA
RAFFLE
RAFTED
RAFTER
SAFARI
SAFELY
SAFEST
SAFETY
SAFIRE
WAFERS
WAFFLE
WAFFLY
WAFTED
ZAFFER
ZAFTIG

•A•F••

BAFFIN
BAFFLE
BAGFUL
BARFLY
CAPFUL
CARFUL
EARFUL
GADFLY
GAFFED
GAFFER
GAFFES
JARFUL
KAFFIR
LAFFER
LAPFUL
LAWFUL
LAYFOR
MANFUL
MAYFLY
PANFRY
PAYFOR
RAFFIA
RAFFLE
RANFOR
SAWFIT
VATFUL
WAFFLE
WAFFLY
ZAFFER

•A••F•

CANIFF
CARAFE
FAROFF
LAYOFF
PACIFY
PAYOFF
RAMIFY
RANOFF
RAREFY
RARIFY
RATIFY
SAWOFF
TAPOFF
TARIFF

•A•••F

CANIFF
FAROFF
LAYOFF
MASSIF
PAYOFF
RANOFF
SAWOFF
TAPOFF
TARIFF

••AF••

ARAFAT
BIAFRA
CHAFED
CHAFES
CHAFFS
CHAFFY
CRAFTS
CRAFTY
DEAFEN
DEAFER
DRAFTS
DRAFTY
GRAFTS
INAFIX
INAFOG
KHAFRE
LEAFED
LOAFED
LOAFER
PIAFFE
QUAFFS
SEAFAN
SEAFOX
SHAFTS
SNAFUS
STAFFS

••A•F•

AMALFI
CHAFFS
CHAFFY
DWARFS
PIAFFE
QUAFFS
SCARFS
STAFFS
WHARFS

••A••F

HEAROF
SHARIF
STAPUF
WHATIF

•••AF•

CARAFE
DECAFS
PILAFS
SCLAFF
SHEAFS
STRAFE
UNSAFE

•••A•F

BEHALF
INHALF
SCLAFF

••••AF

INLEAF

AG••••

AGADIR
AGAMAS
AGARIC
AGASSI
AGATES
AGATHA
AGAVES
AGEING
AGEISM
AGEIST
AGENAS
AGENCY
AGENDA
AGENTS
AGEOLD
AGGIES
AGHAST
AGLAIA
AGLARE
AGLEAM
AGLETS
AGLINT
AGNATE
AGORAE
AGORAS
AGOROT
AGOUTI
AGREED
AGREES

A•G•••

AEGEAN
AFGHAN
AGGIES
AIGRET
ALGORE
ANGELA
ANGELI
ANGELL
ANGELO
ANGELS
ANGERS
ANGKOR
ANGLED
ANGLER
ANGLES
ANGLIA
ANGLOS
ANGOLA
ANGORA
ARGALI
ARGENT
ARGIVE
ARGOSY
ARGOTS
ARGUED
ARGUER
ARGUES
ARGYLE
ARGYLL
ASGARD
AUGEAN
AUGEND
AUGERS
AUGHTS
AUGURS
AUGURY
AUGUST

A••G••

ADAGES
ADAGIO
AIRGUN
ALEGAR
ALEGRE
ALIGHT
ALIGNS
AMIGOS
ANSGAR
APOGEE
ARAGON
ARIGHT
ARTGUM

A•••G•

ALLEGE
ARMAGH
ASSIGN
ATERGO
AURIGA
AVENGE
AWEIGH

A••••G

AAHING
ACHING
ACTING
ADDING
AGEING
AIDING
AILING
AIMING
AIRBAG
AIRING
ALBORG
ANALOG
ARCING
ARMING
ASKING
AWNING

•AG•••

BAGDAD
BAGELS
BAGFUL
BAGGED
BAGGER
BAGGIE
BAGUIO
CAGERS
CAGIER
CAGILY
CAGING
CAGNEY
CAGUAS
DAGAMA
DAGGER
EAGLED
EAGLES
EAGLET
EAGRES
FAGEND
FAGGED
FAGOTS
GAGGED
GAGGLE
GAGING
GAGLAW
GAGMAN
GAGMEN
HAGGIS
HAGGLE
HAGMAN
JAGGED
JAGGER
JAGUAR
KAGERA
LAGASH
LAGERS
LAGGED
LAGGER
LAGOON
LAGUNA
MAGGIE
MAGGIO
MAGMAS
MAGNET
MAGNON
MAGNUM
MAGPIE
MAGUEY
MAGYAR
NAGANO
NAGGED
NAGGER
NAGOYA
PAGANS
PAGERS
PAGING
PAGODA
RAGBAG
RAGGED
RAGING
RAGLAN
RAGMAN
RAGMEN
RAGMOP
RAGOUT
RAGRUG
RAGTAG
RAGTOP
SAGELY
SAGEST
SAGGED
TAGDAY
TAGEND
TAGGED
TAGORE
TAGOUT
TAGSUP
VAGARY
VAGUER
WAGERS
WAGGED
WAGGLE
WAGGLY
WAGGON
WAGING
WAGNER
WAGONS
ZAGGED
ZAGREB

•A•G••

BADGER
BADGES
BADGUY
BAGGED
BAGGER
BAGGIE
BANGED
BANGER
BANGKA
BANGLE
BANGOR
BANGUI
BANGUP
BARGED
BARGES
CADGED
CADGER
CADGES
CAPGUN
CARGOS
CATGUT
CAUGHT
DAGGER
DANGER
DANGLE
DANGLY
DANGME
DAYGLO
FAGGED
FANGED
GADGET
GAGGED
GAGGLE
GANGED
GANGES
GANGLE
GANGLY
GANGUE
GANGUP
GARGLE

GAUGED
GAUGER
GAUGES
HAGGIS
HAGGLE
HAIGHT
HANGAR
HANGED
HANGER
HANGIN
HANGON
HANGUL
HANGUP
JAEGER
JAGGED
JAGGER
JANGLE
JANGLY
JARGON
LAAGER
LAGGED
LAGGER
LANGUR
LARGER
LARGOS
LAUGHS
MAGGIE
MAGGIO
MAJGEN
MANGER
MANGLE
MANGOS
MARGAY
MARGIE
MARGIN
MARGOT
NAGGED
NAGGER
NAUGHT
PARGET
RAGGED
RANGED
RANGER
RANGES
RANGUP
RAYGUN
SAGGED
SAIGAS
SAIGON
SANGER
SANGTO
SARGES
SARGON
SARGOS
SAUGER
TAGGED
TAIGAS
TANGED
TANGLE
TANGLY
TANGOS
TANGUY
TARGES
TARGET
TAUGHT
VAUGHN
WAGGED
WAGGLE
WAGGLY
WAGGON
WANGLE
WARGOD
YANGON
ZAGGED

•A••G•
BADEGG
BAREGE
CAYUGA
DAMAGE
GARAGE
LADOGA
LATIGO
LAVAGE
MALAGA
MALIGN
MANAGE
MANEGE
PAANGA
PAPAGO
RAVAGE
RAWEGG
SAVAGE

•A•••G
AAHING
BAAING
BADEGG
BAKING
BALING
BANDOG
BARING
BARONG
BASING
BATING
BAYING
CAGING
CAKING
CANING
CARING
CASING
CATRIG
CAVING
CAWING
DANANG
DANZIG
DARING
DATING
DATONG
DAZING
EALING
EARING
EARWIG
EASING
EATING
FACING
FADING
FAKING
FARING
FAXING
FAZING
GAGING
GAMING
GAPING
GASBAG
GASLOG
GATING
GAZING
HALING
HARING
HATING
HAVING
HAWING
HAYING
HAZING
JADING
JAPING
JAWING
LACING
LADING
LAMING
LAPDOG
LAVING
LAWING
LAYING
LAZING
MAKING
MATING
MAYTAG
NAMING
OARING
PACING
PADANG
PAGING
PAHANG
PALING
PARANG
PARING
PAVING
PAWING
PAYING
RACING
RAGBAG
RAGING
RAGRUG
RAGTAG
RAKING
RARING
RATEDG
RATING
RAVING
RAWEGG
RAZING
SARONG
SATANG
SATING
SAVING
SAWING
SAWLOG
SAYING
TAKING
TAMING
TAPING
TARING
TAUTOG
TAWING
TAXING
WADING
WAGING
WAKING
WANING
WARING
WAVING
WAXING
YAWING
ZAFTIG

••AG••
ADAGES
ADAGIO
ARAGON
BEAGLE
CRAGGY
DRAGEE
DRAGGY
DRAGIN
DRAGON
FLAGGY
FLAGON
HOAGIE
IMAGED
IMAGER
IMAGES
LAAGER
LEAGUE
MEAGER
MEAGRE
ONAGER
OSAGES
PHAGES
PIAGET
PLAGAL
PLAGES
PLAGIO
PLAGUE
PRAGUE
QUAGGA
QUAGGY
REAGAN
SEAGAL
SHAGGY
SLAGGY
SNAGGY
STAGED
STAGER
STAGES
SWAGED
SWAGES
TRAGIC
UNAGED
USAGES
YEAGER

••A•G•
CHANGE
CHARGE
CLANGS
CRAGGY
DRAGGY
FLAGGY
FLANGE
GRANGE
KIANGS
LIANGS
ORANGE
ORANGS
PAANGA
QUAGGA
QUAGGY
SHAGGY
SLAGGY
SLANGS
SLANGY
SNAGGY
SPARGE
TWANGS
TWANGY
UBANGI

••A••G
ANALOG
BAAING
DIALOG
INAFOG
QUAHOG
SEABAG
SEADOG
STALAG
TEABAG
TUAREG

•••AG•
ARMAGH
BORAGE
CUBAGE
DAMAGE
DEGAGE
DOSAGE
DOTAGE
ENCAGE
ENGAGE
ENRAGE
FORAGE
GARAGE
GULAGS
HOMAGE
ICEAGE
INNAGE
LAVAGE
LESAGE
LINAGE
LOVAGE
MALAGA
MANAGE
MENAGE
MIRAGE
NEWAGE
NONAGE
OUTAGE
PAPAGO
PELAGE
POTAGE
RAVAGE
REBAGS
RETAGS
SAVAGE
SCRAGS
SEWAGE
SILAGE
SOCAGE
SPRAGS
TOBAGO
TOWAGE
TRIAGE
ULLAGE
UNCAGE
VIRAGO
VISAGE
VOYAGE

•••A•G
CHIANG
DANANG
KDLANG
PADANG
PAHANG
PARANG
PENANG
REHANG
SATANG
SPRANG

••••AG
AIRBAG
DOGTAG
GASBAG
GOSTAG
ICEBAG
JETLAG
KITBAG
MAYTAG
RAGBAG
RAGTAG
REDTAG
SEABAG
SONTAG
STALAG
TEABAG
UNSNAG
WIGWAG
ZIGZAG

AH••••
AHCHOO
AHERNE
AHIMSA

A•H•••
AAHING
ABHORS
ACHAEA
ACHEBE
ACHENE
ACHIER
ACHING
ADHERE
AGHAST
ALHIRT
AMHARA
ANHYDR
APHIDS
ASHARP
ASHCAN
ASHIER
ASHLAR
ASHLEY
ASHORE
ASHRAM
ATHAND
ATHENA
ATHENE
ATHENS
ATHOME
AWHILE
AWHIRL

A••H••
AACHEN
ABOHMS
AETHER
AFGHAN
AHCHOO
ALOHAS
ALPHAS
ALTHEA
AMPHID
ANCHOR
ANDHOW
ANTHEM
ANTHER
ANYHOW
ARCHED
ARCHER
ARCHES
ARCHIE
ARCHLY
ARCHON
ARNHEM
ARTHRO
ARTHUR
ASCHAM
ATTHAT
AUGHTS
AUTHOR

A•••H•
AGATHA
ALEPHS
ALIGHT
AMECHE
APACHE
APATHY
ARETHA
ARIGHT
AYESHA

A••••H
ABLUSH
ADOLPH
AFRESH
AMBUSH
ARMAGH
ATTACH
AVOUCH
AWEIGH

•AH•••
AAHING
BAHAMA
BAHIAN
CAHIER
CAHOWS
DAHLIA
KAHLIL
KAHLUA
KAHUNA
LAHORE
MAHDIS
MAHLER
MAHOUT
MAHZOR
PAHANG
PAHARI
RAHRAH
SAHARA
SAHIBS
TAHINI
TAHITI
WAHINE
WAHOOS
WAHWAH
YAHOOS
YAHWEH

•A•H••
AACHEN
BARHOP
BASHED
BASHES
BATHED
BATHER
BATHES
BATHOS
CACHED
CACHES
CACHET
CACHOU
CARHOP
CASHED
CASHES
CASHEW
CASHIN
CATHAY
CATHER
DACHAS
DAPHNE
DASHED
DASHER
DASHES
FATHER
FATHOM
GASHED
GASHES
GATHER
HASHED
HASHES
HATHOR
HAWHAW
JANHUS
KATHIE
LACHES
LAPHAM
LASHED
LASHER
LASHES
LASHIO
LASHUP
LATHED
LATHER
LATHES
MACHES
MACHOS
MASHED
MASHER
MASHES
MASHIE
MATHER
MATHIS
MAYHAP
MAYHEM
NACHOS
NASHUA
NATHAN
PASHAS
PASHTO
PATHAN
PATHOL
PATHOS
RACHEL
RACHIS
RASHAD
RASHER
RASHES
RASHID
RASHLY
RATHER
SACHEM
SACHET
SASHAY
SASHED
SASHES
VACHEL
VASHTI
WARHOL
WASHED
WASHER
WASHES
WASHOE
WASHUP
YACHTS

•A••H•
CANTHI
CATCHY
CAUCHO
CAUGHT
EARTHA
EARTHY
FAITHS
GANDHI
GARTHS
GAUCHE
GAUCHO
HAIGHT
JASCHA
JAWOHL
LANDHO
LAUGHS
MANCHA
MANCHU
MARCHE
MARSHA
MARSHY
MARTHA
NAUGHT
NAVAHO
PANCHO
PATCHY
RAJAHS
RANCHO
SANCHO
SAPPHO
TAICHI
TAUGHT
VAUGHN
XANTHO
YAMAHA

•A•••H
BANISH
BARUCH
CALASH
CALIPH
CASBAH
DALETH
DANISH
FAMISH
FARRAH
GALOSH
GARETH
GARISH
HALVAH
HANNAH
HAUNCH
JARRAH
KALAKH
KASBAH
KAZAKH
LAGASH
LAMECH
LAMEDH
LATISH
LAUNCH
LAVISH
MARIAH
MATZOH
NAMATH
NAUTCH
OAFISH
PALISH
PARAPH
PARIAH
PARISH
PAUNCH
RADISH
RAHRAH
RAKISH
RAVISH
SALISH
SAMEKH
TAKETH
VANISH
WABASH
WAHWAH
WARMTH
YAHWEH

••AH••
BRAHMA
BRAHMS
GRAHAM
OMAHAN
OMAHAS
PEAHEN
QUAHOG
SPAHIS
UTAHAN

••A•H•
AGATHA
APACHE
APATHY
BRASHY
CHACHA
FLASHY
GRAPHS
HEATHS
KWACHA
LOATHE
PEACHY
PLASHY
POACHY
SCATHE
SNATHE
SNATHS
SPATHE
SWATHE
SWATHS
TRASHY
WRATHS

••A••H
BLANCH
BRANCH
DEARTH
EPARCH
EXARCH
HEALTH
HEARTH
INARCH
ISAIAH
KLATCH
SEARCH
SNATCH
STANCH
STARCH
SWARTH
SWATCH
THATCH
WEALTH
WRAITH

•••AH•
EPHAHS
LOTAHS
MYNAHS
NAVAHO
OBEAHS
RAJAHS
SURAHS
TORAHS
YAMAHA

•••A•H
ARMAGH
ATTACH
BLEACH
BREACH
BREATH
BROACH
BYPATH
CALASH
DETACH
EMDASH
ENDASH
INCASH
KALAKH
KAZAKH
LAGASH
NAMATH
ORBACH
PARAPH
PESACH
PLEACH
POTASH
PREACH
REHASH
REWASH
RIYADH
SERAPH
SHEATH
SIWASH
SPLASH
SQUASH
TERAPH
THRASH
UNLASH
WABASH
WREATH

••••AH
BEULAH
CASBAH
ELIJAH
FARRAH
FELLAH
GULLAH
HALVAH
HANNAH
HOOHAH
HOOKAH
HOORAH
HOWDAH
HURRAH
HUZZAH
ISAIAH
JARRAH
JINNAH
JOSIAH
JUBBAH
KASBAH
LOOFAH
MARIAH
MOOLAH
MULLAH
NULLAH
OHYEAH
OOMPAH
PARIAH
PISGAH
PUNKAH
PURDAH
RAHRAH
RUPIAH
SIRRAH
SUKKAH
TUSSAH
UZZIAH
WAHWAH
WHYDAH
ZILPAH

AI••••
AIDING
AIELLO
AIGRET
AIKIDO
AILEEN
AILERS
AILING
AIMING
AIMSAT
AIMSTO
AIRARM
AIRBAG
AIRBUS
AIRDAM
AIRDRY
AIRGUN
AIRIER
AIRILY
AIRING
AIRMAN
AIRMEN
AIROUT
AIRSAC
AIRWAY
AISLES

A•I•••
ABIDED
ABIDES
ACIDIC
ACIDLY
ACINUS
ADIDAS
ADIEUS
ADIEUX
AFIELD
AHIMSA
AKIMBO
AKITAS
ALIBIS
ALIBLE
ALICIA
ALIENS
ALIGHT
ALIGNS
ALINES
ALIOTO
ALISON
AMICES
AMICUS
AMIDES
AMIDOL
AMIDST
AMIENS
AMIGOS
AMINES
AMINOR
AMINUS
ANIMAL
ANIMAS
ANIMES
ANIMUS
ANIONS
ANITRA
APIARY
APICAL
APICES
APIECE
ARIDLY
ARIGHT
ARIOSE
ARIOSO
ARISEN
ARISES
ARISTA
ARISTO
ASIANS
ASIDES
ASIMOV
AVIANS
AVIARY
AVIATE
AVIDLY
AVISOS
AXILLA
AXIOMS
AXIONS

A••I••
AAHING
ACHIER
ACHING
ACTIII
ACTING
ACTINO
ACTION
ACTIUM
ACTIVE
ACUITY
ADDING
ADLIBS
ADMIRE
ADMITS
ADRIAN
ADRIEN
ADRIFT
ADVICE
ADVISE
AEDILE
AERIAL
AERIES
AFFINE
AFFIRM
AFRICA
AGEING
AGEISM
AGEIST
AGGIES
AGLINT
AIDING
AIKIDO
AILING
AIMING
AIRIER
AIRILY
AIRING
ALBINO
ALBION
ALDINE
ALFINE
ALHIRT
ALLIED
ALLIES
ALLIUM
ALNICO
ALOINS
ALPINE
AMBITS
AMNION
ANCIEN
ANOINT
ANTICS
ANVILS
AORIST
APHIDS
APLITE
APPIAN
AQUILA
AQUINO
ARCING
ARGIVE
ARLISS
ARMIES
ARMING
ARNICA
AROIDS
ARRIBA
ARRIVE
ARTIER
ARTIST
ASHIER
ASKING
ASPICS
ASPIRE
ASSIGN
ASSISI
ASSIST
ASSIZE
ASWIRL
ATKINS
ATRIAL
ATRISK
ATRIUM
ATTICA
ATTICS
ATTILA
ATTIRE
ATWILL
AUDIAL
AUDIOS
AUDITS
AURIGA
AUXINS
AVAILS
AVOIDS
AWAITS
AWEIGH
AWHILE
AWHIRL
AWNING

A•••I•
AAFAIR
ABATIS
ABUKIR
ACACIA
ACADIA
ACARID
ACEDIA
ACETIC
ACIDIC
ACQUIT
ACTIII
ADAGIO
ADDSIN
ADELIE
ADJOIN
ADONIS
ADROIT
AENEID
AEOLIA
AEOLIC
AFFAIR
AFLCIO
AFRAID
AGADIR
AGARIC
AGLAIA
ALARIC
ALBEIT
ALBOIN
ALCUIN
ALDRIN
ALEXIA
ALEXIS
ALIBIS
ALICIA
ALTAIC
ALTAIR
AMADIS
AMALIE
AMATIS
AMBLIN
AMEBIC
AMELIA
AMPHID
ANACIN
ANEMIA
ANEMIC
ANGLIA
ANODIC
ANOMIE
ANTRIM
ANUBIS
AODAIS
AORTIC
APULIA
ARABIA
ARABIC
ARALIA
ARAMIS
ARCHIE
ARCTIC
ARMPIT
ARTOIS
ASSAIL
ASTRID
ATOMIC
ATONIC
ATTAIN
ATTRIT
AUFAIT
AUNTIE
AUPAIR
AUSSIE
AUSTIN
AZORIN

A••••I
ACTIII
ADONAI
ADZUKI
AGASSI
AGOUTI
ALEXEI
ALKALI
ALUMNI
AMALFI
ANDREI
ANGELI
ANNULI
ARGALI
ARMANI
ASKARI
ASSISI
AVANTI

•AI•••
BAIKAL
BAILED
BAILEE
BAILER
BAILEY
BAILOR
BAINES
BAIRNS
BAITED
CAICOS
CAIMAN
CAIQUE
CAIRNS
DAIKON
DAILEY
DAIMON
DAIMYO
DAINTY
DAIREN
DAISES
FAILED
FAILLE

FAINTS FAIRED FAIRER FAIRLY FAIRUP FAISAL FAITHS FAIYUM GAIETY GAINED GAINER GAINLY GAINON GAINST GAITED GAITER HAIDAS HAIGHT HAIKOU HAIKUS HAILED HAILEY HAINAN HAINES HAIRDO HAIRED JAILED JAILER JAIPUR KAILUA KAISER LAIDBY LAIDIN LAIDON LAIDTO LAIDUP LAINIE LAIRDS MAIDEN MAIDUS MAILED MAILER MAILES MAILIN MAINLY MAISIE MAITAI MAITRE MAIZES NAIADS NAILED NAILER NAILIN NAIRAS PAIDIN PAIDUP PAILOU PAINED PAINTS PAIRED PAIRUP PAIUTE RAIDED RAIDER RAILAT RAILED RAILER RAINED RAINER RAINES RAIPUR RAISED RAISER RAISES RAISIN SAIGAS SAIGON SAILED SAILOR SAINTE SAINTS SAIPAN TAICHI TAIGAS TAILED TAILLE TAILOR TAINAN TAINOS TAINTS TAIPAN TAIPEI TAIWAN VAINER VAINLY VAISYA WAILED WAILER WAISTS WAITED WAITER WAITON WAITUP WAIVED WAIVER WAIVES

•A•I••

AAHING BAAING BABIED BABIES BAHIAN BAKING BALING BANISH BARING BARITE BARIUM BASICS BASING BASINS BATIKS BATING BAYING CABINS CAGIER CAGILY CAGING CAHIER CAKING CALICO CALIPH CAMINO CAMION CAMISE CANIDS CANIFF CANINE CANING CAPIAS CAPITA CARIBE CARIBS CARIES CARINA CARING CASING CASINO CATION CAVIAR CAVILS CAVING CAVITY CAWING DAMIEN DAMITA DANIEL DANISH DARIEN DARING DARIUS DATING DATIVE DAVIES DAVITS DAZING EALING EARING EASIER EASILY EASING EATING FABIAN FACIAL FACIES FACILE FACING FADING FAJITA FAKING FAKIRS FALINE FAMILY FAMINE FAMISH FANION FARINA FARING FATIMA FAXING FAZING GABION GAGING GAMIER GAMILY GAMINE GAMING GAMINS GAPING GARISH GATING GAVIAL GAZING HABILE HABITS HAKIMS HALIDE HALING HALITE HAMILL HAMITE HARING HATING HAVING HAWING HAYING HAZIER HAZILY HAZING JABIRU JADING JANICE JANINE JAPING JAVIER JAWING KALINE KARIBA LABIAL LABILE LACIER LACING LADIDA LADIES LADING LADINO LAMIAS LAMINA LAMING LANIER LAPINS LARIAT LATIGO LATINA LATINO LATINS LATISH LATIUM LAVING LAVISH LAWING LAXITY LAYING LAZIER LAZILY LAZING MAKING MALIBU MALICE MALIGN MANIAC MANIAS MANILA MANIOC MAOISM MAOIST MARIAH MARIAN MARIEL MARIKO MARILU MARINA MARINE MARINO MARION MARISA MARIST MARIUS MATING MATINS MAXIMA MAXIMS MAXINE MAXIXE NADINE NADIRS NAMING NAPIER NARIAL NATICK NATION NATIVE NAVIES OAFISH OARING OATIER PACIFY PACING PACINO PAGING PALING PALISH PAMIRS PANICS PAPIER PARIAH PARING PARISH PARITY PATINA PATINE PATIOS PAVING PAWING PAYING RABIES RACIAL RACIER RACILY RACINE RACING RADIAL RADIAN RADIOS RADISH RADIUM RADIUS RAGING RAKING RAKISH RAMIES RAMIFY RANIDS RAPIDS RAPIER RAPINE RAPINI RARIFY RARING RARITY RATIFY RATINE RATING RATION RATIOS RATITE RAVINE RAVING RAVISH RAZING SABINE SABINS SAFIRE SAHIBS SALINA SALINE SALISH SALIVA SAMIAM SAMITE SANITY SATING SATINS SATINY SATIRE SAVING SAVIOR SAWING SAYING TAHINI TAHITI TAKING TAKINS TALION TAMILS TAMING TANIST TAOISM TAOIST TAPING TAPINS TAPIRS TARIFF TARING TAWING TAXIED TAXIES TAXING VALISE VALIUM VANIER VANISH VANITY VARIED VARIES WADING WAGING WAHINE WAKING WANING WAPITI WARIER WARILY WARING WAVIER WAVING WAXIER WAXING XAVIER YAKIMA YALIES YAWING ZANIER ZANIES ZANILY ZAYINS

•A••I•

AAFAIR BACKIN BADDIE BAFFIN BAGGIE BAGUIO BALTIC BANDIT BARBIE BARDIC BARKIN BARRIE BARRIO BARRIS BAUCIS CABBIE CADDIE CADDIS CADMIC CALAIS CALLIN CALVIN CAMEIN CANDID CAPRIS CAPSID CARDIN CARDIO CARRIE CASHIN CASSIA CASSIO CASSIS CATKIN CATNIP CATRIG CAVEIN DACOIT DAHLIA DANDIE DANZIG DARNIT DARWIN DASSIN DAYLIT EARWIG EASEIN EATSIN FABRIC FADEIN FAERIE FAFNIR FALLIN FANNIE FASCIA GAELIC GALLIA GALLIC GALOIS GAMBIA GAMBIT GARCIA GARLIC GASKIN GASLIT GATLIN GAVEIN GAWAIN HACKIE HADDIE HADJIS HAGGIS HAJJIS HALOID HAMLIN HANDIN HANGIN HANKIE HARBIN HARRIS HATPIN HATTIE HAWAII IAMBIC IATRIC JACKIE JAMSIN KAFFIR KAHLIL KAOLIN KARMIC KATHIE KAURIS LACTIC LADDIE LAIDIN LAINIE LANAIS LANDIS LANVIN LASHIO LASSIE LATVIA LAURIE LAYSIN MADDIE MADEIT MADRID MAGGIE MAGGIO MAGPIE MAHDIS MAILIN MAISIE MAJLIS MAKEIT MALKIN MALTIN MANNIX MANTIC MANTIS MAORIS MAQUIS MARCIA MARCIE MARGIE MARGIN MARLIN MARNIE MARTIN MARVIN MASAIS MASHIE MASSIF MASTIC MATHIS MATLIN MATRIX MATTIE NAILIN NAPKIN NARNIA NARVIK PAIDIN PALLIA PALLID PANDIT PAPAIN PARNIS PARRIS PARVIS PASSIM PASTIS PATOIS PAYSIN RABBIS RABBIT RACHIS RAFFIA RAISIN RAKEIN RANCID RANKIN RASHID RATLIN SALVIA SAMMIE SANDIA SANTIR SARDIS SAUDIS SAVAII SAVOIE SAVOIR SAWFIT SAYYID TABRIZ TACTIC TAKEIN TALKIE TANNIC TANNIN TARPIT VALOIS WADEIN WALKIE WALKIN WALLIS WANTIN WAVEIN YAQUIS ZADDIK ZAFTIG ZAMBIA

•A•••I

BANGUI BANZAI BATUMI CANTHI CARONI DALASI GANDHI HATARI HAWAII JACOBI JAVARI KABUKI KATMAI LAZULI MAITAI MALAWI MALLEI MALOTI MAOTAI NAPOLI PAHARI PAPYRI QATARI RAPINI SAFARI SALAMI SALUKI SANSEI SATORI SAVAII TAHINI TAHITI TAICHI TAIPEI TATAMI UAKARI VASHTI WAPITI WASABI WATUSI YANQUI

••AI••

AVAILS AWAITS BAAING BLAINE BLAISE BRAIDS BRAILS BRAINS BRAINY BRAISE CHAINE CHAINS CHAIRS CHAISE CLAIMS CLAIRE DRAILS DRAINS ELAINE EMAILS FLAILS FLAIRS FRAISE GLAIRY GRAILS GRAINS GRAINY ISAIAH KRAITS LIAISE PLAICE PLAIDS PLAINS PLAINT PLAITS PRAISE QUAILS QUAINT REAIRS SNAILS STAINS STAIRS SWAINS TRAILS TRAINS TRAITS WRAITH

••A•I•

ABATIS ACACIA ACADIA ACARID ADAGIO AGADIR AGARIC ALARIC AMADIS AMALIE AMATIS ANACIN ARABIA ARABIC ARALIA ARAMIS BEANIE BEATIT BRAZIL CHAPIN CLAVIN COATIS CRANIA CRANIO CYANIC DEALIN DEARIE DRAGIN DRAWIN DYADIC ELAPID ETALIA ETALII FLAVIA GHAZIS GLACIS GOALIE GRACIE GRADIN GRATIA GRATIN GRATIS GRAVID HEADIN HOAGIE ICARIA INAFIX IRANIS IRAQIS ITALIA ITALIC JOANIE KHAKIS KHALID LEADIN MEALIE MEANIE NIACIN OKAPIS OMANIS OXALIS PHATIC PLACID PLAGIO PRAXIS READIN REALIA ROADIE SCALIA SHAMIR SHARIA SHARIF SLAVIC SPADIX SPAHIS SPAVIN STADIA STALIN STASIS STATIC SWAMIS SWAZIS THALIA THATIS TRAGIC TRAVIS URACIL URALIC URANIA URANIC WHATIF

••A••I

AGASSI AMALFI AVANTI BHAKTI BRAZZI CIARDI ETALII QUADRI SCAMPI SHAKTI SMALTI UBANGI

•••AI•

AAFAIR AFFAIR AFRAID AGLAIA ALTAIC ALTAIR AODAIS ASSAIL ATTAIN AUFAIT AUPAIR BELAIR BEWAIL CALAIS DERAIL DETAIL DETAIN DOMAIN ECLAIR ENTAIL GAWAIN HAWAII HOTAIR IMPAIR INLAID INVAIN JUDAIC KUWAIT LANAIS LCHAIM MASAIS MCBAIN MCLAIN MCNAIR MIDAIR MOHAIR MOSAIC OBTAIN ORDAIN OXTAIL PAPAIN PETAIN REGAIN RELAID REMAIL REMAIN RENAIL REPAID REPAIR RETAIL RETAIN ROMAIC SAVAII SERAIS SPRAIN STRAIN STRAIT UJJAIN UNFAIR UNLAID UNPAID UNSAID USMAIL

•••A•I

ALKALI ARGALI ARMANI ASKARI BIHARI BONAMI DALASI DENALI DOMANI DORATI ERNANI FULANI GELATI HATARI HAWAII HEGARI ITHAKI JAVARI KIGALI MALAWI MESABI NEPALI PAHARI QATARI ROMAJI SAFARI SALAMI SAVAII SOMALI SOUARI STRATI TATAMI UAKARI WASABI

••••AI

ADONAI BANZAI BONSAI KATMAI KUBLAI MAITAI MAOTAI NILGAI

AJ••••

AJANTA AJFOYT

A•J•••

ABJECT ABJURE ADJOIN ADJURE ADJUST ANJOUS ARJUNA

A••J••

ACAJOU AMAJOR

•AJ•••

CAJOLE CAJUNS FAJITA HAJJES HAJJIS MAJGEN MAJLIS MAJORS PAJAMA RAJAHS RAJPUT

•A•J••

BANJOS BANJUL FANJET GASJET HADJES HADJIS HAJJES HAJJIS RAMJET

•A••J•

BAROJA NAVAJO

••AJ••

ACAJOU AMAJOR BMAJOR CMAJOR DMAJOR EMAJOR FMAJOR GMAJOR INAJAM PRAJNA TRAJAN

••A••J

SWARAJ

•••AJ•

NAVAJO ROMAJI

••••AJ

SGTMAJ SWARAJ THEHAJ

AK••••

AKELAS AKENES AKIMBO AKITAS AKUAKU

A•K•••

ACKACK AIKIDO ALKALI ALKENE ALKYDS ALKYLS ANKARA ANKLED ANKLES ANKLET ASKARI ASKERS ASKFOR ASKING ASKOUT ATKINS AUKLET

A••K••

ABUKIR ANGKOR AWAKED AWAKEN AWAKES AWOKEN

A•••K•

ADZUKI AKUAKU ALASKA ALECKY

A••••K

ACKACK ADWEEK AMTRAK ANORAK ARAWAK ARRACK ATRISK ATTACK ATWORK

•AK•••

BAKERS BAKERY BAKING CAKING DAKOTA FAKERS FAKERY FAKING FAKIRS HAKIMS KAKAPO LAKERS LAKOTA MAKALU MAKEDO MAKEIT MAKERS MAKEUP MAKING MAKUTA OAKLEY RAKEIN RAKERS RAKEUP RAKING RAKISH SAKERS TAKEIN TAKEON TAKERS TAKETH TAKETO TAKEUP TAKING TAKINS UAKARI WAKENS WAKEUP WAKING YAKIMA YAKKED YAKKER YAKUTS

•A•K••

BABKAS BACKED BACKER BACKIN BACKUP BACKUS BAIKAL BALKAN BALKED BANKED BANKER BANKON BARKED BARKER BARKIN BASKED BASKET

CACKLE
CALKED
CANKER
CATKIN
DAIKON
DANKER
DARKEN
DARKER
DARKLE
DARKLY
FAWKES
GASKET
GASKIN
GAWKED
GAWKER
HACKED
HACKER
HACKIE
HACKLE
HAIKOU
HAIKUS
HANKER
HANKIE
HARKED
HARKEN
HARKER
HAWKED
HAWKER
JACKAL
JACKED
JACKET
JACKIE
JACKUP
KALKAN
LACKED
LACKEY
LANKER
LANKLY
LARKED
LATKES
MALKIN
MARKED
MARKER
MARKET
MARKKA
MARKUP
MASKED
MASKER
NAPKIN
PACKED
PACKER
PACKET
PACKUP
PARKAS
PARKAY
PARKED
PARKER
RACKED
RACKET
RACKUP
RANKED
RANKER
RANKIN
RANKLE
RANKLY
SACKED
SACKER
TACKED
TACKER
TACKLE
TACKON
TALKAT
TALKED
TALKER
TALKIE
TALKTO
TALKUP
TANKAS
TANKED
TANKER
TANKUP
TASKED
WALKED
WALKER
WALKIE
WALKIN
WALKON
WALKUP
YAKKED
YAKKER
YANKED
YANKEE

•A••K•

BAMAKO
BANGKA
BATIKS
CAULKS
HACEKS
JAMOKE
KABUKI
KALAKH
KANAKA
KAYAKS
KAZAKH
KAZAKS
MARIKO
MARKKA
SALUKI
SAMEKH
TANAKA
YAPOKS

•A•••K

BARTOK
DAMASK
FAROUK
GALYAK
KARNAK
MARDUK
NANOOK
NARVIK
NATICK
TANOAK
ZADDIK
ZANUCK

••AK••

AWAKED
AWAKEN
AWAKES
BEAKED
BEAKER
BHAKTI
BRAKED
BRAKES
CRAKES
DRAKES
FLAKED
FLAKER
FLAKES
KHAKIS
KRAKEN
KRAKOW
LEAKED
LEAKER
LEAKEY
PEAKED
QUAKED
QUAKER
QUAKES
SHAKEN
SHAKER
SHAKES
SHAKOS
SHAKTI
SLAKED
SLAKES
SNAKED
SNAKES
SOAKED
SOAKER
SOAKUP
STAKED
STAKES
WEAKEN
WEAKER
WEAKLY

••A•K•

ALASKA
BLACKS
BLANKS
CHALKS
CHALKY
CLACKS
CLANKS
CLANKY
CLARKE
CRACKS
CRANKS
CRANKY
FLACKS
FLANKS
FLASKS
FRANKS
KNACKS
KYACKS
OZARKS
PLANKS
PRANKS
QUACKS
QUARKS
SHACKS
SHANKS
SHARKS
SLACKS
SMACKS
SNACKS
SPANKS
SPANKY
SPARKS
SPARKY
STACKS
STALKS
STALKY
STANKY
SWANKY
THANKS
TRACKS
WHACKS
WHACKY
WRACKS

••A••K

ARAWAK
DRABEK
FRANCK
GDANSK
OCASEK
PLANCK
SPACEK
URALSK

•••AK•

AKUAKU
BAMAKO
BETAKE
BREAKS
CLOAKS
CREAKS
CREAKY
CROAKS
CROAKY
FREAKS
FREAKY
INTAKE
ITHAKI
KALAKH
KANAKA
KAYAKS
KAZAKH
KAZAKS
KULAKS
LUSAKA
MEDAKA
PIKAKE
REMAKE
RETAKE
SEDAKA
SNEAKS
SNEAKY
SPEAKS
STEAKS
STRAKE
TANAKA
TILAKS
TWEAKS
UMIAKS
UNMAKE
UPTAKE
WREAKS

•••A•K

ACKACK
ARRACK
ATTACK
BYTALK
DAMASK
DEBARK
EMBANK
EMBARK
GOBACK
HIJACK
MOHAWK
NEWARK
REMARK
SHRANK
SQUAWK
STMARK
THWACK
UNMASK
UNPACK
UNTACK

••••AK

AMTRAK
ANORAK
ARAWAK
BUROAK
DVORAK
GALYAK
ITZHAK
KARNAK
KODIAK
PINOAK
REDOAK
SCREAK
SENDAK
SLEZAK
SLOVAK
SPIVAK
SQUEAK
STREAK
TANOAK

AL••••

ALAMOS
ALANON
ALARIC
ALARMS
ALARUM
ALASKA
ALATAU
ALBANO
ALBANY
ALBEDO
ALBEIT
ALBERT
ALBINO
ALBION
ALBOIN
ALBORG
ALBUMS
ALCAPP
ALCOTT
ALCOVE
ALCUIN
ALDERS
ALDINE
ALDOSE
ALDOUS
ALDRIN
ALEAST
ALECKY
ALECTO
ALEGAR
ALEGRE
ALEMAN
ALEPHS
ALEPPO
ALERTS
ALEUTS
ALEXEI
ALEXIA
ALEXIS
ALFINE
ALFRED
ALFVEN
ALGORE
ALHIRT
ALIBIS
ALIBLE
ALICIA
ALIENS
ALIGHT
ALIGNS
ALINES
ALIOTO
ALISON
ALKALI
ALKENE
ALKYDS
ALKYLS
ALLAYS
ALLBUT
ALLDAY
ALLEES
ALLEGE
ALLELE
ALLEYS
ALLIED
ALLIES
ALLIUM
ALLMAN
ALLOTS
ALLOUT
ALLOWS
ALLOYS
ALLPRO
ALLSET
ALLUDE
ALLURE
ALLWET
ALMOND
ALMOST
ALNICO
ALOHAS
ALOINS
ALOMAR
ALONSO
ALONZO
ALPACA
ALPERT
ALPHAS
ALPINE
ALSACE
ALTAIC
ALTAIR
ALTARS
ALTERS
ALTHEA
ALTMAN
ALULAE
ALULAR
ALUMNA
ALUMNI
ALWAYS
ALWEST
ALYSSA

A•L•••

ABLATE
ABLAUT
ABLAZE
ABLEST
ABLOOM
ABLUSH
ADLIBS
AFLAME
AFLATS
AFLCIO
AFLOAT
AGLAIA
AGLARE
AGLEAM
AGLETS
AGLINT
AILEEN
AILERS
AILING
ALLAYS
ALLBUT
ALLDAY
ALLEES
ALLEGE
ALLELE
ALLEYS
ALLIED
ALLIES
ALLIUM
ALLMAN
ALLOTS
ALLOUT
ALLOWS
ALLOYS
ALLPRO
ALLSET
ALLUDE
ALLURE
ALLWET
APLITE
APLOMB
ARLENE
ARLISS
ASLANT
ASLEEP
ASLOPE
ATLAST
ATLATL

A••L••

ABELES
ABOLLA
ADDLED
ADDLES
ADELIE
ADELLE
ADOLPH
ADULTS
AEOLIA
AEOLIC
AEOLUS
AIELLO
AISLES
AKELAS
ALULAE
ALULAR
AMALFI
AMALIE
AMBLED
AMBLER
AMBLES
AMBLIN
AMELIA
AMOLES
AMPLER
AMULET
ANALOG
ANGLED
ANGLER
ANGLES
ANGLIA
ANGLOS
ANKLED
ANKLES
ANKLET
ANNLEE
ANOLES
ANTLER
APOLLO
APPLES
APULIA
ARALIA
ARALLU
ARMLET
ASHLAR
ASHLEY
ASYLUM
ATOLLS
ATTLEE
AUKLET
AVALON
AVULSE
AXILLA
AZALEA

A•••L•

ABOLLA
ACIDLY
ADELLE
AEDILE
AFIELD
AGEOLD
AIELLO
AIRILY
ALIBLE
ALKALI
ALKYLS
ALLELE
AMPULE
AMPULS
ANGELA
ANGELI
ANGELL
ANGELO
ANGELS
ANGOLA
ANNALS
ANNULI
ANNULS
ANSELM
ANVILS
APOLLO
APPALL
APPALS
AQUILA
ARABLE
ARALLU
ARBELA
ARCHLY
AREOLA
ARGALI
ARGYLE
ARGYLL
ARIDLY
ARNOLD
ARTELS
ASWELL
ATOLLS
ATTILA
ATWILL
AVAILS
AVIDLY
AWHILE
AXILLA

A••••L

ABORAL
ACETAL
ACETYL
ACTUAL
AERIAL
AMATOL
AMIDOL
AMORAL
AMSTEL
ANGELL
ANIMAL
ANNEAL
ANNUAL
AORTAL
APICAL
APODAL
APPALL
APPEAL
ARGYLL
ARMFUL
ARTFUL
ASSAIL
ASTRAL
ASWELL
ASWIRL
ATLATL
ATONAL
ATRIAL
ATWILL
AUDIAL
AVOWAL
AWHIRL
AXONAL

•AL•••

BALAAM
BALATA
BALBOA
BALDER
BALDLY
BALEEN
BALERS
BALING
BALKAN
BALKED
BALLAD
BALLET
BALLOT
BALLUP
BALSAM
BALTIC
BALZAC
CALAIS
CALASH
CALCES
CALDER
CALICO
CALIPH
CALKED
CALLAO
CALLAS
CALLED
CALLER
CALLES
CALLIN
CALLON
CALLOW
CALLUP
CALLUS
CALMED
CALMER
CALMLY
CALPAC
CALQUE
CALVED
CALVES
CALVIN
CALXES
DALASI
DALETH
DALLAS
DALLES
DALTON
EALING
FALANA
FALCON
FALINE
FALLEN
FALLIN
FALLON
FALLOW
FALLTO
FALSER
FALTER
GALATA
GALAXY
GALEAE
GALENA
GALLED
GALLEY
GALLIA
GALLIC
GALLON
GALLOP
GALLUP
GALOIS
GALOOT
GALOPS
GALORE
GALOSH
GALWAY
GALYAK
HALERS
HALERU
HALEST
HALEVY
HALIDE
HALING
HALITE
HALLEL
HALLEY
HALLOO
HALLOS
HALLOW
HALLUX
HALOED
HALOES
HALOID
HALSEY
HALTED
HALTER
HALVAH
HALVED
HALVES
JALAPA
JALOPY
KALAKH
KALINE
KALKAN
KALMAR
LALALA
MALABO
MALADY
MALAGA
MALATE
MALAWI
MALAYA
MALAYS
MALDEN
MALIBU
MALICE
MALIGN
MALKIN
MALLEE
MALLEI
MALLET
MALLOW
MALONE
MALORY
MALOTI
MALTED
MALTIN
PALACE
PALAEO
PALATE
PALEAE
PALELY
PALEST
PALING
PALISH
PALLAS
PALLED
PALLET
PALLIA
PALLID
PALLOR
PALMAS
PALMED
PALMER
PALOMA
PALPUS
PALTER
PALTRY
SALAAM
SALADS
SALALS
SALAMI
SALARY
SALINA
SALINE
SALISH
SALIVA
SALLET
SALLOW
SALMAN
SALMON
SALOME
SALONS
SALOON
SALSAS
SALTED
SALTEN
SALTER
SALTON
SALUKI
SALUTE
SALVED
SALVER
SALVES
SALVIA
SALVOR
SALVOS
SALYUT
TALBOT
TALCED
TALCUM
TALENT
TALESE
TALION
TALKAT
TALKED
TALKER
TALKIE
TALKTO
TALKUP
TALLER
TALLOW
TALMUD
TALONS
VALDEZ
VALENS
VALENT
VALERY
VALETS
VALISE
VALIUM
VALLEE
VALLEY
VALOIS
VALOUR
VALUED
VALUES
VALVED
VALVES
WALDEN
WALERS
WALESA
WALKED
WALKER
WALKIE
WALKIN
WALKON
WALKUP
WALLED
WALLER
WALLET
WALLIS
WALLOP
WALLOW
WALLUP
WALNUT
WALRUS
WALTER
WALTON
YALIES

•A•L••

BADLOT
BAILED
BAILEE
BAILER
BAILEY
BAILOR
BALLAD
BALLET
BALLOT
BALLUP
BANLON
BARLEY
BAWLED
BAWLER
BAYLOR
CABLED
CABLER
CABLES
CALLAO
CALLAS
CALLED
CALLER
CALLES
CALLIN
CALLON
CALLOW
CALLUP
CALLUS
CAMLET
CAPLET
CARLOS
CARLOT
CAULKS
DAHLIA
DAILEY
DALLAS
DALLES
DAYLIT
EAGLED
EAGLES
EAGLET
EARLAP
FABLED
FABLER
FABLES
FAILED
FAILLE
FALLEN
FALLIN
FALLON
FALLOW
FALLTO
FARLEY
FARLOW
FAULTS
FAULTY
FAWLTY
GABLED
GABLES
GAELIC
GAGLAW
GALLED
GALLEY
GALLIA
GALLIC
GALLON
GALLOP
GALLUP
GARLIC
GASLIT
GASLOG
GATLIN
HAILED
HAILEY
HALLEL
HALLEY
HALLOO
HALLOS
HALLOW
HALLUX
HAMLET
HAMLIN
HARLAN
HARLEM
HARLEY
HARLOW
HAULED
HAULER
HAULUP
HAYLEY
JACLYN
JAILED
JAILER
KAHLIL
KAHLUA
KAILUA
KAOLIN
KAPLAN
LADLED
LADLER
LADLES
LAYLOW
MAHLER
MAILED
MAILER
MAILES
MAILIN
MAJLIS
MALLEE
MALLEI
MALLET
MALLOW
MAPLES
MARLED
MARLEE
MARLEY
MARLIN
MARLON
MATLIN
MAULED
MAULER
NAILED
NAILER
NAILIN
NAPLES
OAKLEY
PABLUM
PAELLA
PAILOU
PALLAS
PALLED
PALLET
PALLIA
PALLID
PALLOR
PARLAY
PARLEY
PARLOR
PAULEY
PAVLOV
RAGLAN
RAILAT
RAILED
RAILER
RATLIN
SABLES
SAILED
SAILOR
SALLET
SALLOW
SAULTS
SAWLOG
TABLAS
TABLED
TABLES
TABLET
TAILED
TAILLE
TAILOR
TALLER
TALLOW
TAYLOR
VACLAV
VALLEE
VALLEY
VARLET
VASLAV
VAULTS
WAILED
WAILER
WALLED
WALLER
WALLET
WALLIS
WALLOP
WALLOW
WALLUP
WAYLAY
WAYLON

•A••L•

BABBLE
BABULS
BACALL
BAFFLE
BAGELS
BALDLY
BANGLE
BARELY
BARFLY
BAROLO
BASALT
BASELY
BATTLE
BAUBLE
CABALA
CABALS
CACKLE
CAGILY
CAJOLE
CALMLY
CAMELS
CANALS
CANDLE
CANOLA
CANTLE
CAROLE
CAROLS
CASALS
CASTLE
CATTLE
CAUDLE
CAVELL
CAVILS
DABBLE
DAMPLY
DANDLE
DANGLE
DANGLY
DAPPLE
DARKLE
DARKLY
DAWDLE
DAYGLO
DAZZLE
EASELS
EASILY
FACILE
FACULA
FAILLE
FAIRLY
FAMILY
FATALE
GABBLE
GADFLY
GAGGLE
GAINLY
GAMBLE
GAMELY
GAMILY
GANGLE
GANGLY
GARBLE
GARGLE
GAVELS
GAYALS
HABILE
HACKLE
HAGGLE
HAMALS
HAMILL
HANDLE
HARDLY
HAROLD
HASSLE
HAZELS
HAZILY
JACALS
JANGLE
JANGLY
KAMALA
LABELS
LABILE
LALALA
LAMELY
LANKLY
LAPELS
LASTLY
LATELY
LAZILY
LAZULI
MABELL
MACULA
MAINLY

MAKALU
MANGLE
MANILA
MANTLE
MARBLE
MARBLY
MARILU
MARPLE
MAYFLY
MAZOLA
NAMELY
NAPOLI
NASALS
NAVELS
PADDLE
PAELLA
PALELY
PAMELA
PANELS
PAROLE
PARTLY
PARULA
PAYOLA
RABBLE
RACILY
RADDLE
RADULA
RAFFLE
RAMBLA
RAMBLE
RANKLE
RANKLY
RAPTLY
RARELY
RASHLY
RASSLE
RATELS
RATTLE
RATTLY
RAVELS
RAZZLE
SADDLE
SAFELY
SAGELY
SALALS
SAMPLE
SANELY
TABULA
TACKLE
TAILLE
TAMALE
TAMELY
TAMILS
TANGLE
TANGLY
TARTLY
TATTLE
TAUTLY
VAINLY
VASTLY
WADDLE
WADDLY
WAFFLE
WAFFLY
WAGGLE
WAGGLY
WAMBLE
WAMBLY
WANGLE
WARBLE
WARILY
WARMLY
WATTLE
YARELY
ZANILY

•A•••L

BACALL
BAGFUL
BAIKAL
BANJUL
BARBEL
BARREL
CANCEL
CANNEL
CAPFUL
CARFUL
CARMEL
CARNAL
CARPAL
CARPEL
CARREL
CARROL
CARTEL
CASUAL
CAUDAL
CAUSAL
CAVELL
DACTYL
DAEDAL
DAMSEL
DANIEL
DARNEL
DARRYL
EARFUL
FACIAL
FAISAL
FAUNAL
GAMBOL
GAVIAL
HALLEL
HAMILL
HANDEL
HANGUL
HANSEL
JACKAL
JAMAAL
JARFUL
JAWOHL
KAHLIL
LABIAL
LAPFUL
LARVAL
LAUREL
LAWFUL
MABELL
MAMMAL
MANFUL
MANTEL
MANUAL
MANUEL
MARCEL
MARIEL
MARTEL
MARVEL
MATTEL
NARIAL
NARWAL
PARCEL
PARREL
PASCAL
PASSEL
PASTEL
PATHOL
PATROL
RACHEL
RACIAL
RADIAL
RAFAEL
RAPPEL
RAQUEL
RASCAL
SACRAL
SAMBAL
SAMUEL
SANDAL
SAUREL
TARSAL
TASSEL
VACHEL
VANDAL
VASSAL
VATFUL
WARHOL

••AL••

AMALFI
AMALIE
ANALOG
ARALIA
ARALLU
AVALON
AZALEA
CHALCO
CHALET
CHALKS
CHALKY
COALER
DEALER
DEALIN
DIALED
DIALER
DIALOG
DUALLY
ETALIA
ETALII
EXALTS
FEALTY
FOALED
GOALIE
HEALED
HEALER
HEALTH
ITALIA
ITALIC
KHALID
KOALAS
LEALTY
MEALIE
NYALAS
ORALES
ORALLY
OXALIS
PEALED
PSALMS
QUALMS
REALER
REALES
REALIA
REALLY
REALMS
REALTY
RIALTO
RVALUE
SCALAR
SCALDS
SCALED
SCALER
SCALES
SCALIA
SCALPS
SEALAB
SEALED
SEALER
SEALUP
SHALES
SHALEY
SHALLY
SHALOM
SKALDS
SLALOM
SMALLS
SMALTI
SMALTO
SPALLS
STALAG
STALED
STALER
STALES
STALIN
STALKS
STALKY
STALLS
SWALES
THALER
THALES
THALIA
TLALOC
TRALEE
URALIC
URALSK
UVALUE
WEALTH
WHALER
WHALES
ZEALOT

••A•L•

ARABLE
ARALLU
AVAILS
BEADLE
BEAGLE
BEATLE
BRAILS
BRAWLS
CHARLY
CRADLE
CRAWLS
CRAWLY
DEADLY
DEARLY
DIABLO
DOABLE
DRABLY
DRAILS
DRAWLS
DUALLY
EMAILS
ENABLE
FLAILS
FLATLY
GLADLY
GNARLS
GNARLY
GRABLE
GRAILS
KRAALS
LEANLY
LIABLE
MEANLY
MEASLY
NEARLY
NEATLY
ORACLE
ORALLY
PEARLS
PEARLY
QUAILS
QUAYLE
REALLY
SEARLE
SHALLY
SHAWLS
SMALLS
SNAILS
SNARLS
SNARLY
SPALLS
STABLE
STABLY
STALLS
STAPLE
TRAILS
TRAWLS
UNABLE
USABLE
USABLY
VIABLE
VIABLY
WEAKLY
YEARLY

••A••L

AMATOL
BRAZIL
CHANEL
CHAPEL
ENAMEL
GRAVEL
HIATAL
ISABEL
IZABAL
PLAGAL
SEAGAL
TEASEL
TRAVEL
URACIL
WEASEL

•••AL•

ALKALI
ANNALS
APPALL
APPALS
ARGALI
BACALL
BASALT
BECALM
BEFALL
BEHALF
BYTALK
CABALA
CABALS
CANALS
CASALS
COBALT
CORALS
DECALS
DEKALB
DENALI
DESALT
DONALD
DUVALL
ENDALL
EQUALS
EXHALE
FATALE
FEMALE
FINALE
FINALS
GAYALS
GERALD
GORALS
HAMALS
HERALD
IDEALS
IMPALA
IMPALE
INHALE
INHALF
JACALS
KAMALA
KERALA
KIGALI
KODALY
KRAALS
KURALT
LALALA
LEGALS
LOCALE
LOCALS
MAKALU
MCHALE
MEDALS
MEGALO
METALS
MORALE
MORALS
MURALS
NASALS
NEPALI
NOSALE
OGLALA
ONCALL
ONSALE
OOLALA
OSWALD
PEDALS
PETALS
PHIALS
PIPALS
RECALL
REGALE
RESALE
RESALT
RIBALD
RIVALS
RIYALS
ROBALO
RONALD
ROYALE
ROYALS
SALALS
SEPALS
SHOALS
SISALS
SOMALI
SQUALL
STEALS
STMALO
TAMALE
TEPALS
THRALE
THRALL
TICALS
TOTALS
TRIALS
TUVALU
TYBALT
URIALS
USUALS
VITALS
VOCALS
YOUALL

•••A•L

APPALL
ASSAIL
ATLATL
BACALL
BEFALL
BEWAIL
DEPAUL
DERAIL
DETAIL
DUVALL
ENDALL
ENTAIL
INHAUL
ISRAEL
JAMAAL
ONCALL
OXTAIL
RAFAEL
RECALL
REMAIL
RENAIL
RETAIL
RUPAUL
SCRAWL
SPRAWL
SQUALL
STPAUL
THRALL
USMAIL
YOUALL

••••AL

ABORAL
ACETAL
ACTUAL
AERIAL
AMORAL
ANIMAL
ANNEAL
ANNUAL
AORTAL
APICAL
APODAL
APPEAL
ASTRAL
ATONAL
ATRIAL
AUDIAL
AVOWAL
AXONAL
BAIKAL
BELIAL
BENGAL
BHOPAL
BOREAL
BRIDAL
BRUMAL
BRUTAL
BUCCAL
BURSAL
CARNAL
CARPAL
CASUAL
CAUDAL
CAUSAL
CEREAL
CHEVAL
CHORAL
COEVAL
CORRAL
COSTAL
CRURAL
CUNEAL
CURIAL
CYMBAL
DAEDAL
DENIAL
DENTAL
DERMAL
DISMAL
DISTAL
DORSAL
DOSSAL
DUCTAL
EPICAL
ESPIAL
FACIAL
FAISAL
FAUNAL
FESTAL
FEUDAL
FILIAL
FINIAL
FISCAL
FLORAL
FONTAL
FORMAL
FRUGAL
GAVIAL
GENIAL
GENUAL
GIMBAL
GLOBAL
HERBAL
HIATAL
HIEMAL
HYETAL
HYMNAL
IRREAL
IZABAL
JACKAL
JAMAAL
JOVIAL
LABIAL
LARVAL
LETHAL
LINEAL
LOREAL
LOWCAL
MAMMAL
MANUAL
MEDIAL
MENIAL
MENSAL
MENTAL
MESCAL
MISSAL
MITRAL
MORTAL
MUSIAL
MUTUAL
MYRDAL
NARIAL
NARWAL
NEURAL
NORMAL
NUCHAL
ORDEAL
OSTEAL
PASCAL
PENPAL
PINEAL
PLAGAL
PLURAL
PORTAL
POSTAL
PRIMAL
RACIAL
RADIAL
RASCAL
REDEAL
REDIAL
REGNAL
REHEAL
RENTAL
REPEAL
RESEAL
RETIAL
RETRAL
REVEAL
RHINAL
RITUAL
SACRAL
SAMBAL
SANDAL
SEAGAL
SEPTAL
SERIAL
SERVAL
SIGNAL
SOCIAL
SPINAL
SPIRAL
SQUEAL
TARSAL
THECAL
TIBIAL
TIMBAL
TINCAL
TRIBAL
TRINAL
UMBRAL
UNCIAL
UNGUAL
UNITAL
UNREAL
UNSEAL
VANDAL
VASSAL
VEINAL
VENIAL
VERBAL
VERNAL
VESTAL
VISUAL
WITHAL

AM••••

AMADIS
AMADOU
AMAJOR
AMALFI
AMALIE
AMANDA
AMATIS
AMATOL
AMAZED
AMAZES
AMAZON
AMBERS
AMBITS
AMBLED
AMBLER
AMBLES
AMBLIN
AMBUSH
AMEBAE
AMEBAS
AMEBIC
AMECHE
AMEDEO
AMEERS
AMELIA
AMENDS
AMENRA
AMENTS
AMERCE
AMHARA
AMICES
AMICUS
AMIDES
AMIDOL
AMIDST
AMIENS
AMIGOS
AMINES
AMINOR
AMINUS
AMNION
AMOEBA
AMOLES
AMORAL
AMOSOZ
AMOUNT
AMOURS
AMPERE
AMPHID
AMPLER
AMPULE
AMPULS
AMSTEL
AMTRAC
AMTRAK
AMULET
AMUSED
AMUSES
AMVETS
AMYTAN

A•M•••

ADMIRE
ADMITS
AIMING
AIMSAT
AIMSTO
ALMOND
ALMOST
ARMADA
ARMAGH
ARMAND
ARMANI
ARMETS
ARMFUL
ARMIES
ARMING
ARMLET
ARMORS
ARMORY
ARMOUR
ARMPIT
ARMURE
ASMARA
ATMOST
AUMONT
AYMARA

A••M••

ABOMBS
ACUMEN
AGAMAS
AHIMSA
AIRMAN
AIRMEN
AKIMBO
ALAMOS
ALEMAN
ALLMAN
ALOMAR
ALTMAN
ALUMNA
ALUMNI
ANEMIA
ANEMIC
ANIMAL
ANIMAS
ANIMES
ANIMUS
ANOMIE
APEMAN
APEMEN
ARAMIS
AROMAS
ASIMOV
ATAMAN
ATEMPO
ATOMIC

A•••M•

ABOHMS
ABRAMS
ABYSMS
ADDAMS
ADEEMS
AFLAME
AFRAME
ALARMS
ALBUMS
APLOMB
ASSUME
ATEAMS
ATHOME
AUTUMN
AXIOMS

A••••M

ABLOOM
ACTIUM
ADYTUM
AFFIRM
AGEISM
AGLEAM
AIRARM
AIRDAM
ALARUM
ALLIUM
ANADEM
ANONYM
ANSELM
ANTHEM
ANTRIM
ANTRUM
ARNHEM
ARTGUM
ASCHAM
ASHRAM
ASYLUM
ATRIUM

•AM•••

BAMAKO
BAMBOO
CAMBER
CAMDEN
CAMEAT
CAMEBY
CAMEIN
CAMELS
CAMEON
CAMEOS
CAMERA
CAMETO
CAMEUP
CAMINO
CAMION
CAMISE
CAMLET
CAMPED
CAMPER
CAMPOS
CAMPUS
DAMAGE
DAMASK
DAMATO
DAMIEN
DAMITA
DAMMAR
DAMMED
DAMNED
DAMONE
DAMORE
DAMOUR
DAMPED
DAMPEN
DAMPER
DAMPLY
DAMSEL
DAMSON
DAMSUP
FAMILY
FAMINE
FAMISH
FAMOUS
GAMAYS
GAMBIA
GAMBIT
GAMBLE
GAMBOL
GAMELY
GAMEST
GAMETE
GAMIER
GAMILY
GAMINE
GAMING
GAMINS
GAMMAS
GAMMON
GAMUTS
HAMALS
HAMILL
HAMITE
HAMLET
HAMLIN
HAMMED
HAMMER
HAMPER
IAMBIC
JAMAAL
JAMMED
JAMMER
JAMOKE
JAMSIN
JAMSUP
JAMUPS
KAMALA
LAMARR
LAMAZE
LAMBDA
LAMBED
LAMECH
LAMEDH
LAMEDS
LAMELY
LAMENT
LAMESA
LAMEST
LAMIAS
LAMINA
LAMING
LAMMAS
LAMMED
LAMONT
LAMOUR
MAMBAS
MAMBOS
MAMMAL
MAMMAS
MAMMON
NAMATH
NAMELY
NAMERS
NAMING
PAMELA
PAMIRS
PAMPAS
PAMPER
RAMADA
RAMATE
RAMBLA
RAMBLE
RAMEAU
RAMIES
RAMIFY
RAMJET
RAMMED
RAMONA
RAMONE
RAMOSE
RAMOUS
RAMPED
RAMROD
RAMSAY
RAMSES
RAMSEY
RAMSON
SAMARA
SAMBAL
SAMBAR
SAMBAS
SAMEKH
SAMIAM
SAMITE
SAMMIE
SAMOAN
SAMOSA
SAMPAN
SAMPLE
SAMSON
SAMUEL
TAMALE
TAMARA
TAMAYO
TAMELY
TAMERS
TAMEST
TAMILS
TAMING
TAMMUZ
TAMPED
TAMPER
TAMTAM
VAMPED
VAMPER
WAMBLE
WAMBLY
WAMPUM
YAMAHA
YAMMER
ZAMBIA

•A•M••

BARMAN
BARMEN
BATMAN
BATMEN
CADMIC
CADMUS
CAIMAN
CALMED
CALMER
CALMLY
CARMAN
CARMEL
CARMEN
CAYMAN
DAIMON
DAIMYO
DAMMAR
DAMMED
FARMED
FARMER
GAGMAN
GAGMEN
GAMMAS
GAMMON
GASMAN
GASMEN
HAEMAT
HAEMON
HAGMAN
HAMMED
HAMMER
HARMED
HARMON
HAYMOW
JAMMED
JAMMER
KALMAR
KARMIC
KATMAI
LAMMAS
LAMMED
LAWMAN
LAWMEN
LAYMAN
LAYMEN
MADMAN
MADMAX
MADMEN
MAGMAS
MAMMAL
MAMMAS
MAMMON
MARMEE
MARMOT
MAUMAU
MAUMEE
PACMAN
PALMAS
PALMED
PALMER
PATMOS
RAGMAN
RAGMEN
RAGMOP
RAMMED
SALMAN
SALMON
SAMMIE
TALMUD
TAMMUZ
TARMAC
TASMAN
TAXMAN
TAXMEN
WARMED
WARMER
WARMLY
WARMTH
WARMUP
YAMMER

•A••M•

BAHAMA
BATUMI
CAROMS
DAGAMA
DANGME
FATIMA
HAKIMS
HAREMS
LARAMS
MADAME
MADAMS
MANAMA
MAXIMA
MAXIMS
MAZUMA
PAJAMA
PALOMA
PANAMA
RACEME
RADOME
SALAMI
SALOME
TACOMA
TATAMI
YAKIMA

•A•••M

BALAAM
BALSAM
BANTAM
BARIUM
BARNUM
BAYRUM
FAIYUM
FANDOM
FATHOM
HANSOM
HARLEM
HASSAM
KABOOM
KAREEM
LABRUM
LAPHAM
LATIUM
MADTOM
MAGNUM
MAOISM
MAYHEM
PABLUM
PASSIM
RADIUM
RANDOM
RANSOM
SACHEM
SACRUM
SADDAM
SALAAM
SAMIAM
TALCUM
TAMTAM

TANDEM TAOISM VACUUM VALIUM WAMPUM

••AM••

AGAMAS ALAMOS ARAMIS ATAMAN BEAMED BEAMUP BLAMED BLAMES CHAMMY CHAMPS CLAMMY CLAMOR CLAMPS CLAMUP CRAMBO CRAMPS DRAMAS EDAMES ENAMEL ENAMOR FLAMBE FLAMED FLAMES FOAMED FRAMED FRAMES GLAMOR GRAMAS GRAMME GRAMMY GRAMPS KRAMER LLAMAS LOAMED NIAMEY REAMED REAMER ROAMED ROAMER SCAMPI SCAMPS SEAMAN SEAMED SEAMEN SEAMUS SHAMAN SHAMED SHAMES SHAMIR SHAMUS STAMEN STAMPS SWAMIS SWAMPS SWAMPY TEAMED TEAMUP THAMES TOAMAN TRAMPS WHAMMO WHAMMY XIAMEN

••A•M•

ALARMS BRAHMA BRAHMS CHACMA CHAMMY CHARMS CHASMS CLAIMS CLAMMY DEARME DHARMA GRAMME GRAMMY MIASMA PLASMA PLASMO PSALMS QUALMS REALMS REARMS SHAWMS SMARMY SPASMS SWARMS TRAUMA UNARMS WHAMMO WHAMMY

••A••M

ALARUM ANADEM DIADEM DIATOM GRAHAM INAJAM MCADAM OMASUM SCARUM SHALOM SHAZAM SLALOM VIACOM

•••AM•

ABRAMS ADDAMS AFLAME AFRAME ATEAMS BAHAMA BECAME BIGAMY BONAMI BREAMS BYNAME CCLAMP CREAMS CREAMY DAGAMA DECAMP DEFAME DREAMS DREAMT DREAMY DYNAMO ENCAMP GLEAMS HBEAMS IBEAMS INFAMY JICAMA LARAMS MADAME MADAMS MANAMA NONAME OGHAMS PAJAMA PANAMA PREAMP PROAMS PYJAMA RENAME REVAMP SALAMI SCRAMS SESAME STEAMS STEAMY TATAMI UGGAMS UNJAMS

•••A•M

AIRARM BALAAM BECALM DISARM LCHAIM REWARM SALAAM

••••AM

AGLEAM AIRDAM ASCHAM ASHRAM BALAAM BALSAM BANTAM BEDLAM BELDAM COBHAM DIGRAM DIRHAM DUNHAM DURHAM ENGRAM GOTHAM GRAHAM HASSAM INAJAM INSEAM JETSAM LAPHAM LOGJAM MCADAM MIRIAM OLDHAM PUTNAM RODHAM SADDAM SALAAM SAMIAM SCREAM SHAZAM SILOAM STREAM TAMTAM WIGWAM

AN••••

ANACIN ANADEM ANALOG ANANDA ANATTO ANCHOR ANCIEN ANCONA ANDEAN ANDHOW ANDREA ANDREI ANDRES ANDREW ANDREY ANDROS ANEMIA ANEMIC ANGELA ANGELI ANGELL ANGELO ANGELS ANGERS ANGKOR ANGLED ANGLER ANGLES ANGLIA ANGLOS ANGOLA ANGORA ANHYDR ANIMAL ANIMAS ANIMES ANIMUS ANIONS ANITRA ANJOUS ANKARA ANKLED ANKLES ANKLET ANNABA ANNALS ANNEAL ANNEXE ANNLEE ANNOYS ANNUAL ANNULI ANNULS ANODES ANODIC ANOINT ANOLES ANOMIE ANONYM ANORAK ANSATE ANSELM ANSGAR ANSWER ANTCOW ANTEED ANTERO ANTEUP ANTHEM ANTHER ANTICS ANTLER ANTONY ANTRES ANTRIM ANTRON ANTRUM ANUBIS ANURAN ANVILS ANYHOW ANYONE ANYWAY

A•N•••

ADNATE AENEAS AENEID AGNATE ALNICO AMNION ANNABA ANNALS ANNEAL ANNEXE ANNLEE ANNOYS ANNUAL ANNULI ANNULS ARNESS ARNETT ARNHEM ARNICA ARNOLD AUNTIE AWNING

A••N••

ACINUS ADONAI ADONIS AGENAS AGENCY AGENDA AGENTS AJANTA AKENES ALANON ALINES ALONSO ALONZO AMANDA AMENDS AMENRA AMENTS AMINES AMINOR AMINUS ANANDA ANONYM ARENAS ARENDT ASANAS ATONAL ATONCE ATONED ATONES ATONIC AVANTI AVENGE AVENUE AXONAL

A•••N•

AAHING ABOUND ABSENT ACCENT ACHENE ACHING ACORNS ACTING ACTINO ACTONE ADDEND ADDING ADDONS ADORNS ADRENO ADVENT AFFINE AGEING AGLINT AHERNE AIDING AILING AIMING AIRING ALBANO ALBANY ALBINO ALDINE ALFINE ALIENS ALIGNS ALKENE ALMOND ALOINS ALPINE ALUMNA ALUMNI AMIENS AMOUNT ANCONA ANIONS ANOINT ANTONY ANYONE APPEND APRONS AQUINO ARCANA ARCANE ARCING ARDENT ARGENT ARJUNA ARLENE ARMAND ARMANI ARMING AROUND ARPENT ARRANT ARSENE ARYANS ASCEND ASCENT ASIANS ASKING ASLANT ASPENS ASSENT ATHAND ATHENA ATHENE ATHENS ATKINS ATTEND ATTUNE AUDENS AUFOND AUGEND AUMONT AUXINS AVAUNT AVERNO AVIANS AWNING AXIONS

A••••N

AACHEN ACTION ACTSON ACUMEN ADDSIN ADDSON ADJOIN ADRIAN ADRIEN AEGEAN AFGHAN AILEEN AIRGUN AIRMAN AIRMEN ALANON ALBION ALBOIN ALCUIN ALDRIN ALEMAN ALFVEN ALISON ALLMAN ALTMAN AMAZON AMBLIN AMNION AMYTAN ANACIN ANCIEN ANDEAN ANTRON ANURAN APEMAN APEMEN APPIAN ARAGON ARCHON ARISEN ARUBAN ASHCAN ASOSAN ASSIGN ASTERN ASWOON ATAMAN ATTAIN AUBURN AUGEAN AUSTEN AUSTIN AUTUMN AVALON AVEDON AWAKEN AWOKEN AZORIN

•AN•••

BANANA BANDED BANDIT BANDOG BANGED BANGER BANGKA BANGLE BANGOR BANGUI BANGUP BANISH BANJOS BANJUL BANKED BANKER BANKON BANLON BANNED BANNER BANQUO BANTAM BANTER BANTUS BANYAN BANZAI CANAAN CANADA CANALS CANAPE CANARD CANARY CANCAN CANCEL CANCUN CANDID CANDLE CANDOR CANERS CANIDS CANIFF CANINE CANING CANKER CANNAE CANNED CANNEL CANNER CANNES CANNON CANNOT CANOED CANOES CANOLA CANONS CANOPY CANOVA CANTAB CANTED CANTER CANTHI CANTLE CANTON CANTOR CANTOS CANUTE CANVAS CANYON DANANG DANAUS DANCED DANCER DANCES DANDER DANDIE DANDLE DANGER DANGLE DANGLY DANGME DANIEL DANISH DANKER DANNAY DANNER DANSON DANTES DANTON DANUBE DANZIG FANDOM FANGED FANION FANJET FANNED FANNIE FANOUT FANTAN GANDER GANDHI GANGED GANGES GANGLE GANGLY GANGUE GANGUP GANNET GANTRY HANDED HANDEL HANDIN HANDLE HANDON HANGAR HANGED HANGER HANGIN HANGON HANGUL HANGUP HANKER HANKIE HANNAH HANSEL HANSOM HANSON JANGLE JANGLY JANHUS JANICE JANINE JANSEN KANAKA KANDER KANSAN KANSAS KANTOR LANAIS LANATE LANCED LANCER LANCES LANCET LANDAU LANDED LANDER LANDHO LANDIS LANDON LANDRY LANGUR LANIER LANKER LANKLY LANOSE LANSON LANVIN MANAGE MANAMA MANANA MANAUS MANCHA MANCHU MANDAN MANDAY MANEGE MANFUL MANGER MANGLE MANGOS MANIAC MANIAS MANILA MANIOC MANNED MANNER MANNIX MANORS MANQUE MANRAY MANSES MANTAS MANTEL MANTIC MANTIS MANTLE MANTRA MANTUA MANUAL MANUEL NANOOK NANSEN NANTES PANADA PANAMA PANCHO PANDAS PANDER PANDIT PANELS PANFRY PANICS PANNED PANNER PANNES PANOUT PANTED PANTRY PANZER QANTAS RANCHO RANCID RANCOR RANDOM RANDRY RANEES RANFOR RANGED RANGER RANGES RANGUP RANIDS RANKED RANKER RANKIN RANKLE RANKLY RANOFF RANOUT RANSOM RANTED RANTER SANCHO SANCTA SANDAL SANDED SANDER SANDIA SANDRA SANELY SANEST SANGER SANGTO SANITY SANNUP SANSEI SANTEE SANTIR SANTOS TANAKA TANDEM TANGED TANGLE TANGLY TANGOS TANGUY TANIST TANKAS TANKED TANKER TANKUP TANNED TANNER TANNIC TANNIN TANOAK TANOAN TANTRA VANDAL VANIER VANISH VANITY VANNED VANRYN WANDER WANERS WANGLE WANING WANNED WANNER WANTAD WANTED WANTIN WANTON WANTTO XANADU XANTHO YANGON YANKED YANKEE YANQUI ZANDER ZANIER ZANIES ZANILY ZANUCK

•A•N••

BAINES BANNED BANNER BARNES BARNEY BARNUM CAGNEY CANNAE CANNED CANNEL CANNER CANNES CANNON CANNOT CAPNUT CARNAL CARNES CARNET CARNEY CARNOT CATNAP CATNIP DABNEY DAINTY DAMNED DANNAY DANNER DARNAY DARNED DARNEL DARNER DARNIT DAUNTS DAWNED EARNED EARNER FAENZA FAFNIR FAINTS FANNED FANNIE FAUNAE FAUNAL FAUNAS FAUNUS FAWNED FAWNER GAINED GAINER GAINLY GAINON GAINST GANNET GARNER GARNET GAYNOR HAINAN HAINES HANNAH HAUNCH HAUNTS JAUNTS JAUNTY KARNAK KAUNAS KAUNDA LAINIE LAUNCH MAENAD MAGNET MAGNON MAGNUM MAINLY MANNED MANNER MANNIX MARNER MARNIE MAUNDY NARNIA PAANGA PAINED PAINTS PANNED PANNER PANNES PARNIS PAUNCH PAWNED PAWNEE PAWNER RADNER RAINED RAINER RAINES SAINTE SAINTS SANNUP SAUNAS TAINAN TAINOS TAINTS TANNED TANNER TANNIC TANNIN TAUNTS VAINER VAINLY VANNED VARNAS VARNEY VAUNTS WAGNER WALNUT WANNED WANNER WAPNER WARNED WARNER WATNEY YARNED YAWNED YAWNER

•A••N•

AAHING BAAING BAIRNS BAKING BALING BANANA BARING BARONG BARONS BARONY BASING BASINS BATING BATONS BAYING CABANA CABINS CADENT CAGING CAIRNS CAJUNS CAKING CAMINO CANINE CANING CANONS CAPONE CAPONS CARINA CARING CARONI CASING CASINO CATENA CAVING CAWING DAMONE DANANG DAPHNE DARING DATING DATONG DAYONE DAZING EALING EARING EASING EATING FACING FADING FAGEND FAKING FALANA FALINE FAMINE FARINA FARING FAXING FAZING GAGING GALENA GAMINE GAMING GAMINS GAPING GATING GAZING HABANA HALING HARING HATING HAVANA HAVENS HAVENT HAVING HAWING HAYING HAZANS HAZING JACANA JADING JANINE JAPANS JAPING JAWING KAHUNA KALINE LACING LACUNA LADING LADINO LAGUNA LAMENT LAMINA LAMING LAMONT LAPINS LARYNX LATENE LATENS LATENT LATINA LATINO LATINS LATONA LAVING LAWING LAYING LAZING MAKING MALONE MANANA MARINA MARINE MARINO MASONS MATING MATINS MAVENS MAXINE MAYANS NADINE NAGANO NAMING NATANT OARING PACING PACINO PADANG PAEANS PAEONS PAGANS PAGING PAHANG PALING PARANA PARANG PARENS PARENT PARING PATENS PATENT PATINA PATINE PAVANE PAVING PAWING PAYING RACINE RACING RACONS RAGING RAKING RAMONA RAMONE RAPINE RAPINI RARING RATINE RATING RAVENS RAVINE RAVING RAYONS RAZING SABENA SABINE SABINS SALINA SALINE SALONS SARANS SARONG SATANG SATING SATINS SATINY SAVANT

SAVING
SAWING
SAXONS
SAXONY
SAYING
TAGEND
TAHINI
TAKING
TAKINS
TALENT
TALONS
TAMING
TAPING
TAPINS
TARING
TAUONS
TAWING
TAXING
VACANT
VALENS
VALENT
VARUNA
WADING
WAGING
WAGONS
WAHINE
WAKENS
WAKING
WANING
WARING
WAVING
WAXING
YAWING
ZAYINS

•A•••N

AACHEN
BABOON
BABSON
BACKIN
BAFFIN
BAHIAN
BALEEN
BALKAN
BANKON
BANLON
BANYAN
BARKIN
BARMAN
BARMEN
BARREN
BARRON
BARTON
BARYON
BARZUN
BATAAN
BATMAN
BATMEN
BATTEN
CAFTAN
CAIMAN
CALLIN
CALLON
CALVIN
CAMDEN
CAMEIN
CAMEON
CAMION
CANAAN
CANCAN
CANCUN
CANNON
CANTON
CANYON
CAPGUN
CAPTAN
CARBON
CARDIN
CAREEN
CARMAN
CARMEN
CARSON
CARTON
CASERN
CASHIN
CASTON
CATION
CATKIN
CATTON
CAVEIN
CAVERN
CAXTON
CAYMAN
DACRON
DAIKON
DAIMON
DAIREN
DALTON
DAMIEN
DAMPEN
DAMSON
DANSON
DANTON
DARIEN
DARKEN
DARREN
DARWIN
DASSIN
DATSUN
DAWSON
DAYTON
EASEIN
EASTON
EATSIN
FABIAN
FADEIN
FALCON
FALLEN
FALLIN
FALLON
FANION
FANTAN
FASTEN
FATTEN
GABION
GAGMAN
GAGMEN
GAINON
GALLON
GAMMON
GARCON
GARDEN
GARSON
GASCON
GASKIN
GASMAN
GASMEN
GASTON
GATLIN
GAVEIN
GAWAIN
HADRON
HAEMON
HAGMAN
HAINAN
HAMLIN
HANDIN
HANDON
HANGIN
HANGON
HANSON
HAPPEN
HARBIN
HARDEN
HARKEN
HARLAN
HARMON
HARPON
HASSAN
HASTEN
HATPIN
HAVEON
HAYDEN
JACLYN
JAMSIN
JANSEN
JARGON
KALKAN
KANSAN
KAOLIN
KAPLAN
LAGOON
LAIDIN
LAIDON
LANDON
LANSON
LANVIN
LARDON
LARSEN
LARSON
LASSEN
LATEEN
LATTEN
LAUREN
LAWMAN
LAWMEN
LAWSON
LAWTON
LAYMAN
LAYMEN
LAYSIN
LAYSON
MACRON
MADDEN
MADMAN
MADMEN
MAGNON
MAIDEN
MAILIN
MAJGEN
MALDEN
MALIGN
MALKIN
MALTIN
MAMMON
MANDAN
MARGIN
MARIAN
MARION
MARLIN
MARLON
MAROON
MARRON
MARTEN
MARTIN
MARVIN
MATLIN
MATRON
NAILIN
NANSEN
NAPKIN
NATHAN
NATION
NATRON
PACMAN
PADUAN
PAIDIN
PAPAIN
PAPUAN
PARDON
PARSON
PARTON
PATHAN
PATRON
PATTEN
PATTON
PAYSIN
PAYSON
RADIAN
RAGLAN
RAGMAN
RAGMEN
RAISIN
RAKEIN
RAMSON
RANKIN
RATION
RATLIN
RATSON
RATTAN
RAYGUN
SADDEN
SAIGON
SAIPAN
SALMAN
SALMON
SALOON
SALTEN
SALTON
SAMOAN
SAMPAN
SAMSON
SARGON
SARTON
SATEEN
SATURN
TACKON
TAINAN
TAIPAN
TAIWAN
TAKEIN
TAKEON
TALION
TANNIN
TANOAN
TAPPAN
TARPAN
TARPON
TARTAN
TARZAN
TASMAN
TAUTEN
TAVERN
TAXMAN
TAXMEN
VANRYN
VARDEN
VAUGHN
WADEIN
WAGGON
WAITON
WALDEN
WALKIN
WALKON
WALTON
WANTIN
WANTON
WARDEN
WARREN
WATSON
WAVEIN
WAYLON
YANGON
YAUPON

••AN••

AJANTA
ALANON
AMANDA
ANANDA
ASANAS
AVANTI
BEANED
BEANIE
BEANOS
BIANCA
BLANCA
BLANCH
BLANDA
BLANKS
BRANCH
BRANDO
BRANDS
BRANDT
BRANDX
BRANDY
BRANTS
BWANAS
CHANCE
CHANCY
CHANEL
CHANEY
CHANGE
CHANTS
CLANCY
CLANGS
CLANKS
CLANKY
CRANED
CRANES
CRANIA
CRANIO
CRANKS
CRANKY
CRANNY
CYANIC
DEANNA
ELANDS
FIANCE
FLANGE
FLANKS
FRANCA
FRANCE
FRANCK
FRANCO
FRANCS
FRANKS
FRANNY
GDANSK
GIANTS
GLANCE
GLANDS
GOANNA
GRANDE
GRANDS
GRANGE
GRANNY
GRANTS
INANER
IRANIS
JEANNE
JOANIE
JOANNA
JOANNE
KIANGS
KRANTZ
KWANZA
LEANED
LEANER
LEANLY
LEANON
LEANTO
LIANAS
LIANGS
LLANOS
LOANED
LOANER
LUANDA
MEANER
MEANIE
MEANLY
MOANED
MOANER
NUANCE
OMANIS
ORANGE
ORANGS
ORANTS
PAANGA
PEANUT
PIANOS
PLANAR
PLANCK
PLANED
PLANER
PLANES
PLANET
PLANKS
PLANON
PLANTE
PLANTS
PRANCE
PRANKS
QUANTA
RUANAS
RUANDA
RWANDA
SCANTS
SCANTY
SEANCE
SHANDY
SHANKS
SHANTY
SLANGS
SLANGY
SLANTS
SPANKS
SPANKY
STANCE
STANCH
STANDS
STANKY
STANZA
SWANEE
SWANKY
THANES
THANKS
TRANCE
TWANGS
TWANGY
UBANGI
UGANDA
URANIA
URANIC
URANUS
USANCE
VIANDS
WEANED

••A•N•

AVAUNT
BAAING
BLAINE
BRAINS
BRAINY
BRAWNY
CHAINE
CHAINS
CRANNY
DEANNA
DRAINS
DWAYNE
ELAINE
ELAYNE
FLAUNT
FRANNY
GOANNA
GRAINS
GRAINY
GRANNY
JEANNE
JOANNA
JOANNE
LEARNS
LEARNT
PLAINS
PLAINT
PRAJNA
PRAWNS
QUAINT
SCARNE
SHAYNE
SPAWNS
STAINS
SWAINS
TRAINS
YEARNS

••A••N

ALANON
AMAZON
ANACIN
ARAGON
ATAMAN
AVALON
AWAKEN
BEACON
BEARON
BEATEN
BEATON
BLAZON
BRAZEN
CHAPIN
CHARON
CLAVIN
CRAVEN
CRAYON
DEACON
DEADEN
DEADON
DEAFEN
DEALIN
DRAGIN
DRAGON
DRAWIN
DRAWON
FLACON
FLAGON
FLAXEN
GRABEN
GRADIN
GRATIN
GRAVEN
HEADIN
HEADON
HEAVEN
IBADAN
KEATON
KLAXON
KRAKEN
LEADEN
LEADIN
LEADON
LEANON
LEAVEN
NEATEN
NIACIN
OMAHAN
PEAHEN
PLANON
PLATEN
PLAYON
READIN
REAGAN
REASON
RYAZAN
SEAFAN
SEAMAN
SEAMEN
SEASON
SHABAN
SHAKEN
SHAMAN
SHARON
SHAVEN
SPAVIN
STALIN
STAMEN
STAYON
TOAMAN
TRAJAN
UTAHAN
WEAKEN
WEAPON
XIAMEN

•••AN•

ALBANO
ALBANY
ARCANA
ARCANE
ARMAND
ARMANI
ARRANT
ARYANS
ASIANS
ASLANT
ATHAND
AVIANS
BANANA
BESANT
BEZANT
BOTANY
BRIAND
BRIANS
BRYANT
BUTANE
BYHAND
CABANA
CETANE
CHIANG
CLEANS
CONANT
CYRANO
DANANG
DECANT
DELANO
DELANY
DEMAND
DISANT
DIVANS
DOMANI
DOPANT
DUNANT
DURANT
EMBANK
ENFANT
ERNANI
ERRAND
ERRANT
ESPANA
ETHANE
EXPAND
EXTANT
FALANA
FULANI
GITANO
GLEANS
GROANS
GUIANA
GUYANA
HABANA
HAVANA
HAZANS
HOGANS
HUMANE
HUMANS
IGUANA
ILEANA
INCANS
INFANT
INHAND
INLAND
INSANE
IOWANS
ISLAND
JACANA
JAPANS
JOHANN
KDLANG
LELAND
LEMANS
LEVANT
LITANY
MANANA
MAYANS
MCCANN
MELANO
MILANO
MORANT
MURANO
MUTANT
NAGANO
NATANT
OCEANS
OCTANE
OCTANT
ONHAND
ONLAND
ORGANA
ORGANS
ORIANA
PADANG
PAEANS
PAGANS
PAHANG
PARANA
PARANG
PAVANE
PECANS
PEDANT
PENANG
PIRANA
PISANS
PLIANT
POLAND
RECANE
RECANT
REDANT
REHANG
REMAND
REMANS
REPAND
RESAND
RIBAND
ROLAND
ROMANO
ROMANS
ROMANY
ROXANA
ROXANE
SARANS
SATANG
SAVANT
SECANT
SEDANS
SEJANT
SHRANK
SKEANS
SLOANE
SOLANS
SOMANY
SONANT
SPRANG
STRAND
SUSANN
TENANT
TEXANS
TIRANA
TIRANE
TISANE
TITANS
TRUANT
TUCANA
TULANE
TYRANT
UCLANS
UHLANS
UNHAND
UNMANS
UPLAND
URBANA
URBANE
UTHANT
VACANT
VEGANS
VIVANT
VOLANS
VOLANT
ZENANA

•••A•N

ATTAIN
BATAAN
CANAAN
DETAIN
DOMAIN
GAWAIN
INVAIN
JOHANN
MCBAIN
MCCANN
MCLAIN
OBTAIN
ORDAIN
PAPAIN
PETAIN
REGAIN
REMAIN
RETAIN
SPRAIN
STRAIN
SUSANN
UJJAIN

••••AN

ADRIAN
AEGEAN
AFGHAN
AIRMAN
ALEMAN
ALLMAN
ALTMAN
AMYTAN
ANDEAN
ANURAN
APEMAN
APPIAN
ARUBAN
ASHCAN
ASOSAN
ATAMAN
AUGEAN
BAHIAN
BALKAN
BANYAN
BARMAN
BATAAN
BATMAN
BEMOAN
BHUTAN
BORMAN
BOWMAN
BROGAN
BUNYAN
BURMAN
BUSMAN
CAFTAN
CAIMAN
CANAAN
CANCAN
CAPTAN
CARMAN
CAYMAN
COLMAN
CONMAN
COOGAN
CORBAN
COWMAN
CRETAN
DEMEAN
DESMAN
DOLMAN
DORIAN
DOTHAN
DUNCAN
DURBAN
DURIAN
ELFMAN
ENDMAN
EOLIAN
EONIAN
FABIAN
FANTAN
FBIMAN
FENIAN
FEZZAN
FIJIAN
FINNAN
FIRMAN
FLYMAN
FORMAN
FRYPAN
FUJIAN
GAGMAN
GASMAN
GENOAN
GERMAN
GIBRAN
GUNMAN
HAGMAN
HAINAN
HARLAN
HASSAN
HERMAN
HETMAN
HITMAN
IBADAN
ICEMAN
INDIAN
INSPAN
IONIAN
JORDAN
JOVIAN
JULIAN
KALKAN
KANSAN
KAPLAN
KEENAN
KENYAN
KERMAN
KIDMAN
KIRMAN
KLIBAN
KOREAN
KORMAN
KURGAN
LAWMAN
LAYMAN
LEGMAN
LIBYAN
LLBEAN
LONGAN
LUCIAN
MADMAN
MANDAN
MARIAN
MCLEAN
MEDIAN
MERMAN
MINOAN
MINYAN
MORGAN
NATHAN
NETMAN
NEUMAN
NEWMAN
NICEAN
NISSAN
NOONAN
NORMAN
NUBIAN
OBIWAN
OBRIAN
OHIOAN
OILCAN
OILMAN
OILPAN
OLDMAN
OMAHAN
ONLOAN
ORPHAN
OSSIAN
OUTRAN
PACMAN
PADUAN
PAPUAN
PATHAN
PENMAN
PIEMAN
PIEPAN
PITMAN
QUMRAN
RADIAN
RAGLAN
RAGMAN
RATTAN
REAGAN
REPLAN
RUDMAN
RUTTAN
RYAZAN
RYOKAN
SAIPAN
SALMAN
SAMOAN
SAMPAN
SEAFAN
SEAMAN
SHABAN
SHAMAN
SHORAN
SIMIAN
SIOUAN
SLOGAN
SOLDAN
STEFAN
STJOAN
SULTAN
SUNTAN
SYLVAN
SYRIAN
TAINAN
TAIPAN
TAIWAN
TANOAN
TAPPAN
TARPAN
TARTAN
TARZAN
TASMAN
TAXMAN
TERRAN
TINCAN
TINMAN
TINPAN
TITIAN
TOAMAN
TODMAN
TONGAN
TOUCAN
TRAJAN
TREPAN
TROJAN
TRUMAN
TUBMAN
TULSAN
TUPIAN
TURBAN
TUSCAN
TYRIAN
UGRIAN
ULLMAN
UTAHAN
VIVIAN
VULCAN
WICCAN
WYSTAN
YEOMAN
YESMAN
YUNNAN
ZEEMAN

AO••••

AODAIS
AORIST
AORTAE
AORTAL
AORTAS
AORTIC
AOUDAD

A•O•••

ABOARD
ABODES
ABOHMS
ABOLLA
ABOMBS
ABORAL
ABORTS
ABOUND
ACORNS
ADOBES
ADOLPH
ADONAI
ADONIS
ADOPTS
ADORED
ADOREE
ADORER
ADORES
ADORNS
AEOLIA
AEOLIC
AEOLUS
AGORAE
AGORAS
AGOROT
AGOUTI
ALOHAS
ALOINS
ALOMAR
ALONSO
ALONZO
AMOEBA
AMOLES
AMORAL
AMOSOZ
AMOUNT
AMOURS
ANODES
ANODIC
ANOINT
ANOLES
ANOMIE
ANONYM
ANORAK
APODAL
APOGEE
APOLLO
AROIDS
AROMAS
AROUND
AROUSE
ASOSAN
ATODDS
ATOLLS
ATOMIC
ATONAL
ATONCE
ATONED
ATONES
ATONIC
AVOCET
AVOIDS
AVOUCH
AVOWAL
AVOWED
AVOWER
AWOKEN
AXONAL
AZODYE
AZORES
AZORIN

A••O••

ABBOTS
ABBOTT
ABHORS
ABLOOM
ABROAD
ABSORB
ACCORD
ACCOST
ACEOUS
ACEOUT
ACROSS
ACTONE
ACTORS
ACTOUT
ADDONS
ADJOIN
ADROIT
ADSORB
AEROBE
AFFORD
AFLOAT
AGEOLD
AIROUT
AJFOYT
ALBOIN
ALBORG
ALCOTT
ALCOVE
ALDOSE
ALDOUS
ALGORE
ALIOTO
ALLOTS
ALLOUT
ALLOWS
ALLOYS
ALMOND
ALMOST
ANCONA
ANGOLA
ANGORA
ANIONS
ANJOUS
ANNOYS
ANTONY
ANYONE
APLOMB
APPOSE
APRONS
ARBORS
ARBOUR
ARDORS
ARDOUR
AREOLA

ARGOSY
ARGOTS
ARIOSE
ARIOSO
ARMORS
ARMORY
ARMOUR
ARNOLD
ARROBA
ARROWS
ARROYO
ARTOIS
ASCOTS
ASHORE
ASKOUT
ASLOPE
ASSORT
ASWOON
ATCOST
ATHOME
ATMOST
ATWOOD
ATWORK
AUFOND
AUMONT
AURORA
AUROUS
AXIOMS
AXIONS

A•••O•

ABLOOM
ABYDOS
ACAJOU
ACTION
ACTSON
ADDSON
AGOROT
AHCHOO
ALAMOS
ALANON
ALBION
ALISON
AMADOU
AMAJOR
AMATOL
AMAZON
AMIDOL
AMIGOS
AMINOR
AMNION
AMOSOZ
ANALOG
ANCHOR
ANDHOW
ANDROS
ANGKOR
ANGLOS
ANTCOW
ANTRON
ANYHOW
ARAGON
ARCHON
ASIMOV
ASKFOR
ASTROS
ASWOON
ATWOOD
AUDIOS
AUTHOR
AVALON
AVEDON
AVISOS

A••••O

ACTINO
ACTTWO
ADAGIO
ADDSTO
ADRENO
AFLCIO
AHCHOO
AIELLO
AIKIDO
AIMSTO
AKIMBO
ALBANO
ALBEDO
ALBINO
ALECTO
ALEPPO
ALIOTO
ALLPRO
ALNICO
ALONSO
ALONZO
AMEDEO
ANATTO
ANGELO
ANTERO
APOLLO
AQUINO
ARCARO
AREZZO
ARIOSO
ARISTO
ARROYO
ARTHRO
ARTURO
ATEMPO
ATERGO
AUSTRO
AVERNO

•AO•••

BAOBAB
KAOLIN
LAOTSE
LAOTZU
MAOISM
MAOIST
MAORIS
MAOTAI
TAOISM
TAOIST

•A•O••

BABOON
BAROJA
BAROLO
BARONG
BARONS
BARONY
BATONS
BAYOUS
CAHOWS
CAJOLE
CANOED
CANOES
CANOLA
CANONS
CANOPY
CANOVA
CAPONE
CAPONS
CAPOTE
CAROBS
CAROLE
CAROLS
CAROMS
CARONI
CAVORT
DACOIT
DADOED
DADOES
DAKOTA
DAMONE
DAMORE
DAMOUR
DATONG
DAYONE
EATOUT
FAGOTS
FAMOUS
FANOUT
FAROFF
FAROUK
FAROUT
FAVORS
FAVOUR
GALOIS
GALOOT
GALOPS
GALORE
GALOSH
GATORS
HALOED
HALOES
HALOID
HAROLD
HAVOCS
JABOTS
JACOBI
JALOPY
JAMOKE
JAWOHL
KABOBS
KABOOM
KAROSS
KAYOED
KAZOOS
LABORS
LABOUR
LADOGA
LAGOON
LAHORE
LAKOTA
LAMONT
LAMOUR
LANOSE
LAROSA
LATONA
LATOUR
LATOYA
LAYOFF
LAYOUT
MAHOUT
MAJORS
MALONE
MALORY
MALOTI
MANORS
MAROON
MASONS
MAXOUT
MAYORS
MAZOLA
NABOBS
NABORS
NAGOYA
NANOOK
NAPOLI
PAEONS
PAGODA
PALOMA
PANOUT
PARODY
PAROLE
PATOIS
PAYOFF
PAYOLA
PAYOUT
RACONS
RADOME
RAGOUT
RAMONA
RAMONE
RAMOSE
RAMOUS
RANOFF
RANOUT
RAYONS
RAZORS
SABOTS
SALOME
SALONS
SALOON
SAMOAN
SAMOSA
SAPORS
SARODS
SARONG
SATORI
SATOUT
SAVOIE
SAVOIR
SAVORS
SAVORY
SAVOUR
SAWOFF
SAWOUT
SAXONS
SAXONY
TABOOS
TABORS
TACOMA
TAGORE
TAGOUT
TALONS
TANOAK
TANOAN
TAPOFF
TAPOUT
TAROTS
TAUONS
VADOSE
VALOIS
VALOUR
VAPORS
VAPOUR
WAGONS
WAHOOS
WAYOUT
YAHOOS
YAPOKS
ZADORA

•A••O•

BABOON
BABSON
BADLOT
BAILOR
BALBOA
BALLOT
BAMBOO
BANDOG
BANGOR
BANJOS
BANKON
BANLON
BARDOT
BARHOP
BARRON
BARROW
BARTOK
BARTON
BARYON
BASSOS
BATBOY
BATHOS
BAYLOR
CACAOS
CACHOU
CAICOS
CALLON
CALLOW
CAMEON
CAMEOS
CAMION
CAMPOS
CANDOR
CANNON
CANNOT
CANTON
CANTOR
CANTOS
CANYON
CAPTOR
CARBON
CARBOY
CARGOS
CARHOP
CARLOS
CARLOT
CARNOT
CARROL
CARROT
CARSON
CARTON
CASTON
CASTOR
CATION
CATTON
CAWDOR
CAXTON
DACRON
DAIKON
DAIMON
DALTON
DAMSON
DANSON
DANTON
DARROW
DAWSON
DAYTON
EASTON
FACTOR
FAEROE
FALCON
FALLON
FALLOW
FANDOM
FANION
FARLOW
FARROW
FATHOM
GABION
GAINON
GALLON
GALLOP
GALOOT
GAMBOL
GAMMON
GARCON
GARSON
GASCON
GASLOG
GASTON
GAYNOR
HADRON
HAEMON
HAIKOU
HALLOO
HALLOS
HALLOW
HANDON
HANGON
HANSOM
HANSON
HARBOR
HARLOW
HARMON
HARPON
HARROW
HATBOX
HATHOR
HAVEON
HAYMOW
JARGON
KABOOM
KANTOR
KARPOV
KARROO
KAZOOS
LAGOON
LAIDON
LANDON
LANSON
LAPDOG
LAPTOP
LARDON
LARGOS
LARSON
LASSOS
LAWSON
LAWTON
LAYFOR
LAYLOW
LAYSON
LAZBOY
MACHOS
MACRON
MACROS
MADTOM
MAGNON
MAHZOR
MALLOW
MAMBOS
MAMMON
MANGOS
MANIOC
MARCOS
MARGOT
MARION
MARLON
MARMOT
MAROON
MARRON
MARROW
MASCOT
MATRON
MATZOH
MATZOS
MAYPOP
NACHOS
NANOOK
NARROW
NATION
NATRON
PAILOU
PALLOR
PARDON
PARLOR
PARROT
PARSON
PARTON
PASEOS
PASTOR
PATHOL
PATHOS
PATIOS
PATMOS
PATROL
PATRON
PATTON
PAVLOV
PAYFOR
PAYSON
RADIOS
RAGMOP
RAGTOP
RAMROD
RAMSON
RANCOR
RANDOM
RANFOR
RANSOM
RAPTOR
RATION
RATIOS
RATSON
SAIGON
SAILOR
SALLOW
SALMON
SALOON
SALTON
SALVOR
SALVOS
SAMSON
SANTOS
SARGON
SARGOS
SARTON
SAVIOR
SAWLOG
SAYSOS
TABOOS
TACKON
TAILOR
TAINOS
TAKEON
TALBOT
TALION
TALLOW
TANGOS
TARPON
TATTOO
TAUTOG
TAYLOR
WAGGON
WAHOOS
WAITON
WALKON
WALLOP
WALLOW
WALTON
WANTON
WARGOD
WARHOL
WASHOE
WATSON
WAYLON
YAHOOS
YANGON
YARROW
YAUPON

•A•••O

BAGUIO
BAMAKO
BAMBOO
BANQUO
BAROLO
BARRIO
CALICO
CALLAO
CAMETO
CAMINO
CARDIO
CARETO
CARUSO
CASINO
CASSIO
CASTRO
CAUCHO
DACAPO
DADDYO
DAIMYO
DAMATO
DARETO
DAYGLO
FALLTO
GABBRO
GASTRO
GAUCHO
GAZEBO
HAIRDO
HALLOO
HASBRO
KAKAPO
KARROO
LADINO
LAIDTO
LANDHO
LAREDO
LASHIO
LATIGO
LATINO
LAVABO
LAYSTO
MACACO
MADEDO
MADERO
MADURO
MAGGIO
MAKEDO
MALABO
MAPUTO
MARIKO
MARINO
NAGANO
NAVAHO
NAVAJO
PACINO
PALAEO
PANCHO
PAPAGO
PARETO
PASHTO
RABATO
RANCHO
SABATO
SANCHO
SANGTO
SAPPHO
SASEBO
TAKETO
TALKTO
TAMAYO
TATTOO
WANTTO
XANTHO

••A•O•

ACAJOU
ALAMOS
ALANON
AMADOU
AMAJOR
AMATOL
AMAZON
ANALOG
ARAGON
AVALON
BEACON
BEANOS
BEARON
BEATON
BLAZON
BMAJOR
BRASOV
BRAVOS
BRAZOS
CHADOR
CHARON
CLAMOR
CLAROS
CMAJOR
CRAYON
DEACON
DEADON
DIALOG
DIATOM
DMAJOR
DRAGON
DRAWON
EMAJOR
ENAMOR
FLACON
FLAGON
FLAVOR
FMAJOR
GLAMOR
GMAJOR
GUACOS
HEADON
HEAROF
INAFOG
INAROW
ISADOR
KEATON
KLAXON
KRAKOW
LEADON
LEANON
LLANOS
MCADOO
MEADOW
ORATOR
PEAPOD
PHAROS
PIANOS
PLANON
PLAYON
QUAHOG
REASON
SEACOW
SEADOG
SEAFOX
SEASON
SHADOW
SHAKOS
SHALOM
SHARON
SLALOM
STATOR
STAYON
TEAPOT
TEAPOY
TLALOC
VIACOM
WEAPON
ZEALOT

••A••O

ADAGIO
ANATTO
BRANDO
CHALCO
CHARRO
CRAMBO
CRANIO
DIABLO
EXACTO
FIASCO
FRANCO
GEARTO
GRAECO
GRASSO
LEADTO
LEANTO
MCADOO
NEARTO
PLAGIO
PLASMO
QUARTO
RIALTO
SMALTO
SNAPTO
SOASTO
WHAMMO

•••AO•

CACAOS
HIVAOA

•••A•O

ALBANO
ARCARO
BAMAKO
BORAXO
CHEAPO
CYRANO
DACAPO
DAMATO
DELANO
DORADO
DYNAMO
ELPASO
FIGARO
GELATO
GITANO
HEMATO
JURADO
KAKAPO
LAVABO
LEGATO
MACACO
MALABO
MEGALO
MELANO
MIKADO
MILANO
MONACO
MURANO
NAGANO
NAVAHO
NAVAJO
NEMATO
OCTAVO
PALAEO
PAPAGO
PICABO
PICARO
POTATO
RABATO
ROBALO
ROMANO
SABATO
SOMATO
STMALO
STRABO
STRATO
TAMAYO
TERATO
TEXACO
TOBAGO
TOMATO
VIRAGO

••••AO

BILBAO
CALLAO
TODDAO

AP••••

APACHE
APATHY
APEMAN
APEMEN
APERCU
APEXES
APHIDS
APIARY
APICAL
APICES
APIECE
APLITE
APLOMB
APODAL
APOGEE
APOLLO
APPALL
APPALS
APPEAL
APPEAR
APPEND
APPIAN
APPLES
APPOSE
APRONS
APTEST
APULIA

A•P•••

ALPACA
ALPERT
ALPHAS
ALPINE
AMPERE
AMPHID
AMPLER
AMPULE
AMPULS
APPALL
APPALS
APPEAL
APPEAR
APPEND
APPIAN
APPLES
APPOSE
ARPENT
ASPECT
ASPENS
ASPERA
ASPICS
ASPIRE
AUPAIR

A••P••

ADAPTS
ADEPTS
ADOPTS
ALEPHS
ALEPPO
ALLPRO
ARMPIT
AUSPEX

A•••P•

ABRUPT
ACCEPT
ADOLPH
ALCAPP
ALEPPO
ASLOPE
ATEMPO

A••••P

ACESUP
ACTSUP
ADDSUP
ALCAPP
ANTEUP
ASHARP
ASLEEP

•AP•••

CAPERS
CAPFUL
CAPGUN
CAPIAS
CAPITA
CAPLET
CAPNUT
CAPONE
CAPONS
CAPOTE
CAPPED
CAPPER
CAPRIS
CAPSID
CAPTAN
CAPTOR
DAPHNE
DAPPED
DAPPER
DAPPLE
GAPERS
GAPING
GAPPED
HAPPEN
JAPANS
JAPERS
JAPERY
JAPING
KAPLAN
KAPPAS
LAPDOG
LAPELS
LAPFUL
LAPHAM
LAPINS
LAPPED
LAPPET
LAPSED
LAPSES
LAPSUP
LAPTEV
LAPTOP
LAPUTA
MAPLES
MAPPED
MAPPER
MAPUTO
NAPERY
NAPIER
NAPKIN
NAPLES
NAPOLI
NAPPED
NAPPER
NAPPES
PAPACY
PAPAGO
PAPAIN
PAPAWS
PAPAYA
PAPERS
PAPERY
PAPIER
PAPPAS
PAPPUS
PAPUAN
PAPYRI
RAPIDS
RAPIER
RAPINE
RAPINI
RAPPED
RAPPEE
RAPPEL
RAPPER
RAPTLY
RAPTOR
SAPORS
SAPPED
SAPPER
SAPPHO
TAPERS
TAPING
TAPINS
TAPIRS
TAPOFF
TAPOUT
TAPPAN
TAPPED
TAPPER
TAPPET
VAPORS
VAPOUR
WAPITI
WAPNER
YAPOKS
YAPPED
ZAPATA
ZAPPED
ZAPPER

•A•P••

CALPAC
CAMPED
CAMPER
CAMPOS
CAMPUS
CAPPED
CAPPER
CARPAL
CARPED
CARPEL
CARPER
CARPET
CARPUS
CASPAR
CASPER
DAMPED
DAMPEN
DAMPER
DAMPLY
DAPPED
DAPPER
DAPPLE
GAPPED
GASPAR
GASPED
HAMPER
HAPPEN
HARPED
HARPER
HARPON
HASPED
HATPIN
JAIPUR
JASPER
KAPPAS
KARPOV
LAPPED
LAPPET
LAUPER
MAGPIE
MAPPED
MAPPER
MARPLE
MAYPOP
NAPPED
NAPPER
NAPPES
PALPUS
PAMPAS
PAMPER
PAPPAS
PAPPUS
PAUPER
PAWPAW
RAIPUR
RAJPUT
RAMPED
RAPPED
RAPPEE
RAPPEL
RAPPER
RASPED
RASPER
SAIPAN
SAMPAN
SAMPLE
SAPPED
SAPPER
SAPPHO
TAIPAN
TAIPEI
TAMPED
TAMPER
TAPPAN
TAPPED
TAPPER
TAPPET
TARPAN
TARPIT
TARPON
TAUPES
VAMPED
VAMPER
WAMPUM
WARPED
YAPPED
YAUPON
YAWPED
YAWPER
ZAPPED
ZAPPER

•A••P•

CALIPH
CANAPE
CANOPY
DACAPO
GALOPS
JALAPA
JALOPY
JAMUPS
KAKAPO
LAYUPS
PARAPH

•A•••P

BACKUP
BALLUP
BANGUP
BARHOP
CALLUP
CAMEUP
CARHOP
CATNAP
CATNIP
CATSUP
DAMSUP
EARLAP
EASEUP
EATSUP
FACEUP
FAIRUP
GALLOP
GALLUP
GANGUP
GASCAP
GAVEUP
HANGUP
HARDUP
HAULUP
JACKUP
JAMSUP
JAZZUP
LACEUP
LAIDUP
LAPSUP
LAPTOP
LARRUP
LASHUP
LAYSUP
MADCAP
MADEUP
MAKEUP
MARKUP
MAYHAP
MAYPOP
PACKUP

PAIDUP
PAIRUP
PASSUP
PAYSUP
RACKUP
RAGMOP
RAGTOP
RAKEUP
RANGUP
SANNUP
SATRAP
SAVEUP
TAGSUP
TAKEUP
TALKUP
TANKUP
WADSUP
WAITUP
WAKEUP
WALKUP
WALLOP
WALLUP
WARMUP
WASHUP

••AP••
ADAPTS
CHAPEL
CHAPIN
COAPTS
CRAPES
DIAPER
DRAPED
DRAPER
DRAPES
ELAPID
ELAPSE
FRAPPE
GRAPES
GRAPHS
GRAPPA
HEAPED
INAPET
LEAPED
LEAPER
OKAPIS
PEAPOD
REAPED
REAPER
SCAPES
SHAPED
SHAPER
SHAPES
SLAPPY
SLAPUP
SNAPAT
SNAPPY
SNAPTO
SNAPUP
SOAPED
SOAPER
STAPES
STAPLE
STAPUF
TEAPOT
TEAPOY
TRAPPY
WEAPON
WRAPUP

••A•P•
CHAMPS
CLAMPS
CLASPS
CRAMPS
FRAPPE
GRAMPS
GRAPPA
GRASPS
SCALPS
SCAMPI
SCAMPS
SCARPS
SCAUPS
SHARPS
SLAPPY
SNAPPY
STAMPS
SWAMPS
SWAMPY
TRAMPS
TRAPPY

••A••P
BEADUP
BEAMUP
BEARUP
BEATUP
CHATUP
CLAMUP
DRAWUP
GEARUP
HEADUP
HEATUP
LEADUP
PLAYUP
REARUP
SEALUP
SLAPUP
SNAPUP
SOAKUP
STAYUP
TEACUP
TEAMUP
TEARUP
WRAPUP

•••AP•
ALCAPP
CANAPE
CHEAPO
DACAPO
ENRAPT
ESCAPE
JALAPA
KAKAPO
LENAPE
ONTAPE
PARAPH
PTRAPS
RECAPS
REMAPS
RETAPE
RETAPS
SCRAPE
SCRAPS
SERAPE
SERAPH
STRAPS
TERAPH
UNCAPS

•••A•P
ALCAPP
ASHARP
BSHARP
CCLAMP
CSHARP
DECAMP
DSHARP
ENCAMP
ESCARP
ESHARP
FSHARP
GSHARP
PREAMP
REVAMP

••••AP
BITMAP
BUMRAP
BURLAP
CATNAP
DEWLAP
EARLAP
ENTRAP
ENWRAP
GASCAP
HOTCAP
HUBCAP
ICECAP
KIDNAP
MADCAP
MAYHAP
MILSAP
MISHAP
MOBCAP
NOSOAP
REDCAP
REWRAP
RIPRAP
SATRAP
SKYCAP
TOECAP
TOETAP
UNSNAP
UNTRAP
UNWRAP

AQ••••
AQUATE
AQUILA
AQUINO

A•Q•••
ACQUIT

•AQ•••
MAQUIS
RAQUEL
YAQUIS

•A•Q••
BANQUO
BARQUE
BASQUE
CAIQUE
CALQUE
CASQUE
MANQUE
MARQUE
MASQUE
SACQUE
YANQUI

•A•••Q
NASDAQ

••AQ••
BRAQUE
CLAQUE
IRAQIS
OPAQUE
PLAQUE

••••AQ
COMPAQ
NASDAQ

AR••••
ARABIA
ARABIC
ARABLE
ARAFAT
ARAGON
ARALIA
ARALLU
ARAMIS
ARARAT
ARAWAK
ARBELA
ARBORS
ARBOUR
ARCADE
ARCANA
ARCANE
ARCARO
ARCHED
ARCHER
ARCHES
ARCHIE
ARCHLY
ARCHON
ARCING
ARCTIC
ARDEBS
ARDENT
ARDORS
ARDOUR
ARECAS
ARENAS
ARENDT
AREOLA
ARETES
ARETHA
AREZZO
ARGALI
ARGENT
ARGIVE
ARGOSY
ARGOTS
ARGUED
ARGUER
ARGUES
ARGYLE
ARGYLL
ARIDLY
ARIGHT
ARIOSE
ARIOSO
ARISEN
ARISES
ARISTA
ARISTO
ARJUNA
ARLENE
ARLISS
ARMADA
ARMAGH
ARMAND
ARMANI
ARMETS
ARMFUL
ARMIES
ARMING
ARMLET
ARMORS
ARMORY
ARMOUR
ARMPIT
ARMURE
ARNESS
ARNETT
ARNHEM
ARNICA
ARNOLD
AROIDS
AROMAS
AROUND
AROUSE
ARPENT
ARRACK
ARRANT
ARRAYS
ARREST
ARRIBA
ARRIVE
ARROBA
ARROWS
ARROYO
ARSENE
ARTELS
ARTERY
ARTFUL
ARTGUM
ARTHRO
ARTHUR
ARTIER
ARTIST
ARTOIS
ARTURO
ARUBAN
ARVADA
ARYANS

A•R•••
ABRADE
ABRAMS
ABROAD
ABRUPT
ACROSS
ADRENO
ADRIAN
ADRIEN
ADRIFT
ADROIT
AERATE
AERIAL
AERIES
AEROBE
AFRAID
AFRAME
AFREET
AFRESH
AFRICA
AGREED
AGREES
AIRARM
AIRBAG
AIRBUS
AIRDAM
AIRDRY
AIRGUN
AIRIER
AIRILY
AIRING
AIRMAN
AIRMEN
AIROUT
AIRSAC
AIRWAY
AORIST
AORTAE
AORTAL
AORTAS
AORTIC
APRONS
ARRACK
ARRANT
ARRAYS
ARREST
ARRIBA
ARRIVE
ARROBA
ARROWS
ARROYO
ATREST
ATREUS
ATRIAL
ATRISK
ATRIUM
AUREUS
AURIGA
AURORA
AUROUS

A••R••
ABORAL
ABORTS
ACARID
ACARUS
ACCRUE
ACORNS
ADORED
ADOREE
ADORER
ADORES
ADORNS
AFFRAY
AGARIC
AGORAE
AGORAS
AGOROT
AHERNE
AIGRET
ALARIC
ALARMS
ALARUM
ALDRIN
ALERTS
ALFRED
AMERCE
AMORAL
AMTRAC
AMTRAK
ANDREA
ANDREI
ANDRES
ANDREW
ANDREY
ANDROS
ANORAK
ANTRES
ANTRIM
ANTRON
ANTRUM
ANURAN
APERCU
ARARAT
ASHRAM
ASTRAL
ASTRAY
ASTRID
ASTROS
ATERGO
ATTRIT
AUBREY
AUDREY
AVERNO
AVERSE
AVERTS
AWARDS
AZORES
AZORIN

A•••R•
ABHORS
ABJURE
ABOARD
ABSORB
ABSURD
ACCORD
ACTORS
ADDERS
ADHERE
ADJURE
ADMIRE
ADSORB
ADVERB
ADVERT
AFFIRM
AFFORD
AGLARE
AILERS
AIRARM
AIRDRY
ALBERT
ALBORG
ALDERS
ALEGRE
ALGORE
ALHIRT
ALLPRO
ALLURE
ALPERT
ALTARS
ALTERS
AMBERS
AMEERS
AMENRA
AMHARA
AMOURS
AMPERE
ANGERS
ANGORA
ANITRA
ANKARA
ANTERO
APIARY
ARBORS
ARCARO
ARDORS
ARMORS
ARMORY
ARMURE
ARTERY
ARTHRO
ARTURO
ASBURY
ASGARD
ASHARP
ASHORE
ASKARI
ASKERS
ASMARA
ASPERA
ASPIRE
ASSERT
ASSORT
ASSURE
ASTERN
ASTERS
ASWIRL
ATTARS
ATTIRE
ATWORK
AUBURN
AUGERS
AUGURS
AUGURY
AURORA
AUSTRO
AVIARY
AWEARY
AWHIRL
AYMARA

A••••R
AAFAIR
ABUKIR
ABUSER
ACHIER
ADORER
AETHER
AFFAIR
AGADIR
AIRIER
ALEGAR
ALOMAR
ALTAIR
ALULAR
AMAJOR
AMBLER
AMINOR
AMPLER
ANCHOR
ANGKOR
ANGLER
ANHYDR
ANSGAR
ANSWER
ANTHER
ANTLER
APPEAR
ARBOUR
ARCHER
ARDOUR
ARGUER
ARMOUR
ARTHUR
ARTIER
ASHIER
ASHLAR
ASKFOR
AUPAIR
AUTEUR
AUTHOR
AVATAR
AVOWER

•AR•••
BARBED
BARBEL
BARBER
BARBET
BARBIE
BARBRA
BARDIC
BARDOT
BAREGE
BARELY
BAREST
BARFLY
BARGED
BARGES
BARHOP
BARING
BARITE
BARIUM
BARKED
BARKER
BARKIN
BARLEY
BARMAN
BARMEN
BARNES
BARNEY
BARNUM
BAROJA
BAROLO
BARONG
BARONS
BARONY
BARQUE
BARRED
BARREL
BARREN
BARRES
BARRIE
BARRIO
BARRIS
BARRON
BARROW
BARTAB
BARTER
BARTOK
BARTON
BARUCH
BARYON
BARZUN
CARAFE
CARATS
CARBON
CARBOY
CARDED
CARDER
CARDIN
CARDIO
CAREEN
CAREER
CARESS
CARETO
CARETS
CARFUL
CARGOS
CARHOP
CARIBE
CARIBS
CARIES
CARINA
CARING
CARLOS
CARLOT
CARMAN
CARMEL
CARMEN
CARNAL
CARNES
CARNET
CARNEY
CARNOT
CAROBS
CAROLE
CAROLS
CAROMS
CARONI
CARPAL
CARPED
CARPEL
CARPER
CARPET
CARPUS
CARREL
CARREY
CARRIE
CARROL
CARROT
CARSON
CARTED
CARTEL
CARTER
CARTES
CARTON
CARUSO
CARVED
CARVER
CARVES
CARVEY
DARETO
DARIEN
DARING
DARIUS
DARKEN
DARKER
DARKLE
DARKLY
DARNAY
DARNED
DARNEL
DARNER
DARNIT
DARREN
DARROW
DARRYL
DARTED
DARTER
DARWIN
EARFUL
EARING
EARLAP
EARNED
EARNER
EARTHA
EARTHY
EARWAX
EARWIG
FARADS
FARCED
FARCES
FARCRY
FARERS
FARINA
FARING
FARLEY
FARLOW
FARMED
FARMER
FAROFF
FAROUK
FAROUT
FARRAH
FARRAR
FARROW
GARAGE
GARBED
GARBLE
GARCIA
GARCON
GARDEN
GARETH
GARGLE
GARISH
GARLIC
GARNER
GARNET
GARRET
GARSON
GARTER
GARTHS
GARVEY
HARARE
HARASS
HARBIN
HARBOR
HARDEN
HARDER
HARDLY
HARDUP
HAREMS
HARING
HARKED
HARKEN
HARKER
HARLAN
HARLEM
HARLEY
HARLOW
HARMED
HARMON
HAROLD
HARPED
HARPER
HARPON
HARRIS
HARROW
HARVEY
JARFUL
JARGON
JARRAH
JARRED
KARATE
KARATS
KAREEM
KARIBA
KARMIC
KARNAK
KAROSS
KARPOV
KARRAS
KARROO
KARSTS
LARAMS
LARDED
LARDER
LARDON
LAREDO
LARGER
LARGOS
LARIAT
LARKED
LAROSA
LARRUP
LARSEN
LARSON
LARVAE
LARVAL
LARVAS
LARYNX
MARACA
MARAUD
MARBLE
MARBLY
MARCEL
MARCHE
MARCIA
MARCIE
MARCOS
MARCUS
MARDUK
MARGAY
MARGIE
MARGIN
MARGOT
MARIAH
MARIAN
MARIEL
MARIKO
MARILU
MARINA
MARINE
MARINO
MARION
MARISA
MARIST
MARIUS
MARKED
MARKER
MARKET
MARKKA
MARKUP
MARLED
MARLEE
MARLEY
MARLIN
MARLON
MARMEE
MARMOT
MARNER
MARNIE
MAROON
MARPLE
MARQUE
MARRED
MARRON
MARROW
MARSHA
MARSHY
MARTEL
MARTEN
MARTHA
MARTIN
MARTYR
MARVEL
MARVIN
NARIAL
NARNIA
NARROW
NARVIK
NARWAL
OARING
PARADE
PARANA
PARANG
PARAPH
PARCAE
PARCEL
PARDON
PARENS
PARENT
PARERS
PARETO
PAREVE
PARGET
PARIAH
PARING
PARISH
PARITY
PARKAS
PARKAY
PARKED
PARKER
PARLAY
PARLEY
PARLOR
PARNIS
PARODY
PAROLE
PARRED
PARREL
PARRIS
PARROT
PARSEC
PARSED
PARSEE
PARSER
PARSES
PARSON
PARTED
PARTLY
PARTON
PARULA
PARURE
PARVIS
RAREFY
RARELY
RAREST
RARIFY
RARING
RARITY
SARANS
SARDIS
SARGES
SARGON
SARGOS
SARODS
SARONG
SARTON
SARTRE
TARAWA
TARGES
TARGET
TARIFF
TARING
TARMAC
TAROTS
TARPAN
TARPIT
TARPON
TARRED
TARSAL
TARSUS
TARTAN
TARTAR
TARTER
TARTLY
TARZAN
VARDEN
VARESE
VARIED
VARIES
VARLET
VARNAS
VARNEY
VARUNA
WARBLE
WARCRY
WARDED
WARDEN
WARDER
WARGOD
WARHOL
WARIER
WARILY
WARING
WARMED
WARMER
WARMLY
WARMTH
WARMUP
WARNED
WARNER
WARPED
WARRED
WARREN
WARSAW
YARDED
YARELY
YARNED
YARROW
ZAREBA

•A•R••
BAIRNS
BARRED
BARREL
BARREN
BARRES
BARRIE
BARRIO
BARRIS
BARRON
BARROW
BAYRUM
CADRES
CAIRNS
CAPRIS
CARREL
CARREY
CARRIE
CARROL
CARROT
CATRIG
DACRON
DAIREN
DARREN
DARROW
DARRYL
EAGRES
FABRAY
FABRIC
FAERIE
FAEROE
FAIRED
FAIRER
FAIRLY
FAIRUP
FARRAH
FARRAR
FARROW
GARRET
HADRON
HAIRDO
HAIRED
HARRIS
HARROW
HATRED
IATRIC
JARRAH
JARRED
JAURES
KARRAS
KARROO
KAURIS
LABREA
LABRET
LABRUM
LAIRDS
LARRUP
LAUREL
LAUREN
LAURIE
MACRAE
MACRON
MACROS
MADRAS
MADRES
MADRID
MANRAY
MAORIS
MARRED
MARRON
MARROW
MATRIX
MATRON
MAURYA
NAIRAS
NARROW
NATRON
PADRES
PAIRED
PAIRUP
PARRED
PARREL
PARRIS
PARROT
PATROL
PATRON
RAGRUG
RAHRAH
RAMROD
SABRAS
SABRES
SACRAL
SACRED
SACRUM
SATRAP
SAUREL
SAWRED
TABRIZ
TARRED
TAURUS
TAYRAS
VANRYN
WALRUS
WARRED
WARREN
YARROW
ZAGREB

•A••R•
BAKERS
BAKERY
BALERS
BARBRA
BAYARD
CABERS
CAGERS
CAMERA
CANARD
CANARY
CANERS
CAPERS
CASERN
CASTRO
CATERS
CAVERN
CAVERS
CAVORT
DAMORE
DATARY

DATERS
DATURA
EATERS
EATERY
FAKERS
FAKERY
FAKIRS
FARCRY
FARERS
FAVORS
GABBRO
GALORE
GANTRY
GAPERS
GASTRO
GATERS
GATORS
HALERS
HALERU
HARARE
HASBRO
HATARI
HATERS
HAZARD
HAZERS
JABIRU
JAPERS
JAPERY
JAVARI
KAGERA
LABORS
LACERS
LADERS
LAGERS
LAHORE
LAKERS
LAMARR
LANDRY
LASERS
LAVERS
LAYERS
MADERO
MADURA
MADURO
MAITRE
MAJORS
MAKERS
MALORY
MANORS
MANTRA
MASERS
MASERU
MATERS
MATURE
MAYORS
MAZERS
NABORS
NADIRS
NAMERS
NAPERY
NATURE
OATERS
PACERS
PAGERS
PAHARI
PALTRY
PAMIRS
PANFRY
PANTRY
PAPERS
PAPERY
PAPYRI
PARERS
PARURE
PASTRY
PAVERS
PAWERS
PAYERS
QATARI
RACERS
RAKERS
RANDRY
RATERS
RAVERS
RAZORS
SABERS
SAFARI
SAFIRE
SAHARA
SAKERS
SALARY
SAMARA
SANDRA
SAPORS
SARTRE
SATIRE
SATORI
SATURN
SATYRS
SAVERS
SAVORS
SAVORY
SAYERS
TABARD
TABORS
TAGORE
TAKERS
TAMARA
TAMERS
TANTRA
TAPERS
TAPIRS
TATARS
TATERS
TAVERN
TAWDRY
TAXERS
UAKARI
VAGARY
VALERY
VAPORS
WADERS
WAFERS
WAGERS
WALERS
WANERS
WARCRY
WATERS
WATERY
WAVERS
WAVERY
WAXERS
ZADORA

•A•••R

AAFAIR
BACKER
BADGER
BAGGER
BAILER
BAILOR
BALDER
BANGER
BANGOR
BANKER
BANNER
BANTER
BARBER
BARKER
BARTER
BASTER
BATHER
BATTER
BAWLER
BAXTER
BAYLOR
BAZAAR
CABLER
CADGER
CAESAR
CAGIER
CAHIER
CALDER
CALLER
CALMER
CAMBER
CAMPER
CANDOR
CANKER
CANNER
CANTER
CANTOR
CAPPER
CAPTOR
CARDER
CAREER
CARPER
CARTER
CARVER
CASPAR
CASPER
CASTER
CASTOR
CATHER
CAVIAR
CAWDOR
DAFTER
DAGGER
DAMMAR
DAMOUR
DAMPER
DANCER
DANDER
DANGER
DANKER
DANNER
DAPPER
DARKER
DARNER
DARTER
DASHER
DAUBER
EARNER
EASIER
EASTER
FABLER
FACTOR
FAFNIR
FAIRER
FALSER
FALTER
FARMER
FARRAR
FASTER
FATHER
FATTER
FAVOUR
FAWNER
GABBER
GADDER
GAFFER
GAINER
GAITER
GAMIER
GANDER
GARNER
GARTER
GASPAR
GASSER
GATHER
GAUGER
GAWKER
GAYNOR
HACKER
HALTER
HAMMER
HAMPER
HANGAR
HANGER
HANKER
HARBOR
HARDER
HARKER
HARPER
HATHOR
HATTER
HAULER
HAWKER
HAWSER
HAZIER
JABBAR
JABBER
JAEGER
JAGGER
JAGUAR
JAILER
JAIPUR
JAMMER
JASPER
JAVIER
KAFFIR
KAISER
KALMAR
KANDER
KANTOR
LAAGER
LABOUR
LACIER
LADDER
LADLER
LAFFER
LAGGER
LAMARR
LAMOUR
LANCER
LANDER
LANGUR
LANIER
LANKER
LARDER
LARGER
LASCAR
LASHER
LASSER
LATHER
LATOUR
LATTER
LAUDER
LAUPER
LAWYER
LAYFOR
LAZIER
MADDER
MAGYAR
MAHLER
MAHZOR
MAILER
MANGER
MANNER
MAPPER
MARKER
MARNER
MARTYR
MASHER
MASKER
MASTER
MATHER
MATTER
MAULER
MAUSER
NABBER
NAGGER
NAILER
NAPIER
NAPPER
NASCAR
NASSER
NATTER
OATIER
PACKER
PADDER
PALLOR
PALMER
PALTER
PAMPER
PANDER
PANNER
PANZER
PAPIER
PARKER
PARLOR
PARSER
PASSER
PASTOR
PATTER
PAUPER
PAWNER
PAYFOR
RACIER
RADNER
RAFTER
RAIDER
RAILER
RAINER
RAIPUR
RAISER
RANCOR
RANFOR
RANGER
RANKER
RANTER
RAPIER
RAPPER
RAPTOR
RASHER
RASPER
RASTER
RATEDR
RATHER
RATTER
SACKER
SADDER
SAILOR
SALTER
SALVER
SALVOR
SAMBAR
SANDER
SANGER
SANTIR
SAPPER
SASSER
SAUCER
SAUGER
SAVIOR
SAVOIR
SAVOUR
SAWYER
TACKER
TAILOR
TALKER
TALLER
TAMPER
TANKER
TANNER
TAPPER
TARTAR
TARTER
TASTER
TATTER
TAUTER
TAYLOR
VAGUER
VAINER
VALOUR
VAMPER
VANIER
VAPOUR
VASSAR
VASTER
WAGNER
WAILER
WAITER
WAIVER
WALKER
WALLER
WALTER
WANDER
WANNER
WAPNER
WARDER
WARIER
WARMER
WARNER
WASHER
WASTER
WAVIER
WAXIER
XAVIER
YAKKER
YAMMER
YASSER
YAWNER
YAWPER
ZAFFER
ZANDER
ZANIER
ZAPPER

••AR••

ACARID
ACARUS
AGARIC
ALARIC
ALARMS
ALARUM
ARARAT
AWARDS
BEARDS
BEARER
BEARON
BEARUP
BLARED
BLARES
BOARDS
CHARGE
CHARLY
CHARMS
CHARON
CHARRO
CHARTS
CIARDI
CLARET
CLARKE
CLAROS
COARSE
DEARER
DEARIE
DEARLY
DEARME
DEARTH
DHARMA
DUARTE
DWARFS
ECARTE
EPARCH
EXARCH
FEARED
FEARER
FLARED
FLARES
GEARED
GEARTO
GEARUP
GHARRY
GLARED
GLARES
GNARLS
GNARLY
GUARDS
HEARER
HEAROF
HEARST
HEARTH
HEARTS
HEARTY
HEARYE
HOARDS
HOARSE
ICARIA
ICARUS
IMARET
INARCH
INAROW
INARUT
JUAREZ
KNARRY
LEARNS
LEARNT
NEARBY
NEARED
NEARER
NEARLY
NEARTO
OZARKS
PEARLS
PEARLY
PHAROS
QUARKS
QUARRY
QUARTO
QUARTS
QUARTZ
REARED
REARER
REARMS
REARUP
ROARED
ROARER
SCARAB
SCARCE
SCARED
SCARER
SCARES
SCARFS
SCARNE
SCARPS
SCARUM
SEARCH
SEARED
SEARLE
SHARDS
SHARED
SHARER
SHARES
SHARIA
SHARIF
SHARKS
SHARON
SHARPS
SMARMY
SMARTS
SMARTY
SNARED
SNARES
SNARLS
SNARLY
SOARED
SOARER
SOARES
SPARED
SPARER
SPARES
SPARGE
SPARKS
SPARKY
SPARSE
SPARTA
STARCH
STARED
STARER
STARES
STARRY
STARTS
STARVE
SWARAJ
SWARDS
SWARMS
SWARTH
TEARAT
TEARED
TEARUP
TIARAS
TUAREG
UNARMS
WEARER
WHARFS
YEARLY
YEARNS

••A•R•

BIAFRA
CHAIRS
CHARRO
CLAIRE
FIACRE
FLAIRS
GHARRY
GLAIRY
GOAWRY
KHAFRE
KNARRY
MEAGRE
QUADRI
QUARRY
REAIRS
STAIRS
STARRY

••A••R

AGADIR
AMAJOR
AVATAR
BEAKER
BEARER
BEATER
BEAVER
BLAZER
BMAJOR
BOATER
BRACER
BRAVER
BRAYER
BRAZER
CHADOR
CHASER
CLAMOR
CLAWER
CMAJOR
COALER
COAXER
CRATER
CRAVER
DEADER
DEAFER
DEALER
DEARER
DIALER
DIAPER
DLAYER
DMAJOR
DRAPER
DRAWER
ELATER
ELAYER
EMAJOR
ENAMOR
ERASER
EVADER
FEARER
FLAKER
FLAVOR
FLAYER
FMAJOR
FRASER
FRAZER
GLAMOR
GLASER
GLAZER
GMAJOR
GNAWER
GRADER
GRATER
GRAVER
GRAYER
GRAZER
HEADER
HEALER
HEARER
HEATER
HEAVER
HOAXER
IMAGER
INANER
IRATER
ISADOR
KRAMER
KRATER
LAAGER
LEADER
LEAKER
LEANER
LEAPER
LEASER
LOADER
LOAFER
LOANER
MEAGER
MEANER
MOANER
NEARER
NEATER
ONAGER
ORATOR
PHASER
PLACER
PLANAR
PLANER
PLATER
PLAYER
PRATER
PRAYER
QUAKER
QUASAR
QUAVER
READER
REALER
REAMER
REAPER
REARER
ROAMER
ROARER
SCALAR
SCALER
SCARER
SEALER
SEATER
SHAKER
SHAMIR
SHAPER
SHARER
SHAVER
SKATER
SLATER
SLAVER
SLAYER
SOAKER
SOAPER
SOARER
SPACER
SPADER
SPARER
STAGER
STALER
STARER
STATER
STATOR
SUAVER
SWAYER
TEASER
THALER
THAYER
TRACER
TRADER
WEAKER
WEARER
WEAVER
WHALER
YEAGER

•••AR•

ABOARD
AGLARE
AIRARM
ALTARS
AMHARA
ANKARA
APIARY
ARCARO
ASGARD
ASHARP
ASKARI
ASMARA
ATTARS
AVIARY
AWEARY
AYMARA
BAYARD
BEWARE
BICARB
BIHARI
BINARY
BLEARS
BLEARY
BOGART
BOVARY
BOYARS
BRIARD
BRIARS
BSHARP
CANARD
CANARY
CEDARS
CESARE
CIGARS
CLEARS
COWARD
CSHARP
CUNARD
CURARE
DATARY
DEBARK
DEBARS
DEPART
DINARS
DISARM
DOTARD
DREARY
DSHARP
EDGARD
EDGARS
EDUARD
EDVARD
EDWARD
EMBARK
ERHARD
ESCARP
ESHARP
FIGARO
FRIARS
FRIARY
FSHARP
FUGARD
GEMARA
GERARD
GIRARD
GOCART
GODARD
GOKART
GSHARP
HARARE
HATARI
HAZARD
HEGARI
HILARY
HOBART
HOWARD
IDCARD
IMPART
INPART
INWARD
IZZARD
JAVARI
LAMARR
LIZARD
MEGARA
MOLARS
MOZART
NEWARK
NONARY
NOTARY
OLEARY
ONWARD
OSCARS
OXCART
OXNARD
PAHARI
PETARD
PICARA
PICARD
PICARO
POPART
QATARI
REBARS
REGARD
REMARK
RETARD
RETARS
REWARD
REWARM
RITARD
ROSARY
ROTARY
SAFARI
SAHARA
SALARY
SAMARA
SENARY
SEWARD
SHEARS
SITARS
SMEARS
SMEARY
SOUARI
SPEARS
SQUARE
STMARK
STUART
SUBARU
SUGARS
SUGARY
SWEARS
TABARD
TAMARA
TATARS
THWART
TOWARD
TULARE
UAKARI
UNBARS
UNWARY
UPWARD
VAGARY
VICARS
VOLARE
VOTARY
WIZARD

•••A•R

AAFAIR
AFFAIR
ALTAIR
AUPAIR
BAZAAR
BELAIR
ECLAIR
HOTAIR
IMPAIR
LAMARR
MCNAIR
MIDAIR
MOHAIR
REPAIR
UNFAIR

••••AR

ALEGAR
ALOMAR
ALULAR
ANSGAR
APPEAR
ASHLAR
AVATAR
BAZAAR
BEGGAR
BOWOAR
BOXCAR
BULGAR
BURSAR
BUSBAR
CAESAR
CASPAR
CAVIAR
CELLAR
CHUKAR
COLLAR
COSTAR
COUGAR
DAMMAR
DEODAR
DISBAR
DOGEAR
DOLLAR
DUNBAR
DURBAR
ENDEAR
FARRAR
FOLIAR
FULMAR
GASPAR
GUITAR
GUNNAR
HANGAR
HOTCAR
HOTWAR
HUSSAR
INGEAR
INGMAR
INSTAR
ISHTAR
ISOBAR
JABBAR
JAGUAR
KALMAR
KEVLAR
LASCAR
LEKVAR
LINEAR
LOTHAR
LUMBAR
MAGYAR
MEDGAR
MEDLAR
MOLNAR
MORTAR
NASCAR
NECTAR
NEWMAR
OCULAR
OVULAR
PEDLAR
PILLAR
PINDAR
PLANAR
POPLAR
PREWAR
PULSAR
QINTAR
QUASAR
REHEAR
SAMBAR
SCALAR
SHOFAR
SIRDAR
STELAR
TARTAR
THENAR
TINEAR
TOWCAR
TROCAR
UPROAR
UVULAR
VASSAR
VULGAR
WEIMAR
WETBAR

AS••••

ASANAS
ASBURY
ASCEND
ASCENT
ASCHAM
ASCOTS
ASGARD
ASHARP
ASHCAN
ASHIER
ASHLAR
ASHLEY
ASHORE
ASHRAM
ASIANS
ASIDES
ASIMOV
ASKARI
ASKERS
ASKFOR
ASKING
ASKOUT
ASLANT
ASLEEP
ASLOPE
ASMARA
ASOSAN
ASPECT
ASPENS
ASPERA
ASPICS
ASPIRE
ASSAIL
ASSAYS
ASSENT
ASSERT
ASSESS
ASSETS
ASSIGN
ASSISI
ASSIST
ASSIZE
ASSORT
ASSUME
ASSURE
ASTERN
ASTERS
ASTRAL
ASTRAY
ASTRID
ASTROS
ASTUTE
ASWELL
ASWIRL
ASWOON
ASYLUM

A•S•••

ABSENT
ABSORB
ABSURD
ADSORB
AISLES
ALSACE
AMSTEL
ANSATE
ANSELM
ANSGAR
ANSWER
ARSENE
ASSAIL
ASSAYS
ASSENT
ASSERT
ASSESS
ASSETS
ASSIGN
ASSISI
ASSIST
ASSIZE
ASSORT
ASSUME
ASSURE
ATSTUD
AUSPEX
AUSSIE
AUSTEN
AUSTIN
AUSTRO
AXSEED

A••S••

ABASED
ABASES
ABUSED
ABUSER
ABUSES
ABYSMS
ACESUP
ACTSON
ACTSUP
ADDSIN
ADDSON
ADDSTO
ADDSUP
ADESTE
AGASSI
AIMSAT
AIMSTO
AIRSAC
ALASKA
ALISON

ALLSET
ALYSSA
AMOSOZ
AMUSED
AMUSES
ARISEN
ARISES
ARISTA
ARISTO
ASOSAN
ATESTS
AUSSIE
AVESTA
AVISOS
AYESHA

A•••S•

ABBESS
ABLEST
ABLUSH
ACCESS
ACCOST
ACCUSE
ACROSS
ADJUST
ADVISE
AFRESH
AGASSI
AGEISM
AGEIST
AGHAST
AHIMSA
ALDOSE
ALEAST
ALMOST
ALONSO
ALWEST
ALYSSA
AMBUSH
AMIDST
AORIST
APPOSE
APTEST
ARGOSY
ARIOSE
ARIOSO
ARLISS
ARNESS
AROUSE
ARREST
ARTIST
ASSESS
ASSISI
ASSIST
ATBEST
ATCOST
ATEASE
ATLAST
ATMOST
ATREST
ATRISK
ATTEST
AUGUST
AVERSE
AVULSE

A••••S

ABACAS
ABACUS
ABASES
ABATES
ABATIS
ABBESS
ABBEYS
ABBOTS
ABELES
ABHORS
ABIDES
ABODES
ABOHMS
ABOMBS
ABORTS
ABRAMS
ABUSES
ABYDOS
ABYSMS
ACARUS
ACCESS
ACEOUS
ACINUS
ACORNS
ACROSS
ACTORS
ADAGES
ADAPTS
ADDAMS
ADDERS
ADDLES
ADDONS
ADEEMS
ADEPTS
ADIDAS
ADIEUS
ADLIBS
ADMITS
ADOBES
ADONIS
ADOPTS
ADORES
ADORNS
ADULTS
AEETES
AENEAS
AEOLUS
AERIES
AFLATS
AGAMAS
AGATES
AGAVES
AGENAS
AGENTS
AGGIES
AGLETS
AGORAS
AGREES
AILERS
AIRBUS
AISLES
AKELAS
AKENES
AKITAS
ALAMOS
ALARMS
ALBUMS
ALDERS
ALDOUS
ALEPHS
ALERTS
ALEUTS
ALEXIS
ALIBIS
ALIENS
ALIGNS
ALINES
ALKYDS
ALKYLS
ALLAYS
ALLEES
ALLEYS
ALLIES
ALLOTS
ALLOWS
ALLOYS
ALOHAS
ALOINS
ALPHAS
ALTARS
ALTERS
ALWAYS
AMADIS
AMATIS
AMAZES
AMBERS
AMBITS
AMBLES
AMEBAS
AMEERS
AMENDS
AMENTS
AMICES
AMICUS
AMIDES
AMIENS
AMIGOS
AMINES
AMINUS
AMOLES
AMOURS
AMPULS
AMUSES
AMVETS
ANDRES
ANDROS
ANGELS
ANGERS
ANGLES
ANGLOS
ANIMAS
ANIMES
ANIMUS
ANIONS
ANJOUS
ANKLES
ANNALS
ANNOYS
ANNULS
ANODES
ANOLES
ANTICS
ANTRES
ANUBIS
ANVILS
AODAIS
AORTAS
APEXES
APHIDS
APICES
APPALS
APPLES
APRONS
ARAMIS
ARBORS
ARCHES
ARDEBS
ARDORS
ARECAS
ARENAS
ARETES
ARGOTS
ARGUES
ARISES
ARLISS
ARMETS
ARMIES
ARMORS
ARNESS
AROIDS
AROMAS
ARRAYS
ARROWS
ARTELS
ARTOIS
ARYANS
ASANAS
ASCOTS
ASIANS
ASIDES
ASKERS
ASPENS
ASPICS
ASSAYS
ASSESS
ASSETS
ASTERS
ASTROS
ATBATS
ATEAMS
ATESTS
ATHENS
ATKINS
ATODDS
ATOLLS
ATONES
ATREUS
ATTARS
ATTICS
AUDENS
AUDIOS
AUDITS
AUGERS
AUGHTS
AUGURS
AUREUS
AUROUS
AUXINS
AVAILS
AVERTS
AVIANS
AVISOS
AVOIDS
AWAITS
AWAKES
AWARDS
AXIOMS
AXIONS
AZORES
AZTECS

•AS•••

BASALT
BASELY
BASEST
BASHED
BASHES
BASICS
BASING
BASINS
BASKED
BASKET
BASQUE
BASSES
BASSET
BASSOS
BASTED
BASTER
BASTES
CASABA
CASALS
CASAVA
CASBAH
CASERN
CASHED
CASHES
CASHEW
CASHIN
CASING
CASINO
CASPAR
CASPER
CASQUE
CASSIA
CASSIO
CASSIS
CASTER
CASTES
CASTLE
CASTON
CASTOR
CASTRO
CASUAL
DASHED
DASHER
DASHES
DASSIN
EASEIN
EASELS
EASEUP
EASIER
EASILY
EASING
EASTER
EASTON
FASCES
FASCIA
FASTED
FASTEN
FASTER
GASBAG
GASCAP
GASCON
GASHED
GASHES
GASJET
GASKET
GASKIN
GASLIT
GASLOG
GASMAN
GASMEN
GASPAR
GASPED
GASSED
GASSER
GASSES
GASTON
GASTRO
HASBRO
HASHED
HASHES
HASPED
HASSAM
HASSAN
HASSLE
HASTEN
HASTES
JASCHA
JASPER
KASBAH
LASCAR
LASERS
LASHED
LASHER
LASHES
LASHIO
LASHUP
LASSEN
LASSER
LASSES
LASSIE
LASSOS
LASTED
LASTEX
LASTLY
MASADA
MASAIS
MASCOT
MASERS
MASERU
MASHED
MASHER
MASHES
MASHIE
MASKED
MASKER
MASONS
MASQUE
MASSED
MASSES
MASSEY
MASSIF
MASTER
MASTIC
NASALS
NASCAR
NASDAQ
NASEBY
NASHUA
NASSAU
NASSER
PASCAL
PASEOS
PASHAS
PASHTO
PASSBY
PASSED
PASSEL
PASSER
PASSES
PASSIM
PASSUP
PASTAS
PASTED
PASTEL
PASTES
PASTIS
PASTOR
PASTRY
RASCAL
RASHAD
RASHER
RASHES
RASHID
RASHLY
RASPED
RASPER
RASSLE
RASTER
SASEBO
SASHAY
SASHED
SASHES
SASSED
SASSER
SASSES
TASKED
TASMAN
TASSEL
TASSES
TASTED
TASTER
TASTES
VASHTI
VASLAV
VASSAL
VASSAR
VASTER
VASTLY
WASABI
WASHED
WASHER
WASHES
WASHOE
WASHUP
WASTED
WASTER
WASTES
YASSER

•A•S••

BABSON
BALSAM
BASSES
BASSET
BASSOS
CAESAR
CAPSID
CARSON
CASSIA
CASSIO
CASSIS
CATSUP
CAUSAL
CAUSED
CAUSES
DAISES
DAMSEL
DAMSON
DAMSUP
DANSON
DASSIN
DATSUN
DAWSON
EATSAT
EATSIN
EATSUP
FAISAL
FALSER
GARSON
GASSED
GASSER
GASSES
GATSBY
HALSEY
HANSEL
HANSOM
HANSON
HASSAM
HASSAN
HASSLE
HAUSAS
HAWSER
HAWSES
JAMSIN
JAMSUP
JANSEN
KAISER
KANSAN
KANSAS
KARSTS
LANSON
LAPSED
LAPSES
LAPSUP
LARSEN
LARSON
LASSEN
LASSER
LASSES
LASSIE
LASSOS
LAWSON
LAYSBY
LAYSIN
LAYSON
LAYSTO
LAYSUP
MAISIE
MANSES
MARSHA
MARSHY
MASSED
MASSES
MASSEY
MASSIF
MAUSER
NANSEN
NASSAU
NASSER
NAUSEA
NAYSAY
PARSEC
PARSED
PARSEE
PARSER
PARSES
PARSON
PASSBY
PASSED
PASSEL
PASSER
PASSES
PASSIM
PASSUP
PAUSED
PAUSES
PAWSAT
PAYSIN
PAYSON
PAYSUP
RAISED
RAISER
RAISES
RAISIN
RAMSAY
RAMSES
RAMSEY
RAMSON
RANSOM
RASSLE
RATSON
SALSAS
SAMSON
SANSEI
SASSED
SASSER
SASSES
SAYSOS
TAGSUP
TARSAL
TARSUS
TASSEL
TASSES
VAISYA
VASSAL
VASSAR
WADSUP
WAISTS
WARSAW
WATSON
WAUSAU
YASSER

•A••S•

BANISH
BAREST
BASEST
CALASH
CAMISE
CARESS
CARUSO
CAYUSE
DALASI
DAMASK
DANISH
FAMISH
GAINST
GALOSH
GAMEST
GARISH
GAYEST
HALEST
HARASS
HAVASU
KAROSS
LAGASH
LAMESA
LAMEST
LANOSE
LAOTSE
LAROSA
LATEST
LATISH
LAVISH
LAXEST
MAOISM
MAOIST
MARISA
MARIST
OAFISH
PALEST
PALISH
PARISH
RADISH
RAKISH
RAMOSE
RAREST
RAVISH
RAWEST
SAFEST
SAGEST
SALISH
SAMOSA
SANEST
TALESE
TAMEST
TANIST
TAOISM
TAOIST
VADOSE
VALISE
VANISH
VARESE
WABASH
WALESA
WATUSI

•A•••S

BABIES
BABKAS
BABULS
BACKUS
BADGES
BAGELS
BAINES
BAIRNS
BAKERS
BALERS
BANJOS
BANTUS
BARGES
BARNES
BARONS
BARRES
BARRIS
BASHES
BASICS
BASINS
BASSES
BASSOS
BASTES
BATHES
BATHOS
BATIKS
BATONS
BAUCIS
BAYOUS
CABALS
CABERS
CABINS
CABLES
CACAOS
CACHES
CACTUS
CADDIS
CADETS
CADGES
CADMUS
CADRES
CAGERS
CAGUAS
CAHOWS
CAICOS
CAIRNS
CAJUNS
CALAIS
CALCES
CALLAS
CALLES
CALLUS
CALVES
CALXES
CAMELS
CAMEOS
CAMPOS
CAMPUS
CANALS
CANERS
CANIDS
CANNES
CANOES
CANONS
CANTOS
CANVAS
CAPERS
CAPIAS
CAPONS
CAPRIS
CARATS
CARESS
CARETS
CARGOS
CARIBS
CARIES
CARLOS
CARNES
CAROBS
CAROLS
CAROMS
CARPUS
CARTES
CARVES
CASALS
CASHES
CASSIS
CASTES
CATERS
CAUCUS
CAULKS
CAUSES
CAVERS
CAVILS
DACHAS
DADOES
DAISES
DALLAS
DALLES
DANAUS
DANCES
DANTES
DARIUS
DASHES
DATERS
DAUBES
DAUNTS
DAVIES
DAVITS
EAGLES
EAGRES
EASELS
EATERS
FABLES
FACETS
FACIES
FAGOTS
FAINTS
FAITHS
FAKERS
FAKIRS
FAMOUS
FARADS
FARCES
FARERS
FASCES
FAUCES
FAULTS
FAUNAS
FAUNUS
FAVORS
FAWKES
GABLES
GAFFES
GALOIS
GALOPS
GAMAYS
GAMINS
GAMMAS
GAMUTS
GANGES
GAPERS
GARTHS
GASHES
GASSES
GATERS
GATORS
GAUGES
GAUZES
GAVELS
GAYALS
HABEAS
HABITS
HACEKS
HADJES
HADJIS
HAGGIS
HAIDAS
HAIKUS
HAINES
HAJJES
HAJJIS
HAKIMS
HALERS
HALLOS
HALOES
HALVES
HAMALS
HARASS
HAREMS
HARRIS
HASHES
HASTES
HATERS
HAUNTS
HAUSAS
HAVENS
HAVOCS
HAWSES
HAZANS
HAZELS
HAZERS
JABOTS
JACALS
JAMUPS
JANHUS
JAPANS
JAPERS
JAUNTS
JAURES
JAZZES
KABOBS
KANSAS
KAPPAS
KARATS
KAROSS
KARRAS
KARSTS
KAUNAS
KAURIS
KAYAKS
KAZAKS
KAZOOS
LABELS
LABORS
LACERS
LACHES
LADERS
LADIES
LADLES
LAGERS
LAIRDS
LAKERS
LAMEDS
LAMIAS
LAMMAS
LANAIS
LANCES
LANDIS
LAPELS
LAPINS
LAPSES
LARAMS
LARGOS
LARVAS
LASERS
LASHES
LASSES
LASSOS
LATENS
LATHES
LATINS
LATKES
LAUGHS
LAVERS
LAYBYS
LAYERS
LAYUPS
MACAWS
MACHES
MACHOS
MACROS
MADAMS
MADRAS
MADRES
MAGMAS
MAHDIS
MAIDUS
MAILES
MAIZES
MAJLIS
MAJORS
MAKERS
MALAYS
MAMBAS
MAMBOS
MAMMAS
MANAUS
MANGOS
MANIAS
MANORS
MANSES
MANTAS
MANTIS
MAORIS
MAPLES
MAQUIS
MARCOS
MARCUS
MARIUS
MASAIS
MASERS
MASHES
MASONS
MASSES
MATERS
MATEYS
MATHIS
MATINS
MATTES
MATZOS
MAUVES
MAVENS
MAXIMS
MAYANS
MAYBES
MAYORS
MAZERS
NABOBS
NABORS
NACHOS
NADIRS
NAIADS
NAIRAS
NAMERS
NANTES
NAPLES
NAPPES
NASALS
NAVELS
NAVIES
NAWABS
OATERS
PACERS
PADRES
PAEANS
PAEONS
PAGANS
PAGERS
PAINTS
PALLAS
PALMAS
PALPUS
PAMIRS
PAMPAS
PANDAS
PANELS
PANICS
PANNES
PAPAWS
PAPERS
PAPPAS
PAPPUS
PARENS
PARERS
PARKAS
PARNIS
PARRIS
PARSES
PARVIS
PASEOS
PASHAS
PASSES
PASTAS
PASTES
PASTIS
PATENS
PATHOS
PATIOS
PATMOS
PATOIS
PAUSES
PAVERS
PAWERS
PAYEES
PAYERS
QANTAS
RABBIS
RABIES
RACERS
RACHIS
RACONS
RADIOS
RADIUS
RAINES
RAISES
RAJAHS
RAKERS
RAMIES
RAMOUS
RAMSES
RANEES
RANGES
RANIDS
RAPIDS
RASHES
RATELS
RATERS
RATIOS
RAVELS
RAVENS
RAVERS
RAYONS
RAZORS
RAZZES
SABERS
SABINS
SABLES
SABOTS
SABRAS
SABRES
SAHIBS
SAIGAS
SAINTS
SAKERS
SALADS
SALALS
SALONS
SALSAS
SALVES
SALVOS
SAMBAS
SANTOS
SAPORS
SARANS
SARDIS
SARGES
SARGOS
SARODS
SASHES
SASSES
SATINS
SATYRS
SAUCES
SAUDIS
SAULTS
SAUNAS
SAUTES
SAVERS
SAVORS
SAXONS
SAYERS
SAYSOS
SAYYES
TABLAS
TABLES
TABOOS
TABORS
TAIGAS
TAINOS
TAINTS
TAKERS
TAKINS
TALONS
TAMERS
TAMILS
TANGOS
TANKAS
TAPERS
TAPINS
TAPIRS
TARGES
TAROTS
TARSUS
TASSES
TASTES
TATARS
TATERS
TAUNTS
TAUONS
TAUPES
TAURUS
TAXERS

TAXIES
TAYRAS
TAZZAS
VALENS
VALETS
VALOIS
VALUES
VALVES
VAPORS
VARIES
VARNAS
VAULTS
VAUNTS
WADERS
WAFERS
WAGERS
WAGONS
WAHOOS
WAISTS
WAIVES
WAKENS
WALERS
WALLIS
WALRUS
WANERS
WASHES
WASTES
WATERS
WAVERS
WAXERS
YACHTS
YAHOOS
YAKUTS
YALIES
YAPOKS
YAQUIS
ZANIES
ZAYINS

••AS••

ABASED
ABASES
AGASSI
ALASKA
BEASTS
BIASED
BIASES
BLASTS
BOASTS
BRASHY
BRASOV
BRASSY
CEASED
CEASES
CHASED
CHASER
CHASES
CHASMS
CHASSE
CHASTE
CLASPS
CLASSY
COASTS
ERASED
ERASER
ERASES
FEASTS
FIASCO
FLASHY
FLASKS
FRASER
GLASER
GLASSY
GRASPS
GRASSO
GRASSY
ITASCA
LEASED
LEASER
LEASES
MEASLY
MIASMA
NYASSA
OCASEK
OCASEY
OMASUM
PHASED
PHASER
PHASES
PLASHY
PLASMA
PLASMO
PLASTY
QUASAR
REASON
ROASTS
SEASON
SHASTA
SOASTO
SPASMS
STASES
STASIS
TEASED
TEASEL
TEASER
TEASES
TEASET
TOASTS
TOASTY
TRASHY
UKASES
WEASEL
WRASSE
YEASTS
YEASTY

••A•S•

AGASSI
BLAISE
BRAISE
BRASSY
CHAISE
CHASSE
CLASSY
CLAUSE
COARSE
ELAPSE
FRAISE
GDANSK
GLASSY
GRASSO
GRASSY
HEARST
HOARSE
LIAISE
NYASSA
PRAISE
SPARSE
URALSK
WRASSE
ZSAZSA

••A••S

ABACAS
ABACUS
ABASES
ABATES
ABATIS
ACARUS
ADAGES
ADAPTS
AGAMAS
AGATES
AGAVES
ALAMOS
ALARMS
AMADIS
AMATIS
AMAZES
ARAMIS
ASANAS
AVAILS
AWAITS
AWAKES
AWARDS
BEANOS
BEARDS
BEASTS
BEAUTS
BIASES
BLACKS
BLADES
BLAMES
BLANKS
BLARES
BLASTS
BLAZES
BOARDS
BOASTS
BRACES
BRACTS
BRAHMS
BRAIDS
BRAILS
BRAINS
BRAKES
BRANDS
BRANTS
BRAVAS
BRAVES
BRAVOS
BRAWLS
BRAZES
BRAZOS
BWANAS
CEASES
CHAFES
CHAFFS
CHAINS
CHAIRS
CHALKS
CHAMPS
CHANTS
CHARMS
CHARTS
CHASES
CHASMS
CLACKS
CLAIMS
CLAMPS
CLANGS
CLANKS
CLAROS
CLASPS
COAPTS
COASTS
COATIS
COAXES
CRACKS
CRAFTS
CRAKES
CRAMPS
CRANES
CRANKS
CRAPES
CRATES
CRAVES
CRAWLS
CRAZES
DRAFTS
DRAILS
DRAINS
DRAKES
DRAMAS
DRAPES
DRAWLS
DWARFS
EDAMES
ELANDS
ELATES
EMAILS
ENACTS
ENATES
ERASES
EVADES
EXACTS
EXALTS
FEASTS
FLACKS
FLAILS
FLAIRS
FLAKES
FLAMES
FLANKS
FLARES
FLASKS
FLAXES
FRACAS
FRAMES
FRANCS
FRANKS
FRAUDS
GHAZIS
GIANTS
GLACES
GLACIS
GLADES
GLADYS
GLANDS
GLARES
GLAZES
GNARLS
GRACES
GRADES
GRADUS
GRAFTS
GRAILS
GRAINS
GRAMAS
GRAMPS
GRANDS
GRANTS
GRAPES
GRAPHS
GRASPS
GRATES
GRATIS
GRAVES
GRAZES
GUACOS
GUARDS
GUAVAS
HEARTS
HEATHS
HEAVES
HIATUS
HOARDS
HOAXES
HYADES
ICARUS
IMAGES
IRANIS
IRAQIS
KHAKIS
KIANGS
KNACKS
KNAVES
KOALAS
KRAALS
KRAITS
KYACKS
LEARNS
LEASES
LEAVES
LIANAS
LIANGS
LLAMAS
LLANOS
LOAVES
NYALAS
OKAPIS
OMAHAS
OMANIS
ORALES
ORANGS
ORANTS
ORATES
OSAGES
OXALIS
OZARKS
PEARLS
PHAGES
PHAROS
PHASES
PIANOS
PLACES
PLAGES
PLAIDS
PLAINS
PLAITS
PLANES
PLANKS
PLANTS
PLATES
PLAYAS
PLAZAS
PRANKS
PRATES
PRAWNS
PRAXES
PRAXIS
PSALMS
QUACKS
QUAFFS
QUAILS
QUAKES
QUALMS
QUARKS
QUARTS
REACTS
REAIRS
REALES
REALMS
REARMS
REATAS
RIATAS
ROASTS
RUANAS
SCALDS
SCALES
SCALPS
SCAMPS
SCANTS
SCAPES
SCARES
SCARFS
SCARPS
SCAUPS
SEAMUS
SHACKS
SHADES
SHAFTS
SHAKES
SHAKOS
SHALES
SHAMES
SHAMUS
SHANKS
SHAPES
SHARDS
SHARES
SHARKS
SHARPS
SHAVES
SHAWLS
SHAWMS
SKALDS
SKATES
SLACKS
SLAKES
SLANGS
SLANTS
SLATES
SLAVES
SMACKS
SMALLS
SMARTS
SNACKS
SNAFUS
SNAILS
SNAKES
SNARES
SNARLS
SNATHS
SOARES
SOAVES
SPACES
SPADES
SPAHIS
SPALLS
SPANKS
SPARES
SPARKS
SPASMS
SPATES
SPAWNS
STACKS
STAFFS
STAGES
STAINS
STAIRS
STAKES
STALES
STALKS
STALLS
STAMPS
STANDS
STAPES
STARES
STARTS
STASES
STASIS
STATES
STATUS
STAVES
SWAGES
SWAINS
SWALES
SWAMIS
SWAMPS
SWARDS
SWARMS
SWATHS
SWAZIS
TEASES
THALES
THAMES
THANES
THANKS
THATIS
TIARAS
TOASTS
TRACES
TRACKS
TRACTS
TRADES
TRAILS
TRAINS
TRAITS
TRAMPS
TRAVIS
TRAWLS
TWANGS
UKASES
UNARMS
URAEUS
URANUS
USAGES
VIANDS
WEAVES
WHACKS
WHALES
WHARFS
WRACKS
WRATHS
YEARNS
YEASTS

•••AS•

AGHAST
ALEAST
ATEASE
ATLAST
BREAST
BYPASS
BYPAST
CALASH
CREASE
CREASY
DALASI
DAMASK
DEBASE
DYNAST
ELPASO
EMDASH
ENCASE
ENDASH
GOEASY
GREASE
GREASY
HARASS
HAVASU
INCASE
INCASH
KUVASZ
LAGASH
LIPASE
MORASS
MUFASA
NLEAST
OBLAST
PHRASE
PLEASE
POTASH
QUEASY
RECAST
REHASH
REPAST
REWASH
SIWASH
SPLASH
SQUASH
STRASS
THRASH
UNCASE
UNEASE
UNEASY
UNLASH
UNMASK
UPCAST
WABASH
ZYMASE

•••A•S

ABRAMS
ADDAMS
AFLATS
ALLAYS
ALTARS
ALWAYS
ANNALS
AODAIS
APPALS
ARRAYS
ARYANS
ASIANS
ASSAYS
ATBATS
ATEAMS
ATTARS
AVIANS
BELAYS
BLEARS
BLEATS
BLOATS
BOYARS
BREADS
BREAKS
BREAMS
BRIANS
BRIARS
BROADS
BYLAWS
BYPASS
BYWAYS
CABALS
CACAOS
CALAIS
CANALS
CARATS
CASALS
CEDARS
CHEATS
CHIAUS
CIGARS
CLEANS
CLEARS
CLEATS
CLOAKS
CORALS
CREAKS
CREAMS
CROAKS
CROATS
CYCADS
DANAUS
DEBARS
DECAFS
DECALS
DECAYS
DEFATS
DELAYS
DINARS
DIVANS
DREADS
DREAMS
DRYADS
DUCATS
EBOATS
ECLATS
EDGARS
EFLATS
EMBAYS
EPHAHS
EQUALS
ESSAYS
FARADS
FINALS
FLOATS
FORAYS
FREAKS
FRIARS
GAMAYS
GAYALS
GLEAMS
GLEANS
GLOATS
GORALS
GREATS
GROANS
GROATS
GULAGS
HAMALS
HARASS
HAZANS
HBEAMS
HEXADS
HODADS
HOGANS
HUMANS
IBEAMS
IDEALS
INCANS
INLAWS
INLAYS
IOWANS
JACALS
JAPANS
JIHADS
JURATS
KARATS
KAYAKS
KAZAKS
KEBABS
KNEADS
KORATS
KOVACS
KRAALS
KULAKS
LANAIS
LARAMS
LEGALS
LEMANS
LILACS
LOCALS
LOTAHS
MACAWS
MADAMS
MALAYS
MANAUS
MASAIS
MAYANS
MEDALS
METALS
MOLARS
MONADS
MORALS
MORASS
MORAYS
MURALS
MYNAHS
NAIADS
NASALS
NAWABS
NOMADS
OBEAHS
OCEANS
OCTADS
OGHAMS
OREADS
ORGANS
OSCARS
PAEANS
PAGANS
PAPAWS
PECANS
PEDALS
PETALS
PHIALS
PILAFS
PIPALS
PISANS
PLEADS
PLEATS
PROAMS
PTRAPS
RAJAHS
REBAGS
REBARS
RECAPS
RELAYS
REMANS
REMAPS
REPAYS
RETAGS
RETAPS
RETARS
RIVALS
RIYALS
ROMANS
ROYALS
SALADS
SALALS
SARANS
SCRAGS
SCRAMS
SCRAPS
SEDANS
SEPALS
SERACS
SERAIS
SHEAFS
SHEARS
SHOALS
SHOATS
SISALS
SITARS
SKEANS
SMEARS
SNEAKS
SOLANS
SPEAKS
SPEARS
SPLATS
SPLAYS
SPRAGS
SPRATS
SPRAYS
SQUABS
SQUADS
SQUATS
STEADS
STEAKS
STEALS
STEAMS
STOATS
STRADS
STRAPS
STRASS
STRAUS
STRAWS
STRAYS
SUGARS
SUMACS
SURAHS
SWEARS
SWEATS
TATARS
TEPALS
TEXANS
TICALS
TILAKS
TITANS
TOKAYS
TORAHS
TOTALS
TREADS
TREATS
TRIADS
TRIALS
TWEAKS
UBOATS
UCLANS
UGGAMS
UHLANS
UMIAKS
UNBARS
UNCAPS
UNIATS
UNJAMS
UNMANS
UNSAYS
URIALS
USUALS
VEGANS
VICARS
VITALS
VOCALS
VOLANS
WHEATS
WREAKS

••••AS

ABACAS
ADIDAS
AENEAS
AGAMAS
AGENAS
AGORAS
AKELAS
AKITAS
ALOHAS
ALPHAS
AMEBAS
ANIMAS
AORTAS
ARECAS
ARENAS
AROMAS
ASANAS
BABKAS
BETTAS
BIOGAS
BIOTAS
BOREAS
BRAVAS
BURGAS
BURSAS
BWANAS
CAGUAS
CALLAS
CANVAS
CAPIAS
CEIBAS
CESTAS
CHELAS
COBIAS
COBRAS
COCOAS
COMMAS
CONGAS
COSTAS
COTTAS
CYCLAS
DACHAS
DALLAS
DEBRAS
DELTAS
DOBLAS
DOBRAS
DOGMAS
DOLMAS
DONNAS
DORCAS
DRAMAS
ESDRAS
EXTRAS
FAUNAS
FELLAS
FLORAS
FORTAS
FOSSAS
FRACAS
GAMMAS
GRAMAS
GUAVAS
HABEAS
HAIDAS
HAUSAS
HELLAS
HENNAS
HOOHAS
HOSTAS
HUZZAS
HYDRAS
HYENAS
JUNTAS
KANSAS
KAPPAS
KARRAS
KAUNAS
KIOWAS
KOALAS
LAMIAS
LAMMAS
LARVAS
LEHUAS
LEMMAS
LIANAS
LLAMAS
MADRAS
MAGMAS
MAMBAS
MAMMAS
MANIAS
MANTAS
MECCAS
MEDIAS
MENSAS
MILPAS
MOCHAS
MOMMAS
MUDRAS
MULLAS
NAIRAS
NINJAS
NORIAS
NYALAS
OMAHAS
OMEGAS
OPERAS
PALLAS
PALMAS
PAMPAS
PANDAS
PAPPAS
PARKAS
PASHAS
PASTAS
PIETAS
PINNAS
PIZZAS
PLAYAS
PLAZAS
POLKAS
POPPAS
QANTAS
QUOTAS
REATAS
RIATAS
RIOJAS
RUANAS
RUMBAS
SABRAS
SAIGAS
SALSAS
SAMBAS
SAUNAS
SCENAS
SCHWAS
SCUBAS
SEENAS
SENNAS
SEPIAS
SIGMAS
SOLFAS
SPICAS
STOMAS
STUPAS
SUCHAS
SUMMAS
SUTRAS
TABLAS
TAIGAS
TANKAS
TAYRAS
TAZZAS
TESLAS
TETRAS
THETAS
THOMAS
THUJAS
TIARAS
TIBIAS
TOBIAS
TOKLAS
ULTRAS
UMBRAS
UNITAS
UVULAS
VARNAS
VESTAS
VILLAS
VIOLAS
VISTAS
VOLVAS
XHOSAS
YENTAS
YUCCAS
ZEBRAS

AT••••

ATAMAN
ATBATS
ATBEST
ATCOST
ATEAMS
ATEASE
ATEMPO
ATERGO
ATESTS
ATHAND
ATHENA
ATHENE
ATHENS
ATHOME
ATKINS
ATLAST
ATLATL
ATMOST
ATODDS
ATOLLS
ATOMIC
ATONAL
ATONCE
ATONED
ATONES
ATONIC
ATREST
ATREUS
ATRIAL
ATRISK
ATRIUM
ATSTUD
ATTACH
ATTACK
ATTAIN
ATTARS
ATTEND
ATTEST
ATTHAT
ATTICA
ATTICS
ATTILA
ATTIRE
ATTLEE
ATTRIT
ATTUNE
ATWILL
ATWOOD
ATWORK

A•T•••

ACTIII
ACTING
ACTINO
ACTION
ACTIUM
ACTIVE
ACTONE
ACTORS
ACTOUT
ACTSON
ACTSUP
ACTTWO
ACTUAL
AETHER
ALTAIC
ALTAIR
ALTARS
ALTERS
ALTHEA
ALTMAN
AMTRAC
AMTRAK
ANTCOW
ANTEED
ANTERO
ANTEUP
ANTHEM
ANTHER
ANTICS
ANTLER
ANTONY
ANTRES
ANTRIM
ANTRON
ANTRUM
APTEST
ARTELS
ARTERY
ARTFUL
ARTGUM
ARTHRO
ARTHUR
ARTIER
ARTIST
ARTOIS
ARTURO
ASTERN
ASTERS
ASTRAL
ASTRAY
ASTRID
ASTROS
ASTUTE
ATTACH
ATTACK
ATTAIN
ATTARS
ATTEND
ATTEST
ATTHAT
ATTICA
ATTICS
ATTILA
ATTIRE
ATTLEE
ATTRIT
ATTUNE
AUTEUR
AUTHOR
AUTUMN
AZTECS

A••T••

ABATED
ABATES
ABATIS
ACETAL

ACETIC
ACETYL
ACTTWO
ADYTUM
AEETES
AGATES
AGATHA
AKITAS
ALATAU
AMATIS
AMATOL
AMSTEL
AMYTAN
ANATTO
ANITRA
AORTAE
AORTAL
AORTAS
AORTIC
APATHY
ARCTIC
ARETES
ARETHA
ATSTUD
AUNTIE
AUSTEN
AUSTIN
AUSTRO
AVATAR

A•••T•
ABBOTS
ABBOTT
ABLATE
ABORTS
ACUATE
ACUITY
ADAPTS
ADDSTO
ADEPTS
ADESTE
ADMITS
ADNATE
ADOPTS
ADULTS
AERATE
AFLATS
AGENTS
AGLETS
AGNATE
AGOUTI
AIMSTO
AJANTA
ALCOTT
ALECTO
ALERTS
ALEUTS
ALIOTO
ALLOTS
AMBITS
AMENTS
AMVETS
ANATTO
ANSATE
APLITE
AQUATE
ARGOTS
ARISTA
ARISTO
ARMETS
ARNETT
ASCOTS
ASSETS
ASTUTE
ATBATS
ATESTS
ATLATL
AUDITS
AUGHTS
AVANTI
AVERTS
AVESTA
AVIATE
AWAITS

A••••T
ABBOTT
ABDUCT
ABJECT
ABLAUT
ABLEST
ABRUPT
ABSENT
ACCENT
ACCEPT
ACCOST
ACEOUT
ACQUIT
ACTOUT
ADDUCT
ADJUST
ADRIFT
ADROIT
ADVENT
ADVERT
AFFECT
AFLOAT
AFREET
AGEIST
AGHAST
AGLINT
AGOROT
AIGRET
AIMSAT
AIROUT
AJFOYT
ALBEIT
ALBERT
ALCOTT
ALEAST
ALHIRT
ALIGHT
ALLBUT
ALLOUT
ALLSET
ALLWET
ALMOST
ALPERT
ALWEST
AMIDST
AMOUNT
AMULET
ANKLET
ANOINT
AORIST
APTEST
ARAFAT
ARARAT
ARDENT
ARENDT
ARGENT
ARIGHT
ARMLET
ARMPIT
ARNETT
ARPENT
ARRANT
ARREST
ARTIST
ASCENT
ASKOUT
ASLANT
ASPECT
ASSENT
ASSERT
ASSIST
ASSORT
ATBEST
ATCOST
ATLAST
ATMOST
ATREST
ATTEST
ATTHAT
ATTRIT
AUFAIT
AUGUST
AUKLET
AUMONT
AVAUNT
AVOCET

•AT•••
BATAAN
BATBOY
BATEAU
BATHED
BATHER
BATHES
BATHOS
BATIKS
BATING
BATMAN
BATMEN
BATONS
BATTED
BATTEN
BATTER
BATTLE
BATTUE
BATUMI
CATCHY
CATENA
CATERS
CATGUT
CATHAY
CATHER
CATION
CATKIN
CATNAP
CATNIP
CATRIG
CATSUP
CATTED
CATTLE
CATTON
DATARY
DATERS
DATING
DATIVE
DATONG
DATSUN
DATURA
EATERS
EATERY
EATING
EATOUT
EATSAT
EATSIN
EATSUP
FATALE
FATCAT
FATHER
FATHOM
FATIMA
FATTED
FATTEN
FATTER
GATEAU
GATERS
GATHER
GATING
GATLIN
GATORS
GATSBY
HATARI
HATBOX
HATERS
HATHOR
HATING
HATPIN
HATRED
HATTED
HATTER
HATTIE
IATRIC
KATHIE
KATMAI
LATEEN
LATELY
LATENE
LATENS
LATENT
LATEST
LATHED
LATHER
LATHES
LATIGO
LATINA
LATINO
LATINS
LATISH
LATIUM
LATKES
LATONA
LATOUR
LATOYA
LATTEN
LATTER
LATVIA
MATERS
MATEYS
MATHER
MATHIS
MATING
MATINS
MATLIN
MATRIX
MATRON
MATTEA
MATTED
MATTEL
MATTER
MATTES
MATTIE
MATURE
MATZOH
MATZOS
NATANT
NATHAN
NATICK
NATION
NATIVE
NATRON
NATTER
NATURE
OATERS
OATIER
PATACA
PATCHY
PATENS
PATENT
PATHAN
PATHOL
PATHOS
PATINA
PATINE
PATIOS
PATMOS
PATOIS
PATROL
PATRON
PATTED
PATTEN
PATTER
PATTON
QATARI
RATEDG
RATEDR
RATEDX
RATELS
RATERS
RATHER
RATIFY
RATINE
RATING
RATION
RATIOS
RATITE
RATLIN
RATSON
RATTAN
RATTED
RATTER
RATTLE
RATTLY
SATANG
SATEEN
SATING
SATINS
SATINY
SATIRE
SATORI
SATOUT
SATRAP
SATURN
SATYRS
TATAMI
TATARS
TATERS
TATTED
TATTER
TATTLE
TATTOO
VATFUL
WATERS
WATERY
WATNEY
WATSON
WATTLE
WATUSI

•A•T••
BAITED
BALTIC
BANTAM
BANTER
BANTUS
BARTAB
BARTER
BARTOK
BARTON
BASTED
BASTER
BASTES
BATTED
BATTEN
BATTER
BATTLE
BATTUE
BAXTER
CACTUS
CAFTAN
CANTAB
CANTED
CANTER
CANTHI
CANTLE
CANTON
CANTOR
CANTOS
CAPTAN
CAPTOR
CARTED
CARTEL
CARTER
CARTES
CARTON
CASTER
CASTES
CASTLE
CASTON
CASTOR
CASTRO
CATTED
CATTLE
CATTON
CAXTON
DACTYL
DAFTER
DALTON
DANTES
DANTON
DARTED
DARTER
DAYTON
EARTHA
EARTHY
EASTER
EASTON
FACTOR
FAITHS
FALTER
FANTAN
FASTED
FASTEN
FASTER
FATTED
FATTEN
FATTER
GAITED
GAITER
GANTRY
GARTER
GARTHS
GASTON
GASTRO
HAFTED
HALTED
HALTER
HASTEN
HASTES
HATTED
HATTER
HATTIE
KANTOR
LACTIC
LAOTSE
LAOTZU
LAPTEV
LAPTOP
LASTED
LASTEX
LASTLY
LATTEN
LATTER
LAWTON
MADTOM
MAITAI
MAITRE
MALTED
MALTIN
MANTAS
MANTEL
MANTIC
MANTIS
MANTLE
MANTRA
MANTUA
MAOTAI
MARTEL
MARTEN
MARTHA
MARTIN
MARTYR
MASTER
MASTIC
MATTEA
MATTED
MATTEL
MATTER
MATTES
MATTIE
MAYTAG
NANTES
NATTER
NAUTCH
PALTER
PALTRY
PANTED
PANTRY
PARTED
PARTLY
PARTON
PASTAS
PASTED
PASTEL
PASTES
PASTIS
PASTOR
PASTRY
PATTED
PATTEN
PATTER
PATTON
QANTAS
RAFTED
RAFTER
RAGTAG
RAGTOP
RANTED
RANTER
RAPTLY
RAPTOR
RASTER
RATTAN
RATTED
RATTER
RATTLE
RATTLY
SALTED
SALTEN
SALTER
SALTON
SANTEE
SANTIR
SANTOS
SARTON
SARTRE
SAUTES
TACTIC
TAMTAM
TANTRA
TARTAN
TARTAR
TARTER
TARTLY
TASTED
TASTER
TASTES
TATTED
TATTER
TATTLE
TATTOO
TAUTEN
TAUTER
TAUTLY
TAUTOG
VASTER
VASTLY
WAFTED
WAITED
WAITER
WAITON
WAITUP
WALTER
WALTON
WANTAD
WANTED
WANTIN
WANTON
WANTTO
WASTED
WASTER
WASTES
WATTLE
XANTHO
ZAFTIG

•A••T•
BALATA
BARITE
CADETS
CAMETO
CANUTE
CAPITA
CAPOTE
CARATS
CARETO
CARETS
CAVETT
CAVITY
DAINTY
DAKOTA
DALETH
DAMATO
DAMITA
DARETO
DAUNTS
DAVITS
FACETS
FAGOTS
FAINTS
FAJITA
FALLTO
FAULTS
FAULTY
FAWLTY
GAIETY
GALATA
GAMETE
GAMUTS
GARETH
HABITS
HALITE
HAMITE
HAUNTS
JABOTS
JAUNTS
JAUNTY
KARATE
KARATS
KARSTS
LAIDTO
LAKOTA
LANATE
LAPUTA
LAXITY
LAYSTO
MAKUTA
MALATE
MALOTI
MAPUTO
NAMATH
PAINTS
PAIUTE
PALATE
PARETO
PARITY
PASHTO
RABATO
RAMATE
RARITY
RATITE
SABATO
SABOTS
SAFETY
SAINTE
SAINTS
SALUTE
SAMITE
SANCTA
SANGTO
SANITY
SAULTS
SAVATE
TAHITI
TAINTS
TAKETH
TAKETO
TALKTO
TAROTS
TAUNTS
VACATE
VALETS
VANITY
VASHTI
VAULTS
VAUNTS
WAISTS
WANTTO
WAPITI
WARMTH
YACHTS
YAKUTS
ZAPATA

•A•••T
BADLOT
BALLET
BALLOT
BANDIT
BARBET
BARDOT
BAREST
BASALT
BASEST
BASKET
BASSET
CACHET
CADENT
CAMEAT
CAMLET
CANNOT
CAPLET
CAPNUT
CARLOT
CARNET
CARNOT
CARPET
CARROT
CATGUT
CAUGHT
CAVEAT
CAVETT
CAVORT
DACOIT
DARNIT
DAYLIT
EAGLET
EATOUT
EATSAT
FANJET
FANOUT
FAROUT
FATCAT
FAUCET
GADGET
GAINST
GALOOT
GAMBIT
GAMEST
GANNET
GARNET
GARRET
GASJET
GASKET
GASLIT
GAYEST
HAEMAT
HAIGHT
HALEST
HAMLET
HAVEAT
HAVENT
JACKET
LABRET
LAMENT
LAMEST
LAMONT
LANCET
LAPPET
LARIAT
LATENT
LATEST
LAXEST
LAYOUT
MADEIT
MAGNET
MAHOUT
MAKEIT
MALLET
MAOIST
MARGOT
MARIST
MARKET
MARMOT
MASCOT
MAXOUT
NATANT
NAUGHT
PACKET
PALEST
PALLET
PANDIT
PANOUT
PARENT
PARGET
PARROT
PATENT
PAWSAT
PAYOUT
RABBET
RABBIT
RACKET
RAGOUT
RAILAT
RAJPUT
RAMJET
RANOUT
RAREST
RAWEST
SACHET
SAFEST
SAGEST
SALLET
SALYUT
SANEST
SATOUT
SAVANT
SAWFIT
SAWOUT
TABLET
TAGOUT
TALBOT
TALENT
TALKAT
TAMEST
TANIST
TAOIST
TAPOUT
TAPPET
TARGET
TARPIT
TAUGHT
VACANT
VALENT
VARLET
WALLET
WALNUT
WAYOUT

••AT••
ABATED
ABATES
ABATIS
AGATES
AGATHA
ALATAU
AMATIS
AMATOL
ANATTO
APATHY
AVATAR
BEATEN
BEATER
BEATIT
BEATLE
BEATON
BEATTY
BEATUP
BLATTY
BOATED
BOATER
BRATTY
CHATTY
CHATUP
COATED
COATIS
CRATED
CRATER
CRATES
DIATOM
ELATED
ELATER
ELATES
ENATES
FLATLY
GOATEE
GRATED
GRATER
GRATES
GRATIA
GRATIN
GRATIS
HEATED
HEATER
HEATHS
HEATUP
HIATAL
HIATUS
IRATER
KEATON
KLATCH
KRATER
LOATHE
MOATED
NEATEN
NEATER
NEATLY
ORATED
ORATES
ORATOR
PHATIC
PLATED
PLATEN
PLATER
PLATES
PLATTE
PRATED
PRATER
PRATES
REATAS
RIATAS
RRATED
SCATHE
SEATED
SEATER
SKATED
SKATER
SKATES
SLATED
SLATER
SLATES
SNATCH
SNATHE
SNATHS
SPATES
SPATHE
STATED
STATER
STATES
STATIC
STATOR
STATUE
STATUS
SWATCH
SWATHE
SWATHS
THATCH
THATIS
TOATEE
WHATIF
WRATHS
XRATED

••A•T•
ADAPTS
AJANTA
ANATTO
AVANTI
AWAITS
BEASTS
BEATTY
BEAUTS
BEAUTY
BHAKTI
BLASTS
BLATTY
BOASTS
BRACTS
BRANTS
BRATTY
CHANTS
CHARTS
CHASTE
CHATTY
COAPTS
COASTS
CRAFTS
CRAFTY
DEARTH
DRAFTS
DRAFTY
DUARTE
ECARTE
ENACTS
EXACTA
EXACTO
EXACTS
EXALTS
FEALTY
FEASTS
GEARTO
GIANTS
GRAFTS
GRANTS
HEALTH
HEARTH
HEARTS
HEARTY
KRAITS
KRANTZ
LEADTO
LEALTY
LEANTO
NEARTO
ORANTS
PLAITS
PLANTE
PLANTS
PLASTY
PLATTE
QUANTA
QUARTO
QUARTS
QUARTZ
REACTS
REALTY
RIALTO
ROASTS
SCANTS
SCANTY
SHAFTS
SHAKTI
SHANTY
SHASTA
SLANTS
SMALTI
SMALTO
SMARTS
SMARTY
SNAPTO
SOASTO
SPARTA
STACTE
STARTS
SWARTH
TOASTS
TOASTY
TRACTS
TRAITS
WEALTH
WRAITH
YEASTS
YEASTY

••A••T
ARAFAT
ARARAT
AVAUNT
BEATIT
BRANDT
CHALET
CLARET
CRAVAT
FLAUNT
GRABAT
HEARST
IMARET
INAPET
INARUT
LEARNT
PEANUT
PIAGET
PLAINT
PLANET
PLAYAT
QUAINT
SNAPAT
STABAT
TEAPOT
TEARAT
TEASET
ZEALOT

•••AT•
ABLATE
ACUATE
ADNATE
AERATE
AFLATS
AGNATE
ANSATE
AQUATE
ATBATS
ATLATL
AVIATE
BALATA
BERATE
BINATE
BLEATS
BLOATS
BORATE
BREATH
BYPATH
CARATS
CERATE
CHEATS
CHOATE
CLEATS
COMATE
CREATE
CROATS
CURATE
DAMATO
DEBATE
DEFATS
DELATE
DILATE
DONATE
DORATI
DUCATS
EBOATS
ECLATS
EFLATS
EQUATE
ERGATE
ERRATA
ERSATZ
ESTATE
FIXATE
FLOATS
GALATA
GELATI
GELATO
GLOATS
GREATS
GROATS
GYRATE
HECATE
HEMATO
IDEATE
IGNATZ
INMATE
INNATE
IODATE
JURATS
KARATE
KARATS
KORATS
LANATE
LEGATE
LEGATO
LIGATE
LOBATE
LOCATE
LUNATE
LUXATE
MALATE
METATE
MUTATE
NAMATH
NEGATE
NEMATO
NOTATE
NUTATE
OBLATE
OFLATE
OLEATE
OPIATE

ORGATE
ORNATE
OUTATE
PALATE
PEDATE
PILATE
PINATA
PIRATE
PLEATS
POTATO
RABATO
RAMATE
REBATE
REDATE
RELATE
RENATA
RERATE
ROTATE
RUGATE
SABATO
SAVATE
SEDATE
SENATE
SHEATH
SHOATS
SOMATA
SOMATO
SONATA
SPLATS
SPRATS
SQUATS
STOATS
STRATA
STRATI
STRATO
SWEATS
SWEATY
TERATO
TODATE
TOMATO
TREATS
TREATY
TUBATE
UBOATS
UMTATA
UNIATE
UNIATS
UPDATE
VACATE
WHEATS
WREATH
YUKATA
ZAPATA
ZONATE

•••A•T
ABLAUT
AGHAST
ALEAST
ARRANT
ASLANT
ATLAST
AUFAIT
BASALT
BESANT
BEZANT
BOGART
BREAST
BRYANT
BYPAST
COBALT
CONANT
DECANT
DEPART
DESALT
DIDACT
DISANT
DOPANT
DREAMT
DUNANT
DURANT
DYNAST
ENFANT
ENRAPT
ERRANT
EXTANT
GOCART
GOKART
HOBART
IMPACT
IMPART
INFACT
INFANT
INPART
INTACT
KURALT
KUWAIT
LEVANT
MORANT
MOZART
MUTANT
NATANT
NLEAST
OBLAST
OCTANT
OUTACT
OXCART
PEDANT
PLIANT
POPART
RECANT
RECAST
REDACT
REDANT
REPAST
RESALT
SAVANT
SECANT
SEJANT
SONANT
STRAIT
STUART
TENANT
THWART
TRUANT
TYBALT
TYRANT
UMLAUT
UPCAST
UTHANT
VACANT
VIVANT
VOLANT

••••AT
AFLOAT
AIMSAT
ARAFAT
ARARAT
ATTHAT
BOBCAT
CAMEAT
CAVEAT
COMBAT
COMEAT
COMSAT
CRAVAT
DEFEAT
DIKTAT
EATSAT
FATCAT
FERMAT
FLEWAT
FOGHAT
FORMAT
GETSAT
GOESAT
GRABAT
HAEMAT
HAVEAT
HEPCAT
HEREAT
HINTAT
HISSAT
HOOTAT
JEERAT
JUMPAT
KEEPAT
KEPTAT
KITKAT
LARIAT
LEERAT
LESTAT
LETSAT
LOOKAT
LOQUAT
LOWFAT
MEDLAT
MUDCAT
MUSCAT
NIPSAT
NONFAT
NOUGAT
NUMBAT
OLDHAT
ORGEAT
OUTEAT
PAWSAT
PECKAT
PEEKAT
PEERAT
PICKAT
PLAYAT
POKEAT
PTBOAT
RAILAT
REDHAT
REHEAT
REPEAT
RESEAT
REXCAT
SETSAT
SEURAT
SHEVAT
SHOTAT
SNAPAT
SNOCAT
SOTHAT
SOWHAT
STABAT
STOMAT
TALKAT
TEARAT
THREAT
THROAT
TINHAT
TOMCAT
TOPCAT
TOPHAT
TOREAT
UNSEAT
UPBEAT
WENTAT
WINKAT
WOMBAT

AU••••
AUBADE
AUBREY
AUBURN
AUDENS
AUDIAL
AUDIOS
AUDITS
AUDREY
AUFAIT
AUFOND
AUGEAN
AUGEND
AUGERS
AUGHTS
AUGURS
AUGURY
AUGUST
AUKLET
AUMONT
AUNTIE
AUPAIR
AUREUS
AURIGA
AURORA
AUROUS
AUSPEX
AUSSIE
AUSTEN
AUSTIN
AUSTRO
AUTEUR
AUTHOR
AUTUMN
AUXINS

A•U•••
ABUKIR
ABUSED
ABUSER
ABUSES
ACUATE
ACUITY
ACUMEN
ADULTS
AKUAKU
ALULAE
ALULAR
ALUMNA
ALUMNI
AMULET
AMUSED
AMUSES
ANUBIS
ANURAN
AOUDAD
APULIA
AQUATE
AQUILA
AQUINO
ARUBAN
AVULSE

A••U••
ABDUCT
ABJURE
ABLUSH
ABOUND
ABRUPT
ABSURD
ACCUSE
ACQUIT
ACTUAL
ADDUCE
ADDUCT
ADJURE
ADJUST
ADZUKI
AGOUTI
ALBUMS
ALCUIN
ALEUTS
ALLUDE
ALLURE
AMBUSH
AMOUNT
AMOURS
AMPULE
AMPULS
ANNUAL
ANNULI
ANNULS
ARGUED
ARGUER
ARGUES
ARJUNA
ARMURE
AROUND
AROUSE
ARTURO
ASBURY
ASSUME
ASSURE
ASTUTE
ATTUNE
AUBURN
AUGURS
AUGURY
AUGUST
AUTUMN
AVAUNT
AVOUCH

A•••U•
ABACUS
ABLAUT
ACARUS
ACCRUE
ACEOUS
ACEOUT
ACESUP
ACINUS
ACTIUM
ACTOUT
ACTSUP
ADDSUP
ADIEUS
ADIEUX
ADYTUM
AEOLUS
AIRBUS
AIRGUN
AIROUT
ALARUM
ALDOUS
ALLBUT
ALLIUM
ALLOUT
AMICUS
AMINUS
ANIMUS
ANJOUS
ANTEUP
ANTRUM
ARBOUR
ARDOUR
ARMFUL
ARMOUR
ARTFUL
ARTGUM
ARTHUR
ASKOUT
ASYLUM
ATREUS
ATRIUM
ATSTUD
AUREUS
AUROUS
AUTEUR
AVENUE

A••••U
ACAJOU
AKUAKU
ALATAU
AMADOU
APERCU
ARALLU

•AU•••
BAUBLE
BAUCIS
CAUCHO
CAUCUS
CAUDAL
CAUDEX
CAUDLE
CAUGHT
CAULKS
CAUSAL
CAUSED
CAUSES
DAUBED
DAUBER
DAUBES
DAUNTS
FAUCES
FAUCET
FAULTS
FAULTY
FAUNAE
FAUNAL
FAUNAS
FAUNUS
GAUCHE
GAUCHO
GAUGED
GAUGER
GAUGES
GAUZED
GAUZES
HAULED
HAULER
HAULUP
HAUNCH
HAUNTS
HAUSAS
JAUNTS
JAUNTY
JAURES
KAUNAS
KAUNDA
KAURIS
LAUDED
LAUDER
LAUGHS
LAUNCH
LAUPER
LAUREL
LAUREN
LAURIE
MAULED
MAULER
MAUMAU
MAUMEE
MAUNDY
MAURYA
MAUSER
MAUVES
NAUGHT
NAUSEA
NAUTCH
PAULEY
PAUNCH
PAUPER
PAUSED
PAUSES
SAUCED
SAUCER
SAUCES
SAUDIS
SAUGER
SAULTS
SAUNAS
SAUREL
SAUTES
TAUGHT
TAUNTS
TAUONS
TAUPES
TAURUS
TAUTEN
TAUTER
TAUTLY
TAUTOG
VAUGHN
VAULTS
VAUNTS
WAUSAU
YAUPON

•A•U••
BABULS
BAGUIO
BARUCH
BATUMI
CAGUAS
CAJUNS
CANUTE
CARUSO
CASUAL
CAYUGA
CAYUSE
DANUBE
DATURA
FACULA
GAMUTS
JAGUAR
JAMUPS
KABUKI
KAHUNA
LACUNA
LAGUNA
LAPUTA
LAYUPS
LAZULI
MACULA
MADURA
MADURO
MAGUEY
MAKUTA
MANUAL
MANUEL
MAPUTO
MAQUIS
MATURE
MAZUMA
NATURE
PADUAN
PAIUTE
PAPUAN
PARULA
PARURE
RADULA
RAQUEL
SALUKI
SALUTE
SAMUEL
SATURN
TABULA
VACUUM
VAGUER
VALUED
VALUES
VARUNA
WATUSI
YAKUTS
YAQUIS
ZANUCK

•A••U•
BACKUP
BACKUS
BADGUY
BAGFUL
BALLUP
BANGUI
BANGUP
BANJUL
BANQUO
BANTUS
BARIUM
BARNUM
BARQUE
BARZUN
BASQUE
BATTUE
BAYEUX
BAYOUS
BAYRUM
CACTUS
CADMUS
CAIQUE
CALLUP
CALLUS
CALQUE
CAMEUP
CAMPUS
CANCUN
CAPFUL
CAPGUN
CAPNUT
CARFUL
CARPUS
CASQUE
CATGUT
CATSUP
CAUCUS
DAMOUR
DAMSUP
DANAUS
DARIUS
DATSUN
EARFUL
EASEUP
EATOUT
EATSUP
FACEUP
FAIRUP
FAIYUM
FAMOUS
FANOUT
FAROUK
FAROUT
FAUNUS
FAVOUR
GALLUP
GANGUE
GANGUP
GAVEUP
HAIKUS
HALLUX
HANGUL
HANGUP
HARDUP
HAULUP
JACKUP
JAIPUR
JAMSUP
JANHUS
JARFUL
JAZZUP
KAHLUA
KAILUA
LABOUR
LABRUM
LACEUP
LAIDUP
LAMOUR
LANGUR
LAPFUL
LAPSUP
LARRUP
LASHUP
LATIUM
LATOUR
LAWFUL
LAYOUT
LAYSUP
MADEUP
MAGNUM
MAHOUT
MAIDUS
MAKEUP
MANAUS
MANFUL
MANQUE
MANTUA
MARAUD
MARCUS
MARDUK
MARIUS
MARKUP
MARQUE
MASQUE
MAXOUT
NASHUA
PABLUM
PACKUP
PAIDUP
PAIRUP
PALPUS
PANOUT
PAPPUS
PASSUP
PAYOUT
PAYSUP
RACKUP
RADIUM
RADIUS
RAGOUT
RAGRUG
RAIPUR
RAJPUT
RAKEUP
RAMOUS
RANGUP
RANOUT
RAYGUN
SACQUE
SACRUM
SALYUT
SANNUP
SATOUT
SAVEUP
SAVOUR
SAWOUT
TAGOUT
TAGSUP
TAKEUP
TALCUM
TALKUP
TALMUD
TAMMUZ
TANGUY
TANKUP
TAPOUT
TARSUS
TAURUS
VACUUM
VALIUM
VALOUR
VAPOUR
VATFUL
WADSUP
WAITUP
WAKEUP
WALKUP
WALLUP
WALNUT
WALRUS
WAMPUM
WARMUP
WASHUP
WAYOUT
YANQUI

•A•••U
BATEAU
CACHOU
GATEAU
HAIKOU
HALERU
HAVASU
JABIRU
LANDAU
LAOTZU
MAKALU
MALIBU
MANCHU
MARILU
MASERU
MAUMAU
NASSAU
PAILOU
RAMEAU
WAUSAU
XANADU

••AU••
AVAUNT
BEAUTS
BEAUTY
CLAUDE
CLAUSE
FLAUNT
FRAUDS
SCAUPS
TRAUMA

••A•U•
ABACUS
ACARUS
ALARUM
BEADUP
BEAMUP
BEARUP
BEATUP
BRAQUE
CHATUP
CLAMUP
CLAQUE
DRAWUP
GEARUP
GRADUS
HEADUP
HEATUP
HIATUS
ICARUS
INARUT
LEADUP
LEAGUE
OMASUM
OPAQUE
PEANUT
PLAGUE
PLAQUE
PLAYUP
PRAGUE
REARUP
RVALUE
SCARUM
SEALUP
SEAMUS
SHAMUS
SLAPUP
SNAFUS
SNAPUP
SOAKUP
STAPUF
STATUE
STATUS
STAYUP
TEACUP
TEAMUP
TEARUP
URAEUS
URANUS
UVALUE
WRAPUP

••A••U
ACAJOU
ALATAU
AMADOU
ARALLU

•••AU•
ABLAUT
BEDAUB
CHIAUS
DANAUS
DEPAUL
DEPAUW
INHAUL
MANAUS
MARAUD
RUPAUL
STPAUL
STRAUS
UMLAUT

•••A•U
AKUAKU
DEJAVU
HAVASU
IGUACU
MAKALU
SUBARU
TUVALU
XANADU

••••AU
ALATAU
BATEAU
BISSAU
BUREAU
GATEAU
JUNEAU
LANDAU
MAUMAU
MOLDAU
MOREAU
NASSAU
RAMEAU
RESEAU
ROSEAU
WAUSAU

AV••••
AVAILS
AVALON
AVANTI
AVATAR
AVAUNT
AVEDON
AVENGE
AVENUE
AVERNO
AVERSE
AVERTS
AVESTA
AVIANS
AVIARY
AVIATE
AVIDLY
AVISOS
AVOCET
AVOIDS
AVOUCH
AVOWAL
AVOWED
AVOWER
AVULSE

A•V•••
ADVENT
ADVERB
ADVERT
ADVICE
ADVISE
AMVETS
ANVILS
ARVADA

A••V••
AGAVES
ALFVEN

A•••V•
ACTIVE
ALCOVE
ARGIVE
ARRIVE

A••••V
ASIMOV

•AV•••
CAVEAT
CAVEIN
CAVELL
CAVERN
CAVERS
CAVETT
CAVIAR
CAVILS
CAVING
CAVITY
CAVORT
DAVIES
DAVITS
FAVORS
FAVOUR
GAVEIN
GAVELS
GAVEUP
GAVIAL
HAVANA
HAVASU
HAVEAT
HAVENS
HAVENT
HAVEON
HAVING
HAVOCS
JAVARI
JAVIER
LAVABO
LAVAGE
LAVERS
LAVING
LAVISH
MAVENS
NAVAHO
NAVAJO
NAVELS
NAVIES
PAVANE
PAVERS
PAVING
PAVLOV
RAVAGE
RAVELS
RAVENS
RAVERS
RAVINE
RAVING
RAVISH
SAVAGE
SAVAII
SAVANT
SAVATE
SAVERS
SAVEUP
SAVING
SAVIOR
SAVOIE
SAVOIR
SAVORS
SAVORY
SAVOUR
TAVERN
WAVEIN
WAVERS
WAVERY
WAVIER
WAVING
XAVIER

•A•V••
CALVED
CALVES
CALVIN
CANVAS
CARVED
CARVER
CARVES
CARVEY
GARVEY
HALVAH
HALVED
HALVES
HARVEY
JAYVEE
LANVIN
LARVAE
LARVAL
LARVAS
LATVIA
MARVEL
MARVIN
MAUVES
NARVIK
PARVIS
SALVED
SALVER
SALVES
SALVIA
SALVOR
SALVOS
VALVED
VALVES
WAIVED
WAIVER
WAIVES

•A••V•
CANOVA
CASAVA
DATIVE
HALEVY
NATIVE
PAREVE
SALIVA

•A•••V
KARPOV
LAPTEV
PAVLOV
VACLAV
VASLAV

••AV••
AGAVES
BEAVER
BRAVAS
BRAVED
BRAVER
BRAVES
BRAVOS
CHAVEZ
CLAVIN
CRAVAT
CRAVED
CRAVEN
CRAVER
CRAVES
FLAVIA
FLAVOR
GRAVED
GRAVEL
GRAVEN
GRAVER
GRAVES
GRAVID
GUAVAS
HEAVED
HEAVEN
HEAVER
HEAVES
KNAVES
LEAVED
LEAVEN
LEAVES
LOAVES
PEAVEY
PRAVDA
QUAVER
SHAVED
SHAVEN
SHAVER
SHAVES
SLAVED
SLAVER
SLAVES
SLAVIC
SOAVES
SPAVIN
STAVED
STAVES
SUAVER
TRAVEL
TRAVIS
WEAVED
WEAVER
WEAVES

••A•V•
STARVE

••A••V
BRASOV

•••AV•
BEHAVE
CASAVA
CLEAVE
DEJAVU
GREAVE
MOHAVE
MOJAVE
MORAVA
OCTAVE
OCTAVO
OTTAVA
REPAVE
SHEAVE
SLEAVE
ZOUAVE

••••AV
GUSTAV
MOSHAV
VACLAV
VASLAV

AW••••
AWAITS
AWAKED
AWAKEN
AWAKES
AWARDS
AWEARY

AWEIGH
AWHILE
AWHIRL
AWNING
AWOKEN

A•W•••
ADWEEK
ALWAYS
ALWEST
ASWELL
ASWIRL
ASWOON
ATWILL
ATWOOD
ATWORK

A••W••
AIRWAY
ALLWET
ANSWER
ANYWAY
ARAWAK
AVOWAL
AVOWED
AVOWER

A•••W•
ACTTWO
ALLOWS
ARROWS

A••••W
ANDHOW
ANDREW
ANTCOW
ANYHOW

•AW•••
BAWLED
BAWLER
CAWDOR
CAWING
DAWDLE
DAWNED
DAWSON
FAWKES
FAWLTY
FAWNED
FAWNER
GAWAIN
GAWKED
GAWKER
HAWAII
HAWHAW
HAWING
HAWKED
HAWKER
HAWSER
HAWSES
JAWING
JAWOHL
LAWFUL
LAWING
LAWMAN
LAWMEN
LAWSON
LAWTON
LAWYER
NAWABS
PAWERS
PAWING
PAWNED
PAWNEE
PAWNER
PAWPAW
PAWSAT
RAWEGG
RAWEST
SAWFIT
SAWING
SAWLOG
SAWOFF
SAWOUT
SAWRED
SAWYER
TAWDRY
TAWING
YAWING
YAWNED
YAWNER
YAWPED
YAWPER

•A•W••
DARWIN
EARWAX
EARWIG
GALWAY
NARWAL
TAIWAN
WAHWAH
YAHWEH

•A••W•
CAHOWS
MACAWS
MALAWI
PAPAWS
TARAWA

•A•••W
BARROW
CALLOW
CASHEW
DARROW
FALLOW
FARLOW
FARROW
GAGLAW
HALLOW
HARLOW
HARROW
HAWHAW
HAYMOW
LAYLOW
MALLOW
MARROW
NARROW
PAWPAW
SALLOW
TALLOW
WALLOW
WARSAW
YARROW

••AW••
ARAWAK
BRAWLS
BRAWNY
CLAWED
CLAWER
CRAWLS
CRAWLY
DRAWER
DRAWIN
DRAWLS
DRAWON
DRAWUP
FLAWED
GNAWED
GNAWER
GOAWAY
GOAWRY
INAWAY
PRAWNS
SEAWAY
SHAWLS
SHAWMS
SPAWNS
THAWED
TRAWLS
UNAWED

••A••W
INAROW
KRAKOW
MEADOW
SEACOW
SHADOW

•••AW•
BYLAWS
INLAWS
MACAWS
MALAWI
MOHAWK
OSHAWA
OTTAWA
PAPAWS
SCRAWL
SPRAWL
SQUAWK
STRAWS
TARAWA
YUKAWA

•••A•W
DEPAUW

••••AW
BOWSAW
BROKAW
CUSHAW
GAGLAW
GEEGAW
GEWGAW
GUFFAW
HAWHAW
HEEHAW
JIGSAW
MCGRAW
OUTLAW
PAWPAW
PITSAW
PRELAW
REDRAW
RIPSAW
SEESAW
UNDRAW
WARSAW

AX••••
AXILLA
AXIOMS
AXIONS
AXONAL
AXSEED

A•X•••
AUXINS

A••X••
ALEXEI
ALEXIA
ALEXIS
APEXES

A•••X•
ANNEXE

A••••X
ADIEUX
AUSPEX

•AX•••
BAXTER
CAXTON
FAXING
LAXEST
LAXITY
MAXIMA
MAXIMS
MAXINE
MAXIXE
MAXOUT
OAXACA
SAXONS
SAXONY
TAXERS
TAXIED
TAXIES
TAXING
TAXMAN
TAXMEN
WAXERS
WAXIER
WAXING

•A•X••
CALXES

•A••X•
GALAXY
MAXIXE

•A•••X
BAYEUX
CAUDEX
EARWAX
HALLUX
HATBOX
LARYNX
LASTEX
MADMAX
MANNIX
MATRIX
RATEDX

••AX••
COAXED
COAXER
COAXES
FLAXEN
FLAXES
HOAXED
HOAXER
HOAXES
KLAXON
PRAXES
PRAXIS

••A••X
BRANDX
INAFIX
SEAFOX
SPADIX

•••AX•
BORAXO
CUNAXA
GALAXY

••••AX
CLIMAX
EARWAX
KOUFAX
MADMAX
PICKAX
POLEAX
PRETAX
PROTAX
SINTAX
SMILAX
SURTAX
SYNTAX
THORAX

AY••••
AYEAYE
AYESHA
AYMARA

A•Y•••
ABYDOS
ABYSMS
ADYTUM
ALYSSA
AMYTAN
ANYHOW
ANYONE
ANYWAY
ARYANS
ASYLUM

A••Y••
ALKYDS
ALKYLS
ANHYDR
ARGYLE
ARGYLL

A•••Y•
ABBEYS
ACETYL
AJFOYT
ALLAYS
ALLEYS
ALLOYS
ALWAYS
ANNOYS
ANONYM
ARRAYS
ARROYO
ASSAYS
AYEAYE
AZODYE

A••••Y
ABBACY
ACIDLY
ACUITY
AFFRAY
AGENCY
AIRDRY
AIRILY
AIRWAY
ALBANY
ALECKY
ALLDAY
ANDREY
ANTONY
ANYWAY
APATHY
APIARY
ARCHLY
ARGOSY
ARIDLY
ARMORY
ARTERY
ASBURY
ASHLEY
ASTRAY
AUBREY
AUDREY
AUGURY
AVIARY
AVIDLY
AWEARY

•AY•••
BAYARD
BAYEUX
BAYING
BAYLOR
BAYOUS
BAYRUM
CAYMAN
CAYUGA
CAYUSE
DAYBED
DAYGLO
DAYLIT
DAYONE
DAYTON
GAYALS
GAYEST
GAYNOR
HAYDEN
HAYING
HAYLEY
HAYMOW
JAYCEE
JAYVEE
KAYAKS
KAYOED
LAYBYS
LAYERS
LAYFOR
LAYING
LAYLOW
LAYMAN
LAYMEN
LAYOFF
LAYOUT
LAYSBY
LAYSIN
LAYSON
LAYSTO
LAYSUP
LAYUPS
MAYANS
MAYBES
MAYDAY
MAYFLY
MAYHAP
MAYHEM
MAYORS
MAYPOP
MAYTAG
NAYSAY
PAYDAY
PAYEES
PAYERS
PAYFOR
PAYING
PAYOFF
PAYOLA
PAYOUT
PAYSIN
PAYSON
PAYSUP
RAYGUN
RAYONS
SAYERS
SAYING
SAYSOS
SAYYES
SAYYID
TAYLOR
TAYRAS
WAYLAY
WAYLON
WAYOUT
ZAYINS

•A•Y••
BANYAN
BARYON
CANYON
FAIYUM
GALYAK
LARYNX
LAWYER
MAGYAR
PAPYRI
SALYUT
SATYRS
SAWYER
SAYYES
SAYYID

•A••Y•
DACTYL
DADDYO
DAIMYO
DARRYL
GAMAYS
JACLYN
LATOYA
LAYBYS
MALAYA
MALAYS
MARTYR
MATEYS
MAURYA
NAGOYA
PAPAYA
TAMAYO
VAISYA
VANRYN

•A•••Y
BADGUY
BAILEY
BAKERY
BALDLY
BARELY
BARFLY
BARLEY
BARNEY
BARONY
BASELY
BATBOY
CAGILY
CAGNEY
CALMLY
CAMEBY
CANARY
CANOPY
CARBOY
CARNEY
CARREY
CARVEY
CATCHY
CATHAY
CAVITY
DABNEY
DAILEY
DAINTY
DAMPLY
DANGLY
DANNAY
DARKLY
DARNAY
DATARY
EARTHY
EASILY
EATERY
FABRAY
FAIRLY
FAKERY
FAMILY
FARCRY
FARLEY
FAULTY
FAWLTY
GADFLY
GAIETY
GAINLY
GALAXY
GALLEY
GALWAY
GAMELY
GAMILY
GANGLY
GANTRY
GARVEY
GATSBY
HAILEY
HALEVY
HALLEY
HALSEY
HARDLY
HARLEY
HARVEY
HAYLEY
HAZILY
JALOPY
JANGLY
JAPERY
JAUNTY
LACKEY
LAIDBY
LAMELY
LANDRY
LANKLY
LASTLY
LATELY
LAXITY
LAYSBY
LAZBOY
LAZILY
MAGUEY
MAINLY
MALADY
MALORY
MANDAY
MANRAY
MARBLY
MARGAY
MARLEY
MARSHY
MASSEY
MAUNDY
MAYDAY
MAYFLY
NAMELY
NAPERY
NASEBY
NAYSAY
OAKLEY
PACIFY
PALELY
PALTRY
PANFRY
PANTRY
PAPACY
PAPERY
PARITY
PARKAY
PARLAY
PARLEY
PARODY
PARTLY
PASSBY
PASTRY
PATCHY
PAULEY
PAYDAY
RACILY
RAMIFY
RAMSAY
RAMSEY
RANDRY
RANKLY
RAPTLY
RAREFY
RARELY
RARIFY
RARITY
RASHLY
RATIFY
RATTLY
SAFELY
SAFETY
SAGELY
SALARY
SANELY
SANITY
SASHAY
SATINY
SAVORY
SAXONY
TAGDAY
TAMELY
TANGLY
TANGUY
TARTLY
TAUTLY
TAWDRY
VAGARY
VAINLY
VALERY
VALLEY
VANITY
VARNEY
VASTLY
WADDLY
WAFFLY
WAGGLY
WAMBLY
WARCRY
WARILY
WARMLY
WATERY
WATNEY
WAVERY
WAYLAY
YARELY
ZANILY

••AY••
BRAYED
BRAYER
CLAYEY
CRAYON
DLAYER
DRAYED
DWAYNE
ELAYER
ELAYNE
FLAYED
FLAYER
FRAYED
GRAYED
GRAYER
OKAYED
PLAYAS
PLAYAT
PLAYED
PLAYER
PLAYON
PLAYUP
PRAYED
PRAYER
QUAYLE
SHAYNE
SLAYED
SLAYER
SPAYED
STAYED
STAYON
STAYUP
SWAYED
SWAYER
SWAYZE
THAYER
XRAYED

••A•Y•
GLADYS
HEARYE

••A••Y
APATHY
BEATTY
BEAUTY
BLABBY
BLATTY
BRAINY
BRANDY
BRASHY
BRASSY
BRATTY
BRAWNY
CHAFFY
CHALKY
CHAMMY
CHANCY
CHANEY
CHARLY
CHATTY
CLAMMY
CLANCY
CLANKY
CLASSY
CLAYEY
CRABBY
CRAFTY
CRAGGY
CRANKY
CRANNY
CRAWLY
DEADLY
DEARLY
DRABLY
DRAFTY
DRAGGY
DUALLY
FEALTY
FLABBY
FLAGGY
FLASHY
FLATLY
FRANNY
GHARRY
GLADLY
GLAIRY
GLASSY
GNARLY
GOAWAY
GOAWRY
GRABBY
GRAINY
GRAMMY
GRANNY
GRASSY
HEARTY
INAWAY
KNARRY
LEAKEY
LEALTY
LEANLY
MEANLY
MEASLY
NEARBY
NEARLY
NEATLY
NIAMEY
OCASEY
ORALLY
PEACHY
PEARLY
PEAVEY
PLASHY
PLASTY
POACHY
QUAGGY
QUARRY
REALLY
REALTY
SCABBY
SCANTY
SEAWAY
SHABBY
SHAGGY
SHALEY
SHALLY
SHANDY
SHANTY
SLAGGY
SLANGY
SLAPPY
SMARMY
SMARTY
SNAGGY
SNAPPY
SNARLY
SNAZZY
SPACEY
SPANKY
SPARKY
STABLY
STALKY
STANKY
STARRY
SWABBY
SWAMPY
SWANKY
TEAPOY
TOASTY
TRACEY
TRAPPY
TRASHY
TWANGY
USABLY
VIABLY
WEAKLY
WHACKY
WHAMMY
YEARLY
YEASTY

•••AY•
ALLAYS
ALWAYS
ARRAYS
ASSAYS
AYEAYE
BELAYS
BYWAYS
DECAYS
DELAYS
EMBAYS
ESSAYS
FORAYS
GAMAYS
INLAYS
MALAYA
MALAYS
MORAYS
PAPAYA
RELAYS
REPAYS
SPLAYS
SPRAYS
STRAYS
TAMAYO
TOKAYS
UNSAYS

•••A•Y
ABBACY
ALBANY
APIARY
AVIARY
AWEARY
BIGAMY
BINARY
BLEARY
BOTANY
BOVARY
CANARY
CREAKY
CREAMY
CREASY
CROAKY
CURACY
DATARY
DELANY
DREAMY
DREARY
FREAKY
FRIARY
GALAXY
GOEASY
GREASY
HILARY
INFAMY
KODALY
LEGACY
LITANY
LUNACY
MALADY
MILADY
NONARY
NOTARY
OLEARY
PAPACY
PIRACY
QUEASY
ROMANY
ROSARY
ROTARY
SALARY
SENARY
SLEAZY
SMEARY
SNEAKY
SOMANY
STEADY
STEAMY
SUGARY
SWEATY
TREATY
UNEASY
UNWARY
VAGARY
VOTARY

••••AY
AFFRAY
AIRWAY
ALLDAY
ANYWAY
ASTRAY
BENDAY
BENGAY
BETRAY
BISCAY
BOMBAY
BYPLAY
CATHAY
CONWAY
CORDAY
DANNAY
DARNAY
DEEJAY
DEFRAY
DELRAY
DISMAY
FABRAY
FLYWAY
FRIDAY
GALWAY
GOAWAY
HEYDAY
HOORAY
HURRAY
ILLSAY
INAWAY
INPLAY
KEYWAY
LEEWAY
MANDAY
MANRAY
MARGAY
MAYDAY
MIDDAY
MIDWAY
MILLAY
MISLAY
MISSAY
MONDAY
MORNAY
MURRAY
NAYSAY
NETPAY
NORGAY
NORWAY
OFFDAY
ONEDAY
ONEWAY
OUTLAY
PARKAY
PARLAY
PAYDAY
PREPAY
RAMSAY
REDBAY
REPLAY
RUNWAY
SASHAY
SEAWAY
SKYWAY
SUBWAY
SUNDAY
SUNRAY
TAGDAY
TWOWAY
VEEJAY
WAYLAY

AZ••••
AZALEA
AZODYE
AZORES
AZORIN
AZTECS

A•Z•••
ADZUKI

A••Z••
AMAZED
AMAZES
AMAZON
AREZZO

A•••Z•
ABLAZE
ALONZO
AREZZO
ASSIZE

A••••Z
AMOSOZ

•AZ•••
BAZAAR
DAZING
DAZZLE
FAZING
GAZEBO
GAZING
HAZANS
HAZARD
HAZELS
HAZERS
HAZIER
HAZILY
HAZING
JAZZED
JAZZES
JAZZUP
KAZAKH
KAZAKS
KAZOOS
LAZBOY
LAZIER
LAZILY
LAZING
LAZULI
MAZERS
MAZOLA
MAZUMA
RAZING
RAZORS
RAZZED
RAZZES
RAZZLE
TAZZAS

•A•Z••
BALZAC
BANZAI
BARZUN
DANZIG
DAZZLE
GAUZED
GAUZES
JAZZED
JAZZES
JAZZUP
MAHZOR
MAIZES
MATZOH
MATZOS
PANZER
RAZZED
RAZZES
RAZZLE
TARZAN
TAZZAS

•A••Z•
FAENZA
LAMAZE
LAOTZU

•A•••Z
TABRIZ
TAMMUZ
VALDEZ

••AZ••
AMAZED
AMAZES
AMAZON
BLAZED
BLAZER
BLAZES
BLAZON
BRAZED
BRAZEN
BRAZER
BRAZES
BRAZIL
BRAZOS
BRAZZA
BRAZZI
CRAZED
CRAZES
FRAZER
GHAZIS
GLAZED
GLAZER
GLAZES
GRAZED

GRAZER
GRAZES
PIAZZA
PLAZAS
RYAZAN
SHAZAM
SNAZZY
SWAZIS
ZSAZSA

••A•Z•
BRAZZA
BRAZZI
KWANZA
PIAZZA
SNAZZY
STANZA
SWAYZE

••A••Z
CHAVEZ
JUAREZ
KRANTZ
QUARTZ

•••AZ•
ABLAZE
BEDAZE
LAMAZE
PIZAZZ
SLEAZE
SLEAZY

•••A•Z
ERSATZ
IGNATZ
KUVASZ
PIZAZZ

••••AZ
SHIRAZ

BA••••
BAAING
BABBLE
BABIED
BABIES
BABKAS
BABOON
BABSON
BABULS
BACALL
BACKED
BACKER
BACKIN
BACKUP
BACKUS
BADDIE
BADEGG
BADGER
BADGES
BADGUY
BADLOT
BAFFIN
BAFFLE
BAGDAD
BAGELS
BAGFUL
BAGGED
BAGGER
BAGGIE
BAGUIO
BAHAMA
BAHIAN
BAIKAL
BAILED
BAILEE
BAILER
BAILEY
BAILOR
BAINES
BAIRNS
BAITED
BAKERS
BAKERY
BAKING
BALAAM
BALATA
BALBOA
BALDER
BALDLY
BALEEN
BALERS
BALING
BALKAN
BALKED
BALLAD
BALLET
BALLOT
BALLUP
BALSAM
BALTIC
BALZAC
BAMAKO
BAMBOO
BANANA
BANDED
BANDIT
BANDOG
BANGED
BANGER
BANGKA
BANGLE
BANGOR
BANGUI
BANGUP
BANISH
BANJOS
BANJUL
BANKED
BANKER
BANKON
BANLON
BANNED
BANNER
BANQUO
BANTAM
BANTER
BANTUS
BANYAN
BANZAI
BAOBAB
BARBED
BARBEL
BARBER
BARBET
BARBIE
BARBRA
BARDIC
BARDOT
BAREGE
BARELY
BAREST
BARFLY
BARGED
BARGES
BARHOP
BARING
BARITE
BARIUM
BARKED
BARKER
BARKIN
BARLEY
BARMAN
BARMEN
BARNES
BARNEY
BARNUM
BAROJA
BAROLO
BARONG
BARONS
BARONY
BARQUE
BARRED
BARREL
BARREN
BARRES
BARRIE
BARRIO
BARRIS
BARRON
BARROW
BARTAB
BARTER
BARTOK
BARTON
BARUCH
BARYON
BARZUN
BASALT
BASELY
BASEST
BASHED
BASHES
BASICS
BASING
BASINS
BASKED
BASKET
BASQUE
BASSES
BASSET
BASSOS
BASTED
BASTER
BASTES
BATAAN
BATBOY
BATEAU
BATHED
BATHER
BATHES
BATHOS
BATIKS
BATING
BATMAN
BATMEN
BATONS
BATTED
BATTEN
BATTER
BATTLE
BATTUE
BATUMI
BAUBLE
BAUCIS
BAWLED
BAWLER
BAXTER
BAYARD
BAYEUX
BAYING
BAYLOR
BAYOUS
BAYRUM
BAZAAR

B•A•••
BAAING
BEACON
BEADED
BEADLE
BEADUP
BEAGLE
BEAKED
BEAKER
BEAMED
BEAMUP
BEANED
BEANIE
BEANOS
BEARDS
BEARER
BEARON
BEARUP
BEASTS
BEATEN
BEATER
BEATIT
BEATLE
BEATON
BEATTY
BEATUP
BEAUTS
BEAUTY
BEAVER
BHAKTI
BIAFRA
BIANCA
BIASED
BIASES
BLABBY
BLACKS
BLADED
BLADES
BLAINE
BLAISE
BLAMED
BLAMES
BLANCA
BLANCH
BLANDA
BLANKS
BLARED
BLARES
BLASTS
BLATTY
BLAZED
BLAZER
BLAZES
BLAZON
BMAJOR
BOARDS
BOASTS
BOATED
BOATER
BRACED
BRACER
BRACES
BRACTS
BRAHMA
BRAHMS
BRAIDS
BRAILS
BRAINS
BRAINY
BRAISE
BRAKED
BRAKES
BRANCH
BRANDO
BRANDS
BRANDT
BRANDX
BRANDY
BRANTS
BRAQUE
BRASHY
BRASOV
BRASSY
BRATTY
BRAVAS
BRAVED
BRAVER
BRAVES
BRAVOS
BRAWLS
BRAWNY
BRAYED
BRAYER
BRAZED
BRAZEN
BRAZER
BRAZES
BRAZIL
BRAZOS
BRAZZA
BRAZZI
BWANAS

B••A••
BACALL
BAHAMA
BALAAM
BALATA
BAMAKO
BANANA
BASALT
BATAAN
BAYARD
BAZAAR
BECALM
BECAME
BEDAUB
BEDAZE
BEFALL
BEHALF
BEHAVE
BELAIR
BELAYS
BERATE
BESANT
BETAKE
BEWAIL
BEWARE
BEZANT
BICARB
BIGAMY
BIHARI
BINARY
BINATE
BLEACH
BLEARS
BLEARY
BLEATS
BLOATS
BOGART
BONAMI
BORAGE
BORATE
BORAXO
BOTANY
BOVARY
BOYARS
BREACH
BREADS
BREAKS
BREAMS
BREAST
BREATH
BRIAND
BRIANS
BRIARD
BRIARS
BROACH
BROADS
BRYANT
BSHARP
BUTANE
BYHAND
BYLAWS
BYNAME
BYPASS
BYPAST
BYPATH
BYTALK
BYWAYS

B•••A•
BABKAS
BAGDAD
BAHIAN
BAIKAL
BALAAM
BALKAN
BALLAD
BALSAM
BALZAC
BANTAM
BANYAN
BANZAI
BAOBAB
BARMAN
BARTAB
BATAAN
BATEAU
BATMAN
BAZAAR
BEDLAM
BEGGAR
BELDAM
BELIAL
BEMOAN
BENDAY
BENGAL
BENGAY
BETRAY
BETTAS
BEULAH
BHOPAL
BHUTAN
BIGMAC
BILBAO
BIOGAS
BIOTAS
BISCAY
BISSAU
BITMAP
BOBCAT
BOMBAY
BONSAI
BOREAL
BOREAS
BORMAN
BOWMAN
BOWOAR
BOWSAW
BOXCAR
BRAVAS
BRIDAL
BROGAN
BROKAW
BRUMAL
BRUTAL
BUCCAL
BULGAR
BULLAE
BUMRAP
BUNYAN
BUREAU
BURGAS
BURLAP
BURMAN
BUROAK
BURSAE
BURSAL
BURSAR
BURSAS
BUSBAR
BUSMAN
BWANAS
BYPLAY
BYROAD

B••••A
BAHAMA
BALATA
BALBOA
BANANA
BANGKA
BARBRA
BAROJA
BELUGA
BERTHA
BETCHA
BIAFRA
BIANCA
BLANCA
BLANDA
BODEGA
BOGOTA
BORGIA
BOSNIA
BRAHMA
BRAZZA
BRENDA
BUDDHA
BULOVA
BUQSHA
BUSHWA

•BA•••
ABACAS
ABACUS
ABASED
ABASES
ABATED
ABATES
ABATIS
IBADAN
UBANGI

•B•A••
ABBACY
ABLATE
ABLAUT
ABLAZE
ABOARD
ABRADE
ABRAMS
EBOATS
HBEAMS
IBEAMS
OBEAHS
OBLAST
OBLATE
OBTAIN
UBOATS

•B••A•
ABACAS
ABORAL
ABROAD
FBIMAN
IBADAN
OBIWAN
OBRIAN

•B•••A
ABOLLA
IBERIA
OBELIA

••BA••
ABBACY
ALBANO
ALBANY
ATBATS
AUBADE
CABALA
CABALS
CABANA
COBALT
CUBAGE
DEBARK
DEBARS
DEBASE
DEBATE
EMBANK
EMBARK
EMBAYS
GOBACK
HABANA
HOBART
KEBABS
LOBATE
MCBAIN
ORBACH
RABATO
REBAGS
REBARS
REBATE
RIBALD
RIBAND
ROBALO
SABATO
SUBARU
TABARD
TOBAGO
TUBATE
TYBALT
UNBARS
URBANA
URBANE
WABASH

••B•A•
BABKAS
BOBCAT
COBHAM
COBIAS
COBRAS
DEBRAS
DOBLAS
DOBRAS
FABIAN
FABRAY
GIBRAN
HABEAS
HUBCAP
JABBAR
JUBBAH
KUBLAI
LABIAL
LIBYAN
LLBEAN
MOBCAP
NUBIAN
PTBOAT
SABRAS
SUBWAY
TABLAS
TIBIAE
TIBIAL
TIBIAS
TOBIAS
TUBMAN
UMBRAE
UMBRAL
UMBRAS
UPBEAT
ZEBRAS

••B••A
ARBELA
CABALA
CABANA
CIBOLA
EUBOEA
FIBULA
HABANA
LABREA
NEBULA
SABENA
TABULA
UMBRIA
URBANA

•••BA•
AIRBAG
AMEBAE
AMEBAS
ARUBAN
BAOBAB
BILBAO
BOMBAY
BUSBAR
CASBAH
CEIBAS
COMBAT
CORBAN
CYMBAL
DISBAR
DUNBAR
DURBAN
DURBAR
FORBAD
GASBAG
GIMBAL
GLOBAL
GRABAT
HERBAL
ICEBAG
ISOBAR
IZABAL
JABBAR
JUBBAH
KASBAH
KITBAG
KLIBAN
LUMBAR
MAMBAS
NOTBAD
NUMBAT
RAGBAG
REDBAY
RUMBAS
SAMBAL
SAMBAR
SAMBAS
SCUBAS
SEABAG
SHABAN
SINBAD
STABAT
TEABAG
TIMBAL
TOMBAC
TOOBAD
TRIBAL
TURBAN
VERBAL
WETBAR
WOMBAT

•••B•A
ARABIA
BALBOA
BARBRA
GAMBIA
JERBOA
LAMBDA
LISBOA
OJIBWA
PHOBIA
PUEBLA
RAMBLA
SERBIA
ZAMBIA

••••BA
AMOEBA
ANNABA
ARRIBA
ARROBA
CASABA
CUIABA
DJERBA
HECUBA
INDABA
JOJOBA
KARIBA
RHUMBA
YORUBA
ZAREBA

BB••••
BBKING

B•B•••
BABBLE
BABIED
BABIES
BABKAS
BABOON
BABSON
BABULS
BEBOPS
BIBBED
BIBLES
BIBLIO
BOBBED
BOBBER
BOBBIE
BOBBIN
BOBBLE
BOBCAT
BOBSUP
BUBBLE
BUBBLY

B••B••
BABBLE
BALBOA
BAMBOO
BAOBAB
BARBED
BARBEL
BARBER
BARBET
BARBIE
BARBRA
BATBOY
BAUBLE
BEDBUG
BERBER
BIBBED
BIGBEN
BIGBOY
BILBAO
BIOBIO
BLABBY
BOBBED
BOBBER
BOBBIE
BOBBIN
BOBBLE
BOMBAY
BOMBED
BOMBER
BOMBES
BONBON
BOOBOO
BOUBOU
BRIBED
BRIBES
BUBBLE
BUBBLY
BULBIL
BULBUL
BUMBLE
BUMBRY
BURBLE
BURBLY
BURBOT
BUSBAR
BUSBOY
BYEBYE

B•••B•
BLABBY
BLURBS

B••••B
BAOBAB
BARTAB
BEDAUB
BENUMB
BICARB

•BB•••
ABBACY
ABBESS
ABBEYS
ABBOTS
ABBOTT
EBBING

•B•B••
IBIBIO

•B••B•
ABOMBS
HBOMBS

•B•••B
ABSORB

••BB••
BABBLE
BIBBED
BOBBED
BOBBER
BOBBIE
BOBBIN
BOBBLE
BUBBLE
BUBBLY
CABBED
CABBIE
COBBLE
DABBED
DABBLE
DEBBIE
DIBBLE
DOBBER
DOBBIN
DUBBED
DUBBIN
DYBBUK
FIBBED
FIBBER
FOBBED
GABBED
GABBER
GABBLE
GABBRO
GIBBED
GIBBER
GIBBET
GIBBON
GOBBLE
HOBBES
HOBBIT
HOBBLE
HUBBLE
HUBBLY
HUBBUB
JABBAR
JABBED
JABBER
JOBBED
JOBBER
JUBBAH
KIBBLE
LIBBED
LIBBER
LOBBED
LOBBER
LUBBER
MOBBED
NABBED
NABBER
NIBBLE
NUBBED
NUBBIN
NUBBLE
PEBBLE
PEBBLY
RABBET
RABBIS
RABBIT
RABBLE
RIBBED
RIBBON
ROBBED
ROBBER
ROBBIE
RUBBED
RUBBER
RUBBLE
RUBBLY
SOBBED
SOBBER
SUBBED
TABBED
TUBBED
WEBBED
WEBBER
WOBBLE
WOBBLY

••B•B•
CUBEBS
IMBIBE
KABOBS
KEBABS
KEBOBS
NABOBS

••B••B
COBWEB
HOBNOB
HUBBUB
SUBDEB
SUBURB

•••BB•
BLABBY
CHUBBY
CLUBBY
CRABBE
CRABBY
FLABBY
GRABBY
GRUBBY
KNOBBY
SCABBY
SHABBY
SNOBBY
STUBBY
SWABBY

•••B•B
BAOBAB
HUBBUB

••••BB
SQUIBB
TYCOBB

B•C•••
BACALL
BACKED
BACKER
BACKIN
BACKUP
BACKUS
BECALM
BECAME
BECKER
BECKET
BECKON
BECOME
BICARB
BICEPS
BICKER
BICORN
BOCCIE
BOCHCO
BUCCAL
BUCKED
BUCKET
BUCKLE
BUCKUP

B••C••
BAUCIS
BEACON
BETCHA
BISCAY
BLACKS
BLOCKS
BLOCKY
BOBCAT
BOCCIE
BOUCLE
BOXCAR
BRACED
BRACER
BRACES
BRACTS
BRECHT
BRICKS
BRICKY
BUCCAL
BUNCHE
BUNCOS

B•••C•
BARUCH
BASICS
BEDECK
BIANCA
BIERCE
BISECT
BLANCA
BLANCH
BLEACH
BLENCH
BLOTCH
BOCHCO
BODICE
BORSCH
BOUNCE
BOUNCY
BRANCH
BREACH
BREECH
BROACH
BRONCO
BRONCS
BROOCH
BRUNCH

B••••C
BALTIC
BALZAC
BARDIC
BELLOC
BIGMAC
BIONIC
BIOTIC

•B•C••
ABACAS
ABACUS

•B••C•
ABBACY
ABDUCT
ABJECT
OBJECT

••BC••
BOBCAT
DUBCEK
HUBCAP
MOBCAP

••B•C•
ABBACY
CUBICS
GOBACK
LUBECK
ORBACH
XEBECS

••B••C
ENBLOC
FABRIC
PUBLIC
RUBRIC

•••B•C
AMEBIC
ARABIC
IAMBIC
PHOBIC
QUEBEC
SORBIC
TOMBAC

B•D•••
BADDIE
BADEGG
BADGER
BADGES
BADGUY
BADLOT
BEDAUB
BEDAZE
BEDBUG
BEDECK
BEDEWS
BEDIMS
BEDLAM
BIDDEN
BIDDER
BIDDLE
BIDING
BIDSIN
BIDSON
BIDSUP
BODEGA
BODICE
BODIED
BODIES
BODILY
BODING
BODKIN
BODONI
BUDDED
BUDDHA
BUDGED
BUDGES
BUDGET
BUDGIE

B••D••
BADDIE
BAGDAD
BALDER
BALDLY
BANDED
BANDIT
BANDOG
BARDIC
BARDOT
BEADED
BEADLE
BEADUP
BELDAM
BENDAY
BENDED
BENDER
BENDIX
BIDDEN
BIDDER
BIDDLE
BINDER
BINDUP
BIRDED
BIRDER
BIRDIE
BLADED
BLADES
BOLDER
BOLDLY
BONDED
BOODLE
BORDEN
BORDER
BOUDIN
BRIDAL
BRIDES
BRIDGE
BRIDLE
BRODIE
BRUDER
BSIDES
BUDDED
BUDDHA
BUNDLE
BURDEN

B•••D•
BEARDS
BESIDE
BETIDE
BIONDI
BIPEDS
BIPODS
BLANDA
BLEEDS
BLENDE
BLENDS
BLINDS
BLONDE
BLONDS
BLOODY
BOARDS
BOLIDE
BORIDE
BOUNDS
BOVIDS
BRAIDS
BRANDO
BRANDS
BRANDT
BRANDX
BRANDY
BREADS
BREEDS
BRENDA
BROADS
BROODS
BROODY
BUILDS

B••••D
BABIED
BACKED
BAGDAD
BAGGED
BAILED
BAITED
BALKED
BALLAD
BANDED
BANGED
BANKED
BANNED
BARBED
BARGED
BARKED
BARRED
BASHED
BASKED
BASTED
BATHED
BATTED
BAWLED
BAYARD
BEADED
BEAKED
BEAMED
BEANED
BEEFED
BEEPED
BEGGED
BEHELD
BEHIND
BEHOLD
BELIED
BELLED
BELTED
BENDED
BESTED
BEYOND
BIASED
BIBBED
BIFFED
BIFOLD
BIGRED
BILKED
BILLED
BINGED
BINNED
BIRDED
BIRLED
BITTED
BLADED
BLAMED
BLARED
BLAZED
BOATED
BOBBED
BODIED
BOFFED
BOGGED
BOILED
BOLTED
BOMBED
BONDED
BONGED
BOOKED
BOOMED
BOOTED
BOPPED
BOSSED
BOWLED
BRACED
BRAKED
BRAVED
BRAYED
BRAZED
BREWED
BRIAND
BRIARD
BRIBED
BRIGID
BRINED
BUCKED
BUDDED
BUDGED
BUFFED
BUGGED
BUGLED
BUJOLD
BULGED
BULKED
BULLED
BUMMED
BUMPED
BUNGED
BUNKED
BUNTED
BUOYED
BURIED
BURLED
BURNED
BURPED
BURRED
BUSHED
BUSIED
BUSSED
BUSTED
BUTTED
BUZZED
BYHAND
BYROAD
BYWORD

•BD•••
ABDUCT

•B•D••
ABIDED
ABIDES
ABODES
ABYDOS
IBADAN
IBIDEM

•B••D•
ABRADE
EBONDS
MBUNDU
TBIRDS
TBONDS

•B•••D
ABASED
ABATED
ABIDED
ABOARD
ABOUND
ABROAD
ABSURD
ABUSED
OBEYED
OBTUND

••BD••
EMBDEN
SUBDEB
SUBDUE

••B•D•
ALBEDO
AUBADE
EMBEDS
EMBODY
LIBIDO
NOBODY
REBIDS

••B••D
AMBLED
BABIED
BIBBED
BOBBED
CABBED
CABLED
CUBOID
DABBED
DUBBED
FABLED
FIBBED
FOBBED
GABBED
GABLED
GIBBED
HYBRID
IMBUED
INBRED
JABBED
JOBBED
KOBOLD
LIBBED
LOBBED
MOBBED
NABBED
NUBBED
REBIND
RIBALD
RIBAND
RIBBED
ROBBED
RUBBED
RUBIED
SOBBED
SUBBED
TABARD
TABBED
TABLED
TUBBED
UNBEND
UNBIND
WEBBED

•••BD•
LAMBDA

•••B•D
BARBED
BIBBED
BOBBED
BOMBED
BRIBED
CABBED
COMBED
CURBED
DABBED
DAUBED
DAYBED
DUBBED
FIBBED
FOBBED
FORBAD
FORBID
GABBED
GARBED
GIBBED
GLOBED
HOTBED
JABBED
JOBBED
LAMBED
LIBBED
LIMBED
LOBBED
MOBBED
MORBID
NABBED
NOTBAD
NUBBED
NUMBED
OUTBID
PROBED
REDBUD
RIBBED
ROBBED
RUBBED
SEABED
SINBAD
SOBBED
SUBBED
TABBED
TOOBAD
TUBBED
TURBID
WEBBED

BE••••
BEACON
BEADED
BEADLE
BEADUP
BEAGLE
BEAKED
BEAKER
BEAMED
BEAMUP
BEANED
BEANIE
BEANOS
BEARDS
BEARER
BEARON
BEARUP
BEASTS
BEATEN
BEATER
BEATIT
BEATLE
BEATON
BEATTY
BEATUP
BEAUTS
BEAUTY
BEAVER
BEBOPS
BECALM
BECAME
BECKER
BECKET
BECKON
BECOME
BEDAUB
BEDAZE
BEDBUG
BEDECK
BEDEWS
BEDIMS
BEDLAM
BEEFED
BEEFUP
BEEGUM
BEEPED
BEEPER
BEETLE
BEEVES
BEFALL
BEFELL
BEFITS
BEFOGS
BEFORE
BEFOUL
BEGETS
BEGGAR
BEGGED
BEGINS
BEGLEY
BEGOFF
BEGONE
BEGUMS
BEHALF
BEHAVE
BEHELD
BEHEST
BEHIND
BEHOLD
BEHOOF
BEIGES
BEINGS
BEIRUT
BEKESY
BELAIR
BELAYS
BELDAM
BELFRY
BELIAL
BELIED
BELIEF
BELIES
BELIZE
BELLED
BELLES
BELLOC
BELLOW
BELOIT
BELONG
BELTED
BELUGA
BEMINE
BEMIRE
BEMOAN
BEMUSE
BENDAY
BENDED
BENDER
BENDIX
BENGAL
BENGAY
BENHUR
BENIGN
BENING
BENITO
BENOIT
BENSON
BENTON
BENUMB
BENZOL
BERATE
BERBER
BEREFT
BERETS
BERGEN
BERING
BERLIN
BERNIE
BERTHA
BERTHS
BERTIE
BESANT
BESETS
BESIDE
BESOMS
BESOTS
BESSER
BESSIE
BESTED
BESTIR
BESTOW
BETAKE
BETCHA
BETELS
BETHEL
BETIDE
BETISE
BETONY
BETOOK
BETRAY
BETSEY
BETTAS
BETTER
BETTOR
BEULAH
BEURRE
BEVELS
BEVIES
BEWAIL
BEWARE
BEYOND
BEZANT
BEZELS

B•E•••
BEEFED
BEEFUP
BEEGUM
BEEPED
BEEPER
BEETLE
BEEVES
BIERCE
BLEACH
BLEARS
BLEARY
BLEATS
BLEEDS
BLEEPS
BLENCH
BLENDE
BLENDS
BLEWIT
BLEWUP
BOEING
BREACH
BREADS
BREAKS
BREAMS
BREAST
BREATH
BRECHT
BREECH
BREEDS
BREEZE
BREEZY
BREMEN
BRENDA
BRENTS
BRETON
BREUER
BREVES
BREVET
BREWED
BREWER
BUENOS
BYEBYE

B••E••
BADEGG
BAGELS
BAKERS
BAKERY
BALEEN
BALERS
BAREGE
BARELY
BAREST
BASELY
BASEST
BATEAU
BAYEUX
BEDECK
BEDEWS
BEFELL
BEGETS
BEHELD
BEHEST
BEKESY
BEREFT
BERETS
BESETS
BETELS
BEVELS
BEZELS
BICEPS
BIKERS
BIPEDS
BIREME
BISECT
BITERS
BLEEDS
BLEEPS
BLUEOX
BLUEST
BLUESY
BLUETS
BODEGA
BOGEYS
BOLERO
BOLEYN
BONERS
BONEUP
BOPEEP
BOREAL
BOREAS
BOREON
BORERS
BOREUP
BOWERS
BOWERY
BOXERS
BREECH
BREEDS
BREEZE
BREEZY
BRIEFS
BRIENZ
BRIERS
BRIERY
BUREAU
BUTENE
BUTEOS
BUYERS

B•••E•
BABIED
BABIES
BACKED
BACKER
BADGER
BADGES
BAGGED
BAGGER
BAILED
BAILEE
BAILER
BAILEY
BAINES
BAITED
BALDER
BALEEN
BALKED
BALLET
BANDED
BANGED
BANGER
BANKED
BANKER
BANNED
BANNER
BANTER
BARBED
BARBEL
BARBER
BARBET
BARGED
BARGES
BARKED
BARKER
BARLEY
BARMEN
BARNES
BARNEY
BARRED
BARREL
BARREN
BARRES
BARTER
BASHED
BASHES
BASKED
BASKET
BASSES
BASSET
BASTED
BASTER
BASTES
BATHED
BATHER
BATHES
BATMEN
BATTED
BATTEN
BATTER
BAWLED
BAWLER
BAXTER
BEADED
BEAKED
BEAKER
BEAMED
BEANED
BEARER
BEATEN
BEATER
BEAVER
BECKER
BECKET
BEEFED
BEEPED
BEEPER
BEEVES
BEGGED
BEGLEY
BEIGES
BELIED
BELIEF
BELIES
BELLED
BELLES
BELTED
BENDED
BENDER
BERBER
BERGEN
BESSER
BESTED
BETHEL
BETSEY
BETTER
BEVIES
BIASED
BIASES
BIBBED
BIBLES
BICKER
BIDDEN
BIDDER
BIFFED
BIGBEN
BIGGER
BIGRED
BIGTEN
BILGES
BILKED
BILLED
BILLET
BINDER
BINGED
BINGES
BINNED
BIOMES
BIRDED
BIRDER
BIRLED
BIRNEY
BISSET
BITTED
BITTEN
BITTER
BLADED
BLADES
BLAMED
BLAMES
BLARED
BLARES
BLAZED
BLAZER
BLAZES
BLIMEY
BLIXEN
BLOKES
BLOOEY
BLOWER
BOATED
BOATER
BOBBED
BOBBER
BODIED
BODIES
BOFFED
BOGGED
BOGIES
BOGLES
BOILED
BOILER
BOITES
BOLDER
BOLGER
BOLTED
BOMBED
BOMBER
BOMBES
BONDED
BONGED
BONIER
BONNES
BONNET
BONZES
BOOKED
BOOKER
BOOMED
BOOMER
BOOTED
BOOTEE
BOOTES
BOPEEP
BOPPED
BOPPER
BORDEN
BORDER
BORNEO
BOSKET
BOSLEY
BOSSED
BOSSES
BOTHER
BOTREE
BOULES
BOULEZ
BOWLED
BOWLER
BOWLES
BOWMEN
BOWNET
BOWSER
BOWYER
BOXSET
BRACED
BRACER
BRACES
BRAKED
BRAKES
BRAVED
BRAVER
BRAVES
BRAYED
BRAYER
BRAZED
BRAZEN
BRAZER
BRAZES
BREMEN
BREUER
BREVES
BREVET
BREWED
BREWER
BRIBED
BRIBES
BRIDES
BRINED
BRINES
BROKEN
BROKER
BRUDER
BRUGES
BRULES
BRUMES
BRUNEI
BRUNET
BRUTES
BSIDES
BUCKED
BUCKET
BUDDED
BUDGED
BUDGES
BUDGET
BUFFED
BUFFER
BUFFET
BUGGED
BUGLED
BUGLER
BUGLES
BULGED
BULGES
BULKED
BULLED
BULLET
BULWER
BUMMED
BUMMER
BUMPED
BUMPER
BUNGED
BUNGEE
BUNKED
BUNKER
BUNSEN
BUNTED
BUNTER
BUNUEL
BUOYED
BURDEN
BURGEE
BURGER
BURIED
BURIES
BURLED
BURLEY
BURNED
BURNER
BURNET
BURNEY
BURPED
BURRED
BURSES
BUSHED
BUSHEL
BUSHES
BUSIED
BUSIER
BUSIES
BUSMEN
BUSSED
BUSSES
BUSTED
BUSTER
BUTLER
BUTTED
BUTTER
BUTTES
BUZZED
BUZZER
BUZZES
BYRNES

B••••E
BABBLE
BADDIE
BAFFLE
BAGGIE
BAILEE
BANGLE
BARBIE
BAREGE
BARITE
BARQUE
BARRIE
BASQUE
BATTLE
BATTUE
BAUBLE
BEADLE
BEAGLE
BEANIE
BEATLE
BECAME
BECOME
BEDAZE
BEETLE
BEFORE
BEGONE
BEHAVE
BELIZE
BEMINE
BEMIRE
BEMUSE
BERATE
BERNIE
BERTIE
BESIDE
BESSIE
BETAKE
BETIDE
BETISE
BEURRE
BEWARE
BIDDLE
BIERCE
BIGGIE
BIGLIE
BIGTOE
BILLIE
BINATE
BIRDIE
BIREME
BISQUE
BLAINE
BLAISE
BLENDE
BLITHE
BLONDE
BLOUSE
BLYTHE
BMOVIE
BOBBIE
BOBBLE
BOCCIE
BODICE
BOGGLE
BOLIDE
BONNIE
BOODLE
BOOGIE
BOOKIE
BOOTEE
BOOTHE
BOOTIE
BORAGE
BORATE
BORIDE
BOTREE
BOTTLE
BOUCLE
BOUFFE
BOULLE
BOUNCE
BOURKE
BOURNE
BOURSE
BOVINE
BOWTIE
BRAISE
BRAQUE
BREEZE
BRIDGE
BRIDLE
BRODIE
BROGUE
BRONTE
BRONZE
BROOKE
BROWNE
BROWSE
BRUISE
BUBBLE
BUCKLE
BUDGIE
BULLAE
BUMBLE
BUNCHE
BUNDLE
BUNGEE
BUNGLE
BURBLE
BURGEE
BURGLE
BURSAE
BUSTLE
BUTANE
BUTENE
BYEBYE
BYGONE
BYJOVE
BYLINE
BYNAME
BYROTE
BYSSHE

•BE•••
ABELES
EBERLY
HBEAMS
IBEAMS
IBERIA
IBEXES
OBEAHS
OBELIA
OBELUS
OBERON
OBEYED

•B•E••
ABBESS
ABBEYS
ABJECT
ABLEST
ABSENT
OBJECT
OBSESS
OBTEST
OBVERT
UBIETY

•B••E•
ABASED
ABASES
ABATED
ABATES
ABELES
ABIDED
ABIDES
ABODES
ABUSED
ABUSER
ABUSES
FBIMEN
IBEXES
IBIDEM
IBISES
OBEYED
OBITER
OBRIEN
OBSTET
TBONES

•B•••E
ABJURE
ABLATE
ABLAZE
ABRADE
OBLATE
OBLIGE
OBTUSE

••BE••
ABBESS
ABBEYS
ALBEDO
ALBEIT
ALBERT
AMBERS
ARBELA
ATBEST
CABERS
CUBEBS
CYBELE
EDBERG
EGBERT
EKBERG
ELBERT
EMBEDS
EMBERS
FIBERS
GIBERS
HABEAS
HUBERT
JOBETH
LABELS
LIBELS
LLBEAN
LUBECK
MABELL
REBELS
RIBEYE
ROBERT
RUBENS
SABENA
SABERS
SEBERG

SOBEIT
SOBERS
TUBERS
UMBELS
UMBERS
UNBELT
UNBEND
UNBENT
UPBEAT
UZBEKS
WEBERN
XEBECS

••B•E•
AMBLED
AMBLER
AMBLES
AUBREY
BABIED
BABIES
BIBBED
BIBLES
BOBBED
BOBBER
CABBED
CABLED
CABLER
CABLES
COBWEB
DABBED
DABNEY
DOBBER
DUBBED
DUBCEK
EMBDEN
EMBLEM
EUBOEA
FABLED
FABLER
FABLES
FIBBED
FIBBER
FIBRES
FOBBED
GABBED
GABBER
GABLED
GABLES
GIBBED
GIBBER
GIBBET
GIBLET
GOBIES
GOBLET
HEBREW
HOBBES
HOBOES
IMBUED
IMBUES
INBRED
JABBED
JABBER
JOBBED
JOBBER
LABREA
LABRET
LIBBED
LIBBER
LOBBED
LOBBER
LUBBER
MOBBED
MOBLEY
NABBED
NABBER
NOBLER
NOBLES
NUBBED
RABBET
RABIES
RIBBED
ROBBED
ROBBER
ROBLES
RUBBED
RUBBER
RUBIED
RUBIES
RUBLES
SABLES
SABRES
SOBBED
SOBBER
SUBBED
SUBDEB
SUBLET
SUBSET
TABBED
TABLED
TABLES
TABLET
TOBIES
TUBBED
VEBLEN
WEBBED
WEBBER

••B••E
AUBADE
BABBLE
BOBBIE
BOBBLE
BUBBLE
CABBIE
COBBLE
CUBAGE
CYBELE
DABBLE
DEBASE
DEBATE
DEBBIE
DEBONE
DIBBLE
GABBLE
GOBBLE
HABILE
HOBBLE
HUBBLE
IMBIBE
IMBRUE
KIBBLE
LABILE
LOBATE
LOBULE
MOBILE
MRBLUE
NIBBLE
NUBBLE
NUBILE
PEBBLE
RABBLE
REBATE
REBUKE
RIBEYE
RIBOSE
ROBBIE
RUBBLE
SABINE
SUBDUE
SUBTLE
TIBIAE
TUBATE
UMBRAE
URBANE
WOBBLE

•••BE•
ADOBES
BARBED
BARBEL
BARBER
BARBET
BERBER
BIBBED
BIGBEN
BOBBED
BOBBER
BOMBED
BOMBER
BOMBES
BRIBED
BRIBES
CABBED
CAMBER
COMBED
COMBER
COMBES
CORBEL
CUMBER
CURBED
DABBED
DAUBED
DAUBER
DAUBES
DAYBED
DOBBER
DRABEK
DUBBED
DUMBER
FERBER
FIBBED
FIBBER
FOBBED
FORBES
GABBED
GABBER
GARBED
GERBER
GIBBED
GIBBER
GIBBET
GIMBEL
GLEBES
GLOBED
GLOBES
GOOBER
GRABEN
GREBES
GUMBEL
HOBBES
HOTBED
ISABEL
JABBED
JABBER
JOBBED
JOBBER
KHYBER
LAMBED
LIBBED
LIBBER
LIMBED
LIMBER
LOBBED
LOBBER
LUBBER
LUMBER
MAYBES
MEMBER
MOBBED
NABBED
NABBER
NUBBED
NUMBED
NUMBER
PLEBES
PROBED
PROBER
PROBES
QUEBEC
RABBET
REUBEN
RIBBED
ROBBED
ROBBER
RUBBED
RUBBER
SEABED
SEABEE
SIMBEL
SOBBED
SOBBER
SOMBER
SORBET
SUBBED
TABBED
THEBES
TIMBER
TREBEK
TRIBES
TUBBED
WEBBED
WEBBER
YOUBET

•••B•E
ALIBLE
AMEBAE
ARABLE
BABBLE
BARBIE
BAUBLE
BOBBIE
BOBBLE
BUBBLE
BUMBLE
BURBLE
BYEBYE
CABBIE
COBBLE
CRABBE
DABBLE
DEBBIE
DIBBLE
DOABLE
DOOBIE
DOUBLE
EDIBLE
ENABLE
FEEBLE
FOIBLE
FUMBLE
GABBLE
GAMBLE
GARBLE
GOBBLE
GRABLE
HEEBIE
HERBIE
HOBBLE
HOMBRE
HUBBLE
HUMBLE
JUMBLE
KIBBLE
LIABLE
MARBLE
MUMBLE
NIBBLE
NIMBLE
NUBBLE
PEBBLE
RABBLE
RAMBLE
ROBBIE
RUBBLE
RUMBLE
SEABEE
SOMBRE
STABLE
TIMBRE
TREBLE
TUMBLE
UNABLE
USABLE
VIABLE
WAMBLE
WARBLE
WIMBLE
WOBBLE
ZOMBIE

••••BE
ACHEBE
AEROBE
CARIBE
CRABBE
DANUBE
ENROBE
EPHEBE
FLAMBE
IMBIBE
JUJUBE
LETSBE
MCCABE
MUGABE
PHOEBE
SCRIBE
STROBE
THISBE
UNROBE

B•F•••
BAFFIN
BAFFLE
BEFALL
BEFELL
BEFITS
BEFOGS
BEFORE
BEFOUL
BIFFED
BIFOLD
BOFFED
BOFFOS
BUFFED
BUFFER
BUFFET
BUFFON
BUFFOS

B••F••
BAFFIN
BAFFLE
BAGFUL
BARFLY
BEEFED
BEEFUP
BELFRY
BIAFRA
BIFFED
BLUFFS
BOFFED
BOFFOS
BOTFLY
BOUFFE
BOWFIN
BOXFUL
BUFFED
BUFFER
BUFFET
BUFFON
BUFFOS

B•••F•
BEGOFF
BEREFT
BITOFF
BLUFFS
BOUFFE
BRIEFS
BUGOFF
BUYOFF

B••••F
BEGOFF
BEHALF
BEHOOF
BELIEF
BITOFF
BUGOFF
BUYOFF

••B•F•
FOBOFF
REBUFF
RUBIFY

••B••F
FOBOFF
REBUFF

BG••••
BGIRLS

B•G•••
BAGDAD
BAGELS
BAGFUL
BAGGED
BAGGER
BAGGIE
BAGUIO
BEGETS
BEGGAR
BEGGED
BEGINS
BEGLEY
BEGOFF
BEGONE
BEGUMS
BIGAMY
BIGBEN
BIGBOY
BIGGER
BIGGIE
BIGGUN
BIGHTS
BIGLIE
BIGMAC
BIGOTS
BIGRED
BIGSUR
BIGTEN
BIGTOE
BIGTOP
BIGWIG
BOGART
BOGEYS
BOGGED
BOGGLE
BOGIES
BOGLES
BOGONG
BOGOTA
BUGGED
BUGLED
BUGLER
BUGLES
BUGOFF
BUGOUT
BYGONE
BYGOSH

B••G••
BADGER
BADGES
BADGUY
BAGGED
BAGGER
BAGGIE
BANGED
BANGER
BANGKA
BANGLE
BANGOR
BANGUI
BANGUP
BARGED
BARGES
BEAGLE
BEEGUM
BEGGAR
BEGGED
BEIGES
BENGAL
BENGAY
BERGEN
BIGGER
BIGGIE
BIGGUN
BILGES
BINGED
BINGES
BIOGAS
BIRGIT
BLIGHT
BOGGED
BOGGLE
BOIGNY
BOLGER
BONGED
BONGOS
BOOGIE
BORGIA
BOUGHS
BOUGHT
BRIGGS
BRIGHT
BRIGID
BROGAN
BROGUE
BRUGES
BUDGED
BUDGES
BUDGET
BUDGIE
BUGGED
BULGAR
BULGED
BULGES
BULGUR
BUNGED
BUNGEE
BUNGLE
BURGAS
BURGEE
BURGER
BURGHS
BURGLE
BURGOO
BURGOS

B•••G•
BADEGG
BAREGE
BEFOGS
BEINGS
BELUGA
BENIGN
BODEGA
BOINGO
BORAGE
BRIDGE
BRIGGS
BRINGS

B••••G
BAAING
BADEGG
BAKING
BALING
BANDOG
BARING
BARONG
BASING
BATING
BAYING
BBKING
BEDBUG
BELONG
BENING
BERING
BIDING
BIGWIG
BIKING
BITING
BLUING
BODING
BOEING
BOGONG
BONING
BOOING
BORING
BOWING
BOXING
BUSING
BUTUNG
BUYING

•B••G•
OBLIGE
UBANGI

•B•••G
BBKING
EBBING
OBLONG

••BG••
SUBGUM

••B•G•
CUBAGE
DEBUGS
REBAGS
TOBAGO

••B••G
ALBORG
COBURG
CUBING
CYBORG
EBBING
EDBERG
EKBERG
GIBING
JIBING
LUBING
ORBING
ROBING
SEBERG
TUBING
VYBORG

•••B•G
AIRBAG
BEDBUG
GASBAG
HUMBUG
ICEBAG
KITBAG
LIEBIG
RAGBAG
SEABAG
SOWBUG
TEABAG

BH••••
BHAKTI
BHOPAL
BHUTAN
BHUTTO

B•H•••
BAHAMA
BAHIAN
BEHALF
BEHAVE
BEHELD
BEHEST
BEHIND
BEHOLD
BEHOOF
BIHARI
BSHARP
BYHAND

B••H••
BARHOP
BASHED
BASHES
BATHED
BATHER
BATHES
BATHOS
BENHUR
BETHEL
BIGHTS
BISHOP
BOCHCO
BOOHOO
BOTHER
BRAHMA
BRAHMS
BUSHED
BUSHEL
BUSHES
BUSHWA

B•••H•
BERTHA
BERTHS
BETCHA
BIRTHS
BLIGHT
BLITHE
BLYTHE
BOOTHE
BOOTHS
BOUGHS
BOUGHT
BRASHY
BRECHT
BRIGHT
BROTHS
BRUSHY
BUDDHA
BUNCHE
BUQSHA
BURGHS
BYSSHE

B••••H
BANISH
BARUCH
BEULAH
BLANCH
BLEACH
BLENCH
BLOTCH
BLUISH
BORSCH
BOYISH
BRANCH
BREACH
BREATH
BREECH
BROACH
BROOCH
BRUNCH
BYGOSH
BYPATH

•BH•••
ABHORS

•B•H••
ABOHMS

•B••H•
OBEAHS

•B•••H
ABLUSH

••BH••
COBHAM
JOBHOP

••B••H
AMBUSH
JOBETH
JUBBAH
KIBOSH
ORBACH
WABASH

•••B•H
CASBAH
JUBBAH
KASBAH

BI••••
BIAFRA
BIANCA
BIASED
BIASES
BIBBED
BIBLES
BIBLIO
BICARB
BICEPS
BICKER
BICORN
BIDDEN
BIDDER
BIDDLE
BIDING
BIDSIN
BIDSON
BIDSUP
BIERCE
BIFFED
BIFOLD
BIGAMY
BIGBEN
BIGBOY
BIGGER
BIGGIE
BIGGUN
BIGHTS
BIGLIE
BIGMAC
BIGOTS
BIGRED
BIGSUR
BIGTEN
BIGTOE
BIGTOP
BIGWIG
BIHARI
BIJOUX
BIKERS
BIKING
BIKINI
BILBAO
BILGES
BILKED
BILLED
BILLET
BILLIE
BILLON
BILLOW
BILOXI
BIMINI
BINARY
BINATE
BINDER
BINDUP
BINGED
BINGES
BINNED
BIOBIO
BIOGAS
BIOMES
BIONDI
BIONIC
BIOTAS
BIOTIC
BIOTIN
BIPEDS
BIPODS
BIRDED
BIRDER
BIRDIE
BIREME
BIRGIT
BIRLED
BIRNEY
BIRTHS
BISCAY
BISECT
BISHOP
BISONS
BISQUE
BISSAU
BISSET
BISTRO
BITERS
BITING
BITMAP
BITOFF
BITTED
BITTEN
BITTER

B•I•••
BAIKAL
BAILED
BAILEE
BAILER
BAILEY
BAILOR
BAINES
BAIRNS
BAITED
BEIGES
BEINGS
BEIRUT
BGIRLS
BLIGHT
BLIMEY
BLIMPS
BLINDS
BLINKS
BLINTZ
BLITHE
BLIXEN
BMINOR
BMINUS
BOIGNY
BOILED
BOILER
BOINGO
BOITES
BRIAND
BRIANS
BRIARD
BRIARS
BRIBED
BRIBES
BRICKS
BRICKY
BRIDAL
BRIDES
BRIDGE
BRIDLE
BRIEFS
BRIENZ
BRIERS
BRIERY
BRIGGS
BRIGHT
BRIGID
BRILLO
BRILLS
BRINED
BRINES
BRINGS
BRINKS
BRITON
BSIDES
BUILDS

B••I••
BAAING
BABIED
BABIES
BAHIAN
BAKING
BALING
BANISH
BARING
BARITE
BARIUM
BASICS
BASING
BASINS
BATIKS
BATING
BAYING
BBKING
BEDIMS
BEFITS
BEGINS
BEHIND
BELIAL
BELIED
BELIEF
BELIES
BELIZE
BEMINE
BEMIRE
BENIGN
BENING
BENITO
BERING
BESIDE
BETIDE
BETISE
BEVIES
BIDING
BIKING
BIKINI
BIMINI
BITING
BLAINE
BLAISE
BLUING
BLUISH
BODICE
BODIED
BODIES
BODILY
BODING
BOEING
BOGIES
BOLIDE
BONIER
BONING
BONITO
BOOING
BORIDE
BORING
BOVIDS
BOVINE
BOWING
BOXING
BOYISH
BRAIDS
BRAILS
BRAINS
BRAINY
BRAISE
BROILS
BRUINS
BRUISE
BRUITS
BUNION
BURIED
BURIES
BURINS
BUSIED
BUSIER
BUSIES
BUSILY
BUSING
BUYING
BYLINE

B•••I•
BACKIN
BADDIE
BAFFIN
BAGGIE
BAGUIO
BALTIC
BANDIT
BARBIE
BARDIC
BARKIN
BARRIE
BARRIO
BARRIS
BAUCIS
BEANIE
BEATIT
BELAIR
BELOIT
BENDIX
BENOIT
BERLIN
BERNIE
BERTIE
BESSIE
BESTIR
BEWAIL
BIBLIO
BIDSIN
BIGGIE
BIGLIE
BIGWIG
BILLIE
BIOBIO
BIONIC
BIOTIC
BIOTIN
BIRDIE
BIRGIT
BLEWIT
BLOWIN
BLOWIT
BMOVIE
BOBBIE
BOBBIN
BOCCIE
BODKIN
BOLLIX
BONNIE
BOOGIE
BOOKIE
BOOTIE
BORGIA
BOSNIA
BOUDIN
BOWFIN
BOWTIE
BRAZIL
BRIGID
BRODIE
BUDGIE
BULBIL
BUSKIN
BUTTIN

B••••I
BANGUI
BANZAI
BATUMI
BHAKTI
BIHARI
BIKINI
BILOXI
BIMINI
BIONDI
BODONI
BONAMI
BONSAI
BORZOI
BRAZZI
BRUNEI
BUSONI

•BI•••
ABIDED
ABIDES
FBIMAN
FBIMEN
IBIBIO
IBIDEM
IBISES
OBISPO
OBITER
OBIWAN
TBILLS
TBIRDS
UBIETY

•B•I••
BBKING
EBBING
OBLIGE
OBOIST
OBRIAN
OBRIEN

•B••I•
ABATIS
ABUKIR
IBERIA
IBIBIO
OBELIA
OBTAIN

•B•••I
UBANGI

••BI••
ALBINO
ALBION
AMBITS

BABIED
BABIES
CABINS
COBIAS
CUBICS
CUBING
CUBISM
CUBIST
CUBITS
CYBILL
DEBITS
EBBING
ERBIUM
FABIAN
GABION
GIBILL
GIBING
GOBIES
HABILE
HABITS
IMBIBE
JABIRU
JIBING
KIBITZ
LABIAL
LABILE
LIBIDO
LUBING
MOBILE
MOBIUS
NUBIAN
NUBILE
ORBING
ORBITS
RABIES
REBIDS
REBIND
ROBING
ROBINS
RUBIED
RUBIES
RUBIFY
SABINE
SABINS
SUBITO
TIBIAE
TIBIAL
TIBIAS
TOBIAS
TOBIES
TUBING
TUBIST
UNBIND

••B•I•
ALBEIT
ALBOIN
AMBLIN
BIBLIO
BOBBIE
BOBBIN
CABBIE
CUBOID
DEBBIE
DEBRIS
DOBBIN
DOBLIN
DUBBIN
DUBLIN
DUBOIS
FABRIC
FIBRIL
FIBRIN
GOBLIN
HOBBIT
HUBRIS
HYBRID
LIBRIS
LUBLIN
MCBAIN
NUBBIN
PUBLIC
RABBIS
RABBIT
REBOIL
ROBBIE
RUBRIC
RUBSIN
SOBEIT
SUBMIT
TABRIZ
UMBRIA

••B••I
KABUKI
KUBLAI

•••BI•
ALIBIS
AMEBIC
ANUBIS
ARABIA
ARABIC
BARBIE
BIOBIO
BOBBIE
BOBBIN
BULBIL
CABBIE
CORBIN
DEBBIE
DOBBIN
DOOBIE
DUBBIN
DURBIN
FORBID
GAMBIA
GAMBIT
GERBIL
GLOBIN
HARBIN
HEEBIE
HENBIT
HERBIE
HOBBIT
IAMBIC
IBIBIO
LIEBIG
MORBID
NUBBIN
ORIBIS
OUTBID
PHOBIA
PHOBIC
RABBIS
RABBIT
ROBBIE
SERBIA
SORBIC
TIDBIT
TITBIT
TURBID
TURBIT
TWOBIT
ZAMBIA
ZOMBIE

••••BI
ITURBI
JACOBI
MESABI
RHOMBI
WASABI

B•J•••
BIJOUX
BUJOLD
BYJOVE

B••J••
BANJOS
BANJUL
BMAJOR
BOOJUM

B•••J•
BAROJA

•BJ•••
ABJECT
ABJURE
OBJECT

B•K•••
BAKERS
BAKERY
BAKING
BBKING
BEKESY
BIKERS
BIKING
BIKINI

B••K••
BABKAS
BACKED
BACKER
BACKIN
BACKUP
BACKUS
BAIKAL
BALKAN
BALKED
BANKED
BANKER
BANKON
BARKED
BARKER
BARKIN
BASKED
BASKET
BEAKED
BEAKER
BECKER
BECKET
BECKON
BHAKTI
BICKER
BILKED
BLOKES
BODKIN
BOOKED
BOOKER
BOOKIE
BOSKET
BRAKED
BRAKES
BROKAW
BROKEN
BROKER
BUCKED
BUCKET
BUCKLE
BUCKUP
BULKED
BUNKED
BUNKER
BUNKOS
BUNKUM
BUSKIN

B•••K•
BAMAKO
BANGKA
BATIKS
BETAKE
BLACKS
BLANKS
BLINKS
BLOCKS
BLOCKY
BOURKE
BREAKS
BRICKS
BRICKY
BRINKS
BROOKE
BROOKS

B••••K
BARTOK
BEDECK
BETOOK
BUROAK
BYTALK

•BK•••
BBKING

•B•K••
ABUKIR

••BK••
BABKAS

••B•K•
KABUKI
REBUKE
UZBEKS

••B••K
DEBARK
DEBUNK
DUBCEK
DYBBUK
EMBANK
EMBARK
GOBACK
INBULK
LUBECK
TOBRUK

•••B•K
DRABEK
DYBBUK
LOMBOK
REEBOK
RHEBOK
TREBEK

BL••••
BLABBY
BLACKS
BLADED
BLADES
BLAINE
BLAISE
BLAMED
BLAMES
BLANCA
BLANCH
BLANDA
BLANKS
BLARED
BLARES
BLASTS
BLATTY
BLAZED
BLAZER
BLAZES
BLAZON
BLEACH
BLEARS
BLEARY
BLEATS
BLEEDS
BLEEPS
BLENCH
BLENDE
BLENDS
BLEWIT
BLEWUP
BLIGHT
BLIMEY
BLIMPS
BLINDS
BLINKS
BLINTZ
BLITHE
BLIXEN
BLOATS
BLOCKS
BLOCKY
BLOKES
BLONDE
BLONDS
BLOODY
BLOOEY
BLOOMS
BLOOMY
BLOOPS
BLOTCH
BLOTTO
BLOUSE
BLOWER
BLOWIN
BLOWIT
BLOWUP
BLOWZY
BLUEOX
BLUEST
BLUESY
BLUETS
BLUFFS
BLUING
BLUISH
BLUNTS
BLURBS
BLURRY
BLURTS
BLYTHE

B•L•••
BALAAM
BALATA
BALBOA
BALDER
BALDLY
BALEEN
BALERS
BALING
BALKAN
BALKED
BALLAD
BALLET
BALLOT
BALLUP
BALSAM
BALTIC
BALZAC
BELAIR
BELAYS
BELDAM
BELFRY
BELIAL
BELIED
BELIEF
BELIES
BELIZE
BELLED
BELLES
BELLOC
BELLOW
BELOIT
BELONG
BELTED
BELUGA
BILBAO
BILGES
BILKED
BILLED
BILLET
BILLIE
BILLON
BILLOW
BILOXI
BOLDER
BOLDLY
BOLERO
BOLEYN
BOLGER
BOLIDE
BOLLIX
BOLTED
BOLTON
BULBIL
BULBUL
BULGAR
BULGED
BULGES
BULGUR
BULKED
BULLAE
BULLED
BULLET
BULOVA
BULWER
BYLAWS
BYLINE

B••L••
BADLOT
BAILED
BAILEE
BAILER
BAILEY
BAILOR
BALLAD
BALLET
BALLOT
BALLUP
BANLON
BARLEY
BAWLED
BAWLER
BAYLOR
BEDLAM
BEGLEY
BELLED
BELLES
BELLOC
BELLOW
BERLIN
BEULAH
BIBLES
BIBLIO
BIGLIE
BILLED
BILLET
BILLIE
BILLON
BILLOW
BIRLED
BOGLES
BOILED
BOILER
BOLLIX
BOSLEY
BOULES
BOULEZ
BOULLE
BOWLED
BOWLER
BOWLES
BRILLO
BRILLS
BROLLY
BRULES
BUGLED
BUGLER
BUGLES
BUILDS
BULLAE
BULLED
BULLET
BURLAP
BURLED
BURLEY
BUTLER
BYPLAY

B•••L•
BABBLE
BABULS
BACALL
BAFFLE
BAGELS
BALDLY
BANGLE
BARELY
BARFLY
BAROLO
BASALT
BASELY
BATTLE
BAUBLE
BEADLE
BEAGLE
BEATLE
BECALM
BEETLE
BEFALL
BEFELL
BEHALF
BEHELD
BEHOLD
BETELS
BEVELS
BEZELS
BGIRLS
BIDDLE
BIFOLD
BOBBLE
BODILY
BOGGLE
BOLDLY
BOODLE
BOTFLY
BOTTLE
BOUCLE
BOULLE
BRAILS
BRAWLS
BRIDLE
BRILLO
BRILLS
BROILS
BROLLY
BUBBLE
BUBBLY
BUCKLE
BUJOLD
BUMBLE
BUNDLE
BUNGLE
BURBLE
BURBLY
BURGLE
BUSILY
BUSTLE
BYTALK

B••••L
BACALL
BAGFUL
BAIKAL
BANJUL
BARBEL
BARREL
BEFALL
BEFELL
BEFOUL
BELIAL
BENGAL
BENZOL
BETHEL
BEWAIL
BHOPAL
BOREAL
BOXFUL
BRAZIL
BRIDAL
BRUMAL
BRUTAL
BUCCAL
BULBIL
BULBUL
BUNUEL
BURSAL
BUSHEL

•BL•••
ABLATE
ABLAUT
ABLAZE
ABLEST
ABLOOM
ABLUSH
OBLAST
OBLATE
OBLIGE
OBLONG

•B•L••
ABELES
ABOLLA
OBELIA
OBELUS
TBILLS
UBOLTS

•B••L•
ABOLLA
EBERLY
TBILLS

•B•••L
ABORAL

••BL••
AMBLED
AMBLER
AMBLES
AMBLIN
BIBLES
BIBLIO
CABLED
CABLER
CABLES
DOBLAS
DOBLIN
DUBLIN
EMBLEM
ENBLOC
FABLED
FABLER
FABLES
GABLED
GABLES
GIBLET
GOBLET
GOBLIN
JOBLOT
KUBLAI
LUBLIN
MOBLEY
MRBLUE
NOBLER
NOBLES
PABLUM
PUBLIC
ROBLES
RUBLES
SABLES
SUBLET
TABLAS
TABLED
TABLES
TABLET
VEBLEN

••B•L•
ARBELA
BABBLE
BABULS
BOBBLE
BUBBLE
BUBBLY
CABALA
CABALS
CIBOLA
COBALT
COBBLE
CYBELE
CYBILL
DABBLE
DIBBLE
FIBULA
GABBLE
GIBILL
GOBBLE
HABILE
HOBBLE
HUBBLE
HUBBLY
INBULK
KIBBLE
KOBOLD
LABELS
LABILE
LIBELS
LOBULE
MABELL
MOBILE
NEBULA
NIBBLE
NUBBLE
NUBILE
PEBBLE
PEBBLY
RABBLE
REBELS
REBOLT
RIBALD
ROBALO
RUBBLE
RUBBLY
SIBYLS
SUBTLE
SUBTLY
TABULA
TYBALT
UMBELS
UNBELT
UNBOLT
WOBBLE
WOBBLY

••B••L
CYBILL
FIBRIL
GIBILL
LABIAL
MABELL
REBOIL
TIBIAL
UMBRAL

•••BL•
ALIBLE
ARABLE
BABBLE
BAUBLE
BOBBLE
BUBBLE
BUBBLY
BUMBLE
BURBLE
BURBLY
COBBLE
DABBLE
DIABLO
DIBBLE
DOABLE
DOUBLE
DOUBLY
DRABLY
DUMBLY
EDIBLE
ENABLE
FEEBLE
FEEBLY
FOIBLE
FUMBLE
GABBLE
GAMBLE
GARBLE
GLIBLY
GOBBLE
GRABLE
HOBBLE
HUBBLE
HUBBLY
HUMBLE
HUMBLY
JUMBLE
KIBBLE
LIABLE
MARBLE
MARBLY
MUMBLE
MUMBLY
NIBBLE
NIMBLE
NIMBLY
NUBBLE
NUMBLY
PEBBLE
PEBBLY
PUEBLA
PUEBLO
RABBLE
RAMBLA
RAMBLE
RUBBLE
RUBBLY
RUMBLE
RUMBLY
STABLE
STABLY
TREBLE
TREBLY
TUMBLE
UNABLE
USABLE
USABLY
VIABLE
VIABLY
WAMBLE
WAMBLY
WARBLE
WIMBLE
WOBBLE
WOBBLY

•••B•L
BARBEL
BULBIL
BULBUL
CORBEL
CYMBAL
GAMBOL
GERBIL
GIMBAL
GIMBEL
GLOBAL
GUMBEL
HERBAL
ISABEL
IZABAL
SAMBAL
SIMBEL
SYMBOL
TIMBAL
TRIBAL
VERBAL

BM••••
BMAJOR
BMINOR
BMINUS
BMOVIE

B•M•••
BAMAKO
BAMBOO
BEMINE
BEMIRE
BEMOAN
BEMUSE
BIMINI
BOMBAY
BOMBED
BOMBER
BOMBES
BUMBLE
BUMBRY
BUMMED
BUMMER
BUMOUT
BUMPED
BUMPER
BUMPPO
BUMPUP
BUMRAP

B••M••
BARMAN
BARMEN
BATMAN
BATMEN
BEAMED
BEAMUP
BIGMAC
BIOMES
BITMAP
BLAMED
BLAMES
BLIMEY
BLIMPS
BONMOT
BOOMED
BOOMER
BORMAN
BOWMAN
BOWMEN
BREMEN
BRUMAL
BRUMES
BUMMED
BUMMER
BURMAN
BUSMAN
BUSMEN

B•••M•
BAHAMA
BATUMI
BECAME
BECOME
BEDIMS
BEGUMS
BENUMB
BESOMS
BIGAMY
BIREME
BLOOMS
BLOOMY
BONAMI
BRAHMA
BRAHMS
BREAMS
BROOMS
BYNAME

B••••M
BALAAM
BALSAM
BANTAM
BARIUM
BARNUM
BAYRUM
BECALM
BEDLAM
BEEGUM
BELDAM
BOOJUM
BOTTOM
BUNKUM

•B•M••
ABOMBS
FBIMAN
FBIMEN
HBOMBS

•B••M•
ABOHMS
ABRAMS
ABYSMS
HBEAMS
IBEAMS

•B•••M
ABLOOM
IBIDEM

••BM••
SUBMIT
TUBMAN

••B•M•
ALBUMS

••B••M
COBHAM
CUBISM
EMBLEM
ERBIUM
KABOOM
LABRUM
PABLUM
SHBOOM
SUBGUM

B•N•••
BANANA
BANDED
BANDIT
BANDOG
BANGED
BANGER
BANGKA
BANGLE
BANGOR
BANGUI
BANGUP
BANISH
BANJOS
BANJUL
BANKED
BANKER
BANKON
BANLON
BANNED
BANNER
BANQUO
BANTAM
BANTER
BANTUS
BANYAN
BANZAI
BENDAY
BENDED
BENDER
BENDIX
BENGAL
BENGAY
BENHUR
BENIGN
BENING
BENITO
BENOIT
BENSON
BENTON
BENUMB
BENZOL
BINARY
BINATE
BINDER
BINDUP
BINGED
BINGES
BINNED
BONAMI
BONBON
BONDED
BONERS
BONEUP
BONGED
BONGOS
BONIER
BONING
BONITO
BONMOT
BONNES
BONNET
BONNIE
BONSAI
BONTON
BONZES
BUNCHE
BUNCOS
BUNDLE
BUNGED
BUNGEE
BUNGLE
BUNION
BUNKED
BUNKER
BUNKOS
BUNKUM
BUNSEN
BUNTED
BUNTER
BUNUEL
BUNYAN
BYNAME

B••N••
BAINES
BANNED
BANNER
BARNES
BARNEY
BARNUM
BEANED
BEANIE
BEANOS
BEINGS
BERNIE
BIANCA
BINNED
BIONDI
BIONIC
BIRNEY
BLANCA
BLANCH
BLANDA
BLANKS
BLENCH
BLENDE
BLENDS
BLINDS
BLINKS
BLINTZ
BLONDE
BLONDS
BLUNTS
BMINOR
BMINUS
BOINGO
BONNES
BONNET
BONNIE
BORNEO
BOSNIA
BOUNCE
BOUNCY
BOUNDS
BOUNTY
BOWNET
BRANCH
BRANDO
BRANDS
BRANDT
BRANDX
BRANDY
BRANTS
BRENDA
BRENTS
BRINED
BRINES
BRINGS
BRINKS
BRONCO
BRONCS
BRONTE
BRONZE
BRONZY
BRUNCH
BRUNEI
BRUNET
BRUNTS
BUENOS
BURNED
BURNER
BURNET
BURNEY
BURNUP
BWANAS
BYRNES

B•••N•
BAAING
BAIRNS
BAKING
BALING
BANANA

BARING
BARONG
BARONS
BARONY
BASING
BASINS
BATING
BATONS
BAYING
BBKING
BEGINS
BEGONE
BEHIND
BELONG
BEMINE
BENING
BERING
BESANT
BETONY
BEYOND
BEZANT
BIDING
BIKING
BIKINI
BIMINI
BISONS
BITING
BLAINE
BLUING
BODING
BODONI
BOEING
BOGONG
BOIGNY
BONING
BOOING
BORING
BOSUNS
BOTANY
BOURNE
BOVINE
BOWING
BOXING
BRAINS
BRAINY
BRAWNY
BRIAND
BRIANS
BRIENZ
BROWNE
BROWNS
BRUINS
BRYANT
BRYONY
BURINS
BUSING
BUSONI
BUTANE
BUTENE
BUTUNG
BUYING
BYGONE
BYHAND
BYLINE

B••••N
BABOON
BABSON
BACKIN
BAFFIN
BAHIAN
BALEEN
BALKAN
BANKON
BANLON
BANYAN
BARKIN
BARMAN
BARMEN
BARREN
BARRON
BARTON
BARYON
BARZUN
BATAAN
BATMAN
BATMEN
BATTEN
BEACON
BEARON
BEATEN
BEATON
BECKON
BEMOAN
BENIGN
BENSON
BENTON
BERGEN
BERLIN
BHUTAN
BICORN
BIDDEN
BIDSIN
BIDSON
BIGBEN
BIGGUN
BIGTEN
BILLON
BIOTIN
BITTEN
BLAZON
BLIXEN
BLOWIN
BOBBIN
BODKIN
BOLEYN
BOLTON
BONBON
BONTON
BORDEN
BOREON
BORMAN
BOSTON
BOUDIN
BOWFIN
BOWMAN
BOWMEN
BRAZEN
BREMEN
BRETON
BRITON
BROGAN
BROKEN
BRYSON
BUFFON
BUNION
BUNSEN
BUNYAN
BURDEN
BURMAN
BURTON
BUSKIN
BUSMAN
BUSMEN
BUTTIN
BUTTON

•B•N••
EBONDS
MBUNDU
TBONDS
TBONES
UBANGI

•B••N•
ABOUND
ABSENT
BBKING
EBBING
OBLONG
OBTUND

•B•••N
FBIMAN
FBIMEN
IBADAN
OBERON
OBIWAN
OBRIAN
OBRIEN
OBTAIN

••BN••
DABNEY
HOBNOB

••B•N•
ALBANO
ALBANY
ALBINO
CABANA
CABINS
CUBING
DEBONE
DEBUNK
EBBING
EMBANK
GIBING
HABANA
JIBING
LUBING
ORBING
REBIND
RIBAND
ROBING
ROBINS
RUBENS
SABENA
SABINE
SABINS
TUBING
UNBEND
UNBENT
UNBIND
URBANA
URBANE

••B••N
ALBION
ALBOIN
AMBLIN
AUBURN
BABOON
BABSON
BOBBIN
COBURN
DOBBIN
DOBLIN
DOBSON
DUBBIN
DUBLIN
EMBDEN
FABIAN
FIBRIN
GABION
GIBBON
GIBRAN
GIBSON
GOBLIN
HOBSON
INBORN
LEBRUN
LIBYAN
LLBEAN
LUBLIN
MCBAIN
NUBBIN
NUBIAN
OSBORN
REBORN
RIBBON
ROBSON
RUBSIN
SUBORN
TUBMAN
UNBORN
VEBLEN
WEBERN

•••B•N
ARUBAN
BIGBEN
BOBBIN
BONBON
CARBON
CORBAN
CORBIN
DOBBIN
DUBBIN
DURBAN
DURBIN
GIBBON
GLOBIN
GRABEN
HARBIN
KLIBAN
LISBON
NUBBIN
REUBEN
RIBBON
SHABAN
TURBAN

BO••••
BOARDS
BOASTS
BOATED
BOATER
BOBBED
BOBBER
BOBBIE
BOBBIN
BOBBLE
BOBCAT
BOBSUP
BOCCIE
BOCHCO
BODEGA
BODICE
BODIED
BODIES
BODILY
BODING
BODKIN
BODONI
BOEING
BOFFED
BOFFOS
BOGART
BOGEYS
BOGGED
BOGGLE
BOGIES
BOGLES
BOGONG
BOGOTA
BOIGNY
BOILED
BOILER
BOINGO
BOITES
BOLDER
BOLDLY
BOLERO
BOLEYN
BOLGER
BOLIDE
BOLLIX
BOLTED
BOLTON
BOMBAY
BOMBED
BOMBER
BOMBES
BONAMI
BONBON
BONDED
BONERS
BONEUP
BONGED
BONGOS
BONIER
BONING
BONITO
BONMOT
BONNES
BONNET
BONNIE
BONSAI
BONTON
BONZES
BOOBOO
BOODLE
BOOGIE
BOOHOO
BOOING
BOOJUM
BOOKED
BOOKER
BOOKIE
BOOMED
BOOMER
BOOSTS
BOOTED
BOOTEE
BOOTES
BOOTHE
BOOTHS
BOOTIE
BOOTSY
BOOTUP
BOPEEP
BOPPED
BOPPER
BORAGE
BORATE
BORAXO
BORDEN
BORDER
BOREAL
BOREAS
BOREON
BORERS
BOREUP
BORGIA
BORIDE
BORING
BORMAN
BORNEO
BORROW
BORSCH
BORZOI
BOSKET
BOSLEY
BOSNIA
BOSSED
BOSSES
BOSTON
BOSUNS
BOTANY
BOTFLY
BOTHER
BOTREE
BOTTLE
BOTTOM
BOUBOU
BOUCLE
BOUDIN
BOUFFE
BOUGHS
BOUGHT
BOULES
BOULEZ
BOULLE
BOUNCE
BOUNCY
BOUNDS
BOUNTY
BOURKE
BOURNE
BOURSE
BOVARY
BOVIDS
BOVINE
BOWERS
BOWERY
BOWFIN
BOWING
BOWLED
BOWLER
BOWLES
BOWMAN
BOWMEN
BOWNET
BOWOAR
BOWOUT
BOWSAW
BOWSER
BOWTIE
BOWWOW
BOWYER
BOXCAR
BOXERS
BOXFUL
BOXING
BOXSET
BOXTOP
BOYARS
BOYISH

B•O•••
BAOBAB
BHOPAL
BIOBIO
BIOGAS
BIOMES
BIONDI
BIONIC
BIOTAS
BIOTIC
BIOTIN
BLOATS
BLOCKS
BLOCKY
BLOKES
BLONDE
BLONDS
BLOODY
BLOOEY
BLOOMS
BLOOMY
BLOOPS
BLOTCH
BLOTTO
BLOUSE
BLOWER
BLOWIN
BLOWIT
BLOWUP
BLOWZY
BMOVIE
BOOBOO
BOODLE
BOOGIE
BOOHOO
BOOING
BOOJUM
BOOKED
BOOKER
BOOKIE
BOOMED
BOOMER
BOOSTS
BOOTED
BOOTEE
BOOTES
BOOTHE
BOOTHS
BOOTIE
BOOTSY
BOOTUP
BROACH
BROADS
BRODIE
BROGAN
BROGUE
BROILS
BROKAW
BROKEN
BROKER
BROLLY
BRONCO
BRONCS
BRONTE
BRONZE
BRONZY
BROOCH
BROODS
BROODY
BROOKE
BROOKS
BROOMS
BROTHS
BROWNE
BROWNS
BROWSE
BUOYED
BUOYUP

B••O••
BABOON
BAROJA
BAROLO
BARONG
BARONS
BARONY
BATONS
BAYOUS
BEBOPS
BECOME
BEFOGS
BEFORE
BEFOUL
BEGOFF
BEGONE
BEHOLD
BEHOOF
BELOIT
BELONG
BEMOAN
BENOIT
BESOMS
BESOTS
BETONY
BETOOK
BEYOND
BICORN
BIFOLD
BIGOTS
BIJOUX
BILOXI
BIPODS
BISONS
BITOFF
BLOODY
BLOOEY
BLOOMS
BLOOMY
BLOOPS
BODONI
BOGONG
BOGOTA
BOWOAR
BOWOUT
BROOCH
BROODS
BROODY
BROOKE
BROOKS
BROOMS
BRYONY
BUGOFF
BUGOUT
BUJOLD
BULOVA
BUMOUT
BUROAK
BUSONI
BUYOFF
BUYOUT
BYGONE
BYGOSH
BYJOVE
BYROAD
BYROTE
BYWORD

B•••O•
BABOON
BABSON
BADLOT
BAILOR
BALBOA
BALLOT
BAMBOO
BANDOG
BANGOR
BANJOS
BANKON
BANLON
BARDOT
BARHOP
BARRON
BARROW
BARTOK
BARTON
BARYON
BASSOS
BATBOY
BATHOS
BAYLOR
BEACON
BEANOS
BEARON
BEATON
BECKON
BEHOOF
BELLOC
BELLOW
BENSON
BENTON
BENZOL
BESTOW
BETOOK
BETTOR
BIDSON
BIGBOY
BIGTOE
BIGTOP
BILLON
BILLOW
BISHOP
BLAZON
BLUEOX
BMAJOR
BMINOR
BOFFOS
BOLTON
BONBON
BONGOS
BONMOT
BONTON
BOOBOO
BOOHOO
BOREON
BORROW
BORZOI
BOSTON
BOTTOM
BOUBOU
BOWWOW
BOXTOP
BRASOV
BRAVOS
BRAZOS
BRETON
BRITON
BRYSON
BUENOS
BUFFON
BUFFOS
BUNCOS
BUNION
BUNKOS
BURBOT
BURGOO
BURGOS
BURROS
BURROW
BURTON
BUSBOY
BUTEOS
BUTTON

B••••O
BAGUIO
BAMAKO
BAMBOO
BANQUO
BAROLO
BARRIO
BENITO
BHUTTO
BIBLIO
BILBAO
BIOBIO
BISTRO
BLOTTO
BOCHCO
BOINGO
BOLERO
BONITO
BOOBOO
BOOHOO
BORAXO
BORNEO
BRANDO
BRILLO
BRONCO
BUMPPO
BURGOO

•BO•••
ABOARD
ABODES
ABOHMS
ABOLLA
ABOMBS
ABORAL
ABORTS
ABOUND
EBOATS
EBONDS
HBOMBS
OBOIST
TBONDS
TBONES
UBOATS
UBOLTS

•B•O••
ABBOTS
ABBOTT
ABHORS
ABLOOM
ABROAD
ABSORB
OBLONG

•B••O•
ABLOOM
ABYDOS
OBERON

•B•••O
IBIBIO
OBISPO

••BO••
ABBOTS
ABBOTT
ALBOIN
ALBORG
ARBORS
ARBOUR
BABOON
BEBOPS
CIBOLA
CUBOID
CYBORG
DEBONE
DUBOIS
ELBOWS
EMBODY
EMBOSS
EUBOEA
FOBOFF
HOBOES
INBORN
JABOTS
KABOBS
KABOOM
KEBOBS
KIBOSH
KOBOLD
LABORS
LABOUR
NABOBS
NABORS
NOBODY
OSBORN
OXBOWS
POBOYS
PTBOAT
REBOIL
REBOLT
REBOOT
REBORN
REBOZO
RIBOSE
ROBOTS
RUBOUT
SABOTS
SHBOOM
SUBORN
TABOOS
TABORS
TOBOOT
UNBOLT
UNBORN
UPBOWS
VYBORG

••B•O•
ALBION
BABOON
BABSON
DEBTOR
DOBROS
DOBSON
ENBLOC
GABION
GIBBON
GIBSON
HOBNOB
HOBSON
JOBHOP
JOBLOT
KABOOM
REBOOT
RIBBON
ROBROY
ROBSON
SHBOOM
TABOOS
TOBOOT

••B••O
ALBANO
ALBEDO
ALBINO
BIBLIO
EMBRYO
GABBRO
LIBIDO
RABATO
REBOZO
ROBALO
SABATO
SUBITO
TOBAGO

•••BO•
BALBOA
BAMBOO
BATBOY
BIGBOY
BONBON
BOOBOO
BOUBOU
BURBOT
BUSBOY
CARBON
CARBOY
COMBOS
COWBOY
FLYBOY
FOGBOW
GAMBOL
GIBBON
GUMBOS
HARBOR
HATBOX
HOTBOX
ICEBOX
JERBOA
JUMBOS
LAZBOY
LESBOS
LIMBOS
LISBOA
LISBON
LOMBOK
LOWBOY
MAMBOS
OLDBOY
PHOBOS
REEBOK
RHEBOK
RIBBON
SKYBOX
SYMBOL
TALBOT
TOMBOY
TURBOS
TURBOT

•••B•O
BAMBOO
BILBAO
BIOBIO
BOOBOO
DIABLO
GABBRO
HASBRO
IBIBIO
PUEBLO

••••BO
AKIMBO
CRAMBO
GAZEBO
LAVABO
MALABO
NINGBO
PHLEBO
PICABO
SASEBO
STRABO

B•P•••
BIPEDS
BIPODS
BOPEEP
BOPPED
BOPPER
BYPASS
BYPAST
BYPATH
BYPLAY

B••P••
BEEPED
BEEPER
BHOPAL
BOPPED
BOPPER
BUMPED
BUMPER
BUMPPO
BUMPUP
BURPED

B•••P•
BEBOPS
BICEPS
BLEEPS
BLIMPS
BLOOPS
BUMPPO

B••••P
BACKUP
BALLUP
BANGUP
BARHOP
BEADUP
BEAMUP
BEARUP
BEATUP
BEEFUP
BIDSUP
BIGTOP
BINDUP
BISHOP
BITMAP
BLEWUP
BLOWUP
BOBSUP
BONEUP
BOOTUP
BOPEEP
BOREUP
BOXTOP
BSHARP
BUCKUP
BUMPUP
BUMRAP
BUOYUP
BURLAP
BURNUP
BUYSUP

•B••P•
ABRUPT
OBISPO

••B•P•
BEBOPS

••B••P
BOBSUP
HUBCAP
JOBHOP
MOBCAP

B•Q•••
BUQSHA

B••Q••
BANQUO
BARQUE
BASQUE
BISQUE
BRAQUE

BR••••
BRACED
BRACER
BRACES
BRACTS
BRAHMA
BRAHMS
BRAIDS
BRAILS
BRAINS
BRAINY
BRAISE
BRAKED
BRAKES
BRANCH
BRANDO
BRANDS
BRANDT
BRANDX
BRANDY
BRANTS
BRAQUE
BRASHY
BRASOV
BRASSY
BRATTY
BRAVAS
BRAVED
BRAVER
BRAVES
BRAVOS
BRAWLS
BRAWNY
BRAYED
BRAYER
BRAZED
BRAZEN
BRAZER
BRAZES
BRAZIL
BRAZOS
BRAZZA
BRAZZI
BREACH
BREADS
BREAKS
BREAMS
BREAST
BREATH
BRECHT
BREECH
BREEDS
BREEZE
BREEZY
BREMEN
BRENDA
BRENTS
BRETON
BREUER
BREVES
BREVET
BREWED
BREWER
BRIAND
BRIANS
BRIARD
BRIARS
BRIBED
BRIBES
BRICKS
BRICKY
BRIDAL
BRIDES
BRIDGE
BRIDLE
BRIEFS
BRIENZ
BRIERS
BRIERY
BRIGGS
BRIGHT
BRIGID
BRILLO
BRILLS
BRINED
BRINES
BRINGS
BRINKS
BRITON
BROACH
BROADS
BRODIE
BROGAN
BROGUE
BROILS
BROKAW
BROKEN
BROKER
BROLLY
BRONCO
BRONCS
BRONTE
BRONZE
BRONZY
BROOCH
BROODS
BROODY
BROOKE
BROOKS
BROOMS
BROTHS
BROWNE
BROWNS
BROWSE
BRUDER
BRUGES
BRUINS
BRUISE
BRUITS
BRULES
BRUMAL
BRUMES

BRUNCH
BRUNEI
BRUNET
BRUNTS
BRUSHY
BRUTAL
BRUTES
BRUTUS
BRYANT
BRYONY
BRYSON

B•R•••
BARBED
BARBEL
BARBER
BARBET
BARBIE
BARBRA
BARDIC
BARDOT
BAREGE
BARELY
BAREST
BARFLY
BARGED
BARGES
BARHOP
BARING
BARITE
BARIUM
BARKED
BARKER
BARKIN
BARLEY
BARMAN
BARMEN
BARNES
BARNEY
BARNUM
BAROJA
BAROLO
BARONG
BARONS
BARONY
BARQUE
BARRED
BARREL
BARREN
BARRES
BARRIE
BARRIO
BARRIS
BARRON
BARROW
BARTAB
BARTER
BARTOK
BARTON
BARUCH
BARYON
BARZUN
BERATE
BERBER
BEREFT
BERETS
BERGEN
BERING
BERLIN
BERNIE
BERTHA
BERTHS
BERTIE
BIRDED
BIRDER
BIRDIE
BIREME
BIRGIT
BIRLED
BIRNEY
BIRTHS
BORAGE
BORATE
BORAXO
BORDEN
BORDER
BOREAL
BOREAS
BOREON
BORERS
BOREUP
BORGIA
BORIDE
BORING
BORMAN
BORNEO
BORROW
BORSCH
BORZOI
BURBLE
BURBLY
BURBOT
BURDEN
BUREAU
BURGAS
BURGEE
BURGER
BURGHS
BURGLE
BURGOO
BURGOS
BURIED
BURIES
BURINS
BURLAP
BURLED
BURLEY
BURMAN
BURNED
BURNER
BURNET
BURNEY
BURNUP
BUROAK
BURPED
BURRED
BURROS
BURROW
BURSAE
BURSAL
BURSAR
BURSAS
BURSES
BURSTS
BURTON
BYRNES
BYROAD
BYROTE

B••R••
BAIRNS
BARRED
BARREL
BARREN
BARRES
BARRIE
BARRIO
BARRIS
BARRON
BARROW
BAYRUM
BEARDS
BEARER
BEARON
BEARUP
BEIRUT
BETRAY
BEURRE
BGIRLS
BIERCE
BIGRED
BLARED
BLARES
BLURBS
BLURRY
BLURTS
BOARDS
BORROW
BOTREE
BOURKE
BOURNE
BOURSE
BUMRAP
BURRED
BURROS
BURROW

B•••R•
BAKERS
BAKERY
BALERS
BARBRA
BAYARD
BEFORE
BELFRY
BEMIRE
BEURRE
BEWARE
BIAFRA
BICARB
BICORN
BIHARI
BIKERS
BINARY
BISTRO
BITERS
BLEARS
BLEARY
BLURRY
BOGART
BOLERO
BONERS
BORERS
BOVARY
BOWERS
BOWERY
BOXERS
BOYARS
BRIARD
BRIARS
BRIERS
BRIERY
BSHARP
BUMBRY
BUYERS
BYWORD

B••••R
BACKER
BADGER
BAGGER
BAILER
BAILOR
BALDER
BANGER
BANGOR
BANKER
BANNER
BANTER
BARBER
BARKER
BARTER
BASTER
BATHER
BATTER
BAWLER
BAXTER
BAYLOR
BAZAAR
BEAKER
BEARER
BEATER
BEAVER
BECKER
BEEPER
BEGGAR
BELAIR
BENDER
BENHUR
BERBER
BESSER
BESTIR
BETTER
BETTOR
BICKER
BIDDER
BIGGER
BIGSUR
BINDER
BIRDER
BITTER
BLAZER
BLOWER
BMAJOR
BMINOR
BOATER
BOBBER
BOILER
BOLDER
BOLGER
BOMBER
BONIER
BOOKER
BOOMER
BOPPER
BORDER
BOTHER
BOWLER
BOWOAR
BOWSER
BOWYER
BOXCAR
BRACER
BRAVER
BRAYER
BRAZER
BREUER
BREWER
BROKER
BRUDER
BUFFER
BUGLER
BULGAR
BULGUR
BULWER
BUMMER
BUMPER
BUNKER
BUNTER
BURGER
BURNER
BURSAR
BUSBAR
BUSIER
BUSTER
BUTLER
BUTTER
BUZZER

•BR•••
ABRADE
ABRAMS
ABROAD
ABRUPT
OBRIAN
OBRIEN

•B•R••
ABORAL
ABORTS
EBERLY
IBERIA
OBERON
TBIRDS

•B••R•
ABHORS
ABJURE
ABOARD
ABSORB
ABSURD
OBVERT

•B•••R
ABUKIR
ABUSER
OBITER

••BR••
AUBREY
COBRAS
DEBRAS
DEBRIS
DOBRAS
DOBROS
ELBRUS
EMBRYO
FABRAY
FABRIC
FIBRES
FIBRIL
FIBRIN
GIBRAN
HEBREW
HUBRIS
HYBRID
IMBRUE
INBRED
LABREA
LABRET
LABRUM
LEBRUN
LIBRIS
ROBROY
RUBRIC
SABRAS
SABRES
TABRIZ
TOBRUK
UMBRAE
UMBRAL
UMBRAS
UMBRIA
ZEBRAS

••B•R•
ALBERT
ALBORG
AMBERS
ARBORS
ASBURY
AUBURN
CABERS
COBURG
COBURN
CYBORG
DEBARK
DEBARS
EDBERG
EGBERT
EKBERG
ELBERT
EMBARK
EMBERS
FIBERS
GABBRO
GIBERS
HOBART
HUBERT
INBORN
JABIRU
LABORS
NABORS
OSBORN
REBARS
REBORN
ROBERT
SABERS
SEBERG
SOBERS
SUBARU
SUBORN
SUBURB
TABARD
TABORS
TUBERS
UMBERS
UNBARS
UNBORN
VYBORG
WEBERN

••B••R
AMBLER
ARBOUR
BOBBER
CABLER
DEBTOR
DOBBER
FABLER
FIBBER
GABBER
GIBBER
JABBAR
JABBER
JOBBER
LABOUR
LIBBER
LOBBER
LUBBER
NABBER
NOBLER
ROBBER
RUBBER
SOBBER
WEBBER

•••BR•
BARBRA
BUMBRY
GABBRO
HASBRO
HOMBRE
SOMBRE
TIMBRE

•••B•R
BARBER
BERBER
BOBBER
BOMBER
BUSBAR
CAMBER
COMBER
CUMBER
DAUBER
DISBAR
DOBBER
DUMBER
DUNBAR
DURBAR
FERBER
FIBBER
GABBER
GERBER
GIBBER
GOOBER
HARBOR
ISOBAR
JABBAR
JABBER
JOBBER
KHYBER
LIBBER
LIMBER
LOBBER
LUBBER
LUMBAR
LUMBER
MEMBER
NABBER
NUMBER
PROBER
ROBBER
RUBBER
SAMBAR
SOBBER
SOMBER
TIMBER
WEBBER
WETBAR
WILBUR

BS••••
BSHARP
BSIDES

B•S•••
BASALT
BASELY
BASEST
BASHED
BASHES
BASICS
BASING
BASINS
BASKED
BASKET
BASQUE
BASSES
BASSET
BASSOS
BASTED
BASTER
BASTES
BESANT
BESETS
BESIDE
BESOMS
BESOTS
BESSER
BESSIE
BESTED
BESTIR
BESTOW
BISCAY
BISECT
BISHOP
BISONS
BISQUE
BISSAU
BISSET
BISTRO
BOSKET
BOSLEY
BOSNIA
BOSSED
BOSSES
BOSTON
BOSUNS
BUSBAR
BUSBOY
BUSHED
BUSHEL
BUSHES
BUSHWA
BUSIED
BUSIER
BUSIES
BUSILY
BUSING
BUSKIN
BUSMAN
BUSMEN
BUSONI
BUSSED
BUSSES
BUSTED
BUSTER
BUSTLE
BYSSHE
BYSSUS

B••S••
BABSON
BALSAM
BASSES
BASSET
BASSOS
BEASTS
BENSON
BESSER
BESSIE
BETSEY
BIASED
BIASES
BIDSIN
BIDSON
BIDSUP
BIGSUR
BISSAU
BISSET
BLASTS
BOASTS
BOBSUP
BONSAI
BOOSTS
BORSCH
BOSSED
BOSSES
BOWSAW
BOWSER
BOXSET
BRASHY
BRASOV
BRASSY
BRUSHY
BRYSON
BUNSEN
BUQSHA
BURSAE
BURSAL
BURSAR
BURSAS
BURSES
BURSTS
BUSSED
BUSSES
BUYSUP
BYSSHE
BYSSUS

B•••S•
BANISH
BAREST
BASEST
BEHEST
BEKESY
BEMUSE
BETISE
BLAISE
BLOUSE
BLUEST
BLUESY
BLUISH
BOOTSY
BOURSE
BOYISH
BRAISE
BRASSY
BREAST
BROWSE
BRUISE
BYGOSH
BYPASS
BYPAST

B••••S
BABIES
BABKAS
BABULS
BACKUS
BADGES
BAGELS
BAINES
BAIRNS
BAKERS
BALERS
BANJOS
BANTUS
BARGES
BARNES
BARONS
BARRES
BARRIS
BASHES
BASICS
BASINS
BASSES
BASSOS
BASTES
BATHES
BATHOS
BATIKS
BATONS
BAUCIS
BAYOUS
BEANOS
BEARDS
BEASTS
BEAUTS
BEBOPS
BEDEWS
BEDIMS
BEEVES
BEFITS
BEFOGS
BEGETS
BEGINS
BEGUMS
BEIGES
BEINGS
BELAYS
BELIES
BELLES
BERETS
BERTHS
BESETS
BESOMS
BESOTS
BETELS
BETTAS
BEVELS
BEVIES
BEZELS
BGIRLS
BIASES
BIBLES
BICEPS
BIGHTS
BIGOTS
BIKERS
BILGES
BINGES
BIOGAS
BIOMES
BIOTAS
BIPEDS
BIPODS
BIRTHS
BISONS
BITERS
BLACKS
BLADES
BLAMES
BLANKS
BLARES
BLASTS
BLAZES
BLEARS
BLEATS
BLEEDS
BLEEPS
BLENDS
BLIMPS
BLINDS
BLINKS
BLOATS
BLOCKS
BLOKES
BLONDS
BLOOMS
BLOOPS
BLUETS
BLUFFS
BLUNTS
BLURBS
BLURTS
BMINUS
BOARDS
BOASTS
BODIES
BOFFOS
BOGEYS
BOGIES
BOGLES
BOITES
BOMBES
BONERS
BONGOS
BONNES
BONZES
BOOSTS
BOOTES
BOOTHS
BOREAS
BORERS
BOSSES
BOSUNS
BOUGHS
BOULES
BOUNDS
BOVIDS
BOWERS
BOWLES
BOXERS
BOYARS
BRACES
BRACTS
BRAHMS
BRAIDS
BRAILS
BRAINS
BRAKES
BRANDS
BRANTS
BRAVAS
BRAVES
BRAVOS
BRAWLS
BRAZES
BRAZOS
BREADS
BREAKS
BREAMS
BREEDS
BRENTS
BREVES
BRIANS
BRIARS
BRIBES
BRICKS
BRIDES
BRIEFS
BRIERS
BRIGGS
BRILLS
BRINES
BRINGS
BRINKS
BROADS
BROILS
BRONCS
BROODS
BROOKS
BROOMS
BROTHS
BROWNS
BRUGES
BRUINS
BRUITS
BRULES
BRUMES
BRUNTS
BRUTES
BRUTUS
BSIDES
BUDGES
BUENOS
BUFFOS
BUGLES
BUILDS
BULGES
BUNCOS
BUNKOS
BURGAS
BURGHS
BURGOS
BURIES
BURINS
BURROS
BURSAS
BURSES
BURSTS
BUSHES
BUSIES
BUSSES
BUTEOS
BUTTES
BUYERS
BUZZES
BWANAS
BYLAWS
BYPASS
BYRNES
BYSSUS
BYWAYS

•BS•••
ABSENT
ABSORB
ABSURD
OBSESS
OBSTET

•B•S••
ABASED
ABASES
ABUSED
ABUSER
ABUSES
ABYSMS
IBISES
OBISPO

•B••S•
ABBESS
ABLEST
ABLUSH
OBLAST
OBOIST
OBSESS
OBTEST
OBTUSE

•B•••S
ABACAS
ABACUS
ABASES
ABATES
ABATIS
ABBESS
ABBEYS
ABBOTS
ABELES
ABHORS
ABIDES
ABODES
ABOHMS
ABOMBS
ABORTS
ABRAMS
ABUSES
ABYDOS
ABYSMS
EBOATS
EBONDS
HBEAMS
HBOMBS
IBEAMS
IBEXES
IBISES
OBEAHS
OBELUS
OBSESS
TBILLS
TBIRDS
TBONDS
TBONES
UBOATS
UBOLTS

••BS••
BABSON
BOBSUP
DOBSON
GIBSON
HOBSON
ROBSON
RUBSIN
SUBSET

••B•S•
ABBESS
AMBUSH
ATBEST
CUBISM
CUBIST
DEBASE
EMBOSS
GOBUST
KIBOSH
RIBOSE
ROBUST
TUBIST
WABASH

••B••S
ABBESS
ABBEYS
ABBOTS
ALBUMS
AMBERS
AMBITS
AMBLES
ARBORS
ATBATS
BABIES
BABKAS
BABULS
BEBOPS
BIBLES
CABALS
CABERS
CABINS
CABLES
COBIAS
COBRAS
CUBEBS
CUBICS
CUBITS
DEBARS
DEBITS
DEBRAS
DEBRIS
DEBUGS
DEBUTS
DOBLAS
DOBRAS
DOBROS
DUBOIS
ELBOWS
ELBRUS
EMBAYS
EMBEDS
EMBERS
EMBOSS
FABLES
FIBERS
FIBRES
GABLES
GIBERS
GOBIES
HABEAS
HABITS
HOBBES
HOBOES
HUBRIS
IMBUES
JABOTS
KABOBS
KEBABS
KEBOBS
LABELS
LABORS
LIBELS
LIBRIS
MOBIUS
NABOBS
NABORS
NOBLES
ORBITS
OXBOWS
POBOYS
RABBIS
RABIES
REBAGS
REBARS
REBELS
REBIDS
REBUTS
ROBINS
ROBLES
ROBOTS
RUBENS
RUBIES
RUBLES
SABERS
SABINS
SABLES
SABOTS
SABRAS
SABRES
SIBYLS
SOBERS
TABLAS
TABLES
TABOOS
TABORS
TIBIAS
TOBIAS
TOBIES
TUBERS
UMBELS
UMBERS
UMBRAS
UNBARS
UPBOWS
UZBEKS
XEBECS
ZEBRAS

•••B•S
ADOBES
AIRBUS
ALIBIS
AMEBAS
ANUBIS
BOMBES
BRIBES
CEIBAS
COMBES
COMBOS
DAUBES
DOUBTS
EREBUS
FLYBYS
FORBES
GLEBES
GLOBES
GREBES
GUMBOS
HOBBES
JUMBOS
LAYBYS
LESBOS
LIMBOS
LIMBUS
MAMBAS
MAMBOS
MAYBES
NIMBUS
ORIBIS
PHOBOS
PLEBES
PROBES
RABBIS
RUMBAS
SAMBAS
SCUBAS
THEBES
TRIBES
TURBOS

••••BS
ABOMBS
ADLIBS
ARDEBS
BLURBS
CARIBS
CAROBS
CELEBS
CLIMBS
CRUMBS
CUBEBS
DEMOBS
DWEEBS
EXURBS
HBOMBS
KABOBS

KEBABS KEBOBS NABOBS NAWABS PLUMBS REDUBS RHOMBS RHUMBS SAHIBS SCRUBS SHRUBS SQUABS SQUIBS THROBS THUMBS

B•T•••
BATAAN BATBOY BATEAU BATHED BATHER BATHES BATHOS BATIKS BATING BATMAN BATMEN BATONS BATTED BATTEN BATTER BATTLE BATTUE BATUMI BETAKE BETCHA BETELS BETHEL BETIDE BETISE BETONY BETOOK BETRAY BETSEY BETTAS BETTER BETTOR BITERS BITING BITMAP BITOFF BITTED BITTEN BITTER BOTANY BOTFLY BOTHER BOTREE BOTTLE BOTTOM BUTANE BUTENE BUTEOS BUTLER BUTTED BUTTER BUTTES BUTTIN BUTTON BUTUNG BYTALK

B••T••
BAITED BALTIC BANTAM BANTER BANTUS BARTAB BARTER BARTOK BARTON BASTED BASTER BASTES BATTED BATTEN BATTER BATTLE BATTUE BAXTER BEATEN BEATER BEATIT BEATLE BEATON BEATTY BEATUP BEETLE BELTED BENTON BERTHA BERTHS BERTIE BESTED BESTIR BESTOW BETTAS BETTER BETTOR BHUTAN BHUTTO BIGTEN BIGTOE BIGTOP BIOTAS BIOTIC BIOTIN BIRTHS BISTRO BITTED BITTEN BITTER BLATTY BLITHE BLOTCH BLOTTO BLYTHE BOATED BOATER BOITES BOLTED BOLTON BONTON BOOTED BOOTEE BOOTES BOOTHE BOOTHS BOOTIE BOOTSY BOOTUP BOSTON BOTTLE BOTTOM BOWTIE BOXTOP BRATTY BRETON BRITON BROTHS BRUTAL BRUTES BRUTUS BUNTED BUNTER BURTON BUSTED BUSTER BUSTLE BUTTED BUTTER BUTTES BUTTIN BUTTON

B•••T•
BALATA BARITE BEASTS BEATTY BEAUTS BEAUTY BEFITS BEGETS BENITO BERATE BERETS BESETS BESOTS BHAKTI BHUTTO BIGHTS BIGOTS BINATE BLASTS BLATTY BLEATS BLINTZ BLOATS BLOTTO BLUETS BLUNTS BLURTS BOASTS BOGOTA BONITO BOOSTS BORATE BOUNTY BRACTS BRANTS BRATTY BREATH BRENTS BRONTE BRUITS BRUNTS BURSTS BYPATH BYROTE

B••••T
BADLOT BALLET BALLOT BANDIT BARBET BARDOT BAREST BASALT BASEST BASKET BASSET BEATIT BECKET BEHEST BEIRUT BELOIT BENOIT BEREFT BESANT BEZANT BILLET BIRGIT BISECT BISSET BLEWIT BLIGHT BLOWIT BLUEST BOBCAT BOGART BONMOT BONNET BOSKET BOUGHT BOWNET BOWOUT BOXSET BRANDT BREAST BRECHT BREVET BRIGHT BRUNET BRYANT BUCKET BUDGET BUFFET BUGOUT BULLET BUMOUT BURBOT BURNET BUYOUT BYPAST

•BT•••
OBTAIN OBTEST OBTUND OBTUSE

•B•T••
ABATED ABATES ABATIS OBITER OBSTET

•B••T•
ABBOTS ABBOTT ABLATE ABORTS EBOATS OBLATE UBIETY UBOATS UBOLTS

•B•••T
ABBOTT ABDUCT ABJECT ABLAUT ABLEST ABRUPT ABSENT OBJECT OBLAST OBOIST OBSTET OBTEST OBVERT

••BT••
DEBTOR SUBTLE SUBTLY

••B•T•
ABBOTS ABBOTT AMBITS ATBATS CUBITS DEBATE DEBITS DEBUTS HABITS JABOTS JOBETH KIBITZ LOBATE ORBITS RABATO REBATE REBUTS ROBOTS SABATO SABOTS SUBITO TUBATE

••B••T
ABBOTT ALBEIT ALBERT ATBEST BOBCAT COBALT CUBIST EGBERT ELBERT GIBBET GIBLET GOBLET GOBUST HOBART HOBBIT HUBERT JOBLOT LABRET PTBOAT RABBET RABBIT REBOLT REBOOT ROBERT ROBUST RUBOUT SOBEIT SUBLET SUBMIT SUBSET TABLET TOBOOT TUBIST TYBALT UNBELT UNBENT UNBOLT UPBEAT

•••BT•
DOUBTS

•••B•T
ALLBUT BARBET BURBOT COMBAT GAMBIT GIBBET GRABAT HENBIT HOBBIT KORBUT NUMBAT RABBET RABBIT SORBET STABAT TALBOT TIDBIT TITBIT TURBIT TURBOT TWOBIT WOMBAT YOUBET

••••BT
INDEBT

BU••••
BUBBLE BUBBLY BUCCAL BUCKED BUCKET BUCKLE BUCKUP BUDDED BUDDHA BUDGED BUDGES BUDGET BUDGIE BUENOS BUFFED BUFFER BUFFET BUFFON BUFFOS BUGGED BUGLED BUGLER BUGLES BUGOFF BUGOUT BUILDS BUJOLD BULBIL BULBUL BULGAR BULGED BULGES BULGUR BULKED BULLAE BULLED BULLET BULOVA BULWER BUMBLE BUMBRY BUMMED BUMMER BUMOUT BUMPED BUMPER BUMPPO BUMPUP BUMRAP BUNCHE BUNCOS BUNDLE BUNGED BUNGEE BUNGLE BUNION BUNKED BUNKER BUNKOS BUNKUM BUNSEN BUNTED BUNTER BUNUEL BUNYAN BUOYED BUOYUP BUQSHA BURBLE BURBLY BURBOT BURDEN BUREAU BURGAS BURGEE BURGER BURGHS BURGLE BURGOO BURGOS BURIED BURIES BURINS BURLAP BURLED BURLEY BURMAN BURNED BURNER BURNET BURNEY BURNUP BUROAK BURPED BURRED BURROS BURROW BURSAE BURSAL BURSAR BURSAS BURSES BURSTS BURTON BUSBAR BUSBOY BUSHED BUSHEL BUSHES BUSHWA BUSIED BUSIER BUSIES BUSILY BUSING BUSKIN BUSMAN BUSMEN BUSONI BUSSED BUSSES BUSTED BUSTER BUSTLE BUTANE BUTENE BUTEOS BUTLER BUTTED BUTTER BUTTES BUTTIN BUTTON BUTUNG BUYERS BUYING BUYOFF BUYOUT BUYSUP BUZZED BUZZER BUZZES

B•U•••
BAUBLE BAUCIS BEULAH BEURRE BHUTAN BHUTTO BLUEOX BLUEST BLUESY BLUETS BLUFFS BLUING BLUISH BLUNTS BLURBS BLURRY BLURTS BOUBOU BOUCLE BOUDIN BOUFFE BOUGHS BOUGHT BOULES BOULEZ BOULLE BOUNCE BOUNCY BOUNDS BOUNTY BOURKE BOURNE BOURSE BRUDER BRUGES BRUINS BRUISE BRUITS BRULES BRUMAL BRUMES BRUNCH BRUNEI BRUNET BRUNTS BRUSHY BRUTAL BRUTES BRUTUS

B••U••
BABULS BAGUIO BARUCH BATUMI BEAUTS BEAUTY BEGUMS BELUGA BEMUSE BENUMB BLOUSE BOSUNS BREUER BUNUEL BUTUNG

B•••U•
BACKUP BACKUS BADGUY BAGFUL BALLUP BANGUI BANGUP BANJUL BANQUO BANTUS BARIUM BARNUM BARQUE BARZUN BASQUE BATTUE BAYEUX BAYOUS BAYRUM BEADUP BEAMUP BEARUP BEATUP BEDAUB BEDBUG BEEFUP BEEGUM BEFOUL BEIRUT BENHUR BIDSUP BIGGUN BIGSUR BIJOUX BINDUP BISQUE BLEWUP BLOWUP BMINUS BOBSUP BONEUP BOOJUM BOOTUP BOREUP BOWOUT BOXFUL BRAQUE BROGUE BRUTUS BUCKUP BUGOUT BULBUL BULGUR BUMOUT BUMPUP BUNKUM BUOYUP BURNUP BUYOUT BUYSUP BYSSUS

B••••U
BATEAU BISSAU BOUBOU BUREAU

•BU•••
ABUKIR ABUSED ABUSER ABUSES MBUNDU

•B•U••
ABDUCT ABJURE ABLUSH ABOUND ABRUPT ABSURD OBTUND OBTUSE

•B••U•
ABACUS ABLAUT OBELUS

•B•••U
MBUNDU

••BU••
ALBUMS AMBUSH ASBURY AUBURN BABULS COBURG COBURN DEBUGS DEBUNK DEBUTS FIBULA GOBUST IMBUED IMBUES INBULK KABUKI LOBULE NEBULA REBUFF REBUKE REBUTS ROBUST SUBURB TABULA

••B•U•
ARBOUR BOBSUP DYBBUK ELBRUS ERBIUM HUBBUB IMBRUE LABOUR LABRUM LEBRUN MOBIUS MRBLUE PABLUM RUBOUT SUBDUE SUBGUM TOBRUK

••B••U
JABIRU SUBARU

•••BU•
AIRBUS ALLBUT BEDBUG BULBUL DYBBUK EREBUS HUBBUB HUMBUG KORBUT LIMBUS NIMBUS REDBUD SOWBUG WILBUR

•••B•U
BOUBOU

••••BU
MALIBU

B•V•••
BEVELS BEVIES BOVARY BOVIDS BOVINE

B••V••
BEAVER BEEVES BMOVIE BRAVAS BRAVED BRAVER BRAVES BRAVOS BREVES BREVET

B•••V•
BEHAVE BULOVA BYJOVE

B••••V
BRASOV

•BV•••
OBVERT

BW••••
BWANAS

B•W•••
BAWLED BAWLER BEWAIL BEWARE BOWERS BOWERY BOWFIN BOWING BOWLED BOWLER BOWLES BOWMAN BOWMEN BOWNET BOWOAR BOWOUT BOWSAW BOWSER BOWTIE BOWWOW BOWYER BYWAYS BYWORD

B••W••
BIGWIG BLEWIT BLEWUP BLOWER BLOWIN BLOWIT BLOWUP BLOWZY BOWWOW BRAWLS BRAWNY BREWED BREWER BROWNE BROWNS BROWSE BULWER

B•••W•
BEDEWS BUSHWA BYLAWS

B••••W
BARROW BELLOW BESTOW BILLOW BORROW BOWSAW BOWWOW BROKAW BURROW

•B•W••
OBIWAN

••BW••
COBWEB SUBWAY

••B•W•
ELBOWS OXBOWS UPBOWS

••B••W
HEBREW

•••BW•
OJIBWA

•••B•W
FOGBOW

B•X•••
BAXTER BOXCAR BOXERS BOXFUL BOXING BOXSET BOXTOP

B••X••
BLIXEN

B•••X•
BILOXI BORAXO

B••••X
BAYEUX BENDIX BIJOUX BLUEOX BOLLIX BRANDX

•B•X••
IBEXES

•••B•X
HATBOX HOTBOX ICEBOX SKYBOX

BY••••
BYEBYE BYGONE BYGOSH BYHAND BYJOVE BYLAWS BYLINE BYNAME BYPASS BYPAST BYPATH BYPLAY BYRNES BYROAD BYROTE BYSSHE BYSSUS BYTALK BYWAYS BYWORD

B•Y•••
BAYARD BAYEUX BAYING BAYLOR BAYOUS BAYRUM BEYOND BLYTHE BOYARS BOYISH BRYANT BRYONY BRYSON BUYERS BUYING BUYOFF BUYOUT BUYSUP

B••Y••
BANYAN BARYON BOWYER BRAYED BRAYER BUNYAN BUOYED BUOYUP

B•••Y•
BELAYS BOGEYS BOLEYN BYEBYE BYWAYS

B••••Y
BADGUY BAILEY BAKERY BALDLY BARELY BARFLY BARLEY BARNEY BARONY BASELY BATBOY BEATTY BEAUTY BEGLEY BEKESY BELFRY BENDAY BENGAY BETONY BETRAY BETSEY BIGAMY BIGBOY BINARY BIRNEY BISCAY BLABBY BLATTY BLEARY BLIMEY BLOCKY BLOODY BLOOEY BLOOMY BLOWZY BLUESY BLURRY BODILY BOIGNY BOLDLY BOMBAY BOOTSY BOSLEY BOTANY BOTFLY BOUNCY BOUNTY BOVARY BOWERY BRAINY BRANDY BRASHY BRASSY BRATTY BRAWNY BREEZY BRICKY BRIERY BROLLY BRONZY BROODY BRUSHY BRYONY BUBBLY BUMBRY BURBLY BURLEY BURNEY BUSBOY BUSILY BYPLAY

•BY•••
ABYDOS ABYSMS

•B•Y••
OBEYED

•B••Y•
ABBEYS

•B•••Y
ABBACY EBERLY UBIETY

••BY••
LIBYAN SIBYLS

••B•Y•
ABBEYS EMBAYS EMBRYO POBOYS RIBEYE

••B••Y
ABBACY ALBANY ASBURY AUBREY BUBBLY DABNEY EMBODY FABRAY HUBBLY MOBLEY NOBODY PEBBLY ROBROY RUBBLY RUBIFY SUBTLY SUBWAY WOBBLY

•••BY•
BYEBYE

FLYBYS
LAYBYS

•••B•Y
BATBOY
BIGBOY
BLABBY
BOMBAY
BUBBLY
BUMBRY
BURBLY
BUSBOY
CARBOY
CHUBBY
CLUBBY
COWBOY
CRABBY
DOUBLY
DRABLY
DUMBLY
FEEBLY
FLABBY
FLYBOY
GLIBLY
GRABBY
GRUBBY
HUBBLY
HUMBLY
KNOBBY
LAZBOY
LOWBOY
MARBLY
MUMBLY
NIMBLY
NUMBLY
OLDBOY
PEBBLY
REDBAY
RUBBLY
RUMBLY
SCABBY
SHABBY
SNOBBY
STABLY
STUBBY
SWABBY
TOMBOY
TREBLY
USABLY
VIABLY
WAMBLY
WOBBLY

••••BY
BLABBY
CAMEBY
CHUBBY
CLUBBY
COMEBY
CRABBY
CROSBY
CRUMBY
DOESBY
DROPBY
FLABBY
GATSBY
GETSBY
GOESBY
GONEBY
GOODBY
GRABBY
GRUBBY
HEREBY
KNOBBY
LAIDBY
LAYSBY
NASEBY
NEARBY
PASSBY
PUTSBY
SCABBY
SETSBY
SHABBY
SNOBBY
STUBBY
SWABBY
TRILBY
WENTBY

B•Z•••
BAZAAR
BEZANT
BEZELS
BUZZED
BUZZER
BUZZES

B••Z••
BALZAC
BANZAI
BARZUN
BENZOL
BLAZED
BLAZER
BLAZES
BLAZON
BONZES
BORZOI
BRAZED
BRAZEN
BRAZER
BRAZES
BRAZIL
BRAZOS
BRAZZA
BRAZZI
BUZZED
BUZZER
BUZZES

B•••Z•
BEDAZE
BELIZE
BLOWZY
BRAZZA
BRAZZI
BREEZE
BREEZY
BRONZE
BRONZY

B••••Z
BLINTZ
BOULEZ
BRIENZ

•B••Z•
ABLAZE

••B•Z•
REBOZO

••B••Z
KIBITZ
TABRIZ

CA••••
CABALA
CABALS
CABANA
CABBED
CABBIE
CABERS
CABINS
CABLED
CABLER
CABLES
CACAOS
CACHED
CACHES
CACHET
CACHOU
CACKLE
CACTUS
CADDIE
CADDIS
CADENT
CADETS
CADGED
CADGER
CADGES
CADMIC
CADMUS
CADRES
CAESAR
CAFTAN
CAGERS
CAGIER
CAGILY
CAGING
CAGNEY
CAGUAS
CAHIER
CAHOWS
CAICOS
CAIMAN
CAIQUE
CAIRNS
CAJOLE
CAJUNS
CAKING
CALAIS
CALASH
CALCES
CALDER
CALICO
CALIPH
CALKED
CALLAO
CALLAS
CALLED
CALLER
CALLES
CALLIN
CALLON
CALLOW
CALLUP
CALLUS
CALMED
CALMER
CALMLY
CALPAC
CALQUE
CALVED
CALVES
CALVIN
CALXES
CAMBER
CAMDEN
CAMEAT
CAMEBY
CAMEIN
CAMELS
CAMEON
CAMEOS
CAMERA
CAMETO
CAMEUP
CAMINO
CAMION
CAMISE
CAMLET
CAMPED
CAMPER
CAMPOS
CAMPUS
CANAAN
CANADA
CANALS
CANAPE
CANARD
CANARY
CANCAN
CANCEL
CANCUN
CANDID
CANDLE
CANDOR
CANERS
CANIDS
CANIFF
CANINE
CANING
CANKER
CANNAE
CANNED
CANNEL
CANNER
CANNES
CANNON
CANNOT
CANOED
CANOES
CANOLA
CANONS
CANOPY
CANOVA
CANTAB
CANTED
CANTER
CANTHI
CANTLE
CANTON
CANTOR
CANTOS
CANUTE
CANVAS
CANYON
CAPERS
CAPFUL
CAPGUN
CAPIAS
CAPITA
CAPLET
CAPNUT
CAPONE
CAPONS
CAPOTE
CAPPED
CAPPER
CAPRIS
CAPSID
CAPTAN
CAPTOR
CARAFE
CARATS
CARBON
CARBOY
CARDED
CARDER
CARDIN
CARDIO
CAREEN
CAREER
CARESS
CARETO
CARETS
CARFUL
CARGOS
CARHOP
CARIBE
CARIBS
CARIES
CARINA
CARING
CARLOS
CARLOT
CARMAN
CARMEL
CARMEN
CARNAL
CARNES
CARNET
CARNEY
CARNOT
CAROBS
CAROLE
CAROLS
CAROMS
CARONI
CARPAL
CARPED
CARPEL
CARPER
CARPET
CARPUS
CARREL
CARREY
CARRIE
CARROL
CARROT
CARSON
CARTED
CARTEL
CARTER
CARTES
CARTON
CARUSO
CARVED
CARVER
CARVES
CARVEY
CASABA
CASALS
CASAVA
CASBAH
CASERN
CASHED
CASHES
CASHEW
CASHIN
CASING
CASINO
CASPAR
CASPER
CASQUE
CASSIA
CASSIO
CASSIS
CASTER
CASTES
CASTLE
CASTON
CASTOR
CASTRO
CASUAL
CATCHY
CATENA
CATERS
CATGUT
CATHAY
CATHER
CATION
CATKIN
CATNAP
CATNIP
CATRIG
CATSUP
CATTED
CATTLE
CATTON
CAUCHO
CAUCUS
CAUDAL
CAUDEX
CAUDLE
CAUGHT
CAULKS
CAUSAL
CAUSED
CAUSES
CAVEAT
CAVEIN
CAVELL
CAVERN
CAVERS
CAVETT
CAVIAR
CAVILS
CAVING
CAVITY
CAVORT
CAWDOR
CAWING
CAXTON
CAYMAN
CAYUGA
CAYUSE

C•A•••
CEASED
CEASES
CHACHA
CHACMA
CHADOR
CHAFED
CHAFES
CHAFFS
CHAFFY
CHAINE
CHAINS
CHAIRS
CHAISE
CHALCO
CHALET
CHALKS
CHALKY
CHAMMY
CHAMPS
CHANCE
CHANCY
CHANEL
CHANEY
CHANGE
CHANTS
CHAPEL
CHAPIN
CHARGE
CHARLY
CHARMS
CHARON
CHARRO
CHARTS
CHASED
CHASER
CHASES
CHASMS
CHASSE
CHASTE
CHATTY
CHATUP
CHAVEZ
CIARDI
CLACKS
CLAIMS
CLAIRE
CLAMMY
CLAMOR
CLAMPS
CLAMUP
CLANCY
CLANGS
CLANKS
CLANKY
CLAQUE
CLARET
CLARKE
CLAROS
CLASPS
CLASSY
CLAUDE
CLAUSE
CLAVIN
CLAWED
CLAWER
CLAYEY
CMAJOR
COALER
COAPTS
COARSE
COASTS
COATED
COATIS
COAXED
COAXER
COAXES
CRABBE
CRABBY
CRACKS
CRADLE
CRAFTS
CRAFTY
CRAGGY
CRAKES
CRAMBO
CRAMPS
CRANED
CRANES
CRANIA
CRANIO
CRANKS
CRANKY
CRANNY
CRAPES
CRATED
CRATER
CRATES
CRAVAT
CRAVED
CRAVEN
CRAVER
CRAVES
CRAWLS
CRAWLY
CRAYON
CRAZED
CRAZES
CYANIC

C••A••
CABALA
CABALS
CABANA
CACAOS
CALAIS
CALASH
CANAAN
CANADA
CANALS
CANAPE
CANARD
CANARY
CARAFE
CARATS
CASABA
CASALS
CASAVA
CCLAMP
CEDARS
CERATE
CESARE
CETANE
CHEAPO
CHEATS
CHIANG
CHIAUS
CHOATE
CICADA
CIGARS
CLEANS
CLEARS
CLEATS
CLEAVE
CLOACA
CLOAKS
COBALT
COLADA
COMATE
CONANT
CORALS
COWARD
CREAKS
CREAKY
CREAMS
CREAMY
CREASE
CREASY
CREATE
CROAKS
CROAKY
CROATS
CSHARP
CUBAGE
CUIABA
CUNARD
CUNAXA
CURACY
CURARE
CURATE
CYCADS
CYRANO

C•••A•
CAESAR
CAFTAN
CAGUAS
CAIMAN
CALLAO
CALLAS
CALPAC
CAMEAT
CANAAN
CANCAN
CANNAE
CANTAB
CANVAS
CAPIAS
CAPTAN
CARMAN
CARNAL
CARPAL
CASBAH
CASPAR
CASUAL
CATHAY
CATNAP
CAUDAL
CAUSAL
CAVEAT
CAVIAR
CAYMAN
CEIBAS
CELLAE
CELLAR
CEREAL
CESTAS
CHELAE
CHELAS
CHEVAL
CHORAL
CHUKAR
CIUDAD
CLIMAX
COBHAM
COBIAS
COBRAS
COCOAS
COEVAL
COGNAC
COLLAR
COLMAN
COMBAT
COMEAT
COMMAS
COMPAQ
COMSAT
CONFAB
CONGAS
CONMAN
CONRAD
CONTAC
CONWAY
COOGAN
CORBAN
CORDAY
CORRAL
COSTAE
COSTAL
COSTAR
COSTAS
COTTAS
COUGAR
COWMAN
CRAVAT
CRETAN
CRURAL
CUNEAL
CURIAE
CURIAL
CUSHAW
CYCLAS
CYMBAL

C••••A
CABALA
CABANA
CAMERA
CANADA
CANOLA
CANOVA
CAPITA
CARINA
CASABA
CASAVA
CASSIA
CATENA
CAYUGA
CESSNA
CHACHA
CHACMA
CHICHA
CHOLLA
CHROMA
CHUKKA
CIBOLA
CICADA
CINEMA
CLOACA
COLADA
COLIMA
CONCHA
CONTRA
COPULA
CORNEA
CORONA
CORYZA
COVINA
COWPEA
CRANIA
CRENNA
CREUSA
CRIMEA
CUESTA
CUIABA
CUNAXA
CUPOLA

•CA•••
ACACIA
ACADIA
ACAJOU
ACARID
ACARUS
ECARTE
ICARIA
ICARUS
MCADAM
MCADOO
OCASEK
OCASEY
SCABBY
SCALAR
SCALDS
SCALED
SCALER
SCALES
SCALIA
SCALPS
SCAMPI
SCAMPS
SCANTS
SCANTY
SCAPES
SCARAB
SCARCE
SCARED
SCARER
SCARES
SCARFS
SCARNE
SCARPS
SCARUM
SCATHE
SCAUPS

•C•A••
ACHAEA
ACKACK
ACUATE
CCLAMP
ECLAIR
ECLATS
ICEAGE
LCHAIM
MCBAIN
MCCABE
MCCANN
MCHALE
MCLAIN
MCNAIR
OCEANS
OCTADS
OCTANE
OCTANT
OCTAVE
OCTAVO
SCLAFF
SCRAGS
SCRAMS
SCRAPE
SCRAPS
SCRAWL
UCLANS

•C••A•
ACETAL
ACTUAL
ICEBAG
ICECAP
ICEMAN
MCADAM
MCGRAW
MCLEAN
OCREAE
OCULAR
SCALAR
SCARAB
SCENAS
SCHWAS
SCREAK
SCREAM
SCUBAS

•C•••A
ACACIA
ACADIA
ACEDIA
ACHAEA
ICARIA
SCALIA
SCHEMA
SCLERA
SCORIA
SCOTIA
SCYLLA

••CA••
ALCAPP
ARCADE
ARCANA
ARCANE
ARCARO
BACALL
BECALM
BECAME
BICARB
CACAOS
CICADA
CYCADS
DACAPO
DECADE
DECAFS
DECALS
DECAMP
DECANT
DECAYS
DUCATS
ENCAGE
ENCAMP
ENCASE
ESCAPE
ESCARP
FACADE
GOCART
HECATE
IDCARD
INCANS
INCASE
INCASH
JACALS
JACANA
JICAMA
LOCALE
LOCALS
LOCATE
MACACO
MACAWS
MCCABE
MCCANN
NICAEA
ONCALL
OSCARS
OXCART
PECANS
PICABO
PICARA
PICARD
PICARO
RECALL
RECANE
RECANT
RECAPS
RECAST
SECANT
SOCAGE
TICALS
TUCANA
UNCAGE
UNCAPS
UNCASE
UPCAST
VACANT
VACATE
VICARS
VOCALS

••C•A•
ASCHAM
BUCCAL
COCOAS
CYCLAS
DACHAS
DUCTAL
FACIAL
JACKAL
LUCIAN
MACRAE
MECCAS
MICMAC
MOCHAS
NECTAR
NICEAN
NUCHAE
NUCHAL
PACMAN
PECKAT
PICKAT
PICKAX
RACIAL
SACRAL
SOCIAL
SUCHAS
TICTAC
UNCIAL
UNCLAD
VACLAV
WICCAN
YUCCAS

••C••A
ANCONA
ARCANA
CICADA
ENCINA
FACULA
HECUBA
ISCHIA
JACANA
JICAMA
LACUNA
MACULA
MUCOSA
NICAEA
NICOLA
OSCULA
PICARA
TACOMA
TUCANA
VICUNA

•••CA•
ABACAS
APICAL
ARECAS
ASHCAN
BISCAY
BOBCAT
BOXCAR
BUCCAL
CANCAN
DORCAS
DUNCAN
EPICAL
FATCAT
FISCAL
FRACAS
GASCAP
HEPCAT
HOTCAP
HOTCAR
HUBCAP
ICECAP
IPECAC
LASCAR
LOWCAL
MADCAP
MECCAS
MESCAL
MOBCAP
MUDCAT
MUSCAT
NASCAR
OILCAN
PARCAE
PASCAL
PLICAE
RASCAL
REDCAP
REXCAT
SKYCAP
SNOCAT
SPICAS
THECAE
THECAL
TINCAL
TINCAN
TOECAP
TOMCAT
TOPCAT
TOUCAN
TOWCAR
TROCAR
TUSCAN
VULCAN
WICCAN
YUCCAS

•••C•A
ACACIA
ALICIA
BETCHA
CHACHA
CHACMA
CHICHA
CONCHA
EJECTA
EXACTA
FASCIA
FLICKA
FULCRA
GARCIA
GOTCHA
JASCHA
KWACHA
MANCHA
MARCIA
MISCHA
MURCIA
PERCHA
SANCTA
TRICIA

••••CA
AFRICA
ALPACA
ARNICA
ATTICA
BIANCA
BLANCA
CLOACA
DESICA
DODECA
EROICA
FRANCA
FRESCA
ITASCA
ITHACA
KONICA
LEXICA
LORICA
MARACA
MONICA
OAXACA
PATACA
SENECA
SILICA
SIRICA
TOLUCA
TUNICA

C•B•••
CABALA
CABALS
CABANA
CABBED
CABBIE
CABERS
CABINS
CABLED
CABLER
CABLES
CIBOLA
COBALT
COBBLE
COBHAM
COBIAS
COBRAS
COBURG
COBURN
COBWEB
CUBAGE
CUBEBS
CUBICS
CUBING
CUBISM
CUBIST
CUBITS
CUBOID
CYBELE
CYBILL
CYBORG

C••B••
CABBED
CABBIE
CAMBER
CARBON
CARBOY
CASBAH
CEIBAS
CHUBBY
CLUBBY
COBBLE
COMBAT
COMBED
COMBER
COMBES
COMBOS
CORBAN
CORBEL
CORBIN
COWBOY
CRABBE
CRABBY
CUMBER
CURBED
CYMBAL

C•••B•
CAMEBY

CARIBE CARIBS CAROBS CASABA CELEBS CHUBBY CLIMBS CLUBBY COMEBY CRABBE CRABBY CRAMBO CROSBY CRUMBS CRUMBY CUBEBS CUIABA

C••••B
CANTAB CHERUB COBWEB CONFAB CONJOB

•CB•••
MCBAIN

•C•B••
ICEBAG ICEBOX SCABBY SCUBAS

•C••B•
ACHEBE MCCABE SCABBY SCRIBE SCRUBS

•C•••B
SCARAB

••C•B•
HECUBA JACOBI MCCABE PICABO TYCOBB

••C••B
BICARB TYCOBB

CC••••
CCLAMP

C•C•••
CACAOS CACHED CACHES CACHET CACHOU CACKLE CACTUS CECILE CICADA CICELY CICERO COCCID COCCUS COCCYX COCHIN COCKED COCKER COCKLE COCOAS COCOON CUCKOO CYCADS CYCLAS CYCLED CYCLER CYCLES CYCLIC CYCLOS

C••C••
CAICOS CALCES CANCAN CANCEL CANCUN CATCHY CAUCHO CAUCUS CHACHA CHACMA CHECKS CHICHA CHICHI CHICKS CHICLE CHOCKS CHUCKS CIRCLE CIRCUM CIRCUS CISCOS CLACKS CLICHE CLICKS CLOCHE CLOCKS CLUCKS COCCID COCCUS COCCYX CONCHA CONCHS CONCUR CRACKS CRECHE CRICKS CROCKS CROCUS CRUCES CZECHS

C•••C•
CALICO CHALCO CHANCE CHANCY CHEECH CHINCH CHOICE CHURCH CIVICS CLANCY CLENCH CLINCH CLOACA CLUTCH COERCE COMICS CONICS CONOCO CRISCO CROUCH CRUNCH CRUTCH CUBICS CURACY CYNICS

C••••C
CADMIC CALPAC CEDRIC CELTIC CITRIC CLERIC CLINIC COGNAC CONTAC COPTIC COSMIC COURIC CRITIC CULTIC CUPRIC CYANIC CYCLIC CYMRIC

•CC•••
ACCEDE ACCENT ACCEPT ACCESS ACCORD ACCOST ACCRUE ACCUSE ECCLES MCCABE MCCANN OCCULT OCCUPY OCCURS

•C•C••
ACACIA ICECAP ICICLE

•C••C•
ACKACK OCLOCK SCARCE SCHICK SCONCE SCORCH SCOTCH SCUTCH

•C•••C
ACETIC ACIDIC ECHOIC ICONIC SCENIC

••CC••
BOCCIE BUCCAL COCCID COCCUS COCCYX HICCUP MECCAS PICCHU SICCED SOCCER SUCCES SUCCOR WICCAN YUCCAS

••C•C•
BOCHCO DECOCT MACACO ROCOCO

••C••C
ARCTIC CYCLIC HECTIC LACTIC MICMAC PECTIC PICNIC TACTIC TICTAC UNCHIC

•••CC•
STUCCO

•••C•C
IPECAC

CD••••
CDROMS

C•D•••
CADDIE CADDIS CADENT CADETS CADGED CADGER CADGES CADMIC CADMUS CADRES CEDARS CEDING CEDRIC CIDERS CODDLE CODERS CODGER CODIFY CODING CODONS CUDDLE CUDDLY CUDGEL CYDERS

C••D••
CADDIE CADDIS CALDER CAMDEN CANDID CANDLE CANDOR CARDED CARDER CARDIN CARDIO CAUDAL CAUDEX CAUDLE CAWDOR CHADOR CHIDED CHIDES CINDER CIUDAD CNIDUS CODDLE COEDIT COLDER COLDLY CONDOR CONDOS COODER CORDAY CORDED CORDON CRADLE CREDIT CREDOS CRUDDY CRUDER CUDDLE CUDDLY CURDED CURDLE

C•••D•
CANADA CANIDS CHILDE CHILDS CHORDS CIARDI CICADA CLAUDE CLOUDS CLOUDY COLADA COMEDY CREEDS CROWDS CRUDDY CUPIDS CYCADS

C••••D
CABBED CABLED CACHED CADGED CALKED CALLED CALMED CALVED CAMPED CANARD CANDID CANNED CANOED CANTED CAPPED CAPSID CARDED CARPED CARTED CARVED CASHED CATTED CAUSED CEASED CEILED CELLED CENSED CERVID CHAFED CHASED CHEWED CHIDED CHIMED CHOKED CHOWED CHUTED CIUDAD CLAWED CLEPED CLEWED CLONED CLOSED CLOYED COATED COAXED COCCID COCKED COGGED COIFED COILED COINED COMBED CONFED CONKED CONNED CONRAD COOKED COOLED COOPED COPIED COPPED CORDED CORKED CORNED COSHED COWARD COWLED COZIED CRANED CRATED CRAVED CRAZED CREWED CROWED CUBOID CUFFED CULLED CUNARD CUPPED CURBED CURDED CURLED CURRED CURSED CURVED CUSPED CUSPID CUSSED CYCLED

•C•D••
ACADIA ACEDIA ACIDIC ACIDLY ICEDIN ICEDUP MCADAM MCADOO

•C••D•
ACCEDE OCTADS SCALDS SCENDS SCOLDS SCRODS

•C•••D
ACARID ACCORD ECHOED SCALED SCARED SCOPED SCORED SCREED

••C•D•
ACCEDE ARCADE CICADA CYCADS DECADE DECIDE DECODE ENCODE ESCUDO FACADE RECEDE RECODE SECEDE

••C••D
ACCORD ARCHED ASCEND BACKED BUCKED CACHED COCCID COCKED CYCLED DECKED DOCKED DUCKED EMCEED ETCHED EUCLID EXCEED FECUND HACKED HOCKED IDCARD INCHED ITCHED JACKED JOCUND KICKED LACKED LICKED LOCKED LUCKED MOCKED MUCKED NECKED NICKED ORCHID PACKED PECKED PICARD PICKED RACKED RECORD RICKED ROCKED RUCKED SACKED SACRED SECOND SICCED SOCKED SUCKED TACKED TICKED TUCKED UNCLAD WICKED

•••C•D
BRACED COCCID DANCED DEICED DEUCED EDUCED FARCED FENCED FORCED GRACED JUICED LANCED MERCED MINCED PIECED PLACED PLACID PRICED RANCID SAUCED SICCED SLICED SPACED SPICED SYNCED TALCED TRACED TRICED VISCID VOICED WINCED

CE••••
CEASED CEASES CECILE CEDARS CEDING CEDRIC CEIBAS CEILED CELEBS CELERY CELINE CELLAE CELLAR CELLED CELLOS CELTIC CEMENT CENOTE CENSED CENSER CENSES CENSOR CENSUS CENTER CENTOS CENTRE CENTRI CENTRO CERATE CEREAL CEREUS CERIPH CERISE CERIUM CERMET CERTIF CERUSE CERVID CESARE CESIUM CESSNA CESTAS CESTOS CESTUS CETANE CEYLON

C•E•••
CAESAR CHEAPO CHEATS CHECKS CHEECH CHEEKS CHEEKY CHEEPS CHEERS CHEERY CHEESE CHEESY CHELAE CHELAS CHEMIN CHENIN CHEOPS CHEQUE CHERIE CHERRY CHERUB CHERYL CHESTS CHESTY CHEVAL CHEVET CHEVRE CHEWED CHEWER CHEWUP CLEANS CLEARS CLEATS CLEAVE CLEEKS CLEESE CLEFTS CLENCH CLEPED CLERGY CLERIC CLERKS CLEVER CLEVES CLEVIS CLEWED COEDIT COELOM COERCE COEVAL CREAKS CREAKY CREAMS CREAMY CREASE CREASY CREATE CRECHE CREDIT CREDOS CREEDS CREEKS CREELS CREEPS CREEPY CREMES CRENEL CRENNA CREOLE CREPES CRESOL CRESTS CRETAN CRETIN CREUSA CREWED CREWEL CUESTA CZECHS CZERNY

C••E••
CABERS CADENT CADETS CAGERS CAMEAT CAMEBY CAMEIN CAMELS CAMEON CAMEOS CAMERA CAMETO CAMEUP CANERS CAPERS CAREEN CAREER CARESS CARETO CARETS CASERN CATENA CATERS CAVEAT CAVEIN CAVELL CAVERN CAVERS CAVETT CELEBS CELERY CEMENT CEREAL CEREUS CHEECH CHEEKS CHEEKY CHEEPS CHEERS CHEERY CHEESE CHEESY CHIEFS CICELY CICERO CIDERS CINEMA CITERS CIVETS CLEEKS CLEESE CLIENT CLUEIN CODERS COGENT COHEIR COHERE COLEUS COMEAT COMEBY COMEDY COMEIN COMELY COMEON COMERS COMETH COMETO COMETS COMEUP CONEYS COOERS CORERS COSELL COVENS COVENT COVERS COVERT COVETS COVEYS COWENS COWERS COYEST COZENS CREEDS CREEKS CREELS CREEPS CREEPY CRIERS CRUETS CUBEBS CULETS CUNEAL CUPELS CURERS CUTEST CUTESY CUVEES CYBELE CYDERS

C•••E•
CABBED CABLED CABLER CABLES CACHED CACHES CACHET CADGED CADGER CADGES CADRES CAGIER CAGNEY CAHIER CALCES CALDER CALKED CALLED CALLER CALLES CALMED CALMER CALVED CALVES CALXES CAMBER CAMDEN CAMLET CAMPED CAMPER CANCEL CANKER CANNED CANNEL CANNER CANNES CANOED CANOES CANTED CANTER CAPLET CAPPED CAPPER CARDED CARDER CAREEN CAREER CARIES CARMEL CARMEN CARNES CARNET CARNEY CARPED CARPEL CARPER CARPET CARREL CARREY CARTED CARTEL CARTER CARTES CARVED CARVER CARVES CARVEY CASHED CASHES CASHEW CASPER CASTER CASTES CATHER CATTED CAUDEX CAUSED CAUSES CEASED CEASES CEILED CELLED CENSED CENSER CENSES CENTER CERMET CHAFED CHAFES CHALET CHANEL CHANEY CHAPEL CHASED CHASER CHASES CHAVEZ CHEVET CHEWED CHEWER CHIDED CHIDES CHIMED CHIMES CHINES CHISEL CHIVES CHOKED CHOKER CHOKES CHOLER CHORES CHOSEN CHOWED CHUTED CHUTES CINDER CIPHER CISKEI CITIES CLARET CLAWED CLAWER CLAYEY CLEPED CLEVER CLEVES CLEWED CLIMES CLINES CLONED CLONES CLOSED CLOSER CLOSES CLOSET CLOVEN CLOVER CLOVES CLOYED CNOTES COALER COATED COAXED COAXER COAXES COBWEB COCKED COCKER CODGER COFFEE COFFER COGGED COIFED COILED COINED COINER COLDER COLLET COLTER COMBED COMBER COMBES COMPEL COMTES CONFED CONFER CONGER CONIES CONKED CONKER CONMEN CONNED CONNER CONTES CONVEX CONVEY COODER COOKED COOKER COOLED COOLER COONEY COOPED COOPER COOTER COPIED COPIER COPIES COPPED COPPER COPSES COPTER COQUET CORBEL CORDED CORKED CORKER CORNEA CORNED CORNEL CORNER CORNET CORREL CORSET CORTES CORTEX CORTEZ CORVEE COSHED COSHES COSIES COSSET COTTEN COTTER COULEE COUPES COUTER COWLED COWLEY COWMEN COWPEA COWPER COZIED COZIER COZIES CRAKES CRANED CRANES CRAPES CRATED CRATER CRATES CRAVED CRAVEN CRAVER CRAVES CRAZED CRAZES CREMES CRENEL CREPES CREWED CREWEL CRIMEA CRIMES CRIPES CRISES CRONES CROWED CROWER CROZES CRUCES CRUDER CRUSES CRUXES CUDGEL CUFFED CULLED CULLEN CULLER CULLET CULVER CUMBER CUPPED CURBED CURDED CURFEW CURLED CURLER CURLEW CURRED CURSED CURSES CURTER CURVED CURVES CURVET CUSPED CUSSED CUSSES CUSTER CUTIES CUTLER CUTLET CUTTER CUVEES CYCLED CYCLER CYCLES CYGNET CYPHER

C••••E
CABBIE CACKLE CADDIE CAIQUE CAJOLE CALQUE CAMISE CANAPE CANDLE CANINE CANNAE CANTLE CANUTE CAPONE CAPOTE

CARAFE
CARIBE
CAROLE
CARRIE
CASQUE
CASTLE
CATTLE
CAUDLE
CAYUSE
CECILE
CELINE
CELLAE
CENOTE
CENTRE
CERATE
CERISE
CERUSE
CESARE
CETANE
CHAINE
CHAISE
CHANCE
CHANGE
CHARGE
CHASSE
CHASTE
CHEESE
CHELAE
CHEQUE
CHERIE
CHEVRE
CHICLE
CHIGOE
CHILDE
CHILOE
CHOATE
CHOICE
CHOOSE
CHROME
CINQUE
CIRCLE
CIRQUE
CLAIRE
CLAQUE
CLARKE
CLAUDE
CLAUSE
CLEAVE
CLEESE
CLICHE
CLIQUE
CLOCHE
CLOQUE
CLOTHE
COARSE
COBBLE
COCKLE
CODDLE
COERCE
COFFEE
COHERE
COHUNE
COLLIE
COMATE
CONNIE
CONTRE
COOKIE
COOTIE
CORVEE
COSINE
COSTAE
COULEE
COUPLE
COURSE
COWRIE
COYOTE
CRABBE
CRADLE
CREASE
CREATE
CRECHE
CREOLE
CRINGE
CROSSE
CROUSE
CROUTE
CRUISE
CRUSOE
CUBAGE
CUDDLE
CUISSE
CURARE
CURATE
CURDLE
CURIAE
CURULE
CYBELE

•CE•••
ACEDIA
ACEOUS
ACEOUT
ACESUP
ACETAL
ACETIC
ACETYL
ECESIS
ICEAGE
ICEBAG
ICEBOX
ICECAP
ICEDIN
ICEDUP
ICEFOG
ICEMAN
ICEMEN
ICEOUT
ICESIN
ICESUP
OCEANS
OCELLI
OCELOT
SCENAS
SCENDS
SCENES
SCENIC
SCENTS

•C•E••
ACCEDE
ACCENT
ACCEPT
ACCESS
ACHEBE
ACHENE
ICIEST
MCLEAN
OCHERS
OCREAE
OCTETS
SCHELL
SCHEMA
SCHEME
SCLERA
SCREAK
SCREAM
SCREED
SCREEN
SCREES
SCREWS
SCREWY

•C••E•
ACHAEA
ACHIER
ACUMEN
ECCLES
ECHOED
ECHOES
ECOLES
ICEMEN
ICKIER
MCGREW
MCKUEN
OCASEK
OCASEY
OCHRES
SCALED
SCALER
SCALES
SCAPES
SCARED
SCARER
SCARES
SCENES
SCHLEP
SCONES
SCOPED
SCOPES
SCORED
SCORER
SCORES
SCOTER
SCREED
SCREEN
SCREES
SCUTES

•C•••E
ACCEDE
ACCRUE
ACCUSE
ACHEBE
ACHENE
ACTIVE
ACTONE
ACUATE
ECARTE
ECTYPE
ICEAGE
ICICLE
MCCABE
MCHALE
OCREAE
OCTANE
OCTAVE
SCARCE
SCARNE
SCATHE
SCHEME
SCONCE
SCRAPE
SCRIBE
SCURVE
SCYTHE

••CE••
ACCEDE
ACCENT
ACCEPT
ACCESS
ASCEND
ASCENT
BICEPS
CICELY
CICERO
DECEIT
DECENT
DICERS
DOCENT
EMCEED
EMCEES
EOCENE
ESCENT
EXCEED
EXCELS
EXCEPT
EXCESS
FACETS
FACEUP
HACEKS
INCEPT
LACERS
LACEUP
LUCENT
LYCEES
LYCEUM
NICEAN
NICELY
NICENE
NICEST
NICETY
NOCENT
PACERS
RACEME
RACERS
RECEDE
RECENT
RECESS
RICERS
SECEDE
SECERN
ULCERS

••C•E•
AACHEN
ANCIEN
ARCHED
ARCHER
ARCHES
BACKED
BACKER
BECKER
BECKET
BICKER
BUCKED
BUCKET
CACHED
CACHES
CACHET
COCKED
COCKER
CYCLED
CYCLER
CYCLES
DECKED
DECKER
DECREE
DICIER
DICKER
DICKEY
DOCKED
DOCKER
DOCKET
DUCKED
ECCLES
EMCEED
EMCEES
ESCHER
ESCHEW
ETCHED
ETCHER
ETCHES
EXCEED
FACIES
FICHES
HACKED
HACKER
HICKEY
HOCKED
HOCKEY
INCHED
INCHES
ITCHED
ITCHES
JACKED
JACKET
JOCKEY
KICKED
KICKER
KUCHEN
LACHES
LACIER
LACKED
LACKEY
LICHEN
LICKED
LOCKED
LOCKER
LOCKET
LUCKED
LYCEES
MACHES
MICKEY
MOCKED
MOCKER
MUCKED
NECKED
NICAEA
NICHES
NICKED
NICKEL
NICKER
NUCLEI
NUCLEO
PACKED
PACKER
PACKET
PECKED
PICKED
PICKER
PICKET
POCKET
PUCKER
RACHEL
RACIER
RACKED
RACKET
RICHEN
RICHER
RICHES
RICKED
RICKEY
ROCHET
ROCKED
ROCKER
ROCKET
RUCHES
RUCKED
SACHEM
SACHET
SACKED
SACKER
SACRED
SECKEL
SECRET
SICCED
SICKEN
SICKER
SOCCER
SOCKED
SOCKET
SOCLES
SUCCES
SUCKED
SUCKER
TACKED
TACKER
TICKED
TICKER
TICKET
TUCKED
TUCKER
TUCKET
UNCLES
VACHEL
WICKED
WICKER
WICKET

••C••E
ACCEDE
ACCRUE
ACCUSE
ALCOVE
ARCADE
ARCANE
ARCHIE
BECAME
BECOME
BOCCIE
BUCKLE
CACKLE
CECILE
COCKLE
DECADE
DECIDE
DECKLE
DECODE
DECREE
DOCILE
ENCAGE
ENCASE
ENCODE
ENCORE
EOCENE
ESCAPE
EUCHRE
EXCISE
EXCITE
EXCUSE
FACADE
FACILE
FICHTE
FICKLE
FOCSLE
HACKIE
HACKLE
HECATE
HECKLE
INCASE
INCISE
INCITE
INCOME
INCUSE
JACKIE
JECKLE
JOCOSE
LOCALE
LOCATE
LUCITE
MACRAE
MCCABE
NICENE
NICOLE
NUCHAE
OOCYTE
OSCINE
PICKLE
RACEME
RACINE
RECANE
RECEDE
RECIFE
RECIPE
RECITE
RECODE
RECUSE
RICHIE
ROCKNE
SACQUE
SECEDE
SECURE
SICKLE
SOCAGE
TACKLE
TECHIE
TICKLE
UNCAGE
UNCASE
VACATE

•••CE•
AMICES
APICES
AVOCET
BRACED
BRACER
BRACES
CALCES
CANCEL
CRUCES
DANCED
DANCER
DANCES
DEICED
DEICER
DEICES
DEUCED
DEUCES
DUBCEK
DULCET
DUNCES
EDUCED
EDUCES
FARCED
FARCES
FASCES
FAUCES
FAUCET
FENCED
FENCER
FENCES
FORCED
FORCER
FORCES
GLACES
GRACED
GRACES
GROCER
JAYCEE
JUICED
JUICER
JUICES
LANCED
LANCER
LANCES
LANCET
MARCEL
MERCED
MERCER
MINCED
MINCER
MINCES
NIECES
NUECES
OUNCES
PARCEL
PENCEL
PIECED
PIECER
PIECES
PINCER
PISCES
PLACED
PLACER
PLACES
PRICED
PRICER
PRICES
PRICEY
SAUCED
SAUCER
SAUCES
SICCED
SLICED
SLICER
SLICES
SOCCER
SPACED
SPACEK
SPACER
SPACES
SPACEY
SPICED
SPICES
SUCCES
SYNCED
TALCED
TERCEL
TERCET
TRACED
TRACER
TRACES
TRACEY
TRICED
TRICES
TRUCES
UNICEF
VOICED
VOICES
WENCES
WINCED
WINCER
WINCES

•••C•E
AMECHE
APACHE
BOCCIE
BOUCLE
BUNCHE
CHICLE
CIRCLE
CLICHE
CLOCHE
CRECHE
FESCUE
FIACRE
FLECHE
GAUCHE
GRACIE
ICICLE
JAYCEE
LOUCHE
MARCHE
MARCIE
MISCUE
MUNCIE
MUSCLE
ORACLE
PARCAE
PLICAE
PROCNE
PSYCHE
QUICHE
RESCUE
ROSCOE
RUNCIE
SEICHE
SIECLE
SPECIE
STACTE
THECAE
THICKE
TOUCHE
TROCHE

••••CE
ADDUCE
ADVICE
ALSACE
AMERCE
APIECE
ATONCE
BIERCE
BODICE
BOUNCE
CHANCE
CHOICE
COERCE
DEDUCE
DEFACE
DEVICE
DRYICE
EFFACE
ELLICE
ENLACE
ENTICE
EUNICE
EVINCE
FIANCE
FIERCE
FLEECE
FRANCE
GLANCE
GREECE
HORACE
IGNACE
INDUCE
JANICE
JOUNCE
MALICE
MENACE
NODICE
NOTICE
NOVICE
NUANCE
OFFICE
PALACE
PEERCE
PIERCE
PLAICE
POLICE
POMACE
POUNCE
PRANCE
PRINCE
PUMICE
PURACE
QUINCE
REDUCE
REFACE
RELACE
SCARCE
SCONCE
SEANCE
SEDUCE
SLUICE
SOLACE
SOURCE
SPLICE
SPRUCE
STANCE
TENACE
THENCE
THRACE
THRICE
TIERCE
TRANCE
UNLACE
USANCE
VELOCE
VENICE
VIVACE
WHENCE

C•F•••
CAFTAN
COFFEE
COFFER
CUFFED

C••F••
CAPFUL
CARFUL
CHAFED
CHAFES
CHAFFS
CHAFFY
CLEFTS
CLIFFS
COFFEE
COFFER
COIFED
COMFIT
CONFAB
CONFED
CONFER
CRAFTS
CRAFTY
CROFTS
CUFFED
CUPFUL
CURFEW

C•••F•
CANIFF
CARAFE
CHAFFS
CHAFFY
CHIEFS
CITIFY
CLIFFS
CODIFY
CRYOFF
CUTOFF

C••••F
CANIFF
CERTIF
CRYOFF
CUTOFF

•C•F••
ICEFOG
SCIFIS
SCOFFS
SCUFFS

•C••F•
SCARFS
SCHIFF
SCLAFF
SCOFFS
SCRUFF
SCUFFS
SCURFY

•C•••F
SCHIFF
SCLAFF
SCRUFF

••C•F•
DECAFS
PACIFY
RECIFE

•••C•F
UNICEF

C•G•••
CAGERS
CAGIER
CAGILY
CAGING
CAGNEY
CAGUAS
CIGARS
COGENT
COGGED
COGNAC
CYGNET
CYGNUS

C••G••
CADGED
CADGER
CADGES
CAPGUN
CARGOS
CATGUT
CAUGHT
CHIGOE
CLOGUP
CODGER
COGGED
CONGAS
CONGER
CONGOU
COOGAN
CORGIS
COUGAR
COUGHS
CRAGGY
CUDGEL

C•••G•
CAYUGA
CHANGE
CHARGE
CHOUGH
CLANGS
CLERGY
CLINGS
CLINGY
COLUGO
COSIGN
CRAGGY
CRINGE
CUBAGE

C••••G
CAGING
CAKING
CANING
CARING
CASING
CATRIG
CAVING
CAWING
CEDING
CHIANG
CITING
CLUING
COBURG
CODING
COMING
COOING
COPING
CORING
COWING
CRYING
CUBING
CURING
CYBORG

•CG•••
MCGRAW
MCGREW

•C••G•
ICEAGE
ICINGS
SCRAGS

•C•••G
ACHING
ACTING
ICEBAG
ICEFOG
ICHING

••C•G•
ENCAGE
SOCAGE
UNCAGE

••C••G
ARCING
DICING
FACING
LACING
PACING
RACING
RICING
UNCLOG

CH••••
CHACHA
CHACMA
CHADOR
CHAFED
CHAFES
CHAFFS
CHAFFY
CHAINE
CHAINS
CHAIRS
CHAISE
CHALCO
CHALET
CHALKS
CHALKY
CHAMMY
CHAMPS
CHANCE
CHANCY
CHANEL
CHANEY
CHANGE
CHANTS
CHAPEL
CHAPIN
CHARGE
CHARLY
CHARMS
CHARON
CHARRO
CHARTS
CHASED
CHASER
CHASES
CHASMS
CHASSE
CHASTE
CHATTY
CHATUP
CHAVEZ
CHEAPO
CHEATS
CHECKS
CHEECH
CHEEKS
CHEEKY
CHEEPS
CHEERS
CHEERY
CHEESE
CHEESY
CHELAE
CHELAS
CHEMIN
CHENIN
CHEOPS
CHEQUE
CHERIE
CHERRY
CHERUB
CHERYL
CHESTS
CHESTY
CHEVAL
CHEVET
CHEVRE
CHEWED
CHEWER
CHEWUP
CHIANG
CHIAUS
CHICHA
CHICHI
CHICKS
CHICLE
CHIDED
CHIDES
CHIEFS
CHIGOE
CHILDE
CHILDS
CHILLS
CHILLY
CHILOE
CHIMED
CHIMES
CHIMPS
CHINCH
CHINES
CHINKS
CHINKY
CHINOS
CHINTZ
CHINUP
CHIPIN
CHIRON
CHIRPS
CHIRPY
CHIRRS
CHISEL
CHISOX
CHITIN
CHITON
CHIVES
CHLORO
CHOATE
CHOCKS
CHOICE
CHOIRS
CHOKED
CHOKER
CHOKES
CHOLER
CHOLLA
CHOMPS
CHOOSE
CHOOSY
CHOOYU
CHOPIN
CHOPPY
CHORAL
CHORDS
CHORES
CHORUS
CHOSEN
CHOUGH
CHOWED
CHRISM
CHROMA
CHROME
CHROMO
CHRONO
CHUBBY
CHUCKS
CHUHSI
CHUKAR
CHUKKA
CHUMMY
CHUMPS
CHUNKS
CHUNKY
CHURCH
CHURLS
CHURNS
CHURRO
CHURRS
CHUTED
CHUTES

C•H•••
CAHIER
CAHOWS
COHEIR
COHERE
COHORT
COHOST
COHUNE
CSHARP

C••H••
CACHED
CACHES
CACHET
CACHOU
CARHOP
CASHED
CASHES
CASHEW
CASHIN
CATHAY
CATHER
CHUHSI
CIPHER
COBHAM
COCHIN
COSHED
COSHES
CUSHAW
CYPHER

C•••H•
CANTHI
CATCHY
CAUCHO
CAUGHT
CHACHA
CHICHA
CHICHI
CLICHE
CLOCHE
CLOTHE
CLOTHO
CLOTHS
CONCHA
CONCHS
COUGHS
CRECHE
CZECHS

C••••H
CALASH
CALIPH
CASBAH
CERIPH
CHEECH
CHINCH
CHOUGH
CHURCH
CLENCH
CLINCH
CLUTCH
COMETH
CROUCH
CRUNCH
CRUTCH

•CH•••
ACHAEA
ACHEBE
ACHENE
ACHIER

ACHING
ECHOED
ECHOES
ECHOIC
ICHING
ICHTHY
LCHAIM
MCHALE
OCHERS
OCHRES
SCHELL
SCHEMA
SCHEME
SCHICK
SCHIFF
SCHISM
SCHIST
SCHLEP
SCHMOO
SCHMOS
SCHNOZ
SCHOOL
SCHORL
SCHULZ
SCHUSS
SCHWAS

•C••H•
ICHTHY
SCATHE
SCYTHE

•C•••H
SCORCH
SCOTCH
SCUTCH

••CH••
AACHEN
AHCHOO
ANCHOR
ARCHED
ARCHER
ARCHES
ARCHIE
ARCHLY
ARCHON
ASCHAM
BOCHCO
CACHED
CACHES
CACHET
CACHOU
COCHIN
DACHAS
DUCHIN
ESCHER
ESCHEW
ETCHED
ETCHER
ETCHES
EUCHRE
FICHES
FICHTE
FICHUS
INCHED
INCHES
INCHON
ISCHIA
ITCHED
ITCHES
KUCHEN
LACHES
LICHEN
MACHES
MACHOS
MOCHAS
NACHOS
NICHES
NUCHAE
NUCHAL
ORCHID
ORCHIL
RACHEL
RACHIS
RICHEN
RICHER
RICHES
RICHIE
RICHLY
ROCHET
RUCHES
SACHEM
SACHET
SUCHAS
TECHIE
TECHNO
TUCHUN
UNCHIC
URCHIN
VACHEL
YACHTS

••C•H•
PICCHU

••C••H
INCASH

•••CH•
AMECHE
APACHE
BETCHA
BRECHT
BUNCHE
CATCHY
CAUCHO
CHACHA
CHICHA
CHICHI
CLICHE
CLOCHE
CONCHA
CONCHS
CRECHE
CZECHS
EPOCHS
FLECHE
GAUCHE
GAUCHO
GOTCHA
HONCHO
JASCHA
KIMCHI
KWACHA
LITCHI
LOUCHE
MANCHA
MANCHU
MARCHE
MISCHA
PANCHO
PATCHY
PEACHY
PERCHA
PICCHU
POACHY
PONCHO
POUCHY
PSYCHE
PSYCHO
PSYCHS
PUNCHY
QUICHE
RANCHO
REECHO
SANCHO
SEICHE
TAICHI
TETCHY
TOUCHE
TOUCHY
TRICHO
TROCHE
WITCHY

••••CH
ATTACH
AVOUCH
BARUCH
BLANCH
BLEACH
BLENCH
BLOTCH
BORSCH
BRANCH
BREACH
BREECH
BROACH
BROOCH
BRUNCH
CHEECH
CHINCH
CHURCH
CLENCH
CLINCH
CLUTCH
CROUCH
CRUNCH
CRUTCH
DETACH
DRENCH
ENRICH
EPARCH
EUNUCH
EXARCH
FLETCH
FLINCH
FLITCH
FRENCH
GLITCH
GRINCH
GROUCH
HAUNCH
HIRSCH
HITECH
INARCH
KIRSCH
KITSCH
KLATCH
KVETCH
LAMECH
LAUNCH
MENSCH
MOLOCH
MUNICH
NAUTCH
ORBACH
PAUNCH
PESACH
PLEACH
PREACH
PUTSCH
QUENCH
SCORCH
SCOTCH
SCUTCH
SEARCH
SKETCH
SKITCH
SLOUCH
SMIRCH
SMOOCH
SMUTCH
SNATCH
SNITCH
SPEECH
STANCH
STARCH
STENCH
STITCH
STORCH
SWATCH
SWITCH
THATCH
TRENCH
TWITCH
VOTECH
WRENCH
WRETCH
ZURICH

CI••••
CIARDI
CIBOLA
CICADA
CICELY
CICERO
CIDERS
CIGARS
CILIUM
CINDER
CINEMA
CINQUE
CIPHER
CIRCLE
CIRCUM
CIRCUS
CIRQUE
CIRRUS
CISCOS
CISKEI
CITERS
CITIES
CITIFY
CITING
CITRIC
CITRON
CITRUS
CIUDAD
CIVETS
CIVICS

C•I•••
CAICOS
CAIMAN
CAIQUE
CAIRNS
CEIBAS
CEILED
CHIANG
CHIAUS
CHICHA
CHICHI
CHICKS
CHICLE
CHIDED
CHIDES
CHIEFS
CHIGOE
CHILDE
CHILDS
CHILLS
CHILLY
CHILOE
CHIMED
CHIMES
CHIMPS
CHINCH
CHINES
CHINKS
CHINKY
CHINOS
CHINTZ
CHINUP
CHIPIN
CHIRON
CHIRPS
CHIRPY
CHIRRS
CHISEL
CHISOX
CHITIN
CHITON
CHIVES
CLICHE
CLICKS
CLIENT
CLIFFS
CLIMAX
CLIMBS
CLIMES
CLINCH
CLINES
CLINGS
CLINGY
CLINIC
CLINKS
CLIPON
CLIQUE
CMINOR
CMINUS
CNIDUS
COIFED
COILED
COILUP
COINED
COINER
CRICKS
CRIERS
CRIMEA
CRIMES
CRIMPS
CRINGE
CRIPES
CRISCO
CRISES
CRISIS
CRISPS
CRISPY
CRITIC
CUIABA
CUISSE

C••I••
CABINS
CAGIER
CAGILY
CAGING
CAHIER
CAKING
CALICO
CALIPH
CAMINO
CAMION
CAMISE
CANIDS
CANIFF
CANINE
CANING
CAPIAS
CAPITA
CARIBE
CARIBS
CARIES
CARINA
CARING
CASING
CASINO
CATION
CAVIAR
CAVILS
CAVING
CAVITY
CAWING
CECILE
CEDING
CELINE
CERIPH
CERISE
CERIUM
CESIUM
CHAINE
CHAINS
CHAIRS
CHAISE
CHOICE
CHOIRS
CHRISM
CILIUM
CITIES
CITIFY
CITING
CIVICS
CLAIMS
CLAIRE
CLUING
COBIAS
CODIFY
CODING
COLIMA
COMICS
COMING
COMITY
CONICS
CONIES
CONIUM
COOING
COPIED
COPIER
COPIES
COPING
CORING
CORIUM
COSIES
COSIGN
COSINE
COVINA
COWING
COZIED
COZIER
COZIES
COZILY
CRUISE
CRYING
CUBICS
CUBING
CUBISM
CUBIST
CUBITS
CUPIDS
CURIAE
CURIAL
CURING
CURIOS
CURIUM
CUTIES
CUTINS
CYBILL
CYNICS

C•••I•
CABBIE
CADDIE
CADDIS
CADMIC
CALAIS
CALLIN
CALVIN
CAMEIN
CANDID
CAPRIS
CAPSID
CARDIN
CARDIO
CARRIE
CASHIN
CASSIA
CASSIO
CASSIS
CATKIN
CATNIP
CATRIG
CAVEIN
CEDRIC
CELTIC
CERTIF
CERVID
CHAPIN
CHEMIN
CHENIN
CHERIE
CHIPIN
CHITIN
CHOPIN
CITRIC
CLAVIN
CLERIC
CLEVIS
CLINIC
CLORIS
CLOVIS
CLUEIN
COATIS
COCCID
COCHIN
COEDIT
COHEIR
COLLIE
COMEIN
COMFIT
COMMIT
COMMIX
CONNIE
COOKIE
COOLIT
COOTIE
COPTIC
CORBIN
CORGIS
COSMIC
COURIC
COUSIN
COWRIE
CRANIA
CRANIO
CREDIT
CRETIN
CRISIS
CRITIC
CRONIN
CUBOID
CULKIN
CULLIS
CULTIC
CUPRIC
CURTIN
CURTIS
CURTIZ
CUSPID
CUTSIN
CYANIC
CYCLIC
CYMRIC

C••••I
CANTHI
CARONI
CENTRI
CHICHI
CHUHSI
CIARDI
CISKEI
CUMULI

•CI•••
ACIDIC
ACIDLY
ACINUS
ICICLE
ICIEST
ICINGS
SCIFIS
SCIONS
SCIPIO

•C•I••
ACHIER
ACHING
ACTIII
ACTING
ACTINO
ACTION
ACTIUM
ACTIVE
ACUITY
ICHING
ICKIER
SCHICK
SCHIFF
SCHISM
SCHIST
SCRIBE
SCRIMP
SCRIMS
SCRIPS
SCRIPT

•C••I•
ACACIA
ACADIA
ACARID
ACEDIA
ACETIC
ACIDIC
ACQUIT
ACTIII
ECESIS
ECHOIC
ECLAIR
ICARIA
ICEDIN
ICESIN
ICONIC
LCHAIM
MCBAIN
MCLAIN
MCNAIR
SCALIA
SCENIC
SCIFIS
SCIPIO
SCORIA
SCOTIA

•C•••I
ACTIII
OCELLI
OCTOPI
OCTROI
SCAMPI

••CI••
ANCIEN
ARCING
CECILE
DECIDE
DICIER
DICING
DOCILE
ENCINA
ENCINO
EXCISE
EXCITE
FACIAL
FACIES
FACILE
FACING
INCISE
INCITE
LACIER
LACING
LUCIAN
LUCITE
LUCIUS
OSCINE
PACIFY
PACING
PACINO
RACIAL
RACIER
RACILY
RACINE
RACING
RECIFE
RECIPE
RECITE
RICING
SICILY
SOCIAL
UNCIAL

••C•I•
ALCUIN
ARCHIE
ARCTIC
BACKIN
BOCCIE
COCCID
COCHIN
CYCLIC
DACOIT
DECEIT
DUCHIN
EUCLID
HACKIE
HECTIC
ISCHIA
JACKIE
KICKIN
LACTIC
LOCKIN
ORCHID
ORCHIL
PECTIC
PECTIN
PICNIC
RACHIS
RECOIL
RICHIE
SOCKIN
SUCKIN
TACTIC
TECHIE
TOCSIN
TUCKIN
UNCHIC
UNCOIL
URCHIN
VICTIM

••C••I
JACOBI
NUCLEI

•••CI•
ACACIA
AFLCIO
ALICIA
ANACIN
BAUCIS
BOCCIE
COCCID
ELICIT
FASCIA
GARCIA
GLACIS
GRACIE
MARCIA
MARCIE
MUNCIE
MURCIA
NIACIN
NUNCIO
PENCIL
PHOCIS
PLACID
PRECIS
RANCID
RUNCIE
SPECIE
TRICIA
URACIL
VISCID

•••C•I
CHICHI
KIMCHI
LITCHI
TAICHI

••••CI
MEDICI

C•J•••
CAJOLE
CAJUNS

C••J••
CMAJOR
CONJOB

•C•J••
ACAJOU

C•K•••
CAKING

C••K••
CACKLE
CALKED
CANKER
CATKIN
CHOKED
CHOKER
CHOKES
CHUKAR
CHUKKA
CISKEI
COCKED
COCKER
COCKLE
CONKED
CONKER
COOKED
COOKER
COOKIE
COOKUP
CORKED
CORKER
CRAKES
CUCKOO
CULKIN

C•••K•
CAULKS
CHALKS
CHALKY
CHECKS
CHEEKS
CHEEKY
CHICKS
CHINKS
CHINKY
CHOCKS
CHUCKS
CHUKKA
CHUNKS
CHUNKY
CLACKS
CLANKS
CLANKY
CLARKE
CLEEKS
CLERKS
CLICKS
CLINKS
CLOAKS
CLOCKS
CLONKS
CLUCKS
CLUNKS
CLUNKY
CRACKS
CRANKS
CRANKY
CREAKS
CREAKY
CREEKS
CRICKS
CROAKS
CROAKY
CROCKS
CROOKS

•CK•••
ACKACK
ICKIER
MCKUEN

•C•••K
ACKACK
OCASEK
OCLOCK
SCHICK
SCREAK

••CK••
BACKED
BACKER
BACKIN
BACKUP
BACKUS
BECKER
BECKET
BECKON
BICKER
BUCKED
BUCKET
BUCKLE
BUCKUP
CACKLE
COCKED
COCKER
COCKLE
CUCKOO
DECKED
DECKER
DECKLE
DICKER
DICKEY
DOCKED
DOCKER
DOCKET
DUCKED
FICKLE
GECKOS
HACKED
HACKER
HACKIE
HACKLE
HECKLE
HICKEY
HICKOK
HOCKED
HOCKEY
JACKAL
JACKED
JACKET
JACKIE
JACKUP
JECKLE
JOCKEY
KICKED
KICKER
KICKIN
KICKUP
LACKED
LACKEY
LICKED
LOCKED
LOCKER
LOCKET
LOCKIN
LOCKUP
LUCKED
MICKEY
MOCKED
MOCKER
MOCKUP
MUCKED
MUCKUP
NECKED
NICKED
NICKEL
NICKER
PACKED
PACKER
PACKET
PACKUP
PECKAT
PECKED
PICKAT
PICKAX
PICKED
PICKER
PICKET
PICKLE
PICKON
PICKUP
POCKET
PUCKER
RACKED
RACKET
RACKUP
RECKON
RICKED
RICKEY
ROCKED
ROCKER
ROCKET
ROCKNE
ROCKYV
RUCKED
RUCKUS
SACKED
SACKER
SECKEL
SICKEN
SICKER
SICKLE
SICKLY
SOCKED
SOCKET
SOCKIN
SUCKED
SUCKER
SUCKIN
TACKED
TACKER
TACKLE
TACKON
TICKED
TICKER
TICKET
TICKLE
TUCKED
TUCKER
TUCKET
TUCKIN
WICKED
WICKER
WICKET

••C•K•
HACEKS

••C••K
HICKOK
RECORK
UNCORK

•••CK•
ALECKY
BLACKS
BLOCKS
BLOCKY
BRICKS
BRICKY
CHECKS
CHICKS
CHOCKS
CHUCKS
CLACKS
CLICKS
CLOCKS
CLUCKS
CRACKS
CRICKS
CROCKS
FLACKS
FLECKS
FLICKA
FLICKS
FLOCKS
FROCKS
KNACKS
KNICKS
KNOCKS
KYACKS
PLUCKS
PLUCKY
PRICKS
QUACKS
SHACKS
SHOCKS
SHUCKS
SLACKS
SLICKS
SMACKS
SMOCKS
SNACKS
SNICKS
SPECKS
STACKS
STICKS
STICKY
STOCKS
STOCKY
THICKE
TRACKS
TRICKS
TRICKY
TRUCKS
VNECKS
WHACKS
WHACKY
WRACKS
WRECKS
YOICKS

•••C•K
DUBCEK
SPACEK

••••CK
ACKACK
ARRACK
ATTACK
BEDECK
FRANCK
GOBACK
HIJACK
INLUCK
KOPECK
LUBECK
MOHOCK
NATICK
OCLOCK
ONDECK
PLANCK
RELOCK
REMICK
SCHICK
SHTICK
STRICK
STRUCK
THWACK
UNLOCK
UNPACK
UNTACK
UPTICK
YORICK
ZANUCK

CL••••
CLACKS
CLAIMS
CLAIRE
CLAMMY
CLAMOR
CLAMPS
CLAMUP
CLANCY
CLANGS
CLANKS
CLANKY
CLAQUE
CLARET
CLARKE
CLAROS
CLASPS
CLASSY
CLAUDE
CLAUSE
CLAVIN
CLAWED
CLAWER
CLAYEY
CLEANS
CLEARS
CLEATS
CLEAVE
CLEEKS
CLEESE
CLEFTS
CLENCH
CLEPED
CLERGY
CLERIC
CLERKS
CLEVER
CLEVES
CLEVIS
CLEWED
CLICHE
CLICKS
CLIENT
CLIFFS
CLIMAX
CLIMBS
CLIMES

CLINCH
CLINES
CLINGS
CLINGY
CLINIC
CLINKS
CLIPON
CLIQUE
CLOACA
CLOAKS
CLOCHE
CLOCKS
CLOGUP
CLOMPS
CLONED
CLONES
CLONKS
CLONUS
CLOQUE
CLORIS
CLOROX
CLOSED
CLOSER
CLOSES
CLOSET
CLOTHE
CLOTHO
CLOTHS
CLOTTY
CLOUDS
CLOUDY
CLOUTS
CLOVEN
CLOVER
CLOVES
CLOVIS
CLOWNS
CLOYED
CLUBBY
CLUCKS
CLUEIN
CLUING
CLUMPS
CLUMPY
CLUMSY
CLUNKS
CLUNKY
CLUTCH

C•L•••

CALAIS
CALASH
CALCES
CALDER
CALICO
CALIPH
CALKED
CALLAO
CALLAS
CALLED
CALLER
CALLES
CALLIN
CALLON
CALLOW
CALLUP
CALLUS
CALMED
CALMER
CALMLY
CALPAC
CALQUE
CALVED
CALVES
CALVIN
CALXES
CCLAMP
CELEBS
CELERY
CELINE
CELLAE
CELLAR
CELLED
CELLOS
CELTIC
CHLORO
CILIUM
COLADA
COLDER
COLDLY
COLEUS
COLIMA
COLLAR
COLLET
COLLIE
COLLOP
COLLOQ
COLMAN
COLONS
COLONY
COLORS
COLOUR
COLTER
COLUGO
COLUMN
CULETS
CULKIN
CULLED
CULLEN
CULLER
CULLET
CULLIS
CULTIC
CULVER

C••L••

CABLED
CABLER
CABLES
CALLAO
CALLAS
CALLED
CALLER
CALLES
CALLIN
CALLON
CALLOW
CALLUP
CALLUS
CAMLET
CAPLET
CARLOS
CARLOT
CAULKS
CEILED
CELLAE
CELLAR
CELLED
CELLOS
CEYLON
CHALCO
CHALET
CHALKS
CHALKY
CHELAE
CHELAS
CHILDE
CHILDS
CHILLS
CHILLY
CHILOE
CHOLER
CHOLLA
COALER
COELOM
COILED
COILUP
COLLAR
COLLET
COLLIE
COLLOP
COLLOQ
COOLED
COOLER
COOLIT
COOLLY
COULEE
COWLED
COWLEY
CULLED
CULLEN
CULLER
CULLET
CULLIS
CURLED
CURLER
CURLEW
CURLUP
CUTLER
CUTLET
CYCLAS
CYCLED
CYCLER
CYCLES
CYCLIC
CYCLOS

C•••L•

CABALA
CABALS
CACKLE
CAGILY
CAJOLE
CALMLY
CAMELS
CANALS
CANDLE
CANOLA
CANTLE
CAROLE
CAROLS
CASALS
CASTLE
CATTLE
CAUDLE
CAVELL
CAVILS
CECILE
CHARLY
CHICLE
CHILLS
CHILLY
CHOLLA
CHURLS
CIBOLA
CICELY
CIRCLE
COBALT
COBBLE
COCKLE
CODDLE
COLDLY
COMELY
COMPLY
COOLLY
COPULA
CORALS
COSELL
COSTLY
COUPLE
COZILY
CRADLE
CRAWLS
CRAWLY
CREELS
CREOLE
CUDDLE
CUDDLY
CUMULI
CUMULO
CUPELS
CUPOLA
CURDLE
CURTLY
CURULE
CYBELE
CYBILL

C••••L

CANCEL
CANNEL
CAPFUL
CARFUL
CARMEL
CARNAL
CARPAL
CARPEL
CARREL
CARROL
CARTEL
CASUAL
CAUDAL
CAUSAL
CAVELL
CEREAL
CHANEL
CHAPEL
CHERYL
CHEVAL
CHISEL
CHORAL
COEVAL
COMPEL
CONSUL
CORBEL
CORNEL
CORRAL
CORREL
COSELL
COSTAL
CRENEL
CRESOL
CREWEL
CRURAL
CUDGEL
CUNEAL
CUPFUL
CURIAL
CYBILL
CYMBAL

•CL•••

CCLAMP
ECLAIR
ECLATS
MCLAIN
MCLEAN
OCLOCK
SCLAFF
SCLERA
UCLANS

•C•L••

ECCLES
ECOLES
OCELLI
OCELOT
OCULAR
SCALAR
SCALDS
SCALED
SCALER
SCALES
SCALIA
SCALPS
SCHLEP
SCOLDS
SCULLS
SCULLY
SCULPT
SCYLLA

•C••L•

ACIDLY
ICICLE
MCHALE
OCCULT
OCELLI
SCHELL
SCHULZ
SCOWLS
SCROLL
SCULLS
SCULLY
SCYLLA

•C•••L

ACETAL
ACETYL
ACTUAL
SCHELL
SCHOOL
SCHORL
SCRAWL
SCROLL

••CL••

CYCLAS
CYCLED
CYCLER
CYCLES
CYCLIC
CYCLOS
ECCLES
EUCLID
JACLYN
NUCLEI
NUCLEO
SOCLES
UNCLAD
UNCLES
UNCLOG
VACLAV

••C•L•

ARCHLY
BACALL
BECALM
BUCKLE
CACKLE
CECILE
CICELY
COCKLE
DECALS
DECKLE
DOCILE
EXCELS
FACILE
FACULA
FICKLE
FOCSLE
HACKLE
HECKLE
INCULT
JACALS
JECKLE
LOCALE
LOCALS
MACULA
NICELY
NICOLA
NICOLE
NICOLO
OCCULT
ONCALL
OSCULA
PICKLE
PICULS
RACILY
RECALL
RICHLY
SICILY
SICKLE
SICKLY
TACKLE
TICALS
TICKLE
VOCALS

••C••L

BACALL
BUCCAL
DACTYL
DUCTAL
FACIAL
JACKAL
MRCOOL
NICKEL
NUCHAL
ONCALL
ORCHIL
RACHEL
RACIAL
RECALL
RECOIL
SACRAL
SECKEL
SOCIAL
UNCIAL
UNCOIL
UNCOOL
UNCURL
VACHEL

•••CL•

BOUCLE
CHICLE
CIRCLE
ICICLE
MUSCLE
MUSCLY
ORACLE
SIECLE

•••C•L

APICAL
BUCCAL
CANCEL
EPICAL
FISCAL
GLYCOL
LOWCAL
MARCEL
MESCAL
PARCEL
PASCAL
PENCEL
PENCIL
RASCAL
TERCEL
THECAL
TINCAL
URACIL

CM••••

CMAJOR
CMINOR
CMINUS

C•M•••

CAMBER
CAMDEN
CAMEAT
CAMEBY
CAMEIN
CAMELS
CAMEON
CAMEOS
CAMERA
CAMETO
CAMEUP
CAMINO
CAMION
CAMISE
CAMLET
CAMPED
CAMPER
CAMPOS
CAMPUS
CEMENT
COMATE
COMBAT
COMBED
COMBER
COMBES
COMBOS
COMEAT
COMEBY
COMEDY
COMEIN
COMELY
COMEON
COMERS
COMETH
COMETO
COMETS
COMEUP
COMFIT
COMICS
COMING
COMITY
COMMAS
COMMIT
COMMIX
COMMON
COMPAQ
COMPEL
COMPLY
COMPOS
COMSAT
COMTES
CUMBER
CUMULI
CUMULO
CYMBAL
CYMRIC

C••M••

CADMIC
CADMUS
CAIMAN
CALMED
CALMER
CALMLY
CARMAN
CARMEL
CARMEN
CAYMAN
CERMET
CHAMMY
CHAMPS
CHEMIN
CHIMED
CHIMES
CHIMPS
CHOMPS
CHUMMY
CHUMPS
CLAMMY
CLAMOR
CLAMPS
CLAMUP
CLIMAX
CLIMBS
CLIMES
CLOMPS
CLUMPS
CLUMPY
CLUMSY
COLMAN
COMMAS
COMMIT
COMMIX
COMMON
CONMAN
CONMEN
COSMIC
COSMOS
COWMAN
COWMEN
CRAMBO
CRAMPS
CREMES
CRIMEA
CRIMES
CRIMPS
CRUMBS
CRUMBY
CRUMMY

C•••M•

CAROMS
CCLAMP
CDROMS
CHACMA
CHAMMY
CHARMS
CHASMS
CHROMA
CHROME
CHROMO
CHUMMY
CINEMA
CLAIMS
CLAMMY
COLIMA
COLUMN
CREAMS
CREAMY
CRUMMY

C••••M

CERIUM
CESIUM
CHRISM
CILIUM
CIRCUM
COBHAM
COELOM
CONIUM
CORIUM
CUBISM
CURIUM
CUSTOM

•C•M••

ACUMEN
ICEMAN
ICEMEN
SCAMPI
SCAMPS
SCHMOO
SCHMOS
SCUMMY

•C••M•

CCLAMP
SCHEMA
SCHEME
SCRAMS
SCRIMP
SCRIMS
SCRUMS
SCUMMY

•C•••M

ACTIUM
LCHAIM
MCADAM
SCARUM
SCHISM
SCREAM

••CM••

MICMAC
PACMAN

••C•M•

BECAME
BECOME
DECAMP
ENCAMP
INCOME
JICAMA
RACEME
TACOMA

••C••M

ASCHAM
BECALM
DICTUM
LYCEUM
SACHEM
SACRUM
VACUUM
VICTIM

•••CM•

CHACMA

•••C•M

CIRCUM
NONCOM
SITCOM
TALCUM
VIACOM

CN••••

CNIDUS
CNOTES

C•N•••

CANAAN
CANADA
CANALS
CANAPE
CANARD
CANARY
CANCAN
CANCEL
CANCUN
CANDID
CANDLE
CANDOR
CANERS
CANIDS
CANIFF
CANINE
CANING
CANKER
CANNAE
CANNED
CANNEL
CANNER
CANNES
CANNON
CANNOT
CANOED
CANOES
CANOLA
CANONS
CANOPY
CANOVA
CANTAB
CANTED
CANTER
CANTHI
CANTLE
CANTON
CANTOR
CANTOS
CANUTE
CANVAS
CANYON
CENOTE
CENSED
CENSER
CENSES
CENSOR
CENSUS
CENTER
CENTOS
CENTRE
CENTRI
CENTRO
CINDER
CINEMA
CINQUE
CONANT
CONCHA
CONCHS
CONCUR
CONDOR
CONDOS
CONEYS
CONFAB
CONFED
CONFER
CONGAS
CONGER
CONGOU
CONICS
CONIES
CONIUM
CONJOB
CONKED
CONKER
CONMAN
CONMEN
CONNED
CONNER
CONNIE
CONNOR
CONOCO
CONRAD
CONROY
CONSUL
CONTAC
CONTES
CONTRA
CONTRE
CONVEX
CONVEY
CONVOY
CONWAY
CUNARD
CUNAXA
CUNEAL
CYNICS

C••N••

CAGNEY
CANNAE
CANNED
CANNEL
CANNER
CANNES
CANNON
CANNOT
CAPNUT
CARNAL
CARNES
CARNET
CARNEY
CARNOT
CATNAP
CATNIP
CHANCE
CHANCY
CHANEL
CHANEY
CHANGE
CHANTS
CHENIN
CHINCH
CHINES
CHINKS
CHINKY
CHINOS
CHINTZ
CHINUP
CHUNKS
CHUNKY
CLANCY
CLANGS
CLANKS
CLANKY
CLENCH
CLINCH
CLINES
CLINGS
CLINGY
CLINIC
CLINKS
CLONED
CLONES
CLONKS
CLONUS
CLUNKS
CLUNKY
CMINOR
CMINUS
COGNAC
COINED
COINER
CONNED
CONNER
CONNIE
CONNOR
COONEY
CORNEA
CORNED
CORNEL
CORNER
CORNET
COUNTS
COUNTY
CPSNOW
CRANED
CRANES
CRANIA
CRANIO
CRANKS
CRANKY
CRANNY
CRENEL
CRENNA
CRINGE
CRONES
CRONIN
CRONUS
CRONYN
CRUNCH
CYANIC
CYGNET
CYGNUS

C•••N•

CABANA
CABINS
CADENT
CAGING
CAIRNS
CAJUNS
CAKING
CAMINO
CANINE
CANING
CANONS
CAPONE
CAPONS
CARINA
CARING
CARONI
CASING
CASINO
CATENA
CAVING
CAWING
CEDING
CELINE
CEMENT
CESSNA
CETANE
CHAINE
CHAINS
CHIANG
CHRONO
CHURNS
CITING
CLEANS
CLIENT
CLOWNS
CLUING
CODING
CODONS
COGENT
COHUNE
COLONS
COLONY
COMING
CONANT
COOING
COPING
CORING
CORONA
COSINE
COVENS
COVENT
COVINA
COWENS
COWING
COZENS
CRANNY
CRENNA
CROONS
CROWNS
CRYING
CUBING
CURING
CUTINS
CYRANO
CZERNY

C••••N

CAFTAN
CAIMAN
CALLIN
CALLON
CALVIN
CAMDEN
CAMEIN
CAMEON
CAMION
CANAAN
CANCAN
CANCUN
CANNON
CANTON
CANYON
CAPGUN
CAPTAN
CARBON
CARDIN
CAREEN
CARMAN
CARMEN
CARSON
CARTON
CASERN
CASHIN
CASTON
CATION
CATKIN
CATTON
CAVEIN
CAVERN
CAXTON
CAYMAN
CEYLON
CHAPIN
CHARON
CHEMIN
CHENIN
CHIPIN
CHIRON
CHITIN
CHITON
CHOPIN
CHOSEN
CITRON
CLAVIN
CLIPON
CLOVEN
CLUEIN
COBURN
COCHIN
COCOON
COLMAN
COLUMN
COMEIN
COMEON
COMMON
CONMAN
CONMEN
COOGAN
CORBAN
CORBIN
CORDON
COSIGN
COTTEN
COTTON
COUPON
COUSIN
COWMAN
COWMEN
CRAVEN
CRAYON
CRETAN
CRETIN
CRONIN
CRONYN
CROTON
CULKIN
CULLEN
CURTIN
CURZON
CUTSIN

•CN•••

MCNAIR

•C•N••

ACINUS
ICINGS
ICONIC
SCANTS
SCANTY
SCENAS
SCENDS
SCENES
SCENIC
SCENTS
SCHNOZ
SCONCE
SCONES

•C••N•

ACCENT
ACHENE
ACHING
ACORNS
ACTING
ACTINO
ACTONE
ICHING
MCCANN
OCEANS
OCTANE
OCTANT
SCARNE
SCIONS
SCORNS
UCLANS

•C•••N

ACTION
ACTSON
ACUMEN
ICEDIN
ICEMAN
ICEMEN
ICESIN
MCBAIN
MCCANN
MCKUEN
MCLAIN
MCLEAN
SCREEN

••CN••

PICNIC

••C•N•

ACCENT
ANCONA
ARCANA
ARCANE
ARCING
ASCEND
ASCENT
DECANT
DECENT
DICING
DOCENT
ENCINA
ENCINO
EOCENE
ESCENT
FACING
FECUND
INCANS
JACANA
JOCUND
LACING
LACUNA
LUCENT
MCCANN
NICENE
NOCENT
OSCINE
PACING
PACINO
PECANS
POCONO
RACINE
RACING
RACONS
RECANE
RECANT
RECENT

RECONS
RICING
ROCKNE
SECANT
SECOND
TECHNO
TUCANA
VACANT
VICUNA

••C••N
AACHEN
ALCUIN
ANCIEN
ARCHON
BACKIN
BECKON
BICORN
COCHIN
COCOON
DACRON
DUCHIN
INCHON
JACLYN
KICKIN
KUCHEN
LICHEN
LOCKIN
LUCIAN
MACRON
MCCANN
MICRON
NICEAN
PACMAN
PECTIN
PICKON
RECKON
RICHEN
SECERN
SICKEN
SOCKIN
SUCKIN
TACKON
TOCSIN
TUCHUN
TUCKIN
TUCSON
TYCOON
URCHIN
WICCAN

•••CN•
PROCNE

•••C•N
ANACIN
ASHCAN
BEACON
CANCAN
CANCUN
DEACON
DUNCAN
FALCON
FLACON
GARCON
GASCON
NIACIN
OILCAN
TINCAN
TOUCAN
TUSCAN
VULCAN
WICCAN
ZIRCON

CO••••
COALER
COAPTS
COARSE
COASTS
COATED
COATIS
COAXED
COAXER
COAXES
COBALT
COBBLE
COBHAM
COBIAS
COBRAS
COBURG
COBURN
COBWEB
COCCID
COCCUS
COCCYX
COCHIN
COCKED
COCKER
COCKLE
COCOAS
COCOON
CODDLE
CODERS
CODGER
CODIFY
CODING
CODONS
COEDIT
COELOM
COERCE
COEVAL
COFFEE
COFFER
COGENT
COGGED
COGNAC
COHEIR
COHERE
COHORT
COHOST
COHUNE
COIFED
COILED
COILUP
COINED
COINER
COLADA
COLDER
COLDLY
COLEUS
COLIMA
COLLAR
COLLET
COLLIE
COLLOP
COLLOQ
COLMAN
COLONS
COLONY
COLORS
COLOUR
COLTER
COLUGO
COLUMN
COMATE
COMBAT
COMBED
COMBER
COMBES
COMBOS
COMEAT
COMEBY
COMEDY
COMEIN
COMELY
COMEON
COMERS
COMETH
COMETO
COMETS
COMEUP
COMFIT
COMICS
COMING
COMITY
COMMAS
COMMIT
COMMIX
COMMON
COMPAQ
COMPEL
COMPLY
COMPOS
COMSAT
COMTES
CONANT
CONCHA
CONCHS
CONCUR
CONDOR
CONDOS
CONEYS
CONFAB
CONFED
CONFER
CONGAS
CONGER
CONGOU
CONICS
CONIES
CONIUM
CONJOB
CONKED
CONKER
CONMAN
CONMEN
CONNED
CONNER
CONNIE
CONNOR
CONOCO
CONRAD
CONROY
CONSUL
CONTAC
CONTES
CONTRA
CONTRE
CONVEX
CONVEY
CONVOY
CONWAY
COODER
COOERS
COOGAN
COOING
COOKED
COOKER
COOKIE
COOKUP
COOLED
COOLER
COOLIT
COOLLY
COONEY
COOPED
COOPER
COOPTS
COOPUP
COOTER
COOTIE
COPIED
COPIER
COPIES
COPING
COPOUT
COPPED
COPPER
COPSES
COPTER
COPTIC
COPULA
COQUET
CORALS
CORBAN
CORBEL
CORBIN
CORDAY
CORDED
CORDON
CORERS
CORGIS
CORING
CORIUM
CORKED
CORKER
CORNEA
CORNED
CORNEL
CORNER
CORNET
CORONA
CORPUS
CORRAL
CORREL
CORSET
CORTES
CORTEX
CORTEZ
CORVEE
CORYZA
COSELL
COSHED
COSHES
COSIES
COSIGN
COSINE
COSMIC
COSMOS
COSSET
COSTAE
COSTAL
COSTAR
COSTAS
COSTLY
COTTAS
COTTEN
COTTER
COTTON
COUGAR
COUGHS
COULEE
COUNTS
COUNTY
COUPES
COUPLE
COUPON
COURIC
COURSE
COURTS
COUSIN
COUTER
COVENS
COVENT
COVERS
COVERT
COVETS
COVEYS
COVINA
COWARD
COWBOY
COWENS
COWERS
COWING
COWLED
COWLEY
COWMAN
COWMEN
COWPEA
COWPER
COWPOX
COWRIE
COYEST
COYOTE
COYPUS
COZENS
COZIED
COZIER
COZIES
COZILY

C•O•••
CHOATE
CHOCKS
CHOICE
CHOIRS
CHOKED
CHOKER
CHOKES
CHOLER
CHOLLA
CHOMPS
CHOOSE
CHOOSY
CHOOYU
CHOPIN
CHOPPY
CHORAL
CHORDS
CHORES
CHORUS
CHOSEN
CHOUGH
CHOWED
CLOACA
CLOAKS
CLOCHE
CLOCKS
CLOGUP
CLOMPS
CLONED
CLONES
CLONKS
CLONUS
CLOQUE
CLORIS
CLOROX
CLOSED
CLOSER
CLOSES
CLOSET
CLOTHE
CLOTHO
CLOTHS
CLOTTY
CLOUDS
CLOUDY
CLOUTS
CLOVEN
CLOVER
CLOVES
CLOVIS
CLOWNS
CLOYED
CNOTES
COODER
COOERS
COOGAN
COOING
COOKED
COOKER
COOKIE
COOKUP
COOLED
COOLER
COOLIT
COOLLY
COONEY
COOPED
COOPER
COOPTS
COOPUP
COOTER
COOTIE
CROAKS
CROAKY
CROATS
CROCKS
CROCUS
CROFTS
CRONES
CRONIN
CRONUS
CRONYN
CROOKS
CROONS
CROPUP
CROSBY
CROSSE
CROTON
CROUCH
CROUPY
CROUSE
CROUTE
CROWDS
CROWED
CROWER
CROWNS
CROZES

C••O••
CAHOWS
CAJOLE
CANOED
CANOES
CANOLA
CANONS
CANOPY
CANOVA
CAPONE
CAPONS
CAPOTE
CAROBS
CAROLE
CAROLS
CAROMS
CARONI
CAVORT
CDROMS
CENOTE
CHEOPS
CHLORO
CHOOSE
CHOOSY
CHOOYU
CHROMA
CHROME
CHROMO
CHRONO
CIBOLA
COCOAS
COCOON
CODONS
COHORT
COHOST
COLONS
COLONY
COLORS
COLOUR
CONOCO
COPOUT
CORONA
COYOTE
CREOLE
CROOKS
CROONS
CRYOFF
CUBOID
CUPOLA
CUTOFF
CUTOUT
CYBORG

C•••O•
CACAOS
CACHOU
CAICOS
CALLON
CALLOW
CAMEON
CAMEOS
CAMION
CAMPOS
CANDOR
CANNON
CANNOT
CANTON
CANTOR
CANTOS
CANYON
CAPTOR
CARBON
CARBOY
CARGOS
CARHOP
CARLOS
CARLOT
CARNOT
CARROL
CARROT
CARSON
CARTON
CASTON
CASTOR
CATION
CATTON
CAWDOR
CAXTON
CELLOS
CENSOR
CENTOS
CESTOS
CEYLON
CHADOR
CHARON
CHIGOE
CHILOE
CHINOS
CHIRON
CHISOX
CHITON
CISCOS
CITRON
CLAMOR
CLAROS
CLIPON
CLOROX
CMAJOR
CMINOR
COCOON
COELOM
COLLOP
COLLOQ
COMBOS
COMEON
COMMON
COMPOS
CONDOR
CONDOS
CONGOU
CONJOB
CONNOR
CONROY
CONVOY
CORDON
COSMOS
COTTON
COUPON
COWBOY
COWPOX
CPSNOW
CRAYON
CREDOS
CRESOL
CROTON
CRUSOE
CUCKOO
CURIOS
CURSOR
CURZON
CUSTOM
CYCLOS

C••••O
CALICO
CALLAO
CAMETO
CAMINO
CARDIO
CARETO
CARUSO
CASINO
CASSIO
CASTRO
CAUCHO
CENTRO
CHALCO
CHARRO
CHEAPO
CHLORO
CHROMO
CHRONO
CHURRO
CICERO
CLOTHO
COLUGO
COMETO
CONOCO
CRAMBO
CRANIO
CRISCO
CRYPTO
CUCKOO
CUMULO
CYRANO

•CO•••
ACORNS
ECOLES
ICONIC
SCOFFS
SCOLDS
SCONCE
SCONES
SCOOPS
SCOOTS
SCOPED
SCOPES
SCORCH
SCORED
SCORER
SCORES
SCORIA
SCORNS
SCOTCH
SCOTER
SCOTIA
SCOTTO
SCOTTY
SCOURS
SCOUTS
SCOWLS

•C•O••
ACCORD
ACCOST
ACEOUS
ACEOUT
ACROSS
ACTONE
ACTORS
ACTOUT
ECHOED
ECHOES
ECHOIC
ICEOUT
OCLOCK
OCTOPI
SCHOOL
SCHORL
SCIONS
SCOOPS
SCOOTS
SCRODS
SCROLL
SCROOP

•C••O•
ACAJOU
ACTION
ACTSON
ICEBOX
ICEFOG
MCADOO
OCELOT
OCTROI
SCHMOO
SCHMOS
SCHNOZ
SCHOOL
SCROOP

•C•••O
ACTINO
ACTTWO
MCADOO
OCTAVO
SCHMOO
SCIPIO
SCOTTO

••CO••
ACCORD
ACCOST
ALCOTT
ALCOVE
ANCONA
ASCOTS
ATCOST
BECOME
BICORN
COCOAS
COCOON
DACOIT
DECOCT
DECODE
DECORS
DECOYS
DICOTS
ENCODE
ENCORE
ESCORT
INCOME
JACOBI
JOCOSE
MRCOOL
MUCOSA
MUCOUS
NICOLA
NICOLE
NICOLO
PICOTS
POCONO
RACONS
RECODE
RECOIL
RECONS
RECOPY
RECORD
RECORK
RECOUP
ROCOCO
SECOND
TACOMA
TYCOBB
TYCOON
UNCOIL
UNCOOL
UNCORK
WICOPY

••C•O•
AHCHOO
ANCHOR
ARCHON
BECKON
CACAOS
CACHOU
COCOON
CUCKOO
CYCLOS
DACRON
DOCTOR
ESCROW
FACTOR
GECKOS
HECTOR
HICKOK
INCHON
LECTOR
LICTOR
MACHOS
MACRON
MACROS
MICRON
MICROS
MRCOOL
NACHOS
PICKON
RECKON
RECTOR
RECTOS
SECTOR
SUCCOR
TACKON
TUCSON
TYCOON
UNCLOG
UNCOOL
VECTOR
VICTOR

••C••O
AHCHOO
ARCARO
BOCHCO
CICERO
CUCKOO
DACAPO
ENCINO
ESCUDO
MACACO
NICOLO
NUCLEO
PACINO
PICABO
PICARO
POCONO
ROCOCO
TECHNO

•••CO•
ANTCOW
BEACON
BUNCOS
CAICOS
CISCOS
DEACON
DISCOS
FALCON
FLACON
GARCON
GASCON
GLYCOL
GUACOS
JUNCOS
MARCOS
MASCOT
MOSCOW
NONCOM
PESCOW
RANCOR
ROSCOE
SEACOW
SITCOM
SUCCOR
TRICOT
VIACOM
ZIRCON

•••C•O
AFLCIO
ALECTO
CAUCHO
EXACTO
GAUCHO
HONCHO
NUNCIO
PANCHO
PONCHO
PSYCHO
RANCHO
REECHO
SANCHO
STUCCO
TRICHO
VELCRO

••••CO
ALNICO
BOCHCO
BRONCO
CALICO
CHALCO
CONOCO
CRISCO
ENESCO
ENRICO
FIASCO
FRANCO
FRESCO
FRISCO
GRAECO
MACACO
MEDICO
MEXICO
MONACO
OROZCO
ROCOCO
STUCCO
SUNOCO
TEXACO
UNESCO
ZYDECO

CP••••
CPSNOW

C•P•••
CAPERS
CAPFUL
CAPGUN
CAPIAS
CAPITA
CAPLET
CAPNUT
CAPONE
CAPONS
CAPOTE
CAPPED
CAPPER
CAPRIS
CAPSID
CAPTAN
CAPTOR
CIPHER
COPIED
COPIER
COPIES
COPING
COPOUT
COPPED
COPPER
COPSES
COPTER
COPTIC
COPULA
CUPELS
CUPFUL
CUPIDS
CUPOLA
CUPPED
CUPRIC
CYPHER
CYPRUS

C••P••
CALPAC
CAMPED
CAMPER
CAMPOS
CAMPUS
CAPPED
CAPPER
CARPAL
CARPED
CARPEL
CARPER
CARPET
CARPUS
CASPAR
CASPER
CHAPEL
CHAPIN
CHIPIN
CHOPIN
CHOPPY
CLEPED
CLIPON
COAPTS
COMPAQ
COMPEL
COMPLY
COMPOS
COOPED
COOPER
COOPTS
COOPUP
COPPED
COPPER
CORPUS
COUPES
COUPLE
COUPON
COWPEA
COWPER
COWPOX
COYPUS
CRAPES
CREPES
CRIPES
CROPUP
CRYPTO
CRYPTS
CUPPED
CUSPED
CUSPID

C•••P•
CALIPH
CANAPE
CANOPY
CERIPH
CHAMPS
CHEAPO
CHEEPS
CHEOPS
CHIMPS
CHIRPS
CHIRPY
CHOMPS
CHOPPY
CHUMPS
CLAMPS
CLASPS
CLOMPS
CLUMPS
CLUMPY
CRAMPS
CREEPS
CREEPY
CRIMPS
CRISPS
CRISPY
CROUPY
CUTUPS

C••••P
CALLUP
CAMEUP
CARHOP
CATNAP
CATNIP
CATSUP
CCLAMP
CHATUP
CHEWUP
CHINUP
CLAMUP
CLOGUP
COILUP
COLLOP
COMEUP
COOKUP
COOPUP
CROPUP
CSHARP
CURLUP
CUTSUP

•C•P••
SCAPES
SCIPIO
SCOPED
SCOPES

•C••P•
ACCEPT
ECTYPE
OCCUPY
OCTOPI
SCALPS
SCAMPI
SCAMPS
SCARPS
SCAUPS
SCOOPS
SCRAPE
SCRAPS
SCRIPS
SCRIPT
SCULPT

•C•••P
ACESUP
ACTSUP
CCLAMP
ICECAP
ICEDUP
ICESUP
SCHLEP
SCRIMP
SCROOP

••C•P•
ACCEPT
ALCAPP
BICEPS
DACAPO
ESCAPE
EXCEPT
INCEPT
OCCUPY
RECAPS
RECIPE
RECOPY
UNCAPS
WICOPY

••C••P
ALCAPP
BACKUP
BUCKUP
DECAMP
ENCAMP
ESCARP
FACEUP
HICCUP
JACKUP
KICKUP
LACEUP
LOCKUP
MOCKUP
MUCKUP
PACKUP
PICKUP
RACKUP
RECOUP

•••C•P
EGGCUP
EYECUP
GASCAP
HICCUP
HOTCAP
HUBCAP
ICECAP
MADCAP
MOBCAP
REDCAP
SKYCAP
TEACUP
TOECAP

C•Q•••
COQUET

C••Q••
CAIQUE
CALQUE
CASQUE
CHEQUE
CINQUE
CIRQUE
CLAQUE
CLIQUE
CLOQUE

C••••Q
COLLOQ

COMPAQ

•CQ•••
ACQUIT

••CQ••
SACQUE

CR••••
CRABBE
CRABBY
CRACKS
CRADLE
CRAFTS
CRAFTY
CRAGGY
CRAKES
CRAMBO
CRAMPS
CRANED
CRANES
CRANIA
CRANIO
CRANKS
CRANKY
CRANNY
CRAPES
CRATED
CRATER
CRATES
CRAVAT
CRAVED
CRAVEN
CRAVER
CRAVES
CRAWLS
CRAWLY
CRAYON
CRAZED
CRAZES
CREAKS
CREAKY
CREAMS
CREAMY
CREASE
CREASY
CREATE
CRECHE
CREDIT
CREDOS
CREEDS
CREEKS
CREELS
CREEPS
CREEPY
CREMES
CRENEL
CRENNA
CREOLE
CREPES
CRESOL
CRESTS
CRETAN
CRETIN
CREUSA
CREWED
CREWEL
CRICKS
CRIERS
CRIMEA
CRIMES
CRIMPS
CRINGE
CRIPES
CRISCO
CRISES
CRISIS
CRISPS
CRISPY
CRITIC
CROAKS
CROAKY
CROATS
CROCKS
CROCUS
CROFTS
CRONES
CRONIN
CRONUS
CRONYN
CROOKS
CROONS
CROPUP
CROSBY
CROSSE
CROTON
CROUCH
CROUPY
CROUSE
CROUTE
CROWDS
CROWED
CROWER
CROWNS
CROZES
CRUCES
CRUDDY
CRUDER
CRUETS
CRUISE
CRUMBS
CRUMBY
CRUMMY
CRUNCH
CRURAL
CRUSES
CRUSOE
CRUSTS
CRUSTY
CRUTCH
CRUXES
CRYING
CRYOFF
CRYPTO
CRYPTS

C•R•••
CARAFE
CARATS
CARBON
CARBOY
CARDED
CARDER
CARDIN
CARDIO
CAREEN
CAREER
CARESS
CARETO
CARETS
CARFUL
CARGOS
CARHOP
CARIBE
CARIBS
CARIES
CARINA
CARING
CARLOS
CARLOT
CARMAN
CARMEL
CARMEN
CARNAL
CARNES
CARNET
CARNEY
CARNOT
CAROBS
CAROLE
CAROLS
CAROMS
CARONI
CARPAL
CARPED
CARPEL
CARPER
CARPET
CARPUS
CARREL
CARREY
CARRIE
CARROL
CARROT
CARSON
CARTED
CARTEL
CARTER
CARTES
CARTON
CARUSO
CARVED
CARVER
CARVES
CARVEY
CDROMS
CERATE
CEREAL
CEREUS
CERIPH
CERISE
CERIUM
CERMET
CERTIF
CERUSE
CERVID
CHRISM
CHROMA
CHROME
CHROMO
CHRONO
CIRCLE
CIRCUM
CIRCUS
CIRQUE
CIRRUS
CORALS
CORBAN
CORBEL
CORBIN
CORDAY
CORDED
CORDON
CORERS
CORGIS
CORING
CORIUM
CORKED
CORKER
CORNEA
CORNED
CORNEL
CORNER
CORNET
CORONA
CORPUS
CORRAL
CORREL
CORSET
CORTES
CORTEX
CORTEZ
CORVEE
CORYZA
CURACY
CURARE
CURATE
CURBED
CURDED
CURDLE
CURERS
CURFEW
CURIAE
CURIAL
CURING
CURIOS
CURIUM
CURLED
CURLER
CURLEW
CURLUP
CURRED
CURSED
CURSES
CURSOR
CURTER
CURTIN
CURTIS
CURTIZ
CURTLY
CURTSY
CURULE
CURVED
CURVES
CURVET
CURZON
CYRANO

C••R••
CADRES
CAIRNS
CAPRIS
CARREL
CARREY
CARRIE
CARROL
CARROT
CATRIG
CEDRIC
CHARGE
CHARLY
CHARMS
CHARON
CHARRO
CHARTS
CHERIE
CHERRY
CHERUB
CHERYL
CHIRON
CHIRPS
CHIRPY
CHIRRS
CHORAL
CHORDS
CHORES
CHORUS
CHURCH
CHURLS
CHURNS
CHURRO
CHURRS
CIARDI
CIRRUS
CITRIC
CITRON
CITRUS
CLARET
CLARKE
CLAROS
CLERGY
CLERIC
CLERKS
CLORIS
CLOROX
COARSE
COBRAS
COERCE
CONRAD
CONROY
CORRAL
CORREL
COURIC
COURSE
COURTS
COWRIE
CRURAL
CUPRIC
CURRED
CYMRIC
CYPRUS
CZERNY

C•••R•
CABERS
CAGERS
CAMERA
CANARD
CANARY
CANERS
CAPERS
CASERN
CASTRO
CATERS
CAVERN
CAVERS
CAVORT
CEDARS
CELERY
CENTRE
CENTRI
CENTRO
CESARE
CHAIRS
CHARRO
CHEERS
CHEERY
CHERRY
CHEVRE
CHIRRS
CHLORO
CHOIRS
CHURRO
CHURRS
CICERO
CIDERS
CIGARS
CITERS
CLAIRE
CLEARS
COBURG
COBURN
CODERS
COHERE
COHORT
COLORS
COMERS
CONTRA
CONTRE
COOERS
CORERS
COVERS
COVERT
COWARD
COWERS
CRIERS
CSHARP
CUNARD
CURARE
CURERS
CYBORG
CYDERS

C••••R
CABLER
CADGER
CAESAR
CAGIER
CAHIER
CALDER
CALLER
CALMER
CAMBER
CAMPER
CANDOR
CANKER
CANNER
CANTER
CANTOR
CAPPER
CAPTOR
CARDER
CAREER
CARPER
CARTER
CARVER
CASPAR
CASPER
CASTER
CASTOR
CATHER
CAVIAR
CAWDOR
CELLAR
CENSER
CENSOR
CENTER
CHADOR
CHASER
CHEWER
CHOKER
CHOLER
CHUKAR
CINDER
CIPHER
CLAMOR
CLAWER
CLEVER
CLOSER
CLOVER
CMAJOR
CMINOR
COALER
COAXER
COCKER
CODGER
COFFER
COHEIR
COINER
COLDER
COLLAR
COLOUR
COLTER
COMBER
CONCUR
CONDOR
CONFER
CONGER
CONKER
CONNER
CONNOR
COODER
COOKER
COOLER
COOPER
COOTER
COPIER
COPPER
COPTER
CORKER
CORNER
COSTAR
COTTER
COUGAR
COUTER
COWPER
COZIER
CRATER
CRAVER
CROWER
CRUDER
CULLER
CULVER
CUMBER
CURLER
CURSOR
CURTER
CUSTER
CUTLER
CUTTER
CYCLER
CYPHER

•CR•••
ACROSS
OCREAE
SCRAGS
SCRAMS
SCRAPE
SCRAPS
SCRAWL
SCREAK
SCREAM
SCREED
SCREEN
SCREES
SCREWS
SCREWY
SCRIBE
SCRIMP
SCRIMS
SCRIPS
SCRIPT
SCRODS
SCROLL
SCROOP
SCRUBS
SCRUFF
SCRUMS

•C•R••
ACARID
ACARUS
ACCRUE
ACORNS
ECARTE
ICARIA
ICARUS
MCGRAW
MCGREW
OCHRES
OCTROI
SCARAB
SCARCE
SCARED
SCARER
SCARES
SCARFS
SCARNE
SCARPS
SCARUM
SCORCH
SCORED
SCORER
SCORES
SCORIA
SCORNS
SCURFY
SCURRY
SCURVE
SCURVY

•C••R•
ACCORD
ACTORS
OCCURS
OCHERS
SCHORL
SCLERA
SCOURS
SCURRY

•C•••R
ACHIER
ECLAIR
ICKIER
MCNAIR
OCULAR
SCALAR
SCALER
SCARER
SCORER
SCOTER

••CR••
ACCRUE
DACRON
DECREE
ESCROW
MACRAE
MACRON
MACROS
MICRON
MICROS
SACRAL
SACRED
SACRUM
SECRET

••C•R•
ACCORD
ARCARO
BICARB
BICORN
CICERO
DECORS
DICERS
ENCORE
ESCARP
ESCORT
EUCHRE
GOCART
IDCARD
INCURS
LACERS
OCCURS
OSCARS
OXCART
PACERS
PICARA
PICARD
PICARO
RACERS
RECORD
RECORK
RECURS
RICERS
SECERN
SECURE
ULCERS
UNCORK
UNCURL
VICARS

••C••R
ANCHOR
ARCHER
BACKER
BECKER
BICKER
COCKER
CYCLER
DECKER
DICIER
DICKER
DOCKER
DOCTOR
ESCHER
ETCHER
FACTOR
HACKER
HECTOR
KICKER
LACIER
LECTOR
LICTOR
LOCKER
MOCKER
NECTAR
NICKER
PACKER
PICKER
PUCKER
RACIER
RECTOR
RICHER
ROCKER
SACKER
SECTOR
SICKER
SOCCER
SUCCOR
SUCKER
TACKER
TICKER
TUCKER
VECTOR
VICTOR
WICKER

•••CR•
DESCRY
FARCRY
FIACRE
FULCRA
OUTCRY
VELCRO
WARCRY

•••C•R
BOXCAR
BRACER
CONCUR
DANCER
DEICER
FENCER
FORCER
GROCER
HOTCAR
JUICER
LANCER
LASCAR
MERCER
MINCER
NASCAR
PIECER
PINCER
PLACER
PRICER
RANCOR
SAUCER
SLICER
SOCCER
SPACER
SUCCOR
TOWCAR
TRACER
TROCAR
WINCER

CS••••
CSHARP

C•S•••
CASABA
CASALS
CASAVA
CASBAH
CASERN
CASHED
CASHES
CASHEW
CASHIN
CASING
CASINO
CASPAR
CASPER
CASQUE
CASSIA
CASSIO
CASSIS
CASTER
CASTES
CASTLE
CASTON
CASTOR
CASTRO
CASUAL
CESARE
CESIUM
CESSNA
CESTAS
CESTOS
CESTUS
CISCOS
CISKEI
COSELL
COSHED
COSHES
COSIES
COSIGN
COSINE
COSMIC
COSMOS
COSSET
COSTAE
COSTAL
COSTAR
COSTAS
COSTLY
CPSNOW
CUSHAW
CUSPED
CUSPID
CUSSED
CUSSES
CUSTER
CUSTOM

C••S••
CAESAR
CAPSID
CARSON
CASSIA
CASSIO
CASSIS
CATSUP
CAUSAL
CAUSED
CAUSES
CEASED
CEASES
CENSED
CENSER
CENSES
CENSOR
CENSUS
CESSNA
CHASED
CHASER
CHASES
CHASMS
CHASSE
CHASTE
CHESTS
CHESTY
CHISEL
CHISOX
CHOSEN
CLASPS
CLASSY
CLOSED
CLOSER
CLOSES
CLOSET
COASTS
COMSAT
CONSUL
COPSES
CORSET
COSSET
COUSIN
CRESOL
CRESTS
CRISCO
CRISES
CRISIS
CRISPS
CRISPY
CROSBY
CROSSE
CRUSES
CRUSOE
CRUSTS
CRUSTY
CUESTA
CUISSE
CURSED
CURSES
CURSOR
CUSSED
CUSSES
CUTSIN
CUTSUP

C•••S•
CALASH
CAMISE
CARESS
CARUSO
CAYUSE
CERISE
CERUSE
CHAISE
CHASSE
CHEESE
CHEESY
CHOOSE
CHOOSY
CHRISM
CHUHSI
CLASSY
CLAUSE
CLEESE
CLUMSY
COARSE
COHOST
COURSE
COYEST
CREASE
CREASY
CREUSA
CROSSE
CROUSE
CRUISE
CUBISM
CUBIST
CUISSE
CURTSY
CUTEST
CUTESY

C••••S
CABALS
CABERS
CABINS
CABLES
CACAOS
CACHES
CACTUS
CADDIS
CADETS
CADGES
CADMUS
CADRES
CAGERS
CAGUAS
CAHOWS
CAICOS
CAIRNS
CAJUNS
CALAIS
CALCES
CALLAS
CALLES
CALLUS
CALVES
CALXES
CAMELS
CAMEOS
CAMPOS
CAMPUS
CANALS
CANERS
CANIDS
CANNES
CANOES
CANONS
CANTOS
CANVAS
CAPERS
CAPIAS
CAPONS
CAPRIS
CARATS
CARESS
CARETS
CARGOS
CARIBS
CARIES
CARLOS
CARNES
CAROBS
CAROLS
CAROMS
CARPUS
CARTES
CARVES
CASALS
CASHES
CASSIS
CASTES
CATERS
CAUCUS
CAULKS
CAUSES
CAVERS
CAVILS
CDROMS
CEASES
CEDARS
CEIBAS
CELEBS
CELLOS
CENSES
CENSUS
CENTOS
CEREUS
CESTAS
CESTOS
CESTUS
CHAFES
CHAFFS
CHAINS
CHAIRS
CHALKS
CHAMPS
CHANTS
CHARMS
CHARTS
CHASES
CHASMS
CHEATS
CHECKS
CHEEKS
CHEEPS
CHEERS
CHELAS
CHEOPS
CHESTS
CHIAUS
CHICKS
CHIDES
CHIEFS
CHILDS
CHILLS
CHIMES
CHIMPS
CHINES
CHINKS
CHINOS
CHIRPS
CHIRRS
CHIVES
CHOCKS
CHOIRS
CHOKES
CHOMPS
CHORDS
CHORES
CHORUS
CHUCKS
CHUMPS
CHUNKS
CHURLS
CHURNS
CHURRS
CHUTES
CIDERS
CIGARS
CIRCUS
CIRRUS
CISCOS
CITERS
CITIES
CITRUS
CIVETS
CIVICS
CLACKS
CLAIMS
CLAMPS
CLANGS
CLANKS
CLAROS
CLASPS
CLEANS
CLEARS
CLEATS
CLEEKS
CLEFTS
CLERKS
CLEVES
CLEVIS
CLICKS
CLIFFS
CLIMBS
CLIMES
CLINES
CLINGS
CLINKS
CLOAKS
CLOCKS
CLOMPS
CLONES
CLONKS
CLONUS
CLORIS
CLOSES
CLOTHS
CLOUDS
CLOUTS
CLOVES
CLOVIS
CLOWNS
CLUCKS
CLUMPS
CLUNKS
CMINUS
CNIDUS
CNOTES
COAPTS
COASTS
COATIS
COAXES
COBIAS
COBRAS
COCCUS
COCOAS
CODERS
CODONS
COLEUS
COLONS
COLORS
COMBES
COMBOS
COMERS
COMETS
COMICS
COMMAS
COMPOS
COMTES
CONCHS
CONDOS
CONEYS
CONGAS
CONICS
CONIES
CONTES
COOERS
COOPTS
COPIES
COPSES
CORALS
CORERS
CORGIS
CORPUS
CORTES
COSHES
COSIES
COSMOS
COSTAS
COTTAS
COUGHS
COUNTS
COUPES
COURTS
COVENS
COVERS
COVETS
COVEYS
COWENS
COWERS
COYPUS
COZENS
COZIES
CRACKS
CRAFTS
CRAKES
CRAMPS
CRANES

CRANKS
CRAPES
CRATES
CRAVES
CRAWLS
CRAZES
CREAKS
CREAMS
CREDOS
CREEDS
CREEKS
CREELS
CREEPS
CREMES
CREPES
CRESTS
CRICKS
CRIERS
CRIMES
CRIMPS
CRIPES
CRISES
CRISIS
CRISPS
CROAKS
CROATS
CROCKS
CROCUS
CROFTS
CRONES
CRONUS
CROOKS
CROONS
CROWDS
CROWNS
CROZES
CRUCES
CRUETS
CRUMBS
CRUSES
CRUSTS
CRUXES
CRYPTS
CUBEBS
CUBICS
CUBITS
CULETS
CULLIS
CUPELS
CUPIDS
CURERS
CURIOS
CURSES
CURTIS
CURVES
CUSSES
CUTIES
CUTINS
CUTUPS
CUVEES
CYCADS
CYCLAS
CYCLES
CYCLOS
CYDERS
CYGNUS
CYNICS
CYPRUS
CZECHS

•C•S••
ACESUP
ACTSON
ACTSUP
ECESIS
ICESIN
ICESUP
OCASEK
OCASEY

•C••S•
ACCESS
ACCOST
ACCUSE
ACROSS
ICIEST
SCHISM
SCHIST
SCHUSS

•C•••S
ACARUS
ACCESS
ACEOUS
ACINUS
ACORNS
ACROSS
ACTORS
ECCLES
ECESIS
ECHOES
ECLATS
ECOLES
ICARUS
ICINGS
OCCURS
OCEANS
OCHERS
OCHRES
OCTADS
OCTETS
SCALDS
SCALES
SCALPS
SCAMPS
SCANTS
SCAPES
SCARES
SCARFS
SCARPS
SCAUPS
SCENAS
SCENDS
SCENES
SCENTS
SCHMOS
SCHUSS
SCHWAS
SCIFIS
SCIONS
SCOFFS
SCOLDS
SCONES
SCOOPS
SCOOTS
SCOPES
SCORES
SCORNS
SCOURS
SCOUTS
SCOWLS
SCRAGS
SCRAMS
SCRAPS
SCREES
SCREWS
SCRIMS
SCRIPS
SCRODS
SCRUBS
SCRUMS
SCUBAS
SCUFFS
SCULLS
SCUTES
UCLANS

••CS••
FOCSLE
TOCSIN
TUCSON

••C•S•
ACCESS
ACCOST
ACCUSE
ATCOST
ENCASE
EXCESS
EXCISE
EXCUSE
INCASE
INCASH
INCISE
INCUSE
JOCOSE
LOCUST
MUCOSA
NICEST
RECAST
RECESS
RECUSE
UNCASE
UPCAST

••C••S
ACCESS
ARCHES
ASCOTS
BACKUS
BICEPS
CACAOS
CACHES
CACTUS
COCCUS
COCOAS
CYCADS
CYCLAS
CYCLES
CYCLOS
DACHAS
DECAFS
DECALS
DECAYS
DECORS
DECOYS
DICERS
DICOTS
DUCATS
ECCLES
EMCEES
ETCHES
EXCELS
EXCESS
FACETS
FACIES
FICHES
FICHUS
GECKOS
HACEKS
INCANS
INCHES
INCURS
ITCHES
JACALS
LACERS
LACHES
LOCALS
LUCIUS
LYCEES
MACAWS
MACHES
MACHOS
MACROS
MECCAS
MICROS
MOCHAS
MUCOUS
NACHOS
NICHES
OCCURS
OSCARS
PACERS
PECANS
PICOTS
PICULS
RACERS
RACHIS
RACONS
RECAPS
RECESS
RECONS
RECTOS
RECTUS
RECURS
RICERS
RICHES
RUCHES
RUCKUS
SOCLES
SUCCES
SUCHAS
TICALS
ULCERS
UNCAPS
UNCLES
VICARS
VOCALS
YACHTS
YUCCAS

•••C•S
ABACAS
ABACUS
AMICES
AMICUS
APICES
ARECAS
BAUCIS
BLACKS
BLOCKS
BRACES
BRACTS
BRICKS
BUNCOS
CAICOS
CALCES
CAUCUS
CHECKS
CHICKS
CHOCKS
CHUCKS
CIRCUS
CISCOS
CLACKS
CLICKS
CLOCKS
CLUCKS
COCCUS
CONCHS
CRACKS
CRICKS
CROCKS
CROCUS
CRUCES
CZECHS
DANCES
DEICES
DEUCES
DISCOS
DISCUS
DORCAS
DUNCES
EDICTS
EDUCES
EJECTS
ELECTS
ENACTS
EPOCHS
ERECTS
ERUCTS
EVICTS
EXACTS
FARCES
FASCES
FAUCES
FENCES
FLACKS
FLECKS
FLICKS
FLOCKS
FORCES
FRACAS
FROCKS
GLACES
GLACIS
GRACES
GUACOS
JUICES
JUNCOS
KNACKS
KNICKS
KNOCKS
KYACKS
LANCES
MARCOS
MARCUS
MECCAS
MINCES
MULCTS
NIECES
NUECES
OUNCES
PHOCIS
PIECES
PISCES
PLACES
PLUCKS
PRECIS
PRICES
PRICKS
PSYCHS
QUACKS
REACTS
SAUCES
SHACKS
SHOCKS
SHUCKS
SLACKS
SLICES
SLICKS
SMACKS
SMOCKS
SNACKS
SNICKS
SPACES
SPECKS
SPICAS
SPICES
STACKS
STICKS
STOCKS
SUCCES
SULCUS
TINCTS
TRACES
TRACKS
TRACTS
TRICES
TRICKS
TRUCES
TRUCKS
VNECKS
VOICES
WENCES
WHACKS
WINCES
WRACKS
WRECKS
YOICKS
YUCCAS

••••CS
ANTICS
ASPICS
ATTICS
AZTECS
BASICS
BRONCS
CIVICS
COMICS
CONICS
CUBICS
CYNICS
DUROCS
ETHICS
FRANCS
HAVOCS
IONICS
KOVACS
LILACS
LYRICS
MEDICS
MIMICS
MODOCS
OLMECS
OPTICS
OSMICS
PANICS
RELICS
SERACS
SONICS
STOICS
SUMACS
TONICS
TOPICS
TOXICS
TUNICS
XEBECS

C•T•••
CATCHY
CATENA
CATERS
CATGUT
CATHAY
CATHER
CATION
CATKIN
CATNAP
CATNIP
CATRIG
CATSUP
CATTED
CATTLE
CATTON
CETANE
CITERS
CITIES
CITIFY
CITING
CITRIC
CITRON
CITRUS
COTTAS
COTTEN
COTTER
COTTON
CUTEST
CUTESY
CUTIES
CUTINS
CUTLER
CUTLET
CUTOFF
CUTOUT
CUTSIN
CUTSUP
CUTTER
CUTUPS

C••T••
CACTUS
CAFTAN
CANTAB
CANTED
CANTER
CANTHI
CANTLE
CANTON
CANTOR
CANTOS
CAPTAN
CAPTOR
CARTED
CARTEL
CARTER
CARTES
CARTON
CASTER
CASTES
CASTLE
CASTON
CASTOR
CASTRO
CATTED
CATTLE
CATTON
CAXTON
CELTIC
CENTER
CENTOS
CENTRE
CENTRI
CENTRO
CERTIF
CESTAS
CESTOS
CESTUS
CHATTY
CHATUP
CHITIN
CHITON
CHUTED
CHUTES
CLOTHE
CLOTHO
CLOTHS
CLOTTY
CLUTCH
CNOTES
COATED
COATIS
COLTER
COMTES
CONTAC
CONTES
CONTRA
CONTRE
COOTER
COOTIE
COPTER
COPTIC
CORTES
CORTEX
CORTEZ
COSTAE
COSTAL
COSTAR
COSTAS
COSTLY
COTTAS
COTTEN
COTTER
COTTON
COUTER
CRATED
CRATER
CRATES
CRETAN
CRETIN
CRITIC
CROTON
CRUTCH
CULTIC
CURTER
CURTIN
CURTIS
CURTIZ
CURTLY
CURTSY
CUSTER
CUSTOM
CUTTER

C•••T•
CADETS
CAMETO
CANUTE
CAPITA
CAPOTE
CARATS
CARETO
CARETS
CAVETT
CAVITY
CENOTE
CERATE
CHANTS
CHARTS
CHASTE
CHATTY
CHEATS
CHESTS
CHESTY
CHINTZ
CHOATE
CIVETS
CLEATS
CLEFTS
CLOTTY
CLOUTS
COAPTS
COASTS
COMATE
COMETH
COMETO
COMETS
COMITY
COOPTS
COUNTS
COUNTY
COURTS
COVETS
COYOTE
CRAFTS
CRAFTY
CREATE
CRESTS
CROATS
CROFTS
CROUTE
CRUETS
CRUSTS
CRUSTY
CRYPTO
CRYPTS
CUBITS
CUESTA
CULETS
CURATE

C••••T
CACHET
CADENT
CAMEAT
CAMLET
CANNOT
CAPLET
CAPNUT
CARLOT
CARNET
CARNOT
CARPET
CARROT
CATGUT
CAUGHT
CAVEAT
CAVETT
CAVORT
CEMENT
CERMET
CHALET
CHEVET
CLARET
CLIENT
CLOSET
COBALT
COEDIT
COGENT
COHORT
COHOST
COLLET
COMBAT
COMEAT
COMFIT
COMMIT
COMSAT
CONANT
COOLIT
COPOUT
COQUET
CORNET
CORSET
COSSET
COVENT
COVERT
COYEST
CRAVAT
CREDIT
CUBIST
CULLET
CURVET
CUTEST
CUTLET
CUTOUT
CYGNET

•CT•••
ACTIII
ACTING
ACTINO
ACTION
ACTIUM
ACTIVE
ACTONE
ACTORS
ACTOUT
ACTSON
ACTSUP
ACTTWO
ACTUAL
ECTYPE
OCTADS
OCTANE
OCTANT
OCTAVE
OCTAVO
OCTETS
OCTOPI
OCTROI

•C•T••
ACETAL
ACETIC
ACETYL
ACTTWO
ICHTHY
SCATHE
SCOTCH
SCOTER
SCOTIA
SCOTTO
SCOTTY
SCUTCH
SCUTES
SCYTHE

•C••T•
ACUATE
ACUITY
ECARTE
ECLATS
OCTETS
SCANTS
SCANTY
SCENTS
SCOOTS
SCOTTO
SCOTTY
SCOUTS

•C•••T
ACCENT
ACCEPT
ACCOST
ACEOUT
ACQUIT
ACTOUT
ICEOUT
ICIEST
OCCULT
OCELOT
OCTANT
SCHIST
SCRIPT
SCULPT

••CT••
ARCTIC
CACTUS
DACTYL
DICTUM
DOCTOR
DUCTAL
FACTOR
HECTIC
HECTOR
LACTIC
LECTOR
LICTOR
NECTAR
PECTIC
PECTIN
RECTOR
RECTOS
RECTUS
SECTOR
TACTIC
TICTAC
VECTOR
VICTIM
VICTOR

••C•T•
ALCOTT
ASCOTS
DICOTS
DUCATS
EXCITE
FACETS
FICHTE
HECATE
INCITE
LOCATE
LUCITE
NICETY
OOCYTE
PICOTS
RECITE
VACATE
YACHTS

••C••T
ACCENT
ACCEPT
ACCOST
ALCOTT
ASCENT
ATCOST
BECKET
BUCKET
CACHET
DACOIT
DECANT
DECEIT
DECENT
DECOCT
DOCENT
DOCKET
ESCENT
ESCORT
EXCEPT
GOCART
INCEPT
INCULT
JACKET
LOCKET
LOCUST
LUCENT
NICEST
NOCENT
OCCULT
OXCART
PACKET
PECKAT
PICKAT
PICKET
POCKET
RACKET
RECANT
RECAST
RECENT
ROCHET
ROCKET
SACHET
SECANT
SECRET
SOCKET
TICKET
TUCKET
UPCAST
VACANT
WICKET

•••CT•
ALECTO
BRACTS
EDICTS
EJECTA
EJECTS
ELECTS
ENACTS
ERECTS
ERUCTS
EVICTS
EXACTA
EXACTO
EXACTS
MULCTS
REACTS
SANCTA
STACTE
TINCTS
TRACTS

•••C•T
AVOCET
BOBCAT
BRECHT
DULCET
ELICIT
FATCAT
FAUCET
HEPCAT
LANCET
MASCOT
MUDCAT
MUSCAT
REXCAT
SNOCAT
TERCET
TOMCAT
TOPCAT
TRICOT

••••CT
ABDUCT
ABJECT
ADDUCT
AFFECT
ASPECT
BISECT
DECOCT
DEDUCT
DEFECT
DEJECT
DELICT
DEPICT
DETECT
DIDACT
DIRECT
EFFECT
EXPECT
IMPACT
INDICT
INDUCT
INFACT
INFECT
INJECT
INSECT
INTACT
OBJECT
OUTACT
REDACT
REJECT
RELICT
RELUCT
RESECT
SELECT
STRICT

CU••••
CUBAGE
CUBEBS
CUBICS
CUBING
CUBISM
CUBIST
CUBITS
CUBOID
CUCKOO
CUDDLE
CUDDLY
CUDGEL
CUESTA
CUFFED
CUIABA
CUISSE
CULETS
CULKIN
CULLED
CULLEN
CULLER
CULLET
CULLIS
CULTIC
CULVER
CUMBER
CUMULI
CUMULO
CUNARD
CUNAXA
CUNEAL
CUPELS
CUPFUL
CUPIDS
CUPOLA
CUPPED
CUPRIC
CURACY
CURARE
CURATE
CURBED
CURDED
CURDLE
CURERS
CURFEW
CURIAE
CURIAL
CURING
CURIOS
CURIUM
CURLED
CURLER
CURLEW
CURLUP
CURRED
CURSED
CURSES
CURSOR
CURTER
CURTIN
CURTIS
CURTIZ
CURTLY
CURTSY
CURULE
CURVED
CURVES
CURVET
CURZON
CUSHAW
CUSPED
CUSPID
CUSSED
CUSSES
CUSTER
CUSTOM
CUTEST
CUTESY
CUTIES
CUTINS
CUTLER
CUTLET
CUTOFF
CUTOUT
CUTSIN
CUTSUP
CUTTER
CUTUPS
CUVEES

C•U•••
CAUCHO
CAUCUS
CAUDAL
CAUDEX
CAUDLE
CAUGHT
CAULKS
CAUSAL
CAUSED
CAUSES
CHUBBY
CHUCKS
CHUHSI
CHUKAR
CHUKKA
CHUMMY
CHUMPS
CHUNKS
CHUNKY
CHURCH
CHURLS
CHURNS
CHURRO
CHURRS
CHUTED
CHUTES
CIUDAD
CLUBBY
CLUCKS
CLUEIN
CLUING
CLUMPS
CLUMPY
CLUMSY
CLUNKS
CLUNKY
CLUTCH
COUGAR
COUGHS
COULEE
COUNTS
COUNTY
COUPES
COUPLE
COUPON
COURIC
COURSE
COURTS
COUSIN
COUTER
CRUCES
CRUDDY
CRUDER
CRUETS
CRUISE
CRUMBS
CRUMBY
CRUMMY
CRUNCH
CRURAL
CRUSES
CRUSOE
CRUSTS
CRUSTY
CRUTCH
CRUXES

C••U••
CAGUAS
CAJUNS
CANUTE
CARUSO
CASUAL
CAYUGA
CAYUSE
CERUSE
CHOUGH
CLAUDE
CLAUSE
CLOUDS
CLOUDY
CLOUTS
COBURG
COBURN
COHUNE
COLUGO

COLUMN
COPULA
COQUET
CREUSA
CROUCH
CROUPY
CROUSE
CROUTE
CUMULI
CUMULO
CURULE
CUTUPS
CRONUS
CROPUP
CUPFUL
CURIUM
CURLUP
CUTOUT
CUTSUP
CYGNUS
CYPRUS

C•••U•
CACTUS
CADMUS
CAIQUE
CALLUP
CALLUS
CALQUE
CAMEUP
CAMPUS
CANCUN
CAPFUL
CAPGUN
CAPNUT
CARFUL
CARPUS
CASQUE
CATGUT
CATSUP
CAUCUS
CENSUS
CEREUS
CERIUM
CESIUM
CESTUS
CHATUP
CHEQUE
CHERUB
CHEWUP
CHIAUS
CHINUP
CHORUS
CILIUM
CINQUE
CIRCUM
CIRCUS
CIRQUE
CIRRUS
CITRUS
CLAMUP
CLAQUE
CLIQUE
CLOGUP
CLONUS
CLOQUE
CMINUS
CNIDUS
COCCUS
COILUP
COLEUS
COLOUR
COMEUP
CONCUR
CONIUM
CONSUL
COOKUP
COOPUP
COPOUT
CORIUM
CORPUS
COYPUS
CROCUS

C••••U
CACHOU
CHOOYU
CONGOU

•CU•••
ACUATE
ACUITY
ACUMEN
OCULAR
SCUBAS
SCUFFS
SCULLS
SCULLY
SCULPT
SCUMMY
SCURFY
SCURRY
SCURVE
SCURVY
SCUTCH
SCUTES
SCUZZY

•C•U••
ACCUSE
ACQUIT
ACTUAL
MCKUEN
OCCULT
OCCUPY
OCCURS
SCAUPS
SCHULZ
SCHUSS
SCOURS
SCOUTS
SCRUBS
SCRUFF
SCRUMS

•C••U•
ACARUS
ACCRUE
ACEOUS
ACEOUT
ACESUP
ACINUS
ACTIUM
ACTOUT
ACTSUP
ICARUS
ICEDUP
ICEOUT
ICESUP
SCARUM

•C•••U
ACAJOU

••CU••
ACCUSE
ALCUIN
ESCUDO
EXCUSE
FACULA
FECUND
HECUBA
INCULT
INCURS
INCUSE
JOCUND
LACUNA
LOCUST
MACULA
OCCULT
OCCUPY
OCCURS
OSCULA
PICULS
RECURS
RECUSE
SECURE
UNCURL
VACUUM
VICUNA

••C•U•
ACCRUE
BACKUP
BACKUS
BUCKUP
CACTUS
COCCUS
DICTUM
FACEUP
FICHUS
HICCUP
JACKUP
KICKUP
LACEUP
LOCKUP
LUCIUS
LYCEUM
MOCKUP
MUCKUP
MUCOUS
PACKUP
PICKUP
RACKUP
RECOUP
RECTUS
RUCKUS
SACQUE
SACRUM
TUCHUN
VACUUM

••C••U
CACHOU
PICCHU

•••CU•
ABACUS
AMICUS
CANCUN
CAUCUS
CIRCUM
CIRCUS
COCCUS
CONCUR
CROCUS
DISCUS
EGGCUP
EYECUP
FESCUE
HICCUP
MARCUS
MISCUE
RESCUE
SULCUS
TALCUM
TEACUP

•••C•U
MANCHU
PICCHU

••••CU
APERCU
IGUACU

C•V•••
CAVEAT
CAVEIN
CAVELL
CAVERN
CAVERS
CAVETT
CAVIAR
CAVILS
CAVING
CAVITY
CAVORT
CIVETS
CIVICS
COVENS
COVENT
COVERS
COVERT
COVETS
COVEYS
COVINA
CUVEES

C••V••
CALVED
CALVES
CALVIN
CANVAS
CARVED
CARVER
CARVES
CARVEY
CERVID
CHAVEZ
CHEVAL
CHEVET
CHEVRE
CHIVES
CLAVIN
CLEVER
CLEVES
CLEVIS
CLOVEN
CLOVER
CLOVES
CLOVIS
COEVAL
CONVEX
CONVEY
CONVOY
CORVEE
CRAVAT
CRAVED
CRAVEN
CRAVER
CRAVES
CULVER
CURVED
CURVES
CURVET

C•••V•
CANOVA
CASAVA
CLEAVE

•C••V•
ACTIVE
OCTAVE
OCTAVO
SCURVE
SCURVY

••C•V•
ALCOVE

••C••V
ROCKYV
VACLAV

C•W•••
CAWDOR
CAWING
COWARD
COWBOY
COWENS
COWERS
COWING
COWLED
COWLEY
COWMAN
COWMEN
COWPEA
COWPER
COWPOX
COWRIE

C••W••
CHEWED
CHEWER
CHEWUP
CHOWED
CLAWED
CLAWER
CLEWED
CLOWNS
COBWEB
CONWAY
CRAWLS
CRAWLY
CREWED
CREWEL
CROWDS
CROWED
CROWER
CROWNS

C•••W•
CAHOWS

C••••W
CALLOW
CASHEW
CPSNOW
CURFEW
CURLEW
CUSHAW

•C•W••
SCHWAS
SCOWLS

•C••W•
ACTTWO
SCRAWL
SCREWS
SCREWY

•C•••W
MCGRAW
MCGREW

••C•W•
MACAWS

••C••W
ESCHEW
ESCROW

•••C•W
ANTCOW
MOSCOW
PESCOW
SEACOW

C•X•••
CAXTON

C••X••
CALXES
COAXED
COAXER
COAXES
CRUXES

C•••X•
CUNAXA

C••••X
CAUDEX
CHISOX
CLIMAX
CLOROX
COCCYX
COMMIX
CONVEX
CORTEX
COWPOX

•C•••X
ICEBOX

••C••X
COCCYX
PICKAX

•••C•X
COCCYX

CY••••
CYANIC
CYBELE
CYBILL
CYBORG
CYCADS
CYCLAS
CYCLED
CYCLER
CYCLES
CYCLIC
CYCLOS
CYDERS
CYGNET
CYGNUS
CYMBAL
CYMRIC
CYNICS
CYPHER
CYPRUS
CYRANO

C•Y•••
CAYMAN
CAYUGA
CAYUSE
CEYLON
COYEST
COYOTE
COYPUS
CRYING
CRYOFF
CRYPTO
CRYPTS

C••Y••
CANYON
CLAYEY
CLOYED
CORYZA
CRAYON

C•••Y•
CHERYL
CHOOYU
COCCYX
CONEYS
COVEYS
CRONYN

C••••Y
CAGILY
CAGNEY
CALMLY
CAMEBY
CANARY
CANOPY
CARBOY
CARNEY
CARREY
CARVEY
CATCHY
CATHAY
CAVITY
CELERY
CHAFFY
CHALKY
CHAMMY
CHANCY
CHANEY
CHARLY
CHATTY
CHEEKY
CHEERY
CHEESY
CHERRY
CHESTY
CHILLY
CHINKY
CHIRPY
CHOOSY
CHOPPY
CHUBBY
CHUMMY
CHUNKY
CICELY
CITIFY
CLAMMY
CLANCY
CLANKY
CLASSY
CLAYEY
CLERGY
CLINGY
CLOTTY
CLOUDY
CLUBBY
CLUMPY
CLUMSY
CLUNKY
CODIFY
COLDLY
COLONY
COMEBY
COMEDY
COMELY
COMITY
COMPLY
CONROY
CONVEY
CONVOY
CONWAY
COOLLY
COONEY
CORDAY
COSTLY
COUNTY
COWBOY
COWLEY
COZILY
CRABBY
CRAFTY
CRAGGY
CRANKY
CRANNY
CRAWLY
CREAKY
CREAMY
CREASY
CREEPY
CRISPY
CROAKY
CROSBY
CROUPY
CRUDDY
CRUMBY
CRUMMY
CRUSTY
CUDDLY
CURACY
CURTLY
CURTSY
CUTESY
CZERNY

•CY•••
SCYLLA
SCYTHE

•C•Y••
ECTYPE

•C••Y•
ACETYL

•C•••Y
ACIDLY
ACUITY
ICHTHY
OCASEY
OCCUPY
SCABBY
SCANTY
SCOTTY
SCREWY
SCULLY
SCUMMY
SCURFY
SCURRY
SCURVY
SCUZZY

••CY••
OOCYTE

••C•Y•
COCCYX
DACTYL
DECAYS
DECOYS
JACLYN
ROCKYV

••C••Y
ARCHLY
CICELY
DICKEY
HICKEY
HOCKEY
JOCKEY
LACKEY
MICKEY
NICELY
NICETY
OCCUPY
PACIFY
RACILY
RECOPY
RICHLY
RICKEY
SICILY
SICKLY
WICOPY

•••CY•
COCCYX

•••C•Y
ALECKY
BISCAY
BLOCKY
BRICKY
CATCHY
DESCRY
FARCRY
MUSCLY
OUTCRY
PATCHY
PEACHY
PLUCKY
POACHY
POUCHY
PRICEY
PUNCHY
SPACEY
STICKY
STOCKY
TETCHY
TOUCHY
TRACEY
TRICKY
WARCRY
WHACKY
WITCHY

••••CY
ABBACY
AGENCY
BOUNCY
CHANCY
CLANCY
CURACY
FLEECY
IDIOCY
JOUNCY
LEGACY
LUNACY
PAPACY
PIRACY
POLICY
QUINCY

CZ••••
CZECHS
CZERNY

C•Z•••
COZENS
COZIED
COZIER
COZIES
COZILY

C••Z••
CRAZED
CRAZES
CROZES
CURZON

C•••Z•
CORYZA

C••••Z
CHAVEZ
CHINTZ
CORTEZ
CURTIZ

•C•Z••
SCUZZY

•C••Z•
SCUZZY

•C•••Z
SCHNOZ
SCHULZ

DA••••
DABBED
DABBLE
DABNEY
DACAPO
DACHAS
DACOIT
DACRON
DACTYL
DADDYO
DADOED
DADOES
DAEDAL
DAFTER
DAGAMA
DAGGER
DAHLIA
DAIKON
DAILEY
DAIMON
DAIMYO
DAINTY
DAIREN
DAISES
DAKOTA
DALASI
DALETH
DALLAS
DALLES
DALTON
DAMAGE
DAMASK
DAMATO
DAMIEN
DAMITA
DAMMAR
DAMMED
DAMNED
DAMONE
DAMORE
DAMOUR
DAMPED
DAMPEN
DAMPER
DAMPLY
DAMSEL
DAMSON
DAMSUP
DANANG
DANAUS
DANCED
DANCER
DANCES
DANDER
DANDIE
DANDLE
DANGER
DANGLE
DANGLY
DANGME
DANIEL
DANISH
DANKER
DANNAY
DANNER
DANSON
DANTES
DANTON
DANUBE
DANZIG
DAPHNE
DAPPED
DAPPER
DAPPLE
DARETO
DARIEN
DARING
DARIUS
DARKEN
DARKER
DARKLE
DARKLY
DARNAY
DARNED
DARNEL
DARNER
DARNIT
DARREN
DARROW
DARRYL
DARTED
DARTER
DARWIN
DASHED
DASHER
DASHES
DASSIN
DATARY
DATERS
DATING
DATIVE
DATONG
DATSUN
DATURA
DAUBED
DAUBER
DAUBES
DAUNTS
DAVIES
DAVITS
DAWDLE
DAWNED
DAWSON
DAYBED
DAYGLO
DAYLIT
DAYONE
DAYTON
DAZING
DAZZLE

D•A•••
DEACON
DEADEN
DEADER
DEADLY
DEADON
DEAFEN
DEAFER
DEALER
DEALIN
DEANNA
DEARER
DEARIE
DEARLY
DEARME
DEARTH
DHARMA
DIABLO
DIADEM
DIALED
DIALER
DIALOG
DIAPER
DIATOM
DLAYER
DMAJOR
DOABLE
DRABEK
DRABLY
DRAFTS
DRAFTY
DRAGEE
DRAGGY
DRAGIN
DRAGON
DRAILS
DRAINS
DRAKES
DRAMAS
DRAPED
DRAPER
DRAPES
DRAWER
DRAWIN
DRAWLS
DRAWON
DRAWUP
DRAYED
DUALLY
DUARTE
DWARFS
DWAYNE
DYADIC

D••A••
DACAPO
DAGAMA
DALASI
DAMAGE
DAMASK
DAMATO
DANANG
DANAUS
DATARY
DEBARK
DEBARS
DEBASE
DEBATE
DECADE
DECAFS
DECALS
DECAMP
DECANT
DECAYS
DEFACE
DEFAME
DEFATS
DEGAGE
DEJAVU
DEKALB
DELANO
DELANY
DELATE
DELAYS
DEMAND
DENALI
DEPART
DEPAUL
DEPAUW
DERAIL
DESALT
DETACH
DETAIL
DETAIN
DIDACT
DILATE
DINARS
DISANT
DISARM
DIVANS
DOMAIN
DOMANI
DONALD
DONATE
DOPANT
DORADO
DORATI
DOSAGE
DOTAGE
DOTARD
DREADS
DREAMS
DREAMT
DREAMY
DREARY
DRYADS
DSHARP
DUCATS
DUNANT
DURANT
DUVALL
DYNAMO
DYNAST

D•••A•
DACHAS
DAEDAL
DALLAS
DAMMAR
DANNAY
DARNAY
DEBRAS
DEEJAY
DEFEAT
DEFRAY
DELRAY
DELTAS
DEMEAN
DENIAL
DENTAL
DEODAR
DERMAL
DESMAN
DEWLAP
DIGRAM
DIKTAT
DIRHAM
DISBAR
DISMAL
DISMAY
DISTAL
DOBLAS
DOBRAS
DOGEAR
DOGMAS
DOGTAG
DOLLAR
DOLMAN
DOLMAS
DONNAS
DOODAD
DORCAS
DORIAN
DORSAL
DOSSAL
DOTHAN
DRAMAS
DUCTAL
DUNBAR
DUNCAN
DUNHAM
DURBAN
DURBAR
DURHAM
DURIAN
DVORAK

D••••A
DAGAMA
DAHLIA
DAKOTA
DAMITA
DATURA
DEANNA
DEFLEA
DESICA
DHARMA
DJERBA
DODECA
DODOMA
DUENNA
DULLEA
DUNERA
DURYEA

•DA•••
ADAGES
ADAGIO
ADAPTS
EDAMES
GDANSK

•D•A••
ADDAMS
ADNATE
EDGARD
EDGARS
EDUARD
EDVARD
EDWARD
IDCARD
IDEALS
IDEATE
KDLANG

•D••A•
ADIDAS
ADONAI
ADRIAN

•D•••A
EDESSA
ODESSA
ODETTA

••DA••
ADDAMS
AODAIS
BEDAUB
BEDAZE
CEDARS
DIDACT
EMDASH
ENDALL
ENDASH
GODARD
HODADS
INDABA
IODATE
JUDAEA
JUDAIC
KODALY
MADAME
MADAMS
MEDAKA
MEDALS
MIDAIR
ORDAIN
PADANG
PEDALS
PEDANT
PEDATE
REDACT
REDANT
REDATE
SEDAKA
SEDANS
SEDATE
TODATE
UPDATE

••D•A•
ANDEAN
AUDIAL
BEDLAM
ENDEAR
ENDMAN
ESDRAS
HYDRAE
HYDRAS
INDIAN
KIDMAN
KIDNAP
KODIAK
MADCAP
MADMAN

MADMAX
MADRAS
MEDGAR
MEDIAL
MEDIAN
MEDIAS
MEDLAR
MEDLAT
MIDDAY
MIDWAY
MUDCAT
MUDRAS
OGDOAD
OLDHAM
OLDHAT
OLDMAN
ORDEAL
PADUAN
PEDLAR
RADIAL
RADIAN
REDBAY
REDCAP
REDEAL
REDHAT
REDIAL
REDOAK
REDRAW
REDTAG
RODHAM
RUDMAN
SADDAM
TODDAO
TODMAN
UNDRAW
ZODIAC

••D••A
ANDREA
BODEGA
BUDDHA
DODECA
DODOMA
EIDOLA
ENDORA
EUDORA
FEDORA
GODIVA
INDABA
INDIRA
JUDAEA
JUDOKA
LADIDA
LADOGA
MADURA
MEDAKA
MEDINA
MEDUSA
MODELA
MODENA
OEDEMA
RADULA
REDSEA
SEDAKA
ZADORA

•••DA•
ADIDAS
AIRDAM
ALLDAY
AOUDAD
APODAL
BAGDAD
BELDAM
BENDAY
BRIDAL
CAUDAL
CIUDAD
CORDAY
DAEDAL
DEODAR
DOODAD
FEUDAL
FRIDAY
HAIDAS
HEYDAY
HOWDAH
IBADAN
JORDAN
LANDAU
MANDAN
MANDAY
MAYDAY
MCADAM
MIDDAY
MOLDAU
MONDAY
MYRDAL
NASDAQ
OFFDAY
ONEDAY
PANDAS
PAYDAY
PINDAR
PURDAH
SADDAM
SANDAL
SENDAK
SIRDAR
SOLDAN
SUNDAE
SUNDAY
TAGDAY
TODDAO
VANDAL
WHYDAH

•••D•A
ACADIA
ACEDIA
BUDDHA
EXEDRA
GRADEA
SANDIA
SANDRA
STADIA
TREDIA
TUNDRA

••••DA
AGENDA
AMANDA
ANANDA
ARMADA
ARVADA
BLANDA
BRENDA
CANADA
CICADA
COLADA
GELADA
GLENDA
IMELDA
JUMADA
KAUNDA
LADIDA
LAMBDA
LERIDA
LUANDA
MASADA
MERIDA
NERUDA
NEVADA
OLINDA
ONEIDA
OREIDA
PAGODA
PANADA
POSADA
PRAVDA
RAMADA
REMUDA
RESEDA
RHONDA
RUANDA
RWANDA
UGANDA
VIGODA

D•B•••
DABBED
DABBLE
DABNEY
DEBARK
DEBARS
DEBASE
DEBATE
DEBBIE
DEBITS
DEBONE
DEBRAS
DEBRIS
DEBTOR
DEBUGS
DEBUNK
DEBUTS
DIBBLE
DOBBER
DOBBIN
DOBLAS
DOBLIN
DOBRAS
DOBROS
DOBSON
DUBBED
DUBBIN
DUBCEK
DUBLIN
DUBOIS
DYBBUK

D••B••
DABBED
DABBLE
DAUBED
DAUBER
DAUBES
DAYBED
DEBBIE
DIABLO
DIBBLE
DISBAR
DOABLE
DOBBER
DOBBIN
DOOBIE
DOUBLE
DOUBLY
DOUBTS
DRABEK
DRABLY
DUBBED
DUBBIN
DUMBER
DUMBLY
DUNBAR
DURBAN
DURBAR
DURBIN
DYBBUK

D•••B•
DANUBE
DEMOBS
DJERBA
DOESBY
DROPBY
DWEEBS

D••••B
DEKALB
DIONEB

•DB•••
EDBERG

•D•B••
ADOBES
EDIBLE

•D••B•
ADLIBS

•D•••B
ADSORB
ADVERB
ODDJOB

••DB••
BEDBUG
OLDBOY
REDBAY
REDBUD
TIDBIT

••D•B•
ARDEBS
INDABA
INDEBT
REDUBS

••D••B
BEDAUB
MIDRIB
ODDJOB

•••DB•
GOODBY
LAIDBY

•••D•B
SUBDEB

D•C•••
DACAPO
DACHAS
DACOIT
DACRON
DACTYL
DECADE
DECAFS
DECALS
DECAMP
DECANT
DECAYS
DECEIT
DECENT
DECIDE
DECKED
DECKER
DECKLE
DECOCT
DECODE
DECORS
DECOYS
DECREE
DICERS
DICIER
DICING
DICKER
DICKEY
DICOTS
DICTUM
DOCENT
DOCILE
DOCKED
DOCKER
DOCKET
DOCTOR
DUCATS
DUCHIN
DUCKED
DUCTAL

D••C••
DANCED
DANCER
DANCES
DEACON
DEICED
DEICER
DEICES
DESCRY
DEUCED
DEUCES
DISCOS
DISCUS
DORCAS
DUBCEK
DULCET
DUNCAN
DUNCES

D•••C•
DECOCT
DEDUCE
DEDUCT
DEFACE
DEFECT
DEJECT
DELICT
DEPICT
DESICA
DETACH
DETECT
DEVICE
DIDACT
DIRECT
DODECA
DRENCH
DRYICE
DUROCS

D••••C
DELTIC
DYADIC

•DC•••
IDCARD

•D•C••
EDICTS
EDUCED
EDUCES

•D••C•
ADDUCE
ADDUCT
ADVICE
IDIOCY

•D•••C
EDENIC

••DC••
MADCAP
MUDCAT
REDCAP

••D•C•
ABDUCT
ADDUCE
ADDUCT
BEDECK
BODICE
DEDUCE
DEDUCT
DIDACT
INDICT
INDUCE
INDUCT
MEDICI
MEDICO
MEDICS
MODOCS
NODICE
ONDECK
REDACT
REDUCE
SEDUCE
ZYDECO

••D••C
CADMIC
CEDRIC
JUDAIC
OLDVIC
ZODIAC

•••D•C
ACIDIC
ANODIC
BARDIC
DYADIC
IRIDIC
NORDIC
OXIDIC
RUNDMC
SYNDIC

D•D•••
DADDYO
DADOED
DADOES
DEDUCE
DEDUCT
DIDACT
DIDDLE
DIDIES
DIDION
DODDER
DODECA
DODGED
DODGER
DODGES
DODODO
DODOES
DODOMA
DUDEEN
DUDLEY

D••D••
DADDYO
DAEDAL
DANDER
DANDIE
DANDLE
DAWDLE
DEADEN
DEADER
DEADLY
DEADON
DEEDED
DEEDEE
DEIDRE
DENDRI
DENDRO
DEODAR
DIADEM
DIDDLE
DIKDIK
DIODES
DODDER
DONDER
DOODAD
DOODLE
DREDGE
DRUDGE
DRYDEN
DUMDUM
DUNDEE
DYADIC

D•••D•
DECADE
DECIDE
DECODE
DELUDE
DEMODE
DENUDE
DERIDE
DIPODY
DIRNDL
DIVIDE
DODODO
DORADO
DOSIDO
DREADS
DROIDS
DRUIDS
DRYADS

D••••D
DABBED
DADOED
DAMMED
DAMNED
DAMPED
DANCED
DAPPED
DARNED
DARTED
DASHED
DAUBED
DAWNED
DAYBED
DECKED
DEEDED
DEEMED
DEFEND
DEFIED
DEICED
DELVED
DEMAND
DEMOND
DENIED
DENNED
DENTED
DEPEND
DEUCED
DEVOID
DIALED
DIETED
DIMMED
DINGED
DINNED
DINTED
DIPPED
DISHED
DISKED
DISSED
DOCKED
DODGED
DOFFED
DOGGED
DOGOOD
DOLLED
DONALD
DONNED
DOODAD
DOOMED
DOSSED
DOTARD
DOTTED
DOUSED
DOWNED
DOWSED
DRAPED
DRAYED
DRONED
DUBBED
DUCKED
DUELED
DULLED
DUMPED
DUNKED
DUNNED
DUSTED

•DD•••
ADDAMS
ADDEND
ADDERS
ADDING
ADDLED
ADDLES
ADDONS
ADDSIN
ADDSON
ADDSTO
ADDSUP
ADDUCE
ADDUCT
EDDIED
EDDIES
EDDOES
ODDEST
ODDITY
ODDJOB
ODDLOT
ODDSON
UDDERS

•D•D••
ADIDAS

•D••D•
IDOIDO

•D•••D
ADDEND
ADDLED
ADORED
EDDIED
EDGARD
EDITED
EDMOND
EDMUND
EDUARD
EDUCED
EDVARD
EDWARD
IDCARD

••DD••
BADDIE
BIDDEN
BIDDER
BIDDLE
BUDDED
BUDDHA
CADDIE
CADDIS
CODDLE
CUDDLE
CUDDLY
DADDYO
DIDDLE
DODDER
FIDDLE
FODDER
FUDDLE
GADDED
GADDER
HADDIE
HEDDLE
HIDDEN
HUDDLE
JUDDER
KIDDED
KIDDER
LADDER
LADDIE
LIDDED
LUDDEN
MADDEN
MADDER
MADDIE
MEDDLE
MIDDAY
MIDDEN
MIDDLE
MUDDED
MUDDER
MUDDLE
NODDED
NODDLE
PADDED
PADDER
PADDLE
PEDDLE
PODDED
PUDDLE
PUDDLY
RADDLE
REDDEN
REDDER
REDDOG
RIDDED
RIDDEN
RIDDLE
RUDDER
RUDDLE
SADDAM
SADDEN
SADDER
SADDLE
SIDDUR
SODDED
SODDEN
SUDDEN
TEDDED
TEDDER
TODDAO
TODDLE
VEDDER
WADDED
WADDLE
WADDLY
WEDDED
ZADDIK

••D•D•
DODODO
HODADS
IODIDE
LADIDA
MADEDO

••D••D
ADDEND
ADDLED
BODIED
BUDDED
BUDGED
CADGED
DADOED
DODGED
EDDIED
ENDUED
FUDGED
GADDED
GODARD
HEDGED
INDEED
JUDGED
KEDGED
KIDDED
KIDVID
LADLED
LIDDED
LODGED
MADRID
MUDDED
NODDED
NUDGED
OGDOAD
PADDED
PODDED
REDBUD
REDYED
RIDDED
RIDGED
SIDLED
SODDED
SUDSED
TEDDED
TIDIED
UNDYED
WADDED
WEDDED
WEDGED

•••DD•
ATODDS
CRUDDY
FREDDY
SHODDY

•••D•D
ABIDED
AOUDAD
BAGDAD
BANDED
BEADED
BENDED
BIRDED
BLADED
BONDED
BUDDED
CANDID
CARDED
CHIDED
CIUDAD
CORDED
CURDED
DEEDED
DOODAD
ELIDED
ELUDED
ERODED
EVADED
EXUDED
FENDED
FEUDED
FOLDED
FORDED
FUNDED
GADDED
GILDED
GIRDED
GLIDED
GOADED
GRADED
GUIDED
HANDED
HEADED
HEEDED
HERDED
HOODED
KIDDED
LANDED
LARDED
LAUDED
LEADED
LIDDED
LOADED
LORDED
MELDED
MENDED
MINDED
MISDID
MOLDED
MUDDED
NEEDED
NODDED
OUTDID
PADDED
PENDED
PODDED
PRIDED
RAIDED
RIDDED
SANDED
SEEDED
SHADED
SODDED
SORDID
SPADED
TEDDED
TENDED
TRADED
VENDED
VOIDED
WADDED
WARDED
WEDDED
WEEDED
WELDED
WENDED
WINDED
WOODED
WORDED
YARDED

DE••••
DEACON
DEADEN
DEADER
DEADLY
DEADON
DEAFEN
DEAFER
DEALER
DEALIN
DEANNA
DEARER
DEARIE
DEARLY
DEARME
DEARTH
DEBARK
DEBARS
DEBASE
DEBATE
DEBBIE
DEBITS
DEBONE
DEBRAS
DEBRIS
DEBTOR
DEBUGS
DEBUNK
DEBUTS
DECADE
DECAFS
DECALS
DECAMP
DECANT
DECAYS
DECEIT
DECENT
DECIDE
DECKED
DECKER
DECKLE
DECOCT
DECODE
DECORS
DECOYS
DECREE
DEDUCE
DEDUCT
DEEDED
DEEDEE
DEEJAY
DEEMED
DEEPEN
DEEPER
DEEPLY
DEFACE
DEFAME
DEFATS
DEFEAT
DEFECT
DEFEND
DEFERS
DEFIED
DEFIES
DEFILE
DEFINE
DEFLEA
DEFOGS
DEFORM
DEFRAY
DEFTER
DEFTLY
DEFUSE
DEGAGE
DEGREE
DEGUST
DEHORN
DEICED
DEICER
DEICES
DEIDRE
DEIGNS
DEIMOS
DEISTS
DEJAVU
DEJECT
DEJURE
DEKALB
DELANO
DELANY
DELATE
DELAYS
DELEON
DELETE
DELFTS
DELICT
DELIST
DELIUS
DELONG
DELPHI
DELRAY
DELRIO
DELTAS
DELTIC
DELUDE
DELUGE
DELUXE
DELVED
DELVER
DELVES
DEMAND
DEMEAN
DEMISE
DEMITS
DEMOBS
DEMODE
DEMOND
DEMONS
DEMOTE
DEMURE
DEMURS
DENALI
DENDRI
DENDRO
DENGUE
DENIAL
DENIED
DENIER
DENIES
DENIMS
DENIRO
DENISE
DENNED
DENNIS
DENOTE
DENOVO
DENSER
DENTAL
DENTED
DENTIL
DENTIN
DENTON
DENUDE
DENVER
DENZEL
DEODAR
DEPART
DEPAUL
DEPAUW
DEPEND
DEPICT
DEPLOY
DEPONE
DEPORT
DEPOSE
DEPOTS
DEPTHS
DEPUTE
DEPUTY
DERAIL
DERIDE
DERIVE
DERMAL
DERMIS
DERRIS
DESALT
DESCRY
DESERT
DESICA
DESIGN
DESILU
DESIRE
DESIST
DESMAN
DESOTO
DESPOT
DESTRY
DETACH
DETAIL
DETAIN
DETECT
DETENT
DETERS
DETEST
DETOUR
DETROP
DEUCED
DEUCES
DEVEIN
DEVEST
DEVICE
DEVILS
DEVINE
DEVISE
DEVITO
DEVOID
DEVOIR
DEVOTE
DEVOTO
DEVOUR
DEVOUT
DEWIER
DEWING
DEWITT
DEWLAP
DEXTER
DEXTRO

D•E•••
DAEDAL
DEEDED
DEEDEE
DEEJAY
DEEMED
DEEPEN
DEEPER
DEEPLY
DIEOFF
DIEOUT
DIEPPE
DIESEL
DIESES
DIESIS
DIETED
DIETER
DJERBA
DOESBY
DOESIN
DOESNT
DOESUP
DREADS
DREAMS
DREAMT
DREAMY
DREARY
DREDGE
DRENCH
DRESSY
DREWIN
DREWON
DREWUP
DREXEL
DUELED
DUELER
DUELLO
DUENNA
DWEEBS
DWELLS
DYEING
DYELOT

D••E••
DALETH
DARETO
DATERS
DECEIT
DECENT
DEFEAT
DEFECT
DEFEND
DEFERS
DEJECT
DELEON
DELETE
DEMEAN
DEPEND
DESERT
DETECT
DETENT
DETERS
DETEST
DEVEIN
DEVEST
DICERS

DIGEST
DINEIN
DINEON
DINERO
DINERS
DIRECT
DIREST
DIVEIN
DIVERS
DIVERT
DIVEST
DOCENT
DODECA
DOGEAR
DONEES
DONEIN
DONETS
DONEUP
DOREMI
DOSERS
DOTELL
DOTEON
DOVEIN
DOWELS
DOWERS
DOYENS
DOZENS
DOZERS
DRIERS
DRIEST
DRYERS
DRYEST
DUDEEN
DUNERA
DUPERY
DURESS
DUVETS
DWEEBS

D•••E•

DABBED
DABNEY
DADOED
DADOES
DAFTER
DAGGER
DAILEY
DAIREN
DAISES
DALLES
DAMIEN
DAMMED
DAMNED
DAMPED
DAMPEN
DAMPER
DAMSEL
DANCED
DANCER
DANCES
DANDER
DANGER
DANIEL
DANKER
DANNER
DANTES
DAPPED
DAPPER
DARIEN
DARKEN
DARKER
DARNED
DARNEL
DARNER
DARREN
DARTED
DARTER
DASHED
DASHER
DASHES
DAUBED
DAUBER
DAUBES
DAVIES
DAWNED
DAYBED
DEADEN
DEADER
DEAFEN
DEAFER
DEALER
DEARER
DECKED
DECKER
DECREE
DEEDED
DEEDEE
DEEMED
DEEPEN
DEEPER
DEFIED
DEFIES
DEFLEA
DEFTER
DEGREE
DEICED
DEICER
DEICES
DELVED
DELVER
DELVES
DENIED
DENIER
DENIES
DENNED
DENSER
DENTED
DENVER
DENZEL
DEUCED
DEUCES
DEWIER
DEXTER
DHOLES
DHOTEL
DIADEM
DIALED
DIALER
DIAPER
DICIER
DICKER
DICKEY
DIDIES
DIESEL
DIESES
DIETED
DIETER
DIFFER
DIGGER
DILLER
DILSEY
DIMMED
DIMMER
DINGED
DINKEY
DINNED
DINNER
DINTED
DIODES
DIONEB
DIPPED
DIPPER
DIRGES
DISHED
DISHES
DISKED
DISMES
DISNEY
DISPEL
DISSED
DITHER
DITZES
DLAYER
DOBBER
DOCKED
DOCKER
DOCKET
DODDER
DODGED
DODGER
DODGES
DODOES
DOFFED
DOGGED
DOGGER
DOGIES
DOGLEG
DOLLED
DOLMEN
DONDER
DONEES
DONKEY
DONNED
DONNEE
DONNER
DOOLEY
DOOMED
DOPIER
DORIES
DORMER
DORSET
DORSEY
DOSSED
DOSSEL
DOSSER
DOSSES
DOTTED
DOURER
DOUSED
DOUSES
DOWNED
DOWNER
DOWNEY
DOWSED
DOWSER
DOWSES
DRABEK
DRAGEE
DRAKES
DRAPED
DRAPER
DRAPES
DRAWER
DRAYED
DREXEL
DRIVEL
DRIVEN
DRIVER
DRIVES
DRONED
DRONER
DRONES
DROVER
DROVES
DRUPES
DRUZES
DRYDEN
DUBBED
DUBCEK
DUCKED
DUDEEN
DUDLEY
DUELED
DUELER
DUFFEL
DUFFER
DUIKER
DULCET
DULLEA
DULLED
DULLER
DULLES
DUMBER
DUMPED
DUMPER
DUNCES
DUNDEE
DUNKED
DUNKER
DUNNED
DUPLEX
DURFEY
DURYEA
DUSTED
DUSTER
DUTIES

D••••E

DABBLE
DAMAGE
DAMONE
DAMORE
DANDIE
DANDLE
DANGLE
DANGME
DANUBE
DAPHNE
DAPPLE
DARKLE
DATIVE
DAWDLE
DAYONE
DAZZLE
DEARIE
DEARME
DEBASE
DEBATE
DEBBIE
DEBONE
DECADE
DECIDE
DECKLE
DECODE
DECREE
DEDUCE
DEEDEE
DEFACE
DEFAME
DEFILE
DEFINE
DEFUSE
DEGAGE
DEGREE
DEIDRE
DEJURE
DELATE
DELETE
DELUDE
DELUGE
DELUXE
DEMISE
DEMODE
DEMOTE
DEMURE
DENGUE
DENISE
DENOTE
DENUDE
DEPONE
DEPOSE
DEPUTE
DERIDE
DERIVE
DESIRE
DEVICE
DEVINE
DEVISE
DEVOTE
DIBBLE
DIDDLE
DIEPPE
DILATE
DILUTE
DIMPLE
DINGLE
DIONNE
DIPOLE
DISUSE
DIVIDE
DIVINE
DOABLE
DOCILE
DOGGIE
DONATE
DONNEE
DOOBIE
DOODLE
DOOGIE
DOOZIE
DOSAGE
DOTAGE
DOTTIE
DOTTLE
DOUBLE
DRAGEE
DREDGE
DROGUE
DROWSE
DRUDGE
DRYICE
DUARTE
DUNDEE
DWAYNE

•DE•••

ADEEMS
ADELIE
ADELLE
ADEPTS
ADESTE
EDENIC
EDERLE
EDESSA
IDEALS
IDEATE
ODENSE
ODESSA
ODETTA
ODETTE

•D•E••

ADDEND
ADDERS
ADEEMS
ADHERE
ADIEUS
ADIEUX
ADRENO
ADVENT
ADVERB
ADVERT
ADWEEK
EDBERG
EDGEIN
EDGERS
EDSELS
IDLERS
IDLEST
ODDEST
UDDERS

•D••E•

ADAGES
ADDLED
ADDLES
ADOBES
ADORED
ADOREE
ADORER
ADORES
ADRIEN
ADWEEK
EDAMES
EDDIED
EDDIES
EDDOES
EDGIER
EDILES
EDITED
EDUCED
EDUCES

•D•••E

ADDUCE
ADELIE
ADELLE
ADESTE
ADHERE
ADJURE
ADMIRE
ADNATE
ADOREE
ADVICE
ADVISE
EDERLE
EDIBLE
IDEATE
ODENSE
ODETTE

••DE••

ADDEND
ADDERS
ALDERS
ANDEAN
ARDEBS
ARDENT
AUDENS
BADEGG
BEDECK
BEDEWS
BODEGA
CADENT
CADETS
CIDERS
CODERS
CYDERS
DODECA
DUDEEN
EIDERS
ELDERS
ELDEST
ENDEAR
ENDERS
FADEIN
GIDEON
GODETS
HIDEHO
HIDEKI
HIDERS
INDEBT
INDEED
INDENE
INDENT
LADERS
LODENS
LUDENS
MADEDO
MADEIT
MADERO
MADEUP
MODELA
MODELS
MODELT
MODEMS
MODENA
MODERN
MODEST
MUDEEL
ODDEST
OEDEMA
OLDEST
ONDECK
ORDEAL
ORDERS
REDEAL
REDEEM
REDEYE
RIDENT
RIDERS
RODENT
RODEOS
RUDELY
RUDEST
RYDELL
SEDERS
SIDERO
SIDERS
TEDEUM
UDDERS
VIDEOS
WADEIN
WADERS
WEDELN
WIDELY
WIDENS
WIDEST
YODELS
ZYDECO

••D•E•

ADDLED
ADDLES
ANDREA
ANDREI
ANDRES
ANDREW
ANDREY
AUDREY
BADGER
BADGES
BIDDEN
BIDDER
BODIED
BODIES
BUDDED
BUDGED
BUDGES
BUDGET
CADGED
CADGER
CADGES
CADRES
CODGER
CUDGEL
DADOED
DADOES
DIDIES
DODDER
DODGED
DODGER
DODGES
DODOES
DUDEEN
DUDLEY
EDDIED
EDDIES
EDDOES
ENDMEN
ENDUED
ENDUES
FIDGET
FODDER
FUDGED
FUDGES
GADDED
GADDER
GADGET
GIDGET
HADJES
HEDGED
HEDGER
HEDGES
HEDREN
HIDDEN
INDEED
INDIES
JUDAEA
JUDDER
JUDGED
JUDGES
KEDGED
KEDGES
KIDDED
KIDDER
KIDNEY
LADDER
LADIES
LADLED
LADLER
LADLES
LEDGER
LEDGES
LIDDED
LODGED
LODGER
LODGES
LUDDEN
MADDEN
MADDER
MADMEN
MADRES
MEDLEY
MIDDEN
MIDGES
MIDGET
MIDLER
MUDDED
MUDDER
MUDEEL
MUDHEN
NODDED
NUDGED
NUDGER
NUDGES
OLDIES
OLDMEN
OODLES
PADDED
PADDER
PADRES
PODDED
RADNER
REDDEN
REDDER
REDEEM
REDOES
REDREW
REDSEA
REDYED
REDYES
RIDDED
RIDDEN
RIDGED
RIDGES
RIDLEY
RODNEY
RUDDER
SADDEN
SADDER
SEDGES
SIDLED
SIDLES
SIDNEY
SODDED
SODDEN
SUDDEN
SUDSED
SUDSES
SYDNEY
TEDDED
TEDDER
TEDKEY
TIDIED
TIDIER
TIDIES
UNDIES
UNDOER
UNDOES
UNDYED
VEDDER
WADDED
WEDDED
WEDGED
WEDGES
WIDGET

••D••E

ADDUCE
AEDILE
ALDINE
ALDOSE
BADDIE
BEDAZE
BIDDLE
BODICE
BUDGIE
CADDIE
CODDLE
CUDDLE
DEDUCE
DIDDLE
ENDIVE
ENDURE
ENDUSE
FIDDLE
FUDDLE
HADDIE
HEDDLE
HUDDLE
HYDRAE
INDENE
INDITE
INDUCE
IODATE
IODIDE
IODINE
IODIZE
LADDIE
MADAME
MADDIE
MEDDLE
MIDDLE
MODINE
MODULE
MUDDLE
MUDPIE
NADINE
NODDLE
NODICE
NODOSE
NODULE
ONDINE
ORDURE
PADDLE
PEDATE
PEDDLE
PUDDLE
RADDLE
RADOME
REDATE
REDEYE
REDONE
REDUCE
RIDDLE
RUDDLE
SADDLE
SEDATE
SEDILE
SEDUCE
TODATE
TODDLE
UNDINE
UNDONE
UPDATE
UPDIKE
VADOSE
WADDLE
WEDGIE

•••DE•

ABIDED
ABIDES
ABODES
AMEDEO
AMIDES
ANADEM
ANODES
ASIDES
BALDER
BANDED
BEADED
BENDED
BENDER
BIDDEN
BIDDER
BINDER
BIRDED
BIRDER
BLADED
BLADES
BOLDER
BONDED
BORDEN
BORDER
BRIDES
BRUDER
BSIDES
BUDDED
BURDEN
CALDER
CAMDEN
CARDED
CARDER
CAUDEX
CHIDED
CHIDES
CINDER
COLDER
COODER
CORDED
CRUDER
CURDED
DANDER
DEADEN
DEADER
DEEDED
DEEDEE
DIADEM
DIODES
DODDER
DONDER
DRYDEN
DUNDEE
ELIDED
ELIDES
ELUDED
ELUDES
EMBDEN
EPODES
ERODED
ERODES
ETUDES
EVADED
EVADER
EVADES
EXUDED
EXUDES
FEEDER
FENDED
FENDER
FEUDED
FINDER
FODDER
FOLDED
FOLDER
FONDER
FORDED
FUNDED
GADDED
GADDER
GANDER
GARDEN
GENDER
GEODES
GILDED
GILDER
GIRDED
GIRDER
GLADES
GLIDED
GLIDER
GLIDES
GOADED
GOLDEN
GOODEN
GRADEA
GRADED
GRADER
GRADES
GUIDED
GUIDES
HANDED
HANDEL
HARDEN
HARDER
HAYDEN
HEADED
HEADER
HEEDED
HEIDEN
HERDED
HERDER
HIDDEN
HINDER
HOLDEN
HOLDER
HOODED
HORDES
HOYDEN
HYADES
IBIDEM
IRIDES
JUDDER
KANDER
KIDDED
KIDDER
KINDER
LADDER
LANDED
LANDER
LARDED
LARDER
LAUDED
LAUDER
LEADED
LEADEN
LEADER
LEIDEN
LENDER
LEWDER
LEYDEN
LIDDED
LIEDER
LINDEN
LOADED
LOADER
LORDED
LOUDEN
LOUDER
LUDDEN
LUNDEN
MADDEN
MADDER
MAIDEN
MALDEN
MELDED
MENDED
MENDEL
MENDER
MENDES
MIDDEN
MILDER
MILDEW
MINDED
MINDER
MOLDED
MOLDER
MUDDED
MUDDER
MURDER
NEEDED
NODDED
OXIDES
PADDED
PADDER
PANDER
PEEDEE
PENDED
PODDED
POLDER
PONDER
POWDER
PRIDED
PRIDES
PRUDES
RAIDED
RAIDER
READER
REDDEN
REDDER
RENDER
RHODES
RIDDED
RIDDEN
RONDEL
RUDDER
SADDEN
SADDER
SANDED
SANDER
SEEDED
SEEDER
SEIDEL
SENDER
SHADED
SHADES
SLIDER
SLIDES
SNIDER
SNYDER
SODDED
SODDEN
SOLDER
SONDES
SPADED
SPADER
SPADES
SPIDER
SUBDEB
SUDDEN
SUEDES
SUNDER
SUNDEW
SWEDEN
SWEDES
TANDEM
TEDDED
TEDDER
TENDED
TENDER
TILDEN
TILDES
TINDER
TRADED
TRADER
TRADES
VALDEZ
VARDEN
VEDDER
VENDED
VENDEE
VOIDED
WADDED
WALDEN
WANDER
WARDED
WARDEN
WARDER
WEDDED
WEEDED
WEEDER
WELDED
WELDER
WENDED
WILDER
WINDED
WINDER
WINDEX
WONDER
WOODED
WOODEN
WORDED
YARDED
YONDER
ZANDER
ZUIDER

•••D•E

AZODYE
BADDIE
BEADLE
BIDDLE
BIRDIE
BOODLE
BRIDGE
BRIDLE
BRODIE
BUNDLE
CADDIE
CANDLE
CAUDLE
CODDLE
CRADLE
CUDDLE
CURDLE
DANDIE
DANDLE
DAWDLE
DEEDEE
DEIDRE
DIDDLE
DOODLE
DREDGE
DRUDGE
DUNDEE
FIDDLE
FLEDGE
FONDLE
FONDUE
FRIDGE
FUDDLE
GIRDLE
GOLDIE
GOODIE
GORDIE
GRUDGE
HADDIE
HANDLE
HEDDLE
HUDDLE
HURDLE
KINDLE
KLUDGE
LADDIE
MADDIE
MEDDLE
MIDDLE
MUDDLE
NEEDLE
NODDLE
NOODLE
ONEDGE
PADDLE
PEDDLE
PEEDEE
PERDUE
PHEDRE
PLEDGE
POODLE
PUDDLE
PURDUE
RADDLE
RIDDLE
ROADIE
RUDDLE
RUNDLE
SADDLE
SLEDGE
SLUDGE
SMUDGE
STODGE
SUBDUE
SUNDAE
TIEDYE
TODDLE
TRUDGE
VENDEE
WADDLE

••••DE

ABRADE
ACCEDE
ALLUDE
ARCADE
AUBADE
BESIDE
BETIDE
BLENDE
BLONDE
BOLIDE
BORIDE
CHILDE
CLAUDE
DECADE
DECIDE
DECODE
DELUDE
DEMODE
DENUDE
DERIDE
DIVIDE
ENCODE
FACADE
GOURDE
GRANDE
HALIDE
IMPEDE
INSIDE
INVADE

IODIDE
ISOLDE
LIPIDE
MRHYDE
ONSIDE
OROIDE
PARADE
POMADE
RECEDE
RECODE
REMADE
RESIDE
SECEDE
STRIDE
STRODE
TIRADE
TRIODE
UNLADE
UNMADE
UPSIDE

D•F•••

DAFTER
DEFACE
DEFAME
DEFATS
DEFEAT
DEFECT
DEFEND
DEFERS
DEFIED
DEFIES
DEFILE
DEFINE
DEFLEA
DEFOGS
DEFORM
DEFRAY
DEFTER
DEFTLY
DEFUSE
DIFFER
DOFFED
DUFFEL
DUFFER

D••F••

DEAFEN
DEAFER
DELFTS
DIFFER
DOFFED
DOOFUS
DRAFTS
DRAFTY
DRIFTS
DRYFLY
DUFFEL
DUFFER
DURFEY

D•••F•

DECAFS
DIEOFF
DRYOFF
DWARFS

D••••F

DIEOFF
DRYOFF

•D••F•

ADRIFT

••DF••

GADFLY
REDFIN
REDFIR
REDFOX

••D•F•

CODIFY
LEDOFF
MODIFY
NODOFF

••D••F

LEDOFF
NODOFF
RUDOLF

•••D•F

KINDOF
TOLDOF

D•G•••

DAGAMA
DAGGER
DEGAGE
DEGREE
DEGUST
DIGEST
DIGGER
DIGITS
DIGLOT
DIGOUT
DIGRAM
DIGSIN
DIGSUP
DOGEAR
DOGGED
DOGGER
DOGGIE
DOGIES
DOGLEG
DOGMAS
DOGONS
DOGOOD
DOGSIT
DOGTAG
DUGONG
DUGOUT

D••G••

DAGGER
DANGER
DANGLE
DANGLY
DANGME
DAYGLO
DEIGNS
DENGUE
DIGGER
DINGED
DINGHY
DINGLE
DINGUS
DIRGES
DODGED
DODGER
DODGES
DOGGED
DOGGER
DOGGIE
DOOGIE
DOUGHS
DOUGHY
DRAGEE
DRAGGY
DRAGIN
DRAGON
DROGUE
DWIGHT

D•••G•

DAMAGE
DEBUGS
DEFOGS
DEGAGE
DELUGE
DESIGN
DIRIGO
DOINGS
DOSAGE
DOTAGE
DRAGGY
DREDGE
DRINGS
DRUDGE

D••••G

DANANG
DANZIG
DARING
DATING
DATONG
DAZING
DELONG
DEWING
DIALOG
DICING
DIKING
DINING
DIVING
DOGLEG
DOGTAG
DOLING
DOMING
DOPING
DOSING
DOTING
DOZING
DRYING
DUGONG
DUKING
DUPING
DURING
DYEING

•DG•••

EDGARD
EDGARS
EDGEIN
EDGERS
EDGIER
EDGILY
EDGING

•D•G••

ADAGES
ADAGIO

•D•••G

ADDING
EDBERG
EDGING
IDLING
KDLANG

••DG••

BADGER
BADGES
BADGUY
BUDGED
BUDGES
BUDGET
BUDGIE
CADGED
CADGER
CADGES
CODGER
CUDGEL
DODGED
DODGER
DODGES
FIDGET
FUDGED
FUDGES
GADGET
GIDGET
HEDGED
HEDGER
HEDGES
JUDGED
JUDGES
KEDGED
KEDGES
LEDGER
LEDGES
LODGED
LODGER
LODGES
MEDGAR
MIDGES
MIDGET
NUDGED
NUDGER
NUDGES
PIDGIN
REDGUM
RIDGED
RIDGES
SEDGES
WEDGED
WEDGES
WEDGIE
WIDGET

••D•G•

BADEGG
BODEGA
INDIGO
LADOGA

••D••G

ADDING
AIDING
BADEGG
BEDBUG
BIDING
BODING
CEDING
CODING
ENDING
FADING
HIDING
JADING
LADING
LUDWIG
PADANG
REDDOG
REDTAG
RIDING
SIDING
TIDING
WADING

•••DG•

BRIDGE
DREDGE
DRUDGE
FLEDGE
FRIDGE
GRUDGE
KLUDGE
ONEDGE
PLEDGE
SLEDGE
SLUDGE
SLUDGY
SMUDGE
SMUDGY
STODGE
STODGY
TRUDGE

•••D•G

BANDOG
GUNDOG
HOTDOG
LAPDOG
PYEDOG
REDDOG
SEADOG
SUNDOG
TOPDOG
TOYDOG

••••DG

RATEDG

DH••••

DHARMA
DHOLES
DHOTEL
DHOTIS

D•H•••

DAHLIA
DEHORN
DRHOOK
DSHARP

D••H••

DACHAS
DAPHNE
DASHED
DASHER
DASHES
DIRHAM
DISHED
DISHES
DITHER
DOTHAN
DUCHIN
DUNHAM
DURHAM

D•••H•

DELPHI
DEPTHS
DINGHY
DOUGHS
DOUGHY
DWIGHT

D••••H

DALETH
DANISH
DEARTH
DETACH
DOVISH
DRENCH
DULUTH

•DH•••

ADHERE

•D•••H

ADOLPH

••DH••

ANDHOW
MUDHEN
OLDHAM
OLDHAT
REDHAT
REDHOT
RODHAM

••D•H•

BUDDHA
HIDEHO
WIDTHS

••D••H

EMDASH
ENDASH
JUDITH
MODISH
OLDISH
RADISH

•••DH•

BUDDHA
GANDHI
LANDHO

•••D•H

HOWDAH
PURDAH
WHYDAH

••••DH

LAMEDH
RIYADH

DI••••

DIABLO
DIADEM
DIALED
DIALER
DIALOG
DIAPER
DIATOM
DIBBLE
DICERS
DICIER
DICING
DICKER
DICKEY
DICOTS
DICTUM
DIDACT
DIDDLE
DIDIES
DIDION
DIEOFF
DIEOUT
DIEPPE
DIESEL
DIESES
DIESIS
DIETED
DIETER
DIFFER
DIGEST
DIGGER
DIGITS
DIGLOT
DIGOUT
DIGRAM
DIGSIN
DIGSUP
DIKDIK
DIKING
DIKTAT
DILATE
DILLER
DILLON
DILSEY
DILUTE
DIMITY
DIMMED
DIMMER
DIMOUT
DIMPLE
DIMPLY
DIMSUM
DIMWIT
DINARS
DINEIN
DINEON
DINERO
DINERS
DINGED
DINGHY
DINGLE
DINGUS
DINING
DINKEY
DINNED
DINNER
DINTED
DIODES
DIONEB
DIONNE
DIOXIN
DIPODY
DIPOLE
DIPPED
DIPPER
DIRECT
DIREST
DIRGES
DIRHAM
DIRIGO
DIRNDL
DISANT
DISARM
DISBAR
DISCOS
DISCUS
DISHED
DISHES
DISKED
DISMAL
DISMAY
DISMES
DISNEY
DISOWN
DISPEL
DISSED
DISTAL
DISTIL
DISUSE
DITHER
DITTOS
DITZES
DIVANS
DIVEIN
DIVERS
DIVERT
DIVEST
DIVIDE
DIVINE
DIVING
DIVOTS
DIXITS

D•I•••

DAIKON
DAILEY
DAIMON
DAIMYO
DAINTY
DAIREN
DAISES
DEICED
DEICER
DEICES
DEIDRE
DEIGNS
DEIMOS
DEISTS
DMINOR
DMINUS
DMITRI
DOINGS
DRIERS
DRIEST
DRIFTS
DRILLS
DRINGS
DRINKS
DRIPPY
DRIVEL
DRIVEN
DRIVER
DRIVES
DUIKER
DWIGHT

D••I••

DAMIEN
DAMITA
DANIEL
DANISH
DARIEN
DARING
DARIUS
DATING
DATIVE
DAVIES
DAVITS
DAZING
DEBITS
DECIDE
DEFIED
DEFIES
DEFILE
DEFINE
DELICT
DELIST
DELIUS
DEMISE
DEMITS
DENIAL
DENIED
DENIER
DENIES
DENIMS
DENIRO
DENISE
DEPICT
DERIDE
DERIVE
DESICA
DESIGN
DESILU
DESIRE
DESIST
DEVICE
DEVILS
DEVINE
DEVISE
DEVITO
DEWIER
DEWING
DEWITT
DICIER
DICING
DIDIES
DIDION
DIGITS
DIKING
DIMITY
DINING
DIRIGO
DIVIDE
DIVINE
DIVING
DIXITS
DOCILE
DOGIES
DOLING
DOMING
DOMINI
DOMINO
DONITZ
DOPIER
DOPING
DORIAN
DORIES
DOSIDO
DOSING
DOTING
DOVISH
DOZILY
DOZING
DRAILS
DRAINS
DROIDS
DROITS
DRUIDS
DRYICE
DRYING
DRYINK
DUKING
DUPING
DURIAN
DURING
DUTIES
DYEING

D•••I•

DACOIT
DAHLIA
DANDIE
DANZIG
DARNIT
DARWIN
DASSIN
DAYLIT
DEALIN
DEARIE
DEBBIE
DEBRIS
DECEIT
DELRIO
DELTIC
DENNIS
DENTIL
DENTIN
DERAIL
DERMIS
DERRIS
DETAIL
DETAIN
DEVEIN
DEVOID
DEVOIR
DHOTIS
DIESIS
DIGSIN
DIKDIK
DIMWIT
DINEIN
DIOXIN
DISTIL
DIVEIN
DOBBIN
DOBLIN
DOESIN
DOGGIE
DOGSIT
DOMAIN
DONEIN
DOOBIE
DOOGIE
DOOZIE
DORRIT
DOTTIE
DOVEIN
DRAGIN
DRAWIN
DREWIN
DROPIN
DROPIT
DUBBIN
DUBLIN
DUBOIS
DUCHIN
DUNLIN
DURBIN
DUSTIN
DYADIC

D••••I

DALASI
DELPHI
DENALI
DENDRI
DMITRI
DOMANI
DOMINI
DORATI
DOREMI
DROMOI

•DI•••

ADIDAS
ADIEUS
ADIEUX
EDIBLE
EDICTS
EDILES
EDISON
EDITED
EDITOR
IDIOCY
IDIOMS
IDIOTS
ODIOUS
ODISTS
ODIUMS

•D•I••

ADDING
ADLIBS
ADMIRE
ADMITS
ADRIAN
ADRIEN
ADRIFT
ADVICE
ADVISE
EDDIED
EDDIES
EDGIER
EDGILY
EDGING
IDLING
IDOIDO
ODDITY

•D••I•

ADAGIO
ADDSIN
ADELIE
ADJOIN
ADONIS
ADROIT
EDENIC
EDGEIN

•D•••I

ADONAI
ADZUKI

••DI••

ADDING
AEDILE
AIDING
ALDINE
AUDIAL
AUDIOS
AUDITS
BEDIMS
BIDING
BODICE
BODIED
BODIES
BODILY
BODING
CEDING
CODIFY
CODING
DIDIES
DIDION
EDDIED
EDDIES
ENDING
ENDIVE
FADING
GODIVA
HIDING
INDIAN
INDICT
INDIES
INDIGO
INDIRA
INDITE
INDIUM
IODIDE
IODINE
IODIZE
JADING
JUDITH
KODIAK
LADIDA
LADIES
LADING
LADINO
MEDIAL
MEDIAN
MEDIAS
MEDICI
MEDICO
MEDICS
MEDINA
MEDIUM
MODIFY
MODINE
MODISH
NADINE
NADIRS
NODICE
NUDIST
NUDITY
ODDITY
OLDIES
OLDISH
ONDINE
PODIUM
RADIAL
RADIAN
RADIOS
RADISH
RADIUM
RADIUS
REDIAL
REDINK
RIDING
SEDILE
SIDING
SODIUM
TEDIUM
TIDIED
TIDIER
TIDIES
TIDILY
TIDING
UNDIES
UNDINE
UPDIKE
WADING
ZODIAC

••D•I•

ADDSIN
ALDRIN
AODAIS
BADDIE
BIDSIN
BODKIN
BUDGIE
CADDIE
CADDIS
CADMIC
CEDRIC
FADEIN
GODWIN
GODWIT
HADDIE
HADJIS
INDRIS
JUDAIC
KIDVID
LADDIE
LUDWIG
MADDIE
MADEIT
MADRID
MIDAIR
MIDRIB
MUDPIE
NUDNIK
OLDVIC
ORDAIN
PIDGIN
REDFIN
REDFIR
TIDBIT
WADEIN
WEDGIE
ZADDIK

••D••I

ANDREI
BODONI
HIDEKI
MEDICI
MIDORI

•••DI•

ACADIA
ACEDIA
ACIDIC
AGADIR
AMADIS
ANODIC
BADDIE
BANDIT
BARDIC
BENDIX
BIRDIE
BOUDIN
BRODIE
CADDIE
CADDIS
CANDID
CARDIN
CARDIO
COEDIT
CREDIT
DANDIE
DIKDIK
DYADIC
GOLDIE
GOODIE
GORDIE
GRADIN
GRODIN
HADDIE
HANDIN
HEADIN
HELDIN
HOLDIT
ICEDIN
IRIDIC
LADDIE
LAIDIN
LANDIS
LEADIN
MADDIE
MAHDIS
MISDID
NORDIC
OUTDID
OXIDIC
PAIDIN
PANDIT
PUNDIT
READIN
REEDIT
ROADIE
SANDIA
SARDIS
SAUDIS
SENDIN
SLIDIN
SORDID
SPADIX
STADIA
STUDIO
SYNDIC
TIEDIN
TOEDIN
TREDIA
VERDIN
ZADDIK

•••D•I

DENDRI
GANDHI
QUADRI

••••DI

BIONDI
CIARDI
SOLIDI
YEHUDI

DJ••••

DJERBA

D•J•••

DEJAVU
DEJECT
DEJURE

D••J••

DEEJAY
DMAJOR
DONJON

•DJ•••

ADJOIN
ADJURE
ADJUST

•D•J••

ODDJOB

••DJ••

HADJES
HADJIS
ODDJOB

D•K•••

DAKOTA
DEKALB
DIKDIK
DIKING
DIKTAT
DUKING

D••K••

DAIKON
DANKER
DARKEN
DARKER
DARKLE
DARKLY
DECKED
DECKER
DECKLE
DICKER
DICKEY
DINKEY
DISKED
DOCKED
DOCKER
DOCKET
DONKEY
DRAKES
DUCKED
DUIKER
DUNKED
DUNKER

D•••K•

DRINKS

D••••K

DAMASK
DEBARK
DEBUNK
DIKDIK
DRABEK
DRHOOK
DRYINK
DUBCEK
DVORAK
DYBBUK

•D••K•

ADZUKI

•D•••K

ADWEEK
GDANSK

••DK••

BODKIN
TEDKEY

••D•K•

HIDEKI
JUDOKA
MEDAKA
SEDAKA
UPDIKE

••D••K

BEDECK
KODIAK
NUDNIK
ONDECK
PODUNK
REDINK
REDOAK
ZADDIK

•••D•K

DIKDIK
MARDUK
SENDAK
ZADDIK

DL••••

DLAYER

D•L•••

DALASI
DALETH
DALLAS
DALLES
DALTON
DELANO

DELANY
DELATE
DELAYS
DELEON
DELETE
DELFTS
DELICT
DELIST
DELIUS
DELONG
DELPHI
DELRAY
DELRIO
DELTAS
DELTIC
DELUDE
DELUGE
DELUXE
DELVED
DELVER
DELVES
DILATE
DILLER
DILLON
DILSEY
DILUTE
DOLING
DOLLAR
DOLLED
DOLLOP
DOLLUP
DOLMAN
DOLMAS
DOLMEN
DOLORS
DULCET
DULLEA
DULLED
DULLER
DULLES
DULUTH

D••L••

DAHLIA
DAILEY
DALLAS
DALLES
DAYLIT
DEALER
DEALIN
DEFLEA
DEPLOY
DEWLAP
DHOLES
DIALED
DIALER
DIALOG
DIGLOT
DILLER
DILLON
DOBLAS
DOBLIN
DOGLEG
DOLLAR
DOLLED
DOLLOP
DOLLUP
DOOLEY
DRILLS
DROLLS
DROLLY
DUALLY
DUBLIN
DUDLEY
DUELED
DUELER
DUELLO
DULLEA
DULLED
DULLER
DULLES
DUNLIN
DUNLOP
DUPLEX
DWELLS
DYELOT

D•••L•

DABBLE
DAMPLY
DANDLE
DANGLE
DANGLY
DAPPLE
DARKLE
DARKLY
DAWDLE
DAYGLO
DAZZLE
DEADLY
DEARLY
DECALS
DECKLE
DEEPLY
DEFILE
DEFTLY
DEKALB
DENALI
DESALT
DESILU
DEVILS
DIABLO
DIBBLE
DIDDLE
DIMPLE
DIMPLY
DINGLE
DIPOLE
DOABLE
DOCILE
DONALD
DOODLE
DOTELL
DOTTLE
DOUBLE
DOUBLY
DOURLY
DOWELS
DOZILY
DRABLY
DRAILS
DRAWLS
DRILLS
DROLLS
DROLLY
DROOLS
DRYFLY
DUALLY
DUELLO
DUMBLY
DUVALL
DWELLS

D••••L

DACTYL
DAEDAL
DAMSEL
DANIEL
DARNEL
DARRYL
DENIAL
DENTAL
DENTIL
DENZEL
DEPAUL
DERAIL
DERMAL
DETAIL
DHOTEL
DIESEL
DIRNDL
DISMAL
DISPEL
DISTAL
DISTIL
DORSAL
DOSSAL
DOSSEL
DOTELL
DREXEL
DRIVEL
DUCTAL
DUFFEL
DUVALL

•DL•••

ADLIBS
IDLERS
IDLEST
IDLING
KDLANG

•D•L••

ADDLED
ADDLES
ADELIE
ADELLE
ADOLPH
ADULTS
EDILES
IDYLLS
ODDLOT

•D••L•

ADELLE
EDERLE
EDGILY
EDIBLE
EDSELS
IDEALS
IDYLLS

••DL••

ADDLED
ADDLES
BADLOT
BEDLAM
DUDLEY
LADLED
LADLER
LADLES
LUDLUM
MEDLAR
MEDLAT
MEDLEY
MIDLER
ODDLOT
OODLES
PEDLAR
RIDLEY
SIDLED
SIDLES

••D•L•

AEDILE
BIDDLE
BODILY
CODDLE
CUDDLE
CUDDLY
DIDDLE
EIDOLA
ENDALL
FIDDLE
FUDDLE
GADFLY
HEDDLE
HUDDLE
KODALY
MEDALS
MEDDLE
MIDDLE
MODELA
MODELS
MODELT
MODULE
MODULO
MUDDLE
NODDLE
NODULE
PADDLE
PEDALS
PEDDLE
PUDDLE
PUDDLY
RADDLE
RADULA
RIDDLE
RUDDLE
RUDELY
RUDOLF
RYDELL
SADDLE
SEDILE
TIDILY
TODDLE
UNDULY
WADDLE
WADDLY
WEDELN
WIDELY
YODELS

••D••L

AUDIAL
CUDGEL
ENDALL
MEDIAL
MUDEEL
ORDEAL
RADIAL
REDEAL
REDIAL
RYDELL

•••DL•

ACIDLY
ARIDLY
AVIDLY
BALDLY
BEADLE
BIDDLE
BOLDLY
BOODLE
BRIDLE
BUNDLE
CANDLE
CAUDLE
CODDLE
COLDLY
CRADLE
CUDDLE
CUDDLY
CURDLE
DANDLE
DAWDLE
DEADLY
DIDDLE
DOODLE
FIDDLE
FONDLE
FONDLY
FUDDLE
GIRDLE
GLADLY
GOODLY
HANDLE
HARDLY
HEDDLE
HUDDLE
HURDLE
KINDLE
KINDLY
LEWDLY
LORDLY
LOUDLY
MEDDLE
MIDDLE
MILDLY
MUDDLE
NEEDLE
NODDLE
NOODLE
PADDLE
PEDDLE
POODLE
PUDDLE
PUDDLY
RADDLE
RIDDLE
RUDDLE
RUNDLE
SADDLE
TODDLE
WADDLE
WADDLY
WILDLY

•••D•L

AMIDOL
APODAL
BRIDAL
CAUDAL
DAEDAL
FEUDAL
HANDEL
MENDEL
MYRDAL
OXYDOL
RONDEL
SANDAL
SEIDEL
VANDAL

••••DL

DIRNDL

DM••••

DMAJOR
DMINOR
DMINUS
DMITRI

D•M•••

DAMAGE
DAMASK
DAMATO
DAMIEN
DAMITA
DAMMAR
DAMMED
DAMNED
DAMONE
DAMORE
DAMOUR
DAMPED
DAMPEN
DAMPER
DAMPLY
DAMSEL
DAMSON
DAMSUP
DEMAND
DEMEAN
DEMISE
DEMITS
DEMOBS
DEMODE
DEMOND
DEMONS
DEMOTE
DEMURE
DEMURS
DIMITY
DIMMED
DIMMER
DIMOUT
DIMPLE
DIMPLY
DIMSUM
DIMWIT
DOMAIN
DOMANI
DOMING
DOMINI
DOMINO
DUMBER
DUMBLY
DUMDUM
DUMONT
DUMPED
DUMPER

D••M••

DAIMON
DAIMYO
DAMMAR
DAMMED
DEEMED
DEIMOS
DERMAL
DERMIS
DESMAN
DIMMED
DIMMER
DISMAL
DISMAY
DISMES
DOGMAS
DOLMAN
DOLMAS
DOLMEN
DOOMED
DORMER
DRAMAS
DROMOI
DROMOS
DRUMUP
DUOMOS

D•••M•

DAGAMA
DANGME
DEARME
DECAMP
DEFAME
DENIMS
DHARMA
DODOMA
DOREMI
DREAMS
DREAMT
DREAMY
DYNAMO

D••••M

DEFORM
DIADEM
DIATOM
DICTUM
DIGRAM
DIMSUM
DIRHAM
DISARM
DORSUM
DUMDUM
DUMDUM
DUNHAM
DURHAM

•DM•••

ADMIRE
ADMITS
EDMOND
EDMUND

•D•M••

EDAMES

•D••M•

ADDAMS
ADEEMS
CDROMS
IDIOMS
ODIUMS

•D•••M

ADYTUM

••DM••

CADMIC
CADMUS
ENDMAN
ENDMEN
KIDMAN
MADMAN
MADMAX
MADMEN
OLDMAN
OLDMEN
RUDMAN
TODMAN

••D•M•

ADDAMS
BEDIMS
DODOMA
MADAME
MADAMS
MODEMS
OEDEMA
RADOME
SEDUMS

••D••M

BEDLAM
INDIUM
LUDLUM
MADTOM
MEDIUM
OLDHAM
PODIUM
RADIUM
REDEEM
REDGUM
RODHAM
SADDAM
SODIUM
TEDEUM
TEDIUM

•••DM•

RUNDMC

•••D•M

AIRDAM
ANADEM
BELDAM
DIADEM
DUMDUM
FANDOM
IBIDEM
MCADAM
RANDOM
SADDAM
SELDOM
TANDEM
WINDOM
WISDOM

D•N•••

DANANG
DANAUS
DANCED
DANCER
DANCES
DANDER
DANDIE
DANDLE
DANGER
DANGLE
DANGLY
DANGME
DANIEL
DANISH
DANKER
DANNAY
DANNER
DANSON
DANTES
DANTON
DANUBE
DANZIG
DENALI
DENDRI
DENDRO
DENGUE
DENIAL
DENIED
DENIER
DENIES
DENIMS
DENIRO
DENISE
DENNED
DENNIS
DENOTE
DENOVO
DENSER
DENTAL
DENTED
DENTIL
DENTIN
DENTON
DENUDE
DENVER
DENZEL
DINARS
DINEIN
DINEON
DINERO
DINERS
DINGED
DINGHY
DINGLE
DINGUS
DINING
DINKEY
DINNED
DINNER
DINTED
DONALD
DONATE
DONDER
DONEES
DONEIN
DONETS
DONEUP
DONITZ
DONJON
DONKEY
DONNAS
DONNED
DONNEE
DONNER
DONORS
DONUTS
DUNANT
DUNBAR
DUNCAN
DUNCES
DUNDEE
DUNERA
DUNHAM
DUNKED
DUNKER
DUNLIN
DUNLOP
DUNNED
DYNAMO
DYNAST

D••N••

DABNEY
DAINTY
DAMNED
DANNAY
DANNER
DARNAY
DARNED
DARNEL
DARNER
DARNIT
DAUNTS
DAWNED
DEANNA
DENNED
DENNIS
DINNED
DINNER
DIONEB
DIONNE
DIRNDL
DISNEY
DMINOR
DMINUS
DOINGS
DONNAS
DONNED
DONNEE
DONNER
DOWNED
DOWNER
DOWNEY
DOWNON
DRENCH
DRINGS
DRINKS
DRONED
DRONER
DRONES
DUENNA
DUNNED

D•••N•

DAMONE
DANANG
DAPHNE
DARING
DATING
DATONG
DAYONE
DAZING
DEANNA
DEBONE
DEBUNK
DECANT
DECENT
DEFEND
DEFINE
DEIGNS
DELANO
DELANY
DELONG
DEMAND
DEMOND
DEMONS
DEPEND
DEPONE
DETENT
DEVINE
DEWING
DICING
DIKING
DINING
DIONNE
DISANT
DIVANS
DIVINE
DIVING
DOCENT
DOESNT
DOGONS
DOLING
DOMANI
DOMING
DOMINI
DOMINO
DOPANT
DOPING
DOSING
DOTING
DOYENS
DOZENS
DOZING
DRAINS
DROWNS
DRYING
DRYINK
DUENNA
DUGONG
DUKING
DUMONT
DUNANT
DUPING
DUPONT
DURANT
DURING
DWAYNE
DYEING

D••••N

DACRON
DAIKON
DAIMON
DAIREN
DALTON
DAMIEN
DAMPEN
DAMSON
DANSON
DANTON
DARIEN
DARKEN
DARREN
DARWIN
DASSIN
DATSUN
DAWSON
DAYTON
DEACON
DEADEN
DEADON
DEAFEN
DEALIN
DEEPEN
DEHORN
DELEON
DEMEAN
DENTIN
DENTON
DESIGN
DESMAN
DETAIN
DEVEIN
DIDION
DIGSIN
DILLON
DINEIN
DINEON
DIOXIN
DISOWN
DIVEIN
DOBBIN
DOBLIN
DOBSON
DOESIN
DOLMAN
DOLMEN
DOMAIN
DONEIN
DONJON
DORIAN
DOTEON
DOTHAN
DOVEIN
DOWNON
DRAGIN
DRAGON
DRAWIN
DRAWON
DREWIN
DREWON
DRIVEN
DROPIN
DRYDEN
DRYRUN
DUBBIN
DUBLIN
DUCHIN
DUDEEN
DUNCAN
DUNLIN
DURBAN
DURBIN
DURIAN
DUSTIN

•DN•••

ADNATE

•D•N••

ADONAI
ADONIS
EDENIC
GDANSK
ODENSE
ODONTO

•D••N•

ADDEND
ADDING
ADDONS
ADORNS
ADRENO
ADVENT
EDGING
EDMOND
EDMUND
EDWYNN
IDLING
KDLANG

•D•••N

ADDSIN
ADDSON
ADJOIN
ADRIAN
ADRIEN
EDGEIN
EDISON
EDWYNN
ODDSON

••DN••

KIDNAP
KIDNEY
NUDNIK
RADNER
RODNEY
SIDNEY
SYDNEY

••D•N•

ADDEND
ADDING
ADDONS
AIDING
ALDINE
ARDENT
AUDENS
BIDING
BODING
BODONI
CADENT
CEDING
CODING
CODONS
ENDING
FADING
HIDING
INDENE
INDENT
IODINE
JADING
LADING
LADINO
LODENS
LUDENS
MEDINA
MODENA
MODINE
NADINE
ONDINE
PADANG
PEDANT
PODUNK
REDANT
REDINK
REDONE
RIDENT
RIDING
RODENT
SEDANS
SIDING
TIDING
UNDINE
UNDONE
WADING
WIDENS

••D••N

ADDSIN
ADDSON
ALDRIN
ANDEAN
BIDDEN
BIDSIN
BIDSON
BODKIN
DIDION
DUDEEN
ENDMAN
ENDMEN
ENDRUN
FADEIN
GIDEON
GODOWN
GODSON
GODWIN
GUDRUN
HADRON
HEDREN
HIDDEN
HUDSON
INDIAN
KIDMAN
LUDDEN
MADDEN
MADMAN
MADMEN
MEDIAN
MIDDEN
MODERN
MUDHEN
ODDSON
OLDMAN
OLDMEN
ORDAIN
PADUAN
PIDGIN
RADIAN
REDDEN
REDFIN
RIDDEN
RUDMAN
SADDEN
SODDEN
SUDDEN
TODMAN
WADEIN
WEDELN

•••DN•

NEEDNT

•••D•N

AVEDON
BIDDEN
BORDEN
BOUDIN
BURDEN
CAMDEN
CARDIN
CORDON
DEADEN
DEADON
DRYDEN
EMBDEN
FEEDON
FELDON
GARDEN
GOLDEN
GOODEN
GORDON
GRADIN
GRODIN
GUIDON
HANDIN
HANDON
HARDEN
HAYDEN
HEADIN
HEADON
HEIDEN
HELDIN
HELDON
HIDDEN
HOLDEN
HOLDON
HOYDEN
IBADAN
ICEDIN
JORDAN
LAIDIN
LAIDON
LANDON
LARDON
LEADEN
LEADIN
LEADON
LEIDEN
LEYDEN
LINDEN
LONDON
LOUDEN
LUDDEN
LUNDEN
LYNDON
MADDEN
MAIDEN
MALDEN
MANDAN
MIDDEN
PAIDIN
PARDON
READIN
REDDEN
RIDDEN
SADDEN
SENDIN
SLIDIN
SODDEN
SOLDAN
SOLDON
SUDDEN
SWEDEN
TENDON
TIEDIN
TILDEN
TOEDIN
VARDEN
VERDIN
VERDON
VERDUN
WALDEN
WARDEN
WOODEN

DO••••

DOABLE
DOBBER
DOBBIN
DOBLAS
DOBLIN
DOBRAS
DOBROS
DOBSON
DOCENT
DOCILE
DOCKED
DOCKER
DOCKET
DOCTOR
DODDER
DODECA
DODGED
DODGER
DODGES
DODODO
DODOES
DODOMA
DOESBY
DOESIN
DOESNT
DOESUP
DOFFED
DOGEAR
DOGGED
DOGGER
DOGGIE
DOGIES
DOGLEG
DOGMAS
DOGONS
DOGOOD
DOGSIT
DOGTAG
DOINGS
DOLING
DOLLAR
DOLLED

DOLLOP
DOLLUP
DOLMAN
DOLMAS
DOLMEN
DOLORS
DOMAIN
DOMANI
DOMING
DOMINI
DOMINO
DONALD
DONATE
DONDER
DONEES
DONEIN
DONETS
DONEUP
DONITZ
DONJON
DONKEY
DONNAS
DONNED
DONNEE
DONNER
DONORS
DONUTS
DOOBIE
DOODAD
DOODLE
DOOFUS
DOOGIE
DOOLEY
DOOMED
DOOWOP
DOOZIE
DOPANT
DOPIER
DOPING
DORADO
DORATI
DORCAS
DOREMI
DORIAN
DORIES
DORMER
DORRIT
DORSAL
DORSET
DORSEY
DORSUM
DOSAGE
DOSERS
DOSIDO
DOSING
DOSSAL
DOSSED
DOSSEL
DOSSER
DOSSES
DOTAGE
DOTARD
DOTELL
DOTEON
DOTHAN
DOTING
DOTTED
DOTTIE
DOTTLE
DOUBLE
DOUBLY
DOUBTS
DOUGHS
DOUGHY
DOURER
DOURLY
DOUSED
DOUSES
DOVEIN
DOVISH
DOWELS
DOWERS
DOWNED
DOWNER
DOWNEY
DOWNON
DOWSED
DOWSER
DOWSES
DOYENS
DOZENS
DOZERS
DOZILY
DOZING

D•O•••

DEODAR
DHOLES
DHOTEL
DHOTIS
DIODES
DIONEB
DIONNE
DIOXIN
DOOBIE
DOODAD
DOODLE
DOOFUS
DOOGIE
DOOLEY
DOOMED
DOOWOP
DOOZIE
DROGUE
DROIDS
DROITS
DROLLS
DROLLY
DROMOI
DROMOS
DRONED
DRONER
DRONES
DROOLS
DROOPS
DROOPY
DROPBY
DROPIN
DROPIT
DROVER
DROVES
DROWNS
DROWSE
DROWSY
DUOMOS
DVORAK

D••O••

DACOIT
DADOED
DADOES
DAKOTA
DAMONE
DAMORE
DAMOUR
DATONG
DAYONE
DEBONE
DECOCT
DECODE
DECORS
DECOYS
DEFOGS
DEFORM
DEHORN
DELONG
DEMOBS
DEMODE
DEMOND
DEMONS
DEMOTE
DENOTE
DENOVO
DEPONE
DEPORT
DEPOSE
DEPOTS
DESOTO
DETOUR
DEVOID
DEVOIR
DEVOTE
DEVOTO
DEVOUR
DEVOUT
DICOTS
DIEOFF
DIEOUT
DIGOUT
DIMOUT
DIPODY
DIPOLE
DISOWN
DIVOTS
DODODO
DODOES
DODOMA
DOGONS
DOGOOD
DOLORS
DONORS
DRHOOK
DROOLS
DROOPS
DROOPY
DRYOFF
DRYOUT
DUBOIS
DUGONG
DUGOUT
DUMONT
DUPONT
DUROCS

D•••O•

DACRON
DAIKON
DAIMON
DALTON
DAMSON
DANSON
DANTON
DARROW
DAWSON
DAYTON
DEACON
DEADON
DEBTOR
DEIMOS
DELEON
DENTON
DEPLOY
DESPOT
DETROP
DIALOG
DIATOM
DIDION
DIGLOT
DILLON
DINEON
DISCOS
DITTOS
DMAJOR
DMINOR
DOBROS
DOBSON
DOCTOR
DOGOOD
DOLLOP
DONJON
DOOWOP
DOTEON
DOWNON
DRAGON
DRAWON
DREWON
DRHOOK
DROMOI
DROMOS
DRYROT
DUNLOP
DUOMOS
DYELOT

D••••O

DACAPO
DADDYO
DAIMYO
DAMATO
DARETO
DAYGLO
DELANO
DELRIO
DENDRO
DENIRO
DENOVO
DESOTO
DEVITO
DEVOTO
DEXTRO
DIABLO
DINERO
DIRIGO
DODODO
DOMINO
DORADO
DOSIDO
DUELLO
DYNAMO

•DO•••

ADOBES
ADOLPH
ADONAI
ADONIS
ADOPTS
ADORED
ADOREE
ADORER
ADORES
ADORNS
IDOIDO
ODONTO
ODOURS

•D•O••

ADDONS
ADJOIN
ADROIT
ADSORB
CDROMS
EDDOES
EDMOND
IDIOCY
IDIOMS
IDIOTS
ODIOUS

•D••O•

ADDSON
EDISON
EDITOR
ODDJOB
ODDLOT
ODDSON

•D•••O

ADAGIO
ADDSTO
ADRENO
IDOIDO
ODONTO

••DO••

ADDONS
ALDOSE
ALDOUS
ARDORS
ARDOUR
BODONI
CODONS
DADOED
DADOES
DODODO
DODOES
DODOMA
EDDOES
EIDOLA
ENDORA
ENDOWS
EUDORA
FEDORA
GODOWN
HIDOUT
INDOOR
JUDOKA
KIDORY
LADOGA
LEDOFF
LEDOUT
MIDORI
MODOCS
NODOFF
NODOSE
OGDOAD
RADOME
REDOAK
REDOES
REDONE
RUDOLF
TUDORS
UNDOER
UNDOES
UNDONE
VADOSE
WIDOWS
ZADORA

••D•O•

ADDSON
ANDHOW
ANDROS
AUDIOS
BADLOT
BIDSON
DIDION
GIDEON
GODSON
HADRON
HUDSON
HYDROS
INDOOR
MADTOM
ODDJOB
ODDLOT
ODDSON
OLDBOY
RADIOS
REDDOG
REDFOX
REDHOT
REDSOX
REDTOP
RODEOS
VIDEOS

••D••O

ADDSTO
DADDYO
DODODO
ENDURO
HIDEHO
INDIGO
LADINO
MADEDO
MADERO
MADURO
MEDICO
MODULO
OLDPRO
SIDERO
TODDAO
ZYDECO

•••DO•

ABYDOS
AMADOU
AMIDOL
AVEDON
BANDOG
BARDOT
CANDOR
CAWDOR
CHADOR
CONDOR
CONDOS
CORDON
CREDOS
DEADON
FANDOM
FEEDON
FELDON
FYODOR
GORDON
GUIDON
GUNDOG
HANDON
HEADON
HELDON
HOLDON
HOODOO
HOTDOG
ISADOR
KINDOF
LAIDON
LANDON
LAPDOG
LARDON
LEADON
LONDON
LYNDON
MCADOO
MEADOW
OXYDOL
PARDON
PYEDOG
RANDOM
REDDOG
RONDOS
SEADOG
SELDOM
SHADOW
SOLDON
SUNDOG
TENDON
TOLDOF
TOPDOG
TOYDOG
VENDOR
VERDON
VOODOO
WINDOM
WINDOW
WISDOM
ZENDOS

•••D•O

AMEDEO
CARDIO
DADDYO
DENDRO
HELDTO
HOLDTO
HOODOO
LAIDTO
LANDHO
LEADTO
MCADOO
STUDIO
TENDTO
TODDAO
USEDTO
VOODOO

••••DO

AIKIDO
ALBEDO
BRANDO
DODODO
DORADO
DOSIDO
ESCUDO
HAIRDO
IDOIDO
JURADO
KOMODO
LAREDO
LIBIDO
MADEDO
MAKEDO
MIKADO
OVERDO
OVIEDO
PSEUDO
TEREDO
TOLEDO
TUXEDO
WEIRDO

D•P•••

DAPHNE
DAPPED
DAPPER
DAPPLE
DEPART
DEPAUL
DEPAUW
DEPEND
DEPICT
DEPLOY
DEPONE
DEPORT
DEPOSE
DEPOTS
DEPTHS
DEPUTE
DEPUTY
DIPODY
DIPOLE
DIPPED
DIPPER
DOPANT
DOPIER
DOPING
DUPERY
DUPING
DUPLEX
DUPONT

D••P••

DAMPED
DAMPEN
DAMPER
DAMPLY
DAPPED
DAPPER
DAPPLE
DEEPEN
DEEPER
DEEPLY
DELPHI
DESPOT
DIAPER
DIEPPE
DIMPLE
DIMPLY
DIPPED
DIPPER
DISPEL
DRAPED
DRAPER
DRAPES
DRIPPY
DROPBY
DROPIN
DROPIT
DRUPES
DUMPED
DUMPER

D•••P•

DACAPO
DIEPPE
DRIPPY
DROOPS
DROOPY

D••••P

DAMSUP
DECAMP
DETROP
DEWLAP
DIGSUP
DOESUP
DOLLOP
DOLLUP
DONEUP
DOOWOP
DRAWUP
DREWUP
DRUMUP
DSHARP
DUNLOP
DUSTUP

•D•P••

ADAPTS
ADEPTS
ADOPTS

•D••P•

ADOLPH

•D•••P

ADDSUP

••DP••

MUDPIE
OLDPRO

••D••P

ADDSUP
BIDSUP
ENDSUP
KIDNAP
MADCAP
MADEUP
REDCAP
REDTOP
TIDYUP
WADSUP

•••D•P

BEADUP
BINDUP
FOLDUP
HARDUP
HEADUP
HELDUP
HOLDUP
ICEDUP
LAIDUP
LEADUP
PAIDUP
SENDUP
SPEDUP
TEEDUP
TIEDUP
USEDUP
WINDUP

•••D•Q

NASDAQ

DR••••

DRABEK
DRABLY
DRAFTS
DRAFTY
DRAGEE
DRAGGY
DRAGIN
DRAGON
DRAILS
DRAINS
DRAKES
DRAMAS
DRAPED
DRAPER
DRAPES
DRAWER
DRAWIN
DRAWLS
DRAWON
DRAWUP
DRAYED
DREADS
DREAMS
DREAMT
DREAMY
DREARY
DREDGE
DRENCH
DRESSY
DREWIN
DREWON
DREWUP
DREXEL
DRHOOK
DRIERS
DRIEST
DRIFTS
DRILLS
DRINGS
DRINKS
DRIPPY
DRIVEL
DRIVEN
DRIVER
DRIVES
DROGUE
DROIDS
DROITS
DROLLS
DROLLY
DROMOI
DROMOS
DRONED
DRONER
DRONES
DROOLS
DROOPS
DROOPY
DROPBY
DROPIN
DROPIT
DROVER
DROVES
DROWNS
DROWSE
DROWSY
DRUDGE
DRUIDS
DRUMUP
DRUPES
DRUZES
DRYADS
DRYDEN
DRYERS
DRYEST
DRYFLY
DRYICE
DRYING
DRYINK
DRYOFF
DRYOUT
DRYROT
DRYRUN

D•R•••

DARETO
DARIEN
DARING
DARIUS
DARKEN
DARKER
DARKLE
DARKLY
DARNAY
DARNED
DARNEL
DARNER
DARNIT
DARREN
DARROW
DARRYL
DARTED
DARTER
DARWIN
DERAIL
DERIDE
DERIVE
DERMAL
DERMIS
DERRIS
DIRECT
DIREST
DIRGES
DIRHAM
DIRIGO
DIRNDL
DORADO
DORATI
DORCAS
DOREMI
DORIAN
DORIES
DORMER
DORRIT
DORSAL
DORSET
DORSEY
DORSUM
DURANT
DURBAN
DURBAR
DURBIN
DURESS
DURFEY
DURHAM
DURIAN
DURING
DUROCS
DURYEA

D••R••

DACRON
DAIREN
DARREN
DARROW
DARRYL
DEARER
DEARIE
DEARLY
DEARME
DEARTH
DEBRAS
DEBRIS
DECREE
DEFRAY
DEGREE
DELRAY
DELRIO
DERRIS
DETROP
DHARMA
DIGRAM
DJERBA
DOBRAS
DOBROS
DORRIT
DOURER
DOURLY
DRYROT
DRYRUN
DUARTE
DVORAK
DWARFS

D•••R•

DAMORE
DATARY
DATERS
DATURA
DEBARK
DEBARS
DECORS
DEFERS
DEFORM
DEHORN
DEIDRE
DEJURE
DEMURE
DEMURS
DENDRI
DENDRO
DENIRO
DEPART
DEPORT
DESCRY
DESERT
DESIRE
DESTRY
DETERS
DEXTRO
DICERS
DINARS
DINERO
DINERS
DISARM
DIVERS
DIVERT
DMITRI
DOLORS
DONORS
DOSERS
DOTARD
DOWERS
DOZERS
DREARY
DRIERS
DRYERS
DSHARP
DUNERA
DUPERY

D••••R

DAFTER
DAGGER
DAMMAR
DAMOUR
DAMPER
DANCER
DANDER
DANGER
DANKER
DANNER
DAPPER
DARKER
DARNER
DARTER
DASHER
DAUBER
DEADER
DEAFER
DEALER
DEARER
DEBTOR
DECKER
DEEPER
DEFTER
DEICER
DELVER
DENIER
DENSER
DENVER
DEODAR
DETOUR
DEVOIR
DEVOUR
DEWIER
DEXTER
DIALER
DIAPER
DICIER
DICKER
DIETER
DIFFER
DIGGER
DILLER
DIMMER
DINNER
DIPPER
DISBAR
DITHER
DLAYER
DMAJOR
DMINOR
DOBBER
DOCKER
DOCTOR
DODDER
DODGER
DOGEAR
DOGGER
DOLLAR
DONDER
DONNER
DOPIER
DORMER
DOSSER
DOURER
DOWNER
DOWSER
DRAPER
DRAWER
DRIVER
DRONER
DROVER
DUELER
DUFFER
DUIKER
DULLER
DUMBER
DUMPER
DUNBAR
DUNKER
DURBAR
DUSTER

•DR•••

ADRENO
ADRIAN
ADRIEN
ADRIFT
ADROIT
CDROMS

•D•R••

ADORED
ADOREE
ADORER
ADORES
ADORNS
EDERLE

•D••R•

ADDERS
ADHERE
ADJURE
ADMIRE
ADSORB
ADVERB
ADVERT
EDBERG
EDGARD
EDGARS
EDGERS
EDUARD
EDVARD
EDWARD
IDCARD
IDLERS
ODOURS
UDDERS

•D•••R

ADORER
EDGIER
EDITOR

••DR••

ALDRIN
ANDREA
ANDREI
ANDRES
ANDREW
ANDREY
ANDROS
AUDREY
CADRES
CEDRIC
ENDRUN
ESDRAS
GUDRUN
HADRON
HEDREN
HYDRAE
HYDRAS
HYDROS
INDRIS
MADRAS
MADRES
MADRID
MIDRIB
MUDRAS
PADRES
REDRAW
REDREW
UNDRAW

••D•R•

ADDERS
ALDERS
ARDORS
CEDARS
CIDERS
CODERS
CYDERS
EIDERS
ELDERS
ENDERS
ENDORA
ENDURE
ENDURO
EUDORA
FEDORA
GODARD
HIDERS
INDIRA
KIDORY
LADERS
MADERO
MADURA
MADURO
MIDORI
MODERN
NADIRS
OLDPRO
ORDERS
ORDURE
RIDERS
SEDERS
SIDERO
SIDERS
TUDORS
UDDERS
WADERS
ZADORA

••D••R

ARDOUR
BADGER
BIDDER
CADGER
CODGER
DODDER
DODGER
ENDEAR
FODDER
GADDER
HEDGER
INDOOR
JUDDER
KIDDER
LADDER
LADLER
LEDGER
LODGER
MADDER
MEDGAR
MEDLAR
MIDAIR
MIDLER
MUDDER
NUDGER
PADDER
PEDLAR
RADNER
REDDER
REDFIR
RUDDER
SADDER
SIDDUR
TEDDER
TIDIER
UNDOER
VEDDER

•••DR•
AIRDRY
DEIDRE
DENDRI
DENDRO
EXEDRA
LANDRY
PHEDRE
QUADRI
RANDRY
RUNDRY
SANDRA
SUNDRY
TAWDRY
TUNDRA

•••D•R
AGADIR
BALDER
BENDER
BIDDER
BINDER
BIRDER
BOLDER
BORDER
BRUDER
CALDER
CANDOR
CARDER
CAWDOR
CHADOR
CINDER
COLDER
CONDOR
COODER
CRUDER
DANDER
DEADER
DEODAR
DODDER
DONDER
EVADER
FEEDER
FENDER
FINDER
FODDER
FOLDER
FONDER
FYODOR
GADDER
GANDER
GENDER
GILDER
GIRDER
GLIDER
GRADER
HARDER
HEADER
HERDER
HINDER
HOLDER
ISADOR
JUDDER
KANDER
KIDDER
KINDER
LADDER
LANDER
LARDER
LAUDER
LEADER
LENDER
LEWDER
LIEDER
LOADER
LOUDER
MADDER
MENDER
MILDER
MINDER
MOLDER
MUDDER
MURDER
PADDER
PANDER
PINDAR
POLDER
PONDER
POWDER
RAIDER
READER
REDDER
RENDER
RUDDER
SADDER
SANDER
SEEDER
SENDER
SIDDUR
SIRDAR
SLIDER
SNIDER
SNYDER
SOLDER
SPADER
SPIDER
SUNDER
TEDDER
TENDER
TINDER
TRADER
VEDDER
VENDOR
WANDER
WARDER
WEEDER
WELDER
WILDER
WINDER
WONDER
YONDER
ZANDER
ZUIDER

••••DR
ANHYDR
RATEDR

DS••••
DSHARP

D•S•••
DASHED
DASHER
DASHES
DASSIN
DESALT
DESCRY
DESERT
DESICA
DESIGN
DESILU
DESIRE
DESIST
DESMAN
DESOTO
DESPOT
DESTRY
DISANT
DISARM
DISBAR
DISCOS
DISCUS
DISHED
DISHES
DISKED
DISMAL
DISMAY
DISMES
DISNEY
DISOWN
DISPEL
DISSED
DISTAL
DISTIL
DISUSE
DOSAGE
DOSERS
DOSIDO
DOSING
DOSSAL
DOSSED
DOSSEL
DOSSER
DOSSES
DUSTED
DUSTER
DUSTIN
DUSTUP

D••S••
DAISES
DAMSEL
DAMSON
DAMSUP
DANSON
DASSIN
DATSUN
DAWSON
DEISTS
DENSER
DIESEL
DIESES
DIESIS
DIGSIN
DIGSUP
DILSEY
DIMSUM
DISSED
DOBSON
DOESBY
DOESIN
DOESNT
DOESUP
DOGSIT
DORSAL
DORSET
DORSEY
DORSUM
DOSSAL
DOSSED
DOSSEL
DOSSER
DOSSES
DOUSED
DOUSES
DOWSED
DOWSER
DOWSES
DRESSY

D•••S•
DALASI
DAMASK
DANISH
DEBASE
DEFUSE
DEGUST
DELIST
DEMISE
DENISE
DEPOSE
DESIST
DETEST
DEVEST
DEVISE
DIGEST
DIREST
DISUSE
DIVEST
DOVISH
DRESSY
DRIEST
DROWSE
DROWSY
DRYEST
DURESS
DYNAST

D••••S
DACHAS
DADOES
DAISES
DALLAS
DALLES
DANAUS
DANCES
DANTES
DARIUS
DASHES
DATERS
DAUBES
DAUNTS
DAVIES
DAVITS
DEBARS
DEBITS
DEBRAS
DEBRIS
DEBUGS
DEBUTS
DECAFS
DECALS
DECAYS
DECORS
DECOYS
DEFATS
DEFERS
DEFIES
DEFOGS
DEICES
DEIGNS
DEIMOS
DEISTS
DELAYS
DELFTS
DELIUS
DELTAS
DELVES
DEMITS
DEMOBS
DEMONS
DEMURS
DENIES
DENIMS
DENNIS
DEPOTS
DEPTHS
DERMIS
DERRIS
DETERS
DEUCES
DEVILS
DHOLES
DHOTIS
DICERS
DICOTS
DIDIES
DIESES
DIESIS
DIGITS
DINARS
DINERS
DINGUS
DIODES
DIRGES
DISCOS
DISCUS
DISHES
DISMES
DITTOS
DITZES
DIVANS
DIVERS
DIVOTS
DIXITS
DMINUS
DOBLAS
DOBRAS
DOBROS
DODGES
DODOES
DOGIES
DOGMAS
DOGONS
DOINGS
DOLMAS
DOLORS
DONEES
DONETS
DONNAS
DONORS
DONUTS
DOOFUS
DORCAS
DORIES
DOSERS
DOSSES
DOUBTS
DOUGHS
DOUSES
DOWELS
DOWERS
DOWSES
DOYENS
DOZENS
DOZERS
DRAFTS
DRAILS
DRAINS
DRAKES
DRAMAS
DRAPES
DRAWLS
DREADS
DREAMS
DRIERS
DRIFTS
DRILLS
DRINGS
DRINKS
DRIVES
DROIDS
DROITS
DROLLS
DROMOS
DRONES
DROOLS
DROOPS
DROVES
DROWNS
DRUIDS
DRUPES
DRUZES
DRYADS
DRYERS
DUBOIS
DUCATS
DULLES
DUNCES
DUOMOS
DURESS
DUROCS
DUTIES
DUVETS
DWARFS
DWEEBS
DWELLS

•DS•••
ADSORB
EDSELS

•D•S••
ADDSIN
ADDSON
ADDSTO
ADDSUP
ADESTE
EDESSA
EDISON
ODDSON
ODESSA
ODISTS

•D••S•
ADJUST
ADVISE
EDESSA
GDANSK
IDLEST
ODDEST
ODENSE
ODESSA

•D•••S
ADAGES
ADAPTS
ADDAMS
ADDERS
ADDLES
ADDONS
ADEEMS
ADEPTS
ADIDAS
ADIEUS
ADLIBS
ADMITS
ADOBES
ADONIS
ADOPTS
ADORES
ADORNS
ADULTS
CDROMS
EDAMES
EDDIES
EDDOES
EDGARS
EDGERS
EDICTS
EDILES
EDSELS
EDUCES
IDEALS
IDIOMS
IDIOTS
IDLERS
IDYLLS
ODIOUS
ODISTS
ODIUMS
ODOURS
UDDERS

••DS••
ADDSIN
ADDSON
ADDSTO
ADDSUP
BIDSIN
BIDSON
BIDSUP
ENDSUP
GODSON
HUDSON
ODDSON
REDSEA
REDSOX
SUDSED
SUDSES
WADSUP

••D•S•
ALDOSE
ELDEST
EMDASH
ENDASH
ENDUSE
MEDUSA
MODEST
MODISH
NODOSE
NUDIST
ODDEST
OLDEST
OLDISH
RADISH
RUDEST
VADOSE
WIDEST

••D••S
ADDAMS
ADDERS
ADDLES
ADDONS
ALDERS
ALDOUS
ANDRES
ANDROS
AODAIS
ARDEBS
ARDORS
AUDENS
AUDIOS
AUDITS
BADGES
BEDEWS
BEDIMS
BODIES
BUDGES
CADDIS
CADETS
CADGES
CADMUS
CADRES
CEDARS
CIDERS
CODERS
CODONS
CYDERS
DADOES
DIDIES
DODGES
DODOES
EDDIES
EDDOES
EIDERS
ELDERS
ENDERS
ENDOWS
ENDUES
ESDRAS
FUDGES
GODETS
HADJES
HADJIS
HEDGES
HIDERS
HODADS
HYDRAS
HYDROS
INDIES
INDRIS
JUDGES
KEDGES
KUDZUS
LADERS
LADIES
LADLES
LEDGES
LODENS
LODGES
LUDENS
MADAMS
MADRAS
MADRES
MEDALS
MEDIAS
MEDICS
MIDGES
MODELS
MODEMS
MODOCS
MUDRAS
NADIRS
NUDGES
OLDIES
OODLES
ORDERS
PADRES
PEDALS
RADIOS
RADIUS
REDOES
REDUBS
REDYES
RIDERS
RIDGES
RODEOS
SEDANS
SEDERS
SEDGES
SEDUMS
SIDERS
SIDLES
SUDSES
TIDIES
TUDORS
UDDERS
UNDIES
UNDOES
VIDEOS
WADERS
WEDGES
WIDENS
WIDOWS
WIDTHS
YODELS

•••DS•
AMIDST
WOODSY

•••D•S
ABIDES
ABODES
ABYDOS
ADIDAS
AMADIS
AMIDES
ANODES
ASIDES
ATODDS
BLADES
BRIDES
BSIDES
CADDIS
CHIDES
CNIDUS
CONDOS
CREDOS
DIODES
ELIDES
ELUDES
EPODES
ERODES
ETUDES
EVADES
EXODUS
EXUDES
GEODES
GLADES
GLADYS
GLIDES
GRADES
GRADUS
GUIDES
HAIDAS
HINDUS
HORDES
HYADES
IRIDES
LANDIS
MAHDIS
MAIDUS
MENDES
OXIDES
PANDAS
PINDUS
PRIDES
PRUDES
RHODES
RONDOS
SARDIS
SAUDIS
SHADES
SLIDES
SONDES
SPADES
SUEDES
SWEDES
TILDES
TRADES
VELDTS
ZENDOS

••••DS
ALKYDS
AMENDS
APHIDS
AROIDS
ATODDS
AVOIDS
AWARDS
BEARDS
BIPEDS
BIPODS
BLEEDS
BLENDS
BLINDS
BLONDS
BOARDS
BOUNDS
BOVIDS
BRAIDS
BRANDS
BREADS
BREEDS
BROADS
BROODS
BUILDS
CANIDS
CHILDS
CHORDS
CLOUDS
CREEDS
CROWDS
CUPIDS
CYCADS
DREADS
DROIDS
DRUIDS
DRYADS
EBONDS
ELANDS
EMBEDS
EMENDS
EPHODS
FARADS
FIELDS
FIENDS
FIORDS
FJELDS
FJORDS
FLOODS
FLUIDS
FOUNDS
FRAUDS
FRONDS
GLANDS
GOURDS
GRANDS
GRINDS
GUARDS
GUILDS
HEXADS
HOARDS
HODADS
HOUNDS
JIHADS
KNEADS
LAIRDS
LAMEDS
LIPIDS
LLOYDS
MONADS
MOPEDS
MOULDS
MOUNDS
NAIADS
NOMADS
OCTADS
OREADS
OVOIDS
PLAIDS
PLEADS
POUNDS
PSEUDS
RANIDS
RAPIDS
REBIDS
RESODS
REWEDS
ROUNDS
SALADS
SARODS
SCALDS
SCENDS
SCOLDS
SCRODS
SHARDS
SHREDS
SKALDS
SNOODS
SOLIDS
SOUNDS
SPEEDS
SPENDS
SQUADS
SQUIDS
STANDS
STEADS
STEEDS
STRADS
SWARDS
SWORDS
SYNODS
TBIRDS
TBONDS
THIRDS
TREADS
TRENDS
TRIADS
TWEEDS
UPENDS
URSIDS
VIANDS
WIELDS
WORLDS
WOUNDS
YIELDS
ZOUNDS

D•T•••
DATARY
DATERS
DATING
DATIVE
DATONG
DATSUN
DATURA
DETACH
DETAIL
DETAIN
DETECT
DETENT
DETERS
DETEST
DETOUR
DETROP
DITHER
DITTOS
DITZES
DOTAGE
DOTARD
DOTELL
DOTEON
DOTHAN
DOTING
DOTTED
DOTTIE
DOTTLE
DUTIES

D••T••
DACTYL
DAFTER
DALTON
DANTES
DANTON
DARTED
DARTER
DAYTON
DEBTOR
DEFTER
DEFTLY
DELTAS
DELTIC
DENTAL
DENTED
DENTIL
DENTIN
DENTON
DEPTHS
DESTRY
DEXTER
DEXTRO
DHOTEL
DHOTIS
DIATOM
DICTUM
DIETED
DIETER
DIKTAT
DINTED
DISTAL
DISTIL
DITTOS
DMITRI
DOCTOR
DOGTAG
DOTTED
DOTTIE
DOTTLE
DUCTAL
DUSTED
DUSTER
DUSTIN
DUSTUP

D•••T•
DAINTY
DAKOTA
DALETH
DAMATO
DAMITA
DARETO
DAUNTS
DAVITS
DEARTH
DEBATE
DEBITS
DEBUTS
DEFATS
DEISTS
DELATE
DELETE
DELFTS
DEMITS
DEMOTE
DENOTE
DEPOTS
DEPUTE
DEPUTY
DESOTO
DEVITO
DEVOTE
DEVOTO
DEWITT
DICOTS
DIGITS
DILATE
DILUTE
DIMITY
DIVOTS
DIXITS
DONATE
DONETS
DONITZ
DONUTS
DORATI
DOUBTS
DRAFTS
DRAFTY
DRIFTS
DROITS
DUARTE
DUCATS
DULUTH
DUVETS

D••••T
DACOIT
DARNIT
DAYLIT
DECANT
DECEIT
DECENT
DECOCT
DEDUCT
DEFEAT
DEFECT
DEGUST
DEJECT
DELICT
DELIST
DEPART
DEPICT
DEPORT
DESALT
DESERT
DESIST
DESPOT
DETECT
DETENT
DETEST
DEVEST
DEVOUT
DEWITT
DIDACT
DIEOUT
DIGEST
DIGLOT
DIGOUT
DIKTAT
DIMOUT
DIMWIT
DIRECT
DIREST
DISANT
DIVERT
DIVEST
DOCENT
DOCKET
DOESNT
DOGSIT
DOPANT
DORRIT
DORSET
DREAMT
DRIEST
DROPIT
DRYEST
DRYOUT
DRYROT
DUGOUT
DULCET
DUMONT
DUNANT
DUPONT
DURANT
DWIGHT
DYELOT
DYNAST

•D•T••
ADYTUM
EDITED
EDITOR
ODETTA
ODETTE

•D••T•
ADAPTS
ADDSTO
ADEPTS
ADESTE
ADMITS
ADNATE
ADOPTS
ADULTS
EDICTS
IDEATE
IDIOTS
ODDITY
ODETTA
ODETTE
ODISTS
ODONTO

•D•••T
ADDUCT
ADJUST
ADRIFT
ADROIT
ADVENT
ADVERT
IDLEST
ODDEST
ODDLOT

••DT••
MADTOM
REDTAG
REDTOP
WIDTHS

••D•T•
ADDSTO
AUDITS
CADETS
GODETS
INDITE
IODATE
JUDITH
NUDITY
ODDITY
PEDATE
REDATE
SEDATE
TODATE
UPDATE

••D••T
ABDUCT
ADDUCT
ARDENT
BADLOT
BUDGET
CADENT
DEDUCT
DIDACT
ELDEST
FIDGET
GADGET
GIDGET
GODWIT
HIDOUT
INDEBT
INDENT
INDICT
INDUCT
LEDOUT
MADEIT
MEDLAT
MIDGET
MODELT
MODEST
MUDCAT
NUDIST
ODDEST
ODDLOT
OLDEST
OLDHAT
PEDANT
REDACT
REDANT
REDHAT
REDHOT
RIDENT
RODENT
RUDEST
TIDBIT
WIDEST
WIDGET

•••DT•
HELDTO
HOLDTO
LAIDTO
LEADTO
TENDTO
USEDTO
VELDTS

•••D•T
AMIDST

BANDIT
BARDOT
COEDIT
CREDIT
HOLDIT
NEEDNT
PANDIT
PUNDIT
REEDIT

••••DT
ARENDT
BRANDT

DU••••
DUALLY
DUARTE
DUBBED
DUBBIN
DUBCEK
DUBLIN
DUBOIS
DUCATS
DUCHIN
DUCKED
DUCTAL
DUDEEN
DUDLEY
DUELED
DUELER
DUELLO
DUENNA
DUFFEL
DUFFER
DUGONG
DUGOUT
DUIKER
DUKING
DULCET
DULLEA
DULLED
DULLER
DULLES
DULUTH
DUMBER
DUMBLY
DUMDUM
DUMONT
DUMPED
DUMPER
DUNANT
DUNBAR
DUNCAN
DUNCES
DUNDEE
DUNERA
DUNHAM
DUNKED
DUNKER
DUNLIN
DUNLOP
DUNNED
DUOMOS
DUPERY
DUPING
DUPLEX
DUPONT
DURANT
DURBAN
DURBAR
DURBIN
DURESS
DURFEY
DURHAM
DURIAN
DURING
DUROCS
DURYEA
DUSTED
DUSTER
DUSTIN
DUSTUP
DUTIES
DUVALL
DUVETS

D•U•••
DAUBED
DAUBER
DAUBES
DAUNTS
DEUCED
DEUCES
DOUBLE
DOUBLY
DOUBTS
DOUGHS
DOUGHY
DOURER
DOURLY
DOUSED
DOUSES
DRUDGE
DRUIDS
DRUMUP
DRUPES
DRUZES

D••U••
DANUBE
DATURA
DEBUGS
DEBUNK
DEBUTS
DEDUCE
DEDUCT
DEFUSE
DEGUST
DEJURE
DELUDE
DELUGE
DELUXE
DEMURE
DEMURS
DENUDE
DEPUTE
DEPUTY
DILUTE
DISUSE
DONUTS
DULUTH

D•••U•
DAMOUR
DAMSUP
DANAUS
DARIUS
DATSUN
DELIUS
DENGUE
DEPAUL
DEPAUW
DETOUR
DEVOUR
DEVOUT
DICTUM
DIEOUT
DIGOUT
DIGSUP
DIMOUT
DIMSUM
DINGUS
DISCUS
DMINUS
DOESUP
DOLLUP
DONEUP
DOOFUS
DORSUM
DRAWUP
DREWUP
DROGUE
DRUMUP
DRYOUT
DRYRUN
DUGOUT
DUMDUM
DUSTUP
DYBBUK

D••••U
DEJAVU
DESILU

•DU•••
ADULTS
EDUARD
EDUCED
EDUCES

•D•U••
ADDUCE
ADDUCT
ADJURE
ADJUST
ADZUKI
EDMUND
ODIUMS
ODOURS

•D••U•
ADDSUP
ADIEUS
ADIEUX
ADYTUM
ODIOUS

••DU••
ABDUCT
ADDUCE
ADDUCT
MAIDUS
DEDUCE
DEDUCT
ENDUED
ENDUES
ENDURE
ENDURO
ENDUSE
INDUCE
INDUCT
MADURA
MADURO
MEDUSA
MODULE
MODULO
NODULE
ORDURE
PADUAN
PODUNK
RADULA
REDUBS
REDUCE
SEDUCE
SEDUMS
UNDULY

••D•U•
ADDSUP
ALDOUS
ARDOUR
BADGUY
BEDAUB
BEDBUG
BIDSUP
CADMUS
ENDRUN
ENDSUP
GUDRUN
HIDOUT
INDIUM
KUDZUS
LEDOUT
LUDLUM
MADEUP
MEDIUM
PODIUM
RADIUM
RADIUS
REDBUD
REDGUM
SIDDUR
SODIUM
TEDEUM
TEDIUM
TIDYUP
WADSUP

•••DU•
BEADUP
BINDUP
CNIDUS
DUMDUM
EXODUS
FOLDUP
FONDUE
GRADUS
HARDUP
HEADUP
HELDUP
HINDUS
HOLDUP
ICEDUP
LAIDUP
LEADUP
MAIDUS
MARDUK
PAIDUP
PERDUE
PINDUS
PURDUE
SENDUP
SIDDUR
SPEDUP
SUBDUE
TEEDUP
TIEDUP
USEDUP
VERDUN
WINDUP

•••D•U
AMADOU
LANDAU
MOLDAU

••••DU
MBUNDU
TELEDU
XANADU

DV••••
DVORAK

D•V•••
DAVIES
DAVITS
DEVEIN
DEVEST
DEVICE
DEVILS
DEVINE
DEVISE
DEVITO
DEVOID
DEVOIR
DEVOTE
DEVOTO
DEVOUR
DEVOUT
DIVANS
DIVEIN
DIVERS
DIVERT
DIVEST
DIVIDE
DIVINE
DIVING
DIVOTS
DOVEIN
DOVISH
DUVALL
DUVETS

D••V••
DELVED
DELVER
DELVES
DENVER
DRIVEL
DRIVEN
DRIVER
DRIVES
DROVER
DROVES

D•••V•
DATIVE
DEJAVU
DENOVO
DERIVE

•DV•••
ADVENT
ADVERB
ADVERT
ADVICE
ADVISE
EDVARD

••DV••
KIDVID
OLDVIC

••D•V•
ENDIVE
GODIVA

DW••••
DWARFS
DWAYNE
DWEEBS
DWELLS
DWIGHT

D•W•••
DAWDLE
DAWNED
DAWSON
DEWIER
DEWING
DEWITT
DEWLAP
DOWELS
DOWERS
DOWNED
DOWNER
DOWNEY
DOWNON
DOWSED
DOWSER
DOWSES

D••W••
DARWIN
DIMWIT
DOOWOP
DRAWER
DRAWIN
DRAWLS
DRAWON
DRAWUP
DREWIN
DREWON
DREWUP
DROWNS
DROWSE
DROWSY

D•••W•
DISOWN

D••••W
DARROW
DEPAUW

•DW•••
ADWEEK
EDWARD
EDWYNN

••DW••
GODWIN
GODWIT
LUDWIG
MIDWAY

••D•W•
BEDEWS
ENDOWS
GODOWN
WIDOWS

••D••W
ANDHOW
ANDREW
REDRAW
REDREW
UNDRAW

•••D•W
MEADOW
MILDEW
SHADOW
SUNDEW
WINDOW

D•X•••
DEXTER
DEXTRO
DIXITS

D••X••
DIOXIN
DREXEL

D•••X•
DELUXE

D••••X
DUPLEX

•D•••X
ADIEUX

••D••X
MADMAX
REDFOX
REDSOX

•••D•X
BENDIX
CAUDEX
SPADIX
WINDEX

••••DX
BRANDX
RATEDX

DY••••
DYADIC
DYBBUK
DYEING
DYELOT
DYNAMO
DYNAST

D•Y•••
DAYBED
DAYGLO
DAYLIT
DAYONE
DAYTON
DOYENS
DRYADS
DRYDEN
DRYERS
DRYEST
DRYFLY
DRYICE
DRYING
DRYINK
DRYOFF
DRYOUT
DRYROT
DRYRUN

D••Y••
DLAYER
DRAYED
DURYEA
DWAYNE

D•••Y•
DACTYL
DADDYO
DAIMYO
DARRYL
DECAYS
DECOYS
DELAYS

D••••Y
DABNEY
DAILEY
DAINTY
DAMPLY
DANGLY
DANNAY
DARKLY
DARNAY
DATARY
DEADLY
DEARLY
DEEJAY
DEEPLY
DEFRAY
DEFTLY
DELANY
DELRAY
DEPLOY
DEPUTY
DESCRY
DESTRY
DICKEY
DILSEY
DIMITY
DIMPLY
DINGHY
DINKEY
DIPODY
DISMAY
DISNEY
DOESBY
DONKEY
DOOLEY
DORSEY
DOUBLY
DOUGHY
DOURLY
DOWNEY
DOZILY
DRABLY
DRAFTY
DRAGGY
DREAMY
DREARY
DRESSY
DRIPPY
DROLLY
DROOPY
DROPBY
DROWSY
DRYFLY
DUALLY
DUDLEY
DUMBLY
DUPERY
DURFEY

•DY•••
ADYTUM
IDYLLS

•D•Y••
EDWYNN

•D•••Y
EDGILY
IDIOCY
ODDITY

••DY••
REDYED
REDYES
TIDYUP
UNDYED

••D•Y•
DADDYO
REDEYE

••D••Y
ANDREY
AUDREY
BADGUY
BODILY
CODIFY
CUDDLY
DUDLEY
GADFLY
KIDNEY
KIDORY
KODALY
MEDLEY
MIDDAY
MIDWAY
MODIFY
NUDITY
ODDITY
OLDBOY
PUDDLY
REDBAY
RIDLEY
RODNEY
RUDELY
SIDNEY
SYDNEY
TEDKEY
TIDILY
UNDULY
WADDLY
WIDELY

•••DY•
AZODYE
DADDYO
GLADYS
TIEDYE

•••D•Y
ACIDLY
AIRDRY
ALLDAY
ARIDLY
AVIDLY
BALDLY
BENDAY
BOLDLY
COLDLY
CORDAY
CRUDDY
CUDDLY
DEADLY
FONDLY
FREDDY
FRIDAY
GLADLY
GOODBY
GOODLY
HARDLY
HEYDAY
KINDLY
LAIDBY
LANDRY
LEWDLY
LORDLY
LOUDLY
MANDAY
MAYDAY
MIDDAY
MILDLY
MONDAY
OFFDAY
ONEDAY
PAYDAY
PUDDLY
RANDRY
RUNDRY
SHODDY
SLUDGY
SMUDGY
STODGY
SUNDAY
SUNDRY
TAGDAY
TAWDRY
WADDLY
WILDLY
WOODSY

••••DY
BLOODY
BRANDY
BROODY
CLOUDY
COMEDY
CRUDDY
DIPODY
EMBODY
FREDDY
GREEDY
GRUNDY
MALADY
MAUNDY
MELODY
MILADY
MONODY
MOULDY
NOBODY
PARODY
REMEDY
SHANDY
SHEEDY
SHINDY
SHODDY
SPEEDY
STEADY
STURDY
TRENDY
TWEEDY
UNTIDY

D•Z•••
DAZING
DAZZLE
DOZENS
DOZERS
DOZILY
DOZING

D••Z••
DANZIG
DAZZLE
DENZEL
DITZES
DOOZIE
DRUZES

D••••Z
DONITZ

•DZ•••
ADZUKI

••DZ••
KUDZUS

••D•Z•
BEDAZE
IODIZE

•••D•Z
VALDEZ

EA••••
EAGLED
EAGLES
EAGLET
EAGRES
EALING
EARFUL
EARING
EARLAP
EARNED
EARNER
EARTHA
EARTHY
EARWAX
EARWIG
EASEIN
EASELS
EASEUP
EASIER
EASILY
EASING
EASTER
EASTON
EATERS
EATERY
EATING
EATOUT
EATSAT
EATSIN
EATSUP

E•A•••
ECARTE
EDAMES
ELAINE
ELANDS
ELAPID
ELAPSE
ELATED
ELATER
ELATES
ELAYER
ELAYNE
EMAILS
EMAJOR
ENABLE
ENACTS
ENAMEL
ENAMOR
ENATES
EPARCH
ERASED
ERASER
ERASES
ETALIA
ETALII
EVADED
EVADER
EVADES
EXACTA
EXACTO
EXACTS
EXALTS
EXARCH

E••A••
EBOATS
ECLAIR
ECLATS
EDGARD
EDGARS
EDUARD
EDVARD
EDWARD
EFFACE
EFLATS
ELPASO
EMBANK
EMBARK
EMBAYS
EMDASH
ENCAGE
ENCAMP
ENCASE
ENDALL
ENDASH
ENFANT
ENGAGE
ENLACE
ENRAGE
ENRAPT
ENTAIL
EPHAHS
EQUALS
EQUATE
ERGATE
ERHARD
ERNANI
ERRAND
ERRANT
ERRATA
ERSATZ
ESCAPE
ESCARP
ESHARP
ESPANA
ESSAYS
ESTATE
ETHANE
EXHALE
EXPAND
EXTANT

E•••A•
EARLAP
EARWAX
EATSAT
ELFMAN
ELIJAH
EMQUAD
ENDEAR
ENDMAN
ENGRAM
ENNEAD
ENQUAD
ENTRAP
ENWRAP
EOLIAN
EONIAN
EPICAL
ESDRAS
ESPIAL
EXTRAS

E••••A
EARTHA
EDESSA
EGERIA
EGESTA
EIDOLA
EJECTA
ELISHA
ELISSA
ELMIRA
ELVIRA
EMILIA
ENCINA
ENDORA
ENIGMA
EROICA
ERRATA
ESPANA
ESPOSA
ETALIA
EUBOEA
EUDORA
EUPNEA
EUREKA
EUROPA
EXACTA
EXEDRA

•EA•••
BEACON
BEADED
BEADLE
BEADUP
BEAGLE
BEAKED
BEAKER
BEAMED
BEAMUP
BEANED
BEANIE
BEANOS
BEARDS
BEARER
BEARON
BEARUP
BEASTS
BEATEN
BEATER
BEATIT
BEATLE
BEATON
BEATTY
BEATUP
BEAUTS
BEAUTY
BEAVER
CEASED
CEASES
DEACON
DEADEN
DEADER
DEADLY
DEADON
DEAFEN
DEAFER
DEALER
DEALIN
DEANNA
DEARER
DEARIE
DEARLY
DEARME
DEARTH
FEALTY
FEARED
FEARER
FEASTS
GEARED
GEARTO
GEARUP
HEADED
HEADER
HEADIN
HEADON
HEADUP
HEALED
HEALER
HEALTH
HEAPED
HEARER
HEAROF
HEARST
HEARTH
HEARTS
HEARTY
HEARYE
HEATED
HEATER
HEATHS
HEATUP
HEAVED
HEAVEN
HEAVER
HEAVES
JEANNE
KEATON
LEADED
LEADEN
LEADER
LEADIN
LEADON
LEADTO
LEADUP
LEAFED
LEAGUE
LEAKED
LEAKER
LEAKEY
LEALTY
LEANED
LEANER
LEANLY
LEANON
LEANTO
LEAPED
LEAPER
LEARNS
LEARNT
LEASED
LEASER
LEASES
LEAVED
LEAVEN
LEAVES
MEADOW
MEAGER
MEAGRE
MEALIE
MEANER
MEANIE
MEANLY
MEASLY
NEARBY
NEARED
NEARER
NEARLY
NEARTO
NEATEN
NEATER
NEATLY
PEACHY
PEAHEN
PEAKED
PEALED
PEANUT
PEAPOD
PEARLS
PEARLY
PEAVEY
REACTS
READER
READIN
REAGAN
REAIRS
REALER
REALES
REALIA
REALLY
REALMS
REALTY
REAMED
REAMER
REAPED
REAPER
REARED
REARER
REARMS
REARUP
REASON
REATAS
SEABAG
SEABED
SEABEE
SEACOW
SEADOG
SEAFAN
SEAFOX
SEAGAL
SEALAB
SEALED
SEALER
SEALUP
SEAMAN
SEAMED
SEAMEN
SEAMUS
SEANCE
SEARCH
SEARED
SEARLE
SEASON
SEATED
SEATER
SEAWAY
TEABAG
TEACUP
TEAMED
TEAMUP
TEAPOT
TEAPOY
TEARAT
TEARED
TEARUP
TEASED
TEASEL
TEASER
TEASES
TEASET
WEAKEN
WEAKER

WEAKLY
WEALTH
WEANED
WEAPON
WEARER
WEASEL
WEAVED
WEAVER
WEAVES
YEAGER
YEARLY
YEARNS
YEASTS
YEASTY
ZEALOT

•E•A••

AERATE
BECALM
BECAME
BEDAUB
BEDAZE
BEFALL
BEHALF
BEHAVE
BELAIR
BELAYS
BERATE
BESANT
BETAKE
BEWAIL
BEWARE
BEZANT
CEDARS
CERATE
CESARE
CETANE
DEBARK
DEBARS
DEBASE
DEBATE
DECADE
DECAFS
DECALS
DECAMP
DECANT
DECAYS
DEFACE
DEFAME
DEFATS
DEGAGE
DEJAVU
DEKALB
DELANO
DELANY
DELATE
DELAYS
DEMAND
DENALI
DEPART
DEPAUL
DEPAUW
DERAIL
DESALT
DETACH
DETAIL
DETAIN
FEMALE
GELADA
GELATI
GELATO
GEMARA
GERALD
GERARD
HECATE
HEGARI
HEMATO
HERALD
HEXADS
KEBABS
KERALA
LEGACY
LEGALS
LEGATE
LEGATO
LELAND
LEMANS
LENAPE
LESAGE
LEVANT
MEDAKA
MEDALS
MEGALO
MEGARA
MELANO
MENACE
MENAGE
MESABI
METALS
METATE
NEGATE
NEMATO
NEPALI
NEVADA
NEWAGE
NEWARK
PECANS
PEDALS
PEDANT
PEDATE
PELAGE
PENANG
PESACH
PETAIN
PETALS
PETARD
REBAGS
REBARS
REBATE
RECALL
RECANE
RECANT
RECAPS
RECAST
REDACT
REDANT
REDATE
REFACE
REGAIN
REGALE
REGARD
REHANG
REHASH
RELACE
RELAID
RELATE
RELAYS
REMADE
REMAIL
REMAIN
REMAKE
REMAND
REMANS
REMAPS
REMARK
RENAIL
RENAME
RENATA
REPAID
REPAIR
REPAND
REPAST
REPAVE
REPAYS
RERATE
RESALE
RESALT
RESAND
RETAGS
RETAIL
RETAIN
RETAKE
RETAPE
RETAPS
RETARD
RETARS
REVAMP
REWARD
REWARM
REWASH
SECANT
SEDAKA
SEDANS
SEDATE
SEJANT
SENARY
SENATE
SEPALS
SERACS
SERAIS
SERAPE
SERAPH
SESAME
SEWAGE
SEWARD
TENACE
TENANT
TEPALS
TERAPH
TERATO
TEXACO
TEXANS
VEGANS
ZENANA

•E••A•

AEGEAN
AENEAS
AERIAL
BEDLAM
BEGGAR
BELDAM
BELIAL
BEMOAN
BENDAY
BENGAL
BENGAY
BETRAY
BETTAS
BEULAH
CEIBAS
CELLAE
CELLAR
CEREAL
CESTAS
DEBRAS
DEEJAY
DEFEAT
DEFRAY
DELRAY
DELTAS
DEMEAN
DENIAL
DENTAL
DEODAR
DERMAL
DESMAN
DEWLAP
FELLAH
FELLAS
FENIAN
FERMAT
FESTAL
FEUDAL
FEZZAN
GEEGAW
GEMMAE
GENIAL
GENOAN
GENUAL
GERMAN
GETSAT
GEWGAW
HEEHAW
HELLAS
HENNAS
HEPCAT
HEPTAD
HERBAL
HEREAT
HERMAN
HETMAN
HEYDAY
JEERAT
JETLAG
JETSAM
KEENAN
KEEPAT
KENYAN
KEPTAT
KERMAN
KEVLAR
KEYPAD
KEYWAY
LEERAT
LEEWAY
LEGMAN
LEHUAS
LEKVAR
LEMMAS
LESTAT
LETHAL
LETSAT
MECCAS
MEDGAR
MEDIAL
MEDIAN
MEDIAS
MEDLAR
MEDLAT
MELMAC
MENIAL
MENSAE
MENSAL
MENSAS
MENTAL
MERMAN
MESCAL
NECTAR
NETMAN
NETPAY
NEUMAN
NEURAL
NEWMAN
NEWMAR
PECKAT
PEDLAR
PEEKAT
PEERAT
PENMAN
PENNAE
PENPAL
PENTAD
REAGAN
REATAS
REDBAY
REDCAP
REDEAL
REDHAT
REDIAL
REDOAK
REDRAW
REDTAG
REGGAE
REGNAL
REHEAL
REHEAR
REHEAT
RELOAD
RENTAL
REPEAL
REPEAT
REPLAN
REPLAY
REREAD
RESEAL
RESEAT
RESEAU
RETIAL
RETRAL
REVEAL
REWRAP
REXCAT
SEABAG
SEAFAN
SEAGAL
SEALAB
SEAMAN
SEAWAY
SEENAS
SEESAW
SENDAK
SENLAC
SENNAS
SEPIAS
SEPTAL
SERIAL
SERVAL
SETSAT
SEURAT
TEABAG
TEARAT
TERRAN
TESLAS
TESTAE
TETRAD
TETRAS
VEEJAY
VEINAL
VENIAL
VERBAL
VERNAL
VESTAL
VESTAS
WEIMAR
WENTAT
WETBAR
YENTAS
YEOMAN
YESMAN
ZEBRAS
ZEEMAN

•E•••A

AEOLIA
BELUGA
BERTHA
BETCHA
CESSNA
DEANNA
DEFLEA
DESICA
FEDORA
FEMORA
GEISHA
GELADA
GEMARA
GENERA
GENEVA
GEZIRA
HECUBA
HEGIRA
HELENA
HESTIA
JERBOA
KERALA
KESHIA
LERIDA
LEXICA
MEDAKA
MEDINA
MEDUSA
MEGARA
MELINA
MERIDA
NEBULA
NERUDA
NESTEA
NEVADA
OEDEMA
PELOTA
PENNIA
PEORIA
PEPITA
PERCHA
PERSIA
PESETA
PETULA
REALIA
REDSEA
REGINA
REMORA
REMUDA
RENATA
RESEDA
RETINA
SEDAKA
SEGURA
SELENA
SENECA
SENEGA
SENORA
SERBIA
SERENA
SEROSA
TEPHRA
TERESA
VERONA
ZENANA
ZEUGMA

••EA••

ALEAST
ATEAMS
ATEASE
AWEARY
AYEAYE
BLEACH
BLEARS
BLEARY
BLEATS
BREACH
BREADS
BREAKS
BREAMS
BREAST
BREATH
CHEAPO
CHEATS
CLEANS
CLEARS
CLEATS
CLEAVE
CREAKS
CREAKY
CREAMS
CREAMY
CREASE
CREASY
CREATE
DREADS
DREAMS
DREAMT
DREAMY
DREARY
FREAKS
FREAKY
GLEAMS
GLEANS
GOEASY
GREASE
GREASY
GREATS
GREAVE
HBEAMS
IBEAMS
ICEAGE
IDEALS
IDEATE
ILEANA
KNEADS
NLEAST
OBEAHS
OCEANS
OLEARY
OLEATE
OREADS
PAEANS
PLEACH
PLEADS
PLEASE
PLEATS
PREACH
PREAMP
QUEASY
SHEAFS
SHEARS
SHEATH
SHEAVE
SKEANS
SLEAVE
SLEAZE
SLEAZY
SMEARS
SMEARY
SNEAKS
SNEAKY
SPEAKS
SPEARS
STEADS
STEADY
STEAKS
STEALS
STEAMS
STEAMY
SWEARS
SWEATS
SWEATY
TREADS
TREATS
TREATY
TWEAKS
UNEASE
UNEASY
WHEATS
WREAKS
WREATH

••E•A•

ACETAL
AGENAS
AKELAS
ALEGAR
ALEMAN
AMEBAE
AMEBAS
APEMAN
ARECAS
ARENAS
CAESAR
CHELAE
CHELAS
CHEVAL
COEVAL
CRETAN
DAEDAL
DEEJAY
FLEWAT
GEEGAW
GOESAT
HAEMAT
HEEHAW
HIEMAL
HYENAS
HYETAL
ICEBAG
ICECAP
ICEMAN
IPECAC
JEERAT
KEENAN
KEEPAT
LEERAT
LEEWAY
MAENAD
OMEGAS
ONEDAY
ONEWAY
OPERAS
PEEKAT
PEERAT
PIEMAN
PIEPAN
PIETAS
PLEIAD
PREFAB
PRELAW
PREPAY
PRETAX
PREWAR
SCENAS
SEENAS
SEESAW
SHEVAT
SLEZAK
STEFAN
STELAE
STELAR
THECAE
THECAL
THEHAJ
THENAR
THETAS
TOECAP
TOETAP
TREPAN
VEEJAY
ZEEMAN

••E••A

ACEDIA
AGENDA
ALEXIA
AMELIA
AMENRA
ANEMIA
AREOLA
ARETHA
AVESTA
AYESHA
BRENDA
CRENNA
CREUSA
CUESTA
DJERBA
DUENNA
EDESSA
EGERIA
EGESTA
EJECTA
EXEDRA
FAENZA
FIESTA
FRESCA
GLENDA
GRETNA
IBERIA
ILEANA
ILESHA
IMELDA
OBELIA
ODESSA
ODETTA
OMERTA
ONEIDA
OREIDA
PAELLA
PLEURA
PNEUMA
PUEBLA
SHEENA
SHEILA
SHERPA
SIENNA
SIERRA
SIESTA
STELLA
STERNA
THELMA
TIERRA
TREDIA
VIENNA

•••EA•

AEGEAN
AENEAS
AGLEAM
ANDEAN
ANNEAL
APPEAL
APPEAR
AUGEAN
BATEAU
BOREAL
BOREAS
BUREAU
CAMEAT
CAVEAT
CEREAL
COMEAT
CUNEAL
DEFEAT
DEMEAN
DOGEAR
ENDEAR
ENNEAD
FOVEAE
GALEAE
GATEAU
GILEAD
HABEAS
HAVEAT
HEREAT
INGEAR
INLEAF
INSEAM
IRREAL
JUNEAU
KOREAN
LINEAL
LINEAR
LLBEAN
LOREAL
MCLEAN
MOREAU
NICEAN
NOLEAD
OCREAE
OHYEAH
ORDEAL
ORGEAT
OSTEAL
OUTEAT
PALEAE
PINEAL
POKEAT
POLEAX
RAMEAU
REDEAL
REHEAL
REHEAR
REHEAT
REPEAL
REPEAT
REREAD
RESEAL
RESEAT
RESEAU
REVEAL
ROSEAU
SCREAK
SCREAM
SINEAD
SPREAD
SQUEAK
SQUEAL
STREAK
STREAM
THREAD
THREAT
TINEAR
TOREAT
UNLEAD
UNREAD
UNREAL
UNSEAL
UNSEAT
UPBEAT

•••E•A

AMOEBA
ANGELA
ARBELA
ASPERA
ATHENA
BODEGA
CAMERA
CATENA
CINEMA
DODECA
DUNERA
EUREKA
GALENA
GENERA
GENEVA
HELENA
KAGERA
LAMESA
MODELA
MODENA
MONERA
MONETA
MULETA
NOVENA
OEDEMA
ORTEGA
PAMELA
PESETA
RESEDA
RIVERA
ROWENA
SABENA
SCHEMA
SCLERA
SELENA
SENECA
SENEGA
SERENA
SHEENA
SISERA
TERESA
TOPEKA
WALESA
XIMENA
ZAREBA

••••EA

ACHAEA
ALTHEA
ANDREA
AZALEA
CORNEA
COWPEA
CRIMEA
DEFLEA
DULLEA
DURYEA
EUBOEA
EUPNEA
GRADEA
GUINEA
HOTTEA
JUDAEA
LABREA
MATTEA
NAUSEA
NESTEA
NICAEA
NOUMEA
REDSEA
SPIREA

EB••••

EBBING
EBERLY
EBOATS
EBONDS

E•B•••

EBBING
EDBERG
EGBERT
EKBERG
ELBERT
ELBOWS
ELBRUS
EMBANK
EMBARK
EMBAYS
EMBDEN
EMBEDS
EMBERS
EMBLEM
EMBODY
EMBOSS
EMBRYO
ENBLOC
ERBIUM
EUBOEA

E••B••

EDIBLE
ENABLE
EREBUS

E•••B•

ENROBE
EPHEBE
EXURBS

•EB•••

BEBOPS
DEBARK
DEBARS
DEBASE
DEBATE
DEBBIE
DEBITS
DEBONE
DEBRAS
DEBRIS
DEBTOR
DEBUGS
DEBUNK
DEBUTS
HEBREW
KEBABS
KEBOBS
LEBRUN
NEBULA
PEBBLE
PEBBLY
REBAGS
REBARS
REBATE
REBELS
REBIDS
REBIND
REBOIL
REBOLT
REBOOT
REBORN
REBOZO
REBUFF
REBUKE
REBUTS
SEBERG
VEBLEN
WEBBED
WEBBER
WEBERN
XEBECS
ZEBRAS

•E•B••

BEDBUG
BERBER
CEIBAS
DEBBIE
FEEBLE
FEEBLY
FERBER
GERBER
GERBIL
HEEBIE
HENBIT
HERBAL
HERBIE
JERBOA
LESBOS
MEMBER
PEBBLE
PEBBLY
REDBAY
REDBUD
REEBOK
REUBEN
SEABAG
SEABED
SEABEE
SERBIA
TEABAG
VERBAL
WEBBED
WEBBER
WETBAR

•E••B•

AEROBE
CELEBS
DEMOBS
GETSBY
HECUBA
HEREBY
KEBABS
KEBOBS
LETSBE
MESABI
NEARBY
REDUBS
SETSBY
WENTBY

•E•••B

BEDAUB
BENUMB
DEKALB
RESORB
REVERB
SEALAB

••EB••

AMEBAE
AMEBAS
AMEBIC
BYEBYE
EREBUS
FEEBLE
FEEBLY
GLEBES
GREBES
HEEBIE
ICEBAG
ICEBOX
LIEBIG
PLEBES
PUEBLA
PUEBLO
QUEBEC
REEBOK
RHEBOK
THEBES
TREBEK
TREBLE
TREBLY

••E•B•

DJERBA
DOESBY
DWEEBS
GOESBY

••E••B

CHERUB
PREFAB

•••EB•

ACHEBE
AMOEBA
ARDEBS
CAMEBY
CELEBS
COMEBY
CUBEBS
DWEEBS
EPHEBE
GAZEBO
GONEBY
HEREBY
INDEBT
NASEBY
PHLEBO
PHOEBE
SASEBO
ZAREBA

•••E•B

ADVERB
REVERB
SUPERB

••••EB

COBWEB
DIONEB
SUBDEB
ZAGREB

EC••••

ECARTE
ECCLES
ECESIS
ECHOED
ECHOES
ECHOIC
ECLAIR
ECLATS
ECOLES
ECTYPE

E•C•••

ECCLES
EMCEED
EMCEES
ENCAGE
ENCAMP
ENCASE
ENCINA
ENCINO
ENCODE
ENCORE
EOCENE
ESCAPE
ESCARP
ESCENT
ESCHER
ESCHEW
ESCORT
ESCROW
ESCUDO
ETCHED
ETCHER
ETCHES
EUCHRE
EUCLID
EXCEED
EXCELS
EXCEPT
EXCESS
EXCISE
EXCITE
EXCUSE

E••C••

EDICTS
EDUCED
EDUCES
EGGCUP
EJECTA
EJECTS
ELECTS
ELICIT
ENACTS
EPICAL
EPOCHS
ERECTS
ERUCTS
EVICTS
EXACTA
EXACTO
EXACTS
EYECUP

E•••C•

EFFACE
EFFECT
ELLICE
ENESCO
ENLACE
ENRICH
ENRICO
ENTICE
EPARCH
EROICA
ETHICS
EUNICE
EUNUCH
EVINCE
EXARCH
EXPECT

E••••C
ECHOIC
EDENIC
ENBLOC
EROTIC
ETHNIC
ETONIC
EXILIC
EXOTIC

•EC•••
BECALM
BECAME
BECKER
BECKET
BECKON
BECOME
CECILE
DECADE
DECAFS
DECALS
DECAMP
DECANT
DECAYS
DECEIT
DECENT
DECIDE
DECKED
DECKER
DECKLE
DECOCT
DECODE
DECORS
DECOYS
DECREE
FECUND
GECKOS
HECATE
HECKLE
HECTIC
HECTOR
HECUBA
JECKLE
LECTOR
MECCAS
NECKED
NECTAR
PECANS
PECKAT
PECKED
PECTIC
PECTIN
RECALL
RECANE
RECANT
RECAPS
RECAST
RECEDE
RECENT
RECESS
RECIFE
RECIPE
RECITE
RECKON
RECODE
RECOIL
RECONS
RECOPY
RECORD
RECORK
RECOUP
RECTOR
RECTOS
RECTUS
RECURS
RECUSE
SECANT
SECEDE
SECERN
SECKEL
SECOND
SECRET
SECTOR
SECURE
TECHIE
TECHNO
VECTOR

•E•C••
BEACON
BETCHA
DEACON
DEICED
DEICER
DEICES
DESCRY
DEUCED
DEUCES
FENCED
FENCER
FENCES
FESCUE
HEPCAT
MECCAS
MERCED
MERCER
MESCAL
PEACHY
PENCEL
PENCIL
PERCHA
PESCOW
REACTS
REDCAP
REECHO
RESCUE
REXCAT
SEACOW
SEICHE
TEACUP
TERCEL
TERCET
TETCHY
VELCRO
WENCES

•E••C•
BEDECK
DECOCT
DEDUCE
DEDUCT
DEFACE
DEFECT
DEJECT
DELICT
DEPICT
DESICA
DETACH
DETECT
DEVICE
LEGACY
LEXICA
MEDICI
MEDICO
MEDICS
MENACE
MENSCH
MEXICO
PEERCE
PESACH
REDACT
REDUCE
REFACE
REJECT
RELACE
RELICS
RELICT
RELOCK
RELUCT
REMICK
RESECT
SEANCE
SEARCH
SEDUCE
SELECT
SENECA
SERACS
TENACE
TEXACO
VELOCE
VENICE
XEBECS

•E•••C
AEOLIC
BELLOC
CEDRIC
CELTIC
DELTIC
FENNEC
FERENC
FERRIC
HECTIC
HEROIC
MELMAC
METRIC
PECTIC
PELVIC
PEPTIC
SENLAC
SEPTIC
TENREC

••EC••
ALECKY
ALECTO
AMECHE
ARECAS
BRECHT
CHECKS
CRECHE
CZECHS
EJECTA
EJECTS
ELECTS
ERECTS
EYECUP
FLECHE
FLECKS
ICECAP
IPECAC
NIECES
NUECES
PIECED
PIECER
PIECES
PRECIS
REECHO
SIECLE
SPECIE
SPECKS
THECAE
THECAL
TOECAP
VNECKS
WRECKS

••E•C•
AGENCY
AMERCE
APERCU
BIERCE
BLEACH
BLENCH
BREACH
BREECH
CHEECH
CLENCH
COERCE
DRENCH
ENESCO
FIERCE
FLEECE
FLEECY
FLETCH
FRENCH
FRESCA
FRESCO
GREECE
KVETCH
PEERCE
PIERCE
PLEACH
PREACH
QUENCH
SKETCH
SPEECH
STENCH
THENCE
TIERCE
TRENCH
UNESCO
WHENCE
WRENCH
WRETCH

••E••C
ACETIC
AMEBIC
ANEMIC
CLERIC
EDENIC
GAELIC
IPECAC
IRENIC
NOETIC
POETIC
QUEBEC
SCENIC
THETIC

•••EC•
ABJECT
AFFECT
APIECE
ASPECT
AZTECS
BEDECK
BISECT
BREECH
CHEECH
DEFECT
DEJECT
DETECT
DIRECT
DODECA
EFFECT
EXPECT
FLEECE
FLEECY
GRAECO
GREECE
HITECH
INFECT
INJECT
INSECT
KOPECK
LAMECH
LUBECK
OBJECT
OLMECS
ONDECK
REJECT
RESECT
SELECT
SENECA
SPEECH
VOTECH
XEBECS
ZYDECO

•••E•C
FERENC
HOMEEC

••••EC
FENNEC
HOMEEC
MIXTEC
ONSPEC
PARSEC
QUEBEC
TENREC
TOLTEC

ED••••
EDAMES
EDBERG
EDDIED
EDDIES
EDDOES
EDENIC
EDERLE
EDESSA
EDGARD
EDGARS
EDGEIN
EDGERS
EDGIER
EDGILY
EDGING
EDIBLE
EDICTS
EDILES
EDISON
EDITED
EDITOR
EDMOND
EDMUND
EDSELS
EDUARD
EDUCED
EDUCES
EDVARD
EDWARD
EDWYNN

E•D•••
EDDIED
EDDIES
EDDOES
EIDERS
EIDOLA
ELDERS
ELDEST
EMDASH
ENDALL
ENDASH
ENDEAR
ENDERS
ENDING
ENDIVE
ENDMAN
ENDMEN
ENDORA
ENDOWS
ENDRUN
ENDSUP
ENDUED
ENDUES
ENDURE
ENDURO
ENDUSE
ESDRAS
EUDORA

E••D••
ELIDED
ELIDES
ELUDED
ELUDES
EMBDEN
EPODES
ERODED
ERODES
ETUDES
EVADED
EVADER
EVADES
EXEDRA
EXODUS
EXUDED
EXUDES

E•••D•
EBONDS
ELANDS
EMBEDS
EMBODY
EMENDS
ENCODE
EPHODS
ESCUDO

E••••D
EAGLED
EARNED
ECHOED
EDDIED
EDGARD
EDITED
EDMOND
EDMUND
EDUARD
EDUCED
EDVARD
EDWARD
ELAPID
ELATED
ELIDED
ELOPED
ELUDED
ELUTED
ELWOOD
EMCEED
EMOTED
EMQUAD
ENDUED
ENFOLD
ENGIRD
ENNEAD
ENQUAD
ENSUED
ENURED
ENVIED
ERASED
ERHARD
ERODED
ERRAND
ESPIED
ETCHED
EUCLID
EVADED
EVENED
EVOKED
EXCEED
EXILED
EXITED
EXPAND
EXPEND
EXTEND
EXUDED
EYELID

•ED•••
AEDILE
BEDAUB
BEDAZE
BEDBUG
BEDECK
BEDEWS
BEDIMS
BEDLAM
CEDARS
CEDING
CEDRIC
DEDUCE
DEDUCT
FEDORA
HEDDLE
HEDGED
HEDGER
HEDGES
HEDREN
KEDGED
KEDGES
LEDGER
LEDGES
LEDOFF
LEDOUT
MEDAKA
MEDALS
MEDDLE
MEDGAR
MEDIAL
MEDIAN
MEDIAS
MEDICI
MEDICO
MEDICS
MEDINA
MEDIUM
MEDLAR
MEDLAT
MEDLEY
MEDUSA
OEDEMA
PEDALS
PEDANT
PEDATE
PEDDLE
PEDLAR
REDACT
REDANT
REDATE
REDBAY
REDBUD
REDCAP
REDDEN
REDDER
REDDOG
REDEAL
REDEEM
REDEYE
REDFIN
REDFIR
REDFOX
REDGUM
REDHAT
REDHOT
REDIAL
REDINK
REDOAK
REDOES
REDONE
REDRAW
REDREW
REDSEA
REDSOX
REDTAG
REDTOP
REDUBS
REDUCE
REDYED
REDYES
SEDAKA
SEDANS
SEDATE
SEDERS
SEDGES
SEDILE
SEDUCE
SEDUMS
TEDDED
TEDDER
TEDEUM
TEDIUM
TEDKEY
VEDDER
WEDDED
WEDELN
WEDGED
WEDGES
WEDGIE

•E•D••
BEADED
BEADLE
BEADUP
BELDAM
BENDAY
BENDED
BENDER
BENDIX
DEADEN
DEADER
DEADLY
DEADON
DEEDED
DEEDEE
DEIDRE
DENDRI
DENDRO
DEODAR
FEEDER
FEEDON
FELDON
FENDED
FENDER
FEUDAL
FEUDED
GENDER
GEODES
HEADED
HEADER
HEADIN
HEADON
HEADUP
HEDDLE
HEEDED
HEIDEN
HELDIN
HELDON
HELDTO
HELDUP
HERDED
HERDER
HEYDAY
LEADED
LEADEN
LEADER
LEADIN
LEADON
LEADTO
LEADUP
LEIDEN
LENDER
LEWDER
LEWDLY
LEYDEN
MEADOW
MEDDLE
MELDED
MENDED
MENDEL
MENDER
MENDES
NEEDED
NEEDLE
NEEDNT
PEDDLE
PEEDEE
PENDED
PERDUE
READER
READIN
REDDEN
REDDER
REDDOG
REEDIT
RENDER
SEADOG
SEEDED
SEEDER
SEIDEL
SELDOM
SENDAK
SENDER
SENDIN
SENDUP
TEDDED
TEDDER
TEEDUP
TENDED
TENDER
TENDON
TENDTO
VEDDER
VELDTS
VENDED
VENDEE
VENDOR
VERDIN
VERDON
VERDUN
WEDDED
WEEDED
WEEDER
WELDED
WELDER
WENDED
ZENDOS

•E••D•
BEARDS
BESIDE
BETIDE
DECADE
DECIDE
DECODE
DELUDE
DEMODE
DENUDE
DERIDE
GELADA
HEXADS
LERIDA
MELODY
MERIDA
NERUDA
NEVADA
REBIDS
RECEDE
RECODE
REMADE
REMEDY
REMUDA
RESEDA
RESIDE
RESODS
REWEDS
SECEDE
TELEDU
TEREDO
WEIRDO
YEHUDI

•E•••D
AENEID
BEADED
BEAKED
BEAMED
BEANED
BEEFED
BEEPED
BEGGED
BEHELD
BEHIND
BEHOLD
BELIED
BELLED
BELTED
BENDED
BESTED
BEYOND
CEASED
CEILED
CELLED
CENSED
CERVID
DECKED
DEEDED
DEEMED
DEFEND
DEFIED
DEICED
DELVED
DEMAND
DEMOND
DENIED
DENNED
DENTED
DEPEND
DEUCED
DEVOID
FEARED
FECUND
FELLED
FELTED
FENCED
FENDED
FERVID
FEUDED
GEARED
GELLED
GEMMED
GERALD
GERARD
GERUND
HEADED
HEALED
HEAPED
HEATED
HEAVED
HEDGED
HEEDED
HEELED
HEFTED
HELMED
HELPED
HEMMED
HEPTAD
HERALD
HERDED
HESIOD
JEERED
JELLED
JERKED
JESTED
JETTED
KEDGED
KEELED
KEENED
KEGGED
KENNED
KERNED
KEYPAD
LEADED
LEAFED
LEAKED
LEANED
LEAPED
LEASED
LEAVED
LEERED
LEGEND
LEGGED
LELAND
LEMOND
LENSED
LEONID
LETTED
LEVEED
LEVIED
MELDED
MELTED
MENDED
MEOWED
MERCED
MERGED
MESHED
MESSED
METHOD
MEWLED
NEARED
NECKED
NEEDED
NEREID
NESTED
NETTED
PEAKED
PEALED
PEAPOD
PECKED
PEEKED
PEELED
PEENED
PEEPED
PEERED
PEEVED
PEGGED
PELTED
PENDED
PENNED
PENROD
PENTAD
PEPPED
PEQUOD
PERIOD
PERKED
PERMED
PERNOD
PETARD
PETTED
REAMED
REAPED
REARED
REBIND
RECORD
REDBUD
REDYED
REEFED
REEKED
REELED
REEVED
REFFED
REFUND
REGARD
REHELD
REINED
RELAID
RELIED
RELOAD
REMAND
REMEND
REMIND
RENTED
REPAID
REPAND
REREAD
RESAND
RESEED
RESEND
RESHOD
RESOLD
RESTED
RETARD
RETIED
RETOLD
REUSED
REVVED
REWARD
REWELD
REWIND
REWORD
SEABED
SEALED
SEAMED
SEARED
SEATED
SECOND
SEEDED
SEEMED
SEEPED
SEERED
SEGUED
SEINED
SEIZED
SENSED
SERVED
SEWARD
TEAMED
TEARED
TEASED
TEDDED
TEEMED
TEHEED
TEMPED
TENDED
TENSED
TENTED
TERMED
TESTED
TETRAD
VEERED
VEGGED
VEILED
VEINED
VENDED
VENTED
VERGED
VERSED
VESPID
VESTED
VETOED
VETTED
WEANED
WEAVED
WEBBED
WEDDED
WEDGED
WEEDED
WELDED
WELLED
WELTED
WENDED
WETTED
YELLED
YELPED
YENNED
YESSED
ZEROED
ZESTED

••ED••
ACEDIA
AMEDEO
AVEDON
COEDIT
CREDIT
CREDOS
DAEDAL
DEEDED
DEEDEE
DREDGE
EXEDRA
FEEDER
FEEDON
FLEDGE
FREDDY
HEEDED
ICEDIN
ICEDUP
LIEDER
NEEDED
NEEDLE
NEEDNT
ONEDAY
ONEDGE
PEEDEE
PHEDRE
PLEDGE
PYEDOG
REEDIT
SEEDED
SEEDER
SLEDGE
SPEDUP
SUEDES
SWEDEN
SWEDES
TEEDUP
TIEDIN
TIEDUP
TIEDYE
TOEDIN
TREDIA
USEDTO
USEDUP
WEEDED
WEEDER

••E•D•
AGENDA
AMENDS
ARENDT
BLEEDS
BLENDE
BLENDS
BREADS
BREEDS
BRENDA
CREEDS
DREADS
EMENDS
FIELDS
FIENDS
FJELDS
FREDDY
GLENDA
GREEDY
IMELDA
KNEADS
ONEIDA
OREADS
OREIDA
OVERDO
PLEADS
PSEUDO
PSEUDS
SCENDS
SHEEDY
SPEEDS
SPEEDY
SPENDS
STEADS
STEADY
STEEDS
TREADS
TRENDS
TRENDY
TWEEDS
TWEEDY
UPENDS
WIELDS
YIELDS

••E••D
AGEOLD
BEEFED
BEEPED
BREWED
CHEWED
CLEPED
CLEWED
CREWED
DEEDED
DEEMED
DIETED
DUELED
EVENED
EYELID
FLEXED
FUELED
GREYED
HEEDED
HEELED
JEERED
KEELED
KEENED
LEERED
MAENAD
NEEDED
OBEYED
OPENED
PEEKED
PEELED
PEENED
PEEPED
PEERED
PEEVED
PIECED
PLEIAD
PREMED
PREYED
QUEUED
REEFED
REEKED
REELED
REEVED
SEEDED
SEEMED
SEEPED
SEERED
SIEGED
SIEVED
SKEWED
SLEWED
SPEWED
STEWED
TEEMED
THEEND
THEFED
THEMED
TIERED
TIEROD
TREPID
USERID
VEERED
VIEWED

WEEDED

•••ED•

ACCEDE
ALBEDO
BIPEDS
BLEEDS
BREEDS
COMEDY
CREEDS
EMBEDS
GREEDY
IMPEDE
LAMEDH
LAMEDS
LAREDO
MADEDO
MAKEDO
MOPEDS
OVIEDO
RATEDG
RATEDR
RATEDX
RECEDE
REMEDY
RESEDA
REWEDS
SECEDE
SHEEDY
SHREDS
SPEEDS
SPEEDY
STEEDS
TELEDU
TEREDO
TOLEDO
TUXEDO
TWEEDS
TWEEDY

•••E•D

ADDEND
AENEID
AFIELD
AGREED
ANTEED
APPEND
ASCEND
ATTEND
AUGEND
AXSEED
BEHELD
DEFEND
DEPEND
EMCEED
ENNEAD
EXCEED
EXPEND
EXTEND
FAGEND
FRIEND
GILEAD
IMPEND
INDEED
INNEED
INTEND
LEGEND
LEVEED
LOWEND
NEREID
NOLEAD
OFFEND
OSTEND
PUREED
REHELD
REMEND
REREAD
RESEED
RESEND
REWELD
SCREED
SHIELD
SHREWD
SINEAD
SPREAD
TAGEND
TEHEED
THEEND
THREAD
THREED
UNBEND
UNHEED
UNLEAD
UNREAD
UPHELD

••••ED

ABASED
ABATED
ABIDED
ABUSED
ADDLED
ADORED
AGREED
ALFRED
ALLIED
AMAZED
AMBLED
AMUSED
ANGLED
ANKLED
ANTEED
ARCHED
ARGUED
ATONED
AVOWED
AWAKED
AXSEED
BABIED
BACKED
BAGGED
BAILED
BAITED
BALKED
BANDED
BANGED
BANKED
BANNED
BARBED
BARGED
BARKED
BARRED
BASHED
BASKED
BASTED
BATHED
BATTED
BAWLED
BEADED
BEAKED
BEAMED
BEANED
BEEFED
BEEPED
BEGGED
BELIED
BELLED
BELTED
BENDED
BESTED
BIASED
BIBBED
BIFFED
BIGRED
BILKED
BILLED
BINGED
BINNED
BIRDED
BIRLED
BITTED
BLADED
BLAMED
BLARED
BLAZED
BOATED
BOBBED
BODIED
BOFFED
BOGGED
BOILED
BOLTED
BOMBED
BONDED
BONGED
BOOKED
BOOMED
BOOTED
BOPPED
BOSSED
BOWLED
BRACED
BRAKED
BRAVED
BRAYED
BRAZED
BREWED
BRIBED
BRINED
BUCKED
BUDDED
BUDGED
BUFFED
BUGGED
BUGLED
BULGED
BULKED
BULLED
BUMMED
BUMPED
BUNGED
BUNKED
BUNTED
BUOYED
BURIED
BURLED
BURNED
BURPED
BURRED
BUSHED
BUSIED
BUSSED
BUSTED
BUTTED
BUZZED
CABBED
CABLED
CACHED
CADGED
CALKED
CALLED
CALMED
CALVED
CAMPED
CANNED
CANOED
CANTED
CAPPED
CARDED
CARPED
CARTED
CARVED
CASHED
CATTED
CAUSED
CEASED
CEILED
CELLED
CENSED
CHAFED
CHASED
CHEWED
CHIDED
CHIMED
CHOKED
CHOWED
CHUTED
CLAWED
CLEPED
CLEWED
CLONED
CLOSED
CLOYED
COATED
COAXED
COCKED
COGGED
COIFED
COILED
COINED
COMBED
CONFED
CONKED
CONNED
COOKED
COOLED
COOPED
COPIED
COPPED
CORDED
CORKED
CORNED
COSHED
COWLED
COZIED
CRANED
CRATED
CRAVED
CRAZED
CREWED
CROWED
CUFFED
CULLED
CUPPED
CURBED
CURDED
CURLED
CURRED
CURSED
CURVED
CUSPED
CUSSED
CYCLED
DABBED
DADOED
DAMMED
DAMNED
DAMPED
DANCED
DAPPED
DARNED
DARTED
DASHED
DAUBED
DAWNED
DAYBED
DECKED
DEEDED
DEEMED
DEFIED
DEICED
DELVED
DENIED
DENNED
DENTED
DEUCED
DIALED
DIETED
DIMMED
DINGED
DINNED
DINTED
DIPPED
DISHED
DISKED
DISSED
DOCKED
DODGED
DOFFED
DOGGED
DOLLED
DONNED
DOOMED
DOSSED
DOTTED
DOUSED
DOWNED
DOWSED
DRAPED
DRAYED
DRONED
DUBBED
DUCKED
DUELED
DULLED
DUMPED
DUNKED
DUNNED
DUSTED
EAGLED
EARNED
ECHOED
EDDIED
EDITED
EDUCED
ELATED
ELIDED
ELOPED
ELUDED
ELUTED
EMCEED
EMOTED
ENDUED
ENSUED
ENURED
ENVIED
ERASED
ERODED
ESPIED
ETCHED
EVADED
EVENED
EVOKED
EXCEED
EXILED
EXITED
EXUDED
FABLED
FAGGED
FAILED
FAIRED
FANGED
FANNED
FARCED
FARMED
FASTED
FATTED
FAWNED
FEARED
FELLED
FELTED
FENCED
FENDED
FEUDED
FIBBED
FILLED
FILMED
FINKED
FINNED
FIRMED
FISHED
FISTED
FITTED
FIZZED
FLAKED
FLAMED
FLARED
FLAWED
FLAYED
FLEXED
FLOWED
FLUTED
FLUXED
FOALED
FOAMED
FOBBED
FOGGED
FOILED
FOLDED
FOOLED
FOOTED
FORCED
FORDED
FORGED
FORKED
FORMED
FOULED
FOWLED
FRAMED
FRAYED
FUDGED
FUELED
FUNDED
FUNKED
FUNNED
FURLED
FURRED
FUSSED
FUZZED
GABBED
GABLED
GADDED
GAFFED
GAGGED
GAINED
GAITED
GALLED
GANGED
GAPPED
GARBED
GASHED
GASPED
GASSED
GAUGED
GAUZED
GAWKED
GEARED
GELLED
GEMMED
GIBBED
GIFTED
GIGGED
GILDED
GILLED
GINNED
GIPPED
GIRDED
GIRTED
GLARED
GLAZED
GLIDED
GLOBED
GLOVED
GLOWED
GNAWED
GOADED
GOLFED
GONGED
GOOFED
GOOSED
GORGED
GOUGED
GOWNED
GRACED
GRADED
GRATED
GRAVED
GRAYED
GRAZED
GREYED
GRIMED
GRIPED
GROPED
GUIDED
GULFED
GULLED
GULPED
GUMMED
GUNNED
GUSHED
GUSTED
GUTTED
GYPPED
HACKED
HAFTED
HAILED
HAIRED
HALOED
HALTED
HALVED
HAMMED
HANDED
HANGED
HARKED
HARMED
HARPED
HASHED
HASPED
HATRED
HATTED
HAULED
HAWKED
HEADED
HEALED
HEAPED
HEATED
HEAVED
HEDGED
HEEDED
HEELED
HEFTED
HELMED
HELPED
HEMMED
HERDED
HILLED
HINGED
HINTED
HIPPED
HISSED
HOAXED
HOCKED
HOGGED
HONIED
HONKED
HOODED
HOOFED
HOOKED
HOOPED
HOOTED
HOPPED
HORNED
HORSED
HOSTED
HOTBED
HOUSED
HOWLED
HUFFED
HUGGED
HULKED
HULLED
HUMMED
HUMPED
HUNTED
HURLED
HUSHED
HUSKED
HUTTED
HYMNED
HYPOED
ILLFED
IMAGED
IMBUED
INBRED
INCHED
INDEED
INNEED
INURED
IRONED
ISSUED
ITCHED
JABBED
JACKED
JAGGED
JAILED
JAMMED
JARRED
JAZZED
JEERED
JELLED
JERKED
JESTED
JETTED
JIGGED
JILTED
JINKED
JINXED
JOBBED
JOGGED
JOINED
JOLTED
JOSHED
JOTTED
JUDGED
JUGGED
JUICED
JUMPED
JUNKED
JUTTED
KAYOED
KEDGED
KEELED
KEENED
KEGGED
KENNED
KERNED
KICKED
KIDDED
KILLED
KILNED
KILTED
KINGED
KINKED
KISSED
KNIFED
LACKED
LADLED
LAGGED
LAMBED
LAMMED
LANCED
LANDED
LAPPED
LAPSED
LARDED
LARKED
LASHED
LASTED
LATHED
LAUDED
LEADED
LEAFED
LEAKED
LEANED
LEAPED
LEASED
LEAVED
LEERED
LEGGED
LENSED
LETTED
LEVEED
LEVIED
LIBBED
LICKED
LIDDED
LIFTED
LILTED
LIMBED
LIMNED
LIMPED
LINKED
LIPPED
LISPED
LISTED
LOADED
LOAFED
LOAMED
LOANED
LOBBED
LOCKED
LODGED
LOFTED
LOGGED
LOLLED
LONGED
LOOKED
LOOMED
LOOPED
LOOSED
LOOTED
LOPPED
LORDED
LOTTED
LOUSED
LUCKED
LUFFED
LUGGED
LULLED
LUMPED
LUNGED
LURKED
LUSTED
MAILED
MALTED
MANNED
MAPPED
MARKED
MARLED
MARRED
MASHED
MASKED
MASSED
MATTED
MAULED
MELDED
MELTED
MENDED
MEOWED
MERCED
MERGED
MESHED
MESSED
MEWLED
MIFFED
MILKED
MILLED
MINCED
MINDED
MINTED
MISLED
MISSED
MISTED
MITRED
MOANED
MOATED
MOBBED
MOCKED
MOILED
MOLDED
MOLTED
MONIED
MOONED
MOORED
MOOTED
MOPPED
MOSSED
MOUSED
MUCKED
MUDDED
MUFFED
MUGGED
MULLED
MUSHED
MUSSED
NABBED
NAGGED
NAILED
NAPPED
NEARED
NECKED
NEEDED
NESTED
NETTED
NICKED
NIPPED
NODDED
NOISED
NOSHED
NUBBED
NUDGED
NULLED
NUMBED
NURSED
NUTTED
OBEYED
OINKED
OKAYED
OPENED
OPINED
ORATED
OUSTED
PACKED
PADDED
PAINED
PAIRED
PALLED
PALMED
PANNED
PANTED
PARKED
PARRED
PARSED
PARTED
PASSED
PASTED
PATTED
PAUSED
PAWNED
PEAKED
PEALED
PECKED
PEEKED
PEELED
PEENED
PEEPED
PEERED
PEEVED
PEGGED
PELTED
PENDED
PENNED
PEPPED
PERKED
PERMED
PETTED
PHASED
PHONED
PHYSED
PICKED
PIECED
PIGGED
PILLED
PINGED
PINKED
PINNED
PIPPED
PIQUED
PITHED
PITIED
PITTED
PLACED
PLANED
PLATED
PLAYED
PLOWED
PLUMED
PODDED
POISED
POLLED
PONIED
POOHED
POOLED
POOPED
POPPED
PORTED
POSTED
POTTED
POURED
POUTED
PRATED
PRAYED
PREMED
PREYED
PRICED
PRIDED
PRIMED
PRIZED
PROBED
PROSED
PROVED
PRUNED
PUFFED
PUGGED
PULLED
PULPED
PULSED
PUMPED
PUNNED
PUNTED
PUREED
PURGED
PURLED
PURRED
PURSED
PUSHED
PUTTED
QUAKED
QUEUED
QUOTED
RACKED
RAFTED
RAGGED
RAIDED
RAILED
RAINED
RAISED
RAMMED
RAMPED
RANGED
RANKED
RANTED
RAPPED
RASPED
RATTED
RAZZED
REAMED
REAPED
REARED
REDYED
REEFED
REEKED
REELED
REEVED
REFFED
REINED
RELIED
RENTED
RESEED
RESTED
RETIED
REUSED
REVVED
RHYMED
RIBBED
RICKED
RIDDED
RIDGED
RIFFED
RIFLED
RIFTED
RIGGED
RIMMED
RINGED
RINSED
RIOTED
RIPPED
RISKED
ROAMED
ROARED
ROBBED
ROCKED
ROILED
ROLLED
ROMPED
ROOFED
ROOKED
ROOMED
ROOTED
ROTTED
ROUGED
ROUSED
ROUTED
RRATED
RUBBED
RUBIED
RUCKED
RUFFED
RUGGED
RUINED
RUSHED
RUSTED
RUTTED
SACKED
SACRED
SAGGED
SAILED
SALTED
SALVED
SANDED
SAPPED
SASHED
SASSED
SAUCED
SAWRED
SCALED
SCARED
SCOPED
SCORED
SCREED
SEABED
SEALED
SEAMED
SEARED
SEATED
SEEDED
SEEMED
SEEPED
SEERED
SEGUED
SEINED
SEIZED
SENSED
SERVED
SHADED
SHAMED
SHAPED
SHARED
SHAVED
SHINED
SHOOED
SHORED
SHOVED
SHOWED
SICCED
SIDLED
SIEGED
SIEVED
SIFTED
SIGHED
SIGNED
SILKED
SILOED
SILTED
SINGED
SINNED
SIPPED
SKATED
SKEWED
SKIVED
SLAKED
SLATED
SLAVED
SLAYED
SLEWED
SLICED
SLIMED
SLOPED
SLOWED
SMILED
SMOKED
SNAKED
SNARED
SNIPED
SNORED
SNOWED
SOAKED
SOAPED
SOARED
SOBBED
SOCKED
SODDED
SOILED
SOLOED
SOLVED
SOPPED
SORTED
SOTTED
SOURED
SOUSED
SPACED
SPADED
SPARED
SPAYED
SPEWED
SPICED
SPIKED
SPINED
SPIRED
SPITED
SPOKED
SPUMED
STAGED
STAKED
STALED
STARED
STATED
STAVED
STAYED
STEWED
STOKED
STONED
STORED
STOWED
STYLED
SUBBED
SUCKED
SUDSED
SUITED
SULKED
SUMMED
SUNNED
SUPPED
SURFED
SURGED
SWAGED
SWAYED
SWIPED
SYNCED
TABBED
TABLED
TACKED
TAGGED
TAILED
TALCED
TALKED
TAMPED
TANGED
TANKED
TANNED
TAPPED
TARRED
TASKED
TASTED
TATTED
TAXIED
TEAMED
TEARED
TEASED
TEDDED
TEEMED
TEHEED
TEMPED
TENDED
TENSED
TENTED
TERMED
TESTED
THAWED
THEFED
THEMED
THREED
TICKED
TIDIED
TIERED
TIFFED
TILLED
TILTED
TINGED
TINNED

TINTED
TIPPED
TITHED
TITLED
TOGAED
TOGGED
TOILED
TOLLED
TOOLED
TOOTED
TOPPED
TOSSED
TOTTED
TOURED
TOUTED
TRACED
TRADED
TRICED
TROWED
TUBBED
TUCKED
TUFTED
TUGGED
TURFED
TURNED
TUSKED
TUTUED
TWINED
UNAGED
UNAWED
UNDYED
UNHEED
UNITED
UNSHED
UNTIED
UNUSED
VALUED
VALVED
VAMPED
VANNED
VARIED
VEERED
VEGGED
VEILED
VEINED
VENDED
VENTED
VERGED
VERSED
VESTED
VETOED
VETTED
VIEWED
VISAED
VOICED
VOIDED
WADDED
WAFTED
WAGGED
WAILED
WAITED
WAIVED
WALKED
WALLED
WANNED
WANTED
WARDED
WARMED
WARNED
WARPED
WARRED
WASHED
WASTED
WEANED

WEAVED
WEBBED
WEDDED
WEDGED
WEEDED
WELDED
WELLED
WELTED
WENDED
WETTED
WHILED
WHINED
WICKED
WIGGED
WILLED
WILTED
WINCED
WINDED
WINGED
WINKED
WISHED
WISPED
WITHED
WITTED
WOLFED
WONNED
WONTED
WOODED
WOOFED
WORDED
WORKED
WORMED
XRATED
XRAYED
YAKKED
YANKED
YAPPED
YARDED
YARNED
YAWNED
YAWPED
YELLED
YELPED
YENNED
YESSED
YIPPED
YOLKED
YOWLED
YOYOED
YUKKED
ZAGGED
ZAPPED
ZEROED
ZESTED
ZIGGED
ZINGED
ZIPPED
ZONKED
ZOOMED

EE••••

EELERS
EELIER
EERIER
EERILY
EEYORE

E•E•••

EBERLY
ECESIS
EDENIC
EDERLE
EDESSA
EGERIA

EGESTA
EGESTS
EJECTA
EJECTS
EKEOUT
ELECTS
ELEGIT
ELEMIS
ELEVEN
ELEVES
EMEERS
EMENDS
EMERGE
ENERGY
ENESCO
EREBUS
ERECTS
ERENOW
ETERNE
EVELYN
EVENED
EVENER
EVENKI
EVENLY
EVENSO
EVENTS
EVENUP
EVERLY
EVERSO
EVERTS
EXEDRA
EXEMPT
EXERTS
EXETER
EXEUNT
EYECUP
EYEFUL
EYEING
EYELET
EYELID

E••E••

EASEIN
EASELS
EASEUP
EATERS
EATERY
EDBERG
EDGEIN
EDGERS
EDSELS
EELERS
EFFECT
EFFETE
EGBERT
EGRESS
EGRETS
EIDERS
EILEEN
EKBERG
ELBERT
ELDERS
ELDEST
ELLERY
ELVERS
EMBEDS
EMBERS
EMCEED
EMCEES
EMEERS
EMMETS
EMMETT
EMPERY
ENDEAR

ENDERS
ENGELS
ENMESH
ENNEAD
ENTERO
ENTERS
EOCENE
EPHEBE
ERNEST
ESCENT
ESKERS
ESSENE
ESTEEM
ESTERS
ETHENE
ETHERS
ETSEQQ
EUGENE
EUREKA
EXCEED
EXCELS
EXCEPT
EXCESS
EXPECT
EXPELS
EXPEND
EXPERT
EXSERT
EXTEND
EXTENT

E•••E•

EAGLED
EAGLES
EAGLET
EAGRES
EARNED
EARNER
EASIER
EASTER
ECCLES
ECHOED
ECHOES
ECOLES
EDAMES
EDDIED
EDDIES
EDDOES
EDGIER
EDILES
EDITED
EDUCED
EDUCES
EELIER
EERIER
EIFFEL
EILEEN
EISNER
EITHER
ELATED
ELATER
ELATES
ELAYER
ELEVEN
ELEVES
ELIDED
ELIDES
ELITES
ELOPED
ELOPER
ELOPES
ELUDED
ELUDES
ELUTED

ELUTES
ELYSEE
EMBDEN
EMBLEM
EMCEED
EMCEES
EMOTED
EMOTER
EMOTES
ENAMEL
ENATES
ENDMEN
ENDUED
ENDUES
ENSUED
ENSUES
ENTREE
ENURED
ENURES
ENVIED
ENVIES
EPODES
EPOPEE
ERASED
ERASER
ERASES
ERODED
ERODES
ESCHER
ESCHEW
ESPIED
ESPIES
ESTEEM
ESTHER
ETCHED
ETCHER
ETCHES
ETUDES
EUBOEA
EUPNEA
EVADED
EVADER
EVADES
EVENED
EVENER
EVILER
EVOKED
EVOKER
EVOKES
EXCEED
EXETER
EXILED
EXILES
EXITED
EXUDED
EXUDES
EYELET
EYRIES

E••••E

ECARTE
ECTYPE
EDERLE
EDIBLE
EEYORE
EFFACE
EFFETE
EFFUSE
ELAINE
ELAPSE
ELAYNE
ELLICE
ELMORE
ELOISE

ELYSEE
EMERGE
EMIGRE
EMPIRE
ENABLE
ENCAGE
ENCASE
ENCODE
ENCORE
ENDIVE
ENDURE
ENDUSE
ENGAGE
ENGINE
ENISLE
ENLACE
ENRAGE
ENROBE
ENSILE
ENSURE
ENTICE
ENTIRE
ENTREE
ENZYME
EOCENE
EPHEBE
EPOPEE
EQUATE
EQUINE
ERGATE
ERMINE
ESCAPE
ESSENE
ESTATE
ETERNE
ETHANE
ETHENE
ETOILE
EUCHRE
EUGENE
EUNICE
EUROPE
EVINCE
EVOLVE
EVONNE
EVULSE
EVZONE
EXCISE
EXCITE
EXCUSE
EXHALE
EXPIRE
EXPOSE
EXWIFE

•EE•••

AEETES
BEEFED
BEEFUP
BEEGUM
BEEPED
BEEPER
BEETLE
BEEVES
DEEDED
DEEDEE
DEEJAY
DEEMED
DEEPEN
DEEPER
DEEPLY
FEEBLE
FEEBLY
FEEDER

FEEDON
FEEING
FEELER
GEEGAW
GEEGEE
GEEING
GEEZER
HEEBIE
HEEDED
HEEHAW
HEELED
HEELER
JEERAT
JEERED
JEERER
JEETER
JEEVES
KEELED
KEELER
KEENAN
KEENED
KEENEN
KEENER
KEENLY
KEEPAT
KEEPER
KEEPIN
KEEPON
KEEPTO
KEEPUP
LEERAT
LEERED
LEERER
LEEWAY
MEEKER
MEEKLY
MEERUT
MEETER
MEETLY
NEEDED
NEEDLE
NEEDNT
NEESON
PEEDEE
PEEKAT
PEEKED
PEELED
PEELER
PEENED
PEEPED
PEEPER
PEERAT
PEERCE
PEERED
PEERIN
PEEVED
PEEVES
PEEWEE
REEBOK
REECHO
REEDIT
REEFED
REEFER
REEKED
REELED
REELIN
REEVED
REEVES
SEEDED
SEEDER
SEEFIT
SEEGER
SEEING
SEEKER

SEEMED
SEEMLY
SEENAS
SEENTO
SEEOFF
SEEOUT
SEEPED
SEEPIN
SEERED
SEESAW
SEESIN
SEESTO
SEETHE
TEEDUP
TEEHEE
TEEING
TEEMED
TEENER
TEENSY
TEEOFF
TEESUP
TEETER
TEETHE
VEEJAY
VEERED
WEEDED
WEEDER
WEEKLY
WEENIE
WEENSY
WEEPER
WEEVIL
ZEEMAN

•E•E••

AEGEAN
AENEAS
AENEID
BEDECK
BEDEWS
BEFELL
BEGETS
BEHELD
BEHEST
BEKESY
BEREFT
BERETS
BESETS
BETELS
BEVELS
BEZELS
CELEBS
CELERY
CEMENT
CEREAL
CEREUS
DECEIT
DECENT
DEFEAT
DEFECT
DEFEND
DEFERS
DEJECT
DELEON
DELETE
DEMEAN
DEPEND
DESERT
DETECT
DETENT
DETERS
DETEST
DEVEIN
DEVEST

EELERS
FERENC
FEVERS
FEWEST
GELEES
GENERA
GENETS
GENEVA
GENEVE
GERENT
HELENA
HELENE
HELENS
HEREAT
HEREBY
HEREIN
HEREOF
HEREON
HERESY
HERETO
HETERO
HEWERS
HEXERS
JEREMY
JEWELS
JEWETT
KEVELS
LEGEND
LEVEED
LEVEES
LEVELS
LEVENE
LEVERS
LEXEME
MELEES
MERELY
MEREST
METEOR
METERS
NENETS
NEREID
NEREIS
NEREUS
NEVERS
NEWELS
NEWEST
OEDEMA
PELEUS
PESETA
PETERS
PEWEES
REBELS
RECEDE
RECENT
RECESS
REDEAL
REDEEM
REDEYE
REFERS
REGENT
REHEAL
REHEAR
REHEAT
REHEEL
REHELD
REHEMS
REJECT
REKEYS
RELENT
RELETS
REMEDY
REMELT
REMEND
RENEGE

RENEWS
REPEAL
REPEAT
REPEGS
REPELS
REPENT
REREAD
RERENT
RESEAL
RESEAT
RESEAU
RESECT
RESEDA
RESEED
RESEEN
RESEES
RESELL
RESEND
RESENT
RESETS
RESEWN
RESEWS
RETELL
RETENE
RETEST
REVEAL
REVELS
REVERB
REVERE
REVERS
REVERT
REVETS
REWEDS
REWELD
SEBERG
SECEDE
SECERN
SEDERS
SELECT
SELENA
SELENE
SEMELE
SENECA
SENEGA
SERENA
SERENE
SEVENS
SEVERE
SEVERN
SEVERS
SEWELL
SEWERS
TEDEUM
TEHEED
TEHEES
TELEDU
TENETS
TEPEES
TEREDO
TERESA
TERETE
TEREUS
VENEER
VENETO
VEREEN
VEXERS
WEBERN
WEDELN
WERENT
XEBECS
YEMENI

•E••E•

AEETES

AERIES
AETHER
BEADED
BEAKED
BEAKER
BEAMED
BEANED
BEARER
BEATEN
BEATER
BEAVER
BECKER
BECKET
BEEFED
BEEPED
BEEPER
BEEVES
BEGGED
BEGLEY
BEIGES
BELIED
BELIEF
BELIES
BELLED
BELLES
BELTED
BENDED
BENDER
BERBER
BERGEN
BESSER
BESTED
BETHEL
BETSEY
BETTER
BEVIES
CEASED
CEASES
CEILED
CELLED
CENSED
CENSER
CENSES
CENTER
CERMET
DEADEN
DEADER
DEAFEN
DEAFER
DEALER
DEARER
DECKED
DECKER
DECREE
DEEDED
DEEDEE
DEEMED
DEEPEN
DEEPER
DEFIED
DEFIES
DEFLEA
DEFTER
DEGREE
DEICED
DEICER
DEICES
DELVED
DELVER
DELVES
DENIED
DENIER
DENIES
DENNED

DENSER
DENTED
DENVER
DENZEL
DEUCED
DEUCES
DEWIER
DEXTER
EELIER
EERIER
FEARED
FEARER
FEEDER
FEELER
FELLED
FELLER
FELTED
FEMMES
FENCED
FENCER
FENCES
FENDED
FENDER
FENNEC
FENNEL
FERBER
FERRER
FERRET
FESSES
FESTER
FETTER
FEUDED
FEZZES
GEARED
GEEGEE
GEEZER
GEIGER
GEISEL
GELEES
GELLED
GELSEY
GEMMED
GENDER
GENIES
GENRES
GEODES
GERBER
GESTES
GETSET
GETTER
GEYSER
HEADED
HEADER
HEALED
HEALER
HEAPED
HEARER
HEATED
HEATER
HEAVED
HEAVEN
HEAVER
HEAVES
HEBREW
HEDGED
HEDGER
HEDGES
HEDREN
HEEDED
HEELED
HEELER
HEFNER
HEFTED
HEIDEN

HEIFER
HELLER
HELMED
HELMET
HELPED
HELPER
HELTER
HELVES
HEMMED
HEMMER
HENLEY
HENNER
HEPPER
HERDED
HERDER
HERMES
HEROES
HERSEY
HESTER
JEERED
JEERER
JEETER
JEEVES
JELLED
JENNER
JENNET
JENSEN
JERKED
JERSEY
JESSEL
JESTED
JESTER
JETSET
JETTED
KEDGED
KEDGES
KEELED
KEELER
KEENED
KEENEN
KEENER
KEEPER
KEGGED
KEGLER
KEITEL
KELLER
KELLEY
KELSEY
KENNED
KENNEL
KEPLER
KERMES
KERNED
KERNEL
KERSEY
KEYNES
LEADED
LEADEN
LEADER
LEAFED
LEAKED
LEAKER
LEAKEY
LEANED
LEANER
LEAPED
LEAPER
LEASED
LEASER
LEASES
LEAVED
LEAVEN
LEAVES
LEDGER

LEDGES
LEERED
LEERER
LEGGED
LEGMEN
LEGREE
LEHRER
LEIDEN
LEMUEL
LENDER
LENSED
LENSES
LENTEN
LEONES
LERNER
LESLEY
LESSEE
LESSEN
LESSER
LESTER
LETTED
LETTER
LEVEED
LEVEES
LEVIED
LEVIER
LEVIES
LEWDER
LEYDEN
MEAGER
MEANER
MEDLEY
MEEKER
MEETER
MELDED
MELEES
MELTED
MEMBER
MENDED
MENDEL
MENDER
MENDES
MENNEN
MEOWED
MERCED
MERCER
MERGED
MERGER
MERGES
MERKEL
MERMEN
MERSEY
MESHED
MESHES
MESMER
MESSED
MESSES
METIER
METRES
MEWLED
MEWLER
NEARED
NEARER
NEATEN
NEATER
NECKED
NEEDED
NEPHEW
NERVES
NESSES
NESTEA
NESTED
NESTER
NETHER

NETMEN
NETTED
NEUMES
NEUTER
NEWLEY
OERTER
PEAHEN
PEAKED
PEALED
PEAVEY
PECKED
PEEDEE
PEEKED
PEELED
PEELER
PEENED
PEEPED
PEEPER
PEERED
PEEVED
PEEVES
PEEWEE
PEGGED
PEGLER
PEKOES
PELLET
PELMET
PELTED
PELTER
PENCEL
PENDED
PENMEN
PENNED
PENNER
PENNEY
PENSEE
PEPPED
PEPPER
PERKED
PERMED
PERTER
PESTER
PETREL
PETTED
PETTER
PEWEES
PEWTER
READER
REALER
REALES
REAMED
REAMER
REAPED
REAPER
REARED
REARER
REDDEN
REDDER
REDEEM
REDOES
REDREW
REDSEA
REDYED
REDYES
REEFED
REEFER
REEKED
REELED
REEVED
REEVES
REFFED
REFLEX
REFUEL
REGLET

REGRET
REHEEL
REINED
REINER
RELIED
RELIEF
RELIES
RENDER
RENNES
RENNET
RENTED
RENTER
REOPEN
RESEED
RESEEN
RESEES
RESTED
RESTER
RETIED
RETIES
REUBEN
REUNES
REUSED
REUSES
REUTER
REVIEW
REVUES
REVVED
SEABED
SEABEE
SEALED
SEALER
SEAMED
SEAMEN
SEARED
SEATED
SEATER
SECKEL
SECRET
SEDGES
SEEDED
SEEDER
SEEGER
SEEKER
SEEMED
SEEPED
SEERED
SEGUED
SEGUES
SEIDEL
SEINED
SEINER
SEINES
SEIZED
SEIZER
SEIZES
SELLER
SELVES
SEMPER
SENDER
SENNET
SENSED
SENSEI
SENSES
SEPTET
SEQUEL
SERGEI
SERGES
SERIES
SERVED
SERVER
SERVES
SESTET
SETTEE
SETTER
SEVRES
SEXIER
SEXTET
TEAMED
TEARED
TEASED
TEASEL
TEASER
TEASES
TEASET
TEDDED
TEDDER
TEDKEY
TEEHEE
TEEMED
TEENER
TEETER
TEHEED
TEHEES
TELLER
TEMPED
TEMPEH
TEMPER
TENDED
TENDER
TENREC
TENSED
TENSER
TENSES
TENTED
TENTER
TEPEES
TERCEL
TERCET
TERKEL
TERMED
TERRET
TERSER
TESTED
TESTEE
TESTER
TETHER
TETZEL
TEXMEX
VEBLEN
VEDDER
VEERED
VEGGED
VEILED
VEINED
VELVET
VENDED
VENDEE
VENEER
VENTED
VENTER
VENUES
VEREEN
VERGED
VERGER
VERGES
VERSED
VERSES
VERTEX
VERVET
VESPER
VESSEL
VESTED
VESTEE
VETOED
VETOER
VETOES
VETTED
WEAKEN
WEAKER
WEANED
WEARER
WEASEL
WEAVED
WEAVER
WEAVES
WEBBED
WEBBER
WEDDED
WEDGED
WEDGES
WEEDED
WEEDER
WEEPER
WELDED
WELDER
WELLED
WELLES
WELTED
WELTER
WENCES
WENDED
WERFEL
WERNER
WESLEY
WESSEX
WETHER
WETTED
WETTER
XERXES
YEAGER
YELLED
YELLER
YELPED
YELPER
YENNED
YEOMEN
YERKES
YESMEN
YESSED
YESSES
YESTER
ZENGER
ZEROED
ZEROES
ZESTED

•E•••E

AEDILE
AERATE
AEROBE
BEADLE
BEAGLE
BEANIE
BEATLE
BECAME
BECOME
BEDAZE
BEETLE
BEFORE
BEGONE
BEHAVE
BELIZE
BEMINE
BEMIRE
BEMUSE
BERATE
BERNIE
BERTIE
BESIDE
BESSIE
BETAKE
BETIDE
BETISE
BEURRE
BEWARE
CECILE
CELINE
CELLAE
CENOTE
CENTRE
CERATE
CERISE
CERUSE
CESARE
CETANE
DEARIE
DEARME
DEBASE
DEBATE
DEBBIE
DEBONE
DECADE
DECIDE
DECKLE
DECODE
DECREE
DEDUCE
DEEDEE
DEFACE
DEFAME
DEFILE
DEFINE
DEFUSE
DEGAGE
DEGREE
DEIDRE
DEJURE
DELATE
DELETE
DELUDE
DELUGE
DELUXE
DEMISE
DEMODE
DEMOTE
DEMURE
DENGUE
DENISE
DENOTE
DENUDE
DEPONE
DEPOSE
DEPUTE
DERIDE
DERIVE
DESIRE
DEVICE
DEVINE
DEVISE
DEVOTE
EEYORE
FEEBLE
FELINE
FELIPE
FELLOE
FEMALE
FERGIE
FERULE
FESCUE
FETTLE
GEEGEE
GEMMAE
GENEVE
GENOME
GENTLE
GEORGE
GERTIE
HEARYE
HECATE
HECKLE
HEDDLE
HEEBIE
HELENE
HERBIE
HETTIE
HEYJOE
JEANNE
JECKLE
JEJUNE
JENNIE
JEROME
JESSIE
KELPIE
KETONE
KETTLE
KEWPIE
LEAGUE
LEGATE
LEGREE
LEGUME
LENAPE
LENNIE
LENORE
LEONIE
LESAGE
LESLIE
LESSEE
LETSBE
LEVENE
LEVINE
LEVITE
LEXEME
MEAGRE
MEALIE
MEANIE
MEDDLE
MENACE
MENAGE
MENSAE
MEROPE
METATE
METOPE
METTLE
NEEDLE
NEGATE
NEISSE
NELLIE
NESSIE
NESTLE
NETTLE
NEWAGE
OENONE
OEUVRE
PEBBLE
PEDATE
PEDDLE
PEEDEE
PEERCE
PEEWEE
PELAGE
PENNAE
PENSEE
PEOPLE
PERDUE
PERUKE
PERUSE
PESTLE
PETITE
PETRIE
PEYOTE
REBATE
REBUKE
RECANE
RECEDE
RECIFE
RECIPE
RECITE
RECODE
RECUSE
REDATE
REDEYE
REDONE
REDUCE
REFACE
REFILE
REFINE
REFUGE
REFUSE
REFUTE
REGALE
REGGAE
REGGIE
REGIME
REGLUE
REHIRE
RELACE
RELATE
RELINE
RELIVE
RELUME
REMADE
REMAKE
REMISE
REMOTE
REMOVE
RENAME
RENEGE
RENNIE
RENOTE
REPAVE
REPINE
REPOSE
REPUTE
RERATE
RESALE
RESCUE
RESHOE
RESIDE
RESILE
RESOLE
RESUME
RETAKE
RETAPE
RETENE
RETILE
RETIME
RETIRE
RETUNE
RETYPE
REVERE
REVILE
REVISE
REVIVE
REVOKE
REWIRE
REWOVE
REZONE
SEABEE
SEANCE
SEARLE
SECEDE
SECURE
SEDATE
SEDILE
SEDUCE
SEETHE
SEICHE
SELENE
SEMELE
SEMITE
SEMPRE
SENATE
SERAPE
SERENE
SERINE
SESAME
SETOSE
SETTEE
SETTLE
SEVERE
SEWAGE
TECHIE
TEEHEE
TEETHE
TEMPLE
TENACE
TENURE
TERETE
TESSIE
TESTAE
TESTEE
VEGGIE
VELOCE
VENDEE
VENICE
VENIRE
VENITE
VERITE
VESTEE
WEDGIE
WEENIE

••EE••

ADEEMS
AMEERS
BLEEDS
BLEEPS
BREECH
BREEDS
BREEZE
BREEZY
CHEECH
CHEEKS
CHEEKY
CHEEPS
CHEERS
CHEERY
CHEESE
CHEESY
CLEEKS
CLEESE
CREEDS
CREEKS
CREELS
CREEPS
CREEPY
DWEEBS
EMEERS
FLEECE
FLEECY
FLEERS
FLEETS
FREELY
FREEST
FREEZE
GREECE
GREEDY
GREEKS
GREENE
GREENS
GREENY
GREETS
KNEELS
OKEEFE
PREENS
QUEENS
SHEEDY
SHEEHY
SHEENA
SHEENS
SHEEPS
SHEERS
SHEETS
SLEEKS
SLEEKY
SLEEPS
SLEEPY
SLEETS
SLEETY
SLEEVE
SNEERS
SNEERY
SNEEZE
SNEEZY
SPEECH
SPEEDS
SPEEDY
STEEDS
STEELE
STEELS
STEELY
STEEPS
STEERS
STEEVE
SWEEPS
SWEETS
THEEND
TWEEDS
TWEEDY
TWEETS
TWEETY
TWEEZE
WHEELS
WHEEZE
WHEEZY

••E•E•

ABELES
AEETES
AKENES
ALEXEI
AMEDEO
APEMEN
APEXES
ARETES
BEEFED
BEEPED
BEEPER
BEEVES
BREMEN
BREUER
BREVES
BREVET
BREWED
BREWER
CHEVET
CHEWED
CHEWER
CLEPED
CLEVER
CLEVES
CLEWED
CREMES
CRENEL
CREPES
CREWED
CREWEL
DEEDED
DEEDEE
DEEMED
DEEPEN
DEEPER
DIESEL
DIESES
DIETED
DIETER
DREXEL
DUELED
DUELER
ELEVEN
ELEVES
EVENED
EVENER
EXETER
EYELET
FEEDER
FEELER
FLEXED
FLEXES
FUELED
FUELER
GEEGEE
GEEZER
GLEBES
GREBES
GRETEL
GREYED
GREYER
HEEDED
HEELED
HEELER
IBEXES
ICEMEN
IRENES
JAEGER
JEERED
JEERER
JEETER
JEEVES
JOETEX
KEELED
KEELER
KEENED
KEENEN
KEENER
KEEPER
KIEFER
LEERED
LEERER
LIEDER
LIEFER
LIEGES
LIENEE
MEEKER
MEETER
NEEDED
NIECES
NUECES
OBEYED
OLEVEL
OMELET
OPENED
OPENER
OXEYES
PEEDEE
PEEKED
PEELED
PEELER
PEENED
PEEPED
PEEPER
PEERED
PEEVED
PEEVES
PEEWEE
PIECED
PIECER
PIECES
PIEMEN
PIETER
PLEBES
PREFER
PREMED
PRESET
PRETER
PREYED
QUEBEC
QUEUED
QUEUER
QUEUES
REEFED
REEFER
REEKED
REELED
REEVED
REEVES
SCENES
SEEDED
SEEDER
SEEGER
SEEKER
SEEMED
SEEPED
SEERED
SHEKEL
SHEREE
SIEGED
SIEGES
SIEVED
SIEVES
SKEWED
SKEWER
SLEWED
SPEWED
STELES
STEREO
STERES
STEVEN
STEWED
STEWER
SUEDES
SWEDEN
SWEDES
TEEHEE
TEEMED
TEENER
TEETER
THEBES
THEFED
THEMED
THEMES
THESES
TIERED
TREBEK
UNEVEN
VEERED
VIEWED
VIEWER
WEEDED
WEEDER
WEEPER
WIENER
WIESEL

••E••E

ADELIE
ADELLE
ADESTE
AHERNE
ALEGRE
AMEBAE
AMECHE
AMERCE
ATEASE
AVENGE
AVENUE
AVERSE
AYEAYE
BEETLE
BIERCE
BLENDE
BREEZE
BYEBYE
CHEESE
CHELAE
CHEQUE
CHERIE
CHEVRE
CLEAVE
CLEESE
COERCE
CREASE
CREATE
CRECHE
CREOLE
DEEDEE
DIEPPE
DREDGE
EDERLE
EMERGE
ETERNE
FAERIE
FAEROE
FEEBLE
FIERCE
FLECHE
FLEDGE
FLEECE
FLENSE
FREEZE
GEEGEE
GOETHE
GREASE
GREAVE
GREECE
GREENE
GREIGE
GUERRE
HEEBIE
ICEAGE
IDEATE
KPELLE
KRESGE
LIENEE
LIERNE
LIEVRE
NEEDLE
ODENSE
ODETTE
OKEEFE
OLEATE
ONEDGE
ORELSE
PEEDEE
PEERCE
PEEWEE
PHEDRE
PIERCE
PIERRE
PLEASE
PLEDGE
PREMIE
PUENTE
SEETHE
SHEAVE
SHELVE
SHEREE
SIECLE
SLEAVE
SLEAZE
SLEDGE
SLEEVE
SNEEZE
SPECIE
STEELE
STEEVE
STELAE
STEPPE
STERNE
STEVIE
SVELTE
SWERVE
TEEHEE
TEETHE
THECAE
THENCE
THEYRE
THEYVE
TIEDYE
TIERCE
TREBLE
TSETSE
TWEEZE
TWELVE
UNEASE
VIENNE
WEENIE
WHEEZE
WHENCE
YVETTE

•••EE•

ADWEEK
AFREET
AGREED
AGREES
AILEEN
ALLEES
ANTEED
ASLEEP
AXSEED
BALEEN
BOPEEP
CAREEN
CAREER
CUVEES
DONEES
DUDEEN
EILEEN
EMCEED
EMCEES
ESTEEM
EXCEED
FUSEES
FUZEES
GELEES
HOMEEC
INDEED
INNEED
KAREEM
LATEEN
LEVEED
LEVEES
LYCEES
MELEES
MOREEN
MUDEEL
PAYEES
PEWEES
POTEEN
PUREED
PUREES
RANEES
REDEEM
REHEEL
RESEED
RESEEN
RESEES
RUPEES
SATEEN
SCREED
SCREEN
SCREES
SPLEEN
SPREES
STREEP
STREET
TEHEED
TEHEES
TEPEES
THREED
THREES
TUREEN
UNHEED
UNMEET
UNREEL
UNSEEN
UPKEEP
VENEER
VEREEN

•••E•E

ACCEDE
ACHEBE
ACHENE
ADHERE
ALKENE
ALLEGE
ALLELE
AMPERE
ANNEXE
APIECE
ARLENE
ARSENE
ATHENE
BAREGE
BIREME
BREEZE
BUTENE
CHEESE
CLEESE
COHERE
CYBELE
DELETE
EFFETE
EOCENE
EPHEBE
ESSENE
ETHENE
EUGENE
FILENE
FLEECE
FOVEAE
FREEZE
FRIEZE
GALEAE
GAMETE
GENEVE
GREECE
GREENE
GRIEVE
GYRENE
HELENE
IMPEDE
INDENE
INHERE
IRLENE
ISMENE
JOLENE
LATENE
LEVENE
LEXEME
MANEGE
NICENE
OCREAE
OKEEFE
OSSETE
PALEAE
PAREVE
PHOEBE
POPEYE
RACEME
RECEDE
REDEYE
RENEGE
RETENE
REVERE
RIBEYE
SCHEME
SECEDE
SELENE
SEMELE
SERENE
SEVERE
SLEEVE
SNEEZE
SPHERE
STEELE
STEEVE
STPETE
SURETE
TALESE
TERETE
THIEVE
TUYERE
TWEEZE
VARESE
WHEEZE
XYLENE

••••EE

ADOREE
ANNLEE
APOGEE
ATTLEE
BAILEE
BOOTEE
BOTREE
BUNGEE
BURGEE
COFFEE
CORVEE
COULEE
DECREE
DEEDEE
DEGREE
DONNEE
DRAGEE
DUNDEE
ELYSEE
ENTREE
EPOPEE
FRISEE
GEEGEE
GOATEE
JAYCEE
JAYVEE
LEGREE
LESSEE
LIENEE
LISTEE
MALLEE
MARLEE
MARMEE
MAUMEE
PARSEE
PAWNEE
PEEDEE
PEEWEE
PENSEE
POMMEE
PONGEE
PUGREE
PUTTEE
RAPPEE
RUSHEE
SANTEE
SEABEE
SETTEE
SHEREE
SIGNEE
SIRREE
SOIREE
SWANEE
TEEHEE
TESTEE
TOATEE
TOFFEE
TOUPEE
TOWHEE
TRALEE
VALLEE
VENDEE
VESTEE
YANKEE
YIPPEE

EF••••

EFFACE
EFFECT
EFFETE
EFFIGY
EFFLUX
EFFORT
EFFUSE
EFLATS

E•F•••

EFFACE
EFFECT
EFFETE
EFFIGY
EFFLUX
EFFORT
EFFUSE
EIFFEL
ELFISH
ELFMAN
ENFANT

ENFOLD
ERFURT

E••F••
EARFUL
EIFFEL
EYEFUL

E•••F•
EXWIFE

E••••F
ENGULF

•EF•••
BEFALL
BEFELL
BEFITS
BEFOGS
BEFORE
BEFOUL
DEFACE
DEFAME
DEFATS
DEFEAT
DEFECT
DEFEND
DEFERS
DEFIED
DEFIES
DEFILE
DEFINE
DEFLEA
DEFOGS
DEFORM
DEFRAY
DEFTER
DEFTLY
DEFUSE
HEFLIN
HEFNER
HEFTED
REFACE
REFERS
REFFED
REFILE
REFILL
REFINE
REFITS
REFLEX
REFLUX
REFORM
REFUEL
REFUGE
REFUND
REFUSE
REFUTE
TEFLON

•E•F••
BEEFED
BEEFUP
BELFRY
DEAFEN
DEAFER
DELFTS
HEIFER
LEAFED
LETFLY
REDFIN
REDFIR
REDFOX
REEFED
REEFER
REFFED
SEAFAN
SEAFOX
SEEFIT
WERFEL
WETFLY

•E••F•
BEGOFF
BEREFT
DECAFS
GETOFF
LEDOFF
LETOFF
REBUFF
RECIFE
SEEOFF
SERIFS
SETOFF
TEEOFF
VERIFY

•E•••F
BEGOFF
BEHALF
BEHOOF
BELIEF
CERTIF
GETOFF
HEAROF
HEREOF
LEDOFF
LETOFF
REBUFF
RELIEF
SEEOFF
SETOFF
TEEOFF

••EF••
BEEFED
BEEFUP
CLEFTS
EYEFUL
ICEFOG
IREFUL
KIEFER
LIEFER
OLEFIN
PREFAB
PREFER
PREFIX
REEFED
REEFER
RUEFUL
SEEFIT
STEFAN
STEFFI
THEFED
THEFTS
USEFUL
WOEFUL

••E•F•
DIEOFF
OKEEFE
SEEOFF
SHEAFS
STEFFI
TEEOFF

••E••F
DIEOFF
SEEOFF
SHERIF
TEEOFF

•••EF•
BEREFT
BRIEFS
CHIEFS
OKEEFE
RAREFY
TUMEFY

•••E•F
HEREOF
IMPERF
INLEAF
ITSELF
MYSELF

••••EF
BELIEF
RELIEF
UNICEF

EG••••
EGBERT
EGERIA
EGESTA
EGESTS
EGGCUP
EGGING
EGGNOG
EGGSON
EGMONT
EGOISM
EGOIST
EGRESS
EGRETS

E•G•••
EAGLED
EAGLES
EAGLET
EAGRES
EDGARD
EDGARS
EDGEIN
EDGERS
EDGIER
EDGILY
EDGING
EGGCUP
EGGING
EGGNOG
EGGSON
EIGHTH
EIGHTS
EIGHTY
ENGAGE
ENGELS
ENGINE
ENGIRD
ENGIRT
ENGLUT
ENGRAM
ENGULF
ERGATE
ERGOTS
EUGENE

E••G••
ELEGIT
EMIGRE
ENIGMA

E•••G•
EFFIGY
ELOIGN
EMERGE
ENCAGE
ENERGY
ENGAGE
ENOUGH
ENRAGE
ENSIGN
ERYNGO
EULOGY

E••••G
EALING
EARING
EARWIG
EASING
EATING
EBBING
EDBERG
EDGING
EGGING
EGGNOG
EKBERG
ENDING
EPILOG
EPPING
ERRING
ERVING
EYEING

•EG•••
AEGEAN
BEGETS
BEGGAR
BEGGED
BEGINS
BEGLEY
BEGOFF
BEGONE
BEGUMS
DEGAGE
DEGREE
DEGUST
HEGARI
HEGIRA
KEGGED
KEGLER
LEGACY
LEGALS
LEGATE
LEGATO
LEGEND
LEGGED
LEGION
LEGIST
LEGMAN
LEGMEN
LEGREE
LEGUME
MEGALO
MEGARA
MEGILP
MEGOHM
NEGATE
PEGGED
PEGLER
PEGTOP
REGAIN
REGALE
REGARD
REGENT
REGGAE
REGGIE
REGIME
REGINA
REGION
REGIUS
REGLET
REGLUE
REGNAL
REGRET
SEGUED
SEGUES
SEGURA
VEGANS
VEGGED
VEGGIE

•E•G••
BEAGLE
BEEGUM
BEGGAR
BEGGED
BEIGES
BENGAL
BENGAY
BERGEN
DEIGNS
DENGUE
FEIGNS
FERGIE
FERGUS
GEEGAW
GEEGEE
GEIGER
GEWGAW
HEDGED
HEDGER
HEDGES
HEIGHT
JETGUN
KEDGED
KEDGES
KEGGED
LEAGUE
LEDGER
LEDGES
LEGGED
LENGTH
MEAGER
MEAGRE
MEDGAR
MERGED
MERGER
MERGES
NEIGHS
PEGGED
PENGHU
REAGAN
REDGUM
REGGAE
REGGIE
REIGNS
SEAGAL
SEDGES
SEEGER
SERGEI
SERGES
SERGIO
VEGGED
VEGGIE
VEIGHT
VERGED
VERGER
VERGES
WEDGED
WEDGES
WEDGIE
WEIGHS
WEIGHT
YEAGER
ZENGER
ZEUGMA

•E••G•
BEFOGS
BEINGS
BELUGA
BENIGN
DEBUGS
DEFOGS
DEGAGE
DELUGE
DESIGN
GEORGE
LEHIGH
LESAGE
LETSGO
MENAGE
NEWAGE
PELAGE
REBAGS
REFUGE
RENEGE
REPEGS
REPUGN
RESIGN
RETAGS
SENEGA
SEWAGE
TELUGU

•E•••G
BEDBUG
BELONG
BENING
BERING
CEDING
DELONG
DEWING
FEEING
FETING
GEEING
GEHRIG
HERZOG
HEWING
HEXING
JETLAG
KENNYG
KEYING
MEKONG
METING
MEWING
PEKING
PENANG
PETROG
REDDOG
REDTAG
REHANG
REHUNG
RESING
SEABAG
SEADOG
SEBERG
SEEING
SEWING
TEABAG
TEEING
VEXING
WETTIG

••EG••
ALEGAR
ALEGRE
BEEGUM
ELEGIT
GEEGAW
GEEGEE
GREGOR
JAEGER
LIEGES
OMEGAS
OREGON
SEEGER
SIEGED
SIEGES

••E•G•
ATERGO
AVENGE
AWEIGH
CLERGY
DREDGE
EMERGE
ENERGY
FLEDGE
GREIGE
ICEAGE
KRESGE
ONEDGE
PLEDGE
SLEDGE
SLEIGH

••E••G
AGEING
BOEING
DYEING
EYEING
FEEING
GEEING
HIEING
HOEING
ICEBAG
ICEFOG
LIEBIG
PYEDOG
SEEING
STENOG
TEEING
TIEING
TOEING

•••EG•
ALLEGE
BADEGG
BAREGE
BODEGA
FOREGO
MANEGE
NONEGO
ORTEGA
OSWEGO
PHLEGM
RAWEGG
RENEGE
REPEGS
SENEGA
UNPEGS

•••E•G
BADEGG
EDBERG
EKBERG
LIPENG
RATEDG
RAWEGG
SEBERG

••••EG
DOGLEG
MUSKEG
NUTMEG
TUAREG

E•H•••
ECHOED
ECHOES
ECHOIC
EPHAHS
EPHEBE
EPHODS
EPHORI
EPHORS
EPHRON
ERHARD
ESHARP
ETHANE
ETHENE
ETHERS
ETHICS
ETHNIC
ETHNOS
EXHALE
EXHORT

E••H••
EIGHTH
EIGHTS
EIGHTY
EITHER
ELOHIM
ESCHER
ESCHEW
ESTHER
ETCHED
ETCHER
ETCHES
EUCHRE

E•••H•
EARTHA
EARTHY
ELISHA
EPHAHS
EPOCHS

E••••H
EIGHTH
ELFISH
ELIJAH
EMDASH
ENDASH
ENMESH
ENOUGH
ENRICH
EOLITH
EPARCH
EUNUCH
EXARCH

•EH•••
BEHALF
BEHAVE
BEHELD
BEHEST
BEHIND
BEHOLD
BEHOOF
DEHORN
GEHRIG
LEHIGH
LEHRER
LEHUAS
REHANG
REHASH
REHEAL
REHEAR
REHEAT
REHEEL
REHELD
REHEMS
REHIRE
REHOOK
REHUNG
TEHEED
TEHEES
YEHUDI

•E•H••
AETHER
BENHUR
BETHEL
HEEHAW
JETHRO
KESHIA
LETHAL
MENHIR
MESHED
MESHES
METHOD
METHYL
NEPHEW
NEPHRO
NETHER
PEAHEN
REDHAT
REDHOT
RESHIP
RESHOD
RESHOE
RESHOT
SENHOR
TECHIE
TECHNO
TEEHEE
TEPHRA
TETHER
TETHYS
WETHER
ZEPHYR

•E••H•
BERTHA
BERTHS
BETCHA
DELPHI
DEPTHS
GEISHA
HEATHS
HEIGHT
MEGOHM
NEIGHS
PEACHY
PENGHU
PERCHA
REECHO
SEETHE
SEICHE
TEETHE
TENTHS
TETCHY
VEIGHT
WEIGHS
WEIGHT

•E•••H
BEULAH
CERIPH
DEARTH
DETACH
FELLAH
FETISH
HEALTH
HEARTH
JEWISH
LEHIGH
LENGTH
MENSCH
NEWISH
PERISH
PESACH
REHASH
RELISH
REWASH
SEARCH
SERAPH
TEMPEH
TERAPH
WEALTH
ZENITH
ZEROTH

••EH••
FOEHNS
HEEHAW
TEEHEE
THEHAJ

••E•H•
ALEPHS
AMECHE
ARETHA
AYESHA
BRECHT
CRECHE
CZECHS
FLECHE
FLESHY
GOETHE
ILESHA
OBEAHS
REECHO
SEETHE
SHEEHY
TEETHE

••E••H
AWEIGH
BLEACH
BLENCH
BREACH
BREATH
BREECH
CHEECH
CLENCH
DRENCH
FLETCH
FRENCH
GUELPH
KVETCH
PLEACH
PREACH
QUENCH
SHEATH
SKETCH
SLEIGH
SLEUTH
SMERSH
SPEECH
STENCH
TRENCH
WREATH
WRENCH
WRETCH

•••EH•
HIDEHO
SHEEHY

•••E•H
AFRESH
BREECH
CHEECH
COMETH
DALETH
ENMESH
GARETH
HITECH
JOBETH
JOSEPH
LAMECH
LAMEDH
OHYEAH
SAMEKH
SPEECH
TAKETH
THRESH
UNMESH
VOTECH

••••EH
TEMPEH
YAHWEH

EI••••
EIDERS
EIDOLA
EIFFEL
EIGHTH
EIGHTS
EIGHTY
EILEEN
EISNER
EITHER

E•I•••
EDIBLE
EDICTS
EDILES
EDISON
EDITED
EDITOR
ELICIT
ELIDED
ELIDES
ELIJAH
ELINOR
ELISHA
ELISSA
ELITES
ELIXIR
EMIGRE
EMILIA
EMILIO
EMINOR
ENIGMA
ENISLE
EPICAL
EPILOG
EPIRUS
ERINYS
EVICTS
EVILER
EVILLY
EVINCE
EXILED
EXILES
EXILIC
EXISTS
EXITED

E••I••
EALING
EARING
EASIER
EASILY
EASING
EATING
EBBING
EDDIED
EDDIES
EDGIER
EDGILY
EDGING
EELIER
EERIER
EERILY
EFFIGY
EGGING
EGOISM
EGOIST
ELAINE
ELFISH
ELLICE
ELLIOT
ELMIRA
ELNINO
ELOIGN
ELOISE
ELVIRA
EMAILS
EMPIRE
ENCINA
ENCINO
ENDING
ENDIVE
ENGINE
ENGIRD
ENGIRT
ENLIST
ENMITY
ENNIUS
ENRICH
ENRICO
ENSIGN
ENSILE
ENTICE
ENTIRE
ENTITY
ENVIED
ENVIES
EOLIAN
EOLITH
EONIAN
EOSINS
EPPING
EQUINE
EQUIPS
EQUITY
ERBIUM
ERMINE
EROICA
ERRING
ERVING
ESKIMO
ESPIAL
ESPIED
ESPIES
ETHICS
ETOILE
EUNICE
EXCISE
EXCITE
EXPIRE
EXPIRY
EXWIFE
EYEING
EYRIES

E•••I•
EARWIG
EASEIN
EATSIN
ECESIS
ECHOIC
ECLAIR
EDENIC
EDGEIN
EGERIA
ELAPID
ELEGIT
ELEMIS
ELICIT
ELIXIR
ELOHIM
EMILIA
EMILIO
ENJOIN
ENOKIS
ENOSIS
ENTAIL
ENVOIS
EROTIC
ESPRIT
ETALIA
ETALII
ETHNIC
ETONIC
EUCLID
EXILIC
EXOTIC
EYELID

E••••I
EPHORI
ERNANI
ETALII
EVENKI

•EI•••
BEIGES
BEINGS
BEIRUT
CEIBAS
CEILED
DEICED
DEICER
DEICES
DEIDRE
DEIGNS
DEIMOS
DEISTS
FEIGNS
FEINTS
FEISTY
GEIGER
GEISEL
GEISHA
HEIDEN
HEIFER
HEIGHT
HEISTS
KEITEL
LEIDEN
NEIGHS
NEISSE
REIGNS
REINED
REINER
REININ
REINKS
SEICHE
SEIDEL
SEINED
SEINER
SEINES
SEISMO
SEISMS
SEIZED
SEIZER
SEIZES
VEIGHT
VEILED
VEINAL
VEINED
WEIGHS
WEIGHT
WEIMAR
WEIRDO

•E•I••
AEDILE
AERIAL
AERIES
BEDIMS
BEFITS
BEGINS
BEHIND
BELIAL
BELIED
BELIEF
BELIES
BELIZE
BEMINE
BEMIRE
BENIGN
BENING
BENITO
BERING
BESIDE
BETIDE
BETISE
BEVIES
CECILE
CEDING
CELINE
CERIPH
CERISE
CERIUM
CESIUM
DEBITS
DECIDE
DEFIED
DEFIES
DEFILE
DEFINE
DELICT
DELIST
DELIUS
DEMISE
DEMITS
DENIAL
DENIED
DENIER
DENIES
DENIMS
DENIRO
DENISE
DEPICT
DERIDE
DERIVE
DESICA
DESIGN
DESILU
DESIRE
DESIST
DEVICE
DEVILS
DEVINE
DEVISE
DEVITO
DEWIER
DEWING
DEWITT
EELIER
EERIER
EERILY
FEEING
FELINE
FELIPE
FENIAN
FETING
FETISH
GEEING
GEMINI
GENIAL
GENIES
GENIUS
GEZIRA
HEGIRA
HELIOS
HELIUM
HERIOT
HESIOD
HEWING
HEXING
JEWISH
KEYING
LEGION
LEGIST
LEHIGH
LENITY
LERIDA
LEVIED
LEVIER
LEVIES
LEVINE
LEVITE
LEVITY
LEXICA
MEDIAL
MEDIAN
MEDIAS
MEDICI
MEDICO
MEDICS
MEDINA
MEDIUM
MEGILP
MELINA
MENIAL
MENINX
MERIDA
MERINO
MERITS
METIER

METING
MEWING
MEXICO
NEVINS
NEWISH
PEKING
PELION
PEPINO
PEPITA
PERILS
PERIOD
PERISH
PETITE
PEWITS
REAIRS
REBIDS
REBIND
RECIFE
RECIPE
RECITE
REDIAL
REDINK
REFILE
REFILL
REFINE
REFITS
REGIME
REGINA
REGION
REGIUS
REHIRE
RELICS
RELICT
RELIED
RELIEF
RELIES
RELINE
RELISH
RELIST
RELIVE
REMICK
REMIND
REMISE
REMISS
REMITS
REOILS
REPINE
RESIDE
RESIGN
RESILE
RESING
RESINS
RESIST
RETIAL
RETIED
RETIES
RETILE
RETIME
RETINA
RETIRE
REVIEW
REVILE
REVISE
REVIVE
REWIND
REWINS
REWIRE
SEDILE
SEEING
SEMITE
SENIOR
SEPIAS
SERIAL
SERIES
SERIFS
SERINE
SERINS
SETINS
SEWING
SEXIER
SEXILY
SEXIST
TEDIUM
TEEING
VENIAL
VENICE
VENIRE
VENITE
VERIFY
VERILY
VERISM
VERITE
VERITY
VEXING
ZENITH

•E••I•

AENEID
AEOLIA
AEOLIC
BEANIE
BEATIT
BELAIR
BELOIT
BENDIX
BENOIT
BERLIN
BERNIE
BERTIE
BESSIE
BESTIR
BEWAIL
CEDRIC
CELTIC
CERTIF
CERVID
DEALIN
DEARIE
DEBBIE
DEBRIS
DECEIT
DELRIO
DELTIC
DENNIS
DENTIL
DENTIN
DERAIL
DERMIS
DERRIS
DETAIL
DETAIN
DEVEIN
DEVOID
DEVOIR
FELLIN
FERGIE
FERRIC
FERRIS
FERVID
GEHRIG
GERBIL
GERTIE
GETSIN
GETSIT
HEADIN
HECTIC
HEEBIE
HEFLIN
HELDIN
HEMSIN
HENBIT
HENNIN
HENRIK
HERBIE
HEREIN
HERMIT
HEROIC
HESTIA
HETTIE
JENNIE
JERKIN
JESSIE
JESUIT
KEEPIN
KELPIE
KELVIN
KEMPIS
KERMIS
KERMIT
KESHIA
KEWPIE
KEYSIN
LEADIN
LENNIE
LENTIL
LEONID
LEONIE
LESLIE
LETSIN
MEALIE
MEANIE
MELVIL
MELVIN
MEMOIR
MENHIR
MENTIS
MERLIN
METRIC
NELLIE
NEREID
NEREIS
NESSIE
PECTIC
PECTIN
PEERIN
PELVIC
PELVIS
PENCIL
PENNIA
PENNIS
PEORIA
PEPSIN
PEPTIC
PERMIT
PERSIA
PETAIN
PETRIE
PETTIT
READIN
REALIA
REBOIL
RECOIL
REDFIN
REDFIR
REEDIT
REELIN
REGAIN
REGGIE
REININ
REJOIN
RELAID
REMAIL
REMAIN
RENAIL
RENNIE
RENNIN
RENOIR
REPAID
REPAIR
RESHIP
RESNIK
RETAIL
RETAIN
RETRIM
REVOIR
SEEFIT
SEEPIN
SEESIN
SENDIN
SENNIT
SENTIN
SEPTIC
SEQUIN
SERAIS
SERBIA
SERGIO
SERKIN
SETSIN
TECHIE
TENNIS
TENPIN
TESSIE
TETRIS
VEGGIE
VERDIN
VERMIN
VESPID
WEDGIE
WEENIE
WEEVIL
WELKIN
WENTIN
WESKIT
WETTIG
YESSIR
ZEROIN
ZEUXIS

•E•••I

CENTRI
DELPHI
DENALI
DENDRI
GELATI
GEMINI
HEGARI
JETSKI
KERNOI
MEDICI
MESABI
NEPALI
NEROLI
SENSEI
SERGEI
SESQUI
YEHUDI
YEMENI

••EI••

AGEING
AGEISM
AGEIST
AWEIGH
BOEING
DYEING
EYEING
FEEING
GEEING
GNEISS
GREIGE
HIEING
HOEING
KLEIST
ONEIDA
ONEILL
OREIDA
PLEIAD
SEEING
SHEIKS
SHEILA
SKEINS
SLEIGH
STEINS
TEEING
THEIRS
THEISM
THEIST
TIEING
TIEINS
TOEING
TOEINS

••E•I•

ACEDIA
ACETIC
ADELIE
ALEXIA
ALEXIS
AMEBIC
AMELIA
ANEMIA
ANEMIC
BLEWIT
CHEMIN
CHENIN
CHERIE
CLERIC
CLEVIS
COEDIT
CREDIT
CRETIN
DIESIS
DOESIN
DREWIN
ECESIS
EDENIC
EGERIA
ELEGIT
ELEMIS
EYELID
FAERIE
FLEWIN
GAELIC
GOESIN
HEEBIE
IBERIA
ICEDIN
ICESIN
IGETIT
IRENIC
ISELIN
KEEPIN
LIEBIG
LIESIN
MYELIN
NOESIS
NOETIC
NOEXIT
OBELIA
OLEFIN
PEERIN
PIETIN
POETIC
PRECIS
PREFIX
PRELIM
PREMIE
PREVIN
REEDIT
REELIN
SCENIC
SEEFIT
SEEPIN
SEESIN
SHERIF
SPECIE
STEPIN
STEVIE
THELIP
THESIS
THESIX
THETIC
THETIS
THEWIZ
TIEDIN
TIEPIN
TIESIN
TMESIS
TOEDIN
TOESIN
TREDIA
TREPID
USERID
WEENIE
WEEViL

••E••I

ALEXEI
EVENKI
NIELLI
OCELLI
STEFFI

•••EI•

AENEID
ALBEIT
CAMEIN
CAVEIN
CLUEIN
COHEIR
COMEIN
DECEIT
DEVEIN
DINEIN
DIVEIN
DONEIN
DOVEIN
EASEIN
EDGEIN
FADEIN
GAVEIN
GIVEIN
HEREIN
LIVEIN
LOMEIN
LOSEIT
LOVEIN
MADEIT
MAKEIT
MOVEIN
NEREID
NEREIS
OSSEIN
PILEIN
RAKEIN
ROPEIN
SOBEIT
SOLEIL
TAKEIN
TUNEIN
UNVEIL
VOTEIN
WADEIN
WAVEIN

•••E•I

ANGELI
DOREMI
HIDEKI
HUMERI
SILENI
YEMENI

••••EI

ALEXEI
ANDREI
BRUNEI
CISKEI
GLUTEI
MALLEI
NUCLEI
PROTEI
SANSEI
SENSEI
SERGEI
TAIPEI

EJ••••

EJECTA
EJECTS

E•J•••

ENJOIN
ENJOYS

E••J••

ELIJAH
EMAJOR

•EJ•••

DEJAVU
DEJECT
DEJURE
JEJUNE
REJECT
REJOIN
SEJANT

•E•J••

DEEJAY
HEYJOE
MENJOU
SELJUK
VEEJAY

••EJ••

DEEJAY
VEEJAY

••E••J

THEHAJ

EK••••

EKBERG
EKEOUT

E•K•••

ESKERS
ESKIMO

E••K••

ENOKIS
EVOKED
EVOKER
EVOKES

E•••K•

EUREKA
EVENKI

E••••K

EMBANK
EMBARK

•EK•••

BEKESY
DEKALB
JEKYLL
LEKVAR
MEKONG
NEKTON
PEKING
PEKOES
REKEYS

•E•K••

BEAKED
BEAKER
BECKER
BECKET
BECKON
DECKED
DECKER
DECKLE
GECKOS
HECKLE
JECKLE
JERKED
JERKIN
LEAKED
LEAKER
LEAKEY
MEEKER
MEEKLY
MERKEL
NECKED
PEAKED
PECKAT
PECKED
PEEKAT
PEEKED
PERKED
PERKUP
RECKON
REEKED
SECKEL
SEEKER
SERKIN
TEDKEY
TERKEL
WEAKEN
WEAKER
WEAKLY
WEEKLY
WELKIN
WESKIT
YERKES

•E••K•

BETAKE
JETSKI
MEDAKA
NEVSKY
PERUKE
REBUKE
REINKS
REMAKE
RETAKE
REVOKE
SEDAKA

•E•••K

BEDECK
BETOOK
DEBARK
DEBUNK
HENRIK
NEWARK
RECORK
REDINK
REDOAK
REEBOK
REHOOK
RELOCK
REMARK
REMICK
RESNIK
RETOOK
REWORK
SELJUK
SENDAK

••EK••

MEEKER
MEEKLY
PEEKAT
PEEKED
REEKED
SEEKER
SHEKEL
WEEKLY

••E•K•

ALECKY
BREAKS
CHECKS
CHEEKS
CHEEKY
CLEEKS
CLERKS
CREAKS
CREAKY
CREEKS
EVENKI
FLECKS
FREAKS
FREAKY
GREEKS
SHEIKS
SLEEKS
SLEEKY
SNEAKS
SNEAKY
SPEAKS
SPECKS
STEAKS
TWEAKS
VNECKS
WHELKS
WREAKS
WRECKS

••E••K

REEBOK
RHEBOK
SLEZAK
TREBEK

•••EK•

CHEEKS
CHEEKY
CLEEKS
CREEKS
EUREKA
GREEKS
HACEKS
HIDEKI
KOPEKS
SAMEKH
SLEEKS
SLEEKY
TOPEKA
UZBEKS

•••E•K

ADWEEK
BEDECK
KOPECK
LUBECK
ONDECK
SCREAK
SQUEAK
STREAK

••••EK

ADWEEK
DRABEK
DUBCEK
OCASEK
SHRIEK
SPACEK
TREBEK

EL••••

ELAINE
ELANDS
ELAPID
ELAPSE
ELATED
ELATER
ELATES
ELAYER
ELAYNE
ELBERT
ELBOWS
ELBRUS
ELDERS
ELDEST
ELECTS
ELEGIT
ELEMIS
ELEVEN
ELEVES
ELFISH
ELFMAN
ELICIT
ELIDED
ELIDES
ELIJAH
ELINOR
ELISHA
ELISSA
ELITES
ELIXIR
ELLERY
ELLICE
ELLIOT
ELMIRA
ELMORE
ELNINO
ELOHIM
ELOIGN
ELOISE
ELOPED
ELOPER
ELOPES
ELPASO
ELUDED
ELUDES
ELUTED
ELUTES
ELVERS
ELVIRA
ELWOOD
ELYSEE

E•L•••

EALING
ECLAIR
ECLATS
EELERS
EELIER
EFLATS
EILEEN
ELLERY
ELLICE
ELLIOT
ENLACE
ENLIST
EOLIAN
EOLITH
EULOGY

E••L••

EAGLED
EAGLES
EAGLET
EARLAP
ECCLES
ECOLES
EDILES
EFFLUX
EMBLEM
EMILIA
EMILIO
EMPLOY
ENBLOC
ENGLUT
EPILOG
ETALIA
ETALII
EUCLID
EVELYN
EVILER
EVILLY
EVOLVE
EVULSE
EXALTS
EXILED
EXILES
EXILIC
EXULTS
EYELET
EYELID

E•••L•

EASELS
EASILY
EBERLY
EDERLE
EDGILY
EDIBLE
EDSELS
EERILY
EIDOLA
EMAILS
ENABLE
ENDALL
ENFOLD
ENGELS
ENGULF
ENISLE
ENROLL
ENSILE
EQUALS
ERROLL
ETOILE
EVENLY
EVERLY
EVILLY
EXCELS
EXHALE
EXPELS
EXTOLS

E••••L

EARFUL
EIFFEL
ENAMEL
ENDALL
ENROLL
ENSOUL
ENTAIL
EPICAL
ERROLL
ESPIAL
ETYMOL
EYEFUL

•EL•••

BELAIR
BELAYS
BELDAM
BELFRY
BELIAL
BELIED
BELIEF
BELIES
BELIZE
BELLED
BELLES
BELLOC
BELLOW
BELOIT
BELONG
BELTED
BELUGA
CELEBS
CELERY
CELINE
CELLAE
CELLAR
CELLED
CELLOS
CELTIC
DELANO
DELANY
DELATE
DELAYS
DELEON
DELETE
DELFTS
DELICT
DELIST
DELIUS
DELONG
DELPHI
DELRAY
DELRIO
DELTAS
DELTIC
DELUDE
DELUGE
DELUXE
DELVED
DELVER
DELVES
EELERS
EELIER
FELDON
FELINE
FELIPE
FELLAH
FELLAS
FELLED
FELLER
FELLIN
FELLOE
FELLOW
FELLTO
FELONS
FELONY
FELTED
GELADA
GELATI
GELATO
GELEES
GELLED
GELSEY
HELDIN
HELDON
HELDTO
HELDUP
HELENA
HELENE
HELENS
HELIOS
HELIUM
HELLAS
HELLER
HELLOS
HELMED
HELMET
HELMUT
HELOTS
HELPED
HELPER
HELTER
HELVES
JELLED
KELLER
KELLEY
KELPIE
KELSEY
KELVIN
LELAND
MELANO
MELDED
MELEES
MELINA
MELLON
MELLOW
MELMAC
MELODY
MELONS
MELOTT
MELTED
MELTON
MELVIL
MELVIN
MELVYN
NELLIE
NELSON
PELAGE
PELEUS
PELION
PELLET
PELMET
PELOPS
PELOTA
PELTED
PELTER
PELTRY
PELVIC
PELVIS
RELACE
RELAID
RELATE
RELAYS
RELENT
RELETS
RELICS
RELICT
RELIED
RELIEF
RELIES
RELINE
RELISH
RELIST
RELIVE
RELOAD
RELOCK
RELUCT
RELUME
SELDOM
SELECT
SELENA
SELENE
SELJUK
SELLER
SELVES
TELEDU
TELLER
TELLON
TELUGU
VELCRO
VELDTS
VELLUM
VELOCE
VELOUR
VELVET
WELDED
WELDER
WELKIN
WELLED
WELLES
WELLUP
WELTED
WELTER
YELLED
YELLER
YELLOW
YELPED
YELPER

•E•L••

AEOLIA
AEOLIC
AEOLUS
BEDLAM
BEGLEY
BELLED
BELLES
BELLOC
BELLOW
BERLIN
BEULAH
CEILED
CELLAE
CELLAR
CELLED
CELLOS
CEYLON
DEALER
DEALIN
DEFLEA
DEPLOY
DEWLAP
FEALTY
FEELER
FELLAH
FELLAS
FELLED
FELLER
FELLIN
FELLOE
FELLOW
FELLTO
GELLED
HEALED
HEALER
HEALTH
HEELED
HEELER
HEFLIN
HELLAS
HELLER
HELLOS
HENLEY
JELLED
JETLAG
KEELED
KEELER
KEGLER
KELLER
KELLEY
KEPLER
KEVLAR
LEALTY
LESLEY
LESLIE
MEALIE
MEDLAR
MEDLAT
MEDLEY
MELLON
MELLOW
MERLIN
MERLON
MERLOT
MEWLED
MEWLER
NELLIE
NEWLEY
PEALED
PEDLAR
PEELED
PEELER
PEGLER
PELLET
PEPLOS
PEPLUM
REALER
REALES
REALIA
REALLY
REALMS
REALTY
REELED
REELIN

REFLEX
REFLUX
REGLET
REGLUE
REPLAN
REPLAY
REPLOW
REVLON
SEALAB
SEALED
SEALER
SEALUP
SELLER
SENLAC
TEFLON
TELLER
TELLON
TESLAS
VEBLEN
VEILED
VELLUM
WEALTH
WELLED
WELLES
WELLUP
WESLEY
YELLED
YELLER
YELLOW
ZEALOT

•E••L•

AEDILE
BEADLE
BEAGLE
BEATLE
BECALM
BEETLE
BEFALL
BEFELL
BEHALF
BEHELD
BEHOLD
BETELS
BEVELS
BEZELS
CECILE
DEADLY
DEARLY
DECALS
DECKLE
DEEPLY
DEFILE
DEFTLY
DEKALB
DENALI
DESALT
DESILU
DEVILS
EERILY
FEEBLE
FEEBLY
FEMALE
FERULE
FETTLE
GENTLE
GENTLY
GERALD
HECKLE
HEDDLE
HERALD
JECKLE
JEKYLL
JEWELS
KEENLY
KERALA
KETTLE
KEVELS
LEANLY
LEGALS
LETFLY
LEVELS
LEWDLY
MEANLY
MEASLY
MEDALS
MEDDLE
MEEKLY
MEETLY
MEGALO
MEGILP
MERELY
METALS
METTLE
NEARLY
NEATLY
NEBULA
NEEDLE
NEPALI
NEROLI
NESTLE
NETTLE
NEWELS
PEARLS
PEARLY
PEBBLE
PEBBLY
PEDALS
PEDDLE
PENULT
PEOPLE
PERILS
PERTLY
PESTLE
PETALS
PETULA
REALLY
REBELS
REBOLT
RECALL
REFILE
REFILL
REGALE
REHELD
REMELT
REOILS
REPELS
REPOLL
RESALE
RESALT
RESELL
RESILE
RESOLD
RESOLE
RESULT
RETELL
RETILE
RETOLD
REVELS
REVILE
REVOLT
REWELD
SEARLE
SEDILE
SEEMLY
SEMELE
SEPALS
SETTLE
SEWELL
SEXILY
TEMPLE
TEPALS
VERILY
WEAKLY
WEDELN
WEEKLY
WETFLY
YEARLY

•E•••L

AERIAL
BEFALL
BEFELL
BEFOUL
BELIAL
BENGAL
BENZOL
BETHEL
BEWAIL
CEREAL
DENIAL
DENTAL
DENTIL
DENZEL
DEPAUL
DERAIL
DERMAL
DETAIL
FENNEL
FESTAL
FEUDAL
GEISEL
GENIAL
GENUAL
GERBIL
HERBAL
JEKYLL
JESSEL
KEITEL
KENNEL
KERNEL
LEMUEL
LENTIL
LETHAL
MEDIAL
MELVIL
MENDEL
MENIAL
MENSAL
MENTAL
MERKEL
MESCAL
METHYL
NEURAL
NEUROL
PENCEL
PENCIL
PENPAL
PETREL
PETROL
REBOIL
RECALL
RECOIL
REDEAL
REDIAL
REFILL
REFUEL
REGNAL
REHEAL
REHEEL
REMAIL
RENAIL
RENTAL
REPEAL
REPOLL
RESEAL
RESELL
RETAIL
RETELL
RETIAL
RETOOL
RETRAL
REVEAL
SEAGAL
SECKEL
SEIDEL
SEPTAL
SEQUEL
SERIAL
SERVAL
SEWELL
TEASEL
TERCEL
TERKEL
TETZEL
VEINAL
VENIAL
VERBAL
VERNAL
VESSEL
VESTAL
WEASEL
WEEVIL
WERFEL

••EL••

ABELES
ADELIE
ADELLE
AIELLO
AKELAS
AMELIA
CHELAE
CHELAS
COELOM
DUELED
DUELER
DUELLO
DWELLS
DYELOT
EVELYN
EYELET
EYELID
FEELER
FIELDS
FJELDS
FUELED
FUELER
GAELIC
GUELPH
HEELED
HEELER
IMELDA
ISELIN
KEELED
KEELER
KNELLS
KPELLE
KVELLS
LIELOW
MYELIN
NIELLI
NIELLO
OBELIA
OBELUS
OCELLI
OCELOT
OKELLY
OMELET
ORELSE
OTELLO
PAELLA
PEELED
PEELER
PRELAW
PRELIM
QUELLS
REELED
REELIN
SHELLS
SHELLY
SHELVE
SMELLS
SMELLY
SMELTS
SNELLS
SPELLS
STELAE
STELAR
STELES
STELLA
STELMO
SVELTE
SWELLS
THELIP
THELMA
TWELVE
WHELKS
WHELPS
WIELDS
YIELDS

••E•L•

ADELLE
AGEOLD
AIELLO
AREOLA
BEETLE
CREELS
CREOLE
DEEPLY
DUELLO
DWELLS
EBERLY
EDERLE
EVENLY
EVERLY
FEEBLE
FEEBLY
FREELY
IDEALS
ISEULT
KEENLY
KNEELS
KNELLS
KPELLE
KVELLS
MEEKLY
MEETLY
NEEDLE
NIELLI
NIELLO
OCELLI
OKELLY
ONEILL
OPENLY
OTELLO
OVERLY
PAELLA
PUEBLA
PUEBLO
QUELLS
SEEMLY
SHEILA
SHELLS
SHELLY
SIECLE
SMELLS
SMELLY
SNELLS
SPELLS
STEALS
STEELE
STEELS
STEELY
STELLA
SWELLS
THEYLL
TREBLE
TREBLY
WEEKLY
WHEELS

••E••L

ACETAL
ACETYL
CHERYL
CHEVAL
COEVAL
CRENEL
CRESOL
CREWEL
DAEDAL
DIESEL
DREXEL
EYEFUL
GRETEL
HIEMAL
HYETAL
IREFUL
OLEVEL
ONEILL
PHENOL
PHENYL
RUEFUL
SHEKEL
STEROL
THECAL
THEYLL
USEFUL
WEEVIL
WIESEL
WOEFUL

•••EL•

AFIELD
ALLELE
ANGELA
ANGELI
ANGELL
ANGELO
ANGELS
ANSELM
ARBELA
ARTELS
ASWELL
BAGELS
BARELY
BASELY
BEFELL
BEHELD
BETELS
BEVELS
BEZELS
CAMELS
CAVELL
CICELY
COMELY
COSELL
CREELS
CUPELS
CYBELE
DOTELL
DOWELS
EASELS
EDSELS
ENGELS
EXCELS
EXPELS
FINELY
FREELY
GAMELY
GAVELS
GIMELS
GRUELS
HAZELS
HOMELY
HOSELS
HOTELS
HOVELS
HOWELL
HUGELY
IMPELS
ITSELF
JEWELS
KEVELS
KNEELS
LABELS
LAMELY
LAPELS
LATELY
LEVELS
LIBELS
LIKELY
LIVELY
LONELY
LOVELL
LOVELY
LOWELL
MABELL
MERELY
MODELA
MODELS
MODELT
MORELS
MOTELS
MUTELY
MYSELF
NAMELY
NAVELS
NEWELS
NICELY
NOVELS
OHWELL
ORIELS
ORWELL
OUSELS
OUZELS
PALELY
PAMELA
PANELS
PIXELS
POMELO
POWELL
PURELY
RARELY
RATELS
RAVELS
REBELS
REHELD
REMELT
REPELS
RESELL
RETELL
REVELS
REWELD
RIPELY
RONELY
ROWELS
RUDELY
RYDELL
SAFELY
SAGELY
SANELY
SCHELL
SEMELE
SEWELL
SHIELD
SOLELY
SORELY
SPIELS
STEELE
STEELS
STEELY
SURELY
TAMELY
TIMELY
TOWELS
TUPELO
UMBELS
UNBELT
UNWELL
UPHELD
UPWELL
VILELY
VOWELS
WEDELN
WHEELS
WIDELY
WIFELY
WISELY
YARELY
YODELS
YOKELS

•••E•L

ANGELL
ANNEAL
APPEAL
ASWELL
BEFELL
BOREAL
CAVELL
CEREAL
COSELL
CUNEAL
DOTELL
HOWELL
IRREAL
LINEAL
LOREAL
LOVELL
LOWELL
MABELL
MUDEEL
OHWELL
ORDEAL
ORWELL
OSTEAL
PINEAL
POWELL
REDEAL
REHEAL
REHEEL
REPEAL
RESEAL
RESELL
RETELL
REVEAL
RYDELL
SCHELL
SEWELL
SHTETL
SOLEIL
SQUEAL
UNREAL
UNREEL
UNSEAL
UNVEIL
UNWELL
UPWELL

••••EL

AMSTEL
BARBEL
BARREL
BETHEL
BUNUEL
BUSHEL
CANCEL
CANNEL
CARMEL
CARPEL
CARREL
CARTEL
CHANEL
CHAPEL
CHISEL
COMPEL
CORBEL
CORNEL
CORREL
CRENEL
CREWEL
CUDGEL
DAMSEL
DANIEL
DARNEL
DENZEL
DHOTEL
DIESEL
DISPEL
DOSSEL
DREXEL
DRIVEL
DUFFEL
EIFFEL
ENAMEL
FENNEL
FUNNEL
GEISEL
GIMBEL
GOSPEL
GRAVEL
GRETEL
GROVEL
GUMBEL
GUNNEL
HALLEL
HANDEL
HANSEL
HILLEL
HORMEL
HOSTEL
IJSSEL
ISABEL
ISOHEL
ISRAEL
JESSEL
KEITEL
KENNEL
KERNEL
KOPPEL
KUMMEL
LAUREL
LEMUEL
LINTEL
LIONEL
LISTEL
MANTEL
MANUEL
MARCEL
MARIEL
MARTEL
MARVEL
MATTEL
MENDEL
MERKEL
MIGUEL
MONTEL
MORSEL
MOSTEL
MUDEEL
MURIEL
MUSSEL
NICKEL
OLEVEL
PARCEL
PARREL
PASSEL
PASTEL
PENCEL
PETREL
POMMEL
PROPEL
PUMMEL
RACHEL
RAFAEL
RAPPEL
RAQUEL
REFUEL
REHEEL
ROMMEL
RONDEL
RUNNEL
SAMUEL
SAUREL
SECKEL
SEIDEL
SEQUEL
SHEKEL
SHOVEL
SIMBEL
SISKEL
SNIVEL
SORREL
SPINEL
STIPEL
SWIVEL
TASSEL
TEASEL
TERCEL
TERKEL
TETZEL
TINSEL
TRAVEL
TROWEL
TUNNEL
UNREEL
VACHEL
VESSEL
WEASEL
WERFEL
WIESEL

EM••••

EMAILS
EMAJOR
EMBANK
EMBARK
EMBAYS
EMBDEN
EMBEDS
EMBERS
EMBLEM
EMBODY
EMBOSS
EMBRYO
EMCEED
EMCEES
EMDASH
EMEERS
EMENDS
EMERGE
EMIGRE
EMILIA
EMILIO
EMINOR
EMMETS
EMMETT
EMOTED
EMOTER
EMOTES
EMPERY
EMPIRE
EMPLOY
EMPTOR
EMQUAD

E•M•••

EDMOND
EDMUND
EGMONT
ELMIRA
ELMORE
EMMETS
EMMETT
ENMESH
ENMITY
ERMINE
EXMOOR

E••M••

EDAMES
ELEMIS
ELFMAN
ENAMEL
ENAMOR
ENDMAN
ENDMEN
ETYMOL
ETYMON
EXEMPT

E•••M•

ENCAMP
ENIGMA
ENZYME
ESKIMO

E••••M

EGOISM
ELOHIM
EMBLEM
ENGRAM
EPONYM
ERBIUM
ESTEEM

•EM•••

BEMINE
BEMIRE
BEMOAN
BEMUSE
CEMENT
DEMAND
DEMEAN
DEMISE
DEMITS
DEMOBS
DEMODE
DEMOND
DEMONS
DEMOTE
DEMURE
DEMURS
FEMALE
FEMMES
FEMORA
FEMURS
GEMARA
GEMINI
GEMMAE
GEMMED
HEMATO
HEMMED
HEMMER
HEMSIN
KEMPIS
LEMANS
LEMMAS
LEMMON
LEMNOS
LEMOND
LEMONS
LEMONY
LEMUEL
LEMURS
MEMBER
MEMNON
MEMOIR
MEMORY
NEMATO
REMADE
REMAIL
REMAIN
REMAKE
REMAND
REMANS
REMAPS
REMARK
REMEDY
REMELT
REMEND
REMICK
REMIND
REMISE
REMISS
REMITS
REMORA
REMOTE
REMOVE
REMOWN
REMOWS
REMUDA
SEMELE
SEMITE
SEMPER
SEMPRE
TEMPED
TEMPEH
TEMPER
TEMPLE
TEMPOS
TEMPTS
YEMENI

•E•M••

BEAMED
BEAMUP
CERMET
DEEMED
DEIMOS
DERMAL
DERMIS
DESMAN
FEMMES
FERMAT
GEMMAE
GEMMED
GERMAN
HELMED
HELMET
HELMUT
HEMMED
HEMMER
HERMAN
HERMES
HERMIT
HERMON
HETMAN
KERMAN
KERMES
KERMIS
KERMIT
LEGMAN
LEGMEN
LEMMAS
LEMMON
MELMAC
MERMAN
MERMEN
MESMER
NETMAN
NETMEN
NEUMAN
NEUMES
NEWMAN
NEWMAR
PELMET
PENMAN
PENMEN
PERMED
PERMIT
REAMED
REAMER
SEAMAN
SEAMED
SEAMEN
SEAMUS
SEEMED
SEEMLY
SERMON
TEAMED
TEAMUP
TEEMED
TERMED
TEXMEX
VERMIN
WEIMAR
WETMOP
YEOMAN
YEOMEN
YESMAN
YESMEN
ZEEMAN

•E••M•

BECAME
BECOME
BEDIMS
BEGUMS
BENUMB
BESOMS
DEARME
DECAMP
DEFAME
DENIMS
GENOME
JEREMY
JEROME
LEGUME
LEXEME
OEDEMA
REALMS
REARMS
REGIME
REHEMS
RELUME
RENAME
RESUME
RETIME
REVAMP
SEDUMS
SEISMO
SEISMS
SERUMS
SESAME
VENOMS
ZEUGMA

•E•••M

BECALM
BEDLAM
BEEGUM
BELDAM
CERIUM
CESIUM
DEFORM
HELIUM
JETSAM
MEDIUM
MEGOHM
PEPLUM
REDEEM
REDGUM
REFORM
RETRIM
REWARM
SELDOM
SEPTUM
TEDEUM
TEDIUM
VELLUM
VERISM

••EM••

ALEMAN
ANEMIA
ANEMIC
APEMAN
APEMEN
ATEMPO
BREMEN
CHEMIN
CREMES
DEEMED
ELEMIS
EXEMPT
HAEMAT
HAEMON
HIEMAL
ICEMAN
ICEMEN
PIEMAN
PIEMEN
PREMED
PREMIE
QUEMOY
SEEMED
SEEMLY
TEEMED
THEMED
THEMES
TREMOR
ZEEMAN

••E•M•

ADEEMS
ATEAMS
BREAMS
CREAMS
CREAMY
DREAMS
DREAMT
DREAMY
GLEAMS
HBEAMS
IBEAMS
PNEUMA
PREAMP
RHEUMS
RHEUMY
STEAMS
STEAMY
STELMO
THELMA
THERMO
THERMS

••E••M

AGEISM
BEEGUM
COELOM
FRENUM
PHENOM
PLENUM
PRELIM
THEISM

•••EM•

ADEEMS
BIREME
CINEMA
DOREMI
GOLEMS
HAREMS
JEREMY
LEXEME
MODEMS
OEDEMA
PROEMS
RACEME
REHEMS
SCHEMA
SCHEME
SOLEMN
TOTEMS

•••E•M

AGLEAM
ANSELM
ESTEEM
INSEAM
KAREEM
LYCEUM
MUSEUM
PHLEGM
PILEUM
REDEEM
SCREAM
STREAM
TEDEUM

••••EM

ANADEM
ANTHEM
ARNHEM
DIADEM
EMBLEM
ESTEEM
HARLEM
IBIDEM
KAREEM
MAYHEM
MOSLEM
PHLOEM
PROTEM
REDEEM
SACHEM
SHOLEM
SYSTEM
TANDEM
WILLEM

EN••••

ENABLE
ENACTS
ENAMEL
ENAMOR
ENATES
ENBLOC
ENCAGE
ENCAMP
ENCASE
ENCINA
ENCINO
ENCODE
ENCORE
ENDALL
ENDASH
ENDEAR
ENDERS
ENDING
ENDIVE
ENDMAN
ENDMEN
ENDORA
ENDOWS
ENDRUN
ENDSUP
ENDUED
ENDUES
ENDURE
ENDURO
ENDUSE
ENERGY
ENESCO
ENFANT
ENFOLD
ENGAGE
ENGELS
ENGINE
ENGIRD
ENGIRT
ENGLUT
ENGRAM
ENGULF
ENIGMA
ENISLE
ENJOIN
ENJOYS
ENLACE
ENLIST
ENMESH
ENMITY
ENNEAD
ENNIUS
ENOKIS
ENOSIS
ENOUGH
ENQUAD
ENRAGE
ENRAPT
ENRICH
ENRICO
ENROBE
ENROLL
ENROOT
ENSIGN
ENSILE
ENSOUL
ENSUED
ENSUES
ENSURE
ENTAIL
ENTERO
ENTERS
ENTICE
ENTIRE
ENTITY
ENTRAP
ENTREE
ENURED
ENURES
ENVIED
ENVIES
ENVOIS
ENVOYS
ENWRAP
ENZYME

E•N•••

ELNINO
ENNEAD
ENNIUS
EONIAN
ERNANI
ERNEST
EUNICE
EUNUCH

E••N••

EARNED
EARNER
EBONDS
EDENIC
EGGNOG
EISNER
ELANDS
ELINOR
EMENDS
EMINOR
EPONYM
ERENOW
ERINYS
ERYNGO
ETHNIC
ETHNOS
ETONIC
EUPNEA
EVENED
EVENER
EVENKI
EVENLY
EVENSO
EVENTS
EVENUP
EVINCE
EVONNE

E•••N•

EALING
EARING
EASING
EATING
EBBING
EDGING
EDMOND
EDMUND
EDWYNN
EGGING
EGMONT
ELAINE
ELAYNE
ELNINO
EMBANK
ENCINA
ENCINO
ENDING
ENFANT
ENGINE
EOCENE
EOSINS
EPPING
EQUINE
ERMINE
ERNANI
ERRAND
ERRANT
ERRING
ERVING
ESCENT
ESPANA
ESSENE
ETERNE
ETHANE
ETHENE
EUGENE
EVONNE
EVZONE
EXEUNT
EXPAND
EXPEND
EXTANT
EXTEND
EXTENT
EYEING

E••••N

EASEIN
EASTON
EATSIN
EDGEIN
EDISON
EDWYNN
EGGSON
EILEEN
ELEVEN
ELFMAN
ELOIGN
EMBDEN
ENDMAN
ENDMEN
ENDRUN
ENJOIN
ENSIGN
EOLIAN
EONIAN
EPHRON
ETYMON
EVELYN

•EN•••

AENEAS
AENEID
BENDAY
BENDED
BENDER
BENDIX
BENGAL
BENGAY
BENHUR
BENIGN
BENING
BENITO
BENOIT
BENSON
BENTON
BENUMB
BENZOL
CENOTE
CENSED
CENSER
CENSES
CENSOR
CENSUS
CENTER
CENTOS
CENTRE
CENTRI
CENTRO
DENALI
DENDRI
DENDRO
DENGUE
DENIAL
DENIED
DENIER
DENIES
DENIMS
DENIRO
DENISE
DENNED
DENNIS
DENOTE
DENOVO
DENSER
DENTAL
DENTED
DENTIL
DENTIN
DENTON
DENUDE
DENVER
DENZEL
FENCED
FENCER
FENCES
FENDED
FENDER
FENIAN
FENNEC
FENNEL
GENDER
GENERA
GENETS
GENEVA
GENEVE
GENIAL
GENIES
GENIUS
GENOAN
GENOME
GENRES
GENTLE
GENTLY
GENTRY
GENUAL
HENBIT
HENLEY
HENNAS
HENNER
HENNIN
HENRIK
HENSON
JENNER
JENNET
JENNIE
JENSEN
KENNED
KENNEL
KENNYG
KENTON
KENYAN
LENAPE
LENDER
LENGTH
LENITY
LENNIE
LENNON
LENORE
LENSED
LENSES
LENTEN
LENTIL
MENACE
MENAGE
MENDED
MENDEL
MENDER
MENDES
MENHIR
MENIAL
MENINX
MENJOU
MENNEN
MENSAE
MENSAL
MENSAS
MENSCH
MENTAL
MENTIS
MENTOR
NENETS
OENONE
PENANG
PENCEL
PENCIL
PENDED
PENGHU
PENMAN
PENMEN
PENNAE
PENNED
PENNER
PENNEY
PENNIA
PENNIS
PENNON
PENPAL
PENROD
PENSEE
PENTAD
PENTUP
PENULT
PENURY
RENAIL
RENAME
RENATA
RENDER
RENEGE
RENEWS
RENNES
RENNET
RENNIE
RENNIN
RENOIR
RENOTE
RENOWN
RENTAL
RENTED
RENTER
SENARY
SENATE
SENDAK
SENDER
SENDIN
SENDUP
SENECA
SENEGA
SENHOR
SENIOR
SENLAC
SENNAS
SENNET
SENNIT
SENORA
SENORS
SENSED
SENSEI
SENSES
SENSOR
SENTIN
SENTRY
SENTUP
TENACE
TENANT
TENDED
TENDER
TENDON
TENDTO
TENETS
TENNIS
TENONS
TENORS
TENPIN
TENREC
TENSED
TENSER
TENSES
TENSOR
TENTED
TENTER
TENTHS
TENURE
TENUTO
VENDED
VENDEE
VENDOR
VENEER
VENETO
VENIAL
VENICE
VENIRE
VENITE
VENOMS
VENOUS
VENTED
VENTER
VENUES
WENCES
WENDED
WENTAT
WENTBY
WENTIN
WENTON
WENTUP
YENNED
YENTAS
ZENANA
ZENDOS
ZENGER
ZENITH

•E•N••

BEANED
BEANIE
BEANOS
BEINGS
BERNIE
DEANNA
DENNED
DENNIS
FEINTS
FENNEC
FENNEL
HEFNER
HENNAS
HENNER
HENNIN
JEANNE
JENNER
JENNET
JENNIE
KEENAN
KEENED
KEENEN
KEENER
KEENLY
KENNED
KENNEL
KENNYG
KERNED
KERNEL
KERNOI
KERNOS
KEYNES
LEANED
LEANER
LEANLY
LEANON
LEANTO
LEMNOS
LENNIE
LENNON
LEONES
LEONID
LEONIE
LERNER
MEANER
MEANIE
MEANLY
MEMNON
MENNEN
PEANUT
PEENED
PENNAE
PENNED
PENNER
PENNEY
PENNIA
PENNIS
PENNON
PERNOD
REGNAL
REINED
REINER
REININ
REINKS
RENNES
RENNET
RENNIE
RENNIN
RESNIK
REUNES
SEANCE
SEENAS
SEENTO
SEINED
SEINER
SEINES
SENNAS
SENNET
SENNIT
SEWNUP
TEENER
TEENSY
TENNIS
VEINAL
VEINED
VERNAL
VERNON
WEANED
WEENIE
WEENSY
WERNER
YENNED

•E••N•

BEGINS
BEGONE
BEHIND
BELONG
BEMINE
BENING
BERING
BESANT
BETONY
BEYOND
BEZANT
CEDING
CELINE
CEMENT
CESSNA
CETANE
DEANNA
DEBONE
DEBUNK
DECANT
DECENT
DEFEND
DEFINE
DEIGNS
DELANO
DELANY
DELONG
DEMAND
DEMOND
DEMONS
DEPEND
DEPONE
DETENT
DEVINE
DEWING
FECUND
FEEING
FEIGNS
FELINE
FELONS
FELONY
FERENC
FETING
GEEING
GEMINI
GERENT
GERONT
GERUND
HELENA
HELENE
HELENS
HERONS
HEWING
HEXING
JEANNE
JEJUNE
KETONE
KEYING
LEARNS
LEARNT
LEGEND
LELAND
LEMANS
LEMOND
LEMONS
LEMONY
LEVANT
LEVENE
LEVINE
MEDINA
MEKONG
MELANO
MELINA
MELONS
MENINX
MERINO
MESONS
METING
MEWING
NEEDNT
NEVINS
OENONE
PECANS
PEDANT
PEKING
PENANG
PEPINO
REBIND
RECANE
RECANT
RECENT
RECONS
REDANT
REDINK
REDONE
REFINE
REFUND
REGENT
REGINA
REHANG
REHUNG
REIGNS
RELENT
RELINE
REMAND
REMANS
REMEND
REMIND
REPAND
REPENT
REPINE
RERENT
RERUNS
RESAND
RESEND
RESENT
RESING
RESINS
RETENE
RETINA
RETUNE
REWIND
REWINS
REZONE
SECANT
SECOND
SEDANS
SEEING
SEJANT
SELENA
SELENE
SERENA
SERENE
SERINE
SERINS
SETINS
SEVENS
SEWING
TECHNO
TEEING
TENANT
TENONS
TETONS
TEXANS
VEGANS
VERONA
VEXING
WERENT
YEARNS
YEMENI
ZENANA

•E•••N

AEGEAN
BEACON
BEARON
BEATEN
BEATON
BECKON
BEMOAN
BENIGN
BENSON
BENTON
BERGEN
BERLIN
CEYLON
DEACON
DEADEN
DEADON
DEAFEN
DEALIN
DEEPEN
DEHORN
DELEON
DEMEAN
DENTIN
DENTON
DESIGN
DESMAN
DETAIN
DEVEIN
FEEDON
FELDON
FELLIN
FENIAN
FEZZAN
GENOAN
GERMAN
GETSIN
GETSON
HEADIN
HEADON
HEAVEN
HEDREN
HEFLIN
HEIDEN
HELDIN
HELDON
HEMSIN
HENNIN
HENSON
HEREIN
HEREON
HERMAN
HERMON
HESTON
HETMAN
JENSEN
JERKIN
JETGUN
JETSON
KEATON
KEENAN
KEENEN
KEEPIN
KEEPON
KELVIN
KENTON
KENYAN
KEPTON
KERMAN
KEYSIN
LEADEN
LEADIN
LEADON
LEANON
LEAVEN
LEBRUN
LEGION
LEGMAN
LEGMEN
LEIDEN
LEMMON
LENNON
LENTEN
LEPTON
LESSEN
LESSON
LETSIN
LETSON
LEYDEN
MEDIAN
MELLON
MELTON
MELVIN
MELVYN
MEMNON
MENNEN
MERLIN
MERLON
MERMAN
MERMEN
MERTON
MERVYN
NEATEN
NEESON
NEKTON
NELSON
NETMAN
NETMEN
NETTON
NEUMAN
NEURON
NEWMAN
NEWTON
PEAHEN
PECTIN
PEERIN
PELION
PENMAN
PENMEN
PENNON
PEPSIN
PERSON
PETAIN
PEYTON
READIN
REAGAN
REASON
REBORN
RECKON
REDDEN
REDFIN
REELIN
REGAIN
REGION
REININ
REJOIN
REMAIN
REMOWN
RENNIN
RENOWN
REOPEN
REPLAN
REPUGN
RESEEN
RESEWN
RESIGN
RESTON
RETAIN
RETTON
RETURN
REUBEN
REVLON
REVSON
SEAFAN
SEAMAN
SEAMEN
SEASON
SECERN
SEEPIN
SEESIN
SENDIN
SENTIN
SEQUIN
SERKIN
SERMON
SETSIN
SETSON
SEVERN
SEWSON
SEXTON
TEFLON
TELLON
TENDON
TENPIN
TERRAN
TEUTON
VEBLEN
VERDIN
VERDON
VERDUN
VEREEN
VERMIN
VERNON
WEAKEN
WEAPON
WEBERN
WEDELN
WELKIN
WENTIN
WENTON
WESSON
YEOMAN
YEOMEN
YESMAN
YESMEN
ZEEMAN
ZEROIN

••EN••

AGENAS
AGENCY
AGENDA
AGENTS
AKENES
AMENDS
AMENRA
AMENTS
ARENAS
ARENDT
AVENGE
AVENUE
BLENCH
BLENDE
BLENDS
BRENDA
BRENTS
BUENOS
CHENIN
CLENCH
CRENEL
CRENNA
DRENCH
DUENNA
EDENIC
EMENDS
ERENOW
EVENED
EVENER
EVENKI
EVENLY
EVENSO
EVENTS
EVENUP
FAENZA
FIENDS
FLENSE
FRENCH
FRENUM
FRENZY
GLENDA
GUENON
HYENAS
IRENES
IRENIC
KEENAN
KEENED
KEENEN
KEENER
KEENLY
LIENEE
MAENAD
ODENSE
OHENRY
OPENED
OPENER
OPENLY
OPENTO
OPENUP
PEENED
PHENOL
PHENOM
PHENYL
PLENTY
PLENUM
PUENTE
QUENCH
SCENAS
SCENDS
SCENES
SCENIC
SCENTS
SEENAS
SEENTO
SIENNA
SPENDS
STENCH
STENOG
STENOS
TEENER
TEENSY
THENAR
THENCE
TRENCH
TRENDS
TRENDY
TWENTY
UPENDS
VIENNA
VIENNE
WEENIE
WEENSY
WHENCE
WIENER
WRENCH

••E•N•

AGEING
AHERNE
AVERNO
BOEING
CLEANS
CRENNA
CZERNY
DOESNT
DUENNA
DYEING
ETERNE
EXEUNT
EYEING
FEEING
FOEHNS
FRESNO
GEEING
GLEANS
GREENE
GREENS
GREENY
GRETNA
HIEING
HOEING
ILEANA
LIERNE
NEEDNT
OCEANS
PAEANS
PAEONS
PREENS
QUEENS
QUERNS
SEEING
SHEENA
SHEENS
SIENNA
SKEANS
SKEINS
STEINS
STERNA
STERNE
STERNO
STERNS
TEEING
THEEND
TIEING
TIEINS
TOEING
TOEINS
VIENNA
VIENNE

••E••N

ALEMAN
APEMAN
APEMEN
AVEDON
BREMEN
BRETON
CHEMIN
CHENIN
CRETAN
CRETIN
DEEPEN
DOESIN
DREWIN
DREWON
ELEVEN
EVELYN
FEEDON
FLEWIN
GOESIN
GOESON
GREWON
GUENON
HAEMON
HIERON
ICEDIN
ICEMAN
ICEMEN
ICESIN
ISELIN
KEENAN
KEENEN
KEEPIN
KEEPON
KMESON
LIESIN
MYELIN
NEESON
OBERON
OLEFIN
OREGON
PEERIN
PIEMAN
PIEMEN
PIEPAN
PIETIN
PREVIN
PREYON

REELIN
SEEPIN
SEESIN
STEFAN
STEPIN
STEPON
STEVEN
SWEDEN
TIEDIN
TIEPIN
TIESIN
TOEDIN
TOESIN
TREPAN
UNEVEN
ZEEMAN

•••EN•
ABSENT
ACCENT
ACHENE
ADDEND
ADRENO
ADVENT
ALIENS
ALKENE
AMIENS
APPEND
ARDENT
ARGENT
ARLENE
ARPENT
ARSENE
ASCEND
ASCENT
ASPENS
ASSENT
ATHENA
ATHENE
ATHENS
ATTEND
AUDENS
AUGEND
BRIENZ
BUTENE
CADENT
CATENA
CEMENT
CLIENT
COGENT
COVENS
COVENT
COWENS
COZENS
DECENT
DEFEND
DEPEND
DETENT
DOCENT
DOYENS
DOZENS
EOCENE
ESCENT
ESSENE
ETHENE
EUGENE
EXPEND
EXTEND
EXTENT
FAGEND
FERENC
FILENE
FLUENT
FOMENT
FRIEND
GALENA
GERENT
GIVENS
GREENE
GREENS
GREENY
GYRENE
HAVENS
HAVENT
HELENA
HELENE
HELENS
IMPEND
INDENE
INDENT
INTEND
INTENS
INTENT
INVENT
IRLENE
ISMENE
JOLENE
LAMENT
LATENE
LATENS
LATENT
LEGEND
LEVENE
LIKENS
LIMENS
LINENS
LIPENG
LIVENS
LODENS
LORENZ
LOWEND
LUCENT
LUDENS
LUMENS
MAVENS
MIZENS
MODENA
MOMENT
MORENO
NICENE
NOCENT
NOLENS
NOVENA
NUGENT
OFFEND
ORIENT
OSTEND
PARENS
PARENT
PATENS
PATENT
POTENT
PREENS
QUEENS
RAVENS
RECENT
REGENT
RELENT
REMEND
REPENT
RERENT
RESEND
RESENT
RETENE
RIDENT
RIPENS
RODENT
ROWENA
ROWENS
RUBENS
RUMENS
SABENA
SELENA
SELENE
SERENA
SERENE
SEVENS
SHEENA
SHEENS
SILENI
SILENT
SIRENS
SOLENT
STHENO
TAGEND
TALENT
THEEND
TOKENS
UNBEND
UNBENT
UNPENS
URGENT
VALENS
VALENT
VIXENS
VOLENS
WAKENS
WERENT
WIDENS
WISENT
WIZENS
WOMENS
XIMENA
XYLENE
YEMENI

•••E•N
AEGEAN
AILEEN
ANDEAN
ASTERN
AUGEAN
BALEEN
BOLEYN
BOREON
CAMEIN
CAMEON
CAREEN
CASERN
CAVEIN
CAVERN
CLUEIN
COMEIN
COMEON
DELEON
DEMEAN
DEVEIN
DINEIN
DINEON
DIVEIN
DONEIN
DOTEON
DOVEIN
DUDEEN
EASEIN
EDGEIN
EILEEN
FADEIN
GAVEIN
GIDEON
GIVEIN
GOVERN
HAVEON
HEREIN
HEREON
HIREON
INTERN
KOREAN
LATEEN
LIVEIN
LIVEON
LLBEAN
LOMEIN
LOVEIN
MCLEAN
MODERN
MOREEN
MOVEIN
NICEAN
OSSEIN
PIGEON
PILEIN
PILEON
POLEYN
POTEEN
RAKEIN
RESEEN
RESEWN
ROPEIN
RULEON
SATEEN
SCREEN
SECERN
SEVERN
SIMEON
SOLEMN
SPLEEN
STREWN
TAKEIN
TAKEON
TAVERN
TUNEIN
TUREEN
UNSEEN
UNSEWN
VEREEN
VOTEIN
WADEIN
WAVEIN
WEBERN
WEDELN
WOREON
WYVERN

••••EN
AACHEN
ACUMEN
ADRIEN
AILEEN
AIRMEN
ALFVEN
ANCIEN
APEMEN
ARISEN
AUSTEN
AWAKEN
AWOKEN
BALEEN
BARMEN
BARREN
BATMEN
BATTEN
BEATEN
BERGEN
BIDDEN
BIGBEN
BIGTEN
BITTEN
BLIXEN
BORDEN
BOWMEN
BRAZEN
BREMEN
BROKEN
BUNSEN
BURDEN
BUSMEN
CAMDEN
CAREEN
CARMEN
CHOSEN
CLOVEN
CONMEN
COTTEN
COWMEN
CRAVEN
CULLEN
DAIREN
DAMIEN
DAMPEN
DARIEN
DARKEN
DARREN
DEADEN
DEAFEN
DEEPEN
DOLMEN
DRIVEN
DRYDEN
DUDEEN
EILEEN
ELEVEN
EMBDEN
ENDMEN
FALLEN
FASTEN
FATTEN
FBIMEN
FLAXEN
FLYMEN
FROZEN
GAGMEN
GARDEN
GASMEN
GLUTEN
GOLDEN
GOODEN
GOSHEN
GOTTEN
GRABEN
GRAVEN
GUNMEN
HAPPEN
HARDEN
HARKEN
HASTEN
HAYDEN
HEAVEN
HEDREN
HEIDEN
HIDDEN
HITMEN
HOLDEN
HOYDEN
HYPHEN
ICEMEN
IMOGEN
JANSEN
JENSEN
KEENEN
KITTEN
KJOLEN
KRAKEN
KUCHEN
LARSEN
LASSEN
LATEEN
LATTEN
LAUREN
LAWMEN
LAYMEN
LEADEN
LEAVEN
LEGMEN
LEIDEN
LENTEN
LESSEN
LEYDEN
LICHEN
LINDEN
LISTEN
LOOSEN
LOUDEN
LUDDEN
LUMPEN
LUNDEN
MADDEN
MADMEN
MAIDEN
MAJGEN
MALDEN
MARTEN
MCKUEN
MENNEN
MERMEN
MIDDEN
MIRREN
MITTEN
MIZZEN
MOLTEN
MOREEN
MORGEN
MUDHEN
NANSEN
NEATEN
NETMEN
NGUYEN
NISSEN
OBRIEN
OILMEN
OLDMEN
ORIGEN
OXYGEN
PATTEN
PEAHEN
PENMEN
PIEMEN
PIGPEN
PINKEN
PITMEN
PLATEN
POLLEN
POTEEN
PROVEN
RAGMEN
REDDEN
REOPEN
RESEEN
REUBEN
RICHEN
RIDDEN
RIPKEN
ROTTEN
SADDEN
SALTEN
SATEEN
SCREEN
SEAMEN
SHAKEN
SHAVEN
SICKEN
SILKEN
SLOVEN
SODDEN
SOFTEN
SPLEEN
SPOKEN
STAMEN
STEVEN
STOLEN
SUDDEN
SULLEN
SUNKEN
SWEDEN
TAUTEN
TAXMEN
TILDEN
TINMEN
TOPTEN
TUREEN
UNEVEN
UNOPEN
UNSEEN
USOPEN
VARDEN
VEBLEN
VEREEN
VIVIEN
WALDEN
WARDEN
WARREN
WEAKEN
WHITEN
WOODEN
WOOLEN
WORSEN
XIAMEN
YEOMEN
YESMEN

EO••••
EOCENE
EOLIAN
EOLITH
EONIAN
EOSINS

E•O•••
EBOATS
EBONDS
ECOLES
EGOISM
EGOIST
ELOHIM
ELOIGN
ELOISE
ELOPED
ELOPER
ELOPES
EMOTED
EMOTER
EMOTES
ENOKIS
ENOSIS
ENOUGH
EPOCHS
EPODES
EPONYM
EPOPEE
ERODED
ERODES
EROICA
EROTIC
ETOILE
ETONIC
EVOKED
EVOKER
EVOKES
EVOLVE
EVONNE
EXODUS
EXOTIC

E••O••
EATOUT
ECHOED
ECHOES
ECHOIC
EDDOES
EDMOND
EEYORE
EFFORT
EGMONT
EIDOLA
EKEOUT
ELBOWS
ELMORE
ELWOOD
EMBODY
EMBOSS
ENCODE
ENCORE
ENDORA
ENDOWS
ENFOLD
ENJOIN
ENJOYS
ENROBE
ENROLL
ENROOT
ENSOUL
ENVOIS
ENVOYS
EPHODS
EPHORI
EPHORS
ERGOTS
ERROLL
ERRORS
ESCORT
ESPOSA
ESPOSO
ESTOPS
EUBOEA
EUDORA
EULOGY
EUROPA
EUROPE
EVZONE
EXHORT
EXMOOR
EXPORT
EXPOSE
EXTOLS
EXTORT
EXVOTO

E•••O•
EASTON
EDISON
EDITOR
EGGNOG
EGGSON
ELINOR
ELLIOT
ELWOOD
EMAJOR
EMINOR
EMPLOY
EMPTOR
ENAMOR
ENBLOC
ENROOT
EPHRON
EPILOG
ERENOW
ESCROW
ETHNOS
ETYMOL
ETYMON
EXMOOR

E••••O
ELNINO
ELPASO
EMBRYO
EMILIO
ENCINO
ENDURO
ENESCO
ENRICO
ENTERO
ERYNGO
ESCUDO
ESKIMO
ESPOSO
EVENSO
EVERSO
EXACTO
EXVOTO

•EO•••
AEOLIA
AEOLIC
AEOLUS
DEODAR
GEODES
GEORGE
LEONES
LEONID
LEONIE
MEOWED
PEOPLE
PEORIA
REOILS
REOPEN
YEOMAN
YEOMEN

•E•O••
AEROBE
BEBOPS
BECOME
BEFOGS
BEFORE
BEFOUL
BEGOFF
BEGONE
BEHOLD
BEHOOF
BELOIT
BELONG
BEMOAN
BENOIT
BESOMS
BESOTS
BETONY
BETOOK
BEYOND
CENOTE
DEBONE
DECOCT
DECODE
DECORS
DECOYS
DEFOGS
DEFORM
DEHORN
DELONG
DEMOBS
DEMODE
DEMOND
DEMONS
DEMOTE
DENOTE
DENOVO
DEPONE
DEPORT
DEPOSE
DEPOTS
DESOTO
DETOUR
DEVOID
DEVOIR
DEVOTE
DEVOTO
DEVOUR
DEVOUT
EEYORE
FEDORA
FELONS
FELONY
FEMORA
GENOAN
GENOME
GERONT
GETOFF
GETOUT
HELOTS
HEROES
HEROIC
HERONS
JEROME
KEBOBS
KETONE
LEDOFF
LEDOUT
LEMOND
LEMONS
LEMONY
LENORE
LETOFF
LETOUT
MEGOHM
MEKONG
MELODY
MELONS
MELOTT
MEMOIR
MEMORY
MEROPE
MESONS
METOPE
NEROLI
OENONE
PEKOES
PELOPS
PELOTA
PEYOTE
REBOIL
REBOLT
REBOOT
REBORN
REBOZO
RECODE
RECOIL
RECONS
RECOPY
RECORD
RECORK
RECOUP
REDOAK
REDOES
REDONE
REFORM
REHOOK
REJOIN
RELOAD
RELOCK
REMORA
REMOTE
REMOVE
REMOWN
REMOWS
RENOIR
RENOTE
RENOWN
REPOLL
REPORT
REPOSE
REPOTS
RESODS
RESOLD
RESOLE
RESORB
RESORT
RETOLD
RETOOK
RETOOL
RETOPS
RETORT
RETOUR
RETOWS
REVOIR
REVOKE
REVOLT
REWORD
REWORK
REWOVE
REZONE
SECOND
SEEOFF
SEEOUT
SENORA
SENORS
SEPOYS
SEROSA
SEROUS
SEROWS
SETOFF
SETOSE
SETOUT
TEEOFF
TENONS
TENORS
TETONS
VELOCE
VELOUR
VENOMS
VENOUS
VERONA
VETOED
VETOER
VETOES
ZEROED
ZEROES
ZEROIN
ZEROTH

•E••O•
BEACON
BEANOS
BEARON
BEATON
BECKON
BEHOOF
BELLOC
BELLOW
BENSON
BENTON
BENZOL
BESTOW
BETOOK
BETTOR
CELLOS
CENSOR
CENTOS
CESTOS
CEYLON
DEACON
DEADON
DEBTOR
DEIMOS
DELEON
DENTON
DEPLOY
DESPOT
DETROP
FEEDON
FELDON
FELLOE
FELLOW
FERVOR
GECKOS
GETSON
HEADON
HEAROF
HECTOR
HELDON
HELIOS
HELLOS
HENSON
HEREOF
HEREON
HERIOT
HERMON
HERZOG
HESIOD
HESTON
HEYJOE
HEYYOU
JERBOA
JETSON
KEATON
KEEPON
KENTON
KEPTON
KERNOI
KERNOS
LEADON
LEANON
LECTOR
LEGION
LEMMON
LEMNOS
LENNON
LEPTON
LESBOS
LESSON
LESSOR
LETSON
MEADOW
MELLON
MELLOW
MELTON
MEMNON
MENJOU
MENTOR
MERLON
MERLOT
MERTON
METEOR
METHOD
METROS
MEZZOS
NEESON
NEKTON
NELSON
NESTOR
NETTON
NEUROL
NEURON
NEWTON
PEAPOD
PEGTOP
PELION
PENNON
PENROD
PEPLOS
PEQUOD
PEQUOT
PERIOD
PERNOD
PERROT
PERSON
PESCOW
PETROG
PETROL
PEYTON
REASON
REBOOT
RECKON
RECTOR
RECTOS
REDDOG
REDFOX
REDHOT
REDSOX
REDTOP
REEBOK
REGION
REHOOK
REPLOW
REPROS
RESHOD
RESHOE
RESHOT
RESTON
RETOOK
RETOOL
RETROS
RETTON
REVLON
REVSON
SEACOW
SEADOG
SEAFOX
SEASON
SECTOR
SELDOM
SENHOR
SENIOR
SENSOR
SERMON
SERVOS
SESTOS
SETSON
SETTOS
SEWSON
SEXTON
TEAPOT
TEAPOY
TEFLON
TELLON
TEMPOS
TENDON
TENSOR
TERROR
TEUTON
VECTOR
VENDOR
VERDON
VERNON
VERSOS
WEAPON
WENTON
WESSON
WETMOP
YELLOW
ZEALOT
ZENDOS

•E•••O
BENITO
CENTRO
DELANO
DELRIO
DENDRO
DENIRO
DENOVO
DESOTO
DEVITO
DEVOTO
DEXTRO
FELLTO
GEARTO
GELATO
GETSTO
HELDTO
HEMATO
HERETO
HETERO
JETHRO
KEEPTO
LEADTO
LEANTO
LEGATO
LETSGO
MEDICO
MEGALO
MELANO
MERINO
MEXICO
NEARTO
NEMATO
NEPHRO
NEXTTO
PEPINO
REBOZO
REECHO
SEENTO
SEESTO
SEISMO
SERGIO
TECHNO
TENDTO
TENUTO
TERATO
TEREDO
TEXACO
VELCRO
VENETO
WEIRDO

••EO••
ACEOUS
ACEOUT
AGEOLD
AREOLA
CHEOPS
CREOLE
DIEOFF
DIEOUT
EKEOUT
ICEOUT
PAEONS
SEEOFF
SEEOUT
TEEOFF
THEORY

••E•O•
AVEDON
BRETON
BUENOS
COELOM
CREDOS
CRESOL
DREWON
DYELOT
ERENOW
FAEROE
FEEDON
FLEXOR
GOESON
GREGOR
GREWON
GUENON
HAEMON
HIERON
HUEVOS
ICEBOX
ICEFOG
KEEPON
KMESON
LIELOW
NEESON
OBERON
OCELOT
OREGON
PHENOL
PHENOM
PLEXOR
PREYON
PYEDOG
QUEMOY
REEBOK
RHEBOK
RHETOR
STENOG
STENOS
STEPON
STEROL
THETOY
TIEROD
TREMOR
TREVOR

••E••O
AIELLO

ALECTO
ALEPPO
AMEDEO
AREZZO
ATEMPO
ATERGO
AVERNO
CHEAPO
DUELLO
ENESCO
EVENSO
EVERSO
FRESCO
FRESNO
GHETTO
KEEPTO
LIESTO
NIELLO
ONETWO
OPENTO
OTELLO
OVERDO
PIETRO
PRESTO
PSEUDO
PUEBLO
PUERTO
REECHO
SEENTO
SEESTO
STELMO
STEREO
STERNO
THERMO
UNESCO
USEDTO

•••EO•

BLUEOX
BOREON
BUTEOS
CAMEON
CAMEOS
COMEON
DELEON
DINEON
DOTEON
GIDEON
HAVEON
HEREOF
HEREON
HIREON
LIVEON
METEOR
MIMEOS
PASEOS
PIGEON
PILEON
RODEOS
ROLEOS
ROMEOS
RULEON
SIMEON
TAKEON
VIDEOS
VIREOS
WOREON

•••E•O

ADRENO
ALBEDO
ANGELO
ANTERO
BOLERO
CAMETO
CARETO
CICERO
COMETO
DARETO
DINERO
ENTERO
FOREGO
GAZEBO
GRAECO
HERETO
HETERO
HIDEHO
HOVETO
LAREDO
MADEDO
MADERO
MAKEDO
MORENO
NONEGO
NUMERO
OSWEGO
OVIEDO
PARETO
PHLEBO
PINERO
POMELO
ROMERO
SASEBO
SIDERO
SOWETO
STHENO
TAKETO
TEREDO
TOLEDO
TORERO
TUPELO
TUXEDO
VENETO
WISETO
ZYDECO

••••EO

AMEDEO
BORNEO
NUCLEO
PALAEO
STEREO

EP••••

EPARCH
EPHAHS
EPHEBE
EPHODS
EPHORI
EPHORS
EPHRON
EPICAL
EPILOG
EPIRUS
EPOCHS
EPODES
EPONYM
EPOPEE
EPPING

E•P•••

ELPASO
EMPERY
EMPIRE
EMPLOY
EMPTOR
EPPING
ESPANA
ESPIAL
ESPIED
ESPIES
ESPOSA
ESPOSO
ESPRIT
EUPNEA
EXPAND
EXPECT
EXPELS
EXPEND
EXPERT
EXPIRE
EXPIRY
EXPORT
EXPOSE

E••P••

ELAPID
ELAPSE
ELOPED
ELOPER
ELOPES
EPOPEE
ERUPTS

E•••P•

ECTYPE
ENRAPT
EQUIPS
ESCAPE
ESTOPS
EUROPA
EUROPE
EXCEPT
EXEMPT

E••••P

EARLAP
EASEUP
EATSUP
EGGCUP
ENCAMP
ENDSUP
ENTRAP
ENWRAP
ESCARP
ESHARP
EVENUP
EYECUP

•EP•••

DEPART
DEPAUL
DEPAUW
DEPEND
DEPICT
DEPLOY
DEPONE
DEPORT
DEPOSE
DEPOTS
DEPTHS
DEPUTE
DEPUTY
HEPCAT
HEPPER
HEPTAD
KEPLER
KEPTAT
KEPTON
KEPTUP
LEPTON
NEPALI
NEPHEW
NEPHRO
PEPINO
PEPITA
PEPLOS
PEPLUM
PEPPED
PEPPER
PEPSIN
PEPSUP
PEPTIC
REPAID
REPAIR
REPAND
REPAST
REPAVE
REPAYS
REPEAL
REPEAT
REPEGS
REPELS
REPENT
REPINE
REPLAN
REPLAY
REPLOW
REPOLL
REPORT
REPOSE
REPOTS
REPROS
REPUGN
REPUTE
SEPALS
SEPIAS
SEPOYS
SEPTAL
SEPTET
SEPTIC
SEPTUM
TEPALS
TEPEES
TEPHRA
ZEPHYR

•E•P••

BEEPED
BEEPER
DEEPEN
DEEPER
DEEPLY
DELPHI
DESPOT
HEAPED
HELPED
HELPER
HEPPER
KEEPAT
KEEPER
KEEPIN
KEEPON
KEEPTO
KEEPUP
KELPIE
KEMPIS
KEWPIE
KEYPAD
LEAPED
LEAPER
NETPAY
PEAPOD
PEEPED
PEEPER
PENPAL
PEOPLE
PEPPED
PEPPER
REAPED
REAPER
REOPEN
SEEPED
SEEPIN
SEMPER
SEMPRE
TEAPOT
TEAPOY
TEMPED
TEMPEH
TEMPER
TEMPLE
TEMPOS
TEMPTS
TENPIN
VESPER
VESPID
WEAPON
WEEPER
YELPED
YELPER

•E••P•

BEBOPS
CERIPH
FELIPE
GETUPS
LENAPE
LETUPS
MEROPE
METOPE
PELOPS
RECAPS
RECIPE
RECOPY
REMAPS
RETAPE
RETAPS
RETOPS
RETYPE
SERAPE
SERAPH
SETUPS
TERAPH

•E•••P

BEADUP
BEAMUP
BEARUP
BEATUP
BEEFUP
DECAMP
DETROP
DEWLAP
FESSUP
GEARUP
GETSUP
HEADUP
HEATUP
HELDUP
KEEPUP
KEPTUP
KEYSUP
LEADUP
LETSUP
MEGILP
MESSUP
PEGTOP
PENTUP
PEPSUP
PERKUP
REARUP
RECOUP
REDCAP
REDTOP
RESHIP
RESTUP
REVAMP
REWRAP
SEALUP
SENDUP
SENTUP
SETSUP
SEWNUP
SEWSUP
TEACUP
TEAMUP
TEARUP
TEEDUP
TEESUP
WELLUP
WENTUP
WETMOP

••EP••

ADEPTS
ALEPHS
ALEPPO
BEEPED
BEEPER
CLEPED
CREPES
DEEPEN
DEEPER
DEEPLY
DIEPPE
KEEPAT
KEEPER
KEEPIN
KEEPON
KEEPTO
KEEPUP
PEEPED
PEEPER
PIEPAN
PREPAY
PREPPY
SEEPED
SEEPIN
STEPIN
STEPON
STEPPE
STEPUP
TIEPIN
TREPAN
TREPID
WEEPER

••E•P•

ALEPPO
ATEMPO
BLEEPS
CHEAPO
CHEEPS
CHEOPS
CREEPS
CREEPY
DIEPPE
EXEMPT
GUELPH
ONEUPS
PREPPY
SHEEPS
SHERPA
SLEEPS
SLEEPY
STEEPS
STEPPE
SWEEPS
TIEUPS
TWERPS
WHELPS

••E••P

ACESUP
BEEFUP
BLEWUP
CHEWUP
DOESUP
DREWUP
EVENUP
EYECUP
GOESUP
GREWUP
ICECAP
ICEDUP
ICESUP
KEEPUP
OPENUP
PREAMP
SPEDUP
STEPUP
TEEDUP
TEESUP
THELIP
TIEDUP
TIESUP
TOECAP
TOETAP
USEDUP
USESUP

•••EP•

ACCEPT
BICEPS
BLEEPS
CHEEPS
CREEPS
CREEPY
EXCEPT
INCEPT
JOSEPH
JULEPS
SHEEPS
SLEEPS
SLEEPY
STEEPS
SWEEPS

•••E•P

ANTEUP
ASLEEP
BONEUP
BOPEEP
BOREUP
CAMEUP
COMEUP
DONEUP
EASEUP
FACEUP
FIREUP
GAVEUP
GIVEUP
HOLEUP
LACEUP
LINEUP
MADEUP
MAKEUP
PILEUP
PIPEUP
RAKEUP
SAVEUP
SIZEUP
STREEP
TAKEUP
TONEUP
TOREUP
TUNEUP
TYPEUP
UPKEEP
WAKEUP
WIPEUP
WISEUP
WOKEUP

••••EP

ASLEEP
BOPEEP
INSTEP
SCHLEP
STREEP
UPKEEP

EQ••••

EQUALS
EQUATE
EQUINE
EQUIPS
EQUITY

E•Q•••

EMQUAD
ENQUAD

E•••Q•

ETSEQQ

E••••Q

ETSEQQ

•EQ•••

PEQUOD
PEQUOT
SEQUEL
SEQUIN

•E•Q••

SESQUI

••EQ••

CHEQUE

•••EQ•

ETSEQQ

•••E•Q

ETSEQQ

••••EQ

SUSIEQ

ER••••

ERASED
ERASER
ERASES
ERBIUM
EREBUS
ERECTS
ERENOW
ERFURT
ERGATE
ERGOTS
ERHARD
ERINYS
ERMINE
ERNANI
ERNEST
ERODED
ERODES
EROICA
EROTIC
ERRAND
ERRANT
ERRATA
ERRING
ERROLL
ERRORS
ERSATZ
ERUCTS
ERUPTS
ERVING
ERYNGO

E•R•••

EARFUL
EARING
EARLAP
EARNED
EARNER
EARTHA
EARTHY
EARWAX
EARWIG
EERIER
EERILY
EGRESS
EGRETS
ENRAGE
ENRAPT
ENRICH
ENRICO
ENROBE
ENROLL
ENROOT
ERRAND
ERRANT
ERRATA
ERRING
ERROLL
ERRORS
EUREKA
EUROPA
EUROPE
EYRIES

E••R••

EAGRES
EBERLY
ECARTE
EDERLE
EGERIA
ELBRUS
EMBRYO
EMERGE
ENDRUN
ENERGY
ENGRAM
ENTRAP
ENTREE
ENURED
ENURES
ENWRAP
EPARCH
EPHRON
EPIRUS
ESCROW
ESDRAS
ESPRIT
ETERNE
EVERLY
EVERSO
EVERTS
EXARCH
EXERTS
EXTRAS
EXURBS

E•••R•

EATERS
EATERY
EDBERG
EDGARD
EDGARS
EDGERS
EDUARD
EDVARD
EDWARD
EELERS
EEYORE
EFFORT
EGBERT
EIDERS
EKBERG
ELBERT
ELDERS
ELLERY
ELMIRA
ELMORE
ELVERS
ELVIRA
EMBARK
EMBERS
EMEERS
EMIGRE
EMPERY
EMPIRE
ENCORE
ENDERS
ENDORA
ENDURE
ENDURO
ENGIRD
ENGIRT
ENSURE
ENTERO
ENTERS
ENTIRE
EPHORI
EPHORS
ERFURT
ERHARD
ERRORS
ESCARP
ESCORT
ESHARP
ESKERS
ESTERS
ETHERS
EUCHRE
EUDORA
EXEDRA
EXHORT
EXPERT
EXPIRE
EXPIRY
EXPORT
EXSERT
EXTORT

E••••R

EARNER
EASIER
EASTER
ECLAIR
EDGIER
EDITOR
EELIER
EERIER
EISNER
EITHER
ELATER
ELAYER
ELINOR
ELIXIR
ELOPER
EMAJOR
EMINOR
EMOTER
EMPTOR
ENAMOR
ENDEAR
ERASER
ESCHER
ESTHER
ETCHER
EVADER
EVENER
EVILER
EVOKER
EXETER
EXMOOR

•ER•••

AERATE
AERIAL
AERIES
AEROBE
BERATE
BERBER
BEREFT
BERETS
BERGEN
BERING
BERLIN
BERNIE
BERTHA
BERTHS
BERTIE
CERATE
CEREAL
CEREUS
CERIPH
CERISE
CERIUM
CERMET
CERTIF
CERUSE
CERVID
DERAIL
DERIDE
DERIVE
DERMAL
DERMIS
DERRIS
EERIER
EERILY
FERBER
FERENC
FERGIE
FERGUS
FERMAT
FERRER
FERRET
FERRIC
FERRIS
FERULE
FERVID
FERVOR
GERALD
GERARD
GERBER
GERBIL
GERENT
GERMAN
GERONT
GERTIE
GERUND
HERALD
HERBAL
HERBIE
HERDED
HERDER
HEREAT
HEREBY
HEREIN
HEREOF
HEREON
HERESY
HERETO
HERIOT
HERMAN
HERMES
HERMIT
HERMON
HEROES
HEROIC
HERONS
HERSEY
HERZOG
JERBOA
JEREMY
JERKED
JERKIN
JEROME
JERSEY
KERALA
KERMAN
KERMES
KERMIS
KERMIT
KERNED
KERNEL
KERNOI
KERNOS
KERSEY
LERIDA
LERNER
MERCED
MERCER
MERELY
MEREST
MERGED
MERGER
MERGES
MERIDA
MERINO
MERITS
MERKEL
MERLIN
MERLON
MERLOT
MERMAN
MERMEN
MEROPE
MERSEY
MERTON
MERVYN
NEREID
NEREIS
NEREUS
NEROLI
NERUDA
NERVES
OERTER
PERCHA
PERDUE
PERILS
PERIOD
PERISH
PERKED
PERKUP
PERMED
PERMIT
PERNOD
PERROT
PERSIA
PERSON
PERTER
PERTLY
PERUKE
PERUSE
RERATE
REREAD
RERENT
RERUNS
SERACS
SERAIS
SERAPE
SERAPH
SERBIA
SERENA
SERENE
SERGEI
SERGES
SERGIO
SERIAL
SERIES
SERIFS
SERINE
SERINS
SERKIN
SERMON
SEROSA
SEROUS
SEROWS
SERUMS
SERVAL
SERVED
SERVER
SERVES
SERVOS
TERAPH
TERATO
TERCEL
TERCET
TEREDO
TERESA
TERETE
TEREUS
TERKEL
TERMED
TERRAN
TERRET
TERROR
TERSER
VERBAL
VERDIN
VERDON
VERDUN
VEREEN
VERGED
VERGER
VERGES
VERIFY
VERILY
VERISM
VERITE
VERITY
VERMIN
VERNAL
VERNON
VERONA
VERSED
VERSES
VERSOS
VERSUS
VERTEX
VERVET
WERENT
WERFEL
WERNER
XERXES
YERKES
ZEROED
ZEROES
ZEROIN
ZEROTH

•E•R••

BEARDS
BEARER
BEARON
BEARUP
BEIRUT
BETRAY
BEURRE
CEDRIC
DEARER
DEARIE
DEARLY
DEARME
DEARTH
DEBRAS
DEBRIS
DECREE
DEFRAY
DEGREE
DELRAY
DELRIO
DERRIS
DETROP
FEARED
FEARER
FERRER
FERRET
FERRIC
FERRIS
GEARED
GEARTO
GEARUP
GEHRIG
GENRES
GEORGE
HEARER
HEAROF
HEARST
HEARTH
HEARTS
HEARTY
HEARYE
HEBREW
HEDREN
HENRIK
JEERAT
JEERED
JEERER
LEARNS
LEARNT
LEBRUN
LEERAT
LEERED
LEERER
LEGREE
LEHRER
MEERUT
METRES
METRIC
METROS
NEARBY
NEARED
NEARER
NEARLY
NEARTO
NEURAL
NEUROL
NEURON
PEARLS
PEARLY
PEERAT
PEERCE
PEERED
PEERIN
PENROD
PEORIA
PERROT
PETREL
PETRIE
PETROG
PETROL
REARED
REARER
REARMS
REARUP
REDRAW
REDREW
REGRET
REPROS
RETRAL
RETRIM
RETROS
REWRAP
SEARCH
SEARED
SEARLE
SECRET
SEERED
SEURAT
SEVRES
TEARAT
TEARED
TEARUP
TENREC
TERRAN
TERRET
TERROR
TETRAD
TETRAS
TETRIS
VEERED
WEARER
WEIRDO
YEARLY
YEARNS
ZEBRAS

•E••R•

BEFORE
BELFRY
BEMIRE

BEURRE
BEWARE
CEDARS
CELERY
CENTRE
CENTRI
CENTRO
CESARE
DEBARK
DEBARS
DECORS
DEFERS
DEFORM
DEHORN
DEIDRE
DEJURE
DEMURE
DEMURS
DENDRI
DENDRO
DENIRO
DEPART
DEPORT
DESCRY
DESERT
DESIRE
DESTRY
DETERS
DEXTRO
EELERS
EEYORE
FEDORA
FEMORA
FEMURS
FEVERS
GEMARA
GENERA
GENTRY
GERARD
GEZIRA
HEGARI
HEGIRA
HETERO
HEWERS
HEXERS
JETHRO
LEMURS
LENORE
LEVERS
MEAGRE
MEGARA
MEMORY
MESSRS
METERS
NEPHRO
NEVERS
NEWARK
OEUVRE
PELTRY
PENURY
PETARD
PETERS
REAIRS
REBARS
REBORN
RECORD
RECORK
RECURS
REFERS
REFORM
REGARD
REHIRE
REMARK
REMORA
REPORT
RESORB
RESORT
RETARD
RETARS
RETIRE
RETORT
RETURN
REVERB
REVERE
REVERS
REVERT
REWARD
REWARM
REWIRE
REWORD
REWORK
SEBERG
SECERN
SECURE
SEDERS
SEGURA
SEMPRE
SENARY
SENORA
SENORS
SENTRY
SEVERE
SEVERN
SEVERS
SEWARD
SEWERS
TENORS
TENURE
TEPHRA
VELCRO
VENIRE
VESTRY
VEXERS
WEBERN

•E•••R

AETHER
BEAKER
BEARER
BEATER
BEAVER
BECKER
BEEPER
BEGGAR
BELAIR
BENDER
BENHUR
BERBER
BESSER
BESTIR
BETTER
BETTOR
CELLAR
CENSER
CENSOR
CENTER
DEADER
DEAFER
DEALER
DEARER
DEBTOR
DECKER
DEEPER
DEFTER
DEICER
DELVER
DENIER
DENSER
DENVER
DEODAR
DETOUR
DEVOIR
DEVOUR
DEWIER
DEXTER
EELIER
EERIER
FEARER
FEEDER
FEELER
FELLER
FENCER
FENDER
FERBER
FERRER
FERVOR
FESTER
FETTER
GEEZER
GEIGER
GENDER
GERBER
GETTER
GEYSER
HEADER
HEALER
HEARER
HEATER
HEAVER
HECTOR
HEDGER
HEELER
HEFNER
HEIFER
HELLER
HELPER
HELTER
HEMMER
HENNER
HEPPER
HERDER
HESTER
JEERER
JEETER
JENNER
JESTER
KEELER
KEENER
KEEPER
KEGLER
KELLER
KEPLER
KEVLAR
LEADER
LEAKER
LEANER
LEAPER
LEASER
LECTOR
LEDGER
LEERER
LEHRER
LEKVAR
LENDER
LERNER
LESSER
LESSOR
LESTER
LETTER
LEVIER
LEWDER
MEAGER
MEANER
MEDGAR
MEDLAR
MEEKER
MEETER
MEMBER
MEMOIR
MENDER
MENHIR
MENTOR
MERCER
MERGER
MESMER
METEOR
METIER
MEWLER
NEARER
NEATER
NECTAR
NESTER
NESTOR
NETHER
NEUTER
NEWMAR
OERTER
PEDLAR
PEELER
PEEPER
PEGLER
PELTER
PENNER
PEPPER
PERTER
PESTER
PETTER
PEWTER
READER
REALER
REAMER
REAPER
REARER
RECTOR
REDDER
REDFIR
REEFER
REHEAR
REINER
RENDER
RENOIR
RENTER
REPAIR
RESTER
RETOUR
REUTER
REVOIR
SEALER
SEATER
SECTOR
SEEDER
SEEGER
SEEKER
SEINER
SEIZER
SELLER
SEMPER
SENDER
SENHOR
SENIOR
SENSOR
SERVER
SETTER
SEXIER
TEASER
TEDDER
TEENER
TEETER
TELLER
TEMPER
TENDER
TENSER
TENSOR
TENTER
TERROR
TERSER
TESTER
TETHER
VECTOR
VEDDER
VELOUR
VENDOR
VENEER
VENTER
VERGER
VESPER
VETOER
WEAKER
WEARER
WEAVER
WEBBER
WEEDER
WEEPER
WEIMAR
WELDER
WELTER
WERNER
WETBAR
WETHER
WETTER
YEAGER
YELLER
YELPER
YESSIR
YESTER
ZENGER
ZEPHYR

••ER••

AHERNE
ALERTS
AMERCE
APERCU
ATERGO
AVERNO
AVERSE
AVERTS
BIERCE
CHERIE
CHERRY
CHERUB
CHERYL
CLERGY
CLERIC
CLERKS
COERCE
CZERNY
DJERBA
EBERLY
EDERLE
EGERIA
EMERGE
ENERGY
ETERNE
EVERLY
EVERSO
EVERTS
EXERTS
FAERIE
FAEROE
FIERCE
GUERRE
HIERON
IBERIA
JEERAT
JEERED
JEERER
LEERAT
LEERED
LEERER
LIERNE
MEERUT
OBERON
OMERTA
OPERAS
OVERDO
OVERLY
PEERAT
PEERCE
PEERED
PEERIN
PIERCE
PIERRE
PUERTO
QUERNS
QWERTY
SEERED
SHEREE
SHERIF
SHERPA
SHERRY
SIERRA
SKERRY
SMERSH
SPERRY
STEREO
STERES
STERNA
STERNE
STERNO
STERNS
STEROL
SWERVE
THERMO
THERMS
TIERCE
TIERED
TIEROD
TIERRA
TWERPS
USERID
VEERED
WHERRY

••E•R•

ALEGRE
AMEERS
AMENRA
AWEARY
BLEARS
BLEARY
CHEERS
CHEERY
CHERRY
CHEVRE
CLEARS
DREARY
EMEERS
EXEDRA
FLEERS
FLEURY
GUERRE
LIEVRE
OHENRY
OLEARY
PHEDRE
PIERRE
PIETRO
PLEURA
POETRY
SHEARS
SHEERS
SHERRY
SIERRA
SKERRY
SMEARS
SMEARY
SNEERS
SNEERY
SPEARS
SPERRY
STEERS
SWEARS
THEIRS
THEORY
THEYRE
TIERRA
WHERRY

••E••R

ALEGAR
BEEPER
BREUER
BREWER
CAESAR
CHEWER
CLEVER
DEEPER
DIETER
DUELER
EVENER
EXETER
FEEDER
FEELER
FLEXOR
FUELER
GEEZER
GREGOR
GREYER
HEELER
JAEGER
JEERER
JEETER
KEELER
KEENER
KEEPER
KIEFER
LEERER
LIEDER
LIEFER
MEEKER
MEETER
OPENER
PEELER
PEEPER
PIECER
PIETER
PLEXOR
PREFER
PRETER
PREWAR
QUEUER
REEFER
RHETOR
SEEDER
SEEGER
SEEKER
SKEWER
STELAR
STEWER
TEENER
TEETER
THENAR
TREMOR
TREVOR
VIEWER
WEEDER
WEEPER
WIENER

•••ER•

ADDERS
ADHERE
ADVERB
ADVERT
AILERS
ALBERT
ALDERS
ALPERT
ALTERS
AMBERS
AMEERS
AMPERE
ANGERS
ANTERO
ARTERY
ASKERS
ASPERA
ASSERT
ASTERN
ASTERS
AUGERS
BAKERS
BAKERY
BALERS
BIKERS
BITERS
BOLERO
BONERS
BORERS
BOWERS
BOWERY
BOXERS
BRIERS
BRIERY
BUYERS
CABERS
CAGERS
CAMERA
CANERS
CAPERS
CASERN
CATERS
CAVERN
CAVERS
CELERY
CHEERS
CHEERY
CICERO
CIDERS
CITERS
CODERS
COHERE
COMERS
COOERS
CORERS
COVERS
COVERT
COWERS
CRIERS
CURERS
CYDERS
DATERS
DEFERS
DESERT
DETERS
DICERS
DINERO
DINERS
DIVERS
DIVERT
DOSERS
DOWERS
DOZERS
DRIERS
DRYERS
DUNERA
DUPERY
EATERS
EATERY
EDBERG
EDGERS
EELERS
EGBERT
EIDERS
EKBERG
ELBERT
ELDERS
ELLERY
ELVERS
EMBERS
EMEERS
EMPERY
ENDERS
ENTERO
ENTERS
ESKERS
ESTERS
ETHERS
EXPERT
EXSERT
FAKERS
FAKERY
FARERS
FEVERS
FIBERS
FIFERS
FILERS
FINERY
FIRERS
FIVERS
FIXERS
FLEERS
FLIERS
FLYERS
FOYERS
FRYERS
GAPERS
GATERS
GENERA
GIBERS
GIVERS
GLUERS
GOFERS
GONERS
GOVERN
HALERS
HALERU
HATERS
HAZERS
HETERO
HEWERS
HEXERS
HIDERS
HIKERS
HIRERS
HOMERS
HOPERS
HOVERS
HUBERT
HUMERI
IDLERS
IMPERF
INFERS
INHERE
INKERS
INSERT
INTERN
INVERT
JAPERS
JAPERY
JIVERS
JOKERS
KAGERA
KHMERS
KITERS
LACERS
LADERS
LAGERS
LAKERS
LASERS
LAVERS
LAYERS
LEVERS
LIFERS
LIGERS
LINERS
LITERS
LIVERS
LIVERY
LONERS
LOPERS
LOSERS
LOVERS
LOWERS
LOWERY
LUGERS
MADERO
MAKERS
MASERS
MASERU
MATERS
MAZERS
METERS
MILERS
MIMERS
MINERS
MISERS
MISERY
MITERS
MIXERS
MODERN
MONERA
MOPERS
MOVERS
MOWERS
MOYERS
MUSERS
NAMERS
NAPERY
NEVERS
NFLERS
NHLERS
NINERS
NITERS
NOTERS
NUMERO
OATERS
OBVERT
OCHERS
OFFERS
OGLERS
OILERS
ORDERS
ORNERY
ORRERY
OSIERS
OTHERS
OTTERS
OWNERS
PACERS
PAGERS
PAPERS
PAPERY
PARERS
PAVERS
PAWERS
PAYERS
PETERS
PIKERS
PINERO
PINERY
PIPERS
PLIERS
POKERS
POKERY
POLERS
POSERS
POWERS
PRIERS
RACERS
RAKERS
RATERS
RAVERS
REFERS
REVERB
REVERE
REVERS
REVERT
RICERS
RIDERS
RISERS
RIVERA
RIVERS
ROBERT
ROGERS
ROMERO
ROPERS
ROVERS
ROWERS
RULERS
RUPERT
SABERS
SAKERS
SAVERS
SAYERS
SCLERA
SEBERG
SECERN
SEDERS
SEVERE
SEVERN
SEVERS
SEWERS
SHEERS
SHOERS
SIDERO
SIDERS
SISERA
SIXERS
SIZERS
SKIERS
SNEERS
SNEERY
SOBERS
SOLERS
SOMERS
SOWERS
SOXERS
SPHERE
SPIERS
STEERS
SUPERB
SUPERS
TAKERS
TAMERS
TAPERS
TATERS
TAVERN
TAXERS
TIGERS
TILERS
TIMERS
TITERS
TONERS
TOPERS
TORERO
TOTERS
TOWERS
TOWERY
TRIERS
TUBERS
TUNERS
TUYERE
TYPERS
UDDERS
ULCERS
UMBERS
UPPERS
URGERS
USHERS
UTTERS
VALERY
VEXERS
VINERY
VIPERS
VOTERS
VOWERS
WADERS
WAFERS
WAGERS
WALERS
WANERS
WATERS
WATERY
WAVERS
WAVERY
WAXERS
WEBERN
WINERY
WIPERS
WIRERS
WOOERS
WYVERN

•••E•R

APPEAR
AUTEUR
CAREER
COHEIR
DOGEAR
ENDEAR
INGEAR
LINEAR
METEOR
POSEUR
RATEDR
REHEAR
TINEAR
VENEER

••••ER

ABUSER
ACHIER
ADORER
AETHER
AIRIER
AMBLER
AMPLER
ANGLER
ANSWER
ANTHER
ANTLER
ARCHER
ARGUER
ARTIER
ASHIER
AVOWER
BACKER
BADGER
BAGGER
BAILER
BALDER
BANGER
BANKER
BANNER
BANTER
BARBER
BARKER
BARTER
BASTER
BATHER
BATTER
BAWLER
BAXTER
BEAKER
BEARER
BEATER
BEAVER
BECKER
BEEPER
BENDER
BERBER
BESSER
BETTER
BICKER
BIDDER
BIGGER
BINDER
BIRDER
BITTER
BLAZER
BLOWER
BOATER
BOBBER
BOILER
BOLDER
BOLGER
BOMBER
BONIER
BOOKER
BOOMER
BOPPER
BORDER
BOTHER
BOWLER
BOWSER
BOWYER
BRACER
BRAVER
BRAYER
BRAZER
BREUER
BREWER
BROKER
BRUDER
BUFFER
BUGLER
BULWER
BUMMER
BUMPER
BUNKER
BUNTER
BURGER
BURNER
BUSIER
BUSTER
BUTLER
BUTTER
BUZZER
CABLER
CADGER
CAGIER
CAHIER
CALDER
CALLER
CALMER
CAMBER
CAMPER
CANKER
CANNER
CANTER
CAPPER
CARDER
CAREER
CARPER
CARTER
CARVER
CASPER
CASTER
CATHER
CENSER
CENTER
CHASER
CHEWER
CHOKER
CHOLER
CINDER
CIPHER
CLAWER
CLEVER
CLOSER
CLOVER
COALER
COAXER
COCKER
CODGER
COFFER
COINER
COLDER
COLTER
COMBER
CONFER
CONGER
CONKER
CONNER
COODER
COOKER
COOLER
COOPER
COOTER
COPIER
COPPER
COPTER
CORKER
CORNER
COTTER
COUTER
COWPER
COZIER
CRATER
CRAVER
CROWER
CRUDER
CULLER
CULVER
CUMBER
CURLER
CURTER
CUSTER
CUTLER
CUTTER
CYCLER
CYPHER
DAFTER
DAGGER
DAMPER
DANCER
DANDER
DANGER
DANKER
DANNER
DAPPER
DARKER
DARNER
DARTER
DASHER
DAUBER
DEADER
DEAFER
DEALER
DEARER
DECKER
DEEPER
DEFTER
DEICER
DELVER
DENIER
DENSER
DENVER
DEWIER
DEXTER
DIALER
DIAPER
DICIER
DICKER
DIETER
DIFFER
DIGGER
DILLER
DIMMER
DINNER
DIPPER
DITHER
DLAYER
DOBBER
DOCKER
DODDER
DODGER
DOGGER
DONDER
DONNER
DOPIER
DORMER
DOSSER
DOURER
DOWNER
DOWSER
DRAPER
DRAWER

DRIVER
DRONER
DROVER
DUELER
DUFFER
DUIKER
DULLER
DUMBER
DUMPER
DUNKER
DUSTER
EARNER
EASIER
EASTER
EDGIER
EELIER
EERIER
EISNER
EITHER
ELATER
ELAYER
ELOPER
EMOTER
ERASER
ESCHER
ESTHER
ETCHER
EVADER
EVENER
EVILER
EVOKER
EXETER
FABLER
FAIRER
FALSER
FALTER
FARMER
FASTER
FATHER
FATTER
FAWNER
FEARER
FEEDER
FEELER
FELLER
FENCER
FENDER
FERBER
FERRER
FESTER
FETTER
FIBBER
FILLER
FILTER
FINDER
FINGER
FIRMER
FISHER
FITTER
FLAKER
FLAYER
FLOWER
FODDER
FOGGER
FOKKER
FOLDER
FONDER
FOOLER
FOOTER
FORCER
FORGER
FORKER
FORMER
FOSTER
FOULER
FOWLER
FOXIER
FRASER
FRAZER
FUELER
FULLER
GABBER
GADDER
GAFFER
GAINER
GAITER
GAMIER
GANDER
GARNER
GARTER
GASSER
GATHER
GAUGER
GAWKER
GEEZER
GEIGER
GENDER
GERBER
GETTER
GEYSER
GIBBER
GILDER
GINGER
GIPPER
GIRDER
GLASER
GLAZER
GLIDER
GLOVER
GLOWER
GNAWER
GOLFER
GOOBER
GOOIER
GOOVER
GOPHER
GORIER
GOUGER
GRADER
GRATER
GRAVER
GRAYER
GRAZER
GREYER
GRIPER
GROCER
GROVER
GROWER
GULPER
GUNNER
GUNTER
GUSHER
GUTTER
GYPPER
HACKER
HALTER
HAMMER
HAMPER
HANGER
HANKER
HARDER
HARKER
HARPER
HATTER
HAULER
HAWKER
HAWSER
HAZIER
HEADER
HEALER
HEARER
HEATER
HEAVER
HEDGER
HEELER
HEFNER
HEIFER
HELLER
HELPER
HELTER
HEMMER
HENNER
HEPPER
HERDER
HESTER
HIGHER
HILLER
HINDER
HINTER
HIPPER
HISSER
HITHER
HITTER
HOAXER
HOKIER
HOLDER
HOLIER
HOLLER
HOMIER
HONKER
HOOFER
HOOPER
HOOTER
HOOVER
HOPPER
HORNER
HOSIER
HOTTER
HOWLER
HUGGER
HULLER
HUMMER
HUNGER
HUNKER
HUNTER
HURLER
HUSKER
ICKIER
IFFIER
IMAGER
INANER
INKIER
IRATER
IRONER
ISOMER
ISSUER
JABBER
JAEGER
JAGGER
JAILER
JAMMER
JASPER
JAVIER
JEERER
JEETER
JENNER
JESTER
JIGGER
JITTER
JOBBER
JOGGER
JOINER
JOYNER
JUDDER
JUICER
JUMPER
JUNKER
JUSTER
KAISER
KANDER
KEELER
KEENER
KEEPER
KEGLER
KELLER
KEPLER
KHYBER
KICKER
KIDDER
KIEFER
KILLER
KILMER
KILTER
KINDER
KIPPER
KISSER
KNOWER
KOHLER
KOSHER
KOTTER
KRAMER
KRATER
KRONER
KRUGER
LAAGER
LACIER
LADDER
LADLER
LAFFER
LAGGER
LANCER
LANDER
LANIER
LANKER
LARDER
LARGER
LASHER
LASSER
LATHER
LATTER
LAUDER
LAUPER
LAWYER
LAZIER
LEADER
LEAKER
LEANER
LEAPER
LEASER
LEDGER
LEERER
LEHRER
LENDER
LERNER
LESSER
LESTER
LETTER
LEVIER
LEWDER
LIBBER
LIEDER
LIEFER
LIFTER
LIMBER
LIMNER
LIMPER
LINGER
LINKER
LINTER
LISTER
LITTER
LOADER
LOAFER
LOANER
LOBBER
LOCKER
LODGER
LOGGER
LOGIER
LOITER
LONGER
LOOKER
LOOPER
LOOSER
LOOTER
LOPPER
LOUDER
LOUVER
LUBBER
LUGGER
LUMBER
LUMPER
LUNKER
LUSHER
LUSTER
LUTHER
MADDER
MAHLER
MAILER
MANGER
MANNER
MAPPER
MARKER
MARNER
MASHER
MASKER
MASTER
MATHER
MATTER
MAULER
MAUSER
MEAGER
MEANER
MEEKER
MEETER
MEMBER
MENDER
MERCER
MERGER
MESMER
METIER
MEWLER
MIDLER
MILDER
MILKER
MILLER
MILNER
MINCER
MINDER
MINTER
MISTER
MOANER
MOCKER
MOILER
MOLDER
MOLTER
MONGER
MOPPER
MOTHER
MOUSER
MUDDER
MUGGER
MULLER
MUMMER
MURDER
MUSHER
MUSTER
MUTTER
NABBER
NAGGER
NAILER
NAPIER
NAPPER
NASSER
NATTER
NEARER
NEATER
NESTER
NETHER
NEUTER
NICKER
NIGHER
NIPPER
NOBLER
NOSHER
NOSIER
NUDGER
NUMBER
NURSER
NUTTER
OATIER
OBITER
OERTER
OILIER
OLIVER
ONAGER
OPENER
OPINER
OSTLER
OUSTER
OYSTER
PACKER
PADDER
PALMER
PALTER
PAMPER
PANDER
PANNER
PANZER
PAPIER
PARKER
PARSER
PASSER
PATTER
PAUPER
PAWNER
PEELER
PEEPER
PEGLER
PELTER
PENNER
PEPPER
PERTER
PESTER
PETTER
PEWTER
PHASER
PICKER
PIECER
PIETER
PILFER
PINCER
PINIER
PINKER
PINNER
PINTER
PITTER
PLACER
PLANER
PLATER
PLAYER
PLOVER
PLOWER
POKIER
POLDER
POLLER
PONDER
POORER
POPPER
PORKER
PORTER
POSHER
POSTER
POTHER
POTTER
POURER
POUTER
POWDER
PRATER
PRAYER
PREFER
PRETER
PRICER
PRIMER
PROBER
PROPER
PROSER
PROVER
PRUNER
PUCKER
PUFFER
PUMPER
PUNIER
PUNKER
PUNTER
PURRER
PURSER
PUTTER
QUAKER
QUAVER
QUEUER
QUIVER
QUOTER
RACIER
RADNER
RAFTER
RAIDER
RAILER
RAINER
RAISER
RANGER
RANKER
RANTER
RAPIER
RAPPER
RASHER
RASPER
RASTER
RATHER
RATTER
READER
REALER
REAMER
REAPER
REARER
REDDER
REEFER
REINER
RENDER
RENTER
RESTER
REUTER
RHYMER
RICHER
RIFLER
RIGGER
RINGER
RIOTER
RIPPER
RISKER
RITTER
ROAMER
ROARER
ROBBER
ROCKER
ROHMER
ROLLER
ROMPER
ROOFER
ROOMER
ROOTER
ROPIER
ROSIER
ROSTER
ROTTER
ROUTER
RUBBER
RUDDER
RUINER
RUMMER
RUNNER
RUTGER
SACKER
SADDER
SALTER
SALVER
SANDER
SANGER
SAPPER
SASSER
SAUCER
SAUGER
SAWYER
SCALER
SCARER
SCORER
SCOTER
SEALER
SEATER
SEEDER
SEEGER
SEEKER
SEINER
SEIZER
SELLER
SEMPER
SENDER
SERVER
SETTER
SEXIER
SHAKER
SHAPER
SHARER
SHAVER
SHINER
SHIRER
SHIVER
SHOVER
SHOWER
SICKER
SIFTER
SIGHER
SIGNER
SILVER
SIMMER
SIMPER
SINGER
SINKER
SINNER
SINTER
SIPPER
SISLER
SISTER
SITTER
SKATER
SKEWER
SKIVER
SLATER
SLAVER
SLAYER
SLICER
SLIDER
SLIVER
SLOWER
SMILER
SMOKER
SNIDER
SNORER
SNYDER
SOAKER
SOAPER
SOARER
SOBBER
SOCCER
SOFTER
SOLDER
SOLVER
SOMBER
SOMMER
SOONER
SORTER
SOURER
SOUTER
SPACER
SPADER
SPARER
SPIDER
SPIKER
SPRIER
SPRYER
STAGER
STALER
STARER
STATER
STEWER
STIVER
STOKER
STONER
STORER
STOVER
STYLER
SUAVER
SUCKER
SUFFER
SULKER
SUMMER
SUMNER
SUMTER
SUNDER
SUPPER
SURFER
SUTLER
SUTTER
SWAYER
SWIPER
TACKER
TALKER
TALLER
TAMPER
TANKER
TANNER
TAPPER
TARTER
TASTER
TATTER
TAUTER
TEASER
TEDDER
TEENER
TEETER
TELLER
TEMPER
TENDER
TENSER
TENTER
TERSER
TESTER
TETHER
THALER
THAYER
TICKER
TIDIER
TIGGER
TILLER
TILTER
TIMBER
TINDER
TINIER
TINKER
TINNER
TINTER
TIPPER
TITHER
TITTER
TOILER
TONIER
TOOTER
TOPPER
TOSSER
TOTHER
TOTTER
TOURER
TOUTER
TOWNER
TRACER
TRADER
TRITER
TUCKER
TUGGER
TURNER
TUSKER
TWOFER
UGLIER
ULSTER
UNDOER
UNITER
USURER
VAGUER
VAINER
VAMPER
VANIER
VASTER
VEDDER
VENEER
VENTER
VERGER
VESPER
VETOER
VIEWER
VIZIER
WAGNER
WAILER
WAITER
WAIVER
WALKER
WALLER
WALTER
WANDER
WANNER
WAPNER
WARDER
WARIER
WARMER
WARNER
WASHER
WASTER
WAVIER
WAXIER
WEAKER
WEARER
WEAVER
WEBBER
WEEDER
WEEPER
WELDER
WELTER
WERNER
WETHER
WETTER
WHALER
WHINER
WHITER
WICKER
WIENER
WILDER
WILIER
WINCER
WINDER
WINGER
WINKER
WINNER
WINTER
WISHER
WISTER
WITHER
WOHLER
WOLPER
WONDER
WOOFER
WORKER
WRITER
WYNTER
XAVIER
XYSTER
YAKKER
YAMMER
YASSER
YAWNER
YAWPER
YEAGER
YELLER
YELPER
YESTER
YONDER
YORKER
ZAFFER
ZANDER
ZANIER
ZAPPER
ZENGER
ZIMMER
ZINGER
ZIPPER
ZITHER
ZONKER
ZUIDER

ES••••

ESCAPE
ESCARP
ESCENT
ESCHER
ESCHEW
ESCORT
ESCROW
ESCUDO
ESDRAS
ESHARP
ESKERS
ESKIMO
ESPANA
ESPIAL
ESPIED
ESPIES
ESPOSA
ESPOSO
ESPRIT
ESSAYS
ESSENE
ESTATE
ESTEEM
ESTERS
ESTHER
ESTOPS

E•S•••

EASEIN
EASELS
EASEUP
EASIER
EASILY
EASING
EASTER
EASTON
EDSELS
EISNER
ENSIGN
ENSILE
ENSOUL
ENSUED
ENSUES
ENSURE
EOSINS
ERSATZ
ESSAYS
ESSENE
ETSEQQ
EXSERT

E••S••

EATSAT
EATSIN
EATSUP
ECESIS
EDESSA
EDISON
EGESTA
EGESTS
EGGSON
ELISHA
ELISSA
ELYSEE
ENDSUP
ENESCO
ENISLE
ENOSIS
ERASED
ERASER
ERASES
EXISTS

E•••S•

EDESSA
EFFUSE
EGOISM
EGOIST
EGRESS
ELAPSE
ELDEST
ELFISH
ELISSA
ELOISE
ELPASO
EMBOSS
EMDASH
ENCASE
ENDASH
ENDUSE
ENLIST
ENMESH
ERNEST
ESPOSA
ESPOSO
EVENSO
EVERSO
EVULSE
EXCESS
EXCISE
EXCUSE
EXPOSE

E••••S

EAGLES
EAGRES
EASELS
EATERS
EBOATS
EBONDS
ECCLES
ECESIS
ECHOES
ECLATS
ECOLES
EDAMES
EDDIES
EDDOES
EDGARS
EDGERS
EDICTS
EDILES
EDSELS
EDUCES
EELERS
EFLATS
EGESTS
EGRESS
EGRETS
EIDERS
EIGHTS
EJECTS
ELANDS
ELATES
ELBOWS
ELBRUS
ELDERS
ELECTS
ELEMIS
ELEVES
ELIDES
ELITES
ELOPES
ELUDES
ELUTES
ELVERS
EMAILS
EMBAYS
EMBEDS
EMBERS
EMBOSS
EMCEES
EMEERS
EMENDS
EMMETS
EMOTES
ENACTS
ENATES
ENDERS
ENDOWS
ENDUES
ENGELS
ENJOYS
ENNIUS
ENOKIS
ENOSIS
ENSUES
ENTERS
ENURES
ENVIES
ENVOIS
ENVOYS
EOSINS
EPHAHS
EPHODS
EPHORS
EPIRUS
EPOCHS
EPODES
EQUALS
EQUIPS
ERASES
EREBUS
ERECTS
ERGOTS
ERINYS
ERODES
ERRORS
ERUCTS
ERUPTS
ESDRAS
ESKERS
ESPIES
ESSAYS
ESTERS
ESTOPS
ETCHES
ETHERS
ETHICS
ETHNOS
ETUDES
EVADES
EVENTS
EVERTS
EVICTS
EVOKES
EXACTS
EXALTS
EXCELS
EXCESS
EXERTS
EXILES
EXISTS
EXODUS
EXPELS
EXTOLS
EXTRAS
EXUDES
EXULTS
EXURBS
EYRIES

•ES•••

BESANT
BESETS
BESIDE
BESOMS
BESOTS
BESSER
BESSIE
BESTED
BESTIR
BESTOW
CESARE
CESIUM
CESSNA
CESTAS
CESTOS
CESTUS
DESALT
DESCRY
DESERT
DESICA
DESIGN
DESILU
DESIRE
DESIST
DESMAN
DESOTO
DESPOT
DESTRY
FESCUE
FESSES
FESSUP
FESTAL
FESTER
FESTUS
GESTES
HESIOD
HESTER
HESTIA
HESTON
JESSEL
JESSIE
JESTED
JESTER
JESUIT
KESHIA
LESAGE
LESBOS
LESLEY
LESLIE
LESSEE
LESSEN
LESSER
LESSON
LESSOR
LESTAT
LESTER
MESABI
MESCAL
MESHED
MESHES
MESMER
MESONS
MESSED
MESSES
MESSRS
MESSUP
NESSES
NESSIE
NESTEA

NESTED
NESTER
NESTLE
NESTOR
PESACH
PESCOW
PESETA
PESTER
PESTLE
RESALE
RESALT
RESAND
RESCUE
RESEAL
RESEAT
RESEAU
RESECT
RESEDA
RESEED
RESEEN
RESEES
RESELL
RESEND
RESENT
RESETS
RESEWN
RESEWS
RESHIP
RESHOD
RESHOE
RESHOT
RESIDE
RESIGN
RESILE
RESING
RESINS
RESIST
RESNIK
RESODS
RESOLD
RESOLE
RESORB
RESORT
RESTED
RESTER
RESTON
RESTUP
RESULT
RESUME
SESAME
SESQUI
SESTET
SESTOS
TESLAS
TESSIE
TESTAE
TESTED
TESTEE
TESTER
VESPER
VESPID
VESSEL
VESTAL
VESTAS
VESTED
VESTEE
VESTRY
WESKIT
WESLEY
WESSEX
WESSON
YESMAN
YESMEN
YESSED
YESSES
YESSIR
YESTER
ZESTED

•E•S••

BEASTS
BENSON
BESSER
BESSIE
BETSEY
CEASED
CEASES
CENSED
CENSER
CENSES
CENSOR
CENSUS
CESSNA
DEISTS
DENSER
FEASTS
FEISTY
FESSES
FESSUP
GEISEL
GEISHA
GELSEY
GETSAT
GETSBY
GETSET
GETSIN
GETSIT
GETSON
GETSTO
GETSUP
GEYSER
HEISTS
HEMSIN
HENSON
HERSEY
JENSEN
JERSEY
JESSEL
JESSIE
JETSAM
JETSET
JETSKI
JETSON
KELSEY
KERSEY
KEYSIN
KEYSUP
LEASED
LEASER
LEASES
LENSED
LENSES
LESSEE
LESSEN
LESSER
LESSON
LESSOR
LETSAT
LETSBE
LETSGO
LETSIN
LETSON
LETSUP
MEASLY
MENSAE
MENSAL
MENSAS
MENSCH
MERSEY
MESSED
MESSES
MESSRS
MESSUP
NEESON
NEISSE
NELSON
NESSES
NESSIE
NEVSKY
PENSEE
PEPSIN
PEPSUP
PERSIA
PERSON
REASON
REDSEA
REDSOX
REUSED
REUSES
REVSON
SEASON
SEESAW
SEESIN
SEESTO
SEISMO
SEISMS
SENSED
SENSEI
SENSES
SENSOR
SETSAT
SETSBY
SETSIN
SETSON
SETSUP
SEWSON
SEWSUP
TEASED
TEASEL
TEASER
TEASES
TEASET
TEESUP
TENSED
TENSER
TENSES
TENSOR
TERSER
TESSIE
VERSED
VERSES
VERSOS
VERSUS
VESSEL
WEASEL
WESSEX
WESSON
YEASTS
YEASTY
YESSED
YESSES
YESSIR

•E••S•

BEHEST
BEKESY
BEMUSE
BETISE
CERISE
CERUSE
DEBASE
DEFUSE
DEGUST
DELIST
DEMISE
DENISE
DEPOSE
DESIST
DETEST
DEVEST
DEVISE
FETISH
FEWEST
HEARST
HERESY
JEWISH
LEGIST
MEDUSA
MEREST
NEISSE
NEWEST
NEWISH
PERISH
PERUSE
RECAST
RECESS
RECUSE
REFUSE
REHASH
RELISH
RELIST
REMISE
REMISS
REPAST
REPOSE
RESIST
RETEST
REVISE
REWASH
SEROSA
SETOSE
SEXIST
TEENSY
TERESA
VERISM
WEENSY

•E•••S

AEETES
AENEAS
AEOLUS
AERIES
BEANOS
BEARDS
BEASTS
BEAUTS
BEBOPS
BEDEWS
BEDIMS
BEEVES
BEFITS
BEFOGS
BEGETS
BEGINS
BEGUMS
BEIGES
BEINGS
BELAYS
BELIES
BELLES
BERETS
BERTHS
BESETS
BESOMS
BESOTS
BETELS
BETTAS
BEVELS
BEVIES
BEZELS
CEASES
CEDARS
CEIBAS
CELEBS
CELLOS
CENSES
CENSUS
CENTOS
CEREUS
CESTAS
CESTOS
CESTUS
DEBARS
DEBITS
DEBRAS
DEBRIS
DEBUGS
DEBUTS
DECAFS
DECALS
DECAYS
DECORS
DECOYS
DEFATS
DEFERS
DEFIES
DEFOGS
DEICES
DEIGNS
DEIMOS
DEISTS
DELAYS
DELFTS
DELIUS
DELTAS
DELVES
DEMITS
DEMOBS
DEMONS
DEMURS
DENIES
DENIMS
DENNIS
DEPOTS
DEPTHS
DERMIS
DERRIS
DETERS
DEUCES
DEVILS
EELERS
FEASTS
FEIGNS
FEINTS
FELLAS
FELONS
FEMMES
FEMURS
FENCES
FERGUS
FERRIS
FESSES
FESTUS
FEVERS
FEZZES
GECKOS
GELEES
GENETS
GENIES
GENIUS
GENRES
GEODES
GESTES
GETUPS
HEARTS
HEATHS
HEAVES
HEDGES
HEISTS
HELENS
HELIOS
HELLAS
HELLOS
HELOTS
HELVES
HENNAS
HERMES
HEROES
HERONS
HEWERS
HEXADS
HEXERS
JEEVES
JEWELS
KEBABS
KEBOBS
KEDGES
KEMPIS
KERMES
KERMIS
KERNOS
KEVELS
KEYNES
LEARNS
LEASES
LEAVES
LEDGES
LEGALS
LEHUAS
LEMANS
LEMMAS
LEMNOS
LEMONS
LEMURS
LENSES
LEONES
LESBOS
LETUPS
LEVEES
LEVELS
LEVERS
LEVIES
MECCAS
MEDALS
MEDIAS
MEDICS
MELEES
MELONS
MENDES
MENSAS
MENTIS
MERGES
MERITS
MESHES
MESONS
MESSES
MESSRS
METALS
METERS
METRES
METROS
MEZZOS
NEIGHS
NENETS
NEREIS
NEREUS
NERVES
NESSES
NEUMES
NEVERS
NEVINS
NEWELS
PEARLS
PECANS
PEDALS
PEEVES
PEKOES
PELEUS
PELOPS
PELVIS
PENNIS
PEPLOS
PERILS
PETALS
PETERS
PEWEES
PEWITS
REACTS
REAIRS
REALES
REALMS
REARMS
REATAS
REBAGS
REBARS
REBELS
REBIDS
REBUTS
RECAPS
RECESS
RECONS
RECTOS
RECTUS
RECURS
REDOES
REDUBS
REDYES
REEVES
REFERS
REFITS
REGIUS
REHEMS
REIGNS
REINKS
REKEYS
RELAYS
RELETS
RELICS
RELIES
REMANS
REMAPS
REMISS
REMITS
REMOWS
RENEWS
RENNES
REOILS
REPAYS
REPEGS
REPELS
REPOTS
REPROS
RERUNS
RESEES
RESETS
RESEWS
RESINS
RESODS
RETAGS
RETAPS
RETARS
RETIES
RETOPS
RETOWS
RETROS
REUNES
REUSES
REVELS
REVERS
REVETS
REVUES
REWEDS
REWINS
SEAMUS
SEDANS
SEDERS
SEDGES
SEDUMS
SEENAS
SEGUES
SEINES
SEISMS
SEIZES
SELVES
SENNAS
SENORS
SENSES
SEPALS
SEPIAS
SEPOYS
SERACS
SERAIS
SERGES
SERIES
SERIFS
SERINS
SEROUS
SEROWS
SERUMS
SERVES
SERVOS
SESTOS
SETINS
SETTOS
SETUPS
SEVENS
SEVERS
SEVRES
SEWERS
TEASES
TEHEES
TEMPOS
TEMPTS
TENETS
TENNIS
TENONS
TENORS
TENSES
TENTHS
TEPALS
TEPEES
TEREUS
TESLAS
TETHYS
TETONS
TETRAS
TETRIS
TEXANS
VEGANS
VELDTS
VENOMS
VENOUS
VENUES
VERGES
VERSES
VERSOS
VERSUS
VESTAS
VETOES
VEXERS
WEAVES
WEDGES
WEIGHS
WELLES
WENCES
XEBECS
XERXES
YEARNS
YEASTS
YENTAS
YERKES
YESSES
ZEBRAS
ZENDOS
ZEROES
ZEUXIS

••ES••

ACESUP
ADESTE
ATESTS
AVESTA
AYESHA
CAESAR
CHESTS
CHESTY
CRESOL
CRESTS
CUESTA
DIESEL
DIESES
DIESIS
DOESBY
DOESIN
DOESNT
DOESUP
DRESSY
ECESIS
EDESSA
EGESTA
EGESTS
ENESCO
FIESTA
FLESHY
FRESCA
FRESCO
FRESNO
GOESAT
GOESBY
GOESIN
GOESON
GOESUP
GUESTS
ICESIN
ICESUP
ILESHA
KMESON
KRESGE
LIESIN
LIESTO
NEESON
NOESIS
ODESSA
PRESET
PRESTO
QUESTS
RHESUS
SEESAW
SEESIN
SEESTO
SIESTA
TEESUP
THESES
THESIS
THESIX
TIESIN
TIESUP
TMESIS
TOESIN
UNESCO
USESUP
WIESEL
WRESTS

••E•S•

AGEISM
AGEIST
ALEAST
ATEASE
AVERSE
BREAST
CHEESE
CHEESY
CLEESE
CREASE
CREASY
CREUSA
DRESSY
EDESSA
EVENSO
EVERSO
FLENSE
FREEST
GNEISS
GOEASY
GREASE
GREASY
KLEIST
NLEAST
ODENSE
ODESSA
ORELSE
PLEASE
QUEASY
SMERSH
TEENSY
THEISM
THEIST
TSETSE
UNEASE
UNEASY
WEENSY

••E••S

ABELES
ACEOUS
ADEEMS
ADEPTS
AEETES
AGENAS
AGENTS
AKELAS
AKENES
ALEPHS
ALERTS
ALEUTS
ALEXIS
AMEBAS
AMEERS
AMENDS
AMENTS
APEXES
ARECAS
ARENAS
ARETES
ATEAMS
ATESTS
AVERTS
BEEVES
BLEARS
BLEATS
BLEEDS
BLEEPS
BLENDS
BREADS
BREAKS
BREAMS
BREEDS
BRENTS
BREVES
BUENOS
CHEATS
CHECKS
CHEEKS
CHEEPS
CHEERS
CHELAS
CHEOPS
CHESTS
CLEANS
CLEARS
CLEATS
CLEEKS
CLEFTS
CLERKS
CLEVES
CLEVIS
CREAKS
CREAMS
CREDOS
CREEDS
CREEKS
CREELS
CREEPS
CREMES
CREPES
CRESTS
CZECHS
DIESES
DIESIS
DREADS
DREAMS
DWEEBS
DWELLS
ECESIS
EGESTS
EJECTS
ELECTS
ELEMIS
ELEVES
EMEERS
EMENDS
EREBUS
ERECTS
EVENTS
EVERTS
EXERTS
FIELDS
FIENDS
FJELDS
FLECKS
FLEERS
FLEETS
FLEXES
FOEHNS
FREAKS
GLEAMS
GLEANS
GLEBES
GNEISS
GREATS
GREBES
GREEKS
GREENS
GREETS
GUESTS
HBEAMS
HUEVOS
HYENAS
IBEAMS
IBEXES
IDEALS
IRENES
JEEVES
KNEADS
KNEELS
KNELLS
KVELLS
LIEGES
LIEUTS
NIECES
NOESIS
NUECES
OBEAHS
OBELUS
OCEANS
OMEGAS
ONEUPS
OPERAS
OREADS
OXEYES
PAEANS
PAEONS
PEEVES
PIECES
PIETAS
PLEADS
PLEATS
PLEBES
PLEXUS
PRECIS
PREENS
PSEUDS
QUEENS
QUELLS
QUERNS
QUESTS
QUEUES
REEVES
RHESUS
RHEUMS
SCENAS
SCENDS
SCENES
SCENTS
SEENAS
SHEAFS
SHEARS
SHEENS
SHEEPS
SHEERS
SHEETS
SHEIKS
SHELLS
SIEGES
SIEVES
SKEANS
SKEINS
SLEEKS
SLEEPS
SLEETS
SMEARS
SMELLS
SMELTS
SNEAKS
SNEERS
SNELLS
SPEAKS
SPEARS
SPECKS
SPEEDS
SPELLS
SPENDS
STEADS
STEAKS
STEALS
STEAMS
STEEDS
STEELS
STEEPS
STEERS
STEINS
STELES
STENOS
STERES
STERNS
SUEDES
SWEARS
SWEATS
SWEDES
SWEEPS
SWEETS
SWELLS
THEBES
THEFTS
THEIRS
THEMES
THERMS
THESES
THESIS
THETAS
THETIS
TIEINS
TIEUPS
TMESIS
TOEINS
TREADS
TREATS
TRENDS
TWEAKS
TWEEDS
TWEETS
TWERPS
UPENDS
VNECKS
WHEATS
WHEELS
WHELKS
WHELPS
WIELDS
WREAKS
WRECKS
WRESTS
YIELDS

•••ES•

ABBESS
ABLEST
ACCESS
AFRESH
ALWEST
APTEST
ARNESS
ARREST
ASSESS
ATBEST
ATREST
ATTEST
BAREST
BASEST
BEHEST
BEKESY
BLUEST
BLUESY
CARESS
CHEESE
CHEESY
CLEESE
COYEST
CUTEST
CUTESY
DETEST
DEVEST
DIGEST
DIREST
DIVEST
DRIEST
DRYEST
DURESS
EGRESS
ELDEST
ENMESH
ERNEST
EXCESS
FEWEST
FINEST
FOREST
FREEST
GAMEST
GAYEST
GOWEST
HALEST
HERESY
HONEST
HUGEST
ICIEST
IDLEST
ILLEST
INFEST
INGEST
INJEST
INNESS
INVEST
IQTEST
LAMESA
LAMEST
LATEST
LAXEST
LOWEST
MEREST
MODEST
MOLEST
MUTEST
NEWEST
NICEST
NLWEST
NOLESS
OBSESS
OBTEST
ODDEST
OGRESS
OLDEST
PALEST
PRIEST
PUREST
RAREST
RAWEST
RECESS
RETEST
RIFEST
RIPEST
RUDEST
SAFEST
SAGEST
SANEST
SHIEST
SHYEST
SLIEST
SLYEST
SOREST
STRESS
SUREST
TALESE
TAMEST
TERESA
THRESH
TRUEST
UNLESS
UNMESH
UNREST
VARESE
VILEST
WALESA
WIDEST
WISEST
WRIEST
WRYEST

•••E•S

ABBESS
ABBEYS
ACCESS
ADDERS
ADEEMS
ADIEUS
AENEAS
AGLETS
AGREES
AILERS
ALDERS
ALIENS
ALLEES
ALLEYS
ALTERS
AMBERS
AMEERS
AMIENS
AMVETS
ANGELS
ANGERS
ARDEBS
ARMETS
ARNESS
ARTELS
ASKERS
ASPENS
ASSESS
ASSETS
ASTERS
ATHENS
ATREUS
AUDENS
AUGERS
AUREUS
AZTECS
BAGELS
BAKERS
BALERS
BEDEWS
BEGETS

BERETS
BESETS
BETELS
BEVELS
BEZELS
BICEPS
BIKERS
BIPEDS
BITERS
BLEEDS
BLEEPS
BLUETS
BOGEYS
BONERS
BOREAS
BORERS
BOWERS
BOXERS
BREEDS
BRIEFS
BRIERS
BUTEOS
BUYERS
CABERS
CADETS
CAGERS
CAMELS
CAMEOS
CANERS
CAPERS
CARESS
CARETS
CATERS
CAVERS
CELEBS
CEREUS
CHEEKS
CHEEPS
CHEERS
CHIEFS
CIDERS
CITERS
CIVETS
CLEEKS
CODERS
COLEUS
COMERS
COMETS
CONEYS
COOERS
CORERS
COVENS
COVERS
COVETS
COVEYS
COWENS
COWERS
COZENS
CREEDS
CREEKS
CREELS
CREEPS
CRIERS
CRUETS
CUBEBS
CULETS
CUPELS
CURERS
CUVEES
CYDERS
DATERS
DEFERS
DETERS
DICERS
DINERS
DIVERS
DONEES
DONETS
DOSERS
DOWELS
DOWERS
DOYENS
DOZENS
DOZERS
DRIERS
DRYERS
DURESS
DUVETS
DWEEBS
EASELS
EATERS
EDGERS
EDSELS
EELERS
EGRESS
EGRETS
EIDERS
ELDERS
ELVERS
EMBEDS
EMBERS
EMCEES
EMEERS
EMMETS
ENDERS
ENGELS
ENTERS
ESKERS
ESTERS
ETHERS
EXCELS
EXCESS
EXPELS
FACETS
FAKERS
FARERS
FEVERS
FIBERS
FIFERS
FILERS
FILETS
FIRERS
FIVERS
FIVEWS
FIXERS
FLEERS
FLEETS
FLIERS
FLYERS
FOGEYS
FOYERS
FRYERS
FUSEES
FUZEES
GAPERS
GATERS
GAVELS
GELEES
GENETS
GIBERS
GIMELS
GIVENS
GIVERS
GLUERS
GODETS
GOFERS
GOLEMS
GONERS
GREEKS
GREENS
GREETS
GRUELS
HABEAS
HACEKS
HALERS
HAREMS
HATERS
HAVENS
HAZELS
HAZERS
HELENS
HEWERS
HEXERS
HIDERS
HIKERS
HIRERS
HOMERS
HONEYS
HOPERS
HOSELS
HOTELS
HOVELS
HOVERS
IDLERS
IMPELS
INFERS
INKERS
INLETS
INNESS
INSETS
INTENS
ISLETS
JAPERS
JEWELS
JIVERS
JOKERS
JULEPS
KEVELS
KHMERS
KITERS
KNEELS
KOPEKS
LABELS
LACERS
LADERS
LAGERS
LAKERS
LAMEDS
LAPELS
LASERS
LATENS
LAVERS
LAYERS
LEVEES
LEVELS
LEVERS
LIBELS
LIFERS
LIGERS
LIKENS
LIMENS
LIMEYS
LINENS
LINERS
LITERS
LIVENS
LIVERS
LODENS
LONERS
LOPERS
LOSERS
LOVERS
LOWERS
LUDENS
LUGERS
LUMENS
LYCEES
MAKERS
MASERS
MATERS
MATEYS
MAVENS
MAZERS
MELEES
METERS
MILERS
MIMEOS
MIMERS
MINERS
MISERS
MITERS
MIXERS
MIZENS
MODELS
MODEMS
MONEYS
MOPEDS
MOPERS
MORELS
MOSEYS
MOTELS
MOTETS
MOVERS
MOWERS
MOYERS
MUSERS
NAMERS
NAVELS
NENETS
NEREIS
NEREUS
NEVERS
NEWELS
NFLERS
NHLERS
NINERS
NITERS
NOLENS
NOLESS
NONETS
NOPETS
NOTERS
NOVELS
OATERS
OBSESS
OCHERS
OCTETS
OFFERS
OGLERS
OGRESS
OILERS
OLMECS
ONSETS
ORDERS
ORIELS
OSIERS
OTHERS
OTTERS
OUSELS
OUZELS
OWLETS
OWNERS
PACERS
PAGERS
PANELS
PAPERS
PARENS
PARERS
PASEOS
PATENS
PAVERS
PAWERS
PAYEES
PAYERS
PELEUS
PETERS
PEWEES
PIKERS
PILEUS
PIPERS
PIXELS
PLIERS
POKERS
POKEYS
POLERS
POSERS
POWERS
PREENS
PRIERS
PROEMS
PUREES
QUEENS
QUIETS
RACERS
RAKERS
RANEES
RATELS
RATERS
RAVELS
RAVENS
RAVERS
REBELS
RECESS
REFERS
REHEMS
REKEYS
RELETS
RENEWS
REPEGS
REPELS
RESEES
RESETS
RESEWS
REVELS
REVERS
REVETS
REWEDS
RICERS
RIDERS
RIPENS
RISERS
RIVERS
RIVETS
RODEOS
ROGERS
ROLEOS
ROMEOS
ROPERS
ROVERS
ROWELS
ROWENS
ROWERS
RUBENS
RULERS
RUMENS
RUPEES
SABERS
SAKERS
SAVERS
SAYERS
SCREES
SCREWS
SEDERS
SEVENS
SEVERS
SEWERS
SHEENS
SHEEPS
SHEERS
SHEETS
SHOERS
SHREDS
SHREWS
SIDERS
SINEWS
SIRENS
SIXERS
SIZERS
SKIERS
SLEEKS
SLEEPS
SLEETS
SNEERS
SOBERS
SOLERS
SOLEUS
SOMERS
SOWERS
SOXERS
SPEEDS
SPIELS
SPIERS
SPREES
STEEDS
STEELS
STEEPS
STEERS
STRESS
STREWS
SUPERS
SWEEPS
SWEETS
TAKERS
TAMERS
TAPERS
TATERS
TAXERS
TEHEES
TENETS
TEPEES
TEREUS
THREES
TIGERS
TILERS
TIMERS
TITERS
TOKENS
TONERS
TOPERS
TOTEMS
TOTERS
TOWELS
TOWERS
TRIERS
TUBERS
TUNERS
TVSETS
TWEEDS
TWEETS
TYPERS
UDDERS
ULCERS
UMBELS
UMBERS
UNLESS
UNPEGS
UNPENS
UNSEWS
UPPERS
UPSETS
URAEUS
URGERS
USHERS
UTTERS
UZBEKS
VALENS
VALETS
VEXERS
VIDEOS
VIPERS
VIREOS
VIXENS
VOLENS
VOTERS
VOWELS
VOWERS
WADERS
WAFERS
WAGERS
WAKENS
WALERS
WANERS
WATERS
WAVERS
WAXERS
WHEELS
WIDENS
WIPERS
WIRERS
WIZENS
WOMENS
WOOERS
XEBECS
YODELS
YOKELS

••••ES

ABASES
ABATES
ABELES
ABIDES
ABODES
ABUSES
ADAGES
ADDLES
ADOBES
ADORES
AEETES
AERIES
AGATES
AGAVES
AGGIES
AGREES
AISLES
AKENES
ALINES
ALLEES
ALLIES
AMAZES
AMBLES
AMICES
AMIDES
AMINES
AMOLES
AMUSES
ANDRES
ANGLES
ANIMES
ANKLES
ANODES
ANOLES
ANTRES
APEXES
APICES
APPLES
ARCHES
ARETES
ARGUES
ARISES
ARMIES
ASIDES
ATONES
AWAKES
AZORES
BABIES
BADGES
BAINES
BARGES
BARNES
BARRES
BASHES
BASSES
BASTES
BATHES
BEEVES
BEIGES
BELIES
BELLES
BEVIES
BIASES
BIBLES
BILGES
BINGES
BIOMES
BLADES
BLAMES
BLARES
BLAZES
BLOKES
BODIES
BOGIES
BOGLES
BOITES
BOMBES
BONNES
BONZES
BOOTES
BOSSES
BOULES
BOWLES
BRACES
BRAKES
BRAVES
BRAZES
BREVES
BRIBES
BRIDES
BRINES
BRUGES
BRULES
BRUMES
BRUTES
BSIDES
BUDGES
BUGLES
BULGES
BURIES
BURSES
BUSHES
BUSIES
BUSSES
BUTTES
BUZZES
BYRNES
CABLES
CACHES
CADGES
CADRES
CALCES
CALLES
CALVES
CALXES
CANNES
CANOES
CARIES
CARNES
CARTES
CARVES
CASHES
CASTES
CAUSES
CEASES
CENSES
CHAFES
CHASES
CHIDES
CHIMES
CHINES
CHIVES
CHOKES
CHORES
CHUTES
CITIES
CLEVES
CLIMES
CLINES
CLONES
CLOSES
CLOVES
CNOTES
COAXES
COMBES
COMTES
CONIES
CONTES
COPIES
COPSES
CORTES
COSHES
COSIES
COUPES
COZIES
CRAKES
CRANES
CRAPES
CRATES
CRAVES
CRAZES
CREMES
CREPES
CRIMES
CRIPES
CRISES
CRONES
CROZES
CRUCES
CRUSES
CRUXES
CURSES
CURVES
CUSSES
CUTIES
CUVEES
CYCLES
DADOES
DAISES
DALLES
DANCES
DANTES
DASHES
DAUBES
DAVIES
DEFIES
DEICES
DELVES
DENIES
DEUCES
DHOLES
DIDIES
DIESES
DIODES
DIRGES
DISHES
DISMES
DITZES
DODGES
DODOES
DOGIES
DONEES
DORIES
DOSSES
DOUSES
DOWSES
DRAKES
DRAPES
DRIVES
DRONES
DROVES
DRUPES
DRUZES
DULLES
DUNCES
DUTIES
EAGLES
EAGRES
ECCLES
ECHOES
ECOLES
EDAMES
EDDIES
EDDOES
EDILES
EDUCES
ELATES
ELEVES
ELIDES
ELITES
ELOPES
ELUDES
ELUTES
EMCEES
EMOTES
ENATES
ENDUES
ENSUES
ENURES
ENVIES
EPODES
ERASES
ERODES
ESPIES
ETCHES
ETUDES
EVADES
EVOKES
EXILES
EXUDES
EYRIES
FABLES
FACIES
FARCES
FASCES
FAUCES
FAWKES
FEMMES
FENCES
FESSES
FEZZES
FIBRES
FICHES
FILLES
FISHES
FIZZES
FLAKES
FLAMES
FLARES
FLAXES
FLEXES
FLORES
FLUKES
FLUMES
FLUTES
FLUXES
FOGIES
FORBES
FORCES
FORGES
FORTES
FOSSES
FOWLES
FRAMES
FRISES
FUDGES
FUGUES
FURIES
FUSEES
FUSSES
FUZEES
FUZZES
GABLES
GAFFES
GANGES
GASHES
GASSES
GAUGES
GAUZES
GELEES
GENIES
GENRES
GEODES
GESTES
GIGUES
GIJOES
GLACES
GLADES
GLARES
GLAZES
GLEBES
GLIDES
GLOBES
GLOVES
GNOMES
GOBIES
GOOSES
GORGES
GORSES
GOUGES
GRACES
GRADES
GRAPES
GRATES
GRAVES
GRAZES
GREBES
GRIMES
GRIPES
GROPES
GROVES
GUIDES
GUILES
GUISES
GUSHES
HADJES
HAINES
HAJJES
HALOES
HALVES
HASHES
HASTES
HAWSES
HEAVES
HEDGES
HELVES
HERMES
HEROES
HINGES
HISSES
HOAXES
HOBBES
HOBOES
HOLMES
HOOVES
HORDES
HORSES
HOUSES
HUGHES
HUSHES
HYADES
IBEXES
IBISES
IMAGES
IMBUES
INCHES
INDIES
INGLES
INGRES
INKLES
INURES
IRENES
IRIDES
IRISES
ISSUES
ISTLES
ITCHES
JAURES
JAZZES
JEEVES
JINXES
JOSHES
JOSSES
JOULES
JUDGES
JUICES
JURIES
KEDGES
KERMES
KEYNES
KISSES
KNAVES
KNIFES
KNIVES
KOPJES
LACHES
LADIES
LADLES
LANCES
LAPSES
LASHES
LASSES
LATHES
LATKES
LEASES
LEAVES
LEDGES
LENSES
LEONES
LEVEES
LEVIES
LIEGES
LILIES
LISLES
LITRES
LIVRES
LOAVES
LODGES
LONGES
LOOSES
LORIES
LOSSES
LOUPES
LOUSES
LUNGES
LYCEES
LYNXES
MACHES
MADRES
MAILES
MAIZES
MANSES
MAPLES
MASHES
MASSES
MATTES
MAUVES
MAYBES
MELEES
MENDES
MERGES
MESHES
MESSES
METRES
MIDGES
MINCES
MINKES
MINXES
MISSES
MITRES
MOINES
MOIRES
MONIES
MOSSES
MOUSES
MOVIES
MURRES
MUSHES
MUSSES
MYOPES
NANTES
NAPLES
NAPPES
NAVIES
NERVES
NESSES
NEUMES
NICHES
NIECES
NITRES
NIXIES
NOBLES
NOISES
NOOSES
NOSHES
NUDGES
NUECES
NURSES
OCHRES
OGIVES
OLDIES
OLIVES
ONUSES
ONYXES
OODLES
OPINES
OPUSES
ORALES
ORATES
ORGIES
ORTLES
ORYXES
OSAGES
OUNCES
OVULES
OXEYES
OXIDES
PADRES
PANNES
PARSES
PASSES
PASTES
PAUSES
PAYEES
PEEVES
PEKOES
PEWEES
PHAGES
PHASES
PHONES
PIECES
PIQUES
PISCES
PITIES
PIXIES
PLACES
PLAGES
PLANES
PLATES
PLEBES
PLUMES
PLUSES
POGIES
POISES
PONIES
PONTES
POSIES
POSSES
PRATES
PRAXES
PRICES
PRIDES
PRIMES
PRIZES
PROBES
PROLES
PROSES
PROVES
PRUDES
PRUNES
PULSES
PUREES
PURGES
PURSES
PUSHES
PUSSES
PYXIES
QUAKES
QUEUES
QUIRES
QUOTES
RABIES
RAINES
RAISES
RAMIES
RAMSES
RANEES
RANGES
RASHES
RAZZES
REALES
REDOES
REDYES
REEVES
RELIES
RENNES
RESEES
RETIES
REUNES
REUSES
REVUES
RHODES
RHYMES
RICHES
RIDGES
RIFLES
RILLES
RINSES
ROBLES
ROGUES
ROUGES
ROUSES
ROUTES
RUBIES
RUBLES
RUCHES
RUPEES
RUSHES
SABLES
SABRES
SALVES
SARGES
SASHES
SASSES
SAUCES
SAUTES
SAYYES
SCALES
SCAPES
SCARES
SCENES
SCONES
SCOPES
SCORES
SCREES
SCUTES
SEDGES
SEGUES
SEINES
SEIZES
SELVES
SENSES
SERGES
SERIES
SERVES
SEVRES
SHADES
SHAKES
SHALES
SHAMES
SHAPES
SHARES
SHAVES

SHINES
SHIRES
SHORES
SHOVES
SIDLES
SIEGES
SIEVES
SINGES
SKATES
SKIVES
SLAKES
SLATES
SLAVES
SLICES
SLIDES
SLIMES
SLOPES
SLYPES
SMILES
SMITES
SMOKES
SNAKES
SNARES
SNIPES
SNOPES
SNORES
SOARES
SOAVES
SOCLES
SOLVES
SONDES
SOUSES
SPACES
SPADES
SPARES
SPATES
SPICES
SPIKES
SPILES
SPINES
SPIRES
SPITES
SPOKES
SPORES
SPREES
SPRUES
SPUMES
STAGES
STAKES
STALES
STAPES
STARES
STASES
STATES
STAVES
STELES
STERES
STILES
STIPES
STOKES
STOLES
STONES
STOPES
STORES
STOVES
STUPES
STYLES
SUCCES
SUDSES
SUEDES
SUITES
SURGES
SWAGES
SWALES

SWEDES
SWIPES
TABLES
TARGES
TASSES
TASTES
TAUPES
TAXIES
TBONES
TEASES
TEHEES
TENSES
TEPEES
THALES
THAMES
THANES
THEBES
THEMES
THESES
THOLES
THREES
THROES
TIDIES
TILDES
TINGES
TITHES
TITLES
TNOTES
TOBIES
TOILES
TONNES
TOQUES
TORIES
TORTES
TOSSES
TRACES
TRADES
TRIBES
TRICES
TRIKES
TRINES
TROPES
TROVES
TRUCES
TULLES
TUQUES
TWINES
UGLIES
UKASES
UNCLES
UNDIES
UNDOES
UNGUES
UNITES
UNTIES
URUSES
USAGES
VALUES
VALVES
VARIES
VENUES
VERGES
VERSES
VETOES
VOGUES
VOICES
VOILES
VOSGES
VSIXES
WAIVES
WASHES
WASTES
WEAVES
WEDGES

WELLES
WENCES
WHALES
WHILES
WHINES
WHITES
WHOLES
WILKES
WINCES
WINZES
WISHES
WITHES
WOLVES
WRITES
XERXES
YALIES
YERKES
YESSES
ZANIES
ZEROES

ET••••
ETALIA
ETALII
ETCHED
ETCHER
ETCHES
ETERNE
ETHANE
ETHENE
ETHERS
ETHICS
ETHNIC
ETHNOS
ETOILE
ETONIC
ETSEQQ
ETUDES
ETYMOL
ETYMON

E•T•••
EATERS
EATERY
EATING
EATOUT
EATSAT
EATSIN
EATSUP
ECTYPE
EITHER
ENTAIL
ENTERO
ENTERS
ENTICE
ENTIRE
ENTITY
ENTRAP
ENTREE
ESTATE
ESTEEM
ESTERS
ESTHER
ESTOPS
EXTANT
EXTEND
EXTENT
EXTOLS
EXTORT
EXTRAS

E••T••
EARTHA
EARTHY

EASTER
EASTON
EDITED
EDITOR
ELATED
ELATER
ELATES
ELITES
ELUTED
ELUTES
EMOTED
EMOTER
EMOTES
EMPTOR
ENATES
EROTIC
EXETER
EXITED
EXOTIC

E•••T•
EBOATS
ECARTE
ECLATS
EDICTS
EFFETE
EFLATS
EGESTA
EGESTS
EGRETS
EIGHTH
EIGHTS
EIGHTY
EJECTA
EJECTS
ELECTS
EMMETS
EMMETT
ENACTS
ENMITY
ENTITY
EOLITH
EQUATE
EQUITY
ERECTS
ERGATE
ERGOTS
ERRATA
ERSATZ
ERUCTS
ERUPTS
ESTATE
EVENTS
EVERTS
EVICTS
EXACTA
EXACTO
EXACTS
EXALTS
EXCITE
EXERTS
EXISTS
EXULTS
EXVOTO

E••••T
EAGLET
EATOUT
EATSAT
EFFECT
EFFORT
EGBERT
EGMONT
EGOIST

EKEOUT
ELBERT
ELDEST
ELEGIT
ELICIT
ELLIOT
EMMETT
ENFANT
ENGIRT
ENGLUT
ENLIST
ENRAPT
ENROOT
ERFURT
ERNEST
ERRANT
ESCENT
ESCORT
ESPRIT
EXCEPT
EXEMPT
EXEUNT
EXHORT
EXPECT
EXPERT
EXPORT
EXSERT
EXTANT
EXTENT
EXTORT
EYELET

•ET•••
AETHER
BETAKE
BETCHA
BETELS
BETHEL
BETIDE
BETISE
BETONY
BETOOK
BETRAY
BETSEY
BETTAS
BETTER
BETTOR
CETANE
DETACH
DETAIL
DETAIN
DETECT
DETENT
DETERS
DETEST
DETOUR
DETROP
FETING
FETISH
FETTER
FETTLE
GETOFF
GETOUT
GETSAT
GETSBY
GETSET
GETSIN
GETSIT
GETSON
GETSTO
GETSUP
GETTER
GETUPS
HETERO

HETMAN
HETTIE
JETGUN
JETHRO
JETLAG
JETSAM
JETSET
JETSKI
JETSON
JETTED
KETONE
KETTLE
LETFLY
LETHAL
LETOFF
LETOUT
LETSAT
LETSBE
LETSGO
LETSIN
LETSON
LETSUP
LETTED
LETTER
LETUPS
METALS
METATE
METEOR
METERS
METHOD
METHYL
METIER
METING
METOPE
METRES
METRIC
METROS
METTLE
NETHER
NETMAN
NETMEN
NETPAY
NETTED
NETTLE
NETTON
PETAIN
PETALS
PETARD
PETERS
PETITE
PETREL
PETRIE
PETROG
PETROL
PETTED
PETTER
PETTIT
PETULA
RETAGS
RETAIL
RETAIN
RETAKE
RETAPE
RETAPS
RETARD
RETARS
RETELL
RETENE
RETEST
RETIAL
RETIED
RETIES
RETILE
RETIME

RETINA
RETIRE
RETOLD
RETOOK
RETOOL
RETOPS
RETORT
RETOUR
RETOWS
RETRAL
RETRIM
RETROS
RETTON
RETUNE
RETURN
RETYPE
SETINS
SETOFF
SETOSE
SETOUT
SETSAT
SETSBY
SETSIN
SETSON
SETSUP
SETTEE
SETTER
SETTLE
SETTOS
SETUPS
TETCHY
TETHER
TETHYS
TETONS
TETRAD
TETRAS
TETRIS
TETZEL
VETOED
VETOER
VETOES
VETTED
WETBAR
WETFLY
WETHER
WETMOP
WETTED
WETTER
WETTIG

•E•T••
AEETES
BEATEN
BEATER
BEATIT
BEATLE
BEATON
BEATTY
BEATUP
BEETLE
BELTED
BENTON
BERTHA
BERTHS
BERTIE
BESTED
BESTIR
BESTOW
BETTAS
BETTER
BETTOR
CELTIC
CENTER
CENTOS

CENTRE
CENTRI
CENTRO
CERTIF
CESTAS
CESTOS
CESTUS
DEBTOR
DEFTER
DEFTLY
DELTAS
DELTIC
DENTAL
DENTED
DENTIL
DENTIN
DENTON
DEPTHS
DESTRY
DEXTER
DEXTRO
FELTED
FESTAL
FESTER
FESTUS
FETTER
FETTLE
GENTLE
GENTLY
GENTRY
GERTIE
GESTES
GETTER
HEATED
HEATER
HEATHS
HEATUP
HECTIC
HECTOR
HEFTED
HELTER
HEPTAD
HESTER
HESTIA
HESTON
HETTIE
JEETER
JESTED
JESTER
JETTED
KEATON
KEITEL
KENTON
KEPTAT
KEPTON
KEPTUP
KETTLE
LECTOR
LENTEN
LENTIL
LEPTON
LESTAT
LESTER
LETTED
LETTER
MEETER
MEETLY
MELTED
MELTON
MENTAL
MENTIS
MENTOR
MERTON
METTLE

NEATEN
NEATER
NEATLY
NECTAR
NEKTON
NESTEA
NESTED
NESTER
NESTLE
NESTOR
NETTED
NETTLE
NETTON
NEUTER
NEWTON
NEXTTO
OERTER
PECTIC
PECTIN
PEGTOP
PELTED
PELTER
PELTRY
PENTAD
PENTUP
PEPTIC
PERTER
PERTLY
PESTER
PESTLE
PETTED
PETTER
PETTIT
PEWTER
PEYTON
REATAS
RECTOR
RECTOS
RECTUS
REDTAG
REDTOP
RENTAL
RENTED
RENTER
RESTED
RESTER
RESTON
RESTUP
RETTON
REUTER
SEATED
SEATER
SECTOR
SEETHE
SENTIN
SENTRY
SENTUP
SEPTAL
SEPTET
SEPTIC
SEPTUM
SESTET
SESTOS
SETTEE
SETTER
SETTLE
SETTOS
SEXTET
SEXTON
TEETER
TEETHE
TENTED
TENTER
TENTHS

TESTAE
TESTED
TESTEE
TESTER
TEUTON
VECTOR
VENTED
VENTER
VERTEX
VESTAL
VESTAS
VESTED
VESTEE
VESTRY
VETTED
WELTED
WELTER
WENTAT
WENTBY
WENTIN
WENTON
WENTUP
WETTED
WETTER
WETTIG
YENTAS
YESTER
ZESTED

•E••T•
AERATE
BEASTS
BEATTY
BEAUTS
BEAUTY
BEFITS
BEGETS
BENITO
BERATE
BERETS
BESETS
BESOTS
CENOTE
CERATE
DEARTH
DEBATE
DEBITS
DEBUTS
DEFATS
DEISTS
DELATE
DELETE
DELFTS
DEMITS
DEMOTE
DENOTE
DEPOTS
DEPUTE
DEPUTY
DESOTO
DEVITO
DEVOTE
DEVOTO
DEWITT
FEALTY
FEASTS
FEINTS
FEISTY
FELLTO
GEARTO
GELATI
GELATO
GENETS
GETSTO

HEALTH
HEARTH
HEARTS
HEARTY
HECATE
HEISTS
HELDTO
HELOTS
HEMATO
HERETO
JEWETT
KEEPTO
LEADTO
LEALTY
LEANTO
LEGATE
LEGATO
LENGTH
LENITY
LEVITE
LEVITY
MELOTT
MERITS
METATE
NEARTO
NEGATE
NEMATO
NENETS
NEXTTO
PEDATE
PELOTA
PEPITA
PESETA
PETITE
PEWITS
PEYOTE
REACTS
REALTY
REBATE
REBUTS
RECITE
REDATE
REFITS
REFUTE
RELATE
RELETS
REMITS
REMOTE
RENATA
RENOTE
REPOTS
REPUTE
RERATE
RESETS
REVETS
SEDATE
SEENTO
SEESTO
SEMITE
SENATE
TEMPTS
TENDTO
TENETS
TENUTO
TERATO
TERETE
VELDTS
VENETO
VENITE
VERITE
VERITY
WEALTH
YEASTS
YEASTY

ZENITH
ZEROTH

•E•••T
BEATIT
BECKET
BEHEST
BEIRUT
BELOIT
BENOIT
BEREFT
BESANT
BEZANT
CEMENT
CERMET
DECANT
DECEIT
DECENT
DECOCT
DEDUCT
DEFEAT
DEFECT
DEGUST
DEJECT
DELICT
DELIST
DEPART
DEPICT
DEPORT
DESALT
DESERT
DESIST
DESPOT
DETECT
DETENT
DETEST
DEVEST
DEVOUT
DEWITT
FERMAT
FERRET
FEWEST
GERENT
GERONT
GETOUT
GETSAT
GETSET
GETSIT
HEARST
HEIGHT
HELMET
HELMUT
HENBIT
HEPCAT
HEREAT
HERIOT
HERMIT
JEERAT
JENNET
JESUIT
JETSET
JEWETT
KEEPAT
KEPTAT
KERMIT
LEARNT
LEDOUT
LEERAT
LEGIST
LESTAT
LETOUT
LETSAT
LEVANT
MEDLAT

MEERUT
MELOTT
MEREST
MERLOT
NEEDNT
NEWEST
PEANUT
PECKAT
PEDANT
PEEKAT
PEERAT
PELLET
PELMET
PENULT
PEQUOT
PERMIT
PERROT
PETTIT
REBOLT
REBOOT
RECANT
RECAST
RECENT
REDACT
REDANT
REDHAT
REDHOT
REEDIT
REGENT
REGLET
REGRET
REHEAT
REJECT
RELENT
RELICT
RELIST
RELUCT
REMELT
RENNET
REPAST
REPEAT
REPENT
REPORT
RERENT
RESALT
RESEAT
RESECT
RESENT
RESHOT
RESIST
RESORT
RESULT
RETEST
RETORT
REVERT
REVOLT
REXCAT
SECANT
SECRET
SEEFIT
SEEOUT
SEJANT
SELECT
SENNET
SENNIT
SEPTET
SESTET
SETOUT
SETSAT
SEURAT
SEXIST
SEXTET
TEAPOT
TEARAT

TEASET
TENANT
TERCET
TERRET
VEIGHT
VELVET
VERVET
WEIGHT
WENTAT
WERENT
WESKIT
ZEALOT

••ET••
ACETAL
ACETIC
ACETYL
AEETES
ARETES
ARETHA
BEETLE
BRETON
CRETAN
CRETIN
DIETED
DIETER
EXETER
FLETCH
FRETTY
GHETTO
GOETHE
GRETEL
GRETNA
HYETAL
IGETIT
JEETER
JOETEX
KVETCH
MEETER
MEETLY
NOETIC
ODETTA
ODETTE
ONETWO
PIETAS
PIETER
PIETIN
PIETRO
POETIC
POETRY
PRETAX
PRETER
PRETTY
RHETOR
SEETHE
SKETCH
TEETER
TEETHE
THETAS
THETIC
THETIS
THETOY
TOETAP
TSETSE
WRETCH
YVETTE

••E•T•
ADEPTS
ADESTE
AGENTS
ALECTO
ALERTS
ALEUTS

AMENTS
ATESTS
AVERTS
AVESTA
BLEATS
BREATH
BRENTS
CHEATS
CHESTS
CHESTY
CLEATS
CLEFTS
CREATE
CRESTS
CUESTA
EGESTA
EGESTS
EJECTA
EJECTS
ELECTS
ERECTS
EVENTS
EVERTS
EXERTS
FIESTA
FLEETS
FRETTY
GHETTO
GREATS
GREETS
GUESTS
IDEATE
KEEPTO
LIESTO
LIEUTS
ODETTA
ODETTE
OLEATE
OMERTA
OPENTO
PLEATS
PLENTY
PRESTO
PRETTY
PUENTE
PUERTO
QUESTS
QWERTY
SCENTS
SEENTO
SEESTO
SHEATH
SHEETS
SIESTA
SLEETS
SLEETY
SLEUTH
SMELTS
SVELTE
SWEATS
SWEATY
SWEETS
THEFTS
TREATS
TREATY
TWEETS
TWEETY
TWENTY
USEDTO
WHEATS
WREATH
WRESTS
YVETTE

••E••T
ACEOUT
AGEIST
ALEAST
ARENDT
BLEWIT
BREAST
BRECHT
BREVET
CHEVET
COEDIT
CREDIT
DIEOUT
DOESNT
DREAMT
DYELOT
EKEOUT
ELEGIT
EXEMPT
EXEUNT
EYELET
FLEWAT
FREEST
GOESAT
HAEMAT
ICEOUT
IGETIT
ISEULT
JEERAT
KEEPAT
KLEIST
LEERAT
MEERUT
NEEDNT
NLEAST
NOEXIT
OCELOT
OMELET
PEEKAT
PEERAT
PRESET
REEDIT
SEEFIT
SEEOUT
SHEVAT
THEIST

•••ET•
AGLETS
AMVETS
ARMETS
ARNETT
ASSETS
BEGETS
BERETS
BESETS
BLUETS
CADETS
CAMETO
CARETO
CARETS
CAVETT
CIVETS
COMETH
COMETO
COMETS
COVETS
CRUETS
CULETS
DALETH
DARETO
DELETE
DONETS
DUVETS
EFFETE
EGRETS
EMMETS
EMMETT
FACETS
FILETS
FLEETS
GAIETY
GAMETE
GARETH
GENETS
GODETS
GREETS
HERETO
HOVETO
INLETS
INSETS
ISLETS
JEWETT
JOBETH
JOWETT
LOVETT
MOIETY
MONETA
MOTETS
MULETA
NENETS
NICETY
NINETY
NONETS
NOPETS
OCTETS
ONSETS
OSSETE
OWLETS
PARETO
PESETA
QUIETS
RELETS
RESETS
REVETS
RIVETS
SAFETY
SHEETS
SHTETL
SLEETS
SLEETY
SOWETO
STPETE
SURETE
SURETY
SWEETS
TAKETH
TAKETO
TENETS
TERETE
TVSETS
TWEETS
TWEETY
UBIETY
UPSETS
VALETS
VENETO
WISETO

•••E•T
ABJECT
ABLEST
ABSENT
ACCENT
ACCEPT
ADVENT
ADVERT
AFFECT
AFREET
ALBEIT
ALBERT
ALPERT
ALWEST
APTEST
ARDENT
ARGENT
ARNETT
ARPENT
ARREST
ASCENT
ASPECT
ASSENT
ASSERT
ATBEST
ATREST
ATTEST
BAREST
BASEST
BEHEST
BEREFT
BISECT
BLUEST
CADENT
CAMEAT
CAVEAT
CAVETT
CEMENT
CLIENT
COGENT
COMEAT
COVENT
COVERT
COYEST
CUTEST
DECEIT
DECENT
DEFEAT
DEFECT
DEJECT
DESERT
DETECT
DETENT
DETEST
DEVEST
DIGEST
DIRECT
DIREST
DIVERT
DIVEST
DOCENT
DRIEST
DRYEST
EFFECT
EGBERT
ELBERT
ELDEST
EMMETT
ERNEST
ESCENT
EXCEPT
EXPECT
EXPERT
EXSERT
EXTENT
FEWEST
FINEST
FLUENT
FOMENT
FOREST
FREEST
GAMEST
GAYEST
GERENT
GOWEST
HALEST
HAVEAT
HAVENT
HEREAT
HONEST
HUBERT
HUGEST
ICIEST
IDLEST
ILLEST
INCEPT
INDEBT
INDENT
INFECT
INFEST
INGEST
INJECT
INJEST
INSECT
INSERT
INTENT
INVENT
INVERT
INVEST
IQTEST
JEWETT
JOWETT
LAMENT
LAMEST
LATENT
LATEST
LAXEST
LOSEIT
LOVETT
LOWEST
LUCENT
MADEIT
MAKEIT
MEREST
MODELT
MODEST
MOLEST
MOMENT
MUTEST
NEWEST
NICEST
NLWEST
NOCENT
NUGENT
OBJECT
OBTEST
OBVERT
ODDEST
OLDEST
ORGEAT
ORIENT
OUTEAT
PALEST
PARENT
PATENT
POKEAT
POTENT
PRIEST
PUREST
RAREST
RAWEST
RECENT
REGENT
REHEAT
REJECT
RELENT
REMELT
REPEAT
REPENT
RERENT
RESEAT
RESECT
RESENT
RETEST
REVERT
RIDENT
RIFEST
RIPEST
ROBERT
RODENT
RUDEST
RUPERT
SAFEST
SAGEST
SANEST
SELECT
SHIEST
SHYEST
SILENT
SLIEST
SLYEST
SOBEIT
SOLENT
SOREST
STREET
SUREST
TALENT
TAMEST
THREAT
TOREAT
TRUEST
UNBELT
UNBENT
UNMEET
UNREST
UNSEAT
UPBEAT
URGENT
VALENT
VILEST
WERENT
WIDEST
WISENT
WISEST
WRIEST
WRYEST

••••ET
AFREET
AIGRET
ALLSET
ALLWET
AMULET
ANKLET
ARMLET
AUKLET
AVOCET
BALLET
BARBET
BASKET
BASSET
BECKET
BILLET
BISSET
BONNET
BOSKET
BOWNET
BOXSET
BREVET
BRUNET
BUCKET
BUDGET
BUFFET
BULLET
BURNET
CACHET
CAMLET
CAPLET
CARNET
CARPET
CERMET
CHALET
CHEVET
CLARET
CLOSET
COLLET
COQUET
CORNET
CORSET
COSSET
CULLET
CURVET
CUTLET
CYGNET
DOCKET
DORSET
DULCET
EAGLET
EYELET
FANJET
FAUCET
FERRET
FIDGET
FILLET
FLORET
FLYNET
FORGET
GADGET
GANNET
GARNET
GARRET
GASJET
GASKET
GETSET
GIBBET
GIBLET
GIDGET
GIMLET
GOBLET
GORGET
GOULET
GRIVET
GULLET
GUSSET
HAMLET
HELMET
HORNET
ILLMET
IMARET
INAPET
JACKET
JENNET
JETSET
JOLIET
JULIET
JUNKET
KISMET
LABRET
LANCET
LAPPET
LIMPET
LINNET
LIONET
LOCKET
MAGNET
MALLET
MARKET
MIDGET
MILLET
MINUET
MOPPET
MULLET
MUPPET
MUSKET
NOTYET
NUGGET
NUTLET
OBSTET
OFFSET
OMELET
OUTLET
OUTSET
PACKET
PALLET
PARGET
PELLET
PELMET
PIAGET
PICKET
PIGLET
PIOLET
PIQUET
PLANET
POCKET
POPPET
POSSET
PRESET
PRIPET
PRIVET
PULLET
PUPPET
RABBET
RACKET
RAMJET
REGLET
REGRET
RENNET
RILLET
ROCHET
ROCKET
RUNLET
RUSSET
SACHET
SALLET
SECRET
SENNET
SEPTET
SESTET
SEXTET
SIGNET
SIPPET
SOCKET
SONNET
SORBET
SOVIET
SPINET
STREET
STYLET
SUBLET
SUBSET
SUNSET
SWIVET
TABLET
TAPPET
TARGET
TEASET
TERCET
TERRET
TICKET
TIPPET
TOILET
TRIVET
TUCKET
TUFFET
TURRET
UNMEET
VARLET
VELVET
VERVET
VIOLET
WALLET
WICKET
WIDGET
WIGLET
WILLET
YOUBET

EU••••
EUBOEA
EUCHRE
EUCLID
EUDORA
EUGENE
EULOGY
EUNICE
EUNUCH
EUPNEA
EUREKA
EUROPA
EUROPE

E•U•••
EDUARD
EDUCED
EDUCES
ELUDED
ELUDES
ELUTED
ELUTES
ENURED
ENURES
EQUALS
EQUATE
EQUINE
EQUIPS
EQUITY
ERUCTS
ERUPTS
ETUDES
EVULSE
EXUDED
EXUDES
EXULTS
EXURBS

E••U••
EDMUND
EFFUSE
EMQUAD
ENDUED
ENDUES
ENDURE
ENDURO
ENDUSE
ENGULF
ENOUGH
ENQUAD
ENSUED
ENSUES
ENSURE
ERFURT
ESCUDO
EUNUCH
EXCUSE
EXEUNT

E•••U•
EARFUL
EASEUP
EATOUT
EATSUP
EFFLUX
EGGCUP
EKEOUT
ELBRUS
ENDRUN
ENDSUP
ENGLUT
ENNIUS
ENSOUL
EPIRUS
ERBIUM
EREBUS
EVENUP
EXODUS
EYECUP
EYEFUL

•EU•••
BEULAH
BEURRE
DEUCED
DEUCES
FEUDAL
FEUDED
NEUMAN
NEUMES
NEURAL
NEUROL
NEURON
NEUTER
OEUVRE
REUBEN
REUNES
REUSED
REUSES
REUTER
SEURAT
TEUTON
ZEUGMA
ZEUXIS

•E•U••
BEAUTS
BEAUTY
BEGUMS
BELUGA
BEMUSE
BENUMB
CERUSE
DEBUGS
DEBUNK
DEBUTS
DEDUCE
DEDUCT
DEFUSE
DEGUST
DEJURE
DELUDE
DELUGE
DELUXE
DEMURE
DEMURS
DENUDE
DEPUTE
DEPUTY
FECUND
FEMURS
FERULE
GENUAL
GERUND
GETUPS
HECUBA
JEJUNE
JESUIT
LEGUME
LEHUAS
LEMUEL
LEMURS
LETUPS
MEDUSA
NEBULA
NERUDA
PENULT
PENURY
PEQUOD
PEQUOT
PERUKE
PERUSE
PETULA
REBUFF
REBUKE
REBUTS
RECURS
RECUSE
REDUBS
REDUCE
REFUEL
REFUGE
REFUND
REFUSE
REFUTE
REHUNG
RELUCT
RELUME
REMUDA
REPUGN
REPUTE
RERUNS
RESULT
RESUME
RETUNE
RETURN
REVUES
SECURE
SEDUCE
SEDUMS
SEGUED
SEGUES
SEGURA
SEQUEL
SEQUIN
SERUMS
SETUPS
TELUGU
TENURE
TENUTO
VENUES
YEHUDI

•E••U•
AEOLUS
BEADUP
BEAMUP
BEARUP
BEATUP
BEDAUB
BEDBUG
BEEFUP
BEEGUM
BEFOUL
BEIRUT
BENHUR
CENSUS
CEREUS
CERIUM
CESIUM
CESTUS
DELIUS
DENGUE
DEPAUL
DEPAUW
DETOUR
DEVOUR
DEVOUT
FERGUS
FESCUE
FESSUP
FESTUS
GEARUP
GENIUS
GETOUT
GETSUP
HEADUP
HEATUP
HELDUP
HELIUM
HELMUT
JETGUN
KEEPUP
KEPTUP
KEYSUP
LEADUP
LEAGUE
LEBRUN
LEDOUT
LETOUT
LETSUP
MEDIUM
MEERUT
MESSUP
NEREUS
PEANUT
PELEUS
PENTUP
PEPLUM
PEPSUP
PERDUE
PERKUP
REARUP
RECOUP
RECTUS
REDBUD
REDGUM
REFLUX
REGIUS
REGLUE
RESCUE
RESTUP
RETOUR
SEALUP
SEAMUS
SEEOUT
SELJUK
SENDUP
SENTUP
SEPTUM
SEROUS
SESQUI
SETOUT
SETSUP
SEWNUP
SEWSUP
TEACUP
TEAMUP
TEARUP
TEDEUM
TEDIUM
TEEDUP
TEESUP
TEREUS
VELLUM
VELOUR
VENOUS
VERDUN
VERSUS
WELLUP
WENTUP

•E•••U
DEJAVU
DESILU
HEYYOU
MENJOU
PENGHU
RESEAU
TELEDU
TELUGU

••EU••
ALEUTS
BREUER
CREUSA
EXEUNT
FLEURY
ISEULT
LIEUTS
ONEUPS
PLEURA
PNEUMA
PSEUDO
PSEUDS
QUEUED
QUEUER
QUEUES
RHEUMS
RHEUMY
SLEUTH
TIEUPS

••E•U•
ACEOUS
ACEOUT
ACESUP
AVENUE
BEEFUP
BEEGUM
BLEWUP
CHEQUE
CHERUB
CHEWUP
DIEOUT
DOESUP
DREWUP
EKEOUT
EREBUS
EVENUP
EYECUP
EYEFUL
FRENUM
GOESUP
GREWUP
ICEDUP
ICEOUT
ICESUP
IREFUL
KEEPUP
MEERUT
OBELUS
OPENUP
PLENUM
PLEXUS
RHESUS
RUEFUL
SEEOUT
SPEDUP
STEPUP
TEEDUP
TEESUP
TIEDUP
TIESUP
USEDUP
USEFUL
USESUP
WOEFUL

••E••U
APERCU

•••EU•
ADIEUS
ADIEUX
ANTEUP
ATREUS
AUREUS
AUTEUR
BAYEUX
BONEUP
BOREUP
CAMEUP
CEREUS
COLEUS
COMEUP
DONEUP
EASEUP
FACEUP
FIREUP
GAVEUP
GIVEUP
HOLEUP
LACEUP
LINEUP
LYCEUM
MADEUP
MAKEUP
MUSEUM
NEREUS
PELEUS
PILEUM
PILEUP
PILEUS
PIPEUP
POSEUR
RAKEUP
SAVEUP
SIZEUP
SOLEUS
TAKEUP
TEDEUM
TEREUS
TONEUP
TOREUP
TUNEUP
TYPEUP
URAEUS
WAKEUP
WIPEUP
WISEUP
WOKEUP

•••E•U
BATEAU
BUREAU
GATEAU
HALERU
JUNEAU
MASERU
MOREAU
RAMEAU
RESEAU
ROSEAU
TELEDU

••••EU
MILIEU

EV••••
EVADED
EVADER
EVADES
EVELYN
EVENED
EVENER
EVENKI
EVENLY
EVENSO
EVENTS
EVENUP
EVERLY
EVERSO
EVERTS
EVICTS
EVILER
EVILLY
EVINCE
EVOKED
EVOKER
EVOKES
EVOLVE
EVONNE
EVULSE
EVZONE

E•V•••
EDVARD
ELVERS
ELVIRA
ENVIED
ENVIES
ENVOIS
ENVOYS
ERVING
EXVOTO

E••V••
ELEVEN
ELEVES

E•••V•
ENDIVE
EVOLVE

•EV•••
BEVELS
BEVIES
DEVEIN
DEVEST
DEVICE
DEVILS
DEVINE
DEVISE
DEVITO
DEVOID
DEVOIR
DEVOTE
DEVOTO
DEVOUR
DEVOUT
FEVERS
KEVELS
KEVLAR
LEVANT
LEVEED
LEVEES
LEVELS
LEVENE
LEVERS
LEVIED
LEVIER
LEVIES
LEVINE
LEVITE
LEVITY
NEVADA
NEVERS
NEVINS
NEVSKY
REVAMP
REVEAL
REVELS
REVERB
REVERE
REVERS
REVERT
REVETS
REVIEW
REVILE
REVISE
REVIVE
REVLON
REVOIR
REVOKE
REVOLT
REVSON
REVUES
REVVED
SEVENS
SEVERE
SEVERN
SEVERS
SEVRES

•E•V••
BEAVER
BEEVES
CERVID
DELVED
DELVER
DELVES
DENVER
FERVID
FERVOR
HEAVED
HEAVEN
HEAVER
HEAVES
HELVES
JEEVES
KELVIN
LEAVED
LEAVEN
LEAVES
LEKVAR
MELVIL
MELVIN
MELVYN
MERVYN
NERVES
OEUVRE
PEAVEY
PEEVED

PEEVES
PELVIC
PELVIS
REEVED
REEVES
REVVED
SELVES
SERVAL
SERVED
SERVER
SERVES
SERVOS
VELVET
VERVET
WEAVED
WEAVER
WEAVES
WEEVIL

•E••V•
BEHAVE
DEJAVU
DENOVO
DERIVE
GENEVA
GENEVE
RELIVE
REMOVE
REPAVE
REVIVE
REWOVE

••EV••
BEEVES
BREVES
BREVET
CHEVAL
CHEVET
CHEVRE
CLEVER
CLEVES
CLEVIS
COEVAL
ELEVEN
ELEVES
HUEVOS
JEEVES
LIEVRE
OLEVEL
PEEVED
PEEVES
PREVIN
REEVED
REEVES
SHEVAT
SIEVED
SIEVES
STEVEN
STEVIE
TREVOR
UNEVEN
WEEVIL

••E•V•
CLEAVE
GREAVE
SHEAVE
SHELVE
SLEAVE
SLEEVE
STEEVE
SWERVE
THEYVE
TWELVE

•••EV•
GENEVA
GENEVE
GRIEVE
HALEVY
PAREVE
SLEEVE
STEEVE
THIEVE

••••EV
KISLEV
LAPTEV

E•W•••
EDWARD
EDWYNN
ELWOOD
ENWRAP
EXWIFE

E••W••
EARWAX
EARWIG

E•••W•
ELBOWS
ENDOWS

E••••W
ERENOW
ESCHEW
ESCROW

•EW•••
BEWAIL
BEWARE
DEWIER
DEWING
DEWITT
DEWLAP
FEWEST
GEWGAW
HEWERS
HEWING
JEWELS
JEWETT
JEWISH
KEWPIE
LEWDER
LEWDLY
MEWING
MEWLED
MEWLER
NEWAGE
NEWARK
NEWELS
NEWEST
NEWISH
NEWLEY
NEWMAN
NEWMAR
NEWTON
PEWEES
PEWITS
PEWTER
REWARD
REWARM
REWASH
REWEDS
REWELD
REWIND
REWINS
REWIRE
REWORD
REWORK
REWOVE
REWRAP
SEWAGE
SEWARD
SEWELL
SEWERS
SEWING
SEWNUP
SEWSON
SEWSUP

•E•W••
KEYWAY
LEEWAY
MEOWED
PEEWEE
SEAWAY

•E••W•
BEDEWS
REMOWN
REMOWS
RENEWS
RENOWN
RESEWN
RESEWS
RETOWS
SEROWS

•E•••W
BELLOW
BESTOW
DEPAUW
FELLOW
GEEGAW
GEWGAW
HEBREW
HEEHAW
MEADOW
MELLOW
NEPHEW
PESCOW
REDRAW
REDREW
REPLOW
REVIEW
SEACOW
SEESAW
YELLOW

••EW••
BLEWIT
BLEWUP
BREWED
BREWER
CHEWED
CHEWER
CHEWUP
CLEWED
CREWED
CREWEL
DREWIN
DREWON
DREWUP
FLEWAT
FLEWIN
GREWON
GREWUP
LEEWAY
ONEWAY
PEEWEE
PREWAR
SKEWED
SKEWER
SLEWED
SPEWED
STEWED
STEWER
THEWIZ
VIEWED
VIEWER

••E•W•
ONETWO

••E••W
ERENOW
GEEGAW
HEEHAW
LIELOW
PRELAW
SEESAW

•••EW•
BEDEWS
FIVEWS
RENEWS
RESEWN
RESEWS
SCREWS
SCREWY
SHREWD
SHREWS
SINEWS
SINEWY
STREWN
STREWS
UNSEWN
UNSEWS

••••EW
ANDREW
CASHEW
CURFEW
CURLEW
ESCHEW
HEBREW
MCGREW
MILDEW
NEPHEW
ONVIEW
REDREW
REVIEW
SUNDEW

EX••••
EXACTA
EXACTO
EXACTS
EXALTS
EXARCH
EXCEED
EXCELS
EXCEPT
EXCESS
EXCISE
EXCITE
EXCUSE
EXEDRA
EXEMPT
EXERTS
EXETER
EXEUNT
EXHALE
EXHORT
EXILED
EXILES
EXILIC
EXISTS
EXITED
EXMOOR
EXODUS
EXOTIC
EXPAND
EXPECT
EXPELS
EXPEND
EXPERT
EXPIRE
EXPIRY
EXPORT
EXPOSE
EXSERT
EXTANT
EXTEND
EXTENT
EXTOLS
EXTORT
EXTRAS
EXUDED
EXUDES
EXULTS
EXURBS
EXVOTO
EXWIFE

E••X••
ELIXIR

E••••X
EARWAX
EFFLUX

•EX•••
DEXTER
DEXTRO
HEXADS
HEXERS
HEXING
LEXEME
LEXICA
MEXICO
NEXTTO
REXCAT
SEXIER
SEXILY
SEXIST
SEXTET
SEXTON
TEXACO
TEXANS
TEXMEX
VEXERS
VEXING

•E•X••
XERXES
ZEUXIS

•E••X•
DELUXE

•E•••X
BENDIX
MENINX
REDFOX
REDSOX
REFLEX
REFLUX
SEAFOX
TEXMEX
VERTEX
WESSEX

••EX••
ALEXEI
ALEXIA
ALEXIS
APEXES
DREXEL
FLEXED
FLEXES
FLEXOR
IBEXES
NOEXIT
PLEXOR
PLEXUS

••E••X
ICEBOX
JOETEX
PREFIX
PRETAX
THESIX

•••EX•
ANNEXE

•••E•X
ADIEUX
BAYEUX
BLUEOX
POLEAX
RATEDX

••••EX
AUSPEX
CAUDEX
CONVEX
CORTEX
DUPLEX
JOETEX
LASTEX
POLLEX
REFLEX
SUSSEX
TEXMEX
UNISEX
VERTEX
VORTEX
WESSEX
WINDEX

EY••••
EYECUP
EYEFUL
EYEING
EYELET
EYELID
EYRIES

E•Y•••
EEYORE
ELYSEE
ERYNGO
ETYMOL
ETYMON

E••Y••
ECTYPE
EDWYNN
ELAYER
ELAYNE
ENZYME

E•••Y•
EMBAYS
EMBRYO
ENJOYS
ENVOYS
EPONYM
ERINYS
ESSAYS
EVELYN

E••••Y
EARTHY
EASILY
EATERY
EBERLY
EDGILY
EERILY
EFFIGY
EIGHTY
ELLERY
EMBODY
EMPERY
EMPLOY
ENERGY
ENMITY
ENTITY
EQUITY
EULOGY
EVENLY
EVERLY
EVILLY
EXPIRY

•EY•••
BEYOND
CEYLON
EEYORE
GEYSER
HEYDAY
HEYJOE
HEYYOU
KEYING
KEYNES
KEYPAD
KEYSIN
KEYSUP
KEYWAY
LEYDEN
PEYOTE
PEYTON

•E•Y••
HEYYOU
JEKYLL
KENYAN
REDYED
REDYES
RETYPE

•E••Y•
BELAYS
DECAYS
DECOYS
DELAYS
HEARYE
KENNYG
MELVYN
MERVYN
METHYL
REDEYE
REKEYS
RELAYS
REPAYS
SEPOYS
TETHYS
ZEPHYR

•E•••Y
BEATTY
BEAUTY
BEGLEY
BEKESY
BELFRY
BENDAY
BENGAY
BETONY
BETRAY
BETSEY
CELERY
DEADLY
DEARLY
DEEJAY
DEEPLY
DEFRAY
DEFTLY
DELANY
DELRAY
DEPLOY
DEPUTY
DESCRY
DESTRY
EERILY
FEALTY
FEEBLY
FEISTY
FELONY
GELSEY
GENTLY
GENTRY
GETSBY
HEARTY
HENLEY
HEREBY
HERESY
HERSEY
HEYDAY
JEREMY
JERSEY
KEENLY
KELLEY
KELSEY
KERSEY
KEYWAY
LEAKEY
LEALTY
LEANLY
LEEWAY
LEGACY
LEMONY
LENITY
LESLEY
LETFLY
LEVITY
LEWDLY
MEANLY
MEASLY
MEDLEY
MEEKLY
MEETLY
MELODY
MEMORY
MERELY
MERSEY
NEARBY
NEARLY
NEATLY
NETPAY
NEVSKY
NEWLEY
PEACHY
PEARLY
PEAVEY
PEBBLY
PELTRY
PENNEY
PENURY
PERTLY
REALLY
REALTY
RECOPY
REDBAY
REMEDY
REPLAY
SEAWAY
SEEMLY
SENARY
SENTRY
SETSBY
SEXILY
TEAPOY
TEDKEY
TEENSY
TETCHY
VEEJAY
VERIFY
VERILY
VERITY
VESTRY
WEAKLY
WEEKLY
WEENSY
WENTBY
WESLEY
WETFLY
YEARLY
YEASTY

••EY••
GREYED
GREYER
OBEYED
OXEYES
PREYED
PREYON
THEYLL
THEYRE
THEYVE

••E•Y•
ACETYL
AYEAYE
BYEBYE
CHERYL
EVELYN
PHENYL
TIEDYE

••E••Y
AGENCY
ALECKY
AWEARY
BLEARY
BREEZY
CHEEKY
CHEERY
CHEESY
CHERRY
CHESTY
CLERGY
CREAKY
CREAMY
CREASY
CREEPY
CZERNY
DEEJAY
DEEPLY
DOESBY
DREAMY
DREARY
DRESSY
EBERLY
ENERGY
EVENLY
EVERLY
FEEBLY
FLEECY
FLESHY
FLEURY
FREAKY
FREDDY
FREELY
FRENZY
FRETTY
GOEASY
GOESBY
GREASY
GREEDY
GREENY
KEENLY
LEEWAY
MEEKLY
MEETLY
OHENRY
OKELLY
OLEARY
ONEDAY
ONEWAY
OPENLY
OVERLY
PLENTY
POETRY
PREPAY
PREPPY
PRETTY
QUEASY
QUEMOY
QWERTY
RHEUMY
SEEMLY
SHEEDY
SHEEHY
SHELLY
SHERRY
SKERRY
SLEAZY
SLEEKY
SLEEPY
SLEETY
SMEARY
SMELLY
SNEAKY
SNEERY
SNEEZY
SPEEDY
SPERRY
STEADY
STEAMY
STEELY
SWEATY
TEENSY
THEORY
THETOY
TREATY
TREBLY
TRENDY
TWEEDY
TWEETY
TWENTY
UNEASY
VEEJAY
WEEKLY
WEENSY
WHEEZY
WHERRY

•••EY•
ABBEYS
ALLEYS
BOGEYS
BOLEYN
CONEYS
COVEYS
FOGEYS
HONEYS
LIMEYS
MATEYS
MONEYS
MOSEYS
POKEYS
POLEYN
POPEYE
REDEYE
REKEYS
RIBEYE

•••E•Y
ARTERY
BAKERY
BARELY
BASELY
BEKESY
BLUESY
BOWERY
BREEZY
BRIERY
CAMEBY
CELERY
CHEEKY
CHEERY
CHEESY
CICELY
COMEBY
COMEDY
COMELY
CREEPY
CUTESY
DUPERY
EATERY
ELLERY
EMPERY
FAKERY
FINELY
FINERY
FLEECY
FREELY
GAIETY
GAMELY
GONEBY
GREEDY
GREENY
HALEVY
HEREBY
HERESY
HOMELY
HUGELY
JAPERY
JEREMY
LAMELY
LATELY
LIKELY
LIVELY
LIVERY
LONELY
LOVELY
LOWERY
MERELY
MISERY
MOIETY
MUTELY
NAMELY
NAPERY
NASEBY
NICELY
NICETY
NINETY
ORNERY
ORRERY
PALELY
PAPERY
PINERY
POKERY
PURELY
RAREFY
RARELY
REMEDY
RIPELY
RONELY
RUDELY
SAFELY
SAFETY
SAGELY
SANELY
SCREWY
SHEEDY
SHEEHY
SINEWY
SLEEKY
SLEEPY
SLEETY
SNEERY
SNEEZY
SOLELY
SORELY
SPEEDY
STEELY
SURELY
SURETY
TAMELY
TIMELY
TOWERY
TUMEFY
TWEEDY
TWEETY
UBIETY
VALERY
VILELY
VINERY
WATERY
WAVERY
WHEEZY
WIDELY
WIFELY
WINERY
WISELY
YARELY

••••EY
ANDREY
ASHLEY
AUBREY
AUDREY
BAILEY
BARLEY
BARNEY
BEGLEY
BETSEY
BIRNEY
BLIMEY
BLOOEY
BOSLEY
BURLEY
BURNEY
CAGNEY
CARNEY
CARREY
CARVEY
CHANEY
CLAYEY
CONVEY
COONEY
COWLEY
DABNEY
DAILEY
DICKEY
DILSEY
DINKEY
DISNEY
DONKEY
DOOLEY
DORSEY
DOWNEY
DUDLEY
DURFEY
FARLEY
FINNEY
FLOOEY
FOSSEY
GALLEY
GARVEY
GELSEY
GURLEY
GURNEY
HAILEY
HALLEY
HALSEY
HARLEY
HARVEY
HAYLEY
HENLEY
HERSEY
HICKEY
HOCKEY
HORNEY
HORSEY
HURLEY
HUXLEY
JERSEY
JITNEY
JOCKEY
KELLEY
KELSEY
KERSEY
KIDNEY
LACKEY
LEAKEY
LESLEY
LINSEY
LOONEY
LOWKEY
LYNLEY
MAGUEY
MARLEY
MASSEY
MEDLEY
MERSEY
MICKEY
MOBLEY
MONKEY
MOONEY
MORLEY
MOTLEY
MOUSEY
MURREY
NEWLEY
NIAMEY
OAKLEY
OCASEY
OFFKEY
ORKNEY
OSPREY
PARLEY
PAULEY
PEAVEY
PENNEY
PHOOEY
POMPEY
PRICEY
PULLEY
PURVEY
RAMSEY
RICKEY
RIDLEY
RIPLEY
RODNEY
ROMNEY
ROONEY
SHALEY
SIDNEY
SMILEY
SMOKEY
SPACEY
STOREY
SURREY
SURVEY
SYDNEY
TEDKEY
TRACEY
TUNNEY
TURKEY
VALLEY
VARNEY
VOLLEY
WATNEY
WESLEY
WIMSEY
WOLSEY
WOOLEY

E•Z•••
ENZYME
EVZONE

E••••Z
ERSATZ

•EZ•••
BEZANT
BEZELS
FEZZAN
FEZZES
GEZIRA
MEZZOS
REZONE

•E•Z••
BENZOL
DENZEL
FEZZAN
FEZZES
GEEZER
HERZOG
MEZZOS
SEIZED
SEIZER
SEIZES
TETZEL

•E••Z•
BEDAZE
BELIZE
REBOZO

••EZ••
AREZZO
GEEZER
SLEZAK

••E•Z•
AREZZO
BREEZE
BREEZY
FAENZA
FREEZE
FRENZY
SLEAZE
SLEAZY
SNEEZE
SNEEZY
TWEEZE
WHEEZE
WHEEZY

••E••Z
THEWIZ

•••EZ•
BREEZE
BREEZY
FREEZE
FRIEZE
SNEEZE
SNEEZY
TWEEZE
WHEEZE
WHEEZY

•••E•Z
BRIENZ
LORENZ

••••EZ
BOULEZ
CHAVEZ
CORTEZ
JUAREZ
MONTEZ
TROPEZ
VALDEZ

FA••••
FABIAN
FABLED
FABLER
FABLES
FABRAY
FABRIC
FACADE
FACETS
FACEUP
FACIAL
FACIES
FACILE
FACING
FACTOR
FACULA
FADEIN

FADING FAENZA FAERIE FAEROE FAFNIR FAGEND FAGGED FAGOTS FAILED FAILLE FAINTS FAIRED FAIRER FAIRLY FAIRUP FAISAL FAITHS FAIYUM FAJITA FAKERS FAKERY FAKING FAKIRS FALANA FALCON FALINE FALLEN FALLIN FALLON FALLOW FALLTO FALSER FALTER FAMILY FAMINE FAMISH FAMOUS FANDOM FANGED FANION FANJET FANNED FANNIE FANOUT FANTAN FARADS FARCED FARCES FARCRY FARERS FARINA FARING FARLEY FARLOW FARMED FARMER FAROFF FAROUK FAROUT FARRAH FARRAR FARROW FASCES FASCIA FASTED FASTEN FASTER FATALE FATCAT FATHER FATHOM FATIMA FATTED FATTEN FATTER FAUCES FAUCET FAULTS FAULTY FAUNAE FAUNAL FAUNAS FAUNUS FAVORS FAVOUR FAWKES FAWLTY FAWNED FAWNER FAXING FAZING

F•A•••

FEALTY FEARED FEARER FEASTS FIACRE FIANCE FIASCO FLABBY FLACKS FLACON FLAGGY FLAGON FLAILS FLAIRS FLAKED FLAKER FLAKES FLAMBE FLAMED FLAMES FLANGE FLANKS FLARED FLARES FLASHY FLASKS FLATLY FLAUNT FLAVIA FLAVOR FLAWED FLAXEN FLAXES FLAYED FLAYER FMAJOR FOALED FOAMED FRACAS FRAISE FRAMED FRAMES FRANCA FRANCE FRANCK FRANCO FRANCS FRANKS FRANNY FRAPPE FRASER FRAUDS FRAYED FRAZER

F••A••

FACADE FALANA FARADS FATALE FEMALE FIGARO FINALE FINALS FIXATE FLOATS FORAGE FORAYS FREAKS FREAKY FRIARS FRIARY FSHARP FUGARD FULANI

F•••A•

FABIAN FABRAY FACIAL FAISAL FANTAN FARRAH FARRAR FATCAT FAUNAE FAUNAL FAUNAS FBIMAN FELLAH FELLAS FENIAN FERMAT FESTAL FEUDAL FEZZAN FIJIAN FILIAL FINIAL FINNAN FIRMAN FISCAL FLEWAT FLORAE FLORAL FLORAS FLYMAN FLYWAY FOGHAT FOLIAR FONTAL FORBAD FORMAL FORMAN FORMAT FORTAS FOSSAE FOSSAS FOVEAE FRACAS FRIDAY FRUGAL FRYPAN FUJIAN FULMAR

F••••A

FACULA FAENZA FAJITA FALANA FARINA FASCIA FATIMA FEDORA FEMORA FIBULA FIESTA FLAVIA FLICKA FRANCA FRESCA FULCRA

•F•A••

AFFAIR AFLAME AFLATS AFRAID AFRAME EFFACE EFLATS OFLATE

•F••A•

AFFRAY AFGHAN AFLOAT OFFDAY

•F•••A

AFRICA SFORZA

••FA••

AAFAIR AFFAIR AUFAIT BEFALL DEFACE DEFAME DEFATS EFFACE ENFANT INFACT INFAMY INFANT MUFASA RAFAEL REFACE SAFARI UNFAIR

••F•A•

AFFRAY CAFTAN DEFEAT DEFRAY ELFMAN GUFFAW OFFDAY

••F••A

DEFLEA MUFASA RAFFIA

•••FA•

ARAFAT CONFAB GUFFAW KOUFAX LOOFAH LOWFAT NONFAT PREFAB SEAFAN SHOFAR SOLFAS STEFAN

•••F•A

BIAFRA RAFFIA

FB••••

FBIMAN FBIMEN

F•B•••

FABIAN FABLED FABLER FABLES FABRAY FABRIC FIBBED FIBBER FIBERS FIBRES FIBRIL FIBRIN FIBULA FOBBED FOBOFF

F••B••

FEEBLE FEEBLY FERBER FIBBED FIBBER FLABBY FLYBOY FLYBYS FOBBED FOGBOW FOIBLE FORBAD FORBES FORBID FUMBLE

F•••B•

FLABBY FLAMBE

•••F•B

CONFAB PREFAB

F•C•••

FACADE FACETS FACEUP FACIAL FACIES FACILE FACING FACTOR FACULA FECUND FICHES FICHTE FICHUS FICKLE FOCSLE

F••C••

FALCON FARCED FARCES FARCRY FASCES FASCIA FATCAT FAUCES FAUCET FENCED FENCER FENCES FESCUE FIACRE FISCAL FLACKS FLACON FLECHE FLECKS FLICKA FLICKS FLOCKS FORCED FORCER FORCES FRACAS FROCKS FULCRA

F•••C•

FIANCE FIASCO FIERCE FLEECE FLEECY FLETCH FLINCH FLITCH FRANCA FRANCE FRANCK FRANCO FRANCS` FRENCH FRESCA FRESCO FRISCO

F••••C

FABRIC FENNEC FERENC FERRIC FINNIC FISTIC FORMIC FROLIC FUSTIC

•F•C••

AFLCIO

•F••C•

AFFECT AFRICA EFFACE EFFECT OFFICE

••F•C•

AFFECT DEFACE DEFECT EFFACE EFFECT INFACT INFECT OFFICE REFACE

•••F•C

UNIFIC

F•D•••

FADEIN FADING FEDORA FIDDLE FIDGET FODDER FUDDLE FUDGED FUDGES

F••D••

FANDOM FEEDER FEEDON FELDON FENDED FENDER FEUDAL FEUDED FIDDLE FINDER FLEDGE FODDER FOLDED FOLDER FOLDUP FONDER FONDLE FONDLY FONDUE FORDED FREDDY FRIDAY FRIDGE FUDDLE FUNDED FYODOR

F•••D•

FACADE FARADS FIELDS FIENDS FIORDS FJELDS FJORDS FLOODS FLUIDS FOUNDS FRAUDS FREDDY FRONDS

F••••D

FABLED FAGEND FAGGED FAILED FAIRED FANGED FANNED FARCED FARMED FASTED FATTED FAWNED FEARED FECUND FELLED FELTED FENCED FENDED FERVID FEUDED FIBBED FILLED FILMED FINKED FINNED FIRMED FISHED FISTED FITTED FIZZED FLAKED FLAMED FLARED FLAWED FLAYED FLEXED FLORID FLOWED FLUTED FLUXED FLYROD FOALED FOAMED FOBBED FOGGED FOILED FOLDED FOOLED FOOTED FORBAD FORBID FORCED FORDED FORGED FORKED FORMED FOULED FOWLED FRAMED FRAYED FRIEND FRIGID FUDGED FUELED FUGARD FUNDED FUNKED FUNNED FURLED FURRED FUSSED FUZZED

•F•D••

OFFDAY

•F•••D

AFFORD AFIELD AFRAID OFFEND

••FD••

OFFDAY

••F••D

AFFORD ALFRED AUFOND BIFFED BIFOLD BOFFED BUFFED CUFFED DEFEND DEFIED DOFFED ENFOLD GAFFED GIFTED HAFTED HEFTED HUFFED INFOLD LIFTED LOFTED LUFFED MIFFED MUFFED OFFEND OXFORD PUFFED RAFTED REFFED REFUND RIFFED RIFLED RIFTED RUFFED SIFTED TIFFED TUFTED UNFOLD WAFTED

•••F•D

BEEFED BIFFED BOFFED BUFFED CHAFED COIFED CONFED CUFFED DOFFED GAFFED GOLFED GOOFED GULFED HOOFED HUFFED ILLFED KNIFED LEAFED LOAFED LUFFED MIFFED MUFFED PUFFED REEFED REFFED RIFFED ROOFED RUFFED SURFED THEFED TIFFED TRIFID TURFED WOLFED WOOFED

FE••••

FEALTY FEARED FEARER FEASTS FECUND FEDORA FEEBLE FEEBLY FEEDER FEEDON FEEING FEELER FEIGNS FEINTS FEISTY FELDON FELINE FELIPE FELLAH FELLAS FELLED FELLER FELLIN FELLOE FELLOW FELLTO FELONS FELONY FELTED FEMALE FEMMES FEMORA FEMURS FENCED FENCER FENCES FENDED FENDER FENIAN FENNEC FENNEL FERBER FERENC FERGIE FERGUS FERMAT FERRER FERRET FERRIC FERRIS FERULE FERVID FERVOR FESCUE FESSES FESSUP FESTAL FESTER FESTUS FETING FETISH FETTER FETTLE FEUDAL FEUDED FEVERS FEWEST FEZZAN FEZZES

F•E•••

FAENZA FAERIE FAEROE FEEBLE FEEBLY FEEDER FEEDON FEEING FEELER FIELDS FIENDS FIERCE FIESTA FJELDS FLECHE FLECKS FLEDGE FLEECE FLEECY FLEERS FLEETS FLENSE FLESHY FLETCH FLEURY FLEWAT FLEWIN FLEXED FLEXES FLEXOR FOEHNS FREAKS FREAKY FREDDY FREELY FREEST FREEZE FRENCH FRENUM FRENZY FRESCA FRESCO FRESNO FRETTY FUELED FUELER

F••E••

FACETS FACEUP FADEIN FAGEND FAKERS FAKERY FARERS FERENC FEVERS FEWEST FIBERS FIFERS FILENE FILERS FILETS FINELY FINERY FINEST FIRERS FIREUP FIVERS FIVEWS FIXERS FLEECE FLEECY FLEERS FLEETS FLIERS FLUENT FLYERS FOGEYS FOMENT FOREGO FOREST FOVEAE FOYERS FREELY FREEST FREEZE FRIEND FRIEZE FRYERS FUSEES FUZEES

F•••E•

FABLED FABLER FABLES FACIES FAGGED FAILED FAIRED FAIRER FALLEN FALSER FALTER FANGED FANJET FANNED FARCED FARCES FARLEY FARMED FARMER FASCES FASTED FASTEN FASTER FATHER FATTED FATTEN FATTER FAUCES FAUCET FAWKES FAWNED FAWNER FBIMEN FEARED FEARER FEEDER FEELER FELLED FELLER FELTED FEMMES FENCED FENCER FENCES FENDED FENDER FENNEC FENNEL FERBER FERRER FERRET FESSES FESTER FETTER FEUDED FEZZES FIBBED FIBBER FIBRES FICHES FIDGET FILLED FILLER FILLES FILLET FILMED FILTER FINDER FINGER FINKED FINNED FINNEY FIRMED FIRMER FISHED FISHER FISHES FISTED FITTED FITTER FIZZED FIZZES FLAKED FLAKER FLAKES FLAMED FLAMES FLARED FLARES FLAWED FLAXEN FLAXES FLAYED FLAYER FLEXED FLEXES FLOOEY FLORES FLORET FLOWED FLOWER FLUKES FLUMES FLUTED FLUTES FLUXED FLUXES FLYMEN FLYNET FOALED FOAMED FOBBED FODDER FOGGED FOGGER FOGIES FOILED FOKKER FOLDED FOLDER FONDER FOOLED FOOLER FOOTED FOOTER FORBES FORCED FORCER FORCES FORDED FORGED FORGER FORGES FORGET FORKED FORKER FORMED FORMER FORTES FOSSES FOSSEY FOSTER FOULED FOULER FOWLED FOWLER FOWLES FOXIER FRAMED FRAMES FRASER FRAYED FRAZER FRISEE FRISES FROZEN FUDGED FUDGES FUELED FUELER FUGUES FULLER FUNDED FUNKED FUNNED FUNNEL FURIES FURLED FURRED FUSEES FUSSED FUSSES FUZEES FUZZED FUZZES

F••••E

FACADE FACILE FAERIE FAEROE FAILLE FALINE FAMINE FANNIE FATALE FAUNAE FEEBLE FELINE FELIPE FELLOE FEMALE FERGIE FERULE FESCUE FETTLE FIACRE FIANCE FICHTE FICKLE FIDDLE FIERCE FIGURE FILENE FILOSE FINALE FINITE FIPPLE FIXATE FIZZLE FLAMBE FLANGE FLECHE FLEDGE FLEECE FLENSE FLORAE FOCSLE FOIBLE FOLKIE FONDLE FONDUE FOOZLE FORAGE FOSSAE FOVEAE FOZZIE FRAISE FRANCE FRAPPE FREEZE FRIDGE FRIEZE FRINGE FRISEE FUDDLE FUMBLE FURORE FUTILE FUTURE

•F•E••

AFFECT AFIELD AFREET AFRESH EFFECT EFFETE NFLERS OFFEND OFFERS

•F••E•

AFREET IFFIER OFFKEY OFFSET

•F•••E

AFFINE AFLAME AFRAME EFFACE EFFETE EFFUSE OFFICE OFLATE

••FE••

AFFECT BEFELL DEFEAT

DEFECT
DEFEND
DEFERS
EFFECT
EFFETE
FIFERS
GOFERS
INFECT
INFERS
INFEST
LIFERS
OFFEND
OFFERS
REFERS
RIFEST
SAFELY
SAFEST
SAFETY
WAFERS
WIFELY

••F•E•
ALFRED
ALFVEN
BIFFED
BOFFED
BUFFED
BUFFER
BUFFET
COFFEE
COFFER
CUFFED
DAFTER
DEFIED
DEFIES
DEFLEA
DEFTER
DIFFER
DOFFED
DUFFEL
DUFFER
EIFFEL
GAFFED
GAFFER
GAFFES
GIFTED
HAFTED
HEFNER
HEFTED
HUFFED
IFFIER
LAFFER
LIFTED
LIFTER
LOFTED
LUFFED
MIFFED
MUFFED
OFFKEY
OFFSET
PUFFED
PUFFER
RAFAEL
RAFTED
RAFTER
REFFED
REFLEX
REFUEL
RIFFED
RIFLED
RIFLER
RIFLES
RIFTED
RUFFED
SIFTED
SIFTER
SOFTEN
SOFTER
SUFFER
TIFFED
TOFFEE
TUFFET
TUFTED
WAFTED
ZAFFER

••F••E
AFFINE
ALFINE
BAFFLE
BEFORE
COFFEE
DEFACE
DEFAME
DEFILE
DEFINE
DEFUSE
EFFACE
EFFETE
EFFUSE
IMFINE
INFUSE
MUFFLE
OFFICE
ONFILE
ONFIRE
PIFFLE
RAFFLE
REFACE
REFILE
REFINE
REFUGE
REFUSE
REFUTE
RIFFLE
RUFFLE
SAFIRE
SOFINE
SOFTIE
TOFFEE
WAFFLE

•••FE•
BEEFED
BIFFED
BOFFED
BUFFED
BUFFER
BUFFET
CHAFED
CHAFES
COFFEE
COFFER
COIFED
CONFED
CONFER
CUFFED
CURFEW
DEAFEN
DEAFER
DIFFER
DOFFED
DUFFEL
DUFFER
DURFEY
EIFFEL
GAFFED
GAFFER
GAFFES
GOLFED
GOLFER
GOOFED
GULFED
HEIFER
HOOFED
HOOFER
HUFFED
ILLFED
KIEFER
KNIFED
KNIFES
LAFFER
LEAFED
LIEFER
LOAFED
LOAFER
LUFFED
MIFFED
MUFFED
PILFER
PREFER
PUFFED
PUFFER
REEFED
REEFER
REFFED
RIFFED
ROOFED
ROOFER
RUFFED
SUFFER
SURFED
SURFER
THEFED
TIFFED
TOFFEE
TUFFET
TURFED
TWOFER
WERFEL
WOLFED
WOOFED
WOOFER
ZAFFER

•••F•E
BAFFLE
BOUFFE
COFFEE
KHAFRE
MUFFLE
PIAFFE
PIFFLE
PURFLE
RAFFLE
RIFFLE
RUFFLE
STIFLE
TOFFEE
TRIFLE
WAFFLE

••••FE
BOUFFE
CARAFE
EXWIFE
OKEEFE
PIAFFE
RECIFE
STRAFE
STRIFE
TOLIFE
UNSAFE

F•F•••
FAFNIR
FIFERS
FIFTHS

F••F••
FITFUL
FLUFFS
FLUFFY

F•••F•
FAROFF
FLUFFS
FLUFFY
FOBOFF

F••••F
FAROFF
FOBOFF

•FF•••
AFFAIR
AFFECT
AFFINE
AFFIRM
AFFORD
AFFRAY
EFFACE
EFFECT
EFFETE
EFFIGY
EFFLUX
EFFORT
EFFUSE
IFFIER
OFFDAY
OFFEND
OFFERS
OFFICE
OFFING
OFFISH
OFFKEY
OFFSET

••FF••
BAFFIN
BAFFLE
BIFFED
BOFFED
BOFFOS
BUFFED
BUFFER
BUFFET
BUFFON
BUFFOS
COFFEE
COFFER
CUFFED
DIFFER
DOFFED
DUFFEL
DUFFER
EIFFEL
GAFFED
GAFFER
GAFFES
GUFFAW
HUFFED
KAFFIR
LAFFER
LUFFED
MIFFED
MUFFED
MUFFIN
MUFFLE
PIFFLE
PUFFED
PUFFER
PUFFIN
RAFFIA
RAFFLE
REFFED
RIFFED
RIFFLE
RUFFED
RUFFLE
RUFFLY
SOFFIT
SUFFER
SUFFIX
TIFFED
TIFFIN
TOFFEE
TUFFET
WAFFLE
WAFFLY
ZAFFER

•••FF•
BLUFFS
BOUFFE
CHAFFS
CHAFFY
CLIFFS
FLUFFS
FLUFFY
PIAFFE
QUAFFS
SCOFFS
SCUFFS
SKIFFS
SNIFFS
SNIFFY
SNUFFS
SNUFFY
SPIFFS
SPIFFY
STAFFS
STEFFI
STIFFS
STUFFS
STUFFY
WHIFFS

••••FF
BEGOFF
BITOFF
BUGOFF
BUYOFF
CANIFF
CRYOFF
CUTOFF
DIEOFF
DRYOFF
FAROFF
FOBOFF
GETOFF
GOTOFF
HOPOFF
LAYOFF
LEDOFF
LETOFF
LOGOFF
NODOFF
PAYOFF
POPOFF
PUTOFF
RANOFF
REBUFF
RIPOFF
RUNOFF
SAWOFF
SCHIFF
SCLAFF
SCRUFF
SEEOFF
SETOFF
TAPOFF
TARIFF
TEEOFF
TIPOFF
TOPOFF

F•G•••
FAGEND
FAGGED
FAGOTS
FIGARO
FIGHTS
FIGURE
FOGBOW
FOGEYS
FOGGED
FOGGER
FOGHAT
FOGIES
FOGSIN
FUGARD
FUGUES

F••G••
FAGGED
FANGED
FEIGNS
FERGIE
FERGUS
FIDGET
FINGER
FIZGIG
FLAGGY
FLAGON
FLIGHT
FOGGED
FOGGER
FORGED
FORGER
FORGES
FORGET
FORGOT
FOUGHT
FRIGHT
FRIGID
FROGGY
FRUGAL
FUDGED
FUDGES
FUNGUS

F•••G•
FLAGGY
FLANGE
FLEDGE
FLINGS
FORAGE
FOREGO
FRIDGE
FRINGE
FRINGY
FROGGY

F••••G
FACING
FADING
FAKING
FARING
FAXING
FAZING
FEEING
FETING
FILING
FINING
FIRING
FIXING
FIZGIG
FLYING
FOXING
FRYING
FUMING
FUSING
FUZING

•FG•••
AFGHAN

•F••G•
EFFIGY

•F•••G
OFFING

••F•G•
BEFOGS
DEFOGS
EFFIGY
REFUGE

••F••G
OFFING
ZAFTIG

•••F•G
ICEFOG
INAFOG

F•H•••
FSHARP

F••H••
FATHER
FATHOM
FICHES
FICHTE
FICHUS
FIGHTS
FISHED
FISHER
FISHES
FOEHNS
FOGHAT
FUZHOU

F•••H•
FAITHS
FIFTHS
FILTHY
FIRTHS
FLASHY
FLECHE
FLESHY
FLIGHT
FOUGHT
FRIGHT
FROTHS
FROTHY

F••••H
FAMISH
FARRAH
FELLAH
FETISH
FINISH
FLETCH
FLINCH
FLITCH
FOURTH
FRENCH

•F•H••
AFGHAN

•F•••H
AFRESH
OFFISH

••F•H•
FIFTHS

••F••H
ELFISH
GOFISH
OAFISH
OFFISH

•••F•H
LOOFAH

FI••••
FIACRE
FIANCE
FIASCO
FIBBED
FIBBER
FIBERS
FIBRES
FIBRIL
FIBRIN
FIBULA
FICHES
FICHTE
FICHUS
FICKLE
FIDDLE
FIDGET
FIELDS
FIENDS
FIERCE
FIESTA
FIFERS
FIFTHS
FIGARO
FIGHTS
FIGURE
FIJIAN
FILENE
FILERS
FILETS
FILIAL
FILING
FILIUS
FILLED
FILLER
FILLES
FILLET
FILLIN
FILLIP
FILLUP
FILMED
FILOSE
FILTER
FILTHY
FINALE
FINALS
FINDER
FINELY
FINERY
FINEST
FINGER
FINIAL
FINING
FINISH
FINITE
FINITO
FINKED
FINNAN
FINNED
FINNEY
FINNIC
FIORDS
FIPPLE
FIRERS
FIREUP
FIRING
FIRKIN
FIRMAN
FIRMED
FIRMER
FIRMLY
FIRMUP
FIRSTS
FIRTHS
FISCAL
FISHED
FISHER
FISHES
FISTED
FISTIC
FITFUL
FITSIN
FITTED
FITTER
FIVERS
FIVEWS
FIXATE
FIXERS
FIXING
FIXITY
FIXUPS
FIZGIG
FIZZED
FIZZES
FIZZLE

F•I•••
FAILED
FAILLE
FAINTS
FAIRED
FAIRER
FAIRLY
FAIRUP
FAISAL
FAITHS
FAIYUM
FBIMAN
FBIMEN
FEIGNS
FEINTS
FEISTY
FLICKA
FLICKS
FLIERS
FLIGHT
FLIMSY
FLINCH
FLINGS
FLINTS
FLINTY
FLIPUP
FLIRTS
FLITCH
FMINOR
FOIBLE
FOILED
FOISTS
FRIARS
FRIARY
FRIDAY
FRIDGE
FRIEND
FRIEZE
FRIGHT
FRIGID
FRIJOL
FRILLS
FRILLY
FRINGE
FRINGY
FRISCO
FRISEE
FRISES
FRISKS
FRISKY
FRITOS
FRIZZY

F••I••
FABIAN
FACIAL
FACIES
FACILE
FACING
FADING
FAJITA
FAKING
FAKIRS
FALINE
FAMILY
FAMINE
FAMISH
FANION
FARINA
FARING
FATIMA
FAXING
FAZING
FEEING
FELINE
FELIPE
FENIAN
FETING
FETISH
FIJIAN
FILIAL
FILING
FILIUS
FINIAL
FINING
FINISH
FINITE
FINITO
FIRING
FIXING
FIXITY
FLAILS
FLAIRS
FLUIDS
FLYING
FOGIES
FOLIAR
FOLIOS
FOLIUM
FORINT
FOXIER
FOXILY
FOXING
FRAISE
FRUITS
FRUITY
FRYING
FUJIAN
FUMING
FURIES
FUSILS
FUSING
FUSION
FUTILE
FUZING

F•••I•
FABRIC
FADEIN
FAERIE
FAFNIR
FALLIN
FANNIE
FASCIA
FELLIN
FERGIE
FERRIC
FERRIS
FERVID
FIBRIL
FIBRIN
FILLIN
FILLIP
FINNIC
FIRKIN
FISTIC
FITSIN
FIZGIG
FLAVIA
FLEWIN
FLORID
FLORIN
FOGSIN
FOLKIE
FORBID
FORMIC
FOSSIL
FOZZIE
FRIGID
FROLIC
FUSTIC

F••••I
FRUTTI
FULANI

•FI•••
AFIELD

•F•I••
AFFINE
AFFIRM
AFRICA
EFFIGY
IFFIER
OFFICE
OFFING
OFFISH

•F••I•
AFFAIR
AFLCIO
AFRAID

••FI••
AFFINE
AFFIRM
ALFINE
BEFITS
DEFIED
DEFIES
DEFILE
DEFINE
EFFIGY
ELFISH
GOFISH
IFFIER
IMFINE
INFIRM
OAFISH
OFFICE
OFFING
OFFISH
ONFILE
ONFIRE
REFILE
REFILL
REFINE
REFITS
SAFIRE
SOFINE
SUFISM
UNFITS

••F•I•
AAFAIR
AFFAIR
AUFAIT
BAFFIN
FAFNIR
HEFLIN
KAFFIR
MUFFIN
MUFTIS
PUFFIN
RAFFIA
SOFFIT
SOFTIE
SUFFIX
TIFFIN
UNFAIR
ZAFTIG

••F••I
SAFARI

•••FI•
BAFFIN
BOWFIN
COMFIT
HOOFIT
INAFIX
KAFFIR
MISFIT
MUFFIN
OLEFIN
OUTFIT
PREFIX
PROFIT
PUFFIN
RAFFIA
REDFIN
REDFIR
SAWFIT
SCIFIS
SEEFIT
SOFFIT
SUFFIX
TIFFIN
TRIFID
UNIFIC

•••F•I
STEFFI

••••FI
AMALFI
STEFFI

FJ••••
FJELDS
FJORDS

F•J•••
FAJITA
FIJIAN
FUJIAN

F••J••
FANJET
FMAJOR
FRIJOL

F•K•••
FAKERS
FAKERY
FAKING
FAKIRS
FOKKER

F••K••
FAWKES
FICKLE
FINKED
FIRKIN
FLAKED
FLAKER
FLAKES
FLUKES
FOKKER
FOLKIE
FOLKSY
FORKED
FORKER
FUNKED

F•••K•
FLACKS
FLANKS
FLASKS
FLECKS
FLICKA
FLICKS
FLOCKS
FLUNKS
FLUNKY
FRANKS
FREAKS
FREAKY
FRISKS
FRISKY
FROCKS

F••••K
FAROUK
FRANCK

•F•K••
OFFKEY

••FK••
OFFKEY

FL••••
FLABBY
FLACKS
FLACON
FLAGGY
FLAGON
FLAILS
FLAIRS
FLAKED
FLAKER
FLAKES
FLAMBE
FLAMED
FLAMES
FLANGE
FLANKS
FLARED
FLARES
FLASHY
FLASKS
FLATLY
FLAUNT
FLAVIA
FLAVOR
FLAWED
FLAXEN
FLAXES
FLAYED
FLAYER
FLECHE
FLECKS
FLEDGE
FLEECE
FLEECY
FLEERS
FLEETS
FLENSE
FLESHY
FLETCH
FLEURY
FLEWAT
FLEWIN
FLEXED
FLEXES
FLEXOR
FLICKA
FLICKS
FLIERS
FLIGHT
FLIMSY
FLINCH
FLINGS
FLINTS
FLINTY
FLIPUP
FLIRTS
FLITCH
FLOATS
FLOCKS
FLOODS
FLOOEY
FLOORS
FLOPPY
FLOPSY
FLORAE
FLORAL
FLORAS
FLORES
FLORET
FLORID
FLORIN
FLOSSY
FLOURS
FLOURY
FLOUTS
FLOWED
FLOWER
FLUENT
FLUFFS
FLUFFY
FLUIDS
FLUKES
FLUMES
FLUNKS
FLUNKY
FLUORO
FLURRY
FLUTED
FLUTES
FLUXED
FLUXES
FLYBOY
FLYBYS
FLYERS
FLYING
FLYMAN
FLYMEN
FLYNET
FLYOUT
FLYROD
FLYWAY

F•L•••
FALANA
FALCON
FALINE
FALLEN
FALLIN
FALLON
FALLOW
FALLTO
FALSER
FALTER
FELDON
FELINE
FELIPE
FELLAH
FELLAS
FELLED
FELLER
FELLIN
FELLOE
FELLOW
FELLTO
FELONS
FELONY
FELTED
FILENE
FILERS
FILETS
FILIAL
FILING
FILIUS
FILLED
FILLER
FILLES
FILLET
FILLIN
FILLIP
FILLUP
FILMED
FILOSE

FILTER FILTHY FOLDED FOLDER FOLDUP FOLIAR FOLIOS FOLIUM FOLKIE FOLKSY FOLLOW FOLSOM FULANI FULCRA FULLER FULMAR FULTON

F••L••

FABLED FABLER FABLES FAILED FAILLE FALLEN FALLIN FALLON FALLOW FALLTO FARLEY FARLOW FAULTS FAULTY FAWLTY FEALTY FEELER FELLAH FELLAS FELLED FELLER FELLIN FELLOE FELLOW FELLTO FIELDS FILLED FILLER FILLES FILLET FILLIN FILLIP FILLUP FJELDS FOALED FOILED FOLLOW FOOLED FOOLER FOULED FOULER FOULLY FOULUP FOWLED FOWLER FOWLES FRILLS FRILLY FROLIC FUELED FUELER FULLER FURLED

F•••L•

FACILE FACULA FAILLE FAIRLY FAMILY FATALE FEEBLE FEEBLY FEMALE FERULE FETTLE FIBULA FICKLE FIDDLE FINALE FINALS FINELY FIPPLE FIRMLY FIZZLE FLAILS FLATLY FOCSLE FOIBLE FONDLE FONDLY FOOZLE FOULLY FOXILY FREELY FRILLS FRILLY FUDDLE FUMBLE FUSILS FUTILE

F••••L

FACIAL FAISAL FAUNAL FENNEL FESTAL FEUDAL FIBRIL FILIAL FINIAL FISCAL FITFUL FLORAL FONTAL FORMAL FOSSIL FRIJOL FRUGAL FUNNEL

•FL•••

AFLAME AFLATS AFLCIO AFLOAT EFLATS NFLERS OFLATE

•F•L••

EFFLUX

•F••L•

AFIELD

••FL••

DEFLEA EFFLUX HEFLIN INFLOW INFLUX REFLEX REFLUX RIFLED RIFLER RIFLES TEFLON

••F•L•

BAFFLE BEFALL BEFELL BIFOLD DEFILE DEFTLY ENFOLD INFOLD INFULL MUFFLE ONFILE PIFFLE RAFFLE REFILE REFILL RIFFLE RUFFLE RUFFLY SAFELY SOFTLY UNFOLD WAFFLE WAFFLY WIFELY

••F••L

BEFALL BEFELL BEFOUL DUFFEL EIFFEL INFULL RAFAEL REFILL REFUEL UNFURL

•••FL•

BAFFLE BARFLY BOTFLY DRYFLY GADFLY LETFLY MAYFLY MUFFLE PIFFLE POPFLY PURFLE RAFFLE RIFFLE RUFFLE RUFFLY STIFLE TRIFLE WAFFLE WAFFLY WETFLY

•••F•L

ARMFUL ARTFUL BAGFUL BOXFUL CAPFUL CARFUL CUPFUL DUFFEL EARFUL EIFFEL EYEFUL FITFUL IREFUL JARFUL JOYFUL JUGFUL LAPFUL LAWFUL MANFUL POTFUL RUEFUL SINFUL USEFUL VATFUL WERFEL WOEFUL

FM••••

FMAJOR FMINOR

F•M•••

FAMILY FAMINE FAMISH FAMOUS FEMALE FEMMES FEMORA FEMURS FOMENT FUMBLE FUMING

F••M••

FARMED FARMER FBIMAN FBIMEN FEMMES FERMAT FILMED FIRMAN FIRMED FIRMER FIRMLY FIRMUP FLAMBE FLAMED FLAMES FLIMSY FLUMES FLYMAN FLYMEN FOAMED FORMAL FORMAN FORMAT FORMED FORMER FORMIC FRAMED FRAMES FRUMPS FRUMPY FULMAR

F•••M•

FATIMA FORUMS

F••••M

FAIYUM FANDOM FATHOM FOLIUM FOLSOM FRENUM

•F••M•

AFLAME AFRAME

•F•••M

AFFIRM

••FM••

ELFMAN

••F•M•

DEFAME INFAMY

••F••M

AFFIRM DEFORM INFIRM INFORM REFORM SUFISM

F•N•••

FANDOM FANGED FANION FANJET FANNED FANNIE FANOUT FANTAN FENCED FENCER FENCES FENDED FENDER FENIAN FENNEC FENNEL FINALE FINALS FINDER FINELY FINERY FINEST FINGER FINIAL FINING FINISH FINITE FINITO FINKED FINNAN FINNED FINNEY FINNIC FONDER FONDLE FONDLY FONDUE FONTAL FUNDED FUNGUS FUNKED FUNNED FUNNEL

F••N••

FAENZA FAFNIR FAINTS FANNED FANNIE FAUNAE FAUNAL FAUNAS FAUNUS FAWNED FAWNER FEINTS FENNEC FENNEL FIANCE FIENDS FINNAN FINNED FINNEY FINNIC FLANGE FLANKS FLENSE FLINCH FLINGS FLINTS FLINTY FLUNKS FLUNKY FLYNET FMINOR FOUNDS FOUNTS FRANCA FRANCE FRANCK FRANCO FRANCS FRANKS FRANNY FRENCH FRENUM FRENZY FRINGE FRINGY FRONDS FRONTS FUNNED FUNNEL

F•••N•

FACING FADING FAGEND FAKING FALANA FALINE FAMINE FARINA FARING FAXING FAZING FECUND FEEING FEIGNS FELINE FELONS FELONY FERENC FETING FILENE FILING FINING FIRING FIXING FLAUNT FLUENT FLYING FOEHNS FOMENT FORINT FOXING FRANNY FRESNO FRIEND FROWNS FRYING FULANI FUMING FUSING FUTONS FUZING

F••••N

FABIAN FADEIN FALCON FALLEN FALLIN FALLON FANION FANTAN FASTEN FATTEN FBIMAN FBIMEN FEEDON FELDON FELLIN FENIAN FEZZAN FIBRIN FIJIAN FILLIN FINNAN FIRKIN FIRMAN FITSIN FLACON FLAGON FLAXEN FLEWIN FLORIN FLYMAN FLYMEN FOGSIN FORMAN FROZEN FRYPAN FUJIAN FULTON FUSION

•F••N•

AFFINE OFFEND OFFING

•F•••N

AFGHAN

••FN••

FAFNIR HEFNER

••F•N•

AFFINE ALFINE AUFOND DEFEND DEFINE ENFANT IMFINE INFANT OFFEND OFFING REFINE REFUND SOFINE

••F••N

ALFVEN BAFFIN BUFFON CAFTAN ELFMAN HEFLIN MUFFIN PUFFIN SOFTEN TEFLON TIFFIN

•••F•N

BAFFIN BOWFIN BUFFON DEAFEN MUFFIN OLEFIN PUFFIN REDFIN SEAFAN STEFAN TIFFIN

FO••••

FOALED FOAMED FOBBED FOBOFF FOCSLE FODDER FOEHNS FOGBOW FOGEYS FOGGED FOGGER FOGHAT FOGIES FOGSIN FOIBLE FOILED FOISTS FOKKER FOLDED FOLDER FOLDUP FOLIAR FOLIOS FOLIUM FOLKIE FOLKSY FOLLOW FOLSOM FOMENT FONDER FONDLE FONDLY FONDUE FONTAL FOOLED FOOLER FOOTED FOOTER FOOZLE FORAGE FORAYS FORBAD FORBES FORBID FORCED FORCER FORCES FORDED FOREGO FOREST FORGED FORGER FORGES FORGET FORGOT FORINT FORKED FORKER FORMAL FORMAN FORMAT FORMED FORMER FORMIC FORTAS FORTES FORUMS FOSSAE FOSSAS FOSSES FOSSEY FOSSIL FOSTER FOUGHT FOULED FOULER FOULLY FOULUP FOUNDS FOUNTS FOURTH FOVEAE FOWLED FOWLER FOWLES FOXIER FOXILY FOXING FOYERS FOZZIE

F•O•••

FIORDS FJORDS FLOATS FLOCKS FLOODS FLOOEY FLOORS FLOPPY FLOPSY FLORAE FLORAL FLORAS FLORES FLORET FLORID FLORIN FLOSSY FLOURS FLOURY FLOUTS FLOWED FLOWER FOOLED FOOLER FOOTED FOOTER FOOZLE FROCKS FROGGY FROLIC FRONDS FRONTS FROSTS FROSTY FROTHS FROTHY FROWNS FROWZY FROZEN FYODOR

F••O••

FAGOTS FAMOUS FANOUT FAROFF FAROUK FAROUT FAVORS FAVOUR FEDORA FELONS FELONY FEMORA FILOSE FLOODS FLOOEY FLOORS FLUORO FLYOUT FOBOFF FSTOPS FTROOP FURORE FURORS FUTONS

F•••O•

FACTOR FAEROE FALCON FALLON FALLOW FANDOM FANION FARLOW FARROW FATHOM FEEDON FELDON FELLOE FELLOW FERVOR FLACON FLAGON FLAVOR FLEXOR FLYBOY FLYROD FMAJOR FMINOR FOGBOW FOLIOS FOLLOW FOLSOM FORGOT FRIJOL FRITOS FTROOP FULTON FURROW FUSION FUZHOU FYODOR

F••••O

FALLTO FELLTO FIASCO FIGARO FINITO FLUORO FOREGO FRANCO FRESCO FRESNO FRISCO

•FO•••

SFORZA

•F•O••

AFFORD AFLOAT EFFORT

•F•••O

AFLCIO

••FO••

AFFORD AJFOYT AUFOND BEFOGS BEFORE BEFOUL BIFOLD DEFOGS DEFORM EFFORT ENFOLD INFOLD INFORM ONFOOT OXFORD REFORM RUFOUS UNFOLD

••F•O•

BOFFOS BUFFON BUFFOS INFLOW ONFOOT TEFLON

•••FO•

ASKFOR BOFFOS BUFFON BUFFOS GUNFOR ICEFOG INAFOG KITFOX LAYFOR OUTFOX PAYFOR RANFOR REDFOX SEAFOX TRYFOR

F•P•••

FIPPLE

F••P••

FIPPLE FLIPUP FLOPPY FLOPSY FRAPPE FRYPAN

F•••P•

FELIPE FIXUPS FLOPPY FRAPPE FRUMPS FRUMPY FSTOPS

F••••P

FACEUP FAIRUP FESSUP FILLIP FILLUP FIREUP FIRMUP FLIPUP FOLDUP FOULUP FSHARP FTROOP

••F••P

LIFTUP

•••F•P

BEEFUP GOOFUP

FR••••

FRACAS FRAISE FRAMED FRAMES FRANCA FRANCE FRANCK FRANCO FRANCS FRANKS FRANNY FRAPPE FRASER FRAUDS FRAYED FRAZER FREAKS FREAKY FREDDY FREELY FREEST FREEZE FRENCH FRENUM FRENZY FRESCA FRESCO FRESNO FRETTY FRIARS FRIARY FRIDAY FRIDGE FRIEND FRIEZE FRIGHT FRIGID FRIJOL FRILLS FRILLY FRINGE FRINGY FRISCO FRISEE FRISES FRISKS FRISKY FRITOS FRIZZY FROCKS FROGGY FROLIC FRONDS FRONTS FROSTS FROSTY FROTHS FROTHY FROWNS FROWZY FROZEN FRUGAL FRUITS FRUITY FRUMPS FRUMPY FRUTTI FRYERS FRYING FRYPAN

F•R•••

FARADS FARCED FARCES FARCRY FARERS FARINA FARING FARLEY FARLOW FARMED FARMER FAROFF FAROUK FAROUT FARRAH FARRAR FARROW FERBER FERENC FERGIE FERGUS FERMAT FERRER FERRET FERRIC FERRIS FERULE FERVID FERVOR FIRERS FIREUP FIRING FIRKIN FIRMAN FIRMED FIRMER FIRMLY FIRMUP FIRSTS FIRTHS FORAGE FORAYS FORBAD FORBES FORBID FORCED FORCER FORCES FORDED FOREGO FOREST FORGED FORGER FORGES FORGET FORGOT FORINT FORKED FORKER FORMAL FORMAN FORMAT FORMED FORMER FORMIC FORTAS FORTES FORUMS FTROOP FURIES FURLED FURORE FURORS FURRED FURROW

F••R••

FABRAY FABRIC FAERIE FAEROE FAIRED FAIRER FAIRLY FAIRUP FARRAH FARRAR FARROW FEARED FEARER FERRER FERRET FERRIC FERRIS FIBRES FIBRIL FIBRIN FIERCE FIORDS FJORDS FLARED FLARES FLIRTS FLORAE FLORAL FLORAS FLORES FLORET FLORID FLORIN FLURRY FLYROD FOURTH FURRED FURROW

F•••R•

FAKERS FAKERY FAKIRS FARCRY FARERS FAVORS FEDORA FEMORA FEMURS FEVERS FIACRE FIBERS FIFERS FIGARO FIGURE FILERS FINERY FIRERS FIVERS FIXERS FLAIRS FLEERS FLEURY FLIERS FLOORS FLOURS FLOURY FLUORO FLURRY FLYERS FOYERS FRIARS FRIARY FRYERS FSHARP FUGARD FULCRA FURORE FURORS FUTURE

F••••R

FABLER FACTOR FAFNIR FAIRER

FALSER
FALTER
FARMER
FARRAR
FASTER
FATHER
FATTER
FAVOUR
FAWNER
FEARER
FEEDER
FEELER
FELLER
FENCER
FENDER
FERBER
FERRER
FERVOR
FESTER
FETTER
FIBBER
FILLER
FILTER
FINDER
FINGER
FIRMER
FISHER
FITTER
FLAKER
FLAVOR
FLAYER
FLEXOR
FLOWER
FMAJOR
FMINOR
FODDER
FOGGER
FOKKER
FOLDER
FOLIAR
FONDER
FOOLER
FOOTER
FORCER
FORGER
FORKER
FORMER
FOSTER
FOULER
FOWLER
FOXIER
FRASER
FRAZER
FUELER
FULLER
FULMAR
FYODOR

•FR•••
AFRAID
AFRAME
AFREET
AFRESH
AFRICA

•F•R••
AFFRAY
SFORZA

•F••R•
AFFIRM
AFFORD
EFFORT
NFLERS
OFFERS

•F•••R
AFFAIR
IFFIER

••FR••
AFFRAY
ALFRED
DEFRAY

••F•R•
AFFIRM
AFFORD
BEFORE
DEFERS
DEFORM
EFFORT
ERFURT
FIFERS
GOFERS
INFERS
INFIRM
INFORM
LIFERS
OFFERS
ONFIRE
OXFORD
REFERS
REFORM
SAFARI
SAFIRE
UNFURL
WAFERS

••F••R
AAFAIR
AFFAIR
BUFFER
COFFER
DAFTER
DEFTER
DIFFER
DUFFER
FAFNIR
GAFFER
HEFNER
IFFIER
KAFFIR
LAFFER
LIFTER
PUFFER
RAFTER
RIFLER
SIFTER
SOFTER
SUFFER
UNFAIR
ZAFFER

•••FR•
BELFRY
BIAFRA
KHAFRE
PANFRY

•••F•R
ASKFOR
BUFFER
COFFER
CONFER
DEAFER
DIFFER
DUFFER
GAFFER
GOLFER
GUNFOR
HEIFER
HOOFER
KAFFIR
KIEFER
LAFFER
LAYFOR
LIEFER
LOAFER
PAYFOR
PILFER
PREFER
PUFFER
RANFOR
REDFIR
REEFER
ROOFER
SHOFAR
SUFFER
SULFUR
SURFER
TRYFOR
TWOFER
WOOFER
ZAFFER

FS••••
FSHARP
FSTOPS

F•S•••
FASCES
FASCIA
FASTED
FASTEN
FASTER
FESCUE
FESSES
FESSUP
FESTAL
FESTER
FESTUS
FISCAL
FISHED
FISHER
FISHES
FISTED
FISTIC
FOSSAE
FOSSAS
FOSSES
FOSSEY
FOSSIL
FOSTER
FUSEES
FUSILS
FUSING
FUSION
FUSSED
FUSSES
FUSTIC

F••S••
FAISAL
FALSER
FEASTS
FEISTY
FESSES
FESSUP
FIASCO
FIESTA
FIRSTS
FITSIN
FLASHY
FLASKS
FLESHY
FLOSSY
FOCSLE
FOGSIN
FOISTS
FOLSOM
FOSSAE
FOSSAS
FOSSES
FOSSEY
FOSSIL
FRASER
FRESCA
FRESCO
FRESNO
FRISCO
FRISEE
FRISES
FRISKS
FRISKY
FROSTS
FROSTY
FUSSED
FUSSES

F•••S•
FAMISH
FETISH
FEWEST
FILOSE
FINEST
FINISH
FLENSE
FLIMSY
FLOPSY
FLOSSY
FOLKSY
FOREST
FRAISE
FREEST

F••••S
FABLES
FACETS
FACIES
FAGOTS
FAINTS
FAITHS
FAKERS
FAKIRS
FAMOUS
FARADS
FARCES
FARERS
FASCES
FAUCES
FAULTS
FAUNAS
FAUNUS
FAVORS
FAWKES
FEASTS
FEIGNS
FEINTS
FELLAS
FELONS
FEMMES
FEMURS
FENCES
FERGUS
FERRIS
FESSES
FESTUS
FEVERS
FEZZES
FIBERS
FIBRES
FICHES
FICHUS
FIELDS
FIENDS
FIFERS
FIFTHS
FIGHTS
FILERS
FILETS
FILIUS
FILLES
FINALS
FIORDS
FIRERS
FIRSTS
FIRTHS
FISHES
FIVERS
FIVEWS
FIXERS
FIXUPS
FIZZES
FJELDS
FJORDS
FLACKS
FLAILS
FLAIRS
FLAKES
FLAMES
FLANKS
FLARES
FLASKS
FLAXES
FLECKS
FLEERS
FLEETS
FLEXES
FLICKS
FLIERS
FLINGS
FLINTS
FLIRTS
FLOATS
FLOCKS
FLOODS
FLOORS
FLORAS
FLORES
FLOURS
FLOUTS
FLUFFS
FLUIDS
FLUKES
FLUMES
FLUNKS
FLUTES
FLUXES
FLYBYS
FLYERS
FOEHNS
FOGEYS
FOGIES
FOISTS
FOLIOS
FORAYS
FORBES
FORCES
FORGES
FORTAS
FORTES
FORUMS
FOSSAS
FOSSES
FOUNDS
FOUNTS
FOWLES
FOYERS
FRACAS
FRAMES
FRANCS
FRANKS
FRAUDS
FREAKS
FRIARS
FRILLS
FRISES
FRISKS
FRITOS
FROCKS
FRONDS
FRONTS
FROSTS
FROTHS
FROWNS
FRUITS
FRUMPS
FRYERS
FSTOPS
FUDGES
FUGUES
FUNGUS
FURIES
FURORS
FUSEES
FUSILS
FUSSES
FUTONS
FUZEES
FUZZES

•F•S••
OFFSET

•F••S•
AFRESH
EFFUSE
OFFISH

•F•••S
AFLATS
EFLATS
NFLERS
OFFERS

••FS••
OFFSET

••F•S•
DEFUSE
EFFUSE
ELFISH
GOFISH
INFEST
INFUSE
MUFASA
OAFISH
OFFISH
REFUSE
RIFEST
SAFEST
SUFISM

••F••S
BEFITS
BEFOGS
BOFFOS
BUFFOS
DEFATS
DEFERS
DEFIES
DEFOGS
FIFERS
FIFTHS
GAFFES
GOFERS
INFERS
LIFERS
MUFTIS
OFFERS
REFERS
REFITS
RIFLES
RUFOUS
UNFITS
WAFERS

•••F•S
BLUFFS
BOFFOS
BUFFOS
CHAFES
CHAFFS
CLEFTS
CLIFFS
CRAFTS
CROFTS
DELFTS
DOOFUS
DRAFTS
DRIFTS
FLUFFS
GAFFES
GRAFTS
KNIFES
QUAFFS
SCIFIS
SCOFFS
SCUFFS
SHAFTS
SHIFTS
SKIFFS
SNAFUS
SNIFFS
SNUFFS
SOLFAS
SPIFFS
STAFFS
STIFFS
STUFFS
SWIFTS
THEFTS
WHIFFS

••••FS
BLUFFS
BRIEFS
CHAFFS
CHIEFS
CLIFFS
DECAFS
DWARFS
FLUFFS
KLOOFS
MOTIFS
PILAFS
PROOFS
QUAFFS
SCARFS
SCOFFS
SCUFFS
SERIFS
SHEAFS
SKIFFS
SMURFS
SNIFFS
SNUFFS
SPIFFS
SPOOFS
STAFFS
STIFFS
STUFFS
WHARFS
WHIFFS
WHOOFS

FT••••
FTROOP

F•T•••
FATALE
FATCAT
FATHER
FATHOM
FATIMA
FATTED
FATTEN
FATTER
FETING
FETISH
FETTER
FETTLE
FITFUL
FITSIN
FITTED
FITTER
FSTOPS
FUTILE
FUTONS
FUTURE

F••T••
FACTOR
FAITHS
FALTER
FANTAN
FASTED
FASTEN
FASTER
FATTED
FATTEN
FATTER
FELTED
FESTAL
FESTER
FESTUS
FETTER
FETTLE
FIFTHS
FILTER
FILTHY
FIRTHS
FISTED
FISTIC
FITTED
FITTER
FLATLY
FLETCH
FLITCH
FLUTED
FLUTES
FONTAL
FOOTED
FOOTER
FORTAS
FORTES
FOSTER
FRETTY
FRITOS
FROTHS
FROTHY
FRUTTI
FULTON
FUSTIC

F•••T•
FACETS
FAGOTS
FAINTS
FAJITA
FALLTO
FAULTS
FAULTY
FAWLTY
FEALTY
FEASTS
FEINTS
FEISTY
FELLTO
FICHTE
FIESTA
FIGHTS
FILETS
FINITE
FINITO
FIRSTS
FIXATE
FIXITY
FLEETS
FLINTS
FLINTY
FLIRTS
FLOATS
FLOUTS
FOISTS
FOUNTS
FOURTH
FRETTY
FRONTS
FROSTS
FROSTY
FRUITS
FRUITY
FRUTTI

F••••T
FANJET
FANOUT
FAROUT
FATCAT
FAUCET
FERMAT
FERRET
FEWEST
FIDGET
FILLET
FINEST
FLAUNT
FLEWAT
FLIGHT
FLORET
FLUENT
FLYNET
FLYOUT
FOGHAT
FOMENT
FOREST
FORGET
FORGOT
FORINT
FORMAT
FOUGHT
FREEST
FRIGHT

•F••T•
AFLATS
EFFETE
EFLATS
OFLATE

•F•••T
AFFECT
AFLOAT
AFREET
EFFECT
EFFORT
OFFSET

••FT••
CAFTAN
DAFTER
DEFTER
DEFTLY
FIFTHS
GIFTED
HAFTED
HEFTED
LIFTED
LIFTER
LIFTUP
LOFTED
MUFTIS
RAFTED
RAFTER
RIFTED
SIFTED
SIFTER
SOFTEN
SOFTER
SOFTIE
SOFTLY
TUFTED
WAFTED
ZAFTIG

••F•T•
BEFITS
DEFATS
EFFETE
REFITS
REFUTE
SAFETY
UNFITS

••F••T
AFFECT
AJFOYT
AUFAIT
BUFFET
DEFEAT
DEFECT
EFFECT
EFFORT
ENFANT
ERFURT
INFACT
INFANT
INFECT
INFEST
OFFSET
ONFOOT
RIFEST
SAFEST
SOFFIT
TUFFET

•••FT•
CLEFTS
CRAFTS
CRAFTY
CROFTS
DELFTS
DRAFTS
DRAFTY
DRIFTS
GRAFTS
SHAFTS
SHIFTS
SHIFTY
SWIFTS
THEFTS

•••F•T
ARAFAT
BUFFET
COMFIT
HOOFIT
LOWFAT
MISFIT
NONFAT
OUTFIT
PROFIT
SAWFIT
SEEFIT
SOFFIT
TUFFET

••••FT
ADRIFT
BEREFT
GOSOFT
SHRIFT
THRIFT
UPLIFT

FU••••
FUDDLE
FUDGED
FUDGES
FUELED
FUELER
FUGARD
FUGUES
FUJIAN
FULANI
FULCRA
FULLER
FULMAR
FULTON
FUMBLE
FUMING
FUNDED
FUNGUS
FUNKED
FUNNED
FUNNEL
FURIES
FURLED
FURORE
FURORS
FURRED
FURROW
FUSEES
FUSILS
FUSING
FUSION
FUSSED
FUSSES
FUSTIC
FUTILE
FUTONS
FUTURE
FUZEES
FUZHOU
FUZING
FUZZED
FUZZES

F•U•••
FAUCES
FAUCET
FAULTS
FAULTY
FAUNAE
FAUNAL
FAUNAS
FAUNUS
FEUDAL
FEUDED
FLUENT
FLUFFS
FLUFFY
FLUIDS
FLUKES
FLUMES
FLUNKS
FLUNKY
FLUORO
FLURRY
FLUTED
FLUTES
FLUXED
FLUXES
FOUGHT
FOULED
FOULER
FOULLY
FOULUP
FOUNDS
FOUNTS
FOURTH
FRUGAL
FRUITS
FRUITY
FRUMPS
FRUMPY
FRUTTI

F••U••
FACULA
FECUND
FEMURS
FERULE
FIBULA
FIGURE
FIXUPS
FLAUNT
FLEURY
FLOURS
FLOURY
FLOUTS
FORUMS
FRAUDS
FUGUES
FUTURE

F•••U•
FACEUP
FAIRUP
FAIYUM
FAMOUS
FANOUT
FAROUK
FAROUT
FAUNUS
FAVOUR
FERGUS
FESCUE
FESSUP
FESTUS
FICHUS
FILIUS
FILLUP
FIREUP
FIRMUP
FITFUL
FLIPUP
FLYOUT
FOLDUP
FOLIUM
FONDUE
FOULUP
FRENUM
FUNGUS

F••••U
FUZHOU

•F•U••
EFFUSE

•F••U•
EFFLUX

••FU••
DEFUSE
EFFUSE
ERFURT
INFULL
INFUSE
REFUEL
REFUGE
REFUND
REFUSE
REFUTE
UNFURL

••F•U•
BEFOUL
EFFLUX
INFLUX
LIFTUP
REFLUX
RUFOUS

•••FU•
ARMFUL
ARTFUL
BAGFUL
BEEFUP
BOXFUL
CAPFUL
CARFUL
CUPFUL
DOOFUS
EARFUL
EYEFUL
FITFUL
GOOFUP
IREFUL
JARFUL
JOYFUL
JUGFUL
LAPFUL
LAWFUL
MANFUL
POTFUL
RUEFUL
SINFUL
SNAFUS
SULFUR
USEFUL
VATFUL
WOEFUL

••••FU
KUNGFU

F•V•••
FAVORS
FAVOUR
FEVERS
FIVERS
FIVEWS
FOVEAE

F••V••
FERVID
FERVOR
FLAVIA
FLAVOR

••FV••
ALFVEN

F•W•••
FAWKES
FAWLTY
FAWNED
FAWNER
FEWEST
FOWLED
FOWLER
FOWLES

F••W••
FLAWED
FLEWAT
FLEWIN
FLOWED
FLOWER
FLYWAY
FROWNS
FROWZY

F•••W•
FIVEWS

F••••W
FALLOW
FARLOW
FARROW
FELLOW
FOGBOW
FOLLOW
FURROW

••F••W
GUFFAW
INFLOW

•••F•W
CURFEW
GUFFAW

F•X•••
FAXING
FIXATE
FIXERS
FIXING
FIXITY
FIXUPS
FOXIER
FOXILY
FOXING

F••X••
FLAXEN
FLAXES
FLEXED
FLEXES
FLEXOR
FLUXED
FLUXES

•F•••X
EFFLUX

••F••X
EFFLUX
INFLUX
REFLEX
REFLUX
SUFFIX

•••F•X
INAFIX
KITFOX
KOUFAX
OUTFOX
PREFIX
REDFOX
SEAFOX
SUFFIX

FY••••
FYODOR

F•Y•••
FLYBOY
FLYBYS
FLYERS
FLYING
FLYMAN
FLYMEN
FLYNET
FLYOUT
FLYROD
FLYWAY
FOYERS
FRYERS
FRYING
FRYPAN

F••Y••
FAIYUM
FLAYED
FLAYER
FRAYED

F•••Y•
FLYBYS
FOGEYS
FORAYS

F••••Y
FABRAY
FAIRLY
FAKERY

FAMILY
FARCRY
FARLEY
FAULTY
FAWLTY
FEALTY
FEEBLY
FEISTY
FELONY
FILTHY
FINELY
FINERY
FINNEY
FIRMLY
FIXITY
FLABBY
FLAGGY
FLASHY
FLATLY
FLEECY
FLESHY
FLEURY
FLIMSY
FLINTY
FLOOEY
FLOPPY
FLOPSY
FLOSSY
FLOURY
FLUFFY
FLUNKY
FLURRY
FLYBOY
FLYWAY
FOLKSY
FONDLY
FOSSEY
FOULLY
FOXILY
FRANNY
FREAKY
FREDDY
FREELY
FRENZY
FRETTY
FRIARY
FRIDAY
FRILLY
FRINGY
FRISKY
FRIZZY
FROGGY
FROSTY
FROTHY
FROWZY
FRUITY
FRUMPY

•F•••Y
AFFRAY
EFFIGY
OFFDAY
OFFKEY

••F•Y•
AJFOYT

••F••Y
AFFRAY
DEFRAY
DEFTLY
EFFIGY
INFAMY
OFFDAY
OFFKEY
RUFFLY
SAFELY
SAFETY
SOFTLY
WAFFLY
WIFELY

•••F•Y
BARFLY
BELFRY
BOTFLY
CHAFFY
CRAFTY
DRAFTY
DRYFLY
DURFEY
FLUFFY
GADFLY
LETFLY
MAYFLY
PANFRY
POPFLY
RUFFLY
SHIFTY
SNIFFY
SNUFFY
SPIFFY
STUFFY
WAFFLY
WETFLY

••••FY
CHAFFY
CITIFY
CODIFY
FLUFFY
MINIFY
MODIFY
NOTIFY
OSSIFY
PACIFY
PURIFY
RAMIFY
RAREFY
RARIFY
RATIFY
RUBIFY
SCURFY
SNIFFY
SNUFFY
SPIFFY
STUFFY
TUMEFY
TYPIFY
UGLIFY
VERIFY
VILIFY
VIVIFY

F•Z•••
FAZING
FEZZAN
FEZZES
FIZGIG
FIZZED
FIZZES
FIZZLE
FOZZIE
FUZEES
FUZHOU
FUZING
FUZZED
FUZZES

F••Z••
FEZZAN
FEZZES
FIZZED
FIZZES
FIZZLE
FOOZLE
FOZZIE
FRAZER
FRIZZY
FROZEN
FUZZED
FUZZES

F•••Z•
FAENZA
FREEZE
FRENZY
FRIEZE
FRIZZY
FROWZY

•F••Z•
SFORZA

GA••••
GABBED
GABBER
GABBLE
GABBRO
GABION
GABLED
GABLES
GADDED
GADDER
GADFLY
GADGET
GAELIC
GAFFED
GAFFER
GAFFES
GAGGED
GAGGLE
GAGING
GAGLAW
GAGMAN
GAGMEN
GAIETY
GAINED
GAINER
GAINLY
GAINON
GAINST
GAITED
GAITER
GALATA
GALAXY
GALEAE
GALENA
GALLED
GALLEY
GALLIA
GALLIC
GALLON
GALLOP
GALLUP
GALOIS
GALOOT
GALOPS
GALORE
GALOSH
GALWAY
GALYAK
GAMAYS
GAMBIA
GAMBIT
GAMBLE
GAMBOL
GAMELY
GAMEST
GAMETE
GAMIER
GAMILY
GAMINE
GAMING
GAMINS
GAMMAS
GAMMON
GAMUTS
GANDER
GANDHI
GANGED
GANGES
GANGLE
GANGLY
GANGUE
GANGUP
GANNET
GANTRY
GAPERS
GAPING
GAPPED
GARAGE
GARBED
GARBLE
GARCIA
GARCON
GARDEN
GARETH
GARGLE
GARISH
GARLIC
GARNER
GARNET
GARRET
GARSON
GARTER
GARTHS
GARVEY
GASBAG
GASCAP
GASCON
GASHED
GASHES
GASJET
GASKET
GASKIN
GASLIT
GASLOG
GASMAN
GASMEN
GASPAR
GASPED
GASSED
GASSER
GASSES
GASTON
GASTRO
GATEAU
GATERS
GATHER
GATING
GATLIN
GATORS
GATSBY
GAUCHE
GAUCHO
GAUGED
GAUGER
GAUGES
GAUZED
GAUZES
GAVEIN
GAVELS
GAVEUP
GAVIAL
GAWAIN
GAWKED
GAWKER
GAYALS
GAYEST
GAYNOR
GAZEBO
GAZING

G•A•••
GDANSK
GEARED
GEARTO
GEARUP
GHARRY
GHAZIS
GIANTS
GLACES
GLACIS
GLADES
GLADLY
GLADYS
GLAIRY
GLAMOR
GLANCE
GLANDS
GLARED
GLARES
GLASER
GLASSY
GLAZED
GLAZER
GLAZES
GMAJOR
GNARLS
GNARLY
GNAWED
GNAWER
GOADED
GOALIE
GOANNA
GOATEE
GOAWAY
GOAWRY
GRABAT
GRABBY
GRABEN
GRABLE
GRACED
GRACES
GRACIE
GRADEA
GRADED
GRADER
GRADES
GRADIN
GRADUS
GRAECO
GRAFTS
GRAHAM
GRAILS
GRAINS
GRAINY
GRAMAS
GRAMME
GRAMMY
GRAMPS
GRANDE
GRANDS
GRANGE
GRANNY
GRANTS
GRAPES
GRAPHS
GRAPPA
GRASPS
GRASSO
GRASSY
GRATED
GRATER
GRATES
GRATIA
GRATIN
GRATIS
GRAVED
GRAVEL
GRAVEN
GRAVER
GRAVES
GRAVID
GRAYED
GRAYER
GRAZED
GRAZER
GRAZES
GUACOS
GUARDS
GUAVAS

G••A••
GALATA
GALAXY
GAMAYS
GARAGE
GAWAIN
GAYALS
GELADA
GELATI
GELATO
GEMARA
GERALD
GERARD
GIRARD
GITANO
GLEAMS
GLEANS
GLOATS
GOBACK
GOCART
GODARD
GOEASY
GOKART
GORALS
GREASE
GREASY
GREATS
GREAVE
GROANS
GROATS
GSHARP
GSTAAD
GUIANA
GULAGS
GUYANA
GYRATE

G•••A•
GAGLAW
GAGMAN
GALEAE
GALWAY
GALYAK
GAMMAS
GASBAG
GASCAP
GASMAN
GASPAR
GATEAU
GAVIAL
GEEGAW
GEMMAE
GENIAL
GENOAN
GENUAL
GERMAN
GETSAT
GEWGAW
GIBRAN
GILEAD
GIMBAL
GLOBAL
GOAWAY
GOESAT
GOSTAG
GOTHAM
GOTMAD
GRABAT
GRAHAM
GRAMAS
GSTAAD
GUAVAS
GUFFAW
GUITAR
GULLAH
GUNMAN
GUNNAR
GUSTAV
GUTTAE

G••••A
GALATA
GALENA
GALLIA
GAMBIA
GARCIA
GEISHA
GELADA
GEMARA
GENERA
GENEVA
GEZIRA
GLENDA
GLINKA
GLORIA
GLOSSA
GOANNA
GODIVA
GOTCHA
GRADEA
GRAPPA
GRATIA
GRETNA
GUIANA
GUINEA
GURKHA
GUYANA

•GA•••
AGADIR
AGAMAS
AGARIC
AGASSI
AGATES
AGATHA
AGAVES
UGANDA

•G•A••
AGHAST
AGLAIA
AGLARE
AGNATE
IGNACE
IGNATZ
IGUACU
IGUANA
OGHAMS
OGLALA
UGGAMS

•G••A•
AGAMAS
AGENAS
AGLEAM
AGORAE
AGORAS
OGDOAD
SGTMAJ
UGRIAN

•G•••A
AGATHA
AGENDA
AGLAIA
EGERIA
EGESTA
IGUANA
OGLALA
UGANDA

••GA••
ARGALI
ASGARD
BIGAMY
BOGART
CIGARS
DAGAMA
DEGAGE
EDGARD
EDGARS
ENGAGE
ERGATE
FIGARO
FUGARD
HEGARI
HOGANS
KIGALI
LAGASH
LEGACY
LEGALS
LEGATE
LEGATO
LIGATE
MEGALO
MEGARA
MUGABE
NAGANO
NEGATE
ORGANA
ORGANS
ORGATE
PAGANS
REGAIN
REGALE
REGARD
RUGATE
SUGARS
SUGARY
TOGAED
UGGAMS
VAGARY
VEGANS

••G•A•
AEGEAN
AFGHAN
AUGEAN
BAGDAD
BEGGAR
BIGMAC
CAGUAS
COGNAC
DIGRAM
DOGEAR
DOGMAS
DOGTAG
ENGRAM
FOGHAT
GAGLAW
GAGMAN
HAGMAN
INGEAR
INGMAR
JAGUAR
JIGSAW
LEGMAN
LOGJAM
MAGMAS
MAGYAR
MCGRAW
ORGEAT
RAGBAG
RAGLAN
RAGMAN
RAGTAG
REGGAE
REGNAL
SIGMAS
SIGNAL
TAGDAY
UNGUAL
WIGWAG
WIGWAM
ZIGZAG

••G••A
ANGELA
ANGLIA
ANGOLA
ANGORA
BOGOTA
DAGAMA
HEGIRA
KAGERA
LAGUNA
LIGULA
LOGGIA
MEGARA
NAGOYA
ORGANA
PAGODA
REGINA
SEGURA
VIGODA

•••GA•
ALEGAR
ANSGAR
BEGGAR
BENGAL
BENGAY
BIOGAS
BROGAN
BULGAR
BURGAS
CONGAS
COOGAN
COUGAR
FRUGAL
GEEGAW
GEWGAW
HANGAR
KURGAN
LONGAN
MARGAY
MEDGAR
MORGAN
NILGAI
NORGAY
NOUGAT
OMEGAS
PISGAH
PLAGAL
REAGAN
REGGAE
SAIGAS
SEAGAL
SLOGAN
TAIGAS
TONGAN
VULGAR

•••G•A
BANGKA
BORGIA
ENIGMA
LINGUA
LOGGIA
QUAGGA
STIGMA
ZEUGMA

••••GA
AURIGA
BELUGA
BODEGA
CAYUGA
LADOGA
MALAGA
ORTEGA
PAANGA
QUAGGA
SENEGA

G•B•••
GABBED
GABBER
GABBLE
GABBRO
GABION
GABLED
GABLES
GIBBED
GIBBER
GIBBET
GIBBON
GIBERS
GIBILL
GIBING
GIBLET
GIBRAN
GIBSON
GOBACK
GOBBLE
GOBIES
GOBLET
GOBLIN
GOBUST

G••B••
GABBED
GABBER
GABBLE
GABBRO
GAMBIA
GAMBIT
GAMBLE
GAMBOL
GARBED
GARBLE
GASBAG
GERBER
GERBIL
GIBBED
GIBBER
GIBBET
GIBBON
GIMBAL
GIMBEL
GLEBES
GLIBLY
GLOBAL
GLOBED
GLOBES
GLOBIN
GOBBLE
GOOBER
GRABAT
GRABBY
GRABEN
GRABLE
GREBES
GRUBBY
GUMBEL
GUMBOS

G•••B•
GATSBY
GAZEBO
GETSBY
GOESBY
GONEBY
GOODBY
GRABBY
GRUBBY

•GB•••
EGBERT

••GB••
BIGBEN
BIGBOY
FOGBOW
RAGBAG

••G•B•
MUGABE

••G••B
ZAGREB

•••GB•
NINGBO

G•C•••
GECKOS
GOCART

G••C••
GARCIA
GARCON
GASCAP
GASCON
GAUCHE
GAUCHO
GLACES
GLACIS
GLYCOL
GOTCHA
GRACED
GRACES
GRACIE
GROCER
GUACOS

G•••C•
GLANCE
GLITCH
GOBACK
GRAECO
GREECE
GRINCH
GROUCH

G••••C
GAELIC
GALLIC
GARLIC
GNOMIC
GOTHIC

•G•C••
EGGCUP

•G••C•
AGENCY
IGNACE
IGUACU

•G•••C
AGARIC

••GC••
EGGCUP

••G•C•
LEGACY

••G••C
BIGMAC
COGNAC

•••G•C
TRAGIC

GD••••
GDANSK

G•D•••
GADDED
GADDER
GADFLY
GADGET
GIDEON
GIDGET
GODARD
GODETS
GODIVA
GODOWN
GODSON
GODWIN
GODWIT
GUDRUN

G••D••
GADDED
GADDER
GANDER
GANDHI
GARDEN
GENDER
GEODES
GILDED
GILDER
GIRDED
GIRDER
GIRDLE
GLADES
GLADLY
GLADYS
GLIDED
GLIDER
GLIDES
GOADED
GOLDEN
GOLDIE
GOODBY
GOODEN
GOODIE
GOODLY
GORDIE
GORDON
GRADEA
GRADED
GRADER
GRADES
GRADIN
GRADUS
GRODIN
GRUDGE
GUIDED
GUIDES
GUIDON
GUNDOG

G•••D•
GELADA
GLANDS
GLENDA
GOURDE
GOURDS
GRANDE
GRANDS
GREEDY
GRINDS
GRUNDY
GUARDS
GUILDS

G••••D
GABBED
GABLED
GADDED
GAFFED
GAGGED
GAINED
GAITED
GALLED
GANGED
GAPPED
GARBED
GASHED
GASPED
GASSED
GAUGED
GAUZED
GAWKED
GEARED
GELLED
GEMMED
GERALD
GERARD
GERUND
GIBBED
GIFTED
GIGGED
GILDED
GILEAD
GILLED
GINNED
GIPPED
GIRARD
GIRDED
GIRTED
GLARED
GLAZED
GLIDED
GLOBED
GLOVED
GLOWED
GNAWED
GOADED
GODARD
GOLFED
GONGED
GOOFED
GOOSED
GORGED
GOTMAD
GOUGED
GOUNOD
GOWILD
GOWNED
GRACED
GRADED
GRATED
GRAVED
GRAVID
GRAYED
GRAZED
GREYED
GRIMED
GRIPED
GROPED
GROUND
GSTAAD
GUIDED
GULFED
GULLED
GULPED
GUMMED
GUNNED
GUSHED
GUSTED
GUTTED
GYPPED

•GD•••
OGDOAD

•G•D••
AGADIR

•G••D•
AGENDA
UGANDA

•G•••D
AGEOLD
AGREED
OGDOAD

••GD••
BAGDAD
TAGDAY

••G•D•
PAGODA
VIGODA

••G••D
ANGLED
ARGUED
ASGARD
AUGEND
BAGDAD
BAGGED
BEGGED
BIGRED
BOGGED
BUGGED
BUGLED
COGGED
DOGGED
DOGOOD
EAGLED
EDGARD
ENGIRD
FAGEND
FAGGED
FOGGED
FUGARD
GAGGED
GIGGED
HOGGED
HUGGED
INGRID
JAGGED
JIGGED
JOGGED
JUGGED
KEGGED
LAGGED
LEGEND
LEGGED
LOGGED
LUGGED
MUGGED
NAGGED
NOGOOD
OSGOOD
PEGGED
PIGGED
PUGGED
RAGGED
REGARD
RIGGED
RUGGED
SAGGED
SEGUED
SIGHED
SIGNED
SIGURD
TAGEND
TAGGED
TOGAED
TOGGED
TUGGED
UNGIRD
VEGGED
WAGGED
WIGGED
ZAGGED
ZIGGED

•••G•D
BAGGED
BANGED
BARGED
BEGGED
BINGED
BOGGED
BONGED
BRIGID
BUDGED
BUGGED
BULGED
BUNGED
CADGED
COGGED
DINGED
DODGED
DOGGED
FAGGED
FANGED
FOGGED
FORGED
FRIGID
FUDGED
GAGGED
GANGED
GAUGED
GIGGED
GONGED
GORGED
GOUGED
HANGED
HEDGED
HINGED
HOGGED
HUGGED
IMAGED
JAGGED
JIGGED
JOGGED
JUDGED
JUGGED
KEDGED
KEGGED
KINGED
LAGGED
LEGGED
LODGED
LOGGED
LONGED
LUGGED
LUNGED
MERGED
MUGGED
NAGGED
NUDGED
PEGGED
PIGGED
PINGED
PONGID
PUGGED
PURGED
RAGGED
RANGED
RIDGED
RIGGED
RINGED
ROUGED
RUGGED
SAGGED
SIEGED
SINGED
STAGED
SUNGOD
SURGED
SWAGED
TAGGED
TANGED
TINGED
TINGOD
TOGGED
TUGGED
TURGID
UNAGED
VEGGED
VERGED
WAGGED
WARGOD
WEDGED
WIGGED
WINGED
ZAGGED
ZIGGED
ZINGED

GE••••
GEARED
GEARTO
GEARUP
GECKOS
GEEGAW
GEEGEE
GEEING
GEEZER
GEHRIG
GEIGER
GEISEL
GEISHA
GELADA
GELATI
GELATO
GELEES
GELLED
GELSEY
GEMARA
GEMINI
GEMMAE
GEMMED
GENDER
GENERA
GENETS
GENEVA
GENEVE
GENIAL
GENIES
GENIUS
GENOAN
GENOME
GENRES
GENTLE
GENTLY
GENTRY
GENUAL
GEODES
GEORGE
GERALD
GERARD
GERBER
GERBIL
GERENT
GERMAN
GERONT
GERTIE
GERUND
GESTES
GETOFF
GETOUT
GETSAT
GETSBY
GETSET
GETSIN
GETSIT
GETSON
GETSTO
GETSUP
GETTER
GETUPS
GEWGAW
GEYSER
GEZIRA

G•E•••
GAELIC
GEEGAW
GEEGEE
GEEING
GEEZER
GHETTO
GLEAMS
GLEANS
GLEBES
GLENDA
GNEISS
GOEASY
GOESAT
GOESBY
GOESIN
GOESON
GOESUP
GOETHE
GREASE
GREASY
GREATS
GREAVE
GREBES
GREECE
GREEDY
GREEKS
GREENE
GREENS
GREENY
GREETS
GREGOR
GREIGE
GRETEL
GRETNA
GREWON
GREWUP
GREYED
GREYER
GUELPH
GUENON
GUERRE
GUESTS

G••E••
GAIETY
GALEAE
GALENA
GAMELY
GAMEST
GAMETE
GAPERS
GARETH
GATEAU
GATERS
GAVEIN
GAVELS
GAVEUP
GAYEST
GAZEBO
GELEES
GENERA
GENETS
GENEVA
GENEVE
GERENT
GIBERS
GIDEON
GILEAD
GIMELS
GIVEIN
GIVENS
GIVERS
GIVEUP
GLUERS
GODETS
GOFERS
GOLEMS
GONEBY
GONERS
GOVERN
GOWEST
GRAECO
GREECE
GREEDY
GREEKS
GREENE
GREENS
GREENY
GREETS
GRIEVE
GRUELS
GYRENE

G•••E•
GABBED
GABBER
GABLED
GABLES
GADDED
GADDER
GADGET
GAFFED
GAFFER
GAFFES
GAGGED
GAGMEN
GAINED
GAINER
GAITED
GAITER
GALLED
GALLEY
GAMIER
GANDER
GANGED
GANGES
GANNET
GAPPED
GARBED
GARDEN
GARNER
GARNET
GARRET
GARTER
GARVEY
GASHED
GASHES
GASJET
GASKET
GASMEN
GASPED
GASSED
GASSER
GASSES
GATHER
GAUGED
GAUGER
GAUGES
GAUZED
GAUZES
GAWKED
GAWKER
GEARED
GEEGEE
GEEZER
GEIGER
GEISEL
GELEES
GELLED
GELSEY
GEMMED
GENDER
GENIES
GENRES
GEODES
GERBER
GESTES
GETSET
GETTER
GEYSER
GIBBED
GIBBER
GIBBET
GIBLET
GIDGET
GIFTED
GIGGED
GIGUES
GIJOES
GILDED
GILDER
GILLED
GIMBEL
GIMLET
GINGER
GINNED
GIPPED
GIPPER
GIRDED
GIRDER
GIRTED
GLACES
GLADES
GLARED
GLARES
GLASER
GLAZED
GLAZER
GLAZES
GLEBES
GLIDED
GLIDER
GLIDES
GLOBED
GLOBES
GLOVED
GLOVER
GLOVES
GLOWED
GLOWER
GLUTEI
GLUTEN
GNAWED
GNAWER
GNOMES
GOADED
GOATEE
GOBIES
GOBLET
GOLDEN
GOLFED
GOLFER
GONGED
GOOBER
GOODEN
GOOFED
GOOIER
GOOSED
GOOSES
GOOVER
GOPHER
GORGED
GORGES
GORGET
GORIER
GORSES
GOSHEN
GOSPEL
GOTTEN
GOUGED
GOUGER
GOUGES
GOULET
GOWNED
GRABEN
GRACED
GRACES
GRADEA
GRADED
GRADER
GRADES
GRAPES
GRATED
GRATER
GRATES
GRAVED
GRAVEL
GRAVEN
GRAVER
GRAVES
GRAYED
GRAYER
GRAZED
GRAZER
GRAZES
GREBES
GRETEL
GREYED
GREYER
GRIMED
GRIMES
GRIPED
GRIPER
GRIPES
GRIVET
GROCER
GROPED
GROPES
GROVEL
GROVER
GROVES
GROWER
GUIDED
GUIDES
GUILES
GUINEA
GUISES
GULFED
GULLED
GULLET
GULPED
GULPER
GUMBEL
GUMMED
GUNMEN
GUNNED
GUNNEL
GUNNER
GUNTER
GURLEY
GURNEY
GUSHED
GUSHER
GUSHES
GUSSET
GUSTED
GUTTED
GUTTER
GYPPED
GYPPER

G••••E
GABBLE
GAGGLE
GALEAE
GALORE
GAMBLE
GAMETE
GAMINE
GANGLE
GANGUE
GARAGE
GARBLE
GARGLE
GAUCHE
GEEGEE
GEMMAE
GENEVE
GENOME
GENTLE
GEORGE
GERTIE
GIGGLE
GILLIE
GIRDLE
GLANCE
GOALIE
GOATEE
GOBBLE
GOETHE
GOGGLE
GOHOME
GOLDIE
GOODIE
GOOGLE
GORDIE
GOURDE
GRABLE
GRACIE
GRAMME
GRANDE
GRANGE
GREASE
GREAVE
GREECE
GREENE
GREIGE
GRIEVE
GRILLE
GRILSE
GRIMKE
GRIPPE
GROOVE
GROSSE
GROUSE
GRUDGE
GRUNGE
GUERRE
GUIMPE
GURGLE
GUTTAE
GUZZLE
GWYNNE
GYRATE
GYRENE
GYROSE

•GE•••
AGEING
AGEISM
AGEIST
AGENAS
AGENCY
AGENDA
AGENTS
AGEOLD
EGERIA
EGESTA
EGESTS
IGETIT

•G•E••
AGLEAM
AGLETS
AGREED
AGREES
EGBERT
EGRESS
EGRETS
OGLERS
OGRESS

•G••E•
AGATES
AGAVES
AGGIES
AGREED
AGREES
NGUYEN
OGIVES
UGLIER
UGLIES

•G•••E
AGLARE
AGNATE
AGORAE
IGNACE
IGNITE
IGNORE

••GE••
AEGEAN
ANGELA
ANGELI
ANGELL
ANGELO
ANGELS
ANGERS
ARGENT
AUGEAN
AUGEND
AUGERS
BAGELS
BEGETS
BOGEYS
CAGERS
COGENT
DIGEST
DOGEAR
EDGEIN
EDGERS
ENGELS
EUGENE
FAGEND
FOGEYS
HUGELY
HUGEST
INGEAR
INGEST
KAGERA
LAGERS
LEGEND
LIGERS
LUGERS
NUGENT
ORGEAT
PAGERS
PIGEON
REGENT
ROGERS
SAGELY
SAGEST
TAGEND
TIGERS
URGENT
URGERS
WAGERS

••G•E•
AGGIES
AIGRET
ANGLED
ANGLER
ANGLES
ARGUED
ARGUER
ARGUES
BAGGED
BAGGER
BEGGED
BEGLEY
BIGBEN
BIGGER
BIGRED
BIGTEN
BOGGED
BOGIES
BOGLES
BUGGED
BUGLED
BUGLER
BUGLES
CAGIER
CAGNEY
COGGED
CYGNET
DAGGER
DEGREE
DIGGER
DOGGED
DOGGER
DOGIES
DOGLEG
EAGLED
EAGLES
EAGLET
EAGRES
EDGIER
FAGGED
FOGGED
FOGGER
FOGIES
FUGUES
GAGGED
GAGMEN
GIGGED
GIGUES
HIGHER
HOGGED
HUGGED
HUGGER
HUGHES
INGLES
INGRES
JAGGED
JAGGER
JIGGED
JIGGER
JOGGED
JOGGER
JUGGED
KEGGED
KEGLER
LAGGED
LAGGER
LEGGED
LEGMEN
LEGREE
LOGGED
LOGGER
LOGIER
LUGGED
LUGGER
MAGNET
MAGUEY
MCGREW
MIGUEL
MUGGED
MUGGER
NAGGED
NAGGER
NIGHER
NUGGET
ORGIES
PEGGED
PEGLER
PIGGED
PIGLET
PIGPEN
POGIES
PUGGED
PUGREE
RAGGED
RAGMEN
REGLET
REGRET
RIGGED
RIGGER
ROGUES
RUGGED
SAGGED
SEGUED
SEGUES
SIGHED
SIGHER
SIGNED
SIGNEE
SIGNER
SIGNET
TAGGED
TIGGER
TOGAED
TOGGED
TUGGED
TUGGER
UNGUES
VAGUER
VEGGED
VOGUES
WAGGED
WAGNER
WIGGED
WIGLET
ZAGGED
ZAGREB
ZIGGED

••G••E
ALGORE
ARGIVE
ARGYLE
BAGGIE
BEGONE
BIGGIE
BIGLIE
BIGTOE
BOGGLE
BYGONE
DEGAGE
DEGREE
DOGGIE
ENGAGE
ENGINE
ERGATE
EUGENE
FIGURE
GAGGLE
GIGGLE
GOGGLE
HAGGLE
HIGGLE
HOGTIE
JIGGLE
JOGGLE
JUGGLE
LEGATE
LEGREE
LEGUME
LIGATE
LIGURE
MAGGIE
MAGPIE
MIGGLE
MUGABE
NEGATE
NIGGLE
ORGATE
PIGGIE
PUGREE
REGALE
REGGAE
REGGIE
REGIME
REGLUE
RUGATE
RUGOSE
SIGNEE
TAGORE
TOGGLE
UNGLUE
VEGGIE
WAGGLE
WIGGLE
ZYGOTE

•••GE•
ADAGES
APOGEE
BADGER
BADGES
BAGGED
BAGGER
BANGED
BANGER
BARGED
BARGES
BEGGED
BEIGES
BERGEN
BIGGER
BILGES
BINGED
BINGES
BOGGED
BOLGER
BONGED
BRUGES
BUDGED
BUDGES
BUDGET
BUGGED
BULGED
BULGES
BUNGED
BUNGEE
BURGEE
BURGER
CADGED
CADGER
CADGES
CODGER
COGGED
CONGER
CUDGEL
DAGGER
DANGER
DIGGER
DINGED
DIRGES
DODGED
DODGER
DODGES
DOGGED
DOGGER
DRAGEE
FAGGED
FANGED
FIDGET
FINGER
FOGGED
FOGGER
FORGED
FORGER
FORGES
FORGET
FUDGED
FUDGES
GADGET
GAGGED
GANGED
GANGES
GAUGED
GAUGER
GAUGES
GEEGEE
GEIGER
GIDGET
GIGGED
GINGER
GONGED
GORGED
GORGES
GORGET
GOUGED
GOUGER
GOUGES
HANGED
HANGER
HEDGED
HEDGER
HEDGES
HINGED
HINGES
HOGGED
HUGGED
HUGGER
HUNGER
IMAGED
IMAGER
IMAGES
IMOGEN
JAEGER
JAGGED
JAGGER
JIGGED
JIGGER
JOGGED
JOGGER
JUDGED
JUDGES
JUGGED
KEDGED
KEDGES
KEGGED
KINGED
KRUGER
LAAGER
LAGGED
LAGGER
LARGER
LEDGER
LEDGES
LEGGED
LIEGES
LINGER
LODGED
LODGER
LODGES
LOGGED
LOGGER
LONGED
LONGER
LONGES
LUGGED
LUGGER
LUNGED
LUNGES
MAJGEN
MANGER
MEAGER
MERGED
MERGER
MERGES
MIDGES
MIDGET
MONGER
MORGEN
MUGGED
MUGGER
NAGGED
NAGGER
NUDGED
NUDGER
NUDGES
NUGGET
ONAGER
ORIGEN
OSAGES
OXYGEN
PARGET
PEGGED
PHAGES
PIAGET
PIGGED
PINGED
PLAGES
PONGEE
PUGGED
PURGED
PURGES
RAGGED
RANGED
RANGER
RANGES
RIDGED
RIDGES
RIGGED
RIGGER
RINGED
RINGER
ROUGED
ROUGES
RUGGED
RUTGER
SAGGED
SANGER
SARGES
SAUGER
SEDGES
SEEGER
SERGEI
SERGES
SIEGED
SIEGES
SINGED
SINGER
SINGES
STAGED
STAGER
STAGES
SURGED
SURGES
SWAGED
SWAGES
TAGGED
TANGED
TARGES
TARGET
TIGGER
TINGED
TINGES
TOGGED
TUGGED
TUGGER
UNAGED
USAGES
VEGGED
VERGED
VERGER
VERGES
VOSGES
WAGGED
WEDGED
WEDGES
WIDGET
WIGGED
WINGED
WINGER
YEAGER
ZAGGED
ZENGER
ZIGGED
ZINGED
ZINGER

•••G•E
ALEGRE
APOGEE
BAGGIE
BANGLE
BEAGLE
BIGGIE
BOGGLE
BOOGIE
BROGUE
BUDGIE
BUNGEE
BUNGLE
BURGEE
BURGLE
CHIGOE
DANGLE
DANGME
DENGUE
DINGLE
DOGGIE
DOOGIE
DRAGEE
DROGUE
EMIGRE
FERGIE
GAGGLE
GANGLE
GANGUE
GARGLE
GEEGEE
GIGGLE
GOGGLE
GOOGLE
GURGLE
HAGGLE
HIGGLE
HOAGIE
JANGLE
JIGGLE
JINGLE
JOGGLE
JUGGLE
JUNGLE
KINGME
LEAGUE
LONGUE
MAGGIE
MANGLE
MARGIE
MEAGRE
MIGGLE
MINGLE
NIGGLE
PIGGIE
PLAGUE
PONGEE
PRAGUE
REGGAE
REGGIE
SINGLE
SOIGNE
STOGIE
TANGLE
TINGLE
TOGGLE
TONGUE
VEGGIE
WAGGLE
WANGLE
WEDGIE
WIGGLE

WOOGIE

••••GE
ALLEGE
AVENGE
BAREGE
BORAGE
BRIDGE
CHANGE
CHARGE
CRINGE
CUBAGE
DAMAGE
DEGAGE
DELUGE
DOSAGE
DOTAGE
DREDGE
DRUDGE
EMERGE
ENCAGE
ENGAGE
ENRAGE
FLANGE
FLEDGE
FORAGE
FRIDGE
FRINGE
GARAGE
GEORGE
GRANGE
GREIGE
GRUDGE
GRUNGE
HOMAGE
ICEAGE
INNAGE
KLUDGE
KRESGE
LAVAGE
LESAGE
LINAGE
LOUNGE
LOVAGE
MANAGE
MANEGE
MENAGE
MIRAGE
NEWAGE
NONAGE
OBLIGE
ONEDGE
ORANGE
OUTAGE
PELAGE
PLEDGE
PLUNGE
POTAGE
RAVAGE
REFUGE
RENEGE
SAVAGE
SEWAGE
SILAGE
SLEDGE
SLUDGE
SMUDGE
SOCAGE
SPARGE
SPONGE
SPURGE
STODGE
STOOGE
TOWAGE
TRIAGE
TRUDGE
TWINGE
ULLAGE
UNCAGE
VISAGE
VOYAGE

G•F•••
GAFFED
GAFFER
GAFFES
GIFTED
GOFERS
GOFISH
GUFFAW

G••F••
GADFLY
GAFFED
GAFFER
GAFFES
GOLFED
GOLFER
GOOFED
GOOFUP
GRAFTS
GUFFAW
GULFED
GUNFOR

G•••F•
GETOFF
GOSOFT
GOTOFF

G••••F
GETOFF
GOTOFF

•G••F•
UGLIFY

••GF••
BAGFUL
JUGFUL

••G•F•
BEGOFF
BUGOFF
LOGOFF

••G••F
BEGOFF
BUGOFF
ENGULF
LOGOFF

•••GF•
KUNGFU

G•G•••
GAGGED
GAGGLE
GAGING
GAGLAW
GAGMAN
GAGMEN
GIGGED
GIGGLE
GIGGLY
GIGOLO
GIGOTS
GIGUES
GOGGLE
GOGGLY

G••G••
GADGET
GAGGED
GAGGLE
GANGED
GANGES
GANGLE
GANGLY
GANGUE
GANGUP
GARGLE
GAUGED
GAUGER
GAUGES
GEEGAW
GEEGEE
GEIGER
GEWGAW
GIDGET
GIGGED
GIGGLE
GIGGLY
GINGER
GLOGGS
GOGGLE
GOGGLY
GONGED
GOOGLE
GOOGLY
GOOGOL
GOOGOO
GORGED
GORGES
GORGET
GORGON
GOUGED
GOUGER
GOUGES
GREGOR
GRIGRI
GROGGY
GUNGHO
GURGLE

G•••G•
GARAGE
GEORGE
GINKGO
GLOGGS
GOINGS
GONOGO
GRANGE
GREIGE
GRINGO
GROGGY
GRUDGE
GRUNGE
GRUNGY
GULAGS

G••••G
GAGING
GAMING
GAPING
GASBAG
GASLOG
GATING
GAZING
GEEING
GEHRIG
GIBING
GIVING
GLUING
GORING
GOSTAG
GUNDOG
GUYING

•GG•••
AGGIES
EGGCUP
EGGING
EGGNOG
EGGSON
UGGAMS

•G•••G
AGEING
EGGING
EGGNOG
OGLING

••GG••
BAGGED
BAGGER
BAGGIE
BEGGAR
BEGGED
BIGGER
BIGGIE
BIGGUN
BOGGED
BOGGLE
BUGGED
COGGED
DAGGER
DIGGER
DOGGED
DOGGER
DOGGIE
FAGGED
FOGGED
FOGGER
GAGGED
GAGGLE
GIGGED
GIGGLE
GIGGLY
GOGGLE
GOGGLY
HAGGIS
HAGGLE
HIGGLE
HOGGED
HUGGED
HUGGER
JAGGED
JAGGER
JIGGED
JIGGER
JIGGLE
JIGGLY
JOGGED
JOGGER
JOGGLE
JUGGED
JUGGLE
KEGGED
LAGGED
LAGGER
LEGGED
LOGGED
LOGGER
LOGGIA
LUGGED
LUGGER
MAGGIE
MAGGIO
MIGGLE
MUGGED
MUGGER
NAGGED
NAGGER
NIGGLE
NOGGIN
NUGGET
PEGGED
PIGGED
PIGGIE
PUGGED
RAGGED
REGGAE
REGGIE
RIGGED
RIGGER
RUGGED
SAGGED
TAGGED
TIGGER
TOGGED
TOGGLE
TUGGED
TUGGER
VEGGED
VEGGIE
WAGGED
WAGGLE
WAGGLY
WAGGON
WIGGED
WIGGLE
WIGGLY
ZAGGED
ZIGGED

••G•G•
DEGAGE
ENGAGE

••G••G
BIGWIG
BOGONG
CAGING
DOGLEG
DOGTAG
DUGONG
EDGING
EGGING
EGGNOG
GAGING
PAGING
RAGBAG
RAGING
RAGRUG
RAGTAG
URGING
WAGING
WIGWAG
ZIGZAG

•••GG•
BRIGGS
CRAGGY
DRAGGY
FLAGGY
FROGGY
GLOGGS
GROGGY
QUAGGA
QUAGGY
SHAGGY
SLAGGY
SLUGGO
SMOGGY
SNAGGY
TWIGGY

•••G•G
FIZGIG

••••GG
BADEGG
RAWEGG

GH••••
GHARRY
GHAZIS
GHETTO
GHOSTS
GHOULS

G•H•••
GEHRIG
GOHOME
GSHARP

G••H••
GASHED
GASHES
GATHER
GOPHER
GOSHEN
GOTHAM
GOTHIC
GRAHAM
GUSHED
GUSHER
GUSHES

G•••H•
GANDHI
GARTHS
GAUCHE
GAUCHO
GEISHA
GIRTHS
GLYPHS
GOETHE
GOTCHA
GRAPHS
GUNGHO
GUNSHY
GURKHA

G••••H
GALOSH
GARETH
GARISH
GLITCH
GOFISH
GOWITH
GRINCH
GROUCH
GROWTH
GUELPH
GULLAH

•GH•••
AGHAST
OGHAMS

•G••H•
AGATHA

••GH••
AFGHAN
AUGHTS
BIGHTS
EIGHTH
EIGHTS
EIGHTY
FIGHTS
FOGHAT
HIGHER
HIGHIQ
HIGHLY
HIGHUP
HUGHES
LIGHTS
MIGHTY
MUGHOS
NIGHER
NIGHTS
NIGHTY
OUGHTS
RIGHTO
RIGHTS
SIGHED
SIGHER
SIGHTS
TIGHTS
WIGHTS

••G•H•
MEGOHM

••G••H
BYGOSH
EIGHTH
LAGASH

•••GH•
ALIGHT
ARIGHT
BLIGHT
BOUGHS
BOUGHT
BRIGHT
BURGHS
CAUGHT
COUGHS
DINGHY
DOUGHS
DOUGHY
DWIGHT
FLIGHT
FOUGHT
FRIGHT
GUNGHO
HAIGHT
HEIGHT
KNIGHT
LAUGHS
NAUGHT
NEIGHS
NOUGHT
PENGHU
PLIGHT
ROUGHS
SLIGHT
SOUGHS
SOUGHT
TAUGHT
THIGHS
TOUGHS
TOUGHY
VAUGHN
VEIGHT
VOIGHT
WEIGHS
WEIGHT
WRIGHT

•••G•H
LENGTH
PISGAH

••••GH
ARMAGH
AWEIGH
CHOUGH
ENOUGH
LEHIGH
ONHIGH
PLOUGH
SLEIGH
SLOUGH
THOUGH
TROUGH

GI••••
GIANTS
GIBBED
GIBBER
GIBBET
GIBBON
GIBERS
GIBILL
GIBING
GIBLET
GIBRAN
GIBSON
GIDEON
GIDGET
GIFTED
GIGGED
GIGGLE
GIGGLY
GIGOLO
GIGOTS
GIGUES
GIJOES
GILDED
GILDER
GILEAD
GILLED
GILLIE
GILLIS
GIMBAL
GIMBEL
GIMELS
GIMLET
GINGER
GINKGO
GINNED
GIOTTO
GIPPED
GIPPER
GIRARD
GIRDED
GIRDER
GIRDLE
GIRTED
GIRTHS
GITANO
GIVEIN
GIVENS
GIVERS
GIVEUP
GIVING
GIZMOS

G•I•••
GAIETY
GAINED
GAINER
GAINLY
GAINON
GAINST
GAITED
GAITER
GEIGER
GEISEL
GEISHA
GLIBLY
GLIDED
GLIDER
GLIDES
GLINKA
GLINTS
GLITCH
GLITZY
GMINOR
GOINGS
GOINTO
GRIEVE
GRIGRI
GRILLE
GRILLS
GRILSE
GRIMED
GRIMES
GRIMKE
GRIMLY
GRINCH
GRINDS
GRINGO
GRIPED
GRIPER
GRIPES
GRIPPE
GRISLY
GRISON
GRISTS
GRITTY
GRIVET
GUIANA
GUIDED
GUIDES
GUIDON
GUILDS
GUILES
GUILTY
GUIMPE
GUINEA
GUISES
GUITAR

G••I••
GABION
GAGING
GAMIER
GAMILY
GAMINE
GAMING
GAMINS
GAPING
GARISH
GATING
GAVIAL
GAZING
GEEING
GEMINI
GENIAL
GENIES
GENIUS
GEZIRA
GIBILL
GIBING
GIVING
GLAIRY
GLUING
GNEISS
GOBIES
GODIVA
GOFISH
GOOIER
GORIER
GORING
GOWILD
GOWITH
GRAILS
GRAINS
GRAINY
GREIGE
GROINS
GSUITS
GUYING

G•••I•
GAELIC
GALLIA
GALLIC
GALOIS
GAMBIA
GAMBIT
GARCIA
GARLIC
GASKIN
GASLIT
GATLIN
GAVEIN
GAWAIN
GEHRIG
GERBIL
GERTIE
GETSIN
GETSIT
GHAZIS
GILLIE
GILLIS
GIVEIN
GLACIS
GLOBIN
GLORIA
GNOMIC
GNOSIS
GOALIE
GOBLIN
GODWIN
GODWIT
GOESIN
GOLDIE
GOODIE
GORDIE
GOSSIP
GOTHIC
GOTOIT
GRACIE
GRADIN
GRATIA
GRATIN
GRATIS
GRAVID
GRODIN

G••••I
GANDHI
GELATI
GEMINI
GLUTEI
GRIGRI

•GI•••
BGIRLS
OGIVES

•G•I••
AGEING
AGEISM
AGEIST
AGGIES
AGLINT
EGGING
EGOISM
EGOIST
IGNITE
OGLING
UGLIER
UGLIES
UGLIFY
UGRIAN

•G••I•
AGADIR
AGARIC
AGLAIA
EGERIA
IGETIT

•G•••I
AGASSI
AGOUTI

••GI••
AGGIES
ARGIVE
BEGINS
BOGIES
CAGIER
CAGILY
CAGING
DIGITS
DOGIES
EDGIER
EDGILY
EDGING
EGGING
ENGINE
ENGIRD
ENGIRT
FOGIES
GAGING
HEGIRA
LEGION
LEGIST
LOGIER
LOGILY
LOGION
MEGILP
MYGIRL
ORGIES
PAGING
POGIES
RAGING
REGIME
REGINA
REGION
REGIUS
SIGILS
UNGIRD
UNGIRT
URGING
VIGILS
WAGING
YOGINI

••G•I•
ANGLIA
BAGGIE
BAGUIO
BIGGIE
BIGLIE
BIGWIG
DIGSIN
DOGGIE
DOGSIT
EDGEIN
FOGSIN
HAGGIS
HIGHIQ
HOGTIE
INGRID
LIGNIN
LOGGIA
LOGSIN
MAGGIE
MAGGIO
MAGPIE
NOGGIN
PIGGIE
REGAIN
REGGIE
SIGNIN
TIGRIS
TUGRIK
UNGUIS
VEGGIE

••G••I
ANGELI
ARGALI
HEGARI
KIGALI
LUGOSI
YOGINI

•••GI•
ADAGIO
BAGGIE
BIGGIE
BIRGIT
BOOGIE
BORGIA
BRIGID
BUDGIE
CORGIS
DOGGIE
DOOGIE
DRAGIN
ELEGIT
FERGIE
FIZGIG
FRIGID
HAGGIS
HANGIN
HOAGIE
HUNGIN
LOGGIA
MAGGIE
MAGGIO
MARGIE
MARGIN
NOGGIN
ORIGIN
PIDGIN
PIGGIE
PLAGIO
PLUGIN
PONGID
REGGIE
SERGIO
STOGIE
TRAGIC
TURGID
VEGGIE
VIRGIL
VIRGIN
WEDGIE
WINGIT
WOOGIE

•••G•I
BANGUI
GRIGRI
MOWGLI
NILGAI
SERGEI

••••GI
UBANGI

G•J•••
GIJOES

G••J••
GASJET
GMAJOR

•G•••J
SGTMAJ

••GJ••
LOGJAM

G•K•••
GOKART

G••K••
GASKET
GASKIN
GAWKED
GAWKER
GECKOS
GINKGO
GURKHA

G•••K•
GLINKA
GREEKS
GRIMKE

G••••K
GALYAK
GDANSK
GOBACK

••GK••
ANGKOR

••G••K
TUGRIK

•••GK•
BANGKA

GL••••
GLACES
GLACIS
GLADES
GLADLY
GLADYS
GLAIRY
GLAMOR
GLANCE
GLANDS
GLARED
GLARES
GLASER
GLASSY
GLAZED
GLAZER
GLAZES
GLEAMS
GLEANS
GLEBES
GLENDA
GLIBLY
GLIDED
GLIDER
GLIDES
GLINKA
GLINTS
GLITCH
GLITZY
GLOATS
GLOBAL
GLOBED
GLOBES
GLOBIN
GLOGGS
GLOOMS
GLOOMY
GLOPPY
GLORIA
GLOSSA
GLOSSY
GLOVED
GLOVER
GLOVES
GLOWED
GLOWER
GLUERS
GLUING
GLUMLY
GLUONS
GLUTEI
GLUTEN
GLYCOL
GLYPHS

G•L•••
GALATA
GALAXY
GALEAE
GALENA
GALLED
GALLEY
GALLIA
GALLIC
GALLON
GALLOP
GALLUP
GALOIS
GALOOT
GALOPS
GALORE
GALOSH
GALWAY
GALYAK
GELADA
GELATI
GELATO
GELEES
GELLED
GELSEY
GILDED
GILDER
GILEAD
GILLED
GILLIE
GILLIS
GOLDEN
GOLDIE
GOLEMS
GOLFED
GOLFER
GOLLUM
GULAGS
GULFED
GULLAH
GULLED
GULLET
GULPED
GULPER

G••L••
GABLED
GABLES
GAELIC
GAGLAW
GALLED
GALLEY
GALLIA
GALLIC
GALLON
GALLOP
GALLUP
GARLIC
GASLIT
GASLOG
GATLIN
GELLED
GIBLET
GILLED
GILLIE
GILLIS
GIMLET
GOALIE
GOBLET
GOBLIN
GOLLUM
GOSLOW
GOULET
GRILLE
GRILLS
GRILSE
GUELPH
GUILDS
GUILES
GUILTY
GULLAH
GULLED
GULLET
GURLEY

G•••L•
GABBLE
GADFLY
GAGGLE
GAINLY
GAMBLE
GAMELY
GAMILY
GANGLE
GANGLY
GARBLE
GARGLE
GAVELS
GAYALS

GENTLE
GENTLY
GERALD
GHOULS
GIBILL
GIGGLE
GIGGLY
GIGOLO
GIMELS
GIRDLE
GLADLY
GLIBLY
GLUMLY
GNARLS
GNARLY
GOBBLE
GOGGLE
GOGGLY
GOODLY
GOOGLE
GOOGLY
GORALS
GOWILD
GRABLE
GRAILS
GRILLE
GRILLS
GRIMLY
GRISLY
GROWLS
GROWLY
GRUELS
GURGLE
GUZZLE

G••••L
GAMBOL
GAVIAL
GEISEL
GENIAL
GENUAL
GERBIL
GIBILL
GIMBAL
GIMBEL
GLOBAL
GLYCOL
GOOGOL
GOSPEL
GRAVEL
GRETEL
GROVEL
GUMBEL
GUNNEL

•GL•••
AGLAIA
AGLARE
AGLEAM
AGLETS
AGLINT
IGLOOS
OGLALA
OGLERS
OGLING
UGLIER
UGLIES
UGLIFY

•G••L•
AGEOLD
BGIRLS
OGLALA

••GL••
ANGLED
ANGLER
ANGLES
ANGLIA
ANGLOS
BEGLEY
BIGLIE
BOGLES
BUGLED
BUGLER
BUGLES
DIGLOT
DOGLEG
EAGLED
EAGLES
EAGLET
ENGLUT
GAGLAW
INGLES
KEGLER
PEGLER
PIGLET
RAGLAN
REGLET
REGLUE
TIGLON
UNGLUE
WIGLET

••G•L•
ANGELA
ANGELI
ANGELL
ANGELO
ANGELS
ANGOLA
ARGALI
ARGYLE
ARGYLL
BAGELS
BOGGLE
CAGILY
EDGILY
ENGELS
ENGULF
GAGGLE
GIGGLE
GIGGLY
GIGOLO
GOGGLE
GOGGLY
HAGGLE
HIGGLE
HIGHLY
HUGELY
JIGGLE
JIGGLY
JOGGLE
JUGGLE
KIGALI
LEGALS
LIGULA
LOGILY
MEGALO
MEGILP
MIGGLE
MOGULS
NIGGLE
REGALE
SAGELY
SIGILS
TOGGLE
VIGILS
WAGGLE
WAGGLY
WIGGLE
WIGGLY

••G••L
ANGELL
ARGYLL
BAGFUL
JUGFUL
MIGUEL
MYGIRL
REGNAL
SIGNAL
UNGUAL

•••GL•
BANGLE
BEAGLE
BOGGLE
BUNGLE
BURGLE
DANGLE
DANGLY
DAYGLO
DINGLE
GAGGLE
GANGLE
GANGLY
GARGLE
GIGGLE
GIGGLY
GOGGLE
GOGGLY
GOOGLE
GOOGLY
GURGLE
HAGGLE
HIGGLE
JANGLE
JANGLY
JIGGLE
JIGGLY
JINGLE
JINGLY
JOGGLE
JUGGLE
JUNGLE
JUNGLY
KINGLY
MANGLE
MIGGLE
MINGLE
MOWGLI
NIGGLE
SINGLE
SINGLY
SMUGLY
SNUGLY
TANGLE
TANGLY
TINGLE
TINGLY
TOGGLE
TRIGLY
WAGGLE
WAGGLY
WANGLE
WIGGLE
WIGGLY
YUNGLO

•••G•L
BENGAL
CUDGEL
FRUGAL
GOOGOL
HANGUL
MONGOL
PLAGAL
SEAGAL
VIRGIL

GM••••
GMAJOR
GMINOR

G•M•••
GAMAYS
GAMBIA
GAMBIT
GAMBLE
GAMBOL
GAMELY
GAMEST
GAMETE
GAMIER
GAMILY
GAMINE
GAMING
GAMINS
GAMMAS
GAMMON
GAMUTS
GEMARA
GEMINI
GEMMAE
GEMMED
GIMBAL
GIMBEL
GIMELS
GIMLET
GUMBEL
GUMBOS
GUMMED
GUMSUP

G••M••
GAGMAN
GAGMEN
GAMMAS
GAMMON
GASMAN
GASMEN
GEMMAE
GEMMED
GERMAN
GIZMOS
GLAMOR
GLUMLY
GNOMES
GNOMIC
GNOMON
GOTMAD
GRAMAS
GRAMME
GRAMMY
GRAMPS
GRIMED
GRIMES
GRIMKE
GRIMLY
GRUMPS
GRUMPY
GUIMPE
GUMMED
GUNMAN
GUNMEN

G•••M•
GENOME
GLEAMS
GLOOMS
GLOOMY
GOHOME
GOLEMS
GRAMME
GRAMMY
GROOMS

G••••M
GOLLUM
GOTHAM
GRAHAM
GYPSUM

•GM•••
EGMONT

•G•M••
AGAMAS
SGTMAJ

•G••M•
OGHAMS
UGGAMS

•G•••M
AGEISM
AGLEAM
EGOISM

••GM••
BIGMAC
DOGMAS
GAGMAN
GAGMEN
HAGMAN
INGMAR
LEGMAN
LEGMEN
MAGMAS
RAGMAN
RAGMEN
RAGMOP
SIGMAS

••G•M•
BEGUMS
BIGAMY
DAGAMA
LEGUME
REGIME
UGGAMS

••G••M
DIGRAM
ENGRAM
LOGJAM
MAGNUM
MEGOHM
WIGWAM

•••GM•
DANGME
ENIGMA
KINGME
STIGMA
ZEUGMA

•••G•M
ARTGUM
BEEGUM
REDGUM
SUBGUM

••••GM
PHLEGM

GN••••
GNARLS
GNARLY
GNAWED
GNAWER
GNEISS
GNOMES
GNOMIC
GNOMON
GNOSIS

G•N•••
GANDER
GANDHI
GANGED
GANGES
GANGLE
GANGLY
GANGUE
GANGUP
GANNET
GANTRY
GENDER
GENERA
GENETS
GENEVA
GENEVE
GENIAL
GENIES
GENIUS
GENOAN
GENOME
GENRES
GENTLE
GENTLY
GENTRY
GENUAL
GINGER
GINKGO
GINNED
GONEBY
GONERS
GONGED
GONOGO
GUNDOG
GUNFOR
GUNGHO
GUNMAN
GUNMEN
GUNNAR
GUNNED
GUNNEL
GUNNER
GUNSHY
GUNTER

G••N••
GAINED
GAINER
GAINLY
GAINON
GAINST
GANNET
GARNER
GARNET
GAYNOR
GDANSK
GIANTS
GINNED
GLANCE
GLANDS
GLENDA
GLINKA
GLINTS
GMINOR
GOANNA
GOINGS
GOINTO
GOUNOD
GOWNED
GRANDE
GRANDS
GRANGE
GRANNY
GRANTS
GRINCH
GRINDS
GRINGO
GRUNDY
GRUNGE
GRUNGY
GRUNTS
GUENON
GUINEA
GUNNAR
GUNNED
GUNNEL
GUNNER
GURNEY
GWYNNE

G•••N•
GAGING
GALENA
GAMINE
GAMING
GAMINS
GAPING
GATING
GAZING
GEEING
GEMINI
GERENT
GERONT
GERUND
GIBING
GITANO
GIVENS
GIVING
GLEANS
GLUING
GLUONS
GOANNA
GORING
GRAINS
GRAINY
GRANNY
GREENE
GREENS
GREENY
GRETNA
GROANS
GROINS
GROUND
GROZNY
GUIANA
GUYANA
GUYING
GWYNNE
GYRENE
GYRONS

G••••N
GABION
GAGMAN
GAGMEN
GAINON
GALLON
GAMMON
GARCON
GARDEN
GARSON
GASCON
GASKIN
GASMAN
GASMEN
GASTON
GATLIN
GAVEIN
GAWAIN
GENOAN
GERMAN
GETSIN
GETSON
GIBBON
GIBRAN
GIBSON
GIDEON
GIVEIN
GLOBIN
GLUTEN
GNOMON
GOBLIN
GODOWN
GODSON
GODWIN
GOESIN
GOESON
GOLDEN
GOODEN
GORDON
GORGON
GOSHEN
GOTTEN
GOVERN
GRABEN
GRADIN
GRATIN
GRAVEN
GREWON
GRISON
GRODIN
GROWON
GUDRUN
GUENON
GUIDON
GUNMAN
GUNMEN

•GN•••
AGNATE
IGNACE
IGNATZ
IGNITE
IGNORE

•G•N••
AGENAS
AGENCY
AGENDA
AGENTS
EGGNOG
UGANDA

•G••N•
AGEING
AGLINT
EGGING
EGMONT
IGUANA
OGLING

•G•••N
EGGSON
NGUYEN
UGRIAN

••GN••
CAGNEY
COGNAC
CYGNET
CYGNUS
EGGNOG
LIGNIN
LUGNUT
MAGNET
MAGNON
MAGNUM
MIGNON
PIGNUT
REGNAL
SIGNAL
SIGNED
SIGNEE
SIGNER
SIGNET
SIGNIN
SIGNON
SIGNOR
SIGNUP
WAGNER

••G•N•
ARGENT
AUGEND
BEGINS
BEGONE
BOGONG
BYGONE
CAGING
COGENT
DOGONS
DUGONG
EDGING
EGGING
ENGINE
EUGENE
FAGEND
GAGING
HOGANS
LAGUNA
LEGEND
NAGANO
NUGENT
ORGANA
ORGANS
PAGANS
PAGING
RAGING
REGENT
REGINA
TAGEND
URGENT
URGING
VEGANS
WAGING
WAGONS
YOGINI

••G••N
AEGEAN
AFGHAN
AUGEAN
BIGBEN
BIGGUN
BIGTEN
DIGSIN
EDGEIN
EGGSON
FOGSIN
GAGMAN
GAGMEN
HAGMAN
LAGOON
LEGION
LEGMAN
LEGMEN
LIGNIN
LOGION
LOGSIN
LOGSON
MAGNON
MIGNON
NOGGIN
PIGEON
PIGPEN
RAGLAN
RAGMAN
RAGMEN
REGAIN
REGION
SIGNIN
SIGNON
TIGLON
WAGGON

•••GN•
ALIGNS
BOIGNY
DEIGNS
FEIGNS
REIGNS
SOIGNE
VSIGNS

•••G•N
AIRGUN
ARAGON
BERGEN
BIGGUN
BROGAN
CAPGUN
COOGAN
DRAGIN
DRAGON
FLAGON
GORGON
HANGIN
HANGON
HUNGIN
HUNGON
IMOGEN
ISOGON
JARGON
JETGUN
KURGAN
LONGAN
MAJGEN
MARGIN
MORGAN
MORGEN
NOGGIN
OREGON
ORIGEN
ORIGIN
OUTGUN
OXYGEN
PIDGIN
PLUGIN
POPGUN
RAYGUN
REAGAN
SAIGON
SARGON
SHOGUN
SIXGUN
SLOGAN
TONGAN
TOPGUN
TRIGON
TROGON
VAUGHN
VIRGIN
WAGGON
YANGON

••••GN
ASSIGN
BENIGN
COSIGN
DESIGN
ELOIGN
ENSIGN
IMPUGN
MALIGN
OPPUGN
REPUGN
RESIGN

GO••••
GOADED
GOALIE
GOANNA
GOATEE
GOAWAY
GOAWRY
GOBACK
GOBBLE
GOBIES
GOBLET
GOBLIN
GOBUST
GOCART
GODARD
GODETS
GODIVA
GODOWN
GODSON
GODWIN
GODWIT
GOEASY
GOESAT
GOESBY
GOESIN
GOESON
GOESUP
GOETHE
GOFERS
GOFISH
GOGGLE
GOGGLY
GOHOME
GOINGS
GOINTO
GOKART
GOLDEN
GOLDIE
GOLEMS
GOLFED
GOLFER
GOLLUM
GONEBY
GONERS
GONGED
GONOGO
GOOBER
GOODBY
GOODEN
GOODIE
GOODLY
GOOFED
GOOFUP
GOOGLE
GOOGLY
GOOGOL
GOOGOO
GOOIER
GOOSED
GOOSES
GOOVER
GOPHER
GORALS
GORDIE
GORDON
GORGED
GORGES
GORGET
GORGON
GORIER
GORING
GORSES
GOSHEN
GOSLOW
GOSOFT
GOSPEL
GOSSIP
GOSTAG
GOTCHA
GOTHAM
GOTHIC
GOTMAD
GOTOFF
GOTOIT
GOTOUT
GOTTEN
GOUGED
GOUGER
GOUGES
GOULET
GOUNOD
GOURDE
GOURDS
GOVERN
GOWEST
GOWILD
GOWITH
GOWNED

G•O•••
GEODES
GEORGE
GHOSTS
GHOULS
GIOTTO
GLOATS
GLOBAL
GLOBED
GLOBES
GLOBIN
GLOGGS
GLOOMS
GLOOMY
GLOPPY
GLORIA
GLOSSA
GLOSSY
GLOVED
GLOVER
GLOVES
GLOWED
GLOWER
GNOMES
GNOMIC
GNOMON
GNOSIS
GOOBER
GOODBY
GOODEN
GOODIE
GOODLY
GOOFED
GOOFUP
GOOGLE
GOOGLY
GOOGOL
GOOGOO
GOOIER
GOOSED
GOOSES
GOOVER
GROANS
GROATS
GROCER
GRODIN
GROGGY
GROINS
GROOMS
GROOVE
GROOVY
GROPED
GROPES
GROSSE
GROSSO
GROSZY
GROTTO
GROTTY
GROUCH
GROUND
GROUPS
GROUSE
GROUTS
GROUTY
GROVEL
GROVER
GROVES
GROWER
GROWLS
GROWLY
GROWON
GROWTH
GROWUP
GROZNY

G••O••
GALOIS
GALOOT
GALOPS
GALORE
GALOSH
GATORS
GENOAN
GENOME
GERONT
GETOFF
GETOUT
GIGOLO
GIGOTS
GIJOES
GLOOMS
GLOOMY
GLUONS
GODOWN
GOHOME
GONOGO
GOSOFT
GOTOFF
GOTOIT
GOTOUT
GROOMS
GROOVE
GROOVY
GUYOTS
GYRONS
GYROSE

G•••O•
GABION
GAINON
GALLON
GALLOP
GALOOT
GAMBOL
GAMMON
GARCON
GARSON
GASCON
GASLOG
GASTON
GAYNOR
GECKOS
GETSON
GIBBON
GIBSON
GIDEON
GIZMOS
GLAMOR
GLYCOL
GMAJOR
GMINOR
GNOMON
GODSON
GOESON
GOOGOL
GOOGOO
GORDON
GORGON
GOSLOW
GOUNOD
GREGOR
GREWON
GRISON
GROWON
GUACOS
GUENON
GUIDON
GUMBOS
GUNDOG
GUNFOR

G••••O
GABBRO
GASTRO
GAUCHO
GAZEBO
GEARTO
GELATO
GETSTO
GHETTO
GIGOLO
GINKGO
GIOTTO
GITANO
GOINTO
GONOGO
GOOGOO
GRAECO
GRASSO
GRINGO
GROSSO
GROTTO
GUNGHO

•GO•••
AGORAE
AGORAS
AGOROT
AGOUTI
EGOISM
EGOIST

•G•O••
AGEOLD
EGMONT
IGLOOS
IGNORE
OGDOAD

•G••O•
AGOROT
EGGNOG
EGGSON
IGLOOS

••GO••
ALGORE
ANGOLA
ANGORA
ARGOSY
ARGOTS
BEGOFF
BEGONE
BIGOTS
BOGONG
BOGOTA
BUGOFF
BUGOUT
BYGONE
BYGOSH
DIGOUT
DOGONS
DOGOOD
DUGONG
DUGOUT
ERGOTS
FAGOTS
GIGOLO
GIGOTS
INGOTS
LAGOON
LOGOFF
LOGOUT
LUGOSI
MEGOHM
NAGOYA
NOGOOD
OSGOOD
PAGODA
PIGOUT
RAGOUT
RIGORS
RIGOUR
RUGOSE
TAGORE

TAGOUT VIGODA VIGOUR WAGONS WIGOUT ZYGOTE

••G•O•

ANGKOR ANGLOS BIGBOY BIGTOE BIGTOP DIGLOT DOGOOD EGGNOG EGGSON FOGBOW LAGOON LEGION LOGION LOGSON MAGNON MIGNON MUGHOS NOGOOD OSGOOD PEGTOP PIGEON RAGMOP RAGTOP REGION SIGNON SIGNOR TIGLON WAGGON

••G••O

ANGELO BAGUIO FIGARO GIGOLO LEGATO MAGGIO MEGALO NAGANO RIGHTO

•••GO•

AMIGOS ARAGON BANGOR BONGOS BURGOO BURGOS CARGOS CHIGOE CONGOU DRAGON FLAGON FORGOT GOOGOL GOOGOO GORGON GREGOR HANGON HUNGON ISOGON JARGON LARGOS MANGOS MARGOT MONGOL MUNGOS OREGON SAIGON SARGON SARGOS SPIGOT SUNGOD TANGOS TINGOD TRIGON TROGON TURGOR WAGGON WARGOD YANGON

•••G•O

ADAGIO BURGOO DAYGLO GOOGOO GUNGHO MAGGIO NINGBO PLAGIO SANGTO SERGIO SINGTO SLUGGO YUNGLO

••••GO

ATERGO BOINGO COLUGO DIRIGO ERYNGO FOREGO GINKGO GONOGO GRINGO INDIGO LATIGO LETSGO NONEGO OLINGO OSWEGO PAPAGO SLUGGO TOBAGO VIRAGO

G•P•••

GAPERS GAPING GAPPED GIPPED GIPPER GOPHER GYPPED GYPPER GYPSUM

G••P••

GAPPED GASPAR GASPED GIPPED GIPPER GLOPPY GLYPHS GOSPEL GRAPES GRAPHS GRAPPA GRIPED GRIPER GRIPES GRIPPE GROPED GROPES GULPED GULPER GYPPED GYPPER

G•••P•

GALOPS GETUPS GLOPPY GRAMPS GRAPPA GRASPS GRIPPE GROUPS GRUMPS GRUMPY GUELPH GUIMPE

G••••P

GALLOP GALLUP GANGUP GASCAP GAVEUP GEARUP GETSUP GIVEUP GOESUP GOOFUP GOSSIP GREWUP GROWUP GSHARP GUMSUP

•G•••P

EGGCUP

••GP••

MAGPIE PIGPEN

••G••P

BIGTOP DIGSUP EGGCUP HIGHUP MEGILP PEGTOP RAGMOP RAGTOP RIGSUP SIGNUP TAGSUP

•••G•P

BANGUP CLOGUP GANGUP HANGUP HUNGUP RANGUP RINGUP RUNGUP

••G••Q

HIGHIQ

GR••••

GRABAT GRABBY GRABEN GRABLE GRACED GRACES GRACIE GRADEA GRADED GRADER GRADES GRADIN GRADUS GRAECO GRAFTS GRAHAM GRAILS GRAINS GRAINY GRAMAS GRAMME GRAMMY GRAMPS GRANDE GRANDS GRANGE GRANNY GRANTS GRAPES GRAPHS GRAPPA GRASPS GRASSO GRASSY GRATED GRATER GRATES GRATIA GRATIN GRATIS GRAVED GRAVEL GRAVEN GRAVER GRAVES GRAVID GRAYED GRAYER GRAZED GRAZER GRAZES GREASE GREASY GREATS GREAVE GREBES GREECE GREEDY GREEKS GREENE GREENS GREENY GREETS GREGOR GREIGE GRETEL GRETNA GREWON GREWUP GREYED GREYER GRIEVE GRIGRI GRILLE GRILLS GRILSE GRIMED GRIMES GRIMKE GRIMLY GRINCH GRINDS GRINGO GRIPED GRIPER GRIPES GRIPPE GRISLY GRISON GRISTS GRITTY GRIVET GROANS GROATS GROCER GRODIN GROGGY GROINS GROOMS GROOVE GROOVY GROPED GROPES GROSSE GROSSO GROSZY GROTTO GROTTY GROUCH GROUND GROUPS GROUSE GROUTS GROUTY GROVEL GROVER GROVES GROWER GROWLS GROWLY GROWON GROWTH GROWUP GROZNY GRUBBY GRUDGE GRUELS GRUMPS GRUMPY GRUNDY GRUNGE GRUNGY GRUNTS

G•R•••

GARAGE GARBED GARBLE GARCIA GARCON GARDEN GARETH GARGLE GARISH GARLIC GARNER GARNET GARRET GARSON GARTER GARTHS GARVEY GERALD GERARD GERBER GERBIL GERENT GERMAN GERONT GERTIE GERUND GIRARD GIRDED GIRDER GIRDLE GIRTED GIRTHS GORALS GORDIE GORDON GORGED GORGES GORGET GORGON GORIER GORING GORSES GURGLE GURKHA GURLEY GURNEY GYRATE GYRENE GYRONS GYROSE

G••R••

GARRET GEARED GEARTO GEARUP GEHRIG GENRES GEORGE GHARRY GIBRAN GLARED GLARES GLORIA GNARLS GNARLY GOURDE GOURDS GUARDS GUDRUN GUERRE

G•••R•

GABBRO GALORE GANTRY GAPERS GASTRO GATERS GATORS GEMARA GENERA GENTRY GERARD GEZIRA GHARRY GIBERS GIRARD GIVERS GLAIRY GLUERS GOAWRY GOCART GODARD GOFERS GOKART GONERS GOVERN GRIGRI GSHARP GUERRE

G••••R

GABBER GADDER GAFFER GAINER GAITER GAMIER GANDER GARNER GARTER GASPAR GASSER GATHER GAUGER GAWKER GAYNOR GEEZER GEIGER GENDER GERBER GETTER GEYSER GIBBER GILDER GINGER GIPPER GIRDER GLAMOR GLASER GLAZER GLIDER GLOVER GLOWER GMAJOR GMINOR GNAWER GOLFER GOOBER GOOIER GOOVER GOPHER GORIER GOUGER GRADER GRATER GRAVER GRAYER GRAZER GREGOR GREYER GRIPER GROCER GROVER GROWER GUITAR GULPER GUNFOR GUNNAR GUNNER GUNTER GUSHER GUTTER GYPPER

•GR•••

AGREED AGREES EGRESS EGRETS OGRESS UGRIAN

•G•R••

AGARIC AGORAE AGORAS AGOROT BGIRLS EGERIA

•G••R•

AGLARE EGBERT IGNORE OGLERS

•G•••R

AGADIR UGLIER

••GR••

AIGRET BIGRED DEGREE DIGRAM EAGRES ENGRAM INGRES INGRID LEGREE MCGRAW MCGREW PUGREE RAGRUG REGRET TIGRIS TUGRIK ZAGREB

••G•R•

ALGORE ANGERS ANGORA ASGARD AUGERS AUGURS AUGURY BOGART CAGERS CIGARS EDGARD EDGARS EDGERS ENGIRD ENGIRT FIGARO FIGURE FUGARD HEGARI HEGIRA KAGERA LAGERS LIGERS LIGURE LUGERS MEGARA MYGIRL PAGERS REGARD RIGORS ROGERS SEGURA SIGURD SUGARS SUGARY TAGORE TIGERS UIGURS UNGIRD UNGIRT URGERS VAGARY WAGERS YOGURT

••G••R

ANGKOR ANGLER ARGUER BAGGER BEGGAR BIGGER BIGSUR BUGLER CAGIER DAGGER DIGGER DOGEAR DOGGER EDGIER FOGGER HIGHER HUGGER INGEAR INGMAR JAGGER JAGUAR JIGGER JOGGER KEGLER LAGGER LOGGER LOGIER LUGGER MAGYAR MUGGER NAGGER NIGHER PEGLER RIGGER RIGOUR SIGHER SIGNER SIGNOR TIGGER TUGGER VAGUER VIGOUR WAGNER

•••GR•

ALEGRE EMIGRE GRIGRI HUNGRY MEAGRE

•••G•R

ALEGAR ANSGAR BADGER BAGGER BANGER BANGOR BEGGAR BIGGER BOLGER BULGAR BULGUR BURGER CADGER CODGER CONGER COUGAR DAGGER DANGER DIGGER DODGER DOGGER FINGER FOGGER FORGER GAUGER GEIGER GINGER GOUGER GREGOR HANGAR HANGER HEDGER HUGGER HUNGER IMAGER JAEGER JAGGER JIGGER JOGGER KRUGER LAAGER LAGGER LANGUR LARGER LEDGER LINGER LODGER LOGGER LONGER LUGGER MANGER MEAGER MEDGAR MERGER MONGER MUGGER NAGGER NUDGER ONAGER RANGER RIGGER RINGER RUTGER SANGER SAUGER SEEGER SINGER STAGER TIGGER TUGGER TURGOR VERGER VULGAR WINGER YEAGER ZENGER ZINGER

GS••••

GSHARP GSTAAD GSUITS

G•S•••

GASBAG GASCAP GASCON GASHED GASHES GASJET GASKET GASKIN GASLIT GASLOG GASMAN GASMEN GASPAR GASPED GASSED GASSER GASSES GASTON GASTRO GESTES GOSHEN GOSLOW GOSOFT GOSPEL GOSSIP GOSTAG GUSHED GUSHER GUSHES GUSSET GUSTAV GUSTED

G••S••

GARSON GASSED GASSER GASSES GATSBY GEISEL GEISHA GELSEY GETSAT GETSBY GETSET GETSIN GETSIT GETSON GETSTO GETSUP GEYSER GHOSTS GIBSON GLASER GLASSY GLOSSA GLOSSY GNOSIS GODSON GOESAT GOESBY GOESIN GOESON GOESUP GOOSED GOOSES GORSES GOSSIP GRASPS GRASSO GRASSY GRISLY GRISON GRISTS GROSSE GROSSO GROSZY GUESTS GUISES GUMSUP GUNSHY GUSSET GYPSUM

G•••S•

GAINST GALOSH GAMEST GARISH GAYEST GDANSK GLASSY GLOSSA GLOSSY GNEISS GOBUST GOEASY GOFISH GOWEST GRASSO GRASSY GREASE GREASY GRILSE GROSSE GROSSO GROUSE GYROSE

G••••S

GABLES GAFFES GALOIS GALOPS GAMAYS GAMINS GAMMAS GAMUTS GANGES GAPERS GARTHS GASHES GASSES GATERS GATORS GAUGES GAUZES GAVELS GAYALS GECKOS GELEES GENETS GENIES GENIUS GENRES GEODES GESTES GETUPS GHAZIS GHOSTS GHOULS GIANTS GIBERS GIGOTS GIGUES GIJOES GILLIS GIMELS GIRTHS GIVENS GIVERS GIZMOS GLACES GLACIS GLADES GLADYS GLANDS GLARES GLAZES GLEAMS GLEANS GLEBES GLIDES GLINTS GLOATS GLOBES GLOGGS GLOOMS GLOVES GLUERS GLUONS GLYPHS GNARLS GNEISS GNOMES GNOSIS GOBIES GODETS GOFERS GOINGS GOLEMS GONERS GOOSES GORALS GORGES GORSES GOUGES GOURDS GRACES GRADES GRADUS GRAFTS GRAILS GRAINS GRAMAS GRAMPS GRANDS GRANTS GRAPES GRAPHS GRASPS GRATES GRATIS GRAVES GRAZES GREATS GREBES GREEKS GREENS GREETS GRILLS GRIMES GRINDS GRIPES GRISTS GROANS GROATS GROINS GROOMS GROPES GROUPS GROUTS GROVES GROWLS GRUELS GRUMPS GRUNTS GSUITS GUACOS GUARDS GUAVAS GUESTS GUIDES GUILDS GUILES GUISES GULAGS GUMBOS GUSHES GUYOTS GYRONS

•G•S••

AGASSI EGESTA EGESTS EGGSON

•G••S•

AGASSI AGEISM AGEIST AGHAST EGOISM EGOIST EGRESS OGRESS

•G•••S

AGAMAS AGATES AGAVES AGENAS AGENTS AGGIES AGLETS AGORAS AGREES BGIRLS EGESTS EGRESS EGRETS IGLOOS OGHAMS OGIVES OGLERS OGRESS UGGAMS UGLIES

••GS••

BIGSUR DIGSIN DIGSUP DOGSIT EGGSON FOGSIN JIGSAW LOGSIN LOGSON PIGSTY RIGSUP TAGSUP

••G•S•

ARGOSY AUGUST BYGOSH DEGUST DIGEST HUGEST INGEST LAGASH LEGIST LUGOSI RUGOSE SAGEST

••G••S

AGGIES ANGELS ANGERS ANGLES ANGLOS ARGOTS ARGUES AUGERS AUGHTS AUGURS BAGELS BEGETS BEGINS BEGUMS BIGHTS BIGOTS BOGEYS BOGIES BOGLES BUGLES CAGERS CAGUAS CIGARS CYGNUS DIGITS DOGIES DOGMAS DOGONS EAGLES EAGRES EDGARS EDGERS EIGHTS ENGELS ERGOTS FAGOTS FIGHTS FOGEYS FOGIES FUGUES GIGOTS GIGUES HAGGIS HOGANS HUGHES INGLES INGOTS INGRES LAGERS LEGALS

LIGERS
LIGHTS
LUGERS
MAGMAS
MOGULS
MUGHOS
NIGHTS
ORGANS
ORGIES
OUGHTS
PAGANS
PAGERS
POGIES
REGIUS
RIGHTS
RIGORS
ROGERS
ROGUES
SEGUES
SIGHTS
SIGILS
SIGMAS
SUGARS
TIGERS
TIGHTS
TIGRIS
UGGAMS
UIGURS
UNGUES
UNGUIS
URGERS
VEGANS
VIGILS
VOGUES
WAGERS
WAGONS
WIGHTS

•••G•S
ADAGES
ALIGNS
AMIGOS
BADGES
BARGES
BEIGES
BILGES
BINGES
BIOGAS
BONGOS
BOUGHS
BRIGGS
BRUGES
BUDGES
BULGES
BURGAS
BURGHS
BURGOS
CADGES
CARGOS
CONGAS
CORGIS
COUGHS
DEIGNS
DINGUS
DIRGES
DODGES
DOUGHS
FEIGNS
FERGUS
FORGES
FUDGES
FUNGUS
GANGES
GAUGES
GLOGGS
GORGES
GOUGES
HAGGIS
HEDGES
HINGES
IMAGES
JUDGES
KEDGES
LARGOS
LAUGHS
LEDGES
LIEGES
LODGES
LONGES
LUNGES
MANGOS
MERGES
MIDGES
MUNGOS
NEIGHS
NUDGES
OMEGAS
OSAGES
PHAGES
PLAGES
PURGES
RANGES
REIGNS
RIDGES
ROUGES
ROUGHS
SAIGAS
SARGES
SARGOS
SEDGES
SERGES
SIEGES
SINGES
SOUGHS
STAGES
SURGES
SWAGES
TAIGAS
TANGOS
TARGES
THIGHS
TINGES
TOUGHS
USAGES
VERGES
VOSGES
VSIGNS
WEDGES
WEIGHS

••••GS
BEFOGS
BEINGS
BRIGGS
BRINGS
CLANGS
CLINGS
DEBUGS
DEFOGS
DOINGS
DRINGS
FLINGS
GLOGGS
GOINGS
GULAGS
HMONGS
ICINGS
KIANGS
LIANGS
ORANGS
ORINGS
PRONGS
REBAGS
REPEGS
RETAGS
SCRAGS
SHRUGS
SLANGS
SLINGS
SPRAGS
SPRIGS
STINGS
SWINGS
THINGS
THONGS
TWANGS
UNPEGS
UNRIGS
WRINGS
WRONGS

G•T•••
GATEAU
GATERS
GATHER
GATING
GATLIN
GATORS
GATSBY
GETOFF
GETOUT
GETSAT
GETSBY
GETSET
GETSIN
GETSIT
GETSON
GETSTO
GETSUP
GETTER
GETUPS
GITANO
GOTCHA
GOTHAM
GOTHIC
GOTMAD
GOTOFF
GOTOIT
GOTOUT
GOTTEN
GSTAAD
GUTTAE
GUTTED
GUTTER

G••T••
GAITED
GAITER
GANTRY
GARTER
GARTHS
GASTON
GASTRO
GENTLE
GENTLY
GENTRY
GERTIE
GESTES
GETTER
GHETTO
GIFTED
GIOTTO
GIRTED
GIRTHS
GLITCH
GLITZY
GLUTEI
GLUTEN
GOATEE
GOETHE
GOSTAG
GOTTEN
GRATED
GRATER
GRATES
GRATIA
GRATIN
GRATIS
GRETEL
GRETNA
GRITTY
GROTTO
GROTTY
GUITAR
GUNTER
GUSTAV
GUSTED
GUTTAE
GUTTED
GUTTER

G•••T•
GAIETY
GALATA
GAMETE
GAMUTS
GARETH
GEARTO
GELATI
GELATO
GENETS
GETSTO
GHETTO
GHOSTS
GIANTS
GIGOTS
GIOTTO
GLINTS
GLOATS
GODETS
GOINTO
GOWITH
GRAFTS
GRANTS
GREATS
GREETS
GRISTS
GRITTY
GROATS
GROTTO
GROTTY
GROUTS
GROUTY
GROWTH
GRUNTS
GSUITS
GUESTS
GUILTY
GUYOTS
GYRATE

G••••T
GADGET
GAINST
GALOOT
GAMBIT
GAMEST
GANNET
GARNET
GARRET
GASJET
GASKET
GASLIT
GAYEST
GERENT
GERONT
GETOUT
GETSAT
GETSET
GETSIT
GIBBET
GIBLET
GIDGET
GIMLET
GOBLET
GOBUST
GOCART
GODWIT
GOESAT
GOKART
GORGET
GOSOFT
GOTOIT
GOTOUT
GOULET
GOWEST
GRABAT
GRIVET
GULLET
GUSSET

•GT•••
SGTMAJ

•G•T••
AGATES
AGATHA
IGETIT

•G••T•
AGENTS
AGLETS
AGNATE
AGOUTI
EGESTA
EGESTS
EGRETS
IGNATZ
IGNITE

•G•••T
AGEIST
AGHAST
AGLINT
AGOROT
EGBERT
EGMONT
EGOIST
IGETIT

••GT••
BIGTEN
BIGTOE
BIGTOP
DOGTAG
HOGTIE
PEGTOP
RAGTAG
RAGTOP

••G•T•
ARGOTS
AUGHTS
BEGETS
BIGHTS
BIGOTS
BOGOTA
DIGITS
EIGHTH
EIGHTS
EIGHTY
ERGATE
ERGOTS
FAGOTS
FIGHTS
GIGOTS
INGOTS
LEGATE
LEGATO
LIGATE
LIGHTS
MIGHTY
NEGATE
NIGHTS
NIGHTY
ORGATE
OUGHTS
PIGSTY
RIGHTO
RIGHTS
RUGATE
SIGHTS
TIGHTS
WIGHTS
ZYGOTE

••G••T
AIGRET
ARGENT
AUGUST
BOGART
BUGOUT
COGENT
CYGNET
DEGUST
DIGEST
DIGLOT
DIGOUT
DOGSIT
DUGOUT
EAGLET
ENGIRT
ENGLUT
FOGHAT
HUGEST
INGEST
LEGIST
LOGOUT
LUGNUT
MAGNET
NUGENT
NUGGET
ORGEAT
PIGLET
PIGNUT
PIGOUT
RAGOUT
REGENT
REGLET
REGRET
SAGEST
SIGNET
TAGOUT
UNGIRT
URGENT
WIGLET
WIGOUT
YOGURT

•••GT•
LENGTH
SANGTO
SINGTO

•••G•T
ALIGHT
ARIGHT
BIRGIT
BLIGHT
BOUGHT
BRIGHT
BUDGET
CATGUT
CAUGHT
DWIGHT
ELEGIT
FIDGET
FLIGHT
FORGET
FORGOT
FOUGHT
FRIGHT
GADGET
GIDGET
GORGET
HAIGHT
HEIGHT
KNIGHT
MARGOT
MIDGET
NAUGHT
NOUGAT
NOUGHT
NUGGET
PARGET
PIAGET
PLIGHT
ROTGUT
SLIGHT
SOUGHT
SPIGOT
TARGET
TAUGHT
VEIGHT
VOIGHT
WEIGHT
WIDGET
WINGIT
WRIGHT

GU••••
GUACOS
GUARDS
GUAVAS
GUDRUN
GUELPH
GUENON
GUERRE
GUESTS
GUFFAW
GUIANA
GUIDED
GUIDES
GUIDON
GUILDS
GUILES
GUILTY
GUIMPE
GUINEA
GUISES
GUITAR
GULAGS
GULFED
GULLAH
GULLED
GULLET
GULPED
GULPER
GUMBEL
GUMBOS
GUMMED
GUMSUP
GUNDOG
GUNFOR
GUNGHO
GUNMAN
GUNMEN
GUNNAR
GUNNED
GUNNEL
GUNNER
GUNSHY
GUNTER
GURGLE
GURKHA
GURLEY
GURNEY
GUSHED
GUSHER
GUSHES
GUSSET
GUSTAV
GUSTED
GUTTAE
GUTTED
GUTTER
GUYANA
GUYING
GUYOTS
GUZZLE

G•U•••
GAUCHE
GAUCHO
GAUGED
GAUGER
GAUGES
GAUZED
GAUZES
GLUERS
GLUING
GLUMLY
GLUONS
GLUTEI
GLUTEN
GOUGED
GOUGER
GOUGES
GOULET
GOUNOD
GOURDE
GOURDS
GRUBBY
GRUDGE
GRUELS
GRUMPS
GRUMPY
GRUNDY
GRUNGE
GRUNGY
GRUNTS
GSUITS

G••U••
GAMUTS
GENUAL
GERUND
GETUPS
GHOULS
GIGUES
GOBUST
GROUCH
GROUND
GROUPS
GROUSE
GROUTS
GROUTY

G•••U•
GALLUP
GANGUE
GANGUP
GAVEUP
GEARUP
GENIUS
GETOUT
GETSUP
GIVEUP
GOESUP
GOLLUM
GOOFUP
GOTOUT
GRADUS
GREWUP
GROWUP
GUDRUN
GUMSUP
GYPSUM

G••••U
GATEAU

•GU•••
IGUACU
IGUANA
NGUYEN

•G•U••
AGOUTI

•G••U•
EGGCUP

•G•••U
IGUACU

••GU••
ARGUED
ARGUER
ARGUES
AUGURS
AUGURY
AUGUST
BAGUIO
BEGUMS
CAGUAS
DEGUST
ENGULF
FIGURE
FUGUES
GIGUES
JAGUAR
LAGUNA
LEGUME
LIGULA
LIGURE
MAGUEY
MIGUEL
MOGULS
ROGUES
SEGUED
SEGUES
SEGURA
SIGURD
UIGURS
UNGUAL
UNGUES
UNGUIS
VAGUER
VOGUES
YOGURT

••G•U•
BAGFUL
BIGGUN
BIGSUR
BUGOUT
CYGNUS
DIGOUT
DIGSUP
DUGOUT
EGGCUP
ENGLUT
HIGHUP
JUGFUL
LOGOUT
LUGNUT
MAGNUM
PIGNUT
PIGOUT
RAGOUT
RAGRUG
REGIUS
REGLUE
RIGOUR
RIGSUP
SIGNUP
TAGOUT
TAGSUP
UNGLUE
VIGOUR
WIGOUT

•••GU•
AIRGUN
ARTGUM
BADGUY
BANGUI
BANGUP
BEEGUM
BIGGUN
BROGUE
BULGUR
CAPGUN
CATGUT
CLOGUP
DENGUE
DINGUS
DROGUE
FERGUS
FUNGUS
GANGUE
GANGUP
HANGUL
HANGUP
HUNGUP
JETGUN
LANGUR
LEAGUE
LINGUA
LONGUE
OUTGUN
PLAGUE
POPGUN
PRAGUE
RANGUP
RAYGUN
REDGUM
RINGUP
ROTGUT
RUNGUP
SHOGUN
SIXGUN
SUBGUM
TANGUY
TONGUE
TOPGUN

•••G•U
CONGOU
HUNGWU
KUNGFU
PENGHU

••••GU
TELUGU

G•V•••
GAVEIN
GAVELS
GAVEUP
GAVIAL
GIVEIN
GIVENS
GIVERS
GIVEUP
GIVING
GOVERN

G••V••
GARVEY
GLOVED
GLOVER
GLOVES
GOOVER
GRAVED
GRAVEL
GRAVEN
GRAVER
GRAVES
GRAVID
GRIVET
GROVEL
GROVER
GROVES
GUAVAS

G•••V•
GENEVA
GENEVE
GODIVA
GREAVE
GRIEVE
GROOVE
GROOVY

G••••V
GUSTAV

•G•V••
AGAVES
OGIVES

••G•V•
ARGIVE

GW••••
GWYNNE

G•W•••
GAWAIN
GAWKED
GAWKER
GEWGAW
GOWEST
GOWILD
GOWITH
GOWNED

G••W••
GALWAY
GLOWED
GLOWER
GNAWED
GNAWER
GOAWAY
GOAWRY
GODWIN
GODWIT
GREWON
GREWUP
GROWER
GROWLS
GROWLY
GROWON
GROWTH
GROWUP

G•••W•
GODOWN

G••••W
GAGLAW
GEEGAW
GEWGAW
GOSLOW
GUFFAW

••GW••
BIGWIG
WIGWAG
WIGWAM

••G••W
FOGBOW
GAGLAW
JIGSAW
MCGRAW
MCGREW

•••GW•
HUNGWU

•••G•W
GEEGAW
GEWGAW

G•••X•
GALAXY

GY••••
GYPPED
GYPPER
GYPSUM
GYRATE
GYRENE
GYRONS
GYROSE

G•Y•••
GAYALS
GAYEST
GAYNOR
GEYSER
GLYCOL
GLYPHS
GUYANA
GUYING
GUYOTS
GWYNNE

G••Y••
GALYAK
GRAYED
GRAYER
GREYED
GREYER

G•••Y•
GAMAYS
GLADYS

G••••Y
GADFLY
GAIETY
GAINLY
GALAXY
GALLEY
GALWAY
GAMELY
GAMILY
GANGLY
GANTRY
GARVEY
GATSBY
GELSEY
GENTLY
GENTRY
GETSBY
GHARRY
GIGGLY
GLADLY
GLAIRY
GLASSY
GLIBLY
GLITZY
GLOOMY
GLOPPY
GLOSSY
GLUMLY
GNARLY
GOAWAY
GOAWRY
GOEASY
GOESBY
GOGGLY
GONEBY
GOODBY
GOODLY
GOOGLY
GRABBY
GRAINY
GRAMMY
GRANNY
GRASSY
GREASY
GREEDY
GREENY
GRIMLY
GRISLY
GRITTY
GROGGY
GROOVY
GROSZY
GROTTY
GROUTY
GROWLY
GROZNY
GRUBBY
GRUMPY
GRUNDY
GRUNGY
GUILTY
GUNSHY
GURLEY
GURNEY

•G•Y••
NGUYEN

•G•••Y
AGENCY
UGLIFY

••GY••
ARGYLE
ARGYLL
MAGYAR

••G•Y•
BOGEYS
FOGEYS
NAGOYA

••G••Y
ARGOSY
AUGURY
BEGLEY
BIGAMY
BIGBOY
CAGILY
CAGNEY
EDGILY
EIGHTY
GIGGLY
GOGGLY
HIGHLY
HUGELY
JIGGLY
LEGACY
LOGILY
MAGUEY
MIGHTY
NIGHTY
PIGSTY
SAGELY
SUGARY
TAGDAY
VAGARY
WAGGLY
WIGGLY

•••G•Y
BADGUY
BENGAY
BOIGNY
CRAGGY
DANGLY
DINGHY
DOUGHY
DRAGGY
FLAGGY
FROGGY
GANGLY
GIGGLY
GOGGLY
GOOGLY
GROGGY
HUNGRY
JANGLY
JIGGLY
JINGLY
JUNGLY
KINGLY
MARGAY
NORGAY
QUAGGY
SHAGGY
SINGLY
SLAGGY
SMOGGY
SMUGLY
SNAGGY
SNUGLY
TANGLY
TANGUY
TINGLY
TOUGHY
TRIGLY
TWIGGY
WAGGLY
WIGGLY

••••GY
CLERGY
CLINGY
CRAGGY
DRAGGY
EFFIGY
ENERGY
EULOGY
FLAGGY
FRINGY
FROGGY
GROGGY
GRUNGY
OOLOGY
QUAGGY
SHAGGY
SLAGGY
SLANGY
SLUDGY
SMOGGY
SMUDGY
SNAGGY
SPONGY
STINGY
STODGY
SWINGY
SYZYGY
TWANGY
TWIGGY

G•Z•••
GAZEBO
GAZING
GEZIRA
GIZMOS
GUZZLE

G••Z••
GAUZED
GAUZES
GEEZER
GHAZIS
GLAZED
GLAZER
GLAZES
GRAZED
GRAZER
GRAZES

GROZNY
GUZZLE

G•••Z•
GLITZY
GROSZY

•G•••Z
IGNATZ

••GZ••
ZIGZAG

HA••••
HABANA
HABEAS
HABILE
HABITS
HACEKS
HACKED
HACKER
HACKIE
HACKLE
HADDIE
HADJES
HADJIS
HADRON
HAEMAT
HAEMON
HAFTED
HAGGIS
HAGGLE
HAGMAN
HAIDAS
HAIGHT
HAIKOU
HAIKUS
HAILED
HAILEY
HAINAN
HAINES
HAIRDO
HAIRED
HAJJES
HAJJIS
HAKIMS
HALERS
HALERU
HALEST
HALEVY
HALIDE
HALING
HALITE
HALLEL
HALLEY
HALLOO
HALLOS
HALLOW
HALLUX
HALOED
HALOES
HALOID
HALSEY
HALTED
HALTER
HALVAH
HALVED
HALVES
HAMALS
HAMILL
HAMITE
HAMLET
HAMLIN
HAMMED
HAMMER
HAMPER
HANDED
HANDEL
HANDIN
HANDLE
HANDON
HANGAR
HANGED
HANGER
HANGIN
HANGON
HANGUL
HANGUP
HANKER
HANKIE
HANNAH
HANSEL
HANSOM
HANSON
HAPPEN
HARARE
HARASS
HARBIN
HARBOR
HARDEN
HARDER
HARDLY
HARDUP
HAREMS
HARING
HARKED
HARKEN
HARKER
HARLAN
HARLEM
HARLEY
HARLOW
HARMED
HARMON
HAROLD
HARPED
HARPER
HARPON
HARRIS
HARROW
HARVEY
HASBRO
HASHED
HASHES
HASPED
HASSAM
HASSAN
HASSLE
HASTEN
HASTES
HATARI
HATBOX
HATERS
HATHOR
HATING
HATPIN
HATRED
HATTED
HATTER
HATTIE
HAULED
HAULER
HAULUP
HAUNCH
HAUNTS
HAUSAS
HAVANA
HAVASU
HAVEAT
HAVENS
HAVENT
HAVEON
HAVING
HAVOCS
HAWAII
HAWHAW
HAWING
HAWKED
HAWKER
HAWSER
HAWSES
HAYDEN
HAYING
HAYLEY
HAYMOW
HAZANS
HAZARD
HAZELS
HAZERS
HAZIER
HAZILY
HAZING

H•A•••
HEADED
HEADER
HEADIN
HEADON
HEADUP
HEALED
HEALER
HEALTH
HEAPED
HEARER
HEAROF
HEARST
HEARTH
HEARTS
HEARTY
HEARYE
HEATED
HEATER
HEATHS
HEATUP
HEAVED
HEAVEN
HEAVER
HEAVES
HIATAL
HIATUS
HOAGIE
HOARDS
HOARSE
HOAXED
HOAXER
HOAXES
HYADES

H••A••
HABANA
HAMALS
HARARE
HARASS
HATARI
HAVANA
HAVASU
HAWAII
HAZANS
HAZARD
HBEAMS
HECATE
HEGARI
HEMATO
HERALD
HEXADS
HIJACK
HILARY
HIVAOA
HOBART
HODADS
HOGANS
HOMAGE
HORACE
HOTAIR
HOWARD
HUMANE
HUMANS

H•••A•
HABEAS
HAEMAT
HAGMAN
HAIDAS
HAINAN
HALVAH
HANGAR
HANNAH
HARLAN
HASSAM
HASSAN
HAUSAS
HAVEAT
HAWHAW
HEEHAW
HELLAS
HENNAS
HEPCAT
HEPTAD
HERBAL
HEREAT
HERMAN
HETMAN
HEYDAY
HIATAL
HIEMAL
HINTAT
HISSAT
HITMAN
HOOHAH
HOOHAS
HOOKAH
HOORAH
HOORAY
HOOTAT
HOSTAS
HOTCAP
HOTCAR
HOTWAR
HOWDAH
HUBCAP
HURRAH
HURRAY
HUSSAR
HUZZAH
HUZZAS
HYDRAE
HYDRAS
HYENAS
HYETAL
HYMNAL

H••••A
HABANA
HAVANA
HECUBA
HEGIRA
HELENA
HESTIA
HIVAOA
HOOPLA
HOTTEA

•HA•••
BHAKTI
CHACHA
CHACMA
CHADOR
CHAFED
CHAFES
CHAFFS
CHAFFY
CHAINE
CHAINS
CHAIRS
CHAISE
CHALCO
CHALET
CHALKS
CHALKY
CHAMMY
CHAMPS
CHANCE
CHANCY
CHANEL
CHANEY
CHANGE
CHANTS
CHAPEL
CHAPIN
CHARGE
CHARLY
CHARMS
CHARON
CHARRO
CHARTS
CHASED
CHASER
CHASES
CHASMS
CHASSE
CHASTE
CHATTY
CHATUP
CHAVEZ
DHARMA
GHARRY
GHAZIS
KHAFRE
KHAKIS
KHALID
PHAGES
PHAROS
PHASED
PHASER
PHASES
PHATIC
SHABAN
SHABBY
SHACKS
SHADED
SHADES
SHADOW
SHAFTS
SHAGGY
SHAKEN
SHAKER
SHAKES
SHAKOS
SHAKTI
SHALES
SHALEY
SHALLY
SHALOM
SHAMAN
SHAMED
SHAMES
SHAMIR
SHAMUS
SHANDY
SHANKS
SHANTY
SHAPED
SHAPER
SHAPES
SHARDS
SHARED
SHARER
SHARES
SHARIA
SHARIF
SHARKS
SHARON
SHARPS
SHASTA
SHAVED
SHAVEN
SHAVER
SHAVES
SHAWLS
SHAWMS
SHAYNE
SHAZAM
THALER
THALES
THALIA
THAMES
THANES
THANKS
THATCH
THATIS
THAWED
THAYER
WHACKS
WHACKY
WHALER
WHALES
WHAMMO
WHAMMY
WHARFS
WHATIF

•H•A••
CHEAPO
CHEATS
CHIANG
CHIAUS
CHOATE
PHIALS
PHRASE
SHEAFS
SHEARS
SHEATH
SHEAVE
SHOALS
SHOATS
SHRANK
THRACE
THRALE
THRALL
THRASH
THWACK
THWART
UHLANS
WHEATS

•H••A•
BHOPAL
BHUTAN
CHELAE
CHELAS
CHEVAL
CHORAL
CHUKAR
OHIOAN
OHYEAH
PHILAE
PHYLAE
RHINAL
SHABAN
SHAMAN
SHAZAM
SHEVAT
SHIRAZ
SHOFAR
SHORAN
SHOTAT
THECAE
THECAL
THEHAJ
THENAR
THETAS
THOMAS
THORAX
THREAD
THREAT
THROAT
THUJAS
WHYDAH
XHOSAS

•H•••A
AHIMSA
CHACHA
CHACMA
CHICHA
CHOLLA
CHROMA
CHUKKA
DHARMA
PHOBIA
RHONDA
RHUMBA
SHARIA
SHASTA
SHEENA
SHEILA
SHERPA
THALIA
THELMA

••HA••
ACHAEA
AGHAST
AMHARA
ASHARP
ATHAND
BAHAMA
BEHALF
BEHAVE
BIHARI
BSHARP
BYHAND
CSHARP
DSHARP
EPHAHS
ERHARD
ESHARP
ETHANE
EXHALE
FSHARP
GSHARP
INHALE
INHALF
INHAND
INHAUL
ITHACA
ITHAKI
JIHADS
JOHANN
LCHAIM
MCHALE
MOHAIR
MOHAVE
MOHAWK
OGHAMS
ONHAND
OSHAWA
PAHANG
PAHARI
REHANG
REHASH
SAHARA
UNHAND
UTHANT

••H•A•
ASHCAN
ASHLAR
ASHRAM
BAHIAN
ISHTAR
LEHUAS
MIHRAB
RAHRAH
REHEAL
REHEAR
REHEAT
SCHWAS
WAHWAH

••H••A
ACHAEA
AMHARA
ATHENA
BAHAMA
DAHLIA
ITHACA
KAHLUA
KAHUNA
OSHAWA
SAHARA
SCHEMA

•••HA•
AFGHAN
ALOHAS
ALPHAS
ASCHAM
ATTHAT
CATHAY
COBHAM
CUSHAW
DACHAS
DIRHAM
DOTHAN
DUNHAM
DURHAM
FOGHAT
GOTHAM
GRAHAM
HAWHAW
HEEHAW
HOOHAH
HOOHAS
ITZHAK
LAPHAM
LETHAL
LOTHAR
MAYHAP
MISHAP
MOCHAS
MOSHAV
NATHAN
NUCHAE
NUCHAL
OLDHAM
OLDHAT
OMAHAN
OMAHAS
ORPHAN
PASHAS
PATHAN
RASHAD
REDHAT
RODHAM
SASHAY
SOTHAT
SOWHAT
SUCHAS
THEHAJ
TINHAT
TOPHAT
UTAHAN
WITHAL

•••H•A
ALTHEA
BRAHMA
BUSHWA
ISCHIA
JOSHUA
KESHIA
NASHUA
PYTHIA
SOPHIA
TEPHRA

••••HA
AGATHA
ARETHA
AYESHA
BERTHA
BETCHA
BUDDHA
BUQSHA
CHACHA
CHICHA
CONCHA
EARTHA
ELISHA
GEISHA
GOTCHA
GURKHA
ILESHA
JASCHA
KWACHA
MANCHA
MARSHA
MARTHA
MISCHA
PERCHA
QUOTHA
TRISHA
YAMAHA

HB••••
HBEAMS
HBOMBS

H•B•••
HABANA
HABEAS
HABILE
HABITS
HEBREW
HOBART
HOBBES
HOBBIT
HOBBLE
HOBNOB
HOBOES
HOBSON
HUBBLE
HUBBLY
HUBBUB
HUBCAP
HUBERT
HUBRIS
HYBRID

H••B••
HARBIN
HARBOR
HASBRO
HATBOX
HEEBIE
HENBIT
HERBAL
HERBIE
HOBBES
HOBBIT
HOBBLE
HOMBRE
HOTBED
HOTBOX
HUBBLE
HUBBLY
HUBBUB
HUMBLE
HUMBLY
HUMBUG

H•••B•
HBOMBS
HECUBA
HEREBY

H••••B
HOBNOB
HOTTUB
HUBBUB

•HB•••
SHBOOM

•H•B••
CHUBBY
KHYBER
PHOBIA
PHOBIC
PHOBOS
RHEBOK
SHABAN
SHABBY
THEBES

•H••B•
CHUBBY
PHLEBO
PHOEBE
RHOMBI
RHOMBS
RHUMBA
RHUMBS
SHABBY
SHRUBS
THISBE
THROBS
THUMBS

•H•••B
CHERUB

••H•B•
ACHEBE
EPHEBE
SAHIBS

••H••B
MIHRAB

H•C•••
HACEKS
HACKED
HACKER
HACKIE
HACKLE
HECATE
HECKLE
HECTIC
HECTOR
HECUBA
HICCUP
HICKEY
HICKOK
HOCKED
HOCKEY

H••C••
HEPCAT
HICCUP
HONCHO
HOTCAP
HOTCAR
HUBCAP

H•••C•
HAUNCH
HAVOCS
HIJACK
HIRSCH
HITECH
HORACE

H••••C
HECTIC
HEROIC
HOMEEC

•HC•••
AHCHOO

•H•C••
CHACHA
CHACMA
CHECKS
CHICHA
CHICHI
CHICKS
CHICLE
CHOCKS
CHUCKS
PHOCIS
SHACKS
SHOCKS
SHUCKS
THECAE
THECAL
THICKE
WHACKS
WHACKY

•H••C•
CHALCO
CHANCE
CHANCY
CHEECH
CHINCH
CHOICE
CHURCH
SHTICK
THATCH
THENCE
THRACE
THRICE
THWACK
WHENCE

•H•••C
PHATIC
PHOBIC
PHONIC
PHOTIC
THETIC

••HC••
ASHCAN

••H•C•
ETHICS
ITHACA
MOHOCK
SCHICK

••H••C
ECHOIC
ETHNIC

•••HC•
BOCHCO

•••H•C
GOTHIC
LITHIC
MYTHIC
ORPHIC
UNCHIC

H•D•••
HADDIE
HADJES
HADJIS
HADRON
HEDDLE
HEDGED
HEDGER
HEDGES
HEDREN
HIDDEN
HIDEHO
HIDEKI
HIDERS
HIDING
HIDOUT
HODADS
HUDDLE
HUDSON
HYDRAE
HYDRAS
HYDROS

H••D••
HADDIE
HAIDAS
HANDED
HANDEL
HANDIN
HANDLE
HANDON
HARDEN
HARDER
HARDLY
HARDUP
HAYDEN
HEADED
HEADER
HEADIN
HEADON
HEADUP
HEDDLE
HEEDED
HEIDEN
HELDIN
HELDON
HELDTO
HELDUP
HERDED
HERDER
HEYDAY
HIDDEN
HINDER
HINDUS
HOLDEN
HOLDER
HOLDIT
HOLDON
HOLDTO
HOLDUP
HOODED
HOODOO
HORDES
HOTDOG
HOWDAH
HOYDEN
HUDDLE
HURDLE
HYADES

H•••D•
HAIRDO
HALIDE
HEXADS
HOARDS
HODADS
HOUNDS

H••••D
HACKED
HAFTED
HAILED
HAIRED
HALOED
HALOID
HALTED
HALVED
HAMMED
HANDED
HANGED
HARKED
HARMED
HAROLD
HARPED
HASHED
HASPED
HATRED
HATTED
HAULED
HAWKED
HAZARD
HEADED
HEALED
HEAPED
HEATED
HEAVED
HEDGED
HEEDED
HEELED
HEFTED
HELMED
HELPED
HEMMED
HEPTAD
HERALD
HERDED
HESIOD
HILLED
HINGED
HINTED
HIPPED
HISPID
HISSED
HOAXED
HOCKED
HOGGED
HONIED
HONKED
HOODED
HOOFED
HOOKED
HOOPED
HOOTED
HOPPED
HORNED
HORRID
HORSED
HOSTED
HOTBED
HOTROD
HOUSED
HOWARD
HOWLED
HUFFED
HUGGED
HULKED
HULLED
HUMMED
HUMPED
HUNTED
HURLED
HUSHED
HUSKED
HUTTED
HYBRID
HYMNED
HYPOED

•H•D••
CHADOR
CHIDED
CHIDES
PHEDRE
RHODES
SHADED
SHADES
SHADOW
SHODDY
WHYDAH

•H••D•
CHILDE
CHILDS
CHORDS
RHONDA
SHANDY
SHARDS
SHEEDY
SHINDY
SHODDY
SHREDS
THIRDS

•H•••D
CHAFED
CHASED
CHEWED
CHIDED
CHIMED
CHOKED
CHOWED
CHUTED
KHALID
PHASED
PHONED
PHYSED
RHYMED
SHADED
SHAMED
SHAPED
SHARED
SHAVED
SHIELD
SHINED
SHOOED
SHORED
SHOULD
SHOVED
SHOWED
SHREWD
SHROUD
THAWED
THEEND
THEFED
THEMED
THREAD
THREED
WHILED
WHINED

••HD••
MAHDIS

••H•D•
ANHYDR
APHIDS
EPHODS
JIHADS
MRHYDE
YEHUDI

••H••D
ATHAND
BEHELD
BEHIND
BEHOLD
BYHAND
ECHOED
ERHARD
INHAND
ONHAND
ONHOLD
REHELD
TEHEED

UNHAND
UNHEED
UPHELD
UPHOLD

•••H•D
AMPHID
ARCHED
BASHED
BATHED
BUSHED
CACHED
CASHED
COSHED
DASHED
DISHED
ETCHED
FISHED
GASHED
GUSHED
HASHED
HUSHED
INCHED
ITCHED
JOSHED
LASHED
LATHED
MASHED
MESHED
METHOD
MUSHED
NOSHED
ORCHID
PITHED
POOHED
PUSHED
RASHAD
RASHID
RESHOD
RUSHED
SASHED
SIGHED
TITHED
UNSHED
UNSHOD
WASHED
WISHED
WITHED

HE••••
HEADED
HEADER
HEADIN
HEADON
HEADUP
HEALED
HEALER
HEALTH
HEAPED
HEARER
HEAROF
HEARST
HEARTH
HEARTS
HEARTY
HEARYE
HEATED
HEATER
HEATHS
HEATUP
HEAVED
HEAVEN
HEAVER
HEAVES
HEBREW
HECATE
HECKLE
HECTIC
HECTOR
HECUBA
HEDDLE
HEDGED
HEDGER
HEDGES
HEDREN
HEEBIE
HEEDED
HEEHAW
HEELED
HEELER
HEFLIN
HEFNER
HEFTED
HEGARI
HEGIRA
HEIDEN
HEIFER
HEIGHT
HEISTS
HELDIN
HELDON
HELDTO
HELDUP
HELENA
HELENE
HELENS
HELIOS
HELIUM
HELLAS
HELLER
HELLOS
HELMED
HELMET
HELMUT
HELOTS
HELPED
HELPER
HELTER
HELVES
HEMATO
HEMMED
HEMMER
HEMSIN
HENBIT
HENLEY
HENNAS
HENNER
HENNIN
HENRIK
HENSON
HEPCAT
HEPPER
HEPTAD
HERALD
HERBAL
HERBIE
HERDED
HERDER
HEREAT
HEREBY
HEREIN
HEREOF
HEREON
HERESY
HERETO
HERIOT
HERMAN
HERMES
HERMIT
HERMON
HEROES
HEROIC
HERONS
HERSEY
HERZOG
HESIOD
HESTER
HESTIA
HESTON
HETERO
HETMAN
HETTIE
HEWERS
HEWING
HEXADS
HEXERS
HEXING
HEYDAY
HEYJOE
HEYYOU

H•E•••
HAEMAT
HAEMON
HBEAMS
HEEBIE
HEEDED
HEEHAW
HEELED
HEELER
HIEING
HIEMAL
HIERON
HOEING
HUEVOS
HYENAS
HYETAL

H••E••
HABEAS
HACEKS
HALERS
HALERU
HALEST
HALEVY
HAREMS
HATERS
HAVEAT
HAVENS
HAVENT
HAVEON
HAZELS
HAZERS
HELENA
HELENE
HELENS
HEREAT
HEREBY
HEREIN
HEREOF
HEREON
HERESY
HERETO
HETERO
HEWERS
HEXERS
HIDEHO
HIDEKI
HIDERS
HIKERS
HIREON
HIRERS
HITECH
HOLEUP
HOMEEC
HOMELY
HOMERS
HONEST
HONEYS
HOPERS
HOSELS
HOTELS
HOVELS
HOVERS
HOVETO
HOWELL
HUBERT
HUGELY
HUGEST
HUMERI

H•••E•
HACKED
HACKER
HADJES
HAFTED
HAILED
HAILEY
HAINES
HAIRED
HAJJES
HALLEL
HALLEY
HALOED
HALOES
HALSEY
HALTED
HALTER
HALVED
HALVES
HAMLET
HAMMED
HAMMER
HAMPER
HANDED
HANDEL
HANGED
HANGER
HANKER
HANSEL
HAPPEN
HARDEN
HARDER
HARKED
HARKEN
HARKER
HARLEM
HARLEY
HARMED
HARPED
HARPER
HARVEY
HASHED
HASHES
HASPED
HASTEN
HASTES
HATRED
HATTED
HATTER
HAULED
HAULER
HAWKED
HAWKER
HAWSER
HAWSES
HAYDEN
HAYLEY
HAZIER
HEADED
HEADER
HEALED
HEALER
HEAPED
HEARER
HEATED
HEATER
HEAVED
HEAVEN
HEAVER
HEAVES
HEBREW
HEDGED
HEDGER
HEDGES
HEDREN
HEEDED
HEELED
HEELER
HEFNER
HEFTED
HEIDEN
HEIFER
HELLER
HELMED
HELMET
HELPED
HELPER
HELTER
HELVES
HEMMED
HEMMER
HENLEY
HENNER
HEPPER
HERDED
HERDER
HERMES
HEROES
HERSEY
HESTER
HICKEY
HIDDEN
HIGHER
HILLED
HILLEL
HILLER
HINDER
HINGED
HINGES
HINTED
HINTER
HIPPED
HIPPER
HISSED
HISSER
HISSES
HITHER
HITMEN
HITTER
HOAXED
HOAXER
HOAXES
HOBBES
HOBOES
HOCKED
HOCKEY
HOGGED
HOKIER
HOLDEN
HOLDER
HOLIER
HOLLER
HOLMES
HOMEEC
HOMIER
HONIED
HONKED
HONKER
HOODED
HOOFED
HOOFER
HOOKED
HOOPED
HOOPER
HOOTED
HOOTER
HOOVER
HOOVES
HOPPED
HOPPER
HORDES
HORMEL
HORNED
HORNER
HORNET
HORNEY
HORSED
HORSES
HORSEY
HOSIER
HOSTED
HOSTEL
HOTBED
HOTTEA
HOTTER
HOUSED
HOUSES
HOWLED
HOWLER
HOYDEN
HUFFED
HUGGED
HUGGER
HUGHES
HULKED
HULLED
HULLER
HUMMED
HUMMER
HUMPED
HUNGER
HUNKER
HUNTED
HUNTER
HURLED
HURLER
HURLEY
HUSHED
HUSHES
HUSKED
HUSKER
HUTTED
HUXLEY
HYADES
HYMNED
HYPHEN
HYPOED

H••••E
HABILE
HACKIE
HACKLE
HADDIE
HAGGLE
HALIDE
HALITE
HAMITE
HANDLE
HANKIE
HARARE
HASSLE
HATTIE
HEARYE
HECATE
HECKLE
HEDDLE
HEEBIE
HELENE
HERBIE
HETTIE
HEYJOE
HIGGLE
HIPPIE
HOAGIE
HOARSE
HOBBLE
HOGTIE
HOMAGE
HOMBRE
HONORE
HOOPLE
HOOPOE
HOPPLE
HORACE
HUBBLE
HUDDLE
HUMANE
HUMBLE
HURDLE
HURTLE
HUSTLE
HYDRAE

•HE•••
AHERNE
CHEAPO
CHEATS
CHECKS
CHEECH
CHEEKS
CHEEKY
CHEEPS
CHEERS
CHEERY
CHEESE
CHEESY
CHELAE
CHELAS
CHEMIN
CHENIN
CHEOPS
CHEQUE
CHERIE
CHERRY
CHERUB
CHERYL
CHESTS
CHESTY
CHEVAL
CHEVET
CHEVRE
CHEWED
CHEWER
CHEWUP
GHETTO
OHENRY
PHEDRE
PHENOL
PHENOM
PHENYL
RHEBOK
RHESUS
RHETOR
RHEUMS
RHEUMY
SHEAFS
SHEARS
SHEATH
SHEAVE
SHEEDY
SHEEHY
SHEENA
SHEENS
SHEEPS
SHEERS
SHEETS
SHEIKS
SHEILA
SHEKEL
SHELLS
SHELLY
SHELVE
SHEREE
SHERIF
SHERPA
SHERRY
SHEVAT
THEBES
THECAE
THECAL
THEEND
THEFED
THEFTS
THEHAJ
THEIRS
THEISM
THEIST
THELIP
THELMA
THEMED
THEMES
THENAR
THENCE
THEORY
THERMO
THERMS
THESES
THESIS
THESIX
THETAS
THETIC
THETIS
THETOY
THEWIZ
THEYLL
THEYRE
THEYVE
WHEATS
WHEELS
WHEEZE
WHEEZY
WHELKS
WHELPS
WHENCE
WHERRY

•H•E••
CHEECH
CHEEKS
CHEEKY
CHEEPS
CHEERS
CHEERY
CHEESE
CHEESY
CHIEFS
KHMERS
NHLERS
OHWELL
OHYEAH
PHLEBO
PHLEGM
PHOEBE
SHEEDY
SHEEHY
SHEENA
SHEENS
SHEEPS
SHEERS
SHEETS
SHIELD
SHIEST
SHOERS
SHREDS
SHREWD
SHREWS
SHTETL
SHYEST
THEEND
THIEVE
THREAD
THREAT
THREED
THREES
THRESH
WHEELS
WHEEZE
WHEEZY

•H••E•
CHAFED
CHAFES
CHALET
CHANEL
CHANEY
CHAPEL
CHASED
CHASER
CHASES
CHAVEZ
CHEVET
CHEWED
CHEWER
CHIDED
CHIDES
CHIMED
CHIMES
CHINES
CHISEL
CHIVES
CHOKED
CHOKER
CHOKES
CHOLER
CHORES
CHOSEN
CHOWED
CHUTED
CHUTES
DHOLES
DHOTEL
KHYBER
PHAGES
PHASED
PHASER
PHASES
PHLOEM
PHONED
PHONES
PHOOEY
PHYSED
RHODES
RHYMED
RHYMER
RHYMES
SHADED
SHADES
SHAKEN
SHAKER
SHAKES
SHALES
SHALEY
SHAMED
SHAMES
SHAPED
SHAPER
SHAPES
SHARED
SHARER
SHARES
SHAVED
SHAVEN
SHAVER
SHAVES
SHEKEL
SHEREE
SHINED
SHINER
SHINES
SHIRER
SHIRES
SHIVER
SHOLEM
SHOOED
SHORED
SHORES
SHOVED
SHOVEL
SHOVER
SHOVES
SHOWED
SHOWER
SHRIEK
THALER
THALES
THAMES
THANES
THAWED
THAYER
THEBES
THEFED
THEMED
THEMES
THESES
THOLES
THREED
THREES
THROES
WHALER
WHALES
WHILED
WHILES
WHINED
WHINER
WHINES
WHITEN
WHITER
WHITES
WHOLES

•H•••E
AHERNE
CHAINE
CHAISE
CHANCE
CHANGE
CHARGE
CHASSE
CHASTE
CHEESE
CHELAE
CHEQUE
CHERIE
CHEVRE
CHICLE
CHIGOE
CHILDE
CHILOE
CHOATE
CHOICE
CHOOSE
CHROME
KHAFRE
LHOTSE
PHEDRE
PHILAE
PHOEBE
PHRASE
PHYLAE
SHAYNE
SHEAVE
SHELVE
SHEREE
SHIITE
SHOPPE
SHOWME
SHRIKE
SHRINE
SHRIVE
SHROVE
THECAE
THENCE
THEYRE
THEYVE
THICKE
THIEVE
THISBE
THORPE
THRACE
THRALE
THRICE
THRIVE
THRONE
THROVE
WHEEZE
WHENCE

••HE••
ACHEBE
ACHENE
ADHERE
ATHENA
ATHENE
ATHENS
BEHELD
BEHEST
COHEIR
COHERE
EPHEBE
ETHENE
ETHERS
INHERE
OCHERS
OTHERS
REHEAL
REHEAR
REHEAT
REHEEL
REHELD
REHEMS
SCHELL
SCHEMA
SCHEME
SPHERE
STHENO
TEHEED
TEHEES
UNHEED
UPHELD
USHERS

••H•E•
ACHAEA
ACHIER
ASHIER
ASHLEY
CAHIER
ECHOED
ECHOES
KOHLER
LEHRER
MAHLER
OCHRES
REHEEL
ROHMER
SCHLEP
TEHEED
TEHEES
UNHEED
WOHLER
YAHWEH

••H••E
ACHEBE
ACHENE
ADHERE
ASHORE
ATHENE
ATHOME
AWHILE
BEHAVE
COHERE
COHUNE
EPHEBE
ETHANE
ETHENE
EXHALE
GOHOME
INHALE
INHERE
INHUME
JOHORE
LAHORE
MCHALE
MOHAVE
MRHYDE
OPHITE
REHIRE
SCHEME
SPHERE
WAHINE

•••HE•
AACHEN
AETHER
ALTHEA
ANTHEM
ANTHER
ARCHED
ARCHER
ARCHES
ARNHEM
BASHED
BASHES
BATHED
BATHER
BATHES
BETHEL
BOTHER
BUSHED
BUSHEL
BUSHES
CACHED
CACHES
CACHET
CASHED
CASHES
CASHEW
CATHER
CIPHER
COSHED
COSHES
CYPHER
DASHED
DASHER
DASHES
DISHED
DISHES
DITHER
EITHER
ESCHER
ESCHEW
ESTHER
ETCHED
ETCHER
ETCHES
FATHER
FICHES
FISHED
FISHER
FISHES
GASHED
GASHES
GATHER
GOPHER
GOSHEN
GUSHED
GUSHER
GUSHES
HASHED
HASHES
HIGHER
HITHER
HUGHES
HUSHED
HUSHES
HYPHEN
INCHED
INCHES
ISOHEL
ITCHED
ITCHES
JOSHED
JOSHES
KOSHER
KUCHEN
LACHES
LASHED
LASHER
LASHES
LATHED
LATHER
LATHES
LICHEN
LUSHER
LUTHER
MACHES
MASHED
MASHER
MASHES
MATHER
MAYHEM
MESHED
MESHES
MOTHER
MUDHEN
MUSHED
MUSHER
MUSHES
NEPHEW
NETHER
NICHES
NIGHER
NOSHED
NOSHER
NOSHES
PEAHEN
PITHED
POOHED
POSHER
POTHER
PUSHED
PUSHES
RACHEL
RASHER
RASHES
RATHER
RICHEN
RICHER
RICHES
ROCHET
RUCHES
RUSHED
RUSHEE
RUSHES
SACHEM
SACHET
SASHED
SASHES
SIGHED
SIGHER
TEEHEE
TETHER
TITHED
TITHER
TITHES
TOTHER
TOWHEE
UNSHED
VACHEL
WASHED
WASHER
WASHES
WETHER
WISHED
WISHER
WISHES
WITHED
WITHER
WITHES
ZITHER

•••H•E
ARCHIE
DAPHNE
EUCHRE
FICHTE
KATHIE
KISHKE
MASHIE
NUCHAE
RESHOE
RICHIE
RUSHEE
SOPHIE
TECHIE
TEEHEE
TOWHEE
WASHOE

••••HE
AMECHE
APACHE
BLITHE
BLYTHE
BOOTHE
BUNCHE
BYSSHE
CLICHE
CLOCHE
CLOTHE
CRECHE
FLECHE
GAUCHE
GOETHE
LOATHE
LOUCHE
MARCHE
PSYCHE
QUICHE
SCATHE
SCYTHE
SEETHE
SEICHE
SNATHE
SOOTHE
SPATHE
SWATHE
TEETHE
TOUCHE
TROCHE
WRITHE

H•F•••
HAFTED
HEFLIN
HEFNER
HEFTED
HUFFED

H••F••
HEIFER
HOOFED
HOOFER
HOOFIT
HUFFED

H•••F•
HOPOFF

H••••F
HEAROF
HEREOF
HOPOFF

•H•F••
CHAFED
CHAFES
CHAFFS
CHAFFY

KHAFRE SHAFTS SHIFTS SHIFTY SHOFAR THEFED THEFTS WHIFFS

•H••F•
CHAFFS CHAFFY CHIEFS SHEAFS SHRIFT THRIFT WHARFS WHIFFS WHOOFS

•H•••F
SHARIF SHERIF WHATIF

••H•F•
SCHIFF

••H••F
BEHALF BEHOOF INHALF SCHIFF

H•G•••
HAGGIS HAGGLE HAGMAN HEGARI HEGIRA HIGGLE HIGHER HIGHIQ HIGHLY HIGHUP HOGANS HOGGED HOGTIE HUGELY HUGEST HUGGED HUGGER HUGHES

H••G••
HAGGIS HAGGLE HAIGHT HANGAR HANGED HANGER HANGIN HANGON HANGUL HANGUP HEDGED HEDGER HEDGES HEIGHT HIGGLE HINGED HINGES HOAGIE HOGGED HUGGED HUGGER HUNGER HUNGIN HUNGON HUNGRY HUNGUP HUNGWU

H•••G•
HMONGS HOMAGE

H••••G
HALING HARING HATING HAVING HAWING HAYING HAZING HERZOG HEWING HEXING HIDING HIEING HIKING HIRING HIVING HOEING HOLING HOMING HONING HOPING HOSING HOTDOG HUMBUG HYPING

•H•G••
CHIGOE PHAGES SHAGGY SHOGUN THIGHS

•H••G•
CHANGE CHARGE CHOUGH PHLEGM SHAGGY SHRUGS THINGS THONGS THOUGH

•H•••G
CHIANG PHOTOG SHYING THRONG

••H•G•
LEHIGH ONHIGH

••H••G
AAHING ACHING GEHRIG ICHING OOHING PAHANG REHANG REHUNG

•••H•G
LITHOG QUAHOG

H•H•••
HOHHOT HOHOHO

H••H••
HASHED HASHES HATHOR HAWHAW HEEHAW HIGHER HIGHIQ HIGHLY HIGHUP HIPHOP HITHER HOHHOT HOOHAH HOOHAS HUGHES HUSHED HUSHES HYPHEN

H•••H•
HAIGHT HEATHS HEIGHT HIDEHO HOHOHO HONCHO HONSHU HUMPHS

H••••H
HALVAH HANNAH HAUNCH HEALTH HEARTH HIRSCH HITECH HOOHAH HOOKAH HOORAH HOWDAH HURRAH HUZZAH

•H•H••
AHCHOO CHUHSI THEHAJ

•H••H•
CHACHA CHICHA CHICHI RHYTHM SHEEHY THIGHS

•H•••H
CHEECH CHINCH CHOUGH CHURCH OHYEAH SHEATH SHILOH THATCH THOUGH THRASH THRESH THRUSH WHOOSH WHYDAH

••HH••
HOHHOT

••H•H•
EPHAHS HOHOHO ICHTHY YOHOHO

••H••H
LEHIGH ONHIGH RAHRAH REHASH WAHWAH YAHWEH

•••H•H
EIGHTH HOOHAH

HI••••
HIATAL HIATUS HICCUP HICKEY HICKOK HIDDEN HIDEHO HIDEKI HIDERS HIDING HIDOUT HIEING HIEMAL HIERON HIGGLE HIGHER HIGHIQ HIGHLY HIGHUP HIJACK HIKERS HIKING HILARY HILLED HILLEL HILLER HILTON HINDER HINDUS HINGED HINGES HINTAT HINTED HINTER HINTON HIPHOP HIPPED HIPPER HIPPIE HIPPOS HIREON HIRERS HIRING HIRSCH HISPID HISSAT HISSED HISSER HISSES HITECH HITHER HITMAN HITMEN HITSIT HITSON HITSUP HITTER HIVAOA HIVING

H•I•••
HAIDAS HAIGHT HAIKOU HAIKUS HAILED HAILEY HAINAN HAINES HAIRDO HAIRED HEIDEN HEIFER HEIGHT HEISTS HOISTS

H••I••
HABILE HABITS HAKIMS HALIDE HALING HALITE HAMILL HAMITE HARING HATING HAVING HAWING HAYING HAZIER HAZILY HAZING HEGIRA HELIOS HELIUM HERIOT HESIOD HEWING HEXING HIDING HIEING HIKING HIRING HIVING HOEING HOKIER HOLIER HOLING HOLISM HOLIST HOMIER HOMILY HOMING HOMINY HONIED HONING HOPING HOSIER HOSING HYPING

H•••I•
HACKIE HADDIE HADJIS HAGGIS HAJJIS HALOID HAMLIN HANDIN HANGIN HANKIE HARBIN HARRIS HATPIN HATTIE HAWAII HEADIN HECTIC HEEBIE HEFLIN HELDIN HEMSIN HENBIT HENNIN HENRIK HERBIE HEREIN HERMIT HEROIC HESTIA HETTIE HIGHIQ HIPPIE HISPID HITSIT HOAGIE HOBBIT HOGTIE HOLDIT HOOFIT HORRID HOTAIR HOTTIP HOURIS HOWLIN HUBRIS HUNGIN HYBRID

H••••I
HATARI HAWAII HEGARI HIDEKI HUMERI

•HI•••
AHIMSA CHIANG CHIAUS CHICHA CHICHI CHICKS CHICLE CHIDED CHIDES CHIEFS CHIGOE CHILDE CHILDS CHILLS CHILLY CHILOE CHIMED CHIMES CHIMPS CHINCH CHINES CHINKS CHINKY CHINOS CHINTZ CHINUP CHIPIN CHIRON CHIRPS CHIRPY CHIRRS CHISEL CHISOX CHITIN CHITON CHIVES OHIOAN PHIALS PHILAE PHILIP PHILLY PHILOL PHILOS RHINAL RHINOS SHIELD SHIEST SHIFTS SHIFTY SHIISM SHIITE SHILLS SHILLY SHILOH SHIMMY SHIMON SHINDY SHINED SHINER SHINES SHINNY SHINTO SHIRAZ SHIRER SHIRES SHIRKS SHIRRS SHIRTS SHIRTY SHIVER THICKE THIEVE THIGHS THILLS THINGS THINKS THINLY THIRDS THIRST THIRTY THISBE WHIFFS WHILED WHILES WHILOM WHILST WHIMSY WHINED WHINER WHINES WHINNY WHIPPY WHIPUP WHIRLS WHIRLY WHIRRS WHISKS WHITEN WHITER WHITES

•H•I••
CHAINE CHAINS CHAIRS CHAISE CHOICE CHOIRS CHRISM SHEIKS SHEILA SHIISM SHIITE SHRIEK SHRIFT SHRIKE SHRILL SHRIMP SHRINE SHRINK SHRIVE SHTICK SHYING THEIRS THEISM THEIST THRICE THRIFT THRILL THRIPS THRIVE

•H••I•
CHAPIN CHEMIN CHENIN CHERIE CHIPIN CHITIN CHOPIN DHOTIS GHAZIS KHAKIS KHALID PHATIC PHILIP PHOBIA PHOBIC PHOCIS PHONIC PHOTIC PHYSIO SHAMIR SHARIA SHARIF SHERIF SHOJIS SHOOIN SHOWIN SHUTIN THALIA THATIS THELIP THESIS THESIX THETIC THETIS THEWIZ WHATIF

•H•••I
BHAKTI CHICHI CHUHSI RHOMBI SHAKTI THYRSI WHOOPI

••HI••
AAHING ACHIER ACHING ALHIRT APHIDS ASHIER AWHILE AWHIRL BAHIAN BEHIND CAHIER ETHICS ICHING LEHIGH NIHILO NOHITS ONHIGH OOHING OPHITE REHIRE SAHIBS SCHICK SCHIFF SCHISM SCHIST SPHINX TAHINI TAHITI TSHIRT UPHILL WAHINE

••H•I•
COHEIR DAHLIA ECHOIC ETHNIC GEHRIG KAHLIL LCHAIM MAHDIS MOHAIR

••H••I
BIHARI EPHORI ITHAKI PAHARI TAHINI TAHITI YEHUDI

•••HI•
AMPHID ARCHIE CASHIN COCHIN DUCHIN ELOHIM GOTHIC HIGHIQ ISCHIA KATHIE KESHIA LASHIO LITHIC MASHIE MATHIS MENHIR MISHIT MUZHIK MYTHIC ORCHID ORCHIL ORPHIC OUTHIT PYTHIA RACHIS RASHID RESHIP RICHIE SOPHIA SOPHIE SPAHIS TECHIE UNCHIC URCHIN WITHIN WITHIT

•••H•I
CHUHSI ISTHMI MYTHOI TISHRI TZUHSI VASHTI

••••HI
CANTHI CHICHI DELPHI GANDHI KIMCHI LITCHI TAICHI

H•J•••
HAJJES HAJJIS HIJACK

H••J••
HADJES HADJIS HAJJES HAJJIS HEYJOE

•H•J••
SHOJIS THUJAS

•H•••J
THEHAJ

•••H•J
THEHAJ

H•K•••
HAKIMS HIKERS HIKING HOKIER HYKSOS

H••K••
HACKED HACKER HACKIE HACKLE HAIKOU HAIKUS HANKER HANKIE HARKED HARKEN HARKER HAWKED HAWKER HECKLE HICKEY HICKOK HOCKED HOCKEY HONKED HONKER HOOKAH HOOKED HOOKUP HULKED HUNKER HUSKED HUSKER

H•••K•
HACEKS HIDEKI

H••••K
HENRIK HICKOK HIJACK

•H•K••
BHAKTI CHOKED CHOKER CHOKES CHUKAR CHUKKA KHAKIS SHAKEN SHAKER SHAKES SHAKOS SHAKTI SHEKEL ZHUKOV

•H••K•
CHALKS CHALKY CHECKS CHEEKS CHEEKY CHICKS CHINKS CHINKY CHOCKS CHUCKS CHUKKA CHUNKS CHUNKY SHACKS SHANKS SHARKS SHEIKS SHIRKS SHOCKS SHOOKS SHRIKE SHUCKS THANKS THICKE THINKS THUNKS WHACKS WHACKY WHELKS WHISKS

•H•••K
RHEBOK SHRANK SHRIEK SHRINK SHRUNK SHTICK THWACK

••H•K•
ITHAKI

••H••K
DRHOOK MOHAWK MOHOCK REHOOK SCHICK UNHOOK

•••HK•
KISHKE ROTHKO

•••H•K
ITZHAK MUZHIK

H•L•••
HALERS HALERU HALEST HALEVY HALIDE HALING HALITE HALLEL HALLEY HALLOO HALLOS HALLOW HALLUX HALOED HALOES HALOID HALSEY HALTED HALTER HALVAH HALVED HALVES HELDIN HELDON HELDTO HELDUP HELENA HELENE HELENS HELIOS HELIUM HELLAS HELLER HELLOS HELMED HELMET HELMUT HELOTS HELPED HELPER HELTER HELVES HILARY HILLED HILLEL HILLER HILTON HOLDEN HOLDER HOLDIT HOLDON HOLDTO HOLDUP HOLEUP HOLIER HOLING HOLISM HOLIST HOLLER HOLLOW HOLMES HULKED HULLED HULLER HULLOS

H••L••
HAILED HAILEY HALLEL HALLEY HALLOO HALLOS HALLOW HALLUX HAMLET HAMLIN HARLAN HARLEM HARLEY HARLOW HAULED HAULER HAULUP HAYLEY HEALED HEALER HEALTH HEELED HEELER HEFLIN HELLAS HELLER HELLOS HENLEY HILLED HILLEL HILLER HOLLER HOLLOW HOWLED HOWLER HOWLIN HULLED HULLER HULLOS HURLED HURLER HURLEY HUXLEY

H•••L•
HABILE HACKLE HAGGLE HAMALS HAMILL HANDLE HARDLY HAROLD HASSLE HAZELS HAZILY HECKLE HEDDLE HERALD HIGGLE HIGHLY HOBBLE HOMELY HOMILY HOOPLA HOOPLE HOPPLE HOSELS HOTELS HOURLY HOVELS HOWELL HUBBLE HUBBLY HUDDLE HUGELY HUMBLE HUMBLY HURDLE HURTLE HUSTLE

H••••L
HALLEL HAMILL HANDEL HANGUL HANSEL HERBAL HIATAL HIEMAL HILLEL HORMEL HOSTEL HOWELL HYETAL HYMNAL

•HL•••
CHLORO NHLERS PHLEBO PHLEGM PHLOEM UHLANS

•H•L••
CHALCO CHALET CHALKS CHALKY CHELAE CHELAS CHILDE CHILDS CHILLS CHILLY CHILOE CHOLER CHOLLA DHOLES KHALID PHILAE PHILIP PHILLY PHILOL PHILOS PHYLAE PHYLLO PHYLUM SHALES SHALEY SHALLY SHALOM SHELLS SHELLY SHELVE SHILLS SHILLY SHILOH SHOLEM SHOLOM THALER THALES THALIA THELIP THELMA THILLS THOLES WHALER WHALES WHELKS WHELPS WHILED WHILES WHILOM WHILST WHOLES WHOLLY

•H••L•
CHARLY CHICLE CHILLS CHILLY CHOLLA CHURLS GHOULS OHWELL PHIALS PHILLY PHYLLO SHALLY SHAWLS SHEILA SHELLS SHELLY SHIELD

SHILLS
SHILLY
SHOALS
SHOULD
SHRILL
THEYLL
THILLS
THINLY
THRALE
THRALL
THRILL
THUSLY
WHEELS
WHIRLS
WHIRLY
WHOLLY
WHORLS

•H•••L
BHOPAL
CHANEL
CHAPEL
CHERYL
CHEVAL
CHISEL
CHORAL
DHOTEL
OHWELL
PHENOL
PHENYL
PHILOL
RHINAL
SHEKEL
SHOVEL
SHRILL
SHTETL
THECAL
THEYLL
THRALL
THRILL

••HL••
ASHLAR
ASHLEY
DAHLIA
KAHLIL
KAHLUA
KOHLER
MAHLER
SCHLEP
WOHLER

••H•L•
AWHILE
BEHALF
BEHELD
BEHOLD
EXHALE
INHALE
INHALF
MCHALE
NIHILO
ONHOLD
REHELD
SCHELL
SCHULZ
UNHOLY
UPHELD
UPHILL
UPHOLD

••H••L
AWHIRL
INHAUL
KAHLIL
REHEAL
REHEEL
SCHELL
SCHOOL
SCHORL
UPHILL

•••HL•
ARCHLY
HIGHLY
LUSHLY
POSHLY
RASHLY
RICHLY

•••H•L
BETHEL
BUSHEL
ISOHEL
LETHAL
METHYL
MYTHOL
NUCHAL
ORCHIL
PATHOL
RACHEL
VACHEL
WARHOL
WITHAL

••••HL
JAWOHL

HM••••
HMONGS

H•M•••
HAMALS
HAMILL
HAMITE
HAMLET
HAMLIN
HAMMED
HAMMER
HAMPER
HEMATO
HEMMED
HEMMER
HEMSIN
HOMAGE
HOMBRE
HOMEEC
HOMELY
HOMERS
HOMIER
HOMILY
HOMING
HOMINY
HUMANE
HUMANS
HUMBLE
HUMBLY
HUMBUG
HUMERI
HUMMED
HUMMER
HUMMUS
HUMORS
HUMOUR
HUMPED
HUMPHS
HYMNAL
HYMNED

H••M••
HAEMAT
HAEMON
HAGMAN
HAMMED
HAMMER
HARMED
HARMON
HAYMOW
HBOMBS
HELMED
HELMET
HELMUT
HEMMED
HEMMER
HERMAN
HERMES
HERMIT
HERMON
HETMAN
HIEMAL
HITMAN
HITMEN
HOLMES
HORMEL
HORMUZ
HUMMED
HUMMER
HUMMUS

H•••M•
HAKIMS
HAREMS
HBEAMS

H••••M
HANSOM
HARLEM
HASSAM
HELIUM
HOLISM

•HM•••
KHMERS

•H•M••
AHIMSA
CHAMMY
CHAMPS
CHEMIN
CHIMED
CHIMES
CHIMPS
CHOMPS
CHUMMY
CHUMPS
RHOMBI
RHOMBS
RHUMBA
RHUMBS
RHYMED
RHYMER
RHYMES
SHAMAN
SHAMED
SHAMES
SHAMIR
SHAMUS
SHIMMY
SHIMON
THAMES
THEMED
THEMES
THOMAS
THUMBS
THUMPS
THYMUS
WHAMMO
WHAMMY
WHIMSY
WHOMPS

•H••M•
CHACMA
CHAMMY
CHARMS
CHASMS
CHROMA
CHROME
CHROMO
CHUMMY
DHARMA
RHEUMS
RHEUMY
SHAWMS
SHIMMY
SHOWME
SHRIMP
THELMA
THERMO
THERMS
THRUMS
WHAMMO
WHAMMY

•H•••M
CHRISM
PHENOM
PHLEGM
PHLOEM
PHYLUM
RHYTHM
SHALOM
SHAZAM
SHBOOM
SHIISM
SHOLEM
SHOLOM
THEISM
WHILOM

••HM••
ROHMER
SCHMOO
SCHMOS

••H•M•
ATHOME
BAHAMA
GOHOME
INHUME
OGHAMS
REHEMS
SCHEMA
SCHEME

••H••M
ASHRAM
LCHAIM
SCHISM

•••HM•
ABOHMS
BRAHMA
BRAHMS
ISTHMI
MYOHMY

•••H•M
ANTHEM
ARNHEM
ASCHAM
COBHAM
DIRHAM
DUNHAM
DURHAM
ELOHIM
FATHOM
GOTHAM
GRAHAM
LAPHAM
MAYHEM
OLDHAM
RODHAM
SACHEM

••••HM
MEGOHM
RHYTHM

H•N•••
HANDED
HANDEL
HANDIN
HANDLE
HANDON
HANGAR
HANGED
HANGER
HANGIN
HANGON
HANGUL
HANGUP
HANKER
HANKIE
HANNAH
HANSEL
HANSOM
HANSON
HENBIT
HENLEY
HENNAS
HENNER
HENNIN
HENRIK
HENSON
HINDER
HINDUS
HINGED
HINGES
HINTAT
HINTED
HINTER
HINTON
HONCHO
HONEST
HONEYS
HONIED
HONING
HONKED
HONKER
HONORE
HONORS
HONOUR
HONSHU
HUNGER
HUNGIN
HUNGON
HUNGRY
HUNGUP
HUNGWU
HUNKER
HUNTED
HUNTER

H••N••
HAINAN
HAINES
HANNAH
HAUNCH
HAUNTS
HEFNER
HENNAS
HENNER
HENNIN
HMONGS
HOBNOB
HORNED
HORNER
HORNET
HORNEY
HOUNDS
HOWNOW
HYENAS
HYMNAL
HYMNED
HYPNOS

H•••N•
HABANA
HALING
HARING
HATING
HAVANA
HAVENS
HAVENT
HAVING
HAWING
HAYING
HAZANS
HAZING
HELENA
HELENE
HELENS
HERONS
HEWING
HEXING
HIDING
HIEING
HIKING
HIRING
HIVING
HOEING
HOGANS
HOLING
HOMING
HOMINY
HONING
HOPING
HOSING
HUMANE
HUMANS
HURONS
HYPING

H••••N
HADRON
HAEMON
HAGMAN
HAINAN
HAMLIN
HANDIN
HANDON
HANGIN
HANGON
HANSON
HAPPEN
HARBIN
HARDEN
HARKEN
HARLAN
HARMON
HARPON
HASSAN
HASTEN
HATPIN
HAVEON
HAYDEN
HEADIN
HEADON
HEAVEN
HEDREN
HEFLIN
HEIDEN
HELDIN
HELDON
HEMSIN
HENNIN
HENSON
HEREIN
HEREON
HERMAN
HERMON
HESTON
HETMAN
HIDDEN
HIERON
HILTON
HINTON
HIREON
HITMAN
HITMEN
HITSON
HOBSON
HOLDEN
HOLDON
HORTON
HOWLIN
HOYDEN
HUDSON
HUNGIN
HUNGON
HUSTON
HUTTON
HYPHEN

•H•N••
CHANCE
CHANCY
CHANEL
CHANEY
CHANGE
CHANTS
CHENIN
CHINCH
CHINES
CHINKS
CHINKY
CHINOS
CHINTZ
CHINUP
CHUNKS
CHUNKY
OHENRY
PHENOL
PHENOM
PHENYL
PHONED
PHONES
PHONIC
PHONON
PHONOS
RHINAL
RHINOS
RHONDA
SHANDY
SHANKS
SHANTY
SHINDY
SHINED
SHINER
SHINES
SHINNY
SHINTO
SHUNTS
THANES
THANKS
THENAR
THENCE
THINGS
THINKS
THINLY
THONGS
THUNKS
WHENCE
WHINED
WHINER
WHINES
WHINNY
WHYNOT

•H••N•
AHERNE
CHAINE
CHAINS
CHIANG
CHRONO
CHURNS
SHAYNE
SHEENA
SHEENS
SHINNY
SHRANK
SHRINE
SHRINK
SHRUNK
SHYING
THEEND
THORNS
THORNY
THRONE
THRONG
UHLANS
WHINNY

•H•••N
BHUTAN
CHAPIN
CHARON
CHEMIN
CHENIN
CHIPIN
CHIRON
CHITIN
CHITON
CHOPIN
CHOSEN
OHIOAN
PHONON
PHOTON
RHYTON
SHABAN
SHAKEN
SHAMAN
SHARON
SHAVEN
SHIMON
SHOGUN
SHOOIN
SHORAN
SHOWIN
SHUTIN
THROWN
WHITEN

••HN••
ETHNIC
ETHNOS
JOHNNY
SCHNOZ

••H•N•
AAHING
ACHENE
ACHING
ATHAND
ATHENA
ATHENE
ATHENS
BEHIND
BYHAND
COHUNE
ETHANE
ETHENE
ICHING
INHAND
JOHANN
JOHNNY
KAHUNA
ONHAND
OOHING
PAHANG
REHANG
REHUNG
SPHINX
STHENO
TAHINI
UNHAND
UTHANT
WAHINE

••H••N
ASHCAN
BAHIAN
DEHORN
EPHRON
JOHANN

•••HN•
DAPHNE
FOEHNS
TECHNO
VISHNU

•••H•N
AACHEN
AFGHAN
ARCHON
CASHIN
COCHIN
DOTHAN
DUCHIN
GOSHEN
HYPHEN
INCHON
KUCHEN
LICHEN
MUDHEN
NATHAN
OMAHAN
ORPHAN
PATHAN
PEAHEN
PUSHON
PYTHON
RICHEN
SIPHON
TUCHUN
URCHIN
UTAHAN
WITHIN

••••HN
STJOHN
VAUGHN

HO••••
HOAGIE
HOARDS
HOARSE
HOAXED
HOAXER
HOAXES
HOBART
HOBBES
HOBBIT
HOBBLE
HOBNOB
HOBOES
HOBSON
HOCKED
HOCKEY
HODADS
HOEING
HOGANS
HOGGED
HOGTIE
HOHHOT
HOHOHO
HOISTS
HOKIER
HOLDEN
HOLDER
HOLDIT
HOLDON
HOLDTO
HOLDUP
HOLEUP
HOLIER
HOLING
HOLISM
HOLIST
HOLLER
HOLLOW
HOLMES
HOMAGE
HOMBRE
HOMEEC
HOMELY
HOMERS
HOMIER
HOMILY
HOMING
HOMINY
HONCHO
HONEST
HONEYS
HONIED
HONING
HONKED
HONKER
HONORE
HONORS
HONOUR
HONSHU
HOODED
HOODOO
HOOFED
HOOFER
HOOFIT
HOOHAH
HOOHAS
HOOKAH
HOOKED
HOOKUP
HOOPED
HOOPER
HOOPLA
HOOPLE
HOOPOE
HOORAH
HOORAY
HOOTAT
HOOTED
HOOTER
HOOVER
HOOVES
HOPERS
HOPING
HOPOFF
HOPPED
HOPPER
HOPPLE
HOPSUP
HORACE
HORDES
HORMEL
HORMUZ
HORNED
HORNER
HORNET
HORNEY
HORRID
HORROR
HORSED
HORSES
HORSEY
HORTON
HOSELS
HOSIER
HOSING
HOSTAS
HOSTED
HOSTEL
HOTAIR
HOTBED
HOTBOX
HOTCAP
HOTCAR
HOTDOG
HOTELS
HOTPOT
HOTROD
HOTTEA
HOTTER
HOTTIP
HOTTUB
HOTWAR
HOUNDS
HOURIS
HOURLY
HOUSED
HOUSES
HOVELS
HOVERS
HOVETO
HOWARD
HOWDAH
HOWELL
HOWLED
HOWLER
HOWLIN
HOWNOW
HOWTOS
HOYDEN

H•O•••
HBOMBS
HMONGS
HOODED
HOODOO
HOOFED
HOOFER
HOOFIT
HOOHAH
HOOHAS
HOOKAH
HOOKED
HOOKUP
HOOPED
HOOPER
HOOPLA
HOOPLE
HOOPOE
HOORAH
HOORAY
HOOTAT
HOOTED
HOOTER
HOOVER
HOOVES

H••O••
HALOED
HALOES
HALOID
HAROLD
HAVOCS
HELOTS
HEROES
HEROIC
HERONS
HIDOUT
HOBOES
HOHOHO
HONORE
HONORS
HONOUR
HOPOFF
HUMORS
HUMOUR
HURONS
HYPOED

H•••O•
HADRON
HAEMON
HAIKOU
HALLOO
HALLOS
HALLOW
HANDON
HANGON
HANSOM
HANSON
HARBOR
HARLOW
HARMON
HARPON
HARROW
HATBOX
HATHOR
HAVEON
HAYMOW
HEADON
HEAROF
HECTOR
HELDON
HELIOS
HELLOS
HENSON
HEREOF
HEREON
HERIOT
HERMON
HERZOG
HESIOD
HESTON
HEYJOE
HEYYOU
HICKOK
HIERON
HILTON
HINTON
HIPHOP
HIPPOS
HIREON
HITSON
HIVAOA
HOBNOB
HOBSON
HOHHOT
HOLDON
HOLLOW
HOODOO
HOOPOE
HORROR
HORTON
HOTBOX
HOTDOG
HOTPOT
HOTROD
HOWNOW
HOWTOS
HUDSON
HUEVOS
HULLOS
HUNGON
HUSTON
HUTTON
HYDROS
HYKSOS
HYPNOS
HYSSOP

H••••O
HAIRDO
HALLOO
HASBRO
HELDTO
HEMATO
HERETO
HETERO
HIDEHO
HOHOHO
HOLDTO
HONCHO
HOODOO
HOVETO

•HO•••
BHOPAL
CHOATE
CHOCKS
CHOICE
CHOIRS
CHOKED
CHOKER
CHOKES
CHOLER
CHOLLA
CHOMPS
CHOOSE
CHOOSY
CHOOYU
CHOPIN
CHOPPY
CHORAL
CHORDS
CHORES
CHORUS
CHOSEN
CHOUGH
CHOWED
DHOLES
DHOTEL
DHOTIS
GHOSTS
GHOULS
LHOTSE
PHOBIA
PHOBIC
PHOBOS
PHOCIS
PHOEBE
PHONED
PHONES
PHONIC
PHONON
PHONOS
PHOOEY
PHOTIC
PHOTOG
PHOTON
PHOTOS
RHODES
RHOMBI
RHOMBS
RHONDA
SHOALS
SHOATS
SHOCKS
SHODDY
SHOERS
SHOFAR
SHOGUN
SHOJIS
SHOLEM
SHOLOM
SHOOED
SHOOIN
SHOOKS
SHOOTS
SHOPPE
SHORAN
SHORED
SHORES
SHORTS
SHORTY
SHOTAT
SHOTUP
SHOULD
SHOUTS
SHOVED
SHOVEL
SHOVER
SHOVES
SHOWED
SHOWER
SHOWIN
SHOWME
SHOWUP
THOLES
THOMAS
THONGS
THORAX
THORNS
THORNY
THORPE
THORPS
THOUGH
WHOLES
WHOLLY
WHOMPS
WHOOFS
WHOOPI
WHOOPS
WHOOSH
WHORLS
XHOSAS

•H•O••
CHEOPS
CHLORO
CHOOSE
CHOOSY
CHOOYU
CHROMA
CHROME
CHROMO
CHRONO
OHIOAN
PHLOEM
PHOOEY
SHBOOM
SHOOED
SHOOIN
SHOOKS
SHOOTS
SHROUD
SHROVE
THEORY
THROAT
THROBS
THROES
THRONE
THRONG
THROVE
THROWN
THROWS
WHOOFS
WHOOPI
WHOOPS
WHOOSH

•H••O•
AHCHOO
CHADOR
CHARON
CHIGOE
CHILOE
CHINOS
CHIRON
CHISOX
CHITON
PHAROS
PHENOL
PHENOM
PHILOL
PHILOS
PHOBOS
PHONON

PHONOS
PHOTOG
PHOTON
PHOTOS
RHEBOK
RHETOR
RHINOS
RHYTON
SHADOW
SHAKOS
SHALOM
SHARON
SHBOOM
SHILOH
SHIMON
SHOLOM
THETOY
WHILOM
WHYNOT
ZHUKOV

•H•••O
AHCHOO
BHUTTO
CHALCO
CHARRO
CHEAPO
CHLORO
CHROMO
CHRONO
CHURRO
GHETTO
PHLEBO
PHYLLO
PHYSIO
SHINTO
THERMO
WHAMMO

••HO••
ABHORS
ASHORE
ATHOME
BEHOLD
BEHOOF
CAHOWS
COHORT
COHOST
DEHORN
DRHOOK
ECHOED
ECHOES
ECHOIC
EPHODS
EPHORI
EPHORS
EXHORT
GOHOME
HOHOHO
JOHORE
LAHORE
MAHOUT
MOHOCK
ONHOLD
REHOOK
SCHOOL
SCHORL
UNHOLY
UNHOOK
UPHOLD
WAHOOS
YAHOOS
YOHOHO

••H•O•
BEHOOF
DRHOOK
EPHRON
ETHNOS
HOHHOT
MAHZOR
REHOOK
SCHMOO
SCHMOS
SCHNOZ
SCHOOL
UNHOOK
WAHOOS
YAHOOS

••H••O
HOHOHO
NIHILO
SCHMOO
STHENO
YOHOHO

•••HO•
AHCHOO
ANCHOR
ANDHOW
ANYHOW
ARCHON
AUTHOR
BARHOP
BATHOS
BISHOP
BOOHOO
CACHOU
CARHOP
FATHOM
FUZHOU
HATHOR
HIPHOP
HOHHOT
INCHON
JOBHOP
LITHOG
LITHOS
LUTHOR
MACHOS
METHOD
MUGHOS
MYTHOI
MYTHOL
MYTHOS
NACHOS
NOSHOW
PATHOL
PATHOS
PUSHON
PYTHON
QUAHOG
REDHOT
RESHOD
RESHOE
RESHOT
SENHOR
SIPHON
TVSHOW
UNSHOD
UPSHOT
WARHOL
WASHOE
YOOHOO

•••H•O
AHCHOO
ARTHRO
BOCHCO
BOOHOO
JETHRO
LASHIO
NEPHRO
PASHTO
RIGHTO
ROTHKO
TECHNO
YOOHOO

••••HO
CAUCHO
CLOTHO
GAUCHO
GUNGHO
HIDEHO
HOHOHO
HONCHO
LANDHO
MORPHO
NAVAHO
PANCHO
PONCHO
PSYCHO
RANCHO
REECHO
SANCHO
SAPPHO
TRICHO
XANTHO
YOHOHO

H•P•••
HAPPEN
HEPCAT
HEPPER
HEPTAD
HIPHOP
HIPPED
HIPPER
HIPPIE
HIPPOS
HOPERS
HOPING
HOPOFF
HOPPED
HOPPER
HOPPLE
HOPSUP
HYPHEN
HYPING
HYPNOS
HYPOED

H••P••
HAMPER
HAPPEN
HARPED
HARPER
HARPON
HASPED
HATPIN
HEAPED
HELPED
HELPER
HEPPER
HIPPED
HIPPER
HIPPIE
HIPPOS
HISPID
HOOPED
HOOPER
HOOPLA
HOOPLE
HOOPOE
HOPPED
HOPPER
HOPPLE
HOTPOT
HUMPED
HUMPHS

H••••P
HANGUP
HARDUP
HAULUP
HEADUP
HEATUP
HELDUP
HICCUP
HIGHUP
HIPHOP
HITSUP
HOLDUP
HOLEUP
HOOKUP
HOPSUP
HOTCAP
HOTTIP
HUBCAP
HUNGUP
HYSSOP

•H•P••
BHOPAL
CHAPEL
CHAPIN
CHIPIN
CHOPIN
CHOPPY
SHAPED
SHAPER
SHAPES
SHOPPE
WHIPPY
WHIPUP

•H••P•
CHAMPS
CHEAPO
CHEEPS
CHEOPS
CHIMPS
CHIRPS
CHIRPY
CHOMPS
CHOPPY
CHUMPS
SHARPS
SHEEPS
SHERPA
SHOPPE
THORPE
THORPS
THRIPS
THUMPS
WHELPS
WHIPPY
WHOMPS
WHOOPI
WHOOPS

•H•••P
CHATUP
CHEWUP
CHINUP
PHILIP
SHOTUP
SHOWUP
SHRIMP
SHUTUP
THELIP
WHIPUP

••H••P
ASHARP
BSHARP
CSHARP
DSHARP
ESHARP
FSHARP
GSHARP
SCHLEP

•••H•P
BARHOP
BISHOP
CARHOP
HIGHUP
HIPHOP
JOBHOP
LASHUP
MAYHAP
MISHAP
PUSHUP
RESHIP
WASHUP

H••••Q
HIGHIQ

•H•Q••
CHEQUE

•••H•Q
HIGHIQ

H•R•••
HARARE
HARASS
HARBIN
HARBOR
HARDEN
HARDER
HARDLY
HARDUP
HAREMS
HARING
HARKED
HARKEN
HARKER
HARLAN
HARLEM
HARLEY
HARLOW
HARMED
HARMON
HAROLD
HARPED
HARPER
HARPON
HARRIS
HARROW
HARVEY
HERALD
HERBAL
HERBIE
HERDED
HERDER
HEREAT
HEREBY
HEREIN
HEREOF
HEREON
HERESY
HERETO
HERIOT
HERMAN
HERMES
HERMIT
HERMON
HEROES
HEROIC
HERONS
HERSEY
HERZOG
HIREON
HIRERS
HIRING
HIRSCH
HORACE
HORDES
HORMEL
HORMUZ
HORNED
HORNER
HORNET
HORNEY
HORRID
HORROR
HORSED
HORSES
HORSEY
HORTON
HURDLE
HURLED
HURLER
HURLEY
HURONS
HURRAH
HURRAY
HURTLE

H••R••
HADRON
HAIRDO
HAIRED
HARRIS
HARROW
HATRED
HEARER
HEAROF
HEARST
HEARTH
HEARTS
HEARTY
HEARYE
HEBREW
HEDREN
HENRIK
HIERON
HOARDS
HOARSE
HOORAH
HOORAY
HORRID
HORROR
HOTROD
HOURIS
HOURLY
HUBRIS
HURRAH
HURRAY
HYBRID
HYDRAE
HYDRAS
HYDROS

H•••R•
HALERS
HALERU
HARARE
HASBRO
HATARI
HATERS
HAZARD
HAZERS
HEGARI
HEGIRA
HETERO
HEWERS
HEXERS
HIDERS
HIKERS
HILARY
HIRERS
HOBART
HOMBRE
HOMERS
HONORE
HONORS
HOPERS
HOVERS
HOWARD
HUBERT
HUMERI
HUMORS
HUNGRY

H••••R
HACKER
HALTER
HAMMER
HAMPER
HANGAR
HANGER
HANKER
HARBOR
HARDER
HARKER
HARPER
HATHOR
HATTER
HAULER
HAWKER
HAWSER
HAZIER
HEADER
HEALER
HEARER
HEATER
HEAVER
HECTOR
HEDGER
HEELER
HEFNER
HEIFER
HELLER
HELPER
HELTER
HEMMER
HENNER
HEPPER
HERDER
HESTER
HIGHER
HILLER
HINDER
HINTER
HIPPER
HISSER
HITHER
HITTER
HOAXER
HOKIER
HOLDER
HOLIER
HOLLER
HOMIER
HONKER
HONOUR
HOOFER
HOOPER
HOOTER
HOOVER
HOPPER
HORNER
HORROR
HOSIER
HOTAIR
HOTCAR
HOTTER
HOTWAR
HOWLER
HUGGER
HULLER
HUMMER
HUMOUR
HUNGER
HUNKER
HUNTER
HURLER
HUSKER
HUSSAR

•HR•••
CHRISM
CHROMA
CHROME
CHROMO
CHRONO
PHRASE
SHRANK
SHREDS
SHREWD
SHREWS
SHRIEK
SHRIFT
SHRIKE
SHRILL
SHRIMP
SHRINE
SHRINK
SHRIVE
SHROUD
SHROVE
SHRUBS
SHRUGS
SHRUNK
THRACE
THRALE
THRALL
THRASH
THREAD
THREAT
THREED
THREES
THRESH
THRICE
THRIFT
THRILL
THRIPS
THRIVE
THROAT
THROBS
THROES
THRONE
THRONG
THROVE
THROWN
THROWS
THRUMS
THRUSH
THRUST

•H•R••
AHERNE
CHARGE
CHARLY
CHARMS
CHARON
CHARRO
CHARTS
CHERIE
CHERRY
CHERUB
CHERYL
CHIRON
CHIRPS
CHIRPY
CHIRRS
CHORAL
CHORDS
CHORES
CHORUS
CHURCH
CHURLS
CHURNS
CHURRO
CHURRS
DHARMA
GHARRY
PHAROS
SHARDS
SHARED
SHARER
SHARES
SHARIA
SHARIF
SHARKS
SHARON
SHARPS
SHEREE
SHERIF
SHERPA
SHERRY
SHIRAZ
SHIRER
SHIRES
SHIRKS
SHIRRS
SHIRTS
SHIRTY
SHORAN
SHORED
SHORES
SHORTS
SHORTY
THERMO
THERMS
THIRDS
THIRST
THIRTY
THORAX
THORNS
THORNY
THORPE
THORPS
THYRSI
WHARFS
WHERRY
WHIRLS
WHIRLY
WHIRRS
WHORLS

•H••R•
CHAIRS
CHARRO
CHEERS
CHEERY
CHERRY
CHEVRE
CHIRRS
CHLORO
CHOIRS
CHURRO
CHURRS
GHARRY
KHAFRE
KHMERS
NHLERS
OHENRY
PHEDRE
SHEARS
SHEERS
SHERRY
SHIRRS
SHOERS
THEIRS
THEORY
THEYRE
THWART
WHERRY
WHIRRS

•H•••R
CHADOR
CHASER
CHEWER
CHOKER
CHOLER
CHUKAR
KHYBER
PHASER
RHETOR
RHYMER
SHAKER
SHAMIR
SHAPER
SHARER
SHAVER
SHINER
SHIRER
SHIVER
SHOFAR
SHOVER
SHOWER
THALER
THAYER
THENAR
WHALER
WHINER
WHITER

••HR••
ASHRAM
EPHRON
GEHRIG
LEHRER
MIHRAB
OCHRES
RAHRAH

••H•R•
ABHORS
ADHERE
ALHIRT
AMHARA
ASHARP
ASHORE
AWHIRL
BIHARI
BSHARP
COHERE
COHORT
CSHARP
DEHORN
DSHARP
EPHORI
EPHORS
ERHARD
ESHARP
ETHERS
EXHORT
FSHARP
GSHARP
INHERE
JOHORE
LAHORE
MOHURS
OCHERS
OTHERS
PAHARI
REHIRE
SAHARA
SCHORL
SPHERE
TSHIRT
UNHURT
USHERS

••H••R
ACHIER
ANHYDR
ASHIER
ASHLAR
CAHIER
COHEIR
ISHTAR
KOHLER
LEHRER
MAHLER
MAHZOR
MOHAIR
REHEAR
ROHMER
WOHLER

•••HR•
ARTHRO
EUCHRE
JETHRO
NEPHRO
TEPHRA
TISHRI

•••H•R
AETHER
ANCHOR
ANTHER
ARCHER
ARTHUR
AUTHOR
BATHER
BENHUR
BOTHER
CATHER
CIPHER
CYPHER
DASHER
DITHER
EITHER
ESCHER
ESTHER
ETCHER
FATHER
FISHER
GATHER
GOPHER
GUSHER
HATHOR
HIGHER
HITHER
KOSHER
LASHER
LATHER
LOTHAR
LUSHER
LUTHER
LUTHOR
MASHER
MATHER
MENHIR
MOTHER
MUSHER
NETHER
NIGHER
NOSHER
POSHER
POTHER
RASHER
RATHER
RICHER
SENHOR
SIGHER
TETHER
TITHER
TOTHER
WASHER
WETHER
WISHER
WITHER
ZEPHYR
ZITHER

H•S•••
HASBRO
HASHED
HASHES
HASPED
HASSAM
HASSAN
HASSLE
HASTEN
HASTES
HESIOD
HESTER
HESTIA
HESTON
HISPID
HISSAT
HISSED
HISSER
HISSES
HOSELS
HOSIER
HOSING
HOSTAS
HOSTED
HOSTEL
HUSHED
HUSHES
HUSKED
HUSKER
HUSSAR
HUSTLE
HUSTON
HYSSOP

H••S••
HALSEY
HANSEL
HANSOM
HANSON
HASSAM
HASSAN
HASSLE
HAUSAS
HAWSER
HAWSES
HEISTS
HEMSIN
HENSON
HERSEY
HIRSCH
HISSAT
HISSED
HISSER
HISSES
HITSIT
HITSON
HITSUP
HOBSON
HOISTS
HONSHU
HOPSUP
HORSED
HORSES
HORSEY
HOUSED
HOUSES
HUDSON
HUSSAR
HYKSOS
HYSSOP

H•••S•
HALEST
HARASS
HAVASU
HEARST
HERESY
HOARSE
HOLISM
HOLIST
HONEST
HUGEST

H••••S
HABEAS
HABITS
HACEKS
HADJES
HADJIS
HAGGIS
HAIDAS
HAIKUS
HAINES
HAJJES
HAJJIS
HAKIMS
HALERS
HALLOS
HALOES
HALVES
HAMALS
HARASS
HAREMS
HARRIS
HASHES
HASTES
HATERS
HAUNTS
HAUSAS
HAVENS
HAVOCS
HAWSES
HAZANS
HAZELS
HAZERS
HBEAMS
HBOMBS
HEARTS
HEATHS
HEAVES
HEDGES
HEISTS
HELENS
HELIOS
HELLAS
HELLOS
HELOTS
HELVES
HENNAS
HERMES
HEROES
HERONS
HEWERS
HEXADS
HEXERS
HIATUS
HIDERS
HIKERS
HINDUS
HINGES
HIPPOS
HIRERS
HISSES
HMONGS
HOARDS
HOAXES
HOBBES
HOBOES
HODADS
HOGANS
HOISTS
HOLMES
HOMERS
HONEYS
HONORS
HOOHAS
HOOVES
HOPERS
HORDES
HORSES
HOSELS
HOSTAS
HOTELS
HOUNDS
HOURIS
HOUSES
HOVELS
HOVERS
HOWTOS
HUBRIS
HUEVOS
HUGHES
HULLOS
HUMANS
HUMMUS
HUMORS
HUMPHS
HURONS
HUSHES
HUZZAS
HYADES
HYDRAS
HYDROS
HYENAS
HYKSOS
HYPNOS

•H•S••
CHASED
CHASER
CHASES
CHASMS
CHASSE
CHASTE
CHESTS
CHESTY
CHISEL
CHISOX
CHOSEN
GHOSTS
PHASED
PHASER
PHASES
PHYSED
PHYSIO
RHESUS
SHASTA
THESES
THESIS
THESIX
THISBE
THUSLY
WHISKS
XHOSAS

•H••S•
AHIMSA
CHAISE
CHASSE
CHEESE
CHEESY
CHOOSE
CHOOSY
CHRISM
CHUHSI
LHOTSE
PHRASE
SHIEST
SHIISM
SHYEST
THEISM
THEIST
THIRST
THRASH
THRESH
THRUSH
THRUST
THYRSI
WHILST
WHIMSY
WHOOSH

•H•••S
CHAFES
CHAFFS
CHAINS
CHAIRS
CHALKS
CHAMPS
CHANTS
CHARMS
CHARTS
CHASES
CHASMS
CHEATS
CHECKS
CHEEKS
CHEEPS
CHEERS
CHELAS
CHEOPS
CHESTS
CHIAUS
CHICKS
CHIDES
CHIEFS
CHILDS
CHILLS
CHIMES
CHIMPS
CHINES
CHINKS
CHINOS
CHIRPS
CHIRRS
CHIVES
CHOCKS
CHOIRS
CHOKES
CHOMPS
CHORDS
CHORES
CHORUS
CHUCKS
CHUMPS
CHUNKS
CHURLS
CHURNS
CHURRS
CHUTES
DHOLES
DHOTIS
GHAZIS
GHOSTS
GHOULS
KHAKIS
KHMERS
NHLERS
PHAGES
PHAROS
PHASES
PHIALS
PHILOS
PHOBOS
PHOCIS
PHONES
PHONOS
PHOTOS
RHESUS
RHEUMS
RHINOS
RHODES
RHOMBS
RHUMBS
RHYMES
SHACKS
SHADES
SHAFTS
SHAKES
SHAKOS
SHALES
SHAMES
SHAMUS
SHANKS
SHAPES
SHARDS
SHARES
SHARKS
SHARPS
SHAVES
SHAWLS
SHAWMS
SHEAFS
SHEARS
SHEENS
SHEEPS
SHEERS
SHEETS
SHEIKS
SHELLS
SHIFTS
SHILLS
SHINES
SHIRES
SHIRKS
SHIRRS
SHIRTS
SHOALS
SHOATS
SHOCKS
SHOERS
SHOJIS
SHOOKS
SHOOTS
SHORES
SHORTS
SHOUTS
SHOVES
SHREDS
SHREWS
SHRUBS
SHRUGS
SHUCKS
SHUNTS
THALES
THAMES
THANES
THANKS
THATIS
THEBES
THEFTS
THEIRS
THEMES
THERMS
THESES
THESIS
THETAS
THETIS
THIGHS
THILLS
THINGS
THINKS
THIRDS
THOLES
THOMAS
THONGS
THORNS
THORPS
THREES
THRIPS
THROBS
THROES
THROWS
THRUMS
THUJAS
THUMBS
THUMPS
THUNKS
THYMUS
UHLANS
WHACKS
WHALES
WHARFS
WHEATS
WHEELS
WHELKS
WHELPS
WHIFFS
WHILES
WHINES
WHIRLS
WHIRRS
WHISKS
WHITES
WHOLES
WHOMPS
WHOOFS
WHOOPS
WHORLS
XHOSAS

••H•S•
AGHAST
BEHEST
COHOST
REHASH
SCHISM
SCHIST
SCHUSS

••H••S
ABHORS
APHIDS
ATHENS
CAHOWS
ECHOES
EPHAHS
EPHODS
EPHORS
ETHERS
ETHICS
ETHNOS
JIHADS
LEHUAS
MAHDIS
MOHURS
NOHITS
OCHERS
OCHRES
OGHAMS
OTHERS
REHEMS
SAHIBS
SCHMOS
SCHUSS
SCHWAS
TEHEES
USHERS
WAHOOS
YAHOOS

•••HS•
CHUHSI
TZUHSI

•••H•S
ABOHMS
ALOHAS
ALPHAS
ARCHES
AUGHTS
BASHES
BATHES
BATHOS
BIGHTS
BRAHMS
BUSHES
CACHES
CASHES
COSHES
DACHAS
DASHES
DISHES
EIGHTS
ETCHES
FICHES
FICHUS
FIGHTS
FISHES
FOEHNS
GASHES
GUSHES
HASHES
HOOHAS
HUGHES
HUSHES
INCHES
ITCHES
JANHUS
JOSHES
LACHES
LASHES
LATHES
LIGHTS
LITHOS
MACHES
MACHOS
MASHES
MATHIS
MESHES
MOCHAS
MUGHOS
MUSHES
MYTHOS
NACHOS
NICHES
NIGHTS
NOSHES
OMAHAS
OUGHTS
PASHAS
PATHOS
PUSHES
RACHIS
RASHES
RICHES
RIGHTS
RUCHES
RUSHES
SASHES
SIGHTS
SPAHIS
SUCHAS
TETHYS
TIGHTS
TITHES
TOPHUS
TYPHUS
WASHES
WIGHTS
WISHES
WITHES
YACHTS

••••HS
ALEPHS
BERTHS
BIRTHS
BOOTHS
BOUGHS
BROTHS
BURGHS
CLOTHS
CONCHS
COUGHS
CZECHS
DEPTHS
DOUGHS
EPHAHS
EPOCHS
FAITHS
FIFTHS
FIRTHS
FROTHS
GARTHS
GIRTHS
GLYPHS
GRAPHS
HEATHS
HUMPHS
LAUGHS
LOTAHS
MONTHS
MORPHS
MOUTHS
MYNAHS
MYRRHS
NEIGHS
NINTHS
NYMPHS
OBEAHS
PSYCHS
RAJAHS
ROUGHS
SIXTHS
SLOTHS
SMITHS
SNATHS
SOUGHS
SURAHS
SWATHS
SYLPHS
TENTHS
THIGHS
TORAHS
TOUGHS
TROTHS
TRUTHS
WEIGHS
WIDTHS
WORTHS
WRATHS
YOUTHS

H•T•••
HATARI
HATBOX
HATERS
HATHOR
HATING
HATPIN
HATRED
HATTED
HATTER
HATTIE
HETERO
HETMAN
HETTIE
HITECH
HITHER
HITMAN
HITMEN
HITSIT
HITSON
HITSUP
HITTER
HOTAIR
HOTBED
HOTBOX
HOTCAP
HOTCAR
HOTDOG
HOTELS
HOTPOT
HOTROD
HOTTEA
HOTTER
HOTTIP
HOTTUB
HOTWAR
HUTTED
HUTTON

H••T••
HAFTED
HALTED
HALTER
HASTEN
HASTES
HATTED
HATTER
HATTIE
HEATED
HEATER
HEATHS
HEATUP
HECTIC
HECTOR
HEFTED
HELTER
HEPTAD
HESTER
HESTIA
HESTON
HETTIE
HIATAL
HIATUS
HILTON
HINTAT
HINTED
HINTER
HINTON
HITTER
HOGTIE
HOOTAT
HOOTED
HOOTER
HORTON
HOSTAS
HOSTED
HOSTEL
HOTTEA
HOTTER
HOTTIP
HOTTUB
HOWTOS
HUNTED
HUNTER
HURTLE
HUSTLE
HUSTON
HUTTED
HUTTON
HYETAL

H•••T•
HABITS
HALITE
HAMITE
HAUNTS
HEALTH
HEARTH
HEARTS
HEARTY
HECATE
HEISTS
HELDTO
HELOTS
HEMATO
HERETO
HOISTS
HOLDTO
HOVETO

H••••T
HAEMAT
HAIGHT
HALEST
HAMLET
HAVEAT
HAVENT
HEARST
HEIGHT
HELMET
HELMUT
HENBIT
HEPCAT
HEREAT
HERIOT
HERMIT
HIDOUT
HINTAT
HISSAT
HITSIT
HOBART
HOBBIT
HOHHOT
HOLDIT
HOLIST
HONEST
HOOFIT
HOOTAT
HORNET
HOTPOT
HUBERT
HUGEST

•HT•••
SHTETL
SHTICK

•H•T••
BHUTAN
BHUTTO
CHATTY
CHATUP
CHITIN
CHITON
CHUTED
CHUTES
DHOTEL
DHOTIS
GHETTO
LHOTSE
PHATIC
PHOTIC
PHOTOG
PHOTON
PHOTOS
RHETOR
RHYTHM
RHYTON
SHOTAT
SHOTUP
SHUTIN
SHUTUP
THATCH
THATIS
THETAS
THETIC
THETIS
THETOY
WHATIF
WHITEN
WHITER
WHITES

•H••T•
BHAKTI
BHUTTO
CHANTS
CHARTS
CHASTE
CHATTY
CHEATS
CHESTS
CHESTY
CHINTZ
CHOATE
GHETTO
GHOSTS
SHAFTS
SHAKTI
SHANTY
SHASTA
SHEATH
SHEETS
SHIFTS
SHIFTY
SHIITE
SHINTO
SHIRTS
SHIRTY
SHOATS
SHOOTS
SHORTS
SHORTY
SHOUTS
SHTETL
SHUNTS
THEFTS
THIRTY
WHEATS

•H•••T
CHALET
CHEVET
SHEVAT
SHIEST
SHOTAT
SHRIFT
SHYEST
THEIST
THIRST
THREAT
THRIFT
THROAT
THRUST
THWART
WHILST
WHYNOT

••HT••
ICHTHY
ISHTAR

••H•T•
NOHITS
OPHITE
TAHITI

••H••T
AGHAST
ALHIRT
BEHEST
COHORT
COHOST
EXHORT
HOHHOT
MAHOUT
REHEAT
SCHIST
TSHIRT
UNHURT
UTHANT

•••HT•
AUGHTS
BIGHTS
EIGHTH
EIGHTS
EIGHTY
FICHTE
FIGHTS
LIGHTS
MIGHTY
NIGHTS
NIGHTY
OUGHTS
PASHTO
RIGHTO
RIGHTS
SIGHTS
TIGHTS
VASHTI
WIGHTS
YACHTS

•••H•T
ATTHAT
CACHET
FOGHAT
HOHHOT
MISHIT
OLDHAT
OUTHIT
REDHAT
REDHOT
RESHOT
ROCHET
SACHET
SOTHAT
SOWHAT
TINHAT
TOPHAT
UPSHOT
WITHIT

••••HT
ALIGHT
ARIGHT
BLIGHT
BOUGHT
BRECHT
BRIGHT
CAUGHT
DWIGHT
FLIGHT
FOUGHT
FRIGHT
HAIGHT
HEIGHT
KNIGHT
NAUGHT
NOUGHT
PLIGHT
SLIGHT
SOUGHT
TAUGHT
VEIGHT
VOIGHT
WEIGHT
WRIGHT

HU••••
HUBBLE
HUBBLY
HUBBUB
HUBCAP
HUBERT
HUBRIS
HUDDLE
HUDSON
HUEVOS
HUFFED
HUGELY
HUGEST
HUGGED
HUGGER
HUGHES
HULKED
HULLED
HULLER
HULLOS
HUMANE
HUMANS
HUMBLE
HUMBLY
HUMBUG
HUMERI
HUMMED
HUMMER
HUMMUS
HUMORS
HUMOUR
HUMPED
HUMPHS
HUNGER
HUNGIN
HUNGON
HUNGRY
HUNGUP
HUNGWU
HUNKER
HUNTED
HUNTER
HURDLE
HURLED
HURLER
HURLEY
HURONS
HURRAH
HURRAY
HURTLE
HUSHED
HUSHES
HUSKED
HUSKER
HUSSAR
HUSTLE
HUSTON
HUTTED
HUTTON
HUXLEY
HUZZAH
HUZZAS

H•U•••
HAULED
HAULER
HAULUP
HAUNCH
HAUNTS
HAUSAS
HOUNDS
HOURIS
HOURLY
HOUSED
HOUSES

H••U••
HECUBA

H•••U•
HAIKUS
HALLUX
HANGUL
HANGUP
HARDUP
HAULUP
HEADUP
HEATUP
HELDUP
HELIUM
HELMUT
HIATUS
HICCUP
HIDOUT
HIGHUP
HINDUS
HITSUP
HOLDUP
HOLEUP
HONOUR
HOOKUP
HOPSUP
HORMUZ
HOTTUB
HUBBUB
HUMBUG
HUMMUS
HUMOUR
HUNGUP

H••••U
HAIKOU
HALERU
HAVASU
HEYYOU
HONSHU
HUNGWU

•HU•••
BHUTAN
BHUTTO
CHUBBY
CHUCKS
CHUHSI
CHUKAR
CHUKKA
CHUMMY
CHUMPS
CHUNKS
CHUNKY
CHURCH
CHURLS
CHURNS
CHURRO
CHURRS
CHUTED
CHUTES
RHUMBA
RHUMBS
SHUCKS
SHUNTS
SHUTIN
SHUTUP
THUJAS
THUMBS
THUMPS
THUNKS
THUSLY
ZHUKOV

•H•U••
CHOUGH
GHOULS
RHEUMS
RHEUMY
SHOULD
SHOUTS
SHRUBS
SHRUGS
SHRUNK
THOUGH
THRUMS
THRUSH
THRUST

•H••U•
CHATUP
CHEQUE
CHERUB
CHEWUP
CHIAUS
CHINUP
CHORUS
PHYLUM
RHESUS
SHAMUS
SHOGUN
SHOTUP
SHOWUP
SHROUD
SHUTUP
THYMUS
WHIPUP

•H•••U
CHOOYU

••HU••
COHUNE
INHUME
KAHUNA
LEHUAS
MOHURS
REHUNG
SCHULZ
SCHUSS
UNHURT
YEHUDI

••H•U•
INHAUL
KAHLUA
MAHOUT

•••HU•
ARTHUR
BENHUR
FICHUS
HIGHUP
JANHUS
JOSHUA
LASHUP
NASHUA
PUSHUP
TOPHUS
TUCHUN
TYPHUS
WASHUP

•••H•U
CACHOU
FUZHOU
VISHNU

••••HU
HONSHU
KYUSHU
MANCHU
PENGHU
PICCHU

H•V•••
HAVANA
HAVASU
HAVEAT
HAVENS
HAVENT
HAVEON
HAVING
HAVOCS
HIVAOA
HIVING
HOVELS
HOVERS
HOVETO

H••V••
HALVAH
HALVED
HALVES
HARVEY
HEAVED
HEAVEN
HEAVER
HEAVES
HELVES
HOOVER
HOOVES
HUEVOS

H•••V•
HALEVY

•H•V••
CHAVEZ
CHEVAL
CHEVET
CHEVRE
CHIVES
SHAVED
SHAVEN
SHAVER
SHAVES
SHEVAT
SHIVER
SHOVED
SHOVEL
SHOVER
SHOVES

•H••V•
SHEAVE
SHELVE
SHRIVE
SHROVE
THEYVE
THIEVE
THRIVE
THROVE

•H•••V
ZHUKOV

••H•V•
BEHAVE
MOHAVE

•••H•V
MOSHAV

H•W•••
HAWAII
HAWHAW
HAWING
HAWKED
HAWKER
HAWSER
HAWSES
HEWERS
HEWING
HOWARD
HOWDAH
HOWELL
HOWLED
HOWLER
HOWLIN
HOWNOW
HOWTOS

H••W••
HOTWAR

H•••W•
HUNGWU

H••••W
HALLOW
HARLOW
HARROW
HAWHAW
HAYMOW
HEBREW
HEEHAW
HOLLOW
HOWNOW

•HW•••
OHWELL
THWACK
THWART

•H•W••
CHEWED
CHEWER
CHEWUP
CHOWED
SHAWLS
SHAWMS
SHOWED
SHOWER
SHOWIN
SHOWME
SHOWUP
THAWED
THEWIZ

•H••W•
SHREWD
SHREWS
THROWN
THROWS

•H•••W
SHADOW

••HW••
SCHWAS
WAHWAH
YAHWEH

••H•W•
CAHOWS
MOHAWK
OSHAWA

•••HW•
BUSHWA

•••H•W
ANDHOW
ANYHOW
CASHEW
CUSHAW
ESCHEW
HAWHAW
HEEHAW
NEPHEW
NOSHOW
TVSHOW

H•X•••
HEXADS
HEXERS
HEXING
HUXLEY

H••X••
HOAXED
HOAXER
HOAXES

H••••X
HALLUX
HATBOX
HOTBOX

•H•••X
CHISOX
THESIX
THORAX

••H••X
SPHINX

HY••••
HYADES
HYBRID
HYDRAE

HYDRAS
HYDROS
HYENAS
HYETAL
HYKSOS
HYMNAL
HYMNED
HYPHEN
HYPING
HYPNOS
HYPOED
HYSSOP

H•Y•••

HAYDEN
HAYING
HAYLEY
HAYMOW
HEYDAY
HEYJOE
HEYYOU
HOYDEN

H••Y••

HEYYOU

H•••Y•

HEARYE
HONEYS

H••••Y

HAILEY
HALEVY
HALLEY
HALSEY
HARDLY
HARLEY
HARVEY
HAYLEY
HAZILY
HEARTY
HENLEY
HEREBY
HERESY
HERSEY
HEYDAY
HICKEY
HIGHLY
HILARY
HOCKEY
HOMELY
HOMILY
HOMINY
HOORAY
HORNEY
HORSEY
HOURLY
HUBBLY
HUGELY
HUMBLY
HUNGRY
HURLEY
HURRAY
HUXLEY

•HY•••

KHYBER
OHYEAH
PHYLAE
PHYLLO
PHYLUM
PHYSED
PHYSIO
RHYMED
RHYMER
RHYMES
RHYTHM
RHYTON
SHYEST
SHYING
THYMUS
THYRSI
WHYDAH
WHYNOT

•H•Y••

SHAYNE
THAYER
THEYLL
THEYRE
THEYVE

•H••Y•

CHERYL
CHOOYU
PHENYL

•H•••Y

CHAFFY
CHALKY
CHAMMY
CHANCY
CHANEY
CHARLY
CHATTY
CHEEKY
CHEERY
CHEESY
CHERRY
CHESTY
CHILLY
CHINKY
CHIRPY
CHOOSY
CHOPPY
CHUBBY
CHUMMY
CHUNKY
GHARRY
OHENRY
PHILLY
PHOOEY
RHEUMY
SHABBY
SHAGGY
SHALEY
SHALLY
SHANDY
SHANTY
SHEEDY
SHEEHY
SHELLY
SHERRY
SHIFTY
SHILLY
SHIMMY
SHINDY
SHINNY
SHIRTY
SHODDY
SHORTY
THEORY
THETOY
THINLY
THIRTY
THORNY
THUSLY
WHACKY
WHAMMY
WHEEZY
WHERRY
WHIMSY
WHINNY
WHIPPY
WHIRLY
WHOLLY

••HY••

ANHYDR
MRHYDE

••H••Y

ASHLEY
ICHTHY
JOHNNY
UNHOLY

•••HY•

METHYL
TETHYS
ZEPHYR

•••H•Y

ARCHLY
CATHAY
EIGHTY
HIGHLY
LUSHLY
MIGHTY
MYOHMY
NIGHTY
POSHLY
RASHLY
RICHLY
SASHAY

••••HY

APATHY
BRASHY
BRUSHY
CATCHY
DINGHY
DOUGHY
EARTHY
FILTHY
FLASHY
FLESHY
FROTHY
GUNSHY
ICHTHY
MARSHY
MOUTHY
MURPHY
PATCHY
PEACHY
PLASHY
PLUSHY
POACHY
POUCHY
PUNCHY
SHEEHY
SLITHY
SLOSHY
SLUSHY
SMITHY
TETCHY
TOOTHY
TOUCHY
TOUGHY
TRASHY
TROPHY
WITCHY
WORTHY

H•Z•••

HAZANS
HAZARD
HAZELS
HAZERS
HAZIER
HAZILY
HAZING
HUZZAH
HUZZAS

H••Z••

HERZOG
HUZZAH
HUZZAS

H••••Z

HORMUZ

•H•Z••

GHAZIS
SHAZAM

•H••Z•

WHEEZE
WHEEZY

•H•••Z

CHAVEZ
CHINTZ
SHIRAZ
THEWIZ

••HZ••

MAHZOR

••H••Z

SCHNOZ
SCHULZ

IA••••

IAMBIC
IATRIC

I•A•••

IBADAN
ICARIA
ICARUS
IMAGED
IMAGER
IMAGES
IMARET
INAFIX
INAFOG
INAJAM
INANER
INAPET
INARCH
INAROW
INARUT
INAWAY
IRANIS
IRAQIS
IRATER
ISABEL
ISADOR
ISAIAH
ITALIA
ITALIC
ITASCA
IZABAL

I••A••

IBEAMS
ICEAGE
IDCARD
IDEALS
IDEATE
IGNACE
IGNATZ
IGUACU
IGUANA
ILEANA
IMPACT
IMPAIR
IMPALA
IMPALE
IMPART
INCANS
INCASE
INCASH
INDABA
INFACT
INFAMY
INFANT
INHALE
INHALF
INHAND
INHAUL
INLAID
INLAND
INLAWS
INLAYS
INMATE
INNAGE
INNATE
INPART
INSANE
INTACT
INTAKE
INVADE
INVAIN
INWARD
IODATE
IOWANS
ISLAND
ISRAEL
ITHACA
ITHAKI
IZZARD

I•••A•

IBADAN
ICEBAG
ICECAP
ICEMAN
ILLSAY
INAJAM
INAWAY
INDIAN
INGEAR
INGMAR
INLEAF
INPLAY
INROAD
INSEAM
INSPAN
INSTAR
IONIAN
IPECAC
IRREAL
ISAIAH
ISHTAR
ISOBAR
ITZHAK
IZABAL

I••••A

IBERIA
ICARIA
IGUANA
ILEANA
ILESHA
IMELDA
IMPALA
INDABA
INDIRA
INTIMA
ISCHIA
ISTRIA
ITALIA
ITASCA
ITHACA

•IA•••

BIAFRA
BIANCA
BIASED
BIASES
CIARDI
DIABLO
DIADEM
DIALED
DIALER
DIALOG
DIAPER
DIATOM
FIACRE
FIANCE
FIASCO
GIANTS
HIATAL
HIATUS
KIANGS
LIABLE
LIAISE
LIANAS
LIANGS
MIASMA
NIACIN
NIAMEY
PIAFFE
PIAGET
PIANOS
PIAZZA
RIALTO
RIATAS
TIARAS
VIABLE
VIABLY
VIACOM
VIANDS
XIAMEN

•I•A••

AIRARM
BICARB
BIGAMY
BIHARI
BINARY
BINATE
CICADA
CIGARS
DIDACT
DILATE
DINARS
DISANT
DISARM
DIVANS
FIGARO
FINALE
FINALS
FIXATE
GIRARD
GITANO
HIJACK
HILARY
HIVAOA
JICAMA
JIHADS
KIGALI
LIGATE
LILACS
LINAGE
LIPASE
LITANY
LIZARD
MIDAIR
MIKADO
MILADY
MILANO
MIRAGE
NICAEA
PICABO
PICARA
PICARD
PICARO
PIKAKE
PILAFS
PILATE
PINATA
PIPALS
PIRACY
PIRANA
PIRATE
PISANS
PIZAZZ
RIBALD
RIBAND
RITARD
RIVALS
RIYADH
RIYALS
SILAGE
SISALS
SITARS
SIWASH
TICALS
TILAKS
TIRADE
TIRANA
TIRANE
TISANE
TITANS
VICARS
VIRAGO
VISAED
VISAGE
VITALS
VIVACE
VIVANT
WIZARD

•I••A•

AIMSAT
AIRBAG
AIRDAM
AIRMAN
AIRSAC
AIRWAY
BIGMAC
BILBAO
BIOGAS
BIOTAS
BISCAY
BISSAU
BITMAP
CIUDAD
DIGRAM
DIKTAT
DIRHAM
DISBAR
DISMAL
DISMAY
DISTAL
FIJIAN
FILIAL
FINIAL
FINNAN
FIRMAN
FISCAL
GIBRAN
GILEAD
GIMBAL
HIATAL
HIEMAL
HINTAT
HISSAT
HITMAN
JIGSAW
JINNAH
KIDMAN
KIDNAP
KIOWAS
KIRMAN
KITBAG
KITKAT
LIANAS
LIBYAN
LINEAL
LINEAR
MICMAC
MIDDAY
MIDWAY
MIHRAB
MILLAY
MILPAS
MILSAP
MINOAN
MINYAN
MIRIAM
MISHAP
MISLAY
MISSAL
MISSAY
MITRAL
NICEAN
NILGAI
NINJAS
NIPSAT
NISSAN
OILCAN
OILMAN
OILPAN
PICKAT
PICKAX
PIEMAN
PIEPAN
PIETAS
PILLAR
PINDAR
PINEAL
PINNAE
PINNAS
PINOAK
PISGAH
PITMAN
PITSAW
PIZZAS
QINTAR
RIATAS
RIOJAS
RIPRAP
RIPSAW
RITUAL
SIGMAS
SIGNAL
SILOAM
SIMIAN
SINBAD
SINEAD
SINTAX
SIOUAN
SIRDAR
SIRRAH
TIARAS
TIBIAE
TIBIAL
TIBIAS
TICTAC
TIMBAL
TINCAL
TINCAN
TINEAR
TINHAT
TINMAN
TINPAN
TITIAN
VILLAS
VIOLAS
VISTAS
VISUAL
VIVIAN
WICCAN
WIGWAG
WIGWAM
WINKAT
WITHAL
ZIGZAG
ZILPAH

•I•••A

BIAFRA
BIANCA
CIBOLA
CICADA
CINEMA
EIDOLA
FIBULA
FIESTA
HIVAOA
JICAMA
LIGULA
LINGUA
LIOTTA
LISBOA
MIASMA
MIKITA
MIMOSA
MINIMA
MISCHA
NICAEA
NICOLA
NIKITA
NIKOLA
PIAZZA
PICARA
PINATA
PIRANA
RIVERA
SIENNA
SIERRA
SIESTA
SILICA
SIRICA
SISERA
TIERRA
TIRANA
VICUNA
VIENNA
VIGODA
VIZSLA
WINONA
XIMENA
ZINNIA

••IA••

APIARY
ASIANS
AVIANS
AVIARY
AVIATE
BRIAND
BRIANS
BRIARD
BRIARS
CHIANG
CHIAUS
CUIABA
FRIARS
FRIARY
GUIANA
NAIADS
OPIATE
ORIANA
PHIALS
PLIANT
TRIADS
TRIAGE
TRIALS
UMIAKS
UNIATE
UNIATS
URIALS

••I•A•

ADIDAS
AKITAS
ANIMAL
ANIMAS
APICAL
BAIKAL
BRIDAL
CAIMAN
CEIBAS
CLIMAX
ELIJAH
EPICAL
FAISAL
FBIMAN
FRIDAY
GUITAR
HAIDAS
HAINAN
KLIBAN
MAITAI
NAIRAS
OBIWAN
OHIOAN
OVISAC
PHILAE
PLICAE
PRIMAL
RAILAT
RHINAL
SAIGAS
SAIPAN
SHIRAZ
SMILAX
SPICAS
SPINAL
SPIRAL
SPIVAK
TAIGAS
TAINAN
TAIPAN
TAIWAN
TRIBAL
TRINAL
UNITAL
UNITAS
UNIVAC
VEINAL
WEIMAR

••I••A

AHIMSA
ALICIA
ANITRA
ARISTA
AXILLA
CHICHA
CRIMEA
CUIABA
ELISHA
ELISSA
EMILIA
ENIGMA
FLICKA
GEISHA
GLINKA
GUIANA
GUINEA
KAILUA
OJIBWA
OLINDA
OLIVIA
ORIANA
ORISSA
QUINOA
SPIREA
STIGMA
TRICIA
TRISHA
TRIVIA
VAISYA

•••IA•

ADRIAN
AERIAL
APPIAN
ATRIAL
AUDIAL
BAHIAN
BELIAL
CAPIAS
CAVIAR
COBIAS
CURIAE
CURIAL
DENIAL
DORIAN
DURIAN
EOLIAN
EONIAN
ESPIAL
FABIAN
FACIAL
FENIAN
FIJIAN
FILIAL
FINIAL
FOLIAR
FUJIAN
GAVIAL
GENIAL
INDIAN
IONIAN
ISAIAH
JOSIAH
JOVIAL
JOVIAN
JULIAN
KODIAK
LABIAL
LAMIAS
LARIAT
LUCIAN
MANIAC
MANIAS
MARIAH
MARIAN
MEDIAL
MEDIAN
MEDIAS
MENIAL
MIRIAM
MUSIAL
MYRIAD
NARIAL
NORIAS
NUBIAN
OBRIAN
OSSIAN
PARIAH
PLEIAD
RACIAL
RADIAL
RADIAN
REDIAL
RETIAL
RUPIAH
SAMIAM
SEPIAS
SERIAL
SIMIAN
SOCIAL
STRIAE
SYRIAN
TIBIAE
TIBIAL
TIBIAS
TITIAN
TOBIAS
TUPIAN
TYRIAN
UGRIAN
UNCIAL
UZZIAH
VENIAL
VIVIAN
ZODIAC

•••I•A

AFRICA
AQUILA
ARNICA
ARRIBA
ATTICA
ATTILA
AURIGA
CAPITA
CARINA
COLIMA
COVINA
DAMITA
DESICA
ELMIRA
ELVIRA
ENCINA
EROICA
FAJITA
FARINA
FATIMA
GEZIRA
GODIVA
HEGIRA
INDIRA
INTIMA
KARIBA
KONICA
LADIDA
LAMINA
LATINA
LERIDA
LEXICA
LOLITA
LORICA
LOUISA
LUMINA
MANILA
MARINA
MARISA
MAXIMA
MEDINA
MELINA
MERIDA
MIKITA
MINIMA
MONICA
MORITA
NIKITA
NUMINA
ONEIDA
OPTIMA
OREIDA
PATINA
PEPITA
PURINA
REGINA
RETINA
ROSITA
RUMINA
SALINA
SALIVA
SHEILA
SILICA
SIRICA
TROIKA
TUNICA
ULTIMA
YAKIMA

••••IA

ACACIA
ACADIA
ACEDIA
AEOLIA
AGLAIA
ALEXIA
ALICIA
AMELIA
ANEMIA
ANGLIA
APULIA
ARABIA
ARALIA
BORGIA
BOSNIA
CASSIA
CRANIA
DAHLIA
EGERIA
EMILIA
ETALIA
FASCIA
FLAVIA
GALLIA
GAMBIA
GARCIA
GLORIA
GRATIA
HESTIA
IBERIA
ICARIA
ISCHIA
ISTRIA
ITALIA
KESHIA
LATVIA
LOGGIA
MARCIA
MURCIA
MYOPIA
NARNIA
NUTRIA
OBELIA
OLIVIA
PALLIA
PENNIA
PEORIA
PERSIA
PHOBIA
PORTIA
PYTHIA
RAFFIA
REALIA
RUSSIA
SALVIA
SANDIA
SCALIA
SCORIA
SCOTIA
SERBIA
SHARIA
SOPHIA
STADIA
STYRIA
SYLVIA
THALIA
TREDIA
TRICIA
TRIVIA
UMBRIA
URANIA
UTOPIA
ZAMBIA
ZINNIA
ZOYSIA

IB••••

IBADAN
IBEAMS
IBERIA
IBEXES
IBIBIO
IBIDEM
IBISES

I•B•••

IMBIBE
IMBRUE
IMBUED
IMBUES
INBORN
INBRED
INBULK

I••B••

IAMBIC
IBIBIO
ICEBAG
ICEBOX
ISABEL
ISOBAR
IZABAL

I•••B•

IMBIBE
INDABA
INDEBT
ITURBI

•IB•••

BIBBED
BIBLES
BIBLIO
CIBOLA
DIBBLE
FIBBED
FIBBER
FIBERS
FIBRES
FIBRIL
FIBRIN
FIBULA
GIBBED
GIBBER
GIBBET
GIBBON
GIBERS
GIBILL
GIBING
GIBLET
GIBRAN
GIBSON
JIBING
KIBBLE
KIBITZ
KIBOSH
LIBBED
LIBBER
LIBELS
LIBIDO
LIBRIS
LIBYAN
NIBBLE
RIBALD
RIBAND
RIBBED
RIBBON
RIBEYE
RIBOSE
SIBYLS
TIBIAE
TIBIAL
TIBIAS

•I•B••

AIRBAG
AIRBUS
BIBBED
BIGBEN
BIGBOY
BILBAO
BIOBIO
DIABLO

DIBBLE
DISBAR
FIBBED
FIBBER
GIBBED
GIBBER
GIBBET
GIBBON
GIMBAL
GIMBEL
KIBBLE
KITBAG
LIABLE
LIBBED
LIBBER
LIEBIG
LIMBED
LIMBER
LIMBOS
LIMBUS
LISBOA
LISBON
NIBBLE
NIMBLE
NIMBLY
NIMBUS
RIBBED
RIBBON
SIMBEL
SINBAD
TIDBIT
TIMBAL
TIMBER
TIMBRE
TITBIT
VIABLE
VIABLY
WILBUR
WIMBLE

•I••B•
NINGBO
PICABO

•I•••B
BICARB
DIONEB
MIDRIB
MIHRAB

••IB••
ALIBIS
ALIBLE
BRIBED
BRIBES
CEIBAS
EDIBLE
FOIBLE
GLIBLY
IBIBIO
KLIBAN
OJIBWA
ORIBIS
TRIBAL
TRIBES

••I•B•
AKIMBO
CLIMBS
CUIABA
LAIDBY
THISBE
TRILBY

•••IB•
ADLIBS
ARRIBA
CARIBE
CARIBS
IMBIBE
KARIBA
MALIBU
SAHIBS
SCRIBE
SQUIBB
SQUIBS

•••I•B
SQUIBB

••••IB
MIDRIB

IC••••
ICARIA
ICARUS
ICEAGE
ICEBAG
ICEBOX
ICECAP
ICEDIN
ICEDUP
ICEFOG
ICEMAN
ICEMEN
ICEOUT
ICESIN
ICESUP
ICHING
ICHTHY
ICICLE
ICIEST
ICINGS
ICKIER
ICONIC

I•C•••
IDCARD
INCANS
INCASE
INCASH
INCEPT
INCHED
INCHES
INCHON
INCISE
INCITE
INCOME
INCULT
INCURS
INCUSE
ISCHIA
ITCHED
ITCHES

I••C••
ICECAP
ICICLE
IPECAC

I•••C•
IDIOCY
IGNACE
IGUACU
IMPACT
INARCH
INDICT
INDUCE
INDUCT
INFACT
INFECT
INJECT
INLUCK
INSECT
INTACT
IONICS
ITASCA
ITHACA

I••••C
IAMBIC
IATRIC
ICONIC
INSYNC
IPECAC
IRENIC
IRIDIC
IRONIC
ITALIC

•IC•••
BICARB
BICEPS
BICKER
BICORN
CICADA
CICELY
CICERO
DICERS
DICIER
DICING
DICKER
DICKEY
DICOTS
DICTUM
FICHES
FICHTE
FICHUS
FICKLE
HICCUP
HICKEY
HICKOK
JICAMA
KICKED
KICKER
KICKIN
KICKUP
LICHEN
LICKED
LICTOR
MICKEY
MICMAC
MICRON
MICROS
NICAEA
NICEAN
NICELY
NICENE
NICEST
NICETY
NICHES
NICKED
NICKEL
NICKER
NICOLA
NICOLE
NICOLO
PICABO
PICARA
PICARD
PICARO
PICCHU
PICKAT
PICKAX
PICKED
PICKER
PICKET
PICKLE
PICKON
PICKUP
PICNIC
PICOTS
PICULS
RICERS
RICHEN
RICHER
RICHES
RICHIE
RICHLY
RICING
RICKED
RICKEY
SICCED
SICILY
SICKEN
SICKER
SICKLE
SICKLY
TICALS
TICKED
TICKER
TICKET
TICKLE
TICTAC
VICARS
VICTIM
VICTOR
VICUNA
WICCAN
WICKED
WICKER
WICKET
WICOPY

•I•C••
BISCAY
CIRCLE
CIRCUM
CIRCUS
CISCOS
DISCOS
DISCUS
FIACRE
FISCAL
HICCUP
KIMCHI
LITCHI
MINCED
MINCER
MINCES
MISCHA
MISCUE
NIACIN
NIECES
OILCAN
PICCHU
PIECED
PIECER
PIECES
PINCER
PISCES
SICCED
SIECLE
SITCOM
TINCAL
TINCAN
TINCTS
VIACOM
VISCID
WICCAN
WINCED
WINCER
WINCES
WITCHY
ZIRCON

•I••C•
BIANCA
BIERCE
BISECT
CIVICS
DIDACT
DIRECT
FIANCE
FIASCO
FIERCE
HIJACK
HIRSCH
HITECH
KIRSCH
KITSCH
LILACS
MIMICS
PIERCE
PIRACY
SILICA
SIRICA
TIERCE
VIVACE

•I•••C
AIRSAC
BIGMAC
BIONIC
BIOTIC
CITRIC
FINNIC
FISTIC
LITHIC
MICMAC
MIXTEC
NITRIC
PICNIC
TICTAC
VITRIC
ZIPLOC

••IC••
ALICIA
AMICES
AMICUS
APICAL
APICES
BRICKS
BRICKY
CAICOS
CHICHA
CHICHI
CHICKS
CHICLE
CLICHE
CLICKS
CRICKS
DEICED
DEICER
DEICES
EDICTS
ELICIT
EPICAL
EVICTS
FLICKA
FLICKS
ICICLE
JUICED
JUICER
JUICES
KNICKS
PLICAE
PRICED
PRICER
PRICES
PRICEY
PRICKS
QUICHE
SEICHE
SLICED
SLICER
SLICES
SLICKS
SNICKS
SPICAS
SPICED
SPICES
STICKS
STICKY
TAICHI
THICKE
TRICED
TRICES
TRICHO
TRICIA
TRICKS
TRICKY
TRICOT
UNICEF
VOICED
VOICES
YOICKS

••I•C•
APIECE
CHINCH
CLINCH
CRISCO
EVINCE
FLINCH
FLITCH
FRISCO
GLITCH
GRINCH
IDIOCY
PRINCE
QUINCE
QUINCY
SKITCH
SMIRCH
SNITCH
STITCH
SWITCH
TWITCH

••I••C
ACIDIC
CLINIC
CRITIC
EXILIC
IRIDIC
OTITIC
OVISAC
OXIDIC
STIVIC
UNIFIC
UNIVAC

•••IC•
ADVICE
AFRICA
ALNICO
ANTICS
ARNICA
ASPICS
ATTICA
ATTICS
BASICS
BODICE
CALICO
CHOICE
CIVICS
COMICS
CONICS
CUBICS
CYNICS
DELICT
DEPICT
DESICA
DEVICE
DRYICE
ELLICE
ENRICH
ENRICO
ENTICE
EROICA
ETHICS
EUNICE
INDICT
IONICS
JANICE
KONICA
LEXICA
LORICA
LYRICS
MALICE
MEDICI
MEDICO
MEDICS
MEXICO
MIMICS
MONICA
MUNICH
NATICK
NODICE
NOTICE
NOVICE
OFFICE
OPTICS
OSMICS
PANICS
PLAICE
POLICE
POLICY
PUMICE
RELICS
RELICT
REMICK
SCHICK
SHTICK
SILICA
SIRICA
SLUICE
SONICS
SPLICE
STOICS
STRICK
STRICT
THRICE
TONICS
TOPICS
TOXICS
TUNICA
TUNICS
UPTICK
VENICE
YORICK
ZURICH

•••I•C
MANIAC
MANIOC
ZODIAC

••••IC
ACETIC
ACIDIC
AEOLIC
AGARIC
ALARIC
ALTAIC
AMEBIC
ANEMIC
ANODIC
AORTIC
ARABIC
ARCTIC
ATOMIC
ATONIC
BALTIC
BARDIC
BIONIC
BIOTIC
CADMIC
CEDRIC
CELTIC
CITRIC
CLERIC
CLINIC
COPTIC
COSMIC
COURIC
CRITIC
CULTIC
CUPRIC
CYANIC
CYCLIC
CYMRIC
DELTIC
DYADIC
ECHOIC
EDENIC
EROTIC
ETHNIC
ETONIC
EXILIC
EXOTIC
FABRIC
FERRIC
FINNIC
FISTIC
FORMIC
FROLIC
FUSTIC
GAELIC
GALLIC
GARLIC
GNOMIC
GOTHIC
HECTIC
HEROIC
IAMBIC
IATRIC
ICONIC
IRENIC
IRIDIC
IRONIC
ITALIC
JUDAIC
KARMIC
LACTIC
LITHIC
MANTIC
MASTIC
METRIC
MOSAIC
MYOPIC
MYSTIC
MYTHIC
NITRIC
NOETIC
NORDIC
OLDVIC
ORPHIC
OTITIC
OXIDIC
OZONIC
PECTIC
PELVIC
PEPTIC
PHATIC
PHOBIC
PHONIC
PHOTIC
PICNIC
POETIC
PONTIC
PUBLIC
PYKNIC
ROMAIC
RUBRIC
RUSTIC
SCENIC
SEPTIC
SLAVIC
SORBIC
STATIC
STIVIC
SYNDIC
TACTIC
TANNIC
THETIC
TRAGIC
TROPIC
TURKIC
UNCHIC
UNIFIC
URALIC
URANIC
VITRIC

ID••••
IDCARD
IDEALS
IDEATE
IDIOCY
IDIOMS
IDIOTS
IDLERS
IDLEST
IDLING
IDOIDO
IDYLLS

I•D•••
INDABA
INDEBT
INDEED
INDENE
INDENT
INDIAN
INDICT
INDIES
INDIGO
INDIRA
INDITE
INDIUM
INDOOR
INDRIS
INDUCE
INDUCT
IODATE
IODIDE
IODINE
IODIZE

I••D••
IBADAN
IBIDEM
ICEDIN
ICEDUP
IRIDES
IRIDIC
ISADOR

I•••D•
IDOIDO
IMELDA
IMPEDE
INSIDE
INVADE
IODIDE
ISOLDE

I••••D
IDCARD
ILLFED
IMAGED
IMBUED
IMPEND
INBRED
INCHED
INDEED
INFOLD
INGRID
INHAND
INKIND
INLAID
INLAND
INNEED
INROAD
INTEND
INURED
INWARD
IRONED
ISLAND
ISOPOD
ISSUED
ITCHED
IZZARD

•ID•••
AIDING
BIDDEN
BIDDER
BIDDLE
BIDING
BIDSIN
BIDSON
BIDSUP
CIDERS
DIDACT
DIDDLE
DIDIES
DIDION
EIDERS
EIDOLA
FIDDLE
FIDGET
GIDEON
GIDGET
HIDDEN
HIDEHO
HIDEKI
HIDERS
HIDING
HIDOUT
KIDDED
KIDDER
KIDMAN
KIDNAP
KIDNEY
KIDORY
KIDVID
LIDDED
MIDAIR
MIDDAY
MIDDEN
MIDDLE
MIDGES
MIDGET
MIDLER
MIDORI
MIDRIB
MIDWAY
PIDGIN
RIDDED
RIDDEN
RIDDLE
RIDENT
RIDERS
RIDGED
RIDGES
RIDING
RIDLEY
SIDDUR
SIDERO
SIDERS
SIDING
SIDLED
SIDLES
SIDNEY
TIDBIT
TIDIED
TIDIER
TIDIES
TIDILY
TIDING
TIDYUP
VIDEOS
WIDELY
WIDENS
WIDEST
WIDGET
WIDOWS
WIDTHS

•I•D••
AIRDAM
AIRDRY
BIDDEN
BIDDER
BIDDLE
BINDER
BINDUP
BIRDED
BIRDER
BIRDIE
CINDER
CIUDAD
DIADEM
DIDDLE
DIKDIK
DIODES
FIDDLE
FINDER
GILDED
GILDER
GIRDED
GIRDER
GIRDLE
HIDDEN
HINDER
HINDUS
KIDDED
KIDDER
KINDER
KINDLE
KINDLY
KINDOF
LIDDED
LIEDER
LINDEN
MIDDAY
MIDDEN
MIDDLE
MILDER
MILDEW
MILDLY
MINDED
MINDER
MISDID
PINDAR
PINDUS
RIDDED
RIDDEN
RIDDLE
SIDDUR
SIRDAR
TIEDIN
TIEDUP
TIEDYE
TILDEN
TILDES
TINDER
WILDER
WILDLY
WINDED
WINDER
WINDEX
WINDOM
WINDOW
WINDUP
WISDOM

•I••D•
AIKIDO
BIONDI
BIPEDS
BIPODS
CIARDI
CICADA
DIPODY
DIRNDL
DIVIDE
FIELDS
FIENDS
FIORDS
JIHADS
LIBIDO
LIPIDE
LIPIDS
MIKADO
MILADY
RIYADH
TIRADE
VIANDS
VIGODA
WIELDS
YIELDS

•I•••D
BIASED
BIBBED
BIFFED
BIFOLD
BIGRED
BILKED
BILLED
BINGED
BINNED
BIRDED
BIRLED
BITTED
CIUDAD
DIALED
DIETED
DIMMED
DINGED
DINNED
DINTED
DIPPED
DISHED
DISKED
DISSED
FIBBED
FILLED
FILMED
FINKED
FINNED
FIRMED
FISHED
FISTED
FITTED
FIZZED
GIBBED
GIFTED
GIGGED
GILDED
GILEAD
GILLED
GINNED
GIPPED
GIRARD
GIRDED
GIRTED
HILLED
HINGED
HINTED
HIPPED
HISPID
HISSED
JIGGED
JILTED
JINKED
JINXED
KICKED
KIDDED
KIDVID
KILLED
KILNED
KILTED
KINGED
KINKED
KISSED
LIBBED
LICKED
LIDDED
LIFTED
LILTED
LIMBED
LIMNED
LIMPED
LIMPID
LINKED
LIPOID
LIPPED
LIQUID
LISPED
LISTED
LIZARD
MIFFED
MILKED
MILLED
MILORD
MINCED
MINDED
MINTED
MISDID
MISLED
MISSED
MISTED
MITRED
NICKED
NIMROD
NIPPED
OINKED
PICARD
PICKED
PIECED
PIGGED
PILLED
PINGED
PINKED
PINNED
PIPPED
PIQUED
PITHED
PITIED
PITTED
RIBALD
RIBAND
RIBBED
RICKED
RIDDED
RIDGED
RIFFED
RIFLED
RIFTED
RIGGED
RIMMED
RINGED
RINSED
RIOTED
RIPPED
RISKED
RITARD
SICCED
SIDLED
SIEGED
SIEVED
SIFTED
SIGHED
SIGNED
SIGURD
SILKED
SILOED
SILTED
SINBAD
SINEAD
SINGED
SINNED
SIPPED
TICKED
TIDIED
TIERED
TIEROD
TIFFED
TILLED
TILTED
TINGED
TINGOD
TINNED
TINTED
TIPPED
TITHED
TITLED
VIEWED
VISAED
VISCID
WICKED
WIGGED
WILLED
WILTED
WINCED
WINDED
WINGED
WINKED
WISHED
WISPED
WITHED
WITTED
WIZARD
YIPPED
ZIGGED
ZINGED
ZIPPED

••ID••
ABIDED
ABIDES
ACIDIC
ACIDLY
ADIDAS
AMIDES
AMIDOL
AMIDST
ARIDLY
ASIDES
AVIDLY
BRIDAL
BRIDES
BRIDGE
BRIDLE
BSIDES
CHIDED
CHIDES
CNIDUS
DEIDRE
ELIDED
ELIDES
FRIDAY
FRIDGE
GLIDED
GLIDER
GLIDES
GUIDED
GUIDES
GUIDON
HAIDAS
HEIDEN
IBIDEM
IRIDES
IRIDIC

LAIDBY
LAIDIN
LAIDON
LAIDTO
LAIDUP
LEIDEN
MAIDEN
MAIDUS
OXIDES
OXIDIC
PAIDIN
PAIDUP
PRIDED
PRIDES
RAIDED
RAIDER
SEIDEL
SLIDER
SLIDES
SLIDIN
SNIDER
SPIDER
VOIDED
ZUIDER

••I•D•

BLINDS
BUILDS
CHILDE
CHILDS
GRINDS
GUILDS
HAIRDO
LAIRDS
NAIADS
OLINDA
OVIEDO
SHINDY
TBIRDS
THIRDS
TRIADS
TRIODE
WEIRDO

••I••D

ABIDED
AFIELD
BAILED
BAITED
BOILED
BRIAND
BRIARD
BRIBED
BRIGID
BRINED
CEILED
CHIDED
CHIMED
COIFED
COILED
COINED
DEICED
EDITED
ELIDED
EXILED
EXITED
FAILED
FAIRED
FOILED
FRIEND
FRIGID
GAINED
GAITED
GLIDED
GRIMED
GRIPED
GUIDED
HAILED
HAIRED
JAILED
JOINED
JUICED
KNIFED
MAILED
MOILED
NAILED
NOISED
OPINED
PAINED
PAIRED
POISED
PRICED
PRIDED
PRIMED
PRIZED
RAIDED
RAILED
RAINED
RAISED
REINED
ROILED
RUINED
SAILED
SEINED
SEIZED
SHIELD
SHINED
SKIVED
SLICED
SLIMED
SMILED
SNIPED
SOILED
SPICED
SPIKED
SPINED
SPIRED
SPITED
SUITED
SWIPED
TAILED
TOILED
TRICED
TRIFID
TRIPOD
TWINED
UNIPOD
UNITED
VEILED
VEINED
VOICED
VOIDED
WAILED
WAITED
WAIVED
WHILED
WHINED

•••ID•

AIKIDO
APHIDS
AROIDS
AVOIDS
BESIDE
BETIDE
BOLIDE
BORIDE
BOVIDS
BRAIDS
CANIDS
CUPIDS
DECIDE
DERIDE
DIVIDE
DOSIDO
DROIDS
DRUIDS
FLUIDS
HALIDE
IDOIDO
INSIDE
IODIDE
LADIDA
LERIDA
LIBIDO
LIPIDE
LIPIDS
MERIDA
ONEIDA
ONSIDE
OREIDA
OROIDE
OVOIDS
PLAIDS
RANIDS
RAPIDS
REBIDS
RESIDE
SOLIDI
SOLIDS
SQUIDS
STRIDE
UNTIDY
UPSIDE
URSIDS

•••I•D

ALLIED
BABIED
BEHIND
BELIED
BODIED
BURIED
BUSIED
COPIED
COZIED
DEFIED
DENIED
EDDIED
ENGIRD
ENVIED
ESPIED
GOWILD
HESIOD
HONIED
INKIND
LEVIED
MONIED
MYRIAD
PERIOD
PITIED
PLEIAD
PONIED
REBIND
RELIED
REMIND
RETIED
REWIND
RUBIED
TAXIED
TIDIED
UNBIND
UNGIRD
UNKIND
UNTIED
UNWIND
UPWIND
VARIED

••••ID

ACARID
AENEID
AFRAID
AMPHID
ASTRID
BRIGID
CANDID
CAPSID
CERVID
COCCID
CUBOID
CUSPID
DEVOID
ELAPID
EUCLID
EYELID
FERVID
FLORID
FORBID
FRIGID
GRAVID
HALOID
HISPID
HORRID
HYBRID
INGRID
INLAID
KHALID
KIDVID
LEONID
LIMPID
LIPOID
LIQUID
MADRID
MISDID
MORBID
NEREID
ORCHID
OUTBID
OUTDID
PALLID
PLACID
PONGID
PUTRID
RANCID
RASHID
RELAID
REPAID
SAYYID
SORDID
STOLID
STUPID
TOROID
TORPID
TORRID
TREPID
TRIFID
TURBID
TURGID
UNLAID
UNPAID
UNSAID
USERID
VESPID
VISCID
XYLOID

I•E•••

IBEAMS
IBERIA
IBEXES
ICEAGE
ICEBAG
ICEBOX
ICECAP
ICEDIN
ICEDUP
ICEFOG
ICEMAN
ICEMEN
ICEOUT
ICESIN
ICESUP
IDEALS
IDEATE
IGETIT
ILEANA
ILESHA
IMELDA
IPECAC
IREFUL
IRENES
IRENIC
ISELIN
ISEULT

I••E••

ICIEST
IDLERS
IDLEST
ILLEST
IMPEDE
IMPELS
IMPEND
IMPERF
INCEPT
INDEBT
INDEED
INDENE
INDENT
INFECT
INFERS
INFEST
INGEAR
INGEST
INHERE
INJECT
INJEST
INKERS
INLEAF
INLETS
INNEED
INNESS
INSEAM
INSECT
INSERT
INSETS
INTEND
INTENS
INTENT
INTERN
INVENT
INVERT
INVEST
IQTEST
IRLENE
IRREAL
ISLETS
ISMENE
ITSELF

I•••E•

IBEXES
IBIDEM
IBISES
ICEMEN
ICKIER
IFFIER
IJSSEL
ILLFED
ILLMET
IMAGED
IMAGER
IMAGES
IMARET
IMBUED
IMBUES
IMOGEN
INANER
INAPET
INBRED
INCHED
INCHES
INDEED
INDIES
INGLES
INGRES
INKIER
INKLES
INNEED
INSTEP
INURED
INURES
IRATER
IRENES
IRIDES
IRISES
IRONED
IRONER
ISABEL
ISOHEL
ISOMER
ISRAEL
ISSUED
ISSUER
ISSUES
ISTLES
ITCHED
ITCHES

I••••E

ICEAGE
ICICLE
IDEATE
IGNACE
IGNITE
IGNORE
ILLUME
ILLUSE
IMBIBE
IMBRUE
IMFINE
IMMUNE
IMMURE
IMPALE
IMPEDE
IMPOSE
IMPURE
IMPUTE
INCASE
INCISE
INCITE
INCOME
INCUSE
INDENE
INDITE
INDUCE
INFUSE
INHALE
INHERE
INHUME
INJOKE
INJURE
INLINE
INLOVE
INMATE
INNAGE
INNATE
INOUYE
INSANE
INSIDE
INSOLE
INSURE
INTAKE
INTIME
INTINE
INTONE
INTUNE
INVADE
INVITE
INVOKE
IODATE
IODIDE
IODINE
IODIZE
IOLITE
IONIZE
IRLENE
IRVINE
ISMENE
ISOLDE

•IE•••

AIELLO
BIERCE
DIEOFF
DIEOUT
DIEPPE
DIESEL
DIESES
DIESIS
DIETED
DIETER
FIELDS
FIENDS
FIERCE
FIESTA
HIEING
HIEMAL
HIERON
KIEFER
LIEBIG
LIEDER
LIEFER
LIEGES
LIELOW
LIENEE
LIERNE
LIESIN
LIESTO
LIEUTS
LIEVRE
NIECES
NIELLI
NIELLO
PIECED
PIECER
PIECES
PIEMAN
PIEMEN
PIEPAN
PIERCE
PIERRE
PIETAS
PIETER
PIETIN
PIETRO
SIECLE
SIEGED
SIEGES
SIENNA
SIERRA
SIESTA
SIEVED
SIEVES
TIEDIN
TIEDUP
TIEDYE
TIEING
TIEINS
TIEPIN
TIERCE
TIERED
TIEROD
TIERRA
TIESIN
TIESUP
TIEUPS
VIENNA
VIENNE
VIEWED
VIEWER
WIELDS
WIENER
WIESEL
YIELDS

•I•E••

AILEEN
AILERS
BICEPS
BIKERS
BIPEDS
BIREME
BISECT
BITERS
CICELY
CICERO
CIDERS
CINEMA
CITERS
CIVETS
DICERS
DIGEST
DINEIN
DINEON
DINERO
DINERS
DIRECT
DIREST
DIVEIN
DIVERS
DIVERT
DIVEST
EIDERS
EILEEN
FIBERS
FIFERS
FILENE
FILERS
FILETS
FINELY
FINERY
FINEST
FIRERS
FIREUP
FIVERS
FIVEWS
FIXERS
GIBERS
GIDEON
GILEAD
GIMELS
GIVEIN
GIVENS
GIVERS
GIVEUP
HIDEHO
HIDEKI
HIDERS
HIKERS
HIREON
HIRERS
HITECH
JIVERS
KITERS
LIBELS
LIFERS
LIGERS
LIKELY
LIKENS
LIMENS
LIMEYS
LINEAL
LINEAR
LINENS
LINERS
LINEUP
LIPENG
LITERS
LIVEIN
LIVELY
LIVENS
LIVEON
LIVERS
LIVERY
MILERS
MIMEOS
MIMERS
MINERS
MISERS
MISERY
MITERS
MIXERS
MIZENS
NICEAN
NICELY
NICENE
NICEST
NICETY
NINERS
NINETY
NITERS
OILERS
PIGEON
PIKERS
PILEIN
PILEON
PILEUM
PILEUP
PILEUS
PINEAL
PINERO
PINERY
PIPERS
PIPEUP
PIXELS
RIBEYE
RICERS
RIDENT
RIDERS
RIFEST
RIPELY
RIPENS
RIPEST
RISERS
RIVERA
RIVERS
RIVETS
SIDERO
SIDERS
SILENI
SILENT
SIMEON
SINEAD
SINEWS
SINEWY
SIRENS
SISERA
SIXERS
SIZERS
SIZEUP
TIGERS
TILERS
TIMELY
TIMERS
TINEAR
TITERS
VIDEOS
VILELY
VILEST
VINERY
VIPERS
VIREOS
VIXENS
WIDELY
WIDENS
WIDEST
WIFELY
WINERY
WIPERS
WIPEUP
WIRERS
WISELY
WISENT
WISEST
WISETO
WISEUP
WIZENS
XIMENA

•I••E•

AIGRET
AILEEN
AIRIER
AIRMEN
AISLES
BIASED
BIASES
BIBBED
BIBLES
BICKER
BIDDEN
BIDDER
BIFFED
BIGBEN
BIGGER
BIGRED
BIGTEN
BILGES
BILKED
BILLED
BILLET
BINDER
BINGED
BINGES
BINNED
BIOMES
BIRDED
BIRDER
BIRLED
BIRNEY
BISSET
BITTED
BITTEN
BITTER
CINDER
CIPHER
CISKEI
CITIES
DIADEM
DIALED
DIALER
DIAPER
DICIER
DICKER
DICKEY
DIDIES
DIESEL
DIESES
DIETED
DIETER
DIFFER
DIGGER
DILLER
DILSEY
DIMMED
DIMMER
DINGED
DINKEY
DINNED
DINNER
DINTED
DIODES
DIONEB
DIPPED
DIPPER
DIRGES
DISHED
DISHES
DISKED
DISMES
DISNEY
DISPEL
DISSED
DITHER
DITZES
EIFFEL
EILEEN
EISNER
EITHER
FIBBED
FIBBER
FIBRES
FICHES
FIDGET
FILLED
FILLER
FILLES
FILLET
FILMED
FILTER
FINDER
FINGER
FINKED
FINNED
FINNEY
FIRMED
FIRMER
FISHED
FISHER
FISHES
FISTED
FITTED
FITTER
FIZZED
FIZZES
GIBBED
GIBBER
GIBBET
GIBLET
GIDGET
GIFTED
GIGGED
GIGUES
GIJOES
GILDED
GILDER
GILLED
GIMBEL
GIMLET
GINGER
GINNED
GIPPED
GIPPER
GIRDED
GIRDER
GIRTED
HICKEY
HIDDEN
HIGHER
HILLED
HILLEL
HILLER
HINDER
HINGED
HINGES
HINTED
HINTER
HIPPED
HIPPER
HISSED
HISSER
HISSES
HITHER
HITMEN
HITTER
JIGGED
JIGGER
JILTED
JINKED
JINXED
JINXES
JITNEY
JITTER
KICKED
KICKER
KIDDED
KIDDER
KIDNEY
KIEFER
KILLED
KILLER
KILMER
KILNED
KILTED
KILTER
KINDER
KINGED
KINKED
KIPPER
KISLEV
KISMET
KISSED
KISSER
KISSES
KITTEN
LIBBED
LIBBER
LICHEN
LICKED
LIDDED
LIEDER
LIEFER
LIEGES
LIENEE
LIFTED
LIFTER
LILIES
LILTED
LIMBED
LIMBER
LIMNED
LIMNER
LIMPED
LIMPER
LIMPET
LINDEN
LINGER
LINKED
LINKER
LINNET
LINSEY
LINTEL
LINTER
LIONEL
LIONET
LIPPED
LISLES
LISPED
LISTED
LISTEE
LISTEL
LISTEN
LISTER
LITRES
LITTER
LIVRES
MICKEY
MIDDEN
MIDGES
MIDGET
MIDLER
MIFFED
MIGUEL
MILDER
MILDEW
MILIEU
MILKED
MILKER
MILLED
MILLER
MILLET
MILNER
MINCED
MINCER
MINCES
MINDED
MINDER
MINKES
MINTED
MINTER
MINUET
MINXES
MIRREN
MISLED
MISSED
MISSES
MISTED
MISTER
MITRED
MITRES
MITTEN
MIXTEC
MIZZEN
NIAMEY
NICAEA
NICHES
NICKED
NICKEL
NICKER
NIECES
NIGHER
NIPPED
NIPPER
NISSEN
NITRES
NIXIES
OILIER
OILMEN
OINKED
PIAGET
PICKED
PICKER
PICKET
PIECED
PIECER
PIECES
PIEMEN
PIETER
PIGGED
PIGLET
PIGPEN
PILFER
PILLED
PINCER
PINGED
PINIER
PINKED
PINKEN
PINKER
PINNED
PINNER
PINTER
PIOLET
PIPPED
PIQUED
PIQUES
PIQUET
PISCES
PITHED
PITIED
PITIES
PITMEN
PITTED
PITTER
PIXIES
RIBBED
RICHEN
RICHER
RICHES
RICKED
RICKEY
RIDDED
RIDDEN
RIDGED
RIDGES
RIDLEY
RIFFED
RIFLED
RIFLER
RIFLES
RIFTED
RIGGED
RIGGER
RILLES
RILLET
RIMMED
RINGED
RINGER
RINSED
RINSES
RIOTED
RIOTER
RIPKEN
RIPLEY
RIPPED
RIPPER
RISKED
RISKER
RITTER
SICCED
SICKEN
SICKER
SIDLED
SIDLES
SIDNEY
SIEGED
SIEGES
SIEVED
SIEVES
SIFTED
SIFTER
SIGHED
SIGHER
SIGNED
SIGNEE
SIGNER
SIGNET
SILKED
SILKEN
SILOED
SILTED
SILVER
SIMBEL
SIMMER
SIMPER
SINGED
SINGER
SINGES
SINKER
SINNED
SINNER
SINTER
SIPPED
SIPPER
SIPPET
SIRREE
SISKEL
SISLER
SISTER
SITTER
TICKED
TICKER
TICKET
TIDIED
TIDIER
TIDIES
TIERED
TIFFED
TIGGER

TILDEN
TILDES
TILLED
TILLER
TILTED
TILTER
TIMBER
TINDER
TINGED
TINGES
TINIER
TINKER
TINMEN
TINNED
TINNER
TINSEL
TINTED
TINTER
TIPPED
TIPPER
TIPPET
TITHED
TITHER
TITHES
TITLED
TITLES
TITTER
VIEWED
VIEWER
VIOLET
VISAED
VIVIEN
VIZIER
WICKED
WICKER
WICKET
WIDGET
WIENER
WIESEL
WIGGED
WIGLET
WILDER
WILIER
WILKES
WILLED
WILLEM
WILLET
WILTED
WIMSEY
WINCED
WINCER
WINCES
WINDED
WINDER
WINDEX
WINGED
WINGER
WINKED
WINKER
WINNER
WINTER
WINZES
WISHED
WISHER
WISHES
WISPED
WISTER
WITHED
WITHER
WITHES
WITTED
XIAMEN
YIPPED
YIPPEE
ZIGGED
ZIMMER
ZINGED
ZINGER
ZIPPED
ZIPPER
ZITHER

•I•••E

BIDDLE
BIERCE
BIGGIE
BIGLIE
BIGTOE
BILLIE
BINATE
BIRDIE
BIREME
BISQUE
CINQUE
CIRCLE
CIRQUE
DIBBLE
DIDDLE
DIEPPE
DILATE
DILUTE
DIMPLE
DINGLE
DIONNE
DIPOLE
DISUSE
DIVIDE
DIVINE
FIACRE
FIANCE
FICHTE
FICKLE
FIDDLE
FIERCE
FIGURE
FILENE
FILOSE
FINALE
FINITE
FIPPLE
FIXATE
FIZZLE
GIGGLE
GILLIE
GIRDLE
HIGGLE
HIPPIE
JIGGLE
JIMMIE
JINGLE
KIBBLE
KILTIE
KINDLE
KINGME
KIRTLE
KISHKE
LIABLE
LIAISE
LIENEE
LIERNE
LIEVRE
LIGATE
LIGURE
LILLIE
LINAGE
LIPASE
LIPIDE
LISTEE
LITTLE
LIZZIE
MIDDLE
MIGGLE
MILLIE
MILTIE
MINGLE
MINNIE
MINUTE
MIRAGE
MISCUE
MISUSE
MIZZLE
NIBBLE
NICENE
NICOLE
NIGGLE
NIMBLE
PIAFFE
PICKLE
PIERCE
PIERRE
PIFFLE
PIGGIE
PIKAKE
PILATE
PILOSE
PINITE
PINKIE
PINNAE
PINOLE
PINTLE
PIRATE
RIBEYE
RIBOSE
RICHIE
RIDDLE
RIFFLE
RIMOSE
RIMPLE
RIPPLE
RISQUE
SICKLE
SIECLE
SIGNEE
SILAGE
SILONE
SIMILE
SIMONE
SIMPLE
SINGLE
SIRREE
SIZZLE
TIBIAE
TICKLE
TIEDYE
TIERCE
TILLIE
TIMBRE
TINGLE
TINKLE
TIPPLE
TIPTOE
TIRADE
TIRANE
TISANE
TISSUE
TITTLE
VIABLE
VIENNE
VIRILE
VIRTUE
VISAGE
VISINE
VIVACE
WIGGLE
WILLIE
WIMBLE
WIMPLE
WINKIE
WINKLE
WINNIE
YIPPEE

••IE••

ADIEUS
ADIEUX
AFIELD
ALIENS
AMIENS
APIECE
BRIEFS
BRIENZ
BRIERS
BRIERY
CHIEFS
CLIENT
CRIERS
DRIERS
DRIEST
FLIERS
FRIEND
FRIEZE
GAIETY
GRIEVE
ICIEST
MOIETY
ORIELS
ORIENT
OSIERS
OVIEDO
PLIERS
PRIERS
PRIEST
QUIETS
SHIELD
SHIEST
SKIERS
SLIEST
SPIELS
SPIERS
THIEVE
TRIERS
UBIETY
WRIEST

••I•E•

ABIDED
ABIDES
ALINES
AMICES
AMIDES
AMINES
ANIMES
APICES
ARISEN
ARISES
ASIDES
BAILED
BAILEE
BAILER
BAILEY
BAINES
BAITED
BEIGES
BLIMEY
BLIXEN
BOILED
BOILER
BOITES
BRIBED
BRIBES
BRIDES
BRINED
BRINES
BSIDES
CEILED
CHIDED
CHIDES
CHIMED
CHIMES
CHINES
CHISEL
CHIVES
CLIMES
CLINES
COIFED
COILED
COINED
COINER
CRIMEA
CRIMES
CRIPES
CRISES
DAILEY
DAIREN
DAISES
DEICED
DEICER
DEICES
DRIVEL
DRIVEN
DRIVER
DRIVES
DUIKER
EDILES
EDITED
ELIDED
ELIDES
ELITES
EVILER
EXILED
EXILES
EXITED
FAILED
FAIRED
FAIRER
FBIMEN
FOILED
FRISEE
FRISES
GAINED
GAINER
GAITED
GAITER
GEIGER
GEISEL
GLIDED
GLIDER
GLIDES
GRIMED
GRIMES
GRIPED
GRIPER
GRIPES
GRIVET
GUIDED
GUIDES
GUILES
GUINEA
GUISES
HAILED
HAILEY
HAINES
HAIRED
HEIDEN
HEIFER
IBIDEM
IBISES
IRIDES
IRISES
JAILED
JAILER
JOINED
JOINER
JUICED
JUICER
JUICES
KAISER
KEITEL
KNIFED
KNIFES
KNIVES
LEIDEN
LOITER
MAIDEN
MAILED
MAILER
MAILES
MAIZES
MOILED
MOILER
MOINES
MOIRES
NAILED
NAILER
NOISED
NOISES
OBITER
OGIVES
OLIVER
OLIVES
OPINED
OPINER
OPINES
ORIGEN
OXIDES
PAINED
PAIRED
POISED
POISES
PRICED
PRICER
PRICES
PRICEY
PRIDED
PRIDES
PRIMED
PRIMER
PRIMES
PRIPET
PRIVET
PRIZED
PRIZES
QUIRES
QUIVER
RAIDED
RAIDER
RAILED
RAILER
RAINED
RAINER
RAINES
RAISED
RAISER
RAISES
REINED
REINER
ROILED
RUINED
RUINER
SAILED
SEIDEL
SEINED
SEINER
SEINES
SEIZED
SEIZER
SEIZES
SHINED
SHINER
SHINES
SHIRER
SHIRES
SHIVER
SKIVED
SKIVER
SKIVES
SLICED
SLICER
SLICES
SLIDER
SLIDES
SLIMED
SLIMES
SLIVER
SMILED
SMILER
SMILES
SMILEY
SMITES
SNIDER
SNIPED
SNIPES
SNIVEL
SOILED
SOIREE
SPICED
SPICES
SPIDER
SPIKED
SPIKER
SPIKES
SPILES
SPINED
SPINEL
SPINES
SPINET
SPIREA
SPIRED
SPIRES
SPITED
SPITES
STILES
STIPEL
STIPES
STIVER
SUITED
SUITES
SWIPED
SWIPER
SWIPES
SWIVEL
SWIVET
TAILED
TAIPEI
TOILED
TOILER
TOILES
TOILET
TRIBES
TRICED
TRICES
TRIKES
TRINES
TRITER
TRIVET
TWINED
TWINES
UNICEF
UNISEX
UNITED
UNITER
UNITES
VAINER
VEILED
VEINED
VOICED
VOICES
VOIDED
VOILES
VSIXES
WAILED
WAILER
WAITED
WAITER
WAIVED
WAIVER
WAIVES
WHILED
WHILES
WHINED
WHINER
WHINES
WHITEN
WHITER
WHITES
WRITER
WRITES
ZUIDER

••I••E

ALIBLE
APIECE
ARIOSE
AVIATE
BAILEE
BLITHE
BRIDGE
BRIDLE
CAIQUE
CHICLE
CHIGOE
CHILDE
CHILOE
CLICHE
CLIQUE
CRINGE
CUISSE
DEIDRE
EDIBLE
EMIGRE
ENISLE
EVINCE
FAILLE
FOIBLE
FRIDGE
FRIEZE
FRINGE
FRISEE
GRIEVE
GRILLE
GRILSE
GRIMKE
GRIPPE
GUIMPE
ICICLE
LAINIE
MAISIE
MAITRE
NEISSE
OPIATE
ORIOLE
OTIOSE
PAIUTE
PHILAE
PLICAE
PLISSE
POINTE
PRINCE
PUISNE
QUICHE
QUINCE
SAINTE
SEICHE
SHIITE
SOIGNE
SOIREE
STIFLE
TAILLE
THICKE
THIEVE
THISBE
TRIAGE
TRIFLE
TRIODE
TRIPLE
TRISTE
TRIUNE
TRIXIE
TUILLE
TWINGE
UNIATE
UNIQUE
WRITHE

•••IE•

ACHIER
ADRIEN
AERIES
AGGIES
AIRIER
ALLIED
ALLIES
ANCIEN
ARMIES
ARTIER
ASHIER
BABIED
BABIES
BELIED
BELIEF
BELIES
BEVIES
BODIED
BODIES
BOGIES
BONIER
BURIED
BURIES
BUSIED
BUSIER
BUSIES
CAGIER
CAHIER
CARIES
CITIES
CONIES
COPIED
COPIER
COPIES
COSIES
COZIED
COZIER
COZIES
CUTIES
DAMIEN
DANIEL
DARIEN
DAVIES
DEFIED
DEFIES
DENIED
DENIER
DENIES
DEWIER
DICIER
DIDIES
DOGIES
DOPIER
DORIES
DUTIES
EASIER
EDDIED
EDDIES
EDGIER
EELIER
EERIER
ENVIED
ENVIES
ESPIED
ESPIES
EYRIES
FACIES
FOGIES
FOXIER
FURIES
GAMIER
GENIES
GOBIES
GOOIER
GORIER
HAZIER
HOKIER
HOLIER
HOMIER
HONIED
HOSIER
ICKIER
IFFIER
INDIES
INKIER
JAVIER
JOLIET
JULIET
JURIES
LACIER
LADIES
LANIER
LAZIER
LEVIED
LEVIER
LEVIES
LILIES
LOGIER
LORIES
MARIEL
METIER
MILIEU
MONIED
MONIES
MOVIES
MURIEL
NAPIER
NAVIES
NIXIES
NOSIER
OATIER
OBRIEN
OILIER
OLDIES
ONVIEW
ORGIES
PAPIER
PINIER
PITIED
PITIES
PIXIES
POGIES
POKIER
PONIED
PONIES
POSIES
PUNIER
PYXIES
RABIES
RACIER
RAMIES
RAPIER
RELIED
RELIEF
RELIES
RETIED
RETIES
REVIEW
ROPIER
ROSIER
RUBIED
RUBIES
SERIES
SEXIER
SHRIEK
SOVIET
SPRIER
SUSIEQ
TAXIED
TAXIES
TIDIED
TIDIER
TIDIES
TINIER
TOBIES
TONIER
TORIES
UGLIER
UGLIES
UNDIES
UNTIED
UNTIES
VANIER
VARIED
VARIES
VIVIEN
VIZIER
WARIER
WAVIER
WAXIER
WILIER
XAVIER
YALIES
ZANIER
ZANIES

•••I•E

ACTIVE
ADMIRE
ADVICE
ADVISE
AEDILE
AFFINE
ALDINE
ALFINE
ALPINE
APLITE
ARGIVE
ARRIVE
ASPIRE
ASSIZE
ATTIRE
AWHILE
BARITE
BELIZE
BEMINE
BEMIRE
BESIDE
BETIDE
BETISE
BLAINE
BLAISE
BODICE
BOLIDE
BORIDE
BOVINE
BRAISE
BRUISE
BYLINE
CAMISE
CANINE
CARIBE
CECILE
CELINE
CERISE
CHAINE
CHAISE
CHOICE
CLAIRE
COSINE
CRUISE
CURIAE
DATIVE
DECIDE
DEFILE
DEFINE
DEMISE
DENISE
DERIDE
DERIVE
DESIRE
DEVICE
DEVINE
DEVISE
DIVIDE
DIVINE
DOCILE
DRYICE
ELAINE
ELLICE
ELOISE
EMPIRE
ENDIVE
ENGINE
ENSILE
ENTICE
ENTIRE
EQUINE
ERMINE
ETOILE
EUNICE
EXCISE
EXCITE
EXPIRE
EXWIFE
FACILE
FALINE
FAMINE
FELINE
FELIPE
FINITE
FRAISE
FUTILE
GAMINE
GREIGE
HABILE
HALIDE
HALITE
HAMITE
IGNITE
IMBIBE
IMFINE
INCISE
INCITE
INDITE
INLINE
INSIDE
INTIME
INTINE
INVITE
IODIDE
IODINE
IODIZE
IOLITE
IONIZE
IRVINE
JANICE
JANINE
KALINE
KURILE
LABILE
LEVINE
LEVITE
LIAISE
LIPIDE
LOUISE
LUCITE
LUPINE
LYSINE
MALICE
MARINE
MAXINE
MAXIXE
MOBILE
MODINE
MOLINE
MOTILE
MOTIVE
MURINE
NADINE
NATIVE
NODICE
NOTICE
NOVICE
NOWISE
NUBILE
OBLIGE
OFFICE
ONDINE
ONFILE
ONFIRE
ONLINE
ONSIDE
ONSITE
ONTIME
OOLITE
OPHITE
OROIDE
ORPINE
OSCINE
PATINE
PETITE
PINITE
PLAICE
POLICE
POLITE
PRAISE
PUMICE
PURINE
PYRITE
RACINE
RAPINE
RATINE
RATITE
RAVINE
RECIFE
RECIPE
RECITE
REFILE
REFINE
REGIME
REHIRE
RELINE
RELIVE
REMISE
REPINE
RESIDE
RESILE
RETILE
RETIME
RETIRE
REVILE
REVISE
REVIVE
REWIRE
RUTILE
SABINE
SAFIRE
SALINE
SAMITE
SATIRE
SCRIBE
SEDILE
SEMITE
SERINE
SHIITE
SHRIKE
SHRINE
SHRIVE
SIMILE
SLUICE
SOFINE
SPLICE
SPLINE
SPRITE
SQUIRE
STRIAE
STRIDE
STRIFE
STRIKE
STRIPE
STRIVE
SUPINE
THRICE
THRIVE
TIBIAE
TOLIFE
TONITE
UMPIRE
UNDINE
UNLIKE
UNPILE
UNRIPE
UNWISE
UPDIKE
UPRISE
UPSIDE
UPTIME
URSINE
VALISE
VENICE
VENIRE
VENITE
VERITE
VIRILE
VISINE
VOTIVE
WAHINE

••••IE

ADELIE
AMALIE
ANOMIE
ARCHIE
AUNTIE
AUSSIE
BADDIE
BAGGIE
BARBIE
BARRIE
BEANIE
BERNIE
BERTIE
BESSIE
BIGGIE
BIGLIE
BILLIE
BIRDIE
BMOVIE
BOBBIE
BOCCIE
BONNIE
BOOGIE
BOOKIE
BOOTIE
BOWTIE
BRODIE
BUDGIE
CABBIE
CADDIE
CARRIE
CHERIE
COLLIE
CONNIE
COOKIE
COOTIE
COWRIE
DANDIE
DEARIE
DEBBIE
DOGGIE
DOOBIE
DOOGIE
DOOZIE
DOTTIE
FAERIE
FANNIE
FERGIE
FOLKIE
FOZZIE
GERTIE
GILLIE
GOALIE
GOLDIE
GOODIE

GORDIE
GRACIE
HACKIE
HADDIE
HANKIE
HATTIE
HEEBIE
HERBIE
HETTIE
HIPPIE
HOAGIE
HOGTIE
JACKIE
JENNIE
JESSIE
JIMMIE
JOANIE
JUNKIE
KATHIE
KELPIE
KEWPIE
KILTIE
KOOKIE
LADDIE
LAINIE
LASSIE
LAURIE
LENNIE
LEONIE
LESLIE
LILLIE
LIZZIE
MADDIE
MAGGIE
MAGPIE
MAISIE
MARCIE
MARGIE
MARNIE
MASHIE
MATTIE
MEALIE
MEANIE
MILLIE
MILTIE
MINNIE
MOMMIE
MUDPIE
MUNCIE
MUSKIE
NELLIE
NESSIE
PETRIE
PIGGIE
PINKIE
POTPIE
PREMIE
PUNKIE
REGGIE
RENNIE
RICHIE
ROADIE
ROBBIE
ROLLIE
RONNIE
ROOKIE
ROOMIE
RUNCIE
SAMMIE
SAVOIE
SKOKIE
SOFTIE
SOPHIE
SORTIE
SPECIE
STEVIE
STOGIE
STYMIE
TALKIE
TECHIE
TESSIE
TILLIE
TOWNIE
TRIXIE
VEGGIE
WALKIE
WEDGIE
WEENIE
WILLIE
WINKIE
WINNIE
WOOGIE
WOOKIE
YUPPIE
ZOMBIE

IF••••
IFFIER

I•F•••
IFFIER
IMFINE
INFACT
INFAMY
INFANT
INFECT
INFERS
INFEST
INFIRM
INFLOW
INFLUX
INFOLD
INFORM
INFULL
INFUSE

I••F••
ICEFOG
ILLFED
INAFIX
INAFOG
IREFUL

I••••F
IMPERF
INHALF
INLEAF
ITSELF

•IF•••
BIFFED
BIFOLD
DIFFER
EIFFEL
FIFERS
FIFTHS
GIFTED
LIFERS
LIFTED
LIFTER
LIFTUP
MIFFED
PIFFLE
RIFEST
RIFFED
RIFFLE
RIFLED
RIFLER
RIFLES
RIFTED
SIFTED
SIFTER
TIFFED
TIFFIN
WIFELY

•I•F••
BIAFRA
BIFFED
DIFFER
EIFFEL
FITFUL
KIEFER
KITFOX
LIEFER
MIFFED
MISFIT
PIAFFE
PIFFLE
PILFER
RIFFED
RIFFLE
SINFUL
TIFFED
TIFFIN

•I••F•
BITOFF
CITIFY
DIEOFF
MINIFY
PIAFFE
PILAFS
RIPOFF
TIPOFF
VILIFY
VIVIFY

•I•••F
BITOFF
DIEOFF
KINDOF
RIPOFF
TIPOFF

••IF••
CLIFFS
COIFED
DRIFTS
HEIFER
KNIFED
KNIFES
SCIFIS
SHIFTS
SHIFTY
SKIFFS
SNIFFS
SNIFFY
SPIFFS
SPIFFY
STIFFS
STIFLE
SWIFTS
TRIFID
TRIFLE
UNIFIC
WHIFFS

••I•F•
BRIEFS
CHIEFS
CLIFFS
SKIFFS
SNIFFS
SNIFFY
SPIFFS
SPIFFY
STIFFS
WHIFFS

••I••F
UNICEF

•••IF•
ADRIFT
CANIFF
CITIFY
CODIFY
EXWIFE
MINIFY
MODIFY
MOTIFS
NOTIFY
OSSIFY
PACIFY
PURIFY
RAMIFY
RARIFY
RATIFY
RECIFE
RUBIFY
SCHIFF
SERIFS
SHRIFT
STRIFE
TARIFF
THRIFT
TOLIFE
TYPIFY
UGLIFY
UPLIFT
VERIFY
VILIFY
VIVIFY

•••I•F
BELIEF
CANIFF
RELIEF
SCHIFF
TARIFF

••••IF
CERTIF
MASSIF
SHARIF
SHERIF
WHATIF

IG••••
IGETIT
IGLOOS
IGNACE
IGNATZ
IGNITE
IGNORE
IGUACU
IGUANA

I•G•••
INGEAR
INGEST
INGLES
INGMAR
INGOTS
INGRES
INGRID

I••G••
IMAGED
IMAGER
IMAGES
IMOGEN
ISOGON

I•••G•
ICEAGE
ICINGS
IMPUGN
INDIGO
INNAGE

I••••G
ICEBAG
ICEFOG
ICHING
IDLING
INAFOG
INKING
INNING
IRKING
IRVING

•IG•••
AIGRET
BIGAMY
BIGBEN
BIGBOY
BIGGER
BIGGIE
BIGGUN
BIGHTS
BIGLIE
BIGMAC
BIGOTS
BIGRED
BIGSUR
BIGTEN
BIGTOE
BIGTOP
BIGWIG
CIGARS
DIGEST
DIGGER
DIGITS
DIGLOT
DIGOUT
DIGRAM
DIGSIN
DIGSUP
EIGHTH
EIGHTS
EIGHTY
FIGARO
FIGHTS
FIGURE
GIGGED
GIGGLE
GIGGLY
GIGOLO
GIGOTS
GIGUES
HIGGLE
HIGHER
HIGHIQ
HIGHLY
HIGHUP
JIGGED
JIGGER
JIGGLE
JIGGLY
JIGSAW
KIGALI
LIGATE
LIGERS
LIGHTS
LIGNIN
LIGULA
LIGURE
MIGGLE
MIGHTY
MIGNON
MIGUEL
NIGGLE
NIGHER
NIGHTS
NIGHTY
PIGEON
PIGGED
PIGGIE
PIGLET
PIGNUT
PIGOUT
PIGPEN
PIGSTY
RIGGED
RIGGER
RIGHTO
RIGHTS
RIGORS
RIGOUR
RIGSUP
SIGHED
SIGHER
SIGHTS
SIGILS
SIGMAS
SIGNAL
SIGNED
SIGNEE
SIGNER
SIGNET
SIGNIN
SIGNON
SIGNOR
SIGNUP
SIGURD
TIGERS
TIGGER
TIGHTS
TIGLON
TIGRIS
UIGURS
VIGILS
VIGODA
VIGOUR
WIGGED
WIGGLE
WIGGLY
WIGHTS
WIGLET
WIGOUT
WIGWAG
WIGWAM
ZIGGED
ZIGZAG

•I•G••
AIRGUN
BIGGER
BIGGIE
BIGGUN
BILGES
BINGED
BINGES
BIOGAS
BIRGIT
DIGGER
DINGED
DINGHY
DINGLE
DINGUS
DIRGES
FIDGET
FINGER
FIZGIG
GIDGET
GIGGED
GIGGLE
GIGGLY
GINGER
HIGGLE
HINGED
HINGES
JIGGED
JIGGER
JIGGLE
JIGGLY
JINGLE
JINGLY
KINGED
KINGLY
KINGME
LIEGES
LINGER
LINGUA
MIDGES
MIDGET
MIGGLE
MINGLE
NIGGLE
NILGAI
NINGBO
PIAGET
PIDGIN
PIGGED
PIGGIE
PINGED
PISGAH
RIDGED
RIDGES
RIGGED
RIGGER
RINGED
RINGER
RINGUP
SIEGED
SIEGES
SINGED
SINGER
SINGES
SINGLE
SINGLY
SINGTO
SIXGUN
TIGGER
TINGED
TINGES
TINGLE
TINGLY
TINGOD
VIRGIL
VIRGIN
WIDGET
WIGGED
WIGGLE
WIGGLY
WINGED
WINGER
WINGIT
ZIGGED
ZINGED
ZINGER

•I••G•
DIRIGO
GINKGO
KIANGS
LIANGS
LINAGE
MIRAGE
SILAGE
VIRAGO
VISAGE

•I•••G
AIDING
AILING
AIMING
AIRBAG
AIRING
BIDING
BIGWIG
BIKING
BITING
CITING
DIALOG
DICING
DIKING
DINING
DIVING
FILING
FINING
FIRING
FIXING
FIZGIG
GIBING
GIVING
HIDING
HIEING
HIKING
HIRING
HIVING
JIBING
JIVING
KITBAG
KITING
LIEBIG
LIKING
LIMING
LINING
LIPENG
LITHOG
LIVING
MIKING
MIMING
MINING
MIRING
MIXING
NIXING
OILING
OILRIG
PIKING
PILING
PINING
PIPING
RICING
RIDING
RILING
RIMING
RISING
RIVING
SIDING
SIRING
SITING
SIXING
SIZING
TIDING
TIEING
TILING
TIMING
TIRING
VIKING
VINING
WIGWAG
WILING
WINING
WIPING
WIRING
ZIGZAG

••IG••
ALIGHT
ALIGNS
AMIGOS
ARIGHT
BEIGES
BLIGHT
BOIGNY
BRIGGS
BRIGHT
BRIGID
CHIGOE
DEIGNS
DWIGHT
EMIGRE
ENIGMA
FEIGNS
FLIGHT
FRIGHT
FRIGID
GEIGER
GRIGRI
HAIGHT
HEIGHT
KNIGHT
NEIGHS
ORIGEN
ORIGIN
PLIGHT
REIGNS
SAIGAS
SAIGON
SLIGHT
SOIGNE
SPIGOT
STIGMA
TAIGAS
THIGHS
TRIGLY
TRIGON
TWIGGY
VEIGHT
VOIGHT
VSIGNS
WEIGHS
WEIGHT
WRIGHT

••I•G•
BEINGS
BOINGO
BRIDGE
BRIGGS
BRINGS
CLINGS
CLINGY
CRINGE
DOINGS
DRINGS
FLINGS
FRIDGE
FRINGE
FRINGY
GOINGS
GRINGO
ICINGS
OLINGO
ORINGS
SLINGS
STINGS
STINGY
SWINGS
SWINGY
THINGS
TRIAGE
TWIGGY
TWINGE
WRINGS

••I••G
CHIANG
EPILOG
SKIING

•••IG•
ASSIGN
AURIGA
AWEIGH
BENIGN
COSIGN
DESIGN
DIRIGO
EFFIGY
ELOIGN
ENSIGN
GREIGE
INDIGO
LATIGO
LEHIGH
MALIGN
OBLIGE
ONHIGH
RESIGN
SLEIGH
SPRIGS
UNRIGS

•••I•G
AAHING
ACHING
ACTING
ADDING
AGEING
AIDING
AILING
AIMING
AIRING
ARCING
ARMING
ASKING
AWNING
BAAING
BAKING
BALING
BARING
BASING
BATING
BAYING
BBKING
BENING
BERING
BIDING
BIKING
BITING
BLUING
BODING
BOEING
BONING
BOOING
BORING
BOWING
BOXING
BUSING
BUYING
CAGING
CAKING
CANING
CARING
CASING
CAVING
CAWING
CEDING
CITING
CLUING
CODING
COMING
COOING
COPING
CORING
COWING
CRYING
CUBING
CURING
DARING
DATING
DAZING
DEWING
DICING
DIKING
DINING
DIVING
DOLING
DOMING
DOPING
DOSING
DOTING
DOZING
DRYING
DUKING
DUPING
DURING
DYEING
EALING
EARING
EASING
EATING
EBBING
EDGING
EGGING
ENDING
EPPING
ERRING
ERVING
EYEING
FACING
FADING
FAKING
FARING
FAXING
FAZING
FEEING
FETING
FILING
FINING
FIRING
FIXING
FLYING
FOXING
FRYING
FUMING
FUSING
FUZING
GAGING
GAMING
GAPING
GATING
GAZING
GEEING
GIBING
GIVING
GLUING
GORING
GUYING
HALING
HARING
HATING
HAVING
HAWING
HAYING
HAZING
HEWING
HEXING
HIDING
HIEING
HIKING
HIRING
HIVING
HOEING
HOLING
HOMING
HONING
HOPING
HOSING
HYPING
ICHING
IDLING
INKING
INNING
IRKING
IRVING
JADING
JAPING
JAWING
JIBING
JIVING
JOKING
JUKING
KEYING
KITING
LACING
LADING
LAMING
LAVING
LAWING
LAYING
LAZING
LIKING
LIMING
LINING
LIVING
LOPING
LOSING
LOVING
LOWING
LUBING
LURING
LUTING
MAKING
MATING
METING
MEWING
MIKING
MIMING
MINING
MIRING
MIXING
MOOING
MOPING
MOVING
MOWING
MUSING
MUTING
NAMING
NIXING
NOSING
NOTING
NUKING
OARING
OFFING
OGLING
OILING
OOHING
OOZING
OPTING
ORBING
OUTING
OWNING
PACING
PAGING
PALING
PARING
PAVING
PAWING
PAYING
PEKING
PIKING
PILING
PINING
PIPING
PLYING
POKING
POLING
PORING
POSING
PRYING
PULING
RACING
RAGING
RAKING
RARING
RATING
RAVING
RAZING
RESING
RICING
RIDING
RILING
RIMING
RISING
RIVING
ROBING
ROPING
ROVING
ROWING
RULING
SATING
SAVING
SAWING
SAYING
SEEING
SEWING
SHYING
SIDING
SIRING
SITING
SIXING
SIZING
SKIING
SKYING
SLUING
SOLING
SOWING
SPRING
SPYING
STRING
TAKING
TAMING
TAPING
TARING
TAWING
TAXING
TEEING
TIDING
TIEING
TILING
TIMING
TIRING
TOEING
TONING
TOTING
TOWING
TOYING
TRUING
TRYING
TUBING
TUNING
TURING
TYPING
UPPING
URGING
VEXING
VIKING
VINING
VOTING
VOWING
WADING
WAGING
WAKING
WANING
WARING
WAVING
WAXING
WILING
WINING
WIPING
WIRING
WOOING
WOWING
YAWING
YOKING
ZONING

••••IG
BIGWIG
CATRIG
DANZIG
EARWIG
FIZGIG
GEHRIG
LIEBIG
LUDWIG
OILRIG
WETTIG
ZAFTIG

I•H•••
ICHING
ICHTHY
INHALE
INHALF
INHAND
INHAUL
INHERE
INHUME
ISHTAR
ITHACA
ITHAKI

I••H••
INCHED
INCHES
INCHON
ISCHIA
ISOHEL
ISTHMI
ITCHED
ITCHES
ITZHAK

I•••H•
ICHTHY
ILESHA

I••••H
IMPISH
INARCH
INCASH
INRUSH
INWITH
IOMOTH
IRTYSH
ISAIAH

•IH•••
BIHARI
JIHADS
MIHRAB
NIHILO

•I•H••
BIGHTS
BISHOP
CIPHER
DIRHAM
DISHED
DISHES
DITHER
EIGHTH
EIGHTS
EIGHTY
EITHER
FICHES
FICHTE
FICHUS
FIGHTS
FISHED
FISHER
FISHES
HIGHER
HIGHIQ
HIGHLY
HIGHUP
HIPHOP
HITHER
KISHKE
LICHEN
LIGHTS
LITHIC
LITHOG

LITHOS
MIGHTY
MISHAP
MISHIT
NICHES
NIGHER
NIGHTS
NIGHTY
PITHED
RICHEN
RICHER
RICHES
RICHIE
RICHLY
RIGHTO
RIGHTS
SIGHED
SIGHER
SIGHTS
SIPHON
TIGHTS
TINHAT
TISHRI
TITHED
TITHER
TITHES
VISHNU
WIGHTS
WISHED
WISHER
WISHES
WITHAL
WITHED
WITHER
WITHES
WITHIN
WITHIT
ZITHER

•I••H•
BIRTHS
DINGHY
FIFTHS
FILTHY
FIRTHS
GIRTHS
HIDEHO
KIMCHI
LITCHI
MISCHA
NINTHS
PICCHU
SIXTHS
WIDTHS
WITCHY

•I•••H
EIGHTH
FINISH
HIRSCH
HITECH
JINNAH
KIBOSH
KIRSCH
KITSCH
LILITH
PISGAH
RIYADH
SIRRAH
SIWASH
ZILPAH
ZIZITH

••I•H•
ALIGHT
ARIGHT
BLIGHT
BLITHE
BRIGHT
CHICHA
CHICHI
CLICHE
DWIGHT
ELISHA
FAITHS
FLIGHT
FRIGHT
GEISHA
HAIGHT
HEIGHT
KNIGHT
NEIGHS
PLIGHT
QUICHE
SEICHE
SLIGHT
SLITHY
SMITHS
SMITHY
TAICHI
THIGHS
TRICHO
TRISHA
VEIGHT
VOIGHT
WEIGHS
WEIGHT
WRIGHT
WRITHE

••I••H
CHINCH
CLINCH
ELIJAH
FLINCH
FLITCH
GLITCH
GRINCH
PLINTH
SHILOH
SKITCH
SMIRCH
SNITCH
SPILTH
STITCH
SWITCH
TWITCH

•••I•H
AWEIGH
BANISH
BLUISH
BOYISH
CALIPH
CERIPH
DANISH
DOVISH
ELFISH
ENRICH
EOLITH
FAMISH
FETISH
FINISH
GARISH
GOFISH
GOWITH
IMPISH
INWITH
ISAIAH
JEWISH
JOSIAH
JUDITH
LATISH
LAVISH
LEHIGH
LILITH
MARIAH
MODISH
MOPISH
MULISH
MUNICH
NEWISH
OAFISH
OFFISH
OLDISH
ONHIGH
OOLITH
ORNITH
OWLISH
PALISH
PARIAH
PARISH
PERISH
POLISH
PUNISH
RADISH
RAKISH
RAVISH
RELISH
RUPIAH
SALISH
SLEIGH
SQUISH
TONISH
UZZIAH
VANISH
WRAITH
ZENITH
ZIZITH
ZURICH

I•I•••
IBIBIO
IBIDEM
IBISES
ICICLE
ICIEST
ICINGS
IDIOCY
IDIOMS
IDIOTS
INIONS
INITIO
IRIDES
IRIDIC
IRISES
IRISIN

I••I••
ICHING
ICKIER
IDLING
IDOIDO
IFFIER
IGNITE
ILLINI
ILOILO
IMBIBE
IMFINE
IMPISH
INCISE
INCITE
INDIAN
INDICT
INDIES
INDIGO
INDIRA
INDITE
INDIUM
INFIRM
INKIER
INKIND
INKING
INLINE
INNING
INSIDE
INSIST
INSITU
INTIMA
INTIME
INTINE
INUITS
INVITE
INVIVO
INWITH
IODIDE
IODINE
IODIZE
IOLITE
IONIAN
IONICS
IONIUM
IONIZE
IRKING
IRVINE
IRVING
ISAIAH

I•••I•
IAMBIC
IATRIC
IBERIA
IBIBIO
ICARIA
ICEDIN
ICESIN
ICONIC
IGETIT
IMPAIR
INAFIX
INDRIS
INGRID
INITIO
INLAID
INTUIT
INVAIN
IRANIS
IRAQIS
IRENIC
IRIDIC
IRISIN
IRONIC
ISCHIA
ISELIN
ISTRIA
ITALIA
ITALIC

I••••I
ILLINI
ISTHMI
ITHAKI
ITURBI

•I•I••
AIDING
AIKIDO
AILING
AIMING
AIRIER
AIRILY
AIRING
BIDING
BIKING
BIKINI
BIMINI
BITING
CILIUM
CITIES
CITIFY
CITING
CIVICS
DICIER
DICING
DIDIES
DIDION
DIGITS
DIKING
DIMITY
DINING
DIRIGO
DIVIDE
DIVINE
DIVING
DIXITS
FIJIAN
FILIAL
FILING
FILIUS
FINIAL
FINING
FINISH
FINITE
FINITO
FIRING
FIXING
FIXITY
GIBILL
GIBING
GIVING
HIDING
HIEING
HIKING
HIRING
HIVING
JIBING
JIMINY
JIVING
KIBITZ
KILIMS
KITING
LIAISE
LIBIDO
LIKING
LILIES
LILITH
LIMING
LIMITS
LINING
LIPIDE
LIPIDS
LIVING
MIKING
MIKITA
MILIEU
MIMICS
MIMING
MINIFY
MINIMA
MINIMS
MINING
MINION
MINIUM
MIRIAM
MIRING
MIXING
NIHILO
NIKITA
NIMINY
NIMITZ
NIXIES
NIXING
OILIER
OILING
PIKING
PILING
PIMINY
PINIER
PINING
PINION
PINITE
PIPING
PIPITS
PITIED
PITIES
PIXIES
QIVIUT
RICING
RIDING
RILING
RIMING
RIMINI
RISING
RIVING
SICILY
SIDING
SIGILS
SILICA
SIMIAN
SIMILE
SIRICA
SIRING
SIRIUS
SITING
SITINS
SIXING
SIZING
TIBIAE
TIBIAL
TIBIAS
TIDIED
TIDIER
TIDIES
TIDILY
TIDING
TIEING
TIEINS
TILING
TIMING
TINIER
TIPINS
TIRING
TITIAN
VIGILS
VIKING
VILIFY
VINING
VIRILE
VISINE
VISION
VISITS
VIVIAN
VIVIEN
VIVIFY
VIZIER
WILIER
WILING
WINING
WIPING
WIRING
ZIZITH

•I••I•
BIBLIO
BIDSIN
BIGGIE
BIGLIE
BIGWIG
BILLIE
BIOBIO
BIONIC
BIOTIC
BIOTIN
BIRDIE
BIRGIT
CITRIC
DIESIS
DIGSIN
DIKDIK
DIMWIT
DINEIN
DIOXIN
DISTIL
DIVEIN
FIBRIL
FIBRIN
FILLIN
FILLIP
FINNIC
FIRKIN
FISTIC
FITSIN
FIZGIG
GILLIE
GILLIS
GIVEIN
HIGHIQ
HIPPIE
HISPID
HITSIT
JIMMIE
KICKIN
KIDVID
KILTIE
LIBRIS
LIEBIG
LIESIN
LIGNIN
LILLIE
LIMPID
LIPOID
LIQUID
LITHIC
LIVEIN
LIZZIE
MIDAIR
MIDRIB
MILLIE
MILTIE
MINNIE
MINUIT
MIOSIS
MISDID
MISFIT
MISHIT
MISSIS
NIACIN
NITRIC
NITWIT
OILRIG
PICNIC
PIDGIN
PIETIN
PIGGIE
PILEIN
PINKIE
PINXIT
PINYIN
PIPKIN
PIPPIN
PIRRIP
PISTIL
RICHIE
SIGNIN
SIKKIM
SINKIN
SISKIN
SITSIN
TIDBIT
TIEDIN
TIEPIN
TIESIN
TIFFIN
TIGRIS
TILLIE
TILLIS
TILSIT
TIPSIN
TITBIT
VICTIM
VIOLIN
VIRGIL
VIRGIN
VISCID
VITRIC
WILLIE
WILLIS
WINGIT
WINKIE
WINNIE
WINWIN
WITHIN
WITHIT
ZINNIA

•I•••I
BIHARI
BIKINI
BILOXI
BIMINI
BIONDI
CIARDI
CISKEI
HIDEKI
KIGALI
KIMCHI
KINSKI
LITCHI
MIDORI
NIELLI
NILGAI
PILOTI
RIMINI
SILENI
TISHRI
TIVOLI

••II••
SHIISM
SHIITE
SKIING

••I•I•
ACIDIC
ALIBIS
ALICIA
BRIGID
CHIPIN
CHITIN
CLINIC
CRISIS
CRITIC
ELICIT
ELIXIR
EMILIA
EMILIO
EXILIC
FRIGID
IBIBIO
INITIO
IRIDIC
IRISIN
JOININ
LAIDIN
LAINIE
MAILIN
MAISIE
NAILIN
OLIVIA
ORIBIS
ORIGIN
OSIRIS
OTITIC
OTITIS
OXIDIC
PAIDIN
PHILIP
QUITIT
RAISIN
REININ
SCIFIS
SCIPIO
SLIDIN
SLIPIN
SPIRIT
STIRIN
STIVIC
TRICIA
TRIFID
TRIVIA
TRIXIE
TWILIT
UNIFIC

••I••I
CHICHI
DMITRI
GRIGRI
MAITAI
PRIORI
TAICHI
TAIPEI

•••II•
ACTIII

•••I•I
ACTIII
ASSISI
BIKINI
BIMINI
DOMINI
GEMINI
ILLINI
MEDICI
RAPINI
RIMINI
ROTINI
SOLIDI
SURIMI
TAHINI
TAHITI
WAPITI
YOGINI

••••II
ACTIII
ETALII
HAWAII
SAVAII

IJ••••
IJSSEL

I•J•••
INJECT
INJEST
INJOKE
INJURE
INJURY

I••J••
INAJAM

•IJ•••
BIJOUX
FIJIAN
GIJOES
HIJACK

•I•J••
NINJAS
RIOJAS

••IJ••
ELIJAH
FRIJOL

I•K•••
ICKIER
INKERS
INKIER
INKIND
INKING
INKLES
IRKING

I•••K•
INJOKE
INTAKE
INVOKE
ITHAKI

I••••K
INBULK
INLUCK
ITZHAK

•IK•••
AIKIDO
BIKERS
BIKING
BIKINI
DIKDIK
DIKING
DIKTAT
HIKERS
HIKING
KIKUYU
LIKELY
LIKENS
LIKING
MIKADO
MIKING
MIKITA
NIKITA
NIKOLA
PIKAKE
PIKERS
PIKING
SIKKIM
VIKING

•I•K••
BICKER
BILKED
CISKEI
DICKER
DICKEY
DINKEY
DISKED
FICKLE
FINKED
FIRKIN
GINKGO
HICKEY
HICKOK
JINKED
KICKED
KICKER
KICKIN
KICKUP
KINKED
KITKAT
LICKED
LINKED
LINKER
LINKUP
MICKEY
MILKED
MILKER
MINKES
NICKED
NICKEL
NICKER
OINKED
PICKAT
PICKAX
PICKED
PICKER
PICKET
PICKLE
PICKON
PICKUP
PINKED
PINKEN
PINKER
PINKIE
PIPKIN
RICKED
RICKEY
RIPKEN
RISKED
RISKER
SICKEN
SICKER
SICKLE
SICKLY
SIKKIM
SILKED
SILKEN
SINKER
SINKIN
SISKEL
SISKIN
TICKED
TICKER
TICKET
TICKLE
TINKER
TINKLE
TINKLY
WICKED
WICKER
WICKET
WILKES
WINKAT
WINKED
WINKER
WINKIE
WINKLE

•I••K•
HIDEKI
KINSKI
KIOSKS
KISHKE
MIWOKS
PIKAKE
RIMSKY
TILAKS

•I•••K
DIKDIK
HICKOK
HIJACK
PINOAK

••IK••
BAIKAL
DAIKON
DUIKER
HAIKOU
HAIKUS
SPIKED
SPIKER
SPIKES
TRIKES

••I•K•
BLINKS
BRICKS
BRICKY
BRINKS
CHICKS
CHINKS
CHINKY
CLICKS
CLINKS
CRICKS
DRINKS
FLICKA
FLICKS
FRISKS
FRISKY
GLINKA
GRIMKE
KNICKS
PLINKS
PRICKS
PRINKS
QUIRKS
QUIRKY
REINKS
SHIRKS
SKINKS
SLICKS
SLINKS
SLINKY
SMIRKS
SMIRKY
SNICKS
SPINKS
STICKS
STICKY
STINKS
STINKY
THICKE
THINKS
TRICKS
TRICKY
UMIAKS
WHISKS
YOICKS

••I••K
SPIVAK

•••IK•
BATIKS
MARIKO
SHEIKS
SHRIKE
STRIKE
TROIKA
UNLIKE
UPDIKE

•••I•K
ATRISK
DRYINK
KODIAK
NATICK
REDINK
REMICK
SCHICK
SHRIEK
SHRINK
SHTICK
STRICK
UNKINK
UNLINK
UPLINK
UPTICK
YORICK

••••IK
DIKDIK
HENRIK
MUZHIK
NARVIK
NUDNIK
RESNIK
SLOVIK
SUSLIK
TUGRIK
ZADDIK

IL••••
ILEANA
ILESHA
ILLEST
ILLFED
ILLINI
ILLMET
ILLSAY
ILLUME
ILLUSE
ILOILO

I•L•••
IDLERS
IDLEST
IDLING
IGLOOS
ILLEST
ILLFED
ILLINI
ILLMET
ILLSAY
ILLUME
ILLUSE
INLAID
INLAND
INLAWS
INLAYS
INLEAF
INLETS
INLINE
INLOVE
INLUCK
IOLITE
IRLENE
ISLAND
ISLETS

I••L••
IDYLLS
IMELDA
INFLOW
INFLUX
INGLES
INKLES
INPLAY
ISELIN
ISOLDE
ISTLES
ITALIA
ITALIC

I•••L•
ICICLE
IDEALS
IDYLLS
ILOILO
IMPALA
IMPALE
IMPELS
INBULK
INCULT
INFOLD
INFULL
INHALE
INHALF
INSOLE
INSULT
ISEULT
ITSELF

I••••L
IJSSEL
INFULL
INHAUL
IREFUL
IRREAL
ISABEL
ISOHEL
ISRAEL
IZABAL

•IL•••
AILEEN
AILERS
AILING
BILBAO
BILGES
BILKED
BILLED
BILLET
BILLIE
BILLON
BILLOW
BILOXI
CILIUM
DILATE
DILLER
DILLON
DILSEY
DILUTE
EILEEN
FILENE
FILERS
FILETS
FILIAL
FILING
FILIUS
FILLED
FILLER
FILLES
FILLET
FILLIN
FILLIP
FILLUP
FILMED
FILOSE
FILTER
FILTHY
GILDED
GILDER
GILEAD
GILLED
GILLIE
GILLIS
HILARY
HILLED
HILLEL
HILLER
HILTON
JILTED
KILIMS
KILLED
KILLER
KILMER
KILNED
KILTED
KILTER
KILTIE
LILACS
LILIES
LILITH
LILLIE
LILTED
MILADY
MILANO
MILDER
MILDEW
MILDLY
MILERS
MILIEU
MILKED
MILKER
MILLAY
MILLED
MILLER
MILLET
MILLIE
MILNER
MILORD

MILOSZ
MILPAS
MILSAP
MILTIE
MILTON
NILGAI
OILCAN
OILERS
OILIER
OILING
OILMAN
OILMEN
OILPAN
OILRIG
PILAFS
PILATE
PILEIN
PILEON
PILEUM
PILEUP
PILEUS
PILFER
PILING
PILLAR
PILLED
PILLOW
PILOSE
PILOTI
PILOTS
RILING
RILLES
RILLET
SILAGE
SILENI
SILENT
SILICA
SILKED
SILKEN
SILOAM
SILOED
SILONE
SILTED
SILVER
TILAKS
TILDEN
TILDES
TILERS
TILING
TILLED
TILLER
TILLIE
TILLIS
TILSIT
TILTED
TILTER
VILELY
VILEST
VILIFY
VILLAS
VILLON
VILLUS
WILBUR
WILDER
WILDLY
WILIER
WILING
WILKES
WILLED
WILLEM
WILLET
WILLIE
WILLIS
WILLOW
WILSON
WILTED
WILTON
ZILPAH

•I•L••

AIELLO
AISLES
BIBLES
BIBLIO
BIGLIE
BILLED
BILLET
BILLIE
BILLON
BILLOW
BIRLED
DIALED
DIALER
DIALOG
DIGLOT
DILLER
DILLON
FIELDS
FILLED
FILLER
FILLES
FILLET
FILLIN
FILLIP
FILLUP
GIBLET
GILLED
GILLIE
GILLIS
GIMLET
HILLED
HILLEL
HILLER
KILLED
KILLER
KISLEV
LIELOW
LILLIE
LISLES
MIDLER
MILLAY
MILLED
MILLER
MILLET
MILLIE
MISLAY
MISLED
NIELLI
NIELLO
PIGLET
PILLAR
PILLED
PILLOW
PIOLET
RIALTO
RIDLEY
RIFLED
RIFLER
RIFLES
RILLES
RILLET
RIPLEY
SIDLED
SIDLES
SISLER
TIGLON
TILLED
TILLER
TILLIE
TILLIS
TITLED
TITLES
VILLAS
VILLON
VILLUS
VIOLAS
VIOLET
VIOLIN
WIELDS
WIGLET
WILLED
WILLEM
WILLET
WILLIE
WILLIS
WILLOW
YIELDS
ZIPLOC

•I••L•

AIELLO
AIRILY
BIDDLE
BIFOLD
CIBOLA
CICELY
CIRCLE
DIABLO
DIBBLE
DIDDLE
DIMPLE
DIMPLY
DINGLE
DIPOLE
EIDOLA
FIBULA
FICKLE
FIDDLE
FINALE
FINALS
FINELY
FIPPLE
FIRMLY
FIZZLE
GIBILL
GIGGLE
GIGGLY
GIGOLO
GIMELS
GIRDLE
HIGGLE
HIGHLY
JIGGLE
JIGGLY
JINGLE
JINGLY
KIBBLE
KIGALI
KINDLE
KINDLY
KINGLY
KIRTLE
LIABLE
LIBELS
LIGULA
LIKELY
LIMPLY
LITTLE
LIVELY
MIDDLE
MIGGLE
MILDLY
MINGLE
MIZZLE
NIBBLE
NICELY
NICOLA
NICOLE
NICOLO
NIELLI
NIELLO
NIGGLE
NIHILO
NIKOLA
NIMBLE
NIMBLY
PICKLE
PICULS
PIFFLE
PINOLE
PINTLE
PIPALS
PIXELS
RIBALD
RICHLY
RIDDLE
RIFFLE
RIMPLE
RIPELY
RIPPLE
RIPPLY
RIVALS
RIYALS
SIBYLS
SICILY
SICKLE
SICKLY
SIECLE
SIGILS
SIMILE
SIMPLE
SIMPLY
SINGLE
SINGLY
SISALS
SIZZLE
TICALS
TICKLE
TIDILY
TIMELY
TINGLE
TINGLY
TINKLE
TINKLY
TIPPLE
TITTLE
TIVOLI
VIABLE
VIABLY
VIGILS
VILELY
VIRILE
VITALS
VIZSLA
WIDELY
WIFELY
WIGGLE
WIGGLY
WILDLY
WIMBLE
WIMPLE
WINKLE
WISELY

•I•••L

DIESEL
DIRNDL
DISMAL
DISPEL
DISTAL
DISTIL
EIFFEL
FIBRIL
FILIAL
FINIAL
FISCAL
FITFUL
GIBILL
GIMBAL
GIMBEL
HIATAL
HIEMAL
HILLEL
LINEAL
LINTEL
LIONEL
LISTEL
MIGUEL
MISSAL
MITRAL
NICKEL
PINEAL
PISTIL
PISTOL
RITUAL
SIGNAL
SIMBEL
SINFUL
SISKEL
TIBIAL
TIMBAL
TINCAL
TINSEL
VIRGIL
VISUAL
WIESEL
WITHAL

••IL••

AXILLA
BAILED
BAILEE
BAILER
BAILEY
BAILOR
BOILED
BOILER
BRILLO
BRILLS
BUILDS
CEILED
CHILDE
CHILDS
CHILLS
CHILLY
CHILOE
COILED
COILUP
DAILEY
DRILLS
EDILES
EMILIA
EMILIO
EPILOG
EVILER
EVILLY
EXILED
EXILES
EXILIC
FAILED
FAILLE
FOILED
FRILLS
FRILLY
GRILLE
GRILLS
GRILSE
GUILDS
GUILES
GUILTY
HAILED
HAILEY
JAILED
JAILER
KAILUA
MAILED
MAILER
MAILES
MAILIN
MOILED
MOILER
NAILED
NAILER
NAILIN
PAILOU
PHILAE
PHILIP
PHILLY
PHILOL
PHILOS
POILUS
QUILLS
QUILTS
RAILAT
RAILED
RAILER
ROILED
SAILED
SAILOR
SHILLS
SHILLY
SHILOH
SKILLS
SMILAX
SMILED
SMILER
SMILES
SMILEY
SOILED
SPILES
SPILLS
SPILTH
STILES
STILLS
STILLY
STILTS
SWILLS
TAILED
TAILLE
TAILOR
TBILLS
THILLS
TOILED
TOILER
TOILES
TOILET
TRILBY
TRILLS
TUILLE
TWILIT
TWILLS
VEILED
VOILES
WAILED
WAILER
WHILED
WHILES
WHILOM
WHILST

••I•L•

ACIDLY
AFIELD
ALIBLE
ARIDLY
AVIDLY
AXILLA
BGIRLS
BRIDLE
BRILLO
BRILLS
CHICLE
CHILLS
CHILLY
DRILLS
EDIBLE
ENISLE
EVILLY
FAILLE
FAIRLY
FOIBLE
FRILLS
FRILLY
GAINLY
GLIBLY
GRILLE
GRILLS
GRIMLY
GRISLY
ICICLE
MAINLY
ORIELS
ORIOLE
PHIALS
PHILLY
PRIMLY
QUILLS
SHIELD
SHILLS
SHILLY
SKILLS
SKIRLS
SLIMLY
SPIELS
SPILLS
STIFLE
STILLS
STILLY
SWILLS
SWIRLS
SWIRLY
TAILLE
TAILLE
TBILLS
THILLS
THINLY
TRIALS
TRIFLE
TRIGLY
TRILLS
TRIMLY
TRIPLE
TRIPLY
TUILLE
TWILLS
TWIRLS
URIALS
VAINLY
WHIRLS
WHIRLY

••I••L

AMIDOL
ANIMAL
APICAL
BAIKAL
BRIDAL
CHISEL
DRIVEL
EPICAL
FAISAL
FRIJOL
GEISEL
KEITEL
PHILOL
PRIMAL
RHINAL
SEIDEL
SNIVEL
SPINAL
SPINEL
SPIRAL
STIPEL
SWIVEL
TRIBAL
TRINAL
UNITAL
VEINAL

•••IL•

AEDILE
AIRILY
ANVILS
AQUILA
ATTILA
ATWILL
AVAILS
AWHILE
BODILY
BRAILS
BROILS
BUSILY
CAGILY
CAVILS
CECILE
COZILY
CYBILL
DEFILE
DESILU
DEVILS
DOCILE
DOZILY
DRAILS
EASILY
EDGILY
EERILY
EMAILS
ENSILE
ETOILE
FACILE
FAMILY
FLAILS
FOXILY
FUSILS
FUTILE
GAMILY
GIBILL
GOWILD
GRAILS
HABILE
HAMILL
HAZILY
HOMILY
ILOILO
KURILE
LABILE
LAZILY
LOGILY
MANILA
MARILU
MEGILP
MOBILE
MOTILE
NIHILO
NOSILY
NUBILE
ONEILL
ONFILE
PERILS
POKILY
PUNILY
PUPILS
QUAILS
RACILY
REFILE
REFILL
REOILS
RESILE
RETILE
REVILE
ROSILY
RUTILE
SEDILE
SEXILY
SHEILA
SHRILL
SICILY
SIGILS
SIMILE
SNAILS
SPOILS
SPOILT
SQUILL
TAMILS
THRILL
TIDILY
TRAILS
UNPILE
UPHILL
VERILY
VIGILS
VIRILE
WARILY
ZANILY
ZORILS

•••I•L

AERIAL
ASWIRL
ATRIAL
ATWILL
AUDIAL
AWHIRL
BELIAL
CURIAL
CYBILL
DANIEL
DENIAL
ESPIAL
FACIAL
FILIAL
FINIAL
GAVIAL
GENIAL
GIBILL
HAMILL
JOVIAL
LABIAL
MARIEL
MEDIAL
MENIAL
MURIEL
MUSIAL
MYGIRL
NARIAL
ONEILL
RACIAL
RADIAL
REDIAL
REFILL
RETIAL
SERIAL
SHRILL
SOCIAL
SQUILL
THRILL
TIBIAL
UNCIAL
UPHILL
VENIAL

••••IL

ASSAIL
BEWAIL
BRAZIL
BULBIL
DENTIL
DERAIL
DETAIL
DISTIL
ENTAIL
FIBRIL
FOSSIL
GERBIL
KAHLIL
LENTIL
MELVIL
NYQUIL
ORCHIL
OXTAIL
PENCIL
PISTIL
REBOIL
RECOIL
REMAIL
RENAIL
RETAIL
SOLEIL
TONSIL
UNCOIL
UNVEIL
URACIL
USMAIL
VIRGIL
WEEVIL

IM••••

IMAGED
IMAGER
IMAGES
IMARET
IMBIBE
IMBRUE
IMBUED
IMBUES
IMELDA
IMFINE
IMMUNE
IMMUNO
IMMURE
IMOGEN
IMPACT
IMPAIR
IMPALA
IMPALE
IMPART
IMPEDE
IMPELS
IMPEND
IMPERF
IMPISH
IMPORT
IMPOSE
IMPOST
IMPROV
IMPUGN
IMPURE
IMPUTE

I•M•••

IAMBIC
IMMUNE
IMMUNO
IMMURE
INMATE
INMOST
IOMOTH
ISMENE

I••M••

ICEMAN
ICEMEN
ILLMET
INGMAR
ISOMER

I•••M•

IBEAMS
IDIOMS
ILLUME
INCOME
INFAMY
INHUME
INTIMA
INTIME
ISTHMI

I••••M

IBIDEM
INAJAM
INDIUM
INFIRM
INFORM
INSEAM
IONIUM

•IM•••

AIMING
AIMSAT
AIMSTO
BIMINI
DIMITY
DIMMED
DIMMER
DIMOUT
DIMPLE
DIMPLY
DIMSUM
DIMWIT
GIMBAL
GIMBEL
GIMELS
GIMLET
JIMINY
JIMMIE
JIMSON
KIMCHI
KIMONO
LIMBED
LIMBER
LIMBOS
LIMBUS
LIMENS
LIMEYS
LIMING
LIMITS
LIMNED
LIMNER
LIMPED
LIMPER
LIMPET
LIMPID
LIMPLY
MIMEOS
MIMERS
MIMICS
MIMING
MIMOSA
NIMBLE
NIMBLY
NIMBUS
NIMINY
NIMITZ
NIMROD
PIMINY
RIMING
RIMINI
RIMMED
RIMOSE
RIMPLE
RIMSKY
SIMBEL
SIMEON
SIMIAN
SIMILE
SIMMER
SIMONE
SIMONY
SIMPER
SIMPLE
SIMPLY
TIMBAL
TIMBER
TIMBRE
TIMELY
TIMERS
TIMING
WIMBLE
WIMPLE
WIMSEY
XIMENA
ZIMMER

•I•M••

AIRMAN
AIRMEN
BIGMAC
BIOMES
BITMAP
DIMMED
DIMMER
DISMAL
DISMAY
DISMES
FILMED
FIRMAN
FIRMED
FIRMER
FIRMLY
FIRMUP
GIZMOS
HIEMAL
HITMAN
HITMEN
JIMMIE
KIDMAN
KILMER
KIRMAN
KISMET
LITMUS
MICMAC
NIAMEY
OILMAN
OILMEN
PIEMAN
PIEMEN
PITMAN
PITMEN
RIMMED
SIGMAS
SIMMER
TINMAN
TINMEN
XIAMEN
ZIMMER

•I••M•

BIGAMY
BIREME
CINEMA
JICAMA
KILIMS
KINGME
MIASMA
MINIMA
MINIMS

•I•••M

AIRARM
AIRDAM
CILIUM
CIRCUM
DIADEM
DIATOM
DICTUM
DIGRAM
DIMSUM
DIRHAM
DISARM
MINIUM
MIRIAM
PILEUM
SIKKIM
SILOAM
SITCOM
VIACOM
VICTIM
WIGWAM
WILLEM
WINDOM
WISDOM

••IM••

AHIMSA
AKIMBO
ANIMAL
ANIMAS
ANIMES
ANIMUS
ASIMOV
BLIMEY
BLIMPS
CAIMAN
CHIMED
CHIMES
CHIMPS
CLIMAX
CLIMBS
CLIMES
CRIMEA
CRIMES
CRIMPS
DAIMON
DAIMYO
DEIMOS
FBIMAN
FBIMEN
FLIMSY
GRIMED
GRIMES
GRIMKE
GRIMLY
GUIMPE
PRIMAL
PRIMED
PRIMER
PRIMES
PRIMLY
PRIMOS
PRIMPS
PRIMUM
PRIMUS
SHIMMY
SHIMON
SKIMPS
SKIMPY
SLIMED
SLIMES
SLIMLY
STIMPY
TRIMLY
WEIMAR
WHIMSY

••I•M•

AXIOMS
ENIGMA
IDIOMS
ODIUMS
PRISMS
SEISMO
SEISMS
SHIMMY
STIGMA

••I••M

FAIYUM
IBIDEM
PRIMUM
SHIISM
WHILOM

•••IM•

BEDIMS
CLAIMS
COLIMA
DENIMS
ESKIMO
FATIMA
HAKIMS
INTIMA
INTIME
KILIMS
MAXIMA
MAXIMS
MINIMA
MINIMS
ONTIME
OPTIMA
REGIME
RETIME
SCRIMP
SCRIMS
SHRIMP
SURIMI
ULTIMA
ULTIMO
UPTIME
YAKIMA

•••I•M

ACTIUM
AFFIRM
AGEISM
ALLIUM
ATRIUM
BARIUM
CERIUM
CESIUM
CHRISM
CILIUM
CONIUM
CORIUM
CUBISM
CURIUM
EGOISM
ERBIUM
FOLIUM
HELIUM
HOLISM
INDIUM
INFIRM
IONIUM
LATIUM
MAOISM
MEDIUM
MINIUM
MIRIAM
MONISM
OMNIUM
OSMIUM
OSTIUM
PODIUM
PURISM
RADIUM
SAMIAM
SCHISM
SHIISM
SODIUM
SQUIRM
SUFISM
TAOISM
TEDIUM
THEISM
TRUISM
VALIUM
VERISM

••••IM

ANTRIM
ELOHIM
LCHAIM
MUSLIM
PASSIM
PRELIM
RETRIM
SIKKIM
VICTIM

IN••••

INAFIX
INAFOG
INAJAM

INANER
INAPET
INARCH
INAROW
INARUT
INAWAY
INBORN
INBRED
INBULK
INCANS
INCASE
INCASH
INCEPT
INCHED
INCHES
INCHON
INCISE
INCITE
INCOME
INCULT
INCURS
INCUSE
INDABA
INDEBT
INDEED
INDENE
INDENT
INDIAN
INDICT
INDIES
INDIGO
INDIRA
INDITE
INDIUM
INDOOR
INDRIS
INDUCE
INDUCT
INFACT
INFAMY
INFANT
INFECT
INFERS
INFEST
INFIRM
INFLOW
INFLUX
INFOLD
INFORM
INFULL
INFUSE
INGEAR
INGEST
INGLES
INGMAR
INGOTS
INGRES
INGRID
INHALE
INHALF
INHAND
INHAUL
INHERE
INHUME
INIONS
INITIO
INJECT
INJEST
INJOKE
INJURE
INJURY
INKERS
INKIER
INKIND
INKING
INKLES
INLAID
INLAND
INLAWS
INLAYS
INLEAF
INLETS
INLINE
INLOVE
INLUCK
INMATE
INMOST
INNAGE
INNATE
INNEED
INNESS
INNING
INOUYE
INPART
INPLAY
INPORT
INPOUR
INPUTS
INROAD
INRUSH
INSANE
INSEAM
INSECT
INSERT
INSETS
INSIDE
INSIST
INSITU
INSOLE
INSPAN
INSTAR
INSTEP
INSULT
INSURE
INSYNC
INTACT
INTAKE
INTEND
INTENS
INTENT
INTERN
INTIMA
INTIME
INTINE
INTONE
INTOTO
INTOWN
INTROS
INTUIT
INTUNE
INTURN
INUITS
INURED
INURES
INVADE
INVAIN
INVENT
INVERT
INVEST
INVITE
INVIVO
INVOKE
INWARD
INWITH

I•N•••

IGNACE
IGNATZ
IGNITE
IGNORE
INNAGE
INNATE
INNEED
INNESS
INNING
IONIAN
IONICS
IONIUM
IONIZE

I••N••

ICINGS
ICONIC
INANER
IRANIS
IRENES
IRENIC
IRONED
IRONER
IRONIC
IRONON

I•••N•

ICHING
IDLING
IGUANA
ILEANA
ILLINI
IMFINE
IMMUNE
IMMUNO
IMPEND
INCANS
INDENE
INDENT
INFANT
INHAND
INIONS
INKIND
INKING
INLAND
INLINE
INNING
INSANE
INSYNC
INTEND
INTENS
INTENT
INTINE
INTONE
INTUNE
INVENT
IODINE
IOWANS
IRKING
IRLENE
IRVINE
IRVING
ISLAND
ISMENE

I••••N

IBADAN
ICEDIN
ICEMAN
ICEMEN
ICESIN
IMOGEN
IMPUGN
INBORN
INCHON
INDIAN
INSPAN
INTERN
INTOWN
INTURN
INVAIN
IONIAN
IRISIN
IRONON
ISELIN
ISOGON

•IN•••

BINARY
BINATE
BINDER
BINDUP
BINGED
BINGES
BINNED
CINDER
CINEMA
CINQUE
DINARS
DINEIN
DINEON
DINERO
DINERS
DINGED
DINGHY
DINGLE
DINGUS
DINING
DINKEY
DINNED
DINNER
DINTED
FINALE
FINALS
FINDER
FINELY
FINERY
FINEST
FINGER
FINIAL
FINING
FINISH
FINITE
FINITO
FINKED
FINNAN
FINNED
FINNEY
FINNIC
GINGER
GINKGO
GINNED
HINDER
HINDUS
HINGED
HINGES
HINTAT
HINTED
HINTER
HINTON
JINGLE
JINGLY
JINKED
JINNAH
JINXED
JINXES
KINDER
KINDLE
KINDLY
KINDOF
KINGED
KINGLY
KINGME
KINKED
KINSKI
LINAGE
LINDEN
LINEAL
LINEAR
LINENS
LINERS
LINEUP
LINGER
LINGUA
LINING
LINKED
LINKER
LINKUP
LINNET
LINSEY
LINTEL
LINTER
MINCED
MINCER
MINCES
MINDED
MINDER
MINERS
MINGLE
MINIFY
MINIMA
MINIMS
MINING
MINION
MINIUM
MINKES
MINNIE
MINNOW
MINOAN
MINORS
MINTED
MINTER
MINUET
MINUIT
MINUTE
MINXES
MINYAN
NINERS
NINETY
NINGBO
NINJAS
NINTHS
OINKED
PINATA
PINCER
PINDAR
PINDUS
PINEAL
PINERO
PINERY
PINGED
PINIER
PINING
PINION
PINITE
PINKED
PINKEN
PINKER
PINKIE
PINNAE
PINNAS
PINNED
PINNER
PINOAK
PINOLE
PINONS
PINOTS
PINSON
PINTER
PINTLE
PINTOS
PINUPS
PINXIT
PINYIN
PINYON
PINZON
QINTAR
RINGED
RINGER
RINGUP
RINSED
RINSES
SINBAD
SINEAD
SINEWS
SINEWY
SINFUL
SINGED
SINGER
SINGES
SINGLE
SINGLY
SINGTO
SINKER
SINKIN
SINNED
SINNER
SINTAX
SINTER
TINCAL
TINCAN
TINCTS
TINDER
TINEAR
TINGED
TINGES
TINGLE
TINGLY
TINGOD
TINHAT
TINIER
TINKER
TINKLE
TINKLY
TINMAN
TINMEN
TINNED
TINNER
TINPAN
TINPOT
TINSEL
TINTED
TINTER
VINERY
VINING
VINOUS
VINTON
WINCED
WINCER
WINCES
WINDED
WINDER
WINDEX
WINDOM
WINDOW
WINDUP
WINERY
WINGED
WINGER
WINGIT
WINING
WINKAT
WINKED
WINKER
WINKIE
WINKLE
WINNER
WINNIE
WINNOW
WINONA
WINOUT
WINSOR
WINTER
WINTRY
WINWIN
WINZES
ZINGED
ZINGER
ZINNIA

•I•N••

BIANCA
BINNED
BIONDI
BIONIC
BIRNEY
DINNED
DINNER
DIONEB
DIONNE
DIRNDL
DISNEY
EISNER
FIANCE
FIENDS
FINNAN
FINNED
FINNEY
FINNIC
GIANTS
GINNED
JINNAH
JITNEY
KIANGS
KIDNAP
KIDNEY
KILNED
LIANAS
LIANGS
LIENEE
LIGNIN
LIMNED
LIMNER
LINNET
LIONEL
LIONET
MIGNON
MILNER
MINNIE
MINNOW
PIANOS
PICNIC
PIGNUT
PINNAE
PINNAS
PINNED
PINNER
SIDNEY
SIENNA
SIGNAL
SIGNED
SIGNEE
SIGNER
SIGNET
SIGNIN
SIGNON
SIGNOR
SIGNUP
SINNED
SINNER
TINNED
TINNER
VIANDS
VIENNA
VIENNE
WIENER
WINNER
WINNIE
WINNOW
ZINNIA

•I••N•

AIDING
AILING
AIMING
AIRING
BIDING
BIKING
BIKINI
BIMINI
BISONS
BITING
CITING
DICING
DIKING
DINING
DIONNE
DISANT
DIVANS
DIVINE
DIVING
FILENE
FILING
FINING
FIRING
FIXING
GIBING
GITANO
GIVENS
GIVING
HIDING
HIEING
HIKING
HIRING
HIVING
JIBING
JIMINY
JIVING
KIMONO
KITING
LIERNE
LIKENS
LIKING
LIMENS
LIMING
LINENS
LINING
LIPENG
LITANY
LIVENS
LIVING
MIKING
MILANO
MIMING
MINING
MIRING
MIXING
MIZENS
NICENE
NIMINY
NIXING
OILING
PIKING
PILING
PIMINY
PINING
PINONS
PIPING
PIRANA
PISANS
PITONS
RIBAND
RICING
RIDENT
RIDING
RILING
RIMING
RIMINI
RIPENS
RISING
RIVING
SIDING
SIENNA
SILENI
SILENT
SILONE
SIMONE
SIMONY
SIRENS
SIRING
SITING
SITINS
SIXING
SIZING
TIDING
TIEING
TIEINS
TILING
TIMING
TIPINS
TIRANA
TIRANE
TIRING
TISANE
TITANS
VICUNA
VIENNA
VIENNE
VIKING
VINING
VISHNU
VISINE
VIVANT
VIXENS
WIDENS
WILING
WINING
WINONA
WIPING
WIRING
WISENT
WIZENS
XIMENA

•I•••N

AILEEN
AIRGUN
AIRMAN
AIRMEN
BICORN
BIDDEN
BIDSIN
BIDSON
BIGBEN
BIGGUN
BIGTEN
BILLON
BIOTIN
BITTEN
CITRON
DIDION
DIGSIN
DILLON
DINEIN
DINEON
DIOXIN
DISOWN
DIVEIN
EILEEN
FIBRIN
FIJIAN
FILLIN
FINNAN
FIRKIN
FIRMAN
FITSIN
GIBBON
GIBRAN
GIBSON
GIDEON
GIVEIN
HIDDEN
HIERON
HILTON
HINTON
HIREON
HITMAN
HITMEN
HITSON
JIMSON
KICKIN
KIDMAN
KIRMAN
KITTEN
LIBYAN
LICHEN
LIESIN
LIGNIN
LINDEN
LIPTON
LISBON
LISTEN
LISTON
LIVEIN
LIVEON
MICRON
MIDDEN
MIGNON
MILTON
MINION
MINOAN
MINYAN
MIRREN
MITTEN
MIZZEN
NIACIN
NICEAN
NIPPON
NISSAN
NISSEN
OILCAN
OILMAN
OILMEN
OILPAN
PICKON
PIDGIN
PIEMAN
PIEMEN
PIEPAN
PIETIN
PIGEON
PIGPEN
PILEIN
PILEON
PINION
PINKEN
PINSON
PINYIN
PINYON
PINZON
PIPKIN
PIPPIN
PISTON
PITMAN
PITMEN
RIBBON
RICHEN
RIDDEN
RIPKEN
SICKEN
SIGNIN
SIGNON
SILKEN
SIMEON
SIMIAN
SINKIN
SIOUAN
SIPHON
SISKIN
SITSIN
SITSON
SIXGUN
TIEDIN
TIEPIN
TIESIN
TIFFIN
TIGLON
TILDEN
TINCAN
TINMAN
TINMEN
TINPAN
TIPSIN
TITIAN
VILLON
VINTON
VIOLIN
VIRGIN
VISION
VIVIAN
VIVIEN
WICCAN
WILSON
WILTON
WINWIN
WITHIN
XIAMEN
ZIRCON

••IN••

ACINUS
ALINES
AMINES
AMINOR
AMINUS
BAINES
BEINGS
BLINDS
BLINKS
BLINTZ
BMINOR
BMINUS
BOINGO
BRINED
BRINES
BRINGS
BRINKS
CHINCH
CHINES
CHINKS
CHINKY
CHINOS
CHINTZ
CHINUP
CLINCH
CLINES
CLINGS
CLINGY
CLINIC
CLINKS
CMINOR
CMINUS
COINED
COINER
CRINGE
DAINTY
DMINOR
DMINUS
DOINGS
DRINGS
DRINKS
ELINOR
EMINOR
ERINYS
EVINCE
FAINTS
FEINTS
FLINCH
FLINGS
FLINTS
FLINTY
FMINOR
FRINGE
FRINGY
GAINED
GAINER
GAINLY
GAINON
GAINST
GLINKA
GLINTS
GMINOR
GOINGS
GOINTO
GRINCH
GRINDS
GRINGO
GUINEA
HAINAN
HAINES
ICINGS
JOINED
JOINER
JOININ
JOINTS
JOINUP
LAINIE
MAINLY
MOINES
OLINDA
OLINGO
OPINED
OPINER
OPINES
ORINGS
PAINED
PAINTS
PLINKS
PLINTH
POINTE
POINTS
POINTY
PRINCE
PRINKS
PRINTS
QUINCE
QUINCY
QUINOA
QUINTS
RAINED
RAINER
RAINES
REINED
REINER
REININ
REINKS
RHINAL
RHINOS
RUINED
RUINER
SAINTE
SAINTS
SEINED
SEINER
SEINES
SHINDY
SHINED
SHINER
SHINES
SHINNY
SHINTO
SKINKS
SKINNY
SLINGS
SLINKS
SLINKY
SPINAL
SPINED
SPINEL
SPINES
SPINET
SPINKS
STINGS
STINGY
STINKS
STINKY
STINTS
SWINGS
SWINGY
TAINAN
TAINOS
TAINTS
THINGS
THINKS
THINLY
TRINAL
TRINES
TWINED
TWINES
TWINGE
VAINER
VAINLY
VEINAL
VEINED
WHINED
WHINER
WHINES
WHINNY
WRINGS

••I•N•

ALIENS
ALIGNS
AMIENS
ANIONS
ASIANS
AVIANS
AXIONS
BAIRNS
BOIGNY
BRIAND
BRIANS
BRIENZ
CAIRNS
CHIANG
CLIENT
DEIGNS
FEIGNS
FRIEND
GUIANA
INIONS
ONIONS
ONIONY
ORIANA
ORIENT
PLIANT
PRIONS
PUISNE
REIGNS
SCIONS
SHINNY
SKIING
SKINNY
SOIGNE
TRIUNE
UNIONS
VSIGNS
WHINNY

••I••N

ALISON
ARISEN
BLIXEN
BRITON
CAIMAN
CHIPIN
CHIRON
CHITIN
CHITON
CLIPON
DAIKON
DAIMON
DAIREN
DRIVEN
EDISON
FBIMAN
FBIMEN
GAINON
GRISON
GUIDON
HAINAN
HEIDEN
IRISIN
JOININ
KLIBAN
LAIDIN
LAIDON
LEIDEN
MAIDEN
MAILIN
NAILIN
NOIRON
OBIWAN
OHIOAN
ORIGEN
ORIGIN
ORISON
PAIDIN
POISON
PRISON
RAISIN
REININ
SAIGON
SAIPAN
SHIMON
SKIRUN
SLIDIN
SLIPIN
SLIPON
STIRIN
TAINAN
TAIPAN
TAIWAN
TRIGON
TRITON
UNISON
WAITON
WHITEN

•••IN•

AAHING
ACHING
ACTING
ACTINO
ADDING
AFFINE
AGEING
AGLINT
AIDING
AILING
AIMING
AIRING
ALBINO
ALDINE
ALFINE
ALOINS
ALPINE
ANOINT
AQUINO
ARCING
ARMING
ASKING
ATKINS
AUXINS
AWNING
BAAING
BAKING
BALING
BARING
BASING
BASINS
BATING
BAYING
BBKING
BEGINS
BEHIND
BEMINE
BENING
BERING
BIDING
BIKING
BIKINI
BIMINI
BITING

BLAINE
BLUING
BODING
BOEING
BONING
BOOING
BORING
BOVINE
BOWING
BOXING
BRAINS
BRAINY
BRUINS
BURINS
BUSING
BUYING
BYLINE
CABINS
CAGING
CAKING
CAMINO
CANINE
CANING
CARINA
CARING
CASING
CASINO
CAVING
CAWING
CEDING
CELINE
CHAINE
CHAINS
CITING
CLUING
CODING
COMING
COOING
COPING
CORING
COSINE
COVINA
COWING
CRYING
CUBING
CURING
CUTINS
DARING
DATING
DAZING
DEFINE
DEVINE
DEWING
DICING
DIKING
DINING
DIVINE
DIVING
DOLING
DOMING
DOMINI
DOMINO
DOPING
DOSING
DOTING
DOZING
DRAINS
DRYING
DRYINK
DUKING
DUPING
DURING
DYEING
EALING

EARING
EASING
EATING
EBBING
EDGING
EGGING
ELAINE
ELNINO
ENCINA
ENCINO
ENDING
ENGINE
EOSINS
EPPING
EQUINE
ERMINE
ERRING
ERVING
EYEING
FACING
FADING
FAKING
FALINE
FAMINE
FARINA
FARING
FAXING
FAZING
FEEING
FELINE
FETING
FILING
FINING
FIRING
FIXING
FLYING
FORINT
FOXING
FRYING
FUMING
FUSING
FUZING
GAGING
GAMINE
GAMING
GAMINS
GAPING
GATING
GAZING
GEEING
GEMINI
GIBING
GIVING
GLUING
GORING
GRAINS
GRAINY
GROINS
GUYING
HALING
HARING
HATING
HAVING
HAWING
HAYING
HAZING
HEWING
HEXING
HIDING
HIEING
HIKING
HIRING
HIVING
HOEING

HOLING
HOMING
HOMINY
HONING
HOPING
HOSING
HYPING
ICHING
IDLING
ILLINI
IMFINE
INKIND
INKING
INLINE
INNING
INTINE
IODINE
IRKING
IRVINE
IRVING
JADING
JANINE
JAPING
JAWING
JIBING
JIMINY
JIVING
JOKING
JUKING
KALINE
KEYING
KITING
LACING
LADING
LADINO
LAMINA
LAMING
LAPINS
LATINA
LATINO
LATINS
LAVING
LAWING
LAYING
LAZING
LEVINE
LIKING
LIMING
LINING
LIVING
LOPING
LOSING
LOVING
LOWING
LUBING
LUMINA
LUPINE
LUPINO
LURING
LUTING
LYSINE
LYSINS
MAKING
MARINA
MARINE
MARINO
MATING
MATINS
MAXINE
MEDINA
MELINA
MENINX
MERINO
METING

MEWING
MIKING
MIMING
MINING
MIRING
MIXING
MODINE
MOLINE
MOOING
MOPING
MOVING
MOWING
MURINE
MUSING
MUTING
MUTINY
NADINE
NAMING
NEVINS
NIMINY
NIXING
NOSING
NOTING
NUKING
NUMINA
OARING
OFFING
OGLING
OILING
ONDINE
ONLINE
OOHING
OOZING
OPTING
ORBING
ORPINE
ORSINO
OSCINE
OUTING
OWNING
PACING
PACINO
PAGING
PALING
PARING
PATINA
PATINE
PAVING
PAWING
PAYING
PEKING
PEPINO
PIKING
PILING
PIMINY
PINING
PIPING
PLAINS
PLAINT
PLYING
POKING
POLING
PORING
POSING
PRYING
PULING
PURINA
PURINE
QUAINT
QUOINS
RACINE
RACING
RAGING
RAKING

RAPINE
RAPINI
RARING
RATINE
RATING
RAVINE
RAVING
RAZING
REBIND
REDINK
REFINE
REGINA
RELINE
REMIND
REPINE
RESING
RESINS
RETINA
REWIND
REWINS
RICING
RIDING
RILING
RIMING
RIMINI
RISING
RIVING
ROBING
ROBINS
ROPING
ROSINS
ROSINY
ROTINI
ROVING
ROWING
RULING
RUMINA
RUNINS
SABINE
SABINS
SALINA
SALINE
SATING
SATINS
SATINY
SAVING
SAWING
SAYING
SEEING
SERINE
SERINS
SETINS
SEWING
SHRINE
SHRINK
SHYING
SIDING
SIRING
SITING
SITINS
SIXING
SIZING
SKEINS
SKIING
SKYING
SLUING
SOFINE
SOLING
SOWING
SPHINX
SPLINE
SPLINT
SPRING
SPRINT

SPYING
SQUINT
STAINS
STEINS
STRING
SUPINE
SWAINS
SYRINX
TAHINI
TAKING
TAKINS
TAMING
TAPING
TAPINS
TARING
TAWING
TAXING
TEEING
TIDING
TIEING
TIEINS
TILING
TIMING
TIPINS
TIRING
TOEING
TOEINS
TONING
TORINO
TOTING
TOWING
TOXINS
TOYING
TRAINS
TRUING
TRYING
TUBING
TUNING
TURING
TYPING
UNBIND
UNDINE
UNKIND
UNKINK
UNLINK
UNPINS
UNWIND
UPLINK
UPPING
UPWIND
URGING
URSINE
VEXING
VIKING
VINING
VISINE
VOTING
VOWING
WADING
WAGING
WAHINE
WAKING
WANING
WARING
WAVING
WAXING
WILING
WINING
WIPING
WIRING
WOOING
WOWING
YAWING
YOGINI
YOKING
ZAYINS
ZONING

•••I•N

ACTION
ADRIAN
ADRIEN
ALBION
AMNION
ANCIEN
APPIAN
ASSIGN
BAHIAN
BENIGN
BUNION
CAMION
CATION
COSIGN
DAMIEN
DARIEN
DESIGN
DIDION
DORIAN
DURIAN
ELOIGN
ENSIGN
EOLIAN
EONIAN
FABIAN
FANION
FENIAN
FIJIAN
FUJIAN
FUSION
GABION
INDIAN
IONIAN
JOVIAN
JULIAN
LEGION
LOGION
LOTION
LUCIAN
MALIGN
MARIAN
MARION
MEDIAN
MINION
MORION
MOTION
NATION
NOTION
NUBIAN
OBRIAN
OBRIEN
OPTION
OSSIAN
PELION
PINION
POTION
RADIAN
RATION
REGION
RESIGN
SIMIAN
SYRIAN
TALION
TITIAN
TUPIAN
TYRIAN
UGRIAN
VISION
VIVIAN
VIVIEN

••••IN

ADDSIN
ADJOIN
ALBOIN
ALCUIN
ALDRIN
AMBLIN
ANACIN
ATTAIN
AUSTIN
AZORIN
BACKIN
BAFFIN
BARKIN
BERLIN
BIDSIN
BIOTIN
BLOWIN
BOBBIN
BODKIN
BOUDIN
BOWFIN
BUSKIN
BUTTIN
CALLIN
CALVIN
CAMEIN
CARDIN
CASHIN
CATKIN
CAVEIN
CHAPIN
CHEMIN
CHENIN
CHIPIN
CHITIN
CHOPIN
CLAVIN
CLUEIN
COCHIN
COMEIN
CORBIN
COUSIN
CRETIN
CRONIN
CULKIN
CURTIN
CUTSIN
DARWIN
DASSIN
DEALIN
DENTIN
DETAIN
DEVEIN
DIGSIN
DINEIN
DIOXIN
DIVEIN
DOBBIN
DOBLIN
DOESIN
DOMAIN
DONEIN
DOVEIN
DRAGIN
DRAWIN
DREWIN
DROPIN
DUBBIN
DUBLIN
DUCHIN
DUNLIN
DURBIN
DUSTIN
EASEIN
EATSIN
EDGEIN
ENJOIN
FADEIN
FALLIN
FELLIN
FIBRIN
FILLIN
FIRKIN
FITSIN
FLEWIN
FLORIN
FOGSIN
GASKIN
GATLIN
GAVEIN
GAWAIN
GETSIN
GIVEIN
GLOBIN
GOBLIN
GODWIN
GOESIN
GRADIN
GRATIN
GRODIN
HAMLIN
HANDIN
HANGIN
HARBIN
HATPIN
HEADIN
HEFLIN
HELDIN
HEMSIN
HENNIN
HEREIN
HOWLIN
HUNGIN
ICEDIN
ICESIN
INVAIN
IRISIN
ISELIN
JAMSIN
JERKIN
JOININ
JOPLIN
JUMPIN
JUSTIN
KAOLIN
KEEPIN
KELVIN
KEYSIN
KICKIN
LAIDIN
LANVIN
LAYSIN
LEADIN
LETSIN
LIESIN
LIGNIN
LIVEIN
LOCKIN
LOGSIN
LOMEIN
LOOKIN
LOVEIN
LUBLIN
MAILIN
MALKIN
MALTIN
MARGIN
MARLIN
MARTIN
MARVIN
MATLIN
MCBAIN
MCLAIN
MELVIN
MERLIN
MOULIN
MOVEIN
MUFFIN
MUNTIN
MUSLIN
MYELIN
MYOSIN
NAILIN
NAPKIN
NIACIN
NOGGIN
NUBBIN
NUTKIN
OBTAIN
OLEFIN
ORDAIN
ORIGIN
OSSEIN
PAIDIN
PAPAIN
PAYSIN
PECTIN
PEERIN
PEPSIN
PETAIN
PIDGIN
PIETIN
PILEIN
PINYIN
PIPKIN
PIPPIN
PLUGIN
POPLIN
POPSIN
POURIN
PREVIN
PUFFIN
PULLIN
PURLIN
PUTSIN
RAISIN
RAKEIN
RANKIN
RATLIN
READIN
REDFIN
REELIN
REGAIN
REININ
REJOIN
REMAIN
RENNIN
RETAIN
ROLLIN
ROPEIN
RUBSIN
RUNSIN
RUSKIN
SEEPIN
SEESIN
SENDIN
SENTIN
SEQUIN
SERKIN
SETSIN
SHOOIN
SHOWIN
SHUTIN
SIGNIN
SINKIN
SISKIN
SITSIN
SLIDIN
SLIPIN
SNOWIN
SOCKIN
SPAVIN
SPRAIN
STALIN
STEPIN
STIRIN
STOPIN
STRAIN
SUCKIN
TAKEIN
TANNIN
TENPIN
TIEDIN
TIEPIN
TIESIN
TIFFIN
TIPSIN
TOCSIN
TOEDIN
TOESIN
TOMLIN
TONKIN
TOOKIN
TUCKIN
TUNEIN
TURNIN
UJJAIN
URCHIN
VERDIN
VERMIN
VIOLIN
VIRGIN
VOTEIN
WADEIN
WALKIN
WANTIN
WAVEIN
WELKIN
WENTIN
WINWIN
WITHIN
WORKIN
ZEROIN

IO••••

IODATE
IODIDE
IODINE
IODIZE
IOLITE
IOMOTH
IONIAN
IONICS
IONIUM
IONIZE
IOWANS

I•O•••

ICONIC
IDOIDO
ILOILO
IMOGEN
INOUYE
IRONED
IRONER
IRONIC
IRONON
ISOBAR
ISOGON
ISOHEL
ISOLDE
ISOMER
ISOPOD

I••O••

ICEOUT
IDIOCY
IDIOMS
IDIOTS
IGLOOS
IGNORE
IMPORT
IMPOSE
IMPOST
INBORN
INCOME
INDOOR
INFOLD
INFORM
INGOTS
INIONS
INJOKE
INLOVE
INMOST
INPORT
INPOUR
INROAD
INSOLE
INTONE
INTOTO
INTOWN
INVOKE
IOMOTH

I•••O•

ICEBOX
ICEFOG
IGLOOS
IMPROV
INAFOG
INAROW
INCHON
INDOOR
INFLOW
INTROS
IRONON
ISADOR
ISOGON
ISOPOD

I••••O

IBIBIO
IDOIDO
ILOILO
IMMUNO
INDIGO
INITIO
INTOTO
INVIVO

•IO•••

BIOBIO
BIOGAS
BIOMES
BIONDI
BIONIC
BIOTAS
BIOTIC
BIOTIN
DIODES
DIONEB
DIONNE
DIOXIN
FIORDS
GIOTTO
KIOSKS
KIOWAS
LIONEL
LIONET
LIOTTA
MIOSIS
PIOLET
RIOJAS
RIOTED
RIOTER
SIOUAN
VIOLAS
VIOLET
VIOLIN

•I•O••

AIROUT
BICORN
BIFOLD
BIGOTS
BIJOUX
BILOXI
BIPODS
BISONS
BITOFF
CIBOLA
DICOTS
DIEOFF
DIEOUT
DIGOUT
DIMOUT
DIPODY
DIPOLE
DISOWN
DIVOTS
EIDOLA
FILOSE
GIGOLO
GIGOTS
GIJOES
HIDOUT
KIBOSH
KIDORY
KIMONO
LIPOID
LITOUT
MIDORI
MILORD
MILOSZ
MIMOSA
MINOAN
MINORS
MIWOKS
NICOLA
NICOLE
NICOLO
NIKOLA
PICOTS
PIGOUT
PILOSE
PILOTI
PILOTS
PINOAK
PINOLE
PINONS
PINOTS
PITONS
PIVOTS
RIBOSE
RIGORS
RIGOUR
RIMOSE
RIPOFF
SILOAM
SILOED
SILONE
SIMONE
SIMONY
SITOUT
TIPOFF
TIVOLI
VIGODA
VIGOUR
VINOUS
VISORS
WICOPY
WIDOWS
WIGOUT
WINONA
WINOUT

•I••O•

BIDSON
BIGBOY
BIGTOE
BIGTOP
BILLON
BILLOW
BISHOP
CISCOS
CITRON
DIALOG
DIATOM
DIDION
DIGLOT
DILLON
DINEON
DISCOS
DITTOS
GIBBON
GIBSON
GIDEON
GIZMOS
HICKOK
HIERON
HILTON
HINTON
HIPHOP
HIPPOS
HIREON
HITSON
HIVAOA
JIMSON
KINDOF
KITFOX
LICTOR
LIELOW
LIMBOS
LIPTON
LIQUOR
LISBOA
LISBON
LISTON
LITHOG
LITHOS
LIVEON
MICRON
MICROS
MIGNON
MILTON
MIMEOS
MINION
MINNOW
MIRROR
NIMROD
NIPPON
PIANOS
PICKON
PIGEON
PILEON
PILLOW
PINION
PINSON
PINTOS
PINYON
PINZON
PISTOL
PISTON
RIBBON
SIGNON
SIGNOR
SIMEON
SIPHON
SITCOM
SITSON
TIEROD
TIGLON
TINGOD
TINPOT
TIPTOE
TIPTOP
VIACOM
VICTOR
VIDEOS
VILLON
VINTON
VIREOS
VISION
WILLOW
WILSON
WILTON
WINDOM
WINDOW
WINNOW
WINSOR
WISDOM
ZIPLOC
ZIRCON

•I•••O

AIELLO
AIKIDO
AIMSTO
BIBLIO
BILBAO
BIOBIO
BISTRO
CICERO
DIABLO
DINERO
DIRIGO
FIASCO
FIGARO
FINITO
GIGOLO
GINKGO
GIOTTO
GITANO
HIDEHO
KIMONO
LIBIDO
LIESTO
MIKADO
MILANO

NICOLO
NIELLO
NIHILO
NINGBO
PICABO
PICARO
PIETRO
PINERO
RIALTO
RIGHTO
SIDERO
SINGTO
VIRAGO
WISETO

••IO••
ALIOTO
ANIONS
ARIOSE
ARIOSO
AXIOMS
AXIONS
IDIOCY
IDIOMS
IDIOTS
INIONS
ODIOUS
OHIOAN
ONIONS
ONIONY
ORIOLE
OTIOSE
PRIONS
PRIORI
PRIORS
PRIORY
SCIONS
TRIODE
UNIONS

••I•O•
ALISON
AMIDOL
AMIGOS
AMINOR
ASIMOV
AVISOS
BAILOR
BMINOR
BRITON
CAICOS
CHIGOE
CHILOE
CHINOS
CHIRON
CHISOX
CHITON
CLIPON
CMINOR
DAIKON
DAIMON
DEIMOS
DMINOR
EDISON
EDITOR
ELINOR
EMINOR
EPILOG
FMINOR
FRIJOL
FRITOS
GAINON
GMINOR
GRISON
GUIDON
HAIKOU
LAIDON
NOIRON
ORISON
PAILOU
PHILOL
PHILOS
POIROT
POISON
PRIMOS
PRISON
QUINOA
RHINOS
SAIGON
SAILOR
SHILOH
SHIMON
SKIROS
SKITOW
SLIPON
SPIGOT
SPIROS
SUITOR
TAILOR
TAINOS
TRICOT
TRIGON
TRIPOD
TRIPOS
TRITON
UNIPOD
UNISON
WAITON
WHILOM

••I••O
AKIMBO
ALIOTO
ARIOSO
ARISTO
BOINGO
BRILLO
CRISCO
DAIMYO
EMILIO
FRISCO
GOINTO
GRINGO
HAIRDO
IBIBIO
INITIO
LAIDTO
OBISPO
OLINGO
OVIEDO
SCIPIO
SEISMO
SHINTO
TRICHO
WEIRDO

•••IO•
ACTION
ALBION
AMNION
AUDIOS
BUNION
CAMION
CATION
CURIOS
DIDION
ELLIOT
FANION
FOLIOS
FUSION
GABION
HELIOS
HERIOT
HESIOD
JOLIOT
JUNIOR
LEGION
LOGION
LOTION
MANIOC
MARION
MINION
MORION
MOTION
NATION
NOTION
OPTION
PATIOS
PELION
PERIOD
PINION
POTION
RADIOS
RATION
RATIOS
REGION
SAVIOR
SENIOR
TALION
VISION

•••I•O
ACTINO
AIKIDO
ALBINO
ALNICO
AQUINO
BENITO
BONITO
CALICO
CAMINO
CASINO
DENIRO
DEVITO
DIRIGO
DOMINO
DOSIDO
ELNINO
ENCINO
ENRICO
ESKIMO
FINITO
IDOIDO
ILOILO
INDIGO
INVIVO
LADINO
LATIGO
LATINO
LIBIDO
LUPINO
MARIKO
MARINO
MEDICO
MERINO
MEXICO
NIHILO
ORSINO
PACINO
PEPINO
SUBITO
TORINO
ULTIMO

••••IO
ADAGIO
AFLCIO
BAGUIO
BARRIO
BIBLIO
BIOBIO
CARDIO
CASSIO
CRANIO
DELRIO
EMILIO
IBIBIO
INITIO
LASHIO
MAGGIO
NUNCIO
PHYSIO
PLAGIO
SCIPIO
SERGIO
STUDIO

IP••••
IPECAC

I•P•••
IMPACT
IMPAIR
IMPALA
IMPALE
IMPART
IMPEDE
IMPELS
IMPEND
IMPERF
IMPISH
IMPORT
IMPOSE
IMPOST
IMPROV
IMPUGN
IMPURE
IMPUTE
INPART
INPLAY
INPORT
INPOUR
INPUTS

I••P••
INAPET
INSPAN
ISOPOD

I•••P•
INCEPT
IRRUPT

I••••P
ICECAP
ICEDUP
ICESUP
INSTEP

•IP•••
BIPEDS
BIPODS
CIPHER
DIPODY
DIPOLE
DIPPED
DIPPER
FIPPLE
GIPPED
GIPPER
HIPHOP
HIPPED
HIPPER
HIPPIE
HIPPOS
KIPPER
KIPPUR
LIPASE
LIPENG
LIPIDE
LIPIDS
LIPOID
LIPPED
LIPTON
NIPPED
NIPPER
NIPPON
NIPPUR
NIPSAT
NIPUPS
PIPALS
PIPERS
PIPEUP
PIPING
PIPITS
PIPKIN
PIPPED
PIPPIN
RIPELY
RIPENS
RIPEST
RIPKEN
RIPLEY
RIPOFF
RIPPED
RIPPER
RIPPLE
RIPPLY
RIPRAP
RIPSAW
RIPSUP
SIPHON
SIPPED
SIPPER
SIPPET
TIPINS
TIPOFF
TIPPED
TIPPER
TIPPET
TIPPLE
TIPSIN
TIPTOE
TIPTOP
TIPUPS
VIPERS
WIPERS
WIPEUP
WIPING
YIPPED
YIPPEE
ZIPLOC
ZIPPED
ZIPPER
ZIPSUP

•I•P••
DIAPER
DIEPPE
DIMPLE
DIMPLY
DIPPED
DIPPER
DISPEL
FIPPLE
GIPPED
GIPPER
HIPPED
HIPPER
HIPPIE
HIPPOS
HISPID
KIPPER
KIPPUR
LIMPED
LIMPER
LIMPET
LIMPID
LIMPLY
LIPPED
LISPED
MILPAS
NIPPED
NIPPER
NIPPON
NIPPUR
OILPAN
PIEPAN
PIGPEN
PIPPED
PIPPIN
RIMPLE
RIPPED
RIPPER
RIPPLE
RIPPLY
SIMPER
SIMPLE
SIMPLY
SIPPED
SIPPER
SIPPET
TIEPIN
TINPAN
TINPOT
TIPPED
TIPPER
TIPPET
TIPPLE
WIMPLE
WISPED
YIPPED
YIPPEE
ZILPAH
ZIPPED
ZIPPER

•I••P•
BICEPS
DIEPPE
FIXUPS
MIXUPS
NIPUPS
PINUPS
SITUPS
TIEUPS
TIPUPS
WICOPY

•I•••P
BIDSUP
BIGTOP
BINDUP
BISHOP
BITMAP
DIGSUP
FILLIP
FILLUP
FIREUP
FIRMUP
GIVEUP
HICCUP
HIGHUP
HIPHOP
HITSUP
KICKUP
KIDNAP
LIFTUP
LINEUP
LINKUP
MILSAP
MISHAP
PICKUP
PILEUP
PIPEUP
PIRRIP
RIGSUP
RINGUP
RIPRAP
RIPSUP
SIGNUP
SITSUP
SIZEUP
TIDYUP
TIEDUP
TIESUP
TIPTOP
WINDUP
WIPEUP
WISEUP
ZIPSUP

••IP••
CHIPIN
CLIPON
CRIPES
DRIPPY
FLIPUP
GRIPED
GRIPER
GRIPES
GRIPPE
JAIPUR
PRIPET
QUIPPY
QUIPUS
RAIPUR
SAIPAN
SCIPIO
SKIPPY
SLIPIN
SLIPON
SLIPUP
SNIPED
SNIPES
SNIPPY
STIPEL
STIPES
SWIPED
SWIPER
SWIPES
TAIPAN
TAIPEI
TRIPLE
TRIPLY
TRIPOD
TRIPOS
TRIPUP
UNIPOD
WHIPPY
WHIPUP

••I•P•
BLIMPS
CHIMPS
CHIRPS
CHIRPY
CRIMPS
CRISPS
CRISPY
DRIPPY
GRIPPE
GUIMPE
OBISPO
PRIMPS
QUIPPY
SKIMPS
SKIMPY
SKIPPY
SNIPPY
STIMPY
WHIPPY

••I••P
CHINUP
COILUP
FAIRUP
FLIPUP
JOINUP
LAIDUP
PAIDUP
PAIRUP
PHILIP
SLIPUP
STIRUP
SUITUP
TRIPUP
WAITUP
WHIPUP

•••IP•
CALIPH
CERIPH
EQUIPS
FELIPE
OXLIPS
RECIPE
SCRIPS
SCRIPT
STRIPE
STRIPS
THRIPS
TULIPS
UNRIPE
UNZIPS

•••I•P
MEGILP
SCRIMP
SHRIMP

••••IP
CATNIP
FILLIP
GOSSIP
HOTTIP
PHILIP
PIRRIP
RESHIP
THELIP
TURNIP

IQ••••
IQTEST

I••Q••
IRAQIS

•IQ•••
LIQUID
LIQUOR
PIQUED
PIQUES
PIQUET

•I•Q••
BISQUE
CINQUE
CIRQUE
RISQUE

•I•••Q
HIGHIQ

••IQ••
CAIQUE
CLIQUE
UNIQUE

•••I•Q
SUSIEQ

••••IQ
HIGHIQ

IR••••
IRANIS
IRAQIS
IRATER
IREFUL
IRENES
IRENIC
IRIDES
IRIDIC
IRISES
IRISIN
IRKING
IRLENE
IRONED
IRONER
IRONIC
IRONON
IRREAL
IRRUPT
IRTYSH
IRVINE
IRVING

I•R•••
INROAD
INRUSH
IRREAL
IRRUPT
ISRAEL

I••R••
IATRIC
IBERIA
ICARIA
ICARUS
IMARET
IMBRUE
IMPROV
INARCH
INAROW
INARUT
INBRED
INDRIS
INGRES
INGRID
INTROS
INURED
INURES
ISTRIA
ITURBI

I•••R•
IDCARD
IDLERS
IGNORE
IMMURE
IMPART
IMPERF
IMPORT
IMPURE
INBORN
INCURS
INDIRA
INFERS
INFIRM
INFORM
INHERE
INJURE
INJURY
INKERS
INPART
INPORT
INSERT
INSURE
INTERN
INTURN
INVERT
INWARD
IZZARD

I••••R
ICKIER
IFFIER
IMAGER
IMPAIR
INANER
INDOOR
INGEAR
INGMAR
INKIER
INPOUR
INSTAR
IRATER
IRONER
ISADOR
ISHTAR
ISOBAR
ISOMER
ISSUER

•IR•••
AIRARM
AIRBAG
AIRBUS
AIRDAM
AIRDRY
AIRGUN
AIRIER
AIRILY
AIRING
AIRMAN
AIRMEN
AIROUT
AIRSAC
AIRWAY
BIRDED
BIRDER
BIRDIE
BIREME
BIRGIT
BIRLED
BIRNEY
BIRTHS
CIRCLE
CIRCUM
CIRCUS
CIRQUE
CIRRUS
DIRECT
DIREST
DIRGES
DIRHAM
DIRIGO
DIRNDL
FIRERS
FIREUP
FIRING
FIRKIN
FIRMAN
FIRMED
FIRMER
FIRMLY
FIRMUP
FIRSTS
FIRTHS
GIRARD
GIRDED
GIRDER
GIRDLE
GIRTED
GIRTHS
HIREON
HIRERS
HIRING
HIRSCH
KIRMAN
KIRSCH
KIRTLE
MIRAGE
MIRIAM
MIRING
MIRREN
MIRROR
PIRACY
PIRANA
PIRATE
PIRRIP
SIRDAR
SIRENS
SIRICA
SIRING
SIRIUS
SIRRAH
SIRREE
TIRADE
TIRANA
TIRANE
TIRING
VIRAGO
VIREOS
VIRGIL
VIRGIN
VIRILE
VIRTUE
VIRTUS
WIRERS
WIRING
ZIRCON

•I•R••
AIGRET
BIERCE
BIGRED
CIARDI
CIRRUS
CITRIC
CITRON
CITRUS
DIGRAM
FIBRES
FIBRIL
FIBRIN
FIERCE
FIORDS
GIBRAN
HIERON
LIBRIS
LIERNE
LITRES
LIVRES
MICRON
MICROS
MIDRIB
MIHRAB
MIRREN
MIRROR
MITRAL
MITRED
MITRES
NIMROD
NITRES
NITRIC
OILRIG
PIERCE
PIERRE
PIRRIP
RIPRAP
SIERRA
SIRRAH
SIRREE
TIARAS
TIERCE
TIERED
TIEROD
TIERRA
TIGRIS
VITRIC

•I••R•
AILERS
AIRARM
AIRDRY
BIAFRA
BICARB
BICORN
BIHARI
BIKERS
BINARY
BISTRO
BITERS
CICERO
CIDERS
CIGARS
CITERS
DICERS
DINARS
DINERO
DINERS
DISARM
DIVERS
DIVERT
EIDERS
FIACRE
FIBERS
FIFERS
FIGARO
FIGURE
FILERS
FINERY
FIRERS
FIVERS
FIXERS
GIBERS
GIRARD
GIVERS
HIDERS
HIKERS
HILARY
HIRERS
JIVERS
KIDORY
KITERS
LIEVRE
LIFERS
LIGERS
LIGURE
LINERS
LITERS
LIVERS
LIVERY
LIZARD
MIDORI
MILERS
MILORD
MIMERS
MINERS
MINORS
MISERS
MISERY
MITERS
MIXERS
NINERS
NITERS
OILERS
PICARA
PICARD
PICARO
PIERRE
PIETRO
PIKERS
PINERO
PINERY
PIPERS
RICERS
RIDERS
RIGORS
RISERS
RITARD
RIVERA
RIVERS
SIDERO
SIDERS
SIERRA
SIGURD
SISERA
SITARS
SIXERS
SIZERS
TIERRA
TIGERS
TILERS
TIMBRE
TIMERS
TISHRI
TITERS
UIGURS
VICARS
VINERY
VIPERS
VISORS
WINERY
WINTRY
WIPERS
WIRERS
WIZARD

•I•••R
AIRIER
BICKER
BIDDER
BIGGER
BIGSUR
BINDER
BIRDER
BITTER
CINDER
CIPHER
DIALER
DIAPER
DICIER
DICKER
DIETER
DIFFER
DIGGER
DILLER
DIMMER
DINNER
DIPPER
DISBAR
DITHER
EISNER
EITHER
FIBBER
FILLER
FILTER
FINDER
FINGER
FIRMER
FISHER
FITTER
GIBBER
GILDER
GINGER
GIPPER
GIRDER
HIGHER
HILLER
HINDER
HINTER
HIPPER
HISSER
HITHER
HITTER
JIGGER
JITTER
KICKER
KIDDER
KIEFER
KILLER
KILMER
KILTER
KINDER
KIPPER
KIPPUR
KISSER
LIBBER
LICTOR
LIEDER
LIEFER
LIFTER
LIMBER
LIMNER
LIMPER
LINEAR
LINGER
LINKER
LINTER
LIQUOR
LISTER
LITTER
MIDAIR
MIDLER
MILDER
MILKER
MILLER
MILNER
MINCER
MINDER
MINTER
MIRROR
MISTER
NICKER
NIGHER
NIPPER
NIPPUR
OILIER
PICKER
PIECER
PIETER
PILFER
PILLAR
PINCER
PINDAR
PINIER
PINKER
PINNER
PINTER
PITTER
QINTAR
RICHER
RIFLER
RIGGER
RIGOUR
RINGER
RIOTER
RIPPER
RISKER
RITTER
SICKER
SIDDUR
SIFTER
SIGHER
SIGNER
SIGNOR
SILVER
SIMMER
SIMPER
SINGER
SINKER
SINNER
SINTER
SIPPER
SIRDAR
SISLER
SISTER
SITTER
TICKER
TIDIER
TIGGER
TILLER
TILTER
TIMBER
TINDER
TINEAR
TINIER

TINKER
TINNER
TINTER
TIPPER
TITHER
TITTER
VICTOR
VIEWER
VIGOUR
VIZIER
WICKER
WIENER
WILBUR
WILDER
WILIER
WINCER
WINDER
WINGER
WINKER
WINNER
WINSOR
WINTER
WISHER
WISTER
WITHER
ZIMMER
ZINGER
ZIPPER
ZITHER

••IR••

BAIRNS
BEIRUT
BGIRLS
CAIRNS
CHIRON
CHIRPS
CHIRPY
CHIRRS
DAIREN
EPIRUS
FAIRED
FAIRER
FAIRLY
FAIRUP
FLIRTS
HAIRDO
HAIRED
LAIRDS
MOIRES
NAIRAS
NOIRON
OSIRIS
PAIRED
PAIRUP
POIROT
QUIRES
QUIRKS
QUIRKY
QUIRTS
SHIRAZ
SHIRER
SHIRES
SHIRKS
SHIRRS
SHIRTS
SHIRTY
SKIRLS
SKIROS
SKIRRS
SKIRTS
SKIRUN
SMIRCH
SMIRKS
SMIRKY
SOIREE
SPIRAL
SPIREA
SPIRED
SPIRES
SPIRIT
SPIROS
STIRIN
STIRUP
SWIRLS
SWIRLY
TBIRDS
THIRDS
THIRST
THIRTY
TWIRLS
WEIRDO
WHIRLS
WHIRLY
WHIRRS

••I•R•

ANITRA
APIARY
AVIARY
BRIARD
BRIARS
BRIERS
BRIERY
CHIRRS
CRIERS
DEIDRE
DMITRI
DRIERS
EMIGRE
FLIERS
FRIARS
FRIARY
GRIGRI
MAITRE
OSIERS
PLIERS
PRIERS
PRIORI
PRIORS
PRIORY
SHIRRS
SKIERS
SKIRRS
SPIERS
TRIERS
WHIRRS

••I••R

AMINOR
BAILER
BAILOR
BMINOR
BOILER
CMINOR
COINER
DEICER
DMINOR
DRIVER
DUIKER
EDITOR
ELINOR
ELIXIR
EMINOR
EVILER
FAIRER
FMINOR
GAINER
GAITER
GEIGER
GLIDER
GMINOR
GRIPER
GUITAR
HEIFER
JAILER
JAIPUR
JOINER
JUICER
KAISER
LOITER
MAILER
MOILER
NAILER
OBITER
OLIVER
OPINER
PRICER
PRIMER
QUIVER
RAIDER
RAILER
RAINER
RAIPUR
RAISER
REINER
RUINER
SAILOR
SEINER
SEIZER
SHINER
SHIRER
SHIVER
SKIVER
SLICER
SLIDER
SLIVER
SMILER
SNIDER
SPIDER
SPIKER
STIVER
SUITOR
SWIPER
TAILOR
TOILER
TRITER
UNITER
VAINER
WAILER
WAITER
WAIVER
WEIMAR
WHINER
WHITER
WRITER
ZUIDER

•••IR•

ADMIRE
AFFIRM
ALHIRT
ASPIRE
ASWIRL
ATTIRE
AWHIRL
BEMIRE
CHAIRS
CHOIRS
CLAIRE
DENIRO
DESIRE
ELMIRA
ELVIRA
EMPIRE
ENGIRD
ENGIRT
ENTIRE
EXPIRE
EXPIRY
FAKIRS
FLAIRS
GEZIRA
GLAIRY
HEGIRA
INDIRA
INFIRM
JABIRU
MYGIRL
NADIRS
ONFIRE
PAMIRS
REAIRS
REHIRE
RETIRE
REWIRE
SAFIRE
SATIRE
SQUIRE
SQUIRM
SQUIRT
STAIRS
TAPIRS
THEIRS
TSHIRT
UMPIRE
UNGIRD
UNGIRT
VENIRE

•••I•R

ACHIER
AIRIER
ARTIER
ASHIER
BONIER
BUSIER
CAGIER
CAHIER
CAVIAR
COPIER
COZIER
DENIER
DEWIER
DICIER
DOPIER
EASIER
EDGIER
EELIER
EERIER
FOLIAR
FOXIER
GAMIER
GOOIER
GORIER
HAZIER
HOKIER
HOLIER
HOMIER
HOSIER
ICKIER
IFFIER
INKIER
JAVIER
JUNIOR
LACIER
LANIER
LAZIER
LEVIER
LOGIER
METIER
NAPIER
NOSIER
OATIER
OILIER
PAPIER
PINIER
POKIER
PUNIER
RACIER
RAPIER
ROPIER
ROSIER
SAVIOR
SENIOR
SEXIER
SPRIER
TIDIER
TINIER
TONIER
UGLIER
VANIER
VIZIER
WARIER
WAVIER
WAXIER
WILIER
XAVIER
ZANIER

••••IR

AAFAIR
ABUKIR
AFFAIR
AGADIR
ALTAIR
AUPAIR
BELAIR
BESTIR
COHEIR
DEVOIR
ECLAIR
ELIXIR
FAFNIR
HOTAIR
IMPAIR
KAFFIR
MCNAIR
MEMOIR
MENHIR
MIDAIR
MOHAIR
REDFIR
RENOIR
REPAIR
REVOIR
SANTIR
SAVOIR
SHAMIR
UNFAIR
YESSIR

IS••••

ISABEL
ISADOR
ISAIAH
ISCHIA
ISELIN
ISEULT
ISHTAR
ISLAND
ISLETS
ISMENE
ISOBAR
ISOGON
ISOHEL
ISOLDE
ISOMER
ISOPOD
ISRAEL
ISSUED
ISSUER
ISSUES
ISTHMI
ISTLES
ISTRIA

I•S•••

IJSSEL
INSANE
INSEAM
INSECT
INSERT
INSETS
INSIDE
INSIST
INSITU
INSOLE
INSPAN
INSTAR
INSTEP
INSULT
INSURE
INSYNC
ISSUED
ISSUER
ISSUES
ITSELF

I••S••

IBISES
ICESIN
ICESUP
IJSSEL
ILESHA
ILLSAY
IRISES
IRISIN
ITASCA

I•••S•

ICIEST
IDLEST
ILLEST
ILLUSE
IMPISH
IMPOSE
IMPOST
INCASE
INCASH
INCISE
INCUSE
INFEST
INFUSE
INGEST
INJEST
INMOST
INNESS
INRUSH
INSIST
INVEST
IQTEST
IRTYSH

I••••S

IBEAMS
IBEXES
IBISES
ICARUS
ICINGS
IDEALS
IDIOMS
IDIOTS
IDLERS
IDYLLS
IGLOOS
IMAGES
IMBUES
IMPELS
INCANS
INCHES
INCURS
INDIES
INDRIS
INFERS
INGLES
INGOTS
INGRES
INIONS
INKERS
INKLES
INLAWS
INLAYS
INLETS
INNESS
INPUTS
INSETS
INTENS
INTROS
INUITS
INURES
IONICS
IOWANS
IRANIS
IRAQIS
IRENES
IRIDES
IRISES
ISLETS
ISSUES
ISTLES
ITCHES

•IS•••

AISLES
BISCAY
BISECT
BISHOP
BISONS
BISQUE
BISSAU
BISSET
BISTRO
CISCOS
CISKEI
DISANT
DISARM
DISBAR
DISCOS
DISCUS
DISHED
DISHES
DISKED
DISMAL
DISMAY
DISMES
DISNEY
DISOWN
DISPEL
DISSED
DISTAL
DISTIL
DISUSE
EISNER
FISCAL
FISHED
FISHER
FISHES
FISTED
FISTIC
HISPID
HISSAT
HISSED
HISSER
HISSES
KISHKE
KISLEV
KISMET
KISSED
KISSER
KISSES
LISBOA
LISBON
LISLES
LISPED
LISTED
LISTEE
LISTEL
LISTEN
LISTER
LISTON
MISCHA
MISCUE
MISDID
MISERS
MISERY
MISFIT
MISHAP
MISHIT
MISLAY
MISLED
MISSAL
MISSAY
MISSED
MISSES
MISSIS
MISSUS
MISTED
MISTER
MISUSE
NISSAN
NISSEN
PISANS
PISCES
PISGAH
PISTIL
PISTOL
PISTON
RISERS
RISING
RISKED
RISKER
RISQUE
SISALS
SISERA
SISKEL
SISKIN
SISLER
SISTER
TISANE
TISHRI
TISSUE
VISAED
VISAGE
VISCID
VISHNU
VISINE
VISION
VISITS
VISORS
VISTAS
VISUAL
WISDOM
WISELY
WISENT
WISEST
WISETO
WISEUP
WISHED
WISHER
WISHES
WISPED
WISTER

•I•S••

AIMSAT
AIMSTO
AIRSAC
BIASED
BIASES
BIDSIN
BIDSON
BIDSUP
BIGSUR
BISSAU
BISSET
DIESEL
DIESES
DIESIS
DIGSIN
DIGSUP
DILSEY
DIMSUM
DISSED
FIASCO
FIESTA
FIRSTS
FITSIN
GIBSON
HIRSCH
HISSAT
HISSED
HISSER
HISSES
HITSIT
HITSON
HITSUP
JIGSAW
JIMSON
KINSKI
KIOSKS
KIRSCH
KISSED
KISSER
KISSES
KITSCH
LIESIN
LIESTO
LINSEY
MIASMA
MILSAP
MIOSIS
MISSAL
MISSAY
MISSED
MISSES
MISSIS
MISSUS
NIPSAT
NISSAN
NISSEN
PIGSTY
PINSON
PITSAW
RIGSUP
RIMSKY
RINSED
RINSES
RIPSAW
RIPSUP
SIESTA
SITSIN
SITSON
SITSUP
TIESIN
TIESUP
TILSIT
TINSEL
TIPSIN
TISSUE
VIZSLA
WIESEL
WILSON
WIMSEY
WINSOR
ZIPSUP

•I••S•

DIGEST
DIREST
DISUSE
DIVEST
FILOSE
FINEST
FINISH
KIBOSH
LIAISE
LIPASE
MILOSZ
MIMOSA
MISUSE
NICEST
PILOSE
RIBOSE
RIFEST
RIMOSE
RIPEST
SIWASH
VILEST
WIDEST
WISEST

•I•••S

AILERS
AIRBUS
AISLES
BIASES
BIBLES
BICEPS
BIGHTS
BIGOTS
BIKERS
BILGES
BINGES
BIOGAS
BIOMES
BIOTAS
BIPEDS
BIPODS
BIRTHS
BISONS
BITERS
CIDERS
CIGARS
CIRCUS
CIRRUS
CISCOS
CITERS
CITIES
CITRUS
CIVETS
CIVICS
DICERS
DICOTS
DIDIES
DIESES
DIESIS
DIGITS
DINARS
DINERS
DINGUS
DIODES
DIRGES
DISCOS
DISCUS
DISHES
DISMES
DITTOS
DITZES
DIVANS
DIVERS
DIVOTS
DIXITS
EIDERS
EIGHTS
FIBERS
FIBRES
FICHES
FICHUS
FIELDS
FIENDS
FIFERS
FIFTHS
FIGHTS
FILERS
FILETS
FILIUS
FILLES
FINALS
FIORDS
FIRERS
FIRSTS
FIRTHS
FISHES
FIVERS
FIVEWS
FIXERS
FIXUPS
FIZZES
GIANTS
GIBERS
GIGOTS
GIGUES
GIJOES
GILLIS
GIMELS
GIRTHS
GIVENS
GIVERS
GIZMOS
HIATUS
HIDERS
HIKERS
HINDUS
HINGES
HIPPOS
HIRERS
HISSES
JIHADS
JINXES
JIVERS
KIANGS
KILIMS
KIOSKS
KIOWAS
KISSES
KITERS
LIANAS
LIANGS
LIBELS
LIBRIS
LIEGES
LIEUTS
LIFERS
LIGERS
LIGHTS
LIKENS
LILACS
LILIES
LIMBOS
LIMBUS
LIMENS
LIMEYS
LIMITS
LINENS
LINERS
LIPIDS
LISLES
LITERS
LITHOS
LITMUS
LITRES
LIVENS
LIVERS
LIVRES
MICROS
MIDGES
MILERS
MILPAS
MIMEOS
MIMERS
MIMICS
MINCES
MINERS
MINIMS
MINKES
MINORS
MINXES
MIOSIS
MISERS
MISSES
MISSIS
MISSUS
MITERS
MITRES
MIWOKS
MIXERS
MIXUPS
MIZENS
NICHES
NIECES
NIGHTS
NIMBUS
NINERS
NINJAS
NINTHS
NIPUPS
NITERS
NITRES
NIXIES
OILERS
PIANOS
PICOTS
PICULS
PIECES
PIETAS
PIKERS
PILAFS
PILEUS
PILOTS
PINDUS
PINNAS
PINONS
PINOTS
PINTOS
PINUPS
PIPALS
PIPERS
PIPITS
PIQUES
PISANS
PISCES
PITIES
PITONS
PIVOTS
PIXELS
PIXIES
PIZZAS
RIATAS
RICERS
RICHES
RIDERS
RIDGES
RIFLES
RIGHTS
RIGORS
RILLES
RINSES
RIOJAS
RIPENS
RISERS
RIVALS
RIVERS
RIVETS
RIYALS
SIBYLS
SIDERS
SIDLES
SIEGES
SIEVES
SIGHTS
SIGILS
SIGMAS
SINEWS
SINGES
SIRENS
SIRIUS
SISALS
SITARS
SITINS
SITUPS
SIXERS
SIXTHS
SIXTUS
SIZERS
TIARAS
TIBIAS
TICALS
TIDIES
TIEINS
TIEUPS
TIGERS
TIGHTS
TIGRIS
TILAKS
TILDES
TILERS
TILLIS
TIMERS
TINCTS
TINGES
TIPINS
TIPUPS
TITANS
TITERS
TITHES
TITLES
UIGURS
VIANDS
VICARS
VIDEOS
VIGILS
VILLAS
VILLUS
VINOUS
VIOLAS
VIPERS
VIREOS
VIRTUS
VISITS
VISORS
VISTAS
VITALS
VIXENS
WIDENS
WIDOWS
WIDTHS
WIELDS
WIGHTS
WILKES
WILLIS
WINCES
WINZES
WIPERS
WIRERS
WISHES
WITHES
WIZENS
YIELDS

••IS••

ALISON
ARISEN
ARISES
ARISTA
ARISTO
AVISOS
CHISEL
CHISOX
CRISCO
CRISES
CRISIS
CRISPS
CRISPY
CUISSE
DAISES
DEISTS
EDISON
ELISHA
ELISSA
ENISLE
EXISTS
FAISAL
FEISTY
FOISTS
FRISCO
FRISEE
FRISES
FRISKS
FRISKY
GEISEL
GEISHA
GRISLY
GRISON
GRISTS
GUISES
HEISTS
HOISTS
IBISES
IRISES
IRISIN
JOISTS
KAISER
MAISIE
NEISSE
NOISED
NOISES
OBISPO
ODISTS
ORISON
ORISSA
OVISAC
PLISSE
POISED
POISES
POISON
PRISMS
PRISON
PRISSY
PUISNE
RAISED
RAISER
RAISES
RAISIN
SEISMO
SEISMS
THISBE
TRISHA
TRISTE
TWISTS
TWISTY
UNISEX
UNISON
VAISYA
WAISTS
WHISKS
WRISTS

••I•S•

AHIMSA
AMIDST
ARIOSE
ARIOSO
CUISSE
DRIEST
ELISSA
FLIMSY
GAINST
GRILSE
ICIEST
NEISSE
ORISSA
OTIOSE
PLISSE
PRIEST
PRISSY
SHIEST
SHIISM
SLIEST
THIRST

WHILST
WHIMSY
WRIEST

••I••S

ABIDES
ACINUS
ADIDAS
ADIEUS
AKITAS
ALIBIS
ALIENS
ALIGNS
ALINES
AMICES
AMICUS
AMIDES
AMIENS
AMIGOS
AMINES
AMINUS
ANIMAS
ANIMES
ANIMUS
ANIONS
APICES
ARISES
ASIANS
ASIDES
AVIANS
AVISOS
AXIOMS
AXIONS
BAINES
BAIRNS
BEIGES
BEINGS
BGIRLS
BLIMPS
BLINDS
BLINKS
BMINUS
BOITES
BRIANS
BRIARS
BRIBES
BRICKS
BRIDES
BRIEFS
BRIERS
BRIGGS
BRILLS
BRINES
BRINGS
BRINKS
BSIDES
BUILDS
CAICOS
CAIRNS
CEIBAS
CHIAUS
CHICKS
CHIDES
CHIEFS
CHILDS
CHILLS
CHIMES
CHIMPS
CHINES
CHINKS
CHINOS
CHIRPS
CHIRRS
CHIVES
CLICKS
CLIFFS
CLIMBS
CLIMES
CLINES
CLINGS
CLINKS
CMINUS
CNIDUS
CRICKS
CRIERS
CRIMES
CRIMPS
CRIPES
CRISES
CRISIS
CRISPS
DAISES
DEICES
DEIGNS
DEIMOS
DEISTS
DMINUS
DOINGS
DRIERS
DRIFTS
DRILLS
DRINGS
DRINKS
DRIVES
EDICTS
EDILES
ELIDES
ELITES
EPIRUS
ERINYS
EVICTS
EXILES
EXISTS
FAINTS
FAITHS
FEIGNS
FEINTS
FLICKS
FLIERS
FLINGS
FLINTS
FLIRTS
FOISTS
FRIARS
FRILLS
FRISES
FRISKS
FRITOS
GLIDES
GLINTS
GOINGS
GRILLS
GRIMES
GRINDS
GRIPES
GRISTS
GUIDES
GUILDS
GUILES
GUISES
HAIDAS
HAIKUS
HAINES
HEISTS
HOISTS
IBISES
ICINGS
IDIOMS
IDIOTS
INIONS
IRIDES
IRISES
JOINTS
JOISTS
JUICES
KNICKS
KNIFES
KNIVES
LAIRDS
MAIDUS
MAILES
MAIZES
MOINES
MOIRES
NAIADS
NAIRAS
NEIGHS
NOISES
ODIOUS
ODISTS
ODIUMS
OGIVES
OLIVES
ONIONS
OPINES
ORIBIS
ORIELS
ORINGS
OSIERS
OSIRIS
OTITIS
OXIDES
PAINTS
PHIALS
PHILOS
PLIERS
PLINKS
POILUS
POINTS
POISES
PRICES
PRICKS
PRIDES
PRIERS
PRIMES
PRIMOS
PRIMPS
PRIMUS
PRINKS
PRINTS
PRIONS
PRIORS
PRISMS
PRIZES
QUIETS
QUILLS
QUILTS
QUINTS
QUIPUS
QUIRES
QUIRKS
QUIRTS
RAINES
RAISES
REIGNS
REINKS
RHINOS
SAIGAS
SAINTS
SCIFIS
SCIONS
SEINES
SEISMS
SEIZES
SHIFTS
SHILLS
SHINES
SHIRES
SHIRKS
SHIRRS
SHIRTS
SKIERS
SKIFFS
SKILLS
SKIMPS
SKINKS
SKIRLS
SKIROS
SKIRRS
SKIRTS
SKIVES
SLICES
SLICKS
SLIDES
SLIMES
SLINGS
SLINKS
SMILES
SMIRKS
SMITES
SMITHS
SNICKS
SNIFFS
SNIPES
SPICAS
SPICES
SPIELS
SPIERS
SPIFFS
SPIKES
SPILES
SPILLS
SPINES
SPINKS
SPIRES
SPIROS
SPITES
STICKS
STIFFS
STILES
STILLS
STILTS
STINGS
STINKS
STINTS
STIPES
SUITES
SWIFTS
SWILLS
SWINGS
SWIPES
SWIRLS
TAIGAS
TAINOS
TAINTS
TBILLS
TBIRDS
THIGHS
THILLS
THINGS
THINKS
THIRDS
TOILES
TRIADS
TRIALS
TRIBES
TRICES
TRICKS
TRIERS
TRIKES
TRILLS
TRINES
TRIPOS
TWILLS
TWINES
TWIRLS
TWISTS
UMIAKS
UNIATS
UNIONS
UNITAS
UNITES
URIALS
VOICES
VOILES
VSIGNS
VSIXES
WAISTS
WAIVES
WEIGHS
WHIFFS
WHILES
WHINES
WHIRLS
WHIRRS
WHISKS
WHITES
WRINGS
WRISTS
WRITES
YOICKS

•••IS•

ADVISE
AGEISM
AGEIST
AORIST
ARLISS
ARTIST
ASSISI
ASSIST
ATRISK
BANISH
BETISE
BLAISE
BLUISH
BOYISH
BRAISE
BRUISE
CAMISE
CERISE
CHAISE
CHRISM
CRUISE
CUBISM
CUBIST
DANISH
DELIST
DEMISE
DENISE
DESIST
DEVISE
DOVISH
EGOISM
EGOIST
ELFISH
ELOISE
ENLIST
EXCISE
FAMISH
FETISH
FINISH
FRAISE
GARISH
GNEISS
GOFISH
HOLISM
HOLIST
IMPISH
INCISE
INSIST
JEWISH
JURIST
KLEIST
KUMISS
LATISH
LAVISH
LEGIST
LIAISE
LOUISA
LOUISE
LUTIST
LYRIST
MAOISM
MAOIST
MARISA
MARIST
MODISH
MONISM
MONIST
MOPISH
MULISH
NEWISH
NOWISE
NUDIST
OAFISH
OBOIST
OFFISH
OLDISH
OWLISH
PALISH
PARISH
PERISH
POLISH
PRAISE
PUNISH
PURISM
PURIST
RADISH
RAKISH
RAVISH
RELISH
RELIST
REMISE
REMISS
RESIST
REVISE
SALISH
SCHISM
SCHIST
SEXIST
SHIISM
SQUISH
SUFISM
TANIST
TAOISM
TAOIST
THEISM
THEIST
TONISH
TRUISM
TUBIST
TYPIST
UNWISE
UPRISE
VALISE
VANISH
VERISM

•••I•S

ADLIBS
ADMITS
AERIES
AGGIES
ALLIES
ALOINS
AMBITS
ANTICS
ANVILS
APHIDS
ARLISS
ARMIES
AROIDS
ASPICS
ATKINS
ATTICS
AUDIOS
AUDITS
AUXINS
AVAILS
AVOIDS
AWAITS
BABIES
BASICS
BASINS
BATIKS
BEDIMS
BEFITS
BEGINS
BELIES
BEVIES
BODIES
BOGIES
BOVIDS
BRAIDS
BRAILS
BRAINS
BROILS
BRUINS
BRUITS
BURIES
BURINS
BUSIES
CABINS
CANIDS
CAPIAS
CARIBS
CARIES
CAVILS
CHAINS
CHAIRS
CHOIRS
CITIES
CIVICS
CLAIMS
COBIAS
COMICS
CONICS
CONIES
COPIES
COSIES
COZIES
CUBICS
CUBITS
CUPIDS
CURIOS
CUTIES
CUTINS
CYNICS
DARIUS
DAVIES
DAVITS
DEBITS
DEFIES
DELIUS
DEMITS
DENIES
DENIMS
DEVILS
DIDIES
DIGITS
DIXITS
DOGIES
DORIES
DRAILS
DRAINS
DROIDS
DROITS
DRUIDS
DUTIES
EDDIES
EMAILS
ENNIUS
ENVIES
EOSINS
EQUIPS
ESPIES
ETHICS
EYRIES
FACIES
FAKIRS
FILIUS
FLAILS
FLAIRS
FLUIDS
FOGIES
FOLIOS
FRUITS
FURIES
FUSILS
GAMINS
GENIES
GENIUS
GNEISS
GOBIES
GRAILS
GRAINS
GROINS
GSUITS
HABITS
HAKIMS
HELIOS
INDIES
INUITS
IONICS
JULIUS
JURIES
KILIMS
KRAITS
KUMISS
LADIES
LAMIAS
LAPINS
LATINS
LEVIES
LILIES
LIMITS
LIPIDS
LORIES
LUCIUS
LYRICS
LYSINS
MANIAS
MARIUS
MATINS
MAXIMS
MEDIAS
MEDICS
MERITS
MIMICS
MINIMS
MOBIUS
MONIES
MOTIFS
MOVIES
NADIRS
NAVIES
NEVINS
NIXIES
NOHITS
NORIAS
OLDIES
OPTICS
ORBITS
ORGIES
OSMICS
OVOIDS
OXLIPS
PAMIRS
PANICS
PATIOS
PERILS
PEWITS
PIPITS
PITIES
PIXIES
PLAIDS
PLAINS
PLAITS
POGIES
PONIES
POSIES
POSITS
PUPILS
PYXIES
QUAILS
QUOINS
QUOITS
RABIES
RADIOS
RADIUS
RAMIES
RANIDS
RAPIDS
RATIOS
REAIRS
REBIDS
REFITS
REGIUS
RELICS
RELIES
REMISS
REMITS
REOILS
RESINS
RETIES
REWINS
ROBINS
ROSINS
RUBIES
RUNINS
SABINS
SAHIBS
SATINS
SCRIMS
SCRIPS
SEPIAS
SERIES
SERIFS
SERINS
SETINS
SHEIKS
SIGILS
SIRIUS
SITINS
SKEINS
SNAILS
SOLIDS
SONICS
SPLITS
SPOILS
SPRIGS
SPRITS
SQUIBS
SQUIDS
STAINS
STAIRS
STEINS
STOICS
STRIPS
SWAINS
TAKINS
TAMILS
TAPINS
TAPIRS
TAXIES
THEIRS
THRIPS
TIBIAS
TIDIES
TIEINS
TIPINS
TOBIAS
TOBIES
TOEINS
TONICS
TOPICS
TORIES
TOXICS
TOXINS
TRAILS
TRAINS
TRAITS
TULIPS
TUNICS
UGLIES
UNDIES
UNFITS
UNPINS
UNRIGS
UNTIES
UNZIPS
URSIDS
VARIES
VIGILS
VISITS
YALIES
ZANIES
ZAYINS
ZORILS

••••IS

ABATIS
ADONIS
ALEXIS
ALIBIS
AMADIS
AMATIS
ANUBIS
AODAIS
ARAMIS
ARTOIS
BARRIS
BAUCIS
CADDIS
CALAIS
CAPRIS
CASSIS
CLEVIS
CLORIS
CLOVIS
COATIS
CORGIS
CRISIS
CULLIS
CURTIS
DEBRIS
DENNIS
DERMIS
DERRIS
DHOTIS
DIESIS
DUBOIS
ECESIS
ELEMIS
ENOKIS
ENOSIS
ENVOIS
FERRIS
GALOIS
GHAZIS
GILLIS
GLACIS
GNOSIS
GRATIS
HADJIS
HAGGIS
HAJJIS
HARRIS
HOURIS
HUBRIS
INDRIS
IRANIS
IRAQIS
KAURIS
KEMPIS
KERMIS
KHAKIS
KUKRIS
LANAIS
LANDIS
LIBRIS
MAHDIS
MAJLIS
MANTIS
MAORIS
MAQUIS
MASAIS
MATHIS
MENTIS
MIOSIS
MISSIS
MORRIS
MUFTIS
NEREIS
NOESIS
NORRIS
OKAPIS
OMANIS
ORIBIS
OSIRIS
OTITIS
OXALIS
PARNIS
PARRIS
PARVIS
PASTIS
PATOIS
PELVIS
PENNIS
PHOCIS
PRAXIS
PRECIS
RABBIS
RACHIS
SARDIS
SAUDIS
SCIFIS
SERAIS
SHOJIS
SPAHIS
STASIS
SUNNIS
SWAMIS
SWAZIS
TENNIS
TETRIS
THATIS
THESIS
THETIS
TIGRIS
TILLIS
TMESIS
TRAVIS
UNGUIS
VALOIS
WALLIS
WILLIS
YAQUIS
ZEUXIS

IT••••

ITALIA
ITALIC
ITASCA
ITCHED
ITCHES
ITHACA
ITHAKI
ITSELF
ITURBI
ITZHAK

I•T•••

IATRIC
INTACT
INTAKE
INTEND
INTENS
INTENT
INTERN
INTIMA
INTIME
INTINE
INTONE
INTOTO
INTOWN
INTROS
INTUIT
INTUNE
INTURN
IQTEST
IRTYSH
ISTHMI
ISTLES
ISTRIA

I••T••

ICHTHY
IGETIT
INITIO
INSTAR
INSTEP
IRATER
ISHTAR

I•••T•

IDEATE
IDIOTS
IGNATZ
IGNITE
IMPUTE
INCITE
INDITE
INGOTS
INLETS
INMATE
INNATE
INPUTS
INSETS
INSITU
INTOTO
INUITS
INVITE
INWITH
IODATE
IOLITE
IOMOTH
ISLETS

I••••T

ICEOUT
ICIEST
IDLEST
IGETIT
ILLEST
ILLMET
IMARET
IMPACT
IMPART
IMPORT
IMPOST
INAPET
INARUT
INCEPT
INCULT
INDEBT
INDENT
INDICT
INDUCT
INFACT
INFANT
INFECT
INFEST
INGEST
INJECT
INJEST
INMOST
INPART
INPORT
INSECT
INSERT
INSIST
INSULT
INTACT
INTENT
INTUIT
INVENT
INVERT
INVEST
IQTEST
IRRUPT
ISEULT

•IT•••

BITERS
BITING
BITMAP
BITOFF
BITTED
BITTEN
BITTER
CITERS
CITIES
CITIFY
CITING
CITRIC
CITRON
CITRUS
DITHER
DITTOS
DITZES
EITHER
FITFUL
FITSIN
FITTED
FITTER
GITANO
HITECH
HITHER
HITMAN
HITMEN
HITSIT
HITSON
HITSUP
HITTER
JITNEY
JITTER
KITBAG
KITERS
KITFOX
KITING
KITKAT
KITSCH
KITTEN
LITANY
LITCHI
LITERS
LITHIC
LITHOG
LITHOS
LITMUS
LITOUT
LITRES
LITTER
LITTLE
MITERS
MITRAL
MITRED
MITRES
MITTEN
NITERS
NITRES
NITRIC
NITWIT
PITHED
PITIED
PITIES
PITMAN
PITMEN
PITONS
PITSAW
PITTED
PITTER
RITARD
RITTER
RITUAL
SITARS
SITCOM
SITING
SITINS
SITOUT
SITSIN
SITSON
SITSUP
SITTER
SITUPS
TITANS
TITBIT
TITERS
TITHED
TITHER
TITHES
TITIAN
TITLED
TITLES
TITTER
TITTLE
VITALS
VITRIC
WITCHY
WITHAL
WITHED
WITHER
WITHES
WITHIN
WITHIT
WITTED
ZITHER

•I•T••

BIGTEN
BIGTOE
BIGTOP
BIOTAS
BIOTIC
BIOTIN
BIRTHS
BISTRO
BITTED
BITTEN
BITTER
DIATOM
DICTUM
DIETED
DIETER
DIKTAT
DINTED
DISTAL
DISTIL
DITTOS
FIFTHS
FILTER
FILTHY
FIRTHS
FISTED
FISTIC
FITTED
FITTER
GIFTED
GIOTTO
GIRTED
GIRTHS
HIATAL
HIATUS
HILTON
HINTAT
HINTED
HINTER

HINTON
HITTER
JILTED
JITTER
KILTED
KILTER
KILTIE
KIRTLE
KITTEN
LICTOR
LIFTED
LIFTER
LIFTUP
LILTED
LINTEL
LINTER
LIOTTA
LIPTON
LISTED
LISTEE
LISTEL
LISTEN
LISTER
LISTON
LITTER
LITTLE
MILTIE
MILTON
MINTED
MINTER
MISTED
MISTER
MITTEN
MIXTEC
NINTHS
PIETAS
PIETER
PIETIN
PIETRO
PINTER
PINTLE
PINTOS
PISTIL
PISTOL
PISTON
PITTED
PITTER
QINTAR
RIATAS
RIFTED
RIOTED
RIOTER
RITTER
SIFTED
SIFTER
SILTED
SINTAX
SINTER
SISTER
SITTER
SIXTHS
SIXTUS
TICTAC
TILTED
TILTER
TINTED
TINTER
TIPTOE
TIPTOP
TITTER
TITTLE
VICTIM
VICTOR
VINTON
VIRTUE
VIRTUS
VISTAS
WIDTHS
WILTED
WILTON
WINTER
WINTRY
WISTER
WITTED

•I••T•

AIMSTO
BIGHTS
BIGOTS
BINATE
CIVETS
DICOTS
DIGITS
DILATE
DILUTE
DIMITY
DIVOTS
DIXITS
EIGHTH
EIGHTS
EIGHTY
FICHTE
FIESTA
FIGHTS
FILETS
FINITE
FINITO
FIRSTS
FIXATE
FIXITY
GIANTS
GIGOTS
GIOTTO
KIBITZ
LIESTO
LIEUTS
LIGATE
LIGHTS
LILITH
LIMITS
LIOTTA
MIGHTY
MIKITA
MINUTE
NICETY
NIGHTS
NIGHTY
NIKITA
NIMITZ
NINETY
PICOTS
PIGSTY
PILATE
PILOTI
PILOTS
PINATA
PINITE
PINOTS
PIPITS
PIRATE
PIVOTS
RIALTO
RIGHTO
RIGHTS
RIVETS
SIESTA
SIGHTS
SINGTO
TIGHTS
TINCTS
VISITS
WIGHTS
WISETO
ZIZITH

•I•••T

AIGRET
AIMSAT
AIROUT
BILLET
BIRGIT
BISECT
BISSET
DIDACT
DIEOUT
DIGEST
DIGLOT
DIGOUT
DIKTAT
DIMOUT
DIMWIT
DIRECT
DIREST
DISANT
DIVERT
DIVEST
FIDGET
FILLET
FINEST
GIBBET
GIBLET
GIDGET
GIMLET
HIDOUT
HINTAT
HISSAT
HITSIT
KISMET
KITKAT
LIMPET
LINNET
LIONET
LITOUT
MIDGET
MILLET
MINUET
MINUIT
MISFIT
MISHIT
NICEST
NIPSAT
NITWIT
PIAGET
PICKAT
PICKET
PIGLET
PIGNUT
PIGOUT
PINXIT
PIOLET
PIQUET
QIVIUT
RIDENT
RIFEST
RILLET
RIPEST
SIGNET
SILENT
SIPPET
SITOUT
TICKET
TIDBIT
TILSIT
TINHAT
TINPOT
TIPPET
TITBIT
VILEST
VIOLET
VIVANT
WICKET
WIDEST
WIDGET
WIGLET
WIGOUT
WILLET
WINGIT
WINKAT
WINOUT
WISENT
WISEST
WITHIT

••IT••

AKITAS
ANITRA
BAITED
BLITHE
BOITES
BRITON
CHITIN
CHITON
CRITIC
DMITRI
EDITED
EDITOR
ELITES
EXITED
FAITHS
FLITCH
FRITOS
GAITED
GAITER
GLITCH
GLITZY
GRITTY
GUITAR
INITIO
KEITEL
LOITER
MAITAI
MAITRE
OBITER
OTITIC
OTITIS
QUITIT
SKITCH
SKITOW
SLITHY
SLITTY
SMITES
SMITHS
SMITHY
SNITCH
SPITED
SPITES
STITCH
SUITED
SUITES
SUITOR
SUITUP
SWITCH
TRITER
TRITON
TWITCH
TWITTY
UNITAL
UNITAS
UNITED
UNITER
UNITES
WAITED
WAITER
WAITON
WAITUP
WHITEN
WHITER
WHITES
WRITER
WRITES
WRITHE

••I•T•

ALIOTO
ARISTA
ARISTO
AVIATE
BLINTZ
CHINTZ
DAINTY
DEISTS
DRIFTS
EDICTS
EVICTS
EXISTS
FAINTS
FEINTS
FEISTY
FLINTS
FLINTY
FLIRTS
FOISTS
GAIETY
GLINTS
GOINTO
GRISTS
GRITTY
GUILTY
HEISTS
HOISTS
IDIOTS
JOINTS
JOISTS
LAIDTO
MOIETY
ODISTS
OPIATE
PAINTS
PAIUTE
PLINTH
POINTE
POINTS
POINTY
PRINTS
QUIETS
QUILTS
QUINTS
QUIRTS
SAINTE
SAINTS
SHIFTS
SHIFTY
SHIITE
SHINTO
SHIRTS
SHIRTY
SKIRTS
SLITTY
SPILTH
STILTS
STINTS
SWIFTS
TAINTS
THIRTY
TRISTE
TWISTS
TWISTY
TWITTY
UBIETY
UNIATE
UNIATS
WAISTS
WRISTS

••I••T

ALIGHT
AMIDST
ARIGHT
BEIRUT
BLIGHT
BRIGHT
CLIENT
DRIEST
DWIGHT
ELICIT
FLIGHT
FRIGHT
GAINST
GRIVET
HAIGHT
HEIGHT
ICIEST
KNIGHT
ORIENT
PLIANT
PLIGHT
POIROT
PRIEST
PRIPET
PRIVET
QUITIT
RAILAT
SHIEST
SLIEST
SLIGHT
SPIGOT
SPINET
SPIRIT
SWIVET
THIRST
TOILET
TRICOT
TRIVET
TWILIT
VEIGHT
VOIGHT
WEIGHT
WHILST
WRIEST
WRIGHT

•••IT•

ACUITY
ADMITS
AMBITS
APLITE
AUDITS
AWAITS
BARITE
BEFITS
BENITO
BONITO
BRUITS
CAPITA
CAVITY
COMITY
CUBITS
DAMITA
DAVITS
DEBITS
DEMITS
DEVITO
DEWITT
DIGITS
DIMITY
DIXITS
DONITZ
DROITS
ENMITY
ENTITY
EOLITH
EQUITY
EXCITE
FAJITA
FINITE
FINITO
FIXITY
FRUITS
FRUITY
GOWITH
GSUITS
HABITS
HALITE
HAMITE
IGNITE
INCITE
INDITE
INSITU
INUITS
INVITE
INWITH
IOLITE
JUDITH
KIBITZ
KRAITS
LAXITY
LENITY
LEVITE
LEVITY
LILITH
LIMITS
LOLITA
LUCITE
MERITS
MIKITA
MORITA
MORITZ
NIKITA
NIMITZ
NOHITS
NUDITY
ODDITY
ONSITE
OOLITE
OOLITH
OPHITE
ORBITS
ORNITH
PARITY
PEPITA
PETITE
PEWITS
PINITE
PIPITS
PLAITS
POLITE
POLITY
POSITS
PURITY
PYRITE
QUOITS
RARITY
RATITE
RECITE
REFITS
REMITS
ROSITA
SAMITE
SANITY
SEMITE
SHIITE
SPLITS
SPRITE
SPRITS
SPRITZ
SUBITO
TAHITI
TONITE
TRAITS
UNFITS
UPPITY
VANITY
VENITE
VERITE
VERITY
VISITS
WAPITI
WRAITH
ZENITH
ZIZITH

•••I•T

ADRIFT
AGEIST
AGLINT
ALHIRT
ANOINT
AORIST
ARTIST
ASSIST
CUBIST
DELICT
DELIST
DEPICT
DESIST
DEWITT
EGOIST
ELLIOT
ENGIRT
ENLIST
FORINT
HERIOT
HOLIST
INDICT
INSIST
JOLIET
JOLIOT
JULIET
JURIST
KLEIST
LARIAT
LEGIST
LUTIST
LYRIST
MAOIST
MARIST
MONIST
NUDIST
OBOIST
PLAINT
PURIST
QIVIUT
QUAINT
RELICT
RELIST
RESIST
SCHIST
SCRIPT
SEXIST
SHRIFT
SOVIET
SPLINT
SPOILT
SPRINT
SQUINT
SQUIRT
STRICT
TANIST
TAOIST
THEIST
THRIFT
TSHIRT
TUBIST
TYPIST
UNGIRT
UPLIFT

••••IT

ACQUIT
ADROIT
ALBEIT
ARMPIT
ATTRIT
AUFAIT
BANDIT
BEATIT
BELOIT
BENOIT
BIRGIT
BLEWIT
BLOWIT
COEDIT
COMFIT
COMMIT
COOLIT
CREDIT
DACOIT
DARNIT
DAYLIT
DECEIT
DIMWIT
DOGSIT
DORRIT
DROPIT
ELEGIT
ELICIT
ESPRIT
GAMBIT
GASLIT
GETSIT
GODWIT
GOTOIT
HENBIT
HERMIT
HITSIT
HOBBIT
HOLDIT
HOOFIT
IGETIT
INTUIT
JESUIT
KERMIT
KUWAIT
LOSEIT
LOSTIT
MADEIT
MAKEIT
MINUIT
MISFIT
MISHIT
NITWIT
NOEXIT
OUTFIT
OUTHIT
OUTWIT
PANDIT
PERMIT
PETTIT
PINXIT
PROFIT
PROSIT
PULPIT
PUNDIT
QUITIT
RABBIT
REEDIT
SAWFIT
SEEFIT
SENNIT
SOBEIT
SOFFIT
SPIRIT
STOPIT
STRAIT
SUBMIT
SUMMIT
SUNLIT
TARPIT
TIDBIT
TILSIT
TITBIT
TOMTIT
TOOKIT
TURBIT
TWILIT
TWOBIT
UNKNIT
WESKIT
WINGIT
WITHIT

I•U•••

IGUACU
IGUANA
INUITS
INURED
INURES
ITURBI

I••U••

ILLUME
ILLUSE
IMBUED
IMBUES
IMMUNE
IMMUNO
IMMURE
IMPUGN
IMPURE
IMPUTE
INBULK
INCULT
INCURS
INCUSE
INDUCE
INDUCT
INFULL
INFUSE
INHUME
INJURE
INJURY
INLUCK
INOUYE
INPUTS
INRUSH
INSULT
INSURE
INTUIT
INTUNE
INTURN
IRRUPT
ISEULT
ISSUED
ISSUER
ISSUES

I•••U•

ICARUS
ICEDUP
ICEOUT
ICESUP
IMBRUE
INARUT
INDIUM
INFLUX
INHAUL
INPOUR
IONIUM
IREFUL

I••••U

IGUACU
INSITU

•IU•••

CIUDAD

•I•U••

DILUTE
DISUSE
FIBULA
FIGURE
FIXUPS
GIGUES
KIKUYU
LIEUTS
LIGULA
LIGURE
LIQUID
LIQUOR
MIGUEL
MINUET
MINUIT
MINUTE
MISUSE
MIXUPS
NIPUPS
PICULS
PINUPS
PIQUED
PIQUES
PIQUET
RITUAL
SIGURD
SIOUAN
SITUPS
TIEUPS
TIPUPS
UIGURS
VICUNA
VISUAL

•I••U•

AIRBUS
AIRGUN
AIROUT
BIDSUP
BIGGUN
BIGSUR
BIJOUX
BINDUP
BISQUE
CILIUM
CINQUE
CIRCUM
CIRCUS
CIRQUE
CIRRUS
CITRUS
DICTUM
DIEOUT
DIGOUT
DIGSUP
DIMOUT
DIMSUM
DINGUS
DISCUS
FICHUS
FILIUS
FILLUP
FIREUP
FIRMUP
FITFUL
GIVEUP
HIATUS
HICCUP
HIDOUT
HIGHUP
HINDUS
HITSUP
KICKUP
KIPPUR
LIFTUP
LIMBUS
LINEUP
LINGUA
LINKUP
LITMUS
LITOUT
MINIUM
MISCUE
MISSUS
NIMBUS
NIPPUR
PICKUP
PIGNUT
PIGOUT
PILEUM
PILEUP
PILEUS
PINDUS
PIPEUP
QIVIUT
RIGOUR
RIGSUP
RINGUP
RIPSUP
RISQUE
SIDDUR
SIGNUP
SINFUL
SIRIUS
SITOUT
SITSUP
SIXGUN
SIXTUS
SIZEUP
TIDYUP
TIEDUP
TIESUP
TISSUE
VIGOUR
VILLUS
VINOUS
VIRTUE
VIRTUS
WIGOUT
WILBUR
WINDUP
WINOUT
WIPEUP
WISEUP
ZIPSUP

•I•••U

BISSAU
KIKUYU
MILIEU
PICCHU
VISHNU

••IU••

ODIUMS
PAIUTE
TRIUNE

••I•U•

ACINUS
ADIEUS
ADIEUX
AMICUS
AMINUS
ANIMUS
BEIRUT
BMINUS
CAIQUE
CHIAUS
CHINUP
CLIQUE
CMINUS
CNIDUS
COILUP
DMINUS
EPIRUS
FAIRUP
FAIYUM
FLIPUP
HAIKUS
JAIPUR
JOINUP
KAILUA
LAIDUP
MAIDUS
ODIOUS
PAIDUP
PAIRUP
POILUS
PRIMUM
PRIMUS
QUIPUS
RAIPUR
SKIRUN
SLIPUP
STIRUP
SUITUP
TRIPUP
UNIQUE
WAITUP
WHIPUP

••I••U

HAIKOU
PAILOU

•••IU•

ACTIUM
ALLIUM
ATRIUM
BARIUM
CERIUM
CESIUM
CILIUM
CONIUM
CORIUM
CURIUM
DARIUS
DELIUS
ENNIUS
ERBIUM
FILIUS
FOLIUM
GENIUS
HELIUM
INDIUM
IONIUM
JULIUS
LATIUM
LUCIUS
MARIUS
MEDIUM
MINIUM
MOBIUS
OMNIUM
OSMIUM
OSTIUM
PODIUM
QIVIUT
RADIUM
RADIUS
REGIUS
SIRIUS
SODIUM
TEDIUM
VALIUM

•••I•U

DESILU
INSITU
JABIRU
MALIBU
MARILU
MILIEU

I•V•••

INVADE
INVAIN
INVENT
INVERT
INVEST
INVITE
INVIVO
INVOKE
IRVINE
IRVING

I•••V•

INLOVE
INVIVO

I••••V

IMPROV

•IV•••

CIVETS
CIVICS
DIVANS
DIVEIN
DIVERS
DIVERT
DIVEST
DIVIDE
DIVINE
DIVING
DIVOTS
FIVERS
FIVEWS
GIVEIN
GIVENS
GIVERS
GIVEUP
GIVING
HIVAOA
HIVING
JIVERS
JIVING
LIVEIN
LIVELY
LIVENS
LIVEON
LIVERS
LIVERY
LIVING
LIVRES
PIVOTS
QIVIUT
RIVALS
RIVERA
RIVERS
RIVETS
RIVING
TIVOLI
VIVACE
VIVANT
VIVIAN
VIVIEN
VIVIFY

•I•V••

KIDVID
LIEVRE
SIEVED
SIEVES
SILVER

•I•••V

KISLEV

••IV••

CHIVES
DRIVEL
DRIVEN
DRIVER
DRIVES
GRIVET
KNIVES
OGIVES
OLIVER
OLIVES
OLIVIA
PRIVET
QUIVER
SHIVER
SKIVED
SKIVER
SKIVES
SKIVVY
SLIVER
SNIVEL
SPIVAK
STIVER

STIVIC
SWIVEL
SWIVET
TRIVET
TRIVIA
UNIVAC
WAIVED
WAIVER
WAIVES

••I•V•
GRIEVE
SKIVVY
THIEVE

••I••V
ASIMOV

•••IV•
ACTIVE
ARGIVE
ARRIVE
DATIVE
DERIVE
ENDIVE
GODIVA
INVIVO
MOTIVE
NATIVE
RELIVE
REVIVE
SALIVA
SHRIVE
STRIVE
THRIVE
VOTIVE

I•W•••
INWARD
INWITH
IOWANS

I••W••
INAWAY

I•••W•
INLAWS
INTOWN

I••••W
INAROW
INFLOW

•IW•••
MIWOKS
SIWASH

•I•W••
AIRWAY
BIGWIG
DIMWIT
KIOWAS
MIDWAY
NITWIT
VIEWED
VIEWER
WIGWAG
WIGWAM
WINWIN

•I••W•
DISOWN
FIVEWS
SINEWS
SINEWY
WIDOWS

•I•••W
BILLOW
JIGSAW
LIELOW
MILDEW
MINNOW
PILLOW
PITSAW
RIPSAW
WILLOW
WINDOW
WINNOW

••IW••
OBIWAN
TAIWAN

••I•W•
OJIBWA

••I••W
SKITOW

•••I•W
ONVIEW
REVIEW

I••X••
IBEXES

I••••X
ICEBOX
INAFIX
INFLUX

•IX•••
DIXITS
FIXATE
FIXERS
FIXING
FIXITY
FIXUPS
MIXERS
MIXING
MIXTEC
MIXUPS
NIXIES
NIXING
PIXELS
PIXIES
SIXERS
SIXGUN
SIXING
SIXTHS
SIXTUS
VIXENS

•I•X••
DIOXIN
JINXED
JINXES
MINXES
PINXIT

•I••X•
BILOXI

•I•••X
BIJOUX
KITFOX
PICKAX
SINTAX
WINDEX

••IX••
BLIXEN
ELIXIR
TRIXIE
VSIXES

••I••X
ADIEUX
CHISOX
CLIMAX
SMILAX
UNISEX

•••IX•
MAXIXE

•••I•X
MENINX
SPHINX
SYRINX

••••IX
BENDIX
BOLLIX
COMMIX
INAFIX
MANNIX
MATRIX
PREFIX
PROLIX
SPADIX
SUFFIX
THESIX
TOMMIX

I•Y•••
IDYLLS

I••Y••
INSYNC
IRTYSH

I•••Y•
INLAYS
INOUYE

I••••Y
ICHTHY
IDIOCY
ILLSAY
INAWAY
INFAMY
INJURY
INPLAY

•IY•••
RIYADH
RIYALS

•I•Y••
LIBYAN
MINYAN
PINYIN
PINYON
SIBYLS
TIDYUP

•I••Y•
KIKUYU
LIMEYS
RIBEYE
TIEDYE

•I•••Y
AIRDRY
AIRILY
AIRWAY
BIGAMY
BIGBOY
BINARY
BIRNEY
BISCAY
CICELY
CITIFY
DICKEY
DILSEY
DIMITY
DIMPLY
DINGHY
DINKEY
DIPODY
DISMAY
DISNEY
EIGHTY
FILTHY
FINELY
FINERY
FINNEY
FIRMLY
FIXITY
GIGGLY
HICKEY
HIGHLY
HILARY
JIGGLY
JIMINY
JINGLY
JITNEY
KIDNEY
KIDORY
KINDLY
KINGLY
LIKELY
LIMPLY
LINSEY
LITANY
LIVELY
LIVERY
MICKEY
MIDDAY
MIDWAY
MIGHTY
MILADY
MILDLY
MILLAY
MINIFY
MISERY
MISLAY
MISSAY
NIAMEY
NICELY
NICETY
NIGHTY
NIMBLY
NIMINY
NINETY
PIGSTY
PIMINY
PINERY
PIRACY
RICHLY
RICKEY
RIDLEY
RIMSKY
RIPELY
RIPLEY
RIPPLY
SICILY
SICKLY
SIDNEY
SIMONY
SIMPLY
SINEWY
SINGLY
TIDILY
TIMELY
TINGLY
TINKLY
VIABLY
VILELY
VILIFY
VINERY
VIVIFY
WICOPY
WIDELY
WIFELY
WIGGLY
WILDLY
WIMSEY
WINERY
WINTRY
WISELY
WITCHY

••IY••
FAIYUM

••I•Y•
DAIMYO
ERINYS
VAISYA

••I••Y
ACIDLY
APIARY
ARIDLY
AVIARY
AVIDLY
BAILEY
BLIMEY
BOIGNY
BRICKY
BRIERY
CHILLY
CHINKY
CHIRPY
CLINGY
CRISPY
DAILEY
DAINTY
DRIPPY
EVILLY
FAIRLY
FEISTY
FLIMSY
FLINTY
FRIARY
FRIDAY
FRILLY
FRINGY
FRISKY
FRIZZY
GAIETY
GAINLY
GLIBLY
GLITZY
GRIMLY
GRISLY
GRITTY
GUILTY
HAILEY
IDIOCY
LAIDBY
MAINLY
MOIETY
ONIONY
PHILLY
POINTY
PRICEY
PRIMLY
PRIORY
PRISSY
QUINCY
QUIPPY
QUIRKY
SHIFTY
SHILLY
SHIMMY
SHINDY
SHINNY
SHIRTY
SKIMPY
SKINNY
SKIPPY
SKIVVY
SLIMLY
SLINKY
SLITHY
SLITTY
SMILEY
SMIRKY
SMITHY
SNIFFY
SNIPPY
SPIFFY
STICKY
STILLY
STIMPY
STINGY
STINKY
SWINGY
SWIRLY
THINLY
THIRTY
TRICKY
TRIGLY
TRILBY
TRIMLY
TRIPLY
TWIGGY
TWISTY
TWITTY
UBIETY
VAINLY
WHIMSY
WHINNY
WHIPPY
WHIRLY

•••I•Y
ACUITY
AIRILY
BODILY
BRAINY
BUSILY
CAGILY
CAVITY
CITIFY
CODIFY
COMITY
COZILY
DIMITY
DOZILY
EASILY
EDGILY
EERILY
EFFIGY
ENMITY
ENTITY
EQUITY
EXPIRY
FAMILY
FIXITY
FOXILY
FRUITY
GAMILY
GLAIRY
GRAINY
HAZILY
HOMILY
HOMINY
JIMINY
LAXITY
LAZILY
LENITY
LEVITY
LOGILY
MINIFY
MODIFY
MUTINY
NIMINY
NOSILY
NOTIFY
NUDITY
ODDITY
OSSIFY
PACIFY
PARITY
PIMINY
POKILY
POLICY
POLITY
PUNILY
PURIFY
PURITY
RACILY
RAMIFY
RARIFY
RARITY
RATIFY
ROSILY
ROSINY
RUBIFY
SANITY
SATINY
SEXILY
SICILY
TIDILY
TYPIFY
UGLIFY
UNTIDY
UPPITY
VANITY
VERIFY
VERILY
VERITY
VILIFY
VIVIFY
WARILY
ZANILY

IZ••••
IZABAL
IZZARD

I•Z•••
ITZHAK
IZZARD

I•••Z•
IODIZE
IONIZE

I••••Z
IGNATZ

•IZ•••
FIZGIG
FIZZED
FIZZES
FIZZLE
GIZMOS
LIZARD
LIZZIE
MIZENS
MIZZEN
MIZZLE
PIZAZZ
PIZZAS
SIZERS
SIZEUP
SIZING
SIZZLE
VIZIER
VIZSLA
WIZARD
WIZENS
ZIZITH

•I•Z••
DITZES
FIZZED
FIZZES
FIZZLE
LIZZIE
MIZZEN
MIZZLE
PIAZZA
PINZON
PIZZAS
SIZZLE
WINZES
ZIGZAG

•I••Z•
PIAZZA
PIZAZZ

•I•••Z
KIBITZ
MILOSZ
NIMITZ
PIZAZZ

••IZ••
FRIZZY
MAIZES
PRIZED
PRIZES
SEIZED
SEIZER
SEIZES

••I•Z•
FRIEZE
FRIZZY
GLITZY

••I••Z
BLINTZ
BRIENZ
CHINTZ
SHIRAZ

•••IZ•
ASSIZE
BELIZE
IODIZE
IONIZE

•••I•Z
DONITZ
KIBITZ
MORITZ
NIMITZ
SPRITZ

••••IZ
CURTIZ
TABRIZ
THEWIZ

JA••••
JABBAR
JABBED
JABBER
JABIRU
JABOTS
JACALS
JACANA
JACKAL
JACKED
JACKET
JACKIE
JACKUP
JACLYN
JACOBI
JADING
JAEGER
JAGGED
JAGGER
JAGUAR
JAILED
JAILER
JAIPUR
JALAPA
JALOPY
JAMAAL
JAMMED
JAMMER
JAMOKE
JAMSIN
JAMSUP
JAMUPS
JANGLE
JANGLY
JANHUS
JANICE
JANINE
JANSEN
JAPANS
JAPERS
JAPERY
JAPING
JARFUL
JARGON
JARRAH
JARRED
JASCHA
JASPER
JAUNTS
JAUNTY
JAURES
JAVARI
JAVIER
JAWING
JAWOHL
JAYCEE
JAYVEE
JAZZED
JAZZES
JAZZUP

J•A•••
JEANNE
JOANIE
JOANNA
JOANNE
JUAREZ

J••A••
JACALS
JACANA
JALAPA
JAMAAL
JAPANS
JAVARI
JICAMA
JIHADS
JOHANN
JUDAEA
JUDAIC
JUMADA
JURADO
JURATS

J•••A•
JABBAR
JACKAL
JAGUAR
JAMAAL
JARRAH
JEERAT
JETLAG
JETSAM
JIGSAW
JINNAH
JORDAN
JOSIAH
JOVIAL
JOVIAN
JUBBAH
JULIAN
JUMPAT
JUNEAU
JUNTAS

J••••A
JACANA
JALAPA
JASCHA
JERBOA
JICAMA
JOANNA
JOJOBA
JOSHUA
JUDAEA
JUDOKA
JUMADA

•JA•••
AJANTA

•J•A••
UJJAIN

•J•••A
AJANTA
DJERBA
EJECTA
OJIBWA

••JA••
DEJAVU
HIJACK
MOJAVE
PAJAMA
PYJAMA
RAJAHS
SEJANT
UJJAIN
UNJAMS

••J•A•
FIJIAN
FUJIAN
STJOAN

••J••A
ARJUNA
FAJITA
JOJOBA
PAJAMA
PYJAMA

•••JA•
DEEJAY
ELIJAH
INAJAM
LOGJAM
NINJAS
PUNJAB
RIOJAS
THUJAS
TRAJAN
TROJAN
VEEJAY

•••J•A
PRAJNA

••••JA
BAROJA

J•B•••
JABBAR
JABBED
JABBER
JABIRU
JABOTS
JIBING
JOBBED
JOBBER
JOBETH
JOBHOP
JOBLOT
JUBBAH

J••B••
JABBAR
JABBED
JABBER
JERBOA
JOBBED
JOBBER
JUBBAH
JUMBLE
JUMBOS

J•••B•
JACOBI
JOJOBA
JUJUBE

•J•B••
OJIBWA

•J••B•
DJERBA

••J•B•
JOJOBA
JUJUBE

•••J•B
CONJOB
ODDJOB
PUNJAB
TOPJOB

J•C•••
JACALS
JACANA
JACKAL
JACKED
JACKET
JACKIE
JACKUP
JACLYN
JACOBI
JECKLE
JICAMA
JOCKEY
JOCOSE
JOCUND

J••C••
JASCHA
JAYCEE
JUICED
JUICER
JUICES
JUNCOS

J•••C•
JANICE
JOUNCE
JOUNCY

J••••C
JUDAIC

•J•C••
EJECTA
EJECTS

••J•C•
ABJECT
DEJECT
HIJACK
INJECT
OBJECT
REJECT

J•D•••
JADING
JUDAEA
JUDAIC
JUDDER
JUDGED
JUDGES
JUDITH
JUDOKA

J••D••
JORDAN
JUDDER

J•••D•
JIHADS
JUMADA
JURADO

J••••D
JABBED
JACKED
JAGGED
JAILED
JAMMED
JARRED
JAZZED
JEERED
JELLED
JERKED
JESTED
JETTED
JIGGED
JILTED
JINKED
JINXED
JOBBED
JOCUND
JOGGED
JOINED
JOLTED
JOSHED
JOTTED
JUDGED
JUGGED
JUICED
JUMPED
JUNKED
JUTTED

•J••D•
FJELDS
FJORDS

••J••D
BUJOLD

JE••••
JEANNE
JECKLE
JEERAT
JEERED
JEERER
JEETER
JEEVES
JEJUNE
JEKYLL
JELLED
JENNER
JENNET
JENNIE
JENSEN
JERBOA
JEREMY
JERKED
JERKIN
JEROME
JERSEY
JESSEL
JESSIE
JESTED
JESTER
JESUIT
JETGUN
JETHRO
JETLAG
JETSAM
JETSET
JETSKI
JETSON
JETTED
JEWELS
JEWETT
JEWISH

J•E•••
JAEGER
JEERAT
JEERED
JEERER
JEETER
JEEVES
JOETEX

J••E••
JAPERS
JAPERY
JEREMY
JEWELS
JEWETT
JIVERS
JOBETH
JOKERS
JOLENE
JOSEPH
JOWETT
JULEPS
JUNEAU

J•••E•
JABBED
JABBER
JACKED
JACKET
JAEGER
JAGGED
JAGGER
JAILED
JAILER
JAMMED
JAMMER
JANSEN
JARRED
JASPER
JAURES
JAVIER
JAYCEE
JAYVEE
JAZZED
JAZZES
JEERED
JEERER
JEETER
JEEVES
JELLED
JENNER
JENNET
JENSEN
JERKED
JERSEY
JESSEL
JESTED
JESTER
JETSET
JETTED
JIGGED
JIGGER
JILTED
JINKED
JINXED
JINXES
JITNEY
JITTER
JOBBED
JOBBER
JOCKEY
JOETEX
JOGGED
JOGGER
JOINED
JOINER
JOLIET
JOLTED
JOSHED
JOSHES
JOSSES
JOTTED
JOULES
JOYNER
JUAREZ
JUDAEA
JUDDER
JUDGED
JUDGES
JUGGED
JUICED
JUICER
JUICES
JULIET
JUMPED
JUMPER
JUNKED
JUNKER
JUNKET
JURIES
JUSTER
JUTTED

J••••E
JACKIE
JAMOKE
JANGLE
JANICE
JANINE
JAYCEE
JAYVEE
JEANNE
JECKLE
JEJUNE
JENNIE
JEROME
JESSIE
JIGGLE
JIMMIE
JINGLE
JOANIE
JOANNE
JOCOSE
JOGGLE
JOHORE
JOLENE
JOSTLE
JOUNCE
JUGGLE
JUJUBE
JUMBLE
JUNGLE
JUNKIE

•JE•••
DJERBA
EJECTA
EJECTS
FJELDS

•J••E•
IJSSEL
KJOLEN

••JE••
ABJECT
DEJECT
INJECT
INJEST
OBJECT
REJECT

••J•E•
GIJOES
HAJJES
MAJGEN

••J••E
ABJURE
ADJURE
BYJOVE
CAJOLE
DEJURE
INJOKE
INJURE
JEJUNE
JUJUBE
MOJAVE

•••JE•
FANJET
GASJET
HADJES
HAJJES
KOPJES
RAMJET

•••J•E
HEYJOE

••••JE
SKOPJE

J••F••
JARFUL
JOYFUL
JUGFUL

•JF•••
AJFOYT

J•G•••
JAGGED
JAGGER
JAGUAR
JIGGED
JIGGER
JIGGLE
JIGGLY
JIGSAW
JOGGED
JOGGER
JOGGLE
JUGFUL
JUGGED
JUGGLE

J••G••
JAEGER
JAGGED
JAGGER
JANGLE
JANGLY
JARGON
JETGUN
JIGGED
JIGGER
JIGGLE
JIGGLY
JINGLE
JINGLY
JOGGED
JOGGER
JOGGLE
JUDGED
JUDGES
JUGGED
JUGGLE
JUNGLE
JUNGLY

J••••G
JADING
JAPING
JAWING
JETLAG
JIBING
JIVING
JOKING
JUKING

••JG••
MAJGEN

J•H•••
JIHADS
JOHANN
JOHNNY
JOHORE

J••H••
JANHUS
JETHRO
JOBHOP
JOSHED
JOSHES
JOSHUA

J•••H•
JASCHA
JAWOHL

J••••H
JARRAH
JEWISH
JINNAH
JOBETH
JOSEPH
JOSIAH
JUBBAH
JUDITH

••J•H•
RAJAHS
STJOHN

•••J•H
ELIJAH

JI••••
JIBING
JICAMA
JIGGED
JIGGER
JIGGLE
JIGGLY
JIGSAW
JIHADS
JILTED
JIMINY
JIMMIE
JIMSON
JINGLE
JINGLY
JINKED
JINNAH
JINXED
JINXES
JITNEY
JITTER
JIVERS
JIVING

J•I•••
JAILED
JAILER
JAIPUR
JOINED
JOINER
JOININ
JOINTS
JOINUP
JOISTS
JUICED
JUICER
JUICES

J••I••
JABIRU
JADING
JANICE
JANINE
JAPING
JAVIER
JAWING
JEWISH
JIBING
JIMINY
JIVING
JOKING
JOLIET
JOLIOT
JOSIAH
JOVIAL
JOVIAN
JUDITH
JUKING
JULIAN
JULIET
JULIUS
JUNIOR
JURIES
JURIST

J•••I•
JACKIE
JAMSIN
JENNIE
JERKIN
JESSIE
JESUIT
JIMMIE
JOANIE
JOININ
JOPLIN
JUDAIC
JUMPIN
JUNKIE
JUSTIN

J••••I
JACOBI
JAVARI
JETSKI

•JI•••
OJIBWA

••J••I
UJJAIN

••JI••
FAJITA
FIJIAN
FUJIAN

••J•I•
ADJOIN
ENJOIN
HAJJIS
MAJLIS
REJOIN
UJJAIN

•••JI•
HADJIS
HAJJIS
SHOJIS

••••JI
ROMAJI

J•J•••
JEJUNE
JOJOBA
JUJUBE

•JJ•••
UJJAIN

••JJ••
HAJJES
HAJJIS

J•K•••
JEKYLL
JOKERS
JOKING
JUKING

J••K••
JACKAL
JACKED
JACKET
JACKIE
JACKUP
JECKLE
JERKED
JERKIN
JINKED
JOCKEY
JUNKED
JUNKER
JUNKET
JUNKIE

J•••K•
JAMOKE
JETSKI
JUDOKA

••J•K•
INJOKE

••J••K
HIJACK

•••JK•
STOJKO

•••J•K
SELJUK

J•L•••
JALAPA
JALOPY
JELLED
JILTED
JOLENE
JOLIET
JOLIOT
JOLSON
JOLTED
JULEPS
JULIAN
JULIET
JULIUS

J••L••
JACLYN
JAILED
JAILER
JELLED
JETLAG
JOBLOT
JOPLIN
JOULES

J•••L•
JACALS
JANGLE
JANGLY
JECKLE
JEKYLL
JEWELS
JIGGLE
JIGGLY
JINGLE
JINGLY
JOGGLE
JOSTLE
JUGGLE
JUMBLE
JUNGLE
JUNGLY
JUSTLY

J••••L
JACKAL
JAMAAL
JARFUL
JAWOHL
JEKYLL
JESSEL
JOVIAL
JOYFUL
JUGFUL

•J•L••
FJELDS
KJOLEN

•J•••L
IJSSEL

••JL••
MAJLIS

••J•L•
BUJOLD
CAJOLE

•••J•L
BANJUL
FRIJOL

J•M•••
JAMAAL
JAMMED
JAMMER
JAMOKE
JAMSIN
JAMSUP
JAMUPS
JIMINY
JIMMIE
JIMSON
JUMADA
JUMBLE
JUMBOS
JUMPAT
JUMPED
JUMPER
JUMPIN
JUMPON
JUMPUP

J••M••
JAMMED
JAMMER
JIMMIE

J•••M•
JEREMY
JEROME
JICAMA
JORUMS

J••••M
JETSAM

••J•M•
PAJAMA
PYJAMA
UNJAMS

•••J•M
BOOJUM
INAJAM
LOGJAM

J•N•••
JANGLE
JANGLY
JANHUS
JANICE
JANINE
JANSEN
JENNER
JENNET
JENNIE
JENSEN
JINGLE
JINGLY
JINKED
JINNAH
JINXED
JINXES
JONSON
JUNCOS
JUNEAU
JUNGLE
JUNGLY
JUNIOR
JUNKED
JUNKER
JUNKET
JUNKIE
JUNTAS
JUNTOS

J••N••
JAUNTS
JAUNTY
JEANNE
JENNER
JENNET
JENNIE
JINNAH
JITNEY
JOANIE
JOANNA
JOANNE
JOHNNY
JOINED
JOINER
JOININ
JOINTS
JOINUP
JOUNCE
JOUNCY
JOYNER

J•••N•
JACANA
JADING
JANINE
JAPANS
JAPING
JAWING
JEANNE
JEJUNE
JIBING
JIMINY
JIVING
JOANNA
JOANNE
JOHANN
JOHNNY
JOKING
JOLENE
JUKING

J••••N
JACLYN
JAMSIN
JANSEN
JARGON
JENSEN
JERKIN
JETGUN
JETSON
JIMSON
JOHANN
JOININ
JOLSON
JONSON
JOPLIN
JORDAN
JOVIAN
JULIAN
JUMPIN
JUMPON
JUSTIN

•J•N••
AJANTA

•J•••N
KJOLEN
UJJAIN

••J•N•
ARJUNA
CAJUNS
JEJUNE
SEJANT

••J••N
ADJOIN
ENJOIN
FIJIAN
FUJIAN
MAJGEN
REJOIN
STJOAN
STJOHN
UJJAIN

•••JN•
PRAJNA

•••J•N
DONJON
TRAJAN
TROJAN

JO••••
JOANIE
JOANNA
JOANNE
JOBBED
JOBBER
JOBETH
JOBHOP
JOBLOT
JOCKEY
JOCOSE
JOCUND
JOETEX
JOGGED
JOGGER
JOGGLE
JOHANN
JOHNNY
JOHORE
JOINED
JOINER
JOININ
JOINTS
JOINUP
JOISTS
JOJOBA
JOKERS
JOKING
JOLENE
JOLIET
JOLIOT
JOLSON
JOLTED
JONSON
JOPLIN
JORDAN
JORUMS
JOSEPH
JOSHED
JOSHES
JOSHUA
JOSIAH
JOSSES
JOSTLE
JOTTED
JOULES
JOUNCE
JOUNCY
JOUSTS
JOVIAL
JOVIAN
JOWETT
JOYFUL
JOYNER
JOYOUS

J••O••
JABOTS
JACOBI
JALOPY
JAMOKE
JAWOHL
JEROME
JOCOSE
JOHORE
JOJOBA
JOYOUS
JUDOKA
JURORS

J•••O•
JARGON
JERBOA
JETSON
JIMSON
JOBHOP
JOBLOT
JOLIOT
JOLSON
JONSON
JUMBOS
JUMPON
JUNCOS
JUNIOR
JUNTOS

J••••O
JETHRO
JURADO

•JO•••
FJORDS
KJOLEN

•J•O••
AJFOYT

••JO••
ADJOIN
ANJOUS
BIJOUX
BUJOLD
BYJOVE
CAJOLE
ENJOIN
ENJOYS
GIJOES
INJOKE
JOJOBA
MAJORS
REJOIN
STJOAN
STJOHN

•••JO•
ACAJOU
AMAJOR
BANJOS
BMAJOR
CMAJOR
CONJOB
DMAJOR
DONJON
EMAJOR
FMAJOR
FRIJOL
GMAJOR
HEYJOE
MENJOU
ODDJOB
TOPJOB

•••J•O
STOJKO

••••JO
NAVAJO

J•P•••
JAPANS
JAPERS
JAPERY
JAPING
JOPLIN

J••P••
JAIPUR
JASPER
JUMPAT
JUMPED
JUMPER
JUMPIN
JUMPON
JUMPUP

J•••P•
JALAPA
JALOPY
JAMUPS
JOSEPH
JULEPS

J••••P
JACKUP
JAMSUP
JAZZUP
JOBHOP
JOINUP
JUMPUP

••JP••
RAJPUT

J•R•••
JARFUL
JARGON
JARRAH
JARRED
JERBOA
JEREMY
JERKED
JERKIN
JEROME
JERSEY
JORDAN
JORUMS
JURADO
JURATS
JURIES
JURIST
JURORS

J••R••
JARRAH
JARRED
JAURES
JEERAT
JEERED
JEERER
JUAREZ

J•••R•
JABIRU
JAPERS
JAPERY
JAVARI
JETHRO
JIVERS
JOHORE
JOKERS
JURORS

J••••R
JABBAR
JABBER
JAEGER
JAGGER
JAGUAR
JAILER
JAIPUR
JAMMER
JASPER
JAVIER
JEERER
JEETER
JENNER
JESTER
JIGGER
JITTER
JOBBER
JOGGER
JOINER
JOYNER
JUDDER
JUICER
JUMPER
JUNIOR
JUNKER
JUSTER

•J•R••
DJERBA
FJORDS

••J•R•
ABJURE
ADJURE
DEJURE
INJURE
INJURY
MAJORS

•••J•R
AMAJOR
BMAJOR
CMAJOR
DMAJOR
EMAJOR
FMAJOR
GMAJOR

J•S•••
JASCHA
JASPER
JESSEL
JESSIE
JESTED
JESTER
JESUIT
JOSEPH
JOSHED
JOSHES
JOSHUA
JOSIAH
JOSSES
JOSTLE
JUSTER
JUSTIN
JUSTLY

J••S••
JAMSIN
JAMSUP
JANSEN
JENSEN
JERSEY
JESSEL
JESSIE
JETSAM
JETSET
JETSKI
JETSON
JIGSAW
JIMSON
JOISTS
JOLSON
JONSON
JOSSES
JOUSTS

J•••S•
JEWISH
JOCOSE
JURIST

J••••S
JABOTS
JACALS
JAMUPS
JANHUS
JAPANS
JAPERS
JAUNTS
JAURES
JAZZES
JEEVES
JEWELS
JIHADS
JINXES
JIVERS
JOINTS
JOISTS
JOKERS
JORUMS
JOSHES
JOSSES
JOULES
JOUSTS
JOYOUS
JUDGES
JUICES
JULEPS
JULIUS
JUMBOS
JUNCOS
JUNTAS
JUNTOS
JURATS
JURIES
JURORS

•JS•••
IJSSEL

•J•S••
IJSSEL

•J•••S
EJECTS
FJELDS
FJORDS

••J•S•
ADJUST
INJEST
UNJUST

••J••S
ANJOUS
CAJUNS
ENJOYS
GIJOES
HAJJES
HAJJIS
MAJLIS
MAJORS
RAJAHS
UNJAMS

•••J•S
BANJOS
HADJES
HADJIS
HAJJES
HAJJIS
KOPJES
NINJAS
RIOJAS
SHOJIS
THUJAS

J•T•••
JETGUN
JETHRO
JETLAG
JETSAM
JETSET
JETSKI
JETSON
JETTED
JITNEY
JITTER
JOTTED
JUTTED

J••T••
JEETER
JESTED
JESTER
JETTED
JILTED
JITTER
JOETEX
JOLTED
JOSTLE
JOTTED
JUNTAS
JUNTOS
JUSTER
JUSTIN
JUSTLY
JUTTED

J•••T•
JABOTS
JAUNTS
JAUNTY
JEWETT
JOBETH
JOINTS
JOISTS
JOUSTS
JOWETT
JUDITH
JURATS

J••••T
JACKET
JEERAT
JENNET
JESUIT
JETSET
JEWETT
JOBLOT
JOLIET
JOLIOT
JOWETT
JULIET
JUMPAT
JUNKET
JURIST

•J••T•
AJANTA
EJECTA
EJECTS

•J•••T
AJFOYT

••J•T•
FAJITA

••J••T
ABJECT
ADJUST
DEJECT
INJECT
INJEST
OBJECT
RAJPUT
REJECT
SEJANT
UNJUST

•••J•T
FANJET
GASJET
RAMJET

JU••••
JUAREZ
JUBBAH
JUDAEA
JUDAIC
JUDDER
JUDGED
JUDGES
JUDITH
JUDOKA
JUGFUL
JUGGED
JUGGLE
JUICED
JUICER
JUICES
JUJUBE
JUKING
JULEPS
JULIAN
JULIET
JULIUS
JUMADA
JUMBLE
JUMBOS
JUMPAT
JUMPED
JUMPER
JUMPIN
JUMPON
JUMPUP
JUNCOS
JUNEAU
JUNGLE
JUNGLY
JUNIOR
JUNKED
JUNKER
JUNKET
JUNKIE
JUNTAS
JUNTOS
JURADO
JURATS
JURIES
JURIST
JURORS
JUSTER
JUSTIN
JUSTLY
JUTTED

J•U•••
JAUNTS
JAUNTY
JAURES
JOULES
JOUNCE
JOUNCY
JOUSTS

J••U••
JAGUAR
JAMUPS
JEJUNE
JESUIT
JOCUND
JORUMS
JUJUBE

J•••U•
JACKUP
JAIPUR
JAMSUP
JANHUS
JARFUL
JAZZUP
JETGUN
JOINUP
JOSHUA
JOYFUL
JOYOUS
JUGFUL
JULIUS
JUMPUP

J••••U
JABIRU
JUNEAU

••JU••
ABJURE
ADJURE

ADJUST
ARJUNA
CAJUNS
DEJURE
INJURE
INJURY
JEJUNE
JUJUBE
UNJUST

••J•U•
ANJOUS
BIJOUX
RAJPUT

••J••U
DEJAVU

•••JU•
BANJUL
BOOJUM
SELJUK

•••J•U
ACAJOU
MENJOU

J•V•••
JAVARI
JAVIER
JIVERS
JIVING
JOVIAL
JOVIAN

J••V••
JAYVEE
JEEVES

••J•V•
BYJOVE
DEJAVU
MOJAVE

J•W•••
JAWING
JAWOHL
JEWELS
JEWETT
JEWISH
JOWETT

J••••W
JIGSAW

•J••W•
OJIBWA

J••X••
JINXED
JINXES

J••••X
JOETEX

••J••X
BIJOUX

J•Y•••
JAYCEE
JAYVEE
JOYFUL
JOYNER
JOYOUS

J••Y••
JEKYLL

J•••Y•
JACLYN

J••••Y
JALOPY
JANGLY
JAPERY
JAUNTY
JEREMY
JERSEY
JIGGLY
JIMINY
JINGLY
JITNEY
JOCKEY
JOHNNY
JOUNCY
JUNGLY
JUSTLY

•J••Y•
AJFOYT

••J•Y•
ENJOYS

••J••Y
INJURY

•••J•Y
DEEJAY
VEEJAY

J•Z•••
JAZZED
JAZZES
JAZZUP

J••Z••
JAZZED
JAZZES
JAZZUP

J••••Z
JUAREZ

KA••••
KABOBS
KABOOM
KABUKI
KAFFIR
KAGERA
KAHLIL
KAHLUA
KAHUNA
KAILUA
KAISER
KAKAPO
KALAKH
KALINE
KALKAN
KALMAR
KAMALA
KANAKA
KANDER
KANSAN
KANSAS
KANTOR
KAOLIN
KAPLAN
KAPPAS
KARATE
KARATS
KAREEM
KARIBA
KARMIC
KARNAK
KAROSS
KARPOV
KARRAS
KARROO
KARSTS
KASBAH
KATHIE
KATMAI
KAUNAS
KAUNDA
KAURIS
KAYAKS
KAYOED
KAZAKH
KAZAKS
KAZOOS

K•A•••
KEATON
KHAFRE
KHAKIS
KHALID
KIANGS
KLATCH
KLAXON
KNACKS
KNARRY
KNAVES
KOALAS
KRAALS
KRAITS
KRAKEN
KRAKOW
KRAMER
KRANTZ
KRATER
KWACHA
KWANZA
KYACKS

K••A••
KAKAPO
KALAKH
KAMALA
KANAKA
KARATE
KARATS
KAYAKS
KAZAKH
KAZAKS
KDLANG
KEBABS
KERALA
KIGALI
KNEADS
KODALY
KORATS
KOVACS
KRAALS
KULAKS
KURALT
KUVASZ
KUWAIT

K•••A•
KALKAN
KALMAR
KANSAN
KANSAS
KAPLAN
KAPPAS
KARNAK
KARRAS
KASBAH
KATMAI
KAUNAS
KEENAN
KEEPAT
KENYAN
KEPTAT
KERMAN
KEVLAR
KEYPAD
KEYWAY
KIDMAN
KIDNAP
KIOWAS
KIRMAN
KITBAG
KITKAT
KLIBAN
KOALAS
KODIAK
KONRAD
KOREAN
KORMAN
KOUFAX
KUBLAI
KURGAN

K••••A
KAGERA
KAHLUA
KAHUNA
KAILUA
KAMALA
KANAKA
KARIBA
KAUNDA
KERALA
KESHIA
KONICA
KORUNA
KWACHA
KWANZA

•KA•••
OKAPIS
OKAYED
SKALDS
SKATED
SKATER
SKATES
UKASES

•K•A••
AKUAKU
SKEANS

•K••A•
AKELAS
AKITAS
SKYCAP
SKYLAB
SKYWAY

••KA••
ACKACK
ALKALI
ANKARA
ASKARI
DEKALB
GOKART
KAKAPO
MAKALU
MIKADO
PIKAKE
TOKAYS
UAKARI
YUKATA
YUKAWA

••K•A•
DIKTAT
LEKVAR
POKEAT
SUKKAH
TOKLAS

••K••A
ANKARA
DAKOTA
LAKOTA
MAKUTA
MIKITA
NIKITA
NIKOLA
YAKIMA
YUKATA
YUKAWA

•••KA•
BABKAS
BAIKAL
BALKAN
BROKAW
CHUKAR
HOOKAH
JACKAL
KALKAN
KITKAT
LOOKAT
PARKAS
PARKAY
PECKAT
PEEKAT
PICKAT
PICKAX
POLKAS
PUNKAH
RYOKAN
SUKKAH
TALKAT
TANKAS
WINKAT

•••K•A
CHUKKA
GURKHA
MARKKA
MOSKVA
QUOKKA

••••KA
ALASKA
BANGKA
CHUKKA
EUREKA
FLICKA
GLINKA
JUDOKA
KANAKA
LUSAKA
MARKKA
MEDAKA
NOOTKA
QUOKKA
SEDAKA
TANAKA
TOPEKA
TROIKA
WOVOKA

K•B•••
KABOBS
KABOOM
KABUKI
KEBABS
KEBOBS
KIBBLE
KIBITZ
KIBOSH
KOBOLD
KUBLAI

K••B••
KASBAH
KHYBER
KIBBLE
KITBAG
KLIBAN
KNOBBY
KORBUT

K•••B•
KABOBS
KARIBA
KEBABS
KEBOBS
KNOBBY

•KB•••
EKBERG

•K•B••
SKYBOX

•K••B•
AKIMBO

•K•••B
SKYLAB

••K••B
DEKALB

K•C•••
KICKED
KICKER
KICKIN
KICKUP
KUCHEN

K••C••
KIMCHI
KNACKS
KNICKS
KNOCKS
KWACHA
KYACKS

K•••C•
KIRSCH
KITSCH
KLATCH
KONICA
KOPECK
KOVACS
KVETCH

K••••C
KARMIC

•K•C••
SKYCAP

•K••C•
SKETCH
SKITCH

••K•C•
ACKACK

••K••C
PYKNIC

•••K•C
TURKIC

KD••••
KDLANG

K•D•••
KEDGED
KEDGES
KIDDED
KIDDER
KIDMAN
KIDNAP
KIDNEY
KIDORY
KIDVID
KODALY
KODIAK
KUDZUS

K••D••
KANDER
KIDDED
KIDDER
KINDER
KINDLE
KINDLY
KINDOF
KLUDGE

K•••D•
KAUNDA
KNEADS
KOMODO

K••••D
KAYOED
KEDGED
KEELED
KEENED
KEGGED
KENNED
KERNED
KEYPAD
KHALID
KICKED
KIDDED
KIDVID
KILLED
KILNED
KILTED
KINGED
KINKED
KISSED
KNIFED
KOBOLD
KONRAD

•K••D•
SKALDS

•K•••D
OKAYED
SKATED
SKEWED
SKIVED

••KD••
DIKDIK

••K•D•
AIKIDO
ALKYDS
MAKEDO
MIKADO

••K••D
ANKLED
INKIND
UNKIND
YAKKED
YUKKED

•••K•D
AWAKED
BACKED
BALKED
BANKED
BARKED
BASKED
BEAKED
BILKED
BOOKED
BRAKED
BUCKED
BULKED
BUNKED
CALKED
CHOKED
COCKED
CONKED
COOKED
CORKED
DECKED
DISKED
DOCKED
DUCKED
DUNKED
EVOKED
FINKED
FLAKED
FORKED
FUNKED
GAWKED
HACKED
HARKED
HAWKED
HOCKED
HONKED
HOOKED
HULKED
HUSKED
JACKED
JERKED
JINKED
JUNKED
KICKED
KINKED
LACKED
LARKED
LEAKED
LICKED
LINKED
LOCKED
LOOKED
LUCKED
LURKED
MARKED
MASKED
MILKED
MOCKED
MUCKED
NECKED
NICKED
OINKED
PACKED
PARKED
PEAKED
PECKED
PEEKED
PERKED
PICKED
PINKED
QUAKED
RACKED
RANKED
REEKED
RICKED
RISKED
ROCKED
ROOKED
RUCKED
SACKED
SILKED
SLAKED
SMOKED
SNAKED
SOAKED
SOCKED
SPIKED
SPOKED
STAKED
STOKED
SUCKED
SULKED
TACKED
TALKED
TANKED
TASKED
TICKED
TUCKED
TUSKED
WALKED
WICKED
WINKED
WORKED
YAKKED
YANKED
YOLKED
YUKKED
ZONKED

KE••••
KEATON
KEBABS
KEBOBS
KEDGED
KEDGES
KEELED
KEELER
KEENAN
KEENED
KEENEN
KEENER
KEENLY
KEEPAT
KEEPER
KEEPIN
KEEPON
KEEPTO
KEEPUP
KEGGED
KEGLER
KEITEL
KELLER
KELLEY
KELPIE
KELSEY
KELVIN
KEMPIS
KENNED
KENNEL
KENNYG
KENTON
KENYAN
KEPLER
KEPTAT
KEPTON
KEPTUP
KERALA
KERMAN
KERMES
KERMIS
KERMIT
KERNED
KERNEL
KERNOI
KERNOS
KERSEY
KESHIA
KETONE
KETTLE
KEVELS
KEVLAR
KEWPIE
KEYING
KEYNES
KEYPAD
KEYSIN
KEYSUP
KEYWAY

K•E•••
KEELED
KEELER
KEENAN
KEENED
KEENEN
KEENER
KEENLY
KEEPAT
KEEPER
KEEPIN
KEEPON
KEEPTO
KEEPUP
KIEFER
KLEIST
KMESON
KNEADS
KNEELS
KNELLS
KPELLE
KRESGE
KVELLS
KVETCH

K••E••
KAGERA
KAREEM
KEVELS
KHMERS
KITERS
KNEELS
KOPECK
KOPEKS
KOREAN

K•••E•
KAISER
KANDER
KAREEM
KAYOED
KEDGED
KEDGES
KEELED
KEELER
KEENED
KEENEN
KEENER
KEEPER
KEGGED
KEGLER
KEITEL
KELLER
KELLEY
KELSEY
KENNED
KENNEL
KEPLER
KERMES
KERNED
KERNEL
KERSEY
KEYNES
KHYBER
KICKED
KICKER
KIDDED
KIDDER
KIDNEY
KIEFER
KILLED
KILLER
KILMER
KILNED
KILTED
KILTER
KINDER
KINGED
KINKED
KIPPER
KISLEV
KISMET
KISSED
KISSER
KISSES
KITTEN
KJOLEN
KNAVES
KNIFED
KNIFES
KNIVES
KNOWER
KOHLER
KOPJES
KOPPEL
KOSHER
KOTTER
KRAKEN
KRAMER
KRATER
KRONER
KRUGER
KUCHEN
KUMMEL

K••••E
KALINE
KARATE
KATHIE
KELPIE
KETONE
KETTLE
KEWPIE
KHAFRE
KIBBLE
KILTIE
KINDLE
KINGME
KIRTLE
KISHKE
KLUDGE
KOOKIE
KPELLE
KRESGE
KURILE

•KE•••
AKELAS
AKENES
EKEOUT
OKEEFE
OKELLY
SKEANS
SKEINS
SKERRY
SKETCH
SKEWED
SKEWER

•K•E••
EKBERG
OKEEFE
SKIERS

•K••E•
AKENES
OKAYED
SKATED
SKATER
SKATES
SKEWED
SKEWER
SKIVED
SKIVER
SKIVES
UKASES

•K•••E
OKEEFE
SKOKIE
SKOPJE

••KE••
ALKENE
ASKERS
BAKERS
BAKERY
BEKESY
BIKERS
ESKERS
FAKERS
FAKERY
HIKERS
INKERS
JOKERS
LAKERS
LIKELY
LIKENS
MAKEDO
MAKEIT
MAKERS
MAKEUP
PIKERS
POKEAT
POKERS
POKERY
POKEYS
RAKEIN
RAKERS
RAKEUP
REKEYS
SAKERS
TAKEIN
TAKEON
TAKERS
TAKETH
TAKETO
TAKEUP
TOKENS
UPKEEP
WAKENS
WAKEUP
WOKEUP
YOKELS

••K•E•
ANKLED
ANKLES
ANKLET
AUKLET
FOKKER
HOKIER
ICKIER
INKIER
INKLES
MCKUEN
OAKLEY
ORKNEY
PEKOES
POKIER
UPKEEP
YAKKED
YAKKER
YUKKED

••K••E
ALKENE
PIKAKE

•••KE•
AWAKED
AWAKEN
AWAKES
AWOKEN
BACKED
BACKER
BALKED
BANKED
BANKER
BARKED
BARKER
BASKED
BASKET
BEAKED
BEAKER
BECKER
BECKET
BICKER
BILKED
BLOKES
BOOKED
BOOKER
BOSKET
BRAKED
BRAKES
BROKEN
BROKER
BUCKED
BUCKET
BULKED
BUNKED
BUNKER
CALKED
CANKER
CHOKED
CHOKER
CHOKES
CISKEI
COCKED
COCKER
CONKED
CONKER
COOKED
COOKER
CORKED
CORKER
CRAKES
DANKER
DARKEN
DARKER
DECKED
DECKER
DICKER
DICKEY
DINKEY
DISKED
DOCKED
DOCKER
DOCKET
DONKEY
DRAKES
DUCKED
DUIKER
DUNKED
DUNKER
EVOKED
EVOKER
EVOKES
FAWKES
FINKED
FLAKED
FLAKER
FLAKES
FLUKES
FOKKER
FORKED
FORKER
FUNKED
GASKET
GAWKED
GAWKER
HACKED
HACKER
HANKER
HARKED
HARKEN
HARKER
HAWKED
HAWKER
HICKEY
HOCKED
HOCKEY
HONKED
HONKER
HOOKED
HULKED
HUNKER
HUSKED
HUSKER
JACKED
JACKET
JERKED
JINKED
JOCKEY
JUNKED
JUNKER
JUNKET
KICKED
KICKER
KINKED
KRAKEN
LACKED
LACKEY
LANKER
LARKED
LATKES
LEAKED
LEAKER
LEAKEY
LICKED
LINKED
LINKER
LOCKED
LOCKER
LOCKET
LOOKED
LOOKER
LOWKEY
LUCKED
LUNKER
LURKED
MARKED
MARKER
MARKET
MASKED
MASKER
MEEKER
MERKEL
MICKEY
MILKED
MILKER
MINKES
MOCKED
MOCKER
MONKEY
MUCKED
MUSKEG
MUSKET
NECKED
NICKED
NICKEL
NICKER
OFFKEY
OINKED
PACKED
PACKER
PACKET
PARKED
PARKER
PEAKED
PECKED
PEEKED
PERKED
PICKED
PICKER
PICKET
PINKED
PINKEN

PINKER
POCKET
PORKER
PUCKER
PUNKER
QUAKED
QUAKER
QUAKES
RACKED
RACKET
RANKED
RANKER
REEKED
RICKED
RICKEY
RIPKEN
RISKED
RISKER
ROCKED
ROCKER
ROCKET
ROOKED
RUCKED
SACKED
SACKER
SECKEL
SEEKER
SHAKEN
SHAKER
SHAKES
SHEKEL
SICKEN
SICKER
SILKED
SILKEN
SINKER
SISKEL
SLAKED
SLAKES
SMOKED
SMOKER
SMOKES
SMOKEY
SNAKED
SNAKES
SOAKED
SOAKER
SOCKED
SOCKET
SPIKED
SPIKER
SPIKES
SPOKED
SPOKEN
SPOKES
STAKED
STAKES
STOKED
STOKER
STOKES
SUCKED
SUCKER
SULKED
SULKER
SUNKEN
TACKED
TACKER
TALKED
TALKER
TANKED
TANKER
TASKED
TEDKEY
TERKEL
TICKED
TICKER
TICKET
TINKER
TRIKES
TUCKED
TUCKER
TUCKET
TURKEY
TUSKED
TUSKER
WALKED
WALKER
WEAKEN
WEAKER
WICKED
WICKER
WICKET
WILKES
WINKED
WINKER
WORKED
WORKER
YAKKED
YAKKER
YANKED
YANKEE
YERKES
YOLKED
YORKER
YUKKED
ZONKED
ZONKER

•••K•E

BOOKIE
BUCKLE
CACKLE
COCKLE
COOKIE
DARKLE
DECKLE
FICKLE
FOLKIE
HACKIE
HACKLE
HANKIE
HECKLE
JACKIE
JECKLE
JUNKIE
KOOKIE
MUSKIE
PICKLE
PINKIE
PUNKIE
RANKLE
ROCKNE
ROOKIE
SICKLE
SKOKIE
TACKLE
TALKIE
TICKLE
TINKLE
WALKIE
WINKIE
WINKLE
WOOKIE
YANKEE

••••KE

BETAKE
BOURKE
BROOKE
CLARKE
GRIMKE
INJOKE
INTAKE
INVOKE
JAMOKE
KISHKE
MOLTKE
PERUKE
PIKAKE
REBUKE
REMAKE
RETAKE
REVOKE
SHRIKE
STLUKE
STRAKE
STRIKE
STROKE
THICKE
UNLIKE
UNMAKE
UNYOKE
UPDIKE
UPTAKE

K•F•••

KAFFIR

K••F••

KAFFIR
KHAFRE
KIEFER
KITFOX
KNIFED
KNIFES
KOUFAX

K•••F•

KLOOFS
KUNGFU

K••••F

KINDOF

•K•F••

SKIFFS

•K••F•

OKEEFE
SKIFFS

••KF••

ASKFOR

K•G•••

KAGERA
KEGGED
KEGLER
KIGALI

K••G••

KEDGED
KEDGES
KEGGED
KINGED
KINGLY
KINGME
KNIGHT
KRUGER
KUNGFU
KURGAN

K•••G•

KIANGS
KLUDGE
KRESGE

K••••G

KDLANG
KENNYG
KEYING
KITBAG
KITING

•K•••G

EKBERG
SKIING
SKYING

••K••G

ASKING
BAKING
BBKING
BIKING
CAKING
DIKING
DUKING
FAKING
HIKING
INKING
IRKING
JOKING
JUKING
LIKING
MAKING
MEKONG
MIKING
NUKING
PEKING
PIKING
POKING
RAKING
TAKING
VIKING
WAKING
YOKING

•••KG•

GINKGO

•••K•G

MUSKEG

KH••••

KHAFRE
KHAKIS
KHALID
KHMERS
KHYBER

K•H•••

KAHLIL
KAHLUA
KAHUNA
KOHLER

K••H••

KATHIE
KESHIA
KISHKE
KOSHER
KUCHEN

K•••H•

KIMCHI
KNIGHT
KWACHA
KYUSHU

K••••H

KALAKH
KASBAH
KAZAKH
KIBOSH
KIRSCH
KITSCH
KLATCH
KVETCH

•K•••H

SKETCH
SKITCH

••K••H

RAKISH
SUKKAH
TAKETH

•••KH•

GURKHA

•••K•H

HOOKAH
PUNKAH
SUKKAH

••••KH

KALAKH
KAZAKH
SAMEKH

KI••••

KIANGS
KIBBLE
KIBITZ
KIBOSH
KICKED
KICKER
KICKIN
KICKUP
KIDDED
KIDDER
KIDMAN
KIDNAP
KIDNEY
KIDORY
KIDVID
KIEFER
KIGALI
KIKUYU
KILIMS
KILLED
KILLER
KILMER
KILNED
KILTED
KILTER
KILTIE
KIMCHI
KIMONO
KINDER
KINDLE
KINDLY
KINDOF
KINGED
KINGLY
KINGME
KINKED
KINSKI
KIOSKS
KIOWAS
KIPPER
KIPPUR
KIRMAN
KIRSCH
KIRTLE
KISHKE
KISLEV
KISMET
KISSED
KISSER
KISSES
KITBAG
KITERS
KITFOX
KITING
KITKAT
KITSCH
KITTEN

K•I•••

KAILUA
KAISER
KEITEL
KLIBAN
KNICKS
KNIFED
KNIFES
KNIGHT
KNIVES

K••I••

KALINE
KARIBA
KEYING
KIBITZ
KILIMS
KITING
KLEIST
KODIAK
KONICA
KRAITS
KUMISS
KURILE

K•••I•

KAFFIR
KAHLIL
KAOLIN
KARMIC
KATHIE
KAURIS
KEEPIN
KELPIE
KELVIN
KEMPIS
KERMIS
KERMIT
KESHIA
KEWPIE
KEYSIN
KHAKIS
KHALID
KICKIN
KIDVID
KILTIE
KOOKIE
KUKRIS
KUWAIT

K••••I

KABUKI
KATMAI
KERNOI
KIGALI
KIMCHI
KINSKI
KUBLAI

•KI•••

AKIMBO
AKITAS
SKIERS
SKIFFS
SKIING
SKILLS
SKIMPS
SKIMPY
SKINKS
SKINNY
SKIPPY
SKIRLS
SKIROS
SKIRRS
SKIRTS
SKIRUN
SKITCH
SKITOW
SKIVED
SKIVER
SKIVES
SKIVVY

•K•I••

SKEINS
SKIING
SKYING

•K••I•

OKAPIS
SKOKIE

••KI••

AIKIDO
ASKING
ATKINS
BAKING
BBKING
BIKING
BIKINI
CAKING
DIKING
DUKING
ESKIMO
FAKING
FAKIRS
HAKIMS
HIKING
HOKIER
ICKIER
INKIER
INKIND
INKING
IRKING
JOKING
JUKING
LIKING
MAKING
MIKING
MIKITA
NIKITA
NUKING
PEKING
PIKING
POKIER
POKILY
POKING
RAKING
RAKISH
TAKING
TAKINS
UNKIND
UNKINK
VIKING
WAKING
YAKIMA
YOKING

••K•I•

DIKDIK
KUKRIS
MAKEIT
PYKNIC
RAKEIN
SIKKIM
TAKEIN
UNKNIT

••K••I

ALKALI
ASKARI
BIKINI
UAKARI

•••KI•

ABUKIR
BACKIN
BARKIN
BODKIN
BOOKIE
BUSKIN
CATKIN
COOKIE
CULKIN
ENOKIS
FIRKIN
FOLKIE
GASKIN
HACKIE
HANKIE
JACKIE
JERKIN
JUNKIE
KHAKIS
KICKIN
KOOKIE
LOCKIN
LOOKIN
MALKIN
MUSKIE
NAPKIN
NUTKIN
PINKIE
PIPKIN
PUNKIE
RANKIN
ROOKIE
RUSKIN
SERKIN
SIKKIM
SINKIN
SISKIN
SKOKIE
SOCKIN
SUCKIN
TALKIE
TONKIN
TOOKIN
TOOKIT
TUCKIN
TURKIC
WALKIE
WALKIN
WELKIN
WESKIT
WINKIE
WOOKIE
WORKIN

•••K•I

BHAKTI
CISKEI
SHAKTI

••••KI

ADZUKI
EVENKI
HIDEKI
ITHAKI
JETSKI
KABUKI
KINSKI
SALUKI
SUZUKI

KJ••••

KJOLEN

K••J••

KOPJES

•K••J•

SKOPJE

K•K•••

KAKAPO
KIKUYU
KOKOMO
KUKRIS

K••K••

KALKAN
KHAKIS
KICKED
KICKER
KICKIN
KICKUP
KINKED
KITKAT
KOOKIE
KRAKEN
KRAKOW

K•••K•

KABUKI
KALAKH
KANAKA
KAYAKS
KAZAKH
KAZAKS
KINSKI
KIOSKS
KISHKE
KNACKS
KNICKS
KNOCKS
KOPEKS
KULAKS
KYACKS

K••••K

KARNAK
KODIAK
KOPECK

•K•K••

SKOKIE

•K••K•

AKUAKU
SKINKS
SKULKS
SKUNKS

••KK••

FOKKER
SIKKIM
SUKKAH
YAKKED
YAKKER
YUKKED

••K•K•

PIKAKE

••K••K

ACKACK
DIKDIK
MUKLUK
UNKINK

•••KK•

CHUKKA
MARKKA
QUOKKA

•••K•K

HICKOK

KL••••

KLATCH
KLAXON
KLEIST
KLIBAN
KLOOFS
KLUDGE
KLUTZY

K•L•••

KALAKH
KALINE
KALKAN
KALMAR
KDLANG
KELLER
KELLEY
KELPIE
KELSEY
KELVIN
KILIMS
KILLED
KILLER
KILMER
KILNED
KILTED
KILTER
KILTIE
KULAKS
KULTUR

K••L••

KAHLIL
KAHLUA
KAILUA
KAOLIN
KAPLAN
KEELED
KEELER
KEGLER
KELLER
KELLEY
KEPLER
KEVLAR
KHALID
KILLED
KILLER
KISLEV
KJOLEN
KNELLS
KNOLLS
KOALAS
KOHLER
KPELLE
KUBLAI
KUNLUN
KVELLS

K•••L•

KAMALA
KEENLY
KERALA
KETTLE
KEVELS
KIBBLE
KIGALI
KINDLE
KINDLY
KINGLY
KIRTLE
KNEELS
KNELLS
KNOLLS
KNURLS
KNURLY
KOBOLD
KODALY
KPELLE
KRAALS
KURALT
KURILE
KVELLS

K••••L

KAHLIL
KEITEL
KENNEL
KERNEL
KOPPEL
KUMMEL

•K•L••

AKELAS
OKELLY
SKALDS
SKILLS
SKULKS
SKULLS
SKYLAB

•K••L•

OKELLY
SKILLS
SKIRLS
SKULLS

••KL••

ANKLED
ANKLES
ANKLET
AUKLET
INKLES
MUKLUK
OAKLEY
TOKLAS

••K•L•

ALKALI
ALKYLS
DEKALB
JEKYLL
LIKELY
MAKALU
NIKOLA
POKILY
YOKELS

••K••L

JEKYLL

•••KL•

BUCKLE
CACKLE
COCKLE
DARKLE
DARKLY
DECKLE
FICKLE
HACKLE
HECKLE
JECKLE
LANKLY
MEEKLY
PICKLE
RANKLE
RANKLY
SICKLE
SICKLY
TACKLE
TICKLE
TINKLE
TINKLY
WEAKLY
WEEKLY
WINKLE

•••K•L

BAIKAL
JACKAL
MERKEL
NICKEL
SECKEL
SHEKEL
SISKEL
TERKEL

KM••••

KMESON

K•M•••

KAMALA
KEMPIS
KHMERS
KIMCHI
KIMONO
KOMODO
KUMISS
KUMMEL

K••M••

KALMAR
KARMIC
KATMAI
KERMAN
KERMES
KERMIS
KERMIT
KIDMAN
KILMER
KIRMAN
KISMET
KORMAN
KRAMER
KUMMEL

K•••M•

KILIMS
KINGME
KOKOMO

K••••M

KABOOM
KAREEM

•K•M••

AKIMBO
SKIMPS
SKIMPY

••K•M•

ESKIMO
HAKIMS
KOKOMO
YAKIMA

••K••M

SIKKIM

•••K•M

BUNKUM
SIKKIM

KN••••

KNACKS
KNARRY
KNAVES
KNEADS
KNEELS
KNELLS
KNICKS
KNIFED
KNIFES
KNIGHT
KNIVES
KNOBBY
KNOCKS
KNOLLS
KNOTTS
KNOTTY
KNOWER
KNOWNS
KNURLS
KNURLY

K•N•••

KANAKA
KANDER
KANSAN
KANSAS
KANTOR
KENNED
KENNEL
KENNYG
KENTON
KENYAN
KINDER
KINDLE
KINDLY
KINDOF
KINGED
KINGLY
KINGME
KINKED
KINSKI
KONICA
KONRAD
KUNGFU
KUNLUN

K••N••

KARNAK
KAUNAS
KAUNDA
KEENAN
KEENED
KEENEN
KEENER
KEENLY
KENNED
KENNEL
KENNYG
KERNED
KERNEL
KERNOI
KERNOS
KEYNES
KIANGS
KIDNAP
KIDNEY
KILNED
KOONTZ
KRANTZ
KRONER
KRONOR
KRONUR
KWANZA

K•••N•

KAHUNA
KALINE
KDLANG
KETONE
KEYING
KIMONO
KITING
KNOWNS
KORUNA

K••••N

KALKAN
KANSAN
KAOLIN
KAPLAN
KEATON
KEENAN
KEENEN
KEEPIN
KEEPON
KELVIN
KENTON
KENYAN
KEPTON
KERMAN
KEYSIN
KICKIN
KIDMAN
KIRMAN
KITTEN
KJOLEN
KLAXON
KLIBAN
KMESON
KOREAN
KORMAN
KRAKEN
KUCHEN
KUNLUN
KURGAN

•K•N••

AKENES
SKINKS
SKINNY
SKUNKS

•K••N•

SKEANS
SKEINS
SKIING
SKINNY
SKYING

•K•••N

SKIRUN

••KN••

ORKNEY
PYKNIC
UNKNIT
UNKNOT

••K•N•

ALKENE
ASKING
ATKINS
BAKING
BBKING
BIKING
BIKINI
CAKING
DIKING
DUKING
FAKING
HIKING
INKIND
INKING
IRKING
JOKING
JUKING
LIKENS
LIKING
MAKING
MEKONG
MIKING
NUKING
PEKING
PIKING
POKING
RAKING
TAKING
TAKINS
TOKENS
UNKIND
UNKINK
VIKING
WAKENS
WAKING
YOKING

••K••N

MCKUEN
NEKTON
RAKEIN
TAKEIN
TAKEON

•••KN•

ROCKNE

•••K•N
AWAKEN
AWOKEN
BACKIN
BALKAN
BANKON
BARKIN
BECKON
BODKIN
BROKEN
BUSKIN
CATKIN
CULKIN
DAIKON
DARKEN
FIRKIN
GASKIN
HARKEN
JERKIN
KALKAN
KICKIN
KRAKEN
LOCKIN
LOOKIN
LOOKON
MALKIN
NAPKIN
NUTKIN
PICKON
PINKEN
PIPKIN
RANKIN
RECKON
RIPKEN
RUSKIN
RYOKAN
SERKIN
SHAKEN
SICKEN
SILKEN
SINKIN
SISKIN
SOCKIN
SPOKEN
SUCKIN
SUNKEN
TACKON
TONKIN
TOOKIN
TOOKON
TUCKIN
WALKIN
WALKON
WEAKEN
WELKIN
WORKIN
WORKON

KO••••
KOALAS
KOBOLD
KODALY
KODIAK
KOHLER
KOKOMO
KOMODO
KONICA
KONRAD
KOOKIE
KOONTZ
KOPECK
KOPEKS
KOPJES
KOPPEL
KORATS
KORBUT
KOREAN
KORMAN
KORUNA
KOSHER
KOTTER
KOUFAX
KOVACS
KOWTOW

K•O•••
KAOLIN
KIOSKS
KIOWAS
KJOLEN
KLOOFS
KNOBBY
KNOCKS
KNOLLS
KNOTTS
KNOTTY
KNOWER
KNOWNS
KOOKIE
KOONTZ
KRONER
KRONOR
KRONUR

K••O••
KABOBS
KABOOM
KAROSS
KAYOED
KAZOOS
KEBOBS
KETONE
KIBOSH
KIDORY
KIMONO
KLOOFS
KOBOLD
KOKOMO
KOMODO

K•••O•
KABOOM
KANTOR
KARPOV
KARROO
KAZOOS
KEATON
KEEPON
KENTON
KEPTON
KERNOI
KERNOS
KINDOF
KITFOX
KLAXON
KMESON
KOWTOW
KRAKOW
KRONOR

K••••O
KAKAPO
KARROO
KEEPTO
KIMONO
KOKOMO
KOMODO

•KO•••
SKOKIE
SKOPJE

•K•O••
EKEOUT

•K••O•
SKIROS
SKITOW
SKYBOX

•K•••O
AKIMBO

••KO••
ASKOUT
DAKOTA
KOKOMO
LAKOTA
MEKONG
NIKOLA
PEKOES

••K•O•
ASKFOR
HYKSOS
NEKTON
TAKEON
UNKNOT

••K••O
AIKIDO
ESKIMO
KAKAPO
KOKOMO
MAKEDO
MIKADO
TAKETO

•••KO•
ANGKOR
BANKON
BECKON
BUNKOS
CUCKOO
DAIKON
GECKOS
HAIKOU
HICKOK
KRAKOW
LOOKON
MUSKOX
PICKON
RECKON
SHAKOS
TACKON
TOOKON
WALKON
WORKON
ZHUKOV

•••K•O
CUCKOO
GINKGO
LOOKTO
TALKTO
TOOKTO

••••KO
BAMAKO
MARIKO
ROTHKO
STOJKO

KP••••
KPELLE

K•P•••
KAPLAN
KAPPAS
KEPLER
KEPTAT
KEPTON
KEPTUP
KIPPER
KIPPUR
KOPECK
KOPEKS
KOPJES
KOPPEL

K••P••
KAPPAS
KARPOV
KEEPAT
KEEPER
KEEPIN
KEEPON
KEEPTO
KEEPUP
KELPIE
KEMPIS
KEWPIE
KEYPAD
KIPPER
KIPPUR
KOPPEL

K•••P•
KAKAPO

K••••P
KEEPUP
KEPTUP
KEYSUP
KICKUP
KIDNAP

•K•P••
OKAPIS
SKIPPY
SKOPJE

•K••P•
SKIMPS
SKIMPY
SKIPPY

•K•••P
SKYCAP

••K•P•
KAKAPO

••K••P
MAKEUP
RAKEUP
TAKEUP
UPKEEP
WAKEUP
WOKEUP

•••K•P
BACKUP
BUCKUP
COOKUP
HOOKUP
JACKUP
KICKUP
LINKUP
LOCKUP
LOOKUP
MARKUP
MOCKUP
MUCKUP
PACKUP
PERKUP
PICKUP
RACKUP
SOAKUP
TALKUP
TANKUP
TOOKUP
WALKUP
WORKUP

KR••••
KRAALS
KRAITS
KRAKEN
KRAKOW
KRAMER
KRANTZ
KRATER
KRESGE
KRONER
KRONOR
KRONUR
KRUGER

K•R•••
KARATE
KARATS
KAREEM
KARIBA
KARMIC
KARNAK
KAROSS
KARPOV
KARRAS
KARROO
KARSTS
KERALA
KERMAN
KERMES
KERMIS
KERMIT
KERNED
KERNEL
KERNOI
KERNOS
KERSEY
KIRMAN
KIRSCH
KIRTLE
KORATS
KORBUT
KOREAN
KORMAN
KORUNA
KURALT
KURGAN
KURILE

K••R••
KARRAS
KARROO
KAURIS
KNARRY
KNURLS
KNURLY
KONRAD
KUKRIS

K•••R•
KAGERA
KHAFRE
KHMERS
KIDORY
KITERS
KNARRY

K••••R
KAFFIR
KAISER
KALMAR
KANDER
KANTOR
KEELER
KEENER
KEEPER
KEGLER
KELLER
KEPLER
KEVLAR
KHYBER
KICKER
KIDDER
KIEFER
KILLER
KILMER
KILTER
KINDER
KIPPER
KIPPUR
KISSER
KNOWER
KOHLER
KOSHER
KOTTER
KRAMER
KRATER
KRONER
KRONOR
KRONUR
KRUGER
KULTUR

•K•R••
SKERRY
SKIRLS
SKIROS
SKIRRS
SKIRTS
SKIRUN

•K••R•
EKBERG
SKERRY
SKIERS
SKIRRS

•K•••R
SKATER
SKEWER
SKIVER

••KR••
KUKRIS

••K•R•
ANKARA
ASKARI
ASKERS
BAKERS
BAKERY
BIKERS
ESKERS
FAKERS
FAKERY
FAKIRS
GOKART
HIKERS
INKERS
JOKERS
LAKERS
MAKERS
PIKERS
POKERS
POKERY
RAKERS
SAKERS
TAKERS
UAKARI

••K••R
ASKFOR
FOKKER
HOKIER
ICKIER
INKIER
LEKVAR
POKIER
YAKKER

•••K•R
ABUKIR
ANGKOR
BACKER
BANKER
BARKER
BEAKER
BECKER
BICKER
BOOKER
BROKER
BUNKER
CANKER
CHOKER
CHUKAR
COCKER
CONKER
COOKER
CORKER
DANKER
DARKER
DECKER
DICKER
DOCKER
DUIKER
DUNKER
EVOKER
FLAKER
FOKKER
FORKER
GAWKER
HACKER
HANKER
HARKER
HAWKER
HONKER
HUNKER
HUSKER
JUNKER
KICKER
LANKER
LEAKER
LINKER
LOCKER
LOOKER
LUNKER
MARKER
MASKER
MEEKER
MILKER
MOCKER
NICKER
PACKER
PARKER
PICKER
PINKER
PORKER
PUCKER
PUNKER
QUAKER
RANKER
RISKER
ROCKER
SACKER
SEEKER
SHAKER
SICKER
SINKER
SMOKER
SOAKER
SPIKER
STOKER
SUCKER
SULKER
TACKER
TALKER
TANKER
TICKER
TINKER
TUCKER
TUSKER
WALKER
WEAKER
WICKER
WINKER
WORKER
YAKKER
YORKER
ZONKER

K•S•••
KASBAH
KESHIA
KISHKE
KISLEV
KISMET
KISSED
KISSER
KISSES
KOSHER

K••S••
KAISER
KANSAN
KANSAS
KARSTS
KELSEY
KERSEY
KEYSIN
KEYSUP
KINSKI
KIOSKS
KIRSCH
KISSED
KISSER
KISSES
KITSCH
KMESON
KRESGE
KYUSHU

K•••S•
KAROSS
KIBOSH
KLEIST
KUMISS
KUVASZ

K••••S
KABOBS
KANSAS
KAPPAS
KARATS
KAROSS
KARRAS
KARSTS
KAUNAS
KAURIS
KAYAKS
KAZAKS
KAZOOS
KEBABS
KEBOBS
KEDGES
KEMPIS
KERMES
KERMIS
KERNOS
KEVELS
KEYNES
KHAKIS
KHMERS
KIANGS
KILIMS
KIOSKS
KIOWAS
KISSES
KITERS
KLOOFS
KNACKS
KNAVES
KNEADS
KNEELS
KNELLS
KNICKS
KNIFES
KNIVES
KNOCKS
KNOLLS
KNOTTS
KNOWNS
KNURLS
KOALAS
KOPEKS
KOPJES
KORATS
KOVACS
KRAALS
KRAITS
KUDZUS
KUKRIS
KULAKS
KUMISS
KVELLS
KYACKS

•K•S••
UKASES

•K•••S
AKELAS
AKENES
AKITAS
OKAPIS
SKALDS
SKATES
SKEANS
SKEINS
SKIERS
SKIFFS
SKILLS
SKIMPS
SKINKS
SKIRLS
SKIROS
SKIRRS
SKIRTS
SKIVES
SKULKS
SKULLS
SKUNKS
UKASES

••KS••
HYKSOS

••K•S•
BEKESY
RAKISH

••K••S
ALKYDS
ALKYLS
ANKLES
ASKERS
ATKINS
BAKERS
BIKERS
ESKERS
FAKERS
FAKIRS
HAKIMS
HIKERS
HYKSOS
INKERS
INKLES
JOKERS
KUKRIS
LAKERS
LIKENS
MAKERS
PEKOES
PIKERS
POKERS
POKEYS
RAKERS
REKEYS
SAKERS
TAKERS
TAKINS
TOKAYS
TOKENS
TOKLAS
WAKENS
YAKUTS
YOKELS
YOKUTS

•••KS•
FOLKSY

•••K•S
AWAKES
BABKAS
BACKUS
BLOKES
BRAKES
BUNKOS
CHOKES
CRAKES
DRAKES
ENOKIS
EVOKES
FAWKES
FLAKES
FLUKES
GECKOS
HAIKUS
KHAKIS
LATKES
MINKES
PARKAS
POLKAS
QUAKES
RUCKUS
SHAKES
SHAKOS
SLAKES
SMOKES
SNAKES
SPIKES
SPOKES
STAKES
STOKES
TANKAS
TRIKES
WILKES
YERKES

••••KS
BATIKS
BLACKS
BLANKS
BLINKS
BLOCKS
BREAKS
BRICKS
BRINKS
BROOKS
CAULKS
CHALKS
CHECKS
CHEEKS
CHICKS
CHINKS
CHOCKS
CHUCKS
CHUNKS
CLACKS
CLANKS
CLEEKS
CLERKS
CLICKS
CLINKS
CLOAKS
CLOCKS
CLONKS
CLUCKS
CLUNKS
CRACKS
CRANKS
CREAKS
CREEKS
CRICKS
CROAKS
CROCKS
CROOKS
DRINKS
FLACKS
FLANKS
FLASKS
FLECKS
FLICKS
FLOCKS
FLUNKS
FRANKS
FREAKS
FRISKS
FROCKS
GREEKS
HACEKS
KAYAKS
KAZAKS
KIOSKS
KNACKS
KNICKS
KNOCKS
KOPEKS
KULAKS
KYACKS
MIWOKS
OZARKS
PLANKS
PLINKS
PLONKS
PLUCKS
PLUNKS
PRANKS
PRICKS
PRINKS
QUACKS
QUARKS
QUIRKS
REINKS
SHACKS
SHANKS
SHARKS
SHEIKS
SHIRKS
SHOCKS
SHOOKS
SHUCKS
SKINKS
SKULKS
SKUNKS
SLACKS
SLEEKS
SLICKS
SLINKS
SMACKS
SMIRKS
SMOCKS
SNACKS
SNEAKS
SNICKS
SNOOKS
SPANKS
SPARKS
SPEAKS
SPECKS
SPINKS
SPOOKS
STACKS
STALKS
STEAKS
STICKS
STINKS
STOCKS
STORKS
THANKS
THINKS
THUNKS
TILAKS
TRACKS
TRICKS
TRUCKS
TRUNKS
TWEAKS
UMIAKS
UZBEKS
VNECKS
WHACKS
WHELKS
WHISKS
WRACKS
WREAKS
WRECKS
YAPOKS
YOICKS
YUROKS

K•T•••
KATHIE
KATMAI
KETONE
KETTLE
KITBAG
KITERS
KITFOX
KITING
KITKAT
KITSCH
KITTEN
KOTTER

K••T••
KANTOR
KEATON
KEITEL
KENTON
KEPTAT
KEPTON
KEPTUP
KETTLE
KILTED
KILTER
KILTIE
KIRTLE
KITTEN
KLATCH
KLUTZY
KNOTTS
KNOTTY
KOTTER
KOWTOW
KRATER
KULTUR
KVETCH

K•••T•
KARATE
KARATS
KARSTS
KEEPTO
KIBITZ
KNOTTS
KNOTTY
KOONTZ
KORATS
KRAITS
KRANTZ

K••••T
KEEPAT
KEPTAT
KERMIT
KISMET
KITKAT
KLEIST
KNIGHT
KORBUT
KURALT
KUWAIT

•K•T••
AKITAS
SKATED
SKATER
SKATES
SKETCH
SKITCH
SKITOW

•K••T•
SKIRTS

•K•••T
EKEOUT

••KT••
DIKTAT
NEKTON

••K•T•
DAKOTA
LAKOTA
MAKUTA
MIKITA
NIKITA
TAKETH
TAKETO
YAKUTS
YOKUTS
YUKATA

••K••T
ANKLET
ASKOUT
AUKLET
DIKTAT
GOKART
MAKEIT
POKEAT
UNKNIT
UNKNOT

•••KT•
BHAKTI
LOOKTO
SHAKTI
TALKTO
TOOKTO

•••K•T
BASKET
BECKET
BOSKET
BUCKET
DOCKET
GASKET
JACKET
JUNKET
KITKAT
LOCKET
LOOKAT
MARKET
MUSKET
PACKET
PECKAT
PEEKAT
PICKAT
PICKET
POCKET
RACKET
ROCKET
SOCKET
TALKAT
TICKET
TOOKIT
TUCKET
WESKIT
WICKET
WINKAT

KU••••
KUBLAI
KUCHEN
KUDZUS
KUKRIS
KULAKS
KULTUR
KUMISS
KUMMEL
KUNGFU
KUNLUN
KURALT
KURGAN
KURILE
KUVASZ
KUWAIT

K•U•••
KAUNAS
KAUNDA
KAURIS
KLUDGE
KLUTZY
KNURLS
KNURLY
KOUFAX
KRUGER
KYUSHU

K••U••
KABUKI
KAHUNA
KIKUYU
KORUNA

K•••U•
KAHLUA
KAILUA
KEEPUP
KEPTUP
KEYSUP
KICKUP
KIPPUR
KORBUT
KRONUR
KUDZUS
KULTUR
KUNLUN

K••••U
KIKUYU
KUNGFU
KYUSHU

•KU•••
AKUAKU
SKULKS
SKULLS
SKUNKS

•K••U•
EKEOUT
SKIRUN

•K•••U
AKUAKU

••KU••
KIKUYU
MAKUTA
MCKUEN
YAKUTS
YOKUTS

••K•U•
ASKOUT
MAKEUP
MUKLUK
RAKEUP
TAKEUP
WAKEUP
WOKEUP

••K••U
KIKUYU
MAKALU

•••KU•
BACKUP
BACKUS
BUCKUP
BUNKUM
COOKUP
HAIKUS
HOOKUP
JACKUP
KICKUP
LINKUP
LOCKUP
LOOKUP
MARKUP
MOCKUP
MUCKUP
PACKUP
PERKUP
PICKUP
RACKUP
RUCKUS
SOAKUP
TALKUP
TANKUP
TOOKUP
WALKUP
WORKUP

•••K•U
HAIKOU
RYUKYU

••••KU
AKUAKU

KV••••
KVELLS
KVETCH

K•V•••
KEVELS
KEVLAR
KOVACS
KUVASZ

K••V••
KELVIN
KIDVID
KNAVES
KNIVES

K••••V
KARPOV
KISLEV

•K•V••
SKIVED
SKIVER
SKIVES
SKIVVY

•K••V•
SKIVVY

••KV••
LEKVAR

•••KV•
MOSKVA

•••K•V
ROCKYV
ZHUKOV

KW••••
KWACHA
KWANZA

K•W•••
KEWPIE
KOWTOW
KUWAIT

K••W••
KEYWAY
KIOWAS
KNOWER
KNOWNS

K••••W
KOWTOW
KRAKOW

•K•W••
SKEWED
SKEWER
SKYWAY

•K•••W
SKITOW

••K•W•
YUKAWA

•••K•W
BROKAW
KRAKOW

K••X••
KLAXON

K••••X
KITFOX
KOUFAX

•K•••X
SKYBOX

•••K•X
MUSKOX
PICKAX

KY••••
KYACKS
KYUSHU

K•Y•••
KAYAKS
KAYOED
KEYING
KEYNES
KEYPAD
KEYSIN
KEYSUP
KEYWAY
KHYBER

K••Y••
KENYAN

K•••Y•
KENNYG
KIKUYU

K••••Y
KEENLY
KELLEY
KELSEY
KERSEY
KEYWAY
KIDNEY
KIDORY
KINDLY
KINGLY
KLUTZY
KNARRY
KNOBBY
KNOTTY
KNURLY
KODALY

•KY•••
SKYBOX
SKYCAP
SKYING
SKYLAB
SKYWAY

•K•Y••
OKAYED

•K•••Y
OKELLY
SKERRY
SKIMPY
SKINNY
SKIPPY
SKIVVY
SKYWAY

••KY••
ALKYDS
ALKYLS
JEKYLL

••K•Y•
KIKUYU
POKEYS
REKEYS
TOKAYS

••K••Y
BAKERY
BEKESY
FAKERY
LIKELY
OAKLEY
ORKNEY
POKERY
POKILY

•••KY•
ROCKYV
RYUKYU

•••K•Y
DARKLY
DICKEY
DINKEY
DONKEY
FOLKSY
HICKEY
HOCKEY
JOCKEY
LACKEY
LANKLY
LEAKEY
LOWKEY
MEEKLY
MICKEY
MONKEY
OFFKEY
PARKAY
RANKLY
RICKEY
SICKLY
SMOKEY
TEDKEY
TINKLY
TURKEY
WEAKLY
WEEKLY

••••KY
ALECKY
BLOCKY
BRICKY
CHALKY
CHEEKY
CHINKY
CHUNKY
CLANKY
CLUNKY
CRANKY
CREAKY
CROAKY
FLUNKY
FREAKY
FRISKY
NEVSKY
PLUCKY
QUIRKY
RIMSKY
SLEEKY
SLINKY
SMIRKY
SNEAKY
SPANKY
SPARKY
SPOOKY
SPUNKY
STALKY
STANKY
STICKY
STINKY
STOCKY
SWANKY
TRICKY
WHACKY

K•Z•••
KAZAKH
KAZAKS
KAZOOS

K••Z••
KUDZUS

K•••Z•
KLUTZY
KWANZA

K••••Z
KIBITZ
KOONTZ
KRANTZ
KUVASZ

LA••••
LAAGER
LABELS
LABIAL
LABILE
LABORS
LABOUR
LABREA
LABRET
LABRUM
LACERS
LACEUP
LACHES
LACIER
LACING
LACKED
LACKEY
LACTIC
LACUNA
LADDER
LADDIE
LADERS
LADIDA
LADIES
LADING
LADINO
LADLED
LADLER
LADLES
LADOGA
LAFFER
LAGASH
LAGERS
LAGGED
LAGGER
LAGOON
LAGUNA
LAHORE
LAIDBY
LAIDIN
LAIDON
LAIDTO
LAIDUP
LAINIE
LAIRDS
LAKERS
LAKOTA
LALALA
LAMARR
LAMAZE
LAMBDA
LAMBED
LAMECH
LAMEDH
LAMEDS
LAMELY
LAMENT
LAMESA
LAMEST
LAMIAS
LAMINA
LAMING
LAMMAS
LAMMED
LAMONT
LAMOUR
LANAIS
LANATE
LANCED
LANCER
LANCES
LANCET
LANDAU
LANDED
LANDER
LANDHO
LANDIS
LANDON
LANDRY
LANGUR
LANIER
LANKER
LANKLY
LANOSE
LANSON
LANVIN
LAOTSE
LAOTZU
LAPDOG
LAPELS
LAPFUL
LAPHAM
LAPINS
LAPPED
LAPPET
LAPSED
LAPSES
LAPSUP
LAPTEV
LAPTOP
LAPUTA
LARAMS
LARDED
LARDER
LARDON
LAREDO
LARGER
LARGOS
LARIAT
LARKED
LAROSA
LARRUP
LARSEN
LARSON
LARVAE
LARVAL
LARVAS
LARYNX
LASCAR
LASERS
LASHED
LASHER
LASHES
LASHIO
LASHUP
LASSEN
LASSER
LASSES
LASSIE
LASSOS
LASTED
LASTEX
LASTLY
LATEEN
LATELY
LATENE
LATENS
LATENT
LATEST
LATHED
LATHER
LATHES
LATIGO
LATINA
LATINO
LATINS
LATISH
LATIUM
LATKES
LATONA
LATOUR
LATOYA
LATTEN
LATTER
LATVIA
LAUDED
LAUDER
LAUGHS
LAUNCH
LAUPER
LAUREL
LAUREN
LAURIE
LAVABO
LAVAGE
LAVERS
LAVING
LAVISH
LAWFUL
LAWING
LAWMAN
LAWMEN
LAWSON
LAWTON
LAWYER
LAXEST
LAXITY
LAYBYS
LAYERS
LAYFOR
LAYING
LAYLOW
LAYMAN
LAYMEN
LAYOFF
LAYOUT
LAYSBY
LAYSIN
LAYSON
LAYSTO
LAYSUP
LAYUPS
LAZBOY
LAZIER
LAZILY
LAZING
LAZULI

L•A•••
LAAGER
LEADED
LEADEN
LEADER
LEADIN
LEADON
LEADTO
LEADUP
LEAFED
LEAGUE
LEAKED
LEAKER
LEAKEY
LEALTY
LEANED
LEANER
LEANLY
LEANON
LEANTO
LEAPED
LEAPER
LEARNS
LEARNT
LEASED
LEASER
LEASES
LEAVED
LEAVEN
LEAVES
LIABLE
LIAISE
LIANAS
LIANGS
LLAMAS
LLANOS
LOADED
LOADER
LOAFED
LOAFER
LOAMED
LOANED
LOANER
LOATHE
LOAVES
LUANDA

L••A••
LAGASH
LALALA
LAMARR
LAMAZE
LANAIS
LANATE
LARAMS
LAVABO
LAVAGE
LCHAIM
LEGACY
LEGALS
LEGATE
LEGATO
LELAND
LEMANS
LENAPE
LESAGE
LEVANT
LIGATE
LILACS
LINAGE
LIPASE
LITANY
LIZARD
LOBATE
LOCALE
LOCALS
LOCATE
LOTAHS
LOVAGE
LUNACY
LUNATE
LUSAKA
LUXATE

L•••A•
LABIAL
LAMIAS
LAMMAS
LANDAU
LAPHAM
LARIAT
LARVAE
LARVAL
LARVAS
LASCAR
LAWMAN
LAYMAN
LEERAT
LEEWAY
LEGMAN
LEHUAS
LEKVAR
LEMMAS
LESTAT
LETHAL
LETSAT
LIANAS
LIBYAN
LINEAL
LINEAR
LLAMAS
LLBEAN
LOGJAM
LONGAN
LOOFAH
LOOKAT
LOQUAT
LOREAL
LOTHAR
LOWCAL
LOWFAT
LUCIAN
LUMBAR

L••••A
LABREA
LACUNA
LADIDA
LADOGA
LAGUNA
LAKOTA
LALALA
LAMBDA
LAMESA
LAMINA
LAPUTA
LAROSA
LATINA
LATONA
LATOYA
LATVIA
LERIDA
LEXICA
LIGULA
LINGUA
LIOTTA
LISBOA
LOGGIA
LOLITA
LORICA
LOUISA
LOYOLA
LUANDA
LUMINA
LUNULA
LUSAKA

•LA•••
ALAMOS
ALANON
ALARIC
ALARMS
ALARUM
ALASKA
ALATAU
BLABBY
BLACKS
BLADED
BLADES
BLAINE
BLAISE
BLAMED
BLAMES
BLANCA
BLANCH
BLANDA
BLANKS
BLARED
BLARES
BLASTS
BLATTY
BLAZED
BLAZER
BLAZES
BLAZON
CLACKS
CLAIMS
CLAIRE
CLAMMY
CLAMOR
CLAMPS
CLAMUP
CLANCY
CLANGS
CLANKS
CLANKY
CLAQUE
CLARET
CLARKE
CLAROS
CLASPS
CLASSY
CLAUDE
CLAUSE
CLAVIN
CLAWED
CLAWER
CLAYEY
DLAYER
ELAINE
ELANDS
ELAPID
ELAPSE
ELATED
ELATER
ELATES
ELAYER
ELAYNE
FLABBY
FLACKS
FLACON
FLAGGY
FLAGON
FLAILS
FLAIRS
FLAKED
FLAKER
FLAKES
FLAMBE
FLAMED
FLAMES
FLANGE
FLANKS
FLARED
FLARES
FLASHY
FLASKS
FLATLY
FLAUNT
FLAVIA
FLAVOR
FLAWED
FLAXEN
FLAXES
FLAYED
FLAYER
GLACES
GLACIS
GLADES
GLADLY
GLADYS
GLAIRY
GLAMOR
GLANCE
GLANDS
GLARED
GLARES
GLASER
GLASSY
GLAZED
GLAZER
GLAZES
KLATCH
KLAXON
LLAMAS
LLANOS
PLACED
PLACER
PLACES
PLACID
PLAGAL
PLAGES
PLAGIO
PLAGUE
PLAICE
PLAIDS
PLAINS
PLAINT
PLAITS
PLANAR
PLANCK
PLANED
PLANER
PLANES
PLANET
PLANKS
PLANON
PLANTE
PLANTS
PLAQUE
PLASHY
PLASMA
PLASMO
PLASTY
PLATED
PLATEN
PLATER
PLATES
PLATTE
PLAYAS
PLAYAT
PLAYED
PLAYER
PLAYON
PLAYUP
PLAZAS
SLACKS
SLAGGY
SLAKED
SLAKES
SLALOM
SLANGS
SLANGY
SLANTS
SLAPPY
SLAPUP
SLATED
SLATER
SLATES
SLAVED
SLAVER
SLAVES
SLAVIC
SLAYED
SLAYER
TLALOC

•L•A••
ALBANO
ALBANY
ALCAPP
ALEAST
ALKALI
ALLAYS
ALPACA
ALSACE
ALTAIC
ALTAIR
ALTARS
ALWAYS
BLEACH
BLEARS
BLEARY
BLEATS
BLOATS
CLEANS
CLEARS
CLEATS
CLEAVE
CLOACA
CLOAKS
ELPASO
FLOATS
GLEAMS
GLEANS
GLOATS
ILEANA
NLEAST
OLEARY
OLEATE
PLEACH
PLEADS
PLEASE
PLEATS
PLIANT
SLEAVE
SLEAZE
SLEAZY
SLOANE
ULLAGE

•L••A•
ALATAU
ALEGAR
ALEMAN
ALLDAY
ALLMAN
ALOHAS
ALOMAR
ALPHAS
ALTMAN
ALULAE
ALULAR
CLIMAX
ELFMAN
ELIJAH
FLEWAT
FLORAE
FLORAL
FLORAS
FLYMAN
FLYWAY
GLOBAL
ILLSAY
KLIBAN
LLAMAS
LLBEAN
OLDHAM
OLDHAT
OLDMAN
PLAGAL
PLANAR
PLAYAS
PLAYAT
PLAZAS
PLEIAD
PLICAE
PLURAL
SLEZAK
SLOGAN
SLOVAK
ULLMAN
ULTRAS

•L•••A
ALASKA
ALEXIA
ALICIA
ALPACA
ALTHEA
ALUMNA
ALYSSA
BLANCA
BLANDA
CLOACA
ELISHA
ELISSA
ELMIRA
ELVIRA
FLAVIA
FLICKA
GLENDA
GLINKA
GLORIA
GLOSSA
ILEANA
ILESHA
OLINDA
OLIVIA
PLASMA
PLEURA
ULTIMA

••LA••
ABLATE
ABLAUT
ABLAZE
AFLAME
AFLATS
AGLAIA
AGLARE
ALLAYS
ASLANT
ATLAST
ATLATL
BALAAM
BALATA
BELAIR
BELAYS
BYLAWS
CALAIS
CALASH
CCLAMP
COLADA
DALASI
DELANO
DELANY
DELATE
DELAYS
DILATE
ECLAIR
ECLATS
EFLATS
ENLACE
FALANA
FULANI
GALATA
GALAXY
GELADA
GELATI
GELATO
GULAGS
HILARY
INLAID
INLAND
INLAWS
INLAYS
ISLAND
JALAPA
KALAKH
KDLANG
KULAKS
LALALA
LELAND
LILACS
MALABO
MALADY
MALAGA
MALATE
MALAWI
MALAYA
MALAYS
MCLAIN
MELANO
MILADY
MILANO
MOLARS
OBLAST
OBLATE
OFLATE
OGLALA
ONLAND
OOLALA
PALACE
PALAEO
PALATE
PELAGE
PILAFS
PILATE
POLAND
RELACE
RELAID
RELATE
RELAYS
ROLAND
SALAAM
SALADS
SALALS
SALAMI
SALARY
SCLAFF
SILAGE
SOLACE
SOLANS
SPLASH
SPLATS
SPLAYS
TILAKS
TULANE
TULARE
UCLANS
UHLANS
ULLAGE
UMLAUT
UNLACE
UNLADE
UNLAID
UNLASH
UPLAND
VOLANS
VOLANT
VOLARE

••L•A•
AFLOAT
AGLEAM
ALLDAY
ALLMAN
BALAAM
BALKAN
BALLAD
BALSAM
BALZAC
BELDAM
BELIAL
BILBAO
BULGAR
BULLAE
CALLAO
CALLAS
CALPAC
CELLAE
CELLAR
COLLAR
COLMAN
DALLAS
DELRAY
DELTAS
DOLLAR
DOLMAN
DOLMAS
EOLIAN
FELLAH
FELLAS
FILIAL
FOLIAR
FULMAR
GALEAE
GALWAY
GALYAK
GILEAD
GULLAH
HALVAH
HELLAS
ILLSAY
INLEAF
JULIAN
KALKAN
KALMAR
MCLEAN
MELMAC

MILLAY
MILPAS
MILSAP
MOLDAU
MOLNAR
MULLAH
MULLAS
NILGAI
NOLEAD
NOLOAD
NULLAH
OILCAN
OILMAN
OILPAN
ONLOAN
PALEAE
PALLAS
PALMAS
PILLAR
POLEAX
POLKAS
PULSAR
RELOAD
SALAAM
SALMAN
SALSAS
SILOAM
SOLDAN
SOLFAS
SULTAN
SYLVAN
TALKAT
TULSAN
ULLMAN
UNLEAD
UNLOAD
UPLOAD
VILLAS
VOLVAS
VULCAN
VULGAR
ZILPAH

••L••A
AGLAIA
BALATA
BALBOA
BELUGA
BULOVA
COLADA
COLIMA
DULLEA
FALANA
FULCRA
GALATA
GALENA
GALLIA
GELADA
HELENA
JALAPA
LALALA
LOLITA
MALAGA
MALAYA
MELINA
MULETA
OGLALA
OOLALA
PALLIA
PALOMA
PELOTA
SALINA
SALIVA
SALVIA
SCLERA
SELENA
SILICA
SYLVIA
TOLUCA
WALESA

•••LA•
AKELAS
ALULAE
ALULAR
ASHLAR
BALLAD
BEDLAM
BEULAH
BULLAE
BURLAP
BYPLAY
CALLAO
CALLAS
CELLAE
CELLAR
CHELAE
CHELAS
COLLAR
CYCLAS
DALLAS
DEWLAP
DOBLAS
DOLLAR
EARLAP
FELLAH
FELLAS
GAGLAW
GULLAH
HARLAN
HELLAS
INPLAY
JETLAG
KAPLAN
KEVLAR
KOALAS
KUBLAI
MEDLAR
MEDLAT
MILLAY
MISLAY
MOOLAH
MULLAH
MULLAS
NULLAH
NYALAS
OCULAR
OUTLAW
OUTLAY
OVULAR
PALLAS
PARLAY
PEDLAR
PHILAE
PHYLAE
PILLAR
POPLAR
PRELAW
RAGLAN
RAILAT
REPLAN
REPLAY
SCALAR
SEALAB
SENLAC
SKYLAB
SMILAX
STALAG
STELAE
STELAR
TABLAS
TESLAS
TOKLAS
UNCLAD
UVULAE
UVULAR
UVULAS
VACLAV
VASLAV
VILLAS
VIOLAS
WAYLAY

•••L•A
ABOLLA
AEOLIA
AMELIA
ANGLIA
APULIA
ARALIA
AXILLA
AZALEA
CHOLLA
DAHLIA
DEFLEA
DULLEA
EMILIA
ETALIA
GALLIA
IMELDA
ITALIA
KAHLUA
KAILUA
OBELIA
PAELLA
PALLIA
PSYLLA
REALIA
SCALIA
SCYLLA
STELLA
THALIA
THELMA

••••LA
ABOLLA
ANGELA
ANGOLA
AQUILA
ARBELA
AREOLA
ATTILA
AXILLA
CABALA
CANOLA
CHOLLA
CIBOLA
COPULA
CUPOLA
EIDOLA
FACULA
FIBULA
HOOPLA
IMPALA
KAMALA
KERALA
LALALA
LIGULA
LOYOLA
LUNULA
MACULA
MANILA
MAZOLA
MODELA
NEBULA
NICOLA
NIKOLA
OGLALA
OOLALA
OSCULA
PAELLA
PAMELA
PARULA
PAYOLA
PETULA
PSYLLA
PUEBLA
RADULA
RAMBLA
ROMOLA
SCYLLA
SHEILA
STELLA
TABULA
URSULA
VIZSLA

L•B•••
LABELS
LABIAL
LABILE
LABORS
LABOUR
LABREA
LABRET
LABRUM
LEBRUN
LIBBED
LIBBER
LIBELS
LIBIDO
LIBRIS
LIBYAN
LLBEAN
LOBATE
LOBBED
LOBBER
LOBULE
LUBBER
LUBECK
LUBING
LUBLIN

L••B••
LAMBDA
LAMBED
LAYBYS
LAZBOY
LESBOS
LIABLE
LIBBED
LIBBER
LIEBIG
LIMBED
LIMBER
LIMBOS
LIMBUS
LISBOA
LISBON
LOBBED
LOBBER
LOMBOK
LOWBOY
LUBBER
LUMBAR
LUMBER

L•••B•
LAIDBY
LAVABO
LAYSBY
LETSBE

•LB•••
ALBANO
ALBANY
ALBEDO
ALBEIT
ALBERT
ALBINO
ALBION
ALBOIN
ALBORG
ALBUMS
ELBERT
ELBOWS
ELBRUS
LLBEAN

•L•B••
ALIBIS
ALIBLE
ALLBUT
BLABBY
CLUBBY
FLABBY
FLYBOY
FLYBYS
GLEBES
GLIBLY
GLOBAL
GLOBED
GLOBES
GLOBIN
KLIBAN
OLDBOY
PLEBES

•L••B•
BLABBY
BLURBS
CLIMBS
CLUBBY
FLABBY
FLAMBE
PLUMBS

••LB••
ALLBUT
BALBOA
BILBAO
BULBIL
BULBUL
TALBOT
WILBUR

••L•B•
ADLIBS
CELEBS
MALABO
MALIBU
PHLEBO

••L••B
APLOMB

•••LB•
TRILBY

•••L•B
SEALAB
SKYLAB

••••LB
DEKALB

LC••••
LCHAIM

L•C•••
LACERS
LACEUP
LACHES
LACIER
LACING
LACKED
LACKEY
LACTIC
LACUNA
LECTOR
LICHEN
LICKED
LICTOR
LOCALE
LOCALS
LOCATE
LOCKED
LOCKER
LOCKET
LOCKIN
LOCKUP
LOCUST
LUCENT
LUCIAN
LUCITE
LUCIUS
LUCKED
LYCEES
LYCEUM

L••C••
LANCED
LANCER
LANCES
LANCET
LASCAR
LITCHI
LOUCHE
LOWCAL

L•••C•
LAMECH
LAUNCH
LEGACY
LEXICA
LILACS
LORICA
LUBECK
LUNACY
LYRICS

L••••C
LACTIC
LITHIC

•LC•••
ALCAPP
ALCOTT
ALCOVE
ALCUIN
ULCERS

•L•C••
ALECKY
ALECTO
ALICIA
BLACKS
BLOCKS
BLOCKY
CLACKS
CLICHE
CLICKS
CLOCHE
CLOCKS
CLUCKS
ELECTS
ELICIT
FLACKS
FLACON
FLECHE
FLECKS
FLICKA
FLICKS
FLOCKS
GLACES
GLACIS
GLYCOL
PLACED
PLACER
PLACES
PLACID
PLICAE
PLUCKS
PLUCKY
SLACKS
SLICED
SLICER
SLICES
SLICKS

•L••C•
ALNICO
ALPACA
ALSACE
BLANCA
BLANCH
BLEACH
BLENCH
BLOTCH
CLANCY
CLENCH
CLINCH
CLOACA
CLUTCH
ELLICE
FLEECE
FLEECY
FLETCH
FLINCH
FLITCH
GLANCE
GLITCH
KLATCH
OLMECS
PLAICE
PLANCK
PLEACH
SLOUCH
SLUICE

•L•••C
ALARIC
ALTAIC
CLERIC
CLINIC
OLDVIC
SLAVIC
TLALOC

••LC••
AFLCIO
CALCES
DULCET
FALCON
FULCRA
MULCTS
OILCAN
SULCUS
TALCED
TALCUM
VELCRO
VULCAN

••L•C•
CALICO
DELICT
ELLICE
ENLACE
INLUCK
LILACS
MALICE
MOLOCH
OCLOCK
PALACE
POLICE
POLICY
RELACE
RELICS
RELICT
RELOCK
RELUCT
SELECT
SILICA
SOLACE
SPLICE
TOLUCA
UNLACE
UNLOCK
VELOCE

••L••C
BALTIC
BALZAC
BELLOC
CALPAC
CELTIC
CULTIC
DELTIC
GALLIC
MELMAC
PELVIC
TOLTEC

•••LC•
CHALCO

•••L•C
AEOLIC
BELLOC
CYCLIC
ENBLOC
EXILIC
FROLIC
GAELIC
GALLIC
GARLIC
ITALIC
PUBLIC
SENLAC
TLALOC
URALIC
ZIPLOC

L•D•••
LADDER
LADDIE
LADERS
LADIDA
LADIES
LADING
LADINO
LADLED
LADLER
LADLES
LADOGA
LEDGER
LEDGES
LEDOFF
LEDOUT
LIDDED
LODENS
LODGED
LODGER
LODGES
LUDDEN
LUDENS
LUDLUM
LUDWIG

L••D••
LADDER
LADDIE
LAIDBY
LAIDIN
LAIDON
LAIDTO
LAIDUP
LANDAU
LANDED
LANDER
LANDHO
LANDIS
LANDON
LANDRY
LAPDOG
LARDED
LARDER
LARDON
LAUDED
LAUDER
LEADED
LEADEN
LEADER
LEADIN
LEADON
LEADTO
LEADUP
LEIDEN
LENDER
LEWDER
LEWDLY
LEYDEN
LIDDED
LIEDER
LINDEN
LOADED
LOADER
LONDON
LORDED
LORDLY
LOUDEN
LOUDER
LOUDLY
LUDDEN
LUNDEN
LYNDON

L•••D•
LADIDA
LAIRDS
LAMBDA
LAMEDH
LAMEDS
LAREDO
LERIDA
LIBIDO
LIPIDE
LIPIDS
LLOYDS
LUANDA

L••••D
LACKED
LADLED
LAGGED
LAMBED
LAMMED
LANCED
LANDED
LAPPED
LAPSED
LARDED
LARKED
LASHED
LASTED
LATHED
LAUDED
LEADED
LEAFED
LEAKED
LEANED
LEAPED
LEASED
LEAVED
LEERED
LEGEND
LEGGED
LELAND
LEMOND
LENSED
LEONID
LETTED
LEVEED
LEVIED
LIBBED
LICKED
LIDDED
LIFTED
LILTED
LIMBED
LIMNED
LIMPED
LIMPID
LINKED
LIPOID
LIPPED
LIQUID
LISPED
LISTED
LIZARD
LOADED
LOAFED
LOAMED
LOANED
LOBBED
LOCKED
LODGED
LOFTED
LOGGED
LOLLED
LOMOND
LONGED
LOOKED
LOOMED
LOOPED
LOOSED
LOOTED
LOPPED
LORDED
LOTTED
LOUSED
LOWEND
LUCKED
LUFFED
LUGGED
LULLED
LUMPED
LUNGED
LURKED
LUSTED
LYNYRD

•LD•••
ALDERS
ALDINE
ALDOSE
ALDOUS
ALDRIN
ELDERS
ELDEST
OLDBOY
OLDEST
OLDHAM
OLDHAT
OLDIES
OLDISH
OLDMAN
OLDMEN
OLDPRO
OLDVIC

•L•D••
ALLDAY
BLADED
BLADES
ELIDED
ELIDES
ELUDED
ELUDES
FLEDGE
GLADES
GLADLY
GLADYS
GLIDED
GLIDER
GLIDES
KLUDGE
PLEDGE
SLEDGE
SLIDER
SLIDES
SLIDIN
SLUDGE
SLUDGY

•L••D•
ALBEDO
ALKYDS
ALLUDE
BLANDA
BLEEDS
BLENDE
BLENDS
BLINDS
BLONDE
BLONDS
BLOODY
CLAUDE
CLOUDS
CLOUDY
ELANDS
FLOODS
FLUIDS
GLANDS
GLENDA
LLOYDS
OLINDA
PLAIDS
PLEADS

•L•••D
ALFRED
ALLIED
ALMOND
BLADED
BLAMED
BLARED
BLAZED
CLAWED
CLEPED
CLEWED
CLONED
CLOSED
CLOYED
ELAPID
ELATED
ELIDED
ELOPED
ELUDED
ELUTED
ELWOOD
FLAKED
FLAMED
FLARED
FLAWED
FLAYED
FLEXED
FLORID
FLOWED
FLUTED
FLUXED
FLYROD
GLARED
GLAZED
GLIDED
GLOBED
GLOVED
GLOWED
ILLFED
PLACED
PLACID
PLANED
PLATED
PLAYED
PLEIAD
PLOWED
PLUMED
SLAKED
SLATED
SLAVED
SLAYED
SLEWED
SLICED
SLIMED
SLOPED
SLOWED

••LD••
ALLDAY
BALDER
BALDLY
BELDAM
BOLDER
BOLDLY
CALDER
COLDER
COLDLY
FELDON
FOLDED
FOLDER
FOLDUP
GILDED
GILDER
GOLDEN
GOLDIE
HELDIN
HELDON
HELDTO
HELDUP
HOLDEN
HOLDER
HOLDIT
HOLDON
HOLDTO
HOLDUP
MALDEN
MELDED
MILDER
MILDEW
MILDLY
MOLDAU
MOLDED
MOLDER
POLDER
SELDOM
SOLDAN
SOLDER
SOLDON
TILDEN
TILDES
TOLDOF
VALDEZ
VELDTS
WALDEN
WELDED
WELDER
WILDER
WILDLY

••L•D•
ALLUDE
BOLIDE
COLADA
DELUDE
GELADA
HALIDE
MALADY
MELODY
MILADY
SALADS
SOLIDI
SOLIDS
TELEDU
TOLEDO
UNLADE

••L••D
ALLIED
BALKED
BALLAD
BELIED
BELLED
BELTED
BILKED
BILLED
BOLTED
BULGED
BULKED
BULLED
CALKED
CALLED
CALMED
CALVED
CELLED
CULLED
DELVED
DOLLED
DULLED
FELLED
FELTED
FILLED
FILMED
FOLDED
GALLED
GELLED
GILDED
GILEAD
GILLED
GOLFED
GULFED
GULLED
GULPED
HALOED
HALOID
HALTED
HALVED
HELMED
HELPED
HILLED
HULKED
HULLED
ILLFED
INLAID
INLAND
ISLAND
JELLED
JILTED
JOLTED
KILLED
KILNED
KILTED
LELAND
LILTED
LOLLED
LULLED
MALTED
MELDED
MELTED
MILKED
MILLED
MILORD
MOLDED
MOLTED
MULLED
NOLEAD
NOLOAD
NULLED
ONLAND
PALLED
PALLID
PALMED
PELTED
PILLED
POLAND
POLLED
PULLED
PULPED
PULSED
RELAID
RELIED
RELOAD
ROLAND
ROLLED
SALTED
SALVED
SILKED
SILOED
SILTED
SOLOED
SOLVED
SULKED
TALCED
TALKED
TALMUD
TILLED
TILTED
TOLLED
UNLAID
UNLEAD
UNLOAD
UPLAND
UPLOAD
VALUED
VALVED
WALKED
WALLED
WELDED
WELLED
WELTED
WILLED
WILTED
WOLFED
XYLOID
YELLED
YELPED
YOLKED

•••LD•
BUILDS
CHILDE
CHILDS
FIELDS
FJELDS
GUILDS
IMELDA
ISOLDE
MOULDS
MOULDY
SCALDS
SCOLDS
SKALDS
WIELDS
WORLDS
YIELDS

•••L•D
ADDLED
AMBLED
ANGLED
ANKLED
BAILED
BALLAD
BAWLED
BELLED
BILLED
BIRLED
BOILED
BOWLED
BUGLED
BULLED
BURLED

CABLED
CALLED
CEILED
CELLED
COILED
COOLED
COWLED
CULLED
CURLED
CYCLED
DIALED
DOLLED
DUELED
DULLED
EAGLED
EUCLID
EXILED
EYELID
FABLED
FAILED
FELLED
FILLED
FOALED
FOILED
FOOLED
FOULED
FOWLED
FUELED
FURLED
GABLED
GALLED
GELLED
GILLED
GULLED
HAILED
HAULED
HEALED
HEELED
HILLED
HOWLED
HULLED
HURLED
JAILED
JELLED
KEELED
KHALID
KILLED
LADLED
LOLLED
LULLED
MAILED
MARLED
MAULED
MEWLED
MILLED
MISLED
MOILED
MULLED
NAILED
NULLED
PALLED
PALLID
PEALED
PEELED
PILLED
POLLED
POOLED
PULLED
PURLED
RAILED
REELED
RIFLED
ROILED
ROLLED
SAILED
SCALED
SEALED
SIDLED
SMILED
SOILED
STALED
STOLID
STYLED
TABLED
TAILED
TILLED
TITLED
TOILED
TOLLED
TOOLED
UNCLAD
VEILED
WAILED
WALLED
WELLED
WHILED
WILLED
YELLED
YOWLED

••••LD

AFIELD
AGEOLD
ARNOLD
BEHELD
BEHOLD
BIFOLD
BUJOLD
DONALD
ENFOLD
GERALD
GOWILD
HAROLD
HERALD
INFOLD
KOBOLD
ONHOLD
OSWALD
REHELD
RESOLD
RETOLD
REWELD
RIBALD
RONALD
SHIELD
SHOULD
UNFOLD
UNSOLD
UNTOLD
UPHELD
UPHOLD

LE••••

LEADED
LEADEN
LEADER
LEADIN
LEADON
LEADTO
LEADUP
LEAFED
LEAGUE
LEAKED
LEAKER
LEAKEY
LEALTY
LEANED
LEANER
LEANLY
LEANON
LEANTO
LEAPED
LEAPER
LEARNS
LEARNT
LEASED
LEASER
LEASES
LEAVED
LEAVEN
LEAVES
LEBRUN
LECTOR
LEDGER
LEDGES
LEDOFF
LEDOUT
LEERAT
LEERED
LEERER
LEEWAY
LEGACY
LEGALS
LEGATE
LEGATO
LEGEND
LEGGED
LEGION
LEGIST
LEGMAN
LEGMEN
LEGREE
LEGUME
LEHIGH
LEHRER
LEHUAS
LEIDEN
LEKVAR
LELAND
LEMANS
LEMMAS
LEMMON
LEMNOS
LEMOND
LEMONS
LEMONY
LEMUEL
LEMURS
LENAPE
LENDER
LENGTH
LENITY
LENNIE
LENNON
LENORE
LENSED
LENSES
LENTEN
LENTIL
LEONES
LEONID
LEONIE
LEPTON
LERIDA
LERNER
LESAGE
LESBOS
LESLEY
LESLIE
LESSEE
LESSEN
LESSER
LESSON
LESSOR
LESTAT
LESTER
LETFLY
LETHAL
LETOFF
LETOUT
LETSAT
LETSBE
LETSGO
LETSIN
LETSON
LETSUP
LETTED
LETTER
LETUPS
LEVANT
LEVEED
LEVEES
LEVELS
LEVENE
LEVERS
LEVIED
LEVIER
LEVIES
LEVINE
LEVITE
LEVITY
LEWDER
LEWDLY
LEXEME
LEXICA
LEYDEN

L•E•••

LEERAT
LEERED
LEERER
LEEWAY
LIEBIG
LIEDER
LIEFER
LIEGES
LIELOW
LIENEE
LIERNE
LIESIN
LIESTO
LIEUTS
LIEVRE

L••E••

LABELS
LACERS
LACEUP
LADERS
LAGERS
LAKERS
LAMECH
LAMEDH
LAMEDS
LAMELY
LAMENT
LAMESA
LAMEST
LAPELS
LAREDO
LASERS
LATEEN
LATELY
LATENE
LATENS
LATENT
LATEST
LAVERS
LAXEST
LAYERS
LEGEND
LEVEED
LEVEES
LEVELS
LEVENE
LEVERS
LEXEME
LIBELS
LIFERS
LIGERS
LIKELY
LIKENS
LIMENS
LIMEYS
LINEAL
LINEAR
LINENS
LINERS
LINEUP
LIPENG
LITERS
LIVEIN
LIVELY
LIVENS
LIVEON
LIVERS
LIVERY
LLBEAN
LODENS
LOMEIN
LONELY
LONERS
LOPERS
LOREAL
LORENZ
LOSEIT
LOSERS
LOVEIN
LOVELL
LOVELY
LOVERS
LOVETT
LOWELL
LOWEND
LOWERS
LOWERY
LOWEST
LUBECK
LUCENT
LUDENS
LUGERS
LUMENS
LYCEES
LYCEUM

L•••E•

LAAGER
LABREA
LABRET
LACHES
LACIER
LACKED
LACKEY
LADDER
LADIES
LADLED
LADLER
LADLES
LAFFER
LAGGED
LAGGER
LAMBED
LAMMED
LANCED
LANCER
LANCES
LANCET
LANDED
LANDER
LANIER
LANKER
LAPPED
LAPPET
LAPSED
LAPSES
LAPTEV
LARDED
LARDER
LARGER
LARKED
LARSEN
LASHED
LASHER
LASHES
LASSEN
LASSER
LASSES
LASTED
LASTEX
LATEEN
LATHED
LATHER
LATHES
LATKES
LATTEN
LATTER
LAUDED
LAUDER
LAUPER
LAUREL
LAUREN
LAWMEN
LAWYER
LAYMEN
LAZIER
LEADED
LEADEN
LEADER
LEAFED
LEAKED
LEAKER
LEAKEY
LEANED
LEANER
LEAPED
LEAPER
LEASED
LEASER
LEASES
LEAVED
LEAVEN
LEAVES
LEDGER
LEDGES
LEERED
LEERER
LEGGED
LEGMEN
LEGREE
LEHRER
LEIDEN
LEMUEL
LENDER
LENSED
LENSES
LENTEN
LEONES
LERNER
LESLEY
LESSEE
LESSEN
LESSER
LESTER
LETTED
LETTER
LEVEED
LEVEES
LEVIED
LEVIER
LEVIES
LEWDER
LEYDEN
LIBBED
LIBBER
LICHEN
LICKED
LIDDED
LIEDER
LIEFER
LIEGES
LIENEE
LIFTED
LIFTER
LILIES
LILTED
LIMBED
LIMBER
LIMNED
LIMNER
LIMPED
LIMPER
LIMPET
LINDEN
LINGER
LINKED
LINKER
LINNET
LINSEY
LINTEL
LINTER
LIONEL
LIONET
LIPPED
LISLES
LISPED
LISTED
LISTEE
LISTEL
LISTEN
LISTER
LITRES
LITTER
LIVRES
LOADED
LOADER
LOAFED
LOAFER
LOAMED
LOANED
LOANER
LOAVES
LOBBED
LOBBER
LOCKED
LOCKER
LOCKET
LODGED
LODGER
LODGES
LOFTED
LOGGED
LOGGER
LOGIER
LOITER
LOLLED
LONGED
LONGER
LONGES
LOOKED
LOOKER
LOOMED
LOONEY
LOOPED
LOOPER
LOOSED
LOOSEN
LOOSER
LOOSES
LOOTED
LOOTER
LOPPED
LOPPER
LORDED
LORIES
LOSSES
LOTTED
LOUDEN
LOUDER
LOUPES
LOUSED
LOUSES
LOUVER
LOWKEY
LUBBER
LUCKED
LUDDEN
LUFFED
LUGGED
LUGGER
LULLED
LUMBER
LUMPED
LUMPEN
LUMPER
LUNDEN
LUNGED
LUNGES
LUNKER
LURKED
LUSHER
LUSTED
LUSTER
LUTHER
LYCEES
LYNLEY
LYNXES

L••••E

LABILE
LADDIE
LAHORE
LAINIE
LAMAZE
LANATE
LANOSE
LAOTSE
LARVAE
LASSIE
LATENE
LAURIE
LAVAGE
LEAGUE
LEGATE
LEGREE
LEGUME
LENAPE
LENNIE
LENORE
LEONIE
LESAGE
LESLIE
LESSEE
LETSBE
LEVENE
LEVINE
LEVITE
LEXEME
LHOTSE
LIABLE
LIAISE
LIENEE
LIERNE
LIEVRE
LIGATE
LIGURE
LILLIE
LINAGE
LIPASE
LIPIDE
LISTEE
LITTLE
LIZZIE
LOATHE
LOBATE
LOBULE
LOCALE
LOCATE
LONGUE
LOUCHE
LOUISE
LOUNGE
LOUVRE
LOVAGE
LUCITE
LUNATE
LUPINE
LUPONE
LUSTRE
LUXATE
LYSINE

•LE•••

ALEAST
ALECKY
ALECTO
ALEGAR
ALEGRE
ALEMAN
ALEPHS
ALEPPO
ALERTS
ALEUTS
ALEXEI
ALEXIA
ALEXIS
BLEACH
BLEARS
BLEARY
BLEATS
BLEEDS
BLEEPS
BLENCH
BLENDE
BLENDS
BLEWIT
BLEWUP
CLEANS
CLEARS
CLEATS
CLEAVE
CLEEKS
CLEESE
CLEFTS
CLENCH
CLEPED
CLERGY
CLERIC
CLERKS
CLEVER
CLEVES
CLEVIS
CLEWED
ELECTS
ELEGIT
ELEMIS
ELEVEN
ELEVES
FLECHE
FLECKS
FLEDGE
FLEECE
FLEECY
FLEERS
FLEETS
FLENSE
FLESHY
FLETCH
FLEURY
FLEWAT
FLEWIN
FLEXED
FLEXES
FLEXOR
GLEAMS
GLEANS
GLEBES
GLENDA
ILEANA
ILESHA
KLEIST
NLEAST
OLEARY
OLEATE
OLEFIN
OLEVEL
PLEACH
PLEADS
PLEASE
PLEATS
PLEBES
PLEDGE
PLEIAD
PLENTY
PLENUM
PLEURA
PLEXOR
PLEXUS
SLEAVE
SLEAZE
SLEAZY
SLEDGE
SLEEKS
SLEEKY
SLEEPS
SLEEPY
SLEETS
SLEETY
SLEEVE
SLEIGH
SLEUTH
SLEWED
SLEZAK

•L•E••

ALBEDO
ALBEIT
ALBERT
ALDERS
ALIENS
ALKENE
ALLEES
ALLEGE
ALLELE
ALLEYS
ALPERT
ALTERS
ALWEST
BLEEDS
BLEEPS
BLUEOX
BLUEST
BLUESY
BLUETS
CLEEKS
CLEESE
CLIENT
CLUEIN
ELBERT
ELDERS
ELDEST
ELLERY
ELVERS
FLEECE
FLEECY
FLEERS
FLEETS
FLIERS
FLUENT
FLYERS
GLUERS
ILLEST
LLBEAN
NLWEST
OLDEST
OLMECS
PLIERS
SLEEKS
SLEEKY
SLEEPS
SLEEPY
SLEETS
SLEETY
SLEEVE
SLIEST
SLYEST
ULCERS

•L••E•

ALEXEI
ALFRED
ALFVEN
ALINES
ALLEES
ALLIED
ALLIES
ALLSET
ALLWET
ALTHEA
BLADED
BLADES
BLAMED
BLAMES
BLARED
BLARES
BLAZED
BLAZER
BLAZES
BLIMEY
BLIXEN
BLOKES
BLOOEY
BLOWER
CLARET
CLAWED
CLAWER
CLAYEY
CLEPED
CLEVER
CLEVES
CLEWED
CLIMES
CLINES
CLONED
CLONES
CLOSED
CLOSER
CLOSES
CLOSET
CLOVEN
CLOVER
CLOVES
CLOYED
DLAYER
ELATED
ELATER
ELATES
ELAYER
ELEVEN
ELEVES
ELIDED
ELIDES
ELITES
ELOPED
ELOPER
ELOPES
ELUDED
ELUDES
ELUTED
ELUTES
ELYSEE
FLAKED
FLAKER
FLAKES
FLAMED
FLAMES
FLARED
FLARES
FLAWED
FLAXEN
FLAXES
FLAYED
FLAYER
FLEXED
FLEXES
FLOOEY
FLORES
FLORET
FLOWED
FLOWER
FLUKES
FLUMES
FLUTED
FLUTES
FLUXED
FLUXES
FLYMEN
FLYNET
GLACES
GLADES
GLARED
GLARES
GLASER
GLAZED
GLAZER
GLAZES
GLEBES
GLIDED
GLIDER
GLIDES
GLOBED
GLOBES
GLOVED
GLOVER
GLOVES
GLOWED
GLOWER
GLUTEI
GLUTEN
ILLFED
ILLMET
OLDIES
OLDMEN
OLEVEL
OLIVER
OLIVES
PLACED
PLACER
PLACES
PLAGES
PLANED
PLANER
PLANES
PLANET
PLATED
PLATEN
PLATER
PLATES
PLAYED
PLAYER
PLEBES
PLOVER
PLOWED
PLOWER
PLUMED
PLUMES
PLUSES
SLAKED
SLAKES
SLATED
SLATER
SLATES
SLAVED
SLAVER
SLAVES
SLAYED
SLAYER
SLEWED
SLICED
SLICER
SLICES
SLIDER
SLIDES
SLIMED
SLIMES
SLIVER
SLOPED
SLOPES
SLOVEN
SLOWED
SLOWER
SLYPES
ULSTER

•L•••E

ALCOVE
ALDINE
ALDOSE
ALEGRE
ALFINE
ALGORE
ALIBLE
ALKENE
ALLEGE
ALLELE
ALLUDE
ALLURE
ALPINE
ALSACE
ALULAE
BLAINE
BLAISE
BLENDE
BLITHE
BLONDE
BLOUSE
BLYTHE
CLAIRE
CLAQUE
CLARKE
CLAUDE
CLAUSE
CLEAVE
CLEESE
CLICHE
CLIQUE
CLOCHE
CLOQUE
CLOTHE
ELAINE
ELAPSE
ELAYNE
ELLICE
ELMORE
ELOISE
ELYSEE
FLAMBE
FLANGE
FLECHE
FLEDGE
FLEECE
FLENSE
FLORAE
GLANCE
ILLUME
ILLUSE
KLUDGE
OLEATE
PLAGUE
PLAICE
PLANTE
PLAQUE
PLATTE
PLEASE
PLEDGE
PLICAE
PLISSE
PLUNGE
SLEAVE
SLEAZE
SLEDGE
SLEEVE
SLOANE
SLUDGE
SLUICE
ULLAGE

••LE••

ABLEST
AGLEAM
AGLETS
AILEEN
AILERS
ALLEES
ALLEGE
ALLELE
ALLEYS
ARLENE
ASLEEP
BALEEN
BALERS
BOLERO
BOLEYN
CELEBS
CELERY
COLEUS
CULETS
DALETH
DELEON
DELETE
EELERS
EILEEN
ELLERY
FILENE
FILERS
FILETS
GALEAE
GALENA
GELEES
GILEAD
GOLEMS
HALERS
HALERU
HALEST
HALEVY
HELENA
HELENE
HELENS
HOLEUP
IDLERS
IDLEST
ILLEST
INLEAF
INLETS
IRLENE
ISLETS
JOLENE
JULEPS
MCLEAN
MELEES
MILERS
MOLEST
MULETA
NFLERS
NHLERS
NOLEAD
NOLENS
NOLESS
OGLERS
OILERS
OWLETS
PALEAE
PALELY
PALEST
PELEUS
PHLEBO
PHLEGM
PILEIN
PILEON
PILEUM
PILEUP

PILEUS
POLEAX
POLERS
POLEYN
RELENT
RELETS
ROLEOS
RULEON
RULERS
SCLERA
SELECT
SELENA
SELENE
SILENI
SILENT
SOLEIL
SOLELY
SOLEMN
SOLENT
SOLERS
SOLEUS
SPLEEN
TALENT
TALESE
TELEDU
TILERS
TOLEDO
UNLEAD
UNLESS
VALENS
VALENT
VALERY
VALETS
VILELY
VILEST
VOLENS
WALERS
WALESA
XYLENE

••L•E•

AILEEN
ALLEES
ALLIED
ALLIES
ALLSET
ALLWET
ASLEEP
BALDER
BALEEN
BALKED
BALLET
BELIED
BELIEF
BELIES
BELLED
BELLES
BELTED
BILGES
BILKED
BILLED
BILLET
BOLDER
BOLGER
BOLTED
BULGED
BULGES
BULKED
BULLED
BULLET
BULWER
CALCES
CALDER
CALKED
CALLED
CALLER
CALLES
CALMED
CALMER
CALVED
CALVES
CALXES
CELLED
COLDER
COLLET
COLTER
CULLED
CULLEN
CULLER
CULLET
CULVER
DALLES
DELVED
DELVER
DELVES
DILLER
DILSEY
DOLLED
DOLMEN
DULCET
DULLEA
DULLED
DULLER
DULLES
EELIER
EILEEN
FALLEN
FALSER
FALTER
FELLED
FELLER
FELTED
FILLED
FILLER
FILLES
FILLET
FILMED
FILTER
FOLDED
FOLDER
FULLER
GALLED
GALLEY
GELEES
GELLED
GELSEY
GILDED
GILDER
GILLED
GOLDEN
GOLFED
GOLFER
GULFED
GULLED
GULLET
GULPED
GULPER
HALLEL
HALLEY
HALOED
HALOES
HALSEY
HALTED
HALTER
HALVED
HALVES
HELLER
HELMED
HELMET
HELPED
HELPER
HELTER
HELVES
HILLED
HILLEL
HILLER
HOLDEN
HOLDER
HOLIER
HOLLER
HOLMES
HULKED
HULLED
HULLER
ILLFED
ILLMET
JELLED
JILTED
JOLIET
JOLTED
JULIET
KELLER
KELLEY
KELSEY
KILLED
KILLER
KILMER
KILNED
KILTED
KILTER
LILIES
LILTED
LOLLED
LULLED
MALDEN
MALLEE
MALLEI
MALLET
MALTED
MELDED
MELEES
MELTED
MILDER
MILDEW
MILIEU
MILKED
MILKER
MILLED
MILLER
MILLET
MILNER
MOLDED
MOLDER
MOLTED
MOLTEN
MOLTER
MULLED
MULLER
MULLET
NULLED
OILIER
OILMEN
PALAEO
PALLED
PALLET
PALMED
PALMER
PALTER
PELLET
PELMET
PELTED
PELTER
PHLOEM
PILFER
PILLED
POLDER
POLLED
POLLEN
POLLER
POLLEX
PULLED
PULLET
PULLEY
PULPED
PULSED
PULSES
RELIED
RELIEF
RELIES
RILLES
RILLET
ROLLED
ROLLER
SALLET
SALTED
SALTEN
SALTER
SALVED
SALVER
SALVES
SELLER
SELVES
SILKED
SILKEN
SILOED
SILTED
SILVER
SOLDER
SOLOED
SOLVED
SOLVER
SOLVES
SPLEEN
SULKED
SULKER
SULLEN
TALCED
TALKED
TALKER
TALLER
TELLER
TILDEN
TILDES
TILLED
TILLER
TILTED
TILTER
TOLLED
TOLTEC
TULLES
UGLIER
UGLIES
VALDEZ
VALLEE
VALLEY
VALUED
VALUES
VALVED
VALVES
VELVET
VOLLEY
WALDEN
WALKED
WALKER
WALLED
WALLER
WALLET
WALTER
WELDED
WELDER
WELLED
WELLES
WELTED
WELTER
WILDER
WILIER
WILKES
WILLED
WILLEM
WILLET
WILTED
WOLFED
WOLPER
WOLSEY
WOLVES
YALIES
YELLED
YELLER
YELPED
YELPER
YOLKED

••L••E

ABLATE
ABLAZE
AFLAME
AGLARE
ALLEGE
ALLELE
ALLUDE
ALLURE
APLITE
ARLENE
ASLOPE
BELIZE
BILLIE
BOLIDE
BULLAE
BYLINE
CALQUE
CELINE
CELLAE
COLLIE
DELATE
DELETE
DELUDE
DELUGE
DELUXE
DILATE
DILUTE
ELLICE
ENLACE
FALINE
FELINE
FELIPE
FELLOE
FILENE
FILOSE
FOLKIE
GALEAE
GALORE
GILLIE
GOLDIE
HALIDE
HALITE
HELENE
ILLUME
ILLUSE
INLINE
INLOVE
IOLITE
IRLENE
JOLENE
KALINE
KELPIE
KILTIE
LILLIE
MALATE
MALICE
MALLEE
MALONE
MILLIE
MILTIE
MOLINE
MOLTKE
NELLIE
OBLATE
OBLIGE
OFLATE
ONLINE
OOLITE
PALACE
PALATE
PALEAE
PELAGE
PILATE
PILOSE
POLICE
POLITE
PULQUE
RELACE
RELATE
RELINE
RELIVE
RELUME
ROLLIE
SALINE
SALOME
SALUTE
SELENE
SILAGE
SILONE
SOLACE
SOLUTE
SPLICE
SPLINE
STLUKE
TALESE
TALKIE
TILLIE
TOLIFE
TULANE
TULARE
ULLAGE
UNLACE
UNLADE
UNLIKE
VALISE
VALLEE
VELOCE
VOLARE
VOLUME
VOLUTE
WALKIE
WILLIE
XYLENE

•••LE•

ABELES
ADDLED
ADDLES
AISLES
AMBLED
AMBLER
AMBLES
AMOLES
AMPLER
AMULET
ANGLED
ANGLER
ANGLES
ANKLED
ANKLES
ANKLET
ANNLEE
ANOLES
ANTLER
APPLES
ARMLET
ASHLEY
ATTLEE
AUKLET
AZALEA
BAILED
BAILEE
BAILER
BAILEY
BALLET
BARLEY
BAWLED
BAWLER
BEGLEY
BELLED
BELLES
BIBLES
BILLED
BILLET
BIRLED
BOGLES
BOILED
BOILER
BOSLEY
BOULES
BOULEZ
BOWLED
BOWLER
BOWLES
BRULES
BUGLED
BUGLER
BUGLES
BULLED
BULLET
BURLED
BURLEY
BUTLER
CABLED
CABLER
CABLES
CALLED
CALLER
CALLES
CAMLET
CAPLET
CEILED
CELLED
CHALET
CHOLER
COALER
COILED
COLLET
COOLED
COOLER
COULEE
COWLED
COWLEY
CULLED
CULLEN
CULLER
CULLET
CURLED
CURLER
CURLEW
CUTLER
CUTLET
CYCLED
CYCLER
CYCLES
DAILEY
DALLES
DEALER
DEFLEA
DHOLES
DIALED
DIALER
DILLER
DOGLEG
DOLLED
DOOLEY
DUDLEY
DUELED
DUELER
DULLEA
DULLED
DULLER
DULLES
DUPLEX
EAGLED
EAGLES
EAGLET
ECCLES
ECOLES
EDILES
EMBLEM
EVILER
EXILED
EXILES
EYELET
FABLED
FABLER
FABLES
FAILED
FALLEN
FARLEY
FEELER
FELLED
FELLER
FILLED
FILLER
FILLES
FILLET
FOALED
FOILED
FOOLED
FOOLER
FOULED
FOULER
FOWLED
FOWLER
FOWLES
FUELED
FUELER
FULLER
FURLED
GABLED
GABLES
GALLED
GALLEY
GELLED
GIBLET
GILLED
GIMLET
GOBLET
GOULET
GUILES
GULLED
GULLET
GURLEY
HAILED
HAILEY
HALLEL
HALLEY
HAMLET
HARLEM
HARLEY
HAULED
HAULER
HAYLEY
HEALED
HEALER
HEELED
HEELER
HELLER
HENLEY
HILLED
HILLEL
HILLER
HOLLER
HOWLED
HOWLER
HULLED
HULLER
HURLED
HURLER
HURLEY
HUXLEY
INGLES
INKLES
ISTLES
JAILED
JAILER
JELLED
JOULES
KEELED
KEELER
KEGLER
KELLER
KELLEY
KEPLER
KILLED
KILLER
KISLEV
KJOLEN
KOHLER
LADLED
LADLER
LADLES
LESLEY
LISLES
LOLLED
LULLED
LYNLEY
MAHLER
MAILED
MAILER
MAILES
MALLEE
MALLEI
MALLET
MAPLES
MARLED
MARLEE
MARLEY
MAULED
MAULER
MEDLEY
MEWLED
MEWLER
MIDLER
MILLED
MILLER
MILLET
MISLED
MOBLEY
MOILED
MOILER
MORLEY
MOSLEM
MOTLEY
MULLED
MULLER
MULLET
NAILED
NAILER
NAPLES
NEWLEY
NOBLER
NOBLES
NUCLEI
NUCLEO
NULLED
NUTLET
OAKLEY
OMELET
OODLES
ORALES
ORTLES
OSTLER
OUTLET
OVULES
PALLED
PALLET
PARLEY
PAULEY
PEALED
PEELED
PEELER
PEGLER
PELLET
PIGLET
PILLED
PIOLET
POLLED
POLLEN
POLLER
POLLEX
POOLED
PROLES
PULLED
PULLET
PULLEY
PURLED
RAILED
RAILER
REALER
REALES
REELED
REFLEX
REGLET
RIDLEY
RIFLED
RIFLER
RIFLES
RILLES
RILLET
RIPLEY
ROBLES
ROILED
ROLLED
ROLLER
RUBLES
RUNLET
SABLES
SAILED
SALLET
SCALED
SCALER
SCALES
SCHLEP
SEALED
SEALER
SELLER
SHALES
SHALEY
SHOLEM
SIDLED
SIDLES
SISLER
SMILED
SMILER
SMILES
SMILEY
SOCLES
SOILED
SPILES
STALED
STALER
STALES
STELES
STILES
STOLEN
STOLES
STYLED
STYLER
STYLES
STYLET
SUBLET
SULLEN
SUTLER
SWALES
TABLED
TABLES
TABLET
TAILED
TALLER
TELLER
THALER
THALES
THOLES
TILLED
TILLER
TITLED
TITLES
TOILED
TOILER
TOILES
TOILET
TOLLED
TOOLED
TRALEE
TULLES
UNCLES
VALLEE
VALLEY
VARLET
VEBLEN
VEILED
VIOLET
VOILES
VOLLEY
WAILED
WAILER
WALLED
WALLER
WALLET
WELLED
WELLES
WESLEY
WHALER
WHALES
WHILED
WHILES
WHOLES
WIGLET
WILLED
WILLEM
WILLET
WOHLER
WOOLEN
WOOLEY
YELLED
YELLER
YOWLED

•••L•E

ADELIE
ADELLE
ALULAE
AMALIE
ANNLEE
ATTLEE
AVULSE
BAILEE
BIGLIE
BILLIE
BOULLE
BULLAE
CELLAE
CHELAE
CHILDE
CHILOE
COLLIE
COULEE
EVOLVE
EVULSE
FAILLE
FELLOE
GILLIE
GOALIE
GRILLE
GRILSE
ISOLDE
KPELLE
LESLIE
LILLIE
MALLEE
MARLEE
MEALIE
MILLIE
MRBLUE
NELLIE
ORELSE
PHILAE
PHYLAE
REGLUE
ROLLIE
RVALUE
SHELVE
STELAE
STOLLE
SVELTE
TAILLE
TILLIE
TRALEE
TUILLE
TWELVE
UNGLUE
UVALUE
UVULAE
VALLEE
WILLIE

••••LE

ADELLE
AEDILE
ALIBLE
ALLELE
AMPULE
ARABLE
ARGYLE
AWHILE
BABBLE
BAFFLE
BANGLE
BATTLE
BAUBLE
BEADLE
BEAGLE
BEATLE
BEETLE
BIDDLE
BOBBLE
BOGGLE
BOODLE
BOTTLE
BOUCLE
BOULLE
BRIDLE
BUBBLE
BUCKLE
BUMBLE
BUNDLE
BUNGLE
BURBLE
BURGLE
BUSTLE
CACKLE
CAJOLE
CANDLE
CANTLE
CAROLE
CASTLE
CATTLE
CAUDLE
CECILE
CHICLE
CIRCLE
COBBLE
COCKLE
CODDLE
COUPLE
CRADLE
CREOLE
CUDDLE
CURDLE
CURULE
CYBELE
DABBLE
DANDLE
DANGLE
DAPPLE
DARKLE
DAWDLE
DAZZLE
DECKLE
DEFILE
DIBBLE
DIDDLE
DIMPLE
DINGLE
DIPOLE
DOABLE
DOCILE
DOODLE
DOTTLE
DOUBLE
EDERLE
EDIBLE
ENABLE
ENISLE
ENSILE
ETOILE
EXHALE
FACILE
FAILLE
FATALE
FEEBLE
FEMALE
FERULE
FETTLE
FICKLE
FIDDLE
FINALE
FIPPLE
FIZZLE
FOCSLE
FOIBLE
FONDLE
FOOZLE
FUDDLE
FUMBLE
FUTILE
GABBLE
GAGGLE
GAMBLE
GANGLE
GARBLE
GARGLE
GENTLE
GIGGLE
GIRDLE
GOBBLE
GOGGLE
GOOGLE
GRABLE
GRILLE
GURGLE
GUZZLE
HABILE
HACKLE
HAGGLE
HANDLE
HASSLE
HECKLE
HEDDLE
HIGGLE
HOBBLE
HOOPLE
HOPPLE
HUBBLE
HUDDLE
HUMBLE
HURDLE
HURTLE
HUSTLE
ICICLE
IMPALE
INHALE
INSOLE
JANGLE
JECKLE
JIGGLE
JINGLE
JOGGLE
JOSTLE
JUGGLE
JUMBLE
JUNGLE
KETTLE
KIBBLE
KINDLE
KIRTLE
KPELLE
KURILE
LABILE
LIABLE
LITTLE
LOBULE
LOCALE
MANGLE
MANTLE
MARBLE
MARPLE
MCHALE
MEDDLE
METTLE
MIDDLE
MIGGLE
MINGLE
MIZZLE
MOBILE
MODULE
MORALE
MOTILE
MOTTLE
MUDDLE
MUFFLE
MUMBLE
MUSCLE
MUZZLE
MYRTLE
NEEDLE
NESTLE
NETTLE
NIBBLE
NICOLE
NIGGLE
NIMBLE
NODDLE
NODULE
NOODLE
NOSALE
NOZZLE
NUBBLE
NUBILE
NUZZLE
ONFILE
ONSALE
ORACLE
ORIOLE
OTOOLE
PADDLE
PAROLE
PEBBLE
PEDDLE
PEOPLE
PESTLE
PICKLE
PIFFLE
PINOLE
PINTLE
POODLE
POPPLE
POTTLE
PUDDLE
PURFLE
PURPLE
PUZZLE
QUAYLE
RABBLE

RADDLE
RAFFLE
RAMBLE
RANKLE
RASSLE
RATTLE
RAZZLE
REFILE
REGALE
RESALE
RESILE
RESOLE
RETILE
REVILE
RIDDLE
RIFFLE
RIMPLE
RIPPLE
ROYALE
RUBBLE
RUDDLE
RUFFLE
RUMBLE
RUMPLE
RUNDLE
RUSTLE
RUTILE
SADDLE
SAMPLE
SEARLE
SEDILE
SEMELE
SETTLE
SICKLE
SIECLE
SIMILE
SIMPLE
SINGLE
SIZZLE
STABLE
STAPLE
STEELE
STIFLE
STOLLE
SUBTLE
SUPPLE
TACKLE
TAILLE
TAMALE
TANGLE
TATTLE
TEMPLE
THRALE
TICKLE
TINGLE
TINKLE
TIPPLE
TITTLE
TODDLE
TOGGLE
TOOTLE
TOPPLE
TOUSLE
TREBLE
TRIFLE
TRIPLE
TUILLE
TUMBLE
TURTLE
TUSSLE
UNABLE
UNPILE
USABLE
VIABLE
VIRILE
WADDLE
WAFFLE
WAGGLE
WAMBLE
WANGLE
WARBLE
WATTLE
WIGGLE
WIMBLE
WIMPLE
WINKLE
WOBBLE

L•F•••
LAFFER
LIFERS
LIFTED
LIFTER
LIFTUP
LOFTED
LUFFED

L••F••
LAFFER
LAPFUL
LAWFUL
LAYFOR
LEAFED
LETFLY
LIEFER
LOAFED
LOAFER
LOOFAH
LOWFAT
LUFFED

L•••F•
LAYOFF
LEDOFF
LETOFF
LOGOFF

L••••F
LAYOFF
LEDOFF
LETOFF
LOGOFF

•LF•••
ALFINE
ALFRED
ALFVEN
ELFISH
ELFMAN

•L•F••
BLUFFS
CLEFTS
CLIFFS
FLUFFS
FLUFFY
ILLFED
OLEFIN

•L••F•
BLUFFS
CLIFFS
FLUFFS
FLUFFY
KLOOFS

••LF••
BELFRY
DELFTS
GOLFED
GOLFER
GULFED
ILLFED
PILFER
SOLFAS
SULFUR
WOLFED

••L•F•
PILAFS
SCLAFF
TOLIFE
UGLIFY
UPLIFT
VILIFY

••L••F
BELIEF
INLEAF
RELIEF
SCLAFF
TOLDOF

•••LF•
AMALFI

••••LF
BEHALF
ENGULF
INHALF
ITSELF
MYSELF
RUDOLF

L•G•••
LAGASH
LAGERS
LAGGED
LAGGER
LAGOON
LAGUNA
LEGACY
LEGALS
LEGATE
LEGATO
LEGEND
LEGGED
LEGION
LEGIST
LEGMAN
LEGMEN
LEGREE
LEGUME
LIGATE
LIGERS
LIGHTS
LIGNIN
LIGULA
LIGURE
LOGGED
LOGGER
LOGGIA
LOGIER
LOGILY
LOGION
LOGJAM
LOGOFF
LOGOUT
LOGSIN
LOGSON
LUGERS
LUGGED
LUGGER
LUGNUT
LUGOSI

L••G••
LAAGER
LAGGED
LAGGER
LANGUR
LARGER
LARGOS
LAUGHS
LEAGUE
LEDGER
LEDGES
LEGGED
LENGTH
LIEGES
LINGER
LINGUA
LODGED
LODGER
LODGES
LOGGED
LOGGER
LOGGIA
LONGAN
LONGED
LONGER
LONGES
LONGUE
LUGGED
LUGGER
LUNGED
LUNGES

L•••G•
LADOGA
LATIGO
LAVAGE
LEHIGH
LESAGE
LETSGO
LIANGS
LINAGE
LOUNGE
LOVAGE

L••••G
LACING
LADING
LAMING
LAPDOG
LAVING
LAWING
LAYING
LAZING
LIEBIG
LIKING
LIMING
LINING
LIPENG
LITHOG
LIVING
LOPING
LOSING
LOVING
LOWING
LUBING
LUDWIG
LURING
LUTING

•LG•••
ALGORE

•L•G••
ALEGAR
ALEGRE
ALIGHT
ALIGNS
BLIGHT
CLOGUP
ELEGIT
FLAGGY
FLAGON
FLIGHT
GLOGGS
PLAGAL
PLAGES
PLAGIO
PLAGUE
PLIGHT
PLUGIN
SLAGGY
SLIGHT
SLOGAN
SLUGGO

•L••G•
ALLEGE
CLANGS
CLERGY
CLINGS
CLINGY
ELOIGN
FLAGGY
FLANGE
FLEDGE
FLINGS
GLOGGS
KLUDGE
OLINGO
PLEDGE
PLOUGH
PLUNGE
SLAGGY
SLANGS
SLANGY
SLEDGE
SLEIGH
SLINGS
SLOUGH
SLUDGE
SLUDGY
SLUGGO
ULLAGE

•L•••G
ALBORG
BLUING
CLUING
FLYING
GLUING
PLYING
SLUING

••LG••
BILGES
BOLGER
BULGAR
BULGED
BULGES
BULGUR
NILGAI
VULGAR

••L•G•
ALLEGE
BELUGA
COLUGO
DELUGE
EULOGY
GULAGS
MALAGA
MALIGN
OBLIGE
OOLOGY
PELAGE
PHLEGM
SILAGE
TELUGU
ULLAGE

••L••G
AILING
BALING
BELONG
DELONG
DOLING
EALING
FILING
HALING
HOLING
IDLING
KDLANG
OBLONG
OGLING
OILING
OILRIG
OOLONG
PALING
PILING
POLING
PULING
RILING
RULING
SOLING
SOLONG
TILING
WILING

•••L•G
ANALOG
DIALOG
DOGLEG
EPILOG
GASLOG
JETLAG
PROLOG
SAWLOG
STALAG
UNCLOG
UNPLUG

LH••••
LHOTSE

L•H•••
LAHORE
LCHAIM
LEHIGH
LEHRER
LEHUAS

L••H••
LACHES
LAPHAM
LASHED
LASHER
LASHES
LASHIO
LASHUP
LATHED
LATHER
LATHES
LETHAL
LICHEN
LIGHTS
LITHIC
LITHOG
LITHOS
LOTHAR
LUSHER
LUSHLY
LUTHER
LUTHOR

L•••H•
LANDHO
LAUGHS
LITCHI
LOATHE
LOTAHS
LOUCHE

L••••H
LAGASH
LAMECH
LAMEDH
LATISH
LAUNCH
LAVISH
LEHIGH
LENGTH
LILITH
LOOFAH

•LH•••
ALHIRT

•L•H••
ALOHAS
ALPHAS
ALTHEA
ELOHIM
OLDHAM
OLDHAT

•L••H•
ALEPHS
ALIGHT
BLIGHT
BLITHE
BLYTHE
CLICHE
CLOCHE
CLOTHE
CLOTHO
CLOTHS
ELISHA
FLASHY
FLECHE
FLESHY
FLIGHT
GLYPHS
ILESHA
PLASHY
PLIGHT
PLUSHY
SLIGHT
SLITHY
SLOSHY
SLOTHS
SLUSHY

•L•••H
BLANCH
BLEACH
BLENCH
BLOTCH
BLUISH
CLENCH
CLINCH
CLUTCH
ELFISH
ELIJAH
FLETCH
FLINCH
FLITCH
GLITCH
KLATCH
OLDISH
PLEACH
PLINTH
PLOUGH
SLEIGH
SLEUTH
SLOUCH
SLOUGH

••L•H•
DELPHI
FILTHY
SYLPHS

••L••H
ABLUSH
CALASH
CALIPH
DALETH
DULUTH
EOLITH
FELLAH
GALOSH
GULLAH
HALVAH
KALAKH
LILITH
MOLOCH
MULISH
MULLAH
NULLAH
OOLITH
OWLISH
PALISH
POLISH
RELISH
SALISH
SPLASH
SPLOSH
UNLASH
ZILPAH

•••L•H
ADOLPH
BEULAH
FELLAH
GUELPH
GULLAH
HEALTH
MOOLAH
MULLAH
NULLAH
SHILOH
SPILTH
WEALTH

LI••••
LIABLE
LIAISE
LIANAS
LIANGS
LIBBED
LIBBER
LIBELS
LIBIDO
LIBRIS
LIBYAN
LICHEN
LICKED
LICTOR
LIDDED
LIEBIG
LIEDER
LIEFER
LIEGES
LIELOW
LIENEE
LIERNE
LIESIN
LIESTO
LIEUTS
LIEVRE
LIFERS
LIFTED
LIFTER
LIFTUP
LIGATE
LIGERS
LIGHTS
LIGNIN
LIGULA
LIGURE
LIKELY
LIKENS
LIKING
LILACS
LILIES
LILITH
LILLIE
LILTED
LIMBED
LIMBER
LIMBOS
LIMBUS
LIMENS
LIMEYS
LIMING
LIMITS
LIMNED
LIMNER
LIMPED
LIMPER
LIMPET
LIMPID
LIMPLY
LINAGE
LINDEN
LINEAL
LINEAR
LINENS
LINERS
LINEUP
LINGER
LINGUA
LINING
LINKED
LINKER
LINKUP
LINNET
LINSEY
LINTEL
LINTER
LIONEL
LIONET
LIOTTA
LIPASE
LIPENG
LIPIDE
LIPIDS
LIPOID
LIPPED
LIPTON
LIQUID
LIQUOR
LISBOA
LISBON
LISLES
LISPED
LISTED
LISTEE
LISTEL
LISTEN
LISTER
LISTON
LITANY
LITCHI
LITERS
LITHIC
LITHOG
LITHOS
LITMUS
LITOUT
LITRES
LITTER
LITTLE
LIVEIN
LIVELY
LIVENS
LIVEON
LIVERS
LIVERY
LIVING
LIVRES
LIZARD
LIZZIE

L•I•••
LAIDBY
LAIDIN
LAIDON
LAIDTO
LAIDUP
LAINIE
LAIRDS
LEIDEN
LOITER

L••I••
LABIAL
LABILE
LACIER
LACING
LADIDA
LADIES
LADING
LADINO
LAMIAS
LAMINA
LAMING
LANIER
LAPINS
LARIAT
LATIGO
LATINA
LATINO
LATINS
LATISH
LATIUM
LAVING
LAVISH
LAWING
LAXITY
LAYING
LAZIER
LAZILY
LAZING
LEGION
LEGIST
LEHIGH
LENITY
LERIDA
LEVIED
LEVIER
LEVIES
LEVINE
LEVITE
LEVITY
LEXICA
LIAISE
LIBIDO
LIKING
LILIES
LILITH
LIMING
LIMITS
LINING
LIPIDE
LIPIDS
LIVING
LOGIER
LOGILY
LOGION
LOLITA
LOPING
LORICA
LORIES
LOSING
LOTION
LOUISA
LOUISE
LOVING
LOWING
LUBING
LUCIAN
LUCITE
LUCIUS
LUMINA
LUPINE
LUPINO
LURING
LUTING
LUTIST
LYRICS
LYRIST
LYSINE
LYSINS

L•••I•
LACTIC
LADDIE
LAIDIN
LAINIE
LANAIS
LANDIS
LANVIN
LASHIO
LASSIE
LATVIA
LAURIE
LAYSIN
LCHAIM
LEADIN
LENNIE
LENTIL
LEONID
LEONIE
LESLIE
LETSIN
LIBRIS
LIEBIG
LIESIN
LIGNIN
LILLIE
LIMPID
LIPOID
LIQUID
LITHIC
LIVEIN
LIZZIE
LOCKIN
LOGGIA
LOGSIN
LOMEIN
LOOKIN
LOSEIT
LOSTIT
LOVEIN
LUBLIN
LUDWIG

L••••I
LAZULI
LITCHI
LUGOSI

•LI•••
ALIBIS
ALIBLE
ALICIA
ALIENS
ALIGHT
ALIGNS
ALINES
ALIOTO
ALISON
BLIGHT
BLIMEY
BLIMPS
BLINDS
BLINKS
BLINTZ
BLITHE
BLIXEN
CLICHE
CLICKS
CLIENT
CLIFFS
CLIMAX
CLIMBS
CLIMES
CLINCH
CLINES
CLINGS
CLINGY
CLINIC
CLINKS
CLIPON
CLIQUE
ELICIT
ELIDED
ELIDES
ELIJAH
ELINOR
ELISHA
ELISSA
ELITES
ELIXIR
FLICKA
FLICKS
FLIERS
FLIGHT
FLIMSY
FLINCH
FLINGS
FLINTS
FLINTY
FLIPUP
FLIRTS
FLITCH
GLIBLY
GLIDED
GLIDER
GLIDES
GLINKA
GLINTS
GLITCH
GLITZY
KLIBAN
OLINDA
OLINGO
OLIVER
OLIVES
OLIVIA
PLIANT
PLICAE
PLIERS
PLIGHT
PLINKS
PLINTH
PLISSE
SLICED
SLICER
SLICES
SLICKS
SLIDER
SLIDES
SLIDIN
SLIEST
SLIGHT
SLIMED
SLIMES
SLIMLY
SLINGS
SLINKS
SLINKY
SLIPIN
SLIPON
SLIPUP
SLITHY
SLITTY
SLIVER

•L•I••
ALBINO
ALBION
ALDINE
ALFINE
ALHIRT
ALLIED
ALLIES
ALLIUM
ALNICO
ALOINS
ALPINE
BLAINE
BLAISE
BLUING
BLUISH
CLAIMS
CLAIRE
CLUING
ELAINE
ELFISH
ELLICE
ELLIOT
ELMIRA
ELNINO
ELOIGN
ELOISE
ELVIRA
FLAILS
FLAIRS
FLUIDS
FLYING
GLAIRY
GLUING
ILLINI
ILOILO
KLEIST
OLDIES
OLDISH
PLAICE
PLAIDS
PLAINS
PLAINT
PLAITS
PLEIAD
PLYING
SLEIGH
SLUICE
SLUING
ULTIMA
ULTIMO

•L••I•
ALARIC
ALBEIT
ALBOIN
ALCUIN
ALDRIN
ALEXIA
ALEXIS
ALIBIS
ALICIA
ALTAIC
ALTAIR
BLEWIT
BLOWIN
BLOWIT
CLAVIN
CLERIC
CLEVIS
CLINIC
CLORIS
CLOVIS
CLUEIN
ELAPID
ELEGIT
ELEMIS
ELICIT
ELIXIR
ELOHIM
FLAVIA
FLEWIN
FLORID
FLORIN
GLACIS
GLOBIN
GLORIA
OLDVIC
OLEFIN
OLIVIA
PLACID
PLAGIO
PLUGIN
SLAVIC
SLIDIN
SLIPIN
SLOVIK

•L•••I
ALEXEI
ALKALI
ALUMNI
GLUTEI
ILLINI

••LI••
ADLIBS
AGLINT
AILING
ALLIED
ALLIES
ALLIUM
APLITE
ARLISS
BALING
BELIAL
BELIED
BELIEF
BELIES
BELIZE
BOLIDE
BYLINE
CALICO
CALIPH
CELINE
CILIUM
COLIMA
DELICT
DELIST
DELIUS
DOLING
EALING
EELIER
ELLICE
ELLIOT
ENLIST
EOLIAN
EOLITH
FALINE
FELINE
FELIPE
FILIAL
FILING
FILIUS
FOLIAR
FOLIOS
FOLIUM
HALIDE
HALING
HALITE
HELIOS
HELIUM
HOLIER
HOLING
HOLISM
HOLIST
IDLING
ILLINI
INLINE
IOLITE
JOLIET
JOLIOT
JULIAN
JULIET

JULIUS
KALINE
KILIMS
LILIES
LILITH
LOLITA
MALIBU
MALICE
MALIGN
MELINA
MILIEU
MOLINE
MULISH
OBLIGE
OGLING
OILIER
OILING
ONLINE
OOLITE
OOLITH
OWLISH
OXLIPS
PALING
PALISH
PELION
PILING
POLICE
POLICY
POLING
POLISH
POLITE
POLITY
PULING
RELICS
RELICT
RELIED
RELIEF
RELIES
RELINE
RELISH
RELIST
RELIVE
RILING
RULING
SALINA
SALINE
SALISH
SALIVA
SILICA
SOLIDI
SOLIDS
SOLING
SPLICE
SPLINE
SPLINT
SPLITS
TALION
TILING
TOLIFE
TULIPS
UGLIER
UGLIES
UGLIFY
UNLIKE
UNLINK
UPLIFT
UPLINK
VALISE
VALIUM
VILIFY
WILIER
WILING
YALIES

••L•I•

AFLCIO
AGLAIA
BALTIC
BELAIR
BELOIT
BILLIE
BOLLIX
BULBIL
CALAIS
CALLIN
CALVIN
CELTIC
COLLIE
CULKIN
CULLIS
CULTIC
DELRIO
DELTIC
ECLAIR
FALLIN
FELLIN
FILLIN
FILLIP
FOLKIE
GALLIA
GALLIC
GALOIS
GILLIE
GILLIS
GOLDIE
HALOID
HELDIN
HOLDIT
INLAID
KELPIE
KELVIN
KILTIE
LILLIE
MALKIN
MALTIN
MCLAIN
MELVIL
MELVIN
MILLIE
MILTIE
NELLIE
OILRIG
PALLIA
PALLID
PELVIC
PELVIS
PILEIN
PULLIN
PULPIT
RELAID
ROLLIE
ROLLIN
SALVIA
SOLEIL
SYLVIA
TALKIE
TILLIE
TILLIS
TILSIT
UNLAID
VALOIS
WALKIE
WALKIN
WALLIS
WELKIN
WILLIE
WILLIS
XYLOID

••L••I

BILOXI
DALASI
DELPHI
FULANI
GELATI
ILLINI
MALAWI
MALLEI
MALOTI
NILGAI
PILOTI
POLLOI
SALAMI
SALUKI
SILENI
SOLIDI

•••LI•

ADELIE
AEOLIA
AEOLIC
AMALIE
AMBLIN
AMELIA
ANGLIA
APULIA
ARALIA
BERLIN
BIBLIO
BIGLIE
BILLIE
BOLLIX
CALLIN
COLLIE
COOLIT
CULLIS
CYCLIC
DAHLIA
DAYLIT
DEALIN
DOBLIN
DUBLIN
DUNLIN
EMILIA
EMILIO
ETALIA
ETALII
EUCLID
EXILIC
EYELID
FALLIN
FELLIN
FILLIN
FILLIP
FROLIC
GAELIC
GALLIA
GALLIC
GARLIC
GASLIT
GATLIN
GILLIE
GILLIS
GOALIE
GOBLIN
HAMLIN
HEFLIN
HOWLIN
ISELIN
ITALIA
ITALIC
JOPLIN
KAHLIL
KAOLIN
KHALID
LESLIE
LILLIE
LUBLIN
MAILIN
MAJLIS
MARLIN
MATLIN
MEALIE
MERLIN
MILLIE
MOULIN
MUSLIM
MUSLIN
MYELIN
NAILIN
NELLIE
OBELIA
OXALIS
PALLIA
PALLID
PHILIP
POPLIN
PRELIM
PROLIX
PUBLIC
PULLIN
PURLIN
RATLIN
REALIA
REELIN
ROLLIE
ROLLIN
SCALIA
STALIN
STOLID
SUNLIT
SUSLIK
THALIA
THELIP
TILLIE
TILLIS
TOMLIN
TWILIT
URALIC
VIOLIN
WALLIS
WILLIE
WILLIS

•••L•I

AMALFI
ETALII
KUBLAI
MALLEI
NIELLI
NUCLEI
OCELLI
POLLOI
SMALTI

••••LI

ALKALI
ANGELI
ANNULI
ARGALI
CUMULI
DENALI
KIGALI
LAZULI
MOWGLI
NAPOLI
NEPALI
NEROLI
NIELLI
OCELLI
POPULI
SOMALI
TIVOLI
TUMULI

L••J••

LOGJAM

•L•J••

ELIJAH

••LJ••

SELJUK

L•K•••

LAKERS
LAKOTA
LEKVAR
LIKELY
LIKENS
LIKING

L••K••

LACKED
LACKEY
LANKER
LANKLY
LARKED
LATKES
LEAKED
LEAKER
LEAKEY
LICKED
LINKED
LINKER
LINKUP
LOCKED
LOCKER
LOCKET
LOCKIN
LOCKUP
LOOKAT
LOOKED
LOOKER
LOOKIN
LOOKON
LOOKTO
LOOKUP
LOWKEY
LUCKED
LUNKER
LURKED

L•••K•

LUSAKA

L••••K

LOMBOK
LUBECK

•LK•••

ALKALI
ALKENE
ALKYDS
ALKYLS

•L•K••

BLOKES
FLAKED
FLAKER
FLAKES
FLUKES
SLAKED
SLAKES

•L••K•

ALASKA
ALECKY
BLACKS
BLANKS
BLINKS
BLOCKS
BLOCKY
CLACKS
CLANKS
CLANKY
CLARKE
CLEEKS
CLERKS
CLICKS
CLINKS
CLOAKS
CLOCKS
CLONKS
CLUCKS
CLUNKS
CLUNKY
FLACKS
FLANKS
FLASKS
FLECKS
FLICKA
FLICKS
FLOCKS
FLUNKS
FLUNKY
GLINKA
PLANKS
PLINKS
PLONKS
PLUCKS
PLUCKY
PLUNKS
SLACKS
SLEEKS
SLEEKY
SLICKS
SLINKS
SLINKY

•L•••K

PLANCK
SLEZAK
SLOVAK
SLOVIK

••LK••

BALKAN
BALKED
BILKED
BULKED
CALKED
CULKIN
FOLKIE
FOLKSY
HULKED
KALKAN
MALKIN
MILKED
MILKER
POLKAS
SILKED
SILKEN
SULKED
SULKER
TALKAT
TALKED
TALKER
TALKIE
TALKTO
TALKUP
WALKED
WALKER
WALKIE
WALKIN
WALKON
WALKUP
WELKIN
WILKES
YOLKED

••L•K•

KALAKH
KULAKS
MOLTKE
SALUKI
STLUKE
TILAKS
UNLIKE

••L••K

GALYAK
INLUCK
OCLOCK
RELOCK
SELJUK
UNLINK
UNLOCK
UPLINK

•••LK•

CAULKS
CHALKS
CHALKY
SKULKS
STALKS
STALKY
WHELKS

•••L•K

MUKLUK
SUSLIK
URALSK

••••LK

BYTALK
INBULK

LL••••

LLAMAS
LLANOS
LLBEAN
LLOYDS

L•L•••

LALALA
LELAND
LILACS
LILIES
LILITH
LILLIE
LILTED
LOLITA
LOLLED
LULLED

L••L••

LADLED
LADLER
LADLES
LAYLOW
LEALTY
LESLEY
LESLIE
LIELOW
LILLIE
LISLES
LOLLED
LUBLIN
LUDLUM
LULLED
LYNLEY

L•••L•

LABELS
LABILE
LALALA
LAMELY
LANKLY
LAPELS
LASTLY
LATELY
LAZILY
LAZULI
LEANLY
LEGALS
LETFLY
LEVELS
LEWDLY
LIABLE
LIBELS
LIGULA
LIKELY
LIMPLY
LITTLE
LIVELY
LOBULE
LOCALE
LOCALS
LOGILY
LONELY
LORDLY
LOUDLY
LOVELL
LOVELY
LOWELL
LOYOLA
LUNULA
LUSHLY

L••••L

LABIAL
LAPFUL
LARVAL
LAUREL
LAWFUL
LEMUEL
LENTIL
LETHAL
LINEAL
LINTEL
LIONEL
LISTEL
LONNOL
LOREAL
LOVELL
LOWCAL
LOWELL

•LL•••

ALLAYS
ALLBUT
ALLDAY
ALLEES
ALLEGE
ALLELE
ALLEYS
ALLIED
ALLIES
ALLIUM
ALLMAN
ALLOTS
ALLOUT
ALLOWS
ALLOYS
ALLPRO
ALLSET
ALLUDE
ALLURE
ALLWET
ELLERY
ELLICE
ELLIOT
ILLEST
ILLFED
ILLINI
ILLMET
ILLSAY
ILLUME
ILLUSE
ULLAGE
ULLMAN

•L•L••

ALULAE
ALULAR
SLALOM
TLALOC

•L••L•

ALIBLE
ALKALI
ALKYLS
ALLELE
FLAILS
FLATLY
GLADLY
GLIBLY
GLUMLY
ILOILO
SLIMLY
SLOWLY

•L•••L

FLORAL
GLOBAL
GLYCOL
OLEVEL
PLAGAL
PLURAL

••LL••

BALLAD
BALLET
BALLOT
BALLUP
BELLED
BELLES
BELLOC
BELLOW
BILLED
BILLET
BILLIE
BILLON
BILLOW
BOLLIX
BULLAE
BULLED
BULLET
CALLAO
CALLAS
CALLED
CALLER
CALLES
CALLIN
CALLON
CALLOW
CALLUP
CALLUS
CELLAE
CELLAR
CELLED
CELLOS
COLLAR
COLLET
COLLIE
COLLOP
COLLOQ
CULLED
CULLEN
CULLER
CULLET
CULLIS
DALLAS
DALLES
DILLER
DILLON
DOLLAR
DOLLED
DOLLOP
DOLLUP
DULLEA
DULLED
DULLER
DULLES
FALLEN
FALLIN
FALLON
FALLOW
FALLTO
FELLAH
FELLAS
FELLED
FELLER
FELLIN
FELLOE
FELLOW
FELLTO
FILLED
FILLER
FILLES
FILLET
FILLIN
FILLIP
FILLUP
FOLLOW
FULLER
GALLED
GALLEY
GALLIA
GALLIC
GALLON
GALLOP
GALLUP
GELLED
GILLED
GILLIE
GILLIS
GOLLUM
GULLAH
GULLED
GULLET
HALLEL
HALLEY
HALLOO
HALLOS
HALLOW
HALLUX
HELLAS
HELLER
HELLOS
HILLED
HILLEL
HILLER
HOLLER
HOLLOW
HULLED
HULLER
HULLOS
JELLED
KELLER
KELLEY
KILLED
KILLER
LILLIE
LOLLED
LULLED
MALLEE
MALLEI
MALLET
MALLOW
MELLON
MELLOW
MILLAY
MILLED
MILLER
MILLET
MILLIE
MULLAH
MULLAS
MULLED
MULLER
MULLET
NELLIE
NULLAH
NULLED
PALLAS
PALLED
PALLET
PALLIA
PALLID
PALLOR
PELLET
PILLAR
PILLED
PILLOW
POLLED
POLLEN
POLLER
POLLEX
POLLOI
POLLUX
PULLED
PULLET
PULLEY
PULLIN
PULLON
PULLUP
RILLES
RILLET
ROLLED
ROLLER
ROLLIE
ROLLIN
ROLLON
ROLLUP
SALLET
SALLOW
SELLER
SULLEN
TALLER
TALLOW
TELLER
TELLON
TILLED
TILLER
TILLIE
TILLIS
TOLLED
TULLES
VALLEE
VALLEY
VELLUM
VILLAS
VILLON
VILLUS
VOLLEY
WALLED
WALLER
WALLET
WALLIS
WALLOP
WALLOW
WALLUP
WELLED
WELLES
WELLUP
WILLED
WILLEM
WILLET
WILLIE
WILLIS
WILLOW
YELLED
YELLER
YELLOW

••L•L•

ALLELE
BALDLY
BOLDLY
CALMLY
COLDLY
LALALA
MILDLY
OGLALA
OOLALA
PALELY
SALALS
SOLELY
VILELY
WILDLY

••L••L

ATLATL
BELIAL
BULBIL
BULBUL
FILIAL
HALLEL
HILLEL
MELVIL
SOLEIL

•••LL•

ABOLLA
ADELLE
AIELLO
APOLLO
ARALLU
ATOLLS
AXILLA
BOULLE
BRILLO
BRILLS
BROLLY
CHILLS
CHILLY
CHOLLA
COOLLY
DRILLS
DROLLS
DROLLY
DUALLY
DUELLO
DWELLS
EVILLY
FAILLE
FOULLY
FRILLS
FRILLY
GRILLE
GRILLS
IDYLLS
KNELLS
KNOLLS
KPELLE
KVELLS
NIELLI
NIELLO
OCELLI
OKELLY
ORALLY
OTELLO
PAELLA
PHILLY
PHYLLO
PSYLLA
QUELLS
QUILLS
REALLY
SCULLS
SCULLY
SCYLLA
SHALLY
SHELLS
SHELLY
SHILLS
SHILLY
SKILLS
SKULLS
SMALLS
SMELLS
SMELLY
SNELLS
SPALLS
SPELLS
SPILLS
STALLS
STELLA
STILLS
STILLY
STOLLE
STULLS
SWELLS
SWILLS
TAILLE
TBILLS
THILLS
TRILLS
TROLLS
TUILLE
TWILLS
WHOLLY
WOOLLY

•••L•L

HALLEL
HILLEL
KAHLIL
PHILOL

••••LL

ANGELL
APPALL
ARGYLL
ASWELL
ATWILL
BACALL
BEFALL
BEFELL
CAVELL
COSELL
CYBILL
DOTELL
DUVALL
ENDALL
ENROLL
ERROLL
GIBILL
HAMILL
HOWELL
INFULL
JEKYLL
LOVELL
LOWELL
MABELL
OHWELL
ONCALL
ONEILL
ORWELL
POWELL
RECALL
REFILL
REPOLL
RESELL
RETELL
RYDELL
SCHELL
SCROLL
SEWELL
SHRILL
SQUALL
SQUILL
STROLL
THEYLL
THRALL
THRILL
UNROLL
UNWELL
UPHILL
UPWELL
YOUALL

L•M•••

LAMARR
LAMAZE
LAMBDA
LAMBED
LAMECH
LAMEDH
LAMEDS
LAMELY
LAMENT
LAMESA
LAMEST
LAMIAS
LAMINA
LAMING
LAMMAS
LAMMED
LAMONT
LAMOUR
LEMANS
LEMMAS
LEMMON
LEMNOS
LEMOND
LEMONS
LEMONY
LEMUEL
LEMURS
LIMBED
LIMBER
LIMBOS
LIMBUS
LIMENS
LIMEYS
LIMING
LIMITS
LIMNED
LIMNER
LIMPED
LIMPER
LIMPET
LIMPID
LIMPLY
LOMBOK
LOMEIN
LOMOND
LUMBAR
LUMBER
LUMENS
LUMINA
LUMMOX
LUMPED
LUMPEN
LUMPER
LUMPUR

L••M••

LAMMAS
LAMMED
LAWMAN
LAWMEN
LAYMAN
LAYMEN
LEGMAN
LEGMEN
LEMMAS
LEMMON
LITMUS
LLAMAS
LOAMED
LOOMED
LUMMOX

L•••M•

LARAMS
LEGUME
LEXEME

L••••M

LABRUM
LAPHAM
LATIUM
LCHAIM
LOGJAM
LUDLUM
LYCEUM

•LM•••
ALMOND
ALMOST
ELMIRA
ELMORE
OLMECS

•L•M••
ALAMOS
ALEMAN
ALLMAN
ALOMAR
ALTMAN
ALUMNA
ALUMNI
BLAMED
BLAMES
BLIMEY
BLIMPS
CLAMMY
CLAMOR
CLAMPS
CLAMUP
CLIMAX
CLIMBS
CLIMES
CLOMPS
CLUMPS
CLUMPY
CLUMSY
ELEMIS
ELFMAN
FLAMBE
FLAMED
FLAMES
FLIMSY
FLUMES
FLYMAN
FLYMEN
GLAMOR
GLUMLY
ILLMET
LLAMAS
OLDMAN
OLDMEN
PLUMBS
PLUMED
PLUMES
PLUMMY
PLUMPS
SLIMED
SLIMES
SLIMLY
SLUMMY
SLUMPS
ULLMAN

•L••M•
ALARMS
ALBUMS
BLOOMS
BLOOMY
CLAIMS
CLAMMY
GLEAMS
GLOOMS
GLOOMY
ILLUME
PLASMA
PLASMO
PLUMMY
SLUMMY
ULTIMA
ULTIMO

•L•••M
ALARUM
ALLIUM
ELOHIM
OLDHAM
PLENUM
SLALOM

••LM••
ALLMAN
CALMED
CALMER
CALMLY
COLMAN
DOLMAN
DOLMAS
DOLMEN
FILMED
FULMAR
HELMED
HELMET
HELMUT
HOLMES
ILLMET
KALMAR
KILMER
MELMAC
OILMAN
OILMEN
PALMAS
PALMED
PALMER
PELMET
SALMAN
SALMON
TALMUD
ULLMAN

••L•M•
AFLAME
APLOMB
CCLAMP
COLIMA
COLUMN
GOLEMS
ILLUME
KILIMS
PALOMA
RELUME
SALAMI
SALOME
SOLEMN
VOLUME

••L••M
ABLOOM
AGLEAM
ALLIUM
BALAAM
BALSAM
BELDAM
CILIUM
FOLIUM
FOLSOM
GOLLUM
HELIUM
HOLISM
PHLEGM
PHLOEM
PILEUM
SALAAM
SELDOM
SILOAM
TALCUM
VALIUM
VELLUM
WILLEM

•••LM•
PSALMS
QUALMS
REALMS
STELMO
THELMA

•••L•M
ASYLUM
BEDLAM
COELOM
EMBLEM
GOLLUM
HARLEM
LUDLUM
MOSLEM
MUSLIM
PABLUM
PEPLUM
PHYLUM
PRELIM
SHALOM
SHOLEM
SHOLOM
SLALOM
VELLUM
WHILOM
WILLEM

••••LM
ANSELM
BECALM

L•N•••
LANAIS
LANATE
LANCED
LANCER
LANCES
LANCET
LANDAU
LANDED
LANDER
LANDHO
LANDIS
LANDON
LANDRY
LANGUR
LANIER
LANKER
LANKLY
LANOSE
LANSON
LANVIN
LENAPE
LENDER
LENGTH
LENITY
LENNIE
LENNON
LENORE
LENSED
LENSES
LENTEN
LENTIL
LINAGE
LINDEN
LINEAL
LINEAR
LINENS
LINERS
LINEUP
LINGER
LINGUA
LINING
LINKED
LINKER
LINKUP
LINNET
LINSEY
LINTEL
LINTER
LONDON
LONELY
LONERS
LONGAN
LONGED
LONGER
LONGES
LONGUE
LONNOL
LUNACY
LUNATE
LUNDEN
LUNGED
LUNGES
LUNKER
LUNULA
LYNDON
LYNLEY
LYNXES
LYNYRD

L••N••
LAINIE
LAUNCH
LEANED
LEANER
LEANLY
LEANON
LEANTO
LEMNOS
LENNIE
LENNON
LEONES
LEONID
LEONIE
LERNER
LIANAS
LIANGS
LIENEE
LIGNIN
LIMNED
LIMNER
LINNET
LIONEL
LIONET
LLANOS
LOANED
LOANER
LONNOL
LOONEY
LOUNGE
LUANDA
LUGNUT

L•••N•
LACING
LACUNA
LADING
LADINO
LAGUNA
LAMENT
LAMINA
LAMING
LAMONT
LAPINS
LARYNX
LATENE
LATENS
LATENT
LATINA
LATINO
LATINS
LATONA
LAVING
LAWING
LAYING
LAZING
LEARNS
LEARNT
LEGEND
LELAND
LEMANS
LEMOND
LEMONS
LEMONY
LEVANT
LEVENE
LEVINE
LIERNE
LIKENS
LIKING
LIMENS
LIMING
LINENS
LINING
LIPENG
LITANY
LIVENS
LIVING
LODENS
LOMOND
LOPING
LORENZ
LOSING
LOVING
LOWEND
LOWING
LUBING
LUCENT
LUDENS
LUMENS
LUMINA
LUPINE
LUPINO
LUPONE
LURING
LUTING
LYSINE
LYSINS

L••••N
LAGOON
LAIDIN
LAIDON
LANDON
LANSON
LANVIN
LARDON
LARSEN
LARSON
LASSEN
LATEEN
LATTEN
LAUREN
LAWMAN
LAWMEN
LAWSON
LAWTON
LAYMAN
LAYMEN
LAYSIN
LAYSON
LEADEN
LEADIN
LEADON
LEANON
LEAVEN
LEBRUN
LEGION
LEGMAN
LEGMEN
LEIDEN
LEMMON
LENNON
LENTEN
LEPTON
LESSEN
LESSON
LETSIN
LETSON
LEYDEN
LIBYAN
LICHEN
LIESIN
LIGNIN
LINDEN
LIPTON
LISBON
LISTEN
LISTON
LIVEIN
LIVEON
LLBEAN
LOCKIN
LOGION
LOGSIN
LOGSON
LOMEIN
LONDON
LONGAN
LOOKIN
LOOKON
LOOSEN
LOTION
LOUDEN
LOVEIN
LUBLIN
LUCIAN
LUDDEN
LUMPEN
LUNDEN
LYNDON
LYTTON

•LN•••
ALNICO
ELNINO

•L•N••
ALANON
ALINES
ALONSO
ALONZO
BLANCA
BLANCH
BLANDA
BLANKS
BLENCH
BLENDE
BLENDS
BLINDS
BLINKS
BLINTZ
BLONDE
BLONDS
BLUNTS
CLANCY
CLANGS
CLANKS
CLANKY
CLENCH
CLINCH
CLINES
CLINGS
CLINGY
CLINIC
CLINKS
CLONED
CLONES
CLONKS
CLONUS
CLUNKS
CLUNKY
ELANDS
ELINOR
FLANGE
FLANKS
FLENSE
FLINCH
FLINGS
FLINTS
FLINTY
FLUNKS
FLUNKY
FLYNET
GLANCE
GLANDS
GLENDA
GLINKA
GLINTS
LLANOS
OLINDA
OLINGO
PLANAR
PLANCK
PLANED
PLANER
PLANES
PLANET
PLANKS
PLANON
PLANTE
PLANTS
PLENTY
PLENUM
PLINKS
PLINTH
PLONKS
PLUNGE
PLUNKS
SLANGS
SLANGY
SLANTS
SLINGS
SLINKS
SLINKY

•L••N•
ALBANO
ALBANY
ALBINO
ALDINE
ALFINE
ALIENS
ALIGNS
ALKENE
ALMOND
ALOINS
ALPINE
ALUMNA
ALUMNI
BLAINE
BLUING
CLEANS
CLIENT
CLOWNS
CLUING
ELAINE
ELAYNE
ELNINO
FLAUNT
FLUENT
FLYING
GLEANS
GLUING
GLUONS
ILEANA
ILLINI
PLAINS
PLAINT
PLIANT
PLYING
SLOANE
SLUING

•L•••N
ALANON
ALBION
ALBOIN
ALCUIN
ALDRIN
ALEMAN
ALFVEN
ALISON
ALLMAN
ALTMAN
BLAZON
BLIXEN
BLOWIN
CLAVIN
CLIPON
CLOVEN
CLUEIN
ELEVEN
ELFMAN
ELOIGN
FLACON
FLAGON
FLAXEN
FLEWIN
FLORIN
FLYMAN
FLYMEN
GLOBIN
GLUTEN
KLAXON
KLIBAN
LLBEAN
OLDMAN
OLDMEN
OLEFIN
PLANON
PLATEN
PLAYON
PLUGIN
SLIDIN
SLIPIN
SLIPON
SLOGAN
SLOVEN
ULLMAN

••LN••
KILNED
MILNER
MOLNAR
WALNUT

••L•N•
AGLINT
AILING
ARLENE
ASLANT
BALING
BELONG
BYLINE
CELINE
COLONS
COLONY
DELANO
DELANY
DELONG
DOLING
EALING
FALANA
FALINE
FELINE
FELONS
FELONY
FILENE
FILING
FULANI
GALENA
HALING
HELENA
HELENE
HELENS
HOLING
IDLING
ILLINI
INLAND
INLINE
IRLENE
ISLAND
JOLENE
KALINE
KDLANG
LELAND
MALONE
MELANO
MELINA
MELONS
MILANO
MOLINE
NOLENS
NYLONS
OBLONG
OGLING
OILING
ONLAND
ONLINE
OOLONG
PALING
PILING
POLAND
POLING
PULING
PYLONS
RELENT
RELINE
RILING
ROLAND
RULING
SALINA
SALINE
SALONS
SELENA
SELENE
SILENI
SILENT
SILONE
SOLANS
SOLENT
SOLING
SOLONG
SPLINE
SPLINT
TALENT
TALONS
TILING
TULANE
UCLANS
UHLANS
UNLINK
UPLAND
UPLINK
VALENS
VALENT
VOLANS
VOLANT
VOLENS
WILING
XYLENE

••L••N
AILEEN
ALLMAN
BALEEN
BALKAN
BILLON
BOLEYN
BOLTON
CALLIN
CALLON
CALVIN
COLMAN
COLUMN
CULKIN
CULLEN
DALTON
DELEON
DILLON
DOLMAN
DOLMEN
EILEEN
EOLIAN
FALCON
FALLEN
FALLIN
FALLON
FELDON
FELLIN
FILLIN
FULTON
GALLON
GOLDEN
HELDIN
HELDON
HILTON
HOLDEN
HOLDON
JOLSON
JULIAN
KALKAN
KELVIN
MALDEN
MALIGN
MALKIN
MALTIN
MCLAIN
MCLEAN
MELLON
MELTON
MELVIN
MELVYN
MILTON
MOLTEN
NELSON
OILCAN
OILMAN
OILMEN
OILPAN
ONLOAN
PELION
PILEIN
PILEON
POLEYN
POLLEN
PULLIN
PULLON
ROLLIN
ROLLON
RULEON
SALMAN
SALMON
SALOON
SALTEN
SALTON
SILKEN
SOLDAN
SOLDON
SOLEMN
SPLEEN
SULLEN
SULTAN
SYLVAN
TALION
TELLON
TILDEN
TULSAN
ULLMAN
VILLON
VULCAN
WALDEN
WALKIN
WALKON
WALTON
WELKIN
WILSON
WILTON

•••L•N
AMBLIN
AVALON
BANLON
BERLIN
BILLON
CALLIN
CALLON
CEYLON
CULLEN
DEALIN
DILLON
DOBLIN
DUBLIN
DUNLIN
EVELYN
FALLEN
FALLIN
FALLON
FELLIN
FILLIN
GALLON
GATLIN
GOBLIN
HAMLIN
HARLAN
HEFLIN
HOWLIN
ISELIN
JACLYN
JOPLIN
KAOLIN
KAPLAN
KJOLEN
KUNLUN
LUBLIN
MAILIN
MARLIN
MARLON
MATLIN
MELLON
MERLIN
MERLON
MOULIN
MUSLIN
MYELIN
NAILIN
POLLEN
POPLIN
PULLIN
PULLON
PURLIN
RAGLAN
RATLIN
REELIN
REPLAN
REVLON
ROLLIN
ROLLON
STALIN
STOLEN
STOLON
SULLEN
TEFLON
TELLON
TIGLON
TOMLIN
TOULON
VEBLEN
VILLON
VIOLIN
WAYLON
WOOLEN

••••LN
WEDELN

LO••••
LOADED
LOADER
LOAFED
LOAFER
LOAMED
LOANED
LOANER
LOATHE
LOAVES
LOBATE
LOBBED
LOBBER
LOBULE
LOCALE
LOCALS
LOCATE
LOCKED
LOCKER
LOCKET
LOCKIN
LOCKUP
LOCUST
LODENS
LODGED
LODGER
LODGES
LOFTED
LOGGED
LOGGER
LOGGIA
LOGIER
LOGILY
LOGION
LOGJAM
LOGOFF
LOGOUT
LOGSIN
LOGSON
LOITER
LOLITA
LOLLED
LOMBOK
LOMEIN
LOMOND
LONDON
LONELY
LONERS
LONGAN
LONGED
LONGER
LONGES
LONGUE
LONNOL
LOOFAH
LOOKAT
LOOKED
LOOKER
LOOKIN
LOOKON
LOOKTO
LOOKUP
LOOMED
LOONEY
LOOPED
LOOPER
LOOSED
LOOSEN
LOOSER
LOOSES
LOOTED
LOOTER
LOPERS
LOPING
LOPPED
LOPPER
LOQUAT
LORDED
LORDLY
LOREAL
LORENZ
LORICA
LORIES
LOSEIT
LOSERS
LOSING
LOSSES
LOSTIT
LOTAHS
LOTHAR
LOTION
LOTTED
LOTTOS
LOUCHE
LOUDEN
LOUDER
LOUDLY
LOUISA
LOUISE
LOUNGE
LOUPES
LOUSED
LOUSES
LOUVER
LOUVRE
LOVAGE
LOVEIN
LOVELL
LOVELY
LOVERS
LOVETT
LOVING
LOWBOY
LOWCAL
LOWELL
LOWEND
LOWERS
LOWERY
LOWEST
LOWFAT
LOWING
LOWKEY
LOYOLA

L•O•••
LAOTSE
LAOTZU
LEONES
LEONID
LEONIE
LHOTSE
LIONEL
LIONET
LIOTTA
LLOYDS
LOOFAH
LOOKAT
LOOKED
LOOKER
LOOKIN
LOOKON
LOOKTO
LOOKUP
LOOMED
LOONEY
LOOPED
LOOPER
LOOSED
LOOSEN
LOOSER
LOOSES
LOOTED
LOOTER

L••O••
LABORS
LABOUR
LADOGA
LAGOON
LAHORE
LAKOTA
LAMONT
LAMOUR
LANOSE
LAROSA
LATONA
LATOUR
LATOYA
LAYOFF
LAYOUT
LEDOFF
LEDOUT
LEMOND
LEMONS
LEMONY
LENORE
LETOFF
LETOUT
LIPOID
LITOUT
LOGOFF
LOGOUT
LOMOND
LOYOLA
LUGOSI
LUPONE

L•••O•
LAGOON
LAIDON
LANDON
LANSON
LAPDOG
LAPTOP
LARDON
LARGOS
LARSON
LASSOS
LAWSON
LAWTON
LAYFOR
LAYLOW
LAYSON
LAZBOY
LEADON
LEANON
LECTOR
LEGION
LEMMON
LEMNOS
LENNON
LEPTON
LESBOS
LESSON
LESSOR
LETSON
LICTOR
LIELOW
LIMBOS
LIPTON
LIQUOR
LISBOA
LISBON
LISTON
LITHOG
LITHOS
LIVEON
LLANOS
LOGION
LOGSON
LOMBOK
LONDON
LONNOL
LOOKON
LOTION
LOTTOS
LOWBOY
LUMMOX

LUTHOR
LYNDON
LYTTON

L••••O
LADINO
LAIDTO
LANDHO
LAREDO
LASHIO
LATIGO
LATINO
LAVABO
LAYSTO
LEADTO
LEANTO
LEGATO
LETSGO
LIBIDO
LIESTO
LOOKTO
LUPINO

•LO•••
ALOHAS
ALOINS
ALOMAR
ALONSO
ALONZO
BLOATS
BLOCKS
BLOCKY
BLOKES
BLONDE
BLONDS
BLOODY
BLOOEY
BLOOMS
BLOOMY
BLOOPS
BLOTCH
BLOTTO
BLOUSE
BLOWER
BLOWIN
BLOWIT
BLOWUP
BLOWZY
CLOACA
CLOAKS
CLOCHE
CLOCKS
CLOGUP
CLOMPS
CLONED
CLONES
CLONKS
CLONUS
CLOQUE
CLORIS
CLOROX
CLOSED
CLOSER
CLOSES
CLOSET
CLOTHE
CLOTHO
CLOTHS
CLOTTY
CLOUDS
CLOUDY
CLOUTS
CLOVEN
CLOVER
CLOVES
CLOVIS
CLOWNS
CLOYED
ELOHIM
ELOIGN
ELOISE
ELOPED
ELOPER
ELOPES
FLOATS
FLOCKS
FLOODS
FLOOEY
FLOORS
FLOPPY
FLOPSY
FLORAE
FLORAL
FLORAS
FLORES
FLORET
FLORID
FLORIN
FLOSSY
FLOURS
FLOURY
FLOUTS
FLOWED
FLOWER
GLOATS
GLOBAL
GLOBED
GLOBES
GLOBIN
GLOGGS
GLOOMS
GLOOMY
GLOPPY
GLORIA
GLOSSA
GLOSSY
GLOVED
GLOVER
GLOVES
GLOWED
GLOWER
ILOILO
KLOOFS
LLOYDS
PLONKS
PLOUGH
PLOVER
PLOWED
PLOWER
SLOANE
SLOGAN
SLOOPS
SLOPED
SLOPES
SLOPPY
SLOSHY
SLOTHS
SLOUCH
SLOUGH
SLOVAK
SLOVEN
SLOVIK
SLOWED
SLOWER
SLOWLY
SLOWUP
ZLOTYS

•L•O••
ALBOIN
ALBORG
ALCOTT
ALCOVE
ALDOSE
ALDOUS
ALGORE
ALIOTO
ALLOTS
ALLOUT
ALLOWS
ALLOYS
ALMOND
ALMOST
BLOODY
BLOOEY
BLOOMS
BLOOMY
BLOOPS
ELBOWS
ELMORE
ELWOOD
FLOODS
FLOOEY
FLOORS
FLUORO
FLYOUT
GLOOMS
GLOOMY
GLUONS
KLOOFS
SLOOPS

•L••O•
ALAMOS
ALANON
ALBION
ALISON
BLAZON
BLUEOX
CLAMOR
CLAROS
CLIPON
CLOROX
ELINOR
ELLIOT
ELWOOD
FLACON
FLAGON
FLAVOR
FLEXOR
FLYBOY
FLYROD
GLAMOR
GLYCOL
KLAXON
LLANOS
OLDBOY
PLANON
PLAYON
PLEXOR
SLALOM
SLIPON
TLALOC

•L•••O
ALBANO
ALBEDO
ALBINO
ALECTO
ALEPPO
ALIOTO
ALLPRO
ALNICO
ALONSO
ALONZO
BLOTTO
CLOTHO
ELNINO
ELPASO
FLUORO
ILOILO
OLDPRO
OLINGO
PLAGIO
PLASMO
SLUGGO
ULTIMO

••LO••
ABLOOM
AFLOAT
ALLOTS
ALLOUT
ALLOWS
ALLOYS
APLOMB
ASLOPE
BELOIT
BELONG
BILOXI
BULOVA
CHLORO
COLONS
COLONY
COLORS
COLOUR
DELONG
DOLORS
EULOGY
FELONS
FELONY
FILOSE
GALOIS
GALOOT
GALOPS
GALORE
GALOSH
HALOED
HALOES
HALOID
HELOTS
IGLOOS
INLOVE
JALOPY
MALONE
MALORY
MALOTI
MELODY
MELONS
MELOTT
MILORD
MILOSZ
MOLOCH
MOLOPO
NOLOAD
NYLONS
OBLONG
OCLOCK
ONLOAN
OOLOGY
OOLONG
ORLOPS
PALOMA
PELOPS
PELOTA
PHLOEM
PILOSE
PILOTI
PILOTS
PYLONS
RELOAD
RELOCK
SALOME
SALONS
SALOON
SILOAM
SILOED
SILONE
SOLOED
SOLONG
SPLOSH
TALONS
UNLOAD
UNLOCK
UPLOAD
VALOIS
VALOUR
VELOCE
VELOUR
XYLOID

••L•O•
ABLOOM
BALBOA
BALLOT
BELLOC
BELLOW
BILLON
BILLOW
BOLTON
CALLON
CALLOW
CELLOS
COLLOP
COLLOQ
DALTON
DELEON
DILLON
DOLLOP
ELLIOT
FALCON
FALLON
FALLOW
FELDON
FELLOE
FELLOW
FOLIOS
FOLLOW
FOLSOM
FULTON
GALLON
GALLOP
GALOOT
HALLOO
HALLOS
HALLOW
HELDON
HELIOS
HELLOS
HILTON
HOLDON
HOLLOW
HULLOS
IGLOOS
JOLIOT
JOLSON
MALLOW
MELLON
MELLOW
MELTON
MILTON
NELSON
PALLOR
PELION
PILEON
PILLOW
POLLOI
POLPOT
PULLON
ROLEOS
ROLLON
RULEON
SALLOW
SALMON
SALOON
SALTON
SALVOR
SALVOS
SELDOM
SOLDON
TALBOT
TALION
TALLOW
TELLON
TOLDOF
VILLON
VOLVOX
WALKON
WALLOP
WALLOW
WALTON
WILLOW
WILSON
WILTON
YELLOW

••L••O
AFLCIO
ALLPRO
BILBAO
BOLERO
CALICO
CALLAO
CHLORO
COLUGO
DELANO
DELRIO
FALLTO
FELLTO
GELATO
HALLOO
HELDTO
HOLDTO
MALABO
MELANO
MILANO
MOLOPO
PALAEO
PHLEBO
TALKTO
TOLEDO
VELCRO

•••LO•
ANALOG
ANGLOS
AVALON
BADLOT
BAILOR
BALLOT
BANLON
BAYLOR
BELLOC
BELLOW
BILLON
BILLOW
CALLON
CALLOW
CARLOS
CARLOT
CELLOS
CEYLON
CHILOE
COELOM
COLLOP
COLLOQ
CYCLOS
DEPLOY
DIALOG
DIGLOT
DILLON
DOLLOP
DUNLOP
DYELOT
EMPLOY
ENBLOC
EPILOG
FALLON
FALLOW
FARLOW
FELLOE
FELLOW
FOLLOW
GALLON
GALLOP
GASLOG
GOSLOW
HALLOO
HALLOS
HALLOW
HARLOW
HELLOS
HOLLOW
HULLOS
INFLOW
JOBLOT
LAYLOW
LIELOW
MALLOW
MARLON
MELLON
MELLOW
MERLON
MERLOT
OCELOT
ODDLOT
PAILOU
PALLOR
PARLOR
PAVLOV
PEPLOS
PHILOL
PHILOS
PILLOW
POLLOI
PROLOG
PULLON
REPLOW
REVLON
ROLLON
SAILOR
SALLOW
SAWLOG
SHALOM
SHILOH
SHOLOM
SLALOM
STOLON
TAILOR
TALLOW
TAYLOR
TEFLON
TELLON
TIGLON
TLALOC
TOULON
UNCLOG
VILLON
WALLOP
WALLOW
WAYLON
WHILOM
WILLOW
YELLOW
ZEALOT
ZIPLOC

•••L•O
AIELLO
APOLLO
BIBLIO
BRILLO
CALLAO
CHALCO
DUELLO
EMILIO
FALLTO
FELLTO
HALLOO
NIELLO
NUCLEO
OTELLO
PHYLLO
RIALTO
SMALTO
STELMO

••••LO
AIELLO
ANGELO
APOLLO
BAROLO
BRILLO
CUMULO
DAYGLO
DIABLO
DUELLO
GIGOLO
ILOILO
MEGALO
MODULO
NICOLO
NIELLO
NIHILO
OTELLO
PHYLLO
POMELO
PUEBLO
ROBALO
STMALO
TUPELO
YUNGLO

L•P•••
LAPDOG
LAPELS
LAPFUL
LAPHAM
LAPINS
LAPPED
LAPPET
LAPSED
LAPSES
LAPSUP
LAPTEV
LAPTOP
LAPUTA
LEPTON
LIPASE
LIPENG
LIPIDE
LIPIDS
LIPOID
LIPPED
LIPTON
LOPERS
LOPING
LOPPED
LOPPER
LUPINE
LUPINO
LUPONE

L••P••
LAPPED
LAPPET
LAUPER
LEAPED
LEAPER
LIMPED
LIMPER
LIMPET
LIMPID
LIMPLY
LIPPED
LISPED
LOOPED
LOOPER
LOPPED
LOPPER
LOUPES
LUMPED
LUMPEN
LUMPER
LUMPUR

L•••P•
LAYUPS
LENAPE
LETUPS

L••••P
LACEUP
LAIDUP
LAPSUP
LAPTOP
LARRUP
LASHUP
LAYSUP
LEADUP
LETSUP
LIFTUP
LINEUP
LINKUP
LOCKUP
LOOKUP

•LP•••
ALPACA
ALPERT
ALPHAS
ALPINE
ELPASO

•L•P••
ALEPHS
ALEPPO
ALLPRO
CLEPED
CLIPON
ELAPID
ELAPSE
ELOPED
ELOPER
ELOPES
FLIPUP
FLOPPY
FLOPSY
GLOPPY
GLYPHS
OLDPRO
SLAPPY
SLAPUP
SLIPIN
SLIPON
SLIPUP
SLOPED
SLOPES
SLOPPY
SLYPES

•L••P•
ALCAPP
ALEPPO
BLEEPS
BLIMPS
BLOOPS
CLAMPS
CLASPS
CLOMPS
CLUMPS
CLUMPY
FLOPPY
GLOPPY
PLUMPS
SLAPPY
SLEEPS
SLEEPY
SLOOPS
SLOPPY
SLUMPS
SLURPS

•L•••P
ALCAPP
BLEWUP
BLOWUP
CLAMUP
CLOGUP
FLIPUP
PLAYUP
SLAPUP
SLIPUP
SLOWUP

••LP••
ALLPRO
CALPAC
DELPHI
GULPED
GULPER
HELPED
HELPER
KELPIE
MILPAS
OILPAN
PALPUS
POLPOT
PULPED
PULPIT
SYLPHS
WOLPER
YELPED
YELPER
ZILPAH

••L•P•
ASLOPE
CALIPH
FELIPE
GALOPS
JALAPA
JALOPY
JULEPS
MOLOPO
ORLOPS
OXLIPS
PELOPS
POLYPS
TULIPS

••L••P
ASLEEP
BALLUP
CALLUP
CCLAMP
COLLOP
DOLLOP
DOLLUP
FILLIP
FILLUP
FOLDUP
GALLOP
GALLUP
HELDUP
HOLDUP
HOLEUP
MILSAP
PILEUP
PULLUP
ROLLUP
TALKUP
WALKUP
WALLOP
WALLUP
WELLUP

•••LP•
ADOLPH
GUELPH
SCALPS
SCULPT
WHELPS

•••L•P
BALLUP
BURLAP
CALLUP
COILUP
COLLOP
CURLUP
DEWLAP
DOLLOP
DOLLUP
DUNLOP
EARLAP
FILLIP
FILLUP
FOULUP
GALLOP
GALLUP
HAULUP
PHILIP
PULLUP
ROLLUP
SCHLEP
SEALUP
THELIP
TOOLUP
WALLOP
WALLUP
WELLUP

••••LP
MEGILP

L•Q•••
LIQUID
LIQUOR
LOQUAT

•L•Q••
CLAQUE
CLIQUE
CLOQUE
PLAQUE

••LQ••
CALQUE
PULQUE

••L••Q
COLLOQ

•••L•Q
COLLOQ

L•R•••
LARAMS
LARDED
LARDER
LARDON
LAREDO
LARGER
LARGOS
LARIAT
LARKED
LAROSA
LARRUP
LARSEN
LARSON
LARVAE
LARVAL
LARVAS
LARYNX
LERIDA
LERNER
LORDED
LORDLY
LOREAL
LORENZ
LORICA
LORIES
LURING
LURKED
LYRICS
LYRIST

L••R••
LABREA
LABRET
LABRUM
LAIRDS
LARRUP
LAUREL
LAUREN
LAURIE
LEARNS
LEARNT
LEBRUN
LEERAT
LEERED
LEERER
LEGREE
LEHRER
LIBRIS
LIERNE
LITRES
LIVRES

L•••R•
LABORS
LACERS
LADERS
LAGERS
LAHORE
LAKERS
LAMARR
LANDRY
LASERS
LAVERS
LAYERS
LEMURS
LENORE
LEVERS
LIEVRE
LIFERS
LIGERS
LIGURE
LINERS
LITERS
LIVERS
LIVERY
LIZARD
LONERS
LOPERS
LOSERS
LOUVRE
LOVERS
LOWERS
LOWERY
LUGERS
LUSTRE
LUXURY
LYNYRD

L••••R
LAAGER
LABOUR
LACIER
LADDER
LADLER
LAFFER
LAGGER
LAMARR
LAMOUR
LANCER
LANDER
LANGUR
LANIER
LANKER
LARDER
LARGER
LASCAR
LASHER
LASSER
LATHER
LATOUR
LATTER
LAUDER
LAUPER
LAWYER
LAYFOR
LAZIER
LEADER
LEAKER
LEANER
LEAPER
LEASER
LECTOR
LEDGER
LEERER
LEHRER
LEKVAR
LENDER
LERNER
LESSER
LESSOR
LESTER
LETTER
LEVIER
LEWDER
LIBBER
LICTOR
LIEDER
LIEFER
LIFTER
LIMBER
LIMNER
LIMPER
LINEAR
LINGER
LINKER
LINTER
LIQUOR
LISTER
LITTER
LOADER
LOAFER
LOANER
LOBBER
LOCKER
LODGER
LOGGER
LOGIER
LOITER
LONGER
LOOKER
LOOPER
LOOSER
LOOTER
LOPPER
LOTHAR
LOUDER
LOUVER
LUBBER
LUGGER
LUMBAR
LUMBER
LUMPER
LUMPUR
LUNKER
LUSHER
LUSTER
LUTHER
LUTHOR

•L•R••
ALARIC
ALARMS
ALARUM
ALDRIN
ALERTS
ALFRED
BLARED
BLARES
BLURBS
BLURRY
BLURTS
CLARET
CLARKE
CLAROS
CLERGY
CLERIC
CLERKS
CLORIS
CLOROX
ELBRUS
FLARED
FLARES
FLIRTS
FLORAE
FLORAL
FLORAS
FLORES
FLORET
FLORID
FLORIN
FLURRY
FLYROD
GLARED
GLARES
GLORIA
PLURAL
SLURPS
SLURRY
ULTRAS

•L••R•
ALBERT
ALBORG
ALDERS
ALEGRE
ALGORE
ALHIRT
ALLPRO
ALLURE
ALPERT
ALTARS
ALTERS
BLEARS
BLEARY
BLURRY
CLAIRE
CLEARS
ELBERT
ELDERS
ELLERY
ELMIRA
ELMORE
ELVERS
ELVIRA
FLAIRS
FLEERS
FLEURY
FLIERS
FLOORS
FLOURS
FLOURY
FLUORO
FLURRY
FLYERS
GLAIRY
GLUERS
OLDPRO
OLEARY
PLEURA
PLIERS
SLURRY
ULCERS

•L•••R
ALEGAR
ALOMAR
ALTAIR
ALULAR
BLAZER
BLOWER
CLAMOR
CLAWER
CLEVER
CLOSER
CLOVER
DLAYER
ELATER
ELAYER
ELINOR
ELIXIR
ELOPER
FLAKER
FLAVOR
FLAYER
FLEXOR
FLOWER
GLAMOR
GLASER
GLAZER
GLIDER
GLOVER
GLOWER
OLIVER
PLACER
PLANAR
PLANER
PLATER
PLAYER
PLEXOR
PLOVER
PLOWER
SLATER
SLAVER
SLAYER
SLICER
SLIDER
SLIVER
SLOWER
ULSTER

••LR••
DELRAY
DELRIO
OILRIG
WALRUS

••L•R•
AGLARE
AILERS
ALLPRO
ALLURE
BALERS
BELFRY
BOLERO
CELERY
CHLORO
COLORS
DOLORS
EELERS
ELLERY
FILERS
FULCRA
GALORE
HALERS
HALERU
HILARY
IDLERS
MALORY
MILERS
MILORD
MOLARS
NFLERS
NHLERS
OGLERS
OILERS
PALTRY
PELTRY
POLERS
RULERS
SALARY
SCLERA
SOLERS
SULTRY
TILERS
TULARE
VALERY
VELCRO
VOLARE
WALERS

••L••R
BALDER
BELAIR
BOLDER
BOLGER
BULGAR
BULGUR
BULWER
CALDER
CALLER
CALMER
CELLAR
COLDER
COLLAR
COLOUR
COLTER
CULLER
CULVER
DELVER
DILLER
DOLLAR
DULLER
ECLAIR
EELIER
FALSER
FALTER
FELLER
FILLER
FILTER
FOLDER
FOLIAR
FULLER
FULMAR
GILDER
GOLFER
GULPER
HALTER
HELLER
HELPER
HELTER
HILLER
HOLDER
HOLIER
HOLLER
HULLER
KALMAR
KELLER
KILLER
KILMER
KILTER
KULTUR
MILDER
MILKER
MILLER
MILNER
MOLDER
MOLNAR
MOLTER
MULLER
OILIER
PALLOR
PALMER
PALTER
PELTER
PILFER
PILLAR
POLDER
POLLER
PULSAR
ROLLER
SALTER
SALVER
SALVOR
SELLER
SILVER
SOLDER
SOLVER
SULFUR
SULKER
TALKER
TALLER
TELLER
TILLER
TILTER
UGLIER
VALOUR
VELOUR
VULGAR
WALKER
WALLER
WALTER
WELDER
WELTER
WILBUR
WILDER
WILIER
WOLPER
YELLER
YELPER

•••L•R
ALULAR
AMBLER
AMPLER
ANGLER
ANTLER
ASHLAR
BAILER
BAILOR
BAWLER
BAYLOR
BOILER
BOWLER
BUGLER
BUTLER
CABLER
CALLER
CELLAR
CHOLER
COALER
COLLAR
COOLER
CULLER
CURLER
CUTLER
CYCLER
DEALER
DIALER
DILLER
DOLLAR
DUELER
DULLER
EVILER
FABLER
FEELER
FELLER
FILLER
FOOLER
FOULER
FOWLER
FUELER
FULLER
HAULER
HEALER
HEELER
HELLER
HILLER
HOLLER
HOWLER
HULLER
HURLER
JAILER
KEELER
KEGLER
KELLER
KEPLER
KEVLAR
KILLER
KOHLER
LADLER
MAHLER
MAILER
MAULER
MEDLAR
MEWLER
MIDLER
MILLER
MOILER
MULLER
NAILER
NOBLER
OCULAR
OSTLER
OVULAR
PALLOR
PARLOR
PEDLAR
PEELER
PEGLER
PILLAR
POLLER
POPLAR
RAILER
REALER
RIFLER
ROLLER
SAILOR
SCALAR
SCALER
SEALER
SELLER
SISLER
SMILER
STALER
STELAR
STYLER
SUTLER
TAILOR
TALLER
TAYLOR
TELLER
THALER
TILLER
TOILER
UVULAR
WAILER
WALLER
WHALER
WOHLER
YELLER

L•S•••
LASCAR
LASERS
LASHED
LASHER
LASHES
LASHIO
LASHUP
LASSEN
LASSER
LASSES
LASSIE
LASSOS
LASTED
LASTEX
LASTLY
LESAGE
LESBOS
LESLEY
LESLIE
LESSEE
LESSEN
LESSER
LESSON
LESSOR
LESTAT
LESTER
LISBOA
LISBON
LISLES
LISPED
LISTED
LISTEE
LISTEL
LISTEN
LISTER
LISTON
LOSEIT
LOSERS
LOSING
LOSSES
LOSTIT
LUSAKA
LUSHER
LUSHLY
LUSTED
LUSTER
LUSTRE
LYSINE
LYSINS

L••S••
LANSON
LAPSED
LAPSES
LAPSUP
LARSEN
LARSON
LASSEN
LASSER
LASSES
LASSIE
LASSOS
LAWSON
LAYSBY
LAYSIN
LAYSON
LAYSTO
LAYSUP
LEASED
LEASER
LEASES
LENSED
LENSES
LÉSSEE
LESSEN
LESSER
LESSON
LESSOR
LETSAT
LETSBE
LETSGO
LETSIN
LETSON
LETSUP
LIESIN
LIESTO
LINSEY
LOGSIN
LOGSON
LOOSED
LOOSEN
LOOSER
LOOSES
LOSSES
LOUSED
LOUSES

L•••S•
LAGASH
LAMESA
LAMEST
LANOSE
LAOTSE
LAROSA
LATEST
LATISH
LAVISH
LAXEST
LEGIST
LHOTSE
LIAISE
LIPASE
LOCUST
LOUISA
LOUISE
LOWEST
LUGOSI
LUTIST
LYRIST

L••••S
LABELS
LABORS
LACERS
LACHES
LADERS
LADIES
LADLES
LAGERS
LAIRDS
LAKERS
LAMEDS
LAMIAS
LAMMAS
LANAIS
LANCES
LANDIS
LAPELS
LAPINS
LAPSES
LARAMS
LARGOS
LARVAS
LASERS
LASHES
LASSES
LASSOS
LATENS
LATHES
LATINS
LATKES
LAUGHS
LAVERS
LAYBYS
LAYERS
LAYUPS
LEARNS
LEASES
LEAVES
LEDGES
LEGALS
LEHUAS
LEMANS
LEMMAS
LEMNOS
LEMONS
LEMURS
LENSES
LEONES
LESBOS
LETUPS
LEVEES
LEVELS
LEVERS
LEVIES
LIANAS
LIANGS
LIBELS
LIBRIS
LIEGES
LIEUTS
LIFERS
LIGERS
LIGHTS
LIKENS
LILACS
LILIES
LIMBOS
LIMBUS
LIMENS
LIMEYS
LIMITS
LINENS
LINERS
LIPIDS
LISLES
LITERS
LITHOS
LITMUS
LITRES
LIVENS
LIVERS
LIVRES
LLAMAS
LLANOS
LLOYDS
LOAVES
LOCALS
LODENS
LODGES
LONERS
LONGES
LOOSES
LOPERS
LORIES
LOSERS
LOSSES
LOTAHS
LOTTOS
LOUPES
LOUSES
LOVERS
LOWERS
LUCIUS
LUDENS
LUGERS
LUMENS
LUNGES
LYCEES
LYNXES
LYRICS
LYSINS

•LS•••
ALSACE
ULSTER

•L•S••
ALASKA
ALISON
ALLSET
ALYSSA
BLASTS
CLASPS
CLASSY
CLOSED
CLOSER
CLOSES
CLOSET
ELISHA
ELISSA
ELYSEE
FLASHY
FLASKS
FLESHY
FLOSSY
GLASER
GLASSY
GLOSSA
GLOSSY
ILESHA
ILLSAY
PLASHY
PLASMA
PLASMO
PLASTY
PLISSE
PLUSES
PLUSHY
SLOSHY
SLUSHY

•L••S•
ALDOSE
ALEAST
ALMOST
ALONSO
ALWEST
ALYSSA
BLAISE
BLOUSE
BLUEST
BLUESY
BLUISH
CLASSY
CLAUSE
CLEESE
CLUMSY
ELAPSE
ELDEST
ELFISH
ELISSA
ELOISE
ELPASO
FLENSE
FLIMSY
FLOPSY
FLOSSY
GLASSY
GLOSSA
GLOSSY
ILLEST
ILLUSE
KLEIST
NLEAST
NLWEST
OLDEST
OLDISH
PLEASE
PLISSE
SLIEST
SLYEST

•L•••S
ALAMOS
ALARMS
ALBUMS
ALDERS
ALDOUS
ALEPHS
ALERTS
ALEUTS
ALEXIS
ALIBIS
ALIENS
ALIGNS
ALINES
ALKYDS
ALKYLS
ALLAYS
ALLEES
ALLEYS
ALLIES
ALLOTS
ALLOWS
ALLOYS
ALOHAS
ALOINS
ALPHAS
ALTARS
ALTERS
ALWAYS
BLACKS
BLADES
BLAMES
BLANKS
BLARES
BLASTS
BLAZES
BLEARS
BLEATS
BLEEDS
BLEEPS
BLENDS
BLIMPS
BLINDS
BLINKS
BLOATS
BLOCKS
BLOKES
BLONDS
BLOOMS
BLOOPS
BLUETS
BLUFFS
BLUNTS
BLURBS
BLURTS
CLACKS
CLAIMS
CLAMPS
CLANGS
CLANKS
CLAROS
CLASPS
CLEANS
CLEARS
CLEATS
CLEEKS
CLEFTS
CLERKS
CLEVES
CLEVIS
CLICKS
CLIFFS
CLIMBS
CLIMES
CLINES
CLINGS
CLINKS
CLOAKS
CLOCKS
CLOMPS
CLONES
CLONKS
CLONUS
CLORIS
CLOSES
CLOTHS
CLOUDS
CLOUTS
CLOVES
CLOVIS
CLOWNS
CLUCKS
CLUMPS
CLUNKS
ELANDS
ELATES
ELBOWS
ELBRUS
ELDERS
ELECTS
ELEMIS
ELEVES
ELIDES
ELITES
ELOPES
ELUDES
ELUTES
ELVERS
FLACKS
FLAILS
FLAIRS
FLAKES
FLAMES
FLANKS
FLARES
FLASKS
FLAXES
FLECKS
FLEERS
FLEETS
FLEXES
FLICKS
FLIERS
FLINGS
FLINTS
FLIRTS
FLOATS
FLOCKS
FLOODS
FLOORS
FLORAS
FLORES
FLOURS
FLOUTS
FLUFFS
FLUIDS
FLUKES
FLUMES
FLUNKS
FLUTES
FLUXES
FLYBYS
FLYERS
GLACES
GLACIS
GLADES
GLADYS
GLANDS
GLARES
GLAZES
GLEAMS
GLEANS
GLEBES
GLIDES
GLINTS
GLOATS
GLOBES
GLOGGS
GLOOMS
GLOVES
GLUERS
GLUONS
GLYPHS
KLOOFS
LLAMAS
LLANOS
LLOYDS
OLDIES
OLIVES
OLMECS
PLACES
PLAGES
PLAIDS
PLAINS
PLAITS
PLANES
PLANKS
PLANTS
PLATES
PLAYAS
PLAZAS
PLEADS
PLEATS
PLEBES
PLEXUS
PLIERS
PLINKS
PLONKS
PLUCKS
PLUMBS
PLUMES
PLUMPS
PLUNKS
PLUSES
SLACKS
SLAKES
SLANGS
SLANTS
SLATES
SLAVES
SLEEKS
SLEEPS
SLEETS
SLICES
SLICKS
SLIDES
SLIMES
SLINGS
SLINKS
SLOOPS
SLOPES
SLOTHS
SLUMPS
SLURPS
SLYPES
ULCERS
ULTRAS
ZLOTYS

••LS••
ALLSET
BALSAM
DILSEY
FALSER
FOLSOM
GELSEY
HALSEY
ILLSAY
JOLSON
KELSEY
MILSAP
NELSON
PULSAR
PULSED
PULSES
SALSAS
TILSIT
TULSAN
WILSON
WOLSEY

••L•S•
ABLEST
ABLUSH
ARLISS
ATLAST
CALASH
DALASI
DELIST
ENLIST
FILOSE
FOLKSY
GALOSH
HALEST
HOLISM
HOLIST
IDLEST
ILLEST
ILLUSE
MILOSZ
MOLEST
MULISH
NOLESS
OBLAST
OWLISH
PALEST
PALISH
PILOSE
POLISH
RELISH
RELIST
SALISH
SPLASH
SPLOSH
TALESE
UNLASH
UNLESS
VALISE
VILEST
WALESA

••L••S
ADLIBS
AFLATS
AGLETS
AILERS
ALLAYS
ALLEES
ALLEYS
ALLIES
ALLOTS
ALLOWS
ALLOYS
ARLISS
BALERS
BELAYS
BELIES
BELLES
BILGES
BULGES
BYLAWS
CALAIS
CALCES
CALLAS
CALLES
CALLUS
CALVES
CALXES
CELEBS
CELLOS
COLEUS
COLONS
COLORS
CULETS
CULLIS
DALLAS
DALLES
DELAYS
DELFTS
DELIUS
DELTAS
DELVES
DOLMAS
DOLORS
DULLES
ECLATS
EELERS
EFLATS
FELLAS
FELONS
FILERS
FILETS
FILIUS
FILLES
FOLIOS
GALOIS
GALOPS
GELEES
GILLIS
GOLEMS
GULAGS
HALERS
HALLOS
HALOES
HALVES
HELENS
HELIOS
HELLAS
HELLOS
HELOTS
HELVES
HOLMES
HULLOS
IDLERS
IGLOOS
INLAWS
INLAYS
INLETS
ISLETS
JULEPS
JULIUS
KILIMS
KULAKS
LILACS
LILIES
MALAYS
MELEES
MELONS
MILERS
MILPAS
MOLARS
MULCTS
MULLAS
NFLERS
NHLERS
NOLENS
NOLESS
NYLONS
OGLERS
OILERS
ORLOPS
OWLETS
OXLIPS
PALLAS
PALMAS
PALPUS
PELEUS
PELOPS
PELVIS
PILAFS
PILEUS
PILOTS
POLERS
POLKAS
POLYPS
PULSES
PYLONS
RELAYS
RELETS
RELICS
RELIES
RILLES
ROLEOS
RULERS
SALADS
SALALS
SALONS
SALSAS
SALVES
SALVOS
SELVES
SOLANS
SOLERS
SOLEUS
SOLFAS
SOLIDS
SOLVES
SPLATS
SPLAYS
SPLITS
SULCUS
SYLPHS
TALONS
TILAKS
TILDES
TILERS
TILLIS
TULIPS
TULLES
UCLANS
UGLIES
UHLANS
UNLESS
VALENS
VALETS
VALOIS
VALUES
VALVES
VELDTS
VILLAS
VILLUS
VOLANS
VOLENS
VOLVAS
WALERS
WALLIS
WALRUS
WELLES
WILKES
WILLIS
WOLVES
YALIES

•••LS•
AVULSE
EVULSE
GRILSE
ORELSE
URALSK
WHILST

•••L•S
ABELES
ADDLES
ADULTS
AEOLUS
AISLES
AKELAS
AMBLES
AMOLES
ANGLES
ANGLOS
ANKLES
ANOLES
APPLES
ATOLLS
BELLES
BIBLES
BOGLES
BOULES
BOWLES
BRILLS
BRULES
BUGLES
BUILDS
CABLES
CALLAS
CALLES

CALLUS
CARLOS
CAULKS
CELLOS
CHALKS
CHELAS
CHILDS
CHILLS
CULLIS
CYCLAS
CYCLES
CYCLOS
DALLAS
DALLES
DHOLES
DOBLAS
DRILLS
DROLLS
DULLES
DWELLS
EAGLES
ECCLES
ECOLES
EDILES
EXALTS
EXILES
EXULTS
FABLES
FAULTS
FELLAS
FIELDS
FILLES
FJELDS
FOWLES
FRILLS
GABLES
GILLIS
GRILLS
GUILDS
GUILES
HALLOS
HELLAS
HELLOS
HULLOS
IDYLLS
INGLES
INKLES
ISTLES
JOULES
KNELLS
KNOLLS
KOALAS
KVELLS
LADLES
LISLES
MAILES
MAJLIS
MAPLES
MOULDS
MOULTS
MULLAS
NAPLES
NOBLES
NYALAS
OBELUS
OODLES
ORALES
ORTLES
OVULES
OXALIS
PALLAS
PEPLOS
PHILOS
POILUS
POULTS
PROLES
PSALMS
QUALMS
QUELLS
QUILLS
QUILTS
REALES
REALMS
RIFLES
RILLES
ROBLES
RUBLES
SABLES
SAULTS
SCALDS
SCALES
SCALPS
SCOLDS
SCULLS
SHALES
SHELLS
SHILLS
SIDLES
SKALDS
SKILLS
SKULKS
SKULLS
SMALLS
SMELLS
SMELTS
SMILES
SNELLS
SOCLES
SPALLS
SPELLS
SPILES
SPILLS
STALES
STALKS
STALLS
STELES
STILES
STILLS
STILTS
STOLES
STULLS
STYLES
STYLUS
SWALES
SWELLS
SWILLS
TABLAS
TABLES
TBILLS
TESLAS
THALES
THILLS
THOLES
TILLIS
TITLES
TOILES
TOKLAS
TRILLS
TROLLS
TULLES
TWILLS
UBOLTS
UNCLES
UVULAS
VAULTS
VILLAS
VILLUS
VIOLAS
VOILES
WALLIS
WELLES
WHALES
WHELKS
WHELPS
WHILES
WHOLES
WIELDS
WILLIS
WORLDS
YIELDS

••••LS

ALKYLS
AMPULS
ANGELS
ANNALS
ANNULS
ANVILS
APPALS
ARTELS
ATOLLS
AVAILS
BABULS
BAGELS
BETELS
BEVELS
BEZELS
BGIRLS
BRAILS
BRAWLS
BRILLS
BROILS
CABALS
CAMELS
CANALS
CAROLS
CASALS
CAVILS
CHILLS
CHURLS
CORALS
CRAWLS
CREELS
CUPELS
DECALS
DEVILS
DOWELS
DRAILS
DRAWLS
DRILLS
DROLLS
DROOLS
DWELLS
EASELS
EDSELS
EMAILS
ENGELS
EQUALS
EXCELS
EXPELS
EXTOLS
FINALS
FLAILS
FRILLS
FUSILS
GAVELS
GAYALS
GHOULS
GIMELS
GNARLS
GORALS
GRAILS
GRILLS
GROWLS
GRUELS
HAMALS
HAZELS
HOSELS
HOTELS
HOVELS
IDEALS
IDYLLS
IMPELS
JACALS
JEWELS
KEVELS
KNEELS
KNELLS
KNOLLS
KNURLS
KRAALS
KVELLS
LABELS
LAPELS
LEGALS
LEVELS
LIBELS
LOCALS
MEDALS
METALS
MODELS
MOGULS
MORALS
MORELS
MOTELS
MURALS
NASALS
NAVELS
NEWELS
NOVELS
ORIELS
OUSELS
OUZELS
PANELS
PEARLS
PEDALS
PERILS
PETALS
PHIALS
PICULS
PIPALS
PIXELS
PROWLS
PUPILS
QUAILS
QUELLS
QUILLS
RATELS
RAVELS
REBELS
REOILS
REPELS
REVELS
RIVALS
RIYALS
ROWELS
ROYALS
SALALS
SCOWLS
SCULLS
SEPALS
SHAWLS
SHELLS
SHILLS
SHOALS
SIBYLS
SIGILS
SISALS
SKILLS
SKIRLS
SKULLS
SMALLS
SMELLS
SNAILS
SNARLS
SNELLS
SOTOLS
SPALLS
SPELLS
SPIELS
SPILLS
SPOILS
SPOOLS
STALLS
STEALS
STEELS
STILLS
STOOLS
STULLS
SWELLS
SWILLS
SWIRLS
TAMILS
TBILLS
TEPALS
THILLS
TICALS
TOTALS
TOWELS
TRAILS
TRAWLS
TRIALS
TRILLS
TROLLS
TWILLS
TWIRLS
UMBELS
URIALS
USUALS
VIGILS
VITALS
VOCALS
VOWELS
WHEELS
WHIRLS
WHORLS
YODELS
YOKELS
ZORILS

L•T•••

LATEEN
LATELY
LATENE
LATENS
LATENT
LATEST
LATHED
LATHER
LATHES
LATIGO
LATINA
LATINO
LATINS
LATISH
LATIUM
LATKES
LATONA
LATOUR
LATOYA
LATTEN
LATTER
LATVIA
LETFLY
LETHAL
LETOFF
LETOUT
LETSAT
LETSBE
LETSGO
LETSIN
LETSON
LETSUP
LETTED
LETTER
LETUPS
LITANY
LITCHI
LITERS
LITHIC
LITHOG
LITHOS
LITMUS
LITOUT
LITRES
LITTER
LITTLE
LOTAHS
LOTHAR
LOTION
LOTTED
LOTTOS
LUTHER
LUTHOR
LUTING
LUTIST
LYTTON

L••T••

LACTIC
LAOTSE
LAOTZU
LAPTEV
LAPTOP
LASTED
LASTEX
LASTLY
LATTEN
LATTER
LAWTON
LECTOR
LENTEN
LENTIL
LEPTON
LESTAT
LESTER
LETTED
LETTER
LHOTSE
LICTOR
LIFTED
LIFTER
LIFTUP
LILTED
LINTEL
LINTER
LIOTTA
LIPTON
LISTED
LISTEE
LISTEL
LISTEN
LISTER
LISTON
LITTER
LITTLE
LOATHE
LOFTED
LOITER
LOOTED
LOOTER
LOSTIT
LOTTED
LOTTOS
LUSTED
LUSTER
LUSTRE
LYTTON

L•••T•

LAIDTO
LAKOTA
LANATE
LAPUTA
LAXITY
LAYSTO
LEADTO
LEALTY
LEANTO
LEGATE
LEGATO
LENGTH
LENITY
LEVITE
LEVITY
LIESTO
LIEUTS
LIGATE
LIGHTS
LILITH
LIMITS
LIOTTA
LOBATE
LOCATE
LOLITA
LOOKTO
LOVETT
LUCITE
LUNATE
LUXATE

L••••T

LABRET
LAMENT
LAMEST
LAMONT
LANCET
LAPPET
LARIAT
LATENT
LATEST
LAXEST
LAYOUT
LEARNT
LEDOUT
LEERAT
LEGIST
LESTAT
LETOUT
LETSAT
LEVANT
LIMPET
LINNET
LIONET
LITOUT
LOCKET
LOCUST
LOGOUT
LOOKAT
LOQUAT
LOSEIT
LOSTIT
LOVETT
LOWEST
LOWFAT
LUCENT
LUGNUT
LUTIST
LYRIST

•LT•••

ALTAIC
ALTAIR
ALTARS
ALTERS
ALTHEA
ALTMAN
ULTIMA
ULTIMO
ULTRAS

•L•T••

ALATAU
BLATTY
BLITHE
BLOTCH
BLOTTO
BLYTHE
CLOTHE
CLOTHO
CLOTHS
CLOTTY
CLUTCH
ELATED
ELATER
ELATES
ELITES
ELUTED
ELUTES
FLATLY
FLETCH
FLITCH
FLUTED
FLUTES
GLITCH
GLITZY
GLUTEI
GLUTEN
KLATCH
KLUTZY
PLATED
PLATEN
PLATER
PLATES
PLATTE
SLATED
SLATER
SLATES
SLITHY
SLITTY
SLOTHS
ULSTER
ZLOTYS

•L••T•

ALCOTT
ALECTO
ALERTS
ALEUTS
ALIOTO
ALLOTS
BLASTS
BLATTY
BLEATS
BLINTZ
BLOATS
BLOTTO
BLUETS
BLUNTS
BLURTS
CLEATS
CLEFTS
CLOTTY
CLOUTS
ELECTS
FLEETS
FLINTS
FLINTY
FLIRTS
FLOATS
FLOUTS
GLINTS
GLOATS
OLEATE
PLAITS
PLANTE
PLANTS
PLASTY
PLATTE
PLEATS
PLENTY
PLINTH
SLANTS
SLEETS
SLEETY
SLEUTH
SLITTY

•L•••T

ALBEIT
ALBERT
ALCOTT
ALEAST
ALHIRT
ALIGHT
ALLBUT
ALLOUT
ALLSET
ALLWET
ALMOST
ALPERT
ALWEST
BLEWIT
BLIGHT
BLOWIT
BLUEST
CLARET
CLIENT
CLOSET
ELBERT
ELDEST
ELEGIT
ELICIT
ELLIOT
FLAUNT
FLEWAT
FLIGHT
FLORET
FLUENT
FLYNET
FLYOUT
ILLEST
ILLMET
KLEIST
NLEAST
NLWEST
OLDEST
OLDHAT
PLAINT
PLANET
PLAYAT
PLIANT
PLIGHT
SLIEST
SLIGHT
SLYEST

••LT••

BALTIC
BELTED
BOLTED
BOLTON
CELTIC
COLTER
CULTIC
DALTON
DELTAS
DELTIC
FALTER
FELTED
FILTER
FILTHY
FULTON
HALTED
HALTER
HELTER
HILTON
JILTED
JOLTED
KILTED
KILTER
KILTIE
KULTUR
LILTED
MALTED
MALTIN
MELTED
MELTON
MILTIE
MILTON
MOLTED
MOLTEN
MOLTER
MOLTKE
PALTER
PALTRY
PELTED
PELTER
PELTRY
SALTED
SALTEN
SALTER
SALTON
SILTED
SULTAN
SULTRY
TILTED
TILTER
TOLTEC
WALTER
WALTON
WELTED
WELTER
WILTED
WILTON

••L•T•

ABLATE
AFLATS
AGLETS
ALLOTS
APLITE
ATLATL
BALATA
CULETS
DALETH
DELATE
DELETE
DELFTS
DILATE
DILUTE
DULUTH
ECLATS
EFLATS
EOLITH
FALLTO
FELLTO
FILETS
GALATA
GELATI
GELATO
HALITE
HELDTO
HELOTS
HOLDTO
INLETS
IOLITE
ISLETS
LILITH
LOLITA
MALATE
MALOTI
MELOTT
MULCTS
MULETA
OBLATE
OFLATE
OOLITE
OOLITH
OWLETS
PALATE
PELOTA
PILATE
PILOTI
PILOTS
POLITE
POLITY
RELATE
RELETS
SALUTE
SOLUTE
SPLATS
SPLITS
TALKTO
VALETS
VELDTS
VOLUTE

••L••T

ABLAUT
ABLEST
AFLOAT
AGLINT
ALLBUT
ALLOUT
ALLSET
ALLWET
ASLANT
ATLAST
BALLET
BALLOT
BELOIT
BILLET
BULLET
COLLET
CULLET
DELICT
DELIST
DULCET
ELLIOT
ENLIST
FILLET
GALOOT
GULLET
HALEST
HELMET
HELMUT
HOLDIT
HOLIST
IDLEST
ILLEST
ILLMET
JOLIET
JOLIOT
JULIET
MALLET
MELOTT
MILLET
MOLEST
MULLET
OBLAST
PALEST
PALLET
PELLET
PELMET
POLPOT
PULLET
PULPIT
RELENT
RELICT
RELIST
RELUCT
RILLET
SALLET
SALYUT
SELECT
SILENT
SOLENT
SPLINT
TALBOT
TALENT
TALKAT
TILSIT
UMLAUT
UPLIFT
VALENT
VELVET
VILEST
VOLANT
WALLET
WALNUT
WILLET

•••LT•

ADULTS
EXALTS
EXULTS
FALLTO
FAULTS
FAULTY
FAWLTY
FEALTY
FELLTO
GUILTY
HEALTH
LEALTY
MOULTS
POULTS
QUILTS
REALTY
RIALTO
SAULTS
SMALTI
SMALTO
SMELTS
SPILTH
STILTS
SVELTE
UBOLTS
VAULTS
WEALTH

•••L•T

AMULET
ANKLET
ARMLET
AUKLET
BADLOT
BALLET
BALLOT
BILLET
BULLET
CAMLET
CAPLET
CARLOT
CHALET
COLLET
COOLIT
CULLET
CUTLET
DAYLIT
DIGLOT
DYELOT
EAGLET
ENGLUT
EYELET
FILLET
GASLIT
GIBLET
GIMLET
GOBLET
GOULET
GULLET
HAMLET
JOBLOT
MALLET
MEDLAT
MERLOT
MILLET
MULLET
NUTLET
OCELOT
ODDLOT
OMELET
OUTLET
PALLET
PELLET
PIGLET
PIOLET
PULLET
RAILAT
REGLET
RILLET
RUNLET
SALLET
SCULPT
STYLET
SUBLET
SUNLIT
TABLET
TOILET
TWILIT
VARLET
VIOLET
WALLET
WHILST
WIGLET
WILLET
ZEALOT

••••LT

BASALT
COBALT
DESALT
INCULT
INSULT
ISEULT
KURALT
MODELT
OCCULT
PENULT
REBOLT
REMELT
RESALT
RESULT
REVOLT
SPOILT
TUMULT
TYBALT
UNBELT
UNBOLT

LU••••

LUANDA
LUBBER
LUBECK
LUBING
LUBLIN
LUCENT
LUCIAN
LUCITE
LUCIUS
LUCKED
LUDDEN
LUDENS
LUDLUM
LUDWIG
LUFFED
LUGERS
LUGGED
LUGGER
LUGNUT
LUGOSI
LULLED
LUMBAR
LUMBER
LUMENS
LUMINA
LUMMOX
LUMPED
LUMPEN
LUMPER
LUMPUR
LUNACY
LUNATE
LUNDEN
LUNGED
LUNGES
LUNKER
LUNULA
LUPINE
LUPINO
LUPONE
LURING
LURKED
LUSAKA
LUSHER
LUSHLY
LUSTED
LUSTER
LUSTRE
LUTHER
LUTHOR
LUTING
LUTIST
LUXATE
LUXURY

L•U•••

LAUDED
LAUDER
LAUGHS
LAUNCH
LAUPER
LAUREL
LAUREN
LAURIE
LOUCHE
LOUDEN
LOUDER
LOUDLY
LOUISA
LOUISE
LOUNGE
LOUPES
LOUSED
LOUSES
LOUVER
LOUVRE

L••U••

LACUNA
LAGUNA
LAPUTA
LAYUPS
LAZULI
LEGUME
LEHUAS
LEMUEL
LEMURS
LETUPS
LIEUTS
LIGULA
LIGURE
LIQUID
LIQUOR
LOBULE
LOCUST
LOQUAT
LUNULA
LUXURY

L•••U•

LABOUR
LABRUM
LACEUP
LAIDUP
LAMOUR
LANGUR
LAPFUL
LAPSUP
LARRUP
LASHUP
LATIUM
LATOUR
LAWFUL
LAYOUT
LAYSUP
LEADUP
LEAGUE

LEBRUN
LEDOUT
LETOUT
LETSUP
LIFTUP
LIMBUS
LINEUP
LINGUA
LINKUP
LITMUS
LITOUT
LOCKUP
LOGOUT
LONGUE
LOOKUP
LUCIUS
LUDLUM
LUGNUT
LUMPUR
LYCEUM

L••••U

LANDAU
LAOTZU

•LU•••

ALULAE
ALULAR
ALUMNA
ALUMNI
BLUEOX
BLUEST
BLUESY
BLUETS
BLUFFS
BLUING
BLUISH
BLUNTS
BLURBS
BLURRY
BLURTS
CLUBBY
CLUCKS
CLUEIN
CLUING
CLUMPS
CLUMPY
CLUMSY
CLUNKS
CLUNKY
CLUTCH
ELUDED
ELUDES
ELUTED
ELUTES
FLUENT
FLUFFS
FLUFFY
FLUIDS
FLUKES
FLUMES
FLUNKS
FLUNKY
FLUORO
FLURRY
FLUTED
FLUTES
FLUXED
FLUXES
GLUERS
GLUING
GLUMLY
GLUONS
GLUTEI
GLUTEN
KLUDGE
KLUTZY
PLUCKS
PLUCKY
PLUGIN
PLUMBS
PLUMED
PLUMES
PLUMMY
PLUMPS
PLUNGE
PLUNKS
PLURAL
PLUSES
PLUSHY
SLUDGE
SLUDGY
SLUGGO
SLUICE
SLUING
SLUMMY
SLUMPS
SLURPS
SLURRY
SLUSHY

•L•U••

ALBUMS
ALCUIN
ALEUTS
ALLUDE
ALLURE
BLOUSE
CLAUDE
CLAUSE
CLOUDS
CLOUDY
CLOUTS
FLAUNT
FLEURY
FLOURS
FLOURY
FLOUTS
ILLUME
ILLUSE
PLEURA
PLOUGH
SLEUTH
SLOUCH
SLOUGH

•L••U•

ALARUM
ALDOUS
ALLBUT
ALLIUM
ALLOUT
BLEWUP
BLOWUP
CLAMUP
CLAQUE
CLIQUE
CLOGUP
CLONUS
CLOQUE
ELBRUS
FLIPUP
FLYOUT
PLAGUE
PLAQUE
PLAYUP
PLENUM
PLEXUS
SLAPUP
SLIPUP
SLOWUP

•L•••U

ALATAU

••LU••

ABLUSH
ALLUDE
ALLURE
BELUGA
COLUGO
COLUMN
DELUDE
DELUGE
DELUXE
DILUTE
DULUTH
ILLUME
ILLUSE
INLUCK
RELUCT
RELUME
SALUKI
SALUTE
SOLUTE
STLUKE
TELUGU
TOLUCA
VALUED
VALUES
VOLUME
VOLUTE

••L•U•

ABLAUT
ALLBUT
ALLIUM
ALLOUT
BALLUP
BULBUL
BULGUR
CALLUP
CALLUS
CALQUE
CILIUM
COLEUS
COLOUR
DELIUS
DOLLUP
FILIUS
FILLUP
FOLDUP
FOLIUM
GALLUP
GOLLUM
HALLUX
HELDUP
HELIUM
HELMUT
HOLDUP
HOLEUP
JULIUS
KULTUR
PALPUS
PELEUS
PILEUM
PILEUP
PILEUS
POLLUX
PULLUP
PULQUE
ROLLUP
SALYUT
SELJUK
SOLEUS
SULCUS
SULFUR
TALCUM
TALKUP
TALMUD
UMLAUT
VALIUM
VALOUR
VELLUM
VELOUR
VILLUS
WALKUP
WALLUP
WALNUT
WALRUS
WELLUP
WILBUR

••L••U

HALERU
MALIBU
MILIEU
MOLDAU
TELEDU
TELUGU

•••LU•

AEOLUS
ASYLUM
BALLUP
CALLUP
CALLUS
COILUP
CURLUP
DOLLUP
EFFLUX
ENGLUT
FILLUP
FOULUP
GALLUP
GOLLUM
HALLUX
HAULUP
INFLUX
KAHLUA
KAILUA
KUNLUN
LUDLUM
MRBLUE
MUKLUK
OBELUS
PABLUM
PEPLUM
PHYLUM
POILUS
POLLUX
PULLUP
REFLUX
REGLUE
ROLLUP
RVALUE
SEALUP
STYLUS
TOOLUP
UNGLUE
UNPLUG
UVALUE
VELLUM
VILLUS
WALLUP
WELLUP

•••L•U

ARALLU
PAILOU

••••LU

ARALLU
DESILU
MAKALU
MARILU
ORMOLU
TUVALU

L•V•••

LAVABO
LAVAGE
LAVERS
LAVING
LAVISH
LEVANT
LEVEED
LEVEES
LEVELS
LEVENE
LEVERS
LEVIED
LEVIER
LEVIES
LEVINE
LEVITE
LEVITY
LIVEIN
LIVELY
LIVENS
LIVEON
LIVERS
LIVERY
LIVING
LIVRES
LOVAGE
LOVEIN
LOVELL
LOVELY
LOVERS
LOVETT
LOVING

L••V••

LANVIN
LARVAE
LARVAL
LARVAS
LATVIA
LEAVED
LEAVEN
LEAVES
LEKVAR
LIEVRE
LOAVES
LOUVER
LOUVRE

L••••V

LAPTEV

•LV•••

ELVERS
ELVIRA

•L•V••

ALFVEN
CLAVIN
CLEVER
CLEVES
CLEVIS
CLOVEN
CLOVER
CLOVES
CLOVIS
ELEVEN
ELEVES
FLAVIA
FLAVOR
GLOVED
GLOVER
GLOVES
OLDVIC
OLEVEL
OLIVER
OLIVES
OLIVIA
PLOVER
SLAVED
SLAVER
SLAVES
SLAVIC
SLIVER
SLOVAK
SLOVEN
SLOVIK

•L••V•

ALCOVE
CLEAVE
SLEAVE
SLEEVE

••LV••

CALVED
CALVES
CALVIN
CULVER
DELVED
DELVER
DELVES
HALVAH
HALVED
HALVES
HELVES
KELVIN
MELVIL
MELVIN
MELVYN
PELVIC
PELVIS
SALVED
SALVER
SALVES
SALVIA
SALVOR
SALVOS
SELVES
SILVER
SOLVED
SOLVER
SOLVES
SYLVAN
SYLVIA
VALVED
VALVES
VELVET
VOLVAS
VOLVOX
WOLVES

••L•V•

BULOVA
HALEVY
INLOVE
RELIVE
SALIVA

•••LV•

EVOLVE
SHELVE
TWELVE

•••L•V

KISLEV
PAVLOV
VACLAV
VASLAV

L•W•••

LAWFUL
LAWING
LAWMAN
LAWMEN
LAWSON
LAWTON
LAWYER
LEWDER
LEWDLY
LOWBOY
LOWCAL
LOWELL
LOWEND
LOWERS
LOWERY
LOWEST
LOWFAT
LOWING
LOWKEY

L••W••

LEEWAY
LUDWIG

L••••W

LAYLOW
LIELOW

•LW•••

ALWAYS
ALWEST
ELWOOD
NLWEST

•L•W••

ALLWET
BLEWIT
BLEWUP
BLOWER
BLOWIN
BLOWIT
BLOWUP
BLOWZY
CLAWED
CLAWER
CLEWED
CLOWNS
FLAWED
FLEWAT
FLEWIN
FLOWED
FLOWER
FLYWAY
GLOWED
GLOWER
PLOWED
PLOWER
SLEWED
SLOWED
SLOWER
SLOWLY
SLOWUP

•L••W•

ALLOWS
ELBOWS

••LW••

ALLWET
BULWER
GALWAY

••L•W•

ALLOWS
BYLAWS
INLAWS
MALAWI

••L••W

BELLOW
BILLOW
CALLOW
FALLOW
FELLOW
FOLLOW
HALLOW
HOLLOW
MALLOW
MELLOW
MILDEW
PILLOW
SALLOW
TALLOW
WALLOW
WILLOW
YELLOW

•••L•W

BELLOW
BILLOW
CALLOW
CURLEW
FALLOW
FARLOW
FELLOW
FOLLOW
GAGLAW
GOSLOW
HALLOW
HARLOW
HOLLOW
INFLOW
LAYLOW
LIELOW
MALLOW
MELLOW
OUTLAW
PILLOW
PRELAW
REPLOW
SALLOW
TALLOW
WALLOW
WILLOW
YELLOW

L•X•••

LAXEST
LAXITY
LEXEME
LEXICA
LUXATE
LUXURY

L••X••

LYNXES

L••••X

LARYNX
LASTEX
LUMMOX

•L•X••

ALEXEI
ALEXIA
ALEXIS
BLIXEN
ELIXIR
FLAXEN
FLAXES
FLEXED
FLEXES
FLEXOR
FLUXED
FLUXES
KLAXON
PLEXOR
PLEXUS

•L•••X

BLUEOX
CLIMAX
CLOROX

••LX••

CALXES

••L•X•

BILOXI
DELUXE
GALAXY

••L••X

BOLLIX
HALLUX
POLEAX
POLLEX
POLLUX
VOLVOX

•••L•X

BOLLIX
DUPLEX
EFFLUX
HALLUX
INFLUX
POLLEX
POLLUX
PROLIX
REFLEX
REFLUX
SMILAX

LY••••

LYCEES
LYCEUM
LYNDON
LYNLEY
LYNXES
LYNYRD
LYRICS
LYRIST
LYSINE
LYSINS
LYTTON

L•Y•••

LAYBYS
LAYERS
LAYFOR
LAYING
LAYLOW
LAYMAN
LAYMEN
LAYOFF
LAYOUT
LAYSBY
LAYSIN
LAYSON
LAYSTO
LAYSUP
LAYUPS
LEYDEN
LOYOLA

L••Y••

LARYNX
LAWYER
LIBYAN
LLOYDS
LYNYRD

L•••Y•

LATOYA
LAYBYS
LIMEYS

L••••Y

LACKEY
LAIDBY
LAMELY
LANDRY
LANKLY
LASTLY
LATELY
LAXITY
LAYSBY
LAZBOY
LAZILY
LEAKEY
LEALTY
LEANLY
LEEWAY
LEGACY
LEMONY
LENITY
LESLEY
LETFLY
LEVITY
LEWDLY
LIKELY
LIMPLY
LINSEY
LITANY
LIVELY
LIVERY
LOGILY
LONELY
LOONEY
LORDLY
LOUDLY
LOVELY
LOWBOY
LOWERY
LOWKEY
LUNACY
LUSHLY
LUXURY
LYNLEY

•LY•••

ALYSSA
BLYTHE
ELYSEE
FLYBOY
FLYBYS
FLYERS
FLYING
FLYMAN
FLYMEN
FLYNET
FLYOUT
FLYROD
FLYWAY
GLYCOL
GLYPHS
PLYING
SLYEST
SLYPES

•L•Y••

ALKYDS
ALKYLS
CLAYEY
CLOYED
DLAYER
ELAYER
ELAYNE
FLAYED
FLAYER
LLOYDS
PLAYAS
PLAYAT
PLAYED
PLAYER
PLAYON
PLAYUP
SLAYED
SLAYER

•L••Y•

ALLAYS
ALLEYS
ALLOYS
ALWAYS
FLYBYS
GLADYS
ZLOTYS

•L•••Y

ALBANY
ALECKY
ALLDAY
BLABBY
BLATTY
BLEARY
BLIMEY
BLOCKY
BLOODY
BLOOEY
BLOOMY
BLOWZY
BLUESY
BLURRY
CLAMMY
CLANCY
CLANKY
CLASSY
CLAYEY
CLERGY
CLINGY
CLOTTY
CLOUDY
CLUBBY
CLUMPY
CLUMSY
CLUNKY
ELLERY
FLABBY
FLAGGY
FLASHY
FLATLY
FLEECY
FLESHY
FLEURY
FLIMSY
FLINTY
FLOOEY
FLOPPY
FLOPSY
FLOSSY
FLOURY
FLUFFY
FLUNKY
FLURRY
FLYBOY
FLYWAY
GLADLY
GLAIRY
GLASSY
GLIBLY
GLITZY
GLOOMY
GLOPPY
GLOSSY
GLUMLY
ILLSAY
KLUTZY
OLDBOY
OLEARY
PLASHY
PLASTY
PLENTY
PLUCKY
PLUMMY
PLUSHY
SLAGGY
SLANGY
SLAPPY
SLEAZY
SLEEKY
SLEEPY
SLEETY
SLIMLY
SLINKY
SLITHY
SLITTY
SLOPPY
SLOSHY
SLOWLY
SLUDGY
SLUMMY
SLURRY
SLUSHY

••LY••

GALYAK
POLYPS
SALYUT

••L•Y•

ALLAYS
ALLEYS
ALLOYS
BELAYS
BOLEYN
DELAYS
INLAYS
MALAYA
MALAYS
MELVYN
POLEYN
RELAYS
SPLAYS

••L••Y

ALLDAY
BALDLY
BELFRY
BOLDLY
CALMLY
CELERY
COLDLY
COLONY
DELANY
DELRAY
DILSEY
ELLERY
EULOGY
FELONY
FILTHY
FOLKSY
GALAXY
GALLEY
GALWAY
GELSEY
HALEVY
HALLEY
HALSEY
HILARY
ILLSAY
JALOPY
KELLEY
KELSEY
MALADY
MALORY
MELODY
MILADY
MILDLY
MILLAY
OOLOGY
PALELY
PALTRY
PELTRY
POLICY
POLITY
PULLEY
SALARY
SOLELY
SULTRY
UGLIFY
VALERY
VALLEY
VILELY
VILIFY
VOLLEY
WILDLY
WOLSEY

•••LY•

EVELYN
JACLYN

•••L•Y

ASHLEY
BAILEY
BARLEY
BEGLEY
BOSLEY
BROLLY
BURLEY
BYPLAY
CHALKY
CHILLY
COOLLY
COWLEY
DAILEY
DEPLOY
DOOLEY
DROLLY
DUALLY
DUDLEY
EMPLOY
EVILLY
FARLEY
FAULTY
FAWLTY
FEALTY
FOULLY
FRILLY
GALLEY
GUILTY
GURLEY
HAILEY
HALLEY
HARLEY
HAYLEY
HENLEY
HURLEY
HUXLEY
INPLAY
KELLEY
LEALTY
LESLEY
LYNLEY
MARLEY
MEDLEY
MILLAY
MISLAY
MOBLEY
MORLEY
MOTLEY
MOULDY
NEWLEY
OAKLEY
OKELLY
ORALLY
OUTLAY
PARLAY
PARLEY
PAULEY
PHILLY
PULLEY
REALLY
REALTY
REPLAY
RIDLEY
RIPLEY
SCULLY
SHALEY
SHALLY
SHELLY
SHILLY
SMELLY
SMILEY
STALKY
STILLY
TRILBY
VALLEY
VOLLEY
WAYLAY
WESLEY
WHOLLY
WOOLEY
WOOLLY

••••LY

ACIDLY
AIRILY
ARCHLY
ARIDLY
AVIDLY
BALDLY
BARELY
BARFLY
BASELY
BODILY
BOLDLY
BOTFLY
BROLLY
BUBBLY
BURBLY
BUSILY
CAGILY
CALMLY
CHARLY
CHILLY
CICELY
COLDLY
COMELY
COMPLY
COOLLY
COSTLY
COZILY
CRAWLY
CUDDLY
CURTLY
DAMPLY
DANGLY
DARKLY
DEADLY
DEARLY
DEEPLY
DEFTLY
DIMPLY
DOUBLY
DOURLY
DOZILY
DRABLY
DROLLY
DRYFLY
DUALLY
DUMBLY
EASILY
EBERLY
EDGILY
EERILY
EVENLY
EVERLY
EVILLY
FAIRLY
FAMILY
FEEBLY
FINELY
FIRMLY
FLATLY
FONDLY
FOULLY
FOXILY
FREELY
FRILLY
GADFLY
GAINLY
GAMELY
GAMILY
GANGLY
GENTLY
GIGGLY
GLADLY
GLIBLY
GLUMLY
GNARLY

GOGGLY
GOODLY
GOOGLY
GRIMLY
GRISLY
GROWLY
HARDLY
HAZILY
HIGHLY
HOMELY
HOMILY
HOURLY
HUBBLY
HUGELY
HUMBLY
JANGLY
JIGGLY
JINGLY
JUNGLY
JUSTLY
KEENLY
KINDLY
KINGLY
KNURLY
KODALY
LAMELY
LANKLY
LASTLY
LATELY
LAZILY
LEANLY
LETFLY
LEWDLY
LIKELY
LIMPLY
LIVELY
LOGILY
LONELY
LORDLY
LOUDLY
LOVELY
LUSHLY
MAINLY
MARBLY
MAYFLY
MEANLY
MEASLY
MEEKLY
MEETLY
MERELY
MILDLY
MOSTLY
MUMBLY
MUSCLY
MUTELY
NAMELY
NEARLY
NEATLY
NICELY
NIMBLY
NOSILY
NUMBLY
OKELLY
OPENLY
ORALLY
OVERLY
PALELY
PARTLY
PEARLY
PEBBLY
PERTLY
PHILLY
POKILY
POORLY

POPFLY
PORTLY
POSHLY
PRIMLY
PUDDLY
PUNILY
PURELY
RACILY
RANKLY
RAPTLY
RARELY
RASHLY
RATTLY
REALLY
RICHLY
RIPELY
RIPPLY
RONELY
ROSILY
RUBBLY
RUDELY
RUFFLY
RUMBLY
RUMPLY
SAFELY
SAGELY
SANELY
SCULLY
SEEMLY
SEXILY
SHALLY
SHELLY
SHILLY
SICILY
SICKLY
SIMPLY
SINGLY
SLIMLY
SLOWLY
SMELLY
SMUGLY
SNARLY
SNUGLY
SOFTLY
SOLELY
SORELY
SOURLY
SPRYLY
STABLY
STEELY
STILLY
SUBTLY
SUPPLY
SURELY
SWIRLY
TAMELY
TANGLY
TARTLY
TAUTLY
THINLY
THUSLY
TIDILY
TIMELY
TINGLY
TINKLY
TREBLY
TRIGLY
TRIMLY
TRIPLY
TWOPLY
UNDULY
UNHOLY
UNRULY
USABLY

VAINLY
VASTLY
VERILY
VIABLY
VILELY
WADDLY
WAFFLY
WAGGLY
WAMBLY
WARILY
WARMLY
WEAKLY
WEEKLY
WETFLY
WHIRLY
WHOLLY
WIDELY
WIFELY
WIGGLY
WILDLY
WISELY
WOBBLY
WOOLLY
YARELY
YEARLY
ZANILY

L•Z•••
LAZBOY
LAZIER
LAZILY
LAZING
LAZULI
LIZARD
LIZZIE

L••Z••
LIZZIE

L•••Z•
LAMAZE
LAOTZU

L••••Z
LORENZ

•L•Z••
BLAZED
BLAZER
BLAZES
BLAZON
GLAZED
GLAZER
GLAZES
PLAZAS
SLEZAK

•L••Z•
ALONZO
BLOWZY
GLITZY
KLUTZY
SLEAZE
SLEAZY

•L•••Z
BLINTZ

••LZ••
BALZAC

••L•Z•
ABLAZE
BELIZE

••L••Z
MILOSZ
VALDEZ

•••L•Z
BOULEZ

••••LZ
SCHULZ

MA••••
MABELL
MACACO
MACAWS
MACHES
MACHOS
MACRAE
MACRON
MACROS
MACULA
MADAME
MADAMS
MADCAP
MADDEN
MADDER
MADDIE
MADEDO
MADEIT
MADERO
MADEUP
MADMAN
MADMAX
MADMEN
MADRAS
MADRES
MADRID
MADTOM
MADURA
MADURO
MAENAD
MAGGIE
MAGGIO
MAGMAS
MAGNET
MAGNON
MAGNUM
MAGPIE
MAGUEY
MAGYAR
MAHDIS
MAHLER
MAHOUT
MAHZOR
MAIDEN
MAIDUS
MAILED
MAILER
MAILES
MAILIN
MAINLY
MAISIE
MAITAI
MAITRE
MAIZES
MAJGEN
MAJLIS
MAJORS
MAKALU
MAKEDO
MAKEIT
MAKERS
MAKEUP
MAKING
MAKUTA
MALABO
MALADY
MALAGA
MALATE
MALAWI
MALAYA
MALAYS
MALDEN
MALIBU
MALICE
MALIGN
MALKIN
MALLEE
MALLEI
MALLET
MALLOW
MALONE
MALORY
MALOTI
MALTED
MALTIN
MAMBAS
MAMBOS
MAMMAL
MAMMAS
MAMMON
MANAGE
MANAMA
MANANA
MANAUS
MANCHA
MANCHU
MANDAN
MANDAY
MANEGE
MANFUL
MANGER
MANGLE
MANGOS
MANIAC
MANIAS
MANILA
MANIOC
MANNED
MANNER
MANNIX
MANORS
MANQUE
MANRAY
MANSES
MANTAS
MANTEL
MANTIC
MANTIS
MANTLE
MANTRA
MANTUA
MANUAL
MANUEL
MAOISM
MAOIST
MAORIS
MAOTAI
MAPLES
MAPPED
MAPPER
MAPUTO
MAQUIS
MARACA
MARAUD
MARBLE
MARBLY
MARCEL
MARCHE
MARCIA
MARCIE
MARCOS
MARCUS
MARDUK
MARGAY
MARGIE
MARGIN
MARGOT
MARIAH
MARIAN
MARIEL
MARIKO
MARILU
MARINA
MARINE
MARINO
MARION
MARISA
MARIST
MARIUS
MARKED
MARKER
MARKET
MARKKA
MARKUP
MARLED
MARLEE
MARLEY
MARLIN
MARLON
MARMEE
MARMOT
MARNER
MARNIE
MAROON
MARPLE
MARQUE
MARRED
MARRON
MARROW
MARSHA
MARSHY
MARTEL
MARTEN
MARTHA
MARTIN
MARTYR
MARVEL
MARVIN
MASADA
MASAIS
MASCOT
MASERS
MASERU
MASHED
MASHER
MASHES
MASHIE
MASKED
MASKER
MASONS
MASQUE
MASSED
MASSES
MASSEY
MASSIF
MASTER
MASTIC
MATERS
MATEYS
MATHER
MATHIS
MATING
MATINS
MATLIN
MATRIX
MATRON
MATTEA
MATTED
MATTEL
MATTER
MATTES
MATTIE
MATURE
MATZOH
MATZOS
MAULED
MAULER
MAUMAU
MAUMEE
MAUNDY
MAURYA
MAUSER
MAUVES
MAVENS
MAXIMA
MAXIMS
MAXINE
MAXIXE
MAXOUT
MAYANS
MAYBES
MAYDAY
MAYFLY
MAYHAP
MAYHEM
MAYORS
MAYPOP
MAYTAG
MAZERS
MAZOLA
MAZUMA

M•A•••
MCADAM
MCADOO
MEADOW
MEAGER
MEAGRE
MEALIE
MEANER
MEANIE
MEANLY
MEASLY
MIASMA
MOANED
MOANER
MOATED

M••A••
MACACO
MACAWS
MADAME
MADAMS
MAKALU
MALABO
MALADY
MALAGA
MALATE
MALAWI
MALAYA
MALAYS
MANAGE
MANAMA
MANANA
MANAUS
MARACA
MARAUD
MASADA
MASAIS
MAYANS
MCCABE
MCCANN
MCHALE
MCLAIN
MCNAIR
MEDAKA
MEDALS
MEGALO
MEGARA
MELANO
MENACE
MENAGE
MESABI
METALS
METATE
MIDAIR
MIKADO
MILADY
MILANO
MIRAGE
MOHAIR
MOHAVE
MOHAWK
MOJAVE
MOLARS
MONACO
MONADS
MORALE
MORALS
MORANT
MORASS
MORAVA
MORAYS
MOSAIC
MOZART
MUFASA
MUGABE
MURALS
MURANO
MUTANT
MUTATE
MYNAHS

M•••A•
MACRAE
MADCAP
MADMAN
MADMAX
MADRAS
MAENAD
MAGMAS
MAGYAR
MAITAI
MAMBAS
MAMMAL
MAMMAS
MANDAN
MANDAY
MANIAC
MANIAS
MANRAY
MANTAS
MANUAL
MAOTAI
MARGAY
MARIAH
MARIAN
MAUMAU
MAYDAY
MAYHAP
MAYTAG
MCADAM
MCGRAW
MCLEAN
MECCAS
MEDGAR
MEDIAL
MEDIAN
MEDIAS
MEDLAR
MEDLAT
MELMAC
MENIAL
MENSAE
MENSAL
MENSAS
MENTAL
MERMAN
MESCAL
MICMAC
MIDDAY
MIDWAY
MIHRAB
MILLAY
MILPAS
MILSAP
MINOAN
MINYAN
MIRIAM
MISHAP
MISLAY
MISSAL
MISSAY
MITRAL
MOBCAP
MOCHAS
MOLDAU
MOLNAR
MOMMAS
MONDAY
MOOLAH
MOREAU
MORGAN
MORNAY
MORTAL
MORTAR
MOSHAV
MUDCAT
MUDRAS
MULLAH
MULLAS
MURRAY
MUSCAT
MUSIAL
MUTUAL
MYRDAL
MYRIAD

M••••A
MACULA
MADURA
MAKUTA
MALAGA
MALAYA
MANAMA
MANANA
MANCHA
MANILA
MANTRA
MANTUA
MARACA
MARCIA
MARINA
MARISA
MARKKA
MARSHA
MARTHA
MASADA
MATTEA
MAURYA
MAXIMA
MAZOLA
MAZUMA
MEDAKA
MEDINA
MEDUSA
MEGARA
MELINA
MERIDA
MIASMA
MIKITA
MIMOSA
MINIMA
MISCHA
MODELA
MODENA
MONERA
MONETA
MONICA
MORAVA
MORITA
MOSKVA
MUCOSA
MUFASA
MULETA
MURCIA
MYOPIA

•MA•••
AMADIS
AMADOU
AMAJOR
AMALFI
AMALIE
AMANDA
AMATIS
AMATOL
AMAZED
AMAZES
AMAZON
BMAJOR
CMAJOR
DMAJOR
EMAILS
EMAJOR
FMAJOR
GMAJOR
IMAGED
IMAGER
IMAGES
IMARET
OMAHAN
OMAHAS
OMANIS
OMASUM
SMACKS
SMALLS
SMALTI
SMALTO
SMARMY
SMARTS
SMARTY

•M•A••
AMHARA
EMBANK
EMBARK
EMBAYS
EMDASH
IMPACT
IMPAIR
IMPALA
IMPALE
IMPART
SMEARS
SMEARY
UMIAKS
UMLAUT
UMTATA

•M••A•
AMEBAE
AMEBAS
AMORAL
AMTRAC
AMTRAK
AMYTAN
EMQUAD
OMAHAN
OMAHAS
OMEGAS
SMILAX
UMBRAE
UMBRAL
UMBRAS

•M•••A
AMANDA
AMELIA
AMENRA
AMHARA
AMOEBA
EMILIA
IMELDA
IMPALA
OMERTA
SMYRNA
UMBRIA
UMTATA

••MA••
ARMADA
ARMAGH
ARMAND
ARMANI
ASMARA
AYMARA
BAMAKO
COMATE
DAMAGE
DAMASK
DAMATO
DEMAND
DOMAIN
DOMANI
FEMALE
GAMAYS
GEMARA
HAMALS
HEMATO
HOMAGE
HUMANE
HUMANS
INMATE
JAMAAL
JUMADA
KAMALA
LAMARR
LAMAZE
LEMANS
NAMATH
NEMATO
NOMADS
POMACE
POMADE
RAMADA
RAMATE
REMADE
REMAIL
REMAIN
REMAKE
REMAND
REMANS
REMAPS
REMARK
ROMAIC
ROMAJI
ROMANO
ROMANS
ROMANY
SAMARA
SOMALI
SOMANY
SOMATA
SOMATO
STMALO
STMARK
SUMACS
TAMALE
TAMARA
TAMAYO
TOMATO
UNMADE
UNMAKE
UNMANS
UNMASK
USMAIL
YAMAHA
ZYMASE

••M•A•
AIMSAT
BEMOAN
BOMBAY
BUMRAP
CAMEAT
COMBAT
COMEAT
COMMAS
COMPAQ
COMSAT
CYMBAL
DAMMAR
DEMEAN
GAMMAS
GEMMAE
GIMBAL
HYMNAL
JAMAAL
JUMPAT
LAMIAS
LAMMAS
LEMMAS
LUMBAR
MAMBAS
MAMMAL
MAMMAS
MOMMAS
NUMBAT
OOMPAH
PAMPAS
QUMRAN
RAMEAU
RAMSAY
RUMBAS
SAMBAL
SAMBAR
SAMBAS
SAMIAM
SAMOAN
SAMPAN
SIMIAN
SUMMAE
SUMMAS
TAMTAM
TIMBAL
TOMBAC
TOMCAT
WOMBAT

••M••A
ARMADA
ASMARA
AYMARA
CAMERA
DAMITA
ELMIRA
FEMORA
GAMBIA
GEMARA
JUMADA
KAMALA
LAMBDA
LAMESA
LAMINA
LUMINA
MIMOSA
NUMINA
PAMELA
POMONA
RAMADA
RAMBLA
RAMONA
REMORA
REMUDA
ROMOLA
RUMINA
SAMARA
SAMOSA
SOMATA
TAMARA
XIMENA
YAMAHA
ZAMBIA

•••MA•
AGAMAS
AIRMAN
ALEMAN
ALLMAN
ALOMAR
ALTMAN
ANIMAL
ANIMAS
APEMAN
AROMAS
ATAMAN
BARMAN
BATMAN
BIGMAC
BITMAP
BORMAN
BOWMAN
BRUMAL
BURMAN
BUSMAN
CAIMAN
CARMAN
CAYMAN
CLIMAX
COLMAN
COMMAS
CONMAN
COWMAN
DAMMAR
DERMAL
DESMAN
DISMAL
DISMAY
DOGMAS
DOLMAN
DOLMAS
DRAMAS
ELFMAN
ENDMAN
FBIMAN
FERMAT
FIRMAN
FLYMAN
FORMAL
FORMAN
FORMAT
FULMAR
GAGMAN
GAMMAS
GASMAN
GEMMAE
GERMAN
GOTMAD
GRAMAS
GUNMAN
HAEMAT
HAGMAN
HERMAN
HETMAN
HIEMAL
HITMAN
ICEMAN
INGMAR
KALMAR
KATMAI
KERMAN
KIDMAN
KIRMAN
KORMAN
LAMMAS
LAWMAN
LAYMAN
LEGMAN
LEMMAS
LLAMAS
MADMAN
MADMAX
MAGMAS
MAMMAL
MAMMAS
MAUMAU
MELMAC
MERMAN
MICMAC
MOMMAS
NETMAN
NEUMAN
NEWMAN
NEWMAR
NORMAL
NORMAN
OILMAN
OLDMAN
PACMAN
PALMAS
PENMAN
PIEMAN
PITMAN
PRIMAL
RAGMAN
RUDMAN
SALMAN
SEAMAN
SGTMAJ
SHAMAN
SIGMAS
STOMAS
STOMAT
SUMMAE
SUMMAS
TARMAC
TASMAN
TAXMAN
THOMAS
TINMAN
TOAMAN
TODMAN
TRUMAN
TUBMAN
ULLMAN
WEIMAR
YEOMAN
YESMAN
ZEEMAN

•••M•A
AHIMSA
ALUMNA
ANEMIA
CRIMEA
NOUMEA
RHUMBA

••••MA
BAHAMA
BRAHMA
CHACMA
CHROMA
CINEMA
COLIMA
DAGAMA
DHARMA
DODOMA
ENIGMA
FATIMA
INTIMA
JICAMA
MANAMA
MAXIMA
MAZUMA
MIASMA
MINIMA
OEDEMA
OPTIMA
PAJAMA
PALOMA
PANAMA
PLASMA
PNEUMA
PYJAMA
SCHEMA
SONOMA
STIGMA
TACOMA
THELMA
TRAUMA
ULTIMA
YAKIMA
YOYOMA
ZEUGMA

MB••••
MBUNDU

M•B•••
MABELL
MCBAIN
MOBBED
MOBCAP
MOBILE
MOBIUS
MOBLEY
MRBLUE

M••B••
MAMBAS
MAMBOS
MARBLE
MARBLY
MAYBES
MEMBER
MOBBED
MORBID
MUMBLE
MUMBLY

M•••B•
MALABO
MALIBU
MCCABE
MESABI
MUGABE

M••••B
MIDRIB
MIHRAB

•MB•••
AMBERS
AMBITS
AMBLED
AMBLER
AMBLES
AMBLIN
AMBUSH
EMBANK
EMBARK
EMBAYS
EMBDEN
EMBEDS
EMBERS
EMBLEM
EMBODY
EMBOSS
EMBRYO
IMBIBE
IMBRUE
IMBUED
IMBUES
UMBELS
UMBERS
UMBRAE
UMBRAL
UMBRAS
UMBRIA

•M•B••
AMEBAE
AMEBAS
AMEBIC

•M••B•
AMOEBA
IMBIBE

••MB••
BAMBOO
BOMBAY
BOMBED
BOMBER
BOMBES
BUMBLE
BUMBRY
CAMBER
COMBAT
COMBED
COMBER
COMBES
COMBOS
CUMBER
CYMBAL
DUMBER
DUMBLY
FUMBLE
GAMBIA
GAMBIT
GAMBLE
GAMBOL
GIMBAL
GIMBEL
GUMBEL
GUMBOS
HOMBRE
HUMBLE
HUMBLY
HUMBUG
IAMBIC
JUMBLE
JUMBOS
LAMBDA
LAMBED
LIMBED
LIMBER
LIMBOS
LIMBUS
LOMBOK
LUMBAR
LUMBER
MAMBAS
MAMBOS
MEMBER
MUMBLE
MUMBLY
NIMBLE
NIMBLY
NIMBUS
NUMBAT
NUMBED
NUMBER
NUMBLY
RAMBLA
RAMBLE
RUMBAS
RUMBLE
RUMBLY
SAMBAL
SAMBAR
SAMBAS
SIMBEL
SOMBER
SOMBRE
SYMBOL
TIMBAL
TIMBER
TIMBRE
TOMBAC
TOMBOY
TUMBLE
WAMBLE
WAMBLY
WIMBLE
WOMBAT
ZAMBIA
ZOMBIE

••M•B•
CAMEBY
COMEBY
DEMOBS

•••MB•
ABOMBS
AKIMBO
CLIMBS
CRAMBO
CRUMBS
CRUMBY
FLAMBE
HBOMBS
PLUMBS
RHOMBI
RHOMBS
RHUMBA
RHUMBS
THUMBS

••••MB
APLOMB
BENUMB

MC••••
MCADAM
MCADOO
MCBAIN
MCCABE
MCCANN
MCGRAW
MCGREW
MCHALE
MCKUEN
MCLAIN
MCLEAN
MCNAIR

M•C•••
MACACO
MACAWS
MACHES
MACHOS
MACRAE
MACRON
MACROS
MACULA
MCCABE
MCCANN
MECCAS
MICKEY
MICMAC
MICRON
MICROS
MOCHAS
MOCKED
MOCKER
MOCKUP
MRCOOL
MUCKED
MUCKUP
MUCOSA
MUCOUS

M••C••
MADCAP
MANCHA
MANCHU
MARCEL
MARCHE
MARCIA
MARCIE
MARCOS
MARCUS
MASCOT
MECCAS
MERCED
MERCER
MESCAL
MINCED
MINCER
MINCES
MISCHA
MISCUE
MOBCAP
MOSCOW
MUDCAT
MULCTS
MUNCIE
MURCIA
MUSCAT
MUSCLE
MUSCLY

M•••C•
MACACO
MALICE
MARACA
MEDICI
MEDICO
MEDICS
MENACE
MENSCH
MEXICO
MIMICS
MODOCS
MOHOCK
MOLOCH
MONACO
MONICA
MUNICH

M••••C
MANIAC
MANIOC
MANTIC
MASTIC
MELMAC
METRIC
MICMAC
MIXTEC
MOSAIC
MYOPIC
MYSTIC
MYTHIC

•MC•••
EMCEED
EMCEES

•M•C••
AMECHE
AMICES
AMICUS
SMACKS
SMOCKS

•M••C•
AMERCE
IMPACT
SMIRCH
SMOOCH
SMUTCH

•M•••C
AMEBIC
AMTRAC

••MC••
KIMCHI
TOMCAT

••M•C•
COMICS
LAMECH
MIMICS
OLMECS
OSMICS
POMACE
PUMICE
REMICK
SUMACS

••M••C
CYMRIC
HOMEEC
IAMBIC
ROMAIC
TOMBAC

•••M•C
ANEMIC
ATOMIC
BIGMAC
CADMIC
COSMIC
FORMIC
GNOMIC
KARMIC
MELMAC
MICMAC
TARMAC

••••MC
RUNDMC

M•D•••
MADAME
MADAMS
MADCAP
MADDEN
MADDER
MADDIE
MADEDO
MADEIT
MADERO
MADEUP
MADMAN
MADMAX
MADMEN
MADRAS
MADRES
MADRID
MADTOM
MADURA
MADURO
MEDAKA
MEDALS
MEDDLE
MEDGAR
MEDIAL
MEDIAN
MEDIAS
MEDICI
MEDICO
MEDICS
MEDINA
MEDIUM
MEDLAR
MEDLAT
MEDLEY
MEDUSA
MIDAIR
MIDDAY
MIDDEN
MIDDLE
MIDGES
MIDGET
MIDLER
MIDORI
MIDRIB
MIDWAY
MODELA
MODELS
MODELT
MODEMS
MODENA
MODERN
MODEST
MODIFY
MODINE
MODISH
MODOCS
MODULE
MODULO
MUDCAT
MUDDED
MUDDER
MUDDLE
MUDEEL
MUDHEN
MUDPIE
MUDRAS

M••D••
MADDEN
MADDER
MADDIE
MAHDIS
MAIDEN
MAIDUS
MALDEN
MANDAN
MANDAY
MARDUK
MAYDAY
MCADAM
MCADOO
MEADOW
MEDDLE
MELDED
MENDED
MENDEL
MENDER
MENDES
MIDDAY
MIDDEN
MIDDLE
MILDER
MILDEW
MILDLY
MINDED
MINDER
MISDID
MOLDAU
MOLDED
MOLDER
MONDAY
MUDDED
MUDDER
MUDDLE
MURDER
MYRDAL

M•••D•
MADEDO
MAKEDO
MALADY
MASADA
MAUNDY
MBUNDU
MELODY
MERIDA
MIKADO
MILADY
MONADS
MONODY
MOPEDS
MOULDS
MOULDY
MOUNDS
MRHYDE

M••••D
MADRID
MAENAD
MAILED
MALTED
MANNED
MAPPED
MARAUD
MARKED
MARLED
MARRED
MASHED
MASKED
MASSED
MATTED
MAULED
MELDED
MELTED
MENDED
MEOWED
MERCED
MERGED
MESHED
MESSED
METHOD
MEWLED
MIFFED
MILKED
MILLED
MILORD
MINCED
MINDED
MINTED
MISDID
MISLED
MISSED
MISTED
MITRED
MOANED
MOATED
MOBBED
MOCKED
MOILED
MOLDED
MOLTED
MONIED
MOONED
MOORED
MOOTED
MOPPED
MORBID
MOSSED
MOUSED
MUCKED
MUDDED
MUFFED
MUGGED
MULLED
MUSHED
MUSSED
MYRIAD
MYWORD

•MD•••
EMDASH

•M•D••
AMADIS
AMADOU
AMEDEO
AMIDES
AMIDOL
AMIDST
EMBDEN
SMUDGE
SMUDGY

•M••D•
AMANDA
AMENDS
EMBEDS
EMBODY
EMENDS
IMELDA
IMPEDE

•M•••D
AMAZED
AMBLED
AMPHID
AMUSED
EMCEED
EMOTED
EMQUAD
IMAGED
IMBUED
IMPEND
SMILED
SMOKED

••MD••
CAMDEN
DUMDUM

••M•D•
ARMADA
COMEDY
DEMODE
JUMADA
KOMODO
LAMBDA
LAMEDH
LAMEDS
NOMADS
POMADE
RAMADA
REMADE
REMEDY
REMUDA
UNMADE

••M••D
ALMOND
ARMAND
BOMBED
BUMMED
BUMPED
CAMPED
COMBED
DAMMED
DAMNED
DAMPED
DEMAND
DEMOND
DIMMED
DUMPED
EDMOND
EDMUND
GEMMED
GUMMED
HAMMED
HEMMED
HUMMED
HUMPED
HYMNED
JAMMED
JUMPED
LAMBED
LAMMED
LEMOND
LIMBED
LIMNED
LIMPED
LIMPID
LOMOND
LUMPED
NIMROD
NUMBED
ORMOND
OSMOND
OSMUND
PUMPED
RAMMED
RAMPED
RAMROD
REMAND
REMEND
REMIND
RIMMED
ROMPED
SUMMED
TAMPED
TEMPED
VAMPED

•••M•D
BEAMED
BLAMED
BOOMED
BUMMED
CALMED
CHIMED
DAMMED
DEEMED
DIMMED
DOOMED
FARMED
FILMED
FIRMED
FLAMED
FOAMED
FORMED
FRAMED
GEMMED
GOTMAD
GRIMED
GUMMED
HAMMED
HARMED
HELMED
HEMMED
HUMMED
JAMMED
LAMMED
LOAMED
LOOMED
PALMED
PERMED
PLUMED
PREMED
PRIMED
RAMMED
REAMED
RHYMED
RIMMED
ROAMED
ROOMED
SEAMED
SEEMED
SHAMED
SLIMED
SPUMED
SUMMED
TALMUD
TEAMED
TEEMED
TERMED
THEMED
WARMED
WORMED
ZOOMED

ME••••
MEADOW
MEAGER
MEAGRE
MEALIE
MEANER
MEANIE
MEANLY
MEASLY
MECCAS
MEDAKA
MEDALS
MEDDLE
MEDGAR
MEDIAL
MEDIAN
MEDIAS
MEDICI
MEDICO
MEDICS
MEDINA
MEDIUM
MEDLAR
MEDLAT
MEDLEY
MEDUSA
MEEKER
MEEKLY
MEERUT
MEETER
MEETLY
MEGALO
MEGARA
MEGILP
MEGOHM
MEKONG
MELANO
MELDED
MELEES
MELINA
MELLON
MELLOW
MELMAC
MELODY
MELONS
MELOTT
MELTED
MELTON
MELVIL
MELVIN
MELVYN
MEMBER
MEMNON
MEMOIR
MEMORY
MENACE
MENAGE
MENDED
MENDEL
MENDER
MENDES
MENHIR
MENIAL
MENINX
MENJOU
MENNEN
MENSAE
MENSAL
MENSAS
MENSCH
MENTAL
MENTIS
MENTOR
MEOWED
MERCED
MERCER
MERELY
MEREST
MERGED
MERGER
MERGES
MERIDA
MERINO
MERITS
MERKEL
MERLIN
MERLON
MERLOT
MERMAN
MERMEN
MEROPE
MERSEY
MERTON
MERVYN
MESABI
MESCAL
MESHED
MESHES
MESMER
MESONS
MESSED
MESSES
MESSRS
MESSUP
METALS
METATE
METEOR
METERS
METHOD
METHYL
METIER
METING
METOPE
METRES
METRIC
METROS
METTLE
MEWING
MEWLED
MEWLER
MEXICO
MEZZOS

M•E•••
MAENAD
MEEKER
MEEKLY
MEERUT
MEETER
MEETLY
MYELIN

M••E••
MABELL
MADEDO
MADEIT
MADERO
MADEUP
MAKEDO
MAKEIT
MAKERS
MAKEUP
MANEGE
MASERS
MASERU
MATERS
MATEYS
MAVENS
MAZERS
MCLEAN
MELEES
MERELY
MEREST
METEOR
METERS
MILERS
MIMEOS
MIMERS
MINERS
MISERS
MISERY
MITERS
MIXERS
MIZENS
MODELA
MODELS
MODELT
MODEMS
MODENA
MODERN
MODEST
MOIETY
MOLEST
MOMENT
MONERA
MONETA
MONEYS
MOPEDS
MOPERS
MOREAU
MOREEN
MORELS
MORENO
MOSEYS
MOTELS
MOTETS
MOVEIN
MOVERS
MOWERS
MOYERS
MUDEEL
MULETA
MUSERS
MUSEUM
MUTELY
MUTEST
MYSELF

M•••E•
MACHES
MADDEN
MADDER
MADMEN
MADRES
MAGNET
MAGUEY
MAHLER
MAIDEN
MAILED
MAILER
MAILES
MAIZES
MAJGEN
MALDEN
MALLEE
MALLEI
MALLET
MALTED
MANGER
MANNED
MANNER
MANSES
MANTEL
MANUEL
MAPLES
MAPPED
MAPPER
MARCEL
MARIEL
MARKED
MARKER
MARKET
MARLED
MARLEE
MARLEY
MARMEE
MARNER
MARRED
MARTEL
MARTEN
MARVEL
MASHED
MASHER
MASHES
MASKED
MASKER
MASSED
MASSES
MASSEY
MASTER
MATHER
MATTEA
MATTED
MATTEL
MATTER
MATTES
MAULED
MAULER
MAUMEE
MAUSER
MAUVES
MAYBES
MAYHEM
MCGREW
MCKUEN
MEAGER
MEANER
MEDLEY
MEEKER
MEETER
MELDED
MELEES
MELTED
MEMBER
MENDED
MENDEL
MENDER
MENDES
MENNEN
MEOWED
MERCED
MERCER
MERGED
MERGER
MERGES
MERKEL
MERMEN
MERSEY
MESHED
MESHES
MESMER
MESSED
MESSES
METIER
METRES
MEWLED
MEWLER
MICKEY
MIDDEN
MIDGES
MIDGET
MIDLER
MIFFED
MIGUEL
MILDER
MILDEW
MILIEU
MILKED
MILKER
MILLED
MILLER
MILLET
MILNER
MINCED
MINCER
MINCES
MINDED
MINDER
MINKES
MINTED
MINTER
MINUET
MINXES
MIRREN
MISLED
MISSED
MISSES
MISTED
MISTER
MITRED
MITRES
MITTEN
MIXTEC
MIZZEN
MOANED
MOANER
MOATED
MOBBED
MOBLEY
MOCKED
MOCKER
MOILED
MOILER
MOINES
MOIRES
MOLDED
MOLDER
MOLTED
MOLTEN
MOLTER
MONGER
MONIED
MONIES
MONKEY
MONTEL
MONTEZ
MOONED
MOONEY
MOORED
MOOTED
MOPPED
MOPPER
MOPPET
MOREEN
MORGEN
MORLEY
MORSEL
MOSLEM
MOSSED
MOSSES
MOSTEL
MOTHER
MOTLEY
MOUSED
MOUSER
MOUSES
MOUSEY
MOVIES
MUCKED
MUDDED
MUDDER
MUDEEL
MUDHEN
MUFFED
MUGGED
MUGGER
MULLED
MULLER
MULLET
MUMMER
MUPPET
MURDER
MURIEL
MURRES
MURREY
MUSHED
MUSHER
MUSHES
MUSKEG
MUSKET
MUSSED
MUSSEL
MUSSES
MUSTER
MUTTER
MYOPES

M••••E
MACRAE
MADAME

MADDIE
MAGGIE
MAGPIE
MAISIE
MAITRE
MALATE
MALICE
MALLEE
MALONE
MANAGE
MANEGE
MANGLE
MANQUE
MANTLE
MARBLE
MARCHE
MARCIE
MARGIE
MARINE
MARLEE
MARMEE
MARNIE
MARPLE
MARQUE
MASHIE
MASQUE
MATTIE
MATURE
MAUMEE
MAXINE
MAXIXE
MCCABE
MCHALE
MEAGRE
MEALIE
MEANIE
MEDDLE
MENACE
MENAGE
MENSAE
MEROPE
METATE
METOPE
METTLE
MIDDLE
MIGGLE
MILLIE
MILTIE
MINGLE
MINNIE
MINUTE
MIRAGE
MISCUE
MISUSE
MIZZLE
MOBILE
MODINE
MODULE
MOHAVE
MOJAVE
MOLINE
MOLTKE
MOMMIE
MONROE
MORALE
MOROSE
MOSQUE
MOTILE
MOTIVE
MOTTLE
MOUSSE
MRBLUE
MRHYDE
MUDDLE
MUDPIE
MUFFLE
MUGABE
MUMBLE
MUNCIE
MURINE
MUSCLE
MUSKIE
MUTATE
MUZZLE
MYRTLE

•ME•••
AMEBAE
AMEBAS
AMEBIC
AMECHE
AMEDEO
AMEERS
AMELIA
AMENDS
AMENRA
AMENTS
AMERCE
EMEERS
EMENDS
EMERGE
IMELDA
KMESON
OMEGAS
OMELET
OMERTA
SMEARS
SMEARY
SMELLS
SMELLY
SMELTS
SMERSH
TMESIS

•M•E••
AMBERS
AMEERS
AMIENS
AMOEBA
AMPERE
AMVETS
EMBEDS
EMBERS
EMCEED
EMCEES
EMEERS
EMMETS
EMMETT
EMPERY
IMPEDE
IMPELS
IMPEND
IMPERF
UMBELS
UMBERS

•M••E•
AMAZED
AMAZES
AMBLED
AMBLER
AMBLES
AMEDEO
AMICES
AMIDES
AMINES
AMOLES
AMPLER
AMSTEL
AMULET
AMUSED
AMUSES
EMBDEN
EMBLEM
EMCEED
EMCEES
EMOTED
EMOTER
EMOTES
IMAGED
IMAGER
IMAGES
IMARET
IMBUED
IMBUES
IMOGEN
OMELET
SMILED
SMILER
SMILES
SMILEY
SMITES
SMOKED
SMOKER
SMOKES
SMOKEY

•M•••E
AMALIE
AMEBAE
AMECHE
AMERCE
AMPERE
AMPULE
BMOVIE
EMERGE
EMIGRE
EMPIRE
IMBIBE
IMBRUE
IMFINE
IMMUNE
IMMURE
IMPALE
IMPEDE
IMPOSE
IMPURE
IMPUTE
SMUDGE
UMBRAE
UMPIRE

••ME••
ARMETS
CAMEAT
CAMEBY
CAMEIN
CAMELS
CAMEON
CAMEOS
CAMERA
CAMETO
CAMEUP
CEMENT
COMEAT
COMEBY
COMEDY
COMEIN
COMELY
COMEON
COMERS
COMETH
COMETO
COMETS
COMEUP
DEMEAN
EMMETS
EMMETT
ENMESH
FOMENT
GAMELY
GAMEST
GAMETE
GIMELS
HOMEEC
HOMELY
HOMERS
HUMERI
ISMENE
KHMERS
LAMECH
LAMEDH
LAMEDS
LAMELY
LAMENT
LAMESA
LAMEST
LIMENS
LIMEYS
LOMEIN
LUMENS
MIMEOS
MIMERS
MOMENT
NAMELY
NAMERS
NUMERO
OLMECS
PAMELA
POMELO
RAMEAU
REMEDY
REMELT
REMEND
ROMEOS
ROMERO
RUMENS
SAMEKH
SEMELE
SIMEON
SOMERS
TAMELY
TAMERS
TAMEST
TIMELY
TIMERS
TUMEFY
UNMEET
UNMESH
WOMENS
XIMENA
YEMENI

••M•E•
ARMIES
ARMLET
BOMBED
BOMBER
BOMBES
BUMMED
BUMMER
BUMPED
BUMPER
CAMBER
CAMDEN
CAMLET
CAMPED
CAMPER
COMBED
COMBER
COMBES
COMPEL
COMTES
CUMBER
DAMIEN
DAMMED
DAMNED
DAMPED
DAMPEN
DAMPER
DAMSEL
DIMMED
DIMMER
DUMBER
DUMPED
DUMPER
FEMMES
GAMIER
GEMMED
GIMBEL
GIMLET
GUMBEL
GUMMED
HAMLET
HAMMED
HAMMER
HAMPER
HEMMED
HEMMER
HOMEEC
HOMIER
HUMMED
HUMMER
HUMPED
HYMNED
JAMMED
JAMMER
JUMPED
JUMPER
KUMMEL
LAMBED
LAMMED
LEMUEL
LIMBED
LIMBER
LIMNED
LIMNER
LIMPED
LIMPER
LIMPET
LUMBER
LUMPED
LUMPEN
LUMPER
MEMBER
MUMMER
NUMBED
NUMBER
PAMPER
POMMEE
POMMEL
POMPEY
PUMMEL
PUMPED
PUMPER
RAMIES
RAMJET
RAMMED
RAMPED
RAMSES
RAMSEY
RIMMED
ROMMEL
ROMNEY
ROMPED
ROMPER
RUMMER
SAMUEL
SEMPER
SIMBEL
SIMMER
SIMPER
SOMBER
SOMMER
SUMMED
SUMMER
SUMNER
SUMTER
TAMPED
TAMPER
TEMPED
TEMPEH
TEMPER
TIMBER
UNMEET
VAMPED
VAMPER
WIMSEY
YAMMER
ZIMMER

••M••E
ADMIRE
ARMURE
BEMINE
BEMIRE
BEMUSE
BUMBLE
CAMISE
COMATE
DAMAGE
DAMONE
DAMORE
DEMISE
DEMODE
DEMOTE
DEMURE
DIMPLE
ELMORE
ERMINE
FAMINE
FEMALE
FUMBLE
GAMBLE
GAMETE
GAMINE
GEMMAE
HAMITE
HOMAGE
HOMBRE
HUMANE
HUMBLE
IMMUNE
IMMURE
INMATE
ISMENE
JAMOKE
JIMMIE
JUMBLE
LAMAZE
MOMMIE
MUMBLE
NIMBLE
NOMORE
OSMOSE
POMACE
POMADE
POMMEE
PUMICE
RAMATE
RAMBLE
RAMONE
RAMOSE
REMADE
REMAKE
REMISE
REMOTE
REMOVE
RIMOSE
RIMPLE
RUMBLE
RUMPLE
SAMITE
SAMMIE
SAMPLE
SEMELE
SEMITE
SEMPRE
SIMILE
SIMONE
SIMPLE
SOMBRE
SUMMAE
TAMALE
TEMPLE
TIMBRE
TUMBLE
UNMADE
UNMAKE
WAMBLE
WIMBLE
WIMPLE
ZOMBIE
ZYMASE

•••ME•
ACUMEN
AIRMEN
ANIMES
APEMEN
BARMEN
BATMEN
BEAMED
BIOMES
BLAMED
BLAMES
BLIMEY
BOOMED
BOOMER
BOWMEN
BREMEN
BRUMES
BUMMED
BUMMER
BUSMEN
CALMED
CALMER
CARMEL
CARMEN
CERMET
CHIMED
CHIMES
CLIMES
CONMEN
COWMEN
CREMES
CRIMEA
CRIMES
DAMMED
DEEMED
DIMMED
DIMMER
DISMES
DOLMEN
DOOMED
DORMER
EDAMES
ENAMEL
ENDMEN
FARMED
FARMER
FBIMEN
FEMMES
FILMED
FIRMED
FIRMER
FLAMED
FLAMES
FLUMES
FLYMEN
FOAMED
FORMED
FORMER
FRAMED
FRAMES
GAGMEN
GASMEN
GEMMED
GNOMES
GRIMED
GRIMES
GUMMED
GUNMEN
HAMMED
HAMMER
HARMED
HELMED
HELMET
HEMMED
HEMMER
HERMES
HITMEN
HOLMES
HORMEL
HUMMED
HUMMER
ICEMEN
ILLMET
ISOMER
JAMMED
JAMMER
KERMES
KILMER
KISMET
KRAMER
KUMMEL
LAMMED
LAWMEN
LAYMEN
LEGMEN
LOAMED
LOOMED
MADMEN
MARMEE
MAUMEE
MERMEN
MESMER
MUMMER
NETMEN
NEUMES
NIAMEY
NOUMEA
NUTMEG
OILMEN
OLDMEN
PALMED
PALMER
PELMET
PENMEN
PERMED
PIEMEN
PITMEN
PLUMED
PLUMES
POMMEE
POMMEL
PREMED
PRIMED
PRIMER
PRIMES
PUMMEL
RAGMEN
RAMMED
REAMED
REAMER
RHYMED
RHYMER
RHYMES
RIMMED
ROAMED
ROAMER
ROHMER
ROMMEL
ROOMED
ROOMER
RUMMER
SEAMED
SEAMEN
SEEMED
SHAMED
SHAMES
SIMMER
SLIMED
SLIMES
SOMMER
SPUMED
SPUMES
STAMEN
SUMMED
SUMMER
TAXMEN
TEAMED
TEEMED
TERMED
TEXMEX
THAMES
THEMED
THEMES
TINMEN
WARMED
WARMER
WORMED
XIAMEN
YAMMER
YEOMEN
YESMEN
ZIMMER
ZOOMED

•••M•E
ANOMIE
FLAMBE
GEMMAE
GRAMME
GRIMKE
GUIMPE
JIMMIE
MARMEE
MAUMEE
MOMMIE
POMMEE
PREMIE
ROOMIE
SAMMIE
STYMIE
SUMMAE
TROMPE

••••ME
AFLAME
AFRAME
ASSUME
ATHOME
BECAME
BECOME
BIREME
BYNAME
CHROME
DANGME
DEARME
DEFAME
ENZYME
GENOME
GOHOME
GRAMME
ILLUME
INCOME
INHUME
INTIME
JEROME
KINGME
LEGUME
LEXEME
MADAME
NONAME
ONTIME
RACEME
RADOME
REGIME
RELUME
RENAME
RESUME
RETIME
SALOME
SCHEME
SESAME
SHOWME
UPTIME
VOLUME

M•F•••
MIFFED
MUFASA
MUFFED
MUFFIN
MUFFLE
MUFTIS

M••F••
MANFUL
MAYFLY
MIFFED
MISFIT
MUFFED
MUFFIN
MUFFLE

M•••F•
MINIFY
MODIFY
MOTIFS

M••••F
MASSIF
MYSELF

•MF•••
IMFINE

•M••F•
AMALFI
SMURFS

•M•••F
IMPERF

••MF••
ARMFUL
COMFIT

••M•F•
RAMIFY
TUMEFY

M•G•••
MAGGIE
MAGGIO
MAGMAS
MAGNET
MAGNON
MAGNUM
MAGPIE
MAGUEY
MAGYAR
MCGRAW
MCGREW
MEGALO
MEGARA
MEGILP
MEGOHM
MIGGLE
MIGHTY
MIGNON
MIGUEL
MOGULS
MUGABE
MUGGED
MUGGER
MUGHOS
MYGIRL

M••G••
MAGGIE
MAGGIO
MAJGEN
MANGER
MANGLE
MANGOS
MARGAY
MARGIE
MARGIN
MARGOT
MEAGER
MEAGRE
MEDGAR
MERGED
MERGER
MERGES
MIDGES
MIDGET
MIGGLE
MINGLE
MONGER
MONGOL
MORGAN
MORGEN
MOWGLI
MUGGED
MUGGER
MUNGOS

M•••G•
MALAGA
MALIGN
MANAGE
MANEGE
MENAGE
MIRAGE

M••••G
MAKING
MATING
MAYTAG
MEKONG
METING
MEWING
MIKING
MIMING
MINING
MIRING
MIXING
MOOING
MOPING
MOVING
MOWING
MUSING
MUSKEG
MUTING

•M•G••
AMIGOS
EMIGRE
IMAGED
IMAGER
IMAGES
IMOGEN
OMEGAS
SMOGGY
SMUGLY

•M••G•
EMERGE
HMONGS
IMPUGN
SMOGGY
SMUDGE
SMUDGY

••M•G•
ARMAGH
DAMAGE
HOMAGE

••M••G
AIMING
ARMING
COMING
DOMING
FUMING
GAMING
HOMING
HUMBUG
LAMING
LIMING
MIMING
NAMING
RIMING
TAMING
TIMING

•••M•G
NUTMEG
WONMUG

M•H•••
MAHDIS
MAHLER
MAHOUT
MAHZOR
MCHALE
MIHRAB
MOHAIR
MOHAVE
MOHAWK
MOHOCK
MOHURS
MRHYDE

M••H••
MACHES
MACHOS
MASHED
MASHER
MASHES
MASHIE
MATHER
MATHIS
MAYHAP
MAYHEM
MENHIR
MESHED
MESHES
METHOD
METHYL
MIGHTY
MISHAP
MISHIT
MOCHAS
MOSHAV
MOTHER
MUDHEN
MUGHOS
MUSHED
MUSHER
MUSHES
MUZHIK
MYOHMY
MYTHIC
MYTHOI
MYTHOL
MYTHOS

M•••H•
MANCHA
MANCHU
MARCHE
MARSHA
MARSHY
MARTHA
MEGOHM
MISCHA
MONTHS
MORPHO
MORPHS
MOUTHS
MOUTHY
MURPHY
MYNAHS
MYRRHS

M••••H
MARIAH
MATZOH
MENSCH
MODISH
MOLOCH
MOOLAH
MOPISH
MULISH
MULLAH
MUNICH

•MH•••
AMHARA

•M•H••
AMPHID
OMAHAN
OMAHAS

•M••H•
AMECHE
SMITHS
SMITHY

•M•••H
AMBUSH
EMDASH
IMPISH
SMERSH
SMIRCH
SMOOCH
SMOOTH
SMUTCH

••M•H•
HUMPHS
KIMCHI
NYMPHS
YAMAHA

••M••H
ARMAGH
COMETH
ENMESH
FAMISH
IOMOTH
LAMECH
LAMEDH
NAMATH
OOMPAH
SAMEKH
TEMPEH
UNMESH

•••M•H
WARMTH

MI••••
MIASMA
MICKEY
MICMAC
MICRON
MICROS
MIDAIR
MIDDAY
MIDDEN
MIDDLE
MIDGES
MIDGET
MIDLER
MIDORI
MIDRIB
MIDWAY
MIFFED
MIGGLE
MIGHTY
MIGNON
MIGUEL
MIHRAB
MIKADO
MIKING
MIKITA
MILADY
MILANO
MILDER
MILDEW
MILDLY
MILERS
MILIEU
MILKED
MILKER
MILLAY
MILLED
MILLER
MILLET
MILLIE
MILNER
MILORD
MILOSZ
MILPAS
MILSAP
MILTIE
MILTON
MIMEOS
MIMERS
MIMICS
MIMING
MIMOSA
MINCED
MINCER
MINCES
MINDED
MINDER
MINERS
MINGLE
MINIFY
MINIMA
MINIMS
MINING
MINION
MINIUM
MINKES
MINNIE
MINNOW
MINOAN
MINORS
MINTED
MINTER
MINUET
MINUIT
MINUTE
MINXES
MINYAN
MIOSIS
MIRAGE
MIRIAM
MIRING
MIRREN
MIRROR
MISCHA
MISCUE
MISDID
MISERS
MISERY
MISFIT
MISHAP
MISHIT
MISLAY
MISLED

MISSAL
MISSAY
MISSED
MISSES
MISSIS
MISSUS
MISTED
MISTER
MISUSE
MITERS
MITRAL
MITRED
MITRES
MITTEN
MIWOKS
MIXERS
MIXING
MIXTEC
MIXUPS
MIZENS
MIZZEN
MIZZLE

M•I•••
MAIDEN
MAIDUS
MAILED
MAILER
MAILES
MAILIN
MAINLY
MAISIE
MAITAI
MAITRE
MAIZES
MOIETY
MOILED
MOILER
MOINES
MOIRES

M••I••
MAKING
MALIBU
MALICE
MALIGN
MANIAC
MANIAS
MANILA
MANIOC
MAOISM
MAOIST
MARIAH
MARIAN
MARIEL
MARIKO
MARILU
MARINA
MARINE
MARINO
MARION
MARISA
MARIST
MARIUS
MATING
MATINS
MAXIMA
MAXIMS
MAXINE
MAXIXE
MEDIAL
MEDIAN
MEDIAS
MEDICI
MEDICO
MEDICS
MEDINA
MEDIUM
MEGILP
MELINA
MENIAL
MENINX
MERIDA
MERINO
MERITS
METIER
METING
MEWING
MEXICO
MIKING
MIKITA
MILIEU
MIMICS
MIMING
MINIFY
MINIMA
MINIMS
MINING
MINION
MINIUM
MIRIAM
MIRING
MIXING
MOBILE
MOBIUS
MODIFY
MODINE
MODISH
MOLINE
MONICA
MONIED
MONIES
MONISM
MONIST
MOOING
MOPING
MOPISH
MORION
MORITA
MORITZ
MOTIFS
MOTILE
MOTION
MOTIVE
MOVIES
MOVING
MOWING
MULISH
MUNICH
MURIEL
MURINE
MUSIAL
MUSING
MUTING
MUTINY
MYGIRL
MYRIAD

M•••I•
MADDIE
MADEIT
MADRID
MAGGIE
MAGGIO
MAGPIE
MAHDIS
MAILIN
MAISIE
MAJLIS
MAKEIT
MALKIN
MALTIN
MANNIX
MANTIC
MANTIS
MAORIS
MAQUIS
MARCIA
MARCIE
MARGIE
MARGIN
MARLIN
MARNIE
MARTIN
MARVIN
MASAIS
MASHIE
MASSIF
MASTIC
MATHIS
MATLIN
MATRIX
MATTIE
MCBAIN
MCLAIN
MCNAIR
MEALIE
MEANIE
MELVIL
MELVIN
MEMOIR
MENHIR
MENTIS
MERLIN
METRIC
MIDAIR
MIDRIB
MILLIE
MILTIE
MINNIE
MINUIT
MIOSIS
MISDID
MISFIT
MISHIT
MISSIS
MOHAIR
MOMMIE
MORBID
MORRIS
MOSAIC
MOULIN
MOVEIN
MUDPIE
MUFFIN
MUFTIS
MUNCIE
MUNTIN
MURCIA
MUSKIE
MUSLIM
MUSLIN
MUZHIK
MYELIN
MYOPIA
MYOPIC
MYOSIN
MYSTIC
MYTHIC

M••••I
MAITAI
MALAWI
MALLEI
MALOTI
MAOTAI
MEDICI
MESABI
MIDORI
MORONI
MOWGLI
MYTHOI

•MI•••
AMICES
AMICUS
AMIDES
AMIDOL
AMIDST
AMIENS
AMIGOS
AMINES
AMINOR
AMINUS
BMINOR
BMINUS
CMINOR
CMINUS
DMINOR
DMINUS
DMITRI
EMIGRE
EMILIA
EMILIO
EMINOR
FMINOR
GMINOR
SMILAX
SMILED
SMILER
SMILES
SMILEY
SMIRCH
SMIRKS
SMIRKY
SMITES
SMITHS
SMITHY
UMIAKS

•M•I••
AMBITS
AMNION
EMAILS
EMPIRE
IMBIBE
IMFINE
IMPISH
OMNIUM
UMPIRE

•M••I•
AMADIS
AMALIE
AMATIS
AMBLIN
AMEBIC
AMELIA
AMPHID
BMOVIE
EMILIA
EMILIO
IMPAIR
OMANIS
TMESIS
UMBRIA

•M•••I
AMALFI
DMITRI
SMALTI

••MI••
ADMIRE
ADMITS
AIMING
ARMIES
ARMING
BEMINE
BEMIRE
BIMINI
CAMINO
CAMION
CAMISE
COMICS
COMING
COMITY
DAMIEN
DAMITA
DEMISE
DEMITS
DIMITY
DOMING
DOMINI
DOMINO
ELMIRA
ENMITY
ERMINE
FAMILY
FAMINE
FAMISH
FUMING
GAMIER
GAMILY
GAMINE
GAMING
GAMINS
GEMINI
HAMILL
HAMITE
HOMIER
HOMILY
HOMING
HOMINY
JIMINY
KUMISS
LAMIAS
LAMINA
LAMING
LIMING
LIMITS
LUMINA
MIMICS
MIMING
NAMING
NIMINY
NIMITZ
NUMINA
OSMICS
OSMIUM
PAMIRS
PIMINY
PUMICE
RAMIES
RAMIFY
REMICK
REMIND
REMISE
REMISS
REMITS
RIMING
RIMINI
RUMINA
SAMIAM
SAMITE
SEMITE
SIMIAN
SIMILE
TAMILS
TAMING
TIMING

••M•I•
ARMPIT
CAMEIN
COMEIN
COMFIT
COMMIT
COMMIX
CYMRIC
DIMWIT
DOMAIN
GAMBIA
GAMBIT
HAMLIN
HEMSIN
IAMBIC
JAMSIN
JIMMIE
JUMPIN
KEMPIS
LIMPID
LOMEIN
MEMOIR
MOMMIE
REMAIL
REMAIN
ROMAIC
SAMMIE
SUMMIT
TOMLIN
TOMMIX
TOMTIT
USMAIL
ZAMBIA
ZOMBIE

••M••I
ARMANI
BIMINI
CUMULI
DOMANI
DOMINI
GEMINI
HUMERI
KIMCHI
RIMINI
ROMAJI
SOMALI
TUMULI
YEMENI

•••MI•
ANEMIA
ANEMIC
ANOMIE
ARAMIS
ATOMIC
CADMIC
CHEMIN
COMMIT
COMMIX
COSMIC
DERMIS
ELEMIS
FORMIC
GNOMIC
HERMIT
JIMMIE
KARMIC
KERMIS
KERMIT
MOMMIE
PERMIT
PREMIE
ROOMIE
SAMMIE
SHAMIR
STYMIE
SUBMIT
SUMMIT
SWAMIS
TOMMIX
VERMIN

•••M•I
ALUMNI
DROMOI
KATMAI
RHOMBI
SCAMPI

••••MI
BATUMI
BONAMI
DOREMI
ISTHMI
SALAMI
SURIMI
TATAMI

M•J•••
MAJGEN
MAJLIS
MAJORS
MOJAVE

M••J••
MENJOU

•M•J••
AMAJOR
BMAJOR
CMAJOR
DMAJOR
EMAJOR
FMAJOR
GMAJOR

••MJ••
RAMJET

••M•J•
ROMAJI

•••M•J
SGTMAJ

M•K•••
MAKALU
MAKEDO
MAKEIT
MAKERS
MAKEUP
MAKING
MAKUTA
MCKUEN
MEKONG
MIKADO
MIKING
MIKITA
MUKLUK

M••K••
MALKIN
MARKED
MARKER
MARKET
MARKKA
MARKUP
MASKED
MASKER
MEEKER
MEEKLY
MERKEL
MICKEY
MILKED
MILKER
MINKES
MOCKED
MOCKER
MOCKUP
MONKEY
MOSKVA
MUCKED
MUCKUP
MUSKEG
MUSKET
MUSKIE
MUSKOX

M•••K•
MARIKO
MARKKA
MEDAKA
MIWOKS
MOLTKE

M••••K
MARDUK
MOHAWK
MOHOCK
MUKLUK
MUZHIK

•M•K••
SMOKED
SMOKER
SMOKES
SMOKEY

•M••K•
SMACKS
SMIRKS
SMIRKY
SMOCKS
UMIAKS

•M•••K
AMTRAK
EMBANK
EMBARK

••M•K•
BAMAKO
JAMOKE
REMAKE
RIMSKY
SAMEKH
UNMAKE

••M••K
DAMASK
LOMBOK
REMARK
REMICK
STMARK
UNMASK

•••MK•
GRIMKE

M•L•••
MALABO
MALADY
MALAGA
MALATE
MALAWI
MALAYA
MALAYS
MALDEN
MALIBU
MALICE
MALIGN
MALKIN
MALLEE
MALLEI
MALLET
MALLOW
MALONE
MALORY
MALOTI
MALTED
MALTIN
MCLAIN
MCLEAN
MELANO
MELDED
MELEES
MELINA
MELLON
MELLOW
MELMAC
MELODY
MELONS
MELOTT
MELTED
MELTON
MELVIL
MELVIN
MELVYN
MILADY
MILANO
MILDER
MILDEW
MILDLY
MILERS
MILIEU
MILKED
MILKER
MILLAY
MILLED
MILLER
MILLET
MILLIE
MILNER
MILORD
MILOSZ
MILPAS
MILSAP
MILTIE
MILTON
MOLARS
MOLDAU
MOLDED
MOLDER
MOLEST
MOLINE
MOLNAR
MOLOCH
MOLOPO
MOLTED
MOLTEN
MOLTER
MOLTKE
MULCTS
MULETA
MULISH
MULLAH
MULLAS
MULLED
MULLER
MULLET

M••L••
MAHLER
MAILED
MAILER
MAILES
MAILIN
MAJLIS
MALLEE
MALLEI
MALLET
MALLOW
MAPLES
MARLED
MARLEE
MARLEY
MARLIN
MARLON
MATLIN
MAULED
MAULER
MEALIE
MEDLAR
MEDLAT
MEDLEY
MELLON
MELLOW
MERLIN
MERLON
MERLOT
MEWLED
MEWLER
MIDLER
MILLAY
MILLED
MILLER
MILLET
MILLIE
MISLAY
MISLED
MOBLEY
MOILED
MOILER
MOOLAH
MORLEY
MOSLEM
MOTLEY
MOULDS
MOULDY
MOULIN
MOULTS
MRBLUE
MUKLUK
MULLAH
MULLAS
MULLED
MULLER
MULLET
MUSLIM
MUSLIN
MYELIN

M•••L•
MABELL
MACULA
MAINLY
MAKALU
MANGLE
MANILA
MANTLE
MARBLE
MARBLY
MARILU
MARPLE
MAYFLY
MAZOLA
MCHALE
MEANLY
MEASLY
MEDALS
MEDDLE
MEEKLY
MEETLY
MEGALO
MEGILP
MERELY
METALS
METTLE
MIDDLE
MIGGLE
MILDLY
MINGLE
MIZZLE
MOBILE
MODELA
MODELS
MODELT
MODULE
MODULO
MOGULS
MORALE
MORALS
MORELS
MOSTLY
MOTELS
MOTILE
MOTTLE
MOWGLI
MUDDLE
MUFFLE
MUMBLE
MUMBLY
MURALS
MUSCLE
MUSCLY
MUTELY
MUZZLE
MYRTLE
MYSELF

M••••L
MABELL
MAMMAL
MANFUL
MANTEL
MANUAL
MANUEL
MARCEL
MARIEL
MARTEL
MARVEL
MATTEL
MEDIAL
MELVIL
MENDEL
MENIAL
MENSAL
MENTAL
MERKEL
MESCAL
METHYL
MIGUEL
MISSAL
MITRAL
MONGOL
MONTEL
MORSEL
MORTAL
MOSTEL
MRCOOL
MUDEEL
MURIEL
MUSIAL
MUSSEL
MUTUAL
MYGIRL
MYRDAL
MYTHOL

•ML•••
UMLAUT

•M•L••
AMALFI
AMALIE
AMBLED
AMBLER
AMBLES
AMBLIN
AMELIA
AMOLES
AMPLER
AMULET
EMBLEM
EMILIA
EMILIO
EMPLOY
IMELDA
OMELET
SMALLS
SMALTI
SMALTO
SMELLS
SMELLY
SMELTS
SMILAX
SMILED
SMILER
SMILES
SMILEY

•M••L•
AMPULE
AMPULS
EMAILS
IMPALA
IMPALE
IMPELS
SMALLS
SMELLS
SMELLY
SMUGLY
UMBELS

•M•••L
AMATOL
AMIDOL
AMORAL
AMSTEL
UMBRAL

••ML••
ARMLET
CAMLET
GIMLET
HAMLET
HAMLIN
TOMLIN

••M•L•
BUMBLE
CAMELS
COMELY
COMPLY
CUMULI
CUMULO
DAMPLY
DIMPLE
DIMPLY
DUMBLY
FAMILY
FEMALE
FUMBLE
GAMBLE
GAMELY
GAMILY
GIMELS
HAMALS
HAMILL
HOMELY
HOMILY
HUMBLE
HUMBLY
JUMBLE
KAMALA
LAMELY
LIMPLY
MUMBLE
MUMBLY
NAMELY
NIMBLE
NIMBLY
NUMBLY
ORMOLU
PAMELA
POMELO
RAMBLA
RAMBLE
REMELT
RIMPLE
ROMOLA
RUMBLE
RUMBLY
RUMPLE
RUMPLY
SAMPLE
SEMELE
SIMILE
SIMPLE
SIMPLY
SOMALI
STMALO
TAMALE
TAMELY
TAMILS
TEMPLE
TIMELY
TUMBLE
TUMULI
TUMULT
WAMBLE
WAMBLY
WIMBLE
WIMPLE

••M••L
ARMFUL
COMPEL
CYMBAL
DAMSEL
GAMBOL
GIMBAL
GIMBEL
GUMBEL
HAMILL
HYMNAL
JAMAAL
KUMMEL
LEMUEL
MAMMAL
POMMEL
PUMMEL
REMAIL
ROMMEL
SAMBAL
SAMUEL
SIMBEL
SYMBOL
TIMBAL
USMAIL

•••ML•
CALMLY
FIRMLY
GLUMLY
GRIMLY
PRIMLY
SEEMLY
SLIMLY
TRIMLY
WARMLY

•••M•L
ANIMAL
BRUMAL
CARMEL
DERMAL
DISMAL
ENAMEL
ETYMOL
FORMAL
HIEMAL
HORMEL
KUMMEL
MAMMAL
NORMAL
POMMEL
PRIMAL
PUMMEL
ROMMEL

M•M•••
MAMBAS
MAMBOS
MAMMAL
MAMMAS
MAMMON
MEMBER
MEMNON
MEMOIR
MEMORY
MIMEOS
MIMERS
MIMICS
MIMING
MIMOSA
MOMENT
MOMMAS
MOMMIE
MRMOTO
MUMBLE
MUMBLY
MUMMER

M••M••
MADMAN
MADMAX
MADMEN
MAGMAS
MAMMAL
MAMMAS
MAMMON
MARMEE
MARMOT
MAUMAU
MAUMEE
MELMAC
MERMAN
MERMEN
MESMER
MICMAC
MOMMAS
MOMMIE
MORMON
MOTMOT
MUMMER
MURMUR
MUUMUU

M•••M•
MADAME
MADAMS
MANAMA
MAXIMA
MAXIMS
MAZUMA
MIASMA
MINIMA
MINIMS
MODEMS
MYOHMY

M••••M
MADTOM
MAGNUM
MAOISM
MAYHEM
MCADAM
MEDIUM
MEGOHM
MINIUM
MIRIAM
MONISM
MOSLEM
MUSEUM
MUSLIM

•MM•••
EMMETS
EMMETT
IMMUNE
IMMUNO
IMMURE

•M••M•
SMARMY

•M••M
EMBLEM
OMASUM
OMNIUM

••MM••
BUMMED
BUMMER
COMMAS
COMMIT
COMMIX
COMMON
DAMMAR
DAMMED
DIMMED
DIMMER
FEMMES
GAMMAS
GAMMON
GEMMAE
GEMMED
GUMMED
HAMMED
HAMMER
HEMMED
HEMMER
HUMMED
HUMMER
HUMMUS
JAMMED
JAMMER
JIMMIE
KUMMEL
LAMMAS
LAMMED
LEMMAS
LEMMON
LUMMOX
MAMMAL
MAMMAS
MAMMON
MOMMAS
MOMMIE
MUMMER
POMMEE
POMMEL
PUMMEL
RAMMED
RIMMED
ROMMEL
RUMMER
SAMMIE
SIMMER
SOMMER
SUMMAE
SUMMAS
SUMMED
SUMMER
SUMMIT
SUMMON
TAMMUZ
TOMMIX
YAMMER
ZIMMER

••M••M
DIMSUM
DUMDUM
OSMIUM
POMPOM
SAMIAM
TAMTAM
TOMTOM
WAMPUM
YUMYUM

•••MM•
CHAMMY
CHUMMY
CLAMMY
CRUMMY
GRAMME
GRAMMY
PLUMMY
SCUMMY
SHIMMY
SLUMMY
WHAMMO
WHAMMY

•••M•M
PRIMUM

M•N•••
MANAGE
MANAMA
MANANA
MANAUS
MANCHA
MANCHU
MANDAN
MANDAY
MANEGE
MANFUL
MANGER
MANGLE
MANGOS
MANIAC
MANIAS
MANILA
MANIOC
MANNED
MANNER
MANNIX
MANORS
MANQUE
MANRAY
MANSES
MANTAS
MANTEL
MANTIC
MANTIS
MANTLE
MANTRA
MANTUA
MANUAL
MANUEL
MCNAIR
MENACE
MENAGE
MENDED
MENDEL
MENDER
MENDES
MENHIR
MENIAL
MENINX
MENJOU
MENNEN
MENSAE
MENSAL
MENSAS
MENSCH
MENTAL
MENTIS
MENTOR
MINCED
MINCER
MINCES
MINDED
MINDER
MINERS
MINGLE
MINIFY
MINIMA
MINIMS
MINING
MINION
MINIUM
MINKES
MINNIE
MINNOW
MINOAN
MINORS
MINTED
MINTER
MINUET
MINUIT
MINUTE
MINXES
MINYAN
MONACO
MONADS
MONDAY
MONERA
MONETA
MONEYS
MONGER
MONGOL
MONICA
MONIED
MONIES
MONISM
MONIST
MONKEY
MONODY
MONROE
MONTEL
MONTEZ
MONTHS
MUNCIE
MUNGOS
MUNICH
MUNTIN
MYNAHS

M••N••
MAENAD
MAGNET
MAGNON
MAGNUM
MAINLY
MANNED
MANNER
MANNIX
MARNER
MARNIE
MAUNDY
MBUNDU
MEANER
MEANIE
MEANLY
MEMNON
MENNEN
MIGNON
MILNER
MINNIE
MINNOW
MOANED
MOANER
MOINES
MOLNAR
MOONED
MOONEY
MORNAY
MOUNDS
MOUNTS
MOUNTY

M•••N•
MAKING
MALONE
MANANA
MARINA
MARINE
MARINO
MASONS
MATING
MATINS
MAVENS
MAXINE
MAYANS
MCCANN
MEDINA
MEKONG
MELANO
MELINA
MELONS
MENINX
MERINO
MESONS
METING
MEWING
MIKING
MILANO
MIMING
MINING
MIRING
MIXING
MIZENS
MODENA
MODINE
MOLINE
MOMENT
MOOING
MOPING
MORANT
MORENO
MORONI
MORONS
MOVING
MOWING
MURANO
MURINE
MUSING
MUSTNT
MUTANT
MUTING
MUTINY

M••••N
MACRON
MADDEN
MADMAN
MADMEN
MAGNON
MAIDEN
MAILIN
MAJGEN
MALDEN
MALIGN
MALKIN
MALTIN
MAMMON
MANDAN
MARGIN
MARIAN
MARION
MARLIN
MARLON
MAROON
MARRON
MARTEN
MARTIN
MARVIN
MATLIN
MATRON
MCBAIN
MCCANN
MCKUEN
MCLAIN
MCLEAN
MEDIAN
MELLON
MELTON
MELVIN
MELVYN
MEMNON
MENNEN
MERLIN
MERLON
MERMAN
MERMEN
MERTON
MERVYN
MICRON
MIDDEN
MIGNON
MILTON
MINION
MINOAN
MINYAN
MIRREN
MITTEN
MIZZEN
MODERN
MOLTEN
MOREEN
MORGAN
MORGEN
MORION
MORMON
MORTON
MOTION
MOTOWN
MOULIN
MOUTON
MOVEIN
MUDHEN
MUFFIN
MUNTIN
MUSLIN
MUTTON
MYELIN
MYOSIN

•MN•••
AMNION
OMNIUM

•M•N••
AMANDA
AMENDS
AMENRA
AMENTS
AMINES
AMINOR
AMINUS
BMINOR
BMINUS
CMINOR
CMINUS
DMINOR
DMINUS
EMENDS
EMINOR
FMINOR
GMINOR
HMONGS
OMANIS

•M••N•
AMIENS
AMOUNT
EMBANK
IMFINE
IMMUNE
IMMUNO
IMPEND
SMYRNA

•M•••N
AMAZON
AMBLIN
AMNION
AMYTAN
EMBDEN
IMOGEN
IMPUGN
KMESON
OMAHAN

••MN••
DAMNED
HYMNAL
HYMNED
LEMNOS
LIMNED
LIMNER
MEMNON
ROMNEY
SUMNER

••M•N•
AIMING
ALMOND
ARMAND
ARMANI
ARMING
AUMONT
BEMINE
BIMINI
CAMINO
CEMENT
COMING
DAMONE
DEMAND
DEMOND
DEMONS
DOMANI
DOMING
DOMINI
DOMINO
DUMONT
EDMOND
EDMUND
EGMONT
ERMINE
FAMINE
FOMENT
FUMING
GAMINE
GAMING
GAMINS
GEMINI
HOMING
HOMINY
HUMANE
HUMANS
IMMUNE
IMMUNO
ISMENE
JIMINY
KIMONO
LAMENT
LAMINA
LAMING
LAMONT
LEMANS
LEMOND
LEMONS
LEMONY
LIMENS
LIMING
LOMOND
LUMENS
LUMINA
MIMING
MOMENT
NAMING
NIMINY
NUMINA
ORMOND
OSMOND
OSMUND
PIMINY
POMONA
RAMONA
RAMONE
REMAND
REMANS
REMEND
REMIND
RIMING
RIMINI
ROMANO
ROMANS
ROMANY
RUMENS
RUMINA
SIMONE
SIMONY
SOMANY
TAMING
TIMING
UNMANS
WOMENS
XIMENA
YEMENI

••M••N
BEMOAN
CAMDEN
CAMEIN
CAMEON
CAMION
COMEIN
COMEON
COMMON
DAMIEN
DAMPEN
DAMSON
DEMEAN
DOMAIN
GAMMON
HAMLIN
HEMSIN
JAMSIN
JIMSON
JUMPIN
JUMPON
LEMMON
LOMEIN
LUMPEN
MAMMON
MEMNON
POMPON
QUMRAN
RAMSON
REMAIN
REMOWN
SAMOAN
SAMPAN
SAMSON
SIMEON
SIMIAN
SUMMON
TOMLIN

•••MN•
ALUMNA
ALUMNI

•••M•N
ACUMEN
AIRMAN
AIRMEN
ALEMAN
ALLMAN
ALTMAN
APEMAN
APEMEN
ATAMAN
BARMAN
BARMEN
BATMAN
BATMEN
BORMAN
BOWMAN
BOWMEN
BREMEN
BURMAN
BUSMAN
BUSMEN
CAIMAN
CARMAN
CARMEN
CAYMAN
CHEMIN
COLMAN
COMMON
CONMAN
CONMEN
COWMAN
COWMEN
DAIMON
DESMAN
DOLMAN
DOLMEN
ELFMAN
ENDMAN
ENDMEN
ETYMON
FBIMAN
FBIMEN
FIRMAN
FLYMAN
FLYMEN
FORMAN
GAGMAN
GAGMEN
GAMMON
GASMAN
GASMEN
GERMAN
GNOMON
GUNMAN
GUNMEN
HAEMON
HAGMAN
HARMON
HERMAN
HERMON
HETMAN
HITMAN
HITMEN
ICEMAN
ICEMEN
KERMAN
KIDMAN
KIRMAN
KORMAN
LAWMAN
LAWMEN
LAYMAN
LAYMEN
LEGMAN
LEGMEN
LEMMON
MADMAN
MADMEN
MAMMON
MERMAN
MERMEN
MORMON
NETMAN
NETMEN
NEUMAN
NEWMAN
NORMAN
OILMAN
OILMEN
OLDMAN
OLDMEN
PACMAN
PENMAN
PENMEN
PIEMAN
PIEMEN
PITMAN
PITMEN
RAGMAN
RAGMEN
RUDMAN
SALMAN
SALMON
SEAMAN
SEAMEN
SERMON
SHAMAN
SHIMON
STAMEN
SUMMON
TASMAN
TAXMAN
TAXMEN
TINMAN
TINMEN
TOAMAN
TODMAN
TRUMAN
TUBMAN
ULLMAN
VERMIN
XIAMEN
YEOMAN
YEOMEN
YESMAN
YESMEN
ZEEMAN

••••MN
AUTUMN
COLUMN
SOLEMN

MO••••
MOANED
MOANER
MOATED
MOBBED
MOBCAP
MOBILE
MOBIUS
MOBLEY
MOCHAS
MOCKED
MOCKER
MOCKUP
MODELA
MODELS
MODELT
MODEMS
MODENA
MODERN
MODEST
MODIFY
MODINE
MODISH
MODOCS
MODULE
MODULO
MOGULS
MOHAIR
MOHAVE
MOHAWK
MOHOCK
MOHURS
MOIETY
MOILED
MOILER
MOINES
MOIRES
MOJAVE
MOLARS
MOLDAU
MOLDED
MOLDER
MOLEST
MOLINE
MOLNAR
MOLOCH
MOLOPO
MOLTED
MOLTEN
MOLTER
MOLTKE
MOMENT
MOMMAS
MOMMIE
MONACO
MONADS
MONDAY
MONERA
MONETA
MONEYS
MONGER
MONGOL
MONICA
MONIED
MONIES
MONISM
MONIST
MONKEY
MONODY
MONROE
MONTEL
MONTEZ
MONTHS
MOOING
MOOLAH
MOONED
MOONEY
MOORED
MOOTED
MOPEDS
MOPERS
MOPING
MOPISH
MOPPED
MOPPER
MOPPET
MOPSUP
MOPUPS
MORALE
MORALS
MORANT
MORASS
MORAVA
MORAYS
MORBID
MOREAU
MOREEN
MORELS
MORENO
MORGAN
MORGEN
MORION
MORITA
MORITZ
MORLEY
MORMON
MORNAY
MORONI
MORONS
MOROSE
MORPHO
MORPHS
MORRIS
MORROW
MORSEL
MORTAL
MORTAR
MORTON
MOSAIC
MOSCOW
MOSEYS
MOSHAV
MOSKVA
MOSLEM
MOSQUE
MOSSED
MOSSES
MOSTEL
MOSTLY
MOTELS
MOTETS
MOTHER
MOTIFS
MOTILE
MOTION
MOTIVE
MOTLEY
MOTMOT
MOTORS
MOTOWN
MOTTLE
MOTTOS
MOULDS
MOULDY
MOULIN
MOULTS
MOUNDS
MOUNTS
MOUNTY
MOUSED
MOUSER
MOUSES
MOUSEY
MOUSSE
MOUTHS
MOUTHY
MOUTON
MOVEIN
MOVERS
MOVIES
MOVING
MOWERS
MOWGLI
MOWING
MOYERS
MOZART

M•O•••
MAOISM
MAOIST
MAORIS
MAOTAI
MEOWED
MIOSIS
MOOING
MOOLAH
MOONED
MOONEY
MOORED
MOOTED
MYOHMY
MYOPES
MYOPIA
MYOPIC
MYOSIN

M••O••
MAHOUT
MAJORS
MALONE
MALORY
MALOTI
MANORS
MAROON
MASONS
MAXOUT
MAYORS
MAZOLA
MEGOHM
MEKONG
MELODY
MELONS
MELOTT
MEMOIR
MEMORY
MEROPE
MESONS
METOPE
MIDORI
MILORD
MILOSZ
MIMOSA
MINOAN
MINORS
MIWOKS
MODOCS
MOHOCK
MOLOCH
MOLOPO
MONODY
MORONI
MORONS
MOROSE
MOTORS
MOTOWN
MRCOOL
MRMOTO
MUCOSA
MUCOUS
MYWORD

M•••O•
MACHOS
MACRON
MACROS
MADTOM
MAGNON
MAHZOR
MALLOW
MAMBOS
MAMMON
MANGOS
MANIOC
MARCOS
MARGOT
MARION
MARLON
MARMOT
MAROON
MARRON
MARROW
MASCOT
MATRON
MATZOH
MATZOS
MAYPOP
MCADOO
MEADOW
MELLON
MELLOW
MELTON
MEMNON
MENJOU
MENTOR
MERLON
MERLOT
MERTON
METEOR
METHOD
METROS
MEZZOS
MICRON
MICROS
MIGNON
MILTON
MIMEOS
MINION
MINNOW
MIRROR
MONGOL
MONROE
MORION
MORMON
MORROW
MORTON
MOSCOW
MOTION
MOTMOT
MOTTOS
MOUTON
MRCOOL
MUGHOS
MUNGOS
MURROW
MUSKOX
MUTTON
MYTHOI
MYTHOL
MYTHOS

M••••O
MACACO
MADEDO
MADERO
MADURO
MAGGIO
MAKEDO
MALABO
MAPUTO
MARIKO
MARINO
MCADOO
MEDICO
MEGALO
MELANO
MERINO
MEXICO
MIKADO
MILANO
MODULO
MOLOPO
MONACO
MORENO
MORPHO
MRMOTO
MURANO

•MO•••
AMOEBA
AMOLES
AMORAL
AMOSOZ
AMOUNT
AMOURS
BMOVIE
EMOTED
EMOTER
EMOTES
HMONGS
IMOGEN
SMOCKS
SMOGGY
SMOKED
SMOKER
SMOKES
SMOKEY
SMOOCH
SMOOTH

•M•O••
EMBODY
EMBOSS
IMPORT
IMPOSE
IMPOST
SMOOCH
SMOOTH

•M••O•
AMADOU
AMAJOR
AMATOL
AMAZON
AMIDOL
AMIGOS
AMINOR
AMNION
AMOSOZ
BMAJOR
BMINOR
CMAJOR
CMINOR
DMAJOR
DMINOR
EMAJOR
EMINOR
EMPLOY
EMPTOR
FMAJOR
FMINOR
GMAJOR
GMINOR
IMPROV
KMESON

•M•••O
AMEDEO
EMBRYO
EMILIO
IMMUNO
SMALTO

••MO••
ALMOND
ALMOST
ARMORS
ARMORY
ARMOUR
ATMOST
AUMONT
BEMOAN
BUMOUT
DAMONE
DAMORE
DAMOUR
DEMOBS
DEMODE
DEMOND
DEMONS
DEMOTE
DIMOUT
DUMONT
EDMOND
EGMONT
ELMORE
EXMOOR
FAMOUS
FEMORA
HUMORS
HUMOUR
INMOST
IOMOTH
JAMOKE
KIMONO
KOMODO
LAMONT
LAMOUR
LEMOND
LEMONS
LEMONY
LOMOND
MEMOIR
MEMORY
MIMOSA

MRMOTO
NOMORE
ORMOLU
ORMOND
OSMOND
OSMOSE
POMONA
RAMONA
RAMONE
RAMOSE
RAMOUS
REMORA
REMOTE
REMOVE
REMOWN
REMOWS
RIMOSE
ROMOLA
RUMORS
RUMOUR
SAMOAN
SAMOSA
SIMONE
SIMONY
UNMOOR
UPMOST
UTMOST

••M•O•
BAMBOO
CAMEON
CAMEOS
CAMION
CAMPOS
COMBOS
COMEON
COMMON
COMPOS
DAMSON
EXMOOR
GAMBOL
GAMMON
GUMBOS
JIMSON
JUMBOS
JUMPON
LEMMON
LEMNOS
LIMBOS
LOMBOK
LUMMOX
MAMBOS
MAMMON
MEMNON
MIMEOS
NIMROD
POMPOM
POMPON
RAMROD
RAMSON
ROMEOS
SAMSON
SIMEON
SUMMON
SYMBOL
TEMPOS
TOMBOY
TOMTOM
UNMOOR

••M••O
AIMSTO
BAMAKO
BAMBOO
BUMPPO
CAMETO
CAMINO
COMETO
CUMULO
DAMATO
DOMINO
HEMATO
IMMUNO
KIMONO
KOMODO
MRMOTO
NEMATO
NUMERO
POMELO
ROMANO
ROMERO
SOMATO
STMALO
TAMAYO
TOMATO

•••MO•
ALAMOS
ASIMOV
BONMOT
CLAMOR
COMMON
COSMOS
DAIMON
DEIMOS
DROMOI
DROMOS
DUOMOS
ENAMOR
ETYMOL
ETYMON
GAMMON
GIZMOS
GLAMOR
GNOMON
HAEMON
HARMON
HAYMOW
HERMON
LEMMON
LUMMOX
MAMMON
MARMOT
MORMON
MOTMOT
PATMOS
PRIMOS
PROMOS
QUEMOY
RAGMOP
SALMON
SCHMOO
SCHMOS
SERMON
SHIMON
SUMMON
TREMOR
WETMOP

•••M•O
AKIMBO
ATEMPO
CRAMBO
DAIMYO
SCHMOO
WHAMMO

••••MO
CHROMO
DYNAMO
ESKIMO
KOKOMO
PLASMO
SEISMO
STELMO
THERMO
ULTIMO
WHAMMO

M•P•••
MAPLES
MAPPED
MAPPER
MAPUTO
MOPEDS
MOPERS
MOPING
MOPISH
MOPPED
MOPPER
MOPPET
MOPSUP
MOPUPS
MUPPET

M••P••
MAGPIE
MAPPED
MAPPER
MARPLE
MAYPOP
MILPAS
MOPPED
MOPPER
MOPPET
MORPHO
MORPHS
MUDPIE
MUPPET
MURPHY
MYOPES
MYOPIA
MYOPIC

M•••P•
MEROPE
METOPE
MIXUPS
MOLOPO
MOPUPS

M••••P
MADCAP
MADEUP
MAKEUP
MARKUP
MAYHAP
MAYPOP
MEGILP
MESSUP
MILSAP
MISHAP
MOBCAP
MOCKUP
MOPSUP
MUCKUP
MUSSUP

•MP•••
AMPERE
AMPHID
AMPLER
AMPULE
AMPULS
EMPERY
EMPIRE
EMPLOY
EMPTOR
IMPACT
IMPAIR
IMPALA
IMPALE
IMPART
IMPEDE
IMPELS
IMPEND
IMPERF
IMPISH
IMPORT
IMPOSE
IMPOST
IMPROV
IMPUGN
IMPURE
IMPUTE
UMPIRE

••MP••
ARMPIT
BUMPED
BUMPER
BUMPPO
BUMPUP
CAMPED
CAMPER
CAMPOS
CAMPUS
COMPAQ
COMPEL
COMPLY
COMPOS
DAMPED
DAMPEN
DAMPER
DAMPLY
DIMPLE
DIMPLY
DUMPED
DUMPER
HAMPER
HUMPED
HUMPHS
JUMPAT
JUMPED
JUMPER
JUMPIN
JUMPON
JUMPUP
KEMPIS
LIMPED
LIMPER
LIMPET
LIMPID
LIMPLY
LUMPED
LUMPEN
LUMPER
LUMPUR
NYMPHS
OOMPAH
PAMPAS
PAMPER
POMPEY
POMPOM
POMPON
PUMPED
PUMPER
PUMPUP
RAMPED
RIMPLE
ROMPED
ROMPER
RUMPLE
RUMPLY
RUMPUS
SAMPAN
SAMPLE
SEMPER
SEMPRE
SIMPER
SIMPLE
SIMPLY
TAMPED
TAMPER
TEMPED
TEMPEH
TEMPER
TEMPLE
TEMPOS
TEMPTS
VAMPED
VAMPER
WAMPUM
WIMPLE

••M•P•
BUMPPO
JAMUPS
REMAPS

••M••P
BUMPUP
BUMRAP
CAMEUP
COMEUP
DAMSUP
GUMSUP
JAMSUP
JUMPUP
PUMPUP
SUMSUP

•••MP•
ATEMPO
BLIMPS
CHAMPS
CHIMPS
CHOMPS
CHUMPS
CLAMPS
CLOMPS
CLUMPS
CLUMPY
CRAMPS
CRIMPS
EXEMPT
FRUMPS
FRUMPY
GRAMPS
GRUMPS
GRUMPY
GUIMPE
PLUMPS
PRIMPS
PROMPT
SCAMPI
SCAMPS
SKIMPS
SKIMPY
SLUMPS
STAMPS
STIMPY
STOMPS
STUMPS
STUMPY
SWAMPS
SWAMPY
THUMPS
TRAMPS
TROMPE
TROMPS
TRUMPS
WHOMPS

•••M•P
BEAMUP
BITMAP
CLAMUP
DRUMUP
FIRMUP
RAGMOP
TEAMUP
WARMUP
WETMOP

••••MP
CCLAMP
DECAMP
ENCAMP
PREAMP
REVAMP
SCRIMP
SHRIMP

M•Q•••
MAQUIS

M••Q••
MANQUE
MARQUE
MASQUE
MOSQUE

•MQ•••
EMQUAD

••M••Q
COMPAQ

MR••••
MRBLUE
MRCOOL
MRHYDE
MRMOTO

M•R•••
MARACA
MARAUD
MARBLE
MARBLY
MARCEL
MARCHE
MARCIA
MARCIE
MARCOS
MARCUS
MARDUK
MARGAY
MARGIE
MARGIN
MARGOT
MARIAH
MARIAN
MARIEL
MARIKO
MARILU
MARINA
MARINE
MARINO
MARION
MARISA
MARIST
MARIUS
MARKED
MARKER
MARKET
MARKKA
MARKUP
MARLED
MARLEE
MARLEY
MARLIN
MARLON
MARMEE
MARMOT
MARNER
MARNIE
MAROON
MARPLE
MARQUE
MARRED
MARRON
MARROW
MARSHA
MARSHY
MARTEL
MARTEN
MARTHA
MARTIN
MARTYR
MARVEL
MARVIN
MERCED
MERCER
MERELY
MEREST
MERGED
MERGER
MERGES
MERIDA
MERINO
MERITS
MERKEL
MERLIN
MERLON
MERLOT
MERMAN
MERMEN
MEROPE
MERSEY
MERTON
MERVYN
MIRAGE
MIRIAM
MIRING
MIRREN
MIRROR
MORALE
MORALS
MORANT
MORASS
MORAVA
MORAYS
MORBID
MOREAU
MOREEN
MORELS
MORENO
MORGAN
MORGEN
MORION
MORITA
MORITZ
MORLEY
MORMON
MORNAY
MORONI
MORONS
MOROSE
MORPHO
MORPHS
MORRIS
MORROW
MORSEL
MORTAL
MORTAR
MORTON
MURALS
MURANO
MURCIA
MURDER
MURIEL
MURINE
MURMUR
MURPHY
MURRAY
MURRES
MURREY
MURROW
MYRDAL
MYRIAD
MYRRHS
MYRTLE

M••R••
MACRAE
MACRON
MACROS
MADRAS
MADRES
MADRID
MANRAY
MAORIS
MARRED
MARRON
MARROW
MATRIX
MATRON
MAURYA
MCGRAW
MCGREW
MEERUT
METRES
METRIC
METROS
MICRON
MICROS
MIDRIB
MIHRAB
MIRREN
MIRROR
MITRAL
MITRED
MITRES
MOIRES
MONROE
MOORED
MORRIS
MORROW
MUDRAS
MURRAY
MURRES
MURREY
MURROW
MYRRHS

M•••R•
MADERO
MADURA
MADURO
MAITRE
MAJORS
MAKERS
MALORY
MANORS
MANTRA
MASERS
MASERU
MATERS
MATURE
MAYORS
MAZERS
MEAGRE
MEGARA
MEMORY
MESSRS
METERS
MIDORI
MILERS
MILORD
MIMERS
MINERS
MINORS
MISERS
MISERY
MITERS
MIXERS
MODERN
MOHURS
MOLARS
MONERA
MOPERS
MOTORS
MOVERS
MOWERS
MOYERS
MOZART
MUSERS
MYGIRL
MYWORD

M••••R
MADDER
MAGYAR
MAHLER
MAHZOR
MAILER
MANGER
MANNER
MAPPER
MARKER
MARNER
MARTYR
MASHER
MASKER
MASTER
MATHER
MATTER
MAULER
MAUSER
MCNAIR
MEAGER
MEANER
MEDGAR
MEDLAR
MEEKER
MEETER
MEMBER
MEMOIR
MENDER
MENHIR
MENTOR
MERCER
MERGER
MESMER
METEOR
METIER
MEWLER
MIDAIR
MIDLER
MILDER
MILKER
MILLER
MILNER
MINCER
MINDER
MINTER
MIRROR
MISTER
MOANER
MOCKER
MOHAIR
MOILER
MOLDER
MOLNAR
MOLTER
MONGER
MOPPER
MORTAR
MOTHER
MOUSER
MUDDER
MUGGER
MULLER
MUMMER
MURDER
MURMUR
MUSHER
MUSTER
MUTTER

•M•R••
AMERCE
AMORAL
AMTRAC
AMTRAK
EMBRYO
EMERGE
IMARET
IMBRUE
IMPROV
OMERTA
SMARMY
SMARTS
SMARTY
SMERSH
SMIRCH
SMIRKS
SMIRKY
SMURFS
SMYRNA
UMBRAE
UMBRAL
UMBRAS
UMBRIA

•M••R•
AMBERS
AMEERS
AMENRA
AMHARA
AMOURS
AMPERE
DMITRI
EMBARK
EMBERS
EMEERS
EMIGRE
EMPERY
EMPIRE
IMMURE
IMPART
IMPERF
IMPORT
IMPURE
SMEARS
SMEARY
UMBERS
UMPIRE

•M•••R
AMAJOR
AMBLER
AMINOR
AMPLER
BMAJOR
BMINOR
CMAJOR
CMINOR
DMAJOR
DMINOR
EMAJOR
EMINOR
EMOTER
EMPTOR
FMAJOR
FMINOR
GMAJOR
GMINOR
IMAGER
IMPAIR
SMILER
SMOKER

••MR••
BUMRAP
CYMRIC
NIMROD
QUMRAN
RAMROD

••M•R•
ADMIRE
ARMORS
ARMORY
ARMURE
ASMARA
AYMARA
BEMIRE
BUMBRY
CAMERA
COMERS
DAMORE
DEMURE
DEMURS
ELMIRA
ELMORE
FEMORA
FEMURS
GEMARA
HOMBRE
HOMERS
HUMERI
HUMORS
IMMURE
KHMERS
LAMARR
LEMURS
MEMORY
MIMERS
NAMERS
NOMORE
NUMERO
PAMIRS
REMARK
REMORA
ROMERO
RUMORS
SAMARA
SEMPRE
SOMBRE
SOMERS
STMARK
TAMARA
TAMERS
TIMBRE
TIMERS

••M••R
ARMOUR
BOMBER
BUMMER
BUMPER
CAMBER
CAMPER
COMBER
CUMBER
DAMMAR
DAMOUR
DAMPER
DIMMER
DUMBER
DUMPER
EXMOOR
GAMIER
HAMMER
HAMPER
HEMMER
HOMIER
HUMMER
HUMOUR
JAMMER
JUMPER
LAMARR
LAMOUR
LIMBER
LIMNER
LIMPER
LUMBAR
LUMBER
LUMPER
LUMPUR
MEMBER
MEMOIR
MUMMER
NUMBER
PAMPER
PUMPER
ROMPER
RUMMER
RUMOUR
SAMBAR
SEMPER
SIMMER
SIMPER
SOMBER
SOMMER
SUMMER
SUMNER
SUMTER
TAMPER
TEMPER
TIMBER
UNMOOR
VAMPER
YAMMER
ZIMMER

•••M•R
ALOMAR
BOOMER
BUMMER
CALMER
CLAMOR
DAMMAR
DIMMER
DORMER
ENAMOR
FARMER
FIRMER
FORMER
FULMAR
GLAMOR
HAMMER
HEMMER
HUMMER
INGMAR
ISOMER
JAMMER
KALMAR
KILMER
KRAMER
MESMER
MUMMER
MURMUR
NEWMAR
PALMER
PRIMER
REAMER
RHYMER
ROAMER
ROHMER
ROOMER
RUMMER
SHAMIR
SIMMER
SOMMER
SUMMER
TREMOR
WARMER
WEIMAR
YAMMER
ZIMMER

M•S•••
MASADA
MASAIS
MASCOT
MASERS
MASERU
MASHED
MASHER
MASHES
MASHIE
MASKED
MASKER
MASONS
MASQUE
MASSED
MASSES
MASSEY
MASSIF
MASTER
MASTIC
MESABI
MESCAL
MESHED
MESHES
MESMER
MESONS
MESSED
MESSES
MESSRS
MESSUP
MISCHA
MISCUE
MISDID
MISERS
MISERY
MISFIT
MISHAP
MISHIT
MISLAY
MISLED
MISSAL
MISSAY
MISSED
MISSES
MISSIS
MISSUS
MISTED
MISTER
MISUSE
MOSAIC
MOSCOW
MOSEYS
MOSHAV
MOSKVA
MOSLEM
MOSQUE
MOSSED
MOSSES
MOSTEL
MOSTLY
MUSCAT
MUSCLE
MUSCLY
MUSERS
MUSEUM
MUSHED
MUSHER
MUSHES
MUSIAL
MUSING
MUSKEG
MUSKET
MUSKIE
MUSKOX
MUSLIM
MUSLIN
MUSSED
MUSSEL
MUSSES
MUSSUP
MUSTER
MUSTNT
MYSELF
MYSTIC

M••S••
MAISIE
MANSES
MARSHA
MARSHY
MASSED
MASSES
MASSEY
MASSIF
MAUSER
MEASLY
MENSAE
MENSAL
MENSAS
MENSCH
MERSEY
MESSED
MESSES
MESSRS
MESSUP
MIASMA
MILSAP
MIOSIS
MISSAL
MISSAY
MISSED
MISSES
MISSIS
MISSUS
MOPSUP
MORSEL
MOSSED
MOSSES
MOUSED
MOUSER
MOUSES
MOUSEY
MOUSSE
MUSSED
MUSSEL
MUSSES
MUSSUP
MYOSIN

M•••S•
MAOISM
MAOIST
MARISA
MARIST
MEDUSA
MEREST
MILOSZ
MIMOSA
MISUSE
MODEST
MODISH
MOLEST
MONISM
MONIST
MOPISH
MORASS
MOROSE
MOUSSE
MUCOSA
MUFASA
MULISH
MUTEST

M••••S
MACAWS
MACHES
MACHOS
MACROS
MADAMS
MADRAS
MADRES
MAGMAS
MAHDIS
MAIDUS
MAILES

MAIZES
MAJLIS
MAJORS
MAKERS
MALAYS
MAMBAS
MAMBOS
MAMMAS
MANAUS
MANGOS
MANIAS
MANORS
MANSES
MANTAS
MANTIS
MAORIS
MAPLES
MAQUIS
MARCOS
MARCUS
MARIUS
MASAIS
MASERS
MASHES
MASONS
MASSES
MATERS
MATEYS
MATHIS
MATINS
MATTES
MATZOS
MAUVES
MAVENS
MAXIMS
MAYANS
MAYBES
MAYORS
MAZERS
MECCAS
MEDALS
MEDIAS
MEDICS
MELEES
MELONS
MENDES
MENSAS
MENTIS
MERGES
MERITS
MESHES
MESONS
MESSES
MESSRS
METALS
METERS
METRES
METROS
MEZZOS
MICROS
MIDGES
MILERS
MILPAS
MIMEOS
MIMERS
MIMICS
MINCES
MINERS
MINIMS
MINKES
MINORS
MINXES
MIOSIS
MISERS
MISSES
MISSIS
MISSUS
MITERS
MITRES
MIWOKS
MIXERS
MIXUPS
MIZENS
MOBIUS
MOCHAS
MODELS
MODEMS
MODOCS
MOGULS
MOHURS
MOINES
MOIRES
MOLARS
MOMMAS
MONADS
MONEYS
MONIES
MONTHS
MOPEDS
MOPERS
MOPUPS
MORALS
MORASS
MORAYS
MORELS
MORONS
MORPHS
MORRIS
MOSEYS
MOSSES
MOTELS
MOTETS
MOTIFS
MOTORS
MOTTOS
MOULDS
MOULTS
MOUNDS
MOUNTS
MOUSES
MOUTHS
MOVERS
MOVIES
MOWERS
MOYERS
MUCOUS
MUDRAS
MUFTIS
MUGHOS
MULCTS
MULLAS
MUNGOS
MURALS
MURRES
MUSERS
MUSHES
MUSSES
MYNAHS
MYOPES
MYRRHS
MYTHOS

•MS•••

AMSTEL

•M•S••

AMOSOZ
AMUSED
AMUSES
KMESON
OMASUM
TMESIS

•M••S•

AMBUSH
AMIDST
EMBOSS
EMDASH
IMPISH
IMPOSE
IMPOST
SMERSH

•M•••S

AMADIS
AMATIS
AMAZES
AMBERS
AMBITS
AMBLES
AMEBAS
AMEERS
AMENDS
AMENTS
AMICES
AMICUS
AMIDES
AMIENS
AMIGOS
AMINES
AMINUS
AMOLES
AMOURS
AMPULS
AMUSES
AMVETS
BMINUS
CMINUS
DMINUS
EMAILS
EMBAYS
EMBEDS
EMBERS
EMBOSS
EMCEES
EMEERS
EMENDS
EMMETS
EMOTES
HMONGS
IMAGES
IMBUES
IMPELS
OMAHAS
OMANIS
OMEGAS
SMACKS
SMALLS
SMARTS
SMEARS
SMELLS
SMELTS
SMILES
SMIRKS
SMITES
SMITHS
SMOCKS
SMOKES
SMURFS
TMESIS
UMBELS
UMBERS
UMBRAS
UMIAKS

••MS••

AIMSAT
AIMSTO
COMSAT
DAMSEL
DAMSON
DAMSUP
DIMSUM
GUMSUP
HEMSIN
JAMSIN
JAMSUP
JIMSON
RAMSAY
RAMSES
RAMSEY
RAMSON
RIMSKY
SAMSON
SUMSUP
WIMSEY

••M•S•

ALMOST
ATMOST
BEMUSE
CAMISE
DAMASK
DEMISE
ENMESH
FAMISH
GAMEST
INMOST
KUMISS
LAMESA
LAMEST
MIMOSA
OSMOSE
RAMOSE
REMISE
REMISS
RIMOSE
SAMOSA
TAMEST
UNMASK
UNMESH
UPMOST
UTMOST
ZYMASE

••M••S

ADMITS
ARMETS
ARMIES
ARMORS
BOMBES
CAMELS
CAMEOS
CAMPOS
CAMPUS
COMBES
COMBOS
COMERS
COMETS
COMICS
COMMAS
COMPOS
COMTES
DEMITS
DEMOBS
DEMONS
DEMURS
EMMETS
FAMOUS
FEMMES
FEMURS
GAMAYS
GAMINS
GAMMAS
GAMUTS
GIMELS
GUMBOS
HAMALS
HOMERS
HUMANS
HUMMUS
HUMORS
HUMPHS
JAMUPS
JUMBOS
KEMPIS
KHMERS
KUMISS
LAMEDS
LAMIAS
LAMMAS
LEMANS
LEMMAS
LEMNOS
LEMONS
LEMURS
LIMBOS
LIMBUS
LIMENS
LIMEYS
LIMITS
LUMENS
MAMBAS
MAMBOS
MAMMAS
MIMEOS
MIMERS
MIMICS
MOMMAS
NAMERS
NIMBUS
NOMADS
NYMPHS
OLMECS
OSMICS
PAMIRS
PAMPAS
RAMIES
RAMOUS
RAMSES
REMANS
REMAPS
REMISS
REMITS
REMOWS
ROMANS
ROMEOS
RUMBAS
RUMENS
RUMORS
RUMPUS
SAMBAS
SOMERS
SUMACS
SUMMAS
TAMERS
TAMILS
TEMPOS
TEMPTS
TIMERS
UNMANS
WOMENS

•••MS•

AHIMSA
CLUMSY
FLIMSY
WHIMSY

•••M•S

ABOMBS
AGAMAS
ALAMOS
ANIMAS
ANIMES
ANIMUS
ARAMIS
AROMAS
BIOMES
BLAMES
BLIMPS
BRUMES
CADMUS
CHAMPS
CHIMES
CHIMPS
CHOMPS
CHUMPS
CLAMPS
CLIMBS
CLIMES
CLOMPS
CLUMPS
COMMAS
COSMOS
CRAMPS
CREMES
CRIMES
CRIMPS
CRUMBS
DEIMOS
DERMIS
DISMES
DOGMAS
DOLMAS
DRAMAS
DROMOS
DUOMOS
EDAMES
ELEMIS
FEMMES
FLAMES
FLUMES
FRAMES
FRUMPS
GAMMAS
GIZMOS
GNOMES
GRAMAS
GRAMPS
GRIMES
GRUMPS
HBOMBS
HERMES
HOLMES
HUMMUS
KERMES
KERMIS
LAMMAS
LEMMAS
LITMUS
LLAMAS
MAGMAS
MAMMAS
MOMMAS
NEUMES
PALMAS
PATMOS
PLUMBS
PLUMES
PLUMPS
PRIMES
PRIMOS
PRIMPS
PRIMUS
PROMOS
RHOMBS
RHUMBS
RHYMES
SCAMPS
SCHMOS
SEAMUS
SHAMES
SHAMUS
SIGMAS
SKIMPS
SLIMES
SLUMPS
SPUMES
STAMPS
STOMAS
STOMPS
STUMPS
SUMMAS
SWAMIS
SWAMPS
THAMES
THEMES
THOMAS
THUMBS
THUMPS
THYMUS
TRAMPS
TROMPS
TRUMPS
WHOMPS

••••MS

ABOHMS
ABRAMS
ABYSMS
ADDAMS
ADEEMS
ALARMS
ALBUMS
ATEAMS
AXIOMS
BEDIMS
BEGUMS
BESOMS
BLOOMS
BRAHMS
BREAMS
BROOMS
CAROMS
CDROMS
CHARMS
CHASMS
CLAIMS
CREAMS
DENIMS
DREAMS
FORUMS
GLEAMS
GLOOMS
GOLEMS
GROOMS
HAKIMS
HAREMS
HBEAMS
IBEAMS
IDIOMS
JORUMS
KILIMS
LARAMS
MADAMS
MAXIMS
MINIMS
MODEMS
ODIUMS
OGHAMS
PRISMS
PROAMS
PROEMS
PSALMS
QUALMS
REALMS
REARMS
REHEMS
RHEUMS
SCRAMS
SCRIMS
SCRUMS
SEDUMS
SEISMS
SERUMS
SHAWMS
SPASMS
STEAMS
STORMS
STRUMS
SWARMS
THERMS
THRUMS
TOTEMS
UGGAMS
UNARMS
UNJAMS
VENOMS
VROOMS

M•T•••

MATERS
MATEYS
MATHER
MATHIS
MATING
MATINS
MATLIN
MATRIX
MATRON
MATTEA
MATTED
MATTEL
MATTER
MATTES
MATTIE
MATURE
MATZOH
MATZOS
METALS
METATE
METEOR
METERS
METHOD
METHYL
METIER
METING
METOPE
METRES
METRIC
METROS
METTLE
MITERS
MITRAL
MITRED
MITRES
MITTEN
MOTELS
MOTETS
MOTHER
MOTIFS
MOTILE
MOTION
MOTIVE
MOTLEY
MOTMOT
MOTORS
MOTOWN
MOTTLE
MOTTOS
MUTANT
MUTATE
MUTELY
MUTEST
MUTING
MUTINY
MUTTER
MUTTON
MUTUAL
MYTHIC
MYTHOI
MYTHOL
MYTHOS

M••T••

MADTOM
MAITAI
MAITRE
MALTED
MALTIN
MANTAS
MANTEL
MANTIC
MANTIS
MANTLE
MANTRA
MANTUA
MAOTAI
MARTEL
MARTEN
MARTHA
MARTIN
MARTYR
MASTER
MASTIC
MATTEA
MATTED
MATTEL
MATTER
MATTES
MATTIE
MAYTAG
MEETER
MEETLY
MELTED
MELTON
MENTAL
MENTIS
MENTOR
MERTON
METTLE
MILTIE
MILTON
MINTED
MINTER
MISTED
MISTER
MITTEN
MIXTEC
MOATED
MOLTED
MOLTEN
MOLTER
MOLTKE
MONTEL
MONTEZ
MONTHS
MOOTED
MORTAL
MORTAR
MORTON
MOSTEL
MOSTLY
MOTTLE
MOTTOS
MOUTHS
MOUTHY
MOUTON
MUFTIS
MUNTIN
MUSTER
MUSTNT
MUTTER
MUTTON
MYRTLE
MYSTIC

M•••T•

MAKUTA
MALATE
MALOTI
MAPUTO
MELOTT
MERITS
METATE
MIGHTY
MIKITA
MINUTE
MOIETY
MONETA
MORITA
MORITZ
MOTETS
MOULTS
MOUNTS
MOUNTY
MRMOTO
MULCTS
MULETA
MUTATE

M••••T

MADEIT
MAGNET
MAHOUT
MAKEIT
MALLET
MAOIST
MARGOT
MARIST
MARKET
MARMOT
MASCOT
MAXOUT
MEDLAT
MEERUT
MELOTT
MEREST
MERLOT
MIDGET
MILLET
MINUET
MINUIT
MISFIT
MISHIT
MODELT
MODEST
MOLEST
MOMENT
MONIST
MOPPET
MORANT
MOTMOT
MOZART
MUDCAT
MULLET
MUPPET
MUSCAT
MUSKET
MUSTNT
MUTANT
MUTEST

•MT•••

AMTRAC
AMTRAK
UMTATA

•M•T••

AMATIS
AMATOL
AMSTEL
AMYTAN
DMITRI
EMOTED
EMOTER
EMOTES
EMPTOR
SMITES
SMITHS
SMITHY
SMUTCH
SMUTTY

•M••T•

AMBITS
AMENTS
AMVETS
EMMETS
EMMETT
IMPUTE
OMERTA
SMALTI
SMALTO
SMARTS
SMARTY
SMELTS
SMOOTH
SMUTTY
UMTATA

•M•••T

AMIDST
AMOUNT
AMULET
EMMETT
IMARET
IMPACT
IMPART
IMPORT
IMPOST
OMELET
UMLAUT

••MT••

COMTES
SUMTER
TAMTAM
TOMTIT
TOMTOM

••M•T•

ADMITS
AIMSTO
ARMETS
CAMETO
COMATE
COMETH
COMETO
COMETS
COMITY
DAMATO
DAMITA
DEMITS
DEMOTE
DIMITY
EMMETS
EMMETT
ENMITY
GAMETE
GAMUTS
HAMITE
HEMATO
INMATE
IOMOTH
LIMITS
MRMOTO
NAMATH
NEMATO
NIMITZ
RAMATE
REMITS
REMOTE
SAMITE
SEMITE
SOMATA
SOMATO
TEMPTS
TOMATO

••M••T

AIMSAT
ALMOST
ARMLET
ARMPIT
ATMOST
AUMONT
BUMOUT
CAMEAT
CAMLET
CEMENT
COMBAT
COMEAT
COMFIT
COMMIT
COMSAT
DIMOUT
DIMWIT
DUMONT
EGMONT
EMMETT
FOMENT
GAMBIT
GAMEST
GIMLET
HAMLET
INMOST
JUMPAT
LAMENT
LAMEST
LAMONT
LIMPET
MOMENT
NUMBAT
RAMJET
REMELT
SUMMIT
TAMEST
TOMCAT
TOMTIT
TUMULT
UNMEET
UPMOST
UTMOST
WOMBAT

•••MT•

WARMTH

•••M•T

BONMOT
CERMET
COMMIT
EXEMPT
FERMAT
FORMAT
HAEMAT
HELMET
HELMUT
HERMIT
ILLMET
KERMIT
KISMET
MARMOT
MOTMOT
PELMET
PERMIT
PROMPT
STOMAT
SUBMIT
SUMMIT

••••MT

DREAMT

MU••••

MUCKED
MUCKUP
MUCOSA
MUCOUS
MUDCAT
MUDDED
MUDDER
MUDDLE
MUDEEL
MUDHEN
MUDPIE
MUDRAS
MUFASA
MUFFED
MUFFIN
MUFFLE
MUFTIS
MUGABE
MUGGED
MUGGER
MUGHOS
MUKLUK
MULCTS
MULETA
MULISH
MULLAH
MULLAS
MULLED
MULLER
MULLET
MUMBLE
MUMBLY
MUMMER
MUNCIE
MUNGOS
MUNICH
MUNTIN
MUPPET
MURALS
MURANO
MURCIA
MURDER
MURIEL
MURINE
MURMUR
MURPHY
MURRAY
MURRES
MURREY
MURROW
MUSCAT
MUSCLE
MUSCLY
MUSERS
MUSEUM
MUSHED
MUSHER
MUSHES
MUSIAL
MUSING
MUSKEG
MUSKET
MUSKIE
MUSKOX
MUSLIM
MUSLIN
MUSSED
MUSSEL
MUSSES
MUSSUP
MUSTER
MUSTNT
MUTANT
MUTATE
MUTELY
MUTEST
MUTING
MUTINY
MUTTER
MUTTON
MUTUAL
MUUMUU
MUZHIK
MUZZLE

M•U•••

MAULED
MAULER
MAUMAU
MAUMEE
MAUNDY
MAURYA
MAUSER
MAUVES
MBUNDU
MOULDS
MOULDY
MOULIN
MOULTS
MOUNDS
MOUNTS
MOUNTY
MOUSED
MOUSER
MOUSES
MOUSEY
MOUSSE
MOUTHS
MOUTHY
MOUTON
MUUMUU

M••U••

MACULA
MADURA
MADURO
MAGUEY
MAKUTA
MANUAL
MANUEL
MAPUTO
MAQUIS
MATURE
MAZUMA
MCKUEN
MEDUSA
MIGUEL
MINUET
MINUIT
MINUTE
MISUSE
MIXUPS
MODULE
MODULO
MOGULS
MOHURS
MOPUPS
MUTUAL

M•••U•

MADEUP
MAGNUM
MAHOUT
MAIDUS
MAKEUP
MANAUS
MANFUL
MANQUE
MANTUA
MARAUD
MARCUS
MARDUK
MARIUS
MARKUP
MARQUE
MASQUE
MAXOUT
MEDIUM
MEERUT
MESSUP
MINIUM
MISCUE
MISSUS
MOBIUS
MOCKUP
MOPSUP
MOSQUE
MRBLUE
MUCKUP
MUCOUS
MUKLUK
MURMUR
MUSEUM
MUSSUP

MUUMUU

M••••U
MAKALU
MALIBU
MANCHU
MARILU
MASERU
MAUMAU
MBUNDU
MENJOU
MILIEU
MOLDAU
MOREAU
MUUMUU

•MU•••
AMULET
AMUSED
AMUSES
SMUDGE
SMUDGY
SMUGLY
SMURFS
SMUTCH
SMUTTY

•M•U••
AMBUSH
AMOUNT
AMOURS
AMPULE
AMPULS
EMQUAD
IMBUED
IMBUES
IMMUNE
IMMUNO
IMMURE
IMPUGN
IMPURE
IMPUTE

•M••U•
AMICUS
AMINUS
BMINUS
CMINUS
DMINUS
IMBRUE
OMASUM
OMNIUM
UMLAUT

•M•••U
AMADOU

••MU••
ARMURE
BEMUSE
CUMULI
CUMULO
DEMURE
DEMURS
EDMUND
FEMURS
GAMUTS
IMMUNE
IMMUNO
IMMURE
JAMUPS
LEMUEL
LEMURS
OSMUND
REMUDA
SAMUEL
TUMULI
TUMULT

••M•U•
ARMFUL
ARMOUR
BUMOUT
BUMPUP
CAMEUP
CAMPUS
COMEUP
DAMOUR
DAMSUP
DIMOUT
DIMSUM
DUMDUM
FAMOUS
GUMSUP
HUMBUG
HUMMUS
HUMOUR
JAMSUP
JUMPUP
LAMOUR
LIMBUS
LUMPUR
NIMBUS
OSMIUM
PUMPUP
RAMOUS
RUMOUR
RUMPUS
SUMSUP
TAMMUZ
WAMPUM
YUMYUM

••M••U
ORMOLU
RAMEAU

•••MU•
ANIMUS
BEAMUP
CADMUS
CLAMUP
DRUMUP
FIRMUP
HELMUT
HORMUZ
HUMMUS
LITMUS
MURMUR
MUUMUU
PRIMUM
PRIMUS
SEAMUS
SHAMUS
TALMUD
TAMMUZ
TEAMUP
THYMUS
WARMUP
WONMUG

•••M•U
MAUMAU
MUUMUU

M•V•••
MAVENS
MOVEIN
MOVERS
MOVIES
MOVING

M••V••
MARVEL
MARVIN
MAUVES
MELVIL
MELVIN
MELVYN
MERVYN

M•••V•
MOHAVE
MOJAVE
MORAVA
MOSKVA
MOTIVE

M••••V
MOSHAV

•MV•••
AMVETS

•M•V••
BMOVIE

•M•••V
IMPROV

••M•V•
REMOVE

•••M•V
ASIMOV

M•W•••
MEWING
MEWLED
MEWLER
MIWOKS
MOWERS
MOWGLI
MOWING
MYWORD

M••W••
MEOWED
MIDWAY

M•••W•
MACAWS
MALAWI
MOHAWK
MOTOWN

M••••W
MALLOW
MARROW
MCGRAW
MCGREW
MEADOW
MELLOW
MILDEW
MINNOW
MORROW
MOSCOW
MURROW

••MW••
DIMWIT

••M•W•
REMOWN
REMOWS

•••M•W
HAYMOW

M•X•••
MAXIMA
MAXIMS
MAXINE
MAXIXE
MAXOUT
MEXICO
MIXERS
MIXING
MIXTEC
MIXUPS

M••X••
MINXES

M•••X•
MAXIXE

M••••X
MADMAX
MANNIX
MATRIX
MENINX
MUSKOX

•M•••X
SMILAX

••M••X
COMMIX
LUMMOX
TOMMIX

•••M•X
CLIMAX
COMMIX
LUMMOX
MADMAX
TEXMEX
TOMMIX

MY••••
MYELIN
MYGIRL
MYNAHS
MYOHMY
MYOPES
MYOPIA
MYOPIC
MYOSIN
MYRDAL
MYRIAD
MYRRHS
MYRTLE
MYSELF
MYSTIC
MYTHIC
MYTHOI
MYTHOL
MYTHOS
MYWORD

M•Y•••
MAYANS
MAYBES
MAYDAY
MAYFLY
MAYHAP
MAYHEM
MAYORS
MAYPOP
MAYTAG
MOYERS

M••Y••
MAGYAR
MINYAN
MRHYDE

M•••Y•
MALAYA
MALAYS
MARTYR
MATEYS
MAURYA
MELVYN
MERVYN
METHYL
MONEYS
MORAYS
MOSEYS

M••••Y
MAGUEY
MAINLY
MALADY
MALORY
MANDAY
MANRAY
MARBLY
MARGAY
MARLEY
MARSHY
MASSEY
MAUNDY
MAYDAY
MAYFLY
MEANLY
MEASLY
MEDLEY
MEEKLY
MEETLY
MELODY
MEMORY
MERELY
MERSEY
MICKEY
MIDDAY
MIDWAY
MIGHTY
MILADY
MILDLY
MILLAY
MINIFY
MISERY
MISLAY
MISSAY
MOBLEY
MODIFY
MOIETY
MONDAY
MONKEY
MONODY
MOONEY
MORLEY
MORNAY
MOSTLY
MOTLEY
MOULDY
MOUNTY
MOUSEY
MOUTHY
MUMBLY
MURPHY
MURRAY
MURREY
MUSCLY
MUTELY
MUTINY
MYOHMY

•MY•••
AMYTAN
SMYRNA

•M••Y•
EMBAYS
EMBRYO

•M•••Y
EMBODY
EMPERY
EMPLOY
SMARMY
SMARTY
SMEARY
SMELLY
SMILEY
SMIRKY
SMITHY
SMOGGY
SMOKEY
SMUDGY
SMUGLY
SMUTTY

••MY••
YUMYUM

••M•Y•
GAMAYS
LIMEYS
TAMAYO

••M••Y
ARMORY
BOMBAY
BUMBRY
CAMEBY
COMEBY
COMEDY
COMELY
COMITY
COMPLY
DAMPLY
DIMITY
DIMPLY
DUMBLY
ENMITY
FAMILY
GAMELY
GAMILY
HOMELY
HOMILY
HOMINY
HUMBLY
JIMINY
LAMELY
LEMONY
LIMPLY
MEMORY
MUMBLY
NAMELY
NIMBLY
NIMINY
NUMBLY
PIMINY
POMPEY
RAMIFY
RAMSAY
RAMSEY
REMEDY
RIMSKY
ROMANY
ROMNEY
RUMBLY
RUMPLY
SIMONY
SIMPLY
SOMANY
TAMELY
TIMELY
TOMBOY
TUMEFY
WAMBLY
WIMSEY

•••MY•
DAIMYO

•••M•Y
BLIMEY
CALMLY
CHAMMY
CHUMMY
CLAMMY
CLUMPY
CLUMSY
CRUMBY
CRUMMY
DISMAY
FIRMLY
FLIMSY
FRUMPY
GLUMLY
GRAMMY
GRIMLY
GRUMPY
NIAMEY
PLUMMY
PRIMLY
QUEMOY
SCUMMY
SEEMLY
SHIMMY
SKIMPY
SLIMLY
SLUMMY
STIMPY
STUMPY
SWAMPY
TRIMLY
WARMLY
WHAMMY
WHIMSY

••••MY
BIGAMY
BLOOMY
CHAMMY
CHUMMY
CLAMMY
CREAMY
CRUMMY
DREAMY
GLOOMY
GRAMMY
INFAMY
JEREMY
MYOHMY
PLUMMY
RHEUMY
SCUMMY
SHIMMY
SLUMMY
SMARMY
STEAMY
STORMY
WHAMMY

M•Z•••
MAZERS
MAZOLA
MAZUMA
MEZZOS
MIZENS
MIZZEN
MIZZLE
MOZART
MUZHIK
MUZZLE

M••Z••
MAHZOR
MAIZES
MATZOH
MATZOS
MEZZOS
MIZZEN
MIZZLE
MUZZLE

M••••Z
MILOSZ
MONTEZ
MORITZ

•M•Z••
AMAZED
AMAZES
AMAZON

•M•••Z
AMOSOZ

••M•Z•
LAMAZE

••M••Z
NIMITZ
TAMMUZ

•••M•Z
HORMUZ
TAMMUZ

NA••••
NABBED
NABBER
NABOBS
NABORS
NACHOS
NADINE
NADIRS
NAGANO
NAGGED
NAGGER
NAGOYA
NAIADS
NAILED
NAILER
NAILIN
NAIRAS
NAMATH
NAMELY
NAMERS
NAMING
NANOOK
NANSEN
NANTES
NAPERY
NAPIER
NAPKIN
NAPLES
NAPOLI
NAPPED
NAPPER
NAPPES
NARIAL
NARNIA
NARROW
NARVIK
NARWAL
NASALS
NASCAR
NASDAQ
NASEBY
NASHUA
NASSAU
NASSER
NATANT
NATHAN
NATICK
NATION
NATIVE
NATRON
NATTER
NATURE
NAUGHT
NAUSEA
NAUTCH
NAVAHO
NAVAJO
NAVELS
NAVIES
NAWABS
NAYSAY

N•A•••
NEARBY
NEARED
NEARER
NEARLY
NEARTO
NEATEN
NEATER
NEATLY
NIACIN
NIAMEY
NUANCE
NYALAS
NYASSA

N••A••
NAGANO
NAIADS
NAMATH
NASALS
NATANT
NAVAHO
NAVAJO
NAWABS
NEGATE
NEMATO
NEPALI
NEVADA
NEWAGE
NEWARK
NICAEA
NLEAST
NOMADS
NONAGE
NONAME
NONARY
NOSALE
NOTARY
NOTATE
NUTATE

N•••A•
NAIRAS
NARIAL
NARWAL
NASCAR
NASDAQ
NASSAU
NATHAN
NAYSAY
NECTAR
NETMAN
NETPAY
NEUMAN
NEURAL
NEWMAN
NEWMAR
NICEAN
NILGAI
NINJAS
NIPSAT
NISSAN
NOLEAD
NOLOAD
NONFAT
NOONAN
NORGAY
NORIAS
NORMAL
NORMAN
NORWAY
NOSOAP
NOTBAD
NOUGAT
NUBIAN
NUCHAE
NUCHAL
NULLAH
NUMBAT
NYALAS

N••••A
NAGOYA
NARNIA
NASHUA
NAUSEA
NEBULA
NERUDA
NESTEA
NEVADA
NICAEA
NICOLA
NIKITA
NIKOLA
NOOTKA
NOUMEA
NOVENA
NUMINA
NUTRIA
NYASSA

•NA•••
ANACIN
ANADEM
ANALOG
ANANDA
ANATTO
ENABLE
ENACTS
ENAMEL
ENAMOR
ENATES
GNARLS
GNARLY
GNAWED
GNAWER
INAFIX
INAFOG
INAJAM
INANER
INAPET
INARCH
INAROW
INARUT
INAWAY
KNACKS
KNARRY
KNAVES
ONAGER
SNACKS
SNAFUS
SNAGGY
SNAILS
SNAKED
SNAKES
SNAPAT
SNAPPY
SNAPTO
SNAPUP
SNARED
SNARES
SNARLS
SNARLY
SNATCH
SNATHE
SNATHS
SNAZZY
UNABLE
UNAGED
UNARMS
UNAWED

•N•A••
ANKARA
ANNABA
ANNALS
ANSATE
ENCAGE
ENCAMP
ENCASE
ENDALL
ENDASH
ENFANT
ENGAGE
ENLACE
ENRAGE
ENRAPT
ENTAIL
INCANS
INCASE
INCASH
INDABA
INFACT
INFAMY
INFANT
INHALE
INHALF
INHAND
INHAUL
INLAID
INLAND
INLAWS
INLAYS
INMATE
INNAGE
INNATE
INPART
INSANE
INTACT
INTAKE
INVADE
INVAIN
INWARD
KNEADS
ONCALL
ONHAND
ONLAND
ONSALE
ONTAPE
ONWARD
SNEAKS
SNEAKY
UNBARS
UNCAGE
UNCAPS
UNCASE
UNEASE
UNEASY
UNFAIR
UNHAND
UNIATE
UNIATS
UNJAMS
UNLACE
UNLADE
UNLAID
UNLASH
UNMADE
UNMAKE
UNMANS
UNMASK
UNPACK
UNPAID
UNSAFE
UNSAID
UNSAYS
UNTACK
UNWARY

•N••A•
ANDEAN
ANIMAL
ANIMAS
ANNEAL
ANNUAL
ANORAK
ANSGAR
ANURAN
ANYWAY
ENDEAR
ENDMAN
ENGRAM
ENNEAD
ENQUAD
ENTRAP
ENWRAP
INAJAM
INAWAY
INDIAN
INGEAR
INGMAR
INLEAF
INPLAY
INROAD
INSEAM
INSPAN
INSTAR
ONEDAY
ONEWAY
ONLOAN
SNAPAT
SNOCAT
UNCIAL
UNCLAD
UNDRAW
UNGUAL
UNITAL
UNITAS
UNIVAC
UNLEAD
UNLOAD
UNREAD
UNREAL
UNSEAL
UNSEAT
UNSNAG
UNSNAP
UNTRAP
UNWRAP

•N•••A
ANANDA
ANCONA
ANDREA
ANEMIA
ANGELA
ANGLIA
ANGOLA
ANGORA
ANITRA
ANKARA
ANNABA
ENCINA
ENDORA
ENIGMA
INDABA
INDIRA
INTIMA
ONEIDA
PNEUMA

••NA••
ADNATE
AGNATE
ANNABA
ANNALS
BANANA
BINARY
BINATE
BONAMI
BYNAME
CANAAN
CANADA
CANALS
CANAPE
CANARD
CANARY
CONANT
CUNARD
CUNAXA
DANANG
DANAUS
DENALI
DINARS
DONALD
DONATE
DUNANT
DYNAMO
DYNAST
ERNANI
FINALE
FINALS
IGNACE
IGNATZ
INNAGE
INNATE
KANAKA
LANAIS
LANATE
LENAPE
LINAGE
LUNACY
LUNATE
MANAGE
MANAMA
MANANA
MANAUS
MCNAIR
MENACE
MENAGE
MONACO
MONADS
MYNAHS
NONAGE
NONAME
NONARY
ORNATE
OXNARD
PANADA
PANAMA
PENANG
PINATA
RENAIL
RENAME
RENATA
RONALD
SENARY
SENATE
SONANT
SONATA
TANAKA
TENACE
TENANT
XANADU
ZENANA
ZONATE

••N•A•
AENEAS
ANNEAL
ANNUAL
BANTAM
BANYAN
BANZAI
BENDAY
BENGAL
BENGAY
BONSAI
BUNYAN
CANAAN
CANCAN
CANNAE
CANTAB
CANVAS
CONFAB
CONGAS
CONMAN
CONRAD
CONTAC
CONWAY
CUNEAL
DANNAY
DENIAL
DENTAL
DONNAS
DUNBAR
DUNCAN
DUNHAM
ENNEAD
EONIAN
FANTAN
FENIAN
FINIAL
FINNAN
FONTAL
GENIAL
GENOAN
GENUAL
GUNMAN
GUNNAR
HANGAR
HANNAH
HENNAS
HINTAT
IONIAN
JINNAH
JUNEAU
JUNTAS
KANSAN
KANSAS
KENYAN
KONRAD
LANDAU
LINEAL
LINEAR
LONGAN
MANDAN
MANDAY
MANIAC
MANIAS
MANRAY
MANTAS
MANUAL
MENIAL
MENSAE
MENSAL
MENSAS
MENTAL
MINOAN
MINYAN
MONDAY
NINJAS
NONFAT
PANDAS
PENMAN
PENNAE
PENPAL
PENTAD
PINDAR
PINEAL
PINNAE
PINNAS
PINOAK
PUNJAB
PUNKAH
QANTAS
QINTAR
RENTAL
RUNWAY
SANDAL
SENDAK
SENLAC
SENNAS

SINBAD
SINEAD
SINTAX
SONTAG
SUNDAE
SUNDAY
SUNRAY
SUNTAN
SYNTAX
TANKAS
TANOAK
TANOAN
TINCAL
TINCAN
TINEAR
TINHAT
TINMAN
TINPAN
TONGAN
VANDAL
VENIAL
WANTAD
WENTAT
WINKAT
YENTAS
YUNNAN

••N••A
ANNABA
ARNICA
BANANA
BANGKA
CANADA
CANOLA
CANOVA
CINEMA
CONCHA
CONTRA
CUNAXA
DUNERA
GENERA
GENEVA
KANAKA
KONICA
LINGUA
LUNULA
MANAMA
MANANA
MANCHA
MANILA
MANTRA
MANTUA
MINIMA
MONERA
MONETA
MONICA
PANADA
PANAMA
PENNIA
PINATA
RENATA
SANCTA
SANDIA
SANDRA
SENECA
SENEGA
SENORA
SONATA
SONOMA
SONORA
TANAKA
TANTRA
TUNDRA
TUNICA
WINONA
ZENANA
ZINNIA

•••NA•
ADONAI
AGENAS
ARENAS
ASANAS
ATONAL
AXONAL
BWANAS
CANNAE
CARNAL
CATNAP
COGNAC
DANNAY
DARNAY
DONNAS
FAUNAE
FAUNAL
FAUNAS
FINNAN
GUNNAR
HAINAN
HANNAH
HENNAS
HYENAS
HYMNAL
JINNAH
KARNAK
KAUNAS
KEENAN
KIDNAP
LIANAS
MAENAD
MOLNAR
MORNAY
NOONAN
PENNAE
PINNAE
PINNAS
PLANAR
PUTNAM
REGNAL
RHINAL
RUANAS
SAUNAS
SCENAS
SEENAS
SENNAS
SIGNAL
SPINAL
TAINAN
THENAR
TRINAL
UNSNAG
UNSNAP
VARNAS
VEINAL
VERNAL
YUNNAN

•••N•A
AGENDA
AJANTA
AMANDA
AMENRA
ANANDA
BIANCA
BLANCA
BLANDA
BOSNIA
BRENDA
CORNEA
CRANIA
CRENNA
DEANNA
DUENNA
EUPNEA
FAENZA
FRANCA
GLENDA
GLINKA
GOANNA
GUINEA
JOANNA
KAUNDA
KWANZA
LUANDA
NARNIA
OLINDA
PAANGA
PENNIA
QUANTA
QUINOA
RHONDA
RUANDA
RWANDA
SIENNA
STANZA
UGANDA
URANIA
VIENNA
ZINNIA

••••NA
ALUMNA
ANCONA
ARCANA
ARJUNA
ATHENA
BANANA
CABANA
CARINA
CATENA
CESSNA
CORONA
COVINA
CRENNA
DEANNA
DUENNA
ENCINA
ESPANA
FALANA
FARINA
GALENA
GOANNA
GRETNA
GUIANA
GUYANA
HABANA
HAVANA
HELENA
IGUANA
ILEANA
JACANA
JOANNA
KAHUNA
KORUNA
LACUNA
LAGUNA
LAMINA
LATINA
LATONA
LUMINA
MANANA
MARINA
MEDINA
MELINA
MODENA
NOVENA
NUMINA
ORGANA
ORIANA
PARANA
PATINA
PIRANA
POMONA
PRAJNA
PURINA
RAMONA
REGINA
RETINA
ROWENA
ROXANA
RUMINA
SABENA
SALINA
SELENA
SERENA
SHEENA
SIENNA
SMYRNA
STERNA
TIRANA
TUCANA
URBANA
VARUNA
VERONA
VICUNA
VIENNA
WINONA
XIMENA
ZENANA

N•B•••
NABBED
NABBER
NABOBS
NABORS
NEBULA
NIBBLE
NOBLER
NOBLES
NOBODY
NUBBED
NUBBIN
NUBBLE
NUBIAN
NUBILE

N••B••
NABBED
NABBER
NIBBLE
NIMBLE
NIMBLY
NIMBUS
NOTBAD
NUBBED
NUBBIN
NUBBLE
NUMBAT
NUMBED
NUMBER
NUMBLY

N•••B•
NABOBS
NASEBY
NAWABS
NEARBY
NINGBO

•NB•••
ENBLOC
INBORN
INBRED
INBULK
UNBARS
UNBELT
UNBEND
UNBENT
UNBIND
UNBOLT
UNBORN

•N•B••
ANUBIS
ENABLE
KNOBBY
SNOBBY
UNABLE

•N••B•
ANNABA
ENROBE
INDABA
INDEBT
KNOBBY
SNOBBY
UNROBE

••NB••
BONBON
DUNBAR
HENBIT
SINBAD

••N•B•
ANNABA
DANUBE
GONEBY
NINGBO
WENTBY

••N••B
BENUMB
CANTAB
CONFAB
CONJOB
PUNJAB

•••N•B
DIONEB
HOBNOB

N•C•••
NACHOS
NECKED
NECTAR
NICAEA
NICEAN
NICELY
NICENE
NICEST
NICETY
NICHES
NICKED
NICKEL
NICKER
NICOLA
NICOLE
NICOLO
NOCENT
NUCHAE
NUCHAL
NUCLEI
NUCLEO

N••C••
NASCAR
NIACIN
NIECES
NONCOM
NUECES
NUNCIO

N•••C•
NATICK
NAUTCH
NODICE
NOTICE
NOVICE
NUANCE

N••••C
NITRIC
NOETIC
NORDIC

•NC•••
ANCHOR
ANCIEN
ANCONA
ENCAGE
ENCAMP
ENCASE
ENCINA
ENCINO
ENCODE
ENCORE
INCANS
INCASE
INCASH
INCEPT
INCHED
INCHES
INCHON
INCISE
INCITE
INCOME
INCULT
INCURS
INCUSE
ONCALL
UNCAGE
UNCAPS
UNCASE
UNCHIC
UNCIAL
UNCLAD
UNCLES
UNCLOG
UNCOIL
UNCOOL
UNCORK
UNCURL

•N•C••
ANACIN
ANTCOW
ENACTS
KNACKS
KNICKS
KNOCKS
SNACKS
SNICKS
SNOCAT
UNICEF
VNECKS

•N••C•
ANTICS
ENESCO
ENLACE
ENRICH
ENRICO
ENTICE
INARCH
INDICT
INDUCE
INDUCT
INFACT
INFECT
INJECT
INLUCK
INSECT
INTACT
ONDECK
SNATCH
SNITCH
UNESCO
UNLACE
UNLOCK
UNPACK
UNTACK

•N•••C
ANEMIC
ANODIC
ENBLOC
GNOMIC
INSYNC
ONSPEC
UNCHIC
UNIFIC
UNIVAC

••NC••
BUNCHE
BUNCOS
CANCAN
CANCEL
CANCUN
CONCHA
CONCHS
CONCUR
DANCED
DANCER
DANCES
DUNCAN
DUNCES
FENCED
FENCER
FENCES
HONCHO
JUNCOS
LANCED
LANCER
LANCES
LANCET
MANCHA
MANCHU
MINCED
MINCER
MINCES
MUNCIE
NONCOM
NUNCIO
OUNCES
PANCHO
PENCEL
PENCIL
PINCER
PONCHO
PUNCHY
RANCHO
RANCID
RANCOR
RUNCIE
SANCHO
SANCTA
SYNCED
TINCAL
TINCAN
TINCTS
WENCES
WINCED
WINCER
WINCES

••N•C•
ALNICO
ARNICA
CONICS
CONOCO
CYNICS
EUNICE
EUNUCH
IGNACE
IONICS
JANICE
KONICA
LUNACY
MENACE
MENSCH
MONACO
MONICA
MUNICH
PANICS
SENECA
SONICS
SUNOCO
TENACE
TONICS
TUNICA
TUNICS
VENICE
ZANUCK

••N••C
CONTAC
FENNEC
FINNIC
MANIAC
MANIOC
MANTIC
PONTIC
RUNDMC
SENLAC
SYNDIC
TANNIC
TENREC

•••NC•
AGENCY
ATONCE
BIANCA
BLANCA
BLANCH
BLENCH
BOUNCE
BOUNCY
BRANCH
BRONCO
BRONCS
BRUNCH
CHANCE
CHANCY
CHINCH
CLANCY
CLENCH
CLINCH
CRUNCH
DRENCH
EVINCE
FIANCE
FLINCH
FRANCA
FRANCE
FRANCK
FRANCO
FRANCS
FRENCH
GLANCE
GRINCH
HAUNCH
JOUNCE
JOUNCY
LAUNCH
NUANCE
PAUNCH
PLANCK
POUNCE
PRANCE
PRINCE
QUENCH
QUINCE
QUINCY
SCONCE
SEANCE
STANCE
STANCH
STENCH
THENCE
TRANCE
TRENCH
USANCE
WHENCE
WRENCH

•••N•C
ATONIC
BIONIC
CLINIC
COGNAC
CYANIC
EDENIC
ETHNIC
ETONIC
FENNEC
FINNIC
ICONIC
IRENIC
IRONIC
OZONIC
PHONIC
PICNIC
PYKNIC
SCENIC
TANNIC
URANIC

••••NC
FERENC
INSYNC

N•D•••
NADINE
NADIRS
NODDED
NODDLE
NODICE
NODOFF
NODOSE
NODULE
NUDGED
NUDGER
NUDGES
NUDIST
NUDITY
NUDNIK

N••D••
NASDAQ
NEEDED
NEEDLE
NEEDNT
NODDED
NODDLE
NOODLE
NORDIC

N•••D•
NAIADS
NERUDA
NEVADA
NOBODY
NOMADS

N••••D
NABBED
NAGGED
NAILED
NAPPED
NEARED
NECKED
NEEDED
NEREID
NESTED
NETTED
NICKED
NIMROD
NIPPED
NODDED
NOGOOD
NOISED
NOLEAD
NOLOAD
NOSHED
NOTBAD
NUBBED
NUDGED
NULLED
NUMBED
NURSED
NUTTED

•ND•••
ANDEAN
ANDHOW
ANDREA
ANDREI
ANDRES
ANDREW
ANDREY
ANDROS
ENDALL
ENDASH
ENDEAR
ENDERS
ENDING
ENDIVE
ENDMAN
ENDMEN
ENDORA
ENDOWS
ENDRUN
ENDSUP
ENDUED
ENDUES
ENDURE
ENDURO
ENDUSE
INDABA
INDEBT
INDEED
INDENE
INDENT
INDIAN
INDICT
INDIES
INDIGO
INDIRA
INDITE
INDIUM
INDOOR
INDRIS
INDUCE
INDUCT
ONDECK
ONDINE
UNDIES
UNDINE
UNDOER
UNDOES
UNDONE
UNDRAW
UNDULY
UNDYED

•N•D••
ANADEM
ANODES
ANODIC
CNIDUS
ONEDAY
ONEDGE
SNIDER
SNYDER

•N••D•
ANANDA
ANHYDR
ENCODE
INSIDE
INVADE
KNEADS
ONEIDA
ONSIDE
SNOODS
UNLADE
UNMADE
UNTIDY

•N•••D
ANGLED
ANKLED
ANTEED
ENDUED
ENFOLD
ENGIRD
ENNEAD
ENQUAD
ENSUED
ENURED
ENVIED
GNAWED
INBRED
INCHED
INDEED
INFOLD
INGRID
INHAND
INKIND
INLAID
INLAND
INNEED
INROAD
INTEND
INURED
INWARD
KNIFED
ONHAND
ONHOLD
ONLAND
ONWARD
SNAKED
SNARED
SNIPED
SNORED
SNOWED
UNAGED
UNAWED
UNBEND
UNBIND
UNCLAD
UNDYED
UNFOLD
UNGIRD
UNHAND
UNHEED
UNIPOD
UNITED
UNKIND
UNLAID
UNLEAD
UNLOAD
UNPAID
UNREAD
UNSAID
UNSHED
UNSHOD
UNSOLD
UNTIED
UNTOLD
UNTROD
UNUSED
UNWIND

••ND••
BANDED
BANDIT
BANDOG
BENDAY
BENDED
BENDER
BENDIX
BINDER
BINDUP
BONDED
BUNDLE
CANDID
CANDLE
CANDOR
CINDER
CONDOR
CONDOS
DANDER
DANDIE
DANDLE
DENDRI
DENDRO
DONDER
DUNDEE
FANDOM
FENDED
FENDER
FINDER
FONDER
FONDLE
FONDLY
FONDUE
FUNDED
GANDER
GANDHI
GENDER
GUNDOG
HANDED
HANDEL
HANDIN
HANDLE
HANDON
HINDER
HINDUS
KANDER
KINDER
KINDLE
KINDLY
KINDOF
LANDAU
LANDED
LANDER
LANDHO
LANDIS
LANDON
LANDRY
LENDER
LINDEN
LONDON
LUNDEN
LYNDON
MANDAN
MANDAY
MENDED
MENDEL
MENDER
MENDES
MINDED
MINDER
MONDAY
PANDAS
PANDER
PANDIT
PENDED
PINDAR
PINDUS
PONDER
PUNDIT
RANDOM
RANDRY
RENDER
RONDEL
RONDOS
RUNDLE
RUNDMC
RUNDRY
SANDAL
SANDED
SANDER
SANDIA
SANDRA
SENDAK
SENDER
SENDIN
SENDUP
SONDES
SUNDAE
SUNDAY
SUNDER
SUNDEW
SUNDOG
SUNDRY
SYNDIC
TANDEM
TENDED
TENDER
TENDON
TENDTO
TINDER
TUNDRA
VANDAL
VENDED
VENDEE
VENDOR
WANDER
WENDED
WINDED
WINDER
WINDEX
WINDOM
WINDOW
WINDUP
WONDER
YONDER
ZANDER
ZENDOS

••N•D•
CANADA
CANIDS
DENUDE
MONADS
MONODY
PANADA
RANIDS
SYNODS
XANADU

••N••D
AENEID
ARNOLD
BANDED
BANGED
BANKED
BANNED
BENDED
BINGED
BINNED
BONDED
BONGED
BUNGED
BUNKED
BUNTED
CANARD
CANDID
CANNED
CANOED
CANTED
CENSED
CONFED
CONKED
CONNED
CONRAD
CUNARD
DANCED
DENIED
DENNED
DENTED
DINGED
DINNED
DINTED
DONALD
DONNED
DUNKED
DUNNED
ENNEAD
FANGED
FANNED
FENCED
FENDED
FINKED
FINNED
FUNDED
FUNKED
FUNNED
GANGED
GINNED
GONGED
GUNNED
HANDED
HANGED
HINGED
HINTED
HONIED
HONKED
HUNTED
INNEED
JINKED
JINXED
JUNKED
KENNED
KINGED
KINKED
KONRAD
LANCED
LANDED
LENSED
LINKED
LONGED
LUNGED
LYNYRD
MANNED
MENDED
MINCED
MINDED
MINTED
MONIED
OINKED
OXNARD
PANNED
PANTED
PENDED
PENNED
PENROD
PENTAD
PINGED
PINKED
PINNED
PONGID
PONIED
PUNNED
PUNTED
RANCID
RANGED
RANKED
RANTED
RENTED
RINGED
RINSED
RONALD
SANDED
SENSED
SINBAD

SINEAD
SINGED
SINNED
SUNGOD
SUNNED
SYNCED
TANGED
TANKED
TANNED
TENDED
TENSED
TENTED
TINGED
TINGOD
TINNED
TINTED
VANNED
VENDED
VENTED
WANNED
WANTAD
WANTED
WENDED
WINCED
WINDED
WINGED
WINKED
WONNED
WONTED
YANKED
YENNED
ZINGED
ZONKED

•••ND•

AGENDA
AMANDA
AMENDS
ANANDA
ARENDT
BIONDI
BLANDA
BLENDE
BLENDS
BLINDS
BLONDE
BLONDS
BOUNDS
BRANDO
BRANDS
BRANDT
BRANDX
BRANDY
BRENDA
DIRNDL
EBONDS
ELANDS
EMENDS
FIENDS
FOUNDS
FRONDS
GLANDS
GLENDA
GRANDE
GRANDS
GRINDS
GRUNDY
HOUNDS
KAUNDA
LUANDA
MAUNDY
MBUNDU
MOUNDS
OLINDA
POUNDS
RHONDA
ROUNDS
RUANDA
RWANDA
SCENDS
SHANDY
SHINDY
SOUNDS
SPENDS
STANDS
TBONDS
TRENDS
TRENDY
UGANDA
UPENDS
VIANDS
WOUNDS
ZOUNDS

•••N•D

ATONED
BANNED
BEANED
BINNED
BRINED
BURNED
CANNED
CLONED
COINED
CONNED
CORNED
CRANED
DAMNED
DARNED
DAWNED
DENNED
DINNED
DONNED
DOWNED
DRONED
DUNNED
EARNED
EVENED
FANNED
FAWNED
FINNED
FUNNED
GAINED
GINNED
GOUNOD
GOWNED
GUNNED
HORNED
HYMNED
IRONED
JOINED
KEENED
KENNED
KERNED
KILNED
LEANED
LEONID
LIMNED
LOANED
MAENAD
MANNED
MOANED
MOONED
OPENED
OPINED
PAINED
PANNED
PAWNED
PEENED
PENNED
PERNOD
PHONED
PINNED
PLANED
PRUNED
PUNNED
RAINED
REINED
RUINED
SEINED
SHINED
SIGNED
SINNED
SPINED
STONED
SUNNED
TANNED
TINNED
TURNED
TWINED
VANNED
VEINED
WANNED
WARNED
WEANED
WHINED
WONNED
YARNED
YAWNED
YENNED

••••ND

ABOUND
ADDEND
ALMOND
APPEND
ARMAND
AROUND
ASCEND
ATHAND
ATTEND
AUFOND
AUGEND
BEHIND
BEYOND
BRIAND
BYHAND
DEFEND
DEMAND
DEMOND
DEPEND
EDMOND
EDMUND
ERRAND
EXPAND
EXPEND
EXTEND
FAGEND
FECUND
FRIEND
GERUND
GROUND
IMPEND
INHAND
INKIND
INLAND
INTEND
ISLAND
JOCUND
LEGEND
LELAND
LEMOND
LOMOND
LOWEND
OBTUND
OFFEND
ONHAND
ONLAND
ORMOND
OSMOND
OSMUND
OSTEND
POLAND
REBIND
REFUND
REMAND
REMEND
REMIND
REPAND
RESAND
RESEND
REWIND
RIBAND
ROLAND
ROTUND
SECOND
STRAND
TAGEND
THEEND
UNBEND
UNBIND
UNHAND
UNKIND
UNWIND
UPLAND
UPWIND

NE••••

NEARBY
NEARED
NEARER
NEARLY
NEARTO
NEATEN
NEATER
NEATLY
NEBULA
NECKED
NECTAR
NEEDED
NEEDLE
NEEDNT
NEESON
NEGATE
NEIGHS
NEISSE
NEKTON
NELLIE
NELSON
NEMATO
NENETS
NEPALI
NEPHEW
NEPHRO
NEREID
NEREIS
NEREUS
NEROLI
NERUDA
NERVES
NESSES
NESSIE
NESTEA
NESTED
NESTER
NESTLE
NESTOR
NETHER
NETMAN
NETMEN
NETPAY
NETTED
NETTLE
NETTON
NEUMAN
NEUMES
NEURAL
NEUROL
NEURON
NEUTER
NEVADA
NEVERS
NEVINS
NEVSKY
NEWAGE
NEWARK
NEWELS
NEWEST
NEWISH
NEWLEY
NEWMAN
NEWMAR
NEWTON
NEXTTO

N•E•••

NEEDED
NEEDLE
NEEDNT
NEESON
NIECES
NIELLI
NIELLO
NLEAST
NOESIS
NOETIC
NOEXIT
NUECES

N••E••

NAMELY
NAMERS
NAPERY
NASEBY
NAVELS
NENETS
NEREID
NEREIS
NEREUS
NEVERS
NEWELS
NEWEST
NFLERS
NHLERS
NICEAN
NICELY
NICENE
NICEST
NICETY
NINERS
NINETY
NITERS
NLWEST
NOCENT
NOLEAD
NOLENS
NOLESS
NONEGO
NONETS
NOPETS
NOTERS
NOVELS
NOVENA
NUGENT
NUMERO

N•••E•

NABBED
NABBER
NAGGED
NAGGER
NAILED
NAILER
NANSEN
NANTES
NAPIER
NAPLES
NAPPED
NAPPER
NAPPES
NASSER
NATTER
NAUSEA
NAVIES
NEARED
NEARER
NEATEN
NEATER
NECKED
NEEDED
NEPHEW
NERVES
NESSES
NESTEA
NESTED
NESTER
NETHER
NETMEN
NETTED
NEUMES
NEUTER
NEWLEY
NGUYEN
NIAMEY
NICAEA
NICHES
NICKED
NICKEL
NICKER
NIECES
NIGHER
NIPPED
NIPPER
NISSEN
NITRES
NIXIES
NOBLER
NOBLES
NODDED
NOISED
NOISES
NOOSES
NOSHED
NOSHER
NOSHES
NOSIER
NOTYET
NOUMEA
NUBBED
NUCLEI
NUCLEO
NUDGED
NUDGER
NUDGES
NUECES
NUGGET
NULLED
NUMBED
NUMBER
NURSED
NURSER
NURSES
NUTLET
NUTMEG
NUTTED
NUTTER

N••••E

NADINE
NATIVE
NATURE
NEEDLE
NEGATE
NEISSE
NELLIE
NESSIE
NESTLE
NETTLE
NEWAGE
NIBBLE
NICENE
NICOLE
NIGGLE
NIMBLE
NODDLE
NODICE
NODOSE
NODULE
NOMORE
NONAGE
NONAME
NOODLE
NOSALE
NOTATE
NOTICE
NOVICE
NOWISE
NOZZLE
NUANCE
NUBBLE
NUBILE
NUCHAE
NUTATE
NUZZLE

•NE•••

ANEMIA
ANEMIC
ENERGY
ENESCO
GNEISS
KNEADS
KNEELS
KNELLS
ONEDAY
ONEDGE
ONEIDA
ONEILL
ONETWO
ONEUPS
ONEWAY
PNEUMA
SNEAKS
SNEAKY
SNEERS
SNEERY
SNEEZE
SNEEZY
SNELLS
UNEASE
UNEASY
UNESCO
UNEVEN
VNECKS

•N•E••

ANDEAN
ANGELA
ANGELI
ANGELL
ANGELO
ANGELS
ANGERS
ANNEAL
ANNEXE
ANSELM
ANTEED
ANTERO
ANTEUP
ENDEAR
ENDERS
ENGELS
ENMESH
ENNEAD
ENTERO
ENTERS
INCEPT
INDEBT
INDEED
INDENE
INDENT
INFECT
INFERS
INFEST
INGEAR
INGEST
INHERE
INJECT
INJEST
INKERS
INLEAF
INLETS
INNEED
INNESS
INSEAM
INSECT
INSERT
INSETS
INTEND
INTENS
INTENT
INTERN
INVENT
INVERT
INVEST
KNEELS
ONDECK
ONSETS
SNEERS
SNEERY
SNEEZE
SNEEZY
UNBELT
UNBEND
UNBENT
UNHEED
UNLEAD
UNLESS
UNMEET
UNMESH
UNPEGS
UNPENS
UNREAD
UNREAL
UNREEL
UNREST
UNSEAL
UNSEAT
UNSEEN
UNSEWN
UNSEWS
UNVEIL
UNWELL

•N••E•

ANADEM
ANCIEN
ANDREA
ANDREI
ANDRES
ANDREW
ANDREY
ANGLED
ANGLER
ANGLES
ANIMES
ANKLED
ANKLES
ANKLET
ANNLEE
ANODES
ANOLES
ANSWER
ANTEED
ANTHEM
ANTHER
ANTLER
ANTRES
CNOTES
ENAMEL
ENATES
ENDMEN
ENDUED
ENDUES
ENSUED
ENSUES
ENTREE
ENURED
ENURES
ENVIED
ENVIES
GNAWED
GNAWER
GNOMES
INANER
INAPET
INBRED
INCHED
INCHES
INDEED
INDIES
INGLES
INGRES
INKIER
INKLES
INNEED
INSTEP
INURED
INURES
KNAVES
KNIFED
KNIFES
KNIVES
KNOWER
ONAGER
ONSPEC
ONUSES
ONVIEW
ONYXES
SNAKED
SNAKES
SNARED
SNARES
SNIDER
SNIPED
SNIPES
SNIVEL
SNOPES
SNORED
SNORER
SNORES
SNOWED
SNYDER
TNOTES
UNAGED
UNAWED
UNCLES
UNDIES
UNDOER
UNDOES
UNDYED
UNEVEN
UNGUES
UNHEED
UNICEF
UNISEX
UNITED
UNITER
UNITES
UNMEET
UNOPEN
UNREEL
UNSEEN
UNSHED
UNTIED
UNTIES
UNUSED

•N•••E

ANNEXE
ANNLEE
ANOMIE
ANSATE
ANYONE
ENABLE
ENCAGE
ENCASE
ENCODE
ENCORE
ENDIVE
ENDURE
ENDUSE
ENGAGE
ENGINE
ENISLE
ENLACE
ENRAGE
ENROBE
ENSILE
ENSURE
ENTICE
ENTIRE
ENTREE
ENZYME
INCASE
INCISE
INCITE
INCOME
INCUSE
INDENE
INDITE
INDUCE
INFUSE
INHALE
INHERE
INHUME
INJOKE
INJURE
INLINE
INLOVE
INMATE
INNAGE
INNATE
INOUYE
INSANE
INSIDE
INSOLE
INSURE
INTAKE
INTIME
INTINE
INTONE
INTUNE
INVADE
INVITE
INVOKE
ONDINE
ONEDGE
ONFILE
ONFIRE
ONLINE
ONSALE
ONSIDE
ONSITE
ONTAPE
ONTIME
SNATHE
SNEEZE
SNOOZE
UNABLE
UNCAGE
UNCASE
UNDINE
UNDONE
UNEASE
UNGLUE
UNIATE
UNIQUE
UNLACE
UNLADE
UNLIKE
UNMADE
UNMAKE
UNPILE
UNRIPE
UNROBE
UNSAFE
UNSURE
UNTRUE
UNTUNE
UNWISE
UNWOVE
UNYOKE

••NE••

AENEAS
AENEID
ANNEAL
ANNEXE
ARNESS
ARNETT
BONERS
BONEUP
CANERS
CINEMA
CONEYS
CUNEAL
DINEIN
DINEON
DINERO
DINERS
DONEES
DONEIN
DONETS
DONEUP
DUNERA
ENNEAD
ERNEST
FINELY
FINERY
FINEST
GENERA
GENETS
GENEVA
GENEVE
GONEBY
GONERS
HONEST
HONEYS
INNEED
INNESS
JUNEAU
LINEAL
LINEAR
LINENS
LINERS
LINEUP
LONELY
LONERS
MANEGE
MINERS
MONERA
MONETA
MONEYS
NENETS
NINERS
NINETY
NONEGO
NONETS
ORNERY
OWNERS
PANELS
PINEAL
PINERO
PINERY
RANEES
RENEGE
RENEWS
RONELY
SANELY
SANEST
SENECA
SENEGA
SINEAD
SINEWS
SINEWY
TENETS
TINEAR
TONERS
TONEUP
TUNEIN
TUNERS
TUNEUP
VENEER
VENETO
VINERY
WANERS
WINERY

••N•E•

ANNLEE
ARNHEM
BANDED
BANGED
BANGER
BANKED
BANKER
BANNED
BANNER
BANTER
BENDED
BENDER
BINDER
BINGED
BINGES
BINNED
BONDED
BONGED
BONIER
BONNES
BONNET
BONZES
BUNGED
BUNGEE
BUNKED
BUNKER
BUNSEN
BUNTED
BUNTER
BUNUEL
CANCEL
CANKER
CANNED
CANNEL
CANNER
CANNES
CANOED
CANOES
CANTED
CANTER
CENSED
CENSER
CENSES
CENTER
CINDER
CONFED
CONFER
CONGER
CONIES
CONKED
CONKER
CONMEN
CONNED
CONNER
CONTES
CONVEX
CONVEY
DANCED
DANCER
DANCES
DANDER
DANGER
DANIEL
DANKER
DANNER
DANTES
DENIED
DENIER
DENIES
DENNED
DENSER
DENTED
DENVER
DENZEL
DINGED
DINKEY
DINNED
DINNER
DINTED
DONDER
DONEES
DONKEY
DONNED
DONNEE
DONNER
DUNCES
DUNDEE
DUNKED
DUNKER
DUNNED
FANGED
FANJET
FANNED
FENCED
FENCER
FENCES
FENDED
FENDER
FENNEC
FENNEL
FINDER
FINGER
FINKED
FINNED
FINNEY
FONDER
FUNDED
FUNKED
FUNNED
FUNNEL
GANDER
GANGED
GANGES
GANNET
GENDER
GENIES
GENRES
GINGER
GINNED
GONGED
GUNMEN
GUNNED
GUNNEL
GUNNER
GUNTER
HANDED
HANDEL
HANGED
HANGER
HANKER
HANSEL
HENLEY
HENNER
HINDER
HINGED
HINGES
HINTED
HINTER
HONIED
HONKED
HONKER
HUNGER
HUNKER
HUNTED
HUNTER
INNEED
JANSEN
JENNER
JENNET
JENSEN
JINKED
JINXED
JINXES
JUNKED
JUNKER
JUNKET
KANDER
KENNED
KENNEL
KINDER
KINGED
KINKED
LANCED
LANCER
LANCES
LANCET
LANDED
LANDER
LANIER
LANKER
LENDER
LENSED
LENSES
LENTEN
LINDEN
LINGER
LINKED
LINKER
LINNET
LINSEY
LINTEL
LINTER
LONGED
LONGER
LONGES
LUNDEN
LUNGED
LUNGES
LUNKER
LYNLEY
LYNXES
MANGER
MANNED
MANNER
MANSES
MANTEL
MANUEL
MENDED
MENDEL
MENDER
MENDES
MENNEN
MINCED
MINCER
MINCES
MINDED
MINDER
MINKES
MINTED
MINTER
MINUET
MINXES
MONGER
MONIED
MONIES
MONKEY
MONTEL
MONTEZ
NANSEN
NANTES
OINKED

OUNCES
PANDER
PANNED
PANNER
PANNES
PANTED
PANZER
PENCEL
PENDED
PENMEN
PENNED
PENNER
PENNEY
PENSEE
PINCER
PINGED
PINIER
PINKED
PINKEN
PINKER
PINNED
PINNER
PINTER
PONDER
PONGEE
PONIED
PONIES
PONTES
PUNIER
PUNKER
PUNNED
PUNTED
PUNTER
RANEES
RANGED
RANGER
RANGES
RANKED
RANKER
RANTED
RANTER
RENDER
RENNES
RENNET
RENTED
RENTER
RINGED
RINGER
RINSED
RINSES
RONDEL
RUNLET
RUNNEL
RUNNER
SANDED
SANDER
SANGER
SANSEI
SANTEE
SENDER
SENNET
SENSED
SENSEI
SENSES
SINGED
SINGER
SINGES
SINKER
SINNED
SINNER
SINTER
SONDES
SONNET
SUNDER
SUNDEW
SUNKEN
SUNNED
SUNSET
SYNCED
TANDEM
TANGED
TANKED
TANKER
TANNED
TANNER
TENDED
TENDER
TENREC
TENSED
TENSER
TENSES
TENTED
TENTER
TINDER
TINGED
TINGES
TINIER
TINKER
TINMEN
TINNED
TINNER
TINSEL
TINTED
TINTER
TONIER
TONNES
TUNNEL
TUNNEY
VANIER
VANNED
VENDED
VENDEE
VENEER
VENTED
VENTER
VENUES
WANDER
WANNED
WANNER
WANTED
WENCES
WENDED
WINCED
WINCER
WINCES
WINDED
WINDER
WINDEX
WINGED
WINGER
WINKED
WINKER
WINNER
WINTER
WINZES
WONDER
WONNED
WONTED
WYNTER
YANKED
YANKEE
YENNED
YONDER
ZANDER
ZANIER
ZANIES
ZENGER
ZINGED
ZINGER
ZONKED
ZONKER

••N••E

ADNATE
AGNATE
ANNEXE
ANNLEE
AUNTIE
BANGLE
BINATE
BONNIE
BUNCHE
BUNDLE
BUNGEE
BUNGLE
BYNAME
CANAPE
CANDLE
CANINE
CANNAE
CANTLE
CANUTE
CENOTE
CENTRE
CINQUE
CONNIE
CONTRE
DANDIE
DANDLE
DANGLE
DANGME
DANUBE
DENGUE
DENISE
DENOTE
DENUDE
DINGLE
DONATE
DONNEE
DUNDEE
EUNICE
FANNIE
FINALE
FINITE
FONDLE
FONDUE
GANGLE
GANGUE
GENEVE
GENOME
GENTLE
HANDLE
HANKIE
HONORE
IGNACE
IGNITE
IGNORE
INNAGE
INNATE
IONIZE
JANGLE
JANICE
JANINE
JENNIE
JINGLE
JUNGLE
JUNKIE
KINDLE
KINGME
LANATE
LANOSE
LENAPE
LENNIE
LENORE
LINAGE
LONGUE
LUNATE
MANAGE
MANEGE
MANGLE
MANQUE
MANTLE
MENACE
MENAGE
MENSAE
MINGLE
MINNIE
MINUTE
MONROE
MUNCIE
NONAGE
NONAME
OENONE
ORNATE
PENNAE
PENSEE
PINITE
PINKIE
PINNAE
PINOLE
PINTLE
PONGEE
PUNKIE
RANKLE
RENAME
RENEGE
RENNIE
RENOTE
RONNIE
RUNCIE
RUNDLE
SANTEE
SENATE
SINGLE
SUNDAE
TANGLE
TENACE
TENURE
TINGLE
TINKLE
TONGUE
TONITE
VENDEE
VENICE
VENIRE
VENITE
WANGLE
WINKIE
WINKLE
WINNIE
YANKEE
ZONATE

•••NE•

AKENES
ALINES
AMINES
ATONED
ATONES
BAINES
BANNED
BANNER
BARNES
BARNEY
BEANED
BINNED
BIRNEY
BONNES
BONNET
BORNEO
BOWNET
BRINED
BRINES
BRUNEI
BRUNET
BURNED
BURNER
BURNET
BURNEY
BYRNES
CAGNEY
CANNED
CANNEL
CANNER
CANNES
CARNES
CARNET
CARNEY
CHANEL
CHANEY
CHINES
CLINES
CLONED
CLONES
COINED
COINER
CONNED
CONNER
COONEY
CORNEA
CORNED
CORNEL
CORNER
CORNET
CRANED
CRANES
CRENEL
CRONES
CYGNET
DABNEY
DAMNED
DANNER
DARNED
DARNEL
DARNER
DAWNED
DENNED
DINNED
DINNER
DIONEB
DISNEY
DONNED
DONNEE
DONNER
DOWNED
DOWNER
DOWNEY
DRONED
DRONER
DRONES
DUNNED
EARNED
EARNER
EISNER
EUPNEA
EVENED
EVENER
FANNED
FAWNED
FAWNER
FENNEC
FENNEL
FINNED
FINNEY
FLYNET
FUNNED
FUNNEL
GAINED
GAINER
GANNET
GARNER
GARNET
GINNED
GOWNED
GUINEA
GUNNED
GUNNEL
GUNNER
GURNEY
HAINES
HEFNER
HENNER
HORNED
HORNER
HORNET
HORNEY
HYMNED
INANER
IRENES
IRONED
IRONER
JENNER
JENNET
JITNEY
JOINED
JOINER
JOYNER
KEENED
KEENEN
KEENER
KENNED
KENNEL
KERNED
KERNEL
KEYNES
KIDNEY
KILNED
KRONER
LEANED
LEANER
LEONES
LERNER
LIENEE
LIMNED
LIMNER
LINNET
LIONEL
LIONET
LOANED
LOANER
LOONEY
MAGNET
MANNED
MANNER
MARNER
MEANER
MENNEN
MILNER
MOANED
MOANER
MOINES
MOONED
MOONEY
OPENED
OPENER
OPINED
OPINER
OPINES
ORKNEY
PAINED
PANNED
PANNER
PANNES
PAWNED
PAWNEE
PAWNER
PEENED
PENNED
PENNER
PENNEY
PHONED
PHONES
PINNED
PINNER
PLANED
PLANER
PLANES
PLANET
PRUNED
PRUNER
PRUNES
PUNNED
RADNER
RAINED
RAINER
RAINES
REINED
REINER
RENNES
RENNET
REUNES
RODNEY
ROMNEY
ROONEY
RUINED
RUINER
RUNNEL
RUNNER
SCENES
SCONES
SEINED
SEINER
SEINES
SENNET
SHINED
SHINER
SHINES
SIDNEY
SIGNED
SIGNEE
SIGNER
SIGNET
SINNED
SINNER
SONNET
SOONER
SPINED
SPINEL
SPINES
SPINET
STONED
STONER
STONES
SUMNER
SUNNED
SWANEE
SYDNEY
TANNED
TANNER
TBONES
TEENER
THANES
TINNED
TINNER
TONNES
TOWNER
TRINES
TUNNEL
TUNNEY
TURNED
TURNER
TWINED
TWINES
VAINER
VANNED
VARNEY
VEINED
WAGNER
WANNED
WANNER
WAPNER
WARNED
WARNER
WATNEY
WEANED
WERNER
WHINED
WHINER
WHINES
WIENER
WINNER
WONNED
YARNED
YAWNED
YAWNER
YENNED

•••N•E

ATONCE
AVENGE
AVENUE
BEANIE
BERNIE
BLENDE
BLONDE
BONNIE
BOUNCE
BRONTE
BRONZE
CANNAE
CHANCE
CHANGE
CONNIE
CRINGE
DIONNE
DONNEE
EVINCE
EVONNE
FANNIE
FAUNAE
FIANCE
FLANGE
FLENSE
FRANCE
FRINGE
GLANCE
GRANDE
GRANGE
GRUNGE
GWYNNE
JEANNE
JENNIE
JOANIE
JOANNE
JOUNCE
LAINIE
LENNIE
LEONIE
LIENEE
LOUNGE
MARNIE
MEANIE
MINNIE
NUANCE
ODENSE
ORANGE
PAWNEE
PENNAE
PINNAE
PLANTE
PLUNGE
POINTE
POUNCE
PRANCE
PRINCE
PRYNNE
PUENTE
QUINCE
RENNIE
RONNIE
SAINTE
SCONCE
SEANCE
SIGNEE
SPONGE
STANCE
SWANEE
THENCE
TOWNIE
TRANCE
TWINGE
USANCE
VIENNE
WEENIE
WHENCE
WINNIE
YVONNE

••••NE

ACHENE
ACTONE
AFFINE
AHERNE
ALDINE
ALFINE
ALKENE
ALPINE
ANYONE
ARCANE
ARLENE
ARSENE
ATHENE
ATTUNE
BEGONE
BEMINE
BLAINE
BOURNE
BOVINE
BROWNE
BUTANE
BUTENE
BYGONE
BYLINE
CANINE
CAPONE
CELINE
CETANE
CHAINE
COHUNE
COSINE
DAMONE
DAPHNE
DAYONE
DEBONE
DEFINE
DEPONE
DEVINE
DIONNE
DIVINE
DWAYNE
ELAINE
ELAYNE
ENGINE
EOCENE
EQUINE
ERMINE
ESSENE
ETERNE
ETHANE
ETHENE
EUGENE
EVONNE
EVZONE
FALINE
FAMINE
FELINE
FILENE
GAMINE
GREENE
GWYNNE
GYRENE
HELENE
HUMANE
IMFINE
IMMUNE
INDENE
INLINE
INSANE
INTINE
INTONE
INTUNE
IODINE
IRLENE
IRVINE
ISMENE
JANINE
JEANNE
JEJUNE
JOANNE
JOLENE
KALINE
KETONE
LATENE
LEVENE
LEVINE
LIERNE
LUPINE
LUPONE
LYSINE
MALONE
MARINE
MAXINE
MODINE
MOLINE
MURINE
NADINE
NICENE
OCTANE
OENONE
ONDINE
ONLINE
ORPINE
OSCINE
PATINE
PAVANE
PROCNE
PRYNNE
PUISNE
PURINE
RACINE
RAMONE
RAPINE
RATINE
RAVINE
RECANE
REDONE
REFINE
RELINE
REPINE
RETENE
RETUNE
REZONE
ROCKNE
ROXANE
SABINE
SALINE
SCARNE
SELENE
SERENE
SERINE
SHAYNE
SHRINE
SILONE
SIMONE
SLOANE
SOFINE
SOIGNE
SPLINE
STERNE
SUPINE
THRONE
TIRANE
TISANE
TRIUNE
TULANE
TYRONE
UNDINE
UNDONE
UNTUNE
URBANE
URSINE
VIENNE
VISINE
WAHINE
XYLENE
YVONNE

NF••••

NFLERS

N••F••

NONFAT

N•••F•

NODOFF
NOTIFY

N••••F

NODOFF

•NF•••

ENFANT
ENFOLD
INFACT
INFAMY
INFANT
INFECT
INFERS
INFEST
INFIRM
INFLOW
INFLUX
INFOLD
INFORM
INFULL
INFUSE
ONFILE
ONFIRE
ONFOOT
UNFAIR
UNFITS
UNFOLD
UNFURL

•N•F••

INAFIX
INAFOG
KNIFED
KNIFES
SNAFUS
SNIFFS
SNIFFY
SNUFFS
SNUFFY
UNIFIC

•N••F•

SNIFFS
SNIFFY
SNUFFS
SNUFFY
UNSAFE

•N•••F

ENGULF
INHALF
INLEAF
UNICEF

••NF••

CONFAB
CONFED
CONFER
GUNFOR
MANFUL
NONFAT
PANFRY
RANFOR
SINFUL

••N•F•

CANIFF
KUNGFU
MINIFY
RANOFF
RUNOFF

••N••F

CANIFF
KINDOF
RANOFF
RUNOFF

NG••••

NGUYEN

N•G•••

NAGANO
NAGGED
NAGGER
NAGOYA
NEGATE
NIGGLE
NIGHER
NIGHTS
NIGHTY
NOGGIN
NOGOOD
NUGENT
NUGGET

N••G••

NAGGED
NAGGER
NAUGHT
NEIGHS
NIGGLE
NILGAI
NINGBO
NOGGIN
NORGAY
NOUGAT
NOUGHT
NUDGED
NUDGER
NUDGES
NUGGET

N•••G•

NEWAGE
NONAGE
NONEGO

N••••G

NAMING
NIXING
NOSING
NOTING
NUKING
NUTMEG

•NG•••

ANGELA
ANGELI
ANGELL
ANGELO
ANGELS
ANGERS
ANGKOR
ANGLED
ANGLER
ANGLES
ANGLIA
ANGLOS
ANGOLA
ANGORA
ENGAGE
ENGELS
ENGINE
ENGIRD
ENGIRT
ENGLUT
ENGRAM
ENGULF
INGEAR
INGEST
INGLES
INGMAR
INGOTS
INGRES
INGRID
UNGIRD
UNGIRT
UNGLUE
UNGUAL
UNGUES
UNGUIS

•N•G••

ANSGAR
ENIGMA
KNIGHT
ONAGER
SNAGGY
SNUGLY
UNAGED

•N••G•

ENCAGE
ENERGY
ENGAGE
ENOUGH
ENRAGE
ENSIGN
INDIGO
INNAGE
ONEDGE
ONHIGH
SNAGGY
UNCAGE
UNPEGS
UNRIGS

•N•••G

ANALOG
ENDING
INAFOG
INKING
INNING
UNCLOG
UNPLUG
UNSNAG
UNSUNG

••NG••

BANGED
BANGER
BANGKA
BANGLE
BANGOR
BANGUI
BANGUP
BENGAL
BENGAY
BINGED
BINGES
BONGED
BONGOS
BUNGED
BUNGEE
BUNGLE
CONGAS
CONGER
CONGOU
DANGER
DANGLE
DANGLY
DANGME
DENGUE
DINGED
DINGHY
DINGLE
DINGUS
FANGED
FINGER
FUNGUS
GANGED
GANGES
GANGLE
GANGLY
GANGUE
GANGUP
GINGER
GONGED
GUNGHO
HANGAR
HANGED
HANGER
HANGIN
HANGON
HANGUL
HANGUP
HINGED
HINGES
HUNGER
HUNGIN
HUNGON
HUNGRY
HUNGUP
HUNGWU
JANGLE
JANGLY
JINGLE
JINGLY
JUNGLE
JUNGLY
KINGED
KINGLY
KINGME
KUNGFU
LANGUR
LENGTH
LINGER
LINGUA
LONGAN
LONGED
LONGER
LONGES
LONGUE
LUNGED
LUNGES
MANGER
MANGLE
MANGOS
MINGLE
MONGER
MONGOL
MUNGOS
NINGBO
PENGHU
PINGED
PONGEE
PONGID
RANGED
RANGER
RANGES
RANGUP
RINGED
RINGER
RINGUP
RUNGUP
SANGER
SANGTO
SINGED
SINGER
SINGES
SINGLE
SINGLY
SINGTO
SUNGOD

TANGED
TANGLE
TANGLY
TANGOS
TANGUY
TINGED
TINGES
TINGLE
TINGLY
TINGOD
TONGAN
TONGUE
WANGLE
WINGED
WINGER
WINGIT
YANGON
YUNGLO
ZENGER
ZINGED
ZINGER

••N•G•

BENIGN
GINKGO
GONOGO
INNAGE
LINAGE
MANAGE
MANEGE
MENAGE
NONAGE
NONEGO
RENEGE
SENEGA

••N••G

AWNING
BANDOG
BENING
BONING
CANING
DANANG
DANZIG
DINING
FINING
GUNDOG
HONING
INNING
KENNYG
LINING
MINING
OWNING
PENANG
PINING
SONTAG
SUNDOG
TONING
TUNING
VINING
WANING
WINING
WONMUG
ZONING

•••NG•

AVENGE
BEINGS
BOINGO
BRINGS
CHANGE
CLANGS
CLINGS
CLINGY
CRINGE
DOINGS
DRINGS
ERYNGO
FLANGE
FLINGS
FRINGE
FRINGY
GOINGS
GRANGE
GRINGO
GRUNGE
GRUNGY
HMONGS
ICINGS
KIANGS
LIANGS
LOUNGE
OLINGO
ORANGE
ORANGS
ORINGS
PAANGA
PLUNGE
PRONGS
SLANGS
SLANGY
SLINGS
SPONGE
SPONGY
STINGS
STINGY
SWINGS
SWINGY
THINGS
THONGS
TWANGS
TWANGY
TWINGE
UBANGI
WRINGS
WRONGS

•••N•G

EGGNOG
KENNYG
STENOG
UNSNAG

••••NG

AAHING
ACHING
ACTING
ADDING
AGEING
AIDING
AILING
AIMING
AIRING
ARCING
ARMING
ASKING
AWNING
BAAING
BAKING
BALING
BARING
BARONG
BASING
BATING
BAYING
BBKING
BELONG
BENING
BERING
BIDING
BIKING
BITING
BLUING
BODING
BOEING
BOGONG
BONING
BOOING
BORING
BOWING
BOXING
BUSING
BUTUNG
BUYING
CAGING
CAKING
CANING
CARING
CASING
CAVING
CAWING
CEDING
CHIANG
CITING
CLUING
CODING
COMING
COOING
COPING
CORING
COWING
CRYING
CUBING
CURING
DANANG
DARING
DATING
DATONG
DAZING
DELONG
DEWING
DICING
DIKING
DINING
DIVING
DOLING
DOMING
DOPING
DOSING
DOTING
DOZING
DRYING
DUGONG
DUKING
DUPING
DURING
DYEING
EALING
EARING
EASING
EATING
EBBING
EDGING
EGGING
ENDING
EPPING
ERRING
ERVING
EYEING
FACING
FADING
FAKING
FARING
FAXING
FAZING
FEEING
FETING
FILING
FINING
FIRING
FIXING
FLYING
FOXING
FRYING
FUMING
FUSING
FUZING
GAGING
GAMING
GAPING
GATING
GAZING
GEEING
GIBING
GIVING
GLUING
GORING
GUYING
HALING
HARING
HATING
HAVING
HAWING
HAYING
HAZING
HEWING
HEXING
HIDING
HIEING
HIKING
HIRING
HIVING
HOEING
HOLING
HOMING
HONING
HOPING
HOSING
HYPING
ICHING
IDLING
INKING
INNING
IRKING
IRVING
JADING
JAPING
JAWING
JIBING
JIVING
JOKING
JUKING
KDLANG
KEYING
KITING
LACING
LADING
LAMING
LAVING
LAWING
LAYING
LAZING
LIKING
LIMING
LINING
LIPENG
LIVING
LOPING
LOSING
LOVING
LOWING
LUBING
LURING
LUTING
MAKING
MATING
MEKONG
METING
MEWING
MIKING
MIMING
MINING
MIRING
MIXING
MOOING
MOPING
MOVING
MOWING
MUSING
MUTING
NAMING
NIXING
NOSING
NOTING
NUKING
OARING
OBLONG
OFFING
OGLING
OILING
OOHING
OOLONG
OOZING
OPTING
ORBING
OUTING
OWNING
PACING
PADANG
PAGING
PAHANG
PALING
PARANG
PARING
PAVING
PAWING
PAYING
PEKING
PENANG
PIKING
PILING
PINING
PIPING
PLYING
POKING
POLING
PORING
POSING
PRYING
PULING
RACING
RAGING
RAKING
RARING
RATING
RAVING
RAZING
REHANG
REHUNG
RESING
RICING
RIDING
RILING
RIMING
RISING
RIVING
ROBING
ROPING
ROVING
ROWING
RULING
SARONG
SATANG
SATING
SAVING
SAWING
SAYING
SEEING
SEWING
SHYING
SIDING
SIRING
SITING
SIXING
SIZING
SKIING
SKYING
SLUING
SOLING
SOLONG
SOWING
SPRANG
SPRING
SPRUNG
SPYING
STRING
STRONG
STRUNG
TAKING
TAMING
TAPING
TARING
TAWING
TAXING
TEEING
THRONG
TIDING
TIEING
TILING
TIMING
TIRING
TOEING
TONING
TOTING
TOWING
TOYING
TRUING
TRYING
TUBING
TUNING
TURING
TYPING
UNSUNG
UPPING
URGING
VEXING
VIKING
VINING
VOTING
VOWING
WADING
WAGING
WAKING
WANING
WARING
WAVING
WAXING
WILING
WINING
WIPING
WIRING
WOOING
WOWING
YAWING
YOKING
ZONING

NH••••

NHLERS

N•H•••

NIHILO
NOHITS

N••H••

NACHOS
NASHUA
NATHAN
NEPHEW
NEPHRO
NETHER
NICHES
NIGHER
NIGHTS
NIGHTY
NOSHED
NOSHER
NOSHES
NOSHOW
NUCHAE
NUCHAL

N•••H•

NAUGHT
NAVAHO
NEIGHS
NINTHS
NOUGHT
NYMPHS

N••••H

NAMATH
NAUTCH
NEWISH
NULLAH

•NH•••

ANHYDR
INHALE
INHALF
INHAND
INHAUL
INHERE
INHUME
ONHAND
ONHIGH
ONHOLD
UNHAND
UNHEED
UNHOLY
UNHOOK
UNHURT

•N•H••

ANCHOR
ANDHOW
ANTHEM
ANTHER
ANYHOW
INCHED
INCHES
INCHON
UNCHIC
UNSHED
UNSHOD

•N••H•

KNIGHT
SNATHE
SNATHS

•N•••H

ENDASH
ENMESH
ENOUGH
ENRICH
INARCH
INCASH
INRUSH
INWITH
ONHIGH
ONRUSH
SNATCH
SNITCH
UNLASH
UNMESH

••NH••

ARNHEM
BENHUR
DUNHAM
JANHUS
MENHIR
SENHOR
TINHAT

••N•H•

BUNCHE
CANTHI
CONCHA
CONCHS
DINGHY
GANDHI
GUNGHO
GUNSHY
HONCHO
HONSHU
LANDHO
MANCHA
MANCHU
MONTHS
MYNAHS
NINTHS
PANCHO
PENGHU
PONCHO
PUNCHY
RANCHO
SANCHO
TENTHS
XANTHO

••N••H

BANISH
DANISH
EUNUCH
FINISH
HANNAH
JINNAH
LENGTH
MENSCH
MUNICH
ORNITH
PUNISH
PUNKAH
TONISH
VANISH
ZENITH

•••N•H

BLANCH
BLENCH
BRANCH
BRUNCH
CHINCH
CLENCH
CLINCH
CRUNCH
DRENCH
FLINCH
FRENCH
GRINCH
HANNAH
HAUNCH
JINNAH
LAUNCH
PAUNCH
PLINTH
QUENCH
STANCH
STENCH
TRENCH
WRENCH

NI••••

NIACIN
NIAMEY
NIBBLE
NICAEA
NICEAN
NICELY
NICENE
NICEST
NICETY
NICHES
NICKED
NICKEL
NICKER
NICOLA
NICOLE
NICOLO
NIECES
NIELLI
NIELLO
NIGGLE
NIGHER
NIGHTS
NIGHTY
NIHILO
NIKITA
NIKOLA
NILGAI
NIMBLE
NIMBLY
NIMBUS
NIMINY
NIMITZ
NIMROD
NINERS
NINETY
NINGBO
NINJAS
NINTHS
NIPPED
NIPPER
NIPPON
NIPPUR
NIPSAT
NIPUPS
NISSAN
NISSEN
NITERS
NITRES
NITRIC
NITWIT
NIXIES
NIXING

N•I•••

NAIADS
NAILED
NAILER
NAILIN
NAIRAS
NEIGHS
NEISSE
NOIRON
NOISED
NOISES

N••I••

NADINE
NADIRS
NAMING
NAPIER
NARIAL
NATICK
NATION
NATIVE
NAVIES
NEVINS
NEWISH
NIHILO
NIKITA
NIMINY
NIMITZ
NIXIES
NIXING
NODICE
NOHITS
NORIAS
NOSIER
NOSILY
NOSING
NOTICE
NOTIFY
NOTING
NOTION
NOVICE
NOWISE
NUBIAN
NUBILE
NUDIST
NUDITY
NUKING
NUMINA

N•••I•

NAILIN
NAPKIN
NARNIA
NARVIK
NELLIE
NEREID
NEREIS
NESSIE
NIACIN
NITRIC
NITWIT
NOESIS
NOETIC
NOEXIT
NOGGIN
NORDIC
NORRIS
NUBBIN
NUDNIK
NUNCIO
NUTKIN
NUTRIA
NYQUIL

N••••I

NAPOLI
NEPALI
NEROLI
NIELLI
NILGAI
NUCLEI

•NI•••

ANIMAL
ANIMAS
ANIMES
ANIMUS
ANIONS
ANITRA
CNIDUS
ENIGMA
ENISLE
INIONS
INITIO
KNICKS
KNIFED
KNIFES
KNIGHT
KNIVES
ONIONS
ONIONY
SNICKS
SNIDER
SNIFFS
SNIFFY
SNIPED
SNIPES
SNIPPY
SNITCH
SNIVEL
UNIATE
UNIATS
UNICEF
UNIFIC
UNIONS
UNIPOD
UNIQUE
UNISEX
UNISON
UNITAL
UNITAS
UNITED
UNITER
UNITES
UNIVAC

•N•I••

ANCIEN
ANOINT
ANTICS
ANVILS
ENCINA
ENCINO
ENDING
ENDIVE
ENGINE
ENGIRD
ENGIRT
ENLIST
ENMITY
ENNIUS
ENRICH
ENRICO
ENSIGN
ENSILE
ENTICE
ENTIRE
ENTITY
ENVIED
ENVIES
GNEISS
INCISE
INCITE
INDIAN
INDICT
INDIES
INDIGO
INDIRA
INDITE
INDIUM
INFIRM
INKIER
INKIND
INKING
INLINE
INNING
INSIDE
INSIST
INSITU
INTIMA
INTIME
INTINE
INUITS
INVITE
INVIVO
INWITH
ONDINE
ONEIDA
ONEILL
ONFILE
ONFIRE
ONHIGH
ONLINE
ONSIDE
ONSITE
ONTIME
ONVIEW
SNAILS
UNBIND
UNCIAL
UNDIES
UNDINE
UNFITS
UNGIRD
UNGIRT
UNKIND
UNKINK
UNLIKE
UNLINK
UNPILE
UNPINS
UNRIGS
UNRIPE
UNTIDY
UNTIED
UNTIES
UNWIND
UNWISE
UNZIPS

•N••I•

ANACIN
ANEMIA
ANEMIC
ANGLIA
ANODIC
ANOMIE
ANTRIM
ANUBIS
ENJOIN
ENOKIS
ENOSIS
ENTAIL
ENVOIS
GNOMIC
GNOSIS
INAFIX
INDRIS
INGRID
INITIO
INLAID
INTUIT
INVAIN
SNOWIN
UNCHIC
UNCOIL
UNFAIR
UNGUIS
UNIFIC
UNKNIT
UNLAID
UNPAID
UNSAID
UNVEIL

•N•••I

ANDREI
ANGELI
ANNULI

••NI••

ALNICO
AMNION
ARNICA
AWNING
BANISH
BENIGN
BENING
BENITO
BONIER
BONING
BONITO
BUNION
CANIDS
CANIFF
CANINE
CANING
CONICS
CONIES
CONIUM
CYNICS
DANIEL
DANISH
DENIAL
DENIED
DENIER
DENIES
DENIMS
DENIRO
DENISE
DINING
DONITZ
ELNINO
ENNIUS
EONIAN
EUNICE
FANION
FENIAN
FINIAL
FINING
FINISH
FINITE
FINITO
GENIAL
GENIES
GENIUS
HONIED
HONING
IGNITE
INNING
IONIAN
IONICS
IONIUM
IONIZE
JANICE
JANINE
JUNIOR
KONICA
LANIER
LENITY
LINING
MANIAC
MANIAS
MANILA
MANIOC
MENIAL
MENINX
MINIFY
MINIMA
MINIMS
MINING
MINION
MINIUM
MONICA
MONIED
MONIES
MONISM
MONIST
MUNICH
OMNIUM
ORNITH
OWNING
PANICS
PINIER
PINING
PINION
PINITE
PONIED
PONIES
PUNIER
PUNILY
PUNISH
RANIDS
RUNINS
SANITY
SENIOR
SONICS
TANIST
TINIER
TONICS
TONIER
TONING
TONISH
TONITE
TUNICA
TUNICS
TUNING
VANIER
VANISH
VANITY
VENIAL
VENICE
VENIRE
VENITE
VINING
WANING
WINING
ZANIER
ZANIES
ZANILY
ZENITH
ZONING

••N•I•

AENEID
AUNTIE
BANDIT
BENDIX
BENOIT
BONNIE
CANDID
CONNIE
DANDIE
DANZIG
DENNIS
DENTIL
DENTIN
DINEIN
DONEIN
DUNLIN
FANNIE
FINNIC
HANDIN
HANGIN
HANKIE
HENBIT
HENNIN
HENRIK
HUNGIN
JENNIE
JUNKIE
LANAIS
LANDIS
LANVIN
LENNIE
LENTIL
MANNIX
MANTIC
MANTIS
MCNAIR
MENHIR
MENTIS
MINNIE
MINUIT
MUNCIE
MUNTIN
NUNCIO
PANDIT
PENCIL
PENNIA
PENNIS
PINKIE
PINXIT
PINYIN
PONGID
PONTIC
PUNDIT
PUNKIE
RANCID
RANKIN
RENAIL
RENNIE

RENNIN
RENOIR
RONNIE
RUNCIE
RUNSIN
SANDIA
SANTIR
SENDIN
SENNIT
SENTIN
SINKIN
SUNLIT
SUNNIS
SYNDIC
TANNIC
TANNIN
TENNIS
TENPIN
TONKIN
TONSIL
TUNEIN
WANTIN
WENTIN
WINGIT
WINKIE
WINNIE
WINWIN
ZINNIA

••N••I
ANNULI
BANGUI
BANZAI
BONAMI
BONSAI
CANTHI
CENTRI
DENALI
DENDRI
ERNANI
GANDHI
KINSKI
SANSEI
SENSEI
YANQUI

•••NI•
ADONIS
ATONIC
BEANIE
BERNIE
BIONIC
BONNIE
BOSNIA
CATNIP
CHENIN
CLINIC
CONNIE
CRANIA
CRANIO
CRONIN
CYANIC
DARNIT
DENNIS
EDENIC
ETHNIC
ETONIC
FAFNIR
FANNIE
FINNIC
HENNIN
ICONIC
IRANIS
IRENIC
IRONIC
JENNIE
JOANIE
JOININ
LAINIE
LENNIE
LEONID
LEONIE
LIGNIN
MANNIX
MARNIE
MEANIE
MINNIE
NARNIA
NUDNIK
OMANIS
OZONIC
PARNIS
PENNIA
PENNIS
PHONIC
PICNIC
PYKNIC
REININ
RENNIE
RENNIN
RESNIK
RONNIE
SCENIC
SENNIT
SIGNIN
SUNNIS
TANNIC
TANNIN
TENNIS
TOWNIE
TURNIN
TURNIP
UNKNIT
URANIA
URANIC
WEENIE
WINNIE
ZINNIA

•••N•I
ADONAI
AVANTI
BIONDI
BRUNEI
EVENKI
KERNOI
UBANGI

••••NI
ALUMNI
ARMANI
BIKINI
BIMINI
BODONI
BUSONI
CARONI
DOMANI
DOMINI
ERNANI
FULANI
GEMINI
ILLINI
MORONI
RAPINI
RIMINI
ROTINI
SILENI
TAHINI
YEMENI
YOGINI

N••J••
NINJAS

N•••J•
NAVAJO

•NJ•••
ANJOUS
ENJOIN
ENJOYS
INJECT
INJEST
INJOKE
INJURE
INJURY
UNJAMS
UNJUST

•N•J••
INAJAM

••NJ••
BANJOS
BANJUL
CONJOB
DONJON
FANJET
MENJOU
NINJAS
PUNJAB

N•K•••
NEKTON
NIKITA
NIKOLA
NUKING

N••K••
NAPKIN
NECKED
NICKED
NICKEL
NICKER
NUTKIN

N•••K•
NEVSKY
NOOTKA

N••••K
NANOOK
NARVIK
NATICK
NEWARK
NUDNIK

•NK•••
ANKARA
ANKLED
ANKLES
ANKLET
INKERS
INKIER
INKIND
INKING
INKLES
UNKIND
UNKINK
UNKNIT
UNKNOT

•N•K••
ANGKOR
ENOKIS
SNAKED
SNAKES

•N••K•
INJOKE
INTAKE
INVOKE
KNACKS
KNICKS
KNOCKS
SNACKS
SNEAKS
SNEAKY
SNICKS
SNOOKS
UNLIKE
UNMAKE
UNYOKE
VNECKS

•N•••K
ANORAK
INBULK
INLUCK
ONDECK
UNCORK
UNHOOK
UNKINK
UNLINK
UNLOCK
UNMASK
UNPACK
UNTACK

••NK••
BANKED
BANKER
BANKON
BUNKED
BUNKER
BUNKOS
BUNKUM
CANKER
CONKED
CONKER
DANKER
DINKEY
DONKEY
DUNKED
DUNKER
FINKED
FUNKED
GINKGO
HANKER
HANKIE
HONKED
HONKER
HUNKER
JINKED
JUNKED
JUNKER
JUNKET
JUNKIE
KINKED
LANKER
LANKLY
LINKED
LINKER
LINKUP
LUNKER
MINKES
MONKEY
OINKED
PINKED
PINKEN
PINKER
PINKIE
PUNKAH
PUNKER
PUNKIE
RANKED
RANKER
RANKIN
RANKLE
RANKLY
SINKER
SINKIN
SUNKEN
TANKAS
TANKED
TANKER
TANKUP
TINKER
TINKLE
TINKLY
TONKIN
WINKAT
WINKED
WINKER
WINKIE
WINKLE
YANKED
YANKEE
ZONKED
ZONKER

••N•K•
BANGKA
KANAKA
KINSKI
TANAKA

••N••K
HENRIK
NANOOK
PINOAK
SENDAK
TANOAK
ZANUCK

•••NK•
BLANKS
BLINKS
BRINKS
CHINKS
CHINKY
CHUNKS
CHUNKY
CLANKS
CLANKY
CLINKS
CLONKS
CLUNKS
CLUNKY
CRANKS
CRANKY
DRINKS
EVENKI
FLANKS
FLUNKS
FLUNKY
FRANKS
GLINKA
PLANKS
PLINKS
PLONKS
PLUNKS
PRANKS
PRINKS
REINKS
SHANKS
SKINKS
SKUNKS
SLINKS
SLINKY
SPANKS
SPANKY
SPINKS
SPUNKY
STANKY
STINKS
STINKY
SWANKY
THANKS
THINKS
THUNKS
TRUNKS

•••N•K
FRANCK
GDANSK
KARNAK
NUDNIK
PLANCK
RESNIK

••••NK
DEBUNK
DRYINK
EMBANK
PODUNK
REDINK
SHRANK
SHRINK
SHRUNK
UNKINK
UNLINK
UPLINK

NL••••
NLEAST
NLWEST

N•L•••
NELLIE
NELSON
NFLERS
NHLERS
NILGAI
NOLEAD
NOLENS
NOLESS
NOLOAD
NULLAH
NULLED
NYLONS

N••L••
NAILED
NAILER
NAILIN
NAPLES
NELLIE
NEWLEY
NIELLI
NIELLO
NOBLER
NOBLES
NUCLEI
NUCLEO
NULLAH
NULLED
NUTLET
NYALAS

N•••L•
NAMELY
NAPOLI
NASALS
NAVELS
NEARLY
NEATLY
NEBULA
NEEDLE
NEPALI
NEROLI
NESTLE
NETTLE
NEWELS
NIBBLE
NICELY
NICOLA
NICOLE
NICOLO
NIELLI
NIELLO
NIGGLE
NIHILO
NIKOLA
NIMBLE
NIMBLY
NODDLE
NODULE
NOODLE
NOSALE
NOSILY
NOVELS
NOZZLE
NUBBLE
NUBILE
NUMBLY
NUZZLE

N••••L
NARIAL
NARWAL
NEURAL
NEUROL
NICKEL
NORMAL
NUCHAL
NYQUIL

•NL•••
ENLACE
ENLIST
INLAID
INLAND
INLAWS
INLAYS
INLEAF
INLETS
INLINE
INLOVE
INLUCK
ONLAND
ONLINE
ONLOAN
UNLACE
UNLADE
UNLAID
UNLASH
UNLEAD
UNLESS
UNLIKE
UNLINK
UNLOAD
UNLOCK

•N•L••
ANALOG
ANGLED
ANGLER
ANGLES
ANGLIA
ANGLOS
ANKLED
ANKLES
ANKLET
ANNLEE
ANOLES
ANTLER
ENBLOC
ENGLUT
INFLOW
INFLUX
INGLES
INKLES
INPLAY
KNELLS
KNOLLS
SNELLS
UNCLAD
UNCLES
UNCLOG
UNGLUE
UNPLUG

•N••L•
ANGELA
ANGELI
ANGELL
ANGELO
ANGELS
ANGOLA
ANNALS
ANNULI
ANNULS
ANSELM
ANVILS
ENABLE
ENDALL
ENFOLD
ENGELS
ENGULF
ENISLE
ENROLL
ENSILE
GNARLS
GNARLY
INBULK
INCULT
INFOLD
INFULL
INHALE
INHALF
INSOLE
INSULT
KNEELS
KNELLS
KNOLLS
KNURLS
KNURLY
ONCALL
ONEILL
ONFILE
ONHOLD
ONSALE
SNAILS
SNARLS
SNARLY
SNELLS
SNUGLY
UNABLE
UNBELT
UNBOLT
UNDULY
UNFOLD
UNHOLY
UNPILE
UNROLL
UNRULY
UNSOLD
UNTOLD
UNWELL

•N•••L
ANGELL
ANIMAL
ANNEAL
ANNUAL
ENAMEL
ENDALL
ENROLL
ENSOUL
ENTAIL
INFULL
INHAUL
ONCALL
ONEILL
SNIVEL
UNCIAL
UNCOIL
UNCOOL
UNCURL
UNFURL
UNGUAL
UNITAL
UNREAL
UNREEL
UNROLL
UNSEAL
UNVEIL
UNWELL

••NL••
ANNLEE
BANLON
DUNLIN
DUNLOP
HENLEY
KUNLUN
LYNLEY
RUNLET
SENLAC
SUNLIT

••N•L•
ANNALS
ANNULI
ANNULS
ARNOLD
BANGLE
BUNDLE
BUNGLE
CANALS
CANDLE
CANOLA
CANTLE
DANDLE
DANGLE
DANGLY
DENALI
DINGLE
DONALD
FINALE
FINALS
FINELY
FONDLE
FONDLY
GANGLE
GANGLY
GENTLE
GENTLY
HANDLE
JANGLE
JANGLY
JINGLE
JINGLY
JUNGLE
JUNGLY
KINDLE
KINDLY
KINGLY
LANKLY
LONELY
LUNULA
MANGLE
MANILA
MANTLE
MINGLE
PANELS
PENULT
PINOLE
PINTLE
PUNILY
RANKLE
RANKLY
RONALD
RONELY
RUNDLE
SANELY
SINGLE
SINGLY
TANGLE
TANGLY
TINGLE
TINGLY
TINKLE
TINKLY
WANGLE
WINKLE
YUNGLO
ZANILY

••N••L
ANNEAL
ANNUAL
BANJUL
BENGAL
BENZOL
BUNUEL
CANCEL
CANNEL
CONSUL
CUNEAL
DANIEL
DENIAL
DENTAL
DENTIL
DENZEL
FENNEL
FINIAL
FONTAL
FUNNEL
GENIAL
GENUAL
GUNNEL
HANDEL
HANGUL
HANSEL
KENNEL
LENTIL
LINEAL
LINTEL
LONNOL
MANFUL
MANTEL
MANUAL
MANUEL
MENDEL
MENIAL
MENSAL
MENTAL
MONGOL
MONTEL
PENCEL
PENCIL
PENPAL
PINEAL
RENAIL
RENTAL
RONDEL
RUNNEL
SANDAL
SINFUL
TINCAL
TINSEL
TONSIL
TUNNEL
VANDAL
VENIAL

•••NL•
EVENLY
GAINLY
KEENLY
LEANLY
MAINLY
MEANLY
OPENLY
THINLY
VAINLY

•••N•L
ATONAL
AXONAL
CANNEL
CARNAL
CHANEL
CORNEL
CRENEL
DARNEL
DIRNDL
FAUNAL
FENNEL
FUNNEL
GUNNEL
HYMNAL
KENNEL
KERNEL
LIONEL
LONNOL
PHENOL
PHENYL
REGNAL
RHINAL
RUNNEL
SIGNAL
SPINAL
SPINEL
TRINAL
TUNNEL
VEINAL
VERNAL

N•M•••
NAMATH
NAMELY
NAMERS
NAMING
NEMATO
NIMBLE
NIMBLY
NIMBUS
NIMINY
NIMITZ
NIMROD
NOMADS
NOMORE
NUMBAT
NUMBED
NUMBER
NUMBLY
NUMERO
NUMINA
NYMPHS

N••M••
NETMAN
NETMEN
NEUMAN
NEUMES
NEWMAN
NEWMAR
NIAMEY
NORMAL
NORMAN
NOUMEA
NUTMEG

N•••M•
NONAME

N••••M
NONCOM

•NM•••
ENMESH
ENMITY
INMATE
INMOST
UNMADE
UNMAKE
UNMANS
UNMASK
UNMEET
UNMESH
UNMOOR

•N•M••
ANEMIA
ANEMIC
ANIMAL
ANIMAS
ANIMES
ANIMUS
ANOMIE
ENAMEL
ENAMOR
ENDMAN
ENDMEN
GNOMES
GNOMIC
GNOMON
INGMAR

•N••M•
ENCAMP
ENIGMA
ENZYME
INCOME
INFAMY
INHUME
INTIMA
INTIME
ONTIME
PNEUMA
UNARMS
UNJAMS

•N•••M
ANADEM
ANONYM
ANSELM
ANTHEM
ANTRIM
ANTRUM
ENGRAM
INAJAM
INDIUM
INFIRM
INFORM
INSEAM

••NM••
BONMOT
CONMAN
CONMEN
GUNMAN
GUNMEN
PENMAN
PENMEN
TINMAN
TINMEN
WONMUG

••N•M•
BENUMB
BONAMI
BYNAME
CINEMA
DANGME
DENIMS
DYNAMO
GENOME
KINGME
MANAMA
MINIMA
MINIMS
NONAME
PANAMA
RENAME
RUNDMC
SONOMA
VENOMS

••N••M
ARNHEM
BANTAM
BUNKUM
CONIUM
DUNHAM
FANDOM
HANSOM
IONIUM
MINIUM
MONISM
NONCOM
OMNIUM
RANDOM
RANSOM
TANDEM
WINDOM

•••N•M
ANONYM
BARNUM
EPONYM
FRENUM
MAGNUM
PHENOM
PLENUM
PUTNAM

N•N•••
NANOOK
NANSEN
NANTES
NENETS
NINERS
NINETY
NINGBO
NINJAS
NINTHS
NONAGE
NONAME
NONARY
NONCOM
NONEGO
NONETS
NONFAT
NUNCIO

N••N••
NARNIA
NOONAN
NOTNOW
NUANCE
NUDNIK

N•••N•
NADINE
NAGANO
NAMING
NATANT
NEEDNT
NEVINS
NICENE
NIMINY
NIXING
NOCENT
NOLENS
NOSING
NOTING
NOVENA
NUGENT
NUKING
NUMINA
NYLONS

N••••N
NAILIN
NANSEN
NAPKIN
NATHAN
NATION
NATRON
NEATEN
NEESON
NEKTON
NELSON
NETMAN
NETMEN
NETTON
NEUMAN
NEURON
NEWMAN
NEWTON
NGUYEN
NIACIN
NICEAN
NIPPON
NISSAN
NISSEN
NOGGIN
NOIRON
NOONAN
NORMAN
NORTON
NOTION
NUBBIN
NUBIAN
NUTKIN

•NN•••
ANNABA
ANNALS
ANNEAL
ANNEXE
ANNLEE
ANNOYS
ANNUAL
ANNULI
ANNULS
ENNEAD
ENNIUS
INNAGE
INNATE
INNEED
INNESS
INNING

•N•N••
ANANDA
ANONYM
INANER
UNKNIT
UNKNOT
UNSNAG
UNSNAP

•N••N•
ANCONA
ANIONS
ANOINT
ANTONY
ANYONE
ENCINA
ENCINO
ENDING
ENFANT
ENGINE
INCANS
INDENE
INDENT
INFANT
INHAND
INIONS
INKIND
INKING
INLAND
INLINE
INNING
INSANE

INSYNC
INTEND
INTENS
INTENT
INTINE
INTONE
INTUNE
INVENT
KNOWNS
ONDINE
ONHAND
ONIONS
ONIONY
ONLAND
ONLINE
UNBEND
UNBENT
UNBIND
UNDINE
UNDONE
UNHAND
UNIONS
UNKIND
UNKINK
UNLINK
UNMANS
UNPENS
UNPINS
UNSUNG
UNTUNE
UNWIND

•N•••N

ANACIN
ANCIEN
ANDEAN
ANTRON
ANURAN
ENDMAN
ENDMEN
ENDRUN
ENJOIN
ENSIGN
GNOMON
INBORN
INCHON
INDIAN
INSPAN
INTERN
INTOWN
INTURN
INVAIN
ONLOAN
SNOWIN
UNBORN
UNEVEN
UNISON
UNOPEN
UNSEEN
UNSEWN
UNSOWN
UNTORN
UNWORN

••NN••

BANNED
BANNER
BINNED
BONNES
BONNET
BONNIE
CANNAE
CANNED
CANNEL
CANNER
CANNES
CANNON
CANNOT
CONNED
CONNER
CONNIE
CONNOR
DANNAY
DANNER
DENNED
DENNIS
DINNED
DINNER
DONNAS
DONNED
DONNEE
DONNER
DUNNED
FANNED
FANNIE
FENNEC
FENNEL
FINNAN
FINNED
FINNEY
FINNIC
FUNNED
FUNNEL
GANNET
GINNED
GUNNAR
GUNNED
GUNNEL
GUNNER
HANNAH
HENNAS
HENNER
HENNIN
JENNER
JENNET
JENNIE
JINNAH
KENNED
KENNEL
KENNYG
LENNIE
LENNON
LINNET
LONNOL
MANNED
MANNER
MANNIX
MENNEN
MINNIE
MINNOW
PANNED
PANNER
PANNES
PENNAE
PENNED
PENNER
PENNEY
PENNIA
PENNIS
PENNON
PINNAE
PINNAS
PINNED
PINNER
PUNNED
RENNES
RENNET
RENNIE
RENNIN
RONNIE
RUNNEL
RUNNER
SANNUP
SENNAS
SENNET
SENNIT
SINNED
SINNER
SONNET
SUNNED
SUNNIS
TANNED
TANNER
TANNIC
TANNIN
TENNIS
TINNED
TINNER
TONNES
TUNNEL
TUNNEY
VANNED
WANNED
WANNER
WINNER
WINNIE
WINNOW
WONNED
YENNED
YUNNAN
ZINNIA

••N•N•

AWNING
BANANA
BENING
BONING
CANINE
CANING
CANONS
CONANT
DANANG
DINING
DUNANT
ELNINO
ERNANI
FINING
HONING
INNING
JANINE
LINENS
LINING
MANANA
MENINX
MINING
OENONE
OWNING
PENANG
PINING
PINONS
RUNINS
RUNONS
SONANT
SUNUNU
TENANT
TENONS
TONING
TUNING
VINING
WANING
WINING
WINONA
ZENANA
ZONING

••N••N

AMNION
BANKON
BANLON
BANYAN
BENIGN
BENSON
BENTON
BONBON
BONTON
BUNION
BUNSEN
BUNYAN
CANAAN
CANCAN
CANCUN
CANNON
CANTON
CANYON
CONMAN
CONMEN
DANSON
DANTON
DENTIN
DENTON
DINEIN
DINEON
DONEIN
DONJON
DUNCAN
DUNLIN
EONIAN
FANION
FANTAN
FENIAN
FINNAN
GENOAN
GUNMAN
GUNMEN
HANDIN
HANDON
HANGIN
HANGON
HANSON
HENNIN
HENSON
HINTON
HUNGIN
HUNGON
IONIAN
JANSEN
JENSEN
JONSON
KANSAN
KENTON
KENYAN
KUNLUN
LANDON
LANSON
LANVIN
LENNON
LENTEN
LINDEN
LONDON
LONGAN
LUNDEN
LYNDON
MANDAN
MENNEN
MINION
MINOAN
MINYAN
MUNTIN
NANSEN
PENMAN
PENMEN
PENNON
PINION
PINKEN
PINSON
PINYIN
PINYON
PINZON
RANKIN
RENNIN
RENOWN
RUNSIN
RUNSON
RUNYON
SENDIN
SENTIN
SINKIN
SUNKEN
SUNTAN
TANNIN
TANOAN
TENDON
TENPIN
TINCAN
TINMAN
TINMEN
TINPAN
TONGAN
TONKIN
TUNEIN
VANRYN
VINTON
WANTIN
WANTON
WENTIN
WENTON
WINWIN
WONTON
WYNTON
YANGON
YUNNAN

•••NN•

CRANNY
CRENNA
DEANNA
DIONNE
DUENNA
EVONNE
FRANNY
GOANNA
GRANNY
GWYNNE
JEANNE
JOANNA
JOANNE
JOHNNY
PRYNNE
SHINNY
SIENNA
SKINNY
VIENNA
VIENNE
WHINNY
YVONNE

•••N•N

ALANON
CANNON
CHENIN
CRONIN
CRONYN
DOWNON
FINNAN
GAINON
GUENON
HAINAN
HENNIN
IRONON
JOININ
KEENAN
KEENEN
LEANON
LENNON
LIGNIN
MAGNON
MEMNON
MENNEN
MIGNON
NOONAN
PENNON
PHONON
PLANON
REININ
RENNIN
SIGNIN
SIGNON
TAINAN
TANNIN
TURNIN
TURNON
VERNON
YUNNAN

••••NN

EDWYNN
JOHANN
MCCANN
SUSANN

NO••••

NOBLER
NOBLES
NOBODY
NOCENT
NODDED
NODDLE
NODICE
NODOFF
NODOSE
NODULE
NOESIS
NOETIC
NOEXIT
NOGGIN
NOGOOD
NOHITS
NOIRON
NOISED
NOISES
NOLEAD
NOLENS
NOLESS
NOLOAD
NOMADS
NOMORE
NONAGE
NONAME
NONARY
NONCOM
NONEGO
NONETS
NONFAT
NOODLE
NOONAN
NOOSES
NOOTKA
NOPETS
NORDIC
NORGAY
NORIAS
NORMAL
NORMAN
NORRIS
NORTON
NORWAY
NOSALE
NOSHED
NOSHER
NOSHES
NOSHOW
NOSIER
NOSILY
NOSING
NOSOAP
NOTARY
NOTATE
NOTBAD
NOTERS
NOTICE
NOTIFY
NOTING
NOTION
NOTNOW
NOTYET
NOUGAT
NOUGHT
NOUMEA
NOVELS
NOVENA
NOVICE
NOWISE
NOZZLE

N•O•••

NOODLE
NOONAN
NOOSES
NOOTKA

N••O••

NABOBS
NABORS
NAGOYA
NANOOK
NAPOLI
NEROLI
NICOLA
NICOLE
NICOLO
NIKOLA
NOBODY
NODOFF
NODOSE
NOGOOD
NOLOAD
NOMORE
NOSOAP
NYLONS

N•••O•

NACHOS
NANOOK
NARROW
NATION
NATRON
NEESON
NEKTON
NELSON
NESTOR
NETTON
NEUROL
NEURON
NEWTON
NIMROD
NIPPON
NOGOOD
NOIRON
NONCOM
NORTON
NOSHOW
NOTION
NOTNOW

N••••O

NAGANO
NAVAHO
NAVAJO
NEARTO
NEMATO
NEPHRO
NEXTTO
NICOLO
NIELLO
NIHILO
NINGBO
NONEGO
NUCLEO
NUMERO
NUNCIO

•NO•••

ANODES
ANODIC
ANOINT
ANOLES
ANOMIE
ANONYM
ANORAK
CNOTES
ENOKIS
ENOSIS
ENOUGH
GNOMES
GNOMIC
GNOMON
GNOSIS
INOUYE
KNOBBY
KNOCKS
KNOLLS
KNOTTS
KNOTTY
KNOWER
KNOWNS
SNOBBY
SNOCAT
SNOODS
SNOOKS
SNOOPS
SNOOPY
SNOOTS
SNOOTY
SNOOZE
SNOPES
SNORED
SNORER
SNORES
SNORTS
SNOUTS
SNOWED
SNOWIN
TNOTES
UNOPEN

•N•O••

ANCONA
ANGOLA
ANGORA
ANIONS
ANJOUS
ANNOYS
ANTONY
ANYONE
ENCODE
ENCORE
ENDORA
ENDOWS
ENFOLD
ENJOIN
ENJOYS
ENROBE
ENROLL
ENROOT
ENSOUL
ENVOIS
ENVOYS
INBORN
INCOME
INDOOR
INFOLD
INFORM
INGOTS
INIONS
INJOKE
INLOVE
INMOST
INPORT
INPOUR
INROAD
INSOLE
INTONE
INTOTO
INTOWN
INVOKE
ONFOOT
ONHOLD
ONIONS
ONIONY
ONLOAN
ONTOUR
SNOODS
SNOOKS
SNOOPS
SNOOPY
SNOOTS
SNOOTY
SNOOZE
UNBOLT
UNBORN
UNCOIL
UNCOOL
UNCORK
UNDOER
UNDOES
UNDONE
UNFOLD
UNHOLY
UNHOOK
UNIONS
UNLOAD
UNLOCK
UNMOOR
UNROBE
UNROLL
UNROOT
UNSOLD
UNSOWN
UNTOLD
UNTORN
UNWORN
UNWOVE
UNYOKE

•N••O•

ANALOG
ANCHOR
ANDHOW
ANDROS
ANGKOR
ANGLOS
ANTCOW
ANTRON
ANYHOW
ENAMOR
ENBLOC
ENROOT
GNOMON
INAFOG
INAROW
INCHON
INDOOR
INFLOW
INTROS
ONFOOT
UNCLOG
UNCOOL
UNHOOK
UNIPOD
UNISON
UNKNOT
UNMOOR
UNROOT
UNSHOD
UNSTOP
UNTROD

•N•••O

ANATTO
ANGELO
ANTERO
ENCINO
ENDURO
ENESCO
ENRICO
ENTERO
INDIGO
INITIO
INTOTO
INVIVO
ONETWO
SNAPTO
UNESCO

••NO••

ANNOYS
ARNOLD
BENOIT
CANOED
CANOES
CANOLA
CANONS
CANOPY
CANOVA
CENOTE
CONOCO
DENOTE
DENOVO
DONORS
FANOUT
GENOAN
GENOME
GONOGO
HONORE
HONORS
HONOUR
IGNORE
LANOSE
LENORE
MANORS
MINOAN
MINORS
MONODY
NANOOK
OENONE
PANOUT
PINOAK
PINOLE
PINONS
PINOTS
RANOFF
RANOUT
RENOIR
RENOTE
RENOWN
RUNOFF
RUNONS
RUNOUT
SENORA
SENORS
SONOMA
SONORA
SUNOCO
SYNODS
TANOAK
TANOAN
TENONS
TENORS
VENOMS
VENOUS
VINOUS
WINONA
WINOUT
WONOUT

••N•O•

AMNION
BANDOG
BANGOR
BANJOS
BANKON
BANLON
BENSON
BENTON
BENZOL
BONBON
BONGOS
BONMOT
BONTON
BUNCOS
BUNION
BUNKOS
CANDOR
CANNON
CANNOT
CANTON
CANTOR
CANTOS
CANYON
CENSOR
CENTOS
CONDOR
CONDOS
CONGOU
CONJOB
CONNOR
CONROY
CONVOY
DANSON
DANTON
DENTON
DINEON
DONJON
DUNLOP
FANDOM
FANION
GUNDOG
GUNFOR
HANDON
HANGON
HANSOM
HANSON
HENSON
HINTON
HUNGON
JONSON
JUNCOS
JUNIOR
JUNTOS
KANTOR
KENTON
KINDOF
LANDON
LANSON
LENNON
LONDON
LONNOL
LYNDON
MANGOS
MANIOC
MENJOU
MENTOR
MINION
MINNOW
MONGOL
MONROE
MUNGOS
NANOOK
NONCOM
PENNON
PENROD
PINION
PINSON
PINTOS
PINYON
PINZON
RANCOR
RANDOM
RANFOR
RANSOM
RONDOS
RUNSON
RUNYON
SANTOS
SENHOR
SENIOR
SENSOR
SUNDOG
SUNGOD
TANGOS
TENDON
TENSOR
TINGOD
TINPOT
VENDOR
VINTON
WANTON
WENTON
WINDOM
WINDOW
WINNOW
WINSOR
WONTON
WYNTON
YANGON
ZENDOS

••N••O

ALNICO
BANQUO
BENITO
BONITO
CENTRO
CONOCO
DENDRO
DENIRO
DENOVO
DINERO
DYNAMO
ELNINO
FINITO
GINKGO
GONOGO
GUNGHO
HONCHO
LANDHO
MONACO
NINGBO
NONEGO
NUNCIO
PANCHO
PINERO
PONCHO
RANCHO
RUNSTO
SANCHO
SANGTO
SINGTO
SUNOCO
TENDTO
TENUTO
VENETO
WANTTO
XANTHO
YUNGLO

•••NO•

ALANON
AMINOR
BEANOS
BMINOR
BUENOS
CANNON
CANNOT
CARNOT
CHINOS
CMINOR
CONNOR
CPSNOW
DMINOR
DOWNON
EGGNOG
ELINOR
EMINOR
ERENOW
ETHNOS
FMINOR
GAINON
GAYNOR
GMINOR
GOUNOD
GUENON
HOBNOB
HOWNOW
HYPNOS
IRONON
KERNOI
KERNOS
KRONOR
LEANON
LEMNOS
LENNON
LLANOS
LONNOL
MAGNON
MEMNON
MIGNON
MINNOW
NOTNOW
PENNON
PERNOD
PHENOL
PHENOM
PHONON
PHONOS
PIANOS
PLANON
QUINOA
RHINOS
SCHNOZ
SIGNON
SIGNOR
STENOG
STENOS
TAINOS
TURNON
UNKNOT
VERNON
WHYNOT
WINNOW

•••N•O

ALONSO
ALONZO
BOINGO
BORNEO
BRANDO
BRONCO
CRANIO
ERYNGO
EVENSO
FRANCO
GOINTO
GRINGO
LEANTO
ODONTO
OLINGO
OPENTO
PRONTO
SEENTO
SHINTO
TURNTO

••••NO

ACTINO
ADRENO
ALBANO
ALBINO
AQUINO
AVERNO
CAMINO
CASINO
CHRONO
CYRANO
DELANO
DOMINO
ELNINO
ENCINO
FRESNO
GITANO
IMMUNO
KIMONO
LADINO
LATINO
LUPINO
MARINO
MELANO
MERINO
MILANO
MORENO
MURANO
NAGANO
ORSINO
PACINO
PEPINO
POCONO
ROMANO
STERNO
STHENO
TECHNO
TORINO

N•P•••

NAPERY
NAPIER
NAPKIN
NAPLES
NAPOLI
NAPPED
NAPPER
NAPPES
NEPALI
NEPHEW
NEPHRO
NIPPED
NIPPER
NIPPON
NIPPUR
NIPSAT
NIPUPS
NOPETS

N••P••

NAPPED
NAPPER
NAPPES
NETPAY
NIPPED
NIPPER
NIPPON
NIPPUR
NYMPHS

N•••P•

NIPUPS

N••••P

NOSOAP

•NP•••

INPART
INPLAY
INPORT
INPOUR
INPUTS
UNPACK
UNPAID
UNPEGS
UNPENS
UNPILE

UNPINS
UNPLUG

•N•P••
INAPET
INSPAN
ONSPEC
SNAPAT
SNAPPY
SNAPTO
SNAPUP
SNIPED
SNIPES
SNIPPY
SNOPES
UNIPOD
UNOPEN

•N••P•
ENRAPT
INCEPT
ONEUPS
ONTAPE
SNAPPY
SNIPPY
SNOOPS
SNOOPY
UNCAPS
UNRIPE
UNZIPS

•N•••P
ANTEUP
ENCAMP
ENDSUP
ENTRAP
ENWRAP
INSTEP
SNAPUP
UNSNAP
UNSTOP
UNTRAP
UNWRAP

••NP••
PENPAL
TENPIN
TINPAN
TINPOT

••N•P•
CANAPE
CANOPY
LENAPE
PINUPS
RUNUPS
SUNUPS

••N••P
BANGUP
BINDUP
BONEUP
DONEUP
DUNLOP
GANGUP
HANGUP
HUNGUP
LINEUP
LINKUP
OWNSUP
PENTUP
PONYUP
RANGUP
RINGUP
RUNGUP
RUNSUP
SANNUP
SENDUP
SENTUP
TANKUP
TONEUP
TUNEUP
WENTUP
WINDUP

•••N•P
BURNUP
CATNAP
CATNIP
CHINUP
EVENUP
JOINUP
KIDNAP
OPENUP
SANNUP
SEWNUP
SIGNUP
TURNIP
TURNUP
UNSNAP

N•Q•••
NYQUIL

N••••Q
NASDAQ

•NQ•••
ENQUAD

•N•Q••
UNIQUE

••NQ••
BANQUO
CINQUE
MANQUE
YANQUI

N•R•••
NARIAL
NARNIA
NARROW
NARVIK
NARWAL
NEREID
NEREIS
NEREUS
NEROLI
NERUDA
NERVES
NORDIC
NORGAY
NORIAS
NORMAL
NORMAN
NORRIS
NORTON
NORWAY
NURSED
NURSER
NURSES

N••R••
NAIRAS
NARROW
NATRON
NEARBY
NEARED
NEARER
NEARLY
NEARTO
NEURAL
NEUROL
NEURON
NIMROD
NITRES
NITRIC
NOIRON
NORRIS
NUTRIA

N•••R•
NABORS
NADIRS
NAMERS
NAPERY
NATURE
NEPHRO
NEVERS
NEWARK
NFLERS
NHLERS
NINERS
NITERS
NOMORE
NONARY
NOTARY
NOTERS
NUMERO

N••••R
NABBER
NAGGER
NAILER
NAPIER
NAPPER
NASCAR
NASSER
NATTER
NEARER
NEATER
NECTAR
NESTER
NESTOR
NETHER
NEUTER
NEWMAR
NICKER
NIGHER
NIPPER
NIPPUR
NOBLER
NOSHER
NOSIER
NUDGER
NUMBER
NURSER
NUTTER

•NR•••
ENRAGE
ENRAPT
ENRICH
ENRICO
ENROBE
ENROLL
ENROOT
INROAD
INRUSH
ONRUSH
UNREAD
UNREAL
UNREEL
UNREST
UNRIGS
UNRIPE
UNROBE
UNROLL
UNROOT
UNRULY

•N•R••
ANDREA
ANDREI
ANDRES
ANDREW
ANDREY
ANDROS
ANORAK
ANTRES
ANTRIM
ANTRON
ANTRUM
ANURAN
ENDRUN
ENERGY
ENGRAM
ENTRAP
ENTREE
ENURED
ENURES
ENWRAP
GNARLS
GNARLY
INARCH
INAROW
INARUT
INBRED
INDRIS
INGRES
INGRID
INTROS
INURED
INURES
KNARRY
KNURLS
KNURLY
SNARED
SNARES
SNARLS
SNARLY
SNORED
SNORER
SNORES
SNORTS
UNARMS
UNDRAW
UNTRAP
UNTROD
UNTRUE
UNWRAP

•N••R•
ANGERS
ANGORA
ANITRA
ANKARA
ANTERO
ENCORE
ENDERS
ENDORA
ENDURE
ENDURO
ENGIRD
ENGIRT
ENSURE
ENTERO
ENTERS
ENTIRE
INBORN
INCURS
INDIRA
INFERS
INFIRM
INFORM
INHERE
INJURE
INJURY
INKERS
INPART
INPORT
INSERT
INSURE
INTERN
INTURN
INVERT
INWARD
KNARRY
ONFIRE
ONWARD
SNEERS
SNEERY
UNBARS
UNBORN
UNCORK
UNCURL
UNFURL
UNGIRD
UNGIRT
UNHURT
UNSURE
UNTORN
UNWARY
UNWORN

•N•••R
ANCHOR
ANGKOR
ANGLER
ANHYDR
ANSGAR
ANSWER
ANTHER
ANTLER
ENAMOR
ENDEAR
GNAWER
INANER
INDOOR
INGEAR
INGMAR
INKIER
INPOUR
INSTAR
KNOWER
ONAGER
ONTOUR
SNIDER
SNORER
SNYDER
UNDOER
UNFAIR
UNITER
UNMOOR

••NR••
CONRAD
CONROY
GENRES
HENRIK
KONRAD
MANRAY
MONROE
PENROD
SUNRAY
TENREC
VANRYN

••N•R•
BINARY
BONERS
CANARD
CANARY
CANERS
CENTRE
CENTRI
CENTRO
CONTRA
CONTRE
CUNARD
DENDRI
DENDRO
DENIRO
DINARS
DINERO
DINERS
DONORS
DUNERA
FINERY
GANTRY
GENERA
GENTRY
GONERS
HONORE
HONORS
HUNGRY
IGNORE
LANDRY
LENORE
LINERS
LONERS
LYNYRD
MANORS
MANTRA
MINERS
MINORS
MONERA
NINERS
NONARY
ORNERY
OWNERS
OXNARD
PANFRY
PANTRY
PENURY
PINERO
PINERY
RANDRY
RUNDRY
SANDRA
SENARY
SENORA
SENORS
SENTRY
SONORA
SUNDRY
TANTRA
TENORS
TENURE
TONERS
TUNDRA
TUNERS
VENIRE
VINERY
WANERS
WINERY
WINTRY

••N••R
BANGER
BANGOR
BANKER
BANNER
BANTER
BENDER
BENHUR
BINDER
BONIER
BUNKER
BUNTER
CANDOR
CANKER
CANNER
CANTER
CANTOR
CENSER
CENSOR
CENTER
CINDER
CONCUR
CONDOR
CONFER
CONGER
CONKER
CONNER
CONNOR
DANCER
DANDER
DANGER
DANKER
DANNER
DENIER
DENSER
DENVER
DINNER
DONDER
DONNER
DUNBAR
DUNKER
FENCER
FENDER
FINDER
FINGER
FONDER
GANDER
GENDER
GINGER
GUNFOR
GUNNAR
GUNNER
GUNTER
HANGAR
HANGER
HANKER
HENNER
HINDER
HINTER
HONKER
HONOUR
HUNGER
HUNKER
HUNTER
JENNER
JUNIOR
JUNKER
KANDER
KANTOR
KINDER
LANCER
LANDER
LANGUR
LANIER
LANKER
LENDER
LINEAR
LINGER
LINKER
LINTER
LONGER
LUNKER
MANGER
MANNER
MCNAIR
MENDER
MENHIR
MENTOR
MINCER
MINDER
MINTER
MONGER
PANDER
PANNER
PANZER
PENNER
PINCER
PINDAR
PINIER
PINKER
PINNER
PINTER
PONDER
PUNIER
PUNKER
PUNTER
QINTAR
RANCOR
RANFOR
RANGER
RANKER
RANTER
RENDER
RENOIR
RENTER
RINGER
RUNNER
SANDER
SANGER
SANTIR
SENDER
SENHOR
SENIOR
SENSOR
SINGER
SINKER
SINNER
SINTER
SUNDER
TANKER
TANNER
TENDER
TENSER
TENSOR
TENTER
TINDER
TINEAR
TINIER
TINKER
TINNER
TINTER
TONIER
VANIER
VENDOR
VENEER
VENTER
WANDER
WANNER
WINCER
WINDER
WINGER
WINKER
WINNER
WINSOR
WINTER
WONDER
WYNTER
YONDER
ZANDER
ZANIER
ZENGER
ZINGER
ZONKER

•••NR•
AMENRA
OHENRY

•••N•R
AMINOR
BANNER
BMINOR
BURNER
CANNER
CMINOR
COINER
CONNER
CONNOR
CORNER
DANNER
DARNER
DINNER
DMINOR
DONNER
DOWNER
DRONER
EARNER
EISNER
ELINOR
EMINOR
EVENER
FAFNIR
FAWNER
FMINOR
GAINER
GARNER
GAYNOR
GMINOR
GUNNAR
GUNNER
HEFNER
HENNER
HORNER
INANER
IRONER
JENNER
JOINER
JOYNER
KEENER
KRONER
KRONOR
KRONUR
LEANER
LERNER
LIMNER
LOANER
MANNER
MARNER
MEANER
MILNER
MOANER
MOLNAR
OPENER
OPINER
PANNER
PAWNER
PENNER
PINNER
PLANAR
PLANER
PRUNER
RADNER
RAINER
REINER
RUINER
RUNNER
SEINER
SHINER
SIGNER
SIGNOR
SINNER
SOONER
STONER
SUMNER
TANNER
TEENER
THENAR
TINNER
TOWNER
TURNER
VAINER
WAGNER
WANNER
WAPNER
WARNER
WERNER
WHINER
WIENER
WINNER
YAWNER

N•S•••
NASALS
NASCAR
NASDAQ
NASEBY
NASHUA
NASSAU
NASSER
NESSES
NESSIE
NESTEA
NESTED
NESTER
NESTLE
NESTOR
NISSAN
NISSEN
NOSALE
NOSHED
NOSHER
NOSHES
NOSHOW
NOSIER
NOSILY
NOSING
NOSOAP

N••S••
NANSEN
NASSAU
NASSER
NAUSEA
NAYSAY
NEESON
NEISSE
NELSON
NESSES
NESSIE
NEVSKY
NIPSAT
NISSAN
NISSEN
NOESIS
NOISED
NOISES
NOOSES
NURSED
NURSER
NURSES
NYASSA

N•••S•
NEISSE
NEWEST
NEWISH
NICEST
NLEAST
NLWEST
NODOSE
NOLESS
NOWISE
NUDIST
NYASSA

N••••S
NABOBS
NABORS
NACHOS
NADIRS
NAIADS
NAIRAS
NAMERS
NANTES
NAPLES
NAPPES
NASALS
NAVELS
NAVIES
NAWABS
NEIGHS
NENETS
NEREIS
NEREUS
NERVES
NESSES
NEUMES
NEVERS
NEVINS
NEWELS
NFLERS
NHLERS
NICHES
NIECES
NIGHTS
NIMBUS
NINERS
NINJAS
NINTHS
NIPUPS
NITERS
NITRES
NIXIES
NOBLES
NOESIS
NOHITS
NOISES
NOLENS
NOLESS
NOMADS
NONETS
NOOSES
NOPETS
NORIAS
NORRIS
NOSHES
NOTERS
NOVELS
NUDGES
NUECES
NURSES
NYALAS
NYLONS
NYMPHS

•NS•••
ANSATE
ANSELM
ANSGAR
ANSWER
ENSIGN
ENSILE
ENSOUL
ENSUED
ENSUES
ENSURE
INSANE
INSEAM
INSECT
INSERT
INSETS
INSIDE
INSIST
INSITU
INSOLE
INSPAN
INSTAR
INSTEP
INSULT
INSURE
INSYNC
ONSALE
ONSETS
ONSIDE
ONSITE
ONSPEC
UNSAFE
UNSAID
UNSAYS
UNSEAL
UNSEAT
UNSEEN
UNSEWN
UNSEWS
UNSHED
UNSHOD
UNSNAG
UNSNAP
UNSOLD
UNSOWN
UNSTOP
UNSUNG
UNSURE

•N•S••
ENDSUP
ENESCO
ENISLE
ENOSIS
GNOSIS
ONUSES
UNESCO
UNISEX
UNISON
UNUSED

•N••S•
ENCASE
ENDASH
ENDUSE
ENLIST
ENMESH
GNEISS
INCASE
INCASH
INCISE
INCUSE
INFEST
INFUSE
INGEST
INJEST
INMOST
INNESS
INRUSH
INSIST
INVEST
ONRUSH
UNCASE
UNEASE
UNEASY
UNJUST
UNLASH
UNLESS
UNMASK
UNMESH
UNREST
UNWISE

•N•••S
ANDRES
ANDROS
ANGELS
ANGERS
ANGLES
ANGLOS
ANIMAS
ANIMES
ANIMUS
ANIONS
ANJOUS
ANKLES
ANNALS
ANNOYS
ANNULS
ANODES
ANOLES
ANTICS
ANTRES
ANUBIS
ANVILS
CNIDUS
CNOTES
ENACTS
ENATES
ENDERS
ENDOWS
ENDUES
ENGELS
ENJOYS
ENNIUS
ENOKIS
ENOSIS
ENSUES
ENTERS
ENURES
ENVIES
ENVOIS
ENVOYS
GNARLS
GNEISS
GNOMES
GNOSIS
INCANS
INCHES
INCURS
INDIES
INDRIS
INFERS
INGLES
INGOTS
INGRES
INIONS
INKERS
INKLES
INLAWS
INLAYS
INLETS
INNESS
INPUTS
INSETS
INTENS
INTROS
INUITS
INURES
KNACKS
KNAVES
KNEADS
KNEELS
KNELLS
KNICKS
KNIFES
KNIVES
KNOCKS
KNOLLS
KNOTTS
KNOWNS
KNURLS
ONEUPS
ONIONS
ONSETS
ONUSES
ONYXES
SNACKS
SNAFUS
SNAILS
SNAKES
SNARES
SNARLS
SNATHS
SNEAKS
SNEERS
SNELLS
SNICKS
SNIFFS
SNIPES
SNOODS
SNOOKS
SNOOPS
SNOOTS
SNOPES
SNORES
SNORTS
SNOUTS
SNUFFS
TNOTES
UNARMS
UNBARS
UNCAPS
UNCLES
UNDIES
UNDOES
UNFITS
UNGUES
UNGUIS
UNIATS
UNIONS
UNITAS
UNITES
UNJAMS
UNLESS
UNMANS
UNPEGS
UNPENS
UNPINS
UNRIGS
UNSAYS
UNSEWS
UNTIES
UNZIPS
VNECKS

••NS••
BENSON
BONSAI
BUNSEN
CENSED
CENSER
CENSES
CENSOR
CENSUS
CONSUL
DANSON
DENSER
GUNSHY
HANSEL
HANSOM
HANSON
HENSON
HONSHU
JANSEN
JENSEN
JONSON
KANSAN
KANSAS
KINSKI
LANSON
LENSED
LENSES
LINSEY
MANSES
MENSAE
MENSAL
MENSAS
MENSCH
NANSEN
OWNSUP
PENSEE
PINSON
RANSOM
RINSED
RINSES
RUNSIN
RUNSON
RUNSTO
RUNSUP
SANSEI
SENSED
SENSEI
SENSES
SENSOR
SUNSET

TENSED
TENSER
TENSES
TENSOR
TINSEL
TONSIL
WINSOR

••N•S•

ARNESS
BANISH
DANISH
DENISE
DYNAST
ERNEST
FINEST
FINISH
HONEST
INNESS
LANOSE
MONISM
MONIST
PUNISH
SANEST
TANIST
TONISH
VANISH

••N••S

AENEAS
ANNALS
ANNOYS
ANNULS
ARNESS
BANJOS
BANTUS
BINGES
BONERS
BONGOS
BONNES
BONZES
BUNCOS
BUNKOS
CANALS
CANERS
CANIDS
CANNES
CANOES
CANONS
CANTOS
CANVAS
CENSES
CENSUS
CENTOS
CONCHS
CONDOS
CONEYS
CONGAS
CONICS
CONIES
CONTES
CYNICS
DANAUS
DANCES
DANTES
DENIES
DENIMS
DENNIS
DINARS
DINERS
DINGUS
DONEES
DONETS
DONNAS
DONORS
DONUTS
DUNCES
ENNIUS
FENCES
FINALS
FUNGUS
GANGES
GENETS
GENIES
GENIUS
GENRES
GONERS
HENNAS
HINDUS
HINGES
HONEYS
HONORS
INNESS
IONICS
JANHUS
JINXES
JUNCOS
JUNTAS
JUNTOS
KANSAS
LANAIS
LANCES
LANDIS
LENSES
LINENS
LINERS
LONERS
LONGES
LUNGES
LYNXES
MANAUS
MANGOS
MANIAS
MANORS
MANSES
MANTAS
MANTIS
MENDES
MENSAS
MENTIS
MINCES
MINERS
MINIMS
MINKES
MINORS
MINXES
MONADS
MONEYS
MONIES
MONTHS
MUNGOS
MYNAHS
NANTES
NENETS
NINERS
NINJAS
NINTHS
NONETS
OUNCES
OWNERS
PANDAS
PANELS
PANICS
PANNES
PENNIS
PINDUS
PINNAS
PINONS
PINOTS
PINTOS
PINUPS
PONIES
PONTES
PONTUS
QANTAS
RANEES
RANGES
RANIDS
RENEWS
RENNES
RINSES
RONDOS
RUNINS
RUNONS
RUNUPS
SANTOS
SENNAS
SENORS
SENSES
SINEWS
SINGES
SONDES
SONICS
SUNNIS
SUNUPS
SYNODS
TANGOS
TANKAS
TENETS
TENNIS
TENONS
TENORS
TENSES
TENTHS
TINCTS
TINGES
TONERS
TONICS
TONNES
TUNERS
TUNICS
VENOMS
VENOUS
VENUES
VINOUS
WANERS
WENCES
WINCES
WINZES
YENTAS
ZANIES
ZENDOS

•••NS•

ALONSO
EVENSO
FLENSE
GAINST
GDANSK
ODENSE
TEENSY
WEENSY

•••N•S

ACINUS
ADONIS
AGENAS
AGENTS
AKENES
ALINES
AMENDS
AMENTS
AMINES
AMINUS
ARENAS
ASANAS
ATONES
BAINES
BARNES
BEANOS
BEINGS
BLANKS
BLENDS
BLINDS
BLINKS
BLONDS
BLUNTS
BMINUS
BONNES
BOUNDS
BRANDS
BRANTS
BRENTS
BRINES
BRINGS
BRINKS
BRONCS
BRUNTS
BUENOS
BWANAS
BYRNES
CANNES
CARNES
CHANTS
CHINES
CHINKS
CHINOS
CHUNKS
CLANGS
CLANKS
CLINES
CLINGS
CLINKS
CLONES
CLONKS
CLONUS
CLUNKS
CMINUS
COUNTS
CRANES
CRANKS
CRONES
CRONUS
CYGNUS
DAUNTS
DENNIS
DMINUS
DOINGS
DONNAS
DRINGS
DRINKS
DRONES
EBONDS
ELANDS
EMENDS
ERINYS
ETHNOS
EVENTS
FAINTS
FAUNAS
FAUNUS
FEINTS
FIENDS
FLANKS
FLINGS
FLINTS
FLUNKS
FOUNDS
FOUNTS
FRANCS
FRANKS
FRONDS
FRONTS
GIANTS
GLANDS
GLINTS
GOINGS
GRANDS
GRANTS
GRINDS
GRUNTS
HAINES
HAUNTS
HENNAS
HMONGS
HOUNDS
HYENAS
HYPNOS
ICINGS
IRANIS
IRENES
JAUNTS
JOINTS
KAUNAS
KERNOS
KEYNES
KIANGS
LEMNOS
LEONES
LIANAS
LIANGS
LLANOS
MOINES
MOUNDS
MOUNTS
OMANIS
OPINES
ORANGS
ORANTS
ORINGS
PAINTS
PANNES
PARNIS
PENNIS
PHONES
PHONOS
PIANOS
PINNAS
PLANES
PLANKS
PLANTS
PLINKS
PLONKS
PLUNKS
POINTS
POUNDS
PRANKS
PRINKS
PRINTS
PRONGS
PRUNES
QUINTS
RAINES
REINKS
RENNES
REUNES
RHINOS
ROUNDS
RUANAS
SAINTS
SAUNAS
SCANTS
SCENAS
SCENDS
SCENES
SCENTS
SCONES
SEENAS
SEINES
SENNAS
SHANKS
SHINES
SHUNTS
SKINKS
SKUNKS
SLANGS
SLANTS
SLINGS
SLINKS
SOUNDS
SPANKS
SPENDS
SPINES
SPINKS
STANDS
STENOS
STINGS
STINKS
STINTS
STONES
STUNTS
SUNNIS
SWINGS
TAINOS
TAINTS
TAUNTS
TBONDS
TBONES
TENNIS
THANES
THANKS
THINGS
THINKS
THONGS
THUNKS
TONNES
TRENDS
TRINES
TRUNKS
TWANGS
TWINES
UPENDS
URANUS
VARNAS
VAUNTS
VIANDS
WHINES
WOUNDS
WRINGS
WRONGS
ZOUNDS

••••NS

ACORNS
ADDONS
ADORNS
ALIENS
ALIGNS
ALOINS
AMIENS
ANIONS
APRONS
ARYANS
ASIANS
ASPENS
ATHENS
ATKINS
AUDENS
AUXINS
AVIANS
AXIONS
BAIRNS
BARONS
BASINS
BATONS
BEGINS
BISONS
BOSUNS
BRAINS
BRIANS
BROWNS
BRUINS
BURINS
CABINS
CAIRNS
CAJUNS
CANONS
CAPONS
CHAINS
CHURNS
CLEANS
CLOWNS
CODONS
COLONS
COVENS
COWENS
COZENS
CROONS
CROWNS
CUTINS
DEIGNS
DEMONS
DIVANS
DOGONS
DOYENS
DOZENS
DRAINS
DROWNS
EOSINS
FEIGNS
FELONS
FOEHNS
FROWNS
FUTONS
GAMINS
GIVENS
GLEANS
GLUONS
GRAINS
GREENS
GROANS
GROINS
GYRONS
HAVENS
HAZANS
HELENS
HERONS
HOGANS
HUMANS
HURONS
INCANS
INIONS
INTENS
IOWANS
JAPANS
KNOWNS
LAPINS
LATENS
LATINS
LEARNS
LEMANS
LEMONS
LIKENS
LIMENS
LINENS
LIVENS
LODENS
LUDENS
LUMENS
LYSINS
MASONS
MATINS
MAVENS
MAYANS
MELONS
MESONS
MIZENS
MORONS
NEVINS
NOLENS
NYLONS
OCEANS
ONIONS
ORGANS
PAEANS
PAEONS
PAGANS
PARENS
PATENS
PECANS
PINONS
PISANS
PITONS
PLAINS
PRAWNS
PREENS
PRIONS
PUTONS
PYLONS
QUEENS
QUERNS
QUOINS
RACONS
RAVENS
RAYONS
RECONS
REIGNS
REMANS
RERUNS
RESINS
REWINS
RIPENS
ROBINS
ROMANS
ROSINS
ROWENS
RUBENS
RUMENS
RUNINS
RUNONS
SABINS
SALONS
SARANS
SATINS
SAXONS
SCIONS
SCORNS
SEDANS
SERINS
SETINS
SEVENS
SHEENS
SIRENS
SITINS
SKEANS
SKEINS
SOLANS
SPAWNS
SPOONS
SPURNS
STAINS
STEINS
STERNS
SWAINS
SWOONS
TAKINS
TALONS
TAPINS
TAUONS
TENONS
TETONS
TEXANS
THORNS
TIEINS
TIPINS
TITANS
TOEINS
TOKENS
TOXINS
TOYONS
TRAINS
UCLANS
UHLANS
UNIONS
UNMANS
UNPENS
UNPINS
UTURNS
VALENS
VEGANS
VIXENS
VOLANS
VOLENS
VSIGNS
WAGONS
WAKENS
WIDENS
WIZENS
WOMENS
YEARNS
ZAYINS

N•T•••

NATANT
NATHAN
NATICK
NATION
NATIVE
NATRON
NATTER
NATURE
NETHER
NETMAN
NETMEN
NETPAY
NETTED
NETTLE
NETTON
NITERS
NITRES
NITRIC
NITWIT
NOTARY
NOTATE
NOTBAD
NOTERS
NOTICE
NOTIFY
NOTING
NOTION
NOTNOW
NOTYET
NUTATE
NUTKIN
NUTLET
NUTMEG
NUTRIA
NUTTED
NUTTER

N••T••

NANTES
NATTER
NAUTCH
NEATEN
NEATER
NEATLY
NECTAR
NEKTON
NESTEA
NESTED
NESTER
NESTLE
NESTOR
NETTED
NETTLE
NETTON
NEUTER
NEWTON
NEXTTO
NINTHS
NOETIC
NOOTKA
NORTON
NUTTED
NUTTER

N•••T•

NAMATH
NEARTO
NEGATE
NEMATO
NENETS
NEXTTO
NICETY
NIGHTS
NIGHTY
NIKITA
NIMITZ
NINETY
NOHITS
NONETS
NOPETS
NOTATE
NUDITY
NUTATE

N••••T

NATANT
NAUGHT
NEEDNT
NEWEST
NICEST
NIPSAT
NITWIT
NLEAST
NLWEST
NOCENT
NOEXIT
NONFAT
NOTYET
NOUGAT
NOUGHT
NUDIST
NUGENT
NUGGET
NUMBAT
NUTLET

•NT•••

ANTCOW
ANTEED
ANTERO
ANTEUP
ANTHEM
ANTHER
ANTICS
ANTLER
ANTONY
ANTRES
ANTRIM
ANTRON
ANTRUM
ENTAIL
ENTERO
ENTERS
ENTICE
ENTIRE
ENTITY
ENTRAP
ENTREE
INTACT
INTAKE
INTEND
INTENS
INTENT
INTERN
INTIMA
INTIME
INTINE
INTONE
INTOTO
INTOWN
INTROS
INTUIT
INTUNE
INTURN
ONTAPE
ONTIME
ONTOUR
UNTACK
UNTIDY
UNTIED
UNTIES
UNTOLD
UNTORN
UNTRAP
UNTROD
UNTRUE
UNTUNE

•N•T••

ANATTO
ANITRA
CNOTES
ENATES
INITIO
INSTAR
INSTEP
KNOTTS
KNOTTY
ONETWO
SNATCH
SNATHE
SNATHS
SNITCH
TNOTES
UNITAL
UNITAS
UNITED
UNITER
UNITES
UNSTOP

•N••T•

ANATTO
ANSATE
ENACTS
ENMITY
ENTITY
INCITE
INDITE
INGOTS
INLETS
INMATE
INNATE
INPUTS
INSETS
INSITU
INTOTO
INUITS
INVITE
INWITH
KNOTTS
KNOTTY
ONSETS
ONSITE
SNAPTO
SNOOTS
SNOOTY
SNORTS
SNOUTS
UNFITS
UNIATE
UNIATS

•N•••T

ANKLET
ANOINT
ENFANT
ENGIRT
ENGLUT
ENLIST
ENRAPT
ENROOT
INAPET
INARUT
INCEPT
INCULT
INDEBT
INDENT
INDICT
INDUCT
INFACT
INFANT
INFECT
INFEST
INGEST
INJECT
INJEST
INMOST
INPART
INPORT
INSECT
INSERT
INSIST
INSULT
INTACT
INTENT
INTUIT
INVENT
INVERT
INVEST
KNIGHT
ONFOOT
SNAPAT
SNOCAT
UNBELT
UNBENT
UNBOLT
UNGIRT
UNHURT
UNJUST
UNKNIT
UNKNOT
UNMEET
UNREST
UNROOT
UNSEAT

••NT••

AUNTIE
BANTAM
BANTER
BANTUS
BENTON
BONTON
BUNTED
BUNTER
CANTAB
CANTED
CANTER
CANTHI
CANTLE
CANTON
CANTOR
CANTOS
CENTER
CENTOS
CENTRE
CENTRI
CENTRO
CONTAC
CONTES
CONTRA
CONTRE
DANTES
DANTON
DENTAL
DENTED
DENTIL
DENTIN
DENTON
DINTED
FANTAN
FONTAL
GANTRY
GENTLE
GENTLY
GENTRY
GUNTER
HINTAT
HINTED
HINTER
HINTON
HUNTED
HUNTER
JUNTAS
JUNTOS
KANTOR
KENTON
LENTEN
LENTIL
LINTEL
LINTER
MANTAS
MANTEL
MANTIC
MANTIS
MANTLE
MANTRA
MANTUA
MENTAL
MENTIS
MENTOR
MINTED
MINTER
MONTEL
MONTEZ
MONTHS
MUNTIN
NANTES
NINTHS
PANTED
PANTRY
PENTAD
PENTUP
PINTER
PINTLE
PINTOS
PONTES
PONTIC
PONTUS
PUNTED
PUNTER
QANTAS
QINTAR
RANTED
RANTER
RENTAL
RENTED
RENTER
SANTEE
SANTIR
SANTOS
SENTIN
SENTRY
SENTUP
SINTAX
SINTER
SONTAG
SUNTAN
SYNTAX
TANTRA
TENTED
TENTER
TENTHS
TINTED
TINTER
VENTED
VENTER
VINTON
WANTAD
WANTED
WANTIN
WANTON
WANTTO
WENTAT
WENTBY
WENTIN
WENTON
WENTUP
WINTER
WINTRY
WONTED
WONTON
WYNTER
WYNTON
XANTHO
YENTAS

••N•T•

ADNATE
AGNATE
ARNETT
BENITO
BINATE
BONITO
CANUTE
CENOTE
DENOTE
DONATE
DONETS
DONITZ
DONUTS
FINITE
FINITO
GENETS
IGNATZ
IGNITE
INNATE
LANATE
LENGTH
LENITY
LUNATE
MINUTE
MONETA
NENETS
NINETY
NONETS
ORNATE
ORNITH
PINATA
PINITE
PINOTS
RENATA
RENOTE
RUNSTO
SANCTA
SANGTO
SANITY
SENATE
SINGTO
SONATA
TENDTO
TENETS
TENUTO
TINCTS
TONITE
VANITY
VENETO
VENITE
WANTTO
ZENITH
ZONATE

••N••T

ARNETT
BANDIT
BENOIT
BONMOT
BONNET
CANNOT
CONANT
DUNANT
DYNAST
ERNEST
FANJET
FANOUT
FINEST

GANNET
HENBIT
HINTAT
HONEST
JENNET
JUNKET
LANCET
LINNET
MINUET
MINUIT
MONIST
NONFAT
PANDIT
PANOUT
PENULT
PINXIT
PUNDIT
RANOUT
RENNET
RUNLET
RUNOUT
SANEST
SENNET
SENNIT
SONANT
SONNET
SUNLIT
SUNSET
TANIST
TENANT
TINHAT
TINPOT
WENTAT
WINGIT
WINKAT
WINOUT
WONOUT

•••NT•
AGENTS
AJANTA
AMENTS
AVANTI
BLINTZ
BLUNTS
BOUNTY
BRANTS
BRENTS
BRONTE
BRUNTS
CHANTS
CHINTZ
COUNTS
COUNTY
DAINTY
DAUNTS
EVENTS
FAINTS
FEINTS
FLINTS
FLINTY
FOUNTS
FRONTS
GIANTS
GLINTS
GOINTO
GRANTS
GRUNTS
HAUNTS
JAUNTS
JAUNTY
JOINTS
KOONTZ
KRANTZ
LEANTO
MOUNTS
MOUNTY
ODONTO
OPENTO
ORANTS
PAINTS
PLANTE
PLANTS
PLENTY
PLINTH
POINTE
POINTS
POINTY
PRINTS
PRONTO
PUENTE
QUANTA
QUINTS
SAINTE
SAINTS
SCANTS
SCANTY
SCENTS
SEENTO
SHANTY
SHINTO
SHUNTS
SLANTS
STINTS
STUNTS
TAINTS
TAUNTS
TURNTO
TWENTY
VAUNTS

•••N•T
ARENDT
BONNET
BOWNET
BRANDT
BRUNET
BURNET
CANNOT
CAPNUT
CARNET
CARNOT
CORNET
CYGNET
DARNIT
FLYNET
GAINST
GANNET
GARNET
HORNET
JENNET
LINNET
LIONET
LUGNUT
MAGNET
PEANUT
PIGNUT
PLANET
RENNET
SENNET
SENNIT
SIGNET
SONNET
SPINET
UNKNIT
UNKNOT
WALNUT
WHYNOT

••••NT
ABSENT
ACCENT
ADVENT
AGLINT
AMOUNT
ANOINT
ARDENT
ARGENT
ARPENT
ARRANT
ASCENT
ASLANT
ASSENT
AUMONT
AVAUNT
BESANT
BEZANT
BRYANT
CADENT
CEMENT
CLIENT
COGENT
CONANT
COVENT
DECANT
DECENT
DETENT
DISANT
DOCENT
DOESNT
DOPANT
DUMONT
DUNANT
DUPONT
DURANT
EGMONT
ENFANT
ERRANT
ESCENT
EXEUNT
EXTANT
EXTENT
FLAUNT
FLUENT
FOMENT
FORINT
GERENT
GERONT
HAVENT
INDENT
INFANT
INTENT
INVENT
LAMENT
LAMONT
LATENT
LEARNT
LEVANT
LUCENT
MOMENT
MORANT
MUSTNT
MUTANT
NATANT
NEEDNT
NOCENT
NUGENT
OCTANT
ORIENT
PARENT
PATENT
PEDANT
PLAINT
PLIANT
POTENT
QUAINT
RECANT
RECENT
REDANT
REGENT
RELENT
REPENT
RERENT
RESENT
RIDENT
RODENT
SAVANT
SECANT
SEJANT
SILENT
SOLENT
SONANT
SPLINT
SPRINT
SQUINT
TALENT
TENANT
TRUANT
TYRANT
UNBENT
URGENT
UTHANT
VACANT
VALENT
VIVANT
VOLANT
WERENT
WISENT

NU••••
NUANCE
NUBBED
NUBBIN
NUBBLE
NUBIAN
NUBILE
NUCHAE
NUCHAL
NUCLEI
NUCLEO
NUDGED
NUDGER
NUDGES
NUDIST
NUDITY
NUDNIK
NUECES
NUGENT
NUGGET
NUKING
NULLAH
NULLED
NUMBAT
NUMBED
NUMBER
NUMBLY
NUMERO
NUMINA
NUNCIO
NURSED
NURSER
NURSES
NUTATE
NUTKIN
NUTLET
NUTMEG
NUTRIA
NUTTED
NUTTER
NUZZLE

N•U•••
NAUGHT
NAUSEA
NAUTCH
NEUMAN
NEUMES
NEURAL
NEUROL
NEURON
NEUTER
NGUYEN
NOUGAT
NOUGHT
NOUMEA

N••U••
NATURE
NEBULA
NERUDA
NIPUPS
NODULE
NYQUIL

N•••U•
NASHUA
NEREUS
NIMBUS
NIPPUR

N••••U
NASSAU

•NU•••
ANUBIS
ANURAN
ENURED
ENURES
INUITS
INURED
INURES
KNURLS
KNURLY
ONUSES
SNUFFS
SNUFFY
SNUGLY
UNUSED

•N•U••
ANNUAL
ANNULI
ANNULS
ENDUED
ENDUES
ENDURE
ENDURO
ENDUSE
ENGULF
ENOUGH
ENQUAD
ENSUED
ENSUES
ENSURE
INBULK
INCULT
INCURS
INCUSE
INDUCE
INDUCT
INFULL
INFUSE
INHUME
INJURE
INJURY
INLUCK
INOUYE
INPUTS
INRUSH
INSULT
INSURE
INTUIT
INTUNE
INTURN
ONEUPS
ONRUSH
PNEUMA
SNOUTS
UNCURL
UNDULY
UNFURL
UNGUAL
UNGUES
UNGUIS
UNHURT
UNJUST
UNRULY
UNSUNG
UNSURE
UNTUNE

•N••U•
ANIMUS
ANJOUS
ANTEUP
ANTRUM
CNIDUS
ENDRUN
ENDSUP
ENGLUT
ENNIUS
ENSOUL
INARUT
INDIUM
INFLUX
INHAUL
INPOUR
ONTOUR
SNAFUS
SNAPUP
UNGLUE
UNIQUE
UNPLUG
UNTRUE

•N•••U
INSITU

••NU••
ANNUAL
ANNULI
ANNULS
BENUMB
BUNUEL
CANUTE
DANUBE
DENUDE
DONUTS
EUNUCH
GENUAL
LUNULA
MANUAL
MANUEL
MINUET
MINUIT
MINUTE
PENULT
PENURY
PINUPS
RUNUPS
SUNUNU
SUNUPS
TENURE
TENUTO
VENUES
ZANUCK

••N•U•
BANGUI
BANGUP
BANJUL
BANQUO
BANTUS
BENHUR
BINDUP
BONEUP
BUNKUM
CANCUN
CENSUS
CINQUE
CONCUR
CONIUM
CONSUL
DANAUS
DENGUE
DINGUS
DONEUP
ENNIUS
FANOUT
FONDUE
FUNGUS
GANGUE
GANGUP
GENIUS
HANGUL
HANGUP
HINDUS
HONOUR
HUNGUP
IONIUM
JANHUS
KUNLUN
LANGUR
LINEUP
LINGUA
LINKUP
LONGUE
MANAUS
MANFUL
MANQUE
MANTUA
MINIUM
OMNIUM
OWNSUP
PANOUT
PENTUP
PINDUS
PONTUS
PONYUP
RANGUP
RANOUT
RINGUP
RUNGUP
RUNOUT
RUNSUP
SANNUP
SENDUP
SENTUP
SINFUL
TANGUY
TANKUP
TONEUP
TONGUE
TUNEUP
VENOUS
VINOUS
WENTUP
WINDUP
WINOUT
WONMUG
WONOUT
YANQUI

••N••U
CONGOU
HONSHU
HUNGWU
JUNEAU
KUNGFU
LANDAU
MANCHU
MENJOU
PENGHU
SUNUNU
XANADU

•••NU•
ACINUS
AMINUS
AVENUE
BARNUM
BMINUS
BURNUP
CAPNUT
CHINUP
CLONUS
CMINUS
CRONUS
CYGNUS
DMINUS
EVENUP
FAUNUS
FRENUM
JOINUP
KRONUR
LUGNUT
MAGNUM
OPENUP
PEANUT
PIGNUT
PLENUM
SANNUP
SEWNUP
SIGNUP
TURNUP
URANUS
WALNUT

•••N•U
MBUNDU

••••NU
SUNUNU
VISHNU

N•V•••
NAVAHO
NAVAJO
NAVELS
NAVIES
NEVADA
NEVERS
NEVINS
NEVSKY
NOVELS
NOVENA
NOVICE

N••V••
NARVIK
NERVES

N•••V•
NATIVE

•NV•••
ANVILS
ENVIED
ENVIES
ENVOIS
ENVOYS
INVADE
INVAIN
INVENT
INVERT
INVEST
INVITE
INVIVO
INVOKE
ONVIEW
UNVEIL

•N•V••
KNAVES
KNIVES
SNIVEL
UNEVEN
UNIVAC

•N••V•
ENDIVE
INLOVE
INVIVO
UNWOVE

••NV••
CANVAS
CONVEX
CONVEY
CONVOY
DENVER
LANVIN

••N•V•
CANOVA
DENOVO
GENEVA
GENEVE

N•W•••
NAWABS
NEWAGE
NEWARK
NEWELS
NEWEST
NEWISH
NEWLEY
NEWMAN
NEWMAR
NEWTON
NLWEST
NOWISE

N••W••
NARWAL
NITWIT
NORWAY

N••••W
NARROW
NEPHEW
NOSHOW
NOTNOW

•NW•••
ENWRAP
INWARD
INWITH
ONWARD
UNWARY
UNWELL
UNWIND
UNWISE
UNWORN
UNWOVE
UNWRAP

•N•W••
ANSWER
ANYWAY
GNAWED
GNAWER
INAWAY
KNOWER
KNOWNS
ONEWAY
SNOWED
SNOWIN
UNAWED

•N••W•
ENDOWS
INLAWS
INTOWN
ONETWO
UNSEWN
UNSEWS
UNSOWN

•N•••W
ANDHOW
ANDREW
ANTCOW
ANYHOW
INAROW
INFLOW
ONVIEW
UNDRAW

••NW••
CONWAY
RUNWAY
WINWIN

••N•W•
HUNGWU
RENEWS
RENOWN
SINEWS
SINEWY

••N••W
MINNOW
SUNDEW
WINDOW
WINNOW

•••N•W
CPSNOW
ERENOW
HOWNOW
MINNOW
NOTNOW
WINNOW

N•X•••
NEXTTO
NIXIES
NIXING

N••X••
NOEXIT

•N•X••
ONYXES

•N••X•
ANNEXE

•N•••X
INAFIX
INFLUX
UNISEX

••NX••
JINXED
JINXES
LYNXES
MINXES
PINXIT

••N•X•
ANNEXE
CUNAXA

••N••X
BENDIX
CONVEX
MANNIX
MENINX
SINTAX
SYNTAX
WINDEX

•••N•X
BRANDX
MANNIX

••••NX
LARYNX
MENINX
SPHINX
SYRINX

NY••••
NYALAS
NYASSA
NYLONS
NYMPHS
NYQUIL

N•Y•••
NAYSAY

N••Y••
NGUYEN
NOTYET

N•••Y•
NAGOYA

N••••Y
NAMELY
NAPERY
NASEBY
NAYSAY
NEARBY
NEARLY
NEATLY
NETPAY
NEVSKY
NEWLEY
NIAMEY
NICELY
NICETY
NIGHTY
NIMBLY
NIMINY
NINETY
NOBODY
NONARY
NORGAY
NORWAY
NOSILY
NOTARY
NOTIFY
NUDITY
NUMBLY

•NY•••
ANYHOW
ANYONE
ANYWAY
ONYXES
SNYDER
UNYOKE

•N•Y••
ANHYDR
ENZYME
INSYNC
UNDYED

•N••Y•
ANNOYS
ANONYM
ENJOYS
ENVOYS
INLAYS
INOUYE
UNSAYS

•N•••Y
ANDREY
ANTONY
ANYWAY
ENERGY
ENMITY
ENTITY
GNARLY
INAWAY
INFAMY
INJURY
INPLAY
KNARRY
KNOBBY
KNOTTY
KNURLY
ONEDAY
ONEWAY
ONIONY
SNAGGY
SNAPPY
SNARLY
SNAZZY
SNEAKY
SNEERY
SNEEZY
SNIFFY
SNIPPY
SNOBBY
SNOOPY
SNOOTY
SNUFFY
SNUGLY
UNDULY
UNEASY
UNHOLY
UNRULY
UNTIDY
UNWARY

••NY••
BANYAN
BUNYAN
CANYON
KENYAN
LYNYRD
MINYAN
PINYIN
PINYON
PONYUP
RUNYON

••N•Y•
ANNOYS
CONEYS
HONEYS
KENNYG
MONEYS
VANRYN

••N••Y
BENDAY
BENGAY
BINARY
CANARY
CANOPY
CONROY
CONVEY
CONVOY
CONWAY
DANGLY
DANNAY
DINGHY
DINKEY
DONKEY
FINELY
FINERY
FINNEY
FONDLY
GANGLY
GANTRY
GENTLY
GENTRY
GONEBY
GUNSHY
HENLEY
HUNGRY
JANGLY
JINGLY
JUNGLY
KINDLY
KINGLY
LANDRY
LANKLY
LENITY
LINSEY
LONELY
LUNACY
LYNLEY
MANDAY
MANRAY
MINIFY
MONDAY
MONKEY
MONODY
NINETY
NONARY
ORNERY
PANFRY
PANTRY
PENNEY
PENURY
PINERY
PUNCHY
PUNILY
RANDRY
RANKLY
RONELY
RUNDRY
RUNWAY
SANELY
SANITY
SENARY
SENTRY
SINEWY
SINGLY
SUNDAY
SUNDRY
SUNRAY
TANGLY
TANGUY
TINGLY
TINKLY
TUNNEY
VANITY
VINERY
WENTBY
WINERY
WINTRY
ZANILY

•••NY•
ANONYM
CRONYN
EPONYM
ERINYS
KENNYG
PHENYL

•••N•Y
AGENCY
BARNEY
BIRNEY
BOUNCY
BOUNTY
BRANDY
BRONZY
BURNEY
CAGNEY
CARNEY
CHANCY
CHANEY
CHINKY
CHUNKY
CLANCY
CLANKY
CLINGY
CLUNKY
COONEY
COUNTY
CRANKY
CRANNY
DABNEY
DAINTY
DANNAY
DARNAY
DISNEY
DOWNEY
EVENLY
FINNEY
FLINTY
FLUNKY
FRANNY
FRENZY
FRINGY
GAINLY
GRANNY
GRUNDY
GRUNGY
GURNEY
HORNEY
JAUNTY
JITNEY
JOHNNY
JOUNCY
KEENLY
KIDNEY
LEANLY
LOONEY
MAINLY
MAUNDY
MEANLY
MOONEY
MORNAY
MOUNTY
OHENRY
OPENLY
ORKNEY
PENNEY
PLENTY
POINTY
QUINCY
RODNEY
ROMNEY
ROONEY
SCANTY
SHANDY
SHANTY
SHINDY
SHINNY
SIDNEY
SKINNY
SLANGY
SLINKY
SPANKY
SPONGY
SPUNKY
STANKY
STINGY
STINKY
SWANKY
SWINGY
SYDNEY
TEENSY
THINLY
TRENDY
TUNNEY
TWANGY
TWENTY
VAINLY
VARNEY
WATNEY
WEENSY
WHINNY

••••NY
ALBANY
ANTONY
BARONY
BETONY

BOIGNY
BOTANY
BRAINY
BRAWNY
BRYONY
COLONY
CRANNY
CZERNY
DELANY
FELONY
FRANNY
GRAINY
GRANNY
GREENY
GROZNY
HOMINY
JIMINY
JOHNNY
LEMONY
LITANY
MUTINY
NIMINY
ONIONY
PIMINY
ROMANY
ROSINY
SATINY
SAXONY
SHINNY
SIMONY
SKINNY
SOMANY
SPOONY
THORNY
WHINNY

N•Z•••
NOZZLE
NUZZLE

N••Z••
NOZZLE
NUZZLE

N••••Z
NIMITZ

•NZ•••
ENZYME
UNZIPS

•N•Z••
SNAZZY

•N••Z•
SNAZZY
SNEEZE
SNEEZY
SNOOZE

••NZ••
BANZAI
BENZOL
BONZES
DANZIG
DENZEL
PANZER
PINZON
WINZES

••N•Z•
IONIZE

••N••Z
DONITZ
IGNATZ
MONTEZ

•••NZ•
ALONZO
BRONZE
BRONZY
FAENZA
FRENZY
KWANZA
STANZA

•••N•Z
BLINTZ
CHINTZ
KOONTZ
KRANTZ
SCHNOZ

••••NZ
BRIENZ
LORENZ

OA••••
OAFISH
OAKLEY
OARING
OATERS
OATIER
OAXACA

O•A•••
OCASEK
OCASEY
OKAPIS
OKAYED
OMAHAN
OMAHAS
OMANIS
OMASUM
ONAGER
OPAQUE
ORACLE
ORALES
ORALLY
ORANGE
ORANGS
ORANTS
ORATED
ORATES
ORATOR
OSAGES
OXALIS
OZARKS

O••A••
OAXACA
OBEAHS
OBLAST
OBLATE
OBTAIN
OCEANS
OCTADS
OCTANE
OCTANT
OCTAVE
OCTAVO
OFLATE
OGHAMS
OGLALA
OLEARY
OLEATE
ONCALL
ONHAND
ONLAND
ONSALE
ONTAPE
ONWARD
OOLALA
OPIATE
ORBACH
ORDAIN
OREADS
ORGANA
ORGANS
ORGATE
ORIANA
ORNATE
OSCARS
OSHAWA
OSWALD
OTTAVA
OTTAWA
OUTACT
OUTAGE
OUTATE
OXCART
OXNARD
OXTAIL

O•••A•
OBIWAN
OBRIAN
OCREAE
OCULAR
OFFDAY
OGDOAD
OHIOAN
OHYEAH
OILCAN
OILMAN
OILPAN
OLDHAM
OLDHAT
OLDMAN
OMAHAN
OMAHAS
OMEGAS
ONEDAY
ONEWAY
ONLOAN
OOMPAH
OPERAS
ORDEAL
ORGEAT
ORPHAN
OSSIAN
OSTEAL
OUTEAT
OUTLAW
OUTLAY
OUTRAN
OVISAC
OVULAR

O••••A
OAXACA
OBELIA
ODESSA
ODETTA
OEDEMA
OGLALA
OJIBWA
OLINDA
OLIVIA
OMERTA
ONEIDA
OOLALA
OPTIMA
OREIDA
ORGANA
ORIANA
ORISSA
ORTEGA
OSCULA
OSHAWA
OTTAVA
OTTAWA

•OA•••
BOARDS
BOASTS
BOATED
BOATER
COALER
COAPTS
COARSE
COASTS
COATED
COATIS
COAXED
COAXER
COAXES
DOABLE
FOALED
FOAMED
GOADED
GOALIE
GOANNA
GOATEE
GOAWAY
GOAWRY
HOAGIE
HOARDS
HOARSE
HOAXED
HOAXER
HOAXES
JOANIE
JOANNA
JOANNE
KOALAS
LOADED
LOADER
LOAFED
LOAFER
LOAMED
LOANED
LOANER
LOATHE
LOAVES
MOANED
MOANER
MOATED
POACHY
ROADIE
ROAMED
ROAMER
ROARED
ROARER
ROASTS
SOAKED
SOAKER
SOAKUP
SOAPED
SOAPER
SOARED
SOARER
SOARES
SOASTO
SOAVES
TOAMAN
TOASTS
TOASTY
TOATEE

•O•A••
AODAIS
BOGART
BONAMI
BORAGE
BORATE
BORAXO
BOTANY
BOVARY
BOYARS
COBALT
COLADA
COMATE
CONANT
CORALS
COWARD
DOMAIN
DOMANI
DONALD
DONATE
DOPANT
DORADO
DORATI
DOSAGE
DOTAGE
DOTARD
FORAGE
FORAYS
GOBACK
GOCART
GODARD
GOEASY
GOKART
GORALS
HOBART
HODADS
HOGANS
HOMAGE
HORACE
HOTAIR
HOWARD
IODATE
IOWANS
JOHANN
KODALY
KORATS
KOVACS
LOBATE
LOCALE
LOCALS
LOCATE
LOTAHS
LOVAGE
MOHAIR
MOHAVE
MOHAWK
MOJAVE
MOLARS
MONACO
MONADS
MORALE
MORALS
MORANT
MORASS
MORAVA
MORAYS
MOSAIC
MOZART
NOMADS
NONAGE
NONAME
NONARY
NOSALE
NOTARY
NOTATE
OOLALA
POLAND
POMACE
POMADE
POPART
POSADA
POTAGE
POTASH
POTATO
ROBALO
ROLAND
ROMAIC
ROMAJI
ROMANO
ROMANS
ROMANY
RONALD
ROSARY
ROTARY
ROTATE
ROXANA
ROXANE
ROYALE
ROYALS
SOCAGE
SOLACE
SOLANS
SOMALI
SOMANY
SOMATA
SOMATO
SONANT
SONATA
SOUARI
TOBAGO
TODATE
TOGAED
TOKAYS
TOMATO
TORAHS
TOTALS
TOWAGE
TOWARD
VOCALS
VOLANS
VOLANT
VOLARE
VOTARY
VOYAGE
YOUALL
ZONATE
ZOUAVE

•O••A•
AORTAE
AORTAL
AORTAS
AOUDAD
BOBCAT
BOMBAY
BONSAI
BOREAL
BOREAS
BORMAN
BOWMAN
BOWOAR
BOWSAW
BOXCAR
COBHAM
COBIAS
COBRAS
COCOAS
COEVAL
COGNAC
COLLAR
COLMAN
COMBAT
COMEAT
COMMAS
COMPAQ
COMSAT
CONFAB
CONGAS
CONMAN
CONRAD
CONTAC
CONWAY
COOGAN
CORBAN
CORDAY
CORRAL
COSTAE
COSTAL
COSTAR
COSTAS
COTTAS
COUGAR
COWMAN
DOBLAS
DOBRAS
DOGEAR
DOGMAS
DOGTAG
DOLLAR
DOLMAN
DOLMAS
DONNAS
DOODAD
DORCAS
DORIAN
DORSAL
DOSSAL
DOTHAN
EOLIAN
EONIAN
FOGHAT
FOLIAR
FONTAL
FORBAD
FORMAL
FORMAN
FORMAT
FORTAS
FOSSAE
FOSSAS
FOVEAE
GOAWAY
GOESAT
GOSTAG
GOTHAM
GOTMAD
HOOHAH
HOOHAS
HOOKAH
HOORAH
HOORAY
HOOTAT
HOSTAS
HOTCAP
HOTCAR
HOTWAR
HOWDAH
IONIAN
JORDAN
JOSIAH
JOVIAL
JOVIAN
KOALAS
KODIAK
KONRAD
KOREAN
KORMAN
KOUFAX
LOGJAM
LONGAN
LOOFAH
LOOKAT
LOQUAT
LOREAL
LOTHAR
LOWCAL
LOWFAT
MOBCAP
MOCHAS
MOLDAU
MOLNAR
MOMMAS
MONDAY
MOOLAH
MOREAU
MORGAN
MORNAY
MORTAL
MORTAR
MOSHAV
NOLEAD
NOLOAD
NONFAT
NOONAN
NORGAY
NORIAS
NORMAL
NORMAN
NORWAY
NOSOAP
NOTBAD
NOUGAT
OOMPAH
POKEAT
POLEAX
POLKAS
POPLAR
POPPAS
PORTAL
POSTAL
RODHAM
ROSEAU
SOCIAL
SOLDAN
SOLFAS
SONTAG
SOTHAT
SOWHAT
TOAMAN
TOBIAS
TODDAO
TODMAN
TOECAP
TOETAP
TOKLAS
TOMBAC
TOMCAT
TONGAN
TOOBAD
TOPCAT
TOPHAT
TOREAT
TOUCAN
TOWCAR
VOLVAS
WOMBAT
ZODIAC

•O•••A
BODEGA
BOGOTA
BORGIA
BOSNIA
COLADA
COLIMA
CONCHA
CONTRA
COPULA
CORNEA
CORONA
CORYZA
COVINA
COWPEA
DODECA
DODOMA
GOANNA
GODIVA
GOTCHA
HOOPLA
HOTTEA
JOANNA
JOJOBA
JOSHUA
KONICA
KORUNA
LOGGIA
LOLITA
LORICA
LOUISA
LOYOLA
MODELA
MODENA
MONERA
MONETA
MONICA
MORAVA
MORITA
MOSKVA
NOOTKA
NOUMEA
NOVENA
OOLALA
POMONA
PORTIA
POSADA
ROMOLA
ROSITA
ROSTRA
ROWENA
ROXANA
SOMATA
SONATA
SONOMA
SONORA
SOPHIA
TOLUCA
TOPEKA
TOYOTA
WOVOKA
YORUBA
YOYOMA
ZOYSIA

••OA••
ABOARD
BLOATS
BROACH
BROADS
CHOATE
CLOACA
CLOAKS
CROAKS
CROAKY
CROATS
EBOATS
FLOATS
GLOATS
GROANS
GROATS
PROAMS
SHOALS
SHOATS
SLOANE
STOATS
UBOATS

••O•A•
ABORAL
ADONAI
AGORAE
AGORAS
ALOHAS
ALOMAR
AMORAL
ANORAK
APODAL
AROMAS
ASOSAN
ATONAL
AVOWAL
AXONAL
BAOBAB
BHOPAL
BIOGAS
BIOTAS
BROGAN
BROKAW
CHORAL
COOGAN
DEODAR
DOODAD
DVORAK
FLORAE
FLORAL
FLORAS
GLOBAL
HOOHAH
HOOHAS
HOOKAH
HOORAH
HOORAY
HOOTAT
ISOBAR
KIOWAS
LOOFAH
LOOKAT
MAOTAI
MOOLAH
NOONAN
PROTAX
QUOTAS
RIOJAS
RYOKAN
SHOFAR
SHORAN
SHOTAT
SIOUAN
SLOGAN
SLOVAK
SNOCAT
STOMAS
STOMAT
THOMAS
THORAX
TOOBAD
TROCAR
TROJAN
TWOWAY
VIOLAS
XHOSAS
YEOMAN

••O••A
ABOLLA
AEOLIA
AMOEBA
CHOLLA
CLOACA
EROICA
GLORIA
GLOSSA
HOOPLA
LIOTTA
MYOPIA
NOOTKA
PEORIA
PHOBIA
QUOKKA
QUOTHA
RHONDA
SCORIA
SCOTIA
SFORZA
TROIKA
UTOPIA

•••OA•
ABROAD
AFLOAT
BEMOAN
BOWOAR
BUROAK
BYROAD
COCOAS
GENOAN
INROAD
MINOAN
NOLOAD
NOSOAP
OGDOAD
OHIOAN
ONLOAN
PINOAK
PTBOAT
REDOAK
RELOAD
SAMOAN
SILOAM
STJOAN
TANOAK
TANOAN
THROAT
UNLOAD
UPLOAD
UPROAR

•••O•A
ANCONA
ANGOLA
ANGORA
AREOLA
ARROBA
AURORA
BAROJA
BOGOTA
BULOVA
CANOLA
CANOVA
CHROMA
CIBOLA
CORONA
CUPOLA
DAKOTA
DODOMA
EIDOLA
ENDORA
ESPOSA
EUBOEA
EUDORA
EUROPA
FEDORA
FEMORA
JOJOBA
JUDOKA
LADOGA
LAKOTA
LAROSA
LATONA
LATOYA
LOYOLA
MAZOLA
MIMOSA
MUCOSA
NAGOYA
NICOLA
NIKOLA
PAGODA
PALOMA
PAYOLA
PELOTA
POMONA
RAMONA
REMORA
ROMOLA
SAMOSA
SENORA
SEROSA
SONOMA
SONORA
TACOMA
TOYOTA
VERONA
VIGODA
WINONA
WOVOKA
YOYOMA
ZADORA

••••OA
BALBOA
HIVAOA
JERBOA
LISBOA
QUINOA

OB••••
OBEAHS
OBELIA
OBELUS
OBERON
OBEYED
OBISPO
OBITER
OBIWAN
OBJECT
OBLAST
OBLATE
OBLIGE
OBLONG
OBOIST
OBRIAN
OBRIEN
OBSESS
OBSTET
OBTAIN
OBTEST
OBTUND
OBTUSE
OBVERT

O•B•••
ORBACH
ORBING
ORBITS
OSBORN
OXBOWS

O••B••
OJIBWA
OLDBOY
ORIBIS
OUTBID

O••••B
ODDJOB

•OB•••
BOBBED
BOBBER
BOBBIE
BOBBIN
BOBBLE
BOBCAT
BOBSUP
COBALT
COBBLE
COBHAM
COBIAS
COBRAS
COBURG
COBURN
COBWEB
DOBBER
DOBBIN
DOBLAS
DOBLIN
DOBRAS
DOBROS
DOBSON
FOBBED
FOBOFF
GOBACK
GOBBLE
GOBIES
GOBLET
GOBLIN
GOBUST
HOBART
HOBBES
HOBBIT
HOBBLE
HOBNOB
HOBOES
HOBSON
JOBBED
JOBBER
JOBETH
JOBHOP
JOBLOT
KOBOLD
LOBATE
LOBBED
LOBBER
LOBULE
MOBBED
MOBCAP
MOBILE
MOBIUS
MOBLEY
NOBLER
NOBLES
NOBODY
POBOYS
ROBALO
ROBBED
ROBBER
ROBBIE
ROBERT
ROBING
ROBINS
ROBLES
ROBOTS
ROBROY
ROBSON
ROBUST
SOBBED
SOBBER
SOBEIT
SOBERS
TOBAGO
TOBIAS
TOBIES
TOBOOT
TOBRUK
WOBBLE
WOBBLY

•O•B••
BOBBED
BOBBER
BOBBIE
BOBBIN
BOBBLE
BOMBAY
BOMBED
BOMBER
BOMBES
BONBON
BOOBOO
BOUBOU
COBBLE
COMBAT
COMBED
COMBER
COMBES
COMBOS
CORBAN
CORBEL
CORBIN
COWBOY
DOABLE
DOBBER
DOBBIN
DOOBIE
DOUBLE
DOUBLY
DOUBTS
FOBBED
FOGBOW
FOIBLE
FORBAD
FORBES
FORBID
GOBBLE
GOOBER
HOBBES
HOBBIT
HOBBLE
HOMBRE
HOTBED
HOTBOX
JOBBED
JOBBER
KORBUT
LOBBED
LOBBER
LOMBOK
LOWBOY
MOBBED
MORBID
NOTBAD
ROBBED
ROBBER
ROBBIE
SOBBED
SOBBER
SOMBER
SOMBRE
SORBET
SORBIC
SOWBUG
TOMBAC
TOMBOY
TOOBAD
WOBBLE
WOBBLY
WOMBAT
YOUBET
ZOMBIE

•O••B•
COMEBY
DOESBY
GOESBY
GONEBY
GOODBY
JOJOBA
YORUBA

•O•••B
COBWEB
CONFAB
CONJOB
HOBNOB
HOTTUB
TOPJOB

••OB••
ADOBES
BAOBAB
BIOBIO
BOOBOO
DOOBIE
GLOBAL
GLOBED
GLOBES
GLOBIN
GOOBER
ISOBAR
KNOBBY
PHOBIA
PHOBIC
PHOBOS
PROBED
PROBER
PROBES
SNOBBY

TOOBAD
TWOBIT

••O•B•
ABOMBS
AMOEBA
CROSBY
DROPBY
GOODBY
HBOMBS
KNOBBY
PHOEBE
RHOMBI
RHOMBS
SNOBBY

••O••B
BAOBAB
DIONEB

•••OB•
AEROBE
ARROBA
CAROBS
DEMOBS
ENROBE
JACOBI
JOJOBA
KABOBS
KEBOBS
NABOBS
STROBE
THROBS
TYCOBB
UNROBE

•••O•B
ABSORB
ADSORB
APLOMB
RESORB
TYCOBB

••••OB
CONJOB
HOBNOB
ODDJOB
TOPJOB

OC••••
OCASEK
OCASEY
OCCULT
OCCUPY
OCCURS
OCEANS
OCELLI
OCELOT
OCHERS
OCHRES
OCLOCK
OCREAE
OCTADS
OCTANE
OCTANT
OCTAVE
OCTAVO
OCTETS
OCTOPI
OCTROI
OCULAR

O•C•••
OCCULT
OCCUPY
OCCURS
ONCALL
OOCYTE
ORCHID
ORCHIL
OSCARS
OSCINE
OSCULA
OXCART

O••C••
OILCAN
ORACLE
OUNCES
OUTCRY

O•••C•
OAXACA
OBJECT
OCLOCK
OFFICE
OLMECS
ONDECK
OPTICS
ORBACH
OROZCO
OSMICS
OUTACT

O••••C
OLDVIC
ONSPEC
ORPHIC
OTITIC
OVISAC
OXIDIC
OZONIC

•OC•••
BOCCIE
BOCHCO
COCCID
COCCUS
COCCYX
COCHIN
COCKED
COCKER
COCKLE
COCOAS
COCOON
DOCENT
DOCILE
DOCKED
DOCKER
DOCKET
DOCTOR
EOCENE
FOCSLE
GOCART
HOCKED
HOCKEY
JOCKEY
JOCOSE
JOCUND
LOCALE
LOCALS
LOCATE
LOCKED
LOCKER
LOCKET
LOCKIN
LOCKUP
LOCUST
MOCHAS
MOCKED
MOCKER
MOCKUP
NOCENT
OOCYTE
POCKET
POCONO
ROCHET
ROCKED
ROCKER
ROCKET
ROCKNE
ROCKYV
ROCOCO
SOCAGE
SOCCER
SOCIAL
SOCKED
SOCKET
SOCKIN
SOCLES
TOCSIN
VOCALS

•O•C••
BOBCAT
BOCCIE
BOUCLE
BOXCAR
COCCID
COCCUS
COCCYX
CONCHA
CONCHS
CONCUR
DORCAS
FORCED
FORCER
FORCES
GOTCHA
HONCHO
HOTCAP
HOTCAR
LOUCHE
LOWCAL
MOBCAP
MOSCOW
NONCOM
POACHY
PONCHO
POUCHY
ROSCOE
SOCCER
TOECAP
TOMCAT
TOPCAT
TOUCAN
TOUCHE
TOUCHY
TOWCAR
VOICED
VOICES
YOICKS

•O••C•
BOCHCO
BODICE
BORSCH
BOUNCE
BOUNCY
COERCE
COMICS
CONICS
CONOCO
DODECA
GOBACK
HORACE
IONICS
JOUNCE
JOUNCY
KONICA
KOPECK
KOVACS
LORICA
MODOCS
MOHOCK
MOLOCH
MONACO
MONICA
NODICE
NOTICE
NOVICE
POLICE
POLICY
POMACE
POUNCE
ROCOCO
SOLACE
SONICS
SOURCE
TOLUCA
TONICS
TOPICS
TOXICS
VOTECH
YORICK

•O•••C
AORTIC
COGNAC
CONTAC
COPTIC
COSMIC
COURIC
FORMIC
GOTHIC
HOMEEC
MOSAIC
NOETIC
NORDIC
POETIC
PONTIC
ROMAIC
SORBIC
TOLTEC
TOMBAC
ZODIAC

••OC••
AVOCET
BLOCKS
BLOCKY
CHOCKS
CLOCHE
CLOCKS
CROCKS
CROCUS
EPOCHS
FLOCKS
FROCKS
GROCER
KNOCKS
PHOCIS
PROCNE
SHOCKS
SMOCKS
SNOCAT
STOCKS
STOCKY
TROCAR
TROCHE

••O•C•
ATONCE
AVOUCH
BLOTCH
BROACH
BRONCO
BRONCS
BROOCH
CHOICE
CLOACA
CROUCH
EROICA
GROUCH
OROZCO
SCONCE
SCORCH
SCOTCH
SLOUCH
SMOOCH
STOICS
STORCH

••O••C
AEOLIC
ANODIC
ATOMIC
ATONIC
BIONIC
BIOTIC
EROTIC
ETONIC
EXOTIC
FROLIC
GNOMIC
ICONIC
IRONIC
MYOPIC
OZONIC
PHOBIC
PHONIC
PHOTIC
TROPIC

•••OC•
BROOCH
CONOCO
DECOCT
DUROCS
HAVOCS
IDIOCY
MODOCS
MOHOCK
MOLOCH
OCLOCK
RELOCK
ROCOCO
SMOOCH
SUNOCO
UNLOCK
VELOCE

•••O•C
ECHOIC
HEROIC

••••OC
BELLOC
ENBLOC
MANIOC
TLALOC
ZIPLOC

OD••••
ODDEST
ODDITY
ODDJOB
ODDLOT
ODDSON
ODENSE
ODESSA
ODETTA
ODETTE
ODIOUS
ODISTS
ODIUMS
ODONTO
ODOURS

O•D•••
ODDEST
ODDITY
ODDJOB
ODDLOT
ODDSON
OEDEMA
OGDOAD
OLDBOY
OLDEST
OLDHAM
OLDHAT
OLDIES
OLDISH
OLDMAN
OLDMEN
OLDPRO
OLDVIC
ONDECK
ONDINE
OODLES
ORDAIN
ORDEAL
ORDERS
ORDURE

O••D••
OFFDAY
ONEDAY
ONEDGE
OUTDID
OXIDES
OXIDIC
OXYDOL

O•••D•
OCTADS
OLINDA
ONEIDA
ONSIDE
OREADS
OREIDA
OROIDE
OVERDO
OVIEDO
OVOIDS

O••••D
OBEYED
OBTUND
OFFEND
OGDOAD
OINKED
OKAYED
ONHAND
ONHOLD
ONLAND
ONWARD
OPENED
OPINED
ORATED
ORCHID
ORMOND
OSGOOD
OSMOND
OSMUND
OSTEND
OSWALD
OUSTED
OUTBID
OUTDID
OXFORD
OXNARD

•OD•••
AODAIS
BODEGA
BODICE
BODIED
BODIES
BODILY
BODING
BODKIN
BODONI
CODDLE
CODERS
CODGER
CODIFY
CODING
CODONS
DODDER
DODECA
DODGED
DODGER
DODGES
DODODO
DODOES
DODOMA
FODDER
GODARD
GODETS
GODIVA
GODOWN
GODSON
GODWIN
GODWIT
HODADS
IODATE
IODIDE
IODINE
IODIZE
KODALY
KODIAK
LODENS
LODGED
LODGER
LODGES
MODELA
MODELS
MODELT
MODEMS
MODENA
MODERN
MODEST
MODIFY
MODINE
MODISH
MODOCS
MODULE
MODULO
NODDED
NODDLE
NODICE
NODOFF
NODOSE
NODULE
OODLES
PODDED
PODIUM
PODUNK
RODENT
RODEOS
RODHAM
RODNEY
SODDED
SODDEN
SODIUM
TODATE
TODDAO
TODDLE
TODMAN
YODELS
ZODIAC

•O•D••
AOUDAD
BOLDER
BOLDLY
BONDED
BOODLE
BORDEN
BORDER
BOUDIN
CODDLE
COEDIT
COLDER
COLDLY
CONDOR
CONDOS
COODER
CORDAY
CORDED
CORDON
DODDER
DONDER
DOODAD
DOODLE
FODDER
FOLDED
FOLDER
FOLDUP
FONDER
FONDLE
FONDLY
FONDUE
FORDED
GOADED
GOLDEN
GOLDIE
GOODBY
GOODEN
GOODIE
GOODLY
GORDIE
GORDON
HOLDEN
HOLDER
HOLDIT
HOLDON
HOLDTO
HOLDUP
HOODED
HOODOO
HORDES
HOTDOG
HOWDAH
HOYDEN
JORDAN
LOADED
LOADER
LONDON
LORDED
LORDLY
LOUDEN
LOUDER
LOUDLY
MOLDAU
MOLDED
MOLDER
MONDAY
NODDED
NODDLE
NOODLE
NORDIC
PODDED
POLDER
PONDER
POODLE
POWDER
ROADIE
RONDEL
RONDOS
SODDED
SODDEN
SOLDAN
SOLDER
SOLDON
SONDES
SORDID
TODDAO
TODDLE
TOEDIN
TOLDOF
TOPDOG
TOYDOG
VOIDED
VOODOO
WONDER
WOODED
WOODEN
WOODSY
WORDED
YONDER

•O••D•
BOARDS
BOLIDE
BORIDE
BOUNDS
BOVIDS
COLADA
COMEDY
DODODO
DORADO
DOSIDO
FOUNDS
GOURDE
GOURDS
HOARDS
HODADS
HOUNDS
IODIDE
KOMODO
MONADS
MONODY
MOPEDS
MOULDS
MOULDY
MOUNDS
NOBODY
NOMADS
POMADE
POSADA
POUNDS
ROUNDS
SOLIDI
SOLIDS
SOUNDS
TOLEDO
WORLDS
WOUNDS
ZOUNDS

•O•••D
AOUDAD
BOATED
BOBBED
BODIED
BOFFED
BOGGED
BOILED
BOLTED
BOMBED
BONDED
BONGED
BOOKED
BOOMED
BOOTED
BOPPED
BOSSED
BOWLED
COATED
COAXED
COCCID
COCKED
COGGED
COIFED
COILED
COINED
COMBED
CONFED
CONKED
CONNED
CONRAD
COOKED
COOLED
COOPED
COPIED
COPPED
CORDED
CORKED
CORNED
COSHED
COWARD
COWLED
COZIED
DOCKED
DODGED
DOFFED
DOGGED
DOGOOD
DOLLED
DONALD
DONNED
DOODAD
DOOMED
DOSSED
DOTARD
DOTTED
DOUSED
DOWNED
DOWSED
FOALED
FOAMED
FOBBED
FOGGED
FOILED
FOLDED
FOOLED
FOOTED
FORBAD
FORBID
FORCED
FORDED
FORGED
FORKED
FORMED
FOULED
FOWLED
GOADED
GODARD
GOLFED
GONGED
GOOFED
GOOSED
GORGED
GOTMAD
GOUGED
GOUNOD
GOWILD
GOWNED
HOAXED
HOCKED
HOGGED
HONIED
HONKED
HOODED
HOOFED
HOOKED
HOOPED
HOOTED
HOPPED
HORNED
HORRID
HORSED
HOSTED
HOTBED
HOTROD
HOUSED
HOWARD
HOWLED
JOBBED
JOCUND
JOGGED
JOINED
JOLTED
JOSHED
JOTTED
KOBOLD
KONRAD
LOADED
LOAFED
LOAMED
LOANED
LOBBED
LOCKED
LODGED
LOFTED
LOGGED
LOLLED
LOMOND
LONGED
LOOKED
LOOMED
LOOPED
LOOSED
LOOTED
LOPPED
LORDED
LOTTED
LOUSED
LOWEND
MOANED
MOATED
MOBBED
MOCKED
MOILED
MOLDED
MOLTED
MONIED
MOONED
MOORED
MOOTED
MOPPED
MORBID
MOSSED
MOUSED
NODDED
NOGOOD
NOISED
NOLEAD
NOLOAD
NOSHED
NOTBAD
PODDED
POISED
POLAND
POLLED
PONGID
PONIED
POOHED
POOLED
POOPED
POPPED
PORTED
POSTED
POTTED
POURED
POUTED
ROAMED
ROARED
ROBBED
ROCKED
ROILED
ROLAND
ROLLED
ROMPED
RONALD
ROOFED
ROOKED
ROOMED
ROOTED
ROTTED
ROTUND
ROUGED
ROUSED
ROUTED
SOAKED
SOAPED
SOARED
SOBBED
SOCKED
SODDED
SOILED
SOLOED
SOLVED
SOPPED
SORDID
SORTED
SOTTED
SOURED
SOUSED
TOGAED
TOGGED
TOILED
TOLLED
TOOBAD
TOOLED
TOOTED
TOPPED
TOROID
TORPID
TORRID
TOSSED
TOTTED
TOURED
TOUTED
TOWARD
VOICED
VOIDED
WOLFED
WONNED
WONTED
WOODED
WOOFED
WORDED
WORKED
WORMED
YOLKED
YOWLED
YOYOED
ZONKED
ZOOMED

••OD••
ABODES
ANODES
ANODIC
APODAL
ATODDS
AZODYE
BOODLE
BRODIE
COODER
DEODAR
DIODES
DOODAD
DOODLE
EPODES
ERODED
ERODES
EXODUS
FYODOR
GEODES
GOODBY
GOODEN
GOODIE
GOODLY
GRODIN
HOODED
HOODOO
NOODLE
POODLE
RHODES
SHODDY
STODGE
STODGY
VOODOO
WOODED
WOODEN
WOODSY

••O•D•
AROIDS
ATODDS
AVOIDS
BIONDI
BLONDE
BLONDS
BLOODY
BROADS
BROODS
BROODY
CHORDS
CLOUDS
CLOUDY
CROWDS
DROIDS
EBONDS
FIORDS
FJORDS
FLOODS
FRONDS
IDOIDO
ISOLDE
LLOYDS
OROIDE
OVOIDS
RHONDA
SCOLDS
SHODDY
SNOODS
SWORDS
TBONDS

••O••D
ABOARD
ABOUND
ADORED
AROUND
ATONED
AVOWED
BOOKED
BOOMED
BOOTED
BUOYED
CHOKED
CHOWED
CLONED
CLOSED
CLOYED
COOKED
COOLED
COOPED
CROWED
DOODAD
DOOMED
DRONED
ELOPED
EMOTED
ERODED
EVOKED
FLORID
FLOWED
FOOLED
FOOTED
GLOBED
GLOVED
GLOWED
GOOFED
GOOSED
GROPED
GROUND
HOODED
HOOFED
HOOKED
HOOPED
HOOTED
IRONED
ISOPOD
LEONID
LOOKED
LOOMED
LOOPED
LOOSED
LOOTED
MEOWED
MOONED
MOORED
MOOTED
PHONED
PLOWED
POOHED
POOLED
POOPED
PROBED
PROSED
PROVED
QUOTED
RIOTED
ROOFED
ROOKED
ROOMED
ROOTED
SCOPED
SCORED
SHOOED
SHORED
SHOULD
SHOVED
SHOWED
SLOPED
SLOWED
SMOKED
SNORED
SNOWED
SPOKED
STOKED
STOLID
STONED
STORED
STOWED
TOOBAD
TOOLED
TOOTED
TROWED
WOODED
WOOFED
ZOOMED

•••OD•
BIPODS
BLOODY
BROODS
BROODY
DECODE
DEMODE
DIPODY
DODODO
EMBODY
ENCODE
EPHODS
FLOODS
KOMODO
MELODY
MONODY
NOBODY
PAGODA
PARODY
RECODE

RESODS
SARODS
SCRODS
SNOODS
STRODE
SYNODS
TRIODE
VIGODA

•••O•D

ABROAD
ACCORD
AFFORD
AGEOLD
ALMOND
ARNOLD
ATWOOD
AUFOND
BEHOLD
BEYOND
BIFOLD
BUJOLD
BYROAD
BYWORD
CANOED
CUBOID
DADOED
DEMOND
DEVOID
DOGOOD
ECHOED
EDMOND
ELWOOD
ENFOLD
HALOED
HALOID
HAROLD
HYPOED
INFOLD
INROAD
KAYOED
KOBOLD
LEMOND
LIPOID
LOMOND
MILORD
MYWORD
NOGOOD
NOLOAD
OGDOAD
ONHOLD
ORMOND
OSGOOD
OSMOND
OXFORD
RECORD
RELOAD
RESOLD
RETOLD
REWORD
SECOND
SHOOED
SHROUD
SILOED
SOLOED
STROUD
TOROID
UNFOLD
UNLOAD
UNSOLD
UNTOLD
UPHOLD
UPLOAD
VETOED
XYLOID
YOYOED
ZEROED

••••OD

ATWOOD
DOGOOD
ELWOOD
FLYROD
GOUNOD
HESIOD
HOTROD
ISOPOD
METHOD
NIMROD
NOGOOD
OSGOOD
PEAPOD
PENROD
PEQUOD
PERIOD
PERNOD
RAMROD
RESHOD
SUNGOD
TIEROD
TINGOD
TRIPOD
UNIPOD
UNSHOD
UNTROD
WARGOD

OE••••

OEDEMA
OENONE
OERTER
OEUVRE

O•E•••

OBEAHS
OBELIA
OBELUS
OBERON
OBEYED
OCEANS
OCELLI
OCELOT
ODENSE
ODESSA
ODETTA
ODETTE
OHENRY
OKEEFE
OKELLY
OLEARY
OLEATE
OLEFIN
OLEVEL
OMEGAS
OMELET
OMERTA
ONEDAY
ONEDGE
ONEIDA
ONEILL
ONETWO
ONEUPS
ONEWAY
OPENED
OPENER
OPENLY
OPENTO
OPENUP
OPERAS
OREADS
OREGON
OREIDA
ORELSE
OTELLO
OVERDO
OVERLY
OXEYES

O••E••

OATERS
OBJECT
OBSESS
OBTEST
OBVERT
OCHERS
OCREAE
OCTETS
ODDEST
OEDEMA
OFFEND
OFFERS
OGLERS
OGRESS
OHWELL
OHYEAH
OILERS
OKEEFE
OLDEST
OLMECS
ONDECK
ONSETS
ORDEAL
ORDERS
ORGEAT
ORIELS
ORIENT
ORNERY
ORRERY
ORTEGA
ORWELL
OSIERS
OSSEIN
OSSETE
OSTEAL
OSTEND
OSWEGO
OTHERS
OTTERS
OUSELS
OUTEAT
OUZELS
OVIEDO
OWLETS
OWNERS

O•••E•

OAKLEY
OATIER
OBEYED
OBITER
OBRIEN
OBSTET
OCASEK
OCASEY
OCHRES
OERTER
OFFKEY
OFFSET
OGIVES
OILIER
OILMEN
OINKED
OKAYED
OLDIES
OLDMEN
OLEVEL
OLIVER
OLIVES
OMELET
ONAGER
ONSPEC
ONUSES
ONVIEW
ONYXES
OODLES
OPENED
OPENER
OPINED
OPINER
OPINES
OPUSES
ORALES
ORATED
ORATES
ORGIES
ORIGEN
ORKNEY
ORTLES
ORYXES
OSAGES
OSPREY
OSTLER
OUNCES
OUSTED
OUSTER
OUTLET
OUTSET
OVULES
OXEYES
OXIDES
OXYGEN
OYSTER

O••••E

OBLATE
OBLIGE
OBTUSE
OCREAE
OCTANE
OCTAVE
ODENSE
ODETTE
OENONE
OEUVRE
OFFICE
OFLATE
OKEEFE
OLEATE
ONDINE
ONEDGE
ONFILE
ONFIRE
ONLINE
ONSALE
ONSIDE
ONSITE
ONTAPE
ONTIME
OOCYTE
OOLITE
OPAQUE
OPHITE
OPIATE
OPPOSE
ORACLE
ORANGE
ORDURE
ORELSE
ORGATE
ORIOLE
ORNATE
OROIDE
ORPINE
OSCINE
OSMOSE
OSSETE
OTIOSE
OTOOLE
OUTAGE
OUTATE

•OE•••

BOEING
COEDIT
COELOM
COERCE
COEVAL
DOESBY
DOESIN
DOESNT
DOESUP
FOEHNS
GOEASY
GOESAT
GOESBY
GOESIN
GOESON
GOESUP
GOETHE
HOEING
JOETEX
NOESIS
NOETIC
NOEXIT
POETIC
POETRY
TOECAP
TOEDIN
TOEING
TOEINS
TOESIN
TOETAP
WOEFUL

•O•E••

BODEGA
BOGEYS
BOLERO
BOLEYN
BONERS
BONEUP
BOPEEP
BOREAL
BOREAS
BOREON
BORERS
BOREUP
BOWERS
BOWERY
BOXERS
CODERS
COGENT
COHEIR
COHERE
COLEUS
COMEAT
COMEBY
COMEDY
COMEIN
COMELY
COMEON
COMERS
COMETH
COMETO
COMETS
COMEUP
CONEYS
COOERS
CORERS
COSELL
COVENS
COVENT
COVERS
COVERT
COVETS
COVEYS
COWENS
COWERS
COYEST
COZENS
DOCENT
DODECA
DOGEAR
DONEES
DONEIN
DONETS
DONEUP
DOREMI
DOSERS
DOTELL
DOTEON
DOVEIN
DOWELS
DOWERS
DOYENS
DOZENS
DOZERS
EOCENE
FOGEYS
FOMENT
FOREGO
FOREST
FOVEAE
FOYERS
GODETS
GOFERS
GOLEMS
GONEBY
GONERS
GOVERN
GOWEST
HOLEUP
HOMEEC
HOMELY
HOMERS
HONEST
HONEYS
HOPERS
HOSELS
HOTELS
HOVELS
HOVERS
HOVETO
HOWELL
JOBETH
JOKERS
JOLENE
JOSEPH
JOWETT
KOPECK
KOPEKS
KOREAN
LODENS
LOMEIN
LONELY
LONERS
LOPERS
LOREAL
LORENZ
LOSEIT
LOSERS
LOVEIN
LOVELL
LOVELY
LOVERS
LOVETT
LOWELL
LOWEND
LOWERS
LOWERY
LOWEST
MODELA
MODELS
MODELT
MODEMS
MODENA
MODERN
MODEST
MOIETY
MOLEST
MOMENT
MONERA
MONETA
MONEYS
MOPEDS
MOPERS
MOREAU
MOREEN
MORELS
MORENO
MOSEYS
MOTELS
MOTETS
MOVEIN
MOVERS
MOWERS
MOYERS
NOCENT
NOLEAD
NOLENS
NOLESS
NONEGO
NONETS
NOPETS
NOTERS
NOVELS
NOVENA
POKEAT
POKERS
POKERY
POKEYS
POLEAX
POLERS
POLEYN
POMELO
POPEYE
POSERS
POSEUR
POTEEN
POTENT
POWELL
POWERS
ROBERT
RODENT
RODEOS
ROGERS
ROLEOS
ROMEOS
ROMERO
RONELY
ROPEIN
ROPERS
ROSEAU
ROVERS
ROWELS
ROWENA
ROWENS
ROWERS
SOBEIT
SOBERS
SOLEIL
SOLELY
SOLEMN
SOLENT
SOLERS
SOLEUS
SOMERS
SORELY
SOREST
SOWERS
SOWETO
SOXERS
TOKENS
TOLEDO
TONERS
TONEUP
TOPEKA
TOPERS
TOREAT
TORERO
TOREUP
TOTEMS
TOTERS
TOWELS
TOWERS
TOWERY
VOLENS
VOTECH
VOTEIN
VOTERS
VOWELS
VOWERS
WOKEUP
WOMENS
WOOERS
WOREON
YODELS
YOKELS

•O••E•

BOATED
BOATER
BOBBED
BOBBER
BODIED
BODIES
BOFFED
BOGGED
BOGIES
BOGLES
BOILED
BOILER
BOITES
BOLDER
BOLGER
BOLTED
BOMBED
BOMBER
BOMBES
BONDED
BONGED
BONIER
BONNES
BONNET
BONZES
BOOKED
BOOKER
BOOMED
BOOMER
BOOTED
BOOTEE
BOOTES
BOPEEP
BOPPED
BOPPER
BORDEN
BORDER
BORNEO
BOSKET
BOSLEY
BOSSED
BOSSES
BOTHER
BOTREE
BOULES
BOULEZ
BOWLED
BOWLER
BOWLES
BOWMEN
BOWNET
BOWSER
BOWYER
BOXSET
COALER
COATED
COAXED
COAXER
COAXES
COBWEB
COCKED
COCKER
CODGER
COFFEE
COFFER
COGGED
COIFED
COILED
COINED
COINER
COLDER
COLLET
COLTER
COMBED
COMBER
COMBES
COMPEL
COMTES
CONFED
CONFER
CONGER
CONIES
CONKED
CONKER
CONMEN
CONNED
CONNER
CONTES
CONVEX
CONVEY
COODER
COOKED
COOKER
COOLED
COOLER
COONEY
COOPED
COOPER
COOTER
COPIED
COPIER
COPIES
COPPED
COPPER
COPSES
COPTER
COQUET
CORBEL
CORDED
CORKED
CORKER
CORNEA
CORNED
CORNEL
CORNER
CORNET
CORREL
CORSET
CORTES
CORTEX
CORTEZ
CORVEE
COSHED
COSHES
COSIES
COSSET
COTTEN
COTTER
COULEE
COUPES
COUTER
COWLED
COWLEY
COWMEN
COWPEA
COWPER
COZIED
COZIER
COZIES
DOBBER
DOCKED
DOCKER
DOCKET
DODDER
DODGED
DODGER
DODGES
DODOES
DOFFED
DOGGED
DOGGER
DOGIES
DOGLEG
DOLLED
DOLMEN
DONDER
DONEES
DONKEY
DONNED
DONNEE
DONNER
DOOLEY
DOOMED
DOPIER
DORIES
DORMER
DORSET
DORSEY
DOSSED
DOSSEL
DOSSER
DOSSES
DOTTED
DOURER
DOUSED
DOUSES
DOWNED
DOWNER
DOWNEY
DOWSED
DOWSER
DOWSES
FOALED
FOAMED
FOBBED
FODDER
FOGGED
FOGGER
FOGIES
FOILED
FOKKER
FOLDED
FOLDER
FONDER
FOOLED
FOOLER
FOOTED
FOOTER
FORBES
FORCED
FORCER
FORCES
FORDED
FORGED
FORGER
FORGES
FORGET
FORKED
FORKER
FORMED
FORMER
FORTES
FOSSES
FOSSEY
FOSTER
FOULED
FOULER
FOWLED
FOWLER
FOWLES
FOXIER
GOADED
GOATEE
GOBIES
GOBLET
GOLDEN
GOLFED
GOLFER
GONGED
GOOBER
GOODEN
GOOFED
GOOIER
GOOSED
GOOSES
GOOVER
GOPHER
GORGED
GORGES
GORGET
GORIER
GORSES
GOSHEN
GOSPEL
GOTTEN
GOUGED
GOUGER
GOUGES
GOULET
GOWNED
HOAXED
HOAXER
HOAXES
HOBBES
HOBOES
HOCKED
HOCKEY
HOGGED
HOKIER
HOLDEN
HOLDER
HOLIER
HOLLER
HOLMES
HOMEEC
HOMIER
HONIED
HONKED
HONKER
HOODED
HOOFED
HOOFER
HOOKED
HOOPED
HOOPER
HOOTED
HOOTER
HOOVER
HOOVES
HOPPED
HOPPER
HORDES
HORMEL
HORNED
HORNER
HORNET
HORNEY
HORSED
HORSES
HORSEY
HOSIER
HOSTED
HOSTEL
HOTBED
HOTTEA
HOTTER
HOUSED
HOUSES
HOWLED
HOWLER
HOYDEN
JOBBED
JOBBER
JOCKEY
JOETEX
JOGGED
JOGGER
JOINED
JOINER
JOLIET
JOLTED
JOSHED
JOSHES
JOSSES
JOTTED
JOULES
JOYNER
KOHLER
KOPJES
KOPPEL
KOSHER
KOTTER
LOADED
LOADER
LOAFED
LOAFER
LOAMED
LOANED
LOANER
LOAVES
LOBBED
LOBBER
LOCKED
LOCKER
LOCKET
LODGED
LODGER
LODGES
LOFTED
LOGGED
LOGGER
LOGIER
LOITER
LOLLED
LONGED
LONGER
LONGES
LOOKED
LOOKER
LOOMED
LOONEY
LOOPED
LOOPER
LOOSED
LOOSEN
LOOSER
LOOSES
LOOTED
LOOTER
LOPPED
LOPPER
LORDED
LORIES
LOSSES
LOTTED
LOUDEN
LOUDER
LOUPES
LOUSED
LOUSES
LOUVER
LOWKEY
MOANED
MOANER
MOATED
MOBBED
MOBLEY
MOCKED
MOCKER
MOILED
MOILER
MOINES
MOIRES
MOLDED
MOLDER
MOLTED
MOLTEN
MOLTER
MONGER
MONIED
MONIES
MONKEY
MONTEL
MONTEZ
MOONED
MOONEY
MOORED
MOOTED
MOPPED
MOPPER
MOPPET
MOREEN
MORGEN
MORLEY
MORSEL
MOSLEM
MOSSED
MOSSES
MOSTEL
MOTHER
MOTLEY
MOUSED
MOUSER
MOUSES
MOUSEY
MOVIES
NOBLER
NOBLES
NODDED
NOISED
NOISES
NOOSES
NOSHED
NOSHER
NOSHES
NOSIER
NOTYET
NOUMEA
OODLES
POCKET
PODDED
POGIES
POISED
POISES
POKIER
POLDER
POLLED
POLLEN
POLLER
POLLEX
POMMEE
POMMEL
POMPEY
PONDER
PONGEE
PONIED
PONIES
PONTES
POOHED
POOLED
POOPED
POORER
POPPED
POPPER
POPPET
PORKER
PORTED
PORTER
POSHER
POSIES
POSSES
POSSET
POSTED
POSTER
POTEEN
POTHER
POTTED
POTTER
POURED
POURER
POUTED
POUTER
POWDER
ROAMED
ROAMER
ROARED
ROARER
ROBBED
ROBBER
ROBLES
ROCHET
ROCKED
ROCKER
ROCKET
RODNEY
ROGUES
ROHMER
ROILED
ROLLED
ROLLER
ROMMEL
ROMNEY
ROMPED
ROMPER
RONDEL
ROOFED
ROOFER
ROOKED
ROOMED
ROOMER
ROONEY
ROOTED
ROOTER
ROPIER
ROSIER
ROSTER
ROTTED
ROTTEN
ROTTER
ROUGED
ROUGES
ROUSED
ROUSES
ROUTED
ROUTER
ROUTES
SOAKED
SOAKER
SOAPED
SOAPER
SOARED
SOARER
SOARES
SOAVES
SOBBED
SOBBER
SOCCER
SOCKED
SOCKET
SOCLES
SODDED
SODDEN
SOFTEN
SOFTER
SOILED
SOIREE
SOLDER
SOLOED
SOLVED
SOLVER

SOLVES
SOMBER
SOMMER
SONDES
SONNET
SOONER
SOPPED
SORBET
SORREL
SORTED
SORTER
SOTTED
SOURED
SOURER
SOUSED
SOUSES
SOUTER
SOVIET
TOATEE
TOBIES
TOFFEE
TOGAED
TOGGED
TOILED
TOILER
TOILES
TOILET
TOLLED
TOLTEC
TONIER
TONNES
TOOLED
TOOTED
TOOTER
TOPPED
TOPPER
TOPTEN
TOQUES
TORIES
TORTES
TOSSED
TOSSER
TOSSES
TOTHER
TOTTED
TOTTER
TOUPEE
TOURED
TOURER
TOUTED
TOUTER
TOWHEE
TOWNER
VOGUES
VOICED
VOICES
VOIDED
VOILES
VOLLEY
VORTEX
VOSGES
WOHLER
WOLFED
WOLPER
WOLSEY
WOLVES
WONDER
WONNED
WONTED
WOODED
WOODEN
WOOFED
WOOFER
WOOLEN
WOOLEY
WORDED
WORKED
WORKER
WORMED
WORSEN
YOLKED
YONDER
YORKER
YOUBET
YOWLED
YOYOED
ZONKED
ZONKER
ZOOMED

•O•••E
AORTAE
BOBBIE
BOBBLE
BOCCIE
BODICE
BOGGLE
BOLIDE
BONNIE
BOODLE
BOOGIE
BOOKIE
BOOTEE
BOOTHE
BOOTIE
BORAGE
BORATE
BORIDE
BOTREE
BOTTLE
BOUCLE
BOUFFE
BOULLE
BOUNCE
BOURKE
BOURNE
BOURSE
BOVINE
BOWTIE
COARSE
COBBLE
COCKLE
CODDLE
COERCE
COFFEE
COHERE
COHUNE
COLLIE
COMATE
CONNIE
CONTRE
COOKIE
COOTIE
CORVEE
COSINE
COSTAE
COULEE
COUPLE
COURSE
COWRIE
COYOTE
DOABLE
DOCILE
DOGGIE
DONATE
DONNEE
DOOBIE
DOODLE
DOOGIE
DOOZIE
DOSAGE
DOTAGE
DOTTIE
DOTTLE
DOUBLE
EOCENE
FOCSLE
FOIBLE
FOLKIE
FONDLE
FONDUE
FOOZLE
FORAGE
FOSSAE
FOVEAE
FOZZIE
GOALIE
GOATEE
GOBBLE
GOETHE
GOGGLE
GOHOME
GOLDIE
GOODIE
GOOGLE
GORDIE
GOURDE
HOAGIE
HOARSE
HOBBLE
HOGTIE
HOMAGE
HOMBRE
HONORE
HOOPLE
HOOPOE
HOPPLE
HORACE
IODATE
IODIDE
IODINE
IODIZE
IOLITE
IONIZE
JOANIE
JOANNE
JOCOSE
JOGGLE
JOHORE
JOLENE
JOSTLE
JOUNCE
KOOKIE
LOATHE
LOBATE
LOBULE
LOCALE
LOCATE
LONGUE
LOUCHE
LOUISE
LOUNGE
LOUVRE
LOVAGE
MOBILE
MODINE
MODULE
MOHAVE
MOJAVE
MOLINE
MOLTKE
MOMMIE
MONROE
MORALE
MOROSE
MOSQUE
MOTILE
MOTIVE
MOTTLE
MOUSSE
NODDLE
NODICE
NODOSE
NODULE
NOMORE
NONAGE
NONAME
NOODLE
NOSALE
NOTATE
NOTICE
NOVICE
NOWISE
NOZZLE
OOCYTE
OOLITE
POINTE
POLICE
POLITE
POMACE
POMADE
POMMEE
PONGEE
POODLE
POPEYE
POPPLE
POTAGE
POTPIE
POTTLE
POUNCE
POUSSE
ROADIE
ROBBIE
ROCKNE
ROLLIE
RONNIE
ROOKIE
ROOMIE
ROSCOE
ROTATE
ROXANE
ROYALE
SOCAGE
SOFINE
SOFTIE
SOIGNE
SOIREE
SOLACE
SOLUTE
SOMBRE
SOOTHE
SOPHIE
SORTIE
SOURCE
TOATEE
TODATE
TODDLE
TOFFEE
TOGGLE
TOLIFE
TONGUE
TONITE
TOOTLE
TOPPLE
TOROSE
TORQUE
TOUCHE
TOUPEE
TOUSLE
TOWAGE
TOWHEE
TOWNIE
VOLARE
VOLUME
VOLUTE
VOTIVE
VOYAGE
WOBBLE
WOOGIE
WOOKIE
ZOMBIE
ZONATE
ZOUAVE

••OE••
AMOEBA
COOERS
PHOEBE
PROEMS
SHOERS
WOOERS

••O•E•
ABODES
ADOBES
ADORED
ADOREE
ADORER
ADORES
AMOLES
ANODES
ANOLES
APOGEE
ATONED
ATONES
AVOCET
AVOWED
AVOWER
AWOKEN
AZORES
BIOMES
BLOKES
BLOOEY
BLOWER
BOOKED
BOOKER
BOOMED
BOOMER
BOOTED
BOOTEE
BOOTES
BROKEN
BROKER
BUOYED
CHOKED
CHOKER
CHOKES
CHOLER
CHORES
CHOSEN
CHOWED
CLONED
CLONES
CLOSED
CLOSER
CLOSES
CLOSET
CLOVEN
CLOVER
CLOVES
CLOYED
CNOTES
COODER
COOKED
COOKER
COOLED
COOLER
COONEY
COOPED
COOPER
COOTER
CRONES
CROWED
CROWER
CROZES
DHOLES
DHOTEL
DIODES
DIONEB
DOOLEY
DOOMED
DRONED
DRONER
DRONES
DROVER
DROVES
ECOLES
ELOPED
ELOPER
ELOPES
EMOTED
EMOTER
EMOTES
EPODES
EPOPEE
ERODED
ERODES
EVOKED
EVOKER
EVOKES
FLOOEY
FLORES
FLORET
FLOWED
FLOWER
FOOLED
FOOLER
FOOTED
FOOTER
FROZEN
GEODES
GLOBED
GLOBES
GLOVED
GLOVER
GLOVES
GLOWED
GLOWER
GNOMES
GOOBER
GOODEN
GOOFED
GOOIER
GOOSED
GOOSES
GOOVER
GROCER
GROPED
GROPES
GROVEL
GROVER
GROVES
GROWER
HOODED
HOOFED
HOOFER
HOOKED
HOOPED
HOOPER
HOOTED
HOOTER
HOOVER
HOOVES
IMOGEN
IRONED
IRONER
ISOHEL
ISOMER
KJOLEN
KNOWER
KRONER
LEONES
LIONEL
LIONET
LOOKED
LOOKER
LOOMED
LOONEY
LOOPED
LOOPER
LOOSED
LOOSEN
LOOSER
LOOSES
LOOTED
LOOTER
MEOWED
MOONED
MOONEY
MOORED
MOOTED
MYOPES
NOOSES
PHONED
PHONES
PHOOEY
PIOLET
PLOVER
PLOWED
PLOWER
POOHED
POOLED
POOPED
POORER
PROBED
PROBER
PROBES
PROLES
PROPEL
PROPER
PROSED
PROSER
PROSES
PROTEI
PROTEM
PROVED
PROVEN
PROVER
PROVES
QUOTED
QUOTER
QUOTES
REOPEN
RHODES
RIOTED
RIOTER
ROOFED
ROOFER
ROOKED
ROOMED
ROOMER
ROONEY
ROOTED
ROOTER
SCONES
SCOPED
SCOPES
SCORED
SCORER
SCORES
SCOTER
SHOLEM
SHOOED
SHORED
SHORES
SHOVED
SHOVEL
SHOVER
SHOVES
SHOWED
SHOWER
SLOPED
SLOPES
SLOVEN
SLOWED
SLOWER
SMOKED
SMOKER
SMOKES
SMOKEY
SNOPES
SNORED
SNORER
SNORES
SNOWED
SOONER
SPOKED
SPOKEN
SPOKES
SPORES
STOKED
STOKER
STOKES
STOLEN
STOLES
STONED
STONER
STONES
STOPES
STORED
STORER
STORES
STOREY
STOVER
STOVES
STOWED
TBONES
THOLES
TNOTES
TOOLED
TOOTED
TOOTER
TROPES
TROPEZ
TROVES
TROWED
TROWEL
TWOFER
UNOPEN
USOPEN
VIOLET
WHOLES
WOODED
WOODEN
WOOFED
WOOFER
WOOLEN
WOOLEY
YEOMEN
ZOOMED

••O••E
ADOREE
AGORAE
ANOMIE
APOGEE
AROUSE
ATONCE
AZODYE
BLONDE
BLOUSE
BMOVIE
BOODLE
BOOGIE
BOOKIE
BOOTEE
BOOTHE
BOOTIE
BRODIE
BROGUE
BRONTE
BRONZE
BROOKE
BROWNE
BROWSE
CHOATE
CHOICE
CHOOSE
CLOCHE
CLOQUE
CLOTHE
COOKIE
COOTIE
CROSSE
CROUSE
CROUTE
DIONNE
DOOBIE
DOODLE
DOOGIE
DOOZIE
DROGUE
DROWSE
ELOISE
EPOPEE
ETOILE
EVOLVE
EVONNE
FLORAE
FOOZLE
GEORGE
GOODIE
GOOGLE
GROOVE
GROSSE
GROUSE
HOOPLE
HOOPOE
INOUYE
ISOLDE
KOOKIE
LAOTSE
LEONIE
LHOTSE
NOODLE
OROIDE
OTOOLE
PEOPLE
PHOEBE
POODLE
PROCNE
PROPRE
PROWSE
ROOKIE
ROOMIE
SCONCE
SHOPPE
SHOWME
SKOKIE
SKOPJE
SLOANE
SNOOZE
SOOTHE
SPONGE
SPOUSE
STODGE
STOGIE
STOLLE
STOOGE
THORPE
TOOTLE
TROCHE
TROMPE
TROUPE
TROUVE
WOOGIE
WOOKIE
YVONNE

•••OE•
BLOOEY
CANOED
CANOES
DADOED
DADOES
DODOES
ECHOED
ECHOES
EDDOES
EUBOEA
FLOOEY
GIJOES
HALOED
HALOES
HEROES
HOBOES
HYPOED
KAYOED
PEKOES
PHLOEM
PHOOEY
REDOES
SHOOED
SILOED
SOLOED
THROES
UNDOER
UNDOES
VETOED
VETOER
VETOES
YOYOED
ZEROED
ZEROES

•••O•E
ACTONE
AEROBE
ALCOVE
ALDOSE
ALGORE
ANYONE
APPOSE
ARIOSE
ASHORE
ASLOPE
ATHOME
BECOME
BEFORE
BEGONE
BROOKE
BYGONE
BYJOVE
BYROTE
CAJOLE
CAPONE
CAPOTE
CAROLE
CENOTE
CHOOSE
CHROME
COYOTE
CREOLE
DAMONE
DAMORE
DAYONE
DEBONE
DECODE
DEMODE
DEMOTE
DENOTE
DEPONE
DEPOSE
DEVOTE
DIPOLE
EEYORE
ELMORE
ENCODE
ENCORE
ENROBE
EUROPE
EVZONE
EXPOSE
FILOSE
FURORE
GALORE
GENOME
GOHOME
GROOVE
GYROSE
HONORE
IGNORE
IMPOSE
INCOME
INJOKE
INLOVE
INSOLE
INTONE
INVOKE
JAMOKE
JEROME
JOCOSE
JOHORE
KETONE
LAHORE
LANOSE
LENORE
LUPONE
MALONE
MEROPE
METOPE
MOROSE
NICOLE
NODOSE
NOMORE
OENONE
OPPOSE
ORIOLE
OSMOSE
OTIOSE
OTOOLE
PAROLE
PEYOTE
PILOSE
PINOLE
RADOME
RAMONE
RAMOSE
RECODE
REDONE
REMOTE
REMOVE
RENOTE
REPOSE
RESOLE
REVOKE
REWOVE
REZONE
RIBOSE
RIMOSE
RUGOSE
SALOME
SAVOIE
SETOSE
SHROVE
SILONE
SIMONE
SNOOZE
STOOGE
STROBE
STRODE
STROKE
STROVE
TAGORE
THRONE
THROVE
TOROSE
TRIODE
TYRONE
UNDONE
UNROBE
UNWOVE
UNYOKE
UPROSE
VADOSE
VELOCE
ZYGOTE

••••OE
BIGTOE
CHIGOE
CHILOE
CRUSOE
FAEROE
FELLOE
HEYJOE
HOOPOE
MONROE
RESHOE
ROSCOE
TIPTOE
WASHOE

OF••••
OFFDAY
OFFEND
OFFERS
OFFICE
OFFING
OFFISH
OFFKEY
OFFSET
OFLATE

O•F•••
OAFISH
OFFDAY
OFFEND
OFFERS
OFFICE
OFFING
OFFISH
OFFKEY
OFFSET
ONFILE
ONFIRE
ONFOOT
OXFORD

O••F••
OLEFIN
OUTFIT
OUTFOX

O•••F•
OKEEFE
OSSIFY

•OF•••
BOFFED
BOFFOS
COFFEE
COFFER
DOFFED
GOFERS
GOFISH
LOFTED
SOFFIT
SOFINE
SOFTEN
SOFTER
SOFTIE
SOFTLY
TOFFEE

•O•F••
BOFFED
BOFFOS
BOTFLY
BOUFFE
BOWFIN
BOXFUL
COFFEE
COFFER
COIFED
COMFIT
CONFAB
CONFED
CONFER
DOFFED
DOOFUS
GOLFED
GOLFER
GOOFED
GOOFUP
HOOFED
HOOFER
HOOFIT
JOYFUL
KOUFAX
LOAFED
LOAFER
LOOFAH
LOWFAT
NONFAT
POPFLY
POTFUL
ROOFED
ROOFER
SOFFIT
SOLFAS
TOFFEE
WOEFUL
WOLFED
WOOFED
WOOFER

•O••F•
BOUFFE
CODIFY
FOBOFF
GOSOFT
GOTOFF
HOPOFF
LOGOFF
MODIFY
MOTIFS
NODOFF
NOTIFY
POPOFF
TOLIFE
TOPOFF

•O•••F
FOBOFF
GOTOFF
HOPOFF
LOGOFF
NODOFF
POPOFF
SORTOF
TOLDOF
TOPOFF

••OF••
CROFTS
DOOFUS
GOOFED
GOOFUP
HOOFED
HOOFER
HOOFIT
LOOFAH
PROFIT
ROOFED
ROOFER
SCOFFS
SHOFAR
TWOFER
WOOFED
WOOFER

••O•F•
KLOOFS
PROOFS
SCOFFS
SPOOFS
WHOOFS

•••OF•
BEGOFF
BITOFF
BUGOFF
BUYOFF
CRYOFF
CUTOFF
DIEOFF
DRYOFF
FAROFF
FOBOFF
GETOFF
GOSOFT
GOTOFF
HOPOFF
KLOOFS
LAYOFF
LEDOFF
LETOFF
LOGOFF
NODOFF
PAYOFF
POPOFF
PROOFS
PUTOFF
RANOFF
RIPOFF
RUNOFF
SAWOFF
SEEOFF
SETOFF
SPOOFS
TAPOFF
TEEOFF
TIPOFF
TOPOFF
WHOOFS

•••O•F
BEGOFF
BEHOOF
BITOFF
BUGOFF
BUYOFF
CRYOFF
CUTOFF
DIEOFF
DRYOFF
FAROFF
FOBOFF
GETOFF
GOTOFF
HOPOFF
LAYOFF
LEDOFF
LETOFF
LOGOFF
NODOFF
PAYOFF
POPOFF
PUTOFF
RANOFF
RIPOFF
RUDOLF
RUNOFF
SAWOFF
SEEOFF
SETOFF
TAPOFF
TEEOFF
TIPOFF
TOPOFF

••••OF
BEHOOF
HEAROF
HEREOF
KINDOF
SORTOF
TOLDOF

OG••••
OGDOAD
OGHAMS
OGIVES
OGLALA
OGLERS
OGLING
OGRESS

O•G•••
ORGANA
ORGANS
ORGATE
ORGEAT
ORGIES
OSGOOD
OUGHTS

O••G••
OMEGAS
ONAGER
OREGON
ORIGEN
ORIGIN
OSAGES
OUTGUN
OXYGEN

O•••G•
OBLIGE
OLINGO
ONEDGE
ONHIGH
OOLOGY
OPPUGN
ORANGE
ORANGS
ORINGS
ORTEGA
OSWEGO
OUTAGE

O••••G
OARING
OBLONG
OFFING
OGLING
OILING
OILRIG
OOHING
OOLONG
OOZING
OPTING
ORBING
OUTING
OWNING

•OG•••
BOGART
BOGEYS
BOGGED
BOGGLE
BOGIES
BOGLES
BOGONG
BOGOTA
COGENT
COGGED
COGNAC
DOGEAR
DOGGED
DOGGER
DOGGIE
DOGIES
DOGLEG
DOGMAS
DOGONS
DOGOOD
DOGSIT
DOGTAG
FOGBOW
FOGEYS
FOGGED
FOGGER
FOGHAT
FOGIES
FOGSIN
GOGGLE
GOGGLY
HOGANS
HOGGED
HOGTIE
JOGGED
JOGGER
JOGGLE
LOGGED
LOGGER
LOGGIA
LOGIER
LOGILY
LOGION
LOGJAM
LOGOFF
LOGOUT
LOGSIN
LOGSON
MOGULS
NOGGIN
NOGOOD
POGIES
ROGERS
ROGUES
TOGAED
TOGGED
TOGGLE
VOGUES
YOGINI
YOGURT

•O•G••
BOGGED
BOGGLE
BOIGNY
BOLGER
BONGED
BONGOS
BOOGIE
BORGIA
BOUGHS
BOUGHT
CODGER
COGGED
CONGAS
CONGER
CONGOU
COOGAN
CORGIS
COUGAR
COUGHS
DODGED
DODGER
DODGES
DOGGED
DOGGER
DOGGIE
DOOGIE
DOUGHS
DOUGHY
FOGGED
FOGGER
FORGED
FORGER
FORGES
FORGET
FORGOT
FOUGHT
GOGGLE
GOGGLY
GONGED
GOOGLE
GOOGLY
GOOGOL
GOOGOO
GORGED
GORGES
GORGET
GORGON
GOUGED
GOUGER
GOUGES
HOAGIE
HOGGED
JOGGED
JOGGER
JOGGLE
LODGED
LODGER
LODGES
LOGGED
LOGGER
LOGGIA
LONGAN
LONGED
LONGER
LONGES
LONGUE
MONGER
MONGOL
MORGAN
MORGEN
MOWGLI
NOGGIN
NORGAY
NOUGAT
NOUGHT
PONGEE
PONGID
POPGUN
ROTGUT
ROUGED
ROUGES
ROUGHS
SOIGNE
SOUGHS
SOUGHT
TOGGED
TOGGLE
TONGAN
TONGUE
TOPGUN
TOUGHS
TOUGHY
VOIGHT
VOSGES
WOOGIE

•O••G•
BODEGA
BOINGO
BORAGE
COLUGO
COSIGN
DOINGS
DOSAGE
DOTAGE
FORAGE
FOREGO
GOINGS
GONOGO
HOMAGE
LOUNGE
LOVAGE
NONAGE
NONEGO
OOLOGY
POTAGE
SOCAGE
TOBAGO
TOWAGE
VOYAGE

•O•••G
BODING
BOEING
BOGONG
BONING
BOOING
BORING
BOWING
BOXING
COBURG
CODING
COMING
COOING
COPING
CORING
COWING
DOGLEG
DOGTAG
DOLING
DOMING
DOPING
DOSING
DOTING
DOZING
FOXING
GORING
GOSTAG
HOEING
HOLING
HOMING
HONING
HOPING
HOSING
HOTDOG
JOKING
LOPING
LOSING
LOVING
LOWING
MOOING
MOPING
MOVING
MOWING
NOSING
NOTING
OOHING
OOLONG
OOZING
POKING
POLING
PORING
POSING
ROBING
ROPING
ROVING
ROWING
SOLING
SOLONG
SONTAG
SOWBUG
SOWING
TOEING
TONING
TOPDOG
TOTING
TOWING
TOYDOG
TOYING
VOTING
VOWING
WONMUG
WOOING
WOWING
YOKING
ZONING

••OG••
APOGEE
BIOGAS
BOOGIE
BROGAN
BROGUE
CLOGUP
COOGAN
DOOGIE
DROGUE
FROGGY
GLOGGS
GOOGLE
GOOGLY
GOOGOL
GOOGOO
GROGGY
IMOGEN
ISOGON
SHOGUN
SLOGAN
SMOGGY
STOGIE
TROGON
WOOGIE

••O•G•
CHOUGH
ELOIGN
ENOUGH
FROGGY
GEORGE
GLOGGS
GROGGY
HMONGS
PLOUGH
PRONGS
SLOUGH
SMOGGY
SPONGE
SPONGY
STODGE
STODGY
STOOGE
THONGS
THOUGH
TROUGH
WRONGS

••O••G
BOOING
COOING
MOOING
PHOTOG
PROLOG
WOOING

•••OG•
BEFOGS
DEFOGS
EULOGY
GONOGO
LADOGA
OOLOGY
STOOGE

•••O•G
ALBORG
BARONG
BELONG
BOGONG
CYBORG
DATONG
DELONG
DUGONG
MEKONG
OBLONG
OOLONG
SARONG
SOLONG
STRONG
THRONG
VYBORG

••••OG
ANALOG
BANDOG
DIALOG
EGGNOG
EPILOG
GASLOG
GUNDOG
HERZOG
HOTDOG
ICEFOG
INAFOG
LAPDOG
LITHOG
PETROG
PHOTOG
PROLOG
PYEDOG
QUAHOG
REDDOG
SAWLOG
SEADOG
STENOG
SUNDOG
TAUTOG
TOPDOG
TOYDOG
UNCLOG

OH••••
OHENRY
OHIOAN
OHWELL
OHYEAH

O•H•••
OCHERS
OCHRES
OGHAMS
ONHAND
ONHIGH
ONHOLD
OOHING
OPHITE
OSHAWA
OTHERS

O••H••
OLDHAM
OLDHAT
OMAHAN
OMAHAS
ORCHID
ORCHIL
ORPHAN
ORPHIC
OUGHTS
OUTHIT

O•••H•
OBEAHS

O••••H
OAFISH
OFFISH
OHYEAH
OLDISH
ONHIGH
ONRUSH
OOLITH
OOMPAH
ORBACH
ORNITH
OWLISH

•OH•••
COHEIR
COHERE
COHORT
COHOST
COHUNE
GOHOME
HOHHOT
HOHOHO
JOHANN
JOHNNY
JOHORE
KOHLER
MOHAIR
MOHAVE
MOHAWK
MOHOCK
MOHURS
NOHITS
OOHING
ROHMER
WOHLER
YOHOHO

•O•H••
BOCHCO
BOOHOO
BOTHER
COBHAM
COCHIN
COSHED
COSHES
DOTHAN
FOEHNS
FOGHAT
GOPHER
GOSHEN
GOTHAM
GOTHIC
HOHHOT
HOOHAH
HOOHAS
JOBHOP
JOSHED
JOSHES
JOSHUA
KOSHER
LOTHAR
MOCHAS
MOSHAV
MOTHER
NOSHED
NOSHER
NOSHES
NOSHOW
POOHED
POSHER
POSHLY
POTHER
ROCHET
RODHAM
ROTHKO
SOPHIA
SOPHIE
SOTHAT
SOWHAT
TOPHAT
TOPHUS
TOTHER
TOWHEE
YOOHOO

•O••H•
BOOTHE
BOOTHS
BOUGHS
BOUGHT
CONCHA
CONCHS
COUGHS
DOUGHS
DOUGHY
FOUGHT
GOETHE
GOTCHA
HOHOHO
HONCHO
HONSHU
LOATHE
LOTAHS
LOUCHE
MONTHS
MORPHO
MORPHS
MOUTHS
MOUTHY
NOUGHT
POACHY
PONCHO
POUCHY
ROUGHS
SOOTHE
SOUGHS
SOUGHT
TOOTHY
TORAHS
TOUCHE
TOUCHY
TOUGHS
TOUGHY
VOIGHT
WORTHS
WORTHY
YOHOHO
YOUTHS

•O•••H
BORSCH
BOYISH
COMETH
DOVISH
EOLITH
FOURTH
GOFISH
GOWITH
HOOHAH
HOOKAH
HOORAH
HOWDAH
IOMOTH
JOBETH
JOSEPH
JOSIAH
LOOFAH
MODISH
MOLOCH
MOOLAH
MOPISH
OOLITH
OOMPAH
POLISH
POTASH
TONISH
VOTECH

••OH••
ABOHMS
ALOHAS
BOOHOO
ELOHIM
HOOHAH
HOOHAS
ISOHEL
MYOHMY
POOHED
YOOHOO

••O•H•
BOOTHE
BOOTHS
BROTHS
CLOCHE
CLOTHE
CLOTHO
CLOTHS
EPOCHS
FROTHS
FROTHY
QUOTHA
SLOSHY
SLOTHS
SOOTHE
TOOTHY
TROCHE
TROPHY
TROTHS

••O••H
ADOLPH
AVOUCH
BLOTCH
BROACH
BROOCH
CHOUGH
CROUCH
ENOUGH
GROUCH
GROWTH
HOOHAH
HOOKAH
HOORAH
LOOFAH
MOOLAH
PLOUGH
SCORCH
SCOTCH
SLOUCH
SLOUGH
SMOOCH
SMOOTH
STORCH
SWOOSH
THOUGH
TROUGH
WHOOSH

•••OH•
HOHOHO
JAWOHL
MEGOHM
STJOHN
YOHOHO

•••O•H
BROOCH
BYGOSH
GALOSH
IOMOTH
KIBOSH
MOLOCH
SMOOCH
SMOOTH
SPLOSH
SWOOSH
WHOOSH
ZEROTH

••••OH
MATZOH
SHILOH

OI••••
OILCAN
OILERS
OILIER
OILING
OILMAN
OILMEN
OILPAN
OILRIG
OINKED

O•I•••
OBISPO
OBITER
OBIWAN
ODIOUS
ODISTS
ODIUMS
OGIVES
OHIOAN
OJIBWA
OLINDA
OLINGO
OLIVER
OLIVES
OLIVIA
ONIONS
ONIONY
OPIATE
OPINED
OPINER
OPINES
ORIANA
ORIBIS
ORIELS
ORIENT
ORIGEN
ORIGIN
ORINGS
ORIOLE
ORISON
ORISSA
OSIERS
OSIRIS
OTIOSE
OTITIC
OTITIS
OVIEDO
OVISAC
OXIDES
OXIDIC

O••I••
OAFISH
OARING
OATIER
OBLIGE
OBOIST
OBRIAN
OBRIEN
ODDITY
OFFICE
OFFING
OFFISH
OGLING
OILIER
OILING
OLDIES
OLDISH
OMNIUM
ONDINE
ONEIDA
ONEILL
ONFILE
ONFIRE
ONHIGH
ONLINE
ONSIDE
ONSITE
ONTIME
ONVIEW
OOHING
OOLITE
OOLITH
OOZING
OPHITE
OPTICS
OPTIMA
OPTING
OPTION
ORBING
ORBITS
OREIDA
ORGIES
ORNITH
OROIDE
ORPINE
ORSINO
OSCINE
OSMICS
OSMIUM
OSSIAN
OSSIFY
OSTIUM
OUTING
OVOIDS
OWLISH
OWNING
OXLIPS

O•••I•
OBELIA
OBTAIN
OILRIG
OKAPIS
OLDVIC
OLEFIN
OLIVIA
OMANIS
ORCHID
ORCHIL
ORDAIN
ORIBIS
ORIGIN
ORPHIC
OSIRIS
OSSEIN
OTITIC
OTITIS
OUTBID
OUTDID
OUTFIT
OUTHIT
OUTWIT
OXALIS
OXIDIC
OXTAIL
OZONIC

O••••I
OCELLI
OCTOPI
OCTROI

•OI•••
BOIGNY
BOILED
BOILER
BOINGO
BOITES
COIFED
COILED
COILUP
COINED
COINER
DOINGS
FOIBLE
FOILED
FOISTS
GOINGS
GOINTO
HOISTS
JOINED
JOINER
JOININ
JOINTS
JOINUP
JOISTS
LOITER
MOIETY
MOILED
MOILER
MOINES
MOIRES
NOIRON
NOISED
NOISES
POILUS
POINTE
POINTS
POINTY
POIROT
POISED
POISES
POISON
ROILED
SOIGNE
SOILED
SOIREE
TOILED
TOILER
TOILES
TOILET
VOICED
VOICES
VOIDED
VOIGHT
VOILES
YOICKS

•O•I••
AORIST
BODICE
BODIED
BODIES
BODILY
BODING
BOEING
BOGIES
BOLIDE
BONIER
BONING
BONITO
BOOING
BORIDE
BORING
BOVIDS
BOVINE
BOWING
BOXING
BOYISH
COBIAS
CODIFY
CODING
COLIMA
COMICS
COMING
COMITY
CONICS
CONIES
CONIUM
COOING
COPIED
COPIER
COPIES
COPING
CORING
CORIUM
COSIES
COSIGN
COSINE
COVINA
COWING
COZIED
COZIER
COZIES
COZILY
DOCILE
DOGIES
DOLING
DOMING
DOMINI
DOMINO
DONITZ
DOPIER
DOPING
DORIAN
DORIES
DOSIDO
DOSING
DOTING
DOVISH
DOZILY
DOZING
EOLIAN
EOLITH
EONIAN
EOSINS
FOGIES
FOLIAR
FOLIOS
FOLIUM
FORINT
FOXIER
FOXILY
FOXING
GOBIES
GODIVA
GOFISH
GOOIER
GORIER
GORING
GOWILD
GOWITH
HOEING
HOKIER
HOLIER
HOLING
HOLISM
HOLIST
HOMIER
HOMILY
HOMING
HOMINY
HONIED
HONING
HOPING
HOSIER
HOSING
IODIDE
IODINE
IODIZE
IOLITE
IONIAN
IONICS
IONIUM
IONIZE
JOKING
JOLIET
JOLIOT
JOSIAH
JOVIAL
JOVIAN
KODIAK
KONICA
LOGIER
LOGILY
LOGION
LOLITA
LOPING
LORICA
LORIES
LOSING
LOTION
LOUISA
LOUISE
LOVING
LOWING
MOBILE
MOBIUS
MODIFY
MODINE
MODISH
MOLINE
MONICA
MONIED
MONIES
MONISM
MONIST
MOOING
MOPING
MOPISH
MORION
MORITA
MORITZ
MOTIFS
MOTILE
MOTION
MOTIVE
MOVIES
MOVING
MOWING
NODICE
NOHITS
NORIAS
NOSIER
NOSILY
NOSING
NOTICE
NOTIFY
NOTING
NOTION
NOVICE
NOWISE
OOHING
OOLITE
OOLITH
OOZING
PODIUM
POGIES
POKIER
POKILY
POKING
POLICE
POLICY
POLING
POLISH
POLITE
POLITY
PONIED
PONIES
PORING
POSIES
POSING
POSITS
POTION
ROBING
ROBINS
ROPIER
ROPING
ROSIER
ROSILY
ROSINS
ROSINY
ROSITA
ROTINI
ROVING
ROWING
SOCIAL
SODIUM
SOFINE
SOLIDI
SOLIDS

SOLING
SONICS
SOVIET
SOWING
TOBIAS
TOBIES
TOEING
TOEINS
TOLIFE
TONICS
TONIER
TONING
TONISH
TONITE
TOPICS
TORIES
TORINO
TOTING
TOWING
TOXICS
TOXINS
TOYING
VOTING
VOTIVE
VOWING
WOOING
WOWING
YOGINI
YOKING
YORICK
ZODIAC
ZONING
ZORILS

•O••I•
AODAIS
AORTIC
BOBBIE
BOBBIN
BOCCIE
BODKIN
BOLLIX
BONNIE
BOOGIE
BOOKIE
BOOTIE
BORGIA
BOSNIA
BOUDIN
BOWFIN
BOWTIE
COATIS
COCCID
COCHIN
COEDIT
COHEIR
COLLIE
COMEIN
COMFIT
COMMIT
COMMIX
CONNIE
COOKIE
COOLIT
COOTIE
COPTIC
CORBIN
CORGIS
COSMIC
COURIC
COUSIN
COWRIE
DOBBIN
DOBLIN
DOESIN
DOGGIE
DOGSIT
DOMAIN
DONEIN
DOOBIE
DOOGIE
DOOZIE
DORRIT
DOTTIE
DOVEIN
FOGSIN
FOLKIE
FORBID
FORMIC
FOSSIL
FOZZIE
GOALIE
GOBLIN
GODWIN
GODWIT
GOESIN
GOLDIE
GOODIE
GORDIE
GOSSIP
GOTHIC
GOTOIT
HOAGIE
HOBBIT
HOGTIE
HOLDIT
HOOFIT
HORRID
HOTAIR
HOTTIP
HOURIS
HOWLIN
JOANIE
JOININ
JOPLIN
KOOKIE
LOCKIN
LOGGIA
LOGSIN
LOMEIN
LOOKIN
LOSEIT
LOSTIT
LOVEIN
MOHAIR
MOMMIE
MORBID
MORRIS
MOSAIC
MOULIN
MOVEIN
NOESIS
NOETIC
NOEXIT
NOGGIN
NORDIC
NORRIS
POETIC
PONGID
PONTIC
POPLIN
POPSIN
PORTIA
POTPIE
POURIN
ROADIE
ROBBIE
ROLLIE
ROLLIN
ROMAIC
RONNIE
ROOKIE
ROOMIE
ROPEIN
SOBEIT
SOCKIN
SOFFIT
SOFTIE
SOLEIL
SOPHIA
SOPHIE
SORBIC
SORDID
SORTIE
TOCSIN
TOEDIN
TOESIN
TOMLIN
TOMMIX
TOMTIT
TONKIN
TONSIL
TOOKIN
TOOKIT
TOROID
TORPID
TORRID
TOWNIE
VOTEIN
WOOGIE
WOOKIE
WORKIN
ZOMBIE
ZOYSIA

•O•••I
BODONI
BONAMI
BONSAI
BORZOI
DOMANI
DOMINI
DORATI
DOREMI
MORONI
MOWGLI
POLLOI
POPULI
POTOSI
ROMAJI
ROTINI
SOLIDI
SOMALI
SOUARI
YOGINI

••OI••
ALOINS
ANOINT
AROIDS
AVOIDS
BOOING
BROILS
CHOICE
CHOIRS
COOING
DROIDS
DROITS
EGOISM
EGOIST
ELOIGN
ELOISE
EROICA
ETOILE
GOOIER
GROINS
IDOIDO
ILOILO
MAOISM
MAOIST
MOOING
OBOIST
OROIDE
OVOIDS
QUOINS
QUOITS
REOILS
SPOILS
SPOILT
STOICS
TAOISM
TAOIST
TROIKA
WOOING

••O•I•
ADONIS
AEOLIA
AEOLIC
ANODIC
ANOMIE
ATOMIC
ATONIC
AZORIN
BIOBIO
BIONIC
BIOTIC
BIOTIN
BLOWIN
BLOWIT
BMOVIE
BOOGIE
BOOKIE
BOOTIE
BRODIE
CHOPIN
CLORIS
CLOVIS
COOKIE
COOLIT
COOTIE
CRONIN
DHOTIS
DIOXIN
DOOBIE
DOOGIE
DOOZIE
DROPIN
DROPIT
ELOHIM
ENOKIS
ENOSIS
EROTIC
ETONIC
EXOTIC
FLORID
FLORIN
FROLIC
GLOBIN
GLORIA
GNOMIC
GNOSIS
GOODIE
GRODIN
HOOFIT
ICONIC
IRONIC
KAOLIN
KOOKIE
LEONID
LEONIE
LOOKIN
MAORIS
MIOSIS
MYOPIA
MYOPIC
MYOSIN
OZONIC
PEORIA
PHOBIA
PHOBIC
PHOCIS
PHONIC
PHOTIC
PROFIT
PROLIX
PROSIT
ROOKIE
ROOMIE
SCORIA
SCOTIA
SHOJIS
SHOOIN
SHOWIN
SKOKIE
SLOVIK
SNOWIN
STOGIE
STOLID
STOPIN
STOPIT
TOOKIN
TOOKIT
TROPIC
TWOBIT
UTOPIA
VIOLIN
WOOGIE
WOOKIE

••O••I
ADONAI
AGOUTI
BIONDI
DROMOI
MAOTAI
PROTEI
RHOMBI
WHOOPI

•••OI•
ADJOIN
ADROIT
ALBOIN
ARTOIS
BELOIT
BENOIT
CUBOID
DACOIT
DEVOID
DEVOIR
DUBOIS
ECHOIC
ENJOIN
ENVOIS
GALOIS
GOTOIT
HALOID
HEROIC
LIPOID
MEMOIR
PATOIS
REBOIL
RECOIL
REJOIN
RENOIR
REVOIR
SAVOIE
SAVOIR
SHOOIN
TOROID
UNCOIL
VALOIS
XYLOID
ZEROIN

•••O•I
BILOXI
BODONI
BUSONI
CARONI
EPHORI
JACOBI
LUGOSI
MALOTI
MIDORI
MORONI
NAPOLI
NEROLI
OCTOPI
PILOTI
POTOSI
PRIORI
SATORI
TIVOLI
WHOOPI

••••OI
BORZOI
DROMOI
KERNOI
MYTHOI
OCTROI
POLLOI

OJ••••
OJIBWA

O•J•••
OBJECT

O••J••
ODDJOB

•OJ•••
JOJOBA
MOJAVE

•O•J••
BOOJUM
CONJOB
DONJON
KOPJES
LOGJAM
TOPJOB

•O••J•
ROMAJI

••OJ••
BOOJUM
RIOJAS
SHOJIS
STOJKO
TROJAN

••O•J•
SKOPJE

•••OJ•
BAROJA

OK••••
OKAPIS
OKAYED
OKEEFE
OKELLY

O•K•••
OAKLEY
ORKNEY

O••K••
OFFKEY
OINKED

O•••K•
OZARKS

O••••K
OCASEK
OCLOCK
ONDECK

•OK•••
FOKKER
GOKART
HOKIER
JOKERS
JOKING
KOKOMO
POKEAT
POKERS
POKERY
POKEYS
POKIER
POKILY
POKING
TOKAYS
TOKENS
TOKLAS
WOKEUP
YOKELS
YOKING
YOKUTS

•O•K••
BODKIN
BOOKED
BOOKER
BOOKIE
BOSKET
COCKED
COCKER
COCKLE
CONKED
CONKER
COOKED
COOKER
COOKIE
COOKUP
CORKED
CORKER
DOCKED
DOCKER
DOCKET
DONKEY
FOKKER
FOLKIE
FOLKSY
FORKED
FORKER
HOCKED
HOCKEY
HONKED
HONKER
HOOKAH
HOOKED
HOOKUP
JOCKEY
KOOKIE
LOCKED
LOCKER
LOCKET
LOCKIN
LOCKUP
LOOKAT
LOOKED
LOOKER
LOOKIN
LOOKON
LOOKTO
LOOKUP
LOWKEY
MOCKED
MOCKER
MOCKUP
MONKEY
MOSKVA
POCKET
POLKAS
PORKER
ROCKED
ROCKER
ROCKET
ROCKNE
ROCKYV
ROOKED
ROOKIE
SOAKED
SOAKER
SOAKUP
SOCKED
SOCKET
SOCKIN
TONKIN
TOOKIN
TOOKIT
TOOKON
TOOKTO
TOOKUP
WOOKIE
WORKED
WORKER
WORKIN
WORKON
WORKUP
YOLKED
YORKER
ZONKED
ZONKER

•O••K•
BOURKE
KOPEKS
MOLTKE
NOOTKA
ROTHKO
TOPEKA
WOVOKA
YOICKS

•O•••K
GOBACK
KODIAK
KOPECK
LOMBOK
MOHAWK
MOHOCK
PODUNK
TOBRUK
VOSTOK
YORICK

••OK••
AWOKEN
BLOKES
BOOKED
BOOKER
BOOKIE
BROKAW
BROKEN
BROKER
CHOKED
CHOKER
CHOKES
COOKED
COOKER
COOKIE
COOKUP
ENOKIS
EVOKED
EVOKER
EVOKES
HOOKAH
HOOKED
HOOKUP
KOOKIE
LOOKAT
LOOKED
LOOKER
LOOKIN
LOOKON
LOOKTO
LOOKUP
QUOKKA
ROOKED
ROOKIE
RYOKAN
SKOKIE
SMOKED
SMOKER
SMOKES
SMOKEY
SPOKED
SPOKEN
SPOKES
STOKED
STOKER
STOKES
TOOKIN
TOOKIT
TOOKON
TOOKTO
TOOKUP
WOOKIE

••O•K•
BLOCKS
BLOCKY
BROOKE
BROOKS
CHOCKS
CLOAKS
CLOCKS
CLONKS
CROAKS
CROAKY
CROCKS
CROOKS
FLOCKS
FROCKS
KIOSKS
KNOCKS
NOOTKA
PLONKS
QUOKKA
SHOCKS
SHOOKS
SMOCKS
SNOOKS
SPOOKS
SPOOKY
STOCKS
STOCKY
STOJKO
STORKS
TROIKA

••O••K
ANORAK
DVORAK
SLOVAK
SLOVIK

•••OK•
BROOKE
BROOKS
CROOKS
INJOKE
INVOKE
JAMOKE
JUDOKA
MIWOKS
REVOKE
SHOOKS
SNOOKS
SPOOKS
SPOOKY
STROKE
UNYOKE
WOVOKA
YAPOKS
YUROKS

•••O•K
ATWORK
BETOOK
BUROAK
DRHOOK
FAROUK
MOHOCK
NANOOK
OCLOCK
PINOAK
RECORK
REDOAK
REHOOK
RELOCK
RETOOK
REWORK
TANOAK
UNCORK
UNHOOK
UNLOCK

••••OK
BARTOK
BETOOK
DRHOOK
HICKOK
LOMBOK
NANOOK
REEBOK
REHOOK
RETOOK
RHEBOK
UNHOOK
VOSTOK

OL••••
OLDBOY
OLDEST
OLDHAM
OLDHAT
OLDIES
OLDISH
OLDMAN
OLDMEN
OLDPRO
OLDVIC
OLEARY
OLEATE
OLEFIN
OLEVEL
OLINDA
OLINGO
OLIVER
OLIVES
OLIVIA
OLMECS

O•L•••
OBLAST
OBLATE
OBLIGE
OBLONG
OCLOCK
OFLATE
OGLALA
OGLERS
OGLING
OILCAN
OILERS
OILIER
OILING
OILMAN
OILMEN
OILPAN
OILRIG
ONLAND
ONLINE
ONLOAN
OOLALA
OOLITE
OOLITH
OOLOGY
OOLONG
ORLOPS
OWLETS
OWLISH
OXLIPS

O••L••
OAKLEY
OBELIA
OBELUS
OCELLI
OCELOT
OCULAR
ODDLOT
OKELLY
OMELET
OODLES
ORALES
ORALLY
ORELSE
ORTLES
OSTLER
OTELLO
OUTLAW
OUTLAY
OUTLET
OVULAR
OVULES
OXALIS

O•••L•
OCCULT
OCELLI
OGLALA
OHWELL
OKELLY
ONCALL
ONEILL
ONFILE
ONHOLD
ONSALE
OOLALA
OPENLY
ORACLE
ORALLY
ORIELS
ORIOLE
ORMOLU
ORWELL
OSCULA
OSWALD
OTELLO
OTOOLE
OUSELS
OUZELS
OVERLY

O••••L
OHWELL
OLEVEL
ONCALL
ONEILL
ORCHIL
ORDEAL
ORWELL
OSTEAL
OXTAIL
OXYDOL

•OL•••
BOLDER
BOLDLY
BOLERO
BOLEYN
BOLGER
BOLIDE
BOLLIX
BOLTED
BOLTON
COLADA
COLDER
COLDLY
COLEUS
COLIMA
COLLAR
COLLET
COLLIE
COLLOP
COLLOQ
COLMAN
COLONS
COLONY
COLORS
COLOUR
COLTER
COLUGO
COLUMN
DOLING
DOLLAR
DOLLED
DOLLOP
DOLLUP
DOLMAN
DOLMAS
DOLMEN
DOLORS
EOLIAN
EOLITH
FOLDED
FOLDER
FOLDUP
FOLIAR
FOLIOS
FOLIUM
FOLKIE
FOLKSY
FOLLOW
FOLSOM
GOLDEN
GOLDIE
GOLEMS
GOLFED
GOLFER
GOLLUM
HOLDEN
HOLDER
HOLDIT
HOLDON
HOLDTO
HOLDUP
HOLEUP
HOLIER
HOLING
HOLISM
HOLIST
HOLLER
HOLLOW
HOLMES
IOLITE
JOLENE
JOLIET
JOLIOT
JOLSON
JOLTED
LOLITA
LOLLED
MOLARS
MOLDAU
MOLDED
MOLDER
MOLEST
MOLINE
MOLNAR
MOLOCH
MOLOPO
MOLTED
MOLTEN
MOLTER
MOLTKE
NOLEAD
NOLENS
NOLESS
NOLOAD
OOLALA
OOLITE
OOLITH
OOLOGY
OOLONG
POLAND
POLDER
POLEAX
POLERS
POLEYN
POLICE
POLICY
POLING
POLISH
POLITE
POLITY
POLKAS
POLLED
POLLEN
POLLER
POLLEX
POLLOI
POLLUX
POLPOT
POLYPS
ROLAND
ROLEOS
ROLLED
ROLLER
ROLLIE
ROLLIN
ROLLON
ROLLUP
SOLACE
SOLANS
SOLDAN
SOLDER
SOLDON
SOLEIL
SOLELY
SOLEMN
SOLENT
SOLERS
SOLEUS
SOLFAS
SOLIDI
SOLIDS
SOLING
SOLOED
SOLONG
SOLUTE
SOLVED
SOLVER
SOLVES
TOLDOF
TOLEDO
TOLIFE
TOLLED
TOLTEC
TOLUCA
VOLANS
VOLANT
VOLARE
VOLENS
VOLLEY
VOLUME
VOLUTE
VOLVAS
VOLVOX
WOLFED
WOLPER
WOLSEY
WOLVES
YOLKED

•O•L••
BOGLES
BOILED
BOILER
BOLLIX
BOSLEY
BOULES
BOULEZ
BOULLE
BOWLED
BOWLER
BOWLES
COALER
COELOM
COILED
COILUP
COLLAR
COLLET
COLLIE
COLLOP
COLLOQ
COOLED
COOLER
COOLIT
COOLLY
COULEE
COWLED
COWLEY
DOBLAS
DOBLIN
DOGLEG
DOLLAR
DOLLED
DOLLOP
DOLLUP
DOOLEY
FOALED
FOILED
FOLLOW
FOOLED
FOOLER
FOULED
FOULER
FOULLY
FOULUP
FOWLED
FOWLER
FOWLES
GOALIE
GOBLET
GOBLIN
GOLLUM
GOSLOW
GOULET
HOLLER
HOLLOW
HOWLED
HOWLER
HOWLIN
JOBLOT
JOPLIN
JOULES
KOALAS
KOHLER
LOLLED
MOBLEY
MOILED
MOILER
MOOLAH
MORLEY
MOSLEM
MOTLEY
MOULDS
MOULDY

MOULIN
MOULTS
NOBLER
NOBLES
OODLES
POILUS
POLLED
POLLEN
POLLER
POLLEX
POLLOI
POLLUX
POOLED
POPLAR
POPLIN
POULTS
ROBLES
ROILED
ROLLED
ROLLER
ROLLIE
ROLLIN
ROLLON
ROLLUP
SOCLES
SOILED
TOILED
TOILER
TOILES
TOILET
TOKLAS
TOLLED
TOMLIN
TOOLED
TOOLUP
TOULON
VOILES
VOLLEY
WOHLER
WOOLEN
WOOLEY
WOOLLY
WORLDS
YOWLED

•O••L•

BOBBLE
BODILY
BOGGLE
BOLDLY
BOODLE
BOTFLY
BOTTLE
BOUCLE
BOULLE
COBALT
COBBLE
COCKLE
CODDLE
COLDLY
COMELY
COMPLY
COOLLY
COPULA
CORALS
COSELL
COSTLY
COUPLE
COZILY
DOABLE
DOCILE
DONALD
DOODLE
DOTELL
DOTTLE
DOUBLE
DOUBLY
DOURLY
DOWELS
DOZILY
FOCSLE
FOIBLE
FONDLE
FONDLY
FOOZLE
FOULLY
FOXILY
GOBBLE
GOGGLE
GOGGLY
GOODLY
GOOGLE
GOOGLY
GORALS
GOWILD
HOBBLE
HOMELY
HOMILY
HOOPLA
HOOPLE
HOPPLE
HOSELS
HOTELS
HOURLY
HOVELS
HOWELL
JOGGLE
JOSTLE
KOBOLD
KODALY
LOBULE
LOCALE
LOCALS
LOGILY
LONELY
LORDLY
LOUDLY
LOVELL
LOVELY
LOWELL
LOYOLA
MOBILE
MODELA
MODELS
MODELT
MODULE
MODULO
MOGULS
MORALE
MORALS
MORELS
MOSTLY
MOTELS
MOTILE
MOTTLE
MOWGLI
NODDLE
NODULE
NOODLE
NOSALE
NOSILY
NOVELS
NOZZLE
OOLALA
POKILY
POMELO
POODLE
POORLY
POPFLY
POPPLE
POPULI
PORTLY
POSHLY
POTTLE
POWELL
ROBALO
ROMOLA
RONALD
RONELY
ROSILY
ROWELS
ROYALE
ROYALS
SOFTLY
SOLELY
SOMALI
SORELY
SOTOLS
SOURLY
TODDLE
TOGGLE
TOOTLE
TOPPLE
TOTALS
TOUSLE
TOWELS
VOCALS
VOWELS
WOBBLE
WOBBLY
WOOLLY
YODELS
YOKELS
YOUALL
ZORILS

•O•••L

AORTAL
BOREAL
BOXFUL
COEVAL
COMPEL
CONSUL
CORBEL
CORNEL
CORRAL
CORREL
COSELL
COSTAL
DORSAL
DOSSAL
DOSSEL
DOTELL
FONTAL
FORMAL
FOSSIL
GOOGOL
GOSPEL
HORMEL
HOSTEL
HOWELL
JOVIAL
JOYFUL
KOPPEL
LONNOL
LOREAL
LOVELL
LOWCAL
LOWELL
MONGOL
MONTEL
MORSEL
MORTAL
MOSTEL
NORMAL
POMMEL
PORTAL
POSTAL
POTFUL
POWELL
ROMMEL
RONDEL
SOCIAL
SOLEIL
SORREL
TONSIL
WOEFUL
YOUALL

••OL••

ABOLLA
ADOLPH
AEOLIA
AEOLIC
AEOLUS
AMOLES
ANOLES
APOLLO
ATOLLS
BROLLY
CHOLER
CHOLLA
COOLED
COOLER
COOLIT
COOLLY
DHOLES
DOOLEY
DROLLS
DROLLY
ECOLES
EVOLVE
FOOLED
FOOLER
FROLIC
ISOLDE
KAOLIN
KJOLEN
KNOLLS
MOOLAH
PIOLET
POOLED
PROLES
PROLIX
PROLOG
SCOLDS
SHOLEM
SHOLOM
STOLEN
STOLES
STOLID
STOLLE
STOLON
THOLES
TOOLED
TOOLUP
TROLLS
UBOLTS
VIOLAS
VIOLET
VIOLIN
WHOLES
WHOLLY
WOOLEN
WOOLEY
WOOLLY

••O•L•

ABOLLA
APOLLO
ATOLLS
BOODLE
BROILS
BROLLY
CHOLLA
COOLLY
DOODLE
DROLLS
DROLLY
DROOLS
ETOILE
FOOZLE
GHOULS
GOODLY
GOOGLE
GOOGLY
GROWLS
GROWLY
HOOPLA
HOOPLE
ILOILO
KNOLLS
NOODLE
OTOOLE
PEOPLE
POODLE
POORLY
PROWLS
REOILS
SCOWLS
SHOALS
SHOULD
SLOWLY
SPOILS
SPOILT
SPOOLS
STOLLE
STOOLS
TOOTLE
TROLLS
TWOPLY
WHOLLY
WHORLS
WOOLLY

••O••L

ABORAL
AMORAL
APODAL
ATONAL
AVOWAL
AXONAL
BHOPAL
CHORAL
DHOTEL
FLORAL
GLOBAL
GOOGOL
GROVEL
ISOHEL
LIONEL
PROPEL
SHOVEL
TROWEL

•••OL•

AGEOLD
ANGOLA
AREOLA
ARNOLD
BAROLO
BEHOLD
BIFOLD
BUJOLD
CAJOLE
CANOLA
CAROLE
CAROLS
CIBOLA
CREOLE
CUPOLA
DIPOLE
DROOLS
EIDOLA
ENFOLD
ENROLL
ERROLL
EXTOLS
GIGOLO
HAROLD
INFOLD
INSOLE
KOBOLD
LOYOLA
MAZOLA
NAPOLI
NEROLI
NICOLA
NICOLE
NICOLO
NIKOLA
ONHOLD
ORIOLE
ORMOLU
OTOOLE
PAROLE
PAYOLA
PINOLE
REBOLT
REPOLL
RESOLD
RESOLE
RETOLD
REVOLT
ROMOLA
RUDOLF
SCROLL
SOTOLS
SPOOLS
STOOLS
STROLL
TIVOLI
UNBOLT
UNFOLD
UNHOLY
UNROLL
UNSOLD
UNTOLD
UPHOLD

•••O•L

BEFOUL
ENROLL
ENSOUL
ERROLL
JAWOHL
MRCOOL
REBOIL
RECOIL
REPOLL
RETOOL
SCHOOL
SCHORL
SCROLL
STROLL
UNCOIL
UNCOOL
UNROLL

••••OL

AMATOL
AMIDOL
BENZOL
CARROL
CRESOL
ETYMOL
FRIJOL
GAMBOL
GLYCOL
GOOGOL
LONNOL
MONGOL
MRCOOL
MYTHOL
NEUROL
OXYDOL
PATHOL
PATROL
PETROL
PHENOL
PHILOL
PISTOL
RETOOL
SCHOOL
STEROL
SYMBOL
UNCOOL
WARHOL

OM••••

OMAHAN
OMAHAS
OMANIS
OMASUM
OMEGAS
OMELET
OMERTA
OMNIUM

O•M•••

OLMECS
OOMPAH
ORMOLU
ORMOND
OSMICS
OSMIUM
OSMOND
OSMOSE
OSMUND

O••M••

OILMAN
OILMEN
OLDMAN
OLDMEN

O•••M•

ODIUMS
OEDEMA
OGHAMS
ONTIME
OPTIMA

O••••M

OLDHAM
OMASUM
OMNIUM
OSMIUM
OSTIUM

•OM•••

BOMBAY
BOMBED
BOMBER
BOMBES
COMATE
COMBAT
COMBED
COMBER
COMBES
COMBOS
COMEAT
COMEBY
COMEDY
COMEIN
COMELY
COMEON
COMERS
COMETH
COMETO
COMETS
COMEUP
COMFIT
COMICS
COMING
COMITY
COMMAS
COMMIT
COMMIX
COMMON
COMPAQ
COMPEL
COMPLY
COMPOS
COMSAT
COMTES
DOMAIN
DOMANI
DOMING
DOMINI
DOMINO
FOMENT
HOMAGE
HOMBRE
HOMEEC
HOMELY
HOMERS
HOMIER
HOMILY
HOMING
HOMINY
IOMOTH
KOMODO
LOMBOK
LOMEIN
LOMOND
MOMENT
MOMMAS
MOMMIE
NOMADS
NOMORE
OOMPAH
POMACE
POMADE
POMELO
POMMEE
POMMEL
POMONA
POMPEY
POMPOM
POMPON
ROMAIC
ROMAJI
ROMANO
ROMANS
ROMANY
ROMEOS
ROMERO
ROMMEL
ROMNEY
ROMOLA
ROMPED
ROMPER
SOMALI
SOMANY
SOMATA
SOMATO
SOMBER
SOMBRE
SOMERS
SOMMER
TOMATO
TOMBAC
TOMBOY
TOMCAT
TOMLIN
TOMMIX
TOMTIT
TOMTOM
WOMBAT
WOMENS
ZOMBIE

•O•M••

BONMOT
BOOMED
BOOMER
BORMAN
BOWMAN
BOWMEN
COLMAN
COMMAS
COMMIT
COMMIX
COMMON
CONMAN
CONMEN
COSMIC
COSMOS
COWMAN
COWMEN
DOGMAS
DOLMAN
DOLMAS
DOLMEN
DOOMED
DORMER
FOAMED
FORMAN
FORMAT
FORMED
FORMER
FORMIC
GOTMAD
HOLMES
HORMEL
HORMUZ
KORMAN
LOAMED
LOOMED
MOMMAS
MOMMIE
MORMON
MOTMOT
NORMAL
NORMAN
NOUMEA
POMMEE
POMMEL
ROAMED
ROAMER
ROHMER
ROMMEL
ROOMED
ROOMER
ROOMIE
SOMMER
TOAMAN
TODMAN
TOMMIX
WONMUG
WORMED
ZOOMED

•O••M•

BONAMI
COLIMA
COLUMN
DODOMA
DOREMI
FORUMS
GOHOME
GOLEMS
JORUMS
KOKOMO
MODEMS
NONAME
SOLEMN
SONOMA
TOTEMS
VOLUME
YOYOMA

•O•••M

BOOJUM
BOTTOM
COBHAM
COELOM
CONIUM
CORIUM
DORSUM
FOLIUM
FOLSOM
GOLLUM
GOTHAM
HOLISM
IONIUM
LOGJAM
MONISM
MOSLEM
NONCOM
PODIUM
POMPOM
POSSUM
RODHAM
SODIUM
TOMTOM

••OM••

ABOMBS
ALOMAR
ANOMIE
AROMAS
ATOMIC
BIOMES
BOOMED
BOOMER
CHOMPS
CLOMPS
DOOMED
DROMOI
DROMOS
DUOMOS
GNOMES
GNOMIC
GNOMON
HBOMBS
ISOMER
LOOMED
PROMOS
PROMPT
RHOMBI
RHOMBS
ROOMED
ROOMER
ROOMIE
STOMAS
STOMAT
STOMPS
THOMAS
TROMPE
TROMPS
WHOMPS
YEOMAN
YEOMEN
ZOOMED

••O•M•

ABOHMS
BLOOMS
BLOOMY
BROOMS
GLOOMS
GLOOMY
GROOMS
MYOHMY
PROAMS
PROEMS
SHOWME
STORMS
STORMY
VROOMS

••O••M

ANONYM
BOOJUM
EGOISM
ELOHIM
EPONYM
MAOISM
PROTEM
QUORUM
SHOLEM
SHOLOM
TAOISM

•••OM•

APLOMB
ATHOME
AXIOMS
BECOME
BESOMS
BLOOMS
BLOOMY
BROOMS
CAROMS
CDROMS
CHROMA
CHROME
CHROMO
DODOMA
GENOME
GLOOMS
GLOOMY
GOHOME
GROOMS
IDIOMS
INCOME
JEROME
KOKOMO
PALOMA
RADOME
SALOME
SONOMA
TACOMA
VENOMS
VROOMS
YOYOMA

•••O•M

ABLOOM
DEFORM
INFORM
KABOOM
MEGOHM
PHLOEM
REFORM
SHBOOM
SILOAM

••••OM

ABLOOM
BOTTOM
COELOM
CUSTOM
DIATOM
FANDOM
FATHOM
FOLSOM
HANSOM
KABOOM
MADTOM
NONCOM
PHENOM
POMPOM
RANDOM
RANSOM
SELDOM
SHALOM
SHBOOM
SHOLOM
SITCOM
SLALOM
TOMTOM
VIACOM
WHILOM
WINDOM
WISDOM

ON••••

ONAGER
ONCALL
ONDECK
ONDINE
ONEDAY
ONEDGE
ONEIDA
ONEILL
ONETWO
ONEUPS
ONEWAY
ONFILE
ONFIRE
ONFOOT
ONHAND
ONHIGH
ONHOLD
ONIONS
ONIONY
ONLAND
ONLINE
ONLOAN
ONRUSH
ONSALE
ONSETS
ONSIDE
ONSITE
ONSPEC
ONTAPE
ONTIME
ONTOUR
ONUSES
ONVIEW
ONWARD
ONYXES

O•N•••

OENONE
OINKED
OMNIUM
ORNATE
ORNERY
ORNITH
OUNCES
OWNERS
OWNING
OWNSUP
OXNARD

O••N••

ODENSE
ODONTO
OHENRY
OLINDA
OLINGO
OMANIS
OPENED
OPENER
OPENLY
OPENTO
OPENUP
OPINED
OPINER
OPINES
ORANGE
ORANGS
ORANTS
ORINGS
ORKNEY
OZONIC

O•••N•

OARING
OBLONG
OBTUND
OCEANS
OCTANE
OCTANT
OENONE
OFFEND
OFFING
OGLING
OILING
ONDINE
ONHAND
ONIONS
ONIONY
ONLAND
ONLINE
OOHING
OOLONG
OOZING
OPTING
ORBING
ORGANA
ORGANS
ORIANA
ORIENT
ORMOND
ORPINE
ORSINO
OSCINE
OSMOND
OSMUND
OSTEND
OUTING
OWNING

O••••N

OBERON
OBIWAN
OBRIAN
OBRIEN
OBTAIN
ODDSON
OHIOAN
OILCAN
OILMAN
OILMEN
OILPAN
OLDMAN
OLDMEN
OLEFIN
OMAHAN
ONLOAN
OPPUGN
OPTION
ORDAIN
OREGON
ORIGEN
ORIGIN
ORISON
ORPHAN
OSBORN
OSSEIN
OSSIAN
OUTGUN
OUTRAN
OUTRUN
OXYGEN

•ON•••

BONAMI
BONBON
BONDED
BONERS
BONEUP
BONGED
BONGOS
BONIER
BONING
BONITO
BONMOT
BONNES
BONNET
BONNIE
BONSAI
BONTON
BONZES
CONANT
CONCHA
CONCHS
CONCUR
CONDOR
CONDOS
CONEYS
CONFAB
CONFED
CONFER
CONGAS
CONGER
CONGOU
CONICS
CONIES
CONIUM
CONJOB
CONKED
CONKER
CONMAN
CONMEN
CONNED
CONNER
CONNIE
CONNOR
CONOCO
CONRAD
CONROY
CONSUL
CONTAC
CONTES
CONTRA
CONTRE
CONVEX
CONVEY
CONVOY
CONWAY
DONALD
DONATE
DONDER
DONEES
DONEIN
DONETS
DONEUP
DONITZ
DONJON
DONKEY
DONNAS
DONNED
DONNEE
DONNER
DONORS
DONUTS
EONIAN
FONDER
FONDLE
FONDLY
FONDUE
FONTAL
GONEBY
GONERS
GONGED
GONOGO
HONCHO
HONEST
HONEYS
HONIED
HONING
HONKED
HONKER
HONORE
HONORS
HONOUR
HONSHU
IONIAN
IONICS
IONIUM
IONIZE
JONSON
KONICA
KONRAD
LONDON

LONELY
LONERS
LONGAN
LONGED
LONGER
LONGES
LONGUE
LONNOL
MONACO
MONADS
MONDAY
MONERA
MONETA
MONEYS
MONGER
MONGOL
MONICA
MONIED
MONIES
MONISM
MONIST
MONKEY
MONODY
MONROE
MONTEL
MONTEZ
MONTHS
NONAGE
NONAME
NONARY
NONCOM
NONEGO
NONETS
NONFAT
PONCHO
PONDER
PONGEE
PONGID
PONIED
PONIES
PONTES
PONTIC
PONTUS
PONYUP
RONALD
RONDEL
RONDOS
RONELY
RONNIE
SONANT
SONATA
SONDES
SONICS
SONNET
SONOMA
SONORA
SONTAG
TONERS
TONEUP
TONGAN
TONGUE
TONICS
TONIER
TONING
TONISH
TONITE
TONKIN
TONNES
TONSIL
WONDER
WONMUG
WONNED
WONOUT
WONTED
WONTON
YONDER
ZONATE
ZONING
ZONKED
ZONKER

•O•N••

BOINGO
BONNES
BONNET
BONNIE
BORNEO
BOSNIA
BOUNCE
BOUNCY
BOUNDS
BOUNTY
BOWNET
COGNAC
COINED
COINER
CONNED
CONNER
CONNIE
CONNOR
COONEY
CORNEA
CORNED
CORNEL
CORNER
CORNET
COUNTS
COUNTY
DOINGS
DONNAS
DONNED
DONNEE
DONNER
DOWNED
DOWNER
DOWNEY
DOWNON
FOUNDS
FOUNTS
GOANNA
GOINGS
GOINTO
GOUNOD
GOWNED
HOBNOB
HORNED
HORNER
HORNET
HORNEY
HOUNDS
HOWNOW
JOANIE
JOANNA
JOANNE
JOHNNY
JOINED
JOINER
JOININ
JOINTS
JOINUP
JOUNCE
JOUNCY
JOYNER
KOONTZ
LOANED
LOANER
LONNOL
LOONEY
LOUNGE
MOANED
MOANER
MOINES
MOLNAR
MOONED
MOONEY
MORNAY
MOUNDS
MOUNTS
MOUNTY
NOONAN
NOTNOW
POINTE
POINTS
POINTY
POUNCE
POUNDS
RODNEY
ROMNEY
RONNIE
ROONEY
ROUNDS
SONNET
SOONER
SOUNDS
TONNES
TOWNER
TOWNIE
WONNED
WOUNDS
ZOUNDS

•O••N•

BODING
BODONI
BOEING
BOGONG
BOIGNY
BONING
BOOING
BORING
BOSUNS
BOTANY
BOURNE
BOVINE
BOWING
BOXING
CODING
CODONS
COGENT
COHUNE
COLONS
COLONY
COMING
CONANT
COOING
COPING
CORING
CORONA
COSINE
COVENS
COVENT
COVINA
COWENS
COWING
COZENS
DOCENT
DOESNT
DOGONS
DOLING
DOMANI
DOMING
DOMINI
DOMINO
DOPANT
DOPING
DOSING
DOTING
DOYENS
DOZENS
DOZING
EOCENE
EOSINS
FOEHNS
FOMENT
FORINT
FOXING
GOANNA
GORING
HOEING
HOGANS
HOLING
HOMING
HOMINY
HONING
HOPING
HOSING
IODINE
IOWANS
JOANNA
JOANNE
JOCUND
JOHANN
JOHNNY
JOKING
JOLENE
KORUNA
LODENS
LOMOND
LOPING
LORENZ
LOSING
LOVING
LOWEND
LOWING
MODENA
MODINE
MOLINE
MOMENT
MOOING
MOPING
MORANT
MORENO
MORONI
MORONS
MOVING
MOWING
NOCENT
NOLENS
NOSING
NOTING
NOVENA
OOHING
OOLONG
OOZING
POCONO
PODUNK
POKING
POLAND
POLING
POMONA
PORING
POSING
POTENT
ROBING
ROBINS
ROCKNE
RODENT
ROLAND
ROMANO
ROMANS
ROMANY
ROPING
ROSINS
ROSINY
ROTINI
ROTUND
ROVING
ROWENA
ROWENS
ROWING
ROXANA
ROXANE
SOFINE
SOIGNE
SOLANS
SOLENT
SOLING
SOLONG
SOMANY
SONANT
SOWING
TOEING
TOEINS
TOKENS
TONING
TORINO
TOTING
TOWING
TOXINS
TOYING
TOYONS
VOLANS
VOLANT
VOLENS
VOTING
VOWING
WOMENS
WOOING
WOWING
YOGINI
YOKING
ZONING

•O•••N

BOBBIN
BODKIN
BOLEYN
BOLTON
BONBON
BONTON
BORDEN
BOREON
BORMAN
BOSTON
BOUDIN
BOWFIN
BOWMAN
BOWMEN
COBURN
COCHIN
COCOON
COLMAN
COLUMN
COMEIN
COMEON
COMMON
CONMAN
CONMEN
COOGAN
CORBAN
CORBIN
CORDON
COSIGN
COTTEN
COTTON
COUPON
COUSIN
COWMAN
COWMEN
DOBBIN
DOBLIN
DOBSON
DOESIN
DOLMAN
DOLMEN
DOMAIN
DONEIN
DONJON
DORIAN
DOTEON
DOTHAN
DOVEIN
DOWNON
EOLIAN
EONIAN
FOGSIN
FORMAN
GOBLIN
GODOWN
GODSON
GODWIN
GOESIN
GOESON
GOLDEN
GOODEN
GORDON
GORGON
GOSHEN
GOTTEN
GOVERN
HOBSON
HOLDEN
HOLDON
HORTON
HOWLIN
HOYDEN
IONIAN
JOHANN
JOININ
JOLSON
JONSON
JOPLIN
JORDAN
JOVIAN
KOREAN
KORMAN
LOCKIN
LOGION
LOGSIN
LOGSON
LOMEIN
LONDON
LONGAN
LOOKIN
LOOKON
LOOSEN
LOTION
LOUDEN
LOVEIN
MODERN
MOLTEN
MOREEN
MORGAN
MORGEN
MORION
MORMON
MORTON
MOTION
MOTOWN
MOULIN
MOUTON
MOVEIN
NOGGIN
NOIRON
NOONAN
NORMAN
NORTON
NOTION
POISON
POLEYN
POLLEN
POMPON
POPGUN
POPLIN
POPSIN
POSTON
POTEEN
POTION
POURIN
ROBSON
ROLLIN
ROLLON
ROPEIN
ROTTEN
SOCKIN
SODDEN
SOFTEN
SOLDAN
SOLDON
SOLEMN
SOSOON
TOAMAN
TOCSIN
TODMAN
TOEDIN
TOESIN
TOMLIN
TONGAN
TONKIN
TOOKIN
TOOKON
TOPGUN
TOPTEN
TOUCAN
TOULON
VOTEIN
WONTON
WOODEN
WOOLEN
WOREON
WORKIN
WORKON
WORSEN

••ON••

ADONAI
ADONIS
ALONSO
ALONZO
ANONYM
ATONAL
ATONCE
ATONED
ATONES
ATONIC
AXONAL
BIONDI
BIONIC
BLONDE
BLONDS
BRONCO
BRONCS
BRONTE
BRONZE
BRONZY
CLONED
CLONES
CLONKS
CLONUS
COONEY
CRONES
CRONIN
CRONUS
CRONYN
DIONEB
DIONNE
DRONED
DRONER
DRONES
EBONDS
EPONYM
ETONIC
EVONNE
FRONDS
FRONTS
HMONGS
ICONIC
IRONED
IRONER
IRONIC
IRONON
KOONTZ
KRONER
KRONOR
KRONUR
LEONES
LEONID
LEONIE
LIONEL
LIONET
LOONEY
MOONED
MOONEY
NOONAN
ODONTO
OZONIC
PHONED
PHONES
PHONIC
PHONON
PHONOS
PLONKS
PRONGS
PRONTO
RHONDA
ROONEY
SCONCE
SCONES
SOONER
SPONGE
SPONGY
STONED
STONER
STONES
TBONDS
TBONES
THONGS
WRONGS
YVONNE

••O•N•

ABOUND
ACORNS
ADORNS
ALOINS
AMOUNT
ANOINT
AROUND
BOOING
BROWNE
BROWNS
CLOWNS
COOING
CROONS
CROWNS
DIONNE
DROWNS
EVONNE
FROWNS
GROANS
GROINS
GROUND
GROZNY
KNOWNS
MOOING
PROCNE
QUOINS
SCORNS
SLOANE
SPOONS
SPOONY
SWOONS
THORNS
THORNY
WOOING
YVONNE

••O••N

ASOSAN
AWOKEN
AZORIN
BIOTIN
BLOWIN
BROGAN
BROKEN
CHOPIN
CHOSEN
CLOVEN
COOGAN
CRONIN
CRONYN
CROTON
DIOXIN
DROPIN
ELOIGN
FLORIN
FROZEN
GLOBIN
GNOMON
GOODEN
GRODIN
GROWON
IMOGEN
IRONON
ISOGON
KAOLIN
KJOLEN
LOOKIN
LOOKON
LOOSEN
MYOSIN
NOONAN
PHONON
PHOTON
PROTON
PROVEN
REOPEN
RYOKAN
SHOGUN
SHOOIN
SHORAN
SHOWIN
SIOUAN
SLOGAN
SLOVEN
SNOWIN
SPOKEN
STOLEN
STOLON
STOPIN
TOOKIN
TOOKON
TROGON
TROJAN
UNOPEN
USOPEN
VIOLIN
WOODEN
WOOLEN
YEOMAN
YEOMEN

•••ON•

ACTONE
ADDONS
ALMOND
ANCONA
ANIONS
ANTONY
ANYONE
APRONS
AUFOND
AUMONT
AXIONS
BARONG
BARONS
BARONY
BATONS
BEGONE
BELONG
BETONY
BEYOND
BISONS
BODONI
BOGONG
BRYONY
BUSONI
BYGONE
CANONS
CAPONE
CAPONS
CARONI
CHRONO
CODONS
COLONS
COLONY
CORONA
CROONS
DAMONE
DATONG
DAYONE
DEBONE
DELONG
DEMOND
DEMONS
DEPONE
DOGONS
DUGONG
DUMONT
DUPONT
EDMOND
EGMONT
EVZONE
FELONS
FELONY
FUTONS
GERONT
GLUONS
GYRONS
HERONS
HURONS
INIONS
INTONE
KETONE
KIMONO
LAMONT
LATONA
LEMOND
LEMONS
LEMONY
LOMOND
LUPONE
MALONE
MASONS
MEKONG
MELONS
MESONS
MORONI
MORONS
NYLONS
OBLONG
OENONE
ONIONS
ONIONY
OOLONG
ORMOND
OSMOND
PAEONS
PINONS
PITONS
POCONO
POMONA
PRIONS
PUTONS
PYLONS
RACONS
RAMONA
RAMONE
RAYONS
RECONS
REDONE
REZONE
RUNONS
SALONS
SARONG
SAXONS
SAXONY
SCIONS
SECOND
SILONE
SIMONE
SIMONY
SOLONG
SPOONS
SPOONY
STRONG
SWOONS
TALONS
TAUONS
TENONS
TETONS
THRONE
THRONG
TOYONS
TYRONE
UNDONE
UNIONS
VERONA
WAGONS
WINONA

•••O•N

ADJOIN
ALBOIN
ASWOON
BABOON
BEMOAN
BICORN
COCOON
DEHORN
DISOWN
ENJOIN
GENOAN
GODOWN
INBORN
INTOWN
LAGOON
MAROON
MINOAN
MOTOWN
OHIOAN
ONLOAN
OSBORN
REBORN
REJOIN
REMOWN
RENOWN
SALOON
SAMOAN
SHOOIN
SOSOON
STJOAN
STJOHN
SUBORN
TANOAN
THROWN
TYCOON
UNBORN
UNSOWN
UNTORN
UNWORN
UPTOWN
ZEROIN

••••ON

ACTION
ACTSON
ADDSON
ALANON
ALBION
ALISON
AMAZON
AMNION
ANTRON
ARAGON
ARCHON
ASWOON
AVALON
AVEDON
BABOON
BABSON
BANKON
BANLON
BARRON
BARTON
BARYON
BEACON
BEARON
BEATON
BECKON
BENSON
BENTON
BIDSON
BILLON
BLAZON
BOLTON
BONBON
BONTON
BOREON
BOSTON
BRETON
BRITON
BRYSON
BUFFON
BUNION
BURTON
BUTTON
CALLON
CAMEON
CAMION
CANNON
CANTON
CANYON
CARBON
CARSON
CARTON
CASTON
CATION
CATTON
CAXTON
CEYLON
CHARON
CHIRON
CHITON
CITRON
CLIPON
COCOON
COMEON
COMMON
CORDON
COTTON
COUPON
CRAYON
CROTON
CURZON
DACRON
DAIKON
DAIMON
DALTON
DAMSON
DANSON
DANTON
DAWSON
DAYTON
DEACON
DEADON
DELEON
DENTON
DIDION
DILLON
DINEON
DOBSON
DONJON
DOTEON
DOWNON
DRAGON
DRAWON
DREWON
EASTON
EDISON
EGGSON
EPHRON
ETYMON
FALCON
FALLON
FANION
FEEDON
FELDON
FLACON
FLAGON
FULTON
FUSION
GABION
GAINON
GALLON
GAMMON
GARCON
GARSON
GASCON
GASTON
GETSON
GIBBON
GIBSON
GIDEON
GNOMON
GODSON
GOESON
GORDON
GORGON
GREWON
GRISON
GROWON
GUENON
GUIDON
HADRON
HAEMON
HANDON
HANGON
HANSON
HARMON
HARPON
HAVEON
HEADON
HELDON
HENSON
HEREON
HERMON
HESTON
HIERON
HILTON
HINTON
HIREON
HITSON
HOBSON
HOLDON
HORTON
HUDSON
HUNGON
HUSTON
HUTTON
INCHON
IRONON
ISOGON
JARGON
JETSON
JIMSON
JOLSON
JONSON
JUMPON
KEATON
KEEPON
KENTON
KEPTON
KLAXON
KMESON
LAGOON
LAIDON
LANDON
LANSON
LARDON
LARSON
LAWSON
LAWTON
LAYSON
LEADON
LEANON
LEGION
LEMMON
LENNON
LEPTON
LESSON
LETSON
LIPTON
LISBON
LISTON
LIVEON
LOGION
LOGSON
LONDON
LOOKON
LOTION
LYNDON
LYTTON
MACRON
MAGNON
MAMMON
MARION
MARLON
MAROON
MARRON
MATRON
MELLON
MELTON
MEMNON
MERLON
MERTON
MICRON
MIGNON
MILTON
MINION
MORION
MORMON
MORTON
MOTION
MOUTON
MUTTON
NATION
NATRON
NEESON
NEKTON
NELSON
NETTON
NEURON
NEWTON
NIPPON
NOIRON
NORTON
NOTION
OBERON
ODDSON
OPTION
OREGON
ORISON
PARDON
PARSON
PARTON
PATRON
PATTON
PAYSON
PELION

PENNON
PERSON
PEYTON
PHONON
PHOTON
PICKON
PIGEON
PILEON
PINION
PINSON
PINYON
PINZON
PISTON
PLANON
PLAYON
POISON
POMPON
POSTON
POTION
PREYON
PRISON
PROTON
PULLON
PUSHON
PUTSON
PYTHON
RAMSON
RATION
RATSON
REASON
RECKON
REGION
RESTON
RETTON
REVLON
REVSON
RHYTON
RIBBON
ROBSON
ROLLON
RULEON
RUNSON
RUNYON
SAIGON
SALMON
SALOON
SALTON
SAMSON
SARGON
SARTON
SEASON
SERMON
SETSON
SEWSON
SEXTON
SHARON
SHIMON
SIGNON
SIMEON
SIPHON
SITSON
SLIPON
SOLDON
SOSOON
SPURON
STAYON
STEPON
STOLON
STYRON
SUMMON
TACKON
TAKEON
TALION
TARPON
TEFLON
TELLON
TENDON
TEUTON
TIGLON
TOOKON
TOULON
TRIGON
TRITON
TROGON
TUCSON
TURNON
TYCOON
UNISON
VERDON
VERNON
VILLON
VINTON
VISION
WAGGON
WAITON
WALKON
WALTON
WANTON
WATSON
WAYLON
WEAPON
WENTON
WESSON
WILSON
WILTON
WONTON
WOREON
WORKON
WYNTON
YANGON
YAUPON
ZIRCON

OO••••
OOCYTE
OODLES
OOHING
OOLALA
OOLITE
OOLITH
OOLOGY
OOLONG
OOMPAH
OOZING

O•O•••
OBOIST
ODONTO
ODOURS
OPORTO
OROIDE
OROZCO
OTOOLE
OVOIDS
OZONIC

O••O••
OBLONG
OCLOCK
OCTOPI
ODIOUS
OENONE
OGDOAD
OHIOAN
ONFOOT
ONHOLD
ONIONS
ONIONY
ONLOAN
ONTOUR
OOLOGY
OOLONG
OPPOSE
OPTOUT
ORIOLE
ORLOPS
ORMOLU
ORMOND
OSBORN
OSGOOD
OSMOND
OSMOSE
OTIOSE
OTOOLE
OXBOWS
OXFORD

O•••O•
OBERON
OCELOT
OCTROI
ODDJOB
ODDLOT
ODDSON
OLDBOY
ONFOOT
OPTION
ORATOR
OREGON
ORISON
OSGOOD
OUTFOX
OXYDOL

O••••O
OBISPO
OCTAVO
ODONTO
OLDPRO
OLINGO
ONETWO
OPENTO
OPORTO
OROZCO
ORSINO
OSWEGO
OTELLO
OVERDO
OVIEDO

•OO•••
BOOBOO
BOODLE
BOOGIE
BOOHOO
BOOING
BOOJUM
BOOKED
BOOKER
BOOKIE
BOOMED
BOOMER
BOOSTS
BOOTED
BOOTEE
BOOTES
BOOTHE
BOOTHS
BOOTIE
BOOTSY
BOOTUP
COODER
COOERS
COOGAN
COOING
COOKED
COOKER
COOKIE
COOKUP
COOLED
COOLER
COOLIT
COOLLY
COONEY
COOPED
COOPER
COOPTS
COOPUP
COOTER
COOTIE
DOOBIE
DOODAD
DOODLE
DOOFUS
DOOGIE
DOOLEY
DOOMED
DOOWOP
DOOZIE
FOOLED
FOOLER
FOOTED
FOOTER
FOOZLE
GOOBER
GOODBY
GOODEN
GOODIE
GOODLY
GOOFED
GOOFUP
GOOGLE
GOOGLY
GOOGOL
GOOGOO
GOOIER
GOOSED
GOOSES
GOOVER
HOODED
HOODOO
HOOFED
HOOFER
HOOFIT
HOOHAH
HOOHAS
HOOKAH
HOOKED
HOOKUP
HOOPED
HOOPER
HOOPLA
HOOPLE
HOOPOE
HOORAH
HOORAY
HOOTAT
HOOTED
HOOTER
HOOVER
HOOVES
KOOKIE
KOONTZ
LOOFAH
LOOKAT
LOOKED
LOOKER
LOOKIN
LOOKON
LOOKTO
LOOKUP
LOOMED
LOONEY
LOOPED
LOOPER
LOOSED
LOOSEN
LOOSER
LOOSES
LOOTED
LOOTER
MOOING
MOOLAH
MOONED
MOONEY
MOORED
MOOTED
NOODLE
NOONAN
NOOSES
NOOTKA
POODLE
POOHED
POOLED
POOPED
POORER
POORLY
ROOFED
ROOFER
ROOKED
ROOKIE
ROOMED
ROOMER
ROOMIE
ROONEY
ROOSTS
ROOTED
ROOTER
SOONER
SOOTHE
TOOBAD
TOOKIN
TOOKIT
TOOKON
TOOKTO
TOOKUP
TOOLED
TOOLUP
TOOTED
TOOTER
TOOTHY
TOOTLE
TOOTOO
TOOTSY
VOODOO
WOODED
WOODEN
WOODSY
WOOERS
WOOFED
WOOFER
WOOGIE
WOOING
WOOKIE
WOOLEN
WOOLEY
WOOLLY
YOOHOO
ZOOMED

•O•O••
BODONI
BOGONG
BOGOTA
BOWOAR
BOWOUT
COCOAS
COCOON
CODONS
COHORT
COHOST
COLONS
COLONY
COLORS
COLOUR
CONOCO
COPOUT
CORONA
COYOTE
DODODO
DODOES
DODOMA
DOGONS
DOGOOD
DOLORS
DONORS
FOBOFF
GODOWN
GOHOME
GONOGO
GOSOFT
GOTOFF
GOTOIT
GOTOUT
HOBOES
HOHOHO
HONORE
HONORS
HONOUR
HOPOFF
IOMOTH
JOCOSE
JOHORE
JOJOBA
JOYOUS
KOBOLD
KOKOMO
KOMODO
LOGOFF
LOGOUT
LOMOND
LOYOLA
MODOCS
MOHOCK
MOLOCH
MOLOPO
MONODY
MORONI
MORONS
MOROSE
MOTORS
MOTOWN
NOBODY
NODOFF
NODOSE
NOGOOD
NOLOAD
NOMORE
NOSOAP
OOLOGY
OOLONG
POBOYS
POCONO
POMONA
POPOFF
POPOUT
POROUS
POTOSI
ROBOTS
ROCOCO
ROMOLA
ROTORS
SOLOED
SOLONG
SONOMA
SONORA
SOPORS
SOSOON
SOTOLS
TOBOOT
TOPOFF
TOPOUT
TOROID
TOROSE
TOYONS
TOYOTA
VOROUS
WONOUT
WOVOKA
YOHOHO
YOYOED
YOYOMA

•O••O•
BOFFOS
BOLTON
BONBON
BONGOS
BONMOT
BONTON
BOOBOO
BOOHOO
BOREON
BORROW
BORZOI
BOSTON
BOTTOM
BOUBOU
BOWWOW
BOXTOP
COCOON
COELOM
COLLOP
COLLOQ
COMBOS
COMEON
COMMON
COMPOS
CONDOR
CONDOS
CONGOU
CONJOB
CONNOR
CONROY
CONVOY
CORDON
COSMOS
COTTON
COUPON
COWBOY
COWPOX
DOBROS
DOBSON
DOCTOR
DOGOOD
DOLLOP
DONJON
DOOWOP
DOTEON
DOWNON
FOGBOW
FOLIOS
FOLLOW
FOLSOM
FORGOT
GODSON
GOESON
GOOGOL
GOOGOO
GORDON
GORGON
GOSLOW
GOUNOD
HOBNOB
HOBSON
HOHHOT
HOLDON
HOLLOW
HOODOO
HOOPOE
HORROR
HORTON
HOTBOX
HOTDOG
HOTPOT
HOTROD
HOWNOW
HOWTOS
JOBHOP
JOBLOT
JOLIOT
JOLSON
JONSON
KOWTOW
LOGION
LOGSON
LOMBOK
LONDON
LONNOL
LOOKON
LOTION
LOTTOS
LOWBOY
MONGOL
MONROE
MORION
MORMON
MORROW
MORTON
MOSCOW
MOTION
MOTMOT
MOTTOS
MOUTON
NOGOOD
NOIRON
NONCOM
NORTON
NOSHOW
NOTION
NOTNOW
POIROT
POISON
POLLOI
POLPOT
POMPOM
POMPON
POPTOP
POSTON
POTION
POTTOS
POWWOW
ROBROY
ROBSON
RODEOS
ROLEOS
ROLLON
ROMEOS
RONDOS
ROSCOE
ROSTOV
SOLDON
SORROW
SORTOF
SOSOON
TOBOOT
TOLDOF
TOMBOY
TOMTOM
TOOKON
TOOTOO
TOPDOG
TOPJOB
TORPOR
TORSOS
TOULON
TOYDOG
VOLVOX
VOODOO
VOSTOK
WONTON
WOREON
WORKON
YOOHOO

•O•••O
BOCHCO
BOINGO
BOLERO
BONITO
BOOBOO
BOOHOO
BORAXO
BORNEO
COLUGO
COMETO
CONOCO
DODODO
DOMINO
DORADO
DOSIDO
FOREGO
GOINTO
GONOGO
GOOGOO
HOHOHO
HOLDTO
HONCHO
HOODOO
HOVETO
KOKOMO
KOMODO
LOOKTO
MODULO
MOLOPO
MONACO
MORENO
MORPHO
NONEGO
POCONO
POMELO
PONCHO
POTATO
ROBALO
ROCOCO
ROMANO
ROMERO
ROTHKO
SOASTO
SOMATO
SOWETO
TOBAGO
TODDAO
TOLEDO
TOMATO
TOOKTO
TOOTOO
TORERO
TORINO
VOODOO
YOHOHO
YOOHOO

••OO••
BLOODY
BLOOEY
BLOOMS
BLOOMY
BLOOPS
BROOCH
BROODS
BROODY
BROOKE
BROOKS
BROOMS
CHOOSE
CHOOSY
CHOOYU
CROOKS
CROONS
DROOLS
DROOPS
DROOPY
FLOODS
FLOOEY
FLOORS
GLOOMS
GLOOMY
GROOMS
GROOVE
GROOVY
KLOOFS
OTOOLE
PHOOEY
PROOFS
SCOOPS
SCOOTS
SHOOED
SHOOIN
SHOOKS
SHOOTS
SLOOPS
SMOOCH
SMOOTH
SNOODS
SNOOKS
SNOOPS
SNOOPY
SNOOTS
SNOOTY
SNOOZE
SPOOFS
SPOOKS
SPOOKY
SPOOLS
SPOONS
SPOONY
SPOORS
STOOGE
STOOLS
STOOPS
SWOONS
SWOOPS
SWOOSH
TROOPS
VROOMS
WHOOFS
WHOOPI
WHOOPS
WHOOSH

••O•O•
AGOROT
AMOSOZ
BOOBOO
BOOHOO
CLOROX
CROTON
DOOWOP
DROMOI
DROMOS
DUOMOS
FYODOR
GNOMON
GOOGOL
GOOGOO
GROWON
HOODOO
HOOPOE
IRONON
ISOGON
ISOPOD
KRONOR
LOOKON
PHOBOS
PHONON
PHONOS
PHOTOG
PHOTON
PHOTOS
PROLOG
PROMOS
PROTON
SHOLOM
STOLON
TOOKON
TOOTOO
TROGON
VOODOO
YOOHOO

••O••O
ALONSO
ALONZO
APOLLO
BIOBIO
BLOTTO
BOOBOO
BOOHOO
BRONCO
CLOTHO
GIOTTO
GOOGOO
GROSSO
GROTTO
HOODOO
IDOIDO
ILOILO
LOOKTO
ODONTO
OPORTO
OROZCO
PRONTO
SCOTTO
STOJKO
TOOKTO
TOOTOO
TROPPO
VOODOO
YOOHOO

•••OO•
ABLOOM
ASWOON
ATWOOD
BABOON
BEHOOF
BETOOK
COCOON
DOGOOD
DRHOOK
ELWOOD
ENROOT
EXMOOR
FTROOP
GALOOT
IGLOOS
INDOOR
KABOOM
KAZOOS
LAGOON
MAROON
MRCOOL
NANOOK
NOGOOD
ONFOOT
OSGOOD
REBOOT
REHOOK
RETOOK
RETOOL
SALOON
SCHOOL
SCROOP
SHBOOM
SOSOON
TABOOS
TOBOOT
TYCOON
UNCOOL
UNHOOK
UNMOOR
UNROOT
UPROOT
WAHOOS
YAHOOS

•••O•O
ALIOTO
ARIOSO
ARROYO
BAROLO
CHLORO
CHROMO
CHRONO
CONOCO
DENOVO
DESOTO
DEVOTO
DODODO
ESPOSO
EXVOTO
FLUORO
GIGOLO
GONOGO
HOHOHO
INTOTO
KIMONO
KOKOMO
KOMODO
MOLOPO
MRMOTO
NICOLO
POCONO
REBOZO
ROCOCO
SUNOCO
YOHOHO

••••OO
AHCHOO
BAMBOO
BOOBOO
BOOHOO
BURGOO
CUCKOO
GOOGOO
HALLOO
HOODOO
KARROO
MCADOO
SCHMOO
TATTOO
TOOTOO
VOODOO
YOOHOO

OP••••
OPAQUE
OPENED
OPENER
OPENLY
OPENTO
OPENUP
OPERAS
OPHITE
OPIATE
OPINED
OPINER
OPINES
OPORTO
OPPOSE
OPPUGN
OPTICS
OPTIMA
OPTING
OPTION
OPTOUT
OPUSES

O•P•••
OPPOSE
OPPUGN
ORPHAN
ORPHIC
ORPINE
OSPREY

O••P••
OILPAN
OKAPIS
OLDPRO
ONSPEC
OOMPAH
OUTPUT

O•••P•
OBISPO
OCCUPY
OCTOPI
ONEUPS
ONTAPE
ORLOPS
OXLIPS

O••••P
OPENUP
OWNSUP

•OP•••
BOPEEP
BOPPED
BOPPER
COPIED
COPIER
COPIES
COPING
COPOUT
COPPED
COPPER
COPSES
COPTER
COPTIC
COPULA
DOPANT
DOPIER
DOPING
GOPHER
HOPERS
HOPING
HOPOFF
HOPPED
HOPPER
HOPPLE
HOPSUP
JOPLIN
KOPECK
KOPEKS
KOPJES
KOPPEL
LOPERS
LOPING
LOPPED
LOPPER
MOPEDS
MOPERS
MOPING
MOPISH
MOPPED
MOPPER
MOPPET
MOPSUP
MOPUPS
NOPETS
POPART
POPEYE
POPFLY
POPGUN
POPLAR
POPLIN
POPOFF
POPOUT
POPPAS
POPPED
POPPER
POPPET
POPPLE
POPSIN
POPSUP
POPTOP
POPULI
POPUPS
ROPEIN
ROPERS
ROPIER
ROPING
SOPHIA
SOPHIE
SOPORS
SOPPED
SOPSUP
TOPCAT
TOPDOG
TOPEKA
TOPERS
TOPGUN
TOPHAT
TOPHUS
TOPICS
TOPJOB
TOPOFF
TOPOUT
TOPPED
TOPPER
TOPPLE
TOPTEN

•O•P••
BOPPED
BOPPER
COAPTS
COMPAQ
COMPEL
COMPLY
COMPOS
COOPED
COOPER
COOPTS
COOPUP
COPPED
COPPER
CORPUS
COUPES
COUPLE
COUPON
COWPEA
COWPER
COWPOX
COYPUS
GOSPEL
HOOPED
HOOPER
HOOPLA
HOOPLE
HOOPOE
HOPPED
HOPPER
HOPPLE
HOTPOT
KOPPEL
LOOPED
LOOPER
LOPPED
LOPPER
LOUPES
MOPPED
MOPPER
MOPPET
MORPHO
MORPHS
OOMPAH
POLPOT
POMPEY
POMPOM
POMPON
POOPED
POPPAS
POPPED
POPPER
POPPET

POPPLE
POTPIE
ROMPED
ROMPER
SOAPED
SOAPER
SOPPED
SOUPUP
TOPPED
TOPPER
TOPPLE
TORPID
TORPOR
TOUPEE
WOLPER

•O••P•
JOSEPH
MOLOPO
MOPUPS
POLYPS
POPUPS

•O•••P
BOBSUP
BONEUP
BOOTUP
BOPEEP
BOREUP
BOXTOP
COILUP
COLLOP
COMEUP
COOKUP
COOPUP
DOESUP
DOLLOP
DOLLUP
DONEUP
DOOWOP
FOLDUP
FOULUP
GOESUP
GOOFUP
GOSSIP
HOLDUP
HOLEUP
HOOKUP
HOPSUP
HOTCAP
HOTTIP
JOBHOP
JOINUP
LOCKUP
LOOKUP
MOBCAP
MOCKUP
MOPSUP
NOSOAP
PONYUP
POPSUP
POPTOP
ROLLUP
SOAKUP
SOPSUP
SOUPUP
TOECAP
TOETAP
TONEUP
TOOKUP
TOOLUP
TOREUP
TOSSUP
TOTSUP
WOKEUP
WORKUP

••OP••
ADOPTS
BHOPAL
CHOPIN
CHOPPY
COOPED
COOPER
COOPTS
COOPUP
CROPUP
DROPBY
DROPIN
DROPIT
ELOPED
ELOPER
ELOPES
EPOPEE
FLOPPY
FLOPSY
GLOPPY
GROPED
GROPES
HOOPED
HOOPER
HOOPLA
HOOPLE
HOOPOE
ISOPOD
LOOPED
LOOPER
MYOPES
MYOPIA
MYOPIC
PEOPLE
POOPED
PROPEL
PROPER
PROPRE
PROPUP
REOPEN
SCOPED
SCOPES
SHOPPE
SKOPJE
SLOPED
SLOPES
SLOPPY
SNOPES
STOPES
STOPIN
STOPIT
STOPUP
TROPES
TROPEZ
TROPHY
TROPIC
TROPPO
TWOPLY
UNOPEN
USOPEN
UTOPIA

••O•P•
ADOLPH
BLOOPS
CHOMPS
CHOPPY
CLOMPS
CROUPY
DROOPS
DROOPY
FLOPPY
GLOPPY
GROUPS
PROMPT
SCOOPS
SHOPPE
SLOOPS
SLOPPY
SNOOPS
SNOOPY
STOMPS
STOOPS
STOUPS
SWOOPS
THORPE
THORPS
TROMPE
TROMPS
TROOPS
TROPPO
TROUPE
WHOMPS
WHOOPI
WHOOPS

••O••P
BLOWUP
BOOTUP
BUOYUP
CLOGUP
COOKUP
COOPUP
CROPUP
DOOWOP
GOOFUP
GROWUP
HOOKUP
LOOKUP
PROPUP
SHOTUP
SHOWUP
SLOWUP
STOPUP
TOOKUP
TOOLUP

•••OP•
ASLOPE
BEBOPS
BLOOPS
CANOPY
CHEOPS
DROOPS
DROOPY
ESTOPS
EUROPA
EUROPE
FSTOPS
GALOPS
JALOPY
MEROPE
METOPE
MOLOPO
OCTOPI
ORLOPS
PELOPS
RECOPY
RETOPS
SCOOPS
SLOOPS
SNOOPS
SNOOPY
STOOPS
STROPS
SWOOPS
TROOPS
WHOOPI
WHOOPS
WICOPY

•••O•P
FTROOP
NOSOAP
RECOUP
SCROOP

••••OP
BARHOP
BIGTOP
BISHOP
BOXTOP
CARHOP
COLLOP
DETROP
DOLLOP
DOOWOP
DUNLOP
FTROOP
GALLOP
HIPHOP
HYSSOP
JOBHOP
LAPTOP
MAYPOP
PEGTOP
POPTOP
RAGMOP
RAGTOP
REDTOP
SCROOP
TIPTOP
UNSTOP
WALLOP
WETMOP

O••Q••
OPAQUE

•OQ•••
COQUET
LOQUAT
TOQUES

•O•Q••
MOSQUE
TORQUE

•O•••Q
COLLOQ
COMPAQ

••OQ••
CLOQUE

••••OQ
COLLOQ

OR••••
ORACLE
ORALES
ORALLY
ORANGE
ORANGS
ORANTS
ORATED
ORATES
ORATOR
ORBACH
ORBING
ORBITS
ORCHID
ORCHIL
ORDAIN
ORDEAL
ORDERS
ORDURE
OREADS
OREGON
OREIDA
ORELSE
ORGANA
ORGANS
ORGATE
ORGEAT
ORGIES
ORIANA
ORIBIS
ORIELS
ORIENT
ORIGEN
ORIGIN
ORINGS
ORIOLE
ORISON
ORISSA
ORKNEY
ORLOPS
ORMOLU
ORMOND
ORNATE
ORNERY
ORNITH
OROIDE
OROZCO
ORPHAN
ORPHIC
ORPINE
ORRERY
ORSINO
ORTEGA
ORTLES
ORWELL
ORYXES

O•R•••
OARING
OBRIAN
OBRIEN
OCREAE
OERTER
OGRESS
ONRUSH
ORRERY

O••R••
OBERON
OCHRES
OCTROI
OILRIG
OMERTA
OPERAS
OPORTO
OSIRIS
OSPREY
OUTRAN
OUTRUN
OVERDO
OVERLY
OZARKS

O•••R•
OATERS
OBVERT
OCCURS
OCHERS
ODOURS
OEUVRE
OFFERS
OGLERS
OHENRY
OILERS
OLDPRO
OLEARY
ONFIRE
ONWARD
ORDERS
ORDURE
ORNERY
ORRERY
OSBORN
OSCARS
OSIERS
OTHERS
OTTERS
OUTCRY
OWNERS
OXCART
OXFORD
OXNARD

O••••R
OATIER
OBITER
OCULAR
OERTER
OILIER
OLIVER
ONAGER
ONTOUR
OPENER
OPINER
ORATOR
OSTLER
OUSTER
OVULAR
OYSTER

•OR•••
AORIST
AORTAE
AORTAL
AORTAS
AORTIC
BORAGE
BORATE
BORAXO
BORDEN
BORDER
BOREAL
BOREAS
BOREON
BORERS
BOREUP
BORGIA
BORIDE
BORING
BORMAN
BORNEO
BORROW
BORSCH
BORZOI
CORALS
CORBAN
CORBEL
CORBIN
CORDAY
CORDED
CORDON
CORERS
CORGIS
CORING
CORIUM
CORKED
CORKER
CORNEA
CORNED
CORNEL
CORNER
CORNET
CORONA
CORPUS
CORRAL
CORREL
CORSET
CORTES
CORTEX
CORTEZ
CORVEE
CORYZA
DORADO
DORATI
DORCAS
DOREMI
DORIAN
DORIES
DORMER
DORRIT
DORSAL
DORSET
DORSEY
DORSUM
FORAGE
FORAYS
FORBAD
FORBES
FORBID
FORCED
FORCER
FORCES
FORDED
FOREGO
FOREST
FORGED
FORGER
FORGES
FORGET
FORGOT
FORINT
FORKED
FORKER
FORMAL
FORMAN
FORMAT
FORMED
FORMER
FORMIC
FORTAS
FORTES
FORUMS
GORALS
GORDIE
GORDON
GORGED
GORGES
GORGET
GORGON
GORIER
GORING
GORSES
HORACE
HORDES
HORMEL
HORMUZ
HORNED
HORNER
HORNET
HORNEY
HORRID
HORROR
HORSED
HORSES
HORSEY
HORTON
JORDAN
JORUMS
KORATS
KORBUT
KOREAN
KORMAN
KORUNA
LORDED
LORDLY
LOREAL
LORENZ
LORICA
LORIES
MORALE
MORALS
MORANT
MORASS
MORAVA
MORAYS
MORBID
MOREAU
MOREEN
MORELS
MORENO
MORGAN
MORGEN
MORION
MORITA
MORITZ
MORLEY
MORMON
MORNAY
MORONI
MORONS
MOROSE
MORPHO
MORPHS
MORRIS
MORROW
MORSEL
MORTAL
MORTAR
MORTON
NORDIC
NORGAY
NORIAS
NORMAL
NORMAN
NORRIS
NORTON
NORWAY
PORING
PORKER
POROUS
PORTAL
PORTED
PORTER
PORTIA
PORTLY
SORBET
SORBIC
SORDID
SORELY
SOREST
SORREL
SORROW
SORTED
SORTER
SORTIE
SORTOF
TORAHS
TOREAT
TORERO
TOREUP
TORIES
TORINO
TOROID
TOROSE
TORPID
TORPOR
TORQUE
TORRID
TORSOS
TORTES
VOROUS
VORTEX
WORDED
WOREON
WORKED
WORKER
WORKIN
WORKON
WORKUP
WORLDS
WORMED
WORSEN
WORSTS
WORTHS
WORTHY
YORICK
YORKER
YORUBA
ZORILS

•O•R••
BOARDS
BORROW
BOTREE
BOURKE
BOURNE
BOURSE
COARSE
COBRAS
COERCE
CONRAD
CONROY
CORRAL
CORREL
COURIC
COURSE
COURTS
COWRIE
DOBRAS
DOBROS
DORRIT
DOURER
DOURLY
FOURTH
GOURDE
GOURDS
HOARDS
HOARSE
HOORAH
HOORAY
HORRID
HORROR
HOTROD
HOURIS
HOURLY
KONRAD
MOIRES
MONROE
MOORED
MORRIS
MORROW
NOIRON
NORRIS
POIROT
POORER
POORLY
POURED
POURER
POURIN
ROARED
ROARER
ROBROY
SOARED
SOARER
SOARES
SOIREE
SORREL
SORROW
SOURCE
SOURED
SOURER
SOURLY
TOBRUK
TORRID
TOURED
TOURER

•O••R•
BOGART
BOLERO
BONERS
BORERS
BOVARY
BOWERS
BOWERY
BOXERS
BOYARS
COBURG
COBURN
CODERS
COHERE
COHORT
COLORS
COMERS
CONTRA
CONTRE
COOERS
CORERS
COVERS
COVERT
COWARD
COWERS
DOLORS
DONORS
DOSERS
DOTARD
DOWERS
DOZERS
FOYERS
GOAWRY
GOCART
GODARD
GOFERS
GOKART
GONERS
GOVERN
HOBART
HOMBRE
HOMERS
HONORE
HONORS
HOPERS
HOVERS
HOWARD
JOHORE
JOKERS
LONERS
LOPERS
LOSERS
LOUVRE
LOVERS
LOWERS
LOWERY
MODERN
MOHURS
MOLARS
MONERA
MOPERS
MOTORS
MOVERS
MOWERS
MOYERS
MOZART
NOMORE
NONARY
NOTARY
NOTERS
POETRY
POKERS
POKERY
POLERS
POPART
POSERS
POWERS
ROBERT
ROGERS
ROMERO
ROPERS
ROSARY
ROSTRA
ROTARY
ROTORS
ROVERS
ROWERS
SOBERS
SOLERS
SOMBRE
SOMERS
SONORA
SOPORS
SOUARI
SOWERS
SOXERS
TONERS
TOPERS
TORERO
TOTERS
TOWARD
TOWERS
TOWERY
VOLARE
VOTARY
VOTERS
VOWERS
WOOERS
YOGURT

•O•••R
BOATER
BOBBER
BOILER
BOLDER
BOLGER
BOMBER
BONIER
BOOKER
BOOMER
BOPPER
BORDER
BOTHER
BOWLER
BOWOAR
BOWSER
BOWYER
BOXCAR
COALER
COAXER
COCKER
CODGER
COFFER
COHEIR
COINER
COLDER
COLLAR
COLOUR
COLTER
COMBER
CONCUR
CONDOR
CONFER
CONGER
CONKER
CONNER
CONNOR
COODER
COOKER
COOLER
COOPER
COOTER
COPIER
COPPER
COPTER
CORKER
CORNER
COSTAR
COTTER
COUGAR
COUTER
COWPER
COZIER
DOBBER
DOCKER
DOCTOR
DODDER
DODGER
DOGEAR
DOGGER
DOLLAR
DONDER
DONNER
DOPIER
DORMER
DOSSER
DOURER
DOWNER
DOWSER
FODDER
FOGGER
FOKKER
FOLDER
FOLIAR
FONDER
FOOLER
FOOTER
FORCER
FORGER
FORKER
FORMER
FOSTER
FOULER
FOWLER
FOXIER
GOLFER
GOOBER
GOOIER
GOOVER
GOPHER
GORIER
GOUGER
HOAXER
HOKIER
HOLDER
HOLIER
HOLLER
HOMIER
HONKER
HONOUR
HOOFER
HOOPER
HOOTER
HOOVER
HOPPER
HORNER
HORROR
HOSIER
HOTAIR
HOTCAR
HOTTER
HOTWAR
HOWLER
JOBBER
JOGGER
JOINER
JOYNER
KOHLER
KOSHER
KOTTER
LOADER
LOAFER
LOANER
LOBBER
LOCKER
LODGER
LOGGER
LOGIER
LOITER
LONGER
LOOKER
LOOPER
LOOSER
LOOTER
LOPPER
LOTHAR
LOUDER
LOUVER
MOANER
MOCKER
MOHAIR
MOILER
MOLDER
MOLNAR
MOLTER
MONGER
MOPPER
MORTAR
MOTHER
MOUSER
NOBLER
NOSHER
NOSIER
POKIER
POLDER
POLLER
PONDER
POORER
POPLAR
POPPER
PORKER
PORTER
POSEUR
POSHER
POSTER
POTHER
POTTER
POURER
POUTER
POWDER
ROAMER
ROARER
ROBBER
ROCKER
ROHMER
ROLLER
ROMPER
ROOFER
ROOMER
ROOTER
ROPIER
ROSIER
ROSTER
ROTTER
ROUTER
SOAKER
SOAPER
SOARER
SOBBER
SOCCER
SOFTER
SOLDER
SOLVER
SOMBER
SOMMER
SOONER
SORTER
SOURER
SOUTER
TOILER
TONIER
TOOTER
TOPPER
TORPOR
TOSSER
TOTHER
TOTTER
TOURER
TOUTER
TOWCAR
TOWNER
WOHLER
WOLPER
WONDER
WOOFER
WORKER
YONDER
YORKER
ZONKER

••OR••
ABORAL
ABORTS
ACORNS
ADORED
ADOREE
ADORER
ADORES
ADORNS
AGORAE
AGORAS
AGOROT
AMORAL
ANORAK
AZORES
AZORIN
CHORAL
CHORDS
CHORES
CHORUS
CLORIS
CLOROX
DVORAK
FIORDS
FJORDS
FLORAE
FLORAL
FLORAS
FLORES
FLORET
FLORID
FLORIN
GEORGE
GLORIA
HOORAH
HOORAY
MAORIS
MOORED
OPORTO
PEORIA
POORER
POORLY
QUORUM
SCORCH
SCORED
SCORER
SCORES
SCORIA
SCORNS
SFORZA
SHORAN
SHORED
SHORES
SHORTS
SHORTY
SNORED
SNORER
SNORES
SNORTS
SPORES
SPORTS
SPORTY
STORCH
STORED
STORER
STORES
STOREY
STORKS
STORMS
STORMY
STORRS
SWORDS
THORAX
THORNS
THORNY
THORPE
THORPS
WHORLS

••O•R•
ABOARD
AMOURS
CHOIRS
COOERS
FLOORS
FLOURS
FLOURY
ODOURS
PROPRE
SCOURS
SHOERS
SPOORS
STORRS
WOOERS

••O••R
ADORER
ALOMAR
AVOWER
BLOWER
BOOKER
BOOMER
BROKER
CHOKER
CHOLER
CLOSER
CLOVER
COODER
COOKER
COOLER
COOPER
COOTER
CROWER
DEODAR
DRONER
DROVER
ELOPER
EMOTER
EVOKER
FLOWER
FOOLER
FOOTER
FYODOR
GLOVER
GLOWER
GOOBER
GOOIER
GOOVER
GROCER
GROVER
GROWER
HOOFER
HOOPER
HOOTER
HOOVER
IRONER
ISOBAR
ISOMER
KNOWER
KRONER
KRONOR
KRONUR
LOOKER
LOOPER
LOOSER
LOOTER
PLOVER
PLOWER
POORER
PROBER
PROPER
PROSER
PROVER
QUOTER
RIOTER
ROOFER
ROOMER
ROOTER
SCORER
SCOTER
SHOFAR
SHOVER
SHOWER
SLOWER
SMOKER
SNORER
SOONER
STOKER
STONER
STORER
STOVER
TOOTER
TROCAR
TWOFER
WOOFER

•••OR•
ABHORS
ABSORB
ACCORD
ACTORS
ADSORB
AFFORD
ALBORG
ALGORE
ANGORA
ARBORS
ARDORS
ARMORS
ARMORY
ASHORE
ASSORT
ATWORK
AURORA
BEFORE
BICORN
BYWORD
CAVORT
CHLORO
COHORT
COLORS
CYBORG
DAMORE
DECORS
DEFORM
DEHORN
DEPORT
DOLORS
DONORS
EEYORE
EFFORT
ELMORE
ENCORE
ENDORA
EPHORI
EPHORS
ERRORS
ESCORT
EUDORA
EXHORT
EXPORT
EXTORT
FAVORS
FEDORA
FEMORA
FLOORS
FLUORO
FURORE
FURORS
GALORE
GATORS
HONORE
HONORS
HUMORS
IGNORE
IMPORT
INBORN
INFORM
INPORT
JOHORE
JURORS
KIDORY
LABORS
LAHORE
LENORE
MAJORS
MALORY
MANORS
MAYORS
MEMORY
MIDORI
MILORD
MINORS
MOTORS
MYWORD
NABORS
NOMORE
OSBORN
OXFORD
PRIORI
PRIORS
PRIORY
RAZORS
REBORN
RECORD
RECORK
REFORM
REMORA
REPORT
RESORB
RESORT
RETORT
REWORD
REWORK
RIGORS
ROTORS
RUMORS
SAPORS
SATORI
SAVORS
SAVORY
SCHORL
SENORA
SENORS
SONORA
SOPORS
SPOORS
SUBORN
TABORS
TAGORE
TENORS
THEORY
TUDORS
TUTORS
UNBORN
UNCORK
UNTORN
UNWORN
VAPORS
VISORS
VYBORG
ZADORA

•••O•R
ARBOUR
ARDOUR
ARMOUR
BOWOAR
COLOUR
DAMOUR
DETOUR
DEVOIR
DEVOUR
EXMOOR
FAVOUR
HONOUR
HUMOUR
INDOOR
INPOUR
LABOUR
LAMOUR
LATOUR
MEMOIR
ONTOUR
RENOIR
RETOUR
REVOIR
RIGOUR
RUMOUR
SAVOIR
SAVOUR
UNDOER
UNMOOR
UPROAR
VALOUR
VAPOUR
VELOUR
VETOER
VIGOUR

••••OR
AMAJOR
AMINOR
ANCHOR
ANGKOR
ASKFOR
AUTHOR
BAILOR
BANGOR
BAYLOR
BETTOR
BMAJOR
BMINOR
CANDOR
CANTOR
CAPTOR
CASTOR
CAWDOR
CENSOR
CHADOR
CLAMOR
CMAJOR
CMINOR
CONDOR
CONNOR
CURSOR
DEBTOR
DMAJOR
DMINOR
DOCTOR
EDITOR
ELINOR
EMAJOR
EMINOR
EMPTOR
ENAMOR
EXMOOR
FACTOR
FERVOR
FLAVOR
FLEXOR
FMAJOR
FMINOR
FYODOR
GAYNOR
GLAMOR
GMAJOR
GMINOR
GREGOR
GUNFOR
HARBOR
HATHOR
HECTOR
HORROR
INDOOR
ISADOR
JUNIOR
KANTOR
KRONOR
LAYFOR
LECTOR
LESSOR
LICTOR
LIQUOR
LUTHOR
MAHZOR
MENTOR
METEOR
MIRROR
NESTOR
ORATOR
PALLOR
PARLOR
PASTOR
PAYFOR
PLEXOR
RANCOR
RANFOR
RAPTOR
RECTOR
RHETOR
SAILOR
SALVOR
SAVIOR
SECTOR
SENHOR
SENIOR
SENSOR
SIGNOR
STATOR
STUPOR
SUCCOR
SUITOR
TAILOR
TAYLOR
TENSOR
TERROR
TORPOR
TREMOR
TREVOR
TRYFOR
TURGOR
UNMOOR
VECTOR
VENDOR
VICTOR
WINSOR

OS••••
OSAGES
OSBORN
OSCARS
OSCINE
OSCULA
OSGOOD
OSHAWA
OSIERS
OSIRIS
OSMICS
OSMIUM
OSMOND
OSMOSE
OSMUND
OSPREY
OSSEIN
OSSETE
OSSIAN
OSSIFY
OSTEAL
OSTEND
OSTIUM
OSTLER
OSWALD
OSWEGO

O•S•••
OBSESS
OBSTET
ONSALE
ONSETS
ONSIDE
ONSITE
ONSPEC
ORSINO
OSSEIN
OSSETE
OSSIAN
OSSIFY
OUSELS
OUSTED
OUSTER
OYSTER

O••S••
OBISPO
OCASEK
OCASEY
ODDSON
ODESSA
ODISTS
OFFSET
OMASUM
ONUSES
OPUSES
ORISON
ORISSA
OUTSET
OVISAC
OWNSUP

O•••S•
OAFISH
OBLAST
OBOIST
OBSESS
OBTEST
OBTUSE
ODDEST
ODENSE
ODESSA
OFFISH
OGRESS
OLDEST
OLDISH
ONRUSH
OPPOSE
ORELSE
ORISSA
OSMOSE
OTIOSE
OWLISH

O••••S
OATERS
OBEAHS
OBELUS
OBSESS
OCCURS
OCEANS
OCHERS
OCHRES
OCTADS
OCTETS
ODIOUS
ODISTS
ODIUMS
ODOURS
OFFERS
OGHAMS
OGIVES
OGLERS
OGRESS
OILERS
OKAPIS
OLDIES
OLIVES
OLMECS
OMAHAS
OMANIS
OMEGAS
ONEUPS
ONIONS
ONSETS
ONUSES
ONYXES
OODLES
OPERAS
OPINES
OPTICS
OPUSES
ORALES
ORANGS
ORANTS
ORATES
ORBITS
ORDERS
OREADS
ORGANS
ORGIES
ORIBIS
ORIELS
ORINGS
ORLOPS
ORTLES
ORYXES
OSAGES
OSCARS
OSIERS
OSIRIS
OSMICS
OTHERS
OTITIS
OTTERS
OUGHTS
OUNCES
OUSELS
OUZELS
OVOIDS
OVULES
OWLETS
OWNERS
OXALIS
OXBOWS
OXEYES
OXIDES
OXLIPS
OZARKS

•OS•••
BOSKET
BOSLEY
BOSNIA
BOSSED
BOSSES
BOSTON
BOSUNS
COSELL
COSHED
COSHES
COSIES
COSIGN
COSINE
COSMIC
COSMOS
COSSET
COSTAE
COSTAL
COSTAR
COSTAS
COSTLY
DOSAGE
DOSERS
DOSIDO
DOSING
DOSSAL
DOSSED
DOSSEL
DOSSER
DOSSES
EOSINS
FOSSAE
FOSSAS
FOSSES
FOSSEY
FOSSIL
FOSTER
GOSHEN
GOSLOW
GOSOFT
GOSPEL
GOSSIP
GOSTAG
HOSELS
HOSIER
HOSING
HOSTAS
HOSTED
HOSTEL
JOSEPH
JOSHED
JOSHES
JOSHUA
JOSIAH
JOSSES
JOSTLE
KOSHER
LOSEIT
LOSERS
LOSING
LOSSES
LOSTIT
MOSAIC
MOSCOW
MOSEYS
MOSHAV
MOSKVA
MOSLEM
MOSQUE
MOSSED
MOSSES
MOSTEL
MOSTLY
NOSALE
NOSHED
NOSHER
NOSHES
NOSHOW
NOSIER
NOSILY
NOSING
NOSOAP
POSADA
POSERS
POSEUR
POSHER
POSHLY
POSIES
POSING
POSITS
POSSES
POSSET
POSSUM
POSTAL
POSTED
POSTER
POSTON
ROSARY
ROSCOE
ROSEAU
ROSIER
ROSILY
ROSINS
ROSINY
ROSITA
ROSTER
ROSTOV
ROSTRA
SOSOON
TOSSED
TOSSER
TOSSES
TOSSUP
VOSGES
VOSTOK

•O•S••
BOASTS
BOBSUP
BONSAI
BOOSTS
BORSCH
BOSSED
BOSSES
BOWSAW
BOWSER
BOXSET
COASTS
COMSAT
CONSUL
COPSES
CORSET
COSSET
COUSIN
DOBSON
DOESBY
DOESIN
DOESNT
DOESUP
DOGSIT
DORSAL
DORSET
DORSEY
DORSUM
DOSSAL
DOSSED
DOSSEL
DOSSER
DOSSES
DOUSED
DOUSES
DOWSED
DOWSER
DOWSES
FOCSLE
FOGSIN
FOISTS
FOLSOM
FOSSAE
FOSSAS
FOSSES
FOSSEY
FOSSIL
GODSON
GOESAT
GOESBY
GOESIN
GOESON
GOESUP
GOOSED
GOOSES
GORSES
GOSSIP
HOBSON
HOISTS
HONSHU
HOPSUP
HORSED
HORSES
HORSEY
HOUSED
HOUSES
JOISTS
JOLSON
JONSON
JOSSES
JOUSTS
LOGSIN
LOGSON
LOOSED
LOOSEN
LOOSER
LOOSES
LOSSES
LOUSED
LOUSES
MOPSUP
MORSEL
MOSSED
MOSSES
MOUSED
MOUSER
MOUSES
MOUSEY
MOUSSE
NOESIS
NOISED
NOISES
NOOSES
POISED
POISES
POISON
POPSIN
POPSUP
POSSES
POSSET
POSSUM
POUSSE
ROASTS
ROBSON
ROOSTS
ROUSED
ROUSES
ROUSTS
SOASTO
SOPSUP
SOUSED
SOUSES
TOASTS
TOASTY
TOCSIN
TOESIN
TONSIL
TORSOS
TOSSED
TOSSER
TOSSES
TOSSUP
TOTSUP
TOUSLE
WOLSEY
WORSEN
WORSTS
ZOYSIA

•O••S•
AORIST
BOOTSY
BOURSE
BOYISH
COARSE
COHOST
COURSE
COYEST
DOVISH
FOLKSY
FOREST
GOBUST
GOEASY
GOFISH
GOWEST
HOARSE
HOLISM
HOLIST
HONEST
JOCOSE
LOCUST
LOUISA
LOUISE
LOWEST
MODEST
MODISH
MOLEST
MONISM
MONIST
MOPISH
MORASS
MOROSE
MOUSSE
NODOSE
NOLESS
NOWISE
POLISH
POTASH
POTOSI
POUSSE
ROBUST
SOREST
TONISH
TOOTSY
TOROSE
WOODSY

•O•••S
AODAIS
AORTAS
BOARDS
BOASTS
BODIES
BOFFOS
BOGEYS
BOGIES
BOGLES
BOITES
BOMBES
BONERS
BONGOS
BONNES
BONZES
BOOSTS
BOOTES
BOOTHS
BOREAS
BORERS
BOSSES
BOSUNS
BOUGHS
BOULES
BOUNDS
BOVIDS
BOWERS
BOWLES
BOXERS
BOYARS
COAPTS
COASTS
COATIS
COAXES
COBIAS
COBRAS
COCCUS
COCOAS
CODERS
CODONS
COLEUS
COLONS
COLORS
COMBES
COMBOS
COMERS
COMETS
COMICS
COMMAS
COMPOS
COMTES
CONCHS
CONDOS
CONEYS
CONGAS
CONICS
CONIES
CONTES
COOERS
COOPTS
COPIES
COPSES
CORALS
CORERS
CORGIS
CORPUS
CORTES
COSHES
COSIES
COSMOS
COSTAS
COTTAS
COUGHS
COUNTS
COUPES
COURTS
COVENS
COVERS
COVETS
COVEYS
COWENS
COWERS
COYPUS
COZENS
COZIES
DOBLAS
DOBRAS
DOBROS
DODGES
DODOES
DOGIES
DOGMAS
DOGONS
DOINGS
DOLMAS
DOLORS
DONEES
DONETS
DONNAS
DONORS
DONUTS
DOOFUS
DORCAS
DORIES
DOSERS
DOSSES
DOUBTS
DOUGHS
DOUSES
DOWELS
DOWERS
DOWSES
DOYENS
DOZENS
DOZERS
EOSINS
FOEHNS
FOGEYS
FOGIES
FOISTS
FOLIOS
FORAYS
FORBES
FORCES
FORGES
FORTAS
FORTES
FORUMS
FOSSAS
FOSSES
FOUNDS
FOUNTS
FOWLES
FOYERS
GOBIES
GODETS
GOFERS
GOINGS
GOLEMS
GONERS
GOOSES
GORALS
GORGES
GORSES
GOUGES
GOURDS
HOARDS
HOAXES
HOBBES
HOBOES
HODADS
HOGANS
HOISTS
HOLMES
HOMERS
HONEYS
HONORS
HOOHAS
HOOVES
HOPERS
HORDES
HORSES
HOSELS
HOSTAS
HOTELS
HOUNDS
HOURIS
HOUSES
HOVELS
HOVERS
HOWTOS
IONICS
IOWANS
JOINTS
JOISTS
JOKERS
JORUMS
JOSHES
JOSSES
JOULES
JOUSTS
JOYOUS
KOALAS
KOPEKS
KOPJES
KORATS
KOVACS
LOAVES
LOCALS
LODENS
LODGES
LONERS
LONGES
LOOSES
LOPERS
LORIES
LOSERS
LOSSES
LOTAHS
LOTTOS
LOUPES
LOUSES
LOVERS
LOWERS
MOBIUS
MOCHAS
MODELS
MODEMS
MODOCS
MOGULS
MOHURS
MOINES
MOIRES
MOLARS
MOMMAS
MONADS
MONEYS
MONIES
MONTHS
MOPEDS
MOPERS
MOPUPS
MORALS
MORASS
MORAYS
MORELS
MORONS
MORPHS
MORRIS
MOSEYS
MOSSES
MOTELS
MOTETS
MOTIFS
MOTORS
MOTTOS
MOULDS
MOULTS
MOUNDS
MOUNTS
MOUSES
MOUTHS
MOVERS
MOVIES
MOWERS
MOYERS
NOBLES
NOESIS
NOHITS
NOISES
NOLENS
NOLESS
NOMADS
NONETS
NOOSES
NOPETS
NORIAS
NORRIS
NOSHES
NOTERS
NOVELS
OODLES
POBOYS
POGIES
POILUS
POINTS
POISES
POKERS
POKEYS
POLERS
POLKAS
POLYPS
PONIES
PONTES
PONTUS
POPPAS
POPUPS
POROUS
POSERS
POSIES
POSITS
POSSES
POTTOS
POULTS
POUNDS

POWERS
ROASTS
ROBINS
ROBLES
ROBOTS
RODEOS
ROGERS
ROGUES
ROLEOS
ROMANS
ROMEOS
RONDOS
ROOSTS
ROPERS
ROSINS
ROTORS
ROUGES
ROUGHS
ROUNDS
ROUSES
ROUSTS
ROUTES
ROVERS
ROWELS
ROWENS
ROWERS
ROYALS
SOARES
SOAVES
SOBERS
SOCLES
SOLANS
SOLERS
SOLEUS
SOLFAS
SOLIDS
SOLVES
SOMERS
SONDES
SONICS
SOPORS
SOTOLS
SOUGHS
SOUNDS
SOUSES
SOWERS
SOXERS
TOASTS
TOBIAS
TOBIES
TOEINS
TOILES
TOKAYS
TOKENS
TOKLAS
TONERS
TONICS
TONNES
TOPERS
TOPHUS
TOPICS
TOQUES
TORAHS
TORIES
TORSOS
TORTES
TOSSES
TOTALS
TOTEMS
TOTERS
TOUGHS
TOWELS
TOWERS
TOXICS
TOXINS
TOYONS
VOCALS
VOGUES
VOICES
VOILES
VOLANS
VOLENS
VOLVAS
VOROUS
VOSGES
VOTERS
VOWELS
VOWERS
WOLVES
WOMENS
WOOERS
WORLDS
WORSTS
WORTHS
WOUNDS
YODELS
YOICKS
YOKELS
YOKUTS
YOUTHS
ZORILS
ZOUNDS

••OS••

AMOSOZ
ASOSAN
BOOSTS
CHOSEN
CLOSED
CLOSER
CLOSES
CLOSET
CROSBY
CROSSE
ENOSIS
FLOSSY
FROSTS
FROSTY
GHOSTS
GLOSSA
GLOSSY
GNOSIS
GOOSED
GOOSES
GROSSE
GROSSO
GROSZY
KIOSKS
LOOSED
LOOSEN
LOOSER
LOOSES
MIOSIS
MYOSIN
NOOSES
PROSED
PROSER
PROSES
PROSIT
ROOSTS
SLOSHY
XHOSAS

••O•S•

ALONSO
AROUSE
BLOUSE
BOOTSY
BROWSE
CHOOSE
CHOOSY
CROSSE
CROUSE
DROWSE
DROWSY
EGOISM
EGOIST
ELOISE
FLOPSY
FLOSSY
GLOSSA
GLOSSY
GROSSE
GROSSO
GROUSE
LAOTSE
LHOTSE
MAOISM
MAOIST
OBOIST
PROUST
PROWSE
SPOUSE
SWOOSH
TAOISM
TAOIST
TOOTSY
WHOOSH
WOODSY

••O••S

ABODES
ABOHMS
ABOMBS
ABORTS
ACORNS
ADOBES
ADONIS
ADOPTS
ADORES
ADORNS
AEOLUS
AGORAS
ALOHAS
ALOINS
AMOLES
AMOURS
ANODES
ANOLES
AROIDS
AROMAS
ATODDS
ATOLLS
ATONES
AVOIDS
AZORES
BIOGAS
BIOMES
BIOTAS
BLOATS
BLOCKS
BLOKES
BLONDS
BLOOMS
BLOOPS
BOOSTS
BOOTES
BOOTHS
BROADS
BROILS
BRONCS
BROODS
BROOKS
BROOMS
BROTHS
BROWNS
CHOCKS
CHOIRS
CHOKES
CHOMPS
CHORDS
CHORES
CHORUS
CLOAKS
CLOCKS
CLOMPS
CLONES
CLONKS
CLONUS
CLORIS
CLOSES
CLOTHS
CLOUDS
CLOUTS
CLOVES
CLOVIS
CLOWNS
CNOTES
COOERS
COOPTS
CROAKS
CROATS
CROCKS
CROCUS
CROFTS
CRONES
CRONUS
CROOKS
CROONS
CROWDS
CROWNS
CROZES
DHOLES
DHOTIS
DIODES
DOOFUS
DROIDS
DROITS
DROLLS
DROMOS
DRONES
DROOLS
DROOPS
DROVES
DROWNS
DUOMOS
EBOATS
EBONDS
ECOLES
ELOPES
EMOTES
ENOKIS
ENOSIS
EPOCHS
EPODES
ERODES
EVOKES
EXODUS
FIORDS
FJORDS
FLOATS
FLOCKS
FLOODS
FLOORS
FLORAS
FLORES
FLOURS
FLOUTS
FROCKS
FRONDS
FRONTS
FROSTS
FROTHS
FROWNS
GEODES
GHOSTS
GHOULS
GLOATS
GLOBES
GLOGGS
GLOOMS
GLOVES
GNOMES
GNOSIS
GOOSES
GROANS
GROATS
GROINS
GROOMS
GROPES
GROUPS
GROUTS
GROVES
GROWLS
HBOMBS
HMONGS
HOOHAS
HOOVES
KIOSKS
KIOWAS
KLOOFS
KNOCKS
KNOLLS
KNOTTS
KNOWNS
LEONES
LLOYDS
LOOSES
MAORIS
MIOSIS
MYOPES
NOOSES
ODOURS
OVOIDS
PHOBOS
PHOCIS
PHONES
PHONOS
PHOTOS
PLONKS
PROAMS
PROBES
PROEMS
PROLES
PROMOS
PRONGS
PROOFS
PROSES
PROVES
PROWLS
QUOINS
QUOITS
QUOTAS
QUOTES
REOILS
RHODES
RHOMBS
RIOJAS
ROOSTS
SCOFFS
SCOLDS
SCONES
SCOOPS
SCOOTS
SCOPES
SCORES
SCORNS
SCOURS
SCOUTS
SCOWLS
SHOALS
SHOATS
SHOCKS
SHOERS
SHOJIS
SHOOKS
SHOOTS
SHORES
SHORTS
SHOUTS
SHOVES
SLOOPS
SLOPES
SLOTHS
SMOCKS
SMOKES
SNOODS
SNOOKS
SNOOPS
SNOOTS
SNOPES
SNORES
SNORTS
SNOUTS
SPOILS
SPOKES
SPOOFS
SPOOKS
SPOOLS
SPOONS
SPOORS
SPORES
SPORTS
SPOUTS
STOATS
STOCKS
STOICS
STOKES
STOLES
STOMAS
STOMPS
STONES
STOOLS
STOOPS
STOPES
STORES
STORKS
STORMS
STORRS
STOUPS
STOUTS
STOVES
SWOONS
SWOOPS
SWORDS
TBONDS
TBONES
THOLES
THOMAS
THONGS
THORNS
THORPS
TNOTES
TROLLS
TROMPS
TROOPS
TROPES
TROTHS
TROUTS
TROVES
UBOATS
UBOLTS
VIOLAS
VROOMS
WHOLES
WHOMPS
WHOOFS
WHOOPS
WHORLS
WOOERS
WRONGS
XHOSAS
ZLOTYS

•••OS•

ACCOST
ACROSS
ALDOSE
ALMOST
APPOSE
ARGOSY
ARIOSE
ARIOSO
ATCOST
ATMOST
BYGOSH
CHOOSE
CHOOSY
COHOST
DEPOSE
EMBOSS
ESPOSA
ESPOSO
EXPOSE
FILOSE
GALOSH
GYROSE
IMPOSE
IMPOST
INMOST
JOCOSE
KAROSS
KIBOSH
LANOSE
LAROSA
LUGOSI
MILOSZ
MIMOSA
MOROSE
MUCOSA
NODOSE
OPPOSE
OSMOSE
OTIOSE
PILOSE
POTOSI
RAMOSE
REPOSE
RIBOSE
RIMOSE
RUGOSE
SAMOSA
SEROSA
SETOSE
SPLOSH
SWOOSH
TOROSE
UPMOST
UPROSE
UTMOST
VADOSE
WHOOSH

•••O•S

ABBOTS
ABHORS
ACEOUS
ACROSS
ACTORS
ADDONS
ALDOUS
ALLOTS
ALLOWS
ALLOYS
ANIONS
ANJOUS
ANNOYS
APRONS
ARBORS
ARDORS
ARGOTS
ARMORS
ARROWS
ARTOIS
ASCOTS
AUROUS
AXIOMS
AXIONS
BARONS
BATONS
BAYOUS
BEBOPS
BEFOGS
BESOMS
BESOTS
BIGOTS
BIPODS
BISONS
BLOOMS
BLOOPS
BROODS
BROOKS
BROOMS
CAHOWS
CANOES
CANONS
CAPONS
CAROBS
CAROLS
CAROMS
CDROMS
CHEOPS
COCOAS
CODONS
COLONS
COLORS
CROOKS
CROONS
DADOES
DECORS
DECOYS
DEFOGS
DEMOBS
DEMONS
DEPOTS
DICOTS
DIVOTS
DODOES
DOGONS
DOLORS
DONORS
DROOLS
DROOPS
DUBOIS
DUROCS
ECHOES
EDDOES
ELBOWS
EMBOSS
ENDOWS
ENJOYS
ENVOIS
ENVOYS
EPHODS
EPHORS
ERGOTS
ERRORS
ESTOPS
EXTOLS
FAGOTS
FAMOUS
FAVORS
FELONS
FLOODS
FLOORS
FSTOPS
FURORS
FUTONS
GALOIS
GALOPS
GATORS
GIGOTS
GIJOES
GLOOMS
GLUONS
GROOMS
GUYOTS
GYRONS
HALOES
HAVOCS
HELOTS
HEROES
HERONS
HOBOES
HONORS
HUMORS
HURONS
IDIOMS
IDIOTS
IGLOOS
INGOTS
INIONS
JABOTS
JOYOUS
JURORS
KABOBS
KAROSS
KAZOOS
KEBOBS
KLOOFS
LABORS
LEMONS
MAJORS
MANORS
MASONS
MAYORS
MELONS
MESONS
MINORS
MIWOKS
MODOCS
MORONS
MOTORS
MUCOUS
NABOBS
NABORS
NYLONS
ODIOUS
ONIONS
ORLOPS
OXBOWS
PAEONS
PATOIS
PEKOES
PELOPS
PICOTS
PILOTS
PINONS
PINOTS
PITONS
PIVOTS
POBOYS
POROUS
PRIONS
PRIORS
PROOFS
PUTONS
PYLONS
RACONS
RAMOUS
RAYONS
RAZORS
RECONS
REDOES
REMOWS
REPOTS
RESODS
RETOPS
RETOWS
RIGORS
ROBOTS
ROTORS
RUFOUS
RUMORS
RUNONS
SABOTS
SALONS
SAPORS
SARODS
SAVORS
SAXONS
SCIONS
SCOOPS
SCOOTS
SCRODS
SENORS
SEPOYS
SEROUS
SEROWS
SHOOKS
SHOOTS
SLOOPS
SNOODS
SNOOKS
SNOOPS
SNOOTS
SOPORS
SOTOLS
SPOOFS
SPOOKS
SPOOLS
SPOONS
SPOORS
STOOLS
STOOPS
STROPS
SWOONS
SWOOPS
SYNODS
TABOOS
TABORS
TALONS
TAROTS
TAUONS
TENONS
TENORS
TETONS
THROBS
THROES
THROWS
TOYONS
TROOPS
TUDORS
TUTORS
UNDOES
UNIONS
UPBOWS
VALOIS
VAPORS
VENOMS
VENOUS
VETOES
VINOUS
VISORS
VOROUS
VROOMS
WAGONS
WAHOOS
WHOOFS
WHOOPS
WIDOWS
YAHOOS
YAPOKS
YUROKS
ZEROES

••••OS

ABYDOS
ALAMOS
AMIGOS
ANDROS
ANGLOS
ASTROS
AUDIOS
AVISOS
BANJOS
BASSOS
BATHOS
BEANOS
BOFFOS
BONGOS
BRAVOS
BRAZOS
BUENOS
BUFFOS
BUNCOS
BUNKOS
BURGOS
BURROS
BUTEOS
CACAOS
CAICOS
CAMEOS
CAMPOS
CANTOS
CARGOS
CARLOS
CELLOS
CENTOS
CESTOS
CHINOS
CISCOS
CLAROS
COMBOS
COMPOS
CONDOS
COSMOS
CREDOS
CURIOS
CYCLOS
DEIMOS
DISCOS
DITTOS
DOBROS
DROMOS
DUOMOS
ETHNOS
FOLIOS
FRITOS
GECKOS
GIZMOS
GUACOS
GUMBOS
HALLOS
HELIOS
HELLOS
HIPPOS
HOWTOS
HUEVOS
HULLOS
HYDROS
HYKSOS
HYPNOS
IGLOOS
INTROS
JUMBOS
JUNCOS
JUNTOS
KAZOOS
KERNOS
LARGOS
LASSOS
LEMNOS
LESBOS
LIMBOS
LITHOS
LLANOS
LOTTOS
MACHOS
MACROS
MAMBOS
MANGOS
MARCOS
MATZOS
METROS
MEZZOS
MICROS
MIMEOS
MOTTOS
MUGHOS
MUNGOS
MYTHOS
NACHOS
PASEOS
PATHOS
PATIOS
PATMOS
PEPLOS
PHAROS
PHILOS
PHOBOS
PHONOS
PHOTOS
PIANOS
PINTOS
POTTOS
PRIMOS
PROMOS
RADIOS
RATIOS
RECTOS
REPROS
RETROS
RHINOS
RODEOS
ROLEOS
ROMEOS
RONDOS
SALVOS
SANTOS
SARGOS
SAYSOS
SCHMOS
SERVOS
SESTOS
SETTOS
SHAKOS
SKIROS
SPIROS
STENOS
TABOOS
TAINOS
TANGOS
TEMPOS
TORSOS
TRIPOS
TURBOS
VERSOS
VIDEOS
VIREOS
WAHOOS
YAHOOS
ZENDOS

OT••••

OTELLO
OTHERS
OTIOSE
OTITIC
OTITIS
OTOOLE
OTTAVA
OTTAWA
OTTERS

O•T•••

OATERS
OATIER
OBTAIN
OBTEST
OBTUND
OBTUSE
OCTADS
OCTANE
OCTANT
OCTAVE
OCTAVO
OCTETS
OCTOPI
OCTROI
ONTAPE
ONTIME
ONTOUR
OPTICS
OPTIMA
OPTING
OPTION
OPTOUT
ORTEGA
ORTLES
OSTEAL
OSTEND
OSTIUM
OSTLER
OTTAVA
OTTAWA
OTTERS
OUTACT
OUTAGE
OUTATE
OUTBID
OUTCRY
OUTDID
OUTEAT
OUTFIT
OUTFOX
OUTGUN
OUTHIT
OUTING
OUTLAW
OUTLAY
OUTLET
OUTPUT
OUTRAN
OUTRUN
OUTSET
OUTWIT
OXTAIL

O••T••

OBITER
OBSTET
ODETTA
ODETTE
OERTER
ONETWO
ORATED
ORATES
ORATOR
OTITIC
OTITIS
OUSTED
OUSTER
OYSTER

O•••T•

OBLATE
OCTETS
ODDITY
ODETTA
ODETTE
ODISTS
ODONTO
OFLATE
OLEATE
OMERTA
ONSETS
ONSITE
OOCYTE
OOLITE
OOLITH
OPENTO
OPHITE
OPIATE
OPORTO
ORANTS
ORBITS
ORGATE
ORNATE
ORNITH
OSSETE
OUGHTS
OUTATE
OWLETS

O••••T

OBJECT
OBLAST
OBOIST
OBSTET
OBTEST
OBVERT
OCCULT
OCELOT
OCTANT
ODDEST
ODDLOT
OFFSET
OLDEST
OLDHAT
OMELET
ONFOOT
OPTOUT
ORGEAT
ORIENT
OUTACT
OUTEAT
OUTFIT
OUTHIT
OUTLET
OUTPUT
OUTSET
OUTWIT
OXCART

•OT•••

BOTANY
BOTFLY
BOTHER
BOTREE
BOTTLE
BOTTOM
COTTAS
COTTEN
COTTER
COTTON
DOTAGE
DOTARD
DOTELL
DOTEON
DOTHAN
DOTING
DOTTED
DOTTIE
DOTTLE
GOTCHA
GOTHAM
GOTHIC
GOTMAD
GOTOFF
GOTOIT
GOTOUT
GOTTEN
HOTAIR
HOTBED
HOTBOX
HOTCAP
HOTCAR
HOTDOG
HOTELS
HOTPOT
HOTROD
HOTTEA
HOTTER
HOTTIP
HOTTUB
HOTWAR
JOTTED
KOTTER

LOTAHS
LOTHAR
LOTION
LOTTED
LOTTOS
MOTELS
MOTETS
MOTHER
MOTIFS
MOTILE
MOTION
MOTIVE
MOTLEY
MOTMOT
MOTORS
MOTOWN
MOTTLE
MOTTOS
NOTARY
NOTATE
NOTBAD
NOTERS
NOTICE
NOTIFY
NOTING
NOTION
NOTNOW
NOTYET
POTAGE
POTASH
POTATO
POTEEN
POTENT
POTFUL
POTHER
POTION
POTOSI
POTPIE
POTTED
POTTER
POTTLE
POTTOS
ROTARY
ROTATE
ROTGUT
ROTHKO
ROTINI
ROTORS
ROTTED
ROTTEN
ROTTER
ROTUND
SOTHAT
SOTOLS
SOTTED
TOTALS
TOTEMS
TOTERS
TOTHER
TOTING
TOTSUP
TOTTED
TOTTER
VOTARY
VOTECH
VOTEIN
VOTERS
VOTING
VOTIVE

•O•T••

AORTAE
AORTAL
AORTAS
AORTIC
BOATED
BOATER
BOITES
BOLTED
BOLTON
BONTON
BOOTED
BOOTEE
BOOTES
BOOTHE
BOOTHS
BOOTIE
BOOTSY
BOOTUP
BOSTON
BOTTLE
BOTTOM
BOWTIE
BOXTOP
COATED
COATIS
COLTER
COMTES
CONTAC
CONTES
CONTRA
CONTRE
COOTER
COOTIE
COPTER
COPTIC
CORTES
CORTEX
CORTEZ
COSTAE
COSTAL
COSTAR
COSTAS
COSTLY
COTTAS
COTTEN
COTTER
COTTON
COUTER
DOCTOR
DOGTAG
DOTTED
DOTTIE
DOTTLE
FONTAL
FOOTED
FOOTER
FORTAS
FORTES
FOSTER
GOATEE
GOETHE
GOSTAG
GOTTEN
HOGTIE
HOOTAT
HOOTED
HOOTER
HORTON
HOSTAS
HOSTED
HOSTEL
HOTTEA
HOTTER
HOTTIP
HOTTUB
HOWTOS
JOETEX
JOLTED
JOSTLE
JOTTED
KOTTER
KOWTOW
LOATHE
LOFTED
LOITER
LOOTED
LOOTER
LOSTIT
LOTTED
LOTTOS
MOATED
MOLTED
MOLTEN
MOLTER
MOLTKE
MONTEL
MONTEZ
MONTHS
MOOTED
MORTAL
MORTAR
MORTON
MOSTEL
MOSTLY
MOTTLE
MOTTOS
MOUTHS
MOUTHY
MOUTON
NOETIC
NOOTKA
NORTON
POETIC
POETRY
PONTES
PONTIC
PONTUS
POPTOP
PORTAL
PORTED
PORTER
PORTIA
PORTLY
POSTAL
POSTED
POSTER
POSTON
POTTED
POTTER
POTTLE
POTTOS
POUTED
POUTER
ROOTED
ROOTER
ROSTER
ROSTOV
ROSTRA
ROTTED
ROTTEN
ROTTER
ROUTED
ROUTER
ROUTES
SOFTEN
SOFTER
SOFTIE
SOFTLY
SONTAG
SOOTHE
SORTED
SORTER
SORTIE
SORTOF
SOTTED
SOUTER
TOATEE
TOETAP
TOLTEC
TOMTIT
TOMTOM
TOOTED
TOOTER
TOOTHY
TOOTLE
TOOTOO
TOOTSY
TOPTEN
TORTES
TOTTED
TOTTER
TOUTED
TOUTER
VORTEX
VOSTOK
WONTED
WONTON
WORTHS
WORTHY
YOUTHS

•O••T•

BOASTS
BOGOTA
BONITO
BOOSTS
BORATE
BOUNTY
COAPTS
COASTS
COMATE
COMETH
COMETO
COMETS
COMITY
COOPTS
COUNTS
COUNTY
COURTS
COVETS
COYOTE
DONATE
DONETS
DONITZ
DONUTS
DORATI
DOUBTS
EOLITH
FOISTS
FOUNTS
FOURTH
GODETS
GOINTO
GOWITH
HOISTS
HOLDTO
HOVETO
IODATE
IOLITE
IOMOTH
JOBETH
JOINTS
JOISTS
JOUSTS
JOWETT
KOONTZ
KORATS
LOBATE
LOCATE
LOLITA
LOOKTO
LOVETT
MOIETY
MONETA
MORITA
MORITZ
MOTETS
MOULTS
MOUNTS
MOUNTY
NOHITS
NONETS
NOPETS
NOTATE
OOCYTE
OOLITE
OOLITH
POINTE
POINTS
POINTY
POLITE
POLITY
POSITS
POTATO
POULTS
ROASTS
ROBOTS
ROOSTS
ROSITA
ROTATE
ROUSTS
SOASTO
SOLUTE
SOMATA
SOMATO
SONATA
SOWETO
TOASTS
TOASTY
TODATE
TOMATO
TONITE
TOOKTO
TOYOTA
VOLUTE
WORSTS
YOKUTS
ZONATE

•O•••T

AORIST
BOBCAT
BOGART
BONMOT
BONNET
BOSKET
BOUGHT
BOWNET
BOWOUT
BOXSET
COBALT
COEDIT
COGENT
COHORT
COHOST
COLLET
COMBAT
COMEAT
COMFIT
COMMIT
COMSAT
CONANT
COOLIT
COPOUT
COQUET
CORNET
CORSET
COSSET
COVENT
COVERT
COYEST
DOCENT
DOCKET
DOESNT
DOGSIT
DOPANT
DORRIT
DORSET
FOGHAT
FOMENT
FOREST
FORGET
FORGOT
FORINT
FORMAT
FOUGHT
GOBLET
GOBUST
GOCART
GODWIT
GOESAT
GOKART
GORGET
GOSOFT
GOTOIT
GOTOUT
GOULET
GOWEST
HOBART
HOBBIT
HOHHOT
HOLDIT
HOLIST
HONEST
HOOFIT
HOOTAT
HORNET
HOTPOT
JOBLOT
JOLIET
JOLIOT
JOWETT
KORBUT
LOCKET
LOCUST
LOGOUT
LOOKAT
LOQUAT
LOSEIT
LOSTIT
LOVETT
LOWEST
LOWFAT
MODELT
MODEST
MOLEST
MOMENT
MONIST
MOPPET
MORANT
MOTMOT
MOZART
NOCENT
NOEXIT
NONFAT
NOTYET
NOUGAT
NOUGHT
POCKET
POIROT
POKEAT
POLPOT
POPART
POPOUT
POPPET
POSSET
POTENT
ROBERT
ROBUST
ROCHET
ROCKET
RODENT
ROTGUT
SOBEIT
SOCKET
SOFFIT
SOLENT
SONANT
SONNET
SORBET
SOREST
SOTHAT
SOUGHT
SOVIET
SOWHAT
TOBOOT
TOILET
TOMCAT
TOMTIT
TOOKIT
TOPCAT
TOPHAT
TOPOUT
TOREAT
VOIGHT
VOLANT
WOMBAT
WONOUT
YOGURT
YOUBET

••OT••

BIOTAS
BIOTIC
BIOTIN
BLOTCH
BLOTTO
BOOTED
BOOTEE
BOOTES
BOOTHE
BOOTHS
BOOTIE
BOOTSY
BOOTUP
BROTHS
CLOTHE
CLOTHO
CLOTHS
CLOTTY
CNOTES
COOTER
COOTIE
CROTON
DHOTEL
DHOTIS
EMOTED
EMOTER
EMOTES
EROTIC
EXOTIC
FOOTED
FOOTER
FROTHS
FROTHY
GIOTTO
GROTTO
GROTTY
HOOTAT
HOOTED
HOOTER
KNOTTS
KNOTTY
LAOTSE
LAOTZU
LHOTSE
LIOTTA
LOOTED
LOOTER
MAOTAI
MOOTED
NOOTKA
PHOTIC
PHOTOG
PHOTON
PHOTOS
PROTAX
PROTEI
PROTEM
PROTON
QUOTAS
QUOTED
QUOTER
QUOTES
QUOTHA
RIOTED
RIOTER
ROOTED
ROOTER
SCOTCH
SCOTER
SCOTIA
SCOTTO
SCOTTY
SHOTAT
SHOTUP
SLOTHS
SOOTHE
SPOTTY
TNOTES
TOOTED
TOOTER
TOOTHY
TOOTLE
TOOTOO
TOOTSY
TROTHS
ZLOTYS

••O•T•

ABORTS
ADOPTS
AGOUTI
BLOATS
BLOTTO
BOOSTS
BRONTE
CHOATE
CLOTTY
CLOUTS
COOPTS
CROATS
CROFTS
CROUTE
DROITS
EBOATS
FLOATS
FLOUTS
FRONTS
FROSTS
FROSTY
GHOSTS
GIOTTO
GLOATS
GROATS
GROTTO
GROTTY
GROUTS
GROUTY
GROWTH
KNOTTS
KNOTTY
KOONTZ
LIOTTA
LOOKTO
ODONTO
OPORTO
PRONTO
QUOITS
ROOSTS
SCOOTS
SCOTTO
SCOTTY
SCOUTS
SHOATS
SHOOTS
SHORTS
SHORTY
SHOUTS
SMOOTH
SNOOTS
SNOOTY
SNORTS
SNOUTS
SPORTS
SPORTY
SPOTTY
SPOUTS
STOATS
STOUTS
TOOKTO
TROUTS
UBOATS
UBOLTS

••O••T

AGOROT
AMOUNT
ANOINT
AVOCET
BLOWIT
CLOSET
COOLIT
DROPIT
EGOIST
FLORET
HOOFIT
HOOTAT
LIONET
LOOKAT
MAOIST
OBOIST
PIOLET
PROFIT
PROMPT
PROSIT
PROUST
SHOTAT
SNOCAT
SPOILT
STOMAT
STOPIT
TAOIST
TOOKIT
TWOBIT
VIOLET

•••OT•

ABBOTS
ABBOTT
ALCOTT
ALIOTO
ALLOTS
ARGOTS
ASCOTS
BESOTS
BIGOTS
BOGOTA
BYROTE
CAPOTE
CENOTE
COYOTE
DAKOTA
DEMOTE
DENOTE
DEPOTS
DESOTO
DEVOTE
DEVOTO
DICOTS
DIVOTS
ERGOTS
EXVOTO
FAGOTS
GIGOTS
GUYOTS
HELOTS
IDIOTS
INGOTS
INTOTO
IOMOTH
JABOTS
LAKOTA
MALOTI
MELOTT
MRMOTO
PELOTA
PEYOTE
PICOTS
PILOTI
PILOTS
PINOTS
PIVOTS
REMOTE
RENOTE
REPOTS
ROBOTS
SABOTS
SCOOTS
SHOOTS
SMOOTH
SNOOTS
SNOOTY
TAROTS
TOYOTA
ZEROTH
ZYGOTE

•••O•T

ABBOTT
ACCOST
ACEOUT
ACTOUT
ADROIT
AFLOAT
AIROUT
AJFOYT
ALCOTT
ALLOUT
ALMOST
ASKOUT
ASSORT
ATCOST
ATMOST
AUMONT
BELOIT
BENOIT
BOWOUT
BUGOUT
BUMOUT
BUYOUT
CAVORT
COHORT
COHOST
COPOUT
CUTOUT
DACOIT
DECOCT
DEPORT
DEVOUT
DIEOUT
DIGOUT
DIMOUT
DRYOUT
DUGOUT
DUMONT
DUPONT
EATOUT
EFFORT
EGMONT
EKEOUT
ENROOT
ESCORT
EXHORT
EXPORT
EXTORT
FANOUT
FAROUT
FLYOUT
GALOOT
GERONT
GETOUT
GOSOFT
GOTOIT
GOTOUT
HIDOUT
ICEOUT
IMPORT
IMPOST
INMOST
INPORT
LAMONT
LAYOUT
LEDOUT
LETOUT
LITOUT
LOGOUT
MAHOUT
MAXOUT
MELOTT
ONFOOT
OPTOUT
PANOUT
PAYOUT
PIGOUT
POPOUT
PTBOAT
PUTOUT
RAGOUT
RANOUT
REBOLT
REBOOT
REPORT
RESORT
RETORT
REVOLT
RUBOUT
RUNOUT
SATOUT
SAWOUT
SEEOUT
SETOUT
SITOUT
SPROUT
TAGOUT
TAPOUT
THROAT
TOBOOT
TOPOUT
TRYOUT
UNBOLT
UNROOT
UPMOST
UPROOT
UTMOST
WAYOUT
WIGOUT
WINOUT
WONOUT

••••OT

AGOROT
BADLOT
BALLOT
BARDOT
BONMOT
BURBOT
CANNOT
CARLOT
CARNOT
CARROT
DESPOT
DIGLOT
DRYROT
DYELOT
ELLIOT
ENROOT
FORGOT
GALOOT
HERIOT
HOHHOT
HOTPOT
JOBLOT
JOLIOT
MARGOT
MARMOT
MASCOT
MERLOT
MOTMOT
OCELOT
ODDLOT
ONFOOT
PARROT
PEQUOT
PERROT
POIROT
POLPOT
REBOOT
REDHOT
RESHOT
SPIGOT
TALBOT
TEAPOT
TINPOT
TOBOOT
TRICOT
TURBOT
UNKNOT
UNROOT
UPROOT
UPSHOT
WHYNOT
ZEALOT

OU••••

OUGHTS
OUNCES
OUSELS
OUSTED
OUSTER
OUTACT
OUTAGE
OUTATE
OUTBID
OUTCRY
OUTDID
OUTEAT
OUTFIT
OUTFOX
OUTGUN
OUTHIT
OUTING
OUTLAW
OUTLAY
OUTLET
OUTPUT
OUTRAN
OUTRUN
OUTSET
OUTWIT
OUZELS

O•U•••

OCULAR
OEUVRE
ONUSES
OPUSES
OVULAR
OVULES

O••U••

OBTUND
OBTUSE
OCCULT
OCCUPY
OCCURS
ODIUMS
ODOURS
ONEUPS
ONRUSH
OPPUGN
ORDURE
OSCULA
OSMUND

O•••U•

OBELUS
ODIOUS
OMASUM
OMNIUM
ONTOUR
OPAQUE
OPENUP
OPTOUT
OSMIUM
OSTIUM
OUTGUN
OUTPUT
OUTRUN
OWNSUP

O••••U

ORMOLU

•OU•••

AOUDAD
BOUBOU
BOUCLE
BOUDIN
BOUFFE
BOUGHS
BOUGHT
BOULES
BOULEZ
BOULLE
BOUNCE
BOUNCY
BOUNDS
BOUNTY
BOURKE
BOURNE
BOURSE
COUGAR
COUGHS
COULEE
COUNTS
COUNTY
COUPES
COUPLE
COUPON
COURIC
COURSE
COURTS
COUSIN
COUTER
DOUBLE
DOUBLY
DOUBTS
DOUGHS
DOUGHY
DOURER
DOURLY
DOUSED
DOUSES
FOUGHT
FOULED
FOULER
FOULLY
FOULUP
FOUNDS
FOUNTS
FOURTH
GOUGED
GOUGER
GOUGES
GOULET
GOUNOD
GOURDE
GOURDS
HOUNDS
HOURIS
HOURLY
HOUSED
HOUSES
JOULES
JOUNCE
JOUNCY
JOUSTS
KOUFAX
LOUCHE
LOUDEN
LOUDER
LOUDLY
LOUISA
LOUISE
LOUNGE
LOUPES
LOUSED
LOUSES
LOUVER
LOUVRE
MOULDS
MOULDY
MOULIN
MOULTS
MOUNDS
MOUNTS
MOUNTY
MOUSED
MOUSER
MOUSES
MOUSEY
MOUSSE
MOUTHS
MOUTHY
MOUTON
NOUGAT
NOUGHT
NOUMEA
POUCHY
POULTS
POUNCE
POUNDS
POURED
POURER
POURIN
POUSSE
POUTED
POUTER
ROUGED
ROUGES
ROUGHS
ROUNDS
ROUSED
ROUSES
ROUSTS
ROUTED
ROUTER
ROUTES
SOUARI
SOUGHS
SOUGHT
SOUNDS
SOUPUP
SOURCE
SOURED
SOURER
SOURLY
SOUSED
SOUSES
SOUTER
TOUCAN
TOUCHE
TOUCHY
TOUGHS
TOUGHY
TOULON
TOUPEE

TOURED
TOURER
TOUSLE
TOUTED
TOUTER
WOUNDS
YOUALL
YOUBET
YOUTHS
ZOUAVE
ZOUNDS

•O•U••
BOSUNS
COBURG
COBURN
COHUNE
COLUGO
COLUMN
COPULA
COQUET
DONUTS
FORUMS
GOBUST
JOCUND
JORUMS
KORUNA
LOBULE
LOCUST
LOQUAT
MODULE
MODULO
MOGULS
MOHURS
MOPUPS
NODULE
PODUNK
POPULI
POPUPS
ROBUST
ROGUES
ROTUND
SOLUTE
TOLUCA
TOQUES
VOGUES
VOLUME
VOLUTE
YOGURT
YOKUTS
YORUBA

•O••U•
BOBSUP
BONEUP
BOOJUM
BOOTUP
BOREUP
BOWOUT
BOXFUL
COCCUS
COILUP
COLEUS
COLOUR
COMEUP
CONCUR
CONIUM
CONSUL
COOKUP
COOPUP
COPOUT
CORIUM
CORPUS
COYPUS
DOESUP
DOLLUP
DONEUP
DOOFUS
DORSUM
FOLDUP
FOLIUM
FONDUE
FOULUP
GOESUP
GOLLUM
GOOFUP
GOTOUT
HOLDUP
HOLEUP
HONOUR
HOOKUP
HOPSUP
HORMUZ
HOTTUB
IONIUM
JOINUP
JOSHUA
JOYFUL
JOYOUS
KORBUT
LOCKUP
LOGOUT
LONGUE
LOOKUP
MOBIUS
MOCKUP
MOPSUP
MOSQUE
PODIUM
POILUS
POLLUX
PONTUS
PONYUP
POPGUN
POPOUT
POPSUP
POROUS
POSEUR
POSSUM
POTFUL
ROLLUP
ROTGUT
SOAKUP
SODIUM
SOLEUS
SOPSUP
SOUPUP
SOWBUG
TOBRUK
TONEUP
TONGUE
TOOKUP
TOOLUP
TOPGUN
TOPHUS
TOPOUT
TOREUP
TORQUE
TOSSUP
TOTSUP
VOROUS
WOEFUL
WOKEUP
WONMUG
WONOUT
WORKUP

•O•••U
BOUBOU
CONGOU
HONSHU
MOLDAU
MOREAU
ROSEAU

••OU••
ABOUND
AGOUTI
AMOUNT
AMOURS
AROUND
AROUSE
AVOUCH
BLOUSE
CHOUGH
CLOUDS
CLOUDY
CLOUTS
CROUCH
CROUPY
CROUSE
CROUTE
ENOUGH
FLOURS
FLOURY
FLOUTS
GHOULS
GROUCH
GROUND
GROUPS
GROUSE
GROUTS
GROUTY
INOUYE
ODOURS
PLOUGH
PROUST
SCOURS
SCOUTS
SHOULD
SHOUTS
SIOUAN
SLOUCH
SLOUGH
SNOUTS
SPOUSE
SPOUTS
STOUPS
STOUTS
THOUGH
TROUGH
TROUPE
TROUTS
TROUVE

••O•U•
AEOLUS
BLOWUP
BOOJUM
BOOTUP
BROGUE
BUOYUP
CHORUS
CLOGUP
CLONUS
CLOQUE
COOKUP
COOPUP
CROCUS
CRONUS
CROPUP
DOOFUS
DROGUE
EXODUS
GOOFUP
GROWUP
HOOKUP
KRONUR
LOOKUP
PROPUP
QUORUM
SHOGUN
SHOTUP
SHOWUP
SLOWUP
STOPUP
TOOKUP
TOOLUP

••O••U
CHOOYU
LAOTZU

•••OU•
ACEOUS
ACEOUT
ACTOUT
AIROUT
ALDOUS
ALLOUT
ANJOUS
ARBOUR
ARDOUR
ARMOUR
ASKOUT
AUROUS
BAYOUS
BEFOUL
BIJOUX
BOWOUT
BUGOUT
BUMOUT
BUYOUT
COLOUR
COPOUT
CUTOUT
DAMOUR
DETOUR
DEVOUR
DEVOUT
DIEOUT
DIGOUT
DIMOUT
DRYOUT
DUGOUT
EATOUT
EKEOUT
ENSOUL
FAMOUS
FANOUT
FAROUK
FAROUT
FAVOUR
FLYOUT
GETOUT
GOTOUT
HIDOUT
HONOUR
HUMOUR
ICEOUT
INPOUR
JOYOUS
LABOUR
LAMOUR
LATOUR
LAYOUT
LEDOUT
LETOUT
LITOUT
LOGOUT
MAHOUT
MAXOUT
MUCOUS
ODIOUS
ONTOUR
OPTOUT
PANOUT
PAYOUT
PIGOUT
POPOUT
POROUS
PUTOUT
RAGOUT
RAMOUS
RANOUT
RECOUP
RETOUR
RIGOUR
RUBOUT
RUFOUS
RUMOUR
RUNOUT
SATOUT
SAVOUR
SAWOUT
SEEOUT
SEROUS
SETOUT
SHROUD
SITOUT
SPROUT
STROUD
TAGOUT
TAPOUT
TOPOUT
TRYOUT
VALOUR
VAPOUR
VELOUR
VENOUS
VIGOUR
VINOUS
VOROUS
WAYOUT
WIGOUT
WINOUT
WONOUT

•••O•U
CHOOYU
ORMOLU

••••OU
ACAJOU
AMADOU
BOUBOU
CACHOU
CONGOU
FUZHOU
HAIKOU
HEYYOU
MENJOU
PAILOU

OV••••
OVERDO
OVERLY
OVIEDO
OVISAC
OVOIDS
OVULAR
OVULES

O•V•••
OBVERT
ONVIEW

O••V••
OEUVRE
OGIVES
OLDVIC
OLEVEL
OLIVER
OLIVES
OLIVIA

O•••V•
OCTAVE
OCTAVO
OTTAVA

•OV•••
BOVARY
BOVIDS
BOVINE
COVENS
COVENT
COVERS
COVERT
COVETS
COVEYS
COVINA
DOVEIN
DOVISH
FOVEAE
GOVERN
HOVELS
HOVERS
HOVETO
JOVIAL
JOVIAN
KOVACS
LOVAGE
LOVEIN
LOVELL
LOVELY
LOVERS
LOVETT
LOVING
MOVEIN
MOVERS
MOVIES
MOVING
NOVELS
NOVENA
NOVICE
ROVERS
ROVING
SOVIET
WOVOKA

•O•V••
COEVAL
CONVEX
CONVEY
CONVOY
CORVEE
GOOVER
HOOVER
HOOVES
LOAVES
LOUVER
LOUVRE
SOAVES
SOLVED
SOLVER
SOLVES
VOLVAS
VOLVOX
WOLVES

•O••V•
GODIVA
MOHAVE
MOJAVE
MORAVA
MOSKVA
MOTIVE
VOTIVE
ZOUAVE

•O•••V
MOSHAV
ROCKYV
ROSTOV

••OV••
BMOVIE
CLOVEN
CLOVER
CLOVES
CLOVIS
DROVER
DROVES
GLOVED
GLOVER
GLOVES
GOOVER
GROVEL
GROVER
GROVES
HOOVER
HOOVES
PLOVER
PROVED
PROVEN
PROVER
PROVES
SHOVED
SHOVEL
SHOVER
SHOVES
SLOVAK
SLOVEN
SLOVIK
STOVER
STOVES
TROVES

••O•V•
EVOLVE
GROOVE
GROOVY
TROUVE

•••OV•
ALCOVE
BULOVA
BYJOVE
CANOVA
DENOVO
GROOVE
GROOVY
INLOVE
REMOVE
REWOVE
SHROVE
STROVE
THROVE
UNWOVE

••••OV
ASIMOV
BRASOV
IMPROV
KARPOV
PAVLOV
ROSTOV
ZHUKOV

OW••••
OWLETS
OWLISH
OWNERS
OWNING
OWNSUP

O•W•••
OHWELL
ONWARD
ORWELL
OSWALD
OSWEGO

O••W••
OBIWAN
ONEWAY
OUTWIT

O•••W•
OJIBWA
ONETWO
OSHAWA
OTTAWA
OXBOWS

O••••W
ONVIEW
OUTLAW

•OW•••
BOWERS
BOWERY
BOWFIN
BOWING
BOWLED
BOWLER
BOWLES
BOWMAN
BOWMEN
BOWNET
BOWOAR
BOWOUT
BOWSAW
BOWSER
BOWTIE
BOWWOW
BOWYER
COWARD
COWBOY
COWENS
COWERS
COWING
COWLED
COWLEY
COWMAN
COWMEN
COWPEA
COWPER
COWPOX
COWRIE
DOWELS
DOWERS
DOWNED
DOWNER
DOWNEY
DOWNON
DOWSED
DOWSER
DOWSES
FOWLED
FOWLER
FOWLES
GOWEST
GOWILD
GOWITH
GOWNED
HOWARD
HOWDAH
HOWELL
HOWLED
HOWLER
HOWLIN
HOWNOW
HOWTOS
IOWANS
JOWETT
KOWTOW
LOWBOY
LOWCAL
LOWELL
LOWEND
LOWERS
LOWERY
LOWEST
LOWFAT
LOWING
LOWKEY
MOWERS
MOWGLI
MOWING
NOWISE
POWDER
POWELL
POWERS
POWWOW
ROWELS
ROWENA
ROWENS
ROWERS
ROWING
SOWBUG
SOWERS
SOWETO
SOWHAT
SOWING
TOWAGE
TOWARD
TOWCAR
TOWELS
TOWERS
TOWERY
TOWHEE
TOWING
TOWNER
TOWNIE
VOWELS
VOWERS
VOWING
WOWING
YOWLED

•O•W••
BOWWOW
COBWEB
CONWAY
DOOWOP
GOAWAY
GOAWRY
GODWIN
GODWIT
HOTWAR
NORWAY
POWWOW

•O••W•
GODOWN
MOHAWK
MOTOWN

•O•••W
BORROW
BOWSAW
BOWWOW
FOGBOW
FOLLOW
GOSLOW
HOLLOW
HOWNOW
KOWTOW
MORROW
MOSCOW
NOSHOW
NOTNOW
POWWOW
SORROW

••OW••
AVOWAL
AVOWED
AVOWER
BLOWER
BLOWIN
BLOWIT
BLOWUP
BLOWZY
BROWNE
BROWNS
BROWSE
CHOWED
CLOWNS
CROWDS
CROWED
CROWER
CROWNS
DOOWOP
DROWNS
DROWSE
DROWSY
FLOWED
FLOWER
FROWNS
FROWZY
GLOWED
GLOWER
GROWER
GROWLS
GROWLY
GROWON
GROWTH
GROWUP
KIOWAS
KNOWER
KNOWNS
MEOWED
PLOWED
PLOWER
PROWLS
PROWSE
SCOWLS
SHOWED
SHOWER
SHOWIN
SHOWME
SHOWUP
SLOWED
SLOWER
SLOWLY
SLOWUP
SNOWED
SNOWIN
STOWED
TROWED
TROWEL
TWOWAY

••O••W
BROKAW

•••OW•
ALLOWS
ARROWS
CAHOWS
DISOWN
ELBOWS
ENDOWS
GODOWN
INTOWN
MOTOWN
OXBOWS
REMOWN
REMOWS
RENOWN
RETOWS
SEROWS
THROWN
THROWS
UNSOWN
UPBOWS
UPTOWN
WIDOWS

••••OW
ANDHOW
ANTCOW
ANYHOW
BARROW
BELLOW
BESTOW
BILLOW
BORROW
BOWWOW
BURROW
CALLOW
CPSNOW
DARROW
ERENOW
ESCROW
FALLOW
FARLOW
FARROW
FELLOW
FOGBOW
FOLLOW
FURROW
GOSLOW
HALLOW
HARLOW
HARROW
HAYMOW
HOLLOW
HOWNOW
INAROW
INFLOW
KOWTOW
KRAKOW
LAYLOW
LIELOW
MALLOW
MARROW
MEADOW
MELLOW
MINNOW
MORROW
MOSCOW
MURROW
NARROW
NOSHOW
NOTNOW
PESCOW
PILLOW
POWWOW
REPLOW
SALLOW
SEACOW
SHADOW
SKITOW
SORROW
TALLOW
TVSHOW
WALLOW
WILLOW
WINDOW
WINNOW
YARROW
YELLOW

OX••••
OXALIS
OXBOWS
OXCART
OXEYES
OXFORD
OXIDES
OXIDIC
OXLIPS
OXNARD
OXTAIL
OXYDOL
OXYGEN

O•X•••
OAXACA

O••X••
ONYXES
ORYXES

O••••X
OUTFOX

•OX•••
BOXCAR
BOXERS
BOXFUL
BOXING
BOXSET
BOXTOP
FOXIER
FOXILY
FOXING
ROXANA
ROXANE
SOXERS
TOXICS
TOXINS

•O•X••
COAXED
COAXER
COAXES
HOAXED
HOAXER
HOAXES
NOEXIT

•O••X•
BORAXO

•O•••X
BOLLIX
COCCYX
COMMIX
CONVEX
CORTEX
COWPOX
HOTBOX
JOETEX
KOUFAX
POLEAX
POLLEX
POLLUX
TOMMIX
VOLVOX
VORTEX

••OX••
DIOXIN

••O••X
CLOROX
PROLIX
PROTAX
THORAX

•••OX•
BILOXI

•••O•X
BIJOUX

••••OX
BLUEOX
CHISOX
CLOROX
COWPOX
HATBOX
HOTBOX
ICEBOX
KITFOX
LUMMOX
MUSKOX
OUTFOX
REDFOX
REDSOX
SEAFOX
SKYBOX
VOLVOX

OY••••
OYSTER

O•Y•••
OHYEAH
ONYXES
ORYXES
OXYDOL
OXYGEN

O••Y••
OBEYED
OKAYED
OOCYTE
OXEYES

O••••Y
OAKLEY
OCASEY
OCCUPY
ODDITY
OFFDAY
OFFKEY
OHENRY
OKELLY
OLDBOY
OLEARY
ONEDAY
ONEWAY
ONIONY
OOLOGY
OPENLY
ORALLY
ORKNEY
ORNERY
ORRERY
OSPREY
OSSIFY
OUTCRY
OUTLAY
OVERLY

•OY•••
BOYARS
BOYISH
COYEST
COYOTE
COYPUS
DOYENS
FOYERS
HOYDEN
JOYFUL
JOYNER
JOYOUS
LOYOLA
MOYERS
ROYALE
ROYALS
TOYDOG
TOYING
TOYONS
TOYOTA
VOYAGE
YOYOED
YOYOMA
ZOYSIA

•O•Y••
BOWYER
CORYZA
NOTYET
OOCYTE
POLYPS
PONYUP

•O••Y•
BOGEYS
BOLEYN
COCCYX
CONEYS
COVEYS
FOGEYS
FORAYS
HONEYS
MONEYS
MORAYS
MOSEYS
POBOYS
POKEYS
POLEYN
POPEYE
ROCKYV
TOKAYS

•O•••Y
BODILY
BOIGNY
BOLDLY
BOMBAY
BOOTSY
BOSLEY
BOTANY
BOTFLY
BOUNCY
BOUNTY
BOVARY
BOWERY
CODIFY
COLDLY
COLONY
COMEBY
COMEDY
COMELY
COMITY
COMPLY
CONROY
CONVEY
CONVOY
CONWAY
COOLLY
COONEY
CORDAY
COSTLY
COUNTY
COWBOY
COWLEY
COZILY
DOESBY
DONKEY
DOOLEY
DORSEY
DOUBLY
DOUGHY
DOURLY
DOWNEY
DOZILY
FOLKSY
FONDLY
FOSSEY
FOULLY
FOXILY
GOAWAY
GOAWRY
GOEASY
GOESBY
GOGGLY
GONEBY
GOODBY
GOODLY
GOOGLY
HOCKEY
HOMELY
HOMILY
HOMINY
HOORAY
HORNEY
HORSEY
HOURLY
JOCKEY
JOHNNY

JOUNCY
KODALY
LOGILY
LONELY
LOONEY
LORDLY
LOUDLY
LOVELY
LOWBOY
LOWERY
LOWKEY
MOBLEY
MODIFY
MOIETY
MONDAY
MONKEY
MONODY
MOONEY
MORLEY
MORNAY
MOSTLY
MOTLEY
MOULDY
MOUNTY
MOUSEY
MOUTHY
NOBODY
NONARY
NORGAY
NORWAY
NOSILY
NOTARY
NOTIFY
OOLOGY
POACHY
POETRY
POINTY
POKERY
POKILY
POLICY
POLITY
POMPEY
POORLY
POPFLY
PORTLY
POSHLY
POUCHY
ROBROY
RODNEY
ROMANY
ROMNEY
RONELY
ROONEY
ROSARY
ROSILY
ROSINY
ROTARY
SOFTLY
SOLELY
SOMANY
SORELY
SOURLY
TOASTY
TOMBOY
TOOTHY
TOOTSY
TOUCHY
TOUGHY
TOWERY
VOLLEY
VOTARY
WOBBLY
WOLSEY
WOODSY
WOOLEY
WOOLLY
WORTHY

••OY••

BUOYED
BUOYUP
CLOYED
LLOYDS

••O•Y•

ANONYM
AZODYE
CHOOYU
CRONYN
EPONYM
INOUYE
ZLOTYS

••O••Y

BLOCKY
BLOODY
BLOOEY
BLOOMY
BLOWZY
BOOTSY
BROLLY
BRONZY
BROODY
CHOOSY
CHOPPY
CLOTTY
CLOUDY
COOLLY
COONEY
CROAKY
CROSBY
CROUPY
DOOLEY
DROLLY
DROOPY
DROPBY
DROWSY
FLOOEY
FLOPPY
FLOPSY
FLOSSY
FLOURY
FROGGY
FROSTY
FROTHY
FROWZY
GLOOMY
GLOPPY
GLOSSY
GOODBY
GOODLY
GOOGLY
GROGGY
GROOVY
GROSZY
GROTTY
GROUTY
GROWLY
GROZNY
HOORAY
KNOBBY
KNOTTY
LOONEY
MOONEY
MYOHMY
PHOOEY
POORLY
ROONEY
SCOTTY
SHODDY
SHORTY
SLOPPY
SLOSHY
SLOWLY
SMOGGY
SMOKEY
SNOBBY
SNOOPY
SNOOTY
SPONGY
SPOOKY
SPOONY
SPORTY
SPOTTY
STOCKY
STODGY
STOREY
STORMY
THORNY
TOOTHY
TOOTSY
TROPHY
TWOPLY
TWOWAY
WHOLLY
WOODSY
WOOLEY
WOOLLY

•••OY•

AJFOYT
ALLOYS
ANNOYS
ARROYO
CHOOYU
DECOYS
ENJOYS
ENVOYS
LATOYA
NAGOYA
POBOYS
SEPOYS

•••O•Y

ANTONY
ARGOSY
ARMORY
BARONY
BETONY
BLOODY
BLOOEY
BLOOMY
BROODY
BRYONY
CANOPY
CHOOSY
COLONY
DIPODY
DROOPY
EMBODY
EULOGY
FELONY
FLOOEY
GLOOMY
GROOVY
IDIOCY
JALOPY
KIDORY
LEMONY
MALORY
MELODY
MEMORY
MONODY
NOBODY
ONIONY
OOLOGY
PARODY
PHOOEY
PRIORY
RECOPY
SAVORY
SAXONY
SIMONY
SNOOPY
SNOOTY
SPOOKY
SPOONY
THEORY
UNHOLY
WICOPY

••••OY

BATBOY
BIGBOY
BUSBOY
CARBOY
CONROY
CONVOY
COWBOY
DEPLOY
EMPLOY
FLYBOY
LAZBOY
LOWBOY
OLDBOY
QUEMOY
ROBROY
TEAPOY
THETOY
TOMBOY

OZ••••

OZARKS
OZONIC

O•Z•••

OOZING
OUZELS

O••Z••

OROZCO

•OZ•••

COZENS
COZIED
COZIER
COZIES
COZILY
DOZENS
DOZERS
DOZILY
DOZING
FOZZIE
MOZART
NOZZLE
OOZING

•O•Z••

BONZES
BORZOI
DOOZIE
FOOZLE
FOZZIE
NOZZLE

•O••Z•

CORYZA
IODIZE
IONIZE

•O•••Z

BOULEZ
CORTEZ
DONITZ
HORMUZ
KOONTZ
LORENZ
MONTEZ
MORITZ

••OZ••

CROZES
DOOZIE
FOOZLE
FROZEN
GROZNY
OROZCO

••O•Z•

ALONZO
BLOWZY
BRONZE
BRONZY
FROWZY
GROSZY
LAOTZU
SFORZA
SNOOZE

••O••Z

AMOSOZ
KOONTZ
TROPEZ

•••OZ•

REBOZO
SNOOZE

•••O•Z

MILOSZ

••••OZ

AMOSOZ
SCHNOZ

PA••••

PAANGA
PABLUM
PACERS
PACIFY
PACING
PACINO
PACKED
PACKER
PACKET
PACKUP
PACMAN
PADANG
PADDED
PADDER
PADDLE
PADRES
PADUAN
PAEANS
PAELLA
PAEONS
PAGANS
PAGERS
PAGING
PAGODA
PAHANG
PAHARI
PAIDIN
PAIDUP
PAILOU
PAINED
PAINTS
PAIRED
PAIRUP
PAIUTE
PAJAMA
PALACE
PALAEO
PALATE
PALEAE
PALELY
PALEST
PALING
PALISH
PALLAS
PALLED
PALLET
PALLIA
PALLID
PALLOR
PALMAS
PALMED
PALMER
PALOMA
PALPUS
PALTER
PALTRY
PAMELA
PAMIRS
PAMPAS
PAMPER
PANADA
PANAMA
PANCHO
PANDAS
PANDER
PANDIT
PANELS
PANFRY
PANICS
PANNED
PANNER
PANNES
PANOUT
PANTED
PANTRY
PANZER
PAPACY
PAPAGO
PAPAIN
PAPAWS
PAPAYA
PAPERS
PAPERY
PAPIER
PAPPAS
PAPPUS
PAPUAN
PAPYRI
PARADE
PARANA
PARANG
PARAPH
PARCAE
PARCEL
PARDON
PARENS
PARENT
PARERS
PARETO
PAREVE
PARGET
PARIAH
PARING
PARISH
PARITY
PARKAS
PARKAY
PARKED
PARKER
PARLAY
PARLEY
PARLOR
PARNIS
PARODY
PAROLE
PARRED
PARREL
PARRIS
PARROT
PARSEC
PARSED
PARSEE
PARSER
PARSES
PARSON
PARTED
PARTLY
PARTON
PARULA
PARURE
PARVIS
PASCAL
PASEOS
PASHAS
PASHTO
PASSBY
PASSED
PASSEL
PASSER
PASSES
PASSIM
PASSUP
PASTAS
PASTED
PASTEL
PASTES
PASTIS
PASTOR
PASTRY
PATACA
PATCHY
PATENS
PATENT
PATHAN
PATHOL
PATHOS
PATINA
PATINE
PATIOS
PATMOS
PATOIS
PATROL
PATRON
PATTED
PATTEN
PATTER
PATTON
PAULEY
PAUNCH
PAUPER
PAUSED
PAUSES
PAVANE
PAVERS
PAVING
PAVLOV
PAWERS
PAWING
PAWNED
PAWNEE
PAWNER
PAWPAW
PAWSAT
PAYDAY
PAYEES
PAYERS
PAYFOR
PAYING
PAYOFF
PAYOLA
PAYOUT
PAYSIN
PAYSON
PAYSUP

P•A•••

PAANGA
PEACHY
PEAHEN
PEAKED
PEALED
PEANUT
PEAPOD
PEARLS
PEARLY
PEAVEY
PHAGES
PHAROS
PHASED
PHASER
PHASES
PHATIC
PIAFFE
PIAGET
PIANOS
PIAZZA
PLACED
PLACER
PLACES
PLACID
PLAGAL
PLAGES
PLAGIO
PLAGUE
PLAICE
PLAIDS
PLAINS
PLAINT
PLAITS
PLANAR
PLANCK
PLANED
PLANER
PLANES
PLANET
PLANKS
PLANON
PLANTE
PLANTS
PLAQUE
PLASHY
PLASMA
PLASMO
PLASTY
PLATED
PLATEN
PLATER
PLATES
PLATTE
PLAYAS
PLAYAT
PLAYED
PLAYER
PLAYON
PLAYUP
PLAZAS
POACHY
PRAGUE
PRAISE
PRAJNA
PRANCE
PRANKS
PRATED
PRATER
PRATES
PRAVDA
PRAWNS
PRAXES
PRAXIS
PRAYED
PRAYER
PSALMS

P••A••

PADANG
PAEANS
PAGANS
PAHANG
PAHARI
PAJAMA
PALACE
PALAEO
PALATE
PANADA
PANAMA
PAPACY
PAPAGO
PAPAIN
PAPAWS
PAPAYA
PARADE
PARANA
PARANG
PARAPH
PATACA
PAVANE
PECANS
PEDALS
PEDANT
PEDATE
PELAGE
PENANG
PESACH
PETAIN
PETALS
PETARD
PHIALS
PHRASE
PICABO
PICARA
PICARD
PICARO
PIKAKE
PILAFS
PILATE
PINATA
PIPALS
PIRACY
PIRANA
PIRATE
PISANS
PIZAZZ
PLEACH
PLEADS
PLEASE
PLEATS
PLIANT
POLAND
POMACE
POMADE
POPART
POSADA
POTAGE
POTASH
POTATO
PREACH
PREAMP
PROAMS
PTBOAT
PTRAPS
PURACE
PYJAMA

P•••A•

PACMAN
PADUAN
PALEAE
PALLAS
PALMAS
PAMPAS
PANDAS
PAPPAS
PAPUAN
PARCAE
PARIAH
PARKAS
PARKAY
PARLAY
PASCAL
PASHAS
PASTAS
PATHAN
PAWPAW
PAWSAT
PAYDAY
PECKAT
PEDLAR
PEEKAT
PEERAT
PENMAN
PENNAE
PENPAL
PENTAD
PHILAE
PHYLAE
PICKAT
PICKAX
PIEMAN
PIEPAN
PIETAS
PILLAR
PINDAR
PINEAL
PINNAE
PINNAS
PINOAK
PISGAH
PITMAN
PITSAW
PIZZAS
PLAGAL
PLANAR
PLAYAS
PLAYAT
PLAZAS
PLEIAD
PLICAE
PLURAL
POKEAT
POLEAX
POLKAS
POPLAR
POPPAS
PORTAL
POSTAL
PREFAB
PRELAW
PREPAY
PRETAX
PREWAR
PRIMAL
PROTAX
PTBOAT
PULSAR
PUNJAB
PUNKAH
PURDAH
PUTNAM

P••••A

PAANGA
PAELLA
PAGODA
PAJAMA
PALLIA
PALOMA
PAMELA
PANADA
PANAMA
PAPAYA
PARANA
PARULA
PATACA
PATINA
PAYOLA
PELOTA
PENNIA
PEORIA
PEPITA
PERCHA
PERSIA
PESETA
PETULA
PHOBIA
PIAZZA
PICARA
PINATA
PIRANA
PLASMA
PLEURA
PNEUMA
POMONA
PORTIA
POSADA
PRAJNA
PRAVDA
PSYLLA
PUEBLA
PURINA
PYJAMA
PYTHIA

•PA•••

APACHE
APATHY
EPARCH
OPAQUE
SPACED
SPACEK
SPACER
SPACES
SPACEY
SPADED
SPADER
SPADES
SPADIX
SPAHIS
SPALLS
SPANKS
SPANKY
SPARED
SPARER
SPARES
SPARGE
SPARKS
SPARKY
SPARSE
SPARTA
SPASMS
SPATES
SPATHE
SPAVIN
SPAWNS
SPAYED

•P•A••

APIARY
APPALL
APPALS
EPHAHS
OPIATE
SPEAKS
SPEARS
SPLASH
SPLATS
SPLAYS
SPRAGS
SPRAIN
SPRANG
SPRATS
SPRAWL
SPRAYS
UPCAST
UPDATE
UPLAND
UPTAKE
UPWARD

•P••A•

APEMAN
APICAL
APODAL
APPEAL
APPEAR
APPIAN
EPICAL
IPECAC
OPERAS
SPICAS
SPINAL
SPIRAL
SPIVAK
SPREAD
UPBEAT
UPLOAD
UPROAR

•P•••A

APULIA
OPTIMA
SPARTA
SPIREA

••PA••

ALPACA
APPALL
APPALS
AUPAIR
BYPASS
BYPAST
BYPATH
DEPART
DEPAUL
DEPAUW
DOPANT
ELPASO
ESPANA
EXPAND
IMPACT
IMPAIR
IMPALA
IMPALE
IMPART
INPART
JAPANS
LIPASE
NEPALI
PAPACY
PAPAGO
PAPAIN
PAPAWS
PAPAYA
PIPALS
POPART
REPAID
REPAIR
REPAND
REPAST
REPAVE
REPAYS
RUPAUL
SEPALS
STPAUL
TEPALS
UNPACK
UNPAID
ZAPATA

••P•A•

ALPHAS
APPEAL
APPEAR
APPIAN
BYPLAY
CAPIAS
CAPTAN
ESPIAL
HEPCAT
HEPTAD
INPLAY
KAPLAN
KAPPAS
KEPTAT
LAPHAM
NIPSAT
ORPHAN
PAPPAS
PAPUAN
POPLAR
POPPAS
REPEAL
REPEAT
REPLAN
REPLAY
RIPRAP
RIPSAW
RUPIAH
SEPIAS
SEPTAL
TAPPAN
TOPCAT
TOPHAT
TUPIAN

••P••A

ALPACA
ASPERA
CAPITA
COPULA
CUPOLA
ESPANA
ESPOSA
EUPNEA
IMPALA
LAPUTA
PAPAYA
PEPITA
SOPHIA
TEPHRA
TOPEKA
ZAPATA

•••PA•

BHOPAL
CALPAC
CARPAL
CASPAR
COMPAQ
FRYPAN
GASPAR
INSPAN
JUMPAT
KAPPAS
KEEPAT
KEYPAD
MILPAS
NETPAY
OILPAN
OOMPAH
PAMPAS
PAPPAS
PAWPAW
PENPAL
PIEPAN
POPPAS
PREPAY
SAIPAN
SAMPAN
SNAPAT
STUPAS
TAIPAN
TAPPAN
TARPAN
TINPAN
TREPAN
ZILPAH

•••P•A

COWPEA
GRAPPA
HOOPLA
MYOPIA
UTOPIA

••••PA

EUROPA
GRAPPA
JALAPA
SHERPA

P•B•••

PABLUM
PEBBLE
PEBBLY
POBOYS
PTBOAT
PUBLIC

P••B••

PEBBLE
PEBBLY
PHOBIA
PHOBIC
PHOBOS
PLEBES
PROBED
PROBER
PROBES
PUEBLA
PUEBLO

P•••B•

PASSBY
PHLEBO
PHOEBE
PICABO
PLUMBS
PUTSBY

P••••B

PREFAB
PUNJAB

•PB•••

UPBEAT
UPBOWS

•P•B••

EPHEBE

•P•••B

APLOMB

••P••B

SUPERB
TOPJOB

•••PB•

DROPBY

P•C•••

PACERS
PACIFY
PACING
PACINO
PACKED
PACKER
PACKET
PACKUP
PACMAN
PECANS
PECKAT
PECKED
PECTIC
PECTIN
PICABO
PICARA
PICARD
PICARO
PICCHU
PICKAT
PICKAX
PICKED
PICKER

PICKET
PICKLE
PICKON
PICKUP
PICNIC
PICOTS
PICULS
POCKET
POCONO
PUCKER

P••C••
PANCHO
PARCAE
PARCEL
PASCAL
PATCHY
PEACHY
PENCEL
PENCIL
PERCHA
PESCOW
PHOCIS
PICCHU
PIECED
PIECER
PIECES
PINCER
PISCES
PLACED
PLACER
PLACES
PLACID
PLICAE
PLUCKS
PLUCKY
POACHY
PONCHO
POUCHY
PRECIS
PRICED
PRICER
PRICES
PRICEY
PRICKS
PROCNE
PSYCHE
PSYCHO
PSYCHS
PUNCHY

P•••C•
PALACE
PANICS
PAPACY
PATACA
PAUNCH
PEERCE
PESACH
PIERCE
PIRACY
PLAICE
PLANCK
PLEACH
POLICE
POLICY
POMACE
POUNCE
PRANCE
PREACH
PRINCE
PUMICE
PURACE
PUTSCH

P••••C
PARSEC
PECTIC
PELVIC
PEPTIC
PHATIC
PHOBIC
PHONIC
PHOTIC
PICNIC
POETIC
PONTIC
PUBLIC
PYKNIC

•PC•••
UPCAST

•P•C••
APACHE
APICAL
APICES
EPICAL
EPOCHS
IPECAC
SPACED
SPACEK
SPACER
SPACES
SPACEY
SPECIE
SPECKS
SPICAS
SPICED
SPICES

•P••C•
APERCU
APIECE
EPARCH
OPTICS
SPEECH
SPLICE
SPRUCE
UPTICK

•P•••C
IPECAC

••PC••
HEPCAT
TOPCAT

••P•C•
ALPACA
ASPECT
ASPICS
DEPICT
EXPECT
IMPACT
KOPECK
PAPACY
TOPICS
UNPACK

••P••C
COPTIC
CUPRIC
ORPHIC
PEPTIC
SEPTIC
ZIPLOC

•••P•C
CALPAC
MYOPIC
ONSPEC
TROPIC

P•D•••
PADANG
PADDED
PADDER
PADDLE
PADRES
PADUAN
PEDALS
PEDANT
PEDATE
PEDDLE
PEDLAR
PIDGIN
PODDED
PODIUM
PODUNK
PUDDLE
PUDDLY

P••D••
PADDED
PADDER
PADDLE
PAIDIN
PAIDUP
PANDAS
PANDER
PANDIT
PARDON
PAYDAY
PEDDLE
PEEDEE
PENDED
PERDUE
PHEDRE
PINDAR
PINDUS
PLEDGE
PODDED
POLDER
PONDER
POODLE
POWDER
PRIDED
PRIDES
PRUDES
PUDDLE
PUDDLY
PUNDIT
PURDAH
PURDUE
PYEDOG

P•••D•
PAGODA
PANADA
PARADE
PARODY
PLAIDS
PLEADS
POMADE
POSADA
POUNDS
PRAVDA
PSEUDO
PSEUDS

P••••D
PACKED
PADDED
PAINED
PAIRED
PALLED
PALLID
PALMED
PANNED
PANTED
PARKED
PARRED
PARSED
PARTED
PASSED
PASTED
PATTED
PAUSED
PAWNED
PEAKED
PEALED
PEAPOD
PECKED
PEEKED
PEELED
PEENED
PEEPED
PEERED
PEEVED
PEGGED
PELTED
PENDED
PENNED
PENROD
PENTAD
PEPPED
PEQUOD
PERIOD
PERKED
PERMED
PERNOD
PETARD
PETTED
PHASED
PHONED
PHYSED
PICARD
PICKED
PIECED
PIGGED
PILLED
PINGED
PINKED
PINNED
PIPPED
PIQUED
PITHED
PITIED
PITTED
PLACED
PLACID
PLANED
PLATED
PLAYED
PLEIAD
PLOWED
PLUMED
PODDED
POISED
POLAND
POLLED
PONGID
PONIED
POOHED
POOLED
POOPED
POPPED
PORTED
POSTED
POTTED
POURED
POUTED
PRATED
PRAYED
PREMED
PREYED
PRICED
PRIDED
PRIMED
PRIZED
PROBED
PROSED
PROVED
PRUNED
PUFFED
PUGGED
PULLED
PULPED
PULSED
PUMPED
PUNNED
PUNTED
PUREED
PURGED
PURLED
PURRED
PURSED
PUSHED
PUTRID
PUTTED

•PD•••
UPDATE
UPDIKE

•P•D••
APODAL
EPODES
SPADED
SPADER
SPADES
SPADIX
SPEDUP
SPIDER

•P••D•
APHIDS
EPHODS
SPEEDS
SPEEDY
SPENDS
UPENDS
UPSIDE

•P•••D
APPEND
OPENED
OPINED
SPACED
SPADED
SPARED
SPAYED
SPEWED
SPICED
SPIKED
SPINED
SPIRED
SPITED
SPOKED
SPREAD
SPUMED
UPHELD
UPHOLD
UPLAND
UPLOAD
UPWARD
UPWIND

••PD••
LAPDOG
TOPDOG

••P•D•
BIPEDS
BIPODS
CUPIDS
DIPODY
IMPEDE
LIPIDE
LIPIDS
MOPEDS
RAPIDS

••P••D
AMPHID
APPEND
BOPPED
CAPPED
CAPSID
COPIED
COPPED
CUPPED
DAPPED
DEPEND
DIPPED
ESPIED
EXPAND
EXPEND
GAPPED
GIPPED
GYPPED
HEPTAD
HIPPED
HOPPED
HYPOED
IMPEND
LAPPED
LAPSED
LIPOID
LIPPED
LOPPED
MAPPED
MOPPED
NAPPED
NIPPED
PEPPED
PIPPED
POPPED
RAPPED
REPAID
REPAND
RIPPED
SAPPED
SIPPED
SOPPED
SUPPED
TAPPED
TIPPED
TOPPED
UNPAID
YAPPED
YIPPED
ZAPPED
ZIPPED

•••P•D
BEEPED
BOPPED
BUMPED
BURPED
CAMPED
CAPPED
CARPED
CLEPED
COOPED
COPPED
CUPPED
CUSPED
CUSPID
DAMPED
DAPPED
DIPPED
DRAPED
DUMPED
ELAPID
ELOPED
GAPPED
GASPED
GIPPED
GRIPED
GROPED
GULPED
GYPPED
HARPED
HASPED
HEAPED
HELPED
HIPPED
HISPID
HOOPED
HOPPED
HUMPED
ISOPOD
JUMPED
KEYPAD
LAPPED
LEAPED
LIMPED
LIMPID
LIPPED
LISPED
LOOPED
LOPPED
LUMPED
MAPPED
MOPPED
NAPPED
NIPPED
PEAPOD
PEEPED
PEPPED
PIPPED
POOPED
POPPED
PULPED
PUMPED
RAMPED
RAPPED
RASPED
REAPED
RIPPED
ROMPED
SAPPED
SCOPED
SEEPED
SHAPED
SIPPED
SLOPED
SNIPED
SOAPED
SOPPED
STUPID
SUPPED
SWIPED
TAMPED
TAPPED
TEMPED
TIPPED
TOPPED
TORPID
TREPID
TRIPOD
UNIPOD
VAMPED
VESPID
WARPED
WISPED
YAPPED
YAWPED
YELPED
YIPPED
ZAPPED
ZIPPED

PE••••
PEACHY
PEAHEN
PEAKED
PEALED
PEANUT
PEAPOD
PEARLS
PEARLY
PEAVEY
PEBBLE
PEBBLY
PECANS
PECKAT
PECKED
PECTIC
PECTIN
PEDALS
PEDANT
PEDATE
PEDDLE
PEDLAR
PEEDEE
PEEKAT
PEEKED
PEELED
PEELER
PEENED
PEEPED
PEEPER
PEERAT
PEERCE
PEERED
PEERIN
PEEVED
PEEVES
PEEWEE
PEGGED
PEGLER
PEGTOP
PEKING
PEKOES
PELAGE
PELEUS
PELION
PELLET
PELMET
PELOPS
PELOTA
PELTED
PELTER
PELTRY
PELVIC
PELVIS
PENANG
PENCEL
PENCIL
PENDED
PENGHU
PENMAN
PENMEN
PENNAE
PENNED
PENNER
PENNEY
PENNIA
PENNIS
PENNON
PENPAL
PENROD
PENSEE
PENTAD
PENTUP
PENULT
PENURY
PEOPLE
PEORIA
PEPINO
PEPITA
PEPLOS
PEPLUM
PEPPED
PEPPER
PEPSIN
PEPSUP
PEPTIC
PEQUOD
PEQUOT
PERCHA
PERDUE
PERILS
PERIOD
PERISH
PERKED
PERKUP
PERMED
PERMIT
PERNOD
PERROT
PERSIA
PERSON
PERTER
PERTLY
PERUKE
PERUSE
PESACH
PESCOW
PESETA
PESTER
PESTLE
PETAIN
PETALS
PETARD
PETERS
PETITE
PETREL
PETRIE
PETROG
PETROL
PETTED
PETTER
PETTIT
PETULA
PEWEES
PEWITS
PEWTER
PEYOTE
PEYTON

P•E•••
PAEANS
PAELLA
PAEONS
PEEDEE
PEEKAT
PEEKED
PEELED
PEELER
PEENED
PEEPED
PEEPER
PEERAT
PEERCE
PEERED
PEERIN
PEEVED
PEEVES
PEEWEE
PHEDRE
PHENOL
PHENOM
PHENYL
PIECED
PIECER
PIECES
PIEMAN
PIEMEN
PIEPAN
PIERCE
PIERRE
PIETAS
PIETER
PIETIN
PIETRO
PLEACH
PLEADS
PLEASE
PLEATS
PLEBES
PLEDGE
PLEIAD
PLENTY
PLENUM
PLEURA
PLEXOR
PLEXUS
PNEUMA
POETIC
POETRY
PREACH
PREAMP
PRECIS
PREENS
PREFAB
PREFER
PREFIX
PRELAW
PRELIM
PREMED
PREMIE
PREPAY
PREPPY
PRESET
PRESTO
PRETAX
PRETER
PRETTY
PREVIN
PREWAR
PREYED
PREYON
PSEUDO
PSEUDS
PUEBLA
PUEBLO
PUENTE
PUERTO
PYEDOG

P••E••
PACERS
PAGERS
PALEAE
PALELY
PALEST
PAMELA
PANELS
PAPERS
PAPERY
PARENS
PARENT
PARERS
PARETO
PAREVE
PASEOS
PATENS
PATENT
PAVERS
PAWERS
PAYEES
PAYERS
PELEUS
PESETA
PETERS
PEWEES
PHLEBO
PHLEGM
PHOEBE
PIGEON
PIKERS
PILEIN
PILEON
PILEUM
PILEUP
PILEUS
PINEAL
PINERO
PINERY
PIPERS
PIPEUP
PIXELS
PLIERS
POKEAT
POKERS
POKERY
POKEYS
POLEAX
POLERS
POLEYN
POMELO
POPEYE
POSERS
POSEUR
POTEEN
POTENT
POWELL
POWERS
PREENS
PRIERS
PRIEST
PROEMS
PUREED
PUREES
PURELY
PUREST

P•••E•
PACKED
PACKER
PACKET
PADDED
PADDER
PADRES
PAINED
PAIRED
PALAEO
PALLED
PALLET
PALMED
PALMER
PALTER
PAMPER
PANDER
PANNED
PANNER
PANNES
PANTED
PANZER
PAPIER
PARCEL
PARGET
PARKED
PARKER
PARLEY
PARRED
PARREL
PARSEC
PARSED
PARSEE
PARSER
PARSES
PARTED
PASSED
PASSEL
PASSER
PASSES
PASTED
PASTEL
PASTES
PATTED
PATTEN
PATTER
PAULEY
PAUPER
PAUSED
PAUSES
PAWNED
PAWNEE
PAWNER
PAYEES
PEAHEN
PEAKED
PEALED
PEAVEY
PECKED
PEEDEE
PEEKED
PEELED
PEELER
PEENED
PEEPED
PEEPER
PEERED
PEEVED
PEEVES
PEEWEE
PEGGED
PEGLER
PEKOES
PELLET
PELMET
PELTED
PELTER
PENCEL
PENDED
PENMEN
PENNED
PENNER
PENNEY
PENSEE
PEPPED
PEPPER
PERKED
PERMED
PERTER
PESTER
PETREL
PETTED
PETTER
PEWEES
PEWTER
PHAGES
PHASED
PHASER
PHASES
PHLOEM
PHONED
PHONES
PHOOEY
PHYSED
PIAGET
PICKED
PICKER
PICKET
PIECED
PIECER
PIECES
PIEMEN
PIETER
PIGGED
PIGLET
PIGPEN
PILFER
PILLED
PINCER
PINGED
PINIER
PINKED
PINKEN
PINKER
PINNED
PINNER
PINTER
PIOLET
PIPPED
PIQUED
PIQUES
PIQUET
PISCES
PITHED
PITIED
PITIES
PITMEN
PITTED
PITTER
PIXIES
PLACED
PLACER
PLACES
PLAGES
PLANED
PLANER
PLANES
PLANET
PLATED
PLATEN
PLATER
PLATES
PLAYED
PLAYER
PLEBES
PLOVER
PLOWED
PLOWER
PLUMED
PLUMES
PLUSES
POCKET
PODDED
POGIES
POISED
POISES
POKIER
POLDER
POLLED
POLLEN
POLLER
POLLEX
POMMEE
POMMEL
POMPEY
PONDER
PONGEE
PONIED
PONIES
PONTES
POOHED
POOLED
POOPED
POORER
POPPED
POPPER
POPPET
PORKER
PORTED
PORTER
POSHER
POSIES
POSSES
POSSET
POSTED
POSTER
POTEEN
POTHER
POTTED
POTTER
POURED
POURER
POUTED
POUTER
POWDER
PRATED
PRATER
PRATES
PRAXES
PRAYED
PRAYER
PREFER
PREMED
PRESET
PRETER
PREYED
PRICED
PRICER
PRICES
PRICEY
PRIDED
PRIDES
PRIMED
PRIMER
PRIMES
PRIPET
PRIVET
PRIZED
PRIZES
PROBED
PROBER
PROBES
PROLES
PROPEL
PROPER
PROSED
PROSER
PROSES
PROTEI
PROTEM
PROVED
PROVEN
PROVER
PROVES
PRUDES
PRUNED
PRUNER
PRUNES
PUCKER
PUFFED
PUFFER
PUGGED
PUGREE
PULLED
PULLET
PULLEY
PULPED
PULSED
PULSES
PUMMEL
PUMPED
PUMPER
PUNIER
PUNKER
PUNNED
PUNTED
PUNTER
PUPPET
PUREED
PUREES
PURGED
PURGES
PURLED
PURRED
PURRER
PURSED
PURSER
PURSES
PURVEY
PUSHED
PUSHES
PUSSES
PUTTED
PUTTEE
PUTTER
PYXIES

P••••E
PADDLE
PAIUTE
PALACE
PALATE
PALEAE
PARADE
PARCAE
PAREVE
PAROLE
PARSEE
PARURE
PATINE
PAVANE
PAWNEE
PEBBLE
PEDATE
PEDDLE
PEEDEE
PEERCE
PEEWEE
PELAGE
PENNAE
PENSEE
PEOPLE
PERDUE
PERUKE
PERUSE
PESTLE
PETITE
PETRIE
PEYOTE
PHEDRE
PHILAE
PHOEBE
PHRASE
PHYLAE
PIAFFE
PICKLE
PIERCE
PIERRE
PIFFLE
PIGGIE
PIKAKE
PILATE
PILOSE
PINITE
PINKIE
PINNAE
PINOLE
PINTLE
PIRATE
PLAGUE
PLAICE
PLANTE
PLAQUE
PLATTE
PLEASE
PLEDGE
PLICAE
PLISSE
PLUNGE
POINTE
POLICE
POLITE
POMACE
POMADE
POMMEE
PONGEE
POODLE
POPEYE
POPPLE
POTAGE
POTPIE
POTTLE
POUNCE
POUSSE
PRAGUE
PRAISE
PRANCE
PREMIE
PRINCE
PROCNE
PROPRE
PROWSE
PRYNNE
PSYCHE
PUDDLE
PUENTE
PUGREE
PUISNE
PULQUE
PUMICE
PUNKIE
PURACE
PURDUE
PURFLE
PURINE
PURPLE
PURSUE
PUTTEE
PUZZLE
PYRITE

•PE•••
APEMAN
APEMEN
APERCU
APEXES
IPECAC
KPELLE
OPENED
OPENER
OPENLY
OPENTO
OPENUP
OPERAS
SPEAKS
SPEARS
SPECIE
SPECKS
SPEDUP
SPEECH
SPEEDS
SPEEDY
SPELLS
SPENDS
SPERRY
SPEWED
UPENDS

•P•E••
APIECE
APPEAL
APPEAR
APPEND
APTEST
EPHEBE
SPEECH
SPEEDS
SPEEDY
SPHERE
SPIELS
SPIERS
SPLEEN
SPREAD
SPREES
UPBEAT
UPHELD
UPKEEP
UPPERS
UPSETS
UPWELL

•P••E•
APEMEN
APEXES
APICES
APOGEE
APPLES
EPODES
EPOPEE
OPENED
OPENER
OPINED
OPINER
OPINES
OPUSES
SPACED
SPACEK
SPACER
SPACES
SPACEY
SPADED
SPADER
SPADES
SPARED
SPARER
SPARES
SPATES
SPAYED
SPEWED
SPICED
SPICES
SPIDER
SPIKED
SPIKER
SPIKES
SPILES
SPINED
SPINEL
SPINES
SPINET
SPIREA
SPIRED
SPIRES
SPITED
SPITES
SPLEEN
SPOKED
SPOKEN
SPOKES
SPORES
SPREES
SPRIER
SPRUES
SPRYER
SPUMED
SPUMES
UPKEEP

•P•••E
APACHE
APIECE
APLITE
APOGEE
APPOSE
EPHEBE
EPOPEE
KPELLE
OPAQUE
OPHITE
OPIATE
OPPOSE
SPARGE
SPARSE
SPATHE
SPECIE
SPHERE
SPLICE
SPLINE
SPONGE
SPOUSE
SPRITE
SPRUCE
SPURGE
UPDATE
UPDIKE
UPRISE
UPROSE
UPSIDE
UPTAKE
UPTIME

••PE••
ALPERT
AMPERE
APPEAL
APPEAR
APPEND
ARPENT
ASPECT
ASPENS
ASPERA
BIPEDS
BOPEEP
CAPERS
CUPELS
DEPEND
DUPERY
EMPERY
EXPECT
EXPELS
EXPEND
EXPERT
GAPERS
HOPERS
IMPEDE
IMPELS
IMPEND
IMPERF
JAPERS
JAPERY
KOPECK
KOPEKS
LAPELS
LIPENG
LOPERS
MOPEDS
MOPERS
NAPERY
NOPETS
PAPERS
PAPERY
PIPERS
PIPEUP
POPEYE
REPEAL
REPEAT
REPEGS
REPELS
REPENT
RIPELY
RIPENS
RIPEST
ROPEIN
ROPERS
RUPEES
RUPERT
STPETE
SUPERB
SUPERS
TAPERS
TEPEES
TOPEKA
TOPERS
TUPELO
TYPERS
TYPEUP
UNPEGS
UNPENS
UPPERS
VIPERS
WIPERS
WIPEUP

••P•E•
AMPLER
APPLES
BOPEEP
BOPPED
BOPPER
CAPLET
CAPPED
CAPPER
CIPHER
COPIED
COPIER
COPIES
COPPED
COPPER
COPSES
COPTER
CUPPED
CYPHER
DAPPED
DAPPER
DIPPED
DIPPER
DOPIER
DUPLEX
ESPIED
ESPIES
EUPNEA
GAPPED
GIPPED
GIPPER
GOPHER
GYPPED
GYPPER
HAPPEN
HEPPER
HIPPED
HIPPER
HOPPED
HOPPER
HYPHEN
HYPOED
KEPLER
KIPPER
KOPJES
KOPPEL
LAPPED
LAPPET
LAPSED
LAPSES
LAPTEV
LIPPED
LOPPED
LOPPER
MAPLES
MAPPED
MAPPER
MOPPED
MOPPER
MOPPET
MUPPET
NAPIER
NAPLES
NAPPED
NAPPER
NAPPES
NEPHEW
NIPPED
NIPPER
OSPREY
PAPIER
PEPPED
PEPPER
PIPPED
POPPED
POPPER
POPPET
PUPPET
RAPIER
RAPPED
RAPPEE
RAPPEL
RAPPER
RIPKEN
RIPLEY
RIPPED
RIPPER
ROPIER
RUPEES
SAPPED
SAPPER
SEPTET
SIPPED
SIPPER
SIPPET
SOPPED
SUPPED
SUPPER
TAPPED
TAPPER
TAPPET
TEPEES
TIPPED
TIPPER
TIPPET
TOPPED
TOPPER
TOPTEN
WAPNER
YAPPED
YIPPED
YIPPEE
ZAPPED
ZAPPER
ZIPPED
ZIPPER

••P••E
ALPINE
AMPERE
AMPULE
APPOSE
ASPIRE
CAPONE
CAPOTE
DAPHNE
DAPPLE
DEPONE
DEPOSE
DEPUTE
DIPOLE
EMPIRE
EXPIRE
EXPOSE
FIPPLE
HIPPIE
HOPPLE
IMPALE
IMPEDE
IMPOSE
IMPURE
IMPUTE
LIPASE
LIPIDE
LUPINE
LUPONE
OPPOSE
ORPINE
POPEYE
POPPLE
RAPINE
RAPPEE
REPAVE
REPINE
REPOSE
REPUTE
RIPPLE
SOPHIE
STPETE
SUPINE
SUPPLE
TIPPLE
TIPTOE
TOPPLE
UMPIRE
UNPILE
YIPPEE
YUPPIE

•••PE•
AUSPEX
BEEPED
BEEPER
BOPPED
BOPPER
BUMPED
BUMPER
BURPED
CAMPED
CAMPER
CAPPED
CAPPER
CARPED
CARPEL
CARPER
CARPET
CASPER
CHAPEL
CLEPED
COMPEL
COOPED
COOPER
COPPED
COPPER
COUPES
COWPEA
COWPER
CRAPES
CREPES
CRIPES
CUPPED
CUSPED
DAMPED
DAMPEN
DAMPER
DAPPED
DAPPER
DEEPEN
DEEPER
DIAPER
DIPPED
DIPPER
DISPEL
DRAPED
DRAPER
DRAPES
DRUPES
DUMPED
DUMPER
ELOPED
ELOPER
ELOPES
EPOPEE
GAPPED
GASPED
GIPPED
GIPPER
GOSPEL
GRAPES
GRIPED
GRIPER
GRIPES
GROPED
GROPES
GULPED
GULPER
GYPPED
GYPPER
HAMPER
HAPPEN
HARPED
HARPER
HASPED
HEAPED
HELPED
HELPER
HEPPER
HIPPED
HIPPER
HOOPED
HOOPER
HOPPED
HOPPER
HUMPED
INAPET
JASPER
JUMPED
JUMPER
KEEPER
KIPPER
KOPPEL
LAPPED
LAPPET
LAUPER
LEAPED
LEAPER
LIMPED
LIMPER
LIMPET
LIPPED
LISPED
LOOPED
LOOPER
LOPPED
LOPPER
LOUPES
LUMPED
LUMPEN
LUMPER
MAPPED
MAPPER
MOPPED
MOPPER
MOPPET
MUPPET
MYOPES
NAPPED
NAPPER
NAPPES
NIPPED
NIPPER
ONSPEC
PAMPER
PAUPER
PEEPED
PEEPER
PEPPED
PEPPER
PIGPEN
PIPPED
POMPEY
POOPED
POPPED
POPPER
POPPET
PRIPET
PROPEL
PROPER
PULPED
PUMPED
PUMPER
PUPPET
RAMPED
RAPPED
RAPPEE
RAPPEL
RAPPER
RASPED
RASPER
REAPED
REAPER
REOPEN
RIPPED
RIPPER
ROMPED
ROMPER
SAPPED
SAPPER
SCAPES
SCOPED
SCOPES
SEEPED
SEMPER
SHAPED
SHAPER
SHAPES
SIMPER
SIPPED
SIPPER
SIPPET
SLOPED
SLOPES
SLYPES
SNIPED
SNIPES
SNOPES
SOAPED
SOAPER
SOPPED
STAPES
STIPEL
STIPES
STOPES
STUPES
SUPPED
SUPPER
SWIPED
SWIPER
SWIPES
TAIPEI
TAMPED
TAMPER
TAPPED
TAPPER
TAPPET
TAUPES
TEMPED
TEMPEH
TEMPER
TIPPED
TIPPER
TIPPET
TOPPED
TOPPER
TOUPEE
TROPES
TROPEZ
UNOPEN
USOPEN
VAMPED
VAMPER
VESPER
WARPED
WEEPER
WISPED
WOLPER
YAPPED
YAWPED
YAWPER
YELPED
YELPER
YIPPED
YIPPEE
ZAPPED
ZAPPER
ZIPPED
ZIPPER

•••P•E
COUPLE
DAPPLE
DIEPPE
DIMPLE
ELAPSE
EPOPEE
FIPPLE
FRAPPE
GRIPPE
HIPPIE
HOOPLE
HOOPOE
HOPPLE
KELPIE
KEWPIE
MAGPIE
MARPLE
MUDPIE
PEOPLE
POPPLE
POTPIE
PROPRE
PURPLE
RAPPEE
RIMPLE
RIPPLE
RUMPLE
SAMPLE
SEMPRE
SHOPPE
SIMPLE
SKOPJE
STAPLE
STEPPE
SUPPLE
TEMPLE
TIPPLE
TOPPLE
TOUPEE
TRIPLE
WIMPLE
YIPPEE
YUPPIE

••••PE
ASLOPE
CANAPE
DIEPPE
ECTYPE
ESCAPE
EUROPE
FELIPE
FRAPPE
GRIPPE
GUIMPE
LENAPE
MEROPE
METOPE
ONTAPE
RECIPE
RETAPE
RETYPE
SCRAPE
SERAPE
SHOPPE
STEPPE
STRIPE
THORPE
TROMPE
TROUPE
UNRIPE

P•F•••
PIFFLE
PUFFED
PUFFER
PUFFIN

P••F••
PANFRY
PAYFOR
PIAFFE
PIFFLE
PILFER
POPFLY
POTFUL
PREFAB
PREFER
PREFIX
PROFIT
PUFFED
PUFFER
PUFFIN
PURFLE

P•••F•
PACIFY
PAYOFF
PIAFFE
PILAFS
POPOFF
PROOFS
PURIFY
PUTOFF

P••••F
PAYOFF
POPOFF
PUTOFF

•P•F••
SPIFFS
SPIFFY

•P••F•
SPIFFS
SPIFFY
SPOOFS
UPLIFT

••PF••
CAPFUL
CUPFUL
LAPFUL
POPFLY

••P•F•
HOPOFF
POPOFF
RIPOFF
TAPOFF
TIPOFF
TOPOFF
TYPIFY

••P••F
HOPOFF
IMPERF
POPOFF
RIPOFF
TAPOFF
TIPOFF
TOPOFF

•••P•F
STAPUF

P•G•••
PAGANS
PAGERS
PAGING
PAGODA
PEGGED
PEGLER
PEGTOP
PIGEON
PIGGED
PIGGIE
PIGLET
PIGNUT
PIGOUT
PIGPEN
PIGSTY
POGIES
PUGGED
PUGREE

P••G••
PARGET
PEGGED
PENGHU
PHAGES
PIAGET
PIDGIN
PIGGED
PIGGIE
PINGED
PISGAH
PLAGAL
PLAGES
PLAGIO
PLAGUE
PLIGHT
PLUGIN
PONGEE
PONGID
POPGUN
PRAGUE
PUGGED
PURGED
PURGES

P•••G•
PAANGA
PAPAGO
PELAGE
PHLEGM
PLEDGE
PLOUGH
PLUNGE
POTAGE
PRONGS

P••••G
PACING
PADANG
PAGING
PAHANG
PALING
PARANG
PARING
PAVING
PAWING
PAYING
PEKING
PENANG
PETROG
PHOTOG
PIKING
PILING
PINING
PIPING
PLYING
POKING
POLING
PORING
POSING
PROLOG
PRYING
PULING
PYEDOG

•P•G••
APOGEE
SPIGOT

•P••G•
OPPUGN
SPARGE
SPONGE
SPONGY
SPRAGS
SPRIGS
SPURGE

•P•••G
EPILOG
EPPING
OPTING
SPRANG
SPRING
SPRUNG
SPYING
UPPING

••PG••
CAPGUN
POPGUN
TOPGUN

••P•G•
IMPUGN
OPPUGN
PAPAGO
REPEGS
REPUGN
UNPEGS

••P••G
COPING
DOPING
DUPING
EPPING
GAPING
HOPING
HYPING
JAPING
LAPDOG
LIPENG
LOPING
MOPING
PIPING
ROPING
TAPING
TOPDOG
TYPING
UNPLUG
UPPING
WIPING

PH••••
PHAGES
PHAROS
PHASED
PHASER
PHASES
PHATIC
PHEDRE
PHENOL
PHENOM
PHENYL
PHIALS
PHILAE
PHILIP
PHILLY
PHILOL
PHILOS
PHLEBO
PHLEGM
PHLOEM
PHOBIA
PHOBIC
PHOBOS
PHOCIS
PHOEBE
PHONED
PHONES
PHONIC
PHONON
PHONOS
PHOOEY
PHOTIC
PHOTOG
PHOTON
PHOTOS
PHRASE
PHYLAE
PHYLLO
PHYLUM
PHYSED
PHYSIO

P•H•••
PAHANG
PAHARI

P••H••
PASHAS
PASHTO
PATHAN
PATHOL
PATHOS
PEAHEN
PITHED
POOHED
POSHER
POSHLY
POTHER
PUSHED
PUSHES
PUSHON
PUSHUP
PYTHIA
PYTHON

P•••H•
PANCHO
PATCHY
PEACHY
PENGHU
PERCHA
PICCHU
PLASHY
PLIGHT
PLUSHY
POACHY
PONCHO
POUCHY
PSYCHE
PSYCHO
PSYCHS
PUNCHY

P••••H
PALISH
PARAPH
PARIAH
PARISH
PAUNCH
PERISH
PESACH
PISGAH
PLEACH
PLINTH
PLOUGH
POLISH
POTASH
PREACH
PUNISH
PUNKAH
PURDAH
PUTSCH

•PH•••
APHIDS

EPHAHS
EPHEBE
EPHODS
EPHORI
EPHORS
EPHRON
OPHITE
SPHERE
SPHINX
UPHELD
UPHILL
UPHOLD

•P•H••
SPAHIS
UPSHOT

•P••H•
APACHE
APATHY
EPHAHS
EPOCHS
SPATHE

•P•••H
EPARCH
SPEECH
SPILTH
SPLASH
SPLOSH
UPRUSH

••PH••
ALPHAS
AMPHID
CIPHER
CYPHER
DAPHNE
GOPHER
HIPHOP
HYPHEN
LAPHAM
NEPHEW
NEPHRO
ORPHAN
ORPHIC
SIPHON
SOPHIA
SOPHIE
TEPHRA
TOPHAT
TOPHUS
TYPHUS
ZEPHYR

••P•H•
DEPTHS
SAPPHO

••P••H
BYPATH
IMPISH
MOPISH
RUPIAH

•••PH•
ALEPHS
DELPHI
GLYPHS
GRAPHS
HUMPHS
MORPHO
MORPHS
MURPHY
NYMPHS
SAPPHO
SYLPHS
TROPHY

•••P•H
OOMPAH
TEMPEH
ZILPAH

••••PH
ADOLPH
CALIPH
CERIPH
GUELPH
JOSEPH
PARAPH
SERAPH
TERAPH

PI••••
PIAFFE
PIAGET
PIANOS
PIAZZA
PICABO
PICARA
PICARD
PICARO
PICCHU
PICKAT
PICKAX
PICKED
PICKER
PICKET
PICKLE
PICKON
PICKUP
PICNIC
PICOTS
PICULS
PIDGIN
PIECED
PIECER
PIECES
PIEMAN
PIEMEN
PIEPAN
PIERCE
PIERRE
PIETAS
PIETER
PIETIN
PIETRO
PIFFLE
PIGEON
PIGGED
PIGGIE
PIGLET
PIGNUT
PIGOUT
PIGPEN
PIGSTY
PIKAKE
PIKERS
PIKING
PILAFS
PILATE
PILEIN
PILEON
PILEUM
PILEUP
PILEUS
PILFER
PILING
PILLAR
PILLED
PILLOW
PILOSE
PILOTI
PILOTS
PIMINY
PINATA
PINCER
PINDAR
PINDUS
PINEAL
PINERO
PINERY
PINGED
PINIER
PINING
PINION
PINITE
PINKED
PINKEN
PINKER
PINKIE
PINNAE
PINNAS
PINNED
PINNER
PINOAK
PINOLE
PINONS
PINOTS
PINSON
PINTER
PINTLE
PINTOS
PINUPS
PINXIT
PINYIN
PINYON
PINZON
PIOLET
PIPALS
PIPERS
PIPEUP
PIPING
PIPITS
PIPKIN
PIPPED
PIPPIN
PIQUED
PIQUES
PIQUET
PIRACY
PIRANA
PIRATE
PIRRIP
PISANS
PISCES
PISGAH
PISTIL
PISTOL
PISTON
PITHED
PITIED
PITIES
PITMAN
PITMEN
PITONS
PITSAW
PITTED
PITTER
PIVOTS
PIXELS
PIXIES
PIZAZZ
PIZZAS

P•I•••
PAIDIN
PAIDUP
PAILOU
PAINED
PAINTS
PAIRED
PAIRUP
PAIUTE
PHIALS
PHILAE
PHILIP
PHILLY
PHILOL
PHILOS
PLIANT
PLICAE
PLIERS
PLIGHT
PLINKS
PLINTH
PLISSE
POILUS
POINTE
POINTS
POINTY
POIROT
POISED
POISES
POISON
PRICED
PRICER
PRICES
PRICEY
PRICKS
PRIDED
PRIDES
PRIERS
PRIEST
PRIMAL
PRIMED
PRIMER
PRIMES
PRIMLY
PRIMOS
PRIMPS
PRIMUM
PRIMUS
PRINCE
PRINKS
PRINTS
PRIONS
PRIORI
PRIORS
PRIORY
PRIPET
PRISMS
PRISON
PRISSY
PRIVET
PRIZED
PRIZES
PUISNE

P••I••
PACIFY
PACING
PACINO
PAGING
PALING
PALISH
PAMIRS
PANICS
PAPIER
PARIAH
PARING
PARISH
PARITY
PATINA
PATINE
PATIOS
PAVING
PAWING
PAYING
PEKING
PELION
PEPINO
PEPITA
PERILS
PERIOD
PERISH
PETITE
PEWITS
PIKING
PILING
PIMINY
PINIER
PINING
PINION
PINITE
PIPING
PIPITS
PITIED
PITIES
PIXIES
PLAICE
PLAIDS
PLAINS
PLAINT
PLAITS
PLEIAD
PLYING
PODIUM
POGIES
POKIER
POKILY
POKING
POLICE
POLICY
POLING
POLISH
POLITE
POLITY
PONIED
PONIES
PORING
POSIES
POSING
POSITS
POTION
PRAISE
PRYING
PULING
PUMICE
PUNIER
PUNILY
PUNISH
PUPILS
PURIFY
PURINA
PURINE
PURISM
PURIST
PURITY
PYRITE
PYXIES

P•••I•
PAIDIN
PALLIA
PALLID
PANDIT
PAPAIN
PARNIS
PARRIS
PARVIS
PASSIM
PASTIS
PATOIS
PAYSIN
PECTIC
PECTIN
PEERIN
PELVIC
PELVIS
PENCIL
PENNIA
PENNIS
PEORIA
PEPSIN
PEPTIC
PERMIT
PERSIA
PETAIN
PETRIE
PETTIT
PHATIC
PHILIP
PHOBIA
PHOBIC
PHOCIS
PHONIC
PHOTIC
PHYSIO
PICNIC
PIDGIN
PIETIN
PIGGIE
PILEIN
PINKIE
PINXIT
PINYIN
PIPKIN
PIPPIN
PIRRIP
PISTIL
PLACID
PLAGIO
PLUGIN
POETIC
PONGID
PONTIC
POPLIN
POPSIN
PORTIA
POTPIE
POURIN
PRAXIS
PRECIS
PREFIX
PRELIM
PREMIE
PREVIN
PROFIT
PROLIX
PROSIT
PUBLIC
PUFFIN
PULLIN
PULPIT
PUNDIT
PUNKIE
PURLIN
PUTRID
PUTSIN
PYKNIC
PYTHIA

P••••I
PAHARI
PAPYRI
PILOTI
POLLOI
POPULI
POTOSI
PRIORI
PROTEI

•PI•••
APIARY
APICAL
APICES
APIECE
EPICAL
EPILOG
EPIRUS
OPIATE
OPINED
OPINER
OPINES
SPICAS
SPICED
SPICES
SPIDER
SPIELS
SPIERS
SPIFFS
SPIFFY
SPIGOT
SPIKED
SPIKER
SPIKES
SPILES
SPILLS
SPILTH
SPINAL
SPINED
SPINEL
SPINES
SPINET
SPINKS
SPIRAL
SPIREA
SPIRED
SPIRES
SPIRIT
SPIROS
SPITED
SPITES
SPIVAK

•P•I••
APHIDS
APLITE
APPIAN
EPPING
OPHITE
OPTICS
OPTIMA
OPTING
OPTION
SPHINX
SPLICE
SPLINE
SPLINT
SPLITS
SPOILS
SPOILT
SPRIER
SPRIGS
SPRING
SPRINT
SPRITE
SPRITS
SPRITZ
SPYING
UPDIKE
UPHILL
UPLIFT
UPLINK
UPPING
UPPITY
UPRISE
UPSIDE
UPTICK
UPTIME
UPWIND

•P••I•
APULIA
SPADIX
SPAHIS
SPAVIN
SPECIE
SPIRIT
SPRAIN

•P•••I
EPHORI

••PI••
ALPINE
APPIAN
ASPICS
ASPIRE
CAPIAS
CAPITA
COPIED
COPIER
COPIES
COPING
CUPIDS
DEPICT
DOPIER
DOPING
DUPING
EMPIRE
EPPING
ESPIAL
ESPIED
ESPIES
EXPIRE
EXPIRY
GAPING
HOPING
HYPING
IMPISH
JAPING
LAPINS
LIPIDE
LIPIDS
LOPING
LUPINE
LUPINO
MOPING
MOPISH
NAPIER
ORPINE
PAPIER
PEPINO
PEPITA
PIPING
PIPITS
PUPILS
RAPIDS
RAPIER
RAPINE
RAPINI
REPINE
ROPIER
ROPING
RUPIAH
SEPIAS
SUPINE
TAPING
TAPINS
TAPIRS
TIPINS
TOPICS
TUPIAN
TYPIFY
TYPING
TYPIST
UMPIRE
UNPILE
UNPINS
UPPING
UPPITY
WAPITI
WIPING

••P•I•
AMPHID
AUPAIR
CAPRIS
CAPSID
COPTIC
CUPRIC
ESPRIT
HIPPIE
IMPAIR
JOPLIN
LIPOID
NAPKIN
ORPHIC
PAPAIN
PEPSIN
PEPTIC
PIPKIN
PIPPIN
POPLIN
POPSIN
REPAID
REPAIR
ROPEIN
SEPTIC
SOPHIA
SOPHIE
TIPSIN
UNPAID
YUPPIE

••P••I
NAPOLI
NEPALI
PAPYRI
POPULI
RAPINI
WAPITI

•••PI•
ARMPIT
CHAPIN
CHIPIN
CHOPIN
CUSPID
DROPIN
DROPIT
ELAPID
HATPIN
HIPPIE
HISPID
JUMPIN
KEEPIN
KELPIE
KEMPIS
KEWPIE
LIMPID
MAGPIE
MUDPIE
MYOPIA
MYOPIC
OKAPIS
PIPPIN
POTPIE
PULPIT
SCIPIO
SEEPIN
SLIPIN
STEPIN
STOPIN
STOPIT
STUPID
TARPIT
TENPIN
TIEPIN
TORPID
TREPID
TROPIC
UTOPIA
VESPID
YUPPIE

•••P•I
DELPHI
TAIPEI

••••PI
OCTOPI
SCAMPI
WHOOPI

P•J•••
PAJAMA
PYJAMA

P••J••
PRAJNA
PUNJAB

••PJ••
KOPJES
TOPJOB

•••PJ•
SKOPJE

P•K•••
PEKING
PEKOES
PIKAKE
PIKERS
PIKING
POKEAT
POKERS
POKERY
POKEYS
POKIER
POKILY
POKING
PYKNIC

P••K••
PACKED
PACKER
PACKET
PACKUP
PARKAS
PARKAY
PARKED
PARKER
PEAKED
PECKAT
PECKED
PEEKAT
PEEKED
PERKED
PERKUP
PICKAT
PICKAX
PICKED
PICKER
PICKET
PICKLE
PICKON
PICKUP
PINKED
PINKEN
PINKER
PINKIE
PIPKIN
POCKET
POLKAS
PORKER
PUCKER
PUNKAH
PUNKER
PUNKIE

P•••K•
PERUKE
PIKAKE
PLANKS
PLINKS
PLONKS
PLUCKS
PLUCKY
PLUNKS
PRANKS
PRICKS
PRINKS

P••••K
PINOAK
PLANCK
PODUNK

•PK•••
UPKEEP

•P•K••
SPIKED
SPIKER
SPIKES
SPOKED
SPOKEN
SPOKES

•P••K•
SPANKS
SPANKY
SPARKS
SPARKY
SPEAKS
SPECKS
SPINKS
SPOOKS
SPOOKY
SPUNKY
UPDIKE
UPTAKE

•P•••K
SPACEK
SPIVAK
UPLINK
UPTICK

••PK••
NAPKIN
PIPKIN
RIPKEN

••P•K•
KOPEKS
TOPEKA
YAPOKS

••P••K
KOPECK
UNPACK

PL••••
PLACED
PLACER
PLACES
PLACID
PLAGAL
PLAGES
PLAGIO
PLAGUE
PLAICE
PLAIDS
PLAINS
PLAINT
PLAITS
PLANAR
PLANCK
PLANED
PLANER
PLANES
PLANET
PLANKS
PLANON
PLANTE
PLANTS
PLAQUE
PLASHY
PLASMA
PLASMO
PLASTY
PLATED
PLATEN
PLATER
PLATES
PLATTE
PLAYAS
PLAYAT
PLAYED
PLAYER
PLAYON
PLAYUP
PLAZAS
PLEACH
PLEADS
PLEASE
PLEATS
PLEBES
PLEDGE
PLEIAD
PLENTY
PLENUM
PLEURA
PLEXOR
PLEXUS
PLIANT
PLICAE
PLIERS
PLIGHT
PLINKS
PLINTH
PLISSE
PLONKS
PLOUGH
PLOVER
PLOWED
PLOWER
PLUCKS
PLUCKY
PLUGIN
PLUMBS
PLUMED
PLUMES
PLUMMY
PLUMPS
PLUNGE
PLUNKS
PLURAL
PLUSES
PLUSHY
PLYING

P•L•••
PALACE
PALAEO
PALATE
PALEAE
PALELY
PALEST
PALING
PALISH
PALLAS
PALLED
PALLET
PALLIA
PALLID
PALLOR
PALMAS
PALMED
PALMER
PALOMA
PALPUS
PALTER
PALTRY
PELAGE
PELEUS
PELION
PELLET
PELMET
PELOPS
PELOTA
PELTED
PELTER
PELTRY
PELVIC
PELVIS
PHLEBO
PHLEGM
PHLOEM
PILAFS
PILATE
PILEIN
PILEON
PILEUM
PILEUP
PILEUS
PILFER
PILING
PILLAR
PILLED
PILLOW
PILOSE
PILOTI
PILOTS
POLAND
POLDER
POLEAX
POLERS
POLEYN
POLICE
POLICY
POLING
POLISH
POLITE
POLITY
POLKAS
POLLED
POLLEN
POLLER
POLLEX
POLLOI
POLLUX
POLPOT
POLYPS
PULING
PULLED
PULLET
PULLEY
PULLIN
PULLON
PULLUP
PULPED
PULPIT
PULQUE
PULSAR
PULSED
PULSES
PYLONS

P••L••
PABLUM
PAELLA
PAILOU
PALLAS
PALLED
PALLET
PALLIA
PALLID
PALLOR
PARLAY
PARLEY
PARLOR
PAULEY
PAVLOV
PEALED
PEDLAR
PEELED
PEELER
PEGLER
PELLET
PEPLOS
PEPLUM
PHILAE
PHILIP
PHILLY
PHILOL
PHILOS
PHYLAE
PHYLLO
PHYLUM
PIGLET
PILLAR
PILLED
PILLOW
PIOLET
POILUS
POLLED
POLLEN
POLLER
POLLEX
POLLOI
POLLUX
POOLED
POPLAR
POPLIN
POULTS
PRELAW
PRELIM
PROLES
PROLIX
PROLOG
PSALMS
PSYLLA
PUBLIC
PULLED
PULLET
PULLEY
PULLIN
PULLON
PULLUP
PURLED
PURLIN

P•••L•
PADDLE
PAELLA
PALELY
PAMELA
PANELS
PAROLE
PARTLY
PARULA
PAYOLA
PEARLS
PEARLY
PEBBLE
PEBBLY
PEDALS
PEDDLE
PENULT
PEOPLE
PERILS
PERTLY
PESTLE
PETALS
PETULA
PHIALS
PHILLY
PHYLLO
PICKLE
PICULS
PIFFLE
PINOLE
PINTLE

PIPALS
PIXELS
POKILY
POMELO
POODLE
POORLY
POPFLY
POPPLE
POPULI
PORTLY
POSHLY
POTTLE
POWELL
PRIMLY
PROWLS
PSYLLA
PUDDLE
PUDDLY
PUEBLA
PUEBLO
PUNILY
PUPILS
PURELY
PURFLE
PURPLE
PUZZLE

P••••L
PARCEL
PARREL
PASCAL
PASSEL
PASTEL
PATHOL
PATROL
PENCEL
PENCIL
PENPAL
PETREL
PETROL
PHENOL
PHENYL
PHILOL
PINEAL
PISTIL
PISTOL
PLAGAL
PLURAL
POMMEL
PORTAL
POSTAL
POTFUL
POWELL
PRIMAL
PROPEL
PUMMEL

•PL•••
APLITE
APLOMB
SPLASH
SPLATS
SPLAYS
SPLEEN
SPLICE
SPLINE
SPLINT
SPLITS
SPLOSH
UPLAND
UPLIFT
UPLINK
UPLOAD

•P•L••
APOLLO
APPLES
APULIA
EPILOG
KPELLE
SPALLS
SPELLS
SPILES
SPILLS
SPILTH

•P••L•
APOLLO
APPALL
APPALS
KPELLE
OPENLY
SPALLS
SPELLS
SPIELS
SPILLS
SPOILS
SPOILT
SPOOLS
SPRYLY
UPHELD
UPHILL
UPHOLD
UPWELL

•P•••L
APICAL
APODAL
APPALL
APPEAL
EPICAL
SPINAL
SPINEL
SPIRAL
SPRAWL
UPHILL
UPWELL

••PL••
AMPLER
APPLES
BYPLAY
CAPLET
DEPLOY
DUPLEX
EMPLOY
INPLAY
JOPLIN
KAPLAN
KEPLER
MAPLES
NAPLES
PEPLOS
PEPLUM
POPLAR
POPLIN
REPLAN
REPLAY
REPLOW
RIPLEY
UNPLUG
ZIPLOC

••P•L•
AMPULE
AMPULS
APPALL
APPALS
COPULA
CUPELS
CUPOLA
DAPPLE
DIPOLE
EXPELS
FIPPLE
HOPPLE
IMPALA
IMPALE
IMPELS
LAPELS
NAPOLI
NEPALI
PIPALS
POPFLY
POPPLE
POPULI
PUPILS
RAPTLY
REPELS
REPOLL
RIPELY
RIPPLE
RIPPLY
SEPALS
SUPPLE
SUPPLY
TEPALS
TIPPLE
TOPPLE
TUPELO
UNPILE

••P••L
APPALL
APPEAL
CAPFUL
CUPFUL
DEPAUL
ESPIAL
KOPPEL
LAPFUL
RAPPEL
REPEAL
REPOLL
RUPAUL
SEPTAL
STPAUL

•••PL•
COMPLY
COUPLE
DAMPLY
DAPPLE
DEEPLY
DIMPLE
DIMPLY
FIPPLE
HOOPLA
HOOPLE
HOPPLE
LIMPLY
MARPLE
PEOPLE
POPPLE
PURPLE
RIMPLE
RIPPLE
RIPPLY
RUMPLE
RUMPLY
SAMPLE
SIMPLE
SIMPLY
STAPLE
SUPPLE
SUPPLY
TEMPLE
TIPPLE
TOPPLE
TRIPLE
TRIPLY
TWOPLY
WIMPLE

•••P•L
BHOPAL
CARPAL
CARPEL
CHAPEL
COMPEL
DISPEL
GOSPEL
KOPPEL
PENPAL
PROPEL
RAPPEL
STIPEL

P•M•••
PAMELA
PAMIRS
PAMPAS
PAMPER
PIMINY
POMACE
POMADE
POMELO
POMMEE
POMMEL
POMONA
POMPEY
POMPOM
POMPON
PUMICE
PUMMEL
PUMPED
PUMPER
PUMPUP

P••M••
PACMAN
PALMAS
PALMED
PALMER
PATMOS
PELMET
PENMAN
PENMEN
PERMED
PERMIT
PIEMAN
PIEMEN
PITMAN
PITMEN
PLUMBS
PLUMED
PLUMES
PLUMMY
PLUMPS
POMMEE
POMMEL
PREMED
PREMIE
PRIMAL
PRIMED
PRIMER
PRIMES
PRIMLY
PRIMOS
PRIMPS
PRIMUM
PRIMUS
PROMOS
PROMPT
PUMMEL

P•••M•
PAJAMA
PALOMA
PANAMA
PLASMA
PLASMO
PLUMMY
PNEUMA
PREAMP
PRISMS
PROAMS
PROEMS
PSALMS
PYJAMA

P••••M
PABLUM
PASSIM
PEPLUM
PHENOM
PHLEGM
PHLOEM
PHYLUM
PILEUM
PLENUM
PODIUM
POMPOM
POSSUM
PRELIM
PRIMUM
PROTEM
PURISM
PUTNAM

•PM•••
UPMOST

•P•M••
APEMAN
APEMEN
SPUMED
SPUMES

•P••M•
APLOMB
OPTIMA
SPASMS
UPTIME

•P•••M
EPONYM

••P••M
GYPSUM
LAPHAM
PEPLUM
SEPTUM

•••P•M
POMPOM
WAMPUM

PN••••
PNEUMA

P•N•••
PANADA
PANAMA
PANCHO
PANDAS
PANDER
PANDIT
PANELS
PANFRY
PANICS
PANNED
PANNER
PANNES
PANOUT
PANTED
PANTRY
PANZER
PENANG
PENCEL
PENCIL
PENDED
PENGHU
PENMAN
PENMEN
PENNAE
PENNED
PENNER
PENNEY
PENNIA
PENNIS
PENNON
PENPAL
PENROD
PENSEE
PENTAD
PENTUP
PENULT
PENURY
PINATA
PINCER
PINDAR
PINDUS
PINEAL
PINERO
PINERY
PINGED
PINIER
PINING
PINION
PINITE
PINKED
PINKEN
PINKER
PINKIE
PINNAE
PINNAS
PINNED
PINNER
PINOAK
PINOLE
PINONS
PINOTS
PINSON
PINTER
PINTLE
PINTOS
PINUPS
PINXIT
PINYIN
PINYON
PINZON
PONCHO
PONDER
PONGEE
PONGID
PONIED
PONIES
PONTES
PONTIC
PONTUS
PONYUP
PUNCHY
PUNDIT
PUNIER
PUNILY
PUNISH
PUNJAB
PUNKAH
PUNKER
PUNKIE
PUNNED
PUNTED
PUNTER

P••N••
PAANGA
PAINED
PAINTS
PANNED
PANNER
PANNES
PARNIS
PAUNCH
PAWNED
PAWNEE
PAWNER
PEANUT
PEENED
PENNAE
PENNED
PENNER
PENNEY
PENNIA
PENNIS
PENNON
PERNOD
PHENOL
PHENOM
PHENYL
PHONED
PHONES
PHONIC
PHONON
PHONOS
PIANOS
PICNIC
PIGNUT
PINNAE
PINNAS
PINNED
PINNER
PLANAR
PLANCK
PLANED
PLANER
PLANES
PLANET
PLANKS
PLANON
PLANTE
PLANTS
PLENTY
PLENUM
PLINKS
PLINTH
PLONKS
PLUNGE
PLUNKS
POINTE
POINTS
POINTY
POUNCE
POUNDS
PRANCE
PRANKS
PRINCE
PRINKS
PRINTS
PRONGS
PRONTO
PRUNED
PRUNER
PRUNES
PRYNNE
PUENTE
PUNNED
PUTNAM
PYKNIC

P•••N•
PACING
PACINO
PADANG
PAEANS
PAEONS
PAGANS
PAGING
PAHANG
PALING
PARANA
PARANG
PARENS
PARENT
PARING
PATENS
PATENT
PATINA
PATINE
PAVANE
PAVING
PAWING
PAYING
PECANS
PEDANT
PEKING
PENANG
PEPINO
PIKING
PILING
PIMINY
PINING
PINONS
PIPING
PIRANA
PISANS
PITONS
PLAINS
PLAINT
PLIANT
PLYING
POCONO
PODUNK
POKING
POLAND
POLING
POMONA
PORING
POSING
POTENT
PRAJNA
PRAWNS
PREENS
PRIONS
PROCNE
PRYING
PRYNNE
PUISNE
PULING
PURINA
PURINE
PUTONS
PYLONS

P••••N
PACMAN
PADUAN
PAIDIN
PAPAIN
PAPUAN
PARDON
PARSON
PARTON
PATHAN
PATRON
PATTEN
PATTON
PAYSIN
PAYSON
PEAHEN
PECTIN
PEERIN
PELION
PENMAN
PENMEN
PENNON
PEPSIN
PERSON
PETAIN
PEYTON
PHONON
PHOTON
PICKON
PIDGIN
PIEMAN
PIEMEN
PIEPAN
PIETIN
PIGEON
PIGPEN
PILEIN
PILEON
PINION
PINKEN
PINSON
PINYIN
PINYON
PINZON
PIPKIN
PIPPIN
PISTON
PITMAN
PITMEN
PLANON
PLATEN
PLAYON
PLUGIN
POISON
POLEYN
POLLEN
POMPON
POPGUN
POPLIN
POPSIN
POSTON
POTEEN
POTION
POURIN
PREVIN
PREYON
PRISON
PROTON
PROVEN
PUFFIN
PULLIN
PULLON
PURLIN
PUSHON
PUTSIN
PUTSON
PYTHON

•P•N••
CPSNOW
EPONYM
OPENED
OPENER
OPENLY
OPENTO
OPENUP
OPINED
OPINER
OPINES
SPANKS
SPANKY
SPENDS
SPINAL
SPINED
SPINEL
SPINES
SPINET
SPINKS
SPONGE
SPONGY
SPUNKY
UPENDS

•P••N•
APPEND
APRONS
EPPING
OPTING
SPAWNS
SPHINX
SPLINE
SPLINT
SPOONS
SPOONY
SPRANG
SPRING
SPRINT
SPRUNG
SPURNS
SPYING
UPLAND
UPLINK
UPPING
UPWIND

•P•••N
APEMAN
APEMEN
APPIAN
EPHRON
OPPUGN
OPTION
SPAVIN
SPLEEN
SPOKEN
SPRAIN
SPURON
UPTOWN
UPTURN

••PN••
CAPNUT
EUPNEA
HYPNOS
WAPNER

••P•N•
ALPINE
APPEND
ARPENT
ASPENS
CAPONE
CAPONS
COPING
DAPHNE
DEPEND
DEPONE
DOPANT
DOPING
DUPING
DUPONT
EPPING
ESPANA
EXPAND
EXPEND
GAPING
HOPING
HYPING
IMPEND
JAPANS
JAPING
LAPINS
LIPENG
LOPING
LUPINE
LUPINO
LUPONE
MOPING
ORPINE
PEPINO
PIPING
RAPINE
RAPINI
REPAND
REPENT
REPINE
RIPENS
ROPING
SUPINE
TAPING
TAPINS
TIPINS
TYPING
UNPENS
UNPINS
UPPING
WIPING

••P••N
APPIAN
CAPGUN
CAPTAN
HAPPEN
HYPHEN
IMPUGN
JOPLIN
KAPLAN
KEPTON
LEPTON
LIPTON
NAPKIN
NIPPON
OPPUGN
ORPHAN
PAPAIN
PAPUAN
PEPSIN
PIPKIN
PIPPIN
POPGUN
POPLIN
POPSIN
REPLAN
REPUGN
RIPKEN
ROPEIN
SIPHON
TAPPAN
TIPSIN
TOPGUN
TOPTEN
TUPIAN

•••P•N
CHAPIN
CHIPIN
CHOPIN
CLIPON
COUPON
DAMPEN
DEEPEN
DROPIN
FRYPAN
HAPPEN
HARPON
HATPIN
INSPAN
JUMPIN
JUMPON
KEEPIN
KEEPON
LUMPEN
NIPPON
OILPAN
PIEPAN
PIGPEN
PIPPIN
POMPON
REOPEN
SAIPAN
SAMPAN
SEEPIN
SLIPIN
SLIPON
STEPIN
STEPON
STOPIN
TAIPAN
TAPPAN
TARPAN
TARPON
TENPIN
TIEPIN
TINPAN
TREPAN
UNOPEN
USOPEN
WEAPON
YAUPON

PO••••
POACHY
POBOYS
POCKET
POCONO
PODDED
PODIUM
PODUNK
POETIC
POETRY
POGIES
POILUS
POINTE
POINTS
POINTY
POIROT
POISED
POISES
POISON
POKEAT
POKERS
POKERY
POKEYS
POKIER
POKILY
POKING
POLAND
POLDER
POLEAX
POLERS
POLEYN
POLICE
POLICY
POLING
POLISH
POLITE
POLITY
POLKAS
POLLED
POLLEN
POLLER
POLLEX
POLLOI
POLLUX
POLPOT
POLYPS
POMACE
POMADE
POMELO
POMMEE
POMMEL
POMONA
POMPEY
POMPOM
POMPON
PONCHO
PONDER
PONGEE
PONGID
PONIED
PONIES
PONTES
PONTIC
PONTUS
PONYUP
POODLE
POOHED
POOLED
POOPED
POORER
POORLY
POPART
POPEYE
POPFLY
POPGUN
POPLAR
POPLIN
POPOFF
POPOUT
POPPAS
POPPED
POPPER
POPPET
POPPLE
POPSIN
POPSUP
POPTOP
POPULI
POPUPS
PORING
PORKER
POROUS
PORTAL
PORTED
PORTER
PORTIA
PORTLY
POSADA
POSERS
POSEUR
POSHER
POSHLY
POSIES
POSING
POSITS
POSSES
POSSET
POSSUM
POSTAL
POSTED
POSTER
POSTON
POTAGE
POTASH
POTATO
POTEEN
POTENT
POTFUL
POTHER
POTION
POTOSI
POTPIE
POTTED
POTTER
POTTLE
POTTOS
POUCHY
POULTS
POUNCE
POUNDS
POURED
POURER
POURIN
POUSSE
POUTED
POUTER
POWDER
POWELL
POWERS
POWWOW

P•O•••
PEOPLE
PEORIA
PHOBIA
PHOBIC
PHOBOS
PHOCIS
PHOEBE
PHONED
PHONES
PHONIC
PHONON
PHONOS
PHOOEY
PHOTIC
PHOTOG
PHOTON
PHOTOS
PIOLET
PLONKS
PLOUGH
PLOVER
PLOWED
PLOWER
POODLE
POOHED
POOLED
POOPED
POORER
POORLY
PROAMS
PROBED
PROBER
PROBES
PROCNE
PROEMS
PROFIT
PROLES
PROLIX
PROLOG
PROMOS
PROMPT
PRONGS
PRONTO
PROOFS
PROPEL
PROPER
PROPRE
PROPUP
PROSED
PROSER
PROSES
PROSIT
PROTAX
PROTEI
PROTEM
PROTON
PROUST
PROVED
PROVEN
PROVER
PROVES
PROWLS
PROWSE

P••O••
PAEONS
PAGODA
PALOMA
PANOUT
PARODY
PAROLE
PATOIS
PAYOFF
PAYOLA
PAYOUT
PEKOES
PELOPS
PELOTA
PEYOTE
PHLOEM
PHOOEY
PICOTS
PIGOUT
PILOSE
PILOTI

PILOTS
PINOAK
PINOLE
PINONS
PINOTS
PITONS
PIVOTS
POBOYS
POCONO
POMONA
POPOFF
POPOUT
POROUS
POTOSI
PRIONS
PRIORI
PRIORS
PRIORY
PROOFS
PTBOAT
PUTOFF
PUTONS
PUTOUT
PYLONS

P•••O•

PAILOU
PALLOR
PARDON
PARLOR
PARROT
PARSON
PARTON
PASEOS
PASTOR
PATHOL
PATHOS
PATIOS
PATMOS
PATROL
PATRON
PATTON
PAVLOV
PAYFOR
PAYSON
PEAPOD
PEGTOP
PELION
PENNON
PENROD
PEPLOS
PEQUOD
PEQUOT
PERIOD
PERNOD
PERROT
PERSON
PESCOW
PETROG
PETROL
PEYTON
PHAROS
PHENOL
PHENOM
PHILOL
PHILOS
PHOBOS
PHONON
PHONOS
PHOTOG
PHOTON
PHOTOS
PIANOS
PICKON
PIGEON
PILEON
PILLOW
PINION
PINSON
PINTOS
PINYON
PINZON
PISTOL
PISTON
PLANON
PLAYON
PLEXOR
POIROT
POISON
POLLOI
POLPOT
POMPOM
POMPON
POPTOP
POSTON
POTION
POTTOS
POWWOW
PREYON
PRIMOS
PRISON
PROLOG
PROMOS
PROTON
PULLON
PUSHON
PUTSON
PYEDOG
PYTHON

P••••O

PACINO
PALAEO
PANCHO
PAPAGO
PARETO
PASHTO
PEPINO
PHLEBO
PHYLLO
PHYSIO
PICABO
PICARO
PIETRO
PINERO
PLAGIO
PLASMO
POCONO
POMELO
PONCHO
POTATO
PRESTO
PRONTO
PSEUDO
PSYCHO
PUEBLO
PUERTO
PUTSTO

•PO•••

APODAL
APOGEE
APOLLO
EPOCHS
EPODES
EPONYM
EPOPEE
OPORTO
SPOILS
SPOILT
SPOKED
SPOKEN
SPOKES
SPONGE
SPONGY
SPOOFS
SPOOKS
SPOOKY
SPOOLS
SPOONS
SPOONY
SPOORS
SPORES
SPORTS
SPORTY
SPOTTY
SPOUSE
SPOUTS

•P•O••

APLOMB
APPOSE
APRONS
EPHODS
EPHORI
EPHORS
OPPOSE
OPTOUT
SPLOSH
SPOOFS
SPOOKS
SPOOKY
SPOOLS
SPOONS
SPOONY
SPOORS
SPROUT
UPBOWS
UPHOLD
UPLOAD
UPMOST
UPROAR
UPROOT
UPROSE
UPTOWN

•P••O•

CPSNOW
EPHRON
EPILOG
OPTION
SPIGOT
SPIROS
SPURON
UPROOT
UPSHOT

•P•••O

APOLLO
OPENTO
OPORTO

••PO••

APPOSE
BIPODS
CAPONE
CAPONS
CAPOTE
COPOUT
CUPOLA
DEPONE
DEPORT
DEPOSE
DEPOTS
DIPODY
DIPOLE
DUPONT
ESPOSA
ESPOSO
EXPORT
EXPOSE
HOPOFF
HYPOED
IMPORT
IMPOSE
IMPOST
INPORT
INPOUR
LIPOID
LUPONE
NAPOLI
OPPOSE
POPOFF
POPOUT
REPOLL
REPORT
REPOSE
REPOTS
RIPOFF
SAPORS
SEPOYS
SOPORS
TAPOFF
TAPOUT
TIPOFF
TOPOFF
TOPOUT
VAPORS
VAPOUR
YAPOKS

••P•O•

CAPTOR
DEPLOY
EMPLOY
EMPTOR
HIPHOP
HIPPOS
HYPNOS
IMPROV
KEPTON
LAPDOG
LAPTOP
LEPTON
LIPTON
NIPPON
PEPLOS
POPTOP
RAPTOR
REPLOW
REPROS
SIPHON
TIPTOE
TIPTOP
TOPDOG
TOPJOB
ZIPLOC

••P••O

ELPASO
ESPOSO
LUPINO
MAPUTO
NEPHRO
PAPAGO
PEPINO
SAPPHO
TUPELO

•••PO•

CAMPOS
CLIPON
COMPOS
COUPON
COWPOX
DESPOT
HARPON
HIPPOS
HOOPOE
HOTPOT
ISOPOD
JUMPON
KARPOV
KEEPON
MAYPOP
NIPPON
PEAPOD
POLPOT
POMPOM
POMPON
SLIPON
STEPON
STUPOR
TARPON
TEAPOT
TEAPOY
TEMPOS
TINPOT
TORPOR
TRIPOD
TRIPOS
UNIPOD
WEAPON
YAUPON

•••P•O

ALEPPO
ALLPRO
BUMPPO
CRYPTO
KEEPTO
MORPHO
OLDPRO
SAPPHO
SCIPIO
SNAPTO
TROPPO

••••PO

ALEPPO
ATEMPO
BUMPPO
CHEAPO
DACAPO
KAKAPO
MOLOPO
OBISPO
TROPPO

P•P•••

PAPACY
PAPAGO
PAPAIN
PAPAWS
PAPAYA
PAPERS
PAPERY
PAPIER
PAPPAS
PAPPUS
PAPUAN
PAPYRI
PEPINO
PEPITA
PEPLOS
PEPLUM
PEPPED
PEPPER
PEPSIN
PEPSUP
PEPTIC
PIPALS
PIPERS
PIPEUP
PIPING
PIPITS
PIPKIN
PIPPED
PIPPIN
POPART
POPEYE
POPFLY
POPGUN
POPLAR
POPLIN
POPOFF
POPOUT
POPPAS
POPPED
POPPER
POPPET
POPPLE
POPSIN
POPSUP
POPTOP
POPULI
POPUPS
PUPILS
PUPPET

P••P••

PALPUS
PAMPAS
PAMPER
PAPPAS
PAPPUS
PAUPER
PAWPAW
PEAPOD
PEEPED
PEEPER
PENPAL
PEOPLE
PEPPED
PEPPER
PIEPAN
PIGPEN
PIPPED
PIPPIN
POLPOT
POMPEY
POMPOM
POMPON
POOPED
POPPAS
POPPED
POPPER
POPPET
POPPLE
POTPIE
PREPAY
PREPPY
PRIPET
PROPEL
PROPER
PROPRE
PROPUP
PULPED
PULPIT
PUMPED
PUMPER
PUMPUP
PUPPET
PURPLE
PUTPUT

P•••P•

PARAPH
PELOPS
PINUPS
PLUMPS
POLYPS
POPUPS
PREPPY
PRIMPS
PROMPT
PTRAPS

P••••P

PACKUP
PAIDUP
PAIRUP
PASSUP
PAYSUP
PEGTOP
PENTUP
PEPSUP
PERKUP
PHILIP
PICKUP
PILEUP
PIPEUP
PIRRIP
PLAYUP
PONYUP
POPSUP
POPTOP
PREAMP
PROPUP
PULLUP
PUMPUP
PUSHUP
PUTSUP

•PP•••

APPALL
APPALS
APPEAL
APPEAR
APPEND
APPIAN
APPLES
APPOSE
EPPING
OPPOSE
OPPUGN
UPPERS
UPPING
UPPITY

•P•P••

EPOPEE

•P•••P

OPENUP
SPEDUP
UPKEEP

••PP••

BOPPED
BOPPER
CAPPED
CAPPER
COPPED
COPPER
CUPPED
DAPPED
DAPPER
DAPPLE
DIPPED
DIPPER
FIPPLE
GAPPED
GIPPED
GIPPER
GYPPED
GYPPER
HAPPEN
HEPPER
HIPPED
HIPPER
HIPPIE
HIPPOS
HOPPED
HOPPER
HOPPLE
KAPPAS
KIPPER
KIPPUR
KOPPEL
LAPPED
LAPPET
LIPPED
LOPPED
LOPPER
MAPPED
MAPPER
MOPPED
MOPPER
MOPPET
MUPPET
NAPPED
NAPPER
NAPPES
NIPPED
NIPPER
NIPPON
NIPPUR
PAPPAS
PAPPUS
PEPPED
PEPPER
PIPPED
PIPPIN
POPPAS
POPPED
POPPER
POPPET
POPPLE
PUPPET
RAPPED
RAPPEE
RAPPEL
RAPPER
RIPPED
RIPPER
RIPPLE
RIPPLY
SAPPED
SAPPER
SAPPHO
SIPPED
SIPPER
SIPPET
SOPPED
SUPPED
SUPPER
SUPPLE
SUPPLY
TAPPAN
TAPPED
TAPPER
TAPPET
TIPPED
TIPPER
TIPPET
TIPPLE
TOPPED
TOPPER
TOPPLE
YAPPED
YIPPED
YIPPEE
YUPPIE
ZAPPED
ZAPPER
ZIPPED
ZIPPER

••P•P•

MOPUPS
NIPUPS
POPUPS
TIPUPS

••P••P

BOPEEP
HIPHOP
HOPSUP
KEPTUP
LAPSUP
LAPTOP
MOPSUP
PEPSUP
PIPEUP
POPSUP
POPTOP
RIPRAP
RIPSUP
SOPSUP
TIPTOP
TYPEUP
WIPEUP
ZIPSUP

•••PP•

ALEPPO
BUMPPO
CHOPPY
DIEPPE
DRIPPY
FLOPPY
FRAPPE
GLOPPY
GRAPPA
GRIPPE
PREPPY
QUIPPY
SHOPPE
SKIPPY
SLAPPY
SLOPPY
SNAPPY
SNIPPY
STEPPE
TRAPPY
TROPPO
WHIPPY

•••P•P

BUMPUP
COOPUP
CROPUP
FLIPUP
JUMPUP
KEEPUP
MAYPOP
PROPUP
PUMPUP
SLAPUP
SLIPUP
SNAPUP
SOUPUP
STEPUP
STOPUP
TRIPUP
WHIPUP
WRAPUP

••••PP

ALCAPP

P•Q•••

PEQUOD
PEQUOT
PIQUED
PIQUES
PIQUET

P••Q••

PLAQUE
PULQUE

•P•Q••

OPAQUE

•••P•Q

COMPAQ

PR••••

PRAGUE
PRAISE
PRAJNA
PRANCE
PRANKS
PRATED
PRATER
PRATES
PRAVDA
PRAWNS
PRAXES
PRAXIS
PRAYED
PRAYER
PREACH
PREAMP
PRECIS
PREENS
PREFAB
PREFER
PREFIX
PRELAW
PRELIM
PREMED
PREMIE
PREPAY
PREPPY
PRESET
PRESTO
PRETAX
PRETER
PRETTY
PREVIN
PREWAR
PREYED
PREYON
PRICED
PRICER
PRICES
PRICEY
PRICKS
PRIDED
PRIDES
PRIERS
PRIEST
PRIMAL
PRIMED
PRIMER
PRIMES
PRIMLY
PRIMOS
PRIMPS
PRIMUM
PRIMUS
PRINCE
PRINKS
PRINTS
PRIONS
PRIORI
PRIORS
PRIORY
PRIPET
PRISMS
PRISON
PRISSY
PRIVET
PRIZED
PRIZES
PROAMS
PROBED
PROBER
PROBES
PROCNE
PROEMS
PROFIT
PROLES
PROLIX
PROLOG
PROMOS
PROMPT
PRONGS
PRONTO
PROOFS
PROPEL
PROPER
PROPRE
PROPUP
PROSED
PROSER
PROSES
PROSIT
PROTAX
PROTEI
PROTEM
PROTON
PROUST
PROVED
PROVEN
PROVER
PROVES
PROWLS
PROWSE
PRUDES
PRUNED
PRUNER
PRUNES
PRYING
PRYNNE

P•R•••

PARADE
PARANA
PARANG
PARAPH
PARCAE
PARCEL
PARDON
PARENS
PARENT
PARERS
PARETO
PAREVE
PARGET
PARIAH
PARING
PARISH
PARITY
PARKAS
PARKAY
PARKED
PARKER
PARLAY
PARLEY
PARLOR
PARNIS
PARODY
PAROLE
PARRED
PARREL
PARRIS
PARROT
PARSEC
PARSED
PARSEE
PARSER
PARSES
PARSON
PARTED
PARTLY
PARTON
PARULA
PARURE
PARVIS
PERCHA
PERDUE
PERILS
PERIOD
PERISH
PERKED
PERKUP
PERMED
PERMIT
PERNOD
PERROT
PERSIA
PERSON
PERTER
PERTLY
PERUKE
PERUSE
PHRASE
PIRACY
PIRANA
PIRATE
PIRRIP
PORING
PORKER
POROUS
PORTAL
PORTED
PORTER
PORTIA
PORTLY
PTRAPS
PURACE
PURDAH
PURDUE
PUREED
PUREES
PURELY
PUREST
PURFLE
PURGED
PURGES
PURIFY
PURINA
PURINE
PURISM
PURIST
PURITY
PURLED
PURLIN
PURPLE
PURRED
PURRER
PURSED
PURSER
PURSES
PURSUE
PURVEY
PYRITE

P••R••

PADRES
PAIRED
PAIRUP
PARRED
PARREL
PARRIS
PARROT
PATROL
PATRON
PEARLS
PEARLY
PEERAT
PEERCE
PEERED
PEERIN
PENROD
PEORIA
PERROT
PETREL
PETRIE
PETROG
PETROL
PHAROS
PIERCE
PIERRE
PIRRIP
PLURAL
POIROT
POORER
POORLY
POURED
POURER
POURIN
PUERTO
PUGREE
PURRED
PURRER
PUTRID

P•••R•

PACERS
PAGERS
PAHARI
PALTRY
PAMIRS
PANFRY
PANTRY
PAPERS
PAPERY
PAPYRI
PARERS
PARURE
PASTRY
PAVERS
PAWERS
PAYERS
PELTRY
PENURY
PETARD
PETERS
PHEDRE
PICARA
PICARD
PICARO
PIERRE
PIETRO
PIKERS
PINERO
PINERY
PIPERS
PLEURA
PLIERS
POETRY
POKERS
POKERY
POLERS
POPART
POSERS
POWERS
PRIERS
PRIORI
PRIORS
PRIORY
PROPRE

P••••R

PACKER
PADDER
PALLOR
PALMER
PALTER
PAMPER
PANDER
PANNER
PANZER
PAPIER
PARKER
PARLOR
PARSER
PASSER
PASTOR
PATTER
PAUPER
PAWNER
PAYFOR
PEDLAR
PEELER
PEEPER
PEGLER
PELTER
PENNER
PEPPER
PERTER
PESTER
PETTER
PEWTER
PHASER
PICKER
PIECER
PIETER
PILFER
PILLAR
PINCER
PINDAR
PINIER
PINKER
PINNER
PINTER
PITTER
PLACER
PLANAR
PLANER
PLATER
PLAYER
PLEXOR
PLOVER
PLOWER
POKIER
POLDER
POLLER
PONDER
POORER
POPLAR
POPPER
PORKER
PORTER
POSEUR
POSHER
POSTER
POTHER
POTTER
POURER
POUTER
POWDER
PRATER
PRAYER
PREFER
PRETER
PREWAR
PRICER
PRIMER
PROBER
PROPER
PROSER
PROVER
PRUNER
PUCKER
PUFFER
PULSAR
PUMPER
PUNIER
PUNKER
PUNTER
PURRER
PURSER
PUTTER

•PR•••

APRONS
SPRAGS
SPRAIN
SPRANG
SPRATS
SPRAWL
SPRAYS
SPREAD
SPREES

SPRIER
SPRIGS
SPRING
SPRINT
SPRITE
SPRITS
SPRITZ
SPROUT
SPRUCE
SPRUES
SPRUNG
SPRYER
SPRYLY
UPRISE
UPROAR
UPROOT
UPROSE
UPRUSH

•P•R••
APERCU
EPARCH
EPHRON
EPIRUS
OPERAS
OPORTO
SPARED
SPARER
SPARES
SPARGE
SPARKS
SPARKY
SPARSE
SPARTA
SPERRY
SPIRAL
SPIREA
SPIRED
SPIRES
SPIRIT
SPIROS
SPORES
SPORTS
SPORTY
SPURGE
SPURNS
SPURON
SPURRY
SPURTS

•P••R•
APIARY
EPHORI
EPHORS
SPEARS
SPERRY
SPHERE
SPIERS
SPOORS
SPURRY
UPPERS
UPTURN
UPWARD

•P•••R
APPEAR
OPENER
OPINER
SPACER
SPADER
SPARER
SPIDER
SPIKER
SPRIER
SPRYER
UPROAR

••PR••
CAPRIS
CUPRIC
CYPRUS
ESPRIT
IMPROV
OSPREY
REPROS
RIPRAP

••P•R•
ALPERT
AMPERE
ASPERA
ASPIRE
CAPERS
DEPART
DEPORT
DUPERY
EMPERY
EMPIRE
EXPERT
EXPIRE
EXPIRY
EXPORT
GAPERS
HOPERS
IMPART
IMPERF
IMPORT
IMPURE
INPART
INPORT
JAPERS
JAPERY
LOPERS
MOPERS
NAPERY
NEPHRO
PAPERS
PAPERY
PAPYRI
PIPERS
POPART
REPORT
ROPERS
RUPERT
SAPORS
SOPORS
SUPERB
SUPERS
TAPERS
TAPIRS
TEPHRA
TOPERS
TYPERS
UMPIRE
UPPERS
VAPORS
VIPERS
WIPERS

••P••R
AMPLER
APPEAR
AUPAIR
BOPPER
CAPPER
CAPTOR
CIPHER
COPIER
COPPER
COPTER
CYPHER
DAPPER
DIPPER
DOPIER
EMPTOR
GIPPER
GOPHER
GYPPER
HEPPER
HIPPER
HOPPER
IMPAIR
INPOUR
KEPLER
KIPPER
KIPPUR
LOPPER
MAPPER
MOPPER
NAPIER
NAPPER
NIPPER
NIPPUR
PAPIER
PEPPER
POPLAR
POPPER
RAPIER
RAPPER
RAPTOR
REPAIR
RIPPER
ROPIER
SAPPER
SIPPER
SUPPER
TAPPER
TIPPER
TOPPER
VAPOUR
WAPNER
ZAPPER
ZEPHYR
ZIPPER

•••PR•
ALLPRO
OLDPRO
PROPRE
SEMPRE

•••P•R
BEEPER
BOPPER
BUMPER
CAMPER
CAPPER
CARPER
CASPAR
CASPER
COOPER
COPPER
COWPER
DAMPER
DAPPER
DEEPER
DIAPER
DIPPER
DRAPER
DUMPER
ELOPER
GASPAR
GIPPER
GRIPER
GULPER
GYPPER
HAMPER
HARPER
HELPER
HEPPER
HIPPER
HOOPER
HOPPER
JAIPUR
JASPER
JUMPER
KEEPER
KIPPER
KIPPUR
LAUPER
LEAPER
LIMPER
LOOPER
LOPPER
LUMPER
LUMPUR
MAPPER
MOPPER
NAPPER
NIPPER
NIPPUR
PAMPER
PAUPER
PEEPER
PEPPER
POPPER
PROPER
PUMPER
RAIPUR
RAPPER
RASPER
REAPER
RIPPER
ROMPER
SAPPER
SEMPER
SHAPER
SIMPER
SIPPER
SOAPER
STUPOR
SUPPER
SWIPER
TAMPER
TAPPER
TEMPER
TIPPER
TOPPER
TORPOR
VAMPER
VESPER
WEEPER
WOLPER
YAWPER
YELPER
ZAPPER
ZIPPER

PS••••
PSALMS
PSEUDO
PSEUDS
PSYCHE
PSYCHO
PSYCHS
PSYLLA

P•S•••
PASCAL
PASEOS
PASHAS
PASHTO
PASSBY
PASSED
PASSEL
PASSER
PASSES
PASSIM
PASSUP
PASTAS
PASTED
PASTEL
PASTES
PASTIS
PASTOR
PASTRY
PESACH
PESCOW
PESETA
PESTER
PESTLE
PISANS
PISCES
PISGAH
PISTIL
PISTOL
PISTON
POSADA
POSERS
POSEUR
POSHER
POSHLY
POSIES
POSING
POSITS
POSSES
POSSET
POSSUM
POSTAL
POSTED
POSTER
POSTON
PUSHED
PUSHES
PUSHON
PUSHUP
PUSSES

P••S••
PARSEC
PARSED
PARSEE
PARSER
PARSES
PARSON
PASSBY
PASSED
PASSEL
PASSER
PASSES
PASSIM
PASSUP
PAUSED
PAUSES
PAWSAT
PAYSIN
PAYSON
PAYSUP
PENSEE
PEPSIN
PEPSUP
PERSIA
PERSON
PHASED
PHASER
PHASES
PHYSED
PHYSIO
PIGSTY
PINSON
PITSAW
PLASHY
PLASMA
PLASMO
PLASTY
PLISSE
PLUSES
PLUSHY
POISED
POISES
POISON
POPSIN
POPSUP
POSSES
POSSET
POSSUM
POUSSE
PRESET
PRESTO
PRISMS
PRISON
PRISSY
PROSED
PROSER
PROSES
PROSIT
PUISNE
PULSAR
PULSED
PULSES
PURSED
PURSER
PURSES
PURSUE
PUSSES
PUTSBY
PUTSCH
PUTSIN
PUTSON
PUTSTO
PUTSUP

P•••S•
PALEST
PALISH
PARISH
PERISH
PERUSE
PHRASE
PILOSE
PLEASE
PLISSE
POLISH
POTASH
POTOSI
POUSSE
PRAISE
PRIEST
PRISSY
PROUST
PROWSE
PUNISH
PUREST
PURISM
PURIST

P••••S
PACERS
PADRES
PAEANS
PAEONS
PAGANS
PAGERS
PAINTS
PALLAS
PALMAS
PALPUS
PAMIRS
PAMPAS
PANDAS
PANELS
PANICS
PANNES
PAPAWS
PAPERS
PAPPAS
PAPPUS
PARENS
PARERS
PARKAS
PARNIS
PARRIS
PARSES
PARVIS
PASEOS
PASHAS
PASSES
PASTAS
PASTES
PASTIS
PATENS
PATHOS
PATIOS
PATMOS
PATOIS
PAUSES
PAVERS
PAWERS
PAYEES
PAYERS
PEARLS
PECANS
PEDALS
PEEVES
PEKOES
PELEUS
PELOPS
PELVIS
PENNIS
PEPLOS
PERILS
PETALS
PETERS
PEWEES
PEWITS
PHAGES
PHAROS
PHASES
PHIALS
PHILOS
PHOBOS
PHOCIS
PHONES
PHONOS
PHOTOS
PIANOS
PICOTS
PICULS
PIECES
PIETAS
PIKERS
PILAFS
PILEUS
PILOTS
PINDUS
PINNAS
PINONS
PINOTS
PINTOS
PINUPS
PIPALS
PIPERS
PIPITS
PIQUES
PISANS
PISCES
PITIES
PITONS
PIVOTS
PIXELS
PIXIES
PIZZAS
PLACES
PLAGES
PLAIDS
PLAINS
PLAITS
PLANES
PLANKS
PLANTS
PLATES
PLAYAS
PLAZAS
PLEADS
PLEATS
PLEBES
PLEXUS
PLIERS
PLINKS
PLONKS
PLUCKS
PLUMBS
PLUMES
PLUMPS
PLUNKS
PLUSES
POBOYS
POGIES
POILUS
POINTS
POISES
POKERS
POKEYS
POLERS
POLKAS
POLYPS
PONIES
PONTES
PONTUS
POPPAS
POPUPS
POROUS
POSERS
POSIES
POSITS
POSSES
POTTOS
POULTS
POUNDS
POWERS
PRANKS
PRATES
PRAWNS
PRAXES
PRAXIS
PRECIS
PREENS
PRICES
PRICKS
PRIDES
PRIERS
PRIMES
PRIMOS
PRIMPS
PRIMUS
PRINKS
PRINTS
PRIONS
PRIORS
PRISMS
PRIZES
PROAMS
PROBES
PROEMS
PROLES
PROMOS
PRONGS
PROOFS
PROSES
PROVES
PROWLS
PRUDES
PRUNES
PSALMS
PSEUDS
PSYCHS
PTRAPS
PULSES
PUPILS
PUREES
PURGES
PURSES
PUSHES
PUSSES
PUTONS
PYLONS
PYXIES

•PS•••
CPSNOW
UPSETS
UPSHOT
UPSIDE

•P•S••
OPUSES
SPASMS

•P••S•
APPOSE
APTEST
OPPOSE
SPARSE
SPLASH
SPLOSH
SPOUSE
UPCAST
UPMOST
UPRISE
UPROSE
UPRUSH

•P•••S
APEXES
APHIDS
APICES
APPALS
APPLES
APRONS
EPHAHS
EPHODS
EPHORS
EPIRUS
EPOCHS
EPODES
OPERAS
OPINES
OPTICS
OPUSES
SPACES
SPADES
SPAHIS
SPALLS
SPANKS
SPARES
SPARKS
SPASMS
SPATES
SPAWNS
SPEAKS
SPEARS
SPECKS
SPEEDS
SPELLS
SPENDS
SPICAS
SPICES
SPIELS
SPIERS
SPIFFS
SPIKES
SPILES
SPILLS
SPINES
SPINKS
SPIRES
SPIROS
SPITES
SPLATS
SPLAYS
SPLITS
SPOILS
SPOKES
SPOOFS
SPOOKS
SPOOLS
SPOONS
SPOORS
SPORES
SPORTS
SPOUTS
SPRAGS
SPRATS
SPRAYS
SPREES
SPRIGS
SPRITS
SPRUES
SPUMES
SPURNS
SPURTS
UPBOWS
UPENDS
UPPERS
UPSETS

••PS••
CAPSID
COPSES
GYPSUM
HOPSUP
LAPSED
LAPSES
LAPSUP
MOPSUP
NIPSAT
PEPSIN
PEPSUP
POPSIN
POPSUP
RIPSAW
RIPSUP
SOPSUP
TIPSIN
ZIPSUP

••P•S•
APPOSE
BYPASS
BYPAST
DEPOSE
ELPASO
ESPOSA
ESPOSO
EXPOSE
IMPISH
IMPOSE
IMPOST
LIPASE
MOPISH
OPPOSE
REPAST
REPOSE
RIPEST
TYPIST

••P••S
ALPHAS
AMPULS
APPALS
APPLES
ASPENS
ASPICS
BIPEDS
BIPODS
BYPASS
CAPERS
CAPIAS
CAPONS
CAPRIS
COPIES
COPSES
CUPELS
CUPIDS
CYPRUS
DEPOTS
DEPTHS
ESPIES
EXPELS
GAPERS
HIPPOS
HOPERS
HYPNOS
IMPELS
INPUTS
JAPANS
JAPERS
KAPPAS
KOPEKS
KOPJES
LAPELS
LAPINS
LAPSES
LIPIDS
LOPERS
MAPLES
MOPEDS
MOPERS
MOPUPS
NAPLES
NAPPES
NIPUPS
NOPETS
PAPAWS
PAPERS
PAPPAS
PAPPUS
PEPLOS
PIPALS
PIPERS
PIPITS
POPPAS
POPUPS
PUPILS
RAPIDS
REPAYS
REPEGS
REPELS
REPOTS
REPROS
RIPENS
ROPERS
RUPEES
SAPORS
SEPALS
SEPIAS
SEPOYS
SOPORS
SUPERS
TAPERS
TAPINS
TAPIRS
TEPALS
TEPEES
TIPINS
TIPUPS
TOPERS
TOPHUS
TOPICS
TYPERS
TYPHUS
UNPEGS
UNPENS
UNPINS
UPPERS
VAPORS
VIPERS
WIPERS
YAPOKS

•••PS•
ELAPSE
FLOPSY

•••P•S
ADAPTS
ADEPTS
ADOPTS
ALEPHS
CAMPOS
CAMPUS
CARPUS
COAPTS
COMPOS
COOPTS
CORPUS
COUPES
COYPUS
CRAPES
CREPES
CRIPES
CRYPTS
DRAPES
DRUPES
ELOPES
ERUPTS
GLYPHS
GRAPES
GRAPHS
GRIPES
GROPES
HIPPOS
HUMPHS
KAPPAS
KEMPIS
LOUPES
MILPAS
MORPHS
MYOPES
NAPPES
NYMPHS
OKAPIS
PALPUS
PAMPAS
PAPPAS
PAPPUS
POPPAS
QUIPUS
RUMPUS
SCAPES
SCOPES
SHAPES
SLOPES
SLYPES
SNIPES
SNOPES
STAPES
STIPES
STOPES
STUPAS
STUPES
SWIPES
SYLPHS
TAUPES
TEMPOS
TEMPTS
TRIPOS
TROPES

••••PS
BEBOPS
BICEPS
BLEEPS
BLIMPS
BLOOPS
CHAMPS
CHEEPS
CHEOPS
CHIMPS
CHIRPS
CHOMPS
CHUMPS
CLAMPS
CLASPS
CLOMPS
CLUMPS
CRAMPS
CREEPS
CRIMPS
CRISPS
CUTUPS
DROOPS
EQUIPS
ESTOPS
FIXUPS
FRUMPS
FSTOPS
GALOPS
GETUPS
GRAMPS
GRASPS
GROUPS
GRUMPS
JAMUPS
JULEPS
LAYUPS
LETUPS
MIXUPS
MOPUPS
NIPUPS
ONEUPS
ORLOPS
OXLIPS
PELOPS
PINUPS
PLUMPS
POLYPS
POPUPS
PRIMPS
PTRAPS
RECAPS
REMAPS
RETAPS
RETOPS
RUNUPS
SCALPS
SCAMPS
SCARPS
SCAUPS
SCOOPS
SCRAPS
SCRIPS
SETUPS
SHARPS
SHEEPS
SITUPS
SKIMPS
SLEEPS
SLOOPS
SLUMPS
SLURPS
SNOOPS
STAMPS
STEEPS
STOMPS
STOOPS
STOUPS
STRAPS
STRIPS
STROPS
STUMPS
SUNUPS
SWAMPS
SWEEPS
SWOOPS
SYRUPS
THORPS
THRIPS
THUMPS
TIEUPS
TIPUPS
TRAMPS
TROMPS
TROOPS
TRUMPS
TULIPS
TWERPS
UNCAPS
UNZIPS
USURPS
WHELPS
WHOMPS
WHOOPS

PT••••
PTBOAT
PTRAPS

P•T•••
PATACA
PATCHY
PATENS
PATENT
PATHAN
PATHOL
PATHOS
PATINA
PATINE
PATIOS
PATMOS
PATOIS
PATROL
PATRON
PATTED
PATTEN
PATTER
PATTON
PETAIN
PETALS
PETARD
PETERS
PETITE
PETREL
PETRIE
PETROG
PETROL
PETTED
PETTER
PETTIT
PETULA
PITHED
PITIED
PITIES
PITMAN
PITMEN
PITONS
PITSAW
PITTED
PITTER
POTAGE
POTASH
POTATO
POTEEN
POTENT
POTFUL
POTHER
POTION
POTOSI
POTPIE
POTTED
POTTER
POTTLE
POTTOS
PUTNAM
PUTOFF
PUTONS
PUTOUT
PUTPUT
PUTRID
PUTSBY
PUTSCH
PUTSIN

PUTSON
PUTSTO
PUTSUP
PUTTED
PUTTEE
PUTTER
PYTHIA
PYTHON

P••T••
PALTER
PALTRY
PANTED
PANTRY
PARTED
PARTLY
PARTON
PASTAS
PASTED
PASTEL
PASTES
PASTIS
PASTOR
PASTRY
PATTED
PATTEN
PATTER
PATTON
PECTIC
PECTIN
PEGTOP
PELTED
PELTER
PELTRY
PENTAD
PENTUP
PEPTIC
PERTER
PERTLY
PESTER
PESTLE
PETTED
PETTER
PETTIT
PEWTER
PEYTON
PHATIC
PHOTIC
PHOTOG
PHOTON
PHOTOS
PIETAS
PIETER
PIETIN
PIETRO
PINTER
PINTLE
PINTOS
PISTIL
PISTOL
PISTON
PITTED
PITTER
PLATED
PLATEN
PLATER
PLATES
PLATTE
POETIC
POETRY
PONTES
PONTIC
PONTUS
POPTOP
PORTAL
PORTED
PORTER
PORTIA
PORTLY
POSTAL
POSTED
POSTER
POSTON
POTTED
POTTER
POTTLE
POTTOS
POUTED
POUTER
PRATED
PRATER
PRATES
PRETAX
PRETER
PRETTY
PROTAX
PROTEI
PROTEM
PROTON
PUNTED
PUNTER
PUTTED
PUTTEE
PUTTER

P•••T•
PAINTS
PAIUTE
PALATE
PARETO
PARITY
PASHTO
PEDATE
PELOTA
PEPITA
PESETA
PETITE
PEWITS
PEYOTE
PICOTS
PIGSTY
PILATE
PILOTI
PILOTS
PINATA
PINITE
PINOTS
PIPITS
PIRATE
PIVOTS
PLAITS
PLANTE
PLANTS
PLASTY
PLATTE
PLEATS
PLENTY
PLINTH
POINTE
POINTS
POINTY
POLITE
POLITY
POSITS
POTATO
POULTS
PRESTO
PRETTY
PRINTS
PRONTO
PUENTE
PUERTO
PURITY
PUTSTO
PYRITE

P••••T
PACKET
PALEST
PALLET
PANDIT
PANOUT
PARENT
PARGET
PARROT
PATENT
PAWSAT
PAYOUT
PEANUT
PECKAT
PEDANT
PEEKAT
PEERAT
PELLET
PELMET
PENULT
PEQUOT
PERMIT
PERROT
PETTIT
PIAGET
PICKAT
PICKET
PIGLET
PIGNUT
PIGOUT
PINXIT
PIOLET
PIQUET
PLAINT
PLANET
PLAYAT
PLIANT
PLIGHT
POCKET
POIROT
POKEAT
POLPOT
POPART
POPOUT
POPPET
POSSET
POTENT
PRESET
PRIEST
PRIPET
PRIVET
PROFIT
PROMPT
PROSIT
PROUST
PTBOAT
PULLET
PULPIT
PUNDIT
PUPPET
PUREST
PURIST
PUTOUT
PUTPUT

•PT•••
APTEST
OPTICS
OPTIMA
OPTING
OPTION
OPTOUT
UPTAKE
UPTICK
UPTIME
UPTOWN
UPTURN

•P•T••
APATHY
SPATES
SPATHE
SPITED
SPITES
SPOTTY

•P••T•
APLITE
OPENTO
OPHITE
OPIATE
OPORTO
SPARTA
SPILTH
SPLATS
SPLITS
SPORTS
SPORTY
SPOTTY
SPOUTS
SPRATS
SPRITE
SPRITS
SPRITZ
SPURTS
UPDATE
UPPITY
UPSETS

•P•••T
APTEST
OPTOUT
SPIGOT
SPINET
SPIRIT
SPLINT
SPOILT
SPRINT
SPROUT
UPBEAT
UPCAST
UPLIFT
UPMOST
UPROOT
UPSHOT

••PT••
CAPTAN
CAPTOR
COPTER
COPTIC
DEPTHS
EMPTOR
HEPTAD
KEPTAT
KEPTON
KEPTUP
LAPTEV
LAPTOP
LEPTON
LIPTON
PEPTIC
POPTOP
RAPTLY
RAPTOR
SEPTAL
SEPTET
SEPTIC
SEPTUM
TIPTOE
TIPTOP
TOPTEN

••P•T•
BYPATH
CAPITA
CAPOTE
DEPOTS
DEPUTE
DEPUTY
IMPUTE
INPUTS
LAPUTA
MAPUTO
NOPETS
PEPITA
PIPITS
REPOTS
REPUTE
STPETE
UPPITY
WAPITI
ZAPATA

••P••T
ALPERT
ARPENT
ASPECT
BYPAST
CAPLET
CAPNUT
COPOUT
DEPART
DEPICT
DEPORT
DOPANT
DUPONT
ESPRIT
EXPECT
EXPERT
EXPORT
HEPCAT
IMPACT
IMPART
IMPORT
IMPOST
INPART
INPORT
KEPTAT
LAPPET
MOPPET
MUPPET
NIPSAT
POPART
POPOUT
POPPET
PUPPET
REPAST
REPEAT
REPENT
REPORT
RIPEST
RUPERT
SEPTET
SIPPET
TAPOUT
TAPPET
TIPPET
TOPCAT
TOPHAT
TOPOUT
TYPIST

•••PT•
ADAPTS
ADEPTS
ADOPTS
COAPTS
COOPTS
CRYPTO
CRYPTS
ERUPTS
KEEPTO
SNAPTO
TEMPTS

•••P•T
ARMPIT
CARPET
DESPOT
DROPIT
HOTPOT
INAPET
JUMPAT
KEEPAT
LAPPET
LIMPET
MOPPET
MUPPET
OUTPUT
POLPOT
POPPET
PRIPET
PULPIT
PUPPET
PUTPUT
RAJPUT
SIPPET
SNAPAT
STOPIT
TAPPET
TARPIT
TEAPOT
TINPOT
TIPPET

••••PT
ABRUPT
ACCEPT
ENRAPT
EXCEPT
EXEMPT
INCEPT
IRRUPT
PROMPT
SCRIPT
SCULPT

PU••••
PUBLIC
PUCKER
PUDDLE
PUDDLY
PUEBLA
PUEBLO
PUENTE
PUERTO
PUFFED
PUFFER
PUFFIN
PUGGED
PUGREE
PUISNE
PULING
PULLED
PULLET
PULLEY
PULLIN
PULLON
PULLUP
PULPED
PULPIT
PULQUE
PULSAR
PULSED
PULSES
PUMICE
PUMMEL
PUMPED
PUMPER
PUMPUP
PUNCHY
PUNDIT
PUNIER
PUNILY
PUNISH
PUNJAB
PUNKAH
PUNKER
PUNKIE
PUNNED
PUNTED
PUNTER
PUPILS
PUPPET
PURACE
PURDAH
PURDUE
PUREED
PUREES
PURELY
PUREST
PURFLE
PURGED
PURGES
PURIFY
PURINA
PURINE
PURISM
PURIST
PURITY
PURLED
PURLIN
PURPLE
PURRED
PURRER
PURSED
PURSER
PURSES
PURSUE
PURVEY
PUSHED
PUSHES
PUSHON
PUSHUP
PUSSES
PUTNAM
PUTOFF
PUTONS
PUTOUT
PUTPUT
PUTRID
PUTSBY
PUTSCH
PUTSIN
PUTSON
PUTSTO
PUTSUP
PUTTED
PUTTEE
PUTTER
PUZZLE

P•U•••
PAULEY
PAUNCH
PAUPER
PAUSED
PAUSES
PLUCKS
PLUCKY
PLUGIN
PLUMBS
PLUMED
PLUMES
PLUMMY
PLUMPS
PLUNGE
PLUNKS
PLURAL
PLUSES
PLUSHY
POUCHY
POULTS
POUNCE
POUNDS
POURED
POURER
POURIN
POUSSE
POUTED
POUTER
PRUDES
PRUNED
PRUNER
PRUNES

P••U••
PADUAN
PAIUTE
PAPUAN
PARULA
PARURE
PENULT
PENURY
PEQUOD
PEQUOT
PERUKE
PERUSE
PETULA
PICULS
PINUPS
PIQUED
PIQUES
PIQUET
PLEURA
PLOUGH
PNEUMA
PODUNK
POPULI
POPUPS
PROUST
PSEUDO
PSEUDS

P•••U•
PABLUM
PACKUP
PAIDUP
PAIRUP
PALPUS
PANOUT
PAPPUS
PASSUP
PAYOUT
PAYSUP
PEANUT
PELEUS
PENTUP
PEPLUM
PEPSUP
PERDUE
PERKUP
PHYLUM
PICKUP
PIGNUT
PIGOUT
PILEUM
PILEUP
PILEUS
PINDUS
PIPEUP
PLAGUE
PLAQUE
PLAYUP
PLENUM
PLEXUS
PODIUM
POILUS
POLLUX
PONTUS
PONYUP
POPGUN
POPOUT
POPSUP
POROUS
POSEUR
POSSUM
POTFUL
PRAGUE
PRIMUM
PRIMUS
PROPUP
PULLUP
PULQUE
PUMPUP
PURDUE
PURSUE
PUSHUP
PUTOUT
PUTPUT
PUTSUP

P••••U
PAILOU
PENGHU
PICCHU

•PU•••
APULIA
OPUSES
SPUMED
SPUMES
SPUNKY
SPURGE
SPURNS
SPURON
SPURRY
SPURTS

•P•U••
OPPUGN
SPOUSE
SPOUTS
SPRUCE
SPRUES
SPRUNG
UPRUSH
UPTURN

•P••U•
EPIRUS
OPAQUE
OPENUP
OPTOUT
SPEDUP
SPROUT

•P•••U
APERCU

••PU••
AMPULE
AMPULS
COPULA
DEPUTE
DEPUTY
IMPUGN
IMPURE
IMPUTE
INPUTS
LAPUTA
MAPUTO
MOPUPS
NIPUPS
OPPUGN
PAPUAN
POPULI
POPUPS
REPUGN
REPUTE
TIPUPS

••P•U•
CAPFUL
CAPGUN
CAPNUT
COPOUT
CUPFUL
CYPRUS
DEPAUL
DEPAUW
GYPSUM
HOPSUP
INPOUR
KEPTUP
KIPPUR
LAPFUL
LAPSUP
MOPSUP
NIPPUR
PAPPUS
PEPLUM
PEPSUP
PIPEUP
POPGUN
POPOUT
POPSUP
RIPSUP
RUPAUL
SEPTUM
SOPSUP
STPAUL
TAPOUT
TOPGUN
TOPHUS
TOPOUT
TYPEUP
TYPHUS
UNPLUG
VAPOUR
WIPEUP
ZIPSUP

•••PU•
BUMPUP
CAMPUS
CARPUS
COOPUP
CORPUS
COYPUS
CROPUP
FLIPUP
JAIPUR
JUMPUP
KEEPUP
KIPPUR
LUMPUR
NIPPUR
OUTPUT
PALPUS
PAPPUS
PROPUP
PUMPUP
PUTPUT
QUIPUS
RAIPUR
RAJPUT
RUMPUS
SLAPUP
SLIPUP
SNAPUP
SOUPUP
STAPUF
STEPUP
STOPUP
TRIPUP
WAMPUM
WHIPUP
WRAPUP

P•V•••
PAVANE
PAVERS
PAVING
PAVLOV
PIVOTS

P••V••
PARVIS
PEAVEY
PEEVED
PEEVES
PELVIC
PELVIS
PLOVER
PRAVDA
PREVIN
PRIVET
PROVED
PROVEN
PROVER
PROVES
PURVEY

P•••V•
PAREVE

P••••V
PAVLOV

•P•V••
SPAVIN
SPIVAK

••P•V•
REPAVE

••P••V
IMPROV
LAPTEV

•••P•V
KARPOV

P•W•••
PAWERS
PAWING
PAWNED
PAWNEE
PAWNER
PAWPAW
PAWSAT
PEWEES
PEWITS
PEWTER
POWDER
POWELL
POWERS
POWWOW

P••W••
PEEWEE
PLOWED
PLOWER
POWWOW
PRAWNS
PREWAR
PROWLS
PROWSE

P•••W•
PAPAWS

P••••W
PAWPAW
PESCOW
PILLOW
PITSAW
POWWOW
PRELAW

•PW•••
UPWARD
UPWELL
UPWIND

•P•W••
SPAWNS
SPEWED

•P••W•
SPRAWL
UPBOWS
UPTOWN

•P•••W
CPSNOW

••P•W•
PAPAWS

••P••W
DEPAUW
NEPHEW
REPLOW
RIPSAW

•••P•W
PAWPAW

P•X•••
PIXELS
PIXIES
PYXIES

P••X••
PINXIT
PLEXOR
PLEXUS
PRAXES
PRAXIS

P••••X
PICKAX
POLEAX
POLLEX
POLLUX
PREFIX
PRETAX
PROLIX
PROTAX

•P•X••
APEXES

•P•••X
SPADIX
SPHINX

••P••X
DUPLEX

•••P•X
AUSPEX
COWPOX

PY••••
PYEDOG
PYJAMA
PYKNIC
PYLONS
PYRITE
PYTHIA
PYTHON
PYXIES

P•Y•••
PAYDAY
PAYEES
PAYERS
PAYFOR
PAYING
PAYOFF
PAYOLA
PAYOUT
PAYSIN
PAYSON
PAYSUP
PEYOTE
PEYTON
PHYLAE
PHYLLO
PHYLUM
PHYSED
PHYSIO
PLYING
PRYING
PRYNNE
PSYCHE
PSYCHO
PSYCHS
PSYLLA

P••Y••
PAPYRI
PINYIN
PINYON
PLAYAS
PLAYAT
PLAYED
PLAYER
PLAYON
PLAYUP
POLYPS
PONYUP
PRAYED
PRAYER
PREYED
PREYON

P•••Y•
PAPAYA
PHENYL
POBOYS
POKEYS
POLEYN
POPEYE

P••••Y
PACIFY
PALELY
PALTRY
PANFRY
PANTRY
PAPACY
PAPERY
PARITY
PARKAY
PARLAY
PARLEY
PARODY
PARTLY
PASSBY
PASTRY
PATCHY
PAULEY
PAYDAY
PEACHY
PEARLY
PEAVEY
PEBBLY
PELTRY
PENNEY
PENURY
PERTLY
PHILLY
PHOOEY
PIGSTY
PIMINY
PINERY
PIRACY
PLASHY
PLASTY
PLENTY
PLUCKY
PLUMMY
PLUSHY
POACHY
POETRY
POINTY
POKERY
POKILY
POLICY
POLITY
POMPEY
POORLY
POPFLY
PORTLY
POSHLY
POUCHY
PREPAY
PREPPY
PRETTY
PRICEY
PRIMLY
PRIORY
PRISSY
PUDDLY
PULLEY
PUNCHY
PUNILY
PURELY
PURIFY
PURITY
PURVEY
PUTSBY

•PY•••
SPYING

•P•Y••
SPAYED
SPRYER
SPRYLY

•P••Y•
EPONYM
SPLAYS
SPRAYS

•P•••Y
APATHY
APIARY
OPENLY
SPACEY
SPANKY
SPARKY
SPEEDY
SPERRY
SPIFFY
SPONGY
SPOOKY
SPOONY
SPORTY
SPOTTY
SPRYLY
SPUNKY
SPURRY
UPPITY

••PY••
PAPYRI

••P•Y•
PAPAYA
POPEYE
REPAYS
SEPOYS
ZEPHYR

••P••Y
BYPLAY
DEPLOY

DEPUTY
DIPODY
DUPERY
EMPERY
EMPLOY
EXPIRY
INPLAY
JAPERY
NAPERY
OSPREY
PAPACY
PAPERY
POPFLY
RAPTLY
REPLAY
RIPELY
RIPLEY
RIPPLY
SUPPLY
TYPIFY
UPPITY

•••P•Y
CHOPPY
COMPLY
DAMPLY
DEEPLY
DIMPLY
DRIPPY
DROPBY
FLOPPY
FLOPSY
GLOPPY
LIMPLY
MURPHY
NETPAY
POMPEY
PREPAY
PREPPY
QUIPPY
RIPPLY
RUMPLY
SIMPLY
SKIPPY
SLAPPY
SLOPPY
SNAPPY
SNIPPY
SUPPLY
TEAPOY
TRAPPY
TRIPLY
TROPHY
TWOPLY
WHIPPY

••••PY
CANOPY
CHIRPY
CHOPPY
CLUMPY
CREEPY
CRISPY
CROUPY
DRIPPY
DROOPY
FLOPPY
FRUMPY
GLOPPY
GRUMPY
JALOPY
OCCUPY
PREPPY
QUIPPY
RECOPY
SKIMPY
SKIPPY
SLAPPY
SLEEPY
SLOPPY
SNAPPY
SNIPPY
SNOOPY
STIMPY
STUMPY
SWAMPY
SYRUPY
TRAPPY
WHIPPY
WICOPY

P•Z•••
PIZAZZ
PIZZAS
PUZZLE

P••Z••
PANZER
PIAZZA
PINZON
PIZZAS
PLAZAS
PRIZED
PRIZES
PUZZLE

P•••Z•
PIAZZA
PIZAZZ

P••••Z
PIZAZZ

•P•••Z
SPRITZ

•••P•Z
TROPEZ

QA••••
QANTAS
QATARI

Q•A•••
QUACKS
QUADRI
QUAFFS
QUAGGA
QUAGGY
QUAHOG
QUAILS
QUAINT
QUAKED
QUAKER
QUAKES
QUALMS
QUANTA
QUARKS
QUARRY
QUARTO
QUARTS
QUARTZ
QUASAR
QUAVER
QUAYLE

Q••A••
QATARI
QUEASY

Q•••A•
QANTAS
QINTAR
QUASAR
QUMRAN
QUOTAS

Q••••A
QUAGGA
QUANTA
QUINOA
QUOKKA
QUOTHA

•Q•A••
AQUATE
EQUALS
EQUATE
SQUABS
SQUADS
SQUALL
SQUARE
SQUASH
SQUATS
SQUAWK

•Q••A•
SQUEAK
SQUEAL

•Q•••A
AQUILA

••Q•A•
EMQUAD
ENQUAD
LOQUAT

••Q••A
BUQSHA

Q••B••
QUEBEC

•Q••B•
SQUABS
SQUIBB
SQUIBS

•Q•••B
SQUIBB

Q••C••
QUACKS
QUICHE

Q•••C•
QUENCH
QUINCE
QUINCY

Q••••C
QUEBEC

Q••D••
QUADRI

Q••••D
QUAKED
QUEUED
QUOTED

•Q••D•
SQUADS
SQUIDS

••Q••D
EMQUAD
ENQUAD
LIQUID
PEQUOD
PIQUED

Q•E•••
QUEASY
QUEBEC
QUEENS
QUELLS
QUEMOY
QUENCH
QUERNS
QUESTS
QUEUED
QUEUER
QUEUES
QWERTY

Q••E••
QUEENS
QUIETS

Q•••E•
QUAKED
QUAKER
QUAKES
QUAVER
QUEBEC
QUEUED
QUEUER
QUEUES
QUIRES
QUIVER
QUOTED
QUOTER
QUOTES

Q••••E
QUAYLE
QUICHE
QUINCE

•Q•E••
IQTEST
SQUEAK
SQUEAL

•Q•••E
AQUATE
EQUATE
EQUINE
SQUARE
SQUIRE

••Q•E•
COQUET
PIQUED
PIQUES
PIQUET
RAQUEL
SEQUEL
TOQUES
TUQUES

•••Q•E
BARQUE
BASQUE
BISQUE
BRAQUE
CAIQUE
CALQUE
CASQUE
CHEQUE
CINQUE
CIRQUE
CLAQUE
CLIQUE
CLOQUE
MANQUE
MARQUE
MASQUE
MOSQUE
OPAQUE
PLAQUE
PULQUE
RISQUE
SACQUE
TORQUE
UNIQUE

Q••F••
QUAFFS

Q•••F•
QUAFFS

Q••G••
QUAGGA
QUAGGY

Q•••G•
QUAGGA
QUAGGY

Q••••G
QUAHOG

Q••H••
QUAHOG

Q•••H•
QUICHE
QUOTHA

Q••••H
QUENCH
QURUSH

•Q•••H
SQUASH
SQUISH

••Q•H•
BUQSHA

QI••••
QINTAR
QIVIUT

Q•I•••
QUICHE
QUIETS
QUILLS
QUILTS
QUINCE
QUINCY
QUINOA
QUINTS
QUIPPY
QUIPUS
QUIRES
QUIRKS
QUIRKY
QUIRTS
QUITIT
QUIVER

Q••I••
QIVIUT
QUAILS
QUAINT
QUOINS
QUOITS

Q•••I•
QUITIT

Q••••I
QATARI
QUADRI

•Q•I••
AQUILA
AQUINO
EQUINE
EQUIPS
EQUITY
SQUIBB
SQUIBS
SQUIDS
SQUILL
SQUINT
SQUIRE
SQUIRM
SQUIRT
SQUISH

••Q•I•
ACQUIT
LIQUID
MAQUIS
NYQUIL
SEQUIN
YAQUIS

•••QI•
IRAQIS

•••Q•I
SESQUI
YANQUI

Q••K••
QUAKED
QUAKER
QUAKES
QUOKKA

Q•••K•
QUACKS
QUARKS
QUIRKS
QUIRKY
QUOKKA

•Q•••K
SQUAWK
SQUEAK

Q••L••
QUALMS
QUELLS
QUILLS
QUILTS

Q•••L•
QUAILS
QUAYLE
QUELLS
QUILLS

•Q••L•
AQUILA
EQUALS
SQUALL
SQUILL

•Q•••L
SQUALL
SQUEAL
SQUILL

••Q••L
NYQUIL
RAQUEL
SEQUEL

Q•M•••
QUMRAN

Q••M••
QUEMOY

Q•••M•
QUALMS

Q••••M
QUORUM

•Q•••M
SQUIRM

Q•N•••
QANTAS
QINTAR

Q••N••
QUANTA
QUENCH
QUINCE
QUINCY
QUINOA
QUINTS

Q•••N•
QUAINT
QUEENS
QUERNS
QUOINS

Q••••N
QUMRAN

•Q••N•
AQUINO
EQUINE
SQUINT

••Q••N
SEQUIN

Q•O•••
QUOINS
QUOITS
QUOKKA
QUORUM
QUOTAS
QUOTED
QUOTER
QUOTES
QUOTHA

Q•••O•
QUAHOG
QUEMOY
QUINOA

Q••••O
QUARTO

•Q•••O
AQUINO

••Q•O•
LIQUOR
PEQUOD
PEQUOT

•••Q•O
BANQUO

Q••P••
QUIPPY
QUIPUS

Q•••P•
QUIPPY

•Q••P•
EQUIPS

••••QQ
ETSEQQ

Q•R•••
QURUSH

Q••R••
QUARKS
QUARRY
QUARTO
QUARTS
QUARTZ
QUERNS
QUIRES
QUIRKS
QUIRKY
QUIRTS
QUMRAN
QUORUM
QWERTY

Q•••R•
QATARI
QUADRI
QUARRY

Q••••R
QINTAR
QUAKER
QUASAR
QUAVER
QUEUER
QUIVER
QUOTER

•Q••R•
SQUARE
SQUIRE
SQUIRM
SQUIRT

••Q••R
LIQUOR

Q••S••
QUASAR
QUESTS

Q•••S•
QUEASY
QURUSH

Q••••S
QANTAS
QUACKS
QUAFFS
QUAILS
QUAKES
QUALMS
QUARKS
QUARTS
QUEENS
QUELLS
QUERNS
QUESTS
QUEUES
QUIETS
QUILLS
QUILTS
QUINTS
QUIPUS
QUIRES
QUIRKS
QUIRTS
QUOINS
QUOITS
QUOTAS
QUOTES

•Q•S••
IQTEST
SQUASH
SQUISH

•Q•••S
EQUALS
EQUIPS
SQUABS
SQUADS
SQUATS
SQUIBS
SQUIDS

••QS••
BUQSHA

••Q••S
MAQUIS
PIQUES
TOQUES
TUQUES
YAQUIS

•••Q•S
IRAQIS

Q•T•••
QATARI

Q••T••
QANTAS
QINTAR
QUITIT
QUOTAS
QUOTED
QUOTER
QUOTES
QUOTHA

Q•••T•
QUANTA
QUARTO
QUARTS
QUARTZ
QUESTS
QUIETS
QUILTS
QUINTS
QUIRTS
QUOITS
QWERTY

Q••••T
QIVIUT
QUAINT
QUITIT

•QT•••
IQTEST

•Q••T•
AQUATE
EQUATE
EQUITY
SQUATS

•Q•••T
IQTEST
SQUINT
SQUIRT

••Q••T
ACQUIT
COQUET
LOQUAT
PEQUOT
PIQUET

QU••••
QUACKS
QUADRI
QUAFFS
QUAGGA
QUAGGY
QUAHOG
QUAILS
QUAINT
QUAKED
QUAKER
QUAKES
QUALMS
QUANTA
QUARKS
QUARRY
QUARTO
QUARTS
QUARTZ
QUASAR
QUAVER
QUAYLE
QUEASY
QUEBEC
QUEENS
QUELLS
QUEMOY
QUENCH
QUERNS
QUESTS
QUEUED
QUEUER
QUEUES
QUICHE
QUIETS
QUILLS
QUILTS
QUINCE
QUINCY
QUINOA
QUINTS
QUIPPY
QUIPUS
QUIRES
QUIRKS
QUIRKY
QUIRTS
QUITIT
QUIVER
QUMRAN
QUOINS
QUOITS
QUOKKA
QUORUM
QUOTAS
QUOTED
QUOTER
QUOTES
QUOTHA
QURUSH

Q••U••
QUEUED
QUEUER
QUEUES
QURUSH

Q•••U•
QIVIUT
QUIPUS
QUORUM

•QU•••
AQUATE
AQUILA
AQUINO
EQUALS
EQUATE
EQUINE
EQUIPS
EQUITY
SQUABS
SQUADS
SQUALL
SQUARE
SQUASH
SQUATS
SQUAWK
SQUEAK
SQUEAL
SQUIBB
SQUIBS
SQUIDS
SQUILL
SQUINT
SQUIRE
SQUIRM
SQUIRT
SQUISH

••QU••
ACQUIT
COQUET
EMQUAD
ENQUAD
LIQUID
LIQUOR
LOQUAT
MAQUIS
NYQUIL
PEQUOD
PEQUOT
PIQUED
PIQUES
PIQUET
RAQUEL
SEQUEL
SEQUIN
TOQUES
TUQUES
YAQUIS

•••QU•
BANQUO
BARQUE
BASQUE
BISQUE
BRAQUE
CAIQUE
CALQUE
CASQUE
CHEQUE
CINQUE
CIRQUE
CLAQUE
CLIQUE
CLOQUE
MANQUE
MARQUE
MASQUE
MOSQUE
OPAQUE
PLAQUE
PULQUE
RISQUE
SACQUE
SESQUI
TORQUE
UNIQUE
YANQUI

Q•V•••
QIVIUT

Q••V••
QUAVER
QUIVER

QW••••
QWERTY

•Q••W•
SQUAWK

Q••Y••
QUAYLE

Q••••Y
QUAGGY
QUARRY
QUEASY
QUEMOY
QUINCY
QUIPPY
QUIRKY
QWERTY

•Q•••Y
EQUITY

Q••••Z
QUARTZ

RA••••
RABATO
RABBET
RABBIS
RABBIT
RABBLE
RABIES
RACEME
RACERS
RACHEL
RACHIS
RACIAL
RACIER
RACILY
RACINE
RACING
RACKED
RACKET
RACKUP
RACONS
RADDLE
RADIAL
RADIAN
RADIOS
RADISH
RADIUM
RADIUS
RADNER
RADOME
RADULA
RAFAEL
RAFFIA
RAFFLE
RAFTED
RAFTER
RAGBAG
RAGGED
RAGING
RAGLAN
RAGMAN
RAGMEN
RAGMOP
RAGOUT
RAGRUG
RAGTAG
RAGTOP
RAHRAH
RAIDED
RAIDER
RAILAT
RAILED
RAILER
RAINED
RAINER
RAINES
RAIPUR
RAISED
RAISER
RAISES
RAISIN
RAJAHS
RAJPUT
RAKEIN
RAKERS
RAKEUP
RAKING
RAKISH
RAMADA
RAMATE
RAMBLA
RAMBLE
RAMEAU
RAMIES
RAMIFY
RAMJET
RAMMED
RAMONA
RAMONE
RAMOSE
RAMOUS
RAMPED
RAMROD
RAMSAY
RAMSES
RAMSEY
RAMSON
RANCHO
RANCID
RANCOR
RANDOM
RANDRY
RANEES
RANFOR
RANGED
RANGER
RANGES
RANGUP
RANIDS
RANKED
RANKER
RANKIN
RANKLE
RANKLY
RANOFF
RANOUT
RANSOM
RANTED
RANTER
RAPIDS
RAPIER
RAPINE
RAPINI
RAPPED
RAPPEE
RAPPEL
RAPPER
RAPTLY
RAPTOR
RAQUEL
RAREFY
RARELY
RAREST
RARIFY
RARING
RARITY
RASCAL
RASHAD
RASHER
RASHES
RASHID
RASHLY
RASPED
RASPER
RASSLE
RASTER
RATEDG
RATEDR
RATEDX
RATELS
RATERS
RATHER
RATIFY
RATINE
RATING
RATION
RATIOS
RATITE
RATLIN
RATSON
RATTAN
RATTED
RATTER
RATTLE
RATTLY
RAVAGE
RAVELS
RAVENS
RAVERS
RAVINE
RAVING
RAVISH
RAWEGG
RAWEST
RAYGUN
RAYONS
RAZING
RAZORS
RAZZED
RAZZES
RAZZLE

R•A•••
REACTS
READER
READIN
REAGAN
REAIRS
REALER
REALES
REALIA
REALLY
REALMS
REALTY
REAMED
REAMER
REAPED
REAPER
REARED
REARER
REARMS
REARUP
REASON
REATAS
RIALTO
RIATAS
ROADIE
ROAMED
ROAMER
ROARED
ROARER
ROASTS
RRATED
RUANAS
RUANDA
RVALUE
RWANDA
RYAZAN

R••A••
RABATO
RAFAEL
RAJAHS
RAMADA
RAMATE
RAVAGE
REBAGS
REBARS
REBATE
RECALL

RECANE
RECANT
RECAPS
RECAST
REDACT
REDANT
REDATE
REFACE
REGAIN
REGALE
REGARD
REHANG
REHASH
RELACE
RELAID
RELATE
RELAYS
REMADE
REMAIL
REMAIN
REMAKE
REMAND
REMANS
REMAPS
REMARK
RENAIL
RENAME
RENATA
REPAID
REPAIR
REPAND
REPAST
REPAVE
REPAYS
RERATE
RESALE
RESALT
RESAND
RETAGS
RETAIL
RETAIN
RETAKE
RETAPE
RETAPS
RETARD
RETARS
REVAMP
REWARD
REWARM
REWASH
RIBALD
RIBAND
RITARD
RIVALS
RIYADH
RIYALS
ROBALO
ROLAND
ROMAIC
ROMAJI
ROMANO
ROMANS
ROMANY
RONALD
ROSARY
ROTARY
ROTATE
ROXANA
ROXANE
ROYALE
ROYALS
RUGATE
RUPAUL

R•••A•

RACIAL
RADIAL
RADIAN
RAGBAG
RAGLAN
RAGMAN
RAGTAG
RAHRAH
RAILAT
RAMEAU
RAMSAY
RASCAL
RASHAD
RATTAN
REAGAN
REATAS
REDBAY
REDCAP
REDEAL
REDHAT
REDIAL
REDOAK
REDRAW
REDTAG
REGGAE
REGNAL
REHEAL
REHEAR
REHEAT
RELOAD
RENTAL
REPEAL
REPEAT
REPLAN
REPLAY
REREAD
RESEAL
RESEAT
RESEAU
RETIAL
RETRAL
REVEAL
REWRAP
REXCAT
RHINAL
RIATAS
RIOJAS
RIPRAP
RIPSAW
RITUAL
RODHAM
ROSEAU
RUANAS
RUDMAN
RUMBAS
RUNWAY
RUPIAH
RUTTAN
RYAZAN
RYOKAN

R••••A

RADULA
RAFFIA
RAMADA
RAMBLA
RAMONA
REALIA
REDSEA
REGINA
REMORA
REMUDA
RENATA
RESEDA
RETINA
RHONDA
RHUMBA
RIVERA
ROMOLA
ROSITA
ROSTRA
ROWENA
ROXANA
RUANDA
RUMINA
RUSSIA
RWANDA

•RA•••

ARABIA
ARABIC
ARABLE
ARAFAT
ARAGON
ARALIA
ARALLU
ARAMIS
ARARAT
ARAWAK
BRACED
BRACER
BRACES
BRACTS
BRAHMA
BRAHMS
BRAIDS
BRAILS
BRAINS
BRAINY
BRAISE
BRAKED
BRAKES
BRANCH
BRANDO
BRANDS
BRANDT
BRANDX
BRANDY
BRANTS
BRAQUE
BRASHY
BRASOV
BRASSY
BRATTY
BRAVAS
BRAVED
BRAVER
BRAVES
BRAVOS
BRAWLS
BRAWNY
BRAYED
BRAYER
BRAZED
BRAZEN
BRAZER
BRAZES
BRAZIL
BRAZOS
BRAZZA
BRAZZI
CRABBE
CRABBY
CRACKS
CRADLE
CRAFTS
CRAFTY
CRAGGY
CRAKES
CRAMBO
CRAMPS
CRANED
CRANES
CRANIA
CRANIO
CRANKS
CRANKY
CRANNY
CRAPES
CRATED
CRATER
CRATES
CRAVAT
CRAVED
CRAVEN
CRAVER
CRAVES
CRAWLS
CRAWLY
CRAYON
CRAZED
CRAZES
DRABEK
DRABLY
DRAFTS
DRAFTY
DRAGEE
DRAGGY
DRAGIN
DRAGON
DRAILS
DRAINS
DRAKES
DRAMAS
DRAPED
DRAPER
DRAPES
DRAWER
DRAWIN
DRAWLS
DRAWON
DRAWUP
DRAYED
ERASED
ERASER
ERASES
FRACAS
FRAISE
FRAMED
FRAMES
FRANCA
FRANCE
FRANCK
FRANCO
FRANCS
FRANKS
FRANNY
FRAPPE
FRASER
FRAUDS
FRAYED
FRAZER
GRABAT
GRABBY
GRABEN
GRABLE
GRACED
GRACES
GRACIE
GRADEA
GRADED
GRADER
GRADES
GRADIN
GRADUS
GRAECO
GRAFTS
GRAHAM
GRAILS
GRAINS
GRAINY
GRAMAS
GRAMME
GRAMMY
GRAMPS
GRANDE
GRANDS
GRANGE
GRANNY
GRANTS
GRAPES
GRAPHS
GRAPPA
GRASPS
GRASSO
GRASSY
GRATED
GRATER
GRATES
GRATIA
GRATIN
GRATIS
GRAVED
GRAVEL
GRAVEN
GRAVER
GRAVES
GRAVID
GRAYED
GRAYER
GRAZED
GRAZER
GRAZES
IRANIS
IRAQIS
IRATER
KRAALS
KRAITS
KRAKEN
KRAKOW
KRAMER
KRANTZ
KRATER
ORACLE
ORALES
ORALLY
ORANGE
ORANGS
ORANTS
ORATED
ORATES
ORATOR
PRAGUE
PRAISE
PRAJNA
PRANCE
PRANKS
PRATED
PRATER
PRATES
PRAVDA
PRAWNS
PRAXES
PRAXIS
PRAYED
PRAYER
RRATED
TRACED
TRACER
TRACES
TRACEY
TRACKS
TRACTS
TRADED
TRADER
TRADES
TRAGIC
TRAILS
TRAINS
TRAITS
TRAJAN
TRALEE
TRAMPS
TRANCE
TRAPPY
TRASHY
TRAUMA
TRAVEL
TRAVIS
TRAWLS
URACIL
URAEUS
URALIC
URALSK
URANIA
URANIC
URANUS
WRACKS
WRAITH
WRAPUP
WRASSE
WRATHS
XRATED
XRAYED

•R•A••

ARCADE
ARCANA
ARCANE
ARCARO
ARGALI
ARMADA
ARMAGH
ARMAND
ARMANI
ARRACK
ARRANT
ARRAYS
ARVADA
ARYANS
BREACH
BREADS
BREAKS
BREAMS
BREAST
BREATH
BRIAND
BRIANS
BRIARD
BRIARS
BROACH
BROADS
BRYANT
CREAKS
CREAKY
CREAMS
CREAMY
CREASE
CREASY
CREATE
CROAKS
CROAKY
CROATS
DREADS
DREAMS
DREAMT
DREAMY
DREARY
DRYADS
ERGATE
ERHARD
ERNANI
ERRAND
ERRANT
ERRATA
ERSATZ
FREAKS
FREAKY
FRIARS
FRIARY
GREASE
GREASY
GREATS
GREAVE
GROANS
GROATS
KRAALS
ORBACH
ORDAIN
OREADS
ORGANA
ORGANS
ORGATE
ORIANA
ORNATE
PREACH
PREAMP
PROAMS
TREADS
TREATS
TREATY
TRIADS
TRIAGE
TRIALS
TRUANT
URBANA
URBANE
URIALS
WREAKS
WREATH

•R••A•

ARAFAT
ARARAT
ARAWAK
ARECAS
ARENAS
AROMAS
ARUBAN
BRAVAS
BRIDAL
BROGAN
BROKAW
BRUMAL
BRUTAL
CRAVAT
CRETAN
CRURAL
DRAMAS
FRACAS
FRIDAY
FRUGAL
FRYPAN
GRABAT
GRAHAM
GRAMAS
IRREAL
ORDEAL
ORGEAT
ORPHAN
PREFAB
PRELAW
PREPAY
PRETAX
PREWAR
PRIMAL
PROTAX
TRAJAN
TREPAN
TRIBAL
TRINAL
TROCAR
TROJAN
TRUMAN

•R•••A

ARABIA
ARALIA
ARBELA
ARCANA
AREOLA
ARETHA
ARISTA
ARJUNA
ARMADA
ARNICA
ARRIBA
ARROBA
ARVADA
BRAHMA
BRAZZA
BRENDA
CRANIA
CRENNA
CREUSA
CRIMEA
EROICA
ERRATA
FRANCA
FRESCA
GRADEA
GRAPPA
GRATIA
GRETNA
OREIDA
ORGANA
ORIANA
ORISSA
ORTEGA
PRAJNA
PRAVDA
TRAUMA
TREDIA
TRICIA
TRISHA
TRIVIA
TROIKA
URANIA
URBANA
URSULA

••RA••

ABRADE
ABRAMS
AERATE
AFRAID
AFRAME
AIRARM
ARRACK
ARRANT
ARRAYS
BERATE
BORAGE
BORATE
BORAXO
CARAFE
CARATS
CERATE
CORALS
CURACY
CURARE
CURATE
CYRANO
DERAIL
DORADO
DORATI
DURANT
ENRAGE
ENRAPT
ERRAND
ERRANT
ERRATA
FARADS
FORAGE
FORAYS
GARAGE
GERALD
GERARD
GIRARD
GORALS
GYRATE
HARARE
HARASS
HERALD
HORACE
ISRAEL
JURADO
JURATS
KARATE
KARATS
KERALA
KORATS
KURALT
LARAMS
MARACA
MARAUD
MIRAGE
MORALE
MORALS
MORANT
MORASS
MORAVA
MORAYS
MURALS
MURANO
PARADE
PARANA
PARANG
PARAPH
PHRASE
PIRACY
PIRANA
PIRATE
PTRAPS
PURACE
RERATE
SARANS
SCRAGS
SCRAMS
SCRAPE
SCRAPS
SCRAWL
SERACS
SERAIS
SERAPE
SERAPH
SHRANK
SPRAGS
SPRAIN
SPRANG
SPRATS
SPRAWL
SPRAYS
STRABO
STRADS
STRAFE
STRAIN
STRAIT
STRAKE
STRAND
STRAPS
STRASS
STRATA
STRATI
STRATO
STRAUS
STRAWS
STRAYS
SURAHS
TARAWA
TERAPH
TERATO
THRACE
THRALE
THRALL
THRASH
TIRADE
TIRANA
TIRANE
TORAHS
TYRANT
VIRAGO

••R•A•

ABROAD
ADRIAN
AERIAL
AIRBAG
AIRDAM
AIRMAN
AIRSAC
AIRWAY
AORTAE
AORTAL
AORTAS
ATRIAL
BARMAN
BARTAB
BOREAL
BOREAS
BORMAN
BUREAU
BURGAS
BURLAP
BURMAN
BUROAK
BURSAE
BURSAL
BURSAR
BURSAS
BYROAD
CARMAN
CARNAL
CARPAL
CEREAL
CORBAN
CORDAY
CORRAL
CURIAE
CURIAL
DARNAY
DERMAL
DIRHAM
DORCAS
DORIAN
DORSAL
DURBAN
DURBAR
DURHAM
DURIAN
EARLAP
EARWAX
FARRAH
FARRAR
FERMAT
FIRMAN
FORBAD
FORMAL
FORMAN
FORMAT
FORTAS
GERMAN
HARLAN
HERBAL
HEREAT
HERMAN
HURRAH
HURRAY
INROAD
IRREAL
JARRAH
JORDAN
KARNAK
KARRAS
KERMAN
KIRMAN
KOREAN
KORMAN
KURGAN
LARIAT
LARVAE
LARVAL
LARVAS
LOREAL
MARGAY
MARIAH
MARIAN
MERMAN
MIRIAM
MOREAU
MORGAN
MORNAY
MORTAL
MORTAR
MURRAY
MYRDAL
MYRIAD
NARIAL
NARWAL
NORGAY
NORIAS
NORMAL
NORMAN
NORWAY
OBRIAN
OCREAE
PARCAE
PARIAH
PARKAS
PARKAY
PARLAY
PORTAL
PURDAH
REREAD
SCREAK
SCREAM
SERIAL
SERVAL
SIRDAR
SIRRAH
SPREAD
STREAK
STREAM
STRIAE
SURTAX
SYRIAN
TARMAC
TARPAN
TARSAL
TARTAN
TARTAR
TARZAN
TERRAN
THREAD
THREAT
THROAT
TOREAT
TURBAN
TYRIAN
UGRIAN
UNREAD
UNREAL
UPROAR
VARNAS
VERBAL
VERNAL
WARSAW

••R••A

AFRICA
ARRIBA
ARROBA
AURIGA
AURORA
BARBRA
BAROJA
BERTHA
BORGIA
CARINA
CHROMA
CORNEA
CORONA
CORYZA
DURYEA
EARTHA
ERRATA
EUREKA
EUROPA
FARINA
GARCIA
GURKHA
JERBOA
KARIBA
KERALA
KORUNA
LAROSA
LERIDA
LORICA
MARACA
MARCIA
MARINA
MARISA
MARKKA
MARSHA
MARTHA
MERIDA
MORAVA
MORITA
MURCIA
NARNIA
NERUDA
PARANA
PARULA
PERCHA
PERSIA
PIRANA
PORTIA
PURINA
SERBIA
SERENA
SEROSA
SIRICA
STRATA
TARAWA
TERESA
TIRANA
VARUNA
VERONA
YORUBA
ZAREBA

•••RA•

ABORAL
AFFRAY
AGORAE
AGORAS
AMORAL
AMTRAC
AMTRAK
ANORAK
ANURAN
ARARAT
ASHRAM
ASTRAL
ASTRAY
BETRAY
BUMRAP
CHORAL
COBRAS
CONRAD
CORRAL
CRURAL
DEBRAS
DEFRAY
DELRAY
DIGRAM
DOBRAS
DVORAK
ENGRAM
ENTRAP
ENWRAP
ESDRAS
EXTRAS
FABRAY
FARRAH
FARRAR
FLORAE
FLORAL
FLORAS
GIBRAN
HOORAH
HOORAY
HURRAH
HURRAY
HYDRAE
HYDRAS
JARRAH
JEERAT
KARRAS
KONRAD
LEERAT
MACRAE
MADRAS
MANRAY
MCGRAW
MIHRAB
MITRAL
MUDRAS
MURRAY
NAIRAS
NEURAL
OPERAS
OUTRAN
PEERAT
PLURAL
QUMRAN
RAHRAH
REDRAW
RETRAL
REWRAP
RIPRAP
SABRAS
SACRAL
SATRAP
SCARAB
SEURAT
SHIRAZ
SHORAN
SIRRAH
SPIRAL
SUNRAY
SUTRAS
SWARAJ
TAYRAS
TEARAT
TERRAN
TETRAD
TETRAS
THORAX
TIARAS
ULTRAS
UMBRAE
UMBRAL
UMBRAS
UNDRAW
UNTRAP
UNWRAP
ZEBRAS

•••R•A

ANDREA
DHARMA
DJERBA
EGERIA
GLORIA
IBERIA
ICARIA
ISTRIA
LABREA
MAURYA
NUTRIA
OMERTA
PEORIA
SCORIA
SFORZA
SHARIA
SHERPA
SIERRA
SMYRNA
SPARTA
SPIREA
STERNA
STYRIA
TIERRA
UMBRIA

••••RA

AMENRA
AMHARA
ANGORA
ANITRA
ANKARA
ASMARA
ASPERA
AURORA
AYMARA
BARBRA
BIAFRA
CAMERA
CONTRA
DATURA
DUNERA
ELMIRA
ELVIRA
ENDORA
EUDORA
EXEDRA
FEDORA
FEMORA
FULCRA
GEMARA
GENERA
GEZIRA
HEGIRA
INDIRA
KAGERA
MADURA
MANTRA
MEGARA
MONERA
PICARA
PLEURA
REMORA
RIVERA
ROSTRA
SAHARA
SAMARA
SANDRA
SCLERA
SEGURA
SENORA
SIERRA
SISERA
SONORA
TAMARA
TANTRA
TEPHRA
TIERRA
TUNDRA
ZADORA

R•B•••

RABATO
RABBET
RABBIS
RABBIT
RABBLE
RABIES
REBAGS
REBARS
REBATE
REBELS
REBIDS
REBIND
REBOIL

REBOLT
REBOOT
REBORN
REBOZO
REBUFF
REBUKE
REBUTS
RIBALD
RIBAND
RIBBED
RIBBON
RIBEYE
RIBOSE
ROBALO
ROBBED
ROBBER
ROBBIE
ROBERT
ROBING
ROBINS
ROBLES
ROBOTS
ROBROY
ROBSON
ROBUST
RUBBED
RUBBER
RUBBLE
RUBBLY
RUBENS
RUBIED
RUBIES
RUBIFY
RUBLES
RUBOUT
RUBRIC
RUBSIN

R••B••
RABBET
RABBIS
RABBIT
RABBLE
RAGBAG
RAMBLA
RAMBLE
REDBAY
REDBUD
REEBOK
REUBEN
RHEBOK
RIBBED
RIBBON
ROBBED
ROBBER
ROBBIE
RUBBED
RUBBER
RUBBLE
RUBBLY
RUMBAS
RUMBLE
RUMBLY

R•••B•
REDUBS
RHOMBI
RHOMBS
RHUMBA
RHUMBS

R••••B
RESORB
REVERB

•RB•••
ARBELA
ARBORS
ARBOUR
ERBIUM
MRBLUE
ORBACH
ORBING
ORBITS
URBANA
URBANE

•R•B••
ARABIA
ARABIC
ARABLE
ARUBAN
BRIBED
BRIBES
CRABBE
CRABBY
DRABEK
DRABLY
EREBUS
GRABAT
GRABBY
GRABEN
GRABLE
GREBES
GRUBBY
ORIBIS
PROBED
PROBER
PROBES
TREBEK
TREBLE
TREBLY
TRIBAL
TRIBES

•R••B•
ARDEBS
ARRIBA
ARROBA
CRABBE
CRABBY
CRAMBO
CROSBY
CRUMBS
CRUMBY
DROPBY
GRABBY
GRUBBY
TRILBY

•R•••B
PREFAB

••RB••
AIRBAG
AIRBUS
BARBED
BARBEL
BARBER
BARBET
BARBIE
BARBRA
BERBER
BURBLE
BURBLY
BURBOT
CARBON
CARBOY
CORBAN
CORBEL
CORBIN
CURBED
DURBAN
DURBAR
DURBIN
FERBER
FORBAD
FORBES
FORBID
GARBED
GARBLE
GERBER
GERBIL
HARBIN
HARBOR
HERBAL
HERBIE
JERBOA
KORBUT
MARBLE
MARBLY
MORBID
SERBIA
SORBET
SORBIC
TURBAN
TURBID
TURBIT
TURBOS
TURBOT
VERBAL
WARBLE

••R•B•
AEROBE
ARRIBA
ARROBA
CARIBE
CARIBS
CAROBS
ENROBE
HEREBY
KARIBA
SCRIBE
SCRUBS
SHRUBS
STRABO
STROBE
THROBS
UNROBE
YORUBA
ZAREBA

••R••B
BARTAB

•••RB•
BLURBS
DJERBA
EXURBS
ITURBI
NEARBY

•••R•B
CHERUB
MIDRIB
MIHRAB
SCARAB
ZAGREB

••••RB
ABSORB
ADSORB
ADVERB
BICARB
RESORB
REVERB
SUBURB
SUPERB

R•C•••
RACEME
RACERS
RACHEL
RACHIS
RACIAL
RACIER
RACILY
RACINE
RACING
RACKED
RACKET
RACKUP
RACONS
RECALL
RECANE
RECANT
RECAPS
RECAST
RECEDE
RECENT
RECESS
RECIFE
RECIPE
RECITE
RECKON
RECODE
RECOIL
RECONS
RECOPY
RECORD
RECORK
RECOUP
RECTOR
RECTOS
RECTUS
RECURS
RECUSE
RICERS
RICHEN
RICHER
RICHES
RICHIE
RICHLY
RICING
RICKED
RICKEY
ROCHET
ROCKED
ROCKER
ROCKET
ROCKNE
ROCKYV
ROCOCO
RUCHES
RUCKED
RUCKUS

R••C••
RANCHO
RANCID
RANCOR
RASCAL
REACTS
REDCAP
REECHO
RESCUE
REXCAT
ROSCOE
RUNCIE

R•••C•
REDACT
REDUCE
REFACE
REJECT
RELACE
RELICS
RELICT
RELOCK
RELUCT
REMICK
RESECT
ROCOCO

R••••C
ROMAIC
RUBRIC
RUNDMC
RUSTIC

•RC•••
ARCADE
ARCANA
ARCANE
ARCARO
ARCHED
ARCHER
ARCHES
ARCHIE
ARCHLY
ARCHON
ARCING
ARCTIC
MRCOOL
ORCHID
ORCHIL
URCHIN

•R•C••
ARECAS
BRACED
BRACER
BRACES
BRACTS
BRECHT
BRICKS
BRICKY
CRACKS
CRECHE
CRICKS
CROCKS
CROCUS
CRUCES
ERECTS
ERUCTS
FRACAS
FROCKS
GRACED
GRACES
GRACIE
GROCER
ORACLE
PRECIS
PRICED
PRICER
PRICES
PRICEY
PRICKS
PROCNE
TRACED
TRACER
TRACES
TRACEY
TRACKS
TRACTS
TRICED
TRICES
TRICHO
TRICIA
TRICKS
TRICKY
TRICOT
TROCAR
TROCHE
TRUCES
TRUCKS
URACIL
WRACKS
WRECKS

•R••C•
ARNICA
ARRACK
BRANCH
BREACH
BREECH
BROACH
BRONCO
BRONCS
BROOCH
BRUNCH
CRISCO
CROUCH
CRUNCH
CRUTCH
DRENCH
DRYICE
EROICA
FRANCA
FRANCE
FRANCK
FRANCO
FRANCS
FRENCH
FRESCA
FRESCO
FRISCO
GRAECO
GREECE
GRINCH
GROUCH
ORBACH
OROZCO
PRANCE
PREACH
PRINCE
TRANCE
TRENCH
WRENCH
WRETCH

•R•••C
ARABIC
ARCTIC
CRITIC
EROTIC
FROLIC
IRENIC
IRIDIC
IRONIC
ORPHIC
TRAGIC
TROPIC
URALIC
URANIC

••RC••
CIRCLE
CIRCUM
CIRCUS
DORCAS
FARCED
FARCES
FARCRY
FORCED
FORCER
FORCES
GARCIA
GARCON
MARCEL
MARCHE
MARCIA
MARCIE
MARCOS
MARCUS
MERCED
MERCER
MURCIA
PARCAE
PARCEL
PERCHA
TERCEL
TERCET
WARCRY
ZIRCON

••R•C•
AFRICA
ARRACK
BARUCH
BORSCH
CURACY
DIRECT
DUROCS
ENRICH
ENRICO
HIRSCH
HORACE
KIRSCH
LORICA
LYRICS
MARACA
PIRACY
PURACE
SERACS
SIRICA
SPRUCE
STRICK
STRICT
STRUCK
THRACE
THRICE
YORICK
ZURICH

••R••C
AIRSAC
AORTIC
BARDIC
FERENC
FERRIC
FORMIC
GARLIC
HEROIC
KARMIC
NORDIC
PARSEC
SORBIC
TARMAC
TURKIC

•••RC•
AMERCE
APERCU
BIERCE
CHURCH
COERCE
EPARCH
EXARCH
FIERCE
INARCH
PEERCE
PIERCE
SCARCE
SCORCH
SEARCH
SMIRCH
SOURCE
STARCH
STORCH
TIERCE

•••R•C
AGARIC
ALARIC
AMTRAC
CEDRIC
CITRIC
CLERIC
COURIC
CUPRIC
CYMRIC
FABRIC
FERRIC
IATRIC
METRIC
NITRIC
RUBRIC
TENREC
VITRIC

R•D•••
RADDLE
RADIAL
RADIAN
RADIOS
RADISH
RADIUM
RADIUS
RADNER
RADOME
RADULA
REDACT
REDANT
REDATE
REDBAY
REDBUD
REDCAP
REDDEN
REDDER
REDDOG
REDEAL
REDEEM
REDEYE
REDFIN
REDFIR
REDFOX
REDGUM
REDHAT
REDHOT
REDIAL
REDINK
REDOAK
REDOES
REDONE
REDRAW
REDREW
REDSEA
REDSOX
REDTAG
REDTOP
REDUBS
REDUCE
REDYED
REDYES
RIDDED
RIDDEN
RIDDLE
RIDENT
RIDERS
RIDGED
RIDGES
RIDING
RIDLEY
RODENT
RODEOS
RODHAM
RODNEY
RUDDER
RUDDLE
RUDELY
RUDEST
RUDMAN
RUDOLF
RYDELL

R••D••
RADDLE
RAIDED
RAIDER
RANDOM
RANDRY
READER
READIN
REDDEN
REDDER
REDDOG
REEDIT
RENDER
RHODES
RIDDED
RIDDEN
RIDDLE
ROADIE
RONDEL
RONDOS
RUDDER
RUDDLE
RUNDLE
RUNDMC
RUNDRY

R•••D•
RAMADA
RANIDS
RAPIDS
RATEDG
RATEDR
RATEDX
REBIDS
RECEDE
RECODE
REMADE
REMEDY
REMUDA
RESEDA
RESIDE
RESODS
REWEDS
RHONDA
RIYADH
ROUNDS
RUANDA
RWANDA

R••••D
RACKED
RAFTED
RAGGED
RAIDED
RAILED
RAINED
RAISED
RAMMED
RAMPED
RAMROD
RANCID
RANGED
RANKED
RANTED
RAPPED
RASHAD
RASHID
RASPED
RATTED
RAZZED
REAMED
REAPED
REARED
REBIND
RECORD
REDBUD
REDYED
REEFED
REEKED
REELED
REEVED
REFFED
REFUND
REGARD
REHELD
REINED
RELAID
RELIED
RELOAD
REMAND
REMEND
REMIND
RENTED
REPAID
REPAND
REREAD
RESAND
RESEED
RESEND
RESHOD
RESOLD
RESTED
RETARD
RETIED
RETOLD
REUSED
REVVED
REWARD
REWELD
REWIND
REWORD
RHYMED
RIBALD
RIBAND
RIBBED
RICKED
RIDDED
RIDGED
RIFFED
RIFLED
RIFTED
RIGGED
RIMMED
RINGED
RINSED
RIOTED
RIPPED
RISKED
RITARD
ROAMED
ROARED
ROBBED
ROCKED
ROILED
ROLAND
ROLLED
ROMPED
RONALD
ROOFED
ROOKED
ROOMED
ROOTED
ROTTED
ROTUND
ROUGED
ROUSED
ROUTED
RRATED
RUBBED
RUBIED
RUCKED
RUFFED
RUGGED
RUINED
RUSHED
RUSTED
RUTTED

•RD•••
ARDEBS
ARDENT
ARDORS
ARDOUR
ORDAIN
ORDEAL
ORDERS
ORDURE

•R•D••
ARIDLY
BRIDAL
BRIDES
BRIDGE
BRIDLE
BRODIE
BRUDER
CRADLE
CREDIT
CREDOS
CRUDDY
CRUDER
DREDGE
DRUDGE
DRYDEN
ERODED
ERODES
FREDDY
FRIDAY
FRIDGE
GRADEA
GRADED
GRADER
GRADES
GRADIN
GRADUS
GRODIN
GRUDGE
IRIDES
IRIDIC
PRIDED
PRIDES
PRUDES
TRADED
TRADER
TRADES
TREDIA
TRUDGE

•R••D•
ARCADE
ARENDT
ARMADA
AROIDS
ARVADA
BRAIDS
BRANDO
BRANDS
BRANDT
BRANDX
BRANDY
BREADS
BREEDS
BRENDA
BROADS
BROODS
BROODY
CREEDS
CROWDS
CRUDDY
DREADS
DROIDS
DRUIDS
DRYADS
FRAUDS
FREDDY
FRONDS
GRANDE
GRANDS
GREEDY
GRINDS
GRUNDY
MRHYDE
OREADS
OREIDA
OROIDE
PRAVDA
TREADS
TRENDS
TRENDY
TRIADS
TRIODE
URSIDS

•R•••D
ARCHED
ARGUED
ARMAND
ARNOLD
AROUND
BRACED
BRAKED
BRAVED
BRAYED
BRAZED
BREWED
BRIAND
BRIARD
BRIBED
BRIGID
BRINED
CRANED
CRATED
CRAVED
CRAZED
CREWED
CROWED
DRAPED
DRAYED
DRONED
ERASED
ERHARD
ERODED
ERRAND
FRAMED
FRAYED
FRIEND
FRIGID
GRACED
GRADED
GRATED
GRAVED
GRAVID
GRAYED
GRAZED
GREYED
GRIMED
GRIPED
GROPED
GROUND
IRONED
ORATED
ORCHID
ORMOND
PRATED
PRAYED
PREMED
PREYED
PRICED
PRIDED
PRIMED
PRIZED
PROBED
PROSED
PROVED
PRUNED
RRATED
TRACED
TRADED
TREPID
TRICED
TRIFID
TRIPOD
TROWED
XRATED
XRAYED

••RD••
AIRDAM
AIRDRY
BARDIC
BARDOT
BIRDED
BIRDER
BIRDIE
BORDEN
BORDER
BURDEN
CARDED
CARDER
CARDIN
CARDIO
CORDAY
CORDED
CORDON
CURDED
CURDLE
FORDED
GARDEN
GIRDED
GIRDER
GIRDLE
GORDIE
GORDON
HARDEN
HARDER
HARDLY
HARDUP
HERDED
HERDER
HORDES
HURDLE
JORDAN
LARDED
LARDER
LARDON
LORDED
LORDLY
MARDUK
MURDER
MYRDAL
NORDIC
PARDON
PERDUE
PURDAH
PURDUE
SARDIS
SIRDAR
SORDID
VARDEN
VERDIN
VERDON
VERDUN
WARDED
WARDEN
WARDER
WORDED
YARDED

••R•D•
ABRADE
BORIDE
DERIDE
DIRNDL
DORADO
FARADS
JURADO
LAREDO
LERIDA
MERIDA
NERUDA
PARADE
PARODY
SARODS
SCRODS
SHREDS
STRADS
STRIDE
STRODE
TEREDO
TIRADE
WORLDS

••R••D
ABROAD
AFRAID
AGREED
BARBED
BARGED
BARKED
BARRED
BIRDED
BIRLED
BURIED
BURLED
BURNED
BURPED
BURRED
BYROAD
CARDED
CARPED
CARTED
CARVED
CERVID
CORDED
CORKED
CORNED
CURBED
CURDED
CURLED
CURRED
CURSED
CURVED
DARNED
DARTED
EARNED
ERRAND
FARCED
FARMED
FERVID
FIRMED
FORBAD
FORBID
FORCED
FORDED
FORGED
FORKED
FORMED
FURLED
FURRED
GARBED
GERALD
GERARD
GERUND
GIRARD
GIRDED
GIRTED
GORGED
HARKED
HARMED
HAROLD
HARPED
HERALD
HERDED
HORNED
HORRID
HORSED
HURLED
INROAD
JARRED
JERKED
KERNED
LARDED
LARKED
LORDED

LURKED
MARAUD
MARKED
MARLED
MARRED
MERCED
MERGED
MORBID
MYRIAD
NEREID
NURSED
PARKED
PARRED
PARSED
PARTED
PERIOD
PERKED
PERMED
PERNOD
PORTED
PUREED
PURGED
PURLED
PURRED
PURSED
REREAD
SCREED
SERVED
SHREWD
SHROUD
SORDID
SORTED
SPREAD
STRAND
STROUD
SURFED
SURGED
TARRED
TERMED
THREAD
THREED
TOROID
TORPID
TORRID
TURBID
TURFED
TURGID
TURNED
UNREAD
VARIED
VERGED
VERSED
WARDED
WARGOD
WARMED
WARNED
WARPED
WARRED
WORDED
WORKED
WORMED
YARDED
YARNED
ZEROED

•••RD•
AWARDS
BEARDS
BOARDS
CHORDS
CIARDI
FIORDS
FJORDS
GOURDE
GOURDS
GUARDS
HAIRDO
HOARDS
LAIRDS
OVERDO
SHARDS
STURDY
SWARDS
SWORDS
TBIRDS
THIRDS
WEIRDO

•••R•D
ACARID
ADORED
ALFRED
ASTRID
BARRED
BIGRED
BLARED
BURRED
CONRAD
CURRED
ENURED
FAIRED
FEARED
FLARED
FLORID
FLYROD
FURRED
GEARED
GLARED
HAIRED
HATRED
HORRID
HOTROD
HYBRID
INBRED
INGRID
INURED
JARRED
JEERED
KONRAD
LEERED
MADRID
MARRED
MITRED
MOORED
NEARED
NIMROD
PAIRED
PARRED
PEERED
PENROD
POURED
PURRED
PUTRID
RAMROD
REARED
ROARED
SACRED
SAWRED
SCARED
SCORED
SEARED
SEERED
SHARED
SHORED
SNARED
SNORED
SOARED
SOURED
SPARED
SPIRED
STARED
STORED
TARRED
TEARED
TETRAD
TIERED
TIEROD
TORRID
TOURED
UNTROD
USERID
VEERED
WARRED

••••RD
ABOARD
ABSURD
ACCORD
AFFORD
ASGARD
BAYARD
BRIARD
BYWORD
CANARD
COWARD
CUNARD
DOTARD
EDGARD
EDUARD
EDVARD
EDWARD
ENGIRD
ERHARD
FUGARD
GERARD
GIRARD
GODARD
HAZARD
HOWARD
IDCARD
INWARD
IZZARD
LIZARD
LYNYRD
MILORD
MYWORD
ONWARD
OXFORD
OXNARD
PETARD
PICARD
RECORD
REGARD
RETARD
REWARD
REWORD
RITARD
SEWARD
SIGURD
TABARD
TOWARD
UNGIRD
UPWARD
WIZARD

RE••••
REACTS
READER
READIN
REAGAN
REAIRS
REALER
REALES
REALIA
REALLY
REALMS
REALTY
REAMED
REAMER
REAPED
REAPER
REARED
REARER
REARMS
REARUP
REASON
REATAS
REBAGS
REBARS
REBATE
REBELS
REBIDS
REBIND
REBOIL
REBOLT
REBOOT
REBORN
REBOZO
REBUFF
REBUKE
REBUTS
RECALL
RECANE
RECANT
RECAPS
RECAST
RECEDE
RECENT
RECESS
RECIFE
RECIPE
RECITE
RECKON
RECODE
RECOIL
RECONS
RECOPY
RECORD
RECORK
RECOUP
RECTOR
RECTOS
RECTUS
RECURS
RECUSE
REDACT
REDANT
REDATE
REDBAY
REDBUD
REDCAP
REDDEN
REDDER
REDDOG
REDEAL
REDEEM
REDEYE
REDFIN
REDFIR
REDFOX
REDGUM
REDHAT
REDHOT
REDIAL
REDINK
REDOAK
REDOES
REDONE
REDRAW
REDREW
REDSEA
REDSOX
REDTAG
REDTOP
REDUBS
REDUCE
REDYED
REDYES
REEBOK
REECHO
REEDIT
REEFED
REEFER
REEKED
REELED
REELIN
REEVED
REEVES
REFACE
REFERS
REFFED
REFILE
REFILL
REFINE
REFITS
REFLEX
REFLUX
REFORM
REFUEL
REFUGE
REFUND
REFUSE
REFUTE
REGAIN
REGALE
REGARD
REGENT
REGGAE
REGGIE
REGIME
REGINA
REGION
REGIUS
REGLET
REGLUE
REGNAL
REGRET
REHANG
REHASH
REHEAL
REHEAR
REHEAT
REHEEL
REHELD
REHEMS
REHIRE
REHOOK
REHUNG
REIGNS
REINED
REINER
REININ
REINKS
REJECT
REJOIN
REKEYS
RELACE
RELAID
RELATE
RELAYS
RELENT
RELETS
RELICS
RELICT
RELIED
RELIEF
RELIES
RELINE
RELISH
RELIST
RELIVE
RELOAD
RELOCK
RELUCT
RELUME
REMADE
REMAIL
REMAIN
REMAKE
REMAND
REMANS
REMAPS
REMARK
REMEDY
REMELT
REMEND
REMICK
REMIND
REMISE
REMISS
REMITS
REMORA
REMOTE
REMOVE
REMOWN
REMOWS
REMUDA
RENAIL
RENAME
RENATA
RENDER
RENEGE
RENEWS
RENNES
RENNET
RENNIE
RENNIN
RENOIR
RENOTE
RENOWN
RENTAL
RENTED
RENTER
REOILS
REOPEN
REPAID
REPAIR
REPAND
REPAST
REPAVE
REPAYS
REPEAL
REPEAT
REPEGS
REPELS
REPENT
REPINE
REPLAN
REPLAY
REPLOW
REPOLL
REPORT
REPOSE
REPOTS
REPROS
REPUGN
REPUTE
RERATE
REREAD
RERENT
RERUNS
RESALE
RESALT
RESAND
RESCUE
RESEAL
RESEAT
RESEAU
RESECT
RESEDA
RESEED
RESEEN
RESEES
RESELL
RESEND
RESENT
RESETS
RESEWN
RESEWS
RESHIP
RESHOD
RESHOE
RESHOT
RESIDE
RESIGN
RESILE
RESING
RESINS
RESIST
RESNIK
RESODS
RESOLD
RESOLE
RESORB
RESORT
RESTED
RESTER
RESTON
RESTUP
RESULT
RESUME
RETAGS
RETAIL
RETAIN
RETAKE
RETAPE
RETAPS
RETARD
RETARS
RETELL
RETENE
RETEST
RETIAL
RETIED
RETIES
RETILE
RETIME
RETINA
RETIRE
RETOLD
RETOOK
RETOOL
RETOPS
RETORT
RETOUR
RETOWS
RETRAL
RETRIM
RETROS
RETTON
RETUNE
RETURN
RETYPE
REUBEN
REUNES
REUSED
REUSES
REUTER
REVAMP
REVEAL
REVELS
REVERB
REVERE
REVERS
REVERT
REVETS
REVIEW
REVILE
REVISE
REVIVE
REVLON
REVOIR
REVOKE
REVOLT
REVSON
REVUES
REVVED
REWARD
REWARM
REWASH
REWEDS
REWELD
REWIND
REWINS
REWIRE
REWORD
REWORK
REWOVE
REWRAP
REXCAT
REZONE

R•E•••
REEBOK
REECHO
REEDIT
REEFED
REEFER
REEKED
REELED
REELIN
REEVED
REEVES
RHEBOK
RHESUS
RHETOR
RHEUMS
RHEUMY
RUEFUL

R••E••
RACEME
RACERS
RAKEIN
RAKERS
RAKEUP
RAMEAU
RANEES
RAREFY
RARELY
RAREST
RATEDG
RATEDR
RATEDX
RATELS
RATERS
RAVELS
RAVENS
RAVERS
RAWEGG
RAWEST
REBELS
RECEDE
RECENT
RECESS
REDEAL
REDEEM
REDEYE
REFERS
REGENT
REHEAL
REHEAR
REHEAT
REHEEL
REHELD
REHEMS
REJECT
REKEYS
RELENT
RELETS
REMEDY
REMELT
REMEND
RENEGE
RENEWS
REPEAL
REPEAT
REPEGS
REPELS
REPENT
REREAD
RERENT
RESEAL
RESEAT
RESEAU
RESECT
RESEDA
RESEED
RESEEN
RESEES
RESELL
RESEND
RESENT
RESETS
RESEWN
RESEWS
RETELL
RETENE
RETEST
REVEAL
REVELS
REVERB
REVERE
REVERS
REVERT
REVETS
REWEDS
REWELD
RIBEYE
RICERS
RIDENT
RIDERS
RIFEST
RIPELY
RIPENS
RIPEST
RISERS
RIVERA
RIVERS
RIVETS
ROBERT
RODENT
RODEOS
ROGERS
ROLEOS
ROMEOS
ROMERO
RONELY
ROPEIN
ROPERS
ROSEAU
ROVERS
ROWELS
ROWENA
ROWENS
ROWERS
RUBENS
RUDELY
RUDEST
RULEON
RULERS
RUMENS
RUPEES
RUPERT
RYDELL

R•••E•
RABBET
RABIES
RACHEL
RACIER
RACKED
RACKET
RADNER
RAFAEL
RAFTED
RAFTER
RAGGED
RAGMEN
RAIDED
RAIDER
RAILED
RAILER
RAINED
RAINER
RAINES
RAISED
RAISER
RAISES
RAMIES
RAMJET
RAMMED
RAMPED
RAMSES
RAMSEY
RANEES
RANGED
RANGER
RANGES
RANKED
RANKER
RANTED
RANTER
RAPIER
RAPPED
RAPPEE
RAPPEL
RAPPER
RAQUEL
RASHER
RASHES
RASPED
RASPER
RASTER
RATHER
RATTED
RATTER
RAZZED
RAZZES
READER
REALER
REALES
REAMED
REAMER
REAPED
REAPER
REARED
REARER
REDDEN
REDDER
REDEEM
REDOES
REDREW
REDSEA
REDYED
REDYES
REEFED
REEFER
REEKED
REELED
REEVED
REEVES
REFFED
REFLEX
REFUEL
REGLET
REGRET
REHEEL
REINED
REINER
RELIED
RELIEF
RELIES
RENDER
RENNES
RENNET
RENTED
RENTER
REOPEN
RESEED
RESEEN
RESEES
RESTED
RESTER
RETIED
RETIES
REUBEN
REUNES
REUSED
REUSES
REUTER
REVIEW
REVUES
REVVED
RHODES
RHYMED
RHYMER
RHYMES
RIBBED
RICHEN
RICHER
RICHES
RICKED
RICKEY
RIDDED
RIDDEN
RIDGED
RIDGES
RIDLEY
RIFFED
RIFLED
RIFLER
RIFLES
RIFTED
RIGGED
RIGGER
RILLES
RILLET
RIMMED
RINGED
RINGER
RINSED
RINSES
RIOTED
RIOTER
RIPKEN
RIPLEY
RIPPED
RIPPER
RISKED
RISKER
RITTER
ROAMED
ROAMER
ROARED
ROARER
ROBBED
ROBBER
ROBLES
ROCHET
ROCKED
ROCKER
ROCKET
RODNEY
ROGUES
ROHMER
ROILED
ROLLED
ROLLER
ROMMEL
ROMNEY
ROMPED
ROMPER
RONDEL
ROOFED
ROOFER
ROOKED
ROOMED
ROOMER
ROONEY
ROOTED
ROOTER
ROPIER
ROSIER
ROSTER
ROTTED
ROTTEN
ROTTER
ROUGED
ROUGES
ROUSED
ROUSES
ROUTED
ROUTER
ROUTES
RRATED
RUBBED
RUBBER
RUBIED
RUBIES
RUBLES
RUCHES
RUCKED
RUDDER
RUFFED
RUGGED
RUINED
RUINER
RUMMER
RUNLET
RUNNEL
RUNNER
RUPEES
RUSHED
RUSHEE
RUSHES
RUSSET
RUSTED
RUTGER
RUTTED

R••••E
RABBLE
RACEME
RACINE
RADDLE
RADOME
RAFFLE
RAMATE
RAMBLE
RAMONE
RAMOSE
RANKLE
RAPINE
RAPPEE
RASSLE
RATINE
RATITE
RATTLE
RAVAGE
RAVINE
RAZZLE
REBATE
REBUKE
RECANE
RECEDE
RECIFE
RECIPE
RECITE
RECODE
RECUSE
REDATE
REDEYE
REDONE
REDUCE
REFACE
REFILE
REFINE
REFUGE
REFUSE
REFUTE
REGALE
REGGAE
REGGIE
REGIME
REGLUE
REHIRE
RELACE
RELATE
RELINE
RELIVE
RELUME
REMADE
REMAKE
REMISE
REMOTE
REMOVE
RENAME
RENEGE
RENNIE
RENOTE
REPAVE
REPINE
REPOSE
REPUTE
RERATE
RESALE
RESCUE
RESHOE
RESIDE
RESILE
RESOLE
RESUME
RETAKE
RETAPE
RETENE
RETILE
RETIME
RETIRE
RETUNE
RETYPE
REVERE
REVILE
REVISE
REVIVE
REVOKE
REWIRE
REWOVE
REZONE
RIBEYE
RIBOSE
RICHIE
RIDDLE
RIFFLE
RIMOSE
RIMPLE
RIPPLE
RISQUE
ROADIE
ROBBIE
ROCKNE
ROLLIE
RONNIE
ROOKIE
ROOMIE
ROSCOE
ROTATE
ROXANE
ROYALE
RUBBLE
RUDDLE
RUFFLE
RUGATE
RUGOSE
RUMBLE
RUMPLE
RUNCIE
RUNDLE
RUSHEE
RUSTLE
RUTILE
RVALUE

•RE•••
ARECAS
ARENAS
ARENDT
AREOLA
ARETES
ARETHA
AREZZO
BREACH
BREADS
BREAKS
BREAMS
BREAST
BREATH
BRECHT
BREECH
BREEDS
BREEZE
BREEZY
BREMEN
BRENDA
BRENTS
BRETON
BREUER
BREVES
BREVET
BREWED
BREWER
CREAKS
CREAKY
CREAMS
CREAMY
CREASE
CREASY
CREATE
CRECHE
CREDIT
CREDOS
CREEDS
CREEKS
CREELS
CREEPS
CREEPY
CREMES
CRENEL
CRENNA
CREOLE
CREPES
CRESOL
CRESTS
CRETAN
CRETIN
CREUSA
CREWED
CREWEL
DREADS
DREAMS
DREAMT
DREAMY
DREARY
DREDGE
DRENCH
DRESSY
DREWIN
DREWON
DREWUP
DREXEL
EREBUS
ERECTS
ERENOW
FREAKS
FREAKY
FREDDY
FREELY
FREEST
FREEZE
FRENCH

FRENUM
FRENZY
FRESCA
FRESCO
FRESNO
FRETTY
GREASE
GREASY
GREATS
GREAVE
GREBES
GREECE
GREEDY
GREEKS
GREENE
GREENS
GREENY
GREETS
GREGOR
GREIGE
GRETEL
GRETNA
GREWON
GREWUP
GREYED
GREYER
IREFUL
IRENES
IRENIC
KRESGE
OREADS
OREGON
OREIDA
ORELSE
PREACH
PREAMP
PRECIS
PREENS
PREFAB
PREFER
PREFIX
PRELAW
PRELIM
PREMED
PREMIE
PREPAY
PREPPY
PRESET
PRESTO
PRETAX
PRETER
PRETTY
PREVIN
PREWAR
PREYED
PREYON
TREADS
TREATS
TREATY
TREBEK
TREBLE
TREBLY
TREDIA
TREMOR
TRENCH
TRENDS
TRENDY
TREPAN
TREPID
TREVOR
WREAKS
WREATH
WRECKS
WRENCH
WRESTS
WRETCH

•R•E••

ARBELA
ARDEBS
ARDENT
ARGENT
ARLENE
ARMETS
ARNESS
ARNETT
ARPENT
ARREST
ARSENE
ARTELS
ARTERY
BREECH
BREEDS
BREEZE
BREEZY
BRIEFS
BRIENZ
BRIERS
BRIERY
CREEDS
CREEKS
CREELS
CREEPS
CREEPY
CRIERS
CRUETS
DRIERS
DRIEST
DRYERS
DRYEST
ERNEST
FREELY
FREEST
FREEZE
FRIEND
FRIEZE
FRYERS
GRAECO
GREECE
GREEDY
GREEKS
GREENE
GREENS
GREENY
GREETS
GRIEVE
GRUELS
IRLENE
IRREAL
ORDEAL
ORDERS
ORGEAT
ORIELS
ORIENT
ORNERY
ORRERY
ORTEGA
ORWELL
PREENS
PRIERS
PRIEST
PROEMS
TRIERS
TRUEST
URAEUS
URGENT
URGERS
WRIEST
WRYEST

•R••E•

ARCHED
ARCHER
ARCHES
ARETES
ARGUED
ARGUER
ARGUES
ARISEN
ARISES
ARMIES
ARMLET
ARNHEM
ARTIER
BRACED
BRACER
BRACES
BRAKED
BRAKES
BRAVED
BRAVER
BRAVES
BRAYED
BRAYER
BRAZED
BRAZEN
BRAZER
BRAZES
BREMEN
BREUER
BREVES
BREVET
BREWED
BREWER
BRIBED
BRIBES
BRIDES
BRINED
BRINES
BROKEN
BROKER
BRUDER
BRUGES
BRULES
BRUMES
BRUNEI
BRUNET
BRUTES
CRAKES
CRANED
CRANES
CRAPES
CRATED
CRATER
CRATES
CRAVED
CRAVEN
CRAVER
CRAVES
CRAZED
CRAZES
CREMES
CRENEL
CREPES
CREWED
CREWEL
CRIMEA
CRIMES
CRIPES
CRISES
CRONES
CROWED
CROWER
CROZES
CRUCES
CRUDER
CRUSES
CRUXES
DRABEK
DRAGEE
DRAKES
DRAPED
DRAPER
DRAPES
DRAWER
DRAYED
DREXEL
DRIVEL
DRIVEN
DRIVER
DRIVES
DRONED
DRONER
DRONES
DROVER
DROVES
DRUPES
DRUZES
DRYDEN
ERASED
ERASER
ERASES
ERODED
ERODES
FRAMED
FRAMES
FRASER
FRAYED
FRAZER
FRISEE
FRISES
FROZEN
GRABEN
GRACED
GRACES
GRADEA
GRADED
GRADER
GRADES
GRAPES
GRATED
GRATER
GRATES
GRAVED
GRAVEL
GRAVEN
GRAVER
GRAVES
GRAYED
GRAYER
GRAZED
GRAZER
GRAZES
GREBES
GRETEL
GREYED
GREYER
GRIMED
GRIMES
GRIPED
GRIPER
GRIPES
GRIVET
GROCER
GROPED
GROPES
GROVEL
GROVER
GROVES
GROWER
IRATER
IRENES
IRIDES
IRISES
IRONED
IRONER
KRAKEN
KRAMER
KRATER
KRONER
KRUGER
ORALES
ORATED
ORATES
ORGIES
ORIGEN
ORKNEY
ORTLES
ORYXES
PRATED
PRATER
PRATES
PRAXES
PRAYED
PRAYER
PREFER
PREMED
PRESET
PRETER
PREYED
PRICED
PRICER
PRICES
PRICEY
PRIDED
PRIDES
PRIMED
PRIMER
PRIMES
PRIPET
PRIVET
PRIZED
PRIZES
PROBED
PROBER
PROBES
PROLES
PROPEL
PROPER
PROSED
PROSER
PROSES
PROTEI
PROTEM
PROVED
PROVEN
PROVER
PROVES
PRUDES
PRUNED
PRUNER
PRUNES
RRATED
TRACED
TRACER
TRACES
TRACEY
TRADED
TRADER
TRADES
TRALEE
TRAVEL
TREBEK
TRIBES
TRICED
TRICES
TRIKES
TRINES
TRITER
TRIVET
TROPES
TROPEZ
TROVES
TROWED
TROWEL
TRUCES
URUSES
WRITER
WRITES
XRATED
XRAYED

•R•••E

ARABLE
ARCADE
ARCANE
ARCHIE
ARGIVE
ARGYLE
ARIOSE
ARLENE
ARMURE
AROUSE
ARRIVE
ARSENE
BRAISE
BRAQUE
BREEZE
BRIDGE
BRIDLE
BRODIE
BROGUE
BRONTE
BRONZE
BROOKE
BROWNE
BROWSE
BRUISE
CRABBE
CRADLE
CREASE
CREATE
CRECHE
CREOLE
CRINGE
CROSSE
CROUSE
CROUTE
CRUISE
CRUSOE
DRAGEE
DREDGE
DROGUE
DROWSE
DRUDGE
DRYICE
ERGATE
ERMINE
FRAISE
FRANCE
FRAPPE
FREEZE
FRIDGE
FRIEZE
FRINGE
FRISEE
GRABLE
GRACIE
GRAMME
GRANDE
GRANGE
GREASE
GREAVE
GREECE
GREENE
GREIGE
GRIEVE
GRILLE
GRILSE
GRIMKE
GRIPPE
GROOVE
GROSSE
GROUSE
GRUDGE
GRUNGE
IRLENE
IRVINE
KRESGE
MRBLUE
MRHYDE
ORACLE
ORANGE
ORDURE
ORELSE
ORGATE
ORIOLE
ORNATE
OROIDE
ORPINE
PRAGUE
PRAISE
PRANCE
PREMIE
PRINCE
PROCNE
PROPRE
PROWSE
PRYNNE
TRALEE
TRANCE
TREBLE
TRIAGE
TRIFLE
TRIODE
TRIPLE
TRISTE
TRIUNE
TRIXIE
TROCHE
TROMPE
TROUPE
TROUVE
TRUDGE
URBANE
URSINE
WRASSE
WRITHE

••RE••

ADRENO
AFREET
AFRESH
AGREED
AGREES
ARREST
ATREST
ATREUS
AUREUS
BAREGE
BARELY
BAREST
BEREFT
BERETS
BIREME
BOREAL
BOREAS
BOREON
BORERS
BOREUP
BUREAU
CAREEN
CAREER
CARESS
CARETO
CARETS
CEREAL
CEREUS
CORERS
CURERS
DARETO
DIRECT
DIREST
DOREMI
DURESS
EGRESS
EGRETS
EUREKA
FARERS
FERENC
FIRERS
FIREUP
FOREGO
FOREST
GARETH
GERENT
GYRENE
HAREMS
HEREAT
HEREBY
HEREIN
HEREOF
HEREON
HERESY
HERETO
HIREON
HIRERS
IRREAL
JEREMY
KAREEM
KOREAN
LAREDO
LOREAL
LORENZ
MERELY
MEREST
MOREAU
MOREEN
MORELS
MORENO
NEREID
NEREIS
NEREUS
OCREAE
OGRESS
ORRERY
PARENS
PARENT
PARERS
PARETO
PAREVE
PUREED
PUREES
PURELY
PUREST
RAREFY
RARELY
RAREST
REREAD
RERENT
SCREAK
SCREAM
SCREED
SCREEN
SCREES
SCREWS
SCREWY
SERENA
SERENE
SHREDS
SHREWD
SHREWS
SIRENS
SORELY
SOREST
SPREAD
SPREES
STREAK
STREAM
STREEP
STREET
STRESS
STREWN
STREWS
SURELY
SUREST
SURETE
SURETY
TEREDO
TERESA
TERETE
TEREUS
THREAD
THREAT
THREED
THREES
THRESH
TOREAT
TORERO
TOREUP
TUREEN
UNREAD
UNREAL
UNREEL
UNREST
VARESE
VEREEN
VIREOS
WERENT
WIRERS
WOREON
YARELY
ZAREBA

••R•E•

ADRIEN
AERIES
AFREET
AGREED
AGREES
AIRIER
AIRMEN
BARBED
BARBEL
BARBER
BARBET
BARGED
BARGES
BARKED
BARKER
BARLEY
BARMEN
BARNES
BARNEY
BARRED
BARREL
BARREN
BARRES
BARTER
BERBER
BERGEN
BIRDED
BIRDER
BIRLED
BIRNEY
BORDEN
BORDER
BORNEO
BURDEN
BURGEE
BURGER
BURIED
BURIES
BURLED
BURLEY
BURNED
BURNER
BURNET
BURNEY
BURPED
BURRED
BURSES
BYRNES
CARDED
CARDER
CAREEN
CAREER
CARIES
CARMEL
CARMEN
CARNES
CARNET
CARNEY
CARPED
CARPEL
CARPER
CARPET
CARREL
CARREY
CARTED
CARTEL
CARTER
CARTES
CARVED
CARVER
CARVES
CARVEY
CERMET
CORBEL
CORDED
CORKED
CORKER
CORNEA
CORNED
CORNEL
CORNER
CORNET
CORREL
CORSET
CORTES
CORTEX
CORTEZ
CORVEE
CURBED
CURDED
CURFEW
CURLED
CURLER
CURLEW
CURRED
CURSED
CURSES
CURTER
CURVED
CURVES
CURVET
DARIEN
DARKEN
DARKER
DARNED
DARNEL
DARNER
DARREN
DARTED
DARTER
DIRGES
DORIES
DORMER
DORSET
DORSEY
DURFEY
DURYEA
EARNED
EARNER
EERIER
EYRIES
FARCED
FARCES
FARLEY
FARMED
FARMER
FERBER
FERRER
FERRET
FIRMED
FIRMER
FORBES
FORCED
FORCER
FORCES
FORDED
FORGED
FORGER
FORGES
FORGET
FORKED
FORKER
FORMED
FORMER
FORTES
FURIES
FURLED
FURRED
GARBED
GARDEN
GARNER
GARNET
GARRET
GARTER
GARVEY
GERBER
GIRDED
GIRDER
GIRTED
GORGED
GORGES
GORGET
GORIER
GORSES
GURLEY
GURNEY
HARDEN
HARDER
HARKED
HARKEN
HARKER
HARLEM
HARLEY
HARMED
HARPED
HARPER
HARVEY
HERDED
HERDER
HERMES
HEROES
HERSEY
HORDES
HORMEL
HORNED
HORNER
HORNET
HORNEY
HORSED
HORSES
HORSEY
HURLED
HURLER
HURLEY
ISRAEL
JARRED
JERKED
JERSEY
JURIES
KAREEM
KERMES
KERNED
KERNEL
KERSEY
LARDED
LARDER
LARGER
LARKED
LARSEN
LERNER
LORDED
LORIES
LURKED
MARCEL
MARIEL
MARKED
MARKER
MARKET
MARLED
MARLEE
MARLEY
MARMEE
MARNER
MARRED
MARTEL
MARTEN
MARVEL
MERCED
MERCER
MERGED
MERGER
MERGES
MERKEL
MERMEN
MERSEY
MIRREN
MOREEN
MORGEN
MORLEY
MORSEL
MURDER
MURIEL
MURRES
MURREY
NERVES
NURSED
NURSER
NURSES
OBRIEN
OERTER
PARCEL
PARGET
PARKED
PARKER
PARLEY
PARRED
PARREL
PARSEC
PARSED
PARSEE
PARSER
PARSES
PARTED
PERKED
PERMED
PERTER
PORKER
PORTED
PORTER
PUREED
PUREES
PURGED
PURGES
PURLED
PURRED
PURRER
PURSED
PURSER
PURSES
PURVEY
SARGES
SCREED
SCREEN
SCREES
SERGEI
SERGES
SERIES
SERVED
SERVER
SERVES
SHRIEK
SIRREE
SORBET
SORREL
SORTED
SORTER
SPREES
SPRIER
SPRUES
SPRYER
STREEP
STREET
SURFED
SURFER
SURGED
SURGES
SURREY
SURVEY
TARGES
TARGET
TARRED
TARTER
TERCEL
TERCET
TERKEL
TERMED
TERRET
TERSER
THREED
THREES
THROES
TORIES
TORTES
TUREEN
TURFED
TURKEY
TURNED
TURNER
TURRET
UNREEL
VARDEN
VARIED
VARIES
VARLET
VARNEY
VEREEN
VERGED
VERGER
VERGES
VERSED
VERSES
VERTEX
VERVET
VORTEX
WARDED
WARDEN
WARDER
WARIER
WARMED
WARMER
WARNED
WARNER
WARPED
WARRED
WARREN
WERFEL
WERNER
WORDED
WORKED
WORKER
WORMED
WORSEN
XERXES
YARDED
YARNED
YERKES
YORKER
ZEROED
ZEROES

••R••E

ABRADE
AERATE
AEROBE
AFRAME
AORTAE
ARRIVE
BARBIE
BAREGE
BARITE
BARQUE
BARRIE
BERATE
BERNIE
BERTIE
BIRDIE
BIREME
BORAGE
BORATE
BORIDE
BURBLE
BURGEE
BURGLE
BURSAE
BYROTE
CARAFE
CARIBE
CAROLE
CARRIE
CERATE
CERISE
CERUSE
CHROME
CIRCLE
CIRQUE
CORVEE
CURARE
CURATE
CURDLE
CURIAE
CURULE
DARKLE
DERIDE
DERIVE
ENRAGE
ENROBE
EUROPE
FERGIE
FERULE
FORAGE
FURORE
GARAGE
GARBLE
GARGLE
GERTIE
GIRDLE
GORDIE
GURGLE
GYRATE
GYRENE
GYROSE
HARARE
HERBIE
HORACE
HURDLE
HURTLE
JEROME
KARATE
KIRTLE
KURILE
LARVAE
MARBLE
MARCHE
MARCIE
MARGIE
MARINE
MARLEE
MARMEE
MARNIE
MARPLE
MARQUE
MEROPE
MIRAGE
MORALE
MOROSE

MURINE
MYRTLE
OCREAE
PARADE
PARCAE
PAREVE
PAROLE
PARSEE
PARURE
PERDUE
PERUKE
PERUSE
PHRASE
PIRATE
PURACE
PURDUE
PURFLE
PURINE
PURPLE
PURSUE
PYRITE
RERATE
SARTRE
SCRAPE
SCRIBE
SERAPE
SERENE
SERINE
SHRIKE
SHRINE
SHRIVE
SHROVE
SIRREE
SORTIE
SPRITE
SPRUCE
STRAFE
STRAKE
STRIAE
STRIDE
STRIFE
STRIKE
STRIPE
STRIVE
STROBE
STRODE
STROKE
STROVE
SURETE
TERETE
THRACE
THRALE
THRICE
THRIVE
THRONE
THROVE
TIRADE
TIRANE
TOROSE
TORQUE
TURTLE
TYRONE
UNRIPE
UNROBE
UPRISE
UPROSE
VARESE
VERITE
VIRILE
VIRTUE
WARBLE

•••RE•
ADORED
ADOREE
ADORER
ADORES
AIGRET
ALFRED
ANDREA
ANDREI
ANDRES
ANDREW
ANDREY
ANTRES
AUBREY
AUDREY
AZORES
BARRED
BARREL
BARREN
BARRES
BEARER
BIGRED
BLARED
BLARES
BOTREE
BURRED
CADRES
CARREL
CARREY
CHORES
CLARET
CORREL
CURRED
DAIREN
DARREN
DEARER
DECREE
DEGREE
DOURER
EAGRES
ENTREE
ENURED
ENURES
FAIRED
FAIRER
FEARED
FEARER
FERRER
FERRET
FIBRES
FLARED
FLARES
FLORES
FLORET
FURRED
GARRET
GEARED
GENRES
GLARED
GLARES
HAIRED
HATRED
HEARER
HEBREW
HEDREN
IMARET
INBRED
INGRES
INURED
INURES
JARRED
JAURES
JEERED
JEERER
JUAREZ
LABREA
LABRET
LAUREL
LAUREN
LEERED
LEERER
LEGREE
LEHRER
LITRES
LIVRES
MADRES
MARRED
MCGREW
METRES
MIRREN
MITRED
MITRES
MOIRES
MOORED
MURRES
MURREY
NEARED
NEARER
NITRES
OCHRES
OSPREY
PADRES
PAIRED
PARRED
PARREL
PEERED
PETREL
POORER
POURED
POURER
PUGREE
PURRED
PURRER
QUIRES
REARED
REARER
REDREW
REGRET
ROARED
ROARER
SABRES
SACRED
SAUREL
SAWRED
SCARED
SCARER
SCARES
SCORED
SCORER
SCORES
SEARED
SECRET
SEERED
SEVRES
SHARED
SHARER
SHARES
SHEREE
SHIRER
SHIRES
SHORED
SHORES
SIRREE
SNARED
SNARES
SNORED
SNORER
SNORES
SOARED
SOARER
SOARES
SOIREE
SORREL
SOURED
SOURER
SPARED
SPARER
SPARES
SPIREA
SPIRED
SPIRES
SPORES
STARED
STARER
STARES
STEREO
STERES
STORED
STORER
STORES
STOREY
SURREY
TARRED
TEARED
TENREC
TERRET
TIERED
TOURED
TOURER
TUAREG
TURRET
USURER
VEERED
WARRED
WARREN
WEARER
ZAGREB

•••R•E
ACCRUE
ADOREE
AGORAE
AHERNE
AMERCE
AVERSE
BARRIE
BEURRE
BIERCE
BOTREE
BOURKE
BOURNE
BOURSE
CARRIE
CHARGE
CHERIE
CLARKE
COARSE
COERCE
COURSE
COWRIE
DEARIE
DEARME
DECREE
DEGREE
DUARTE
ECARTE
EDERLE
EMERGE
ENTREE
ETERNE
FAERIE
FAEROE
FIERCE
FLORAE
GEORGE
GOURDE
GUERRE
HEARYE
HOARSE
HYDRAE
IMBRUE
LAURIE
LEGREE
LIERNE
MACRAE
MONROE
PEERCE
PETRIE
PIERCE
PIERRE
PUGREE
SCARCE
SCARNE
SCURVE
SEARLE
SHEREE
SIRREE
SOIREE
SOURCE
SPARGE
SPARSE
SPURGE
STARVE
STERNE
SWERVE
THORPE
TIERCE
UMBRAE
UNTRUE

••••RE
ABJURE
ADHERE
ADJURE
ADMIRE
AGLARE
ALEGRE
ALGORE
ALLURE
AMPERE
ARMURE
ASHORE
ASPIRE
ASSURE
ATTIRE
BEFORE
BEMIRE
BEURRE
BEWARE
CENTRE
CESARE
CHEVRE
CLAIRE
COHERE
CONTRE
CURARE
DAMORE
DEIDRE
DEJURE
DEMURE
DESIRE
EEYORE
ELMORE
EMIGRE
EMPIRE
ENCORE
ENDURE
ENSURE
ENTIRE
EUCHRE
EXPIRE
FIACRE
FIGURE
FURORE
FUTURE
GALORE
GUERRE
HARARE
HOMBRE
HONORE
IGNORE
IMMURE
IMPURE
INHERE
INJURE
INSURE
JOHORE
KHAFRE
LAHORE
LENORE
LIEVRE
LIGURE
LOUVRE
LUSTRE
MAITRE
MATURE
MEAGRE
NATURE
NOMORE
OEUVRE
ONFIRE
ORDURE
PARURE
PHEDRE
PIERRE
PROPRE
REHIRE
RETIRE
REVERE
REWIRE
SAFIRE
SARTRE
SATIRE
SECURE
SEMPRE
SEVERE
SOMBRE
SPHERE
SQUARE
SQUIRE
SUTURE
TAGORE
TENURE
THEYRE
TIMBRE
TULARE
TUYERE
UMPIRE
UNSURE
VENIRE
VOLARE

R•F•••
RAFAEL
RAFFIA
RAFFLE
RAFTED
RAFTER
REFACE
REFERS
REFFED
REFILE
REFILL
REFINE
REFITS
REFLEX
REFLUX
REFORM
REFUEL
REFUGE
REFUND
REFUSE
REFUTE
RIFEST
RIFFED
RIFFLE
RIFLED
RIFLER
RIFLES
RIFTED
RUFFED
RUFFLE
RUFFLY
RUFOUS

R••F••
RAFFIA
RAFFLE
RANFOR
REDFIN
REDFIR
REDFOX
REEFED
REEFER
REFFED
RIFFED
RIFFLE
ROOFED
ROOFER
RUEFUL
RUFFED
RUFFLE
RUFFLY

R•••F•
RAMIFY
RANOFF
RAREFY
RARIFY
RATIFY
REBUFF
RECIFE
RIPOFF
RUBIFY
RUNOFF

R••••F
RANOFF
REBUFF
RELIEF
RIPOFF
RUDOLF
RUNOFF

•RF•••
ERFURT

•R•F••
ARAFAT
ARMFUL
ARTFUL
CRAFTS
CRAFTY
CROFTS
DRAFTS
DRAFTY
DRIFTS
DRYFLY
GRAFTS
IREFUL
PREFAB
PREFER
PREFIX
PROFIT
TRIFID
TRIFLE
TRYFOR

•R••F•
BRIEFS
CRYOFF
DRYOFF
PROOFS

•R•••F
CRYOFF
DRYOFF

••RF••
BARFLY
CARFUL
CURFEW
DURFEY
EARFUL
JARFUL
PURFLE
SURFED
SURFER
TURFED
WERFEL

••R•F•
ADRIFT
BEREFT
CARAFE
FAROFF
PURIFY
RAREFY
RARIFY
SCRUFF
SERIFS
SHRIFT
STRAFE
STRIFE
TARIFF
THRIFT
VERIFY

••R••F
CERTIF
FAROFF
HEREOF
SCRUFF
SORTOF
TARIFF

•••RF•
DWARFS
SCARFS
SCURFY
SMURFS
WHARFS

•••R•F
HEAROF
SHARIF
SHERIF

••••RF
IMPERF

R•G•••
RAGBAG
RAGGED
RAGING
RAGLAN
RAGMAN
RAGMEN
RAGMOP
RAGOUT
RAGRUG
RAGTAG
RAGTOP
REGAIN
REGALE
REGARD
REGENT
REGGAE
REGGIE
REGIME
REGINA
REGION
REGIUS
REGLET
REGLUE
REGNAL
REGRET
RIGGED
RIGGER
RIGHTO
RIGHTS
RIGORS
RIGOUR
RIGSUP
ROGERS
ROGUES
RUGATE
RUGGED
RUGOSE

R••G••
RAGGED
RANGED
RANGER
RANGES
RANGUP
RAYGUN
REAGAN
REDGUM
REGGAE
REGGIE
REIGNS
RIDGED
RIDGES
RIGGED
RIGGER
RINGED
RINGER
RINGUP
ROTGUT
ROUGED
ROUGES
ROUGHS
RUGGED
RUNGUP
RUTGER

R•••G•
RAVAGE
RAWEGG
REBAGS
REFUGE
RENEGE
REPEGS
REPUGN
RESIGN
RETAGS

R••••G
RACING
RAGBAG
RAGING
RAGRUG
RAGTAG
RAKING
RARING
RATEDG
RATING
RAVING
RAWEGG
RAZING
REDDOG
REDTAG
REHANG
REHUNG
RESING
RICING
RIDING
RILING
RIMING
RISING
RIVING
ROBING
ROPING
ROVING
ROWING
RULING

•RG•••
ARGALI
ARGENT
ARGIVE
ARGOSY
ARGOTS
ARGUED
ARGUER
ARGUES
ARGYLE
ARGYLL
ERGATE
ERGOTS
ORGANA
ORGANS
ORGATE
ORGEAT
ORGIES
URGENT
URGERS
URGING

•R•G••
ARAGON
ARIGHT
ARTGUM
BRIGGS
BRIGHT
BRIGID
BROGAN
BROGUE
BRUGES
CRAGGY
DRAGEE
DRAGGY
DRAGIN
DRAGON
DROGUE
FRIGHT
FRIGID
FROGGY
FRUGAL
GREGOR
GRIGRI
GROGGY
KRUGER
OREGON
ORIGEN
ORIGIN
PRAGUE
TRAGIC
TRIGLY
TRIGON
TROGON
WRIGHT

•R••G•
ARMAGH
BRIDGE
BRIGGS
BRINGS
CRAGGY
CRINGE
DRAGGY
DREDGE
DRINGS
DRUDGE
ERYNGO
FRIDGE
FRINGE
FRINGY
FROGGY
GRANGE
GREIGE
GRINGO
GROGGY
GRUDGE
GRUNGE
GRUNGY
KRESGE
ORANGE
ORANGS
ORINGS
ORTEGA
PRONGS
TRIAGE
TROUGH
TRUDGE
WRINGS
WRONGS

•R•••G
ARCING
ARMING
CRYING
DRYING
ERRING
ERVING
FRYING
IRKING
IRVING
ORBING
PROLOG
PRYING
TRUING
TRYING
URGING

••RG••
AIRGUN
BARGED
BARGES
BERGEN
BIRGIT
BORGIA
BURGAS
BURGEE
BURGER
BURGHS
BURGLE
BURGOO
BURGOS
CARGOS
CORGIS
DIRGES
FERGIE
FERGUS
FORGED
FORGER
FORGES
FORGET
FORGOT
GARGLE
GORGED
GORGES
GORGET
GORGON
GURGLE
JARGON
KURGAN
LARGER
LARGOS
MARGAY
MARGIE
MARGIN
MARGOT
MERGED
MERGER
MERGES
MORGAN
MORGEN
NORGAY
PARGET
PURGED
PURGES
SARGES
SARGON
SARGOS
SERGEI
SERGES
SERGIO
SURGED
SURGES
TARGES
TARGET
TURGID
TURGOR
VERGED
VERGER
VERGES
VIRGIL
VIRGIN
WARGOD

••R•G•
AURIGA
BAREGE
BORAGE
DIRIGO
ENRAGE
FORAGE
FOREGO
GARAGE
MIRAGE
SCRAGS
SHRUGS
SPRAGS
SPRIGS
UNRIGS
VIRAGO

••R••G
AIRBAG
AIRING
BARING
BARONG
BERING
BORING
CARING
CORING
CURING
DARING
DURING
EARING
EARWIG
ERRING
FARING
FIRING
GORING
HARING
HERZOG
HIRING
LURING
MIRING
OARING
PARANG
PARING
PORING
RARING
SARONG
SIRING
SPRANG
SPRING
SPRUNG
STRING
STRONG
STRUNG
TARING
THRONG
TIRING
TURING
WARING
WIRING

•••RG•
ATERGO
CHARGE
CLERGY
EMERGE
ENERGY
GEORGE
SPARGE
SPURGE

•••R•G
CATRIG
GEHRIG
OILRIG
PETROG
RAGRUG
TUAREG

••••RG
ALBORG
COBURG
CYBORG
EDBERG
EKBERG
SEBERG
VYBORG

RH••••
RHEBOK
RHESUS
RHETOR
RHEUMS
RHEUMY
RHINAL
RHINOS
RHODES
RHOMBI
RHOMBS
RHONDA
RHUMBA
RHUMBS
RHYMED
RHYMER
RHYMES
RHYTHM
RHYTON

R•H•••
RAHRAH
REHANG
REHASH
REHEAL
REHEAR
REHEAT
REHEEL
REHELD
REHEMS
REHIRE
REHOOK
REHUNG
ROHMER

R••H••
RACHEL
RACHIS
RASHAD
RASHER
RASHES
RASHID
RASHLY
RATHER
REDHAT
REDHOT
RESHIP
RESHOD
RESHOE
RESHOT
RICHEN
RICHER
RICHES
RICHIE
RICHLY
RIGHTO
RIGHTS
ROCHET
RODHAM
ROTHKO
RUCHES
RUSHED
RUSHEE
RUSHES

R•••H•
RAJAHS
RANCHO
REECHO
RHYTHM
ROUGHS

R••••H
RADISH
RAHRAH
RAKISH
RAVISH
REHASH
RELISH
REWASH
RIYADH
RUPIAH

•RH•••
DRHOOK
ERHARD
MRHYDE

•R•H••
ARCHED
ARCHER
ARCHES
ARCHIE
ARCHLY
ARCHON
ARNHEM
ARTHRO
ARTHUR
BRAHMA
BRAHMS
GRAHAM
ORCHID
ORCHIL
ORPHAN
ORPHIC
URCHIN

•R••H•
ARETHA
ARIGHT
BRASHY
BRECHT
BRIGHT
BROTHS
BRUSHY
CRECHE
FRIGHT
FROTHS
FROTHY
GRAPHS
TRASHY
TRICHO
TRISHA
TROCHE
TROPHY
TROTHS
TRUTHS
WRATHS
WRIGHT
WRITHE

•R•••H
ARMAGH
BRANCH
BREACH
BREATH
BREECH
BROACH
BROOCH
BRUNCH
CROUCH
CRUNCH
CRUTCH
DRENCH
FRENCH
GRINCH
GROUCH
GROWTH
IRTYSH
ORBACH

ORNITH
PREACH
TRENCH
TROUGH
WRAITH
WREATH
WRENCH
WRETCH

••RH••
BARHOP
CARHOP
DIRHAM
DURHAM
WARHOL

••R•H•
BERTHA
BERTHS
BIRTHS
BURGHS
EARTHA
EARTHY
FIRTHS
GARTHS
GIRTHS
GURKHA
MARCHE
MARSHA
MARSHY
MARTHA
MORPHO
MORPHS
MURPHY
MYRRHS
PERCHA
SURAHS
TORAHS
WORTHS
WORTHY

••R••H
AFRESH
BARUCH
BORSCH
CERIPH
ENRICH
FARRAH
GARETH
GARISH
HIRSCH
HURRAH
INRUSH
JARRAH
KIRSCH
MARIAH
ONRUSH
PARAPH
PARIAH
PARISH
PERISH
PURDAH
QURUSH
SERAPH
SIRRAH
TERAPH
THRASH
THRESH
THRUSH
UPRUSH
WARMTH
ZEROTH
ZURICH

•••RH•
MYRRHS

•••R•H
CHURCH
DEARTH
EPARCH
EXARCH
FARRAH
FOURTH
HEARTH
HOORAH
HURRAH
INARCH
JARRAH
RAHRAH
SCORCH
SEARCH
SIRRAH
SMERSH
SMIRCH
STARCH
STORCH
SWARTH

RI••••
RIALTO
RIATAS
RIBALD
RIBAND
RIBBED
RIBBON
RIBEYE
RIBOSE
RICERS
RICHEN
RICHER
RICHES
RICHIE
RICHLY
RICING
RICKED
RICKEY
RIDDED
RIDDEN
RIDDLE
RIDENT
RIDERS
RIDGED
RIDGES
RIDING
RIDLEY
RIFEST
RIFFED
RIFFLE
RIFLED
RIFLER
RIFLES
RIFTED
RIGGED
RIGGER
RIGHTO
RIGHTS
RIGORS
RIGOUR
RIGSUP
RILING
RILLES
RILLET
RIMING
RIMINI
RIMMED
RIMOSE
RIMPLE
RIMSKY
RINGED
RINGER
RINGUP
RINSED
RINSES
RIOJAS
RIOTED
RIOTER
RIPELY
RIPENS
RIPEST
RIPKEN
RIPLEY
RIPOFF
RIPPED
RIPPER
RIPPLE
RIPPLY
RIPRAP
RIPSAW
RIPSUP
RISERS
RISING
RISKED
RISKER
RISQUE
RITARD
RITTER
RITUAL
RIVALS
RIVERA
RIVERS
RIVETS
RIVING
RIYADH
RIYALS

R•I•••
RAIDED
RAIDER
RAILAT
RAILED
RAILER
RAINED
RAINER
RAINES
RAIPUR
RAISED
RAISER
RAISES
RAISIN
REIGNS
REINED
REINER
REININ
REINKS
RHINAL
RHINOS
ROILED
RUINED
RUINER

R••I••
RABIES
RACIAL
RACIER
RACILY
RACINE
RACING
RADIAL
RADIAN
RADIOS
RADISH
RADIUM
RADIUS
RAGING
RAKING
RAKISH
RAMIES
RAMIFY
RANIDS
RAPIDS
RAPIER
RAPINE
RAPINI
RARIFY
RARING
RARITY
RATIFY
RATINE
RATING
RATION
RATIOS
RATITE
RAVINE
RAVING
RAVISH
RAZING
REAIRS
REBIDS
REBIND
RECIFE
RECIPE
RECITE
REDIAL
REDINK
REFILE
REFILL
REFINE
REFITS
REGIME
REGINA
REGION
REGIUS
REHIRE
RELICS
RELICT
RELIED
RELIEF
RELIES
RELINE
RELISH
RELIST
RELIVE
REMICK
REMIND
REMISE
REMISS
REMITS
REOILS
REPINE
RESIDE
RESIGN
RESILE
RESING
RESINS
RESIST
RETIAL
RETIED
RETIES
RETILE
RETIME
RETINA
RETIRE
REVIEW
REVILE
REVISE
REVIVE
REWIND
REWINS
REWIRE
RICING
RIDING
RILING
RIMING
RIMINI
RISING
RIVING
ROBING
ROBINS
ROPIER
ROPING
ROSIER
ROSILY
ROSINS
ROSINY
ROSITA
ROTINI
ROVING
ROWING
RUBIED
RUBIES
RUBIFY
RULING
RUMINA
RUNINS
RUPIAH
RUTILE

R•••I•
RABBIS
RABBIT
RACHIS
RAFFIA
RAISIN
RAKEIN
RANCID
RANKIN
RASHID
RATLIN
READIN
REALIA
REBOIL
RECOIL
REDFIN
REDFIR
REEDIT
REELIN
REGAIN
REGGIE
REININ
REJOIN
RELAID
REMAIL
REMAIN
RENAIL
RENNIE
RENNIN
RENOIR
REPAID
REPAIR
RESHIP
RESNIK
RETAIL
RETAIN
RETRIM
REVOIR
RICHIE
ROADIE
ROBBIE
ROLLIE
ROLLIN
ROMAIC
RONNIE
ROOKIE
ROOMIE
ROPEIN
RUBRIC
RUBSIN
RUNCIE
RUNSIN
RUSKIN
RUSSIA
RUSTIC

R••••I
RAPINI
RHOMBI
RIMINI
ROMAJI
ROTINI

•RI•••
ARIDLY
ARIGHT
ARIOSE
ARIOSO
ARISEN
ARISES
ARISTA
ARISTO
BRIAND
BRIANS
BRIARD
BRIARS
BRIBED
BRIBES
BRICKS
BRICKY
BRIDAL
BRIDES
BRIDGE
BRIDLE
BRIEFS
BRIENZ
BRIERS
BRIERY
BRIGGS
BRIGHT
BRIGID
BRILLO
BRILLS
BRINED
BRINES
BRINGS
BRINKS
BRITON
CRICKS
CRIERS
CRIMEA
CRIMES
CRIMPS
CRINGE
CRIPES
CRISCO
CRISES
CRISIS
CRISPS
CRISPY
CRITIC
DRIERS
DRIEST
DRIFTS
DRILLS
DRINGS
DRINKS
DRIPPY
DRIVEL
DRIVEN
DRIVER
DRIVES
ERINYS
FRIARS
FRIARY
FRIDAY
FRIDGE
FRIEND
FRIEZE
FRIGHT
FRIGID
FRIJOL
FRILLS
FRILLY
FRINGE
FRINGY
FRISCO
FRISEE
FRISES
FRISKS
FRISKY
FRITOS
FRIZZY
GRIEVE
GRIGRI
GRILLE
GRILLS
GRILSE
GRIMED
GRIMES
GRIMKE
GRIMLY
GRINCH
GRINDS
GRINGO
GRIPED
GRIPER
GRIPES
GRIPPE
GRISLY
GRISON
GRISTS
GRITTY
GRIVET
IRIDES
IRIDIC
IRISES
IRISIN
ORIANA
ORIBIS
ORIELS
ORIENT
ORIGEN
ORIGIN
ORINGS
ORIOLE
ORISON
ORISSA
PRICED
PRICER
PRICES
PRICEY
PRICKS
PRIDED
PRIDES
PRIERS
PRIEST
PRIMAL
PRIMED
PRIMER
PRIMES
PRIMLY
PRIMOS
PRIMPS
PRIMUM
PRIMUS
PRINCE
PRINKS
PRINTS
PRIONS
PRIORI
PRIORS
PRIORY
PRIPET
PRISMS
PRISON
PRISSY
PRIVET
PRIZED
PRIZES
TRIADS
TRIAGE
TRIALS
TRIBAL
TRIBES
TRICED
TRICES
TRICHO
TRICIA
TRICKS
TRICKY
TRICOT
TRIERS
TRIFID
TRIFLE
TRIGLY
TRIGON
TRIKES
TRILBY
TRILLS
TRIMLY
TRINAL
TRINES
TRIODE
TRIPLE
TRIPLY
TRIPOD
TRIPOS
TRIPUP
TRISHA
TRISTE
TRITER
TRITON
TRIUNE
TRIVET
TRIVIA
TRIXIE
URIALS
WRIEST
WRIGHT
WRINGS
WRISTS
WRITER
WRITES
WRITHE

•R•I••
ARCING
ARGIVE
ARLISS
ARMIES
ARMING
ARNICA
AROIDS
ARRIBA
ARRIVE
ARTIER
ARTIST
BRAIDS
BRAILS
BRAINS
BRAINY
BRAISE
BROILS
BRUINS
BRUISE
BRUITS
CRUISE
CRYING
DRAILS
DRAINS
DROIDS
DROITS
DRUIDS
DRYICE
DRYING
DRYINK
ERBIUM
ERMINE
EROICA
ERRING
ERVING
FRAISE
FRUITS
FRUITY
FRYING
GRAILS
GRAINS
GRAINY
GREIGE
GROINS
IRKING
IRVINE
IRVING
KRAITS
ORBING
ORBITS
OREIDA
ORGIES
ORNITH
OROIDE
ORPINE
ORSINO
PRAISE
PRYING
TRAILS
TRAINS
TRAITS
TROIKA
TRUING
TRUISM
TRYING
URGING
URSIDS
URSINE
WRAITH

•R••I•
ARABIA
ARABIC
ARALIA
ARAMIS
ARCHIE
ARCTIC
ARMPIT
ARTOIS
BRAZIL
BRIGID
BRODIE
CRANIA
CRANIO
CREDIT
CRETIN
CRISIS
CRITIC
CRONIN
DRAGIN
DRAWIN
DREWIN
DROPIN
DROPIT
EROTIC
FRIGID
FROLIC
GRACIE
GRADIN
GRATIA
GRATIN
GRATIS
GRAVID
GRODIN
IRANIS
IRAQIS
IRENIC
IRIDIC
IRISIN
IRONIC
ORCHID
ORCHIL
ORDAIN
ORIBIS
ORIGIN
ORPHIC
PRAXIS
PRECIS
PREFIX
PRELIM
PREMIE
PREVIN
PROFIT
PROLIX
PROSIT
TRAGIC
TRAVIS
TREDIA
TREPID
TRICIA
TRIFID
TRIVIA
TRIXIE
TROPIC
URACIL
URALIC
URANIA
URANIC
URCHIN

•R•••I
ARGALI
ARMANI
BRAZZI
BRUNEI
DROMOI
ERNANI
FRUTTI
GRIGRI
PRIORI
PROTEI

••RI••
ADRIAN
ADRIEN
ADRIFT
AERIAL
AERIES
AFRICA
AIRIER
AIRILY
AIRING
AORIST
ARRIBA
ARRIVE
ATRIAL
ATRISK
ATRIUM
AURIGA
BARING
BARITE
BARIUM
BERING
BORIDE
BORING
BURIED
BURIES
BURINS
CARIBE
CARIBS
CARIES
CARINA
CARING
CERIPH
CERISE
CERIUM
CHRISM
CORING
CORIUM
CURIAE
CURIAL
CURING
CURIOS
CURIUM
DARIEN
DARING
DARIUS
DERIDE
DERIVE
DIRIGO
DORIAN
DORIES
DURIAN
DURING
EARING
EERIER
EERILY
ENRICH
ENRICO
ERRING
EYRIES
FARINA
FARING
FIRING
FORINT
FURIES
GARISH
GORIER
GORING
HARING
HERIOT
HIRING
JURIES
JURIST
KARIBA
KURILE
LARIAT
LERIDA
LORICA
LORIES
LURING
LYRICS
LYRIST
MARIAH
MARIAN
MARIEL
MARIKO
MARILU
MARINA
MARINE
MARINO
MARION
MARISA
MARIST
MARIUS
MERIDA
MERINO
MERITS
MIRIAM
MIRING
MORION
MORITA
MORITZ
MURIEL
MURINE
MYRIAD
NARIAL
NORIAS
OARING
OBRIAN
OBRIEN
PARIAH
PARING
PARISH
PARITY
PERILS
PERIOD
PERISH
PORING
PURIFY
PURINA
PURINE
PURISM
PURIST
PURITY
PYRITE
RARIFY
RARING
RARITY
SCRIBE
SCRIMP
SCRIMS
SCRIPS
SCRIPT
SERIAL
SERIES
SERIFS
SERINE
SERINS
SHRIEK
SHRIFT
SHRIKE
SHRILL
SHRIMP
SHRINE
SHRINK
SHRIVE
SIRICA
SIRING
SIRIUS
SPRIER
SPRIGS
SPRING
SPRINT
SPRITE
SPRITS
SPRITZ
STRIAE
STRICK
STRICT
STRIDE
STRIFE
STRIKE
STRING
STRIPE
STRIPS
STRIVE
SURIMI
SYRIAN
SYRINX
TARIFF
TARING
THRICE
THRIFT
THRILL
THRIPS
THRIVE
TIRING
TORIES
TORINO
TURING
TYRIAN
UGRIAN
UNRIGS
UNRIPE
UPRISE
VARIED
VARIES
VERIFY
VERILY
VERISM
VERITE
VERITY
VIRILE
WARIER
WARILY
WARING
WIRING
YORICK
ZORILS
ZURICH

••R•I•
ADROIT
AFRAID
AORTIC
BARBIE
BARDIC
BARKIN
BARRIE
BARRIO
BARRIS
BERLIN
BERNIE
BERTIE
BIRDIE
BIRGIT
BORGIA
CARDIN
CARDIO
CARRIE
CERTIF
CERVID
CORBIN
CORGIS
CURTIN
CURTIS
CURTIZ
DARNIT
DARWIN
DERAIL
DERMIS
DERRIS
DORRIT
DURBIN
EARWIG
FERGIE
FERRIC
FERRIS
FERVID
FIRKIN
FORBID
FORMIC
GARCIA
GARLIC
GERBIL
GERTIE
GORDIE
HARBIN
HARRIS
HERBIE
HEREIN
HERMIT
HEROIC
HORRID
JERKIN
KARMIC
KERMIS
KERMIT
MARCIA
MARCIE
MARGIE
MARGIN
MARLIN
MARNIE
MARTIN
MARVIN
MERLIN
MORBID
MORRIS
MURCIA
NARNIA
NARVIK
NEREID
NEREIS
NORDIC
NORRIS
PARNIS
PARRIS
PARVIS
PERMIT
PERSIA
PIRRIP
PORTIA
PURLIN
SARDIS
SERAIS
SERBIA
SERGIO
SERKIN
SORBIC
SORDID
SORTIE
SPRAIN
STRAIN
STRAIT
TARPIT
TOROID
TORPID
TORRID
TURBID
TURBIT
TURGID
TURKIC
TURNIN
TURNIP
VERDIN
VERMIN
VIRGIL
VIRGIN
WORKIN
ZEROIN

••R••I
BORZOI
CARONI
DORATI
DOREMI
KERNOI
MORONI
NEROLI
SERGEI
STRATI
SURIMI

•••RI•
ACARID
AGARIC
ALARIC
ALDRIN
ANTRIM
ASTRID
ATTRIT
AZORIN
BARRIE
BARRIO
BARRIS
CAPRIS
CARRIE
CATRIG
CEDRIC
CHERIE
CITRIC
CLERIC
CLORIS
COURIC
COWRIE
CUPRIC
CYMRIC
DEARIE
DEBRIS
DELRIO
DERRIS
DORRIT
EGERIA
ESPRIT
FABRIC
FAERIE
FERRIC
FERRIS
FIBRIL
FIBRIN
FLORID
FLORIN
GEHRIG
GLORIA
HARRIS
HENRIK
HORRID
HOURIS
HUBRIS
HYBRID
IATRIC
IBERIA
ICARIA

INDRIS
INGRID
ISTRIA
KAURIS
KUKRIS
LAURIE
LIBRIS
MADRID
MAORIS
MATRIX
METRIC
MIDRIB
MORRIS
NITRIC
NORRIS
NUTRIA
OILRIG
OSIRIS
PARRIS
PEERIN
PEORIA
PETRIE
PIRRIP
POURIN
PUTRID
RETRIM
RUBRIC
SCORIA
SHARIA
SHARIF
SHERIF
SPIRIT
STIRIN
STYRIA
TABRIZ
TETRIS
TIGRIS
TORRID
TUGRIK
UMBRIA
USERID
VITRIC

•••R•I
ANDREI
CIARDI
ITURBI
OCTROI
THYRSI

••••RI
ASKARI
BIHARI
CENTRI
DENDRI
DMITRI
EPHORI
GRIGRI
HATARI
HEGARI
HUMERI
JAVARI
MIDORI
PAHARI
PAPYRI
PRIORI
QATARI
QUADRI
SAFARI
SATORI
SOUARI
TISHRI
UAKARI

R•J•••
RAJAHS
RAJPUT
REJECT
REJOIN

R••J••
RAMJET
RIOJAS

R•••J•
ROMAJI

•RJ•••
ARJUNA

•R•J••
FRIJOL
PRAJNA
TRAJAN
TROJAN

••R•J•
BAROJA

•••R•J
SWARAJ

R•K•••
RAKEIN
RAKERS
RAKEUP
RAKING
RAKISH
REKEYS

R••K••
RACKED
RACKET
RACKUP
RANKED
RANKER
RANKIN
RANKLE
RANKLY
RECKON
REEKED
RICKED
RICKEY
RIPKEN
RISKED
RISKER
ROCKED
ROCKER
ROCKET
ROCKNE
ROCKYV
ROOKED
ROOKIE
RUCKED
RUCKUS
RUSKIN
RYOKAN
RYUKYU

R•••K•
REBUKE
REINKS
REMAKE
RETAKE
REVOKE
RIMSKY
ROTHKO

R••••K
RECORK
REDINK
REDOAK
REEBOK
REHOOK
RELOCK
REMARK
REMICK
RESNIK
RETOOK
REWORK
RHEBOK

•RK•••
IRKING
ORKNEY

•R•K••
BRAKED
BRAKES
BROKAW
BROKEN
BROKER
CRAKES
DRAKES
KRAKEN
KRAKOW
TRIKES

•R••K•
BREAKS
BRICKS
BRICKY
BRINKS
BROOKE
BROOKS
CRACKS
CRANKS
CRANKY
CREAKS
CREAKY
CREEKS
CRICKS
CROAKS
CROAKY
CROCKS
CROOKS
DRINKS
FRANKS
FREAKS
FREAKY
FRISKS
FRISKY
FROCKS
GREEKS
GRIMKE
PRANKS
PRICKS
PRINKS
TRACKS
TRICKS
TRICKY
TROIKA
TRUCKS
TRUNKS
WRACKS
WREAKS
WRECKS

•R•••K
ARAWAK
ARRACK
DRABEK
DRHOOK
DRYINK
FRANCK
TREBEK
URALSK

••RK••
BARKED
BARKER
BARKIN
CORKED
CORKER
DARKEN
DARKER
DARKLE
DARKLY
FIRKIN
FORKED
FORKER
GURKHA
HARKED
HARKEN
HARKER
JERKED
JERKIN
LARKED
LURKED
MARKED
MARKER
MARKET
MARKKA
MARKUP
MERKEL
PARKAS
PARKAY
PARKED
PARKER
PERKED
PERKUP
PORKER
SERKIN
TERKEL
TURKEY
TURKIC
WORKED
WORKER
WORKIN
WORKON
WORKUP
YERKES
YORKER

••R•K•
EUREKA
MARIKO
MARKKA
PERUKE
SHRIKE
STRAKE
STRIKE
STROKE
YUROKS

••R••K
ARRACK
ATRISK
BARTOK
BUROAK
FAROUK
KARNAK
MARDUK
NARVIK
SCREAK
SHRANK
SHRIEK
SHRINK
SHRUNK
STREAK
STRICK
STRUCK
YORICK

•••RK•
BOURKE
CLARKE
CLERKS
OZARKS
QUARKS
QUIRKS
QUIRKY
SHARKS
SHIRKS
SMIRKS
SMIRKY
SPARKS
SPARKY
STORKS

•••R•K
AMTRAK
ANORAK
DVORAK
HENRIK
TOBRUK
TUGRIK

••••RK
ATWORK
DEBARK
EMBARK
NEWARK
RECORK
REMARK
REWORK
STMARK
UNCORK

R•L•••
RELACE
RELAID
RELATE
RELAYS
RELENT
RELETS
RELICS
RELICT
RELIED
RELIEF
RELIES
RELINE
RELISH
RELIST
RELIVE
RELOAD
RELOCK
RELUCT
RELUME
RILING
RILLES
RILLET
ROLAND
ROLEOS
ROLLED
ROLLER
ROLLIE
ROLLIN
ROLLON
ROLLUP
RULEON
RULERS
RULING

R••L••
RAGLAN
RAILAT
RAILED
RAILER
RATLIN
REALER
REALES
REALIA
REALLY
REALMS
REALTY
REELED
REELIN
REFLEX
REFLUX
REGLET
REGLUE
REPLAN
REPLAY
REPLOW
REVLON
RIALTO
RIDLEY
RIFLED
RIFLER
RIFLES
RILLES
RILLET
RIPLEY
ROBLES
ROILED
ROLLED
ROLLER
ROLLIE
ROLLIN
ROLLON
ROLLUP
RUBLES
RUNLET
RVALUE

R•••L•
RABBLE
RACILY
RADDLE
RADULA
RAFFLE
RAMBLA
RAMBLE
RANKLE
RANKLY
RAPTLY
RARELY
RASHLY
RASSLE
RATELS
RATTLE
RATTLY
RAVELS
RAZZLE
REALLY
REBELS
REBOLT
RECALL
REFILE
REFILL
REGALE
REHELD
REMELT
REOILS
REPELS
REPOLL
RESALE
RESALT
RESELL
RESILE
RESOLD
RESOLE
RESULT
RETELL
RETILE
RETOLD
REVELS
REVILE
REVOLT
REWELD
RIBALD
RICHLY
RIDDLE
RIFFLE
RIMPLE
RIPELY
RIPPLE
RIPPLY
RIVALS
RIYALS
ROBALO
ROMOLA
RONALD
RONELY
ROSILY
ROWELS
ROYALE
ROYALS
RUBBLE
RUBBLY
RUDDLE
RUDELY
RUDOLF
RUFFLE
RUFFLY
RUMBLE
RUMBLY
RUMPLE
RUMPLY
RUNDLE
RUSTLE
RUTILE
RYDELL

R••••L
RACHEL
RACIAL
RADIAL
RAFAEL
RAPPEL
RAQUEL
RASCAL
REBOIL
RECALL
RECOIL
REDEAL
REDIAL
REFILL
REFUEL
REGNAL
REHEAL
REHEEL
REMAIL
RENAIL
RENTAL
REPEAL
REPOLL
RESEAL
RESELL
RETAIL
RETELL
RETIAL
RETOOL
RETRAL
REVEAL
RHINAL
RITUAL
ROMMEL
RONDEL
RUEFUL
RUNNEL
RUPAUL
RYDELL

•RL•••
ARLENE
ARLISS
IRLENE
ORLOPS

•R•L••
ARALIA
ARALLU
ARMLET
BRILLO
BRILLS
BROLLY
BRULES
DRILLS
DROLLS
DROLLY
FRILLS
FRILLY
FROLIC
GRILLE
GRILLS
GRILSE
MRBLUE
ORALES
ORALLY
ORELSE
ORTLES
PRELAW
PRELIM
PROLES
PROLIX
PROLOG
TRALEE
TRILBY
TRILLS
TROLLS
URALIC
URALSK

•R••L•
ARABLE
ARALLU
ARBELA
ARCHLY
AREOLA
ARGALI
ARGYLE
ARGYLL
ARIDLY
ARNOLD
ARTELS
BRAILS
BRAWLS
BRIDLE
BRILLO
BRILLS
BROILS
BROLLY
CRADLE
CRAWLS
CRAWLY
CREELS
CREOLE
DRABLY
DRAILS
DRAWLS
DRILLS
DROLLS
DROLLY
DROOLS
DRYFLY
ERROLL
FREELY
FRILLS
FRILLY
GRABLE
GRAILS
GRILLE
GRILLS
GRIMLY
GRISLY
GROWLS
GROWLY
GRUELS
KRAALS
ORACLE
ORALLY
ORIELS
ORIOLE
ORMOLU
ORWELL
PRIMLY
PROWLS
TRAILS
TRAWLS
TREBLE
TREBLY
TRIALS
TRIFLE
TRIGLY
TRILLS
TRIMLY
TRIPLE
TRIPLY
TROLLS
URIALS
URSULA

•R•••L
ARGYLL
ARMFUL
ARTFUL
BRAZIL
BRIDAL
BRUMAL
BRUTAL
CRENEL
CRESOL
CREWEL
CRURAL
DREXEL
DRIVEL
ERROLL
FRIJOL
FRUGAL
GRAVEL
GRETEL
GROVEL
IREFUL
IRREAL
MRCOOL
ORCHIL
ORDEAL
ORWELL
PRIMAL
PROPEL
TRAVEL
TRIBAL
TRINAL
TROWEL
URACIL

••RL••
BARLEY
BERLIN
BIRLED
BURLAP
BURLED
BURLEY
CARLOS
CARLOT
CURLED
CURLER
CURLEW
CURLUP
EARLAP
FARLEY
FARLOW
FURLED
GARLIC
GURLEY
HARLAN
HARLEM
HARLEY
HARLOW
HURLED
HURLER
HURLEY
MARLED
MARLEE
MARLEY
MARLIN
MARLON
MERLIN
MERLON
MERLOT
MORLEY
PARLAY
PARLEY
PARLOR
PURLED
PURLIN
VARLET
WORLDS

••R•L•
AIRILY
BARELY
BARFLY
BAROLO
BURBLE
BURBLY
BURGLE
CAROLE
CAROLS
CIRCLE
CORALS
CURDLE
CURTLY
CURULE
DARKLE
DARKLY
EERILY
ENROLL
ERROLL
FERULE
FIRMLY
GARBLE
GARGLE
GERALD
GIRDLE
GORALS
GURGLE
HARDLY
HAROLD
HERALD
HURDLE
HURTLE
KERALA
KIRTLE
KURALT
KURILE
LORDLY
MARBLE
MARBLY
MARILU
MARPLE
MERELY
MORALE
MORALS
MORELS
MURALS
MYRTLE
NEROLI
PAROLE
PARTLY
PARULA
PERILS
PERTLY
PORTLY
PURELY
PURFLE
PURPLE
RARELY
SCROLL
SHRILL
SORELY
SPRYLY
STROLL
SURELY
TARTLY
THRALE
THRALL
THRILL
TURTLE
UNROLL
UNRULY
VERILY
VIRILE
WARBLE
WARILY
WARMLY
YARELY
ZORILS

••R••L
AERIAL
AORTAL
ATRIAL
BARBEL
BARREL
BOREAL
BURSAL
CARFUL
CARMEL
CARNAL
CARPAL
CARPEL
CARREL
CARROL
CARTEL
CEREAL
CORBEL
CORNEL
CORRAL
CORREL
CURIAL
DARNEL
DARRYL
DERAIL
DERMAL
DIRNDL
DORSAL
EARFUL
ENROLL
ERROLL
FORMAL
GERBIL
HERBAL
HORMEL
IRREAL
ISRAEL
JARFUL
KERNEL
LARVAL
LOREAL
MARCEL
MARIEL
MARTEL
MARVEL
MERKEL
MORSEL
MORTAL
MURIEL
MYRDAL
NARIAL
NARWAL
NORMAL
PARCEL
PARREL
PORTAL
SCRAWL
SCROLL
SERIAL
SERVAL
SHRILL
SORREL
SPRAWL
STROLL
TARSAL
TERCEL
TERKEL
THRALL
THRILL
UNREAL
UNREEL
UNROLL
VERBAL
VERNAL
VIRGIL
WARHOL
WERFEL

•••RL•
BGIRLS
CHARLY
CHURLS
DEARLY
DOURLY
EBERLY
EDERLE
EVERLY
FAIRLY
GNARLS
GNARLY
HOURLY
KNURLS
KNURLY
NEARLY
OVERLY
PEARLS
PEARLY
POORLY
SEARLE
SKIRLS
SNARLS
SNARLY
SOURLY
SWIRLS
SWIRLY
TWIRLS
WHIRLS
WHIRLY
WHORLS
YEARLY

•••R•L
ABORAL
AMORAL
ASTRAL
BARREL
CARREL
CARROL
CHERYL
CHORAL
CORRAL
CORREL
CRURAL
DARRYL
FIBRIL
FLORAL
LAUREL
MITRAL
NEURAL
NEUROL
PARREL
PATROL
PETREL
PETROL
PLURAL
RETRAL
SACRAL
SAUREL
SORREL
SPIRAL
STEROL
UMBRAL

••••RL
ASWIRL
AWHIRL
MYGIRL
SCHORL
UNCURL
UNFURL

R•M•••
RAMADA
RAMATE
RAMBLA
RAMBLE
RAMEAU
RAMIES
RAMIFY
RAMJET
RAMMED
RAMONA
RAMONE
RAMOSE
RAMOUS
RAMPED
RAMROD
RAMSAY
RAMSES
RAMSEY
RAMSON
REMADE
REMAIL
REMAIN
REMAKE
REMAND
REMANS
REMAPS
REMARK
REMEDY
REMELT
REMEND
REMICK
REMIND
REMISE
REMISS
REMITS
REMORA
REMOTE
REMOVE
REMOWN
REMOWS
REMUDA
RIMING
RIMINI
RIMMED
RIMOSE
RIMPLE
RIMSKY
ROMAIC
ROMAJI
ROMANO
ROMANS
ROMANY
ROMEOS
ROMERO
ROMMEL
ROMNEY
ROMOLA
ROMPED
ROMPER
RUMBAS
RUMBLE
RUMBLY
RUMENS
RUMINA
RUMMER
RUMORS
RUMOUR
RUMPLE
RUMPLY
RUMPUS

R••M••
RAGMAN
RAGMEN
RAGMOP
RAMMED
REAMED
REAMER
RHOMBI
RHOMBS
RHUMBA
RHUMBS
RHYMED
RHYMER
RHYMES
RIMMED
ROAMED
ROAMER
ROHMER
ROMMEL
ROOMED
ROOMER
ROOMIE
RUDMAN
RUMMER

R•••M•
RACEME
RADOME
REALMS
REARMS
REGIME
REHEMS
RELUME
RENAME
RESUME
RETIME
REVAMP
RHEUMS
RHEUMY
RUNDMC

R••••M
RADIUM
RANDOM
RANSOM
REDEEM
REDGUM
REFORM
RETRIM
REWARM
RHYTHM
RODHAM

•RM•••
ARMADA
ARMAGH
ARMAND
ARMANI
ARMETS
ARMFUL
ARMIES
ARMING
ARMLET
ARMORS
ARMORY
ARMOUR
ARMPIT
ARMURE
ERMINE
MRMOTO
ORMOLU
ORMOND

•R•M••
ARAMIS
AROMAS
BREMEN
BRUMAL
BRUMES
CRAMBO
CRAMPS
CREMES
CRIMEA
CRIMES
CRIMPS
CRUMBS

CRUMBY
CRUMMY
DRAMAS
DROMOI
DROMOS
DRUMUP
FRAMED
FRAMES
FRUMPS
FRUMPY
GRAMAS
GRAMME
GRAMMY
GRAMPS
GRIMED
GRIMES
GRIMKE
GRIMLY
GRUMPS
GRUMPY
KRAMER
PREMED
PREMIE
PRIMAL
PRIMED
PRIMER
PRIMES
PRIMLY
PRIMOS
PRIMPS
PRIMUM
PRIMUS
PROMOS
PROMPT
TRAMPS
TREMOR
TRIMLY
TROMPE
TROMPS
TRUMAN
TRUMPS

•R••M•
BRAHMA
BRAHMS
BREAMS
BROOMS
CREAMS
CREAMY
CRUMMY
DREAMS
DREAMT
DREAMY
GRAMME
GRAMMY
GROOMS
PREAMP
PRISMS
PROAMS
PROEMS
TRAUMA
VROOMS

•R•••M
ARNHEM
ARTGUM
ERBIUM
FRENUM
GRAHAM
PRELIM
PRIMUM
PROTEM
TRUISM

••RM••
AIRMAN
AIRMEN
BARMAN
BARMEN
BORMAN
BURMAN
CARMAN
CARMEL
CARMEN
CERMET
DERMAL
DERMIS
DORMER
FARMED
FARMER
FERMAT
FIRMAN
FIRMED
FIRMER
FIRMLY
FIRMUP
FORMAL
FORMAN
FORMAT
FORMED
FORMER
FORMIC
GERMAN
HARMED
HARMON
HERMAN
HERMES
HERMIT
HERMON
HORMEL
HORMUZ
KARMIC
KERMAN
KERMES
KERMIS
KERMIT
KIRMAN
KORMAN
MARMEE
MARMOT
MERMAN
MERMEN
MORMON
MURMUR
NORMAL
NORMAN
PERMED
PERMIT
SERMON
TARMAC
TERMED
VERMIN
WARMED
WARMER
WARMLY
WARMTH
WARMUP
WORMED

••R•M•
ABRAMS
AFRAME
BIREME
CAROMS
CDROMS
CHROMA
CHROME
CHROMO
DOREMI
FORUMS
HAREMS
JEREMY
JEROME
JORUMS
LARAMS
SCRAMS
SCRIMP
SCRIMS
SCRUMS
SERUMS
SHRIMP
STRUMS
SURIMI
THRUMS

••R••M
AIRARM
AIRDAM
ATRIUM
BARIUM
BARNUM
CERIUM
CHRISM
CIRCUM
CORIUM
CURIUM
DIRHAM
DORSUM
DURHAM
HARLEM
KAREEM
MIRIAM
PURISM
SCREAM
STREAM
VERISM

•••RM•
ALARMS
CHARMS
DEARME
DHARMA
REARMS
SMARMY
STORMS
STORMY
SWARMS
THERMO
THERMS
UNARMS

•••R•M
ALARUM
ANTRIM
ANTRUM
ASHRAM
BAYRUM
DIGRAM
ENGRAM
LABRUM
QUORUM
RETRIM
SACRUM
SCARUM

••••RM
AFFIRM
AIRARM
DEFORM
DISARM
INFIRM
INFORM
REFORM
REWARM
SQUIRM

R•N•••
RANCHO
RANCID
RANCOR
RANDOM
RANDRY
RANEES
RANFOR
RANGED
RANGER
RANGES
RANGUP
RANIDS
RANKED
RANKER
RANKIN
RANKLE
RANKLY
RANOFF
RANOUT
RANSOM
RANTED
RANTER
RENAIL
RENAME
RENATA
RENDER
RENEGE
RENEWS
RENNES
RENNET
RENNIE
RENNIN
RENOIR
RENOTE
RENOWN
RENTAL
RENTED
RENTER
RINGED
RINGER
RINGUP
RINSED
RINSES
RONALD
RONDEL
RONDOS
RONELY
RONNIE
RUNCIE
RUNDLE
RUNDMC
RUNDRY
RUNGUP
RUNINS
RUNLET
RUNNEL
RUNNER
RUNOFF
RUNONS
RUNOUT
RUNSIN
RUNSON
RUNSTO
RUNSUP
RUNUPS
RUNWAY
RUNYON

R••N••
RADNER
RAINED
RAINER
RAINES
REGNAL
REINED
REINER
REININ
REINKS
RENNES
RENNET
RENNIE
RENNIN
RESNIK
REUNES
RHINAL
RHINOS
RHONDA
RODNEY
ROMNEY
RONNIE
ROONEY
ROUNDS
RUANAS
RUANDA
RUINED
RUINER
RUNNEL
RUNNER
RWANDA

R•••N•
RACINE
RACING
RACONS
RAGING
RAKING
RAMONA
RAMONE
RAPINE
RAPINI
RARING
RATINE
RATING
RAVENS
RAVINE
RAVING
RAYONS
RAZING
REBIND
RECANE
RECANT
RECENT
RECONS
REDANT
REDINK
REDONE
REFINE
REFUND
REGENT
REGINA
REHANG
REHUNG
REIGNS
RELENT
RELINE
REMAND
REMANS
REMEND
REMIND
REPAND
REPENT
REPINE
RERENT
RERUNS
RESAND
RESEND
RESENT
RESING
RESINS
RETENE
RETINA
RETUNE
REWIND
REWINS
REZONE
RIBAND
RICING
RIDENT
RIDING
RILING
RIMING
RIMINI
RIPENS
RISING
RIVING
ROBING
ROBINS
ROCKNE
RODENT
ROLAND
ROMANO
ROMANS
ROMANY
ROPING
ROSINS
ROSINY
ROTINI
ROTUND
ROVING
ROWENA
ROWENS
ROWING
ROXANA
ROXANE
RUBENS
RULING
RUMENS
RUMINA
RUNINS
RUNONS

R••••N
RADIAN
RAGLAN
RAGMAN
RAGMEN
RAISIN
RAKEIN
RAMSON
RANKIN
RATION
RATLIN
RATSON
RATTAN
RAYGUN
READIN
REAGAN
REASON
REBORN
RECKON
REDDEN
REDFIN
REELIN
REGAIN
REGION
REININ
REJOIN
REMAIN
REMOWN
RENNIN
RENOWN
REOPEN
REPLAN
REPUGN
RESEEN
RESEWN
RESIGN
RESTON
RETAIN
RETTON
RETURN
REUBEN
REVLON
REVSON
RHYTON
RIBBON
RICHEN
RIDDEN
RIPKEN
ROBSON
ROLLIN
ROLLON
ROPEIN
ROTTEN
RUBSIN
RUDMAN
RULEON
RUNSIN
RUNSON
RUNYON
RUSKIN
RUTTAN
RYAZAN
RYOKAN

•RN•••
ARNESS
ARNETT
ARNHEM
ARNICA
ARNOLD
ERNANI
ERNEST
ORNATE
ORNERY
ORNITH

•R•N••
ARENAS
ARENDT
BRANCH
BRANDO
BRANDS
BRANDT
BRANDX
BRANDY
BRANTS
BRENDA
BRENTS
BRINED
BRINES
BRINGS
BRINKS
BRONCO
BRONCS
BRONTE
BRONZE
BRONZY
BRUNCH
BRUNEI
BRUNET
BRUNTS
CRANED
CRANES
CRANIA
CRANIO
CRANKS
CRANKY
CRANNY
CRENEL
CRENNA
CRINGE
CRONES
CRONIN
CRONUS
CRONYN
CRUNCH
DRENCH
DRINGS
DRINKS
DRONED
DRONER
DRONES
ERENOW
ERINYS
ERYNGO
FRANCA
FRANCE
FRANCK
FRANCO
FRANCS
FRANKS
FRANNY
FRENCH
FRENUM
FRENZY
FRINGE
FRINGY
FRONDS
FRONTS
GRANDE
GRANDS
GRANGE
GRANNY
GRANTS
GRINCH
GRINDS
GRINGO
GRUNDY
GRUNGE
GRUNGY
GRUNTS
IRANIS
IRENES
IRENIC
IRONED
IRONER
IRONIC
IRONON
KRANTZ
KRONER
KRONOR
KRONUR
ORANGE
ORANGS
ORANTS
ORINGS
ORKNEY
PRANCE
PRANKS
PRINCE
PRINKS
PRINTS
PRONGS
PRONTO
PRUNED
PRUNER
PRUNES
PRYNNE
TRANCE
TRENCH
TRENDS
TRENDY
TRINAL
TRINES
TRUNKS
URANIA
URANIC
URANUS
WRENCH
WRINGS
WRONGS

•R••N•
ARCANA
ARCANE
ARCING
ARDENT
ARGENT
ARJUNA
ARLENE
ARMAND
ARMANI
ARMING
AROUND
ARPENT
ARRANT
ARSENE
ARYANS
BRAINS
BRAINY
BRAWNY
BRIAND
BRIANS
BRIENZ
BROWNE
BROWNS
BRUINS
BRYANT
BRYONY
CRANNY
CRENNA
CROONS
CROWNS
CRYING
DRAINS
DROWNS
DRYING
DRYINK
ERMINE
ERNANI
ERRAND
ERRANT
ERRING
ERVING
FRANNY
FRESNO
FRIEND
FROWNS
FRYING
GRAINS
GRAINY
GRANNY
GREENE
GREENS
GREENY
GRETNA
GROANS
GROINS
GROUND
GROZNY
IRKING
IRLENE
IRVINE
IRVING
ORBING
ORGANA
ORGANS
ORIANA
ORIENT
ORMOND
ORPINE
ORSINO
PRAJNA
PRAWNS
PREENS
PRIONS
PROCNE
PRYING
PRYNNE
TRAINS
TRIUNE
TRUANT
TRUING
TRYING
URBANA
URBANE
URGENT
URGING
URSINE

•R•••N
ARAGON
ARCHON
ARISEN
ARUBAN
BRAZEN
BREMEN
BRETON
BRITON
BROGAN
BROKEN
BRYSON
CRAVEN
CRAYON
CRETAN
CRETIN
CRONIN
CRONYN
CROTON
DRAGIN
DRAGON
DRAWIN
DRAWON
DREWIN
DREWON
DRIVEN
DROPIN
DRYDEN
DRYRUN
FROZEN
FRYPAN
GRABEN
GRADIN
GRATIN
GRAVEN
GREWON
GRISON
GRODIN
GROWON
IRISIN
IRONON
KRAKEN
ORDAIN
OREGON
ORIGEN
ORIGIN
ORISON
ORPHAN
PREVIN
PREYON
PRISON
PROTON
PROVEN
TRAJAN
TREPAN
TRIGON
TRITON
TROGON
TROJAN
TRUMAN
URCHIN

••RN••
BARNES
BARNEY
BARNUM
BERNIE
BIRNEY
BORNEO
BURNED
BURNER
BURNET
BURNEY
BURNUP
BYRNES
CARNAL
CARNES
CARNET
CARNEY
CARNOT
CORNEA
CORNED
CORNEL
CORNER
CORNET
DARNAY
DARNED
DARNEL
DARNER
DARNIT
DIRNDL
EARNED
EARNER
GARNER
GARNET
GURNEY
HORNED
HORNER
HORNET
HORNEY
KARNAK
KERNED
KERNEL
KERNOI
KERNOS
LERNER
MARNER
MARNIE
MORNAY
NARNIA
PARNIS
PERNOD
TURNED
TURNER
TURNIN
TURNIP
TURNON
TURNTO
TURNUP
VARNAS
VARNEY
VERNAL
VERNON
WARNED
WARNER
WERNER
YARNED

••R•N•
ADRENO
AIRING
APRONS
ARRANT
BARING
BARONG
BARONS
BARONY
BERING
BORING
BURINS
CARINA
CARING
CARONI
CHRONO
CORING
CORONA
CURING
CYRANO
DARING
DURANT
DURING
EARING
ERRAND
ERRANT
ERRING
FARINA
FARING
FERENC
FIRING
FORINT
GERENT
GERONT
GERUND
GORING
GYRENE
GYRONS
HARING
HERONS
HIRING
HURONS
KORUNA
LARYNX
LORENZ
LURING
MARINA
MARINE
MARINO
MERINO
MIRING
MORANT
MORENO
MORONI
MORONS
MURANO
MURINE
OARING
PARANA
PARANG
PARENS
PARENT
PARING
PIRANA
PORING
PURINA
PURINE
RARING
RERENT
RERUNS
SARANS
SARONG
SERENA
SERENE
SERINE
SERINS
SHRANK
SHRINE
SHRINK
SHRUNK
SIRENS
SIRING
SPRANG
SPRING
SPRINT
SPRUNG
STRAND
STRING
STRONG
STRUNG
SYRINX
TARING
THRONE
THRONG
TIRANA
TIRANE
TIRING
TORINO
TURING
TYRANT
TYRONE
VARUNA
VERONA
WARING
WERENT
WIRING

••R••N
ADRIAN
ADRIEN
AIRGUN
AIRMAN
AIRMEN
BARKIN
BARMAN
BARMEN
BARREN
BARRON
BARTON
BARYON
BARZUN
BERGEN
BERLIN
BORDEN
BOREON
BORMAN
BURDEN
BURMAN
BURTON
CARBON
CARDIN
CAREEN
CARMAN
CARMEN
CARSON
CARTON
CORBAN
CORBIN
CORDON
CURTIN
CURZON
DARIEN
DARKEN
DARREN
DARWIN
DORIAN
DURBAN
DURBIN
DURIAN
FIRKIN
FIRMAN
FORMAN
GARCON
GARDEN
GARSON
GERMAN
GORDON
GORGON
HARBIN
HARDEN
HARKEN
HARLAN
HARMON
HARPON
HEREIN
HEREON
HERMAN
HERMON
HIREON
HORTON
JARGON
JERKIN
JORDAN
KERMAN
KIRMAN
KOREAN
KORMAN
KURGAN
LARDON
LARSEN
LARSON
MARGIN
MARIAN
MARION
MARLIN
MARLON
MAROON
MARRON
MARTEN
MARTIN
MARVIN
MERLIN
MERLON
MERMAN
MERMEN
MERTON
MERVYN
MIRREN
MOREEN
MORGAN
MORGEN
MORION
MORMON
MORTON
NORMAN
NORTON
OBRIAN
OBRIEN
PARDON
PARSON
PARTON
PERSON
PURLIN
SARGON
SARTON
SCREEN
SERKIN
SERMON
SPRAIN
STRAIN
STREWN
SYRIAN
TARPAN
TARPON
TARTAN
TARZAN
TERRAN
THROWN
TURBAN
TUREEN
TURNIN
TURNON
TYRIAN
UGRIAN
VARDEN
VERDIN
VERDON
VERDUN
VEREEN
VERMIN
VERNON
VIRGIN
WARDEN
WARREN
WOREON
WORKIN
WORKON
WORSEN
ZEROIN
ZIRCON

•••RN•
ACORNS
ADORNS
AHERNE
AVERNO
BAIRNS
BOURNE
CAIRNS
CHURNS
CZERNY
ETERNE
LEARNS
LEARNT
LIERNE
QUERNS
SCARNE
SCORNS
SMYRNA
SPURNS
STERNA
STERNE
STERNO
STERNS
THORNS
THORNY
UTURNS
YEARNS

•••R•N
ALDRIN
ANTRON
ANURAN

AZORIN BARREN BARRON BEARON CHARON CHIRON CITRON DACRON DAIREN DARREN DRYRUN ENDRUN EPHRON FIBRIN FLORIN GIBRAN GUDRUN HADRON HEDREN HIERON LAUREN LEBRUN MACRON MARRON MATRON MICRON MIRREN NATRON NEURON NOIRON OBERON OUTRAN OUTRUN PATRON PEERIN POURIN QUMRAN SHARON SHORAN SKIRUN SPURON STIRIN STYRON TERRAN VANRYN WARREN

••••RN

ASTERN AUBURN BICORN CASERN CAVERN COBURN DEHORN GOVERN INBORN INTERN INTURN MODERN OSBORN REBORN RETURN SATURN SECERN SEVERN SUBORN TAVERN UNBORN UNTORN UNWORN UPTURN WEBERN WYVERN

RO••••

ROADIE ROAMED ROAMER ROARED ROARER ROASTS ROBALO ROBBED ROBBER ROBBIE ROBERT ROBING ROBINS ROBLES ROBOTS ROBROY ROBSON ROBUST ROCHET ROCKED ROCKER ROCKET ROCKNE ROCKYV ROCOCO RODENT RODEOS RODHAM RODNEY ROGERS ROGUES ROHMER ROILED ROLAND ROLEOS ROLLED ROLLER ROLLIE ROLLIN ROLLON ROLLUP ROMAIC ROMAJI ROMANO ROMANS ROMANY ROMEOS ROMERO ROMMEL ROMNEY ROMOLA ROMPED ROMPER RONALD RONDEL RONDOS RONELY RONNIE ROOFED ROOFER ROOKED ROOKIE ROOMED ROOMER ROOMIE ROONEY ROOSTS ROOTED ROOTER ROPEIN ROPERS ROPIER ROPING

ROSARY ROSCOE ROSEAU ROSIER ROSILY ROSINS ROSINY ROSITA ROSTER ROSTOV ROSTRA ROTARY ROTATE ROTGUT ROTHKO ROTINI ROTORS ROTTED ROTTEN ROTTER ROTUND ROUGED ROUGES ROUGHS ROUNDS ROUSED ROUSES ROUSTS ROUTED ROUTER ROUTES ROVERS ROVING ROWELS ROWENA ROWENS ROWERS ROWING ROXANA ROXANE ROYALE ROYALS

R•O•••

REOILS REOPEN RHODES RHOMBI RHOMBS RHONDA RIOJAS RIOTED RIOTER ROOFED ROOFER ROOKED ROOKIE ROOMED ROOMER ROOMIE ROONEY ROOSTS ROOTED ROOTER RYOKAN

R••O••

RACONS RADOME RAGOUT RAMONA RAMONE RAMOSE RAMOUS

RANOFF RANOUT RAYONS RAZORS REBOIL REBOLT REBOOT REBORN REBOZO RECODE RECOIL RECONS RECOPY RECORD RECORK RECOUP REDOAK REDOES REDONE REFORM REHOOK REJOIN RELOAD RELOCK REMORA REMOTE REMOVE REMOWN REMOWS RENOIR RENOTE RENOWN REPOLL REPORT REPOSE REPOTS RESODS RESOLD RESOLE RESORB RESORT RETOLD RETOOK RETOOL RETOPS RETORT RETOUR RETOWS REVOIR REVOKE REVOLT REWORD REWORK REWOVE REZONE RIBOSE RIGORS RIGOUR RIMOSE RIPOFF ROBOTS ROCOCO ROMOLA ROTORS RUBOUT RUDOLF RUFOUS RUGOSE RUMORS RUMOUR RUNOFF RUNONS RUNOUT

R•••O•

RADIOS RAGMOP RAGTOP RAMROD RAMSON RANCOR RANDOM RANFOR RANSOM RAPTOR RATION RATIOS RATSON REASON REBOOT RECKON RECTOR RECTOS REDDOG REDFOX REDHOT REDSOX REDTOP REEBOK REGION REHOOK REPLOW REPROS RESHOD RESHOE RESHOT RESTON RETOOK RETOOL RETROS RETTON REVLON REVSON RHEBOK RHETOR RHINOS RHYTON RIBBON ROBROY ROBSON RODEOS ROLEOS ROLLON ROMEOS RONDOS ROSCOE ROSTOV RULEON RUNSON RUNYON

R••••O

RABATO RANCHO REBOZO REECHO RIALTO RIGHTO ROBALO ROCOCO ROMANO ROMERO ROTHKO RUNSTO

•RO•••

AROIDS AROMAS AROUND AROUSE BROACH BROADS BRODIE BROGAN BROGUE BROILS BROKAW BROKEN BROKER BROLLY BRONCO BRONCS BRONTE BRONZE BRONZY BROOCH BROODS BROODY BROOKE BROOKS BROOMS BROTHS BROWNE BROWNS BROWSE CROAKS CROAKY CROATS CROCKS CROCUS CROFTS CRONES CRONIN CRONUS CRONYN CROOKS CROONS CROPUP CROSBY CROSSE CROTON CROUCH CROUPY CROUSE CROUTE CROWDS CROWED CROWER CROWNS CROZES DROGUE DROIDS DROITS DROLLS DROLLY DROMOI DROMOS DRONED DRONER DRONES DROOLS DROOPS DROOPY DROPBY DROPIN DROPIT DROVER DROVES DROWNS DROWSE DROWSY ERODED

ERODES EROICA EROTIC FROCKS FROGGY FROLIC FRONDS FRONTS FROSTS FROSTY FROTHS FROTHY FROWNS FROWZY FROZEN GROANS GROATS GROCER GRODIN GROGGY GROINS GROOMS GROOVE GROOVY GROPED GROPES GROSSE GROSSO GROSZY GROTTO GROTTY GROUCH GROUND GROUPS GROUSE GROUTS GROUTY GROVEL GROVER GROVES GROWER GROWLS GROWLY GROWON GROWTH GROWUP GROZNY IRONED IRONER IRONIC IRONON KRONER KRONOR KRONUR OROIDE OROZCO PROAMS PROBED PROBER PROBES PROCNE PROEMS PROFIT PROLES PROLIX PROLOG PROMOS PROMPT PRONGS PRONTO PROOFS PROPEL PROPER PROPRE

PROPUP PROSED PROSER PROSES PROSIT PROTAX PROTEI PROTEM PROTON PROUST PROVED PROVEN PROVER PROVES PROWLS PROWSE TROCAR TROCHE TROGON TROIKA TROJAN TROLLS TROMPE TROMPS TROOPS TROPES TROPEZ TROPHY TROPIC TROPPO TROTHS TROUGH TROUPE TROUTS TROUVE TROVES TROWED TROWEL VROOMS WRONGS

•R•O••

ARBORS ARBOUR ARDORS ARDOUR AREOLA ARGOSY ARGOTS ARIOSE ARIOSO ARMORS ARMORY ARMOUR ARNOLD ARROBA ARROWS ARROYO ARTOIS BROOCH BROODS BROODY BROOKE BROOKS BROOMS BRYONY CREOLE CROOKS CROONS CRYOFF DRHOOK DROOLS DROOPS DROOPY

DRYOFF DRYOUT ERGOTS ERROLL ERRORS GROOMS GROOVE GROOVY MRCOOL MRMOTO ORIOLE ORLOPS ORMOLU ORMOND PRIONS PRIORI PRIORS PRIORY PROOFS TRIODE TROOPS TRYOUT VROOMS

•R••O•

ARAGON ARCHON BRASOV BRAVOS BRAZOS BRETON BRITON BRYSON CRAYON CREDOS CRESOL CROTON CRUSOE DRAGON DRAWON DREWON DRHOOK DROMOI DROMOS DRYROT ERENOW FRIJOL FRITOS GREGOR GREWON GRISON GROWON IRONON KRAKOW KRONOR MRCOOL ORATOR OREGON ORISON PREYON PRIMOS PRISON PROLOG PROMOS PROTON TREMOR TREVOR TRICOT TRIGON TRIPOD TRIPOS TRITON TROGON TRYFOR

•R•••O

ARCARO AREZZO ARIOSO ARISTO ARROYO ARTHRO ARTURO BRANDO BRILLO BRONCO CRAMBO CRANIO CRISCO CRYPTO ERYNGO FRANCO FRESCO FRESNO FRISCO GRAECO GRASSO GRINGO GROSSO GROTTO MRMOTO OROZCO ORSINO PRESTO PRONTO TRICHO TROPPO

••RO••

ABROAD ACROSS ADROIT AEROBE AIROUT APRONS ARROBA ARROWS ARROYO AURORA AUROUS BAROJA BAROLO BARONG BARONS BARONY BUROAK BYROAD BYROTE CAROBS CAROLE CAROLS CAROMS CARONI CDROMS CHROMA CHROME CHROMO CHRONO CORONA DUROCS ENROBE ENROLL ENROOT ERROLL ERRORS EUROPA EUROPE FAROFF FAROUK

FAROUT FTROOP FURORE FURORS GERONT GYRONS GYROSE HAROLD HEROES HEROIC HERONS HURONS INROAD JEROME JURORS KAROSS LAROSA MAROON MEROPE MORONI MORONS MOROSE NEROLI PARODY PAROLE POROUS SARODS SARONG SCRODS SCROLL SCROOP SEROSA SEROUS SEROWS SHROUD SHROVE SPROUT STROBE STRODE STROKE STROLL STRONG STROPS STROUD STROVE TAROTS THROAT THROBS THROES THRONE THRONG THROVE THROWN THROWS TOROID TOROSE TYRONE UNROBE UNROLL UNROOT UPROAR UPROOT UPROSE VERONA VOROUS YUROKS ZEROED ZEROES ZEROIN ZEROTH

••R•O•

BARDOT BARHOP BARRON BARROW BARTOK BARTON BARYON BOREON BORROW BORZOI BURBOT BURGOO BURGOS BURROS BURROW BURTON CARBON CARBOY CARGOS CARHOP CARLOS CARLOT CARNOT CARROL CARROT CARSON CARTON CORDON CURIOS CURSOR CURZON DARROW ENROOT FARLOW FARROW FERVOR FORGOT FTROOP FURROW GARCON GARSON GORDON GORGON HARBOR HARLOW HARMON HARPON HARROW HEREOF HEREON HERIOT HERMON HERZOG HIREON HORROR HORTON JARGON JERBOA KARPOV KARROO KERNOI KERNOS LARDON LARGOS LARSON MARCOS MARGOT MARION MARLON MARMOT MAROON MARRON MARROW MERLON MERLOT MERTON

MIRROR MORION MORMON MORROW MORTON MURROW NARROW NORTON PARDON PARLOR PARROT PARSON PARTON PERIOD PERNOD PERROT PERSON SARGON SARGOS SARTON SCROOP SERMON SERVOS SORROW SORTOF TARPON TERROR TORPOR TORSOS TURBOS TURBOT TURGOR TURNON UNROOT UPROOT VERDON VERNON VERSOS VIREOS WARGOD WARHOL WOREON WORKON YARROW ZIRCON

••R••O

ADRENO ARROYO BAROLO BARRIO BORAXO BORNEO BURGOO CARDIO CARETO CARUSO CHROMO CHRONO CYRANO DARETO DIRIGO DORADO ENRICO FOREGO HERETO JURADO KARROO LAREDO MARIKO MARINO MERINO MORENO MORPHO

MURANO PARETO SERGIO STRABO STRATO TERATO TEREDO TORERO TORINO TURNTO VIRAGO

•••RO•

AGOROT ANDROS ANTRON ASTROS BARRON BARROW BEARON BORROW BURROS BURROW CARROL CARROT CHARON CHIRON CITRON CLAROS CLOROX CONROY DACRON DARROW DETROP DOBROS DRYROT EPHRON ESCROW FAEROE FARROW FLYROD FURROW HADRON HARROW HEAROF HIERON HORROR HOTROD HYDROS IMPROV INAROW INTROS KARROO MACRON MACROS MARRON MARROW MATRON METROS MICRON MICROS MIRROR MONROE MORROW MURROW NARROW NATRON NEUROL NEURON NIMROD NOIRON OBERON OCTROI PARROT

PATROL PATRON PENROD PERROT PETROG PETROL PHAROS POIROT RAMROD REPROS RETROS ROBROY SHARON SKIROS SORROW SPIROS SPURON STEROL STYRON TERROR TIEROD UNTROD YARROW

•••R•O

ATERGO AVERNO BARRIO CHARRO CHURRO DELRIO EMBRYO EVERSO GEARTO HAIRDO KARROO NEARTO OPORTO OVERDO PUERTO QUARTO STEREO STERNO THERMO WEIRDO

••••RO

ALLPRO ANTERO ARCARO ARTHRO ARTURO AUSTRO BISTRO BOLERO CASTRO CENTRO CHARRO CHLORO CHURRO CICERO DENDRO DENIRO DEXTRO DINERO ENDURO ENTERO FIGARO FLUORO GABBRO GASTRO HASBRO HETERO JETHRO

MADERO
MADURO
NEPHRO
NUMERO
OLDPRO
PICARO
PIETRO
PINERO
ROMERO
SIDERO
TORERO
VELCRO

R•P•••

RAPIDS
RAPIER
RAPINE
RAPINI
RAPPED
RAPPEE
RAPPEL
RAPPER
RAPTLY
RAPTOR
REPAID
REPAIR
REPAND
REPAST
REPAVE
REPAYS
REPEAL
REPEAT
REPEGS
REPELS
REPENT
REPINE
REPLAN
REPLAY
REPLOW
REPOLL
REPORT
REPOSE
REPOTS
REPROS
REPUGN
REPUTE
RIPELY
RIPENS
RIPEST
RIPKEN
RIPLEY
RIPOFF
RIPPED
RIPPER
RIPPLE
RIPPLY
RIPRAP
RIPSAW
RIPSUP
ROPEIN
ROPERS
ROPIER
ROPING
RUPAUL
RUPEES
RUPERT
RUPIAH

R••P••

RAIPUR
RAJPUT
RAMPED
RAPPED
RAPPEE
RAPPEL
RAPPER
RASPED
RASPER
REAPED
REAPER
REOPEN
RIMPLE
RIPPED
RIPPER
RIPPLE
RIPPLY
ROMPED
ROMPER
RUMPLE
RUMPLY
RUMPUS

R•••P•

RECAPS
RECIPE
RECOPY
REMAPS
RETAPE
RETAPS
RETOPS
RETYPE
RUNUPS

R••••P

RACKUP
RAGMOP
RAGTOP
RAKEUP
RANGUP
REARUP
RECOUP
REDCAP
REDTOP
RESHIP
RESTUP
REVAMP
REWRAP
RIGSUP
RINGUP
RIPRAP
RIPSUP
ROLLUP
RUNGUP
RUNSUP

•RP•••

ARPENT
ORPHAN
ORPHIC
ORPINE

•R•P••

ARMPIT
CRAPES
CREPES
CRIPES
CROPUP
CRYPTO
CRYPTS
DRAPED
DRAPER
DRAPES
DRIPPY
DROPBY
DROPIN
DROPIT
DRUPES
ERUPTS
FRAPPE
FRYPAN
GRAPES
GRAPHS
GRAPPA
GRIPED
GRIPER
GRIPES
GRIPPE
GROPED
GROPES
PREPAY
PREPPY
PRIPET
PROPEL
PROPER
PROPRE
PROPUP
TRAPPY
TREPAN
TREPID
TRIPLE
TRIPLY
TRIPOD
TRIPOS
TRIPUP
TROPES
TROPEZ
TROPHY
TROPIC
TROPPO
WRAPUP

•R••P•

CRAMPS
CREEPS
CREEPY
CRIMPS
CRISPS
CRISPY
CROUPY
DRIPPY
DROOPS
DROOPY
FRAPPE
FRUMPS
FRUMPY
GRAMPS
GRAPPA
GRASPS
GRIPPE
GROUPS
GRUMPS
GRUMPY
IRRUPT
ORLOPS
PREPPY
PRIMPS
PROMPT
TRAMPS
TRAPPY
TROMPE
TROMPS
TROOPS
TROPPO
TROUPE
TRUMPS

•R•••P

CROPUP
DRAWUP
DREWUP
DRUMUP
GREWUP
GROWUP
PREAMP
PROPUP
TRIPUP
WRAPUP

••RP••

BURPED
CARPAL
CARPED
CARPEL
CARPER
CARPET
CARPUS
CORPUS
HARPED
HARPER
HARPON
KARPOV
MARPLE
MORPHO
MORPHS
MURPHY
PURPLE
TARPAN
TARPIT
TARPON
TORPID
TORPOR
WARPED

••R•P•

ABRUPT
CERIPH
ENRAPT
EUROPA
EUROPE
IRRUPT
MEROPE
PARAPH
PTRAPS
SCRAPE
SCRAPS
SCRIPS
SCRIPT
SERAPE
SERAPH
STRAPS
STRIPE
STRIPS
STROPS
SYRUPS
SYRUPY
TERAPH
THRIPS
UNRIPE

••R••P

BARHOP
BOREUP
BURLAP
BURNUP
CARHOP
CURLUP
EARLAP
FIREUP
FIRMUP
FTROOP
HARDUP
LARRUP
MARKUP
PERKUP
PIRRIP
SCRIMP
SCROOP
SHRIMP
STREEP
TOREUP
TURNIP
TURNUP
WARMUP
WORKUP

•••RP•

CHIRPS
CHIRPY
SCARPS
SHARPS
SHERPA
SLURPS
THORPE
THORPS
TWERPS
USURPS

•••R•P

BEARUP
BUMRAP
DETROP
ENTRAP
ENWRAP
FAIRUP
GEARUP
LARRUP
PAIRUP
PIRRIP
REARUP
REWRAP
RIPRAP
SATRAP
STIRUP
TEARUP
UNTRAP
UNWRAP

••••RP

ASHARP
BSHARP
CSHARP
DSHARP
ESCARP
ESHARP
FSHARP
GSHARP

R•Q•••

RAQUEL

R••Q••

RISQUE

•R•Q••

BRAQUE
IRAQIS

••RQ••

BARQUE
CIRQUE
MARQUE
TORQUE

RR••••

RRATED

R•R•••

RAREFY
RARELY
RAREST
RARIFY
RARING
RARITY
RERATE
REREAD
RERENT
RERUNS

R••R••

RAGRUG
RAHRAH
RAMROD
REARED
REARER
REARMS
REARUP
REDRAW
REDREW
REGRET
REPROS
RETRAL
RETRIM
RETROS
REWRAP
RIPRAP
ROARED
ROARER
ROBROY
RUBRIC

R•••R•

RACERS
RAKERS
RANDRY
RATERS
RAVERS
RAZORS
REAIRS
REBARS
REBORN
RECORD
RECORK
RECURS
REFERS
REFORM
REGARD
REHIRE
REMARK
REMORA
REPORT
RESORB
RESORT
RETARD
RETARS
RETIRE
RETORT
RETURN
REVERB
REVERE
REVERS
REVERT
REWARD
REWARM
REWIRE
REWORD
REWORK
RICERS
RIDERS
RIGORS
RISERS
RITARD
RIVERA
RIVERS
ROBERT
ROGERS
ROMERO
ROPERS
ROSARY
ROSTRA
ROTARY
ROTORS
ROVERS
ROWERS
RULERS
RUMORS
RUNDRY
RUPERT

R••••R

RACIER
RADNER
RAFTER
RAIDER
RAILER
RAINER
RAIPUR
RAISER
RANCOR
RANFOR
RANGER
RANKER
RANTER
RAPIER
RAPPER
RAPTOR
RASHER
RASPER
RASTER
RATEDR
RATHER
RATTER
READER
REALER
REAMER
REAPER
REARER
RECTOR
REDDER
REDFIR
REEFER
REHEAR
REINER
RENDER
RENOIR
RENTER
REPAIR
RESTER
RETOUR
REUTER
REVOIR
RHETOR
RHYMER
RICHER
RIFLER
RIGGER
RIGOUR
RINGER
RIOTER
RIPPER
RISKER
RITTER
ROAMER
ROARER
ROBBER
ROCKER
ROHMER
ROLLER
ROMPER
ROOFER
ROOMER
ROOTER
ROPIER
ROSIER
ROSTER
ROTTER
ROUTER
RUBBER
RUDDER
RUINER
RUMMER
RUMOUR
RUNNER
RUTGER

•RR•••

ARRACK
ARRANT
ARRAYS
ARREST
ARRIBA
ARRIVE
ARROBA
ARROWS
ARROYO
ERRAND
ERRANT
ERRATA
ERRING
ERROLL
ERRORS
IRREAL
IRRUPT
ORRERY

•R•R••

ARARAT
CRURAL
DRYROT
DRYRUN

•R••R•

ARBORS
ARCARO
ARDORS
ARMORS
ARMORY
ARMURE
ARTERY
ARTHRO
ARTURO
BRIARD
BRIARS
BRIERS
BRIERY
CRIERS
DREARY
DRIERS
DRYERS
ERFURT
ERHARD
ERRORS
FRIARS
FRIARY
FRYERS
GRIGRI
ORDERS
ORDURE
ORNERY
ORRERY
PRIERS
PRIORI
PRIORS
PRIORY
PROPRE
TRIERS
URGERS

•R•••R

ARBOUR
ARCHER
ARDOUR
ARGUER
ARMOUR
ARTHUR
ARTIER
BRACER
BRAVER
BRAYER
BRAZER
BREUER
BREWER
BROKER
BRUDER
CRATER
CRAVER
CROWER
CRUDER
DRAPER
DRAWER
DRIVER
DRONER
DROVER
ERASER
FRASER
FRAZER
GRADER
GRATER
GRAVER
GRAYER
GRAZER
GREGOR
GREYER
GRIPER
GROCER
GROVER
GROWER
IRATER
IRONER
KRAMER
KRATER
KRONER
KRONOR
KRONUR
KRUGER
ORATOR
PRATER
PRAYER
PREFER
PRETER
PREWAR
PRICER
PRIMER
PROBER
PROPER
PROSER
PROVER
PRUNER
TRACER
TRADER
TREMOR
TREVOR
TRITER
TROCAR
TRYFOR
WRITER

••RR••

BARRED
BARREL
BARREN
BARRES
BARRIE
BARRIO
BARRIS
BARRON
BARROW
BORROW
BURRED
BURROS
BURROW
CARREL
CARREY
CARRIE
CARROL
CARROT
CIRRUS
CORRAL
CORREL
CURRED
DARREN
DARROW
DARRYL
DERRIS
DORRIT
FARRAH
FARRAR
FARROW
FERRER
FERRET
FERRIC
FERRIS
FURRED
FURROW
GARRET
HARRIS
HARROW
HORRID
HORROR
HURRAH
HURRAY
JARRAH
JARRED
KARRAS
KARROO
LARRUP
MARRED
MARRON
MARROW
MIRREN
MIRROR
MORRIS
MORROW
MURRAY
MURRES
MURREY
MURROW
MYRRHS
NARROW
NORRIS
PARRED
PARREL
PARRIS
PARROT
PERROT
PIRRIP
PURRED
PURRER
SIRRAH
SIRREE
SORREL
SORROW
SURREY
TARRED
TERRAN
TERRET
TERROR
TORRID
TURRET
WARRED
WARREN
YARROW

••R•R•

AIRARM
AIRDRY
AURORA
BARBRA
BORERS
CORERS
CURARE
CURERS
ERRORS
FARCRY
FARERS
FIRERS
FURORE
FURORS
GERARD
GIRARD
HARARE
HIRERS
JURORS
ORRERY
PARERS
PARURE
SARTRE
TORERO
WARCRY
WIRERS

••R••R

AIRIER
BARBER
BARKER
BARTER
BERBER
BIRDER
BORDER
BURGER
BURNER
BURSAR
CARDER
CAREER
CARPER
CARTER
CARVER
CORKER
CORNER
CURLER
CURSOR
CURTER
DARKER
DARNER
DARTER
DORMER
DURBAR
EARNER
EERIER
FARMER
FARRAR
FERBER
FERRER
FERVOR
FIRMER
FORCER
FORGER
FORKER
FORMER
GARNER
GARTER
GERBER
GIRDER
GORIER
HARBOR
HARDER
HARKER
HARPER
HERDER
HORNER
HORROR
HURLER
LARDER
LARGER
LERNER
MARKER
MARNER
MARTYR
MERCER
MERGER
MIRROR
MORTAR
MURDER
MURMUR
NURSER
OERTER
PARKER
PARLOR
PARSER
PERTER
PORKER
PORTER
PURRER
PURSER
SERVER
SIRDAR
SORTER
SPRIER
SPRYER
SURFER
TARTAR
TARTER
TERROR
TERSER
TORPOR
TURGOR
TURNER
UPROAR
VERGER
WARDER
WARIER
WARMER
WARNER
WERNER
WORKER
YORKER

•••RR•

BEURRE
BLURRY
CHARRO
CHERRY
CHIRRS
CHURRO
CHURRS
FLURRY
GHARRY
GUERRE
KNARRY
PIERRE
QUARRY
SCURRY
SHERRY
SHIRRS
SIERRA
SKERRY
SKIRRS
SLURRY
SPERRY
SPURRY
STARRY
STORRS
TIERRA
WHERRY
WHIRRS

•••R•R

ADORER
BEARER
DEARER
DOURER
FAIRER
FARRAR
FEARER
FERRER
HEARER
HORROR
JEERER
LEERER
LEHRER
MIRROR
NEARER
POORER
POURER
PURRER
REARER
ROARER
SCARER
SCORER
SHARER
SHIRER
SNORER
SOARER
SOURER
SPARER
STARER
STORER
TERROR
TOURER
USURER
WEARER

••••RR

LAMARR

R•S•••

RASCAL
RASHAD
RASHER
RASHES
RASHID
RASHLY
RASPED
RASPER
RASSLE
RASTER
RESALE
RESALT
RESAND
RESCUE
RESEAL
RESEAT
RESEAU
RESECT
RESEDA
RESEED
RESEEN
RESEES
RESELL
RESEND
RESENT
RESETS
RESEWN
RESEWS
RESHIP
RESHOD
RESHOE
RESHOT
RESIDE
RESIGN
RESILE
RESING
RESINS
RESIST
RESNIK
RESODS
RESOLD
RESOLE
RESORB
RESORT
RESTED
RESTER
RESTON
RESTUP
RESULT
RESUME
RISERS
RISING
RISKED
RISKER
RISQUE
ROSARY
ROSCOE
ROSEAU
ROSIER
ROSILY
ROSINS
ROSINY
ROSITA
ROSTER
ROSTOV
ROSTRA
RUSHED
RUSHEE
RUSHES
RUSKIN
RUSSET
RUSSIA
RUSTED
RUSTIC
RUSTLE

R••S••

RAISED
RAISER
RAISES
RAISIN
RAMSAY
RAMSES
RAMSEY
RAMSON
RANSOM
RASSLE
RATSON
REASON
REDSEA
REDSOX
REUSED
REUSES
REVSON
RHESUS
RIGSUP
RIMSKY
RINSED
RINSES
RIPSAW
RIPSUP
ROASTS
ROBSON
ROOSTS
ROUSED
ROUSES
ROUSTS
RUBSIN
RUNSIN
RUNSON
RUNSTO
RUNSUP
RUSSET
RUSSIA

R•••S•

RADISH
RAKISH
RAMOSE
RAREST
RAVISH
RAWEST
RECAST
RECESS
RECUSE
REFUSE
REHASH
RELISH
RELIST
REMISE
REMISS
REPAST
REPOSE
RESIST
RETEST
REVISE
REWASH
RIBOSE
RIFEST
RIMOSE
RIPEST
ROBUST
RUDEST
RUGOSE

R••••S

RABBIS
RABIES
RACERS
RACHIS
RACONS
RADIOS
RADIUS
RAINES
RAISES
RAJAHS
RAKERS
RAMIES
RAMOUS
RAMSES
RANEES
RANGES
RANIDS
RAPIDS
RASHES

RATELS
RATERS
RATIOS
RAVELS
RAVENS
RAVERS
RAYONS
RAZORS
RAZZES
REACTS
REAIRS
REALES
REALMS
REARMS
REATAS
REBAGS
REBARS
REBELS
REBIDS
REBUTS
RECAPS
RECESS
RECONS
RECTOS
RECTUS
RECURS
REDOES
REDUBS
REDYES
REEVES
REFERS
REFITS
REGIUS
REHEMS
REIGNS
REINKS
REKEYS
RELAYS
RELETS
RELICS
RELIES
REMANS
REMAPS
REMISS
REMITS
REMOWS
RENEWS
RENNES
REOILS
REPAYS
REPEGS
REPELS
REPOTS
REPROS
RERUNS
RESEES
RESETS
RESEWS
RESINS
RESODS
RETAGS
RETAPS
RETARS
RETIES
RETOPS
RETOWS
RETROS
REUNES
REUSES
REVELS
REVERS
REVETS
REVUES
REWEDS

REWINS
RHESUS
RHEUMS
RHINOS
RHODES
RHOMBS
RHUMBS
RHYMES
RIATAS
RICERS
RICHES
RIDERS
RIDGES
RIFLES
RIGHTS
RIGORS
RILLES
RINSES
RIOJAS
RIPENS
RISERS
RIVALS
RIVERS
RIVETS
RIYALS
ROASTS
ROBINS
ROBLES
ROBOTS
RODEOS
ROGERS
ROGUES
ROLEOS
ROMANS
ROMEOS
RONDOS
ROOSTS
ROPERS
ROSINS
ROTORS
ROUGES
ROUGHS
ROUNDS
ROUSES
ROUSTS
ROUTES
ROVERS
ROWELS
ROWENS
ROWERS
ROYALS
RUANAS
RUBENS
RUBIES
RUBLES
RUCHES
RUCKUS
RUFOUS
RULERS
RUMBAS
RUMENS
RUMORS
RUMPUS
RUNINS
RUNONS
RUNUPS
RUPEES
RUSHES

•RS•••

ARSENE
ERSATZ
ORSINO
URSIDS

URSINE
URSULA

•R•S••

ARISEN
ARISES
ARISTA
ARISTO
BRASHY
BRASOV
BRASSY
BRUSHY
BRYSON
CRESOL
CRESTS
CRISCO
CRISES
CRISIS
CRISPS
CRISPY
CROSBY
CROSSE
CRUSES
CRUSOE
CRUSTS
CRUSTY
DRESSY
ERASED
ERASER
ERASES
FRASER
FRESCA
FRESCO
FRESNO
FRISCO
FRISEE
FRISES
FRISKS
FRISKY
FROSTS
FROSTY
GRASPS
GRASSO
GRASSY
GRISLY
GRISON
GRISTS
GROSSE
GROSSO
GROSZY
IRISES
IRISIN
KRESGE
ORISON
ORISSA
PRESET
PRESTO
PRISMS
PRISON
PRISSY
PROSED
PROSER
PROSES
PROSIT
TRASHY
TRISHA
TRISTE
TRUSTS
TRUSTY
TRYSTS
URUSES
WRASSE
WRESTS
WRISTS

•R••S•

ARGOSY
ARIOSE
ARIOSO
ARLISS
ARNESS
AROUSE
ARREST
ARTIST
BRAISE
BRASSY
BREAST
BROWSE
BRUISE
CREASE
CREASY
CREUSA
CROSSE
CROUSE
CRUISE
DRESSY
DRIEST
DROWSE
DROWSY
DRYEST
ERNEST
FRAISE
FREEST
GRASSO
GRASSY
GREASE
GREASY
GRILSE
GROSSE
GROSSO
GROUSE
IRTYSH
ORELSE
ORISSA
PRAISE
PRIEST
PRISSY
PROUST
PROWSE
TRUEST
TRUISM
URALSK
WRASSE
WRIEST
WRYEST

•R•••S

ARAMIS
ARBORS
ARCHES
ARDEBS
ARDORS
ARECAS
ARENAS
ARETES
ARGOTS
ARGUES
ARISES
ARLISS
ARMETS
ARMIES
ARMORS
ARNESS
AROIDS
AROMAS
ARRAYS
ARROWS
ARTELS
ARTOIS

ARYANS
BRACES
BRACTS
BRAHMS
BRAIDS
BRAILS
BRAINS
BRAKES
BRANDS
BRANTS
BRAVAS
BRAVES
BRAVOS
BRAWLS
BRAZES
BRAZOS
BREADS
BREAKS
BREAMS
BREEDS
BRENTS
BREVES
BRIANS
BRIARS
BRIBES
BRICKS
BRIDES
BRIEFS
BRIERS
BRIGGS
BRILLS
BRINES
BRINGS
BRINKS
BROADS
BROILS
BRONCS
BROODS
BROOKS
BROOMS
BROTHS
BROWNS
BRUGES
BRUINS
BRUITS
BRULES
BRUMES
BRUNTS
BRUTES
BRUTUS
CRACKS
CRAFTS
CRAKES
CRAMPS
CRANES
CRANKS
CRAPES
CRATES
CRAVES
CRAWLS
CRAZES
CREAKS
CREAMS
CREDOS
CREEDS
CREEKS
CREELS
CREEPS
CREMES
CREPES
CRESTS
CRICKS
CRIERS
CRIMES

CRIMPS
CRIPES
CRISES
CRISIS
CRISPS
CROAKS
CROATS
CROCKS
CROCUS
CROFTS
CRONES
CRONUS
CROOKS
CROONS
CROWDS
CROWNS
CROZES
CRUCES
CRUETS
CRUMBS
CRUSES
CRUSTS
CRUXES
CRYPTS
DRAFTS
DRAILS
DRAINS
DRAKES
DRAMAS
DRAPES
DRAWLS
DREADS
DREAMS
DRIERS
DRIFTS
DRILLS
DRINGS
DRINKS
DRIVES
DROIDS
DROITS
DROLLS
DROMOS
DRONES
DROOLS
DROOPS
DROVES
DROWNS
DRUIDS
DRUPES
DRUZES
DRYADS
DRYERS
ERASES
EREBUS
ERECTS
ERGOTS
ERINYS
ERODES
ERRORS
ERUCTS
ERUPTS
FRACAS
FRAMES
FRANCS
FRANKS
FRAUDS
FREAKS
FRIARS
FRILLS
FRISES
FRISKS
FRITOS
FROCKS

FRONDS
FRONTS
FROSTS
FROTHS
FROWNS
FRUITS
FRUMPS
FRYERS
GRACES
GRADES
GRADUS
GRAFTS
GRAILS
GRAINS
GRAMAS
GRAMPS
GRANDS
GRANTS
GRAPES
GRAPHS
GRASPS
GRATES
GRATIS
GRAVES
GRAZES
GREATS
GREBES
GREEKS
GREENS
GREETS
GRILLS
GRIMES
GRINDS
GRIPES
GRISTS
GROANS
GROATS
GROINS
GROOMS
GROPES
GROUPS
GROUTS
GROVES
GROWLS
GRUELS
GRUMPS
GRUNTS
IRANIS
IRAQIS
IRENES
IRIDES
IRISES
KRAALS
KRAITS
ORALES
ORANGS
ORANTS
ORATES
ORBITS
ORDERS
OREADS
ORGANS
ORGIES
ORIBIS
ORIELS
ORINGS
ORLOPS
ORTLES
ORYXES
PRANKS
PRATES
PRAWNS
PRAXES
PRAXIS

PRECIS
PREENS
PRICES
PRICKS
PRIDES
PRIERS
PRIMES
PRIMOS
PRIMPS
PRIMUS
PRINKS
PRINTS
PRIONS
PRIORS
PRISMS
PRIZES
PROAMS
PROBES
PROEMS
PROLES
PROMOS
PRONGS
PROOFS
PROSES
PROVES
PROWLS
PRUDES
PRUNES
TRACES
TRACKS
TRACTS
TRADES
TRAILS
TRAINS
TRAITS
TRAMPS
TRAVIS
TRAWLS
TREADS
TREATS
TRENDS
TRIADS
TRIALS
TRIBES
TRICES
TRICKS
TRIERS
TRIKES
TRILLS
TRINES
TRIPOS
TROLLS
TROMPS
TROOPS
TROPES
TROTHS
TROUTS
TROVES
TRUCES
TRUCKS
TRUMPS
TRUNKS
TRUSTS
TRUTHS
TRYSTS
URAEUS
URANUS
URGERS
URIALS
URSIDS
URUSES
VROOMS
WRACKS
WRATHS

WREAKS
WRECKS
WRESTS
WRINGS
WRISTS
WRITES
WRONGS

••RS••

AIRSAC
BORSCH
BURSAE
BURSAL
BURSAR
BURSAS
BURSES
BURSTS
CARSON
CORSET
CURSED
CURSES
CURSOR
DORSAL
DORSET
DORSEY
DORSUM
FIRSTS
GARSON
GORSES
HERSEY
HIRSCH
HORSED
HORSES
HORSEY
JERSEY
KARSTS
KERSEY
KIRSCH
LARSEN
LARSON
MARSHA
MARSHY
MERSEY
MORSEL
NURSED
NURSER
NURSES
PARSEC
PARSED
PARSEE
PARSER
PARSES
PARSON
PERSIA
PERSON
PURSED
PURSER
PURSES
PURSUE
TARSAL
TARSUS
TERSER
TORSOS
VERSED
VERSES
VERSOS
VERSUS
WARSAW
WORSEN
WORSTS
WURSTS

••R•S•

ACROSS

AFRESH
AORIST
ARREST
ATREST
ATRISK
BAREST
CARESS
CARUSO
CERISE
CERUSE
CHRISM
CURTSY
DIREST
DURESS
EGRESS
FOREST
GARISH
GYROSE
HARASS
HERESY
INRUSH
JURIST
KAROSS
LAROSA
LYRIST
MARISA
MARIST
MEREST
MORASS
MOROSE
OGRESS
ONRUSH
PARISH
PERISH
PERUSE
PHRASE
PUREST
PURISM
PURIST
QURUSH
RAREST
SEROSA
SOREST
STRASS
STRESS
SUREST
TERESA
THRASH
THRESH
THRUSH
THRUST
TOROSE
UNREST
UPRISE
UPROSE
UPRUSH
VARESE
VERISM

••R••S

ABRAMS
ACROSS
AERIES
AGREES
AIRBUS
AORTAS
APRONS
ARRAYS
ARROWS
ATREUS
AUREUS
AUROUS
BARGES
BARNES

BARONS
BARRES
BARRIS
BERETS
BERTHS
BIRTHS
BOREAS
BORERS
BURGAS
BURGHS
BURGOS
BURIES
BURINS
BURROS
BURSAS
BURSES
BURSTS
BYRNES
CARATS
CARESS
CARETS
CARGOS
CARIBS
CARIES
CARLOS
CARNES
CAROBS
CAROLS
CAROMS
CARPUS
CARTES
CARVES
CDROMS
CEREUS
CIRCUS
CIRRUS
CORALS
CORERS
CORGIS
CORPUS
CORTES
CURERS
CURIOS
CURSES
CURTIS
CURVES
DARIUS
DERMIS
DERRIS
DIRGES
DORCAS
DORIES
DURESS
DUROCS
EGRESS
EGRETS
ERRORS
EYRIES
FARADS
FARCES
FARERS
FERGUS
FERRIS
FIRERS
FIRSTS
FIRTHS
FORAYS
FORBES
FORCES
FORGES
FORTAS
FORTES
FORUMS
FURIES

FURORS
GARTHS
GIRTHS
GORALS
GORGES
GORSES
GYRONS
HARASS
HAREMS
HARRIS
HERMES
HEROES
HERONS
HIRERS
HORDES
HORSES
HURONS
JORUMS
JURATS
JURIES
JURORS
KARATS
KAROSS
KARRAS
KARSTS
KERMES
KERMIS
KERNOS
KORATS
LARAMS
LARGOS
LARVAS
LORIES
LYRICS
MARCOS
MARCUS
MARIUS
MERGES
MERITS
MORALS
MORASS
MORAYS
MORELS
MORONS
MORPHS
MORRIS
MURALS
MURRES
MYRRHS
NEREIS
NEREUS
NERVES
NORIAS
NORRIS
NURSES
OGRESS
PARENS
PARERS
PARKAS
PARNIS
PARRIS
PARSES
PARVIS
PERILS
POROUS
PTRAPS
PUREES
PURGES
PURSES
RERUNS
SARANS
SARDIS
SARGES
SARGOS

SARODS
SCRAGS
SCRAMS
SCRAPS
SCREES
SCREWS
SCRIMS
SCRIPS
SCRODS
SCRUBS
SCRUMS
SERACS
SERAIS
SERGES
SERIES
SERIFS
SERINS
SEROUS
SEROWS
SERUMS
SERVES
SERVOS
SHREDS
SHREWS
SHRUBS
SHRUGS
SIRENS
SIRIUS
SPRAGS
SPRATS
SPRAYS
SPREES
SPRIGS
SPRITS
SPRUES
STRADS
STRAPS
STRASS
STRAUS
STRAWS
STRAYS
STRESS
STREWS
STRIPS
STROPS
STRUMS
STRUTS
SURAHS
SURGES
SYRUPS
TARGES
TAROTS
TARSUS
TEREUS
THREES
THRIPS
THROBS
THROES
THROWS
THRUMS
TORAHS
TORIES
TORSOS
TORTES
TURBOS
UNRIGS
VARIES
VARNAS
VERGES
VERSES
VERSOS
VERSUS
VIREOS
VIRTUS

VOROUS
WIRERS
WORLDS
WORSTS
WORTHS
WURSTS
XERXES
YERKES
YUROKS
ZEROES
ZORILS

•••RS•

AVERSE
BOURSE
COARSE
COURSE
EVERSO
HEARST
HOARSE
SMERSH
SPARSE
THIRST
THYRSI

•••R•S

ABORTS
ACARUS
ACORNS
ADORES
ADORNS
AGORAS
ALARMS
ALERTS
ANDRES
ANDROS
ANTRES
ASTROS
AVERTS
AWARDS
AZORES
BAIRNS
BARRES
BARRIS
BEARDS
BGIRLS
BLARES
BLURBS
BLURTS
BOARDS
BURROS
CADRES
CAIRNS
CAPRIS
CHARMS
CHARTS
CHIRPS
CHIRRS
CHORDS
CHORES
CHORUS
CHURLS
CHURNS
CHURRS
CIRRUS
CITRUS
CLAROS
CLERKS
CLORIS
COBRAS
COURTS
CYPRUS
DEBRAS
DEBRIS

DERRIS
DOBRAS
DOBROS
DWARFS
EAGRES
ELBRUS
ENURES
EPIRUS
ESDRAS
EVERTS
EXERTS
EXTRAS
EXURBS
FERRIS
FIBRES
FIORDS
FJORDS
FLARES
FLIRTS
FLORAS
FLORES
GENRES
GLARES
GNARLS
GOURDS
GUARDS
HARRIS
HEARTS
HOARDS
HOURIS
HUBRIS
HYDRAS
HYDROS
ICARUS
INDRIS
INGRES
INTROS
INURES
JAURES
KARRAS
KAURIS
KNURLS
KUKRIS
LAIRDS
LEARNS
LIBRIS
LITRES
LIVRES
MACROS
MADRAS
MADRES
MAORIS
METRES
METROS
MICROS
MITRES
MOIRES
MORRIS
MUDRAS
MURRES
MYRRHS
NAIRAS
NITRES
NORRIS
OCHRES
OPERAS
OSIRIS
OZARKS
PADRES
PARRIS
PEARLS
PHAROS
QUARKS
QUARTS

QUERNS
QUIRES
QUIRKS
QUIRTS
REARMS
REPROS
RETROS
SABRAS
SABRES
SCARES
SCARFS
SCARPS
SCORES
SCORNS
SEVRES
SHARDS
SHARES
SHARKS
SHARPS
SHIRES
SHIRKS
SHIRRS
SHIRTS
SHORES
SHORTS
SKIRLS
SKIROS
SKIRRS
SKIRTS
SLURPS
SMARTS
SMIRKS
SMURFS
SNARES
SNARLS
SNORES
SNORTS
SOARES
SPARES
SPARKS
SPIRES
SPIROS
SPORES
SPORTS
SPURNS
SPURTS
STARES
STARTS
STERES
STERNS
STORES
STORKS
STORMS
STORRS
SUTRAS
SWARDS
SWARMS
SWIRLS
SWORDS
TAURUS
TAYRAS
TBIRDS
TETRAS
TETRIS
THERMS
THIRDS
THORNS
THORPS
TIARAS
TIGRIS
TWERPS
TWIRLS
ULTRAS
UMBRAS

UNARMS
USURPS
UTURNS
WALRUS
WHARFS
WHIRLS
WHIRRS
WHORLS
YEARNS
ZEBRAS

••••RS

ABHORS
ACTORS
ADDERS
AILERS
ALDERS
ALTARS
ALTERS
AMBERS
AMEERS
AMOURS
ANGERS
ARBORS
ARDORS
ARMORS
ASKERS
ASTERS
ATTARS
AUGERS
AUGURS
BAKERS
BALERS
BIKERS
BITERS
BLEARS
BONERS
BORERS
BOWERS
BOXERS
BOYARS
BRIARS
BRIERS
BUYERS
CABERS
CAGERS
CANERS
CAPERS
CATERS
CAVERS
CEDARS
CHAIRS
CHEERS
CHIRRS
CHOIRS
CHURRS
CIDERS
CIGARS
CITERS
CLEARS
CODERS
COLORS
COMERS
COOERS
CORERS
COVERS
COWERS
CRIERS
CURERS
CYDERS
DATERS
DEBARS
DECORS
DEFERS

DEMURS
DETERS
DICERS
DINARS
DINERS
DIVERS
DOLORS
DONORS
DOSERS
DOWERS
DOZERS
DRIERS
DRYERS
EATERS
EDGARS
EDGERS
EELERS
EIDERS
ELDERS
ELVERS
EMBERS
EMEERS
ENDERS
ENTERS
EPHORS
ERRORS
ESKERS
ESTERS
ETHERS
FAKERS
FAKIRS
FARERS
FAVORS
FEMURS
FEVERS
FIBERS
FIFERS
FILERS
FIRERS
FIVERS
FIXERS
FLAIRS
FLEERS
FLIERS
FLOORS
FLOURS
FLYERS
FOYERS
FRIARS
FRYERS
FURORS
GAPERS
GATERS
GATORS
GIBERS
GIVERS
GLUERS
GOFERS
GONERS
HALERS
HATERS
HAZERS
HEWERS
HEXERS
HIDERS
HIKERS
HIRERS
HOMERS
HONORS
HOPERS
HOVERS
HUMORS
IDLERS
INCURS

INFERS
INKERS
JAPERS
JIVERS
JOKERS
JURORS
KHMERS
KITERS
LABORS
LACERS
LADERS
LAGERS
LAKERS
LASERS
LAVERS
LAYERS
LEMURS
LEVERS
LIFERS
LIGERS
LINERS
LITERS
LIVERS
LONERS
LOPERS
LOSERS
LOVERS
LOWERS
LUGERS
MAJORS
MAKERS
MANORS
MASERS
MATERS
MAYORS
MAZERS
MESSRS
METERS
MILERS
MIMERS
MINERS
MINORS
MISERS
MITERS
MIXERS
MOHURS
MOLARS
MOPERS
MOTORS
MOVERS
MOWERS
MOYERS
MUSERS
NABORS
NADIRS
NAMERS
NEVERS
NFLERS
NHLERS
NINERS
NITERS
NOTERS
OATERS
OCCURS
OCHERS
ODOURS
OFFERS
OGLERS
OILERS
ORDERS
OSCARS
OSIERS
OTHERS
OTTERS

OWNERS
PACERS
PAGERS
PAMIRS
PAPERS
PARERS
PAVERS
PAWERS
PAYERS
PETERS
PIKERS
PIPERS
PLIERS
POKERS
POLERS
POSERS
POWERS
PRIERS
PRIORS
RACERS
RAKERS
RATERS
RAVERS
RAZORS
REAIRS
REBARS
RECURS
REFERS
RETARS
REVERS
RICERS
RIDERS
RIGORS
RISERS
RIVERS
ROGERS
ROPERS
ROTORS
ROVERS
ROWERS
RULERS
RUMORS
SABERS
SAKERS
SAPORS
SATYRS
SAVERS
SAVORS
SAYERS
SCOURS
SEDERS
SENORS
SEVERS
SEWERS
SHEARS
SHEERS
SHIRRS
SHOERS
SIDERS
SITARS
SIXERS
SIZERS
SKIERS
SKIRRS
SMEARS
SNEERS
SOBERS
SOLERS
SOMERS
SOPORS
SOWERS
SOXERS
SPEARS
SPIERS

SPOORS
STAIRS
STEERS
STORRS
SUGARS
SUPERS
SWEARS
TABORS
TAKERS
TAMERS
TAPERS
TAPIRS
TATARS
TATERS
TAXERS
TENORS
THEIRS
TIGERS
TILERS
TIMERS
TITERS
TONERS
TOPERS
TOTERS
TOWERS
TRIERS
TUBERS
TUDORS
TUNERS
TUTORS
TYPERS
UDDERS
UIGURS
ULCERS
UMBERS
UNBARS
UPPERS
URGERS
USHERS
UTTERS
VAPORS
VEXERS
VICARS
VIPERS
VISORS
VOTERS
VOWERS
WADERS
WAFERS
WAGERS
WALERS
WANERS
WATERS
WAVERS
WAXERS
WHIRRS
WIPERS
WIRERS
WOOERS

R•T•••

RATEDG
RATEDR
RATEDX
RATELS
RATERS
RATHER
RATIFY
RATINE
RATING
RATION
RATIOS
RATITE
RATLIN

RATSON
RATTAN
RATTED
RATTER
RATTLE
RATTLY
RETAGS
RETAIL
RETAIN
RETAKE
RETAPE
RETAPS
RETARD
RETARS
RETELL
RETENE
RETEST
RETIAL
RETIED
RETIES
RETILE
RETIME
RETINA
RETIRE
RETOLD
RETOOK
RETOOL
RETOPS
RETORT
RETOUR
RETOWS
RETRAL
RETRIM
RETROS
RETTON
RETUNE
RETURN
RETYPE
RITARD
RITTER
RITUAL
ROTARY
ROTATE
ROTGUT
ROTHKO
ROTINI
ROTORS
ROTTED
ROTTEN
ROTTER
ROTUND
RUTGER
RUTILE
RUTTAN
RUTTED

R••T••

RAFTED
RAFTER
RAGTAG
RAGTOP
RANTED
RANTER
RAPTLY
RAPTOR
RASTER
RATTAN
RATTED
RATTER
RATTLE
RATTLY
REATAS
RECTOR
RECTOS

RECTUS
REDTAG
REDTOP
RENTAL
RENTED
RENTER
RESTED
RESTER
RESTON
RESTUP
RETTON
REUTER
RHETOR
RHYTHM
RHYTON
RIATAS
RIFTED
RIOTED
RIOTER
RITTER
ROOTED
ROOTER
ROSTER
ROSTOV
ROSTRA
ROTTED
ROTTEN
ROTTER
ROUTED
ROUTER
ROUTES
RRATED
RUSTED
RUSTIC
RUSTLE
RUTTAN
RUTTED

R•••T•

RABATO
RAMATE
RARITY
RATITE
REACTS
REALTY
REBATE
REBUTS
RECITE
REDATE
REFITS
REFUTE
RELATE
RELETS
REMITS
REMOTE
RENATA
RENOTE
REPOTS
REPUTE
RERATE
RESETS
REVETS
RIALTO
RIGHTO
RIGHTS
RIVETS
ROASTS
ROBOTS
ROOSTS
ROSITA
ROTATE
ROUSTS
RUGATE
RUNSTO

R••••T

RABBET
RABBIT
RACKET
RAGOUT
RAILAT
RAJPUT
RAMJET
RANOUT
RAREST
RAWEST
REBOLT
REBOOT
RECANT
RECAST
RECENT
REDACT
REDANT
REDHAT
REDHOT
REEDIT
REGENT
REGLET
REGRET
REHEAT
REJECT
RELENT
RELICT
RELIST
RELUCT
REMELT
RENNET
REPAST
REPEAT
REPENT
REPORT
RERENT
RESALT
RESEAT
RESECT
RESENT
RESHOT
RESIST
RESORT
RESULT
RETEST
RETORT
REVERT
REVOLT
REXCAT
RIDENT
RIFEST
RILLET
RIPEST
ROBERT
ROBUST
ROCHET
ROCKET
RODENT
ROTGUT
RUBOUT
RUDEST
RUNLET
RUNOUT
RUPERT
RUSSET

•RT•••

ARTELS
ARTERY
ARTFUL
ARTGUM
ARTHRO
ARTHUR

ARTIER
ARTIST
ARTOIS
ARTURO
IRTYSH
ORTEGA
ORTLES

•R•T••

ARCTIC
ARETES
ARETHA
BRATTY
BRETON
BRITON
BROTHS
BRUTAL
BRUTES
BRUTUS
CRATED
CRATER
CRATES
CRETAN
CRETIN
CRITIC
CROTON
CRUTCH
EROTIC
FRETTY
FRITOS
FROTHS
FROTHY
FRUTTI
GRATED
GRATER
GRATES
GRATIA
GRATIN
GRATIS
GRETEL
GRETNA
GRITTY
GROTTO
GROTTY
IRATER
KRATER
ORATED
ORATES
ORATOR
PRATED
PRATER
PRATES
PRETAX
PRETER
PRETTY
PROTAX
PROTEI
PROTEM
PROTON
RRATED
TRITER
TRITON
TROTHS
TRUTHS
WRATHS
WRETCH
WRITER
WRITES
WRITHE
XRATED

•R••T•

ARGOTS
ARISTA

ARISTO
ARMETS
ARNETT
BRACTS
BRANTS
BRATTY
BREATH
BRENTS
BRONTE
BRUITS
BRUNTS
CRAFTS
CRAFTY
CREATE
CRESTS
CROATS
CROFTS
CROUTE
CRUETS
CRUSTS
CRUSTY
CRYPTO
CRYPTS
DRAFTS
DRAFTY
DRIFTS
DROITS
ERECTS
ERGATE
ERGOTS
ERRATA
ERSATZ
ERUCTS
ERUPTS
FRETTY
FRONTS
FROSTS
FROSTY
FRUITS
FRUITY
FRUTTI
GRAFTS
GRANTS
GREATS
GREETS
GRISTS
GRITTY
GROATS
GROTTO
GROTTY
GROUTS
GROUTY
GROWTH
GRUNTS
KRAITS
KRANTZ
MRMOTO
ORANTS
ORBITS
ORGATE
ORNATE
ORNITH
PRESTO
PRETTY
PRINTS
PRONTO
TRACTS
TRAITS
TREATS
TREATY
TRISTE
TROUTS
TRUSTS
TRUSTY

TRYSTS
WRAITH
WREATH
WRESTS
WRISTS

•R•••T

ARAFAT
ARARAT
ARDENT
ARENDT
ARGENT
ARIGHT
ARMLET
ARMPIT
ARNETT
ARPENT
ARRANT
ARREST
ARTIST
BRANDT
BREAST
BRECHT
BREVET
BRIGHT
BRUNET
BRYANT
CRAVAT
CREDIT
DREAMT
DRIEST
DROPIT
DRYEST
DRYOUT
DRYROT
ERFURT
ERNEST
ERRANT
FREEST
FRIGHT
GRABAT
GRIVET
IRRUPT
ORGEAT
ORIENT
PRESET
PRIEST
PRIPET
PRIVET
PROFIT
PROMPT
PROSIT
PROUST
TRICOT
TRIVET
TRUANT
TRUEST
TRYOUT
URGENT
WRIEST
WRIGHT
WRYEST

••RT••

AORTAE
AORTAL
AORTAS
AORTIC
BARTAB
BARTER
BARTOK
BARTON
BERTHA
BERTHS

BERTIE
BIRTHS
BURTON
CARTED
CARTEL
CARTER
CARTES
CARTON
CERTIF
CORTES
CORTEX
CORTEZ
CURTER
CURTIN
CURTIS
CURTIZ
CURTLY
CURTSY
DARTED
DARTER
EARTHA
EARTHY
FIRTHS
FORTAS
FORTES
GARTER
GARTHS
GERTIE
GIRTED
GIRTHS
HORTON
HURTLE
KIRTLE
MARTEL
MARTEN
MARTHA
MARTIN
MARTYR
MERTON
MORTAL
MORTAR
MORTON
MYRTLE
NORTON
OERTER
PARTED
PARTLY
PARTON
PERTER
PERTLY
PORTAL
PORTED
PORTER
PORTIA
PORTLY
SARTON
SARTRE
SORTED
SORTER
SORTIE
SORTOF
SURTAX
TARTAN
TARTAR
TARTER
TARTLY
TORTES
TURTLE
VERTEX
VIRTUE
VIRTUS
VORTEX
WORTHS
WORTHY

••R•T•

AERATE
BARITE
BERATE
BERETS
BORATE
BURSTS
BYROTE
CARATS
CARETO
CARETS
CERATE
CURATE
DARETO
DORATI
EGRETS
ERRATA
FIRSTS
GARETH
GYRATE
HERETO
JURATS
KARATE
KARATS
KARSTS
KORATS
MERITS
MORITA
MORITZ
PARETO
PARITY
PIRATE
PURITY
PYRITE
RARITY
RERATE
SPRATS
SPRITE
SPRITS
SPRITZ
STRATA
STRATI
STRATO
STRUTS
SURETE
SURETY
TAROTS
TERATO
TERETE
TURNTO
VERITE
VERITY
WARMTH
WORSTS
WURSTS
ZEROTH

••R••T

ABRUPT
ADRIFT
ADROIT
AFREET
AIROUT
AORIST
ARRANT
ARREST
ATREST
BARBET
BARDOT
BAREST
BEREFT
BIRGIT
BURBOT
BURNET

CARLOT
CARNET
CARNOT
CARPET
CARROT
CERMET
CORNET
CORSET
CURVET
DARNIT
DIRECT
DIREST
DORRIT
DORSET
DURANT
ENRAPT
ENROOT
ERRANT
FAROUT
FERMAT
FERRET
FOREST
FORGET
FORGOT
FORINT
FORMAT
GARNET
GARRET
GERENT
GERONT
GORGET
HEREAT
HERIOT
HERMIT
HORNET
IRRUPT
JURIST
KERMIT
KORBUT
KURALT
LARIAT
LYRIST
MARGOT
MARIST
MARKET
MARMOT
MEREST
MERLOT
MORANT
PARENT
PARGET
PARROT
PERMIT
PERROT
PUREST
PURIST
RAREST
RERENT
SCRIPT
SHRIFT
SORBET
SOREST
SPRINT
SPROUT
STRAIT
STREET
STRICT
SUREST
TARGET
TARPIT
TERCET
TERRET
THREAT
THRIFT

THROAT
THRUST
TOREAT
TURBIT
TURBOT
TURRET
TYRANT
UNREST
UNROOT
UPROOT
VARLET
VERVET
WERENT

•••RT•
ABORTS
ALERTS
AVERTS
BLURTS
CHARTS
COURTS
DEARTH
DUARTE
ECARTE
EVERTS
EXERTS
FLIRTS
FOURTH
GEARTO
HEARTH
HEARTS
HEARTY
NEARTO
OMERTA
OPORTO
PUERTO
QUARTO
QUARTS
QUARTZ
QUIRTS
QWERTY
SHIRTS
SHIRTY
SHORTS
SHORTY
SKIRTS
SMARTS
SMARTY
SNORTS
SPARTA
SPORTS
SPORTY
SPURTS
STARTS
SWARTH
THIRTY

•••R•T
AGOROT
AIGRET
ARARAT
ATTRIT
BEIRUT
CARROT
CLARET
DORRIT
DRYROT
ESPRIT
FERRET
FLORET
GARRET
HEARST
IMARET
INARUT
JEERAT
LABRET
LEARNT
LEERAT
MEERUT
PARROT
PEERAT
PERROT
POIROT
REGRET
SECRET
SEURAT
SPIRIT
TEARAT
TERRET
THIRST
TURRET

••••RT
ADVERT
ALBERT
ALHIRT
ALPERT
ASSERT
ASSORT
BOGART
CAVORT
COHORT
COVERT
DEPART
DEPORT
DESERT
DIVERT
EFFORT
EGBERT
ELBERT
ENGIRT
ERFURT
ESCORT
EXHORT
EXPERT
EXPORT
EXSERT
EXTORT
GOCART
GOKART
HOBART
HUBERT
IMPART
IMPORT
INPART
INPORT
INSERT
INVERT
MOZART
OBVERT
OXCART
POPART
REPORT
RESORT
RETORT
REVERT
ROBERT
RUPERT
SQUIRT
STUART
THWART
TSHIRT
UNGIRT
UNHURT
YOGURT

RU••••
RUANAS
RUANDA
RUBBED
RUBBER
RUBBLE
RUBBLY
RUBENS
RUBIED
RUBIES
RUBIFY
RUBLES
RUBOUT
RUBRIC
RUBSIN
RUCHES
RUCKED
RUCKUS
RUDDER
RUDDLE
RUDELY
RUDEST
RUDMAN
RUDOLF
RUEFUL
RUFFED
RUFFLE
RUFFLY
RUFOUS
RUGATE
RUGGED
RUGOSE
RUINED
RUINER
RULEON
RULERS
RULING
RUMBAS
RUMBLE
RUMBLY
RUMENS
RUMINA
RUMMER
RUMORS
RUMOUR
RUMPLE
RUMPLY
RUMPUS
RUNCIE
RUNDLE
RUNDMC
RUNDRY
RUNGUP
RUNINS
RUNLET
RUNNEL
RUNNER
RUNOFF
RUNONS
RUNOUT
RUNSIN
RUNSON
RUNSTO
RUNSUP
RUNUPS
RUNWAY
RUNYON
RUPAUL
RUPEES
RUPERT
RUPIAH
RUSHED
RUSHEE
RUSHES
RUSKIN
RUSSET
RUSSIA
RUSTED
RUSTIC
RUSTLE
RUTGER
RUTILE
RUTTAN
RUTTED

R•U•••
REUBEN
REUNES
REUSED
REUSES
REUTER
RHESUS
RHUMBA
RHUMBS
ROUGED
ROUGES
ROUGHS
ROUNDS
ROUSED
ROUSES
ROUSTS
ROUTED
ROUTER
ROUTES
RYUKYU

R••U••
RADULA
RAQUEL
REBUFF
REBUKE
REBUTS
RECURS
RECUSE
REDUBS
REDUCE
REFUEL
REFUGE
REFUND
REFUSE
REFUTE
REHUNG
RELUCT
RELUME
REMUDA
REPUGN
REPUTE
RERUNS
RESULT
RESUME
RETUNE
RETURN
REVUES
RHEUMS
RHEUMY
RITUAL
ROBUST
ROGUES
ROTUND
RUNUPS

R•••U•
RACKUP
RADIUM
RADIUS
RAGOUT
RAGRUG
RAIPUR
RAJPUT
RAKEUP
RAMOUS
RANGUP
RANOUT
RAYGUN
REARUP
RECOUP
RECTUS
REDBUD
REDGUM
REFLUX
REGIUS
REGLUE
RESCUE
RESTUP
RETOUR
RHESUS
RIGOUR
RIGSUP
RINGUP
RIPSUP
RISQUE
ROLLUP
ROTGUT
RUBOUT
RUCKUS
RUEFUL
RUFOUS
RUMOUR
RUMPUS
RUNGUP
RUNOUT
RUNSUP
RUPAUL
RVALUE

R••••U
RAMEAU
RESEAU
ROSEAU
RYUKYU

•RU•••
ARUBAN
BRUDER
BRUGES
BRUINS
BRUISE
BRUITS
BRULES
BRUMAL
BRUMES
BRUNCH
BRUNEI
BRUNET
BRUNTS
BRUSHY
BRUTAL
BRUTES
BRUTUS
CRUCES
CRUDDY
CRUDER
CRUETS
CRUISE
CRUMBS
CRUMBY
CRUMMY
CRUNCH
CRURAL
CRUSES
CRUSOE
CRUSTS
CRUSTY
CRUTCH
CRUXES
DRUDGE
DRUIDS
DRUMUP
DRUPES
DRUZES
ERUCTS
ERUPTS
FRUGAL
FRUITS
FRUITY
FRUMPS
FRUMPY
FRUTTI
GRUBBY
GRUDGE
GRUELS
GRUMPS
GRUMPY
GRUNDY
GRUNGE
GRUNGY
GRUNTS
KRUGER
PRUDES
PRUNED
PRUNER
PRUNES
TRUANT
TRUCES
TRUCKS
TRUDGE
TRUEST
TRUING
TRUISM
TRUMAN
TRUMPS
TRUNKS
TRUSTS
TRUSTY
TRUTHS
URUSES

•R•U••
ARGUED
ARGUER
ARGUES
ARJUNA
ARMURE
AROUND
AROUSE
ARTURO
BREUER
CREUSA
CROUCH
CROUPY
CROUSE
CROUTE
ERFURT
FRAUDS
GROUCH
GROUND
GROUPS
GROUSE
GROUTS
GROUTY
IRRUPT
ORDURE
PROUST
TRAUMA
TRIUNE
TROUGH
TROUPE
TROUTS
TROUVE
URSULA

•R••U•
ARBOUR
ARDOUR
ARMFUL
ARMOUR
ARTFUL
ARTGUM
ARTHUR
BRAQUE
BROGUE
BRUTUS
CROCUS
CRONUS
CROPUP
DRAWUP
DREWUP
DROGUE
DRUMUP
DRYOUT
DRYRUN
ERBIUM
EREBUS
FRENUM
GRADUS
GREWUP
GROWUP
IREFUL
KRONUR
MRBLUE
PRAGUE
PRIMUM
PRIMUS
PROPUP
TRIPUP
TRYOUT
URAEUS
URANUS
WRAPUP

•R•••U
ARALLU
ORMOLU

••RU••
ABRUPT
BARUCH
CARUSO
CERUSE
CURULE
FERULE
FORUMS
GERUND
INRUSH
IRRUPT
JORUMS
KORUNA
NERUDA
ONRUSH
PARULA
PARURE
PERUKE
PERUSE
QURUSH
RERUNS
SCRUBS
SCRUFF
SCRUMS
SERUMS
SHRUBS
SHRUGS
SHRUNK
SPRUCE
SPRUES
SPRUNG
STRUCK
STRUMS
STRUNG
STRUTS
SYRUPS
SYRUPY
THRUMS
THRUSH
THRUST
UNRULY
UPRUSH
VARUNA
YORUBA

••R•U•
AIRBUS
AIRGUN
AIROUT
ATREUS
ATRIUM
AUREUS
AUROUS
BARIUM
BARNUM
BARQUE
BARZUN
BOREUP
BURNUP
CARFUL
CARPUS
CEREUS
CERIUM
CIRCUM
CIRCUS
CIRQUE
CIRRUS
CORIUM
CORPUS
CURIUM
CURLUP
DARIUS
DORSUM
EARFUL
FAROUK
FAROUT
FERGUS
FIREUP
FIRMUP
HARDUP
HORMUZ
JARFUL
KORBUT
LARRUP
MARAUD
MARCUS
MARDUK
MARIUS
MARKUP
MARQUE
MURMUR
NEREUS
PERDUE
PERKUP
POROUS
PURDUE
PURSUE
SEROUS
SHROUD
SIRIUS
SPROUT
STRAUS
STROUD
TARSUS
TEREUS
TOREUP
TORQUE
TURNUP
VERDUN
VERSUS
VIRTUE
VIRTUS
VOROUS
WARMUP
WORKUP

••R••U
BUREAU
MARILU
MOREAU

•••RU•
ACARUS
ACCRUE
ALARUM
ANTRUM
BAYRUM
BEARUP
BEIRUT
CHERUB
CHORUS
CIRRUS
CITRUS
CYPRUS
DRYRUN
ELBRUS
ENDRUN
EPIRUS
FAIRUP
GEARUP
GUDRUN
ICARUS
IMBRUE
INARUT
LABRUM
LARRUP
LEBRUN
MEERUT
OUTRUN
PAIRUP
QUORUM
RAGRUG
REARUP
SACRUM
SCARUM
SKIRUN
STIRUP
TAURUS
TEARUP
TOBRUK
UNTRUE
WALRUS

•••R•U
APERCU

••••RU
HALERU
JABIRU
MASERU
SUBARU

RV••••
RVALUE

R•V•••
RAVAGE
RAVELS
RAVENS
RAVERS
RAVINE
RAVING
RAVISH
REVAMP
REVEAL
REVELS
REVERB
REVERE
REVERS
REVERT
REVETS
REVIEW
REVILE
REVISE
REVIVE
REVLON
REVOIR
REVOKE
REVOLT
REVSON
REVUES
REVVED
RIVALS
RIVERA
RIVERS
RIVETS
RIVING
ROVERS
ROVING

R••V••
REEVED
REEVES
REVVED

R•••V•
RELIVE
REMOVE
REPAVE
REVIVE
REWOVE

R••••V
ROCKYV
ROSTOV

•RV•••
ARVADA
ERVING
IRVINE
IRVING

•R•V••
BRAVAS
BRAVED
BRAVER
BRAVES
BRAVOS
BREVES
BREVET
CRAVAT
CRAVED
CRAVEN
CRAVER
CRAVES
DRIVEL
DRIVEN
DRIVER
DRIVES
DROVER
DROVES
GRAVED
GRAVEL
GRAVEN
GRAVER
GRAVES
GRAVID
GRIVET
GROVEL
GROVER
GROVES
PRAVDA
PREVIN
PRIVET
PROVED
PROVEN
PROVER
PROVES
TRAVEL
TRAVIS
TREVOR
TRIVET
TRIVIA
TROVES

•R••V•
ARGIVE
ARRIVE
GREAVE
GRIEVE
GROOVE
GROOVY
TROUVE

•R•••V
BRASOV

••RV••
CARVED
CARVER
CARVES
CARVEY
CERVID
CORVEE
CURVED
CURVES
CURVET
FERVID
FERVOR
GARVEY
HARVEY
LARVAE
LARVAL
LARVAS
MARVEL
MARVIN
MERVYN
NARVIK
NERVES
PARVIS
PURVEY
SERVAL
SERVED
SERVER
SERVES
SERVOS
SURVEY
VERVET

••R•V•
ARRIVE
DERIVE
MORAVA
PAREVE
SHRIVE
SHROVE
STRIVE
STROVE
THRIVE
THROVE

••R••V
KARPOV

•••RV•
SCURVE
SCURVY
STARVE
SWERVE

•••R•V
IMPROV

RW••••
RWANDA

R•W•••
RAWEGG
RAWEST
REWARD
REWARM
REWASH
REWEDS
REWELD
REWIND
REWINS
REWIRE
REWORD
REWORK
REWOVE
REWRAP
ROWELS
ROWENA
ROWENS
ROWERS
ROWING

R••W••
RUNWAY

R•••W•
REMOWN
REMOWS
RENEWS
RENOWN
RESEWN
RESEWS
RETOWS

R••••W
REDRAW
REDREW
REPLOW
REVIEW
RIPSAW

•RW•••
ORWELL

•R•W••
ARAWAK
BRAWLS
BRAWNY
BREWED
BREWER
BROWNE
BROWNS
BROWSE
CRAWLS
CRAWLY
CREWED
CREWEL
CROWDS
CROWED
CROWER
CROWNS
DRAWER
DRAWIN
DRAWLS
DRAWON
DRAWUP
DREWIN
DREWON
DREWUP
DROWNS
DROWSE
DROWSY
FROWNS
FROWZY
GREWON
GREWUP
GROWER
GROWLS
GROWLY
GROWON
GROWTH
GROWUP
PRAWNS
PREWAR
PROWLS
PROWSE
TRAWLS
TROWED
TROWEL

•R••W•
ARROWS

•R•••W
BROKAW
ERENOW
KRAKOW
PRELAW

••RW••
AIRWAY
DARWIN
EARWAX
EARWIG
NARWAL
NORWAY

••R•W•
ARROWS
SCRAWL
SCREWS
SCREWY
SEROWS
SHREWD
SHREWS
SPRAWL
STRAWS
STREWN
STREWS
TARAWA
THROWN
THROWS

••R••W
BARROW
BORROW
BURROW
CURFEW
CURLEW
DARROW
FARLOW
FARROW
FURROW
HARLOW
HARROW
MARROW
MORROW
MURROW
NARROW
SORROW
WARSAW
YARROW

•••R•W
ANDREW
BARROW
BORROW
BURROW
DARROW
ESCROW
FARROW
FURROW
HARROW
HEBREW
INAROW
MARROW
MCGRAW
MCGREW
MORROW
MURROW
NARROW
REDRAW
REDREW
SORROW
UNDRAW
YARROW

R•X•••
REXCAT
ROXANA
ROXANE

R••••X
RATEDX
REDFOX
REDSOX
REFLEX
REFLUX

•R•X••
CRUXES
DREXEL
ORYXES
PRAXES
PRAXIS
TRIXIE

•R•••X
BRANDX
PREFIX
PRETAX
PROLIX
PROTAX

••RX••
XERXES

••R•X•
BORAXO

••R••X
CORTEX
EARWAX
LARYNX
SURTAX
SYRINX
VERTEX
VORTEX

•••R•X
CLOROX
MATRIX
THORAX

RY••••
RYAZAN
RYDELL
RYOKAN
RYUKYU

R•Y•••
RAYGUN
RAYONS
RHYMED
RHYMER
RHYMES
RHYTHM
RHYTON
RIYADH
RIYALS
ROYALE
ROYALS

R••Y••
REDYED
REDYES
RETYPE
RUNYON

R•••Y•
REDEYE
REKEYS
RELAYS
REPAYS
RIBEYE
ROCKYV
RYUKYU

R••••Y
RACILY
RAMIFY
RAMSAY
RAMSEY
RANDRY
RANKLY
RAPTLY
RAREFY
RARELY
RARIFY
RARITY
RASHLY
RATIFY
RATTLY
REALLY
REALTY
RECOPY
REDBAY
REMEDY
REPLAY
RHEUMY
RICHLY
RICKEY
RIDLEY
RIMSKY
RIPELY
RIPLEY

RIPPLY
ROBROY
RODNEY
ROMANY
ROMNEY
RONELY
ROONEY
ROSARY
ROSILY
ROSINY
ROTARY
RUBBLY
RUBIFY
RUDELY
RUFFLY
RUMBLY
RUMPLY
RUNDRY
RUNWAY

•RY•••

ARYANS
BRYANT
BRYONY
BRYSON
CRYING
CRYOFF
CRYPTO
CRYPTS
DRYADS
DRYDEN
DRYERS
DRYEST
DRYFLY
DRYICE
DRYING
DRYINK
DRYOFF
DRYOUT
DRYROT
DRYRUN
ERYNGO
FRYERS
FRYING
FRYPAN
ORYXES
PRYING
PRYNNE
TRYFOR
TRYING
TRYOUT
TRYSTS
WRYEST

•R•Y••

ARGYLE
ARGYLL
BRAYED
BRAYER
CRAYON
DRAYED
FRAYED
GRAYED
GRAYER
GREYED
GREYER
IRTYSH
MRHYDE
PRAYED
PRAYER
PREYED
PREYON
XRAYED

•R••Y•

ARRAYS
ARROYO
CRONYN
ERINYS

•R•••Y

ARCHLY
ARGOSY
ARIDLY
ARMORY
ARTERY
BRAINY
BRANDY
BRASHY
BRASSY
BRATTY
BRAWNY
BREEZY
BRICKY
BRIERY
BROLLY
BRONZY
BROODY
BRUSHY
BRYONY
CRABBY
CRAFTY
CRAGGY
CRANKY
CRANNY
CRAWLY
CREAKY
CREAMY
CREASY
CREEPY
CRISPY
CROAKY
CROSBY
CROUPY
CRUDDY
CRUMBY
CRUMMY
CRUSTY
DRABLY
DRAFTY
DRAGGY
DREAMY
DREARY
DRESSY
DRIPPY
DROLLY
DROOPY
DROPBY
DROWSY
DRYFLY
FRANNY
FREAKY
FREDDY
FREELY
FRENZY
FRETTY
FRIARY
FRIDAY
FRILLY
FRINGY
FRISKY
FRIZZY
FROGGY
FROSTY
FROTHY
FROWZY
FRUITY
FRUMPY
GRABBY
GRAINY
GRAMMY
GRANNY
GRASSY
GREASY
GREEDY
GREENY
GRIMLY
GRISLY
GRITTY
GROGGY
GROOVY
GROSZY
GROTTY
GROUTY
GROWLY
GROZNY
GRUBBY
GRUMPY
GRUNDY
GRUNGY
ORALLY
ORKNEY
ORNERY
ORRERY
PREPAY
PREPPY
PRETTY
PRICEY
PRIMLY
PRIORY
PRISSY
TRACEY
TRAPPY
TRASHY
TREATY
TREBLY
TRENDY
TRICKY
TRIGLY
TRILBY
TRIMLY
TRIPLY
TROPHY
TRUSTY

••RY••

BARYON
CORYZA
DURYEA
LARYNX
SPRYER
SPRYLY

••R•Y•

ARRAYS
ARROYO
DARRYL
FORAYS
MARTYR
MERVYN
MORAYS
SPRAYS
STRAYS

••R••Y

AIRDRY
AIRILY
AIRWAY
BARELY
BARFLY
BARLEY
BARNEY
BARONY
BIRNEY
BURBLY
BURLEY
BURNEY
CARBOY
CARNEY
CARREY
CARVEY
CORDAY
CURACY
CURTLY
CURTSY
DARKLY
DARNAY
DORSEY
DURFEY
EARTHY
EERILY
FARCRY
FARLEY
FIRMLY
GARVEY
GURLEY
GURNEY
HARDLY
HARLEY
HARVEY
HEREBY
HERESY
HERSEY
HORNEY
HORSEY
HURLEY
HURRAY
JEREMY
JERSEY
KERSEY
LORDLY
MARBLY
MARGAY
MARLEY
MARSHY
MERELY
MERSEY
MORLEY
MORNAY
MURPHY
MURRAY
MURREY
NORGAY
NORWAY
ORRERY
PARITY
PARKAY
PARLAY
PARLEY
PARODY
PARTLY
PERTLY
PIRACY
PORTLY
PURELY
PURIFY
PURITY
PURVEY
RAREFY
RARELY
RARIFY
RARITY
SCREWY
SORELY
SPRYLY
SURELY
SURETY
SURREY
SURVEY
SYRUPY
TARTLY
TURKEY
UNRULY
VARNEY
VERIFY
VERILY
VERITY
WARCRY
WARILY
WARMLY
WORTHY
YARELY

•••RY•

CHERYL
DARRYL
EMBRYO
HEARYE
MAURYA
VANRYN

•••R•Y

AFFRAY
ANDREY
ASTRAY
AUBREY
AUDREY
BETRAY
BLURRY
CARREY
CHARLY
CHERRY
CHIRPY
CLERGY
CONROY
CZERNY
DEARLY
DEFRAY
DELRAY
DOURLY
EBERLY
ENERGY
EVERLY
FABRAY
FAIRLY
FLURRY
GHARRY
GNARLY
HEARTY
HOORAY
HOURLY
HURRAY
KNARRY
KNURLY
MANRAY
MURRAY
MURREY
NEARBY
NEARLY
OSPREY
OVERLY
PEARLY
POORLY
QUARRY
QUIRKY
QWERTY
ROBROY
SCURFY
SCURRY
SCURVY
SHERRY
SHIRTY
SHORTY
SKERRY
SLURRY
SMARMY
SMARTY
SMIRKY
SNARLY
SOURLY
SPARKY
SPERRY
SPORTY
SPURRY
STARRY
STOREY
STORMY
STURDY
SUNRAY
SURREY
SWIRLY
THIRTY
THORNY
WHERRY
WHIRLY
YEARLY

••••RY

AIRDRY
APIARY
ARMORY
ARTERY
ASBURY
AUGURY
AVIARY
AWEARY
BAKERY
BELFRY
BINARY
BLEARY
BLURRY
BOVARY
BOWERY
BRIERY
BUMBRY
CANARY
CELERY
CHEERY
CHERRY
DATARY
DESCRY
DESTRY
DREARY
DUPERY
EATERY
ELLERY
EMPERY
EXPIRY
FAKERY
FARCRY
FINERY
FLEURY
FLOURY
FLURRY
FRIARY
GANTRY
GENTRY
GHARRY
GLAIRY
GOAWRY
HILARY
HUNGRY
INJURY
JAPERY
KIDORY
KNARRY
LANDRY
LIVERY
LOWERY
LUXURY
MALORY
MEMORY
MISERY
NAPERY
NONARY
NOTARY
OHENRY
OLEARY
ORNERY
ORRERY
OUTCRY
PALTRY
PANFRY
PANTRY
PAPERY
PASTRY
PELTRY
PENURY
PINERY
POETRY
POKERY
PRIORY
QUARRY
RANDRY
ROSARY
ROTARY
RUNDRY
SALARY
SAVORY
SCURRY
SENARY
SENTRY
SHERRY
SKERRY
SLURRY
SMEARY
SNEERY
SPERRY
SPURRY
STARRY
SUGARY
SULTRY
SUNDRY
TAWDRY
THEORY
TOWERY
UNWARY
VAGARY
VALERY
VESTRY
VINERY
VOTARY
WARCRY
WATERY
WAVERY
WHERRY
WINERY
WINTRY

R••Z••

RAZZED
RAZZES
RAZZLE
RYAZAN

R•••Z•

REBOZO

•R•Z••

AREZZO
BRAZED
BRAZEN
BRAZER
BRAZES
BRAZIL
BRAZOS
BRAZZA
BRAZZI
CRAZED
CRAZES
CROZES
DRUZES
FRAZER
FRIZZY
FROZEN
GRAZED
GRAZER
GRAZES
GROZNY
OROZCO
PRIZED
PRIZES

•R••Z•

AREZZO
BRAZZA
BRAZZI
BREEZE
BREEZY
BRONZE
BRONZY
FREEZE
FRENZY
FRIEZE
FRIZZY
FROWZY
GROSZY

•R•••Z

BRIENZ
ERSATZ
KRANTZ
TROPEZ

••RZ••

BARZUN
BORZOI
CURZON
HERZOG
TARZAN

••R•Z•

CORYZA

R•Z•••

RAZING
RAZORS
RAZZED
RAZZES
RAZZLE
REZONE

•••RZ•

SFORZA

•••R•Z

JUAREZ
QUARTZ
SHIRAZ
TABRIZ

SA••••

SABATO
SABENA
SABERS
SABINE
SABINS
SABLES
SABOTS
SABRAS
SABRES
SACHEM
SACHET
SACKED
SACKER
SACQUE
SACRAL
SACRED
SACRUM
SADDAM
SADDEN
SADDER
SADDLE
SAFARI
SAFELY
SAFEST
SAFETY
SAFIRE
SAGELY
SAGEST
SAGGED
SAHARA
SAHIBS
SAIGAS
SAIGON
SAILED
SAILOR
SAINTE
SAINTS
SAIPAN
SAKERS
SALAAM
SALADS
SALALS
SALAMI
SALARY
SALINA
SALINE
SALISH
SALIVA
SALLET
SALLOW
SALMAN
SALMON
SALOME
SALONS
SALOON
SALSAS
SALTED
SALTEN
SALTER
SALTON
SALUKI
SALUTE
SALVED
SALVER
SALVES
SALVIA
SALVOR
SALVOS
SALYUT
SAMARA
SAMBAL
SAMBAR
SAMBAS
SAMEKH
SAMIAM
SAMITE
SAMMIE
SAMOAN
SAMOSA
SAMPAN
SAMPLE
SAMSON
SAMUEL
SANCHO
SANCTA
SANDAL
SANDED
SANDER
SANDIA
SANDRA
SANELY
SANEST
SANGER
SANGTO
SANITY
SANNUP
SANSEI
SANTEE
SANTIR
SANTOS
SAPORS
SAPPED
SAPPER
SAPPHO
SARANS
SARDIS
SARGES
SARGON
SARGOS
SARODS
SARONG
SARTON
SARTRE
SASEBO
SASHAY
SASHED
SASHES
SASSED
SASSER
SASSES
SATANG
SATEEN
SATING
SATINS
SATINY
SATIRE
SATORI
SATOUT
SATRAP
SATURN
SATYRS
SAUCED
SAUCER
SAUCES
SAUDIS
SAUGER
SAULTS
SAUNAS
SAUREL
SAUTES
SAVAGE
SAVAII
SAVANT
SAVATE
SAVERS
SAVEUP
SAVING
SAVIOR
SAVOIE
SAVOIR
SAVORS
SAVORY
SAVOUR
SAWFIT
SAWING
SAWLOG
SAWOFF
SAWOUT
SAWRED
SAWYER
SAXONS
SAXONY
SAYERS
SAYING
SAYSOS
SAYYES
SAYYID

S•A•••

SCABBY
SCALAR
SCALDS
SCALED
SCALER
SCALES
SCALIA
SCALPS
SCAMPI
SCAMPS
SCANTS
SCANTY
SCAPES
SCARAB
SCARCE
SCARED
SCARER
SCARES
SCARFS
SCARNE
SCARPS
SCARUM
SCATHE
SCAUPS
SEABAG
SEABED
SEABEE
SEACOW
SEADOG
SEAFAN
SEAFOX
SEAGAL
SEALAB
SEALED
SEALER
SEALUP
SEAMAN
SEAMED
SEAMEN
SEAMUS
SEANCE
SEARCH
SEARED
SEARLE
SEASON
SEATED
SEATER
SEAWAY
SHABAN
SHABBY
SHACKS
SHADED
SHADES
SHADOW
SHAFTS
SHAGGY
SHAKEN
SHAKER
SHAKES
SHAKOS
SHAKTI
SHALES
SHALEY
SHALLY
SHALOM
SHAMAN
SHAMED
SHAMES
SHAMIR
SHAMUS
SHANDY
SHANKS
SHANTY
SHAPED
SHAPER
SHAPES
SHARDS
SHARED
SHARER
SHARES
SHARIA
SHARIF
SHARKS
SHARON
SHARPS
SHASTA
SHAVED
SHAVEN
SHAVER
SHAVES
SHAWLS
SHAWMS
SHAYNE
SHAZAM
SKALDS
SKATED
SKATER
SKATES
SLACKS
SLAGGY
SLAKED
SLAKES
SLALOM
SLANGS
SLANGY
SLANTS
SLAPPY
SLAPUP
SLATED
SLATER
SLATES
SLAVED
SLAVER
SLAVES
SLAVIC
SLAYED
SLAYER
SMACKS
SMALLS
SMALTI
SMALTO
SMARMY
SMARTS
SMARTY
SNACKS
SNAFUS
SNAGGY
SNAILS
SNAKED
SNAKES
SNAPAT
SNAPPY
SNAPTO
SNAPUP
SNARED
SNARES
SNARLS
SNARLY
SNATCH
SNATHE
SNATHS
SNAZZY
SOAKED
SOAKER
SOAKUP
SOAPED
SOAPER
SOARED
SOARER
SOARES
SOASTO
SOAVES
SPACED
SPACEK
SPACER
SPACES
SPACEY
SPADED
SPADER
SPADES
SPADIX
SPAHIS
SPALLS
SPANKS
SPANKY
SPARED
SPARER
SPARES
SPARGE
SPARKS
SPARKY
SPARSE
SPARTA
SPASMS
SPATES
SPATHE
SPAVIN
SPAWNS
SPAYED
STABAT
STABLE
STABLY
STACKS
STACTE
STADIA
STAFFS
STAGED
STAGER
STAGES
STAINS
STAIRS
STAKED
STAKES
STALAG
STALED
STALER
STALES
STALIN
STALKS
STALKY
STALLS
STAMEN
STAMPS
STANCE
STANCH
STANDS
STANKY
STANZA
STAPES
STAPLE
STAPUF
STARCH
STARED
STARER
STARES
STARRY
STARTS
STARVE
STASES
STASIS
STATED
STATER
STATES
STATIC
STATOR
STATUE
STATUS
STAVED
STAVES
STAYED
STAYON
STAYUP
SUAVER
SWABBY
SWAGED
SWAGES
SWAINS
SWALES
SWAMIS
SWAMPS
SWAMPY
SWANEE
SWANKY
SWARAJ
SWARDS
SWARMS
SWARTH
SWATCH
SWATHE
SWATHS
SWAYED
SWAYER
SWAYZE
SWAZIS

S••A••

SABATO
SAFARI
SAHARA
SALAAM
SALADS
SALALS
SALAMI
SALARY
SAMARA
SARANS
SATANG
SAVAGE
SAVAII
SAVANT
SAVATE
SCLAFF
SCRAGS
SCRAMS
SCRAPE
SCRAPS
SCRAWL
SECANT
SEDAKA
SEDANS
SEDATE
SEJANT
SENARY
SENATE
SEPALS
SERACS
SERAIS
SERAPE
SERAPH
SESAME
SEWAGE
SEWARD
SHEAFS
SHEARS
SHEATH
SHEAVE
SHOALS
SHOATS
SHRANK
SILAGE
SISALS
SITARS
SIWASH
SKEANS
SLEAVE
SLEAZE
SLEAZY
SLOANE
SMEARS
SMEARY
SNEAKS
SNEAKY
SOCAGE
SOLACE
SOLANS
SOMALI
SOMANY
SOMATA
SOMATO
SONANT
SONATA
SOUARI
SPEAKS
SPEARS
SPLASH
SPLATS
SPLAYS
SPRAGS
SPRAIN
SPRANG
SPRATS
SPRAWL
SPRAYS
SQUABS
SQUADS
SQUALL
SQUARE
SQUASH
SQUATS

SQUAWK
STEADS
STEADY
STEAKS
STEALS
STEAMS
STEAMY
STMALO
STMARK
STOATS
STPAUL
STRABO
STRADS
STRAFE
STRAIN
STRAIT
STRAKE
STRAND
STRAPS
STRASS
STRATA
STRATI
STRATO
STRAUS
STRAWS
STRAYS
STUART
SUBARU
SUGARS
SUGARY
SUMACS
SURAHS
SUSANN
SWEARS
SWEATS
SWEATY

S•••A•

SABRAS
SACRAL
SADDAM
SAIGAS
SAIPAN
SALAAM
SALMAN
SALSAS
SAMBAL
SAMBAR
SAMBAS
SAMIAM
SAMOAN
SAMPAN
SANDAL
SASHAY
SATRAP
SAUNAS
SCALAR
SCARAB
SCENAS
SCHWAS
SCREAK
SCREAM
SCUBAS
SEABAG
SEAFAN
SEAGAL
SEALAB
SEAMAN
SEAWAY
SEENAS
SEESAW
SENDAK
SENLAC
SENNAS
SEPIAS
SEPTAL
SERIAL
SERVAL
SETSAT
SEURAT
SGTMAJ
SHABAN
SHAMAN
SHAZAM
SHEVAT
SHIRAZ
SHOFAR
SHORAN
SHOTAT
SIGMAS
SIGNAL
SILOAM
SIMIAN
SINBAD
SINEAD
SINTAX
SIOUAN
SIRDAR
SIRRAH
SKYCAP
SKYLAB
SKYWAY
SLEZAK
SLOGAN
SLOVAK
SMILAX
SNAPAT
SNOCAT
SOCIAL
SOLDAN
SOLFAS
SONTAG
SOTHAT
SOWHAT
SPICAS
SPINAL
SPIRAL
SPIVAK
SPREAD
SQUEAK
SQUEAL
STABAT
STALAG
STEFAN
STELAE
STELAR
STJOAN
STOMAS
STOMAT
STREAK
STREAM
STRIAE
STUPAS
SUBWAY
SUCHAS
SUKKAH
SULTAN
SUMMAE
SUMMAS
SUNDAE
SUNDAY
SUNRAY
SUNTAN
SURTAX
SUTRAS
SWARAJ
SYLVAN
SYNTAX
SYRIAN

S••••A

SABENA
SAHARA
SALINA
SALIVA
SALVIA
SAMARA
SAMOSA
SANCTA
SANDIA
SANDRA
SCALIA
SCHEMA
SCLERA
SCORIA
SCOTIA
SCYLLA
SEDAKA
SEGURA
SELENA
SENECA
SENEGA
SENORA
SERBIA
SERENA
SEROSA
SFORZA
SHARIA
SHASTA
SHEENA
SHEILA
SHERPA
SIENNA
SIERRA
SIESTA
SILICA
SIRICA
SISERA
SMYRNA
SOMATA
SONATA
SONOMA
SONORA
SOPHIA
SPARTA
SPIREA
STADIA
STANZA
STELLA
STERNA
STIGMA
STRATA
STYRIA
SYLVIA

•SA•••

ASANAS
ISABEL
ISADOR
ISAIAH
OSAGES
PSALMS
USABLE
USABLY
USAGES
USANCE
ZSAZSA

•S•A••

ASGARD
ASHARP
ASIANS
ASKARI
ASLANT
ASMARA
ASSAIL
ASSAYS
BSHARP
CSHARP
DSHARP
ESCAPE
ESCARP
ESHARP
ESPANA
ESSAYS
ESTATE
FSHARP
GSHARP
GSTAAD
ISLAND
ISRAEL
OSCARS
OSHAWA
OSWALD
USMAIL
USUALS

•S••A•

ASANAS
ASCHAM
ASHCAN
ASHLAR
ASHRAM
ASOSAN
ASTRAL
ASTRAY
ESDRAS
ESPIAL
GSTAAD
ISAIAH
ISHTAR
ISOBAR
OSSIAN
OSTEAL

•S•••A

ASMARA
ASPERA
ESPANA
ESPOSA
ISCHIA
ISTRIA
OSCULA
OSHAWA
PSYLLA
ZSAZSA

••SA••

ALSACE
ANSATE
ASSAIL
ASSAYS
BASALT
BESANT
CASABA
CASALS
CASAVA
CESARE
DESALT
DISANT
DISARM
DOSAGE
ERSATZ
ESSAYS
INSANE
LESAGE
LUSAKA
MASADA
MASAIS
MESABI
MOSAIC
NASALS
NOSALE
ONSALE
PESACH
PISANS
POSADA
RESALE
RESALT
RESAND
ROSARY
SESAME
SISALS
SUSANN
TISANE
UNSAFE
UNSAID
UNSAYS
VISAED
VISAGE
WASABI

••S•A•

ANSGAR
BISCAY
BISSAU
BUSBAR
BUSMAN
CASBAH
CASPAR
CASUAL
CESTAS
COSTAE
COSTAL
COSTAR
COSTAS
CUSHAW
DESMAN
DISBAR
DISMAL
DISMAY
DISTAL
DOSSAL
FESTAL
FISCAL
FOSSAE
FOSSAS
GASBAG
GASCAP
GASMAN
GASPAR
GOSTAG
GUSTAV
HASSAM
HASSAN
HISSAT
HOSTAS
HUSSAR
INSEAM
INSPAN
INSTAR
JOSIAH
KASBAH
LASCAR
LESTAT
MESCAL
MISHAP
MISLAY
MISSAL
MISSAY
MOSHAV
MUSCAT
MUSIAL
NASCAR
NASDAQ
NASSAU
NISSAN
NOSOAP
OSSIAN
PASCAL
PASHAS
PASTAS
PISGAH
POSTAL
RASCAL
RASHAD
RESEAL
RESEAT
RESEAU
ROSEAU
SASHAY
TASMAN
TESLAS
TESTAE
TUSCAN
TUSSAH
UNSEAL
UNSEAT
UNSNAG
UNSNAP
VASLAV
VASSAL
VASSAR
VESTAL
VESTAS
VISTAS
VISUAL
WYSTAN
YESMAN

••S••A

BOSNIA
BUSHWA
CASABA
CASAVA
CASSIA
CESSNA
DESICA
FASCIA
HESTIA
JASCHA
JOSHUA
KESHIA
LISBOA
LUSAKA
MASADA
MISCHA
MOSKVA
NASHUA
NESTEA
PESETA
POSADA
RESEDA
ROSITA
ROSTRA
RUSSIA
SISERA
URSULA

•••SA•

AIMSAT
AIRSAC
ASOSAN
BALSAM
BISSAU
BONSAI
BOWSAW
BURSAE
BURSAL
BURSAR
BURSAS
CAESAR
CAUSAL
COMSAT
DORSAL
DOSSAL
EATSAT
FAISAL
FOSSAE
FOSSAS
GETSAT
GOESAT
HASSAM
HASSAN
HAUSAS
HISSAT
HUSSAR
ILLSAY
JETSAM
JIGSAW
KANSAN
KANSAS
LETSAT
MENSAE
MENSAL
MENSAS
MILSAP
MISSAL
MISSAY
NASSAU
NAYSAY
NIPSAT
NISSAN
OVISAC
PAWSAT
PITSAW
PULSAR
QUASAR
RAMSAY
RIPSAW
SALSAS
SEESAW
SETSAT
TARSAL
TULSAN
TUSSAH
VASSAL
VASSAR
WARSAW
WAUSAU
XHOSAS

•••S•A

ALASKA
ALYSSA
ARISTA
AVESTA
AYESHA
BUQSHA
CASSIA
CESSNA
CUESTA
EDESSA
EGESTA
ELISHA
ELISSA
FIESTA
FRESCA
GEISHA
GLOSSA
ILESHA
ITASCA
MARSHA
MIASMA
NAUSEA
NYASSA
ODESSA
ORISSA
PERSIA
PLASMA
REDSEA
RUSSIA
SHASTA
SIESTA
TRISHA
VAISYA
VIZSLA
ZOYSIA

••••SA

AHIMSA
ALYSSA
CREUSA
EDESSA
ELISSA
ESPOSA
GLOSSA
LAMESA
LAROSA
LOUISA
MARISA
MEDUSA
MIMOSA
MUCOSA
MUFASA
NYASSA
ODESSA
ORISSA
SAMOSA
SEROSA
TERESA
WALESA
ZSAZSA

S•B•••

SABATO
SABENA
SABERS
SABINE
SABINS
SABLES
SABOTS
SABRAS
SABRES
SEBERG
SHBOOM
SIBYLS
SOBBED
SOBBER
SOBEIT
SOBERS
SUBARU
SUBBED
SUBDEB
SUBDUE
SUBGUM
SUBITO
SUBLET
SUBMIT
SUBORN
SUBSET
SUBTLE
SUBTLY
SUBURB
SUBWAY

S••B••

SAMBAL
SAMBAR
SAMBAS
SCABBY
SCUBAS
SEABAG
SEABED
SEABEE
SERBIA
SHABAN
SHABBY
SIMBEL
SINBAD
SKYBOX
SNOBBY
SOBBED
SOBBER
SOMBER
SOMBRE
SORBET
SORBIC
SOWBUG
STABAT
STABLE
STABLY
STUBBY
SUBBED
SWABBY
SYMBOL

S•••B•

SAHIBS
SASEBO
SCABBY
SCRIBE
SCRUBS
SETSBY
SHABBY
SHRUBS
SNOBBY
SQUABS
SQUIBB
SQUIBS
STRABO
STROBE
STUBBY
SWABBY

S••••B

SCARAB
SEALAB
SKYLAB
SQUIBB
SUBDEB
SUBURB
SUPERB

•SB•••

ASBURY
OSBORN

•S•B••

ISABEL
ISOBAR
USABLE
USABLY

••SB••

BUSBAR
BUSBOY
CASBAH
DISBAR
GASBAG
HASBRO
KASBAH
LESBOS
LISBOA
LISBON

••S•B•

CASABA
MESABI
NASEBY
PASSBY
SASEBO
WASABI

••S••B

ABSORB
ADSORB
RESORB

•••SB•

CROSBY
DOESBY
GATSBY
GETSBY
GOESBY
LAYSBY
LETSBE
PASSBY
PUTSBY
SETSBY
THISBE

SC••••

SCABBY
SCALAR
SCALDS
SCALED
SCALER
SCALES
SCALIA
SCALPS
SCAMPI
SCAMPS
SCANTS
SCANTY
SCAPES
SCARAB
SCARCE
SCARED
SCARER
SCARES
SCARFS
SCARNE
SCARPS
SCARUM
SCATHE
SCAUPS
SCENAS
SCENDS
SCENES
SCENIC
SCENTS
SCHELL
SCHEMA
SCHEME
SCHICK
SCHIFF
SCHISM
SCHIST
SCHLEP
SCHMOO
SCHMOS
SCHNOZ
SCHOOL
SCHORL
SCHULZ
SCHUSS
SCHWAS
SCIFIS
SCIONS
SCIPIO
SCLAFF
SCLERA
SCOFFS
SCOLDS
SCONCE
SCONES
SCOOPS
SCOOTS
SCOPED
SCOPES
SCORCH
SCORED
SCORER
SCORES
SCORIA
SCORNS
SCOTCH
SCOTER
SCOTIA
SCOTTO
SCOTTY
SCOURS
SCOUTS
SCOWLS
SCRAGS
SCRAMS
SCRAPE
SCRAPS
SCRAWL
SCREAK
SCREAM
SCREED
SCREEN
SCREES
SCREWS
SCREWY
SCRIBE
SCRIMP
SCRIMS
SCRIPS
SCRIPT
SCRODS
SCROLL
SCROOP
SCRUBS
SCRUFF
SCRUMS
SCUBAS
SCUFFS
SCULLS
SCULLY
SCULPT
SCUMMY
SCURFY
SCURRY
SCURVE
SCURVY
SCUTCH
SCUTES
SCUZZY
SCYLLA
SCYTHE

S•C•••

SACHEM
SACHET
SACKED
SACKER
SACQUE
SACRAL
SACRED
SACRUM
SECANT
SECEDE
SECERN
SECKEL
SECOND
SECRET
SECTOR
SECURE
SICCED
SICILY
SICKEN
SICKER
SICKLE
SICKLY
SOCAGE
SOCCER
SOCIAL
SOCKED
SOCKET
SOCKIN
SOCLES
SUCCES
SUCCOR
SUCHAS
SUCKED
SUCKER
SUCKIN

S••C••

SANCHO
SANCTA
SAUCED
SAUCER
SAUCES
SEACOW
SEICHE
SHACKS
SHOCKS
SHUCKS
SICCED
SIECLE
SITCOM
SKYCAP
SLACKS
SLICED
SLICER
SLICES
SLICKS
SMACKS
SMOCKS
SNACKS
SNICKS
SNOCAT
SOCCER
SPACED
SPACEK
SPACER
SPACES
SPACEY
SPECIE
SPECKS
SPICAS
SPICED
SPICES
STACKS
STACTE
STICKS
STICKY
STOCKS
STOCKY
STUCCO
SUCCES
SUCCOR
SULCUS
SYNCED

S•••C•

SCARCE
SCHICK
SCONCE
SCORCH
SCOTCH
SCUTCH
SEANCE
SEARCH
SEDUCE
SELECT
SENECA
SERACS
SHTICK
SILICA
SIRICA
SKETCH
SKITCH
SLOUCH
SLUICE
SMIRCH
SMOOCH
SMUTCH
SNATCH
SNITCH
SOLACE
SONICS
SOURCE
SPEECH
SPLICE
SPRUCE
STANCE
STANCH
STARCH
STENCH
STITCH
STOICS
STORCH
STRICK
STRICT
STRUCK
STUCCO
SUMACS
SUNOCO
SWATCH
SWITCH

S••••C

SCENIC
SENLAC
SEPTIC
SLAVIC
SORBIC
STATIC
STIVIC
SYNDIC

•SC•••

ASCEND
ASCENT
ASCHAM
ASCOTS
ESCAPE
ESCARP
ESCENT
ESCHER
ESCHEW
ESCORT
ESCROW
ESCUDO
ISCHIA
OSCARS
OSCINE
OSCULA

•S•C••

ASHCAN
PSYCHE
PSYCHO
PSYCHS

•S••C•

ASPECT
ASPICS
OSMICS
USANCE

••SC••

BISCAY
CISCOS
DESCRY
DISCOS
DISCUS
FASCES
FASCIA
FESCUE
FISCAL
GASCAP
GASCON
JASCHA
LASCAR
MASCOT
MESCAL
MISCHA
MISCUE
MOSCOW
MUSCAT
MUSCLE
MUSCLY
NASCAR
PASCAL
PESCOW
PISCES
RASCAL
RESCUE
ROSCOE
TUSCAN
VISCID

••S•C•

ALSACE
BASICS
BISECT
DESICA
INSECT
PESACH
RESECT

••S••C

COSMIC
FISTIC
FUSTIC
INSYNC
MASTIC
MOSAIC
MYSTIC
ONSPEC
RUSTIC

•••SC•

BORSCH
CRISCO
ENESCO
FIASCO
FRESCA
FRESCO
FRISCO
HIRSCH
ITASCA
KIRSCH
KITSCH
MENSCH
PUTSCH
UNESCO

•••S•C

AIRSAC
OVISAC
PARSEC

S•D•••

SADDAM
SADDEN
SADDER
SADDLE
SEDAKA
SEDANS
SEDATE
SEDERS
SEDGES
SEDILE
SEDUCE
SEDUMS
SIDDUR
SIDERO
SIDERS
SIDING
SIDLED
SIDLES
SIDNEY
SODDED
SODDEN
SODIUM
SUDDEN
SUDSED
SUDSES
SYDNEY

S••D••

SADDAM
SADDEN
SADDER
SADDLE
SANDAL
SANDED
SANDER
SANDIA
SANDRA
SARDIS
SAUDIS
SEADOG
SEEDED
SEEDER
SEIDEL
SELDOM
SENDAK
SENDER
SENDIN
SENDUP
SHADED
SHADES

SHADOW
SHODDY
SIDDUR
SIRDAR
SLEDGE
SLIDER
SLIDES
SLIDIN
SLUDGE
SLUDGY
SMUDGE
SMUDGY
SNIDER
SNYDER
SODDED
SODDEN
SOLDAN
SOLDER
SOLDON
SONDES
SORDID
SPADED
SPADER
SPADES
SPADIX
SPEDUP
SPIDER
STADIA
STODGE
STODGY
STUDIO
SUBDEB
SUBDUE
SUDDEN
SUEDES
SUNDAE
SUNDAY
SUNDER
SUNDEW
SUNDOG
SUNDRY
SWEDEN
SWEDES
SYNDIC

S•••D•

SALADS
SARODS
SCALDS
SCENDS
SCOLDS
SCRODS
SECEDE
SHANDY
SHARDS
SHEEDY
SHINDY
SHODDY
SHREDS
SKALDS
SNOODS
SOLIDI
SOLIDS
SOUNDS
SPEEDS
SPEEDY
SPENDS
SQUADS
SQUIDS
STANDS
STEADS
STEADY
STEEDS
STRADS
STRIDE
STRODE
STURDY
SWARDS
SWORDS
SYNODS

S••••D

SACKED
SACRED
SAGGED
SAILED
SALTED
SALVED
SANDED
SAPPED
SASHED
SASSED
SAUCED
SAWRED
SAYYID
SCALED
SCARED
SCOPED
SCORED
SCREED
SEABED
SEALED
SEAMED
SEARED
SEATED
SECOND
SEEDED
SEEMED
SEEPED
SEERED
SEGUED
SEINED
SEIZED
SENSED
SERVED
SEWARD
SHADED
SHAMED
SHAPED
SHARED
SHAVED
SHIELD
SHINED
SHOOED
SHORED
SHOULD
SHOVED
SHOWED
SHREWD
SHROUD
SICCED
SIDLED
SIEGED
SIEVED
SIFTED
SIGHED
SIGNED
SIGURD
SILKED
SILOED
SILTED
SINBAD
SINEAD
SINGED
SINNED
SIPPED
SKATED
SKEWED
SKIVED
SLAKED
SLATED
SLAVED
SLAYED
SLEWED
SLICED
SLIMED
SLOPED
SLOWED
SMILED
SMOKED
SNAKED
SNARED
SNIPED
SNORED
SNOWED
SOAKED
SOAPED
SOARED
SOBBED
SOCKED
SODDED
SOILED
SOLOED
SOLVED
SOPPED
SORDID
SORTED
SOTTED
SOURED
SOUSED
SPACED
SPADED
SPARED
SPAYED
SPEWED
SPICED
SPIKED
SPINED
SPIRED
SPITED
SPOKED
SPREAD
SPUMED
STAGED
STAKED
STALED
STARED
STATED
STAVED
STAYED
STEWED
STOKED
STOLID
STONED
STORED
STOWED
STRAND
STROUD
STUPID
STYLED
SUBBED
SUCKED
SUDSED
SUITED
SULKED
SUMMED
SUNGOD
SUNNED
SUPPED
SURFED
SURGED
SWAGED
SWAYED
SWIPED
SYNCED

•SD•••

ESDRAS

•S•D••

ASIDES
BSIDES
ISADOR
USEDTO
USEDUP

•S••D•

ESCUDO
ISOLDE
PSEUDO
PSEUDS

•S•••D

ASCEND
ASGARD
ASTRID
ESPIED
GSTAAD
ISLAND
ISOPOD
ISSUED
OSGOOD
OSMOND
OSMUND
OSTEND
OSWALD
USERID

••SD••

MISDID
NASDAQ
WISDOM

••S•D•

BESIDE
DOSIDO
INSIDE
MASADA
ONSIDE
POSADA
RESEDA
RESIDE
RESODS
UPSIDE
URSIDS

••S••D

ABSURD
ATSTUD
AXSEED
BASHED
BASKED
BASTED
BESTED
BOSSED
BUSHED
BUSIED
BUSSED
BUSTED
CASHED
COSHED
CUSPED
CUSPID
CUSSED
DASHED
DISHED
DISKED
DISSED
DOSSED
DUSTED
ENSUED
FASTED
FISHED
FISTED
FUSSED
GASHED
GASPED
GASSED
GUSHED
GUSTED
HASHED
HASPED
HESIOD
HISPID
HISSED
HOSTED
HUSHED
HUSKED
ISSUED
JESTED
JOSHED
KISSED
LASHED
LASTED
LISPED
LISTED
LUSTED
MASHED
MASKED
MASSED
MESHED
MESSED
MISDID
MISLED
MISSED
MISTED
MOSSED
MUSHED
MUSSED
NESTED
NOSHED
OUSTED
PASSED
PASTED
POSTED
PUSHED
RASHAD
RASHID
RASPED
RESAND
RESEED
RESEND
RESHOD
RESOLD
RESTED
RISKED
RUSHED
RUSTED
SASHED
SASSED
TASKED
TASTED
TESTED
TOSSED
TUSKED
UNSAID
UNSHED
UNSHOD
UNSOLD
VESPID
VESTED
VISAED
VISCID
WASHED
WASTED
WISHED
WISPED
YESSED
ZESTED

•••S•D

ABASED
ABUSED
AMUSED
BIASED
BOSSED
BUSSED
CAPSID
CAUSED
CEASED
CENSED
CHASED
CLOSED
CURSED
CUSSED
DISSED
DOSSED
DOUSED
DOWSED
ERASED
FUSSED
GASSED
GOOSED
HISSED
HORSED
HOUSED
KISSED
LAPSED
LEASED
LENSED
LOOSED
LOUSED
MASSED
MESSED
MISSED
MOSSED
MOUSED
MUSSED
NOISED
NURSED
PARSED
PASSED
PAUSED
PHASED
PHYSED
POISED
PROSED
PULSED
PURSED
RAISED
REUSED
RINSED
ROUSED
SASSED
SENSED
SOUSED
SUDSED
TEASED
TENSED
TOSSED
UNUSED
VERSED
YESSED

SE••••

SEABAG
SEABED
SEABEE
SEACOW
SEADOG
SEAFAN
SEAFOX
SEAGAL
SEALAB
SEALED
SEALER
SEALUP
SEAMAN
SEAMED
SEAMEN
SEAMUS
SEANCE
SEARCH
SEARED
SEARLE
SEASON
SEATED
SEATER
SEAWAY
SEBERG
SECANT
SECEDE
SECERN
SECKEL
SECOND
SECRET
SECTOR
SECURE
SEDAKA
SEDANS
SEDATE
SEDERS
SEDGES
SEDILE
SEDUCE
SEDUMS
SEEDED
SEEDER
SEEFIT
SEEGER
SEEING
SEEKER
SEEMED
SEEMLY
SEENAS
SEENTO
SEEOFF
SEEOUT
SEEPED
SEEPIN
SEERED
SEESAW
SEESIN
SEESTO
SEETHE
SEGUED
SEGUES
SEGURA
SEICHE
SEIDEL
SEINED
SEINER
SEINES
SEISMO
SEISMS
SEIZED
SEIZER
SEIZES
SEJANT
SELDOM
SELECT
SELENA
SELENE
SELJUK
SELLER
SELVES
SEMELE
SEMITE
SEMPER
SEMPRE
SENARY
SENATE
SENDAK
SENDER
SENDIN
SENDUP
SENECA
SENEGA
SENHOR
SENIOR
SENLAC
SENNAS
SENNET
SENNIT
SENORA
SENORS
SENSED
SENSEI
SENSES
SENSOR
SENTIN
SENTRY
SENTUP
SEPALS
SEPIAS
SEPOYS
SEPTAL
SEPTET
SEPTIC
SEPTUM
SEQUEL
SEQUIN
SERACS
SERAIS
SERAPE
SERAPH
SERBIA
SERENA
SERENE
SERGEI
SERGES
SERGIO
SERIAL
SERIES
SERIFS
SERINE
SERINS
SERKIN
SERMON
SEROSA
SEROUS
SEROWS
SERUMS
SERVAL
SERVED
SERVER
SERVES
SERVOS
SESAME
SESQUI
SESTET
SESTOS
SETINS
SETOFF
SETOSE
SETOUT
SETSAT
SETSBY
SETSIN
SETSON
SETSUP
SETTEE
SETTER
SETTLE
SETTOS
SETUPS
SEURAT
SEVENS
SEVERE
SEVERN
SEVERS
SEVRES
SEWAGE
SEWARD
SEWELL
SEWERS
SEWING
SEWNUP
SEWSON
SEWSUP
SEXIER
SEXILY
SEXIST
SEXTET
SEXTON

S•E•••

SCENAS
SCENDS
SCENES
SCENIC
SCENTS
SEEDED
SEEDER
SEEFIT
SEEGER
SEEING
SEEKER
SEEMED
SEEMLY
SEENAS
SEENTO
SEEOFF
SEEOUT
SEEPED
SEEPIN
SEERED
SEESAW
SEESIN
SEESTO
SEETHE
SHEAFS
SHEARS
SHEATH
SHEAVE
SHEEDY
SHEEHY
SHEENA
SHEENS
SHEEPS
SHEERS
SHEETS
SHEIKS
SHEILA
SHEKEL
SHELLS
SHELLY
SHELVE
SHEREE
SHERIF
SHERPA
SHERRY
SHEVAT
SIECLE
SIEGED
SIEGES
SIENNA
SIERRA
SIESTA
SIEVED
SIEVES
SKEANS
SKEINS
SKERRY
SKETCH
SKEWED
SKEWER
SLEAVE
SLEAZE
SLEAZY
SLEDGE
SLEEKS
SLEEKY
SLEEPS
SLEEPY
SLEETS
SLEETY
SLEEVE
SLEIGH
SLEUTH
SLEWED
SLEZAK
SMEARS
SMEARY
SMELLS
SMELLY
SMELTS
SMERSH
SNEAKS
SNEAKY
SNEERS
SNEERY
SNEEZE
SNEEZY
SNELLS
SPEAKS
SPEARS
SPECIE
SPECKS
SPEDUP
SPEECH
SPEEDS
SPEEDY
SPELLS
SPENDS
SPERRY
SPEWED
STEADS
STEADY
STEAKS
STEALS
STEAMS
STEAMY
STEEDS
STEELE
STEELS
STEELY
STEEPS
STEERS
STEEVE
STEFAN
STEFFI
STEINS
STELAE
STELAR
STELES
STELLA
STELMO
STENCH
STENOG
STENOS
STEPIN
STEPON
STEPPE
STEPUP
STEREO
STERES
STERNA
STERNE
STERNO
STERNS
STEROL
STEVEN
STEVIE
STEWED
STEWER
SUEDES
SVELTE
SWEARS
SWEATS
SWEATY
SWEDEN
SWEDES
SWEEPS
SWEETS
SWELLS
SWERVE

S••E••

SABENA
SABERS
SAFELY
SAFEST
SAFETY
SAGELY
SAGEST
SAKERS
SAMEKH
SANELY
SANEST
SASEBO
SATEEN
SAVERS
SAVEUP
SAYERS
SCHELL
SCHEMA
SCHEME
SCLERA
SCREAK
SCREAM
SCREED
SCREEN
SCREES
SCREWS
SCREWY
SEBERG
SECEDE
SECERN
SEDERS
SELECT
SELENA
SELENE
SEMELE
SENECA
SENEGA
SERENA
SERENE
SEVENS
SEVERE
SEVERN
SEVERS
SEWELL
SEWERS
SHEEDY
SHEEHY
SHEENA
SHEENS
SHEEPS
SHEERS
SHEETS
SHIELD
SHIEST
SHOERS
SHREDS
SHREWD
SHREWS
SHTETL
SHYEST
SIDERO
SIDERS
SILENI
SILENT
SIMEON
SINEAD
SINEWS
SINEWY
SIRENS
SISERA
SIXERS
SIZERS
SIZEUP
SKIERS
SLEEKS
SLEEKY
SLEEPS
SLEEPY
SLEETS
SLEETY
SLEEVE
SLIEST
SLYEST
SNEERS
SNEERY
SNEEZE
SNEEZY
SOBEIT
SOBERS
SOLEIL
SOLELY
SOLEMN
SOLENT
SOLERS
SOLEUS
SOMERS
SORELY
SOREST
SOWERS
SOWETO
SOXERS
SPEECH
SPEEDS
SPEEDY
SPHERE
SPIELS
SPIERS
SPLEEN
SPREAD
SPREES
SQUEAK
SQUEAL
STEEDS
STEELE
STEELS
STEELY
STEEPS
STEERS
STEEVE
STHENO
STPETE
STREAK
STREAM
STREEP
STREET
STRESS
STREWN
STREWS
SUPERB
SUPERS
SURELY
SUREST
SURETE
SURETY
SWEEPS
SWEETS

S•••E•

SABLES
SABRES
SACHEM
SACHET
SACKED
SACKER
SACRED
SADDEN
SADDER
SAGGED
SAILED
SALLET
SALTED
SALTEN
SALTER
SALVED
SALVER
SALVES
SAMUEL
SANDED
SANDER
SANGER
SANSEI
SANTEE
SAPPED
SAPPER
SARGES
SASHED
SASHES
SASSED
SASSER
SASSES
SATEEN
SAUCED
SAUCER
SAUCES
SAUGER
SAUREL
SAUTES
SAWRED
SAWYER
SAYYES
SCALED
SCALER
SCALES
SCAPES
SCARED
SCARER
SCARES
SCENES
SCHLEP
SCONES
SCOPED
SCOPES
SCORED
SCORER
SCORES
SCOTER
SCREED
SCREEN
SCREES
SCUTES
SEABED
SEABEE
SEALED
SEALER
SEAMED
SEAMEN
SEARED
SEATED
SEATER
SECKEL
SECRET
SEDGES
SEEDED
SEEDER
SEEGER
SEEKER
SEEMED
SEEPED
SEERED
SEGUED
SEGUES
SEIDEL
SEINED
SEINER
SEINES
SEIZED
SEIZER
SEIZES
SELLER
SELVES
SEMPER
SENDER
SENNET
SENSED
SENSEI
SENSES
SEPTET
SEQUEL
SERGEI
SERGES
SERIES
SERVED
SERVER
SERVES
SESTET
SETTEE
SETTER
SEVRES
SEXIER
SEXTET
SHADED
SHADES
SHAKEN
SHAKER
SHAKES
SHALES
SHALEY
SHAMED
SHAMES
SHAPED
SHAPER
SHAPES
SHARED
SHARER
SHARES
SHAVED
SHAVEN
SHAVER
SHAVES
SHEKEL
SHEREE
SHINED
SHINER
SHINES
SHIRER
SHIRES
SHIVER
SHOLEM
SHOOED
SHORED
SHORES
SHOVED
SHOVEL
SHOVER
SHOVES
SHOWED
SHOWER
SHRIEK
SICCED
SICKEN
SICKER
SIDLED
SIDLES
SIDNEY
SIEGED
SIEGES
SIEVED
SIEVES
SIFTED
SIFTER
SIGHED
SIGHER
SIGNED
SIGNEE
SIGNER
SIGNET
SILKED
SILKEN
SILOED
SILTED
SILVER
SIMBEL
SIMMER
SIMPER
SINGED
SINGER
SINGES
SINKER
SINNED
SINNER
SINTER
SIPPED
SIPPER
SIPPET
SIRREE
SISKEL
SISLER
SISTER
SITTER
SKATED
SKATER

SKATES SKEWED SKEWER SKIVED SKIVER SKIVES SLAKED SLAKES SLATED SLATER SLATES SLAVED SLAVER SLAVES SLAYED SLAYER SLEWED SLICED SLICER SLICES SLIDER SLIDES SLIMED SLIMES SLIVER SLOPED SLOPES SLOVEN SLOWED SLOWER SLYPES SMILED SMILER SMILES SMILEY SMITES SMOKED SMOKER SMOKES SMOKEY SNAKED SNAKES SNARED SNARES SNIDER SNIPED SNIPES SNIVEL SNOPES SNORED SNORER SNORES SNOWED SNYDER SOAKED SOAKER SOAPED SOAPER SOARED SOARER SOARES SOAVES SOBBED SOBBER SOCCER SOCKED SOCKET SOCLES SODDED SODDEN SOFTEN SOFTER SOILED SOIREE

SOLDER SOLOED SOLVED SOLVER SOLVES SOMBER SOMMER SONDES SONNET SOONER SOPPED SORBET SORREL SORTED SORTER SOTTED SOURED SOURER SOUSED SOUSES SOUTER SOVIET SPACED SPACEK SPACER SPACES SPACEY SPADED SPADER SPADES SPARED SPARER SPARES SPATES SPAYED SPEWED SPICED SPICES SPIDER SPIKED SPIKER SPIKES SPILES SPINED SPINEL SPINES SPINET SPIREA SPIRED SPIRES SPITED SPITES SPLEEN SPOKED SPOKEN SPOKES SPORES SPREES SPRIER SPRUES SPRYER SPUMED SPUMES STAGED STAGER STAGES STAKED STAKES STALED STALER STALES STAMEN STAPES STARED

STARER STARES STASES STATED STATER STATES STAVED STAVES STAYED STELES STEREO STERES STEVEN STEWED STEWER STILES STIPEL STIPES STIVER STOKED STOKER STOKES STOLEN STOLES STONED STONER STONES STOPES STORED STORER STORES STOREY STOVER STOVES STOWED STREEP STREET STUPES STYLED STYLER STYLES STYLET SUAVER SUBBED SUBDEB SUBLET SUBSET SUCCES SUCKED SUCKER SUDDEN SUDSED SUDSES SUEDES SUFFER SUITED SUITES SULKED SULKER SULLEN SUMMED SUMMER SUMNER SUMTER SUNDER SUNDEW SUNKEN SUNNED SUNSET SUPPED SUPPER SURFED SURFER SURGED

SURGES SURREY SURVEY SUSIEQ SUSSEX SUTLER SUTTER SWAGED SWAGES SWALES SWANEE SWAYED SWAYER SWEDEN SWEDES SWIPED SWIPER SWIPES SWIVEL SWIVET SYDNEY SYNCED SYSTEM

S••••E

SABINE SACQUE SADDLE SAFIRE SAINTE SALINE SALOME SALUTE SAMITE SAMMIE SAMPLE SANTEE SARTRE SATIRE SAVAGE SAVATE SAVOIE SCARCE SCARNE SCATHE SCHEME SCONCE SCRAPE SCRIBE SCURVE SCYTHE SEABEE SEANCE SEARLE SECEDE SECURE SEDATE SEDILE SEDUCE SEETHE SEICHE SELENE SEMELE SEMITE SEMPRE SENATE SERAPE SERENE SERINE SESAME SETOSE SETTEE SETTLE SEVERE

SEWAGE SHAYNE SHEAVE SHELVE SHEREE SHIITE SHOPPE SHOWME SHRIKE SHRINE SHRIVE SHROVE SICKLE SIECLE SIGNEE SILAGE SILONE SIMILE SIMONE SIMPLE SINGLE SIRREE SIZZLE SKOKIE SKOPJE SLEAVE SLEAZE SLEDGE SLEEVE SLOANE SLUDGE SLUICE SMUDGE SNATHE SNEEZE SNOOZE SOCAGE SOFINE SOFTIE SOIGNE SOIREE SOLACE SOLUTE SOMBRE SOOTHE SOPHIE SORTIE SOURCE SPARGE SPARSE SPATHE SPECIE SPHERE SPLICE SPLINE SPONGE SPOUSE SPRITE SPRUCE SPURGE SQUARE SQUIRE STABLE STACTE STANCE STAPLE STARVE STATUE STEELE STEEVE STELAE STEPPE STERNE STEVIE

STIFLE STLUKE STODGE STOGIE STOLLE STOOGE STPETE STRAFE STRAKE STRIAE STRIDE STRIFE STRIKE STRIPE STRIVE STROBE STRODE STROKE STROVE STYMIE SUBDUE SUBTLE SUMMAE SUNDAE SUPINE SUPPLE SURETE SUTURE SVELTE SWANEE SWATHE SWAYZE SWERVE

•SE•••

ISELIN ISEULT PSEUDO PSEUDS TSETSE USEDTO USEDUP USEFUL USERID USESUP

•S•E••

ASCEND ASCENT ASKERS ASLEEP ASPECT ASPENS ASPERA ASSENT ASSERT ASSESS ASSETS ASTERN ASTERS ASWELL ESCENT ESKERS ESSENE ESTEEM ESTERS ISLETS ISMENE OSIERS OSSEIN OSSETE OSTEAL OSTEND OSWEGO

USHERS

•S••E•

ASHIER ASHLEY ASIDES ASLEEP BSIDES ESCHER ESCHEW ESPIED ESPIES ESTEEM ESTHER ISABEL ISOHEL ISOMER ISRAEL ISSUED ISSUER ISSUES ISTLES OSAGES OSPREY OSTLER USAGES USOPEN USURER VSIXES

•S•••E

ASHORE ASLOPE ASPIRE ASSIZE ASSUME ASSURE ASTUTE ESCAPE ESSENE ESTATE ISMENE ISOLDE OSCINE OSMOSE OSSETE PSYCHE TSETSE USABLE USANCE

••SE••

ABSENT ANSELM ARSENE ASSENT ASSERT ASSESS ASSETS AXSEED BASELY BASEST BESETS BISECT CASERN COSELL DESERT DOSERS EASEIN EASELS EASEUP EDSELS ESSENE ETSEQQ

EXSERT FUSEES HOSELS INSEAM INSECT INSERT INSETS ITSELF JOSEPH LASERS LOSEIT LOSERS MASERS MASERU MISERS MISERY MOSEYS MUSERS MUSEUM MYSELF NASEBY OBSESS ONSETS OSSEIN OSSETE OUSELS PASEOS PESETA POSERS POSEUR RESEAL RESEAT RESEAU RESECT RESEDA RESEED RESEEN RESEES RESELL RESEND RESENT RESETS RESEWN RESEWS RISERS ROSEAU SASEBO SISERA TVSETS UNSEAL UNSEAT UNSEEN UNSEWN UNSEWS UPSETS WISELY WISENT WISEST WISETO WISEUP

••S•E•

AISLES AMSTEL ANSWER AUSPEX AUSTEN AXSEED BASHED BASHES BASKED BASKET BASSES BASSET

BASTED BASTER BASTES BESSER BESTED BISSET BOSKET BOSLEY BOSSED BOSSES BUSHED BUSHEL BUSHES BUSIED BUSIER BUSIES BUSMEN BUSSED BUSSES BUSTED BUSTER CASHED CASHES CASHEW CASPER CASTER CASTES CISKEI COSHED COSHES COSIES COSSET CUSPED CUSSED CUSSES CUSTER DASHED DASHER DASHES DISHED DISHES DISKED DISMES DISNEY DISPEL DISSED DOSSED DOSSEL DOSSER DOSSES DUSTED DUSTER EASIER EASTER EISNER ENSUED ENSUES FASCES FASTED FASTEN FASTER FESSES FESTER FISHED FISHER FISHES FISTED FOSSES FOSSEY FOSTER FUSEES FUSSED FUSSES GASHED

GASHES GASJET GASKET GASMEN GASPED GASSED GASSER GASSES GESTES GOSHEN GOSPEL GUSHED GUSHER GUSHES GUSSET GUSTED HASHED HASHES HASPED HASTEN HASTES HESTER HISSED HISSER HISSES HOSIER HOSTED HOSTEL HUSHED HUSHES HUSKED HUSKER IJSSEL INSTEP ISSUED ISSUER ISSUES JASPER JESSEL JESTED JESTER JOSHED JOSHES JOSSES JUSTER KISLEV KISMET KISSED KISSER KISSES KOSHER LASHED LASHER LASHES LASSEN LASSER LASSES LASTED LASTEX LESLEY LESSEE LESSEN LESSER LESTER LISLES LISPED LISTED LISTEE LISTEL LISTEN LISTER LOSSES LUSHER LUSTED

LUSTER MASHED MASHER MASHES MASKED MASKER MASSED MASSES MASSEY MASTER MESHED MESHES MESMER MESSED MESSES MISLED MISSED MISSES MISTED MISTER MOSLEM MOSSED MOSSES MOSTEL MUSHED MUSHER MUSHES MUSKEG MUSKET MUSSED MUSSEL MUSSES MUSTER NASSER NESSES NESTEA NESTED NESTER NISSEN NOSHED NOSHER NOSHES NOSIER OBSTET ONSPEC OUSTED OUSTER OYSTER PASSED PASSEL PASSER PASSES PASTED PASTEL PASTES PESTER PISCES POSHER POSIES POSSES POSSET POSTED POSTER PUSHED PUSHES PUSSES RASHER RASHES RASPED RASPER RASTER RESEED RESEEN RESEES

RESTED RESTER RISKED RISKER ROSIER ROSTER RUSHED RUSHEE RUSHES RUSSET RUSTED SASHED SASHES SASSED SASSER SASSES SESTET SISKEL SISLER SISTER SUSIEQ SUSSEX SYSTEM TASKED TASSEL TASSES TASTED TASTER TASTES TESTED TESTEE TESTER TOSSED TOSSER TOSSES TUSKED TUSKER ULSTER UNSEEN UNSHED VASTER VESPER VESSEL VESTED VESTEE VISAED VOSGES WASHED WASHER WASHES WASTED WASTER WASTES WESLEY WESSEX WISHED WISHER WISHES WISPED WISTER XYSTER YASSER YESMEN YESSED YESSES YESTER ZESTED

••S••E

ALSACE ANSATE ARSENE ASSIZE ASSUME

ASSURE AUSSIE BASQUE BESIDE BESSIE BISQUE BUSTLE BYSSHE CASQUE CASTLE CESARE COSINE COSTAE DESIRE DISUSE DOSAGE ENSILE ENSURE ESSENE FESCUE FOSSAE HASSLE HUSTLE INSANE INSIDE INSOLE INSURE JESSIE JOSTLE KISHKE LASSIE LESAGE LESLIE LESSEE LISTEE LUSTRE LYSINE MASHIE MASQUE MISCUE MISUSE MOSQUE MUSCLE MUSKIE NESSIE NESTLE NOSALE ONSALE ONSIDE ONSITE OSSETE PESTLE RASSLE RESALE RESCUE RESHOE RESIDE RESILE RESOLE RESUME RISQUE ROSCOE RUSHEE RUSTLE SESAME TESSIE TESTAE TESTEE TISANE TISSUE TUSSLE UNSAFE UNSURE UPSIDE

URSINE VESTEE VISAGE VISINE WASHOE

•••SE•

ABASED ABASES ABUSED ABUSER ABUSES ALLSET AMUSED AMUSES ARISEN ARISES BASSES BASSET BESSER BETSEY BIASED BIASES BISSET BOSSED BOSSES BOWSER BOXSET BUNSEN BURSES BUSSED BUSSES CAUSED CAUSES CEASED CEASES CENSED CENSER CENSES CHASED CHASER CHASES CHISEL CHOSEN CLOSED CLOSER CLOSES CLOSET COPSES CORSET COSSET CRISES CRUSES CURSED CURSES CUSSED CUSSES DAISES DAMSEL DENSER DIESEL DIESES DILSEY DISSED DORSET DORSEY DOSSED DOSSEL DOSSER DOSSES DOUSED DOUSES DOWSED DOWSER

DOWSES ELYSEE ERASED ERASER ERASES FALSER FESSES FOSSES FOSSEY FRASER FRISEE FRISES FUSSED FUSSES GASSED GASSER GASSES GEISEL GELSEY GETSET GEYSER GLASER GOOSED GOOSES GORSES GUISES GUSSET HALSEY HANSEL HAWSER HAWSES HERSEY HISSED HISSER HISSES HORSED HORSES HORSEY HOUSED HOUSES IBISES IJSSEL IRISES JANSEN JENSEN JERSEY JESSEL JETSET JOSSES KAISER KELSEY KERSEY KISSED KISSER KISSES LAPSED LAPSES LARSEN LASSEN LASSER LASSES LEASED LEASER LEASES LENSED LENSES LESSEE LESSEN LESSER LINSEY LOOSED LOOSEN LOOSER LOOSES

LOSSES
LOUSED
LOUSES
MANSES
MASSED
MASSES
MASSEY
MAUSER
MERSEY
MESSED
MESSES
MISSED
MISSES
MORSEL
MOSSED
MOSSES
MOUSED
MOUSER
MOUSES
MOUSEY
MUSSED
MUSSEL
MUSSES
NANSEN
NASSER
NAUSEA
NESSES
NISSEN
NOISED
NOISES
NOOSES
NURSED
NURSER
NURSES
OCASEK
OCASEY
OFFSET
ONUSES
OPUSES
OUTSET
PARSEC
PARSED
PARSEE
PARSER
PARSES
PASSED
PASSEL
PASSER
PASSES
PAUSED
PAUSES
PENSEE
PHASED
PHASER
PHASES
PHYSED
PLUSES
POISED
POISES
POSSES
POSSET
PRESET
PROSED
PROSER
PROSES
PULSED
PULSES
PURSED
PURSER
PURSES
PUSSES
RAISED
RAISER
RAISES
RAMSES
RAMSEY
REDSEA
REUSED
REUSES
RINSED
RINSES
ROUSED
ROUSES
RUSSET
SANSEI
SASSED
SASSER
SASSES
SENSED
SENSEI
SENSES
SOUSED
SOUSES
STASES
SUBSET
SUDSED
SUDSES
SUNSET
SUSSEX
TASSEL
TASSES
TEASED
TEASEL
TEASER
TEASES
TEASET
TENSED
TENSER
TENSES
TERSER
THESES
TINSEL
TOSSED
TOSSER
TOSSES
UKASES
UNISEX
UNUSED
URUSES
VERSED
VERSES
VESSEL
WEASEL
WESSEX
WIESEL
WIMSEY
WOLSEY
WORSEN
YASSER
YESSED
YESSES

•••S•E
ADESTE
AUSSIE
BESSIE
BURSAE
BYSSHE
CHASSE
CHASTE
CROSSE
CRUSOE
CUISSE
ELYSEE
ENISLE
FOCSLE
FOSSAE
FRISEE
GROSSE
HASSLE
JESSIE
KRESGE
LASSIE
LESSEE
LETSBE
MAISIE
MENSAE
MOUSSE
NEISSE
NESSIE
PARSEE
PENSEE
PLISSE
POUSSE
PUISNE
PURSUE
RASSLE
TESSIE
THISBE
TISSUE
TOUSLE
TRISTE
TUSSLE
WRASSE

••••SE
ACCUSE
ADVISE
ALDOSE
APPOSE
ARIOSE
AROUSE
ATEASE
AVERSE
AVULSE
BEMUSE
BETISE
BLAISE
BLOUSE
BOURSE
BRAISE
BROWSE
BRUISE
CAMISE
CAYUSE
CERISE
CERUSE
CHAISE
CHASSE
CHEESE
CHOOSE
CLAUSE
CLEESE
COARSE
COURSE
CREASE
CROSSE
CROUSE
CRUISE
CUISSE
DEBASE
DEFUSE
DEMISE
DENISE
DEPOSE
DEVISE
DISUSE
DROWSE
EFFUSE
ELAPSE
ELOISE
ENCASE
ENDUSE
EVULSE
EXCISE
EXCUSE
EXPOSE
FILOSE
FLENSE
FRAISE
GREASE
GRILSE
GROSSE
GROUSE
GYROSE
HOARSE
ILLUSE
IMPOSE
INCASE
INCISE
INCUSE
INFUSE
JOCOSE
LANOSE
LAOTSE
LHOTSE
LIAISE
LIPASE
LOUISE
MISUSE
MOROSE
MOUSSE
NEISSE
NODOSE
NOWISE
OBTUSE
ODENSE
OPPOSE
ORELSE
OSMOSE
OTIOSE
PERUSE
PHRASE
PILOSE
PLEASE
PLISSE
POUSSE
PRAISE
PROWSE
RAMOSE
RECUSE
REFUSE
REMISE
REPOSE
REVISE
RIBOSE
RIMOSE
RUGOSE
SETOSE
SPARSE
SPOUSE
TALESE
TOROSE
TSETSE
UNCASE
UNEASE
UNWISE
UPRISE
UPROSE
VADOSE
VALISE
VARESE
WRASSE
ZYMASE

SF••••
SFORZA

S•F•••
SAFARI
SAFELY
SAFEST
SAFETY
SAFIRE
SIFTED
SIFTER
SOFFIT
SOFINE
SOFTEN
SOFTER
SOFTIE
SOFTLY
SUFFER
SUFFIX
SUFISM

S••F••
SAWFIT
SCIFIS
SCOFFS
SCUFFS
SEAFAN
SEAFOX
SEEFIT
SHAFTS
SHIFTS
SHIFTY
SHOFAR
SINFUL
SKIFFS
SNAFUS
SNIFFS
SNIFFY
SNUFFS
SNUFFY
SOFFIT
SOLFAS
SPIFFS
SPIFFY
STAFFS
STEFAN
STEFFI
STIFFS
STIFLE
STUFFS
STUFFY
SUFFER
SUFFIX
SULFUR
SURFED
SURFER
SWIFTS

S•••F•
SAWOFF
SCARFS
SCHIFF
SCLAFF
SCOFFS
SCRUFF
SCUFFS
SCURFY
SEEOFF
SERIFS
SETOFF
SHEAFS
SHRIFT
SKIFFS
SMURFS
SNIFFS
SNIFFY
SNUFFS
SNUFFY
SPIFFS
SPIFFY
SPOOFS
STAFFS
STEFFI
STIFFS
STRAFE
STRIFE
STUFFS
STUFFY

S••••F
SAWOFF
SCHIFF
SCLAFF
SCRUFF
SEEOFF
SETOFF
SHARIF
SHERIF
SORTOF
STAPUF

•S•F••
ASKFOR
USEFUL

•S••F•
OSSIFY

••SF••
MISFIT

••S•F•
GOSOFT
OSSIFY
UNSAFE

••S••F
ITSELF
MASSIF
MYSELF

•••S•F
MASSIF

SG••••
SGTMAJ

S•G•••
SAGELY
SAGEST
SAGGED
SEGUED
SEGUES
SEGURA
SIGHED
SIGHER
SIGHTS
SIGILS
SIGMAS
SIGNAL
SIGNED
SIGNEE
SIGNER
SIGNET
SIGNIN
SIGNON
SIGNOR
SIGNUP
SIGURD
SUGARS
SUGARY

S••G••
SAGGED
SAIGAS
SAIGON
SANGER
SANGTO
SARGES
SARGON
SARGOS
SAUGER
SEAGAL
SEDGES
SEEGER
SERGEI
SERGES
SERGIO
SHAGGY
SHOGUN
SIEGED
SIEGES
SINGED
SINGER
SINGES
SINGLE
SINGLY
SINGTO
SIXGUN
SLAGGY
SLIGHT
SLOGAN
SLUGGO
SMOGGY
SMUGLY
SNAGGY
SNUGLY
SOIGNE
SOUGHS
SOUGHT
SPIGOT
STAGED
STAGER
STAGES
STIGMA
STOGIE
SUBGUM
SUNGOD
SURGED
SURGES
SWAGED
SWAGES

S•••G•
SAVAGE
SCRAGS
SENEGA
SEWAGE
SHAGGY
SHRUGS
SILAGE
SLAGGY
SLANGS
SLANGY
SLEDGE
SLEIGH
SLINGS
SLOUGH
SLUDGE
SLUDGY
SLUGGO
SMOGGY
SMUDGE
SMUDGY
SNAGGY
SOCAGE
SPARGE
SPONGE
SPONGY
SPRAGS
SPRIGS
SPURGE
STINGS
STINGY
STODGE
STODGY
STOOGE
SWINGS
SWINGY
SYZYGY

S••••G
SARONG
SATANG
SATING
SAVING
SAWING
SAWLOG
SAYING
SEABAG
SEADOG
SEBERG
SEEING
SEWING
SHYING
SIDING
SIRING
SITING
SIXING
SIZING
SKIING
SKYING
SLUING
SOLING
SOLONG
SONTAG
SOWBUG
SOWING
SPRANG
SPRING
SPRUNG
SPYING
STALAG
STENOG
STRING
STRONG
STRUNG
SUNDOG

•SG•••
ASGARD
OSGOOD

•S•G••
ISOGON
OSAGES
USAGES
VSIGNS

•S••G•
ASSIGN
OSWEGO

•S•••G
ASKING

••SG••
ANSGAR
PISGAH
VOSGES

••S•G•
ASSIGN
COSIGN
DESIGN
DOSAGE
ENSIGN
LESAGE
RESIGN
VISAGE

••S••G
BASING
BUSING
CASING
DOSING
EASING
FUSING
GASBAG
GASLOG
GOSTAG
HOSING
LOSING
MUSING
MUSKEG
NOSING
POSING
RESING
RISING
UNSNAG
UNSUNG

•••SG•
KRESGE
LETSGO

SH••••
SHABAN
SHABBY
SHACKS
SHADED
SHADES
SHADOW
SHAFTS
SHAGGY
SHAKEN
SHAKER
SHAKES
SHAKOS
SHAKTI
SHALES
SHALEY
SHALLY
SHALOM
SHAMAN
SHAMED
SHAMES
SHAMIR
SHAMUS
SHANDY
SHANKS
SHANTY
SHAPED
SHAPER
SHAPES
SHARDS
SHARED
SHARER
SHARES
SHARIA
SHARIF
SHARKS
SHARON
SHARPS
SHASTA
SHAVED
SHAVEN
SHAVER
SHAVES
SHAWLS
SHAWMS
SHAYNE
SHAZAM
SHBOOM
SHEAFS
SHEARS
SHEATH
SHEAVE
SHEEDY
SHEEHY
SHEENA
SHEENS
SHEEPS
SHEERS
SHEETS
SHEIKS
SHEILA
SHEKEL
SHELLS
SHELLY
SHELVE
SHEREE
SHERIF
SHERPA
SHERRY
SHEVAT
SHIELD
SHIEST
SHIFTS
SHIFTY
SHIISM
SHIITE
SHILLS
SHILLY
SHILOH
SHIMMY
SHIMON
SHINDY
SHINED
SHINER
SHINES
SHINNY
SHINTO
SHIRAZ
SHIRER
SHIRES
SHIRKS
SHIRRS
SHIRTS
SHIRTY
SHIVER
SHOALS
SHOATS
SHOCKS
SHODDY
SHOERS
SHOFAR
SHOGUN
SHOJIS
SHOLEM
SHOLOM
SHOOED
SHOOIN
SHOOKS
SHOOTS
SHOPPE
SHORAN
SHORED
SHORES
SHORTS
SHORTY
SHOTAT
SHOTUP
SHOULD
SHOUTS
SHOVED
SHOVEL
SHOVER
SHOVES
SHOWED
SHOWER
SHOWIN
SHOWME
SHOWUP
SHRANK
SHREDS
SHREWD
SHREWS
SHRIEK
SHRIFT
SHRIKE
SHRILL
SHRIMP
SHRINE
SHRINK
SHRIVE
SHROUD
SHROVE
SHRUBS
SHRUGS
SHRUNK
SHTETL
SHTICK
SHUCKS
SHUNTS
SHUTIN
SHUTUP
SHYEST
SHYING

S•H•••
SAHARA
SAHIBS
SCHELL
SCHEMA
SCHEME
SCHICK
SCHIFF
SCHISM
SCHIST
SCHLEP
SCHMOO
SCHMOS
SCHNOZ
SCHOOL
SCHORL
SCHULZ
SCHUSS
SCHWAS
SPHERE
SPHINX
STHENO

S••H••
SACHEM
SACHET
SASHAY
SASHED
SASHES
SENHOR
SIGHED
SIGHER
SIGHTS
SIPHON
SOPHIA
SOPHIE
SOTHAT
SOWHAT
SPAHIS
SUCHAS

S•••H•
SANCHO
SAPPHO
SCATHE
SCYTHE
SEETHE
SEICHE
SHEEHY
SIXTHS
SLIGHT
SLITHY
SLOSHY
SLOTHS
SLUSHY
SMITHS
SMITHY
SNATHE
SNATHS
SOOTHE
SOUGHS
SOUGHT
SPATHE
STJOHN
SURAHS
SWATHE
SWATHS
SYLPHS

S••••H
SALISH
SAMEKH
SCORCH
SCOTCH
SCUTCH
SEARCH
SERAPH
SHEATH
SHILOH
SIRRAH
SIWASH
SKETCH
SKITCH
SLEIGH
SLEUTH
SLOUCH
SLOUGH
SMERSH
SMIRCH
SMOOCH
SMOOTH
SMUTCH
SNATCH
SNITCH
SPEECH
SPILTH
SPLASH
SPLOSH
SQUASH
SQUISH
STANCH
STARCH
STENCH
STITCH
STORCH
SUKKAH
SWARTH
SWATCH
SWITCH
SWOOSH

•SH•••
ASHARP
ASHCAN
ASHIER
ASHLAR
ASHLEY
ASHORE
ASHRAM
BSHARP
CSHARP
DSHARP
ESHARP
FSHARP
GSHARP
ISHTAR
OSHAWA
TSHIRT
USHERS

•S•H••
ASCHAM
ESCHER
ESCHEW
ESTHER
ISCHIA
ISOHEL
ISTHMI

•S••H•
PSYCHE
PSYCHO
PSYCHS

•S•••H
ISAIAH

••SH••
BASHED
BASHES
BISHOP
BUSHED
BUSHEL
BUSHES
BUSHWA
CASHED
CASHES
CASHEW
CASHIN
COSHED
COSHES
CUSHAW
DASHED
DASHER
DASHES
DISHED
DISHES
FISHED
FISHER
FISHES
GASHED
GASHES
GOSHEN
GUSHED
GUSHER
GUSHES
HASHED
HASHES
HUSHED
HUSHES
JOSHED
JOSHES
JOSHUA
KESHIA
KISHKE
KOSHER
LASHED
LASHER
LASHES
LASHIO
LASHUP
LUSHER
LUSHLY
MASHED
MASHER
MASHES
MASHIE
MESHED
MESHES
MISHAP
MISHIT
MOSHAV
MUSHED
MUSHER
MUSHES
NASHUA
NOSHED
NOSHER
NOSHES
NOSHOW
PASHAS
PASHTO
POSHER
POSHLY
PUSHED
PUSHES
PUSHON
PUSHUP
RASHAD
RASHER
RASHES
RASHID
RASHLY
RESHIP
RESHOD
RESHOE
RESHOT
RUSHED
RUSHEE
RUSHES
SASHAY
SASHED
SASHES
TISHRI
TVSHOW
UNSHED
UNSHOD
UPSHOT
VASHTI
VISHNU
WASHED
WASHER
WASHES
WASHOE
WASHUP
WISHED
WISHER
WISHES

••S•H•
BYSSHE
JASCHA
MISCHA

••S••H
CASBAH
JOSEPH
JOSIAH
KASBAH
PESACH
PISGAH
TUSSAH

•••SH•
AYESHA
BRASHY
BRUSHY
BUQSHA
BYSSHE
ELISHA
FLASHY
FLESHY
GEISHA
GUNSHY
HONSHU
ILESHA
KYUSHU
MARSHA
MARSHY
PLASHY
PLUSHY
SLOSHY
SLUSHY
TRASHY
TRISHA

•••S•H
BORSCH
HIRSCH
KIRSCH
KITSCH
MENSCH
PUTSCH
TUSSAH

••••SH
ABLUSH
AFRESH
AMBUSH
BANISH
BLUISH
BOYISH
BYGOSH
CALASH
DANISH
DOVISH
ELFISH
EMDASH
ENDASH
ENMESH
FAMISH
FETISH
FINISH
GALOSH
GARISH
GOFISH
IMPISH
INCASH
INRUSH
IRTYSH
JEWISH
KIBOSH
LAGASH

LATISH
LAVISH
MODISH
MOPISH
MULISH
NEWISH
OAFISH
OFFISH
OLDISH
ONRUSH
OWLISH
PALISH
PARISH
PERISH
POLISH
POTASH
PUNISH
QURUSH
RADISH
RAKISH
RAVISH
REHASH
RELISH
REWASH
SALISH
SIWASH
SMERSH
SPLASH
SPLOSH
SQUASH
SQUISH
SWOOSH
THRASH
THRESH
THRUSH
TONISH
UNLASH
UNMESH
UPRUSH
VANISH
WABASH
WHOOSH

SI••••
SIBYLS
SICCED
SICILY
SICKEN
SICKER
SICKLE
SICKLY
SIDDUR
SIDERO
SIDERS
SIDING
SIDLED
SIDLES
SIDNEY
SIECLE
SIEGED
SIEGES
SIENNA
SIERRA
SIESTA
SIEVED
SIEVES
SIFTED
SIFTER
SIGHED
SIGHER
SIGHTS
SIGILS
SIGMAS
SIGNAL
SIGNED
SIGNEE
SIGNER
SIGNET
SIGNIN
SIGNON
SIGNOR
SIGNUP
SIGURD
SIKKIM
SILAGE
SILENI
SILENT
SILICA
SILKED
SILKEN
SILOAM
SILOED
SILONE
SILTED
SILVER
SIMBEL
SIMEON
SIMIAN
SIMILE
SIMMER
SIMONE
SIMONY
SIMPER
SIMPLE
SIMPLY
SINBAD
SINEAD
SINEWS
SINEWY
SINFUL
SINGED
SINGER
SINGES
SINGLE
SINGLY
SINGTO
SINKER
SINKIN
SINNED
SINNER
SINTAX
SINTER
SIOUAN
SIPHON
SIPPED
SIPPER
SIPPET
SIRDAR
SIRENS
SIRICA
SIRING
SIRIUS
SIRRAH
SIRREE
SISALS
SISERA
SISKEL
SISKIN
SISLER
SISTER
SITARS
SITCOM
SITING
SITINS
SITOUT
SITSIN
SITSON
SITSUP
SITTER
SITUPS
SIWASH
SIXERS
SIXGUN
SIXING
SIXTHS
SIXTUS
SIZERS
SIZEUP
SIZING
SIZZLE

S•I•••
SAIGAS
SAIGON
SAILED
SAILOR
SAINTE
SAINTS
SAIPAN
SCIFIS
SCIONS
SCIPIO
SEICHE
SEIDEL
SEINED
SEINER
SEINES
SEISMO
SEISMS
SEIZED
SEIZER
SEIZES
SHIELD
SHIEST
SHIFTS
SHIFTY
SHIISM
SHIITE
SHILLS
SHILLY
SHILOH
SHIMMY
SHIMON
SHINDY
SHINED
SHINER
SHINES
SHINNY
SHINTO
SHIRAZ
SHIRER
SHIRES
SHIRKS
SHIRRS
SHIRTS
SHIRTY
SHIVER
SKIERS
SKIFFS
SKIING
SKILLS
SKIMPS
SKIMPY
SKINKS
SKINNY
SKIPPY
SKIRLS
SKIROS
SKIRRS
SKIRTS
SKIRUN
SKITCH
SKITOW
SKIVED
SKIVER
SKIVES
SKIVVY
SLICED
SLICER
SLICES
SLICKS
SLIDER
SLIDES
SLIDIN
SLIEST
SLIGHT
SLIMED
SLIMES
SLIMLY
SLINGS
SLINKS
SLINKY
SLIPIN
SLIPON
SLIPUP
SLITHY
SLITTY
SLIVER
SMILAX
SMILED
SMILER
SMILES
SMILEY
SMIRCH
SMIRKS
SMIRKY
SMITES
SMITHS
SMITHY
SNICKS
SNIDER
SNIFFS
SNIFFY
SNIPED
SNIPES
SNIPPY
SNITCH
SNIVEL
SOIGNE
SOILED
SOIREE
SPICAS
SPICED
SPICES
SPIDER
SPIELS
SPIERS
SPIFFS
SPIFFY
SPIGOT
SPIKED
SPIKER
SPIKES
SPILES
SPILLS
SPILTH
SPINAL
SPINED
SPINEL
SPINES
SPINET
SPINKS
SPIRAL
SPIREA
SPIRED
SPIRES
SPIRIT
SPIROS
SPITED
SPITES
SPIVAK
STICKS
STICKY
STIFFS
STIFLE
STIGMA
STILES
STILLS
STILLY
STILTS
STIMPY
STINGS
STINGY
STINKS
STINKY
STINTS
STIPEL
STIPES
STIRIN
STIRUP
STITCH
STIVER
STIVIC
SUITED
SUITES
SUITOR
SUITUP
SWIFTS
SWILLS
SWINGS
SWINGY
SWIPED
SWIPER
SWIPES
SWIRLS
SWIRLY
SWITCH
SWIVEL
SWIVET

S••I••
SABINE
SABINS
SAFIRE
SAHIBS
SALINA
SALINE
SALISH
SALIVA
SAMIAM
SAMITE
SANITY
SATING
SATINS
SATINY
SATIRE
SAVING
SAVIOR
SAWING
SAYING
SCHICK
SCHIFF
SCHISM
SCHIST
SCRIBE
SCRIMP
SCRIMS
SCRIPS
SCRIPT
SEDILE
SEEING
SEMITE
SENIOR
SEPIAS
SERIAL
SERIES
SERIFS
SERINE
SERINS
SETINS
SEWING
SEXIER
SEXILY
SEXIST
SHEIKS
SHEILA
SHIISM
SHIITE
SHRIEK
SHRIFT
SHRIKE
SHRILL
SHRIMP
SHRINE
SHRINK
SHRIVE
SHTICK
SHYING
SICILY
SIDING
SIGILS
SILICA
SIMIAN
SIMILE
SIRICA
SIRING
SIRIUS
SITING
SITINS
SIXING
SIZING
SKEINS
SKIING
SKYING
SLEIGH
SLUICE
SLUING
SNAILS
SOCIAL
SODIUM
SOFINE
SOLIDI
SOLIDS
SOLING
SONICS
SOVIET
SOWING
SPHINX
SPLICE
SPLINE
SPLINT
SPLITS
SPOILS
SPOILT
SPRIER
SPRIGS
SPRING
SPRINT
SPRITE
SPRITS
SPRITZ
SPYING
SQUIBB
SQUIBS
SQUIDS
SQUILL
SQUINT
SQUIRE
SQUIRM
SQUIRT
SQUISH
STAINS
STAIRS
STEINS
STOICS
STRIAE
STRICK
STRICT
STRIDE
STRIFE
STRIKE
STRING
STRIPE
STRIPS
STRIVE
SUBITO
SUFISM
SUPINE
SURIMI
SUSIEQ
SWAINS
SYRIAN
SYRINX

S•••I•
SALVIA
SAMMIE
SANDIA
SANTIR
SARDIS
SAUDIS
SAVAII
SAVOIE
SAVOIR
SAWFIT
SAYYID
SCALIA
SCENIC
SCIFIS
SCIPIO
SCORIA
SCOTIA
SEEFIT
SEEPIN
SEESIN
SENDIN
SENNIT
SENTIN
SEPTIC
SEQUIN
SERAIS
SERBIA
SERGIO
SERKIN
SETSIN
SHAMIR
SHARIA
SHARIF
SHERIF
SHOJIS
SHOOIN
SHOWIN
SHUTIN
SIGNIN
SIKKIM
SINKIN
SISKIN
SITSIN
SKOKIE
SLAVIC
SLIDIN
SLIPIN
SLOVIK
SNOWIN
SOBEIT
SOCKIN
SOFFIT
SOFTIE
SOLEIL
SOPHIA
SOPHIE
SORBIC
SORDID
SORTIE
SPADIX
SPAHIS
SPAVIN
SPECIE
SPIRIT
SPRAIN
STADIA
STALIN
STASIS
STATIC
STEPIN
STEVIE
STIRIN
STIVIC
STOGIE
STOLID
STOPIN
STOPIT
STRAIN
STRAIT
STUDIO
STUPID
STYMIE
STYRIA
SUBMIT
SUCKIN
SUFFIX
SUMMIT
SUNLIT
SUNNIS
SUSLIK
SWAMIS
SWAZIS
SYLVIA
SYNDIC

S••••I
SAFARI
SALAMI
SALUKI
SANSEI
SATORI
SAVAII
SCAMPI
SENSEI
SERGEI
SESQUI
SHAKTI
SILENI
SMALTI
SOLIDI
SOMALI
SOUARI
STEFFI
STRATI
SURIMI
SUZUKI

•SI•••
ASIANS
ASIDES
ASIMOV
BSIDES
OSIERS
OSIRIS
VSIGNS
VSIXES

•S•I••
ASHIER
ASKING
ASPICS
ASPIRE
ASSIGN
ASSISI
ASSIST
ASSIZE
ASWIRL
ESKIMO
ESPIAL
ESPIED
ESPIES
GSUITS
ISAIAH
OSCINE
OSMICS
OSMIUM
OSSIAN
OSSIFY
OSTIUM
TSHIRT

•S••I•
ASSAIL
ASTRID
ESPRIT
ISCHIA
ISELIN
ISTRIA
OSIRIS
OSSEIN
USERID
USMAIL

•S•••I
ASKARI
ASSISI
ISTHMI

••SI••
ASSIGN
ASSISI
ASSIST
ASSIZE
BASICS
BASING
BASINS
BESIDE
BUSIED
BUSIER
BUSIES
BUSILY
BUSING
CASING
CASINO
CESIUM
COSIES
COSIGN
COSINE
DESICA
DESIGN
DESILU
DESIRE
DESIST
DOSIDO
DOSING
EASIER
EASILY
EASING
ENSIGN
ENSILE
EOSINS
FUSILS
FUSING
FUSION
HESIOD
HOSIER
HOSING
INSIDE
INSIST
INSITU
JOSIAH
LOSING
LYSINE
LYSINS
MUSIAL
MUSING
NOSIER
NOSILY
NOSING
ONSIDE
ONSITE
ORSINO
OSSIAN
OSSIFY
POSIES
POSING
POSITS
RESIDE
RESIGN
RESILE
RESING
RESINS
RESIST
RISING
ROSIER
ROSILY
ROSINS
ROSINY
ROSITA
SUSIEQ
UPSIDE
URSIDS
URSINE
VISINE
VISION
VISITS

••S•I•
ASSAIL
AUSSIE
AUSTIN
BESSIE
BESTIR
BOSNIA
BUSKIN
CASHIN
CASSIA
CASSIO
CASSIS
COSMIC
CUSPID
DASSIN
DISTIL
DUSTIN
EASEIN
FASCIA
FISTIC
FOSSIL
FUSTIC
GASKIN
GASLIT
GOSSIP
HESTIA
HISPID
JESSIE
JESUIT
JUSTIN
KESHIA
LASHIO
LASSIE
LESLIE
LOSEIT
LOSTIT
MASAIS
MASHIE
MASSIF
MASTIC
MISDID
MISFIT
MISHIT
MISSIS
MOSAIC
MUSKIE
MUSLIM
MUSLIN
MYSTIC
NESSIE
OSSEIN
PASSIM
PASTIS
PISTIL
RASHID
RESHIP
RESNIK
RUSKIN
RUSSIA
RUSTIC
SISKIN
SUSLIK
TESSIE
UNSAID
VESPID
VISCID
WESKIT
YESSIR

••S••I
ASSISI
BUSONI
CISKEI
MESABI
SESQUI
TISHRI
VASHTI
WASABI

•••SI•
ADDSIN
AUSSIE
BESSIE
BIDSIN
CAPSID
CASSIA
CASSIO
CASSIS
COUSIN
CRISIS
CUTSIN
DASSIN
DIESIS
DIGSIN
DOESIN
DOGSIT
EATSIN
ECESIS
ENOSIS
FITSIN
FOGSIN
FOSSIL
GETSIN
GETSIT
GNOSIS
GOESIN
GOSSIP
HEMSIN
HITSIT
ICESIN
IRISIN
JAMSIN
JESSIE
KEYSIN
LASSIE
LAYSIN
LETSIN
LIESIN
LOGSIN
MAISIE
MASSIF
MIOSIS
MISSIS
MYOSIN
NESSIE
NOESIS
PASSIM
PAYSIN
PEPSIN
PERSIA
PHYSIO
POPSIN
PROSIT
PUTSIN
RAISIN
RUBSIN
RUNSIN
RUSSIA
SEESIN
SETSIN
SITSIN
STASIS
TESSIE
THESIS
THESIX
TIESIN
TILSIT
TIPSIN
TMESIS
TOCSIN
TOESIN
TONSIL
YESSIR
ZOYSIA

•••S•I
AGASSI
BONSAI
JETSKI
KINSKI
SANSEI
SENSEI

••••SI
AGASSI
ASSISI
CHUHSI
DALASI
LUGOSI
POTOSI
THYRSI
TZUHSI
WATUSI

S•J•••
SEJANT
STJOAN
STJOHN

S••J••
SELJUK
SHOJIS
STOJKO

S•••J•
SKOPJE

S••••J
SGTMAJ
SWARAJ

••SJ••
GASJET

SK••••
SKALDS
SKATED
SKATER
SKATES
SKEANS
SKEINS
SKERRY
SKETCH
SKEWED
SKEWER
SKIERS
SKIFFS
SKIING
SKILLS
SKIMPS
SKIMPY
SKINKS
SKINNY
SKIPPY
SKIRLS
SKIROS
SKIRRS
SKIRTS
SKIRUN
SKITCH
SKITOW
SKIVED
SKIVER
SKIVES
SKIVVY
SKOKIE
SKOPJE
SKULKS
SKULLS
SKUNKS
SKYBOX
SKYCAP
SKYING
SKYLAB
SKYWAY

S•K•••
SAKERS
SIKKIM
SUKKAH

S••K••
SACKED
SACKER
SECKEL
SEEKER
SERKIN
SHAKEN
SHAKER
SHAKES
SHAKOS
SHAKTI
SHEKEL
SICKEN
SICKER
SICKLE
SICKLY
SIKKIM
SILKED
SILKEN
SINKER
SINKIN
SISKEL
SISKIN
SKOKIE
SLAKED
SLAKES
SMOKED
SMOKER
SMOKES
SMOKEY
SNAKED
SNAKES
SOAKED
SOAKER
SOAKUP
SOCKED
SOCKET
SOCKIN
SPIKED
SPIKER
SPIKES
SPOKED
SPOKEN
SPOKES
STAKED
STAKES
STOKED
STOKER
STOKES
SUCKED
SUCKER
SUCKIN
SUKKAH
SULKED
SULKER
SUNKEN

S•••K•
SALUKI
SAMEKH
SEDAKA
SHACKS
SHANKS
SHARKS
SHEIKS
SHIRKS
SHOCKS
SHOOKS
SHRIKE
SHUCKS
SKINKS
SKULKS
SKUNKS
SLACKS
SLEEKS
SLEEKY
SLICKS
SLINKS
SLINKY
SMACKS
SMIRKS
SMIRKY
SMOCKS
SNACKS
SNEAKS
SNEAKY
SNICKS
SNOOKS
SPANKS
SPANKY
SPARKS
SPARKY
SPEAKS
SPECKS
SPINKS
SPOOKS
SPOOKY
SPUNKY
STACKS
STALKS
STALKY
STANKY
STEAKS
STICKS
STICKY
STINKS
STINKY
STLUKE
STOCKS
STOCKY
STOJKO
STORKS
STRAKE
STRIKE
STROKE
SUZUKI
SWANKY

S••••K
SCHICK
SCREAK
SELJUK
SENDAK
SHRANK
SHRIEK
SHRINK
SHRUNK
SHTICK
SLEZAK
SLOVAK
SLOVIK
SPACEK
SPIVAK
SQUAWK
SQUEAK
STMARK
STREAK
STRICK
STRUCK
SUSLIK

•SK•••
ASKARI
ASKERS
ASKFOR
ASKING
ASKOUT
ESKERS

ESKIMO

••SK••
BASKED
BASKET
BOSKET
BUSKIN
CISKEI
DISKED
GASKET
GASKIN
HUSKED
HUSKER
MASKED
MASKER
MOSKVA
MUSKEG
MUSKET
MUSKIE
MUSKOX
RISKED
RISKER
RUSKIN
SISKEL
SISKIN
TASKED
TUSKED
TUSKER
WESKIT

••S•K•
KISHKE
LUSAKA

••S••K
RESNIK
SUSLIK
VOSTOK

•••SK•
ALASKA
FLASKS
FRISKS
FRISKY
JETSKI
KINSKI
KIOSKS
NEVSKY
RIMSKY
WHISKS

•••S•K
OCASEK

••••SK
ATRISK
DAMASK
GDANSK
UNMASK
URALSK

SL••••
SLACKS
SLAGGY
SLAKED
SLAKES
SLALOM
SLANGS
SLANGY
SLANTS
SLAPPY
SLAPUP
SLATED
SLATER
SLATES
SLAVED
SLAVER
SLAVES
SLAVIC
SLAYED
SLAYER
SLEAVE
SLEAZE
SLEAZY
SLEDGE
SLEEKS
SLEEKY
SLEEPS
SLEEPY
SLEETS
SLEETY
SLEEVE
SLEIGH
SLEUTH
SLEWED
SLEZAK
SLICED
SLICER
SLICES
SLICKS
SLIDER
SLIDES
SLIDIN
SLIEST
SLIGHT
SLIMED
SLIMES
SLIMLY
SLINGS
SLINKS
SLINKY
SLIPIN
SLIPON
SLIPUP
SLITHY
SLITTY
SLIVER
SLOANE
SLOGAN
SLOOPS
SLOPED
SLOPES
SLOPPY
SLOSHY
SLOTHS
SLOUCH
SLOUGH
SLOVAK
SLOVEN
SLOVIK
SLOWED
SLOWER
SLOWLY
SLOWUP
SLUDGE
SLUDGY
SLUGGO
SLUICE
SLUING
SLUMMY
SLUMPS
SLURPS
SLURRY
SLUSHY
SLYEST
SLYPES

S•L•••
SALAAM
SALADS
SALALS
SALAMI
SALARY
SALINA
SALINE
SALISH
SALIVA
SALLET
SALLOW
SALMAN
SALMON
SALOME
SALONS
SALOON
SALSAS
SALTED
SALTEN
SALTER
SALTON
SALUKI
SALUTE
SALVED
SALVER
SALVES
SALVIA
SALVOR
SALVOS
SALYUT
SCLAFF
SCLERA
SELDOM
SELECT
SELENA
SELENE
SELJUK
SELLER
SELVES
SILAGE
SILENI
SILENT
SILICA
SILKED
SILKEN
SILOAM
SILOED
SILONE
SILTED
SILVER
SOLACE
SOLANS
SOLDAN
SOLDER
SOLDON
SOLEIL
SOLELY
SOLEMN
SOLENT
SOLERS
SOLEUS
SOLFAS
SOLIDI
SOLIDS
SOLING
SOLOED
SOLONG
SOLUTE
SOLVED
SOLVER
SOLVES
SPLASH
SPLATS
SPLAYS
SPLEEN
SPLICE
SPLINE
SPLINT
SPLITS
SPLOSH
STLUKE
SULCUS
SULFUR
SULKED
SULKER
SULLEN
SULTAN
SULTRY
SYLPHS
SYLVAN
SYLVIA

S••L••
SABLES
SAILED
SAILOR
SALLET
SALLOW
SAULTS
SAWLOG
SCALAR
SCALDS
SCALED
SCALER
SCALES
SCALIA
SCALPS
SCHLEP
SCOLDS
SCULLS
SCULLY
SCULPT
SCYLLA
SEALAB
SEALED
SEALER
SEALUP
SELLER
SENLAC
SHALES
SHALEY
SHALLY
SHALOM
SHELLS
SHELLY
SHELVE
SHILLS
SHILLY
SHILOH
SHOLEM
SHOLOM
SIDLED
SIDLES
SISLER
SKALDS
SKILLS
SKULKS
SKULLS
SKYLAB
SLALOM
SMALLS
SMALTI
SMALTO
SMELLS
SMELLY
SMELTS
SMILAX
SMILED
SMILER
SMILES
SMILEY
SNELLS
SOCLES
SOILED
SPALLS
SPELLS
SPILES
SPILLS
SPILTH
STALAG
STALED
STALER
STALES
STALIN
STALKS
STALKY
STALLS
STELAE
STELAR
STELES
STELLA
STELMO
STILES
STILLS
STILLY
STILTS
STOLEN
STOLES
STOLID
STOLLE
STOLON
STULLS
STYLED
STYLER
STYLES
STYLET
STYLUS
SUBLET
SULLEN
SUNLIT
SUSLIK
SUTLER
SVELTE
SWALES
SWELLS
SWILLS

S•••L•
SADDLE
SAFELY
SAGELY
SALALS
SAMPLE
SANELY
SCHELL
SCHULZ
SCOWLS
SCROLL
SCULLS
SCULLY
SCYLLA
SEARLE
SEDILE
SEEMLY
SEMELE
SEPALS
SETTLE
SEWELL
SEXILY
SHALLY
SHAWLS
SHEILA
SHELLS
SHELLY
SHIELD
SHILLS
SHILLY
SHOALS
SHOULD
SHRILL
SIBYLS
SICILY
SICKLE
SICKLY
SIECLE
SIGILS
SIMILE
SIMPLE
SIMPLY
SINGLE
SINGLY
SISALS
SIZZLE
SKILLS
SKIRLS
SKULLS
SLIMLY
SLOWLY
SMALLS
SMELLS
SMELLY
SMUGLY
SNAILS
SNARLS
SNARLY
SNELLS
SNUGLY
SOFTLY
SOLELY
SOMALI
SORELY
SOTOLS
SOURLY
SPALLS
SPELLS
SPIELS
SPILLS
SPOILS
SPOILT
SPOOLS
SPRYLY
SQUALL
SQUILL
STABLE
STABLY
STALLS
STAPLE
STEALS
STEELE
STEELS
STEELY
STELLA
STIFLE
STILLS
STILLY
STMALO
STOLLE
STOOLS
STROLL
STULLS
SUBTLE
SUBTLY
SUPPLE
SUPPLY
SURELY
SWELLS
SWILLS
SWIRLS
SWIRLY

S••••L
SACRAL
SAMBAL
SAMUEL
SANDAL
SAUREL
SCHELL
SCHOOL
SCHORL
SCRAWL
SCROLL
SEAGAL
SECKEL
SEIDEL
SEPTAL
SEQUEL
SERIAL
SERVAL
SEWELL
SHEKEL
SHOVEL
SHRILL
SHTETL
SIGNAL
SIMBEL
SINFUL
SISKEL
SNIVEL
SOCIAL
SOLEIL
SORREL
SPINAL
SPINEL
SPIRAL
SPRAWL
SQUALL
SQUEAL
SQUILL
STEROL
STIPEL
STPAUL
STROLL
SWIVEL
SYMBOL

•SL•••
ASLANT
ASLEEP
ASLOPE
ISLAND
ISLETS

•S•L••
ASHLAR
ASHLEY
ASYLUM
ISELIN
ISOLDE
ISTLES
OSTLER
PSALMS
PSYLLA

•S••L•
ASWELL
ISEULT
OSCULA
OSWALD
PSYLLA
USABLE
USABLY
USUALS

•S•••L
ASSAIL
ASTRAL
ASWELL
ASWIRL
ESPIAL
ISABEL
ISOHEL
ISRAEL
OSTEAL
USEFUL
USMAIL

••SL••
AISLES
BOSLEY
GASLIT
GASLOG
GOSLOW
KISLEV
LESLEY
LESLIE
LISLES
MISLAY
MISLED
MOSLEM
MUSLIM
MUSLIN
SISLER
SUSLIK
TESLAS
VASLAV
WESLEY

••S•L•
ANSELM
BASALT
BASELY
BUSILY
BUSTLE
CASALS
CASTLE
COSELL
COSTLY
DESALT
DESILU
EASELS
EASILY
EDSELS
ENSILE
FUSILS
HASSLE
HOSELS
HUSTLE
INSOLE
INSULT
ITSELF
JOSTLE
JUSTLY
LASTLY
LUSHLY
MOSTLY
MUSCLE
MUSCLY
MYSELF
NASALS
NESTLE
NOSALE
NOSILY
ONSALE
OUSELS
PESTLE
POSHLY
RASHLY
RASSLE
RESALE
RESALT
RESELL
RESILE
RESOLD
RESOLE
RESULT
ROSILY
RUSTLE
SISALS
TUSSLE
UNSOLD
URSULA
VASTLY
WISELY

••S••L
AMSTEL
ASSAIL
BUSHEL
CASUAL
COSELL
COSTAL
DISMAL
DISPEL
DISTAL
DISTIL
DOSSAL
DOSSEL
ENSOUL
FESTAL
FISCAL
FOSSIL
GOSPEL
HOSTEL
IJSSEL
JESSEL
LISTEL
MESCAL
MISSAL
MOSTEL
MUSIAL
MUSSEL
PASCAL
PASSEL
PASTEL
PISTIL
PISTOL
POSTAL
RASCAL
RESEAL
RESELL
SISKEL
TASSEL
UNSEAL
VASSAL
VESSEL
VESTAL
VISUAL

•••SL•
ENISLE
FOCSLE
GRISLY
HASSLE
MEASLY
RASSLE
THUSLY
TOUSLE
TUSSLE
VIZSLA

•••S•L
BURSAL
CAUSAL
CHISEL
CONSUL
CRESOL
DAMSEL
DIESEL
DORSAL
DOSSAL
DOSSEL
FAISAL
FOSSIL
GEISEL
HANSEL
IJSSEL
JESSEL
MENSAL
MISSAL
MORSEL
MUSSEL
PASSEL
TARSAL
TASSEL
TEASEL
TINSEL
TONSIL
VASSAL
VESSEL
WEASEL
WIESEL

SM••••
SMACKS
SMALLS
SMALTI
SMALTO
SMARMY
SMARTS
SMARTY
SMEARS
SMEARY
SMELLS
SMELLY
SMELTS
SMERSH
SMILAX
SMILED
SMILER
SMILES
SMILEY
SMIRCH
SMIRKS
SMIRKY
SMITES
SMITHS
SMITHY
SMOCKS
SMOGGY
SMOKED
SMOKER
SMOKES
SMOKEY
SMOOCH
SMOOTH
SMUDGE
SMUDGY
SMUGLY
SMURFS
SMUTCH
SMUTTY
SMYRNA

S•M•••
SAMARA
SAMBAL
SAMBAR
SAMBAS
SAMEKH
SAMIAM
SAMITE
SAMMIE
SAMOAN
SAMOSA
SAMPAN
SAMPLE
SAMSON
SAMUEL
SEMELE
SEMITE
SEMPER
SEMPRE
SIMBEL
SIMEON
SIMIAN
SIMILE
SIMMER
SIMONE
SIMONY
SIMPER
SIMPLE
SIMPLY
SOMALI
SOMANY
SOMATA
SOMATO
SOMBER
SOMBRE
SOMERS
SOMMER
STMALO
STMARK
SUMACS
SUMMAE
SUMMAS
SUMMED
SUMMER
SUMMIT
SUMMON
SUMNER
SUMSUP
SUMTER
SYMBOL

S••M••
SALMAN
SALMON
SAMMIE
SCAMPI
SCAMPS
SCHMOO
SCHMOS
SCUMMY
SEAMAN
SEAMED
SEAMEN
SEAMUS
SEEMED
SEEMLY
SERMON
SGTMAJ
SHAMAN
SHAMED
SHAMES
SHAMIR
SHAMUS
SHIMMY
SHIMON
SIGMAS
SIMMER
SKIMPS
SKIMPY
SLIMED
SLIMES
SLIMLY
SLUMMY
SLUMPS
SOMMER
SPUMED
SPUMES
STAMEN
STAMPS
STIMPY
STOMAS
STOMAT
STOMPS
STUMPS
STUMPY
STYMIE
SUBMIT
SUMMAE
SUMMAS
SUMMED
SUMMER
SUMMIT
SUMMON
SWAMIS
SWAMPS
SWAMPY

S•••M•
SALAMI
SALOME
SCHEMA
SCHEME
SCRAMS
SCRIMP
SCRIMS
SCRUMS
SCUMMY
SEDUMS
SEISMO
SEISMS
SERUMS
SESAME
SHAWMS
SHIMMY
SHOWME
SHRIMP
SLUMMY
SMARMY
SOLEMN
SONOMA
SPASMS
STEAMS
STEAMY
STELMO
STIGMA
STORMS
STORMY
STRUMS
SURIMI
SWARMS

S••••M
SACHEM
SACRUM
SADDAM
SALAAM
SAMIAM
SCARUM
SCHISM
SCREAM
SELDOM
SEPTUM
SHALOM
SHAZAM
SHBOOM
SHIISM
SHOLEM
SHOLOM
SIKKIM
SILOAM
SITCOM
SLALOM
SODIUM
SQUIRM
STREAM
SUBGUM
SUFISM
SYSTEM

•SM•••
ASMARA
ISMENE
OSMICS
OSMIUM
OSMOND
OSMOSE
OSMUND
USMAIL

•S•M••
ASIMOV
ISOMER

•S••M•
ASSUME
ESKIMO
ISTHMI
PSALMS

•S•••M
ASCHAM
ASHRAM
ASYLUM
ESTEEM
OSMIUM
OSTIUM

••SM••
BUSMAN
BUSMEN
COSMIC
COSMOS
DESMAN
DISMAL
DISMAY
DISMES
GASMAN
GASMEN
KISMET
MESMER
TASMAN
YESMAN
YESMEN

••S•M•
ASSUME
BESOMS
RESUME
SESAME

••S••M
ANSELM
CESIUM
CUSTOM
DISARM
HASSAM
INSEAM
MOSLEM
MUSEUM
MUSLIM
PASSIM
POSSUM
SYSTEM
WISDOM

•••SM•
ABYSMS
CHASMS
MIASMA
PLASMA
PLASMO
PRISMS
SEISMO
SEISMS
SPASMS

•••S•M
BALSAM
DIMSUM
DORSUM
FOLSOM
GYPSUM
HANSOM
HASSAM
JETSAM
OMASUM
PASSIM
POSSUM
RANSOM

••••SM
AGEISM
CHRISM
CUBISM
EGOISM
HOLISM
MAOISM
MONISM
PURISM
SCHISM
SHIISM
SUFISM
TAOISM
THEISM
TRUISM
VERISM

SN••••
SNACKS
SNAFUS
SNAGGY
SNAILS
SNAKED
SNAKES
SNAPAT
SNAPPY
SNAPTO
SNAPUP
SNARED
SNARES
SNARLS
SNARLY
SNATCH
SNATHE
SNATHS
SNAZZY
SNEAKS
SNEAKY
SNEERS
SNEERY
SNEEZE
SNEEZY
SNELLS
SNICKS
SNIDER
SNIFFS
SNIFFY
SNIPED
SNIPES
SNIPPY
SNITCH
SNIVEL
SNOBBY
SNOCAT
SNOODS
SNOOKS
SNOOPS
SNOOPY
SNOOTS
SNOOTY
SNOOZE
SNOPES
SNORED
SNORER
SNORES
SNORTS
SNOUTS
SNOWED
SNOWIN
SNUFFS
SNUFFY
SNUGLY
SNYDER

S•N•••
SANCHO
SANCTA
SANDAL
SANDED
SANDER
SANDIA
SANDRA
SANELY
SANEST
SANGER
SANGTO
SANITY
SANNUP
SANSEI
SANTEE
SANTIR
SANTOS
SENARY
SENATE
SENDAK
SENDER
SENDIN
SENDUP
SENECA
SENEGA
SENHOR
SENIOR
SENLAC
SENNAS
SENNET
SENNIT
SENORA
SENORS

SENSED
SENSEI
SENSES
SENSOR
SENTIN
SENTRY
SENTUP
SINBAD
SINEAD
SINEWS
SINEWY
SINFUL
SINGED
SINGER
SINGES
SINGLE
SINGLY
SINGTO
SINKER
SINKIN
SINNED
SINNER
SINTAX
SINTER
SONANT
SONATA
SONDES
SONICS
SONNET
SONOMA
SONORA
SONTAG
SUNDAE
SUNDAY
SUNDER
SUNDEW
SUNDOG
SUNDRY
SUNGOD
SUNKEN
SUNLIT
SUNNED
SUNNIS
SUNOCO
SUNRAY
SUNSET
SUNTAN
SUNUNU
SUNUPS
SYNCED
SYNDIC
SYNODS
SYNTAX

S••N••
SAINTE
SAINTS
SANNUP
SAUNAS
SCANTS
SCANTY
SCENAS
SCENDS
SCENES
SCENIC
SCENTS
SCHNOZ
SCONCE
SCONES
SEANCE
SEENAS
SEENTO
SEINED
SEINER
SEINES
SENNAS
SENNET
SENNIT
SEWNUP
SHANDY
SHANKS
SHANTY
SHINDY
SHINED
SHINER
SHINES
SHINNY
SHINTO
SHUNTS
SIDNEY
SIENNA
SIGNAL
SIGNED
SIGNEE
SIGNER
SIGNET
SIGNIN
SIGNON
SIGNOR
SIGNUP
SINNED
SINNER
SKINKS
SKINNY
SKUNKS
SLANGS
SLANGY
SLANTS
SLINGS
SLINKS
SLINKY
SONNET
SOONER
SOUNDS
SPANKS
SPANKY
SPENDS
SPINAL
SPINED
SPINEL
SPINES
SPINET
SPINKS
SPONGE
SPONGY
SPUNKY
STANCE
STANCH
STANDS
STANKY
STANZA
STENCH
STENOG
STENOS
STINGS
STINGY
STINKS
STINKY
STINTS
STONED
STONER
STONES
STUNTS
SUMNER
SUNNED
SUNNIS
SWANEE
SWANKY
SWINGS
SWINGY
SYDNEY

S•••N•
SABENA
SABINE
SABINS
SALINA
SALINE
SALONS
SARANS
SARONG
SATANG
SATING
SATINS
SATINY
SAVANT
SAVING
SAWING
SAXONS
SAXONY
SAYING
SCARNE
SCIONS
SCORNS
SECANT
SECOND
SEDANS
SEEING
SEJANT
SELENA
SELENE
SERENA
SERENE
SERINE
SERINS
SETINS
SEVENS
SEWING
SHAYNE
SHEENA
SHEENS
SHINNY
SHRANK
SHRINE
SHRINK
SHRUNK
SHYING
SIDING
SIENNA
SILENI
SILENT
SILONE
SIMONE
SIMONY
SIRENS
SIRING
SITING
SITINS
SIXING
SIZING
SKEANS
SKEINS
SKIING
SKINNY
SKYING
SLOANE
SLUING
SMYRNA
SOFINE
SOIGNE
SOLANS
SOLENT
SOLING
SOLONG
SOMANY
SONANT
SOWING
SPAWNS
SPHINX
SPLINE
SPLINT
SPOONS
SPOONY
SPRANG
SPRING
SPRINT
SPRUNG
SPURNS
SPYING
SQUINT
STAINS
STEINS
STERNA
STERNE
STERNO
STERNS
STHENO
STRAND
STRING
STRONG
STRUNG
SUNUNU
SUPINE
SUSANN
SWAINS
SWOONS
SYRINX

S••••N
SADDEN
SAIGON
SAIPAN
SALMAN
SALMON
SALOON
SALTEN
SALTON
SAMOAN
SAMPAN
SAMSON
SARGON
SARTON
SATEEN
SATURN
SCREEN
SEAFAN
SEAMAN
SEAMEN
SEASON
SECERN
SEEPIN
SEESIN
SENDIN
SENTIN
SEQUIN
SERKIN
SERMON
SETSIN
SETSON
SEVERN
SEWSON
SEXTON
SHABAN
SHAKEN
SHAMAN
SHARON
SHAVEN
SHIMON
SHOGUN
SHOOIN
SHORAN
SHOWIN
SHUTIN
SICKEN
SIGNIN
SIGNON
SILKEN
SIMEON
SIMIAN
SINKIN
SIOUAN
SIPHON
SISKIN
SITSIN
SITSON
SIXGUN
SKIRUN
SLIDIN
SLIPIN
SLIPON
SLOGAN
SLOVEN
SNOWIN
SOCKIN
SODDEN
SOFTEN
SOLDAN
SOLDON
SOLEMN
SOSOON
SPAVIN
SPLEEN
SPOKEN
SPRAIN
SPURON
STALIN
STAMEN
STAYON
STEFAN
STEPIN
STEPON
STEVEN
STIRIN
STJOAN
STJOHN
STOLEN
STOLON
STOPIN
STRAIN
STREWN
STYRON
SUBORN
SUCKIN
SUDDEN
SULLEN
SULTAN
SUMMON
SUNKEN
SUNTAN
SUSANN
SWEDEN
SYLVAN
SYRIAN

•S•N••
ASANAS
USANCE

•S••N•
ASCEND
ASCENT
ASIANS
ASKING
ASLANT
ASPENS
ASSENT
ESCENT
ESPANA
ESSENE
ISLAND
ISMENE
OSCINE
OSMOND
OSMUND
OSTEND
VSIGNS

•S•••N
ASHCAN
ASOSAN
ASSIGN
ASTERN
ASWOON
ISELIN
ISOGON
OSBORN
OSSEIN
OSSIAN
USOPEN

••SN••
BOSNIA
CPSNOW
DISNEY
EISNER
RESNIK
UNSNAG
UNSNAP

••S•N•
ABSENT
ARSENE
ASSENT
BASING
BASINS
BESANT
BISONS
BOSUNS
BUSING
BUSONI
CASING
CASINO
CESSNA
COSINE
DISANT
DOSING
EASING
EOSINS
ESSENE
FUSING
HOSING
INSANE
INSYNC
LOSING
LYSINE
LYSINS
MASONS
MESONS
MUSING
MUSTNT
NOSING
ORSINO
PISANS
POSING
RESAND
RESEND
RESENT
RESING
RESINS
RISING
ROSINS
ROSINY
SUSANN
TISANE
UNSUNG
URSINE
VISHNU
VISINE
WISENT

••S••N
ASSIGN
AUSTEN
AUSTIN
BOSTON
BUSKIN
BUSMAN
BUSMEN
CASERN
CASHIN
CASTON
COSIGN
DASSIN
DESIGN
DESMAN
DISOWN
DUSTIN
EASEIN
EASTON
ENSIGN
FASTEN
FUSION
GASCON
GASKIN
GASMAN
GASMEN
GASTON
GOSHEN
HASSAN
HASTEN
HESTON
HUSTON
INSPAN
JUSTIN
LASSEN
LESSEN
LESSON
LISBON
LISTEN
LISTON
MUSLIN
NISSAN
NISSEN
OSSEIN
OSSIAN
PISTON
POSTON
PUSHON
RESEEN
RESEWN
RESIGN
RESTON
RUSKIN
SISKIN
SOSOON
SUSANN
TASMAN
TUSCAN
UNSEEN
UNSEWN
UNSOWN
VISION
WESSON
WYSTAN
YESMAN
YESMEN

•••SN•
CESSNA
DOESNT
FRESNO
PUISNE

•••S•N
ACTSON
ADDSIN
ADDSON
ALISON
ARISEN
ASOSAN
BABSON
BENSON
BIDSIN
BIDSON
BRYSON
BUNSEN
CARSON
CHOSEN
COUSIN
CUTSIN
DAMSON
DANSON
DASSIN
DATSUN
DAWSON
DIGSIN
DOBSON
DOESIN
EATSIN
EDISON
EGGSON
FITSIN
FOGSIN
GARSON
GETSIN
GETSON
GIBSON
GODSON
GOESIN
GOESON
GRISON
HANSON
HASSAN
HEMSIN
HENSON
HITSON
HOBSON
HUDSON
ICESIN
IRISIN
JAMSIN
JANSEN
JENSEN
JETSON
JIMSON
JOLSON
JONSON
KANSAN
KEYSIN
KMESON
LANSON
LARSEN
LARSON
LASSEN
LAWSON
LAYSIN
LAYSON
LESSEN
LESSON
LETSIN
LETSON
LIESIN
LOGSIN
LOGSON
LOOSEN
MYOSIN
NANSEN
NEESON
NELSON
NISSAN
NISSEN
ODDSON
ORISON
PARSON
PAYSIN
PAYSON
PEPSIN
PERSON
PINSON
POISON
POPSIN
PRISON
PUTSIN
PUTSON
RAISIN
RAMSON
RATSON
REASON
REVSON
ROBSON
RUBSIN
RUNSIN
RUNSON
SAMSON
SEASON
SEESIN
SETSIN
SETSON
SEWSON
SITSIN
SITSON
TIESIN
TIPSIN
TOCSIN
TOESIN
TUCSON
TULSAN
UNISON
WATSON
WESSON
WILSON
WORSEN

SO••••
SOAKED
SOAKER
SOAKUP
SOAPED
SOAPER
SOARED
SOARER
SOARES
SOASTO
SOAVES
SOBBED
SOBBER
SOBEIT
SOBERS
SOCAGE
SOCCER
SOCIAL
SOCKED
SOCKET
SOCKIN
SOCLES
SODDED
SODDEN
SODIUM
SOFFIT
SOFINE
SOFTEN
SOFTER
SOFTIE
SOFTLY
SOIGNE
SOILED
SOIREE
SOLACE
SOLANS
SOLDAN
SOLDER
SOLDON
SOLEIL
SOLELY
SOLEMN
SOLENT
SOLERS
SOLEUS
SOLFAS
SOLIDI
SOLIDS
SOLING
SOLOED
SOLONG
SOLUTE
SOLVED
SOLVER
SOLVES
SOMALI
SOMANY
SOMATA
SOMATO
SOMBER
SOMBRE
SOMERS
SOMMER
SONANT
SONATA
SONDES
SONICS
SONNET
SONOMA
SONORA
SONTAG
SOONER
SOOTHE
SOPHIA
SOPHIE
SOPORS
SOPPED
SOPSUP
SORBET
SORBIC
SORDID
SORELY
SOREST
SORREL
SORROW
SORTED
SORTER
SORTIE
SORTOF
SOSOON
SOTHAT
SOTOLS
SOTTED
SOUARI
SOUGHS
SOUGHT
SOUNDS
SOUPUP
SOURCE
SOURED
SOURER
SOURLY
SOUSED
SOUSES
SOUTER
SOVIET
SOWBUG
SOWERS
SOWETO
SOWHAT
SOWING
SOXERS

S•O•••
SCOFFS
SCOLDS
SCONCE
SCONES
SCOOPS
SCOOTS
SCOPED
SCOPES
SCORCH
SCORED
SCORER
SCORES
SCORIA
SCORNS
SCOTCH
SCOTER
SCOTIA
SCOTTO
SCOTTY
SCOURS
SCOUTS
SCOWLS
SFORZA
SHOALS
SHOATS
SHOCKS
SHODDY
SHOERS
SHOFAR
SHOGUN
SHOJIS
SHOLEM
SHOLOM
SHOOED
SHOOIN
SHOOKS
SHOOTS
SHOPPE
SHORAN
SHORED
SHORES
SHORTS
SHORTY
SHOTAT
SHOTUP
SHOULD
SHOUTS
SHOVED
SHOVEL
SHOVER
SHOVES
SHOWED
SHOWER
SHOWIN
SHOWME
SHOWUP
SIOUAN
SKOKIE
SKOPJE
SLOANE
SLOGAN
SLOOPS
SLOPED
SLOPES
SLOPPY
SLOSHY
SLOTHS
SLOUCH
SLOUGH
SLOVAK
SLOVEN
SLOVIK
SLOWED
SLOWER
SLOWLY
SLOWUP
SMOCKS
SMOGGY
SMOKED
SMOKER
SMOKES
SMOKEY
SMOOCH
SMOOTH
SNOBBY
SNOCAT
SNOODS
SNOOKS
SNOOPS
SNOOPY
SNOOTS
SNOOTY
SNOOZE
SNOPES
SNORED
SNORER
SNORES
SNORTS
SNOUTS
SNOWED
SNOWIN
SOONER
SOOTHE
SPOILS
SPOILT
SPOKED
SPOKEN
SPOKES
SPONGE
SPONGY
SPOOFS
SPOOKS
SPOOKY
SPOOLS
SPOONS
SPOONY
SPOORS
SPORES
SPORTS
SPORTY
SPOTTY
SPOUSE
SPOUTS
STOATS
STOCKS
STOCKY
STODGE
STODGY
STOGIE
STOICS
STOJKO
STOKED
STOKER
STOKES
STOLEN
STOLES
STOLID
STOLLE
STOLON
STOMAS
STOMAT
STOMPS
STONED
STONER
STONES
STOOGE
STOOLS
STOOPS
STOPES
STOPIN
STOPIT
STOPUP
STORCH
STORED
STORER
STORES
STOREY
STORKS
STORMS
STORMY
STORRS
STOUPS
STOUTS
STOVER
STOVES
STOWED
SWOONS
SWOOPS
SWOOSH
SWORDS

S••O••
SABOTS
SALOME
SALONS
SALOON
SAMOAN
SAMOSA
SAPORS
SARODS
SARONG
SATORI
SATOUT
SAVOIE
SAVOIR
SAVORS
SAVORY
SAVOUR
SAWOFF
SAWOUT
SAXONS
SAXONY
SCHOOL
SCHORL
SCIONS
SCOOPS
SCOOTS
SCRODS
SCROLL
SCROOP
SECOND
SEEOFF
SEEOUT
SENORA
SENORS
SEPOYS
SEROSA
SEROUS
SEROWS
SETOFF
SETOSE
SETOUT
SHBOOM
SHOOED
SHOOIN
SHOOKS
SHOOTS
SHROUD
SHROVE
SILOAM
SILOED
SILONE
SIMONE
SIMONY
SITOUT
SLOOPS
SMOOCH
SMOOTH
SNOODS
SNOOKS
SNOOPS
SNOOPY
SNOOTS
SNOOTY
SNOOZE
SOLOED
SOLONG
SONOMA
SONORA
SOPORS
SOSOON
SOTOLS
SPLOSH
SPOOFS
SPOOKS
SPOOKY
SPOOLS
SPOONS
SPOONY
SPOORS
SPROUT
STJOAN
STJOHN
STOOGE
STOOLS
STOOPS
STROBE
STRODE
STROKE
STROLL
STRONG
STROPS
STROUD
STROVE
SUBORN
SUNOCO
SWOONS
SWOOPS
SWOOSH
SYNODS

S•••O•
SAIGON
SAILOR
SALLOW
SALMON
SALOON
SALTON
SALVOR
SALVOS
SAMSON
SANTOS
SARGON
SARGOS
SARTON
SAVIOR
SAWLOG
SAYSOS
SCHMOO
SCHMOS
SCHNOZ
SCHOOL
SCROOP
SEACOW
SEADOG
SEAFOX
SEASON
SECTOR
SELDOM
SENHOR
SENIOR
SENSOR
SERMON
SERVOS
SESTOS
SETSON
SETTOS
SEWSON
SEXTON
SHADOW
SHAKOS
SHALOM
SHARON
SHBOOM
SHILOH
SHIMON
SHOLOM
SIGNON
SIGNOR
SIMEON
SIPHON
SITCOM
SITSON
SKIROS
SKITOW
SKYBOX
SLALOM
SLIPON
SOLDON
SORROW
SORTOF
SOSOON
SPIGOT
SPIROS
SPURON
STATOR
STAYON
STENOG
STENOS
STEPON
STEROL
STOLON
STUPOR

STYRON
SUCCOR
SUITOR
SUMMON
SUNDOG
SUNGOD
SYMBOL

S••••O
SABATO
SANCHO
SANGTO
SAPPHO
SASEBO
SCHMOO
SCIPIO
SCOTTO
SEENTO
SEESTO
SEISMO
SERGIO
SHINTO
SIDERO
SINGTO
SLUGGO
SMALTO
SNAPTO
SOASTO
SOMATO
SOWETO
STELMO
STEREO
STERNO
STHENO
STMALO
STOJKO
STRABO
STRATO
STUCCO
STUDIO
SUBITO
SUNOCO

•SO•••
ASOSAN
ISOBAR
ISOGON
ISOHEL
ISOLDE
ISOMER
ISOPOD
USOPEN

•S•O••
ASCOTS
ASHORE
ASKOUT
ASLOPE
ASSORT
ASWOON
ESCORT
ESPOSA
ESPOSO
ESTOPS
FSTOPS
OSBORN
OSGOOD
OSMOND
OSMOSE

•S••O•
ASIMOV
ASKFOR
ASTROS
ASWOON
ESCROW
ISADOR
ISOGON
ISOPOD
OSGOOD

•S•••O
ESCUDO
ESKIMO
ESPOSO
OSWEGO
PSEUDO
PSYCHO
USEDTO

••SO••
ABSORB
ADSORB
ASSORT
BESOMS
BESOTS
BISONS
BUSONI
DESOTO
DISOWN
ENSOUL
GOSOFT
INSOLE
MASONS
MESONS
NOSOAP
RESODS
RESOLD
RESOLE
RESORB
RESORT
SOSOON
UNSOLD
UNSOWN
VISORS

••S•O•
BASSOS
BESTOW
BISHOP
BOSTON
BUSBOY
CASTON
CASTOR
CESTOS
CISCOS
COSMOS
CPSNOW
CUSTOM
DESPOT
DISCOS
EASTON
FUSION
GASCON
GASLOG
GASTON
GOSLOW
HESIOD
HESTON
HUSTON
HYSSOP
LASSOS
LESBOS
LESSON
LESSOR
LISBOA
LISBON
LISTON
MASCOT
MOSCOW
MUSKOX
NESTOR
NOSHOW
PASEOS
PASTOR
PESCOW
PISTOL
PISTON
POSTON
PUSHON
RESHOD
RESHOE
RESHOT
RESTON
ROSCOE
ROSTOV
SESTOS
SOSOON
TVSHOW
UNSHOD
UNSTOP
UPSHOT
VISION
VOSTOK
WASHOE
WESSON
WISDOM

••S••O
AUSTRO
BISTRO
CASINO
CASSIO
CASTRO
DESOTO
DOSIDO
GASTRO
HASBRO
LASHIO
ORSINO
PASHTO
SASEBO
WISETO

•••SO•
ACTSON
ADDSON
ALISON
AMOSOZ
AVISOS
BABSON
BASSOS
BENSON
BIDSON
BRASOV
BRYSON
CARSON
CENSOR
CHISOX
CRESOL
CRUSOE
CURSOR
DAMSON
DANSON
DAWSON
DOBSON
EDISON
EGGSON
FOLSOM
GARSON
GETSON
GIBSON
GODSON
GOESON
GRISON
HANSOM
HANSON
HENSON
HITSON
HOBSON
HUDSON
HYKSOS
HYSSOP
JETSON
JIMSON
JOLSON
JONSON
KMESON
LANSON
LARSON
LASSOS
LAWSON
LAYSON
LESSON
LESSOR
LETSON
LOGSON
NEESON
NELSON
ODDSON
ORISON
PARSON
PAYSON
PERSON
PINSON
POISON
PRISON
PUTSON
RAMSON
RANSOM
RATSON
REASON
REDSOX
REVSON
ROBSON
RUNSON
SAMSON
SAYSOS
SEASON
SENSOR
SETSON
SEWSON
SITSON
TENSOR
TORSOS
TUCSON
UNISON
VERSOS
WATSON
WESSON
WILSON
WINSOR

•••S•O
ADDSTO
AIMSTO
ARISTO
CASSIO
CRISCO
ENESCO
FIASCO
FRESCO
FRESNO
FRISCO
GETSTO
GRASSO
GROSSO
LAYSTO
LETSGO
LIESTO
OBISPO
PHYSIO
PLASMO
PRESTO
PUTSTO
RUNSTO
SEESTO
SEISMO
SOASTO
UNESCO

••••SO
ALONSO
ARIOSO
CARUSO
ELPASO
ESPOSO
EVENSO
EVERSO
GRASSO
GROSSO

SP••••
SPACED
SPACEK
SPACER
SPACES
SPACEY
SPADED
SPADER
SPADES
SPADIX
SPAHIS
SPALLS
SPANKS
SPANKY
SPARED
SPARER
SPARES
SPARGE
SPARKS
SPARKY
SPARSE
SPARTA
SPASMS
SPATES
SPATHE
SPAVIN
SPAWNS
SPAYED
SPEAKS
SPEARS
SPECIE
SPECKS
SPEDUP
SPEECH
SPEEDS
SPEEDY
SPELLS
SPENDS
SPERRY
SPEWED
SPHERE
SPHINX
SPICAS
SPICED
SPICES
SPIDER
SPIELS
SPIERS
SPIFFS
SPIFFY
SPIGOT
SPIKED
SPIKER
SPIKES
SPILES
SPILLS
SPILTH
SPINAL
SPINED
SPINEL
SPINES
SPINET
SPINKS
SPIRAL
SPIREA
SPIRED
SPIRES
SPIRIT
SPIROS
SPITED
SPITES
SPIVAK
SPLASH
SPLATS
SPLAYS
SPLEEN
SPLICE
SPLINE
SPLINT
SPLITS
SPLOSH
SPOILS
SPOILT
SPOKED
SPOKEN
SPOKES
SPONGE
SPONGY
SPOOFS
SPOOKS
SPOOKY
SPOOLS
SPOONS
SPOONY
SPOORS
SPORES
SPORTS
SPORTY
SPOTTY
SPOUSE
SPOUTS
SPRAGS
SPRAIN
SPRANG
SPRATS
SPRAWL
SPRAYS
SPREAD
SPREES
SPRIER
SPRIGS
SPRING
SPRINT
SPRITE
SPRITS
SPRITZ
SPROUT
SPRUCE
SPRUES
SPRUNG
SPRYER
SPRYLY
SPUMED
SPUMES
SPUNKY
SPURGE
SPURNS
SPURON
SPURRY
SPURTS
SPYING

S•P•••
SAPORS
SAPPED
SAPPER
SAPPHO
SEPALS
SEPIAS
SEPOYS
SEPTAL
SEPTET
SEPTIC
SEPTUM
SIPHON
SIPPED
SIPPER
SIPPET
SOPHIA
SOPHIE
SOPORS
SOPPED
SOPSUP
STPAUL
STPETE
SUPERB
SUPERS
SUPINE
SUPPED
SUPPER
SUPPLE
SUPPLY

S••P••
SAIPAN
SAMPAN
SAMPLE
SAPPED
SAPPER
SAPPHO
SCAPES
SCIPIO
SCOPED
SCOPES
SEEPED
SEEPIN
SEMPER
SEMPRE
SHAPED
SHAPER
SHAPES
SHOPPE
SIMPER
SIMPLE
SIMPLY
SIPPED
SIPPER
SIPPET
SKIPPY
SKOPJE
SLAPPY
SLAPUP
SLIPIN
SLIPON
SLIPUP
SLOPED
SLOPES
SLOPPY
SLYPES
SNAPAT
SNAPPY
SNAPTO
SNAPUP
SNIPED
SNIPES
SNIPPY
SNOPES
SOAPED
SOAPER
SOPPED
SOUPUP
STAPES
STAPLE
STAPUF
STEPIN
STEPON
STEPPE
STEPUP
STIPEL
STIPES
STOPES
STOPIN
STOPIT
STOPUP
STUPAS
STUPES
STUPID
STUPOR
SUPPED
SUPPER
SUPPLE
SUPPLY
SWIPED
SWIPER
SWIPES
SYLPHS

S•••P•
SCALPS
SCAMPI
SCAMPS
SCARPS
SCAUPS
SCOOPS
SCRAPE
SCRAPS
SCRIPS
SCRIPT
SCULPT
SERAPE
SERAPH
SETUPS
SHARPS
SHEEPS
SHERPA
SHOPPE
SITUPS
SKIMPS
SKIMPY
SKIPPY
SLAPPY
SLEEPS
SLEEPY
SLOOPS
SLOPPY
SLUMPS
SLURPS
SNAPPY
SNIPPY
SNOOPS
SNOOPY
STAMPS
STEEPS
STEPPE
STIMPY
STOMPS
STOOPS
STOUPS
STRAPS
STRIPE
STRIPS
STROPS
STUMPS
STUMPY
SUNUPS
SWAMPS
SWAMPY
SWEEPS
SWOOPS
SYRUPS
SYRUPY

S••••P
SANNUP
SATRAP
SAVEUP
SCHLEP
SCRIMP
SCROOP
SEALUP
SENDUP
SENTUP
SETSUP
SEWNUP
SEWSUP
SHOTUP
SHOWUP
SHRIMP
SHUTUP
SIGNUP
SITSUP
SIZEUP
SKYCAP
SLAPUP
SLIPUP
SLOWUP
SNAPUP
SOAKUP
SOPSUP
SOUPUP
SPEDUP
STAYUP
STEPUP
STIRUP
STOPUP
STREEP
SUITUP
SUMSUP

•SP•••
ASPECT
ASPENS
ASPERA
ASPICS
ASPIRE
ESPANA
ESPIAL
ESPIED
ESPIES
ESPOSA
ESPOSO
ESPRIT
OSPREY

•S•P••
ISOPOD
USOPEN

•S••P•
ASLOPE
ESCAPE
ESTOPS
FSTOPS
USURPS

•S•••P
ASHARP
ASLEEP
BSHARP
CSHARP
DSHARP
ESCARP
ESHARP
FSHARP
GSHARP
USEDUP
USESUP

••SP••
AUSPEX
CASPAR
CASPER
CUSPED
CUSPID
DESPOT
DISPEL
GASPAR
GASPED
GOSPEL
HASPED
HISPID
INSPAN
JASPER
LISPED
ONSPEC
RASPED
RASPER
VESPER
VESPID
WISPED

••S•P•
JOSEPH

••S••P
BISHOP
DUSTUP
EASEUP
FESSUP
GASCAP
GOSSIP
HYSSOP
INSTEP
LASHUP
MESSUP
MISHAP
MUSSUP
NOSOAP
PASSUP
PUSHUP
RESHIP
RESTUP
TOSSUP
UNSNAP
UNSTOP
WASHUP
WISEUP

•••SP•
CLASPS
CRISPS
CRISPY
GRASPS
OBISPO

•••S•P
ACESUP
ACTSUP
ADDSUP
BIDSUP
BOBSUP
BUYSUP
CATSUP
CUTSUP
DAMSUP
DIGSUP
DOESUP
EATSUP
ENDSUP
FESSUP
GETSUP
GOESUP
GOSSIP
GUMSUP
HITSUP
HOPSUP
HYSSOP
ICESUP
JAMSUP
KEYSUP
LAPSUP
LAYSUP
LETSUP
MESSUP
MILSAP
MOPSUP
MUSSUP
OWNSUP
PASSUP
PAYSUP
PEPSUP
POPSUP
PUTSUP
RIGSUP
RIPSUP
RUNSUP
SETSUP
SEWSUP
SITSUP
SOPSUP
SUMSUP
TAGSUP
TEESUP
TIESUP
TOSSUP
TOTSUP
USESUP
WADSUP
ZIPSUP

SQ••••
SQUABS
SQUADS
SQUALL
SQUARE
SQUASH
SQUATS
SQUAWK
SQUEAK
SQUEAL
SQUIBB
SQUIBS
SQUIDS
SQUILL
SQUINT
SQUIRE
SQUIRM
SQUIRT
SQUISH

S•Q•••
SEQUEL
SEQUIN

S••Q••
SACQUE
SESQUI

S••••Q
SUSIEQ

••SQ••
BASQUE
BISQUE
CASQUE
MASQUE
MOSQUE
RISQUE
SESQUI

••S•Q•
ETSEQQ

••S••Q
ETSEQQ
NASDAQ
SUSIEQ

S•R•••
SARANS
SARDIS
SARGES
SARGON
SARGOS
SARODS
SARONG
SARTON
SARTRE
SCRAGS
SCRAMS
SCRAPE
SCRAPS
SCRAWL
SCREAK
SCREAM
SCREED
SCREEN
SCREES
SCREWS
SCREWY
SCRIBE
SCRIMP
SCRIMS
SCRIPS
SCRIPT
SCRODS
SCROLL
SCROOP
SCRUBS
SCRUFF
SCRUMS
SERACS
SERAIS
SERAPE
SERAPH
SERBIA
SERENA
SERENE
SERGEI
SERGES
SERGIO
SERIAL
SERIES
SERIFS
SERINE
SERINS
SERKIN
SERMON
SEROSA
SEROUS
SEROWS
SERUMS
SERVAL
SERVED
SERVER
SERVES
SERVOS
SHRANK
SHREDS
SHREWD
SHREWS
SHRIEK
SHRIFT
SHRIKE
SHRILL
SHRIMP
SHRINE
SHRINK
SHRIVE
SHROUD
SHROVE
SHRUBS
SHRUGS
SHRUNK
SIRDAR
SIRENS
SIRICA
SIRING
SIRIUS
SIRRAH
SIRREE
SORBET
SORBIC
SORDID
SORELY
SOREST
SORREL
SORROW
SORTED
SORTER
SORTIE
SORTOF
SPRAGS
SPRAIN
SPRANG
SPRATS
SPRAWL
SPRAYS
SPREAD
SPREES
SPRIER
SPRIGS
SPRING
SPRINT
SPRITE
SPRITS
SPRITZ
SPROUT
SPRUCE
SPRUES
SPRUNG
SPRYER
SPRYLY
STRABO
STRADS
STRAFE
STRAIN
STRAIT
STRAKE
STRAND
STRAPS
STRASS
STRATA
STRATI
STRATO
STRAUS
STRAWS
STRAYS
STREAK
STREAM
STREEP
STREET
STRESS
STREWN
STREWS
STRIAE
STRICK
STRICT
STRIDE
STRIFE
STRIKE
STRING
STRIPE
STRIPS
STRIVE
STROBE
STRODE
STROKE
STROLL
STRONG
STROPS
STROUD
STROVE
STRUCK
STRUMS
STRUNG
STRUTS
SURAHS
SURELY
SUREST
SURETE
SURETY
SURFED
SURFER
SURGED
SURGES
SURIMI
SURREY
SURTAX
SURVEY
SYRIAN
SYRINX
SYRUPS
SYRUPY

S••R••
SABRAS
SABRES
SACRAL
SACRED
SACRUM
SATRAP
SAUREL
SAWRED
SCARAB
SCARCE
SCARED
SCARER
SCARES
SCARFS
SCARNE
SCARPS
SCARUM
SCORCH
SCORED
SCORER
SCORES
SCORIA
SCORNS
SCURFY
SCURRY
SCURVE
SCURVY
SEARCH
SEARED
SEARLE
SECRET
SEERED
SEURAT
SEVRES
SFORZA
SHARDS
SHARED
SHARER
SHARES
SHARIA
SHARIF
SHARKS
SHARON
SHARPS
SHEREE
SHERIF
SHERPA
SHERRY
SHIRAZ
SHIRER
SHIRES
SHIRKS
SHIRRS
SHIRTS
SHIRTY
SHORAN
SHORED
SHORES
SHORTS
SHORTY
SIERRA
SIRRAH
SIRREE
SKERRY
SKIRLS
SKIROS
SKIRRS
SKIRTS
SKIRUN
SLURPS
SLURRY
SMARMY
SMARTS
SMARTY
SMERSH
SMIRCH
SMIRKS
SMIRKY
SMURFS
SMYRNA
SNARED
SNARES

SNARLS
SNARLY
SNORED
SNORER
SNORES
SNORTS
SOARED
SOARER
SOARES
SOIREE
SORREL
SORROW
SOURCE
SOURED
SOURER
SOURLY
SPARED
SPARER
SPARES
SPARGE
SPARKS
SPARKY
SPARSE
SPARTA
SPERRY
SPIRAL
SPIREA
SPIRED
SPIRES
SPIRIT
SPIROS
SPORES
SPORTS
SPORTY
SPURGE
SPURNS
SPURON
SPURRY
SPURTS
STARCH
STARED
STARER
STARES
STARRY
STARTS
STARVE
STEREO
STERES
STERNA
STERNE
STERNO
STERNS
STEROL
STIRIN
STIRUP
STORCH
STORED
STORER
STORES
STOREY
STORKS
STORMS
STORMY
STORRS
STURDY
STYRIA
STYRON
SUNRAY
SURREY
SUTRAS
SWARAJ
SWARDS
SWARMS
SWARTH
SWERVE
SWIRLS
SWIRLY
SWORDS

S•••R•

SABERS
SAFARI
SAFIRE
SAHARA
SAKERS
SALARY
SAMARA
SANDRA
SAPORS
SARTRE
SATIRE
SATORI
SATURN
SATYRS
SAVERS
SAVORS
SAVORY
SAYERS
SCHORL
SCLERA
SCOURS
SCURRY
SEBERG
SECERN
SECURE
SEDERS
SEGURA
SEMPRE
SENARY
SENORA
SENORS
SENTRY
SEVERE
SEVERN
SEVERS
SEWARD
SEWERS
SHEARS
SHEERS
SHERRY
SHIRRS
SHOERS
SIDERO
SIDERS
SIERRA
SIGURD
SISERA
SITARS
SIXERS
SIZERS
SKERRY
SKIERS
SKIRRS
SLURRY
SMEARS
SMEARY
SNEERS
SNEERY
SOBERS
SOLERS
SOMBRE
SOMERS
SONORA
SOPORS
SOUARI
SOWERS
SOXERS
SPEARS
SPERRY
SPHERE
SPIERS
SPOORS
SPURRY
SQUARE
SQUIRE
SQUIRM
SQUIRT
STAIRS
STARRY
STEERS
STMARK
STORRS
STUART
SUBARU
SUBORN
SUBURB
SUGARS
SUGARY
SULTRY
SUNDRY
SUPERB
SUPERS
SUTURE
SWEARS

S••••R

SACKER
SADDER
SAILOR
SALTER
SALVER
SALVOR
SAMBAR
SANDER
SANGER
SANTIR
SAPPER
SASSER
SAUCER
SAUGER
SAVIOR
SAVOIR
SAVOUR
SAWYER
SCALAR
SCALER
SCARER
SCORER
SCOTER
SEALER
SEATER
SECTOR
SEEDER
SEEGER
SEEKER
SEINER
SEIZER
SELLER
SEMPER
SENDER
SENHOR
SENIOR
SENSOR
SERVER
SETTER
SEXIER
SHAKER
SHAMIR
SHAPER
SHARER
SHAVER
SHINER
SHIRER
SHIVER
SHOFAR
SHOVER
SHOWER
SICKER
SIDDUR
SIFTER
SIGHER
SIGNER
SIGNOR
SILVER
SIMMER
SIMPER
SINGER
SINKER
SINNER
SINTER
SIPPER
SIRDAR
SISLER
SISTER
SITTER
SKATER
SKEWER
SKIVER
SLATER
SLAVER
SLAYER
SLICER
SLIDER
SLIVER
SLOWER
SMILER
SMOKER
SNIDER
SNORER
SNYDER
SOAKER
SOAPER
SOARER
SOBBER
SOCCER
SOFTER
SOLDER
SOLVER
SOMBER
SOMMER
SOONER
SORTER
SOURER
SOUTER
SPACER
SPADER
SPARER
SPIDER
SPIKER
SPRIER
SPRYER
STAGER
STALER
STARER
STATER
STATOR
STELAR
STEWER
STIVER
STOKER
STONER
STORER
STOVER
STUPOR
STYLER
SUAVER
SUCCOR
SUCKER
SUFFER
SUITOR
SULFUR
SULKER
SUMMER
SUMNER
SUMTER
SUNDER
SUPPER
SURFER
SUTLER
SUTTER
SWAYER
SWIPER

•SR•••

ISRAEL

•S•R••

ASHRAM
ASTRAL
ASTRAY
ASTRID
ASTROS
ESCROW
ESDRAS
ESPRIT
ISTRIA
OSIRIS
OSPREY
USERID
USURER
USURPS

•S••R•

ASBURY
ASGARD
ASHARP
ASHORE
ASKARI
ASKERS
ASMARA
ASPERA
ASPIRE
ASSERT
ASSORT
ASSURE
ASTERN
ASTERS
ASWIRL
BSHARP
CSHARP
DSHARP
ESCARP
ESCORT
ESHARP
ESKERS
ESTERS
FSHARP
GSHARP
OSBORN
OSCARS
OSIERS
TSHIRT
USHERS

•S•••R

ASHIER
ASHLAR
ASKFOR
ESCHER
ESTHER
ISADOR
ISHTAR
ISOBAR
ISOMER
ISSUER
OSTLER
USURER

••S•R•

ABSORB
ABSURD
ADSORB
ASSERT
ASSORT
ASSURE
AUSTRO
BISTRO
CASERN
CASTRO
CESARE
DESCRY
DESERT
DESIRE
DESTRY
DISARM
DOSERS
ENSURE
EXSERT
GASTRO
HASBRO
INSERT
INSURE
LASERS
LOSERS
LUSTRE
MASERS
MASERU
MESSRS
MISERS
MISERY
MUSERS
PASTRY
POSERS
RESORB
RESORT
RISERS
ROSARY
ROSTRA
SISERA
TISHRI
UNSURE
VESTRY
VISORS

••S••R

ANSGAR
ANSWER
BASTER
BESSER
BESTIR
BUSBAR
BUSIER
BUSTER
CASPAR
CASPER
CASTER
CASTOR
COSTAR
CUSTER
DASHER
DISBAR
DOSSER
DUSTER
EASIER
EASTER
EISNER
FASTER
FESTER
FISHER
FOSTER
GASPAR
GASSER
GUSHER
HESTER
HISSER
HOSIER
HUSKER
HUSSAR
INSTAR
ISSUER
JASPER
JESTER
JUSTER
KISSER
KOSHER
LASCAR
LASHER
LASSER
LESSER
LESSOR
LESTER
LISTER
LUSHER
LUSTER
MASHER
MASKER
MASTER
MESMER
MISTER
MUSHER
MUSTER
NASCAR
NASSER
NESTER
NESTOR
NOSHER
NOSIER
OUSTER
OYSTER
PASSER
PASTOR
PESTER
POSEUR
POSHER
POSTER
RASHER
RASPER
RASTER
RESTER
RISKER
ROSIER
ROSTER
SASSER
SISLER
SISTER
TASTER
TESTER
TOSSER
TUSKER
ULSTER
VASSAR
VASTER
VESPER
WASHER
WASTER
WISHER
WISTER
XYSTER
YASSER
YESSIR
YESTER

•••SR•

MESSRS

•••S•R

ABUSER
BESSER
BIGSUR
BOWSER
BURSAR
CAESAR
CENSER
CENSOR
CHASER
CLOSER
CURSOR
DENSER
DOSSER
DOWSER
ERASER
FALSER
FRASER
GASSER
GEYSER
GLASER
HAWSER
HISSER
HUSSAR
KAISER
KISSER
LASSER
LEASER
LESSER
LESSOR
LOOSER
MAUSER
MOUSER
NASSER
NURSER
PARSER
PASSER
PHASER
PROSER
PULSAR
PURSER
QUASAR
RAISER
SASSER
SENSOR
TEASER
TENSER
TENSOR
TERSER
TOSSER
VASSAR
WINSOR
YASSER
YESSIR

S•S•••

SASEBO
SASHAY
SASHED
SASHES
SASSED
SASSER
SASSES
SESAME
SESQUI
SESTET
SESTOS
SISALS
SISERA
SISKEL
SISKIN
SISLER
SISTER
SOSOON
SUSANN
SUSIEQ
SUSLIK
SUSSEX
SYSTEM

S••S••

SALSAS
SAMSON
SANSEI
SASSED
SASSER
SASSES
SAYSOS
SEASON
SEESAW
SEESIN
SEESTO
SEISMO
SEISMS
SENSED
SENSEI
SENSES
SENSOR
SETSAT
SETSBY
SETSIN
SETSON
SETSUP
SEWSON
SEWSUP
SHASTA
SIESTA
SITSIN
SITSON
SITSUP
SLOSHY
SLUSHY
SOASTO
SOPSUP
SOUSED
SOUSES
SPASMS
STASES
STASIS
SUBSET
SUDSED
SUDSES
SUMSUP
SUNSET
SUSSEX

S•••S•

SAFEST
SAGEST
SALISH
SAMOSA
SANEST
SCHISM
SCHIST
SCHUSS
SEROSA
SETOSE
SEXIST
SHIEST
SHIISM
SHYEST
SIWASH
SLIEST
SLYEST
SMERSH
SOREST
SPARSE
SPLASH
SPLOSH
SPOUSE
SQUASH
SQUISH
STRASS
STRESS
SUFISM
SUREST
SWOOSH

S••••S

SABERS
SABINS
SABLES
SABOTS
SABRAS
SABRES
SAHIBS
SAIGAS
SAINTS
SAKERS
SALADS
SALALS
SALONS
SALSAS
SALVES
SALVOS
SAMBAS
SANTOS
SAPORS
SARANS
SARDIS
SARGES
SARGOS
SARODS
SASHES
SASSES
SATINS
SATYRS
SAUCES
SAUDIS
SAULTS
SAUNAS
SAUTES
SAVERS
SAVORS
SAXONS
SAYERS
SAYSOS
SAYYES
SCALDS
SCALES
SCALPS
SCAMPS
SCANTS
SCAPES
SCARES
SCARFS
SCARPS
SCAUPS
SCENAS
SCENDS
SCENES
SCENTS
SCHMOS
SCHUSS
SCHWAS
SCIFIS
SCIONS
SCOFFS
SCOLDS
SCONES
SCOOPS
SCOOTS
SCOPES
SCORES
SCORNS
SCOURS
SCOUTS
SCOWLS
SCRAGS
SCRAMS
SCRAPS
SCREES
SCREWS
SCRIMS
SCRIPS
SCRODS
SCRUBS
SCRUMS
SCUBAS
SCUFFS
SCULLS
SCUTES
SEAMUS
SEDANS
SEDERS
SEDGES
SEDUMS
SEENAS
SEGUES
SEINES
SEISMS
SEIZES
SELVES
SENNAS
SENORS
SENSES
SEPALS
SEPIAS
SEPOYS
SERACS
SERAIS
SERGES
SERIES
SERIFS
SERINS
SEROUS
SEROWS
SERUMS
SERVES
SERVOS
SESTOS
SETINS
SETTOS
SETUPS
SEVENS
SEVERS
SEVRES
SEWERS
SHACKS
SHADES
SHAFTS
SHAKES
SHAKOS
SHALES
SHAMES
SHAMUS
SHANKS
SHAPES
SHARDS
SHARES
SHARKS
SHARPS
SHAVES
SHAWLS
SHAWMS
SHEAFS
SHEARS
SHEENS
SHEEPS
SHEERS
SHEETS
SHEIKS
SHELLS
SHIFTS
SHILLS
SHINES
SHIRES
SHIRKS
SHIRRS
SHIRTS
SHOALS
SHOATS
SHOCKS
SHOERS
SHOJIS
SHOOKS
SHOOTS
SHORES
SHORTS
SHOUTS
SHOVES
SHREDS
SHREWS
SHRUBS
SHRUGS
SHUCKS
SHUNTS
SIBYLS
SIDERS
SIDLES
SIEGES
SIEVES
SIGHTS
SIGILS
SIGMAS
SINEWS
SINGES
SIRENS
SIRIUS
SISALS
SITARS
SITINS
SITUPS
SIXERS
SIXTHS
SIXTUS
SIZERS
SKALDS
SKATES
SKEANS
SKEINS
SKIERS
SKIFFS
SKILLS
SKIMPS
SKINKS
SKIRLS
SKIROS
SKIRRS
SKIRTS
SKIVES
SKULKS
SKULLS
SKUNKS
SLACKS
SLAKES
SLANGS
SLANTS
SLATES
SLAVES
SLEEKS
SLEEPS
SLEETS
SLICES
SLICKS
SLIDES
SLIMES
SLINGS
SLINKS
SLOOPS
SLOPES
SLOTHS
SLUMPS
SLURPS
SLYPES
SMACKS
SMALLS
SMARTS
SMEARS
SMELLS
SMELTS
SMILES
SMIRKS
SMITES
SMITHS
SMOCKS
SMOKES
SMURFS
SNACKS
SNAFUS
SNAILS
SNAKES
SNARES
SNARLS
SNATHS
SNEAKS
SNEERS
SNELLS
SNICKS
SNIFFS
SNIPES
SNOODS
SNOOKS
SNOOPS
SNOOTS
SNOPES
SNORES
SNORTS
SNOUTS
SNUFFS
SOARES
SOAVES
SOBERS
SOCLES
SOLANS
SOLERS
SOLEUS
SOLFAS
SOLIDS
SOLVES
SOMERS
SONDES
SONICS
SOPORS
SOTOLS
SOUGHS
SOUNDS
SOUSES
SOWERS
SOXERS
SPACES
SPADES
SPAHIS
SPALLS
SPANKS
SPARES
SPARKS
SPASMS
SPATES
SPAWNS
SPEAKS
SPEARS
SPECKS
SPEEDS
SPELLS
SPENDS
SPICAS
SPICES
SPIELS
SPIERS
SPIFFS
SPIKES
SPILES
SPILLS
SPINES
SPINKS
SPIRES
SPIROS
SPITES
SPLATS
SPLAYS
SPLITS
SPOILS
SPOKES
SPOOFS
SPOOKS
SPOOLS
SPOONS
SPOORS
SPORES
SPORTS
SPOUTS
SPRAGS
SPRATS
SPRAYS
SPREES
SPRIGS
SPRITS
SPRUES
SPUMES
SPURNS
SPURTS
SQUABS
SQUADS
SQUATS
SQUIBS
SQUIDS
STACKS
STAFFS
STAGES
STAINS
STAIRS
STAKES
STALES
STALKS
STALLS
STAMPS
STANDS
STAPES
STARES
STARTS
STASES
STASIS
STATES
STATUS
STAVES
STEADS
STEAKS
STEALS
STEAMS
STEEDS
STEELS
STEEPS
STEERS
STEINS
STELES
STENOS
STERES
STERNS
STICKS
STIFFS
STILES
STILLS
STILTS
STINGS
STINKS
STINTS
STIPES
STOATS
STOCKS
STOICS
STOKES
STOLES
STOMAS
STOMPS
STONES
STOOLS
STOOPS
STOPES
STORES
STORKS
STORMS
STORRS
STOUPS
STOUTS
STOVES
STRADS
STRAPS
STRASS
STRAUS
STRAWS
STRAYS
STRESS
STREWS
STRIPS
STROPS
STRUMS
STRUTS
STUFFS
STULLS
STUMPS
STUNTS
STUPAS
STUPES
STYLES
STYLUS
SUCCES
SUCHAS
SUDSES
SUEDES
SUGARS
SUITES
SULCUS
SUMACS
SUMMAS

SUNNIS
SUNUPS
SUPERS
SURAHS
SURGES
SUTRAS
SWAGES
SWAINS
SWALES
SWAMIS
SWAMPS
SWARDS
SWARMS
SWATHS
SWAZIS
SWEARS
SWEATS
SWEDES
SWEEPS
SWEETS
SWELLS
SWIFTS
SWILLS
SWINGS
SWIPES
SWIRLS
SWOONS
SWOOPS
SWORDS
SYLPHS
SYNODS
SYRUPS

•SS•••

ASSAIL
ASSAYS
ASSENT
ASSERT
ASSESS
ASSETS
ASSIGN
ASSISI
ASSIST
ASSIZE
ASSORT
ASSUME
ASSURE
ESSAYS
ESSENE
ISSUED
ISSUER
ISSUES
OSSEIN
OSSETE
OSSIAN
OSSIFY

•S•S••

ASOSAN
USESUP

•S••S•

ASSESS
ASSISI
ASSIST
ESPOSA
ESPOSO
OSMOSE
TSETSE
ZSAZSA

•S•••S

ASANAS
ASCOTS
ASIANS
ASIDES
ASKERS
ASPENS
ASPICS
ASSAYS
ASSESS
ASSETS
ASTERS
ASTROS
BSIDES
ESDRAS
ESKERS
ESPIES
ESSAYS
ESTERS
ESTOPS
FSTOPS
GSUITS
ISLETS
ISSUES
ISTLES
OSAGES
OSCARS
OSIERS
OSIRIS
OSMICS
PSALMS
PSEUDS
PSYCHS
USAGES
USHERS
USUALS
USURPS
VSIGNS
VSIXES

••SS••

AUSSIE
BASSES
BASSET
BASSOS
BESSER
BESSIE
BISSAU
BISSET
BOSSED
BOSSES
BUSSED
BUSSES
BYSSHE
BYSSUS
CASSIA
CASSIO
CASSIS
CESSNA
COSSET
CUSSED
CUSSES
DASSIN
DISSED
DOSSAL
DOSSED
DOSSEL
DOSSER
DOSSES
FESSES
FESSUP
FOSSAE
FOSSAS
FOSSES
FOSSEY
FOSSIL
FUSSED
FUSSES
GASSED
GASSER
GASSES
GOSSIP
GUSSET
HASSAM
HASSAN
HASSLE
HISSAT
HISSED
HISSER
HISSES
HUSSAR
HYSSOP
IJSSEL
JESSEL
JESSIE
JOSSES
KISSED
KISSER
KISSES
LASSEN
LASSER
LASSES
LASSIE
LASSOS
LESSEE
LESSEN
LESSER
LESSON
LESSOR
LOSSES
MASSED
MASSES
MASSEY
MASSIF
MESSED
MESSES
MESSRS
MESSUP
MISSAL
MISSAY
MISSED
MISSES
MISSIS
MISSUS
MOSSED
MOSSES
MUSSED
MUSSEL
MUSSES
MUSSUP
NASSAU
NASSER
NESSES
NESSIE
NISSAN
NISSEN
PASSBY
PASSED
PASSEL
PASSER
PASSES
PASSIM
PASSUP
POSSES
POSSET
POSSUM
PUSSES
RASSLE
RUSSET
RUSSIA
SASSED
SASSER
SASSES
SUSSEX
TASSEL
TASSES
TESSIE
TISSUE
TOSSED
TOSSER
TOSSES
TOSSUP
TUSSAH
TUSSLE
VASSAL
VASSAR
VESSEL
WESSEX
WESSON
YASSER
YESSED
YESSES
YESSIR

••S•S•

ASSESS
ASSISI
ASSIST
BASEST
DESIST
DISUSE
INSIST
MISUSE
OBSESS
RESIST
WISEST

••S••S

AISLES
ASSAYS
ASSESS
ASSETS
BASHES
BASICS
BASINS
BASSES
BASSOS
BASTES
BESETS
BESOMS
BESOTS
BISONS
BOSSES
BOSUNS
BUSHES
BUSIES
BUSSES
BYSSUS
CASALS
CASHES
CASSIS
CASTES
CESTAS
CESTOS
CESTUS
CISCOS
COSHES
COSIES
COSMOS
COSTAS
CUSSES
DASHES
DISCOS
DISCUS
DISHES
DISMES
DOSERS
DOSSES
EASELS
EDSELS
ENSUES
EOSINS
ESSAYS
FASCES
FESSES
FESTUS
FISHES
FOSSAS
FOSSES
FUSEES
FUSILS
FUSSES
GASHES
GASSES
GESTES
GUSHES
HASHES
HASTES
HISSES
HOSELS
HOSTAS
HUSHES
INSETS
ISSUES
JOSHES
JOSSES
KISSES
LASERS
LASHES
LASSES
LASSOS
LESBOS
LISLES
LOSERS
LOSSES
LYSINS
MASAIS
MASERS
MASHES
MASONS
MASSES
MESHES
MESONS
MESSES
MESSRS
MISERS
MISSES
MISSIS
MISSUS
MOSEYS
MOSSES
MUSERS
MUSHES
MUSSES
NASALS
NESSES
NOSHES
OBSESS
ONSETS
OUSELS
PASEOS
PASHAS
PASSES
PASTAS
PASTES
PASTIS
PISANS
PISCES
POSERS
POSIES
POSITS
POSSES
PUSHES
PUSSES
RASHES
RESEES
RESETS
RESEWS
RESINS
RESODS
RISERS
ROSINS
RUSHES
SASHES
SASSES
SESTOS
SISALS
TASSES
TASTES
TESLAS
TOSSES
TVSETS
UNSAYS
UNSEWS
UPSETS
URSIDS
VESTAS
VISITS
VISORS
VISTAS
VOSGES
WASHES
WASTES
WISHES
YESSES

•••SS•

AGASSI
ALYSSA
BRASSY
CHASSE
CLASSY
CROSSE
CUISSE
DRESSY
EDESSA
ELISSA
FLOSSY
GLASSY
GLOSSA
GLOSSY
GRASSO
GRASSY
GROSSE
GROSSO
MOUSSE
NEISSE
NYASSA
ODESSA
ORISSA
PLISSE
POUSSE
PRISSY
WRASSE

•••S•S

ABASES
ABUSES
ABYSMS
AMUSES
ARISES
ATESTS
AVISOS
BASSES
BASSOS
BEASTS
BIASES
BLASTS
BOASTS
BOOSTS
BOSSES
BURSAS
BURSES
BURSTS
BUSSES
BYSSUS
CASSIS
CAUSES
CEASES
CENSES
CENSUS
CHASES
CHASMS
CHESTS
CLASPS
CLOSES
COASTS
COPSES
CRESTS
CRISES
CRISIS
CRISPS
CRUSES
CRUSTS
CURSES
CUSSES
DAISES
DEISTS
DIESES
DIESIS
DOSSES
DOUSES
DOWSES
ECESIS
EGESTS
ENOSIS
ERASES
EXISTS
FEASTS
FESSES
FIRSTS
FLASKS
FOISTS
FOSSAS
FOSSES
FRISES
FRISKS
FROSTS
FUSSES
GASSES
GHOSTS
GNOSIS
GOOSES
GORSES
GRASPS
GRISTS
GUESTS
GUISES
HAUSAS
HAWSES
HEISTS
HISSES
HOISTS
HORSES
HOUSES
HYKSOS
IBISES
IRISES
JOISTS
JOSSES
JOUSTS
KANSAS
KARSTS
KIOSKS
KISSES
LAPSES
LASSES
LASSOS
LEASES
LENSES
LOOSES
LOSSES
LOUSES
MANSES
MASSES
MENSAS
MESSES
MESSRS
MIOSIS
MISSES
MISSIS
MISSUS
MOSSES
MOUSES
MUSSES
NESSES
NOESIS
NOISES
NOOSES
NURSES
ODISTS
ONUSES
OPUSES
PARSES
PASSES
PAUSES
PHASES
PLUSES
POISES
POSSES
PRISMS
PROSES
PULSES
PURSES
PUSSES
QUESTS
RAISES
RAMSES
REUSES
RHESUS
RINSES
ROASTS
ROOSTS
ROUSES
ROUSTS
SALSAS
SASSES
SAYSOS
SEISMS
SENSES
SOUSES
SPASMS
STASES
STASIS
SUDSES
TARSUS
TASSES
TEASES
TENSES
THESES
THESIS
TMESIS
TOASTS
TORSOS
TOSSES
TRUSTS
TRYSTS
TWISTS
UKASES
URUSES
VERSES
VERSOS
VERSUS
WAISTS
WHISKS
WORSTS
WRESTS
WRISTS
WURSTS
XHOSAS
YEASTS
YESSES

••••SS

ABBESS
ACCESS
ACROSS
ARLISS
ARNESS
ASSESS
BYPASS
CARESS
DURESS
EGRESS
EMBOSS
EXCESS
GNEISS
HARASS
INNESS
KAROSS
KUMISS
MORASS
NOLESS
OBSESS
OGRESS
RECESS
REMISS
SCHUSS
STRASS
STRESS
UNLESS

ST••••

STABAT
STABLE
STABLY
STACKS
STACTE
STADIA
STAFFS
STAGED
STAGER
STAGES
STAINS
STAIRS
STAKED
STAKES
STALAG
STALED
STALER
STALES
STALIN
STALKS
STALKY
STALLS
STAMEN
STAMPS
STANCE
STANCH
STANDS
STANKY
STANZA
STAPES
STAPLE
STAPUF
STARCH
STARED
STARER
STARES
STARRY
STARTS
STARVE
STASES
STASIS
STATED
STATER
STATES
STATIC
STATOR
STATUE
STATUS
STAVED
STAVES
STAYED
STAYON
STAYUP
STEADS
STEADY
STEAKS
STEALS
STEAMS
STEAMY
STEEDS
STEELE
STEELS
STEELY
STEEPS
STEERS
STEEVE
STEFAN
STEFFI
STEINS
STELAE
STELAR
STELES
STELLA
STELMO
STENCH
STENOG
STENOS
STEPIN
STEPON
STEPPE
STEPUP
STEREO
STERES
STERNA
STERNE
STERNO
STERNS
STEROL
STEVEN
STEVIE
STEWED
STEWER
STHENO
STICKS
STICKY
STIFFS
STIFLE
STIGMA
STILES
STILLS
STILLY
STILTS
STIMPY
STINGS
STINGY
STINKS
STINKY
STINTS
STIPEL
STIPES
STIRIN
STIRUP
STITCH
STIVER
STIVIC
STJOAN
STJOHN
STLUKE
STMALO
STMARK
STOATS
STOCKS
STOCKY
STODGE
STODGY
STOGIE
STOICS
STOJKO
STOKED
STOKER
STOKES
STOLEN
STOLES
STOLID
STOLLE
STOLON
STOMAS
STOMAT
STOMPS
STONED
STONER
STONES
STOOGE
STOOLS
STOOPS
STOPES
STOPIN
STOPIT
STOPUP
STORCH
STORED
STORER
STORES
STOREY
STORKS
STORMS
STORMY
STORRS
STOUPS
STOUTS
STOVER
STOVES
STOWED
STPAUL
STPETE
STRABO
STRADS
STRAFE
STRAIN
STRAIT
STRAKE
STRAND
STRAPS
STRASS
STRATA
STRATI
STRATO
STRAUS
STRAWS
STRAYS
STREAK
STREAM
STREEP
STREET
STRESS
STREWN
STREWS
STRIAE
STRICK
STRICT
STRIDE
STRIFE
STRIKE
STRING
STRIPE
STRIPS
STRIVE
STROBE
STRODE
STROKE
STROLL
STRONG
STROPS
STROUD
STROVE
STRUCK
STRUMS
STRUNG
STRUTS
STUART
STUBBY
STUCCO
STUDIO
STUFFS
STUFFY
STULLS
STUMPS
STUMPY
STUNTS
STUPAS
STUPES
STUPID
STUPOR
STURDY
STYLED
STYLER
STYLES
STYLET
STYLUS
STYMIE
STYRIA
STYRON

S•T•••

SATANG
SATEEN
SATING
SATINS
SATINY
SATIRE
SATORI
SATOUT
SATRAP
SATURN
SATYRS
SETINS
SETOFF
SETOSE
SETOUT
SETSAT
SETSBY
SETSIN
SETSON
SETSUP
SETTEE
SETTER
SETTLE
SETTOS
SETUPS
SGTMAJ
SHTETL
SHTICK
SITARS
SITCOM
SITING
SITINS
SITOUT
SITSIN
SITSON
SITSUP
SITTER
SITUPS
SOTHAT
SOTOLS
SOTTED
SUTLER
SUTRAS
SUTTER
SUTURE

S••T••

SALTED
SALTEN
SALTER
SALTON
SANTEE
SANTIR
SANTOS
SARTON
SARTRE
SAUTES
SCATHE
SCOTCH
SCOTER
SCOTIA
SCOTTO
SCOTTY
SCUTCH
SCUTES
SCYTHE
SEATED
SEATER
SECTOR
SEETHE
SENTIN
SENTRY
SENTUP
SEPTAL
SEPTET
SEPTIC
SEPTUM
SESTET
SESTOS
SETTEE
SETTER
SETTLE
SETTOS
SEXTET
SEXTON
SHOTAT
SHOTUP
SHUTIN
SHUTUP
SIFTED
SIFTER
SILTED
SINTAX
SINTER
SISTER
SITTER
SIXTHS
SIXTUS
SKATED
SKATER
SKATES
SKETCH
SKITCH
SKITOW
SLATED
SLATER
SLATES
SLITHY
SLITTY
SLOTHS
SMITES
SMITHS
SMITHY
SMUTCH
SMUTTY
SNATCH
SNATHE
SNATHS
SNITCH
SOFTEN
SOFTER
SOFTIE
SOFTLY
SONTAG
SOOTHE
SORTED
SORTER
SORTIE
SORTOF
SOTTED
SOUTER
SPATES
SPATHE
SPITED
SPITES
SPOTTY
STATED
STATER
STATES
STATIC
STATOR
STATUE
STATUS
STITCH
SUBTLE
SUBTLY
SUITED
SUITES
SUITOR
SUITUP
SULTAN
SULTRY
SUMTER
SUNTAN
SURTAX
SUTTER
SWATCH
SWATHE
SWATHS
SWITCH
SYNTAX
SYSTEM

S•••T•

SABATO
SABOTS
SAFETY
SAINTE
SAINTS
SALUTE
SAMITE
SANCTA
SANGTO
SANITY
SAULTS
SAVATE
SCANTS
SCANTY
SCENTS
SCOOTS
SCOTTO
SCOTTY
SCOUTS
SEDATE
SEENTO
SEESTO
SEMITE
SENATE
SHAFTS
SHAKTI
SHANTY
SHASTA
SHEATH
SHEETS
SHIFTS
SHIFTY
SHIITE
SHINTO
SHIRTS
SHIRTY
SHOATS
SHOOTS
SHORTS
SHORTY
SHOUTS
SHTETL
SHUNTS
SIESTA
SIGHTS
SINGTO
SKIRTS
SLANTS
SLEETS
SLEETY
SLEUTH
SLITTY
SMALTI
SMALTO
SMARTS
SMARTY
SMELTS
SMOOTH
SMUTTY
SNAPTO
SNOOTS
SNOOTY
SNORTS
SNOUTS
SOASTO
SOLUTE
SOMATA
SOMATO

SONATA
SOWETO
SPARTA
SPILTH
SPLATS
SPLITS
SPORTS
SPORTY
SPOTTY
SPOUTS
SPRATS
SPRITE
SPRITS
SPRITZ
SPURTS
SQUATS
STACTE
STARTS
STILTS
STINTS
STOATS
STOUTS
STPETE
STRATA
STRATI
STRATO
STRUTS
STUNTS
SUBITO
SURETE
SURETY
SVELTE
SWARTH
SWEATS
SWEATY
SWEETS
SWIFTS

S••••T

SACHET
SAFEST
SAGEST
SALLET
SALYUT
SANEST
SATOUT
SAVANT
SAWFIT
SAWOUT
SCHIST
SCRIPT
SCULPT
SECANT
SECRET
SEEFIT
SEEOUT
SEJANT
SELECT
SENNET
SENNIT
SEPTET
SESTET
SETOUT
SETSAT
SEURAT
SEXIST
SEXTET
SHEVAT
SHIEST
SHOTAT
SHRIFT
SHYEST
SIGNET
SILENT
SIPPET
SITOUT
SLIEST
SLIGHT
SLYEST
SNAPAT
SNOCAT
SOBEIT
SOCKET
SOFFIT
SOLENT
SONANT
SONNET
SORBET
SOREST
SOTHAT
SOUGHT
SOVIET
SOWHAT
SPIGOT
SPINET
SPIRIT
SPLINT
SPOILT
SPRINT
SPROUT
SQUINT
SQUIRT
STABAT
STOMAT
STOPIT
STRAIT
STREET
STRICT
STUART
STYLET
SUBLET
SUBMIT
SUBSET
SUMMIT
SUNLIT
SUNSET
SUREST
SWIVET

•ST•••

ASTERN
ASTERS
ASTRAL
ASTRAY
ASTRID
ASTROS
ASTUTE
ESTATE
ESTEEM
ESTERS
ESTHER
ESTOPS
FSTOPS
GSTAAD
ISTHMI
ISTLES
ISTRIA
OSTEAL
OSTEND
OSTIUM
OSTLER

•S•T••

ISHTAR
TSETSE

•S••T•

ASCOTS
ASSETS
ASTUTE
ESTATE
GSUITS
ISLETS
OSSETE
USEDTO

•S•••T

ASCENT
ASKOUT
ASLANT
ASPECT
ASSENT
ASSERT
ASSIST
ASSORT
ESCENT
ESCORT
ESPRIT
ISEULT
TSHIRT

••ST••

AMSTEL
ATSTUD
AUSTEN
AUSTIN
AUSTRO
BASTED
BASTER
BASTES
BESTED
BESTIR
BESTOW
BISTRO
BOSTON
BUSTED
BUSTER
BUSTLE
CASTER
CASTES
CASTLE
CASTON
CASTOR
CASTRO
CESTAS
CESTOS
CESTUS
COSTAE
COSTAL
COSTAR
COSTAS
COSTLY
CUSTER
CUSTOM
DESTRY
DISTAL
DISTIL
DUSTED
DUSTER
DUSTIN
DUSTUP
EASTER
EASTON
FASTED
FASTEN
FASTER
FESTAL
FESTER
FESTUS
FISTED
FISTIC
FOSTER
FUSTIC
GASTON
GASTRO
GESTES
GOSTAG
GUSTAV
GUSTED
HASTEN
HASTES
HESTER
HESTIA
HESTON
HOSTAS
HOSTED
HOSTEL
HUSTLE
HUSTON
INSTAR
INSTEP
JESTED
JESTER
JOSTLE
JUSTER
JUSTIN
JUSTLY
LASTED
LASTEX
LASTLY
LESTAT
LESTER
LISTED
LISTEE
LISTEL
LISTEN
LISTER
LISTON
LOSTIT
LUSTED
LUSTER
LUSTRE
MASTER
MASTIC
MISTED
MISTER
MOSTEL
MOSTLY
MUSTER
MUSTNT
MYSTIC
NESTEA
NESTED
NESTER
NESTLE
NESTOR
OBSTET
OUSTED
OUSTER
OYSTER
PASTAS
PASTED
PASTEL
PASTES
PASTIS
PASTOR
PASTRY
PESTER
PESTLE
PISTIL
PISTOL
PISTON
POSTAL
POSTED
POSTER
POSTON
RASTER
RESTED
RESTER
RESTON
RESTUP
ROSTER
ROSTOV
ROSTRA
RUSTED
RUSTIC
RUSTLE
SESTET
SESTOS
SISTER
SYSTEM
TASTED
TASTER
TASTES
TESTAE
TESTED
TESTEE
TESTER
ULSTER
UNSTOP
VASTER
VASTLY
VESTAL
VESTAS
VESTED
VESTEE
VESTRY
VISTAS
VOSTOK
WASTED
WASTER
WASTES
WISTER
WYSTAN
XYSTER
YESTER
ZESTED

••S•T•

ANSATE
ASSETS
BESETS
BESOTS
DESOTO
ERSATZ
INSETS
INSITU
ONSETS
ONSITE
OSSETE
PASHTO
PESETA
POSITS
RESETS
ROSITA
TVSETS
UPSETS
VASHTI
VISITS
WISETO

••S••T

ABSENT
ASSENT
ASSERT
ASSIST
ASSORT
BASALT
BASEST
BASKET
BASSET
BESANT
BISECT
BISSET
BOSKET
COSSET
DESALT
DESERT
DESIST
DESPOT
DISANT
EXSERT
GASJET
GASKET
GASLIT
GOSOFT
GUSSET
HISSAT
INSECT
INSERT
INSIST
INSULT
JESUIT
KISMET
LESTAT
LOSEIT
LOSTIT
MASCOT
MISFIT
MISHIT
MUSCAT
MUSKET
MUSTNT
OBSTET
POSSET
RESALT
RESEAT
RESECT
RESENT
RESHOT
RESIST
RESORT
RESULT
RUSSET
SESTET
UNSEAT
UPSHOT
WESKIT
WISENT
WISEST

•••ST•

ADDSTO
ADESTE
AIMSTO
ARISTA
ARISTO
ATESTS
AVESTA
BEASTS
BLASTS
BOASTS
BOOSTS
BURSTS
CHASTE
CHESTS
CHESTY
COASTS
CRESTS
CRUSTS
CRUSTY
CUESTA
DEISTS
EGESTA
EGESTS
EXISTS
FEASTS
FEISTY
FIESTA
FIRSTS
FOISTS
FROSTS
FROSTY
GETSTO
GHOSTS
GRISTS
GUESTS
HEISTS
HOISTS
JOISTS
JOUSTS
KARSTS
LAYSTO
LIESTO
ODISTS
PIGSTY
PLASTY
PRESTO
PUTSTO
QUESTS
ROASTS
ROOSTS
ROUSTS
RUNSTO
SEESTO
SHASTA
SIESTA
SOASTO
TOASTS
TOASTY
TRISTE
TRUSTS
TRUSTY
TRYSTS
TWISTS
TWISTY
WAISTS
WORSTS
WRESTS
WRISTS
WURSTS
YEASTS
YEASTY

•••S•T

AIMSAT
ALLSET
BASSET
BISSET
BOXSET
CLOSET
COMSAT
CORSET
COSSET
DOESNT
DOGSIT
DORSET
EATSAT
GETSAT
GETSET
GETSIT
GOESAT
GUSSET
HISSAT
HITSIT
JETSET
LETSAT
NIPSAT
OFFSET
OUTSET
PAWSAT
POSSET
PRESET
PROSIT
RUSSET
SETSAT
SUBSET
SUNSET
TEASET
TILSIT

••••ST

ABLEST
ACCOST
ADJUST
AGEIST
AGHAST
ALEAST
ALMOST
ALWEST
AMIDST
AORIST
APTEST
ARREST
ARTIST
ASSIST
ATBEST
ATCOST
ATLAST
ATMOST
ATREST
ATTEST
AUGUST
BAREST
BASEST
BEHEST
BLUEST
BREAST
BYPAST
COHOST
COYEST
CUBIST
CUTEST
DEGUST
DELIST
DESIST
DETEST
DEVEST
DIGEST
DIREST
DIVEST
DRIEST
DRYEST
DYNAST
EGOIST
ELDEST
ENLIST
ERNEST
FEWEST
FINEST
FOREST
FREEST
GAINST
GAMEST
GAYEST
GOBUST
GOWEST
HALEST
HEARST
HOLIST
HONEST
HUGEST
ICIEST
IDLEST
ILLEST
IMPOST
INFEST
INGEST
INJEST
INMOST
INSIST
INVEST
IQTEST
JURIST
KLEIST
LAMEST
LATEST
LAXEST
LEGIST
LOCUST
LOWEST
LUTIST
LYRIST
MAOIST
MARIST
MEREST
MODEST
MOLEST
MONIST
MUTEST
NEWEST
NICEST
NLEAST
NLWEST
NUDIST
OBLAST
OBOIST
OBTEST
ODDEST
OLDEST
PALEST
PRIEST
PROUST
PUREST
PURIST
RAREST
RAWEST
RECAST
RELIST
REPAST
RESIST
RETEST
RIFEST
RIPEST
ROBUST
RUDEST
SAFEST
SAGEST
SANEST
SCHIST
SEXIST
SHIEST
SHYEST
SLIEST
SLYEST
SOREST
SUREST
TAMEST
TANIST
TAOIST
THEIST
THIRST
THRUST
TRUEST
TUBIST
TYPIST
UNJUST
UNREST
UPCAST
UPMOST
UTMOST
VILEST
WHILST
WIDEST
WISEST
WRIEST
WRYEST

SU••••

SUAVER
SUBARU
SUBBED
SUBDEB
SUBDUE
SUBGUM
SUBITO
SUBLET
SUBMIT
SUBORN
SUBSET
SUBTLE
SUBTLY
SUBURB
SUBWAY
SUCCES
SUCCOR
SUCHAS
SUCKED
SUCKER
SUCKIN
SUDDEN
SUDSED
SUDSES
SUEDES
SUFFER
SUFFIX
SUFISM
SUGARS
SUGARY
SUITED
SUITES
SUITOR
SUITUP
SUKKAH
SULCUS
SULFUR
SULKED
SULKER
SULLEN
SULTAN
SULTRY
SUMACS
SUMMAE
SUMMAS
SUMMED
SUMMER
SUMMIT
SUMMON
SUMNER
SUMSUP
SUMTER
SUNDAE
SUNDAY
SUNDER
SUNDEW
SUNDOG
SUNDRY
SUNGOD
SUNKEN
SUNLIT
SUNNED
SUNNIS
SUNOCO
SUNRAY
SUNSET
SUNTAN
SUNUNU
SUNUPS
SUPERB
SUPERS
SUPINE
SUPPED
SUPPER
SUPPLE
SUPPLY
SURAHS
SURELY
SUREST
SURETE
SURETY
SURFED
SURFER
SURGED
SURGES
SURIMI
SURREY
SURTAX
SURVEY
SUSANN
SUSIEQ
SUSLIK
SUSSEX
SUTLER
SUTRAS
SUTTER
SUTURE
SUZUKI

S•U•••

SAUCED
SAUCER
SAUCES
SAUDIS
SAUGER
SAULTS
SAUNAS
SAUREL
SAUTES
SCUBAS
SCUFFS
SCULLS
SCULLY
SCULPT
SCUMMY
SCURFY
SCURRY
SCURVE
SCURVY
SCUTCH
SCUTES
SCUZZY
SEURAT
SHUCKS
SHUNTS
SHUTIN
SHUTUP
SKULKS
SKULLS
SKUNKS
SLUDGE
SLUDGY
SLUGGO
SLUICE
SLUING
SLUMMY
SLUMPS
SLURPS
SLURRY
SLUSHY
SMUDGE
SMUDGY
SMUGLY
SMURFS
SMUTCH
SMUTTY
SNUFFS
SNUFFY
SNUGLY
SOUARI
SOUGHS
SOUGHT
SOUNDS
SOUPUP
SOURCE
SOURED
SOURER
SOURLY
SOUSED
SOUSES
SOUTER
SPUMED
SPUMES
SPUNKY
SPURGE
SPURNS
SPURON
SPURRY
SPURTS
SQUABS
SQUADS
SQUALL
SQUARE
SQUASH
SQUATS
SQUAWK
SQUEAK
SQUEAL
SQUIBB
SQUIBS
SQUIDS
SQUILL
SQUINT
SQUIRE
SQUIRM
SQUIRT
SQUISH
STUART
STUBBY
STUCCO
STUDIO
STUFFS
STUFFY
STULLS
STUMPS
STUMPY
STUNTS
STUPAS
STUPES
STUPID
STUPOR
STURDY

S••U••

SALUKI
SALUTE
SAMUEL
SATURN
SCAUPS
SCHULZ
SCHUSS
SCOURS
SCOUTS
SCRUBS
SCRUFF
SCRUMS
SECURE
SEDUCE
SEDUMS
SEGUED
SEGUES
SEGURA
SEQUEL
SEQUIN
SERUMS
SETUPS
SHOULD
SHOUTS
SHRUBS
SHRUGS
SHRUNK
SIGURD
SIOUAN
SITUPS
SLEUTH
SLOUCH
SLOUGH
SNOUTS
SOLUTE
SPOUSE
SPOUTS
SPRUCE
SPRUES
SPRUNG
STLUKE
STOUPS
STOUTS
STRUCK
STRUMS
STRUNG
STRUTS
SUBURB
SUNUNU
SUNUPS
SUTURE
SUZUKI
SYRUPS
SYRUPY

S•••U•

SACQUE
SACRUM
SALYUT
SANNUP
SATOUT
SAVEUP
SAVOUR
SAWOUT
SCARUM
SEALUP
SEAMUS
SEEOUT
SELJUK
SENDUP
SENTUP
SEPTUM
SEROUS
SESQUI
SETOUT
SETSUP
SEWNUP
SEWSUP
SHAMUS
SHOGUN
SHOTUP
SHOWUP
SHROUD
SHUTUP
SIDDUR
SIGNUP
SINFUL
SIRIUS
SITOUT
SITSUP
SIXGUN
SIXTUS
SIZEUP
SKIRUN
SLAPUP
SLIPUP
SLOWUP
SNAFUS
SNAPUP
SOAKUP
SODIUM
SOLEUS
SOPSUP
SOUPUP
SOWBUG
SPEDUP
SPROUT
STAPUF
STATUE
STATUS
STAYUP
STEPUP
STIRUP
STOPUP
STPAUL
STRAUS
STROUD
STYLUS
SUBDUE
SUBGUM
SUITUP
SULCUS
SULFUR
SUMSUP

S••••U

SUBARU
SUNUNU

•SU•••

GSUITS
USUALS
USURER
USURPS

•S•U••

ASBURY
ASSUME
ASSURE
ASTUTE
ESCUDO
ISEULT
ISSUED
ISSUER
ISSUES
OSCULA
OSMUND
PSEUDO
PSEUDS

•S••U•

ASKOUT
ASYLUM
OSMIUM
OSTIUM
USEDUP
USEFUL
USESUP

••SU••

ABSURD
ASSUME
ASSURE
BOSUNS
CASUAL
DISUSE
ENSUED
ENSUES
ENSURE
INSULT
INSURE
ISSUED
ISSUER
ISSUES
JESUIT
MISUSE
RESULT
RESUME
UNSUNG
UNSURE
URSULA
VISUAL

••S•U•

ATSTUD
BASQUE
BISQUE
BYSSUS
CASQUE
CESIUM
CESTUS
DISCUS
DUSTUP
EASEUP
ENSOUL
FESCUE
FESSUP
FESTUS
JOSHUA
LASHUP
MASQUE
MESSUP
MISCUE
MISSUS
MOSQUE
MUSEUM
MUSSUP
NASHUA
PASSUP
POSEUR
POSSUM
PUSHUP
RESCUE
RESTUP
RISQUE
SESQUI
TISSUE
TOSSUP
WASHUP
WISEUP

••S••U

BISSAU
DESILU
INSITU
MASERU
NASSAU

RESEAU
ROSEAU
VISHNU

•••SU•
ACESUP
ACTSUP
ADDSUP
BIDSUP
BIGSUR
BOBSUP
BUYSUP
BYSSUS
CATSUP
CENSUS
CONSUL
CUTSUP
DAMSUP
DATSUN
DIGSUP
DIMSUM
DOESUP
DORSUM
EATSUP
ENDSUP
FESSUP
GETSUP
GOESUP
GUMSUP
GYPSUM
HITSUP
HOPSUP
ICESUP
JAMSUP
KEYSUP
LAPSUP
LAYSUP
LETSUP
MESSUP
MISSUS
MOPSUP
MUSSUP
OMASUM
OWNSUP
PASSUP
PAYSUP
PEPSUP
POPSUP
POSSUM
PURSUE
PUTSUP
RHESUS
RIGSUP
RIPSUP
RUNSUP
SETSUP
SEWSUP
SITSUP
SOPSUP
SUMSUP
TAGSUP
TARSUS
TEESUP
TIESUP
TISSUE
TOSSUP
TOTSUP
USESUP
VERSUS
WADSUP
ZIPSUP

•••S•U
BISSAU
HONSHU
KYUSHU
NASSAU
WAUSAU

••••SU
HAVASU

SV••••
SVELTE

S•V•••
SAVAGE
SAVAII
SAVANT
SAVATE
SAVERS
SAVEUP
SAVING
SAVIOR
SAVOIE
SAVOIR
SAVORS
SAVORY
SAVOUR
SEVENS
SEVERE
SEVERN
SEVERS
SEVRES
SOVIET

S••V••
SALVED
SALVER
SALVES
SALVIA
SALVOR
SALVOS
SELVES
SERVAL
SERVED
SERVER
SERVES
SERVOS
SHAVED
SHAVEN
SHAVER
SHAVES
SHEVAT
SHIVER
SHOVED
SHOVEL
SHOVER
SHOVES
SIEVED
SIEVES
SILVER
SKIVED
SKIVER
SKIVES
SKIVVY
SLAVED
SLAVER
SLAVES
SLAVIC
SLIVER
SLOVAK
SLOVEN
SLOVIK
SNIVEL
SOAVES
SOLVED
SOLVER
SOLVES
SPAVIN
SPIVAK
STAVED
STAVES
STEVEN
STEVIE
STIVER
STIVIC
STOVER
STOVES
SUAVER
SURVEY
SWIVEL
SWIVET
SYLVAN
SYLVIA

S•••V•
SALIVA
SCURVE
SCURVY
SHEAVE
SHELVE
SHRIVE
SHROVE
SKIVVY
SLEAVE
SLEEVE
STARVE
STEEVE
STRIVE
STROVE
SWERVE

•S•••V
ASIMOV

••S•V•
CASAVA
MOSKVA

••S••V
GUSTAV
KISLEV
MOSHAV
ROSTOV
VASLAV

•••S•V
BRASOV

SW••••
SWABBY
SWAGED
SWAGES
SWAINS
SWALES
SWAMIS
SWAMPS
SWAMPY
SWANEE
SWANKY
SWARAJ
SWARDS
SWARMS
SWARTH
SWATCH
SWATHE
SWATHS
SWAYED
SWAYER
SWAYZE
SWAZIS
SWEARS
SWEATS
SWEATY
SWEDEN
SWEDES
SWEEPS
SWEETS
SWELLS
SWERVE
SWIFTS
SWILLS
SWINGS
SWINGY
SWIPED
SWIPER
SWIPES
SWIRLS
SWIRLY
SWITCH
SWIVEL
SWIVET
SWOONS
SWOOPS
SWOOSH
SWORDS

S•W•••
SAWFIT
SAWING
SAWLOG
SAWOFF
SAWOUT
SAWRED
SAWYER
SEWAGE
SEWARD
SEWELL
SEWERS
SEWING
SEWNUP
SEWSON
SEWSUP
SIWASH
SOWBUG
SOWERS
SOWETO
SOWHAT
SOWING

S••W••
SCHWAS
SCOWLS
SEAWAY
SHAWLS
SHAWMS
SHOWED
SHOWER
SHOWIN
SHOWME
SHOWUP
SKEWED
SKEWER
SKYWAY
SLEWED
SLOWED
SLOWER
SLOWLY
SLOWUP
SNOWED
SNOWIN
SPAWNS
SPEWED
STEWED
STEWER
STOWED
SUBWAY

S•••W•
SCRAWL
SCREWS
SCREWY
SEROWS
SHREWD
SHREWS
SINEWS
SINEWY
SPRAWL
SQUAWK
STRAWS
STREWN
STREWS

S••••W
SALLOW
SEACOW
SEESAW
SHADOW
SKITOW
SORROW
SUNDEW

•SW•••
ASWELL
ASWIRL
ASWOON
OSWALD
OSWEGO

•S•W••
OSHAWA

•S•••W
ESCHEW
ESCROW

••SW••
ANSWER

••S•W•
BUSHWA
DISOWN
RESEWN
RESEWS
UNSEWN
UNSEWS
UNSOWN

••S••W
BESTOW
CASHEW
CPSNOW
CUSHAW
GOSLOW
MOSCOW
NOSHOW
PESCOW
TVSHOW

•••S•W
BOWSAW
JIGSAW
PITSAW
RIPSAW
SEESAW
WARSAW

S•X•••
SAXONS
SAXONY
SEXIER
SEXILY
SEXIST
SEXTET
SEXTON
SIXERS
SIXGUN
SIXING
SIXTHS
SIXTUS
SOXERS

S••••X
SEAFOX
SINTAX
SKYBOX
SMILAX
SPADIX
SPHINX
SUFFIX
SURTAX
SUSSEX
SYNTAX
SYRINX

•S•X••
VSIXES

••S••X
AUSPEX
LASTEX
MUSKOX
SUSSEX
WESSEX

•••S•X
CHISOX
REDSOX
SUSSEX
THESIX
UNISEX
WESSEX

SY••••
SYDNEY
SYLPHS
SYLVAN
SYLVIA
SYMBOL
SYNCED
SYNDIC
SYNODS
SYNTAX
SYRIAN
SYRINX
SYRUPS
SYRUPY
SYSTEM
SYZYGY

S•Y•••
SAYERS
SAYING
SAYSOS
SAYYES
SAYYID
SCYLLA
SCYTHE
SHYEST
SHYING
SKYBOX
SKYCAP
SKYING
SKYLAB
SKYWAY
SLYEST
SLYPES
SMYRNA
SNYDER
SPYING
STYLED
STYLER
STYLES
STYLET
STYLUS
STYMIE
STYRIA
STYRON

S••Y••
SALYUT
SATYRS
SAWYER
SAYYES
SAYYID
SHAYNE
SIBYLS
SLAYED
SLAYER
SPAYED
SPRYER
SPRYLY
STAYED
STAYON
STAYUP
SWAYED
SWAYER
SWAYZE
SYZYGY

S•••Y•
SEPOYS
SPLAYS
SPRAYS
STRAYS

S••••Y
SAFELY
SAFETY
SAGELY
SALARY
SANELY
SANITY
SASHAY
SATINY
SAVORY
SAXONY
SCABBY
SCANTY
SCOTTY
SCREWY
SCULLY
SCUMMY
SCURFY
SCURRY
SCURVY
SCUZZY
SEAWAY
SEEMLY
SENARY
SENTRY
SETSBY
SEXILY
SHABBY
SHAGGY
SHALEY
SHALLY
SHANDY
SHANTY
SHEEDY
SHEEHY
SHELLY
SHERRY
SHIFTY
SHILLY
SHIMMY
SHINDY
SHINNY
SHIRTY
SHODDY
SHORTY
SICILY
SICKLY
SIDNEY
SIMONY
SIMPLY
SINEWY
SINGLY
SKERRY
SKIMPY
SKINNY
SKIPPY
SKIVVY
SKYWAY
SLAGGY
SLANGY
SLAPPY
SLEAZY
SLEEKY
SLEEPY
SLEETY
SLIMLY
SLINKY
SLITHY
SLITTY
SLOPPY
SLOSHY
SLOWLY
SLUDGY
SLUMMY
SLURRY
SLUSHY
SMARMY
SMARTY
SMEARY
SMELLY
SMILEY
SMIRKY
SMITHY
SMOGGY
SMOKEY
SMUDGY
SMUGLY
SMUTTY
SNAGGY
SNAPPY
SNARLY
SNAZZY
SNEAKY
SNEERY
SNEEZY
SNIFFY
SNIPPY
SNOBBY
SNOOPY
SNOOTY
SNUFFY
SNUGLY
SOFTLY
SOLELY
SOMANY
SORELY
SOURLY
SPACEY
SPANKY
SPARKY
SPEEDY
SPERRY
SPIFFY
SPONGY
SPOOKY
SPOONY
SPORTY
SPOTTY
SPRYLY
SPUNKY
SPURRY
STABLY
STALKY
STANKY
STARRY
STEADY
STEAMY
STEELY
STICKY
STILLY
STIMPY
STINGY
STINKY
STOCKY
STODGY
STOREY
STORMY
STUBBY
STUFFY
STUMPY
STURDY
SUBTLY
SUBWAY
SUGARY
SULTRY
SUNDAY
SUNDRY
SUNRAY
SUPPLY
SURELY
SURETY
SURREY
SURVEY
SWABBY
SWAMPY
SWANKY
SWEATY
SWINGY
SWIRLY
SYDNEY
SYRUPY
SYZYGY

•SY•••
ASYLUM
PSYCHE
PSYCHO
PSYCHS
PSYLLA

•S••Y•
ASSAYS
ESSAYS

•S•••Y
ASBURY
ASHLEY
ASTRAY
OSPREY
OSSIFY
USABLY

••SY••
INSYNC

••S•Y•
ASSAYS
ESSAYS
MOSEYS
UNSAYS

••S••Y
BASELY
BISCAY
BOSLEY
BUSBOY
BUSILY
COSTLY
DESCRY
DESTRY
DISMAY
DISNEY
EASILY
FOSSEY
JUSTLY
LASTLY
LESLEY
LUSHLY
MASSEY
MISERY
MISLAY
MISSAY
MOSTLY
MUSCLY
NASEBY
NOSILY
OSSIFY
PASSBY
PASTRY
POSHLY
RASHLY
ROSARY
ROSILY
ROSINY
SASHAY
VASTLY
VESTRY
WESLEY
WISELY

•••SY•
VAISYA

•••S•Y
BETSEY
BRASHY
BRASSY
BRUSHY
CHESTY
CLASSY
CRISPY
CROSBY
CRUSTY
DILSEY
DOESBY
DORSEY
DRESSY
FEISTY
FLASHY
FLESHY
FLOSSY
FOSSEY
FRISKY
FROSTY
GATSBY
GELSEY
GETSBY
GLASSY
GLOSSY
GOESBY
GRASSY
GRISLY
GROSZY
GUNSHY
HALSEY
HERSEY
HORSEY
ILLSAY
JERSEY
KELSEY
KERSEY
LAYSBY
LINSEY
MARSHY
MASSEY
MEASLY
MERSEY
MISSAY
MOUSEY
NAYSAY
NEVSKY
OCASEY
PASSBY
PIGSTY
PLASHY
PLASTY
PLUSHY
PRISSY
PUTSBY
RAMSAY
RAMSEY
RIMSKY
SETSBY
SLOSHY
SLUSHY
THUSLY
TOASTY
TRASHY
TRUSTY
TWISTY
WIMSEY
WOLSEY
YEASTY

••••SY
ARGOSY
BEKESY
BLUESY
BOOTSY
BRASSY
BRASSY
CHEESY
CHOOSY
CLASSY
CLUMSY
CREASY
CURTSY
CUTESY
DRESSY
DROWSY
FLIMSY
FLOPSY
FLOSSY
FOLKSY
GLASSY
GLOSSY
GOEASY
GRASSY
GREASY
HERESY
PRISSY
QUEASY
TEENSY
TOOTSY
UNEASY
WEENSY
WHIMSY
WOODSY

S•Z•••
SIZERS
SIZEUP
SIZING
SIZZLE
SUZUKI
SYZYGY

S••Z••
SCUZZY
SEIZED
SEIZER
SEIZES
SHAZAM
SIZZLE
SLEZAK
SNAZZY
SWAZIS

S•••Z•
SCUZZY
SFORZA
SLEAZE
SLEAZY
SNAZZY
SNEEZE
SNEEZY
SNOOZE
STANZA
SWAYZE

S••••Z
SCHNOZ
SCHULZ
SHIRAZ
SPRITZ

•S•Z••
ZSAZSA

•S••Z•
ASSIZE

••S•Z•
ASSIZE

••S••Z
ERSATZ

•••SZ•
GROSZY

•••S•Z
AMOSOZ

••••SZ
KUVASZ
MILOSZ

TA••••
TABARD
TABBED
TABLAS
TABLED
TABLES
TABLET
TABOOS
TABORS
TABRIZ
TABULA
TACKED
TACKER
TACKLE
TACKON
TACOMA
TACTIC
TAGDAY
TAGEND
TAGGED
TAGORE
TAGOUT
TAGSUP
TAHINI
TAHITI
TAICHI
TAIGAS
TAILED
TAILLE
TAILOR
TAINAN
TAINOS
TAINTS
TAIPAN
TAIPEI
TAIWAN
TAKEIN
TAKEON
TAKERS
TAKETH
TAKETO
TAKEUP
TAKING
TAKINS
TALBOT
TALCED
TALCUM
TALENT
TALESE
TALION
TALKAT
TALKED
TALKER
TALKIE
TALKTO
TALKUP
TALLER
TALLOW
TALMUD
TALONS
TAMALE
TAMARA
TAMAYO
TAMELY
TAMERS
TAMEST
TAMILS
TAMING
TAMMUZ
TAMPED
TAMPER
TAMTAM
TANAKA
TANDEM
TANGED
TANGLE
TANGLY
TANGOS
TANGUY
TANIST
TANKAS
TANKED
TANKER
TANKUP
TANNED
TANNER
TANNIC
TANNIN
TANOAK
TANOAN
TANTRA
TAOISM
TAOIST
TAPERS
TAPING
TAPINS
TAPIRS
TAPOFF
TAPOUT
TAPPAN
TAPPED
TAPPER
TAPPET
TARAWA
TARGES
TARGET
TARIFF
TARING
TARMAC
TAROTS
TARPAN
TARPIT
TARPON
TARRED
TARSAL
TARSUS
TARTAN
TARTAR
TARTER
TARTLY
TARZAN
TASKED
TASMAN
TASSEL
TASSES
TASTED
TASTER
TASTES
TATAMI
TATARS
TATERS
TATTED
TATTER
TATTLE
TATTOO
TAUGHT
TAUNTS
TAUONS
TAUPES
TAURUS
TAUTEN
TAUTER
TAUTLY
TAUTOG
TAVERN
TAWDRY
TAWING
TAXERS
TAXIED
TAXIES
TAXING
TAXMAN
TAXMEN
TAYLOR
TAYRAS
TAZZAS

T•A•••
TEABAG
TEACUP
TEAMED
TEAMUP
TEAPOT
TEAPOY
TEARAT
TEARED
TEARUP
TEASED
TEASEL
TEASER
TEASES
TEASET
THALER
THALES
THALIA
THAMES
THANES
THANKS
THATCH
THATIS
THAWED
THAYER
TIARAS
TLALOC
TOAMAN
TOASTS
TOASTY
TOATEE
TRACED
TRACER
TRACES
TRACEY
TRACKS
TRACTS
TRADED
TRADER
TRADES
TRAGIC
TRAILS
TRAINS
TRAITS
TRAJAN
TRALEE
TRAMPS
TRANCE
TRAPPY
TRASHY
TRAUMA
TRAVEL
TRAVIS
TRAWLS
TUAREG
TWANGS
TWANGY

T••A••
TABARD
TAMALE
TAMARA
TAMAYO
TANAKA
TARAWA
TATAMI
TATARS
TENACE
TENANT

TEPALS
TERAPH
TERATO
TEXACO
TEXANS
THRACE
THRALE
THRALL
THRASH
THWACK
THWART
TICALS
TILAKS
TIRADE
TIRANA
TIRANE
TISANE
TITANS
TOBAGO
TODATE
TOGAED
TOKAYS
TOMATO
TORAHS
TOTALS
TOWAGE
TOWARD
TREADS
TREATS
TREATY
TRIADS
TRIAGE
TRIALS
TRUANT
TUBATE
TUCANA
TULANE
TULARE
TUVALU
TWEAKS
TYBALT
TYRANT

T•••A•

TABLAS
TAGDAY
TAIGAS
TAINAN
TAIPAN
TAIWAN
TALKAT
TAMTAM
TANKAS
TANOAK
TANOAN
TAPPAN
TARMAC
TARPAN
TARSAL
TARTAN
TARTAR
TARZAN
TASMAN
TAXMAN
TAYRAS
TAZZAS
TEABAG
TEARAT
TERRAN
TESLAS
TESTAE
TETRAD
TETRAS
THECAE
THECAL
THEHAJ
THENAR
THETAS
THOMAS
THORAX
THREAD
THREAT
THROAT
THUJAS
TIARAS
TIBIAE
TIBIAL
TIBIAS
TICTAC
TIMBAL
TINCAL
TINCAN
TINEAR
TINHAT
TINMAN
TINPAN
TITIAN
TOAMAN
TOBIAS
TODDAO
TODMAN
TOECAP
TOETAP
TOKLAS
TOMBAC
TOMCAT
TONGAN
TOOBAD
TOPCAT
TOPHAT
TOREAT
TOUCAN
TOWCAR
TRAJAN
TREPAN
TRIBAL
TRINAL
TROCAR
TROJAN
TRUMAN
TUBMAN
TULSAN
TUPIAN
TURBAN
TUSCAN
TUSSAH
TWOWAY
TYRIAN

T••••A

TABULA
TACOMA
TAMARA
TANAKA
TANTRA
TARAWA
TEPHRA
TERESA
THALIA
THELMA
TIERRA
TIRANA
TOLUCA
TOPEKA
TOYOTA
TRAUMA
TREDIA
TRICIA
TRISHA
TRIVIA
TROIKA
TUCANA
TUNDRA
TUNICA

•TA•••

ATAMAN
ETALIA
ETALII
ITALIA
ITALIC
ITASCA
STABAT
STABLE
STABLY
STACKS
STACTE
STADIA
STAFFS
STAGED
STAGER
STAGES
STAINS
STAIRS
STAKED
STAKES
STALAG
STALED
STALER
STALES
STALIN
STALKS
STALKY
STALLS
STAMEN
STAMPS
STANCE
STANCH
STANDS
STANKY
STANZA
STAPES
STAPLE
STAPUF
STARCH
STARED
STARER
STARES
STARRY
STARTS
STARVE
STASES
STASIS
STATED
STATER
STATES
STATIC
STATOR
STATUE
STATUS
STAVED
STAVES
STAYED
STAYON
STAYUP
UTAHAN

•T•A••

ATBATS
ATEAMS
ATEASE
ATHAND
ATLAST
ATLATL
ATTACH
ATTACK
ATTAIN
ATTARS
ETHANE
ITHACA
ITHAKI
OTTAVA
OTTAWA
PTRAPS
STEADS
STEADY
STEAKS
STEALS
STEAMS
STEAMY
STMALO
STMARK
STOATS
STPAUL
STRABO
STRADS
STRAFE
STRAIN
STRAIT
STRAKE
STRAND
STRAPS
STRASS
STRATA
STRATI
STRATO
STRAUS
STRAWS
STRAYS
STUART
UTHANT

•T••A•

ATAMAN
ATONAL
ATRIAL
ATTHAT
ITZHAK
PTBOAT
STABAT
STALAG
STEFAN
STELAE
STELAR
STJOAN
STOMAS
STOMAT
STREAK
STREAM
STRIAE
STUPAS
UTAHAN

•T•••A

ATHENA
ATTICA
ATTILA
ETALIA
ITALIA
ITASCA
ITHACA
OTTAVA
OTTAWA
STADIA
STANZA
STELLA
STERNA
STIGMA
STRATA
STYRIA
UTOPIA

••TA••

ALTAIC
ALTAIR
ALTARS
ATTACH
ATTACK
ATTAIN
ATTARS
BATAAN
BETAKE
BOTANY
BUTANE
BYTALK
CETANE
DATARY
DETACH
DETAIL
DETAIN
DOTAGE
DOTARD
ENTAIL
ESTATE
EXTANT
FATALE
GITANO
GSTAAD
HATARI
HOTAIR
INTACT
INTAKE
LITANY
LOTAHS
METALS
METATE
MUTANT
MUTATE
NATANT
NOTARY
NOTATE
NUTATE
OBTAIN
OCTADS
OCTANE
OCTANT
OCTAVE
OCTAVO
ONTAPE
OTTAVA
OTTAWA
OUTACT
OUTAGE
OUTATE
OXTAIL
PATACA
PETAIN
PETALS
PETARD
POTAGE
POTASH
POTATO
QATARI
RETAGS
RETAIL
RETAIN
RETAKE
RETAPE
RETAPS
RETARD
RETARS
RITARD
ROTARY
ROTATE
SATANG
SITARS
TATAMI
TATARS
TITANS
TOTALS
UMTATA
UNTACK
UPTAKE
VITALS
VOTARY

••T•A•

ACTUAL
ALTMAN
AMTRAC
AMTRAK
ASTRAL
ASTRAY
ATTHAT
BATAAN
BATEAU
BATMAN
BETRAY
BETTAS
BITMAP
CATHAY
CATNAP
COTTAS
DOTHAN
EATSAT
ENTRAP
EXTRAS
FATCAT
GATEAU
GETSAT
GOTHAM
GOTMAD
GSTAAD
GUTTAE
HETMAN
HITMAN
HOTCAP
HOTCAR
HOTWAR
JETLAG
JETSAM
KATMAI
KITBAG
KITKAT
LETHAL
LETSAT
LOTHAR
MITRAL
MUTUAL
NATHAN
NETMAN
NETPAY
NOTBAD
OSTEAL
OUTEAT
OUTLAW
OUTLAY
OUTRAN
PATHAN
PITMAN
PITSAW
PUTNAM
RATTAN
RETIAL
RETRAL
RITUAL
RUTTAN
SATRAP
SETSAT
SGTMAJ
SOTHAT
SUTRAS
TETRAD
TETRAS
TITIAN
ULTRAS
UNTRAP
WETBAR
WITHAL

••T••A

ALTHEA
ATTICA
ATTILA
BETCHA
CATENA
DATURA
FATIMA
GOTCHA
HOTTEA
INTIMA
ISTRIA
LATINA
LATONA
LATOYA
LATVIA
MATTEA
NUTRIA
OPTIMA
ORTEGA
OTTAVA
OTTAWA
PATACA
PATINA
PETULA
PYTHIA
RETINA
ULTIMA
UMTATA

•••TA•

ACETAL
AKITAS
ALATAU
AMYTAN
AORTAE
AORTAL
AORTAS
AVATAR
BANTAM
BARTAB
BETTAS
BHUTAN
BIOTAS
BRUTAL
CAFTAN
CANTAB
CAPTAN
CESTAS
CONTAC
COSTAE
COSTAL
COSTAR
COSTAS
COTTAS
CRETAN
DELTAS
DENTAL
DIKTAT
DISTAL
DOGTAG
DUCTAL
FANTAN
FESTAL
FONTAL
FORTAS
GOSTAG
GUITAR
GUSTAV
GUTTAE
HEPTAD
HIATAL
HINTAT
HOOTAT
HOSTAS
HYETAL
INSTAR
ISHTAR
JUNTAS
KEPTAT
LESTAT
MAITAI
MANTAS
MAOTAI
MAYTAG
MENTAL
MORTAL
MORTAR
NECTAR
PASTAS
PENTAD
PIETAS
PORTAL
POSTAL
PRETAX
PROTAX
QANTAS
QINTAR
QUOTAS
RAGTAG
RATTAN
REATAS
REDTAG
RENTAL
RIATAS
RUTTAN
SEPTAL
SHOTAT
SINTAX
SONTAG
SULTAN
SUNTAN
SURTAX
SYNTAX
TAMTAM
TARTAN
TARTAR
TESTAE
THETAS
TICTAC
TOETAP
UNITAL
UNITAS
VESTAL
VESTAS
VISTAS
WANTAD
WENTAT
WYSTAN
YENTAS

•••T•A

AGATHA
ANITRA
ARETHA
BERTHA
CONTRA
EARTHA
GRATIA
GRETNA
HESTIA
HOTTEA
LIOTTA
MANTRA
MANTUA
MARTHA
MATTEA
NESTEA
NOOTKA
ODETTA
PORTIA
QUOTHA
ROSTRA
SCOTIA
TANTRA

••••TA

AJANTA
ARISTA
AVESTA
BALATA
BOGOTA
CAPITA
CUESTA
DAKOTA
DAMITA
EGESTA
EJECTA
ERRATA
EXACTA
FAJITA
FIESTA
GALATA
LAKOTA
LAPUTA
LIOTTA
LOLITA
MAKUTA
MIKITA
MONETA
MORITA
MULETA
NIKITA
ODETTA
OMERTA
PELOTA
PEPITA
PESETA
PINATA
QUANTA
RENATA
ROSITA
SANCTA
SHASTA
SIESTA
SOMATA
SONATA
SPARTA
STRATA
TOYOTA
UMTATA
YUKATA
ZAPATA

TB••••

TBILLS
TBIRDS
TBONDS
TBONES

T•B•••

TABARD
TABBED
TABLAS
TABLED
TABLES
TABLET
TABOOS
TABORS
TABRIZ
TABULA
TIBIAE
TIBIAL
TIBIAS
TOBAGO
TOBIAS
TOBIES
TOBOOT
TOBRUK
TUBATE
TUBBED
TUBERS
TUBING
TUBIST
TUBMAN
TYBALT

T••B••

TABBED
TALBOT
TEABAG
THEBES
TIDBIT
TIMBAL
TIMBER
TIMBRE
TITBIT
TOMBAC
TOMBOY
TOOBAD
TREBEK
TREBLE
TREBLY
TRIBAL
TRIBES
TUBBED
TUMBLE
TURBAN
TURBID
TURBIT
TURPOS
TURBOT
TWOBIT

T•••B•

THISBE
THROBS
THUMBS
TRILBY
TYCOBB

T••••B

TOPJOB
TYCOBB

•TB•••

ATBATS
ATBEST
PTBOAT

•T•B••

STABAT
STABLE
STABLY
STUBBY

•T••B•

ITURBI
STRABO
STROBE
STUBBY

••TB••

BATBOY
HATBOX
HOTBED
HOTBOX
KITBAG
NOTBAD
OUTBID
TITBIT
WETBAR

••T•B•

GATSBY
GETSBY
LETSBE
PUTSBY
SETSBY

••T••B

HOTTUB

•••TB•

WENTBY

•••T•B

BARTAB
CANTAB
HOTTUB

T•C•••

TACKED
TACKER
TACKLE
TACKON
TACOMA
TACTIC
TECHIE
TECHNO
TICALS
TICKED
TICKER
TICKET
TICKLE
TICTAC
TOCSIN
TUCANA
TUCHUN
TUCKED
TUCKER
TUCKET
TUCKIN
TUCSON
TYCOBB
TYCOON

T••C••

TAICHI
TALCED
TALCUM
TEACUP
TERCEL
TERCET
TETCHY
THECAE
THECAL
THICKE
TINCAL
TINCAN
TINCTS
TOECAP
TOMCAT
TOPCAT
TOUCAN
TOUCHE
TOUCHY
TOWCAR
TRACED
TRACER
TRACES
TRACEY
TRACKS
TRACTS
TRICED
TRICES
TRICHO
TRICIA
TRICKS
TRICKY
TRICOT
TROCAR
TROCHE
TRUCES
TRUCKS
TUSCAN

T•••C•

TENACE
TEXACO
THATCH
THENCE
THRACE
THRICE
THWACK
TIERCE
TOLUCA
TONICS
TOPICS
TOXICS
TRANCE
TRENCH
TUNICA
TUNICS
TWITCH

T••••C

TACTIC
TANNIC
TARMAC
TENREC
THETIC
TICTAC
TLALOC
TOLTEC
TOMBAC
TRAGIC
TROPIC
TURKIC

•TC•••

ATCOST
ETCHED
ETCHER
ETCHES
ITCHED
ITCHES

•T•C••

STACKS
STACTE
STICKS
STICKY
STOCKS
STOCKY
STUCCO

•T••C•

ATONCE
ATTACH
ATTACK
ATTICA
ATTICS
ETHICS
ITASCA
ITHACA
STANCE
STANCH
STARCH
STENCH
STITCH
STOICS
STORCH
STRICK
STRICT
STRUCK
STUCCO

•T•••C

ATOMIC
ATONIC
ETHNIC
ETONIC
ITALIC
OTITIC
STATIC
STIVIC

••TC••

ANTCOW
BETCHA
CATCHY
FATCAT
GOTCHA
HOTCAP
HOTCAR
LITCHI
OUTCRY
PATCHY
SITCOM
TETCHY
WITCHY

••T•C•

ANTICS
ATTACH
ATTACK
ATTICA
ATTICS
AZTECS
DETACH
DETECT
ENTICE
HITECH
INTACT
KITSCH
NATICK
NOTICE
OPTICS
OUTACT
PATACA
PUTSCH
SHTICK
UNTACK
UPTICK
VOTECH

••T••C

ALTAIC
AMTRAC
CITRIC
GOTHIC
IATRIC
LITHIC
METRIC
MYTHIC
NITRIC
VITRIC

•••TC•

BLOTCH
CLUTCH
CRUTCH
FLETCH
FLITCH
GLITCH
KLATCH
KVETCH
NAUTCH
SCOTCH
SCUTCH
SKETCH
SKITCH
SMUTCH
SNATCH
SNITCH
STITCH
SWATCH
SWITCH
THATCH
TWITCH
WRETCH

•••T•C

ACETIC
AORTIC
ARCTIC
BALTIC
BIOTIC
CELTIC
CONTAC
COPTIC
CRITIC
CULTIC
DELTIC
EROTIC
EXOTIC
FISTIC
FUSTIC
HECTIC
LACTIC
MANTIC
MASTIC
MIXTEC
MYSTIC
NOETIC
OTITIC
PECTIC
PEPTIC
PHATIC
PHOTIC
POETIC
PONTIC
RUSTIC
SEPTIC
STATIC
TACTIC
THETIC
TICTAC
TOLTEC

T•D•••

TEDDED
TEDDER
TEDEUM
TEDIUM
TEDKEY
TIDBIT
TIDIED
TIDIER
TIDIES
TIDILY
TIDING
TIDYUP
TODATE
TODDAO
TODDLE
TODMAN
TUDORS

T••D••

TAGDAY
TANDEM
TAWDRY
TEDDED
TEDDER
TEEDUP
TENDED
TENDER
TENDON
TENDTO
TIEDIN
TIEDUP
TIEDYE
TILDEN
TILDES
TINDER
TODDAO
TODDLE
TOEDIN
TOLDOF
TOPDOG
TOYDOG
TRADED
TRADER
TRADES
TREDIA
TRUDGE
TUNDRA

T•••D•

TBIRDS
TBONDS
TELEDU
TEREDO
THIRDS
TIRADE
TOLEDO
TREADS
TRENDS
TRENDY
TRIADS
TRIODE
TUXEDO
TWEEDS
TWEEDY

T••••D
TABARD
TABBED
TABLED
TACKED
TAGEND
TAGGED
TAILED
TALCED
TALKED
TALMUD
TAMPED
TANGED
TANKED
TANNED
TAPPED
TARRED
TASKED
TASTED
TATTED
TAXIED
TEAMED
TEARED
TEASED
TEDDED
TEEMED
TEHEED
TEMPED
TENDED
TENSED
TENTED
TERMED
TESTED
TETRAD
THAWED
THEEND
THEFED
THEMED
THREAD
THREED
TICKED
TIDIED
TIERED
TIEROD
TIFFED
TILLED
TILTED
TINGED
TINGOD
TINNED
TINTED
TIPPED
TITHED
TITLED
TOGAED
TOGGED
TOILED
TOLLED
TOOBAD
TOOLED
TOOTED
TOPPED
TOROID
TORPID
TORRID
TOSSED
TOTTED
TOURED
TOUTED
TOWARD
TRACED
TRADED
TREPID
TRICED
TRIFID
TRIPOD
TROWED
TUBBED
TUCKED
TUFTED
TUGGED
TURBID
TURFED
TURGID
TURNED
TUSKED
TUTUED
TWINED

•T•D••
ATODDS
ETUDES
STADIA
STODGE
STODGY
STUDIO

•T••D•
ATODDS
STANDS
STEADS
STEADY
STEEDS
STRADS
STRIDE
STRODE
STURDY

•T•••D
ATHAND
ATONED
ATSTUD
ATTEND
ATWOOD
ETCHED
ITCHED
STAGED
STAKED
STALED
STARED
STATED
STAVED
STAYED
STEWED
STOKED
STOLID
STONED
STORED
STOWED
STRAND
STROUD
STUPID
STYLED

••TD••
HOTDOG
OUTDID

••T•D•
BETIDE
OCTADS
RATEDG
RATEDR
RATEDX
UNTIDY

••T••D
ANTEED
ASTRID
ATTEND
BATHED
BATTED
BITTED
BUTTED
CATTED
DOTARD
DOTTED
EXTEND
FATTED
FITTED
GOTMAD
GSTAAD
GUTTED
HATRED
HATTED
HOTBED
HOTROD
HUTTED
INTEND
JETTED
JOTTED
JUTTED
LATHED
LETTED
LOTTED
MATTED
METHOD
MITRED
NETTED
NOTBAD
NUTTED
OBTUND
OSTEND
OUTBID
OUTDID
PATTED
PETARD
PETTED
PITHED
PITIED
PITTED
POTTED
PUTRID
PUTTED
RATTED
RETARD
RETIED
RETOLD
RITARD
ROTTED
ROTUND
RUTTED
SOTTED
TATTED
TETRAD
TITHED
TITLED
TOTTED
TUTUED
UNTIED
UNTOLD
UNTROD
VETOED
VETTED
WETTED
WITHED
WITTED

•••T•D
ABATED
ATSTUD
BAITED
BASTED
BATTED
BELTED
BESTED
BITTED
BOATED
BOLTED
BOOTED
BUNTED
BUSTED
BUTTED
CANTED
CARTED
CATTED
CHUTED
COATED
CRATED
DARTED
DENTED
DIETED
DINTED
DOTTED
DUSTED
EDITED
ELATED
ELUTED
EMOTED
EXITED
FASTED
FATTED
FELTED
FISTED
FITTED
FLUTED
FOOTED
GAITED
GIFTED
GIRTED
GRATED
GUSTED
GUTTED
HAFTED
HALTED
HATTED
HEATED
HEFTED
HEPTAD
HINTED
HOOTED
HOSTED
HUNTED
HUTTED
JESTED
JETTED
JILTED
JOLTED
JOTTED
JUTTED
KILTED
LASTED
LETTED
LIFTED
LILTED
LISTED
LOFTED
LOOTED
LOTTED
LUSTED
MALTED
MATTED
MELTED
MINTED
MISTED
MOATED
MOLTED
MOOTED
NESTED
NETTED
NUTTED
ORATED
OUSTED
PANTED
PARTED
PASTED
PATTED
PELTED
PENTAD
PETTED
PITTED
PLATED
PORTED
POSTED
POTTED
POUTED
PRATED
PUNTED
PUTTED
QUOTED
RAFTED
RANTED
RATTED
RENTED
RESTED
RIFTED
RIOTED
ROOTED
ROTTED
ROUTED
RRATED
RUSTED
RUTTED
SALTED
SEATED
SIFTED
SILTED
SKATED
SLATED
SORTED
SOTTED
SPITED
STATED
SUITED
TASTED
TATTED
TENTED
TESTED
TILTED
TINTED
TOOTED
TOTTED
TOUTED
TUFTED
UNITED
VENTED
VESTED
VETTED
WAFTED
WAITED
WANTAD
WANTED
WASTED
WELTED
WETTED
WILTED
WITTED
WONTED
XRATED
ZESTED

TE••••
TEABAG
TEACUP
TEAMED
TEAMUP
TEAPOT
TEAPOY
TEARAT
TEARED
TEARUP
TEASED
TEASEL
TEASER
TEASES
TEASET
TECHIE
TECHNO
TEDDED
TEDDER
TEDEUM
TEDIUM
TEDKEY
TEEDUP
TEEHEE
TEEING
TEEMED
TEENER
TEENSY
TEEOFF
TEESUP
TEETER
TEETHE
TEFLON
TEHEED
TEHEES
TELEDU
TELLER
TELLON
TELUGU
TEMPED
TEMPEH
TEMPER
TEMPLE
TEMPOS
TEMPTS
TENACE
TENANT
TENDED
TENDER
TENDON
TENDTO
TENETS
TENNIS
TENONS
TENORS
TENPIN
TENREC
TENSED
TENSER
TENSES
TENSOR
TENTED
TENTER
TENTHS
TENURE
TENUTO
TEPALS
TEPEES
TEPHRA
TERAPH
TERATO
TERCEL
TERCET
TEREDO
TERESA
TERETE
TEREUS
TERKEL
TERMED
TERRAN
TERRET
TERROR
TERSER
TESLAS
TESSIE
TESTAE
TESTED
TESTEE
TESTER
TETCHY
TETHER
TETHYS
TETONS
TETRAD
TETRAS
TETRIS
TETZEL
TEUTON
TEXACO
TEXANS
TEXMEX

T•E•••
TEEDUP
TEEHEE
TEEING
TEEMED
TEENER
TEENSY
TEEOFF
TEESUP
TEETER
TEETHE
THEBES
THECAE
THECAL
THEEND
THEFED
THEFTS
THEHAJ
THEIRS
THEISM
THEIST
THELIP
THELMA
THEMED
THEMES
THENAR
THENCE
THEORY
THERMO
THERMS
THESES
THESIS
THESIX
THETAS
THETIC
THETIS
THETOY
THEWIZ
THEYLL
THEYRE
THEYVE
TIEDIN
TIEDUP
TIEDYE
TIEING
TIEINS
TIEPIN
TIERCE
TIERED
TIEROD
TIERRA
TIESIN
TIESUP
TIEUPS
TMESIS
TOECAP
TOEDIN
TOEING
TOEINS
TOESIN
TOETAP
TREADS
TREATS
TREATY
TREBEK
TREBLE
TREBLY
TREDIA
TREMOR
TRENCH
TRENDS
TRENDY
TREPAN
TREPID
TREVOR
TSETSE
TWEAKS
TWEEDS
TWEEDY
TWEETS
TWEETY
TWEEZE
TWELVE
TWENTY
TWERPS

T••E••
TAGEND
TAKEIN
TAKEON
TAKERS
TAKETH
TAKETO
TAKEUP
TALENT
TALESE
TAMELY
TAMERS
TAMEST
TAPERS
TATERS
TAVERN
TAXERS
TEDEUM
TEHEED
TEHEES
TELEDU
TENETS
TEPEES
TEREDO
TERESA
TERETE
TEREUS
THEEND
THIEVE
THREAD
THREAT
THREED
THREES
THRESH
TIGERS
TILERS
TIMELY
TIMERS
TINEAR
TITERS
TOKENS
TOLEDO
TONERS
TONEUP
TOPEKA
TOPERS
TOREAT
TORERO
TOREUP
TOTEMS
TOTERS
TOWELS
TOWERS
TOWERY
TRIERS
TRUEST
TUBERS
TUMEFY
TUNEIN
TUNERS
TUNEUP
TUPELO
TUREEN
TUXEDO
TUYERE
TVSETS
TWEEDS
TWEEDY
TWEETS
TWEETY
TWEEZE
TYPERS
TYPEUP

T•••E•
TABBED
TABLED
TABLES
TABLET
TACKED
TACKER
TAGGED
TAILED
TAIPEI
TALCED
TALKED
TALKER
TALLER
TAMPED
TAMPER
TANDEM
TANGED
TANKED
TANKER
TANNED
TANNER
TAPPED
TAPPER
TAPPET
TARGES
TARGET
TARRED
TARTER
TASKED
TASSEL
TASSES
TASTED
TASTER
TASTES
TATTED
TATTER
TAUPES
TAUTEN
TAUTER
TAXIED
TAXIES
TAXMEN
TBONES
TEAMED
TEARED
TEASED
TEASEL
TEASER
TEASES
TEASET
TEDDED
TEDDER
TEDKEY
TEEHEE
TEEMED
TEENER
TEETER
TEHEED
TEHEES
TELLER
TEMPED
TEMPEH
TEMPER
TENDED
TENDER
TENREC
TENSED
TENSER
TENSES
TENTED
TENTER
TEPEES
TERCEL
TERCET
TERKEL
TERMED
TERRET
TERSER
TESTED
TESTEE
TESTER
TETHER
TETZEL
TEXMEX
THALER
THALES
THAMES
THANES
THAWED
THAYER
THEBES
THEFED
THEMED
THEMES
THESES
THOLES
THREED
THREES
THROES
TICKED
TICKER
TICKET
TIDIED
TIDIER
TIDIES
TIERED
TIFFED
TIGGER
TILDEN
TILDES
TILLED
TILLER
TILTED
TILTER
TIMBER
TINDER
TINGED
TINGES
TINIER
TINKER
TINMEN
TINNED
TINNER
TINSEL
TINTED
TINTER
TIPPED
TIPPER
TIPPET
TITHED
TITHER
TITHES
TITLED
TITLES
TITTER
TNOTES
TOATEE
TOBIES
TOFFEE
TOGAED
TOGGED
TOILED
TOILER
TOILES
TOILET
TOLLED
TOLTEC
TONIER
TONNES
TOOLED
TOOTED
TOOTER
TOPPED
TOPPER
TOPTEN
TOQUES
TORIES
TORTES
TOSSED
TOSSER
TOSSES
TOTHER
TOTTED
TOTTER
TOUPEE
TOURED
TOURER
TOUTED
TOUTER
TOWHEE
TOWNER
TRACED
TRACER
TRACES
TRACEY
TRADED
TRADER
TRADES
TRALEE
TRAVEL
TREBEK
TRIBES
TRICED
TRICES
TRIKES
TRINES
TRITER
TRIVET
TROPES
TROPEZ
TROVES
TROWED
TROWEL
TRUCES
TUAREG
TUBBED
TUCKED
TUCKER
TUCKET
TUFFET
TUFTED
TUGGED
TUGGER
TULLES
TUNNEL
TUNNEY
TUQUES
TUREEN
TURFED
TURKEY
TURNED
TURNER
TURRET
TUSKED
TUSKER
TUTUED
TWINED
TWINES
TWOFER

T••••E
TACKLE
TAGORE
TAILLE
TALESE
TALKIE
TAMALE
TANGLE
TATTLE
TECHIE
TEEHEE
TEETHE
TEMPLE
TENACE
TENURE
TERETE
TESSIE
TESTAE
TESTEE
THECAE
THENCE
THEYRE
THEYVE
THICKE
THIEVE
THISBE
THORPE
THRACE
THRALE
THRICE
THRIVE
THRONE
THROVE
TIBIAE
TICKLE
TIEDYE
TIERCE
TILLIE
TIMBRE
TINGLE
TINKLE
TIPPLE
TIPTOE
TIRADE
TIRANE
TISANE
TISSUE
TITTLE
TOATEE
TODATE
TODDLE
TOFFEE
TOGGLE
TOLIFE
TONGUE
TONITE
TOOTLE
TOPPLE
TOROSE
TORQUE
TOUCHE
TOUPEE
TOUSLE
TOWAGE
TOWHEE
TOWNIE
TRALEE
TRANCE
TREBLE
TRIAGE
TRIFLE
TRIODE
TRIPLE
TRISTE
TRIUNE
TRIXIE
TROCHE
TROMPE
TROUPE
TROUVE
TRUDGE
TSETSE
TUBATE
TUILLE
TULANE
TULARE
TUMBLE
TURTLE
TUSSLE
TUYERE
TWEEZE
TWELVE
TWINGE
TYRONE

•TE•••
ATEAMS
ATEASE
ATEMPO
ATERGO
ATESTS
ETERNE
OTELLO
STEADS
STEADY
STEAKS
STEALS
STEAMS
STEAMY
STEEDS
STEELE
STEELS
STEELY
STEEPS
STEERS
STEEVE
STEFAN
STEFFI
STEINS
STELAE
STELAR
STELES
STELLA
STELMO
STENCH
STENOG
STENOS
STEPIN
STEPON
STEPPE
STEPUP
STEREO
STERES
STERNA
STERNE
STERNO
STERNS
STEROL
STEVEN
STEVIE
STEWED
STEWER

•T•E••
ATBEST
ATHENA
ATHENE
ATHENS
ATREST
ATREUS
ATTEND
ATTEST
ETHENE
ETHERS
ETSEQQ
ITSELF
OTHERS
OTTERS
STEEDS
STEELE
STEELS
STEELY
STEEPS
STEERS
STEEVE
STHENO
STPETE
STREAK
STREAM
STREEP
STREET
STRESS
STREWN
STREWS
UTTERS

•T••E•
ATONED
ATONES
ATTLEE
ETCHED
ETCHER
ETCHES
ETUDES
ITCHED
ITCHES
STAGED
STAGER
STAGES
STAKED
STAKES
STALED
STALER
STALES
STAMEN
STAPES
STARED
STARER
STARES
STASES
STATED
STATER
STATES
STAVED
STAVES
STAYED
STELES
STEREO
STERES
STEVEN
STEWED
STEWER
STILES
STIPEL
STIPES
STIVER
STOKED
STOKER
STOKES
STOLEN
STOLES
STONED
STONER
STONES
STOPES
STORED
STORER
STORES
STOREY
STOVER
STOVES
STOWED
STREEP
STREET
STUPES
STYLED
STYLER
STYLES
STYLET

•T•••E
ATEASE
ATHENE
ATHOME
ATONCE
ATTIRE
ATTLEE
ATTUNE
ETERNE
ETHANE
ETHENE
ETOILE
OTIOSE
OTOOLE
STABLE
STACTE
STANCE

STAPLE
STARVE
STATUE
STEELE
STEEVE
STELAE
STEPPE
STERNE
STEVIE
STIFLE
STLUKE
STODGE
STOGIE
STOLLE
STOOGE
STPETE
STRAFE
STRAKE
STRIAE
STRIDE
STRIFE
STRIKE
STRIPE
STRIVE
STROBE
STRODE
STROKE
STROVE
STYMIE

••TE••

ALTERS
ANTEED
ANTERO
ANTEUP
APTEST
ARTELS
ARTERY
ASTERN
ASTERS
ATTEND
ATTEST
AUTEUR
AZTECS
BATEAU
BETELS
BITERS
BUTENE
BUTEOS
CATENA
CATERS
CITERS
CUTEST
CUTESY
DATERS
DETECT
DETENT
DETERS
DETEST
DOTELL
DOTEON
EATERS
EATERY
ENTERO
ENTERS
ESTEEM
ESTERS
EXTEND
EXTENT
GATEAU
GATERS
HATERS
HETERO
HITECH
HOTELS
INTEND
INTENS
INTENT
INTERN
IQTEST
KITERS
LATEEN
LATELY
LATENE
LATENS
LATENT
LATEST
LITERS
MATERS
MATEYS
METEOR
METERS
MITERS
MOTELS
MOTETS
MUTELY
MUTEST
NITERS
NOTERS
OATERS
OBTEST
OCTETS
ORTEGA
OSTEAL
OSTEND
OTTERS
OUTEAT
PATENS
PATENT
PETERS
POTEEN
POTENT
RATEDG
RATEDR
RATEDX
RATELS
RATERS
RETELL
RETENE
RETEST
SATEEN
SHTETL
TATERS
TITERS
TOTEMS
TOTERS
UTTERS
VOTECH
VOTEIN
VOTERS
WATERS
WATERY

••T•E•

AETHER
ALTHEA
ANTEED
ANTHEM
ANTHER
ANTLER
ANTRES
ARTIER
ATTLEE
BATHED
BATHER
BATHES
BATMEN
BATTED
BATTEN
BATTER
BETHEL
BETSEY
BETTER
BITTED
BITTEN
BITTER
BOTHER
BOTREE
BUTLER
BUTTED
BUTTER
BUTTES
CATHER
CATTED
CITIES
COTTEN
COTTER
CUTIES
CUTLER
CUTLET
CUTTER
DITHER
DITZES
DOTTED
DUTIES
EITHER
ENTREE
ESTEEM
ESTHER
FATHER
FATTED
FATTEN
FATTER
FETTER
FITTED
FITTER
GATHER
GETSET
GETTER
GOTTEN
GUTTED
GUTTER
HATRED
HATTED
HATTER
HITHER
HITMEN
HITTER
HOTBED
HOTTEA
HOTTER
HUTTED
ISTLES
JETSET
JETTED
JITNEY
JITTER
JOTTED
JUTTED
KITTEN
KOTTER
LATEEN
LATHED
LATHER
LATHES
LATKES
LATTEN
LATTER
LETTED
LETTER
LITRES
LITTER
LOTTED
LUTHER
MATHER
MATTEA
MATTED
MATTEL
MATTER
MATTES
METIER
METRES
MITRED
MITRES
MITTEN
MOTHER
MOTLEY
MUTTER
NATTER
NETHER
NETMEN
NETTED
NITRES
NOTYET
NUTLET
NUTMEG
NUTTED
NUTTER
OATIER
ORTLES
OSTLER
OUTLET
OUTSET
PATTED
PATTEN
PATTER
PETREL
PETTED
PETTER
PITHED
PITIED
PITIES
PITMEN
PITTED
PITTER
POTEEN
POTHER
POTTED
POTTER
PUTTED
PUTTEE
PUTTER
RATHER
RATTED
RATTER
RETIED
RETIES
RITTER
ROTTED
ROTTEN
ROTTER
RUTGER
RUTTED
SATEEN
SETTEE
SETTER
SITTER
SOTTED
SUTLER
SUTTER
TATTED
TATTER
TETHER
TETZEL
TITHED
TITHER
TITHES
TITLED
TITLES
TITTER
TOTHER
TOTTED
TOTTER
TUTUED
UNTIED
UNTIES
VETOED
VETOER
VETOES
VETTED
WATNEY
WETHER
WETTED
WETTER
WITHED
WITHER
WITHES
WITTED
ZITHER

••T••E

ACTIVE
ACTONE
ASTUTE
ATTIRE
ATTLEE
ATTUNE
BATTLE
BATTUE
BETAKE
BETIDE
BETISE
BOTREE
BOTTLE
BUTANE
BUTENE
CATTLE
CETANE
DATIVE
DOTAGE
DOTTIE
DOTTLE
ECTYPE
ENTICE
ENTIRE
ENTREE
ESTATE
FATALE
FETTLE
FUTILE
FUTURE
GUTTAE
HATTIE
HETTIE
INTAKE
INTIME
INTINE
INTONE
INTUNE
KATHIE
KETONE
KETTLE
LATENE
LETSBE
LITTLE
MATTIE
MATURE
METATE
METOPE
METTLE
MOTILE
MOTIVE
MOTTLE
MUTATE
NATIVE
NATURE
NETTLE
NOTATE
NOTICE
NUTATE
OBTUSE
OCTANE
OCTAVE
ONTAPE
ONTIME
OUTAGE
OUTATE
PATINE
PETITE
PETRIE
POTAGE
POTPIE
POTTLE
PUTTEE
RATINE
RATITE
RATTLE
RETAKE
RETAPE
RETENE
RETILE
RETIME
RETIRE
RETUNE
RETYPE
ROTATE
RUTILE
SATIRE
SETOSE
SETTEE
SETTLE
SUTURE
TATTLE
TITTLE
UNTRUE
UNTUNE
UPTAKE
UPTIME
VOTIVE
WATTLE

•••TE•

ABATED
ABATES
AEETES
AGATES
AMSTEL
ARETES
AUSTEN
BAITED
BANTER
BARTER
BASTED
BASTER
BASTES
BATTED
BATTEN
BATTER
BAXTER
BEATEN
BEATER
BELTED
BESTED
BETTER
BIGTEN
BITTED
BITTEN
BITTER
BOATED
BOATER
BOITES
BOLTED
BOOTED
BOOTEE
BOOTES
BRUTES
BUNTED
BUNTER
BUSTED
BUSTER
BUTTED
BUTTER
BUTTES
CANTED
CANTER
CARTED
CARTEL
CARTER
CARTES
CASTER
CASTES
CATTED
CENTER
CHUTED
CHUTES
CNOTES
COATED
COLTER
COMTES
CONTES
COOTER
COPTER
CORTES
CORTEX
CORTEZ
COTTEN
COTTER
COUTER
CRATED
CRATER
CRATES
CURTER
CUSTER
CUTTER
DAFTER
DANTES
DARTED
DARTER
DEFTER
DENTED
DEXTER
DHOTEL
DIETED
DIETER
DINTED
DOTTED
DUSTED
DUSTER
EASTER
EDITED
ELATED
ELATER
ELATES
ELITES
ELUTED
ELUTES
EMOTED
EMOTER
EMOTES
ENATES
EXETER
EXITED
FALTER
FASTED
FASTEN
FASTER
FATTED
FATTEN
FATTER
FELTED
FESTER
FETTER
FILTER
FISTED
FITTED
FITTER
FLUTED
FLUTES
FOOTED
FOOTER
FORTES
FOSTER
GAITED
GAITER
GARTER
GESTES
GETTER
GIFTED
GIRTED
GLUTEI
GLUTEN
GOATEE
GOTTEN
GRATED
GRATER
GRATES
GRETEL
GUNTER
GUSTED
GUTTED
GUTTER
HAFTED
HALTED
HALTER
HASTEN
HASTES
HATTED
HATTER
HEATED
HEATER
HEFTED
HELTER
HESTER
HINTED
HINTER
HITTER
HOOTED
HOOTER
HOSTED
HOSTEL
HOTTEA
HOTTER
HUNTED
HUNTER
HUTTED
INSTEP
IRATER
JEETER
JESTED
JESTER
JETTED
JILTED
JITTER
JOETEX
JOLTED
JOTTED
JUSTER
JUTTED
KEITEL
KILTED
KILTER
KITTEN
KOTTER
KRATER
LAPTEV
LASTED
LASTEX
LATTEN
LATTER
LENTEN
LESTER
LETTED
LETTER
LIFTED
LIFTER
LILTED
LINTEL
LINTER
LISTED
LISTEE
LISTEL
LISTEN
LISTER
LITTER
LOFTED
LOITER
LOOTED
LOOTER
LOTTED
LUSTED
LUSTER
MALTED
MANTEL
MARTEL
MARTEN
MASTER
MATTEA
MATTED
MATTEL
MATTER
MATTES
MEETER
MELTED
MINTED
MINTER
MISTED
MISTER
MITTEN
MIXTEC
MOATED
MOLTED
MOLTEN
MOLTER
MONTEL
MONTEZ
MOOTED
MOSTEL
MUSTER
MUTTER
NANTES
NATTER
NEATEN
NEATER
NESTEA
NESTED
NESTER
NETTED
NEUTER
NUTTED
NUTTER
OBITER
OBSTET
OERTER
ORATED
ORATES
OUSTED
OUSTER
OYSTER
PALTER
PANTED
PARTED
PASTED
PASTEL
PASTES
PATTED
PATTEN
PATTER
PELTED
PELTER
PERTER
PESTER
PETTED
PETTER
PEWTER
PIETER
PINTER
PITTED
PITTER
PLATED
PLATEN
PLATER
PLATES
PONTES
PORTED
PORTER
POSTED
POSTER
POTTED
POTTER
POUTED
POUTER
PRATED
PRATER
PRATES
PRETER
PROTEI
PROTEM
PUNTED
PUNTER
PUTTED
PUTTEE
PUTTER
QUOTED
QUOTER
QUOTES
RAFTED
RAFTER
RANTED
RANTER
RASTER
RATTED
RATTER
RENTED
RENTER
RESTED
RESTER
REUTER
RIFTED
RIOTED
RIOTER
RITTER
ROOTED
ROOTER
ROSTER
ROTTED
ROTTEN
ROTTER
ROUTED
ROUTER
ROUTES
RRATED
RUSTED
RUTTED
SALTED
SALTEN
SALTER
SANTEE
SAUTES
SCOTER
SCUTES
SEATED
SEATER
SEPTET
SESTET
SETTEE
SETTER
SEXTET
SIFTED
SIFTER
SILTED
SINTER
SISTER
SITTER
SKATED
SKATER
SKATES
SLATED
SLATER
SLATES
SMITES
SOFTEN
SOFTER
SORTED
SORTER
SOTTED
SOUTER
SPATES
SPITED
SPITES
STATED
STATER
STATES
SUITED
SUITES
SUMTER
SUTTER
SYSTEM
TARTER
TASTED
TASTER
TASTES
TATTED
TATTER
TAUTEN
TAUTER
TEETER
TENTED
TENTER
TESTED
TESTEE
TESTER
TILTED
TILTER
TINTED
TINTER
TITTER
TNOTES
TOATEE
TOLTEC
TOOTED
TOOTER
TOPTEN
TORTES
TOTTED
TOTTER
TOUTED
TOUTER
TRITER
TUFTED
ULSTER
UNITED
UNITER
UNITES
VASTER
VENTED
VENTER
VERTEX
VESTED
VESTEE
VETTED
VORTEX
WAFTED
WAITED
WAITER
WALTER
WANTED
WASTED
WASTER
WASTES
WELTED
WELTER
WETTED
WETTER
WHITEN
WHITER
WHITES
WILTED
WINTER
WISTER
WITTED
WONTED
WRITER
WRITES
WYNTER
XRATED
XYSTER
YESTER
ZESTED

•••T•E

AORTAE
AUNTIE
BATTLE
BATTUE
BEATLE
BEETLE
BERTIE
BIGTOE
BLITHE
BLYTHE
BOOTEE
BOOTHE
BOOTIE
BOTTLE
BOWTIE
BUSTLE
CANTLE
CASTLE
CATTLE
CENTRE
CLOTHE
CONTRE
COOTIE
COSTAE
DOTTIE
DOTTLE
FETTLE
GENTLE
GERTIE
GOATEE
GOETHE
GUTTAE
HATTIE
HETTIE
HOGTIE
HURTLE
HUSTLE
JOSTLE
KETTLE
KILTIE
KIRTLE
LAOTSE
LHOTSE
LISTEE
LITTLE
LOATHE
LUSTRE
MAITRE
MANTLE
MATTIE
METTLE
MILTIE
MOLTKE
MOTTLE
MYRTLE
NESTLE
NETTLE
ODETTE
PESTLE
PINTLE
PLATTE
POTTLE
PUTTEE
RATTLE
RUSTLE
SANTEE
SARTRE
SCATHE
SCYTHE
SEETHE
SETTEE
SETTLE
SNATHE
SOFTIE
SOOTHE
SORTIE
SPATHE
STATUE
SUBTLE
SWATHE
TATTLE
TEETHE
TESTAE
TESTEE
TIPTOE
TITTLE
TOATEE
TOOTLE
TSETSE
TURTLE
VESTEE
VIRTUE
WATTLE
WRITHE
YVETTE

••••TE

ABLATE
ACUATE
ADESTE
ADNATE
AERATE
AGNATE
ANSATE
APLITE
AQUATE
ASTUTE
AVIATE
BARITE
BERATE
BINATE
BORATE
BRONTE
BYROTE
CANUTE
CAPOTE
CENOTE
CERATE
CHASTE
CHOATE
COMATE
COYOTE
CREATE
CROUTE
CURATE
DEBATE
DELATE
DELETE
DEMOTE
DENOTE
DEPUTE
DEVOTE
DILATE
DILUTE
DONATE
DUARTE
ECARTE
EFFETE
EQUATE
ERGATE
ESTATE
EXCITE
FICHTE
FINITE
FIXATE
GAMETE
GYRATE
HALITE
HAMITE
HECATE
IDEATE
IGNITE
IMPUTE
INCITE
INDITE
INMATE
INNATE
INVITE
IODATE
IOLITE
KARATE
LANATE
LEGATE
LEVITE
LIGATE
LOBATE
LOCATE
LUCITE
LUNATE
LUXATE
MALATE
METATE
MINUTE
MUTATE
NEGATE
NOTATE
NUTATE
OBLATE
ODETTE
OFLATE
OLEATE
ONSITE
OOCYTE
OOLITE
OPHITE
OPIATE
ORGATE
ORNATE
OSSETE
OUTATE
PAIUTE
PALATE
PEDATE
PETITE
PEYOTE
PILATE
PINITE
PIRATE
PLANTE
PLATTE
POINTE
POLITE
PUENTE
PYRITE
RAMATE
RATITE
REBATE
RECITE
REDATE
REFUTE
RELATE
REMOTE
RENOTE
REPUTE
RERATE
ROTATE
RUGATE
SAINTE
SALUTE
SAMITE
SAVATE
SEDATE
SEMITE
SENATE
SHIITE
SOLUTE
SPRITE
STACTE
STPETE
SURETE
SVELTE
TERETE
TODATE
TONITE
TRISTE
TUBATE
UNIATE
UPDATE
VACATE
VENITE

VERITE
VOLUTE
YVETTE
ZONATE
ZYGOTE

T•F•••
TEFLON
TIFFED
TIFFIN
TOFFEE
TUFFET
TUFTED

T••F••
THEFED
THEFTS
TIFFED
TIFFIN
TOFFEE
TRIFID
TRIFLE
TRYFOR
TUFFET
TURFED
TWOFER

T•••F•
TAPOFF
TARIFF
TEEOFF
THRIFT
TIPOFF
TOLIFE
TOPOFF
TUMEFY
TYPIFY

T••••F
TAPOFF
TARIFF
TEEOFF
TIPOFF
TOLDOF
TOPOFF

•T•F••
STAFFS
STEFAN
STEFFI
STIFFS
STIFLE
STUFFS
STUFFY

•T••F•
STAFFS
STEFFI
STIFFS
STRAFE
STRIFE
STUFFS
STUFFY

•T•••F
ITSELF
STAPUF

••TF••
ARTFUL
BOTFLY
FITFUL
KITFOX
LETFLY
OUTFIT
OUTFOX
POTFUL
VATFUL
WETFLY

••T•F•
BITOFF
CITIFY
CUTOFF
GETOFF
GOTOFF
LETOFF
MOTIFS
NOTIFY
PUTOFF
RATIFY
SETOFF

••T••F
BITOFF
CUTOFF
GETOFF
GOTOFF
LETOFF
PUTOFF
SETOFF

•••T•F
CERTIF
SORTOF
WHATIF

T•G•••
TAGDAY
TAGEND
TAGGED
TAGORE
TAGOUT
TAGSUP
TIGERS
TIGGER
TIGHTS
TIGLON
TIGRIS
TOGAED
TOGGED
TOGGLE
TUGGED
TUGGER
TUGRIK

T••G••
TAGGED
TAIGAS
TANGED
TANGLE
TANGLY
TANGOS
TANGUY
TARGES
TARGET
TAUGHT
THIGHS
TIGGER
TINGED
TINGES
TINGLE
TINGLY
TINGOD
TOGGED
TOGGLE
TONGAN
TONGUE
TOPGUN
TOUGHS
TOUGHY
TRAGIC
TRIGLY
TRIGON
TROGON
TUGGED
TUGGER
TURGID
TURGOR
TWIGGY

T•••G•
TELUGU
THINGS
THONGS
THOUGH
TOBAGO
TOWAGE
TRIAGE
TROUGH
TRUDGE
TWANGS
TWANGY
TWIGGY
TWINGE

T••••G
TAKING
TAMING
TAPING
TARING
TAUTOG
TAWING
TAXING
TEABAG
TEEING
THRONG
TIDING
TIEING
TILING
TIMING
TIRING
TOEING
TONING
TOPDOG
TOTING
TOWING
TOYDOG
TOYING
TRUING
TRYING
TUAREG
TUBING
TUNING
TURING
TYPING

•T•G••
STAGED
STAGER
STAGES
STIGMA
STOGIE

•T••G•
ATERGO
STINGS
STINGY
STODGE
STODGY
STOOGE

•T•••G
STALAG
STENOG
STRING
STRONG
STRUNG

••TG••
ARTGUM
CATGUT
JETGUN
OUTGUN
ROTGUT
RUTGER

••T•G•
DOTAGE
LATIGO
LETSGO
ORTEGA
OUTAGE
POTAGE
RETAGS

••T••G
ACTING
BATING
BITING
BUTUNG
CATRIG
CITING
DATING
DATONG
DOTING
EATING
FETING
GATING
HATING
HOTDOG
JETLAG
KITBAG
KITING
LITHOG
LUTING
MATING
METING
MUTING
NOTING
NUTMEG
OPTING
OUTING
PETROG
RATEDG
RATING
SATANG
SATING
SITING
TOTING
VOTING
WETTIG

•••T•G
DOGTAG
GOSTAG
MAYTAG
PHOTOG
RAGTAG
REDTAG
SONTAG
TAUTOG
WETTIG
ZAFTIG

TH••••
THALER
THALES
THALIA
THAMES
THANES
THANKS
THATCH
THATIS
THAWED
THAYER
THEBES
THECAE
THECAL
THEEND
THEFED
THEFTS
THEHAJ
THEIRS
THEISM
THEIST
THELIP
THELMA
THEMED
THEMES
THENAR
THENCE
THEORY
THERMO
THERMS
THESES
THESIS
THESIX
THETAS
THETIC
THETIS
THETOY
THEWIZ
THEYLL
THEYRE
THEYVE
THICKE
THIEVE
THIGHS
THILLS
THINGS
THINKS
THINLY
THIRDS
THIRST
THIRTY
THISBE
THOLES
THOMAS
THONGS
THORAX
THORNS
THORNY
THORPE
THORPS
THOUGH
THRACE
THRALE
THRALL
THRASH
THREAD
THREAT
THREED
THREES
THRESH
THRICE
THRIFT
THRILL
THRIPS
THRIVE
THROAT
THROBS
THROES
THRONE
THRONG
THROVE
THROWN
THROWS
THRUMS
THRUSH
THRUST
THUJAS
THUMBS
THUMPS
THUNKS
THUSLY
THWACK
THWART
THYMUS
THYRSI

T•H•••
TAHINI
TAHITI
TEHEED
TEHEES
TSHIRT

T••H••
TECHIE
TECHNO
TEEHEE
TEPHRA
TETHER
TETHYS
THEHAJ
TIGHTS
TINHAT
TISHRI
TITHED
TITHER
TITHES
TOPHAT
TOPHUS
TOTHER
TOWHEE
TUCHUN
TVSHOW
TYPHUS
TZUHSI

T•••H•
TAICHI
TAUGHT
TEETHE
TENTHS
TETCHY
THIGHS
TOOTHY
TORAHS
TOUCHE
TOUCHY
TOUGHS
TOUGHY
TRASHY
TRICHO
TRISHA
TROCHE
TROPHY
TROTHS
TRUTHS

T••••H
TAKETH
TEMPEH
TERAPH
THATCH
THOUGH
THRASH
THRESH
THRUSH
TONISH
TRENCH
TROUGH
TUSSAH
TWITCH

•TH•••
ATHAND
ATHENA
ATHENE
ATHENS
ATHOME
ETHANE
ETHENE
ETHERS
ETHICS
ETHNIC
ETHNOS
ITHACA
ITHAKI
OTHERS
STHENO
UTHANT

•T•H••
ATTHAT
ETCHED
ETCHER
ETCHES
ITCHED
ITCHES
ITZHAK
UTAHAN

•T••H•
STJOHN

•T•••H
ATTACH
STANCH
STARCH
STENCH
STITCH
STORCH

••TH••
AETHER
ALTHEA
ANTHEM
ANTHER
ARTHRO
ARTHUR
ATTHAT
AUTHOR
BATHED
BATHER
BATHES
BATHOS
BETHEL
BOTHER
CATHAY
CATHER
DITHER
DOTHAN
EITHER
ESTHER
FATHER
FATHOM
GATHER
GOTHAM
GOTHIC
HATHOR
HITHER
ISTHMI
JETHRO
KATHIE
LATHED
LATHER
LATHES
LETHAL
LITHIC
LITHOG
LITHOS
LOTHAR
LUTHER
LUTHOR
MATHER
MATHIS
METHOD
METHYL
MOTHER
MYTHIC
MYTHOI
MYTHOL
MYTHOS
NATHAN
NETHER
OUTHIT
PATHAN
PATHOL
PATHOS
PITHED
POTHER
PYTHIA
PYTHON
RATHER
ROTHKO
SOTHAT
TETHER
TETHYS
TITHED
TITHER
TITHES
TOTHER
WETHER
WITHAL
WITHED
WITHER
WITHES
WITHIN
WITHIT
ZITHER

••T•H•
BETCHA
CATCHY
GOTCHA
LITCHI
LOTAHS
PATCHY
TETCHY
WITCHY

••T••H
ATTACH
DETACH
FETISH
HITECH
IRTYSH
KITSCH
LATISH
MATZOH
POTASH
PUTSCH
VOTECH

•••TH•
AGATHA
APATHY
ARETHA
BERTHA
BERTHS
BIRTHS
BLITHE
BLYTHE
BOOTHE
BOOTHS
BROTHS
CANTHI
CLOTHE
CLOTHO
CLOTHS
DEPTHS
EARTHA
EARTHY
FAITHS
FIFTHS
FILTHY
FIRTHS
FROTHS
FROTHY
GARTHS
GIRTHS
GOETHE
HEATHS
ICHTHY
LOATHE
MARTHA
MONTHS
MOUTHS
MOUTHY
NINTHS
QUOTHA
RHYTHM
SCATHE
SCYTHE
SEETHE
SIXTHS
SLITHY
SLOTHS
SMITHS
SMITHY
SNATHE
SNATHS
SOOTHE
SPATHE
SWATHE
SWATHS
TEETHE
TENTHS
TOOTHY
TROTHS
TRUTHS
WIDTHS
WORTHS
WORTHY
WRATHS
WRITHE
XANTHO
YOUTHS

•••T•H
BLOTCH
CLUTCH
CRUTCH
FLETCH
FLITCH
GLITCH
KLATCH
KVETCH
NAUTCH
SCOTCH
SCUTCH
SKETCH
SKITCH
SMUTCH
SNATCH
SNITCH
STITCH
SWATCH
SWITCH
THATCH
TWITCH
WRETCH

••••TH
BREATH
BYPATH
COMETH
DALETH
DEARTH
DULUTH
EIGHTH
EOLITH
FOURTH
GARETH
GOWITH
GROWTH
HEALTH
HEARTH
INWITH
IOMOTH
JOBETH
JUDITH
LENGTH
LILITH
NAMATH
OOLITH
ORNITH
PLINTH
SHEATH
SLEUTH
SMOOTH
SPILTH
SWARTH
TAKETH
WARMTH
WEALTH
WRAITH
WREATH
ZENITH
ZEROTH
ZIZITH

TI••••
TIARAS
TIBIAE
TIBIAL
TIBIAS
TICALS
TICKED
TICKER
TICKET
TICKLE
TICTAC
TIDBIT
TIDIED
TIDIER
TIDIES
TIDILY
TIDING
TIDYUP
TIEDIN
TIEDUP
TIEDYE
TIEING
TIEINS
TIEPIN
TIERCE
TIERED
TIEROD
TIERRA
TIESIN
TIESUP
TIEUPS
TIFFED
TIFFIN
TIGERS
TIGGER
TIGHTS
TIGLON
TIGRIS
TILAKS
TILDEN
TILDES
TILERS
TILING
TILLED
TILLER
TILLIE
TILLIS
TILSIT
TILTED
TILTER
TIMBAL
TIMBER
TIMBRE
TIMELY
TIMERS
TIMING
TINCAL
TINCAN
TINCTS
TINDER
TINEAR
TINGED
TINGES
TINGLE
TINGLY
TINGOD
TINHAT
TINIER
TINKER
TINKLE
TINKLY
TINMAN
TINMEN
TINNED
TINNER
TINPAN
TINPOT
TINSEL
TINTED
TINTER
TIPINS
TIPOFF
TIPPED
TIPPER
TIPPET
TIPPLE
TIPSIN
TIPTOE
TIPTOP
TIPUPS
TIRADE
TIRANA
TIRANE
TIRING
TISANE
TISHRI
TISSUE
TITANS
TITBIT
TITERS
TITHED
TITHER
TITHES
TITIAN
TITLED
TITLES
TITTER
TITTLE
TIVOLI

T•I•••
TAICHI
TAIGAS
TAILED
TAILLE
TAILOR
TAINAN
TAINOS
TAINTS
TAIPAN
TAIPEI
TAIWAN
TBILLS
TBIRDS
THICKE
THIEVE
THIGHS
THILLS
THINGS
THINKS
THINLY
THIRDS
THIRST
THIRTY
THISBE
TOILED
TOILER
TOILES
TOILET
TRIADS
TRIAGE
TRIALS
TRIBAL
TRIBES
TRICED
TRICES
TRICHO
TRICIA
TRICKS
TRICKY
TRICOT
TRIERS
TRIFID
TRIFLE
TRIGLY
TRIGON
TRIKES
TRILBY
TRILLS
TRIMLY
TRINAL
TRINES
TRIODE
TRIPLE
TRIPLY
TRIPOD
TRIPOS
TRIPUP
TRISHA
TRISTE
TRITER
TRITON
TRIUNE
TRIVET
TRIVIA
TRIXIE
TUILLE
TWIGGY
TWILIT
TWILLS
TWINED
TWINES
TWINGE
TWIRLS
TWISTS
TWISTY
TWITCH
TWITTY

T••I••
TAHINI
TAHITI
TAKING
TAKINS
TALION
TAMILS
TAMING
TANIST
TAOISM
TAOIST
TAPING
TAPINS
TAPIRS
TARIFF
TARING
TAWING
TAXIED
TAXIES
TAXING
TEDIUM
TEEING
THEIRS
THEISM
THEIST
THRICE
THRIFT
THRILL
THRIPS
THRIVE
TIBIAE
TIBIAL
TIBIAS
TIDIED
TIDIER
TIDIES
TIDILY
TIDING
TIEING
TIEINS
TILING
TIMING
TINIER
TIPINS
TIRING
TITIAN
TOBIAS
TOBIES
TOEING
TOEINS
TOLIFE
TONICS
TONIER
TONING
TONISH
TONITE
TOPICS
TORIES
TORINO
TOTING
TOWING
TOXICS
TOXINS
TOYING
TRAILS
TRAINS
TRAITS
TROIKA
TRUING
TRUISM
TRYING
TSHIRT
TUBING
TUBIST
TULIPS
TUNICA
TUNICS
TUNING
TUPIAN
TURING
TYPIFY
TYPING
TYPIST
TYRIAN

T•••I•
TABRIZ
TACTIC
TAKEIN
TALKIE
TANNIC
TANNIN
TARPIT
TECHIE
TENNIS
TENPIN
TESSIE
TETRIS
THALIA
THATIS
THELIP
THESIS
THESIX
THETIC
THETIS
THEWIZ
TIDBIT
TIEDIN
TIEPIN
TIESIN
TIFFIN
TIGRIS
TILLIE
TILLIS
TILSIT
TIPSIN
TITBIT
TMESIS
TOCSIN
TOEDIN
TOESIN
TOMLIN
TOMMIX
TOMTIT
TONKIN
TONSIL
TOOKIN
TOOKIT
TOROID
TORPID
TORRID
TOWNIE
TRAGIC
TRAVIS
TREDIA
TREPID
TRICIA
TRIFID
TRIVIA
TRIXIE
TROPIC
TUCKIN
TUGRIK
TUNEIN
TURBID
TURBIT
TURGID
TURKIC
TURNIN
TURNIP
TWILIT
TWOBIT

T••••I
TAHINI
TAHITI
TAICHI
TAIPEI
TATAMI
THYRSI
TISHRI
TIVOLI
TUMULI
TZUHSI

•TI•••
OTIOSE
OTITIC
OTITIS
STICKS
STICKY
STIFFS
STIFLE
STIGMA
STILES
STILLS
STILLY
STILTS
STIMPY
STINGS
STINGY
STINKS
STINKY
STINTS
STIPEL
STIPES
STIRIN
STIRUP
STITCH
STIVER
STIVIC

•T•I••
ATKINS

ATRIAL
ATRISK
ATRIUM
ATTICA
ATTICS
ATTILA
ATTIRE
ATWILL
ETHICS
ETOILE
STAINS
STAIRS
STEINS
STOICS
STRIAE
STRICK
STRICT
STRIDE
STRIFE
STRIKE
STRING
STRIPE
STRIPS
STRIVE
ARTIST
ATTICA
ATTICS
ATTILA
ATTIRE
BATIKS
BATING
BETIDE
BETISE
BITING
CATION
CITIES
CITIFY
CITING
CUTIES
CUTINS
DATING
DATIVE
DOTING
DUTIES
EATING
ENTICE
ENTIRE
ENTITY
FATIMA
FETING
FETISH
FUTILE
GATING
HATING
INTIMA
INTIME
INTINE
KITING
LATIGO
LATINA
LATINO
LATINS
LATISH
LATIUM
LOTION
LUTING
LUTIST
MATING
MATINS
METIER
METING
MOTIFS
MOTILE
MOTION
MOTIVE
MUTING
MUTINY
NATICK
NATION
NATIVE
NOTICE
NOTIFY
NOTING
NOTION
OATIER
ONTIME
OPTICS
OPTIMA
OPTING
OPTION
OSTIUM
OUTING
PATINA
PATINE
PATIOS
PETITE
PITIED
PITIES
POTION
RATIFY
RATINE
RATING
RATION
RATIOS
RATITE
RETIAL
RETIED
RETIES
RETILE
RETIME
RETINA
RETIRE
ROTINI
RUTILE
SATING
SATINS
SATINY
SATIRE
SETINS
SHTICK
SITING
SITINS
TITIAN
TOTING
ULTIMA
ULTIMO
UNTIDY
UNTIED
UNTIES
UPTICK
UPTIME
VOTING
VOTIVE

•T••I•
ATOMIC
ATONIC
ATTAIN
ATTRIT
ETALIA
ETALII
ETHNIC
ETONIC
ITALIA
ITALIC
OTITIC
OTITIS
STADIA
STALIN
STASIS
STATIC
STEPIN
STEVIE
STIRIN
STIVIC
STOGIE
STOLID
STOPIN
STOPIT
STRAIN
STRAIT
STUDIO
STUPID
STYMIE
STYRIA
UTOPIA

•T•••I
ETALII
ITHAKI
ITURBI
STEFFI
STRATI

••TI••
ACTIII
ACTING
ACTINO
ACTION
ACTIUM
ACTIVE
ANTICS
ARTIER

••T•I•
ACTIII
ALTAIC
ALTAIR
ANTRIM
ARTOIS
ASTRID
ATTAIN
ATTRIT
BUTTIN
CATKIN
CATNIP
CATRIG
CITRIC
CUTSIN
DETAIL
DETAIN
DOTTIE
EATSIN
ENTAIL
FITSIN
GATLIN
GETSIN
GETSIT
GOTHIC
GOTOIT
HATPIN
HATTIE
HETTIE
HITSIT
HOTAIR
HOTTIP
IATRIC
INTUIT
ISTRIA
KATHIE
LATVIA
LETSIN
LITHIC
MATHIS
MATLIN
MATRIX
MATTIE
METRIC
MYTHIC
NITRIC
NITWIT
NUTKIN
NUTRIA
OBTAIN
OUTBID
OUTDID
OUTFIT
OUTHIT
OUTWIT
OXTAIL
PATOIS
PETAIN
PETRIE
PETTIT
POTPIE
PUTRID
PUTSIN
PYTHIA
RATLIN
RETAIL
RETAIN
RETRIM
SETSIN
SITSIN
TETRIS
TITBIT
VITRIC
VOTEIN
WETTIG
WITHIN
WITHIT

••T••I
ACTIII
BATUMI
HATARI
ISTHMI
JETSKI
KATMAI
LITCHI
MYTHOI
OCTOPI
OCTROI
POTOSI
QATARI
ROTINI
SATORI
TATAMI
WATUSI

•••TI•
ABATIS
ACETIC
AMATIS
AORTIC
ARCTIC
AUNTIE
AUSTIN
BALTIC
BEATIT
BERTIE
BESTIR
BIOTIC
BIOTIN
BOOTIE
BOWTIE
BUTTIN
CELTIC
CERTIF
CHITIN
COATIS
COOTIE
COPTIC
CRETIN
CRITIC
CULTIC
CURTIN
CURTIS
CURTIZ
DELTIC
DENTIL
DENTIN
DHOTIS
DISTIL
DOTTIE
DUSTIN
EROTIC
EXOTIC
FISTIC
FUSTIC
GERTIE
GRATIA
GRATIN
GRATIS
HATTIE
HECTIC
HESTIA
HETTIE
HOGTIE
HOTTIP
IGETIT
INITIO
JUSTIN
KILTIE
LACTIC
LENTIL
LOSTIT
MALTIN
MANTIC
MANTIS
MARTIN
MASTIC
MATTIE
MENTIS
MILTIE
MUFTIS
MUNTIN
MYSTIC
NOETIC
OTITIC
OTITIS
PASTIS
PECTIC
PECTIN
PEPTIC
PETTIT
PHATIC
PHOTIC
PIETIN
PISTIL
POETIC
PONTIC
PORTIA
QUITIT
RUSTIC
SANTIR
SCOTIA
SENTIN
SEPTIC
SHUTIN
SOFTIE
SORTIE
STATIC
TACTIC
THATIS
THETIC
THETIS
TOMTIT
VICTIM
WANTIN
WENTIN
WETTIG
WHATIF
ZAFTIG

•••T•I
CANTHI
CENTRI
DMITRI
FRUTTI
GLUTEI
MAITAI
MAOTAI
PROTEI

••••TI
AGOUTI
AVANTI
BHAKTI
DORATI
FRUTTI
GELATI
MALOTI
PILOTI
SHAKTI
SMALTI
STRATI
TAHITI
VASHTI
WAPITI

T••J••
THUJAS
TOPJOB
TRAJAN
TROJAN

T••••J
THEHAJ

•TJ•••
STJOAN
STJOHN

•T•J••
STOJKO

••T••J
SGTMAJ

T•K•••
TAKEIN
TAKEON
TAKERS
TAKETH
TAKETO
TAKEUP
TAKING
TAKINS
TOKAYS
TOKENS
TOKLAS

T••K••
TACKED
TACKER
TACKLE
TACKON
TALKAT
TALKED
TALKER
TALKIE
TALKTO
TALKUP
TANKAS
TANKED
TANKER
TANKUP
TASKED
TEDKEY
TERKEL
TICKED
TICKER
TICKET
TICKLE
TINKER
TINKLE
TINKLY
TONKIN
TOOKIN
TOOKIT
TOOKON
TOOKTO
TOOKUP
TRIKES
TUCKED
TUCKER
TUCKET
TUCKIN
TURKEY
TURKIC
TUSKED
TUSKER

T•••K•
TANAKA
THANKS
THICKE
THINKS
THUNKS
TILAKS
TOPEKA
TRACKS
TRICKS
TRICKY
TROIKA
TRUCKS
TRUNKS
TWEAKS

T••••K
TANOAK
THWACK
TOBRUK
TREBEK
TUGRIK

•TK•••
ATKINS

•T•K••
STAKED
STAKES
STOKED
STOKER
STOKES

•T••K•
ITHAKI
STACKS
STALKS
STALKY
STANKY
STEAKS
STICKS
STICKY
STINKS
STINKY
STLUKE
STOCKS
STOCKY
STOJKO
STORKS
STRAKE
STRIKE
STROKE

•T•••K
ATRISK
ATTACK
ATWORK
ITZHAK
STMARK
STREAK
STRICK
STRUCK

••TK••
CATKIN
KITKAT
LATKES
NUTKIN

••T•K•
BATIKS
BETAKE
INTAKE
JETSKI
RETAKE
ROTHKO
UPTAKE

••T••K
AMTRAK
ATTACK
BETOOK
BYTALK
NATICK
RETOOK
SHTICK
UNTACK
UPTICK

•••TK•
MOLTKE
NOOTKA

•••T•K
BARTOK
VOSTOK

TL••••
TLALOC

T•L•••
TALBOT
TALCED
TALCUM
TALENT
TALESE
TALION
TALKAT
TALKED
TALKER
TALKIE
TALKTO
TALKUP
TALLER
TALLOW
TALMUD
TALONS
TELEDU
TELLER
TELLON
TELUGU
TILAKS
TILDEN
TILDES
TILERS
TILING
TILLED
TILLER
TILLIE
TILLIS
TILSIT
TILTED
TILTER
TOLDOF
TOLEDO
TOLIFE
TOLLED
TOLTEC
TOLUCA
TULANE
TULARE
TULIPS
TULLES
TULSAN

T••L••
TABLAS
TABLED
TABLES
TABLET
TAILED
TAILLE
TAILOR
TALLER
TALLOW
TAYLOR
TBILLS
TEFLON
TELLER
TELLON
TESLAS
THALER
THALES
THALIA
THELIP
THELMA
THILLS
THOLES
TIGLON
TILLED
TILLER
TILLIE
TILLIS
TITLED
TITLES
TLALOC
TOILED
TOILER
TOILES
TOILET
TOKLAS
TOLLED
TOMLIN
TOOLED
TOOLUP
TOULON
TRALEE
TRILBY
TRILLS
TROLLS
TUILLE
TULLES
TWELVE
TWILIT
TWILLS

T•••L•
TABULA
TACKLE
TAILLE
TAMALE
TAMELY
TAMILS
TANGLE
TANGLY
TARTLY
TATTLE
TAUTLY
TBILLS
TEMPLE
TEPALS
THEYLL
THILLS
THINLY
THRALE
THRALL
THRILL
THUSLY
TICALS
TICKLE
TIDILY
TIMELY
TINGLE
TINGLY
TINKLE
TINKLY
TIPPLE
TITTLE
TIVOLI
TODDLE
TOGGLE
TOOTLE
TOPPLE
TOTALS
TOUSLE
TOWELS
TRAILS
TRAWLS
TREBLE
TREBLY
TRIALS
TRIFLE
TRIGLY
TRILLS
TRIMLY
TRIPLE
TRIPLY
TROLLS
TUILLE
TUMBLE
TUMULI
TUMULT
TUPELO
TURTLE
TUSSLE
TUVALU
TWILLS
TWIRLS
TWOPLY
TYBALT

T••••L
TARSAL
TASSEL
TEASEL
TERCEL
TERKEL
TETZEL
THECAL
THEYLL
THRALL
THRILL
TIBIAL
TIMBAL
TINCAL
TINSEL
TONSIL
TRAVEL
TRIBAL
TRINAL
TROWEL
TUNNEL

•TL•••
ATLAST
ATLATL
STLUKE

•T•L••
ATOLLS
ATTLEE
ETALIA
ETALII
ITALIA
ITALIC
OTELLO
STALAG
STALED
STALER
STALES
STALIN
STALKS
STALKY
STALLS
STELAE
STELAR
STELES
STELLA
STELMO
STILES
STILLS
STILLY
STILTS
STOLEN
STOLES
STOLID
STOLLE
STOLON
STULLS
STYLED
STYLER
STYLES
STYLET
STYLUS

•T••L•
ATOLLS
ATTILA
ATWILL
ETOILE
ITSELF
OTELLO
OTOOLE
STABLE
STABLY
STALLS
STAPLE
STEALS
STEELE
STEELS
STEELY
STELLA
STIFLE
STILLS
STILLY
STMALO
STOLLE
STOOLS
STROLL
STULLS

•T•••L
ATLATL
ATONAL
ATRIAL
ATWILL
ETYMOL
STEROL
STIPEL
STPAUL
STROLL

••TL••
ANTLER
ATTLEE
BUTLER
CUTLER
CUTLET
GATLIN
ISTLES
JETLAG
MATLIN
MOTLEY
NUTLET
ORTLES
OSTLER
OUTLAW
OUTLAY
OUTLET
RATLIN
SUTLER
TITLED
TITLES

••T•L•
ARTELS
ATTILA
BATTLE
BETELS
BOTFLY
BOTTLE
BYTALK
CATTLE
DOTELL
DOTTLE
EXTOLS
FATALE
FETTLE
FUTILE
HOTELS
KETTLE
LATELY
LETFLY
LITTLE
METALS
METTLE
MOTELS
MOTILE
MOTTLE
MUTELY
NETTLE
PETALS
PETULA
POTTLE
RATELS
RATTLE
RATTLY
RETELL
RETILE
RETOLD
RUTILE
SETTLE
SOTOLS
TATTLE
TITTLE
TOTALS
UNTOLD
VITALS
WATTLE
WETFLY

••T••L
ACTUAL
ARTFUL
ASTRAL
BETHEL
DETAIL
DOTELL
ENTAIL
FITFUL
LETHAL
MATTEL
METHYL
MITRAL
MUTUAL
MYTHOL
OSTEAL
OXTAIL
PATHOL
PATROL
PETREL
PETROL
POTFUL
RETAIL
RETELL
RETIAL
RETOOL
RETRAL
RITUAL
SHTETL
TETZEL
VATFUL
WITHAL

•••TL•
BATTLE
BEATLE
BEETLE
BOTTLE
BUSTLE
CANTLE
CASTLE
CATTLE
COSTLY
CURTLY
DEFTLY
DOTTLE
FETTLE
FLATLY
GENTLE
GENTLY
HURTLE
HUSTLE
JOSTLE
JUSTLY
KETTLE
KIRTLE
LASTLY
LITTLE
MANTLE
MEETLY
METTLE
MOSTLY
MOTTLE
MYRTLE
NEATLY
NESTLE
NETTLE
PARTLY
PERTLY
PESTLE
PINTLE
PORTLY
POTTLE
RAPTLY
RATTLE
RATTLY
RUSTLE
SETTLE
SOFTLY
SUBTLE
SUBTLY
TARTLY
TATTLE
TAUTLY
TITTLE
TOOTLE
TURTLE
VASTLY
WATTLE

•••T•L
ACETAL
ACETYL
AMATOL
AMSTEL
AORTAL
BRUTAL
CARTEL
COSTAL
DACTYL
DENTAL
DENTIL
DHOTEL
DISTAL
DISTIL
DUCTAL
FESTAL
FONTAL
GRETEL
HIATAL
HOSTEL
HYETAL
KEITEL
LENTIL
LINTEL
LISTEL
MANTEL
MARTEL
MATTEL
MENTAL
MONTEL
MORTAL
MOSTEL
PASTEL
PISTIL
PISTOL
PORTAL
POSTAL
RENTAL
SEPTAL
UNITAL
VESTAL

••••TL
ATLATL
SHTETL

TM••••
TMESIS

T•M•••
TAMALE
TAMARA
TAMAYO
TAMELY
TAMERS
TAMEST
TAMILS
TAMING
TAMMUZ
TAMPED
TAMPER
TAMTAM
TEMPED
TEMPEH
TEMPER
TEMPLE
TEMPOS
TEMPTS
TIMBAL
TIMBER
TIMBRE
TIMELY
TIMERS
TIMING
TOMATO
TOMBAC
TOMBOY
TOMCAT
TOMLIN
TOMMIX
TOMTIT
TOMTOM
TUMBLE
TUMEFY
TUMULI
TUMULT

T••M••
TALMUD
TAMMUZ
TARMAC
TASMAN
TAXMAN
TAXMEN
TEAMED
TEAMUP
TEEMED
TERMED
TEXMEX
THAMES
THEMED
THEMES
THOMAS

THUMBS THUMPS THYMUS TINMAN TINMEN TOAMAN TODMAN TOMMIX TRAMPS TREMOR TRIMLY TROMPE TROMPS TRUMAN TRUMPS TUBMAN

T•••M•

TACOMA TATAMI THELMA THERMO THERMS THRUMS TOTEMS TRAUMA

T••••M

TALCUM TAMTAM TANDEM TAOISM TEDEUM TEDIUM THEISM TOMTOM TRUISM

•TM•••

ATMOST STMALO STMARK UTMOST

•T•M••

ATAMAN ATEMPO ATOMIC ETYMOL ETYMON STAMEN STAMPS STIMPY STOMAS STOMAT STOMPS STUMPS STUMPY STYMIE

•T••M•

ATEAMS ATHOME STEAMS STEAMY STELMO STIGMA STORMS STORMY STRUMS

•T•••M

ATRIUM STREAM

••TM••

ALTMAN BATMAN BATMEN BITMAP GOTMAD HETMAN HITMAN HITMEN KATMAI LITMUS MOTMOT NETMAN NETMEN NUTMEG PATMOS PITMAN PITMEN SGTMAJ WETMOP

••T•M•

AUTUMN BATUMI FATIMA INTIMA INTIME ISTHMI ONTIME OPTIMA RETIME TATAMI TOTEMS ULTIMA ULTIMO UPTIME

••T••M

ACTIUM ANTHEM ANTRIM ANTRUM ARTGUM BOTTOM ESTEEM FATHOM GOTHAM JETSAM LATIUM OSTIUM PUTNAM RETRIM SITCOM

•••T•M

ADYTUM BANTAM BOTTOM CUSTOM DIATOM DICTUM MADTOM PROTEM RHYTHM SEPTUM SYSTEM TAMTAM TOMTOM VICTIM

TN••••

TNOTES

T•N•••

TANAKA TANDEM TANGED TANGLE TANGLY TANGOS TANGUY TANIST TANKAS TANKED TANKER TANKUP TANNED TANNER TANNIC TANNIN TANOAK TANOAN TANTRA TENACE TENANT TENDED TENDER TENDON TENDTO TENETS TENNIS TENONS TENORS TENPIN TENREC TENSED TENSER TENSES TENSOR TENTED TENTER TENTHS TENURE TENUTO TINCAL TINCAN TINCTS TINDER TINEAR TINGED TINGES TINGLE TINGLY TINGOD TINHAT TINIER TINKER TINKLE TINKLY TINMAN TINMEN TINNED TINNER TINPAN TINPOT TINSEL TINTED TINTER TONERS TONEUP TONGAN TONGUE TONICS TONIER TONING TONISH TONITE TONKIN TONNES TONSIL TUNDRA TUNEIN TUNERS TUNEUP TUNICA TUNICS TUNING TUNNEL TUNNEY

T••N••

TAINAN TAINOS TAINTS TANNED TANNER TANNIC TANNIN TAUNTS TBONDS TBONES TEENER TEENSY TENNIS THANES THANKS THENAR THENCE THINGS THINKS THINLY THONGS THUNKS TINNED TINNER TONNES TOWNER TOWNIE TRANCE TRENCH TRENDS TRENDY TRINAL TRINES TRUNKS TUNNEL TUNNEY TURNED TURNER TURNIN TURNIP TURNON TURNTO TURNUP TWANGS TWANGY TWENTY TWINED TWINES TWINGE

T•••N•

TAGEND TAHINI TAKING TAKINS TALENT TALONS TAMING TAPING TAPINS TARING TAUONS TAWING TAXING TECHNO TEEING TENANT TENONS TETONS TEXANS THEEND THORNS THORNY THRONE THRONG TIDING TIEING TIEINS TILING TIMING TIPINS TIRANA TIRANE TIRING TISANE TITANS TOEING TOEINS TOKENS TONING TORINO TOTING TOWING TOXINS TOYING TOYONS TRAINS TRIUNE TRUANT TRUING TRYING TUBING TUCANA TULANE TUNING TURING TYPING TYRANT TYRONE

T••••N

TACKON TAINAN TAIPAN TAIWAN TAKEIN TAKEON TALION TANNIN TANOAN TAPPAN TARPAN TARPON TARTAN TARZAN TASMAN TAUTEN TAVERN TAXMAN TAXMEN TEFLON TELLON TENDON TENPIN TERRAN TEUTON THROWN TIEDIN TIEPIN TIESIN TIFFIN TIGLON TILDEN TINCAN TINMAN TINMEN TINPAN TIPSIN TITIAN TOAMAN TOCSIN TODMAN TOEDIN TOESIN TOMLIN TONGAN TONKIN TOOKIN TOOKON TOPGUN TOPTEN TOUCAN TOULON TRAJAN TREPAN TRIGON TRITON TROGON TROJAN TRUMAN TUBMAN TUCHUN TUCKIN TUCSON TULSAN TUNEIN TUPIAN TURBAN TUREEN TURNIN TURNON TUSCAN TYCOON TYRIAN

•T•N••

ATONAL ATONCE ATONED ATONES ATONIC ETHNIC ETHNOS ETONIC STANCE STANCH STANDS STANKY STANZA STENCH STENOG STENOS STINGS STINGY STINKS STINKY STINTS STONED STONER STONES STUNTS

•T••N•

ATHAND ATHENA ATHENE ATHENS ATKINS ATTEND ATTUNE ETERNE ETHANE ETHENE STAINS STEINS STERNA STERNE STERNO STERNS STHENO STRAND STRING STRONG STRUNG UTHANT UTURNS

•T•••N

ATAMAN ATTAIN ETYMON STALIN STAMEN STAYON STEFAN STEPIN STEPON STEVEN STIRIN STJOAN STJOHN STOLEN STOLON STOPIN STRAIN STREWN STYRON UTAHAN

••TN••

CATNAP CATNIP JITNEY NOTNOW PUTNAM WATNEY

••T•N•

ACTING ACTINO ACTONE ANTONY ATTEND ATTUNE BATING BATONS BETONY BITING BOTANY BUTANE BUTENE BUTUNG CATENA CETANE CITING CUTINS DATING DATONG DETENT DOTING EATING EXTANT EXTEND EXTENT FETING FUTONS GATING GITANO HATING INTEND INTENS INTENT INTINE INTONE INTUNE KETONE KITING LATENE LATENS LATENT LATINA LATINO LATINS LATONA LITANY LUTING MATING MATINS METING MUTANT MUTING MUTINY NATANT NOTING OBTUND OCTANE OCTANT OPTING OSTEND OUTING PATENS PATENT PATINA PATINE PITONS POTENT PUTONS RATINE RATING RETENE RETINA RETUNE ROTINI ROTUND SATANG SATING SATINS SATINY SETINS SITING SITINS TETONS TITANS TOTING UNTUNE VOTING

••T••N

ACTION ACTSON ALTMAN ANTRON ASTERN ATTAIN AUTUMN BATAAN BATMAN BATMEN BATTEN BITTEN BUTTIN BUTTON CATION CATKIN CATTON CITRON COTTEN COTTON CUTSIN DATSUN DETAIN DOTEON DOTHAN EATSIN FATTEN FITSIN GATLIN GETSIN GETSON GOTTEN HATPIN HETMAN HITMAN HITMEN HITSON HUTTON INTERN INTOWN INTURN JETGUN JETSON KITTEN LATEEN LATTEN LETSIN LETSON LOTION LYTTON MATLIN MATRON MITTEN MOTION MOTOWN MUTTON NATHAN NATION NATRON NETMAN NETMEN NETTON NOTION NUTKIN OBTAIN OPTION OUTGUN OUTRAN OUTRUN PATHAN PATRON PATTEN PATTON PETAIN PITMAN PITMEN POTEEN POTION PUTSIN PUTSON PYTHON RATION RATLIN RATSON RATTAN RETAIN RETTON RETURN ROTTEN RUTTAN SATEEN SATURN SETSIN SETSON SITSIN SITSON TITIAN UNTORN UPTOWN UPTURN VOTEIN WATSON WITHIN

•••TN•

GRETNA MUSTNT

•••T•N

AMYTAN AUSTEN AUSTIN BARTON BATTEN BEATEN BEATON BENTON BHUTAN BIGTEN BIOTIN BITTEN BOLTON BONTON BOSTON BRETON BRITON BURTON BUTTIN BUTTON CAFTAN CANTON CAPTAN CARTON CASTON CATTON CAXTON CHITIN CHITON COTTEN COTTON CRETAN CRETIN CROTON CURTIN DALTON DANTON DAYTON DENTIN DENTON DUSTIN EASTON FANTAN FASTEN FATTEN FULTON GASTON GLUTEN GOTTEN GRATIN HASTEN HESTON HILTON HINTON HORTON HUSTON HUTTON JUSTIN KEATON KENTON KEPTON KITTEN LATTEN LAWTON LENTEN LEPTON LIPTON LISTEN LISTON LYTTON MALTIN MARTEN MARTIN MELTON MERTON MILTON MITTEN MOLTEN MORTON MOUTON MUNTIN MUTTON NEATEN NEKTON NETTON NEWTON NORTON PARTON PATTEN PATTON PECTIN PEYTON PHOTON PIETIN PISTON PLATEN POSTON PROTON RATTAN RESTON RETTON RHYTON ROTTEN RUTTAN SALTEN SALTON SARTON SENTIN SEXTON SHUTIN SOFTEN SULTAN SUNTAN TARTAN TAUTEN TEUTON TOPTEN TRITON VINTON WAITON WALTON WANTIN WANTON WENTIN WENTON WHITEN WILTON WONTON WYNTON WYSTAN

TO••••

TOAMAN TOASTS TOASTY TOATEE TOBAGO TOBIAS TOBIES TOBOOT TOBRUK TOCSIN TODATE TODDAO TODDLE TODMAN TOECAP TOEDIN TOEING TOEINS TOESIN TOETAP TOFFEE TOGAED TOGGED TOGGLE TOILED TOILER TOILES TOILET TOKAYS TOKENS TOKLAS TOLDOF TOLEDO TOLIFE TOLLED TOLTEC TOLUCA TOMATO TOMBAC TOMBOY TOMCAT TOMLIN TOMMIX TOMTIT TOMTOM TONERS TONEUP TONGAN TONGUE TONICS TONIER TONING TONISH TONITE TONKIN TONNES TONSIL TOOBAD TOOKIN TOOKIT TOOKON TOOKTO TOOKUP TOOLED TOOLUP TOOTED TOOTER TOOTHY TOOTLE TOOTOO TOOTSY TOPCAT TOPDOG TOPEKA TOPERS TOPGUN TOPHAT TOPHUS TOPICS TOPJOB TOPOFF TOPOUT TOPPED TOPPER TOPPLE TOPTEN TOQUES TORAHS TOREAT TORERO TOREUP TORIES TORINO TOROID TOROSE TORPID TORPOR TORQUE TORRID TORSOS TORTES TOSSED TOSSER TOSSES TOSSUP TOTALS TOTEMS TOTERS TOTHER TOTING TOTSUP TOTTED TOTTER TOUCAN TOUCHE TOUCHY TOUGHS TOUGHY TOULON TOUPEE TOURED TOURER TOUSLE TOUTED TOUTER TOWAGE TOWARD TOWCAR TOWELS TOWERS TOWERY TOWHEE TOWING TOWNER TOWNIE TOXICS TOXINS TOYDOG TOYING TOYONS TOYOTA

T•O•••

TAOISM TAOIST TBONDS TBONES THOLES THOMAS THONGS THORAX THORNS THORNY THORPE THORPS THOUGH TNOTES TOOBAD TOOKIN TOOKIT TOOKON TOOKTO TOOKUP TOOLED TOOLUP TOOTED TOOTER TOOTHY TOOTLE TOOTOO TOOTSY TROCAR TROCHE TROGON TROIKA TROJAN TROLLS TROMPE TROMPS TROOPS TROPES TROPEZ TROPHY TROPIC TROPPO TROTHS TROUGH TROUPE TROUTS TROUVE TROVES TROWED TROWEL TWOBIT TWOFER TWOPLY TWOWAY

T••O••

TABOOS TABORS TACOMA TAGORE TAGOUT TALONS TANOAK TANOAN TAPOFF TAPOUT TAROTS TAUONS TEEOFF TENONS TENORS TETONS THEORY THROAT THROBS THROES THRONE THRONG THROVE THROWN THROWS TIPOFF TIVOLI TOBOOT TOPOFF TOPOUT TOROID TOROSE TOYONS TOYOTA TRIODE TROOPS TRYOUT TUDORS TUTORS TYCOBB TYCOON TYRONE

T•••O•

TABOOS TACKON TAILOR TAINOS TAKEON TALBOT TALION TALLOW TANGOS TARPON TATTOO TAUTOG TAYLOR TEAPOT TEAPOY TEFLON TELLON TEMPOS TENDON TENSOR TERROR TEUTON THETOY TIEROD TIGLON TINGOD TINPOT TIPTOE TIPTOP TLALOC TOBOOT TOLDOF TOMBOY

TOMTOM
TOOKON
TOOTOO
TOPDOG
TOPJOB
TORPOR
TORSOS
TOULON
TOYDOG
TREMOR
TREVOR
TRICOT
TRIGON
TRIPOD
TRIPOS
TRITON
TROGON
TRYFOR
TUCSON
TURBOS
TURBOT
TURGOR
TURNON
TVSHOW
TYCOON

T••••O
TAKETO
TALKTO
TAMAYO
TATTOO
TECHNO
TENDTO
TENUTO
TERATO
TEREDO
TEXACO
THERMO
TOBAGO
TODDAO
TOLEDO
TOMATO
TOOKTO
TOOTOO
TORERO
TORINO
TRICHO
TROPPO
TUPELO
TURNTO
TUXEDO

•TO•••
ATODDS
ATOLLS
ATOMIC
ATONAL
ATONCE
ATONED
ATONES
ATONIC
ETOILE
ETONIC
OTOOLE
STOATS
STOCKS
STOCKY
STODGE
STODGY
STOGIE
STOICS
STOJKO
STOKED
STOKER
STOKES
STOLEN
STOLES
STOLID
STOLLE
STOLON
STOMAS
STOMAT
STOMPS
STONED
STONER
STONES
STOOGE
STOOLS
STOOPS
STOPES
STOPIN
STOPIT
STOPUP
STORCH
STORED
STORER
STORES
STOREY
STORKS
STORMS
STORMY
STORRS
STOUPS
STOUTS
STOVER
STOVES
STOWED
UTOPIA

•T•O••
ATCOST
ATHOME
ATMOST
ATWOOD
ATWORK
FTROOP
OTIOSE
OTOOLE
PTBOAT
STJOAN
STJOHN
STOOGE
STOOLS
STOOPS
STROBE
STRODE
STROKE
STROLL
STRONG
STROPS
STROUD
STROVE
UTMOST

•T••O•
ATWOOD
ETHNOS
ETYMOL
ETYMON
FTROOP
STATOR
STAYON
STENOG
STENOS
STEPON
STEROL
STOLON
STUPOR
STYRON

•T•••O
ATEMPO
ATERGO
OTELLO
STELMO
STEREO
STERNO
STHENO
STMALO
STOJKO
STRABO
STRATO
STUCCO
STUDIO

••TO••
ACTONE
ACTORS
ACTOUT
ANTONY
ARTOIS
BATONS
BETONY
BETOOK
BITOFF
CUTOFF
CUTOUT
DATONG
DETOUR
EATOUT
ESTOPS
EXTOLS
EXTORT
FSTOPS
FUTONS
GATORS
GETOFF
GETOUT
GOTOFF
GOTOIT
GOTOUT
INTONE
INTOTO
INTOWN
KETONE
LATONA
LATOUR
LATOYA
LETOFF
LETOUT
LITOUT
METOPE
MOTORS
MOTOWN
OCTOPI
ONTOUR
OPTOUT
PATOIS
PITONS
POTOSI
PUTOFF
PUTONS
PUTOUT
RETOLD
RETOOK
RETOOL
RETOPS
RETORT
RETOUR
RETOWS
ROTORS
SATORI
SATOUT
SETOFF
SETOSE
SETOUT
SITOUT
SOTOLS
TETONS
TUTORS
UNTOLD
UNTORN
UPTOWN
VETOED
VETOER
VETOES

••T•O•
ACTION
ACTSON
ANTCOW
ANTRON
ASTROS
AUTHOR
BATBOY
BATHOS
BETOOK
BETTOR
BOTTOM
BUTEOS
BUTTON
CATION
CATTON
CITRON
COTTON
DETROP
DITTOS
DOTEON
FATHOM
GETSON
HATBOX
HATHOR
HITSON
HOTBOX
HOTDOG
HOTPOT
HOTROD
HUTTON
INTROS
JETSON
KITFOX
LETSON
LITHOG
LITHOS
LOTION
LOTTOS
LUTHOR
LYTTON
MATRON
MATZOH
MATZOS
METEOR
METHOD
METROS
MOTION
MOTMOT
MOTTOS
MUTTON
MYTHOI
MYTHOL
MYTHOS
NATION
NATRON
NETTON
NOTION
NOTNOW
OCTROI
OPTION
OUTFOX
PATHOL
PATHOS
PATIOS
PATMOS
PATROL
PATRON
PATTON
PETROG
PETROL
POTION
POTTOS
PUTSON
PYTHON
RATION
RATIOS
RATSON
RETOOK
RETOOL
RETROS
RETTON
SETSON
SETTOS
SITCOM
SITSON
TATTOO
UNTROD
WATSON
WETMOP

••T••O
ACTINO
ACTTWO
ANTERO
ARTHRO
ARTURO
ENTERO
GETSTO
GITANO
HETERO
INTOTO
JETHRO
LATIGO
LATINO
LETSGO
OCTAVO
POTATO
PUTSTO
ROTHKO
TATTOO
ULTIMO

•••TO•
AMATOL
BARTOK
BARTON
BEATON
BENTON
BESTOW
BETTOR
BIGTOE
BIGTOP
BOLTON
BONTON
BOSTON
BOTTOM
BOXTOP
BRETON
BRITON
BURTON
BUTTON
CANTON
CANTOR
CANTOS
CAPTOR
CARTON
CASTON
CASTOR
CATTON
CAXTON
CENTOS
CESTOS
CHITON
COTTON
CROTON
CUSTOM
DALTON
DANTON
DAYTON
DEBTOR
DENTON
DIATOM
DITTOS
DOCTOR
EASTON
EDITOR
EMPTOR
FACTOR
FRITOS
FULTON
GASTON
HECTOR
HESTON
HILTON
HINTON
HORTON
HOWTOS
HUSTON
HUTTON
JUNTOS
KANTOR
KEATON
KENTON
KEPTON
KOWTOW
LAPTOP
LAWTON
LECTOR
LEPTON
LICTOR
LIPTON
LISTON
LOTTOS
LYTTON
MADTOM
MELTON
MENTOR
MERTON
MILTON
MORTON
MOTTOS
MOUTON
MUTTON
NEKTON
NESTOR
NETTON
NEWTON
NORTON
ORATOR
PARTON
PASTOR
PATTON
PEGTOP
PEYTON
PHOTOG
PHOTON
PHOTOS
PINTOS
PISTOL
PISTON
POPTOP
POSTON
POTTOS
PROTON
RAGTOP
RAPTOR
RECTOR
RECTOS
REDTOP
RESTON
RETTON
RHETOR
RHYTON
ROSTOV
SALTON
SANTOS
SARTON
SECTOR
SESTOS
SETTOS
SEXTON
SKITOW
SORTOF
STATOR
SUITOR
TATTOO
TAUTOG
TEUTON
THETOY
TIPTOE
TIPTOP
TOMTOM
TOOTOO
TRITON
UNSTOP
VECTOR
VICTOR
VINTON
VOSTOK
WAITON
WALTON
WANTON
WENTON
WILTON
WONTON
WYNTON

•••T•O
ACTTWO
ANATTO
AUSTRO
BHUTTO
BISTRO
BLOTTO
CASTRO
CENTRO
CLOTHO
DEXTRO
GASTRO
GHETTO
GIOTTO
GROTTO
INITIO
NEXTTO
ONETWO
PIETRO
SCOTTO
TATTOO
TOOTOO
WANTTO
XANTHO

••••TO
ADDSTO
AIMSTO
ALECTO
ALIOTO
ANATTO
ARISTO
BENITO
BHUTTO
BLOTTO
BONITO
CAMETO
CARETO
COMETO
CRYPTO
DAMATO
DARETO
DESOTO
DEVITO
DEVOTO
EXACTO
EXVOTO
FALLTO
FELLTO
FINITO
GEARTO
GELATO
GETSTO
GHETTO
GIOTTO
GOINTO
GROTTO
HELDTO
HEMATO
HERETO
HOLDTO
HOVETO
INTOTO
KEEPTO
LAIDTO
LAYSTO
LEADTO
LEANTO
LEGATO
LIESTO
LOOKTO
MAPUTO
MRMOTO
NEARTO
NEMATO
NEXTTO
ODONTO
OPENTO
OPORTO
PARETO
PASHTO
POTATO
PRESTO
PRONTO
PUERTO
PUTSTO
QUARTO
RABATO
RIALTO
RIGHTO
RUNSTO
SABATO
SANGTO
SCOTTO
SEENTO
SEESTO
SHINTO
SINGTO
SMALTO
SNAPTO
SOASTO
SOMATO
SOWETO
STRATO
SUBITO
TAKETO
TALKTO
TENDTO
TENUTO
TERATO
TOMATO
TOOKTO
TURNTO
USEDTO
VENETO
WANTTO
WISETO

T•P•••
TAPERS
TAPING
TAPINS
TAPIRS
TAPOFF
TAPOUT
TAPPAN
TAPPED
TAPPER
TAPPET
TEPALS
TEPEES
TEPHRA
TIPINS
TIPOFF
TIPPED
TIPPER
TIPPET
TIPPLE
TIPSIN
TIPTOE
TIPTOP
TIPUPS
TOPCAT
TOPDOG
TOPEKA
TOPERS
TOPGUN
TOPHAT
TOPHUS
TOPICS
TOPJOB
TOPOFF
TOPOUT
TOPPED
TOPPER
TOPPLE
TOPTEN
TUPELO
TUPIAN
TYPERS
TYPEUP
TYPHUS
TYPIFY
TYPING
TYPIST

T••P••
TAIPAN
TAIPEI
TAMPED
TAMPER
TAPPAN
TAPPED
TAPPER
TAPPET
TARPAN
TARPIT
TARPON
TAUPES
TEAPOT
TEAPOY
TEMPED
TEMPEH
TEMPER
TEMPLE
TEMPOS
TEMPTS
TENPIN
TIEPIN
TINPAN
TINPOT
TIPPED
TIPPER
TIPPET
TIPPLE
TOPPED
TOPPER
TOPPLE
TORPID
TORPOR
TOUPEE
TRAPPY
TREPAN
TREPID
TRIPLE
TRIPLY
TRIPOD
TRIPOS
TRIPUP
TROPES
TROPEZ
TROPHY
TROPIC
TROPPO
TWOPLY

T•••P•
TERAPH
THORPE
THORPS
THRIPS
THUMPS
TIEUPS
TIPUPS
TRAMPS
TRAPPY
TROMPE
TROMPS
TROOPS
TROPPO
TROUPE
TRUMPS
TULIPS
TWERPS

T••••P
TAGSUP
TAKEUP
TALKUP
TANKUP
TEACUP
TEAMUP
TEARUP
TEEDUP
TEESUP
THELIP
TIDYUP
TIEDUP
TIESUP
TIPTOP
TOECAP
TOETAP
TONEUP
TOOKUP
TOOLUP
TOREUP
TOSSUP
TOTSUP
TRIPUP
TUNEUP
TURNIP
TURNUP
TYPEUP

•TP•••
STPAUL
STPETE

•T•P••
STAPES
STAPLE
STAPUF
STEPIN
STEPON
STEPPE
STEPUP
STIPEL
STIPES
STOPES
STOPIN
STOPIT
STOPUP
STUPAS
STUPES
STUPID
STUPOR
UTOPIA

•T••P•
ATEMPO
PTRAPS
STAMPS
STEEPS
STEPPE
STIMPY
STOMPS
STOOPS
STOUPS
STRAPS
STRIPE
STRIPS
STROPS
STUMPS
STUMPY

•T•••P
FTROOP
STAYUP
STEPUP
STIRUP
STOPUP
STREEP

••TP••
HATPIN
HOTPOT
NETPAY
OUTPUT
POTPIE
PUTPUT

••T•P•
CUTUPS
ECTYPE
ESTOPS
FSTOPS
GETUPS
LETUPS
METOPE
OCTOPI
ONTAPE
RETAPE
RETAPS
RETOPS
RETYPE
SETUPS
SITUPS

••T••P
ACTSUP
ANTEUP
BITMAP
CATNAP
CATNIP
CATSUP
CUTSUP
DETROP
EATSUP
ENTRAP
GETSUP
HITSUP
HOTCAP
HOTTIP
LETSUP
PUTSUP
SATRAP
SETSUP
SITSUP
TOTSUP
UNTRAP
WETMOP

•••T•P
BEATUP
BIGTOP
BOOTUP
BOXTOP
CHATUP
DUSTUP
HEATUP
HOTTIP
INSTEP
KEPTUP
LAPTOP
LIFTUP
PEGTOP
PENTUP
POPTOP
RAGTOP
REDTOP
RESTUP
SENTUP
SHOTUP
SHUTUP
SUITUP
TIPTOP
TOETAP
UNSTOP
WAITUP
WENTUP

T•Q•••
TOQUES
TUQUES

T••Q••
TORQUE

•T••Q•
ETSEQQ

•T•••Q
ETSEQQ

TR••••
TRACED
TRACER
TRACES
TRACEY
TRACKS
TRACTS
TRADED
TRADER
TRADES
TRAGIC
TRAILS
TRAINS
TRAITS
TRAJAN
TRALEE
TRAMPS
TRANCE
TRAPPY
TRASHY
TRAUMA
TRAVEL
TRAVIS
TRAWLS
TREADS
TREATS
TREATY
TREBEK
TREBLE
TREBLY
TREDIA
TREMOR
TRENCH
TRENDS
TRENDY
TREPAN
TREPID
TREVOR
TRIADS
TRIAGE
TRIALS
TRIBAL
TRIBES
TRICED
TRICES
TRICHO
TRICIA
TRICKS
TRICKY
TRICOT
TRIERS
TRIFID
TRIFLE
TRIGLY
TRIGON
TRIKES
TRILBY
TRILLS
TRIMLY
TRINAL
TRINES
TRIODE
TRIPLE
TRIPLY
TRIPOD
TRIPOS
TRIPUP
TRISHA
TRISTE
TRITER
TRITON
TRIUNE
TRIVET
TRIVIA
TRIXIE
TROCAR
TROCHE
TROGON
TROIKA
TROJAN
TROLLS
TROMPE
TROMPS
TROOPS
TROPES
TROPEZ
TROPHY
TROPIC
TROPPO
TROTHS
TROUGH
TROUPE
TROUTS
TROUVE
TROVES
TROWED
TROWEL
TRUANT
TRUCES
TRUCKS
TRUDGE
TRUEST
TRUING
TRUISM
TRUMAN
TRUMPS
TRUNKS
TRUSTS
TRUSTY
TRUTHS
TRYFOR
TRYING
TRYOUT
TRYSTS

T•R•••
TARAWA
TARGES
TARGET
TARIFF
TARING
TARMAC
TAROTS
TARPAN
TARPIT
TARPON
TARRED
TARSAL
TARSUS
TARTAN
TARTAR
TARTER
TARTLY
TARZAN
TERAPH
TERATO
TERCEL
TERCET
TEREDO
TERESA
TERETE
TEREUS
TERKEL
TERMED
TERRAN
TERRET
TERROR
TERSER
THRACE
THRALE
THRALL
THRASH
THREAD
THREAT
THREED
THREES
THRESH
THRICE
THRIFT
THRILL
THRIPS
THRIVE
THROAT
THROBS
THROES
THRONE
THRONG
THROVE
THROWN
THROWS
THRUMS
THRUSH
THRUST
TIRADE
TIRANA
TIRANE
TIRING
TORAHS
TOREAT
TORERO
TOREUP
TORIES
TORINO
TOROID
TOROSE
TORPID
TORPOR
TORQUE
TORRID
TORSOS
TORTES
TURBAN
TURBID
TURBIT
TURBOS
TURBOT
TUREEN
TURFED
TURGID
TURGOR
TURING
TURKEY
TURKIC
TURNED
TURNER
TURNIN
TURNIP
TURNON
TURNTO
TURNUP
TURRET

TURTLE
TYRANT
TYRIAN
TYRONE

T••R••
TABRIZ
TARRED
TAURUS
TAYRAS
TBIRDS
TEARAT
TEARED
TEARUP
TENREC
TERRAN
TERRET
TERROR
TETRAD
TETRAS
TETRIS
THERMO
THERMS
THIRDS
THIRST
THIRTY
THORAX
THORNS
THORNY
THORPE
THORPS
THYRSI
TIARAS
TIERCE
TIERED
TIEROD
TIERRA
TIGRIS
TOBRUK
TORRID
TOURED
TOURER
TUAREG
TUGRIK
TURRET
TWERPS
TWIRLS

T•••R•
TABARD
TABORS
TAGORE
TAKERS
TAMARA
TAMERS
TANTRA
TAPERS
TAPIRS
TATARS
TATERS
TAVERN
TAWDRY
TAXERS
TENORS
TENURE
TEPHRA
THEIRS
THEORY
THEYRE
THWART
TIERRA
TIGERS
TILERS
TIMBRE
TIMERS
TISHRI
TITERS
TONERS
TOPERS
TORERO
TOTERS
TOWARD
TOWERS
TOWERY
TRIERS
TSHIRT
TUBERS
TUDORS
TULARE
TUNDRA
TUNERS
TUTORS
TUYERE
TYPERS

T••••R
TACKER
TAILOR
TALKER
TALLER
TAMPER
TANKER
TANNER
TAPPER
TARTAR
TARTER
TASTER
TATTER
TAUTER
TAYLOR
TEASER
TEDDER
TEENER
TEETER
TELLER
TEMPER
TENDER
TENSER
TENSOR
TENTER
TERROR
TERSER
TESTER
TETHER
THALER
THAYER
THENAR
TICKER
TIDIER
TIGGER
TILLER
TILTER
TIMBER
TINDER
TINEAR
TINIER
TINKER
TINNER
TINTER
TIPPER
TITHER
TITTER
TOILER
TONIER
TOOTER
TOPPER
TORPOR
TOSSER
TOTHER
TOTTER
TOURER
TOUTER
TOWCAR
TOWNER
TRACER
TRADER
TREMOR
TREVOR
TRITER
TROCAR
TRYFOR
TUCKER
TUGGER
TURGOR
TURNER
TUSKER
TWOFER

•TR•••
ATREST
ATREUS
ATRIAL
ATRISK
ATRIUM
FTROOP
PTRAPS
STRABO
STRADS
STRAFE
STRAIN
STRAIT
STRAKE
STRAND
STRAPS
STRASS
STRATA
STRATI
STRATO
STRAUS
STRAWS
STRAYS
STREAK
STREAM
STREEP
STREET
STRESS
STREWN
STREWS
STRIAE
STRICK
STRICT
STRIDE
STRIFE
STRIKE
STRING
STRIPE
STRIPS
STRIVE
STROBE
STRODE
STROKE
STROLL
STRONG
STROPS
STROUD
STROVE
STRUCK
STRUMS
STRUNG
STRUTS

•T•R••
ATERGO
ATTRIT
ETERNE
ITURBI
STARCH
STARED
STARER
STARES
STARRY
STARTS
STARVE
STEREO
STERES
STERNA
STERNE
STERNO
STERNS
STEROL
STIRIN
STIRUP
STORCH
STORED
STORER
STORES
STOREY
STORKS
STORMS
STORMY
STORRS
STURDY
STYRIA
STYRON
UTURNS

•T••R•
ATTARS
ATTIRE
ATWORK
ETHERS
OTHERS
OTTERS
STAIRS
STARRY
STEERS
STMARK
STORRS
STUART
UTTERS

•T•••R
ETCHER
STAGER
STALER
STARER
STATER
STATOR
STELAR
STEWER
STIVER
STOKER
STONER
STORER
STOVER
STUPOR
STYLER

••TR••
AMTRAC
AMTRAK
ANTRES
ANTRIM
ANTRON
ANTRUM
ASTRAL
ASTRAY
ASTRID
ASTROS
ATTRIT
BETRAY
BOTREE
CATRIG
CITRIC
CITRON
CITRUS
DETROP
ENTRAP
ENTREE
EXTRAS
HATRED
HOTROD
IATRIC
INTROS
ISTRIA
LITRES
MATRIX
MATRON
METRES
METRIC
METROS
MITRAL
MITRED
MITRES
NATRON
NITRES
NITRIC
NUTRIA
OCTROI
OUTRAN
OUTRUN
PATROL
PATRON
PETREL
PETRIE
PETROG
PETROL
PUTRID
RETRAL
RETRIM
RETROS
SATRAP
SUTRAS
TETRAD
TETRAS
TETRIS
ULTRAS
UNTRAP
UNTROD
UNTRUE
VITRIC

••T•R•
ACTORS
ALTARS
ALTERS
ANTERO
ARTERY
ARTHRO
ARTURO
ASTERN
ASTERS
ATTARS
ATTIRE
BITERS
CATERS
CITERS
DATARY
DATERS
DATURA
DETERS
DOTARD
EATERS
EATERY
ENTERO
ENTERS
ENTIRE
ESTERS
EXTORT
FUTURE
GATERS
GATORS
HATARI
HATERS
HETERO
INTERN
INTURN
JETHRO
KITERS
LITERS
MATERS
MATURE
METERS
MITERS
MOTORS
NATURE
NITERS
NOTARY
NOTERS
OATERS
OTTERS
OUTCRY
PETARD
PETERS
QATARI
RATERS
RETARD
RETARS
RETIRE
RETORT
RETURN
RITARD
ROTARY
ROTORS
SATIRE
SATORI
SATURN
SATYRS
SITARS
SUTURE
TATARS
TATERS
TITERS
TOTERS
TUTORS
UNTORN
UPTURN
UTTERS
VOTARY
VOTERS
WATERS
WATERY

••T••R
AETHER
ALTAIR
ANTHER
ANTLER
ARTHUR
ARTIER
AUTEUR
AUTHOR
BATHER
BATTER
BETTER
BETTOR
BITTER
BOTHER
BUTLER
BUTTER
CATHER
COTTER
CUTLER
CUTTER
DETOUR
DITHER
EITHER
ESTHER
FATHER
FATTER
FETTER
FITTER
GATHER
GETTER
GUTTER
HATHOR
HATTER
HITHER
HITTER
HOTAIR
HOTCAR
HOTTER
HOTWAR
JITTER
KOTTER
LATHER
LATOUR
LATTER
LETTER
LITTER
LOTHAR
LUTHER
LUTHOR
MATHER
MATTER
METEOR
METIER
MOTHER
MUTTER
NATTER
NETHER
NUTTER
OATIER
ONTOUR
OSTLER
PATTER
PETTER
PITTER
POTHER
POTTER
PUTTER
RATEDR
RATHER
RATTER
RETOUR
RITTER
ROTTER
RUTGER
SETTER
SITTER
SUTLER
SUTTER
TATTER
TETHER
TITHER
TITTER
TOTHER
TOTTER
VETOER
WETBAR
WETHER
WETTER
WITHER
ZITHER

•••TR•
ANITRA
AUSTRO
BISTRO
CASTRO
CENTRE
CENTRI
CENTRO
CONTRA
CONTRE
DESTRY
DEXTRO
DMITRI
GANTRY
GASTRO
GENTRY
LUSTRE
MAITRE
MANTRA
PALTRY
PANTRY
PASTRY
PELTRY
PIETRO
POETRY
ROSTRA
SARTRE
SENTRY
SULTRY
TANTRA
VESTRY
WINTRY

•••T•R
AVATAR
BANTER
BARTER
BASTER
BATTER
BAXTER
BEATER
BESTIR
BETTER
BETTOR
BITTER
BOATER
BUNTER
BUSTER
BUTTER
CANTER
CANTOR
CAPTOR
CARTER
CASTER
CASTOR
CENTER
COLTER
COOTER
COPTER
COSTAR
COTTER
COUTER
CRATER
CURTER
CUSTER
CUTTER
DAFTER
DARTER
DEBTOR
DEFTER
DEXTER
DIETER
DOCTOR
DUSTER
EASTER
EDITOR
ELATER
EMOTER
EMPTOR
EXETER
FACTOR
FALTER
FASTER
FATTER
FESTER
FETTER
FILTER
FITTER
FOOTER
FOSTER
GAITER
GARTER
GETTER
GRATER
GUITAR
GUNTER
GUTTER
HALTER
HATTER
HEATER
HECTOR
HELTER
HESTER
HINTER
HITTER
HOOTER
HOTTER
HUNTER
INSTAR
IRATER
ISHTAR
JEETER
JESTER
JITTER
JUSTER
KANTOR
KILTER
KOTTER
KRATER
KULTUR
LATTER
LECTOR
LESTER
LETTER
LICTOR
LIFTER
LINTER
LISTER
LITTER
LOITER
LOOTER
LUSTER
MARTYR
MASTER
MATTER
MEETER
MENTOR
MINTER
MISTER
MOLTER
MORTAR
MUSTER
MUTTER
NATTER
NEATER
NECTAR
NESTER
NESTOR
NEUTER
NUTTER
OBITER
OERTER
ORATOR
OUSTER
OYSTER
PALTER
PASTOR
PATTER
PELTER
PERTER
PESTER
PETTER
PEWTER
PIETER
PINTER
PITTER
PLATER
PORTER
POSTER
POTTER
POUTER
PRATER
PRETER
PUNTER
PUTTER
QINTAR
QUOTER
RAFTER
RANTER
RAPTOR
RASTER
RATTER
RECTOR
RENTER
RESTER
REUTER
RHETOR
RIOTER
RITTER
ROOTER
ROSTER
ROTTER
ROUTER
SALTER
SANTIR
SCOTER
SEATER
SECTOR
SETTER
SIFTER
SINTER
SISTER
SITTER
SKATER
SLATER
SOFTER
SORTER
SOUTER
STATER
STATOR
SUITOR
SUMTER
SUTTER
TARTAR
TARTER
TASTER
TATTER
TAUTER
TEETER
TENTER
TESTER
TILTER
TINTER
TITTER
TOOTER
TOTTER
TOUTER
TRITER
ULSTER
UNITER
VASTER
VECTOR
VENTER
VICTOR
WAITER
WALTER
WASTER
WELTER
WETTER
WHITER
WINTER
WISTER
WRITER
WYNTER
XYSTER
YESTER

TS••••
TSETSE
TSHIRT

T•S•••
TASKED
TASMAN
TASSEL
TASSES
TASTED
TASTER
TASTES
TESLAS
TESSIE
TESTAE
TESTED
TESTEE
TESTER
TISANE
TISHRI
TISSUE
TOSSED
TOSSER
TOSSES
TOSSUP
TUSCAN
TUSKED
TUSKER
TUSSAH
TUSSLE
TVSETS
TVSHOW

T••S••
TAGSUP
TARSAL
TARSUS
TASSEL
TASSES
TEASED
TEASEL
TEASER
TEASES
TEASET
TEESUP
TENSED
TENSER
TENSES
TENSOR
TERSER
TESSIE
THESES
THESIS
THESIX
THISBE
THUSLY
TIESIN
TIESUP
TILSIT
TINSEL
TIPSIN
TISSUE
TMESIS
TOASTS
TOASTY
TOCSIN
TOESIN
TONSIL
TORSOS
TOSSED
TOSSER
TOSSES
TOSSUP
TOTSUP
TOUSLE
TRASHY
TRISHA
TRISTE
TRUSTS
TRUSTY
TRYSTS
TUCSON
TULSAN
TUSSAH
TUSSLE
TWISTS
TWISTY

T•••S•
TALESE
TAMEST
TANIST
TAOISM
TAOIST
TEENSY
TERESA
THEISM
THEIST
THIRST
THRASH
THRESH
THRUSH
THRUST
THYRSI
TONISH
TOOTSY
TOROSE
TRUEST
TRUISM
TSETSE
TUBIST
TYPIST
TZUHSI

T••••S
TABLAS
TABLES
TABOOS
TABORS
TAIGAS
TAINOS
TAINTS
TAKERS
TAKINS
TALONS
TAMERS
TAMILS
TANGOS
TANKAS
TAPERS
TAPINS
TAPIRS
TARGES
TAROTS
TARSUS
TASSES
TASTES
TATARS
TATERS
TAUNTS
TAUONS
TAUPES
TAURUS
TAXERS
TAXIES
TAYRAS
TAZZAS
TBILLS
TBIRDS
TBONDS
TBONES
TEASES
TEHEES
TEMPOS
TEMPTS
TENETS
TENNIS
TENONS
TENORS
TENSES
TENTHS
TEPALS
TEPEES
TEREUS
TESLAS
TETHYS
TETONS
TETRAS
TETRIS
TEXANS
THALES
THAMES
THANES
THANKS
THATIS
THEBES
THEFTS
THEIRS
THEMES
THERMS
THESES
THESIS
THETAS
THETIS
THIGHS
THILLS
THINGS
THINKS
THIRDS
THOLES
THOMAS
THONGS
THORNS
THORPS
THREES
THRIPS
THROBS
THROES
THROWS
THRUMS
THUJAS
THUMBS
THUMPS
THUNKS
THYMUS
TIARAS
TIBIAS
TICALS
TIDIES
TIEINS
TIEUPS
TIGERS
TIGHTS
TIGRIS
TILAKS
TILDES
TILERS
TILLIS
TIMERS
TINCTS
TINGES
TIPINS
TIPUPS
TITANS
TITERS
TITHES
TITLES
TMESIS
TNOTES
TOASTS
TOBIAS
TOBIES
TOEINS
TOILES
TOKAYS
TOKENS
TOKLAS
TONERS
TONICS
TONNES
TOPERS
TOPHUS
TOPICS
TOQUES
TORAHS
TORIES
TORSOS
TORTES
TOSSES
TOTALS
TOTEMS
TOTERS
TOUGHS
TOWELS
TOWERS
TOXICS
TOXINS
TOYONS
TRACES
TRACKS
TRACTS
TRADES
TRAILS
TRAINS
TRAITS
TRAMPS
TRAVIS
TRAWLS
TREADS
TREATS
TRENDS
TRIADS
TRIALS
TRIBES
TRICES
TRICKS
TRIERS
TRIKES
TRILLS
TRINES
TRIPOS
TROLLS
TROMPS
TROOPS
TROPES
TROTHS
TROUTS
TROVES
TRUCES
TRUCKS
TRUMPS
TRUNKS
TRUSTS
TRUTHS
TRYSTS
TUBERS
TUDORS
TULIPS
TULLES
TUNERS
TUNICS
TUQUES
TURBOS
TUTORS
TVSETS
TWANGS
TWEAKS
TWEEDS
TWEETS
TWERPS
TWILLS
TWINES
TWIRLS
TWISTS
TYPERS
TYPHUS

•TS•••
ATSTUD
ETSEQQ
ITSELF

•T•S••
ATESTS
ITASCA
STASES
STASIS

•T••S•
ATBEST
ATCOST
ATEASE
ATLAST
ATMOST
ATREST
ATRISK

ATTEST
OTIOSE
STRASS
STRESS
UTMOST

•T•••S
ATBATS
ATEAMS
ATESTS
ATHENS
ATKINS
ATODDS
ATOLLS
ATONES
ATREUS
ATTARS
ATTICS
ETCHES
ETHERS
ETHICS
ETHNOS
ETUDES
ITCHES
OTHERS
OTITIS
OTTERS
PTRAPS
STACKS
STAFFS
STAGES
STAINS
STAIRS
STAKES
STALES
STALKS
STALLS
STAMPS
STANDS
STAPES
STARES
STARTS
STASES
STASIS
STATES
STATUS
STAVES
STEADS
STEAKS
STEALS
STEAMS
STEEDS
STEELS
STEEPS
STEERS
STEINS
STELES
STENOS
STERES
STERNS
STICKS
STIFFS
STILES
STILLS
STILTS
STINGS
STINKS
STINTS
STIPES
STOATS
STOCKS
STOICS
STOKES
STOLES
STOMAS
STOMPS
STONES
STOOLS
STOOPS
STOPES
STORES
STORKS
STORMS
STORRS
STOUPS
STOUTS
STOVES
STRADS
STRAPS
STRASS
STRAUS
STRAWS
STRAYS
STRESS
STREWS
STRIPS
STROPS
STRUMS
STRUTS
STUFFS
STULLS
STUMPS
STUNTS
STUPAS
STUPES
STYLES
STYLUS
UTTERS
UTURNS

••TS••
ACTSON
ACTSUP
BETSEY
CATSUP
CUTSIN
CUTSUP
DATSUN
EATSAT
EATSIN
EATSUP
FITSIN
GATSBY
GETSAT
GETSBY
GETSET
GETSIN
GETSIT
GETSON
GETSTO
GETSUP
HITSIT
HITSON
HITSUP
JETSAM
JETSET
JETSKI
JETSON
KITSCH
LETSAT
LETSBE
LETSGO
LETSIN
LETSON
LETSUP
OUTSET
PITSAW
PUTSBY
PUTSCH
PUTSIN
PUTSON
PUTSTO
PUTSUP
RATSON
SETSAT
SETSBY
SETSIN
SETSON
SETSUP
SITSIN
SITSON
SITSUP
TOTSUP
WATSON

••T•S•
APTEST
ARTIST
ATTEST
BETISE
CUTEST
CUTESY
DETEST
FETISH
IQTEST
IRTYSH
LATEST
LATISH
LUTIST
MUTEST
OBTEST
OBTUSE
POTASH
POTOSI
RETEST
SETOSE
WATUSI

••T••S
ACTORS
ALTARS
ALTERS
ANTICS
ANTRES
ARTELS
ARTOIS
ASTERS
ASTROS
ATTARS
ATTICS
AZTECS
BATHES
BATHOS
BATIKS
BATONS
BETELS
BETTAS
BITERS
BUTEOS
BUTTES
CATERS
CITERS
CITIES
CITRUS
COTTAS
CUTIES
CUTINS
CUTUPS
DATERS
DETERS
DITTOS
DITZES
DUTIES
EATERS
ENTERS
ESTERS
ESTOPS
EXTOLS
EXTRAS
FSTOPS
FUTONS
GATERS
GATORS
GETUPS
HATERS
HOTELS
INTENS
INTROS
ISTLES
KITERS
LATENS
LATHES
LATINS
LATKES
LETUPS
LITERS
LITHOS
LITMUS
LITRES
LOTAHS
LOTTOS
MATERS
MATEYS
MATHIS
MATINS
MATTES
MATZOS
METALS
METERS
METRES
METROS
MITERS
MITRES
MOTELS
MOTETS
MOTIFS
MOTORS
MOTTOS
MYTHOS
NITERS
NITRES
NOTERS
OATERS
OCTADS
OCTETS
OPTICS
ORTLES
OTTERS
PATENS
PATHOS
PATIOS
PATMOS
PATOIS
PETALS
PETERS
PITIES
PITONS
POTTOS
PUTONS
RATELS
RATERS
RATIOS
RETAGS
RETAPS
RETARS
RETIES
RETOPS
RETOWS
RETROS
ROTORS
SATINS
SATYRS
SETINS
SETTOS
SETUPS
SITARS
SITINS
SITUPS
SOTOLS
SUTRAS
TATARS
TATERS
TETHYS
TETONS
TETRAS
TETRIS
TITANS
TITERS
TITHES
TITLES
TOTALS
TOTEMS
TOTERS
TUTORS
ULTRAS
UNTIES
UTTERS
VETOES
VITALS
VOTERS
WATERS
WITHES

•••TS•
BOOTSY
CURTSY
LAOTSE
LHOTSE
TOOTSY
TSETSE

•••T•S
ABATES
ABATIS
AEETES
AGATES
AKITAS
AMATIS
AORTAS
ARETES
BANTUS
BASTES
BERTHS
BETTAS
BIOTAS
BIRTHS
BOITES
BOOTES
BOOTHS
BROTHS
BRUTES
BRUTUS
BUTTES
CACTUS
CANTOS
CARTES
CASTES
CENTOS
CESTAS
CESTOS
CESTUS
CHUTES
CLOTHS
CNOTES
COATIS
COMTES
CONTES
CORTES
COSTAS
COTTAS
CRATES
CURTIS
DANTES
DELTAS
DEPTHS
DHOTIS
DITTOS
ELATES
ELITES
ELUTES
EMOTES
ENATES
FAITHS
FESTUS
FIFTHS
FIRTHS
FLUTES
FORTAS
FORTES
FRITOS
FROTHS
GARTHS
GESTES
GIRTHS
GRATES
GRATIS
HASTES
HEATHS
HIATUS
HOSTAS
HOWTOS
JUNTAS
JUNTOS
KNOTTS
LOTTOS
MANTAS
MANTIS
MATTES
MENTIS
MONTHS
MOTTOS
MOUTHS
MUFTIS
NANTES
NINTHS
ORATES
OTITIS
PASTAS
PASTES
PASTIS
PHOTOS
PIETAS
PINTOS
PLATES
PONTES
PONTUS
POTTOS
PRATES
QANTAS
QUOTAS
QUOTES
REATAS
RECTOS
RECTUS
RIATAS
ROUTES
SANTOS
SAUTES
SCUTES
SESTOS
SETTOS
SIXTHS
SIXTUS
SKATES
SLATES
SLOTHS
SMITES
SMITHS
SNATHS
SPATES
SPITES
STATES
STATUS
SUITES
SWATHS
TASTES
TENTHS
THATIS
THETAS
THETIS
TNOTES
TORTES
TROTHS
TRUTHS
UNITAS
UNITES
VESTAS
VIRTUS
VISTAS
WASTES
WHITES
WIDTHS
WORTHS
WRATHS
WRITES
YENTAS
YOUTHS
ZLOTYS

••••TS
ABBOTS
ABORTS
ADAPTS
ADEPTS
ADMITS
ADOPTS
ADULTS
AFLATS
AGENTS
AGLETS
ALERTS
ALEUTS
ALLOTS
AMBITS
AMENTS
AMVETS
ARGOTS
ARMETS
ASCOTS
ASSETS
ATBATS
ATESTS
AUDITS
AUGHTS
AVERTS
AWAITS
BEASTS
BEAUTS
BEFITS
BEGETS
BERETS
BESETS
BESOTS
BIGHTS
BIGOTS
BLASTS
BLEATS
BLOATS
BLUETS
BLUNTS
BLURTS
BOASTS
BOOSTS
BRACTS
BRANTS
BRENTS
BRUITS
BRUNTS
BURSTS
CADETS
CARATS
CARETS
CHANTS
CHARTS
CHEATS
CHESTS
CIVETS
CLEATS
CLEFTS
CLOUTS
COAPTS
COASTS
COMETS
COOPTS
COUNTS
COURTS
COVETS
CRAFTS
CRESTS
CROATS
CROFTS
CRUETS
CRUSTS
CRYPTS
CUBITS
CULETS
DAUNTS
DAVITS
DEBITS
DEBUTS
DEFATS
DEISTS
DELFTS
DEMITS
DEPOTS
DICOTS
DIGITS
DIVOTS
DIXITS
DONETS
DONUTS
DOUBTS
DRAFTS
DRIFTS
DROITS
DUCATS
DUVETS
EBOATS
ECLATS
EDICTS
EFLATS
EGESTS
EGRETS
EIGHTS
EJECTS
ELECTS
EMMETS
ENACTS
ERECTS
ERGOTS
ERUCTS
ERUPTS
EVENTS
EVERTS
EVICTS
EXACTS
EXALTS
EXERTS
EXISTS
EXULTS
FACETS
FAGOTS
FAINTS
FAULTS
FEASTS
FEINTS
FIGHTS
FILETS
FIRSTS
FLEETS
FLINTS
FLIRTS
FLOATS
FLOUTS
FOISTS
FOUNTS
FRONTS
FROSTS
FRUITS
GAMUTS
GENETS
GHOSTS
GIANTS
GIGOTS
GLINTS
GLOATS
GODETS
GRAFTS
GRANTS
GREATS
GREETS
GRISTS
GROATS
GROUTS
GRUNTS
GSUITS
GUESTS
GUYOTS
HABITS
HAUNTS
HEARTS
HEISTS
HELOTS
HOISTS
IDIOTS
INGOTS
INLETS
INPUTS
INSETS
INUITS
ISLETS
JABOTS
JAUNTS
JOINTS
JOISTS
JOUSTS
JURATS
KARATS
KARSTS
KNOTTS
KORATS
KRAITS
LIEUTS
LIGHTS
LIMITS
MERITS
MOTETS
MOULTS
MOUNTS
MULCTS
NENETS
NIGHTS
NOHITS
NONETS
NOPETS
OCTETS
ODISTS
ONSETS
ORANTS
ORBITS
OUGHTS
OWLETS
PAINTS
PEWITS
PICOTS
PILOTS
PINOTS
PIPITS
PIVOTS
PLAITS
PLANTS
PLEATS
POINTS
POSITS
POULTS
PRINTS
QUARTS
QUESTS
QUIETS
QUILTS
QUINTS
QUIRTS
QUOITS
REACTS
REBUTS
REFITS
RELETS
REMITS
REPOTS
RESETS
REVETS
RIGHTS
RIVETS
ROASTS
ROBOTS
ROOSTS
ROUSTS
SABOTS
SAINTS
SAULTS
SCANTS
SCENTS
SCOOTS
SCOUTS
SHAFTS
SHEETS
SHIFTS
SHIRTS
SHOATS
SHOOTS
SHORTS
SHOUTS
SHUNTS
SIGHTS
SKIRTS
SLANTS
SLEETS
SMARTS
SMELTS
SNOOTS
SNORTS
SNOUTS
SPLATS
SPLITS
SPORTS
SPOUTS
SPRATS
SPRITS
SPURTS
SQUATS
STARTS
STILTS
STINTS
STOATS
STOUTS
STRUTS
STUNTS
SWEATS
SWEETS
SWIFTS
TAINTS
TAROTS
TAUNTS
TEMPTS
TENETS
THEFTS
TIGHTS
TINCTS
TOASTS
TRACTS
TRAITS
TREATS
TROUTS
TRUSTS
TRYSTS
TVSETS
TWEETS
TWISTS
UBOATS
UBOLTS
UNFITS
UNIATS
UPSETS
VALETS
VAULTS
VAUNTS
VELDTS
VISITS
WAISTS
WHEATS
WIGHTS
WORSTS
WRESTS
WRISTS
WURSTS
YACHTS
YAKUTS
YEASTS
YOKUTS

T•T•••
TATAMI
TATARS
TATERS
TATTED
TATTER
TATTLE
TATTOO
TETCHY
TETHER
TETHYS
TETONS
TETRAD
TETRAS
TETRIS
TETZEL
TITANS
TITBIT
TITERS
TITHED
TITHER
TITHES
TITIAN
TITLED
TITLES
TITTER
TITTLE
TOTALS
TOTEMS
TOTERS
TOTHER
TOTING
TOTSUP
TOTTED
TOTTER
TUTORS
TUTTUT
TUTUED

T••T••
TACTIC
TAMTAM
TANTRA
TARTAN
TARTAR
TARTER
TARTLY
TASTED
TASTER
TASTES
TATTED
TATTER
TATTLE
TATTOO
TAUTEN
TAUTER
TAUTLY
TAUTOG
TEETER
TEETHE
TENTED
TENTER
TENTHS
TESTAE
TESTED
TESTEE
TESTER
TEUTON
THATCH
THATIS
THETAS
THETIC
THETIS
THETOY
TICTAC
TILTED
TILTER
TINTED
TINTER
TIPTOE
TIPTOP
TITTER
TITTLE
TNOTES
TOATEE
TOETAP
TOLTEC
TOMTIT
TOMTOM
TOOTED
TOOTER
TOOTHY
TOOTLE
TOOTOO
TOOTSY
TOPTEN
TORTES
TOTTED
TOTTER
TOUTED
TOUTER
TRITER
TRITON
TROTHS
TRUTHS
TSETSE
TUFTED
TURTLE
TUTTUT
TWITCH
TWITTY

T•••T•
TAHITI
TAINTS
TAKETH
TAKETO
TALKTO
TAROTS
TAUNTS
TEMPTS
TENDTO
TENETS
TENUTO
TERATO
TERETE
THEFTS
THIRTY
TIGHTS
TINCTS
TOASTS
TOASTY
TODATE
TOMATO
TONITE
TOOKTO
TOYOTA
TRACTS
TRAITS
TREATS
TREATY
TRISTE
TROUTS
TRUSTS
TRUSTY
TRYSTS
TUBATE
TURNTO
TVSETS
TWEETS
TWEETY
TWENTY
TWISTS
TWISTY
TWITTY

T••••T
TABLET
TAGOUT
TALBOT
TALENT
TALKAT
TAMEST
TANIST
TAOIST
TAPOUT
TAPPET
TARGET
TARPIT
TAUGHT
TEAPOT
TEARAT
TEASET
TENANT
TERCET
TERRET
THEIST
THIRST
THREAT
THRIFT
THROAT
THRUST
THWART
TICKET
TIDBIT
TILSIT
TINHAT
TINPOT
TIPPET
TITBIT
TOBOOT
TOILET
TOMCAT
TOMTIT
TOOKIT
TOPCAT
TOPHAT
TOPOUT
TOREAT
TRICOT
TRIVET
TRUANT
TRUEST
TRYOUT
TSHIRT
TUBIST
TUCKET
TUFFET
TUMULT
TURBIT
TURBOT
TURRET
TUTTUT
TWILIT
TWOBIT
TYBALT
TYPIST
TYRANT

•TT•••
ATTACH
ATTACK
ATTAIN
ATTARS
ATTEND
ATTEST
ATTHAT
ATTICA
ATTICS
ATTILA
ATTIRE
ATTLEE
ATTRIT
ATTUNE
OTTAVA
OTTAWA
OTTERS
UTTERS

•T•T••
ATSTUD
OTITIC
OTITIS
STATED
STATER
STATES
STATIC
STATOR
STATUE
STATUS
STITCH

•T••T•
ATBATS
ATESTS
ATLATL
STACTE
STARTS
STILTS
STINTS
STOATS
STOUTS
STPETE
STRATA
STRATI
STRATO
STRUTS
STUNTS

•T•••T
ATBEST
ATCOST
ATLAST
ATMOST
ATREST
ATTEST
ATTHAT
ATTRIT
PTBOAT
STABAT
STOMAT
STOPIT
STRAIT
STREET
STRICT
STUART
STYLET
UTHANT
UTMOST

••TT••
ACTTWO
BATTED
BATTEN
BATTER
BATTLE
BATTUE
BETTAS
BETTER
BETTOR

BITTED
BITTEN
BITTER
BOTTLE
BOTTOM
BUTTED
BUTTER
BUTTES
BUTTIN
BUTTON
CATTED
CATTLE
CATTON
COTTAS
COTTEN
COTTER
COTTON
CUTTER
DITTOS
DOTTED
DOTTIE
DOTTLE
FATTED
FATTEN
FATTER
FETTER
FETTLE
FITTED
FITTER
GETTER
GOTTEN
GUTTAE
GUTTED
GUTTER
HATTED
HATTER
HATTIE
HETTIE
HITTER
HOTTEA
HOTTER
HOTTIP
HOTTUB
HUTTED
HUTTON
JETTED
JITTER
JOTTED
JUTTED
KETTLE
KITTEN
KOTTER
LATTEN
LATTER
LETTED
LETTER
LITTER
LITTLE
LOTTED
LOTTOS
LYTTON
MATTEA
MATTED
MATTEL
MATTER
MATTES
MATTIE
METTLE
MITTEN
MOTTLE
MOTTOS
MUTTER
MUTTON
NATTER
NETTED
NETTLE
NETTON
NUTTED
NUTTER
PATTED
PATTEN
PATTER
PATTON
PETTED
PETTER
PETTIT
PITTED
PITTER
POTTED
POTTER
POTTLE
POTTOS
PUTTED
PUTTEE
PUTTER
RATTAN
RATTED
RATTER
RATTLE
RATTLY
RETTON
RITTER
ROTTED
ROTTEN
ROTTER
RUTTAN
RUTTED
SETTEE
SETTER
SETTLE
SETTOS
SITTER
SOTTED
SUTTER
TATTED
TATTER
TATTLE
TATTOO
TITTER
TITTLE
TOTTED
TOTTER
TUTTUT
VETTED
WATTLE
WETTED
WETTER
WETTIG
WITTED

••T•T•
ASTUTE
ENTITY
ESTATE
GETSTO
INTOTO
METATE
MOTETS
MUTATE
NOTATE
NUTATE
OCTETS
OUTATE
PETITE
POTATO
PUTSTO
RATITE
ROTATE
SHTETL
UMTATA

••T••T
ACTOUT
APTEST
ARTIST
ATTEST
ATTHAT
ATTRIT
CATGUT
CUTEST
CUTLET
CUTOUT
DETECT
DETENT
DETEST
EATOUT
EATSAT
EXTANT
EXTENT
EXTORT
FATCAT
GETOUT
GETSAT
GETSET
GETSIT
GOTOIT
GOTOUT
HITSIT
HOTPOT
INTACT
INTENT
INTUIT
IQTEST
JETSET
KITKAT
LATENT
LATEST
LETOUT
LETSAT
LITOUT
LUTIST
MOTMOT
MUTANT
MUTEST
NATANT
NITWIT
NOTYET
NUTLET
OBTEST
OCTANT
OPTOUT
OUTACT
OUTEAT
OUTFIT
OUTHIT
OUTLET
OUTPUT
OUTSET
OUTWIT
PATENT
PETTIT
POTENT
PUTOUT
PUTPUT
RETEST
RETORT
ROTGUT
SATOUT
SETOUT
SETSAT
SITOUT
SOTHAT
TITBIT
TUTTUT
WITHIT

•••TT•
ANATTO
BEATTY
BHUTTO
BLATTY
BLOTTO
BRATTY
CHATTY
CLOTTY
FRETTY
FRUTTI
GHETTO
GIOTTO
GRITTY
GROTTO
GROTTY
KNOTTS
KNOTTY
LIOTTA
NEXTTO
ODETTA
ODETTE
PLATTE
PRETTY
SCOTTO
SCOTTY
SLITTY
SMUTTY
SPOTTY
TWITTY
WANTTO
YVETTE

•••T•T
BEATIT
DIKTAT
HINTAT
HOOTAT
IGETIT
KEPTAT
LESTAT
LOSTIT
MUSTNT
OBSTET
PETTIT
QUITIT
SEPTET
SESTET
SEXTET
SHOTAT
TOMTIT
TUTTUT
WENTAT

••••TT
ABBOTT
ALCOTT
ARNETT
CAVETT
DEWITT
EMMETT
JEWETT
JOWETT
LOVETT
MELOTT

TU••••
TUAREG
TUBATE
TUBBED
TUBERS
TUBING
TUBIST
TUBMAN
TUCANA
TUCHUN
TUCKED
TUCKER
TUCKET
TUCKIN
TUCSON
TUDORS
TUFFET
TUFTED
TUGGED
TUGGER
TUGRIK
TUILLE
TULANE
TULARE
TULIPS
TULLES
TULSAN
TUMBLE
TUMEFY
TUMULI
TUMULT
TUNDRA
TUNEIN
TUNERS
TUNEUP
TUNICA
TUNICS
TUNING
TUNNEL
TUNNEY
TUPELO
TUPIAN
TUQUES
TURBAN
TURBID
TURBIT
TURBOS
TURBOT
TUREEN
TURFED
TURGID
TURGOR
TURING
TURKEY
TURKIC
TURNED
TURNER
TURNIN
TURNIP
TURNON
TURNTO
TURNUP
TURRET
TURTLE
TUSCAN
TUSKED
TUSKER
TUSSAH
TUSSLE
TUTORS
TUTTUT
TUTUED
TUVALU
TUXEDO
TUYERE

T•U•••
TAUGHT
TAUNTS
TAUONS
TAUPES
TAURUS
TAUTEN
TAUTER
TAUTLY
TAUTOG
TEUTON
THUJAS
THUMBS
THUMPS
THUNKS
THUSLY
TOUCAN
TOUCHE
TOUCHY
TOUGHS
TOUGHY
TOULON
TOUPEE
TOURED
TOURER
TOUSLE
TOUTED
TOUTER
TRUANT
TRUCES
TRUCKS
TRUDGE
TRUEST
TRUING
TRUISM
TRUMAN
TRUMPS
TRUNKS
TRUSTS
TRUSTY
TRUTHS
TZUHSI

T••U••
TABULA
TELUGU
TENURE
TENUTO
THOUGH
THRUMS
THRUSH
THRUST
TIEUPS
TIPUPS
TOLUCA
TOQUES
TRAUMA
TRIUNE
TROUGH
TROUPE
TROUTS
TROUVE
TUMULI
TUMULT
TUQUES
TUTUED

T•••U•
TAGOUT
TAGSUP
TAKEUP
TALCUM
TALKUP
TALMUD
TAMMUZ
TANGUY
TANKUP
TAPOUT
TARSUS
TAURUS
TEACUP
TEAMUP
TEARUP
TEDEUM
TEDIUM
TEEDUP
TEESUP
TEREUS
THYMUS
TIDYUP
TIEDUP
TIESUP
TISSUE
TOBRUK
TONEUP
TONGUE
TOOKUP
TOOLUP
TOPGUN
TOPHUS
TOPOUT
TOREUP
TORQUE
TOSSUP
TOTSUP
TRIPUP
TRYOUT
TUCHUN
TUNEUP
TURNUP
TUTTUT
TYPEUP
TYPHUS

T••••U
TELEDU
TELUGU
TUVALU

•TU•••
ETUDES
ITURBI
STUART
STUBBY
STUCCO
STUDIO
STUFFS
STUFFY
STULLS
STUMPS
STUMPY
STUNTS
STUPAS
STUPES
STUPID
STUPOR
STURDY
UTURNS

•T•U••
ATTUNE
STLUKE
STOUPS
STOUTS
STRUCK
STRUMS
STRUNG
STRUTS

•T••U•
ATREUS
ATRIUM
ATSTUD
STAPUF
STATUE
STATUS
STAYUP
STEPUP
STIRUP
STOPUP
STPAUL
STRAUS
STROUD
STYLUS

••TU••
ACTUAL
ARTURO
ASTUTE
ATTUNE
AUTUMN
BATUMI
BUTUNG
CUTUPS
DATURA
FUTURE
GETUPS
INTUIT
INTUNE
INTURN
LETUPS
MATURE
MUTUAL
NATURE
OBTUND
OBTUSE
PETULA
RETUNE
RETURN
RITUAL
ROTUND
SATURN
SETUPS
SITUPS
SUTURE
TUTUED
UNTUNE
UPTURN
WATUSI

••T•U•
ACTIUM
ACTOUT
ACTSUP
ANTEUP
ANTRUM
ARTFUL
ARTGUM
ARTHUR
AUTEUR
BATTUE
CATGUT
CATSUP
CITRUS
CUTOUT
CUTSUP
DATSUN
DETOUR
EATOUT
EATSUP
FITFUL
GETOUT
GETSUP
GOTOUT
HITSUP
HOTTUB
JETGUN
LATIUM
LATOUR
LETOUT
LETSUP
LITMUS
LITOUT
ONTOUR
OPTOUT
OSTIUM
OUTGUN
OUTPUT
OUTRUN
POTFUL
PUTOUT
PUTPUT
PUTSUP
RETOUR
ROTGUT
SATOUT
SETOUT
SETSUP
SITOUT
SITSUP
TOTSUP
TUTTUT
UNTRUE
VATFUL

••T••U
BATEAU
GATEAU

•••TU•
ADYTUM
ATSTUD
BANTUS
BATTUE
BEATUP
BOOTUP
BRUTUS
CACTUS
CESTUS
CHATUP
DICTUM
DUSTUP
FESTUS
HEATUP
HIATUS
HOTTUB
KEPTUP
KULTUR
LIFTUP
MANTUA
PENTUP
PONTUS
RECTUS
RESTUP
SENTUP
SEPTUM
SHOTUP
SHUTUP
SIXTUS
STATUE
STATUS
SUITUP
TUTTUT
VIRTUE
VIRTUS
WAITUP
WENTUP

•••T•U
ALATAU
LAOTZU

••••TU
INSITU

TV••••
TVSETS
TVSHOW

T•V•••
TAVERN
TIVOLI
TUVALU

T••V••
TRAVEL
TRAVIS
TREVOR
TRIVET
TRIVIA
TROVES

T•••V•
THEYVE
THIEVE
THRIVE
THROVE
TROUVE
TWELVE

•T•V••
STAVED
STAVES
STEVEN
STEVIE
STIVER
STIVIC
STOVER
STOVES

•T••V•
OTTAVA
STARVE
STEEVE
STRIVE
STROVE

••TV••
LATVIA

••T•V•
ACTIVE
DATIVE
MOTIVE
NATIVE
OCTAVE
OCTAVO
OTTAVA
VOTIVE

•••T•V
GUSTAV
LAPTEV
ROSTOV

TW••••
TWANGS
TWANGY
TWEAKS
TWEEDS
TWEEDY
TWEETS
TWEETY
TWEEZE
TWELVE
TWENTY
TWERPS
TWIGGY
TWILIT
TWILLS
TWINED
TWINES
TWINGE
TWIRLS
TWISTS
TWISTY
TWITCH
TWITTY
TWOBIT
TWOFER
TWOPLY
TWOWAY

T•W•••
TAWDRY
TAWING
THWACK
THWART
TOWAGE
TOWARD
TOWCAR
TOWELS
TOWERS
TOWERY
TOWHEE
TOWING
TOWNER
TOWNIE

T••W••
TAIWAN
THAWED
THEWIZ
TRAWLS
TROWED
TROWEL
TWOWAY

T•••W•
TARAWA
THROWN
THROWS

T••••W
TALLOW
TVSHOW

•TW•••
ATWILL
ATWOOD
ATWORK

•T•W••
STEWED
STEWER
STOWED

•T••W•
OTTAWA
STRAWS
STREWN
STREWS

••TW••
HOTWAR
NITWIT
OUTWIT

••T•W•
ACTTWO
INTOWN
MOTOWN
OTTAWA
RETOWS
UPTOWN

••T••W
ANTCOW
NOTNOW
OUTLAW
PITSAW

•••TW•
ACTTWO
ONETWO

•••T•W
BESTOW
KOWTOW
SKITOW

T•X•••
TAXERS
TAXIED
TAXIES
TAXING
TAXMAN
TAXMEN
TEXACO
TEXANS
TEXMEX
TOXICS
TOXINS
TUXEDO

T••X••
TRIXIE

T••••X
TEXMEX
THESIX
THORAX
TOMMIX

••T••X
HATBOX
HOTBOX
KITFOX
MATRIX
OUTFOX
RATEDX

•••T•X
CORTEX
JOETEX
LASTEX
PRETAX
PROTAX
SINTAX
SURTAX
SYNTAX
VERTEX
VORTEX

TY••••
TYBALT
TYCOBB
TYCOON
TYPERS
TYPEUP
TYPHUS
TYPIFY
TYPING
TYPIST
TYRANT
TYRIAN
TYRONE

T•Y•••
TAYLOR
TAYRAS
THYMUS
THYRSI
TOYDOG
TOYING
TOYONS
TOYOTA
TRYFOR
TRYING
TRYOUT
TRYSTS
TUYERE

T••Y••
THAYER
THEYLL
THEYRE
THEYVE
TIDYUP

T•••Y•
TAMAYO
TETHYS
TIEDYE
TOKAYS

T••••Y
TAGDAY
TAMELY
TANGLY
TANGUY
TARTLY
TAUTLY
TAWDRY
TEAPOY
TEDKEY
TEENSY
TETCHY
THEORY
THETOY
THINLY
THIRTY
THORNY
THUSLY
TIDILY
TIMELY
TINGLY
TINKLY
TOASTY
TOMBOY
TOOTHY
TOOTSY
TOUCHY
TOUGHY
TOWERY
TRACEY
TRAPPY
TRASHY
TREATY
TREBLY
TRENDY
TRICKY
TRIGLY
TRILBY
TRIMLY
TRIPLY
TROPHY
TRUSTY
TUMEFY
TUNNEY
TURKEY
TWANGY
TWEEDY
TWEETY
TWENTY
TWIGGY
TWISTY
TWITTY
TWOPLY
TWOWAY
TYPIFY

•TY•••
ETYMOL
ETYMON
STYLED
STYLER
STYLES
STYLET
STYLUS
STYMIE
STYRIA
STYRON

•T•Y••
STAYED
STAYON
STAYUP

•T••Y•
STRAYS

•T•••Y
STABLY
STALKY
STANKY
STARRY
STEADY
STEAMY
STEELY
STICKY
STILLY
STIMPY
STINGY
STINKY
STOCKY
STODGY
STOREY
STORMY
STUBBY
STUFFY
STUMPY
STURDY

••TY••
ECTYPE
IRTYSH
NOTYET
RETYPE
SATYRS

••T•Y•
LATOYA
MATEYS
METHYL
TETHYS

••T••Y
ANTONY
ARTERY
ASTRAY
BATBOY
BETONY
BETRAY
BETSEY
BOTANY
BOTFLY
CATCHY
CATHAY
CITIFY
CUTESY
DATARY
EATERY
ENTITY
GATSBY
GETSBY
JITNEY
LATELY
LETFLY
LITANY
MOTLEY
MUTELY
MUTINY
NETPAY
NOTARY
NOTIFY
OUTCRY
OUTLAY
PATCHY
PUTSBY
RATIFY
RATTLY
ROTARY
SATINY
SETSBY
TETCHY
UNTIDY
VOTARY
WATERY
WATNEY
WETFLY
WITCHY

•••TY•
ACETYL
DACTYL
MARTYR
ZLOTYS

•••T•Y
APATHY
BEATTY
BLATTY
BOOTSY
BRATTY
CHATTY
CLOTTY
COSTLY
CURTLY
CURTSY
DEFTLY
DESTRY
EARTHY
FILTHY
FLATLY
FRETTY
FROTHY
GANTRY
GENTLY
GENTRY
GLITZY

GRITTY
GROTTY
ICHTHY
JUSTLY
KLUTZY
KNOTTY
LASTLY
MEETLY
MOSTLY
MOUTHY
NEATLY
PALTRY
PANTRY
PARTLY
PASTRY
PELTRY
PERTLY
POETRY
PORTLY
PRETTY
RAPTLY
RATTLY
SCOTTY
SENTRY
SLITHY
SLITTY
SMITHY
SMUTTY
SOFTLY
SPOTTY
SUBTLY
SULTRY
TARTLY
TAUTLY
THETOY
TOOTHY
TOOTSY
TWITTY
VASTLY
VESTRY
WENTBY
WINTRY
WORTHY

••••TY

ACUITY
BEATTY
BEAUTY
BLATTY
BOUNTY
BRATTY
CAVITY
CHATTY
CHESTY
CLOTTY
COMITY
COUNTY
CRAFTY
CRUSTY
DAINTY
DEPUTY
DIMITY
DRAFTY
EIGHTY
ENMITY
ENTITY
EQUITY
FAULTY
FAWLTY
FEALTY
FEISTY
FIXITY
FLINTY
FRETTY
FROSTY
FRUITY
GAIETY
GRITTY
GROTTY
GROUTY
GUILTY
HEARTY
JAUNTY
KNOTTY
LAXITY
LEALTY
LENITY
LEVITY
MIGHTY
MOIETY
MOUNTY
NICETY
NIGHTY
NINETY
NUDITY
ODDITY
PARITY
PIGSTY
PLASTY
PLENTY
POINTY
POLITY
PRETTY
PURITY
QWERTY
RARITY
REALTY
SAFETY
SANITY
SCANTY
SCOTTY
SHANTY
SHIFTY
SHIRTY
SHORTY
SLEETY
SLITTY
SMARTY
SMUTTY
SNOOTY
SPORTY
SPOTTY
SURETY
SWEATY
THIRTY
TOASTY
TREATY
TRUSTY
TWEETY
TWENTY
TWISTY
TWITTY
UBIETY
UPPITY
VANITY
VERITY
YEASTY

TZ••••

TZUHSI

T•Z•••

TAZZAS

T••Z••

TARZAN
TAZZAS
TETZEL

T•••Z•

TWEEZE

T••••Z

TABRIZ
TAMMUZ
THEWIZ
TROPEZ

•TZ•••

ITZHAK

•T••Z•

STANZA

••TZ••

DITZES
MATZOH
MATZOS
TETZEL

•••TZ•

GLITZY
KLUTZY
LAOTZU

•••T•Z

CORTEZ
CURTIZ
MONTEZ

••••TZ

BLINTZ
CHINTZ
DONITZ
ERSATZ
IGNATZ
KIBITZ
KOONTZ
KRANTZ
MORITZ
NIMITZ
QUARTZ
SPRITZ

UA••••

UAKARI

U•A•••

UBANGI
UGANDA
UKASES
UNABLE
UNAGED
UNARMS
UNAWED
URACIL
URAEUS
URALIC
URALSK
URANIA
URANIC
URANUS
USABLE
USABLY
USAGES
USANCE
UTAHAN
UVALUE

U••A••

UAKARI
UBOATS
UCLANS
UGGAMS
UHLANS
UJJAIN
ULLAGE
UMIAKS
UMLAUT
UMTATA
UNBARS
UNCAGE
UNCAPS
UNCASE
UNEASE
UNEASY
UNFAIR
UNHAND
UNIATE
UNIATS
UNJAMS
UNLACE
UNLADE
UNLAID
UNLASH
UNMADE
UNMAKE
UNMANS
UNMASK
UNPACK
UNPAID
UNSAFE
UNSAID
UNSAYS
UNTACK
UNWARY
UPCAST
UPDATE
UPLAND
UPTAKE
UPWARD
URBANA
URBANE
URIALS
USMAIL
USUALS
UTHANT

U•••A•

UGRIAN
ULLMAN
ULTRAS
UMBRAE
UMBRAL
UMBRAS
UNCIAL
UNCLAD
UNDRAW
UNGUAL
UNITAL
UNITAS
UNIVAC
UNLEAD
UNLOAD
UNREAD
UNREAL
UNSEAL
UNSEAT
UNSNAG
UNSNAP
UNTRAP
UNWRAP
UPBEAT
UPLOAD
UPROAR
UTAHAN
UVULAE
UVULAR
UVULAS
UZZIAH

U••••A

UGANDA
ULTIMA
UMBRIA
UMTATA
URANIA
URBANA
URSULA
UTOPIA

•UA•••

DUALLY
DUARTE
GUACOS
GUARDS
GUAVAS
JUAREZ
LUANDA
NUANCE
QUACKS
QUADRI
QUAFFS
QUAGGA
QUAGGY
QUAHOG
QUAILS
QUAINT
QUAKED
QUAKER
QUAKES
QUALMS
QUANTA
QUARKS
QUARRY
QUARTO
QUARTS
QUARTZ
QUASAR
QUAVER
QUAYLE
RUANAS
RUANDA
SUAVER
TUAREG

•U•A••

AUBADE
AUFAIT
AUPAIR
BUTANE
CUBAGE
CUIABA
CUNARD
CUNAXA
CURACY
CURARE
CURATE
DUCATS
DUNANT
DURANT
DUVALL
FUGARD
FULANI
GUIANA
GULAGS
GUYANA
HUMANE
HUMANS
JUDAEA
JUDAIC
JUMADA
JURADO
JURATS
KULAKS
KURALT
KUVASZ
KUWAIT
LUNACY
LUNATE
LUSAKA
LUXATE
MUFASA
MUGABE
MURALS
MURANO
MUTANT
MUTATE
NUTATE
OUTACT
OUTAGE
OUTATE
PURACE
QUEASY
RUGATE
RUPAUL
SUBARU
SUGARS
SUGARY
SUMACS
SURAHS
SUSANN
TUBATE
TUCANA
TULANE
TULARE
TUVALU
YUKATA
YUKAWA

•U••A•

AUDIAL
AUGEAN
BUCCAL
BULGAR
BULLAE
BUMRAP
BUNYAN
BUREAU
BURGAS
BURLAP
BURMAN
BUROAK
BURSAE
BURSAL
BURSAR
BURSAS
BUSBAR
BUSMAN
CUNEAL
CURIAE
CURIAL
CUSHAW
DUCTAL
DUNBAR
DUNCAN
DUNHAM
DURBAN
DURBAR
DURHAM
DURIAN
FUJIAN
FULMAR
GUAVAS
GUFFAW
GUITAR
GULLAH
GUNMAN
GUNNAR
GUSTAV
GUTTAE
HUBCAP
HURRAH
HURRAY
HUSSAR
HUZZAH
HUZZAS
JUBBAH
JULIAN
JUMPAT
JUNEAU
JUNTAS
KUBLAI
KURGAN
LUCIAN
LUMBAR
MUDCAT
MUDRAS
MULLAH
MULLAS
MURRAY
MUSCAT
MUSIAL
MUTUAL
NUBIAN
NUCHAE
NUCHAL
NULLAH
NUMBAT
OUTEAT
OUTLAW
OUTLAY
OUTRAN
PULSAR
PUNJAB
PUNKAH
PURDAH
PUTNAM
QUASAR
QUMRAN
QUOTAS
RUANAS
RUDMAN
RUMBAS
RUNWAY
RUPIAH
RUTTAN
SUBWAY
SUCHAS
SUKKAH
SULTAN
SUMMAE
SUMMAS
SUNDAE
SUNDAY
SUNRAY
SUNTAN
SURTAX
SUTRAS
TUBMAN
TULSAN
TUPIAN
TURBAN
TUSCAN
TUSSAH
VULCAN
VULGAR
YUCCAS
YUNNAN

•U•••A

AURIGA
AURORA
BUDDHA
BULOVA
BUQSHA
BUSHWA
CUESTA
CUIABA
CUNAXA
CUPOLA
DUENNA
DULLEA
DUNERA
DURYEA
EUBOEA
EUDORA
EUPNEA
EUREKA
EUROPA
FULCRA
GUIANA
GUINEA
GURKHA
GUYANA
JUDAEA
JUDOKA
JUMADA
LUANDA
LUMINA
LUNULA
LUSAKA
MUCOSA
MUFASA
MULETA
MURCIA
NUMINA
NUTRIA
PUEBLA
PURINA
QUAGGA
QUANTA
QUINOA
QUOKKA
QUOTHA
RUANDA
RUMINA
RUSSIA
TUCANA
TUNDRA
TUNICA
YUKATA
YUKAWA

••UA••

ACUATE
AKUAKU
AQUATE
EDUARD
EQUALS
EQUATE
IGUACU
IGUANA
SOUARI
SQUABS
SQUADS
SQUALL
SQUARE
SQUASH
SQUATS
SQUAWK
STUART
TRUANT
USUALS
YOUALL
ZOUAVE

••U•A•

ALULAE
ALULAR
ANURAN
AOUDAD
ARUBAN
BEULAH
BHUTAN
BRUMAL
BRUTAL
CAUDAL
CAUSAL
CHUKAR
CIUDAD
COUGAR
CRURAL
FAUNAE
FAUNAL
FAUNAS
FEUDAL
FRUGAL
HAUSAS
KAUNAS
KOUFAX
MAUMAU
NEUMAN
NEURAL
NOUGAT
OCULAR
OVULAR
PLURAL
SAUNAS
SCUBAS
SEURAT
SQUEAK
SQUEAL
STUPAS
THUJAS
TOUCAN
TRUMAN
UVULAE
UVULAR
UVULAS
WAUSAU

••U••A

ALUMNA
APULIA
AQUILA
CHUKKA
IGUANA
KAUNDA
LOUISA
MAURYA
NAUSEA
NOUMEA
RHUMBA
ZEUGMA

•••UA•

ACTUAL
ANNUAL
CAGUAS
CASUAL
EMQUAD
ENQUAD
GENUAL
JAGUAR
LEHUAS
LOQUAT
MANUAL
MUTUAL
PADUAN
PAPUAN
RITUAL
SIOUAN
UNGUAL
VISUAL

•••U•A

ARJUNA
BELUGA
CAYUGA
COPULA
CREUSA
DATURA
FACULA
FIBULA
HECUBA
KAHUNA
KORUNA
LACUNA
LAGUNA
LAPUTA
LIGULA
LUNULA
MACULA
MADURA
MAKUTA
MAZUMA
MEDUSA
NEBULA
NERUDA
OSCULA
PARULA
PETULA
PLEURA
PNEUMA
RADULA
REMUDA
SEGURA
TABULA
TOLUCA
TRAUMA
URSULA
VARUNA
VICUNA
YORUBA

••••UA

JOSHUA
KAHLUA
KAILUA
LINGUA
MANTUA
NASHUA

UB••••

UBANGI
UBIETY
UBOATS
UBOLTS

U•B•••

UMBELS
UMBERS
UMBRAE
UMBRAL
UMBRAS
UMBRIA
UNBARS
UNBELT
UNBEND
UNBENT
UNBIND
UNBOLT
UNBORN
UPBEAT
UPBOWS
URBANA
URBANE
UZBEKS

U••B••

UNABLE
USABLE
USABLY

U•••B•

UNROBE

•UB•••

AUBADE
AUBREY
AUBURN
BUBBLE
BUBBLY
CUBAGE
CUBEBS
CUBICS
CUBING
CUBISM
CUBIST
CUBITS
CUBOID
DUBBED
DUBBIN
DUBCEK
DUBLIN
DUBOIS
EUBOEA
HUBBLE
HUBBLY
HUBBUB
HUBCAP
HUBERT
HUBRIS
JUBBAH
KUBLAI
LUBBER
LUBECK
LUBING
LUBLIN
NUBBED
NUBBIN
NUBBLE
NUBIAN
NUBILE
PUBLIC
RUBBED
RUBBER
RUBBLE
RUBBLY
RUBENS
RUBIED
RUBIES
RUBIFY
RUBLES
RUBOUT
RUBRIC
RUBSIN
SUBARU
SUBBED
SUBDEB
SUBDUE
SUBGUM
SUBITO
SUBLET
SUBMIT
SUBORN
SUBSET
SUBTLE
SUBTLY
SUBURB
SUBWAY
TUBATE
TUBBED
TUBERS
TUBING
TUBIST
TUBMAN

•U•B••

BUBBLE
BUBBLY
BULBIL
BULBUL
BUMBLE
BUMBRY
BURBLE
BURBLY
BURBOT
BUSBAR
BUSBOY
CUMBER
CURBED
DUBBED
DUBBIN
DUMBER
DUMBLY
DUNBAR
DURBAN
DURBAR
DURBIN
FUMBLE
GUMBEL
GUMBOS
HUBBLE
HUBBLY
HUBBUB
HUMBLE
HUMBLY
HUMBUG
JUBBAH
JUMBLE
JUMBOS
LUBBER
LUMBAR
LUMBER
MUMBLE
MUMBLY
NUBBED
NUBBIN
NUBBLE
NUMBAT
NUMBED
NUMBER
NUMBLY
OUTBID
PUEBLA
PUEBLO
QUEBEC
RUBBED
RUBBER
RUBBLE
RUBBLY
RUMBAS
RUMBLE
RUMBLY
SUBBED
TUBBED
TUMBLE
TURBAN
TURBID
TURBIT
TURBOS
TURBOT

•U••B•

CUBEBS
CUIABA
JUJUBE
MUGABE
PUTSBY

•U•••B

HUBBUB
PUNJAB
SUBDEB
SUBURB
SUPERB

••UB••

ANUBIS
ARUBAN
BAUBLE
BOUBOU
CHUBBY
CLUBBY
DAUBED
DAUBER
DAUBES
DOUBLE
DOUBLY
DOUBTS
GRUBBY
REUBEN
SCUBAS
STUBBY
YOUBET

••U•B•

BLURBS
CHUBBY
CLUBBY
CRUMBS
CRUMBY
EXURBS
GRUBBY
ITURBI
PLUMBS
RHUMBA
RHUMBS
SQUABS
SQUIBB
SQUIBS
STUBBY
THUMBS

••U••B

SQUIBB

•••UB•

DANUBE
HECUBA
JUJUBE
REDUBS
SCRUBS
SHRUBS
YORUBA

•••U•B

BENUMB
SUBURB

••••UB

BEDAUB
CHERUB
HOTTUB
HUBBUB

UC••••

UCLANS

U•C•••

ULCERS
UNCAGE
UNCAPS
UNCASE
UNCHIC
UNCIAL
UNCLAD
UNCLES
UNCLOG
UNCOIL
UNCOOL
UNCORK
UNCURL
UPCAST
URCHIN

U••C••

UNICEF
URACIL

U•••C•

UNESCO
UNLACE
UNLOCK
UNPACK
UNTACK
UPTICK
USANCE

U••••C

UNCHIC
UNIFIC
UNIVAC
URALIC
URANIC

•UC•••

BUCCAL
BUCKED
BUCKET
BUCKLE
BUCKUP
CUCKOO
DUCATS
DUCHIN
DUCKED
DUCTAL
EUCHRE
EUCLID
KUCHEN
LUCENT
LUCIAN
LUCITE
LUCIUS
LUCKED
MUCKED
MUCKUP
MUCOSA
MUCOUS
NUCHAE
NUCHAL
NUCLEI
NUCLEO
PUCKER
RUCHES
RUCKED
RUCKUS
SUCCES
SUCCOR
SUCHAS
SUCKED
SUCKER
SUCKIN
TUCANA
TUCHUN
TUCKED
TUCKER
TUCKET
TUCKIN
TUCSON
YUCCAS

•U•C••

BUCCAL
BUNCHE
BUNCOS
DUBCEK
DULCET
DUNCAN
DUNCES
FULCRA
GUACOS
HUBCAP
JUICED
JUICER
JUICES
JUNCOS
MUDCAT
MULCTS
MUNCIE
MURCIA
MUSCAT
MUSCLE
MUSCLY
NUECES
NUNCIO
OUNCES
OUTCRY
PUNCHY
QUACKS
QUICHE
RUNCIE
SUCCES
SUCCOR
SULCUS
TUSCAN
VULCAN
YUCCAS

•U••C•

CUBICS
CURACY
DUROCS
EUNICE
EUNUCH
LUBECK
LUNACY
MUNICH
NUANCE
OUTACT
PUMICE
PURACE
PUTSCH
QUENCH
QUINCE
QUINCY
SUMACS
SUNOCO
TUNICA
TUNICS

ZURICH

•U•••C

CULTIC
CUPRIC
FUSTIC
JUDAIC
PUBLIC
QUEBEC
RUBRIC
RUNDMC
RUSTIC
TURKIC

••UC••

BAUCIS
BOUCLE
CAUCHO
CAUCUS
CHUCKS
CLUCKS
CRUCES
DEUCED
DEUCES
EDUCED
EDUCES
ERUCTS
FAUCES
FAUCET
GAUCHE
GAUCHO
LOUCHE
PLUCKS
PLUCKY
POUCHY
SAUCED
SAUCER
SAUCES
SHUCKS
STUCCO
TOUCAN
TOUCHE
TOUCHY
TRUCES
TRUCKS

••U•C•

BOUNCE
BOUNCY
BRUNCH
CHURCH
CLUTCH
CRUNCH
CRUTCH
HAUNCH
IGUACU
JOUNCE
JOUNCY
LAUNCH
NAUTCH
PAUNCH
POUNCE
SCUTCH
SLUICE
SMUTCH
SOURCE
STUCCO

••U••C

COURIC

•••UC•

ABDUCT
ADDUCE
ADDUCT
AVOUCH
BARUCH
CROUCH
DEDUCE
DEDUCT
EUNUCH
GROUCH
INDUCE
INDUCT
INLUCK
REDUCE
RELUCT
SEDUCE
SLOUCH
SPRUCE
STRUCK
TOLUCA
ZANUCK

UD••••

UDDERS

U•D•••

UDDERS
UNDIES
UNDINE
UNDOER
UNDOES
UNDONE
UNDRAW
UNDULY
UNDYED
UPDATE
UPDIKE

U••D••

USEDTO
USEDUP

U•••D•

UGANDA
UNLADE
UNMADE
UNTIDY
UPENDS
UPSIDE
URSIDS

U••••D

UNAGED
UNAWED
UNBEND
UNBIND
UNCLAD
UNDYED
UNFOLD
UNGIRD
UNHAND
UNHEED
UNIPOD
UNITED
UNKIND
UNLAID
UNLEAD
UNLOAD
UNPAID
UNREAD
UNSAID
UNSHED
UNSHOD
UNSOLD
UNTIED
UNTOLD
UNTROD
UNUSED
UNWIND
UPHELD
UPHOLD
UPLAND
UPLOAD
UPWARD
UPWIND
USERID

•UD•••

AUDENS
AUDIAL
AUDIOS
AUDITS
AUDREY
BUDDED
BUDDHA
BUDGED
BUDGES
BUDGET
BUDGIE
CUDDLE
CUDDLY
CUDGEL
DUDEEN
DUDLEY
EUDORA
FUDDLE
FUDGED
FUDGES
GUDRUN
HUDDLE
HUDSON
JUDAEA
JUDAIC
JUDDER
JUDGED
JUDGES
JUDITH
JUDOKA
KUDZUS
LUDDEN
LUDENS
LUDLUM
LUDWIG
MUDCAT
MUDDED
MUDDER
MUDDLE
MUDEEL
MUDHEN
MUDPIE
MUDRAS
NUDGED
NUDGER
NUDGES
NUDIST
NUDITY
NUDNIK
PUDDLE
PUDDLY
RUDDER
RUDDLE
RUDELY
RUDEST
RUDMAN
RUDOLF
SUDDEN
SUDSED
SUDSES
TUDORS

•U•D••

BUDDED
BUDDHA
BUNDLE
BURDEN
CUDDLE
CUDDLY
CURDED
CURDLE
DUMDUM
DUNDEE
FUDDLE
FUNDED
GUIDED
GUIDES
GUIDON
GUNDOG
HUDDLE
HURDLE
JUDDER
LUDDEN
LUNDEN
MUDDED
MUDDER
MUDDLE
MURDER
OUTDID
PUDDLE
PUDDLY
PUNDIT
PURDAH
PURDUE
QUADRI
RUDDER
RUDDLE
RUNDLE
RUNDMC
RUNDRY
SUBDEB
SUBDUE
SUDDEN
SUEDES
SUNDAE
SUNDAY
SUNDER
SUNDEW
SUNDOG
SUNDRY
TUNDRA
ZUIDER

•U••D•

AUBADE
BUILDS
CUPIDS
GUARDS
GUILDS
JUMADA
JURADO
LUANDA
RUANDA
TUXEDO

•U•••D

AUFOND
AUGEND
BUCKED
BUDDED
BUDGED
BUFFED
BUGGED
BUGLED
BUJOLD
BULGED
BULKED
BULLED
BUMMED
BUMPED
BUNGED
BUNKED
BUNTED
BUOYED
BURIED
BURLED
BURNED
BURPED
BURRED
BUSHED
BUSIED
BUSSED
BUSTED
BUTTED
BUZZED
CUBOID
CUFFED
CULLED
CUNARD
CUPPED
CURBED
CURDED
CURLED
CURRED
CURSED
CURVED
CUSPED
CUSPID
CUSSED
DUBBED
DUCKED
DUELED
DULLED
DUMPED
DUNKED
DUNNED
DUSTED
EUCLID
FUDGED
FUELED
FUGARD
FUNDED
FUNKED
FUNNED
FURLED
FURRED
FUSSED
FUZZED
GUIDED
GULFED
GULLED
GULPED
GUMMED
GUNNED
GUSHED
GUSTED
GUTTED
HUFFED
HUGGED
HULKED
HULLED
HUMMED
HUMPED
HUNTED
HURLED
HUSHED
HUSKED
HUTTED
JUDGED
JUGGED
JUICED
JUMPED
JUNKED
JUTTED
LUCKED
LUFFED
LUGGED
LULLED
LUMPED
LUNGED
LURKED
LUSTED
MUCKED
MUDDED
MUFFED
MUGGED
MULLED
MUSHED
MUSSED
NUBBED
NUDGED
NULLED
NUMBED
NURSED
NUTTED
OUSTED
OUTBID
OUTDID
PUFFED
PUGGED
PULLED
PULPED
PULSED
PUMPED
PUNNED
PUNTED
PUREED
PURGED
PURLED
PURRED
PURSED
PUSHED
PUTRID
PUTTED
QUAKED
QUEUED
QUOTED
RUBBED
RUBIED
RUCKED
RUFFED
RUGGED
RUINED
RUSHED
RUSTED
RUTTED
SUBBED
SUCKED
SUDSED
SUITED
SULKED
SUMMED
SUNGOD
SUNNED
SUPPED
SURFED
SURGED
TUBBED
TUCKED
TUFTED
TUGGED
TURBID
TURFED
TURGID
TURNED
TUSKED
TUTUED
YUKKED

••UD••

AOUDAD
BOUDIN
BRUDER
CAUDAL
CAUDEX
CAUDLE
CIUDAD
CRUDDY
CRUDER
DRUDGE
ELUDED
ELUDES
ETUDES
EXUDED
EXUDES
FEUDAL
FEUDED
GRUDGE
KLUDGE
LAUDED
LAUDER
LOUDEN
LOUDER
LOUDLY
PRUDES
SAUDIS
SLUDGE
SLUDGY
SMUDGE
SMUDGY
STUDIO
TRUDGE

••U•D•

BOUNDS
CRUDDY
DRUIDS
FLUIDS
FOUNDS
GOURDE
GOURDS
GRUNDY
HOUNDS
KAUNDA
MAUNDY
MBUNDU
MOULDS
MOULDY
MOUNDS
POUNDS
ROUNDS
SOUNDS
SQUADS
SQUIDS
STURDY
WOUNDS
ZOUNDS

••U••D

ABUSED
AMUSED
AOUDAD
CAUSED
CHUTED
CIUDAD
DAUBED
DEUCED
DOUSED
EDUARD
EDUCED
ELUDED
ELUTED
ENURED
EXUDED
FEUDED
FLUTED
FLUXED
FOULED
GAUGED
GAUZED
GOUGED
GOUNOD
HAULED
HOUSED
INURED
LAUDED
LOUSED
MAULED
MOUSED
PAUSED
PLUMED
POURED
POUTED
PRUNED
REUSED
ROUGED
ROUSED
ROUTED
SAUCED
SOURED
SOUSED
SPUMED
STUPID
TOURED
TOUTED
UNUSED

•••UD•

ALLUDE
CLAUDE
CLOUDS
CLOUDY
DELUDE
DENUDE
ESCUDO
FRAUDS
NERUDA
PSEUDO
PSEUDS
REMUDA
YEHUDI

•••U•D

ABOUND
ABSURD
ARGUED
AROUND
EDMUND
EMQUAD
ENDUED
ENQUAD
ENSUED
FECUND
GERUND
GROUND
IMBUED
ISSUED
JOCUND
LIQUID
OBTUND
OSMUND
PEQUOD
PIQUED
QUEUED
REFUND
ROTUND
SEGUED
SHOULD
SIGURD
TUTUED
VALUED

••••UD

ATSTUD
MARAUD
REDBUD
SHROUD
STROUD
TALMUD

U•E•••

UNEASE
UNEASY
UNESCO
UNEVEN
UPENDS
USEDTO
USEDUP
USEFUL
USERID
USESUP

U••E••

UBIETY
UDDERS
ULCERS
UMBELS
UMBERS
UNBELT
UNBEND
UNBENT
UNHEED
UNLEAD
UNLESS
UNMEET
UNMESH
UNPEGS
UNPENS
UNREAD
UNREAL
UNREEL
UNREST
UNSEAL
UNSEAT
UNSEEN
UNSEWN
UNSEWS
UNVEIL
UNWELL
UPBEAT
UPHELD
UPKEEP
UPPERS
UPSETS
UPWELL
URAEUS
URGENT
URGERS
USHERS
UTTERS
UZBEKS

U•••E•

UGLIER
UGLIES
UKASES
ULSTER
UNAGED
UNAWED
UNCLES
UNDIES
UNDOER
UNDOES
UNDYED
UNEVEN
UNGUES
UNHEED
UNICEF
UNISEX
UNITED
UNITER
UNITES
UNMEET
UNOPEN
UNREEL
UNSEEN
UNSHED
UNTIED
UNTIES
UNUSED
UPKEEP
URUSES
USAGES
USOPEN
USURER

U••••E

ULLAGE
UMBRAE
UMPIRE
UNABLE
UNCAGE
UNCASE
UNDINE
UNDONE
UNEASE
UNGLUE
UNIATE
UNIQUE
UNLACE
UNLADE
UNLIKE
UNMADE
UNMAKE
UNPILE
UNRIPE
UNROBE
UNSAFE
UNSURE
UNTRUE
UNTUNE
UNWISE
UNWOVE
UNYOKE
UPDATE
UPDIKE
UPRISE
UPROSE
UPSIDE
UPTAKE
UPTIME
URBANE
URSINE
USABLE
USANCE
UVALUE
UVULAE

•UE•••

BUENOS
CUESTA
DUELED
DUELER
DUELLO
DUENNA
FUELED
FUELER
GUELPH
GUENON
GUERRE
GUESTS
HUEVOS
NUECES
PUEBLA
PUEBLO
PUENTE
PUERTO
QUEASY
QUEBEC
QUEENS
QUELLS
QUEMOY
QUENCH
QUERNS
QUESTS
QUEUED
QUEUER
QUEUES
RUEFUL
SUEDES

•U•E••

AUDENS
AUGEAN
AUGEND
AUGERS
AUREUS
AUTEUR
BUREAU
BUTENE
BUTEOS
BUYERS
CUBEBS
CULETS
CUNEAL
CUPELS
CURERS
CUTEST
CUTESY
CUVEES
DUDEEN
DUNERA
DUPERY
DURESS
DUVETS
EUGENE
EUREKA
FUSEES
FUZEES
HUBERT
HUGELY
HUGEST
HUMERI
JULEPS
JUNEAU
LUBECK
LUCENT
LUDENS
LUGERS
LUMENS
MUDEEL
MULETA
MUSERS
MUSEUM
MUTELY
MUTEST
NUGENT
NUMERO
OUSELS
OUTEAT
OUZELS
PUREED
PUREES
PURELY
PUREST
QUEENS
QUIETS
RUBENS
RUDELY
RUDEST
RULEON
RULERS
RUMENS
RUPEES
RUPERT
SUPERB
SUPERS
SURELY
SUREST
SURETE
SURETY
TUBERS
TUMEFY
TUNEIN
TUNERS
TUNEUP
TUPELO
TUREEN
TUXEDO
TUYERE

•U••E•

AUBREY
AUDREY
AUKLET
AUSPEX
AUSTEN
BUCKED
BUCKET
BUDDED
BUDGED
BUDGES
BUDGET
BUFFED
BUFFER
BUFFET
BUGGED
BUGLED
BUGLER
BUGLES
BULGED
BULGES
BULKED
BULLED
BULLET
BULWER
BUMMED
BUMMER
BUMPED
BUMPER
BUNGED
BUNGEE
BUNKED
BUNKER
BUNSEN
BUNTED
BUNTER
BUNUEL
BUOYED
BURDEN
BURGEE
BURGER
BURIED
BURIES
BURLED
BURLEY
BURNED
BURNER
BURNET
BURNEY
BURPED
BURRED
BURSES
BUSHED
BUSHEL
BUSHES
BUSIED
BUSIER
BUSIES
BUSMEN
BUSSED
BUSSES
BUSTED
BUSTER
BUTLER
BUTTED
BUTTER
BUTTES
BUZZED
BUZZER
BUZZES
CUDGEL
CUFFED
CULLED
CULLEN
CULLER
CULLET
CULVER
CUMBER
CUPPED
CURBED
CURDED
CURFEW
CURLED
CURLER
CURLEW
CURRED
CURSED
CURSES
CURTER
CURVED
CURVES
CURVET
CUSPED
CUSSED
CUSSES
CUSTER
CUTIES
CUTLER
CUTLET
CUTTER
CUVEES
DUBBED
DUBCEK
DUCKED
DUDEEN
DUDLEY
DUELED
DUELER
DUFFEL
DUFFER
DUIKER
DULCET
DULLEA
DULLED
DULLER
DULLES
DUMBER
DUMPED
DUMPER
DUNCES
DUNDEE
DUNKED
DUNKER
DUNNED
DUPLEX
DURFEY
DURYEA
DUSTED
DUSTER
DUTIES
EUBOEA
EUPNEA
FUDGED
FUDGES
FUELED
FUELER
FUGUES
FULLER
FUNDED
FUNKED
FUNNED
FUNNEL
FURIES
FURLED
FURRED
FUSEES
FUSSED
FUSSES
FUZEES
FUZZED
FUZZES
GUIDED
GUIDES
GUILES
GUINEA
GUISES
GULFED
GULLED
GULLET
GULPED
GULPER
GUMBEL
GUMMED
GUNMEN
GUNNED
GUNNEL
GUNNER
GUNTER
GURLEY
GURNEY
GUSHED
GUSHER
GUSHES
GUSSET
GUSTED
GUTTED
GUTTER
HUFFED
HUGGED
HUGGER
HUGHES
HULKED
HULLED
HULLER
HUMMED
HUMMER
HUMPED
HUNGER
HUNKER
HUNTED
HUNTER
HURLED
HURLER
HURLEY
HUSHED
HUSHES
HUSKED
HUSKER
HUTTED
HUXLEY
JUAREZ
JUDAEA
JUDDER
JUDGED
JUDGES
JUGGED
JUICED
JUICER
JUICES
JULIET
JUMPED
JUMPER
JUNKED
JUNKER
JUNKET
JURIES
JUSTER
JUTTED
KUCHEN
KUMMEL
LUBBER
LUCKED
LUDDEN
LUFFED
LUGGED
LUGGER
LULLED
LUMBER
LUMPED
LUMPEN
LUMPER
LUNDEN
LUNGED
LUNGES
LUNKER
LURKED
LUSHER
LUSTED
LUSTER
LUTHER
MUCKED
MUDDED
MUDDER
MUDEEL
MUDHEN
MUFFED
MUGGED
MUGGER
MULLED
MULLER
MULLET
MUMMER
MUPPET
MURDER
MURIEL
MURRES
MURREY
MUSHED
MUSHER

MUSHES
MUSKEG
MUSKET
MUSSED
MUSSEL
MUSSES
MUSTER
MUTTER
NUBBED
NUCLEI
NUCLEO
NUDGED
NUDGER
NUDGES
NUECES
NUGGET
NULLED
NUMBED
NUMBER
NURSED
NURSER
NURSES
NUTLET
NUTMEG
NUTTED
NUTTER
OUNCES
OUSTED
OUSTER
OUTLET
OUTSET
PUCKER
PUFFED
PUFFER
PUGGED
PUGREE
PULLED
PULLET
PULLEY
PULPED
PULSED
PULSES
PUMMEL
PUMPED
PUMPER
PUNIER
PUNKER
PUNNED
PUNTED
PUNTER
PUPPET
PUREED
PUREES
PURGED
PURGES
PURLED
PURRED
PURRER
PURSED
PURSER
PURSES
PURVEY
PUSHED
PUSHES
PUSSES
PUTTED
PUTTEE
PUTTER
QUAKED
QUAKER
QUAKES
QUAVER
QUEBEC
QUEUED
QUEUER
QUEUES
QUIRES
QUIVER
QUOTED
QUOTER
QUOTES
RUBBED
RUBBER
RUBIED
RUBIES
RUBLES
RUCHES
RUCKED
RUDDER
RUFFED
RUGGED
RUINED
RUINER
RUMMER
RUNLET
RUNNEL
RUNNER
RUPEES
RUSHED
RUSHEE
RUSHES
RUSSET
RUSTED
RUTGER
RUTTED
SUAVER
SUBBED
SUBDEB
SUBLET
SUBSET
SUCCES
SUCKED
SUCKER
SUDDEN
SUDSED
SUDSES
SUEDES
SUFFER
SUITED
SUITES
SULKED
SULKER
SULLEN
SUMMED
SUMMER
SUMNER
SUMTER
SUNDER
SUNDEW
SUNKEN
SUNNED
SUNSET
SUPPED
SUPPER
SURFED
SURFER
SURGED
SURGES
SURREY
SURVEY
SUSIEQ
SUSSEX
SUTLER
SUTTER
TUAREG
TUBBED
TUCKED
TUCKER
TUCKET
TUFFET
TUFTED
TUGGED
TUGGER
TULLES
TUNNEL
TUNNEY
TUQUES
TUREEN
TURFED
TURKEY
TURNED
TURNER
TURRET
TUSKED
TUSKER
TUTUED
YUKKED
ZUIDER

•U•••E

AUBADE
AUNTIE
AUSSIE
BUBBLE
BUCKLE
BUDGIE
BULLAE
BUMBLE
BUNCHE
BUNDLE
BUNGEE
BUNGLE
BURBLE
BURGEE
BURGLE
BURSAE
BUSTLE
BUTANE
BUTENE
CUBAGE
CUDDLE
CUISSE
CURARE
CURATE
CURDLE
CURIAE
CURULE
DUARTE
DUNDEE
EUCHRE
EUGENE
EUNICE
EUROPE
FUDDLE
FUMBLE
FURORE
FUTILE
FUTURE
GUERRE
GUIMPE
GURGLE
GUTTAE
GUZZLE
HUBBLE
HUDDLE
HUMANE
HUMBLE
HURDLE
HURTLE
HUSTLE
JUGGLE
JUJUBE
JUMBLE
JUNGLE
JUNKIE
KURILE
LUCITE
LUNATE
LUPINE
LUPONE
LUSTRE
LUXATE
MUDDLE
MUDPIE
MUFFLE
MUGABE
MUMBLE
MUNCIE
MURINE
MUSCLE
MUSKIE
MUTATE
MUZZLE
NUANCE
NUBBLE
NUBILE
NUCHAE
NUTATE
NUZZLE
OUTAGE
OUTATE
PUDDLE
PUENTE
PUGREE
PUISNE
PULQUE
PUMICE
PUNKIE
PURACE
PURDUE
PURFLE
PURINE
PURPLE
PURSUE
PUTTEE
PUZZLE
QUAYLE
QUICHE
QUINCE
RUBBLE
RUDDLE
RUFFLE
RUGATE
RUGOSE
RUMBLE
RUMPLE
RUNCIE
RUNDLE
RUSHEE
RUSTLE
RUTILE
SUBDUE
SUBTLE
SUMMAE
SUNDAE
SUPINE
SUPPLE
SURETE
SUTURE
TUBATE
TUILLE
TULANE
TULARE
TUMBLE
TURTLE
TUSSLE
TUYERE
YUPPIE

••UE••

BLUEOX
BLUEST
BLUESY
BLUETS
CLUEIN
CRUETS
FLUENT
GLUERS
GRUELS
SQUEAK
SQUEAL
TRUEST

••U•E•

ABUSED
ABUSER
ABUSES
ACUMEN
AMULET
AMUSED
AMUSES
BOULES
BOULEZ
BRUDER
BRUGES
BRULES
BRUMES
BRUNEI
BRUNET
BRUTES
CAUDEX
CAUSED
CAUSES
CHUTED
CHUTES
COULEE
COUPES
COUTER
CRUCES
CRUDER
CRUSES
CRUXES
DAUBED
DAUBER
DAUBES
DEUCED
DEUCES
DOURER
DOUSED
DOUSES
DRUPES
DRUZES
EDUCED
EDUCES
ELUDED
ELUDES
ELUTED
ELUTES
ENURED
ENURES
ETUDES
EXUDED
EXUDES
FAUCES
FAUCET
FEUDED
FLUKES
FLUMES
FLUTED
FLUTES
FLUXED
FLUXES
FOULED
FOULER
GAUGED
GAUGER
GAUGES
GAUZED
GAUZES
GLUTEI
GLUTEN
GOUGED
GOUGER
GOUGES
GOULET
HAULED
HAULER
HOUSED
HOUSES
INURED
INURES
JAURES
JOULES
KRUGER
LAUDED
LAUDER
LAUPER
LAUREL
LAUREN
LOUDEN
LOUDER
LOUPES
LOUSED
LOUSES
LOUVER
MAULED
MAULER
MAUMEE
MAUSER
MAUVES
MOUSED
MOUSER
MOUSES
MOUSEY
NAUSEA
NEUMES
NEUTER
NGUYEN
NOUMEA
ONUSES
OPUSES
OVULES
PAULEY
PAUPER
PAUSED
PAUSES
PLUMED
PLUMES
PLUSES
POURED
POURER
POUTED
POUTER
PRUDES
PRUNED
PRUNER
PRUNES
REUBEN
REUNES
REUSED
REUSES
REUTER
ROUGED
ROUGES
ROUSED
ROUSES
ROUTED
ROUTER
ROUTES
SAUCED
SAUCER
SAUCES
SAUGER
SAUREL
SAUTES
SCUTES
SOURED
SOURER
SOUSED
SOUSES
SOUTER
SPUMED
SPUMES
STUPES
TAUPES
TAUTEN
TAUTER
TOUPEE
TOURED
TOURER
TOUTED
TOUTER
TRUCES
UNUSED
URUSES
USURER
YOUBET

••U••E

ACUATE
ALULAE
AQUATE
AVULSE
BAUBLE
BEURRE
BOUCLE
BOUFFE
BOULLE
BOUNCE
BOURKE
BOURNE
BOURSE
BRUISE
CAUDLE
COULEE
COUPLE
COURSE
CRUISE
CRUSOE
DOUBLE
DRUDGE
EQUATE
EQUINE
EVULSE
FAUNAE
GAUCHE
GOURDE
GRUDGE
GRUNGE
JOUNCE
KLUDGE
LAURIE
LOUCHE
LOUISE
LOUNGE
LOUVRE
MAUMEE
MOUSSE
OEUVRE
PLUNGE
POUNCE
POUSSE
SCURVE
SLUDGE
SLUICE
SMUDGE
SOURCE
SPURGE
SQUARE
SQUIRE
TOUCHE
TOUPEE
TOUSLE
TRUDGE
UVULAE
ZOUAVE

•••UE•

ARGUED
ARGUER
ARGUES
BREUER
BUNUEL
COQUET
ENDUED
ENDUES
ENSUED
ENSUES
FUGUES
GIGUES
IMBUED
IMBUES
ISSUED
ISSUER
ISSUES
LEMUEL
MAGUEY
MANUEL
MCKUEN
MIGUEL
MINUET
PIQUED
PIQUES
PIQUET
QUEUED
QUEUER
QUEUES
RAQUEL
REFUEL
REVUES
ROGUES
SAMUEL
SEGUED
SEGUES
SEQUEL
SPRUES
TOQUES
TUQUES
TUTUED
UNGUES
VAGUER
VALUED
VALUES
VENUES
VOGUES

•••U•E

ABJURE
ACCUSE
ADDUCE
ADJURE
ALLUDE
ALLURE
AMPULE
ARMURE
AROUSE
ASSUME
ASSURE
ASTUTE
ATTUNE
BEMUSE
BLOUSE
CANUTE
CAYUSE
CERUSE
CLAUDE
CLAUSE
COHUNE
CROUSE
CROUTE
CURULE
DANUBE
DEDUCE
DEFUSE
DEJURE
DELUDE
DELUGE
DELUXE
DEMURE
DENUDE
DEPUTE
DILUTE
DISUSE
EFFUSE
ENDURE
ENDUSE
ENSURE
EXCUSE
FERULE
FIGURE
FUTURE
GROUSE
ILLUME
ILLUSE
IMMUNE
IMMURE
IMPURE
IMPUTE
INCUSE
INDUCE
INFUSE
INHUME
INJURE
INOUYE
INSURE
INTUNE
JEJUNE
JUJUBE
LEGUME
LIGURE
LOBULE
MATURE
MINUTE
MISUSE
MODULE
NATURE
NODULE
OBTUSE
ORDURE
PAIUTE
PARURE
PERUKE
PERUSE
REBUKE
RECUSE
REDUCE
REFUGE
REFUSE
REFUTE
RELUME
REPUTE
RESUME
RETUNE
SALUTE
SECURE
SEDUCE
SOLUTE
SPOUSE
SPRUCE
STLUKE
SUTURE
TENURE
TRIUNE
TROUPE
TROUVE
UNSURE
UNTUNE
VOLUME
VOLUTE

••••UE

ACCRUE
AVENUE
BARQUE
BASQUE
BATTUE
BISQUE
BRAQUE
BROGUE
CAIQUE
CALQUE
CASQUE
CHEQUE
CINQUE
CIRQUE
CLAQUE
CLIQUE
CLOQUE
DENGUE
DROGUE
FESCUE
FONDUE
GANGUE
IMBRUE
LEAGUE
LONGUE
MANQUE
MARQUE
MASQUE
MISCUE
MOSQUE
MRBLUE
OPAQUE
PERDUE
PLAGUE
PLAQUE
PRAGUE
PULQUE
PURDUE
PURSUE
REGLUE
RESCUE
RISQUE
RVALUE
SACQUE
STATUE
SUBDUE
TISSUE
TONGUE
TORQUE
UNGLUE
UNIQUE
UNTRUE
UVALUE
VIRTUE

U•F•••

UNFAIR
UNFITS
UNFOLD
UNFURL

U••F••

UNIFIC
USEFUL

U•••F•

UGLIFY
UNSAFE
UPLIFT

U••••F

UNICEF

•UF•••

AUFAIT
AUFOND
BUFFED
BUFFER
BUFFET
BUFFON
BUFFOS
CUFFED
DUFFEL
DUFFER
GUFFAW
HUFFED
LUFFED
MUFASA
MUFFED
MUFFIN
MUFFLE
MUFTIS
PUFFED
PUFFER
PUFFIN
RUFFED
RUFFLE
RUFFLY
RUFOUS
SUFFER
SUFFIX
SUFISM
TUFFET
TUFTED

•U•F••

BUFFED
BUFFER
BUFFET
BUFFON
BUFFOS
CUFFED
CUPFUL
CURFEW
DUFFEL
DUFFER
DURFEY
GUFFAW
GULFED
GUNFOR
HUFFED
JUGFUL
LUFFED
MUFFED
MUFFIN
MUFFLE
OUTFIT
OUTFOX
PUFFED
PUFFER
PUFFIN
PURFLE
QUAFFS
RUEFUL
RUFFED
RUFFLE
RUFFLY
SUFFER
SUFFIX
SULFUR
SURFED
SURFER
TUFFET
TURFED

•U••F•

BUGOFF
BUYOFF
CUTOFF
KUNGFU
PURIFY
PUTOFF
QUAFFS
RUBIFY
RUNOFF
TUMEFY

•U•••F

BUGOFF
BUYOFF
CUTOFF
PUTOFF
RUDOLF
RUNOFF

••UF••

BLUFFS
BOUFFE
FLUFFS
FLUFFY
KOUFAX
SCUFFS
SNUFFS
SNUFFY
STUFFS
STUFFY

••U•F•

BLUFFS
BOUFFE
FLUFFS
FLUFFY
SCUFFS
SCURFY
SMURFS
SNUFFS
SNUFFY
STUFFS
STUFFY

•••UF•

REBUFF
SCRUFF

•••U•F

ENGULF
REBUFF
SCRUFF

••••UF

STAPUF

UG••••

UGANDA
UGGAMS
UGLIER
UGLIES
UGLIFY
UGRIAN

U•G•••

UGGAMS
UIGURS
UNGIRD
UNGIRT
UNGLUE
UNGUAL
UNGUES
UNGUIS
URGENT
URGERS
URGING

U••G••

UNAGED
USAGES

U•••G•

UBANGI
ULLAGE
UNCAGE
UNPEGS
UNRIGS

U••••G

UNCLOG
UNPLUG
UNSNAG
UNSUNG
UPPING
URGING

•UG•••

AUGEAN
AUGEND
AUGERS
AUGHTS
AUGURS
AUGURY
AUGUST
BUGGED
BUGLED
BUGLER
BUGLES
BUGOFF
BUGOUT
DUGONG
DUGOUT
EUGENE
FUGARD
FUGUES
HUGELY
HUGEST
HUGGED
HUGGER
HUGHES
JUGFUL
JUGGED
JUGGLE
LUGERS
LUGGED
LUGGER
LUGNUT
LUGOSI
MUGABE
MUGGED
MUGGER
MUGHOS
NUGENT
NUGGET
OUGHTS
PUGGED
PUGREE
RUGATE
RUGGED
RUGOSE
SUGARS
SUGARY
TUGGED
TUGGER
TUGRIK

•U•G••

BUDGED
BUDGES
BUDGET
BUDGIE
BUGGED
BULGAR
BULGED
BULGES
BULGUR
BUNGED
BUNGEE
BUNGLE
BURGAS
BURGEE
BURGER
BURGHS
BURGLE
BURGOO
BURGOS
CUDGEL
FUDGED
FUDGES
FUNGUS
GUNGHO
GURGLE
HUGGED
HUGGER
HUNGER
HUNGIN
HUNGON
HUNGRY
HUNGUP
HUNGWU
JUDGED
JUDGES
JUGGED
JUGGLE
JUNGLE
JUNGLY
KUNGFU
KURGAN
LUGGED
LUGGER
LUNGED
LUNGES
MUGGED
MUGGER
MUNGOS
NUDGED
NUDGER
NUDGES
NUGGET
OUTGUN
PUGGED
PURGED
PURGES
QUAGGA
QUAGGY
RUGGED
RUNGUP
RUTGER
SUBGUM
SUNGOD
SURGED
SURGES
TUGGED
TUGGER
TURGID
TURGOR
VULGAR
YUNGLO

•U••G•

AURIGA
CUBAGE
EULOGY
GULAGS
OUTAGE
QUAGGA
QUAGGY

•U•••G

BUSING
BUTUNG
BUYING
CUBING
CURING
DUGONG
DUKING
DUPING
DURING
FUMING
FUSING
FUZING
GUNDOG
GUYING
HUMBUG
JUKING
LUBING
LUDWIG
LURING
LUTING
MUSING
MUSKEG
MUTING
NUKING
NUTMEG
OUTING
PULING
QUAHOG
RULING
SUNDOG
TUAREG
TUBING
TUNING
TURING

••UG••

BOUGHS
BOUGHT
BRUGES
CAUGHT
COUGAR
COUGHS
DOUGHS
DOUGHY

FOUGHT
FRUGAL
GAUGED
GAUGER
GAUGES
GOUGED
GOUGER
GOUGES
KRUGER
LAUGHS
NAUGHT
NOUGAT
NOUGHT
PLUGIN
ROUGED
ROUGES
ROUGHS
SAUGER
SLUGGO
SMUGLY
SNUGLY
SOUGHS
SOUGHT
TAUGHT
TOUGHS
TOUGHY
VAUGHN
ZEUGMA

••U•G•
DRUDGE
GRUDGE
GRUNGE
GRUNGY
KLUDGE
LOUNGE
PLUNGE
SLUDGE
SLUDGY
SLUGGO
SMUDGE
SMUDGY
SPURGE
TRUDGE

••U••G
BLUING
CLUING
GLUING
SLUING
TAUTOG
TRUING

•••UG•
BELUGA
CAYUGA
CHOUGH
COLUGO
DEBUGS
DELUGE
ENOUGH
IMPUGN
OPPUGN
PLOUGH
REFUGE
REPUGN
SHRUGS
SLOUGH
TELUGU
THOUGH
TROUGH

•••U•G
BUTUNG
COBURG
REHUNG
SPRUNG
STRUNG
UNSUNG

••••UG
BEDBUG
HUMBUG
RAGRUG
SOWBUG
UNPLUG
WONMUG

UH••••
UHLANS

U•H•••
UNHAND
UNHEED
UNHOLY
UNHOOK
UNHURT
UPHELD
UPHILL
UPHOLD
USHERS
UTHANT

U••H••
UNCHIC
UNSHED
UNSHOD
UPSHOT
URCHIN
UTAHAN

U••••H
UNLASH
UNMESH
UPRUSH
UZZIAH

•U•H••
AUGHTS
AUTHOR
BUSHED
BUSHEL
BUSHES
BUSHWA
CUSHAW
DUCHIN
DUNHAM
DURHAM
EUCHRE
FUZHOU
GUSHED
GUSHER
GUSHES
HUGHES
HUSHED
HUSHES
KUCHEN
LUSHER
LUSHLY
LUTHER
LUTHOR
MUDHEN
MUGHOS
MUSHED
MUSHER
MUSHES
MUZHIK
NUCHAE
NUCHAL
OUGHTS
OUTHIT
PUSHED
PUSHES
PUSHON
PUSHUP
QUAHOG
RUCHES
RUSHED
RUSHEE
RUSHES
SUCHAS
TUCHUN

•U••H•
BUDDHA
BUNCHE
BUQSHA
BURGHS
GUNGHO
GUNSHY
GURKHA
HUMPHS
MURPHY
PUNCHY
QUICHE
QUOTHA
SURAHS

•U•••H
DULUTH
EUNUCH
GUELPH
GULLAH
HURRAH
HUZZAH
JUBBAH
JUDITH
MULISH
MULLAH
MUNICH
NULLAH
PUNISH
PUNKAH
PURDAH
PUTSCH
QUENCH
QURUSH
RUPIAH
SUKKAH
TUSSAH
ZURICH

••UH••
CHUHSI
TZUHSI

••U•H•
BOUGHS
BOUGHT
BRUSHY
CAUCHO
CAUGHT
COUGHS
DOUGHS
DOUGHY
FOUGHT
GAUCHE
GAUCHO
KYUSHU
LAUGHS
LOUCHE
MOUTHS
MOUTHY
NAUGHT
NOUGHT
PLUSHY
POUCHY
ROUGHS
SLUSHY
SOUGHS
SOUGHT
TAUGHT
TOUCHE
TOUCHY
TOUGHS
TOUGHY
TRUTHS
VAUGHN
YOUTHS

••U••H
BEULAH
BLUISH
BRUNCH
CHURCH
CLUTCH
CRUNCH
CRUTCH
FOURTH
HAUNCH
LAUNCH
NAUTCH
PAUNCH
SCUTCH
SMUTCH
SQUASH
SQUISH

•••U•H
ABLUSH
AMBUSH
AVOUCH
BARUCH
CHOUGH
CROUCH
DULUTH
ENOUGH
EUNUCH
GROUCH
INRUSH
ONRUSH
PLOUGH
QURUSH
SLEUTH
SLOUCH
SLOUGH
THOUGH
THRUSH
TROUGH
UPRUSH

UI••••
UIGURS

U•I•••
UBIETY
UMIAKS
UNIATE
UNIATS
UNICEF
UNIFIC
UNIONS
UNIPOD
UNIQUE
UNISEX
UNISON
UNITAL
UNITAS
UNITED
UNITER
UNITES
UNIVAC
URIALS

U••I••
UGLIER
UGLIES
UGLIFY
UGRIAN
ULTIMA
ULTIMO
UMPIRE
UNBIND
UNCIAL
UNDIES
UNDINE
UNFITS
UNGIRD
UNGIRT
UNKIND
UNKINK
UNLIKE
UNLINK
UNPILE
UNPINS
UNRIGS
UNRIPE
UNTIDY
UNTIED
UNTIES
UNWIND
UNWISE
UNZIPS
UPDIKE
UPHILL
UPLIFT
UPLINK
UPPING
UPPITY
UPRISE
UPSIDE
UPTICK
UPTIME
UPWIND
URGING
URSIDS
URSINE
UZZIAH

U•••I•
UJJAIN
UMBRIA
UNCHIC
UNCOIL
UNFAIR
UNGUIS
UNIFIC
UNKNIT
UNLAID
UNPAID
UNSAID
UNVEIL
URACIL
URALIC
URANIA
URANIC
URCHIN
USERID
USMAIL
UTOPIA

U••••I
UAKARI
UBANGI

•UI•••
BUILDS
CUIABA
CUISSE
DUIKER
GUIANA
GUIDED
GUIDES
GUIDON
GUILDS
GUILES
GUILTY
GUIMPE
GUINEA
GUISES
GUITAR
JUICED
JUICER
JUICES
PUISNE
QUICHE
QUIETS
QUILLS
QUILTS
QUINCE
QUINCY
QUINOA
QUINTS
QUIPPY
QUIPUS
QUIRES
QUIRKS
QUIRKY
QUIRTS
QUITIT
QUIVER
RUINED
RUINER
SUITED
SUITES
SUITOR
SUITUP
TUILLE
ZUIDER

•U•I••
AUDIAL
AUDIOS
AUDITS
AURIGA
AUXINS
BUNION
BURIED
BURIES
BURINS
BUSIED
BUSIER
BUSIES
BUSILY
BUSING
BUYING
CUBICS
CUBING
CUBISM
CUBIST
CUBITS
CUPIDS
CURIAE
CURIAL
CURING
CURIOS
CURIUM
CUTIES
CUTINS
DUKING
DUPING
DURIAN
DURING
DUTIES
EUNICE
FUJIAN
FUMING
FURIES
FUSILS
FUSING
FUSION
FUTILE
FUZING
GUYING
JUDITH
JUKING
JULIAN
JULIET
JULIUS
JUNIOR
JURIES
JURIST
KUMISS
KURILE
LUBING
LUCIAN
LUCITE
LUCIUS
LUMINA
LUPINE
LUPINO
LURING
LUTING
LUTIST
MULISH
MUNICH
MURIEL
MURINE
MUSIAL
MUSING
MUTING
MUTINY
NUBIAN
NUBILE
NUDIST
NUDITY
NUKING
NUMINA
OUTING
PULING
PUMICE
PUNIER
PUNILY
PUNISH
PUPILS
PURIFY
PURINA
PURINE
PURISM
PURIST
PURITY
QUAILS
QUAINT
QUOINS
QUOITS
RUBIED
RUBIES
RUBIFY
RULING
RUMINA
RUNINS
RUPIAH
RUTILE
SUBITO
SUFISM
SUPINE
SURIMI
SUSIEQ
TUBING
TUBIST
TULIPS
TUNICA
TUNICS
TUNING
TUPIAN
TURING
ZURICH

•U••I•
AUFAIT
AUNTIE
AUPAIR
AUSSIE
AUSTIN
BUDGIE
BULBIL
BUSKIN
BUTTIN
CUBOID
CULKIN
CULLIS
CULTIC
CUPRIC
CURTIN
CURTIS
CURTIZ
CUSPID
CUTSIN
DUBBIN
DUBLIN
DUBOIS
DUCHIN
DUNLIN
DURBIN
DUSTIN
EUCLID
FUSTIC
HUBRIS
HUNGIN
JUDAIC
JUMPIN
JUNKIE
JUSTIN
KUKRIS
KUWAIT
LUBLIN
LUDWIG
MUDPIE
MUFFIN
MUFTIS
MUNCIE
MUNTIN
MURCIA
MUSKIE
MUSLIM
MUSLIN
MUZHIK
NUBBIN
NUDNIK
NUNCIO
NUTKIN
NUTRIA
OUTBID
OUTDID
OUTFIT
OUTHIT
OUTWIT
PUBLIC
PUFFIN
PULLIN
PULPIT
PUNDIT
PUNKIE
PURLIN
PUTRID
PUTSIN
QUITIT
RUBRIC
RUBSIN
RUNCIE
RUNSIN
RUSKIN
RUSSIA
RUSTIC
SUBMIT
SUCKIN
SUFFIX
SUMMIT
SUNLIT
SUNNIS
SUSLIK
TUCKIN
TUGRIK
TUNEIN
TURBID
TURBIT
TURGID
TURKIC
TURNIN
TURNIP
YUPPIE

•U•••I
BUSONI
CUMULI
FULANI
HUMERI
KUBLAI
LUGOSI
NUCLEI
QUADRI
SURIMI
SUZUKI
TUMULI

••UI••
ACUITY
AQUILA
AQUINO
BLUING
BLUISH
BRUINS
BRUISE
BRUITS
CLUING
CRUISE
DRUIDS
EQUINE
EQUIPS
EQUITY
FLUIDS
FRUITS
FRUITY
GLUING
GSUITS
INUITS
LOUISA
LOUISE
SLUICE
SLUING
SQUIBB
SQUIBS
SQUIDS
SQUILL
SQUINT
SQUIRE
SQUIRM
SQUIRT
SQUISH
TRUING
TRUISM

••U•I•
ABUKIR
ANUBIS
APULIA
BAUCIS
BOUDIN
CLUEIN
COURIC
COUSIN
HOURIS
KAURIS
LAURIE
MOULIN
PLUGIN
POURIN
SAUDIS
SHUTIN
STUDIO
STUPID
ZEUXIS

••U••I
ALUMNI
BRUNEI
CHUHSI
FRUTTI
GLUTEI
ITURBI
SOUARI
TZUHSI

•••UI•
ACQUIT
ALCUIN
BAGUIO
INTUIT
JESUIT
LIQUID
MAQUIS
MINUIT
NYQUIL
SEQUIN
UNGUIS
YAQUIS

•••U•I
ADZUKI
AGOUTI
ANNULI
BATUMI
CUMULI
KABUKI
LAZULI
POPULI
SALUKI
SUZUKI
TUMULI
WATUSI
YEHUDI

••••UI
BANGUI
SESQUI
YANQUI

UJ••••
UJJAIN

U•J•••
UJJAIN
UNJAMS
UNJUST

•UJ•••
BUJOLD
FUJIAN
JUJUBE

•U•J••
PUNJAB

••UJ••
THUJAS

UK••••
UKASES

U•K•••
UAKARI
UNKIND
UNKINK
UNKNIT
UNKNOT
UPKEEP

U•••K•
UMIAKS
UNLIKE
UNMAKE
UNYOKE
UPDIKE
UPTAKE
UZBEKS

U••••K
UNCORK
UNHOOK
UNKINK
UNLINK
UNLOCK
UNMASK
UNPACK
UNTACK
UPLINK
UPTICK
URALSK

•UK•••
AUKLET
DUKING
JUKING
KUKRIS
MUKLUK
NUKING
SUKKAH
YUKATA
YUKAWA
YUKKED

•U•K••
BUCKED
BUCKET
BUCKLE
BUCKUP
BULKED
BUNKED
BUNKER
BUNKOS
BUNKUM
BUSKIN
CUCKOO
CULKIN
DUCKED
DUIKER
DUNKED
DUNKER
FUNKED
GURKHA
HULKED
HUNKER
HUSKED
HUSKER
JUNKED
JUNKER
JUNKET
JUNKIE
LUCKED
LUNKER
LURKED
MUCKED
MUCKUP
MUSKEG
MUSKET
MUSKIE
MUSKOX
NUTKIN
PUCKER
PUNKAH
PUNKER
PUNKIE
QUAKED
QUAKER
QUAKES
QUOKKA
RUCKED
RUCKUS
RUSKIN
SUCKED
SUCKER
SUCKIN
SUKKAH
SULKED
SULKER
SUNKEN
TUCKED
TUCKER
TUCKET
TUCKIN
TURKEY
TURKIC
TUSKED
TUSKER
YUKKED

•U••K•
EUREKA
JUDOKA
KULAKS
LUSAKA
QUACKS
QUARKS
QUIRKS
QUIRKY
QUOKKA
SUZUKI
YUROKS

•U•••K
BUROAK
DUBCEK
LUBECK
MUKLUK
MUZHIK
NUDNIK
SUSLIK
TUGRIK

••UK••
ABUKIR
CHUKAR
CHUKKA
FLUKES
RYUKYU
ZHUKOV

••U•K•
AKUAKU
BOURKE
CAULKS
CHUCKS
CHUKKA
CHUNKS
CHUNKY
CLUCKS
CLUNKS
CLUNKY
FLUNKS
FLUNKY
PLUCKS
PLUCKY
PLUNKS
SHUCKS
SKULKS
SKUNKS
SPUNKY
THUNKS
TRUCKS
TRUNKS

••U••K
SQUAWK
SQUEAK

•••UK•
ADZUKI
KABUKI
PERUKE
REBUKE
SALUKI
STLUKE
SUZUKI

•••U•K
DEBUNK
INBULK
INLUCK
PODUNK
SHRUNK
STRUCK
ZANUCK

••••UK
DYBBUK
FAROUK
MARDUK
MUKLUK
SELJUK
TOBRUK

UL••••
ULCERS
ULLAGE
ULLMAN
ULSTER
ULTIMA
ULTIMO
ULTRAS

U•L•••
UCLANS
UGLIER
UGLIES
UGLIFY
UHLANS
ULLAGE
ULLMAN
UMLAUT
UNLACE
UNLADE
UNLAID
UNLASH
UNLEAD
UNLESS
UNLIKE
UNLINK
UNLOAD
UNLOCK
UPLAND
UPLIFT
UPLINK
UPLOAD

U••L••
UBOLTS
UNCLAD
UNCLES
UNCLOG
UNGLUE
UNPLUG
URALIC
URALSK
UVALUE
UVULAE
UVULAR
UVULAS

U•••L•
UMBELS
UNABLE
UNBELT
UNBOLT
UNDULY
UNFOLD
UNHOLY
UNPILE
UNROLL
UNRULY
UNSOLD
UNTOLD
UNWELL
UPHELD
UPHILL
UPHOLD
UPWELL
URIALS
URSULA
USABLE
USABLY
USUALS

U••••L
UMBRAL
UNCIAL
UNCOIL
UNCOOL
UNCURL
UNFURL
UNGUAL
UNITAL
UNREAL
UNREEL
UNROLL
UNSEAL
UNVEIL
UNWELL
UPHILL
UPWELL
URACIL
USEFUL
USMAIL

•UL•••
BULBIL
BULBUL
BULGAR
BULGED
BULGES
BULGUR
BULKED
BULLAE
BULLED
BULLET
BULOVA
BULWER
CULETS
CULKIN
CULLED
CULLEN
CULLER
CULLET
CULLIS
CULTIC
CULVER
DULCET
DULLEA
DULLED
DULLER
DULLES
DULUTH
EULOGY
FULANI
FULCRA
FULLER
FULMAR
FULTON
GULAGS
GULFED
GULLAH
GULLED
GULLET
GULPED
GULPER
HULKED
HULLED
HULLER
HULLOS
JULEPS
JULIAN
JULIET
JULIUS
KULAKS
KULTUR
LULLED
MULCTS
MULETA
MULISH
MULLAH
MULLAS
MULLED

MULLER
MULLET
NULLAH
NULLED
PULING
PULLED
PULLET
PULLEY
PULLIN
PULLON
PULLUP
PULPED
PULPIT
PULQUE
PULSAR
PULSED
PULSES
RULEON
RULERS
RULING
SULCUS
SULFUR
SULKED
SULKER
SULLEN
SULTAN
SULTRY
TULANE
TULARE
TULIPS
TULLES
TULSAN
VULCAN
VULGAR

•U•L••

AUKLET
BUGLED
BUGLER
BUGLES
BUILDS
BULLAE
BULLED
BULLET
BURLAP
BURLED
BURLEY
BUTLER
CULLED
CULLEN
CULLER
CULLET
CULLIS
CURLED
CURLER
CURLEW
CURLUP
CUTLER
CUTLET
DUALLY
DUBLIN
DUDLEY
DUELED
DUELER
DUELLO
DULLEA
DULLED
DULLER
DULLES
DUNLIN
DUNLOP
DUPLEX
EUCLID
FUELED

FUELER
FULLER
FURLED
GUELPH
GUILDS
GUILES
GUILTY
GULLAH
GULLED
GULLET
GURLEY
HULLED
HULLER
HULLOS
HURLED
HURLER
HURLEY
HUXLEY
KUBLAI
KUNLUN
LUBLIN
LUDLUM
LULLED
MUKLUK
MULLAH
MULLAS
MULLED
MULLER
MULLET
MUSLIM
MUSLIN
NUCLEI
NUCLEO
NULLAH
NULLED
NUTLET
OUTLAW
OUTLAY
OUTLET
PUBLIC
PULLED
PULLET
PULLEY
PULLIN
PULLON
PULLUP
PURLED
PURLIN
QUALMS
QUELLS
QUILLS
QUILTS
RUBLES
RUNLET
SUBLET
SULLEN
SUNLIT
SUSLIK
SUTLER
TUILLE
TULLES

•U••L•

BUBBLE
BUBBLY
BUCKLE
BUJOLD
BUMBLE
BUNDLE
BUNGLE
BURBLE
BURBLY
BURGLE
BUSILY

BUSTLE
CUDDLE
CUDDLY
CUMULI
CUMULO
CUPELS
CUPOLA
CURDLE
CURTLY
CURULE
DUALLY
DUELLO
DUMBLY
DUVALL
FUDDLE
FUMBLE
FUSILS
FUTILE
GURGLE
GUZZLE
HUBBLE
HUBBLY
HUDDLE
HUGELY
HUMBLE
HUMBLY
HURDLE
HURTLE
HUSTLE
JUGGLE
JUMBLE
JUNGLE
JUNGLY
JUSTLY
KURALT
KURILE
LUNULA
LUSHLY
MUDDLE
MUFFLE
MUMBLE
MUMBLY
MURALS
MUSCLE
MUSCLY
MUTELY
MUZZLE
NUBBLE
NUBILE
NUMBLY
NUZZLE
OUSELS
OUZELS
PUDDLE
PUDDLY
PUEBLA
PUEBLO
PUNILY
PUPILS
PURELY
PURFLE
PURPLE
PUZZLE
QUAILS
QUAYLE
QUELLS
QUILLS
RUBBLE
RUBBLY
RUDDLE
RUDELY
RUDOLF
RUFFLE
RUFFLY

RUMBLE
RUMBLY
RUMPLE
RUMPLY
RUNDLE
RUSTLE
RUTILE
SUBTLE
SUBTLY
SUPPLE
SUPPLY
SURELY
TUILLE
TUMBLE
TUMULI
TUMULT
TUPELO
TURTLE
TUSSLE
TUVALU
YUNGLO

•U•••L

AUDIAL
BUCCAL
BULBIL
BULBUL
BUNUEL
BURSAL
BUSHEL
CUDGEL
CUNEAL
CUPFUL
CURIAL
DUCTAL
DUFFEL
DUVALL
FUNNEL
GUMBEL
GUNNEL
JUGFUL
KUMMEL
MUDEEL
MURIEL
MUSIAL
MUSSEL
MUTUAL
NUCHAL
PUMMEL
RUEFUL
RUNNEL
RUPAUL
TUNNEL

••UL••

ADULTS
ALULAE
ALULAR
AMULET
APULIA
AVULSE
BEULAH
BOULES
BOULEZ
BOULLE
BRULES
CAULKS
COULEE
EVULSE
EXULTS
FAULTS
FAULTY
FOULED
FOULER

FOULLY
FOULUP
GOULET
HAULED
HAULER
HAULUP
JOULES
MAULED
MAULER
MOULDS
MOULDY
MOULIN
MOULTS
OCULAR
OVULAR
OVULES
PAULEY
POULTS
SAULTS
SCULLS
SCULLY
SCULPT
SKULKS
SKULLS
STULLS
TOULON
UVULAE
UVULAR
UVULAS
VAULTS

••U•L•

AQUILA
BAUBLE
BOUCLE
BOULLE
CAUDLE
CHURLS
COUPLE
DOUBLE
DOUBLY
DOURLY
EQUALS
FOULLY
GLUMLY
GRUELS
HOURLY
KNURLS
KNURLY
LOUDLY
SCULLS
SCULLY
SKULLS
SMUGLY
SNUGLY
SOURLY
SQUALL
SQUILL
STULLS
TAUTLY
THUSLY
TOUSLE
USUALS
YOUALL

••U••L

BRUMAL
BRUTAL
CAUDAL
CAUSAL
CRURAL
FAUNAL
FEUDAL
FRUGAL

LAUREL
NEURAL
NEUROL
PLURAL
SAUREL
SQUALL
SQUEAL
SQUILL
YOUALL

•••UL•

AMPULE
AMPULS
ANNULI
ANNULS
BABULS
COPULA
CUMULI
CUMULO
CURULE
ENGULF
FACULA
FERULE
FIBULA
GHOULS
INBULK
INCULT
INFULL
INSULT
ISEULT
LAZULI
LIGULA
LOBULE
LUNULA
MACULA
MODULE
MODULO
MOGULS
NEBULA
NODULE
OCCULT
OSCULA
PARULA
PENULT
PETULA
PICULS
POPULI
RADULA
RESULT
SCHULZ
SHOULD
TABULA
TUMULI
TUMULT
UNDULY
UNRULY
URSULA

•••U•L

ACTUAL
ANNUAL
BUNUEL
CASUAL
GENUAL
INFULL
LEMUEL
MANUAL
MANUEL
MIGUEL
MUTUAL
NYQUIL
RAQUEL
REFUEL
RITUAL

SAMUEL
SEQUEL
UNCURL
UNFURL
UNGUAL
VISUAL

••••UL

ARMFUL
ARTFUL
BAGFUL
BANJUL
BEFOUL
BOXFUL
BULBUL
CAPFUL
CARFUL
CONSUL
CUPFUL
DEPAUL
EARFUL
ENSOUL
EYEFUL
FITFUL
HANGUL
INHAUL
IREFUL
JARFUL
JOYFUL
JUGFUL
LAPFUL
LAWFUL
MANFUL
POTFUL
RUEFUL
RUPAUL
SINFUL
STPAUL
USEFUL
VATFUL
WOEFUL

UM••••

UMBELS
UMBERS
UMBRAE
UMBRAL
UMBRAS
UMBRIA
UMIAKS
UMLAUT
UMPIRE
UMTATA

U•M•••

UNMADE
UNMAKE
UNMANS
UNMASK
UNMEET
UNMESH
UNMOOR
UPMOST
USMAIL
UTMOST

U••M••

ULLMAN

U•••M•

UGGAMS
ULTIMA
ULTIMO
UNARMS

UNJAMS
UPTIME

•UM•••

AUMONT
BUMBLE
BUMBRY
BUMMED
BUMMER
BUMOUT
BUMPED
BUMPER
BUMPPO
BUMPUP
BUMRAP
CUMBER
CUMULI
CUMULO
DUMBER
DUMBLY
DUMDUM
DUMONT
DUMPED
DUMPER
FUMBLE
FUMING
GUMBEL
GUMBOS
GUMMED
GUMSUP
HUMANE
HUMANS
HUMBLE
HUMBLY
HUMBUG
HUMERI
HUMMED
HUMMER
HUMMUS
HUMORS
HUMOUR
HUMPED
HUMPHS
JUMADA
JUMBLE
JUMBOS
JUMPAT
JUMPED
JUMPER
JUMPIN
JUMPON
JUMPUP
KUMISS
KUMMEL
LUMBAR
LUMBER
LUMENS
LUMINA
LUMMOX
LUMPED
LUMPEN
LUMPER
LUMPUR
MUMBLE
MUMBLY
MUMMER
NUMBAT
NUMBED
NUMBER
NUMBLY
NUMERO
NUMINA
PUMICE
PUMMEL

PUMPED
PUMPER
PUMPUP
QUMRAN
RUMBAS
RUMBLE
RUMBLY
RUMENS
RUMINA
RUMMER
RUMORS
RUMOUR
RUMPLE
RUMPLY
RUMPUS
SUMACS
SUMMAE
SUMMAS
SUMMED
SUMMER
SUMMIT
SUMMON
SUMNER
SUMSUP
SUMTER
TUMBLE
TUMEFY
TUMULI
TUMULT
YUMYUM

•U•M••

BUMMED
BUMMER
BURMAN
BUSMAN
BUSMEN
DUOMOS
FULMAR
GUIMPE
GUMMED
GUNMAN
GUNMEN
HUMMED
HUMMER
HUMMUS
KUMMEL
LUMMOX
MUMMER
MURMUR
MUUMUU
NUTMEG
PUMMEL
QUEMOY
RUDMAN
RUMMER
SUBMIT
SUMMAE
SUMMAS
SUMMED
SUMMER
SUMMIT
SUMMON
TUBMAN

•U••M•

AUTUMN
QUALMS
RUNDMC
SURIMI

•U•••M

BUNKUM
CUBISM

CURIUM
CUSTOM
DUMDUM
DUNHAM
DURHAM
LUDLUM
MUSEUM
MUSLIM
PURISM
PUTNAM
QUORUM
SUBGUM
SUFISM
YUMYUM

••UM••

ACUMEN
ALUMNA
ALUMNI
BRUMAL
BRUMES
CHUMMY
CHUMPS
CLUMPS
CLUMPY
CLUMSY
CRUMBS
CRUMBY
CRUMMY
DRUMUP
FLUMES
FRUMPS
FRUMPY
GLUMLY
GRUMPS
GRUMPY
MAUMAU
MAUMEE
MUUMUU
NEUMAN
NEUMES
NOUMEA
PLUMBS
PLUMED
PLUMES
PLUMMY
PLUMPS
RHUMBA
RHUMBS
SCUMMY
SLUMMY
SLUMPS
SPUMED
SPUMES
STUMPS
STUMPY
THUMBS
THUMPS
TRUMAN
TRUMPS

••U•M•

CHUMMY
CRUMMY
PLUMMY
SCUMMY
SLUMMY
ZEUGMA

••U••M

SQUIRM
TRUISM

•••UM•

ALBUMS
ASSUME
AUTUMN
BATUMI
BEGUMS
BENUMB
COLUMN
FORUMS
ILLUME
INHUME
JORUMS
LEGUME
MAZUMA
ODIUMS
PNEUMA
RELUME
RESUME
RHEUMS
RHEUMY
SCRUMS
SEDUMS
SERUMS
STRUMS
THRUMS
TRAUMA
VOLUME

•••U•M

VACUUM

••••UM

ACTIUM
ADYTUM
ALARUM
ALLIUM
ANTRUM
ARTGUM
ASYLUM
ATRIUM
BARIUM
BARNUM
BAYRUM
BEEGUM
BOOJUM
BUNKUM
CERIUM
CESIUM
CILIUM
CIRCUM
CONIUM
CORIUM
CURIUM
DICTUM
DIMSUM
DORSUM
DUMDUM
ERBIUM
FAIYUM
FOLIUM
FRENUM
GOLLUM
GYPSUM
HELIUM
INDIUM
IONIUM
LABRUM
LATIUM
LUDLUM
LYCEUM
MAGNUM
MEDIUM
MINIUM
MUSEUM

OMASUM
OMNIUM
OSMIUM
OSTIUM
PABLUM
PEPLUM
PHYLUM
PILEUM
PLENUM
PODIUM
POSSUM
PRIMUM
QUORUM
RADIUM
REDGUM
SACRUM
SCARUM
SEPTUM
SODIUM
SUBGUM
TALCUM
TEDEUM
TEDIUM
VACUUM
VALIUM
VELLUM
WAMPUM
YUMYUM

UN••••

UNABLE
UNAGED
UNARMS
UNAWED
UNBARS
UNBELT
UNBEND
UNBENT
UNBIND
UNBOLT
UNBORN
UNCAGE
UNCAPS
UNCASE
UNCHIC
UNCIAL
UNCLAD
UNCLES
UNCLOG
UNCOIL
UNCOOL
UNCORK
UNCURL
UNDIES
UNDINE
UNDOER
UNDOES
UNDONE
UNDRAW
UNDULY
UNDYED
UNEASE
UNEASY
UNESCO
UNEVEN
UNFAIR
UNFITS
UNFOLD
UNFURL
UNGIRD
UNGIRT
UNGLUE
UNGUAL
UNGUES

UNGUIS
UNHAND
UNHEED
UNHOLY
UNHOOK
UNHURT
UNIATE
UNIATS
UNICEF
UNIFIC
UNIONS
UNIPOD
UNIQUE
UNISEX
UNISON
UNITAL
UNITAS
UNITED
UNITER
UNITES
UNIVAC
UNJAMS
UNJUST
UNKIND
UNKINK
UNKNIT
UNKNOT
UNLACE
UNLADE
UNLAID
UNLASH
UNLEAD
UNLESS
UNLIKE
UNLINK
UNLOAD
UNLOCK
UNMADE
UNMAKE
UNMANS
UNMASK
UNMEET
UNMESH
UNMOOR
UNOPEN
UNPACK
UNPAID
UNPEGS
UNPENS
UNPILE
UNPINS
UNPLUG
UNREAD
UNREAL
UNREEL
UNREST
UNRIGS
UNRIPE
UNROBE
UNROLL
UNROOT
UNRULY
UNSAFE
UNSAID
UNSAYS
UNSEAL
UNSEAT
UNSEEN
UNSEWN
UNSEWS
UNSHED
UNSHOD
UNSNAG
UNSNAP

UNSOLD
UNSOWN
UNSTOP
UNSUNG
UNSURE
UNTACK
UNTIDY
UNTIED
UNTIES
UNTOLD
UNTORN
UNTRAP
UNTROD
UNTRUE
UNTUNE
UNUSED
UNVEIL
UNWARY
UNWELL
UNWIND
UNWISE
UNWORN
UNWOVE
UNWRAP
UNYOKE
UNZIPS

U••N••

UBANGI
UGANDA
UNKNIT
UNKNOT
UNSNAG
UNSNAP
UPENDS
URANIA
URANIC
URANUS
USANCE

U•••N•

UCLANS
UHLANS
UNBEND
UNBENT
UNBIND
UNDINE
UNDONE
UNHAND
UNIONS
UNKIND
UNKINK
UNLINK
UNMANS
UNPENS
UNPINS
UNSUNG
UNTUNE
UNWIND
UPLAND
UPLINK
UPPING
UPWIND
URBANA
URBANE
URGENT
URGING
URSINE
UTHANT
UTURNS

U••••N

UGRIAN
UJJAIN

ULLMAN
UNBORN
UNEVEN
UNISON
UNOPEN
UNSEEN
UNSEWN
UNSOWN
UNTORN
UNWORN
UPTOWN
UPTURN
URCHIN
USOPEN
UTAHAN

•UN•••

AUNTIE
BUNCHE
BUNCOS
BUNDLE
BUNGED
BUNGEE
BUNGLE
BUNION
BUNKED
BUNKER
BUNKOS
BUNKUM
BUNSEN
BUNTED
BUNTER
BUNUEL
BUNYAN
CUNARD
CUNAXA
CUNEAL
DUNANT
DUNBAR
DUNCAN
DUNCES
DUNDEE
DUNERA
DUNHAM
DUNKED
DUNKER
DUNLIN
DUNLOP
DUNNED
EUNICE
EUNUCH
FUNDED
FUNGUS
FUNKED
FUNNED
FUNNEL
GUNDOG
GUNFOR
GUNGHO
GUNMAN
GUNMEN
GUNNAR
GUNNED
GUNNEL
GUNNER
GUNSHY
GUNTER
HUNGER
HUNGIN
HUNGON
HUNGRY
HUNGUP
HUNGWU
HUNKER

HUNTED
HUNTER
JUNCOS
JUNEAU
JUNGLE
JUNGLY
JUNIOR
JUNKED
JUNKER
JUNKET
JUNKIE
JUNTAS
JUNTOS
KUNGFU
KUNLUN
LUNACY
LUNATE
LUNDEN
LUNGED
LUNGES
LUNKER
LUNULA
MUNCIE
MUNGOS
MUNICH
MUNTIN
NUNCIO
OUNCES
PUNCHY
PUNDIT
PUNIER
PUNILY
PUNISH
PUNJAB
PUNKAH
PUNKER
PUNKIE
PUNNED
PUNTED
PUNTER
RUNCIE
RUNDLE
RUNDMC
RUNDRY
RUNGUP
RUNINS
RUNLET
RUNNEL
RUNNER
RUNOFF
RUNONS
RUNOUT
RUNSIN
RUNSON
RUNSTO
RUNSUP
RUNUPS
RUNWAY
RUNYON
SUNDAE
SUNDAY
SUNDER
SUNDEW
SUNDOG
SUNDRY
SUNGOD
SUNKEN
SUNLIT
SUNNED
SUNNIS
SUNOCO
SUNRAY
SUNSET
SUNTAN
SUNUNU
SUNUPS
TUNDRA
TUNEIN
TUNERS
TUNEUP
TUNICA
TUNICS
TUNING
TUNNEL
TUNNEY
YUNGLO
YUNNAN

•U•N••

BUENOS
BURNED
BURNER
BURNET
BURNEY
BURNUP
DUENNA
DUNNED
EUPNEA
FUNNED
FUNNEL
GUENON
GUINEA
GUNNAR
GUNNED
GUNNEL
GUNNER
GURNEY
LUANDA
LUGNUT
NUANCE
NUDNIK
PUENTE
PUNNED
PUTNAM
QUANTA
QUENCH
QUINCE
QUINCY
QUINOA
QUINTS
RUANAS
RUANDA
RUINED
RUINER
RUNNEL
RUNNER
SUMNER
SUNNED
SUNNIS
TUNNEL
TUNNEY
TURNED
TURNER
TURNIN
TURNIP
TURNON
TURNTO
TURNUP
YUNNAN

•U••N•

AUDENS
AUFOND
AUGEND
AUMONT
AUXINS
BURINS
BUSING
BUSONI
BUTANE
BUTENE
BUTUNG
BUYING
CUBING
CURING
CUTINS
DUENNA
DUGONG
DUKING
DUMONT
DUNANT
DUPING
DUPONT
DURANT
DURING
EUGENE
FULANI
FUMING
FUSING
FUTONS
FUZING
GUIANA
GUYANA
GUYING
HUMANE
HUMANS
HURONS
JUKING
LUBING
LUCENT
LUDENS
LUMENS
LUMINA
LUPINE
LUPINO
LUPONE
LURING
LUTING
MURANO
MURINE
MUSING
MUSTNT
MUTANT
MUTING
MUTINY
NUGENT
NUKING
NUMINA
OUTING
PUISNE
PULING
PURINA
PURINE
PUTONS
QUAINT
QUEENS
QUERNS
QUOINS
RUBENS
RULING
RUMENS
RUMINA
RUNINS
RUNONS
SUNUNU
SUPINE
SUSANN
TUBING
TUCANA
TULANE
TUNING
TURING

•U•••N

AUBURN
AUGEAN
AUSTEN
AUSTIN
AUTUMN
BUFFON
BUNION
BUNSEN
BUNYAN
BURDEN
BURMAN
BURTON
BUSKIN
BUSMAN
BUSMEN
BUTTIN
BUTTON
CULKIN
CULLEN
CURTIN
CURZON
CUTSIN
DUBBIN
DUBLIN
DUCHIN
DUDEEN
DUNCAN
DUNLIN
DURBAN
DURBIN
DURIAN
DUSTIN
FUJIAN
FULTON
FUSION
GUDRUN
GUENON
GUIDON
GUNMAN
GUNMEN
HUDSON
HUNGIN
HUNGON
HUSTON
HUTTON
JULIAN
JUMPIN
JUMPON
JUSTIN
KUCHEN
KUNLUN
KURGAN
LUBLIN
LUCIAN
LUDDEN
LUMPEN
LUNDEN
MUDHEN
MUFFIN
MUNTIN
MUSLIN
MUTTON
NUBBIN
NUBIAN
NUTKIN
OUTGUN
OUTRAN
OUTRUN
PUFFIN
PULLIN
PULLON
PURLIN
PUSHON
PUTSIN
PUTSON
QUMRAN
RUBSIN
RUDMAN
RULEON
RUNSIN
RUNSON
RUNYON
RUSKIN
RUTTAN
SUBORN
SUCKIN
SUDDEN
SULLEN
SULTAN
SUMMON
SUNKEN
SUNTAN
SUSANN
TUBMAN
TUCHUN
TUCKIN
TUCSON
TULSAN
TUNEIN
TUPIAN
TURBAN
TUREEN
TURNIN
TURNON
TUSCAN
VULCAN
YUNNAN

••UN••

BLUNTS
BOUNCE
BOUNCY
BOUNDS
BOUNTY
BRUNCH
BRUNEI
BRUNET
BRUNTS
CHUNKS
CHUNKY
CLUNKS
CLUNKY
COUNTS
COUNTY
CRUNCH
DAUNTS
FAUNAE
FAUNAL
FAUNAS
FAUNUS
FLUNKS
FLUNKY
FOUNDS
FOUNTS
GOUNOD
GRUNDY
GRUNGE
GRUNGY
GRUNTS
HAUNCH
HAUNTS
HOUNDS
JAUNTS
JAUNTY
JOUNCE
JOUNCY
KAUNAS
KAUNDA
LAUNCH
LOUNGE
MAUNDY
MBUNDU
MOUNDS
MOUNTS
MOUNTY
PAUNCH
PLUNGE
PLUNKS
POUNCE
POUNDS
PRUNED
PRUNER
PRUNES
REUNES
ROUNDS
SAUNAS
SHUNTS
SKUNKS
SOUNDS
SPUNKY
STUNTS
TAUNTS
THUNKS
TRUNKS
VAUNTS
WOUNDS
ZOUNDS

••U•N•

ALUMNA
ALUMNI
AQUINO
BLUING
BOURNE
BRUINS
CHURNS
CLUING
EQUINE
FLUENT
GLUING
GLUONS
IGUANA
SLUING
SPURNS
SQUINT
TAUONS
TRUANT
TRUING
UTURNS

••U••N

ACUMEN
ANURAN
ARUBAN
BHUTAN
BOUDIN
CLUEIN
COUPON
COUSIN
GLUTEN
LAUREN
LOUDEN
MOULIN
MOUTON
NEUMAN
NEURON
NGUYEN
PLUGIN
POURIN
REUBEN
SHUTIN
SPURON
TAUTEN
TEUTON
TOUCAN
TOULON
TRUMAN
VAUGHN
YAUPON

•••UN•

ABOUND
AMOUNT
ARJUNA
AROUND
ATTUNE
AVAUNT
BOSUNS
BUTUNG
CAJUNS
COHUNE
DEBUNK
EDMUND
EXEUNT
FECUND
FLAUNT
GERUND
GROUND
IMMUNE
IMMUNO
INTUNE
JEJUNE
JOCUND
KAHUNA
KORUNA
LACUNA
LAGUNA
OBTUND
OSMUND
PODUNK
REFUND
REHUNG
RERUNS
RETUNE
ROTUND
SHRUNK
SPRUNG
STRUNG
SUNUNU
TRIUNE
UNSUNG
UNTUNE
VARUNA
VICUNA

•••U•N

ALCUIN
AUBURN
AUTUMN
COBURN
COLUMN
IMPUGN
INTURN
MCKUEN
OPPUGN
PADUAN
PAPUAN
REPUGN
RETURN
SATURN
SEQUIN
SIOUAN
UPTURN

••••UN

AIRGUN
BARZUN
BIGGUN
CANCUN
CAPGUN
DATSUN
DRYRUN
ENDRUN
GUDRUN
JETGUN
KUNLUN
LEBRUN
OUTGUN
OUTRUN
POPGUN
RAYGUN
SHOGUN
SIXGUN
SKIRUN
TOPGUN
TUCHUN
VERDUN

U•O•••

UBOATS
UBOLTS
UNOPEN
USOPEN
UTOPIA

U••O••

UNBOLT
UNBORN
UNCOIL
UNCOOL
UNCORK
UNDOER
UNDOES
UNDONE
UNFOLD
UNHOLY
UNHOOK
UNIONS
UNLOAD
UNLOCK
UNMOOR
UNROBE
UNROLL
UNROOT
UNSOLD
UNSOWN
UNTOLD
UNTORN
UNWORN
UNWOVE
UNYOKE
UPBOWS
UPHOLD
UPLOAD
UPMOST
UPROAR
UPROOT
UPROSE
UPTOWN
UTMOST

U•••O•

UNCLOG
UNCOOL
UNHOOK
UNIPOD
UNISON
UNKNOT
UNMOOR
UNROOT
UNSHOD
UNSTOP
UNTROD
UPROOT
UPSHOT

U••••O

ULTIMO
UNESCO
USEDTO

•UO•••

BUOYED
BUOYUP
DUOMOS
QUOINS
QUOITS
QUOKKA
QUORUM
QUOTAS
QUOTED
QUOTER
QUOTES
QUOTHA

•U•O••

AUFOND
AUMONT
AURORA
AUROUS
BUGOFF
BUGOUT
BUJOLD
BULOVA
BUMOUT
BUROAK
BUSONI
BUYOFF
BUYOUT
CUBOID
CUPOLA
CUTOFF
CUTOUT
DUBOIS
DUGONG
DUGOUT
DUMONT
DUPONT
DUROCS
EUBOEA
EUDORA
EULOGY
EUROPA
EUROPE
FURORE
FURORS
FUTONS
GUYOTS
HUMORS
HUMOUR
HURONS
JUDOKA
JURORS
LUGOSI
LUPONE
MUCOSA
MUCOUS
PUTOFF
PUTONS
PUTOUT
RUBOUT
RUDOLF
RUFOUS
RUGOSE
RUMORS
RUMOUR
RUNOFF
RUNONS
RUNOUT
SUBORN
SUNOCO
TUDORS
TUTORS
YUROKS

•U••O•

AUDIOS
AUTHOR
BUENOS
BUFFON
BUFFOS
BUNCOS
BUNION
BUNKOS
BURBOT
BURGOO
BURGOS
BURROS
BURROW
BURTON
BUSBOY
BUTEOS
BUTTON
CUCKOO
CURIOS
CURSOR
CURZON
CUSTOM
DUNLOP
DUOMOS
FULTON
FURROW
FUSION
FUZHOU
GUACOS
GUENON
GUIDON
GUMBOS
GUNDOG
GUNFOR
HUDSON
HUEVOS
HULLOS
HUNGON
HUSTON
HUTTON
JUMBOS
JUMPON
JUNCOS
JUNIOR
JUNTOS
LUMMOX
LUTHOR
MUGHOS
MUNGOS
MURROW
MUSKOX
MUTTON
OUTFOX
PULLON
PUSHON
PUTSON
QUAHOG
QUEMOY
QUINOA
RULEON
RUNSON
RUNYON
SUCCOR
SUITOR
SUMMON
SUNDOG
SUNGOD
TUCSON
TURBOS
TURBOT
TURGOR
TURNON

•U•••O

AUSTRO
BUMPPO
BURGOO
CUCKOO
CUMULO
DUELLO
GUNGHO
JURADO
LUPINO
MURANO
NUCLEO
NUMERO
NUNCIO
PUEBLO
PUERTO
PUTSTO
QUARTO
RUNSTO
SUBITO
SUNOCO
TUPELO
TURNTO
TUXEDO
YUNGLO

••UO••

FLUORO
GLUONS
TAUONS

••U•O•

BLUEOX
BOUBOU
COUPON
CRUSOE
GOUNOD
MOUTON
NEUROL
NEURON
SPURON
STUPOR
TAUTOG
TEUTON
TOULON
YAUPON
ZHUKOV

••U••O

AQUINO
BHUTTO
CAUCHO
CHURRO
FLUORO
GAUCHO
SLUGGO
STUCCO
STUDIO

•••UO•

LIQUOR
PEQUOD
PEQUOT

•••U•O

ARTURO
BAGUIO
CARUSO
COLUGO
CUMULO
ENDURO
ESCUDO
IMMUNO
MADURO
MAPUTO
MODULO
PSEUDO
TENUTO

••••UO

BANQUO

UP••••

UPBEAT
UPBOWS
UPCAST
UPDATE
UPDIKE
UPENDS
UPHELD
UPHILL
UPHOLD
UPKEEP
UPLAND
UPLIFT
UPLINK
UPLOAD
UPMOST
UPPERS
UPPING
UPPITY
UPRISE
UPROAR
UPROOT
UPROSE
UPRUSH
UPSETS
UPSHOT
UPSIDE
UPTAKE
UPTICK
UPTIME
UPTOWN
UPTURN
UPWARD
UPWELL
UPWIND

U•P•••

UMPIRE
UNPACK
UNPAID
UNPEGS
UNPENS
UNPILE
UNPINS
UNPLUG
UPPERS
UPPING
UPPITY

U••P••

UNIPOD
UNOPEN
USOPEN
UTOPIA

U•••P•

UNCAPS
UNRIPE
UNZIPS
USURPS

U••••P

UNSNAP
UNSTOP
UNTRAP
UNWRAP
UPKEEP
USEDUP
USESUP

•UP•••

AUPAIR
CUPELS
CUPFUL
CUPIDS
CUPOLA
CUPPED
CUPRIC
DUPERY
DUPING
DUPLEX
DUPONT
EUPNEA
LUPINE
LUPINO
LUPONE
MUPPET
PUPILS
PUPPET
RUPAUL
RUPEES
RUPERT
RUPIAH
SUPERB
SUPERS
SUPINE
SUPPED
SUPPER
SUPPLE
SUPPLY
TUPELO
TUPIAN
YUPPIE

•U•P••

AUSPEX
BUMPED
BUMPER
BUMPPO
BUMPUP
BURPED
CUPPED
CUSPED
CUSPID
DUMPED
DUMPER
GULPED
GULPER
HUMPED
HUMPHS
JUMPAT
JUMPED
JUMPER
JUMPIN
JUMPON
JUMPUP
LUMPED
LUMPEN
LUMPER
LUMPUR
MUDPIE
MUPPET
MURPHY
OUTPUT
PULPED
PULPIT
PUMPED
PUMPER
PUMPUP
PUPPET
PURPLE
PUTPUT
QUIPPY
QUIPUS
RUMPLE
RUMPLY
RUMPUS
SUPPED
SUPPER
SUPPLE
SUPPLY
YUPPIE

•U••P•

BUMPPO
CUTUPS
EUROPA
EUROPE
GUELPH
GUIMPE
JULEPS
QUIPPY
RUNUPS
SUNUPS
TULIPS

•U•••P

BUCKUP
BUMPUP
BUMRAP
BUOYUP
BURLAP
BURNUP
BUYSUP
CURLUP
CUTSUP
DUNLOP
DUSTUP
GUMSUP
HUBCAP
HUNGUP
JUMPUP
MUCKUP
MUSSUP
PULLUP
PUMPUP
PUSHUP
PUTSUP
RUNGUP
RUNSUP
SUITUP
SUMSUP
TUNEUP
TURNIP
TURNUP

••UP••

COUPES
COUPLE
COUPON
DRUPES
ERUPTS
LAUPER
LOUPES
PAUPER
SOUPUP
STUPAS
STUPES
STUPID
STUPOR
TAUPES
TOUPEE
YAUPON

••U•P•

CHUMPS
CLUMPS
CLUMPY
EQUIPS
FRUMPS
FRUMPY
GRUMPS
GRUMPY
PLUMPS
SCULPT
SLUMPS
SLURPS
STUMPS
STUMPY
THUMPS
TRUMPS
USURPS

••U••P

DRUMUP
FOULUP
HAULUP
SHUTUP
SOUPUP

•••UP•

ABRUPT
CROUPY
CUTUPS
FIXUPS
GETUPS
GROUPS
IRRUPT
JAMUPS
LAYUPS
LETUPS
MIXUPS
MOPUPS
NIPUPS
OCCUPY
ONEUPS
PINUPS
POPUPS
RUNUPS
SCAUPS
SETUPS
SITUPS
STOUPS
SUNUPS
SYRUPS
SYRUPY
TIEUPS
TIPUPS
TROUPE

••••UP

ACESUP
ACTSUP
ADDSUP
ANTEUP

BACKUP
BALLUP
BANGUP
BEADUP
BEAMUP
BEARUP
BEATUP
BEEFUP
BIDSUP
BINDUP
BLEWUP
BLOWUP
BOBSUP
BONEUP
BOOTUP
BOREUP
BUCKUP
BUMPUP
BUOYUP
BURNUP
BUYSUP
CALLUP
CAMEUP
CATSUP
CHATUP
CHEWUP
CHINUP
CLAMUP
CLOGUP
COILUP
COMEUP
COOKUP
COOPUP
CROPUP
CURLUP
CUTSUP
DAMSUP
DIGSUP
DOESUP
DOLLUP
DONEUP
DRAWUP
DREWUP
DRUMUP
DUSTUP
EASEUP
EATSUP
EGGCUP
ENDSUP
EVENUP
EYECUP
FACEUP
FAIRUP
FESSUP
FILLUP
FIREUP
FIRMUP
FLIPUP
FOLDUP
FOULUP
GALLUP
GANGUP
GAVEUP
GEARUP
GETSUP
GIVEUP
GOESUP
GOOFUP
GREWUP
GROWUP
GUMSUP
HANGUP
HARDUP
HAULUP
HEADUP
HEATUP
HELDUP
HICCUP
HIGHUP
HITSUP
HOLDUP
HOLEUP
HOOKUP
HOPSUP
HUNGUP
ICEDUP
ICESUP
JACKUP
JAMSUP
JAZZUP
JOINUP
JUMPUP
KEEPUP
KEPTUP
KEYSUP
KICKUP
LACEUP
LAIDUP
LAPSUP
LARRUP
LASHUP
LAYSUP
LEADUP
LETSUP
LIFTUP
LINEUP
LINKUP
LOCKUP
LOOKUP
MADEUP
MAKEUP
MARKUP
MESSUP
MOCKUP
MOPSUP
MUCKUP
MUSSUP
OPENUP
OWNSUP
PACKUP
PAIDUP
PAIRUP
PASSUP
PAYSUP
PENTUP
PEPSUP
PERKUP
PICKUP
PILEUP
PIPEUP
PLAYUP
PONYUP
POPSUP
PROPUP
PULLUP
PUMPUP
PUSHUP
PUTSUP
RACKUP
RAKEUP
RANGUP
REARUP
RECOUP
RESTUP
RIGSUP
RINGUP
RIPSUP
ROLLUP
RUNGUP
RUNSUP
SANNUP
SAVEUP
SEALUP
SENDUP
SENTUP
SETSUP
SEWNUP
SEWSUP
SHOTUP
SHOWUP
SHUTUP
SIGNUP
SITSUP
SIZEUP
SLAPUP
SLIPUP
SLOWUP
SNAPUP
SOAKUP
SOPSUP
SOUPUP
SPEDUP
STAYUP
STEPUP
STIRUP
STOPUP
SUITUP
SUMSUP
TAGSUP
TAKEUP
TALKUP
TANKUP
TEACUP
TEAMUP
TEARUP
TEEDUP
TEESUP
TIDYUP
TIEDUP
TIESUP
TONEUP
TOOKUP
TOOLUP
TOREUP
TOSSUP
TOTSUP
TRIPUP
TUNEUP
TURNUP
TYPEUP
USEDUP
USESUP
WADSUP
WAITUP
WAKEUP
WALKUP
WALLUP
WARMUP
WASHUP
WELLUP
WENTUP
WHIPUP
WINDUP
WIPEUP
WISEUP
WOKEUP
WORKUP
WRAPUP
ZIPSUP

U••Q••
UNIQUE

•UQ•••
BUQSHA
TUQUES

•U•Q••
PULQUE

•U•••Q
SUSIEQ

UR••••
URACIL
URAEUS
URALIC
URALSK
URANIA
URANIC
URANUS
URBANA
URBANE
URCHIN
URGENT
URGERS
URGING
URIALS
URSIDS
URSINE
URSULA
URUSES

U•R•••
UGRIAN
UNREAD
UNREAL
UNREEL
UNREST
UNRIGS
UNRIPE
UNROBE
UNROLL
UNROOT
UNRULY
UPRISE
UPROAR
UPROOT
UPROSE
UPRUSH

U••R••
ULTRAS
UMBRAE
UMBRAL
UMBRAS
UMBRIA
UNARMS
UNDRAW
UNTRAP
UNTROD
UNTRUE
UNWRAP
USERID
USURER
USURPS
UTURNS

U•••R•
UAKARI
UDDERS
UIGURS
ULCERS
UMBERS
UMPIRE
UNBARS
UNBORN
UNCORK
UNCURL
UNFURL
UNGIRD
UNGIRT
UNHURT
UNSURE
UNTORN
UNWARY
UNWORN
UPPERS
UPTURN
UPWARD
URGERS
USHERS
UTTERS

U••••R
UGLIER
ULSTER
UNDOER
UNFAIR
UNITER
UNMOOR
UPROAR
USURER
UVULAR

•UR•••
AUREUS
AURIGA
AURORA
AUROUS
BURBLE
BURBLY
BURBOT
BURDEN
BUREAU
BURGAS
BURGEE
BURGER
BURGHS
BURGLE
BURGOO
BURGOS
BURIED
BURIES
BURINS
BURLAP
BURLED
BURLEY
BURMAN
BURNED
BURNER
BURNET
BURNEY
BURNUP
BUROAK
BURPED
BURRED
BURROS
BURROW
BURSAE
BURSAL
BURSAR
BURSAS
BURSES
BURSTS
BURTON
CURACY
CURARE
CURATE
CURBED
CURDED
CURDLE
CURERS
CURFEW
CURIAE
CURIAL
CURING
CURIOS
CURIUM
CURLED
CURLER
CURLEW
CURLUP
CURRED
CURSED
CURSES
CURSOR
CURTER
CURTIN
CURTIS
CURTIZ
CURTLY
CURTSY
CURULE
CURVED
CURVES
CURVET
CURZON
DURANT
DURBAN
DURBAR
DURBIN
DURESS
DURFEY
DURHAM
DURIAN
DURING
DUROCS
DURYEA
EUREKA
EUROPA
EUROPE
FURIES
FURLED
FURORE
FURORS
FURRED
FURROW
GURGLE
GURKHA
GURLEY
GURNEY
HURDLE
HURLED
HURLER
HURLEY
HURONS
HURRAH
HURRAY
HURTLE
JURADO
JURATS
JURIES
JURIST
JURORS
KURALT
KURGAN
KURILE
LURING
LURKED
MURALS
MURANO
MURCIA
MURDER
MURIEL
MURINE
MURMUR
MURPHY
MURRAY
MURRES
MURREY
MURROW
NURSED
NURSER
NURSES
PURACE
PURDAH
PURDUE
PUREED
PUREES
PURELY
PUREST
PURFLE
PURGED
PURGES
PURIFY
PURINA
PURINE
PURISM
PURIST
PURITY
PURLED
PURLIN
PURPLE
PURRED
PURRER
PURSED
PURSER
PURSES
PURSUE
PURVEY
QURUSH
SURAHS
SURELY
SUREST
SURETE
SURETY
SURFED
SURFER
SURGED
SURGES
SURIMI
SURREY
SURTAX
SURVEY
TURBAN
TURBID
TURBIT
TURBOS
TURBOT
TUREEN
TURFED
TURGID
TURGOR
TURING
TURKEY
TURKIC
TURNED
TURNER
TURNIN
TURNIP
TURNON
TURNTO
TURNUP
TURRET
TURTLE
WURSTS
YUROKS
ZURICH

•U•R••
AUBREY
AUDREY
BUMRAP
BURRED
BURROS
BURROW
CUPRIC
CURRED
DUARTE
FURRED
FURROW
GUARDS
GUDRUN
GUERRE
HUBRIS
HURRAH
HURRAY
JUAREZ
KUKRIS
MUDRAS
MURRAY
MURRES
MURREY
MURROW
NUTRIA
OUTRAN
OUTRUN
PUERTO
PUGREE
PURRED
PURRER
PUTRID
QUARKS
QUARRY
QUARTO
QUARTS
QUARTZ
QUERNS
QUIRES
QUIRKS
QUIRKY
QUIRTS
QUMRAN
QUORUM
RUBRIC
SUNRAY
SURREY
SUTRAS
TUAREG
TUGRIK
TURRET

•U••R•
AUBURN
AUGERS
AUGURS
AUGURY
AURORA
AUSTRO
BUMBRY
BUYERS
CUNARD
CURARE
CURERS
DUNERA
DUPERY
EUCHRE
EUDORA
FUGARD
FULCRA
FURORE
FURORS
FUTURE
GUERRE
HUBERT
HUMERI
HUMORS
HUNGRY
JURORS
LUGERS
LUSTRE
LUXURY
MUSERS
NUMERO
OUTCRY
QUADRI
QUARRY
RULERS
RUMORS
RUNDRY
RUPERT
SUBARU
SUBORN
SUBURB
SUGARS
SUGARY
SULTRY
SUNDRY
SUPERB
SUPERS
SUTURE
TUBERS
TUDORS
TULARE
TUNDRA
TUNERS
TUTORS
TUYERE

•U•••R
AUPAIR
AUTEUR
AUTHOR
BUFFER
BUGLER
BULGAR
BULGUR
BULWER
BUMMER
BUMPER
BUNKER
BUNTER
BURGER
BURNER
BURSAR
BUSBAR
BUSIER
BUSTER
BUTLER
BUTTER
BUZZER
CULLER
CULVER
CUMBER
CURLER
CURSOR
CURTER
CUSTER
CUTLER
CUTTER
DUELER
DUFFER
DUIKER
DULLER
DUMBER
DUMPER
DUNBAR
DUNKER
DURBAR
DUSTER
FUELER
FULLER
FULMAR
GUITAR
GULPER
GUNFOR
GUNNAR
GUNNER
GUNTER
GUSHER
GUTTER
HUGGER
HULLER
HUMMER
HUMOUR
HUNGER
HUNKER
HUNTER
HURLER
HUSKER
HUSSAR
JUDDER
JUICER
JUMPER
JUNIOR
JUNKER
JUSTER
KULTUR
LUBBER
LUGGER
LUMBAR
LUMBER
LUMPER
LUMPUR
LUNKER
LUSHER
LUSTER
LUTHER
LUTHOR
MUDDER
MUGGER
MULLER
MUMMER
MURDER
MURMUR
MUSHER
MUSTER
MUTTER
NUDGER
NUMBER
NURSER
NUTTER
OUSTER
PUCKER
PUFFER
PULSAR
PUMPER
PUNIER
PUNKER
PUNTER
PURRER
PURSER
PUTTER
QUAKER
QUASAR
QUAVER
QUEUER
QUIVER
QUOTER
RUBBER
RUDDER
RUINER
RUMMER
RUMOUR
RUNNER
RUTGER
SUAVER
SUCCOR
SUCKER
SUFFER
SUITOR
SULFUR
SULKER
SUMMER
SUMNER
SUMTER
SUNDER
SUPPER
SURFER
SUTLER
SUTTER
TUCKER
TUGGER
TURGOR
TURNER
TUSKER
VULGAR
ZUIDER

••UR••
ANURAN
BEURRE
BLURBS
BLURRY
BLURTS
BOURKE
BOURNE
BOURSE
CHURCH
CHURLS
CHURNS
CHURRO
CHURRS
COURIC
COURSE
COURTS
CRURAL
DOURER
DOURLY
ENURED
ENURES
EXURBS
FLURRY
FOURTH
GOURDE
GOURDS
HOURIS
HOURLY
INURED
INURES
ITURBI
JAURES
KAURIS
KNURLS
KNURLY
LAUREL
LAUREN
LAURIE
MAURYA
NEURAL
NEUROL
NEURON
PLURAL
POURED
POURER
POURIN
SAUREL
SCURFY
SCURRY
SCURVE
SCURVY
SEURAT
SLURPS
SLURRY
SMURFS
SOURCE
SOURED
SOURER
SOURLY
SPURGE
SPURNS
SPURON
SPURRY
SPURTS
STURDY
TAURUS
TOURED
TOURER
USURER
USURPS
UTURNS

••U•R•
BEURRE
BLURRY
CHURRO
CHURRS
EDUARD
FLUORO
FLURRY
GLUERS
LOUVRE
OEUVRE
SCURRY
SLURRY
SOUARI
SPURRY
SQUARE
SQUIRE
SQUIRM
SQUIRT
STUART

••U••R
ABUKIR
ABUSER
ALULAR
BRUDER
CHUKAR
COUGAR
COUTER
CRUDER
DAUBER
DOURER
FOULER
GAUGER
GOUGER
HAULER
KRUGER
LAUDER
LAUPER
LOUDER
LOUVER
MAULER
MAUSER
MOUSER
NEUTER
OCULAR
OVULAR
PAUPER
POURER
POUTER
PRUNER
REUTER
ROUTER
SAUCER
SAUGER
SOURER
SOUTER
STUPOR
TAUTER
TOURER
TOUTER
USURER
UVULAR

•••UR•
ABJURE
ABSURD
ADJURE
ALLURE
AMOURS
ARMURE
ARTURO
ASBURY
ASSURE
AUBURN
AUGURS
AUGURY
COBURG
COBURN
DATURA
DEJURE
DEMURE
DEMURS
ENDURE
ENDURO
ENSURE
ERFURT
FEMURS
FIGURE
FLEURY
FLOURS
FLOURY
FUTURE
IMMURE
IMPURE
INCURS
INJURE
INJURY
INSURE
INTURN
LEMURS
LIGURE
LUXURY
MADURA
MADURO
MATURE
MOHURS
NATURE
OCCURS
ODOURS
ORDURE
PARURE
PENURY
PLEURA
RECURS
RETURN
SATURN
SCOURS
SECURE
SEGURA
SIGURD
SUBURB
SUTURE
TENURE
UIGURS
UNCURL
UNFURL
UNHURT
UNSURE
UPTURN
YOGURT

•••U•R
ARGUER
BREUER
ISSUER
JAGUAR
LIQUOR
QUEUER
VAGUER

••••UR
ARBOUR
ARDOUR
ARMOUR
ARTHUR
AUTEUR
BENHUR
BIGSUR
BULGUR
COLOUR
CONCUR
DAMOUR
DETOUR
DEVOUR
FAVOUR
HONOUR
HUMOUR
INPOUR
JAIPUR
KIPPUR
KRONUR
KULTUR
LABOUR
LAMOUR
LANGUR
LATOUR
LUMPUR
MURMUR
NIPPUR
ONTOUR
POSEUR
RAIPUR
RETOUR
RIGOUR
RUMOUR
SAVOUR
SIDDUR
SULFUR
VALOUR
VAPOUR
VELOUR
VIGOUR
WILBUR

US••••
USABLE
USABLY
USAGES
USANCE
USEDTO
USEDUP
USEFUL
USERID
USESUP
USHERS
USMAIL
USOPEN
USUALS
USURER
USURPS

U•S•••
ULSTER
UNSAFE
UNSAID
UNSAYS
UNSEAL
UNSEAT
UNSEEN
UNSEWN
UNSEWS
UNSHED
UNSHOD
UNSNAG
UNSNAP
UNSOLD
UNSOWN
UNSTOP
UNSUNG
UNSURE
UPSETS
UPSHOT
UPSIDE
URSIDS
URSINE
URSULA

U••S••
UKASES
UNESCO
UNISEX
UNISON
UNUSED
URUSES
USESUP

U•••S•
UNCASE
UNEASE
UNEASY
UNJUST
UNLASH
UNLESS
UNMASK
UNMESH
UNREST
UNWISE
UPCAST
UPMOST
UPRISE
UPROSE
UPRUSH
URALSK
UTMOST

U••••S
UBOATS
UBOLTS
UCLANS
UDDERS
UGGAMS
UGLIES
UHLANS
UIGURS
UKASES
ULCERS
ULTRAS
UMBELS

UMBERS
UMBRAS
UMIAKS
UNARMS
UNBARS
UNCAPS
UNCLES
UNDIES
UNDOES
UNFITS
UNGUES
UNGUIS
UNIATS
UNIONS
UNITAS
UNITES
UNJAMS
UNLESS
UNMANS
UNPEGS
UNPENS
UNPINS
UNRIGS
UNSAYS
UNSEWS
UNTIES
UNZIPS
UPBOWS
UPENDS
UPPERS
UPSETS
URAEUS
URANUS
URGERS
URIALS
URSIDS
URUSES
USAGES
USHERS
USUALS
USURPS
UTTERS
UTURNS
UVULAS
UZBEKS

•US•••

AUSPEX
AUSSIE
AUSTEN
AUSTIN
AUSTRO
BUSBAR
BUSBOY
BUSHED
BUSHEL
BUSHES
BUSHWA
BUSIED
BUSIER
BUSIES
BUSILY
BUSING
BUSKIN
BUSMAN
BUSMEN
BUSONI
BUSSED
BUSSES
BUSTED
BUSTER
BUSTLE
CUSHAW
CUSPED
CUSPID
CUSSED
CUSSES
CUSTER
CUSTOM
DUSTED
DUSTER
DUSTIN
DUSTUP
FUSEES
FUSILS
FUSING
FUSION
FUSSED
FUSSES
FUSTIC
GUSHED
GUSHER
GUSHES
GUSSET
GUSTAV
GUSTED
HUSHED
HUSHES
HUSKED
HUSKER
HUSSAR
HUSTLE
HUSTON
JUSTER
JUSTIN
JUSTLY
LUSAKA
LUSHER
LUSHLY
LUSTED
LUSTER
LUSTRE
MUSCAT
MUSCLE
MUSCLY
MUSERS
MUSEUM
MUSHED
MUSHER
MUSHES
MUSIAL
MUSING
MUSKEG
MUSKET
MUSKIE
MUSKOX
MUSLIM
MUSLIN
MUSSED
MUSSEL
MUSSES
MUSSUP
MUSTER
MUSTNT
OUSELS
OUSTED
OUSTER
PUSHED
PUSHES
PUSHON
PUSHUP
PUSSES
RUSHED
RUSHEE
RUSHES
RUSKIN
RUSSET
RUSSIA
RUSTED
RUSTIC
RUSTLE
SUSANN
SUSIEQ
SUSLIK
SUSSEX
TUSCAN
TUSKED
TUSKER
TUSSAH
TUSSLE

•U•S••

AUSSIE
BUNSEN
BUQSHA
BURSAE
BURSAL
BURSAR
BURSAS
BURSES
BURSTS
BUSSED
BUSSES
BUYSUP
CUESTA
CUISSE
CURSED
CURSES
CURSOR
CUSSED
CUSSES
CUTSIN
CUTSUP
FUSSED
FUSSES
GUESTS
GUISES
GUMSUP
GUNSHY
GUSSET
HUDSON
HUSSAR
MUSSED
MUSSEL
MUSSES
MUSSUP
NURSED
NURSER
NURSES
OUTSET
PUISNE
PULSAR
PULSED
PULSES
PURSED
PURSER
PURSES
PURSUE
PUSSES
PUTSBY
PUTSCH
PUTSIN
PUTSON
PUTSTO
PUTSUP
QUASAR
QUESTS
RUBSIN
RUNSIN
RUNSON
RUNSTO
RUNSUP
RUSSET
RUSSIA
SUBSET
SUDSED
SUDSES
SUMSUP
SUNSET
SUSSEX
TUCSON
TULSAN
TUSSAH
TUSSLE
WURSTS

•U••S•

AUGUST
CUBISM
CUBIST
CUISSE
CURTSY
CUTEST
CUTESY
DURESS
HUGEST
JURIST
KUMISS
KUVASZ
LUGOSI
LUTIST
MUCOSA
MUFASA
MULISH
MUTEST
NUDIST
PUNISH
PUREST
PURISM
PURIST
QUEASY
QURUSH
RUDEST
RUGOSE
SUFISM
SUREST
TUBIST

•U•••S

AUDENS
AUDIOS
AUDITS
AUGERS
AUGHTS
AUGURS
AUREUS
AUROUS
AUXINS
BUDGES
BUENOS
BUFFOS
BUGLES
BUILDS
BULGES
BUNCOS
BUNKOS
BURGAS
BURGHS
BURGOS
BURIES
BURINS
BURROS
BURSAS
BURSES
BURSTS
BUSHES
BUSIES
BUSSES
BUTEOS
BUTTES
BUYERS
BUZZES
CUBEBS
CUBICS
CUBITS
CULETS
CULLIS
CUPELS
CUPIDS
CURERS
CURIOS
CURSES
CURTIS
CURVES
CUSSES
CUTIES
CUTINS
CUTUPS
CUVEES
DUBOIS
DUCATS
DULLES
DUNCES
DUOMOS
DURESS
DUROCS
DUTIES
DUVETS
FUDGES
FUGUES
FUNGUS
FURIES
FURORS
FUSEES
FUSILS
FUSSES
FUTONS
FUZEES
FUZZES
GUACOS
GUARDS
GUAVAS
GUESTS
GUIDES
GUILDS
GUILES
GUISES
GULAGS
GUMBOS
GUSHES
GUYOTS
HUBRIS
HUEVOS
HUGHES
HULLOS
HUMANS
HUMMUS
HUMORS
HUMPHS
HURONS
HUSHES
HUZZAS
JUDGES
JUICES
JULEPS
JULIUS
JUMBOS
JUNCOS
JUNTAS
JUNTOS
JURATS
JURIES
JURORS
KUDZUS
KUKRIS
KULAKS
KUMISS
LUCIUS
LUDENS
LUGERS
LUMENS
LUNGES
MUCOUS
MUDRAS
MUFTIS
MUGHOS
MULCTS
MULLAS
MUNGOS
MURALS
MURRES
MUSERS
MUSHES
MUSSES
NUDGES
NUECES
NURSES
OUGHTS
OUNCES
OUSELS
OUZELS
PULSES
PUPILS
PUREES
PURGES
PURSES
PUSHES
PUSSES
PUTONS
QUACKS
QUAFFS
QUAILS
QUAKES
QUALMS
QUARKS
QUARTS
QUEENS
QUELLS
QUERNS
QUESTS
QUEUES
QUIETS
QUILLS
QUILTS
QUINTS
QUIPUS
QUIRES
QUIRKS
QUIRTS
QUOINS
QUOITS
QUOTAS
QUOTES
RUANAS
RUBENS
RUBIES
RUBLES
RUCHES
RUCKUS
RUFOUS
RULERS
RUMBAS
RUMENS
RUMORS
RUMPUS
RUNINS
RUNONS
RUNUPS
RUPEES
RUSHES
SUCCES
SUCHAS
SUDSES
SUEDES
SUGARS
SUITES
SULCUS
SUMACS
SUMMAS
SUNNIS
SUNUPS
SUPERS
SURAHS
SURGES
SUTRAS
TUBERS
TUDORS
TULIPS
TULLES
TUNERS
TUNICS
TUQUES
TURBOS
TUTORS
WURSTS
YUCCAS
YUROKS

••US••

ABUSED
ABUSER
ABUSES
AMUSED
AMUSES
BRUSHY
CAUSAL
CAUSED
CAUSES
COUSIN
CRUSES
CRUSOE
CRUSTS
CRUSTY
DOUSED
DOUSES
HAUSAS
HOUSED
HOUSES
JOUSTS
KYUSHU
LOUSED
LOUSES
MAUSER
MOUSED
MOUSER
MOUSES
MOUSEY
MOUSSE
NAUSEA
ONUSES
OPUSES
PAUSED
PAUSES
PLUSES
PLUSHY
POUSSE
REUSED
REUSES
ROUSED
ROUSES
ROUSTS
SLUSHY
SOUSED
SOUSES
THUSLY
TOUSLE
TRUSTS
TRUSTY
UNUSED
URUSES
WAUSAU

••U•S•

AVULSE
BLUEST
BLUESY
BLUISH
BOURSE
BRUISE
CHUHSI
CLUMSY
COURSE
CRUISE
EVULSE
LOUISA
LOUISE
MOUSSE
POUSSE
SQUASH
SQUISH
TRUEST
TRUISM
TZUHSI

••U••S

ABUSES
ADULTS
AMUSES
ANUBIS
BAUCIS
BLUETS
BLUFFS
BLUNTS
BLURBS
BLURTS
BOUGHS
BOULES
BOUNDS
BRUGES
BRUINS
BRUITS
BRULES
BRUMES
BRUNTS
BRUTES
BRUTUS
CAUCUS
CAULKS
CAUSES
CHUCKS
CHUMPS
CHUNKS
CHURLS
CHURNS
CHURRS
CHUTES
CLUCKS
CLUMPS
CLUNKS
COUGHS
COUNTS
COUPES
COURTS
CRUCES
CRUETS
CRUMBS
CRUSES
CRUSTS
CRUXES
DAUBES
DAUNTS
DEUCES
DOUBTS
DOUGHS
DOUSES
DRUIDS
DRUPES
DRUZES
EDUCES
ELUDES
ELUTES
ENURES
EQUALS
EQUIPS
ERUCTS
ERUPTS
ETUDES
EXUDES
EXULTS
EXURBS
FAUCES
FAULTS
FAUNAS
FAUNUS
FLUFFS
FLUIDS
FLUKES
FLUMES
FLUNKS
FLUTES
FLUXES
FOUNDS
FOUNTS
FRUITS
FRUMPS
GAUGES
GAUZES
GLUERS
GLUONS
GOUGES
GOURDS
GRUELS
GRUMPS
GRUNTS
GSUITS
HAUNTS
HAUSAS
HOUNDS
HOURIS
HOUSES
INUITS
INURES
JAUNTS
JAURES
JOULES
JOUSTS
KAUNAS
KAURIS
KNURLS
LAUGHS
LOUPES
LOUSES
MAUVES
MOULDS
MOULTS
MOUNDS
MOUNTS
MOUSES
MOUTHS
NEUMES
ONUSES
OPUSES
OVULES
PAUSES
PLUCKS
PLUMBS
PLUMES
PLUMPS
PLUNKS
PLUSES
POULTS
POUNDS
PRUDES
PRUNES
REUNES
REUSES
RHUMBS
ROUGES
ROUGHS
ROUNDS
ROUSES
ROUSTS
ROUTES
SAUCES
SAUDIS
SAULTS
SAUNAS
SAUTES
SCUBAS
SCUFFS
SCULLS
SCUTES
SHUCKS
SHUNTS
SKULKS
SKULLS
SKUNKS
SLUMPS
SLURPS
SMURFS
SNUFFS
SOUGHS
SOUNDS
SOUSES
SPUMES
SPURNS
SPURTS
SQUABS
SQUADS
SQUATS
SQUIBS
SQUIDS
STUFFS
STULLS
STUMPS
STUNTS
STUPAS
STUPES
TAUNTS
TAUONS
TAUPES
TAURUS
THUJAS
THUMBS
THUMPS
THUNKS
TOUGHS
TRUCES
TRUCKS
TRUMPS
TRUNKS
TRUSTS
TRUTHS
URUSES
USUALS
USURPS
UTURNS
UVULAS
VAULTS
VAUNTS
WOUNDS
YOUTHS
ZEUXIS
ZOUNDS

•••US•

ABLUSH
ACCUSE
ADJUST
AMBUSH
AROUSE
AUGUST
BEMUSE
BLOUSE
CARUSO
CAYUSE
CERUSE
CLAUSE
CREUSA
CROUSE
DEFUSE
DEGUST
DISUSE
EFFUSE
ENDUSE
EXCUSE
GOBUST
GROUSE
ILLUSE
INCUSE
INFUSE
INRUSH
LOCUST
MEDUSA
MISUSE
OBTUSE
ONRUSH
PERUSE
PROUST
QURUSH
RECUSE
REFUSE
ROBUST
SCHUSS
SPOUSE
THRUSH
THRUST
UNJUST
UPRUSH
WATUSI

•••U•S

ALBUMS
ALEUTS
AMOURS
AMPULS
ANNULS
ARGUES
AUGURS
BABULS
BEAUTS
BEGUMS
BOSUNS
CAGUAS
CAJUNS
CLOUDS
CLOUTS
CUTUPS
DEBUGS
DEBUTS
DEMURS
DONUTS
ENDUES
ENSUES
FEMURS
FIXUPS
FLOURS
FLOUTS
FORUMS
FRAUDS
FUGUES
GAMUTS
GETUPS
GHOULS
GIGUES
GROUPS
GROUTS
IMBUES
INCURS
INPUTS
ISSUES
JAMUPS
JORUMS
LAYUPS
LEHUAS
LEMURS
LETUPS
LIEUTS
MAQUIS
MIXUPS
MOGULS
MOHURS
MOPUPS
NIPUPS
OCCURS
ODIUMS
ODOURS
ONEUPS
PICULS
PINUPS
PIQUES
POPUPS
PSEUDS
QUEUES
REBUTS
RECURS
REDUBS
RERUNS
REVUES
RHEUMS
ROGUES
RUNUPS
SCAUPS
SCHUSS
SCOURS
SCOUTS
SCRUBS
SCRUMS
SEDUMS
SEGUES
SERUMS
SETUPS
SHOUTS
SHRUBS
SHRUGS
SITUPS
SNOUTS
SPOUTS
SPRUES
STOUPS
STOUTS
STRUMS
STRUTS
SUNUPS
SYRUPS
THRUMS
TIEUPS
TIPUPS
TOQUES
TROUTS
TUQUES
UIGURS
UNGUES
UNGUIS
VALUES
VENUES
VOGUES
YAKUTS
YAQUIS
YOKUTS

••••US

ABACUS
ACARUS
ACEOUS
ACINUS
ADIEUS
AEOLUS
AIRBUS
ALDOUS
AMICUS
AMINUS
ANIMUS
ANJOUS
ATREUS
AUREUS
AUROUS
BACKUS
BANTUS
BAYOUS
BMINUS
BRUTUS
BYSSUS
CACTUS
CADMUS
CALLUS
CAMPUS
CARPUS
CAUCUS
CENSUS
CEREUS
CESTUS
CHIAUS
CHORUS
CIRCUS
CIRRUS
CITRUS
CLONUS
CMINUS
CNIDUS
COCCUS
COLEUS
CORPUS
COYPUS
CROCUS
CRONUS
CYGNUS
CYPRUS
DANAUS
DARIUS
DELIUS
DINGUS
DISCUS
DMINUS
DOOFUS
ELBRUS
ENNIUS
EPIRUS
EREBUS
EXODUS
FAMOUS
FAUNUS
FERGUS
FESTUS
FICHUS
FILIUS
FUNGUS
GENIUS
GRADUS
HAIKUS
HIATUS
HINDUS
HUMMUS
ICARUS
JANHUS
JOYOUS
JULIUS
KUDZUS
LIMBUS
LITMUS
LUCIUS
MAIDUS
MANAUS
MARCUS
MARIUS
MISSUS
MOBIUS
MUCOUS
NEREUS
NIMBUS
OBELUS
ODIOUS
PALPUS
PAPPUS
PELEUS
PILEUS
PINDUS
PLEXUS
POILUS
PONTUS
POROUS
PRIMUS
QUIPUS
RADIUS
RAMOUS
RECTUS
REGIUS
RHESUS
RUCKUS
RUFOUS
RUMPUS
SEAMUS
SEROUS
SHAMUS
SIRIUS
SIXTUS
SNAFUS
SOLEUS
STATUS
STRAUS
STYLUS
SULCUS
TARSUS
TAURUS
TEREUS
THYMUS
TOPHUS
TYPHUS
URAEUS
URANUS
VENOUS
VERSUS
VILLUS
VINOUS
VIRTUS
VOROUS
WALRUS

UT••••

UTAHAN
UTHANT
UTMOST
UTOPIA
UTTERS
UTURNS

U•T•••

ULTIMA
ULTIMO
ULTRAS
UMTATA
UNTACK
UNTIDY
UNTIED
UNTIES
UNTOLD
UNTORN
UNTRAP
UNTROD
UNTRUE
UNTUNE
UPTAKE
UPTICK
UPTIME
UPTOWN
UPTURN
UTTERS

U••T••

ULSTER
UNITAL
UNITAS
UNITED
UNITER
UNITES
UNSTOP

U•••T•

UBIETY
UBOATS
UBOLTS
UMTATA
UNFITS
UNIATE
UNIATS
UPDATE
UPPITY
UPSETS
USEDTO

U••••T

UMLAUT
UNBELT
UNBENT
UNBOLT
UNGIRT
UNHURT
UNJUST
UNKNIT
UNKNOT

UNMEET
UNREST
UNROOT
UNSEAT
UPBEAT
UPCAST
UPLIFT
UPMOST
UPROOT
UPSHOT
URGENT
UTHANT
UTMOST

•UT•••
AUTEUR
AUTHOR
AUTUMN
BUTANE
BUTENE
BUTEOS
BUTLER
BUTTED
BUTTER
BUTTES
BUTTIN
BUTTON
BUTUNG
CUTEST
CUTESY
CUTIES
CUTINS
CUTLER
CUTLET
CUTOFF
CUTOUT
CUTSIN
CUTSUP
CUTTER
CUTUPS
DUTIES
FUTILE
FUTONS
FUTURE
GUTTAE
GUTTED
GUTTER
HUTTED
HUTTON
JUTTED
LUTHER
LUTHOR
LUTING
LUTIST
MUTANT
MUTATE
MUTELY
MUTEST
MUTING
MUTINY
MUTTER
MUTTON
MUTUAL
NUTATE
NUTKIN
NUTLET
NUTMEG
NUTRIA
NUTTED
NUTTER
OUTACT
OUTAGE
OUTATE
OUTBID
OUTCRY
OUTDID
OUTEAT
OUTFIT
OUTFOX
OUTGUN
OUTHIT
OUTING
OUTLAW
OUTLAY
OUTLET
OUTPUT
OUTRAN
OUTRUN
OUTSET
OUTWIT
PUTNAM
PUTOFF
PUTONS
PUTOUT
PUTPUT
PUTRID
PUTSBY
PUTSCH
PUTSIN
PUTSON
PUTSTO
PUTSUP
PUTTED
PUTTEE
PUTTER
RUTGER
RUTILE
RUTTAN
RUTTED
SUTLER
SUTRAS
SUTTER
SUTURE
TUTORS
TUTTUT
TUTUED

•U•T••
AUNTIE
AUSTEN
AUSTIN
AUSTRO
BUNTED
BUNTER
BURTON
BUSTED
BUSTER
BUSTLE
BUTTED
BUTTER
BUTTES
BUTTIN
BUTTON
CULTIC
CURTER
CURTIN
CURTIS
CURTIZ
CURTLY
CURTSY
CUSTER
CUSTOM
CUTTER
DUCTAL
DUSTED
DUSTER
DUSTIN
DUSTUP
FULTON
FUSTIC
GUITAR
GUNTER
GUSTAV
GUSTED
GUTTAE
GUTTED
GUTTER
HUNTED
HUNTER
HURTLE
HUSTLE
HUSTON
HUTTED
HUTTON
JUNTAS
JUNTOS
JUSTER
JUSTIN
JUSTLY
JUTTED
KULTUR
LUSTED
LUSTER
LUSTRE
MUFTIS
MUNTIN
MUSTER
MUSTNT
MUTTER
MUTTON
NUTTED
NUTTER
OUSTED
OUSTER
PUNTED
PUNTER
PUTTED
PUTTEE
PUTTER
QUITIT
QUOTAS
QUOTED
QUOTER
QUOTES
QUOTHA
RUSTED
RUSTIC
RUSTLE
RUTTAN
RUTTED
SUBTLE
SUBTLY
SUITED
SUITES
SUITOR
SUITUP
SULTAN
SULTRY
SUMTER
SUNTAN
SURTAX
SUTTER
TUFTED
TURTLE
TUTTUT

•U••T•
AUDITS
AUGHTS
BURSTS
CUBITS
CUESTA
CULETS
CURATE
DUARTE
DUCATS
DULUTH
DUVETS
GUESTS
GUILTY
GUYOTS
JUDITH
JURATS
LUCITE
LUNATE
LUXATE
MULCTS
MULETA
MUTATE
NUDITY
NUTATE
OUGHTS
OUTATE
PUENTE
PUERTO
PURITY
PUTSTO
QUANTA
QUARTO
QUARTS
QUARTZ
QUESTS
QUIETS
QUILTS
QUINTS
QUIRTS
QUOITS
RUGATE
RUNSTO
SUBITO
SURETE
SURETY
TUBATE
TURNTO
WURSTS
YUKATA

•U•••T
AUFAIT
AUGUST
AUKLET
AUMONT
BUCKET
BUDGET
BUFFET
BUGOUT
BULLET
BUMOUT
BURBOT
BURNET
BUYOUT
CUBIST
CULLET
CURVET
CUTEST
CUTLET
CUTOUT
DUGOUT
DULCET
DUMONT
DUNANT
DUPONT
DURANT
GULLET
GUSSET
HUBERT
HUGEST
JULIET
JUMPAT
JUNKET
JURIST
KURALT
KUWAIT
LUCENT
LUGNUT
LUTIST
MUDCAT
MULLET
MUPPET
MUSCAT
MUSKET
MUSTNT
MUTANT
MUTEST
NUDIST
NUGENT
NUGGET
NUMBAT
NUTLET
OUTACT
OUTEAT
OUTFIT
OUTHIT
OUTLET
OUTPUT
OUTSET
OUTWIT
PULLET
PULPIT
PUNDIT
PUPPET
PUREST
PURIST
PUTOUT
PUTPUT
QUAINT
QUITIT
RUBOUT
RUDEST
RUNLET
RUNOUT
RUPERT
RUSSET
SUBLET
SUBMIT
SUBSET
SUMMIT
SUNLIT
SUNSET
SUREST
TUBIST
TUCKET
TUFFET
TUMULT
TURBIT
TURBOT
TURRET
TUTTUT

••UT••
BHUTAN
BHUTTO
BRUTAL
BRUTES
BRUTUS
CHUTED
CHUTES
CLUTCH
COUTER
CRUTCH
ELUTED
ELUTES
FLUTED
FLUTES
FRUTTI
GLUTEI
GLUTEN
KLUTZY
MOUTHS
MOUTHY
MOUTON
NAUTCH
NEUTER
POUTED
POUTER
REUTER
ROUTED
ROUTER
ROUTES
SAUTES
SCUTCH
SCUTES
SHUTIN
SHUTUP
SMUTCH
SMUTTY
SOUTER
TAUTEN
TAUTER
TAUTLY
TAUTOG
TEUTON
TOUTED
TOUTER
TRUTHS
YOUTHS

••U•T•
ACUATE
ACUITY
ADULTS
AQUATE
BHUTTO
BLUETS
BLUNTS
BLURTS
BOUNTY
BRUITS
BRUNTS
COUNTS
COUNTY
COURTS
CRUETS
CRUSTS
CRUSTY
DAUNTS
DOUBTS
EQUATE
EQUITY
ERUCTS
ERUPTS
EXULTS
FAULTS
FAULTY
FOUNTS
FOURTH
FRUITS
FRUITY
FRUTTI
GRUNTS
GSUITS
HAUNTS
INUITS
JAUNTS
JAUNTY
JOUSTS
MOULTS
MOUNTS
MOUNTY
POULTS
ROUSTS
SAULTS
SHUNTS
SMUTTY
SPURTS
SQUATS
STUNTS
TAUNTS
TRUSTS
TRUSTY
VAULTS
VAUNTS

••U••T
AMULET
BLUEST
BOUGHT
BRUNET
CAUGHT
FAUCET
FLUENT
FOUGHT
GOULET
NAUGHT
NOUGAT
NOUGHT
SCULPT
SEURAT
SOUGHT
SQUINT
SQUIRT
STUART
TAUGHT
TRUANT
TRUEST
YOUBET

•••UT•
AGOUTI
ALEUTS
ASTUTE
BEAUTS
BEAUTY
CANUTE
CLOUTS
CROUTE
DEBUTS
DEPUTE
DEPUTY
DILUTE
DONUTS
DULUTH
FLOUTS
GAMUTS
GROUTS
GROUTY
IMPUTE
INPUTS
LAPUTA
LIEUTS
MAKUTA
MAPUTO
MINUTE
PAIUTE
REBUTS
REFUTE
REPUTE
SALUTE
SCOUTS
SHOUTS
SLEUTH
SNOUTS
SOLUTE
SPOUTS
STOUTS
STRUTS
TENUTO
TROUTS
VOLUTE
YAKUTS
YOKUTS

•••U•T
ABDUCT
ABRUPT
ACQUIT
ADDUCT
ADJUST
AMOUNT
AUGUST
AVAUNT
COQUET
DEDUCT
DEGUST
ERFURT
EXEUNT
FLAUNT
GOBUST
INCULT
INDUCT
INSULT
INTUIT
IRRUPT
ISEULT
JESUIT
LOCUST
LOQUAT
MINUET
MINUIT
OCCULT
PENULT
PEQUOT
PIQUET
PROUST
RELUCT
RESULT
ROBUST
THRUST
TUMULT
UNHURT
UNJUST
YOGURT

••••UT
ABLAUT
ACEOUT
ACTOUT
AIROUT
ALLBUT
ALLOUT
ASKOUT
BEIRUT
BOWOUT
BUGOUT
BUMOUT
BUYOUT
CAPNUT
CATGUT
COPOUT
CUTOUT
DEVOUT
DIEOUT
DIGOUT
DIMOUT
DRYOUT
DUGOUT
EATOUT
EKEOUT
ENGLUT
FANOUT
FAROUT
FLYOUT
GETOUT
GOTOUT
HELMUT
HIDOUT
ICEOUT
INARUT
KORBUT
LAYOUT
LEDOUT
LETOUT
LITOUT
LOGOUT
LUGNUT
MAHOUT
MAXOUT
MEERUT
OPTOUT
OUTPUT
PANOUT
PAYOUT
PEANUT
PIGNUT
PIGOUT
POPOUT
PUTOUT
PUTPUT
QIVIUT
RAGOUT
RAJPUT
RANOUT
ROTGUT
RUBOUT
RUNOUT
SALYUT
SATOUT
SAWOUT
SEEOUT
SETOUT
SITOUT
SPROUT
TAGOUT
TAPOUT
TOPOUT
TRYOUT
TUTTUT
UMLAUT
WALNUT
WAYOUT
WIGOUT
WINOUT
WONOUT

U•U•••
UNUSED
URUSES
USUALS
USURER
USURPS
UTURNS
UVULAE
UVULAR
UVULAS

U••U••
UIGURS
UNCURL
UNDULY
UNFURL
UNGUAL
UNGUES
UNGUIS
UNHURT
UNJUST
UNRULY
UNSUNG
UNSURE
UNTUNE
UPRUSH
UPTURN
URSULA

U•••U•
UMLAUT
UNGLUE
UNIQUE
UNPLUG
UNTRUE
URAEUS
URANUS
USEDUP
USEFUL
USESUP
UVALUE

•UU•••
MUUMUU

•U•U••
AUBURN
AUGURS
AUGURY
AUGUST
AUTUMN
BUNUEL
BUTUNG
CUMULI
CUMULO
CURULE
CUTUPS
DULUTH
EUNUCH
FUGUES
FUTURE
JUJUBE
LUNULA
LUXURY
MUTUAL
QUEUED
QUEUER
QUEUES
QURUSH
RUNUPS
SUBURB
SUNUNU
SUNUPS
SUTURE
SUZUKI
TUMULI
TUMULT
TUQUES
TUTUED

•U••U•
AUREUS
AUROUS
AUTEUR
BUCKUP
BUGOUT
BULBUL
BULGUR
BUMOUT
BUMPUP
BUNKUM
BUOYUP
BURNUP
BUYOUT
BUYSUP
CUPFUL
CURIUM
CURLUP
CUTOUT
CUTSUP
DUGOUT
DUMDUM
DUSTUP
FUNGUS
GUDRUN
GUMSUP
HUBBUB
HUMBUG
HUMMUS
HUMOUR
HUNGUP
JUGFUL
JULIUS
JUMPUP
KUDZUS
KULTUR
KUNLUN
LUCIUS
LUDLUM
LUGNUT
LUMPUR
MUCKUP
MUCOUS
MUKLUK
MURMUR
MUSEUM
MUSSUP
MUUMUU
OUTGUN
OUTPUT
OUTRUN
PULLUP
PULQUE
PUMPUP
PURDUE
PURSUE
PUSHUP
PUTOUT
PUTPUT
PUTSUP
QUIPUS
QUORUM
RUBOUT
RUCKUS
RUEFUL
RUFOUS
RUMOUR
RUMPUS
RUNGUP
RUNOUT
RUNSUP
RUPAUL
SUBDUE
SUBGUM
SUITUP
SULCUS
SULFUR
SUMSUP
TUCHUN
TUNEUP
TURNUP
TUTTUT
YUMYUM

•U•••U
BUREAU
FUZHOU
HUNGWU
JUNEAU
KUNGFU
MUUMUU
SUBARU
SUNUNU
TUVALU

••U•U•
BRUTUS
CAUCUS
DRUMUP
FAUNUS
FOULUP
HAULUP
MUUMUU
SHUTUP
SOUPUP
TAURUS

••U••U
AKUAKU
BOUBOU
IGUACU
KYUSHU
MAUMAU
MBUNDU
MUUMUU
RYUKYU
WAUSAU

•••UU•
VACUUM

•••U•U
KIKUYU
SUNUNU
TELUGU

••••UU
MUUMUU

UV••••
UVALUE
UVULAE
UVULAR
UVULAS

U•V•••
UNVEIL

U••V••
UNEVEN
UNIVAC

U•••V•
UNWOVE

•UV•••
CUVEES
DUVALL
DUVETS
KUVASZ
TUVALU

•U•V••
CULVER
CURVED
CURVES
CURVET
GUAVAS
HUEVOS
PURVEY
QUAVER
QUIVER
SUAVER
SURVEY

•U••V•
BULOVA

•U•••V
GUSTAV

••UV••
LOUVER
LOUVRE
MAUVES
OEUVRE

••U•V•
SCURVE
SCURVY
ZOUAVE

••U••V
ZHUKOV

•••UV•
TROUVE

U•W•••
UNWARY
UNWELL
UNWIND
UNWISE
UNWORN
UNWOVE
UNWRAP
UPWARD
UPWELL
UPWIND

U••W••
UNAWED

U•••W•
UNSEWN
UNSEWS
UNSOWN
UPBOWS
UPTOWN

U••••W
UNDRAW

•UW•••
KUWAIT

•U•W••
BULWER
LUDWIG
OUTWIT
RUNWAY
SUBWAY

•U••W•
BUSHWA
HUNGWU
YUKAWA

•U•••W
BURROW
CURFEW
CURLEW
CUSHAW
FURROW
GUFFAW
MURROW
OUTLAW
SUNDEW

••U•W•
SQUAWK

••••UW
DEPAUW

U••••X
UNISEX

•UX•••
AUXINS
HUXLEY
LUXATE
LUXURY
TUXEDO

•U••X•
CUNAXA

•U•••X
AUSPEX
DUPLEX
LUMMOX
MUSKOX
OUTFOX
SUFFIX
SURTAX
SUSSEX

••UX••
CRUXES
FLUXED
FLUXES
ZEUXIS

••U••X
BLUEOX
CAUDEX
KOUFAX

•••UX•
DELUXE

••••UX
ADIEUX
BAYEUX
BIJOUX
EFFLUX
HALLUX
INFLUX
POLLUX
REFLUX

U•Y•••
UNYOKE

U••Y••
UNDYED

U•••Y•
UNSAYS

U••••Y
UBIETY
UGLIFY
UNDULY
UNEASY
UNHOLY
UNRULY
UNTIDY
UNWARY
UPPITY
USABLY

•UY•••
BUYERS
BUYING
BUYOFF
BUYOUT
BUYSUP
GUYANA
GUYING
GUYOTS
TUYERE

•U•Y••
BUNYAN
BUOYED
BUOYUP
DURYEA
QUAYLE
RUNYON
YUMYUM

•U•••Y
AUBREY
AUDREY
AUGURY
BUBBLY
BUMBRY
BURBLY
BURLEY
BURNEY
BUSBOY
BUSILY
CUDDLY
CURACY
CURTLY
CURTSY
CUTESY
DUALLY
DUDLEY
DUMBLY
DUPERY
DURFEY
EULOGY
GUILTY
GUNSHY
GURLEY
GURNEY
HUBBLY
HUGELY
HUMBLY
HUNGRY
HURLEY
HURRAY
HUXLEY
JUNGLY
JUSTLY
LUNACY
LUSHLY
LUXURY
MUMBLY
MURPHY
MURRAY
MURREY

MUSCLY
MUTELY
MUTINY
NUDITY
NUMBLY
OUTCRY
OUTLAY
PUDDLY
PULLEY
PUNCHY
PUNILY
PURELY
PURIFY
PURITY
PURVEY
PUTSBY
QUAGGY
QUARRY
QUEASY
QUEMOY
QUINCY
QUIPPY
QUIRKY
RUBBLY
RUBIFY
RUDELY
RUFFLY
RUMBLY
RUMPLY
RUNDRY
RUNWAY
SUBTLY
SUBWAY
SUGARY
SULTRY
SUNDAY
SUNDRY
SUNRAY
SUPPLY
SURELY
SURETY
SURREY
SURVEY
TUMEFY
TUNNEY
TURKEY

••UY••
NGUYEN

••U•Y•
MAURYA
RYUKYU

••U••Y
ACUITY
BLUESY
BLURRY
BOUNCY
BOUNTY
BRUSHY
CHUBBY
CHUMMY
CHUNKY
CLUBBY
CLUMPY
CLUMSY
CLUNKY
COUNTY
CRUDDY
CRUMBY
CRUMMY
CRUSTY
DOUBLY
DOUGHY
DOURLY
EQUITY
FAULTY
FLUFFY
FLUNKY
FLURRY
FOULLY
FRUITY
FRUMPY
GLUMLY
GRUBBY
GRUMPY
GRUNDY
GRUNGY
HOURLY
JAUNTY
JOUNCY
KLUTZY
KNURLY
LOUDLY
MAUNDY
MOULDY
MOUNTY
MOUSEY
MOUTHY
PAULEY
PLUCKY
PLUMMY
PLUSHY
POUCHY
SCULLY
SCUMMY
SCURFY
SCURRY
SCURVY
SCUZZY
SLUDGY
SLUMMY
SLURRY
SLUSHY
SMUDGY
SMUGLY
SMUTTY
SNUFFY
SNUGLY
SOURLY
SPUNKY
SPURRY
STUBBY
STUFFY
STUMPY
STURDY
TAUTLY
THUSLY
TOUCHY
TOUGHY
TRUSTY

•••UY•
INOUYE
KIKUYU

•••U•Y
ASBURY
AUGURY
BEAUTY
CLOUDY
CROUPY
DEPUTY
FLEURY
FLOURY
GROUTY
INJURY
LUXURY
MAGUEY
OCCUPY
PENURY
RHEUMY
SYRUPY
UNDULY
UNRULY

••••UY
BADGUY
TANGUY

UZ••••
UZBEKS
UZZIAH

U•Z•••
UNZIPS
UZZIAH

•UZ•••
BUZZED
BUZZER
BUZZES
FUZEES
FUZHOU
FUZING
FUZZED
FUZZES
GUZZLE
HUZZAH
HUZZAS
MUZHIK
MUZZLE
NUZZLE
OUZELS
PUZZLE
SUZUKI

•U•Z••
BUZZED
BUZZER
BUZZES
CURZON
FUZZED
FUZZES
GUZZLE
HUZZAH
HUZZAS
KUDZUS
MUZZLE
NUZZLE
PUZZLE

•U•••Z
CURTIZ
JUAREZ
KUVASZ
QUARTZ

••UZ••
DRUZES
GAUZED
GAUZES
SCUZZY

••U•Z•
KLUTZY
SCUZZY

••U••Z
BOULEZ

•••U•Z
SCHULZ

••••UZ
HORMUZ
TAMMUZ

VA••••
VACANT
VACATE
VACHEL
VACLAV
VACUUM
VADOSE
VAGARY
VAGUER
VAINER
VAINLY
VAISYA
VALDEZ
VALENS
VALENT
VALERY
VALETS
VALISE
VALIUM
VALLEE
VALLEY
VALOIS
VALOUR
VALUED
VALUES
VALVED
VALVES
VAMPED
VAMPER
VANDAL
VANIER
VANISH
VANITY
VANNED
VANRYN
VAPORS
VAPOUR
VARDEN
VARESE
VARIED
VARIES
VARLET
VARNAS
VARNEY
VARUNA
VASHTI
VASLAV
VASSAL
VASSAR
VASTER
VASTLY
VATFUL
VAUGHN
VAULTS
VAUNTS

V•A•••
VIABLE
VIABLY
VIACOM
VIANDS

V••A••
VACANT
VACATE
VAGARY
VEGANS
VICARS
VIRAGO
VISAED
VISAGE
VITALS
VIVACE
VIVANT
VOCALS
VOLANS
VOLANT
VOLARE
VOTARY
VOYAGE

V•••A•
VACLAV
VANDAL
VARNAS
VASLAV
VASSAL
VASSAR
VEEJAY
VEINAL
VENIAL
VERBAL
VERNAL
VESTAL
VESTAS
VILLAS
VIOLAS
VISTAS
VISUAL
VIVIAN
VOLVAS
VULCAN
VULGAR

V••••A
VAISYA
VARUNA
VERONA
VICUNA
VIENNA
VIGODA
VIZSLA

•VA•••
AVAILS
AVALON
AVANTI
AVATAR
AVAUNT
EVADED
EVADER
EVADES
RVALUE
UVALUE

•V•A••
AVIANS
AVIARY
AVIATE

•V••A•
AVATAR
AVOWAL
DVORAK
OVISAC
OVULAR
UVULAE
UVULAR
UVULAS

•V•••A
AVESTA

••VA••
ARVADA
BOVARY
DIVANS
DUVALL
EDVARD
HAVANA
HAVASU
HIVAOA
INVADE
INVAIN
JAVARI
KOVACS
KUVASZ
LAVABO
LAVAGE
LEVANT
LOVAGE
NAVAHO
NAVAJO
NEVADA
PAVANE
RAVAGE
REVAMP
RIVALS
SAVAGE
SAVAII
SAVANT
SAVATE
TUVALU
VIVACE
VIVANT

••V•A•
CAVEAT
CAVIAR
FOVEAE
GAVIAL
HAVEAT
JOVIAL
JOVIAN
KEVLAR
REVEAL
VIVIAN

••V••A
ARVADA
COVINA
ELVIRA
HAVANA
HIVAOA
NEVADA
NOVENA
RIVERA
WOVOKA

•••VA•
BRAVAS
CANVAS
CHEVAL
COEVAL
CRAVAT
GUAVAS
HALVAH
LARVAE
LARVAL
LARVAS
LEKVAR
SERVAL
SHEVAT
SLOVAK
SPIVAK
SYLVAN
UNIVAC
VOLVAS

•••V•A
FLAVIA
LATVIA
OLIVIA
PRAVDA
SALVIA
SYLVIA
TRIVIA

••••VA
BULOVA
CANOVA
CASAVA
GENEVA
GODIVA
MORAVA
MOSKVA
OTTAVA
SALIVA

V•B•••
VEBLEN
VYBORG

V••B••
VERBAL
VIABLE
VIABLY

••V•B•
LAVABO

••V••B
ADVERB
REVERB

V•C•••
VACANT
VACATE
VACHEL
VACLAV
VACUUM
VECTOR
VICARS
VICTIM
VICTOR
VICUNA
VOCALS

V••C••
VELCRO
VIACOM
VISCID
VNECKS
VOICED
VOICES
VULCAN

V•••C•
VELOCE
VENICE
VIVACE
VOTECH

V••••C
VITRIC

•V•C••
AVOCET
EVICTS

•V••C•
AVOUCH
EVINCE
KVETCH

•V•••C
OVISAC

••V•C•
ADVICE
CIVICS
DEVICE
HAVOCS
KOVACS
NOVICE
VIVACE

•••V•C
OLDVIC
PELVIC
SLAVIC
STIVIC
UNIVAC

V•D•••
VADOSE
VEDDER
VIDEOS

V••D••
VALDEZ
VANDAL
VARDEN
VEDDER
VELDTS
VENDED
VENDEE
VENDOR
VERDIN
VERDON
VERDUN
VOIDED
VOODOO

V•••D•
VIANDS
VIGODA

V••••D
VALUED
VALVED
VAMPED
VANNED
VARIED
VEERED
VEGGED
VEILED
VEINED
VENDED
VENTED
VERGED
VERSED
VESPID
VESTED
VETOED
VETTED
VIEWED
VISAED
VISCID
VOICED
VOIDED

•V•D••
AVEDON
AVIDLY
EVADED
EVADER
EVADES

•V••D•
AVOIDS
OVERDO
OVIEDO
OVOIDS

•V•••D
AVOWED
EVADED
EVENED
EVOKED

••V•D•
ARVADA
BOVIDS
DIVIDE
INVADE
NEVADA

••V••D
DEVOID
EDVARD
ENVIED
LEVEED
LEVIED
REVVED

•••VD•
PRAVDA

•••V•D
BRAVED
CALVED
CARVED
CERVID
CRAVED
CURVED
DELVED
FERVID
GLOVED
GRAVED
GRAVID
HALVED
HEAVED
KIDVID
LEAVED
PEEVED
PROVED
REEVED
REVVED
SALVED
SERVED
SHAVED
SHOVED
SIEVED
SKIVED
SLAVED
SOLVED
STAVED
VALVED
WAIVED
WEAVED

VE••••
VEBLEN
VECTOR
VEDDER
VEEJAY
VEERED
VEGANS
VEGGED
VEGGIE
VEIGHT
VEILED
VEINAL
VEINED
VELCRO
VELDTS
VELLUM
VELOCE
VELOUR
VELVET
VENDED
VENDEE
VENDOR
VENEER
VENETO
VENIAL
VENICE
VENIRE
VENITE
VENOMS
VENOUS
VENTED
VENTER
VENUES
VERBAL
VERDIN
VERDON
VERDUN
VEREEN
VERGED
VERGER
VERGES
VERIFY
VERILY
VERISM
VERITE
VERITY
VERMIN
VERNAL
VERNON
VERONA
VERSED
VERSES
VERSOS
VERSUS
VERTEX
VERVET
VESPER
VESPID
VESSEL
VESTAL
VESTAS
VESTED
VESTEE
VESTRY
VETOED
VETOER
VETOES
VETTED
VEXERS
VEXING

V•E•••
VEEJAY
VEERED
VIENNA
VIENNE
VIEWED
VIEWER
VNECKS

V••E••
VALENS
VALENT
VALERY
VALETS
VARESE
VENEER
VENETO
VEREEN
VEXERS
VIDEOS
VILELY
VILEST
VINERY
VIPERS
VIREOS
VIXENS
VOLENS
VOTECH
VOTEIN
VOTERS
VOWELS
VOWERS

V•••E•
VACHEL
VAGUER
VAINER
VALDEZ
VALLEE
VALLEY
VALUED
VALUES
VALVED
VALVES
VAMPED
VAMPER
VANIER
VANNED
VARDEN
VARIED
VARIES
VARLET
VARNEY
VASTER
VEBLEN
VEDDER
VEERED
VEGGED
VEILED
VEINED
VELVET
VENDED
VENDEE
VENEER
VENTED
VENTER
VENUES
VEREEN
VERGED
VERGER
VERGES
VERSED
VERSES
VERTEX
VERVET
VESPER
VESSEL
VESTED
VESTEE
VETOED
VETOER
VETOES
VETTED
VIEWED
VIEWER
VIOLET
VISAED
VIVIEN
VIZIER
VOGUES
VOICED
VOICES
VOIDED
VOILES
VOLLEY
VORTEX
VOSGES
VSIXES

V••••E
VACATE
VADOSE
VALISE
VALLEE
VARESE
VEGGIE
VELOCE
VENDEE
VENICE
VENIRE
VENITE
VERITE
VESTEE
VIABLE
VIENNE
VIRILE
VIRTUE
VISAGE
VISINE
VIVACE
VOLARE
VOLUME
VOLUTE
VOTIVE
VOYAGE

•VE•••
AVEDON
AVENGE
AVENUE
AVERNO
AVERSE
AVERTS
AVESTA
EVELYN
EVENED
EVENER
EVENKI
EVENLY
EVENSO
EVENTS
EVENUP
EVERLY
EVERSO
EVERTS
KVELLS
KVETCH
OVERDO
OVERLY
SVELTE
YVETTE

•V•E••
OVIEDO
TVSETS

•V••E•
AVOCET
AVOWED
AVOWER
EVADED
EVADER
EVADES
EVENED
EVENER
EVILER
EVOKED
EVOKER
EVOKES
OVULES

•V•••E
AVENGE
AVENUE
AVERSE
AVIATE
AVULSE
EVINCE
EVOLVE
EVONNE
EVULSE
EVZONE
RVALUE
SVELTE
UVALUE
UVULAE
YVETTE
YVONNE

••VE••
ADVENT
ADVERB
ADVERT
AMVETS
BEVELS
CAVEAT
CAVEIN
CAVELL
CAVERN
CAVERS
CAVETT
CIVETS
COVENS
COVENT
COVERS
COVERT
COVETS
COVEYS
CUVEES
DEVEIN
DEVEST
DIVEIN
DIVERS
DIVERT
DIVEST
DOVEIN
DUVETS
ELVERS
FEVERS
FIVERS
FIVEWS
FOVEAE
GAVEIN
GAVELS
GAVEUP
GIVEIN
GIVENS
GIVERS
GIVEUP
GOVERN
HAVEAT
HAVENS
HAVENT
HAVEON
HOVELS
HOVERS
HOVETO
INVENT
INVERT
INVEST
JIVERS
KEVELS
LAVERS
LEVEED
LEVEES
LEVELS
LEVENE
LEVERS
LIVEIN
LIVELY
LIVENS
LIVEON
LIVERS
LIVERY
LOVEIN
LOVELL
LOVELY
LOVERS
LOVETT
MAVENS
MOVEIN
MOVERS
NAVELS
NEVERS
NOVELS
NOVENA
OBVERT
PAVERS
RAVELS
RAVENS
RAVERS
REVEAL
REVELS
REVERB
REVERE
REVERS
REVERT
REVETS
RIVERA
RIVERS
RIVETS
ROVERS
SAVERS
SAVEUP
SEVENS
SEVERE
SEVERN
SEVERS
TAVERN
UNVEIL
WAVEIN
WAVERS
WAVERY
WYVERN

••V•E•
BEVIES
CUVEES
DAVIES
ENVIED
ENVIES
JAVIER
LEVEED
LEVEES
LEVIED
LEVIER
LEVIES
LIVRES
MOVIES
NAVIES
ONVIEW
REVIEW
REVUES
REVVED
SEVRES
SOVIET
VIVIEN
WAVIER
XAVIER

••V••E
ADVICE
ADVISE
BOVINE
DEVICE
DEVINE
DEVISE
DEVOTE
DIVIDE
DIVINE
FOVEAE
INVADE
INVITE
INVOKE
IRVINE
LAVAGE
LEVENE
LEVINE
LEVITE
LOVAGE
NOVICE
PAVANE
RAVAGE
RAVINE
REVERE
REVILE
REVISE
REVIVE
REVOKE
SAVAGE
SAVATE
SAVOIE
SEVERE
VIVACE

•••VE•
AGAVES
ALFVEN
BEAVER
BEEVES
BRAVED
BRAVER
BRAVES
BREVES
BREVET
CALVED
CALVES
CARVED
CARVER
CARVES
CARVEY
CHAVEZ
CHEVET
CHIVES
CLEVER
CLEVES
CLOVEN
CLOVER

CLOVES
CONVEX
CONVEY
CORVEE
CRAVED
CRAVEN
CRAVER
CRAVES
CULVER
CURVED
CURVES
CURVET
DELVED
DELVER
DELVES
DENVER
DRIVEL
DRIVEN
DRIVER
DRIVES
DROVER
DROVES
ELEVEN
ELEVES
GARVEY
GLOVED
GLOVER
GLOVES
GOOVER
GRAVED
GRAVEL
GRAVEN
GRAVER
GRAVES
GRIVET
GROVEL
GROVER
GROVES
HALVED
HALVES
HARVEY
HEAVED
HEAVEN
HEAVER
HEAVES
HELVES
HOOVER
HOOVES
JAYVEE
JEEVES
KNAVES
KNIVES
LEAVED
LEAVEN
LEAVES
LOAVES
LOUVER
MARVEL
MAUVES
NERVES
OGIVES
OLEVEL
OLIVER
OLIVES
PEAVEY
PEEVED
PEEVES
PLOVER
PRIVET
PROVED
PROVEN
PROVER
PROVES
PURVEY

QUAVER
QUIVER
REEVED
REEVES
REVVED
SALVED
SALVER
SALVES
SELVES
SERVED
SERVER
SERVES
SHAVED
SHAVEN
SHAVER
SHAVES
SHIVER
SHOVED
SHOVEL
SHOVER
SHOVES
SIEVED
SIEVES
SILVER
SKIVED
SKIVER
SKIVES
SLAVED
SLAVER
SLAVES
SLIVER
SLOVEN
SNIVEL
SOAVES
SOLVED
SOLVER
SOLVES
STAVED
STAVES
STEVEN
STIVER
STOVER
STOVES
SUAVER
SURVEY
SWIVEL
SWIVET
TRAVEL
TRIVET
TROVES
UNEVEN
VALVED
VALVES
VELVET
VERVET
WAIVED
WAIVER
WAIVES
WEAVED
WEAVER
WEAVES
WOLVES

•••V•E
BMOVIE
CHEVRE
CORVEE
JAYVEE
LARVAE
LIEVRE
LOUVRE
OEUVRE
STEVIE

••••VE
ACTIVE
ALCOVE
ARGIVE
ARRIVE
BEHAVE
BYJOVE
CLEAVE
DATIVE
DERIVE
ENDIVE
EVOLVE
GENEVE
GREAVE
GRIEVE
GROOVE
INLOVE
MOHAVE
MOJAVE
MOTIVE
NATIVE
OCTAVE
PAREVE
RELIVE
REMOVE
REPAVE
REVIVE
REWOVE
SCURVE
SHEAVE
SHELVE
SHRIVE
SHROVE
SLEAVE
SLEEVE
STARVE
STEEVE
STRIVE
STROVE
SWERVE
THEYVE
THIEVE
THRIVE
THROVE
TROUVE
TWELVE
UNWOVE
VOTIVE
ZOUAVE

V••F••
VATFUL

V•••F•
VERIFY
VILIFY
VIVIFY

••V•F•
VIVIFY

V•G•••
VAGARY
VAGUER
VEGANS
VEGGED
VEGGIE
VIGILS
VIGODA
VIGOUR
VOGUES

V••G••
VAUGHN
VEGGED
VEGGIE
VEIGHT
VERGED
VERGER
VERGES
VIRGIL
VIRGIN
VOIGHT
VOSGES
VSIGNS
VULGAR

V•••G•
VIRAGO
VISAGE
VOYAGE

V••••G
VEXING
VIKING
VINING
VOTING
VOWING
VYBORG

•V••G•
AVENGE

••V•G•
LAVAGE
LOVAGE
RAVAGE
SAVAGE

••V••G
CAVING
DIVING
ERVING
GIVING
HAVING
HIVING
IRVING
JIVING
LAVING
LIVING
LOVING
MOVING
PAVING
RAVING
RIVING
ROVING
SAVING
WAVING

V••H••
VACHEL
VASHTI
VISHNU

V•••H•
VAUGHN
VEIGHT
VOIGHT

V••••H
VANISH
VOTECH

•V•H••
TVSHOW

•V•••H
AVOUCH
KVETCH

••V•H•
NAVAHO

••V••H
DOVISH
LAVISH
RAVISH

•••V•H
HALVAH

VI••••
VIABLE
VIABLY
VIACOM
VIANDS
VICARS
VICTIM
VICTOR
VICUNA
VIDEOS
VIENNA
VIENNE
VIEWED
VIEWER
VIGILS
VIGODA
VIGOUR
VIKING
VILELY
VILEST
VILIFY
VILLAS
VILLON
VILLUS
VINERY
VINING
VINOUS
VINTON
VIOLAS
VIOLET
VIOLIN
VIPERS
VIRAGO
VIREOS
VIRGIL
VIRGIN
VIRILE
VIRTUE
VIRTUS
VISAED
VISAGE
VISCID
VISHNU
VISINE
VISION
VISITS
VISORS
VISTAS
VISUAL
VITALS
VITRIC
VIVACE
VIVANT
VIVIAN
VIVIEN
VIVIFY
VIXENS
VIZIER
VIZSLA

V•I•••
VAINER
VAINLY
VAISYA
VEIGHT
VEILED
VEINAL
VEINED
VOICED
VOICES
VOIDED
VOIGHT
VOILES
VSIGNS
VSIXES

V••I••
VALISE
VALIUM
VANIER
VANISH
VANITY
VARIED
VARIES
VENIAL
VENICE
VENIRE
VENITE
VERIFY
VERILY
VERISM
VERITE
VERITY
VEXING
VIGILS
VIKING
VILIFY
VINING
VIRILE
VISINE
VISION
VISITS
VIVIAN
VIVIEN
VIVIFY
VIZIER
VOTING
VOTIVE
VOWING

V•••I•
VALOIS
VEGGIE
VERDIN
VERMIN
VESPID
VICTIM
VIOLIN
VIRGIL
VIRGIN
VISCID
VITRIC
VOTEIN

V••••I
VASHTI

•VI•••
AVIANS
AVIARY
AVIATE
AVIDLY
AVISOS
EVICTS
EVILER
EVILLY
EVINCE
OVIEDO
OVISAC

•V•I••
AVAILS
AVOIDS
OVOIDS

•V•••I
AVANTI
EVENKI

••VI••
ADVICE
ADVISE
ANVILS
BEVIES
BOVIDS
BOVINE
CAVIAR
CAVILS
CAVING
CAVITY
CIVICS
COVINA
DAVIES
DAVITS
DEVICE
DEVILS
DEVINE
DEVISE
DEVITO
DIVIDE
DIVINE
DIVING
DOVISH
ELVIRA
ENVIED
ENVIES
ERVING
GAVIAL
GIVING
HAVING
HIVING
INVITE
INVIVO
IRVINE
IRVING
JAVIER
JIVING
JOVIAL
JOVIAN
LAVING
LAVISH
LEVIED
LEVIER
LEVIES
LEVINE
LEVITE
LEVITY
LIVING
LOVING
MOVIES
MOVING
NAVIES
NEVINS
NOVICE
ONVIEW
PAVING
QIVIUT
RAVINE
RAVING
RAVISH
REVIEW
REVILE
REVISE
REVIVE
RIVING
ROVING
SAVING
SAVIOR
SOVIET
VIVIAN
VIVIEN
VIVIFY
WAVIER
WAVING
XAVIER

••V•I•
CAVEIN
DEVEIN
DEVOID
DEVOIR
DIVEIN
DOVEIN
ENVOIS
GAVEIN
GIVEIN
INVAIN
LIVEIN
LOVEIN
MOVEIN
REVOIR
SAVAII
SAVOIE
SAVOIR
UNVEIL
WAVEIN

••V••I
JAVARI
SAVAII
TIVOLI

•••VI•
BMOVIE
CALVIN
CERVID
CLAVIN
CLEVIS
CLOVIS
FERVID
FLAVIA
GRAVID
KELVIN
KIDVID
LANVIN
LATVIA
MARVIN
MELVIL
MELVIN
NARVIK
OLDVIC
OLIVIA
PARVIS
PELVIC
PELVIS
PREVIN
SALVIA
SLAVIC
SLOVIK
SPAVIN
STEVIE
STIVIC
SYLVIA
TRAVIS
TRIVIA
WEEVIL

V••J••
VEEJAY

••V•J•
NAVAJO

V•K•••
VIKING

V•••K•
VNECKS

V••••K
VOSTOK

•V•K••
EVOKED
EVOKER
EVOKES

•V••K•
EVENKI

•V•••K
DVORAK

••V•K•
INVOKE
NEVSKY
REVOKE
WOVOKA

•••V•K
NARVIK
SLOVAK
SLOVIK
SPIVAK

V•L•••
VALDEZ
VALENS
VALENT
VALERY
VALETS
VALISE
VALIUM
VALLEE
VALLEY
VALOIS
VALOUR
VALUED
VALUES
VALVED
VALVES
VELCRO
VELDTS
VELLUM
VELOCE
VELOUR
VELVET
VILELY
VILEST
VILIFY
VILLAS
VILLON
VILLUS
VOLANS
VOLANT
VOLARE
VOLENS
VOLLEY
VOLUME
VOLUTE
VOLVAS
VOLVOX
VULCAN
VULGAR

V••L••
VACLAV
VALLEE
VALLEY
VARLET
VASLAV
VAULTS
VEBLEN
VEILED
VELLUM
VILLAS
VILLON
VILLUS
VIOLAS
VIOLET
VIOLIN
VOILES
VOLLEY

V•••L•
VAINLY
VASTLY
VERILY
VIABLE
VIABLY
VIGILS
VILELY
VIRILE
VITALS
VIZSLA
VOCALS
VOWELS

V••••L
VACHEL
VANDAL
VASSAL
VATFUL
VEINAL
VENIAL
VERBAL
VERNAL
VESSEL
VESTAL
VIRGIL
VISUAL

•V•L••
AVALON
AVULSE
EVELYN
EVILER
EVILLY
EVOLVE
EVULSE
KVELLS
OVULAR
OVULES
RVALUE
SVELTE
UVALUE
UVULAE
UVULAR
UVULAS

•V••L•
AVAILS
AVIDLY
EVENLY
EVERLY
EVILLY
KVELLS
OVERLY

•V•••L
AVOWAL

••VL••
KEVLAR
PAVLOV
REVLON

••V•L•
ANVILS
BEVELS
CAVELL
CAVILS
DEVILS
DUVALL
GAVELS
HOVELS
KEVELS
LEVELS
LIVELY
LOVELL
LOVELY
NAVELS
NOVELS
RAVELS
REVELS
REVILE
REVOLT
RIVALS
TIVOLI
TUVALU

••V••L
CAVELL
DUVALL
GAVIAL
JOVIAL
LOVELL
REVEAL
UNVEIL

•••V•L
CHEVAL
COEVAL
DRIVEL
GRAVEL
GROVEL
LARVAL
MARVEL
MELVIL
OLEVEL
SERVAL
SHOVEL
SNIVEL
SWIVEL
TRAVEL
WEEVIL

V•M•••
VAMPED
VAMPER

V••M••
VERMIN

V•••M•
VENOMS
VOLUME
VROOMS

V••••M
VACUUM
VALIUM
VELLUM
VERISM
VIACOM
VICTIM

••V•M•
REVAMP

VN••••
VNECKS

V•N•••
VANDAL
VANIER
VANISH
VANITY
VANNED
VANRYN
VENDED
VENDEE
VENDOR
VENEER
VENETO
VENIAL
VENICE
VENIRE
VENITE
VENOMS
VENOUS
VENTED
VENTER
VENUES
VINERY
VINING
VINOUS
VINTON

V••N••
VAINER
VAINLY
VANNED
VARNAS
VARNEY
VAUNTS
VEINAL
VEINED
VERNAL
VERNON
VIANDS
VIENNA
VIENNE

V•••N•
VACANT
VALENS
VALENT
VARUNA
VEGANS
VERONA
VEXING
VICUNA
VIENNA
VIENNE
VIKING
VINING
VISHNU
VISINE
VIVANT
VIXENS
VOLANS
VOLANT
VOLENS
VOTING
VOWING
VSIGNS

V••••N
VANRYN
VARDEN
VAUGHN
VEBLEN
VERDIN
VERDON
VERDUN
VEREEN
VERMIN
VERNON
VILLON
VINTON
VIOLIN
VIRGIN
VISION
VIVIAN
VIVIEN
VOTEIN
VULCAN

•V•N••
AVANTI
AVENGE
AVENUE
EVENED
EVENER
EVENKI
EVENLY
EVENSO
EVENTS
EVENUP
EVINCE
EVONNE
YVONNE

•V••N•
AVAUNT
AVERNO
AVIANS
EVONNE
EVZONE
YVONNE

•V•••N
AVALON
AVEDON
EVELYN

••V•N•
ADVENT
BOVINE
CAVING
COVENS
COVENT
COVINA
DEVINE
DIVANS
DIVINE
DIVING
ERVING
GIVENS
GIVING
HAVANA
HAVENS
HAVENT
HAVING
HIVING
INVENT
IRVINE
IRVING
JIVING
LAVING
LEVANT
LEVENE
LEVINE
LIVENS
LIVING
LOVING
MAVENS
MOVING
NEVINS
NOVENA
PAVANE
PAVING
RAVENS
RAVINE
RAVING
RIVING
ROVING
SAVANT
SAVING
SEVENS
VIVANT
WAVING

••V••N
CAVEIN
CAVERN
DEVEIN
DIVEIN
DOVEIN
GAVEIN
GIVEIN
GOVERN
HAVEON
INVAIN
JOVIAN
LIVEIN
LIVEON
LOVEIN
MOVEIN
REVLON
REVSON
SEVERN
TAVERN
VIVIAN
VIVIEN
WAVEIN
WYVERN

•••V•N
ALFVEN
CALVIN
CLAVIN
CLOVEN
CRAVEN
DRIVEN
ELEVEN
GRAVEN
HEAVEN
KELVIN
LANVIN
LEAVEN
MARVIN
MELVIN
MELVYN
MERVYN
PREVIN
PROVEN
SHAVEN
SLOVEN
SPAVIN
STEVEN
SYLVAN
UNEVEN

VO••••
VOCALS
VOGUES
VOICED
VOICES
VOIDED
VOIGHT
VOILES
VOLANS
VOLANT
VOLARE
VOLENS
VOLLEY
VOLUME
VOLUTE
VOLVAS
VOLVOX
VOODOO
VOROUS
VORTEX
VOSGES
VOSTOK
VOTARY
VOTECH
VOTEIN
VOTERS
VOTING
VOTIVE
VOWELS
VOWERS
VOWING
VOYAGE

V•O•••
VIOLAS
VIOLET
VIOLIN
VOODOO
VROOMS

V••O••
VADOSE
VALOIS
VALOUR
VAPORS
VAPOUR
VELOCE
VELOUR
VENOMS
VENOUS
VERONA
VETOED
VETOER
VETOES
VIGODA
VIGOUR
VINOUS
VISORS
VOROUS
VROOMS
VYBORG

V•••O•
VECTOR
VENDOR

VERDON
VERNON
VERSOS
VIACOM
VICTOR
VIDEOS
VILLON
VINTON
VIREOS
VISION
VOLVOX
VOODOO
VOSTOK

V••••O
VELCRO
VENETO
VIRAGO
VOODOO

•VO•••
AVOCET
AVOIDS
AVOUCH
AVOWAL
AVOWED
AVOWER
DVORAK
EVOKED
EVOKER
EVOKES
EVOLVE
EVONNE
OVOIDS
YVONNE

•V•O••
EVZONE

•V••O•
AVALON
AVEDON
AVISOS
TVSHOW

•V•••O
AVERNO
EVENSO
EVERSO
OVERDO
OVIEDO

••VO••
CAVORT
DEVOID
DEVOIR
DEVOTE
DEVOTO
DEVOUR
DEVOUT
DIVOTS
ENVOIS
ENVOYS
EXVOTO
FAVORS
FAVOUR
HAVOCS
INVOKE
PIVOTS
REVOIR
REVOKE
REVOLT
SAVOIE
SAVOIR
SAVORS
SAVORY
SAVOUR
TIVOLI
WOVOKA

••V•O•
HAVEON
HIVAOA
LIVEON
PAVLOV
REVLON
REVSON
SAVIOR

••V••O
DEVITO
DEVOTO
EXVOTO
HOVETO
INVIVO
LAVABO
NAVAHO
NAVAJO

•••VO•
BRAVOS
CONVOY
FERVOR
FLAVOR
HUEVOS
SALVOR
SALVOS
SERVOS
TREVOR
VOLVOX

••••VO
DENOVO
INVIVO
OCTAVO

V•P•••
VAPORS
VAPOUR
VIPERS

V••P••
VAMPED
VAMPER
VESPER
VESPID

•V•••P
EVENUP

••V••P
GAVEUP
GIVEUP
REVAMP
SAVEUP

VR••••
VROOMS

V•R•••
VARDEN
VARESE
VARIED
VARIES
VARLET
VARNAS
VARNEY
VARUNA
VERBAL
VERDIN
VERDON
VERDUN
VEREEN
VERGED
VERGER
VERGES
VERIFY
VERILY
VERISM
VERITE
VERITY
VERMIN
VERNAL
VERNON
VERONA
VERSED
VERSES
VERSOS
VERSUS
VERTEX
VERVET
VIRAGO
VIREOS
VIRGIL
VIRGIN
VIRILE
VIRTUE
VIRTUS
VOROUS
VORTEX

V••R••
VANRYN
VEERED
VITRIC

V•••R•
VAGARY
VALERY
VAPORS
VELCRO
VENIRE
VESTRY
VEXERS
VICARS
VINERY
VIPERS
VISORS
VOLARE
VOTARY
VOTERS
VOWERS
VYBORG

V••••R
VAGUER
VAINER
VALOUR
VAMPER
VANIER
VAPOUR
VASSAR
VASTER
VECTOR
VEDDER
VELOUR
VENDOR
VENEER
VENTER
VERGER
VESPER
VETOER
VICTOR
VIEWER
VIGOUR
VIZIER
VULGAR

•V•R••
AVERNO
AVERSE
AVERTS
DVORAK
EVERLY
EVERSO
EVERTS
OVERDO
OVERLY

•V••R•
AVIARY

•V•••R
AVATAR
AVOWER
EVADER
EVENER
EVILER
EVOKER
OVULAR
UVULAR

••VR••
LIVRES
SEVRES

••V•R•
ADVERB
ADVERT
BOVARY
CAVERN
CAVERS
CAVORT
COVERS
COVERT
DIVERS
DIVERT
EDVARD
ELVERS
ELVIRA
FAVORS
FEVERS
FIVERS
GIVERS
GOVERN
HOVERS
INVERT
JAVARI
JIVERS
LAVERS
LEVERS
LIVERS
LIVERY
LOVERS
MOVERS
NEVERS
OBVERT
PAVERS
RAVERS
REVERB
REVERE
REVERS
REVERT
RIVERA
RIVERS
ROVERS
SAVERS
SAVORS
SAVORY
SEVERE
SEVERN
SEVERS
TAVERN
WAVERS
WAVERY
WYVERN

••V••R
CAVIAR
DEVOIR
DEVOUR
FAVOUR
JAVIER
KEVLAR
LEVIER
REVOIR
SAVIOR
SAVOIR
SAVOUR
WAVIER
XAVIER

•••VR•
CHEVRE
LIEVRE
LOUVRE
OEUVRE

•••V•R
BEAVER
BRAVER
CARVER
CLEVER
CLOVER
CRAVER
CULVER
DELVER
DENVER
DRIVER
DROVER
FERVOR
FLAVOR
GLOVER
GOOVER
GRAVER
GROVER
HEAVER
HOOVER
LEKVAR
LOUVER
OLIVER
PLOVER
PROVER
QUAVER
QUIVER
SALVER
SALVOR
SERVER
SHAVER
SHIVER
SHOVER
SILVER
SKIVER
SLAVER
SLIVER
SOLVER
STIVER
STOVER
SUAVER
TREVOR
WAIVER
WEAVER

VS••••
VSIGNS
VSIXES

V•S•••
VASHTI
VASLAV
VASSAL
VASSAR
VASTER
VASTLY
VESPER
VESPID
VESSEL
VESTAL
VESTAS
VESTED
VESTEE
VESTRY
VISAED
VISAGE
VISCID
VISHNU
VISINE
VISION
VISITS
VISORS
VISTAS
VISUAL
VOSGES
VOSTOK

V••S••
VAISYA
VASSAL
VASSAR
VERSED
VERSES
VERSOS
VERSUS
VESSEL
VIZSLA

V•••S•
VADOSE
VALISE
VANISH
VARESE
VERISM
VILEST

V••••S
VALENS
VALETS
VALOIS
VALUES
VALVES
VAPORS
VARIES
VARNAS
VAULTS
VAUNTS
VEGANS
VELDTS
VENOMS
VENOUS
VENUES
VERGES
VERSES
VERSOS
VERSUS
VESTAS
VETOES
VEXERS
VIANDS
VICARS
VIDEOS
VIGILS
VILLAS
VILLUS
VINOUS
VIOLAS
VIPERS
VIREOS
VIRTUS
VISITS
VISORS
VISTAS
VITALS
VIXENS
VNECKS
VOCALS
VOGUES
VOICES
VOILES
VOLANS
VOLENS
VOLVAS
VOROUS
VOSGES
VOTERS
VOWELS
VOWERS
VROOMS
VSIGNS
VSIXES

•VS•••
TVSETS
TVSHOW

•V•S••
AVESTA
AVISOS
OVISAC

•V••S•
AVERSE
AVULSE
EVENSO
EVERSO
EVULSE

•V•••S
AVAILS
AVERTS
AVIANS
AVISOS
AVOIDS
EVADES
EVENTS
EVERTS
EVICTS
EVOKES
KVELLS
OVOIDS
OVULES
TVSETS
UVULAS

••VS••
NEVSKY
REVSON

••V•S•
ADVISE
DEVEST
DEVISE
DIVEST
DOVISH
HAVASU
INVEST
KUVASZ
LAVISH
RAVISH
REVISE

••V••S
AMVETS
ANVILS
BEVELS
BEVIES
BOVIDS
CAVERS
CAVILS
CIVETS
CIVICS
COVENS
COVERS
COVETS
COVEYS
CUVEES
DAVIES
DAVITS
DEVILS
DIVANS
DIVERS
DIVOTS
DUVETS
ELVERS
ENVIES
ENVOIS
ENVOYS
FAVORS
FEVERS
FIVERS
FIVEWS
GAVELS
GIVENS
GIVERS
HAVENS
HAVOCS
HOVELS
HOVERS
JIVERS
KEVELS
KOVACS
LAVERS
LEVEES
LEVELS
LEVERS
LEVIES
LIVENS
LIVERS
LIVRES
LOVERS
MAVENS
MOVERS
MOVIES
NAVELS
NAVIES
NEVERS
NEVINS
NOVELS
PAVERS
PIVOTS
RAVELS
RAVENS
RAVERS
REVELS
REVERS
REVETS
REVUES
RIVALS
RIVERS
RIVETS
ROVERS
SAVERS
SAVORS
SEVENS
SEVERS
SEVRES
WAVERS

•••V•S
AGAVES
BEEVES
BRAVAS
BRAVES
BRAVOS
BREVES
CALVES
CANVAS
CARVES
CHIVES
CLEVES
CLEVIS
CLOVES
CLOVIS
CRAVES
CURVES
DELVES
DRIVES
DROVES
ELEVES
GLOVES
GRAVES
GROVES
GUAVAS
HALVES
HEAVES
HELVES
HOOVES
HUEVOS
JEEVES
KNAVES
KNIVES
LARVAS
LEAVES
LOAVES
MAUVES
NERVES
OGIVES
OLIVES
PARVIS
PEEVES
PELVIS
PROVES
REEVES
SALVES
SALVOS
SELVES
SERVES
SERVOS
SHAVES
SHOVES
SIEVES
SKIVES
SLAVES
SOAVES
SOLVES
STAVES
STOVES
TRAVIS
TROVES
VALVES
VOLVAS
WAIVES
WEAVES
WOLVES

V•T•••
VATFUL
VETOED
VETOER
VETOES
VETTED
VITALS
VITRIC
VOTARY
VOTECH
VOTEIN
VOTERS
VOTING
VOTIVE

V••T••
VASTER
VASTLY
VECTOR
VENTED
VENTER
VERTEX
VESTAL
VESTAS
VESTED
VESTEE
VESTRY
VETTED
VICTIM
VICTOR
VINTON
VIRTUE
VIRTUS
VISTAS
VORTEX
VOSTOK

V•••T•
VACATE
VALETS
VANITY
VASHTI
VAULTS
VAUNTS
VELDTS
VENETO
VENITE
VERITE
VERITY
VISITS
VOLUTE

V••••T
VACANT
VALENT
VARLET
VEIGHT
VELVET
VERVET
VILEST
VIOLET
VIVANT
VOIGHT
VOLANT

•V•T••
AVATAR
KVETCH
YVETTE

•V••T•
AVANTI
AVERTS
AVESTA
AVIATE
EVENTS
EVERTS
EVICTS
SVELTE
TVSETS
YVETTE

•V•••T
AVAUNT
AVOCET

••V•T•
AMVETS
CAVETT
CAVITY
CIVETS
COVETS
DAVITS
DEVITO
DEVOTE
DEVOTO
DIVOTS
DUVETS
EXVOTO
HOVETO
INVITE
LEVITE
LEVITY
LOVETT
PIVOTS
REVETS
RIVETS
SAVATE

••V••T
ADVENT
ADVERT
CAVEAT
CAVETT
CAVORT
COVENT
COVERT
DEVEST
DEVOUT
DIVERT
DIVEST
HAVEAT
HAVENT
INVENT
INVERT
INVEST
LEVANT
LOVETT
OBVERT
QIVIUT
REVERT
REVOLT
SAVANT
SOVIET
VIVANT

•••V•T
BREVET
CHEVET
CRAVAT
CURVET
GRIVET
PRIVET
SHEVAT
SWIVET
TRIVET
VELVET
VERVET

VU••••
VULCAN
VULGAR

V•U•••
VAUGHN
VAULTS
VAUNTS

V••U••
VACUUM
VAGUER
VALUED
VALUES
VARUNA
VENUES
VICUNA
VISUAL
VOGUES
VOLUME
VOLUTE

V•••U•
VACUUM
VALIUM
VALOUR
VAPOUR
VATFUL
VELLUM
VELOUR
VENOUS
VERDUN
VERSUS
VIGOUR
VILLUS
VINOUS
VIRTUE
VIRTUS
VOROUS

V••••U
VISHNU

•VU•••
AVULSE
EVULSE
OVULAR
OVULES
UVULAE
UVULAR
UVULAS

•V•U••
AVAUNT
AVOUCH

•V••U•
AVENUE
EVENUP
RVALUE
UVALUE

••VU••
REVUES

••V•U•
DEVOUR
DEVOUT
FAVOUR
GAVEUP
GIVEUP
QIVIUT
SAVEUP
SAVOUR

••V••U
HAVASU
TUVALU

••••VU
DEJAVU

V•V•••
VIVACE
VIVANT
VIVIAN
VIVIEN
VIVIFY

V••V••
VALVED
VALVES
VELVET
VERVET
VOLVAS
VOLVOX

V•••V•
VOTIVE

V••••V
VACLAV
VASLAV

•V••V•
EVOLVE

••VV••
REVVED

••V•V•
INVIVO
REVIVE

••V••V
PAVLOV

•••VV•
SKIVVY

V•W•••
VOWELS
VOWERS
VOWING

V••W••
VIEWED
VIEWER

•V•W••
AVOWAL
AVOWED
AVOWER

•V•••W
TVSHOW

••V•W•
FIVEWS

••V••W
ONVIEW
REVIEW

V•X•••
VEXERS
VEXING
VIXENS

V••X••
VSIXES

V••••X
VERTEX
VOLVOX
VORTEX

•••V•X
CONVEX
VOLVOX

VY••••
VYBORG

V•Y•••
VOYAGE

V•••Y•
VAISYA
VANRYN

V••••Y
VAGARY
VAINLY
VALERY
VALLEY
VANITY
VARNEY
VASTLY
VEEJAY
VERIFY
VERILY
VERITY
VESTRY
VIABLY
VILELY
VILIFY
VINERY
VIVIFY
VOLLEY
VOTARY

•V••Y•
EVELYN

•V•••Y
AVIARY
AVIDLY
EVENLY
EVERLY
EVILLY
OVERLY

••V•Y•
COVEYS
ENVOYS

••V••Y
BOVARY
CAVITY
LEVITY
LIVELY
LIVERY
LOVELY
NEVSKY
SAVORY
VIVIFY
WAVERY

•••VY•
MELVYN
MERVYN

•••V•Y
CARVEY
CONVEY
CONVOY
GARVEY
HARVEY
PEAVEY
PURVEY
SKIVVY
SURVEY

••••VY
GROOVY
HALEVY
SCURVY
SKIVVY

V•Z•••
VIZIER
VIZSLA

V••••Z
VALDEZ

•VZ•••
EVZONE

••V••Z
KUVASZ

•••V•Z
CHAVEZ

WA••••
WABASH
WADDED
WADDLE
WADDLY
WADEIN
WADERS
WADING
WADSUP
WAFERS
WAFFLE
WAFFLY
WAFTED
WAGERS
WAGGED
WAGGLE
WAGGLY
WAGGON
WAGING
WAGNER
WAGONS
WAHINE
WAHOOS
WAHWAH
WAILED
WAILER
WAISTS
WAITED
WAITER
WAITON
WAITUP
WAIVED

WAIVER
WAIVES
WAKENS
WAKEUP
WAKING
WALDEN
WALERS
WALESA
WALKED
WALKER
WALKIE
WALKIN
WALKON
WALKUP
WALLED
WALLER
WALLET
WALLIS
WALLOP
WALLOW
WALLUP
WALNUT
WALRUS
WALTER
WALTON
WAMBLE
WAMBLY
WAMPUM
WANDER
WANERS
WANGLE
WANING
WANNED
WANNER
WANTAD
WANTED
WANTIN
WANTON
WANTTO
WAPITI
WAPNER
WARBLE
WARCRY
WARDED
WARDEN
WARDER
WARGOD
WARHOL
WARIER
WARILY
WARING
WARMED
WARMER
WARMLY
WARMTH
WARMUP
WARNED
WARNER
WARPED
WARRED
WARREN
WARSAW
WASABI
WASHED
WASHER
WASHES
WASHOE
WASHUP
WASTED
WASTER
WASTES
WATERS
WATERY
WATNEY
WATSON
WATTLE
WATUSI
WAUSAU
WAVEIN
WAVERS
WAVERY
WAVIER
WAVING
WAXERS
WAXIER
WAXING
WAYLAY
WAYLON
WAYOUT

W•A•••
WEAKEN
WEAKER
WEAKLY
WEALTH
WEANED
WEAPON
WEARER
WEASEL
WEAVED
WEAVER
WEAVES
WHACKS
WHACKY
WHALER
WHALES
WHAMMO
WHAMMY
WHARFS
WHATIF
WRACKS
WRAITH
WRAPUP
WRASSE
WRATHS

W••A••
WABASH
WASABI
WHEATS
WIZARD
WREAKS
WREATH

W•••A•
WAHWAH
WANTAD
WARSAW
WAUSAU
WAYLAY
WEIMAR
WENTAT
WETBAR
WHYDAH
WICCAN
WIGWAG
WIGWAM
WINKAT
WITHAL
WOMBAT
WYSTAN

W••••A
WALESA
WINONA
WOVOKA

•WA•••
AWAITS
AWAKED
AWAKEN
AWAKES
AWARDS
BWANAS
DWARFS
DWAYNE
KWACHA
KWANZA
RWANDA
SWABBY
SWAGED
SWAGES
SWAINS
SWALES
SWAMIS
SWAMPS
SWAMPY
SWANEE
SWANKY
SWARAJ
SWARDS
SWARMS
SWARTH
SWATCH
SWATHE
SWATHS
SWAYED
SWAYER
SWAYZE
SWAZIS
TWANGS
TWANGY

•W•A••
AWEARY
SWEARS
SWEATS
SWEATY
TWEAKS

•W••A•
BWANAS
SWARAJ
TWOWAY

•W•••A
KWACHA
KWANZA
RWANDA

••WA••
ALWAYS
BEWAIL
BEWARE
BYWAYS
COWARD
EDWARD
GAWAIN
HAWAII
HOWARD
INWARD
IOWANS
KUWAIT
NAWABS
NEWAGE
NEWARK
ONWARD
OSWALD
REWARD
REWARM
REWASH
SEWAGE
SEWARD
SIWASH
THWACK
THWART
TOWAGE
TOWARD
UNWARY
UPWARD

••W•A•
BOWMAN
BOWOAR
BOWSAW
COWMAN
DEWLAP
ENWRAP
GEWGAW
HAWHAW
HOWDAH
LAWMAN
LOWCAL
LOWFAT
NEWMAN
NEWMAR
PAWPAW
PAWSAT
REWRAP
SOWHAT
TOWCAR
UNWRAP

••W••A
COWPEA
ROWENA

•••WA•
AIRWAY
ANYWAY
ARAWAK
AVOWAL
CONWAY
EARWAX
FLEWAT
FLYWAY
GALWAY
GOAWAY
HOTWAR
INAWAY
KEYWAY
KIOWAS
LEEWAY
MIDWAY
NARWAL
NORWAY
OBIWAN
ONEWAY
PREWAR
RUNWAY
SCHWAS
SEAWAY
SKYWAY
SUBWAY
TAIWAN
TWOWAY
WAHWAH
WIGWAG
WIGWAM

••••WA
BUSHWA
OJIBWA
OSHAWA
OTTAWA
TARAWA
YUKAWA

W•B•••
WABASH
WEBBED
WEBBER
WEBERN
WOBBLE
WOBBLY

W••B••
WAMBLE
WAMBLY
WARBLE
WEBBED
WEBBER
WETBAR
WILBUR
WIMBLE
WOBBLE
WOBBLY
WOMBAT

W•••B•
WASABI
WENTBY

•W•B••
SWABBY
TWOBIT

•W••B•
DWEEBS
SWABBY

••WB••
COWBOY
LOWBOY
SOWBUG

••W•B•
NAWABS

•••W•B
COBWEB

W•C•••
WICCAN
WICKED
WICKER
WICKET
WICOPY

W••C••
WARCRY
WENCES
WHACKS
WHACKY
WICCAN
WINCED
WINCER
WINCES
WITCHY
WRACKS
WRECKS

W•••C•
WHENCE
WRENCH
WRETCH

•W•C••
KWACHA

•W••C•
SWATCH
SWITCH
TWITCH

••WC••
LOWCAL
TOWCAR

••W•C•
THWACK

W•D•••
WADDED
WADDLE
WADDLY
WADEIN
WADERS
WADING
WADSUP
WEDDED
WEDELN
WEDGED
WEDGES
WEDGIE
WIDELY
WIDENS
WIDEST
WIDGET
WIDOWS
WIDTHS

W••D••
WADDED
WADDLE
WADDLY
WALDEN
WANDER
WARDED
WARDEN
WARDER
WEDDED
WEEDED
WEEDER
WELDED
WELDER
WENDED
WHYDAH
WILDER
WILDLY
WINDED
WINDER
WINDEX
WINDOM
WINDOW
WINDUP
WISDOM
WONDER
WOODED
WOODEN
WOODSY
WORDED

W•••D•
WEIRDO
WIELDS
WORLDS
WOUNDS

W••••D
WADDED
WAFTED
WAGGED
WAILED
WAITED
WAIVED
WALKED
WALLED
WANNED
WANTAD
WANTED
WARDED
WARGOD
WARMED
WARNED
WARPED
WARRED
WASHED
WASTED
WEANED
WEAVED
WEBBED
WEDDED
WEDGED
WEEDED
WELDED
WELLED
WELTED
WENDED
WETTED
WHILED
WHINED
WICKED
WIGGED
WILLED
WILTED
WINCED
WINDED
WINGED
WINKED
WISHED
WISPED
WITHED
WITTED
WIZARD
WOLFED
WONNED
WONTED
WOODED
WOOFED
WORDED
WORKED
WORMED

•W•D••
SWEDEN
SWEDES

•W••D•
AWARDS
RWANDA
SWARDS
SWORDS
TWEEDS
TWEEDY

••WD••
CAWDOR
DAWDLE
HOWDAH
LEWDER
LEWDLY
POWDER
TAWDRY

••W•D•
REWEDS

••W••D
ATWOOD
BAWLED
BOWLED
BYWORD
COWARD
COWLED
DAWNED
DOWNED
DOWSED
EDWARD
ELWOOD
FAWNED
FOWLED
GAWKED
GOWILD
GOWNED
HAWKED
HOWARD
HOWLED
INWARD
LOWEND
MEWLED
MYWORD
ONWARD
OSWALD
PAWNED
REWARD
REWELD
REWIND
REWORD
SAWRED
SEWARD
TOWARD
UNWIND
UPWARD
UPWIND
YAWNED
YAWPED
YOWLED

•••WD•
CROWDS

•••W•D
AVOWED
BREWED
CHEWED
CHOWED
CLAWED
CLEWED
CREWED
CROWED
FLAWED
FLOWED
GLOWED
GNAWED
MEOWED
PLOWED
SHOWED
SKEWED
SLEWED
SLOWED
SNOWED
SPEWED
STEWED
STOWED
THAWED
TROWED
UNAWED
VIEWED

••••WD
SHREWD

WE••••
WEAKEN
WEAKER
WEAKLY
WEALTH
WEANED
WEAPON
WEARER
WEASEL
WEAVED
WEAVER
WEAVES
WEBBED
WEBBER
WEBERN
WEDDED
WEDELN
WEDGED
WEDGES
WEDGIE
WEEDED
WEEDER
WEEKLY
WEENIE
WEENSY
WEEPER
WEEVIL
WEIGHS
WEIGHT
WEIMAR
WEIRDO
WELDED
WELDER
WELKIN
WELLED
WELLES
WELLUP
WELTED
WELTER
WENCES
WENDED
WENTAT
WENTBY
WENTIN
WENTON
WENTUP
WERENT
WERFEL
WERNER
WESKIT
WESLEY
WESSEX
WESSON
WETBAR
WETFLY
WETHER
WETMOP
WETTED
WETTER
WETTIG

W•E•••
WEEDED
WEEDER
WEEKLY
WEENIE
WEENSY
WEEPER
WEEVIL
WHEATS
WHEELS
WHEEZE
WHEEZY
WHELKS
WHELPS
WHENCE
WHERRY
WIELDS
WIENER
WIESEL
WOEFUL
WREAKS
WREATH
WRECKS
WRENCH
WRESTS
WRETCH

W••E••
WADEIN
WADERS
WAFERS
WAGERS
WAKENS
WAKEUP
WALERS
WALESA
WANERS
WATERS
WATERY
WAVEIN
WAVERS
WAVERY
WAXERS
WEBERN
WEDELN
WERENT
WHEELS
WHEEZE
WHEEZY
WIDELY
WIDENS
WIDEST
WIFELY
WINERY
WIPERS
WIPEUP
WIRERS
WISELY
WISENT
WISEST
WISETO
WISEUP
WIZENS
WOKEUP
WOMENS
WOOERS
WOREON
WRIEST
WRYEST
WYVERN

W•••E•
WADDED
WAFTED
WAGGED
WAGNER
WAILED
WAILER
WAITED
WAITER
WAIVED
WAIVER
WAIVES
WALDEN
WALKED
WALKER
WALLED
WALLER
WALLET
WALTER
WANDER
WANNED
WANNER
WANTED
WAPNER
WARDED
WARDEN
WARDER
WARIER
WARMED
WARMER
WARNED
WARNER
WARPED
WARRED
WARREN
WASHED
WASHER
WASHES
WASTED
WASTER
WASTES
WATNEY
WAVIER
WAXIER
WEAKEN
WEAKER
WEANED
WEARER
WEASEL
WEAVED
WEAVER
WEAVES
WEBBED
WEBBER
WEDDED
WEDGED
WEDGES
WEEDED
WEEDER
WEEPER
WELDED
WELDER
WELLED
WELLES
WELTED
WELTER
WENCES
WENDED
WERFEL
WERNER
WESLEY
WESSEX
WETHER
WETTED
WETTER
WHALER
WHALES
WHILED
WHILES
WHINED
WHINER
WHINES
WHITEN
WHITER
WHITES
WHOLES
WICKED
WICKER
WICKET
WIDGET
WIENER
WIESEL
WIGGED
WIGLET
WILDER
WILIER
WILKES
WILLED
WILLEM
WILLET
WILTED
WIMSEY
WINCED
WINCER
WINCES
WINDED
WINDER
WINDEX
WINGED
WINGER
WINKED
WINKER
WINNER
WINTER
WINZES
WISHED
WISHER
WISHES
WISPED
WISTER
WITHED
WITHER
WITHES
WITTED
WOHLER
WOLFED
WOLPER
WOLSEY
WOLVES
WONDER
WONNED
WONTED
WOODED
WOODEN
WOOFED
WOOFER
WOOLEN
WOOLEY
WORDED
WORKED
WORKER
WORMED
WORSEN
WRITER
WRITES
WYNTER

W••••E
WADDLE
WAFFLE
WAGGLE
WAHINE
WALKIE
WAMBLE
WANGLE
WARBLE
WASHOE
WATTLE
WEDGIE
WEENIE
WHEEZE
WHENCE
WIGGLE
WILLIE
WIMBLE
WIMPLE
WINKIE
WINKLE
WINNIE
WOBBLE
WOOGIE
WOOKIE
WRASSE
WRITHE

•WE•••
AWEARY
AWEIGH
DWEEBS
DWELLS
QWERTY
SWEARS
SWEATS
SWEATY
SWEDEN
SWEDES
SWEEPS
SWEETS
SWELLS
SWERVE
TWEAKS
TWEEDS
TWEEDY
TWEETS
TWEETY
TWEEZE
TWELVE
TWENTY
TWERPS

•W•E••
DWEEBS
OWLETS
OWNERS
SWEEPS
SWEETS
TWEEDS
TWEEDY
TWEETS
TWEETY
TWEEZE

•W••E•
AWAKED
AWAKEN
AWAKES
AWOKEN
SWAGED
SWAGES
SWALES
SWANEE
SWAYED
SWAYER
SWEDEN
SWEDES
SWIPED
SWIPER
SWIPES
SWIVEL
SWIVET
TWINED
TWINES
TWOFER

•W•••E
AWHILE
DWAYNE
GWYNNE
SWANEE
SWATHE
SWAYZE
SWERVE
TWEEZE
TWELVE
TWINGE

••WE••
ADWEEK
ALWEST
ASWELL
BOWERS
BOWERY
COWENS
COWERS
DOWELS
DOWERS
FEWEST
GOWEST
HEWERS
HOWELL
JEWELS
JEWETT
JOWETT
LOWELL
LOWEND
LOWERS
LOWERY
LOWEST
MOWERS
NEWELS
NEWEST
NLWEST
OHWELL
ORWELL
OSWEGO
PAWERS
PEWEES
POWELL
POWERS
RAWEGG
RAWEST
REWEDS
REWELD
ROWELS
ROWENA
ROWENS
ROWERS
SEWELL
SEWERS
SOWERS
SOWETO
TOWELS
TOWERS
TOWERY
UNWELL
UPWELL
VOWELS
VOWERS

••W•E•
ADWEEK
BAWLED
BAWLER
BOWLED
BOWLER
BOWLES
BOWMEN
BOWNET
BOWSER
BOWYER
COWLED
COWLEY
COWMEN
COWPEA
COWPER
DAWNED
DEWIER
DOWNED
DOWNER
DOWNEY
DOWSED
DOWSER
DOWSES
FAWKES
FAWNED
FAWNER
FOWLED
FOWLER
FOWLES
GAWKED
GAWKER
GOWNED
HAWKED
HAWKER
HAWSER
HAWSES
HOWLED
HOWLER
LAWMEN
LAWYER
LEWDER
LOWKEY
MEWLED
MEWLER
NEWLEY
PAWNED
PAWNEE
PAWNER
PEWEES
PEWTER
POWDER
SAWRED
SAWYER
TOWHEE
TOWNER
YAWNED
YAWNER
YAWPED
YAWPER
YOWLED

••W••E
BEWARE
BOWTIE
COWRIE
DAWDLE
EXWIFE
KEWPIE
NEWAGE
NOWISE
PAWNEE
REWIRE
REWOVE
SEWAGE
TOWAGE
TOWHEE
TOWNIE
UNWISE

UNWOVE

•••WE•
ALLWET
ANSWER
AVOWED
AVOWER
BLOWER
BREWED
BREWER
BULWER
CHEWED
CHEWER
CHOWED
CLAWED
CLAWER
CLEWED
COBWEB
CREWED
CREWEL
CROWED
CROWER
DRAWER
FLAWED
FLOWED
FLOWER
GLOWED
GLOWER
GNAWED
GNAWER
GROWER
KNOWER
MEOWED
PEEWEE
PLOWED
PLOWER
SHOWED
SHOWER
SKEWED
SKEWER
SLEWED
SLOWED
SLOWER
SNOWED
SPEWED
STEWED
STEWER
STOWED
THAWED
TROWED
TROWEL
UNAWED
VIEWED
VIEWER
YAHWEH

•••W•E
BROWNE
BROWSE
DROWSE
PEEWEE
PROWSE
SHOWME

W•F•••
WAFERS
WAFFLE
WAFFLY
WAFTED
WIFELY

W••F••
WAFFLE
WAFFLY
WERFEL
WETFLY
WHIFFS
WOEFUL
WOLFED
WOOFED
WOOFER

W•••F•
WHARFS
WHIFFS
WHOOFS

W••••F
WHATIF

•W•F••
SWIFTS
TWOFER

•W••F•
DWARFS

••WF••
BOWFIN
LAWFUL
LOWFAT
SAWFIT

••W•F•
EXWIFE
SAWOFF

••W••F
SAWOFF

W•G•••
WAGERS
WAGGED
WAGGLE
WAGGLY
WAGGON
WAGING
WAGNER
WAGONS
WIGGED
WIGGLE
WIGGLY
WIGHTS
WIGLET
WIGOUT
WIGWAG
WIGWAM

W••G••
WAGGED
WAGGLE
WAGGLY
WAGGON
WANGLE
WARGOD
WEDGED
WEDGES
WEDGIE
WEIGHS
WEIGHT
WIDGET
WIGGED
WIGGLE
WIGGLY
WINGED
WINGER
WINGIT
WOOGIE
WRIGHT

W•••G•
WRINGS
WRONGS

W••••G
WADING
WAGING
WAKING
WANING
WARING
WAVING
WAXING
WETTIG
WIGWAG
WILING
WINING
WIPING
WIRING
WONMUG
WOOING
WOWING

•W•G••
DWIGHT
SWAGED
SWAGES
TWIGGY

•W••G•
AWEIGH
SWINGS
SWINGY
TWANGS
TWANGY
TWIGGY
TWINGE

•W•••G
AWNING
OWNING

••WG••
GEWGAW
MOWGLI

••W•G•
NEWAGE
OSWEGO
RAWEGG
SEWAGE
TOWAGE

••W••G
BOWING
CAWING
COWING
DEWING
HAWING
HEWING
JAWING
LAWING
LOWING
MEWING
MOWING
PAWING
RAWEGG
ROWING
SAWING
SAWLOG
SEWING
SOWBUG
SOWING
TAWING
TOWING
VOWING
WOWING
YAWING

•••W•G
BIGWIG
EARWIG
LUDWIG
WIGWAG

WH••••
WHACKS
WHACKY
WHALER
WHALES
WHAMMO
WHAMMY
WHARFS
WHATIF
WHEATS
WHEELS
WHEEZE
WHEEZY
WHELKS
WHELPS
WHENCE
WHERRY
WHIFFS
WHILED
WHILES
WHILOM
WHILST
WHIMSY
WHINED
WHINER
WHINES
WHINNY
WHIPPY
WHIPUP
WHIRLS
WHIRLY
WHIRRS
WHISKS
WHITEN
WHITER
WHITES
WHOLES
WHOLLY
WHOMPS
WHOOFS
WHOOPI
WHOOPS
WHOOSH
WHORLS
WHYDAH
WHYNOT

W•H•••
WAHINE
WAHOOS
WAHWAH
WOHLER

W••H••
WARHOL
WASHED
WASHER
WASHES
WASHOE
WASHUP
WETHER
WIGHTS
WISHED
WISHER
WISHES
WITHAL
WITHED
WITHER
WITHES
WITHIN
WITHIT

W•••H•
WEIGHS
WEIGHT
WIDTHS
WITCHY
WORTHS
WORTHY
WRATHS
WRIGHT
WRITHE

W••••H
WABASH
WAHWAH
WARMTH
WEALTH
WHOOSH
WHYDAH
WRAITH
WREATH
WRENCH
WRETCH

•WH•••
AWHILE
AWHIRL

•W••H•
DWIGHT
KWACHA
SWATHE
SWATHS

•W•••H
AWEIGH
OWLISH
SWARTH
SWATCH
SWITCH
SWOOSH
TWITCH

••WH••
HAWHAW
SOWHAT
TOWHEE

••W•H•
JAWOHL

••W••H
GOWITH
HOWDAH
INWITH
JEWISH
NEWISH
REWASH
SIWASH

•••W•H
GROWTH
WAHWAH
YAHWEH

WI••••
WICCAN
WICKED
WICKER
WICKET
WICOPY
WIDELY
WIDENS
WIDEST
WIDGET
WIDOWS
WIDTHS
WIELDS
WIENER
WIESEL
WIFELY
WIGGED
WIGGLE
WIGGLY
WIGHTS
WIGLET
WIGOUT
WIGWAG
WIGWAM
WILBUR
WILDER
WILDLY
WILIER
WILING
WILKES
WILLED
WILLEM
WILLET
WILLIE
WILLIS
WILLOW
WILSON
WILTED
WILTON
WIMBLE
WIMPLE
WIMSEY
WINCED
WINCER
WINCES
WINDED
WINDER
WINDEX
WINDOM
WINDOW
WINDUP
WINERY
WINGED
WINGER
WINGIT
WINING
WINKAT
WINKED
WINKER
WINKIE
WINKLE
WINNER
WINNIE
WINNOW
WINONA
WINOUT
WINSOR
WINTER
WINTRY
WINWIN
WINZES
WIPERS
WIPEUP
WIPING
WIRERS
WIRING
WISDOM
WISELY
WISENT
WISEST
WISETO
WISEUP
WISHED
WISHER
WISHES
WISPED
WISTER
WITCHY
WITHAL
WITHED
WITHER
WITHES
WITHIN
WITHIT
WITTED
WIZARD
WIZENS

W•I•••
WAILED
WAILER
WAISTS
WAITED
WAITER
WAITON
WAITUP
WAIVED
WAIVER
WAIVES
WEIGHS
WEIGHT
WEIMAR
WEIRDO
WHIFFS
WHILED
WHILES
WHILOM
WHILST
WHIMSY
WHINED
WHINER
WHINES
WHINNY
WHIPPY
WHIPUP
WHIRLS
WHIRLY
WHIRRS
WHISKS
WHITEN
WHITER
WHITES
WRIEST
WRIGHT
WRINGS
WRISTS
WRITER
WRITES
WRITHE

W••I••
WADING
WAGING
WAHINE
WAKING
WANING
WAPITI
WARIER
WARILY
WARING
WAVIER
WAVING
WAXIER
WAXING
WILIER
WILING
WINING
WIPING
WIRING
WOOING
WOWING
WRAITH

W•••I•
WADEIN
WALKIE
WALKIN
WALLIS
WANTIN
WAVEIN
WEDGIE
WEENIE
WEEVIL
WELKIN
WENTIN
WESKIT
WETTIG
WHATIF
WILLIE
WILLIS
WINGIT
WINKIE
WINNIE
WINWIN
WITHIN
WITHIT
WOOGIE
WOOKIE
WORKIN

W••••I
WAPITI
WASABI
WATUSI
WHOOPI

•WI•••
DWIGHT
SWIFTS
SWILLS
SWINGS
SWINGY
SWIPED
SWIPER
SWIPES
SWIRLS
SWIRLY
SWITCH
SWIVEL
SWIVET
TWIGGY
TWILIT
TWILLS
TWINED
TWINES
TWINGE
TWIRLS
TWISTS
TWISTY
TWITCH
TWITTY

•W•I••
AWAITS
AWEIGH
AWHILE
AWHIRL
AWNING
OWLISH
OWNING
SWAINS

•W••I•
SWAMIS
SWAZIS
TWILIT
TWOBIT

••WI••
ASWIRL
ATWILL
BOWING
CAWING
COWING
DEWIER
DEWING
DEWITT
EXWIFE
GOWILD
GOWITH
HAWING
HEWING
INWITH
JAWING
JEWISH
LAWING
LOWING
MEWING
MOWING
NEWISH
NOWISE
PAWING
PEWITS
REWIND
REWINS
REWIRE
ROWING
SAWING
SEWING
SOWING
TAWING
TOWING
UNWIND
UNWISE
UPWIND
VOWING
WOWING
YAWING

••W•I•
BEWAIL
BOWFIN
BOWTIE
COWRIE
GAWAIN
HAWAII
HOWLIN
KEWPIE
KUWAIT
SAWFIT
TOWNIE

••W••I
HAWAII
MOWGLI

•••WI•
BIGWIG
BLEWIT
BLOWIN
BLOWIT
DARWIN
DIMWIT
DRAWIN
DREWIN
EARWIG
FLEWIN
GODWIN
GODWIT
LUDWIG
NITWIT
OUTWIT
SHOWIN
SNOWIN
THEWIZ
WINWIN

••••WI
MALAWI

•W•••J
SWARAJ

W•K•••
WAKENS
WAKEUP
WAKING
WOKEUP

W••K••
WALKED
WALKER
WALKIE
WALKIN
WALKON
WALKUP
WEAKEN
WEAKER
WEAKLY
WEEKLY
WELKIN
WESKIT
WICKED
WICKER
WICKET
WILKES
WINKAT
WINKED
WINKER
WINKIE
WINKLE
WOOKIE
WORKED
WORKER
WORKIN
WORKON
WORKUP

W•••K•
WHACKS
WHACKY
WHELKS
WHISKS
WOVOKA
WRACKS
WREAKS
WRECKS

•W•K••
AWAKED
AWAKEN
AWAKES
AWOKEN

•W••K•
SWANKY
TWEAKS

••WK••
FAWKES
GAWKED
GAWKER
HAWKED
HAWKER
LOWKEY

••W•K•
MIWOKS

••W••K
ADWEEK
ATWORK
NEWARK
REWORK
THWACK

•••W•K
ARAWAK

••••WK
MOHAWK
SQUAWK

W•L•••
WALDEN
WALERS
WALESA
WALKED
WALKER
WALKIE
WALKIN
WALKON
WALKUP
WALLED
WALLER
WALLET
WALLIS
WALLOP
WALLOW
WALLUP
WALNUT
WALRUS
WALTER
WALTON
WELDED
WELDER
WELKIN
WELLED
WELLES
WELLUP
WELTED
WELTER
WILBUR
WILDER
WILDLY
WILIER
WILING
WILKES
WILLED
WILLEM
WILLET
WILLIE
WILLIS
WILLOW
WILSON
WILTED
WILTON
WOLFED
WOLPER
WOLSEY
WOLVES

W••L••
WAILED
WAILER
WALLED
WALLER
WALLET
WALLIS
WALLOP
WALLOW
WALLUP
WAYLAY
WAYLON
WEALTH
WELLED
WELLES
WELLUP
WESLEY
WHALER
WHALES
WHELKS
WHELPS
WHILED
WHILES
WHILOM
WHILST
WHOLES
WHOLLY
WIELDS
WIGLET
WILLED
WILLEM
WILLET
WILLIE
WILLIS
WILLOW
WOHLER
WOOLEN
WOOLEY
WOOLLY
WORLDS

W•••L•
WADDLE
WADDLY
WAFFLE
WAFFLY
WAGGLE
WAGGLY
WAMBLE
WAMBLY
WANGLE
WARBLE
WARILY
WARMLY
WATTLE
WEAKLY
WEDELN
WEEKLY
WETFLY
WHEELS
WHIRLS
WHIRLY
WHOLLY
WHORLS
WIDELY
WIFELY
WIGGLE
WIGGLY
WILDLY
WIMBLE
WIMPLE
WINKLE
WISELY
WOBBLE
WOBBLY
WOOLLY

W••••L
WARHOL
WEASEL
WEEVIL
WERFEL
WIESEL
WITHAL
WOEFUL

•WL•••
OWLETS
OWLISH

•W•L••
DWELLS
SWALES
SWELLS
SWILLS
TWELVE
TWILIT
TWILLS

•W••L•
AWHILE
DWELLS
SWELLS
SWILLS
SWIRLS
SWIRLY
TWILLS
TWIRLS
TWOPLY

•W•••L
AWHIRL
SWIVEL

••WL••
BAWLED
BAWLER
BOWLED
BOWLER
BOWLES
COWLED
COWLEY
DEWLAP
FAWLTY
FOWLED
FOWLER
FOWLES
HOWLED
HOWLER
HOWLIN
MEWLED
MEWLER
NEWLEY
SAWLOG
YOWLED

••W•L•
ASWELL
ATWILL
DAWDLE
DOWELS
GOWILD
HOWELL
JEWELS
LEWDLY
LOWELL
MOWGLI
NEWELS
OHWELL
ORWELL
OSWALD
POWELL
REWELD
ROWELS
SEWELL
TOWELS
UNWELL
UPWELL
VOWELS

••W••L
ASWELL
ASWIRL
ATWILL
BEWAIL
HOWELL
JAWOHL
LAWFUL
LOWCAL
LOWELL
OHWELL
ORWELL
POWELL
SEWELL
UNWELL
UPWELL

•••WL•
BRAWLS
CRAWLS
CRAWLY
DRAWLS
GROWLS
GROWLY
PROWLS
SCOWLS
SHAWLS
SLOWLY
TRAWLS

•••W•L
AVOWAL
CREWEL
NARWAL
TROWEL

••••WL
SCRAWL
SPRAWL

W•M•••
WAMBLE
WAMBLY
WAMPUM
WIMBLE
WIMPLE
WIMSEY
WOMBAT
WOMENS

W••M••
WARMED
WARMER
WARMLY
WARMTH
WARMUP
WEIMAR
WETMOP
WHAMMO
WHAMMY
WHIMSY
WHOMPS
WONMUG
WORMED

W•••M•
WHAMMO
WHAMMY

W••••M
WAMPUM
WHILOM
WIGWAM
WILLEM
WINDOM
WISDOM

•W•M••
SWAMIS
SWAMPS
SWAMPY

•W••M•
SWARMS

••WM••
BOWMAN
BOWMEN
COWMAN
COWMEN
LAWMAN
LAWMEN
NEWMAN
NEWMAR

••W••M
REWARM

•••WM•
SHAWMS
SHOWME

•••W•M
WIGWAM

W•N•••
WANDER
WANERS
WANGLE
WANING
WANNED
WANNER
WANTAD
WANTED
WANTIN
WANTON
WANTTO
WENCES
WENDED
WENTAT
WENTBY
WENTIN
WENTON
WENTUP
WINCED
WINCER
WINCES
WINDED

WINDER WINDEX WINDOM WINDOW WINDUP WINERY WINGED WINGER WINGIT WINING WINKAT WINKED WINKER WINKIE WINKLE WINNER WINNIE WINNOW WINONA WINOUT WINSOR WINTER WINTRY WINWIN WINZES WONDER WONMUG WONNED WONOUT WONTED WONTON WYNTER WYNTON

W••N••
WAGNER WALNUT WANNED WANNER WAPNER WARNED WARNER WATNEY WEANED WEENIE WEENSY WERNER WHENCE WHINED WHINER WHINES WHINNY WHYNOT WIENER WINNER WINNIE WINNOW WONNED WOUNDS WRENCH WRINGS WRONGS

W•••N•
WADING WAGING WAGONS WAHINE WAKENS WAKING WANING WARING WAVING WAXING WERENT WHINNY WIDENS WILING WINING WINONA WIPING WIRING WISENT WIZENS WOMENS WOOING WOWING

W••••N
WADEIN WAGGON WAITON WALDEN WALKIN WALKON WALTON WANTIN WANTON WARDEN WARREN WATSON WAVEIN WAYLON WEAKEN WEAPON WEBERN WEDELN WELKIN WENTIN WENTON WESSON WHITEN WICCAN WILSON WILTON WINWIN WITHIN WONTON WOODEN WOOLEN WOREON WORKIN WORKON WORSEN WYNTON WYSTAN WYVERN

•WN•••
AWNING OWNERS OWNING OWNSUP

•W•N••
BWANAS GWYNNE KWANZA RWANDA SWANEE SWANKY SWINGS SWINGY TWANGS TWANGY TWENTY TWINED TWINES TWINGE

•W••N•
AWNING DWAYNE GWYNNE OWNING SWAINS SWOONS

•W•••N
AWAKEN AWOKEN SWEDEN

••WN••
BOWNET DAWNED DOWNED DOWNER DOWNEY DOWNON FAWNED FAWNER GOWNED HOWNOW PAWNED PAWNEE PAWNER SEWNUP TOWNER TOWNIE YAWNED YAWNER

••W•N•
BOWING CAWING COWENS COWING DEWING EDWYNN HAWING HEWING IOWANS JAWING LAWING LOWEND LOWING MEWING MOWING PAWING REWIND REWINS ROWENA ROWENS ROWING SAWING SEWING SOWING TAWING TOWING UNWIND UPWIND VOWING WOWING YAWING

••W••N
ASWOON BOWFIN BOWMAN BOWMEN COWMAN COWMEN DAWSON DOWNON EDWYNN GAWAIN HOWLIN LAWMAN LAWMEN LAWSON LAWTON NEWMAN NEWTON SEWSON UNWORN

•••WN•
BRAWNY BROWNE BROWNS CLOWNS CROWNS DROWNS FROWNS KNOWNS PRAWNS SPAWNS

•••W•N
BLOWIN DARWIN DRAWIN DRAWON DREWIN DREWON FLEWIN GODWIN GREWON GROWON OBIWAN SHOWIN SNOWIN TAIWAN WINWIN

••••WN
DISOWN GODOWN INTOWN MOTOWN REMOWN RENOWN RESEWN STREWN THROWN UNSEWN UNSOWN UPTOWN

WO••••
WOBBLE WOBBLY WOEFUL WOHLER WOKEUP WOLFED WOLPER WOLSEY WOLVES WOMBAT WOMENS WONDER WONMUG WONNED WONOUT WONTED WONTON WOODED WOODEN WOODSY WOOERS WOOFED WOOFER WOOGIE WOOING WOOKIE WOOLEN WOOLEY WOOLLY WORDED WOREON WORKED WORKER WORKIN WORKON WORKUP WORLDS WORMED WORSEN WORSTS WORTHS WORTHY WOUNDS WOVOKA WOWING

W•O•••
WHOLES WHOLLY WHOMPS WHOOFS WHOOPI WHOOPS WHOOSH WHORLS WOODED WOODEN WOODSY WOOERS WOOFED WOOFER WOOGIE WOOING WOOKIE WOOLEN WOOLEY WOOLLY WRONGS

W••O••
WAGONS WAHOOS WAYOUT WHOOFS WHOOPI WHOOPS WHOOSH WICOPY WIDOWS WIGOUT WINONA WINOUT WONOUT WOVOKA

W•••O•
WAGGON WAHOOS WAITON WALKON WALLOP WALLOW WALTON WANTON WARGOD WARHOL WASHOE WATSON WAYLON WEAPON WENTON WESSON WETMOP WHILOM WHYNOT WILLOW WILSON WILTON WINDOM WINDOW WINNOW WINSOR WISDOM WONTON WOREON WORKON WYNTON

W••••O
WANTTO WEIRDO WHAMMO WISETO

•WO•••
AWOKEN SWOONS SWOOPS SWOOSH SWORDS TWOBIT TWOFER TWOPLY TWOWAY

•W•O••
SWOONS SWOOPS SWOOSH

••WO••
ASWOON ATWOOD ATWORK BOWOAR BOWOUT BYWORD ELWOOD JAWOHL MIWOKS MYWORD REWORD REWORK REWOVE SAWOFF SAWOUT UNWORN UNWOVE

••W•O•
ASWOON ATWOOD BOWWOW CAWDOR COWBOY COWPOX DAWSON DOWNON ELWOOD HOWNOW HOWTOS KOWTOW LAWSON LAWTON LOWBOY NEWTON POWWOW SAWLOG SEWSON

••W••O
OSWEGO SOWETO

•••WO•
BOWWOW DOOWOP DRAWON DREWON GREWON GROWON POWWOW

••••WO
ACTTWO ONETWO

W•P•••
WAPITI WAPNER WIPERS WIPEUP WIPING

W••P••
WAMPUM WARPED WEAPON WEEPER WHIPPY WHIPUP WIMPLE WISPED WOLPER WRAPUP

W•••P•
WHELPS WHIPPY WHOMPS WHOOPI WHOOPS WICOPY

W••••P
WADSUP WAITUP WAKEUP WALKUP WALLOP WALLUP WARMUP WASHUP WELLUP WENTUP WETMOP WHIPUP WINDUP WIPEUP WISEUP WOKEUP WORKUP WRAPUP

•W•P••
SWIPED SWIPER SWIPES TWOPLY

•W••P•
SWAMPS SWAMPY SWEEPS SWOOPS TWERPS

•W•••P
OWNSUP

••WP••
COWPEA COWPER COWPOX KEWPIE PAWPAW YAWPED YAWPER

••W••P
DEWLAP ENWRAP REWRAP SEWNUP SEWSUP UNWRAP

•••W•P
BLEWUP BLOWUP CHEWUP DOOWOP DRAWUP DREWUP GREWUP GROWUP SHOWUP SLOWUP

WR••••
WRACKS WRAITH WRAPUP WRASSE WRATHS WREAKS WREATH WRECKS WRENCH WRESTS WRETCH WRIEST WRIGHT WRINGS WRISTS WRITER WRITES WRITHE WRONGS WRYEST

W•R•••
WARBLE WARCRY WARDED WARDEN WARDER WARGOD WARHOL WARIER WARILY WARING WARMED WARMER WARMLY WARMTH WARMUP WARNED WARNER WARPED WARRED WARREN WARSAW WERENT WERFEL WERNER WIRERS WIRING WORDED WOREON WORKED WORKER WORKIN WORKON WORKUP WORLDS WORMED WORSEN WORSTS WORTHS WORTHY WURSTS

W••R••
WALRUS WARRED WARREN WEARER WEIRDO WHARFS WHERRY WHIRLS WHIRLY WHIRRS WHORLS

W•••R•
WADERS WAFERS WAGERS WALERS WANERS WARCRY WATERS WATERY WAVERS WAVERY WAXERS WEBERN WHERRY WHIRRS WINERY WINTRY WIPERS WIRERS WIZARD WOOERS WYVERN

W••••R
WAGNER WAILER WAITER WAIVER WALKER WALLER WALTER WANDER WANNER WAPNER WARDER WARIER WARMER WARNER WASHER WASTER WAVIER WAXIER WEAKER WEARER WEAVER WEBBER WEEDER WEEPER WEIMAR WELDER WELTER WERNER WETBAR WETHER WETTER WHALER WHINER WHITER WICKER WIENER WILBUR WILDER WILIER WINCER WINDER WINGER WINKER WINNER WINSOR WINTER WISHER WISTER WITHER WOHLER WOLPER WONDER WOOFER WORKER WRITER WYNTER

•W•R••
AWARDS DWARFS QWERTY SWARAJ SWARDS SWARMS SWARTH SWERVE SWIRLS SWIRLY SWORDS TWERPS TWIRLS

•W••R•
AWEARY AWHIRL OWNERS SWEARS

•W•••R
SWAYER SWIPER TWOFER

••WR••
COWRIE ENWRAP REWRAP SAWRED UNWRAP

••W•R•
ASWIRL ATWORK BEWARE BOWERS BOWERY BYWORD COWARD COWERS DOWERS EDWARD HEWERS HOWARD INWARD LOWERS LOWERY MOWERS MYWORD NEWARK ONWARD PAWERS POWERS REWARD REWARM REWIRE REWORD REWORK ROWERS SEWARD SEWERS SOWERS TAWDRY THWART TOWARD TOWERS TOWERY UNWARY UNWORN UPWARD VOWERS

••W••R
BAWLER BOWLER BOWOAR BOWSER BOWYER CAWDOR COWPER DEWIER DOWNER DOWSER FAWNER FOWLER GAWKER HAWKER HAWSER HOWLER LAWYER LEWDER MEWLER NEWMAR PAWNER PEWTER POWDER SAWYER TOWCAR TOWNER YAWNER YAWPER

•••WR•
GOAWRY

•••W•R
ANSWER AVOWER BLOWER BREWER BULWER CHEWER CLAWER CROWER DRAWER FLOWER GLOWER GNAWER GROWER HOTWAR KNOWER PLOWER PREWAR SHOWER SKEWER SLOWER STEWER VIEWER

W•S•••
WASABI WASHED WASHER WASHES WASHOE WASHUP WASTED WASTER WASTES WESKIT WESLEY WESSEX WESSON WISDOM WISELY WISENT WISEST WISETO WISEUP WISHED WISHER WISHES WISPED WISTER WYSTAN

W••S••
WADSUP WAISTS WARSAW WATSON WAUSAU WEASEL WESSEX WESSON WHISKS WIESEL WILSON WIMSEY WINSOR WOLSEY WORSEN WORSTS WRASSE WRESTS WRISTS WURSTS

W•••S•
WABASH WALESA WATUSI WEENSY WHILST WHIMSY WHOOSH WIDEST WISEST WOODSY WRASSE WRIEST WRYEST

W••••S
WADERS WAFERS WAGERS WAGONS WAHOOS WAISTS WAIVES WAKENS WALERS WALLIS WALRUS WANERS WASHES WASTES WATERS WAVERS WAXERS WEAVES WEDGES WEIGHS WELLES WENCES WHACKS WHALES WHARFS WHEATS WHEELS WHELKS WHELPS WHIFFS WHILES WHINES WHIRLS WHIRRS WHISKS WHITES WHOLES WHOMPS WHOOFS WHOOPS WHORLS WIDENS WIDOWS WIDTHS WIELDS WIGHTS WILKES WILLIS WINCES WINZES WIPERS WIRERS WISHES WITHES WIZENS WOLVES WOMENS WOOERS WORLDS WORSTS WORTHS WOUNDS WRACKS WRATHS WREAKS WRECKS WRESTS WRINGS WRISTS WRITES WRONGS WURSTS

•W•S••
OWNSUP TWISTS TWISTY

•W••S•
OWLISH SWOOSH

•W•••S
AWAITS AWAKES AWARDS BWANAS DWARFS DWEEBS DWELLS OWLETS OWNERS SWAGES SWAINS SWALES SWAMIS SWAMPS SWARDS SWARMS SWATHS SWAZIS SWEARS SWEATS SWEDES SWEEPS SWEETS SWELLS SWIFTS SWILLS SWINGS SWIPES SWIRLS SWOONS SWOOPS SWORDS TWANGS TWEAKS TWEEDS TWEETS TWERPS TWILLS TWINES TWIRLS TWISTS

••WS••
BOWSAW BOWSER DAWSON DOWSED DOWSER DOWSES HAWSER HAWSES LAWSON PAWSAT SEWSON SEWSUP

••W•S•
ALWEST FEWEST GOWEST JEWISH LOWEST NEWEST NEWISH NLWEST NOWISE RAWEST REWASH SIWASH UNWISE

••W••S
ALWAYS BOWERS BOWLES BYWAYS COWENS COWERS DOWELS DOWERS DOWSES FAWKES FOWLES HAWSES HEWERS HOWTOS IOWANS JEWELS LOWERS MIWOKS MOWERS NAWABS NEWELS PAWERS PEWEES PEWITS POWERS REWEDS REWINS ROWELS ROWENS ROWERS SEWERS

SOWERS TOWELS TOWERS VOWELS VOWERS

•••WS•
BROWSE DROWSE DROWSY PROWSE

•••W•S
BRAWLS BROWNS CLOWNS CRAWLS CROWDS CROWNS DRAWLS DROWNS FROWNS GROWLS KIOWAS KNOWNS PRAWNS PROWLS SCHWAS SCOWLS SHAWLS SHAWMS SPAWNS TRAWLS

••••WS
ALLOWS ARROWS BEDEWS BYLAWS CAHOWS ELBOWS ENDOWS FIVEWS INLAWS MACAWS OXBOWS PAPAWS REMOWS RENEWS RESEWS RETOWS SCREWS SEROWS SHREWS SINEWS STRAWS STREWS THROWS UNSEWS UPBOWS WIDOWS

W•T•••
WATERS WATERY WATNEY WATSON WATTLE WATUSI WETBAR WETFLY WETHER WETMOP WETTED WETTER WETTIG WITCHY WITHAL WITHED WITHER WITHES WITHIN WITHIT WITTED

W••T••
WAFTED WAITED WAITER WAITON WAITUP WALTER WALTON WANTAD WANTED WANTIN WANTON WANTTO WASTED WASTER WASTES WATTLE WELTED WELTER WENTAT WENTBY WENTIN WENTON WENTUP WETTED WETTER WETTIG WHATIF WHITEN WHITER WHITES WIDTHS WILTED WILTON WINTER WINTRY WISTER WITTED WONTED WONTON WORTHS WORTHY WRATHS WRETCH WRITER WRITES WRITHE WYNTER WYNTON WYSTAN

W•••T•
WAISTS WANTTO WAPITI WARMTH WEALTH WHEATS WIGHTS WISETO WORSTS WRAITH WREATH WRESTS WRISTS WURSTS

W••••T
WALLET WALNUT WAYOUT WEIGHT WENTAT WERENT WESKIT WHILST WHYNOT WICKET WIDEST WIDGET WIGLET WIGOUT WILLET WINGIT WINKAT WINOUT WISENT WISEST WITHIT WOMBAT WONOUT WRIEST WRIGHT WRYEST

•W•T••
SWATCH SWATHE SWATHS SWITCH TWITCH TWITTY

•W••T•
AWAITS OWLETS QWERTY SWARTH SWEATS SWEATY SWEETS SWIFTS TWEETS TWEETY TWENTY TWISTS TWISTY TWITTY

•W•••T
DWIGHT SWIVET TWILIT TWOBIT

••WT••
BOWTIE HOWTOS KOWTOW LAWTON NEWTON PEWTER

••W•T•
DEWITT FAWLTY GOWITH INWITH JEWETT JOWETT PEWITS SOWETO

••W••T
ALWEST BOWNET BOWOUT DEWITT FEWEST GOWEST JEWETT JOWETT KUWAIT LOWEST LOWFAT NEWEST NLWEST PAWSAT RAWEST SAWFIT SAWOUT SOWHAT THWART

•••WT•
GROWTH

•••W•T
ALLWET BLEWIT BLOWIT DIMWIT FLEWAT GODWIT NITWIT OUTWIT

WU••••
WURSTS

W•U•••
WAUSAU WOUNDS

W••U••
WATUSI

W•••U•
WADSUP WAITUP WAKEUP WALKUP WALLUP WALNUT WALRUS WAMPUM WARMUP WASHUP WAYOUT WELLUP WENTUP WHIPUP WIGOUT WILBUR WINDUP WINOUT WIPEUP WISEUP WOEFUL WOKEUP WONMUG WONOUT WORKUP WRAPUP

W••••U
WAUSAU

•W••U•
OWNSUP

••W•U•
BOWOUT LAWFUL SAWOUT SEWNUP SEWSUP SOWBUG

•••WU•
BLEWUP BLOWUP CHEWUP DRAWUP DREWUP GREWUP GROWUP SHOWUP SLOWUP

••••WU
HUNGWU

W•V•••
WAVEIN WAVERS WAVERY WAVIER WAVING WOVOKA WYVERN

W••V••
WAIVED WAIVER WAIVES WEAVED WEAVER WEAVES WEEVIL WOLVES

•W•V••
SWIVEL SWIVET

•W••V•
SWERVE TWELVE

••W•V•
REWOVE UNWOVE

W•W•••
WOWING

W••W••
WAHWAH WIGWAG WIGWAM WINWIN

W•••W•
WIDOWS

W••••W
WALLOW WARSAW WINDOW WINNOW

•W•W••
TWOWAY

••WW••
BOWWOW POWWOW

••W••W
BOWSAW BOWWOW GEWGAW HAWHAW HOWNOW KOWTOW PAWPAW POWWOW

•••W•W
BOWWOW POWWOW

W•X•••
WAXERS WAXIER WAXING

W••••X
WESSEX WINDEX

••W••X
COWPOX

•••W•X
EARWAX

WY••••
WYNTER WYNTON WYSTAN WYVERN

W•Y•••
WAYLAY WAYLON WAYOUT WHYDAH WHYNOT WRYEST

W••••Y
WADDLY WAFFLY WAGGLY WAMBLY WARCRY WARILY WARMLY WATERY WATNEY WAVERY WAYLAY WEAKLY WEEKLY WEENSY WENTBY WESLEY WETFLY WHACKY WHAMMY WHEEZY WHERRY WHIMSY WHINNY WHIPPY WHIRLY WHOLLY WICOPY WIDELY WIFELY WIGGLY WILDLY WIMSEY WINERY WINTRY WISELY WITCHY WOBBLY WOLSEY WOODSY WOOLEY WOOLLY WORTHY

•WY•••
GWYNNE

•W•Y••
DWAYNE SWAYED SWAYER SWAYZE

•W•••Y
AWEARY QWERTY SWABBY SWAMPY SWANKY SWEATY SWINGY SWIRLY TWANGY TWEEDY TWEETY TWENTY TWIGGY TWISTY TWITTY TWOPLY TWOWAY

••WY••
BOWYER EDWYNN LAWYER SAWYER

••W•Y•
ALWAYS BYWAYS

••W••Y
BOWERY COWBOY COWLEY DOWNEY FAWLTY LEWDLY LOWBOY LOWERY LOWKEY NEWLEY TAWDRY TOWERY UNWARY

•••W•Y
AIRWAY ANYWAY BLOWZY BRAWNY CONWAY CRAWLY DROWSY FLYWAY FROWZY GALWAY GOAWAY GOAWRY GROWLY INAWAY KEYWAY LEEWAY MIDWAY NORWAY ONEWAY RUNWAY SEAWAY SKYWAY SLOWLY SUBWAY TWOWAY

••••WY
SCREWY SINEWY

W•Z•••
WIZARD WIZENS

W••Z••
WINZES

W•••Z•
WHEEZE WHEEZY

•W•Z••
SWAZIS

•W••Z•
KWANZA SWAYZE TWEEZE

•••WZ•
BLOWZY FROWZY

•••W•Z
THEWIZ

XA••••
XANADU XANTHO XAVIER

X•A•••
XIAMEN XRATED XRAYED

X••A••
XANADU

X•••A•
XHOSAS

X••••A
XIMENA

•XA•••
EXACTA EXACTO EXACTS EXALTS EXARCH OXALIS

•X•A••
EXHALE EXPAND EXTANT OXCART OXNARD OXTAIL

•X••A•
AXONAL EXTRAS

•X•••A
AXILLA EXACTA EXEDRA

••XA••
FIXATE HEXADS LUXATE OAXACA ROXANA ROXANE TEXACO TEXANS

••X•A•
BOXCAR REXCAT TAXMAN

••X••A
LEXICA MAXIMA OAXACA ROXANA

•••X•A
ALEXIA

••••XA
CUNAXA

X•B•••
XEBECS

•XB•••
OXBOWS

•X••B•
EXURBS

X•••C•
XEBECS

•XC•••
EXCEED EXCELS EXCEPT EXCESS EXCISE EXCITE EXCUSE OXCART

•X•C••
EXACTA EXACTO EXACTS

•X••C•
EXARCH EXPECT

•X•••C
EXILIC EXOTIC OXIDIC

••XC••
BOXCAR REXCAT

••X•C•
LEXICA MEXICO OAXACA TEXACO TOXICS

••X••C
MIXTEC

X•••D•
XANADU

X••••D
XRATED XRAYED XYLOID

•X•D••
EXEDRA EXODUS EXUDED EXUDES OXIDES OXIDIC OXYDOL

•X•••D
AXSEED EXCEED EXILED EXITED EXPAND EXPEND EXTEND EXUDED OXFORD OXNARD

••X•D•
HEXADS TUXEDO

••X••D
TAXIED

•••X•D
COAXED FLEXED FLUXED HOAXED JINXED

XE••••
XEBECS XERXES

X••E••
XEBECS XIMENA XYLENE

X•••E•
XAVIER XERXES XIAMEN XRATED XRAYED XYSTER

X••••E
XYLENE

•XE•••
EXEDRA EXEMPT EXERTS EXETER EXEUNT OXEYES

•X•E••
AXSEED EXCEED EXCELS EXCEPT EXCESS EXPECT EXPELS EXPEND EXPERT EXSERT EXTEND EXTENT

•X••E•
AXSEED EXCEED EXETER EXILED EXILES EXITED EXUDED EXUDES OXEYES OXIDES OXYGEN

•X•••E
EXCISE EXCITE EXCUSE EXHALE EXPIRE EXPOSE EXWIFE

••XE••
BOXERS FIXERS HEXERS LAXEST LEXEME MIXERS PIXELS SIXERS SOXERS TAXERS TUXEDO VEXERS VIXENS WAXERS

••X•E•
BAXTER BOXSET DEXTER FOXIER HUXLEY MIXTEC NIXIES PIXIES PYXIES SEXIER SEXTET TAXIED TAXIES TAXMEN TEXMEX WAXIER

••X••E
FIXATE LEXEME LUXATE MAXINE MAXIXE ROXANE

•••XE•
ALEXEI APEXES BLIXEN CALXES COAXED COAXER COAXES CRUXES DREXEL FLAXEN FLAXES FLEXED FLEXES FLUXED FLUXES HOAXED HOAXER HOAXES IBEXES JINXED JINXES LYNXES MINXES ONYXES ORYXES PRAXES VSIXES XERXES

•••X•E
TRIXIE

••••XE
ANNEXE DELUXE MAXIXE

•XF•••
OXFORD

•X••F•
EXWIFE

••XF••
BOXFUL

•X•G••
OXYGEN

••XG••
SIXGUN

••X••G
BOXING FAXING FIXING FOXING HEXING MIXING NIXING SIXING TAXING VEXING WAXING

XH••••
XHOSAS

X•••H•
XANTHO

•XH•••
EXHALE EXHORT

•X•••H
EXARCH

••X•H•
SIXTHS

XI••••
XIAMEN XIMENA

X••I••
XAVIER

X•••I•
XYLOID

•XI•••
AXILLA AXIOMS AXIONS EXILED EXILES EXILIC EXISTS EXITED OXIDES OXIDIC

•X•I••
EXCISE EXCITE EXPIRE EXPIRY EXWIFE OXLIPS

•X••I•
EXILIC EXOTIC OXALIS OXIDIC OXTAIL

••XI••
AUXINS BOXING DIXITS FAXING FIXING FIXITY FOXIER FOXILY FOXING HEXING LAXITY LEXICA MAXIMA MAXIMS MAXINE MAXIXE MEXICO MIXING NIXIES NIXING PIXIES PYXIES SEXIER SEXILY SEXIST SIXING TAXIED TAXIES TAXING TOXICS TOXINS VEXING WAXIER WAXING

•••XI•
ALEXIA ALEXIS DIOXIN ELIXIR NOEXIT PINXIT PRAXIS TRIXIE ZEUXIS

•••X•I
ALEXEI

••••XI
BILOXI

X•L•••
XYLENE XYLOID

•XL•••
OXLIPS

•X•L••
AXILLA EXALTS EXILED EXILES EXILIC EXULTS OXALIS

•X••L•
AXILLA EXCELS EXHALE EXPELS EXTOLS

•X•••L
AXONAL OXTAIL OXYDOL

••XL••
HUXLEY

••X•L•
FOXILY PIXELS SEXILY

••X••L
BOXFUL

•••X•L
DREXEL

X•M•••
XIMENA

X••M••
XIAMEN

•XM•••
EXMOOR

•X•M••
EXEMPT

•X••M•
AXIOMS

••XM••
TAXMAN TAXMEN TEXMEX

••X•M•
LEXEME MAXIMA MAXIMS

X•N•••
XANADU XANTHO

X•••N•
XIMENA XYLENE

X••••N
XIAMEN

•XN•••
OXNARD

•X•N••
AXONAL

•X••N•
AXIONS
EXEUNT
EXPAND
EXPEND
EXTANT
EXTEND
EXTENT

•X•••N
OXYGEN

••X•N•
AUXINS
BOXING
FAXING
FIXING
FOXING
HEXING
MAXINE
MIXING
NIXING
ROXANA
ROXANE
SAXONS
SAXONY
SIXING
TAXING
TEXANS
TOXINS
VEXING
VIXENS
WAXING

••X••N
CAXTON
SEXTON
SIXGUN
TAXMAN
TAXMEN

•••X•N
BLIXEN
DIOXIN
FLAXEN
KLAXON

X•O•••
XHOSAS

X••O••
XYLOID

X••••O
XANTHO

•XO•••
AXONAL
EXODUS
EXOTIC

•X•O••
AXIOMS
AXIONS
EXHORT
EXMOOR
EXPORT
EXPOSE
EXTOLS
EXTORT
EXVOTO
OXBOWS
OXFORD

•X••O•
EXMOOR
OXYDOL

•X•••O
EXACTO
EXVOTO

••XO••
MAXOUT
SAXONS
SAXONY

••X•O•
BOXTOP
CAXTON
SEXTON

••X••O
DEXTRO
MEXICO
NEXTTO
TEXACO
TUXEDO

•••XO•
FLEXOR
KLAXON
PLEXOR

••••XO
BORAXO

•XP•••
EXPAND
EXPECT
EXPELS
EXPEND
EXPERT
EXPIRE
EXPIRY
EXPORT
EXPOSE

•X••P•
EXCEPT
EXEMPT
OXLIPS

••X•P•
FIXUPS
MIXUPS

••X••P
BOXTOP

XR••••
XRATED
XRAYED

X•R•••
XERXES

X••••R
XAVIER
XYSTER

•X•R••
EXARCH
EXERTS
EXTRAS
EXURBS

•X••R•
EXEDRA
EXHORT
EXPERT
EXPIRE
EXPIRY
EXPORT
EXSERT
EXTORT
OXCART
OXFORD
OXNARD

•X•••R
EXETER
EXMOOR

••X•R•
BOXERS
DEXTRO
FIXERS
HEXERS
LUXURY
MIXERS
SIXERS
SOXERS
TAXERS
VEXERS
WAXERS

••X••R
BAXTER
BOXCAR
DEXTER
FOXIER
SEXIER
WAXIER

•••X•R
COAXER
ELIXIR
FLEXOR
HOAXER
PLEXOR

X•S•••
XYSTER

X••S••
XHOSAS

X••••S
XEBECS
XERXES
XHOSAS

•XS•••
AXSEED
EXSERT

•X•S••
EXISTS

•X••S•
EXCESS
EXCISE
EXCUSE
EXPOSE

•X•••S
AXIOMS
AXIONS
EXACTS
EXALTS
EXCELS
EXCESS
EXERTS
EXILES
EXISTS
EXODUS
EXPELS
EXTOLS
EXTRAS
EXUDES
EXULTS
EXURBS
OXALIS
OXBOWS
OXEYES
OXIDES
OXLIPS

••XS••
BOXSET

••X•S•
LAXEST
SEXIST

••X••S
AUXINS
BOXERS
DIXITS
FIXERS
FIXUPS
HEXADS
HEXERS
MAXIMS
MIXERS
MIXUPS
NIXIES
PIXELS
PIXIES
PYXIES
SAXONS
SIXERS
SIXTHS
SIXTUS
SOXERS
TAXERS
TAXIES
TEXANS
TOXICS
TOXINS
VEXERS
VIXENS
WAXERS

•••X•S
ALEXIS
APEXES
CALXES
COAXES
CRUXES
FLAXES
FLEXES
FLUXES
HOAXES
IBEXES
JINXES
LYNXES
MINXES
ONYXES
ORYXES
PLEXUS
PRAXES
PRAXIS
VSIXES
XERXES
ZEUXIS

X••T••
XANTHO
XRATED
XYSTER

•XT•••
EXTANT
EXTEND
EXTENT
EXTOLS
EXTORT
EXTRAS
OXTAIL

•X•T••
EXETER
EXITED
EXOTIC

•X••T•
EXACTA
EXACTO
EXACTS
EXALTS
EXCITE
EXERTS
EXISTS
EXULTS
EXVOTO

•X•••T
EXCEPT
EXEMPT
EXEUNT
EXHORT
EXPECT
EXPERT
EXPORT
EXSERT
EXTANT
EXTENT
EXTORT
OXCART

••XT••
BAXTER
BOXTOP
CAXTON
DEXTER
DEXTRO
MIXTEC
NEXTTO
SEXTET
SEXTON
SIXTHS
SIXTUS

••X•T•
DIXITS
FIXATE
FIXITY
LAXITY
LUXATE
NEXTTO

••X••T
BOXSET
LAXEST
MAXOUT
REXCAT
SEXIST
SEXTET

•••X•T
NOEXIT
PINXIT

X••••U
XANADU

•XU•••
EXUDED
EXUDES
EXULTS
EXURBS

•X•U••
EXCUSE
EXEUNT

•X••U•
EXODUS

••XU••
FIXUPS
LUXURY
MIXUPS

••X•U•
BOXFUL
MAXOUT
SIXGUN
SIXTUS

•••XU•
PLEXUS

X•V•••
XAVIER

•XV•••
EXVOTO

•XW•••
EXWIFE

•X••W•
OXBOWS

X••X••
XERXES

••X•X•
MAXIXE

••X••X
TEXMEX

XY••••
XYLENE
XYLOID
XYSTER

X••Y••
XRAYED

•XY•••
OXYDOL
OXYGEN

•X•Y••
OXEYES

•X•••Y
EXPIRY

••X••Y
FIXITY
FOXILY
HUXLEY
LAXITY
LUXURY
SAXONY
SEXILY

••••XY
GALAXY

YA••••
YACHTS
YAHOOS
YAHWEH
YAKIMA
YAKKED
YAKKER
YAKUTS
YALIES
YAMAHA
YAMMER
YANGON
YANKED
YANKEE
YANQUI
YAPOKS
YAPPED
YAQUIS
YARDED
YARELY
YARNED
YARROW
YASSER
YAUPON
YAWING
YAWNED
YAWNER
YAWPED
YAWPER

Y•A•••
YEAGER
YEARLY
YEARNS
YEASTS
YEASTY

Y••A••
YAMAHA
YOUALL
YUKATA
YUKAWA

Y•••A•
YENTAS
YEOMAN
YESMAN
YUCCAS
YUNNAN

Y••••A
YAKIMA
YAMAHA
YORUBA
YOYOMA
YUKATA
YUKAWA

•YA•••
CYANIC
DYADIC
HYADES
KYACKS
NYALAS
NYASSA
RYAZAN

•Y•A••
AYEAYE
AYMARA
BYHAND
BYLAWS
BYNAME
BYPASS
BYPAST
BYPATH
BYTALK
BYWAYS
CYCADS
CYRANO
DYNAMO
DYNAST
GYRATE
MYNAHS
PYJAMA
TYBALT
TYRANT
ZYMASE

•Y••A•
BYPLAY
BYROAD
CYCLAS
CYMBAL
HYDRAE
HYDRAS
HYENAS
HYETAL
HYMNAL
MYRDAL
MYRIAD
NYALAS
RYAZAN
RYOKAN
SYLVAN
SYNTAX
SYRIAN
TYRIAN
WYSTAN

•Y•••A
AYESHA
AYMARA
MYOPIA
NYASSA
PYJAMA
PYTHIA
SYLVIA

••YA••
ARYANS
BAYARD
BOYARS
BRYANT
DRYADS
GAYALS
GUYANA
KAYAKS
MAYANS
RIYADH
RIYALS
ROYALE
ROYALS
VOYAGE

••Y•A•
AMYTAN
ANYWAY
CAYMAN
FLYMAN
FLYWAY
FRYPAN
HEYDAY
KEYPAD
KEYWAY
LAYMAN
MAYDAY
MAYHAP
MAYTAG
NAYSAY
OHYEAH
PAYDAY
PHYLAE
SKYCAP
SKYLAB
SKYWAY
TAYRAS
WAYLAY
WHYDAH

••Y••A
ALYSSA
CAYUGA
GUYANA
LOYOLA
PAYOLA
PSYLLA
SCYLLA
SMYRNA
STYRIA
TOYOTA
YOYOMA
ZOYSIA

•••YA•
BANYAN
BUNYAN
GALYAK
KENYAN
LIBYAN
MAGYAR
MINYAN
PLAYAS
PLAYAT

•••Y•A
CORYZA
DURYEA

••••YA
LATOYA
MALAYA
MAURYA
NAGOYA
PAPAYA
VAISYA

Y••B••
YOUBET

Y•••B•
YORUBA

•YB•••
CYBELE
CYBILL
CYBORG
DYBBUK
HYBRID
TYBALT
VYBORG

•Y•B••
BYEBYE
CYMBAL
DYBBUK
SYMBOL

•Y••B•
TYCOBB

•Y•••B
TYCOBB

••YB••
DAYBED
FLYBOY
FLYBYS
KHYBER
LAYBYS
MAYBES
SKYBOX

••Y•B•
LAYSBY

••Y••B
SKYLAB

Y•C•••
YACHTS
YUCCAS

Y••C••
YOICKS
YUCCAS

Y•••C•
YORICK

•YC•••
CYCADS
CYCLAS
CYCLED
CYCLER
CYCLES
CYCLIC
CYCLOS
LYCEES
LYCEUM
TYCOBB
TYCOON

•Y•C••
EYECUP
KYACKS
SYNCED

•Y••C•
CYNICS
LYRICS
ZYDECO

•Y•••C
CYANIC
CYCLIC
CYMRIC
DYADIC
MYOPIC
MYSTIC
MYTHIC
PYKNIC
SYNDIC

••YC••
GLYCOL
JAYCEE
PSYCHE
PSYCHO
PSYCHS
SKYCAP

••Y•C•
DRYICE

•••Y•C
INSYNC

Y•D•••
YODELS

Y••D••
YARDED
YONDER

Y•••D•
YEHUDI
YIELDS

Y••••D
YAKKED
YANKED
YAPPED
YARDED
YARNED
YAWNED
YAWPED
YELLED
YELPED
YENNED
YESSED
YIPPED
YOLKED
YOWLED
YOYOED
YUKKED

•YD•••
CYDERS
HYDRAE
HYDRAS
HYDROS
RYDELL
SYDNEY
ZYDECO

•Y•D••
DYADIC
FYODOR
HYADES
LYNDON
MYRDAL
PYEDOG
SYNDIC

•Y••D•
CYCADS
SYNODS

•Y•••D
BYHAND
BYROAD
BYWORD
CYCLED
EYELID
GYPPED
HYBRID
HYMNED
HYPOED
LYNYRD
MYRIAD
MYWORD
SYNCED
XYLOID

••YD••
ABYDOS
DRYDEN
HAYDEN
HEYDAY
HOYDEN
LEYDEN
MAYDAY
OXYDOL
PAYDAY
SNYDER
TOYDOG
WHYDAH

••Y•D•
DRYADS
RIYADH

••Y••D
BAYARD
BEYOND
DAYBED
FLYROD
KAYOED
KEYPAD
PHYSED
RHYMED
SAYYID
STYLED
YOYOED

•••YD•
ALKYDS
ANHYDR
LLOYDS
MRHYDE

•••Y•D
BRAYED
BUOYED
CLOYED
DRAYED
FLAYED
FRAYED
GRAYED
GREYED
LYNYRD
OBEYED
OKAYED
PLAYED
PRAYED
PREYED
REDYED
SAYYID
SLAYED
SPAYED
STAYED
SWAYED
UNDYED
XRAYED

YE••••
YEAGER
YEARLY
YEARNS
YEASTS
YEASTY
YEHUDI
YELLED
YELLER
YELLOW
YELPED
YELPER
YEMENI
YENNED
YENTAS
YEOMAN
YEOMEN
YERKES
YESMAN
YESMEN
YESSED
YESSES
YESSIR
YESTER

Y•E•••
YIELDS
YVETTE

Y••E••
YARELY
YEMENI
YODELS
YOKELS

Y•••E•
YAHWEH
YAKKED
YAKKER
YALIES
YAMMER
YANKED
YANKEE
YAPPED
YARDED
YARNED
YASSER
YAWNED
YAWNER
YAWPED
YAWPER
YEAGER
YELLED
YELLER
YELPED
YELPER
YENNED
YEOMEN
YERKES
YESMEN
YESSED
YESSES
YESTER
YIPPED
YIPPEE
YOLKED
YONDER
YORKER
YOUBET
YOWLED
YOYOED
YUKKED

Y••••E
YANKEE
YIPPEE
YUPPIE
YVETTE
YVONNE

•YE•••
AYEAYE
AYESHA
BYEBYE
DYEING
DYELOT
EYECUP
EYEFUL
EYEING
EYELET
EYELID
HYENAS
HYETAL
MYELIN
PYEDOG

•Y•E••
CYBELE
CYDERS
GYRENE
LYCEES
LYCEUM
MYSELF
RYDELL
TYPERS
TYPEUP
WYVERN
XYLENE
ZYDECO

•Y••E•
BYRNES
CYCLED
CYCLER
CYCLES
CYGNET
CYPHER
EYELET
EYRIES
GYPPED
GYPPER
HYADES
HYMNED
HYPHEN
HYPOED
LYCEES
LYNLEY
LYNXES
MYOPES
OYSTER
PYXIES
SYDNEY
SYNCED
SYSTEM
WYNTER
XYSTER

•Y•••E
AYEAYE
BYEBYE
BYGONE
BYJOVE
BYLINE
BYNAME
BYROTE
BYSSHE
CYBELE
GYRATE
GYRENE
GYROSE
HYDRAE
LYSINE
MYRTLE
PYRITE
TYRONE
XYLENE
ZYGOTE
ZYMASE

••YE••
BAYEUX
BUYERS
COYEST
DOYENS
DRYERS
DRYEST
FLYERS
FOYERS
FRYERS
GAYEST
LAYERS
MOYERS
OHYEAH
PAYEES
PAYERS
SAYERS
SHYEST
SLYEST
TUYERE
WRYEST

••Y•E•
DAYBED
DRYDEN
ELYSEE
FLYMEN
FLYNET
GEYSER
HAYDEN
HAYLEY
HOYDEN
JAYCEE
JAYVEE
JOYNER
KAYOED
KEYNES
KHYBER
LAYMEN
LEYDEN
MAYBES
MAYHEM
ONYXES
ORYXES
OXYGEN
PAYEES
PHYSED
RHYMED
RHYMER
RHYMES
SAYYES
SLYPES
SNYDER
STYLED
STYLER
STYLES
STYLET
YOYOED

••Y••E
ANYONE
BLYTHE
CAYUSE
COYOTE
DAYONE
DRYICE
EEYORE
ELYSEE
GWYNNE

HEYJOE
JAYCEE
JAYVEE
PEYOTE
PHYLAE
PRYNNE
PSYCHE
ROYALE
SCYTHE
STYMIE
TUYERE
UNYOKE
VOYAGE

•••YE•
BOWYER
BRAYED
BRAYER
BUOYED
CLAYEY
CLOYED
DLAYER
DRAYED
DURYEA
ELAYER
FLAYED
FLAYER
FRAYED
GRAYED
GRAYER
GREYED
GREYER
LAWYER
NGUYEN
NOTYET
OBEYED
OKAYED
OXEYES
PLAYED
PLAYER
PRAYED
PRAYER
PREYED
REDYED
REDYES
SAWYER
SAYYES
SLAYED
SLAYER
SPAYED
SPRYER
STAYED
SWAYED
SWAYER
THAYER
UNDYED
XRAYED

•••Y•E
ARGYLE
DWAYNE
ECTYPE
ELAYNE
ENZYME
MRHYDE
OOCYTE
QUAYLE
RETYPE
SHAYNE
SWAYZE
THEYRE
THEYVE

••••YE
AYEAYE
AZODYE
BYEBYE
HEARYE
INOUYE
POPEYE
REDEYE
RIBEYE
TIEDYE

•YF••
EYEFUL

•Y••F•
TYPIFY

•Y•••F
MYSELF

••YF••
DRYFLY
JOYFUL
LAYFOR
MAYFLY
PAYFOR
TRYFOR

••Y•F•
BUYOFF
CRYOFF
DRYOFF
LAYOFF
PAYOFF

••Y••F
BUYOFF
CRYOFF
DRYOFF
LAYOFF
PAYOFF

Y•G•••
YOGINI
YOGURT

Y••G••
YANGON
YEAGER
YUNGLO

Y••••G
YAWING
YOKING

•YG•••
BYGONE
BYGOSH
CYGNET
CYGNUS
MYGIRL
ZYGOTE

•Y••G•
SYZYGY

•Y•••G
CYBORG
DYEING
EYEING
HYPING
PYEDOG
TYPING
VYBORG

••YG••
DAYGLO
OXYGEN
RAYGUN

••Y•G•
CAYUGA
ERYNGO
VOYAGE

••Y••G
BAYING
BUYING
CRYING
DRYING
FLYING
FRYING
GUYING
HAYING
KEYING
LAYING
MAYTAG
PAYING
PLYING
PRYING
SAYING
SHYING
SKYING
SPYING
TOYDOG
TOYING
TRYING

•••YG•
SYZYGY

••••YG
KENNYG

Y•H•••
YAHOOS
YAHWEH
YEHUDI
YOHOHO

Y••H••
YACHTS
YOOHOO

Y•••H•
YAMAHA
YOHOHO
YOUTHS

Y••••H
YAHWEH

•YH•••
BYHAND

•Y•H••
CYPHER
HYPHEN
MYOHMY
MYTHIC
MYTHOI
MYTHOL
MYTHOS
PYTHIA
PYTHON
TYPHUS

•Y••H•
AYESHA
BYSSHE
KYUSHU
MYNAHS
MYRRHS
NYMPHS
SYLPHS

•Y•••H
BYGOSH
BYPATH

••YH••
ANYHOW
MAYHAP
MAYHEM

••Y•H•
BLYTHE
GLYPHS
PSYCHE
PSYCHO
PSYCHS
RHYTHM
SCYTHE

••Y••H
BOYISH
OHYEAH
RIYADH
WHYDAH

•••Y•H
IRTYSH

YI••••
YIELDS
YIPPED
YIPPEE

Y•I•••
YOICKS

Y••I••
YAKIMA
YALIES
YAWING
YOGINI
YOKING
YORICK

Y•••I•
YAQUIS
YESSIR
YUPPIE

Y••••I
YANQUI
YEHUDI
YEMENI
YOGINI

•Y•I••
BYLINE
CYBILL
CYNICS
DYEING
EYEING
EYRIES
HYPING
LYRICS
LYRIST
LYSINE
LYSINS
MYGIRL
MYRIAD
PYRITE
PYXIES
SYRIAN
SYRINX
TYPIFY
TYPING
TYPIST
TYRIAN

•Y••I•
CYANIC
CYCLIC
CYMRIC
DYADIC
EYELID
HYBRID
MYELIN
MYOPIA
MYOPIC
MYOSIN
MYSTIC
MYTHIC
NYQUIL
PYKNIC
PYTHIA
SYLVIA
SYNDIC
XYLOID

•Y•••I
MYTHOI

••YI••
BAYING
BOYISH
BUYING
CRYING
DRYICE
DRYING
DRYINK
FLYING
FRYING
GUYING
HAYING
KEYING
LAYING
PAYING
PLYING
PRYING
SAYING
SHYING
SKYING
SPYING
TOYING
TRYING
ZAYINS

••Y•I•
DAYLIT
KEYSIN
LAYSIN
PAYSIN
PHYSIO
SAYYID
STYMIE
STYRIA
ZOYSIA

••Y••I
THYRSI

•••YI•
PINYIN
SAYYID

•••Y•I
PAPYRI

•YJ•••
BYJOVE
PYJAMA

••YJ••
HEYJOE

Y•K•••
YAKIMA
YAKKED
YAKKER
YAKUTS
YOKELS
YOKING
YOKUTS
YUKATA
YUKAWA
YUKKED

Y••K••
YAKKED
YAKKER
YANKED
YANKEE
YERKES
YOLKED
YORKER
YUKKED

Y•••K•
YAPOKS
YOICKS
YUROKS

Y••••K
YORICK

•YK•••
HYKSOS
PYKNIC

•Y•K••
RYOKAN
RYUKYU

•Y••K•
KYACKS

•Y•••K
BYTALK
DYBBUK

••Y•K•
KAYAKS
UNYOKE

••Y••K
DRYINK

•••Y•K
GALYAK

Y•L•••
YALIES
YELLED
YELLER
YELLOW
YELPED
YELPER
YOLKED

Y••L••
YELLED
YELLER
YELLOW
YIELDS
YOWLED

Y•••L•
YARELY
YEARLY
YODELS
YOKELS
YOUALL
YUNGLO

Y••••L
YOUALL

•YL•••
BYLAWS
BYLINE
NYLONS
PYLONS
SYLPHS
SYLVAN
SYLVIA
XYLENE
XYLOID

•Y•L••
BYPLAY
CYCLAS
CYCLED
CYCLER
CYCLES
CYCLIC
CYCLOS
DYELOT
EYELET
EYELID
LYNLEY
MYELIN
NYALAS

•Y••L•
BYTALK
CYBELE
CYBILL
MYRTLE
MYSELF
RYDELL
TYBALT

•Y•••L
CYBILL
CYMBAL
EYEFUL
HYETAL
HYMNAL
MYGIRL
MYRDAL
MYTHOL
NYQUIL
RYDELL
SYMBOL

••YL••
ASYLUM
BAYLOR
CEYLON
DAYLIT
HAYLEY
IDYLLS
LAYLOW
PHYLAE
PHYLLO
PHYLUM
PSYLLA
SCYLLA
SKYLAB
STYLED
STYLER
STYLES
STYLET
STYLUS
TAYLOR
WAYLAY
WAYLON

••Y•L•
DAYGLO
DRYFLY
GAYALS
IDYLLS
LOYOLA
MAYFLY
PAYOLA
PHYLLO
PSYLLA
RIYALS
ROYALE
ROYALS
SCYLLA

••Y••L
ETYMOL
GLYCOL
JOYFUL
OXYDOL

•••YL•
ALKYLS
ARGYLE
ARGYLL
JEKYLL
QUAYLE
SIBYLS
SPRYLY
THEYLL

•••Y•L
ARGYLL
JEKYLL
THEYLL

••••YL
ACETYL
CHERYL
DACTYL
DARRYL
METHYL
PHENYL

Y•M•••
YAMAHA
YAMMER
YEMENI
YUMYUM

Y••M••
YAMMER
YEOMAN
YEOMEN
YESMAN
YESMEN

Y•••M•
YAKIMA
YOYOMA

Y••••M
YUMYUM

•YM•••
AYMARA
CYMBAL
CYMRIC
HYMNAL
HYMNED
NYMPHS
SYMBOL
ZYMASE

•Y•M••
BYNAME
DYNAMO
MYOHMY
PYJAMA

•Y•••M
GYPSUM
LYCEUM
SYSTEM

••YM••
CAYMAN
ETYMOL
ETYMON
FLYMAN
FLYMEN
HAYMOW
LAYMAN
LAYMEN
RHYMED
RHYMER
RHYMES
STYMIE
THYMUS

••Y•M•
ABYSMS
YOYOMA

••Y••M
ADYTUM
ASYLUM
BAYRUM
MAYHEM
PHYLUM
RHYTHM

•••YM•
ENZYME

•••Y•M
FAIYUM
YUMYUM

••••YM
ANONYM
EPONYM

Y•N•••
YANGON
YANKED
YANKEE
YANQUI
YENNED
YENTAS
YONDER
YUNGLO
YUNNAN

Y••N••
YARNED
YAWNED
YAWNER
YENNED
YUNNAN
YVONNE

Y•••N•
YAWING
YEARNS
YEMENI
YOGINI
YOKING
YVONNE

Y••••N
YANGON
YAUPON
YEOMAN
YEOMEN
YESMAN
YESMEN
YUNNAN

•YN•••
BYNAME
CYNICS
DYNAMO
DYNAST
LYNDON
LYNLEY
LYNXES
LYNYRD
MYNAHS
SYNCED
SYNDIC
SYNODS
SYNTAX
WYNTER
WYNTON

•Y•N••
BYRNES
CYANIC
CYGNET
CYGNUS
HYENAS
HYMNAL
HYMNED
HYPNOS
PYKNIC
SYDNEY

•Y••N•
BYGONE
BYHAND
BYLINE
CYRANO
DYEING
EYEING
GYRENE
GYRONS
HYPING
LYSINE
LYSINS
NYLONS
PYLONS
SYRINX
TYPING
TYRANT
TYRONE
XYLENE

•Y•••N
HYPHEN
LYNDON
LYTTON
MYELIN
MYOSIN
PYTHON
RYAZAN
RYOKAN
SYLVAN
SYRIAN
TYCOON
TYRIAN
WYNTON
WYSTAN
WYVERN

••YN••
ERYNGO
FLYNET
GAYNOR
GWYNNE
JOYNER
KEYNES
PRYNNE
WHYNOT

••Y•N•
ANYONE
ARYANS
BAYING
BEYOND
BRYANT
BRYONY
BUYING
CRYING
DAYONE
DOYENS
DRYING
DRYINK
FLYING
FRYING
GUYANA
GUYING
GWYNNE
HAYING
KEYING
LAYING
MAYANS
PAYING
PLYING
PRYING
PRYNNE
RAYONS
SAYING
SHYING
SKYING
SMYRNA
SPYING
TOYING
TOYONS
TRYING
ZAYINS

••Y••N
AMYTAN
BRYSON
CAYMAN
CEYLON
DAYTON
DRYDEN
DRYRUN
ETYMON
FLYMAN
FLYMEN
FRYPAN
HAYDEN
HOYDEN
KEYSIN
LAYMAN
LAYMEN
LAYSIN
LAYSON
LEYDEN
OXYGEN
PAYSIN
PAYSON
PEYTON
RAYGUN
RHYTON
STYRON
WAYLON

•••YN•
DWAYNE
EDWYNN
ELAYNE
INSYNC
LARYNX
SHAYNE

•••Y•N
BANYAN
BARYON
BUNYAN
CANYON
CRAYON
EDWYNN
KENYAN
LIBYAN
MINYAN
NGUYEN
PINYIN
PINYON
PLAYON
PREYON
RUNYON
STAYON

••••YN
BOLEYN
CRONYN
EVELYN
JACLYN
MELVYN
MERVYN
POLEYN
VANRYN

YO••••
YODELS
YOGINI
YOGURT
YOHOHO
YOICKS
YOKELS
YOKING
YOKUTS
YOLKED
YONDER
YOOHOO
YORICK
YORKER
YORUBA
YOUALL
YOUBET
YOUTHS
YOWLED
YOYOED
YOYOMA

Y•O•••
YEOMAN
YEOMEN
YOOHOO
YVONNE

Y••O••
YAHOOS
YAPOKS
YOHOHO
YOYOED
YOYOMA
YUROKS

Y•••O•
YAHOOS
YANGON
YARROW
YAUPON
YELLOW
YOOHOO

Y••••O
YOHOHO
YOOHOO
YUNGLO

•YO•••
FYODOR
MYOHMY
MYOPES
MYOPIA
MYOPIC
MYOSIN
RYOKAN

•Y•O••
BYGONE
BYGOSH
BYJOVE
BYROAD
BYROTE
BYWORD
CYBORG
GYRONS
GYROSE
HYPOED
MYWORD
NYLONS
PYLONS
SYNODS
TYCOBB
TYCOON
TYRONE
VYBORG
XYLOID
ZYGOTE

•Y••O•
CYCLOS
DYELOT
FYODOR
HYDROS
HYKSOS
HYPNOS
HYSSOP
LYNDON
LYTTON
MYTHOI
MYTHOL
MYTHOS
PYEDOG
PYTHON
SYMBOL
TYCOON
WYNTON

•Y•••O
CYRANO
DYNAMO
ZYDECO

••YO••
ANYONE
BAYOUS
BEYOND
BRYONY
BUYOFF
BUYOUT
COYOTE
CRYOFF
DAYONE
DRYOFF
DRYOUT
EEYORE
FLYOUT
GUYOTS
JOYOUS
KAYOED
LAYOFF
LAYOUT
LOYOLA
MAYORS
PAYOFF
PAYOLA
PAYOUT
PEYOTE
RAYONS
TOYONS
TOYOTA
TRYOUT
UNYOKE
WAYOUT
YOYOED
YOYOMA

••Y•O•
ABYDOS
ANYHOW
BAYLOR
BRYSON
CEYLON
DAYTON
DRYROT
ETYMOL
ETYMON
FLYBOY
FLYROD
GAYNOR
GLYCOL
HAYMOW
HEYJOE
HEYYOU
LAYFOR
LAYLOW
LAYSON
MAYPOP
OXYDOL
PAYFOR
PAYSON
PEYTON
RHYTON
SAYSOS
SKYBOX
STYRON
TAYLOR
TOYDOG
TRYFOR
WAYLON
WHYNOT

••Y••O
CRYPTO
DAYGLO
ERYNGO
LAYSTO
PHYLLO
PHYSIO
PSYCHO

•••YO•
BARYON
CANYON
CRAYON
HEYYOU
PINYON
PLAYON
PREYON
RUNYON
STAYON

••••YO
ARROYO
DADDYO
DAIMYO
EMBRYO
TAMAYO

Y•P•••
YAPOKS
YAPPED
YIPPED
YIPPEE
YUPPIE

Y••P••
YAPPED
YAUPON
YAWPED
YAWPER
YELPED
YELPER
YIPPED
YIPPEE
YUPPIE

•YP•••
BYPASS
BYPAST
BYPATH
BYPLAY
CYPHER
CYPRUS
GYPPED
GYPPER
GYPSUM
HYPHEN
HYPING
HYPNOS
HYPOED
TYPERS
TYPEUP
TYPHUS
TYPIFY
TYPING
TYPIST

•Y•P••
GYPPED GYPPER MYOPES MYOPIA MYOPIC NYMPHS SYLPHS

•Y••P•
SYRUPS SYRUPY

•Y•••P
EYECUP HYSSOP TYPEUP

••YP••
COYPUS CRYPTO CRYPTS FRYPAN GLYPHS KEYPAD MAYPOP SLYPES

••Y•P•
LAYUPS

••Y••P
BUYSUP KEYSUP LAYSUP MAYHAP MAYPOP PAYSUP SKYCAP

•••YP•
ECTYPE POLYPS RETYPE

•••Y•P
BUOYUP PLAYUP PONYUP STAYUP TIDYUP

Y•Q•••
YAQUIS

Y••Q••
YANQUI

•YQ•••
NYQUIL

Y•R•••
YARDED YARELY YARNED YARROW YERKES YORICK YORKER YORUBA YUROKS

Y••R••
YARROW YEARLY YEARNS

Y•••R•
YOGURT

Y••••R
YAKKER YAMMER YASSER YAWNER YAWPER YEAGER YELLER YELPER YESSIR YESTER YONDER YORKER

•YR•••
BYRNES BYROAD BYROTE CYRANO EYRIES GYRATE GYRENE GYRONS GYROSE LYRICS LYRIST MYRDAL MYRIAD MYRRHS MYRTLE PYRITE SYRIAN SYRINX SYRUPS SYRUPY TYRANT TYRIAN TYRONE

•Y•R••
CYMRIC CYPRUS HYBRID HYDRAE HYDRAS HYDROS MYRRHS

•Y••R•
AYMARA BYWORD CYBORG CYDERS LYNYRD MYGIRL MYWORD TYPERS VYBORG WYVERN

•Y•••R
CYCLER CYPHER FYODOR GYPPER OYSTER WYNTER XYSTER

••YR••
BAYRUM DRYROT DRYRUN FLYROD SMYRNA STYRIA STYRON TAYRAS THYRSI

••Y•R•
BAYARD BOYARS BUYERS DRYERS EEYORE FLYERS FOYERS FRYERS LAYERS MAYORS MOYERS PAYERS SAYERS TUYERE

••Y••R
BAYLOR GAYNOR GEYSER JOYNER KHYBER LAYFOR PAYFOR RHYMER SNYDER STYLER TAYLOR TRYFOR

•••YR•
LYNYRD PAPYRI SATYRS THEYRE

•••Y•R
ANHYDR BOWYER BRAYER DLAYER ELAYER FLAYER GRAYER GREYER LAWYER MAGYAR PLAYER PRAYER SAWYER SLAYER SPRYER SWAYER THAYER

••••YR
MARTYR ZEPHYR

Y•S•••
YASSER YESMAN YESMEN YESSED YESSES YESSIR YESTER

Y••S••
YASSER YEASTS YEASTY YESSED YESSES YESSIR

Y••••S
YACHTS YAHOOS YAKUTS YALIES YAPOKS YAQUIS YEARNS YEASTS YENTAS YERKES YESSES YIELDS YODELS YOICKS YOKELS YOKUTS YOUTHS YUCCAS YUROKS

•YS•••
BYSSHE BYSSUS HYSSOP LYSINE LYSINS MYSELF MYSTIC OYSTER SYSTEM WYSTAN XYSTER

•Y•S••
AYESHA BYSSHE BYSSUS GYPSUM HYKSOS HYSSOP KYUSHU MYOSIN NYASSA

•Y••S•
BYGOSH BYPASS BYPAST DYNAST GYROSE LYRIST NYASSA TYPIST ZYMASE

•Y•••S
BYLAWS BYPASS BYRNES BYSSUS BYWAYS CYCADS CYCLAS CYCLES CYCLOS CYDERS CYGNUS CYNICS CYPRUS EYRIES GYRONS HYADES HYDRAS HYDROS HYENAS HYKSOS HYPNOS KYACKS LYCEES LYNXES LYRICS LYSINS MYNAHS MYOPES MYRRHS MYTHOS NYALAS NYLONS NYMPHS PYLONS PYXIES SYLPHS SYNODS SYRUPS TYPERS TYPHUS

••YS••
ABYSMS ALYSSA BRYSON BUYSUP ELYSEE GEYSER KEYSIN KEYSUP LAYSBY LAYSIN LAYSON LAYSTO LAYSUP NAYSAY PAYSIN PAYSON PAYSUP PHYSED PHYSIO SAYSOS TRYSTS ZOYSIA

••Y•S•
ALYSSA BOYISH CAYUSE COYEST DRYEST GAYEST SHYEST SLYEST THYRSI WRYEST

••Y••S
ABYDOS ABYSMS ARYANS BAYOUS BOYARS BUYERS COYPUS CRYPTS DOYENS DRYADS DRYERS FLYBYS FLYERS FOYERS FRYERS GAYALS GLYPHS GUYOTS IDYLLS JOYOUS KAYAKS KEYNES LAYBYS LAYERS LAYUPS MAYANS MAYBES MAYORS MOYERS ONYXES ORYXES PAYEES PAYERS PSYCHS RAYONS RHYMES RIYALS ROYALS SAYERS SAYSOS SAYYES SLYPES STYLES STYLUS TAYRAS THYMUS TOYONS TRYSTS ZAYINS

•••YS•
IRTYSH

•••Y•S
ALKYDS ALKYLS LLOYDS OXEYES PLAYAS POLYPS REDYES SATYRS SAYYES SIBYLS

••••YS
ABBEYS ALLAYS ALLEYS ALLOYS ALWAYS ANNOYS ARRAYS ASSAYS BELAYS BOGEYS BYWAYS CONEYS COVEYS DECAYS DECOYS DELAYS EMBAYS ENJOYS ENVOYS ERINYS ESSAYS FLYBYS FOGEYS FORAYS GAMAYS GLADYS HONEYS INLAYS LAYBYS LIMEYS MALAYS MATEYS MONEYS MORAYS MOSEYS POBOYS POKEYS REKEYS RELAYS REPAYS SEPOYS SPLAYS SPRAYS STRAYS TETHYS TOKAYS UNSAYS ZLOTYS

Y••T••
YENTAS YESTER YOUTHS YVETTE

Y•••T•
YACHTS YAKUTS YEASTS YEASTY YOKUTS YUKATA YVETTE

Y••••T
YOGURT YOUBET

•YT•••
BYTALK LYTTON MYTHIC MYTHOI MYTHOL MYTHOS PYTHIA PYTHON

•Y•T••
HYETAL LYTTON MYRTLE MYSTIC OYSTER SYNTAX SYSTEM WYNTER WYNTON WYSTAN XYSTER

•Y••T•
BYPATH BYROTE GYRATE PYRITE ZYGOTE

•Y•••T
BYPAST CYGNET DYELOT DYNAST EYELET LYRIST TYBALT TYPIST TYRANT

••YT••
ADYTUM AMYTAN BLYTHE DAYTON MAYTAG PEYTON RHYTHM RHYTON SCYTHE

••Y•T•
COYOTE CRYPTO CRYPTS GUYOTS LAYSTO PEYOTE TOYOTA TRYSTS

••Y••T
BRYANT BUYOUT COYEST DAYLIT DRYEST DRYOUT DRYROT FLYNET FLYOUT GAYEST LAYOUT PAYOUT SHYEST SLYEST STYLET TRYOUT WAYOUT WHYNOT WRYEST

•••YT•
OOCYTE

•••Y•T
NOTYET PLAYAT SALYUT

••••YT
AJFOYT

YU••••
YUCCAS YUKATA YUKAWA YUKKED YUMYUM YUNGLO YUNNAN YUPPIE YUROKS

Y•U•••
YAUPON YOUALL YOUBET YOUTHS

Y••U••
YAKUTS YAQUIS YEHUDI YOGURT YOKUTS YORUBA

Y•••U•
YANQUI YUMYUM

•YU•••
KYUSHU RYUKYU

•Y•U••
NYQUIL SYRUPS SYRUPY

•Y••U•
BYSSUS CYGNUS CYPRUS DYBBUK EYECUP EYEFUL GYPSUM LYCEUM TYPEUP TYPHUS

•Y•••U
KYUSHU RYUKYU

••YU••
CAYUGA CAYUSE LAYUPS

••Y•U•
ADYTUM ASYLUM BAYEUX BAYOUS BAYRUM BUYOUT BUYSUP COYPUS DRYOUT DRYRUN FLYOUT JOYFUL JOYOUS KEYSUP LAYOUT LAYSUP PAYOUT PAYSUP PHYLUM RAYGUN STYLUS THYMUS TRYOUT WAYOUT

••Y••U
HEYYOU

•••YU•
BUOYUP FAIYUM PLAYUP PONYUP SALYUT STAYUP TIDYUP YUMYUM

•••Y•U
HEYYOU

••••YU
CHOOYU KIKUYU RYUKYU

YV••••
YVETTE YVONNE

•YV•••
WYVERN

•Y•V••
SYLVAN SYLVIA

•Y••V•
BYJOVE

••YV••
JAYVEE

•••YV•
THEYVE

••••YV
ROCKYV

Y•W•••
YAWING YAWNED YAWNER YAWPED YAWPER YOWLED

Y••W••
YAHWEH

Y•••W•
YUKAWA

Y••••W
YARROW YELLOW

•YW•••
BYWAYS BYWORD MYWORD

•Y••W•
BYLAWS

••YW••
ANYWAY FLYWAY KEYWAY SKYWAY

••Y••W
ANYHOW HAYMOW LAYLOW

•YX•••
PYXIES

•Y•X••
LYNXES

•Y•••X
SYNTAX SYRINX

••YX••
ONYXES ORYXES

••Y••X
BAYEUX SKYBOX

•••Y•X
LARYNX

••••YX
COCCYX

Y•Y•••
YOYOED YOYOMA

Y••Y••
YUMYUM

Y••••Y
YARELY YEARLY YEASTY

•Y•Y••
LYNYRD SYZYGY

•Y••Y•
AYEAYE BYEBYE BYWAYS RYUKYU

•Y•••Y
BYPLAY LYNLEY MYOHMY SYDNEY SYRUPY SYZYGY TYPIFY

••YY••
HEYYOU SAYYES SAYYID

••Y•Y•
FLYBYS LAYBYS

••Y••Y
ANYWAY BRYONY DRYFLY FLYBOY FLYWAY HAYLEY HEYDAY KEYWAY LAYSBY MAYDAY MAYFLY NAYSAY PAYDAY SKYWAY WAYLAY

•••Y•Y
CLAYEY SPRYLY SYZYGY

•YZ•••
SYZYGY

•Y•Z••
RYAZAN

•••YZ•
CORYZA SWAYZE

ZA••••
ZADDIK ZADORA ZAFFER ZAFTIG ZAGGED ZAGREB ZAMBIA ZANDER ZANIER ZANIES ZANILY ZANUCK ZAPATA ZAPPED ZAPPER ZAREBA ZAYINS

Z•A•••
ZEALOT ZSAZSA

Z••A••
ZAPATA ZENANA ZONATE ZOUAVE ZYMASE

Z•••A•
ZEBRAS ZEEMAN ZIGZAG ZILPAH ZODIAC

Z••••A
ZADORA ZAMBIA ZAPATA ZAREBA ZENANA ZEUGMA ZINNIA ZOYSIA ZSAZSA

•ZA•••
AZALEA IZABAL OZARKS

•Z•A••
IZZARD

•Z••A•
IZABAL UZZIAH

•Z•••A
AZALEA

••ZA••
BAZAAR BEZANT HAZANS HAZARD IZZARD KAZAKH KAZAKS LIZARD MOZART PIZAZZ WIZARD

••Z•A•
BAZAAR FEZZAN HUZZAH HUZZAS ITZHAK PIZZAS TAZZAS UZZIAH

••Z••A
GEZIRA MAZOLA MAZUMA VIZSLA

•••ZA•
BALZAC BANZAI FEZZAN HUZZAH HUZZAS PIZZAS PLAZAS RYAZAN SHAZAM SLEZAK TARZAN TAZZAS ZIGZAG

•••Z•A
BRAZZA PIAZZA ZSAZSA

••••ZA
BRAZZA CORYZA FAENZA KWANZA PIAZZA SFORZA STANZA

Z•B•••
ZEBRAS

Z••B••
ZAMBIA ZOMBIE

Z•••B•
ZAREBA

Z••••B
ZAGREB

•ZB•••
UZBEKS

•Z•B••
IZABAL

••ZB••
LAZBOY

••Z•B•
GAZEBO

Z••C••
ZIRCON

Z•••C•
ZANUCK ZURICH ZYDECO

Z••••C
ZIPLOC ZODIAC

•Z•C••
CZECHS

•Z••C•
AZTECS

•Z•••C
OZONIC

•••ZC•
OROZCO

•••Z•C
BALZAC

Z•D•••
ZADDIK ZADORA ZODIAC ZYDECO

Z••D••
ZADDIK ZANDER ZENDOS ZUIDER

Z•••D•
ZOUNDS

Z••••D
ZAGGED ZAPPED ZEROED ZESTED ZIGGED ZINGED ZIPPED ZONKED ZOOMED

•Z•D••
AZODYE

•Z•••D
IZZARD

••Z••D
BUZZED COZIED FIZZED FUZZED HAZARD IZZARD JAZZED LIZARD RAZZED WIZARD

•••Z•D
AMAZED BLAZED BRAZED BUZZED CRAZED FIZZED FUZZED GAUZED GLAZED GRAZED JAZZED PRIZED RAZZED SEIZED

ZE••••
ZEALOT ZEBRAS ZEEMAN ZENANA ZENDOS ZENGER ZENITH ZEPHYR ZEROED ZEROES ZEROIN ZEROTH ZESTED

ZEUGMA
ZEUXIS

Z•E•••
ZEEMAN

Z••E••
ZAREBA
ZYDECO

Z•••E•
ZAFFER
ZAGGED
ZAGREB
ZANDER
ZANIER
ZANIES
ZAPPED
ZAPPER
ZENGER
ZEROED
ZEROES
ZESTED
ZIGGED
ZIMMER
ZINGED
ZINGER
ZIPPED
ZIPPER
ZITHER
ZONKED
ZONKER
ZOOMED
ZUIDER

Z••••E
ZOMBIE
ZONATE
ZOUAVE
ZYGOTE
ZYMASE

•ZE•••
CZECHS
CZERNY

•Z•E••
AZTECS
UZBEKS

•Z••E•
AZALEA
AZORES

•Z•••E
AZODYE

••ZE••
BEZELS
COZENS
DOZENS
DOZERS
FUZEES
GAZEBO
HAZELS
HAZERS
MAZERS
MIZENS
OUZELS
SIZERS
SIZEUP
WIZENS

••Z•E•
BUZZED
BUZZER
BUZZES
COZIED
COZIER
COZIES
FEZZES
FIZZED
FIZZES
FUZEES
FUZZED
FUZZES
HAZIER
JAZZED
JAZZES
LAZIER
MIZZEN
RAZZED
RAZZES
VIZIER

••Z••E
DAZZLE
ENZYME
EVZONE
FIZZLE
FOZZIE
GUZZLE
LIZZIE
MIZZLE
MUZZLE
NOZZLE
NUZZLE
PUZZLE
RAZZLE
REZONE
SIZZLE

•••ZE•
AMAZED
AMAZES
BLAZED
BLAZER
BLAZES
BONZES
BRAZED
BRAZEN
BRAZER
BRAZES
BUZZED
BUZZER
BUZZES
CRAZED
CRAZES
CROZES
DENZEL
DITZES
DRUZES
FEZZES
FIZZED
FIZZES
FRAZER
FROZEN
FUZZED
FUZZES
GAUZED
GAUZES
GEEZER
GLAZED
GLAZER
GLAZES
GRAZED
GRAZER
GRAZES
JAZZED
JAZZES
MAIZES
MIZZEN
PANZER
PRIZED
PRIZES
RAZZED
RAZZES
SEIZED
SEIZER
SEIZES
TETZEL
WINZES

•••Z•E
DAZZLE
DOOZIE
FIZZLE
FOOZLE
FOZZIE
GUZZLE
LIZZIE
MIZZLE
MUZZLE
NOZZLE
NUZZLE
PUZZLE
RAZZLE
SIZZLE

••••ZE
ABLAZE
ASSIZE
BEDAZE
BELIZE
BREEZE
BRONZE
FREEZE
FRIEZE
IODIZE
IONIZE
LAMAZE
SLEAZE
SNEEZE
SNOOZE
SWAYZE
TWEEZE
WHEEZE

Z•F•••
ZAFFER
ZAFTIG

Z••F••
ZAFFER

Z•G•••
ZAGGED
ZAGREB
ZIGGED
ZIGZAG
ZYGOTE

Z••G••
ZAGGED
ZENGER
ZEUGMA
ZIGGED
ZINGED
ZINGER

Z••••G
ZAFTIG
ZIGZAG
ZONING

••ZG••
FIZGIG

••Z•G•
SYZYGY

••Z••G
DAZING
DOZING
FAZING
FIZGIG
FUZING
GAZING
HAZING
LAZING
OOZING
RAZING
SIZING

•••Z•G
DANZIG
HERZOG
ZIGZAG

ZH••••
ZHUKOV

Z••H••
ZEPHYR
ZITHER

Z••••H
ZENITH
ZEROTH
ZILPAH
ZIZITH
ZURICH

•Z•H••
TZUHSI

•Z••H•
CZECHS

•Z•••H
UZZIAH

••ZH••
FUZHOU
ITZHAK
MUZHIK

••Z••H
HUZZAH
KAZAKH
UZZIAH
ZIZITH

•••Z•H
HUZZAH
MATZOH

ZI••••
ZIGGED
ZIGZAG
ZILPAH
ZIMMER
ZINGED
ZINGER
ZINNIA
ZIPLOC
ZIPPED
ZIPPER
ZIPSUP
ZIRCON
ZITHER
ZIZITH

Z•I•••
ZUIDER

Z••I••
ZANIER
ZANIES
ZANILY
ZAYINS
ZENITH
ZIZITH
ZODIAC
ZONING
ZORILS
ZURICH

Z•••I•
ZADDIK
ZAFTIG
ZAMBIA
ZEROIN
ZEUXIS
ZINNIA
ZOMBIE
ZOYSIA

•Z•I••
UZZIAH

•Z••I•
AZORIN
OZONIC

•Z•••I
TZUHSI

••ZI••
COZIED
COZIER
COZIES
COZILY
DAZING
DOZILY
DOZING
FAZING
FUZING
GAZING
GEZIRA
HAZIER
HAZILY
HAZING
LAZIER
LAZILY
LAZING
OOZING
RAZING
SIZING
UNZIPS
UZZIAH
VIZIER
ZIZITH

••Z•I•
FIZGIG
FOZZIE
LIZZIE
MUZHIK

••Z••I
ADZUKI
LAZULI
SUZUKI

•••ZI•
BRAZIL
DANZIG
DOOZIE
FOZZIE
GHAZIS
LIZZIE
SWAZIS

•••Z•I
BANZAI
BORZOI
BRAZZI

••••ZI
BRAZZI

Z••K••
ZHUKOV
ZONKED
ZONKER

Z••••K
ZADDIK
ZANUCK

•Z••K•
OZARKS
UZBEKS

••Z•K•
ADZUKI
KAZAKH
KAZAKS
SUZUKI

••Z••K
ITZHAK
MUZHIK

•••Z•K
SLEZAK

ZL••••
ZLOTYS

Z•L•••
ZILPAH

Z••L••
ZEALOT
ZIPLOC

Z•••L•
ZANILY
ZORILS

•Z•L••
AZALEA

•Z•••L
IZABAL

••Z•L•
BEZELS
COZILY
DAZZLE
DOZILY
FIZZLE
GUZZLE
HAZELS
HAZILY
LAZILY
LAZULI
MAZOLA
MIZZLE
MUZZLE
NOZZLE
NUZZLE
OUZELS
PUZZLE
RAZZLE
SIZZLE
VIZSLA

•••ZL•
DAZZLE
FIZZLE
FOOZLE
GUZZLE
MIZZLE
MUZZLE
NOZZLE
NUZZLE
PUZZLE
RAZZLE
SIZZLE

•••Z•L
BENZOL
BRAZIL
DENZEL
TETZEL

Z•M•••
ZAMBIA
ZIMMER
ZOMBIE
ZYMASE

Z••M••
ZEEMAN
ZIMMER
ZOOMED

Z•••M•
ZEUGMA

••ZM••
GIZMOS

••Z•M•
ENZYME
MAZUMA

•••Z•M
SHAZAM

Z•N•••
ZANDER
ZANIER
ZANIES
ZANILY
ZANUCK
ZENANA
ZENDOS
ZENGER
ZENITH
ZINGED
ZINGER
ZINNIA
ZONATE
ZONING
ZONKED
ZONKER

Z••N••
ZINNIA
ZOUNDS

Z•••N•
ZAYINS
ZENANA
ZONING

Z••••N
ZEEMAN
ZEROIN
ZIRCON

•Z•N••
OZONIC

•Z••N•
CZERNY

•Z•••N
AZORIN

••Z•N•
BEZANT
COZENS
DAZING
DOZENS
DOZING
EVZONE
FAZING
FUZING
GAZING
HAZANS
HAZING
LAZING
MIZENS
OOZING
RAZING
REZONE
SIZING
WIZENS

••Z••N
FEZZAN
MIZZEN

•••ZN•
GROZNY

•••Z•N
AMAZON
BARZUN
BLAZON
BRAZEN
CURZON
FEZZAN
FROZEN
MIZZEN
PINZON
RYAZAN
TARZAN

ZO••••
ZODIAC
ZOMBIE
ZONATE
ZONING
ZONKED
ZONKER
ZOOMED
ZORILS
ZOUAVE
ZOUNDS
ZOYSIA

Z•O•••
ZLOTYS
ZOOMED

Z••O••
ZADORA
ZEROED
ZEROES
ZEROIN
ZEROTH
ZYGOTE

Z•••O•
ZEALOT
ZENDOS
ZHUKOV
ZIPLOC
ZIRCON

Z••••O
ZYDECO

•ZO•••
AZODYE
AZORES
AZORIN
OZONIC

••ZO••
EVZONE
KAZOOS
MAZOLA
RAZORS
REZONE

••Z•O•
FUZHOU
GIZMOS
KAZOOS
LAZBOY
MEZZOS

••Z••O
GAZEBO

•••ZO•
AMAZON
BENZOL
BLAZON
BORZOI
BRAZOS
CURZON
HERZOG
MAHZOR
MATZOH
MATZOS
MEZZOS
PINZON

•••Z•O
AREZZO
OROZCO

••••ZO
ALONZO
AREZZO
REBOZO

Z•P•••
ZAPATA
ZAPPED
ZAPPER
ZEPHYR
ZIPLOC
ZIPPED
ZIPPER
ZIPSUP

Z••P••
ZAPPED
ZAPPER
ZILPAH
ZIPPED
ZIPPER

Z••••P
ZIPSUP

••Z•P•
UNZIPS

••Z••P
JAZZUP
SIZEUP

•••Z•P
JAZZUP

Z•R•••
ZAREBA
ZEROED
ZEROES
ZEROIN
ZEROTH
ZIRCON
ZORILS
ZURICH

Z••R••
ZAGREB
ZEBRAS

Z•••R•
ZADORA

Z••••R
ZAFFER
ZANDER
ZANIER
ZAPPER
ZENGER
ZEPHYR
ZIMMER
ZINGER
ZIPPER
ZITHER
ZONKER
ZUIDER

•Z•R••
AZORES
AZORIN
CZERNY
OZARKS

•Z••R•
IZZARD

••Z•R•
DOZERS
GEZIRA
HAZARD
HAZERS
IZZARD
LIZARD
MAZERS
MOZART
RAZORS
SIZERS
WIZARD

••Z••R
BAZAAR
BUZZER
COZIER
HAZIER
LAZIER
VIZIER

•••Z•R
BLAZER
BRAZER
BUZZER
FRAZER
GEEZER
GLAZER
GRAZER
MAHZOR
PANZER
SEIZER

ZS••••
ZSAZSA

Z•S•••
ZESTED

Z••S••
ZIPSUP
ZOYSIA

Z•••S•
ZSAZSA
ZYMASE

Z••••S
ZANIES
ZAYINS
ZEBRAS
ZENDOS
ZEROES
ZEUXIS
ZLOTYS
ZORILS
ZOUNDS

•Z••S•
TZUHSI

•Z•••S
AZORES
AZTECS
CZECHS
OZARKS
UZBEKS

••ZS••
VIZSLA

••Z••S
BEZELS
BUZZES
COZENS
COZIES
DOZENS
DOZERS
FEZZES
FIZZES
FUZEES
FUZZES
GIZMOS
HAZANS
HAZELS
HAZERS
HUZZAS
JAZZES
KAZAKS
KAZOOS
MAZERS
MEZZOS
MIZENS
OUZELS
PIZZAS
RAZORS
RAZZES
SIZERS
TAZZAS
UNZIPS
WIZENS

•••ZS•
ZSAZSA

•••Z•S
AMAZES
BLAZES
BONZES
BRAZES
BRAZOS
BUZZES
CRAZES
CROZES
DITZES
DRUZES
FEZZES
FIZZES
FUZZES
GAUZES
GHAZIS
GLAZES
GRAZES
HUZZAS
JAZZES
KUDZUS
MAIZES
MATZOS
MEZZOS
PIZZAS
PLAZAS
PRIZES
RAZZES
SEIZES
SWAZIS
TAZZAS
WINZES

Z•T•••
ZITHER

Z••T••
ZAFTIG
ZESTED
ZLOTYS

Z•••T•
ZAPATA
ZENITH
ZEROTH
ZIZITH
ZONATE
ZYGOTE

Z••••T
ZEALOT

•ZT•••
AZTECS

••Z•T•
ZIZITH

••Z••T
BEZANT
MOZART

ZU••••
ZUIDER
ZURICH

Z•U•••
ZEUGMA
ZEUXIS
ZHUKOV
ZOUAVE
ZOUNDS

Z••U••
ZANUCK

Z•••U•
ZIPSUP

•ZU•••
TZUHSI

••ZU••
ADZUKI
LAZULI
MAZUMA
SUZUKI

••Z•U•
JAZZUP
SIZEUP

••Z••U
FUZHOU

•••ZU•
BARZUN
JAZZUP
KUDZUS

••••ZU
LAOTZU

Z•••V•
ZOUAVE

Z••••V
ZHUKOV

Z••X••
ZEUXIS

ZY••••
ZYDECO
ZYGOTE
ZYMASE

Z•Y•••
ZAYINS
ZOYSIA

Z•••Y•
ZEPHYR
ZLOTYS

Z••••Y
ZANILY

•Z••Y•
AZODYE

•Z•••Y
CZERNY

••ZY••
ENZYME
SYZYGY

••Z••Y
COZILY
DOZILY
HAZILY
LAZBOY
LAZILY
SYZYGY

•••Z•Y
FRIZZY
GROZNY
SCUZZY
SNAZZY

••••ZY
BLOWZY
BREEZY
BRONZY
FRENZY
FRIZZY
FROWZY
GLITZY
GROSZY
KLUTZY
SCUZZY
SLEAZY
SNAZZY
SNEEZY
WHEEZY

Z•Z•••
ZIZITH

Z••Z••
ZIGZAG
ZSAZSA

•ZZ•••
IZZARD
UZZIAH

••ZZ••
BUZZED
BUZZER
BUZZES
DAZZLE
FEZZAN
FEZZES
FIZZED
FIZZES
FIZZLE
FOZZIE
FUZZED
FUZZES
GUZZLE
HUZZAH
HUZZAS
JAZZED
JAZZES
JAZZUP
LIZZIE
MEZZOS
MIZZEN
MIZZLE
MUZZLE
NOZZLE
NUZZLE
PIZZAS
PUZZLE
RAZZED
RAZZES
RAZZLE
SIZZLE
TAZZAS

••Z•Z•
PIZAZZ

••Z••Z
PIZAZZ

•••ZZ•
AREZZO
BRAZZA
BRAZZI
FRIZZY
PIAZZA
SCUZZY
SNAZZY

••••ZZ
PIZAZZ

7

AA•••••
AAMILNE

A•A••••
ABALONE
ABANDON
ABASHED
ABASHES
ABASING
ABATING
ACACIAS
ACADEME
ACADEMY
ACADIAN
ACANTHI
ACARIDS
ADAGIOS
ADAMANT
ADAMITE
ADAMSON
ADAPTED
ADAPTER
ADAPTOR
AGAINST
AGAKHAN
AGASSIZ
ALABAMA
ALADDIN
ALAKING
ALAMEDA
ALAMEIN
ALAMODE
ALARCON
ALARMED
ALARMER
ALARUMS
ALASKAN
AMADEUS
AMALGAM
AMAPOLA
AMASSED
AMASSES
AMATEUR
AMATIVE
AMATORY
AMAZING
AMAZONS
ANADEMS
ANAEMIA
ANAGRAM
ANAHEIM
ANAHUAC
ANALOGS
ANALOGY
ANALYSE
ANALYST
ANALYZE
ANANIAS
ANAPEST
ANARCHY
ANASAZI
ANATOLE
ANATOMY
APACHES
APATITE
ARABIAN
ARACHNE
ARALSEA
ARAMAIC
ARAMEAN
ARAPAHO
ARAWAKS
ATACAMA
ATALOSS
ATAMANS
ATATURK
ATAVISM
ATAVIST
AVAILED
AVARICE
AVATARS
AWAITED
AWAKENS
AWAKING
AWARDED
AWARDEE
AWARDER
AWAREOF
AZALEAS

A••A•••
ABLATED
ABLATES
ABLAUTS
ABNAKIS
ABRADED
ABRADES
ABRAHAM
ABSALOM
ACHATES
ACKACKS
ACTABLE
ACTAEON
ADDABLE
ADVANCE
AERATED
AERATES
AERATOR
AFFABLE
AFFABLY
AFFAIRE
AFFAIRS
AFRAMES
AGNATES
AGRAFFE
AHEADOF
ALBANIA
ALCAZAR
ALFALFA
ALIASES
ALKALIS
ALLAYED
ALLAYER
ALMAATA
ALMADEN
ALMANAC
ALPACAS
ALVAREZ
AMHARIC
AMIABLE
AMIABLY
AMRADIO
ANDANTE
ANNABEL
ANNALEE
ANNATTO
ANTACID
ANTAEUS
ANTARES
APPALLS
APPAREL
AQUARIA
AQUATIC
AQUAVIT
ARCADES
ARCADIA
AREARUG
AREAWAY
ARIADNE
ARMADAS
ARRAIGN
ARRANGE
ARRASES
ARRAYED
ASFARAS
ASHAMED
ASHANTI
ASIATIC
ASKANCE
ASSAILS
ASSAULT
ASSAYED
ASSAYER
ASTAIRE
ASTARTE
ATFAULT
ATLANTA
ATLARGE
ATLASES
ATLATLS
ATTACHE
ATTACKS
ATTAINS
AUBADES
AURALEE
AURALLY
AVIANCA
AVIATED
AVIATES
AVIATOR
AXIALLY
AYEAYES

A•••A••
ABELARD
ABENAKI
ABIGAIL
ABREAST
ABSTAIN
ABUBAKR
ACCLAIM
ACETATE
ACREAGE
ACTUARY
ACTUATE
ADAMANT
ADONAIS
ADULATE
AERIALS
AFFRAYS
AFGHANI
AFGHANS
AGESAGO
AGITATE
AIRBAGS
AIRBALL
AIRBASE
AIRDAMS
AIRDATE
AIRFARE
AIRLANE
AIRMAIL
AIRMASS
AIRRAID
AIRSACS
AIRTAXI
AIRWAVE
AIRWAYS
ALABAMA
ALIBABA
ALIDADE
ALLEARS
ALLHAIL
ALMAATA
ALOHAOE
ALREADY
AMYLASE
ANASAZI
ANDEANS
ANIMALS
ANIMATE
ANIMATO
ANNEALS
ANNUALS
ANOMALY
ANORAKS
ANSPACH
ANTFARM
ANTIART
AOUDADS
APPEALS
APPEARS
APPEASE
APPLAUD
ARAMAIC
ARAPAHO
ARAWAKS
ARCHAIC
ARCLAMP
ARIKARA
ARMBAND
ARMYANT
ARREARS
ARTWARE
ASHCANS
ASHLAND
ASHLARS
ASHRAMS
ASPHALT
ASSUAGE
ATACAMA
ATAMANS
ATHEART
ATHWART
ATLEAST
ATPEACE
ATSTAKE
ATTRACT
AUREATE
AVATARS
AVERAGE
AVOCADO
AVOWALS
AWKWARD
AYNRAND

A••••A•
ABOREAL
ABRAHAM
ABUTTAL
ABYSMAL
ACACIAS
ACADIAN
ACCRUAL
ACROBAT
ADMIRAL
ADRENAL
AEOLIAN
AEROBAT
AFRICAN
AGAKHAN
AGENDAS
AIMEDAT
AIRBOAT
AIRHEAD
AIRPLAY
ALASKAN
ALCAZAR
ALLHEAL
ALLSTAR
ALMANAC
ALPACAS
ALSORAN
ALTOSAX
ALUMNAE
ALUMNAL
AMALGAM
AMOEBAE
AMOEBAS
AMSCRAY
ANAGRAM
ANAHUAC
ANANIAS
ANDREAS
ANGOLAN
ANGORAS
ANGULAR
ANNULAR
ANTBEAR
ANTIWAR
AQUINAS
ARABIAN
ARAMEAN
ARCHWAY
AREAWAY
AREOLAE
AREOLAR
AREOLAS
ARISTAE
ARISTAS
ARMADAS
ARMLOAD
ARNICAS
AROUSAL
ARRIVAL
ARROBAS
ARSENAL
ARTISAN
ASFARAS
ASHTRAY
ASOCIAL
ASSEGAI
ASTOLAT
ASUSUAL
AUGURAL
AURORAE
AURORAL
AURORAS
AUSTRAL
AUTOMAT
AXILLAE
AZALEAS
AZTECAN

A•••••A
ACEROLA
ADDENDA
AGRIPPA
ALABAMA
ALAMEDA
ALBANIA
ALBERTA
ALFALFA
ALGEBRA
ALGERIA
ALIBABA
ALLUVIA
ALMAATA
ALTOONA
ALYOSHA
AMAPOLA
AMERICA
AMERIKA
AMMONIA
AMNESIA
AMPHORA
ANAEMIA
ANDORRA
ANOSMIA
ANTENNA
ANTIGUA
ANTONIA
APHELIA
AQUARIA
ARALSEA
ARCADIA
ARIETTA
ARIKARA
ARIZONA
ARMENIA
ARUGULA
ASSYRIA
ASTORIA
ATACAMA
ATLANTA
AUGUSTA
AUREOLA
AUSTRIA
AVIANCA
AVONLEA

•AA••••
HAARLEM
LAAGERS

•A•A•••
BABASSU
BACARDI
BAHAMAS
BALANCE
BALATON
BANALLY
BANANAS
BARANOF
BASALLY
BASALTS
BAVARIA
BAZAARS
CABALAS
CABANAS
CABARET
CANAPES
CANARDS
CANASTA
CAPABLE
CAPABLY
CAPAPIE
CARACAL
CARACAS
CARAFES
CARAMBA
CARAMEL
CARAMIA
CARAVAN
CARAVEL
CARAWAY
CASABAS
CATALAN
CATALOG
CATALPA
CATAWBA
CAVALRY
DADAISM
DADAIST
DAMAGED
DAMAGES
DAMASKS
DATASET
EARACHE
EATABLE
EATAWAY
FABARES
FACADES
FALAFEL
FANATIC
FARADAY
FARAWAY
GAGARIN
GALAHAD
GALATEA
GALATIA
GARAGED
GARAGES
HAVARTI
HAZARDS
JACANAS
JAIALAI
JAKARTA
JAMAICA
JANACEK
JAVAMAN
KANAKAS
KARACHI
KARAJAN
KARAKUL
KARAKUM
KARAOKE
KARASEA
KAYAKED
KAYAKER
KAZAKHS
LABAMBA
LAFARGE
LALAKER
LALANNE
LAMAISM
LAMAIST
LAMARCK
LAPALMA
LARAINE
LARAMIE
LASAGNA
LASAGNE
LASALLE
LAVALSE
LAYAWAY
LAZARUS
MACABRE
MACADAM
MACAQUE
MADAMEX
MAHALIA
MAHARIS
MAHATMA
MALABAR
MALACCA
MALACHI
MALAISE
MALAMUD
MALAREN
MALAYAN
MANACLE
MANAGED
MANAGER
MANAGES
MANAGUA
MANANAS
MANATEE
MARABOU
MARACAS
MARAUDS
MATADOR
MAYALIN
NAIADES
NASALLY
NATALIA
NATALIE
NATASHA
NAVAHOS
NAVAJOS
NAVARRE
PAJAMAS
PALACES
PALADIN
PALANCE
PALATAL
PALATES
PALAVER
PALAZZI
PALAZZO
PANACEA
PANACHE
PANAMAS
PAPADOC
PAPAGOS
PAPAYAS
PARABLE
PARADED
PARADES
PARADOX
PARAGON
PARAPET
PARAPHS
PARASOL
PATAKES
PAVANES
PAYABLE
RADAMES
RAMADAN
RAMADAS
RANAWAY
RAPANUI
RATABLE
RATAFIA
RATATAT
RAVAGED
RAVAGES
SAFARIS
SAHARAN
SALAAMS
SALABLE
SALADIN
SALAMIS
SALAZAR
SAMARIA
SARACEN
SARALEE
SARANAC
SARAWAK
SARAZEN
SAVABLE
SAVAGED
SAVAGER
SAVAGES
SAVALAS

SAVANNA
SAVANTS
SAVARIN
TABARDS
TABASCO
TAGALOG
TALARIA
TAMABLE
TAMALES
TAMARIN
TANAGER
TARANTO
TATAMIS
TAXABLE
VACANCY
VACATED
VACATES
VALANCE
WASATCH

•A••A••

BABBAGE
BAGGAGE
BAHRAIN
BAKLAVA
BALKANS
BALLADE
BALLADS
BALLARD
BALLAST
BALSAMS
BANDAGE
BANDAID
BANDANA
BANTAMS
BANYANS
BAOBABS
BARBARA
BARBARY
BARGAIN
BARMAID
BARNARD
BARRACK
BARRAGE
BATEAUX
BAZAARS
CABBAGE
CAESARS
CAFTANS
CAIMANS
CALGARY
CALPACS
CALVARY
CAMPARI
CANCANS
CANTATA
CANVASS
CAPEANN
CAPTAIN
CARCASS
CARFARE
CARPALS
CARTAGE
CARWASH
CASCADE
CASCARA
CASSATT
CASSAVA
CASUALS
CATCALL
CATHAIR
CATNAPS
CATTAIL
CATWALK
CAVEART
CAVEATS
DABHAND
DARKAGE
DASTARD
DAYCAMP
DAYCARE
EARHART
EARMARK
FACIALS
FALLACY
FANFARE
FANMAIL
FANTAIL
FANTASY
FAREAST
FARRAGO
FATBACK
FATCATS
GALLANT
GALVANI
GARBAGE
GARLAND
GASBAGS
GASCAPS
GASMAIN
GATEAUX
GAUTAMA
GAVIALS
GAZZARA
HAEMATO
HAGGARD
HALYARD
HANGARS
HANSARP
HARVARD
HATRACK
HAULAGE
HAWHAWS
HAYRACK
HAYWARD
JACKALS
JACKASS
JAGUARS
JAMPACK
JANUARY
JAYWALK
JAZZAGE
KAFTANS
KAMPALA
KANSANS
LABIALS
LABIATE
LACTASE
LACTATE
LAGGARD
LAMBADA
LANDAUS
LANTANA
LANYARD
LAPLACE
LAPLAND
LAPLATA
LARIATS
LASCALA
LASCAUX
MACRAME
MADCAPS
MAENADS
MAGNATE
MAGYARS
MAITAIS
MALEATE
MALLARD
MALRAUX
MAMMALS
MANDALA
MANDANS
MANDATE
MANDAYS
MANIACS
MANMADE
MANSARD
MANUALS
MARGATE
MARGAUX
MARGAYS
MARIANA
MARMARA
MARSALA
MARYANN
MASCARA
MASSAGE
MASTABA
MAXBAER
MAYDAYS
MAYFAIR
MAYNARD
NAHUATL
NARRATE
NARWALS
NASTASE
NAYSAID
NAYSAYS
OAKLAND
OAKLAWN
PACKAGE
PACKARD
PAGEANT
PAHLAVI
PAISANO
PALMATE
PANCAKE
PAPUANS
PARFAIT
PARIAHS
PARLAYS
PARTAKE
PASSAGE
PASSANT
PAWPAWS
PAYCASH
PAYDAYS
RADIALS
RADIANS
RADIANT
RADIATE
RAGLANS
RAMPAGE
RAMPANT
RAMPART
RANDALL
RANLATE
RANSACK
RAPHAEL
RASCALS
RATPACK
RATRACE
RATTAIL
RATTANS
RAWDATA
SABBATH
SADSACK
SAGUARO
SALAAMS
SALVAGE
SAMBAED
SAMBARS
SAMOANS
SAMPANS
SAMSARA
SANDALS
SANTAFE
SANTANA
SAPSAGO
SARCASM
SASHAYS
SATIATE
SATRAPS
SAUSAGE
TAGSALE
TAIPANS
TAKEAIM
TAMBALA
TAMMANY
TAMTAMS
TANKARD
TANOAKS
TANTARA
TARBABY
TARMACS
TARSALS
TARTANS
TARTARE
TARTARS
TARZANA
TATIANA
TAXRATE
VACCARO
VAGRANT
VALIANT
VALUATE
VANDALS
VANTAGE
VANZANT
VARIANT
VASSALS
WAGTAIL
WALLABY
WALLACE
WALLACH
WALMART
WANNABE
WANTADS
WARFARE
WARGAME
WARPATH
WARRANT
WASSAIL
WASTAGE
WATTAGE
WAYLAID
WAYLAYS
WAYWARD
YARDAGE
YARDARM
ZACHARY

•A•••A•

BABYSAT
BACKBAY
BAGHDAD
BAHAMAS
BALBOAS
BALIHAI
BANANAS
BANDSAW
BARKSAT
BARSOAP
BASEMAN
BASEPAY
BATEMAN
BATHMAT
BATSMAN
BAYLEAF
CABALAS
CABANAS
CADDOAN
CALIBAN
CAMERAS
CAPITAL
CAPITAN
CAPSHAW
CAPSTAN
CARACAL
CARACAS
CARAVAN
CARAWAY
CARCOAT
CARINAS
CARLOAD
CARSEAT
CASABAS
CASELAW
CASHBAR
CASPIAN
CASSIAS
CATALAN
CATBOAT
CATENAE
CATHEAD
CATSCAN
CATSPAW
CAVEMAN
CAYUGAS
DAHLIAS
DAKOTAN
DAKOTAS
DANELAW
DARESAY
DARKMAN
DAYSTAR
EARFLAP
EASTMAN
EATAWAY
EATENAT
FACTUAL
FADIMAN
FAIRWAY
FAJITAS
FARADAY
FARAWAY
FASCIAS
FATHEAD
FAUXPAS
FAYWRAY
GAINSAY
GALAHAD
GAMBIAN
GAMELAW
GANGSAW
GANGWAY
GATEMAN
GATEWAY
GAVEWAY
HABITAT
HACKMAN
HACKSAW
HADRIAN
HAITIAN
HALFDAN
HALFWAY
HALIFAX
HALLWAY
HANDBAG
HANDCAR
HANDSAW
HANGMAN
HANUKAH
HARDHAT
HARDPAN
HARTMAN
JACANAS
JACKDAW
JACKTAR
JAIALAI
JANEWAY
JAVAMAN
JAZZMAN
KAHUNAS
KANAKAS
KARAJAN
LABCOAT
LACTEAL
LACUNAE
LACUNAL
LACUNAS
LADYDAY
LAGUNAS
LAKOTAS
LAMBDAS
LAMBEAU
LAMINAE
LAMINAL
LAMINAR
LAMINAS
LANDSAT
LAOTIAN
LATERAL
LATERAN
LATIFAH
LATINAS
LATVIAN
LAUGHAT
LAYAWAY
MACADAM
MACGRAW
MACULAE
MADEHAY
MADEWAY
MAGICAL
MAILBAG
MAKEHAY
MAKEPAR
MAKEWAY
MALABAR
MALAYAN
MANANAS
MANOWAR
MANTRAP
MANTRAS
MANXCAT
MANXMAN
MANYEAR
MARACAS
MARCEAU
MARINAS
MARITAL
MARKHAM
MARKKAA
MARSHAL
MARTIAL
MARTIAN
MARYKAY
MATEWAN
MATHIAS
MATTHAU
MAUGHAM
MAXIMAL
MAYORAL
NAMEDAY
NAMETAG
NARWHAL
NATURAL
OAKLEAF
OATMEAL
PACECAR
PACKRAT
PADUCAH
PAGODAS
PAJAMAS
PALATAL
PALOMAR
PANAMAS
PANCHAX
PAPAYAS
PARKWAY
PARTIAL
PARTWAY
PASCHAL
PATHWAY
PATINAS
PAWEDAT
PAYLOAD
PAYOLAS
RACECAR
RACEWAY
RADICAL
RAILSAT
RAILWAY
RAINHAT
RAINMAN
RAMADAN
RAMADAS
RAMBEAU
RANAWAY
RAREGAS
RARITAN
RATATAT
RATTRAP
RAWDEAL
RAYOVAC
SAGINAW
SAHARAN
SALAZAR
SAMEDAY
SAMOVAR
SAMPRAS
SAMURAI
SANDBAG
SANDBAR
SANDMAN
SANJUAN
SARANAC
SARAWAK
SAROYAN
SAURIAN
SAVALAS
TABLEAU
TABULAR
TALKSAT
TAXICAB
TAXIWAY
VALJEAN
VATICAN
VAUGHAN
WALKMAN
WALKWAY
WASHRAG
WATTEAU
WAXBEAN
XANTHAN
YARDMAN
YASHMAK
ZAMBIAN
ZAREBAS

•A••••A

BAKLAVA
BANDANA
BARBARA
BARBUDA
BARETTA
BATISTA
BAVARIA
BAZOOKA
CADENZA
CAESURA
CALDERA
CAMELIA
CANASTA
CANDELA
CANDIDA
CANTATA
CANTINA
CAPELLA
CARAMBA
CARAMIA
CARIOCA
CARNERA
CASCARA
CASSAVA
CATALPA
CATAWBA
DAYTONA
GALATEA
GALATIA
GANGLIA
GANGSTA
GAUTAMA
GAZZARA
IACOCCA
JAKARTA
JAMAICA
KACHINA
KAMPALA
KARASEA
LABAMBA
LAJOLLA
LAMBADA
LAMOTTA
LANTANA
LAPALMA
LAPLATA
LASAGNA
LASCALA
LASORDA
LAVINIA
MACHINA
MADEIRA
MADONNA
MADRONA
MAGENTA
MAHALIA
MAHATMA
MAJORCA
MALACCA
MANAGUA
MANDALA
MANDELA
MARIANA
MARIMBA
MARKKAA
MARKOVA
MARMARA
MARSALA
MARTINA
MASCARA
MASTABA
MATILDA
MAXILLA
MAZURKA
NAMIBIA
NAPHTHA
NATALIA
NATASHA
PALOOKA
PANACEA
PANDORA
PANETTA
PAPILLA
PAPRIKA
PARTITA
PASTINA
PATELLA
PAULINA
PAVLOVA
RATAFIA
RAVENNA
RAWDATA
SABRINA
SALSODA
SAMARIA
SAMSARA
SANGRIA
SANTANA
SATSUMA
SAVANNA
TABITHA
TAFFETA
TALARIA
TAMBALA
TANTARA
TAPIOCA
TARZANA
TATIANA
VANESSA
VANILLA

••A•A••

ADAMANT
ALABAMA
ANASAZI
ARAMAIC
ARAPAHO
ARAWAKS
ATACAMA
ATAMANS
AVATARS
BLATANT
BRAVADO
CHAGALL
CHAPATI
CHARADE
CRAVATS
DEADAIR
DIAHANN
DRAYAGE
EMANATE
GRAHAME
GRAHAMS
GRANADA
GRANARY
GUANACO
GUARANI
HEALALL
IMAMATE
INADAZE
JEANARP
KLAMATH
LEAKAGE
MBABANE
NIAGARA
OCANADA
ONADARE
ONADATE
PEASANT
PHALANX
PHARAOH
PLACARD
PLACATE
PLAYACT
QUASARS
REAMASS
REAVAIL
SCALARS
SCARABS
SEABAGS
SEABASS
SEAFANS
SEAGATE
SEALABS
SEALANE
SEALANT
SEASALT
SEAWALL
SEAWARD
SEAWAYS
SHALALA
SHAMANS
SHANANA
STALAGS
TEABAGS
TEABALL
TEACAKE
TEACART
TRALALA
TRAVAIL
UNAWARE
UTAHANS
ZEALAND

••A••A•

ACACIAS
ACADIAN
AGAKHAN
ALASKAN
AMALGAM
ANAGRAM
ANAHUAC
ANANIAS
ARABIAN
ARAMEAN
AZALEAS
BEANBAG
BEARCAT
BEARPAW
BOATMAN
BRAHMAN
BRAHMAS
CHACHAS
CHAPEAU
CHAPMAN
CHATEAU
CHATHAM
COALCAR
COALGAS
COALTAR
COASTAL
COAXIAL
CRANIAL
CRAWDAD
CZARDAS
DEADPAN
DIAGRAM
DRAWBAR
FLAGDAY
FLAGMAN
FLATCAR
FRACTAL
GLACIAL
GOAHEAD
GRABBAG
GRABSAT
GRACIAS
GRADUAL
GRAMMAR
GRANDAM
HEADMAN
HEADWAY
HEARSAY
HIALEAH
IDAHOAN
INAHEAP
IRANIAN
ITALIAN
KHAYYAM
KWACHAS
KWANZAS
MIAMIAN
MIASMAS
MUAMMAR
MYANMAR
OBADIAH
ONATEAR
PEABEAN
PEACOAT
PIAZZAS
PLANTAR
PLASMAS
PLATEAU
PLAYSAT
QUAGGAS
ROADMAP
ROADWAY
RUANDAN
RWANDAN
SCANDAL
SEAGRAM
SEASTAR
SHANKAR
SHAWWAL
SNAPSAT
SPARTAN
SPATIAL
STANZAS
STAREAT
STARMAN
STARMAP
TEALEAF
TEARGAS
TEARSAT
TEATRAY
TRAMCAR
TRAMPAS
TRAUMAS
UGANDAN
YEATEAM

••A•••A

ALABAMA
ALAMEDA
AMAPOLA
ANAEMIA
ARALSEA
ATACAMA
BRAVURA
CLAUDIA
CRAYOLA
CZARINA
DEADSEA
DRACHMA
DRACULA
GRANADA
GRANDMA
GRANDPA
GRANOLA
IPANEMA
ISADORA
NIAGARA
OCANADA
OCARINA
PHAEDRA
SCAPULA
SHALALA
SHANANA
SPATULA
STAMINA
TRACHEA
TRALALA
TSARINA
TZARINA
ULANOVA

•••AA••

ALMAATA
BAZAARS
SALAAMS

•••A•A•

ABRAHAM
ALCAZAR
ALMANAC
ALPACAS
AREAWAY
ARMADAS
ASFARAS
BAHAMAS
BANANAS
BENATAR
BETAMAX
BETARAY
BROADAX
CABALAS
CABANAS
CARACAL
CARACAS
CARAVAN
CARAWAY
CASABAS
CATALAN
CICADAE
CICADAS
CURACAO
CUTAWAY
DUNAWAY
EATAWAY
FARADAY
FARAWAY
FLEABAG
FLYAWAY
GALAHAD
GELADAS
GETAWAY
GOTAWAY
IGUANAS
IMPALAS
ITHACAN
JACANAS
JAIALAI
JAVAMAN
JICAMAS
KANAKAS
KARAJAN
LAYAWAY
MACADAM
MALABAR
MALAYAN
MANANAS
MARACAS
MIRAMAR
MIRAMAX
MUBARAK
NEVADAN
OGLALAS
OTTAWAS
PAJAMAS
PALATAL
PANAMAS
PAPAYAS
PHRASAL
PINATAS
PITAPAT
POSADAS
PUTAWAY
PYJAMAS
RAMADAN
RAMADAS
RANAWAY
RATATAT
RUNAWAY
SAHARAN
SALAZAR
SARANAC
SARAWAK
SAVALAS
SONATAS
SWEARAT
TOWAWAY
YUCATAN
ZENANAS

•••A••A

ALBANIA
ALFALFA
ALMAATA
AQUARIA
ARCADIA
ATLANTA
AVIANCA
BAVARIA
BONANZA
CANASTA
CARAMBA
CARAMIA
CATALPA
CATAWBA
CROATIA
DEPALMA
EURASIA
GALATEA
GALATIA
HOSANNA
INFANTA
JAKARTA

JAMAICA
JOCASTA
JOHANNA
KARASEA
KILAUEA
LABAMBA
LAPALMA
LASAGNA
MAHALIA
MAHATMA
MALACCA
MANAGUA
MIRANDA
MORAVIA
NATALIA
NATASHA
OCEANIA
OCTAVIA
ORGANZA
PANACEA
PIRANHA
RATAFIA
REGALIA
REGATTA
ROMANIA
ROSANNA
SAMARIA
SAVANNA
SEDALIA
SINATRA
SOLARIA
SOMALIA
SUMATRA
SUSANNA
TALARIA
TITANIA
VEDANTA
VERANDA
VIDALIA

••••AA•
ROLVAAG
YESMAAM

••••A•A
ALABAMA
ALIBABA
ALMAATA
ARIKARA
ATACAMA
BAKLAVA
BANDANA
BARBARA
BOKHARA
CANTATA
CASCARA
CASSAVA
CHICANA
DIORAMA
DOGMATA
ESTRADA
GAUTAMA
GAZZARA
GRANADA
GRENADA
GUEVARA
IKEBANA
INDIANA
JULIANA
KAMPALA
LAMBADA
LANTANA
LAPLATA
LASCALA
MANDALA
MARIANA
MARMARA
MARSALA
MASCARA
MASTABA
MESSALA
MOMBASA
MONTANA
MORGANA
MUSTAFA
NIAGARA
NIRVANA
OCANADA
OKINAWA
PRORATA
RAWDATA
SAMSARA
SANTANA
SHALALA
SHANANA
SMETANA
STOMATA
SULTANA
TAMBALA
TANTARA
TARZANA
TATIANA
TIJUANA
TOCCATA
TOSTADA
TRALALA
TYMPANA
UPPSALA

•••••AA
MARKKAA
RUFIYAA

AB•••••
ABALONE
ABANDON
ABASHED
ABASHES
ABASING
ABATING
ABDOMEN
ABDUCTS
ABELARD
ABENAKI
ABETTED
ABETTOR
ABIDEBY
ABIDING
ABIGAIL
ABILENE
ABILITY
ABJURED
ABJURES
ABLATED
ABLATES
ABLAUTS
ABNAKIS
ABOLISH
ABOREAL
ABORTED
ABOUNDS
ABRADED
ABRADES
ABRAHAM
ABREAST
ABRIDGE
ABSALOM
ABSCOND
ABSENCE
ABSENTS
ABSOLUT
ABSOLVE
ABSORBS
ABSTAIN
ABUBAKR
ABUSERS
ABUSING
ABUSIVE
ABUTTAL
ABUTTED
ABYSMAL
ABYSSES

A•B••••
ALBANIA
ALBEDOS
ALBENIZ
ALBERTA
ALBERTO
ALBINOS
ALBUMEN
ALBUMIN
AMBIENT
AMBLERS
AMBLING
AMBRIES
AMBROSE
ARBITER
ARBORED
ARBOURS
ARBUTUS
AUBADES
AUBURNS

A••B•••
ABUBAKR
AIRBAGS
AIRBALL
AIRBASE
AIRBOAT
ALABAMA
ALIBABA
AMIBLUE
ANTBEAR
ANYBODY
ARABIAN
ARMBAND
ASHBURY

A•••B••
ACERBIC
ACROBAT
ACTABLE
ADDABLE
AEROBAT
AEROBES
AEROBIC
AFFABLE
AFFABLY
ALEMBIC
ALGEBRA
AMIABLE
AMIABLY
AMOEBAE
AMOEBAS
AMOEBIC
ANNABEL
ANTIBES
ARROBAS
AUDIBLE
AUDIBLY
AUDUBON

A••••B•
ABIDEBY
ABSORBS
ADSORBS
ADVERBS
ALIBABA
ASCRIBE

•AB••••
BABASSU
BABBAGE
BABBITT
BABBLED
BABBLES
BABETTE
BABOONS
BABYING
BABYISH
BABYLON
BABYSAT
BABYSIT
CABALAS
CABANAS
CABARET
CABBAGE
CABBIES
CABINET
CABLERS
CABLETV
CABLING
CABOOSE
DABBING
DABBLED
DABBLER
DABBLES
DABHAND
FABARES
FABERGE
FABRICS
GABBERS
GABBIER
GABBING
GABBLED
GABBLES
GABBROS
GABFEST
GABRIEL
HABITAT
HABITED
HABITUE
JABBERS
JABBING
JABIRUS
KABUKIS
LABAMBA
LABCOAT
LABELED
LABELER
LABELLE
LABIALS
LABIATE
LABORED
LABORER
LABOURS
LABRETS
NABBERS
NABBING
NABISCO
NABOKOV
PABLUMS
PABULUM
RABBETS
RABBITS
RABBITT
RABBLES
SABBATH
SABINES
SABRINA
TABARDS
TABASCO
TABBIES
TABBING
TABITHA
TABLEAU
TABLETS
TABLING
TABLOID
TABORET
TABULAR

•A•B•••
BABBAGE
BABBITT
BABBLED
BABBLES
BALBOAS
BAMBINO
BAMBOOS
BAOBABS
BARBARA
BARBARY
BARBELL
BARBELS
BARBERS
BARBING
BARBUDA
BATBOYS
BAUBLES
CABBAGE
CABBIES
CADBURY
CAMBERS
CAMBIUM
CAMBRIC
CARBIDE
CARBINE
CARBONS
CARBOYS
CATBIRD
CATBOAT
DABBING
DABBLED
DABBLER
DABBLES
DASBOOT
DAUBERS
DAUBING
DAYBEDS
DAYBOOK
FANBELT
FATBACK
GABBERS
GABBIER
GABBING
GABBLED
GABBLES
GABBROS
GAMBIAN
GAMBITS
GAMBLED
GAMBLER
GAMBLES
GAMBOLS
GAMBREL
GARBAGE
GARBING
GARBLED
GARBLES
GASBAGS
HAMBURG
HARBORS
HARBOUR
HASBEEN
HAUBERK
JABBERS
JABBING
JAWBONE
JAYBIRD
LAMBADA
LAMBDAS
LAMBEAU
LAMBENT
LAMBERT
LAPBELT
MACBETH
MAMBOED
MARBLED
MARBLES
MAXBAER
MAXBORN
NABBERS
NABBING
PAMBIES
PARBOIL
RABBETS
RABBITS
RABBITT
RABBLES
RAMBEAU
RAMBLED
RAMBLER
RAMBLES
RAYBURN
SABBATH
SAMBAED
SAMBARS
SANBORN
SAWBUCK
TABBIES
TABBING
TAMBALA
TAMBOUR
TARBABY
TARBELL
WAMBLED
WAMBLES
WARBLED
WARBLER
WARBLES
WAXBEAN
WAYBILL
ZAMBEZI
ZAMBIAN

•A••B••
BACKBAY
BACKBIT
BALLBOY
BANDBOX
CALIBAN
CALIBER
CALIBRE
CALLBOX
CAPABLE
CAPABLY
CARIBES
CARIBOU
CASABAS
CASHBAR
CASHBOX
EATABLE
GAZEBOS
HALIBUT
HANDBAG
HAUTBOY
JACOBIN
LADYBUG
MACABRE
MAILBAG
MAILBOX
MALABAR
MARABOU
NAMIBIA
PAGEBOY
PARABLE
PARIBUS
PAYABLE
RAINBOW
RAREBIT
RATABLE
SALABLE
SALTBOX
SANDBAG
SANDBAR
SANDBOX
SANIBEL
SAVABLE
TALKBIG
TAMABLE
TAXABLE
ZAREBAS

•A•••B•
BAOBABS
CARAMBA
CATAWBA
EARLOBE
LABAMBA
LAPROBE
LAZENBY
MADLIBS
MARIMBA
MASTABA
NAIROBI
TARBABY
WALLABY
WANNABE

•A••••B
BACKRUB
BATHTUB
TAXICAB
WASHTUB

••AB•••
ALABAMA
ARABIAN
BLABBED
BLABBER
CHABLIS
CLABBER
CRABBED
CRABBER
DRABBER
ENABLED
ENABLES
GOABOUT
GRABBAG
GRABBED
GRABBER
GRABSAT
MBABANE
PEABEAN
PEABODY
SEABAGS
SEABASS
SEABEDS
SEABEES
SEABIRD
SEABORG
SLABBED
STABBED
STABILE
STABLED
STABLER
STABLES
SWABBED
TEABAGS
TEABALL
TRABERT

••A•B••
BEANBAG
BLABBED
BLABBER
BRAMBLE
BRAMBLY
CHAMBER
CLABBER
CLAMBER
COALBIN
CRABBED
CRABBER
DRABBER
DRAWBAR
FLAMBED
FLAMBES
FLATBED
GEARBOX
GRABBAG
GRABBED
GRABBER
PEATBOG
PLAYBOY
ROADBED
SHAMBLE
SLABBED
SOAPBOX
STABBED
SWABBED
TRAUBEL

••A••B•
BYANDBY
PLACEBO
SCARABS
SEALABS
STANDBY

•••AB••
ACTABLE
ADDABLE
AFFABLE
AFFABLY
AMIABLE
AMIABLY
ANNABEL
BELABOR
BUGABOO
BUYABLE
CAPABLE
CAPABLY
CASABAS
CITABLE
COHABIT
DISABLE
DURABLE
DURABLY
EATABLE
EQUABLE
EQUABLY
FIXABLE
FLEABAG
FRIABLE
HIRABLE
ICHABOD
INHABIT
LIEABED
LIKABLE
LIVABLE
LOVABLE
MACABRE
MALABAR
MARABOU
MINABLE
MIXABLE
MOVABLE
MUTABLE
MUTABLY
NOTABIT
NOTABLE
NOTABLY
PARABLE
PAYABLE
PLIABLE
PLIABLY
POTABLE
RATABLE
SALABLE
SAVABLE
SIZABLE
SIZABLY
SOFABED
TAMABLE
TAXABLE
TENABLE
TENABLY
USEABLE

•••A•B•
BEDAUBS
CARAMBA
CATAWBA
LABAMBA
MOGAMBO
SWEARBY

••••AB•
ALIBABA
BAOBABS
CONFABS
CRYBABY
HUSHABY
LULLABY
MASTABA
PREFABS
PUNJABI
SCARABS
SEALABS
SYLLABI
TARBABY
THEBABE
WALLABY
WANNABE

••••A•B
RHUBARB

•••••AB
CHEMLAB
GODTHAB
PULLTAB
SHECRAB
TAXICAB

AC•••••
ACACIAS
ACADEME
ACADEMY
ACADIAN
ACANTHI
ACARIDS
ACCEDED
ACCEDER
ACCEDES
ACCENTS
ACCEPTS
ACCLAIM
ACCORDS
ACCOSTS
ACCOUNT
ACCRETE
ACCRUAL
ACCRUED
ACCRUES
ACCURST
ACCUSED
ACCUSER
ACCUSES
ACEDOUT
ACERBIC
ACEROLA
ACEROSE
ACESOUT
ACETATE
ACETONE
ACHATES
ACHENES
ACHERON
ACHESON
ACHIEST
ACHIEVE
ACHTUNG
ACIDIFY
ACIDITY
ACKACKS
ACOLYTE
ACONITE
ACQUIRE
ACQUITS
ACREAGE
ACRIDLY
ACROBAT
ACRONYM
ACRYLIC
ACTABLE
ACTAEON
ACTEDUP
ACTINIC
ACTIONS
ACTIVES
ACTRESS
ACTSOUT
ACTUARY
ACTUATE
ACTUPON
ACUTELY

A•C••••
ACCEDED
ACCEDER
ACCEDES
ACCENTS
ACCEPTS
ACCLAIM
ACCORDS
ACCOSTS
ACCOUNT
ACCRETE
ACCRUAL
ACCRUED
ACCRUES
ACCURST
ACCUSED
ACCUSER
ACCUSES
ALCAZAR
ALCHEMY
ALCOHOL
ALCOVES
ANCHORS
ANCHOVY
ANCIENT
ARCADES
ARCADIA
ARCHAIC
ARCHERS
ARCHERY
ARCHIES
ARCHING
ARCHIVE
ARCHONS
ARCHWAY
ARCLAMP
ARCSINE
ASCENDS
ASCENTS
ASCETIC
ASCRIBE
AUCTION

A••C•••
ABSCOND
ACACIAS
AIRCOOL
AIRCREW
AITCHES
AMSCRAY
ANTCOWS
APACHES
APOCOPE
ARACHNE
ASHCANS
ASOCIAL
ATACAMA
ATECROW
AVOCADO
AVOCETS

A•••C••
ABDUCTS
ACKACKS
ADDUCED
ADDUCES
ADDUCTS
AFFECTS
AFRICAN
ALARCON
ALENCON
ALPACAS
AMERCED
AMERCES
ANARCHY
ANTACID
APERCUS
APRICOT
ARNICAS
ARTICLE
ASPECTS
ATTACHE
ATTACKS
ATTICUS
ATTUCKS
AURICLE
AUROCHS
AZTECAN

A••••C•
ABSENCE
ADJUNCT
ADVANCE
AFFLICT
AIRLOCK
AIRSACS
AIRSOCK
ALDRICH
AMERICA
ANSPACH
ANTIOCH
ARDENCY
ARMLOCK
ARTDECO
ASKANCE
ATPEACE
ATTRACT
AUSPICE
AVARICE
AVIANCA

A•••••C
ACERBIC
ACRYLIC
ACTINIC
AELFRIC
AEROBIC
ALEMBIC
ALMANAC
AMHARIC
AMOEBIC
ANAHUAC
ANGELIC
ANOSMIC
AQUATIC
ARAMAIC
ARCHAIC
ARSENIC
ASCETIC
ASEPTIC
ASIATIC

•AC••••
BACARDI
BACCHUS
BACILLI
BACKBAY
BACKBIT
BACKEND
BACKERS
BACKHOE
BACKING
BACKLIT
BACKLOG
BACKOFF
BACKOUT
BACKRUB
BACKSIN
BACKSUP
BACKUPS
CACHETS
CACHING
CACHOUS
CACKLED
CACKLER
CACKLES
DACTYLS
FACADES
FACEOFF
FACETED
FACIALS
FACINGS
FACTION
FACTORS
FACTORY
FACTUAL
FACULTY
HACKERS
HACKETT
HACKIES
HACKING
HACKLES
HACKMAN
HACKNEY
HACKSAW
IACOCCA
JACANAS
JACCUSE
JACINTO
JACKALS
JACKASS
JACKDAW
JACKETS
JACKING
JACKPOT
JACKSON
JACKSUP
JACKTAR
JACOBIN
JACONET
JACQUES
JACUZZI
KACHINA
LACEDUP
LACESUP
LACIEST
LACINGS
LACKEYS
LACKING
LACONIC
LACOSTE
LACQUER
LACTASE
LACTATE
LACTEAL
LACTOSE
LACUNAE
LACUNAL
LACUNAS
MACABRE
MACADAM
MACAQUE
MACBETH
MACDUFF
MACGRAW
MACHETE
MACHINA
MACHINE
MACRAME

MACRONS
MACULAE
NACELLE
PACECAR
PACHISI
PACIFIC
PACKAGE
PACKARD
PACKERS
PACKETS
PACKICE
PACKING
PACKRAT
PACKSUP
RACCOON
RACECAR
RACEMES
RACEWAY
RACIEST
RACKETS
RACKING
RACKSUP
RACQUET
SACHEMS
SACHETS
SACKERS
SACKFUL
SACKING
SACKOUT
TACITLY
TACITUS
TACKERS
TACKIER
TACKILY
TACKING
TACKLED
TACKLER
TACKLES
TACKSON
TACTFUL
TACTICS
TACTILE
VACANCY
VACATED
VACATES
VACCARO
VACCINE
VACUITY
VACUOLE
VACUOUS
VACUUMS
WACKIER
WACKILY
YACHTED
ZACHARY

•A•C•••

BACCHUS
BADCOLD
BALCONY
BARCODE
BATCHED
BATCHES
BAYCITY
CALCIFY
CALCITE
CALCIUM
CANCANS
CANCELS
CARCASS
CARCOAT
CASCADE
CASCARA
CATCALL
CATCHER
CATCHES
CATCHON
CATCHUP
DANCERS
DANCING
DAYCAMP
DAYCARE
EATCROW
FALCONS
FANCIED
FANCIER
FANCIES
FANCILY
FASCIAS
FASCISM
FASCIST
FATCATS
FATCITY
FAUCETS
FAWCETT
GARCONS
GASCAPS
GASCONS
GAUCHER
GAUCHOS
HALCYON
HANCOCK
HATCHED
HATCHER
HATCHES
HATCHET
JACCUSE
JAYCEES
LABCOAT
LANCERS
LANCETS
LAOCOON
LARCENY
LARCHES
LASCALA
LASCAUX
LATCHED
LATCHES
MADCAPS
MADCHEN
MALCOLM
MANCINI
MARCEAU
MARCELS
MARCHED
MARCHEN
MARCHER
MARCHES
MARCHON
MARCONI
MASCARA
MASCOTS
MATCHED
MATCHES
MATCHUP
NASCENT
NATCHEZ
PANCAKE
PANCHAX
PARCELS
PARCHED
PARCHES
PASCHAL
PATCHED
PATCHES
PATCHUP
PAUCITY
PAYCASH
RACCOON
RANCHED
RANCHER
RANCHES
RANCHOS
RANCOUR
RASCALS
RATCHET
RAUCOUS
SALCHOW
SANCTUM
SARCASM
SATCHEL
SATCHMO
SAUCERS
SAUCIER
SAUCILY
VACCARO
VACCINE
WALCOTT
WATCHED
WATCHER
WATCHES
WATCHIT

•A••C••

CADUCEI
CALICOS
CALYCES
CAPECOD
CARACAL
CARACAS
CASHCOW
CATSCAN
EARACHE
HAIRCUT
HANDCAR
HARICOT
IACOCCA
JANACEK
KARACHI
LAROCHE
LATICES
MAGICAL
MALACCA
MALACHI
MANACLE
MANXCAT
MARACAS
PACECAR
PADUCAH
PALACES
PANACEA
PANACHE
PANICKY
PANICLE
PAUNCHY
RACECAR
RADICAL
RADICES
RADICLE
SARACEN
TAXICAB
VANOCUR
VATICAN

•A•••C•

BALANCE
BANNOCK
BARRACK
CADENCE
CALPACS
CALTECH
CANDICE
CANSECO
CAPRICE
CARIOCA
CARRICK
CASSOCK
DAVINCI
EARLOCK
FABRICS
FAIENCE
FALLACY
FATBACK
GALLICO
GARRICK
HADDOCK
HAMHOCK
HAMMOCK
HANCOCK
HASSOCK
HATRACK
HAYRACK
IACOCCA
JALISCO
JAMAICA
JAMPACK
LAMARCK
LAPLACE
LATENCY
LATTICE
MAJORCA
MALACCA
MANIACS
MASTICS
MATLOCK
MATTOCK
MAURICE
NABISCO
OARLOCK
PACKICE
PADDOCK
PADLOCK
PALANCE
PANDECT
PARSECS
PATRICE
PATRICK
RANSACK
RATPACK
RATRACE
SADSACK
SAWBUCK
TABASCO
TACTICS
TAMPICO
TAPIOCA
TARMACS
VACANCY
VALANCE
VALENCE
VANDYCK
VANEYCK
WALLACE
WALLACH
WARLOCK
WARWICK
WASATCH

•A••••C

BALDRIC
CALORIC
CAMBRIC
CANONIC
CAUSTIC
FANATIC
GASTRIC
HAMITIC
LACONIC
LAENNEC
LAUTREC
MALEFIC
MANTRIC
MASONIC
PACIFIC
PAPADOC
RAYKROC
RAYOVAC
SARANAC
SATIRIC
XANTHIC
ZAPOTEC

••AC•••

ACACIAS
APACHES
ARACHNE
ATACAMA
BEACHED
BEACHES
BEACONS
BLACKED
BLACKEN
BLACKER
BLACKLY
BRACERS
BRACEUP
BRACING
BRACKEN
BRACKET
CHACHAS
CLACKED
COACHED
COACHES
CRACKED
CRACKER
CRACKLE
CRACKUP
DEACONS
DRACHMA
DRACULA
EDACITY
ENACTED
ENACTOR
EVACUEE
EXACTED
EXACTER
EXACTLY
EXACTOR
FIACRES
FLACCID
FLACONS
FRACTAL
GIACOMO
GLACEED
GLACIAL
GLACIER
GRACIAS
GRACILE
GRACING
GRACKLE
JOACHIM
KWACHAS
LEACHED
LEACHES
LEACOCK
LOACHES
OPACITY
ORACLES
PEACHED
PEACHES
PEACOAT
PEACOCK
PLACARD
PLACATE
PLACEBO
PLACERS
PLACIDO
PLACING
PLACKET
POACHED
POACHER
POACHES
QUACKED
REACHED
REACHES
REACTED
REACTOR
REACTTO
ROACHED
ROACHES
SEACOWS
SHACKLE
SLACKED
SLACKEN
SLACKER
SMACKED
SMACKER
SNACKED
SNACKER
SPACERS
SPACIER
SPACING
SPACKLE
STACKED
STACKUP
TEACAKE
TEACART
TEACHER
TEACHES
TEACHIN
TEACUPS
TRACERS
TRACERY
TRACHEA
TRACING
TRACKED
TRACKER
TRACTOR
WHACKED
WRACKED

••A•C••

ALARCON
ANARCHY
BEARCAT
BLANCHE
CHANCED
CHANCEL
CHANCES
CHAUCER
COALCAR
EPARCHS
FIANCEE
FIANCES
FIASCOS
FLACCID
FLATCAR
FRAICHE
FRANCES
FRANCIS
GLANCED
GLANCES
NUANCED
NUANCES
PLAICES
PRANCED
PRANCER
PRANCES
SCARCER
SEANCES
STANCES
STARCHY
THATCHY
TRAMCAR
TRANCES

••A••C•

AVARICE
CHALICE
CLARICE
DIALECT
GUANACO
ITALICS
KLATSCH
LEACOCK
PEACOCK
PLAYACT
SEASICK
STATICE
STATICS
STAUNCH
TRADUCE
UNAVOCE
VIADUCT

••A•••C

ANAHUAC
ARAMAIC
CHAOTIC
CLASSIC
DRASTIC
EDAPHIC
ELASTIC
FRANTIC
GRAPHIC
JEANLUC
MIASMIC
PLASTIC
STANNIC
TRAFFIC

•••AC••

ACKACKS
ALPACAS
ANTACID
ATTACHE
ATTACKS
CARACAL
CARACAS
CURACAO
DEBACLE
DEFACED
DEFACES
DEFACTO
DIDACTS
EARACHE
EFFACED
EFFACES
ENLACED
ENLACES
GOUACHE
HIBACHI
HIJACKS
HITACHI
HYRACES
IMPACTS
INVACUO
ITHACAN
JANACEK
KARACHI
KOLACKY
MALACCA
MALACHI
MANACLE
MARACAS
MENACED
MENACES
MIRACLE
OUTACTS
PALACES
PANACEA
PANACHE
PREACHY
REDACTS
REFACED
REFACES
RELACED
RELACES
SARACEN
SOLACES
TENACES
THWACKS
TOBACCO
TREACLE
TREACLY
UNLACED
UNLACES
UNPACKS
UNTACKS

•••A•C•

ADVANCE
ASKANCE
AVIANCA
BALANCE
DEBAUCH
DURANCE
ENHANCE
FINANCE
INFANCY
JAMAICA
LAMARCK
MALACCA
MONARCH
MOSAICS
PALANCE
PENANCE
PLIANCY
ROMANCE
SCRATCH
TABASCO
TENANCY
TOBACCO
TRUANCY
UNLATCH
VACANCY
VALANCE
WASATCH

•••A••C

ALMANAC
AMHARIC
AQUATIC
ASIATIC
CERAMIC
DYNAMIC
ERRATIC
FANATIC
HEPATIC
ISLAMIC
LUNATIC
NOMADIC
OCEANIC
ORGANIC
PAPADOC
PELAGIC
PIRATIC
SARANAC
SOMATIC
TITANIC
VOCALIC

••••AC•

AIRSACS
ANSPACH
ATPEACE
ATTRACT
BARRACK
CALPACS
COGNACS
COMPACT
CONRACK
CONTACT
COSSACK
CUTBACK
DETRACT
DOGFACE
EMBRACE
EXTRACT
FALLACY
FATBACK
FURNACE
GETBACK
GOTBACK
GRIMACE
GUANACO
HATRACK
HAYRACK
HOGBACK
ICEPACK
IMPEACH
INEXACT
INPEACE
INPLACE
JAMPACK
LAPLACE
MANIACS
MICMACS
MUDPACK
OUTBACK
OUTFACE
OUTPACE
OUTRACE
OVERACT
PINNACE
PLAYACT
PREFACE
PRIMACY
PRIVACY
RANSACK
RATPACK
RATRACE
REENACT
REFRACT
REPLACE
RETEACH
RETRACE
RETRACK
RETRACT
RIOTACT
RUNBACK
SADSACK
SETBACK
SIXPACK
SKYJACK
SPINACH
STOMACH
SURFACE
TARMACS
TEDMACK
TERRACE
TICTACS
TIERACK
TIETACK
TOURACO
UNSTACK
WALLACE
WALLACH
ZODIACS

••••A•C

ARAMAIC
ARCHAIC
DELTAIC
HEBRAIC
PROSAIC
VOLTAIC

•••••AC

ALMANAC
ANAHUAC
BIVOUAC
ELEGIAC
KEROUAC
MEDEVAC
PONTIAC
POTOMAC
RAYOVAC
SARANAC
SHELLAC

AD•••••

ADAGIOS
ADAMANT
ADAMITE
ADAMSON
ADAPTED
ADAPTER
ADAPTOR
ADDABLE
ADDEDIN
ADDEDON
ADDEDTO
ADDEDUP
ADDENDA
ADDENDS
ADDISON
ADDLING
ADDONTO
ADDRESS
ADDUCED
ADDUCES
ADDUCTS
ADDUPTO
ADELINE
ADENINE
ADEPTLY
ADHERED
ADHERES
ADIPOSE
ADJOINS
ADJOURN
ADJUDGE
ADJUNCT
ADJURED
ADJURES
ADJUSTS
ADMIRAL
ADMIRED
ADMIRER
ADMIRES
ADMIXED
ADMIXES
ADOLPHE
ADONAIS
ADOPTED
ADOPTEE
ADOPTER
ADORERS
ADORING
ADORNED
ADRENAL
ADSORBS
ADULATE
ADVANCE
ADVENTS
ADVERBS
ADVERSE
ADVERTS
ADVISED
ADVISER
ADVISES
ADVISOR

A•D••••

ABDOMEN
ABDUCTS
ADDABLE
ADDEDIN
ADDEDON
ADDEDTO
ADDEDUP
ADDENDA
ADDENDS
ADDISON
ADDLING
ADDONTO
ADDRESS
ADDUCED
ADDUCES
ADDUCTS
ADDUPTO
AEDILES
ALDENTE
ALDRICH
ANDANTE
ANDEANS
ANDIRON
ANDORRA
ANDOVER
ANDREAS
ANDRESS
ANDREWS
ANDROID
ANDSOON
ANDYKIM
ARDENCY
ARDMORE
ARDOURS
ARDUOUS
AUDIBLE
AUDIBLY
AUDITED
AUDITOR
AUDUBON

A••D•••

ABIDEBY
ABIDING
ACADEME
ACADEMY
ACADIAN
ACEDOUT
ACIDIFY
ACIDITY
AIRDAMS
AIRDATE
AIRDROP
ALADDIN
ALIDADE
AMADEUS
ANADEMS
ANODIZE
ANODYNE
AOUDADS
ARIDEST
ARIDITY
ARTDECO
AVIDITY

A•••D••

ABANDON
ABRADED
ABRADES
ABRIDGE
ACCEDED
ACCEDER
ACCEDES
ACRIDLY
ACTEDUP
ADDEDIN
ADDEDON
ADDEDTO
ADDEDUP
ADJUDGE
AGENDAS
AHEADOF
AIMEDAT
AIMEDTO
ALADDIN
ALBEDOS
ALLUDED
ALLUDES
ALMADEN
AMENDED
AMRADIO
ANTEDUP
APSIDES
ARCADES
ARCADIA
ARIADNE
ARLEDGE
ARMADAS
ASUNDER
AUBADES
AVOIDED
AWARDED
AWARDEE
AWARDER

A••••D•

ABOUNDS
ACARIDS
ACCORDS
ADDENDA
ADDENDS
AFFORDS
ALAMEDA
ALAMODE
ALFREDO
ALIDADE
ALLENDE
ALMONDS
ALREADY
ANYBODY
AOUDADS
APPENDS
ASCENDS
ASTRIDE
ATTENDS
AUGENDS
AVOCADO

A•••••D

ABASHED
ABELARD
ABETTED
ABJURED
ABLATED
ABORTED
ABRADED
ABSCOND
ABUTTED
ACCEDED
ACCRUED
ACCUSED
ADAPTED
ADDUCED
ADHERED
ADJURED
ADMIRED
ADMIXED
ADOPTED
ADORNED
ADVISED
AERATED
AFFIXED
AGROUND
AIRHEAD
AIRRAID
ALARMED
ALERTED
ALIGNED
ALLAYED
ALLEGED
ALLOWED
ALLOYED
ALLTOLD
ALLUDED
ALLURED
ALTERED
AMASSED
AMENDED
AMERCED
AMERIND
ANDROID
ANEROID
ANGERED
ANISEED
ANNELID
ANNEXED
ANNOYED
ANTACID
APPLAUD
APPLIED
APPOSED
APRONED
ARBORED
ARMBAND

ARMLOAD
ARMORED
AROUSED
ARRAYED
ARRIVED
ASHAMED
ASHFORD
ASHLAND
ASPIRED
ASSAYED
ASSUMED
ASSURED
ASTOUND
ATTIRED
ATTUNED
AUDITED
AUGURED
AVAILED
AVENGED
AVERRED
AVERTED
AVIATED
AVOIDED
AVULSED
AWAITED
AWARDED
AWKWARD
AYKROYD
AYNRAND

•AD••••

BADCOLD
BADDIES
BADEGGS
BADGERS
BADGUYS
BADNESS
CADBURY
CADDIED
CADDIES
CADDOAN
CADENCE
CADENZA
CADETTE
CADGERS
CADGING
CADMIUM
CADUCEI
DADAISM
DADAIST
DADDIES
FADDISH
FADDISM
FADDIST
FADEDIN
FADEINS
FADEOUT
FADESIN
FADIMAN
GADDING
GADGETS
GADGETY
GADSDEN
HADDOCK
HADRIAN
JADEDLY
JADEITE
KADDISH
LADDERS
LADDIES
LADINOS
LADLERS
LADLING
LADYBUG
LADYDAY
MADAMEX
MADCAPS
MADCHEN
MADDENS
MADDERS
MADDEST
MADDING
MADEFOR
MADEHAY
MADEIRA
MADEOFF
MADEOUT
MADEWAY
MADISON
MADLIBS
MADNESS
MADONNA
MADRONA
PADDERS
PADDIES
PADDING
PADDLED
PADDLER
PADDLES
PADDOCK
PADLOCK
PADRONE
PADRONI
PADUCAH
RADAMES
RADDLED
RADDLES
RADIALS
RADIANS
RADIANT
RADIATE
RADICAL
RADICES
RADICLE
RADIOED
SADDENS
SADDEST
SADDLED
SADDLER
SADDLES
SADNESS
SADSACK
TADPOLE
WADDING
WADDLED
WADDLER
WADDLES
WADESIN

•A•D•••

BADDIES
BALDEST
BALDING
BALDRIC
BALDWIN
BANDAGE
BANDAID
BANDANA
BANDBOX
BANDIED
BANDIES
BANDING
BANDITO
BANDITS
BANDSAW
BAWDIER
BAWDILY
CADDIED
CADDIES
CADDOAN
CALDERA
CALDRON
CANDELA
CANDICE
CANDIDA
CANDIDE
CANDIDS
CANDIED
CANDIES
CANDLES
CANDOUR
CARDERS
CARDING
CARDOZO
DADDIES
DANDERS
DANDIER
DANDIES
DANDLED
DANDLES
DAWDLED
DAWDLER
DAWDLES
EARDROP
EARDRUM
FADDISH
FADDISM
FADDIST
GADDING
GANDERS
GARDENS
GARDNER
GAUDENS
GAUDIER
GAUDILY
HADDOCK
HANDBAG
HANDCAR
HANDFUL
HANDGUN
HANDIER
HANDILY
HANDING
HANDLED
HANDLER
HANDLES
HANDOFF
HANDOUT
HANDSAW
HANDSET
HANDSIN
HANDSON
HANDSUP
HARDENS
HARDEST
HARDHAT
HARDHIT
HARDIER
HARDILY
HARDING
HARDPAN
HARDPUT
HARDSET
HARDTOP
HARDWON
KADDISH
LADDERS
LADDIES
LAIDFOR
LAIDLOW
LAIDOFF
LAIDOUT
LANDAUS
LANDERS
LANDING
LANDSAT
LAPDOGS
LARDERS
LARDING
LARDNER
LARDONS
LAUDING
LAYDOWN
MACDUFF
MADDENS
MADDERS
MADDEST
MADDING
MAIDENS
MANDALA
MANDANS
MANDATE
MANDAYS
MANDELA
MANDREL
MANDRIL
MAUDLIN
MAYDAYS
PADDERS
PADDIES
PADDING
PADDLED
PADDLER
PADDLES
PADDOCK
PAIDFOR
PAIDOFF
PAIDOUT
PANDECT
PANDERS
PANDITS
PANDORA
PARDNER
PARDONS
PAYDAYS
PAYDIRT
RADDLED
RADDLES
RAGDOLL
RAIDERS
RAIDING
RANDALL
RANDIER
RAWDATA
RAWDEAL
SADDENS
SADDEST
SADDLED
SADDLER
SADDLES
SANDALS
SANDBAG
SANDBAR
SANDBOX
SANDERS
SANDFLY
SANDHOG
SANDIER
SANDING
SANDLOT
SANDMAN
SANDMEN
SARDINE
SATDOWN
SAWDUST
TANDEMS
TARDIER
TARDILY
VANDALS
VANDINE
VANDYCK
VANDYKE
WADDING
WADDLED
WADDLER
WADDLES
WALDORF
WANDERS
WARDENS
WARDERS
WARDING
WARDOFF
YARDAGE
YARDARM
YARDMAN
YARDMEN
ZANDERS

•A••D••

BAGHDAD
CAVEDIN
DATEDLY
DAZEDLY
EARLDOM
EASEDIN
EASEDUP
FACADES
FADEDIN
FARADAY
GADSDEN
HAIRDOS
HAIRDYE
HALFDAN
HANGDOG
HASIDIM
JACKDAW
JADEDLY
JANEDOE
KATYDID
LACEDUP
LADYDAY
LAMBDAS
LANGDON
LAUNDER
LAUNDRY
MACADAM
MALODOR
MATADOR
MAULDIN
MAUNDER
NAIADES
NAKEDLY
NAMEDAY
PAGODAS
PALADIN
PALEDRY
PAPADOC
PARADED
PARADES
PARADOX
PASTDUE
PAWEDAT
RAKEDIN
RAKEDUP
RAMADAN
RAMADAS
RAPIDER
RAPIDLY
SALADIN
SAMEDAY
SAVEDUP
VALIDLY
VAPIDLY
WAVEDIN

•A•••D•

BACARDI
BALLADE
BALLADS
BARBUDA
BARCODE
CALENDS
CANARDS
CANDIDA
CANDIDE
CANDIDS
CARBIDE
CASCADE
CASSIDY
CATHODE
DAYBEDS
FAGENDS
HAYRIDE
HAZARDS
LAMBADA
LASORDA
MAENADS
MAKESDO
MALTEDS
MANMADE
MARAUDS
MATILDA
RAGGEDY
RAMRODS
RAWHIDE
SALSODA
TABARDS
TAGENDS
WANTADS
WARGODS
WAYSIDE
YAOUNDE

•A••••D

BABBLED
BACKEND
BADCOLD
BAFFLED
BAGHDAD
BAGNOLD
BALLARD
BANDAID
BANDIED
BARMAID
BARNARD
BARTEND
BATCHED
BATIKED
BATTLED
CACKLED
CADDIED
CAJOLED
CAMEOED
CANDIED
CAPECOD
CAPERED
CARLOAD
CAROLED
CAROMED
CAROTID
CARRIED
CASTLED
CATBIRD
CATERED
CATHEAD
CAULKED
CAVILED
DABBLED
DABHAND
DAGWOOD
DALLIED
DAMAGED
DANDLED
DANGLED
DAPPLED
DASTARD
DAUNTED
DAWDLED
DAZZLED
EASTEND
FACETED
FAGOTED
FAINTED
FANCIED
FATHEAD
FAULTED
FAVORED
GABBLED
GALAHAD
GAMBLED
GANGLED
GARAGED
GARBLED
GARGLED
GARLAND
GAVELED
GAYLORD
HABITED
HAGGARD
HAGGLED
HALYARD
HAMMOND
HANDLED
HARRIED
HARVARD
HASSLED
HATCHED
HAUNTED
HAYSEED
HAYWARD
JANGLED
JAUNTED
JAYBIRD
KATYDID
KAYAKED
LABELED
LABORED
LAGGARD
LANFORD
LANGUID
LANYARD
LAPELED
LAPLAND
LASSOED
LATCHED
LAUGHED
LAWFORD
LAYERED
MAITRED
MAJORED
MALAMUD
MALLARD
MAMBOED
MANAGED
MANFRED
MANGLED
MANHOOD
MANKIND
MANSARD
MANTLED
MARBLED
MARCHED
MARRIED
MASTOID
MATCHED
MATURED
MAYNARD
NATURED
NAYSAID
OAKLAND
PACKARD
PADDLED
PAINTED
PANELED
PAPERED
PARADED
PARCHED
PAROLED
PARRIED
PARTIED
PATCHED
PAYLOAD
RADDLED
RADIOED
RAFFLED
RAGWEED
RALLIED
RAMBLED
RANCHED
RANKLED
RASSLED
RATTLED
RAVAGED
RAVELED
RAVENED
RAYMOND
RAZORED
SADDLED
SAINTED
SALLIED
SALUTED
SAMBAED
SAMOYED
SAMPLED
SANFORD
SAUTEED
SAVAGED
SAVORED
SAWWOOD
TABLOID
TACKLED
TAILEND
TAINTED
TALLIED
TALONED
TANGLED
TANGOED
TANKARD
TAPERED
TARRIED
TATTLED
TAUNTED
VACATED
VAULTED
VAUNTED
WADDLED
WAFFLED
WAGERED
WAGGLED
WAISTED
WAKENED
WALTZED
WAMBLED
WANGLED
WARBLED
WARLORD
WATCHED
WATERED
WAVERED
WAYLAID
WAYWARD
YACHTED

••AD•••

ACADEME
ACADEMY
ACADIAN
ALADDIN
AMADEUS
ANADEMS
BEADIER
BEADING
BEADLES
BEADSUP
BLADDER
BRADLEE
BRADLEY
CRADLED
CRADLES
DEADAIR
DEADEND
DEADENS
DEADEYE
DEADPAN
DEADSEA
DEADSET
DIADEMS
EVADERS
EVADING
GLADDEN
GLADDER
GLADEYE
GOADING
GRADERS
GRADING
GRADUAL
HEADERS
HEADIER
HEADILY
HEADING
HEADMAN
HEADMEN
HEADOFF
HEADOUT
HEADPIN
HEADSET
HEADSIN
HEADSUP
HEADWAY
INADAZE
ISADORA
LEADERS
LEADING
LEADINS
LEADOFF
LEADOUT
LEADSIN
LEADSON
LEADSTO
LEADSUP
LOADERS
LOADING
MEADOWS
MEADOWY
OBADIAH
ONADARE
ONADATE
ONADIET
READERS
READIED
READIER
READIES
READILY
READING
READMIT
READOUT
READSIN
ROADBED
ROADHOG
ROADIES
ROADMAP
ROADWAY
SEADOGS
SEADUTY
SHADIER
SHADILY
SHADING
SHADOOF
SHADOWS
SHADOWY
SPADERS
SPADING
STADIUM
SWADDLE
TOADIED
TOADIES
TRADEIN
TRADEON
TRADERS
TRADEUP
TRADING
TRADUCE
TWADDLE
VIADUCT

••A•D••

ABANDON
ALADDIN
AWARDED
AWARDEE
AWARDER
BEARDED
BLADDER
BLANDER
BLANDLY
BOARDED
BOARDER
BRAIDED
BRAIDER
BRANDED
BRANDER
BRANDON
BYANDBY
CLAUDIA
CLAUDIO
CRAWDAD
CZARDAS
CZARDOM
EVANDER
FLAGDAY
GLADDEN
GLADDER
GRANDAM
GRANDEE
GRANDER
GRANDLY
GRANDMA
GRANDPA
GUARDED
HEARDOF
HOARDED
HOARDER
LEANDER
MEANDER
ONANDON
PHAEDRA
PLAUDIT
PLAYDOH
PSANDQS
REARDON
RUANDAN
RWANDAN
SCALDED
SCANDAL
SHAHDOM
SLANDER
SOANDSO
SPANDEX
STAIDER
STAIDLY
STANDBY
STANDEE
STANDIN
STANDON
STANDUP
STARDOM
SWADDLE
TWADDLE
UGANDAN
UNAIDED
WHAUDEN
WYANDOT

••A••D•

ACARIDS
ALAMEDA
ALAMODE
BRAVADO
CHARADE
ELAPIDS
GRANADA
OCANADA
PEABODY
PEAPODS
PLACIDO
SEABEDS
SEASIDE
TRAGEDY

••A•••D

ABASHED
ADAPTED
ALARMED
AMASSED
AVAILED
AWAITED
AWARDED
BEACHED
BEARDED
BIASSED
BLABBED
BLACKED
BLANKED
BLASTED
BLATTED
BOARDED
BOASTED
BRAGGED
BRAIDED
BRAINED
BRAISED
BRANDED
BRAWLED
CHAINED
CHAIRED
CHALKED
CHAMPED
CHANCED
CHANGED
CHANTED
CHAPPED
CHARGED
CHARMED
CHARRED
CHARTED
CHATTED
CLACKED
CLAIMED
CLAMMED
CLAMPED
CLANGED
CLANKED
CLAPPED
CLASHED
CLASPED
CLASSED
COACHED
COASTED
CRABBED
CRACKED
CRADLED
CRAFTED
CRAMMED
CRAMPED
CRANKED
CRASHED
CRAWDAD
CRAWLED
DEADEND
DIAMOND
DRAFTED
DRAGGED
DRAINED
DRATTED
DRAWLED
DWARFED
ELAPSED
ENABLED
ENACTED
EXACTED
EXALTED
FEASTED
FLACCID
FLAGGED
FLAILED
FLAMBED
FLANKED
FLAPPED
FLASHED
FLATBED
FLATTED
FRANKED
GLACEED
GLANCED
GLASSED
GNARLED
GNARRED
GNASHED
GOAHEAD
GOATEED
GRABBED
GRAFTED
GRAINED
GRANTED
GRAPHED
GRASPED
GRASSED
GUARDED
HOARDED
INAWORD
LEACHED
LEARNED
LEASHED
LIAISED
LOATHED
NUANCED
PEACHED
PEARLED
PLACARD
PLAGUED
PLAITED
PLANKED
PLANNED
PLANTED
PLASHED
POACHED
PRAISED
PRANCED
PRANKED
PSALMED
QUACKED
QUAFFED
QUAILED
QUASHED
REACHED
REACTED
READIED
REAIRED
REAREND
REARMED
ROACHED
ROADBED
ROASTED
SCALDED
SCALPED
SCAMMED
SCAMPED
SCANNED
SCANTED
SCARFED
SCARPED
SCARRED
SCATHED
SCATTED
SEABIRD
SEAFOOD
SEAWARD
SEAWEED
SHAFTED
SHAGGED
SHAMMED
SHANKED
SHARPED
SLABBED
SLACKED
SLAMMED
SLANTED
SLAPPED
SLASHED

SLATTED
SMACKED
SMARTED
SMASHED
SNACKED
SNAFUED
SNAGGED
SNAPPED
SNARLED
SPALLED
SPANKED
SPANNED
SPARGED
SPARKED
SPARRED
SPATTED
SPAWNED
STABBED
STABLED
STACKED
STAFFED
STAGGED
STAINED
STALKED
STALLED
STAMPED
STAPLED
STARRED
STARTED
STARVED
STASHED
SWABBED
SWAMPED
SWAPPED
SWARMED
SWATHED
SWATTED
THANKED
TOADIED
TOASTED
TRACKED
TRAILED
TRAINED
TRAMPED
TRAPPED
TRASHED
TRAWLED
TWANGED
UNAIDED
UNAIMED
UNAIRED
UNARMED
UNASKED
WEARIED
WHACKED
WHAMMED
WHARFED
WRACKED
WRAPPED
YEAREND
YEARNED
ZEALAND

•••AD••

ABRADED
ABRADES
AHEADOF
ALMADEN
AMRADIO
ARCADES
ARCADIA
ARIADNE
ARMADAS
AUBADES
BREADED
BREADTH
BROADAX
BROADEN
BROADER
BROADLY
CBRADIO
CELADON
CICADAE
CICADAS
CITADEL
DECADES
DREADED
ECUADOR
FACADES
FARADAY
FMRADIO
GELADAS
INVADED
INVADER
INVADES
KNEADED
KNEADER
MACADAM
MATADOR
MIKADOS
MIRADOR
NAIADES
NEVADAN
NOMADIC
PALADIN
PAPADOC
PARADED
PARADES
PARADOX
PICADOR
PLEADED
PLEADER
POMADED
POMADES
POSADAS
RAMADAN
RAMADAS
SALADIN
TIRADES
TREADED
TREADER
TREADLE
UNLADES

•••A•D•

BACARDI
BRIARDS
CANARDS
COWARDS
DEMANDS
EDWARDS
ENGARDE
ERRANDS
EXPANDS
GERALDO
HAZARDS
HERALDS
HOWARDS
IDCARDS
INNARDS
INWARDS
ISLANDS
LIZARDS
MARAUDS
MIRANDA
NOCANDO
ONWARDS
ORGANDY
ORLANDO
ORMANDY
PETARDS
REGARDS
REMANDS
RESANDS
RETARDS
REWARDS
RIBANDS
RICARDO
ROBARDS
ROLAIDS
STRANDS
TABARDS
TOWARDS
UNHANDS
UNHANDY
UPLANDS
UPWARDS
VERANDA
VIVALDI
WCHANDY
WIZARDS

•••A••D

ABLATED
ABRADED
AERATED
ALLAYED
ANTACID
ARRAYED
ASHAMED
ASSAYED
AVIATED
BEHAVED
BELATED
BELAYED
BERATED
BLEARED
BLEATED
BLOATED
BREADED
CHEATED
CLEANED
CLEARED
CLEAVED
CLOAKED
CREAKED
CREAMED
CREASED
CREATED
CROAKED
DAMAGED
DEBASED
DEBATED
DECAPOD
DECAYED
DEFACED
DEFAMED
DELAYED
DILATED
DONATED
DREADED
DREAMED
EFFACED
ENCAGED
ENCASED
ENGAGED
ENLACED
ENRAGED
EQUALED
EQUATED
ESCAPED
ESSAYED
EXHALED
FIXATED
FLOATED
FORAGED
FREAKED
GALAHAD
GARAGED
GLEAMED
GLEANED
GLOATED
GREASED
GROANED
GYRATED
ICHABOD
IDEATED
IMPALED
INHALED
INVADED
INVALID
KAYAKED
KNEADED
LIEABED
LIGATED
LOCATED
LUXATED
MALAMUD
MANAGED
MEDALED
MENACED
MUTATED
NEGATED
NOTATED
OCEANID
PARADED
PEDALED
PETALED
PHRASED
PIRATED
PLEADED
PLEASED
PLEATED
POMADED
PYRAMID
RAVAGED
REBATED
RECANED
REDATED
REFACED
REGALED
RELACED
RELATED
RELAXED
RELAYED
RENAMED
REPAVED
RERATED
RETAPED
RETAXED
REWAXED
RIVALED
ROTATED
SAVAGED
SCRAPED
SHEARED
SHEAVED
SMEARED
SNEAKED
SOFABED
SPEARED
SPLAYED
SPRAYED
SQUALID
SQUARED
STEAMED
STRAFED
STRAYED
SUGARED
SWEATED
TOTALED
TREADED
TREATED
TWEAKED
UNBAKED
UNCAGED
UNCASED
UNDATED
UNFAZED
UNLACED
UNNAMED
UNPAVED
UNRATED
UNSATED
UNTAMED
UNTAPED
UPDATED
VACATED
VOYAGED
WREAKED

••••AD•

ALIDADE
ALREADY
AOUDADS
AVOCADO
BALLADE
BALLADS
BRAVADO
BRIGADE
BROCADE
BYROADS
CASCADE
CHARADE
COCKADE
COMRADE
CRUSADE
CRUZADO
DEGRADE
DOODADS
ENNEADS
ESTRADA
FORBADE
GRANADA
GRENADA
GRENADE
HEPTADS
INROADS
KEYPADS
LAMBADA
LIMEADE
MAENADS
MANMADE
MYRIADS
OCANADA
OGDOADS
PENTADS
PERVADE
REGRADE
RELOADS
REREADS
RETRADE
ROULADE
SPREADS
TETRADS
THREADS
THREADY
TORNADO
TOSTADA
UNLOADS
UNREADY
UPGRADE
UPLOADS
WANTADS

••••A•D

ABELARD
AIRRAID
APPLAUD
ARMBAND
ASHLAND
AWKWARD
AYNRAND
BALLARD
BANDAID
BARMAID
BARNARD
BERNARD
BIGBAND
BOMBARD
BRIGAND
BUSTARD
BUZZARD
COLLARD
COMMAND
CONGAED
COPLAND
COWHAND
CUECARD
CUSTARD
DABHAND
DASTARD
DEFRAUD
DIEHARD
DILLARD
DISBAND
DISCARD
DULLARD
EDOUARD
EMERALD
ENGLAND
FINLAND
FORWARD
FOULARD
FROWARD
GARLAND
GIZZARD
GODDARD
GOTLAND
HAGGARD
HALYARD
HARVARD
HAYWARD
HENNAED
HOLLAND
HUBBARD
HUSBAND
IBNSAUD
ICELAND
INBOARD
IRELAND
JUGBAND
JUTLAND
KEYCARD
KOOLAID
LAGGARD
LANYARD
LAPLAND
LEEWARD
LEONARD
LEOPARD
LEOTARD
LOMBARD
LOWLAND
LOWPAID
MALLARD
MANSARD
MAYNARD
MERMAID
MIDLAND
MILHAUD
MILLAND
MILLARD
MISLAID
MONTAND
MUSTARD
NAYSAID
NIGGARD
NORMAND
OAKLAND
OFFHAND
OLDHAND
OLDMAID
ONBOARD
ONGUARD
OPERAND
ORCHARD
OUTLAID
OUTLAND
OUTWARD
PACKARD
PEPPARD
PICCARD
PIEBALD
PLACARD
POLKAED
PONIARD
PREPAID
REHEARD
REYNARD
RICHARD
RIMBAUD
ROSTAND
RUDYARD
RUMBAED
SAMBAED
SEAWARD
SHEPARD
SKYWARD
STEWARD
SUNMAID
TANKARD
TOYLAND
TUSSAUD
UNHEARD
UPBRAID
WAYLAID
WAYWARD
WELLAND
WETLAND
WILLARD
WOODARD
ZEALAND

•••••AD

AIRHEAD
ARMLOAD
BAGHDAD
BIGHEAD
CARLOAD
CATHEAD
CRAWDAD
EGGHEAD
FATHEAD
FOOTPAD
GALAHAD
GOAHEAD
GOESBAD
HELIPAD
HOTHEAD
INSTEAD
JUGHEAD
KNEEPAD
LIKEMAD
LILYPAD
LIPREAD
LOWROAD
MISLEAD
MISREAD
NOTEPAD
OFFLOAD
OFFROAD
PAYLOAD
PINHEAD
PRELOAD
REDHEAD
RETREAD
SOLEDAD
SUBHEAD
TOWHEAD
WENTBAD

AE•••••

AEDILES
AELFRIC
AEOLIAN
AERATED
AERATES
AERATOR
AERIALS
AERIEST
AEROBAT
AEROBES
AEROBIC
AEROSOL

A•E••••

ABELARD
ABENAKI
ABETTED
ABETTOR
ACEDOUT
ACERBIC
ACEROLA
ACEROSE
ACESOUT
ACETATE
ACETONE
ADELINE
ADENINE
ADEPTLY
AGEISTS
AGELESS
AGENDAS
AGESAGO
AHEADOF
ALEMBIC
ALENCON
ALERTED
ALERTER
ALERTLY
ALEWIFE
AMENDED
AMENITY
AMERCED
AMERCES
AMERICA
AMERIGO
AMERIKA
AMERIND
ANEMONE
ANEROID
APELIKE
APERCUS
APERIES
AREARUG
AREAWAY
AREOLAE
AREOLAR
AREOLAS
ASEPSIS
ASEPTIC
ATECROW
ATELIER
AVENGED
AVENGER
AVENGES
AVENUES
AVERAGE
AVERRED
AVERTED
AWELESS
AWESOME
AYEAYES

A••E•••

ABREAST
ABSENCE
ABSENTS
ACCEDED
ACCEDER
ACCEDES
ACCENTS
ACCEPTS
ACHENES
ACHERON
ACHESON
ACREAGE
ACTEDUP
ADDEDIN
ADDEDON
ADDEDTO
ADDEDUP
ADDENDA
ADDENDS
ADHERED
ADHERES
ADRENAL
ADVENTS
ADVERBS
ADVERSE
ADVERTS
AFFECTS
AFREETS
AGREETO
AILERON
AIMEDAT
AIMEDTO
ALBEDOS
ALBENIZ
ALBERTA
ALBERTO
ALDENTE
ALGEBRA
ALGERIA
ALIENEE
ALIENOR
ALKENES
ALLEARS
ALLEGED
ALLEGER
ALLEGES
ALLEGRO
ALLELES
ALLENDE
ALLERGY
ALLEYES
ALREADY
ALTERED
ALTERER
ALVEOLI
AMHERST
AMMETER
AMNESIA
AMNESTY
AMOEBAE
AMOEBAS
AMOEBIC
AMPERES
ANAEMIA
ANDEANS
ANGELES
ANGELIC
ANGELOU
ANGELUS
ANGERED
ANNEALS
ANNELID
ANNETTE
ANNEXED
ANNEXES
ANTEDUP
ANTEING
ANTENNA
ANTESUP
APHELIA
APHESES
APLENTY
APPEALS
APPEARS
APPEASE
APPENDS
AQUEOUS
ARDENCY
ARIETTA
ARLEDGE
ARMENIA
ARREARS
ARRESTS
ARSENAL
ARSENIC
ARSENIO
ARTEMIS
ARTEMUS
ASCENDS
ASCENTS
ASCETIC
ASPECTS
ASPERSE
ASSEGAI
ASSENTS
ASSERTS
ATHEART
ATHEISM
ATHEIST
ATLEAST
ATPEACE
ATTEMPT
ATTENDS
ATTESTS
AUGENDS
AUREATE
AUREOLA
AUREOLE
AUTEURS
AZTECAN

A•••E••

ABIDEBY
ABILENE
ABOREAL
ABUSERS
ACADEME
ACADEMY
ACCRETE
ACHIEST
ACHIEVE
ACTAEON
ACTRESS
ACUTELY
ADDRESS
ADORERS
AERIEST
AFREETS
AGELESS
AGGRESS
AGILELY
AGREETO
AIGRETS
AILMENT
AIMLESS
AIRHEAD
AIRIEST
AIRLESS
ALAMEDA
ALAMEIN
ALCHEMY
ALFIERI
ALFREDO
ALGIERS
ALIMENT
ALLHEAL
ALLHERE
AMADEUS
AMATEUR
AMBIENT
AMBLERS
AMPLEST
AMULETS
ANADEMS
ANAHEIM
ANAPEST
ANCIENT
ANDREAS
ANDRESS
ANDREWS
ANGLERS
ANISEED
ANKLETS
ANSWERS
ANTAEUS
ANTBEAR
ANTHEMS
ANTHERS
ANTLERS
ANTWERP
ANXIETY
APOGEES
APTNESS
ARAMEAN
ARCHERS
ARCHERY
ARGUERS
ARIDEST
ARMLESS
ARMLETS
ARMREST
ARRIERE
ARTDECO
ARTIEST
ARTLESS
ASHIEST
ASHLESS
ATHLETE
AUGMENT
AUKLETS
AUSTERE
AVOCETS
AVOWERS
AWAKENS
AWAREOF
AWELESS
AZALEAS

A••••E•

ABASHED
ABASHES
ABDOMEN
ABETTED
ABJURED
ABJURES
ABLATED
ABLATES
ABORTED
ABRADED
ABRADES
ABUTTED
ABYSSES
ACCEDED
ACCEDER
ACCEDES
ACCRUED
ACCRUES
ACCUSED
ACCUSER
ACCUSES
ACHATES
ACHENES
ACTIVES
ADAPTED
ADAPTER
ADDUCED
ADDUCES
ADHERED
ADHERES
ADJURED
ADJURES
ADMIRED
ADMIRER
ADMIRES
ADMIXED
ADMIXES
ADOPTED
ADOPTEE
ADOPTER
ADORNED
ADVISED
ADVISER
ADVISES
AEDILES
AERATED
AERATES
AEROBES
AFFINES
AFFIXED
AFFIXES
AFRAMES
AGNATES
AIRCREW
AITCHES
ALARMED
ALARMER
ALBUMEN
ALCOVES
ALERTED
ALERTER
ALIASES
ALIENEE
ALIGNED
ALIGNER
ALKENES
ALLAYED
ALLAYER
ALLEGED
ALLEGER
ALLEGES
ALLELES
ALLEYES
ALLOVER
ALLOWED
ALLOYED
ALLUDED
ALLUDES
ALLURED
ALLURES
ALMADEN
ALTERED
ALTERER
ALUNSER
ALVAREZ
AMASSED
AMASSES
AMBRIES
AMENDED
AMERCED
AMERCES
AMMETER
AMPERES
AMPULES
ANDOVER
ANGELES
ANGERED
ANGRIER
ANISEED
ANNABEL
ANNALEE
ANNEXED
ANNEXES
ANNOYED
ANOTHER
ANTARES
ANTIBES
ANTIGEN
ANTSIER
APACHES
APERIES
APHESES
APOGEES
APOTHEM
APPAREL
APPLIED
APPLIES
APPOSED
APPOSES
APRONED
APSIDES
AQUIFER
AQUIVER
ARALSEA

ARBITER
ARBORED
ARCADES
ARCHIES
ARGIVES
ARGYLES
ARMORED
ARMORER
AROUSED
AROUSES
ARRASES
ARRAYED
ARRISES
ARRIVED
ARRIVER
ARRIVES
ASHAMED
ASPIRED
ASPIRER
ASPIRES
ASSAYED
ASSAYER
ASSIZES
ASSUMED
ASSUMES
ASSURED
ASSURES
ASUNDER
ATELIER
ATHOMES
ATLASES
ATOMIES
ATTIMES
ATTIRED
ATTIRES
ATTUNED
ATTUNES
AUBADES
AUDITED
AUGURED
AUNTIES
AURALEE
AUSSIES
AVAILED
AVENGED
AVENGER
AVENGES
AVENUES
AVERRED
AVERTED
AVIATED
AVIATES
AVOIDED
AVONLEA
AVULSED
AVULSES
AWAITED
AWARDED
AWARDEE
AWARDER
AYEAYES

A•••••E

AAMILNE
ABALONE
ABILENE
ABRIDGE
ABSENCE
ABSOLVE
ABUSIVE
ACADEME
ACCRETE
ACEROSE
ACETATE
ACETONE
ACHIEVE
ACOLYTE
ACONITE
ACQUIRE
ACREAGE
ACTABLE
ACTUATE
ADAMITE
ADDABLE
ADELINE
ADENINE
ADIPOSE
ADJUDGE
ADOLPHE
ADOPTEE
ADULATE
ADVANCE
ADVERSE
AFFABLE
AFFAIRE
AGITATE
AGONIZE
AGRAFFE
AIRBASE
AIRDATE
AIRFARE
AIRHOLE
AIRLANE
AIRLINE
AIRMILE
AIRTIME
AIRWAVE
ALAMODE
ALDENTE
ALEWIFE
ALIDADE
ALIENEE
ALLENDE
ALLGONE
ALLHERE
ALLOFME
ALLTIME
ALOHAOE
ALUMNAE
AMATIVE
AMBROSE
AMIABLE
AMIBLUE
AMOEBAE
AMPOULE
AMYLASE
ANALYSE
ANALYZE
ANATOLE
ANDANTE
ANEMONE
ANILINE
ANIMATE
ANNALEE
ANNETTE
ANODIZE
ANODYNE
ANTIQUE
ANTOINE
ANYMORE
ANYTIME
APATITE
APELIKE
APOCOPE
APOSTLE
APPEASE
APPRISE
APPRIZE
APPROVE
ARACHNE
ARCHIVE
ARCSINE
ARDMORE
AREOLAE
ARGONNE
ARIADNE
ARISTAE
ARLEDGE
ARMHOLE
ARMOIRE
ARRANGE
ARRIERE
ARTICLE
ARTISTE
ARTWARE
ASCRIBE
ASININE
ASKANCE
ASPERSE
ASSUAGE
ASTAIRE
ASTARTE
ASTRIDE
ATHLETE
ATINGLE
ATISSUE
ATLARGE
ATOMIZE
ATPEACE
ATSTAKE
ATTACHE
ATTRITE
AUDIBLE
AUGUSTE
AURALEE
AUREATE
AUREOLE
AURICLE
AURORAE
AUSPICE
AUSTERE
AVARICE
AVERAGE
AWARDEE
AWESOME
AXILLAE
AXLROSE
AZURITE

•AE••••

CAESARS
CAESURA
HAEMATO
JAEGERS
LAENNEC
LAERTES
MAENADS
MAESTRI
MAESTRO
MAEWEST

•A•E•••

BABETTE
BADEGGS
BAKEOFF
BALEENS
BALEFUL
BANEFUL
BARENTS
BARETTA
BASEHIT
BASEMAN
BASEMEN
BASENJI
BASEPAY
BATEAUX
BATEMAN
CADENCE
CADENZA
CADETTE
CAKEMIX
CALENDS
CAMELIA
CAMELOT
CAMEOED
CAMEOFF
CAMEOUT
CAMERAS
CAMERON
CAPEANN
CAPECOD
CAPELET
CAPELLA
CAPERED
CAREENS
CAREERS
CAREFOR
CAREFUL
CASELAW
CASERNS
CATENAE
CATERED
CATERER
CAVEART
CAVEATS
CAVEDIN
CAVEINS
CAVEMAN
CAVEMEN
CAVERNS
CAVESIN
CAYENNE
DANELAW
DARESAY
DARESTO
DATEDLY
DAZEDLY
EAGERER
EAGERLY
EASEDIN
EASEDUP
EASEOFF
EASESIN
EASESUP
EATENAT
EATENUP
FABERGE
FACEOFF
FACETED
FADEDIN
FADEINS
FADEOUT
FADESIN
FAGENDS
FAIENCE
FAKEFUR
FAREAST
FATEFUL
GAMELAW
GAMETES
GASEOUS
GATEAUX
GATELEG
GATEMAN
GATEMEN
GATEWAY
GAVELED
GAVEOFF
GAVEOUT
GAVEWAY
GAZEBOS
GAZELLE
GAZETTE
HAMELIN
HATEFUL
HAVENOT
JADEDLY
JADEITE
JAMESON
JANEDOE
JANEIRO
JANEWAY
JAVELIN
LABELED
LABELER
LABELLE
LACEDUP
LACESUP
LAMENTS
LAPELED
LATEENS
LATENCY
LATENTS
LATERAL
LATERAN
LATERON
LATEXES
LAVERNE
LAYERED
LAYETTE
LAZENBY
MADEFOR
MADEHAY
MADEIRA
MADEOFF
MADEOUT
MADEWAY
MAGENTA
MAJESTE
MAJESTY
MAJEURE
MAKEFOR
MAKEHAY
MAKEOFF
MAKEOUT
MAKEPAR
MAKESDO
MAKESIT
MAKESUP
MAKEUPS
MAKEWAY
MALEATE
MALEFIC
MANEGES
MATEWAN
NACELLE
NAKEDLY
NAMEDAY
NAMETAG
NANETTE
PACECAR
PAGEANT
PAGEBOY
PAGEFUL
PALEDRY
PALERMO
PALETTE
PANELED
PANETTA
PAPEETE
PAPERED
PAPERER
PARENTS
PATELLA
PATENTS
PATERNO
PAWEDAT
RACECAR
RACEMES
RACEWAY
RAKEDIN
RAKEDUP
RAKEOFF
RAKESIN
RAKESUP
RALEIGH
RAMEKIN
RAMESES
RAREBIT
RAREGAS
RAVELED
RAVENED
RAVENNA
SALERNO
SAMEDAY
SAVEDUP
SAVESUP
TAGENDS
TAKEAIM
TAKENIN
TAKENON
TAKEOFF
TAKEONE
TAKEOUT
TAKESIN
TAKESON
TAKESTO
TAKESUP
TAKETEN
TALENTS
TAPERED
TAVERNS
VALENCE
VALERIE
VANESSA
VANEYCK
WADESIN
WAGERED
WAGERER
WAKEFUL
WAKENED
WAKENER
WAKESUP
WATERED
WATERER
WAVEDIN
WAVELET
WAVEOFF
WAVERED
WAVERER
WAVESIN
ZAREBAS

•A••E••

BACKEND
BACKERS
BADGERS
BADNESS
BAGGERS
BAILEES
BAILERS
BAILEYS
BALDEST
BALEENS
BALLETS
BANKERS
BANNERS
BANTERS
BARBELL
BARBELS
BARBERS
BARGEIN
BARKEEP
BARKERS
BARLEYS
BARNEYS
BARRELS
BARRENS
BARRETT
BARTEND
BARTERS
BASKETS
BASSETS
BASTERS
BATHERS
BATTENS
BATTERS
BATTERY
BAWLERS
BAYLEAF
CABLERS
CABLETV
CACHETS
CADGERS
CAGIEST
CAHIERS
CALDERA
CALLERS
CALMEST
CALTECH
CALVERT
CAMBERS
CAMPERS
CANCELS
CANDELA
CANKERS
CANNERS
CANNERY
CANSECO
CANTEEN
CANTERS
CAPLESS
CAPLETS
CAPPERS
CARDERS
CAREENS
CAREERS
CARLESS
CARNERA
CARNETS
CARPERS
CARPETS
CARRELS
CARRERE
CARSEAT
CARTELS
CARTERS
CARVERS
CASHEWS
CASTERS
CATHEAD
CATSEYE
DAFTEST
DAGGERS
DAMPENS
DAMPERS
DAMPEST
DAMSELS
DANCERS
DANDERS
DANGERS
DANIELS
DANKEST
DANSEUR
DARKENS
DARKEST
DARLEEN
DARLENE
DARNERS
DARRELL
DARTERS
DASHERS
DAUBERS
DAYBEDS
EAGLETS
EARNERS
EARNEST
EASIEST
EASTEND
EASTERN
EASTERS
FAIREST
FALSELY
FALSEST
FALTERS
FALWELL
FANBELT
FANJETS
FARLEFT
FARMERS
FARWEST
FASTENS
FASTEST
FATHEAD
FATHERS
FATLESS
FATNESS
FATTENS
FATTEST
FAUCETS
FAWCETT
FAWNERS
GABBERS
GABFEST
GADGETS
GADGETY
GAFFERS
GAINERS
GAITERS
GALLEON
GALLERY
GALLEYS
GAMIEST
GANDERS
GANNETS
GANNETT
GARDENS
GARMENT
GARNERS
GARNETS
GARRETS
GARRETT
GARTERS
GASJETS
GASKETS
GASSERS
GATHERS
GAUDENS
GAUGERS
GAWKERS
HACKERS
HACKETT
HALTERS
HAMLETS
HAMMERS
HAMMETT
HAMPERS
HANGERS
HANKERS
HAPLESS
HAPPENS
HARDENS
HARDEST
HARKENS
HARNESS
HARPERS
HARVEST
HASBEEN
HASTENS
HATLESS
HATTERS
HAUBERK
HAULERS
HAUTEUR
HAWKERS
HAWKEYE
HAWSERS
HAYSEED
HAZIEST
JABBERS
JACKETS
JAEGERS
JAGLESS
JAILERS
JAMMERS
JAPHETH
JASPERS
JAYCEES
JAYLENO
JAYVEES
KAISERS
LAAGERS
LABRETS
LACIEST
LACKEYS
LACTEAL
LADDERS
LADLERS
LAGGERS
LAMBEAU
LAMBENT
LAMBERT
LANCERS
LANCETS
LANDERS
LANKEST
LANTERN
LAPBELT
LAPPETS
LARCENY
LARDERS
LARGELY
LARGESS
LARGEST
LASHERS
LATEENS
LATHERS
LATHERY
LATTENS
LAURELS
LAURENT
LAWLESS
LAWYERS
LAXNESS
LAZIEST
MACBETH
MACHETE
MADDENS
MADDERS
MADDEST
MADNESS
MAEWEST
MAGNETO
MAGNETS
MAGUEYS
MAIDENS
MAILERS
MALLETS
MALTEDS
MALTESE
MANDELA
MANGERS
MANNERS
MANTELS
MANYEAR
MAPPERS
MARCEAU
MARCELS
MARKERS
MARKETS
MARLENE
MARTENS
MARVELS
MASHERS
MASKERS
MASSEUR
MASTERS
MASTERY
MATHERS
MATHEWS
MATTERS
MAUREEN
MAXWELL
MAYHEMS
NABBERS
NAILERS
NAIVELY
NAIVETE
NANKEEN
NAPPERS
NASCENT
NATTERS
OAKFERN
OAKLEAF
OARLESS
OATMEAL
PACKERS
PACKETS
PADDERS
PALLETS
PALTERS
PAMPERS
PANDECT
PANDERS
PANNERS
PANZERS
PAPEETE
PARCELS
PARGETS
PARLEYS
PARNELL
PARSECS
PARSEES
PARSERS
PARVENU
PASSELS
PASSERS
PASSEUL
PASTELS
PASTERN
PASTEUP
PASTEUR
PATIENT
PATNESS
PATTENS
PATTERN
PATTERS
PAUPERS
PAWNEES
PAWNERS
PAYMENT
RABBETS
RACIEST
RACKETS
RAFTERS
RAGGEDY
RAGWEED
RAIDERS
RAILERS
RAIMENT
RAISERS
RAISEUP
RAMBEAU
RAMJETS
RANGERS
RANKERS
RANKEST
RANTERS
RAPIERS
RAPPELS
RAPPERS
RASHERS
RASHEST
RASPERS
RASTERS
RATTERS
RAWDEAL
RAWNESS
SACHEMS
SACHETS
SACKERS
SADDENS
SADDEST
SADNESS
SALIENT
SALIERI
SALTERS
SALVERS
SANDERS
SANREMO
SAPIENS
SAPIENT
SAPPERS
SARGENT
SASSERS
SATIETY
SAUCERS
SAUTEED
SAWYERS
TABLEAU
TABLETS
TACKERS
TAFFETA
TAILEND
TALKERS
TALLEST
TAMPERS
TANDEMS
TANGELO
TANGENT
TANGERE
TANKERS
TANNERS
TANNERY
TANNEST
TAPPERS
TAPPETS
TARBELL
TARGETS
TARHEEL
TARTEST
TASSELS
TASTERS
TATTERS
TAUTENS
TAUTEST
VAGUELY
VAGUEST
VAINEST
VALJEAN
VALLEYS
VAMPERS
VAQUERO
VARIETY
VARLETS
VASTEST
WAGGERY
WAILERS
WAITERS
WAIVERS
WALKERS
WALLETS
WALLEYE
WALTERS
WANDERS
WARDENS
WARDERS
WARIEST
WARMEST
WARRENS
WASHERS
WASTERS
WATTEAU
WAVIEST
WAXBEAN
WAXIEST
YAKKERS
YAMMERS
YANKEES
YAPPERS
YAWNERS
YAWPERS
ZAMBEZI
ZANDERS
ZANIEST
ZAPPERS

•A•••E•

BABBLED
BABBLES
BADDIES
BAFFLED
BAFFLER
BAFFLES
BAGGIER
BAGGIES
BAILEES
BALKIER
BALMIER
BALONEY
BANDIED
BANDIES
BANGLES
BANJOES
BANQUET
BANSHEE
BARKEEP
BARMIER
BARONET
BARRIER
BASEMEN
BASQUES
BATCHED
BATCHES
BATIKED
BATSMEN
BATTIER
BATTLED
BATTLER
BATTLES
BAUBLES
BAWDIER
BAYONET
CABARET
CABBIES
CABINET
CACKLED
CACKLER
CACKLES
CADDIED
CADDIES
CADUCEI
CAIQUES
CAJOLED
CAJOLER
CAJOLES
CALIBER
CALIPER
CALOMEL
CALUMET
CALYCES
CALYXES
CAMEOED
CAMISES
CAMPIER
CANAPES
CANDIED
CANDIES
CANDLES
CANINES
CANNIER
CANTEEN
CANTLES
CAPELET
CAPERED
CAPULET
CARAFES
CARAMEL
CARAVEL
CARGOES
CARIBES
CARNIES
CAROLED
CAROLER
CAROLES
CAROMED
CARRIED
CARRIER
CARRIES

CARTIER
CASHIER
CASTLED
CASTLES
CATCHER
CATCHES
CATERED
CATERER
CATTIER
CAULKED
CAULKER
CAVEMEN
CAVILED
CAVILER
CAYUSES
DABBLED
DABBLER
DABBLES
DADDIES
DAFFIER
DAHOMEY
DAILIES
DAIMLER
DAIRIES
DAISIES
DALLIED
DALLIER
DALLIES
DALTREY
DAMAGED
DAMAGES
DANDIER
DANDIES
DANDLED
DANDLES
DANGLED
DANGLER
DANGLES
DAPPLED
DAPPLES
DARLEEN
DATASET
DAUMIER
DAUNTED
DAWDLED
DAWDLER
DAWDLES
DAZZLED
DAZZLER
DAZZLES
EAGERER
EARLIER
EARTHEN
FABARES
FACADES
FACETED
FAGOTED
FAINTED
FAINTER
FAIRIES
FALAFEL
FANCIED
FANCIER
FANCIES
FARRIER
FARTHER
FAULTED
FAVORED
GABBIER
GABBLED
GABBLES
GABRIEL
GADSDEN
GAGGLES
GAGSTER
GALATEA
GALILEE
GALILEI
GALILEO
GAMBLED
GAMBLER
GAMBLES
GAMBREL
GAMETES
GAMINES
GANGLED
GANTLET
GARAGED
GARAGES
GARBLED
GARBLES
GARDNER
GARGLED
GARGLES
GATELEG
GATEMEN
GAUCHER
GAUDIER
GAUNTER
GAUZIER
GAVELED
GAWKIER
HAARLEM
HABITED
HACKIES
HACKLES
HACKNEY
HAGGLED
HAGGLER
HAGGLES
HAIRIER
HAIRNET
HALITES
HALOGEN
HAMITES
HAMSTER
HANDIER
HANDLED
HANDLER
HANDLES
HANDSET
HANGMEN
HANGTEN
HANKIES
HANOVER
HAPPIER
HARDIER
HARDSET
HARPIES
HARRIED
HARRIER
HARRIES
HARRIET
HARSHEN
HARSHER
HASBEEN
HASSLED
HASSLES
HASTIER
HATCHED
HATCHER
HATCHES
HATCHET
HAUNTED
HAYSEED
JACONET
JACQUES
JANACEK
JANGLED
JANGLES
JANSSEN
JANTZEN
JANVIER
JAUNTED
JAYCEES
JAYVEES
JAZZIER
JAZZMEN
KAISHEK
KARASEA
KAYAKED
KAYAKER
LABELED
LABELER
LABORED
LABORER
LACQUER
LADDIES
LAENNEC
LAERTES
LAISSEZ
LALAKER
LAMPREY
LANGLEY
LANKIER
LAPELED
LARCHES
LARDNER
LASSIES
LASSOED
LASSOER
LASSOES
LATCHED
LATCHES
LATEXES
LATICES
LAUGHED
LAUGHER
LAUNDER
LAUTREC
LAYERED
LAYOVER
MADAMEX
MADCHEN
MAGPIES
MAHONEY
MAIGRET
MAITRED
MAJORED
MALAREN
MALMSEY
MAMBOED
MANAGED
MANAGER
MANAGES
MANATEE
MANDREL
MANEGES
MANFRED
MANGIER
MANGLED
MANGLES
MANGOES
MANLIER
MANTLED
MANTLES
MANXMEN
MARBLED
MARBLES
MARCHED
MARCHEN
MARCHER
MARCHES
MARGRET
MARINER
MARINES
MARQUEE
MARQUES
MARQUEZ
MARRIED
MARRIES
MARSHES
MASHIES
MASQUES
MATCHED
MATCHES
MATINEE
MATTHEW
MATURED
MATURER
MATURES
MAUNDER
MAUREEN
MAXBAER
NAIADES
NAILSET
NANKEEN
NANNIES
NARTHEX
NASTIER
NATCHEZ
NATIVES
NATTIER
NATURED
NATURES
OAKTREE
PADDIES
PADDLED
PADDLER
PADDLES
PAINTED
PAINTER
PAISLEY
PAIUTES
PALACES
PALATES
PALAVER
PALFREY
PALJOEY
PALMIER
PAMBIES
PANACEA
PANELED
PANNIER
PANSIES
PANTHER
PAPERED
PAPERER
PARADED
PARADES
PARAPET
PARCHED
PARCHES
PARDNER
PAROLED
PAROLEE
PAROLES
PARQUET
PARRIED
PARRIES
PARSEES
PARSLEY
PARTIED
PARTIES
PARTNER
PARURES
PASSKEY
PASTIER
PATAKES
PATCHED
PATCHES
PATSIES
PATTIES
PAULSEN
PAVANES
PAWNEES
RABBLES
RACEMES
RACQUET
RADAMES
RADDLED
RADDLES
RADICES
RADIOED
RAFFLED
RAFFLER
RAFFLES
RAGGIER
RAGWEED
RAINIER
RALLIED
RALLIES
RAMBLED
RAMBLER
RAMBLES
RAMESES
RANCHED
RANCHER
RANCHES
RANDIER
RANGIER
RANKLED
RANKLES
RANOVER
RAPHAEL
RAPIDER
RAPINES
RASPIER
RASSLED
RASSLES
RATCHET
RATITES
RATTIER
RATTLED
RATTLER
RATTLES
RAVAGED
RAVAGES
RAVELED
RAVENED
RAVINES
RAZORED
SABINES
SADDLED
SADDLER
SADDLES
SAGGIER
SAINTED
SALLIED
SALLIES
SALTIER
SALUTED
SALUTES
SALVOES
SAMBAED
SAMISEN
SAMITES
SAMOYED
SAMPLED
SAMPLER
SAMPLES
SANDIER
SANDMEN
SANIBEL
SAPPIER
SARACEN
SARALEE
SARAZEN
SASSIER
SASSIES
SATCHEL
SATIRES
SAUCIER
SAUNTER
SAUTEED
SAVAGED
SAVAGER
SAVAGES
SAVORED
SAVVIER
SAYWHEN
TABBIES
TABORET
TACKIER
TACKLED
TACKLER
TACKLES
TAFFIES
TAILLES
TAINTED
TAKETEN
TALKIES
TALLIED
TALLIES
TALONED
TALUSES
TAMALES
TANAGER
TANGIER
TANGLED
TANGLES
TANGOED
TANSIES
TAPERED
TAPSTER
TARDIER
TARHEEL
TARRIED
TARRIES
TARSIER
TASTIER
TATTIER
TATTLED
TATTLER
TATTLES
TAUNTED
TAWNIER
TAXFREE
VACATED
VACATES
VALISES
VAULTED
VAULTER
VAUNTED
VAUNTER
WACKIER
WADDLED
WADDLER
WADDLES
WAFFLED
WAFFLER
WAFFLES
WAGERED
WAGERER
WAGGLED
WAGGLES
WAGONER
WAHINES
WAISTED
WAKENED
WAKENER
WALTZED
WALTZER
WALTZES
WAMBLED
WAMBLES
WANGLED
WANGLER
WANGLES
WARBLED
WARBLER
WARBLES
WASTREL
WATCHED
WATCHER
WATCHES
WATERED
WATERER
WATTLES
WAVELET
WAVERED
WAVERER
YACHTED
YAHTZEE
YANKEES
YARDMEN
ZAPOTEC
ZATOPEK

•A••••E

AAMILNE
BABBAGE
BABETTE
BACKHOE
BAGGAGE
BAGPIPE
BALANCE
BALLADE
BANDAGE
BANSHEE
BAPTIZE
BARCODE
BAROQUE
BARRAGE
BATISTE
BAUXITE
CABBAGE
CABOOSE
CADENCE
CADETTE
CALCITE
CALIBRE
CALORIE
CALZONE
CAMILLE
CANDICE
CANDIDE
CANZONE
CAPABLE
CAPAPIE
CAPRICE
CAPSIZE
CAPSULE
CAPTIVE
CAPTURE
CARBIDE
CARBINE
CARFARE
CARLYLE
CARMINE
CAROUSE
CARRERE
CARTAGE
CASCADE
CASTILE
CATENAE
CATHODE
CATLIKE
CATSEYE
CAYENNE
DARKAGE
DARLENE
DAYCARE
DAYTIME
EARACHE
EARLOBE
EATABLE
FABERGE
FAIENCE
FAILURE
FANFARE
FANZINE
FARGONE
FASTONE
FATIGUE
GAGLINE
GAGRULE
GALILEE
GARBAGE
GARONNE
GAVOTTE
GAZELLE
GAZETTE
HABITUE
HAIRDYE
HAULAGE
HAWKEYE
HAYRIDE
HAYWIRE
JACCUSE
JADEITE
JANEDOE
JASMINE
JAWBONE
JAWLINE
JAZZAGE
KARAOKE
LABELLE
LABIATE
LACOSTE
LACTASE
LACTATE
LACTOSE
LACUNAE
LAFARGE
LAFITTE
LALANNE
LALIQUE
LAMINAE
LAPLACE
LAPORTE
LAPROBE
LARAINE
LARAMIE
LAROCHE
LASAGNE
LASALLE
LATTICE
LAVALSE
LAVERNE
LAYETTE
MACABRE
MACAQUE
MACHETE
MACHINE
MACRAME
MACULAE
MAGNATE
MAJESTE
MAJEURE
MALAISE
MALEATE
MALTESE
MALTOSE
MANACLE
MANATEE
MANDATE
MANHOLE
MANIPLE
MANMADE
MARGATE
MARLENE
MARLOWE
MARQUEE
MARRYME
MASSAGE
MASSIVE
MATINEE
MATISSE
MAURICE
MAYPOLE
MAYTIME
MAYWINE
NACELLE
NAIVETE
NANETTE
NAPTIME
NARRATE
NASTASE
NATALIE
NAVARRE
OAKTREE
PACKAGE
PACKICE
PADRONE
PALANCE
PALETTE
PALMATE
PANACHE
PANCAKE
PANICLE
PANPIPE
PANURGE
PAPEETE
PAPOOSE
PARABLE
PAROLEE
PARTAKE
PARTITE
PASSAGE
PASSIVE
PASTDUE
PASTIME
PASTURE
PATRICE
PAULINE
PAYABLE
RADIATE
RADICLE
RAGTIME
RAMPAGE
RANLATE
RAPTURE
RATABLE
RATHOLE
RATLINE
RATRACE
RAWHIDE
SALABLE
SALTINE
SALVAGE
SANJOSE
SANTAFE
SAOTOME
SARALEE
SARDINE
SATIATE
SAUSAGE
SAVABLE
TACTILE
TADPOLE
TAGLINE
TAGSALE
TAKEONE
TAMABLE
TANGERE
TANLINE
TARTARE
TAURINE
TAXABLE
TAXFREE
TAXRATE
VACCINE
VACUOLE
VALANCE
VALENCE
VALERIE
VALUATE
VAMOOSE
VAMPIRE
VANDINE
VANDYKE
VANTAGE
WALLACE
WALLEYE
WALPOLE
WANNABE
WARFARE
WARGAME
WARLIKE
WARTIME
WASTAGE
WATTAGE
WAYSIDE
YAHTZEE
YANGTZE
YAOUNDE
YARDAGE

••AE•••

ANAEMIA
PHAEDRA
PHAETON
PRAETOR

••A•E••

ACADEME
ACADEMY
ALAMEDA
ALAMEIN
AMADEUS
AMATEUR
ANADEMS
ANAHEIM
ANAPEST
ARAMEAN
AWAKENS
AWAREOF
AZALEAS
BEAKERS
BEANERY
BEARERS
BEATERS
BEAVERS
BLAZERS
BOATERS
BRACERS
BRACEUP
BRAVELY
BRAVERY
BRAVEST
BRAYERS
CHALETS
CHAPEAU
CHAPELS
CHASERS
CHATEAU
CLARETS
CLAVELL
CLAWERS
COALERS
COAXERS
CRATERS
CRAVENS
CRAVERS
DEADEND
DEADENS
DEADEYE
DEAFENS
DEAFEST
DEALERS
DEAREST
DIADEMS
DIALECT
DIALERS
DIAPERS
DRAPERS
DRAPERY
DRAWERS
ELATERS
ENAMELS
ERASERS
ETAGERE
EVADERS
FEARERS
FLAKERS
FLANEUR
FLAREUP
FRAMEUP
GLACEED
GLADEYE
GLAZERS
GNAWERS
GOAHEAD
GOATEED
GOATEES
GRADERS
GRATERS
GRAVELS
GRAVELY
GRAVEST
GRAYEST
GRAZERS
HEADERS
HEALERS
HEARERS
HEATERS
HEAVEHO
HEAVENS
HEAVERS
HEAVETO
HIALEAH
HOAXERS
IMAGERS
IMAGERY
IMARETS
INAHEAP
INAMESS
INANELY
INANEST
INAWEOF
IPANEMA
IRATELY
IRATEST
KNAVERY
KRATERS
LAAGERS
LEADERS
LEAKERS
LEANERS
LEANEST
LEAPERS
LEASERS
LEAVENS
LOADERS
LOAFERS
LOANERS
MEANEST
MOANERS
NEAREST
NEATENS
NEATEST
ONAGERS
ONATEAR
PEABEAN
PEAHENS
PEAVEYS
PHASEIN
PHASERS
PLACEBO
PLACERS
PLANERS
PLANETS
PLATEAU
PLATENS
PLATERS
PLAYERS
PRATERS
PRAYERS
QUAKERS
QUAVERS
QUAVERY
READERS
REAGENT
REAMERS
REAPERS
REAREND
REARERS
ROAMERS
ROARERS
SCALENE
SCALERS
SCARERS
SCAREUP
SEABEDS
SEABEES
SEALEGS
SEALERS
SEATERS
SEAWEED
SHAKERS
SHAKEUP
SHAPELY
SHAPERS
SHAPEUP
SHAREIN
SHARERS
SHAVERS
SIAMESE
SKATERS
SLAVERS
SLAVERY
SLAYERS
SOAKERS
SOAPERS
SOARERS
SPACERS
SPADERS
SPARELY
SPAREST
STAGERS
STALEST
STAMENS
STAREAT
STARERS
STARETS
STATELY
SUAVELY
SUAVEST
SWAYERS
TEALEAF
TEASELS
TEASERS
TEASETS
THALERS
TRABERT
TRACERS
TRACERY
TRADEIN
TRADEON
TRADERS
TRADEUP
TRAGEDY
TRAPEZE
TRAVELS
TRAVERS
TUAREGS
WEAKENS
WEAKEST
WEARERS
WEASELS
WEAVERS
WHALERS
YEAREND
YEATEAM

••A••E•

ABASHED
ABASHES
ADAPTED
ADAPTER
ALARMED
ALARMER
AMASSED
AMASSES
APACHES
ARALSEA
AVAILED
AWAITED

AWARDED
AWARDEE
AWARDER
BEACHED
BEACHES
BEADIER
BEADLES
BEAGLES
BEAMIER
BEANIES
BEARDED
BEATLES
BIALIES
BIASSED
BLABBED
BLABBER
BLACKED
BLACKEN
BLACKER
BLADDER
BLANDER
BLANKED
BLANKER
BLANKET
BLARNEY
BLASTED
BLASTER
BLATHER
BLATTED
BOARDED
BOARDER
BOASTED
BOASTER
BOATMEN
BRACKEN
BRACKET
BRADLEE
BRADLEY
BRAGGED
BRAGGER
BRAIDED
BRAIDER
BRAINED
BRAISED
BRAISES
BRANDED
BRANDER
BRASHER
BRASSES
BRAVOES
BRAWLED
BRAWLER
BRAZIER
CHAINED
CHAIRED
CHAISES
CHALKED
CHAMBER
CHAMFER
CHAMPED
CHANCED
CHANCEL
CHANCES
CHANGED
CHANGER
CHANGES
CHANNEL
CHANTED
CHANTER
CHANTEY
CHAPLET
CHAPMEN
CHAPPED

CHAPTER
CHARGED
CHARGER
CHARGES
CHARIER
CHARLES
CHARLEY
CHARMED
CHARMER
CHARRED
CHARTED
CHARTER
CHASSES
CHASTEN
CHASTER
CHATTED
CHATTEL
CHATTER
CHAUCER
CLABBER
CLACKED
CLAIMED
CLAIMER
CLAMBER
CLAMMED
CLAMMER
CLAMPED
CLANGED
CLANKED
CLAPPED
CLAPPER
CLAQUES
CLASHED
CLASHES
CLASPED
CLASSED
CLASSES
CLATTER
CLAUSES
CLAVIER
CLAYIER
COACHED
COACHES
COARSEN
COARSER
COASTED
COASTER
CRABBED
CRABBER
CRACKED
CRACKER
CRADLED
CRADLES
CRAFTED
CRAFTER
CRAMMED
CRAMMER
CRAMPED
CRANKED
CRASHED
CRASHES
CRASSER
CRAWLED
CRAWLER
CRAZIER
CRAZIES
DEADSEA
DEADSET
DIARIES
DRABBER
DRAFTED
DRAFTEE
DRAGGED

DRAGNET
DRAINED
DRAINER
DRATTED
DRAWLED
DWARFED
DWARVES
EDASNER
ELAPSED
ELAPSES
EMANUEL
ENABLED
ENABLES
ENACTED
EPAULET
EVACUEE
EVANDER
EVANGEL
EXACTED
EXACTER
EXALTED
FEASTED
FEATHER
FIACRES
FIANCEE
FIANCES
FLAGGED
FLAGMEN
FLAILED
FLAKIER
FLAMBED
FLAMBES
FLANGES
FLANKED
FLANKER
FLANNEL
FLAPPED
FLAPPER
FLASHED
FLASHER
FLASHES
FLATBED
FLATTED
FLATTEN
FLATTER
FOAMIER
FRAILER
FRAISES
FRANCES
FRANKED
FRANKER
FRAPPES
FRASIER
FRAWLEY
FRAZIER
GLACEED
GLACIER
GLADDEN
GLADDER
GLANCED
GLANCES
GLASSED
GLASSES
GLAZIER
GNARLED
GNARRED
GNASHED
GNASHES
GOALIES
GOATEED
GOATEES
GRABBED
GRABBER

GRAFTED
GRAINED
GRAMMER
GRAMMES
GRANDEE
GRANDER
GRANGER
GRANGES
GRANTED
GRANTEE
GRAPHED
GRAPNEL
GRASPED
GRASSED
GRASSES
GRAVIES
GUARDED
HAARLEM
HEADIER
HEADMEN
HEADSET
HEARKEN
HEARTEN
HEATHEN
HEATHER
HEATTER
HEAVIER
HEAVIES
HOAGIES
HOARDED
HOARDER
HOARIER
HOARSEN
HOARSER
IMAGOES
INASTEW
LEACHED
LEACHES
LEAFIER
LEAFLET
LEAGUER
LEAGUES
LEAKIER
LEANDER
LEARJET
LEARNED
LEARNER
LEASHED
LEASHES
LEATHER
LIAISED
LIAISES
LOACHES
LOAMIER
LOATHED
LOATHES
MEALIER
MEALIES
MEANDER
MEANIES
MEASLES
MEATIER
NUANCED
NUANCES
ONADIET
OPAQUES
ORACLES
ORANGES
PEACHED
PEACHES
PEARLED
PIASTER
PLACKET

PLAGUED
PLAGUES
PLAICES
PLAINER
PLAINES
PLAITED
PLANKED
PLANNED
PLANNER
PLANTED
PLANTER
PLAQUES
PLASHED
PLASHES
PLASTER
PLATTER
PLAYLET
PLAYPEN
POACHED
POACHER
POACHES
PRAISED
PRAISER
PRAISES
PRANCED
PRANCER
PRANCES
PRANKED
PSALMED
PSALTER
QUACKED
QUAFFED
QUAFFER
QUAILED
QUARREL
QUARTER
QUARTET
QUASHED
QUASHES
REACHED
REACHES
REACTED
READIED
READIER
READIES
REAIRED
REARMED
ROACHED
ROACHES
ROADBED
ROADIES
ROASTED
ROASTER
SCALDED
SCALIER
SCALPED
SCALPEL
SCALPER
SCAMMED
SCAMPED
SCAMPER
SCANNED
SCANNER
SCANTED
SCANTER
SCARCER
SCARFED
SCARIER
SCARLET
SCARPED
SCARRED
SCARVES
SCATHED

SCATHES
SCATTED
SCATTER
SEABEES
SEAMIER
SEANCES
SEAWEED
SHADIER
SHAFFER
SHAFTED
SHAGGED
SHAKIER
SHAKOES
SHAMMED
SHANKED
SHANTER
SHARKEY
SHARPED
SHARPEI
SHARPEN
SHARPER
SHATNER
SHATTER
SHAWNEE
SLABBED
SLACKED
SLACKEN
SLACKER
SLAMMED
SLAMMER
SLANDER
SLANTED
SLAPPED
SLASHED
SLASHER
SLASHES
SLATHER
SLATIER
SLATTED
SMACKED
SMACKER
SMALLER
SMARTED
SMARTEN
SMARTER
SMASHED
SMASHER
SMASHES
SMATTER
SNACKED
SNACKER
SNAFUED
SNAGGED
SNAKIER
SNAPPED
SNAPPER
SNARLED
SOAPIER
SPACIER
SPALLED
SPANDEX
SPANIEL
SPANKED
SPANKER
SPANNED
SPANNER
SPARGED
SPARGES
SPARKED
SPARRED
SPARSER
SPATTED
SPATTER

SPAWNED
STABBED
STABLED
STABLER
STABLES
STACKED
STAFFED
STAFFER
STAGGED
STAGGER
STAGIER
STAIDER
STAINED
STAINER
STALKED
STALKER
STALLED
STAMMER
STAMPED
STANCES
STANDEE
STANLEE
STANLEY
STAPLED
STAPLER
STAPLES
STARKER
STARLET
STARRED
STARTED
STARTER
STARVED
STARVES
STASHED
STASHES
STASSEN
STATUES
SWABBED
SWAGGER
SWAMPED
SWANKER
SWAPPED
SWAPPER
SWARMED
SWATHED
SWATHES
SWATTED
SWATTER
TEACHER
TEACHES
TEARIER
THANKED
TOADIED
TOADIES
TOASTED
TOASTER
TRACHEA
TRACKED
TRACKER
TRAILED
TRAILER
TRAINED
TRAINEE
TRAINER
TRAMMEL
TRAMPED
TRANCES
TRAPPED
TRAPPER
TRASHED
TRASHES
TRAUBEL
TRAWLED

TRAWLER
TWANGED
UNAIDED
UNAIMED
UNAIRED
UNARMED
UNASKED
UPATREE
WEARIED
WEARIER
WEARIES
WEATHER
WHACKED
WHAMMED
WHARFED
WHARVES
WHAUDEN
WRACKED
WRAPPED
WRAPPER
YEARNED
YEARNER

••A•••E

ABALONE
ACADEME
ADAMITE
ALAMODE
AMATIVE
ANALYSE
ANALYZE
ANATOLE
APATITE
ARACHNE
AVARICE
AWARDEE
BEASTIE
BEATTIE
BLANCHE
BRADLEE
BRAILLE
BRAMBLE
BRASSIE
BYANOSE
CHALICE
CHARADE
CHARLIE
CLARICE
CRACKLE
CRAPPIE
DEADEYE
DRAFTEE
DRAYAGE
EGALITE
EMANATE
ERASURE
ETAGERE
ETAMINE
EVACUEE
EVASIVE
EXAMINE
EXAMPLE
FEATURE
FIANCEE
FRAGILE
FRAICHE
FRANKIE
FRAZZLE
GLADEYE
GRACILE
GRACKLE
GRAHAME
GRANDEE
GRANITE
GRANTEE
GRANULE
GRAPPLE
GRAVURE
GUANINE
HYALINE
IMAGINE
IMAMATE
INADAZE
IVANHOE
JEANNIE
LEAKAGE
MBABANE
MEASURE
ONADARE
ONADATE
OPALINE
PIASTRE
PLACATE
PRAIRIE
PRALINE
PRATTLE
REALIZE
REARGUE
ROANOKE
SCALENE
SEAGATE
SEALANE
SEASIDE
SEATTLE
SHACKLE
SHAMBLE
SHAWNEE
SIAMESE
SNAFFLE
SPACKLE
SPANGLE
SPARKLE
STABILE
STANDEE
STANLEE
STARTLE
STATICE
STATURE
STATUTE
SWADDLE
TEACAKE
TEAROSE
TEATIME
TRADUCE
TRAINEE
TRAIPSE
TRAMPLE
TRAPEZE
TWADDLE
ULALUME
UNALIKE
UNAVOCE
UNAWARE
UPATREE
URANITE
WRANGLE

•••AE••

ACTAEON
ANTAEUS
ISRAELI
PIRAEUS

•••A•E•

ABLATED
ABLATES
ABRADED
ABRADES
ACHATES
AERATED
AERATES
AFRAMES
AGNATES
ALIASES
ALLAYED
ALLAYER
ALMADEN
ALVAREZ
ANNABEL
ANNALEE
ANTARES
APPAREL
ARCADES
ARRASES
ARRAYED
ASHAMED
ASSAYED
ASSAYER
ATLASES
AUBADES
AURALEE
AVIATED
AVIATES
AYEAYES
BEHAVED
BEHAVES
BELATED
BELAYED
BERATED
BERATES
BETAKEN
BETAKES
BLEAKER
BLEARED
BLEATED
BLOATED
BORATES
BREADED
BREAKER
BROADEN
BROADER
CABARET
CANAPES
CARAFES
CARAMEL
CARAVEL
CHEAPEN
CHEAPER
CHEATED
CHEATER
CITADEL
CLEANED
CLEANER
CLEARED
CLEARER
CLEAVED
CLEAVER
CLEAVES
CLOAKED
CREAKED
CREAMED
CREAMER
CREASED
CREASES
CREATED
CREATES
CROAKED
CURATES
DAMAGED

DAMAGES
DATASET
DEBAKEY
DEBASED
DEBASES
DEBATED
DEBATER
DEBATES
DECADES
DECAYED
DEFACED
DEFACES
DEFAMED
DEFAMES
DELANEY
DELAYED
DELAYER
DILATED
DILATES
DONATED
DONATES
DOSAGES
DOWAGER
DREADED
DREAMED
DREAMER
EFFACED
EFFACES
EMPANEL
ENCAGED
ENCAGES
ENCASED
ENCASES
ENGAGED
ENGAGES
ENLACED
ENLACES
ENRAGED
ENRAGES
EQUALED
EQUATED
EQUATES
ESCAPED
ESCAPEE
ESCAPES
ESSAYED
ESTATES
EXHALED
EXHALES
FABARES
FACADES
FALAFEL
FEMALES
FINALES
FIXATED
FIXATES
FLOATED
FLOATER
FORAGED
FORAGER
FORAGES
FREAKED
GALATEA
GARAGED
GARAGES
GLEAMED
GLEANED
GLEANER
GLOATED
GREASED
GREASER
GREASES
GREATER

GREAVES
GROANED
GROANER
GYRATED
GYRATES
HYRACES
HYRAXES
ICEAGES
ICEAXES
IDEATED
IDEATES
IMPALED
IMPALES
IMPANEL
INHALED
INHALER
INHALES
INMATES
INTAKES
INVADED
INVADER
INVADES
IODATES
JANACEK
KARASEA
KAYAKED
KAYAKER
KILAUEA
KNEADED
KNEADER
LALAKER
LEGATEE
LEGATES
LIEABED
LIGATED
LIGATES
LINAGES
LOCALES
LOCATED
LOCATER
LOCATES
LUXATED
LUXATES
MADAMEX
MALAREN
MANAGED
MANAGER
MANAGES
MANATEE
MEDALED
MENACED
MENACES
MENAGES
METATES
MINARET
MIRAGES
MORALES
MUTAGEN
MUTATED
MUTATES
NAIADES
NEGATED
NEGATES
NEWAGER
NOGALES
NOTATED
NOTATES
OBLATES
OCTANES
OCTAVES
OLEATES
ONPAPER
OPIATES

OUTAGES
PALACES
PALATES
PALAVER
PANACEA
PARADED
PARADES
PARAPET
PATAKES
PAVANES
PDJAMES
PEDALED
PELAGES
PENATES
PETALED
PHRASED
PHRASES
PIRATED
PIRATES
PLEADED
PLEADER
PLEASED
PLEASER
PLEASES
PLEATED
POMADED
POMADES
POTAGES
PUTAMEN
RADAMES
RAVAGED
RAVAGES
REBATED
REBATES
RECANED
RECANES
REDATED
REDATES
REFACED
REFACES
REGALED
REGALES
RELACED
RELACES
RELATED
RELATES
RELAXED
RELAXES
RELAYED
REMAKES
RENAMED
RENAMES
REPAPER
REPAVED
REPAVES
RERATED
RERATES
RESALES
RETAKEN
RETAKES
RETAPED
RETAPES
RETAXED
RETAXES
REWAXED
REWAXES
RIVALED
ROTATED
ROTATES
SARACEN
SARALEE
SARAZEN
SAVAGED

SAVAGER
SAVAGES
SCRAPED
SCRAPER
SCRAPES
SEDATER
SENATES
SERAPES
SESAMES
SHEARED
SHEARER
SHEAVED
SHEAVES
SMEARED
SNEAKED
SNEAKER
SOFABED
SOLACES
SPEAKER
SPEARED
SPLAYED
SPRAYED
SPRAYER
SQUARED
SQUARER
SQUARES
STEAMED
STEAMER
STRAFED
STRAFES
STRAYED
SUGARED
SWEARER
SWEATED
SWEATER
TAMALES
TANAGER
TENACES
THEATER
TIRADES
TISANES
TOPAZES
TOTALED
TREADED
TREADER
TREATED
TWEAKED
UNBAKED
UNCAGED
UNCAGES
UNCASED
UNCASES
UNDATED
UNFAZED
UNLACED
UNLACES
UNLADES
UNMAKES
UNNAMED
UNPAVED
UNRATED
UNRAVEL
UNSATED
UNTAMED
UNTAPED
UPDATED
UPDATES
UPTAKES
URBANER
VACATED
VACATES
VISAGES
VOYAGED
VOYAGER
VOYAGES
WREAKED
ZOUAVES

•••A••E

ACTABLE
ADDABLE
ADVANCE
AFFABLE
AFFAIRE
AGRAFFE
AMIABLE
ANDANTE
ANNALEE
ARIADNE
ARRANGE
ASKANCE
ASTAIRE
ASTARTE
ATLARGE
ATTACHE
AURALEE
BALANCE
BECAUSE
BIVALVE
BIZARRE
BREATHE
BUYABLE
CAPABLE
CAPAPIE
CEZANNE
CHEAPIE
CICADAE
CITABLE
CLEANSE
DEBACLE
DEBARGE
DEFARGE
DEVALUE
DISABLE
DONAHUE
DURABLE
DURANCE
DURANTE
EARACHE
EATABLE
ENGARDE
ENHANCE
ENLARGE
ENMASSE
EQUABLE
ESCAPEE
EXPANSE
EXPARTE
FINAGLE
FINANCE
FIXABLE
FRIABLE
GIRAFFE
GOUACHE
HILAIRE
HIRABLE
IMPASSE
INHASTE
KARAOKE
LAFARGE
LALANNE
LARAINE
LARAMIE
LASAGNE
LASALLE
LAVALSE
LECARRE
LEGATEE
LEHAVRE
LIKABLE
LIVABLE
LOVABLE
MACABRE
MACAQUE
MALAISE
MANACLE
MANATEE
MELANGE
MELANIE
MINABLE
MIRACLE
MIXABLE
MORAINE
MOVABLE
MUTABLE
NATALIE
NAVARRE
NOTABLE
PALANCE
PANACHE
PARABLE
PAYABLE
PENANCE
PICANTE
PLIABLE
POTABLE
RATABLE
REBASTE
RELAPSE
REPASTE
RERAISE
REVALUE
ROMAINE
ROMANCE
ROSALIE
ROSANNE
ROXANNE
SALABLE
SARALEE
SAVABLE
SHEATHE
SIZABLE
STRANGE
STRASSE
SUSANNE
SUZANNE
SYNAPSE
TAMABLE
TAXABLE
TENABLE
THEATRE
TREACLE
TREADLE
UKRAINE
UPRAISE
USEABLE
VALANCE
WREATHE

••••AE•

CONGAED
HENNAED
ISHMAEL
MAXBAER
MICHAEL
POLKAED
RAPHAEL
RUMBAED
SAMBAED
SUNDAES

••••A•E

ACETATE
ACREAGE
ACTUATE
ADULATE
AGITATE
AIRBASE
AIRDATE
AIRFARE
AIRLANE
AIRWAVE
ALIDADE
ALOHAOE
AMYLASE
ANIMATE
APPEASE
ARTWARE
ASSUAGE
ATPEACE
ATSTAKE
AUREATE
AVERAGE
BABBAGE
BAGGAGE
BALLADE
BANDAGE
BARRAGE
BELDAME
BELTANE
BEREAVE
BIGGAME
BIGNAME
BIPLANE
BONDAGE
BRIGADE
BROCADE
BROMATE
BUSFARE
CABBAGE
CARFARE
CARTAGE
CASCADE
CHARADE
CHORALE
CILIATE
CITRATE
CLIMATE
COCKADE
COGNATE
COINAGE
COLGATE
COLLAGE
COLLATE
COMPARE
COMRADE
CONCAVE
CONGAME
CORDAGE
CORDATE
CORKAGE
CORSAGE
COTTAGE
COURAGE
CRUSADE
CUPCAKE
CUTRATE
DARKAGE
DAYCARE
DECLARE
DEFLATE
DEGRADE
DENTATE
DEPLANE
DEPRAVE
DEVIATE
DICTATE
DISEASE
DOCKAGE
DOGFACE
DRAYAGE
DUEDATE
EDUCATE
EGGCASE
ELEVATE
EMANATE
EMBRACE
EMIRATE
EMULATE
ENCLAVE
ENDGAME
ENGRAVE
ENPLANE
ENSLAVE
ENSNARE
EXPIATE
FANFARE
FERRATE
FOLIAGE
FOLIATE
FOOTAGE
FORBADE
FORGAVE
FORSAKE
FORSALE
FRIGATE
FROMAGE
FURNACE
GARBAGE
GERMANE
GESTATE
GOESAPE
GRAHAME
GRENADE
GRIMACE
GUNWALE
GUSTAVE
HAULAGE
HECTARE
HENBANE
HERBAGE
HOECAKE
HOSTAGE
HOTCAKE
HYDRATE
IMAMATE
IMITATE
INADAZE
INFLAME
INFLATE
INGRATE
INPEACE
INPHASE
INPLACE
INSCAPE
INSHAPE
INSTATE
IRONAGE
ISOLATE
ITERATE
JAZZAGE
KILDARE
LABIATE
LACTASE
LACTATE
LAPLACE
LEAKAGE
LIMEADE
LINEAGE
LINEATE
LINKAGE
LUGGAGE
MACRAME
MAGNATE
MALEATE
MANDATE
MANMADE
MARGATE
MASSAGE
MBABANE
MEDIATE
MESSAGE
METHANE
MIGRATE
MILEAGE
MISDATE
MISMATE
MISNAME
MISTAKE
MONDALE
MONTAGE
MONTANE
MOORAGE
MOULAGE
MUNDANE
NARRATE
NASTASE
NEONATE
NESCAFE
NEWGATE
NEWWAVE
NITRATE
OBVIATE
OFFBASE
OILCAKE
ONADARE
ONADATE
ONLEAVE
ONSTAGE
OPERATE
OUTFACE
OUTPACE
OUTRACE
OUTRAGE
OUTTAKE
OVERAGE
OVERATE
OVERAWE
OXIDASE
PACKAGE
PALMATE
PANCAKE
PARTAKE
PASSAGE
PEERAGE
PELTATE
PENNAME
PENNATE
PEONAGE
PERCALE
PERVADE
PETNAME
PICKAXE
PILLAGE
PINNACE
PINNATE
PINWALE
PLACATE
PLUMAGE
POLEAXE
PORTAGE
POSTAGE
POTTAGE
PREDATE
PREFACE
PRELATE
PREPARE
PRESAGE
PRESALE
PRETAPE
PRIMATE
PRIVATE
PROBATE
PROFANE
PROPANE
PRORATE
PULSATE
RADIATE
RAMPAGE
RANLATE
RATRACE
RECLAME
REDTAPE
REFRAME
REGRADE
RELEASE
REPLACE
REPLATE
RESCALE
RESTAGE
RESTATE
RETRACE
RETRADE
REWEAVE
RIBCAGE
ROSEATE
ROULADE
RUMMAGE
SALVAGE
SANTAFE
SATIATE
SAUSAGE
SEAGATE
SEALANE
SELVAGE
SENSATE
SERIATE
SERRATE
SINKAGE
SITUATE
SORBATE
SOUTANE
SPOKANE
STORAGE
STRIATE
SUCRASE
SULFATE
SURFACE
SURNAME
TAGSALE
TARTARE
TAXRATE
TEACAKE
TEENAGE
TERNATE
TERRACE
THEBABE
TILLAGE
TIMBALE
TITRATE
TONNAGE
TOSCALE
TOSPARE
TSQUARE
TWOBASE
ULULATE
UMBRAGE
UNAWARE
UNCRATE
UNDRAPE
UNWEAVE
UPGRADE
UPSCALE
UPSTAGE
UPSTATE
VALUATE
VANTAGE
VIBRATE
VILLAGE
VINTAGE
VIOLATE
VITIATE
VOLTAGE
VULGATE
WALLACE
WANNABE
WARFARE
WARGAME
WASTAGE
WATTAGE
WELFARE
WENTAPE
YARDAGE

•••••AE

ALUMNAE
AMOEBAE
AREOLAE
ARISTAE
AURORAE
AXILLAE
CATENAE
CICADAE
CORONAE
FIBULAE
GLOSSAE
LACUNAE
LAMINAE
MACULAE
MEDUSAE
NEBULAE
RETINAE
SHEILAE

AF•••••

AFFABLE
AFFABLY
AFFAIRE
AFFAIRS
AFFECTS
AFFINES
AFFIRMS
AFFIXED
AFFIXES
AFFLICT
AFFORDS
AFFRAYS
AFFRONT
AFGHANI
AFGHANS
AFRAMES
AFREETS
AFRICAN

A•F••••

AFFABLE
AFFABLY
AFFAIRE
AFFAIRS
AFFECTS
AFFINES
AFFIRMS
AFFIXED
AFFIXES
AFFLICT
AFFORDS
AFFRAYS
AFFRONT
ALFALFA
ALFIERI
ALFONSO
ALFREDO
ASFARAS
ATFAULT
AWFULLY

A••F•••

AELFRIC
AIRFARE
AIRFLOW
AIRFOIL
ANTFARM
ARMFULS
ARTFILM
ARTFORM
ASHFORD
ASOFNOW

A•••F••

AGRAFFE
ALLOFME
ALOOFLY
AQUIFER
ASKSFOR

A••••F•

ACIDIFY
AGRAFFE
AIRLIFT
ALEWIFE
ALFALFA
AMPLIFY

A•••••F

AHEADOF
AIRWOLF
AWAREOF

•AF••••

BAFFLED
BAFFLER
BAFFLES
CAFTANS
DAFFIER
DAFFILY
DAFTEST
GAFFERS
GAFFING
HAFNIUM
KAFTANS
LAFARGE
LAFITTE
MAFIOSO
RAFFISH
RAFFLED
RAFFLER
RAFFLES
RAFTERS
RAFTING
SAFARIS
SAFFRON
TAFFETA
TAFFIES
WAFFLED
WAFFLER
WAFFLES
WAFTING

•A•F•••

BAFFLED
BAFFLER
BAFFLES
BAGFULS
BALFOUR
CAPFULS
CARFARE
CARFULS
CATFISH
DAFFIER
DAFFILY
EARFLAP
EARFULS
FANFARE
GABFEST
GAFFERS
GAFFING
HALFDAN
HALFWAY
HALFWIT
HAYFORK
JARFULS
LANFORD
LAPFULS
LAWFORD
MANFRED
MAYFAIR
OAKFERN
PALFREY
PANFISH
PARFAIT
RAFFISH
RAFFLED
RAFFLER
RAFFLES
RATFINK
SAFFRON
SANFORD
SAWFISH
TAFFETA
TAFFIES
TAXFREE
VATFULS
WAFFLED
WAFFLER
WAFFLES
WARFARE

•A••F••

BALEFUL
BANEFUL
BASHFUL
CALLFOR
CARAFES
CAREFOR
CAREFUL
FAKEFUR
FALAFEL
FALLFOR
FATEFUL
GAINFUL
HALIFAX
HANDFUL
HARMFUL
HATEFUL
LAIDFOR
LATIFAH
LAYOFFS
LAYSFOR
MADEFOR
MAKEFOR
MALEFIC
PACIFIC
PAGEFUL
PAIDFOR
PAILFUL
PAINFUL
PASSFOR
PAYOFFS
PAYSFOR
RATAFIA
SACKFUL
SANDFLY
TACTFUL
TAILFIN
TANKFUL
TARIFFS
WAKEFUL

•A•••F•

BACKOFF
BAILIFF
BAKEOFF
CALCIFY
CALLOFF
CAMEOFF
CASTOFF
DASHOFF
EARMUFF
EASEOFF
FACEOFF
FAIROFF
FALLOFF
FALSIFY
FARLEFT
GAVEOFF
HANDOFF
HANGOFF
HAULOFF
HAYLOFT
KARLOFF
LAIDOFF
LAYOFFS
LAYSOFF
MACDUFF
MADEOFF
MAGNIFY
MAKEOFF
MARKOFF
MASSIFS
MASTIFF
PAIDOFF
PAIROFF
PALMOFF
PASSOFF
PAWNOFF
PAYOFFS
PAYSOFF
RAKEOFF
SALSIFY
SANTAFE
SATISFY
TAILOFF
TAKEOFF
TARIFFS
WARDOFF
WASHOFF
WAVEOFF

•A••••F

BACKOFF
BAILIFF
BAKEOFF
BARANOF
BAYLEAF
CALLOFF
CAMEOFF
CASTOFF
DASHOFF
EARMUFF
EASEOFF
FACEOFF
FAIROFF
FALLOFF
GAVEOFF
HANDOFF
HANGOFF
HAULOFF
KARLOFF
LAIDOFF
LAYSOFF
MACDUFF
MADEOFF
MAKEOFF
MARKOFF
MASTIFF
OAKLEAF
PAIDOFF
PAIROFF
PALMOFF
PASSOFF
PAWNOFF
PAYSOFF
RAKEOFF
TAILOFF
TAKEOFF
WALDORF
WARDOFF
WASHOFF
WAVEOFF

••AF•••

CHAFING
CRAFTED
CRAFTER
CRAFTSY
DEAFENS
DEAFEST
DRAFTED
DRAFTEE
GRAFTED
LEAFIER
LEAFING
LEAFLET
LOAFERS
LOAFING
PEAFOWL
QUAFFED
QUAFFER
REAFFIX
SEAFANS
SEAFOOD
SHAFFER
SHAFTED
SNAFFLE
SNAFUED
STAFFED
STAFFER
TRAFFIC

••A•F••

CHAMFER
DWARFED
FEARFUL
PLAYFUL
PRAYFOR
QUAFFED
QUAFFER
REAFFIX
SCARFED
SHAFFER
SNAFFLE
STAFFED
STAFFER
TEARFUL
TRAFFIC
TRAYFUL
WHARFED
WHATFOR

••A••F•

BEAROFF
BEATIFY
BRANIFF
CLARIFY
GRATIFY
HEADOFF
LEADOFF
PLAYOFF
QUALIFY
SCARIFY
SEALOFF
TEAROFF
WEAROFF

••A•••F

AWAREOF
BEAROFF
BRANIFF
HEADOFF
HEARDOF
HEARSOF
INAWEOF
LEADOFF
PLAYOFF
SEALOFF
SHADOOF
TEALEAF
TEAROFF
WEAROFF

•••AF••

AGRAFFE
CARAFES
FALAFEL
GIRAFFE
RATAFIA
STRAFED
STRAFES

•••A•F•

AGRAFFE
ALFALFA
GIRAFFE

•••A••F

AHEADOF
BARANOF
BYWAYOF
SPEAKOF

••••AF•
DISTAFF
ENGRAFT
MUSTAFA
NESCAFE
SANTAFE
UPDRAFT

••••A•F
DISTAFF

•••••AF
BAYLEAF
FIGLEAF
FLYLEAF
OAKLEAF
TEALEAF

AG•••••
AGAINST
AGAKHAN
AGASSIZ
AGEISTS
AGELESS
AGENDAS
AGESAGO
AGGRESS
AGILELY
AGILITY
AGITATE
AGNATES
AGONIST
AGONIZE
AGOUTIS
AGRAFFE
AGREETO
AGRIPPA
AGROUND

A•G••••
AFGHANI
AFGHANS
AGGRESS
AIGRETS
ALGEBRA
ALGERIA
ALGIERS
ANGELES
ANGELIC
ANGELOU
ANGELUS
ANGERED
ANGLERS
ANGLING
ANGOLAN
ANGORAS
ANGRIER
ANGRILY
ANGULAR
ARGIVES
ARGONNE
ARGUERS
ARGUING
ARGYLES
AUGENDS
AUGMENT
AUGURAL
AUGURED
AUGUSTA
AUGUSTE

A••G•••
ABIGAIL
ADAGIOS
AIRGUNS
ALIGHTS
ALIGNED
ALIGNER
ALLGONE
ANAGRAM
APOGEES
ARUGULA
AVIGNON

A•••G••
ALLEGED
ALLEGER
ALLEGES
ALLEGRO
ALRIGHT
AMALGAM
AMONGST
ANTIGEN
ANTIGUA
ASSEGAI
ASSIGNS
ATINGLE
AVENGED
AVENGER
AVENGES

A••••G•
ABRIDGE
ACREAGE
ADJUDGE
AGESAGO
AIRBAGS
AIRINGS
ALLERGY
AMERIGO
ANALOGS
ANALOGY
APOLOGY
ARLEDGE
ARRAIGN
ARRANGE
ASSUAGE
ATLARGE
AVERAGE
AWNINGS

A•••••G
ABASING
ABATING
ABIDING
ABUSING
ACHTUNG
ADDLING
ADORING
ALAKING
ALLYING
AMAZING
AMBLING
AMUSING
ANGLING
ANTEING
ANTILOG
ARCHING
AREARUG
ARGUING
ARISING
ARTSONG
ATONING
AVOWING
AWAKING

•AG••••
BAGFULS
BAGGAGE
BAGGERS
BAGGIER
BAGGIES
BAGGILY
BAGGING
BAGHDAD
BAGNOLD
BAGPIPE
CAGIEST
DAGGERS
DAGWOOD
EAGERER
EAGERLY
EAGLETS
EAGLING
FAGENDS
FAGGING
FAGOTED
GAGARIN
GAGGING
GAGGLES
GAGLINE
GAGRULE
GAGSTER
HAGGARD
HAGGLED
HAGGLER
HAGGLES
JAGGING
JAGLESS
JAGUARS
LAGGARD
LAGGERS
LAGGING
LAGOONS
LAGUNAS
MAGENTA
MAGICAL
MAGINOT
MAGNATE
MAGNETO
MAGNETS
MAGNIFY
MAGNUMS
MAGPIES
MAGUEYS
MAGYARS
NAGGING
PAGEANT
PAGEBOY
PAGEFUL
PAGODAS
RAGDOLL
RAGGEDY
RAGGIER
RAGGING
RAGLANS
RAGMOPS
RAGOUTS
RAGRUGS
RAGTIME
RAGTOPS
RAGWEED
SAGGIER
SAGGING
SAGINAW
SAGUARO
TAGALOG
TAGENDS
TAGGING
TAGLINE
TAGSALE
TAGSOUT
VAGRANT
VAGUELY
VAGUEST
WAGERED
WAGERER
WAGGERY
WAGGING
WAGGISH
WAGGLED
WAGGLES
WAGGONS
WAGONER
WAGTAIL
ZAGGING

•A•G•••
BADGERS
BADGUYS
BAGGAGE
BAGGERS
BAGGIER
BAGGIES
BAGGILY
BAGGING
BANGING
BANGKOK
BANGLES
BANGSUP
BARGAIN
BARGEIN
BARGING
CADGERS
CADGING
CALGARY
CAPGUNS
CARGOES
DAGGERS
DANGERS
DANGLED
DANGLER
DANGLES
FAGGING
FARGONE
GADGETS
GADGETY
GAGGING
GAGGLES
GANGING
GANGLED
GANGLIA
GANGSAW
GANGSTA
GANGSUP
GANGWAY
GARGLED
GARGLES
GAUGERS
GAUGING
GAUGUIN
HAGGARD
HAGGLED
HAGGLER
HAGGLES
HANGARS
HANGDOG
HANGERS
HANGING
HANGMAN
HANGMEN
HANGOFF
HANGOUT
HANGSIN
HANGSON
HANGSUP
HANGTEN
HANGUPS
HAUGHTY
JAEGERS
JAGGING
JANGLED
JANGLES
JARGONS
LAAGERS
LAGGARD
LAGGERS
LAGGING
LANGDON
LANGLEY
LANGTRY
LANGUID
LANGUOR
LANGURS
LARGELY
LARGESS
LARGEST
LAUGHAT
LAUGHED
LAUGHER
LAUGHIN
MACGRAW
MAIGRET
MANGERS
MANGIER
MANGLED
MANGLES
MANGOES
MARGATE
MARGAUX
MARGAYS
MARGINS
MARGRET
MAUGHAM
NAGGING
NAUGHTS
NAUGHTY
PARGETS
RAGGEDY
RAGGIER
RAGGING
RANGERS
RANGIER
RANGING
RANGOON
RAYGUNS
SAGGIER
SAGGING
SANGOUT
SANGRIA
SARGENT
TAGGING
TANGELO
TANGENT
TANGERE
TANGIER
TANGLED
TANGLES
TANGOED
TARGETS
VANGOGH
VAUGHAN
WAGGERY
WAGGING
WAGGISH
WAGGLED
WAGGLES
WAGGONS
WANGLED
WANGLER
WANGLES
WARGAME
WARGODS
YANGTZE
ZAGGING

•A••G••
BADEGGS
CAYUGAS
DAMAGED
DAMAGES
FALLGUY
FATIGUE
GARAGED
GARAGES
HALOGEN
HANDGUN
LASAGNA
LASAGNE
MALIGNS
MANAGED
MANAGER
MANAGES
MANAGUA
MANEGES
PAPAGOS
PARAGON
RAREGAS
RAVAGED
RAVAGES
SAVAGED
SAVAGER
SAVAGES
TANAGER

•A•••G•
BABBAGE
BADEGGS
BAGGAGE
BANDAGE
BARONGS
BARRAGE
CABBAGE
CARTAGE
CASINGS
DARKAGE
EARWIGS
FABERGE
FACINGS
FARRAGO
GARBAGE
GASBAGS
HAULAGE
HAZINGS
JAZZAGE
LACINGS
LAFARGE
LAPDOGS
MAKINGS
MASSAGE
PACKAGE
PANURGE
PARINGS
PASSAGE
RAGRUGS
RALEIGH
RAMPAGE
RATINGS
RAVINGS
SALVAGE
SAPSAGO
SARONGS
SAUSAGE
SAVINGS
SAWLOGS
SAYINGS
TAPINGS
VANGOGH
VANTAGE
WASTAGE
WATTAGE
YARDAGE

•A••••G
BABYING
BACKING
BACKLOG
BAGGING
BAILING
BAITING
BALDING
BALKING
BANDING
BANGING
BANKING
BANNING
BARBING
BARGING
BARKING
BARRING
BASHING
BASKING
BASTING
BATHING
BATTING
BATWING
BAWLING
CABLING
CACHING
CADGING
CALKING
CALLING
CALMING
CALVING
CAMPING
CANNING
CANTING
CAPPING
CARDING
CARPING
CARTING
CARVING
CASHING
CASTING
CATALOG
CATTING
CAUSING
DABBING
DAMMING
DAMNING
DAMPING
DANCING
DAPPING
DARLING
DARNING
DARTING
DASHING
DAUBING
DAWNING
DAYLONG
EAGLING
EARNING
EARPLUG
EARRING
FAGGING
FAILING
FAIRING
FALLING
FANNING
FARMING
FASTING
FAWNING
GABBING
GADDING
GAFFING
GAGGING
GAINING
GAITING
GALLING
GANGING
GAPPING
GARBING
GASHING
GASPING
GATELEG
GATLING
GAUGING
GAWKING
HACKING
HAILING
HALOING
HALTING
HALVING
HAMBURG
HAMMING
HANDBAG
HANDING
HANGDOG
HANGING
HARDING
HARKING
HARMING
HARPING
HASHING
HASTING
HATTING
HAULING
HAWKING
JABBING
JACKING
JAGGING
JAILING
JAMMING
JARRING
JAZZING
KAYOING
LACKING
LADLING
LADYBUG
LAGGING
LAMMING
LANDING
LANSING
LAPPING
LAPSING
LAPWING
LARDING
LASHING
LASTING
LATHING
LAUDING
MADDING
MAILBAG
MAILING
MALTING
MANNING
MAPPING
MARKING
MARRING
MASHING
MASKING
MASSING
MATTING
MAULING
NABBING
NAGGING
NAILING
NAMETAG
NAPPING
PACKING
PADDING
PAIRING
PALLING
PALMING
PANNING
PANTING
PARKING
PARRING
PARSING
PARTING
PASSING
PASTING
PATTING
PAULING
PAUSING
PAWNING
RACKING
RAFTING
RAGGING
RAIDING
RAILING
RAINING
RAISING
RAMMING
RANGING
RANKING
RANTING
RAPPING
RASPING
RATTING
RAZZING
SACKING
SAGGING
SAILING
SALTING
SALVING
SAMSUNG
SANDBAG
SANDHOG
SANDING
SAPLING
SAPPING
SASSING
TABBING
TABLING
TACKING
TAGALOG
TAGGING
TAILING
TALKBIG
TALKING
TAMPING
TANKING
TANNING
TAPPING
TARRING
TASKING
TASTING
TATTING
TAXIING
VALUING
VAMPING
VARYING
WADDING
WAFTING
WAGGING
WAILING
WAITING
WAIVING
WALKING
WALLING
WANTING
WARDING
WARMING
WARNING
WARPING
WARRING
WARTHOG
WASHING
WASHRAG
WASTING
WAXWING
YAKKING
YANKING
YAPPING
YARNING
YAWNING
ZAGGING
ZAPPING

••AG•••
ADAGIOS
ANAGRAM
BEAGLES
BRAGGED
BRAGGER
CHAGALL
CHAGRIN
DIAGRAM
DRAGGED
DRAGNET
DRAGONS
DRAGOON
DRAGOUT
DRAGSIN
DRAGSON
ETAGERE
FLAGDAY
FLAGGED
FLAGMAN
FLAGMEN
FLAGONS
FRAGILE
HOAGIES
IMAGERS
IMAGERY
IMAGINE
IMAGING
IMAGOES
LAAGERS
LEAGUER
LEAGUES
NIAGARA
ONAGERS
PLAGUED
PLAGUES
QUAGGAS
REAGENT
SEAGATE
SEAGIRT
SEAGRAM
SEAGULL
SHAGGED
SNAGGED
STAGERS
STAGGED
STAGGER
STAGIER
STAGILY
STAGING
SWAGGER
TRAGEDY

••A•G••
AMALGAM
BRAGGED
BRAGGER
CHANGED
CHANGER
CHANGES
CHARGED
CHARGER
CHARGES
CLANGED
CLANGOR
COALGAS
DRAGGED
DRAUGHT
EVANGEL
FLAGGED
FLANGES
FRAUGHT
GLASGOW
GRANGER
GRANGES
GUARGUM
ORANGES
QUAGGAS
REARGUE
SHAGGED
SHANGRI
SNAGGED
SPANGLE
SPANGLY
SPARGED
SPARGES
STAGGED
STAGGER
SWAGGER
TEARGAS
TWANGED
WRANGLE

••A••G•
ANALOGS
ANALOGY
DIALOGS
DRAYAGE
LEAKAGE
QUAHOGS
SEABAGS
SEADOGS
SEALEGS
STALAGS
TEABAGS
TUAREGS

••A•••G
ABASING
ABATING
ALAKING
AMAZING
AWAKING
BEADING
BEAMING
BEANBAG
BEANING
BEARHUG
BEARING
BEATING
BIASING
BLAMING
BLARING
BLAZING
BOATING
BRACING
BRAKING
BRAVING
BRAYING
BRAZING
CEASING
CHAFING
CHASING
CLAWING
COATING
COAXING
CRANING
CRATING
CRAVING
CRAZING
DEALING
DIALING
DRAPING
DRAWING
DRAYING
ELATING
ERASING
EVADING
FEARING
FLAKING
FLAMING
FLARING
FLAWING
FLAYING
FOALING
FOAMING
FRAMING
FRAYING
GEARING
GLARING
GLAZING
GNAWING
GOADING
GOALONG
GRABBAG
GRACING
GRADING
GRATING
GRAVING
GRAYING
GRAZING
HEADING
HEALING
HEAPING
HEARING
HEATING
HEAVING
HOAXING
IMAGING
LEADING
LEAFING
LEAKING
LEANING
LEAPING
LEASING
LEAVING
LOADING
LOAFING
LOAMING
LOANING
MEANING
MOANING
NEARING
OKAYING
ORATING
PEAKING
PEALING
PEATBOG
PHASING
PLACING
PLANING
PLATING
PLAYING
PRATING
PRAYING
QUAKING
READING
REAMING
REAPING
REARING
ROADHOG
ROAMING
ROARING
SCALING
SCARING
SEABORG
SEALING
SEAMING
SEARING
SEASLUG
SEATING
SHADING
SHAKING
SHAMING
SHAPING
SHARING
SHAVING
SKATING
SLAKING
SLATING
SLAVING
SNAKING
SNARING
SOAKING
SOAPING
SOARING
SPACING
SPADING
SPARING
SPAYING
STAGING
STAKING
STARING
STATING
STAVING
STAYING
SWAYING
TEAMING
TEARING
TEASING
THAWING
TRACING
TRADING
WEANING
WEARING
WEAVING
WHALING
XRATING
XRAYING

•••AG••

DAMAGED DAMAGES DECAGON DOSAGES DOWAGER ENCAGED ENCAGES ENGAGED ENGAGES ENRAGED ENRAGES FINAGLE FORAGED FORAGER FORAGES GARAGED GARAGES HEXAGON ICEAGES LASAGNA LASAGNE LINAGES MANAGED MANAGER MANAGES MANAGUA MENAGES MIRAGES MRMAGOO MUTAGEN NEWAGER NONAGON OCTAGON OUTAGES PAPAGOS PARAGON PELAGES PELAGIC POTAGES RAVAGED RAVAGES SAVAGED SAVAGER SAVAGES SCRAGGY TANAGER UNCAGED UNCAGES VIRAGOS VISAGES VOYAGED VOYAGER VOYAGES

•••A•G•

ARRAIGN ARRANGE ATLARGE DEBARGE DEFARGE DURANGO EMBARGO ENLARGE HIDALGO LAFARGE MELANGE REHANGS SCRAGGY STRANGE

•••A••G

AREARUG CATALOG DECALOG FLEABAG RDLAING TAGALOG

••••AG•

ACREAGE AGESAGO AIRBAGS ASSUAGE AVERAGE BABBAGE BAGGAGE BANDAGE BARRAGE BONDAGE CABBAGE CARTAGE CHICAGO COINAGE COLLAGE CORDAGE CORKAGE CORSAGE COTTAGE COURAGE DARKAGE DOCKAGE DOGTAGS DRAYAGE FARRAGO FOLIAGE FOOTAGE FROMAGE GARBAGE GASBAGS HAULAGE HERBAGE HOSTAGE ICEBAGS IRONAGE JAZZAGE KITBAGS LEAKAGE LINEAGE LINKAGE LONGAGO LUGGAGE LUMBAGO MASSAGE MESSAGE MILEAGE MONTAGE MOORAGE MOULAGE ONSTAGE OUTRAGE OVERAGE PACKAGE PASSAGE PEERAGE PEONAGE PILLAGE PLUMAGE PORTAGE POSTAGE POTTAGE PRESAGE RAMPAGE RESTAGE RIBCAGE RUMMAGE SALVAGE SAPSAGO SAUSAGE SEABAGS SELVAGE SINKAGE STALAGS STORAGE TEABAGS TEENAGE TILLAGE TONNAGE UMBRAGE UNSNAGS UPSTAGE VANTAGE VILLAGE VINTAGE VOLTAGE WASTAGE WATTAGE WIGWAGS YARDAGE ZHIVAGO ZIGZAGS

••••A•G

BIGBANG MUSTANG ROLVAAG SHEBANG

•••••AG

BEANBAG DISHRAG FEEDBAG FLEABAG FREITAG GRABBAG HANDBAG MAILBAG NAMETAG NOSEBAG REDFLAG ROLVAAG SANDBAG TIMELAG TOTEBAG WASHRAG WINDBAG

AH•••••

AHEADOF

A•H••••

ACHATES ACHENES ACHERON ACHESON ACHIEST ACHIEVE ACHTUNG ADHERED ADHERES AMHARIC AMHERST APHELIA APHESES ASHAMED ASHANTI ASHBURY ASHCANS ASHFORD ASHIEST ASHLAND ASHLARS ASHLESS ASHRAMS ASHTRAY ATHEART ATHEISM ATHEIST ATHIRST ATHLETE ATHOMES ATHWART

A••H•••

AFGHANI AFGHANS AIRHEAD AIRHOLE AKIHITO ALCHEMY ALLHAIL ALLHEAL ALLHERE ALOHAOE AMPHORA ANAHEIM ANAHUAC ANCHORS ANCHOVY ANTHEMS ANTHERS ANTHILL ANTHONY ARCHAIC ARCHERS ARCHERY ARCHIES ARCHING ARCHIVE ARCHONS ARCHWAY ARMHOLE ASPHALT AUTHORS

A•••H••

ABASHED ABASHES ABRAHAM AGAKHAN AIRSHIP AIRSHOW AITCHES ALCOHOL ALIGHTS ANOTHER APACHES APISHLY APOTHEM ARACHNE

A••••H•

ACANTHI ADOLPHE ALRIGHT ALYOSHA ANARCHY ARAPAHO ATROPHY ATTACHE AUROCHS

A•••••H

ABOLISH ALDRICH ALWORTH ANOUILH ANSPACH ANTIOCH AZIMUTH

•AH••••

BAHAMAS BAHRAIN CAHIERS CAHOOTS DAHLIAS DAHOMEY HAHNIUM KAHUNAS MAHALIA MAHARIS MAHATMA MAHONEY MAHOUTS NAHUATL PAHLAVI SAHARAN WAHINES YAHTZEE

•A•H•••

BAGHDAD BARHOPS BASHFUL BASHING BATHERS BATHING BATHMAT BATHOIL BATHTUB CACHETS CACHING CACHOUS CALHOUN CARHOPS CASHBAR CASHBOX CASHCOW CASHEWS CASHIER CASHING CASHOUT CATHAIR CATHEAD CATHODE DABHAND DAPHNIS DASHERS DASHIKI DASHING DASHOFF EARHART FASHION FATHEAD FATHERS FATHOMS GASHING GATHERS HAMHOCK HASHING HAWHAWS JAPHETH KACHINA KASHMIR KATHRYN LASHERS LASHING LASHUPS LATHERS LATHERY LATHING MACHETE MACHINA MACHINE MANHOLE MANHOOD MANHOUR MANHUNT MASHERS MASHIES MASHING MATHERS MATHEWS MATHIAS MAYHEMS NAPHTHA PACHISI PATHWAY RAPHAEL RASHERS RASHEST RATHOLE RAWHIDE SACHEMS SACHETS SAMHILL SASHAYS SASHIMI SAXHORN TARHEEL WASHERS WASHING WASHOFF WASHOUT WASHRAG WASHTUB YACHTED YASHMAK ZACHARY

•A••H••

BACCHUS BACKHOE BALIHAI BANSHEE BASEHIT BATCHED BATCHES CAMPHOR CAPSHAW CATCHER CATCHES CATCHON CATCHUP DAUPHIN EARSHOT EARTHEN EARTHLY FARTHER GALAHAD GASOHOL GAUCHER GAUCHOS HARDHAT HARDHIT HARSHEN HARSHER HARSHLY HATCHED HATCHER HATCHES HATCHET HAUGHTY KAISHEK LARCHES LATCHED LATCHES LAUGHAT LAUGHED LAUGHER LAUGHIN MADCHEN MADEHAY MAKEHAY MALTHUS MARCHED MARCHEN MARCHER MARCHES MARCHON MARKHAM MARKHOR MARSHAL MARSHES MATCHED MATCHES MATCHUP MATTHAU MATTHEW MAUGHAM NARTHEX NARWHAL NATCHEZ NAUGHTS NAUGHTY NAVAHOS PANCHAX PANTHER PARCHED PARCHES PASCHAL PATCHED PATCHES PATCHUP RAINHAT RANCHED RANCHER RANCHES RANCHOS RATCHET SALCHOW SANDHOG SATCHEL SATCHMO SAYWHEN VAUGHAN WARSHIP WARTHOG WATCHED WATCHER WATCHES WATCHIT XANTHAN XANTHIC

•A•••H•

CALIPHS EARACHE KARACHI KAZAKHS LAROCHE MALACHI MATZOHS NAPHTHA NATASHA PANACHE PARAPHS PARIAHS PAUNCHY TABITHA TALLYHO

•A••••H

BABYISH CALTECH CARWASH CATFISH CATTISH DAMPISH DARKISH FADDISH GALUMPH GARNISH HANUKAH HAWKISH JAPHETH KADDISH LATIFAH MACBETH MAMMOTH MANNISH MAWKISH PADUCAH PANFISH PAYCASH RAFFISH RALEIGH SABBATH SAWFISH TALLISH TANNISH TARNISH VANGOGH VARNISH WAGGISH WALLACH WARMISH WARPATH WASATCH WASPISH

••AH•••

ANAHEIM ANAHUAC BRAHMAN BRAHMAS BRAHMIN DIAHANN GOAHEAD GRAHAME GRAHAMS IDAHOAN INAHEAP PEAHENS QUAHOGS SHAHDOM SWAHILI UTAHANS

••A•H••

ABASHED ABASHES AGAKHAN APACHES ARACHNE BEACHED BEACHES BEARHUG BLATHER BRASHER BRASHLY CHACHAS CHATHAM CLASHED CLASHES COACHED COACHES CRASHED CRASHES DRACHMA EDAPHIC FEATHER FLASHED FLASHER FLASHES GNASHED GNASHES GRAPHED GRAPHIC HEATHEN HEATHER IVANHOE JOACHIM KWACHAS LEACHED LEACHES LEASHED LEASHES LEATHER LOACHES LOATHED LOATHES PEACHED PEACHES PLASHED PLASHES POACHED POACHER POACHES QUASHED QUASHES REACHED REACHES ROACHED ROACHES ROADHOG SCATHED SCATHES SLASHED SLASHER SLASHES SLATHER SMASHED SMASHER SMASHES SMASHUP STASHED STASHES SWATHED SWATHES TEACHER TEACHES TEACHIN TEASHOP TRACHEA TRASHED TRASHES WEATHER

••A••H•

ACANTHI ANARCHY ARAPAHO BLANCHE DEARTHS DRAUGHT EPARCHS FRAICHE FRAUGHT HEALTHY HEARTHS HEAVEHO STARCHY SWARTHY THATCHY WEALTHY WRAITHS

••A•••H

BEARISH GOATISH HIALEAH INARUSH KLAMATH KLATSCH KNAVISH OBADIAH PHARAOH PLAYDOH SLAVISH SPANISH STAUNCH WEAKISH

•••AH••

ABRAHAM DONAHUE GALAHAD MCMAHON NAVAHOS

•••A•H•

ATTACHE BREATHE BREATHS BREATHY BYPATHS EARACHE EMPATHY GOUACHE HIBACHI HITACHI KARACHI KAZAKHS MALACHI NATASHA PANACHE PARAPHS PIRANHA PREACHY SERAPHS SHEATHE SHEATHS SPLASHY TERAPHS WREATHE WREATHS

•••A••H

BREADTH DEBAUCH HOGARTH MONARCH ROMANSH SCRATCH STEALTH UNEARTH UNLATCH WASATCH

••••AH•

ARAPAHO HOOHAHS HOOKAHS HOWDAHS HURRAHS HUZZAHS LOOFAHS MULLAHS OOMPAHS PARIAHS PUNKAHS PURDAHS RUPIAHS WHYDAHS

••••A•H

ANSPACH BENEATH BONEASH CARWASH DIGRAPH EYELASH EYEWASH GOLIATH GOULASH HOGWASH IMPEACH JETWASH KLAMATH NEWMATH PAYCASH PHARAOH PREWASH RETEACH SABBATH SPINACH STOMACH SUNBATH TOWPATH UNLEASH WALLACH WARPATH

•••••AH

CHEETAH DEBORAH DELILAH HANUKAH HIALEAH LATIFAH MENORAH MESSIAH MITZVAH OBADIAH PADUCAH POOHBAH REBEKAH SHEILAH

AI•••••

AIGRETS AILERON AILMENT AIMEDAT AIMEDTO AIMLESS AIRBAGS AIRBALL AIRBASE AIRBOAT AIRCOOL AIRCREW AIRDAMS AIRDATE AIRDROP AIRFARE AIRFLOW AIRFOIL AIRGUNS AIRHEAD AIRHOLE AIRIEST AIRINGS AIRLANE AIRLESS AIRLIFT AIRLINE AIRLOCK AIRMAIL AIRMASS AIRMILE AIRPLAY AIRPORT AIRPUMP AIRRAID AIRSACS AIRSHIP AIRSHOW AIRSOCK AIRSOUT AIRTAXI AIRTIME AIRWAVE AIRWAYS AIRWOLF AITCHES

A•I••••

ABIDEBY ABIDING ABIGAIL ABILENE ABILITY ACIDIFY ACIDITY ADIPOSE AGILELY AGILITY AGITATE AKIHITO ALIASES ALIBABA ALIDADE ALIENEE ALIENOR ALIGHTS ALIGNED ALIGNER ALIMENT ALIMONY AMIABLE AMIABLY AMIBLUE ANILINE ANIMALS ANIMATE ANIMATO ANIMISM ANIMIST ANISEED APISHLY ARIADNE ARIDEST ARIDITY ARIETTA ARIKARA ARIOSOS ARIOSTO ARISING ARISTAE ARISTAS ARISTOS ARIZONA ASIATIC ASININE ATINGLE ATISSUE AVIANCA AVIATED AVIATES AVIATOR AVIDITY AVIGNON AXIALLY AXILLAE AZIMUTH

A••I•••

AAMILNE ABRIDGE ACHIEST ACHIEVE ACRIDLY ACTINIC ACTIONS ACTIVES ADDISON ADMIRAL ADMIRED ADMIRER ADMIRES ADMIXED ADMIXES ADVISED ADVISER ADVISES ADVISOR AEDILES AERIALS AERIEST AFFINES AFFIRMS AFFIXED AFFIXES AFRICAN AGAINST AGEISTS AGRIPPA AIRIEST AIRINGS ALBINOS ALFIERI ALGIERS ALLISON ALRIGHT

AMBIENT
AMNIONS
ANCIENT
ANDIRON
ANOINTS
ANTIART
ANTIBES
ANTIGEN
ANTIGUA
ANTILOG
ANTIOCH
ANTIQUE
ANTIWAR
ANXIETY
ANXIOUS
AORISTS
APRICOT
APRIORI
APSIDES
AQUIFER
AQUINAS
AQUIVER
ARBITER
ARGIVES
ARNICAS
ARRIERE
ARRISES
ARRIVAL
ARRIVED
ARRIVER
ARRIVES
ARTICLE
ARTIEST
ARTISAN
ARTISTE
ARTISTS
ASHIEST
ASPIRED
ASPIRER
ASPIRES
ASPIRIN
ASSIGNS
ASSISTS
ASSIZES
ATHIRST
ATRIUMS
ATTICUS
ATTIMES
ATTIRED
ATTIRES
AUDIBLE
AUDIBLY
AUDITED
AUDITOR
AURICLE
AVAILED
AVOIDED
AWAITED
AWNINGS

A•••I••

ABASING
ABATING
ABIDING
ABILITY
ABOLISH
ABUSING
ABUSIVE
ACACIAS
ACADIAN
ACARIDS
ACIDIFY
ACIDITY
ACONITE
ACQUIRE
ACQUITS
ADAGIOS
ADAMITE
ADDLING
ADELINE
ADENINE
ADJOINS
ADORING
AEOLIAN
AFFAIRE
AFFAIRS
AFFLICT
AGILITY
AGONIST
AGONIZE
AIRLIFT
AIRLINE
AIRMILE
AIRTIME
AKIHITO
ALAKING
ALDRICH
ALEWIFE
ALLTIME
ALLYING
AMATIVE
AMAZING
AMBLING
AMBRIES
AMENITY
AMERICA
AMERIGO
AMERIKA
AMERIND
AMPLIFY
AMUSING
ANANIAS
ANGLING
ANGRIER
ANGRILY
ANILINE
ANIMISM
ANIMIST
ANNUITY
ANODIZE
ANOUILH
ANTEING
ANTHILL
ANTLION
ANTOINE
ANTSIER
ANYTIME
APATITE
APELIKE
APERIES
APPLIED
APPLIES
APPOINT
APPRISE
APPRIZE
ARABIAN
ARCHIES
ARCHING
ARCHIVE
ARCSINE
ARGUING
ARIDITY
ARISING
ARMOIRE
ARMPITS
ARRAIGN
ARTFILM
ASCRIBE
ASININE
ASOCIAL
ASSAILS
ASTAIRE
ASTRIDE
ATAVISM
ATAVIST
ATELIER
ATHEISM
ATHEIST
ATOMIES
ATOMIZE
ATONING
ATTAINS
ATTRITE
ATTRITS
AUCTION
AUNTIES
AUSPICE
AUSSIES
AVARICE
AVIDITY
AVOWING
AWAKING
AZURITE

A••••I•

ABIGAIL
ABNAKIS
ABSTAIN
ACCLAIM
ACERBIC
ACRYLIC
ACTINIC
ADDEDIN
ADONAIS
AELFRIC
AEROBIC
AGASSIZ
AGOUTIS
AIRFOIL
AIRMAIL
AIRRAID
AIRSHIP
ALADDIN
ALAMEIN
ALBANIA
ALBENIZ
ALBUMIN
ALEMBIC
ALGERIA
ALKALIS
ALLHAIL
ALLUVIA
AMHARIC
AMMONIA
AMNESIA
AMOEBIC
AMRADIO
ANAEMIA
ANAHEIM
ANDROID
ANDYKIM
ANEROID
ANGELIC
ANNELID
ANOSMIA
ANOSMIC
ANTACID
ANTONIA
ANTONIN
ANTONIO
APHELIA
AQUARIA
AQUATIC
AQUAVIT
ARAMAIC
ARCADIA
ARCHAIC
ARMENIA
ARSENIC
ARSENIO
ARTEMIS
ASCETIC
ASEPSIS
ASEPTIC
ASIATIC
ASPIRIN
ASSYRIA
ASTORIA
AUSTRIA

A•••••I

ABENAKI
ACANTHI
AFGHANI
AIRTAXI
ALFIERI
ALVEOLI
ANASAZI
APRIORI
ASHANTI
ASSEGAI

•AI••••

BAILEES
BAILERS
BAILEYS
BAILIFF
BAILING
BAILORS
BAILOUT
BAITING
CAIMANS
CAIQUES
CAISSON
DAILIES
DAIMLER
DAIRIES
DAISIES
FAIENCE
FAILING
FAILURE
FAINTED
FAINTER
FAINTLY
FAIREST
FAIRIES
FAIRING
FAIROFF
FAIRSUP
FAIRWAY
GAINERS
GAINFUL
GAINING
GAINSAY
GAINSON
GAITERS
GAITING
HAILING
HAIRCUT
HAIRDOS
HAIRDYE
HAIRIER
HAIRNET
HAIRPIN
HAITIAN
JAIALAI
JAILERS
JAILING
KAISERS
KAISHEK
LAIDFOR
LAIDLOW
LAIDOFF
LAIDOUT
LAISSEZ
MAIDENS
MAIGRET
MAILBAG
MAILBOX
MAILERS
MAILING
MAILLOT
MAINTOP
MAITAIS
MAITRED
NAIADES
NAILERS
NAILING
NAILSET
NAIROBI
NAIVELY
NAIVETE
PAIDFOR
PAIDOFF
PAIDOUT
PAILFUL
PAILOUS
PAINFUL
PAINTED
PAINTER
PAIRING
PAIROFF
PAIRSUP
PAISANO
PAISLEY
PAIUTES
RAIDERS
RAIDING
RAILERS
RAILING
RAILSAT
RAILWAY
RAIMENT
RAINBOW
RAINHAT
RAINIER
RAINING
RAINMAN
RAINOUT
RAISERS
RAISEUP
RAISING
RAISINS
SAILING
SAILORS
SAINTED
SAINTLY
TAILEND
TAILFIN
TAILING
TAILLES
TAILOFF
TAILORS
TAINTED
TAIPANS
VAINEST
WAIKIKI
WAILERS
WAILING
WAISTED
WAITERS
WAITING
WAITOUT
WAITSON
WAITSUP
WAIVERS
WAIVING

•A•I•••

AAMILNE
BACILLI
BALIHAI
BATIKED
BATISTA
BATISTE
CABINET
CAGIEST
CAHIERS
CALIBAN
CALIBER
CALIBRE
CALICOS
CALIPER
CALIPHS
CAMILLE
CAMISES
CANINES
CAPITAL
CAPITAN
CAPITOL
CARIBES
CARIBOU
CARINAS
CARIOCA
CASINGS
CASINOS
CATIONS
CAVILED
CAVILER
DANIELS
DAVINCI
EASIEST
FACIALS
FACINGS
FADIMAN
FAJITAS
FANIONS
FATIGUE
GALILEE
GALILEI
GALILEO
GAMIEST
GAMINES
GAVIALS
HABITAT
HABITED
HABITUE
HALIBUT
HALIFAX
HALITES
HAMITES
HAMITIC
HAMITUP
HARICOT
HASIDIM
HAZIEST
HAZINGS
JABIRUS
JACINTO
JALISCO
JANITOR
LABIALS
LABIATE
LACIEST
LACINGS
LADINOS
LAFITTE
LALIQUE
LAMINAE
LAMINAL
LAMINAR
LAMINAS
LARIATS
LATICES
LATIFAH
LATINAS
LATINOS
LAVINIA
LAYINTO
LAZIEST
MADISON
MAFIOSO
MAGICAL
MAGINOT
MAKINGS
MALIGNS
MANIACS
MANILOW
MANIPLE
MANITOU
MAOISTS
MARIANA
MARILYN
MARIMBA
MARINAS
MARINER
MARINES
MARITAL
MATILDA
MATINEE
MATISSE
MAXILLA
MAXIMAL
MAXIMUM
MAXIMUS
NABISCO
NAMIBIA
NATIONS
NATIVES
PACIFIC
PANICKY
PANICLE
PAPILLA
PARIAHS
PARIBUS
PARINGS
PATIENT
PATINAS
PAVIOUR
RACIEST
RADIALS
RADIANS
RADIANT
RADIATE
RADICAL
RADICES
RADICLE
RADIOED
RANINTO
RAPIDER
RAPIDLY
RAPIERS
RAPINES
RARITAN
RATINGS
RATIONS
RATITES
RAVINES
RAVINGS
RAVIOLI
SABINES
SAGINAW
SALIENT
SALIERI
SAMISEN
SAMITES
SANIBEL
SAPIENS
SAPIENT
SATIATE
SATIETY
SATIRES
SATIRIC
SATISFY
SAVINGS
SAVIORS
SAYINGS
TABITHA
TACITLY
TACITUS
TAOISTS
TAPINGS
TAPIOCA
TARIFFS
TATIANA
TAXICAB
TAXIING
TAXIWAY
VALIANT
VALIDLY
VALISES
VANILLA
VANILLI
VAPIDLY
VARIANT
VARIETY
VARIOUS
VATICAN
WAHINES
WAPITIS
WARIEST
WAVIEST
WAXIEST
ZANIEST

•A••I••

BABBITT
BABYING
BABYISH
BACKING
BADDIES
BAGGIER
BAGGIES
BAGGILY
BAGGING
BAGPIPE
BAILIFF
BAILING
BAITING
BALDING
BALKIER
BALKING
BALMIER
BAMBINO
BANDIED
BANDIES
BANDING
BANDITO
BANDITS
BANGING
BANKING
BANNING
BAPTISM
BAPTIST
BAPTIZE
BARBING
BARGING
BARKING
BARMIER
BARRIER
BARRING
BARRIOS
BASHING
BASKING
BASSIST
BASTING
BASTION
BATHING
BATTIER
BATTING
BATWING
BAUXITE
BAWDIER
BAWDILY
BAWLING
BAYCITY
CABBIES
CABLING
CACHING
CADDIED
CADDIES
CADGING
CADMIUM
CALCIFY
CALCITE
CALCIUM
CALKING
CALKINS
CALLING
CALLINS
CALMING
CALVING
CAMBIUM
CAMPIER
CAMPING
CAMPION
CANDICE
CANDIDA
CANDIDE
CANDIDS
CANDIED
CANDIES
CANNIER
CANNILY
CANNING
CANTINA
CANTING
CAPPING
CAPRICE
CAPSIZE
CAPTION
CAPTIVE
CARBIDE
CARBINE
CARDING
CARMINE
CARNIES
CARPING
CARRICK
CARRIED
CARRIER
CARRIES
CARRION
CARTIER
CARTING
CARVING
CASHIER
CASHING
CASPIAN
CASSIAS
CASSIDY
CASSINI
CASSIUS
CASTILE
CASTING
CATBIRD
CATFISH
CATKINS
CATLIKE
CATNIPS
CATTIER
CATTILY
CATTING
CATTISH
CAUSING
CAUTION
CAVEINS
DABBING
DADAISM
DADAIST
DADDIES
DAFFIER
DAFFILY
DAHLIAS
DAILIES
DAIRIES
DAISIES
DALLIED
DALLIER
DALLIES
DAMMING
DAMNING
DAMPING
DAMPISH
DANCING
DANDIER
DANDIES
DAPPING
DARKISH
DARLING
DARNING
DARTING
DASHIKI
DASHING
DAUBING
DAUMIER
DAWKINS
DAWNING
DAYLILY
DAYSINN
DAYTIME
EAGLING
EARLIER
EARNING
EARRING
EARWIGS
FABRICS
FACTION
FADDISH
FADDISM
FADDIST
FADEINS
FAGGING
FAILING
FAIRIES
FAIRING
FALLING
FALSIFY
FALSITY
FANCIED
FANCIER
FANCIES
FANCILY
FANNING
FANZINE
FARMING
FARRIER
FASCIAS
FASCISM
FASCIST
FASHION
FASTING
FATCITY
FATUITY
FAUVISM
FAUVIST
FAWNING
GABBIER
GABBING
GABRIEL
GADDING
GAFFING
GAGGING
GAGLINE
GAINING
GAITING
GALLICO
GALLING
GALLIUM
GAMBIAN
GAMBITS
GANGING
GAPPING
GARBING
GARNISH
GARRICK
GASHING
GASKINS
GASPING
GATLING
GAUDIER
GAUDILY
GAUGING
GAUZIER
GAUZILY
GAWKIER
GAWKING
HACKIES
HACKING
HADRIAN
HAFNIUM
HAHNIUM
HAILING
HAIRIER
HAITIAN
HALOING
HALTING
HALVING
HAMMILY
HAMMING
HANDIER
HANDILY
HANDING
HANGING
HANKIES
HAPPIER
HAPPILY
HARDIER
HARDILY
HARDING
HARKING
HARMING
HARPIES
HARPING
HARPIST
HARRIED
HARRIER
HARRIES
HARRIET
HASHING
HASTIER
HASTILY
HASTING
HATPINS
HATTING
HAULING
HAWKING
HAWKINS
HAWKISH
HAYRIDE
HAYWIRE
JABBING
JACKING
JADEITE
JAGGING
JAILING
JAMAICA
JAMMING
JANEIRO
JANVIER
JARRING
JASMINE
JAWLINE
JAYBIRD
JAZZIER
JAZZILY
JAZZING
KACHINA
KADDISH
KAYOING
LACKING
LADDIES
LADLING
LAGGING
LAMAISM
LAMAIST
LAMMING
LANDING
LANKIER
LANKILY
LANSING
LAOTIAN
LAPPING
LAPSING
LAPWING
LARAINE
LARDING
LASHING
LASSIES
LASTING
LATHING
LATTICE
LATVIAN
LAUDING
MACHINA
MACHINE
MADDING
MADEIRA
MADLIBS
MAGNIFY
MAGPIES
MAILING
MALAISE
MALTING
MANCINI
MANGIER
MANKIND
MANLIER
MANNING
MANNISH
MANSION
MAPPING
MARGINS
MARKING
MARLINS
MARMION
MARRIED
MARRIES
MARRING
MARTIAL
MARTIAN
MARTINA
MARTINI
MARTINO
MARTINS
MARXISM
MASHIES
MASHING
MASKING
MASSIFS
MASSING
MASSIVE
MASTICS
MASTIFF
MATHIAS
MATTING
MAULING
MAURICE
MAWKISH
MAYTIME
MAYWINE
NABBING
NAGGING
NAILING
NANNIES
NAPKINS
NAPPING
NAPTIME
NASTIER
NASTILY
NATRIUM
NATTIER
NATTILY
PACHISI
PACKICE
PACKING
PADDIES
PADDING
PAIRING
PALLING
PALLIUM
PALMIER
PALMING
PALMIST
PAMBIES
PANDITS
PANFISH
PANNIER
PANNING

PANPIPE
PANSIES
PANTING
PAPRIKA
PARKING
PARRIED
PARRIES
PARRING
PARSING
PARTIAL
PARTIED
PARTIES
PARTING
PARTITA
PARTITE
PASSING
PASSION
PASSIVE
PASTIER
PASTIME
PASTINA
PASTING
PATRICE
PATRICK
PATRIOT
PATSIES
PATTIES
PATTING
PAUCITY
PAULINA
PAULINE
PAULING
PAULIST
PAUSING
PAWNING
PAYDIRT
RABBITS
RABBITT
RACKING
RAFFISH
RAFTING
RAGGIER
RAGGING
RAGTIME
RAIDING
RAILING
RAINIER
RAINING
RAISING
RAISINS
RALEIGH
RALLIED
RALLIES
RAMMING
RANDIER
RANGIER
RANGING
RANKING
RANRIOT
RANTING
RAPPING
RASPIER
RASPING
RATFINK
RATLINE
RATTIER
RATTING
RAWHIDE
RAWSILK
RAZZING
SABRINA
SACKING
SAGGIER

SAGGING
SAILING
SALLIED
SALLIES
SALSIFY
SALTIER
SALTILY
SALTINE
SALTING
SALVING
SAMHILL
SANDIER
SANDING
SANTINI
SANTIRS
SAPLING
SAPPIER
SAPPING
SARDINE
SASHIMI
SASSIER
SASSIES
SASSILY
SASSING
SAUCIER
SAUCILY
SAURIAN
SAVVIER
SAVVILY
SAWFISH
SAWMILL
TABBIES
TABBING
TABLING
TACKIER
TACKILY
TACKING
TACTICS
TACTILE
TAFFIES
TAGGING
TAGLINE
TAILING
TALKIES
TALKING
TALLIED
TALLIES
TALLISH
TAMPICO
TAMPING
TANGIER
TANKING
TANLINE
TANNING
TANNINS
TANNISH
TANSIES
TAPPING
TARDIER
TARDILY
TARNISH
TARPITS
TARRIED
TARRIES
TARRING
TARSIER
TASKING
TASTIER
TASTILY
TASTING
TATTIER
TATTING
TAURINE

TAWNIER
TAXIING
VACCINE
VACUITY
VALUING
VAMPING
VAMPIRE
VANDINE
VARMINT
VARNISH
VARSITY
VARYING
WACKIER
WACKILY
WADDING
WAFTING
WAGGING
WAGGISH
WAIKIKI
WAILING
WAITING
WAIVING
WALKING
WALKINS
WALLING
WANTING
WARDING
WARLIKE
WARMING
WARMISH
WARNING
WARPING
WARRING
WARRIOR
WARTIME
WARWICK
WASHING
WASPISH
WASTING
WAXWING
WAYBILL
WAYSIDE
YAKKING
YANKING
YAPPING
YARNING
YAWNING
ZAGGING
ZAMBIAN
ZAPPING

•A•••I•

BABYSIT
BACKBIT
BACKLIT
BACKSIN
BAHRAIN
BALDRIC
BALDWIN
BANDAID
BARGAIN
BARGEIN
BARMAID
BASEHIT
BATHOIL
BAVARIA
CAKEMIX
CALLSIN
CALORIC
CALORIE
CAMBRIC
CAMELIA
CANONIC
CAPAPIE
CAPTAIN
CARAMIA
CAROTID
CATHAIR
CATTAIL
CAUSTIC
CAVEDIN
CAVESIN
DAPHNIS
DAUPHIN
DAYTRIP
EASEDIN
EASESIN
FADEDIN
FADESIN
FALLSIN
FANATIC
FANMAIL
FANTAIL
GAGARIN
GALATIA
GANGLIA
GASMAIN
GASTRIC
GAUGUIN
HAIRPIN
HALFWIT
HAMELIN
HAMITIC
HANDSIN
HANGSIN
HARDHIT
HASIDIM
JACOBIN
JAVELIN
KABUKIS
KASHMIR
KATYDID
LACONIC
LAMPOIL
LANGUID
LANOLIN
LARAMIE
LAUGHIN
LAVINIA
LAWSUIT
MAHALIA
MAHARIS
MAITAIS
MAKESIT
MALEFIC
MANDRIL
MANTRIC
MANUMIT
MARQUIS
MASONIC
MASTOID
MAUDLIN
MAULDIN
MAUROIS
MAYALIN
MAYFAIR
NAMIBIA
NATALIA
NATALIE
NAYSAID
PACIFIC
PALADIN
PALMOIL
PARBOIL
PARFAIT
PARSNIP
RAKEDIN
RAKESIN
RAMEKIN
RAREBIT
RATAFIA
RATTAIL
SAFARIS
SALADIN
SALAMIS
SALUKIS
SAMARIA
SANGRIA
SANLUIS
SATIRIC
SAVARIN
TABLOID
TAILFIN
TAKEAIM
TAKENIN
TAKESIN
TALARIA
TALKBIG
TAMARIN
TATAMIS
VALERIE
WADESIN
WAGTAIL
WANTSIN
WAPITIS
WARSHIP
WASSAIL
WATCHIT
WAVEDIN
WAVESIN
WAYLAID
XANTHIC

•A••••I

BACARDI
BACILLI
BALIHAI
BASENJI
CADUCEI
CAMPARI
CANNOLI
CASSINI
DASHIKI
DAVINCI
GALILEI
GALVANI
HAVARTI
JACUZZI
JAIALAI
KARACHI
KAROLYI
MAESTRI
MALACHI
MANCINI
MARCONI
MARTINI
NAIROBI
PACHISI
PADRONI
PAHLAVI
PALAZZI
RAPANUI
RAVIOLI
SALIERI
SAMURAI
SANTINI
SASHIMI
VANILLI
WAIKIKI
ZAMBEZI

••AI•••

AGAINST
AVAILED
AWAITED
BRAIDED
BRAIDER
BRAILLE
BRAINED
BRAISED
BRAISES
CHAINED
CHAIRED
CHAISES
CLAIMED
CLAIMER
CLAIROL
DRAINED
DRAINER
FLAILED
FRAICHE
FRAILER
FRAILTY
FRAISES
GRAINED
LIAISED
LIAISES
LIAISON
PLAICES
PLAINER
PLAINES
PLAINLY
PLAINTS
PLAITED
PRAIRIE
PRAISED
PRAISER
PRAISES
QUAILED
REAIRED
STAIDER
STAIDLY
STAINED
STAINER
TRAILED
TRAILER
TRAINED
TRAINEE
TRAINER
TRAIPSE
TRAITOR
UNAIDED
UNAIMED
UNAIRED
WRAITHS

••A•I••

ABASING
ABATING
ACACIAS
ACADIAN
ACARIDS
ADAGIOS
ADAMITE
ALAKING
AMATIVE
AMAZING
ANANIAS
APATITE
ARABIAN
ATAVISM
ATAVIST
AVARICE
AWAKING
BEADIER
BEADING
BEAMIER
BEAMING
BEANIES
BEANING
BEARING
BEARISH
BEATIFY
BEATING
BIALIES
BIASING
BLAMING
BLARING
BLAZING
BOATING
BRACING
BRAKING
BRANIFF
BRAVING
BRAYING
BRAZIER
BRAZING
CEASING
CHAFING
CHALICE
CHARIER
CHARILY
CHARIOT
CHARITY
CHASING
CLARICE
CLARIFY
CLARION
CLARITY
CLAVIER
CLAWING
CLAYIER
COATING
COAXIAL
COAXING
CRANIAL
CRANING
CRANIUM
CRATING
CRAVING
CRAZIER
CRAZIES
CRAZILY
CRAZING
CZARINA
CZARISM
CZARIST
DEALING
DIALING
DIARIES
DRAPING
DRAWING
DRAYING
DUALITY
EDACITY
EGALITE
ELAPIDS
ELATING
ELATION
ERASING
ETAMINE
EVADING
EVASION
EVASIVE
EXAMINE
FEARING
FLAKIER
FLAKING
FLAMING
FLARING
FLAWING
FLAYING
FOALING
FOAMIER
FOAMING
FRAGILE
FRAMING
FRASIER
FRAYING
FRAZIER
GEARING
GLACIAL
GLACIER
GLARING
GLAZIER
GLAZING
GNAWING
GOADING
GOALIES
GOATISH
GRACIAS
GRACILE
GRACING
GRADING
GRANITE
GRATIFY
GRATING
GRAVIES
GRAVING
GRAVITY
GRAYING
GRAZING
GUANINE
HEADIER
HEADILY
HEADING
HEALING
HEAPING
HEARING
HEATING
HEAVIER
HEAVIES
HEAVILY
HEAVING
HOAGIES
HOARIER
HOAXING
HYALINE
IMAGINE
IMAGING
IRANIAN
ITALIAN
ITALICS
KNAVISH
KRATION
LEADING
LEADINS
LEAFIER
LEAFING
LEAKIER
LEAKING
LEANING
LEAPING
LEASING
LEAVING
LOADING
LOAFING
LOAMIER
LOAMING
LOANING
MEALIER
MEALIES
MEANIES
MEANING
MEATIER
MIAMIAN
MOANING
NEARING
OBADIAH
OCARINA
OKAYING
ONADIET
OPACITY
OPALINE
ORATING
ORATION
OVATION
PEAKING
PEALING
PHASING
PIANISM
PIANIST
PLACIDO
PLACING
PLANING
PLATING
PLAYING
PRALINE
PRATING
PRAYING
QUAKING
QUALIFY
QUALITY
READIED
READIER
READIES
READILY
READING
REALISM
REALIST
REALITY
REALIZE
REAMING
REAPING
REARING
ROADIES
ROAMING
ROARING
SCALIER
SCALING
SCARIER
SCARIFY
SCARILY
SCARING
SEABIRD
SEAGIRT
SEALILY
SEALING
SEALION
SEAMIER
SEAMING
SEARING
SEASICK
SEASIDE
SEATING
SHADIER
SHADILY
SHADING
SHAKIER
SHAKILY
SHAKING
SHAMING
SHAPING
SHAPIRO
SHARING
SHAVING
SKATING
SLAKING
SLATIER
SLATING
SLAVING
SLAVISH
SNAKIER
SNAKING
SNARING
SOAKING
SOAPIER
SOAPING
SOARING
SPACIER
SPACING
SPADING
SPANIEL
SPANISH
SPARING
SPATIAL
SPAVINS
SPAYING
STABILE
STADIUM
STAGIER
STAGILY
STAGING
STAKING
STAMINA
STARING
STATICE
STATICS
STATING
STATION
STATIST
STAVING
STAYING
SUASION
SUAVITY
SWAHILI
SWAYING
TEAMING
TEARIER
TEARILY
TEARING
TEASING
TEATIME
THAWING
TOADIED
TOADIES
TRACING
TRADING
TSARINA
TSARIST
TZARINA
UNALIKE
URANITE
URANIUM
WEAKISH
WEANING
WEARIED
WEARIER
WEARIES
WEARILY
WEARING
WEAVING
WHALING
XRATING
XRAYING

••A••I•

AGASSIZ
ALADDIN
ALAMEIN
ANAEMIA
ANAHEIM
ARAMAIC
BEASTIE
BEATNIK
BEATRIX
BEATSIT
BEATTIE
BRAHMIN
BRASSIE
CHABLIS
CHAGRIN
CHALLIS
CHAMOIS
CHAOTIC
CHAPLIN
CHARLIE
CHARMIN
CHASSIS
CLASSIC
CLAUDIA
CLAUDIO
COALBIN
COALOIL
CRAPPIE
DEADAIR
DEALSIN
DEALTIN
DEARSIR
DRAGSIN
DRASTIC
DRAWNIN
DRAWSIN
EDAPHIC
ELASTIC
FLACCID
FRANCIS
FRANKIE
FRANTIC
GRAPHIC
HEADPIN
HEADSIN
INASNIT
INASPIN
JEANNIE
JOACHIM
JOAQUIN
LEADSIN
MIASMIC
ONASSIS
PHASEIN
PLASTIC
PLAUDIT
PRAIRIE
READMIT
READSIN
REAFFIX
REAVAIL
SHAREIN
SLATKIN
STANDIN
STANNIC
STARLIT
TEACHIN
THATSIT
TRADEIN
TRAFFIC
TRANSIT
TRAVAIL
TRAVOIS

••A•••I

ACANTHI
ANASAZI
CHAPATI
GUARANI
PLATYPI
SHANGRI
SHARPEI
SHASTRI
SWAHILI

•••AI••

AFFAIRE
AFFAIRS
ARRAIGN
ASSAILS
ASTAIRE
ATTAINS
BEWAILS
DADAISM
DADAIST
DERAILS
DETAILS
DETAINS
DOMAINS
ECLAIRS
ENTAILS
GERAINT
HILAIRE
IMPAIRS
JAMAICA
JUDAISM
KUWAITI
LAMAISM
LAMAIST
LARAINE
MALAISE
MOHAIRS
MORAINE
MOSAICS
OBTAINS
ORDAINS
RDLAING
REGAINS
REMAILS
REMAINS
RENAILS
REPAINT
REPAIRS
RERAISE
RETAILS
RETAINS
ROLAIDS
ROMAINE
SPRAINS
STRAINS
STRAITS
TUBAIST
UKRAINE
UPRAISE

•••A•I•

ABNAKIS
ALBANIA
ALKALIS
AMHARIC
AMRADIO
ANTACID
AQUARIA
AQUATIC
AQUAVIT
ARCADIA
ASIATIC
BAVARIA
BENAZIR
BREAKIN
CAPAPIE
CARAMIA
CBRADIO
CERAMIC
CHEAPIE
COHABIT
CROATIA
DUKAKIS
DYNAMIC
ERRATIC
EURASIA
FANATIC
FMRADIO
GAGARIN
GALATIA
GELATIN
GELATIS
HEPARIN
HEPATIC
HORATIO
IDIAMIN
INHABIT
INVALID
ISLAMIC
KERATIN
KIWANIS
LARAMIE
LUNATIC
MAHALIA
MAHARIS
MAYALIN
MCGAVIN
MELANIE
MELANIN
MORANIS
MORAVIA
MUTATIS
NATALIA
NATALIE
NEPALIS
NOMADIC
NOTABIT
OCEANIA
OCEANIC
OCEANID
OCTAVIA
ONTARIO
ORGANIC
PALADIN
PELAGIC
PIRATIC
POLARIS
PYRAMID
RATAFIA
REGALIA
ROMANIA
ROSALIE
SAFARIS
SALADIN
SALAMIS
SAMARIA
SAVARIN
SEDALIA
SERAPIS
SNEAKIN
SOLARIA

SOMALIA
SOMALIS
SOMATIC
SQUALID
SWEARIN
TALARIA
TAMARIN
TATAMIS
TELAVIV
TITANIA
TITANIC
VIDALIA
VISAVIS
VITAMIN
VOCALIC

•••A••I
ASHANTI
BACARDI
CHIANTI
HAVARTI
HIBACHI
HITACHI
ISRAELI
JAIALAI
JUMANJI
KARACHI
KUWAITI
MALACHI
PALAZZI
PULASKI
RAPANUI
SCHATZI
VIVALDI

••••AI•
ABIGAIL
ABSTAIN
ACCLAIM
ADONAIS
AIRMAIL
AIRRAID
ALLHAIL
ARAMAIC
ARCHAIC
BAHRAIN
BANDAID
BARGAIN
BARMAID
BIDFAIR
BOBTAIL
BRITAIN
CAPTAIN
CATHAIR
CATTAIL
CERTAIN
CONTAIN
CORSAIR
COSTAIN
CURTAIL
CURTAIN
DEADAIR
DECLAIM
DELTAIC
DESPAIR
DETRAIN
DISDAIN
ENCHAIN
ENTRAIN
EXCLAIM
EXPLAIN
FANMAIL
FANTAIL
FOXTAIL
FUNFAIR
GASMAIN
HEBRAIC
HOBNAIL
INGRAIN
KOOLAID
LOWPAID
MAITAIS
MAYFAIR
MERMAID
MIKHAIL
MISLAID
NAYSAID
OLDMAID
OPENAIR
OUTLAID
PARFAIT
PERTAIN
PIGTAIL
PINTAIL
PREPAID
PREVAIL
PROSAIC
RATTAIL
REAVAIL
RECLAIM
REDHAIR
REFRAIN
RESTAIN
RETRAIN
SETSAIL
SUNMAID
SUSTAIN
TAKEAIM
TERRAIN
THINAIR
TOENAIL
TOPSAIL
TRAVAIL
UNCHAIN
UPBRAID
VILLAIN
VOLTAIC
WAGTAIL
WASSAIL
WAYLAID
YOPLAIT

•••••A•I
ABENAKI
AFGHANI
AIRTAXI
ANASAZI
BENGALI
CAMPARI
CHAPATI
FERRARI
GALVANI
GOURAMI
GUARANI
OMPHALI
ORIGAMI
PAHLAVI
PUNJABI
SYLLABI
TOPKAPI
TSUNAMI
TYMPANI

••••••AI
ASSEGAI
BALIHAI
HYUNDAI
JAIALAI
KUTENAI
MOLOKAI
NIKOLAI
OLDUVAI
SAMURAI

A•J••••
ABJURED
ABJURES
ADJOINS
ADJOURN
ADJUDGE
ADJUNCT
ADJURED
ADJURES
ADJUSTS

•AJ••••
CAJOLED
CAJOLER
CAJOLES
FAJITAS
LAJOLLA
MAJESTE
MAJESTY
MAJEURE
MAJORCA
MAJORED
PAJAMAS

•A•J•••
BANJOES
FANJETS
GASJETS
PALJOEY
RAMJETS
SANJOSE
SANJUAN
VALJEAN

•A••J••
KARAJAN
NAVAJOS

•A•••J•
BASENJI

••A•J••
LEARJET

•••AJ••
KARAJAN
NAVAJOS

•••A•J•
JUMANJI

AK•••••
AKIHITO

A•K••••
ACKACKS
ALKALIS
ALKENES
ANKLETS
ASKANCE
ASKSFOR
ASKSOUT
AUKLETS
AWKWARD
AYKROYD

A••K•••
AGAKHAN
ALAKING
ARIKARA
AWAKENS
AWAKING

A•••K••
ABNAKIS
ALASKAN
ANDYKIM

A••••K•
ABENAKI
ABUBAKR
ACKACKS
AMERIKA
ANORAKS
APELIKE
ARAWAKS
ATSTAKE
ATTACKS
ATTUCKS

A•••••K
AIRLOCK
AIRSOCK
ARMLOCK
ARTWORK
ATATURK

•AK••••
BAKEOFF
BAKLAVA
CAKEMIX
DAKOTAN
DAKOTAS
FAKEFUR
JAKARTA
LAKOTAS
MAKEFOR
MAKEHAY
MAKEOFF
MAKEOUT
MAKEPAR
MAKESDO
MAKESIT
MAKESUP
MAKEUPS
MAKEWAY
MAKINGS
NAKEDLY
OAKFERN
OAKLAND
OAKLAWN
OAKLEAF
OAKMOSS
OAKTREE
RAKEDIN
RAKEDUP
RAKEOFF
RAKESIN
RAKESUP
TAKEAIM
TAKENIN
TAKENON
TAKEOFF
TAKEONE
TAKEOUT
TAKESIN
TAKESON
TAKESTO
TAKESUP
TAKETEN
WAKEFUL
WAKENED
WAKENER
WAKESUP
YAKKERS
YAKKING
YAKUTSK

•A•K•••
BACKBAY
BACKBIT
BACKEND
BACKERS
BACKHOE
BACKING
BACKLIT
BACKLOG
BACKOFF
BACKOUT
BACKRUB
BACKSIN
BACKSUP
BACKUPS
BALKANS
BALKIER
BALKING
BANKERS
BANKING
BANKSON
BARKEEP
BARKERS
BARKING
BARKSAT
BASKETS
BASKING
CACKLED
CACKLER
CACKLES
CALKING
CALKINS
CANKERS
CATKINS
DANKEST
DARKAGE
DARKENS
DARKEST
DARKISH
DARKMAN
DAWKINS
GASKETS
GASKINS
GAWKERS
GAWKIER
GAWKING
HACKERS
HACKETT
HACKIES
HACKING
HACKLES
HACKMAN
HACKNEY
HACKSAW
HANKERS
HANKIES
HARKENS
HARKING
HAWKERS
HAWKEYE
HAWKING
HAWKINS
HAWKISH
JACKALS
JACKASS
JACKDAW
JACKETS
JACKING
JACKPOT
JACKSON
JACKSUP
JACKTAR
LACKEYS
LACKING
LANKEST
LANKIER
LANKILY
MANKIND
MARKERS
MARKETS
MARKHAM
MARKHOR
MARKING
MARKKAA
MARKOFF
MARKOVA
MARKSUP
MARKUPS
MASKERS
MASKING
MAWKISH
NANKEEN
NAPKINS
PACKAGE
PACKARD
PACKERS
PACKETS
PACKICE
PACKING
PACKRAT
PACKSUP
PARKING
PARKWAY
RACKETS
RACKING
RACKSUP
RANKERS
RANKEST
RANKING
RANKLED
RANKLES
RAYKROC
SACKERS
SACKFUL
SACKING
SACKOUT
TACKERS
TACKIER
TACKILY
TACKING
TACKLED
TACKLER
TACKLES
TACKSON
TALKBIG
TALKERS
TALKIES
TALKING
TALKOUT
TALKSAT
TALKSTO
TALKSUP
TANKARD
TANKERS
TANKFUL
TANKING
TANKSUP
TANKTOP
TASKING
WACKIER
WACKILY
WAIKIKI
WALKERS
WALKING
WALKINS
WALKMAN
WALKONS
WALKOUT
WALKUPS
WALKWAY
YAKKERS
YAKKING
YANKEES
YANKING
YANKTON

•A••K••
BANGKOK
BATIKED
CAULKED
CAULKER
HANUKAH
KABUKIS
KANAKAS
KARAKUL
KARAKUM
KAYAKED
KAYAKER
KAZAKHS
LALAKER
MARKKAA
MARYKAY
NABOKOV
PASSKEY
PATAKES
RAMEKIN
SALUKIS

•A•••K•
BAZOOKA
CATLIKE
DAMASKS
DASHIKI
KARAOKE
MAZURKA
PALOOKA
PANCAKE
PANICKY
PAPRIKA
PARTAKE
TANOAKS
VANDYKE
WAIKIKI
WARLIKE

•A••••K
BANGKOK
BANNOCK
BARRACK
CARRICK
CASSOCK
CATWALK
DAYBOOK
EARLOCK
EARMARK
FATBACK
GARRICK
HADDOCK
HAMHOCK
HAMMOCK
HANCOCK
HASSOCK
HATRACK
HAUBERK
HAYFORK
HAYRACK
JAMPACK
JANACEK
JAYWALK
KAISHEK
LAMARCK
MATLOCK
MATTOCK
OARLOCK
PADDOCK
PADLOCK
PARTOOK
PATRICK
RANSACK
RATFINK
RATPACK
RAWSILK
SADSACK
SARAWAK
SAWBUCK
VANDYCK
VANEYCK
WARLOCK
WARWICK
WAXWORK
YAKUTSK
YASHMAK
ZATOPEK

••AK•••
AGAKHAN
ALAKING
AWAKENS
AWAKING
BEAKERS
BRAKING
FLAKERS
FLAKIER
FLAKING
LEAKAGE
LEAKERS
LEAKIER
LEAKING
PEAKING
QUAKERS
QUAKING
SHAKERS
SHAKEUP
SHAKIER
SHAKILY
SHAKING
SHAKOES
SLAKING
SNAKIER
SNAKING
SOAKERS
SOAKING
SOAKSUP
STAKING
WEAKENS
WEAKEST
WEAKISH

••A•K••
ALASKAN
BLACKED
BLACKEN
BLACKER
BLACKLY
BLANKED
BLANKER
BLANKET
BLANKLY
BRACKEN
BRACKET
CHALKED
CHALKUP
CLACKED
CLANKED
CRACKED
CRACKER
CRACKLE
CRACKUP
CRANKED
CRANKUP
FLANKED
FLANKER
FRANKED
FRANKER
FRANKIE
FRANKLY
FRANKOZ
GRACKLE
HEARKEN
PLACKET
PLANKED
PRANKED
QUACKED
SHACKLE
SHANKAR
SHANKED
SHARKEY
SLACKED
SLACKEN
SLACKER
SLATKIN
SMACKED
SMACKER
SNACKED
SNACKER
SPACKLE
SPANKED
SPANKER
SPARKED
SPARKLE
STACKED
STACKUP
STALKED
STALKER
STARKER
STARKLY
SWANKER
THANKED
TRACKED
TRACKER
UNASKED
WHACKED
WRACKED

••A••K•
ARAWAKS
ROANOKE
SPASSKY
TEACAKE
UNALIKE

••A•••K
ATATURK
BEATNIK
LEACOCK
PEACOCK
SEASICK

•••AK••
ABNAKIS
BELAKUN
BETAKEN
BETAKES
BLEAKER
BLEAKLY
BREAKER
BREAKIN
BREAKUP
CLOAKED
CONAKRY
CREAKED
CROAKED
DEBAKEY
DUKAKIS
FREAKED
INTAKES
KANAKAS
KARAKUL
KARAKUM
KAYAKED
KAYAKER
KAZAKHS
LALAKER
PATAKES
REMAKES
RETAKEN
RETAKES
SNEAKED
SNEAKER
SNEAKIN
SPEAKER
SPEAKOF
SPEAKUP
TWEAKED
UNBAKED
UNMAKES
UPTAKES
WREAKED

•••A•K•
ACKACKS
ATTACKS
DAMASKS
DEBARKS
EMBANKS
EMBARKS
HIJACKS
KARAOKE
KOLACKY
MOHAWKS
PULASKI
REMARKS
SQUAWKS
THWACKS
UNMASKS
UNPACKS
UNTACKS

•••A••K
JANACEK
LAMARCK
MUBARAK
RUNAMOK
SARAWAK

••••AK•
ABENAKI
ABUBAKR
ANORAKS
ARAWAKS
ATSTAKE
BUROAKS
CUPCAKE
FORSAKE
HOECAKE
HOTCAKE
KODIAKS
MISTAKE
OILCAKE
OUTTAKE
PANCAKE
PARTAKE
PINOAKS
REDOAKS
SCREAKS
SLOVAKS
SQUEAKS
SQUEAKY
STREAKS
STREAKY
TANOAKS
TEACAKE

••••A•K
BARRACK
BULWARK
BURBANK
CATWALK
CONRACK
COSSACK
CUTBACK
DENMARK
EARMARK
EYEBANK
FATBACK
FOGBANK
GETBACK
GOSHAWK
GOTBACK
HATRACK
HAYRACK
HOGBACK
HOLYARK
ICEPACK
JAMPACK
JAYWALK
JOBBANK
MUDPACK
OUTBACK
OUTRANK
OUTTALK
PEPTALK
RANSACK
RATPACK
RECHALK
RETRACK
RUNBACK
SADSACK
SETBACK
SIXPACK
SKIMASK
SKYJACK
SKYLARK
TEDMACK
TIERACK
TIETACK
UNSTACK
WIDMARK

•••••AK
BESPEAK
HOLMOAK
LIVEOAK
MUBARAK
OFFPEAK
PRESOAK
SARAWAK
UNCLOAK
WOZNIAK
YASHMAK
YITZHAK

AL•••••
ALABAMA
ALADDIN
ALAKING
ALAMEDA
ALAMEIN
ALAMODE
ALARCON
ALARMED
ALARMER
ALARUMS
ALASKAN
ALBANIA
ALBEDOS
ALBENIZ
ALBERTA
ALBERTO
ALBINOS
ALBUMEN
ALBUMIN
ALCAZAR
ALCHEMY
ALCOHOL
ALCOVES
ALDENTE
ALDRICH
ALEMBIC
ALENCON
ALERTED
ALERTER
ALERTLY
ALEWIFE
ALFALFA
ALFIERI
ALFONSO
ALFREDO
ALGEBRA
ALGERIA
ALGIERS
ALIASES
ALIBABA
ALIDADE
ALIENEE
ALIENOR
ALIGHTS
ALIGNED
ALIGNER
ALIMENT
ALIMONY
ALKALIS
ALKENES
ALLAYED
ALLAYER
ALLEARS
ALLEGED
ALLEGER
ALLEGES
ALLEGRO
ALLELES
ALLENDE
ALLERGY
ALLEYES
ALLGONE
ALLHAIL
ALLHEAL
ALLHERE
ALLISON
ALLOFME
ALLOVER
ALLOWED
ALLOYED
ALLSTAR
ALLSTON
ALLTIME
ALLTOLD
ALLUDED
ALLUDES
ALLURED
ALLURES
ALLUVIA
ALLYING
ALLYSON
ALMAATA
ALMADEN
ALMANAC
ALMONDS
ALOHAOE
ALOOFLY
ALPACAS
ALREADY
ALRIGHT
ALSORAN
ALTERED
ALTERER
ALTOONA
ALTOSAX
ALUMNAE
ALUMNAL
ALUMNUS
ALUNSER
ALVAREZ
ALVEOLI
ALWORTH
ALYOSHA
ALYSSUM

A•L••••
ABLATED
ABLATES
ABLAUTS
AELFRIC
AILERON
AILMENT
ALLAYED
ALLAYER
ALLEARS
ALLEGED
ALLEGER
ALLEGES
ALLEGRO
ALLELES
ALLENDE
ALLERGY
ALLEYES
ALLGONE
ALLHAIL
ALLHEAL
ALLHERE
ALLISON
ALLOFME
ALLOVER
ALLOWED
ALLOYED
ALLSTAR
ALLSTON
ALLTIME

ALLTOLD
ALLUDED
ALLUDES
ALLURED
ALLURES
ALLUVIA
ALLYING
ALLYSON
APLENTY
ARLEDGE
ATLANTA
ATLARGE
ATLASES
ATLATLS
ATLEAST
AXLROSE

A••L•••

ABALONE
ABELARD
ABILENE
ABILITY
ABOLISH
ACCLAIM
ACOLYTE
ADDLING
ADELINE
ADOLPHE
ADULATE
AEOLIAN
AFFLICT
AGELESS
AGILELY
AGILITY
AIMLESS
AIRLANE
AIRLESS
AIRLIFT
AIRLINE
AIRLOCK
AMALGAM
AMBLERS
AMBLING
AMPLEST
AMPLIFY
AMULETS
AMYLASE
ANALOGS
ANALOGY
ANALYSE
ANALYST
ANALYZE
ANGLERS
ANGLING
ANILINE
ANKLETS
ANTLERS
ANTLION
APELIKE
APOLOGY
APPLAUD
APPLIED
APPLIES
ARALSEA
ARCLAMP
ARMLESS
ARMLETS
ARMLOAD
ARMLOCK
ARTLESS
ASHLAND
ASHLARS
ASHLESS
ASYLUMS
ATALOSS
ATELIER
ATHLETE
AUKLETS
AVULSED
AVULSES
AWELESS
AXILLAE
AXOLOTL
AZALEAS

A•••L••

AAMILNE
ABSALOM
ABSOLUT
ABSOLVE
ACRYLIC
AEDILES
AIRFLOW
AIRPLAY
ALFALFA
ALKALIS
ALLELES
AMIBLUE
AMPULES
ANGELES
ANGELIC
ANGELOU
ANGELUS
ANGOLAN
ANGULAR
ANNALEE
ANNELID
ANNULAR
ANNULUS
ANTILOG
APHELIA
APPALLS
AREOLAE
AREOLAR
AREOLAS
ARGYLES
ASTOLAT
AURALEE
AURALLY
AVAILED
AVONLEA
AWFULLY
AXIALLY
AXILLAE

A••••L•

ACEROLA
ACRIDLY
ACTABLE
ACUTELY
ADDABLE
ADEPTLY
AERIALS
AFFABLE
AFFABLY
AGILELY
AIRBALL
AIRHOLE
AIRMILE
AIRWOLF
ALERTLY
ALLTOLD
ALOOFLY
ALVEOLI
AMAPOLA
AMIABLE
AMIABLY
AMPOULE
ANATOLE
ANGRILY
ANIMALS
ANNEALS
ANNUALS
ANOMALY
ANOUILH
ANTHILL
APISHLY
APOSTLE
APPALLS
APPEALS
ARMFULS
ARMHOLE
ARTFILM
ARTICLE
ARUGULA
ASPHALT
ASSAILS
ASSAULT
ATFAULT
ATINGLE
ATLATLS
AUDIBLE
AUDIBLY
AURALLY
AUREOLA
AUREOLE
AURICLE
AVOWALS
AWFULLY
AXIALLY

A•••••L

ABIGAIL
ABOREAL
ABUTTAL
ABYSMAL
ACCRUAL
ADMIRAL
ADRENAL
AEROSOL
AIRBALL
AIRCOOL
AIRFOIL
AIRMAIL
ALCOHOL
ALLHAIL
ALLHEAL
ALUMNAL
ANNABEL
ANTHILL
APPAREL
AROUSAL
ARRIVAL
ARSENAL
ASOCIAL
ASUSUAL
AUGURAL
AURORAL
AUSTRAL
AXOLOTL

•AL••••

BALANCE
BALATON
BALBOAS
BALCONY
BALDEST
BALDING
BALDRIC
BALDWIN
BALEENS
BALEFUL
BALFOUR
BALIHAI
BALKANS
BALKIER
BALKING
BALLADE
BALLADS
BALLARD
BALLAST
BALLBOY
BALLETS
BALLOON
BALLOTS
BALLSUP
BALMIER
BALONEY
BALSAMS
CALCIFY
CALCITE
CALCIUM
CALDERA
CALDRON
CALENDS
CALGARY
CALHOUN
CALIBAN
CALIBER
CALIBRE
CALICOS
CALIPER
CALIPHS
CALKING
CALKINS
CALLBOX
CALLERS
CALLFOR
CALLING
CALLINS
CALLOFF
CALLOUS
CALLOUT
CALLSIN
CALLSON
CALLSUP
CALMEST
CALMING
CALOMEL
CALORIC
CALORIE
CALPACS
CALTECH
CALUMET
CALUMNY
CALVARY
CALVERT
CALVING
CALYCES
CALYPSO
CALYXES
CALZONE
DALLIED
DALLIER
DALLIES
DALTREY
FALAFEL
FALCONS
FALLACY
FALLFOR
FALLGUY
FALLING
FALLOFF
FALLOUT
FALLOWS
FALLSIN
FALLSON
FALLSTO
FALSELY
FALSEST
FALSIFY
FALSITY
FALTERS
FALWELL
GALAHAD
GALATEA
GALATIA
GALILEE
GALILEI
GALILEO
GALLANT
GALLEON
GALLERY
GALLEYS
GALLICO
GALLING
GALLIUM
GALLONS
GALLOPS
GALOOTS
GALUMPH
GALVANI
HALCYON
HALFDAN
HALFWAY
HALFWIT
HALIBUT
HALIFAX
HALITES
HALLOWS
HALLWAY
HALOGEN
HALOING
HALSTON
HALTERS
HALTING
HALVING
HALYARD
JALISCO
LALAKER
LALANNE
LALIQUE
MALABAR
MALACCA
MALACHI
MALAISE
MALAMUD
MALAREN
MALAYAN
MALCOLM
MALEATE
MALEFIC
MALIGNS
MALLARD
MALLETS
MALLOWS
MALMSEY
MALODOR
MALRAUX
MALTEDS
MALTESE
MALTHUS
MALTING
MALTOSE
PALACES
PALADIN
PALANCE
PALATAL
PALATES
PALAVER
PALAZZI
PALAZZO
PALEDRY
PALERMO
PALETTE
PALFREY
PALJOEY
PALLETS
PALLING
PALLIUM
PALMATE
PALMIER
PALMING
PALMIST
PALMOFF
PALMOIL
PALOMAR
PALOOKA
PALTERS
RALEIGH
RALLIED
RALLIES
RALLYTO
RALSTON
SALAAMS
SALABLE
SALADIN
SALAMIS
SALAZAR
SALCHOW
SALERNO
SALIENT
SALIERI
SALLIED
SALLIES
SALMONS
SALOONS
SALSIFY
SALSODA
SALTBOX
SALTERS
SALTIER
SALTILY
SALTINE
SALTING
SALUKIS
SALUTED
SALUTES
SALVAGE
SALVERS
SALVING
SALVOES
TALARIA
TALENTS
TALKBIG
TALKERS
TALKIES
TALKING
TALKOUT
TALKSAT
TALKSTO
TALKSUP
TALLEST
TALLIED
TALLIES
TALLISH
TALLOWS
TALLYHO
TALLYUP
TALONED
TALUSES
VALANCE
VALENCE
VALERIE
VALIANT
VALIDLY
VALISES
VALJEAN
VALLEYS
VALOURS
VALUATE
VALUING
WALCOTT
WALDORF
WALKERS
WALKING
WALKINS
WALKMAN
WALKONS
WALKOUT
WALKUPS
WALKWAY
WALLABY
WALLACE
WALLACH
WALLETS
WALLEYE
WALLING
WALLOON
WALLOPS
WALLOWS
WALLSUP
WALMART
WALNUTS
WALPOLE
WALTERS
WALTZED
WALTZER
WALTZES

•A•L•••

BAILEES
BAILERS
BAILEYS
BAILIFF
BAILING
BAILORS
BAILOUT
BAKLAVA
BALLADE
BALLADS
BALLARD
BALLAST
BALLBOY
BALLETS
BALLOON
BALLOTS
BALLSUP
BARLEYS
BAWLERS
BAWLING
BAWLOUT
BAYLEAF
CABLERS
CABLETV
CABLING
CALLBOX
CALLERS
CALLFOR
CALLING
CALLINS
CALLOFF
CALLOUS
CALLOUT
CALLSIN
CALLSON
CALLSUP
CAPLESS
CAPLETS
CARLESS
CARLOAD
CARLSON
CARLTON
CARLYLE
CATLIKE
CAULKED
CAULKER
DAHLIAS
DAILIES
DALLIED
DALLIER
DALLIES
DARLEEN
DARLENE
DARLING
DAYLILY
DAYLONG
EAGLETS
EAGLING
EARLDOM
EARLIER
EARLOBE
EARLOCK
EARLYON
FAILING
FAILURE
FALLACY
FALLFOR
FALLGUY
FALLING
FALLOFF
FALLOUT
FALLOWS
FALLSIN
FALLSON
FALLSTO
FARLEFT
FATLESS
FAULTED
GAGLINE
GALLANT
GALLEON
GALLERY
GALLEYS
GALLICO
GALLING
GALLIUM
GALLONS
GALLOPS
GARLAND
GATLING
GAYLORD
HAILING
HALLOWS
HALLWAY
HAMLETS
HAPLESS
HATLESS
HAULAGE
HAULERS
HAULING
HAULOFF
HAULSUP
HAYLOFT
JAGLESS
JAILERS
JAILING
JAWLINE
JAYLENO
KARLOFF
LADLERS
LADLING
LAPLACE
LAPLAND
LAPLATA
LAWLESS
MADLIBS
MAILBAG
MAILBOX
MAILERS
MAILING
MAILLOT
MALLARD
MALLETS
MALLOWS
MANLIER
MARLENE
MARLINS
MARLOWE
MATLOCK
MAULDIN
MAULING
NAILERS
NAILING
NAILSET
OAKLAND
OAKLAWN
OAKLEAF
OARLESS
OARLOCK
PABLUMS
PADLOCK
PAHLAVI
PAILFUL
PAILOUS
PALLETS
PALLING
PALLIUM
PARLAYS
PARLEYS
PARLORS
PARLOUR
PARLOUS
PAULINA
PAULINE
PAULING
PAULIST
PAULSEN
PAVLOVA
PAYLOAD
RAGLANS
RAILERS
RAILING
RAILSAT
RAILWAY
RALLIED
RALLIES
RALLYTO
RANLATE
RATLINE
SAILING
SAILORS
SALLIED
SALLIES
SANLUIS
SAPLING
SAWLOGS
TABLEAU
TABLETS
TABLING
TABLOID
TAGLINE
TAILEND
TAILFIN
TAILING
TAILLES
TAILOFF
TAILORS
TALLEST
TALLIED
TALLIES
TALLISH
TALLOWS
TALLYHO
TALLYUP
TANLINE
VALLEYS
VARLETS
VAULTED
VAULTER
WAILERS
WAILING
WALLABY
WALLACE
WALLACH
WALLETS
WALLEYE
WALLING
WALLOON
WALLOPS
WALLOWS
WALLSUP
WARLIKE
WARLOCK
WARLORD
WAYLAID
WAYLAYS

•A••L••

AAMILNE
BABBLED
BABBLES
BABYLON
BACILLI
BACKLIT
BACKLOG
BAFFLED
BAFFLER
BAFFLES
BANALLY
BANGLES
BASALLY
BASALTS
BATTLED
BATTLER
BATTLES
BAUBLES
CABALAS
CACKLED
CACKLER
CACKLES
CAJOLED
CAJOLER
CAJOLES
CAMELIA
CAMELOT
CAMILLE
CANDLES
CANTLES
CAPELET
CAPELLA
CAPULET
CAROLED
CAROLER
CAROLES
CAROLUS
CAROLYN
CASELAW
CASTLED
CASTLES
CATALAN
CATALOG
CATALPA
CAVALRY
CAVILED
CAVILER
DABBLED
DABBLER
DABBLES
DAIMLER
DANDLED
DANDLES
DANELAW
DANGLED
DANGLER
DANGLES
DAPPLED
DAPPLES
DAWDLED
DAWDLER
DAWDLES
DAZZLED
DAZZLER
DAZZLES
EARFLAP
EARPLUG
FACULTY
FAMULUS
GABBLED
GABBLES
GAGGLES
GALILEE
GALILEI
GALILEO
GAMBLED
GAMBLER
GAMBLES
GAMELAW
GANGLED
GANGLIA
GANTLET
GARBLED
GARBLES
GARGLED
GARGLES
GATELEG
GAVELED
GAZELLE
HAARLEM
HACKLES
HAGGLED
HAGGLER
HAGGLES
HAMELIN
HANDLED
HANDLER
HANDLES
HASSLED
HASSLES
JAIALAI
JANGLED
JANGLES
JAVELIN
KAROLYI
LABELED
LABELER
LABELLE
LAIDLOW
LAJOLLA
LANGLEY
LANOLIN
LAPALMA
LAPELED
LASALLE
LAVALSE
LAYSLOW
MACULAE
MAHALIA
MAILLOT
MANGLED
MANGLES
MANILOW
MANTLED
MANTLES
MARBLED
MARBLES
MARILYN
MARYLOU
MATILDA
MAUDLIN
MAXILLA
MAYALIN
NACELLE
NASALLY
NATALIA
NATALIE
PABULUM
PADDLED
PADDLER
PADDLES
PAISLEY
PANELED
PAPILLA
PAROLED
PAROLEE
PAROLES
PARSLEY
PATELLA
PAYOLAS
RABBLES
RADDLED
RADDLES
RAFFLED
RAFFLER
RAFFLES
RAMBLED
RAMBLER
RAMBLES
RANKLED
RANKLES
RASSLED
RASSLES
RATTLED
RATTLER
RATTLES
RAVELED
SADDLED
SADDLER
SADDLES
SAMPLED
SAMPLER
SAMPLES
SANDLOT
SARALEE
SAVALAS
TABULAR
TACKLED
TACKLER
TACKLES
TAGALOG
TAILLES
TAMALES
TANGLED
TANGLES
TATTLED
TATTLER
TATTLES
VANILLA
VANILLI
WADDLED
WADDLER
WADDLES
WAFFLED
WAFFLER
WAFFLES
WAGGLED
WAGGLES
WAMBLED
WAMBLES
WANGLED
WANGLER
WANGLES
WARBLED
WARBLER
WARBLES
WATTLES
WAVELET

•A•••L•

BACILLI
BADCOLD
BAGFULS
BAGGILY
BAGNOLD
BANALLY
BARBELL
BARBELS
BARRELS
BASALLY
BAWDILY
CAMILLE
CANCELS
CANDELA
CANNILY
CANNOLI
CAPABLE
CAPABLY
CAPELLA
CAPFULS
CAPSULE
CARFULS
CARLYLE
CARPALS
CARRELS
CARROLL
CARTELS
CASTILE
CASUALS
CATCALL
CATTILY
CATWALK
DACTYLS
DAFFILY
DAMSELS
DANIELS
DARRELL
DATEDLY
DAYLILY
DAZEDLY

EAGERLY
EARFULS
EARTHLY
EATABLE
FACIALS
FAINTLY
FALSELY
FALWELL
FANBELT
FANCILY
GAGRULE
GAMBOLS
GAUDILY
GAUNTLY
GAUZILY
GAVIALS
GAZELLE
HAMMILY
HANDILY
HANSOLO
HAPPILY
HARDILY
HARSHLY
HASTILY
JACKALS
JADEDLY
JARFULS
JAYWALK
JAZZILY
KAMPALA
LABELLE
LABIALS
LAJOLLA
LANKILY
LAPBELT
LAPFULS
LARGELY
LASALLE
LASCALA
LAURELS
MALCOLM
MAMMALS
MANACLE
MANDALA
MANDELA
MANHOLE
MANIPLE
MANTELS
MANUALS
MARCELS
MARSALA
MARVELS
MAXILLA
MAXWELL
MAYPOLE
NACELLE
NAIVELY
NAKEDLY
NARWALS
NASALLY
NASTILY
NATTILY
PANICLE
PANOPLY
PAPILLA
PARABLE
PARCELS
PARNELL
PASSELS
PASTELS
PATELLA
PATROLS
PAYABLE
PAYROLL
RADIALS
RADICLE
RAGDOLL
RANDALL
RAPIDLY
RAPPELS
RASCALS
RATABLE
RATHOLE
RAVIOLI
RAWSILK
SAINTLY
SALABLE
SALTILY
SAMHILL
SANDALS
SANDFLY
SASSILY
SAUCILY
SAVABLE
SAVVILY
SAWMILL
TACITLY
TACKILY
TACTILE
TADPOLE
TAGSALE
TAMABLE
TAMBALA
TANGELO
TARBELL
TARDILY
TARSALS
TASSELS
TASTILY
TAXABLE
VACUOLE
VAGUELY
VALIDLY
VANDALS
VANILLA
VANILLI
VAPIDLY
VASSALS
VATFULS
WACKILY
WALPOLE
WAYBILL

•A••••L

BALEFUL
BANEFUL
BARBELL
BARNOWL
BASHFUL
BATHOIL
CALOMEL
CAPITAL
CAPITOL
CARACAL
CARAMEL
CARAVEL
CAREFUL
CARPOOL
CARROLL
CATCALL
CATTAIL
DARRELL
FACTUAL
FALAFEL
FALWELL
FANMAIL
FANTAIL
FATEFUL
GABRIEL
GAINFUL
GAMBREL
GASOHOL
HANDFUL
HARMFUL
HATEFUL
KARAKUL
LACTEAL
LACUNAL
LAMINAL
LAMPOIL
LATERAL
MAGICAL
MANDREL
MANDRIL
MARITAL
MARSHAL
MARTIAL
MAXIMAL
MAXWELL
MAYORAL
NAHUATL
NARWHAL
NATURAL
OATMEAL
PAGEFUL
PAILFUL
PAINFUL
PALATAL
PALMOIL
PARASOL
PARBOIL
PARNELL
PARTIAL
PASCHAL
PASSEUL
PAYROLL
RADICAL
RAGDOLL
RANDALL
RAPHAEL
RATTAIL
RAWDEAL
SACKFUL
SAMHILL
SANIBEL
SATCHEL
SAWMILL
TACTFUL
TANKFUL
TARBELL
TARHEEL
VANPOOL
WAGTAIL
WAKEFUL
WASSAIL
WASTREL
WAYBILL

••AL•••

ABALONE
AMALGAM
ANALOGS
ANALOGY
ANALYSE
ANALYST
ANALYZE
ARALSEA
ATALOSS
AZALEAS
BIALIES
CHALETS
CHALICE
CHALKED
CHALKUP
CHALLIS
COALBIN
COALCAR
COALERS
COALGAS
COALOIL
COALTAR
DEALERS
DEALING
DEALOUT
DEALSIN
DEALTIN
DIALECT
DIALERS
DIALING
DIALOGS
DUALITY
EGALITE
EXALTED
FOALING
GOALIES
GOALONG
HEALALL
HEALERS
HEALING
HEALTHY
HIALEAH
HYALINE
ITALIAN
ITALICS
JEALOUS
MEALIER
MEALIES
OPALINE
PEALING
PHALANX
PRALINE
PSALMED
PSALTER
QUALIFY
QUALITY
REALISM
REALIST
REALITY
REALIZE
REALTOR
SCALARS
SCALDED
SCALENE
SCALERS
SCALIER
SCALING
SCALLOP
SCALPED
SCALPEL
SCALPER
SEALABS
SEALANE
SEALANT
SEALEGS
SEALERS
SEALILY
SEALING
SEALION
SEALOFF
SEALSUP
SHALALA
SHALLOT
SHALLOW
SHALOMS
SLALOMS
SMALLER
SMALTOS
SPALLED
STALAGS
STALEST
STALKED
STALKER
STALLED
SWALLOW
TEALEAF
THALERS
TRALALA
ULALUME
UNALIKE
WEALTHY
WHALERS
WHALING
ZEALAND
ZEALOTS
ZEALOUS

••A•L••

AVAILED
BEADLES
BEAGLES
BEATLES
BRADLEE
BRADLEY
BRAILLE
BRAWLED
BRAWLER
CHABLIS
CHALLIS
CHAPLET
CHAPLIN
CHARLES
CHARLEY
CHARLIE
CRADLED
CRADLES
CRAWLED
CRAWLER
DRAWLED
ENABLED
ENABLES
EPAULET
FLAILED
FRAILER
FRAILTY
FRAWLEY
GNARLED
HAARLEM
JEANLUC
LEAFLET
MEASLES
ORACLES
PEARLED
PLAYLET
QUAILED
SCALLOP
SCARLET
SEASLUG
SHALLOT
SHALLOW
SMALLER
SNARLED
SPALLED
STABLED
STABLER
STABLES
STALLED
STANLEE
STANLEY
STAPLED
STAPLER
STAPLES
STARLET
STARLIT
SWALLOW
TRAILED
TRAILER
TRAWLED
TRAWLER

••A••L•

AMAPOLA
ANATOLE
BEASTLY
BLACKLY
BLANDLY
BLANKLY
BRAILLE
BRAMBLE
BRAMBLY
BRASHLY
BRAVELY
CHAGALL
CHAPELS
CHARILY
CLAVELL
CRACKLE
CRASSLY
CRAYOLA
CRAZILY
DRACULA
ENAMELS
EXACTLY
EXAMPLE
FRAGILE
FRANKLY
FRAZZLE
GHASTLY
GRACILE
GRACKLE
GRANDLY
GRANOLA
GRANULE
GRAPPLE
GRAVELS
GRAVELY
HEADILY
HEALALL
HEAVILY
INANELY
INAPTLY
IRATELY
ONAROLL
PLAINLY
PRATTLE
READILY
SCANTLY
SCAPULA
SCARILY
SEAGULL
SEALILY
SEASALT
SEATTLE
SEAWALL
SHACKLE
SHADILY
SHAKILY
SHALALA
SHAMBLE
SHAPELY
SHARPLY
SMARTLY
SNAFFLE
SPACKLE
SPANGLE
SPANGLY
SPARELY
SPARKLE
SPATULA
STABILE
STAGILY
STAIDLY
STARKLY
STARTLE
STATELY
SUAVELY
SWADDLE
SWAHILI
TEABALL
TEARILY
TEASELS
TRALALA
TRAMPLE
TRAVELS
TWADDLE
WEARILY
WEASELS
WRANGLE

••A•••L

CHAGALL
CHANCEL
CHANNEL
CHATTEL
CLAIROL
CLAVELL
COALOIL
COASTAL
COAXIAL
CRANIAL
EMANUEL
EVANGEL
FEARFUL
FLANNEL
FRACTAL
GLACIAL
GRADUAL
GRAPNEL
HEALALL
ONAROLL
PEAFOWL
PLAYFUL
QUARREL
REAVAIL
SCALPEL
SCANDAL
SEAGULL
SEAWALL
SHAWWAL
SPANIEL
SPATIAL
TEABALL
TEARFUL
TRAMMEL
TRAUBEL
TRAVAIL
TRAYFUL

•••AL••

ABSALOM
ALFALFA
ALKALIS
ANNALEE
APPALLS
AURALEE
AURALLY
AXIALLY
BANALLY
BASALLY
BASALTS
BECALMS
BEFALLS
BIVALVE
BUGALOO
CABALAS
CATALAN
CATALOG
CATALPA
CAVALRY
DECALOG
DEDALUS
DEPALMA
DESALTS
DEVALUE
EQUALED
EQUALLY
EXHALED
EXHALES
FEMALES
FINALES
FINALLY
GERALDO
HERALDS
HIDALGO
IDEALLY
IMPALAS
IMPALED
IMPALES
INGALLS
INHALED
INHALER
INHALES
INVALID
JAIALAI
LAPALMA
LASALLE
LAVALSE
LEGALLY
LOCALES
LOCALLY
LOYALLY
LOYALTY
MAHALIA
MAYALIN
MCCALLS
MEDALED
MISALLY
MORALES
MORALLY
NASALLY
NATALIA
NATALIE
NEPALIS
NOGALES
OGLALAS
PEDALED
PENALTY
PETALED
RECALLS
REGALED
REGALES
REGALIA
REGALLY
RESALES
RESALTS
REVALUE
RIVALED
RIVALRY
ROSALIE
ROYALLY
ROYALTY
SARALEE
SAVALAS
SEDALIA
SOMALIA
SOMALIS
SQUALID
SQUALLS
SQUALOR
STEALTH
TAGALOG
TAMALES
THRALLS
TONALLY
TOTALED
TOTALLY
USUALLY
VIDALIA
VITALLY
VIVALDI
VOCALIC
VOCALLY
ZONALLY

•••A•L•

ACTABLE
ADDABLE
AFFABLE
AFFABLY
AMIABLE
AMIABLY
APPALLS
ASSAILS
ASSAULT
ATFAULT
ATLATLS
AURALLY
AXIALLY
BANALLY
BASALLY
BEFALLS
BEWAILS
BLEAKLY
BROADLY
BUYABLE
CAPABLE
CAPABLY
CHEAPLY
CITABLE
CLEANLY
CLEARLY
DEBACLE
DECARLO
DEFAULT
DERAILS
DETAILS
DISABLE
DURABLE
DURABLY
EATABLE
ENTAILS
EQUABLE
EQUABLY
EQUALLY
FINAGLE
FINALLY
FIXABLE
FRIABLE
GREATLY
HIRABLE
HUMANLY
IDEALLY
INGALLS
ISRAELI
LASALLE
LEGALLY
LIKABLE
LIVABLE
LOCALLY
LOVABLE
LOYALLY
MANACLE
MCCALLS
MINABLE
MIRACLE
MISALLY
MIXABLE
MORALLY
MOVABLE
MUTABLE
MUTABLY
NASALLY
NOFAULT
NOTABLE
NOTABLY
PARABLE
PAYABLE
PLIABLE
PLIABLY
POTABLE
RATABLE
RECALLS
REGALLY
REMAILS
RENAILS
RENAULT
RETAILS
ROYALLY
SALABLE
SAVABLE
SCRAWLS
SCRAWLY
SIZABLE
SIZABLY
SPRAWLS
SQUALLS
TAMABLE
TAXABLE
TENABLE
TENABLY
THRALLS
TONALLY
TOTALLY
TREACLE
TREACLY
TREADLE
USEABLE
USUALLY
VITALLY
VOCALLY
WOMANLY
ZONALLY

•••A••L

ANNABEL
APPAREL
CARACAL
CARAMEL
CARAVEL
CITADEL
EMPANEL
ESPANOL
ETHANOL
FALAFEL
GIRASOL
IMPANEL
KARAKUL
PALATAL
PARASOL
PHRASAL
UNRAVEL

••••AL•

AERIALS
AIRBALL
ANIMALS
ANNEALS
ANNUALS
ANOMALY
APPEALS
ASPHALT
AVOWALS
BEEBALM
BEEFALO
BENGALI
BENGALS
BRIDALS
BUFFALO
CARPALS
CASUALS
CATCALL
CATWALK
CEMBALO
CEREALS
CHAGALL
CHORALE
CHORALS
COEVALS
CORRALS
CUEBALL
CUREALL
CYMBALS
DENIALS
DORSALS
DOSSALS
DRYWALL
EMERALD
ESPIALS
EYEBALL
FACIALS
FINIALS
FLYBALL
FORMALS
FORSALE
FURBALL
GAVIALS
GESTALT
GIMBALS
GOODALL
GUMBALL
GUNWALE
HEALALL
HERBALS
HYMNALS
INSTALL
JACKALS
JAYWALK
KAMPALA
KENDALL
KIMBALL
LABIALS
LASCALA
LIPBALM
LOWBALL
MAMMALS
MANDALA
MANUALS
MARSALA
MENIALS
MESCALS
MESSALA
MISCALL
MISSALS
MONDALE
MORTALS
MUTUALS
NARWALS
NORMALS
ODDBALL
OMPHALI
ORDEALS
OUTTALK
OVERALL
PENPALS
PEPTALK
PERCALE
PIEBALD
PINBALL
PINWALE
PITFALL
PLURALS
PORTALS
PRESALE
RADIALS
RANDALL
RASCALS
RECHALK
REDEALS
REDEALT
REDIALS
REHEALS
RENTALS
REPEALS
RESCALE
RESEALS
REVEALS
RITUALS
SANDALS
SEASALT
SEAWALL
SERIALS
SERVALS
SHALALA
SIGNALS
SOCIALS
SPIRALS
SQUEALS
TAGSALE
TAMBALA
TARSALS
TEABALL
TELLALL
TIMBALE
TIMBALS
TOOTALL
TOSCALE
TRALALA
UNCIALS
UNSEALS
UPPSALA
UPSCALE
VANDALS
VASSALS
VERBALS
VISUALS

••••A•L

ABIGAIL
AIRBALL
AIRMAIL
ALLHAIL
BOBTAIL
CATCALL
CATTAIL
CHAGALL
CUEBALL
CUREALL
CURTAIL
DRYWALL
ENSNARL
EYEBALL
FANMAIL
FANTAIL
FLYBALL
FOXTAIL
FURBALL
GOODALL
GUMBALL
HEALALL
HOBNAIL
INSTALL
ISHMAEL
KENDALL
KIMBALL
LESPAUL
LOWBALL
MICHAEL
MIKHAIL
MISCALL
NAHUATL
ODDBALL
OVERALL
PIGTAIL
PINBALL
PINTAIL
PITFALL
PREVAIL
RANDALL
RAPHAEL
RATTAIL
REAVAIL
SEAWALL
SETSAIL
TEABALL
TELLALL
TOENAIL
TOOTALL
TOPSAIL
TRAVAIL
UNSNARL
WAGTAIL
WASSAIL

•••••AL

ABOREAL
ABUTTAL
ABYSMAL
ACCRUAL
ADMIRAL
ADRENAL
ALLHEAL
ALUMNAL
AROUSAL
ARRIVAL
ARSENAL
ASOCIAL
ASUSUAL
AUGURAL
AURORAL

AUSTRAL
BESTIAL
BIFOCAL
BIGDEAL
BIMODAL
BIPEDAL
CAPITAL
CARACAL
CENTRAL
CHLORAL
COASTAL
COAXIAL
COEQUAL
COMICAL
CONCEAL
CONGEAL
CONICAL
CORDIAL
CORNEAL
CRANIAL
CRUCIAL
CRYSTAL
CYNICAL
DECIMAL
DEPOSAL
DIGITAL
DIURNAL
DONEGAL
ESTIVAL
ETERNAL
ETHICAL
FACTUAL
FEDERAL
FEMORAL
FLUVIAL
FORREAL
FRACTAL
FRONTAL
FURSEAL
GENERAL
GLACIAL
GLOTTAL
GRADUAL
HELICAL
HUMERAL
ILLEGAL
IMMORAL
INITIAL
JOURNAL
JUVENAL
LACTEAL
LACUNAL
LAMINAL
LATERAL
LEXICAL
LIBERAL
LINGUAL
LITERAL
LOGICAL
LYRICAL
MAGICAL
MARITAL
MARSHAL
MARTIAL
MAXIMAL
MAYORAL
MEDICAL
MINERAL
MINIMAL
MISDEAL
MISDIAL
MISTRAL
MUSICAL
NARWHAL
NATURAL
NEUTRAL
NEWDEAL
NOMINAL
NUMERAL
NUPTIAL
OATMEAL
OEDIPAL
ONTRIAL
OPTICAL
OPTIMAL
ORBITAL
ORDINAL
OVOIDAL
PALATAL
PARTIAL
PASCHAL
PERUSAL
PHRASAL
PIVOTAL
PLUVIAL
QUETZAL
RADICAL
RAWDEAL
RECITAL
REFUSAL
REMOVAL
RENEWAL
RETINAL
RETRIAL
REVIVAL
RORQUAL
SCANDAL
SEMINAL
SENEGAL
SENSUAL
SEVERAL
SHAWWAL
SORORAL
SPATIAL
SPECIAL
SPOUSAL
STERNAL
STOICAL
SUNDIAL
SURREAL
SYNODAL
TERTIAL
TEXTUAL
THERMAL
TOPICAL
TRIVIAL
TRUCIAL
TYPICAL
UNEQUAL
UNUSUAL
UXORIAL
VEGETAL
VENTRAL
VICTUAL
VIRTUAL
WOLFGAL

AM•••••

AMADEUS
AMALGAM
AMAPOLA
AMASSED
AMASSES
AMATEUR
AMATIVE
AMATORY
AMAZING
AMAZONS
AMBIENT
AMBLERS
AMBLING
AMBRIES
AMBROSE
AMENDED
AMENITY
AMERCED
AMERCES
AMERICA
AMERIGO
AMERIKA
AMERIND
AMHARIC
AMHERST
AMIABLE
AMIABLY
AMIBLUE
AMMETER
AMMONIA
AMNESIA
AMNESTY
AMNIONS
AMOEBAE
AMOEBAS
AMOEBIC
AMONGST
AMOROUS
AMOUNTS
AMPERES
AMPHORA
AMPLEST
AMPLIFY
AMPOULE
AMPULES
AMRADIO
AMSCRAY
AMULETS
AMUSING
AMYLASE

A•M••••

AAMILNE
ADMIRAL
ADMIRED
ADMIRER
ADMIRES
ADMIXED
ADMIXES
AIMEDAT
AIMEDTO
AIMLESS
ALMAATA
ALMADEN
ALMANAC
ALMONDS
AMMETER
AMMONIA
ARMADAS
ARMBAND
ARMENIA
ARMFULS
ARMHOLE
ARMLESS
ARMLETS
ARMLOAD
ARMLOCK
ARMOIRE
ARMORED
ARMORER
ARMOURS
ARMPITS
ARMREST
ARMYANT

A••M•••

ADAMANT
ADAMITE
ADAMSON
AILMENT
AIRMAIL
AIRMASS
AIRMILE
ALAMEDA
ALAMEIN
ALAMODE
ALEMBIC
ALIMENT
ALIMONY
ALUMNAE
ALUMNAL
ALUMNUS
ANEMONE
ANIMALS
ANIMATE
ANIMATO
ANIMISM
ANIMIST
ANOMALY
ANYMORE
ARAMAIC
ARAMEAN
ARDMORE
ATAMANS
ATOMIES
ATOMIZE
AUGMENT
AZIMUTH

A•••M••

ABDOMEN
ABYSMAL
AFRAMES
ALARMED
ALARMER
ALBUMEN
ALBUMIN
ANAEMIA
ANOSMIA
ANOSMIC
ARTEMIS
ARTEMUS
ASHAMED
ASSUMED
ASSUMES
ATHOMES
ATTEMPT
ATTIMES
AUTOMAT
AUTUMNS

A••••M•

ACADEME
ACADEMY
AFFIRMS
AIRDAMS
AIRPUMP
AIRTIME
ALABAMA
ALARUMS
ALCHEMY
ALLOFME
ALLTIME
ANADEMS
ANATOMY
ANONYMS
ANTHEMS
ANYTIME
ARCLAMP
ASHRAMS
ASYLUMS
ATACAMA
ATRIUMS
AWESOME

A•••••M

ABRAHAM
ABSALOM
ACCLAIM
ACRONYM
ALYSSUM
AMALGAM
ANAGRAM
ANAHEIM
ANDYKIM
ANIMISM
ANTFARM
ANTONYM
APOTHEM
ARTFILM
ARTFORM
ATAVISM
ATHEISM

•AM••••

AAMILNE
BAMBINO
BAMBOOS
CAMBERS
CAMBIUM
CAMBRIC
CAMELIA
CAMELOT
CAMEOED
CAMEOFF
CAMEOUT
CAMERAS
CAMERON
CAMILLE
CAMISES
CAMPARI
CAMPERS
CAMPHOR
CAMPIER
CAMPING
CAMPION
CAMPOUT
DAMAGED
DAMAGES
DAMASKS
DAMMING
DAMNING
DAMPENS
DAMPERS
DAMPEST
DAMPING
DAMPISH
DAMSELS
DAMSONS
FAMULUS
GAMBIAN
GAMBITS
GAMBLED
GAMBLER
GAMBLES
GAMBOLS
GAMBREL
GAMELAW
GAMETES
GAMIEST
GAMINES
GAMMONS
HAMBURG
HAMELIN
HAMHOCK
HAMITES
HAMITIC
HAMITUP
HAMLETS
HAMMERS
HAMMETT
HAMMILY
HAMMING
HAMMOCK
HAMMOND
HAMPERS
HAMPTON
HAMSTER
JAMAICA
JAMESON
JAMMERS
JAMMING
JAMPACK
KAMPALA
LAMAISM
LAMAIST
LAMARCK
LAMBADA
LAMBDAS
LAMBEAU
LAMBENT
LAMBERT
LAMENTS
LAMINAE
LAMINAL
LAMINAR
LAMINAS
LAMMING
LAMOTTA
LAMPOIL
LAMPOON
LAMPREY
MAMBOED
MAMMALS
MAMMOTH
NAMEDAY
NAMETAG
NAMIBIA
PAMBIES
PAMPERS
RAMADAN
RAMADAS
RAMBEAU
RAMBLED
RAMBLER
RAMBLES
RAMEKIN
RAMESES
RAMJETS
RAMMING
RAMPAGE
RAMPANT
RAMPART
RAMRODS
SAMARIA
SAMBAED
SAMBARS
SAMEDAY
SAMHILL
SAMISEN
SAMITES
SAMNUNN
SAMOANS
SAMOVAR
SAMOYED
SAMPANS
SAMPLED
SAMPLER
SAMPLES
SAMPRAS
SAMPSON
SAMSARA
SAMSUNG
SAMURAI
TAMABLE
TAMALES
TAMARIN
TAMBALA
TAMBOUR
TAMMANY
TAMPERS
TAMPICO
TAMPING
TAMTAMS
VAMOOSE
VAMPERS
VAMPING
VAMPIRE
WAMBLED
WAMBLES
YAMMERS
ZAMBEZI
ZAMBIAN

•A•M•••

BALMIER
BARMAID
BARMIER
CADMIUM
CAIMANS
CALMEST
CALMING
CARMINE
DAIMLER
DAMMING
DAUMIER
EARMARK
EARMUFF
FANMAIL
FARMERS
FARMING
FARMOUT
GAMMONS
GARMENT
GASMAIN
HAEMATO
HAMMERS
HAMMETT
HAMMILY
HAMMING
HAMMOCK
HAMMOND
HARMFUL
HARMING
HARMONY
HAYMOWS
JAMMERS
JAMMING
JASMINE
LAMMING
MALMSEY
MAMMALS
MAMMOTH
MANMADE
MARMARA
MARMION
MARMOTS
OAKMOSS
OATMEAL
PALMATE
PALMIER
PALMING
PALMIST
PALMOFF
PALMOIL
PAYMENT
RAGMOPS
RAIMENT
RAMMING
RAYMOND
SALMONS
SAWMILL
TAMMANY
TARMACS
VARMINT
WALMART
WARMEST
WARMING
WARMISH
WARMSUP
WARMUPS
YAMMERS

•A••M••

BAHAMAS
BASEMAN
BASEMEN
BATEMAN
BATHMAT
BATSMAN
BATSMEN
CAKEMIX
CALOMEL
CALUMET
CALUMNY
CARAMBA
CARAMEL
CARAMIA
CAROMED
CAVEMAN
CAVEMEN
DAHOMEY
DARKMAN
EASTMAN
FADIMAN
GALUMPH
GATEMAN
GATEMEN
HACKMAN
HANGMAN
HANGMEN
HARTMAN
JAVAMAN
JAZZMAN
JAZZMEN
KASHMIR
LABAMBA
LARAMIE
MADAMEX
MALAMUD
MANUMIT
MANXMAN
MANXMEN
MARIMBA
MAXIMAL
MAXIMUM
MAXIMUS
PAJAMAS
PALOMAR
PANAMAS
RACEMES
RADAMES
RAINMAN
SALAMIS
SANDMAN
SANDMEN
TATAMIS
WALKMAN
YARDMAN
YARDMEN
YASHMAK

•A•••M•

BALSAMS
BANTAMS
DAYCAMP
DAYTIME
FATHOMS
GASPUMP
GAUTAMA
HANSOMS
LAPALMA
MACRAME
MAGNUMS
MAHATMA
MARRYME
MAYHEMS
MAYTIME
NAPTIME
PABLUMS
PALERMO
PASTIME
RAGTIME
RANSOMS
SACHEMS
SALAAMS
SANREMO
SAOTOME
SASHIMI
SATCHMO
SATSUMA
TAMTAMS
TANDEMS
VACUUMS
WARGAME
WARTIME

•A••••M

BAPTISM
BARROOM
CADMIUM
CALCIUM
CAMBIUM
DADAISM
DAYROOM
EARDRUM
EARLDOM
FADDISM
FASCISM
FAUVISM
GALLIUM
HAARLEM
HAFNIUM
HAHNIUM
HASIDIM
KARAKUM
LAMAISM
MACADAM
MALCOLM
MARKHAM
MARXISM
MAUGHAM
MAXIMUM
NATRIUM
PABULUM
PALLIUM
SANCTUM
SARCASM
TAKEAIM
TANTRUM
TAPROOM
YARDARM

••AM•••

ADAMANT
ADAMITE
ADAMSON
ALAMEDA
ALAMEIN
ALAMODE
ARAMAIC
ARAMEAN
ATAMANS
BEAMIER
BEAMING
BEAMSUP
BLAMING
BRAMBLE
BRAMBLY
CHAMBER
CHAMFER
CHAMOIS
CHAMPED
CLAMBER
CLAMMED
CLAMMER
CLAMORS
CLAMPED
CLAMSUP
CRAMMED
CRAMMER
CRAMPED
CRAMPON
DIAMOND
ENAMELS
ENAMORS
ENAMOUR
ETAMINE
EXAMINE
EXAMPLE
FLAMBED
FLAMBES
FLAMING
FOAMIER
FOAMING
FRAMEUP
FRAMING
GLAMOUR
GRAMMAR
GRAMMER
GRAMMES
GRAMPUS
IMAMATE
INAMESS
KLAMATH
LOAMIER
LOAMING
MIAMIAN
MUAMMAR
REAMASS
REAMERS
REAMING
ROAMERS
ROAMING
SCAMMED
SCAMPED
SCAMPER
SEAMIER
SEAMING
SEAMOSS
SHAMANS
SHAMBLE
SHAMING
SHAMMED
SHAMPOO
SIAMESE
SLAMMED
SLAMMER
STAMENS
STAMINA
STAMMER
STAMPED
SWAMPED
TEAMING
TEAMSUP
TRAMCAR
TRAMMEL
TRAMPAS
TRAMPED
TRAMPLE
WHAMMED

••A•M••

ALARMED
ALARMER
ANAEMIA
BOATMAN
BOATMEN
BRAHMAN
BRAHMAS
BRAHMIN
CHAPMAN
CHAPMEN
CHARMED
CHARMER
CHARMIN
CLAIMED
CLAIMER
CLAMMED
CLAMMER
CRAMMED
CRAMMER
ERASMUS
FLAGMAN
FLAGMEN
GRAMMAR
GRAMMER
GRAMMES
HEADMAN
HEADMEN
MIASMAS
MIASMIC
MUAMMAR
MYANMAR
PLASMAS
PSALMED
READMIT
REARMED
ROADMAP
SCAMMED
SHAMMED
SLAMMED
SLAMMER
STAMMER
STARMAN
STARMAP
SWARMED
TRAMMEL
TRAUMAS
UNAIMED
UNARMED
WHAMMED

••A••M•

ACADEME
ACADEMY
ALABAMA
ALARUMS
ANADEMS
ANATOMY
ATACAMA
DIADEMS
DIATOMS
DRACHMA
GIACOMO
GRAHAME
GRAHAMS
GRANDMA
IPANEMA
SHALOMS
SLALOMS
TEATIME
ULALUME

••A•••M

AMALGAM
ANAGRAM
ANAHEIM
ATAVISM
CHATHAM
CRANIUM
CZARDOM
CZARISM
DIAGRAM
GRANDAM
GUARGUM
HAARLEM
JOACHIM
KHAYYAM
PHANTOM
PIANISM
QUANTUM
REALISM
SEAGRAM
SHAHDOM
STADIUM
STARDOM
TEAROOM
TRANSOM
URANIUM
YEATEAM

•••AM••

AFRAMES
ASHAMED
BAHAMAS
BETAMAX
CARAMBA
CARAMEL
CARAMIA
CCLAMPS
CERAMIC
CREAMED
CREAMER
DECAMPS
DEFAMED
DEFAMES
DREAMED
DREAMER
DREAMON
DREAMUP
DYNAMIC
DYNAMOS
ENCAMPS
GLEAMED
IDIAMIN
ISLAMIC
JAVAMAN
JICAMAS
LABAMBA
LARAMIE
MADAMEX
MALAMUD
MIRAMAR
MIRAMAX
MOGAMBO
MYMAMMY
PAJAMAS
PANAMAS
PDJAMES
PREAMPS
PUTAMEN
PYJAMAS
PYRAMID
PYRAMUS
RADAMES
RENAMED
RENAMES
REVAMPS
RUNAMOK
SALAMIS
SESAMES
STEAMED
STEAMER
TATAMIS
UNNAMED
UNTAMED
VITAMIN

•••A•M•

BECALMS
DEPALMA
DISARMS
LAPALMA
MAHATMA
MYMAMMY
REWARMS
SALAAMS

•••A••M

ABRAHAM
ABSALOM
DADAISM
ERRATUM
JUDAISM
KARAKUM
LAMAISM
MACADAM
ORGANUM
STRATUM

••••AM•

AIRDAMS
ALABAMA
ARCLAMP
ASHRAMS
ATACAMA
BALSAMS
BANTAMS
BEDLAMP
BELDAME

BELDAMS
BELLAMY
BIGGAME
BIGNAME
CONGAME
DAYCAMP
DIORAMA
ENDGAME
ENGRAMS
GAUTAMA
GOURAMI
GRAHAME
GRAHAMS
INFLAME
INSEAMS
JIMJAMS
LOGJAMS
MACRAME
MISNAME
OFFRAMP
OILLAMP
ORIGAMI
PENNAME
PETNAME
RECLAME
REFRAME
RESTAMP
SALAAMS
SCREAMS
STREAMS
SUNLAMP
SURNAME
TAMTAMS
TSUNAMI
WARGAME
WIGWAMS

••••A•M

ACCLAIM
ANTFARM
BEEBALM
DECLAIM
EXCLAIM
FIREARM
FOREARM
LIPBALM
RECLAIM
SARCASM
SIDEARM
TAKEAIM
TONEARM
YARDARM
YESMAAM

•••••AM

ABRAHAM
AMALGAM
ANAGRAM
BEECHAM
BENTHAM
BINGHAM
BRIGHAM
BUCKRAM
CHATHAM
CULTJAM
DIAGRAM
EPIGRAM
FLOTSAM
FORDHAM
GINGHAM
GRANDAM
GRISHAM
KETCHAM
KHAYYAM
LOWBEAM
MACADAM
MARKHAM
MAUGHAM
MILLDAM
MINICAM
POTSDAM
PROGRAM
SEAGRAM
SUNBEAM
SURINAM
TRIGRAM
VIETNAM
WILLIAM
WOLFRAM
YEATEAM
YESMAAM

AN•••••

ANADEMS
ANAEMIA
ANAGRAM
ANAHEIM
ANAHUAC
ANALOGS
ANALOGY
ANALYSE
ANALYST
ANALYZE
ANANIAS
ANAPEST
ANARCHY
ANASAZI
ANATOLE
ANATOMY
ANCHORS
ANCHOVY
ANCIENT
ANDANTE
ANDEANS
ANDIRON
ANDORRA
ANDOVER
ANDREAS
ANDRESS
ANDREWS
ANDROID
ANDSOON
ANDYKIM
ANEMONE
ANEROID
ANGELES
ANGELIC
ANGELOU
ANGELUS
ANGERED
ANGLERS
ANGLING
ANGOLAN
ANGORAS
ANGRIER
ANGRILY
ANGULAR
ANILINE
ANIMALS
ANIMATE
ANIMATO
ANIMISM
ANIMIST
ANISEED
ANKLETS
ANNABEL
ANNALEE
ANNATTO
ANNEALS
ANNELID
ANNETTE
ANNEXED
ANNEXES
ANNOYED
ANNUALS
ANNUITY
ANNULAR
ANNULUS
ANODIZE
ANODYNE
ANOINTS
ANOMALY
ANONYMS
ANORAKS
ANOSMIA
ANOSMIC
ANOTHER
ANOUILH
ANSPACH
ANSWERS
ANTACID
ANTAEUS
ANTARES
ANTBEAR
ANTCOWS
ANTEDUP
ANTEING
ANTENNA
ANTESUP
ANTFARM
ANTHEMS
ANTHERS
ANTHILL
ANTHONY
ANTIART
ANTIBES
ANTIGEN
ANTIGUA
ANTILOG
ANTIOCH
ANTIQUE
ANTIWAR
ANTLERS
ANTLION
ANTOINE
ANTONIA
ANTONIN
ANTONIO
ANTONYM
ANTSIER
ANTWERP
ANXIETY
ANXIOUS
ANYBODY
ANYMORE
ANYTIME

A•N••••

ABNAKIS
AGNATES
AMNESIA
AMNESTY
AMNIONS
ANNABEL
ANNALEE
ANNATTO
ANNEALS
ANNELID
ANNETTE
ANNEXED
ANNEXES
ANNOYED
ANNUALS
ANNUITY
ANNULAR
ANNULUS
ARNICAS
AUNTIES
AWNINGS
AYNRAND

A••N•••

ABANDON
ABENAKI
ACANTHI
ACONITE
ADENINE
ADONAIS
AGENDAS
AGONIST
AGONIZE
ALENCON
ALUNSER
AMENDED
AMENITY
AMONGST
ANANIAS
ANONYMS
APTNESS
ASININE
ASUNDER
ATINGLE
ATONING
AVENGED
AVENGER
AVENGES
AVENUES
AVONLEA

A•••N••

ABOUNDS
ABSENCE
ABSENTS
ACCENTS
ACHENES
ACRONYM
ACTINIC
ADDENDA
ADDENDS
ADDONTO
ADJUNCT
ADORNED
ADRENAL
ADVANCE
ADVENTS
AFFINES
AGAINST
AIRINGS
ALBANIA
ALBENIZ
ALBINOS
ALDENTE
ALFONSO
ALIENEE
ALIENOR
ALIGNED
ALIGNER
ALKENES
ALLENDE
ALMANAC
ALMONDS
ALUMNAE
ALUMNAL
ALUMNUS
AMMONIA
AMOUNTS
ANDANTE
ANOINTS
ANTENNA
ANTONIA
ANTONIN
ANTONIO
ANTONYM
APLENTY
APPENDS
APRONED
AQUINAS
ARDENCY
ARGONNE
ARMENIA
ARRANGE
ARSENAL
ARSENIC
ARSENIO
ASCENDS
ASCENTS
ASHANTI
ASKANCE
ASOFNOW
ASSENTS
ATLANTA
ATTENDS
ATTUNED
ATTUNES
AUGENDS
AVIANCA
AVIGNON
AWNINGS

A••••N•

AAMILNE
ABALONE
ABASING
ABATING
ABIDING
ABILENE
ABSCOND
ABUSING
ACCOUNT
ACETONE
ACHTUNG
ACTIONS
ADAMANT
ADDLING
ADELINE
ADENINE
ADJOINS
ADORING
AFFRONT
AFGHANI
AFGHANS
AGROUND
AILMENT
AIRGUNS
AIRLANE
AIRLINE
ALAKING
ALIMENT
ALIMONY
ALLGONE
ALLYING
ALTOONA
AMAZING
AMAZONS
AMBIENT
AMBLING
AMERIND
AMNIONS
AMUSING
ANCIENT
ANDEANS
ANEMONE
ANGLING
ANILINE
ANODYNE
ANTEING
ANTENNA
ANTHONY
ANTOINE
APPOINT
ARACHNE
ARCHING
ARCHONS
ARCSINE
ARGONNE
ARGUING
ARIADNE
ARISING
ARIZONA
ARMBAND
ARMYANT
ARTSONG
ASHCANS
ASHLAND
ASININE
ASSIGNS
ASTOUND
ATAMANS
ATONING
ATTAINS
AUBURNS
AUGMENT
AUTUMNS
AVOWING
AWAKENS
AWAKING
AYNRAND

A•••••N

ABANDON
ABDOMEN
ABSTAIN
ACADIAN
ACHERON
ACHESON
ACTAEON
ACTUPON
ADAMSON
ADDEDIN
ADDEDON
ADDISON
ADJOURN
AEOLIAN
AFRICAN
AGAKHAN
AILERON
ALADDIN
ALAMEIN
ALARCON
ALASKAN
ALBUMEN
ALBUMIN
ALENCON
ALLISON
ALLSTON
ALLYSON
ALMADEN
ALSORAN
ANDIRON
ANDSOON
ANGOLAN
ANTIGEN
ANTLION
ANTONIN
ARABIAN
ARAMEAN
ARRAIGN
ARTISAN
ASPIRIN
AUCTION
AUDUBON
AVIGNON
AZTECAN

•AN••••

BANALLY
BANANAS
BANDAGE
BANDAID
BANDANA
BANDBOX
BANDIED
BANDIES
BANDING
BANDITO
BANDITS
BANDSAW
BANEFUL
BANGING
BANGKOK
BANGLES
BANGSUP
BANJOES
BANKERS
BANKING
BANKSON
BANNERS
BANNING
BANNOCK
BANQUET
BANSHEE
BANTAMS
BANTERS
BANYANS
CANAPES
CANARDS
CANASTA
CANCANS
CANCELS
CANDELA
CANDICE
CANDIDA
CANDIDE
CANDIDS
CANDIED
CANDIES
CANDLES
CANDOUR
CANINES
CANKERS
CANNERS
CANNERY
CANNIER
CANNILY
CANNING
CANNOLI
CANNONS
CANONIC
CANOPUS
CANSECO
CANTATA
CANTEEN
CANTERS
CANTINA
CANTING
CANTLES
CANTONS
CANTORS
CANVASS
CANYONS
CANZONE
DANCERS
DANCING
DANDERS
DANDIER
DANDIES
DANDLED
DANDLES
DANELAW
DANGERS
DANGLED
DANGLER
DANGLES
DANIELS
DANKEST
DANSEUR
FANATIC
FANBELT
FANCIED
FANCIER
FANCIES
FANCILY
FANFARE
FANIONS
FANJETS
FANMAIL
FANNING
FANSOUT
FANTAIL
FANTASY
FANZINE
GANDERS
GANGING
GANGLED
GANGLIA
GANGSAW
GANGSTA
GANGSUP
GANGWAY
GANNETS
GANNETT
GANTLET
HANCOCK
HANDBAG
HANDCAR
HANDFUL
HANDGUN
HANDIER
HANDILY
HANDING
HANDLED
HANDLER
HANDLES
HANDOFF
HANDOUT
HANDSAW
HANDSET
HANDSIN
HANDSON
HANDSUP
HANGARS
HANGDOG
HANGERS
HANGING
HANGMAN
HANGMEN
HANGOFF
HANGOUT
HANGSIN
HANGSON
HANGSUP
HANGTEN
HANGUPS
HANKERS
HANKIES
HANOVER
HANSARP
HANSOLO
HANSOMS
HANUKAH
JANACEK
JANEDOE
JANEIRO
JANEWAY
JANGLED
JANGLES
JANITOR
JANSSEN
JANTZEN
JANUARY
JANVIER
KANAKAS
KANSANS
LANCERS
LANCETS
LANDAUS
LANDERS
LANDING
LANDSAT
LANFORD
LANGDON
LANGLEY
LANGTRY
LANGUID
LANGUOR
LANGURS
LANKEST
LANKIER
LANKILY
LANOLIN
LANSING
LANTANA
LANTERN
LANYARD
MANACLE
MANAGED
MANAGER
MANAGES
MANAGUA
MANANAS
MANATEE
MANCINI
MANDALA
MANDANS
MANDATE
MANDAYS
MANDELA
MANDREL
MANDRIL
MANEGES
MANFRED
MANGERS
MANGIER
MANGLED
MANGLES
MANGOES
MANHOLE
MANHOOD
MANHOUR
MANHUNT
MANIACS
MANILOW
MANIPLE
MANITOU
MANKIND
MANLIER
MANMADE
MANNERS
MANNING
MANNISH
MANOWAR
MANSARD
MANSION
MANTELS
MANTLED
MANTLES
MANTRAP
MANTRAS
MANTRIC
MANUALS
MANUMIT
MANXCAT
MANXMAN
MANXMEN
MANYEAR
NANETTE
NANKEEN
NANNIES
PANACEA
PANACHE
PANAMAS
PANCAKE
PANCHAX
PANDECT
PANDERS
PANDITS
PANDORA
PANELED
PANETTA
PANFISH
PANICKY
PANICLE
PANNERS
PANNIER
PANNING
PANOPLY
PANPIPE
PANSIES
PANSOUT
PANTHER
PANTING
PANURGE
PANZERS
RANAWAY
RANCHED
RANCHER
RANCHES
RANCHOS
RANCOUR
RANDALL
RANDIER
RANGERS
RANGIER
RANGING
RANGOON
RANINTO
RANKERS
RANKEST
RANKING
RANKLED
RANKLES
RANLATE
RANOVER
RANRIOT
RANSACK
RANSOMS
RANTERS
RANTING
SANBORN
SANCTUM
SANDALS
SANDBAG
SANDBAR
SANDBOX
SANDERS
SANDFLY
SANDHOG
SANDIER
SANDING
SANDLOT
SANDMAN
SANDMEN
SANFORD
SANGOUT
SANGRIA
SANIBEL
SANJOSE
SANJUAN
SANLUIS
SANREMO
SANTAFE
SANTANA
SANTINI
SANTIRS
TANAGER
TANDEMS
TANGELO
TANGENT
TANGERE
TANGIER
TANGLED
TANGLES
TANGOED
TANKARD
TANKERS
TANKFUL
TANKING
TANKSUP
TANKTOP
TANLINE
TANNERS
TANNERY
TANNEST
TANNING
TANNINS
TANNISH
TANOAKS
TANSIES
TANTARA
TANTRUM
VANDALS
VANDINE
VANDYCK
VANDYKE
VANESSA
VANEYCK
VANGOGH
VANILLA
VANILLI
VANOCUR
VANPOOL
VANTAGE
VANZANT
WANDERS
WANGLED
WANGLER
WANGLES
WANNABE
WANTADS
WANTING
WANTOUT
WANTSIN
WANTSTO
XANTHAN
XANTHIC
YANGTZE
YANKEES
YANKING
YANKTON
ZANDERS
ZANIEST

•A•N•••

BADNESS
BAGNOLD
BANNERS
BANNING
BANNOCK
BARNARD
BARNEYS
BARNOWL
CANNERS
CANNERY
CANNIER
CANNILY
CANNING
CANNOLI
CANNONS
CAPNUTS
CARNERA
CARNETS
CARNIES
CATNAPS
CATNIPS
DAMNING
DARNERS
DARNING
DAUNTED
DAWNING
EARNERS
EARNEST
EARNING
FAINTED
FAINTER
FAINTLY
FANNING
FATNESS
FAWNERS
FAWNING
GAINERS
GAINFUL
GAINING
GAINSAY
GAINSON
GANNETS
GANNETT
GARNERS
GARNETS
GARNISH
GAUNTER
GAUNTLY
HAFNIUM
HAHNIUM
HARNESS
HAUNTED
JAUNTED
LAENNEC
LAUNDER
LAUNDRY
LAXNESS
MADNESS
MAENADS
MAGNATE
MAGNETO
MAGNETS
MAGNIFY
MAGNUMS
MAINTOP
MANNERS
MANNING
MANNISH
MAUNDER
MAYNARD
NANNIES
PAINFUL
PAINTED
PAINTER
PANNERS
PANNIER
PANNING
PARNELL
PATNESS
PAUNCHY
PAWNEES
PAWNERS
PAWNING
PAWNOFF
RAINBOW
RAINHAT
RAINIER
RAINING
RAINMAN
RAINOUT
RAWNESS
SADNESS
SAINTED
SAINTLY
SAMNUNN
SAUNTER
TAINTED
TANNERS
TANNERY
TANNEST
TANNING
TANNINS
TANNISH
TARNISH
TAUNTED
TAWNIER
VAINEST
VARNISH
VAUNTED
VAUNTER
WALNUTS
WANNABE
WARNING
YARNING
YAWNERS
YAWNING

•A••N••

BALANCE
BALONEY
BANANAS
BARANOF
BARENTS
BARONET
BARONGS
BASENJI

BAYONET
CABANAS
CABINET
CADENCE
CADENZA
CALENDS
CANINES
CANONIC
CARINAS
CASINGS
CASINOS
CATENAE
CAYENNE
DAPHNIS
DAVINCI
EATENAT
EATENUP
FACINGS
FAGENDS
FAIENCE
GAMINES
GARDNER
GARONNE
HACKNEY
HAIRNET
HAVENOT
HAZINGS
JACANAS
JACINTO
JACONET
KAHUNAS
LACINGS
LACONIC
LACUNAE
LACUNAL
LACUNAS
LADINOS
LAENNEC
LAGUNAS
LALANNE
LAMENTS
LAMINAE
LAMINAL
LAMINAR
LAMINAS
LARDNER
LATENCY
LATENTS
LATINAS
LATINOS
LAVINIA
LAYINTO
LAZENBY
MADONNA
MAGENTA
MAGINOT
MAHONEY
MAKINGS
MANANAS
MARINAS
MARINER
MARINES
MASONIC
MASONRY
MATINEE
PALANCE
PARDNER
PARENTS
PARINGS
PARSNIP
PARTNER
PATENTS
PATINAS
PAVANES
RANINTO
RAPANUI
RAPINES
RATINGS
RAVENED
RAVENNA
RAVINES
RAVINGS
SABINES
SAGINAW
SARANAC
SARONGS
SAVANNA
SAVANTS
SAVINGS
SAYINGS
TAGENDS
TAKENIN
TAKENON
TALENTS
TALONED
TAPINGS
TARANTO
VACANCY
VALANCE
VALENCE
WAGONER
WAHINES
WAKENED
WAKENER
YAOUNDE

•A•••N•

AAMILNE
BABOONS
BABYING
BACKEND
BACKING
BAGGING
BAILING
BAITING
BALCONY
BALDING
BALEENS
BALKANS
BALKING
BAMBINO
BANDANA
BANDING
BANGING
BANKING
BANNING
BANYANS
BARBING
BARGING
BARKING
BARRENS
BARRING
BARTEND
BARYONS
BASHING
BASKING
BASTING
BATHING
BATTENS
BATTING
BATWING
BAWLING
CABLING
CACHING
CADGING
CAFTANS
CAIMANS
CALKING
CALKINS
CALLING
CALLINS
CALMING
CALUMNY
CALVING
CALZONE
CAMPING
CANCANS
CANNING
CANNONS
CANTINA
CANTING
CANTONS
CANYONS
CANZONE
CAPEANN
CAPGUNS
CAPPING
CARBINE
CARBONS
CARDING
CAREENS
CARMINE
CARPING
CARTING
CARTONS
CARVING
CASERNS
CASHING
CASSINI
CASTING
CATIONS
CATKINS
CATTING
CAUSING
CAVEINS
CAVERNS
CAYENNE
DABBING
DABHAND
DAMMING
DAMNING
DAMPENS
DAMPING
DAMSONS
DANCING
DAPPING
DARKENS
DARLENE
DARLING
DARNING
DARTING
DASHING
DAUBING
DAWKINS
DAWNING
DAYLONG
DAYSINN
DAYTONA
EAGLING
EARNING
EARRING
EASTEND
FADEINS
FAGGING
FAILING
FAIRING
FALCONS
FALLING
FANIONS
FANNING
FANZINE
FARGONE
FARMING
FASTENS
FASTING
FASTONE
FATTENS
FAWNING
GABBING
GADDING
GAFFING
GAGGING
GAGLINE
GAINING
GAITING
GALLANT
GALLING
GALLONS
GALVANI
GAMMONS
GANGING
GAPPING
GARBING
GARCONS
GARDENS
GARLAND
GARMENT
GARONNE
GASCONS
GASHING
GASKINS
GASPING
GATLING
GAUDENS
GAUGING
GAWKING
HACKING
HAILING
HALOING
HALTING
HALVING
HAMMING
HAMMOND
HANDING
HANGING
HAPPENS
HARDENS
HARDING
HARKENS
HARKING
HARMING
HARMONY
HARPING
HASHING
HASTENS
HASTING
HATPINS
HATTING
HAULING
HAWKING
HAWKINS
JABBING
JACKING
JAGGING
JAILING
JAMMING
JARGONS
JARRING
JASMINE
JAWBONE
JAWLINE
JAYLENO
JAZZING
KACHINA
KAFTANS
KANSANS
KAYOING
LACKING
LADLING
LAGGING
LAGOONS
LALANNE
LAMBENT
LAMMING
LANDING
LANSING
LANTANA
LAPLAND
LAPPING
LAPSING
LAPWING
LARAINE
LARCENY
LARDING
LARDONS
LASAGNA
LASAGNE
LASHING
LASTING
LATEENS
LATHING
LATTENS
LAUDING
LAURENT
LAVERNE
MACHINA
MACHINE
MACRONS
MADDENS
MADDING
MADONNA
MADRONA
MAIDENS
MAILING
MALIGNS
MALTING
MANCINI
MANDANS
MANHUNT
MANKIND
MANNING
MAPPING
MARCONI
MARGINS
MARIANA
MARKING
MARLENE
MARLINS
MAROONS
MARRING
MARTENS
MARTINA
MARTINI
MARTINO
MARTINS
MARYANN
MASHING
MASKING
MASSING
MATRONS
MATTING
MAULING
MAYWINE
NABBING
NAGGING
NAILING
NAPKINS
NAPPING
NASCENT
NATIONS
OAKLAND
PACKING
PADDING
PADRONE
PADRONI
PAGEANT
PAIRING
PAISANO
PALLING
PALMING
PANNING
PANTING
PAPUANS
PARDONS
PARKING
PARRING
PARSING
PARSONS
PARTING
PARVENU
PASSANT
PASSING
PASTINA
PASTING
PATERNO
PATIENT
PATRONS
PATTENS
PATTING
PAULINA
PAULINE
PAULING
PAUSING
PAWNING
PAYMENT
RACKING
RADIANS
RADIANT
RAFTING
RAGGING
RAGLANS
RAIDING
RAILING
RAIMENT
RAINING
RAISING
RAISINS
RAMMING
RAMPANT
RANGING
RANKING
RANTING
RAPPING
RASPING
RATFINK
RATIONS
RATLINE
RATTANS
RATTING
RAVENNA
RAYGUNS
RAYMOND
RAZZING
SABRINA
SACKING
SADDENS
SAGGING
SAILING
SALERNO
SALIENT
SALMONS
SALOONS
SALTINE
SALTING
SALVING
SAMNUNN
SAMOANS
SAMPANS
SAMSUNG
SANDING
SANTANA
SANTINI
SAPIENS
SAPIENT
SAPLING
SAPPING
SARDINE
SARGENT
SASSING
SAVANNA
TABBING
TABLING
TACKING
TAGGING
TAGLINE
TAILEND
TAILING
TAIPANS
TAKEONE
TALKING
TAMMANY
TAMPING
TANGENT
TANKING
TANLINE
TANNING
TANNINS
TAPPING
TARPONS
TARRING
TARTANS
TARZANA
TASKING
TASTING
TATIANA
TATTING
TAURINE
TAUTENS
TAVERNS
TAXIING
VACCINE
VAGRANT
VALIANT
VALUING
VAMPING
VANDINE
VANZANT
VARIANT
VARMINT
VARYING
WADDING
WAFTING
WAGGING
WAGGONS
WAILING
WAITING
WAIVING
WALKING
WALKINS
WALKONS
WALLING
WANTING
WARDENS
WARDING
WARMING
WARNING
WARPING
WARRANT
WARRENS
WARRING
WASHING
WASTING
WAXWING
YAKKING
YANKING
YAPPING
YARNING
YAUPONS
YAWNING
ZAGGING
ZAPPING

•A••••N

BABYLON
BACKSIN
BAHRAIN
BALATON
BALDWIN
BALLOON
BANKSON
BARGAIN
BARGEIN
BASEMAN
BASEMEN
BASSOON
BASTION
BATEMAN
BATSMAN
BATSMEN
CADDOAN
CAISSON
CALDRON
CALHOUN
CALIBAN
CALLSIN
CALLSON
CAMERON
CAMPION
CANTEEN
CAPEANN
CAPITAN
CAPSTAN
CAPTAIN
CAPTION
CARAVAN
CARLSON
CARLTON
CAROLYN
CARRION
CARRYON
CARTOON
CASPIAN
CATALAN
CATCHON
CATSCAN
CAUTION
CAVEDIN
CAVEMAN
CAVEMEN
CAVESIN
DAKOTAN
DARKMAN
DARLEEN
DAUPHIN
DAYSINN
EARLYON
EARTHEN
EASEDIN
EASESIN
EASTERN
EASTMAN
FACTION
FADEDIN
FADESIN
FADIMAN
FALLSIN
FALLSON
FASHION
GADSDEN
GAGARIN
GAINSON
GALLEON
GAMBIAN
GASMAIN
GATEMAN
GATEMEN
GAUGUIN
HACKMAN
HADRIAN
HAIRPIN
HAITIAN
HALCYON
HALFDAN
HALOGEN
HALSTON
HAMELIN
HAMPTON
HANDGUN
HANDSIN
HANDSON
HANGMAN
HANGMEN
HANGSIN
HANGSON
HANGTEN
HARDPAN
HARDWON
HARPOON
HARPSON
HARSHEN
HARTMAN
HASBEEN
JACKSON
JACOBIN
JAMESON
JANSSEN
JANTZEN
JAVAMAN
JAVELIN
JAZZMAN
JAZZMEN
KARAJAN
KATHRYN
LAMPOON
LANGDON
LANOLIN
LANTERN
LAOCOON
LAOTIAN
LATERAN
LATERON
LATVIAN
LAUGHIN
LAYDOWN
MADCHEN
MADISON
MALAREN
MALAYAN
MANSION
MANXMAN
MANXMEN
MARCHEN
MARCHON
MARILYN
MARMION
MARTIAN
MARYANN
MATEWAN
MAUDLIN
MAULDIN
MAUREEN
MAXBORN
MAYALIN
NANKEEN
OAKFERN
OAKLAWN
PALADIN
PARAGON
PASSION
PASTERN
PATROON
PATTERN
PAULSEN
RACCOON
RAINMAN
RAKEDIN
RAKESIN
RALSTON
RAMADAN
RAMEKIN
RANGOON
RARITAN
RAYBURN
SAFFRON
SAHARAN
SALADIN
SAMISEN
SAMNUNN
SAMPSON
SANBORN
SANDMAN
SANDMEN
SANJUAN
SARACEN
SARAZEN
SAROYAN
SASSOON
SATDOWN
SAURIAN
SAVARIN
SAXHORN
SAYWHEN
TACKSON
TAILFIN
TAKENIN
TAKENON
TAKESIN
TAKESON
TAKETEN
TAMARIN
VALJEAN
VATICAN
VAUGHAN
WADESIN
WAITSON
WALKMAN
WALLOON
WANTSIN
WAVEDIN
WAVESIN
WAXBEAN
WAYWORN
XANTHAN
YANKTON
YARDMAN
YARDMEN
ZAMBIAN

••AN•••

ABANDON
ACANTHI
ANANIAS
BEANBAG
BEANERY
BEANIES
BEANING
BLANCHE
BLANDER
BLANDLY
BLANKED
BLANKER
BLANKET
BLANKLY
BRANDED
BRANDER
BRANDON
BRANIFF
BRANSON
BYANDBY
BYANOSE
CHANCED
CHANCEL
CHANCES
CHANGED
CHANGER
CHANGES
CHANNEL
CHANSON
CHANTED
CHANTER
CHANTEY
CLANGED
CLANGOR
CLANKED
CRANIAL
CRANING
CRANIUM
CRANKED
CRANKUP
EMANATE
EMANUEL
EVANDER
EVANGEL
FIANCEE
FIANCES
FLANEUR
FLANGES
FLANKED
FLANKER
FLANNEL
FRANCES
FRANCIS
FRANKED
FRANKER
FRANKIE
FRANKLY
FRANKOZ
FRANTIC
GLANCED
GLANCES
GRANADA
GRANARY
GRANDAM
GRANDEE
GRANDER
GRANDLY
GRANDMA
GRANDPA
GRANGER
GRANGES
GRANITE
GRANOLA
GRANTED
GRANTEE
GRANTOR
GRANULE
GUANACO
GUANINE
INANELY
INANEST
IPANEMA
IRANIAN
IVANHOE
JEANARP
JEANLUC
JEANNIE
KWANZAS
LEANDER
LEANERS
LEANEST
LEANING
LEANSON
LEANTOS
LOANERS
LOANING
MEANDER
MEANEST
MEANIES
MEANING
MOANERS
MOANING
MYANMAR
NUANCED
NUANCES
OCANADA
ONANDON
ORANGES
PEANUTS
PHANTOM
PIANISM
PIANIST
PLANERS
PLANETS
PLANING
PLANKED
PLANNED
PLANNER
PLANSON
PLANTAR
PLANTED
PLANTER
PRANCED
PRANCER
PRANCES
PRANKED
PSANDQS
QUANTUM
ROANOKE
RUANDAN
RWANDAN
SCANDAL
SCANNED
SCANNER
SCANTED
SCANTER
SCANTLY
SEANCES
SHANANA
SHANGRI
SHANKAR
SHANKED
SHANNON
SHANTER
SLANDER
SLANTED
SOANDSO
SPANDEX
SPANGLE
SPANGLY
SPANIEL
SPANISH
SPANKED
SPANKER
SPANNED
SPANNER
STANCES
STANDBY
STANDEE
STANDIN
STANDON
STANDUP
STANLEE
STANLEY
STANNIC
STANTON
STANZAS
SWANKER
SWANSON
THANKED
TRANCES
TRANSIT
TRANSOM
TWANGED
UGANDAN
ULANOVA
URANITE
URANIUM
WEANING
WRANGLE
WYANDOT

••A•N••

AGAINST
BEATNIK
BLARNEY
BRAINED
CHAINED
CHANNEL
DRAGNET
DRAINED
DRAINER
DRAWNIN
DRAWNON
DRAWNUP
EDASNER
FLANNEL
FLAUNTS
GRAINED
GRAPNEL
INASNIT
JEANNIE
LEARNED
LEARNER
PLAINER
PLAINES
PLAINLY
PLAINTS
PLANNED
PLANNER

SCANNED
SCANNER
SHANNON
SHATNER
SHAWNEE
SPANNED
SPANNER
SPAWNED
STAINED
STAINER
STANNIC
STAUNCH
TRAINED
TRAINEE
TRAINER
WHATNOT
YEARNED
YEARNER
YEARNTO

••A••N•

ABALONE
ABASING
ABATING
ADAMANT
ALAKING
AMAZING
AMAZONS
ARACHNE
ATAMANS
AWAKENS
AWAKING
BEACONS
BEADING
BEAMING
BEANING
BEARING
BEATING
BIASING
BLAMING
BLARING
BLATANT
BLAZING
BLAZONS
BOATING
BRACING
BRAKING
BRAVING
BRAYING
BRAZING
CEASING
CHAFING
CHASING
CLAWING
COATING
COAXING
CRANING
CRATING
CRAVENS
CRAVING
CRAYONS
CRAZING
CZARINA
DEACONS
DEADEND
DEADENS
DEAFENS
DEALING
DIAHANN
DIALING
DIAMOND
DRAGONS
DRAPING
DRAWING
DRAYING
ELATING
ERASING
ETAMINE
EVADING
EXAMINE
FEARING
FLACONS
FLAGONS
FLAKING
FLAMING
FLARING
FLAWING
FLAYING
FOALING
FOAMING
FRAMING
FRAYING
GEARING
GLARING
GLAZING
GNAWING
GOADING
GOALONG
GRACING
GRADING
GRATING
GRAVING
GRAYING
GRAZING
GUANINE
GUARANI
HEADING
HEALING
HEAPING
HEARING
HEATING
HEAVENS
HEAVING
HOAXING
HYALINE
IMAGINE
IMAGING
KLAXONS
LEADING
LEADINS
LEAFING
LEAKING
LEANING
LEAPING
LEASING
LEAVENS
LEAVING
LOADING
LOAFING
LOAMING
LOANING
MBABANE
MEANING
MOANING
NEARING
NEATENS
OCARINA
OKAYING
OPALINE
ORATING
PEAHENS
PEAKING
PEALING
PEASANT
PHALANX
PHARYNX
PHASING
PLACING
PLANING
PLATENS
PLATING
PLAYING
PRALINE
PRATING
PRAYING
QUAKING
READING
REAGENT
REAMING
REAPING
REAREND
REARING
REASONS
ROAMING
ROARING
SCALENE
SCALING
SCARING
SEAFANS
SEALANE
SEALANT
SEALING
SEAMING
SEARING
SEASONS
SEATING
SHADING
SHAKING
SHAMANS
SHAMING
SHANANA
SHAPING
SHARING
SHAVING
SKATING
SLAKING
SLATING
SLAVING
SNAKING
SNAPONS
SNARING
SOAKING
SOAPING
SOARING
SPACING
SPADING
SPARING
SPAVINS
SPAYING
STAGING
STAKING
STAMENS
STAMINA
STARING
STATING
STAVING
STAYING
SWAYING
TEAMING
TEARING
TEASING
THAWING
TRACING
TRADING
TSARINA
TZARINA
UTAHANS
WEAKENS
WEANING
WEAPONS
WEARING
WEAVING
WHALING
XRATING
XRAYING
YEAREND
ZEALAND

••A•••N

ABANDON
ACADIAN
ADAMSON
AGAKHAN
ALADDIN
ALAMEIN
ALARCON
ALASKAN
ARABIAN
ARAMEAN
BEARSON
BLACKEN
BOATMAN
BOATMEN
BRACKEN
BRAHMAN
BRAHMIN
BRANDON
BRANSON
BRAXTON
CHAGRIN
CHANSON
CHAPLIN
CHAPMAN
CHAPMEN
CHARMIN
CHASTEN
CLAPTON
CLARION
CLAYTON
COALBIN
COARSEN
CRAMPON
DEADPAN
DEALSIN
DEALTIN
DIAHANN
DRAGOON
DRAGSIN
DRAGSON
DRAWNIN
DRAWNON
DRAWSIN
DRAWSON
ELATION
EVASION
FLAGMAN
FLAGMEN
FLATTEN
GLADDEN
GRAYSON
HEADMAN
HEADMEN
HEADPIN
HEADSIN
HEARKEN
HEARTEN
HEATHEN
HOARSEN
IDAHOAN
INASPIN
IRANIAN
ITALIAN
JOAQUIN
KRATION
LEADSIN
LEADSON
LEANSON
LIAISON
MIAMIAN
ONANDON
ORATION
OVATION
PEABEAN
PEARSON
PHAETON
PHASEIN
PLANSON
PLATOON
PLAYPEN
PLAYSON
READSIN
REARDON
RUANDAN
RWANDAN
SEALION
SHANNON
SHAREIN
SHARPEN
SLACKEN
SLATKIN
SLAYTON
SMARTEN
SPARTAN
STANDIN
STANDON
STANTON
STARMAN
STASSEN
STATION
SUASION
SWANSON
TEACHIN
TRADEIN
TRADEON
UGANDAN
WHARTON
WHAUDEN

•••AN••

ADVANCE
ALBANIA
ALMANAC
ANDANTE
ARRANGE
ASHANTI
ASKANCE
ATLANTA
AVIANCA
BALANCE
BANANAS
BARANOF
BONANZA
CABANAS
CEZANNE
CHIANTI
CLEANED
CLEANER
CLEANLY
CLEANSE
CLEANUP
DECANTS
DELANEY
DEMANDS
DURANCE
DURANGO
DURANTE
ELEANOR
EMBANKS
EMPANEL
ENHANCE
ERRANDS
ESPANOL
ETHANOL
EXPANDS
EXPANSE
FINANCE
GLEANED
GLEANER
GROANED
GROANER
HOSANNA
HUMANLY
IGUANAS
IMPANEL
INCANTS
INFANCY
INFANTA
INFANTS
ISLANDS
JACANAS
JOHANNA
JUMANJI
KIWANIS
LALANNE
LEBANON
LEPANTO
MANANAS
MELANGE
MELANIE
MELANIN
MIRANDA
MORANIS
MUTANTS
NOCANDO
OCEANIA
OCEANIC
OCEANID
OCEANUS
OCTANES
OCTANTS
ORGANDY
ORGANIC
ORGANON
ORGANUM
ORGANZA
ORLANDO
ORMANDY
OTRANTO
PALANCE
PAVANES
PEDANTS
PENANCE
PICANTE
PIRANHA
PLIANCY
RAPANUI
RECANED
RECANES
RECANTS
REDANTS
REHANGS
REMANDS
RESANDS
RIBANDS
ROMANCE
ROMANIA
ROMANOV
ROMANSH
ROSANNA
ROSANNE
ROXANNE
SARANAC
SAVANNA
SAVANTS
SECANTS
SQUANTO
STRANDS
STRANGE
SUSANNA
SUSANNE
SUZANNE
TARANTO
TENANCY
TENANTS
TETANUS
TISANES
TITANIA
TITANIC
TRUANCY
TRUANTS
TYRANNY
TYRANTS
ULYANOV
UNCANNY
UNHANDS
UNHANDY
UPLANDS
URBANER
VACANCY
VALANCE
VEDANTA
VERANDA
WCHANDY
WOMANLY
ZENANAS

•••A•N•

ARIADNE
ATTAINS
CEZANNE
DETAINS
DOMAINS
GERAINT
HOSANNA
JOHANNA
LALANNE
LARAINE
LASAGNA
LASAGNE
MORAINE
OBTAINS
ORDAINS
RDLAING
REGAINS
REMAINS
REPAINT
RETAINS
ROMAINE
ROSANNA
ROSANNE
ROXANNE
SAVANNA
SCRAWNY
SPRAINS
STRAINS
SUKARNO
SUSANNA
SUSANNE
SUZANNE
TYRANNY
UKRAINE
UNCANNY

•••A••N

ACTAEON
ALMADEN
ARRAIGN
BALATON
BELAKUN
BETAKEN
BREAKIN
BROADEN
CARAVAN
CATALAN
CELADON
CHEAPEN
CLEAVON
CORAZON
DECAGON
DREAMON
GAGARIN
GELATIN
GLEASON
HEPARIN
HEXAGON
IDIAMIN
ITHACAN
JAVAMAN
KARAJAN
KERATIN
LEBANON
LEBARON
MALAREN
MALAYAN
MAYALIN
MCGAVIN
MCMAHON
MELANIN
MUTAGEN
NEVADAN
NONAGON
OCTAGON
ORGANON
PALADIN
PARAGON
PUTAMEN
RAMADAN
RETAKEN
SAHARAN
SALADIN
SARACEN
SARAZEN
SAVARIN
SNEAKIN
SWEARIN
TAMARIN
TREASON
VITAMIN
WHEATON
YUCATAN

••••AN•

ADAMANT
AFGHANI
AFGHANS
AIRLANE
ANDEANS
ARMBAND
ARMYANT
ASHCANS
ASHLAND
ATAMANS
AYNRAND
BALKANS
BANDANA
BANYANS
BELTANE
BEMOANS
BETHANY
BIGBAND
BIGBANG
BIPLANE
BLATANT
BOITANO
BRIGAND
BROGANS
BUOYANT
BURBANK
CAFTANS
CAIMANS
CANCANS
CAPEANN
CHICANA
CHICANO
CINZANO
COMMAND
COMPANY
COOLANT
COPLAND
COURANT
COWHAND
CRETANS
CURRANT
DABHAND
DEFIANT
DEMEANS
DEPLANE
DESCANT
DEVIANT
DIAHANN
DISBAND
DISTANT
DITTANY
DOLMANS
DORMANT
ELEGANT
ENCHANT
ENGLAND
ENPLANE
ENTRANT
EYEBANK
FIJIANS
FINLAND
FIREANT
FOGBANK
FONDANT
FRYPANS
GALLANT
GALVANI
GARLAND
GERMANE
GERMANS
GERMANY
GOTLAND
GUARANI
HENBANE
HERMANN
HETMANS
HISPANO
HOLLAND
HUSBAND
HYDRANT
ICELAND
IKEBANA
IMPLANT
INDIANA
INDIANS
INSPANS
INSTANT
IRELAND
ITERANT
JOBBANK
JUGBAND
JULIANA
JUTLAND
KAFTANS
KANSANS
KENYANS
KIRMANS
KOREANS
LANTANA
LAPLAND
LENFANT
LIBYANS
LOWLAND
LUCIANO
MANDANS
MARIANA
MARYANN
MBABANE
MEDIANS
MEDIANT
METHANE
MIDLAND
MIGRANT
MILLAND
MINOANS
MONTANA
MONTAND
MONTANE
MORDANT
MORGANA
MORGANS
MUNDANE
MUSTANG
NIRVANA
NITTANY
NORMAND
NORMANS
NUBIANS
OAKLAND
OFFHAND
OHIOANS
OILCANS
OILPANS
OLDHAND
OPERAND
OREGANO
ORLEANS
ORPHANS
OUTLAND
OUTRANK
OXIDANT
PAGEANT
PAISANO
PAPUANS
PASSANT
PEASANT
PECCANT
PENDANT
PENNANT
PHALANX
PIEPANS
PIQUANT
POMPANO
PROFANE
PROPANE
RADIANS
RADIANT
RAGLANS
RAMPANT
RATTANS
REGNANT
RELIANT
REMNANT
REPLANS
REPLANT
ROSTAND
SAMOANS
SAMPANS
SANTANA
SEAFANS
SEALANE
SEALANT
SERVANT
SEXTANS
SEXTANT
SHAMANS
SHANANA
SHEBANG
SIMIANS
SIOUANS
SLOGANS
SMETANA
SOPRANO
SOUTANE
SPIRANT
SPOKANE
SULTANA
SULTANS
SUNTANS
SYLVANS
SYRIANS
TAIPANS
TAMMANY
TARTANS
TARZANA
TATIANA
TIFFANY
TIJUANA
TINCANS
TONGANS
TOUCANS
TOYLAND
TREPANS
TROJANS
TULSANS
TURBANS
TUSCANY
TYMPANA
TYMPANI
ULLMANN
ULULANT
UTAHANS
VAGRANT
VALIANT
VANZANT
VARIANT
VERDANT
VIBRANT
VOLCANO
VULCANS
WARRANT
WELLAND
WETLAND
YOUMANS
ZEALAND

••••A•N

ABSTAIN
BAHRAIN
BARGAIN
BRITAIN
CAPEANN
CAPTAIN
CERTAIN
CONTAIN
COSTAIN
CURTAIN
DETRAIN
DIAHANN
DISDAIN
ENCHAIN
ENTRAIN
EXPLAIN
GASMAIN
HERMANN
INGRAIN
MARYANN
OAKLAWN
PERTAIN
PREDAWN
REDRAWN
REFRAIN
RELEARN
RESTAIN
RETRAIN
SUSTAIN
TERRAIN
ULLMANN
UNCHAIN
UNDRAWN
UNLEARN
VILLAIN

•••••AN

ACADIAN
AEOLIAN
AFRICAN
AGAKHAN
ALASKAN
ALSORAN
ANGOLAN
ARABIAN
ARAMEAN
ARTISAN
AZTECAN
BASEMAN
BATEMAN
BATSMAN
BELGIAN
BELLMAN
BERGMAN
BESTMAN
BIRDMAN
BKLIBAN
BOATMAN
BONDMAN
BOOLEAN
BRAHMAN
BRENDAN
BRENNAN
BROSNAN
BUSHMAN
CADDOAN
CALIBAN
CAPITAN
CAPSTAN
CARAVAN
CASPIAN
CATALAN
CATSCAN
CAVEMAN
CHAPMAN
CHILEAN
COCHRAN
COLEMAN
CREWMAN
CRIMEAN
DAKOTAN
DARKMAN
DEADPAN
DISHPAN
DONJUAN
DONOVAN
DOORMAN
DRIPPAN
DRISTAN
DUSTPAN
EASTMAN
ELYSIAN
ETESIAN
ETONIAN
EXURBAN
FADIMAN
FELDMAN
FEYNMAN
FIREMAN
FLAGMAN
FOOTMAN
FOREMAN
FORERAN
FORTRAN
FREEMAN
FRIEDAN
FRISIAN
FROGMAN
FUSTIAN
GAMBIAN
GATEMAN
GENTIAN
GOODMAN
GORDIAN
GRECIAN
HACKMAN
HADRIAN
HAITIAN
HALFDAN
HANGMAN
HARDPAN
HARTMAN
HEADMAN
HELLMAN
HESHVAN
HESSIAN
HICKMAN
HOFFMAN
HOUSMAN
IBERIAN
IDAHOAN
INHUMAN
IRANIAN
IRONMAN
ITALIAN
ITHACAN
JAVAMAN
JAZZMAN
JILLIAN
JOURDAN
JUNKMAN
KARAJAN
KEESHAN
KINGMAN
KINSMAN
KLUGMAN
LAOTIAN
LATERAN
LATVIAN
LILLIAN

LINEMAN
MALAYAN
MANXMAN
MARTIAN
MATEWAN
MCLUHAN
MEGRYAN
MEXICAN
MIAMIAN
MILKMAN
MINIVAN
MOHICAN
MRCLEAN
NEVADAN
NEWSMAN
ORPHEAN
ORTOLAN
OTTOMAN
OVERRAN
OXONIAN
PEABEAN
PELICAN
PEMICAN
PERLMAN
PERSIAN
PIKEMAN
PITTMAN
PLOWMAN
POSTMAN
PROPMAN
PROTEAN
PULLMAN
PURITAN
RAINMAN
RAMADAN
RARITAN
RECLEAN
REPOMAN
RICHMAN
ROMULAN
ROYBEAN
RUANDAN
RUFFIAN
RUSSIAN
RWANDAN
SAHARAN
SANDMAN
SANJUAN
SAROYAN
SAURIAN
SERBIAN
SHERMAN
SHIPMAN
SHOWMAN
SICHUAN
SIDEMAN
SIOBHAN
SNOWMAN
SOYBEAN
SPARTAN
SPORRAN
STARMAN
STYGIAN
STYRIAN
SYNGMAN
TEHERAN
TELERAN
TESTBAN
THINMAN
THURMAN
TIBETAN
TRISTAN
TUCHMAN
UGANDAN
UMBRIAN
UNCLEAN
UTOPIAN
VALJEAN
VATICAN
VAUGHAN
VETERAN
VIRGOAN
WALKMAN
WAXBEAN
WHITMAN
WISEMAN
WOLFMAN
WORKMAN
XANTHAN
YARDMAN
YEREVAN
YUCATAN
ZAMBIAN

AO•••••

AORISTS
AOUDADS

A•O••••

ABOLISH
ABOREAL
ABORTED
ABOUNDS
ACOLYTE
ACONITE
ADOLPHE
ADONAIS
ADOPTED
ADOPTEE
ADOPTER
ADORERS
ADORING
ADORNED
AEOLIAN
AGONIST
AGONIZE
AGOUTIS
ALOHAOE
ALOOFLY
AMOEBAE
AMOEBAS
AMOEBIC
AMONGST
AMOROUS
AMOUNTS
ANODIZE
ANODYNE
ANOINTS
ANOMALY
ANONYMS
ANORAKS
ANOSMIA
ANOSMIC
ANOTHER
ANOUILH
APOCOPE
APOGEES
APOLOGY
APOSTLE
APOTHEM
AROUSAL
AROUSED
AROUSES
ASOCIAL
ASOFNOW
ATOMIES
ATOMIZE
ATONING
AVOCADO
AVOCETS
AVOIDED
AVONLEA
AVOWALS
AVOWERS
AVOWING
AXOLOTL

A••O•••

ABDOMEN
ABSOLUT
ABSOLVE
ABSORBS
ACCORDS
ACCOSTS
ACCOUNT
ACROBAT
ACRONYM
ADDONTO
ADJOINS
ADJOURN
ADSORBS
AEROBAT
AEROBES
AEROBIC
AEROSOL
AFFORDS
AGROUND
ALCOHOL
ALCOVES
ALFONSO
ALLOFME
ALLOVER
ALLOWED
ALLOYED
ALMONDS
ALOOFLY
ALSORAN
ALTOONA
ALTOSAX
ALWORTH
ALYOSHA
AMMONIA
AMPOULE
ANDORRA
ANDOVER
ANGOLAN
ANGORAS
ANNOYED
ANTOINE
ANTONIA
ANTONIN
ANTONIO
ANTONYM
APPOINT
APPOSED
APPOSES
APRONED
APROPOS
ARBORED
ARBOURS
ARDOURS
AREOLAE
AREOLAR
AREOLAS
ARGONNE
ARIOSOS
ARIOSTO
ARMOIRE
ARMORED
ARMORER
ARMOURS
ARROBAS
ARROYOS
ASSORTS
ASTOLAT
ASTORIA
ASTOUND
ATHOMES
ATROPHY
ATWORST
AUROCHS
AURORAE
AURORAL
AURORAS
AUTOMAT

A•••O••

ABALONE
ABSCOND
ACEDOUT
ACEROLA
ACEROSE
ACESOUT
ACETONE
ACTIONS
ACTSOUT
ADIPOSE
AFFRONT
AIRBOAT
AIRCOOL
AIRFOIL
AIRHOLE
AIRLOCK
AIRPORT
AIRSOCK
AIRSOUT
AIRWOLF
ALAMODE
ALIMONY
ALLGONE
ALLTOLD
ALTOONA
ALVEOLI
AMAPOLA
AMATORY
AMAZONS
AMBROSE
AMNIONS
AMOROUS
AMPHORA
ANALOGS
ANALOGY
ANATOLE
ANATOMY
ANCHORS
ANCHOVY
ANDROID
ANDSOON
ANEMONE
ANEROID
ANTCOWS
ANTHONY
ANTIOCH
ANXIOUS
ANYBODY
ANYMORE
APOCOPE
APOLOGY
APPROVE
APRIORI
AQUEOUS
ARCHONS
ARDMORE
ARDUOUS
ARIZONA
ARMHOLE
ARMLOAD
ARMLOCK
ARTFORM
ARTSONG
ARTWORK
ASHFORD
ASKSOUT
ATALOSS
AUREOLA
AUREOLE
AUTHORS
AWESOME
AXLROSE
AXOLOTL
AYKROYD

A••••O•

ABANDON
ABETTOR
ABSALOM
ACHERON
ACHESON
ACTAEON
ACTUPON
ADAGIOS
ADAMSON
ADAPTOR
ADDEDON
ADDISON
ADVISOR
AERATOR
AEROSOL
AHEADOF
AILERON
AIRCOOL
AIRDROP
AIRFLOW
AIRSHOW
ALARCON
ALBEDOS
ALBINOS
ALCOHOL
ALENCON
ALIENOR
ALLISON
ALLSTON
ALLYSON
ALOHAOE
ANDIRON
ANDSOON
ANGELOU
ANTILOG
ANTLION
APRICOT
APROPOS
ARIOSOS
ARISTOS
ARROYOS
ASKSFOR
ASOFNOW
ATECROW
AUCTION
AUDITOR
AUDUBON
AVIATOR
AVIGNON
AWAREOF

A•••••O

ADDEDTO
ADDONTO
ADDUPTO
AGESAGO
AGREETO
AIMEDTO
AKIHITO
ALBERTO
ALFONSO
ALFREDO
ALLEGRO
AMERIGO
AMRADIO
ANIMATO
ANNATTO
ANTONIO
ARAPAHO
ARIOSTO
ARSENIO
ARTDECO
AVOCADO

•AO••••

BAOBABS
LAOCOON
LAOTIAN
MAOISTS
SAOTOME
TAOISTS
YAOUNDE

•A•O•••

BABOONS
BALONEY
BARONET
BARONGS
BAROQUE
BAYONET
BAZOOKA
CABOOSE
CAHOOTS
CAJOLED
CAJOLER
CAJOLES
CALOMEL
CALORIC
CALORIE
CANONIC
CANOPUS
CAROLED
CAROLER
CAROLES
CAROLUS
CAROLYN
CAROMED
CAROTID
CAROUSE
CAVORTS
DAHOMEY
DAKOTAN
DAKOTAS
FAGOTED
FAVORED
FAVOURS
GALOOTS
GARONNE
GASOHOL
GAVOTTE
HALOGEN
HALOING
HANOVER
IACOCCA
JACOBIN
JACONET
KAROLYI
KAYOING
LABORED
LABORER
LABOURS
LACONIC
LACOSTE
LAGOONS
LAJOLLA
LAKOTAS
LAMOTTA
LANOLIN
LAPORTE
LAROCHE
LASORDA
LAYOFFS
LAYOUTS
LAYOVER
MADONNA
MAHONEY
MAHOUTS
MAJORCA
MAJORED
MALODOR
MANOWAR
MAROONS
MASONIC
MASONRY
MAYORAL
NABOKOV
PAGODAS
PALOMAR
PALOOKA
PANOPLY
PAPOOSE
PAROLED
PAROLEE
PAROLES
PAYOFFS
PAYOLAS
PAYOUTS
RAGOUTS
RANOVER
RAYOVAC
RAZORED
SALOONS
SAMOANS
SAMOVAR
SAMOYED
SARONGS
SAROYAN
SAVORED
SAVOURS
SAVOURY
TABORET
TALONED
TANOAKS
VALOURS
VAMOOSE
VANOCUR
VAPOURS
WAGONER
ZAPOTEC
ZATOPEK

•A••O••

BABOONS
BACKOFF
BACKOUT
BADCOLD
BAGNOLD
BAILORS
BAILOUT
BAKEOFF
BALBOAS
BALCONY
BALFOUR
BALLOON
BALLOTS
BAMBOOS
BANJOES
BANNOCK
BARCODE
BARHOPS
BARNOWL
BARROOM
BARROWS
BARSOAP
BARYONS
BASSOON
BATBOYS
BATHOIL
BAWLOUT
BAZOOKA
CABOOSE
CACHOUS
CADDOAN
CAHOOTS
CALHOUN
CALLOFF
CALLOUS
CALLOUT
CALZONE
CAMEOED
CAMEOFF
CAMEOUT
CAMPOUT
CANDOUR
CANNOLI
CANNONS
CANTONS
CANTORS
CANYONS
CANZONE
CAPTORS
CARBONS
CARBOYS
CARCOAT
CARDOZO
CARGOES
CARHOPS
CARIOCA
CARLOAD
CARPOOL
CARPORT
CARROLL
CARROTS
CARTONS
CARTOON
CASHOUT
CASSOCK
CASTOFF
CASTOUT
CATBOAT
CATHODE
CATIONS
DAGWOOD
DAMSONS
DASBOOT
DASHOFF
DAYBOOK
DAYLONG
DAYROOM
DAYTONA
EARLOBE
EARLOCK
EASEOFF
EATSOUT
FACEOFF
FACTORS
FACTORY
FADEOUT
FAIROFF
FALCONS
FALLOFF
FALLOUT
FALLOWS
FANIONS
FANSOUT
FARGONE
FARMOUT
FARROWS
FASTONE
FATHOMS
FATUOUS
GALLONS
GALLOPS
GALOOTS
GAMBOLS
GAMMONS
GARCONS
GASCONS
GASEOUS
GAVEOFF
GAVEOUT
GAYLORD
HADDOCK
HALLOWS
HAMHOCK
HAMMOCK
HAMMOND
HANCOCK
HANDOFF
HANDOUT
HANGOFF
HANGOUT
HANSOLO
HANSOMS
HARBORS
HARBOUR
HARMONY
HARPOON
HARROWS
HASSOCK
HAULOFF
HAYFORK
HAYLOFT
HAYMOWS
JARGONS
JAWBONE
KARAOKE
KARLOFF
LABCOAT
LACTOSE
LAGOONS
LAIDOFF
LAIDOUT
LAMPOIL
LAMPOON
LANFORD
LAOCOON
LAPDOGS
LAPROBE
LAPTOPS
LARDONS
LASSOED
LASSOER
LASSOES
LASTORY
LAWFORD
LAYDOWN
LAYSOFF
LAYSOUT
MACRONS
MADEOFF
MADEOUT
MADRONA
MAFIOSO
MAKEOFF
MAKEOUT
MALCOLM
MALLOWS
MALTOSE
MAMBOED
MAMMOTH
MANGOES
MANHOLE
MANHOOD
MANHOUR
MARCONI
MARKOFF
MARKOVA
MARLOWE
MARMOTS
MAROONS
MARROWS
MASCOTS
MASTOID
MATLOCK
MATRONS
MATTOCK
MATZOHS
MAUROIS
MAXBORN
MAYPOLE
NAIROBI
NARROWS
NATIONS
OAKMOSS
OARLOCK
PADDOCK
PADLOCK
PADRONE
PADRONI
PAIDOFF
PAIDOUT
PAILOUS
PAIROFF
PALJOEY
PALMOFF
PALMOIL
PALOOKA
PANDORA
PANSOUT
PAPOOSE
PARBOIL
PARDONS
PARLORS
PARLOUR
PARLOUS
PARROTS
PARSONS
PARTOOK
PARTOUT
PASSOFF
PASSOUT
PASTORS
PATROLS
PATRONS
PATROON
PAVIOUR
PAVLOVA
PAWNOFF
PAYLOAD
PAYROLL
PAYSOFF
PAYSOUT
RACCOON
RADIOED
RAGDOLL
RAGMOPS
RAGTOPS
RAINOUT
RAKEOFF
RAMRODS
RANCOUR
RANGOON
RANSOMS
RAPPORT
RAPTORS
RATHOLE
RATIONS
RAUCOUS
RAVIOLI
RAYMOND
SACKOUT
SAILORS
SALMONS
SALOONS
SALSODA
SALVOES
SANBORN
SANFORD
SANGOUT
SANJOSE
SAOTOME
SAPPORO
SASSOON
SATDOWN
SAVIORS
SAWLOGS
SAWWOOD
SAXHORN
TABLOID
TADPOLE
TAGSOUT
TAILOFF
TAILORS
TAKEOFF
TAKEONE
TAKEOUT
TALKOUT
TALLOWS
TAMBOUR
TANGOED
TAPIOCA
TAPROOM
TAPROOT
TAPSOUT
TARPONS
TATTOOS
VACUOLE
VACUOUS
VAMOOSE
VANGOGH
VANPOOL
VARIOUS
WAGGONS
WAITOUT
WALCOTT
WALDORF
WALKONS
WALKOUT
WALLOON
WALLOPS
WALLOWS
WALPOLE
WANTOUT
WARDOFF
WARGODS
WARLOCK
WARLORD
WASHOFF
WASHOUT
WAVEOFF
WAXWORK
WAYWORN
YARROWS
YAUPONS

•A•••O•

BABYLON
BACKHOE
BACKLOG
BALATON
BALLBOY
BALLOON
BAMBOOS
BANDBOX
BANGKOK
BANKSON
BARANOF
BARRIOS
BARROOM
BASSOON
BASTION
CAISSON
CALDRON
CALICOS
CALLBOX
CALLFOR
CALLSON
CAMELOT
CAMERON
CAMPHOR
CAMPION
CAPECOD
CAPITOL
CAPTION
CAREFOR
CARIBOU
CARLSON
CARLTON
CARPOOL
CARRION
CARRYON
CARTOON
CASHBOX
CASHCOW
CASINOS
CATALOG
CATCHON
CAUTION
DAGWOOD
DASBOOT
DAYBOOK
DAYROOM
EARDROP
EARLDOM
EARLYON
EARSHOT
EATCROW
FACTION
FALLFOR
FALLSON
FASHION
GABBROS
GAINSON
GALLEON
GASOHOL
GAUCHOS
GAZEBOS
HAIRDOS
HALCYON
HALSTON
HAMPTON
HANDSON
HANGDOG
HANGSON
HARDTOP
HARDWON
HARICOT
HARPOON
HARPSON
HAUTBOY
HAVENOT
JACKPOT
JACKSON
JAMESON
JANEDOE
JANITOR
LADINOS
LAIDFOR
LAIDLOW
LAMPOON
LANGDON
LANGUOR
LAOCOON
LATERON
LATINOS
LAYSFOR
LAYSLOW
MADEFOR
MADISON
MAGINOT
MAILBOX
MAILLOT
MAINTOP
MAKEFOR
MALODOR
MANHOOD
MANILOW
MANITOU
MANSION
MARABOU
MARCHON
MARKHOR
MARMION
MARYLOU
MATADOR
NABOKOV
NAVAHOS
NAVAJOS
PAGEBOY
PAIDFOR
PAPADOC
PAPAGOS
PARADOX
PARAGON
PARASOL
PARTOOK
PASSFOR
PASSION
PATRIOT
PATROON
PAYSFOR
RACCOON
RAINBOW
RALSTON

RANCHOS
RANGOON
RANRIOT
RAYKROC
SAFFRON
SALCHOW
SALTBOX
SAMPSON
SANDBOX
SANDHOG
SANDLOT
SASSOON
SAWWOOD
TACKSON
TAGALOG
TAKENON
TAKESON
TANKTOP
TAPROOM
TAPROOT
TATTOOS
VANPOOL
WAITSON
WALLOON
WARRIOR
WARTHOG
YANKTON

•A••••O
BAMBINO
BANDITO
CALYPSO
CANSECO
CARDOZO
DARESTO
FALLSTO
FARRAGO
GALILEO
GALLICO
HAEMATO
HANSOLO
JACINTO
JALISCO
JANEIRO
JAYLENO
LAYINTO
MAESTRO
MAFIOSO
MAGNETO
MAKESDO
MARTINO
NABISCO
PAISANO
PALAZZO
PALERMO
PATERNO
RALLYTO
RANINTO
SAGUARO
SALERNO
SANREMO
SAPPORO
SAPSAGO
SATCHMO
TABASCO
TAKESTO
TALKSTO
TALLYHO
TAMPICO
TANGELO
TARANTO
VACCARO
VAQUERO
WANTSTO

••AO•••
CHAOTIC

••A•O••
ABALONE
ALAMODE
AMAPOLA
AMATORY
AMAZONS
ANALOGS
ANALOGY
ANATOLE
ANATOMY
ATALOSS
BEACONS
BEAROFF
BEAROUT
BEATOUT
BLAZONS
BRAVOES
BYANOSE
CHAMOIS
CLAMORS
COALOIL
CRAYOLA
CRAYONS
DEACONS
DEALOUT
DIALOGS
DIAMOND
DIATOMS
DRAGONS
DRAGOON
DRAGOUT
DRAWOUT
ENAMORS
ENAMOUR
FLACONS
FLAGONS
FLATOUT
FLAVORS
FLAVOUR
GIACOMO
GLAMOUR
GOABOUT
GOALONG
GRANOLA
HEADOFF
HEADOUT
HEAROUT
IDAHOAN
IMAGOES
INAWORD
ISADORA
JEALOUS
KLAXONS
LEACOCK
LEADOFF
LEADOUT
MEADOWS
MEADOWY
OFASORT
ONAROLL
ORATORS
ORATORY
PEABODY
PEACOAT
PEACOCK
PEAFOWL
PEAPODS
PEASOUP
PLATOON
PLAYOFF
PLAYOUT
QUAHOGS
READOUT
REASONS
ROANOKE
SEABORG
SEACOWS
SEADOGS
SEAFOOD
SEALOFF
SEAMOSS
SEAPORT
SEASONS
SHADOOF
SHADOWS
SHADOWY
SHAKOES
SHALOMS
SLALOMS
SNAPONS
STATORS
TEAPOTS
TEAPOYS
TEAROFF
TEAROOM
TEAROSE
TRAVOIS
ULANOVA
UNAVOCE
WEAPONS
WEAROFF
WEAROUT
ZEALOTS
ZEALOUS

••A••O•
ABANDON
ADAGIOS
ADAMSON
ADAPTOR
ALARCON
AWAREOF
BEARSON
BRANDON
BRANSON
BRAXTON
CHANSON
CHARIOT
CLAIROL
CLANGOR
CLAPTON
CLARION
CLAYTON
CRAMPON
CZARDOM
DRAGOON
DRAGSON
DRAWNON
DRAWSON
ELATION
ENACTOR
EVASION
EXACTOR
FIASCOS
FLATTOP
FRANKOZ
GEARBOX
GLASGOW
GRANTOR
GRAYSON
HEARDOF
HEARSOF
INASPOT
INAWEOF
IVANHOE
KRATION
LEADSON
LEANSON
LEANTOS
LIAISON
NEARYOU
ONANDON
ORATION
OVATION
PEARSON
PEATBOG
PHAETON
PHANTOM
PHARAOH
PLANSON
PLATOON
PLAYBOY
PLAYDOH
PLAYSON
PRAETOR
PRAYFOR
QUARTOS
REACTOR
REALTOR
REARDON
ROADHOG
SCALLOP
SEAFOOD
SEALION
SHADOOF
SHAHDOM
SHALLOT
SHALLOW
SHAMPOO
SHANNON
SLAYTON
SMALTOS
SOAPBOX
SPARROW
STANDON
STANTON
STARDOM
STATION
SUASION
SWALLOW
SWANSON
TEAROOM
TEASHOP
TRACTOR
TRADEON
TRAITOR
TRANSOM
WHARTON
WHATFOR
WHATNOT
WYANDOT

••A•••O
ARAPAHO
BRAVADO
CLAUDIO
GEARSTO
GIACOMO
GUANACO
HEAVEHO
HEAVETO
LEADSTO
PLACEBO
PLACIDO
PRAYSTO
REACTTO
SHAMPOO
SHAPIRO
SNAPSTO
SOANDSO
YEARNTO

•••AO••
KARAOKE

•••A•O•
ABSALOM
ACTAEON
AERATOR
AHEADOF
AVIATOR
BALATON
BARANOF
BELABOR
BUGABOO
BUGALOO
BYWAYOF
CATALOG
CELADON
CLEAVON
CORAZON
CREATOR
CURATOR
DECAGON
DECALOG
DECAPOD
DISAVOW
DONATOR
DREAMON
DYNAMOS
ECUADOR
ELEANOR
EQUATOR
ESPANOL
ETHANOL
GIRASOL
GLEASON
GYRATOR
HEXAGON
ICHABOD
INFAVOR
LEBANON
LEBARON
LEGATOS
LOCATOR
MARABOU
MATADOR
MCMAHON
MIKADOS
MIRADOR
MRMAGOO
NAVAHOS
NAVAJOS
NEGATOR
NONAGON
OCTAGON
OCTAVOS
ORGANON
PAPADOC
PAPAGOS
PARADOX
PARAGON
PARASOL
PICADOR
PICAROS
ROMANOV
ROTATOR
RUNAMOK
SENATOR
SODAPOP
SPEAKOF
SQUALOR
TAGALOG
TREASON
ULYANOV
VIRAGOS
WHEATON

•••A••O
AMRADIO
ANNATTO
BUGABOO
BUGALOO
CBRADIO
CURACAO
DECARLO
DEFACTO
DURANGO
EMBARGO
FMRADIO
GERALDO
HIDALGO
HORATIO
IMPASTO
INVACUO
LEPANTO
MOGAMBO
MRMAGOO
NOCANDO
NOVARRO
ONTARIO
ORLANDO
OTRANTO
PALAZZO
PICASSO
PIZARRO
RICARDO
SQUANTO
SUKARNO
SWEARTO
TABASCO
TARANTO
TOBACCO

••••AO•
ALOHAOE
PHARAOH

••••A•O
AGESAGO
ANIMATO
ARAPAHO
AVOCADO
BEEFALO
BOITANO
BRAVADO
BUFFALO
CEMBALO
CENTAVO
CHICAGO
CHICANO
CINZANO
CRUZADO
FARRAGO
FERRARO
GENNARO
GUANACO
HAEMATO
HISPANO
LONGAGO
LUCIANO
LUMBAGO
OREGANO
PAISANO
POMPANO
SAGUARO
SAPSAGO
SOPRANO
TORNADO
TOURACO
VACCARO
VIBRATO
VOLCANO
ZHIVAGO

•••••AO
CURACAO
LINBIAO

AP•••••
APACHES
APATITE
APELIKE
APERCUS
APERIES
APHELIA
APHESES
APISHLY
APLENTY
APOCOPE
APOGEES
APOLOGY
APOSTLE
APOTHEM
APPALLS
APPAREL
APPEALS
APPEARS
APPEASE
APPENDS
APPLAUD
APPLIED
APPLIES
APPOINT
APPOSED
APPOSES
APPRISE
APPRIZE
APPROVE
APRICOT
APRIORI
APRONED
APROPOS
APSIDES
APTNESS

A•P••••
ALPACAS
AMPERES
AMPHORA
AMPLEST
AMPLIFY
AMPOULE
AMPULES
APPALLS
APPAREL
APPEALS
APPEARS
APPEASE
APPENDS
APPLAUD
APPLIED
APPLIES
APPOINT
APPOSED
APPOSES
APPRISE
APPRIZE
APPROVE
ASPECTS
ASPERSE
ASPHALT
ASPIRED
ASPIRER
ASPIRES
ASPIRIN
ATPEACE

A••P•••
ADAPTED
ADAPTER
ADAPTOR
ADEPTLY
ADIPOSE
ADOPTED
ADOPTEE
ADOPTER
AIRPLAY
AIRPORT
AIRPUMP
AMAPOLA
ANAPEST
ANSPACH
ARAPAHO
ARMPITS
ASEPSIS
ASEPTIC
AUSPICE

A•••P••
ACCEPTS
ACTUPON
ADDUPTO
ADOLPHE
AGRIPPA
APROPOS
ATROPHY

A••••P•
AGRIPPA
APOCOPE
ATTEMPT

A•••••P
ACTEDUP
ADDEDUP
AIRDROP
AIRPUMP
AIRSHIP
ANTEDUP
ANTESUP
ANTWERP
ARCLAMP

•AP••••
BAPTISM
BAPTIST
BAPTIZE
CAPABLE
CAPABLY
CAPAPIE
CAPEANN
CAPECOD
CAPELET
CAPELLA
CAPERED
CAPFULS
CAPGUNS
CAPITAL
CAPITAN
CAPITOL
CAPLESS
CAPLETS
CAPNUTS
CAPPERS
CAPPING
CAPRICE
CAPSHAW
CAPSIZE
CAPSTAN
CAPSULE
CAPTAIN
CAPTION
CAPTIVE
CAPTORS
CAPTURE
CAPULET
DAPHNIS
DAPPING
DAPPLED
DAPPLES
GAPPING
HAPLESS
HAPPENS
HAPPIER
HAPPILY
JAPHETH
LAPALMA
LAPBELT
LAPDOGS
LAPELED
LAPFULS
LAPLACE
LAPLAND
LAPLATA
LAPORTE
LAPPETS
LAPPING
LAPROBE
LAPSING
LAPTOPS
LAPWING
MAPPERS
MAPPING
NAPHTHA
NAPKINS
NAPPERS
NAPPING
NAPTIME
PAPADOC
PAPAGOS
PAPAYAS
PAPEETE
PAPERED
PAPERER
PAPILLA
PAPOOSE
PAPRIKA
PAPUANS
PAPYRUS
RAPANUI
RAPHAEL
RAPIDER
RAPIDLY
RAPIERS
RAPINES
RAPPELS
RAPPERS
RAPPING
RAPPORT
RAPTORS
RAPTURE
SAPIENS
SAPIENT
SAPLING
SAPPERS
SAPPIER
SAPPING
SAPPORO
SAPSAGO
TAPERED
TAPINGS
TAPIOCA
TAPPERS
TAPPETS
TAPPING
TAPROOM
TAPROOT
TAPSOUT
TAPSTER
VAPIDLY
VAPOURS
WAPITIS
YAPPERS
YAPPING
ZAPOTEC
ZAPPERS
ZAPPING

•A•P•••
BAGPIPE
CALPACS
CAMPARI
CAMPERS
CAMPHOR
CAMPIER
CAMPING
CAMPION
CAMPOUT
CAPPERS
CAPPING
CARPALS
CARPERS
CARPETS
CARPING
CARPOOL
CARPORT
CASPIAN
DAMPENS
DAMPERS
DAMPEST
DAMPING
DAMPISH
DAPPING
DAPPLED
DAPPLES
DAUPHIN
EARPLUG
GAPPING
GASPING
GASPUMP
HAMPERS
HAMPTON
HAPPENS
HAPPIER
HAPPILY
HARPERS
HARPIES
HARPING
HARPIST
HARPOON
HARPSON
HATPINS
JAMPACK
JASPERS
KAMPALA
LAMPOIL
LAMPOON
LAMPREY
LAPPETS
LAPPING
MAGPIES
MAPPERS
MAPPING
MAYPOLE
NAPPERS
NAPPING
PAMPERS
PANPIPE
PAUPERS
PAWPAWS
RAMPAGE
RAMPANT
RAMPART
RAPPELS
RAPPERS
RAPPING
RAPPORT
RASPERS
RASPIER
RASPING
RATPACK
SAMPANS
SAMPLED
SAMPLER
SAMPLES
SAMPRAS
SAMPSON
SAPPERS
SAPPIER
SAPPING
SAPPORO
TADPOLE
TAIPANS
TAMPERS
TAMPICO
TAMPING
TAPPERS
TAPPETS
TAPPING
TARPITS
TARPONS
VAMPERS
VAMPING
VAMPIRE
VANPOOL
WALPOLE
WARPATH
WARPING
WASPISH
YAPPERS
YAPPING
YAUPONS
YAWPERS
ZAPPERS
ZAPPING

•A••P••
BASEPAY
CALIPER
CALIPHS
CALYPSO
CANAPES
CANOPUS
CAPAPIE
CATSPAW
FAUXPAS
HAIRPIN
HARDPAN
HARDPUT
JACKPOT
MAKEPAR
MANIPLE
PANOPLY
PARAPET
PARAPHS
ZATOPEK

•A•••P•
BACKUPS
BAGPIPE
BARHOPS
CARHOPS
CATALPA
CATNAPS
CATNIPS
GALLOPS
GALUMPH
GASCAPS
HANGUPS
LAPTOPS
LARRUPS
LASHUPS
MADCAPS
MAKEUPS
MARKUPS
PANPIPE
RAGMOPS
RAGTOPS
SATRAPS
WALKUPS
WALLOPS
WARMUPS

•A••••P
BACKSUP
BALLSUP
BANGSUP
BARKEEP
BARSOAP
CALLSUP
CATCHUP
DAYCAMP
DAYTRIP
EARDROP
EARFLAP
EASEDUP
EASESUP
EATENUP
FAIRSUP
GANGSUP
GASPUMP
HAMITUP
HANDSUP
HANGSUP
HANSARP
HARDTOP
HAULSUP
JACKSUP
LACEDUP
LACESUP
MAINTOP
MAKESUP
MANTRAP
MARKSUP
MATCHUP
PACKSUP
PAIRSUP
PARSNIP
PASTEUP
PATCHUP
RACKSUP
RAISEUP
RAKEDUP
RAKESUP
RATTRAP
SAVEDUP
SAVESUP
TAKESUP
TALKSUP
TALLYUP
TANKSUP
TANKTOP
WAITSUP
WAKESUP
WALLSUP
WARMSUP
WARSHIP

••AP•••
ADAPTED
ADAPTER
ADAPTOR
AMAPOLA
ANAPEST
ARAPAHO
CHAPATI
CHAPEAU
CHAPELS
CHAPLET
CHAPLIN
CHAPMAN
CHAPMEN
CHAPPED
CHAPTER
CLAPPED
CLAPPER
CLAPTON
CRAPPIE
DIAPERS
DRAPERS
DRAPERY
DRAPING
EDAPHIC
ELAPIDS
ELAPSED
ELAPSES
FLAPPED
FLAPPER
FRAPPES
GRAPHED
GRAPHIC
GRAPNEL
GRAPPLE
HEAPING
INAPTLY
LEAPERS
LEAPING
PEAPODS
REAPERS
REAPING
SCAPULA
SEAPORT
SHAPELY
SHAPERS
SHAPEUP
SHAPING
SHAPIRO
SLAPPED
SNAPONS
SNAPPED

SNAPPER
SNAPSAT
SNAPSTO
SNAPSUP
SOAPBOX
SOAPERS
SOAPIER
SOAPING
STAPLED
STAPLER
STAPLES
SWAPPED
SWAPPER
TEAPOTS
TEAPOYS
TRAPEZE
TRAPPED
TRAPPER
WEAPONS
WRAPPED
WRAPPER
WRAPSUP
WRAPUPS

••A•P••
BEARPAW
CHAMPED
CHAPPED
CLAMPED
CLAPPED
CLAPPER
CLASPED
CRAMPED
CRAMPON
CRAPPIE
DEADPAN
EXAMPLE
FLAPPED
FLAPPER
FRAPPES
GRAMPUS
GRAPPLE
GRASPED
HEADPIN
INASPIN
INASPOT
PLAYPEN
SCALPED
SCALPEL
SCALPER
SCAMPED
SCAMPER
SCARPED
SHAMPOO
SHARPED
SHARPEI
SHARPEN
SHARPER
SHARPLY
SLAPPED
SNAPPED
SNAPPER
STAMPED
STAYPUT
SWAMPED
SWAPPED
SWAPPER
TRAIPSE
TRAMPAS
TRAMPED
TRAMPLE
TRAPPED
TRAPPER
WRAPPED
WRAPPER

••A••P•
GRANDPA
PLATYPI
TEACUPS
WRAPUPS

••A•••P
BEADSUP
BEAMSUP
BEARSUP
BEATSUP
BRACEUP
CHALKUP
CHATSUP
CLAMSUP
CRACKUP
CRANKUP
DRAWNUP
DRAWSUP
FLAREUP
FLATTOP
FRAMEUP
GEARSUP
HEADSUP
HEATSUP
INAHEAP
JEANARP
LEADSUP
PEASOUP
PLAYSUP
REARSUP
ROADMAP
SCALLOP
SCAREUP
SEALSUP
SHAKEUP
SHAPEUP
SMASHUP
SNAPSUP
SOAKSUP
STACKUP
STANDUP
STARMAP
STARTUP
STAYSUP
TEAMSUP
TEARSUP
TEASHOP
TRADEUP
WRAPSUP

•••AP••
CANAPES
CAPAPIE
CHEAPEN
CHEAPER
CHEAPIE
CHEAPLY
DECAPOD
ESCAPED
ESCAPEE
ESCAPES
ONPAPER
PARAPET
PARAPHS
PITAPAT
RELAPSE
REPAPER
RETAPED
RETAPES
SCRAPED
SCRAPER
SCRAPES
SCRAPPY
SERAPES
SERAPHS
SERAPIS
SODAPOP
SYNAPSE
TERAPHS
UNHAPPY
UNTAPED

•••A•P•
CATALPA
CCLAMPS
DECAMPS
ENCAMPS
ESCARPS
PREAMPS
REVAMPS
SCRAPPY
UNHAPPY

•••A••P
BREAKUP
CLEANUP
CLEARUP
DREAMUP
SODAPOP
SPEAKUP

••••AP•
BITMAPS
BURLAPS
CATNAPS
DEWLAPS
DIGRAPH
ENTRAPS
ENWRAPS
GASCAPS
GOESAPE
HOTCAPS
HUBCAPS
ICECAPS
INSCAPE
INSHAPE
KIDNAPS
MADCAPS
MISHAPS
MOBCAPS
PERHAPS
PRETAPE
REDCAPS
REDTAPE
REWRAPS
RIPRAPS
RUNLAPS
SATRAPS
SCHNAPS
SKYCAPS
THERAPY
TOECAPS
TOETAPS
TOPKAPI
UNDRAPE
UNSNAPS
UNTRAPS
UNWRAPS
WENTAPE

••••A•P
ARCLAMP
BEDLAMP
DAYCAMP
HANSARP
JEANARP
OFFRAMP
OILLAMP
RESTAMP
SUNLAMP
UNCLASP

•••••AP
BARSOAP
EARFLAP
FLYTRAP
GIDDYAP
HEELTAP
INAHEAP
INKYCAP
KNEECAP
MANTRAP
OLDCHAP
OVERLAP
PINESAP
RATTRAP
ROADMAP
SNOWCAP
STARMAP
STOPGAP
UNSTRAP
WINESAP
WIRETAP

AQ•••••
AQUARIA
AQUATIC
AQUAVIT
AQUEOUS
AQUIFER
AQUINAS
AQUIVER

A•Q••••
ACQUIRE
ACQUITS

A•••Q••
ANTIQUE

•AQ••••
VAQUERO

•A•Q•••
BANQUET
BASQUES
CAIQUES
JACQUES
LACQUER
MARQUEE
MARQUES
MARQUEZ
MARQUIS
MASQUES
PARQUET
RACQUET

•A••Q••
BAROQUE
LALIQUE
MACAQUE

••AQ•••
CLAQUES
JOAQUIN
OPAQUES
PLAQUES

••A••Q•
PSANDQS

•••AQ••
MACAQUE

AR•••••
ARABIAN
ARACHNE
ARALSEA
ARAMAIC
ARAMEAN
ARAPAHO
ARAWAKS
ARBITER
ARBORED
ARBOURS
ARBUTUS
ARCADES
ARCADIA
ARCHAIC
ARCHERS
ARCHERY
ARCHIES
ARCHING
ARCHIVE
ARCHONS
ARCHWAY
ARCLAMP
ARCSINE
ARDENCY
ARDMORE
ARDOURS
ARDUOUS
AREARUG
AREAWAY
AREOLAE
AREOLAR
AREOLAS
ARGIVES
ARGONNE
ARGUERS
ARGUING
ARGYLES
ARIADNE
ARIDEST
ARIDITY
ARIETTA
ARIKARA
ARIOSOS
ARIOSTO
ARISING
ARISTAE
ARISTAS
ARISTOS
ARIZONA
ARLEDGE
ARMADAS
ARMBAND
ARMENIA
ARMFULS
ARMHOLE
ARMLESS
ARMLETS
ARMLOAD
ARMLOCK
ARMOIRE
ARMORED
ARMORER
ARMOURS
ARMPITS
ARMREST
ARMYANT
ARNICAS
AROUSAL
AROUSED
AROUSES
ARRAIGN
ARRANGE
ARRASES
ARRAYED
ARREARS
ARRESTS
ARRIERE
ARRISES
ARRIVAL
ARRIVED
ARRIVER
ARRIVES
ARROBAS
ARROYOS
ARSENAL
ARSENIC
ARSENIO
ARTDECO
ARTEMIS
ARTEMUS
ARTFILM
ARTFORM
ARTICLE
ARTIEST
ARTISAN
ARTISTE
ARTISTS
ARTLESS
ARTSONG
ARTWARE
ARTWORK
ARUGULA

A•R••••
ABRADED
ABRADES
ABRAHAM
ABREAST
ABRIDGE
ACREAGE
ACRIDLY
ACROBAT
ACRONYM
ACRYLIC
ADRENAL
AERATED
AERATES
AERATOR
AERIALS
AERIEST
AEROBAT
AEROBES
AEROBIC
AEROSOL
AFRAMES
AFREETS
AFRICAN
AGRAFFE
AGREETO
AGRIPPA
AGROUND
AIRBAGS
AIRBALL
AIRBASE
AIRBOAT
AIRCOOL
AIRCREW
AIRDAMS
AIRDATE
AIRDROP
AIRFARE
AIRFLOW
AIRFOIL
AIRGUNS
AIRHEAD
AIRHOLE
AIRIEST
AIRINGS
AIRLANE
AIRLESS
AIRLIFT
AIRLINE
AIRLOCK
AIRMAIL
AIRMASS
AIRMILE
AIRPLAY
AIRPORT
AIRPUMP
AIRRAID
AIRSACS
AIRSHIP
AIRSHOW
AIRSOCK
AIRSOUT
AIRTAXI
AIRTIME
AIRWAVE
AIRWAYS
AIRWOLF
ALREADY
ALRIGHT
AMRADIO
AORISTS
APRICOT
APRIORI
APRONED
APROPOS
ARRAIGN
ARRANGE
ARRASES
ARRAYED
ARREARS
ARRESTS
ARRIERE
ARRISES
ARRIVAL
ARRIVED
ARRIVER
ARRIVES
ARROBAS
ARROYOS
ATRIUMS
ATROPHY
AURALEE
AURALLY
AUREATE
AUREOLA
AUREOLE
AURICLE
AUROCHS
AURORAE
AURORAL
AURORAS

A••R•••
ABOREAL
ABORTED
ACARIDS
ACCRETE
ACCRUAL
ACCRUED
ACCRUES
ACERBIC
ACEROLA
ACEROSE
ACTRESS
ADDRESS
ADORERS
ADORING
ADORNED
AFFRAYS
AFFRONT
AGGRESS
AIGRETS
AIRRAID
ALARCON
ALARMED
ALARMER
ALARUMS
ALDRICH
ALERTED
ALERTER
ALERTLY
ALFREDO
AMBRIES
AMBROSE
AMERCED
AMERCES
AMERICA
AMERIGO
AMERIKA
AMERIND
AMOROUS
ANARCHY
ANDREAS
ANDRESS
ANDREWS
ANDROID
ANEROID
ANGRIER
ANGRILY
ANORAKS
APERCUS
APERIES
APPRISE
APPRIZE
APPROVE
ARMREST
ASCRIBE
ASHRAMS
ASTRIDE
ATTRACT
ATTRITE
ATTRITS
AVARICE
AVERAGE
AVERRED
AVERTED
AWARDED
AWARDEE
AWARDER
AWAREOF
AXLROSE
AYKROYD
AYNRAND
AZURITE

A•••R••
ABJURED
ABJURES
ABSORBS
ACCORDS
ACCURST
ACHERON
ADHERED
ADHERES
ADJURED
ADJURES
ADMIRAL
ADMIRED
ADMIRER
ADMIRES
ADSORBS
ADVERBS
ADVERSE
ADVERTS
AELFRIC
AFFIRMS
AFFORDS
AILERON
AIRCREW
AIRDROP
ALBERTA
ALBERTO
ALGERIA
ALLERGY
ALLURED
ALLURES
ALSORAN
ALTERED
ALTERER
ALVAREZ
ALWORTH
AMHARIC
AMHERST
AMPERES
AMSCRAY
ANAGRAM
ANDIRON
ANDORRA
ANGERED
ANGORAS
ANTARES
APPAREL
AQUARIA
ARBORED
AREARUG
ARMORED
ARMORER
ASFARAS
ASHTRAY
ASPERSE
ASPIRED
ASPIRER
ASPIRES
ASPIRIN
ASSERTS
ASSORTS
ASSURED
ASSURES
ASSYRIA
ASTARTE
ASTORIA
ATECROW
ATHIRST
ATLARGE
ATTIRED
ATTIRES
ATWORST
AUBURNS
AUGURAL
AUGURED
AURORAE
AURORAL
AURORAS
AUSTRAL
AUSTRIA
AVERRED

A••••R•
ABELARD
ABUSERS
ACQUIRE
ACTUARY
ADJOURN
ADORERS
AFFAIRE
AFFAIRS
AIRFARE
AIRPORT
ALFIERI
ALGEBRA
ALGIERS
ALLEARS
ALLEGRO
ALLHERE
AMATORY
AMBLERS
AMPHORA
ANCHORS
ANDORRA
ANGLERS
ANSWERS
ANTFARM
ANTHERS
ANTIART
ANTLERS
ANTWERP
ANYMORE
APPEARS
APRIORI
ARBOURS
ARCHERS
ARCHERY
ARDMORE
ARDOURS
ARGUERS
ARIKARA
ARMOIRE
ARMOURS
ARREARS
ARRIERE
ARTFORM
ARTWARE
ARTWORK
ASHBURY
ASHFORD
ASHLARS
ASTAIRE
ATATURK
ATHEART
ATHWART
AUSTERE
AUTEURS
AUTHORS
AVATARS
AVOWERS
AWKWARD

A•••••R
ABETTOR
ABUBAKR
ACCEDER
ACCUSER
ADAPTER
ADAPTOR
ADMIRER
ADOPTER
ADVISER
ADVISOR
AERATOR
ALARMER
ALCAZAR
ALERTER
ALIENOR
ALIGNER
ALLAYER
ALLEGER
ALLOVER
ALLSTAR
ALTERER
ALUNSER
AMATEUR
AMMETER
ANDOVER
ANGRIER
ANGULAR
ANNULAR
ANOTHER
ANTBEAR
ANTIWAR
ANTSIER
AQUIFER
AQUIVER
ARBITER
AREOLAR
ARMORER
ARRIVER
ASKSFOR
ASPIRER
ASSAYER
ASUNDER
ATELIER
AUDITOR
AVENGER
AVIATOR
AWARDER

•AR••••
BARANOF
BARBARA
BARBARY
BARBELL
BARBELS
BARBERS
BARBING
BARBUDA
BARCODE
BARENTS
BARETTA
BARGAIN
BARGEIN
BARGING
BARHOPS
BARKEEP
BARKERS
BARKING
BARKSAT
BARLEYS
BARMAID
BARMIER
BARNARD
BARNEYS
BARNOWL
BARONET
BARONGS
BAROQUE
BARRACK
BARRAGE
BARRELS
BARRENS
BARRETT
BARRIER
BARRING
BARRIOS
BARROOM
BARROWS
BARSOAP
BARTEND
BARTERS
BARYONS
CARACAL
CARACAS
CARAFES
CARAMBA
CARAMEL
CARAMIA
CARAVAN
CARAVEL
CARAWAY
CARBIDE
CARBINE
CARBONS
CARBOYS
CARCASS
CARCOAT
CARDERS
CARDING
CARDOZO
CAREENS
CAREERS
CAREFOR
CAREFUL
CARFARE
CARFULS
CARGOES
CARHOPS
CARIBES
CARIBOU
CARINAS
CARIOCA
CARLESS
CARLOAD
CARLSON
CARLTON
CARLYLE
CARMINE
CARNERA
CARNETS
CARNIES
CAROLED
CAROLER
CAROLES
CAROLUS
CAROLYN
CAROMED
CAROTID
CAROUSE
CARPALS
CARPERS
CARPETS
CARPING
CARPOOL
CARPORT
CARRELS
CARRERE
CARRICK
CARRIED
CARRIER
CARRIES
CARRION
CARROLL
CARROTS
CARRYON
CARSEAT
CARTAGE
CARTELS
CARTERS
CARTIER
CARTING
CARTONS
CARTOON
CARVERS
CARVING
CARWASH
DARESAY
DARESTO
DARKAGE
DARKENS
DARKEST
DARKISH
DARKMAN
DARLEEN
DARLENE
DARLING
DARNERS
DARNING
DARRELL
DARTERS
DARTING
EARACHE
EARDROP
EARDRUM
EARFLAP
EARFULS
EARHART
EARLDOM
EARLIER
EARLOBE
EARLOCK
EARLYON
EARMARK
EARMUFF
EARNERS
EARNEST
EARNING
EARPLUG
EARRING
EARSHOT
EARTHEN
EARTHLY
EARWIGS
FARADAY
FARAWAY
FAREAST
FARGONE
FARLEFT
FARMERS
FARMING
FARMOUT
FARRAGO
FARRIER
FARROWS
FARTHER
FARWEST
GARAGED
GARAGES
GARBAGE
GARBING
GARBLED
GARBLES
GARCONS
GARDENS
GARDNER
GARGLED
GARGLES

GARLAND
GARMENT
GARNERS
GARNETS
GARNISH
GARONNE
GARRETS
GARRETT
GARRICK
GARTERS
HARBORS
HARBOUR
HARDENS
HARDEST
HARDHAT
HARDHIT
HARDIER
HARDILY
HARDING
HARDPAN
HARDPUT
HARDSET
HARDTOP
HARDWON
HARICOT
HARKENS
HARKING
HARMFUL
HARMING
HARMONY
HARNESS
HARPERS
HARPIES
HARPING
HARPIST
HARPOON
HARPSON
HARRIED
HARRIER
HARRIES
HARRIET
HARROWS
HARSHEN
HARSHER
HARSHLY
HARTMAN
HARVARD
HARVEST
JARFULS
JARGONS
JARRING
KARACHI
KARAJAN
KARAKUL
KARAKUM
KARAOKE
KARASEA
KARLOFF
KAROLYI
LARAINE
LARAMIE
LARCENY
LARCHES
LARDERS
LARDING
LARDNER
LARDONS
LARGELY
LARGESS
LARGEST
LARIATS
LAROCHE
LARRUPS
MARABOU
MARACAS
MARAUDS
MARBLED
MARBLES
MARCEAU
MARCELS
MARCHED
MARCHEN
MARCHER
MARCHES
MARCHON
MARCONI
MARGATE
MARGAUX
MARGAYS
MARGINS
MARGRET
MARIANA
MARILYN
MARIMBA
MARINAS
MARINER
MARINES
MARITAL
MARKERS
MARKETS
MARKHAM
MARKHOR
MARKING
MARKKAA
MARKOFF
MARKOVA
MARKSUP
MARKUPS
MARLENE
MARLINS
MARLOWE
MARMARA
MARMION
MARMOTS
MAROONS
MARQUEE
MARQUES
MARQUEZ
MARQUIS
MARRIED
MARRIES
MARRING
MARROWS
MARRYME
MARSALA
MARSHAL
MARSHES
MARTENS
MARTIAL
MARTIAN
MARTINA
MARTINI
MARTINO
MARTINS
MARTYRS
MARVELS
MARXISM
MARYANN
MARYKAY
MARYLOU
NARRATE
NARROWS
NARTHEX
NARWALS
NARWHAL
OARLESS
OARLOCK
PARABLE
PARADED
PARADES
PARADOX
PARAGON
PARAPET
PARAPHS
PARASOL
PARBOIL
PARCELS
PARCHED
PARCHES
PARDNER
PARDONS
PARENTS
PARFAIT
PARGETS
PARIAHS
PARIBUS
PARINGS
PARKING
PARKWAY
PARLAYS
PARLEYS
PARLORS
PARLOUR
PARLOUS
PARNELL
PAROLED
PAROLEE
PAROLES
PARQUET
PARRIED
PARRIES
PARRING
PARROTS
PARSECS
PARSEES
PARSERS
PARSING
PARSLEY
PARSNIP
PARSONS
PARTAKE
PARTIAL
PARTIED
PARTIES
PARTING
PARTITA
PARTITE
PARTNER
PARTOOK
PARTOUT
PARTWAY
PARURES
PARVENU
RAREBIT
RAREGAS
RARITAN
SARACEN
SARALEE
SARANAC
SARAWAK
SARAZEN
SARCASM
SARDINE
SARGENT
SARONGS
SAROYAN
TARANTO
TARBABY
TARBELL
TARDIER
TARDILY
TARGETS
TARHEEL
TARIFFS
TARMACS
TARNISH
TARPITS
TARPONS
TARRIED
TARRIES
TARRING
TARSALS
TARSIER
TARTANS
TARTARE
TARTARS
TARTEST
TARZANA
VARIANT
VARIETY
VARIOUS
VARLETS
VARMINT
VARNISH
VARSITY
VARYING
WARBLED
WARBLER
WARBLES
WARDENS
WARDERS
WARDING
WARDOFF
WARFARE
WARGAME
WARGODS
WARIEST
WARLIKE
WARLOCK
WARLORD
WARMEST
WARMING
WARMISH
WARMSUP
WARMUPS
WARNING
WARPATH
WARPING
WARRANT
WARRENS
WARRING
WARRIOR
WARSHIP
WARTHOG
WARTIME
WARWICK
YARDAGE
YARDARM
YARDMAN
YARDMEN
YARNING
YARROWS
ZAREBAS

•A•R•••

BAHRAIN
BARRACK
BARRAGE
BARRELS
BARRENS
BARRETT
BARRIER
BARRING
BARRIOS
BARROOM
BARROWS
CAPRICE
CARRELS
CARRERE
CARRICK
CARRIED
CARRIER
CARRIES
CARRION
CARROLL
CARROTS
CARRYON
DAIRIES
DARRELL
DAYROOM
EARRING
FABRICS
FAIREST
FAIRIES
FAIRING
FAIROFF
FAIRSUP
FAIRWAY
FARRAGO
FARRIER
FARROWS
GABRIEL
GAGRULE
GARRETS
GARRETT
GARRICK
HAARLEM
HADRIAN
HAIRCUT
HAIRDOS
HAIRDYE
HAIRIER
HAIRNET
HAIRPIN
HARRIED
HARRIER
HARRIES
HARRIET
HARROWS
HATRACK
HAYRACK
HAYRIDE
JARRING
LABRETS
LAERTES
LAPROBE
LARRUPS
LAURELS
LAURENT
MACRAME
MACRONS
MADRONA
MALRAUX
MARRIED
MARRIES
MARRING
MARROWS
MARRYME
MATRONS
MAUREEN
MAURICE
MAUROIS
NAIROBI
NARRATE
NARROWS
NATRIUM
PADRONE
PADRONI
PAIRING
PAIROFF
PAIRSUP
PAPRIKA
PARRIED
PARRIES
PARRING
PARROTS
PATRICE
PATRICK
PATRIOT
PATROLS
PATRONS
PATROON
PAYROLL
RAGRUGS
RAMRODS
RANRIOT
RATRACE
SABRINA
SANREMO
SATRAPS
SAURIAN
TAPROOM
TAPROOT
TARRIED
TARRIES
TARRING
TAURINE
TAXRATE
VAGRANT
WARRANT
WARRENS
WARRING
WARRIOR
YARROWS

•A••R••

BACARDI
BACKRUB
BALDRIC
BAVARIA
CABARET
CALDRON
CALORIC
CALORIE
CAMBRIC
CAMERAS
CAMERON
CANARDS
CAPERED
CASERNS
CATERED
CATERER
CAVERNS
CAVORTS
DALTREY
DAYTRIP
EAGERER
EAGERLY
EARDROP
EARDRUM
EATCROW
FABARES
FABERGE
FAVORED
FAYWRAY
GABBROS
GAGARIN
GAMBREL
GASTRIC
HAVARTI
HAZARDS
JABIRUS
JAKARTA
KATHRYN
LABORED
LABORER
LAFARGE
LAMARCK
LAMPREY
LAPORTE
LASORDA
LATERAL
LATERAN
LATERON
LAUTREC
LAVERNE
LAYERED
LAZARUS
MACGRAW
MAHARIS
MAIGRET
MAITRED
MAJORCA
MAJORED
MALAREN
MANDREL
MANDRIL
MANFRED
MANTRAP
MANTRAS
MANTRIC
MARGRET
MATURED
MATURER
MATURES
MAYORAL
MAZURKA
NATURAL
NATURED
NATURES
NAVARRE
OAKTREE
PACKRAT
PALERMO
PALFREY
PANURGE
PAPERED
PAPERER
PAPYRUS
PARURES
PATERNO
RATTRAP
RAYKROC
RAZORED
SAFARIS
SAFFRON
SAHARAN
SALERNO
SAMARIA
SAMPRAS
SAMURAI
SANGRIA
SATIRES
SATIRIC
SAVARIN
SAVORED
TABARDS
TABORET
TALARIA
TAMARIN
TANTRUM
TAPERED
TAVERNS
TAXFREE
VALERIE
WAGERED
WAGERER
WASHRAG
WASTREL
WATERED
WATERER
WAVERED
WAVERER

•A•••R•

BACKERS
BADGERS
BAGGERS
BAILERS
BAILORS
BALLARD
BANKERS
BANNERS
BANTERS
BARBARA
BARBARY
BARBERS
BARKERS
BARNARD
BARTERS
BASTERS
BATHERS
BATTERS
BATTERY
BAWLERS
BAZAARS
CABLERS
CADBURY
CADGERS
CAESARS
CAESURA
CAHIERS
CALDERA
CALGARY
CALIBRE
CALLERS
CALVARY
CALVERT
CAMBERS
CAMPARI
CAMPERS
CANKERS
CANNERS
CANNERY
CANTERS
CANTORS
CAPPERS
CAPTORS
CAPTURE
CARDERS
CAREERS
CARFARE
CARNERA
CARPERS
CARPORT
CARRERE
CARTERS
CARVERS
CASCARA
CASTERS
CATBIRD
CAVALRY
CAVEART
DAGGERS
DAMPERS
DANCERS
DANDERS
DANGERS
DARNERS
DARTERS
DASHERS
DASTARD
DAUBERS
DAYCARE
EARHART
EARMARK
EARNERS
EASTERN
EASTERS
FACTORS
FACTORY
FAILURE
FALTERS
FANFARE
FARMERS
FATHERS
FAVOURS
FAWNERS
GABBERS
GAFFERS
GAINERS
GAITERS
GALLERY
GANDERS
GARNERS
GARTERS
GASSERS
GATHERS
GAUGERS
GAWKERS
GAYLORD
GAZZARA
HACKERS
HAGGARD
HALTERS
HALYARD
HAMBURG
HAMMERS
HAMPERS
HANGARS
HANGERS
HANKERS
HANSARP
HARBORS
HARPERS
HARVARD
HATTERS
HAUBERK
HAULERS
HAWKERS
HAWSERS
HAYFORK
HAYWARD
HAYWIRE
JABBERS
JAEGERS
JAGUARS
JAILERS
JAMMERS
JANEIRO
JANUARY
JASPERS
JAYBIRD
KAISERS
LAAGERS
LABOURS
LADDERS
LADLERS
LAGGARD
LAGGERS
LAMBERT
LANCERS
LANDERS
LANFORD
LANGTRY
LANGURS
LANTERN
LANYARD
LARDERS
LASHERS
LASTORY
LATHERS
LATHERY
LAUNDRY
LAWFORD
LAWYERS
MACABRE
MADDERS
MADEIRA
MAESTRI
MAESTRO
MAGYARS
MAILERS
MAJEURE
MALLARD
MANGERS
MANNERS
MANSARD
MAPPERS
MARKERS
MARMARA
MARTYRS
MASCARA
MASHERS
MASKERS
MASONRY
MASTERS
MASTERY
MATHERS
MATTERS
MAXBORN
MAYNARD
NABBERS
NAILERS
NAPPERS
NATTERS
NAVARRE
OAKFERN
PACKARD
PACKERS
PADDERS
PALEDRY
PALTERS
PAMPERS
PANDERS
PANDORA
PANNERS
PANZERS
PARLORS
PARSERS
PASSERS
PASTERN
PASTORS
PASTURE
PATTERN
PATTERS
PAUPERS
PAWNERS
PAYDIRT
RAFTERS
RAIDERS
RAILERS
RAISERS
RAMPART
RANGERS
RANKERS
RANTERS
RAPIERS
RAPPERS
RAPPORT
RAPTORS
RAPTURE
RASHERS
RASPERS
RASTERS
RATTERS
RAYBURN
SACKERS
SAGUARO
SAILORS
SALIERI
SALTERS
SALVERS
SAMBARS
SAMSARA
SANBORN
SANDERS
SANFORD
SANTIRS
SAPPERS
SAPPORO
SASSERS
SAUCERS
SAVIORS
SAVOURS
SAVOURY
SAWYERS
SAXHORN
TACKERS
TAILORS
TALKERS
TAMPERS
TANGERE
TANKARD
TANKERS
TANNERS
TANNERY
TANTARA
TAPPERS
TARTARE
TARTARS
TASTERS
TATTERS
VACCARO
VALOURS
VAMPERS
VAMPIRE
VAPOURS
VAQUERO
WAGGERY
WAILERS
WAITERS
WAIVERS
WALDORF
WALKERS
WALMART
WALTERS
WANDERS
WARDERS
WARFARE
WARLORD
WASHERS
WASTERS
WAXWORK
WAYWARD
WAYWORN
YAKKERS
YAMMERS
YAPPERS
YARDARM
YAWNERS
YAWPERS
ZACHARY
ZANDERS
ZAPPERS

•A••••R

BAFFLER
BAGGIER
BALFOUR
BALKIER
BALMIER
BARMIER
BARRIER
BATTIER
BATTLER
BAWDIER
CACKLER
CAJOLER
CALIBER
CALIPER
CALLFOR
CAMPHOR
CAMPIER
CANDOUR
CANNIER
CAREFOR
CAROLER
CARRIER
CARTIER
CASHBAR
CASHIER
CATCHER
CATERER
CATHAIR
CATTIER
CAULKER
CAVILER
DABBLER
DAFFIER
DAIMLER
DALLIER
DANDIER
DANGLER
DANSEUR
DAUMIER
DAWDLER
DAYSTAR
DAZZLER
EAGERER
EARLIER
FAINTER
FAKEFUR
FALLFOR
FANCIER
FARRIER
FARTHER
GABBIER
GAGSTER
GAMBLER
GARDNER
GAUCHER
GAUDIER
GAUNTER
GAUZIER
GAWKIER
HAGGLER
HAIRIER
HAMSTER
HANDCAR
HANDIER
HANDLER
HANOVER
HAPPIER
HARBOUR
HARDIER
HARRIER
HARSHER
HASTIER
HATCHER
HAUTEUR
JACKTAR
JANITOR
JANVIER
JAZZIER
KASHMIR
KAYAKER
LABELER
LABORER
LACQUER
LAIDFOR
LALAKER
LAMINAR
LANGUOR
LANKIER
LARDNER
LASSOER
LAUGHER
LAUNDER
LAYOVER
LAYSFOR
MADEFOR
MAKEFOR
MAKEPAR
MALABAR
MALODOR
MANAGER
MANGIER
MANHOUR
MANLIER
MANOWAR
MANYEAR
MARCHER
MARINER
MARKHOR
MASSEUR
MATADOR
MATURER
MAUNDER
MAXBAER
MAYFAIR
NASTIER
NATTIER
PACECAR
PADDLER
PAIDFOR
PAINTER
PALAVER
PALMIER
PALOMAR
PANNIER
PANTHER
PAPERER
PARDNER
PARLOUR
PARTNER
PASSFOR
PASTEUR
PASTIER

PAVIOUR
PAYSFOR
RACECAR
RAFFLER
RAGGIER
RAINIER
RAMBLER
RANCHER
RANCOUR
RANDIER
RANGIER
RANOVER
RAPIDER
RASPIER
RATTIER
RATTLER
SADDLER
SAGGIER
SALAZAR
SALTIER
SAMOVAR
SAMPLER
SANDBAR
SANDIER
SAPPIER
SASSIER
SAUCIER
SAUNTER
SAVAGER
SAVVIER
TABULAR
TACKIER
TACKLER
TAMBOUR
TANAGER
TANGIER
TAPSTER
TARDIER
TARSIER
TASTIER
TATTIER
TATTLER
TAWNIER
VANOCUR
VAULTER
VAUNTER
WACKIER
WADDLER
WAFFLER
WAGERER
WAGONER
WAKENER
WALTZER
WANGLER
WARBLER
WARRIOR
WATCHER
WATERER
WAVERER

••AR•••

ACARIDS
ALARCON
ALARMED
ALARMER
ALARUMS
ANARCHY
AVARICE
AWARDED
AWARDEE
AWARDER
AWAREOF
BEARCAT
BEARDED
BEARERS
BEARHUG
BEARING
BEARISH
BEAROFF
BEAROUT
BEARPAW
BEARSON
BEARSUP
BLARING
BLARNEY
BOARDED
BOARDER
CHARADE
CHARGED
CHARGER
CHARGES
CHARIER
CHARILY
CHARIOT
CHARITY
CHARLES
CHARLEY
CHARLIE
CHARMED
CHARMER
CHARMIN
CHARRED
CHARTED
CHARTER
CLARETS
CLARICE
CLARIFY
CLARION
CLARITY
COARSEN
COARSER
CZARDAS
CZARDOM
CZARINA
CZARISM
CZARIST
DEAREST
DEARSIR
DEARTHS
DIARIES
DWARFED
DWARVES
EPARCHS
FEARERS
FEARFUL
FEARING
FLAREUP
FLARING
GEARBOX
GEARING
GEARSTO
GEARSUP
GLARING
GNARLED
GNARRED
GUARANI
GUARDED
GUARGUM
HAARLEM
HEARDOF
HEARERS
HEARING
HEARKEN
HEAROUT
HEARSAY
HEARSOF
HEARTEN
HEARTHS
HOARDED
HOARDER
HOARIER
HOARSEN
HOARSER
IMARETS
INARUSH
LEARJET
LEARNED
LEARNER
NEAREST
NEARING
NEARYOU
OCARINA
ONAROLL
PEARLED
PEARSON
PHARAOH
PHARYNX
QUARREL
QUARTER
QUARTET
QUARTOS
REARDON
REAREND
REARERS
REARGUE
REARING
REARMED
REARSUP
ROARERS
ROARING
SCARABS
SCARCER
SCARERS
SCAREUP
SCARFED
SCARIER
SCARIFY
SCARILY
SCARING
SCARLET
SCARPED
SCARRED
SCARVES
SEARING
SHAREIN
SHARERS
SHARING
SHARKEY
SHARPED
SHARPEI
SHARPEN
SHARPER
SHARPLY
SMARTED
SMARTEN
SMARTER
SMARTLY
SNARING
SNARLED
SOARERS
SOARING
SPARELY
SPAREST
SPARGED
SPARGES
SPARING
SPARKED
SPARKLE
SPARRED
SPARROW
SPARSER
SPARTAN
STARCHY
STARDOM
STAREAT
STARERS
STARETS
STARING
STARKER
STARKLY
STARLET
STARLIT
STARMAN
STARMAP
STARRED
STARTED
STARTER
STARTLE
STARTUP
STARVED
STARVES
SWARMED
SWARTHY
TEARFUL
TEARGAS
TEARIER
TEARILY
TEARING
TEAROFF
TEAROOM
TEAROSE
TEARSAT
TEARSUP
TSARINA
TSARIST
TUAREGS
TZARINA
UNARMED
WEARERS
WEARIED
WEARIER
WEARIES
WEARILY
WEARING
WEAROFF
WEAROUT
WHARFED
WHARTON
WHARVES
YEAREND
YEARNED
YEARNER
YEARNTO

••A•R••

ANAGRAM
BEATRIX
CHAGRIN
CHAIRED
CHARRED
CLAIROL
DIAGRAM
FIACRES
GNARRED
PRAIRIE
QUARREL
REAIRED
SCARRED
SEAGRAM
SPARRED
SPARROW
STARRED
TEATRAY
UNAIRED
UPATREE

••A••R•

AMATORY
ATATURK
AVATARS
BEAKERS
BEANERY
BEARERS
BEATERS
BEAVERS
BLAZERS
BOATERS
BRACERS
BRAVERY
BRAVURA
BRAYERS
CHASERS
CLAMORS
CLAWERS
COALERS
COAXERS
CRATERS
CRAVERS
DEALERS
DIALERS
DIAPERS
DRAPERS
DRAPERY
DRAWERS
ELATERS
ENAMORS
ERASERS
ERASURE
ETAGERE
EVADERS
FEARERS
FEATURE
FLAKERS
FLAVORS
GLAZERS
GNAWERS
GRADERS
GRANARY
GRATERS
GRAVURE
GRAZERS
HEADERS
HEALERS
HEARERS
HEATERS
HEAVERS
HOAXERS
IMAGERS
IMAGERY
INAWORD
ISADORA
JEANARP
KNAVERY
KRATERS
LAAGERS
LEADERS
LEAKERS
LEANERS
LEAPERS
LEASERS
LOADERS
LOAFERS
LOANERS
MEASURE
MOANERS
NIAGARA
OFASORT
ONADARE
ONAGERS
ORATORS
ORATORY
PHAEDRA
PHASERS
PIASTRE
PLACARD
PLACERS
PLANERS
PLATERS
PLAYERS
PRATERS
PRAYERS
QUAKERS
QUASARS
QUAVERS
QUAVERY
READERS
REAMERS
REAPERS
REARERS
ROAMERS
ROARERS
SCALARS
SCALERS
SCARERS
SEABIRD
SEABORG
SEAGIRT
SEALERS
SEAPORT
SEATERS
SEAWARD
SHAKERS
SHANGRI
SHAPERS
SHAPIRO
SHARERS
SHASTRI
SHAVERS
SKATERS
SLAVERS
SLAVERY
SLAYERS
SOAKERS
SOAPERS
SOARERS
SPACERS
SPADERS
STAGERS
STARERS
STATORS
STATURE
SWAYERS
TEACART
TEASERS
THALERS
TRABERT
TRACERS
TRACERY
TRADERS
TRAVERS
UNAWARE
WEARERS
WEAVERS
WHALERS

••A•••R

ADAPTER
ADAPTOR
ALARMER
AMATEUR
AWARDER
BEADIER
BEAMIER
BLABBER
BLACKER
BLADDER
BLANDER
BLANKER
BLASTER
BLATHER
BOARDER
BOASTER
BRAGGER
BRAIDER
BRANDER
BRASHER
BRAWLER
BRAZIER
CHAMBER
CHAMFER
CHANGER
CHANTER
CHAPTER
CHARGER
CHARIER
CHARMER
CHARTER
CHASTER
CHATTER
CHAUCER
CLABBER
CLAIMER
CLAMBER
CLAMMER
CLANGOR
CLAPPER
CLATTER
CLAVIER
CLAYIER
COALCAR
COALTAR
COARSER
COASTER
CRABBER
CRACKER
CRAFTER
CRAMMER
CRASSER
CRAWLER
CRAZIER
DEADAIR
DEARSIR
DRABBER
DRAINER
DRAWBAR
EDASNER
ENACTOR
ENAMOUR
EVANDER
EXACTER
EXACTOR
FEATHER
FLAKIER
FLANEUR
FLANKER
FLAPPER
FLASHER
FLATCAR
FLATTER
FLAVOUR
FOAMIER
FRAILER
FRANKER
FRASIER
FRAZIER
GLACIER
GLADDER
GLAMOUR
GLAZIER
GRABBER
GRAMMAR
GRAMMER
GRANDER
GRANGER
GRANTOR
HEADIER
HEATHER
HEATTER
HEAVIER
HOARDER
HOARIER
HOARSER
LEAFIER
LEAGUER
LEAKIER
LEANDER
LEARNER
LEATHER
LOAMIER
MEALIER
MEANDER
MEATIER
MUAMMAR
MYANMAR
ONATEAR
PIASTER
PLAINER
PLANNER
PLANTAR
PLANTER
PLASTER
PLATTER
POACHER
PRAETOR
PRAISER
PRANCER
PRAYFOR
PSALTER
QUAFFER
QUARTER
REACTOR
READIER
REALTOR
ROASTER
SCALIER
SCALPER
SCAMPER
SCANNER
SCANTER
SCARCER
SCARIER
SCATTER
SEAMIER
SEASTAR
SHADIER
SHAFFER
SHAKIER
SHANKAR
SHANTER
SHARPER
SHATNER
SHATTER
SLACKER
SLAMMER
SLANDER
SLASHER
SLATHER
SLATIER
SMACKER
SMALLER
SMARTER
SMASHER
SMATTER
SNACKER
SNAKIER
SNAPPER
SOAPIER
SPACIER
SPANKER
SPANNER
SPARSER
SPATTER
STABLER
STAFFER
STAGGER
STAGIER
STAIDER
STAINER
STALKER
STAMMER
STAPLER
STARKER
STARTER
SWAGGER
SWANKER
SWAPPER
SWATTER
TEACHER
TEARIER
TOASTER
TRACKER
TRACTOR
TRAILER
TRAINER
TRAITOR
TRAMCAR
TRAPPER
TRAWLER
WEARIER
WEATHER
WHATFOR
WRAPPER
YEARNER

•••AR••

ALVAREZ
AMHARIC
ANTARES
APPAREL
AQUARIA
AREARUG
ASFARAS
ASTARTE
ATLARGE
BACARDI
BAVARIA
BETARAY
BIZARRE
BLEARED
BRIARDS
CABARET
CANARDS
CLEARED
CLEARER
CLEARLY
CLEARUP
COWARDS
DEBARGE
DEBARKS
DECARLO
DEFARGE
DEPARTS
DISARMS
DUBARRY
EDWARDS
EMBARGO
EMBARKS
ENGARDE
ENLARGE
ESCARPS
EXPARTE
FABARES
GAGARIN
GOCARTS
GOKARTS
HAVARTI
HAZARDS
HEPARIN
HOGARTH
HOWARDS
IDCARDS
IMPARTS
INNARDS
INWARDS
JAKARTA
LAFARGE
LAMARCK
LAZARUS
LEBARON
LECARRE
LIZARDS
MAHARIS
MALAREN
MINARET
MONARCH
MUBARAK
NAVARRE
NOVARRO
ONTARIO
ONWARDS
OXCARTS
PETARDS
PICAROS
PIZARRO
POLARIS
REGARDS
REMARKS
REMARRY
RETARDS
REWARDS
REWARMS
RICARDO
ROBARDS
SAFARIS
SAHARAN
SAMARIA
SAVARIN
SHEARED
SHEARER
SMEARED
SOLARIA
SPEARED
SQUARED
SQUARER
SQUARES
SUGARED
SUKARNO
SWEARAT
SWEARBY
SWEARER
SWEARIN
SWEARTO
TABARDS
TALARIA
TAMARIN
THWARTS
TOWARDS
UNEARTH
UPWARDS
WIZARDS

•••A•R•

AFFAIRE
AFFAIRS
ASTAIRE
BAZAARS
BIZARRE
CAVALRY
CONAKRY
DUBARRY
ECLAIRS
HILAIRE
IMPAIRS
LECARRE
LEHAVRE
MACABRE
MOHAIRS
NAVARRE
NOVARRO
PIZARRO
REMARRY
REPAIRS
RIVALRY
SINATRA
SUMATRA
THEATRE

•••A••R

AERATOR
ALCAZAR
ALLAYER
ASSAYER
AVIATOR
BELABOR
BENATAR
BENAZIR
BLEAKER
BREAKER
BROADER
CHEAPER
CHEATER
CLEANER
CLEARER
CLEAVER
CREAMER
CREATOR
CURATOR
DEBATER
DELAYER
DONATOR
DOWAGER
DREAMER
ECUADOR
ELEANOR
EQUATOR
FLOATER
FORAGER
GLEANER
GREASER
GREATER
GROANER
GYRATOR
INFAVOR
INHALER
INVADER
KAYAKER
KNEADER
LALAKER
LOCATER
LOCATOR
MALABAR
MANAGER
MATADOR
MIRADOR
MIRAMAR
NEGATOR
NEWAGER
ONPAPER
PALAVER
PICADOR
PLEADER
PLEASER
REPAPER
ROTATOR
SALAZAR
SAVAGER
SCRAPER
SEDATER
SENATOR
SHEARER
SNEAKER
SPEAKER
SPRAYER
SQUALOR
SQUARER
STEAMER
SWEARER
SWEATER
TANAGER
THEATER
TREADER
URBANER
VOYAGER

••••AR•

ABELARD
ACTUARY
AIRFARE
ALLEARS
ANTFARM
ANTIART
APPEARS
ARIKARA
ARREARS
ARTWARE
ASHLARS
ATHEART
ATHWART
AVATARS
AWKWARD
BALLARD
BARBARA
BARBARY
BARNARD
BAZAARS
BEGGARS
BERNARD
BITPART
BOKHARA
BOMBARD
BOXCARS
BULGARS
BULWARK
BURSARS
BUSFARE
BUSTARD
BUZZARD
BYHEART
CAESARS
CALGARY
CALVARY
CAMPARI
CARFARE
CASCARA
CAVEART
CELLARS
CLIPART
COLLARD
COLLARS
COMPARE
COSTARS
COUGARS
CUECARD
CUSTARD
DASTARD
DAYCARE
DECLARE
DENMARK
DEODARS
DIEHARD
DIETARY
DILLARD
DISBARS
DISCARD
DOGCART
DOGEARS
DOLLARS
DULLARD
EARHART
EARMARK
ECKHART
EDOUARD
ELKHART
ENDEARS
ENSNARE
ENSNARL
ESTUARY
FANFARE
FERRARI
FERRARO
FINEART
FIREARM
FOLKART
FOREARM
FORWARD
FOULARD
FROWARD
GAZZARA
GENNARO
GIZZARD
GODDARD
GRANARY
GUEVARA
GUITARS
HAGGARD
HALYARD
HANGARS
HANSARP
HARVARD
HAYWARD
HECTARE
HILLARY
HOLYARK
HOTCARS
HOTWARS
HUBBARD
HUNGARY
HUSSARS
INBOARD

ISOBARS
JAGUARS
JANUARY
JEANARP
JUNKART
KEYCARD
KILDARE
LAGGARD
LANYARD
LEEWARD
LEONARD
LEOPARD
LEOTARD
LIBRARY
LOMBARD
LUMBARS
MAGYARS
MALLARD
MANSARD
MARMARA
MASCARA
MAYNARD
MILLARD
MORTARS
MUSTARD
NECTARS
NEWHART
NIAGARA
NIGGARD
ONADARE
ONBOARD
ONGUARD
ORCHARD
OUTWARD
PACKARD
PECCARY
PEDLARS
PEPPARD
PICCARD
PILLARS
PLACARD
PLENARY
PONIARD
POPLARS
POPTART
PREPARE
PRIMARY
PULSARS
QINTARS
QUASARS
RAMPART
REHEARD
REHEARS
RELEARN
RESTART
REYNARD
RHUBARB
RICHARD
RUDYARD
SAGUARO
SAMBARS
SAMSARA
SCALARS
SEAWARD
SHEPARD
SHOFARS
SIDEARM
SKYLARK
SKYWARD
STEWARD
STEWART
SUMMARY
TANKARD
TANTARA
TARTARE
TARTARS
TEACART
TERNARY
TINEARS
TONEARM
TOPIARY
TOSPARE
TOWCARS
TRENARY
TROCARS
TSQUARE
UNAWARE
UNHEARD
UNITARY
UNLEARN
UNSNARL
UPROARS
UPSTART
VACCARO
WALMART
WARFARE
WAYWARD
WELFARE
WETBARS
WIDMARK
WILLARD
WOODARD
YARDARM
ZACHARY

••••A•R

ABUBAKR
BIDFAIR
CATHAIR
CENTAUR
CORSAIR
DEADAIR
DESPAIR
FUNFAIR
MAXBAER
MAYFAIR
OPENAIR
REDHAIR
THINAIR

•••••AR

ALCAZAR
ALLSTAR
ANGULAR
ANNULAR
ANTBEAR
ANTIWAR
AREOLAR
BELLJAR
BENATAR
BESMEAR
BIPOLAR
BOERWAR
BOLIVAR
BUGBEAR
BURGLAR
CASHBAR
CHEDDAR
CLUBCAR
COALCAR
COALTAR
COLDWAR
CROWBAR
DAYSTAR
DIPOLAR
DOGSTAR
DOVEBAR
DRAWBAR
FLATCAR
FORBEAR
GOODBAR
GRAMMAR
HANDCAR
HOLYWAR
INGEMAR
INSOFAR
INSULAR
JACKTAR
JOCULAR
JUGULAR
LAMINAR
LOWGEAR
MAKEPAR
MALABAR
MANOWAR
MANYEAR
MIDYEAR
MIRAMAR
MISHEAR
MODULAR
MUAMMAR
MYANMAR
NEBULAR
NEWYEAR
NODULAR
NUCLEAR
OFFYEAR
ONATEAR
OPENBAR
OUTWEAR
PACECAR
PALOMAR
PINETAR
PLANTAR
POPULAR
POSTWAR
RACECAR
REDSTAR
REGULAR
ROLLBAR
SALAZAR
SAMOVAR
SANDBAR
SCHOLAR
SEASTAR
SECULAR
SEMINAR
SHANKAR
SIDEBAR
SIDECAR
SIMILAR
SLOTCAR
STELLAR
TABULAR
TELSTAR
TEMPLAR
THUSFAR
TINSTAR
TITULAR
TRAMCAR
TUBULAR
TUTELAR
TWOSTAR
UNCLEAR
UPTOPAR
VINEGAR
WINEBAR
YESDEAR

AS•••••

ASCENDS
ASCENTS
ASCETIC
ASCRIBE
ASEPSIS
ASEPTIC
ASFARAS
ASHAMED
ASHANTI
ASHBURY
ASHCANS
ASHFORD
ASHIEST
ASHLAND
ASHLARS
ASHLESS
ASHRAMS
ASHTRAY
ASIATIC
ASININE
ASKANCE
ASKSFOR
ASKSOUT
ASOCIAL
ASOFNOW
ASPECTS
ASPERSE
ASPHALT
ASPIRED
ASPIRER
ASPIRES
ASPIRIN
ASSAILS
ASSAULT
ASSAYED
ASSAYER
ASSEGAI
ASSENTS
ASSERTS
ASSIGNS
ASSISTS
ASSIZES
ASSORTS
ASSUAGE
ASSUMED
ASSUMES
ASSURED
ASSURES
ASSYRIA
ASTAIRE
ASTARTE
ASTOLAT
ASTORIA
ASTOUND
ASTRIDE
ASUNDER
ASUSUAL
ASYLUMS

A•S••••

ABSALOM
ABSCOND
ABSENCE
ABSENTS
ABSOLUT
ABSOLVE
ABSORBS
ABSTAIN
ADSORBS
ALSORAN
AMSCRAY
ANSPACH
ANSWERS
APSIDES
ARSENAL
ARSENIC
ARSENIO
ASSAILS
ASSAULT
ASSAYED
ASSAYER
ASSEGAI
ASSENTS
ASSERTS
ASSIGNS
ASSISTS
ASSIZES
ASSORTS
ASSUAGE
ASSUMED
ASSUMES
ASSURED
ASSURES
ASSYRIA
ATSTAKE
AUSPICE
AUSSIES
AUSTERE
AUSTRAL
AUSTRIA

A••S•••

ABASHED
ABASHES
ABASING
ABUSERS
ABUSING
ABUSIVE
ABYSMAL
ABYSSES
ACESOUT
ACTSOUT
AGASSIZ
AGESAGO
AIRSACS
AIRSHIP
AIRSHOW
AIRSOCK
AIRSOUT
ALASKAN
ALLSTAR
ALLSTON
ALYSSUM
AMASSED
AMASSES
AMUSING
ANASAZI
ANDSOON
ANISEED
ANOSMIA
ANOSMIC
ANTSIER
APISHLY
APOSTLE
ARCSINE
ARISING
ARISTAE
ARISTAS
ARISTOS
ARTSONG
ASKSFOR
ASKSOUT
ASUSUAL
ATISSUE
AUSSIES
AWESOME

A•••S••

ABYSSES
ACCOSTS
ACCUSED
ACCUSER
ACCUSES
ACHESON
ADAMSON
ADDISON
ADJUSTS
ADVISED
ADVISER
ADVISES
ADVISOR
AEROSOL
AGASSIZ
AGEISTS
ALIASES
ALLISON
ALLYSON
ALTOSAX
ALUNSER
ALYOSHA
ALYSSUM
AMASSED
AMASSES
AMNESIA
AMNESTY
ANTESUP
AORISTS
APHESES
APPOSED
APPOSES
ARALSEA
ARIOSOS
ARIOSTO
AROUSAL
AROUSED
AROUSES
ARRASES
ARRESTS
ARRISES
ARTISAN
ARTISTE
ARTISTS
ASEPSIS
ASSISTS
ATISSUE
ATLASES
ATTESTS
AUGUSTA
AUGUSTE
AVULSED
AVULSES

A••••S•

ABOLISH
ABREAST
ACCURST
ACEROSE
ACHIEST
ACTRESS
ADDRESS
ADIPOSE
ADVERSE
AERIEST
AGAINST
AGELESS
AGGRESS
AGONIST
AIMLESS
AIRBASE
AIRIEST
AIRLESS
AIRMASS
ALFONSO
AMBROSE
AMHERST
AMONGST
AMPLEST
AMYLASE
ANALYSE
ANALYST
ANAPEST
ANDRESS
ANIMISM
ANIMIST
APPEASE
APPRISE
APTNESS
ARIDEST
ARMLESS
ARMREST
ARTIEST
ARTLESS
ASHIEST
ASHLESS
ASPERSE
ATALOSS
ATAVISM
ATAVIST
ATHEISM
ATHEIST
ATHIRST
ATLEAST
ATWORST
AWELESS
AXLROSE

A•••••S

ABASHES
ABDUCTS
ABJURES
ABLATES
ABLAUTS
ABNAKIS
ABOUNDS
ABRADES
ABSENTS
ABSORBS
ABUSERS
ABYSSES
ACACIAS
ACARIDS
ACCEDES
ACCENTS
ACCEPTS
ACCORDS
ACCOSTS
ACCRUES
ACCUSES
ACHATES
ACHENES
ACKACKS
ACQUITS
ACTIONS
ACTIVES
ACTRESS
ADAGIOS
ADDENDS
ADDRESS
ADDUCES
ADDUCTS
ADHERES
ADJOINS
ADJURES
ADJUSTS
ADMIRES
ADMIXES
ADONAIS
ADORERS
ADSORBS
ADVENTS
ADVERBS
ADVERTS
ADVISES
AEDILES
AERATES
AERIALS
AEROBES
AFFAIRS
AFFECTS
AFFINES
AFFIRMS
AFFIXES
AFFORDS
AFFRAYS
AFGHANS
AFRAMES
AFREETS
AGEISTS
AGELESS
AGENDAS
AGGRESS
AGNATES
AGOUTIS
AIGRETS
AIMLESS
AIRBAGS
AIRDAMS
AIRGUNS
AIRINGS
AIRLESS
AIRMASS
AIRSACS
AIRWAYS
AITCHES
ALARUMS
ALBEDOS
ALBINOS
ALCOVES
ALGIERS
ALIASES
ALIGHTS
ALKALIS
ALKENES
ALLEARS
ALLEGES
ALLELES
ALLEYES
ALLUDES
ALLURES
ALMONDS
ALPACAS
ALUMNUS
AMADEUS
AMASSES
AMAZONS
AMBLERS
AMBRIES
AMERCES
AMNIONS
AMOEBAS
AMOROUS
AMOUNTS
AMPERES
AMPULES
AMULETS
ANADEMS
ANALOGS
ANANIAS
ANCHORS
ANDEANS
ANDREAS
ANDRESS
ANDREWS
ANGELES
ANGELUS
ANGLERS
ANGORAS
ANIMALS
ANKLETS
ANNEALS
ANNEXES
ANNUALS
ANNULUS
ANOINTS
ANONYMS
ANORAKS
ANSWERS
ANTAEUS
ANTARES
ANTCOWS
ANTHEMS
ANTHERS
ANTIBES
ANTLERS
ANXIOUS
AORISTS
AOUDADS
APACHES
APERCUS
APERIES
APHESES
APOGEES
APPALLS
APPEALS
APPEARS
APPENDS
APPLIES
APPOSES
APROPOS
APSIDES
APTNESS
AQUEOUS
AQUINAS
ARAWAKS
ARBOURS
ARBUTUS
ARCADES
ARCHERS
ARCHIES
ARCHONS
ARDOURS
ARDUOUS
AREOLAS
ARGIVES
ARGUERS
ARGYLES
ARIOSOS
ARISTAS
ARISTOS
ARMADAS
ARMFULS
ARMLESS
ARMLETS
ARMOURS
ARMPITS
ARNICAS
AROUSES
ARRASES
ARREARS
ARRESTS
ARRISES
ARRIVES
ARROBAS
ARROYOS
ARTEMIS
ARTEMUS
ARTISTS
ARTLESS
ASCENDS
ASCENTS
ASEPSIS
ASFARAS
ASHCANS
ASHLARS
ASHLESS
ASHRAMS
ASPECTS
ASPIRES
ASSAILS
ASSENTS
ASSERTS
ASSIGNS
ASSISTS
ASSIZES
ASSORTS
ASSUMES
ASSURES
ASYLUMS
ATALOSS
ATAMANS
ATHOMES
ATLASES
ATLATLS
ATOMIES
ATRIUMS
ATTACKS
ATTAINS
ATTENDS
ATTESTS
ATTICUS
ATTIMES
ATTIRES
ATTRITS
ATTUCKS
ATTUNES
AUBADES
AUBURNS
AUGENDS
AUKLETS
AUNTIES
AUROCHS
AURORAS
AUSSIES
AUTEURS
AUTHORS
AUTUMNS
AVATARS
AVENGES
AVENUES
AVIATES
AVOCETS
AVOWALS
AVOWERS
AVULSES
AWAKENS
AWELESS
AWNINGS
AYEAYES
AZALEAS

•AS••••

BASALLY
BASALTS
BASEHIT
BASEMAN
BASEMEN
BASENJI
BASEPAY
BASHFUL
BASHING
BASKETS
BASKING
BASQUES
BASSETS
BASSIST
BASSOON
BASTERS
BASTING
BASTION
CASABAS
CASCADE
CASCARA
CASELAW
CASERNS
CASHBAR
CASHBOX
CASHCOW
CASHEWS
CASHIER
CASHING
CASHOUT
CASINGS
CASINOS
CASPIAN
CASSATT
CASSAVA
CASSIAS
CASSIDY
CASSINI
CASSIUS
CASSOCK
CASTERS
CASTILE
CASTING
CASTLED
CASTLES
CASTOFF
CASTOUT
CASUALS
DASBOOT
DASHERS
DASHIKI
DASHING
DASHOFF
DASTARD
EASEDIN
EASEDUP
EASEOFF
EASESIN
EASESUP
EASIEST
EASTEND
EASTERN
EASTERS
EASTMAN
FASCIAS
FASCISM
FASCIST
FASHION
FASTENS
FASTEST
FASTING
FASTONE
GASBAGS
GASCAPS
GASCONS
GASEOUS
GASHING
GASJETS
GASKETS
GASKINS
GASMAIN
GASOHOL
GASPING
GASPUMP
GASSERS
GASTRIC
HASBEEN
HASHING
HASIDIM
HASSLED
HASSLES
HASSOCK
HASTENS
HASTIER
HASTILY
HASTING
JASMINE
JASPERS
KASHMIR
LASAGNA
LASAGNE
LASALLE
LASCALA
LASCAUX
LASHERS
LASHING
LASHUPS
LASORDA
LASSIES
LASSOED
LASSOER
LASSOES
LASTING
LASTORY
MASCARA
MASCOTS
MASHERS
MASHIES
MASHING
MASKERS
MASKING
MASONIC
MASONRY
MASQUES
MASSAGE
MASSEUR
MASSIFS
MASSING
MASSIVE
MASTABA
MASTERS
MASTERY
MASTICS
MASTIFF
MASTOID
NASALLY
NASCENT
NASTASE
NASTIER
NASTILY
PASCHAL
PASSAGE
PASSANT
PASSELS
PASSERS
PASSEUL
PASSFOR
PASSING
PASSION
PASSIVE
PASSKEY
PASSOFF
PASSOUT
PASTDUE
PASTELS
PASTERN
PASTEUP
PASTEUR
PASTIER
PASTIME
PASTINA
PASTING
PASTORS
PASTURE
RASCALS
RASHERS
RASHEST
RASPERS
RASPIER
RASPING
RASSLED
RASSLES
RASTERS
SASHAYS
SASHIMI
SASSERS
SASSIER
SASSIES
SASSILY
SASSING
SASSOON
TASKING
TASSELS
TASTERS
TASTIER
TASTILY
TASTING
VASSALS
VASTEST
WASATCH
WASHERS
WASHING
WASHOFF
WASHOUT
WASHRAG
WASHTUB
WASPISH
WASSAIL
WASTAGE
WASTERS
WASTING
WASTREL
YASHMAK

•A•S•••

BALSAMS
BANSHEE
BARSOAP
BASSETS
BASSIST
BASSOON
BATSMAN
BATSMEN
CAESARS
CAESURA
CAISSON
CANSECO
CAPSHAW

CAPSIZE
CAPSTAN
CAPSULE
CARSEAT
CASSATT
CASSAVA
CASSIAS
CASSIDY
CASSINI
CASSIUS
CASSOCK
CATSCAN
CATSEYE
CATSPAW
CAUSING
CAUSTIC
DAISIES
DAMSELS
DAMSONS
DANSEUR
DAYSINN
DAYSTAR
EARSHOT
EATSOUT
FALSELY
FALSEST
FALSIFY
FALSITY
FANSOUT
FAUSTUS
GADSDEN
GAGSTER
GASSERS
HALSTON
HAMSTER
HANSARP
HANSOLO
HANSOMS
HARSHEN
HARSHER
HARSHLY
HASSLED
HASSLES
HASSOCK
HAWSERS
HAYSEED
JANSSEN
KAISERS
KAISHEK
KANSANS
LAISSEZ
LANSING
LAPSING
LASSIES
LASSOED
LASSOER
LASSOES
LAWSUIT
LAYSFOR
LAYSLOW
LAYSOFF
LAYSOUT
MAESTRI
MAESTRO
MANSARD
MANSION
MARSALA
MARSHAL
MARSHES
MASSAGE
MASSEUR
MASSIFS
MASSING

MASSIVE
NAYSAID
NAYSAYS
PAISANO
PAISLEY
PANSIES
PANSOUT
PARSECS
PARSEES
PARSERS
PARSING
PARSLEY
PARSNIP
PARSONS
PASSAGE
PASSANT
PASSELS
PASSERS
PASSEUL
PASSFOR
PASSING
PASSION
PASSIVE
PASSKEY
PASSOFF
PASSOUT
PATSIES
PAUSING
PAYSFOR
PAYSOFF
PAYSOUT
RAISERS
RAISEUP
RAISING
RAISINS
RALSTON
RANSACK
RANSOMS
RASSLED
RASSLES
RAWSILK
SADSACK
SALSIFY
SALSODA
SAMSARA
SAMSUNG
SAPSAGO
SASSERS
SASSIER
SASSIES
SASSILY
SASSING
SASSOON
SATSUMA
SAUSAGE
TAGSALE
TAGSOUT
TANSIES
TAPSOUT
TAPSTER
TARSALS
TARSIER
TASSELS
VARSITY
VASSALS
WAISTED
WARSHIP
WASSAIL
WAYSIDE

•A••S••

BABASSU
BABYSAT
BABYSIT
BACKSIN
BACKSUP
BALLSUP
BANDSAW
BANGSUP
BANKSON
BARKSAT
BATISTA
BATISTE
CAISSON
CALLSIN
CALLSON
CALLSUP
CAMISES
CANASTA
CARLSON
CAVESIN
CAYUSES
DAMASKS
DARESAY
DARESTO
DATASET
EASESIN
EASESUP
FADESIN
FAIRSUP
FALLSIN
FALLSON
FALLSTO
GAINSAY
GAINSON
GANGSAW
GANGSTA
GANGSUP
HACKSAW
HANDSAW
HANDSET
HANDSIN
HANDSON
HANDSUP
HANGSIN
HANGSON
HANGSUP
HARDSET
HARPSON
HAULSUP
JACKSON
JACKSUP
JALISCO
JAMESON
JANSSEN
KARASEA
LACESUP
LACOSTE
LAISSEZ
LANDSAT
MADISON
MAJESTE
MAJESTY
MAKESDO
MAKESIT
MAKESUP
MALMSEY
MAOISTS
MARKSUP
MATISSE
NABISCO
NAILSET
NATASHA
PACKSUP
PAIRSUP
PARASOL
PAULSEN
RACKSUP
RAILSAT
RAKESIN
RAKESUP
RAMESES
SAMISEN
SAMPSON
SATISFY
SAVESUP
TABASCO
TACKSON
TAKESIN
TAKESON
TAKESTO
TAKESUP
TALKSAT
TALKSTO
TALKSUP
TALUSES
TANKSUP
TAOISTS
VALISES
VANESSA
WADESIN
WAITSON
WAITSUP
WAKESUP
WALLSUP
WANTSIN
WANTSTO
WARMSUP
WAVESIN

•A•••S•

BABASSU
BABYISH
BADNESS
BALDEST
BALLAST
BAPTISM
BAPTIST
BASSIST
CABOOSE
CAGIEST
CALMEST
CALYPSO
CANVASS
CAPLESS
CARCASS
CARLESS
CAROUSE
CARWASH
CATFISH
CATTISH
DADAISM
DADAIST
DAFTEST
DAMPEST
DAMPISH
DANKEST
DARKEST
DARKISH
EARNEST
EASIEST
FADDISH
FADDISM
FADDIST
FAIREST
FALSEST
FANTASY
FAREAST
FARWEST
FASCISM
FASCIST
FASTEST
FATLESS
FATNESS
FATTEST
FAUVISM
FAUVIST
GABFEST
GAMIEST
GARNISH
HAPLESS
HARDEST
HARNESS
HARPIST
HARVEST
HATLESS
HAWKISH
HAZIEST
JACCUSE
JACKASS
JAGLESS
KADDISH
LACIEST
LACTASE
LACTOSE
LAMAISM
LAMAIST
LANKEST
LARGESS
LARGEST
LAVALSE
LAWLESS
LAXNESS
LAZIEST
MADDEST
MADNESS
MAEWEST
MAFIOSO
MALAISE
MALTESE
MALTOSE
MANNISH
MARXISM
MATISSE
MAWKISH
NASTASE
OAKMOSS
OARLESS
PACHISI
PALMIST
PANFISH
PAPOOSE
PATNESS
PAULIST
PAYCASH
RACIEST
RAFFISH
RANKEST
RASHEST
RAWNESS
SADDEST
SADNESS
SANJOSE
SARCASM
SAWDUST
SAWFISH
TALLEST
TALLISH
TANNEST
TANNISH
TARNISH
TARTEST
TAUTEST
VAGUEST
VAINEST
VAMOOSE
VANESSA
VARNISH
VASTEST
WAGGISH
WARIEST
WARMEST
WARMISH
WASPISH
WAVIEST
WAXIEST
YAKUTSK
ZANIEST

•A••••S

BABBLES
BABOONS
BACCHUS
BACKERS
BACKUPS
BADDIES
BADEGGS
BADGERS
BADGUYS
BADNESS
BAFFLES
BAGFULS
BAGGERS
BAGGIES
BAHAMAS
BAILEES
BAILERS
BAILEYS
BAILORS
BALBOAS
BALEENS
BALKANS
BALLADS
BALLETS
BALLOTS
BALSAMS
BAMBOOS
BANANAS
BANDIES
BANDITS
BANGLES
BANJOES
BANKERS
BANNERS
BANTAMS
BANTERS
BANYANS
BAOBABS
BARBELS
BARBERS
BARENTS
BARHOPS
BARKERS
BARLEYS
BARNEYS
BARONGS
BARRELS
BARRENS
BARRIOS
BARROWS
BARTERS
BARYONS
BASALTS
BASKETS
BASQUES
BASSETS
BASTERS
BATBOYS
BATCHES
BATHERS
BATTENS
BATTERS
BATTLES
BAUBLES
BAWLERS
BAZAARS
CABALAS
CABANAS
CABBIES
CABLERS
CACHETS
CACHOUS
CACKLES
CADDIES
CADGERS
CAESARS
CAFTANS
CAHIERS
CAHOOTS
CAIMANS
CAIQUES
CAJOLES
CALENDS
CALICOS
CALIPHS
CALKINS
CALLERS
CALLINS
CALLOUS
CALPACS
CALYCES
CALYXES
CAMBERS
CAMERAS
CAMISES
CAMPERS
CANAPES
CANARDS
CANCANS
CANCELS
CANDIDS
CANDIES
CANDLES
CANINES
CANKERS
CANNERS
CANNONS
CANOPUS
CANTERS
CANTLES
CANTONS
CANTORS
CANVASS
CANYONS
CAPFULS
CAPGUNS
CAPLESS
CAPLETS
CAPNUTS
CAPPERS
CAPTORS
CARACAS
CARAFES
CARBONS
CARBOYS
CARCASS
CARDERS
CAREENS
CAREERS
CARFULS
CARGOES
CARHOPS
CARIBES
CARINAS
CARLESS
CARNETS
CARNIES
CAROLES
CAROLUS
CARPALS
CARPERS
CARPETS
CARRELS
CARRIES
CARROTS
CARTELS
CARTERS
CARTONS
CARVERS
CASABAS
CASERNS
CASHEWS
CASINGS
CASINOS
CASSIAS
CASSIUS
CASTERS
CASTLES
CASUALS
CATCHES
CATIONS
CATKINS
CATNAPS
CATNIPS
CAVEATS
CAVEINS
CAVERNS
CAVORTS
CAYUGAS
CAYUSES
DABBLES
DACTYLS
DADDIES
DAGGERS
DAHLIAS
DAILIES
DAIRIES
DAISIES
DAKOTAS
DALLIES
DAMAGES
DAMASKS
DAMPENS
DAMPERS
DAMSELS
DAMSONS
DANCERS
DANDERS
DANDIES
DANDLES
DANGERS
DANGLES
DANIELS
DAPHNIS
DAPPLES
DARKENS
DARNERS
DARTERS
DASHERS
DAUBERS
DAWDLES
DAWKINS
DAYBEDS
DAZZLES
EAGLETS
EARFULS
EARNERS
EARWIGS
EASTERS
FABARES
FABRICS
FACADES
FACIALS
FACINGS
FACTORS
FADEINS
FAGENDS
FAIRIES
FAJITAS
FALCONS
FALLOWS
FALTERS
FAMULUS
FANCIES
FANIONS
FANJETS
FARMERS
FARROWS
FASCIAS
FASTENS
FATCATS
FATHERS
FATHOMS
FATLESS
FATNESS
FATTENS
FATUOUS
FAUCETS
FAUSTUS
FAUXPAS
FAVOURS
FAWNERS
GABBERS
GABBLES
GABBROS
GADGETS
GAFFERS
GAGGLES
GAINERS
GAITERS
GALLEYS
GALLONS
GALLOPS
GALOOTS
GAMBITS
GAMBLES
GAMBOLS
GAMETES
GAMINES
GAMMONS
GANDERS
GANNETS
GARAGES
GARBLES
GARCONS
GARDENS
GARGLES
GARNERS
GARNETS
GARRETS
GARTERS
GASBAGS
GASCAPS
GASCONS
GASEOUS
GASJETS
GASKETS
GASKINS
GASSERS
GATHERS
GAUCHOS
GAUDENS
GAUGERS
GAVIALS
GAWKERS
GAZEBOS
HACKERS
HACKIES
HACKLES
HAGGLES
HAIRDOS
HALITES
HALLOWS
HALTERS
HAMITES
HAMLETS
HAMMERS
HAMPERS
HANDLES
HANGARS
HANGERS
HANGUPS
HANKERS
HANKIES
HANSOMS
HAPLESS
HAPPENS
HARBORS
HARDENS
HARKENS
HARNESS
HARPERS
HARPIES
HARRIES
HARROWS
HASSLES
HASTENS
HATCHES
HATLESS
HATPINS
HATTERS
HAULERS
HAWHAWS
HAWKERS
HAWKINS
HAWSERS
HAYMOWS
HAZARDS
HAZINGS
JABBERS
JABIRUS
JACANAS
JACKALS
JACKASS
JACKETS
JACQUES
JAEGERS
JAGLESS
JAGUARS
JAILERS
JAMMERS
JANGLES
JARFULS
JARGONS
JASPERS
JAYCEES
JAYVEES
KABUKIS
KAFTANS
KAHUNAS
KAISERS
KANAKAS
KANSANS
KAZAKHS
LAAGERS
LABIALS
LABOURS
LABRETS
LACINGS
LACKEYS
LACUNAS
LADDERS
LADDIES
LADINOS
LADLERS
LAERTES
LAGGERS
LAGOONS
LAGUNAS
LAKOTAS
LAMBDAS
LAMENTS
LAMINAS
LANCERS
LANCETS
LANDAUS
LANDERS
LANGURS
LAPDOGS
LAPFULS
LAPPETS
LAPTOPS
LARCHES
LARDERS
LARDONS
LARGESS
LARIATS
LARRUPS
LASHERS
LASHUPS
LASSIES
LASSOES
LATCHES
LATEENS
LATENTS
LATEXES
LATHERS
LATICES
LATINAS
LATINOS
LATTENS
LAURELS
LAWLESS
LAWYERS
LAXNESS
LAYOFFS
LAYOUTS
LAZARUS
MACRONS
MADCAPS
MADDENS
MADDERS
MADLIBS
MADNESS
MAENADS
MAGNETS
MAGNUMS
MAGPIES
MAGUEYS
MAGYARS
MAHARIS
MAHOUTS
MAIDENS
MAILERS
MAITAIS
MAKEUPS
MAKINGS
MALIGNS
MALLETS
MALLOWS
MALTEDS
MALTHUS
MAMMALS
MANAGES
MANANAS
MANDANS
MANDAYS
MANEGES
MANGERS
MANGLES
MANGOES
MANIACS
MANNERS
MANTELS
MANTLES
MANTRAS
MANUALS
MAOISTS
MAPPERS
MARACAS
MARAUDS
MARBLES
MARCELS
MARCHES
MARGAYS
MARGINS
MARINAS
MARINES
MARKERS
MARKETS
MARKUPS
MARLINS
MARMOTS
MAROONS
MARQUES
MARQUIS
MARRIES
MARROWS
MARSHES
MARTENS
MARTINS
MARTYRS
MARVELS
MASCOTS
MASHERS
MASHIES
MASKERS
MASQUES
MASSIFS
MASTERS
MASTICS
MATCHES
MATHERS
MATHEWS
MATHIAS
MATRONS
MATTERS
MATURES
MATZOHS
MAUROIS
MAXIMUS
MAYDAYS
MAYHEMS
NABBERS
NAIADES
NAILERS
NANNIES
NAPKINS
NAPPERS
NARROWS
NARWALS
NATIONS
NATIVES
NATTERS
NATURES
NAUGHTS
NAVAHOS
NAVAJOS
NAYSAYS
OAKMOSS
OARLESS
PABLUMS
PACKERS
PACKETS
PADDERS
PADDIES
PADDLES
PAGODAS
PAILOUS
PAIUTES
PAJAMAS
PALACES
PALATES
PALLETS
PALTERS
PAMBIES
PAMPERS
PANAMAS
PANDERS
PANDITS
PANNERS
PANSIES
PANZERS
PAPAGOS
PAPAYAS
PAPUANS
PAPYRUS
PARADES
PARAPHS
PARCELS
PARCHES
PARDONS
PARENTS
PARGETS
PARIAHS
PARIBUS
PARINGS
PARLAYS
PARLEYS
PARLORS
PARLOUS
PAROLES
PARRIES
PARROTS
PARSECS
PARSEES
PARSERS
PARSONS
PARTIES
PARURES
PASSELS
PASSERS
PASTELS
PASTORS
PATAKES
PATCHES

PATENTS
PATINAS
PATNESS
PATROLS
PATRONS
PATSIES
PATTENS
PATTERS
PATTIES
PAUPERS
PAVANES
PAWNEES
PAWNERS
PAWPAWS
PAYDAYS
PAYOFFS
PAYOLAS
PAYOUTS
RABBETS
RABBITS
RABBLES
RACEMES
RACKETS
RADAMES
RADDLES
RADIALS
RADIANS
RADICES
RAFFLES
RAFTERS
RAGLANS
RAGMOPS
RAGOUTS
RAGRUGS
RAGTOPS
RAIDERS
RAILERS
RAISERS
RAISINS
RALLIES
RAMADAS
RAMBLES
RAMESES
RAMJETS
RAMRODS
RANCHES
RANCHOS
RANGERS
RANKERS
RANKLES
RANSOMS
RANTERS
RAPIERS
RAPINES
RAPPELS
RAPPERS
RAPTORS
RAREGAS
RASCALS
RASHERS
RASPERS
RASSLES
RASTERS
RATINGS
RATIONS
RATITES
RATTANS
RATTERS
RATTLES
RAUCOUS
RAVAGES
RAVINES
RAVINGS
RAWNESS
RAYGUNS
SABINES
SACHEMS
SACHETS
SACKERS
SADDENS
SADDLES
SADNESS
SAFARIS
SAILORS
SALAAMS
SALAMIS
SALLIES
SALMONS
SALOONS
SALTERS
SALUKIS
SALUTES
SALVERS
SALVOES
SAMBARS
SAMITES
SAMOANS
SAMPANS
SAMPLES
SAMPRAS
SANDALS
SANDERS
SANLUIS
SANTIRS
SAPIENS
SAPPERS
SARONGS
SASHAYS
SASSERS
SASSIES
SATIRES
SATRAPS
SAUCERS
SAVAGES
SAVALAS
SAVANTS
SAVINGS
SAVIORS
SAVOURS
SAWLOGS
SAWYERS
SAYINGS
TABARDS
TABBIES
TABLETS
TACITUS
TACKERS
TACKLES
TACTICS
TAFFIES
TAGENDS
TAILLES
TAILORS
TAIPANS
TALENTS
TALKERS
TALKIES
TALLIES
TALLOWS
TALUSES
TAMALES
TAMPERS
TAMTAMS
TANDEMS
TANGLES
TANKERS
TANNERS
TANNINS
TANOAKS
TANSIES
TAOISTS
TAPINGS
TAPPERS
TAPPETS
TARGETS
TARIFFS
TARMACS
TARPITS
TARPONS
TARRIES
TARSALS
TARTANS
TARTARS
TASSELS
TASTERS
TATAMIS
TATTERS
TATTLES
TATTOOS
TAUTENS
TAVERNS
VACATES
VACUOUS
VACUUMS
VALISES
VALLEYS
VALOURS
VAMPERS
VANDALS
VAPOURS
VARIOUS
VARLETS
VASSALS
VATFULS
WADDLES
WAFFLES
WAGGLES
WAGGONS
WAHINES
WAILERS
WAITERS
WAIVERS
WALKERS
WALKINS
WALKONS
WALKUPS
WALLETS
WALLOPS
WALLOWS
WALNUTS
WALTERS
WALTZES
WAMBLES
WANDERS
WANGLES
WANTADS
WAPITIS
WARBLES
WARDENS
WARDERS
WARGODS
WARMUPS
WARRENS
WASHERS
WASTERS
WATCHES
WATTLES
WAYLAYS
YAKKERS
YAMMERS
YANKEES
YAPPERS
YARROWS
YAUPONS
YAWNERS
YAWPERS
ZANDERS
ZAPPERS
ZAREBAS

••AS•••

ABASHED
ABASHES
ABASING
AGASSIZ
ALASKAN
AMASSED
AMASSES
ANASAZI
BEASTIE
BEASTLY
BIASING
BIASSED
BLASTED
BLASTER
BOASTED
BOASTER
BRASHER
BRASHLY
BRASSES
BRASSIE
CEASING
CHASERS
CHASING
CHASSES
CHASSIS
CHASTEN
CHASTER
CLASHED
CLASHES
CLASPED
CLASSED
CLASSES
CLASSIC
COASTAL
COASTED
COASTER
CRASHED
CRASHES
CRASSER
CRASSLY
CRASSUS
DRASTIC
EDASNER
ELASTIC
ERASERS
ERASING
ERASMUS
ERASURE
EVASION
EVASIVE
FEASTED
FIASCOS
FLASHED
FLASHER
FLASHES
FRASIER
GHASTLY
GLASGOW
GLASSED
GLASSES
GNASHED
GNASHES
GRASPED
GRASSED
GRASSES
INASNIT
INASPIN
INASPOT
INASTEW
LEASERS
LEASHED
LEASHES
LEASING
MEASLES
MEASURE
MIASMAS
MIASMIC
OFASORT
ONASSIS
PEASANT
PEASOUP
PHASEIN
PHASERS
PHASING
PIASTER
PIASTRE
PLASHED
PLASHES
PLASMAS
PLASTER
PLASTIC
QUASARS
QUASHED
QUASHES
REASONS
ROASTED
ROASTER
SEASALT
SEASICK
SEASIDE
SEASLUG
SEASONS
SEASTAR
SHASTRI
SLASHED
SLASHER
SLASHES
SMASHED
SMASHER
SMASHES
SMASHUP
SPASSKY
STASHED
STASHES
STASSEN
SUASION
TEASELS
TEASERS
TEASETS
TEASHOP
TEASING
TOASTED
TOASTER
TRASHED
TRASHES
UNASKED
WEASELS

••A•S••

ADAMSON
AGASSIZ
AMASSED
AMASSES
ARALSEA
BEADSUP
BEAMSUP
BEARSON
BEARSUP
BEATSIT
BEATSUP
BIASSED
BRAISED
BRAISES
BRANSON
BRASSES
BRASSIE
CHAISES
CHANSON
CHASSES
CHASSIS
CHATSUP
CLAMSUP
CLASSED
CLASSES
CLASSIC
CLAUSES
COARSEN
COARSER
CRASSER
CRASSLY
CRASSUS
DEADSEA
DEADSET
DEALSIN
DEARSIR
DRAGSIN
DRAGSON
DRAWSIN
DRAWSON
DRAWSUP
ELAPSED
ELAPSES
FRAISES
GEARSTO
GEARSUP
GLASSED
GLASSES
GRABSAT
GRASSED
GRASSES
GRAYSON
HEADSET
HEADSIN
HEADSUP
HEARSAY
HEARSOF
HEATSUP
HOARSEN
HOARSER
KLATSCH
LEADSIN
LEADSON
LEADSTO
LEADSUP
LEANSON
LIAISED
LIAISES
LIAISON
ONASSIS
PEARSON
PLANSON
PLAYSAT
PLAYSON
PLAYSUP
PRAISED
PRAISER
PRAISES
PRAYSTO
READSIN
REARSUP
SEALSUP
SNAPSAT
SNAPSTO
SNAPSUP
SOAKSUP
SPARSER
SPASSKY
STASSEN
STAYSUP
SWANSON
TEAMSUP
TEARSAT
TEARSUP
THATSIT
TRANSIT
TRANSOM
WRAPSUP

••A••S•

AGAINST
ANALYSE
ANALYST
ANAPEST
ATALOSS
ATAVISM
ATAVIST
BEARISH
BRAVEST
BYANOSE
CRAFTSY
CZARISM
CZARIST
DEAFEST
DEAREST
GOATISH
GRAVEST
GRAYEST
INAMESS
INANEST
INARUSH
IRATEST
KNAVISH
LEANEST
MEANEST
NEAREST
NEATEST
PIANISM
PIANIST
REALISM
REALIST
REAMASS
SEABASS
SEAMOSS
SIAMESE
SLAVISH
SOANDSO
SPANISH
SPAREST
STALEST
STATIST
SUAVEST
TEAROSE
TRAIPSE
TSARIST
WEAKEST
WEAKISH

••A•••S

ABASHES
ACACIAS
ACARIDS
ADAGIOS
ALARUMS
AMADEUS
AMASSES
AMAZONS
ANADEMS
ANALOGS
ANANIAS
APACHES
ARAWAKS
ATALOSS
ATAMANS
AVATARS
AWAKENS
AZALEAS
BEACHES
BEACONS
BEADLES
BEAGLES
BEAKERS
BEANIES
BEARERS
BEATERS
BEATLES
BEAVERS
BIALIES
BLAZERS
BLAZONS
BOATERS
BRACERS
BRAHMAS
BRAISES
BRASSES
BRAVOES
BRAYERS
CHABLIS
CHACHAS
CHAISES
CHALETS
CHALLIS
CHAMOIS
CHANCES
CHANGES
CHAPELS
CHARGES
CHARLES
CHASERS
CHASSES
CHASSIS
CLAMORS
CLAQUES
CLARETS
CLASHES
CLASSES
CLAUSES
CLAWERS
COACHES
COALERS
COALGAS
COAXERS
CRADLES
CRASHES
CRASSUS
CRATERS
CRAVATS
CRAVENS
CRAVERS
CRAYONS
CRAZIES
CZARDAS
DEACONS
DEADENS
DEAFENS
DEALERS
DEARTHS
DIADEMS
DIALERS
DIALOGS
DIAPERS
DIARIES
DIATOMS
DRAGONS
DRAPERS
DRAWERS
DWARVES
ELAPIDS
ELAPSES
ELATERS
ENABLES
ENAMELS
ENAMORS
EPARCHS
ERASERS
ERASMUS
EVADERS
FEARERS
FIACRES
FIANCES
FIASCOS
FLACONS
FLAGONS
FLAKERS
FLAMBES
FLANGES
FLASHES
FLAUNTS
FLAVORS
FRAISES
FRANCES
FRANCIS
FRAPPES
GLANCES
GLASSES
GLAZERS
GNASHES
GNAWERS
GOALIES
GOATEES
GRACIAS
GRADERS
GRAHAMS
GRAMMES
GRAMPUS
GRANGES
GRASSES
GRATERS
GRAVELS
GRAVIES
GRAZERS
HEADERS
HEALERS
HEARERS
HEARTHS
HEATERS
HEAVENS
HEAVERS
HEAVIES
HOAGIES
HOAXERS
IMAGERS
IMAGOES
IMARETS
INAMESS
ITALICS
JEALOUS
KLAXONS
KRATERS
KWACHAS
KWANZAS
LAAGERS
LEACHES
LEADERS
LEADINS
LEAGUES
LEAKERS
LEANERS
LEANTOS
LEAPERS
LEASERS
LEASHES
LEAVENS
LIAISES
LOACHES
LOADERS
LOAFERS
LOANERS
LOATHES
MEADOWS
MEALIES
MEANIES
MEASLES
MIASMAS
MOANERS
NEATENS
NUANCES
ONAGERS
ONASSIS
OPAQUES
ORACLES
ORANGES
ORATORS
PEACHES
PEAHENS
PEANUTS
PEAPODS
PEAVEYS
PHASERS
PIAZZAS
PLACERS
PLAGUES
PLAICES
PLAINES
PLAINTS
PLANERS
PLANETS
PLAQUES
PLASHES
PLASMAS
PLATENS
PLATERS
PLAUTUS
PLAYERS
POACHES
PRAISES
PRANCES
PRATERS
PRAYERS
PSANDQS
QUAGGAS
QUAHOGS
QUAKERS
QUARTOS
QUASARS
QUASHES
QUAVERS
REACHES
READERS
READIES
REAMASS
REAMERS
REAPERS
REARERS
REASONS
ROACHES
ROADIES
ROAMERS
ROARERS
SCALARS
SCALERS
SCARABS
SCARERS
SCARVES
SCATHES
SEABAGS
SEABASS
SEABEDS
SEABEES
SEACOWS
SEADOGS
SEAFANS
SEALABS
SEALEGS
SEALERS
SEAMOSS
SEANCES
SEASONS
SEATERS
SEAWAYS
SHADOWS
SHAKERS
SHAKOES
SHALOMS
SHAMANS
SHAPERS
SHARERS
SHAVERS
SKATERS
SLALOMS
SLASHES
SLAVERS
SLAYERS
SMALTOS
SMASHES
SNAPONS
SOAKERS
SOAPERS
SOARERS
SPACERS
SPADERS
SPARGES
SPAVINS
STABLES
STAGERS
STALAGS
STAMENS
STANCES
STANZAS
STAPLES
STARERS
STARETS
STARVES
STASHES
STATICS
STATORS
STATUES
SWATHES
SWAYERS
TEABAGS
TEACHES
TEACUPS
TEAPOTS
TEAPOYS
TEARGAS
TEASELS
TEASERS
TEASETS
THALERS
TOADIES
TRACERS
TRADERS
TRAMPAS
TRANCES
TRASHES
TRAUMAS
TRAVELS
TRAVERS
TRAVOIS
TUAREGS
UTAHANS
WEAKENS
WEAPONS
WEARERS
WEARIES
WEASELS
WEAVERS
WHALERS
WHARVES
WRAITHS
WRAPUPS
ZEALOTS
ZEALOUS

•••AS••

ALIASES
ARRASES
ATLASES
BABASSU
BREASTS
CANASTA
CREASED
CREASES
DAMASKS
DATASET
DEBASED
DEBASES
DYNASTS
DYNASTY
EMBASSY
ENCASED
ENCASES
ENMASSE
EURASIA
GIRASOL
GLEASON
GREASED
GREASER
GREASES
IMPASSE
IMPASTO
INHASTE
JOCASTA
KARASEA
NATASHA
OBLASTS
PARASOL
PEGASUS
PHRASAL
PHRASED
PHRASES
PICASSO
PLEASED
PLEASER
PLEASES
PULASKI
REBASTE
RECASTS
REPASTE
REPASTS
SPLASHY
STRASSE
TABASCO
TREASON
UNCASED
UNCASES
UNMASKS

•••A•S•

BABASSU
BECAUSE
CLEANSE
DADAISM
DADAIST
DEGAUSS
EMBASSY
ENMASSE
EXHAUST
EXPANSE
IMPASSE
JUDAISM
KOMATSU
LAMAISM
LAMAIST
LAVALSE
MALAISE
PICASSO
RELAPSE
RERAISE
ROMANSH
SHIATSU
STRASSE
STRAUSS
SYNAPSE
TUBAIST
UPRAISE

•••A••S

ABLATES
ABLAUTS
ABNAKIS
ABRADES
ACHATES
ACKACKS
AERATES
AFFAIRS
AFRAMES
AGNATES
ALIASES
ALKALIS
ALPACAS
ANTAEUS
ANTARES
APPALLS
ARCADES
ARMADAS
ARRASES
ASFARAS
ASSAILS
ATLASES
ATLATLS
ATTACKS
ATTAINS
AUBADES
AVIATES
AYEAYES
BAHAMAS
BANANAS
BASALTS

BAZAARS
BECALMS
BEDAUBS
BEFALLS
BEHAVES
BERATES
BETAKES
BEWAILS
BORATES
BREASTS
BREATHS
BRIARDS
BYPATHS
CABALAS
CABANAS
CANAPES
CANARDS
CARACAS
CARAFES
CASABAS
CCLAMPS
CICADAS
CLEAVES
COWARDS
CREASES
CREATES
CURATES
DAMAGES
DAMASKS
DEBARKS
DEBASES
DEBATES
DECADES
DECAMPS
DECANTS
DEDALUS
DEFACES
DEFAMES
DEGAUSS
DEMANDS
DEPARTS
DERAILS
DESALTS
DETAILS
DETAINS
DIDACTS
DILATES
DISARMS
DOMAINS
DONATES
DOSAGES
DUKAKIS
DYNAMOS
DYNASTS
ECLAIRS
EDWARDS
EFFACES
EMBANKS
EMBARKS
ENCAGES
ENCAMPS
ENCASES
ENGAGES
ENLACES
ENRAGES
ENTAILS
EQUATES
ERRANDS
ESCAPES
ESCARPS
ESTATES
EXHALES
EXPANDS

FABARES
FACADES
FEMALES
FINALES
FIXATES
FORAGES
GARAGES
GELADAS
GELATIS
GOCARTS
GOKARTS
GREASES
GREAVES
GYRATES
HAZARDS
HERALDS
HIJACKS
HOWARDS
HYRACES
HYRAXES
ICEAGES
ICEAXES
IDCARDS
IDEATES
IGUANAS
IMPACTS
IMPAIRS
IMPALAS
IMPALES
IMPARTS
INCANTS
INFANTS
INGALLS
INHALES
INMATES
INNARDS
INTAKES
INVADES
INWARDS
IODATES
ISLANDS
JACANAS
JICAMAS
KANAKAS
KAZAKHS
KIWANIS
LAZARUS
LEGATES
LEGATOS
LIGATES
LINAGES
LIZARDS
LOCALES
LOCATES
LUXATES
MAHARIS
MANAGES
MANANAS
MARACAS
MARAUDS
MCCALLS
MENACES
MENAGES
METATES
MIKADOS
MIRAGES
MOHAIRS
MOHAWKS
MORALES
MORANIS
MOSAICS
MUTANTS
MUTATES

MUTATIS
NAIADES
NAVAHOS
NAVAJOS
NEGATES
NEPALIS
NOGALES
NOTATES
OBLASTS
OBLATES
OBTAINS
OCEANUS
OCTANES
OCTANTS
OCTAVES
OCTAVOS
OGLALAS
OLEATES
ONWARDS
OPIATES
ORDAINS
OTTAWAS
OUTACTS
OUTAGES
OXCARTS
PAJAMAS
PALACES
PALATES
PANAMAS
PAPAGOS
PAPAYAS
PARADES
PARAPHS
PATAKES
PAVANES
PDJAMES
PEDANTS
PEGASUS
PELAGES
PENATES
PETARDS
PHRASES
PICAROS
PINATAS
PIRAEUS
PIRATES
PLEASES
POLARIS
POMADES
POSADAS
POTAGES
PREAMPS
PYJAMAS
PYRAMUS
RADAMES
RAMADAS
RAVAGES
REBATES
RECALLS
RECANES
RECANTS
RECASTS
REDACTS
REDANTS
REDATES
REFACES
REGAINS
REGALES
REGARDS
REHANGS
RELACES
RELATES
RELAXES

REMAILS
REMAINS
REMAKES
REMANDS
REMARKS
RENAILS
RENAMES
REPAIRS
REPASTS
REPAVES
RERATES
RESALES
RESALTS
RESANDS
RETAILS
RETAINS
RETAKES
RETAPES
RETARDS
RETAXES
REVAMPS
REWARDS
REWARMS
REWAXES
RIBANDS
ROBARDS
ROLAIDS
ROTATES
SAFARIS
SALAAMS
SALAMIS
SAVAGES
SAVALAS
SAVANTS
SCRAPES
SCRAWLS
SECANTS
SENATES
SERAPES
SERAPHS
SERAPIS
SESAMES
SHEATHS
SHEAVES
SOLACES
SOMALIS
SONATAS
SPRAINS
SPRAWLS
SQUALLS
SQUARES
SQUAWKS
STRAFES
STRAINS
STRAITS
STRANDS
STRATUS
STRAUSS
TABARDS
TAMALES
TATAMIS
TENACES
TENANTS
TERAPHS
TETANUS
THRALLS
THWACKS
THWARTS
TIRADES
TISANES
TOPAZES
TOWARDS
TRUANTS

TYRANTS
UMLAUTS
UNCAGES
UNCASES
UNHANDS
UNLACES
UNLADES
UNMAKES
UNMASKS
UNPACKS
UNTACKS
UPDATES
UPLANDS
UPTAKES
UPWARDS
VACATES
VIRAGOS
VISAGES
VISAVIS
VOYAGES
WIZARDS
WREATHS
ZENANAS
ZOUAVES

••••AS•

ABREAST
AIRBASE
AIRMASS
AMYLASE
APPEASE
ATLEAST
BALLAST
BELFAST
BIOMASS
BOMBAST
BONEASH
CANVASS
CARCASS
CARWASH
COMPASS
CUIRASS
CUTLASS
DECLASS
DISEASE
ECSTASY
EGGCASE
EYELASH
EYEWASH
FANTASY
FAREAST
FLYCAST
FLYPAST
GOULASH
GYMNAST
HOGWASH
INPHASE
JACKASS
JETWASH
LACTASE
MIDEAST
MISCAST
MOMBASA
NASTASE
OFFBASE
OUTCAST
OUTLAST
OXIDASE
PAYCASH
PRECAST
PREWASH
REAMASS
RELEASE

SARCASM
SEABASS
SKIMASK
SUCRASE
SURPASS
TOPMAST
TWOBASE
UNCLASP
UNLEASH

••••A•S

ADONAIS
AERIALS
AFFRAYS
AFGHANS
AIRBAGS
AIRDAMS
AIRMASS
AIRSACS
AIRWAYS
ALLEARS
ANDEANS
ANIMALS
ANNEALS
ANNUALS
ANORAKS
AOUDADS
APPEALS
APPEARS
ARAWAKS
ARREARS
ASHCANS
ASHLARS
ASHRAMS
ATAMANS
AVATARS
AVOWALS
BALKANS
BALLADS
BALSAMS
BANTAMS
BANYANS
BAOBABS
BAZAARS
BEGGARS
BELDAMS
BEMOANS
BENGALS
BETRAYS
BIOMASS
BITMAPS
BOBCATS
BOWSAWS
BOXCARS
BRIDALS
BROGANS
BULGARS
BUREAUS
BURLAPS
BUROAKS
BURSARS
BYPLAYS
BYROADS
CAESARS
CAFTANS
CAIMANS
CALPACS
CANCANS
CANVASS
CARCASS
CARPALS
CASUALS
CATNAPS

CAVEATS
CELLARS
CEREALS
CHORALS
COEVALS
COGNACS
COLLARS
COMBATS
COMPASS
CONFABS
CORRALS
COSTARS
COUGARS
CRAVATS
CRETANS
CUIRASS
CUSHAWS
CUTLASS
CYMBALS
DECLASS
DEEJAYS
DEFEATS
DEFRAYS
DEMEANS
DENIALS
DEODARS
DEWLAPS
DIKTATS
DISBARS
DISMAYS
DOGDAYS
DOGEARS
DOGTAGS
DOLLARS
DOLMANS
DOODADS
DORSALS
DOSSALS
ENDEARS
ENDWAYS
ENGRAMS
ENNEADS
ENTRAPS
ENWRAPS
ESPIALS
ESTRAYS
FACIALS
FATCATS
FIJIANS
FINIALS
FLYWAYS
FORMALS
FORMATS
FRIDAYS
FRYPANS
GASBAGS
GASCAPS
GAVIALS
GEEGAWS
GERMANS
GEWGAWS
GIMBALS
GRAHAMS
GUFFAWS
GUITARS
HANGARS
HAWHAWS
HEEHAWS
HEPCATS
HEPTADS
HERBALS
HETMANS
HEYDAYS

HOOHAHS
HOOKAHS
HOTCAPS
HOTCARS
HOTWARS
HOWDAHS
HUBCAPS
HURRAHS
HUSSARS
HUZZAHS
HYMNALS
ICEBAGS
ICECAPS
INDIANS
INROADS
INSEAMS
INSPANS
ISOBARS
JACKALS
JACKASS
JAGUARS
JIGSAWS
JIMJAMS
KAFTANS
KANSANS
KENYANS
KEYPADS
KIDNAPS
KIRMANS
KITBAGS
KODIAKS
KOREANS
LABIALS
LANDAUS
LARIATS
LIBYANS
LOGJAMS
LOOFAHS
LOQUATS
LUMBARS
MADCAPS
MAENADS
MAGYARS
MAITAIS
MAMMALS
MANDANS
MANDAYS
MANIACS
MANUALS
MARGAYS
MAYDAYS
MEDIANS
MENIALS
MESCALS
MICMACS
MIDDAYS
MIDWAYS
MINOANS
MISHAPS
MISLAYS
MISSALS
MOBCAPS
MONDAYS
MORGANS
MORTALS
MORTARS
MULLAHS
MUSCATS
MUTUALS
MYRIADS
NARWALS
NAYSAYS
NECTARS

NORMALS
NORMANS
NOUGATS
NUBIANS
NUMBATS
OGDOADS
OHIOANS
OILCANS
OILPANS
OLDDAYS
OOMPAHS
ORDEALS
ORLEANS
ORPHANS
OUTEATS
OUTLAWS
OUTLAYS
PAPUANS
PARIAHS
PARLAYS
PAWPAWS
PAYDAYS
PEDLARS
PENPALS
PENTADS
PERHAPS
PIEPANS
PILLARS
PINOAKS
PITSAWS
PLURALS
POPLARS
PORTALS
PREFABS
PREPAYS
PTBOATS
PULSARS
PUNKAHS
PURDAHS
QINTARS
QUASARS
RADIALS
RADIANS
RAGLANS
RASCALS
RATTANS
REAMASS
REDCAPS
REDEALS
REDHATS
REDIALS
REDOAKS
REDRAWS
REHEALS
REHEARS
REHEATS
RELOADS
RENTALS
REPEALS
REPEATS
REPLANS
REPLAYS
REREADS
RESEALS
RESEATS
REVEALS
REWRAPS
REXCATS
RIPRAPS
RIPSAWS
RITUALS
RUNLAPS
RUNWAYS

RUPIAHS
SALAAMS
SAMBARS
SAMOANS
SAMPANS
SANDALS
SASHAYS
SATRAPS
SCALARS
SCARABS
SCHNAPS
SCREAKS
SCREAMS
SEABAGS
SEABASS
SEAFANS
SEALABS
SEAWAYS
SEESAWS
SERIALS
SERVALS
SEXTANS
SHAMANS
SHOFARS
SIGNALS
SIMIANS
SIOUANS
SKYCAPS
SKYWAYS
SLOGANS
SLOVAKS
SNOCATS
SOCIALS
SPIRALS
SPREADS
SQUEAKS
SQUEALS
STALAGS
STREAKS
STREAMS
SUBWAYS
SULTANS
SUNDAES
SUNDAYS
SUNRAYS
SUNTANS
SURPASS
SYLVANS
SYRIANS
TAIPANS
TAMTAMS
TANOAKS
TARMACS
TARSALS
TARTANS
TARTARS
TEABAGS
TETRADS
THREADS
THREATS
THROATS
TICTACS
TIMBALS
TINCANS
TINEARS
TINHATS
TOECAPS
TOETAPS
TOMCATS
TONGANS
TOPHATS
TOUCANS
TOWCARS

TREPANS
TROCARS
TROJANS
TULSANS
TURBANS
UNCIALS
UNLOADS
UNSEALS
UNSEATS
UNSNAGS
UNSNAPS
UNTRAPS
UNWRAPS
UPBEATS
UPLOADS
UPROARS
UTAHANS
VANDALS
VASSALS
VEEJAYS
VERBALS
VISUALS
VULCANS
WANTADS
WAYLAYS
WETBARS
WHYDAHS
WIGWAGS
WIGWAMS
WOMBATS
YOUMANS
ZIGZAGS
ZODIACS

•••••AS

ACACIAS
AGENDAS
ALPACAS
AMOEBAS
ANANIAS
ANDREAS
ANGORAS
AQUINAS
AREOLAS
ARISTAS
ARMADAS
ARNICAS
ARROBAS
ASFARAS
AURORAS
AZALEAS
BAHAMAS
BALBOAS
BANANAS
BODEGAS
BRAHMAS
BUDDHAS
CABALAS
CABANAS
CAMERAS
CARACAS
CARINAS
CASABAS
CASSIAS
CAYUGAS
CHACHAS
CHOLLAS
CHUKKAS
CICADAS
CINEMAS
COALGAS
CONTRAS
CORNEAS

CORONAS
COWPEAS
CUPOLAS
CZARDAS
DAHLIAS
DAKOTAS
DOUGLAS
DUENNAS
ENIGMAS
ESPOSAS
FAJITAS
FASCIAS
FAUXPAS
FEDORAS
FIBULAS
FIESTAS
GEISHAS
GELADAS
GILBLAS
GLORIAS
GOTCHAS
GRACIAS
GUINEAS
GURKHAS
HEGIRAS
HOOPLAS
IGUANAS
IMPALAS
JACANAS
JERBOAS
JICAMAS
KAHUNAS
KANAKAS
KORUNAS
KWACHAS
KWANZAS
LACUNAS
LAGUNAS
LAKOTAS
LAMBDAS
LAMINAS
LATINAS
LOGGIAS
MANANAS
MANTRAS
MARACAS
MARINAS
MATHIAS
MEDUSAS
MIASMAS
MIMOSAS
MITHRAS
MODELAS
MULETAS
NEBULAS
NICOLAS
NOVENAS
NUTRIAS
OGLALAS
OJIBWAS
ONEIDAS
OTTAWAS
PAGODAS
PAJAMAS
PANAMAS
PAPAYAS
PATINAS
PAYOLAS
PELOTAS
PESETAS
PHIDIAS
PHINEAS
PHOBIAS

PIAZZAS
PINATAS
PINCHAS
PLASMAS
POSADAS
PYJAMAS
PYTHIAS
QUAGGAS
QUINOAS
QUOKKAS
RAMADAS
RAREGAS
REMORAS
REMUDAS
RETINAS
RHUMBAS
SAMPRAS
SAVALAS
SCHEMAS
SCLERAS
SENECAS
SENORAS
SHEILAS
SHERPAS
SIENNAS
SIERRAS
SIESTAS
SILICAS
SONATAS
SPIREAS
STANZAS
STIGMAS
TEARGAS
TIMEWAS
TRAMPAS
TRAUMAS
TROIKAS
TSONGAS
TUNDRAS
UTOPIAS
VICUNAS
VIZSLAS
WHEREAS
ZAREBAS
ZENANAS
ZEUGMAS
ZINNIAS
ZOYSIAS

AT•••••

ATACAMA
ATALOSS
ATAMANS
ATATURK
ATAVISM
ATAVIST
ATECROW
ATELIER
ATFAULT
ATHEART
ATHEISM
ATHEIST
ATHIRST
ATHLETE
ATHOMES
ATHWART
ATINGLE
ATISSUE
ATLANTA
ATLARGE
ATLASES
ATLATLS
ATLEAST

ATOMIES
ATOMIZE
ATONING
ATPEACE
ATRIUMS
ATROPHY
ATSTAKE
ATTACHE
ATTACKS
ATTAINS
ATTEMPT
ATTENDS
ATTESTS
ATTICUS
ATTIMES
ATTIRED
ATTIRES
ATTRACT
ATTRITE
ATTRITS
ATTUCKS
ATTUNED
ATTUNES
ATWORST

A•T••••

ACTABLE
ACTAEON
ACTEDUP
ACTINIC
ACTIONS
ACTIVES
ACTRESS
ACTSOUT
ACTUARY
ACTUATE
ACTUPON
AITCHES
ALTERED
ALTERER
ALTOONA
ALTOSAX
ANTACID
ANTAEUS
ANTARES
ANTBEAR
ANTCOWS
ANTEDUP
ANTEING
ANTENNA
ANTESUP
ANTFARM
ANTHEMS
ANTHERS
ANTHILL
ANTHONY
ANTIART
ANTIBES
ANTIGEN
ANTIGUA
ANTILOG
ANTIOCH
ANTIQUE
ANTIWAR
ANTLERS
ANTLION
ANTOINE
ANTONIA
ANTONIN
ANTONIO
ANTONYM
ANTSIER
ANTWERP
APTNESS
ARTDECO
ARTEMIS
ARTEMUS
ARTFILM
ARTFORM
ARTICLE
ARTIEST
ARTISAN
ARTISTE
ARTISTS
ARTLESS
ARTSONG
ARTWARE
ARTWORK
ASTAIRE
ASTARTE
ASTOLAT
ASTORIA
ASTOUND
ASTRIDE
ATTACHE
ATTACKS
ATTAINS
ATTEMPT
ATTENDS
ATTESTS
ATTICUS
ATTIMES
ATTIRED
ATTIRES
ATTRACT
ATTRITE
ATTRITS
ATTUCKS
ATTUNED
ATTUNES
AUTEURS
AUTHORS
AUTOMAT
AUTUMNS
AZTECAN

A••T•••

ABATING
ABETTED
ABETTOR
ABSTAIN
ABUTTAL
ABUTTED
ACETATE
ACETONE
ACHTUNG
ACUTELY
AGITATE
AIRTAXI
AIRTIME
ALLTIME
ALLTOLD
AMATEUR
AMATIVE
AMATORY
ANATOLE
ANATOMY
ANOTHER
ANYTIME
APATITE
APOTHEM
ASHTRAY
ATATURK
ATSTAKE
AUCTION
AUNTIES
AUSTERE
AUSTRAL
AUSTRIA
AVATARS

A•••T••

ABETTED
ABETTOR
ABLATED
ABLATES
ABORTED
ABUTTAL
ABUTTED
ACANTHI
ACHATES
ADAPTED
ADAPTER
ADAPTOR
ADEPTLY
ADOPTED
ADOPTEE
ADOPTER
AERATED
AERATES
AERATOR
AGNATES
AGOUTIS
ALERTED
ALERTER
ALERTLY
ALLSTAR
ALLSTON
AMMETER
ANNATTO
ANNETTE
APOSTLE
AQUATIC
ARBITER
ARBUTUS
ARIETTA
ARISTAE
ARISTAS
ARISTOS
ASCETIC
ASEPTIC
ASIATIC
ATLATLS
AUDITED
AUDITOR
AVERTED
AVIATED
AVIATES
AVIATOR
AWAITED

A••••T•

ABDUCTS
ABILITY
ABLAUTS
ABSENTS
ACCENTS
ACCEPTS
ACCOSTS
ACCRETE
ACETATE
ACIDITY
ACOLYTE
ACONITE
ACQUITS
ACTUATE
ADAMITE
ADDEDTO
ADDONTO
ADDUCTS
ADDUPTO
ADJUSTS
ADULATE
ADVENTS
ADVERTS
AFFECTS
AFREETS
AGEISTS
AGILITY
AGITATE
AGREETO
AIGRETS
AIMEDTO
AIRDATE
AKIHITO
ALBERTA
ALBERTO
ALDENTE
ALIGHTS
ALMAATA
ALWORTH
AMENITY
AMNESTY
AMOUNTS
AMULETS
ANDANTE
ANIMATE
ANIMATO
ANKLETS
ANNATTO
ANNETTE
ANNUITY
ANOINTS
ANXIETY
AORISTS
APATITE
APLENTY
ARIDITY
ARIETTA
ARIOSTO
ARMLETS
ARMPITS
ARRESTS
ARTISTE
ARTISTS
ASCENTS
ASHANTI
ASPECTS
ASSENTS
ASSERTS
ASSISTS
ASSORTS
ASTARTE
ATHLETE
ATLANTA
ATTESTS
ATTRITE
ATTRITS
AUGUSTA
AUGUSTE
AUKLETS
AUREATE
AVIDITY
AVOCETS
AXOLOTL
AZIMUTH
AZURITE

A•••••T

ABREAST
ABSOLUT
ACCOUNT
ACCURST
ACEDOUT
ACESOUT
ACHIEST
ACROBAT
ACTSOUT
ADAMANT
ADJUNCT
AERIEST
AEROBAT
AFFLICT
AFFRONT
AGAINST
AGONIST
AILMENT
AIMEDAT
AIRBOAT
AIRIEST
AIRLIFT
AIRPORT
AIRSOUT
ALIMENT
ALRIGHT
AMBIENT
AMHERST
AMONGST
AMPLEST
ANALYST
ANAPEST
ANCIENT
ANIMIST
ANTIART
APPOINT
APRICOT
AQUAVIT
ARIDEST
ARMREST
ARMYANT
ARTIEST
ASHIEST
ASKSOUT
ASPHALT
ASSAULT
ASTOLAT
ATAVIST
ATFAULT
ATHEART
ATHEIST
ATHIRST
ATHWART
ATLEAST
ATTEMPT
ATTRACT
ATWORST
AUGMENT
AUTOMAT

•AT••••

BATBOYS
BATCHED
BATCHES
BATEAUX
BATEMAN
BATHERS
BATHING
BATHMAT
BATHOIL
BATHTUB
BATIKED
BATISTA
BATISTE
BATSMAN
BATSMEN
BATTENS
BATTERS
BATTERY
BATTIER
BATTING
BATTLED
BATTLER
BATTLES
BATWING
CATALAN
CATALOG
CATALPA
CATAWBA
CATBIRD
CATBOAT
CATCALL
CATCHER
CATCHES
CATCHON
CATCHUP
CATENAE
CATERED
CATERER
CATFISH
CATHAIR
CATHEAD
CATHODE
CATIONS
CATKINS
CATLIKE
CATNAPS
CATNIPS
CATSCAN
CATSEYE
CATSPAW
CATTAIL
CATTIER
CATTILY
CATTING
CATTISH
CATWALK
DATASET
DATEDLY
EATABLE
EATAWAY
EATCROW
EATENAT
EATENUP
EATSOUT
FATBACK
FATCATS
FATCITY
FATEFUL
FATHEAD
FATHERS
FATHOMS
FATIGUE
FATLESS
FATNESS
FATTENS
FATTEST
FATUITY
FATUOUS
GATEAUX
GATELEG
GATEMAN
GATEMEN
GATEWAY
GATHERS
GATLING
HATCHED
HATCHER
HATCHES
HATCHET
HATEFUL
HATLESS
HATPINS
HATRACK
HATTERS
HATTING
KATHRYN
KATYDID
LATCHED
LATCHES
LATEENS
LATENCY
LATENTS
LATERAL
LATERAN
LATERON
LATEXES
LATHERS
LATHERY
LATHING
LATICES
LATIFAH
LATINAS
LATINOS
LATTENS
LATTICE
LATVIAN
MATADOR
MATCHED
MATCHES
MATCHUP
MATEWAN
MATHERS
MATHEWS
MATHIAS
MATILDA
MATINEE
MATISSE
MATLOCK
MATRONS
MATTERS
MATTHAU
MATTHEW
MATTING
MATTOCK
MATURED
MATURER
MATURES
MATZOHS
NATALIA
NATALIE
NATASHA
NATCHEZ
NATIONS
NATIVES
NATRIUM
NATTERS
NATTIER
NATTILY
NATURAL
NATURED
NATURES
OATMEAL
PATAKES
PATCHED
PATCHES
PATCHUP
PATELLA
PATENTS
PATERNO
PATHWAY
PATIENT
PATINAS
PATNESS
PATRICE
PATRICK
PATRIOT
PATROLS
PATRONS
PATROON
PATSIES
PATTENS
PATTERN
PATTERS
PATTIES
PATTING
RATABLE
RATAFIA
RATATAT
RATCHET
RATFINK
RATHOLE
RATINGS
RATIONS
RATITES
RATLINE
RATPACK
RATRACE
RATTAIL
RATTANS
RATTERS
RATTIER
RATTING
RATTLED
RATTLER
RATTLES
RATTRAP
SATCHEL
SATCHMO
SATDOWN
SATIATE
SATIETY
SATIRES
SATIRIC
SATISFY
SATRAPS
SATSUMA
TATAMIS
TATIANA
TATTERS
TATTIER
TATTING
TATTLED
TATTLER
TATTLES
TATTOOS
VATFULS
VATICAN
WATCHED
WATCHER
WATCHES
WATCHIT
WATERED
WATERER
WATTAGE
WATTEAU
WATTLES
ZATOPEK

•A•T•••

BAITING
BANTAMS
BANTERS
BAPTISM
BAPTIST
BAPTIZE
BARTEND
BARTERS
BASTERS
BASTING
BASTION
BATTENS
BATTERS
BATTERY
BATTIER
BATTING
BATTLED
BATTLER
BATTLES
CAFTANS
CALTECH
CANTATA
CANTEEN
CANTERS
CANTINA
CANTING
CANTLES
CANTONS
CANTORS
CAPTAIN
CAPTION
CAPTIVE
CAPTORS
CAPTURE
CARTAGE
CARTELS
CARTERS
CARTIER
CARTING
CARTONS
CARTOON
CASTERS
CASTILE
CASTING
CASTLED
CASTLES
CASTOFF
CASTOUT
CATTAIL
CATTIER
CATTILY
CATTING
CATTISH
CAUTION
DACTYLS
DAFTEST
DALTREY
DARTERS
DARTING
DASTARD
DAYTIME
DAYTONA
DAYTRIP
EARTHEN
EARTHLY
EASTEND
EASTERN
EASTERS
EASTMAN
FACTION
FACTORS
FACTORY
FACTUAL
FALTERS
FANTAIL
FANTASY
FARTHER
FASTENS
FASTEST
FASTING
FASTONE
FATTENS
FATTEST
GAITERS
GAITING
GANTLET
GARTERS
GASTRIC
GAUTAMA
HAITIAN
HALTERS
HALTING
HARTMAN
HASTENS
HASTIER
HASTILY
HASTING
HATTERS
HATTING
HAUTBOY
HAUTEUR
JANTZEN
KAFTANS
LACTASE
LACTATE
LACTEAL
LACTOSE
LANTANA
LANTERN
LAOTIAN
LAPTOPS
LASTING
LASTORY
LATTENS
LATTICE
LAUTREC
MAITAIS
MAITRED
MALTEDS
MALTESE
MALTHUS
MALTING
MALTOSE
MANTELS
MANTLED
MANTLES
MANTRAP
MANTRAS
MANTRIC
MARTENS
MARTIAL
MARTIAN
MARTINA
MARTINI
MARTINO
MARTINS
MARTYRS
MASTABA
MASTERS
MASTERY
MASTICS
MASTIFF
MASTOID
MATTERS
MATTHAU
MATTHEW
MATTING
MATTOCK
MAYTIME
NAPTIME
NARTHEX
NASTASE
NASTIER
NASTILY
NATTERS
NATTIER
NATTILY
OAKTREE
PALTERS
PANTHER
PANTING
PARTAKE
PARTIAL
PARTIED
PARTIES
PARTING
PARTITA
PARTITE
PARTNER
PARTOOK
PARTOUT
PARTWAY
PASTDUE
PASTELS
PASTERN
PASTEUP
PASTEUR
PASTIER
PASTIME
PASTINA
PASTING
PASTORS
PASTURE
PATTENS
PATTERN
PATTERS
PATTIES
PATTING
RAFTERS
RAFTING
RAGTIME
RAGTOPS
RANTERS
RANTING
RAPTORS
RAPTURE
RASTERS
RATTAIL
RATTANS
RATTERS
RATTIER
RATTING
RATTLED
RATTLER
RATTLES
RATTRAP
SALTBOX
SALTERS
SALTIER
SALTILY
SALTINE
SALTING
SANTAFE
SANTANA
SANTINI
SANTIRS
SAOTOME
SAUTEED
TACTFUL
TACTICS
TACTILE
TAMTAMS
TANTARA
TANTRUM
TARTANS
TARTARE
TARTARS
TARTEST
TASTERS
TASTIER
TASTILY
TASTING
TATTERS
TATTIER
TATTING
TATTLED
TATTLER
TATTLES
TATTOOS
TAUTENS
TAUTEST
VANTAGE
VASTEST
WAFTING
WAGTAIL
WAITERS
WAITING
WAITOUT
WAITSON
WAITSUP
WALTERS
WALTZED
WALTZER
WALTZES
WANTADS
WANTING
WANTOUT
WANTSIN
WANTSTO
WARTHOG
WARTIME
WASTAGE
WASTERS
WASTING
WASTREL
WATTAGE
WATTEAU
WATTLES
XANTHAN
XANTHIC
YAHTZEE

•A••T••

BABETTE
BALATON
BARETTA
BATHTUB
CADETTE
CAPITAL
CAPITAN
CAPITOL
CAPSTAN
CARLTON
CAROTID
CAUSTIC
DAKOTAN
DAKOTAS
DAUNTED
DAYSTAR
FACETED
FAGOTED
FAINTED
FAINTER
FAINTLY
FAJITAS
FANATIC
FAULTED
FAUSTUS
GAGSTER
GALATEA
GALATIA
GAMETES
GAUNTER
GAUNTLY
GAVOTTE
GAZETTE
HABITAT
HABITED
HABITUE
HALITES
HALSTON
HAMITES
HAMITIC
HAMITUP
HAMPTON
HAMSTER
HANGTEN
HARDTOP
HAUNTED
JACKTAR
JANITOR
JAUNTED
LAERTES
LAFITTE
LAKOTAS
LAMOTTA
LANGTRY
LAYETTE
MAESTRI
MAESTRO
MAHATMA
MAINTOP
MANATEE
MANITOU
MARITAL
NAMETAG
NANETTE
NAPHTHA
PAINTED
PAINTER
PAIUTES
PALATAL
PALATES
PALETTE
PANETTA
RALSTON
RARITAN
RATATAT
RATITES
SAINTED
SAINTLY
SALUTED
SALUTES
SAMITES
SANCTUM
SAUNTER
TABITHA
TACITLY
TACITUS
TAINTED
TAKETEN
TANKTOP
TAPSTER
TAUNTED
VACATED
VACATES
VAULTED
VAULTER
VAUNTED
VAUNTER

WAISTED
WAPITIS
WASATCH
WASHTUB
YACHTED
YAKUTSK
YANGTZE
YANKTON
ZAPOTEC

•A•••T•

BABBITT
BABETTE
BALLETS
BALLOTS
BANDITO
BANDITS
BARENTS
BARETTA
BARRETT
BASALTS
BASKETS
BASSETS
BATISTA
BATISTE
BAUXITE
BAYCITY
CABLETV
CACHETS
CADETTE
CAHOOTS
CALCITE
CANASTA
CANTATA
CAPLETS
CAPNUTS
CARNETS
CARPETS
CARROTS
CASSATT
CAVEATS
CAVORTS
DARESTO
EAGLETS
FACULTY
FALLSTO
FALSITY
FANJETS
FATCATS
FATCITY
FATUITY
FAUCETS
FAWCETT
GADGETS
GADGETY
GALOOTS
GAMBITS
GANGSTA
GANNETS
GANNETT
GARNETS
GARRETS
GARRETT
GASJETS
GASKETS
GAVOTTE
GAZETTE
HACKETT
HAEMATO
HAMLETS
HAMMETT
HAUGHTY
HAVARTI
JACINTO
JACKETS
JADEITE
JAKARTA
JAPHETH
LABIATE
LABRETS
LACOSTE
LACTATE
LAFITTE
LAMENTS
LAMOTTA
LANCETS
LAPLATA
LAPORTE
LAPPETS
LARIATS
LATENTS
LAYETTE
LAYINTO
LAYOUTS
MACBETH
MACHETE
MAGENTA
MAGNATE
MAGNETO
MAGNETS
MAHOUTS
MAJESTE
MAJESTY
MALEATE
MALLETS
MAMMOTH
MANDATE
MAOISTS
MARGATE
MARKETS
MARMOTS
MASCOTS
NAHUATL
NAIVETE
NANETTE
NARRATE
NAUGHTS
NAUGHTY
PACKETS
PALETTE
PALLETS
PALMATE
PANDITS
PANETTA
PAPEETE
PARENTS
PARGETS
PARROTS
PARTITA
PARTITE
PATENTS
PAUCITY
PAYOUTS
RABBETS
RABBITS
RABBITT
RACKETS
RADIATE
RAGOUTS
RALLYTO
RAMJETS
RANINTO
RANLATE
RAWDATA
SABBATH
SACHETS
SATIATE
SATIETY
SAVANTS
TABLETS
TAFFETA
TAKESTO
TALENTS
TALKSTO
TAOISTS
TAPPETS
TARANTO
TARGETS
TARPITS
TAXRATE
VACUITY
VALUATE
VARIETY
VARLETS
VARSITY
WALCOTT
WALLETS
WALNUTS
WANTSTO
WARPATH

•A••••T

BABBITT
BABYSAT
BABYSIT
BACKBIT
BACKLIT
BACKOUT
BAILOUT
BALDEST
BALLAST
BANQUET
BAPTIST
BARKSAT
BARONET
BARRETT
BASEHIT
BASSIST
BATHMAT
BAWLOUT
BAYONET
CABARET
CABINET
CAGIEST
CALLOUT
CALMEST
CALUMET
CALVERT
CAMELOT
CAMEOUT
CAMPOUT
CAPELET
CAPULET
CARCOAT
CARPORT
CARSEAT
CASHOUT
CASSATT
CASTOUT
CATBOAT
CAVEART
DADAIST
DAFTEST
DAMPEST
DANKEST
DARKEST
DASBOOT
DATASET
EARHART
EARNEST
EARSHOT
EASIEST
EATENAT
EATSOUT
FADDIST
FADEOUT
FAIREST
FALLOUT
FALSEST
FANBELT
FANSOUT
FAREAST
FARLEFT
FARMOUT
FARWEST
FASCIST
FASTEST
FATTEST
FAUVIST
FAWCETT
GABFEST
GALLANT
GAMIEST
GANNETT
GANTLET
GARMENT
GARRETT
GAVEOUT
HABITAT
HACKETT
HAIRCUT
HAIRNET
HALFWIT
HALIBUT
HAMMETT
HANDOUT
HANDSET
HANGOUT
HARDEST
HARDHAT
HARDHIT
HARDPUT
HARDSET
HARICOT
HARPIST
HARRIET
HARVEST
HATCHET
HAVENOT
HAYLOFT
HAZIEST
JACKPOT
JACONET
LABCOAT
LACIEST
LAIDOUT
LAMAIST
LAMBENT
LAMBERT
LANDSAT
LANKEST
LAPBELT
LARGEST
LAUGHAT
LAURENT
LAWSUIT
LAYSOUT
LAZIEST
MADDEST
MADEOUT
MAEWEST
MAGINOT
MAIGRET
MAILLOT
MAKEOUT
MAKESIT
MANHUNT
MANUMIT
MANXCAT
MARGRET
NAILSET
NASCENT
PACKRAT
PAGEANT
PAIDOUT
PALMIST
PANDECT
PANSOUT
PARAPET
PARFAIT
PARQUET
PARTOUT
PASSANT
PASSOUT
PATIENT
PATRIOT
PAULIST
PAWEDAT
PAYDIRT
PAYMENT
PAYSOUT
RABBITT
RACIEST
RACQUET
RADIANT
RAILSAT
RAIMENT
RAINHAT
RAINOUT
RAMPANT
RAMPART
RANKEST
RANRIOT
RAPPORT
RAREBIT
RASHEST
RATATAT
RATCHET
SACKOUT
SADDEST
SALIENT
SANDLOT
SANGOUT
SAPIENT
SARGENT
SAWDUST
TABORET
TAGSOUT
TAKEOUT
TALKOUT
TALKSAT
TALLEST
TANGENT
TANNEST
TAPROOT
TAPSOUT
TARTEST
TAUTEST
VAGRANT
VAGUEST
VAINEST
VALIANT
VANZANT
VARIANT
VARMINT
VASTEST
WAITOUT
WALCOTT
WALKOUT
WALMART
WANTOUT
WARIEST
WARMEST
WARRANT
WASHOUT
WATCHIT
WAVELET
WAVIEST
WAXIEST
ZANIEST

••AT•••

ABATING
AMATEUR
AMATIVE
AMATORY
ANATOLE
ANATOMY
APATITE
ATATURK
AVATARS
BEATERS
BEATIFY
BEATING
BEATLES
BEATNIK
BEATOUT
BEATRIX
BEATSIT
BEATSUP
BEATTIE
BLATANT
BLATHER
BLATTED
BOATERS
BOATING
BOATMAN
BOATMEN
CHATEAU
CHATHAM
CHATSUP
CHATTED
CHATTEL
CHATTER
CLATTER
COATING
CRATERS
CRATING
DIATOMS
DRATTED
ELATERS
ELATING
ELATION
FEATHER
FEATURE
FLATBED
FLATCAR
FLATOUT
FLATTED
FLATTEN
FLATTER
FLATTOP
GOATEED
GOATEES
GOATISH
GRATERS
GRATIFY
GRATING
HEATERS
HEATHEN
HEATHER
HEATING
HEATSUP
HEATTER
IRATELY
IRATEST
KLATSCH
KRATERS
KRATION
LEATHER
LOATHED
LOATHES
MEATIER
NEATENS
NEATEST
ONATEAR
ORATING
ORATION
ORATORS
ORATORY
OVATION
PEATBOG
PLATEAU
PLATENS
PLATERS
PLATING
PLATOON
PLATTER
PLATYPI
PRATERS
PRATING
PRATTLE
SCATHED
SCATHES
SCATTED
SCATTER
SEATERS
SEATING
SEATTLE
SHATNER
SHATTER
SKATERS
SKATING
SLATHER
SLATIER
SLATING
SLATKIN
SLATTED
SMATTER
SPATIAL
SPATTED
SPATTER
SPATULA
STATELY
STATICE
STATICS
STATING
STATION
STATIST
STATORS
STATUES
STATURE
STATUTE
SWATHED
SWATHES
SWATTED
SWATTER
TEATIME
TEATRAY
THATCHY
THATSIT
UPATREE
WEATHER
WHATFOR
WHATNOT
XRATING
YEATEAM

••A•T••

ACANTHI
ADAPTED
ADAPTER
ADAPTOR
AWAITED
BEASTIE
BEASTLY
BEATTIE
BLASTED
BLASTER
BLATTED
BOASTED
BOASTER
BRAXTON
CHANTED
CHANTER
CHANTEY
CHAOTIC
CHAPTER
CHARTED
CHARTER
CHASTEN
CHASTER
CHATTED
CHATTEL
CHATTER
CLAPTON
CLATTER
CLAYTON
COALTAR
COASTAL
COASTED
COASTER
CRAFTED
CRAFTER
CRAFTSY
DEALTIN
DEARTHS
DRAFTED
DRAFTEE
DRASTIC
DRATTED
ELASTIC
ENACTED
ENACTOR
EXACTED
EXACTER
EXACTLY
EXACTOR
EXALTED
FEASTED
FLATTED
FLATTEN
FLATTER
FLATTOP
FRACTAL
FRANTIC
GHASTLY
GRAFTED
GRANTED
GRANTEE
GRANTOR
HEALTHY
HEARTEN
HEARTHS
HEATTER
INAPTLY
INASTEW
LEANTOS
PHAETON
PHANTOM
PIASTER
PIASTRE
PLAITED
PLANTAR
PLANTED
PLANTER
PLASTER
PLASTIC
PLATTER
PLAUTUS
PRAETOR
PRATTLE
PSALTER
QUANTUM
QUARTER
QUARTET
QUARTOS
REACTED
REACTOR
REACTTO
REALTOR
ROASTED
ROASTER
SCANTED
SCANTER
SCANTLY
SCATTED
SCATTER
SEASTAR
SEATTLE
SHAFTED
SHANTER
SHASTRI
SHATTER
SLANTED
SLATTED
SLAYTON
SMALTOS
SMARTED
SMARTEN
SMARTER
SMARTLY
SMATTER
SPARTAN
SPATTED
SPATTER
STANTON
STARTED
STARTER
STARTLE
STARTUP
SWARTHY
SWATTED
SWATTER
TOASTED
TOASTER
TRACTOR
TRAITOR
WEALTHY
WHARTON
WRAITHS

••A••T•

ADAMITE
APATITE
CHALETS
CHAPATI
CHARITY
CLARETS
CLARITY
CRAVATS
DUALITY
EDACITY
EGALITE
EMANATE
FLAUNTS
FRAILTY
GEARSTO
GRANITE
GRAVITY
HEAVETO
IMAMATE
IMARETS
KLAMATH
LEADSTO
ONADATE
OPACITY
PEANUTS
PLACATE
PLAINTS
PLANETS
PRAYSTO
QUALITY
REACTTO
REALITY
SEADUTY
SEAGATE
SNAPSTO
STARETS
STATUTE
SUAVITY
TEAPOTS
TEASETS
URANITE
YEARNTO
ZEALOTS

••A•••T

ADAMANT
AGAINST
ANALYST
ANAPEST
ATAVIST
BEARCAT
BEAROUT
BEATOUT
BEATSIT
BLANKET
BLATANT
BRACKET
BRAVEST
CHAPLET
CHARIOT
CZARIST
DEADSET
DEAFEST
DEALOUT
DEAREST
DIALECT
DRAGNET
DRAGOUT
DRAUGHT
DRAWOUT
EPAULET
FLATOUT
FRAUGHT
GOABOUT
GRABSAT
GRAVEST
GRAYEST
HEADOUT
HEADSET
HEAROUT
INANEST
INASNIT
INASPOT
IRATEST
LEADOUT
LEAFLET
LEANEST
LEARJET
MEANEST
NEAREST
NEATEST
OFASORT
ONADIET
PEACOAT
PEASANT
PIANIST
PLACKET
PLAUDIT
PLAYACT
PLAYLET
PLAYOUT
PLAYSAT
QUARTET
READMIT
READOUT
REAGENT
REALIST
SCARLET
SEAGIRT
SEALANT
SEAPORT
SEASALT
SHALLOT
SNAPSAT
SPAREST
STALEST
STAREAT
STARLET
STARLIT
STATIST
STAYPUT
SUAVEST
TEACART
TEARSAT
THATSIT
TRABERT
TRANSIT
TSARIST
VIADUCT
WEAKEST
WEAROUT
WHATNOT
WYANDOT

•••AT••

ABLATED
ABLATES
ACHATES
AERATED
AERATES
AERATOR
AGNATES
ANNATTO
AQUATIC
ASIATIC
ATLATLS
AVIATED
AVIATES
AVIATOR
BALATON
BELATED
BENATAR
BERATED
BERATES
BLEATED
BLOATED
BORATES
BREATHE
BREATHS
BREATHY
BYPATHS
CHEATED
CHEATER
CREATED
CREATES
CREATOR
CROATIA
CURATES
CURATOR
DEBATED
DEBATER
DEBATES
DILATED
DILATES
DONATED
DONATES
DONATOR
EMPATHY
EQUATED
EQUATES
EQUATOR
ERRATIC
ERRATUM
ESTATES
FANATIC
FIXATED
FIXATES
FLOATED
FLOATER
GALATEA
GALATIA
GELATIN
GELATIS
GLOATED
GREATER
GREATLY
GYRATED
GYRATES
GYRATOR
HEPATIC
HORATIO
IDEATED
IDEATES
INMATES
IODATES
KERATIN
KOMATSU
LEGATEE
LEGATES
LEGATOS
LIGATED
LIGATES
LOCATED
LOCATER
LOCATES
LOCATOR
LUNATIC
LUXATED
LUXATES
MAHATMA
MANATEE
METATES
MUTATED
MUTATES
MUTATIS
NEGATED
NEGATES
NEGATOR
NOTATED
NOTATES
OBLATES
OLEATES
OPIATES
PALATAL
PALATES
PENATES
PINATAS
PIRATED
PIRATES
PIRATIC
PLEATED
RATATAT
REBATED
REBATES
REDATED
REDATES
REGATTA
RELATED
RELATES
RERATED
RERATES
ROTATED
ROTATES
ROTATOR
SCHATZI
SCRATCH
SEDATER
SENATES
SENATOR
SHEATHE
SHEATHS
SHIATSU
SINATRA
SOMATIC
SONATAS
STRATUM
STRATUS
SUMATRA
SWEATED
SWEATER
THEATER
THEATRE
TREATED
UNDATED
UNLATCH
UNRATED
UNSATED
UPDATED
UPDATES
VACATED
VACATES
WASATCH
WHEATON
WREATHE
WREATHS
YUCATAN

•••A•T•

ABLAUTS
ALMAATA
ANDANTE
ANNATTO
ASHANTI
ASTARTE
ATLANTA
BASALTS

BREADTH
BREASTS
CANASTA
CHIANTI
DECANTS
DEFACTO
DEPARTS
DESALTS
DIDACTS
DURANTE
DYNASTS
DYNASTY
EXPARTE
GOCARTS
GOKARTS
HAVARTI
HOGARTH
IMPACTS
IMPARTS
IMPASTO
INCANTS
INFANTA
INFANTS
INHASTE
JAKARTA
JOCASTA
KUWAITI
LEPANTO
LOYALTY
MUTANTS
OBLASTS
OCTANTS
OTRANTO
OUTACTS
OXCARTS
PEDANTS
PENALTY
PICANTE
REBASTE
RECANTS
RECASTS
REDACTS
REDANTS
REGATTA
REPASTE
REPASTS
RESALTS
ROYALTY
SAVANTS
SECANTS
SQUANTO
STEALTH
STRAITS
SWEARTO
TARANTO
TENANTS
THWARTS
TRUANTS
TYRANTS
UMLAUTS
UNEARTH
VEDANTA

•••A••T

AQUAVIT
ASSAULT
ATFAULT
CABARET
COHABIT
DADAIST
DATASET
DEFAULT
EXHAUST
GERAINT
INHABIT
LAMAIST
MINARET
NOFAULT
NOTABIT
PARAPET
PITAPAT
RATATAT
RENAULT
REPAINT
SWEARAT
TUBAIST

••••AT•

ACETATE
ACTUATE
ADULATE
AGITATE
AIRDATE
ALMAATA
ANIMATE
ANIMATO
AUREATE
BENEATH
BOBCATS
BROMATE
CANTATA
CASSATT
CAVEATS
CHAPATI
CILIATE
CITRATE
CLIMATE
COGNATE
COLGATE
COLLATE
COMBATS
CORDATE
CRAVATS
CUTRATE
DEFEATS
DEFLATE
DENTATE
DEVIATE
DICTATE
DIKTATS
DOGMATA
DUEDATE
EDUCATE
ELEVATE
EMANATE
EMIRATE
EMULATE
EXPIATE
FATCATS
FERRATE
FOLIATE
FORMATS
FRIGATE
GESTATE
GOLIATH
HAEMATO
HEPCATS
HYDRATE
IMAMATE
IMITATE
INFLATE
INGRATE
INSTATE
ISOLATE
ITERATE
KKKKATY
KLAMATH
LABIATE
LACTATE
LAPLATA
LARIATS
LINEATE
LOQUATS
MAGNATE
MALEATE
MANDATE
MARGATE
MEDIATE
MIGRATE
MISDATE
MISMATE
MUSCATS
NAHUATL
NARRATE
NEONATE
NEWGATE
NEWMATH
NITRATE
NOUGATS
NUMBATS
OBVIATE
ONADATE
OPERATE
OUTEATS
OVERATE
PALMATE
PELTATE
PENNATE
PINNATE
PLACATE
PREDATE
PRELATE
PRIMATE
PRIVATE
PROBATE
PRORATA
PRORATE
PTBOATS
PULSATE
RADIATE
RANLATE
RAWDATA
REDHATS
REHEATS
REPEATS
REPLATE
RESEATS
RESTATE
REXCATS
ROSEATE
SABBATH
SATIATE
SEAGATE
SENSATE
SERIATE
SERRATE
SITUATE
SNOCATS
SORBATE
STOMATA
STRIATE
SULFATE
SUNBATH
TAXRATE
TERNATE
THREATS
THROATS
THROATY
TINHATS
TITRATE
TOCCATA
TOMCATS
TOPHATS
TOWPATH
ULULATE
UNCRATE
UNSEATS
UPBEATS
UPSTATE
VALUATE
VIBRATE
VIBRATO
VIOLATE
VITIATE
VULGATE
WARPATH
WOMBATS
ZERMATT

••••A•T

ABREAST
ADAMANT
ANTIART
ARMYANT
ASPHALT
ATHEART
ATHWART
ATLEAST
ATTRACT
BALLAST
BELFAST
BITPART
BLATANT
BOMBAST
BUOYANT
BYHEART
CASSATT
CAVEART
CLIPART
COMPACT
CONTACT
COOLANT
COURANT
CURRANT
DEFIANT
DESCANT
DETRACT
DEVIANT
DISTANT
DOGCART
DORMANT
EARHART
ECKHART
ELEGANT
ELKHART
ENCHANT
ENGRAFT
ENTRANT
EXTRACT
FAREAST
FINEART
FIREANT
FLYCAST
FLYPAST
FOLKART
FONDANT
GALLANT
GESTALT
GYMNAST
HYDRANT
IMPLANT
INEXACT
INSTANT
ITERANT
JUNKART
LENFANT
MEDIANT
MIDEAST
MIGRANT
MISCAST
MORDANT
NEWHART
OUTCAST
OUTLAST
OVERACT
OXIDANT
PAGEANT
PARFAIT
PASSANT
PEASANT
PECCANT
PENDANT
PENNANT
PIQUANT
PLAYACT
POPTART
PRECAST
RADIANT
RAMPANT
RAMPART
REDEALT
REENACT
REFRACT
REGNANT
RELIANT
REMNANT
REPLANT
RESTART
RETRACT
RIOTACT
SEALANT
SEASALT
SERVANT
SEXTANT
SPIRANT
STEWART
TEACART
TOPMAST
ULULANT
UPDRAFT
UPSTART
VAGRANT
VALIANT
VANZANT
VARIANT
VERDANT
VIBRANT
WALMART
WARRANT
YOPLAIT
ZERMATT

•••••AT

ACROBAT
AEROBAT
AIMEDAT
AIRBOAT
ASTOLAT
AUTOMAT
BABYSAT
BARKSAT
BATHMAT
BEARCAT
BLINKAT
BODYFAT
BOXSEAT
BRILLAT
CARCOAT
CARSEAT
CATBOAT
COMESAT
COONCAT
COPYCAT
DEEPFAT
DINGBAT
DOORMAT
DOWNPAT
DRIVEAT
EATENAT
ENTREAT
ESCHEAT
FLIESAT
FROWNAT
GOINGAT
GRABSAT
GUNBOAT
HABITAT
HARDHAT
HELLCAT
HIGHHAT
HINTSAT
HOOTSAT
HOTSEAT
ICEBOAT
JEERSAT
JETBOAT
JUMPSAT
KEEPSAT
KINGRAT
KUMQUAT
LABCOAT
LANDSAT
LAUGHAT
LEERSAT
LOOKSAT
LUNGEAT
MANXCAT
MUSKRAT
NOSWEAT
NUTMEAT
OFFBEAT
OVEREAT
PACKRAT
PAWEDAT
PEACOAT
PECKSAT
PEEKSAT
PEERSAT
PICKSAT
PITAPAT
PLAYSAT
POKEDAT
POKESAT
POLECAT
PREHEAT
RAILSAT
RAINHAT
RATATAT
REDCOAT
REDHEAT
REDMEAT
RETREAT
RICERAT
ROWBOAT
SHOOTAT
SILKHAT
SNAPSAT
SNEERAT
SNIFFAT
SNIPEAT
STAREAT
SURCOAT
SWEARAT
SWOREAT
TALKSAT
TEARSAT
THEREAT
TOPCOAT
TREERAT
TUGBOAT
WHEREAT
WILDCAT
WINKSAT
YELLSAT

AU•••••

AUBADES
AUBURNS
AUCTION
AUDIBLE
AUDIBLY
AUDITED
AUDITOR
AUDUBON
AUGENDS
AUGMENT
AUGURAL
AUGURED
AUGUSTA
AUGUSTE
AUKLETS
AUNTIES
AURALEE
AURALLY
AUREATE
AUREOLA
AUREOLE
AURICLE
AUROCHS
AURORAE
AURORAL
AURORAS
AUSPICE
AUSSIES
AUSTERE
AUSTRAL
AUSTRIA
AUTEURS
AUTHORS
AUTOMAT
AUTUMNS

A•U••••

ABUBAKR
ABUSERS
ABUSING
ABUSIVE
ABUTTAL
ABUTTED
ACUTELY
ADULATE
ALUMNAE
ALUMNAL
ALUMNUS
ALUNSER
AMULETS
AMUSING
AOUDADS
AQUARIA
AQUATIC
AQUAVIT
AQUEOUS
AQUIFER
AQUINAS
AQUIVER
ARUGULA
ASUNDER
ASUSUAL
AVULSED
AVULSES
AZURITE

A••U•••

ABDUCTS
ABJURED
ABJURES
ABOUNDS
ACCURST
ACCUSED
ACCUSER
ACCUSES
ACQUIRE
ACQUITS
ACTUARY
ACTUATE
ACTUPON
ADDUCED
ADDUCES
ADDUCTS
ADDUPTO
ADJUDGE
ADJUNCT
ADJURED
ADJURES
ADJUSTS
AGOUTIS
ALBUMEN
ALBUMIN
ALLUDED
ALLUDES
ALLURED
ALLURES
ALLUVIA
AMOUNTS
AMPULES
ANGULAR
ANNUALS
ANNUITY
ANNULAR
ANNULUS
ANOUILH
ARBUTUS
ARDUOUS
ARGUERS
ARGUING
AROUSAL
AROUSED
AROUSES
ASSUAGE
ASSUMED
ASSUMES
ASSURED
ASSURES
ATTUCKS
ATTUNED
ATTUNES
AUBURNS
AUDUBON
AUGURAL
AUGURED
AUGUSTA
AUGUSTE
AUTUMNS
AWFULLY

A•••U••

ABLAUTS
ACCOUNT
ACCRUAL
ACCRUED
ACCRUES
ACHTUNG
ADJOURN
AGROUND
AIRGUNS
AIRPUMP
ALARUMS
AMPOULE
ANAHUAC
ARBOURS
ARDOURS
ARMFULS
ARMOURS
ARUGULA
ASHBURY
ASSAULT
ASTOUND
ASUSUAL
ASYLUMS
ATATURK
ATFAULT
ATRIUMS
AUTEURS
AVENUES
AZIMUTH

A••••U•

ABSOLUT
ACEDOUT
ACESOUT
ACTEDUP
ACTSOUT
ADDEDUP
AIRSOUT
ALUMNUS
ALYSSUM
AMADEUS
AMATEUR
AMIBLUE
AMOROUS
ANGELUS
ANNULUS
ANTAEUS
ANTEDUP
ANTESUP
ANTIGUA
ANTIQUE
ANXIOUS
APERCUS
APPLAUD
AQUEOUS
ARBUTUS
ARDUOUS
AREARUG
ARTEMUS
ASKSOUT
ATISSUE
ATTICUS

A•••••U

ANGELOU

•AU••••

BAUBLES
BAUXITE
CAULKED
CAULKER
CAUSING
CAUSTIC
CAUTION
DAUBERS
DAUBING
DAUMIER
DAUNTED
DAUPHIN
FAUCETS
FAULTED
FAUSTUS
FAUVISM
FAUVIST
FAUXPAS
GAUCHER
GAUCHOS
GAUDENS
GAUDIER
GAUDILY
GAUGERS
GAUGING
GAUGUIN
GAUNTER
GAUNTLY
GAUTAMA
GAUZIER
GAUZILY
HAUBERK
HAUGHTY
HAULAGE
HAULERS
HAULING
HAULOFF
HAULSUP
HAUNTED
HAUTBOY
HAUTEUR
JAUNTED
LAUDING
LAUGHAT
LAUGHED
LAUGHER
LAUGHIN
LAUNDER
LAUNDRY
LAURELS
LAURENT
LAUTREC
MAUDLIN
MAUGHAM
MAULDIN
MAULING
MAUNDER
MAUREEN
MAURICE
MAUROIS
NAUGHTS
NAUGHTY
PAUCITY
PAULINA
PAULINE
PAULING
PAULIST
PAULSEN
PAUNCHY
PAUPERS
PAUSING
RAUCOUS
SAUCERS
SAUCIER
SAUCILY
SAUNTER
SAURIAN
SAUSAGE
SAUTEED
TAUNTED
TAURINE
TAUTENS
TAUTEST
VAUGHAN
VAULTED
VAULTER
VAUNTED
VAUNTER
YAUPONS

•A•U•••

CADUCEI
CALUMET
CALUMNY
CAPULET
CASUALS
CAYUGAS
CAYUSES
FACULTY
FAMULUS
FATUITY
FATUOUS
GALUMPH
HANUKAH
JACUZZI
JAGUARS
JANUARY
KABUKIS
KAHUNAS
LACUNAE
LACUNAL
LACUNAS
LAGUNAS
MACULAE
MAGUEYS
MANUALS
MANUMIT
MATURED
MATURER
MATURES
MAZURKA
NAHUATL
NATURAL
NATURED
NATURES
PABULUM
PADUCAH
PAIUTES
PANURGE
PAPUANS
PARURES
SAGUARO
SALUKIS
SALUTED
SALUTES
SAMURAI
TABULAR
TALUSES
VACUITY
VACUOLE
VACUOUS
VACUUMS
VAGUELY
VAGUEST
VALUATE
VALUING
VAQUERO
YAKUTSK
YAOUNDE

•A••U••

BACKUPS
BADGUYS
BAGFULS
BANQUET
BARBUDA
BASQUES
CADBURY
CAESURA
CAIQUES
CAPFULS
CAPGUNS
CAPNUTS
CAPSULE
CAPTURE
CARFULS
CAROUSE
EARFULS
EARMUFF
FACTUAL
FAILURE
FAVOURS
GAGRULE
GASPUMP
GAUGUIN
HAMBURG
HANGUPS
JACCUSE
JACQUES
JARFULS
LABOURS
LACQUER
LANGUID
LANGUOR
LANGURS
LAPFULS
LARRUPS
LASHUPS
LAWSUIT
LAYOUTS
MACDUFF
MAGNUMS
MAHOUTS
MAJEURE
MAKEUPS
MANHUNT
MARAUDS
MARKUPS
MARQUEE
MARQUES
MARQUEZ
MARQUIS
MASQUES
PABLUMS
PARQUET
PASTURE
PAYOUTS
RACQUET
RAGOUTS
RAGRUGS
RAPTURE
RAYBURN
RAYGUNS
SAMNUNN
SAMSUNG
SANJUAN
SANLUIS
SATSUMA
SAVOURS
SAVOURY
SAWBUCK
SAWDUST
VACUUMS
VALOURS
VAPOURS
VATFULS
WALKUPS
WALNUTS
WARMUPS

•A•••U•

BACCHUS
BACKOUT
BACKRUB
BACKSUP
BAILOUT
BALEFUL
BALFOUR
BALLSUP
BANEFUL
BANGSUP
BAROQUE
BASHFUL
BATEAUX
BATHTUB
BAWLOUT
CACHOUS
CADMIUM
CALCIUM
CALHOUN
CALLOUS
CALLOUT
CALLSUP
CAMBIUM
CAMEOUT
CAMPOUT
CANDOUR
CANOPUS
CAREFUL
CAROLUS
CASHOUT
CASSIUS
CASTOUT
CATCHUP
DANSEUR
EARDRUM
EARPLUG
EASEDUP
EASESUP
EATENUP
EATSOUT
FADEOUT
FAIRSUP
FAKEFUR
FALLGUY
FALLOUT
FAMULUS
FANSOUT
FARMOUT
FATEFUL
FATIGUE
FATUOUS
FAUSTUS
GAINFUL
GALLIUM
GANGSUP
GASEOUS
GATEAUX
GAVEOUT
HABITUE
HAFNIUM
HAHNIUM
HAIRCUT
HALIBUT
HAMITUP
HANDFUL

HANDGUN
HANDOUT
HANDSUP
HANGOUT
HANGSUP
HARBOUR
HARDPUT
HARMFUL
HATEFUL
HAULSUP
HAUTEUR
JABIRUS
JACKSUP
KARAKUL
KARAKUM
LACEDUP
LACESUP
LADYBUG
LAIDOUT
LALIQUE
LANDAUS
LASCAUX
LAYSOUT
LAZARUS
MACAQUE
MADEOUT
MAKEOUT
MAKESUP
MALAMUD
MALRAUX
MALTHUS
MANAGUA
MANHOUR
MARGAUX
MARKSUP
MASSEUR
MATCHUP
MAXIMUM
MAXIMUS
NATRIUM
PABULUM
PACKSUP
PAGEFUL
PAIDOUT
PAILFUL
PAILOUS
PAINFUL
PAIRSUP
PALLIUM
PANSOUT
PAPYRUS
PARIBUS
PARLOUR
PARLOUS
PARTOUT
PASSEUL
PASSOUT
PASTDUE
PASTEUP
PASTEUR
PATCHUP
PAVIOUR
PAYSOUT
RACKSUP
RAINOUT
RAISEUP
RAKEDUP
RAKESUP
RANCOUR
RAPANUI
RAUCOUS
SACKFUL
SACKOUT
SANCTUM
SANGOUT
SAVEDUP
SAVESUP
TACITUS
TACTFUL
TAGSOUT
TAKEOUT
TAKESUP
TALKOUT
TALKSUP
TALLYUP
TAMBOUR
TANKFUL
TANKSUP
TANTRUM
TAPSOUT
VACUOUS
VANOCUR
VARIOUS
WAITOUT
WAITSUP
WAKEFUL
WAKESUP
WALKOUT
WALLSUP
WANTOUT
WARMSUP
WASHOUT
WASHTUB

•A••••U

BABASSU
CARIBOU
LAMBEAU
MANITOU
MARABOU
MARCEAU
MARYLOU
MATTHAU
PARVENU
RAMBEAU
TABLEAU
WATTEAU

••AU•••

CHAUCER
CLAUDIA
CLAUDIO
CLAUSES
DRAUGHT
EPAULET
FLAUNTS
FRAUGHT
PLAUDIT
PLAUTUS
STAUNCH
TRAUBEL
TRAUMAS
WHAUDEN

••A•U••

ALARUMS
ANAHUAC
ATATURK
BRAVURA
CLAQUES
DRACULA
EMANUEL
ERASURE
EVACUEE
FEATURE
GRADUAL
GRANULE
GRAVURE
INARUSH
JOAQUIN
LEAGUER
LEAGUES
MEASURE
OPAQUES
PEANUTS
PLAGUED
PLAGUES
PLAQUES
SCAPULA
SEADUTY
SEAGULL
SNAFUED
SPATULA
STATUES
STATURE
STATUTE
TEACUPS
TRADUCE
ULALUME
VIADUCT
WRAPUPS

••A••U•

AMADEUS
AMATEUR
BEADSUP
BEAMSUP
BEARHUG
BEAROUT
BEARSUP
BEATOUT
BEATSUP
BRACEUP
CHALKUP
CHATSUP
CLAMSUP
CRACKUP
CRANIUM
CRANKUP
CRASSUS
DEALOUT
DRAGOUT
DRAWNUP
DRAWOUT
DRAWSUP
ENAMOUR
ERASMUS
FEARFUL
FLANEUR
FLAREUP
FLATOUT
FLAVOUR
FRAMEUP
GEARSUP
GLAMOUR
GOABOUT
GRAMPUS
GUARGUM
HEADOUT
HEADSUP
HEAROUT
HEATSUP
JEALOUS
JEANLUC
LEADOUT
LEADSUP
PEASOUP
PLAUTUS
PLAYFUL
PLAYOUT
PLAYSUP
QUANTUM
READOUT
REARGUE
REARSUP
SCAREUP
SEALSUP
SEASLUG
SHAKEUP
SHAPEUP
SMASHUP
SNAPSUP
SOAKSUP
STACKUP
STADIUM
STANDUP
STARTUP
STAYPUT
STAYSUP
TEAMSUP
TEARFUL
TEARSUP
TRADEUP
TRAYFUL
URANIUM
WEAROUT
WRAPSUP
ZEALOUS

••A•••U

CHAPEAU
CHATEAU
NEARYOU
PLATEAU

•••AU••

ABLAUTS
ASSAULT
ATFAULT
BECAUSE
BEDAUBS
DEBAUCH
DEFAULT
DEGAUSS
EXHAUST
KILAUEA
MARAUDS
NOFAULT
RENAULT
STRAUSS
UMLAUTS

•••A•U•

ANTAEUS
AREARUG
BELAKUN
BREAKUP
CLEANUP
CLEARUP
DEDALUS
DEVALUE
DONAHUE
DREAMUP
ERRATUM
INVACUO
KARAKUL
KARAKUM
LAZARUS
MACAQUE
MALAMUD
MANAGUA
OCEANUS
ORGANUM
PEGASUS
PIRAEUS
PYRAMUS
RAPANUI
REVALUE
SPEAKUP
STRATUM
STRATUS
TETANUS

•••A••U

BABASSU
KOMATSU
MARABOU
SHIATSU

••••AU•

APPLAUD
BATEAUX
BUREAUS
CENTAUR
DEFRAUD
GATEAUX
IBNSAUD
LANDAUS
LASCAUX
LESPAUL
MALRAUX
MARGAUX
MILHAUD
RIMBAUD
TUSSAUD

•••••AU

CHAPEAU
CHATEAU
COCTEAU
FRENEAU
HOFBRAU
LAMBEAU
MARCEAU
MATTHAU
NOUVEAU
PLATEAU
RAMBEAU
RONDEAU
TABLEAU
THOREAU
TONNEAU
TRUDEAU
WATTEAU

AV•••••

AVAILED
AVARICE
AVATARS
AVENGED
AVENGER
AVENGES
AVENUES
AVERAGE
AVERRED
AVERTED
AVIANCA
AVIATED
AVIATES
AVIATOR
AVIDITY
AVIGNON
AVOCADO
AVOCETS
AVOIDED
AVONLEA
AVOWALS
AVOWERS
AVOWING
AVULSED
AVULSES

A•V••••

ADVANCE
ADVENTS
ADVERBS
ADVERSE
ADVERTS
ADVISED
ADVISER
ADVISES
ADVISOR
ALVAREZ
ALVEOLI

A••V•••

ATAVISM
ATAVIST

A•••V••

ACTIVES
ALCOVES
ALLOVER
ALLUVIA
ANDOVER
AQUAVIT
AQUIVER
ARGIVES
ARRIVAL
ARRIVED
ARRIVER
ARRIVES

A••••V•

ABSOLVE
ABUSIVE
ACHIEVE
AIRWAVE
AMATIVE
ANCHOVY
APPROVE
ARCHIVE

•AV••••

BAVARIA
CAVALRY
CAVEART
CAVEATS
CAVEDIN
CAVEINS
CAVEMAN
CAVEMEN
CAVERNS
CAVESIN
CAVILED
CAVILER
CAVORTS
DAVINCI
FAVORED
FAVOURS
GAVELED
GAVEOFF
GAVEOUT
GAVEWAY
GAVIALS
GAVOTTE
HAVARTI
HAVENOT
JAVAMAN
JAVELIN
LAVALSE
LAVERNE
LAVINIA
NAVAHOS
NAVAJOS
NAVARRE
PAVANES
PAVIOUR
PAVLOVA
RAVAGED
RAVAGES
RAVELED
RAVENED
RAVENNA
RAVINES
RAVINGS
RAVIOLI
SAVABLE
SAVAGED
SAVAGER
SAVAGES
SAVALAS
SAVANNA
SAVANTS
SAVARIN
SAVEDUP
SAVESUP
SAVINGS
SAVIORS
SAVORED
SAVOURS
SAVOURY
SAVVIER
SAVVILY
TAVERNS
WAVEDIN
WAVELET
WAVEOFF
WAVERED
WAVERER
WAVESIN
WAVIEST

•A•V•••

CALVARY
CALVERT
CALVING
CANVASS
CARVERS
CARVING
FAUVISM
FAUVIST
GALVANI
HALVING
HARVARD
HARVEST
JANVIER
JAYVEES
LATVIAN
MARVELS
NAIVELY
NAIVETE
PARVENU
SALVAGE
SALVERS
SALVING
SALVOES
SAVVIER
SAVVILY
WAIVERS
WAIVING

•A••V••

CARAVAN
CARAVEL
HANOVER
LAYOVER
NATIVES
PALAVER
RANOVER
RAYOVAC
SAMOVAR

•A•••V•

BAKLAVA
CAPTIVE
CASSAVA
MARKOVA
MASSIVE
PAHLAVI
PASSIVE
PAVLOVA

•A••••V

CABLETV
NABOKOV

••AV•••

ATAVISM
ATAVIST
BEAVERS
BRAVADO
BRAVELY
BRAVERY
BRAVEST
BRAVING
BRAVOES
BRAVURA
CLAVELL
CLAVIER
CRAVATS
CRAVENS
CRAVERS
CRAVING
FLAVORS
FLAVOUR
GRAVELS
GRAVELY
GRAVEST
GRAVIES
GRAVING
GRAVITY
GRAVURE
HEAVEHO
HEAVENS
HEAVERS
HEAVETO
HEAVIER
HEAVIES
HEAVILY
HEAVING
KNAVERY
KNAVISH
LEAVENS
LEAVING
PEAVEYS
QUAVERS
QUAVERY
REAVAIL
SHAVERS
SHAVING
SLAVERS
SLAVERY
SLAVING
SLAVISH
SPAVINS
STAVING
SUAVELY
SUAVEST
SUAVITY
TRAVAIL
TRAVELS
TRAVERS
TRAVOIS
UNAVOCE
WEAVERS
WEAVING

••A•V••

DWARVES
SCARVES
STARVED
STARVES
WHARVES

••A••V•

AMATIVE
EVASIVE
ULANOVA

•••AV••

AQUAVIT
BEHAVED
BEHAVES
CARAVAN
CARAVEL
CLEAVED
CLEAVER
CLEAVES
CLEAVON
DISAVOW
GREAVES
INFAVOR
LEHAVRE
MCGAVIN
MORAVIA
OCTAVES
OCTAVIA
OCTAVOS
PALAVER
REPAVED
REPAVES
SHEAVED
SHEAVES
TELAVIV
UNPAVED
UNRAVEL
VISAVIS
ZOUAVES

•••A•V•

BIVALVE

•••A••V

ROMANOV
TELAVIV
ULYANOV

••••AV•

AIRWAVE
BAKLAVA
BEREAVE
CASSAVA
CENTAVO
CONCAVE
DEPRAVE
ENCLAVE
ENGRAVE
ENSLAVE
FORGAVE
GUSTAVE
NEWWAVE
ONLEAVE
PAHLAVI
REWEAVE
UNWEAVE

AW•••••

AWAITED
AWAKENS
AWAKING
AWARDED
AWARDEE
AWARDER
AWAREOF
AWELESS
AWESOME
AWFULLY
AWKWARD
AWNINGS

A•W••••

ALWORTH
ATWORST

A••W•••

AIRWAVE
AIRWAYS
AIRWOLF
ALEWIFE
ANSWERS
ANTWERP
ARAWAKS
ARTWARE
ARTWORK
ATHWART
AVOWALS
AVOWERS
AVOWING
AWKWARD

A•••W••

ALLOWED
ANTIWAR
ARCHWAY
AREAWAY

A••••W•

ANDREWS
ANTCOWS

A•••••W

AIRCREW
AIRFLOW
AIRSHOW
ASOFNOW
ATECROW

•AW••••

BAWDIER
BAWDILY
BAWLERS
BAWLING
BAWLOUT
DAWDLED
DAWDLER
DAWDLES
DAWKINS
DAWNING
FAWCETT
FAWNERS
FAWNING
GAWKERS
GAWKIER
GAWKING
HAWHAWS
HAWKERS
HAWKEYE
HAWKING
HAWKINS
HAWKISH
HAWSERS
JAWBONE
JAWLINE
LAWFORD
LAWLESS
LAWSUIT
LAWYERS
MAWKISH
PAWEDAT
PAWNEES
PAWNERS
PAWNING
PAWNOFF
PAWPAWS
RAWDATA
RAWDEAL
RAWHIDE
RAWNESS
RAWSILK
SAWBUCK
SAWDUST
SAWFISH
SAWLOGS
SAWMILL
SAWWOOD
SAWYERS
TAWNIER
YAWNERS
YAWNING
YAWPERS

•A•W•••

BATWING
CARWASH
CATWALK
DAGWOOD
EARWIGS
FALWELL
FARWEST
FAYWRAY
HAYWARD
HAYWIRE
JAYWALK
LAPWING
MAEWEST
MAXWELL
MAYWINE
NARWALS
NARWHAL
RAGWEED
SAWWOOD
SAYWHEN
WARWICK
WAXWING
WAXWORK
WAYWARD
WAYWORN

•A••W••

BALDWIN
CARAWAY
CATAWBA
EATAWAY
FAIRWAY
FARAWAY
GANGWAY
GATEWAY
GAVEWAY
HALFWAY
HALFWIT
HALLWAY
HARDWON
JANEWAY
LAYAWAY
MADEWAY
MAKEWAY
MANOWAR
MATEWAN
PARKWAY
PARTWAY
PATHWAY
RACEWAY
RAILWAY
RANAWAY
SARAWAK
TAXIWAY
WALKWAY

•A•••W•

BARNOWL
BARROWS
CASHEWS
FALLOWS
FARROWS
HALLOWS
HARROWS
HAWHAWS
HAYMOWS
LAYDOWN
MALLOWS
MARLOWE
MARROWS
MATHEWS
NARROWS
OAKLAWN
PAWPAWS
SATDOWN
TALLOWS
WALLOWS
YARROWS

•A••••W

BANDSAW
CAPSHAW
CASELAW
CASHCOW
CATSPAW
DANELAW
EATCROW
GAMELAW
GANGSAW
HACKSAW
HANDSAW
JACKDAW
LAIDLOW
LAYSLOW
MACGRAW
MANILOW
MATTHEW
RAINBOW
SAGINAW
SALCHOW

••AW•••

ARAWAKS
BRAWLED
BRAWLER
CLAWERS
CLAWING
CRAWDAD
CRAWLED
CRAWLER
DRAWBAR
DRAWERS
DRAWING
DRAWLED
DRAWNIN
DRAWNON
DRAWNUP
DRAWOUT
DRAWSIN
DRAWSON
DRAWSUP
FLAWING
FRAWLEY
GNAWERS
GNAWING
INAWEOF
INAWORD
SEAWALL
SEAWARD
SEAWAYS
SEAWEED
SHAWNEE
SHAWWAL
SPAWNED
THAWING
TRAWLED
TRAWLER
UNAWARE

••A•W••

HEADWAY
ROADWAY
SHAWWAL

••A••W•

MEADOWS
MEADOWY
PEAFOWL
SEACOWS
SHADOWS
SHADOWY

••A•••W

BEARPAW
GLASGOW
INASTEW
SHALLOW
SPARROW
SWALLOW

•••AW••

AREAWAY
CARAWAY
CATAWBA
CUTAWAY
DUNAWAY
EATAWAY
FARAWAY
FLYAWAY
GETAWAY
GOTAWAY
LAYAWAY
MOHAWKS
OTTAWAS
PUTAWAY
RANAWAY
RUNAWAY

SARAWAK
SCRAWLS
SCRAWLY
SCRAWNY
SPRAWLS
SQUAWKS
TOWAWAY

•••A••W
DISAVOW

••••AW•
BOWSAWS
CUSHAWS
GEEGAWS
GEWGAWS
GOSHAWK
GUFFAWS
HAWHAWS
HEEHAWS
JIGSAWS
OAKLAWN
OKINAWA
OUTLAWS
OVERAWE
PAWPAWS
PITSAWS
PREDAWN
REDRAWN
REDRAWS
RIPSAWS
SEESAWS
UNDRAWN

•••••AW
BANDSAW
BEARPAW
BLUELAW
BUCKSAW
BUZZSAW
CAPSHAW
CASELAW
CATSPAW
CHOCTAW
DANELAW
DEWCLAW
FOREPAW
FORESAW
FRETSAW
GAMELAW
GANGSAW
HACKSAW
HANDSAW
JACKDAW
MACGRAW
OUTDRAW
OVERSAW
SAGINAW
WHIPSAW

AX•••••
AXIALLY
AXILLAE
AXLROSE
AXOLOTL

A•X••••
ANXIETY
ANXIOUS

A•••X••
ADMIXED
ADMIXES
AFFIXED
AFFIXES
ANNEXED
ANNEXES

A••••X•
AIRTAXI

A•••••X
ALTOSAX

•AX••••
LAXNESS
MAXBAER
MAXBORN
MAXILLA
MAXIMAL
MAXIMUM
MAXIMUS
MAXWELL
SAXHORN
TAXABLE
TAXFREE
TAXICAB
TAXIING
TAXIWAY
TAXRATE
WAXBEAN
WAXIEST
WAXWING
WAXWORK

•A•X•••
BAUXITE
FAUXPAS
MANXCAT
MANXMAN
MANXMEN
MARXISM

•A••X••
CALYXES
LATEXES

•A••••X
BANDBOX
BATEAUX
CAKEMIX
CALLBOX
CASHBOX
GATEAUX
HALIFAX
LASCAUX
MADAMEX
MAILBOX
MALRAUX
MARGAUX
NARTHEX
PANCHAX
PARADOX
SALTBOX
SANDBOX

••AX•••
BRAXTON
COAXERS
COAXIAL
COAXING
HOAXERS
HOAXING
KLAXONS

••A•••X
BEATRIX
GEARBOX
PHALANX
PHARYNX
REAFFIX
SOAPBOX
SPANDEX

•••AX••
HYRAXES
ICEAXES
RELAXED
RELAXES
RETAXED
RETAXES
REWAXED
REWAXES

•••A••X
BETAMAX
BROADAX
MADAMEX
MIRAMAX
PARADOX

••••AX•
AIRTAXI
PICKAXE
POLEAXE

••••A•X
BATEAUX
GATEAUX
LASCAUX
MALRAUX
MARGAUX
PHALANX

•••••AX
ALTOSAX
BEESWAX
BETAMAX
BROADAX
CINEMAX
HALIFAX
MIRAMAX
PANCHAX
POLLTAX

AY•••••
AYEAYES
AYKROYD
AYNRAND

A•Y••••
ABYSMAL
ABYSSES
ALYOSHA
ALYSSUM
AMYLASE
ANYBODY
ANYMORE
ANYTIME
ASYLUMS

A••Y•••
ACRYLIC
ALLYING
ALLYSON
ANDYKIM
ARGYLES
ARMYANT
ASSYRIA

A•••Y••
ACOLYTE
ALLAYED
ALLAYER
ALLEYES
ALLOYED
ANALYSE
ANALYST
ANALYZE
ANNOYED
ANODYNE
ANONYMS
ARRAYED
ARROYOS
ASSAYED
ASSAYER
AYEAYES

A••••Y•
ACRONYM
AFFRAYS
AIRWAYS
ANTONYM
AYKROYD

A•••••Y
ABIDEBY
ABILITY
ACADEMY
ACIDIFY
ACIDITY
ACRIDLY
ACTUARY
ACUTELY
ADEPTLY
AFFABLY
AGILELY
AGILITY
AIRPLAY
ALCHEMY
ALERTLY
ALIMONY
ALLERGY
ALOOFLY
ALREADY
AMATORY
AMENITY
AMIABLY
AMNESTY
AMPLIFY
AMSCRAY
ANALOGY
ANARCHY
ANATOMY
ANCHOVY
ANGRILY
ANNUITY
ANOMALY
ANTHONY
ANXIETY
ANYBODY
APISHLY
APLENTY
APOLOGY
ARCHERY
ARCHWAY
ARDENCY
AREAWAY
ARIDITY
ASHBURY
ASHTRAY
ATROPHY
AUDIBLY
AURALLY
AVIDITY
AWFULLY
AXIALLY

•AY••••
BAYCITY
BAYLEAF
BAYONET
CAYENNE
CAYUGAS
CAYUSES
DAYBEDS
DAYBOOK
DAYCAMP
DAYCARE
DAYLILY
DAYLONG
DAYROOM
DAYSINN
DAYSTAR
DAYTIME
DAYTONA
DAYTRIP
FAYWRAY
GAYLORD
HAYFORK
HAYLOFT
HAYMOWS
HAYRACK
HAYRIDE
HAYSEED
HAYWARD
HAYWIRE
JAYBIRD
JAYCEES
JAYLENO
JAYVEES
JAYWALK
KAYAKED
KAYAKER
KAYOING
LAYAWAY
LAYDOWN
LAYERED
LAYETTE
LAYINTO
LAYOFFS
LAYOUTS
LAYOVER
LAYSFOR
LAYSLOW
LAYSOFF
LAYSOUT
MAYALIN
MAYDAYS
MAYFAIR
MAYHEMS
MAYNARD
MAYORAL
MAYPOLE
MAYTIME
MAYWINE
NAYSAID
NAYSAYS
PAYABLE
PAYCASH
PAYDAYS
PAYDIRT
PAYLOAD
PAYMENT
PAYOFFS
PAYOLAS
PAYOUTS
PAYROLL
PAYSFOR
PAYSOFF
PAYSOUT
RAYBURN
RAYGUNS
RAYKROC
RAYMOND
RAYOVAC
SAYINGS
SAYWHEN
WAYBILL
WAYLAID
WAYLAYS
WAYSIDE
WAYWARD
WAYWORN

•A•Y•••
BABYING
BABYISH
BABYLON
BABYSAT
BABYSIT
BANYANS
BARYONS
CALYCES
CALYPSO
CALYXES
CANYONS
HALYARD
KATYDID
LADYBUG
LADYDAY
LANYARD
LAWYERS
MAGYARS
MANYEAR
MARYANN
MARYKAY
MARYLOU
PAPYRUS
SAWYERS
VARYING

•A••Y••
CARLYLE
CARRYON
DACTYLS
EARLYON
HALCYON
MALAYAN
MARRYME
MARTYRS
PAPAYAS
RALLYTO
SAMOYED
SAROYAN
TALLYHO
TALLYUP
VANDYCK
VANDYKE
VANEYCK

•A•••Y•
BADGUYS
BAILEYS
BARLEYS
BARNEYS
BATBOYS
CARBOYS
CAROLYN
CATSEYE
GALLEYS
HAIRDYE
HAWKEYE
KAROLYI
KATHRYN
LACKEYS
MAGUEYS
MANDAYS
MARGAYS
MARILYN
MAYDAYS
NAYSAYS
PARLAYS
PARLEYS
PAYDAYS
SASHAYS
VALLEYS
WALLEYE
WAYLAYS

•A••••Y
BACKBAY
BAGGILY
BALCONY
BALLBOY
BALONEY
BANALLY
BARBARY
BASALLY
BASEPAY
BATTERY
BAWDILY
BAYCITY
CADBURY
CALCIFY
CALGARY
CALUMNY
CALVARY
CANNERY
CANNILY
CAPABLY
CARAWAY
CASSIDY
CATTILY
CAVALRY
DAFFILY
DAHOMEY
DALTREY
DARESAY
DATEDLY
DAYLILY
DAZEDLY
EAGERLY
EARTHLY
EATAWAY
FACTORY
FACULTY
FAINTLY
FAIRWAY
FALLACY
FALLGUY
FALSELY
FALSIFY
FALSITY
FANCILY
FANTASY
FARADAY
FARAWAY
FATCITY
FATUITY
FAYWRAY
GADGETY
GAINSAY
GALLERY
GANGWAY
GATEWAY
GAUDILY
GAUNTLY
GAUZILY
GAVEWAY
HACKNEY
HALFWAY
HALLWAY
HAMMILY
HANDILY
HAPPILY
HARDILY
HARMONY
HARSHLY
HASTILY
HAUGHTY
HAUTBOY
JADEDLY
JANEWAY
JANUARY
JAZZILY
LADYDAY
LAMPREY
LANGLEY
LANGTRY
LANKILY
LARCENY
LARGELY
LASTORY
LATENCY
LATHERY
LAUNDRY
LAYAWAY
LAZENBY
MADEHAY
MADEWAY
MAGNIFY
MAHONEY
MAJESTY
MAKEHAY
MAKEWAY
MALMSEY
MARYKAY
MASONRY
MASTERY
NAIVELY
NAKEDLY
NAMEDAY
NASALLY
NASTILY
NATTILY
NAUGHTY
PAGEBOY
PAISLEY
PALEDRY
PALFREY
PALJOEY
PANICKY
PANOPLY
PARKWAY
PARSLEY
PARTWAY
PASSKEY
PATHWAY
PAUCITY
PAUNCHY
RACEWAY
RAGGEDY
RAILWAY
RANAWAY
RAPIDLY
SAINTLY
SALSIFY
SALTILY
SAMEDAY
SANDFLY
SASSILY
SATIETY
SATISFY
SAUCILY
SAVOURY
SAVVILY
TACITLY
TACKILY
TAMMANY
TANNERY
TARBABY
TARDILY
TASTILY
TAXIWAY
VACANCY
VACUITY
VAGUELY
VALIDLY
VAPIDLY
VARIETY
VARSITY
WACKILY
WAGGERY
WALKWAY
WALLABY
ZACHARY

••AY•••
BRAYERS
BRAYING
CLAYIER
CLAYTON
CRAYOLA
CRAYONS
DRAYAGE
DRAYING
FLAYING
FRAYING
GRAYEST
GRAYING
GRAYSON
KHAYYAM
OKAYING
PLAYACT
PLAYBOY
PLAYDOH
PLAYERS
PLAYFUL
PLAYING
PLAYLET
PLAYOFF
PLAYOUT
PLAYPEN
PLAYSAT
PLAYSON
PLAYSUP
PRAYERS
PRAYFOR
PRAYING
PRAYSTO
SLAYERS
SLAYTON
SPAYING
STAYING
STAYPUT
STAYSUP
SWAYERS
SWAYING
TRAYFUL
XRAYING

••A•Y••
ANALYSE
ANALYST
ANALYZE
KHAYYAM
NEARYOU
PHARYNX
PLATYPI

••A••Y•
DEADEYE
GLADEYE
PEAVEYS
SEAWAYS
TEAPOYS

••A•••Y
ACADEMY
AMATORY
ANALOGY
ANARCHY
ANATOMY
BEANERY
BEASTLY
BEATIFY
BLACKLY
BLANDLY
BLANKLY
BLARNEY
BRADLEY
BRAMBLY
BRASHLY
BRAVELY
BRAVERY
BYANDBY
CHANTEY
CHARILY
CHARITY
CHARLEY
CLARIFY
CLARITY
CRAFTSY
CRASSLY
CRAZILY
DRAPERY
DUALITY
EDACITY
EXACTLY
FLAGDAY
FRAILTY
FRANKLY
FRAWLEY
GHASTLY
GRANARY
GRANDLY
GRATIFY
GRAVELY
GRAVITY
HEADILY
HEADWAY
HEALTHY
HEARSAY
HEAVILY
IMAGERY
INANELY
INAPTLY
IRATELY
KNAVERY
MEADOWY
OPACITY
ORATORY
PEABODY
PLAINLY
PLAYBOY
QUALIFY
QUALITY
QUAVERY
READILY
REALITY
ROADWAY
SCANTLY
SCARIFY
SCARILY
SEADUTY
SEALILY
SHADILY
SHADOWY
SHAKILY
SHAPELY
SHARKEY
SHARPLY
SLAVERY
SMARTLY
SPANGLY
SPARELY
SPASSKY
STAGILY
STAIDLY
STANDBY
STANLEY
STARCHY
STARKLY
STATELY
SUAVELY
SUAVITY
SWARTHY
TEARILY
TEATRAY
THATCHY
TRACERY
TRAGEDY
WEALTHY
WEARILY

•••AY••
ALLAYED
ALLAYER
ARRAYED
ASSAYED
ASSAYER
AYEAYES
BELAYED
BYWAYOF
DECAYED
DELAYED
DELAYER
ESSAYED
MALAYAN
PAPAYAS
RELAYED
SPLAYED
SPRAYED
SPRAYER
STRAYED

•••A••Y
AFFABLY
AMIABLY
AREAWAY
AURALLY
AXIALLY
BANALLY
BASALLY
BETARAY
BLEAKLY
BREATHY
BROADLY
CAPABLY
CARAWAY
CAVALRY
CHEAPLY
CLEANLY
CLEARLY
CONAKRY
CUTAWAY
DEBAKEY
DELANEY
DUBARRY
DUNAWAY
DURABLY
DYNASTY
EATAWAY
EMBASSY
EMPATHY
EQUABLY
EQUALLY
FARADAY
FARAWAY
FINALLY
FLYAWAY
GETAWAY
GOTAWAY
GREATLY
HUMANLY
IDEALLY
INFANCY
KOLACKY
LAYAWAY
LEGALLY
LOCALLY
LOYALLY
LOYALTY
MISALLY
MORALLY
MUTABLY
MYMAMMY
NASALLY
NOTABLY
ORGANDY
ORMANDY
PENALTY
PLIABLY
PLIANCY
PREACHY
PUTAWAY
RANAWAY
REGALLY
REMARRY
RIVALRY
ROYALLY
ROYALTY
RUNAWAY
SCRAGGY
SCRAPPY
SCRAWLY
SCRAWNY
SIZABLY
SPLASHY
SWEARBY
TENABLY
TENANCY
TONALLY
TOTALLY
TOWAWAY
TREACLY
TRUANCY
TYRANNY
UNCANNY
UNHANDY
UNHAPPY
USUALLY
VACANCY
VITALLY
VOCALLY
WCHANDY
WOMANLY
ZONALLY

••••AY•
AFFRAYS
AIRWAYS
BETRAYS
BYPLAYS
DEEJAYS
DEFRAYS
DISMAYS
DOGDAYS
ENDWAYS
ESTRAYS
FLYWAYS
FRIDAYS
HEYDAYS
MANDAYS
MARGAYS
MAYDAYS
MIDDAYS
MIDWAYS
MISLAYS
MONDAYS
NAYSAYS
OLDDAYS
OUTLAYS
PARLAYS
PAYDAYS
PREPAYS
REPLAYS
RUNWAYS
SASHAYS
SEAWAYS
SKYWAYS
SUBWAYS
SUNDAYS
SUNRAYS
VEEJAYS
WAYLAYS

••••A•Y
ACTUARY
ALREADY
ANOMALY
BARBARY
BELLAMY
BETHANY
CALGARY
CALVARY
COMPANY
CRYBABY
DIETARY
DITTANY
ECSTASY
ESTUARY
FALLACY
FANTASY
GERMANY
GRANARY
HILLARY

HUNGARY
HUSHABY
JANUARY
KKKKATY
LIBRARY
LULLABY
NITTANY
PECCARY
PLENARY
PRIMACY
PRIMARY
PRIVACY
SQUEAKY
STREAKY
SUMMARY
TAMMANY
TARBABY
TERNARY
THERAPY
THREADY
THROATY
TIFFANY
TOPIARY
TRENARY
TUSCANY
UNITARY
UNREADY
WALLABY
ZACHARY

•••••AY
AIRPLAY
AMSCRAY
ARCHWAY
AREAWAY
ASHTRAY
BACKBAY
BASEPAY
BELTWAY
BETARAY
BIKEWAY
BLUEJAY
CARAWAY
CUTAWAY
DARESAY
DISPLAY
DOORWAY
DUNAWAY
EATAWAY
ENDPLAY
FAIRWAY
FARADAY
FARAWAY
FAYWRAY
FLAGDAY
FLYAWAY
FREEWAY
GAINSAY
GANGWAY
GATEWAY
GAVEWAY
GETAWAY
GIVEWAY
GOTAWAY
GUNPLAY
HALFWAY
HALLWAY
HEADWAY
HEARSAY
HIGHWAY
HOLIDAY
INNOWAY
JANEWAY
JOHNGAY
JOHNJAY
LADYDAY
LAYAWAY
LINDSAY
MADEHAY
MADEWAY
MAKEHAY
MAKEWAY
MARYKAY
MISPLAY
NAMEDAY
NEWSDAY
NOONDAY
NOSEGAY
OJIBWAY
OUTPLAY
OVERLAY
PARKWAY
PARTWAY
PATHWAY
PORTRAY
PUTAWAY
RACEWAY
RAILWAY
RANAWAY
RIDGWAY
ROADWAY
RUNAWAY
SAMEDAY
SICKBAY
SICKPAY
SNOWDAY
SOMEDAY
SOMEWAY
TAXIWAY
TEATRAY
THRUWAY
TOLLWAY
TOWAWAY
TUESDAY
URUGUAY
WALKWAY
WEEKDAY
WORKDAY

AZ•••••
AZALEAS
AZIMUTH
AZTECAN
AZURITE

A••Z•••
AMAZING
AMAZONS
ARIZONA

A•••Z••
ALCAZAR
ASSIZES

A••••Z•
AGONIZE
ANALYZE
ANASAZI
ANODIZE
APPRIZE
ATOMIZE

A•••••Z
AGASSIZ
ALBENIZ
ALVAREZ

•AZ••••
BAZAARS
BAZOOKA
DAZEDLY
DAZZLED
DAZZLER
DAZZLES
GAZEBOS
GAZELLE
GAZETTE
GAZZARA
HAZARDS
HAZIEST
HAZINGS
JAZZAGE
JAZZIER
JAZZILY
JAZZING
JAZZMAN
JAZZMEN
KAZAKHS
LAZARUS
LAZENBY
LAZIEST
MAZURKA
RAZORED
RAZZING

•A•Z•••
CALZONE
CANZONE
DAZZLED
DAZZLER
DAZZLES
FANZINE
GAUZIER
GAUZILY
GAZZARA
JAZZAGE
JAZZIER
JAZZILY
JAZZING
JAZZMAN
JAZZMEN
MATZOHS
PANZERS
RAZZING
TARZANA
VANZANT

•A••Z••
JACUZZI
JANTZEN
PALAZZI
PALAZZO
SALAZAR
SARAZEN
WALTZED
WALTZER
WALTZES
YAHTZEE

•A•••Z•
BAPTIZE
CADENZA
CAPSIZE
CARDOZO
JACUZZI
PALAZZI
PALAZZO
YANGTZE
ZAMBEZI

•A••••Z
LAISSEZ
MARQUEZ
NATCHEZ

••AZ•••
AMAZING
AMAZONS
BLAZERS
BLAZING
BLAZONS
BRAZIER
BRAZING
CRAZIER
CRAZIES
CRAZILY
CRAZING
FRAZIER
FRAZZLE
GLAZERS
GLAZIER
GLAZING
GRAZERS
GRAZING
PIAZZAS

••A•Z••
FRAZZLE
KWANZAS
PIAZZAS
STANZAS

••A••Z•
ANALYZE
ANASAZI
INADAZE
REALIZE
TRAPEZE

••A•••Z
AGASSIZ
FRANKOZ

•••AZ••
ALCAZAR
BENAZIR
CORAZON
PALAZZI
PALAZZO
SALAZAR
SARAZEN
TOPAZES
UNFAZED

•••A•Z•
BONANZA
ORGANZA
PALAZZI
PALAZZO
SCHATZI

•••A••Z
ALVAREZ

••••AZ•
ANASAZI
INADAZE
PIZZAZZ

••••A•Z
PIZZAZZ

BA•••••
BABASSU
BABBAGE
BABBITT
BABBLED
BABBLES
BABETTE
BABOONS
BABYING
BABYISH
BABYLON
BABYSAT
BABYSIT
BACARDI
BACCHUS
BACILLI
BACKBAY
BACKBIT
BACKEND
BACKERS
BACKHOE
BACKING
BACKLIT
BACKLOG
BACKOFF
BACKOUT
BACKRUB
BACKSIN
BACKSUP
BACKUPS
BADCOLD
BADDIES
BADEGGS
BADGERS
BADGUYS
BADNESS
BAFFLED
BAFFLER
BAFFLES
BAGFULS
BAGGAGE
BAGGERS
BAGGIER
BAGGIES
BAGGILY
BAGGING
BAGHDAD
BAGNOLD
BAGPIPE
BAHAMAS
BAHRAIN
BAILEES
BAILERS
BAILEYS
BAILIFF
BAILING
BAILORS
BAILOUT
BAITING
BAKEOFF
BAKLAVA
BALANCE
BALATON
BALBOAS
BALCONY
BALDEST
BALDING
BALDRIC
BALDWIN
BALEENS
BALEFUL
BALFOUR
BALIHAI
BALKANS
BALKIER
BALKING
BALLADE
BALLADS
BALLARD
BALLAST
BALLBOY
BALLETS
BALLOON
BALLOTS
BALLSUP
BALMIER
BALONEY
BALSAMS
BAMBINO
BAMBOOS
BANALLY
BANANAS
BANDAGE
BANDAID
BANDANA
BANDBOX
BANDIED
BANDIES
BANDING
BANDITO
BANDITS
BANDSAW
BANEFUL
BANGING
BANGKOK
BANGLES
BANGSUP
BANJOES
BANKERS
BANKING
BANKSON
BANNERS
BANNING
BANNOCK
BANQUET
BANSHEE
BANTAMS
BANTERS
BANYANS
BAOBABS
BAPTISM
BAPTIST
BAPTIZE
BARANOF
BARBARA
BARBARY
BARBELL
BARBELS
BARBERS
BARBING
BARBUDA
BARCODE
BARENTS
BARETTA
BARGAIN
BARGEIN
BARGING
BARHOPS
BARKEEP
BARKERS
BARKING
BARKSAT
BARLEYS
BARMAID
BARMIER
BARNARD
BARNEYS
BARNOWL
BARONET
BARONGS
BAROQUE
BARRACK
BARRAGE
BARRELS
BARRENS
BARRETT
BARRIER
BARRING
BARRIOS
BARROOM
BARROWS
BARSOAP
BARTEND
BARTERS
BARYONS
BASALLY
BASALTS
BASEHIT
BASEMAN
BASEMEN
BASENJI
BASEPAY
BASHFUL
BASHING
BASKETS
BASKING
BASQUES
BASSETS
BASSIST
BASSOON
BASTERS
BASTING
BASTION
BATBOYS
BATCHED
BATCHES
BATEAUX
BATEMAN
BATHERS
BATHING
BATHMAT
BATHOIL
BATHTUB
BATIKED
BATISTA
BATISTE
BATSMAN
BATSMEN
BATTENS
BATTERS
BATTERY
BATTIER
BATTING
BATTLED
BATTLER
BATTLES
BATWING
BAUBLES
BAUXITE
BAVARIA
BAWDIER
BAWDILY
BAWLERS
BAWLING
BAWLOUT
BAYCITY
BAYLEAF
BAYONET
BAZAARS
BAZOOKA

B•A••••
BEACHED
BEACHES
BEACONS
BEADIER
BEADING
BEADLES
BEADSUP
BEAGLES
BEAKERS
BEAMIER
BEAMING
BEAMSUP
BEANBAG
BEANERY
BEANIES
BEANING
BEARCAT
BEARDED
BEARERS
BEARHUG
BEARING
BEARISH
BEAROFF
BEAROUT
BEARPAW
BEARSON
BEARSUP
BEASTIE
BEASTLY
BEATERS
BEATIFY
BEATING
BEATLES
BEATNIK
BEATOUT
BEATRIX
BEATSIT
BEATSUP
BEATTIE
BEAVERS
BIALIES
BIASING
BIASSED
BLABBED
BLABBER
BLACKED
BLACKEN
BLACKER
BLACKLY
BLADDER
BLAMING
BLANCHE
BLANDER
BLANDLY
BLANKED
BLANKER
BLANKET
BLANKLY
BLARING
BLARNEY
BLASTED
BLASTER
BLATANT
BLATHER
BLATTED
BLAZERS
BLAZING
BLAZONS
BOARDED
BOARDER
BOASTED
BOASTER
BOATERS
BOATING
BOATMAN
BOATMEN
BRACERS
BRACEUP
BRACING
BRACKEN
BRACKET
BRADLEE
BRADLEY
BRAGGED
BRAGGER
BRAHMAN
BRAHMAS
BRAHMIN
BRAIDED
BRAIDER
BRAILLE
BRAINED
BRAISED
BRAISES
BRAKING
BRAMBLE
BRAMBLY
BRANDED
BRANDER
BRANDON
BRANIFF
BRANSON
BRASHER
BRASHLY
BRASSES
BRASSIE
BRAVADO
BRAVELY
BRAVERY
BRAVEST
BRAVING
BRAVOES
BRAVURA
BRAWLED
BRAWLER
BRAXTON
BRAYERS
BRAYING
BRAZIER
BRAZING
BYANDBY
BYANOSE

B••A•••
BABASSU
BACARDI
BAHAMAS
BALANCE
BALATON
BANALLY
BANANAS
BARANOF
BASALLY
BASALTS
BAVARIA
BAZAARS
BECALMS
BECAUSE
BEDAUBS
BEFALLS
BEHAVED
BEHAVES
BELABOR
BELAKUN
BELATED
BELAYED
BENATAR
BENAZIR
BERATED
BERATES
BETAKEN
BETAKES
BETAMAX
BETARAY
BEWAILS
BIVALVE
BIZARRE
BLEAKER
BLEAKLY
BLEARED
BLEATED
BLOATED
BONANZA
BORATES
BREADED
BREADTH
BREAKER
BREAKIN
BREAKUP
BREASTS
BREATHE
BREATHS
BREATHY
BRIARDS
BROADAX
BROADEN
BROADER
BROADLY
BUGABOO
BUGALOO
BUYABLE
BYPATHS
BYWAYOF

B•••A••
BABBAGE
BAGGAGE
BAHRAIN
BAKLAVA
BALKANS
BALLADE
BALLADS
BALLARD
BALLAST
BALSAMS
BANDAGE
BANDAID
BANDANA
BANTAMS
BANYANS
BAOBABS
BARBARA
BARBARY
BARGAIN
BARMAID
BARNARD
BARRACK
BARRAGE
BATEAUX
BAZAARS
BEDLAMP
BEEBALM
BEEFALO
BEGGARS
BELDAME
BELDAMS
BELFAST
BELLAMY
BELTANE
BEMOANS
BENEATH
BENGALI
BENGALS
BEREAVE
BERNARD
BETHANY
BETRAYS
BIDFAIR
BIGBAND
BIGBANG
BIGGAME
BIGNAME
BIOMASS
BIPLANE
BITMAPS
BITPART
BLATANT
BOBCATS
BOBTAIL
BOITANO
BOKHARA
BOMBARD
BOMBAST
BONDAGE
BONEASH
BOWSAWS
BOXCARS
BRAVADO
BRIDALS
BRIGADE
BRIGAND
BRITAIN
BROCADE
BROGANS
BROMATE
BUFFALO
BULGARS
BULWARK
BUOYANT
BURBANK
BUREAUS
BURLAPS
BUROAKS
BURSARS
BUSFARE
BUSTARD
BUZZARD
BYHEART
BYPLAYS
BYROADS

B••••A•
BABYSAT
BACKBAY
BAGHDAD
BAHAMAS
BALBOAS
BALIHAI
BANANAS
BANDSAW
BARKSAT
BARSOAP
BASEMAN
BASEPAY
BATEMAN
BATHMAT
BATSMAN
BAYLEAF
BEANBAG
BEARCAT
BEARPAW
BEECHAM
BEESWAX
BELGIAN
BELLJAR
BELLMAN
BELTWAY
BENATAR
BENTHAM
BERGMAN
BESMEAR
BESPEAK
BESTIAL
BESTMAN
BETAMAX
BETARAY
BIFOCAL
BIGDEAL
BIGHEAD
BIKEWAY
BIMODAL
BINGHAM
BIPEDAL
BIPOLAR
BIRDMAN
BIVOUAC
BKLIBAN
BLINKAT
BLUEJAY
BLUELAW
BOATMAN
BODEGAS
BODYFAT
BOERWAR
BOLIVAR
BONDMAN
BOOLEAN
BOXSEAT
BRAHMAN
BRAHMAS
BRENDAN
BRENNAN
BRIGHAM
BRILLAT
BROADAX
BROSNAN
BUCKRAM
BUCKSAW
BUDDHAS
BUGBEAR
BURGLAR
BUSHMAN
BUZZSAW

B•••••A
BAKLAVA
BANDANA
BARBARA
BARBUDA
BARETTA
BATISTA
BAVARIA
BAZOOKA
BEDELIA
BEGONIA
BEGORRA
BELINDA
BERETTA
BERMUDA
BIRETTA
BOBVILA
BOHEMIA
BOKHARA
BOLIVIA
BOLOGNA
BONANZA
BOTHNIA
BRAVURA
BURKINA

•BA••••
ABALONE
ABANDON
ABASHED
ABASHES
ABASING
ABATING
MBABANE
OBADIAH

•B•A•••
ABLATED
ABLATES
ABLAUTS
ABNAKIS
ABRADED
ABRADES
ABRAHAM
ABSALOM
CBRADIO
OBLASTS
OBLATES
OBTAINS

•B••A••
ABELARD
ABENAKI
ABIGAIL
ABREAST
ABSTAIN
ABUBAKR
IBNSAUD
MBABANE
OBVIATE

•B•••A•
ABOREAL
ABRAHAM
ABUTTAL
ABYSMAL
IBERIAN
OBADIAH

••BA•••
ALBANIA
AUBADES
BABASSU
CABALAS
CABANAS
CABARET
DEBACLE
DEBAKEY
DEBARGE
DEBARKS
DEBASED
DEBASES
DEBATED
DEBATER
DEBATES
DEBAUCH
DUBARRY
EMBANKS
EMBARGO
EMBARKS
EMBASSY

FABARES
HIBACHI
LABAMBA
LEBANON
LEBARON
MUBARAK
REBASTE
REBATED
REBATES
RIBANDS
ROBARDS
TABARDS
TABASCO
TOBACCO
TUBAIST
UNBAKED
URBANER

••B•A••
BABBAGE
BOBCATS
BOBTAIL
CABBAGE
DABHAND
EMBRACE
HEBRAIC
HOBNAIL
HUBBARD
HUBCAPS
INBOARD
JOBBANK
LABIALS
LABIATE
LIBRARY
LIBYANS
MOBCAPS
NUBIANS
ONBOARD
PTBOATS
RIBCAGE
SABBATH
SUBWAYS
UMBRAGE
UPBEATS
UPBRAID
VIBRANT
VIBRATE
VIBRATO

••B••A•
BABYSAT
CABALAS
CABANAS
DEBORAH
FIBULAE
FIBULAS
HABITAT
LABCOAT
LIBERAL
MUBARAK
NEBULAE
NEBULAR
NEBULAS
ORBITAL
REBEKAH
SUBHEAD
TABLEAU
TABULAR
TIBETAN
TUBULAR
UMBRIAN

••B•••A
ALBANIA
ALBERTA
BOBVILA
CIBORIA
LABAMBA
LIBERIA
REBECCA
ROBERTA
ROBUSTA
SABRINA
SIBERIA
SUBROSA
TABITHA

•••BA••
ABUBAKR
AIRBAGS
AIRBALL
AIRBASE
ALABAMA
ALIBABA
ARMBAND
BABBAGE
BAOBABS
BARBARA
BARBARY
BEEBALM
BIGBAND
BIGBANG
BOMBARD
BOMBAST
BURBANK
CABBAGE
CEMBALO
COMBATS
CRYBABY
CUEBALL
CUTBACK
CYMBALS
DISBAND
DISBARS
EYEBALL
EYEBANK
FATBACK
FLYBALL
FOGBANK
FORBADE
FURBALL
GARBAGE
GASBAGS
GETBACK
GIMBALS
GOTBACK
GUMBALL
HENBANE
HERBAGE
HERBALS
HOGBACK
HUBBARD
HUSBAND
ICEBAGS
IKEBANA
ISOBARS
JOBBANK
JUGBAND
KIMBALL
KITBAGS
LAMBADA
LIPBALM
LOMBARD
LOWBALL
LUMBAGO
LUMBARS
MAXBAER
MBABANE
MOMBASA
NUMBATS
ODDBALL
OFFBASE
OUTBACK
PIEBALD
PINBALL
PROBATE
RHUBARB
RIMBAUD
RUMBAED
RUNBACK
SABBATH
SAMBAED
SAMBARS
SEABAGS
SEABASS
SETBACK
SHEBANG
SORBATE
SUNBATH
TAMBALA
TARBABY
TEABAGS
TEABALL
THEBABE
TIMBALE
TIMBALS
TURBANS
TWOBASE
VERBALS
WETBARS
WOMBATS

•••B•A•
AIRBOAT
ANTBEAR
ARABIAN
BALBOAS
BUGBEAR
CATBOAT
CLUBCAR
FORBEAR
GAMBIAN
GILBLAS
GRABBAG
GRABSAT
GUNBOAT
HOFBRAU
ICEBOAT
JERBOAS
JETBOAT
LAMBDAS
LAMBEAU
LINBIAO
LOWBEAM
OFFBEAT
OJIBWAS
OJIBWAY
PEABEAN
PHOBIAS
RAMBEAU
ROWBOAT
ROYBEAN
SERBIAN
SIOBHAN
SOYBEAN
SUNBEAM
TUGBOAT
WAXBEAN
ZAMBIAN

•••B••A
ALABAMA
ALIBABA
BARBARA
BARBUDA
HERBTEA
IKEBANA
LAMBADA
MOMBASA
TAMBALA
VERBENA

••••BA•
ACROBAT
AEROBAT
AMOEBAE
AMOEBAS
ARROBAS
BACKBAY
BEANBAG
BKLIBAN
CALIBAN
CASABAS
CASHBAR
CROWBAR
DINGBAT
DOVEBAR
DRAWBAR
EXURBAN
FEEDBAG
FLEABAG
GOESBAD
GOODBAR
GRABBAG
HANDBAG
MAILBAG
MALABAR
NOSEBAG
OPENBAR
POOHBAH
RHUMBAS
ROLLBAR
SANDBAG
SANDBAR
SICKBAY
SIDEBAR
TESTBAN
TOTEBAG
WENTBAD
WINDBAG
WINEBAR
ZAREBAS

••••B•A
ALGEBRA
CEREBRA
CULEBRA
EXURBIA
NAMIBIA
ZENOBIA

•••••BA
ALIBABA
CARAMBA
CATAWBA
CORDOBA
LABAMBA
MARIMBA
MASTABA
TOSHIBA

B•B••••
BABASSU
BABBAGE
BABBITT
BABBLED
BABBLES
BABETTE
BABOONS
BABYING
BABYISH
BABYLON
BABYSAT
BABYSIT
BIBELOT
BOBBERS
BOBBIES
BOBBING
BOBBINS
BOBBLED
BOBBLES
BOBCATS
BOBDOLE
BOBHOPE
BOBSLED
BOBTAIL
BOBVILA
BUBBLED
BUBBLES

B••B•••
BABBAGE
BABBITT
BABBLED
BABBLES
BALBOAS
BAMBINO
BAMBOOS
BAOBABS
BARBARA
BARBARY
BARBELL
BARBELS
BARBERS
BARBING
BARBUDA
BATBOYS
BAUBLES
BEDBUGS
BEEBALM
BERBERS
BIGBAND
BIGBANG
BIGBEND
BIGBIRD
BIGBOYS
BILBOES
BLABBED
BLABBER
BLUBBER
BOBBERS
BOBBIES
BOBBING
BOBBINS
BOBBLED
BOBBLES
BOMBARD
BOMBAST
BOMBECK
BOMBERS
BOMBING
BONBONS
BOOBIES
BOOBOOS
BRIBERY
BRIBING
BRUBECK
BUBBLED
BUBBLES
BUGBEAR
BULBLET
BULBOUS
BULBULS
BUMBLED
BUMBLER
BUMBLES
BURBANK
BURBLED
BURBLES
BURBOTS
BUSBIES
BUSBOYS

B•••B••
BACKBAY
BACKBIT
BALLBOY
BANDBOX
BEANBAG
BELABOR
BELLBOY
BESTBOY
BKLIBAN
BLABBED
BLABBER
BLUBBER
BLUEBOY
BOOMBOX
BOURBON
BRAMBLE
BRAMBLY
BUGABOO
BUNKBED
BUYABLE

B••••B•
BAOBABS
BEDAUBS
BENUMBS
BYANDBY
BYTHEBY

B•••••B
BACKRUB
BATHTUB

•BB••••
EBBTIDE

•B•B•••
ABUBAKR
MBABANE

•B•••B•
ABIDEBY
ABSORBS

••BB•••
BABBAGE
BABBITT
BABBLED
BABBLES
BOBBERS
BOBBIES
BOBBING
BOBBINS
BOBBLED
BOBBLES
BUBBLED
BUBBLES
CABBAGE
CABBIES
COBBLED
COBBLER
COBBLES
CUBBIES
DABBING
DABBLED
DABBLER
DABBLES
DIBBLED
DIBBLES
DOBBINS
DUBBERS
DUBBING
DYBBUKS
FIBBERS
FIBBING
FOBBING
GABBERS
GABBIER
GABBING
GABBLED
GABBLES
GABBROS
GIBBERS
GIBBETS
GIBBONS
GIBBOUS
GOBBLED
GOBBLER
GOBBLES
HOBBIES
HOBBITS
HOBBLED
HOBBLES
HUBBARD
HUBBELL
HUBBIES
HUBBUBS
JABBERS
JABBING
JIBBOOM
JOBBANK
JOBBERS
JOBBING
KIBBLED
KIBBLES
KIBBUTZ
LIBBERS
LIBBING
LOBBERS
LOBBIED
LOBBIES
LOBBING
LOBBYER
LUBBERS
LUBBOCK
MOBBING
NABBERS
NABBING
NEBBISH
NIBBLED
NIBBLER
NIBBLES
NUBBIER
NUBBINS
NUBBLES
PEBBLED
PEBBLES
RABBETS
RABBITS
RABBITT
RABBLES
RIBBING
RIBBONS
ROBBERS
ROBBERY
ROBBING
ROBBINS
RUBBERS
RUBBERY
RUBBING
RUBBISH
RUBBLES
SABBATH
SOBBERS
SOBBING
SUBBING
TABBIES
TABBING
TUBBIER
WEBBING
WOBBLED
WOBBLES

••B•B••
IMBIBED
IMBIBES

••B••B•
COBWEBS
HOBNOBS
HUBBUBS
LABAMBA
SUBDEBS
SUBURBS

•••BB••
BLABBED
BLABBER
BLUBBER
CLABBER
CLOBBER
CLUBBED
CRABBED
CRABBER
CRIBBED
DRABBER
DRIBBLE
DRUBBED
FLUBBED
GLIBBER
GRABBAG
GRABBED
GRABBER
GRUBBED
KNOBBED
QUIBBLE
SLABBED
SLOBBER
SNUBBED
STABBED
STUBBED
STUBBLE
STUBBLY
SWABBED

•••B•B•
ALIBABA
BAOBABS
CRYBABY
HUBBUBS
TARBABY
THEBABE

•••B••B
DIMBULB
RHUBARB
THEBLOB

••••BB•
ENTEBBE
SCRUBBY
SHRUBBY

B•C••••
BACARDI
BACCHUS
BACILLI
BACKBAY
BACKBIT
BACKEND
BACKERS
BACKHOE
BACKING
BACKLIT
BACKLOG
BACKOFF
BACKOUT
BACKRUB
BACKSIN
BACKSUP
BACKUPS
BECALMS
BECAUSE
BECKETT
BECKONS
BECLOUD
BECOMES
BICKERS
BICOLOR
BICYCLE
BUCKETS
BUCKEYE
BUCKING
BUCKLED
BUCKLER
BUCKLES
BUCKLEY
BUCKOES
BUCKRAM
BUCKSAW
BUCKSUP
BUCOLIC

B••C•••
BACCHUS
BADCOLD
BALCONY
BARCODE
BATCHED
BATCHES
BAYCITY
BEACHED
BEACHES
BEACONS
BEECHAM
BEECHER
BEECHES
BELCHED
BELCHES
BENCHED
BENCHES
BIRCHED
BIRCHES
BISCUIT
BLACKED
BLACKEN
BLACKER
BLACKLY
BLOCKED
BLOCKER
BOBCATS
BOKCHOY
BOTCHED
BOTCHES
BOXCARS
BOYCOTT
BRACERS
BRACEUP
BRACING
BRACKEN
BRACKET
BRICKED
BROCADE
BUNCHED
BUNCHES
BUNCOED
BUTCHER

B•••C••
BEARCAT
BEDECKS
BICYCLE
BIFOCAL
BISECTS
BLANCHE
BLOTCHY
BODICES
BORSCHT
BOUNCED
BOUNCER
BOUNCES
BRIOCHE
BRONCHI
BRONCOS

B••••C•
BALANCE
BANNOCK
BARRACK
BEDROCK
BERNICE
BESEECH
BEWITCH
BIONICS
BOMBECK
BRUBECK
BULLOCK
BURDOCK
BYFORCE

B•••••C
BALDRIC
BIVOUAC
BUCOLIC

•B•C•••
ABSCOND
OBSCENE
OBSCURE

•B••C••
ABDUCTS
OBJECTS

•B•••C•
ABSENCE

••BC•••
BOBCATS
HUBCAPS
LABCOAT
MOBCAPS
RIBCAGE

••B•C••
CUBICLE
DEBACLE
HIBACHI
REBECCA
ROBOCOP
RUBICON
TOBACCO

••B••C•
DEBAUCH
DEBOUCH
EMBRACE
FABRICS
KUBRICK
LUBBOCK
NABISCO
NIBLICK
PUBLICS
REBECCA
RUBRICS
SUBJECT
TABASCO
TOBACCO

••B•••C
HEBRAIC
ROBOTIC

•••BC••
CLUBCAR
CURBCUT

•••B•C•
BOMBECK
BRUBECK
CUTBACK
FATBACK
GETBACK
GOTBACK
HOGBACK
LUBBOCK
OUTBACK
PHOBICS
ROEBUCK
RUNBACK
SAWBUCK
SETBACK

•••B••C
CAMBRIC

••••B•C
ACERBIC
AEROBIC
ALEMBIC
AMOEBIC

B•D••••
BADCOLD
BADDIES
BADEGGS
BADGERS
BADGUYS
BADNESS
BEDAUBS
BEDBUGS
BEDDING
BEDDOWN
BEDECKS
BEDELIA
BEDEVIL
BEDEWED
BEDIZEN
BEDLAMP
BEDOUIN
BEDPOST
BEDREST
BEDROCK
BEDROLL
BEDROOM
BEDSIDE
BEDTIME
BIDDERS
BIDDIES
BIDDING
BIDFAIR
BODEGAS
BODEREK
BODICES
BODKINS
BODYFAT
BUDDHAS
BUDDIES
BUDDING
BUDDYUP
BUDGETS
BUDGIES
BUDGING

B••D•••
BADDIES
BALDEST
BALDING
BALDRIC
BALDWIN
BANDAGE
BANDAID
BANDANA
BANDBOX
BANDIED
BANDIES
BANDING
BANDITO
BANDITS
BANDSAW
BAWDIER
BAWDILY
BEADIER
BEADING
BEADLES
BEADSUP
BEDDING
BEDDOWN
BELDAME
BELDAMS
BENDERS
BENDING
BIDDERS
BIDDIES
BIDDING
BIGDEAL
BINDERS
BINDERY
BINDING
BINDSUP
BIRDDOG
BIRDERS
BIRDIED
BIRDIES
BIRDING
BIRDMAN
BIRDMEN
BLADDER
BOBDOLE
BOGDOWN
BOLDEST
BONDAGE
BONDING
BONDMAN
BONDMEN
BOODLES
BORDERS
BOUDOIR
BOWDLER
BOYDORR
BRADLEE
BRADLEY
BRIDALS
BRIDGED
BRIDGES
BRIDGET
BRIDLED
BRIDLES
BUDDHAS
BUDDIES
BUDDING
BUDDYUP
BUNDLED
BUNDLES
BURDENS
BURDOCK

B•••D••
BAGHDAD
BEARDED
BESIDES
BETIDED
BETIDES
BIMODAL
BIPEDAL
BIRDDOG
BLADDER
BLANDER
BLANDLY
BLENDED
BLENDER
BLINDED
BLINDER
BLINDLY
BLONDER
BLONDES
BLONDIE
BLOODED
BLOWDRY
BLUNDER
BOARDED
BOARDER
BOLIDES
BONEDRY
BONEDUP
BOREDOM
BORODIN
BOULDER
BOUNDED
BOUNDER
BOUNDTO
BOUNDUP
BOXEDIN
BOXEDUP
BRAIDED
BRAIDER

BRANDED
BRANDER
BRANDON
BREADED
BREADTH
BREEDER
BRENDAN
BRINDLE
BROADAX
BROADEN
BROADER
BROADLY
BROODED
BROODER
BUILDER
BUILDIN
BUILDON
BUILDUP
BULLDOG
BYANDBY

B••••D•

BACARDI
BALLADE
BALLADS
BARBUDA
BARCODE
BEDSIDE
BEHOLDS
BELINDA
BERMUDA
BRAVADO
BRIARDS
BRIGADE
BROCADE
BROMIDE
BUSHIDO
BYROADS
BYWORDS

B•••••D

BABBLED
BACKEND
BADCOLD
BAFFLED
BAGHDAD
BAGNOLD
BALLARD
BANDAID
BANDIED
BARMAID
BARNARD
BARTEND
BATCHED
BATIKED
BATTLED
BEACHED
BEARDED
BECLOUD
BEDEWED
BEHAVED
BELATED
BELAYED
BELCHED
BELLIED
BELOVED
BEMIRED
BEMUSED
BENCHED
BERATED
BERNARD
BERRIED
BERTHED
BETIDED
BEVELED
BIASSED
BIGBAND
BIGBEND
BIGBIRD
BIGHEAD
BIGOTED
BIRCHED
BIRDIED
BIRTHED
BLABBED
BLACKED
BLANKED
BLASTED
BLATTED
BLEARED
BLEATED
BLEEPED
BLENDED
BLESSED
BLINDED
BLINKED
BLIPPED
BLITZED
BLOATED
BLOCKED
BLOODED
BLOOMED
BLOOPED
BLOTTED
BLOUSED
BLUFFED
BLUNTED
BLURRED
BLURTED
BLUSHED
BOARDED
BOASTED
BOBBLED
BOBSLED
BOGEYED
BOGGLED
BOMBARD
BOOGIED
BOOKEND
BOOSTED
BOTCHED
BOTTLED
BOUNCED
BOUNDED
BOWERED
BOXWOOD
BOYHOOD
BRAGGED
BRAIDED
BRAINED
BRAISED
BRANDED
BRAWLED
BREADED
BREEZED
BRICKED
BRIDGED
BRIDLED
BRIEFED
BRIGAND
BRIMMED
BROILED
BRONZED
BROODED
BROOKED
BROWNED
BROWSED
BRUISED
BRUITED
BRUSHED
BUBBLED
BUCKLED
BUGEYED
BULLIED
BUMBLED
BUNCHED
BUNCOED
BUNDLED
BUNGLED
BUNKBED
BUNKOED
BURBLED
BURGLED
BUSTARD
BUSTLED
BUZZARD
BYLINED

•BD••••

ABDOMEN
ABDUCTS

•B•D•••

ABIDEBY
ABIDING
OBADIAH

•B••D••

ABANDON
ABRADED
ABRADES
ABRIDGE
CBRADIO

•B•••D•

ABOUNDS
EBBTIDE
OBTRUDE
OBTUNDS

•B••••D

ABASHED
ABELARD
ABETTED
ABJURED
ABLATED
ABORTED
ABRADED
ABSCOND
ABUTTED
IBNSAUD
OBLIGED

••BD•••

BOBDOLE
RUBDOWN
SUBDEBS
SUBDUED
SUBDUER
SUBDUES

••B•D••

ALBEDOS
AUBADES
LIBIDOS
RUBYDEE

••B••D•

EBBTIDE
HYBRIDS
KOBOLDS
REBINDS
RIBANDS
ROBARDS
SUBSIDE
SUBSIDY
TABARDS
UNBENDS
UNBINDS

••B•••D

ARBORED
BABBLED
BOBBLED
BOBSLED
BUBBLED
COBBLED
DABBLED
DABHAND
DEBASED
DEBATED
DEBITED
DEBONED
DEBUTED
DIBBLED
ELBOWED
GABBLED
GOBBLED
HABITED
HOBBLED
HUBBARD
IMBIBED
IMBRUED
INBOARD
INBOUND
INBREED
KIBBLED
LABELED
LABORED
LIBELED
LOBBIED
NIBBLED
ONBOARD
ORBITED
OXBLOOD
PEBBLED
REBATED
REBOUND
REBUILD
REBUKED
SOBERED
SUBDUED
SUBHEAD
SUBTEND
TABLOID
UNBAKED
UNBOUND
UNBOWED
UNBOXED
UPBRAID
WEBTOED
WOBBLED

•••BD••

LAMBDAS

•••B•D•

ANYBODY
BARBUDA
CARBIDE
DAYBEDS
FORBADE
FORBIDS
HOTBEDS
LAMBADA
OUTBIDS
PEABODY
REDBUDS
SEABEDS

•••B••D

ARMBAND
BABBLED
BIGBAND
BIGBEND
BIGBIRD
BLABBED
BOBBLED
BOMBARD
BUBBLED
BUMBLED
BURBLED
CATBIRD
CLUBBED
COBBLED
COWBIRD
CRABBED
CRIBBED
DABBLED
DIBBLED
DISBAND
DOUBLED
DOUBTED
DRUBBED
ENABLED
FLUBBED
FUMBLED
GABBLED
GAMBLED
GARBLED
GOBBLED
GRABBED
GRUBBED
HOBBLED
HUBBARD
HUMBLED
HUSBAND
ILLBRED
JAYBIRD
JUGBAND
JUMBLED
KIBBLED
KNOBBED
LOBBIED
LOMBARD
LOWBRED
MAMBOED
MARBLED
MUMBLED
NIBBLED
PEBBLED
PIEBALD
PREBEND
RAMBLED
REDBIRD
RIMBAUD
RUMBAED
RUMBLED
SAMBAED
SEABIRD
SLABBED
SNUBBED
STABBED
STABLED
STUBBED
SWABBED
TREBLED
TUMBLED
WAMBLED
WARBLED
WOBBLED

••••B•D

BLABBED
BUNKBED
CLIMBED
CLUBBED
CRABBED
CRIBBED
DRUBBED
ENROBED
FLAMBED
FLATBED
FLUBBED
GOESBAD
GRABBED
GRUBBED
ICHABOD
IMBIBED
KNOBBED
LIEABED
PLUMBED
ROADBED
ROSEBUD
SEEDBED
SLABBED
SNUBBED
SOFABED
STABBED
STUBBED
SWABBED
THUMBED
TWINBED
UNROBED
WENTBAD

BE•••••

BEACHED
BEACHES
BEACONS
BEADIER
BEADING
BEADLES
BEADSUP
BEAGLES
BEAKERS
BEAMIER
BEAMING
BEAMSUP
BEANBAG
BEANERY
BEANIES
BEANING
BEARCAT
BEARDED
BEARERS
BEARHUG
BEARING
BEARISH
BEAROFF
BEAROUT
BEARPAW
BEARSON
BEARSUP
BEASTIE
BEASTLY
BEATERS
BEATIFY
BEATING
BEATLES
BEATNIK
BEATOUT
BEATRIX
BEATSIT
BEATSUP
BEATTIE
BEAVERS
BECALMS
BECAUSE
BECKETT
BECKONS
BECLOUD
BECOMES
BEDAUBS
BEDBUGS
BEDDING
BEDDOWN
BEDECKS
BEDELIA
BEDEVIL
BEDEWED
BEDIZEN
BEDLAMP
BEDOUIN
BEDPOST
BEDREST
BEDROCK
BEDROLL
BEDROOM
BEDSIDE
BEDTIME
BEEBALM
BEECHAM
BEECHER
BEECHES
BEEFALO
BEEFIER
BEEFING
BEEFSUP
BEEGEES
BEEHIVE
BEELINE
BEEPERS
BEEPING
BEESWAX
BEETLES
BEETREE
BEFALLS
BEFOULS
BEGGARS
BEGGING
BEGONIA
BEGORRA
BEGRIME
BEGSOFF
BEGUILE
BEGUINE
BEHAVED
BEHAVES
BEHESTS
BEHOLDS
BEHOOVE
BEIJING
BELABOR
BELAKUN
BELATED
BELAYED
BELCHED
BELCHES
BELDAME
BELDAMS
BELFAST
BELGIAN
BELGIUM
BELIEFS
BELIEVE
BELINDA
BELLAMY
BELLBOY
BELLHOP
BELLIED
BELLIES
BELLING
BELLINI
BELLJAR
BELLMAN
BELLMEN
BELLOWS
BELLYUP
BELMONT
BELONGS
BELOVED
BELTANE
BELTING
BELTWAY
BELUSHI
BELYING
BEMIRED
BEMIRES
BEMOANS
BEMUSED
BEMUSES
BENATAR
BENAZIR
BENCHED
BENCHES
BENDERS
BENDING
BENEATH
BENEFIT
BENGALI
BENGALS
BENISON
BENNETT
BENTHAM
BENTLEY
BENTSEN
BENUMBS
BENZENE
BEOWULF
BEQUEST
BERATED
BERATES
BERBERS
BEREAVE
BERETTA
BERGERE
BERGMAN
BERGSON
BERLIOZ
BERLITZ
BERMUDA
BERNARD
BERNESE
BERNICE
BERNSEN
BERRIED
BERRIES
BERSERK
BERTHED
BERTOLT
BESEECH
BESEEMS
BESIDES
BESIEGE
BESMEAR
BESPEAK
BESPOKE
BESTBOY
BESTIAL
BESTING
BESTIRS
BESTMAN
BESTMEN
BESTOWS
BESTREW
BETAKEN
BETAKES
BETAMAX
BETARAY
BETHANY
BETHELS
BETHINK
BETIDED
BETIDES
BETIMES
BETOKEN
BETRAYS
BETROTH
BETTERS
BETTING
BETTORS
BETWEEN
BETWIXT
BEVELED
BEVERLY
BEWAILS
BEWITCH
BEZIERS
BEZIQUE

B•E••••

BEEBALM
BEECHAM
BEECHER
BEECHES
BEEFALO
BEEFIER
BEEFING
BEEFSUP
BEEGEES
BEEHIVE
BEELINE
BEEPERS
BEEPING
BEESWAX
BEETLES
BEETREE
BIENTOT
BLEAKER
BLEAKLY
BLEARED
BLEATED
BLEEPED
BLEEPER
BLEMISH
BLENDED
BLENDER
BLERIOT
BLESSED
BLESSES
BLEWOFF
BLEWOUT
BOERWAR
BREADED
BREADTH
BREAKER
BREAKIN
BREAKUP
BREASTS
BREATHE
BREATHS
BREATHY
BREEDER
BREEZED
BREEZES
BRENDAN
BRENNAN
BRENNER
BRERFOX
BRESLIN
BRESSON
BRETONS
BREVETS
BREVITY
BREWERS
BREWERY
BREWING

B••E•••

BABETTE
BADEGGS
BAKEOFF
BALEENS
BALEFUL
BANEFUL
BARENTS
BARETTA
BASEHIT
BASEMAN
BASEMEN
BASENJI
BASEPAY
BATEAUX
BATEMAN
BEDECKS
BEDELIA
BEDEVIL
BEDEWED
BEHESTS
BENEATH
BENEFIT
BEREAVE
BERETTA
BESEECH
BESEEMS
BEVELED
BEVERLY
BIBELOT
BIGELOW
BIGEYES
BIKEWAY
BILEVEL
BIPEDAL
BIREMES
BIRETTA
BISECTS
BITEOFF
BLEEPED
BLEEPER
BLUEBOY
BLUEFIN
BLUEFLU
BLUEFOX
BLUEING
BLUEJAY
BLUELAW
BLUESKY
BODEGAS
BODEREK
BOGEYED
BOHEMIA
BOLEROS
BONEASH
BONEDRY
BONEDUP
BONESUP
BOREDOM
BOREOUT
BOWERED
BOXEDIN
BOXEDUP
BOXESIN
BOXESUP
BREEDER
BREEZED
BREEZES
BRIEFED
BRIEFER
BRIEFLY
BRUEGEL
BUGEYED
BUREAUS
BURETTE
BYHEART

B•••E••

BACKEND
BACKERS
BADGERS
BADNESS
BAGGERS
BAILEES
BAILERS
BAILEYS
BALDEST
BALEENS
BALLETS
BANKERS
BANNERS
BANTERS
BARBELL
BARBELS
BARBERS
BARGEIN
BARKEEP
BARKERS
BARLEYS
BARNEYS
BARRELS
BARRENS
BARRETT
BARTEND
BARTERS
BASKETS
BASSETS
BASTERS
BATHERS
BATTENS
BATTERS
BATTERY
BAWLERS
BAYLEAF
BEAKERS
BEANERY
BEARERS
BEATERS
BEAVERS
BECKETT
BEDREST
BEEGEES
BEEPERS
BELIEFS
BELIEVE
BENDERS
BENNETT
BENZENE
BEQUEST
BERBERS
BERGERE
BERNESE
BERSERK
BESEECH
BESEEMS
BESIEGE
BESMEAR
BESPEAK
BETHELS
BETTERS
BETWEEN
BEZIERS
BICKERS
BIDDERS
BIGBEND
BIGDEAL
BIGFEET
BIGGERS
BIGGEST
BIGHEAD
BIGNESS
BILLETS
BINDERS
BINDERY
BIOGENY
BIRDERS
BITTERN
BITTERS
BLAZERS
BLOWERS
BOATERS
BOBBERS
BOILERS
BOLDEST
BOMBECK
BOMBERS
BONIEST
BONKERS
BONNETS
BOOKEND
BOOLEAN
BOOMERS
BOOTEES
BOPPERS
BORDERS
BORNEUP
BOSKETS
BOSWELL
BOTHERS
BOWLERS
BOWYERS
BOXSEAT
BRACERS
BRACEUP
BRAVELY
BRAVERY
BRAVEST
BRAYERS
BREVETS
BREWERS
BREWERY
BRIBERY
BROKEIN
BROKERS
BROKEUP
BRUBECK
BRUNETS
BUCKETS
BUCKEYE
BUDGETS
BUFFERS
BUFFETS
BUFFETT
BUGBEAR
BUGLERS
BULLETS
BUMMERS
BUMPERS
BUNGEES
BUNKERS
BURDENS
BURGEES
BURGEON
BURGERS
BURGESS
BURMESE
BURNERS
BURNETT
BUSHELS
BUSIEST
BUTLERS
BUTTERS
BUTTERY
BUZZERS
BYTHEBY

B••••E•

BABBLED
BABBLES
BADDIES
BAFFLED
BAFFLER
BAFFLES
BAGGIER
BAGGIES
BAILEES
BALKIER
BALMIER
BALONEY
BANDIED
BANDIES
BANGLES
BANJOES
BANQUET
BANSHEE
BARKEEP
BARMIER
BARONET
BARRIER
BASEMEN
BASQUES
BATCHED
BATCHES
BATIKED
BATSMEN
BATTIER
BATTLED
BATTLER
BATTLES
BAUBLES
BAWDIER
BAYONET
BEACHED
BEACHES
BEADIER
BEADLES
BEAGLES
BEAMIER
BEANIES
BEARDED

BEATLES
BECOMES
BEDEWED
BEDIZEN
BEECHER
BEECHES
BEEFIER
BEEGEES
BEETLES
BEETREE
BEHAVED
BEHAVES
BELATED
BELAYED
BELCHED
BELCHES
BELLIED
BELLIES
BELLMEN
BELOVED
BEMIRED
BEMIRES
BEMUSED
BEMUSES
BENCHED
BENCHES
BENTLEY
BENTSEN
BERATED
BERATES
BERNSEN
BERRIED
BERRIES
BERTHED
BESIDES
BESTMEN
BESTREW
BETAKEN
BETAKES
BETIDED
BETIDES
BETIMES
BETOKEN
BETWEEN
BEVELED
BIALIES
BIASSED
BIDDIES
BIGEYES
BIGFEET
BIGGIES
BIGOTED
BIGTOES
BILBOES
BILEVEL
BILLIES
BINGOES
BIRCHED
BIRCHES
BIRDIED
BIRDIES
BIRDMEN
BIREMES
BIRTHED
BISQUES
BITTIER
BITUMEN
BLABBED
BLABBER
BLACKED
BLACKEN
BLACKER
BLADDER
BLANDER
BLANKED
BLANKER
BLANKET
BLARNEY
BLASTED
BLASTER
BLATHER
BLATTED
BLEAKER
BLEARED
BLEATED
BLEEPED
BLEEPER
BLENDED
BLENDER
BLESSED
BLESSES
BLINDED
BLINDER
BLINKED
BLINKER
BLIPPED
BLISTER
BLITHER
BLITZED
BLITZEN
BLITZES
BLOATED
BLOCKED
BLOCKER
BLONDER
BLONDES
BLOODED
BLOOMED
BLOOMER
BLOOPED
BLOOPER
BLOTTED
BLOTTER
BLOUSED
BLOUSES
BLOWIER
BLUBBER
BLUFFED
BLUFFER
BLUNDER
BLUNTED
BLUNTER
BLURRED
BLURTED
BLUSHED
BLUSHER
BLUSHES
BLUSTER
BMOVIES
BOARDED
BOARDER
BOASTED
BOASTER
BOATMEN
BOBBIES
BOBBLED
BOBBLES
BOBSLED
BODEREK
BODICES
BOGEYED
BOGGLED
BOGGLER
BOGGLES
BOLIDES
BOLSTER
BOLUSES
BONDMEN
BONGOES
BONNIER
BONUSES
BOOBIES
BOODLES
BOOGIED
BOOGIES
BOOKIES
BOOKLET
BOONIES
BOOSLER
BOOSTED
BOOSTER
BOOTEES
BOOTIES
BOOTLEG
BORATES
BOSSIER
BOTCHED
BOTCHES
BOTTLED
BOTTLER
BOTTLES
BOULDER
BOUNCED
BOUNCER
BOUNCES
BOUNDED
BOUNDER
BOUQUET
BOURREE
BOVINES
BOWDLER
BOWERED
BOWTIES
BOXSTEP
BRACKEN
BRACKET
BRADLEE
BRADLEY
BRAGGED
BRAGGER
BRAIDED
BRAIDER
BRAINED
BRAISED
BRAISES
BRANDED
BRANDER
BRASHER
BRASSES
BRAVOES
BRAWLED
BRAWLER
BRAZIER
BREADED
BREAKER
BREEDER
BREEZED
BREEZES
BRENNER
BRICKED
BRIDGED
BRIDGES
BRIDGET
BRIDLED
BRIDLES
BRIEFED
BRIEFER
BRIMMED
BRINGER
BRINIER
BRIQUET
BRISKER
BRISKET
BRITTEN
BROADEN
BROADER
BROGUES
BROILED
BROILER
BRONZED
BRONZES
BROODED
BROODER
BROOKED
BROTHER
BROWNED
BROWNER
BROWSED
BROWSER
BROWSES
BRUEGEL
BRUISED
BRUISER
BRUISES
BRUITED
BRUSHED
BRUSHES
BRYNNER
BUBBLED
BUBBLES
BUCKLED
BUCKLER
BUCKLES
BUCKLEY
BUCKOES
BUDDIES
BUDGIES
BUGEYED
BUGGIER
BUGGIES
BUILDER
BULBLET
BULKIER
BULLIED
BULLIES
BULLPEN
BUMBLED
BUMBLER
BUMBLES
BUMPIER
BUNCHED
BUNCHES
BUNCOED
BUNDLED
BUNDLES
BUNGEES
BUNGLED
BUNGLER
BUNGLES
BUNKBED
BUNKOED
BUNNIES
BURBLED
BURBLES
BURGEES
BURGHER
BURGLED
BURGLES
BURLIER
BUSBIES
BUSHIER
BUSHMEN
BUSTLED
BUSTLES
BUTCHER
BYGONES
BYLINED
BYLINES

B•••••E

BABBAGE
BABETTE
BACKHOE
BAGGAGE
BAGPIPE
BALANCE
BALLADE
BANDAGE
BANSHEE
BAPTIZE
BARCODE
BAROQUE
BARRAGE
BATISTE
BAUXITE
BEASTIE
BEATTIE
BECAUSE
BEDSIDE
BEDTIME
BEEHIVE
BEELINE
BEETREE
BEGRIME
BEGUILE
BEGUINE
BEHOOVE
BELDAME
BELIEVE
BELTANE
BENZENE
BEREAVE
BERGERE
BERNESE
BERNICE
BESIEGE
BESPOKE
BEZIQUE
BICYCLE
BIGGAME
BIGNAME
BIGTIME
BIPLANE
BIVALVE
BIZARRE
BLANCHE
BLONDIE
BOBDOLE
BOBHOPE
BOGHOLE
BOLOTIE
BONDAGE
BONFIRE
BOURREE
BOWLINE
BOXKITE
BRADLEE
BRAILLE
BRAMBLE
BRASSIE
BREATHE
BRIGADE
BRINDLE
BRIOCHE
BRISTLE
BRITTLE
BROCADE
BROMATE
BROMIDE
BROMINE
BROWNIE
BRUSQUE
BUCKEYE
BURETTE
BURMESE
BUSFARE
BUSLINE
BUYABLE
BUYTIME
BYANOSE
BYFORCE

•BE••••

ABELARD
ABENAKI
ABETTED
ABETTOR
IBERIAN
OBELISK
OBELIZE
OBERLIN
OBEYING

•B•E•••

ABREAST
ABSENCE
ABSENTS
OBJECTS
OBREGON
OBSERVE
OBVERSE
OBVERTS

•B••E••

ABIDEBY
ABILENE
ABOREAL
ABUSERS
OBSCENE

•B•••E•

ABASHED
ABASHES
ABDOMEN
ABETTED
ABJURED
ABJURES
ABLATED
ABLATES
ABORTED
ABRADED
ABRADES
ABUTTED
ABYSSES
EBONIES
OBLATES
OBLIGED
OBLIGES
OBTUSER

•B••••E

ABALONE
ABILENE
ABRIDGE
ABSENCE
ABSOLVE
ABUSIVE
EBBTIDE
EBONITE
EBWHITE
MBABANE
OBELIZE
OBLIQUE
OBSCENE
OBSCURE
OBSERVE
OBTRUDE
OBVERSE
OBVIATE

••BE•••

ALBEDOS
ALBENIZ
ALBERTA
ALBERTO
BABETTE
BIBELOT
DEBEERS
FABERGE
LABELED
LABELER
LABELLE
LIBELED
LIBELER
LIBERAL
LIBERIA
LIBERTY
PUBERTY
REBECCA
REBEKAH
RIBEYES
ROBERTA
ROBERTO
ROBERTS
ROBESON
SIBERIA
SOBERED
SOBERER
SOBERLY
TIBETAN
UMBERTO
UNBENDS
UPBEATS
WOBEGON

••B•E••

AMBIENT
AMBLERS
BOBBERS
CABLERS
CABLETV
COBWEBS
DEBEERS
DUBBERS
DUBIETY
EMBLEMS
FIBBERS
GABBERS
GABFEST
GIBBERS
GIBBETS
GIBLETS
GOBLETS
HEBREWS
HUBBELL
INBREED
JABBERS
JOBBERS
KOBLENZ
LABRETS
LIBBERS
LOBBERS
LUBBERS
NABBERS
NOBLEST
RABBETS
ROBBERS
ROBBERY
RUBBERS
RUBBERY
SOBBERS
SUBDEBS
SUBHEAD
SUBJECT
SUBLETS
SUBSETS
SUBTEND
SUBTEXT
SUBVERT
SUBZERO
TABLEAU
TABLETS
UNBLEST
WEBFEET

••B••E•

ALBUMEN
AMBRIES
ARBITER
ARBORED
AUBADES
BABBLED
BABBLES
BOBBIES
BOBBLED
BOBBLES
BOBSLED
BUBBLED
BUBBLES
CABARET
CABBIES
CABINET
COBBLED
COBBLER
COBBLES
CUBBIES
DABBLED
DABBLER
DABBLES
DEBAKEY
DEBASED
DEBASES
DEBATED
DEBATER
DEBATES
DEBITED
DEBONED
DEBONES
DEBRIEF
DEBUTED
DIBBLED
DIBBLES
ELBOWED
FABARES
GABBIER
GABBLED
GABBLES
GABRIEL
GIBLUES
GOBBLED
GOBBLER
GOBBLES
HABITED
HOBBIES
HOBBLED
HOBBLES
HOBOKEN
HUBBIES
IMBIBED
IMBIBES
IMBRUED
IMBRUES
INBREED
INBRIEF
JUBILEE
KIBBLED
KIBBLES
LABELED
LABELER
LABORED
LABORER
LIBELED
LIBELER
LOBBIED
LOBBIES
LOBBYER
LOBSTER
MOBILES
MOBSTER
MRBONES
NIBBLED
NIBBLER
NIBBLES
NUBBIER
NUBBLES
ORBITED
ORBITER
PEBBLED
PEBBLES
POBOXES
RABBLES
REBATED
REBATES
REBUKED
REBUKES
REBUSES
RIBEYES
RUBBLES
RUBYDEE
SABINES
SOBERED
SOBERER
SUBDUED
SUBDUER
SUBDUES
SUBTLER
TABBIES
TABORET
TUBBIER
UNBAKED
UNBOWED
UNBOXED
UNBOXES
URBANER
WEBFEET
WEBSTER
WEBTOED
WOBBLED
WOBBLES

••B•••E

AMBROSE
BABBAGE
BABETTE
BOBDOLE
BOBHOPE
CABBAGE
CABOOSE
CUBICLE
DEBACLE
DEBARGE
DUBUQUE
EBBTIDE
EMBRACE
FABERGE
FEBRILE
FIBULAE
GOBROKE
HABITUE
JUBILEE
LABELLE
LABIATE
NEBULAE
OSBORNE
REBASTE
RIBCAGE
ROBLOWE
RUBYDEE
SUBLIME
SUBSIDE
SUBSUME
UMBRAGE
UPBORNE
VIBRATE
WEBSITE

•••BE••

ANTBEAR
BARBELL
BARBELS
BARBERS
BERBERS
BIGBEND
BOBBERS
BOMBECK
BOMBERS
BRIBERY
BRUBECK
BUGBEAR
CAMBERS
COLBERT
COMBERS
CORBELS
CORBETT
COWBELL
DAUBERS
DAYBEDS
DELBERT
DUBBERS
DUMBEST
FANBELT
FIBBERS
FILBERT
FORBEAR
GABBERS
GIBBERS
GIBBETS
GILBERT
GOOBERS
HASBEEN
HAUBERK
HERBERT
HOLBEIN
HOTBEDS
HOWBEIT
HUBBELL
ICEBERG
JABBERS
JOBBERS
LAMBEAU
LAMBENT
LAMBERT
LAPBELT
LIBBERS
LIMBERS
LOBBERS
LOWBEAM
LUBBERS
LUMBERS
MACBETH
MEMBERS
NABBERS
NUMBERS
NUMBEST
OFFBEAT
PEABEAN
PREBEND
PROBERS
RABBETS
RAMBEAU
REUBENS
ROBBERS
ROBBERY
ROYBEAN
RUBBERS
RUBBERY
SEABEDS
SEABEES
SHUBERT
SOBBERS
SORBETS
SOYBEAN
SUNBEAM
SUNBELT
TARBELL
TIMBERS
TRABERT
VERBENA
WAXBEAN
ZAMBEZI

•••B•E•

BABBLED
BABBLES
BAUBLES
BILBOES
BLABBED
BLABBER
BLUBBER
BOBBIES
BOBBLED
BOBBLES
BOOBIES
BUBBLED
BUBBLES
BULBLET
BUMBLED
BUMBLER
BUMBLES
BURBLED
BURBLES
BUSBIES
CABBIES
CLABBER
CLOBBER
CLUBBED
COBBLED
COBBLER
COBBLES
CRABBED
CRABBER
CRIBBED
CUBBIES
DABBLED
DABBLER
DABBLES
DERBIES
DIBBLED
DIBBLES
DOUBLED
DOUBLES
DOUBLET
DOUBLEU
DOUBTED
DOUBTER
DRABBER
DRIBLET
DRUBBED
EDIBLES
ENABLED
ENABLES
FEEBLER
FLUBBED
FOIBLES
FUMBLED
FUMBLER
FUMBLES
GABBIER
GABBLED
GABBLES
GAMBLED
GAMBLER
GAMBLES
GAMBREL
GARBLED
GARBLES
GLIBBER
GOBBLED
GOBBLER
GOBBLES
GRABBED
GRABBER
GRUBBED
HASBEEN
HERBTEA
HOBBIES
HOBBLED
HOBBLES
HOMBRES
HUBBIES
HUMBLED
HUMBLER
HUMBLES
ILLBRED
JEEBIES
JUMBLED
JUMBLES
KEEBLER
KIBBLED
KIBBLES
KNOBBED
LOBBIED
LOBBIES
LOBBYER
LOWBRED
MAMBOED
MARBLED
MARBLES
MAXBAER
MUMBLED
MUMBLER
MUMBLES
NIBBLED
NIBBLER
NIBBLES
NIMBLER
NUBBIER
NUBBLES
PAMBIES
PEBBLED
PEBBLES
PROBLEM
RABBLES
RAMBLED
RAMBLER
RAMBLES
RUBBLES
RUMBAED
RUMBLED
RUMBLES
SAMBAED
SEABEES
SLABBED
SLOBBER
SNUBBED
STABBED
STABLED
STABLER
STABLES
STUBBED
SWABBED
TABBIES
TIMBRES
TREBLED
TREBLES
TUBBIER
TUMBLED
TUMBLER
TUMBLES
TUMBREL
WAMBLED
WAMBLES
WARBLED
WARBLER
WARBLES
WOBBLED
WOBBLES
ZOMBIES

•••B••E

AIRBASE
AMIBLUE
BABBAGE
CABBAGE
CARBIDE
CARBINE
COMBINE
DRIBBLE
FORBADE
FORBORE
GARBAGE
GLOBULE
HENBANE
HERBAGE
HIPBONE
ICEBLUE
JAWBONE
MBABANE
OFFBASE
PROBATE
QUIBBLE
SKYBLUE
SORBATE
STABILE
STUBBLE
THEBABE
TIMBALE
TRIBUNE
TRIBUTE

TURBINE
TWOBASE
VERBOSE

••••BE•
AEROBES
ANNABEL
ANTIBES
BLABBED
BLABBER
BLUBBER
BUNKBED
CALIBER
CARIBES
CELEBES
CHAMBER
CLABBER
CLAMBER
CLIMBED
CLIMBER
CLOBBER
CLUBBED
CRABBED
CRABBER
CRIBBED
DECIBEL
DELIBES
DISOBEY
DRABBER
DRUBBED
ENROBED
ENROBES
FLAMBED
FLAMBES
FLATBED
FLUBBED
FNUMBER
FREEBEE
FRISBEE
GLIBBER
GRABBED
GRABBER
GRUBBED
IMBIBED
IMBIBES
JEZEBEL
JUJUBES
KNOBBED
LIEABED
OCTOBER
PHOEBES
PLUMBED
PLUMBER
ROADBED
SANIBEL
SCRIBES
SEEDBED
SHERBET
SIDEBET
SLABBED
SLOBBER
SLUMBER
SNUBBED
SOFABED
STABBED
STEUBEN
STROBES
STUBBED
SWABBED
THUMBED
THURBER
TOYNBEE
TRAUBEL
TWINBED
UNROBED
UNROBES

••••B•E
ACTABLE
ADDABLE
AFFABLE
AMIABLE
AMOEBAE
AUDIBLE
BRAMBLE
BUYABLE
CALIBRE
CAPABLE
CELEBRE
CITABLE
CRUMBLE
DISABLE
DRIBBLE
DURABLE
EATABLE
ENNOBLE
ENTEBBE
EQUABLE
FIXABLE
FREEBEE
FREEBIE
FRIABLE
FRISBEE
GOODBYE
GRUMBLE
HIRABLE
IGNOBLE
LEGIBLE
LIKABLE
LIVABLE
LOVABLE
MACABRE
MINABLE
MIXABLE
MOVABLE
MUTABLE
NOTABLE
PARABLE
PAYABLE
PLIABLE
POTABLE
QUIBBLE
RATABLE
RISIBLE
SALABLE
SAVABLE
SHAMBLE
SIZABLE
SOLUBLE
STUBBLE
STUMBLE
TAMABLE
TAXABLE
TENABLE
THIMBLE
TOYNBEE
TREMBLE
TROUBLE
USEABLE
VISIBLE
VOLUBLE

•••••BE
ASCRIBE
DISROBE
EARLOBE
ENTEBBE
ICECUBE
LAPROBE
LETITBE
MICROBE
THEBABE
WANNABE
WOULDBE

B•F••••
BAFFLED
BAFFLER
BAFFLES
BEFALLS
BEFOULS
BIFOCAL
BUFFALO
BUFFERS
BUFFETS
BUFFETT
BUFFING
BUFFOON
BYFORCE

B••F•••
BAFFLED
BAFFLER
BAFFLES
BAGFULS
BALFOUR
BEEFALO
BEEFIER
BEEFING
BEEFSUP
BELFAST
BIDFAIR
BIGFEET
BIGFOOT
BLUFFED
BLUFFER
BLUFFLY
BONFIRE
BOWFINS
BOXFULS
BUFFALO
BUFFERS
BUFFETS
BUFFETT
BUFFING
BUFFOON
BUSFARE

B•••F••
BALEFUL
BANEFUL
BASHFUL
BENEFIT
BLOWFLY
BLUEFIN
BLUEFLU
BLUEFOX
BLUFFED
BLUFFER
BLUFFLY
BODYFAT
BOWLFUL
BRERFOX
BRIEFED
BRIEFER
BRIEFLY
BRIMFUL

B••••F•
BACKOFF
BAILIFF
BAKEOFF
BEAROFF
BEATIFY
BEGSOFF
BELIEFS
BITEOFF
BLEWOFF
BLOWOFF
BRANIFF
BUGSOFF
BUYSOFF
BUZZOFF

B•••••F
BACKOFF
BAILIFF
BAKEOFF
BARANOF
BAYLEAF
BEAROFF
BEGSOFF
BEOWULF
BITEOFF
BLEWOFF
BLOWOFF
BRANIFF
BUGSOFF
BUYSOFF
BUZZOFF
BYWAYOF

••BF•••
GABFEST
WEBFEET
WEBFOOT

••B•F••
REBUFFS

••B••F•
FOBSOFF
REBUFFS

••B•••F
DEBRIEF
FOBSOFF
INBRIEF

B•G••••
BAGFULS
BAGGAGE
BAGGERS
BAGGIER
BAGGIES
BAGGILY
BAGGING
BAGHDAD
BAGNOLD
BAGPIPE
BEGGARS
BEGGING
BEGONIA
BEGORRA
BEGRIME
BEGSOFF
BEGUILE
BEGUINE
BIGBAND
BIGBANG
BIGBEND
BIGBIRD
BIGBOYS
BIGDEAL
BIGELOW
BIGEYES
BIGFEET
BIGFOOT
BIGGAME
BIGGERS
BIGGEST
BIGGIES
BIGGUNS
BIGHEAD
BIGHORN
BIGJOHN
BIGNAME
BIGNESS
BIGOTED
BIGOTRY
BIGSHOT
BIGTIME
BIGTOES
BIGTOPS
BIGWIGS
BOGDOWN
BOGEYED
BOGGING
BOGGLED
BOGGLER
BOGGLES
BOGHOLE
BUGABOO
BUGALOO
BUGBEAR
BUGEYED
BUGGIER
BUGGIES
BUGGING
BUGLERS
BUGLING
BUGSOFF
BUGSOUT
BYGONES

B••G•••
BADGERS
BADGUYS
BAGGAGE
BAGGERS
BAGGIER
BAGGIES
BAGGILY
BAGGING
BANGING
BANGKOK
BANGLES
BANGSUP
BARGAIN
BARGEIN
BARGING
BEAGLES
BEEGEES
BEGGARS
BEGGING
BELGIAN
BELGIUM
BENGALI
BENGALS
BERGERE
BERGMAN
BERGSON
BIGGAME
BIGGERS
BIGGEST
BIGGIES
BIGGUNS
BINGHAM
BINGING
BINGOES
BIOGENY
BLIGHTS
BOGGING
BOGGLED
BOGGLER
BOGGLES
BONGING
BONGOES
BOOGIED
BOOGIES
BRAGGED
BRAGGER
BRIGADE
BRIGAND
BRIGHAM
BROGANS
BROGUES
BUDGETS
BUDGIES
BUDGING
BUGGIER
BUGGIES
BUGGING
BULGARS
BULGHUR
BULGING
BUNGEES
BUNGING
BUNGLED
BUNGLER
BUNGLES
BURGEES
BURGEON
BURGERS
BURGESS
BURGHER
BURGLAR
BURGLED
BURGLES
BURGOOS

B•••G••
BADEGGS
BLOWGUN
BODEGAS
BOLOGNA
BRAGGED
BRAGGER
BRIDGED
BRIDGES
BRIDGET
BRINGER
BRINGIN
BRINGON
BRINGTO
BRINGUP
BROUGHT
BRUEGEL
BURPGUN

B••••G•
BABBAGE
BADEGGS
BAGGAGE
BANDAGE
BARONGS
BARRAGE
BEDBUGS
BELONGS
BESIEGE
BIGWIGS
BIOLOGY
BONDAGE
BOROUGH

B•••••G
BABYING
BACKING
BACKLOG
BAGGING
BAILING
BAITING
BALDING
BALKING
BANDING
BANGING
BANKING
BANNING
BARBING
BARGING
BARKING
BARRING
BASHING
BASKING
BASTING
BATHING
BATTING
BATWING
BAWLING
BEADING
BEAMING
BEANBAG
BEANING
BEARHUG
BEARING
BEATING
BEDDING
BEEFING
BEEPING
BEGGING
BEIJING
BELLING
BELTING
BELYING
BENDING
BESTING
BETTING
BIASING
BIDDING
BIGBANG
BILKING
BILLING
BINDING
BINGING
BINNING
BIRDDOG
BIRDING
BIRLING
BITTING
BLAMING
BLARING
BLAZING
BLOWING
BLUEING
BOATING
BOBBING
BOGGING
BOILING
BOLTING
BOMBING
BONDING
BONGING
BOOKING
BOOMING
BOOTING
BOOTLEG
BOPPING
BOSSING
BOWLING
BRACING
BRAKING
BRAVING
BRAYING
BRAZING
BREWING
BRIBING
BRINING
BUCKING
BUDDING
BUDGING
BUFFING
BUGGING
BUGLING
BULGING
BULKING
BULLDOG
BULLING
BUMMING
BUMPING
BUNGING
BUNKING
BUNTING
BUOYING
BURLING
BURNING
BURPING
BURYING
BUSHHOG
BUSHING
BUSHPIG
BUSSING
BUSTING
BUSYING
BUTTING
BUZZING

•B•G•••
ABIGAIL

•B••G••
OBLIGED
OBLIGES
OBREGON

•B•••G•
ABRIDGE
OBLONGS

•B••••G
ABASING
ABATING
ABIDING
ABUSING
OBEYING

••B•G••
WOBEGON

••B••G•
BABBAGE
CABBAGE
CYBORGS
DEBARGE
EMBARGO
FABERGE
RIBCAGE
UMBRAGE

••B•••G
AMBLING
BABYING
BOBBING
CABLING
DABBING
DUBBING
FIBBING
FOBBING
GABBING
HOBOING
IMBUING
JABBING
JOBBING
LIBBING
LOBBING
MOBBING
NABBING
RIBBING
ROBBING
RUBBING
SIBLING
SOBBING
SUBBING
TABBING
TABLING
WEBBING

•••B•G•
AIRBAGS
BABBAGE
BEDBUGS
CABBAGE
GARBAGE
GASBAGS
HERBAGE
HUMBUGS
ICEBAGS
KITBAGS
LUMBAGO
SEABAGS
SOWBUGS
TEABAGS

•••B••G
BARBING
BIGBANG
BOBBING
BOMBING
BRIBING
COMBING
CURBING
DABBING
DAUBING
DUBBING
FIBBING
FOBBING
GABBING
GARBING
GRABBAG
HAMBURG
HOMBURG
ICEBERG
JABBING
JOBBING
LIBBING
LIMBING
LOBBING
MOBBING
NABBING
NUMBING
PROBING
RIBBING
ROBBING
RUBBING
SEABORG
SHEBANG
SOBBING
SUBBING
TABBING
WEBBING

••••B•G
BEANBAG
FEEDBAG
FIREBUG
FLEABAG
GOLDBUG
GRABBAG
HANDBAG
JUNEBUG
LADYBUG
LOVEBUG
MAILBAG
NOSEBAG
OVERBIG
PEATBOG
PILLBUG
SANDBAG
TALKBIG
TOTEBAG
WINDBAG

B•H••••
BAHAMAS
BAHRAIN
BEHAVED
BEHAVES
BEHESTS
BEHOLDS
BEHOOVE
BOHEMIA
BYHEART

B••H•••
BAGHDAD
BARHOPS
BASHFUL
BASHING
BATHERS
BATHING
BATHMAT
BATHOIL
BATHTUB
BEEHIVE
BETHANY
BETHELS
BETHINK
BIGHEAD
BIGHORN
BISHOPS
BOBHOPE
BOGHOLE
BOKHARA
BOOHOOS
BOTHERS
BOTHNIA
BOYHOOD
BRAHMAN
BRAHMAS
BRAHMIN
BUSHELS
BUSHHOG
BUSHIDO
BUSHIER
BUSHING
BUSHMAN
BUSHMEN
BUSHPIG
BYTHEBY

B•••H••
BACCHUS
BACKHOE
BALIHAI
BANSHEE
BASEHIT
BATCHED
BATCHES
BEACHED
BEACHES
BEARHUG
BEECHAM
BEECHER
BEECHES
BELCHED
BELCHES
BELLHOP
BENCHED
BENCHES
BENTHAM
BERTHED
BIGSHOT
BINGHAM
BIRCHED
BIRCHES
BIRTHED
BLATHER
BLIGHTS
BLITHER
BLUSHED
BLUSHER
BLUSHES
BOKCHOY
BOLSHOI
BOTCHED
BOTCHES
BRASHER
BRASHLY
BRIGHAM
BROTHER
BRUSHED
BRUSHES
BRUSHUP
BUDDHAS
BULGHUR
BUNCHED
BUNCHES
BURGHER
BUSHHOG
BUTCHER

B••••H•
BELUSHI
BIGJOHN
BLANCHE
BLOTCHY
BORSCHT
BREATHE
BREATHS
BREATHY
BRIOCHE
BRONCHI
BROUGHT
BYPATHS

B•••••H
BABYISH
BEARISH
BENEATH
BESEECH
BETROTH
BEWITCH
BISMUTH
BLEMISH
BONEASH
BOOKISH
BOORISH
BOROUGH
BREADTH
BRITISH
BRUTISH
BULLISH
BULRUSH
BURNISH

•B•H•••
EBWHITE

•B••H••
ABASHED
ABASHES
ABRAHAM

•B••••H
ABOLISH
OBADIAH

••BH•••
BOBHOPE
DABHAND
JOBHOPS
JOBHUNT
NOBHILL
SUBHEAD

••B••H•
HIBACHI
TABITHA

••B•••H
BABYISH
DEBAUCH
DEBORAH
DEBOUCH
NEBBISH
PUBLISH
REBEKAH
REBIRTH
RUBBISH
SABBATH

•••BH••
SIOBHAN

•••B•H•
NIEBUHR

••••B•H
FURBISH
MACBETH
NEBBISH
RUBBISH
SABBATH
SUNBATH

••••B•H
POOHBAH

BI•••••
BIALIES
BIASING
BIASSED
BIBELOT
BICKERS
BICOLOR
BICYCLE
BIDDERS
BIDDIES
BIDDING
BIDFAIR
BIENTOT
BIFOCAL
BIGBAND
BIGBANG
BIGBEND
BIGBIRD
BIGBOYS
BIGDEAL
BIGELOW
BIGEYES
BIGFEET
BIGFOOT
BIGGAME
BIGGERS
BIGGEST
BIGGIES
BIGGUNS
BIGHEAD
BIGHORN
BIGJOHN
BIGNAME
BIGNESS
BIGOTED
BIGOTRY
BIGSHOT
BIGTIME
BIGTOES
BIGTOPS
BIGWIGS
BIKEWAY
BIKINIS
BILBOES
BILEVEL
BILIOUS
BILKING
BILLETS
BILLIES
BILLING
BILLION
BILLOWS
BILLOWY
BIMODAL
BINDERS
BINDERY
BINDING
BINDSUP
BINGHAM
BINGING
BINGOES
BINNING
BIOGENY
BIOLOGY
BIOMASS
BIONICS
BIPEDAL
BIPLANE
BIPOLAR
BIRCHED

BIRCHES
BIRDDOG
BIRDERS
BIRDIED
BIRDIES
BIRDING
BIRDMAN
BIRDMEN
BIREMES
BIRETTA
BIRLING
BIRTHED
BISCUIT
BISECTS
BISHOPS
BISMUTH
BISQUES
BISTROS
BITEOFF
BITMAPS
BITPART
BITTERN
BITTERS
BITTIER
BITTING
BITUMEN
BIVALVE
BIVOUAC
BIZARRE

B•I••••

BAILEES
BAILERS
BAILEYS
BAILIFF
BAILING
BAILORS
BAILOUT
BAITING
BEIJING
BLIGHTS
BLINDED
BLINDER
BLINDLY
BLINKAT
BLINKED
BLINKER
BLIPPED
BLISTER
BLITHER
BLITZED
BLITZEN
BLITZES
BOILERS
BOILING
BOITANO
BRIARDS
BRIBERY
BRIBING
BRICKED
BRIDALS
BRIDGED
BRIDGES
BRIDGET
BRIDLED
BRIDLES
BRIEFED
BRIEFER
BRIEFLY
BRIGADE
BRIGAND
BRIGHAM
BRILLAT
BRIMFUL
BRIMMED
BRINDLE
BRINGER
BRINGIN
BRINGON
BRINGTO
BRINGUP
BRINIER
BRINING
BRIOCHE
BRIQUET
BRISKER
BRISKET
BRISKLY
BRISTLE
BRISTLY
BRISTOL
BRITAIN
BRITISH
BRITONS
BRITTEN
BRITTLE
BRITTON
BUILDER
BUILDIN
BUILDON
BUILDUP
BUILTIN
BUILTON
BUILTUP

B••I•••

BACILLI
BALIHAI
BATIKED
BATISTA
BATISTE
BEDIZEN
BELIEFS
BELIEVE
BELINDA
BEMIRED
BEMIRES
BENISON
BESIDES
BESIEGE
BETIDED
BETIDES
BETIMES
BEWITCH
BEZIERS
BEZIQUE
BIKINIS
BILIOUS
BKLIBAN
BODICES
BOLIDES
BOLIVAR
BOLIVIA
BONIEST
BONITOS
BOVINES
BRAIDED
BRAIDER
BRAILLE
BRAINED
BRAISED
BRAISES
BROILED
BROILER
BRUISED
BRUISER
BRUISES
BRUITED
BUNIONS
BUSIEST
BYLINED
BYLINES

B•••I••

BABBITT
BABYING
BABYISH
BACKING
BADDIES
BAGGIER
BAGGIES
BAGGILY
BAGGING
BAGPIPE
BAILIFF
BAILING
BAITING
BALDING
BALKIER
BALKING
BALMIER
BAMBINO
BANDIED
BANDIES
BANDING
BANDITO
BANDITS
BANGING
BANKING
BANNING
BAPTISM
BAPTIST
BAPTIZE
BARBING
BARGING
BARKING
BARMIER
BARRIER
BARRING
BARRIOS
BASHING
BASKING
BASSIST
BASTING
BASTION
BATHING
BATTIER
BATTING
BATWING
BAUXITE
BAWDIER
BAWDILY
BAWLING
BAYCITY
BEADIER
BEADING
BEAMIER
BEAMING
BEANIES
BEANING
BEARING
BEARISH
BEATIFY
BEATING
BEDDING
BEDSIDE
BEDTIME
BEEFIER
BEEFING
BEEHIVE
BEELINE
BEEPING
BEGGING
BEGRIME
BEGUILE
BEGUINE
BEIJING
BELGIAN
BELGIUM
BELLIED
BELLIES
BELLING
BELLINI
BELTING
BELYING
BENDING
BERLIOZ
BERLITZ
BERNICE
BERRIED
BERRIES
BESTIAL
BESTING
BESTIRS
BETHINK
BETTING
BETWIXT
BEWAILS
BIALIES
BIASING
BIDDIES
BIDDING
BIGBIRD
BIGGIES
BIGTIME
BIGWIGS
BILKING
BILLIES
BILLING
BILLION
BINDING
BINGING
BINNING
BIONICS
BIRDIED
BIRDIES
BIRDING
BIRLING
BITTIER
BITTING
BLAMING
BLARING
BLAZING
BLEMISH
BLERIOT
BLOWIER
BLOWING
BLUEING
BMOVIES
BOATING
BOBBIES
BOBBING
BOBBINS
BOBVILA
BODKINS
BOGGING
BOILING
BOLTING
BOMBING
BONDING
BONFIRE
BONGING
BONNIER
BONNILY
BOOBIES
BOOGIED
BOOGIES
BOOKIES
BOOKING
BOOKISH
BOOMING
BOONIES
BOORISH
BOOTIES
BOOTING
BOPPING
BOSSIER
BOSSILY
BOSSING
BOWFINS
BOWLINE
BOWLING
BOWTIES
BOXKITE
BRACING
BRAKING
BRANIFF
BRAVING
BRAYING
BRAZIER
BRAZING
BREVITY
BREWING
BRIBING
BRINIER
BRINING
BRITISH
BROMIDE
BROMINE
BRUTISH
BUCKING
BUDDIES
BUDDING
BUDGIES
BUDGING
BUFFING
BUGGIER
BUGGIES
BUGGING
BUGLING
BULGING
BULKIER
BULKING
BULLIED
BULLIES
BULLING
BULLION
BULLISH
BULLITT
BUMMING
BUMPIER
BUMPING
BUNGING
BUNKING
BUNNIES
BUNTING
BUOYING
BURKINA
BURLIER
BURLING
BURNING
BURNISH
BURPING
BURRITO
BURYING
BUSBIES
BUSHIDO
BUSHIER
BUSHING
BUSKINS
BUSLINE
BUSSING
BUSTING
BUSYING
BUTTING
BUYTIME
BUZZING

B••••I•

BABYSIT
BACKBIT
BACKLIT
BACKSIN
BAHRAIN
BALDRIC
BALDWIN
BANDAID
BARGAIN
BARGEIN
BARMAID
BASEHIT
BATHOIL
BAVARIA
BEASTIE
BEATNIK
BEATRIX
BEATSIT
BEATTIE
BEDELIA
BEDEVIL
BEDOUIN
BEGONIA
BENAZIR
BENEFIT
BIDFAIR
BIKINIS
BISCUIT
BLONDIE
BLOWSIN
BLOWSIT
BLUEFIN
BOBTAIL
BOHEMIA
BOLIVIA
BOLOTIE
BONSOIR
BORODIN
BORZOIS
BOTHNIA
BOUDOIR
BOXEDIN
BOXESIN
BRAHMIN
BRASSIE
BREAKIN
BRESLIN
BRINGIN
BRITAIN
BROKEIN
BROWNIE
BUCOLIC
BUILDIN
BUILTIN
BUMPKIN
BUSHPIG
BUTTSIN

B•••••I

BACARDI
BACILLI
BALIHAI
BASENJI
BELLINI
BELUSHI
BENGALI
BOLSHOI
BONJOVI
BRONCHI

•BI••••

ABIDEBY
ABIDING
ABIGAIL
ABILENE
ABILITY
TBILISI

•B•I•••

ABRIDGE
OBLIGED
OBLIGES
OBLIQUE
OBOISTS
OBVIATE
OBVIOUS

•B••I••

ABASING
ABATING
ABIDING
ABILITY
ABOLISH
ABUSING
ABUSIVE
EBBTIDE
EBONIES
EBONITE
EBWHITE
IBERIAN
OBADIAH
OBELISK
OBELIZE
OBEYING
OBTAINS
TBILISI

•B•••I•

ABIGAIL
ABNAKIS
ABSTAIN
CBRADIO
OBERLIN

•B••••I

ABENAKI
TBILISI

••BI•••

ALBINOS
AMBIENT
ARBITER
CABINET
CUBICLE
CUBISTS
DEBITED
DUBIETY
DUBIOUS
HABITAT
HABITED
HABITUE
IMBIBED
IMBIBES
JABIRUS
JUBILEE
LABIALS
LABIATE
LIBIDOS
MOBILES
NABISCO
NUBIANS
ORBISON
ORBITAL
ORBITED
ORBITER
REBINDS
REBIRTH
RUBICON
RUBITIN
SABINES
TABITHA
TUBISTS
UNBINDS

••B•I••

AMBLING
AMBRIES
BABBITT
BABYING
BABYISH
BOBBIES
BOBBING
BOBBINS
BOBVILA
CABBIES
CABLING
CUBBIES
DABBING
DEBRIEF
DOBBINS
DUBBING
EBBTIDE
FABRICS
FEBRILE
FIBBING
FIBRILS
FOBBING
GABBIER
GABBING
GABRIEL
GOBLINS
HOBBIES
HOBBITS
HOBOING
HUBBIES
HYBRIDS
IMBUING
INBRIEF
JABBING
JOBBING
KUBRICK
LIBBING
LOBBIED
LOBBIES
LOBBING
MOBBING
NABBING
NEBBISH
NIBLICK
NOBHILL
NUBBIER
NUBBINS
PUBLICS
PUBLISH
RABBITS
RABBITT
REBOILS
REBUILD
REBUILT
RIBBING
ROBBING
ROBBINS
RUBBING
RUBBISH
RUBRICS
SABRINA
SIBLING
SOBBING
SUBBING
SUBLIME
SUBMITS
SUBSIDE
SUBSIDY
SUBSIST
TABBIES
TABBING
TABLING
TUBAIST
TUBBIER
UMBRIAN
WEBBING
WEBSITE

••B••I•

ALBANIA
ALBENIZ
ALBUMIN
BABYSIT
BOBTAIL
CIBORIA
EMBROIL
HEBRAIC
HOBNAIL
KABUKIS
LIBERIA
ROBOTIC
RUBITIN
SIBERIA
SUBJOIN
SUBSOIL
SUBUNIT
TABLOID
UPBRAID

••B•••I

HIBACHI

•••BI••

ARABIAN
BABBITT
BAMBINO
BARBING
BIGBIRD
BOBBIES
BOBBING
BOBBINS
BOMBING
BOOBIES
BRIBING
BUSBIES
CABBIES
CAMBIUM
CARBIDE
CARBINE
CATBIRD
COMBINE
COMBING
COWBIRD
CUBBIES
CURBING
DABBING
DAUBING
DERBIES
DOBBINS
DUBBING
FIBBING
FOBBING
FORBIDS
FURBISH
GABBIER
GABBING
GAMBIAN
GAMBITS
GARBING
GERBILS
HENBITS
HOBBIES
HOBBITS
HUBBIES
JABBING
JAYBIRD
JEEBIES
JOBBING
LIBBING
LIMBING
LINBIAO
LOBBIED
LOBBIES
LOBBING
MOBBING
NABBING
NEBBISH
NIOBIUM
NUBBIER
NUBBINS
NUMBING
OUTBIDS
PAMBIES
PHOBIAS
PHOBICS
PROBING
PROBITY
RABBITS
RABBITT
REDBIRD
RIBBING
ROBBING
ROBBINS
RUBBING
RUBBISH
SEABIRD
SERBIAN
SOBBING
STABILE
SUBBING
TABBIES
TABBING
TERBIUM
TIDBITS
TITBITS
TUBBIER
TURBINE
TWOBITS
WAYBILL
WEBBING
ZAMBIAN
ZOMBIES

•••B•I•

CAMBRIC
CHABLIS
CONBRIO
HOLBEIN
HOWBEIT
LEIBNIZ
PARBOIL

•••B••I

ZAMBEZI

••••BI•

ACERBIC
AEROBIC
ALEMBIC
AMOEBIC
BACKBIT
COALBIN
COHABIT
EXHIBIT
EXURBIA
FREEBIE
INHABIT
INHIBIT
INORBIT
JACOBIN
NAMIBIA
NOTABIT
OVERBIG
PHILBIN
RAREBIT
SHOWBIZ
TALKBIG
ZENOBIA

•••••BI

NAIROBI
PUNJABI
SYLLABI

B••J•••

BANJOES
BEIJING
BIGJOHN
BONJOUR
BONJOVI

B•••J••

BELLJAR
BLUEJAY

B••••J•

BASENJI

•BJ••••

ABJURED
ABJURES
OBJECTS

••BJ•••

SUBJECT
SUBJOIN

BK•••••

BKLIBAN

B•K••••

BAKEOFF
BAKLAVA
BIKEWAY
BIKINIS
BOKCHOY
BOKHARA

B••K•••

BACKBAY
BACKBIT
BACKEND
BACKERS
BACKHOE
BACKING
BACKLIT
BACKLOG
BACKOFF
BACKOUT
BACKRUB
BACKSIN
BACKSUP
BACKUPS
BALKANS
BALKIER
BALKING
BANKERS
BANKING
BANKSON
BARKEEP
BARKERS
BARKING
BARKSAT
BASKETS
BASKING
BEAKERS
BECKETT
BECKONS
BICKERS
BILKING
BODKINS
BONKERS
BOOKEND
BOOKIES
BOOKING
BOOKISH
BOOKLET
BOSKETS
BOWKNOT
BOXKITE
BRAKING
BROKEIN
BROKERS
BROKEUP
BUCKETS
BUCKEYE
BUCKING
BUCKLED
BUCKLER
BUCKLES
BUCKLEY
BUCKOES
BUCKRAM
BUCKSAW
BUCKSUP
BULKIER
BULKING
BUNKBED
BUNKERS
BUNKING
BUNKOED
BURKINA
BUSKINS

B•••K••

BANGKOK
BATIKED
BELAKUN
BETAKEN
BETAKES
BETOKEN
BLACKED
BLACKEN
BLACKER
BLACKLY
BLANKED
BLANKER
BLANKET
BLANKLY
BLEAKER
BLEAKLY
BLINKAT
BLINKED
BLINKER
BLOCKED
BLOCKER
BRACKEN
BRACKET
BREAKER
BREAKIN
BREAKUP
BRICKED
BRISKER
BRISKET
BRISKLY
BROOKED
BUMPKIN

B••••K•

BAZOOKA
BEDECKS
BESPOKE
BLUESKY
BUROAKS

B•••••K

BANGKOK
BANNOCK
BARRACK
BEATNIK
BEDROCK
BERSERK
BESPEAK
BETHINK
BODEREK
BOMBECK
BRUBECK
BULLOCK
BULWARK
BURBANK
BURDOCK

•B••K••

ABNAKIS

•B•••K•

ABENAKI
ABUBAKR

•B••••K

OBELISK

••B•K••

DEBAKEY
HOBOKEN
KABUKIS
NABOKOV
REBEKAH
REBUKED
REBUKES
UNBAKED

••B••K•

DEBARKS

DEBUNKS
DYBBUKS
EMBANKS
EMBARKS
GOBROKE

••B•••K
JOBBANK
KUBRICK
LUBBOCK
MUBARAK
NIBLICK

•••B•K•
ABUBAKR
DYBBUKS

•••B••K
BOMBECK
BRUBECK
BURBANK
CUTBACK
DAYBOOK
EYEBANK
FATBACK
FOGBANK
GETBACK
GOTBACK
HAUBERK
HOGBACK
JOBBANK
LOGBOOK
LUBBOCK
OUTBACK
REDBOOK
ROEBUCK
RUNBACK
SAWBUCK
SETBACK

••••B•K
GEMSBOK

BL•••••
BLABBED
BLABBER
BLACKED
BLACKEN
BLACKER
BLACKLY
BLADDER
BLAMING
BLANCHE
BLANDER
BLANDLY
BLANKED
BLANKER
BLANKET
BLANKLY
BLARING
BLARNEY
BLASTED
BLASTER
BLATANT
BLATHER
BLATTED
BLAZERS
BLAZING
BLAZONS
BLEAKER
BLEAKLY
BLEARED
BLEATED
BLEEPED
BLEEPER
BLEMISH
BLENDED
BLENDER
BLERIOT
BLESSED
BLESSES
BLEWOFF
BLEWOUT
BLIGHTS
BLINDED
BLINDER
BLINDLY
BLINKAT
BLINKED
BLINKER
BLIPPED
BLISTER
BLITHER
BLITZED
BLITZEN
BLITZES
BLOATED
BLOCKED
BLOCKER
BLONDER
BLONDES
BLONDIE
BLOODED
BLOOMED
BLOOMER
BLOOPED
BLOOPER
BLOSSOM
BLOTCHY
BLOTOUT
BLOTTED
BLOTTER
BLOUSED
BLOUSES
BLOUSON
BLOWDRY
BLOWERS
BLOWFLY
BLOWGUN
BLOWIER
BLOWING
BLOWNUP
BLOWOFF
BLOWOUT
BLOWSIN
BLOWSIT
BLOWSUP
BLOWUPS
BLUBBER
BLUEBOY
BLUEFIN
BLUEFLU
BLUEFOX
BLUEING
BLUEJAY
BLUELAW
BLUESKY
BLUFFED
BLUFFER
BLUFFLY
BLUNDER
BLUNTED
BLUNTER
BLUNTLY
BLURRED
BLURTED
BLUSHED
BLUSHER
BLUSHES
BLUSTER

B•L••••
BALANCE
BALATON
BALBOAS
BALCONY
BALDEST
BALDING
BALDRIC
BALDWIN
BALEENS
BALEFUL
BALFOUR
BALIHAI
BALKANS
BALKIER
BALKING
BALLADE
BALLADS
BALLARD
BALLAST
BALLBOY
BALLETS
BALLOON
BALLOTS
BALLSUP
BALMIER
BALONEY
BALSAMS
BELABOR
BELAKUN
BELATED
BELAYED
BELCHED
BELCHES
BELDAME
BELDAMS
BELFAST
BELGIAN
BELGIUM
BELIEFS
BELIEVE
BELINDA
BELLAMY
BELLBOY
BELLHOP
BELLIED
BELLIES
BELLING
BELLINI
BELLJAR
BELLMAN
BELLMEN
BELLOWS
BELLYUP
BELMONT
BELONGS
BELOVED
BELTANE
BELTING
BELTWAY
BELUSHI
BELYING
BILBOES
BILEVEL
BILIOUS
BILKING
BILLETS
BILLIES
BILLING
BILLION
BILLOWS
BILLOWY
BKLIBAN
BOLDEST
BOLEROS
BOLIDES
BOLIVAR
BOLIVIA
BOLOGNA
BOLOTIE
BOLSHOI
BOLSTER
BOLTING
BOLUSES
BULBLET
BULBOUS
BULBULS
BULGARS
BULGHUR
BULGING
BULKIER
BULKING
BULLDOG
BULLETS
BULLIED
BULLIES
BULLING
BULLION
BULLISH
BULLITT
BULLOCK
BULLPEN
BULLRUN
BULRUSH
BULWARK
BYLINED
BYLINES

B••L•••
BAILEES
BAILERS
BAILEYS
BAILIFF
BAILING
BAILORS
BAILOUT
BAKLAVA
BALLADE
BALLADS
BALLARD
BALLAST
BALLBOY
BALLETS
BALLOON
BALLOTS
BALLSUP
BARLEYS
BAWLERS
BAWLING
BAWLOUT
BAYLEAF
BECLOUD
BEDLAMP
BEELINE
BELLAMY
BELLBOY
BELLHOP
BELLIED
BELLIES
BELLING
BELLINI
BELLJAR
BELLMAN
BELLMEN
BELLOWS
BELLYUP
BERLIOZ
BERLITZ
BIALIES
BILLETS
BILLIES
BILLING
BILLION
BILLOWS
BILLOWY
BIOLOGY
BIPLANE
BIRLING
BOILERS
BOILING
BOOLEAN
BOULDER
BOWLERS
BOWLFUL
BOWLINE
BOWLING
BRILLAT
BUGLERS
BUGLING
BUILDER
BUILDIN
BUILDON
BUILDUP
BUILTIN
BUILTON
BUILTUP
BULLDOG
BULLETS
BULLIED
BULLIES
BULLING
BULLION
BULLISH
BULLITT
BULLOCK
BULLPEN
BULLRUN
BURLAPS
BURLIER
BURLING
BUSLINE
BUTLERS
BYPLAYS

B•••L••
BABBLED
BABBLES
BABYLON
BACILLI
BACKLIT
BACKLOG
BAFFLED
BAFFLER
BAFFLES
BANALLY
BANGLES
BASALLY
BASALTS
BATTLED
BATTLER
BATTLES
BAUBLES
BEADLES
BEAGLES
BEATLES
BECALMS
BEDELIA
BEETLES
BEFALLS
BEHOLDS
BENTLEY
BEVELED
BIBELOT
BICOLOR
BIGELOW
BIPOLAR
BIVALVE
BLUELAW
BOBBLED
BOBBLES
BOBSLED
BOGGLED
BOGGLER
BOGGLES
BOODLES
BOOKLET
BOOSLER
BOOTLEG
BOTTLED
BOTTLER
BOTTLES
BOWDLER
BRADLEE
BRADLEY
BRAILLE
BRAWLED
BRAWLER
BRESLIN
BRIDLED
BRIDLES
BRILLAT
BROILED
BROILER
BUBBLED
BUBBLES
BUCKLED
BUCKLER
BUCKLES
BUCKLEY
BUCOLIC
BUGALOO
BULBLET
BUMBLED
BUMBLER
BUMBLES
BUNDLED
BUNDLES
BUNGLED
BUNGLER
BUNGLES
BURBLED
BURBLES
BURGLAR
BURGLED
BURGLES
BUSTLED
BUSTLES

B••••L•
BACILLI
BADCOLD
BAGFULS
BAGGILY
BAGNOLD
BANALLY
BARBELL
BARBELS
BARRELS
BASALLY
BAWDILY
BEASTLY
BEDROLL
BEEBALM
BEEFALO
BEFALLS
BEFOULS
BEGUILE
BENGALI
BENGALS
BEOWULF
BERTOLT
BETHELS
BEVERLY
BEWAILS
BICYCLE
BLACKLY
BLANDLY
BLANKLY
BLEAKLY
BLINDLY
BLOWFLY
BLUEFLU
BLUFFLY
BLUNTLY
BOBDOLE
BOBVILA
BOGHOLE
BONNILY
BOSSILY
BOSWELL
BOXFULS
BRAILLE
BRAMBLE
BRAMBLY
BRASHLY
BRAVELY
BRIDALS
BRIEFLY
BRINDLE
BRISKLY
BRISTLE
BRISTLY
BRITTLE
BROADLY
BUFFALO
BULBULS
BUSHELS
BUYABLE

B•••••L
BALEFUL
BANEFUL
BARBELL
BARNOWL
BASHFUL
BATHOIL
BEDEVIL
BEDROLL
BESTIAL
BIFOCAL
BIGDEAL
BILEVEL
BIMODAL
BIPEDAL
BOBTAIL
BOSWELL
BOWLFUL
BRIMFUL
BRISTOL
BRUEGEL

•BL••••
ABLATED
ABLATES
ABLAUTS
OBLASTS
OBLATES
OBLIGED
OBLIGES
OBLIQUE
OBLONGS
OBLOQUY

•B•L•••
ABALONE
ABELARD
ABILENE
ABILITY
ABOLISH
OBELISK
OBELIZE
TBILISI

•B••L••
ABSALOM
ABSOLUT
ABSOLVE
OBERLIN

•B••••L
ABIGAIL
ABOREAL
ABUTTAL
ABYSMAL

••BL•••
AMBLERS
AMBLING
CABLERS
CABLETV
CABLING
EMBLEMS
GIBLETS
GIBLUES
GOBLETS
GOBLINS
INBLOOM
JOBLOTS
KOBLENZ
NIBLICK
NOBLEST
OXBLOOD
PABLUMS
PUBLICS
PUBLISH
REBLOOM
ROBLOWE
SIBLING
SUBLETS
SUBLIME
TABLEAU
TABLETS
TABLING
TABLOID
UNBLEST

••B•L••
BABBLED
BABBLES
BABYLON
BIBELOT
BOBBLED
BOBBLES
BOBSLED
BUBBLED
BUBBLES
CABALAS
COBBLED
COBBLER
COBBLES
DABBLED
DABBLER
DABBLES
DIBBLED
DIBBLES
FIBULAE
FIBULAS
GABBLED
GABBLES
GOBBLED
GOBBLER
GOBBLES
HOBBLED
HOBBLES
JUBILEE
KIBBLED
KIBBLES
KOBOLDS
LABELED
LABELER
LABELLE
LIBELED
LIBELER
MOBILES
NEBULAE
NEBULAR
NEBULAS
NIBBLED
NIBBLER
NIBBLES
NUBBLES
PABULUM
PEBBLED
PEBBLES
RABBLES
REBOLTS
RUBBLES
SUBPLOT
SUBTLER
TABULAR
TUBULAR
UNBOLTS
WOBBLED
WOBBLES
ZEBULON

••B••L•
BOBDOLE
BOBVILA
CUBICLE
DEBACLE
FEBRILE
FIBRILS
HUBBELL
LABELLE
LABIALS
NOBHILL
REBOILS
REBUILD
REBUILT
SOBERLY

••B•••L
BOBTAIL
EMBROIL
GABRIEL
HOBNAIL
HUBBELL
LIBERAL
NOBHILL
ORBITAL
SUBSOIL

•••BL••
AMIBLUE
BABBLED
BABBLES
BAUBLES
BOBBLED
BOBBLES
BUBBLED
BUBBLES
BULBLET
BUMBLED
BUMBLER
BUMBLES
BURBLED
BURBLES
CHABLIS
COBBLED
COBBLER
COBBLES
DABBLED
DABBLER
DABBLES
DIBBLED
DIBBLES
DOUBLED
DOUBLES
DOUBLET
DOUBLEU
DRIBLET
EDIBLES
ENABLED
ENABLES
FEEBLER
FOIBLES
FUMBLED
FUMBLER
FUMBLES
GABBLED
GABBLES
GAMBLED
GAMBLER
GAMBLES
GARBLED
GARBLES
GILBLAS
GOBBLED
GOBBLER
GOBBLES
HOBBLED
HOBBLES
HUMBLED
HUMBLER
HUMBLES
ICEBLUE
INKBLOT
JOEBLOW
JUMBLED
JUMBLES
KEEBLER
KIBBLED
KIBBLES
LOWBLOW
MARBLED
MARBLES
MUMBLED
MUMBLER
MUMBLES
NIBBLED
NIBBLER
NIBBLES
NIMBLER
NUBBLES
PEBBLED
PEBBLES
PROBLEM
PUEBLOS
RABBLES
RAMBLED
RAMBLER
RAMBLES
RUBBLES
RUMBLED
RUMBLES
SKYBLUE
STABLED
STABLER
STABLES
TEMBLOR
THEBLOB
TREBLED
TREBLES
TUMBLED
TUMBLER
TUMBLES
WAMBLED
WAMBLES
WARBLED
WARBLER
WARBLES
WOBBLED
WOBBLES

•••B•L•
AIRBALL
BARBELL
BARBELS
BEEBALM
BULBULS
CEMBALO
CORBELS
COWBELL
CUEBALL
CYMBALS
DIMBULB
DRIBBLE
EYEBALL
EYEBOLT
FANBELT
FLYBALL
FURBALL
GAMBOLS
GERBILS
GIMBALS
GLOBULE
GUMBALL
HERBALS
HUBBELL
KIMBALL
LAPBELT
LIPBALM
LOWBALL
ODDBALL
PIEBALD
PINBALL
PITBULL
QUIBBLE
STABILE
STUBBLE
STUBBLY
SUNBELT
SYMBOLS
TAMBALA
TARBELL
TEABALL
TIMBALE
TIMBALS
VERBALS
WAYBILL

•••B••L
AIRBALL
BARBELL
COWBELL
CUEBALL
EYEBALL
FLYBALL
FURBALL
GAMBREL
GUMBALL
HUBBELL
KIMBALL
LOWBALL
ODDBALL
PARBOIL
PINBALL
PITBULL
TARBELL
TEABALL
TUMBREL
WAYBILL

••••BL•
ACTABLE
ADDABLE
AFFABLE
AFFABLY
AMIABLE
AMIABLY
AUDIBLE
AUDIBLY
BRAMBLE
BRAMBLY
BUYABLE
CAPABLE
CAPABLY
CITABLE
CRUMBLE
CRUMBLY
DISABLE
DRIBBLE
DURABLE
DURABLY
EATABLE
ENNOBLE
EQUABLE
EQUABLY
FIXABLE
FRIABLE
GRUMBLE
HIRABLE
IGNOBLE
IGNOBLY
LEGIBLE
LEGIBLY
LIKABLE
LIVABLE
LOVABLE
MINABLE
MIXABLE
MOVABLE
MUTABLE
MUTABLY
NOTABLE
NOTABLY
PARABLE
PAYABLE
PLIABLE
PLIABLY
POTABLE
QUIBBLE
RATABLE
RISIBLE
SALABLE
SAVABLE
SHAMBLE
SIZABLE
SIZABLY
SOLUBLE
STUBBLE
STUBBLY
STUMBLE
TAMABLE
TAXABLE
TENABLE
TENABLY
THIMBLE
TREMBLE
TREMBLY
TROUBLE
USEABLE
VISIBLE
VISIBLY
VOLUBLE
VOLUBLY

••••B•L
ANNABEL
DECIBEL
JEZEBEL
SANIBEL
TRAUBEL

BM•••••
BMOVIES

B•M••••
BAMBINO
BAMBOOS
BEMIRED
BEMIRES
BEMOANS
BEMUSED
BEMUSES
BIMODAL
BOMBARD
BOMBAST
BOMBECK
BOMBERS
BOMBING
BUMBLED
BUMBLER
BUMBLES
BUMMERS
BUMMING
BUMPERS
BUMPIER
BUMPING
BUMPKIN
BUMPSUP
BUMSOUT

B••M•••
BALMIER
BARMAID
BARMIER
BEAMIER

BEAMING
BEAMSUP
BELMONT
BERMUDA
BESMEAR
BIOMASS
BISMUTH
BITMAPS
BLAMING
BLEMISH
BOOMBOX
BOOMERS
BOOMING
BRAMBLE
BRAMBLY
BRIMFUL
BRIMMED
BROMATE
BROMIDE
BROMINE
BUMMERS
BUMMING
BURMESE

B•••M••

BAHAMAS
BASEMAN
BASEMEN
BATEMAN
BATHMAT
BATSMAN
BATSMEN
BECOMES
BELLMAN
BELLMEN
BENUMBS
BERGMAN
BESTMAN
BESTMEN
BETAMAX
BETIMES
BIRDMAN
BIRDMEN
BIREMES
BITUMEN
BLOOMED
BLOOMER
BOATMAN
BOATMEN
BOHEMIA
BONDMAN
BONDMEN
BRAHMAN
BRAHMAS
BRAHMIN
BRIMMED
BUSHMAN
BUSHMEN

B••••M•

BALSAMS
BANTAMS
BECALMS
BEDLAMP
BEDTIME
BEGRIME
BELDAME
BELDAMS
BELLAMY
BESEEMS
BIGGAME
BIGNAME
BIGTIME
BOTTOMS
BUYTIME

B•••••M

BAPTISM
BARROOM
BEDROOM
BEEBALM
BEECHAM
BELGIUM
BENTHAM
BINGHAM
BLOSSOM
BOREDOM
BRIGHAM
BUCKRAM

•B••M••

ABDOMEN
ABYSMAL

•B••••M

ABRAHAM
ABSALOM

••BM•••

SUBMITS

••B•M••

ALBUMEN
ALBUMIN
LABAMBA

••B••M•

EMBLEMS
PABLUMS
SUBLIME
SUBSUME

••B•••M

INBLOOM
JIBBOOM
PABULUM
REBLOOM

•••B•M•

ALABAMA

•••B••M

BEEBALM
CAMBIUM
JIBBOOM
LIPBALM
LOWBEAM
NIOBIUM
PROBLEM
SUNBEAM
TERBIUM

B•N••••

BANALLY
BANANAS
BANDAGE
BANDAID
BANDANA
BANDBOX
BANDIED
BANDIES
BANDING
BANDITO
BANDITS
BANDSAW
BANEFUL
BANGING
BANGKOK
BANGLES
BANGSUP
BANJOES
BANKERS
BANKING
BANKSON
BANNERS
BANNING
BANNOCK
BANQUET
BANSHEE
BANTAMS
BANTERS
BANYANS
BENATAR
BENAZIR
BENCHED
BENCHES
BENDERS
BENDING
BENEATH
BENEFIT
BENGALI
BENGALS
BENISON
BENNETT
BENTHAM
BENTLEY
BENTSEN
BENUMBS
BENZENE
BINDERS
BINDERY
BINDING
BINDSUP
BINGHAM
BINGING
BINGOES
BINNING
BONANZA
BONBONS
BONDAGE
BONDING
BONDMAN
BONDMEN
BONEASH
BONEDRY
BONEDUP
BONESUP
BONFIRE
BONGING
BONGOES
BONIEST
BONITOS
BONJOUR
BONJOVI
BONKERS
BONNETS
BONNIER
BONNILY
BONSOIR
BONUSES
BUNCHED
BUNCHES
BUNCOED
BUNDLED
BUNDLES
BUNGEES
BUNGING
BUNGLED
BUNGLER
BUNGLES
BUNIONS
BUNKBED
BUNKERS
BUNKING
BUNKOED
BUNNIES
BUNTING

B••N•••

BADNESS
BAGNOLD
BANNERS
BANNING
BANNOCK
BARNARD
BARNEYS
BARNOWL
BEANBAG
BEANERY
BEANIES
BEANING
BENNETT
BERNARD
BERNESE
BERNICE
BERNSEN
BIENTOT
BIGNAME
BIGNESS
BINNING
BIONICS
BLANCHE
BLANDER
BLANDLY
BLANKED
BLANKER
BLANKET
BLANKLY
BLENDED
BLENDER
BLINDED
BLINDER
BLINDLY
BLINKAT
BLINKED
BLINKER
BLONDER
BLONDES
BLONDIE
BLUNDER
BLUNTED
BLUNTER
BLUNTLY
BONNETS
BONNIER
BONNILY
BOONIES
BORNEUP
BOUNCED
BOUNCER
BOUNCES
BOUNDED
BOUNDER
BOUNDTO
BOUNDUP
BRANDED
BRANDER
BRANDON
BRANIFF
BRANSON
BRENDAN
BRENNAN
BRENNER
BRINDLE
BRINGER
BRINGIN
BRINGON
BRINGTO
BRINGUP
BRINIER
BRINING
BRONCHI
BRONCOS
BRONSON
BRONZED
BRONZES
BRUNETS
BRYNNER
BUNNIES
BURNERS
BURNETT
BURNING
BURNISH
BURNOUT
BURNSUP
BURNTUP
BYANDBY
BYANOSE

B•••N••

BALANCE
BALONEY
BANANAS
BARANOF
BARENTS
BARONET
BARONGS
BASENJI
BAYONET
BEATNIK
BEGONIA
BELINDA
BELONGS
BIKINIS
BLARNEY
BLOWNUP
BONANZA
BOTHNIA
BOVINES
BOWKNOT
BRAINED
BRENNAN
BRENNER
BROSNAN
BROWNED
BROWNER
BROWNIE
BRYNNER
BYGONES
BYLINED
BYLINES

B••••N•

BABOONS
BABYING
BACKEND
BACKING
BAGGING
BAILING
BAITING
BALCONY
BALDING
BALEENS
BALKANS
BALKING
BAMBINO
BANDANA
BANDING
BANGING
BANKING
BANNING
BANYANS
BARBING
BARGING
BARKING
BARRENS
BARRING
BARTEND
BARYONS
BASHING
BASKING
BASTING
BATHING
BATTENS
BATTING
BATWING
BAWLING
BEACONS
BEADING
BEAMING
BEANING
BEARING
BEATING
BECKONS
BEDDING
BEEFING
BEELINE
BEEPING
BEGGING
BEGUINE
BEIJING
BELLING
BELLINI
BELMONT
BELTANE
BELTING
BELYING
BEMOANS
BENDING
BENZENE
BESTING
BETHANY
BETHINK
BETTING
BIASING
BIDDING
BIGBAND
BIGBANG
BIGBEND
BIGGUNS
BILKING
BILLING
BINDING
BINGING
BINNING
BIOGENY
BIPLANE
BIRDING
BIRLING
BITTING
BLAMING
BLARING
BLATANT
BLAZING
BLAZONS
BLOWING
BLUEING
BOATING
BOBBING
BOBBINS
BODKINS
BOGGING
BOILING
BOITANO
BOLOGNA
BOLTING
BOMBING
BONBONS
BONDING
BONGING
BOOKEND
BOOKING
BOOMING
BOOTING
BOPPING
BOSSING
BOWFINS
BOWLINE
BOWLING
BRACING
BRAKING
BRAVING
BRAYING
BRAZING
BRETONS
BREWING
BRIBING
BRIGAND
BRINING
BRITONS
BROGANS
BROMINE
BUCKING
BUDDING
BUDGING
BUFFING
BUGGING
BUGLING
BULGING
BULKING
BULLING
BUMMING
BUMPING
BUNGING
BUNIONS
BUNKING
BUNTING
BUOYANT
BUOYING
BURBANK
BURDENS
BURKINA
BURLING
BURNING
BURPING
BURYING
BUSHING
BUSKINS
BUSLINE
BUSSING
BUSTING
BUSYING
BUTTING
BUTTONS
BUZZING
BYTURNS

B•••••N

BABYLON
BACKSIN
BAHRAIN
BALATON
BALDWIN
BALLOON
BANKSON
BARGAIN
BARGEIN
BASEMAN
BASEMEN
BASSOON
BASTION
BATEMAN
BATSMAN
BATSMEN
BEARSON
BEDDOWN
BEDIZEN
BEDOUIN
BELAKUN
BELGIAN
BELLMAN
BELLMEN
BENISON
BENTSEN
BERGMAN
BERGSON
BERNSEN
BESTMAN
BESTMEN
BETAKEN
BETOKEN
BETWEEN
BIGHORN
BIGJOHN
BILLION
BIRDMAN
BIRDMEN
BITTERN
BITUMEN
BKLIBAN
BLACKEN
BLITZEN
BLOUSON
BLOWGUN
BLOWSIN
BLUEFIN
BOATMAN
BOATMEN
BOGDOWN
BONDMAN
BONDMEN
BOOLEAN
BORODIN
BOURBON
BOXEDIN
BOXESIN
BRACKEN
BRAHMAN
BRAHMIN
BRANDON
BRANSON
BRAXTON
BREAKIN
BRENDAN
BRENNAN
BRESLIN
BRESSON
BRINGIN
BRINGON
BRITAIN
BRITTEN
BRITTON
BROADEN
BROKEIN
BRONSON
BROSNAN
BUFFOON
BUILDIN
BUILDON
BUILTIN
BUILTON
BULLION
BULLPEN
BULLRUN
BUMPKIN
BURGEON
BURPGUN
BURSTYN
BUSHMAN
BUSHMEN
BUTTSIN

•BN••••

ABNAKIS
IBNSAUD

•B•N•••

ABANDON
ABENAKI
EBONIES
EBONITE

•B••N••

ABOUNDS
ABSENCE
ABSENTS
OBLONGS
OBTUNDS

•B•••N•

ABALONE
ABASING
ABATING
ABIDING
ABILENE
ABSCOND
ABUSING
MBABANE
OBEYING
OBSCENE
OBTAINS

•B••••N

ABANDON
ABDOMEN
ABSTAIN
IBERIAN
OBERLIN
OBREGON

••BN•••

HOBNAIL
HOBNOBS

••B•N••

ALBANIA
ALBENIZ
ALBINOS
CABANAS
CABINET
DEBONED
DEBONES
DEBUNKS
EMBANKS
LEBANON
MRBONES
REBINDS
RIBANDS
SABINES
SUBUNIT
UNBENDS
UNBINDS
URBANER

••B••N•

AMBIENT
AMBLING
AUBURNS
BABOONS
BABYING
BOBBING
BOBBINS
CABLING
DABBING
DABHAND
DOBBINS
DUBBING
FIBBING
FOBBING
GABBING
GIBBONS
GOBLINS
HOBOING
IMBUING
INBOUND
JABBING
JOBBANK
JOBBING
JOBHUNT
KOBLENZ
LIBBING
LIBYANS
LOBBING
MOBBING
NABBING
NUBBINS
NUBIANS
OSBORNE
REBOUND
RIBBING
RIBBONS
ROBBING
ROBBINS
RUBBING
SABRINA
SIBLING
SOBBING
SUBBING
SUBORNS
SUBTEND
TABBING
TABLING
UNBOUND
UPBORNE
VIBRANT
WEBBING

••B•••N

ALBUMEN
ALBUMIN
BABYLON
HOBOKEN
LEBANON
LEBARON
ORBISON
ROBESON
RUBDOWN
RUBICON
RUBITIN
SUBJOIN
TIBETAN
UMBRIAN
WOBEGON
ZEBULON

•••BN••

LEIBNIZ

•••B•N•

ARMBAND
BAMBINO
BARBING
BIGBAND
BIGBANG
BIGBEND
BOBBING
BOBBINS
BOMBING
BONBONS
BRIBING
BURBANK
CARBINE
CARBONS
COMBINE
COMBING
CUIBONO
CURBING
DABBING
DAUBING
DISBAND
DOBBINS
DUBBING
EYEBANK
FIBBING
FOBBING
FOGBANK
GABBING
GARBING
GIBBONS
HENBANE
HIPBONE
HUSBAND
IKEBANA
JABBING
JAWBONE
JOBBANK
JOBBING
JUGBAND
LAMBENT
LIBBING
LIMBING
LOBBING
MBABANE
MOBBING
NABBING
NUBBINS
NUMBING
PREBEND
PROBING
PROBONO
REUBENS
RIBBING
RIBBONS
ROBBING
ROBBINS
RUBBING
SHEBANG
SOBBING
SUBBING
TABBING
TRIBUNE
TURBANS
TURBINE
VERBENA
WEBBING

•••B••N

ARABIAN
CLIBURN
COGBURN
GAMBIAN
HASBEEN
HEPBURN
HOLBEIN
LOWBORN
MAXBORN
NEWBORN
PEABEAN
RAYBURN
ROYBEAN
SANBORN
SERBIAN
SIOBHAN
SOYBEAN
SUNBURN
WAXBEAN
ZAMBIAN

••••B•N

AUDUBON
BKLIBAN
BOURBON
CALIBAN
COALBIN
EXURBAN
JACOBIN
PHILBIN
STEUBEN
TESTBAN

BO•••••

BOARDED
BOARDER
BOASTED
BOASTER
BOATERS
BOATING
BOATMAN
BOATMEN
BOBBERS
BOBBIES
BOBBING
BOBBINS
BOBBLED
BOBBLES
BOBCATS
BOBDOLE
BOBHOPE
BOBSLED
BOBTAIL
BOBVILA
BODEGAS
BODEREK
BODICES
BODKINS
BODYFAT
BOERWAR
BOGDOWN
BOGEYED
BOGGING
BOGGLED
BOGGLER
BOGGLES
BOGHOLE
BOHEMIA
BOILERS
BOILING
BOITANO
BOKCHOY
BOKHARA
BOLDEST
BOLEROS
BOLIDES
BOLIVAR
BOLIVIA
BOLOGNA
BOLOTIE
BOLSHOI
BOLSTER
BOLTING
BOLUSES
BOMBARD
BOMBAST
BOMBECK
BOMBERS
BOMBING
BONANZA
BONBONS
BONDAGE
BONDING
BONDMAN
BONDMEN
BONEASH
BONEDRY
BONEDUP
BONESUP
BONFIRE
BONGING
BONGOES
BONIEST
BONITOS
BONJOUR
BONJOVI
BONKERS
BONNETS
BONNIER
BONNILY
BONSOIR
BONUSES
BOOBIES
BOOBOOS
BOODLES
BOOGIED
BOOGIES
BOOHOOS
BOOKEND
BOOKIES
BOOKING
BOOKISH
BOOKLET
BOOLEAN
BOOMBOX
BOOMERS
BOOMING
BOONIES
BOORISH
BOOSLER
BOOSTED
BOOSTER
BOOSTUP
BOOTEES
BOOTIES
BOOTING
BOOTLEG
BOOTOUT
BOOTSUP
BOPPERS
BOPPING
BORATES

BORDERS
BOREDOM
BOREOUT
BORNEUP
BORODIN
BOROUGH
BORROWS
BORSCHT
BORZOIS
BOSKETS
BOSSIER
BOSSILY
BOSSING
BOSWELL
BOTCHED
BOTCHES
BOTHERS
BOTHNIA
BOTTLED
BOTTLER
BOTTLES
BOTTOMS
BOUDOIR
BOULDER
BOUNCED
BOUNCER
BOUNCES
BOUNDED
BOUNDER
BOUNDTO
BOUNDUP
BOUQUET
BOURBON
BOURREE
BOUTROS
BOVINES
BOWDLER
BOWERED
BOWFINS
BOWKNOT
BOWLERS
BOWLFUL
BOWLINE
BOWLING
BOWSAWS
BOWSOUT
BOWTIES
BOWWOWS
BOWYERS
BOXCARS
BOXEDIN
BOXEDUP
BOXESIN
BOXESUP
BOXFULS
BOXKITE
BOXSEAT
BOXSTEP
BOXTOPS
BOXWOOD
BOYCOTT
BOYDORR
BOYHOOD

B•O••••

BAOBABS
BEOWULF
BIOGENY
BIOLOGY
BIOMASS
BIONICS
BLOATED
BLOCKED
BLOCKER
BLONDER
BLONDES
BLONDIE
BLOODED
BLOOMED
BLOOMER
BLOOPED
BLOOPER
BLOSSOM
BLOTCHY
BLOTOUT
BLOTTED
BLOTTER
BLOUSED
BLOUSES
BLOUSON
BLOWDRY
BLOWERS
BLOWFLY
BLOWGUN
BLOWIER
BLOWING
BLOWNUP
BLOWOFF
BLOWOUT
BLOWSIN
BLOWSIT
BLOWSUP
BLOWUPS
BMOVIES
BOOBIES
BOOBOOS
BOODLES
BOOGIED
BOOGIES
BOOHOOS
BOOKEND
BOOKIES
BOOKING
BOOKISH
BOOKLET
BOOLEAN
BOOMBOX
BOOMERS
BOOMING
BOONIES
BOORISH
BOOSLER
BOOSTED
BOOSTER
BOOSTUP
BOOTEES
BOOTIES
BOOTING
BOOTLEG
BOOTOUT
BOOTSUP
BROADAX
BROADEN
BROADER
BROADLY
BROCADE
BROGANS
BROGUES
BROILED
BROILER
BROKEIN
BROKERS
BROKEUP
BROMATE
BROMIDE
BROMINE
BRONCHI
BRONCOS
BRONSON
BRONZED
BRONZES
BROODED
BROODER
BROOKED
BROSNAN
BROTHER
BROUGHT
BROWNED
BROWNER
BROWNIE
BROWSED
BROWSER
BROWSES
BUOYANT
BUOYING
BUOYSUP

B••O•••

BABOONS
BALONEY
BARONET
BARONGS
BAROQUE
BAYONET
BAZOOKA
BECOMES
BEDOUIN
BEFOULS
BEGONIA
BEGORRA
BEHOLDS
BEHOOVE
BELONGS
BELOVED
BEMOANS
BETOKEN
BICOLOR
BIFOCAL
BIGOTED
BIGOTRY
BIMODAL
BIPOLAR
BIVOUAC
BLOODED
BLOOMED
BLOOMER
BLOOPED
BLOOPER
BOLOGNA
BOLOTIE
BORODIN
BOROUGH
BRIOCHE
BROODED
BROODER
BROOKED
BUCOLIC
BUROAKS
BUYOUTS
BYFORCE
BYGONES
BYROADS
BYWORDS

B•••O••

BABOONS
BACKOFF
BACKOUT
BADCOLD
BAGNOLD
BAILORS
BAILOUT
BAKEOFF
BALBOAS
BALCONY
BALFOUR
BALLOON
BALLOTS
BAMBOOS
BANJOES
BANNOCK
BARCODE
BARHOPS
BARNOWL
BARROOM
BARROWS
BARSOAP
BARYONS
BASSOON
BATBOYS
BATHOIL
BAWLOUT
BAZOOKA
BEACONS
BEAROFF
BEAROUT
BEATOUT
BECKONS
BECLOUD
BEDDOWN
BEDPOST
BEDROCK
BEDROLL
BEDROOM
BEGSOFF
BEHOOVE
BELLOWS
BELMONT
BERTOLT
BESPOKE
BESTOWS
BETROTH
BETTORS
BIGBOYS
BIGFOOT
BIGHORN
BIGJOHN
BIGTOES
BIGTOPS
BILBOES
BILIOUS
BILLOWS
BILLOWY
BINGOES
BIOLOGY
BISHOPS
BITEOFF
BLAZONS
BLEWOFF
BLEWOUT
BLOTOUT
BLOWOFF
BLOWOUT
BOBDOLE
BOBHOPE
BOGDOWN
BOGHOLE
BONBONS
BONGOES
BONJOUR
BONJOVI
BONSOIR
BOOBOOS
BOOHOOS
BOOTOUT
BOREOUT
BORROWS
BORZOIS
BOTTOMS
BOUDOIR
BOWSOUT
BOWWOWS
BOXTOPS
BOXWOOD
BOYCOTT
BOYDORR
BOYHOOD
BRAVOES
BRETONS
BRITONS
BUCKOES
BUFFOON
BUGSOFF
BUGSOUT
BULBOUS
BULLOCK
BUMSOUT
BUNCOED
BUNIONS
BUNKOED
BURBOTS
BURDOCK
BURGOOS
BURNOUT
BURROWS
BUSBOYS
BUSTOUT
BUTTONS
BUTTOUT
BUYSOFF
BUYSOUT
BUZZOFF
BYANOSE

B••••O•

BABYLON
BACKHOE
BACKLOG
BALATON
BALLBOY
BALLOON
BAMBOOS
BANDBOX
BANGKOK
BANKSON
BARANOF
BARRIOS
BARROOM
BASSOON
BASTION
BEARSON
BEDROOM
BELABOR
BELLBOY
BELLHOP
BENISON
BERGSON
BERLIOZ
BESTBOY
BIBELOT
BICOLOR
BIENTOT
BIGELOW
BIGFOOT
BIGSHOT
BILLION
BIRDDOG
BISTROS
BLERIOT
BLOSSOM
BLOUSON
BLUEBOY
BLUEFOX
BOKCHOY
BOLEROS
BOLSHOI
BONITOS
BOOBOOS
BOOHOOS
BOOMBOX
BOREDOM
BOURBON
BOUTROS
BOWKNOT
BOXWOOD
BOYHOOD
BRANDON
BRANSON
BRAXTON
BRERFOX
BRESSON
BRINGON
BRISTOL
BRITTON
BRONCOS
BRONSON
BUFFOON
BUGABOO
BUGALOO
BUILDON
BUILTON
BULLDOG
BULLION
BURGEON
BURGOOS
BUSHHOG
BUSSTOP
BYWAYOF

B•••••O

BAMBINO
BANDITO
BEEFALO
BOITANO
BOUNDTO
BRAVADO
BRINGTO
BUFFALO
BUGABOO
BUGALOO
BURRITO
BUSHIDO

•BO••••

ABOLISH
ABOREAL
ABORTED
ABOUNDS
EBONIES
EBONITE
OBOISTS

•B•O•••

ABDOMEN
ABSOLUT
ABSOLVE
ABSORBS
OBLONGS
OBLOQUY

•B••O••

ABALONE
ABSCOND
OBVIOUS

•B•••O•

ABANDON
ABETTOR
ABSALOM
OBREGON

•B••••O

CBRADIO

••BO•••

ARBORED
ARBOURS
BABOONS
CABOOSE
CIBORIA
CYBORGS
DEBONED
DEBONES
DEBORAH
DEBOUCH
ELBOWED
HOBOING
HOBOKEN
INBOARD
INBOUND
KOBOLDS
LABORED
LABORER
LABOURS
MRBONES
NABOKOV
ONBOARD
OSBORNE
POBOXES
PTBOATS
REBOILS
REBOLTS
REBOOTS
REBOUND
REBOZOS
ROBOCOP
ROBOTIC
SUBORNS
TABORET
UNBOLTS
UNBOUND
UNBOWED
UNBOXED
UNBOXES
UPBORNE

••B•O••

AMBROSE
BABOONS
BOBDOLE
BOBHOPE
CABOOSE
DEBTORS
DUBIOUS
EMBROIL
FIBROUS
FOBSOFF
GIBBONS
GIBBOUS
GOBROKE
HOBNOBS
INBLOOM
JIBBOOM
JOBHOPS
JOBLOTS
LABCOAT
LUBBOCK
OXBLOOD
REBLOOM
REBOOTS
RIBBONS
ROBLOWE
ROBROYS
RUBDOWN
RUBSOUT
SUBJOIN
SUBROSA
SUBSOIL
TABLOID
WEBFOOT
WEBTOED

••B••O•

ALBEDOS
ALBINOS
BABYLON
BIBELOT
EMBRYOS
GABBROS
HOBOING
INBLOOM
JIBBOOM
LEBANON
LEBARON
LIBIDOS
NABOKOV
ORBISON
OXBLOOD
REBLOOM
REBOZOS
ROBESON
ROBOCOP
RUBICON
SUBPLOT
WEBFOOT
WOBEGON
ZEBULON

••B•••O

ALBERTO
EMBARGO
NABISCO
ROBERTO
SUBZERO
TABASCO
TOBACCO
UMBERTO
VIBRATO

•••BO••

AIRBOAT
ANYBODY
BALBOAS
BAMBOOS
BATBOYS
BIGBOYS
BILBOES
BONBONS
BOOBOOS
BULBOUS
BURBOTS
BUSBOYS
CARBONS
CARBOYS
CATBOAT
COWBOYS
CUIBONO
DASBOOT
DAYBOOK
EYEBOLT
FLYBOYS
FOGBOWS
FORBORE
GAMBOLS
GIBBONS
GIBBOUS
GOABOUT
GUNBOAT
HARBORS
HARBOUR
HIPBONE
HIPBOOT
ICEBOAT
JAWBONE
JERBOAS
JETBOAT
JIBBOOM
LOGBOOK
LOWBORN
LOWBOYS
LUBBOCK
MAMBOED
MAXBORN
NEWBORN
PARBOIL
PEABODY
PITBOSS
PROBONO
REDBOOK
RIBBONS
ROWBOAT
SANBORN
SEABORG
SKIBOOT
SYMBOLS
TAMBOUR
TOMBOYS
TUGBOAT
TURBOTS
VERBOSE

•••B•O•

BAMBOOS
BOOBOOS
DASBOOT
DAYBOOK
EYEBROW
GABBROS
HIPBOOT
INKBLOT
JIBBOOM
JOEBLOW
LOGBOOK
LOWBLOW
LOWBROW
PUEBLOS
REDBOOK
SKIBOOT
TEMBLOR
THEBLOB

•••B••O

BAMBINO
CEMBALO
CONBRIO
CUIBONO
LINBIAO
LUMBAGO
PROBONO

••••BO•

AUDUBON
BALLBOY
BANDBOX
BELABOR
BELLBOY
BESTBOY
BLUEBOY
BOOMBOX
BOURBON
BUGABOO
CALLBOX
CARIBOU
CASHBOX
COPYBOY
DOWNBOW
FIREBOX
GAZEBOS
GEARBOX
GEMSBOK
HAUTBOY
HIGHBOY
ICHABOD
JUKEBOX
LOCKBOX
LONGBOW
MAILBOX
MARABOU
NEWSBOY
PAGEBOY
PEATBOG
PILLBOX
PLAYBOY
PLOWBOY
POORBOX
POORBOY
POSTBOX
RAINBOW
SALTBOX
SANDBOX
SHOEBOX
SOAPBOX
TOOLBOX

••••B•O

BUGABOO

•••••BO

COLUMBO
MOGAMBO
PLACEBO
RIOLOBO

B•P••••

BAPTISM
BAPTIST
BAPTIZE
BIPEDAL
BIPLANE
BIPOLAR
BOPPERS
BOPPING
BYPATHS
BYPLAYS

B••P•••

BAGPIPE
BEDPOST
BEEPERS
BEEPING
BESPEAK
BESPOKE
BITPART
BLIPPED
BOPPERS
BOPPING
BUMPERS
BUMPIER
BUMPING
BUMPKIN
BUMPSUP
BURPGUN
BURPING

B•••P••

BASEPAY
BEARPAW
BLEEPED
BLEEPER
BLIPPED
BLOOPED
BLOOPER
BULLPEN
BUSHPIG

B••••P•

BACKUPS
BAGPIPE
BARHOPS
BIGTOPS
BISHOPS
BITMAPS
BLOWUPS
BOBHOPE
BOXTOPS
BURLAPS

B•••••P

BACKSUP
BALLSUP
BANGSUP
BARKEEP
BARSOAP
BEADSUP
BEAMSUP
BEARSUP
BEATSUP
BEDLAMP
BEEFSUP
BELLHOP
BELLYUP
BINDSUP
BLOWNUP
BLOWSUP
BONEDUP
BONESUP
BOOSTUP
BOOTSUP
BORNEUP
BOUNDUP
BOXEDUP
BOXESUP
BOXSTEP
BRACEUP
BREAKUP
BRINGUP
BROKEUP
BRUSHUP
BUCKSUP
BUDDYUP
BUILDUP
BUILTUP
BUMPSUP
BUOYSUP
BURNSUP
BURNTUP
BUSSTOP

••BP•••

SUBPLOT

••B••P•

BOBHOPE
HUBCAPS
JOBHOPS
MOBCAPS

••B•••P

ROBOCOP

••••B•P

SCRUBUP

B•Q••••

BEQUEST

B••Q•••

BANQUET
BASQUES
BISQUES
BOUQUET
BRIQUET

B•••Q••

BAROQUE
BEZIQUE
BRUSQUE

•B••Q••

OBLIQUE
OBLOQUY

••B•Q••

DUBUQUE

BR•••••

BRACERS
BRACEUP
BRACING
BRACKEN
BRACKET
BRADLEE
BRADLEY
BRAGGED
BRAGGER
BRAHMAN
BRAHMAS
BRAHMIN
BRAIDED
BRAIDER
BRAILLE
BRAINED
BRAISED
BRAISES
BRAKING
BRAMBLE
BRAMBLY
BRANDED
BRANDER
BRANDON
BRANIFF
BRANSON
BRASHER
BRASHLY
BRASSES
BRASSIE
BRAVADO
BRAVELY
BRAVERY
BRAVEST
BRAVING
BRAVOES
BRAVURA
BRAWLED
BRAWLER
BRAXTON
BRAYERS
BRAYING
BRAZIER
BRAZING
BREADED
BREADTH
BREAKER
BREAKIN
BREAKUP
BREASTS
BREATHE
BREATHS
BREATHY
BREEDER
BREEZED
BREEZES
BRENDAN
BRENNAN
BRENNER
BRERFOX
BRESLIN
BRESSON
BRETONS
BREVETS
BREVITY
BREWERS
BREWERY
BREWING
BRIARDS
BRIBERY
BRIBING
BRICKED
BRIDALS
BRIDGED
BRIDGES
BRIDGET
BRIDLED
BRIDLES
BRIEFED
BRIEFER
BRIEFLY
BRIGADE
BRIGAND
BRIGHAM
BRILLAT
BRIMFUL
BRIMMED
BRINDLE
BRINGER
BRINGIN
BRINGON
BRINGTO
BRINGUP
BRINIER
BRINING
BRIOCHE
BRIQUET
BRISKER
BRISKET
BRISKLY
BRISTLE
BRISTLY
BRISTOL
BRITAIN

BRITISH
BRITONS
BRITTEN
BRITTLE
BRITTON
BROADAX
BROADEN
BROADER
BROADLY
BROCADE
BROGANS
BROGUES
BROILED
BROILER
BROKEIN
BROKERS
BROKEUP
BROMATE
BROMIDE
BROMINE
BRONCHI
BRONCOS
BRONSON
BRONZED
BRONZES
BROODED
BROODER
BROOKED
BROSNAN
BROTHER
BROUGHT
BROWNED
BROWNER
BROWNIE
BROWSED
BROWSER
BROWSES
BRUBECK
BRUEGEL
BRUISED
BRUISER
BRUISES
BRUITED
BRUNETS
BRUSHED
BRUSHES
BRUSHUP
BRUSQUE
BRUTISH
BRYNNER

B•R••••

BARANOF
BARBARA
BARBARY
BARBELL
BARBELS
BARBERS
BARBING
BARBUDA
BARCODE
BARENTS
BARETTA
BARGAIN
BARGEIN
BARGING
BARHOPS
BARKEEP
BARKERS
BARKING
BARKSAT
BARLEYS
BARMAID
BARMIER
BARNARD
BARNEYS
BARNOWL
BARONET
BARONGS
BAROQUE
BARRACK
BARRAGE
BARRELS
BARRENS
BARRETT
BARRIER
BARRING
BARRIOS
BARROOM
BARROWS
BARSOAP
BARTEND
BARTERS
BARYONS
BERATED
BERATES
BERBERS
BEREAVE
BERETTA
BERGERE
BERGMAN
BERGSON
BERLIOZ
BERLITZ
BERMUDA
BERNARD
BERNESE
BERNICE
BERNSEN
BERRIED
BERRIES
BERSERK
BERTHED
BERTOLT
BIRCHED
BIRCHES
BIRDDOG
BIRDERS
BIRDIED
BIRDIES
BIRDING
BIRDMAN
BIRDMEN
BIREMES
BIRETTA
BIRLING
BIRTHED
BORATES
BORDERS
BOREDOM
BOREOUT
BORNEUP
BORODIN
BOROUGH
BORROWS
BORSCHT
BORZOIS
BURBANK
BURBLED
BURBLES
BURBOTS
BURDENS
BURDOCK
BUREAUS
BURETTE
BURGEES
BURGEON
BURGERS
BURGESS
BURGHER
BURGLAR
BURGLED
BURGLES
BURGOOS
BURKINA
BURLAPS
BURLIER
BURLING
BURMESE
BURNERS
BURNETT
BURNING
BURNISH
BURNOUT
BURNSUP
BURNTUP
BUROAKS
BURPGUN
BURPING
BURRITO
BURROWS
BURSARS
BURSTYN
BURYING
BYROADS

B••R•••

BAHRAIN
BARRACK
BARRAGE
BARRELS
BARRENS
BARRETT
BARRIER
BARRING
BARRIOS
BARROOM
BARROWS
BEARCAT
BEARDED
BEARERS
BEARHUG
BEARING
BEARISH
BEAROFF
BEAROUT
BEARPAW
BEARSON
BEARSUP
BEDREST
BEDROCK
BEDROLL
BEDROOM
BEGRIME
BERRIED
BERRIES
BETRAYS
BETROTH
BLARING
BLARNEY
BLERIOT
BLURRED
BLURTED
BOARDED
BOARDER
BOERWAR
BOORISH
BORROWS
BOURBON
BOURREE
BRERFOX
BULRUSH
BURRITO
BURROWS

B•••R••

BACARDI
BACKRUB
BALDRIC
BAVARIA
BEATRIX
BEETREE
BEGORRA
BEMIRED
BEMIRES
BESTREW
BETARAY
BEVERLY
BISTROS
BIZARRE
BLEARED
BLURRED
BODEREK
BOLEROS
BOURREE
BOUTROS
BOWERED
BRIARDS
BUCKRAM
BULLRUN
BYFORCE
BYTURNS
BYWORDS

B••••R•

BACKERS
BADGERS
BAGGERS
BAILERS
BAILORS
BALLARD
BANKERS
BANNERS
BANTERS
BARBARA
BARBARY
BARBERS
BARKERS
BARNARD
BARTERS
BASTERS
BATHERS
BATTERS
BATTERY
BAWLERS
BAZAARS
BEAKERS
BEANERY
BEARERS
BEATERS
BEAVERS
BEEPERS
BEGGARS
BEGORRA
BENDERS
BERBERS
BERGERE
BERNARD
BERSERK
BESTIRS
BETTERS
BETTORS
BEZIERS
BICKERS
BIDDERS
BIGBIRD
BIGGERS
BIGHORN
BIGOTRY
BINDERS
BINDERY
BIRDERS
BITPART
BITTERN
BITTERS
BIZARRE
BLAZERS
BLOWDRY
BLOWERS
BOATERS
BOBBERS
BOILERS
BOKHARA
BOMBARD
BOMBERS
BONEDRY
BONFIRE
BONKERS
BOOMERS
BOPPERS
BORDERS
BOTHERS
BOWLERS
BOWYERS
BOXCARS
BOYDORR
BRACERS
BRAVERY
BRAVURA
BRAYERS
BREWERS
BREWERY
BRIBERY
BROKERS
BUFFERS
BUGLERS
BULGARS
BULWARK
BUMMERS
BUMPERS
BUNKERS
BURGERS
BURNERS
BURSARS
BUSFARE
BUSTARD
BUTLERS
BUTTERS
BUTTERY
BUZZARD
BUZZERS
BYHEART

B•••••R

BAFFLER
BAGGIER
BALFOUR
BALKIER
BALMIER
BARMIER
BARRIER
BATTIER
BATTLER
BAWDIER
BEADIER
BEAMIER
BEECHER
BEEFIER
BELABOR
BELLJAR
BENATAR
BENAZIR
BESMEAR
BICOLOR
BIDFAIR
BIPOLAR
BITTIER
BLABBER
BLACKER
BLADDER
BLANDER
BLANKER
BLASTER
BLATHER
BLEAKER
BLEEPER
BLENDER
BLINDER
BLINKER
BLISTER
BLITHER
BLOCKER
BLONDER
BLOOMER
BLOOPER
BLOTTER
BLOWIER
BLUBBER
BLUFFER
BLUNDER
BLUNTER
BLUSHER
BLUSTER
BOARDER
BOASTER
BOERWAR
BOGGLER
BOLIVAR
BOLSTER
BONJOUR
BONNIER
BONSOIR
BOOSLER
BOOSTER
BOSSIER
BOTTLER
BOUDOIR
BOULDER
BOUNCER
BOUNDER
BOWDLER
BOYDORR
BRAGGER
BRAIDER
BRANDER
BRASHER
BRAWLER
BRAZIER
BREAKER
BREEDER
BRENNER
BRIEFER
BRINGER
BRINIER
BRISKER
BROADER
BROILER
BROODER
BROTHER
BROWNER
BROWSER
BRUISER
BRYNNER
BUCKLER
BUGBEAR
BUGGIER
BUILDER
BULGHUR
BULKIER
BUMBLER
BUMPIER
BUNGLER
BURGHER
BURGLAR
BURLIER
BUSHIER
BUTCHER

•BR••••

ABRADED
ABRADES
ABRAHAM
ABREAST
ABRIDGE
CBRADIO
OBREGON

•B•R•••

ABOREAL
ABORTED
IBERIAN
OBERLIN
OBTRUDE

•B••R••

ABJURED
ABJURES
ABSORBS
OBSERVE
OBVERSE
OBVERTS

•B•••R•

ABELARD
ABUSERS
OBSCURE

•B••••R

ABETTOR
ABUBAKR
OBTUSER

••BR•••

AMBRIES
AMBROSE
DEBRIEF
EMBRACE
EMBROIL
EMBRYOS
FABRICS
FEBRILE
FIBRILS
FIBROUS
GABRIEL
GOBROKE
HEBRAIC
HEBREWS
HYBRIDS
IMBRUED
IMBRUES
INBREED
INBRIEF
KUBRICK
LABRETS
LIBRARY
ROBROYS
RUBRICS
SABRINA
SUBROSA
UMBRAGE
UMBRIAN
UPBRAID
VIBRANT
VIBRATE
VIBRATO

••B•R••

ALBERTA
ALBERTO
ARBORED
AUBURNS
CABARET
CIBORIA
CYBORGS
DEBARGE
DEBARKS
DEBORAH
DUBARRY
EMBARGO
EMBARKS
FABARES
FABERGE
GABBROS
JABIRUS
LABORED
LABORER
LEBARON
LIBERAL
LIBERIA
LIBERTY
MUBARAK
OSBORNE
PUBERTY
REBIRTH
ROBARDS
ROBERTA
ROBERTO
ROBERTS
SIBERIA
SOBERED
SOBERER
SOBERLY
SUBORNS
SUBURBS
TABARDS
TABORET
UMBERTO
UPBORNE

••B••R•

AMBLERS
ARBOURS
BOBBERS
CABLERS
DEBEERS
DEBTORS
DUBARRY
DUBBERS
FIBBERS
GABBERS
GIBBERS
HUBBARD
INBOARD
JABBERS
JOBBERS
LABOURS
LIBBERS
LIBRARY
LOBBERS
LUBBERS
NABBERS
ONBOARD
ROBBERS
ROBBERY
RUBBERS
RUBBERY
SOBBERS
SUBVERT
SUBZERO

••B•••R

ARBITER
COBBLER
DABBLER
DEBATER
GABBIER
GOBBLER
LABELER
LABORER
LIBELER
LOBBYER
LOBSTER
MOBSTER
NEBULAR
NIBBLER
NUBBIER
ORBITER
SOBERER
SUBDUER
SUBTLER
TABULAR
TUBBIER
TUBULAR
URBANER
WEBSTER

•••BR••

CAMBRIC
CONBRIO
EYEBROW
GABBROS
GAMBREL
HOFBRAU
HOMBRES
ILLBRED
LOWBRED
LOWBROW
TIMBRES
TUMBREL

•••B•R•

ASHBURY
BARBARA
BARBARY
BARBERS
BERBERS
BIGBIRD
BOBBERS
BOMBARD
BOMBERS
BRIBERY
CADBURY
CAMBERS
CATBIRD
CLIBURN
COGBURN
COLBERT
COMBERS
COWBIRD
DAUBERS
DELBERT
DISBARS
DUBBERS
FIBBERS
FILBERT
FORBORE
GABBERS
GIBBERS
GILBERT
GOOBERS
HAMBURG
HARBORS
HAUBERK
HEPBURN
HERBERT
HOMBURG
HUBBARD
ICEBERG
ISOBARS
JABBERS
JAYBIRD
JOBBERS
LAMBERT
LIBBERS
LIMBERS
LOBBERS
LOMBARD
LOWBORN
LUBBERS
LUMBARS
LUMBERS
MAXBORN
MEMBERS
NABBERS
NEWBORN
NUMBERS
PROBERS
RAYBURN
REDBIRD
RHUBARB
ROBBERS
ROBBERY
RUBBERS
RUBBERY
SAMBARS
SANBORN
SEABIRD
SEABORG
SHUBERT
SOBBERS
SUDBURY
SUNBURN
TIMBERS
TRABERT
WETBARS

•••B••R

ABUBAKR
ANTBEAR
BLABBER
BLUBBER
BUGBEAR
BUMBLER
CLABBER
CLOBBER
CLUBCAR
COBBLER
CRABBER
DABBLER
DOUBTER
DRABBER
FEEBLER
FORBEAR
FUMBLER
GABBIER
GAMBLER
GLIBBER
GOBBLER
GRABBER
HARBOUR
HUMBLER
KEEBLER
LOBBYER
MAXBAER
MUMBLER
NIBBLER
NIEBUHR
NIMBLER
NUBBIER
RAMBLER
SLOBBER
STABLER
TAMBOUR
TEMBLOR
TUBBIER
TUMBLER
WARBLER

••••BR•

ALGEBRA
CALIBRE
CELEBRE
CEREBRA
CULEBRA
MACABRE

••••B•R

BELABOR
BLABBER
BLUBBER
CALIBER
CASHBAR
CHAMBER
CLABBER
CLAMBER
CLIMBER
CLOBBER
CRABBER
CROWBAR
DOVEBAR
DRABBER
DRAWBAR
FNUMBER
GLIBBER
GOODBAR
GRABBER
MALABAR
OCTOBER
OPENBAR
PLUMBER
ROLLBAR
SANDBAR
SIDEBAR
SLOBBER
SLUMBER
THURBER
WINEBAR

B•S••••

BASALLY
BASALTS
BASEHIT
BASEMAN
BASEMEN
BASENJI
BASEPAY
BASHFUL
BASHING
BASKETS
BASKING
BASQUES
BASSETS
BASSIST
BASSOON
BASTERS
BASTING
BASTION
BESEECH
BESEEMS
BESIDES
BESIEGE
BESMEAR
BESPEAK
BESPOKE
BESTBOY
BESTIAL
BESTING
BESTIRS
BESTMAN
BESTMEN
BESTOWS
BESTREW
BISCUIT
BISECTS
BISHOPS
BISMUTH
BISQUES
BISTROS
BOSKETS
BOSSIER
BOSSILY
BOSSING
BOSWELL
BUSBIES
BUSBOYS
BUSFARE
BUSHELS
BUSHHOG
BUSHIDO
BUSHIER
BUSHING
BUSHMAN
BUSHMEN
BUSHPIG
BUSIEST
BUSKINS
BUSLINE
BUSSING
BUSSTOP
BUSTARD
BUSTING
BUSTLED
BUSTLES
BUSTOUT
BUSYING

B••S•••

BALSAMS
BANSHEE
BARSOAP
BASSETS
BASSIST
BASSOON
BATSMAN
BATSMEN
BEASTIE
BEASTLY
BEDSIDE
BEESWAX
BEGSOFF
BERSERK
BIASING
BIASSED
BIGSHOT
BLASTED
BLASTER
BLESSED
BLESSES
BLISTER
BLOSSOM
BLUSHED
BLUSHER
BLUSHES
BLUSTER
BOASTED
BOASTER
BOBSLED
BOLSHOI
BOLSTER
BONSOIR
BOOSLER
BOOSTED
BOOSTER
BOOSTUP
BORSCHT
BOSSIER
BOSSILY
BOSSING
BOWSAWS
BOWSOUT
BOXSEAT
BOXSTEP
BRASHER
BRASHLY
BRASSES
BRASSIE
BRESLIN
BRESSON
BRISKER
BRISKET
BRISKLY
BRISTLE
BRISTLY
BRISTOL
BROSNAN
BRUSHED
BRUSHES
BRUSHUP
BRUSQUE
BUGSOFF
BUGSOUT
BUMSOUT
BURSARS
BURSTYN
BUSSING
BUSSTOP
BUYSOFF
BUYSOUT

B•••S••

BABASSU
BABYSAT
BABYSIT
BACKSIN
BACKSUP
BALLSUP
BANDSAW
BANGSUP
BANKSON

BARKSAT
BATISTA
BATISTE
BEADSUP
BEAMSUP
BEARSON
BEARSUP
BEATSIT
BEATSUP
BEEFSUP
BEHESTS
BELUSHI
BEMUSED
BEMUSES
BENISON
BENTSEN
BERGSON
BERNSEN
BIASSED
BINDSUP
BLESSED
BLESSES
BLOSSOM
BLOUSED
BLOUSES
BLOUSON
BLOWSIN
BLOWSIT
BLOWSUP
BLUESKY
BOLUSES
BONESUP
BONUSES
BOOTSUP
BOXESIN
BOXESUP
BRAISED
BRAISES
BRANSON
BRASSES
BRASSIE
BREASTS
BRESSON
BRONSON
BROWSED
BROWSER
BROWSES
BRUISED
BRUISER
BRUISES
BUCKSAW
BUCKSUP
BUMPSUP
BUOYSUP
BURNSUP
BUTTSIN
BUZZSAW

B••••S•

BABASSU
BABYISH
BADNESS
BALDEST
BALLAST
BAPTISM
BAPTIST
BASSIST
BEARISH
BECAUSE
BEDPOST
BEDREST
BELFAST
BEQUEST
BERNESE
BIGGEST
BIGNESS
BIOMASS
BLEMISH
BOLDEST
BOMBAST
BONEASH
BONIEST
BOOKISH
BOORISH
BRAVEST
BRITISH
BRUTISH
BULLISH
BULRUSH
BURGESS
BURMESE
BURNISH
BUSIEST
BYANOSE

B•••••S

BABBLES
BABOONS
BACCHUS
BACKERS
BACKUPS
BADDIES
BADEGGS
BADGERS
BADGUYS
BADNESS
BAFFLES
BAGFULS
BAGGERS
BAGGIES
BAHAMAS
BAILEES
BAILERS
BAILEYS
BAILORS
BALBOAS
BALEENS
BALKANS
BALLADS
BALLETS
BALLOTS
BALSAMS
BAMBOOS
BANANAS
BANDIES
BANDITS
BANGLES
BANJOES
BANKERS
BANNERS
BANTAMS
BANTERS
BANYANS
BAOBABS
BARBELS
BARBERS
BARENTS
BARHOPS
BARKERS
BARLEYS
BARNEYS
BARONGS
BARRELS
BARRENS
BARRIOS
BARROWS
BARTERS
BARYONS
BASALTS
BASKETS
BASQUES
BASSETS
BASTERS
BATBOYS
BATCHES
BATHERS
BATTENS
BATTERS
BATTLES
BAUBLES
BAWLERS
BAZAARS
BEACHES
BEACONS
BEADLES
BEAGLES
BEAKERS
BEANIES
BEARERS
BEATERS
BEATLES
BEAVERS
BECALMS
BECKONS
BECOMES
BEDAUBS
BEDBUGS
BEDECKS
BEECHES
BEEGEES
BEEPERS
BEETLES
BEFALLS
BEFOULS
BEGGARS
BEHAVES
BEHESTS
BEHOLDS
BELCHES
BELDAMS
BELIEFS
BELLIES
BELLOWS
BELONGS
BEMIRES
BEMOANS
BEMUSES
BENCHES
BENDERS
BENGALS
BENUMBS
BERATES
BERBERS
BERRIES
BESEEMS
BESIDES
BESTIRS
BESTOWS
BETAKES
BETHELS
BETIDES
BETIMES
BETRAYS
BETTERS
BETTORS
BEWAILS
BEZIERS
BIALIES
BICKERS
BIDDERS
BIDDIES
BIGBOYS
BIGEYES
BIGGERS
BIGGIES
BIGGUNS
BIGNESS
BIGTOES
BIGTOPS
BIGWIGS
BIKINIS
BILBOES
BILIOUS
BILLETS
BILLIES
BILLOWS
BINDERS
BINGOES
BIOMASS
BIONICS
BIRCHES
BIRDERS
BIRDIES
BIREMES
BISECTS
BISHOPS
BISQUES
BISTROS
BITMAPS
BITTERS
BLAZERS
BLAZONS
BLESSES
BLIGHTS
BLITZES
BLONDES
BLOUSES
BLOWERS
BLOWUPS
BLUSHES
BMOVIES
BOATERS
BOBBERS
BOBBIES
BOBBINS
BOBBLES
BOBCATS
BODEGAS
BODICES
BODKINS
BOGGLES
BOILERS
BOLEROS
BOLIDES
BOLUSES
BOMBERS
BONBONS
BONGOES
BONITOS
BONKERS
BONNETS
BONUSES
BOOBIES
BOOBOOS
BOODLES
BOOGIES
BOOHOOS
BOOKIES
BOOMERS
BOONIES
BOOTEES
BOOTIES
BOPPERS
BORATES
BORDERS
BORROWS
BORZOIS
BOSKETS
BOTCHES
BOTHERS
BOTTLES
BOTTOMS
BOUNCES
BOUTROS
BOVINES
BOWFINS
BOWLERS
BOWSAWS
BOWTIES
BOWWOWS
BOWYERS
BOXCARS
BOXFULS
BOXTOPS
BRACERS
BRAHMAS
BRAISES
BRASSES
BRAVOES
BRAYERS
BREASTS
BREATHS
BREEZES
BRETONS
BREVETS
BREWERS
BRIARDS
BRIDALS
BRIDGES
BRIDLES
BRITONS
BROGANS
BROGUES
BROKERS
BRONCOS
BRONZES
BROWSES
BRUISES
BRUNETS
BRUSHES
BUBBLES
BUCKETS
BUCKLES
BUCKOES
BUDDHAS
BUDDIES
BUDGETS
BUDGIES
BUFFERS
BUFFETS
BUGGIES
BUGLERS
BULBOUS
BULBULS
BULGARS
BULLETS
BULLIES
BUMBLES
BUMMERS
BUMPERS
BUNCHES
BUNDLES
BUNGEES
BUNGLES
BUNIONS
BUNKERS
BUNNIES
BURBLES
BURBOTS
BURDENS
BUREAUS
BURGEES
BURGERS
BURGESS
BURGLES
BURGOOS
BURLAPS
BURNERS
BUROAKS
BURROWS
BURSARS
BUSBIES
BUSBOYS
BUSHELS
BUSKINS
BUSTLES
BUTLERS
BUTTERS
BUTTONS
BUYOUTS
BUZZERS
BYGONES
BYLINES
BYPATHS
BYPLAYS
BYROADS
BYTURNS
BYWORDS

•BS••••

ABSALOM
ABSCOND
ABSENCE
ABSENTS
ABSOLUT
ABSOLVE
ABSORBS
ABSTAIN
OBSCENE
OBSCURE
OBSERVE

•B•S•••

ABASHED
ABASHES
ABASING
ABUSERS
ABUSING
ABUSIVE
ABYSMAL
ABYSSES
IBNSAUD

•B••S••

ABYSSES
OBLASTS
OBOISTS
OBTUSER

•B•••S•

ABOLISH
ABREAST
OBELISK
OBVERSE
TBILISI

•B••••S

ABASHES
ABDUCTS
ABJURES
ABLATES
ABLAUTS
ABNAKIS
ABOUNDS
ABRADES
ABSENTS
ABSORBS
ABUSERS
ABYSSES
EBONIES
OBJECTS
OBLASTS
OBLATES
OBLIGES
OBLONGS
OBOISTS
OBTAINS
OBTUNDS
OBVERTS
OBVIOUS

••BS•••

BOBSLED
FOBSOFF
LOBSTER
MOBSTER
RUBSOUT
SUBSETS
SUBSIDE
SUBSIDY
SUBSIST
SUBSOIL
SUBSUME
WEBSITE
WEBSTER

••B•S••

BABASSU
BABYSAT
BABYSIT
CUBISTS
DEBASED
DEBASES
DEBUSSY
EMBASSY
NABISCO
ORBISON
REBASTE
REBUSES
ROBESON
ROBUSTA
TABASCO
TUBISTS

••B••S•

AMBROSE
BABASSU
BABYISH
CABOOSE
DEBUSSY
EMBASSY
GABFEST
NEBBISH
NOBLEST
PUBLISH
RUBBISH
SUBROSA
SUBSIST
TUBAIST
UNBLEST

••B•••S

ALBEDOS
ALBINOS
AMBLERS
AMBRIES
ARBOURS
ARBUTUS
AUBADES
AUBURNS
BABBLES
BABOONS
BOBBERS
BOBBIES
BOBBINS
BOBBLES
BOBCATS
BUBBLES
CABALAS
CABANAS
CABBIES
CABLERS
COBBLES
COBWEBS
CUBBIES
CUBISTS
CYBORGS
DABBLES
DEBARKS
DEBASES
DEBATES
DEBEERS
DEBONES
DEBTORS
DEBUNKS
DIBBLES
DOBBINS
DUBBERS
DUBIOUS
DYBBUKS
EMBANKS
EMBARKS
EMBLEMS
EMBRYOS
FABARES
FABRICS
FIBBERS
FIBRILS
FIBROUS
FIBULAS
GABBERS
GABBLES
GABBROS
GIBBERS
GIBBETS
GIBBONS
GIBBOUS
GIBLETS
GIBLUES
GOBBLES
GOBLETS
GOBLINS
HEBREWS
HOBBIES
HOBBITS
HOBBLES
HOBNOBS
HUBBIES
HUBBUBS
HUBCAPS
HYBRIDS
IMBIBES
IMBRUES
JABBERS
JABIRUS
JOBBERS
JOBHOPS
JOBLOTS
KABUKIS
KIBBLES
KOBOLDS
LABIALS
LABOURS
LABRETS
LIBBERS
LIBIDOS
LIBYANS
LOBBERS
LOBBIES
LUBBERS
MOBCAPS
MOBILES
MRBONES
NABBERS
NEBULAS
NIBBLES
NUBBINS
NUBBLES
NUBIANS
PABLUMS
PEBBLES
POBOXES
PTBOATS
PUBLICS
RABBETS
RABBITS
RABBLES
REBATES
REBINDS
REBOILS
REBOLTS
REBOOTS
REBOZOS
REBUFFS
REBUKES
REBUSES
RIBANDS
RIBBONS
RIBEYES
ROBARDS
ROBBERS
ROBBINS
ROBERTS
ROBROYS
RUBBERS
RUBBLES
RUBRICS
SABINES
SOBBERS
SUBDEBS
SUBDUES
SUBLETS
SUBMITS
SUBORNS
SUBSETS
SUBURBS
SUBWAYS
TABARDS
TABBIES
TABLETS
TUBISTS
UNBENDS
UNBINDS
UNBOLTS
UNBOXES
UPBEATS
WOBBLES

•••BS••

GRABSAT

•••B•S•

AIRBASE
BOMBAST
COMBUST
DUMBEST
FURBISH
MOMBASA
NEBBISH
NUMBEST
OFFBASE
PITBOSS
RUBBISH
SEABASS
TWOBASE
VERBOSE

•••B••S

AIRBAGS
BABBLES
BALBOAS
BAMBOOS
BAOBABS
BARBELS
BARBERS
BATBOYS
BAUBLES
BEDBUGS
BERBERS
BIGBOYS
BILBOES
BOBBERS
BOBBIES
BOBBINS
BOBBLES
BOMBERS
BONBONS
BOOBIES
BOOBOOS
BUBBLES
BULBOUS
BULBULS
BUMBLES
BURBLES
BURBOTS
BUSBIES
BUSBOYS
CABBIES
CAMBERS
CARBONS
CARBOYS
CHABLIS
COBBLES
COMBATS
COMBERS
CORBELS
COWBOYS
CUBBIES
CYMBALS
DABBLES
DAUBERS
DAYBEDS
DERBIES
DIBBLES
DISBARS
DOBBINS
DOUBLES
DUBBERS
DYBBUKS
EDIBLES
ENABLES
FIBBERS
FLYBOYS
FOGBOWS
FOIBLES
FORBIDS
FUMBLES
GABBERS
GABBLES
GABBROS
GAMBITS
GAMBLES
GAMBOLS
GARBLES
GASBAGS
GERBILS
GIBBERS
GIBBETS
GIBBONS
GIBBOUS
GILBLAS
GIMBALS
GOBBLES
GOOBERS
HARBORS
HENBITS
HERBALS
HOBBIES
HOBBITS
HOBBLES
HOMBRES
HOTBEDS
HUBBIES
HUBBUBS
HUMBLES
HUMBUGS
ICEBAGS
ISOBARS
JABBERS
JEEBIES
JERBOAS
JOBBERS
JUMBLES
KIBBLES
KITBAGS
LAMBDAS
LIBBERS
LIMBERS
LOBBERS
LOBBIES
LOWBOYS
LUBBERS
LUMBARS
LUMBERS
MARBLES
MEMBERS
MUMBLES
NABBERS
NIBBLES
NUBBINS
NUBBLES
NUMBATS
NUMBERS
OJIBWAS
OUTBIDS
PAMBIES
PEBBLES
PHOBIAS
PHOBICS
PITBOSS
PROBERS
PUEBLOS
RABBETS
RABBITS
RABBLES
RAMBLES
REDBUDS
REUBENS
RIBBONS
ROBBERS
ROBBINS
RUBBERS
RUBBLES
RUMBLES
SAMBARS
SEABAGS
SEABASS
SEABEDS
SEABEES
SOBBERS
SORBETS
SOWBUGS
STABLES
SYMBOLS
TABBIES
TEABAGS
TIDBITS
TIMBALS
TIMBERS
TIMBRES
TITBITS
TOMBOYS
TREBLES
TUMBLES
TURBANS
TURBOTS
TWOBITS
VERBALS
WAMBLES
WARBLES
WETBARS
WOBBLES
WOMBATS
ZOMBIES

••••B•S

AEROBES
AMOEBAS
ANTIBES
ARROBAS
CARIBES
CASABAS
CELEBES
COLOBUS
DELIBES
ENROBES
FLAMBES
GAZEBOS
GOODBYS
IMBIBES
JUJUBES
MINIBUS
OMNIBUS
PARIBUS
PHOEBES
PHOEBUS
RHOMBUS
RHUMBAS
SCRIBES
STROBES
UNROBES
ZAREBAS

•••••BS

ABSORBS
ADSORBS
ADVERBS
BAOBABS
BEDAUBS
BENUMBS
CHERUBS
COBWEBS
CONFABS
CONJOBS
HOBNOBS
HOTTUBS
HUBBUBS
MADLIBS
MIDRIBS
ODDJOBS
PREFABS
RESORBS
REVERBS
SCARABS
SEALABS
SUBDEBS
SUBURBS

B•T••••

BATBOYS
BATCHED
BATCHES
BATEAUX
BATEMAN
BATHERS
BATHING
BATHMAT
BATHOIL
BATHTUB
BATIKED
BATISTA
BATISTE
BATSMAN
BATSMEN
BATTENS
BATTERS
BATTERY
BATTIER
BATTING
BATTLED
BATTLER
BATTLES
BATWING
BETAKEN
BETAKES
BETAMAX
BETARAY
BETHANY
BETHELS
BETHINK
BETIDED
BETIDES
BETIMES
BETOKEN
BETRAYS
BETROTH
BETTERS
BETTING
BETTORS
BETWEEN
BETWIXT
BITEOFF
BITMAPS
BITPART
BITTERN
BITTERS
BITTIER
BITTING
BITUMEN
BOTCHED

BOTCHES
BOTHERS
BOTHNIA
BOTTLED
BOTTLER
BOTTLES
BOTTOMS
BUTCHER
BUTLERS
BUTTERS
BUTTERY
BUTTING
BUTTONS
BUTTOUT
BUTTSIN
BYTHEBY
BYTURNS

B••T•••
BAITING
BANTAMS
BANTERS
BAPTISM
BAPTIST
BAPTIZE
BARTEND
BARTERS
BASTERS
BASTING
BASTION
BATTENS
BATTERS
BATTERY
BATTIER
BATTING
BATTLED
BATTLER
BATTLES
BEATERS
BEATIFY
BEATING
BEATLES
BEATNIK
BEATOUT
BEATRIX
BEATSIT
BEATSUP
BEATTIE
BEDTIME
BEETLES
BEETREE
BELTANE
BELTING
BELTWAY
BENTHAM
BENTLEY
BENTSEN
BERTHED
BERTOLT
BESTBOY
BESTIAL
BESTING
BESTIRS
BESTMAN
BESTMEN
BESTOWS
BESTREW
BETTERS
BETTING
BETTORS
BIGTIME
BIGTOES
BIGTOPS
BIRTHED
BISTROS
BITTERN
BITTERS
BITTIER
BITTING
BLATANT
BLATHER
BLATTED
BLITHER
BLITZED
BLITZEN
BLITZES
BLOTCHY
BLOTOUT
BLOTTED
BLOTTER
BOATERS
BOATING
BOATMAN
BOATMEN
BOBTAIL
BOITANO
BOLTING
BOOTEES
BOOTIES
BOOTING
BOOTLEG
BOOTOUT
BOOTSUP
BOTTLED
BOTTLER
BOTTLES
BOTTOMS
BOUTROS
BOWTIES
BOXTOPS
BRETONS
BRITAIN
BRITISH
BRITONS
BRITTEN
BRITTLE
BRITTON
BROTHER
BRUTISH
BUNTING
BUSTARD
BUSTING
BUSTLED
BUSTLES
BUSTOUT
BUTTERS
BUTTERY
BUTTING
BUTTONS
BUTTOUT
BUTTSIN
BUYTIME

B•••T••
BABETTE
BALATON
BARETTA
BATHTUB
BEASTIE
BEASTLY
BEATTIE
BELATED
BENATAR
BERATED
BERATES
BERETTA
BEWITCH
BIENTOT
BIGOTED
BIGOTRY
BIRETTA
BLASTED
BLASTER
BLATTED
BLEATED
BLISTER
BLOATED
BLOTTED
BLOTTER
BLUNTED
BLUNTER
BLUNTLY
BLURTED
BLUSTER
BOASTED
BOASTER
BOLOTIE
BOLSTER
BONITOS
BOOSTED
BOOSTER
BOOSTUP
BORATES
BOXSTEP
BRAXTON
BREATHE
BREATHS
BREATHY
BRISTLE
BRISTLY
BRISTOL
BRITTEN
BRITTLE
BRITTON
BRUITED
BUILTIN
BUILTON
BUILTUP
BURETTE
BURNTUP
BURSTYN
BUSSTOP
BYPATHS

B••••T•
BABBITT
BABETTE
BALLETS
BALLOTS
BANDITO
BANDITS
BARENTS
BARETTA
BARRETT
BASALTS
BASKETS
BASSETS
BATISTA
BATISTE
BAUXITE
BAYCITY
BECKETT
BEHESTS
BENEATH
BENNETT
BERETTA
BERLITZ
BETROTH
BILLETS
BIRETTA
BISECTS
BISMUTH
BLIGHTS
BOBCATS
BONNETS
BOSKETS
BOUNDTO
BOXKITE
BOYCOTT
BREADTH
BREASTS
BREVETS
BREVITY
BRINGTO
BROMATE
BRUNETS
BUCKETS
BUDGETS
BUFFETS
BUFFETT
BULLETS
BULLITT
BURBOTS
BURETTE
BURNETT
BURRITO
BUYOUTS

B•••••T
BABBITT
BABYSAT
BABYSIT
BACKBIT
BACKLIT
BACKOUT
BAILOUT
BALDEST
BALLAST
BANQUET
BAPTIST
BARKSAT
BARONET
BARRETT
BASEHIT
BASSIST
BATHMAT
BAWLOUT
BAYONET
BEARCAT
BEAROUT
BEATOUT
BEATSIT
BECKETT
BEDPOST
BEDREST
BELFAST
BELMONT
BENEFIT
BENNETT
BEQUEST
BERTOLT
BETWIXT
BIBELOT
BIENTOT
BIGFEET
BIGFOOT
BIGGEST
BIGSHOT
BISCUIT
BITPART
BLANKET
BLATANT
BLERIOT
BLEWOUT
BLINKAT
BLOTOUT
BLOWOUT
BLOWSIT
BODYFAT
BOLDEST
BOMBAST
BONIEST
BOOKLET
BOOTOUT
BOREOUT
BORSCHT
BOUQUET
BOWKNOT
BOWSOUT
BOXSEAT
BOYCOTT
BRACKET
BRAVEST
BRIDGET
BRILLAT
BRIQUET
BRISKET
BROUGHT
BUFFETT
BUGSOUT
BULBLET
BULLITT
BUMSOUT
BUOYANT
BURNETT
BURNOUT
BUSIEST
BUSTOUT
BUTTOUT
BUYSOUT
BYHEART

•BT••••
OBTAINS
OBTRUDE
OBTUNDS
OBTUSER

•B•T•••
ABATING
ABETTED
ABETTOR
ABSTAIN
ABUTTAL
ABUTTED
EBBTIDE

•B••T••
ABETTED
ABETTOR
ABLATED
ABLATES
ABORTED
ABUTTAL
ABUTTED
OBLATES

•B•••T•
ABDUCTS
ABILITY
ABLAUTS
ABSENTS
EBONITE
EBWHITE
OBJECTS
OBLASTS
OBOISTS
OBVERTS
OBVIATE

•B••••T
ABREAST
ABSOLUT

••BT•••
BOBTAIL
DEBTORS
EBBTIDE
SUBTEND
SUBTEXT
SUBTLER
WEBTOED

••B•T••
ARBITER
ARBUTUS
BABETTE
DEBATED
DEBATER
DEBATES
DEBITED
DEBUTED
HABITAT
HABITED
HABITUE
LOBSTER
MOBSTER
ORBITAL
ORBITED
ORBITER
REBATED
REBATES
ROBOTIC
RUBITIN
TABITHA
TIBETAN
WEBSTER

••B••T•
ALBERTA
ALBERTO
BABBITT
BABETTE
BOBCATS
CABLETV
CUBISTS
DUBIETY
GIBBETS
GIBLETS
GOBLETS
HOBBITS
JOBLOTS
KIBBUTZ
LABIATE
LABRETS
LIBERTY
PTBOATS
PUBERTY
RABBETS
RABBITS
RABBITT
REBASTE
REBIRTH
REBOLTS
REBOOTS
ROBERTA
ROBERTO
ROBERTS
ROBUSTA
SABBATH
SUBLETS
SUBMITS
SUBSETS
TABLETS
TUBISTS
UMBERTO
UNBOLTS
UPBEATS
VIBRATE
VIBRATO
WEBSITE

••B•••T
AMBIENT
BABBITT
BABYSAT
BABYSIT
BIBELOT
CABARET
CABINET
GABFEST
HABITAT
JOBHUNT
LABCOAT
NOBLEST
RABBITT
REBUILT
RUBSOUT
SUBJECT
SUBPLOT
SUBSIST
SUBTEXT
SUBUNIT
SUBVERT
TABORET
TUBAIST
UNBLEST
VIBRANT
WEBFEET
WEBFOOT

•••BT••
DOUBTED
DOUBTER
HERBTEA

•••B•T•
BABBITT
BURBOTS
COMBATS
CORBETT
GAMBITS
GIBBETS
HENBITS
HOBBITS
KIBBUTZ
MACBETH
NUMBATS
PROBATE
PROBITY
RABBETS
RABBITS
RABBITT
SABBATH
SORBATE
SORBETS
SUNBATH
TIDBITS
TITBITS
TRIBUTE
TURBOTS
TWOBITS
WOMBATS

•••B••T
AIRBOAT
BABBITT
BOMBAST
BULBLET
CATBOAT
COLBERT
COMBUST
CORBETT
CURBCUT
DASBOOT
DELBERT
DOUBLET
DRIBLET
DUMBEST
EYEBOLT
FANBELT
FILBERT
GILBERT
GOABOUT
GRABSAT
GUNBOAT
HERBERT
HIPBOOT
HOWBEIT
ICEBOAT
INKBLOT
JETBOAT
LAMBENT
LAMBERT
LAPBELT
NUMBEST
OFFBEAT
RABBITT
ROWBOAT
SHUBERT
SKIBOOT
SUNBELT
TRABERT
TUGBOAT

••••B•T
ACROBAT
AEROBAT
BACKBIT
COHABIT
DINGBAT
EXHIBIT
HALIBUT
INHABIT
INHIBIT
INORBIT
NOTABIT
RAREBIT
SHERBET
SIDEBET

•••••BT
INDOUBT
NODOUBT
REDOUBT

BU•••••
BUBBLED
BUBBLES
BUCKETS
BUCKEYE
BUCKING
BUCKLED
BUCKLER
BUCKLES
BUCKLEY
BUCKOES
BUCKRAM
BUCKSAW
BUCKSUP
BUCOLIC
BUDDHAS
BUDDIES
BUDDING
BUDDYUP
BUDGETS
BUDGIES
BUDGING
BUFFALO
BUFFERS
BUFFETS
BUFFETT
BUFFING
BUFFOON
BUGABOO
BUGALOO
BUGBEAR
BUGEYED
BUGGIER
BUGGIES
BUGGING
BUGLERS
BUGLING
BUGSOFF
BUGSOUT
BUILDER
BUILDIN
BUILDON
BUILDUP
BUILTIN
BUILTON
BUILTUP
BULBLET
BULBOUS
BULBULS
BULGARS
BULGHUR
BULGING
BULKIER
BULKING
BULLDOG
BULLETS
BULLIED
BULLIES
BULLING
BULLION
BULLISH
BULLITT
BULLOCK
BULLPEN
BULLRUN
BULRUSH
BULWARK
BUMBLED
BUMBLER
BUMBLES
BUMMERS
BUMMING
BUMPERS
BUMPIER
BUMPING
BUMPKIN
BUMPSUP
BUMSOUT
BUNCHED
BUNCHES
BUNCOED
BUNDLED
BUNDLES
BUNGEES
BUNGING
BUNGLED
BUNGLER
BUNGLES
BUNIONS
BUNKBED
BUNKERS
BUNKING
BUNKOED
BUNNIES
BUNTING
BUOYANT
BUOYING
BUOYSUP
BURBANK
BURBLED
BURBLES
BURBOTS
BURDENS
BURDOCK
BUREAUS
BURETTE
BURGEES
BURGEON
BURGERS
BURGESS
BURGHER
BURGLAR
BURGLED
BURGLES
BURGOOS
BURKINA
BURLAPS
BURLIER
BURLING
BURMESE
BURNERS
BURNETT
BURNING
BURNISH
BURNOUT
BURNSUP
BURNTUP
BUROAKS
BURPGUN
BURPING
BURRITO
BURROWS
BURSARS
BURSTYN
BURYING
BUSBIES
BUSBOYS
BUSFARE
BUSHELS
BUSHHOG
BUSHIDO
BUSHIER
BUSHING
BUSHMAN
BUSHMEN
BUSHPIG
BUSIEST
BUSKINS
BUSLINE
BUSSING
BUSSTOP
BUSTARD
BUSTING
BUSTLED
BUSTLES
BUSTOUT
BUSYING
BUTCHER
BUTLERS
BUTTERS
BUTTERY
BUTTING
BUTTONS
BUTTOUT
BUTTSIN
BUYABLE
BUYOUTS
BUYSOFF
BUYSOUT
BUYTIME
BUZZARD
BUZZERS
BUZZING
BUZZOFF
BUZZSAW

B•U••••
BAUBLES
BAUXITE
BLUBBER
BLUEBOY
BLUEFIN
BLUEFLU
BLUEFOX
BLUEING
BLUEJAY
BLUELAW
BLUESKY
BLUFFED
BLUFFER
BLUFFLY
BLUNDER
BLUNTED
BLUNTER
BLUNTLY
BLURRED
BLURTED
BLUSHED
BLUSHER
BLUSHES
BLUSTER
BOUDOIR
BOULDER
BOUNCED
BOUNCER
BOUNCES
BOUNDED
BOUNDER
BOUNDTO
BOUNDUP
BOUQUET
BOURBON
BOURREE
BOUTROS
BRUBECK
BRUEGEL
BRUISED
BRUISER
BRUISES
BRUITED
BRUNETS
BRUSHED
BRUSHES
BRUSHUP
BRUSQUE
BRUTISH

B••U•••
BEGUILE
BEGUINE
BELUSHI
BEMUSED
BEMUSES
BENUMBS
BEQUEST
BITUMEN
BLOUSED
BLOUSES
BLOUSON
BOLUSES
BONUSES
BROUGHT
BYTURNS

B•••U••
BACKUPS
BADGUYS
BAGFULS
BANQUET
BARBUDA
BASQUES
BECAUSE
BEDAUBS
BEDBUGS
BEDOUIN
BEFOULS
BEOWULF
BERMUDA
BIGGUNS
BISCUIT
BISMUTH
BISQUES
BIVOUAC
BLOWUPS
BOROUGH
BOUQUET
BOXFULS
BRAVURA
BRIQUET
BROGUES
BULBULS
BULRUSH
BUYOUTS

B••••U•
BACCHUS
BACKOUT
BACKRUB
BACKSUP
BAILOUT
BALEFUL
BALFOUR
BALLSUP
BANEFUL
BANGSUP
BAROQUE
BASHFUL
BATEAUX
BATHTUB
BAWLOUT
BEADSUP
BEAMSUP
BEARHUG
BEAROUT
BEARSUP
BEATOUT
BEATSUP
BECLOUD
BEEFSUP
BELAKUN
BELGIUM
BELLYUP
BEZIQUE
BILIOUS
BINDSUP
BLEWOUT
BLOTOUT
BLOWGUN
BLOWNUP
BLOWOUT
BLOWSUP
BONEDUP
BONESUP
BONJOUR
BOOSTUP
BOOTOUT
BOOTSUP
BOREOUT
BORNEUP
BOUNDUP
BOWLFUL
BOWSOUT
BOXEDUP
BOXESUP
BRACEUP
BREAKUP
BRIMFUL
BRINGUP
BROKEUP
BRUSHUP
BRUSQUE
BUCKSUP
BUDDYUP
BUGSOUT
BUILDUP
BUILTUP
BULBOUS
BULGHUR
BULLRUN
BUMPSUP
BUMSOUT
BUOYSUP
BUREAUS
BURNOUT
BURNSUP
BURNTUP
BURPGUN
BUSTOUT
BUTTOUT
BUYSOUT

B•••••U
BABASSU
BLUEFLU

•BU••••
ABUBAKR
ABUSERS
ABUSING
ABUSIVE
ABUTTAL
ABUTTED

•B•U•••
ABDUCTS
ABJURED
ABJURES
ABOUNDS
OBTUNDS
OBTUSER

•B••U••
ABLAUTS

OBSCURE
OBTRUDE

•B•••U•
ABSOLUT
IBNSAUD
OBLIQUE
OBLOQUY
OBVIOUS

••BU•••
ALBUMEN
ALBUMIN
ARBUTUS
AUBURNS
DEBUNKS
DEBUSSY
DEBUTED
DUBUQUE
FIBULAE
FIBULAS
IMBUING
KABUKIS
NEBULAE
NEBULAR
NEBULAS
PABULUM
REBUFFS
REBUILD
REBUILT
REBUKED
REBUKES
REBUSES
ROBUSTA
SUBUNIT
SUBURBS
TABULAR
TUBULAR
ZEBULON

••B•U••
ARBOURS
DEBAUCH
DEBOUCH
DYBBUKS
GIBLUES
HUBBUBS
IMBRUED
IMBRUES
INBOUND
JOBHUNT
KIBBUTZ
LABOURS
PABLUMS
REBOUND
SUBDUED
SUBDUER
SUBDUES
SUBSUME
UNBOUND

••B••U•
ARBUTUS
DUBIOUS
DUBUQUE
FIBROUS
GIBBOUS
HABITUE
JABIRUS
PABULUM
RUBSOUT

••B•••U
BABASSU
TABLEAU

•••BU••
ASHBURY
BARBUDA
BEDBUGS
BULBULS
CADBURY
CLIBURN
COGBURN
COMBUST
DIMBULB
DYBBUKS
GLOBULE
HAMBURG
HEPBURN
HOMBURG
HUBBUBS
HUMBUGS
KIBBUTZ
NIEBUHR
PITBULL
RAYBURN
REDBUDS
ROEBUCK
SAWBUCK
SOWBUGS
SUDBURY
SUNBURN
TRIBUNE
TRIBUTE

•••B•U•
AMIBLUE
BULBOUS
CAMBIUM
CURBCUT
GIBBOUS
GOABOUT
HARBOUR
ICEBLUE
NIOBIUM
RIMBAUD
SKYBLUE
TAMBOUR
TERBIUM

•••B••U
DOUBLEU
HOFBRAU
LAMBEAU
RAMBEAU

••••BU•
COLOBUS
FIREBUG
GOLDBUG
HALIBUT
JUNEBUG
LADYBUG
LOVEBUG
MINIBUS
OMNIBUS
OVERBUY
PARIBUS
PHOEBUS
PILLBUG
RHOMBUS
ROSEBUD
SCRUBUP

••••B•U
CARIBOU
MARABOU

B•V••••
BAVARIA
BEVELED
BEVERLY
BIVALVE
BIVOUAC
BOVINES

B••V•••
BEAVERS
BMOVIES
BOBVILA
BRAVADO
BRAVELY
BRAVERY
BRAVEST
BRAVING
BRAVOES
BRAVURA
BREVETS
BREVITY

B•••V••
BEDEVIL
BEHAVED
BEHAVES
BELOVED
BILEVEL
BOLIVAR
BOLIVIA

B••••V•
BAKLAVA
BEEHIVE
BEHOOVE
BELIEVE
BEREAVE
BIVALVE
BONJOVI

•BV••••
OBVERSE
OBVERTS
OBVIATE
OBVIOUS

•B•••V•
ABSOLVE
ABUSIVE
OBSERVE

••BV•••
BOBVILA
SUBVERT

••B•••V
CABLETV
NABOKOV

B•W••••
BAWDIER
BAWDILY
BAWLERS
BAWLING
BAWLOUT
BEWAILS
BEWITCH
BOWDLER
BOWERED
BOWFINS
BOWKNOT
BOWLERS
BOWLFUL
BOWLINE
BOWLING
BOWSAWS
BOWSOUT
BOWTIES
BOWWOWS
BOWYERS
BYWAYOF
BYWORDS

B••W•••
BATWING
BEOWULF
BETWEEN
BETWIXT
BIGWIGS
BLEWOFF
BLEWOUT
BLOWDRY
BLOWERS
BLOWFLY
BLOWGUN
BLOWIER
BLOWING
BLOWNUP
BLOWOFF
BLOWOUT
BLOWSIN
BLOWSIT
BLOWSUP
BLOWUPS
BOSWELL
BOWWOWS
BOXWOOD
BRAWLED
BRAWLER
BREWERS
BREWERY
BREWING
BROWNED
BROWNER
BROWNIE
BROWSED
BROWSER
BROWSES
BULWARK

B•••W••
BALDWIN
BEDEWED
BEESWAX
BELTWAY
BIKEWAY
BOERWAR

B••••W•
BARNOWL
BARROWS
BEDDOWN
BELLOWS
BESTOWS
BILLOWS
BILLOWY
BOGDOWN
BORROWS
BOWSAWS
BOWWOWS
BURROWS

B•••••W
BANDSAW
BEARPAW
BESTREW
BIGELOW
BLUELAW
BUCKSAW
BUZZSAW

•BW••••
EBWHITE

••BW•••
COBWEBS
SUBWAYS

••B•W••
ELBOWED
UNBOWED

••B••W•
HEBREWS
ROBLOWE
RUBDOWN

•••BW••
OJIBWAS
OJIBWAY

•••B•W•
FOGBOWS

•••B••W
EYEBROW
JOEBLOW
LOWBLOW
LOWBROW

••••B•W
DOWNBOW
LONGBOW
RAINBOW

B•X••••
BOXCARS
BOXEDIN
BOXEDUP
BOXESIN
BOXESUP
BOXFULS
BOXKITE
BOXSEAT
BOXSTEP
BOXTOPS
BOXWOOD

B••X•••
BAUXITE
BRAXTON

B••••X•
BETWIXT

B•••••X
BANDBOX
BATEAUX
BEATRIX
BEESWAX
BETAMAX
BLUEFOX
BOOMBOX
BRERFOX
BROADAX

••B•X••
POBOXES
UNBOXED
UNBOXES

••B••X•
SUBTEXT

••••B•X
BANDBOX
BOOMBOX
CALLBOX
CASHBOX
FIREBOX
GEARBOX
JUKEBOX
LOCKBOX
MAILBOX
PILLBOX
POORBOX
POSTBOX
SALTBOX
SANDBOX
SHOEBOX
SOAPBOX
TOOLBOX

BY•••••
BYANDBY
BYANOSE
BYFORCE
BYGONES
BYHEART
BYLINED
BYLINES
BYPATHS
BYPLAYS
BYROADS
BYTHEBY
BYTURNS
BYWAYOF
BYWORDS

B•Y••••
BAYCITY
BAYLEAF
BAYONET
BOYCOTT
BOYDORR
BOYHOOD
BRYNNER
BUYABLE
BUYOUTS
BUYSOFF
BUYSOUT
BUYTIME

B••Y•••
BABYING
BABYISH
BABYLON
BABYSAT
BABYSIT
BANYANS
BARYONS
BELYING
BICYCLE
BODYFAT
BOWYERS
BRAYERS
BRAYING
BUOYANT
BUOYING
BUOYSUP
BURYING
BUSYING

B•••Y••
BELAYED
BELLYUP
BIGEYES
BOGEYED
BUDDYUP
BUGEYED
BYWAYOF

B••••Y•
BADGUYS
BAILEYS
BARLEYS
BARNEYS
BATBOYS
BETRAYS
BIGBOYS
BUCKEYE
BURSTYN
BUSBOYS
BYPLAYS

B•••••Y
BACKBAY
BAGGILY
BALCONY
BALLBOY
BALONEY
BANALLY
BARBARY
BASALLY
BASEPAY
BATTERY
BAWDILY
BAYCITY
BEANERY
BEASTLY
BEATIFY
BELLAMY
BELLBOY
BELTWAY
BENTLEY
BESTBOY
BETARAY
BETHANY
BEVERLY
BIGOTRY
BIKEWAY
BILLOWY
BINDERY
BIOGENY
BIOLOGY
BLACKLY
BLANDLY
BLANKLY
BLARNEY
BLEAKLY
BLINDLY
BLOTCHY
BLOWDRY
BLOWFLY
BLUEBOY
BLUEJAY
BLUESKY
BLUFFLY
BLUNTLY
BOKCHOY
BONEDRY
BONNILY
BOSSILY
BRADLEY
BRAMBLY
BRASHLY
BRAVELY
BRAVERY
BREATHY
BREVITY
BREWERY
BRIBERY
BRIEFLY
BRISKLY
BRISTLY
BROADLY
BUCKLEY
BUTTERY
BYANDBY
BYTHEBY

•BY••••
ABYSMAL
ABYSSES

•B•Y•••
OBEYING

•B••••Y
ABIDEBY
ABILITY
OBLOQUY

••BY•••
BABYING
BABYISH
BABYLON
BABYSAT
BABYSIT
LIBYANS
RUBYDEE

••B•Y••
EMBRYOS
LOBBYER
RIBEYES

••B••Y•
ROBROYS
SUBWAYS

••B•••Y
DEBAKEY
DEBUSSY
DUBARRY
DUBIETY
EMBASSY
LIBERTY
LIBRARY
PUBERTY
ROBBERY
RUBBERY
SOBERLY
SUBSIDY

•••BY••
LOBBYER

•••B•Y•
BATBOYS
BIGBOYS
BUSBOYS
CARBOYS
COWBOYS
FLYBOYS
LOWBOYS
TOMBOYS

•••B••Y
ANYBODY
ASHBURY
BARBARY
BRIBERY
CADBURY
CRYBABY
OJIBWAY
PEABODY
PROBITY
ROBBERY
RUBBERY
STUBBLY
SUDBURY
TARBABY

••••BY•
GOODBYE
GOODBYS

••••B•Y
AFFABLY
AMIABLY
AUDIBLY
BACKBAY
BALLBOY
BELLBOY
BESTBOY
BLUEBOY
BRAMBLY
CAPABLY
COPYBOY
CRUMBLY
DISOBEY
DURABLY
EQUABLY
HAUTBOY
HIGHBOY
IGNOBLY
LEGIBLY
MUTABLY
NEWSBOY
NOTABLY
OVERBUY
PAGEBOY
PLAYBOY
PLIABLY
PLOWBOY
POORBOY
SCRUBBY
SHRUBBY
SICKBAY
SIZABLY
STUBBLY
TENABLY
TREMBLY
VISIBLY
VOLUBLY

•••••BY
ABIDEBY
BYANDBY
BYTHEBY
COMESBY
CRYBABY
DROPSBY
GOINGBY
HORNSBY
HUSHABY
LAZENBY
LULLABY
MORESBY
SCRUBBY
SHRUBBY
STANDBY
STOODBY
SWEARBY
SWINGBY
SWOREBY
TARBABY
THEREBY
WALLABY
WHEREBY

B•Z••••
BAZAARS
BAZOOKA
BEZIERS
BEZIQUE
BIZARRE
BUZZARD
BUZZERS
BUZZING
BUZZOFF
BUZZSAW

B••Z•••
BENZENE
BLAZERS
BLAZING
BLAZONS
BORZOIS
BRAZIER
BRAZING
BUZZARD
BUZZERS
BUZZING
BUZZOFF
BUZZSAW

B•••Z••
BEDIZEN
BENAZIR
BLITZED
BLITZEN
BLITZES
BREEZED
BREEZES
BRONZED
BRONZES

B••••Z•
BAPTIZE
BONANZA

B•••••Z
BERLIOZ
BERLITZ

•B•••Z•
OBELIZE

••BZ•••
SUBZERO

••B•Z••
REBOZOS

••B•••Z
ALBENIZ
KIBBUTZ
KOBLENZ

•••B•Z•
ZAMBEZI

•••B••Z
KIBBUTZ
LEIBNIZ

••••B•Z
SHOWBIZ

CA•••••
CABALAS
CABANAS
CABARET
CABBAGE
CABBIES
CABINET
CABLERS
CABLETV
CABLING
CABOOSE
CACHETS
CACHING
CACHOUS
CACKLED
CACKLER
CACKLES
CADBURY
CADDIED
CADDIES
CADDOAN
CADENCE
CADENZA
CADETTE
CADGERS
CADGING
CADMIUM
CADUCEI
CAESARS
CAESURA
CAFTANS
CAGIEST
CAHIERS
CAHOOTS
CAIMANS
CAIQUES
CAISSON
CAJOLED
CAJOLER
CAJOLES
CAKEMIX
CALCIFY
CALCITE
CALCIUM
CALDERA
CALDRON
CALENDS
CALGARY
CALHOUN
CALIBAN
CALIBER
CALIBRE
CALICOS
CALIPER
CALIPHS
CALKING
CALKINS
CALLBOX
CALLERS
CALLFOR
CALLING
CALLINS
CALLOFF
CALLOUS
CALLOUT
CALLSIN
CALLSON
CALLSUP
CALMEST
CALMING
CALOMEL
CALORIC
CALORIE
CALPACS
CALTECH
CALUMET
CALUMNY
CALVARY
CALVERT
CALVING
CALYCES
CALYPSO
CALYXES
CALZONE
CAMBERS
CAMBIUM
CAMBRIC
CAMELIA
CAMELOT
CAMEOED
CAMEOFF
CAMEOUT
CAMERAS
CAMERON
CAMILLE
CAMISES
CAMPARI
CAMPERS
CAMPHOR
CAMPIER
CAMPING
CAMPION
CAMPOUT
CANAPES
CANARDS
CANASTA
CANCANS
CANCELS
CANDELA
CANDICE
CANDIDA
CANDIDE
CANDIDS
CANDIED
CANDIES
CANDLES
CANDOUR
CANINES
CANKERS
CANNERS
CANNERY
CANNIER
CANNILY
CANNING
CANNOLI
CANNONS
CANONIC
CANOPUS
CANSECO
CANTATA
CANTEEN
CANTERS
CANTINA
CANTING
CANTLES
CANTONS
CANTORS
CANVASS
CANYONS
CANZONE
CAPABLE
CAPABLY
CAPAPIE
CAPEANN
CAPECOD
CAPELET
CAPELLA
CAPERED
CAPFULS
CAPGUNS
CAPITAL
CAPITAN
CAPITOL
CAPLESS
CAPLETS
CAPNUTS
CAPPERS
CAPPING
CAPRICE
CAPSHAW
CAPSIZE
CAPSTAN
CAPSULE
CAPTAIN
CAPTION
CAPTIVE
CAPTORS
CAPTURE
CAPULET
CARACAL
CARACAS
CARAFES
CARAMBA
CARAMEL
CARAMIA
CARAVAN
CARAVEL
CARAWAY
CARBIDE
CARBINE
CARBONS
CARBOYS
CARCASS
CARCOAT
CARDERS
CARDING
CARDOZO
CAREENS
CAREERS
CAREFOR
CAREFUL
CARFARE
CARFULS
CARGOES
CARHOPS
CARIBES
CARIBOU
CARINAS
CARIOCA
CARLESS
CARLOAD
CARLSON
CARLTON
CARLYLE
CARMINE
CARNERA
CARNETS
CARNIES
CAROLED

CAROLER
CAROLES
CAROLUS
CAROLYN
CAROMED
CAROTID
CAROUSE
CARPALS
CARPERS
CARPETS
CARPING
CARPOOL
CARPORT
CARRELS
CARRERE
CARRICK
CARRIED
CARRIER
CARRIES
CARRION
CARROLL
CARROTS
CARRYON
CARSEAT
CARTAGE
CARTELS
CARTERS
CARTIER
CARTING
CARTONS
CARTOON
CARVERS
CARVING
CARWASH
CASABAS
CASCADE
CASCARA
CASELAW
CASERNS
CASHBAR
CASHBOX
CASHCOW
CASHEWS
CASHIER
CASHING
CASHOUT
CASINGS
CASINOS
CASPIAN
CASSATT
CASSAVA
CASSIAS
CASSIDY
CASSINI
CASSIUS
CASSOCK
CASTERS
CASTILE
CASTING
CASTLED
CASTLES
CASTOFF
CASTOUT
CASUALS
CATALAN
CATALOG
CATALPA
CATAWBA
CATBIRD
CATBOAT
CATCALL
CATCHER
CATCHES
CATCHON
CATCHUP
CATENAE
CATERED
CATERER
CATFISH
CATHAIR
CATHEAD
CATHODE
CATIONS
CATKINS
CATLIKE
CATNAPS
CATNIPS
CATSCAN
CATSEYE
CATSPAW
CATTAIL
CATTIER
CATTILY
CATTING
CATTISH
CATWALK
CAULKED
CAULKER
CAUSING
CAUSTIC
CAUTION
CAVALRY
CAVEART
CAVEATS
CAVEDIN
CAVEINS
CAVEMAN
CAVEMEN
CAVERNS
CAVESIN
CAVILED
CAVILER
CAVORTS
CAYENNE
CAYUGAS
CAYUSES

C•A••••
CEASING
CHABLIS
CHACHAS
CHAFING
CHAGALL
CHAGRIN
CHAINED
CHAIRED
CHAISES
CHALETS
CHALICE
CHALKED
CHALKUP
CHALLIS
CHAMBER
CHAMFER
CHAMOIS
CHAMPED
CHANCED
CHANCEL
CHANCES
CHANGED
CHANGER
CHANGES
CHANNEL
CHANSON
CHANTED
CHANTER
CHANTEY
CHAOTIC
CHAPATI
CHAPEAU
CHAPELS
CHAPLET
CHAPLIN
CHAPMAN
CHAPMEN
CHAPPED
CHAPTER
CHARADE
CHARGED
CHARGER
CHARGES
CHARIER
CHARILY
CHARIOT
CHARITY
CHARLES
CHARLEY
CHARLIE
CHARMED
CHARMER
CHARMIN
CHARRED
CHARTED
CHARTER
CHASERS
CHASING
CHASSES
CHASSIS
CHASTEN
CHASTER
CHATEAU
CHATHAM
CHATSUP
CHATTED
CHATTEL
CHATTER
CHAUCER
CLABBER
CLACKED
CLAIMED
CLAIMER
CLAIROL
CLAMBER
CLAMMED
CLAMMER
CLAMORS
CLAMPED
CLAMSUP
CLANGED
CLANGOR
CLANKED
CLAPPED
CLAPPER
CLAPTON
CLAQUES
CLARETS
CLARICE
CLARIFY
CLARION
CLARITY
CLASHED
CLASHES
CLASPED
CLASSED
CLASSES
CLASSIC
CLATTER
CLAUDIA
CLAUDIO
CLAUSES
CLAVELL
CLAVIER
CLAWERS
CLAWING
CLAYIER
CLAYTON
COACHED
COACHES
COALBIN
COALCAR
COALERS
COALGAS
COALOIL
COALTAR
COARSEN
COARSER
COASTAL
COASTED
COASTER
COATING
COAXERS
COAXIAL
COAXING
CRABBED
CRABBER
CRACKED
CRACKER
CRACKLE
CRACKUP
CRADLED
CRADLES
CRAFTED
CRAFTER
CRAFTSY
CRAMMED
CRAMMER
CRAMPED
CRAMPON
CRANIAL
CRANING
CRANIUM
CRANKED
CRANKUP
CRAPPIE
CRASHED
CRASHES
CRASSER
CRASSLY
CRASSUS
CRATERS
CRATING
CRAVATS
CRAVENS
CRAVERS
CRAVING
CRAWDAD
CRAWLED
CRAWLER
CRAYOLA
CRAYONS
CRAZIER
CRAZIES
CRAZILY
CRAZING
CZARDAS
CZARDOM
CZARINA
CZARISM
CZARIST

C••A•••
CABALAS
CABANAS
CABARET
CANAPES
CANARDS
CANASTA
CAPABLE
CAPABLY
CAPAPIE
CARACAL
CARACAS
CARAFES
CARAMBA
CARAMEL
CARAMIA
CARAVAN
CARAVEL
CARAWAY
CASABAS
CATALAN
CATALOG
CATALPA
CATAWBA
CAVALRY
CBRADIO
CCLAMPS
CELADON
CERAMIC
CEZANNE
CHEAPEN
CHEAPER
CHEAPIE
CHEAPLY
CHEATED
CHEATER
CHIANTI
CICADAE
CICADAS
CITABLE
CITADEL
CLEANED
CLEANER
CLEANLY
CLEANSE
CLEANUP
CLEARED
CLEARER
CLEARLY
CLEARUP
CLEAVED
CLEAVER
CLEAVES
CLEAVON
CLOAKED
COHABIT
CONAKRY
CORAZON
COWARDS
CREAKED
CREAMED
CREAMER
CREASED
CREASES
CREATED
CREATES
CREATOR
CROAKED
CROATIA
CURACAO
CURATES
CURATOR
CUTAWAY

C•••A••
CABBAGE
CAESARS
CAFTANS
CAIMANS
CALGARY
CALPACS
CALVARY
CAMPARI
CANCANS
CANTATA
CANVASS
CAPEANN
CAPTAIN
CARCASS
CARFARE
CARPALS
CARTAGE
CARWASH
CASCADE
CASCARA
CASSATT
CASSAVA
CASUALS
CATCALL
CATHAIR
CATNAPS
CATTAIL
CATWALK
CAVEART
CAVEATS
CELLARS
CEMBALO
CENTAUR
CENTAVO
CEREALS
CERTAIN
CHAGALL
CHAPATI
CHARADE
CHICAGO
CHICANA
CHICANO
CHORALE
CHORALS
CILIATE
CINZANO
CITRATE
CLIMATE
CLIPART
COCKADE
COEVALS
COGNACS
COGNATE
COINAGE
COLGATE
COLLAGE
COLLARD
COLLARS
COLLATE
COMBATS
COMMAND
COMPACT
COMPANY
COMPARE
COMPASS
COMRADE
CONCAVE
CONFABS
CONGAED
CONGAME
CONRACK
CONTACT
CONTAIN
COOLANT
COPLAND
CORDAGE
CORDATE
CORKAGE
CORRALS
CORSAGE
CORSAIR
COSSACK
COSTAIN
COSTARS
COTTAGE
COUGARS
COURAGE
COURANT
COWHAND
CRAVATS
CRETANS
CRUSADE
CRUZADO
CRYBABY
CUEBALL
CUECARD
CUIRASS
CUPCAKE
CUREALL
CURRANT
CURTAIL
CURTAIN
CUSHAWS
CUSTARD
CUTBACK
CUTLASS
CUTRATE
CYMBALS

C••••A•
CABALAS
CABANAS
CADDOAN
CALIBAN
CAMERAS
CAPITAL
CAPITAN
CAPSHAW
CAPSTAN
CARACAL
CARACAS
CARAVAN
CARAWAY
CARCOAT
CARINAS
CARLOAD
CARSEAT
CASABAS
CASELAW
CASHBAR
CASPIAN
CASSIAS
CATALAN
CATBOAT
CATENAE
CATHEAD
CATSCAN
CATSPAW
CAVEMAN
CAYUGAS
CENTRAL
CHACHAS
CHAPEAU
CHAPMAN
CHATEAU
CHATHAM
CHEDDAR
CHEETAH
CHEMLAB
CHILEAN
CHLORAL
CHOCTAW
CHOLLAS
CHUKKAS
CICADAE
CICADAS
CINEMAS
CINEMAX
CLUBCAR
COALCAR
COALGAS
COALTAR
COASTAL
COAXIAL
COCHRAN
COCTEAU
COEQUAL
COLDWAR
COLEMAN
COMESAT
COMICAL
CONCEAL
CONGEAL
CONICAL
CONTRAS
COONCAT
COPYCAT
CORDIAL
CORNEAL
CORNEAS
CORONAE
CORONAS
COWPEAS
CRANIAL
CRAWDAD
CREWMAN
CRIMEAN
CROWBAR
CRUCIAL
CRYSTAL
CULTJAM
CUPOLAS
CURACAO
CUTAWAY
CYNICAL
CZARDAS

C•••••A
CADENZA
CAESURA
CALDERA
CAMELIA
CANASTA
CANDELA
CANDIDA
CANTATA
CANTINA
CAPELLA
CARAMBA
CARAMIA
CARIOCA
CARNERA
CASCARA
CASSAVA
CATALPA
CATAWBA
CECILIA
CEDILLA
CELESTA
CEREBRA
CHELSEA
CHICANA
CHIMERA
CIBORIA
CLAUDIA
COCHLEA
COLONNA
COPPOLA
CORDOBA
CORETTA
COROLLA
CORRIDA
CORSICA
CRAYOLA
CREMONA
CROATIA
CULEBRA
CYNTHIA
CZARINA

•CA••••
ACACIAS
ACADEME
ACADEMY
ACADIAN
ACANTHI
ACARIDS
OCANADA
OCARINA
SCALARS
SCALDED
SCALENE
SCALERS
SCALIER
SCALING
SCALLOP
SCALPED
SCALPEL
SCALPER
SCAMMED
SCAMPED
SCAMPER
SCANDAL
SCANNED
SCANNER
SCANTED
SCANTER
SCANTLY
SCAPULA
SCARABS
SCARCER
SCARERS
SCAREUP
SCARFED
SCARIER
SCARIFY
SCARILY
SCARING
SCARLET
SCARPED
SCARRED
SCARVES
SCATHED
SCATHES
SCATTED
SCATTER

•C•A•••
ACHATES
ACKACKS
ACTABLE
ACTAEON
CCLAMPS
ECLAIRS
ECUADOR
ICEAGES
ICEAXES
ICHABOD
MCCALLS
MCGAVIN
MCMAHON
OCEANIA
OCEANIC
OCEANID
OCEANUS
OCTAGON
OCTANES
OCTANTS
OCTAVES
OCTAVIA
OCTAVOS
SCHATZI
SCRAGGY
SCRAPED
SCRAPER
SCRAPES
SCRAPPY
SCRATCH
SCRAWLS
SCRAWLY
SCRAWNY
WCHANDY

•C••A••
ACCLAIM
ACETATE
ACREAGE
ACTUARY
ACTUATE
ECKHART
ECSTASY
ICEBAGS
ICECAPS
ICELAND
ICEPACK
OCANADA
SCALARS
SCARABS
SCHNAPS
SCREAKS
SCREAMS

•C•••A•
ACACIAS
ACADIAN
ACCRUAL
ACROBAT
ICEBOAT
MCLUHAN
SCANDAL
SCHEMAS
SCHOLAR
SCLERAS

•C••••A
ACEROLA
ECHIDNA
ICEDTEA
OCANADA
OCARINA
OCEANIA
OCTAVIA
SCAPULA
SCHIRRA

••CA•••
ALCAZAR
ARCADES
ARCADIA
BACARDI
BECALMS
BECAUSE
CICADAE
CICADAS
DECADES
DECAGON
DECALOG
DECAMPS
DECANTS
DECAPOD
DECARLO
DECAYED
ENCAGED
ENCAGES
ENCAMPS
ENCASED
ENCASES
ESCAPED
ESCAPEE
ESCAPES
ESCARPS
FACADES
GOCARTS
IDCARDS
INCANTS
JACANAS
JICAMAS
JOCASTA
LECARRE
LOCALES
LOCALLY
LOCATED
LOCATER
LOCATES
LOCATOR
MACABRE
MACADAM
MACAQUE
MCCALLS
NOCANDO
OXCARTS
PICADOR
PICANTE
PICAROS
PICASSO
RECALLS
RECANED
RECANES
RECANTS
RECASTS
RICARDO
SECANTS
UNCAGED
UNCAGES
UNCANNY
UNCASED
UNCASES
VACANCY
VACATED
VACATES
VOCALIC
VOCALLY
YUCATAN

••C•A••
ACCLAIM
ARCHAIC
ARCLAMP
COCKADE
DECLAIM
DECLARE
DECLASS
DICTATE
DOCKAGE
ENCHAIN
ENCHANT
ENCLAVE
EXCLAIM
FACIALS
HECTARE
JACKALS
JACKASS
LACTASE
LACTATE
LUCIANO
MACRAME
MICHAEL
MICMACS
NECTARS
ORCHARD
PACKAGE
PACKARD
PECCANT
PECCARY
PICCARD
PICKAXE
RECHALK
RECLAIM
RECLAME
RICHARD
SOCIALS
SUCRASE
TICTACS
TOCCATA
UNCHAIN
UNCIALS
UNCLASP
UNCRATE
VACCARO
ZACHARY

••C••A•
ACCRUAL
ALCAZAR
ARCHWAY
BACKBAY
BUCKRAM
BUCKSAW
CICADAE
CICADAS
COCHRAN
COCTEAU
DECIMAL
ESCHEAT
FACTUAL
HACKMAN
HACKSAW
HICKMAN
JACANAS
JACKDAW
JACKTAR
JICAMAS
JOCULAR
LACTEAL
LACUNAE
LACUNAL
LACUNAS
MACADAM
MACGRAW
MACULAE
MRCLEAN
NICOLAS
NUCLEAR
PACECAR
PACKRAT
PECKSAT
PICKSAT
RACECAR
RACEWAY
RECITAL
RECLEAN
RICERAT
RICHMAN
SECULAR
SICHUAN
SICKBAY
SICKPAY
TUCHMAN
UNCLEAN
UNCLEAR
UNCLOAK
VICTUAL
VICUNAS
YUCATAN

••C•••A
ARCADIA
CECILIA
COCHLEA
ENCOMIA
FUCHSIA
IACOCCA
JOCASTA
KACHINA
MACHINA
NICOSIA
OSCEOLA
RICKSHA
RICOTTA
TOCCATA
WICHITA

•••CA••
ASHCANS
ATACAMA
AVOCADO
BOBCATS
BOXCARS
BROCADE
CANCANS
CARCASS
CASCADE
CASCARA
CATCALL
CHICAGO
CHICANA
CHICANO
CONCAVE
CUECARD
CUPCAKE
DAYCAMP
DAYCARE
DESCANT
DISCARD
DOGCART
EDUCATE
EGGCASE
FATCATS
FLYCAST
GASCAPS
HEPCATS
HOECAKE
HOTCAKE
HOTCAPS

HOTCARS
HUBCAPS
ICECAPS
INSCAPE
KEYCARD
LASCALA
LASCAUX
MADCAPS
MASCARA
MESCALS
MISCALL
MISCAST
MOBCAPS
MUSCATS
NESCAFE
OILCAKE
OILCANS
OUTCAST
PANCAKE
PAYCASH
PECCANT
PECCARY
PERCALE
PICCARD
PLACARD
PLACATE
PRECAST
RASCALS
REDCAPS
RESCALE
REXCATS
RIBCAGE
SARCASM
SKYCAPS
SNOCATS
TEACAKE
TEACART
TINCANS
TOCCATA
TOECAPS
TOMCATS
TOSCALE
TOUCANS
TOWCARS
TROCARS
TUSCANY
UPSCALE
VACCARO
VOLCANO
VULCANS

•••C•A•

ACACIAS
AMSCRAY
ASOCIAL
BEECHAM
CARCOAT
CHACHAS
CHOCTAW
CONCEAL
CRUCIAL
DEWCLAW
FASCIAS
FRACTAL
GLACIAL
GOTCHAS
GRACIAS
GRECIAN
KETCHAM
KWACHAS
LABCOAT
MARCEAU
OLDCHAP
PANCHAX
PASCHAL
PEACOAT
PINCHAS
REDCOAT
SHECRAB
SPECIAL
SURCOAT
TOPCOAT
TRUCIAL

•••C••A

ATACAMA
CASCARA
CHICANA
DRACHMA
DRACULA
ELECTRA
INOCULA
LASCALA
MASCARA
PLECTRA
QUECHUA
SPECTRA
TOCCATA
TRACHEA
VISCERA

••••CA•

AFRICAN
ALPACAS
ARNICAS
AZTECAN
BEARCAT
BIFOCAL
CARACAL
CARACAS
CATSCAN
CLUBCAR
COALCAR
COMICAL
CONICAL
COONCAT
COPYCAT
CURACAO
CYNICAL
ETHICAL
FLATCAR
HANDCAR
HELICAL
HELLCAT
INKYCAP
ITHACAN
KNEECAP
LEXICAL
LOGICAL
LYRICAL
MAGICAL
MANXCAT
MARACAS
MEDICAL
MEXICAN
MINICAM
MOHICAN
MUSICAL
OPTICAL
PACECAR
PADUCAH
PELICAN
PEMICAN
POLECAT
RACECAR
RADICAL
SENECAS
SIDECAR
SILICAS
SLOTCAR
SNOWCAP
STOICAL
TAXICAB
TOPICAL
TRAMCAR
TYPICAL
VATICAN
WILDCAT

••••C•A

FELICIA
FELUCCA
IACOCCA
INDICIA
MALACCA
PANACEA
REBECCA
STLUCIA

•••••CA

AMERICA
AVIANCA
CARIOCA
CORSICA
EROTICA
EXOTICA
FELUCCA
FORMICA
IACOCCA
JAMAICA
JESSICA
MAJORCA
MALACCA
MINORCA
REBECCA
REPLICA
TAPIOCA

CB•••••

CBRADIO

C•B••••

CABALAS
CABANAS
CABARET
CABBAGE
CABBIES
CABINET
CABLERS
CABLETV
CABLING
CABOOSE
CIBORIA
COBBLED
COBBLER
COBBLES
COBWEBS
CUBBIES
CUBICLE
CUBISTS
CYBORGS

C••B•••

CABBAGE
CABBIES
CADBURY
CAMBERS
CAMBIUM
CAMBRIC
CARBIDE
CARBINE
CARBONS
CARBOYS
CATBIRD
CATBOAT
CEMBALO
CHABLIS
CLABBER
CLIBURN
CLOBBER
CLUBBED
CLUBCAR
COBBLED
COBBLER
COBBLES
COGBURN
COLBERT
COMBATS
COMBERS
COMBINE
COMBING
COMBUST
CONBRIO
CORBELS
CORBETT
COWBELL
COWBIRD
COWBOYS
CRABBED
CRABBER
CRIBBED
CRYBABY
CUBBIES
CUEBALL
CUIBONO
CURBCUT
CURBING
CUTBACK
CYMBALS

C•••B••

CALIBAN
CALIBER
CALIBRE
CALLBOX
CAPABLE
CAPABLY
CARIBES
CARIBOU
CASABAS
CASHBAR
CASHBOX
CELEBES
CELEBRE
CEREBRA
CHAMBER
CITABLE
CLABBER
CLAMBER
CLIMBED
CLIMBER
CLOBBER
CLUBBED
COALBIN
COHABIT
COLOBUS
COPYBOY
CRABBED
CRABBER
CRIBBED
CROWBAR
CRUMBLE
CRUMBLY
CULEBRA

C••••B•

CARAMBA
CATAWBA
CHERUBS
COBWEBS
COLUMBO
COMESBY
CONFABS
CONJOBS
CORDOBA
CRYBABY

C•••••B

CHEMLAB
CORNCOB
COULOMB
COXCOMB

•C•B•••

ICEBAGS
ICEBERG
ICEBLUE
ICEBOAT

•C••B••

ACERBIC
ACROBAT
ACTABLE
ICHABOD
OCTOBER
SCRIBES
SCRUBBY
SCRUBUP

•C•••B•

ICECUBE
SCARABS
SCRUBBY

••CB•••

MACBETH

••C•B••

BACKBAY
BACKBIT
DECIBEL
JACOBIN
LOCKBOX
MACABRE
SICKBAY

••C••B•

ASCRIBE
MICROBE

••C•••B

BACKRUB
SUCCUMB

•••C•B•

ICECUBE
PLACEBO

•••C••B

COXCOMB
KEYCLUB
SHECRAB
SUCCUMB

••••C•B

CORNCOB
LIONCUB
TAXICAB

CC•••••

CCLAMPS

C•C••••

CACHETS
CACHING
CACHOUS
CACKLED
CACKLER
CACKLES
CECILIA
CICADAE
CICADAS
COCHERE
COCHISE
COCHLEA
COCHRAN
COCKADE
COCKIER
COCKILY
COCKING
COCKLES
COCKNEY
COCKPIT
COCONUT
COCOONS
COCTEAU
CUCKOOS
CYCLERS
CYCLING
CYCLIST
CYCLONE
CYCLOPS

C••C•••

CALCIFY
CALCITE
CALCIUM
CANCANS
CANCELS
CARCASS
CARCOAT
CASCADE
CASCARA
CATCALL
CATCHER
CATCHES
CATCHON
CATCHUP
CHACHAS
CHECHEN
CHECKED
CHECKER
CHECKIN
CHECKUP
CHICAGO
CHICANA
CHICANO
CHICHEN
CHICKEN
CHICORY
CHOCTAW
CHUCKED
CHUCKLE
CINCHED
CINCHES
CIRCLED
CIRCLES
CIRCLET
CIRCUIT
CIRCUSY
CLACKED
CLICHES
CLICKED
CLOCHES
CLOCKED
CLOCKER
CLOCKIN
CLUCKED
COACHED
COACHES
CONCAVE
CONCEAL
CONCEDE
CONCEIT
CONCEPT
CONCERN
CONCERT
CONCHES
CONCISE
CONCOCT
CONCORD
CONCURS
COUCHED
COUCHES
COXCOMB
CRACKED
CRACKER
CRACKLE
CRACKUP
CRECHES
CRICKED
CRICKET
CROCHET
CRUCIAL
CUECARD
CUPCAKE

C•••C••

CADUCEI
CALICOS
CALYCES
CAPECOD
CARACAL
CARACAS
CASHCOW
CATSCAN
CEVICHE
CHANCED
CHANCEL
CHANCES
CHAUCER
CHOICER
CHOICES
CLUBCAR
COALCAR
CODICES
CODICIL
COERCED
COERCES
COLDCUT
COMICAL
CONICAL
COONCAT
COPYCAT
CORNCOB
COUNCIL
CREWCUT
CRUNCHY
CUBICLE
CURACAO
CURBCUT
CUTICLE
CYNICAL

C••••C•

CADENCE
CALPACS
CALTECH
CANDICE
CANSECO
CAPRICE
CARIOCA
CARRICK
CASSOCK
CELTICS
CHALICE
CLARICE
CLERICS
CLINICS
COGENCY
COGNACS
COLLECT
COMPACT
CONCOCT
CONDUCE
CONDUCT
CONNECT
CONNICK
CONRACK
CONTACT
CONVICT
COPPICE
CORNICE
CORRECT
CORSICA
COSSACK
COWLICK
CREVICE
CRITICS
CUTBACK

C•••••C

CALORIC
CAMBRIC
CANONIC
CAUSTIC
CENTRIC
CERAMIC
CHAOTIC
CHRONIC
CLASSIC
COMEDIC
CRYPTIC

•CC••••

ACCEDED
ACCEDER
ACCEDES
ACCENTS
ACCEPTS
ACCLAIM
ACCORDS
ACCOSTS
ACCOUNT
ACCRETE
ACCRUAL
ACCRUED
ACCRUES
ACCURST
ACCUSED
ACCUSER
ACCUSES
MCCALLS
OCCIPUT
OCCLUDE
OCCULTS
UCCELLO

•C•C•••

ACACIAS
ICECAPS
ICECOLD
ICECUBE
ICICLES

•C••C••

ACKACKS
SCARCER
SCONCES

•C•••C•

ICEPACK
ICEPICK
SCHLOCK
SCIENCE
SCRATCH
SCREECH
SCRUNCH

•C••••C

ACERBIC
ACRYLIC
ACTINIC
OCEANIC

••CC•••

BACCHUS
HICCUPS
JACCUSE
NICCOLO
PECCANT
PECCARY
PICCARD
PICCOLO
PUCCINI
RACCOON
SICCING
SUCCEED
SUCCESS
SUCCORS
SUCCOUR
SUCCUMB
TOCCATA
VACCARO
VACCINE

••C•C••

BICYCLE
DECOCTS
IACOCCA
PACECAR
RACECAR
RECYCLE

••C••C•

IACOCCA
LICENCE
MICMACS
PACKICE
PICNICS
RECENCY
RECHECK
SECRECY
TACTICS
TICTACS
VACANCY

••C•••C

ARCHAIC
ASCETIC
BUCOLIC
LACONIC
NUCLEIC
PACIFIC
VOCALIC

•••CC••

FLACCID
GNOCCHI
REOCCUR
STUCCOS

•••C•C•

CONCOCT
HANCOCK
LEACOCK
PEACOCK
PETCOCK

•••C••C

PSYCHIC

••••CC•

FELUCCA
IACOCCA
MALACCA
MOROCCO
REBECCA
SIROCCO
TOBACCO

C•D••••

CADBURY
CADDIED
CADDIES
CADDOAN
CADENCE
CADENZA
CADETTE
CADGERS
CADGING
CADMIUM
CADUCEI
CEDILLA
CODDLED
CODDLER
CODDLES
CODEINE
CODFISH
CODGERS
CODICES
CODICIL
CUDDLED
CUDDLES
CUDGELS

C••D•••

CADDIED
CADDIES
CADDOAN
CALDERA
CALDRON
CANDELA
CANDICE
CANDIDA
CANDIDE
CANDIDS
CANDIED
CANDIES
CANDLES
CANDOUR
CARDERS
CARDING
CARDOZO
CHEDDAR
CHIDING
CINDERS
CODDLED
CODDLER
CODDLES
COEDITS
COLDCUT
COLDEST
COLDWAR
CONDEMN
CONDIGN
CONDOLE
CONDONE
CONDORS
CONDUCE
CONDUCT
CONDUIT
CORDAGE
CORDATE
CORDELL
CORDERO
CORDIAL
CORDING
CORDITE
CORDOBA
CORDONS
CRADLED
CRADLES
CREDITS
CRUDELY
CRUDEST
CRUDITY
CUDDLED
CUDDLES
CURDING
CURDLED
CURDLES
CUTDOWN

C•••D••

CAVEDIN
CBRADIO
CELADON
CHEDDAR
CHOWDER
CICADAE
CICADAS
CITADEL
CLAUDIA
CLAUDIO
CLOUDED
CLOWDER
CLUEDIN
COMEDIC
COMEDUE
CORNDOG
COULDNT
CRAWDAD
CROWDED
CZARDAS
CZARDOM

C••••D•

CALENDS
CANARDS
CANDIDA
CANDIDE
CANDIDS
CARBIDE
CASCADE
CASSIDY
CATHODE
CHARADE
COCKADE
COLLIDE
COLLODI
COLLUDE
COMMODE
COMRADE
CONCEDE
CONFIDE
CORRIDA
CORRODE
COWARDS
COWHIDE
CRUSADE
CRUZADO
CUSPIDS
CUSTODY

C•••••D

CACKLED
CADDIED
CAJOLED
CAMEOED
CANDIED
CAPECOD
CAPERED
CARLOAD
CAROLED
CAROMED
CAROTID
CARRIED
CASTLED
CATBIRD
CATERED
CATHEAD
CAULKED
CAVILED
CENTRED
CHAINED
CHAIRED
CHALKED
CHAMPED
CHANCED
CHANGED
CHANTED
CHAPPED
CHARGED
CHARMED
CHARRED
CHARTED
CHATTED
CHEATED
CHECKED
CHEEPED
CHEERED
CHEVIED
CHILLED
CHINKED
CHINNED
CHIPPED
CHIRPED
CHOMPED
CHOPPED
CHUCKED
CHUGGED
CHUMMED
CHURNED
CINCHED
CIRCLED
CLACKED
CLAIMED
CLAMMED
CLAMPED
CLANGED
CLANKED
CLAPPED
CLASHED
CLASPED
CLASSED
CLEANED
CLEARED
CLEAVED
CLERKED
CLICKED
CLIMBED
CLINKED
CLIPPED
CLOAKED
CLOCKED
CLOGGED
CLOPPED
CLOTHED
CLOTTED
CLOUDED
CLOUTED
CLOWNED
CLUBBED
CLUCKED
CLUMPED
CLUNKED
COACHED
COASTED
COBBLED
CODDLED
COERCED
COHERED
COLLARD
COLLOID
COLORED
COMMAND
COMMEND
CONCORD
CONGAED
CONREID
CONTEND
COOPTED
COPLAND
CORNFED
COUCHED
COUGHED
COUNTED
COUPLED
COURSED
COURTED
COVERED
COVETED
COWBIRD
COWERED
COWHAND
COWHERD
COZENED
CRABBED
CRACKED
CRADLED
CRAFTED
CRAMMED
CRAMPED
CRANKED
CRASHED
CRAWDAD
CRAWLED
CREAKED

CREAMED
CREASED
CREATED
CREEPED
CRESTED
CRIBBED
CRICKED
CRIMPED
CRINGED
CRINOID
CRISPED
CROAKED
CROOKED
CROONED
CROPPED
CROSSED
CROWDED
CROWNED
CRUISED
CRUSHED
CRUSTED
CUDDLED
CUECARD
CURDLED
CURRIED
CUSTARD

•CD••••
ECDYSES
ECDYSIS

•C•D•••
ACADEME
ACADEMY
ACADIAN
ACEDOUT
ACIDIFY
ACIDITY
ICEDTEA
SCUDDED

•C••D••
ACCEDED
ACCEDER
ACCEDES
ACRIDLY
ACTEDUP
ECHIDNA
ECUADOR
SCALDED
SCANDAL
SCENDED
SCOLDED
SCOLDER
SCUDDED

•C•••D•
ACARIDS
ACCORDS
OCANADA
OCCLUDE
SCHMIDT
SCREEDS
WCHANDY

•C••••D
ACCEDED
ACCRUED
ACCUSED
ICECOLD
ICELAND
ICHABOD
OCEANID
OCTOPOD
SCALDED
SCALPED
SCAMMED
SCAMPED
SCANNED
SCANTED
SCARFED
SCARPED
SCARRED
SCATHED
SCATTED
SCENDED
SCENTED
SCHEMED
SCOFFED
SCOLDED
SCOOPED
SCOOTED
SCORNED
SCOURED
SCOUTED
SCOWLED
SCRAPED
SCREWED
SCUDDED
SCUFFED
SCULLED
SCYTHED

••CD•••
MACDUFF

••C•D••
ACCEDED
ACCEDER
ACCEDES
ARCADES
ARCADIA
CICADAE
CICADAS
DECADES
DECIDED
DECIDES
DECODED
DECODER
DECODES
ENCODED
ENCODER
ENCODES
ESCUDOS
FACADES
INCUDES
JACKDAW
LACEDUP
LUCIDLY
MACADAM
PICADOR
RECEDED
RECEDES
RECODED
RECODES
SECEDED
SECEDER
SECEDES

••C••D•
ACCORDS
ASCENDS
BACARDI
COCKADE
EXCEEDS
EXCLUDE
IDCARDS
INCLUDE
NOCANDO
NUCLIDE
OCCLUDE
ORCHIDS
RECORDS
RICARDO
SECLUDE
SECONDS

••C•••D
ACCEDED
ACCRUED
ACCUSED
BACKEND
BECLOUD
BUCKLED
CACKLED
DECAPOD
DECAYED
DECIDED
DECODED
DECOYED
DECREED
DECRIED
ENCAGED
ENCASED
ENCODED
ESCAPED
EUCHRED
EXCISED
EXCITED
EXCUSED
FACETED
FOCUSED
HECKLED
INCISED
INCITED
LOCATED
ORCHARD
PACKARD
PICCARD
PICKLED
RECANED
RECEDED
RECITED
RECODED
RECUSED
RICHARD
SECEDED
SECURED
SUCCEED
TACKLED
TICKLED
UNCAGED
UNCASED
VACATED
YACHTED

•••C•D•
AVOCADO
BARCODE
BROCADE
CASCADE
CONCEDE
PLACIDO
PRECEDE
ZIPCODE

•••C••D
ABSCOND
BADCOLD
BATCHED
BEACHED
BELCHED
BENCHED
BIRCHED
BLACKED
BLOCKED
BOTCHED
BRICKED
BUNCHED
BUNCOED
CHECKED
CHUCKED
CINCHED
CIRCLED
CLACKED
CLICKED
CLOCKED
CLUCKED
COACHED
CONCORD
COUCHED
CRACKED
CRICKED
CUECARD
DESCEND
DISCARD
DISCOED
DISCORD
DITCHED
EJECTED
ELECTED
ENACTED
ERECTED
ERUCTED
EVICTED
EXACTED
FANCIED
FETCHED
FILCHED
FLACCID
FLECKED
FLICKED
FLOCKED
FROCKED
GLACEED
HATCHED
HITCHED
HUNCHED
ICECOLD
KEYCARD
KNOCKED
LATCHED
LEACHED
LEECHED
LUNCHED
LURCHED
MARCHED
MATCHED
MISCUED
MOOCHED
MULCHED
MULCTED
MUNCHED
MUSCLED
NOTCHED
PARCHED
PATCHED
PEACHED
PERCHED
PICCARD
PINCHED
PITCHED
PLACARD
PLUCKED
POACHED
POUCHED
PRICKED
PROCEED
PSYCHED
PUNCHED
QUACKED
RANCHED
REACHED
REACTED
RESCIND
RESCUED
RIPCORD
ROACHED
SHOCKED
SHUCKED
SLACKED
SLICKED
SMACKED
SNACKED
STACKED
STOCKED
SUCCEED
SYNCHED
TETCHED
TORCHED
TOUCHED
TRACKED
TRICKED
TRUCKED
VOUCHED
WATCHED
WELCHED
WHACKED
WINCHED
WRACKED
WRECKED

••••C•D
ADDUCED
AMERCED
ANTACID
BOUNCED
CAPECOD
CHANCED
COERCED
DEDUCED
DEFACED
EFFACED
ENLACED
ENTICED
EVINCED
FLACCID
FLEECED
GLANCED
INDUCED
JOUNCED
MENACED
NOTICED
NUANCED
PIERCED
POLICED
POUNCED
PRANCED
REDUCED
REFACED
RELACED
SEDUCED
SLUICED
SOURCED
SPLICED
SPRUCED
UNLACED

CE•••••
CEASING
CECILIA
CEDILLA
CEILING
CELADON
CELEBES
CELEBRE
CELESTA
CELESTE
CELLARS
CELLINI
CELLIST
CELSIUS
CELTICS
CEMBALO
CEMENTS
CENSERS
CENSING
CENSORS
CENSURE
CENTAUR
CENTAVO
CENTERS
CENTIME
CENTIMO
CENTRAL
CENTRED
CENTRES
CENTRIC
CENTURY
CEPHEUS
CERAMIC
CEREALS
CEREBRA
CERIPHS
CERTAIN
CERTIFY
CERUMEN
CESSION
CEVICHE
CEZANNE

C•E••••
CAESARS
CAESURA
CHEAPEN
CHEAPER
CHEAPIE
CHEAPLY
CHEATED
CHEATER
CHECHEN
CHECKED
CHECKER
CHECKIN
CHECKUP
CHEDDAR
CHEEPED
CHEERED
CHEERIO
CHEERUP
CHEESES
CHEETAH
CHEETOS
CHEEVER
CHEKHOV
CHELSEA
CHEMISE
CHEMIST
CHEMLAB
CHENIER
CHEQUER
CHEQUES
CHERISH
CHEROOT
CHERUBS
CHERVIL
CHESTER
CHETRUM
CHEVIED
CHEVIES
CHEVIOT
CHEVRES
CHEVRON
CHEWERS
CHEWIER
CHEWING
CHEWOUT
CHEWSUP
CLEANED
CLEANER
CLEANLY
CLEANSE
CLEANUP
CLEARED
CLEARER
CLEARLY
CLEARUP
CLEAVED
CLEAVER
CLEAVES
CLEAVON
CLEMENS
CLEMENT
CLEMSON
CLERICS
CLERKED
COEDITS
COEQUAL
COERCED
COERCES
COEVALS
COEXIST
CREAKED
CREAMED
CREAMER
CREASED
CREASES
CREATED
CREATES
CREATOR
CRECHES
CREDITS
CREEPED
CREEPER
CREEPUP
CREMONA
CRENELS
CREOLES
CREOSOL
CRESSES
CRESTED
CRETANS
CRETINS
CREVICE
CREWCUT
CREWELS
CREWING
CREWMAN
CREWMEN
CUEBALL
CUECARD

C••E•••
CADENCE
CADENZA
CADETTE
CAKEMIX
CALENDS
CAMELIA
CAMELOT
CAMEOED
CAMEOFF
CAMEOUT
CAMERAS
CAMERON
CAPEANN
CAPECOD
CAPELET
CAPELLA
CAPERED
CAREENS
CAREERS
CAREFOR
CAREFUL
CASELAW
CASERNS
CATENAE
CATERED
CATERER
CAVEART
CAVEATS
CAVEDIN
CAVEINS
CAVEMAN
CAVEMEN
CAVERNS
CAVESIN
CAYENNE
CELEBES
CELEBRE
CELESTA
CELESTE
CEMENTS
CEREALS
CEREBRA
CHEEPED
CHEERED
CHEERIO
CHEERUP
CHEESES
CHEETAH
CHEETOS
CHEEVER
CHIEFLY
CINEMAS
CINEMAX
CLIENTS
CLUEDIN
CLUEING
CLUESIN
CODEINE
COGENCY
COHEIRS
COHERED
COHERES
COLEMAN
COLETTE
COMEDIC
COMEDUE
COMEOFF
COMEONS
COMEOUT
COMESAT
COMESBY
COMESIN
COMESON
COMESTO
COMESUP
CORELLI
CORETTA
COTERIE
COVERED
COVERUP
COVETED
COWERED
COZENED
CREEPED
CREEPER
CREEPUP
CROESUS
CRUELER
CRUELLY
CSLEWIS
CULEBRA
CUREALL

C•••E••
CABLERS
CABLETV
CACHETS
CADGERS
CAGIEST
CAHIERS
CALDERA
CALLERS
CALMEST
CALTECH
CALVERT
CAMBERS
CAMPERS
CANCELS
CANDELA
CANKERS
CANNERS
CANNERY
CANSECO
CANTEEN
CANTERS
CAPLESS
CAPLETS
CAPPERS
CARDERS
CAREENS
CAREERS
CARLESS
CARNERA
CARNETS
CARPERS
CARPETS
CARRELS
CARRERE
CARSEAT
CARTELS
CARTERS
CARVERS
CASHEWS
CASTERS
CATHEAD
CATSEYE
CENSERS
CENTERS
CEPHEUS
CHALETS
CHAPEAU
CHAPELS
CHASERS
CHATEAU
CHEWERS
CHILEAN
CHIMERA
CHINESE
CHISELS
CHOKERS
CHOKEUP
CINDERS
CIPHERS
CISTERN
CLARETS
CLAVELL
CLAWERS
CLEMENS
CLEMENT
CLORETS
CLOSEIN
CLOSELY
CLOSEST
CLOSETS
CLOSEUP
CLOVERS
COALERS
COAXERS
COBWEBS
COCHERE
COCTEAU
CODGERS
COFFEES
COFFERS
COINERS
COLBERT
COLDEST
COLLECT
COLLEEN
COLLEGE
COLLETS
COMBERS
COMMEND
COMMENT
COMPEER
COMPELS
COMPETE
CONCEAL
CONCEDE
CONCEIT
CONCEPT
CONCERN
CONCERT
CONDEMN
CONFERS
CONFESS
CONGEAL
CONGERS
CONGEST
CONKERS
CONNECT
CONNERY
CONREID
CONSENT
CONTEMN
CONTEND
CONTENT
CONTEST
CONTEXT
CONVENE
CONVENT
CONVERT
CONVEYS
COOKERS
COOKERY
COOLERS
COOLEST
COOPERS
COPIERS
COPPERS
COPPERY
COPTERS
CORBELS
CORBETT
CORDELL
CORDERO
CORKERS
CORNEAL
CORNEAS
CORNELL
CORNERS
CORNETS
CORRECT
CORSETS
CORTEGE
CORYELL
COSSETS
COTTERS
COULEES
COWBELL
COWHERD
COWPEAS
COYNESS
COZIEST
COZZENS
CRATERS
CRAVENS
CRAVERS
CRENELS
CREWELS
CRIMEAN
CROWERS
CRUDELY
CRUDEST
CUDGELS
CULVERT
CURFEWS
CURLERS
CURLEWS
CURRENT
CURTEST
CURVETS
CUTLERS
CUTLERY
CUTLETS
CUTTERS
CYCLERS
CYGNETS
CYPHERS
CYPRESS

C••••E•
CABARET
CABBIES
CABINET
CACKLED
CACKLER
CACKLES
CADDIED
CADDIES
CADUCEI
CAIQUES
CAJOLED
CAJOLER
CAJOLES
CALIBER
CALIPER
CALOMEL
CALUMET
CALYCES
CALYXES
CAMEOED
CAMISES
CAMPIER
CANAPES
CANDIED
CANDIES
CANDLES
CANINES
CANNIER
CANTEEN
CANTLES
CAPELET
CAPERED
CAPULET
CARAFES
CARAMEL
CARAVEL
CARGOES
CARIBES
CARNIES
CAROLED
CAROLER
CAROLES
CAROMED
CARRIED
CARRIER
CARRIES
CARTIER
CASHIER
CASTLED
CASTLES
CATCHER
CATCHES
CATERED
CATERER
CATTIER
CAULKED
CAULKER
CAVEMEN
CAVILED
CAVILER
CAYUSES
CELEBES
CENTRED
CENTRES
CERUMEN
CHAINED
CHAIRED
CHAISES
CHALKED
CHAMBER
CHAMFER
CHAMPED
CHANCED
CHANCEL
CHANCES
CHANGED
CHANGER
CHANGES
CHANNEL
CHANTED
CHANTER
CHANTEY
CHAPLET
CHAPMEN
CHAPPED
CHAPTER
CHARGED
CHARGER
CHARGES
CHARIER
CHARLES
CHARLEY
CHARMED
CHARMER
CHARRED
CHARTED
CHARTER
CHASSES
CHASTEN
CHASTER
CHATTED
CHATTEL
CHATTER
CHAUCER
CHEAPEN
CHEAPER
CHEATED
CHEATER
CHECHEN
CHECKED
CHECKER
CHEEPED
CHEERED
CHEESES
CHEEVER
CHELSEA
CHENIER
CHEQUER
CHEQUES
CHESTER
CHEVIED
CHEVIES
CHEVRES
CHEWIER
CHICHEN
CHICKEN
CHIGGER
CHILIES
CHILLED
CHILLER
CHIMNEY
CHINKED
CHINNED
CHIPPED
CHIPPER
CHIRPED
CHITTER
CHOICER
CHOICES
CHOMPED
CHOOSER
CHOOSES
CHOPPED
CHOPPER
CHOWDER
CHROMES
CHUCKED
CHUGGED
CHUKKER
CHUMMED
CHUNNEL
CHURNED
CHUTNEY
CINCHED
CINCHES
CIRCLED
CIRCLES
CIRCLET
CIRQUES
CITADEL
CITIZEN
CITROEN
CIVVIES
CLABBER
CLACKED

CLAIMED
CLAIMER
CLAMBER
CLAMMED
CLAMMER
CLAMPED
CLANGED
CLANKED
CLAPPED
CLAPPER
CLAQUES
CLASHED
CLASHES
CLASPED
CLASSED
CLASSES
CLATTER
CLAUSES
CLAVIER
CLAYIER
CLEANED
CLEANER
CLEARED
CLEARER
CLEAVED
CLEAVER
CLEAVES
CLERKED
CLICHES
CLICKED
CLIMBED
CLIMBER
CLINKED
CLINKER
CLIPPED
CLIPPER
CLIQUES
CLOAKED
CLOBBER
CLOCHES
CLOCKED
CLOCKER
CLOGGED
CLOONEY
CLOPPED
CLOQUES
CLOTHED
CLOTHES
CLOTTED
CLOUDED
CLOUTED
CLOWDER
CLOWNED
CLUBBED
CLUCKED
CLUMPED
CLUNKED
CLUNKER
CLUSTER
CLUTTER
CNTOWER
COACHED
COACHES
COARSEN
COARSER
COASTED
COASTER
COBBLED
COBBLER
COBBLES
COCHLEA
COCKIER
COCKLES
COCKNEY
CODDLED
CODDLER
CODDLES
CODICES
COERCED
COERCES
COFFEES
COHERED
COHERES
COLLEEN
COLLIER
COLLIES
COLLYER
COLONEL
COLONES
COLORED
COMFIER
COMFREY
COMPEER
COMPLEX
CONCHES
CONGAED
CONIFER
CONQUER
COOKIES
COOPTED
COOTIES
CORNFED
CORNIER
CORONET
COSINES
COSTNER
COUCHED
COUCHES
COUGHED
COULEES
COULTER
COUNSEL
COUNTED
COUNTER
COUPLED
COUPLES
COUPLET
COURIER
COURSED
COURSER
COURSES
COURTED
COVERED
COVETED
COWERED
COWRIES
COYOTES
COZENED
COZUMEL
CRABBED
CRABBER
CRACKED
CRACKER
CRADLED
CRADLES
CRAFTED
CRAFTER
CRAMMED
CRAMMER
CRAMPED
CRANKED
CRASHED
CRASHES
CRASSER
CRAWLED
CRAWLER
CRAZIER
CRAZIES
CREAKED
CREAMED
CREAMER
CREASED
CREASES
CREATED
CREATES
CRECHES
CREEPED
CREEPER
CREOLES
CRESSES
CRESTED
CREWMEN
CRIBBED
CRICKED
CRICKET
CRIMPED
CRIMPER
CRINGED
CRINGES
CRISPED
CRISPER
CRITTER
CROAKED
CROCHET
CRONIES
CROOKED
CROONED
CROONER
CROPPED
CROPPER
CROQUET
CROSIER
CROSSED
CROSSER
CROSSES
CROWDED
CROWNED
CRUELER
CRUISED
CRUISER
CRUISES
CRULLER
CRUMPET
CRUSHED
CRUSHER
CRUSHES
CRUSTED
CRYOGEN
CUBBIES
CUDDLED
CUDDLES
CURATES
CURDLED
CURDLES
CURLIER
CURRIED
CURRIER
CURRIES
CURTSEY
CURVIER
CUSHIER
CUSSLER

C•••••E

CABBAGE
CABOOSE
CADENCE
CADETTE
CALCITE
CALIBRE
CALORIE
CALZONE
CAMILLE
CANDICE
CANDIDE
CANZONE
CAPABLE
CAPAPIE
CAPRICE
CAPSIZE
CAPSULE
CAPTIVE
CAPTURE
CARBIDE
CARBINE
CARFARE
CARLYLE
CARMINE
CAROUSE
CARRERE
CARTAGE
CASCADE
CASTILE
CATENAE
CATHODE
CATLIKE
CATSEYE
CAYENNE
CELEBRE
CELESTE
CENSURE
CENTIME
CEVICHE
CEZANNE
CHALICE
CHARADE
CHARLIE
CHEAPIE
CHEMISE
CHINESE
CHORALE
CHORINE
CHORTLE
CHUCKLE
CICADAE
CILIATE
CITABLE
CITRATE
CITRINE
CLARICE
CLEANSE
CLIMATE
CLOSURE
CLOTURE
COCHERE
COCHISE
COCKADE
CODEINE
COGNATE
COINAGE
COLETTE
COLGATE
COLLAGE
COLLATE
COLLEGE
COLLIDE
COLLUDE
COLOGNE
COMBINE
COMEDUE
COMIQUE
COMMODE
COMMOVE
COMMUNE
COMMUTE
COMPARE
COMPETE
COMPILE
COMPOSE
COMPOTE
COMPUTE
COMRADE
CONCAVE
CONCEDE
CONCISE
CONDOLE
CONDONE
CONDUCE
CONFIDE
CONFINE
CONFUSE
CONFUTE
CONGAME
CONJURE
CONNIVE
CONNOTE
CONSOLE
CONSUME
CONTUSE
CONVENE
CONVOKE
COPPICE
CORDAGE
CORDATE
CORDITE
CORKAGE
CORNICE
CORONAE
CORRODE
CORSAGE
CORTEGE
COSTUME
COTERIE
COTTAGE
COURAGE
COUTURE
COWHIDE
COWPOKE
CRACKLE
CRAPPIE
CREVICE
CRINKLE
CRUMBLE
CRUMPLE
CRUSADE
CUBICLE
CUISINE
CULOTTE
CULTURE
CUPCAKE
CURSIVE
CUTICLE
CUTRATE
CUTTIME
CYCLONE

•CE•••••

ACEDOUT
ACERBIC
ACEROLA
ACEROSE
ACESOUT
ACETATE
ACETONE
ICEAGES
ICEAXES
ICEBAGS
ICEBERG
ICEBLUE
ICEBOAT
ICECAPS
ICECOLD
ICECUBE
ICEDTEA
ICEFLOE
ICEFREE
ICELAND
ICELESS
ICEMILK
ICEPACK
ICEPICK
ICERINK
ICESHOW
MCENROE
OCEANIA
OCEANIC
OCEANID
OCEANUS
OCELOTS
SCENDED
SCENERY
SCENTED
SCEPTER
SCEPTRE

•C•E•••

ACCEDED
ACCEDER
ACCEDES
ACCENTS
ACCEPTS
ACHENES
ACHERON
ACHESON
ACREAGE
ACTEDUP
ECHELON
SCHEMAS
SCHEMED
SCHEMER
SCHEMES
SCHERZI
SCHERZO
SCIENCE
SCLERAS
SCREAKS
SCREAMS
SCREECH
SCREEDS
SCREENS
SCREWED
SCREWUP
UCCELLO

•C••E••

ACADEME
ACADEMY
ACCRETE
ACHIEST
ACHIEVE
ACTAEON
ACTRESS
ACUTELY
ICEBERG
ICELESS
ICINESS
ICKIEST
MCQUEEN
NCWYETH
SCALENE
SCALERS
SCARERS
SCAREUP
SCENERY
SCHLEPP
SCHLEPS
SCHMEER
SCORERS
SCOTERS
SCREECH
SCREEDS
SCREENS

•C•••E•

ACCEDED
ACCEDER
ACCEDES
ACCRUED
ACCRUES
ACCUSED
ACCUSER
ACCUSES
ACHATES
ACHENES
ACTIVES
ECDYSES
ECTYPES
ICEAGES
ICEAXES
ICEDTEA
ICEFREE
ICICLES
MCQUEEN
OCTANES
OCTAVES
OCTOBER
SCALDED
SCALIER
SCALPED
SCALPEL
SCALPER
SCAMMED
SCAMPED
SCAMPER
SCANNED
SCANNER
SCANTED
SCANTER
SCARCER
SCARFED
SCARIER
SCARLET
SCARPED
SCARRED
SCARVES
SCATHED
SCATHES
SCATTED
SCATTER
SCENDED
SCENTED
SCEPTER
SCHEMED
SCHEMER
SCHEMES
SCHMEER
SCHMOES
SCOFFED
SCOFFER
SCOLDED
SCOLDER
SCONCES
SCOOPED
SCOOPER
SCOOTED
SCOOTER
SCORNED
SCOURED
SCOURER
SCOUTED
SCOUTER
SCOWLED
SCOWLER
SCRAPED
SCRAPER
SCRAPES
SCREWED
SCRIBES
SCRIVEN
SCUDDED
SCUFFED
SCULLED
SCULLER
SCUPPER
SCURVES
SCYTHED
SCYTHES

•C••••E

ACADEME
ACCRETE
ACEROSE
ACETATE
ACETONE
ACHIEVE
ACOLYTE
ACONITE
ACQUIRE
ACREAGE
ACTABLE
ACTUATE
ECLIPSE
ECLOGUE
ICEBLUE
ICECUBE
ICEFLOE
ICEFREE
MCENROE
MCGUIRE
MCSWINE
OCCLUDE
OCTUPLE
SCALENE
SCEPTRE
SCIENCE
SCOTTIE
SCOURGE
SCROOGE
SCRUPLE
SCUFFLE
SCUTTLE

••CE•••

ACCEDED
ACCEDER
ACCEDES
ACCENTS
ACCEPTS
ASCENDS
ASCENTS
ASCETIC
DECEITS
DECEIVE
DOCENTS
EXCEEDS
EXCEPTS
EXCERPT
FACEOFF
FACETED
INCENSE
INCEPTS
LACEDUP
LACESUP
LICENCE
LICENSE
LUCERNE
LYCEUMS
NACELLE
OSCEOLA
PACECAR
RACECAR
RACEMES
RACEWAY
RECEDED
RECEDES
RECEIPT
RECEIVE
RECENCY
RICERAT
SECEDED
SECEDER
SECEDES
UCCELLO
VICEROY

••C•E••

ACCRETE
ALCHEMY
ANCIENT
ARCHERS
ARCHERY
BACKEND
BACKERS
BECKETT
BICKERS
BUCKETS
BUCKEYE
CACHETS
COCHERE
COCTEAU
CYCLERS
DECREED
DECREES
DICIEST
DICKENS
DICKERS
DICKEYS
DOCKERS
DOCKETS
DUCHESS
ESCHEAT
ESCHEWS
ETCHERS
EXCEEDS
EXCRETE
HACKERS
HACKETT
IPCRESS
JACKETS
JOCKEYS
KICKERS
LACIEST
LACKEYS
LACTEAL
LECTERN
LICHENS
LICKETY
LOCKERS
LOCKETS
MACBETH
MACHETE
MICHELE
MOCKERS
MOCKERY
MRCLEAN
NECKERS
NICKELS
NICKERS
NUCLEAR
NUCLEIC
NUCLEON
NUCLEUS
PACKERS
PACKETS
PICKENS
PICKERS
PICKETS
PICKETT
POCKETS
PUCKERS
PUCKETT
RACIEST
RACKETS
RECHECK
RECLEAN
RICHEST
RICKETY
RICKEYS
ROCKERS
ROCKETS
SACHEMS
SACHETS
SACKERS
SECRECY
SECRETE
SECRETS
SICKENS
SICKEST
SOCIETY
SOCKETS
SOCKEYE
SUCCEED
SUCCESS
SUCKERS
TACKERS
TICKERS
TICKETS
TUCKERS
UNCLEAN
UNCLEAR
WICKERS
WICKETS
WYCHELM

••C••E•

ACCEDED
ACCEDER
ACCEDES
ACCRUED
ACCRUES
ACCUSED
ACCUSER
ACCUSES
ALCOVES
ARCADES
ARCHIES
BECOMES
BUCKLED
BUCKLER
BUCKLES
BUCKLEY
BUCKOES
CACKLED
CACKLER
CACKLES
COCHLEA
COCKIER
COCKLES
COCKNEY
DECADES
DECAYED
DECIBEL
DECIDED
DECIDES
DECKLES
DECODED
DECODER
DECODES
DECOYED
DECREED
DECREES
DECRIED
DECRIES
DICKIES
DUCHIES
DUCKIER
ENCAGED
ENCAGES
ENCASED
ENCASES
ENCODED
ENCODER
ENCODES
ENCORES
ESCAPED
ESCAPEE
ESCAPES
EUCHRED
EUCHRES
EXCISED
EXCISES
EXCITED
EXCITES
EXCUSED
EXCUSES
FACADES
FACETED
FICKLER
FICUSES
FOCSLES
FOCUSED
FOCUSES
GECKOES
HACKIES
HACKLES
HACKNEY
HECKLED
HECKLER
HECKLES
INCISED
INCISES
INCITED
INCITER
INCITES
INCOMES
INCUDES
ITCHIER
JACONET
JACQUES
LACQUER
LOCALES
LOCATED
LOCATER
LOCATES
LUCIFER
LUCKIER
MICHAEL
OOCYTES
OSCINES
PICKIER
PICKLED
PICKLES
RACEMES
RACQUET
RECANED
RECANES
RECEDED
RECEDES
RECIPES
RECITED
RECITER
RECITES
RECODED
RECODES
RECOVER
RECUSED
RECUSES
RICHTER
RICKLES
ROCKIER
ROCKIES
SECEDED
SECEDER
SECEDES
SECURED
SECURER
SECURES
SICKLES
SUCCEED
TACKIER
TACKLED
TACKLER
TACKLES
TECHIES
TICKLED
TICKLER
TICKLES
UNCAGED
UNCAGES
UNCASED
UNCASES
UNCOVER
VACATED
VACATES
WACKIER
YACHTED
YUCKIER

••C•••E

ACCRETE
ARCHIVE
ARCSINE
ASCRIBE
BACKHOE
BECAUSE
BICYCLE
BUCKEYE
CICADAE
COCHERE
COCHISE
COCKADE
CYCLONE
DECEIVE
DECLARE
DECLINE
DICTATE
DOCKAGE
DUCTILE
ENCLAVE
ENCLOSE
ESCAPEE
EXCLUDE
EXCRETE
FICTIVE
HECTARE
INCENSE
INCLINE
INCLOSE
INCLUDE
JACCUSE
LACOSTE
LACTASE
LACTATE
LACTOSE
LACUNAE
LECARRE
LECTURE
LICENCE
LICENSE
LUCERNE
LUCILLE
MACABRE
MACAQUE
MACHETE
MACHINE
MACRAME
MACULAE
MICHELE
MICROBE
NACELLE
NECKTIE
NUCLIDE
OCCLUDE
PACKAGE
PACKICE
PICANTE
PICKAXE
PICTURE
RECEIVE
RECHOSE
RECLAME
RECLINE
RECLUSE
RECYCLE
SECLUDE
SECRETE
SOCKEYE
SUCRASE
SUCROSE
TACTILE
UNCLOSE
UNCRATE
UPCLOSE
VACCINE
VACUOLE

•••CE••

AVOCETS
BRACERS
BRACEUP
CANCELS
CONCEAL
CONCEDE
CONCEIT
CONCEPT
CONCERN
CONCERT
DANCERS
DEICERS

DESCEND
DESCENT
DIOCESE
DISCERN
DRYCELL
EPICENE
FAUCETS
FAWCETT
FENCERS
FORCEPS
FORCERS
GLACEED
GROCERS
GROCERY
JAYCEES
JUICERS
JUICEUP
LANCERS
LANCETS
LARCENY
MARCEAU
MARCELS
MINCERS
MIOCENE
NASCENT
OBSCENE
PARCELS
PERCENT
PIECERS
PINCERS
PLACEBO
PLACERS
PRECEDE
PRECEPT
PRICERS
PROCEED
PROCESS
PURCELL
REDCELL
REDCENT
SAUCERS
SINCERE
SLICERS
SORCERY
SPACERS
SPICEUP
SUCCEED
SUCCESS
TERCELS
TERCETS
TRACERS
TRACERY
TRICEPS
VINCENT
VISCERA
WETCELL
WINCERS

•••C•E•

AIRCREW
AITCHES
APACHES
BATCHED
BATCHES
BEACHED
BEACHES
BEECHER
BEECHES
BELCHED
BELCHES
BENCHED
BENCHES
BIRCHED
BIRCHES
BLACKED
BLACKEN
BLACKER
BLOCKED
BLOCKER
BOTCHED
BOTCHES
BRACKEN
BRACKET
BRICKED
BUNCHED
BUNCHES
BUNCOED
BUTCHER
CATCHER
CATCHES
CHECHEN
CHECKED
CHECKER
CHICHEN
CHICKEN
CHUCKED
CINCHED
CINCHES
CIRCLED
CIRCLES
CIRCLET
CLACKED
CLICHES
CLICKED
CLOCHES
CLOCKED
CLOCKER
CLUCKED
COACHED
COACHES
CONCHES
COUCHED
COUCHES
CRACKED
CRACKER
CRECHES
CRICKED
CRICKET
CROCHET
DISCOED
DITCHED
DITCHES
DOGCHEW
DRUCKER
EJECTED
ELECTED
ELECTEE
ENACTED
ERECTED
ERECTER
ERUCTED
EVACUEE
EVICTED
EXACTED
EXACTER
FANCIED
FANCIER
FANCIES
FETCHED
FETCHES
FIACRES
FILCHED
FILCHER
FILCHES
FINCHES
FISCHER
FITCHES
FLECHES
FLECKED
FLICKED
FLICKER
FLOCKED
FROCKED
GAUCHER
GLACEED
GLACIER
GULCHES
HATCHED
HATCHER
HATCHES
HATCHET
HITCHED
HITCHER
HITCHES
HUNCHED
HUNCHES
HUTCHES
ICICLES
JAYCEES
JIMCHEE
JUICIER
JUNCOES
KETCHES
KITCHEN
KNOCKED
KNOCKER
LARCHES
LATCHED
LATCHES
LEACHED
LEACHES
LEECHED
LEECHES
LOACHES
LUNCHED
LUNCHER
LUNCHES
LURCHED
LURCHES
MADCHEN
MARCHED
MARCHEN
MARCHER
MARCHES
MATCHED
MATCHES
MENCKEN
MERCIES
MISCUED
MISCUES
MOOCHED
MOOCHER
MOOCHES
MULCHED
MULCHES
MULCTED
MUNCHED
MUNCHER
MUNCHES
MUSCLED
MUSCLES
NATCHEZ
NOTCHED
NOTCHES
ORACLES
PARCHED
PARCHES
PATCHED
PATCHES
PEACHED
PEACHES
PERCHED
PERCHES
PINCHED
PINCHER
PINCHES
PITCHED
PITCHER
PITCHES
PLACKET
PLUCKED
POACHED
POACHER
POACHES
POOCHES
PORCHES
POUCHED
POUCHES
PRICIER
PRICKED
PROCEED
PSYCHED
PSYCHES
PUNCHED
PUNCHER
PUNCHES
QUACKED
QUICHES
QUICKEN
QUICKER
RANCHED
RANCHER
RANCHES
RATCHET
REACHED
REACHES
REACTED
RESCUED
RESCUER
RESCUES
ROACHED
ROACHES
SATCHEL
SAUCIER
SEICHES
SHOCKED
SHOCKER
SHUCKED
SHUCKER
SLACKED
SLACKEN
SLACKER
SLICKED
SLICKER
SMACKED
SMACKER
SNACKED
SNACKER
SNICKER
SPACIER
SPECIES
SPECTER
SPICIER
STACKED
STICHES
STICKER
STOCKED
SUCCEED
SYNCHED
SYNCHES
TEACHER
TEACHES
TEICHER
TETCHED
THICKEN
THICKER
THICKET
TORCHED
TORCHES
TOUCHED
TOUCHES
TRACHEA
TRACKED
TRACKER
TRICKED
TRICKER
TROCHEE
TROCHES
TRUCKED
TRUCKEE
TRUCKER
UNSCREW
VETCHES
VOUCHED
VOUCHER
VOUCHES
WATCHED
WATCHER
WATCHES
WELCHED
WELCHES
WENCHES
WHACKED
WINCHED
WINCHES
WITCHES
WRACKED
WRECKED
WRECKER
ZILCHES

•••C••E

APOCOPE
ARACHNE
BARCODE
BROCADE
CALCITE
CASCADE
CHUCKLE
CONCAVE
CONCEDE
CONCISE
CRACKLE
CUPCAKE
DAYCARE
DIOCESE
EDUCATE
EGGCASE
ELECTEE
EPICENE
EPICURE
EVACUEE
EXECUTE
FRECKLE
FRICKIE
GLUCOSE
GRACILE
GRACKLE
HERCULE
HOECAKE
HOTCAKE
HOWCOME
ICECUBE
INSCAPE
JACCUSE
JIMCHEE
KNUCKLE
MIOCENE
NESCAFE
OBSCENE
OBSCURE
OILCAKE
OUTCOME
PANCAKE
PERCALE
PISCINE
PLACATE
PORCINE
PRECEDE
PRECISE
PRICKLE
PROCURE
QUICKIE
RESCALE
RIBCAGE
RITCHIE
SHACKLE
SINCERE
SNOCONE
SPACKLE
SPECKLE
SPECTRE
TEACAKE
TOSCALE
TRICKLE
TROCHEE
TRUCKEE
TRUCKLE
UPSCALE
VACCINE
WELCOME
ZIPCODE

••••CE•

ADDUCED
ADDUCES
AMERCED
AMERCES
BODICES
BOUNCED
BOUNCER
BOUNCES
CADUCEI
CALYCES
CHANCED
CHANCEL
CHANCES
CHAUCER
CHOICER
CHOICES
CODICES
COERCED
COERCES
DEDUCED
DEDUCES
DEFACED
DEFACES
DEVICES
EFFACED
EFFACES
ENLACED
ENLACES
ENTICED
ENTICER
ENTICES
EVINCED
EVINCES
FIANCEE
FIANCES
FIERCER
FLEECED
FLEECES
FRANCES
GLANCED
GLANCES
HELICES
HYRACES
INDICES
INDUCED
INDUCER
INDUCES
JANACEK
JOUNCED
JOUNCES
LATICES
MENACED
MENACES
NOTICED
NOTICES
NOVICES
NUANCED
NUANCES
OFFICER
OFFICES
PALACES
PANACEA
PEDICEL
PIERCED
PIERCES
PLAICES
POLICED
POLICES
POUNCED
POUNCER
POUNCES
PRANCED
PRANCER
PRANCES
PRINCES
PUMICES
QUINCES
RADICES
REDUCED
REDUCER
REDUCES
REFACED
REFACES
RELACED
RELACES
SARACEN
SCARCER
SCONCES
SEANCES
SEDUCED
SEDUCER
SEDUCES
SLUICED
SLUICES
SOLACES
SOURCED
SOURCES
SPENCER
SPLICED
SPLICER
SPLICES
SPRUCED
SPRUCER
SPRUCES
STANCES
TENACES
TRANCES
UNLACED
UNLACES

••••C•E

ARTICLE
ATTACHE
AURICLE
BICYCLE
BLANCHE
BRIOCHE
CEVICHE
CUBICLE
CUTICLE
DEBACLE
DEPECHE
EARACHE
FIANCEE
FRAICHE
GOUACHE
LAROCHE
MANACLE
MIRACLE
MONOCLE
OSSICLE
PANACHE
PANICLE
PEDICLE
PENUCHE
PINOCLE
PORSCHE
RADICLE
RECYCLE
RETICLE
TREACLE
TUNICLE
VEHICLE

•••••CE

ABSENCE
ADVANCE
ASKANCE
ATPEACE
AUSPICE
AVARICE
BALANCE
BERNICE
BYFORCE
CADENCE
CANDICE
CAPRICE
CHALICE
CLARICE
CONDUCE
COPPICE
CORNICE
CREVICE
DEFENCE
DEHISCE
DENIECE
DIVORCE
DOGFACE
DORMICE
DURANCE
EDIFICE
EMBRACE
ENFORCE
ENHANCE
ENOUNCE
ESSENCE
FAIENCE
FINANCE
FLOUNCE
FURNACE
GRIMACE
HOSPICE
INFORCE
INPEACE
INPLACE
INVOICE
JUSTICE
LAPLACE
LATTICE
LETTUCE
LICENCE
MAURICE
OFFENCE
ORIFICE
OUTFACE
OUTPACE
OUTRACE
PACKICE
PALANCE
PATRICE
PENANCE
PINNACE
PREFACE
PRODUCE
RATRACE
REJOICE
REPLACE
REPRICE
RETRACE
REVOICE
ROMANCE
SCIENCE
SERVICE
SILENCE
STATICE
SUFFICE
SURFACE
TERENCE
TERRACE
THINICE
TITMICE
TRADUCE
TROUNCE
UNAVOCE
VALANCE
VALENCE
WALLACE

C•F••••

CAFTANS
COFFEES
COFFERS
CUFFING

C••F•••

CAPFULS
CARFARE
CARFULS
CATFISH
CHAFING
CHIFFON
CLIFTON
CODFISH
COFFEES
COFFERS
COIFING
COMFIER
COMFITS
COMFORT
COMFREY
CONFABS
CONFERS
CONFESS
CONFIDE
CONFINE
CONFIRM
CONFORM
CONFUSE
CONFUTE
CRAFTED
CRAFTER
CRAFTSY
CUFFING
CUPFULS
CURFEWS

C•••F••

CALLFOR
CARAFES
CAREFOR
CAREFUL
CHAMFER
CHIEFLY
CHIFFON
CONIFER
CORNFED
CUTOFFS

C••••F•

CALCIFY
CALLOFF
CAMEOFF
CASTOFF
CERTIFY
CLARIFY
COMEOFF
CONNIFF
COOKOFF
CUTOFFS
CUTSOFF

C•••••F

CALLOFF
CAMEOFF
CASTOFF
COMEOFF
CONNIFF
COOKOFF
CRYWOLF
CUTSOFF

•C•F•••

ICEFLOE
ICEFREE
SCOFFED
SCOFFER
SCUFFED
SCUFFLE

•C••F••

SCARFED
SCOFFED
SCOFFER
SCRUFFS
SCRUFFY
SCUFFED
SCUFFLE

•C•••F•

ACIDIFY
SCARIFY
SCRUFFS
SCRUFFY

••C•F••

LUCIFER
PACIFIC
SACKFUL
TACTFUL

••C••F•

BACKOFF
FACEOFF
KICKOFF
MACDUFF
PICKOFF
RECTIFY
TICKOFF

••C•••F

BACKOFF
FACEOFF
KICKOFF
MACDUFF
PICKOFF
TICKOFF

•••C•F•

CALCIFY
NESCAFE
SPECIFY

C•G••••

CAGIEST
COGBURN
COGENCY
COGNACS
COGNATE
CYGNETS

C••G•••

CADGERS
CADGING
CALGARY
CAPGUNS
CARGOES
CHAGALL
CHAGRIN
CHIGGER
CHIGNON
CHUGGED
CLOGGED
CLOGSUP
CODGERS
COLGATE
CONGAED
CONGAME
CONGEAL
CONGERS
CONGEST
COUGARS
COUGHED
COUGHUP
COWGIRL
CUDGELS

C•••G••

CAYUGAS
CHANGED
CHANGER
CHANGES
CHARGED
CHARGER
CHARGES
CHIGGER
CHUGGED
CLANGED
CLANGOR
CLINGTO
CLOGGED
COALGAS
COLOGNE
COSIGNS
CRINGED
CRINGES
CRYOGEN

C••••G•

CABBAGE
CARTAGE
CASINGS
CHICAGO
COINAGE
COLLAGE
COLLEGE
COMINGS
CONDIGN
CONSIGN
CORDAGE
CORKAGE
CORSAGE
CORTEGE
COTTAGE
COURAGE
CYBORGS

C•••••G

CABLING
CACHING
CADGING
CALKING
CALLING
CALMING
CALVING
CAMPING
CANNING
CANTING
CAPPING
CARDING
CARPING
CARTING
CARVING
CASHING
CASTING
CATALOG
CATTING
CAUSING
CEASING
CEILING
CENSING
CHAFING
CHASING
CHEWING
CHIDING
CHIMING
CLAWING
CLONING
CLOSING
CLOYING
CLUEING
COATING
COAXING
COCKING
COIFING
COILING
COINING
COMBING
CONKING
CONNING
COOKING
COOLING
COOPING
COPPING
COPYING
CORDING
CORKING
CORNDOG
CORNING
COSTING
COWLING
COZYING
CRANING
CRATING
CRAVING
CRAZING
CREWING
CROWING
CUFFING
CULLING
CUNNING
CUPPING
CURBING
CURDING
CURLING
CURSING
CURVING
CUSSING
CUTTING
CYCLING
CYYOUNG

•CG••••

MCGAVIN
MCGUIRE

•C••G••

ECLOGUE
ICEAGES
ICINGIN
OCTAGON
SCRAGGY

•C•••G•

ACREAGE
ECOLOGY
ICEBAGS
SCOURGE
SCRAGGY
SCROOGE

•C••••G

ACHTUNG
ECHOING
ICEBERG
SCALING
SCARING
SCOPING
SCORING

••CG•••

MACGRAW

••C•G••

DECAGON
ENCAGED
ENCAGES
UNCAGED
UNCAGES

••C••G•

DOCKAGE
FACINGS
LACINGS
PACKAGE
UNCLOGS

••C•••G
ARCHING
BACKING
BACKLOG
BUCKING
CACHING
COCKING
CYCLING
DECALOG
DECKING
DOCKING
DUCKING
DUCTING
ETCHING
HACKING
HOCKING
INCHING
ITCHING
JACKING
KICKING
LACKING
LICKING
LOCKING
LUCKING
MOCKING
MUCKING
NECKING
NICKING
PACKING
PECKING
PICKING
RACKING
ROCKING
RUCHING
RUCKING
SACKING
SICCING
SOCKING
SUCKING
TACKING
TICKING
TUCKING

•••C•G•
CHICAGO
RIBCAGE

•••C••G
BRACING
DANCING
DEICING
EDUCING
FENCING
FORCING
GRACING
JUICING
MINCING
PIECING
PLACING
PRICING
SICCING
SLICING
SPACING
SPICING
SYNCING
TRACING
VOICING
WINCING

CH•••••
CHABLIS
CHACHAS
CHAFING
CHAGALL
CHAGRIN
CHAINED
CHAIRED
CHAISES
CHALETS
CHALICE
CHALKED
CHALKUP
CHALLIS
CHAMBER
CHAMFER
CHAMOIS
CHAMPED
CHANCED
CHANCEL
CHANCES
CHANGED
CHANGER
CHANGES
CHANNEL
CHANSON
CHANTED
CHANTER
CHANTEY
CHAOTIC
CHAPATI
CHAPEAU
CHAPELS
CHAPLET
CHAPLIN
CHAPMAN
CHAPMEN
CHAPPED
CHAPTER
CHARADE
CHARGED
CHARGER
CHARGES
CHARIER
CHARILY
CHARIOT
CHARITY
CHARLES
CHARLEY
CHARLIE
CHARMED
CHARMER
CHARMIN
CHARRED
CHARTED
CHARTER
CHASERS
CHASING
CHASSES
CHASSIS
CHASTEN
CHASTER
CHATEAU
CHATHAM
CHATSUP
CHATTED
CHATTEL
CHATTER
CHAUCER
CHEAPEN
CHEAPER
CHEAPIE
CHEAPLY
CHEATED
CHEATER
CHECHEN
CHECKED
CHECKER
CHECKIN
CHECKUP
CHEDDAR
CHEEPED
CHEERED
CHEERIO
CHEERUP
CHEESES
CHEETAH
CHEETOS
CHEEVER
CHEKHOV
CHELSEA
CHEMISE
CHEMIST
CHEMLAB
CHENIER
CHEQUER
CHEQUES
CHERISH
CHEROOT
CHERUBS
CHERVIL
CHESTER
CHETRUM
CHEVIED
CHEVIES
CHEVIOT
CHEVRES
CHEVRON
CHEWERS
CHEWIER
CHEWING
CHEWOUT
CHEWSUP
CHIANTI
CHICAGO
CHICANA
CHICANO
CHICHEN
CHICKEN
CHICORY
CHIDING
CHIEFLY
CHIFFON
CHIGGER
CHIGNON
CHILEAN
CHILIES
CHILLED
CHILLER
CHIMERA
CHIMING
CHIMNEY
CHINESE
CHINKED
CHINNED
CHINOOK
CHINTZY
CHINUPS
CHIPPED
CHIPPER
CHIPSIN
CHIRPED
CHISELS
CHITTER
CHLORAL
CHOCTAW
CHOICER
CHOICES
CHOKERS
CHOKEUP
CHOLLAS
CHOMPED
CHOMSKY
CHOOSER
CHOOSES
CHOPPED
CHOPPER
CHORALE
CHORALS
CHORINE
CHORIZO
CHORTLE
CHOWDER
CHRISMS
CHRISTI
CHRISTO
CHRISTY
CHROMES
CHRONIC
CHUCKED
CHUCKLE
CHUGGED
CHUKKAS
CHUKKER
CHUMMED
CHUNNEL
CHURNED
CHUTNEY

C•H••••
CAHIERS
CAHOOTS
COHABIT
COHEIRS
COHERED
COHERES
COHORTS
COHOSTS

C••H•••
CACHETS
CACHING
CACHOUS
CALHOUN
CARHOPS
CASHBAR
CASHBOX
CASHCOW
CASHEWS
CASHIER
CASHING
CASHOUT
CATHAIR
CATHEAD
CATHODE
CEPHEUS
CIPHERS
COCHERE
COCHISE
COCHLEA
COCHRAN
COWHAND
COWHERD
COWHIDE
CUSHAWS
CUSHIER
CUSHION
CYPHERS

C•••H••
CAMPHOR
CAPSHAW
CATCHER
CATCHES
CATCHON
CATCHUP
CHACHAS
CHATHAM
CHECHEN
CHEKHOV
CHICHEN
CINCHED
CINCHES
CLASHED
CLASHES
CLICHES
CLOCHES
CLOTHED
CLOTHES
COACHED
COACHES
CONCHES
COUCHED
COUCHES
COUGHED
COUGHUP
CRASHED
CRASHES
CRECHES
CROCHET
CRUSHED
CRUSHER
CRUSHES
CYNTHIA

C••••H•
CALIPHS
CERIPHS
CEVICHE
CRUNCHY

C•••••H
CALTECH
CARWASH
CATFISH
CATTISH
CHEETAH
CHERISH
CODFISH
COLTISH
CORINTH
CORNISH
CULTISH

•CH••••
ACHATES
ACHENES
ACHERON
ACHESON
ACHIEST
ACHIEVE
ACHTUNG
ECHELON
ECHIDNA
ECHINUS
ECHOING
ICHABOD
SCHATZI
SCHEMAS
SCHEMED
SCHEMER
SCHEMES
SCHERZI
SCHERZO
SCHIRRA
SCHISMS
SCHLEPP
SCHLEPS
SCHLOCK
SCHMEER
SCHMIDT
SCHMOES
SCHMOOS
SCHNAPS
SCHOLAR
SCHOOLS
SCHWINN
WCHANDY

•C•H•••
ECKHART

•C••H••
ICESHOW
MCLUHAN
MCMAHON
SCATHED
SCATHES
SCYTHED
SCYTHES

•C•••H•
ACANTHI

•C••••H
NCWYETH
SCRATCH
SCREECH
SCRUNCH

••CH•••
ALCHEMY
ANCHORS
ANCHOVY
ARCHAIC
ARCHERS
ARCHERY
ARCHIES
ARCHING
ARCHIVE
ARCHONS
ARCHWAY
CACHETS
CACHING
CACHOUS
COCHERE
COCHISE
COCHLEA
COCHRAN
DUCHESS
DUCHIES
ENCHAIN
ENCHANT
ESCHEAT
ESCHEWS
ETCHERS
ETCHING
EUCHRED
EUCHRES
FUCHSIA
INCHING
ITCHIER
ITCHING
KACHINA
LICHENS
MACHETE
MACHINA
MACHINE
MICHAEL
MICHELE
MRCHIPS
NICHOLS
ORCHARD
ORCHIDS
PACHISI
RECHALK
RECHECK
RECHOSE
RICHARD
RICHEST
RICHMAN
RICHTER
RUCHING
SACHEMS
SACHETS
SICHUAN
TECHIES
TUCHMAN
UNCHAIN
URCHINS
WICHITA
WYCHELM
YACHTED
ZACHARY

••C•H••
ALCOHOL
BACCHUS
BACKHOE

••C••H•
RICKSHA

••C•••H
MACBETH
PECKISH
PUCKISH
UNCOUTH

•••CH••
AITCHES
APACHES
ARACHNE
BACCHUS
BATCHED
BATCHES
BEACHED
BEACHES
BEECHAM
BEECHER
BEECHES
BELCHED
BELCHES
BENCHED
BENCHES
BIRCHED
BIRCHES
BOKCHOY
BOTCHED
BOTCHES
BUNCHED
BUNCHES
BUTCHER
CATCHER
CATCHES
CATCHON
CATCHUP
CHACHAS
CHECHEN
CHICHEN
CINCHED
CINCHES
CLICHES
CLOCHES
COACHED
COACHES
CONCHES
COUCHED
COUCHES
CRECHES
CROCHET
DITCHED
DITCHES
DOGCHEW
DOGCHOW
DRACHMA
FETCHED
FETCHES
FILCHED
FILCHER
FILCHES
FINCHES
FISCHER
FITCHES
FLECHES
GAUCHER
GAUCHOS
GOTCHAS
GULCHES
HATCHED
HATCHER
HATCHES
HATCHET
HITCHED
HITCHER
HITCHES
HONCHOS
HUNCHED
HUNCHES
HUTCHES
JIMCHEE
JOACHIM
KERCHOO
KETCHAM
KETCHES
KETCHUP
KITCHEN
KWACHAS
LARCHES
LATCHED
LATCHES
LEACHED
LEACHES
LEECHED
LEECHES
LITCHIS
LOACHES
LUNCHED
LUNCHER
LUNCHES
LURCHED
LURCHES
MADCHEN
MARCHED
MARCHEN
MARCHER
MARCHES
MARCHON
MATCHED
MATCHES
MATCHUP
MITCHUM
MOOCHED
MOOCHER
MOOCHES
MULCHED
MULCHES
MUNCHED
MUNCHER
MUNCHES
NATCHEZ
NOTCHED
NOTCHES
OLDCHAP
PANCHAX
PARCHED
PARCHES
PASCHAL
PATCHED
PATCHES
PATCHUP
PEACHED
PEACHES
PERCHED
PERCHES
PINCHAS
PINCHED
PINCHER
PINCHES
PITCHED
PITCHER
PITCHES
PITCHIN
POACHED
POACHER
POACHES
PONCHOS
POOCHES
PORCHES
POUCHED
POUCHES
PSYCHED
PSYCHES
PSYCHIC
PSYCHUP
PUNCHED
PUNCHER
PUNCHES
PUNCHIN
PUNCHUP
PYNCHON
QUECHUA
QUICHES
RANCHED
RANCHER
RANCHES
RANCHOS
RATCHET
REACHED
REACHES
RITCHIE
ROACHED
ROACHES
SALCHOW
SATCHEL
SATCHMO
SEICHES
STICHES
SYNCHED
SYNCHES
TEACHER
TEACHES
TEACHIN
TEICHER
TETCHED
TORCHED
TORCHES
TOUCHED
TOUCHES
TOUCHON
TOUCHUP
TRACHEA
TROCHEE
TROCHES
VETCHES
VOUCHED
VOUCHER
VOUCHES
WATCHED
WATCHER
WATCHES
WATCHIT
WELCHED
WELCHES
WENCHES
WINCHED
WINCHES
WITCHES
ZILCHES

•••C•H•
GNOCCHI

•••C••H
PAYCASH

••••CH•
ANARCHY
ATTACHE
AUROCHS
BLANCHE
BLOTCHY
BORSCHT
BRIOCHE
BRONCHI
CEVICHE
CRUNCHY
DEPECHE
EARACHE
EPARCHS
EUNUCHS
FRAICHE
GNOCCHI
GOUACHE
GROUCHO
GROUCHY
HIBACHI
HITACHI
HOOTCHY
JERICHO
KARACHI
KITSCHY
KOOTCHY
LAROCHE
MALACHI
NOGUCHI
PANACHE
PAUNCHY
PENUCHE
PORSCHE
PREACHY
SKETCHY
SLOUCHY
STARCHY
THATCHY
TWITCHY
UTRECHT
VOTECHS

••••C•H
PADUCAH

•••••CH
ALDRICH
ANSPACH
ANTIOCH
BESEECH
BEWITCH
CALTECH
DEBAUCH
DEBOUCH
DIPTYCH
EHRLICH
GODUTCH
IMPEACH
INDUTCH
IPSWICH
KLATSCH
LOWTECH
MONARCH
MURDOCH
OSTRICH
RETEACH
RETOUCH
SCRATCH
SCREECH
SCRUNCH
SPINACH
SPLOTCH
SQUELCH
SQUINCH
STAUNCH
STOMACH
STRETCH
UNHITCH
UNLATCH
WALLACH
WASATCH

CI•••••
CIBORIA
CICADAE
CICADAS
CILIATE
CINCHED
CINCHES
CINDERS
CINEMAS
CINEMAX
CINZANO
CIPHERS
CIRCLED
CIRCLES
CIRCLET
CIRCUIT
CIRCUSY
CIRQUES
CISTERN
CITABLE
CITADEL
CITIZEN
CITRATE
CITRINE
CITROEN
CITRONS
CIVILLY
CIVVIES

C•I••••
CAIMANS
CAIQUES
CAISSON
CEILING
CHIANTI
CHICAGO
CHICANA
CHICANO
CHICHEN
CHICKEN
CHICORY
CHIDING
CHIEFLY
CHIFFON
CHIGGER
CHIGNON
CHILEAN
CHILIES
CHILLED
CHILLER
CHIMERA
CHIMING
CHIMNEY
CHINESE
CHINKED
CHINNED
CHINOOK
CHINTZY
CHINUPS
CHIPPED
CHIPPER
CHIPSIN
CHIRPED
CHISELS
CHITTER
CLIBURN
CLICHES
CLICKED
CLIENTS
CLIFTON
CLIMATE
CLIMBED
CLIMBER
CLINGTO
CLINICS
CLINKED
CLINKER
CLINTON
CLIPART
CLIPONS
CLIPPED
CLIPPER
CLIQUES
COIFING
COILING
COILSUP
COINAGE
COINERS
COINING
CRIBBED
CRICKED
CRICKET
CRIMEAN
CRIMPED
CRIMPER
CRIMSON
CRINGED
CRINGES
CRINKLE
CRINKLY
CRINOID
CRISPED
CRISPER
CRISPIN
CRISPLY
CRISPUS
CRITICS
CRITTER
CUIBONO
CUIRASS
CUISINE

C••I•••
CABINET
CAGIEST
CAHIERS
CALIBAN
CALIBER
CALIBRE
CALICOS
CALIPER
CALIPHS
CAMILLE
CAMISES
CANINES
CAPITAL
CAPITAN
CAPITOL
CARIBES
CARIBOU
CARINAS
CARIOCA
CASINGS
CASINOS
CATIONS
CAVILED
CAVILER
CECILIA
CEDILLA
CERIPHS
CEVICHE
CHAINED
CHAIRED
CHAISES
CHOICER
CHOICES
CHRISMS
CHRISTI
CHRISTO
CHRISTY
CILIATE
CITIZEN
CIVILLY
CLAIMED
CLAIMER
CLAIROL
CODICES
CODICIL
COMICAL
COMINGS
COMIQUE
CONICAL
CONIFER
COPIERS
COPILOT
COPIOUS
CORINTH
COSIGNS
COSINES
COZIEST
CRUISED
CRUISER
CRUISES
CUBICLE
CUBISTS
CURIOUS
CUTICLE
CUTINTO
CYNICAL

C•••I••
CABBIES

CABLING
CACHING
CADDIED
CADDIES
CADGING
CADMIUM
CALCIFY
CALCITE
CALCIUM
CALKING
CALKINS
CALLING
CALLINS
CALMING
CALVING
CAMBIUM
CAMPIER
CAMPING
CAMPION
CANDICE
CANDIDA
CANDIDE
CANDIDS
CANDIED
CANDIES
CANNIER
CANNILY
CANNING
CANTINA
CANTING
CAPPING
CAPRICE
CAPSIZE
CAPTION
CAPTIVE
CARBIDE
CARBINE
CARDING
CARMINE
CARNIES
CARPING
CARRICK
CARRIED
CARRIER
CARRIES
CARRION
CARTIER
CARTING
CARVING
CASHIER
CASHING
CASPIAN
CASSIAS
CASSIDY
CASSINI
CASSIUS
CASTILE
CASTING
CATBIRD
CATFISH
CATKINS
CATLIKE
CATNIPS
CATTIER
CATTILY
CATTING
CATTISH
CAUSING
CAUTION
CAVEINS
CEASING
CEILING
CELLINI
CELLIST
CELSIUS
CELTICS
CENSING
CENTIME
CENTIMO
CERTIFY
CESSION
CHAFING
CHALICE
CHARIER
CHARILY
CHARIOT
CHARITY
CHASING
CHEMISE
CHEMIST
CHENIER
CHERISH
CHEVIED
CHEVIES
CHEVIOT
CHEWIER
CHEWING
CHIDING
CHILIES
CHIMING
CHORINE
CHORIZO
CITRINE
CIVVIES
CLARICE
CLARIFY
CLARION
CLARITY
CLAVIER
CLAWING
CLAYIER
CLERICS
CLINICS
CLONING
CLOSING
CLOYING
CLUEING
COATING
COAXIAL
COAXING
COCHISE
COCKIER
COCKILY
COCKING
CODEINE
CODFISH
COEDITS
COEXIST
COHEIRS
COIFING
COILING
COINING
COLLIDE
COLLIER
COLLIES
COLLINS
COLTISH
COMBINE
COMBING
COMFIER
COMFITS
COMMITS
COMPILE
CONCISE
CONDIGN
CONFIDE
CONFINE
CONFIRM
CONKING
CONNICK
CONNIFF
CONNING
CONNIVE
CONSIGN
CONSIST
CONVICT
COOKIES
COOKING
COOLING
COOPING
COOTIES
COPPICE
COPPING
COPYING
COPYIST
CORDIAL
CORDING
CORDITE
CORKING
CORNICE
CORNIER
CORNILY
CORNING
CORNISH
CORRIDA
CORSICA
COSTING
COURIER
COUSINS
COWBIRD
COWGIRL
COWHIDE
COWLICK
COWLING
COWRIES
COZYING
CRANIAL
CRANING
CRANIUM
CRATING
CRAVING
CRAZIER
CRAZIES
CRAZILY
CRAZING
CREDITS
CRETINS
CREVICE
CREWING
CRITICS
CRONIES
CROSIER
CROWING
CRUCIAL
CRUDITY
CUBBIES
CUFFING
CUISINE
CULLING
CULTISH
CULTISM
CULTIST
CUNNING
CUPPING
CURBING
CURDING
CURLIER
CURLING
CURRIED
CURRIER
CURRIES
CURSING
CURSIVE
CURVIER
CURVING
CUSHIER
CUSHION
CUSPIDS
CUSSING
CUTTIME
CUTTING
CYCLING
CYCLIST
CYPRIOT
CZARINA
CZARISM
CZARIST

C••••I•
CAKEMIX
CALLSIN
CALORIC
CALORIE
CAMBRIC
CAMELIA
CANONIC
CAPAPIE
CAPTAIN
CARAMIA
CAROTID
CATHAIR
CATTAIL
CAUSTIC
CAVEDIN
CAVESIN
CBRADIO
CECILIA
CENTRIC
CERAMIC
CERTAIN
CHABLIS
CHAGRIN
CHALLIS
CHAMOIS
CHAOTIC
CHAPLIN
CHARLIE
CHARMIN
CHASSIS
CHEAPIE
CHECKIN
CHEERIO
CHERVIL
CHIPSIN
CHRONIC
CIBORIA
CIRCUIT
CLASSIC
CLAUDIA
CLAUDIO
CLOCKIN
CLOSEIN
CLUEDIN
CLUESIN
COALBIN
COALOIL
COCKPIT
CODICIL
COHABIT
COLLOID
COMEDIC
COMESIN
CONBRIO
CONCEIT
CONDUIT
CONJOIN
CONREID
CONTAIN
COOLSIT
CORNOIL
CORSAIR
COSTAIN
COTERIE
COUNCIL
COWSLIP
CRAPPIE
CRINOID
CRISPIN
CROATIA
CRYPTIC
CSLEWIS
CULPRIT
CURTAIL
CURTAIN
CYNTHIA

C•••••I
CADUCEI
CAMPARI
CANNOLI
CASSINI
CELLINI
CHAPATI
CHIANTI
CHRISTI
COLLODI
COLOSSI
CORELLI

•CI••••
ACIDIFY
ACIDITY
ICICLES
ICINESS
ICINGIN
SCIENCE
SCISSOR

•C•I•••
ACHIEST
ACHIEVE
ACRIDLY
ACTINIC
ACTIONS
ACTIVES
ECHIDNA
ECHINUS
ECLIPSE
ICKIEST
OCCIPUT
SCHIRRA
SCHISMS
SCRIBES
SCRIMPS
SCRIMPY
SCRIPPS
SCRIPTS
SCRIVEN

•C••I••
ACACIAS
ACADIAN
ACARIDS
ACIDIFY
ACIDITY
ACONITE
ACQUIRE
ACQUITS
ECHOING
ECLAIRS
ICEMILK
ICEPICK
ICERINK
MCGUIRE
MCSWINE
OCARINA
OCULIST
SCALIER
SCALING
SCARIER
SCARIFY
SCARILY
SCARING
SCHMIDT
SCHWINN
SCOPING
SCORING

•C•••I•
ACCLAIM
ACERBIC
ACRYLIC
ACTINIC
ECDYSIS
ICINGIN
MCGAVIN
OCEANIA
OCEANIC
OCEANID
OCTAVIA
SCORPIO
SCOTTIE

•C••••I
ACANTHI
SCHATZI
SCHERZI

••CI•••
ANCIENT
BACILLI
CECILIA
DECIBEL
DECIDED
DECIDES
DECIMAL
DICIEST
EXCISED
EXCISES
EXCITED
EXCITES
FACIALS
FACINGS
INCIPIT
INCISED
INCISES
INCISOR
INCITED
INCITER
INCITES
INCIVIL
JACINTO
LACIEST
LACINGS
LICITLY
LUCIANO
LUCIDLY
LUCIFER
LUCILLE
OCCIPUT
OSCINES
PACIFIC
RACIEST
RECIPES
RECITAL
RECITED
RECITER
RECITES
SOCIALS
SOCIETY
TACITLY
TACITUS
UNCIALS
UNCIVIL
VICIOUS

••C•I••
ARCHIES
ARCHING
ARCHIVE
ARCSINE
ASCRIBE
AUCTION
BACKING
BUCKING
CACHING
COCHISE
COCKIER
COCKILY
COCKING
CYCLING
CYCLIST
DECEITS
DECEIVE
DECKING
DECLINE
DECRIED
DECRIES
DICKIES
DICTION
DOCKING
DUCHIES
DUCKIER
DUCKING
DUCTILE
DUCTING
ETCHING
FACTION
FICTION
FICTIVE
HACKIES
HACKING
HOCKING
INCHING
INCLINE
ITCHIER
ITCHING
JACKING
KACHINA
KICKING
LACKING
LICKING
LOCKING
LOCKINS
LUCKIER
LUCKILY
LUCKING
MACHINA
MACHINE
MOCKING
MRCHIPS
MUCKING
NECKING
NICKING
NUCLIDE
ORCHIDS
PACHISI
PACKICE
PACKING
PECKING
PECKISH
PECTINS
PICKIER
PICKING
PICNICS
PUCCINI
PUCKISH
RACKING
RECEIPT
RECEIVE
RECLINE
RECOILS
RECTIFY
ROCKIER
ROCKIES
ROCKING
RUCHING
RUCKING
RUCTION
SACKING
SECTION
SICCING
SOCKING
SUCKING
SUCTION
TACKIER
TACKILY
TACKING
TACTICS
TACTILE
TECHIES
TICKING
TOCSINS
TUCKING
UNCOILS
UNCTION
URCHINS
VACCINE
VACUITY
VICTIMS
WACKIER
WACKILY
WICHITA
WICKIUP
YUCKIER

••C••I•
ACCLAIM
ARCADIA
ARCHAIC
ASCETIC
BACKBIT
BACKLIT
BACKSIN
BUCOLIC
CECILIA
COCKPIT
DECLAIM
DUCKPIN
ENCHAIN
ENCOMIA
EXCLAIM
FUCHSIA
INCIPIT
INCIVIL
JACOBIN
KICKSIN
LACONIC
NECKTIE
NICOSIA
NUCLEIC
PACIFIC
RECLAIM
RECRUIT
ROCKYII
ROCKYIV
SOCKSIN
STCROIX
SUCKSIN
TUCKSIN
UNCHAIN
UNCIVIL
VOCALIC

••C•••I
BACARDI
BACILLI
JACUZZI
PACHISI
PUCCINI
ROCKYII

•••CI••
ACACIAS
ASOCIAL
BAYCITY
BRACING
CALCIFY
CALCITE
CALCIUM
CONCISE
CRUCIAL
DANCING
DEICING
EDACITY
EDUCING
ELICITS
FANCIED
FANCIER
FANCIES
FANCILY
FASCIAS
FASCISM
FASCIST
FATCITY
FENCING
FORCING
GLACIAL
GLACIER
GRACIAS
GRACILE
GRACING
GRECIAN
JUICIER
JUICILY
JUICING
MANCINI
MERCIES
MINCING
NUNCIOS
OPACITY
PAUCITY
PENCILS
PIECING
PISCINE
PLACIDO
PLACING
PORCINE
PRECISE
PRICIER
PRICING
PUCCINI
RESCIND
SAUCIER
SAUCILY
SICCING
SLICING
SPACIER
SPACING
SPECIAL
SPECIES
SPECIFY
SPICIER
SPICING
SUNCITY
SYNCING
TRACING
TRUCIAL
VACCINE
VOICING
WINCING

•••C•I•
BISCUIT
CHECKIN
CIRCUIT
CLOCKIN
CONCEIT
FLACCID
FRICKIE
JOACHIM
LITCHIS
PITCHIN
PSYCHIC
PUNCHIN
QUICKIE
RITCHIE
TEACHIN
TIECLIP
WATCHIT

•••C••I
GNOCCHI
MANCINI
MARCONI
PUCCINI

••••CI•
ANTACID
CODICIL
COUNCIL
DEFICIT
FELICIA
FLACCID
FRANCIS
ILLICIT
INDICIA
SOLICIT
STENCIL
STLUCIA

••••C•I
BRONCHI
CADUCEI
DELICTI
GNOCCHI
HIBACHI
HITACHI
KARACHI
MALACHI
NOGUCHI

•••••CI
DAVINCI
MENISCI

C•J••••
CAJOLED
CAJOLER
CAJOLES

C••J•••
CONJOBS
CONJOIN
CONJURE

C•••J••
CULTJAM

••C•••J
LLCOOLJ

C•K••••
CAKEMIX

C••K•••
CACKLED
CACKLER
CACKLES
CALKING
CALKINS
CANKERS
CATKINS
CHEKHOV
CHOKERS
CHOKEUP
CHUKKAS
CHUKKER
COCKADE
COCKIER
COCKILY
COCKING
COCKLES
COCKNEY
COCKPIT
CONKERS
CONKING
CONKOUT
COOKERS
COOKERY
COOKIES
COOKING
COOKOFF
COOKOUT
COOKSUP
CORKAGE
CORKERS
CORKING
CUCKOOS

C•••K••
CAULKED
CAULKER
CHALKED
CHALKUP
CHECKED
CHECKER
CHECKIN
CHECKUP
CHICKEN
CHINKED
CHUCKED
CHUCKLE
CHUKKAS
CHUKKER
CLACKED
CLANKED
CLERKED
CLICKED
CLINKED
CLINKER
CLOAKED
CLOCKED
CLOCKER
CLOCKIN
CLUCKED
CLUNKED
CLUNKER
CONAKRY
CRACKED
CRACKER
CRACKLE
CRACKUP
CRANKED
CRANKUP
CREAKED
CRICKED
CRICKET
CRINKLE
CRINKLY
CROAKED
CROOKED

C••••K•
CATLIKE
CHOMSKY
CONVOKE
COWPOKE
CUPCAKE

C•••••K
CARRICK
CASSOCK
CATWALK
CHINOOK
CONNICK
CONRACK
COSSACK
COWLICK
CUTBACK

•CK••••
ACKACKS
ECKHART
ICKIEST

•C•••K•
ACKACKS
SCREAKS

•C••••K
ICEMILK
ICEPACK
ICEPICK
ICERINK
SCHLOCK

••CK•••
BACKBAY
BACKBIT
BACKEND
BACKERS
BACKHOE
BACKING
BACKLIT
BACKLOG
BACKOFF
BACKOUT
BACKRUB
BACKSIN
BACKSUP
BACKUPS
BECKETT
BECKONS
BICKERS
BUCKETS
BUCKEYE
BUCKING
BUCKLED
BUCKLER
BUCKLES
BUCKLEY
BUCKOES
BUCKRAM
BUCKSAW
BUCKSUP
CACKLED
CACKLER
CACKLES
COCKADE
COCKIER
COCKILY
COCKING
COCKLES
COCKNEY
COCKPIT
CUCKOOS
DECKING
DECKLES
DECKOUT
DICKENS
DICKERS
DICKEYS
DICKIES
DOCKAGE
DOCKERS
DOCKETS
DOCKING
DUCKIER
DUCKING
DUCKPIN
FICKLER
GECKOES
HACKERS
HACKETT
HACKIES
HACKING
HACKLES
HACKMAN
HACKNEY
HACKSAW
HECKLED
HECKLER
HECKLES
HICKMAN
HICKORY
HOCKING
JACKALS
JACKASS
JACKDAW
JACKETS
JACKING
JACKPOT
JACKSON
JACKSUP
JACKTAR
JOCKEYS
KICKERS
KICKING

KICKOFF
KICKOUT
KICKSIN
KICKSUP
KICKUPS
LACKEYS
LACKING
LICKETY
LICKING
LOCKBOX
LOCKERS
LOCKETS
LOCKING
LOCKINS
LOCKNUT
LOCKOUT
LOCKSUP
LOCKUPS
LUCKIER
LUCKILY
LUCKING
LUCKOUT
MOCKERS
MOCKERY
MOCKING
MOCKUPS
MUCKING
MUCKSUP
NECKERS
NECKING
NECKTIE
NICKELS
NICKERS
NICKING
PACKAGE
PACKARD
PACKERS
PACKETS
PACKICE
PACKING
PACKRAT
PACKSUP
PECKING
PECKISH
PECKSAT
PICKAXE
PICKENS
PICKERS
PICKETS
PICKETT
PICKIER
PICKING
PICKLED
PICKLES
PICKOFF
PICKOUT
PICKSAT
PICKSON
PICKSUP
PICKUPS
POCKETS
PUCKERS
PUCKETT
PUCKISH
RACKETS
RACKING
RACKSUP
RECKONS
RICKETY
RICKEYS
RICKLES
RICKSHA
ROCKERS
ROCKETS
ROCKIER
ROCKIES
ROCKING
ROCKYII
ROCKYIV
RUCKING
SACKERS
SACKFUL
SACKING
SACKOUT
SICKBAY
SICKENS
SICKEST
SICKLES
SICKOUT
SICKPAY
SOCKETS
SOCKEYE
SOCKING
SOCKSIN
SUCKERS
SUCKING
SUCKSIN
TACKERS
TACKIER
TACKILY
TACKING
TACKLED
TACKLER
TACKLES
TACKSON
TICKERS
TICKETS
TICKING
TICKLED
TICKLER
TICKLES
TICKOFF
TUCKERS
TUCKING
TUCKSIN
WACKIER
WACKILY
WICKERS
WICKETS
WICKIUP
YUCKIER

••C••K•

RECORKS
UNCORKS

••C•••K

RECHALK
RECHECK
UNCLOAK

•••CK••

BLACKED
BLACKEN
BLACKER
BLACKLY
BLOCKED
BLOCKER
BRACKEN
BRACKET
BRICKED
CHECKED
CHECKER
CHECKIN
CHECKUP
CHICKEN
CHUCKED
CHUCKLE
CLACKED
CLICKED
CLOCKED
CLOCKER
CLOCKIN
CLUCKED
CRACKED
CRACKER
CRACKLE
CRACKUP
CRICKED
CRICKET
DRUCKER
FLECKED
FLICKED
FLICKER
FLOCKED
FLOCKTO
FRECKLE
FRICKIE
FROCKED
GRACKLE
IRECKON
KNOCKED
KNOCKER
KNUCKLE
MENCKEN
PLACKET
PLUCKED
PRICKED
PRICKLE
PRICKLY
QUACKED
QUICKEN
QUICKER
QUICKIE
QUICKLY
SHACKLE
SHOCKED
SHOCKER
SHUCKED
SHUCKER
SLACKED
SLACKEN
SLACKER
SLICKED
SLICKER
SLICKLY
SMACKED
SMACKER
SNACKED
SNACKER
SNICKER
SPACKLE
SPECKLE
STACKED
STACKUP
STICKER
STICKTO
STICKUP
STOCKED
STOCKUP
STUCKTO
STUCKUP
THICKEN
THICKER
THICKET
THICKLY
TRACKED
TRACKER
TRICKED
TRICKER
TRICKLE
TRUCKED
TRUCKEE
TRUCKER
TRUCKLE
WHACKED
WRACKED
WRECKED
WRECKER

•••C•K•

CUPCAKE
HOECAKE
HOTCAKE
OILCAKE
PANCAKE
TEACAKE

•••C••K

FRYCOOK
HANCOCK
LEACOCK
PEACOCK
PETCOCK
PRECOOK

••••CK•

ACKACKS
ATTACKS
ATTUCKS
BEDECKS
FINICKY
HIJACKS
KOLACKY
KOPECKS
PANICKY
RELOCKS
SHTICKS
THWACKS
UNLOCKS
UNLUCKY
UNPACKS
UNTACKS
UPTICKS

••••C•K

JANACEK

•••••CK

AIRLOCK
AIRSOCK
ARMLOCK
BANNOCK
BARRACK
BEDROCK
BOMBECK
BRUBECK
BULLOCK
BURDOCK
CARRICK
CASSOCK
CONNICK
CONRACK
COSSACK
COWLICK
CUTBACK
DEFROCK
DERRICK
DRSPOCK
DRYDOCK
EARLOCK
FATBACK
FETLOCK
FOSDICK
GARRICK
GETBACK
GIMMICK
GOTBACK
GUNLOCK
HADDOCK
HAMHOCK
HAMMOCK
HANCOCK
HASSOCK
HATRACK
HAYRACK
HEMLOCK
HENPECK
HILLOCK
HOGBACK
HUMMOCK
ICEPACK
ICEPICK
INSTOCK
JAMPACK
KUBRICK
LAMARCK
LEACOCK
LOWNECK
LUBBOCK
MATLOCK
MATTOCK
MRSPOCK
MUDPACK
NIBLICK
NITPICK
OARLOCK
OLDNICK
OUTBACK
PADDOCK
PADLOCK
PATRICK
PEACOCK
PETCOCK
PETROCK
POLLOCK
POTLUCK
RANSACK
RATPACK
RECHECK
RESTOCK
RETRACK
RIDDICK
ROEBUCK
ROLLICK
RUNBACK
SADSACK
SAWBUCK
SCHLOCK
SEASICK
SELLECK
SETBACK
SHYLOCK
SIXPACK
SKYJACK
SUNDECK
TEDMACK
TIERACK
TIETACK
TOPKICK
TUSSOCK
UNFROCK
UNSTACK
UNSTICK
UNSTUCK
VANDYCK
VANEYCK
VEENECK
WARLOCK
WARWICK
WEDLOCK
WOZZECK

CL•••••

CLABBER
CLACKED
CLAIMED
CLAIMER
CLAIROL
CLAMBER
CLAMMED
CLAMMER
CLAMORS
CLAMPED
CLAMSUP
CLANGED
CLANGOR
CLANKED
CLAPPED
CLAPPER
CLAPTON
CLAQUES
CLARETS
CLARICE
CLARIFY
CLARION
CLARITY
CLASHED
CLASHES
CLASPED
CLASSED
CLASSES
CLASSIC
CLATTER
CLAUDIA
CLAUDIO
CLAUSES
CLAVELL
CLAVIER
CLAWERS
CLAWING
CLAYIER
CLAYTON
CLEANED
CLEANER
CLEANLY
CLEANSE
CLEANUP
CLEARED
CLEARER
CLEARLY
CLEARUP
CLEAVED
CLEAVER
CLEAVES
CLEAVON
CLEMENS
CLEMENT
CLEMSON
CLERICS
CLERKED
CLIBURN
CLICHES
CLICKED
CLIENTS
CLIFTON
CLIMATE
CLIMBED
CLIMBER
CLINGTO
CLINICS
CLINKED
CLINKER
CLINTON
CLIPART
CLIPONS
CLIPPED
CLIPPER
CLIQUES
CLOAKED
CLOBBER
CLOCHES
CLOCKED
CLOCKER
CLOCKIN
CLOGGED
CLOGSUP
CLONING
CLOONEY
CLOPPED
CLOQUES
CLORETS
CLOSEIN
CLOSELY
CLOSEST
CLOSETS
CLOSEUP
CLOSING
CLOSURE
CLOTHED
CLOTHES
CLOTTED
CLOTURE
CLOUDED
CLOUTED
CLOVERS
CLOWDER
CLOWNED
CLOYING
CLUBBED
CLUBCAR
CLUCKED
CLUEDIN
CLUEING
CLUESIN
CLUMPED
CLUNKED
CLUNKER
CLUSTER
CLUTTER

C•L••••

CALCIFY
CALCITE
CALCIUM
CALDERA
CALDRON
CALENDS
CALGARY
CALHOUN
CALIBAN
CALIBER
CALIBRE
CALICOS
CALIPER
CALIPHS
CALKING
CALKINS
CALLBOX
CALLERS
CALLFOR
CALLING
CALLINS
CALLOFF
CALLOUS
CALLOUT
CALLSIN
CALLSON
CALLSUP
CALMEST
CALMING
CALOMEL
CALORIC
CALORIE
CALPACS
CALTECH
CALUMET
CALUMNY
CALVARY
CALVERT
CALVING
CALYCES
CALYPSO
CALYXES
CALZONE
CCLAMPS
CELADON
CELEBES
CELEBRE
CELESTA
CELESTE
CELLARS
CELLINI
CELLIST
CELSIUS
CELTICS
CHLORAL
CILIATE
COLBERT
COLDCUT
COLDEST
COLDWAR
COLEMAN
COLETTE
COLGATE
COLLAGE
COLLARD
COLLARS
COLLATE
COLLECT
COLLEEN
COLLEGE
COLLETS
COLLIDE
COLLIER
COLLIES
COLLINS
COLLODI
COLLOID
COLLOPS
COLLUDE
COLLYER
COLOBUS
COLOGNE
COLONEL
COLONES
COLONNA
COLORED
COLOSSI
COLOURS
COLTISH
COLUMBO
COLUMNS
CSLEWIS
CULEBRA
CULLING
CULOTTE
CULPRIT
CULTISH
CULTISM
CULTIST
CULTJAM
CULTURE
CULVERT

C••L•••

CABLERS
CABLETV
CABLING
CALLBOX
CALLERS
CALLFOR
CALLING
CALLINS
CALLOFF
CALLOUS
CALLOUT
CALLSIN
CALLSON
CALLSUP
CAPLESS
CAPLETS
CARLESS
CARLOAD
CARLSON
CARLTON
CARLYLE
CATLIKE
CAULKED
CAULKER
CEILING
CELLARS
CELLINI
CELLIST
CHALETS
CHALICE
CHALKED
CHALKUP
CHALLIS
CHELSEA
CHILEAN
CHILIES
CHILLED
CHILLER
CHOLLAS
COALBIN
COALCAR
COALERS
COALGAS
COALOIL
COALTAR
COILING
COILSUP
COLLAGE
COLLARD
COLLARS
COLLATE
COLLECT
COLLEEN
COLLEGE
COLLETS
COLLIDE
COLLIER
COLLIES
COLLINS
COLLODI
COLLOID
COLLOPS
COLLUDE
COLLYER
COOLANT
COOLERS
COOLEST
COOLING
COOLSIT
COPLAND
COULDNT
COULEES
COULOMB
COULTER
COWLICK
COWLING
CRULLER
CULLING
CURLERS
CURLEWS
CURLIER
CURLING
CURLSUP
CUTLASS
CUTLERS
CUTLERY
CUTLETS
CYCLERS
CYCLING
CYCLIST
CYCLONE
CYCLOPS

C•••L••

CABALAS
CACKLED
CACKLER
CACKLES
CAJOLED
CAJOLER
CAJOLES
CAMELIA
CAMELOT
CAMILLE
CANDLES
CANTLES
CAPELET
CAPELLA
CAPULET
CAROLED
CAROLER
CAROLES
CAROLUS
CAROLYN
CASELAW
CASTLED
CASTLES
CATALAN
CATALOG
CATALPA
CAVALRY
CAVILED
CAVILER
CECILIA
CEDILLA
CHABLIS
CHALLIS
CHAPLET
CHAPLIN
CHARLES
CHARLEY
CHARLIE
CHEMLAB
CHILLED
CHILLER
CHOLLAS
CIRCLED
CIRCLES
CIRCLET
CIVILLY
COBBLED
COBBLER
COBBLES
COCHLEA
COCKLES
CODDLED
CODDLER
CODDLES
COMPLEX
COPILOT
CORELLI
COROLLA
COUPLED
COUPLES
COUPLET
COWSLIP
CRADLED
CRADLES
CRAWLED
CRAWLER
CREOLES
CRUELER
CRUELLY
CRULLER
CUDDLED
CUDDLES
CUMULUS
CUPOLAS
CURDLED
CURDLES
CUSSLER

C••••L•

CAMILLE
CANCELS
CANDELA
CANNILY
CANNOLI
CAPABLE
CAPABLY
CAPELLA
CAPFULS
CAPSULE
CARFULS
CARLYLE
CARPALS
CARRELS
CARROLL
CARTELS
CASTILE
CASUALS
CATCALL
CATTILY
CATWALK
CEDILLA
CEMBALO
CEREALS
CHAGALL
CHAPELS
CHARILY
CHEAPLY
CHIEFLY
CHISELS
CHORALE
CHORALS
CHORTLE
CHUCKLE
CITABLE
CIVILLY
CLAVELL
CLEANLY
CLEARLY
CLOSELY
COCKILY
COEVALS
COMPELS
COMPILE
CONDOLE
CONSOLE
CONSULS
CONSULT
COPPOLA
CORBELS
CORDELL
CORELLI
CORNELL
CORNILY
COROLLA
CORRALS
CORYELL
COURTLY
COWBELL
CRACKLE
CRASSLY
CRAYOLA
CRAZILY
CRENELS
CREWELS
CRINKLE
CRINKLY
CRISPLY
CROSSLY
CRUDELY
CRUELLY
CRUMBLE
CRUMBLY
CRUMPLE
CRUMPLY
CRYWOLF
CUBICLE
CUDGELS
CUEBALL
CUPFULS
CUREALL
CUTICLE
CYMBALS

C•••••L

CALOMEL
CAPITAL
CAPITOL
CARACAL
CARAMEL
CARAVEL
CAREFUL
CARPOOL
CARROLL
CATCALL
CATTAIL
CENTRAL
CHAGALL
CHANCEL
CHANNEL
CHATTEL
CHERVIL
CHLORAL
CHUNNEL
CITADEL
CLAIROL
CLAVELL
COALOIL
COASTAL
COAXIAL
CODICIL
COEQUAL
COLONEL
COMICAL
CONCEAL
CONGEAL
CONICAL
CONTROL
CORDELL
CORDIAL
CORNEAL
CORNELL
CORNOIL
CORYELL
COUNCIL
COUNSEL
COWBELL
COWGIRL
COZUMEL
CRANIAL
CREOSOL
CRUCIAL
CRYSTAL
CUEBALL
CUREALL
CURTAIL
CYNICAL

•CL••••

CCLAMPS
ECLAIRS
ECLIPSE
ECLOGUE
MCLUHAN
SCLERAS

•C•L•••

ACCLAIM
ACOLYTE
ECOLOGY
ICELAND
ICELESS
OCCLUDE
OCELOTS
OCULIST
SCALARS
SCALDED
SCALENE
SCALERS
SCALIER
SCALING
SCALLOP
SCALPED
SCALPEL
SCALPER
SCHLEPP
SCHLEPS
SCHLOCK
SCOLDED
SCOLDER
SCULLED
SCULLER
SCULPTS

•C••L••

ACRYLIC
ECHELON
ICEBLUE
ICEFLOE
ICICLES

MCCALLS
OCCULTS
SCALLOP
SCARLET
SCHOLAR
SCOWLED
SCOWLER
SCROLLS
SCULLED
SCULLER
UCCELLO

•C•••L•

ACEROLA
ACRIDLY
ACTABLE
ACUTELY
ICECOLD
ICEMILK
MCCALLS
OCTUPLE
SCANTLY
SCAPULA
SCARILY
SCHOOLS
SCRAWLS
SCRAWLY
SCROLLS
SCRUPLE
SCUFFLE
SCUTTLE
UCCELLO

•C••••L

ACCRUAL
SCALPEL
SCANDAL

••CL•••

ACCLAIM
ARCLAMP
BECLOUD
CYCLERS
CYCLING
CYCLIST
CYCLONE
CYCLOPS
DECLAIM
DECLARE
DECLASS
DECLINE
ENCLAVE
ENCLOSE
EXCLAIM
EXCLUDE
INCLINE
INCLOSE
INCLUDE
MRCLEAN
NUCLEAR
NUCLEIC
NUCLEON
NUCLEUS
NUCLIDE
OCCLUDE
RECLAIM
RECLAME
RECLEAN
RECLINE
RECLUSE
SECLUDE
UNCLASP
UNCLEAN
UNCLEAR
UNCLOAK
UNCLOGS
UNCLOSE
UPCLOSE

••C•L••

BACILLI
BACKLIT
BACKLOG
BECALMS
BICOLOR
BUCKLED
BUCKLER
BUCKLES
BUCKLEY
BUCOLIC
CACKLED
CACKLER
CACKLES
CECILIA
COCHLEA
COCKLES
DECALOG
DECKLES
FACULTY
FICKLER
FOCSLES
HACKLES
HECKLED
HECKLER
HECKLES
JOCULAR
LOCALES
LOCALLY
LUCILLE
MACULAE
MCCALLS
NACELLE
NICOLAS
OCCULTS
PICKLED
PICKLES
RECALLS
RECOLOR
RICKLES
SECULAR
SICKLES
TACKLED
TACKLER
TACKLES
TICKLED
TICKLER
TICKLES
UCCELLO
VOCALIC
VOCALLY

••C••L•

BACILLI
BICYCLE
COCKILY
DACTYLS
DECARLO
DUCTILE
FACIALS
JACKALS
LICITLY
LLCOOLJ
LOCALLY
LUCIDLY
LUCILLE
LUCKILY
MCCALLS
MICHELE
NACELLE
NICCOLO
NICHOLS
NICKELS
OSCEOLA
PICCOLO
RECALLS
RECHALK
RECOILS
RECYCLE
SOCIALS
TACITLY
TACKILY
TACTILE
UCCELLO
UNCIALS
UNCOILS
UNCURLS
VACUOLE
VOCALLY
WACKILY
WYCHELM

••C•••L

ACCRUAL
ALCOHOL
DECIBEL
DECIMAL
FACTUAL
INCIVIL
LACTEAL
LACUNAL
MICHAEL
RECITAL
SACKFUL
TACTFUL
UNCIVIL
VICTUAL

•••CL••

CIRCLED
CIRCLES
CIRCLET
DEWCLAW
ICICLES
KEYCLUB
MUSCLED
MUSCLES
ORACLES
TIECLIP

•••C•L•

BADCOLD
BLACKLY
CANCELS
CATCALL
CHUCKLE
CRACKLE
DRACULA
DRYCELL
ERECTLY
EXACTLY
FANCILY
FRECKLE
GRACILE
GRACKLE
HERCULE
ICECOLD
INOCULA
JUICILY
KNUCKLE
LASCALA
LINCOLN
MALCOLM
MARCELS
MESCALS
MISCALL
NICCOLO
PARCELS
PENCILS
PERCALE
PICCOLO
PRICKLE
PRICKLY
PURCELL
QUICKLY
RASCALS
REDCELL
RESCALE
SAUCILY
SHACKLE
SLICKLY
SPACKLE
SPECKLE
TERCELS
THICKLY
TOSCALE
TRICKLE
TRUCKLE
UPSCALE
WETCELL

•••C••L

AIRCOOL
ASOCIAL
CATCALL
CONCEAL
CRUCIAL
DRYCELL
FRACTAL
GLACIAL
MISCALL
PASCHAL
PINCURL
PRECOOL
PURCELL
REDCELL
SATCHEL
SPECIAL
TRUCIAL
WETCELL

••••CL•

ARTICLE
AURICLE
BICYCLE
CUBICLE
CUTICLE
DEBACLE
MANACLE
MIRACLE
MONOCLE
OSSICLE
PANICLE
PEDICLE
PINOCLE
RADICLE
RECYCLE
RETICLE
TREACLE
TREACLY
TUNICLE
VEHICLE

••••C•L

BIFOCAL
CARACAL
CHANCEL
CODICIL
COMICAL
CONICAL
COUNCIL
CYNICAL
ETHICAL
HELICAL
LEXICAL
LOGICAL
LYRICAL
MAGICAL
MEDICAL
MUSICAL
OPTICAL
PEDICEL
RADICAL
STENCIL
STOICAL
TOPICAL
TYPICAL

C•M••••

CAMBERS
CAMBIUM
CAMBRIC
CAMELIA
CAMELOT
CAMEOED
CAMEOFF
CAMEOUT
CAMERAS
CAMERON
CAMILLE
CAMISES
CAMPARI
CAMPERS
CAMPHOR
CAMPIER
CAMPING
CAMPION
CAMPOUT
CEMBALO
CEMENTS
COMBATS
COMBERS
COMBINE
COMBING
COMBUST
COMEDIC
COMEDUE
COMEOFF
COMEONS
COMEOUT
COMESAT
COMESBY
COMESIN
COMESON
COMESTO
COMESUP
COMFIER
COMFITS
COMFORT
COMFREY
COMICAL
COMINGS
COMIQUE
COMMAND
COMMEND
COMMENT
COMMITS
COMMODE
COMMONS
COMMOVE
COMMUNE
COMMUTE
COMOROS
COMPACT
COMPANY
COMPARE
COMPASS
COMPEER
COMPELS
COMPETE
COMPILE
COMPLEX
COMPORT
COMPOSE
COMPOST
COMPOTE
COMPUTE
COMRADE
CUMULUS
CYMBALS

C••M•••

CADMIUM
CAIMANS
CALMEST
CALMING
CARMINE
CHAMBER
CHAMFER
CHAMOIS
CHAMPED
CHEMISE
CHEMIST
CHEMLAB
CHIMERA
CHIMING
CHIMNEY
CHOMPED
CHOMSKY
CHUMMED
CLAMBER
CLAMMED
CLAMMER
CLAMORS
CLAMPED
CLAMSUP
CLEMENS
CLEMENT
CLEMSON
CLIMATE
CLIMBED
CLIMBER
CLUMPED
COMMAND
COMMEND
COMMENT
COMMITS
COMMODE
COMMONS
COMMOVE
COMMUNE
COMMUTE
CRAMMED
CRAMMER
CRAMPED
CRAMPON
CREMONA
CRIMEAN
CRIMPED
CRIMPER
CRIMSON
CRUMBLE
CRUMBLY
CRUMPET
CRUMPLE
CRUMPLY

C•••M••

CAKEMIX
CALOMEL
CALUMET
CALUMNY
CARAMBA
CARAMEL
CARAMIA
CAROMED
CAVEMAN
CAVEMEN
CCLAMPS
CERAMIC
CERUMEN
CHAPMAN
CHAPMEN
CHARMED
CHARMER
CHARMIN
CHROMES
CHUMMED
CINEMAS
CINEMAX
CLAIMED
CLAIMER
CLAMMED
CLAMMER
COLEMAN
COLUMBO
COLUMNS
COZUMEL
CRAMMED
CRAMMER
CREAMED
CREAMER
CREWMAN
CREWMEN

C••••M•

CENTIME
CENTIMO
CHRISMS
CONDEMN
CONGAME
CONSUME
CONTEMN
COSTUME
COULOMB
COXCOMB
CUSTOMS
CUTTIME

C•••••M

CADMIUM
CALCIUM
CAMBIUM
CHATHAM
CHETRUM
CONFIRM
CONFORM
CRANIUM
CULTISM
CULTJAM
CZARDOM
CZARISM

•CM••••

MCMAHON

•C•M•••

ICEMILK
SCAMMED
SCAMPED
SCAMPER
SCHMEER
SCHMIDT
SCHMOES
SCHMOOS

•C••M••

CCLAMPS
SCAMMED
SCHEMAS
SCHEMED
SCHEMER
SCHEMES
SCRIMPS
SCRIMPY

•C•••M•

ACADEME
ACADEMY
ECONOMY
SCHISMS
SCREAMS

•C••••M

ACCLAIM
ACRONYM

••CM•••

MICMACS

••C•M••

BECOMES
DECAMPS
DECIMAL
ENCAMPS
ENCOMIA
HACKMAN
HICKMAN
INCOMES
JICAMAS
RACEMES
RICHMAN
TUCHMAN

••C••M•

ALCHEMY
ARCLAMP
BECALMS
DICTUMS
LYCEUMS
MACRAME
RECLAME
SACHEMS
SUCCUMB
VACUUMS
VICTIMS

••C•••M

ACCLAIM
BUCKRAM
DECLAIM
DECORUM
EXCLAIM
MACADAM
RECLAIM
RECROOM
WYCHELM

•••C•M•

ATACAMA
COXCOMB
DAYCAMP
DRACHMA
GIACOMO
HOWCOME
NONCOMS
OUTCOME
SATCHMO
SITCOMS
SUCCUMB
WELCOME

•••C••M

BEECHAM
CALCIUM
FASCISM
FULCRUM
JOACHIM
KETCHAM
MALCOLM
MITCHUM
SANCTUM
SARCASM

••••C•M

MINICAM
MODICUM

CN•••••

CNTOWER

C•N••••

CANAPES
CANARDS
CANASTA
CANCANS
CANCELS
CANDELA
CANDICE
CANDIDA
CANDIDE
CANDIDS
CANDIED
CANDIES
CANDLES
CANDOUR
CANINES
CANKERS
CANNERS
CANNERY
CANNIER
CANNILY
CANNING
CANNOLI
CANNONS
CANONIC
CANOPUS
CANSECO
CANTATA
CANTEEN
CANTERS
CANTINA
CANTING
CANTLES
CANTONS
CANTORS
CANVASS
CANYONS
CANZONE
CENSERS
CENSING
CENSORS
CENSURE
CENTAUR
CENTAVO
CENTERS
CENTIME
CENTIMO
CENTRAL
CENTRED
CENTRES
CENTRIC
CENTURY
CINCHED
CINCHES
CINDERS
CINEMAS
CINEMAX
CINZANO
CONAKRY
CONBRIO
CONCAVE
CONCEAL
CONCEDE
CONCEIT
CONCEPT
CONCERN
CONCERT
CONCHES
CONCISE
CONCOCT
CONCORD
CONCURS
CONDEMN
CONDIGN
CONDOLE
CONDONE
CONDORS
CONDUCE
CONDUCT
CONDUIT
CONFABS
CONFERS
CONFESS
CONFIDE
CONFINE
CONFIRM
CONFORM
CONFUSE
CONFUTE
CONGAED
CONGAME
CONGEAL
CONGERS
CONGEST
CONICAL
CONIFER
CONJOBS
CONJOIN
CONJURE
CONKERS
CONKING
CONKOUT
CONNECT
CONNERY
CONNICK
CONNIFF
CONNING
CONNIVE
CONNORS
CONNOTE
CONQUER
CONRACK
CONREID
CONSENT
CONSIGN
CONSIST
CONSOLE
CONSORT
CONSULS
CONSULT
CONSUME
CONTACT
CONTAIN
CONTEMN
CONTEND
CONTENT
CONTEST
CONTEXT
CONTORT
CONTOUR
CONTRAS
CONTROL
CONTUSE
CONVENE
CONVENT
CONVERT
CONVEYS
CONVICT
CONVOKE
CONVOYS
CUNNING
CYNICAL
CYNTHIA

C••N•••

CANNERS
CANNERY
CANNIER
CANNILY
CANNING
CANNOLI
CANNONS
CAPNUTS
CARNERA
CARNETS
CARNIES
CATNAPS
CATNIPS
CHANCED
CHANCEL
CHANCES
CHANGED
CHANGER
CHANGES
CHANNEL
CHANSON
CHANTED
CHANTER
CHANTEY
CHENIER
CHINESE
CHINKED
CHINNED
CHINOOK
CHINTZY
CHINUPS
CHUNNEL
CLANGED
CLANGOR
CLANKED
CLINGTO
CLINICS
CLINKED
CLINKER
CLINTON
CLONING
CLUNKED
CLUNKER
COGNACS
COGNATE
COINAGE
COINERS
COINING
CONNECT
CONNERY
CONNICK
CONNIFF
CONNING
CONNIVE
CONNORS
CONNOTE
COONCAT
CORNCOB
CORNDOG
CORNEAL
CORNEAS
CORNELL
CORNERS
CORNETS
CORNFED
CORNICE
CORNIER
CORNILY
CORNING
CORNISH
CORNOIL
CORNROW
COUNCIL
COUNSEL
COUNTED
COUNTER
COUNTON
COUNTRY
COYNESS
CRANIAL
CRANING
CRANIUM
CRANKED
CRANKUP
CRENELS
CRINGED
CRINGES
CRINKLE
CRINKLY
CRINOID
CRONIES
CRUNCHY
CUNNING
CYGNETS

C•••N••

CABANAS
CABINET
CADENCE
CADENZA
CALENDS
CANINES
CANONIC
CARINAS
CASINGS
CASINOS
CATENAE
CAYENNE
CEMENTS
CEZANNE
CHAINED
CHANNEL
CHIANTI
CHIGNON
CHIMNEY
CHINNED
CHRONIC
CHUNNEL
CHURNED
CHUTNEY
CLEANED
CLEANER
CLEANLY
CLEANSE
CLEANUP
CLIENTS
CLOONEY
CLOWNED
COCKNEY
COCONUT
COGENCY
COLONEL
COLONES
COLONNA
COMINGS
CORINTH
CORONAE
CORONAS
CORONET
COSINES
COSTNER
COZENED
CROONED
CROONER
CROWNED
CUTINTO

C••••N•

CABLING
CACHING
CADGING
CAFTANS
CAIMANS
CALKING
CALKINS
CALLING
CALLINS
CALMING
CALUMNY
CALVING
CALZONE
CAMPING
CANCANS
CANNING
CANNONS
CANTINA
CANTING
CANTONS
CANYONS
CANZONE
CAPEANN
CAPGUNS
CAPPING
CARBINE
CARBONS
CARDING
CAREENS
CARMINE
CARPING
CARTING
CARTONS
CARVING
CASERNS
CASHING
CASSINI

CASTING
CATIONS
CATKINS
CATTING
CAUSING
CAVEINS
CAVERNS
CAYENNE
CEASING
CEILING
CELLINI
CENSING
CEZANNE
CHAFING
CHASING
CHEWING
CHICANA
CHICANO
CHIDING
CHIMING
CHORINE
CINZANO
CITRINE
CITRONS
CLAWING
CLEMENS
CLEMENT
CLIPONS
CLONING
CLOSING
CLOYING
CLUEING
COATING
COAXING
COCKING
COCOONS
CODEINE
COIFING
COILING
COINING
COLLINS
COLOGNE
COLONNA
COLUMNS
COMBINE
COMBING
COMEONS
COMMAND
COMMEND
COMMENT
COMMONS
COMMUNE
COMPANY
CONDONE
CONFINE
CONKING
CONNING
CONSENT
CONTEND
CONTENT
CONVENE
CONVENT
COOKING
COOLANT
COOLING
COOPING
COPLAND
COPPING
COPYING
CORDING
CORDONS
CORKING
CORNING
COSIGNS
COSTING
COTTONS
COTTONY
COULDNT
COUPONS
COURANT
COUSINS
COWHAND
COWLING
COZYING
COZZENS
CRANING
CRATING
CRAVENS
CRAVING
CRAYONS
CRAZING
CREMONA
CRETANS
CRETINS
CREWING
CROWING
CUFFING
CUIBONO
CUISINE
CULLING
CUNNING
CUPPING
CURBING
CURDING
CURLING
CURRANT
CURRENT
CURSING
CURVING
CUSSING
CUTTING
CYCLING
CYCLONE
CYYOUNG
CZARINA

C•••••N

CADDOAN
CAISSON
CALDRON
CALHOUN
CALIBAN
CALLSIN
CALLSON
CAMERON
CAMPION
CANTEEN
CAPEANN
CAPITAN
CAPSTAN
CAPTAIN
CAPTION
CARAVAN
CARLSON
CARLTON
CAROLYN
CARRION
CARRYON
CARTOON
CASPIAN
CATALAN
CATCHON
CATSCAN
CAUTION
CAVEDIN
CAVEMAN
CAVEMEN
CAVESIN
CELADON
CERTAIN
CERUMEN
CESSION
CHAGRIN
CHANSON
CHAPLIN
CHAPMAN
CHAPMEN
CHARMIN
CHASTEN
CHEAPEN
CHECHEN
CHECKIN
CHEVRON
CHICHEN
CHICKEN
CHIFFON
CHIGNON
CHILEAN
CHIPSIN
CISTERN
CITIZEN
CITROEN
CLAPTON
CLARION
CLAYTON
CLEAVON
CLEMSON
CLIBURN
CLIFTON
CLINTON
CLOCKIN
CLOSEIN
CLUEDIN
CLUESIN
COALBIN
COARSEN
COCHRAN
COGBURN
COLEMAN
COLLEEN
COMESIN
COMESON
CONCERN
CONDEMN
CONDIGN
CONJOIN
CONSIGN
CONTAIN
CONTEMN
CORAZON
COSTAIN
COUNTON
COWTOWN
CRAMPON
CREWMAN
CREWMEN
CRIMEAN
CRIMSON
CRISPIN
CROUTON
CRYOGEN
CURTAIN
CUSHION
CUTDOWN

•C•N•••

ACANTHI
ACONITE
ECONOMY
ICINESS
ICINGIN
MCENROE
OCANADA
OCONNOR
SCANDAL
SCANNED
SCANNER
SCANTED
SCANTER
SCANTLY
SCENDED
SCENERY
SCENTED
SCHNAPS
SCONCES

•C••N••

ACCENTS
ACHENES
ACRONYM
ACTINIC
ECHINUS
OCEANIA
OCEANIC
OCEANID
OCEANUS
OCONNOR
OCTANES
OCTANTS
SCANNED
SCANNER
SCIENCE
SCORNED
SCRUNCH
WCHANDY

•C•••N•

ACCOUNT
ACETONE
ACHTUNG
ACTIONS
ECHIDNA
ECHOING
ICELAND
ICERINK
MCSWINE
OCARINA
SCALENE
SCALING
SCARING
SCHWINN
SCOPING
SCORING
SCRAWNY
SCREENS

•C••••N

ACADIAN
ACHERON
ACHESON
ACTAEON
ACTUPON
ECHELON
ICINGIN
MCGAVIN
MCLUHAN
MCMAHON
MCQUEEN
OCTAGON
SCHWINN
SCRIVEN

••CN•••

PICNICS

••C•N••

ACCENTS
ASCENDS
ASCENTS
COCKNEY
COCONUT
DECANTS
DOCENTS
FACINGS
HACKNEY
INCANTS
INCENSE
JACANAS
JACINTO
JACONET
LACINGS
LACONIC
LACUNAE
LACUNAL
LACUNAS
LICENCE
LICENSE
LOCKNUT
NOCANDO
OSCINES
PICANTE
POCONOS
RECANED
RECANES
RECANTS
RECENCY
SECANTS
SECONDS
UNCANNY
VACANCY
VICUNAS

••C••N•

ACCOUNT
ANCIENT
ARCHING
ARCHONS
ARCSINE
BACKEND
BACKING
BECKONS
BUCKING
CACHING
COCKING
COCOONS
CYCLING
CYCLONE
DECKING
DECLINE
DICKENS
DOCKING
DUCKING
DUCTING
ENCHANT
ETCHING
HACKING
HOCKING
INCHING
INCLINE
ITCHING
JACKING
KACHINA
KICKING
LACKING
LICHENS
LICKING
LOCKING
LOCKINS
LUCERNE
LUCIANO
LUCKING
MACHINA
MACHINE
MACRONS
MICRONS
MOCKING
MUCKING
NECKING
NICKING
PACKING
PECCANT
PECKING
PECTINS
PICKENS
PICKING
PUCCINI
RACKING
RECKONS
RECLINE
RECOUNT
ROCKING
RUCHING
RUCKING
SACKING
SICCING
SICKENS
SOCKING
SUCKING
TACKING
TICKING
TOCSINS
TUCKING
TYCOONS
UNCANNY
URCHINS
VACCINE

••C•••N

AUCTION
BACKSIN
COCHRAN
DECAGON
DICTION
DUCKPIN
ENCHAIN
FACTION
FICTION
HACKMAN
HICKMAN
JACKSON
JACOBIN
KICKSIN
LECTERN
MRCLEAN
NOCTURN
NUCLEON
PICKSON
RACCOON
RECLEAN
RICHMAN
RUCTION
SECTION
SICHUAN
SOCKSIN
SUCKSIN
SUCTION
TACKSON
TUCHMAN
TUCKSIN
UNCHAIN
UNCLEAN
UNCTION
YUCATAN

•••C•N•

ABSCOND
ARACHNE
ASHCANS
BALCONY
BEACONS
BRACING
CANCANS
CHICANA
CHICANO
DANCING
DEACONS
DEICING
DESCANT
DESCEND
DESCENT
EDUCING
EPICENE
FALCONS
FENCING
FLACONS
FORCING
GARCONS
GASCONS
GRACING
JUICING
LARCENY
MANCINI
MARCONI
MINCING
MIOCENE
NASCENT
OBSCENE
OILCANS
PECCANT
PERCENT
PIECING
PISCINE
PLACING
PORCINE
PRICING
PUCCINI
REDCENT
RESCIND
SICCING
SLICING
SNOCONE
SPACING
SPICING
SYNCING
TINCANS
TOUCANS
TRACING
TUSCANY
VACCINE
VINCENT
VOICING
VOLCANO
VULCANS
WINCING
ZIRCONS

•••C••N

BLACKEN
BRACKEN
CATCHON
CHECHEN
CHECKIN
CHICHEN
CHICKEN
CLOCKIN
CONCERN
DISCERN
ERICSON
GRECIAN
HALCYON
IRECKON
KITCHEN
LAOCOON
LINCOLN
MADCHEN
MARCHEN
MARCHON
MENCKEN
OMICRON
PITCHIN
POPCORN
PROCYON
PUNCHIN
PYNCHON
QUICKEN
RACCOON
SLACKEN
TEACHIN
THICKEN
TOUCHON
TRICORN
UNICORN

••••C•N

AFRICAN
ALARCON
ALENCON
AZTECAN
CATSCAN
HELICON
ITHACAN
LEXICON
MEXICAN
MOHICAN
PELICAN
PEMICAN
RUBICON
SARACEN
SILICON
SOUPCON
VATICAN

CO•••••

COACHED
COACHES
COALBIN
COALCAR
COALERS
COALGAS
COALOIL
COALTAR
COARSEN
COARSER
COASTAL
COASTED
COASTER
COATING
COAXERS
COAXIAL
COAXING
COBBLED
COBBLER
COBBLES
COBWEBS
COCHERE
COCHISE
COCHLEA
COCHRAN
COCKADE
COCKIER
COCKILY
COCKING
COCKLES
COCKNEY
COCKPIT
COCONUT
COCOONS
COCTEAU
CODDLED
CODDLER
CODDLES
CODEINE
CODFISH
CODGERS
CODICES
CODICIL
COEDITS
COEQUAL
COERCED
COERCES
COEVALS
COEXIST
COFFEES
COFFERS
COGBURN
COGENCY
COGNACS
COGNATE
COHABIT
COHEIRS
COHERED
COHERES
COHORTS
COHOSTS
COIFING
COILING
COILSUP
COINAGE
COINERS
COINING
COLBERT
COLDCUT
COLDEST
COLDWAR
COLEMAN
COLETTE
COLGATE
COLLAGE
COLLARD
COLLARS
COLLATE
COLLECT
COLLEEN
COLLEGE
COLLETS
COLLIDE
COLLIER
COLLIES
COLLINS
COLLODI
COLLOID
COLLOPS
COLLUDE
COLLYER
COLOBUS
COLOGNE
COLONEL
COLONES
COLONNA
COLORED
COLOSSI
COLOURS
COLTISH
COLUMBO
COLUMNS
COMBATS
COMBERS
COMBINE
COMBING
COMBUST
COMEDIC
COMEDUE
COMEOFF
COMEONS
COMEOUT
COMESAT
COMESBY
COMESIN
COMESON
COMESTO
COMESUP
COMFIER
COMFITS
COMFORT
COMFREY
COMICAL
COMINGS
COMIQUE
COMMAND
COMMEND
COMMENT
COMMITS
COMMODE
COMMONS
COMMOVE
COMMUNE
COMMUTE
COMOROS
COMPACT
COMPANY
COMPARE
COMPASS
COMPEER
COMPELS
COMPETE
COMPILE
COMPLEX
COMPORT
COMPOSE
COMPOST
COMPOTE
COMPUTE
COMRADE
CONAKRY
CONBRIO
CONCAVE
CONCEAL
CONCEDE
CONCEIT
CONCEPT
CONCERN
CONCERT
CONCHES
CONCISE
CONCOCT
CONCORD
CONCURS
CONDEMN
CONDIGN
CONDOLE
CONDONE
CONDORS
CONDUCE
CONDUCT
CONDUIT
CONFABS
CONFERS
CONFESS
CONFIDE
CONFINE
CONFIRM
CONFORM
CONFUSE
CONFUTE
CONGAED
CONGAME
CONGEAL
CONGERS
CONGEST
CONICAL
CONIFER
CONJOBS
CONJOIN
CONJURE
CONKERS
CONKING
CONKOUT
CONNECT
CONNERY
CONNICK
CONNIFF
CONNING
CONNIVE
CONNORS
CONNOTE
CONQUER
CONRACK
CONREID
CONSENT
CONSIGN
CONSIST
CONSOLE
CONSORT
CONSULS
CONSULT
CONSUME
CONTACT
CONTAIN
CONTEMN
CONTEND
CONTENT
CONTEST
CONTEXT
CONTORT
CONTOUR
CONTRAS
CONTROL
CONTUSE
CONVENE
CONVENT
CONVERT
CONVEYS
CONVICT
CONVOKE
CONVOYS
COOKERS
COOKERY
COOKIES
COOKING
COOKOFF
COOKOUT
COOKSUP
COOLANT
COOLERS
COOLEST
COOLING
COOLSIT
COONCAT
COOPERS
COOPING
COOPSUP
COOPTED
COOTIES
COPIERS
COPILOT
COPIOUS
COPLAND
COPOUTS
COPPERS
COPPERY
COPPICE
COPPING
COPPOLA
COPSOUT
COPTERS
COPYBOY
COPYCAT
COPYING
COPYIST
CORAZON
CORBELS
CORBETT
CORDAGE
CORDATE
CORDELL
CORDERO
CORDIAL
CORDING
CORDITE
CORDOBA
CORDONS
CORELLI
CORETTA
CORINTH
CORKAGE
CORKERS
CORKING
CORNCOB
CORNDOG
CORNEAL
CORNEAS
CORNELL
CORNERS
CORNETS
CORNFED
CORNICE
CORNIER
CORNILY
CORNING
CORNISH
CORNOIL
CORNROW
COROLLA
CORONAE
CORONAS
CORONET
CORRALS
CORRECT
CORRIDA
CORRODE
CORRUPT
CORSAGE
CORSAIR
CORSETS
CORSICA
CORTEGE
CORYELL
COSIGNS
COSINES
COSSACK
COSSETS
COSTAIN
COSTARS
COSTING
COSTNER
COSTUME
COTERIE
COTTAGE
COTTERS
COTTONS
COTTONY
COUCHED
COUCHES
COUGARS
COUGHED
COUGHUP
COULDNT
COULEES
COULOMB
COULTER
COUNCIL
COUNSEL
COUNTED
COUNTER
COUNTON
COUNTRY
COUPLED
COUPLES
COUPLET
COUPONS
COURAGE
COURANT
COURIER
COURSED
COURSER
COURSES
COURTED
COURTLY
COUSINS
COUTURE
COVERED
COVERUP
COVETED
COWARDS
COWBELL
COWBIRD
COWBOYS
COWERED
COWGIRL
COWHAND
COWHERD
COWHIDE
COWLICK
COWLING
COWPEAS
COWPOKE
COWRIES
COWSLIP
COWTOWN
COXCOMB
COYNESS
COYOTES
COZENED
COZIEST
COZUMEL
COZYING
COZZENS

C•O••••
CHOCTAW
CHOICER
CHOICES
CHOKERS
CHOKEUP
CHOLLAS
CHOMPED
CHOMSKY
CHOOSER
CHOOSES
CHOPPED
CHOPPER
CHORALE
CHORALS
CHORINE
CHORIZO
CHORTLE
CHOWDER
CLOAKED
CLOBBER
CLOCHES
CLOCKED
CLOCKER
CLOCKIN
CLOGGED
CLOGSUP
CLONING
CLOONEY
CLOPPED
CLOQUES
CLORETS
CLOSEIN
CLOSELY
CLOSEST
CLOSETS
CLOSEUP
CLOSING
CLOSURE
CLOTHED
CLOTHES
CLOTTED
CLOTURE
CLOUDED
CLOUTED
CLOVERS
CLOWDER
CLOWNED
CLOYING
COOKERS
COOKERY
COOKIES
COOKING
COOKOFF
COOKOUT
COOKSUP
COOLANT
COOLERS
COOLEST
COOLING
COOLSIT
COONCAT
COOPERS
COOPING
COOPSUP
COOPTED
COOTIES
CROAKED
CROATIA
CROCHET
CROESUS
CRONIES
CROOKED
CROONED
CROONER
CROPPED
CROPPER
CROPSUP
CROQUET
CROSIER
CROSSED
CROSSER
CROSSES
CROSSLY
CROSSUP
CROUTON
CROWBAR
CROWDED
CROWERS
CROWING
CROWNED

C••O•••
CABOOSE
CAHOOTS
CAJOLED
CAJOLER
CAJOLES
CALOMEL
CALORIC
CALORIE
CANONIC
CANOPUS
CAROLED
CAROLER
CAROLES
CAROLUS
CAROLYN
CAROMED
CAROTID
CAROUSE
CAVORTS
CHAOTIC
CHLORAL
CHOOSER
CHOOSES
CHROMES
CHRONIC
CIBORIA
CLOONEY
CNTOWER
COCONUT
COCOONS
COHORTS
COHOSTS
COLOBUS
COLOGNE
COLONEL
COLONES
COLONNA
COLORED
COLOSSI
COLOURS
COMOROS
COPOUTS
COROLLA
CORONAE
CORONAS
CORONET
COYOTES
CREOLES
CREOSOL
CROOKED
CROONED
CROONER
CRYOGEN
CULOTTE
CUPOLAS
CUTOFFS
CUTOUTS
CYBORGS
CYYOUNG

C•••O••
CABOOSE
CACHOUS
CADDOAN
CAHOOTS
CALHOUN
CALLOFF
CALLOUS
CALLOUT
CALZONE
CAMEOED
CAMEOFF
CAMEOUT
CAMPOUT
CANDOUR
CANNOLI
CANNONS
CANTONS
CANTORS
CANYONS
CANZONE
CAPTORS
CARBONS
CARBOYS
CARCOAT
CARDOZO
CARGOES
CARHOPS
CARIOCA
CARLOAD
CARPOOL
CARPORT
CARROLL
CARROTS
CARTONS
CARTOON
CASHOUT
CASSOCK
CASTOFF
CASTOUT
CATBOAT
CATHODE
CATIONS
CENSORS
CHAMOIS
CHEROOT
CHEWOUT
CHICORY
CHINOOK
CITROEN
CITRONS
CLAMORS
CLIPONS
COALOIL
COCOONS
COLLODI
COLLOID
COLLOPS
COMEOFF
COMEONS
COMEOUT
COMFORT
COMMODE
COMMONS
COMMOVE
COMPORT
COMPOSE
COMPOST
COMPOTE
CONCOCT
CONCORD
CONDOLE
CONDONE
CONDORS
CONFORM
CONJOBS
CONJOIN
CONKOUT
CONNORS
CONNOTE
CONSOLE
CONSORT
CONTORT
CONTOUR
CONVOKE
CONVOYS
COOKOFF
COOKOUT
COPIOUS
COPPOLA
COPSOUT
CORDOBA
CORDONS
CORNOIL
CORRODE
COTTONS
COTTONY
COULOMB
COUPONS
COWBOYS
COWPOKE
COWTOWN
COXCOMB
CRAYOLA
CRAYONS
CREMONA
CRINOID
CRYWOLF
CUCKOOS
CUIBONO
CURIOUS
CURSORS
CURSORY
CUSTODY
CUSTOMS
CUTDOWN
CUTSOFF
CUTSOUT
CYCLONE
CYCLOPS

C••••O•
CAISSON
CALDRON
CALICOS
CALLBOX
CALLFOR
CALLSON
CAMELOT
CAMERON
CAMPHOR
CAMPION
CAPECOD
CAPITOL
CAPTION
CAREFOR
CARIBOU
CARLSON
CARLTON
CARPOOL
CARRION
CARRYON
CARTOON
CASHBOX
CASHCOW
CASINOS
CATALOG
CATCHON
CAUTION
CELADON
CESSION
CHANSON
CHARIOT
CHEETOS
CHEKHOV
CHEROOT
CHEVIOT
CHEVRON
CHIFFON
CHIGNON
CHINOOK
CLAIROL
CLANGOR
CLAPTON
CLARION
CLAYTON
CLEAVON
CLEMSON
CLIFTON
CLINTON
COMESON
COMOROS
CONTROL
COPILOT
COPYBOY
CORAZON
CORNCOB
CORNDOG
CORNROW
COUNTON
CRAMPON
CREATOR
CREOSOL
CRIMSON
CROUTON
CRYPTOS
CUCKOOS
CURATOR
CUSHION
CYPRIOT
CZARDOM

C•••••O
CALYPSO
CANSECO
CARDOZO
CBRADIO
CEMBALO
CENTAVO
CENTIMO
CHEERIO
CHICAGO
CHICANO
CHORIZO
CHRISTO
CINZANO
CLAUDIO
CLINGTO
COLUMBO
COMESTO
CONBRIO
CORDERO
CRUZADO
CUIBONO
CURACAO
CUTINTO

•CO••••
ACOLYTE
ACONITE
ECOLOGY
ECONOMY
OCONNOR
SCOFFED
SCOFFER
SCOLDED
SCOLDER
SCONCES
SCOOPED
SCOOPER
SCOOTED
SCOOTER
SCOPING
SCORERS
SCORING
SCORNED
SCORPIO
SCOTERS
SCOTTIE
SCOURED
SCOURER
SCOURGE
SCOUTED
SCOUTER
SCOWLED
SCOWLER

•C•O•••
ACCORDS
ACCOSTS
ACCOUNT
ACROBAT
ACRONYM
ECHOING
ECLOGUE
OCTOBER
OCTOPOD
OCTOPUS
SCHOLAR
SCHOOLS
SCOOPED
SCOOPER
SCOOTED
SCOOTER
SCROLLS
SCROOGE

•C••O••
ACEDOUT
ACEROLA
ACEROSE
ACESOUT
ACETONE
ACTIONS
ACTSOUT
ECOLOGY
ECONOMY
ICEBOAT
ICECOLD
OCELOTS
SCHLOCK
SCHMOES
SCHMOOS
SCHOOLS
SCROOGE

•C•••O•
ACHERON
ACHESON
ACTAEON
ACTUPON
ECHELON
ECUADOR
ICEFLOE
ICESHOW
ICHABOD
MCENROE
MCMAHON
OCONNOR
OCTAGON
OCTAVOS
OCTOPOD
SCALLOP
SCHMOOS
SCISSOR

•C••••O
SCHERZO
SCORPIO
UCCELLO

••CO•••
ACCORDS
ACCOSTS
ACCOUNT
ALCOHOL
ALCOVES
BECOMES
BICOLOR
BUCOLIC
COCONUT
COCOONS
DECOCTS
DECODED
DECODER
DECODES
DECORUM
DECOYED
ENCODED
ENCODER
ENCODES
ENCOMIA
ENCORES
ESCORTS
IACOCCA
INCOMES
JACOBIN
JACONET
LACONIC
LACOSTE
LLCOOLJ
NICOLAS
NICOSIA
POCONOS
RECODED
RECODES
RECOILS
RECOLOR
RECORDS
RECORKS
RECOUNT
RECOUPS
RECOVER
RICOTTA
SECONDS
TYCOONS
UNCOILS
UNCORKS
UNCOUTH
UNCOVER

••C•O••
ANCHORS
ANCHOVY
ARCHONS
BACKOFF
BACKOUT
BECKONS
BECLOUD
BUCKOES
CACHOUS
COCOONS
CUCKOOS
CYCLONE
CYCLOPS
DECKOUT
DOCTORS
ENCLOSE
ESCROWS
FACEOFF
FACTORS
FACTORY
GECKOES
HECTORS
HICKORY
INCLOSE
KICKOFF
KICKOUT
LACTOSE
LECTORS
LLCOOLJ
LOCKOUT
LUCKOUT
MACRONS
MICROBE
MICRONS
NICCOLO
NICHOLS
NOCUOUS
OSCEOLA
PICCOLO
PICKOFF
PICKOUT
RACCOON
RECHOSE
RECKONS
RECROOM
RECROSS
RECTORS
RECTORY
SACKOUT
SECTORS
SICKOUT
STCROIX
SUCCORS
SUCCOUR
SUCROSE
TICKOFF
TYCOONS
UNCLOAK
UNCLOGS
UNCLOSE
UPCLOSE
VACUOLE
VACUOUS
VECTORS
VICIOUS
VICTORS
VICTORY

••C••O•
ALCOHOL
AUCTION
BACKHOE
BACKLOG
BICOLOR
CUCKOOS
DECAGON
DECALOG
DECAPOD
DICTION
ESCUDOS
FACTION
FICTION
INCISOR
JACKPOT
JACKSON
LOCATOR
LOCKBOX
NUCLEON
PICADOR
PICAROS
PICKSON
POCONOS
RACCOON
RECOLOR
RECROOM
RUCTION
SECTION
SUCTION
TACKSON
UNCTION
VICEROY

••C•••O
DECARLO
JACINTO
LUCIANO
NICCOLO
NOCANDO
PICASSO
PICCOLO
RICARDO
UCCELLO
VACCARO

•••CO••
ABSCOND
AIRCOOL
ANTCOWS
APOCOPE
BADCOLD
BALCONY
BARCODE
BEACONS
BOYCOTT
BUNCOED
CARCOAT
CHICORY
CONCOCT
CONCORD
COXCOMB
DEACONS
DISCOED
DISCORD
FALCONS
FLACONS
FRYCOOK
GARCONS
GASCONS
GIACOMO
GLUCOSE
HANCOCK
HENCOOP
HOWCOME
ICECOLD
JUNCOES
LABCOAT
LAOCOON
LEACOCK
LINCOLN
MALCOLM
MARCONI
MASCOTS
MUSCOVY
NICCOLO
NONCOMS
OUTCOME
PEACOAT
PEACOCK
PETCOCK
PICCOLO
PISCOPO
POPCORN
PRECOOK
PRECOOL
RACCOON
RANCOUR
RAUCOUS
REDCOAT
RIPCORD
SEACOWS
SITCOMS
SNOCONE
SUCCORS
SUCCOUR
SURCOAT
TOPCOAT
TRICORN
TRICOTS
UNICORN
VISCOUS
WALCOTT
WELCOME
ZIPCODE
ZIRCONS

•••C•O•
AIRCOOL
ATECROW
BOKCHOY
CATCHON
DOGCHOW
EATCROW
ELECTOR
ENACTOR
ERECTOR
ERICSON
EXACTOR
FRYCOOK
GAUCHOS
HALCYON
HENCOOP
HONCHOS
IRECKON
KERCHOO
LAOCOON
MARCHON
NUNCIOS
OMICRON
OUTCROP
PONCHOS
PRECOOK
PRECOOL
PROCTOR
PROCYON
PYNCHON
RACCOON
RANCHOS
REACTOR
SALCHOW
SPECTOR
STUCCOS
TOUCHON
TRACTOR

•••C••O
AVOCADO
CHICAGO
CHICANO
ELECTRO
FLOCKTO
GIACOMO
KERCHOO
NICCOLO
PICCOLO
PISCOPO
PLACEBO
PLACIDO
REACTTO
SATCHMO
STICKTO
STUCKTO
VACCARO
VOLCANO

••••CO•
ALARCON
ALENCON
APRICOT
BRONCOS
CALICOS
CAPECOD
CASHCOW
CORNCOB
DOVECOT
FIASCOS
FRESCOS
HARICOT
HELICON
HOLYCOW
LEXICON
MEDICOS
MILKCOW
MONOCOT
ROBOCOP
RUBICON
SILICON
SOUPCON
STUCCOS
TIMECOP

••••C•O
CURACAO
DEFACTO
GROUCHO
INVACUO
JERICHO
MOROCCO
SIROCCO
TOBACCO

•••••CO
ARTDECO
CANSECO
ELGRECO
GALLICO
GUANACO
IONESCO
JALISCO
MOROCCO
NABISCO
ORINOCO
PIMLICO
PORTICO
SERPICO
SIROCCO
TABASCO
TAMPICO
TOBACCO
TOURACO

C•P••••
CAPABLE
CAPABLY
CAPAPIE
CAPEANN
CAPECOD
CAPELET
CAPELLA
CAPERED
CAPFULS
CAPGUNS
CAPITAL
CAPITAN
CAPITOL
CAPLESS
CAPLETS
CAPNUTS
CAPPERS
CAPPING
CAPRICE
CAPSHAW
CAPSIZE
CAPSTAN
CAPSULE
CAPTAIN
CAPTION
CAPTIVE
CAPTORS
CAPTURE
CAPULET
CEPHEUS
CIPHERS
COPIERS
COPILOT
COPIOUS
COPLAND
COPOUTS
COPPERS
COPPERY
COPPICE
COPPING
COPPOLA
COPSOUT
COPTERS
COPYBOY
COPYCAT
COPYING
COPYIST
CUPCAKE
CUPFULS
CUPOLAS
CUPPING
CYPHERS
CYPRESS
CYPRIOT

C••P•••
CALPACS
CAMPARI
CAMPERS
CAMPHOR
CAMPIER
CAMPING
CAMPION
CAMPOUT
CAPPERS
CAPPING
CARPALS
CARPERS
CARPETS
CARPING
CARPOOL
CARPORT
CASPIAN
CHAPATI
CHAPEAU
CHAPELS
CHAPLET
CHAPLIN
CHAPMAN
CHAPMEN
CHAPPED
CHAPTER
CHIPPED
CHIPPER
CHIPSIN
CHOPPED
CHOPPER
CLAPPED
CLAPPER
CLAPTON
CLIPART
CLIPONS
CLIPPED
CLIPPER
CLOPPED
COMPACT
COMPANY
COMPARE
COMPASS
COMPEER
COMPELS
COMPETE
COMPILE
COMPLEX
COMPORT
COMPOSE
COMPOST
COMPOTE
COMPUTE
COOPERS
COOPING
COOPSUP
COOPTED
COPPERS
COPPERY
COPPICE
COPPING
COPPOLA
COUPLED
COUPLES
COUPLET
COUPONS
COWPEAS
COWPOKE
CRAPPIE
CROPPED
CROPPER
CROPSUP
CRYPTIC
CRYPTOS
CULPRIT
CUPPING
CUSPIDS

C•••P••
CALIPER
CALIPHS
CALYPSO
CANAPES
CANOPUS
CAPAPIE
CATSPAW
CERIPHS
CHAMPED
CHAPPED
CHEAPEN
CHEAPER
CHEAPIE
CHEAPLY
CHEEPED
CHIPPED
CHIPPER
CHIRPED
CHOMPED
CHOPPED
CHOPPER
CLAMPED
CLAPPED
CLAPPER
CLASPED
CLIPPED
CLIPPER
CLOPPED
CLUMPED
COCKPIT
CRAMPED
CRAMPON
CRAPPIE
CREEPED
CREEPER
CREEPUP
CRIMPED
CRIMPER
CRISPED
CRISPER
CRISPIN
CRISPLY
CRISPUS
CROPPED
CROPPER
CRUMPET
CRUMPLE
CRUMPLY

C••••P•
CARHOPS
CATALPA
CATNAPS
CATNIPS
CCLAMPS
CHINUPS
COLLOPS
CONCEPT
CORRUPT
CYCLOPS

C•••••P
CALLSUP
CATCHUP
CHALKUP
CHATSUP
CHECKUP
CHEERUP
CHEWSUP
CHOKEUP
CLAMSUP
CLEANUP
CLEARUP
CLOGSUP
CLOSEUP
COILSUP
COMESUP
COOKSUP
COOPSUP
COUGHUP
COVERUP
COWSLIP
CRACKUP
CRANKUP
CREEPUP
CROPSUP
CROSSUP
CURLSUP

•C•P•••
ICEPACK
ICEPICK
SCAPULA
SCEPTER
SCEPTRE
SCOPING
SCUPPER

•C••P••
ACCEPTS
ACTUPON
ECLIPSE
ECTYPES
OCCIPUT
OCTOPOD
OCTOPUS
OCTUPLE
SCALPED
SCALPEL
SCALPER
SCAMPED
SCAMPER
SCARPED
SCOOPED
SCOOPER
SCORPIO
SCRAPED
SCRAPER
SCRAPES
SCRAPPY
SCRIPPS
SCRIPTS
SCRUPLE
SCULPTS
SCUPPER

•C•••P•
CCLAMPS
ICECAPS
SCHLEPP
SCHLEPS
SCHNAPS
SCRAPPY
SCRIMPS
SCRIMPY
SCRIPPS

•C••••P
ACTEDUP
SCALLOP
SCAREUP
SCHLEPP
SCREWUP
SCRUBUP

••C•P••
ACCEPTS
COCKPIT
DECAPOD
DUCKPIN
ESCAPED
ESCAPEE
ESCAPES
EXCEPTS
INCEPTS
INCIPIT
JACKPOT
OCCIPUT
RECIPES
SICKPAY

••C••P•
BACKUPS
CYCLOPS
DECAMPS
DECRYPT
ENCAMPS
ENCRYPT
ESCARPS
EXCERPT
HICCUPS
KICKUPS
LOCKUPS
MOCKUPS
MRCHIPS
PICKUPS
RECEIPT
RECOUPS

••C•••P
ARCLAMP
BACKSUP
BUCKSUP
JACKSUP
KICKSUP
LACEDUP
LACESUP
LOCKSUP
MUCKSUP
PACKSUP
PICKSUP
RACKSUP
UNCLASP
WICKIUP

•••C•P•
APOCOPE
CONCEPT
EGGCUPS
EYECUPS
FORCEPS
GASCAPS
HICCUPS
HOTCAPS
HUBCAPS
ICECAPS
INSCAPE
MADCAPS
MOBCAPS
PISCOPO
PRECEPT
REDCAPS
SKYCAPS
TEACUPS
TOECAPS
TRICEPS

•••C••P
BRACEUP
CATCHUP
CHECKUP
CRACKUP
DAYCAMP
HENCOOP
JUICEUP
KETCHUP
MATCHUP
OLDCHAP
OUTCROP
PATCHUP
PSYCHUP
PUNCHUP
SPICEUP
STACKUP
STICKUP
STOCKUP
STUCKUP
TIECLIP
TOUCHUP

••••C•P
INKYCAP
KNEECAP
ROBOCOP
SNOWCAP
TIMECOP

C••Q•••
CAIQUES
CHEQUER
CHEQUES
CIRQUES
CLAQUES
CLIQUES
CLOQUES
COEQUAL
CONQUER
CROQUET

C•••Q••
COMIQUE

•CQ••••
ACQUIRE
ACQUITS
MCQUEEN

••CQ•••
JACQUES
LACQUER
RACQUET

••C•Q••
MACAQUE

CR•••••
CRABBED
CRABBER
CRACKED
CRACKER
CRACKLE
CRACKUP
CRADLED
CRADLES
CRAFTED
CRAFTER
CRAFTSY
CRAMMED
CRAMMER
CRAMPED
CRAMPON
CRANIAL
CRANING
CRANIUM
CRANKED
CRANKUP
CRAPPIE
CRASHED
CRASHES
CRASSER
CRASSLY
CRASSUS
CRATERS
CRATING
CRAVATS
CRAVENS
CRAVERS
CRAVING
CRAWDAD
CRAWLED
CRAWLER
CRAYOLA
CRAYONS
CRAZIER
CRAZIES
CRAZILY
CRAZING
CREAKED
CREAMED
CREAMER
CREASED
CREASES
CREATED
CREATES
CREATOR
CRECHES
CREDITS
CREEPED
CREEPER
CREEPUP
CREMONA
CRENELS
CREOLES
CREOSOL
CRESSES
CRESTED
CRETANS
CRETINS
CREVICE
CREWCUT
CREWELS
CREWING
CREWMAN
CREWMEN
CRIBBED
CRICKED
CRICKET
CRIMEAN
CRIMPED
CRIMPER
CRIMSON
CRINGED
CRINGES
CRINKLE
CRINKLY
CRINOID
CRISPED
CRISPER
CRISPIN
CRISPLY
CRISPUS
CRITICS
CRITTER
CROAKED
CROATIA
CROCHET
CROESUS
CRONIES
CROOKED
CROONED
CROONER
CROPPED
CROPPER
CROPSUP
CROQUET
CROSIER
CROSSED
CROSSER
CROSSES
CROSSLY
CROSSUP
CROUTON
CROWBAR
CROWDED
CROWERS
CROWING
CROWNED
CRUCIAL
CRUDELY
CRUDEST
CRUDITY
CRUELER
CRUELLY
CRUISED
CRUISER
CRUISES
CRULLER
CRUMBLE
CRUMBLY
CRUMPET
CRUMPLE
CRUMPLY
CRUNCHY
CRUSADE
CRUSHED
CRUSHER
CRUSHES
CRUSTED
CRUZADO
CRYBABY
CRYOGEN
CRYPTIC
CRYPTOS
CRYSTAL
CRYWOLF

C•R••••
CARACAL
CARACAS
CARAFES
CARAMBA
CARAMEL
CARAMIA
CARAVAN
CARAVEL
CARAWAY
CARBIDE
CARBINE
CARBONS
CARBOYS
CARCASS
CARCOAT
CARDERS
CARDING
CARDOZO
CAREENS
CAREERS
CAREFOR
CAREFUL
CARFARE
CARFULS
CARGOES
CARHOPS
CARIBES
CARIBOU
CARINAS
CARIOCA
CARLESS
CARLOAD
CARLSON
CARLTON
CARLYLE
CARMINE
CARNERA
CARNETS
CARNIES
CAROLED
CAROLER
CAROLES
CAROLUS
CAROLYN
CAROMED
CAROTID
CAROUSE
CARPALS
CARPERS
CARPETS
CARPING
CARPOOL
CARPORT
CARRELS
CARRERE
CARRICK
CARRIED
CARRIER
CARRIES
CARRION
CARROLL
CARROTS
CARRYON
CARSEAT
CARTAGE
CARTELS
CARTERS
CARTIER
CARTING
CARTONS
CARTOON
CARVERS
CARVING
CARWASH
CBRADIO
CERAMIC
CEREALS
CEREBRA
CERIPHS
CERTAIN
CERTIFY
CERUMEN
CHRISMS
CHRISTI
CHRISTO
CHRISTY
CHROMES
CHRONIC
CIRCLED
CIRCLES
CIRCLET
CIRCUIT
CIRCUSY
CIRQUES
CORAZON
CORBELS
CORBETT
CORDAGE
CORDATE
CORDELL
CORDERO
CORDIAL
CORDING
CORDITE
CORDOBA
CORDONS
CORELLI
CORETTA
CORINTH
CORKAGE
CORKERS
CORKING
CORNCOB
CORNDOG
CORNEAL
CORNEAS
CORNELL
CORNERS
CORNETS
CORNFED
CORNICE
CORNIER
CORNILY
CORNING
CORNISH
CORNOIL
CORNROW
COROLLA
CORONAE
CORONAS
CORONET
CORRALS
CORRECT
CORRIDA
CORRODE
CORRUPT
CORSAGE
CORSAIR
CORSETS
CORSICA
CORTEGE
CORYELL
CURACAO
CURATES
CURATOR
CURBCUT
CURBING
CURDING
CURDLED
CURDLES
CUREALL
CURFEWS
CURIOUS
CURLERS
CURLEWS
CURLIER
CURLING
CURLSUP
CURRANT
CURRENT
CURRIED
CURRIER
CURRIES
CURSING
CURSIVE
CURSORS
CURSORY
CURTAIL
CURTAIN
CURTEST
CURTSEY
CURVETS
CURVIER
CURVING

C••R•••
CAPRICE
CARRELS
CARRERE
CARRICK
CARRIED
CARRIER
CARRIES
CARRION
CARROLL
CARROTS
CARRYON
CHARADE
CHARGED
CHARGER
CHARGES
CHARIER
CHARILY
CHARIOT
CHARITY
CHARLES
CHARLEY
CHARLIE
CHARMED
CHARMER
CHARMIN
CHARRED
CHARTED
CHARTER
CHERISH
CHEROOT
CHERUBS
CHERVIL
CHIRPED
CHORALE
CHORALS
CHORINE
CHORIZO
CHORTLE
CHURNED
CITRATE
CITRINE
CITROEN
CITRONS
CLARETS
CLARICE
CLARIFY
CLARION
CLARITY
CLERICS
CLERKED
CLORETS
COARSEN
COARSER
COERCED
COERCES
COMRADE
CONRACK
CONREID
CORRALS
CORRECT
CORRIDA
CORRODE
CORRUPT
COURAGE
COURANT
COURIER
COURSED
COURSER
COURSES
COURTED
COURTLY
COWRIES
CUIRASS
CURRANT
CURRENT
CURRIED
CURRIER
CURRIES
CUTRATE
CYPRESS
CYPRIOT
CZARDAS
CZARDOM
CZARINA
CZARISM
CZARIST

C•••R••
CABARET
CALDRON
CALORIC
CALORIE
CAMBRIC
CAMERAS
CAMERON
CANARDS
CAPERED
CASERNS
CATERED
CATERER
CAVERNS
CAVORTS
CENTRAL
CENTRED
CENTRES
CENTRIC
CHAGRIN
CHAIRED
CHARRED
CHEERED
CHEERIO
CHEERUP
CHETRUM
CHEVRES
CHEVRON
CHLORAL
CIBORIA
CLAIROL
CLEARED
CLEARER
CLEARLY
CLEARUP
COCHRAN
COHERED
COHERES
COHORTS
COLORED
COMFREY
COMOROS
CONBRIO
CONTRAS
CONTROL
CORNROW
COTERIE
COVERED
COVERUP
COWARDS
COWERED
CULPRIT
CYBORGS

C••••R•
CABLERS
CADBURY
CADGERS
CAESARS
CAESURA
CAHIERS
CALDERA
CALGARY
CALIBRE
CALLERS
CALVARY
CALVERT
CAMBERS
CAMPARI
CAMPERS
CANKERS
CANNERS
CANNERY
CANTERS
CANTORS
CAPPERS
CAPTORS
CAPTURE
CARDERS
CAREERS
CARFARE
CARNERA
CARPERS
CARPORT
CARRERE
CARTERS
CARVERS
CASCARA
CASTERS
CATBIRD
CAVALRY
CAVEART
CELEBRE
CELLARS
CENSERS
CENSORS
CENSURE
CENTERS
CENTURY
CEREBRA
CHASERS
CHEWERS
CHICORY
CHIMERA
CHOKERS
CINDERS
CIPHERS
CISTERN
CLAMORS
CLAWERS
CLIBURN
CLIPART
CLOSURE
CLOTURE
CLOVERS
COALERS
COAXERS
COCHERE
CODGERS
COFFERS
COGBURN
COHEIRS
COINERS
COLBERT
COLLARD
COLLARS
COLOURS
COMBERS
COMFORT
COMPARE
COMPORT
CONAKRY
CONCERN
CONCERT
CONCORD
CONCURS
CONDORS
CONFERS
CONFIRM
CONFORM
CONGERS
CONJURE
CONKERS
CONNERY
CONNORS
CONSORT
CONTORT
CONVERT
COOKERS
COOKERY
COOLERS
COOPERS
COPIERS
COPPERS
COPPERY
COPTERS
CORDERO
CORKERS
CORNERS
COSTARS
COTTERS
COUGARS
COUNTRY
COUTURE
COWBIRD
COWGIRL
COWHERD
CRATERS
CRAVERS
CROWERS
CUECARD
CULEBRA
CULTURE
CULVERT
CURLERS
CURSORS
CURSORY
CUSTARD
CUTLERS
CUTLERY
CUTTERS
CYCLERS
CYPHERS

C•••••R
CACKLER
CAJOLER
CALIBER
CALIPER
CALLFOR
CAMPHOR
CAMPIER
CANDOUR
CANNIER
CAREFOR
CAROLER
CARRIER
CARTIER
CASHBAR
CASHIER
CATCHER
CATERER
CATHAIR
CATTIER
CAULKER
CAVILER
CENTAUR
CHAMBER
CHAMFER
CHANGER
CHANTER
CHAPTER
CHARGER
CHARIER
CHARMER
CHARTER
CHASTER
CHATTER
CHAUCER
CHEAPER
CHEATER
CHECKER
CHEDDAR
CHEEVER
CHENIER
CHEQUER
CHESTER
CHEWIER
CHIGGER
CHILLER
CHIPPER
CHITTER
CHOICER
CHOOSER
CHOPPER
CHOWDER
CHUKKER
CLABBER
CLAIMER
CLAMBER
CLAMMER
CLANGOR
CLAPPER
CLATTER
CLAVIER
CLAYIER
CLEANER
CLEARER
CLEAVER
CLIMBER
CLINKER
CLIPPER
CLOBBER
CLOCKER
CLOWDER
CLUBCAR
CLUNKER
CLUSTER
CLUTTER
CNTOWER
COALCAR
COALTAR
COARSER
COASTER
COBBLER
COCKIER
CODDLER

COLDWAR
COLLIER
COLLYER
COMFIER
COMPEER
CONIFER
CONQUER
CONTOUR
CORNIER
CORSAIR
COSTNER
COULTER
COUNTER
COURIER
COURSER
CRABBER
CRACKER
CRAFTER
CRAMMER
CRASSER
CRAWLER
CRAZIER
CREAMER
CREATOR
CREEPER
CRIMPER
CRISPER
CRITTER
CROONER
CROPPER
CROSIER
CROSSER
CROWBAR
CRUELER
CRUISER
CRULLER
CRUSHER
CURATOR
CURLIER
CURRIER
CURVIER
CUSHIER
CUSSLER

•CR••••
ACREAGE
ACRIDLY
ACROBAT
ACRONYM
ACRYLIC
SCRAGGY
SCRAPED
SCRAPER
SCRAPES
SCRAPPY
SCRATCH
SCRAWLS
SCRAWLY
SCRAWNY
SCREAKS
SCREAMS
SCREECH
SCREEDS
SCREENS
SCREWED
SCREWUP
SCRIBES
SCRIMPS
SCRIMPY
SCRIPPS
SCRIPTS
SCRIVEN
SCROLLS
SCROOGE
SCRUBBY
SCRUBUP
SCRUFFS
SCRUFFY
SCRUNCH
SCRUPLE

•C•R•••
ACARIDS
ACCRETE
ACCRUAL
ACCRUED
ACCRUES
ACERBIC
ACEROLA
ACEROSE
ACTRESS
ICERINK
OCARINA
SCARABS
SCARCER
SCARERS
SCAREUP
SCARFED
SCARIER
SCARIFY
SCARILY
SCARING
SCARLET
SCARPED
SCARRED
SCARVES
SCORERS
SCORING
SCORNED
SCORPIO
SCURVES

•C••R••
ACCORDS
ACCURST
ACHERON
ICEFREE
MCENROE
SCARRED
SCHERZI
SCHERZO
SCHIRRA
SCLERAS
SCOURED
SCOURER
SCOURGE

•C•••R•
ACQUIRE
ACTUARY
ECKHART
ECLAIRS
ICEBERG
MCGUIRE
SCALARS
SCALERS
SCARERS
SCENERY
SCEPTRE
SCHIRRA
SCORERS
SCOTERS

•C••••R
ACCEDER
ACCUSER
ECUADOR
OCONNOR
OCTOBER
SCALIER
SCALPER
SCAMPER
SCANNER
SCANTER
SCARCER
SCARIER
SCATTER
SCEPTER
SCHEMER
SCHMEER
SCHOLAR
SCISSOR
SCOFFER
SCOLDER
SCOOPER
SCOOTER
SCOURER
SCOUTER
SCOWLER
SCRAPER
SCULLER
SCUPPER

••CR•••
ACCRETE
ACCRUAL
ACCRUED
ACCRUES
ASCRIBE
DECREED
DECREES
DECRIED
DECRIES
DECRYPT
ENCRUST
ENCRYPT
ESCROWS
EXCRETE
IPCRESS
MACRAME
MACRONS
MICROBE
MICRONS
RECROOM
RECROSS
RECRUIT
SECRECY
SECRETE
SECRETS
STCROIX
SUCRASE
SUCROSE
UNCRATE

••C•R••
ACCORDS
ACCURST
BACARDI
BACKRUB
BUCKRAM
COCHRAN
DECARLO
DECORUM
ENCORES
ESCARPS
ESCORTS
EUCHRED
EUCHRES
EXCERPT
GOCARTS
IDCARDS
LECARRE
LUCERNE
MACGRAW
OXCARTS
PACKRAT
PICAROS
RECORDS
RECORKS
RICARDO
RICERAT
SECURED
SECURER
SECURES
UNCORKS
UNCURLS
VICEROY

••C••R•
ANCHORS
ARCHERS
ARCHERY
BACKERS
BICKERS
COCHERE
CYCLERS
DECLARE
DICKERS
DOCKERS
DOCTORS
ETCHERS
FACTORS
FACTORY
HACKERS
HECTARE
HECTORS
HICKORY
KICKERS
LECARRE
LECTERN
LECTORS
LECTURE
LOCKERS
MACABRE
MOCKERS
MOCKERY
NECKERS
NECTARS
NICKERS
NOCTURN
ORCHARD
PACKARD
PACKERS
PECCARY
PICCARD
PICKERS
PICTURE
PUCKERS
RECTORS
RECTORY
RICHARD
ROCKERS
SACKERS
SECTORS
SUCCORS
SUCKERS
TACKERS
TICKERS
TUCKERS
VACCARO
VECTORS
VICTORS
VICTORY
WICKERS
ZACHARY

••C•••R
ACCEDER
ACCUSER
ALCAZAR
BICOLOR
BUCKLER
CACKLER
COCKIER
DECODER
DUCKIER
ENCODER
FICKLER
HECKLER
INCISOR
INCITER
ITCHIER
JACKTAR
JOCULAR
LACQUER
LOCATER
LOCATOR
LUCIFER
LUCKIER
NUCLEAR
PACECAR
PICADOR
PICKIER
RACECAR
RECITER
RECOLOR
RECOVER
RICHTER
ROCKIER
SECEDER
SECULAR
SECURER
SUCCOUR
TACKIER
TACKLER
TICKLER
UNCLEAR
UNCOVER
WACKIER
YUCKIER

•••CR••
AIRCREW
AMSCRAY
ATECROW
EATCROW
FIACRES
FULCRUM
OMICRON
OUTCROP
SHECRAB
UNSCREW

•••C•R•
BOXCARS
BRACERS
CASCARA
CHICORY
CONCERN
CONCERT
CONCORD
CONCURS
CUECARD
DANCERS
DAYCARE
DEICERS
DISCARD
DISCERN
DISCORD
DOGCART
ELECTRA
ELECTRO
EPICURE
FENCERS
FORCERS
GROCERS
GROCERY
HOTCARS
JUICERS
KEYCARD
LANCERS
MASCARA
MERCURY
MINCERS
OBSCURE
PECCARY
PICCARD
PIECERS
PINCERS
PINCURL
PLACARD
PLACERS
PLECTRA
POPCORN
PRICERS
PROCURE
RIPCORD
SAUCERS
SINCERE
SLICERS
SORCERY
SPACERS
SPECTRA
SPECTRE
SUCCORS
TEACART
TOWCARS
TRACERS
TRACERY
TRICORN
TROCARS
UNICORN
VACCARO
VISCERA
WINCERS

•••C••R
BEECHER
BLACKER
BLOCKER
BUTCHER
CATCHER
CHECKER
CLOCKER
CRACKER
DRUCKER
ELECTOR
ENACTOR
ERECTER
ERECTOR
EXACTER
EXACTOR
FANCIER
FILCHER
FISCHER
FLICKER
GAUCHER
GLACIER
HATCHER
HITCHER
JUICIER
KNOCKER
LUNCHER
MARCHER
MOOCHER
MUNCHER
PINCHER
PITCHER
POACHER
PRICIER
PROCTOR
PUNCHER
QUICKER
RANCHER
RANCOUR
REACTOR
REOCCUR
RESCUER
SAUCIER
SHOCKER
SHUCKER
SLACKER
SLICKER
SMACKER
SNACKER
SNICKER
SPACIER
SPECTER
SPECTOR
SPICIER
STICKER
SUCCOUR
TEACHER
TEICHER
THICKER
TRACKER
TRACTOR
TRICKER
TRUCKER
VOUCHER
WATCHER
WRECKER

••••CR•
MIMICRY

••••C•R
BOUNCER
CHAUCER
CHOICER
CLUBCAR
COALCAR
ENTICER
FIERCER
FLATCAR
HANDCAR
INDUCER
OFFICER
PACECAR
POUNCER
PRANCER
RACECAR
REDUCER
REOCCUR
SCARCER
SEDUCER
SIDECAR
SLOTCAR
SPENCER
SPLICER
SPRUCER
TRAMCAR
VANOCUR

CS•••••
CSLEWIS

C•S••••
CASABAS
CASCADE
CASCARA
CASELAW
CASERNS
CASHBAR
CASHBOX
CASHCOW
CASHEWS
CASHIER
CASHING
CASHOUT
CASINGS
CASINOS
CASPIAN
CASSATT
CASSAVA
CASSIAS
CASSIDY
CASSINI
CASSIUS
CASSOCK
CASTERS
CASTILE
CASTING
CASTLED
CASTLES
CASTOFF
CASTOUT
CASUALS
CESSION
CISTERN
COSIGNS
COSINES
COSSACK
COSSETS
COSTAIN
COSTARS
COSTING
COSTNER
COSTUME
CUSHAWS
CUSHIER
CUSHION
CUSPIDS
CUSSING
CUSSLER
CUSTARD
CUSTODY
CUSTOMS

C••S•••
CAESARS
CAESURA
CAISSON
CANSECO
CAPSHAW
CAPSIZE
CAPSTAN
CAPSULE
CARSEAT
CASSATT
CASSAVA
CASSIAS
CASSIDY
CASSINI
CASSIUS
CASSOCK
CATSCAN
CATSEYE
CATSPAW
CAUSING
CAUSTIC
CEASING
CELSIUS
CENSERS
CENSING
CENSORS
CENSURE
CESSION
CHASERS
CHASING
CHASSES
CHASSIS
CHASTEN
CHASTER
CHESTER
CHISELS
CLASHED
CLASHES
CLASPED
CLASSED
CLASSES
CLASSIC
CLOSEIN
CLOSELY
CLOSEST
CLOSETS
CLOSEUP
CLOSING
CLOSURE
CLUSTER
COASTAL
COASTED
COASTER
CONSENT
CONSIGN
CONSIST
CONSOLE
CONSORT
CONSULS
CONSULT
CONSUME
COPSOUT
CORSAGE
CORSAIR
CORSETS
CORSICA
COSSACK
COSSETS
COUSINS
COWSLIP
CRASHED
CRASHES
CRASSER
CRASSLY
CRASSUS
CRESSES
CRESTED
CRISPED
CRISPER
CRISPIN
CRISPLY
CRISPUS
CROSIER
CROSSED
CROSSER
CROSSES
CROSSLY
CROSSUP
CRUSADE
CRUSHED
CRUSHER
CRUSHES
CRUSTED
CRYSTAL
CUISINE
CURSING
CURSIVE
CURSORS
CURSORY
CUSSING
CUSSLER
CUTSOFF
CUTSOUT

C•••S••
CAISSON
CALLSIN
CALLSON
CALLSUP
CAMISES
CANASTA
CARLSON
CAVESIN
CAYUSES
CELESTA
CELESTE
CHAISES
CHANSON
CHASSES
CHASSIS
CHATSUP
CHEESES
CHELSEA
CHEWSUP
CHIPSIN
CHOMSKY
CHOOSER
CHOOSES
CHRISMS
CHRISTI
CHRISTO
CHRISTY
CLAMSUP
CLASSED
CLASSES
CLASSIC
CLAUSES
CLEMSON
CLOGSUP
CLUESIN
COARSEN
COARSER
COHOSTS
COILSUP
COLOSSI
COMESAT
COMESBY
COMESIN
COMESON
COMESTO
COMESUP
COOKSUP
COOLSIT
COOPSUP
COUNSEL
COURSED
COURSER
COURSES
CRASSER
CRASSLY
CRASSUS
CREASED
CREASES
CREOSOL
CRESSES
CRIMSON
CROESUS
CROPSUP
CROSSED
CROSSER
CROSSES
CROSSLY
CROSSUP
CRUISED
CRUISER
CRUISES
CUBISTS
CURLSUP
CURTSEY

C••••S•
CABOOSE
CAGIEST
CALMEST
CALYPSO
CANVASS
CAPLESS
CARCASS
CARLESS
CAROUSE
CARWASH
CATFISH
CATTISH
CELLIST
CHEMISE
CHEMIST
CHERISH
CHINESE
CIRCUSY
CLEANSE
CLOSEST
COCHISE
CODFISH
COEXIST
COLDEST
COLOSSI
COLTISH
COMBUST
COMPASS
COMPOSE
COMPOST
CONCISE
CONFESS
CONFUSE
CONGEST
CONSIST
CONTEST
CONTUSE
COOLEST
COPYIST
CORNISH
COYNESS
COZIEST
CRAFTSY
CRUDEST
CUIRASS
CULTISH
CULTISM
CULTIST
CURTEST
CUTLASS
CYCLIST
CYPRESS
CZARISM
CZARIST

C•••••S
CABALAS
CABANAS
CABBIES
CABLERS
CACHETS
CACHOUS
CACKLES
CADDIES
CADGERS
CAESARS
CAFTANS
CAHIERS
CAHOOTS
CAIMANS
CAIQUES
CAJOLES
CALENDS
CALICOS
CALIPHS
CALKINS
CALLERS
CALLINS
CALLOUS
CALPACS
CALYCES
CALYXES
CAMBERS
CAMERAS
CAMISES
CAMPERS
CANAPES
CANARDS
CANCANS
CANCELS
CANDIDS
CANDIES
CANDLES
CANINES
CANKERS
CANNERS
CANNONS
CANOPUS
CANTERS
CANTLES
CANTONS
CANTORS
CANVASS
CANYONS
CAPFULS
CAPGUNS
CAPLESS
CAPLETS
CAPNUTS
CAPPERS
CAPTORS
CARACAS
CARAFES
CARBONS
CARBOYS
CARCASS
CARDERS
CAREENS
CAREERS
CARFULS
CARGOES
CARHOPS
CARIBES
CARINAS
CARLESS
CARNETS
CARNIES
CAROLES
CAROLUS
CARPALS
CARPERS
CARPETS
CARRELS
CARRIES
CARROTS
CARTELS
CARTERS
CARTONS
CARVERS
CASABAS
CASERNS
CASHEWS
CASINGS
CASINOS
CASSIAS
CASSIUS
CASTERS
CASTLES
CASUALS
CATCHES
CATIONS
CATKINS
CATNAPS
CATNIPS
CAVEATS
CAVEINS
CAVERNS
CAVORTS
CAYUGAS
CAYUSES
CCLAMPS
CELEBES
CELLARS
CELSIUS
CELTICS
CEMENTS
CENSERS
CENSORS
CENTERS
CENTRES
CEPHEUS
CEREALS
CERIPHS
CHABLIS
CHACHAS
CHAISES
CHALETS
CHALLIS
CHAMOIS
CHANCES
CHANGES
CHAPELS
CHARGES
CHARLES
CHASERS
CHASSES
CHASSIS
CHEESES
CHEETOS
CHEQUES
CHERUBS
CHEVIES
CHEVRES
CHEWERS
CHILIES
CHINUPS
CHISELS
CHOICES

CHOKERS
CHOLLAS
CHOOSES
CHORALS
CHRISMS
CHROMES
CHUKKAS
CICADAS
CINCHES
CINDERS
CINEMAS
CIPHERS
CIRCLES
CIRQUES
CITRONS
CIVVIES
CLAMORS
CLAQUES
CLARETS
CLASHES
CLASSES
CLAUSES
CLAWERS
CLEAVES
CLEMENS
CLERICS
CLICHES
CLIENTS
CLINICS
CLIPONS
CLIQUES
CLOCHES
CLOQUES
CLORETS
CLOSETS
CLOTHES
CLOVERS
COACHES
COALERS
COALGAS
COAXERS
COBBLES
COBWEBS
COCKLES
COCOONS
CODDLES
CODGERS
CODICES
COEDITS
COERCES
COEVALS
COFFEES
COFFERS
COGNACS
COHEIRS
COHERES
COHORTS
COHOSTS
COINERS
COLLARS
COLLETS
COLLIES
COLLINS
COLLOPS
COLOBUS
COLONES
COLOURS
COLUMNS
COMBATS
COMBERS
COMEONS
COMFITS
COMINGS
COMMITS
COMMONS
COMOROS
COMPASS
COMPELS
CONCHES
CONCURS
CONDORS
CONFABS
CONFERS
CONFESS
CONGERS
CONJOBS
CONKERS
CONNORS
CONSULS
CONTRAS
CONVEYS
CONVOYS
COOKERS
COOKIES
COOLERS
COOPERS
COOTIES
COPIERS
COPIOUS
COPOUTS
COPPERS
COPTERS
CORBELS
CORDONS
CORKERS
CORNEAS
CORNERS
CORNETS
CORONAS
CORRALS
CORSETS
COSIGNS
COSINES
COSSETS
COSTARS
COTTERS
COTTONS
COUCHES
COUGARS
COULEES
COUPLES
COUPONS
COURSES
COUSINS
COWARDS
COWBOYS
COWPEAS
COWRIES
COYNESS
COYOTES
COZZENS
CRADLES
CRASHES
CRASSUS
CRATERS
CRAVATS
CRAVENS
CRAVERS
CRAYONS
CRAZIES
CREASES
CREATES
CRECHES
CREDITS
CRENELS
CREOLES
CRESSES
CRETANS
CRETINS
CREWELS
CRINGES
CRISPUS
CRITICS
CROESUS
CRONIES
CROSSES
CROWERS
CRUISES
CRUSHES
CRYPTOS
CSLEWIS
CUBBIES
CUBISTS
CUCKOOS
CUDDLES
CUDGELS
CUIRASS
CUMULUS
CUPFULS
CUPOLAS
CURATES
CURDLES
CURFEWS
CURIOUS
CURLERS
CURLEWS
CURRIES
CURSORS
CURVETS
CUSHAWS
CUSPIDS
CUSTOMS
CUTLASS
CUTLERS
CUTLETS
CUTOFFS
CUTOUTS
CUTTERS
CYBORGS
CYCLERS
CYCLOPS
CYGNETS
CYMBALS
CYPHERS
CYPRESS
CZARDAS

•CS••••

ECSTASY
MCSWINE

•C•S•••

ACESOUT
ACTSOUT
ICESHOW
SCISSOR

•C••S••

ACCOSTS
ACCUSED
ACCUSER
ACCUSES
ACHESON
ECDYSES
ECDYSIS
SCHISMS
SCISSOR

•C•••S•

ACCURST
ACEROSE
ACHIEST
ACTRESS
ECLIPSE
ECSTASY
ICELESS
ICINESS
ICKIEST
OCULIST

•C••••S

ACACIAS
ACARIDS
ACCEDES
ACCENTS
ACCEPTS
ACCORDS
ACCOSTS
ACCRUES
ACCUSES
ACHATES
ACHENES
ACKACKS
ACQUITS
ACTIONS
ACTIVES
ACTRESS
CCLAMPS
ECDYSES
ECDYSIS
ECHINUS
ECLAIRS
ECTYPES
ICEAGES
ICEAXES
ICEBAGS
ICECAPS
ICELESS
ICICLES
ICINESS
MCCALLS
OCCULTS
OCEANUS
OCELOTS
OCTANES
OCTANTS
OCTAVES
OCTAVOS
OCTOPUS
SCALARS
SCALERS
SCARABS
SCARERS
SCARVES
SCATHES
SCHEMAS
SCHEMES
SCHISMS
SCHLEPS
SCHMOES
SCHMOOS
SCHNAPS
SCHOOLS
SCLERAS
SCONCES
SCORERS
SCOTERS
SCRAPES
SCRAWLS
SCREAKS
SCREAMS
SCREEDS
SCREENS
SCRIBES
SCRIMPS
SCRIPPS
SCRIPTS
SCROLLS
SCRUFFS
SCULPTS
SCURVES
SCYTHES

••CS•••

ARCSINE
FOCSLES
TOCSINS

••C•S••

ACCOSTS
ACCUSED
ACCUSER
ACCUSES
BACKSIN
BACKSUP
BUCKSAW
BUCKSUP
ENCASED
ENCASES
EXCISED
EXCISES
EXCUSED
EXCUSES
FICUSES
FOCUSED
FOCUSES
FUCHSIA
HACKSAW
INCISED
INCISES
INCISOR
JACKSON
JACKSUP
JOCASTA
KICKSIN
KICKSUP
LACESUP
LACOSTE
LOCKSUP
LOCUSTS
MUCKSUP
NICOSIA
PACKSUP
PECKSAT
PICASSO
PICKSAT
PICKSON
PICKSUP
RACKSUP
RECASTS
RECUSED
RECUSES
RICKSHA
SOCKSIN
SUCKSIN
TACKSON
TUCKSIN
UNCASED
UNCASES

••C••S•

ACCURST
BECAUSE
COCHISE
CYCLIST
DECLASS
DICIEST
DUCHESS
ENCLOSE
ENCRUST
INCENSE
INCLOSE
IPCRESS
JACCUSE
JACKASS
LACIEST
LACTASE
LACTOSE
LICENSE
PACHISI
PECKISH
PICASSO
PUCKISH
RACIEST
RECHOSE
RECLUSE
RECROSS
RICHEST
SICKEST
SUCCESS
SUCRASE
SUCROSE
UNCLASP
UNCLOSE
UPCLOSE

••C•••S

ACCEDES
ACCENTS
ACCEPTS
ACCORDS
ACCOSTS
ACCRUES
ACCUSES
ALCOVES
ANCHORS
ARCADES
ARCHERS
ARCHIES
ARCHONS
ASCENDS
ASCENTS
BACCHUS
BACKERS
BACKUPS
BECALMS
BECKONS
BECOMES
BICKERS
BUCKETS
BUCKLES
BUCKOES
CACHETS
CACHOUS
CACKLES
CICADAS
COCKLES
COCOONS
CUCKOOS
CYCLERS
CYCLOPS
DACTYLS
DECADES
DECAMPS
DECANTS
DECEITS
DECIDES
DECKLES
DECLASS
DECOCTS
DECODES
DECREES
DECRIES
DICKENS
DICKERS
DICKEYS
DICKIES
DICTUMS
DOCENTS
DOCKERS
DOCKETS
DOCTORS
DUCHESS
DUCHIES
ENCAGES
ENCAMPS
ENCASES
ENCODES
ENCORES
ESCAPES
ESCARPS
ESCHEWS
ESCORTS
ESCROWS
ESCUDOS
ETCHERS
EUCHRES
EXCEEDS
EXCEPTS
EXCISES
EXCITES
EXCUSES
FACADES
FACIALS
FACINGS
FACTORS
FICUSES
FOCSLES
FOCUSES
GECKOES
GOCARTS
HACKERS
HACKIES
HACKLES
HECKLES
HECTORS
HICCUPS
IDCARDS
INCANTS
INCEPTS
INCISES
INCITES
INCOMES
INCUDES
IPCRESS
JACANAS
JACKALS
JACKASS
JACKETS
JACQUES
JICAMAS
JOCKEYS
KICKERS
KICKUPS
LACINGS
LACKEYS
LACUNAS
LECTORS
LICHENS
LOCALES
LOCATES
LOCKERS
LOCKETS
LOCKINS
LOCKUPS
LOCUSTS
LYCEUMS
MACRONS
MCCALLS
MICMACS
MICRONS
MOCKERS
MOCKUPS
MRCHIPS
NECKERS
NECTARS
NICHOLS
NICKELS
NICKERS
NICOLAS
NOCUOUS
NUCLEUS
OCCULTS
OOCYTES
ORCHIDS
OSCINES
OXCARTS
PACKERS
PACKETS
PECTINS
PICAROS
PICKENS
PICKERS
PICKETS
PICKLES
PICKUPS
PICNICS
POCKETS
POCONOS
PUCKERS
RACEMES
RACKETS
RECALLS
RECANES
RECANTS
RECASTS
RECEDES
RECIPES
RECITES
RECKONS
RECODES
RECOILS
RECORDS
RECORKS
RECOUPS
RECROSS
RECTORS
RECUSES
RICKEYS
RICKLES
ROCKERS
ROCKETS
ROCKIES
SACHEMS
SACHETS
SACKERS
SECANTS
SECEDES
SECONDS
SECRETS
SECTORS
SECURES
SICKENS
SICKLES
SOCIALS
SOCKETS
SUCCESS
SUCCORS
SUCKERS
TACITUS
TACKERS
TACKLES
TACTICS
TECHIES
TICKERS
TICKETS
TICKLES
TICTACS
TOCSINS
TUCKERS
TYCOONS
UNCAGES
UNCASES
UNCIALS
UNCLOGS
UNCOILS
UNCORKS
UNCURLS
URCHINS
VACATES
VACUOUS
VACUUMS
VECTORS
VICIOUS
VICTIMS
VICTORS
VICUNAS
WICKERS
WICKETS

•••CS••

ERICSON

•••C•S•

CARCASS
CIRCUSY
CONCISE
DIOCESE
DISCUSS
EGGCASE
FASCISM
FASCIST
FLYCAST
GLUCOSE
JACCUSE
MISCAST
OUTCAST
PAYCASH
PRECAST
PRECISE
PROCESS
SARCASM
SUCCESS

•••C••S

ACACIAS
AITCHES
ANTCOWS
APACHES
ASHCANS
AVOCETS
BACCHUS
BATCHES
BEACHES
BEACONS
BEECHES
BELCHES
BENCHES
BIRCHES
BOBCATS
BOTCHES
BOXCARS
BRACERS
BUNCHES
CANCANS
CANCELS
CARCASS
CATCHES
CHACHAS
CINCHES
CIRCLES
CLICHES
CLOCHES
COACHES
CONCHES
CONCURS
COUCHES
CRECHES
DANCERS
DEACONS
DEICERS
DISCUSS
DITCHES
EGGCUPS
ELICITS
EYECUPS
FALCONS
FANCIES
FASCIAS
FATCATS
FAUCETS
FENCERS
FETCHES
FIACRES
FILCHES
FINCHES
FITCHES
FLACONS
FLECHES
FORCEPS
FORCERS
GARCONS
GASCAPS
GASCONS
GAUCHOS
GOTCHAS
GRACIAS
GROCERS
GULCHES
HATCHES
HEPCATS
HICCUPS
HITCHES
HONCHOS
HOTCAPS
HOTCARS
HUBCAPS
HUNCHES
HUTCHES
ICECAPS
ICICLES
JAYCEES
JUICERS
JUNCOES
KETCHES
KWACHAS
LANCERS
LANCETS
LARCHES
LATCHES
LEACHES
LEECHES
LITCHIS
LOACHES
LUNCHES
LURCHES
MADCAPS
MARCELS
MARCHES
MASCOTS
MATCHES
MERCIES
MESCALS
MINCERS
MISCUES
MOBCAPS
MOOCHES
MULCHES
MUNCHES
MUSCATS
MUSCLES
NONCOMS
NOTCHES
NUNCIOS
OILCANS
ORACLES
PARCELS
PARCHES
PATCHES
PEACHES
PENCILS
PERCHES
PIECERS
PINCERS
PINCHAS
PINCHES
PITCHES
PLACERS
POACHES
PONCHOS
POOCHES
PORCHES
POUCHES
PRICERS
PROCESS
PSYCHES
PUNCHES
QUICHES
RANCHES
RANCHOS
RASCALS
RAUCOUS
REACHES
REDCAPS
RESCUES
REXCATS
ROACHES
SAUCERS
SEACOWS
SEICHES
SITCOMS
SKYCAPS
SLICERS
SNOCATS
SPACERS
SPECIES
STICHES
STUCCOS
SUCCESS
SUCCORS
SYNCHES
TEACHES
TEACUPS
TERCELS
TERCETS
TINCANS
TOECAPS
TOMCATS
TORCHES
TOUCANS
TOUCHES
TOWCARS
TRACERS
TRICEPS
TRICOTS
TROCARS
TROCHES
VETCHES
VISCOUS
VOUCHES
VULCANS
WATCHES
WELCHES
WENCHES
WINCERS
WINCHES
WITCHES
ZILCHES
ZIRCONS

••••C•S

ABDUCTS
ACKACKS
ADDUCES
ADDUCTS
AFFECTS
ALPACAS
AMERCES
APERCUS
ARNICAS
ASPECTS
ATTACKS
ATTICUS
ATTUCKS
AUROCHS
BEDECKS
BISECTS
BODICES
BOUNCES
BRONCOS
CALICOS
CALYCES
CARACAS
CHANCES
CHOICES
CODICES
COERCES
DECOCTS
DEDUCES
DEDUCTS
DEFACES
DEFECTS
DEJECTS
DELICTS
DEPICTS
DETECTS
DEVICES
DIDACTS
DIRECTS
EFFACES
EFFECTS
ENLACES
ENTICES
EPARCHS
EUNUCHS
EVINCES
EXPECTS
FIANCES
FIASCOS
FLEECES
FRANCES
FRANCIS
FRESCOS
GLANCES
HELICES
HIJACKS
HYRACES
IMPACTS
INDICES
INDICTS
INDUCES
INDUCTS
INFECTS
INFOCUS
INJECTS
INSECTS
JOUNCES
KOPECKS
LATICES
MARACAS
MEDICOS
MENACES
NOTICES
NOVICES
NUANCES
OBJECTS
OFFICES
OUTACTS
PALACES
PIERCES
PLAICES
POLICES
POUNCES
PRANCES
PRINCES
PUMICES
QUINCES
RADICES
REDACTS
REDUCES
REFACES
REJECTS
RELACES
RELICTS
RELOCKS
RESECTS
SCONCES
SEANCES
SEDUCES
SELECTS
SENECAS
SHTICKS
SILICAS
SLUICES
SOLACES
SOURCES
SPLICES
SPRUCES
STANCES
STUCCOS
TENACES
THWACKS
TRANCES
UNLACES
UNLOCKS
UNPACKS
UNTACKS
UPTICKS

VOTECHS

•••••CS
AIRSACS
BIONICS
CALPACS
CELTICS
CLERICS
CLINICS
COGNACS
CRITICS
ETHNICS
EXOTICS
FABRICS
FROLICS
FUSTICS
GOTHICS
HEROICS
ITALICS
MANIACS
MASTICS
METRICS
MICMACS
MOSAICS
MYSTICS
NOETICS
NORDICS
PARSECS
PHOBICS
PHONICS
PHYSICS
PICNICS
POETICS
PUBLICS
RUBRICS
RUSTICS
STATICS
TACTICS
TARMACS
TICTACS
TOLTECS
TROPICS
ZODIACS

C•T••••
CATALAN
CATALOG
CATALPA
CATAWBA
CATBIRD
CATBOAT
CATCALL
CATCHER
CATCHES
CATCHON
CATCHUP
CATENAE
CATERED
CATERER
CATFISH
CATHAIR
CATHEAD
CATHODE
CATIONS
CATKINS
CATLIKE
CATNAPS
CATNIPS
CATSCAN
CATSEYE
CATSPAW
CATTAIL
CATTIER
CATTILY
CATTING
CATTISH
CATWALK
CITABLE
CITADEL
CITIZEN
CITRATE
CITRINE
CITROEN
CITRONS
CNTOWER
COTERIE
COTTAGE
COTTERS
COTTONS
COTTONY
CUTAWAY
CUTBACK
CUTDOWN
CUTICLE
CUTINTO
CUTLASS
CUTLERS
CUTLERY
CUTLETS
CUTOFFS
CUTOUTS
CUTRATE
CUTSOFF
CUTSOUT
CUTTERS
CUTTIME
CUTTING

C••T•••
CAFTANS
CALTECH
CANTATA
CANTEEN
CANTERS
CANTINA
CANTING
CANTLES
CANTONS
CANTORS
CAPTAIN
CAPTION
CAPTIVE
CAPTORS
CAPTURE
CARTAGE
CARTELS
CARTERS
CARTIER
CARTING
CARTONS
CARTOON
CASTERS
CASTILE
CASTING
CASTLED
CASTLES
CASTOFF
CASTOUT
CATTAIL
CATTIER
CATTILY
CATTING
CATTISH
CAUTION
CELTICS
CENTAUR
CENTAVO
CENTERS
CENTIME
CENTIMO
CENTRAL
CENTRED
CENTRES
CENTRIC
CENTURY
CERTAIN
CERTIFY
CHATEAU
CHATHAM
CHATSUP
CHATTED
CHATTEL
CHATTER
CHETRUM
CHITTER
CHUTNEY
CISTERN
CLATTER
CLOTHED
CLOTHES
CLOTTED
CLOTURE
CLUTTER
COATING
COCTEAU
COLTISH
CONTACT
CONTAIN
CONTEMN
CONTEND
CONTENT
CONTEST
CONTEXT
CONTORT
CONTOUR
CONTRAS
CONTROL
CONTUSE
COOTIES
COPTERS
CORTEGE
COSTAIN
COSTARS
COSTING
COSTNER
COSTUME
COTTAGE
COTTERS
COTTONS
COTTONY
COUTURE
COWTOWN
CRATERS
CRATING
CRETANS
CRETINS
CRITICS
CRITTER
CULTISH
CULTISM
CULTIST
CULTJAM
CULTURE
CURTAIL
CURTAIN
CURTEST
CURTSEY
CUSTARD
CUSTODY
CUSTOMS
CUTTERS
CUTTIME
CUTTING
CYNTHIA

C•••T••
CADETTE
CAPITAL
CAPITAN
CAPITOL
CAPSTAN
CARLTON
CAROTID
CAUSTIC
CHANTED
CHANTER
CHANTEY
CHAOTIC
CHAPTER
CHARTED
CHARTER
CHASTEN
CHASTER
CHATTED
CHATTEL
CHATTER
CHEATED
CHEATER
CHEETAH
CHEETOS
CHESTER
CHINTZY
CHITTER
CHOCTAW
CHORTLE
CLAPTON
CLATTER
CLAYTON
CLIFTON
CLINTON
CLOTTED
CLOUTED
CLUSTER
CLUTTER
COALTAR
COASTAL
COASTED
COASTER
COLETTE
COOPTED
CORETTA
COULTER
COUNTED
COUNTER
COUNTON
COUNTRY
COURTED
COURTLY
COVETED
COYOTES
CRAFTED
CRAFTER
CRAFTSY
CREATED
CREATES
CREATOR
CRESTED
CRITTER
CROATIA
CROUTON
CRUSTED
CRYPTIC
CRYPTOS
CRYSTAL
CULOTTE
CURATES
CURATOR

C••••T•
CABLETV
CACHETS
CADETTE
CAHOOTS
CALCITE
CANASTA
CANTATA
CAPLETS
CAPNUTS
CARNETS
CARPETS
CARROTS
CASSATT
CAVEATS
CAVORTS
CELESTA
CELESTE
CEMENTS
CHALETS
CHAPATI
CHARITY
CHIANTI
CHRISTI
CHRISTO
CHRISTY
CILIATE
CITRATE
CLARETS
CLARITY
CLIENTS
CLIMATE
CLINGTO
CLORETS
CLOSETS
COEDITS
COGNATE
COHORTS
COHOSTS
COLETTE
COLGATE
COLLATE
COLLETS
COMBATS
COMESTO
COMFITS
COMMITS
COMMUTE
COMPETE
COMPOTE
COMPUTE
CONFUTE
CONNOTE
COPOUTS
CORBETT
CORDATE
CORDITE
CORETTA
CORINTH
CORNETS
CORSETS
COSSETS
CRAVATS
CREDITS
CRUDITY
CUBISTS
CULOTTE
CURVETS
CUTINTO
CUTLETS
CUTOUTS
CUTRATE
CYGNETS

C•••••T
CABARET
CABINET
CAGIEST
CALLOUT
CALMEST
CALUMET
CALVERT
CAMELOT
CAMEOUT
CAMPOUT
CAPELET
CAPULET
CARCOAT
CARPORT
CARSEAT
CASHOUT
CASSATT
CASTOUT
CATBOAT
CAVEART
CELLIST
CHAPLET
CHARIOT
CHEMIST
CHEROOT
CHEVIOT
CHEWOUT
CIRCLET
CIRCUIT
CLEMENT
CLIPART
CLOSEST
COCKPIT
COCONUT
COEXIST
COHABIT
COLBERT
COLDCUT
COLDEST
COLLECT
COMBUST
COMEOUT
COMESAT
COMFORT
COMMENT
COMPACT
COMPORT
COMPOST
CONCEIT
CONCEPT
CONCERT
CONCOCT
CONDUCT
CONDUIT
CONGEST
CONKOUT
CONNECT
CONSENT
CONSIST
CONSORT
CONSULT
CONTACT
CONTENT
CONTEST
CONTEXT
CONTORT
CONVENT
CONVERT
CONVICT
COOKOUT
COOLANT
COOLEST
COOLSIT
COONCAT
COPILOT
COPSOUT
COPYCAT
COPYIST
CORBETT
CORONET
CORRECT
CORRUPT
COULDNT
COUPLET
COURANT
COZIEST
CREWCUT
CRICKET
CROCHET
CROQUET
CRUDEST
CRUMPET
CULPRIT
CULTIST
CULVERT
CURBCUT
CURRANT
CURRENT
CURTEST
CUTSOUT
CYCLIST
CYPRIOT
CZARIST

•CT••••
ACTABLE
ACTAEON
ACTEDUP
ACTINIC
ACTIONS
ACTIVES
ACTRESS
ACTSOUT
ACTUARY
ACTUATE
ACTUPON
ECTYPES
OCTAGON
OCTANES
OCTANTS
OCTAVES
OCTAVIA
OCTAVOS
OCTOBER
OCTOPOD
OCTOPUS
OCTUPLE

•C•T•••
ACETATE
ACETONE
ACHTUNG
ACUTELY
ECSTASY
SCATHED
SCATHES
SCATTED
SCATTER
SCOTERS
SCOTTIE
SCUTTLE
SCYTHED
SCYTHES

•C••T••
ACANTHI
ACHATES
ICEDTEA
SCANTED
SCANTER
SCANTLY
SCATTED
SCATTER
SCENTED
SCEPTER
SCEPTRE
SCHATZI
SCOOTED
SCOOTER
SCOTTIE
SCOUTED
SCOUTER
SCRATCH
SCUTTLE

•C•••T•
ACCENTS
ACCEPTS
ACCOSTS
ACCRETE
ACETATE
ACIDITY
ACOLYTE
ACONITE
ACQUITS
ACTUATE
NCWYETH
OCCULTS
OCELOTS
OCTANTS
SCRIPTS
SCULPTS

•C••••T
ACCOUNT
ACCURST
ACEDOUT
ACESOUT
ACHIEST
ACROBAT
ACTSOUT
ECKHART
ICEBOAT
ICKIEST
OCCIPUT
OCULIST
SCARLET
SCHMIDT

••CT•••
AUCTION
COCTEAU
DACTYLS
DICTATE
DICTION
DICTUMS
DOCTORS
DUCTILE
DUCTING
FACTION
FACTORS
FACTORY
FACTUAL
FICTION
FICTIVE
HECTARE
HECTORS
LACTASE
LACTATE
LACTEAL
LACTOSE
LECTERN
LECTORS
LECTURE
NECTARS
NOCTURN
PECTINS
PICTURE
RECTIFY
RECTORS
RECTORY
RUCTION
SECTION
SECTORS
SUCTION
TACTFUL
TACTICS
TACTILE
TICTACS
UNCTION
VECTORS
VICTIMS
VICTORS
VICTORY
VICTUAL

••C•T••
ASCETIC
EXCITED
EXCITES
FACETED
INCITED
INCITER
INCITES
JACKTAR
LICITLY
LOCATED
LOCATER
LOCATES
LOCATOR
NECKTIE
OOCYTES
RECITAL
RECITED
RECITER
RECITES
RICHTER
RICOTTA
TACITLY
TACITUS
VACATED
VACATES
YACHTED
YUCATAN

••C••T•
ACCENTS
ACCEPTS
ACCOSTS
ACCRETE
ASCENTS
BECKETT
BUCKETS
CACHETS
DECANTS
DECEITS
DECOCTS
DICTATE
DOCENTS
DOCKETS
ESCORTS
EXCEPTS
EXCRETE
FACULTY
GOCARTS
HACKETT
INCANTS
INCEPTS
JACINTO
JACKETS
JOCASTA
LACOSTE
LACTATE
LICKETY
LOCKETS
LOCUSTS
MACBETH
MACHETE
OCCULTS
OXCARTS
PACKETS
PICANTE
PICKETS
PICKETT
POCKETS
PUCKETT
RACKETS
RECANTS
RECASTS
RICKETY
RICOTTA
ROCKETS
SACHETS
SECANTS
SECRETE
SECRETS
SOCIETY
SOCKETS
TICKETS
TOCCATA
UNCOUTH
UNCRATE
VACUITY
WICHITA
WICKETS

••C•••T
ACCOUNT
ACCURST
ANCIENT
BACKBIT
BACKLIT
BACKOUT
BECKETT
COCKPIT
COCONUT
CYCLIST
DECKOUT
DECRYPT
DICIEST
ENCHANT
ENCRUST
ENCRYPT
ESCHEAT
EXCERPT
HACKETT
INCIPIT
JACKPOT
JACONET
KICKOUT
LACIEST
LOCKNUT
LOCKOUT
LUCKOUT
OCCIPUT
PACKRAT
PECCANT
PECKSAT
PICKETT
PICKOUT
PICKSAT
PUCKETT
RACIEST
RACQUET
RECEIPT
RECOUNT
RECRUIT
RICERAT
RICHEST
SACKOUT
SICKEST
SICKOUT

•••CT••
CHOCTAW
EJECTED
ELECTED
ELECTEE
ELECTOR
ELECTRA
ELECTRO
ENACTED
ENACTOR
ERECTED
ERECTER
ERECTLY
ERECTOR
ERUCTED
EVICTED
EXACTED
EXACTER
EXACTLY
EXACTOR
FRACTAL
MULCTED
PLECTRA
PROCTOR
REACTED
REACTOR
REACTTO
SANCTUM
SPECTER
SPECTOR
SPECTRA
SPECTRE
TRACTOR

•••C•T•
AVOCETS
BAYCITY
BOBCATS
BOYCOTT
CALCITE
EDACITY
EDUCATE
ELICITS
EXECUTE
FATCATS
FATCITY
FAUCETS
FAWCETT
FLOCKTO
HEPCATS
LANCETS
MASCOTS
MUSCATS
OPACITY
PAUCITY
PLACATE
REACTTO
REXCATS
SNOCATS
STICKTO
STUCKTO
SUNCITY
TERCETS
TOCCATA
TOMCATS
TRICOTS
WALCOTT

•••C••T
BISCUIT
BOYCOTT
BRACKET
CARCOAT
CIRCLET
CIRCUIT
CONCEIT
CONCEPT
CONCERT
CONCOCT
CRICKET
CROCHET
DESCANT
DESCENT
DOGCART
FASCIST
FAWCETT
FLYCAST
HATCHET
LABCOAT
MISCAST
NASCENT
OUTCAST
PEACOAT
PECCANT
PERCENT
PLACKET
PRECAST
PRECEPT
RATCHET
REDCENT
REDCOAT
SURCOAT
TEACART
THICKET
TOPCOAT
VINCENT
WALCOTT
WATCHIT

••••CT•
ABDUCTS
ADDUCTS
AFFECTS
ASPECTS
BISECTS
DECOCTS
DEDUCTS
DEFACTO
DEFECTS
DEJECTS
DELICTI
DELICTS
DEPICTS
DETECTS
DIDACTS
DIRECTS
EFFECTS
EXPECTS
IMPACTS
INDICTS
INDUCTS
INFECTS
INJECTS
INSECTS
OBJECTS
OUTACTS
REDACTS
REJECTS
RELICTS
RESECTS
SELECTS

••••C•T
APRICOT
BEARCAT
BORSCHT
COLDCUT
COONCAT
COPYCAT
CREWCUT
CURBCUT
DEFICIT
DOVECOT
HAIRCUT
HARICOT
HELLCAT
ILLICIT
JUMPCUT
MANXCAT
MONOCOT
POLECAT
SOLICIT
UTRECHT
WILDCAT
WOODCUT

•••••CT
ADJUNCT
AFFLICT
ATTRACT
COLLECT
COMPACT
CONCOCT
CONDUCT
CONNECT
CONTACT
CONVICT
CORRECT
DEFLECT
DEFUNCT
DETRACT
DIALECT
DISSECT
EXTINCT
EXTRACT
INEXACT
INFLECT
INFLICT
INSPECT
NEGLECT
OVERACT
PANDECT
PERFECT

PLAYACT
PREDICT
PREFECT
PRODUCT
PROJECT
PROTECT
REELECT
REENACT
REFLECT
REFRACT
RESPECT
RETRACT
RIOTACT
SUBJECT
SUSPECT
TRISECT
VERDICT
VIADUCT

CU•••••
CUBBIES
CUBICLE
CUBISTS
CUCKOOS
CUDDLED
CUDDLES
CUDGELS
CUEBALL
CUECARD
CUFFING
CUIBONO
CUIRASS
CUISINE
CULEBRA
CULLING
CULOTTE
CULPRIT
CULTISH
CULTISM
CULTIST
CULTJAM
CULTURE
CULVERT
CUMULUS
CUNNING
CUPCAKE
CUPFULS
CUPOLAS
CUPPING
CURACAO
CURATES
CURATOR
CURBCUT
CURBING
CURDING
CURDLED
CURDLES
CUREALL
CURFEWS
CURIOUS
CURLERS
CURLEWS
CURLIER
CURLING
CURLSUP
CURRANT
CURRENT
CURRIED
CURRIER
CURRIES
CURSING
CURSIVE
CURSORS
CURSORY
CURTAIL
CURTAIN
CURTEST
CURTSEY
CURVETS
CURVIER
CURVING
CUSHAWS
CUSHIER
CUSHION
CUSPIDS
CUSSING
CUSSLER
CUSTARD
CUSTODY
CUSTOMS
CUTAWAY
CUTBACK
CUTDOWN
CUTICLE
CUTINTO
CUTLASS
CUTLERS
CUTLERY
CUTLETS
CUTOFFS
CUTOUTS
CUTRATE
CUTSOFF
CUTSOUT
CUTTERS
CUTTIME
CUTTING

C•U••••
CAULKED
CAULKER
CAUSING
CAUSTIC
CAUTION
CHUCKED
CHUCKLE
CHUGGED
CHUKKAS
CHUKKER
CHUMMED
CHUNNEL
CHURNED
CHUTNEY
CLUBBED
CLUBCAR
CLUCKED
CLUEDIN
CLUEING
CLUESIN
CLUMPED
CLUNKED
CLUNKER
CLUSTER
CLUTTER
COUCHED
COUCHES
COUGARS
COUGHED
COUGHUP
COULDNT
COULEES
COULOMB
COULTER
COUNCIL
COUNSEL
COUNTED
COUNTER
COUNTON
COUNTRY
COUPLED
COUPLES
COUPLET
COUPONS
COURAGE
COURANT
COURIER
COURSED
COURSER
COURSES
COURTED
COURTLY
COUSINS
COUTURE
CRUCIAL
CRUDELY
CRUDEST
CRUDITY
CRUELER
CRUELLY
CRUISED
CRUISER
CRUISES
CRULLER
CRUMBLE
CRUMBLY
CRUMPET
CRUMPLE
CRUMPLY
CRUNCHY
CRUSADE
CRUSHED
CRUSHER
CRUSHES
CRUSTED
CRUZADO

C••U•••
CADUCEI
CALUMET
CALUMNY
CAPULET
CASUALS
CAYUGAS
CAYUSES
CERUMEN
CHAUCER
CLAUDIA
CLAUDIO
CLAUSES
CLOUDED
CLOUTED
COLUMBO
COLUMNS
COZUMEL
CROUTON
CUMULUS

C•••U••
CADBURY
CAESURA
CAIQUES
CAPFULS
CAPGUNS
CAPNUTS
CAPSULE
CAPTURE
CARFULS
CAROUSE
CENSURE
CENTURY
CHEQUER
CHEQUES
CHERUBS
CHINUPS
CIRCUIT
CIRCUSY
CIRQUES
CLAQUES
CLIBURN
CLIQUES
CLOQUES
CLOSURE
CLOTURE
COEQUAL
COGBURN
COLLUDE
COLOURS
COMBUST
COMMUNE
COMMUTE
COMPUTE
CONCURS
CONDUCE
CONDUCT
CONDUIT
CONFUSE
CONFUTE
CONJURE
CONQUER
CONSULS
CONSULT
CONSUME
CONTUSE
COPOUTS
CORRUPT
COSTUME
COUTURE
CROQUET
CULTURE
CUPFULS
CUTOUTS
CYYOUNG

C••••U•
CACHOUS
CADMIUM
CALCIUM
CALHOUN
CALLOUS
CALLOUT
CALLSUP
CAMBIUM
CAMEOUT
CAMPOUT
CANDOUR
CANOPUS
CAREFUL
CAROLUS
CASHOUT
CASSIUS
CASTOUT
CATCHUP
CELSIUS
CENTAUR
CEPHEUS
CHALKUP
CHATSUP
CHECKUP
CHEERUP
CHETRUM
CHEWOUT
CHEWSUP
CHOKEUP
CLAMSUP
CLEANUP
CLEARUP
CLOGSUP
CLOSEUP
COCONUT
COILSUP
COLDCUT
COLOBUS
COMEDUE
COMEOUT
COMESUP
COMIQUE
CONKOUT
CONTOUR
COOKOUT
COOKSUP
COOPSUP
COPIOUS
COPSOUT
COUGHUP
COVERUP
CRACKUP
CRANIUM
CRANKUP
CRASSUS
CREEPUP
CREWCUT
CRISPUS
CROESUS
CROPSUP
CROSSUP
CUMULUS
CURBCUT
CURIOUS
CURLSUP
CUTSOUT

C•••••U
CARIBOU
CHAPEAU
CHATEAU
COCTEAU

•CU••••
ACUTELY
ECUADOR
OCULIST
SCUDDED
SCUFFED
SCUFFLE
SCULLED
SCULLER
SCULPTS
SCUPPER
SCURVES
SCUTTLE

•C•U•••
ACCURST
ACCUSED
ACCUSER
ACCUSES
ACQUIRE
ACQUITS
ACTUARY
ACTUATE
ACTUPON
MCGUIRE
MCLUHAN
MCQUEEN
OCCULTS
OCTUPLE
SCOURED
SCOURER
SCOURGE
SCOUTED
SCOUTER
SCRUBBY
SCRUBUP
SCRUFFS
SCRUFFY
SCRUNCH
SCRUPLE

•C••U••
ACCOUNT
ACCRUAL
ACCRUED
ACCRUES
ACHTUNG
ICECUBE
OCCLUDE
SCAPULA

•C•••U•
ACEDOUT
ACESOUT
ACTEDUP
ACTSOUT
ECHINUS
ECLOGUE
ICEBLUE
OCCIPUT
OCEANUS
OCTOPUS
SCAREUP
SCREWUP
SCRUBUP

••CU•••
ACCURST
ACCUSED
ACCUSER
ACCUSES
ESCUDOS
EXCUSED
EXCUSES
FACULTY
FICUSES
FOCUSED
FOCUSES
INCUDES
JACUZZI
JOCULAR
LACUNAE
LACUNAL
LACUNAS
LOCUSTS
MACULAE
NOCUOUS
OCCULTS
RECUSED
RECUSES
SECULAR
SECURED
SECURER
SECURES
UNCURLS
VACUITY
VACUOLE
VACUOUS
VACUUMS
VICUNAS

••C•U••
ACCOUNT
ACCRUAL
ACCRUED
ACCRUES
BACKUPS
BECAUSE
DICTUMS
ENCRUST
EXCLUDE
FACTUAL
HICCUPS
INCLUDE
JACCUSE
JACQUES
KICKUPS
LACQUER
LECTURE
LOCKUPS
LYCEUMS
MACDUFF
MOCKUPS
NOCTURN
OCCLUDE
PICKUPS
PICTURE
RACQUET
RECLUSE
RECOUNT
RECOUPS
RECRUIT
SECLUDE
SICHUAN
SUCCUMB
UNCOUTH
VACUUMS
VICTUAL

••C••U•
BACCHUS
BACKOUT
BACKRUB
BACKSUP
BECLOUD
BUCKSUP
CACHOUS
COCONUT
DECKOUT
DECORUM
JACKSUP
KICKOUT
KICKSUP
LACEDUP
LACESUP
LOCKNUT
LOCKOUT
LOCKSUP
LUCKOUT
MACAQUE
MUCKSUP
NOCUOUS
NUCLEUS
OCCIPUT
PACKSUP
PICKOUT
PICKSUP
RACKSUP
SACKFUL
SACKOUT
SICKOUT
SUCCOUR
TACITUS
TACTFUL
VACUOUS
VICIOUS
WICKIUP

••C•••U
COCTEAU

•••CU••
BISCUIT
CIRCUIT
CIRCUSY
CONCURS
DISCUSS
DRACULA
EGGCUPS
EPICURE
EVACUEE
EXECUTE
EYECUPS
HERCULE
HICCUPS
ICECUBE
INOCULA
JACCUSE
MERCURY
MISCUED
MISCUES
OBSCURE
PINCURL
PROCURE
RESCUED
RESCUER
RESCUES
SUCCUMB
TEACUPS

•••C•U•
BACCHUS
BRACEUP
CALCIUM
CATCHUP
CHECKUP
CRACKUP
FULCRUM
JUICEUP
KETCHUP
KEYCLUB
LASCAUX
MATCHUP
MITCHUM
PATCHUP
PSYCHUP
PUNCHUP
QUECHUA
RANCOUR
RAUCOUS
REOCCUR
SANCTUM
SPICEUP
STACKUP
STICKUP
STOCKUP
STUCKUP
SUCCOUR
TOUCHUP
VISCOUS

•••C••U
MARCEAU

••••CU•
APERCUS
ATTICUS
COLDCUT
CREWCUT
CURBCUT
HAIRCUT
INFOCUS
INVACUO
JUMPCUT
LIONCUB
MODICUM
REOCCUR
VANOCUR
WOODCUT

•••••CU
ILIESCU

C•V••••
CAVALRY
CAVEART
CAVEATS
CAVEDIN
CAVEINS
CAVEMAN
CAVEMEN
CAVERNS
CAVESIN
CAVILED
CAVILER
CAVORTS
CEVICHE
CIVILLY
CIVVIES
COVERED
COVERUP
COVETED

C••V•••
CALVARY
CALVERT
CALVING
CANVASS
CARVERS
CARVING
CHEVIED
CHEVIES
CHEVIOT
CHEVRES
CHEVRON
CIVVIES
CLAVELL
CLAVIER
CLOVERS
COEVALS
CONVENE
CONVENT
CONVERT
CONVEYS
CONVICT
CONVOKE
CONVOYS
CRAVATS
CRAVENS
CRAVERS
CRAVING
CREVICE
CULVERT
CURVETS
CURVIER
CURVING

C•••V••
CARAVAN
CARAVEL
CHEEVER
CHERVIL
CLEAVED
CLEAVER
CLEAVES
CLEAVON

C••••V•
CAPTIVE
CASSAVA
CENTAVO
COMMOVE
CONCAVE
CONNIVE
CURSIVE

C•••••V
CABLETV
CHEKHOV

•C••V••
ACTIVES
MCGAVIN
OCTAVES
OCTAVIA
OCTAVOS
SCARVES
SCRIVEN
SCURVES

•C•••V•
ACHIEVE

••C•V••
ALCOVES
INCIVIL
RECOVER
UNCIVIL
UNCOVER

••C••V•
ANCHOVY
ARCHIVE
DECEIVE
ENCLAVE
FICTIVE
RECEIVE

••C•••V
ROCKYIV

•••C•V•
CONCAVE
MUSCOVY

C•W••••
COWARDS
COWBELL
COWBIRD
COWBOYS
COWERED
COWGIRL
COWHAND
COWHERD
COWHIDE
COWLICK
COWLING
COWPEAS
COWPOKE
COWRIES
COWSLIP
COWTOWN

C••W•••
CARWASH
CATWALK
CHEWERS
CHEWIER
CHEWING
CHEWOUT
CHEWSUP
CHOWDER
CLAWERS
CLAWING
CLOWDER
CLOWNED
COBWEBS
CRAWDAD
CRAWLED
CRAWLER
CREWCUT
CREWELS
CREWING
CREWMAN
CREWMEN
CROWBAR
CROWDED
CROWERS
CROWING
CROWNED
CRYWOLF

C•••W••
CARAWAY
CATAWBA
CNTOWER
COLDWAR
CSLEWIS
CUTAWAY

C••••W•
CASHEWS
COWTOWN
CURFEWS
CURLEWS
CUSHAWS
CUTDOWN

C•••••W
CAPSHAW
CASELAW
CASHCOW
CATSPAW
CHOCTAW
CORNROW

•CW••••
NCWYETH

•C•W•••
MCSWINE
SCHWINN
SCOWLED
SCOWLER

•C••W••
SCRAWLS
SCRAWLY
SCRAWNY
SCREWED
SCREWUP

•C••••W
ICESHOW

••C•W••
ARCHWAY
RACEWAY

••C••W•
ESCHEWS
ESCROWS

••C•••W
BUCKSAW
HACKSAW
JACKDAW
MACGRAW

•••C•W•
ANTCOWS
SEACOWS

•••C••W
AIRCREW
ATECROW
CHOCTAW
DEWCLAW
DOGCHEW
DOGCHOW
EATCROW
SALCHOW
UNSCREW

••••C•W
CASHCOW
HOLYCOW
MILKCOW

C•X••••
COXCOMB

C••X•••
COAXERS
COAXIAL
COAXING
COEXIST

C•••X••
CALYXES

C••••X•
CONTEXT

C•••••X
CAKEMIX
CALLBOX
CASHBOX
CINEMAX
COMPLEX

•C••X••
ICEAXES

••C••X•
PICKAXE

••C•••X
LOCKBOX
STCROIX

•••C••X
LASCAUX
PANCHAX

CY•••••
CYBORGS
CYCLERS
CYCLING
CYCLIST
CYCLONE
CYCLOPS
CYGNETS
CYMBALS
CYNICAL
CYNTHIA
CYPHERS
CYPRESS
CYPRIOT
CYYOUNG

C•Y••••
CAYENNE
CAYUGAS
CAYUSES
COYNESS
COYOTES
CRYBABY
CRYOGEN
CRYPTIC
CRYPTOS
CRYSTAL
CRYWOLF
CYYOUNG

C••Y•••
CALYCES
CALYPSO
CALYXES
CANYONS
CLAYIER
CLAYTON
CLOYING
COPYBOY
COPYCAT
COPYING
COPYIST
CORYELL
COZYING
CRAYOLA
CRAYONS

C•••Y••
CARLYLE
CARRYON
COLLYER

C••••Y•
CARBOYS
CAROLYN
CATSEYE
CONVEYS
CONVOYS
COWBOYS

C•••••Y
CADBURY
CALCIFY
CALGARY
CALUMNY
CALVARY
CANNERY
CANNILY
CAPABLY
CARAWAY
CASSIDY
CATTILY
CAVALRY
CENTURY
CERTIFY
CHANTEY

CHARILY
CHARITY
CHARLEY
CHEAPLY
CHICORY
CHIEFLY
CHIMNEY
CHINTZY
CHOMSKY
CHRISTY
CHUTNEY
CIRCUSY
CIVILLY
CLARIFY
CLARITY
CLEANLY
CLEARLY
CLOONEY
CLOSELY
COCKILY
COCKNEY
COGENCY
COMESBY
COMFREY
COMPANY
CONAKRY
CONNERY
COOKERY
COPPERY
COPYBOY
CORNILY
COTTONY
COUNTRY
COURTLY
CRAFTSY
CRASSLY
CRAZILY
CRINKLY
CRISPLY
CROSSLY
CRUDELY
CRUDITY
CRUELLY
CRUMBLY
CRUMPLY
CRUNCHY
CRYBABY
CURSORY
CURTSEY
CUSTODY
CUTAWAY
CUTLERY

•CY••••
SCYTHED
SCYTHES

•C•Y•••
ACRYLIC
ECDYSES
ECDYSIS
ECTYPES
NCWYETH

•C••Y••
ACOLYTE

•C•••Y•
ACRONYM

•C••••Y
ACADEMY
ACIDIFY
ACIDITY
ACRIDLY
ACTUARY
ACUTELY
ECOLOGY
ECONOMY
ECSTASY
SCANTLY
SCARIFY
SCARILY
SCENERY
SCRAGGY
SCRAPPY
SCRAWLY
SCRAWNY
SCRIMPY
SCRUBBY
SCRUFFY
WCHANDY

••CY•••
BICYCLE
OOCYTES
RECYCLE

••C•Y••
DACTYLS
DECAYED
DECOYED
DECRYPT
ENCRYPT
ROCKYII
ROCKYIV

••C••Y•
BUCKEYE
DICKEYS
JOCKEYS
LACKEYS
RICKEYS
SOCKEYE

••C•••Y
ALCHEMY
ANCHOVY
ARCHERY
ARCHWAY
BACKBAY
BUCKLEY
COCKILY
COCKNEY
FACTORY
FACULTY
HACKNEY
HICKORY
LICITLY
LICKETY
LOCALLY
LUCIDLY
LUCKILY
MOCKERY
PECCARY
RACEWAY
RECENCY
RECTIFY
RECTORY
RICKETY
SECRECY
SICKBAY
SICKPAY
SOCIETY
TACITLY
TACKILY
UNCANNY
VACANCY
VACUITY
VICEROY
VICTORY
VOCALLY
WACKILY
ZACHARY

•••CY••
HALCYON
PROCYON

•••C••Y
AMSCRAY
BALCONY
BAYCITY
BLACKLY
BOKCHOY
CALCIFY
CHICORY
CIRCUSY
EDACITY
ERECTLY
EXACTLY
FANCILY
FATCITY
GROCERY
JUICILY
LARCENY
MERCURY
MUSCOVY
OPACITY
PAUCITY
PECCARY
PRICKLY
QUICKLY
SAUCILY
SLICKLY
SORCERY
SPECIFY
SUNCITY
THICKLY
TRACERY
TUSCANY

••••C•Y
ANARCHY
BLOTCHY
CRUNCHY
FINICKY
GROUCHY
HOOTCHY
KITSCHY
KOLACKY
KOOTCHY
MIMICRY
PANICKY
PAUNCHY
PREACHY
SKETCHY
SLOUCHY
STARCHY
THATCHY
TREACLY
TWITCHY
UNLUCKY

•••••CY
ARDENCY
COGENCY
FALLACY
FLUENCY
INFANCY
LATENCY
PLIANCY
POTENCY
PRIMACY
PRIVACY
RECENCY
REGENCY
SECRECY
TENANCY
TRUANCY
URGENCY
VACANCY

CZ•••••
CZARDAS
CZARDOM
CZARINA
CZARISM
CZARIST

C•Z••••
CEZANNE
COZENED
COZIEST
COZUMEL
COZYING
COZZENS

C••Z•••
CALZONE
CANZONE
CINZANO
COZZENS
CRAZIER
CRAZIES
CRAZILY
CRAZING
CRUZADO

C•••Z••
CITIZEN
CORAZON

C••••Z•
CADENZA
CAPSIZE
CARDOZO
CHINTZY
CHORIZO

•C•••Z•
SCHATZI
SCHERZI
SCHERZO

••C•Z••
ALCAZAR
JACUZZI

••C••Z•
JACUZZI

•••C••Z
NATCHEZ

DA•••••
DABBING
DABBLED
DABBLER
DABBLES
DABHAND
DACTYLS
DADAISM
DADAIST
DADDIES
DAFFIER
DAFFILY
DAFTEST
DAGGERS
DAGWOOD
DAHLIAS
DAHOMEY
DAILIES
DAIMLER
DAIRIES
DAISIES
DAKOTAN
DAKOTAS
DALLIED
DALLIER
DALLIES
DALTREY
DAMAGED
DAMAGES
DAMASKS
DAMMING
DAMNING
DAMPENS
DAMPERS
DAMPEST
DAMPING
DAMPISH
DAMSELS
DAMSONS
DANCERS
DANCING
DANDERS
DANDIER
DANDIES
DANDLED
DANDLES
DANELAW
DANGERS
DANGLED
DANGLER
DANGLES
DANIELS
DANKEST
DANSEUR
DAPHNIS
DAPPING
DAPPLED
DAPPLES
DARESAY
DARESTO
DARKAGE
DARKENS
DARKEST
DARKISH
DARKMAN
DARLEEN
DARLENE
DARLING
DARNERS
DARNING
DARRELL
DARTERS
DARTING
DASBOOT
DASHERS
DASHIKI
DASHING
DASHOFF
DASTARD
DATASET
DATEDLY
DAUBERS
DAUBING
DAUMIER
DAUNTED
DAUPHIN
DAVINCI
DAWDLED
DAWDLER
DAWDLES
DAWKINS
DAWNING
DAYBEDS
DAYBOOK
DAYCAMP
DAYCARE
DAYLILY
DAYLONG
DAYROOM
DAYSINN
DAYSTAR
DAYTIME
DAYTONA
DAYTRIP
DAZEDLY
DAZZLED
DAZZLER
DAZZLES

D•A••••
DEACONS
DEADAIR
DEADEND
DEADENS
DEADEYE
DEADPAN
DEADSEA
DEADSET
DEAFENS
DEAFEST
DEALERS
DEALING
DEALOUT
DEALSIN
DEALTIN
DEAREST
DEARSIR
DEARTHS
DIADEMS
DIAGRAM
DIAHANN
DIALECT
DIALERS
DIALING
DIALOGS
DIAMOND
DIAPERS
DIARIES
DIATOMS
DRABBER
DRACHMA
DRACULA
DRAFTED
DRAFTEE
DRAGGED
DRAGNET
DRAGONS
DRAGOON
DRAGOUT
DRAGSIN
DRAGSON
DRAINED
DRAINER
DRAPERS
DRAPERY
DRAPING
DRASTIC
DRATTED
DRAUGHT
DRAWBAR
DRAWERS
DRAWING
DRAWLED
DRAWNIN
DRAWNON
DRAWNUP
DRAWOUT
DRAWSIN
DRAWSON
DRAWSUP
DRAYAGE
DRAYING
DUALITY
DWARFED
DWARVES

D••A•••
DADAISM
DADAIST
DAMAGED
DAMAGES
DAMASKS
DATASET
DEBACLE
DEBAKEY
DEBARGE
DEBARKS
DEBASED
DEBASES
DEBATED
DEBATER
DEBATES
DEBAUCH
DECADES
DECAGON
DECALOG
DECAMPS
DECANTS
DECAPOD
DECARLO
DECAYED
DEDALUS
DEFACED
DEFACES
DEFACTO
DEFAMED
DEFAMES
DEFARGE
DEFAULT
DEGAUSS
DELANEY
DELAYED
DELAYER
DEMANDS
DEPALMA
DEPARTS
DERAILS
DESALTS
DETAILS
DETAINS
DEVALUE
DIDACTS
DILATED
DILATES
DISABLE
DISARMS
DISAVOW
DOMAINS
DONAHUE
DONATED
DONATES
DONATOR
DOSAGES
DOWAGER
DREADED
DREAMED
DREAMER
DREAMON
DREAMUP
DUBARRY
DUKAKIS
DUNAWAY
DURABLE
DURABLY
DURANCE
DURANGO
DURANTE
DYNAMIC
DYNAMOS
DYNASTS
DYNASTY

D•••A••
DABHAND
DARKAGE
DASTARD
DAYCAMP
DAYCARE
DEADAIR
DECLAIM
DECLARE
DECLASS
DEEJAYS
DEFEATS
DEFIANT
DEFLATE
DEFRAUD
DEFRAYS
DEGRADE
DELTAIC
DEMEANS
DENIALS
DENMARK
DENTATE
DEODARS
DEPLANE
DEPRAVE
DESCANT
DESPAIR
DETRACT
DETRAIN
DEVIANT
DEVIATE
DEWLAPS
DIAHANN
DICTATE
DIEHARD
DIETARY
DIGRAPH
DIKTATS
DILLARD
DIORAMA
DISBAND
DISBARS
DISCARD
DISDAIN
DISEASE
DISMAYS
DISTAFF
DISTANT
DITTANY
DOCKAGE
DOGCART
DOGDAYS
DOGEARS
DOGFACE
DOGMATA
DOGTAGS
DOLLARS
DOLMANS
DOODADS
DORMANT
DORSALS
DOSSALS
DRAYAGE
DRYWALL
DUEDATE
DULLARD

D••••A•
DAHLIAS
DAKOTAN
DAKOTAS
DANELAW
DARESAY
DARKMAN
DAYSTAR
DEADPAN
DEBORAH
DECIMAL
DEEPFAT
DELILAH
DEPOSAL
DEWCLAW
DIAGRAM
DIGITAL
DINGBAT
DIPOLAR
DISHPAN
DISHRAG
DISPLAY
DIURNAL
DOGSTAR
DONEGAL
DONJUAN
DONOVAN
DOORMAN
DOORMAT
DOORWAY
DOUGLAS
DOVEBAR
DOWNPAT
DRAWBAR
DRIPPAN
DRISTAN
DRIVEAT
DUENNAS
DUNAWAY
DUSTPAN

D•••••A
DAYTONA
DEADSEA
DEEPSEA
DELIRIA
DEPALMA
DILEMMA
DIORAMA
DIPLOMA
DOGMATA
DRACHMA
DRACULA
DUODENA
DYKSTRA

•DA••••
ADAGIOS
ADAMANT
ADAMITE
ADAMSON
ADAPTED
ADAPTER
ADAPTOR
EDACITY
EDAPHIC
EDASNER
IDAHOAN

•D•A•••
ADDABLE
ADVANCE
EDWARDS
IDCARDS
IDEALLY
IDEATED
IDEATES
IDIAMIN
PDJAMES
RDLAING

•D••A••
ADAMANT
ADONAIS
ADULATE
EDOUARD
EDUCATE
ODDBALL

•D•••A•
ADMIRAL
ADRENAL
IDAHOAN

•D••••A
ADDENDA

••DA•••
ADDABLE
ANDANTE
BEDAUBS
DADAISM
DADAIST
DEDALUS
DIDACTS
HIDALGO
IODATES
JUDAISM
MADAMEX
MEDALED
ORDAINS
PEDALED
PEDANTS
RADAMES
REDACTS
REDANTS
REDATED
REDATES
SEDALIA
SEDATER
SODAPOP
UNDATED
UPDATED
UPDATES
VEDANTA
VIDALIA

••D•A••
ANDEANS
BEDLAMP
BIDFAIR
ENDEARS
ENDGAME
ENDWAYS
GODDARD
HYDRANT
HYDRATE
INDIANA
INDIANS
KIDNAPS
KODIAKS
MADCAPS
MEDIANS
MEDIANT
MEDIATE
MIDDAYS
MIDEAST
MIDLAND
MIDWAYS
MUDPACK
ODDBALL
OGDOADS
OLDDAYS
OLDHAND
OLDMAID
ORDEALS
PEDLARS
RADIALS
RADIANS
RADIANT
RADIATE
REDCAPS
REDEALS
REDEALT
REDHAIR
REDHATS
REDIALS
REDOAKS
REDRAWN
REDRAWS
REDTAPE
RUDYARD
SADSACK
SIDEARM
TEDMACK
UNDRAPE
UNDRAWN
UPDRAFT
WIDMARK
ZODIACS

••D••A•
ANDREAS
BODEGAS
BODYFAT
BUDDHAS
CADDOAN
ENDPLAY
FADIMAN
FEDERAL
FEDORAS
GIDDYAP
GODTHAB
HADRIAN
LADYDAY
MADEHAY
MADEWAY
MEDEVAC
MEDICAL
MEDUSAE
MEDUSAS
MIDYEAR
MODELAS
MODULAR
NODULAR
OEDIPAL
OLDCHAP
OLDUVAI
ORDINAL
PADUCAH
RADICAL
REDCOAT
REDFLAG
REDHEAD
REDHEAT
REDMEAT
REDSTAR
RIDGWAY
SIDEBAR
SIDECAR
SIDEMAN

••D•••A
ADDENDA
ANDORRA
BEDELIA
CADENZA
CEDILLA
INDIANA
INDICIA
KEDROVA
MADEIRA
MADONNA
MADRONA
MEDULLA
PODRIDA
SEDALIA
VEDANTA
VIDALIA

•••DA••
AIRDAMS
AIRDATE
ALIDADE
AOUDADS
BANDAGE
BANDAID
BANDANA
BELDAME
BELDAMS
BONDAGE
BRIDALS
CORDAGE
CORDATE
DEADAIR
DEODARS
DISDAIN
DOGDAYS
DOODADS
DUEDATE
FONDANT
FRIDAYS
GODDARD
GOODALL
HEYDAYS
HOWDAHS
INADAZE
KENDALL
KILDARE
LANDAUS
MANDALA
MANDANS
MANDATE
MANDAYS
MAYDAYS
MIDDAYS
MISDATE
MONDALE
MONDAYS
MORDANT
MUNDANE
OLDDAYS
ONADARE
ONADATE
OXIDANT
OXIDASE
PAYDAYS
PENDANT
PREDATE
PREDAWN
PURDAHS
RANDALL
RAWDATA
SANDALS
SUNDAES
SUNDAYS
VANDALS
VERDANT
WHYDAHS
WOODARD
YARDAGE
YARDARM

•••D•A•
ACADIAN
BANDSAW
BIGDEAL
BIRDMAN
BONDMAN
BUDDHAS
CADDOAN
CHEDDAR
COLDWAR
CORDIAL
DEADPAN
FEEDBAG
FELDMAN
FORDHAM
GIDDYAP
GOODBAR
GOODMAN
GORDIAN
GRADUAL
HANDBAG
HANDCAR
HANDSAW
HARDHAT
HARDPAN
HEADMAN
HEADWAY
LANDSAT
LINDSAY
MISDEAL
MISDIAL
NEWDEAL
OBADIAH
OUTDRAW
PHIDIAS
RAWDEAL
ROADMAP
ROADWAY
RONDEAU
SANDBAG
SANDBAR
SANDMAN
SUNDIAL

TRUDEAU
TUNDRAS
WILDCAT
WINDBAG
YARDMAN
YESDEAR

•••D••A
BANDANA
CALDERA
CANDELA
CANDIDA
CORDOBA
DEADSEA
DUODENA
GONDOLA
ICEDTEA
ISADORA
MANDALA
MANDELA
MENDOZA
PANDORA
RAWDATA

••••DA•
AGENDAS
AIMEDAT
ARMADAS
BAGHDAD
BIMODAL
BIPEDAL
BRENDAN
BROADAX
CHEDDAR
CICADAE
CICADAS
CRAWDAD
CZARDAS
FARADAY
FLAGDAY
FRIEDAN
GELADAS
GRANDAM
HALFDAN
HOLIDAY
HYUNDAI
JACKDAW
JOURDAN
LADYDAY
LAMBDAS
MACADAM
MILLDAM
NAMEDAY
NEVADAN
NEWSDAY
NOONDAY
ONEIDAS
OVOIDAL
PAGODAS
PAWEDAT
POKEDAT
POSADAS
POTSDAM
RAMADAN
RAMADAS
REMUDAS
RUANDAN
RWANDAN
SAMEDAY
SCANDAL
SNOWDAY
SOLEDAD
SOMEDAY
SYNODAL
TUESDAY
UGANDAN
WEEKDAY
WORKDAY

••••D•A
ARCADIA
CLAUDIA
ECHIDNA
GRANDMA
GRANDPA
PHAEDRA

•••••DA
ADDENDA
ALAMEDA
BARBUDA
BELINDA
BERMUDA
CANDIDA
CORRIDA
ESTRADA
FLORIDA
GRANADA
GRENADA
LAMBADA
LASORDA
MATILDA
MELINDA
MIRANDA
OCANADA
PODRIDA
RIGVEDA
ROTUNDA
SALSODA
TOSTADA
VERANDA

D•B••••
DABBING
DABBLED
DABBLER
DABBLES
DABHAND
DEBACLE
DEBAKEY
DEBARGE
DEBARKS
DEBASED
DEBASES
DEBATED
DEBATER
DEBATES
DEBAUCH
DEBEERS
DEBITED
DEBONED
DEBONES
DEBORAH
DEBOUCH
DEBRIEF
DEBTORS
DEBUNKS
DEBUSSY
DEBUTED
DIBBLED
DIBBLES
DOBBINS
DUBARRY
DUBBERS
DUBBING
DUBIETY
DUBIOUS
DUBUQUE
DYBBUKS

D••B•••
DABBING
DABBLED
DABBLER
DABBLES
DASBOOT
DAUBERS
DAUBING
DAYBEDS
DAYBOOK
DELBERT
DERBIES
DIBBLED
DIBBLES
DIMBULB
DISBAND
DISBARS
DOBBINS
DOUBLED
DOUBLES
DOUBLET
DOUBLEU
DOUBTED
DOUBTER
DRABBER
DRIBBLE
DRIBLET
DRUBBED
DUBBERS
DUBBING
DUMBEST
DYBBUKS

D•••B••
DECIBEL
DELIBES
DINGBAT
DISABLE
DISOBEY
DOVEBAR
DOWNBOW
DRABBER
DRAWBAR
DRIBBLE
DRUBBED
DURABLE
DURABLY

D••••B•
DISROBE
DROPSBY

D•••••B
DIMBULB
DISTURB

•D•B•••
EDIBLES
ODDBALL

•D••B••
ADDABLE

•D•••B•
ADSORBS
ADVERBS
ODDJOBS

••DB•••
BEDBUGS
CADBURY
ODDBALL
REDBIRD
REDBOOK
REDBUDS
SUDBURY
TIDBITS

••D•B••
ADDABLE
AUDIBLE
AUDIBLY
AUDUBON
LADYBUG
SIDEBAR
SIDEBET

••D••B•
BEDAUBS
INDOUBT
MADLIBS
MIDRIBS
NODOUBT
ODDJOBS
REDOUBT

••D•••B
GODTHAB

•••DB••
BANDBOX
FEEDBAG
GOLDBUG
GOODBAR
GOODBYE
GOODBYS
HANDBAG
ROADBED
SANDBAG
SANDBAR
SANDBOX
SEEDBED
WINDBAG

•••D•B•
ABIDEBY
CORDOBA
SUBDEBS

•••D••B
FOODWEB
GOODJOB

••••DB•
BYANDBY
STANDBY
STOODBY
WOULDBE

••••D•B
OVERDUB

D•C••••
DACTYLS
DECADES
DECAGON
DECALOG
DECAMPS
DECANTS
DECAPOD
DECARLO
DECAYED
DECEITS
DECEIVE
DECIBEL
DECIDED
DECIDES
DECIMAL
DECKING
DECKLES
DECKOUT
DECLAIM
DECLARE
DECLASS
DECLINE
DECOCTS
DECODED
DECODER
DECODES
DECORUM
DECOYED
DECREED
DECREES
DECRIED
DECRIES
DECRYPT
DICIEST
DICKENS
DICKERS
DICKEYS
DICKIES
DICTATE
DICTION
DICTUMS
DOCENTS
DOCKAGE
DOCKERS
DOCKETS
DOCKING
DOCTORS
DUCHESS
DUCHIES
DUCKIER
DUCKING
DUCKPIN
DUCTILE
DUCTING

D••C•••
DANCERS
DANCING
DAYCAMP
DAYCARE
DEACONS
DEICERS
DEICING
DESCANT
DESCEND
DESCENT
DEWCLAW
DIOCESE
DISCARD
DISCERN
DISCOED
DISCORD
DISCUSS
DITCHED
DITCHES
DOGCART
DOGCHEW
DOGCHOW
DRACHMA
DRACULA
DRUCKER
DRYCELL

D•••C••
DEBACLE
DECOCTS
DEDUCED
DEDUCES
DEDUCTS
DEFACED
DEFACES
DEFACTO
DEFECTS
DEFICIT
DEJECTS
DELICTI
DELICTS
DEPECHE
DEPICTS
DETECTS
DEVICES
DIDACTS
DIRECTS
DOVECOT

D••••C•
DAVINCI
DEBAUCH
DEBOUCH
DEFENCE
DEFLECT
DEFROCK
DEFUNCT
DEHISCE
DENIECE
DERRICK
DETRACT
DIALECT
DIPTYCH
DISSECT
DIVORCE
DOGFACE
DORMICE
DRSPOCK
DRYDOCK
DURANCE

D•••••C
DELTAIC
DEMONIC
DRASTIC
DYNAMIC

•DC••••
IDCARDS

•D•C•••
EDACITY
EDUCATE
EDUCING

•D••C••
ADDUCED
ADDUCES
ADDUCTS

•D•••C•
ADJUNCT
ADVANCE
EDIFICE

•D••••C
EDAPHIC
IDENTIC
IDIOTIC
IDYLLIC

••DC•••
BADCOLD
MADCAPS
MADCHEN
OLDCHAP
REDCAPS
REDCELL
REDCENT
REDCOAT

••D•C••
ABDUCTS
ADDUCED
ADDUCES
ADDUCTS
BEDECKS
BODICES
CADUCEI
CODICES
CODICIL
DEDUCED
DEDUCES
DEDUCTS
DIDACTS
INDICES
INDICIA
INDICTS
INDUCED
INDUCER
INDUCES
INDUCTS
MEDICAL
MEDICOS
MODICUM
PADUCAH
PEDICEL
PEDICLE
RADICAL
RADICES
RADICLE
REDACTS
REDUCED
REDUCER
REDUCES
SEDUCED
SEDUCER
SEDUCES
SIDECAR

••D••C•
ALDRICH
ARDENCY
BEDROCK
CADENCE
GODUTCH
HADDOCK
INDUTCH
MUDPACK
OLDNICK
PADDOCK
PADLOCK
RIDDICK
SADSACK
TEDMACK
WEDLOCK
ZODIACS

••D•••C
ENDEMIC
MEDEVAC
MIDDLEC

•••DC••
COLDCUT
HANDCAR
WILDCAT
WOODCUT

•••D•C•
ARTDECO
BURDOCK
CANDICE
CONDUCE
CONDUCT
DRYDOCK
FOSDICK
HADDOCK
MURDOCH
NORDICS
PADDOCK
PANDECT
PREDICT
PRODUCE
PRODUCT
RIDDICK
SUNDECK
TRADUCE
VANDYCK
VERDICT
VIADUCT

•••D••C
BALDRIC
FREDRIC
MIDDLEC

••••D•C
COMEDIC
JURIDIC
MELODIC
NOMADIC
PAPADOC
SYNODIC

D•D••••
DADAISM
DADAIST
DADDIES
DEDALUS
DEDUCED
DEDUCES
DEDUCTS
DIDACTS
DIDDLED
DIDDLES
DIDDLEY
DIDEROT
DIDGOOD
DIDOVER
DODDERS
DODGERS
DODGING
DODGSON
DUDDIES
DUDEDUP
DUDGEON

D••D•••
DADDIES
DANDERS
DANDIER
DANDIES
DANDLED
DANDLES
DAWDLED
DAWDLER
DAWDLES
DEADAIR
DEADEND
DEADENS
DEADEYE
DEADPAN
DEADSEA
DEADSET
DEEDING
DENDRON
DEODARS
DEWDROP
DIADEMS
DIDDLED
DIDDLES
DIDDLEY
DIEDOFF
DIEDOUT
DIEDOWN
DIKDIKS
DISDAIN
DODDERS
DOGDAYS
DOODADS
DOODLED
DOODLER
DOODLES
DOWDIER
DOWDILY
DREDGED
DREDGER
DREDGES
DRUDGED
DRUDGES
DRYDOCK
DUDDIES
DUEDATE
DUMDUMS
DUODENA

D•••D••
DATEDLY
DAZEDLY
DECADES
DECIDED
DECIDES
DECODED
DECODER
DECODES
DELUDED
DELUDES
DENUDED
DENUDES
DERIDED
DERIDES
DINEDIN
DINEDON
DIRNDLS
DIVIDED
DIVIDER
DIVIDES
DOORDIE
DOSIDOS
DOTEDON
DREADED
DREIDEL
DRESDEN
DRIEDUP
DRIPDRY
DUDEDUP
DUKEDOM
DWINDLE

D••••D•
DAYBEDS
DEFENDS
DEGRADE
DEMANDS
DEPENDS
DEWILDE
DIOMEDE
DIOXIDE
DOODADS

D•••••D
DABBLED
DABHAND
DAGWOOD
DALLIED
DAMAGED
DANDLED
DANGLED
DAPPLED
DASTARD
DAUNTED
DAWDLED
DAZZLED
DEADEND
DEBASED
DEBATED
DEBITED
DEBONED
DEBUTED
DECAPOD
DECAYED
DECIDED
DECODED
DECOYED
DECREED
DECRIED
DEDUCED
DEEPEND
DEFACED
DEFAMED
DEFILED
DEFINED
DEFRAUD
DEFUSED
DEIFIED
DEIGNED
DELAYED
DELETED
DELTOID
DELUDED
DELUGED
DEMIGOD
DEMISED
DEMOTED
DENOTED
DENUDED
DEPONED
DEPOSED
DEPUTED
DERIDED
DERIVED
DESCEND
DESIRED
DESMOND
DEVILED
DEVISED
DEVOTED
DIAMOND
DIBBLED
DIDDLED
DIDGOOD
DIEHARD
DILATED
DILLARD
DILUTED
DIMPLED
DIPLOID
DIRTIED
DISBAND
DISCARD
DISCOED
DISCORD
DISTEND
DISUSED
DITCHED
DITTOED
DIVIDED
DIVINED
DIVVIED
DIZZIED
DOGSLED
DOGWOOD
DOLLIED
DONATED
DOODLED
DOUBLED
DOUBTED
DRAFTED
DRAGGED
DRAINED
DRATTED
DRAWLED
DREADED
DREAMED
DREDGED
DRESSED
DRIFTED
DRILLED
DRIPPED
DROOLED
DROOPED
DROPPED
DROWNED
DROWSED
DRUBBED
DRUDGED
DRUGGED
DRUMMED
DRYEYED
DULLARD
DUMMIED
DWARFED
DWELLED

•DD••••
ADDABLE
ADDEDIN
ADDEDON
ADDEDTO
ADDEDUP
ADDENDA
ADDENDS
ADDISON
ADDLING
ADDONTO
ADDRESS
ADDUCED
ADDUCES
ADDUCTS
ADDUPTO
EDDYING
ODDBALL
ODDJOBS
ODDLOTS
ODDMENT
ODDNESS

•D••D••
ADDEDIN
ADDEDON
ADDEDTO
ADDEDUP
ADJUDGE
EDGEDIN

•D•••D•
ADDENDA
ADDENDS
EDWARDS
IDCARDS

•D••••D
ADAPTED
ADDUCED
ADHERED
ADJURED
ADMIRED
ADMIXED
ADOPTED
ADORNED
ADVISED
EDIFIED
EDOUARD
IDEATED

••DD•••
BADDIES
BEDDING
BEDDOWN
BIDDERS
BIDDIES
BIDDING
BUDDHAS
BUDDIES
BUDDING
BUDDYUP
CADDIED
CADDIES
CADDOAN
CODDLED
CODDLER
CODDLES
CUDDLED
CUDDLES
DADDIES
DIDDLED
DIDDLES
DIDDLEY
DODDERS
DUDDIES
FADDISH
FADDISM
FADDIST
FIDDLED
FIDDLER
FIDDLES
FODDERS
FUDDLED
FUDDLES
GADDING
GIDDIER
GIDDILY
GIDDYAP
GIDDYUP
GODDARD
GODDESS
HADDOCK
HEDDLES
HUDDLED
HUDDLES
JUDDERS
KADDISH
KIDDERS
KIDDIES
KIDDING
LADDERS
LADDIES
MADDENS
MADDERS
MADDEST
MADDING
MEDDLED
MEDDLER
MEDDLES
MIDDAYS
MIDDENS
MIDDIES
MIDDLEC
MIDDLES
MUDDERS
MUDDIED
MUDDIER
MUDDIES
MUDDLED
MUDDLER
MUDDLES
NODDERS
NODDING
OLDDAYS
PADDERS
PADDIES
PADDING
PADDLED
PADDLER
PADDLES
PADDOCK
PEDDLED
PEDDLER
PEDDLES
PUDDING
PUDDLED
PUDDLES
RADDLED
RADDLES
REDDEER
REDDENS
REDDEST
REDDING
REDDISH
REDDOGS
RIDDICK
RIDDING
RIDDLED
RIDDLER
RIDDLES
RUDDERS
RUDDIER
SADDENS
SADDEST
SADDLED
SADDLER
SADDLES
SODDING
TEDDERS
TEDDIES
TEDDING
TODDIES
TODDLED

TODDLER
TODDLES
WADDING
WADDLED
WADDLER
WADDLES
WEDDING
YIDDISH

••D•D••
ADDEDIN
ADDEDON
ADDEDTO
ADDEDUP
DUDEDUP
FADEDIN
GADSDEN
IODIDES
JADEDLY
LADYDAY

••D••D•
ADDENDA
ADDENDS
BEDSIDE
OGDOADS
PODRIDA
REDBUDS

••D•••D
ADDUCED
ANDROID
AUDITED
BADCOLD
BEDEWED
CADDIED
CODDLED
CUDDLED
DEDUCED
DIDDLED
DIDGOOD
ENDOWED
ENDURED
FIDDLED
FUDDLED
GODDARD
GODSEND
HUDDLED
INDEXED
INDITED
INDUCED
IODIZED
MEDALED
MEDDLED
MIDLAND
MODELED
MUDDIED
MUDDLED
OLDGOLD
OLDHAND
OLDMAID
ORDERED
PADDLED
PEDALED
PEDDLED
PUDDLED
RADDLED
RADIOED
REDATED
REDBIRD
REDFORD
REDHEAD
REDOUND
REDUCED
REDWOOD
RIDDLED
RUDYARD
SADDLED
SEDUCED
TODDLED
UNDATED
UPDATED
WADDLED
WIDENED
WIDOWED
YODELED

•••DD••
ALADDIN
BIRDDOG
BLADDER
CHEDDAR
FREDDIE
GLADDEN
GLADDER
GRIDDED
GRIDDER
GRIDDLE
PLODDED
PLODDER
PRODDED
PRODDER
SCUDDED
SHODDEN
SHUDDER
SKIDDED
SKIDDER
SKIDDOO
SLEDDED
SLEDDER
SLEDDOG
STUDDED
SWADDLE
THUDDED
TRODDEN
TWADDLE
TWIDDLE

•••D•D•
ALIDADE
AOUDADS
CANDIDA
CANDIDE
CANDIDS
DOODADS

•••D••D
BANDAID
BANDIED
BIRDIED
BRIDGED
BRIDLED
BUNDLED
CADDIED
CANDIED
CODDLED
CRADLED
CUDDLED
CURDLED
DANDLED
DAWDLED
DEADEND
DIDDLED
DOODLED
DREDGED
DRUDGED
FIDDLED
FLEDGED
FONDLED
FUDDLED
GIRDLED
GODDARD
GRIDDED
GRUDGED
HANDLED
HUDDLED
HUNDRED
HURDLED
KINDLED
KINDRED
LINDIED
MEDDLED
MILDRED
MISDEED
MORDRED
MUDDIED
MUDDLED
NEEDLED
PADDLED
PEDDLED
PLEDGED
PLODDED
PRODDED
PUDDLED
RADDLED
READIED
RIDDLED
ROADBED
SADDLED
SCUDDED
SEEDBED
SEEDPOD
SKIDDED
SLEDDED
SMUDGED
STUDDED
STUDIED
SUBDUED
THUDDED
TIEDYED
TOADIED
TODDLED
TRUDGED
WADDLED
WOODARD

••••D•D
ABRADED
ACCEDED
ALLUDED
AMENDED
AVOIDED
AWARDED
BAGHDAD
BEARDED
BETIDED
BLENDED
BLINDED
BLOODED
BOARDED
BOUNDED
BRAIDED
BRANDED
BREADED
BROODED
CLOUDED
CRAWDAD
CROWDED
DECIDED
DECODED
DELUDED
DENUDED
DERIDED
DIVIDED
DREADED
EMENDED
ENCODED
FIELDED
FLOODED
FOUNDED
GRIDDED
GUARDED
HOARDED
HOUNDED
IMPEDED
INVADED
KATYDID
KNEADED
MOULDED
MOUNDED
OVERDID
PARADED
PLEADED
PLODDED
POMADED
POUNDED
PRODDED
RECEDED
RECODED
RESIDED
ROUNDED
SCALDED
SCENDED
SCOLDED
SCUDDED
SECEDED
SKIDDED
SLEDDED
SOLEDAD
SOUNDED
SPEEDED
STUDDED
THUDDED
TREADED
TRENDED
UNAIDED
UNENDED
UPENDED
WIELDED
WOUNDED
YIELDED

DE•••••
DEACONS
DEADAIR
DEADEND
DEADENS
DEADEYE
DEADPAN
DEADSEA
DEADSET
DEAFENS
DEAFEST
DEALERS
DEALING
DEALOUT
DEALSIN
DEALTIN
DEAREST
DEARSIR
DEARTHS
DEBACLE
DEBAKEY
DEBARGE
DEBARKS
DEBASED
DEBASES
DEBATED
DEBATER
DEBATES
DEBAUCH
DEBEERS
DEBITED
DEBONED
DEBONES
DEBORAH
DEBOUCH
DEBRIEF
DEBTORS
DEBUNKS
DEBUSSY
DEBUTED
DECADES
DECAGON
DECALOG
DECAMPS
DECANTS
DECAPOD
DECARLO
DECAYED
DECEITS
DECEIVE
DECIBEL
DECIDED
DECIDES
DECIMAL
DECKING
DECKLES
DECKOUT
DECLAIM
DECLARE
DECLASS
DECLINE
DECOCTS
DECODED
DECODER
DECODES
DECORUM
DECOYED
DECREED
DECREES
DECRIED
DECRIES
DECRYPT
DEDALUS
DEDUCED
DEDUCES
DEDUCTS
DEEDING
DEEJAYS
DEEMING
DEEPEND
DEEPENS
DEEPEST
DEEPFAT
DEEPFRY
DEEPSEA
DEEPSET
DEEPSIX
DEERFLY
DEFACED
DEFACES
DEFACTO
DEFAMED
DEFAMES
DEFARGE
DEFAULT
DEFEATS
DEFECTS
DEFENCE
DEFENDS
DEFENSE
DEFIANT
DEFICIT
DEFILED
DEFILER
DEFILES
DEFINED
DEFINES
DEFLATE
DEFLECT
DEFORMS
DEFRAUD
DEFRAYS
DEFROCK
DEFROST
DEFTEST
DEFUNCT
DEFUSED
DEFUSES
DEFYING
DEGAUSS
DEGRADE
DEGREES
DEHISCE
DEHORNS
DEICERS
DEICING
DEIFIED
DEIFIES
DEIGNED
DEITIES
DEJECTS
DEKLERK
DEKOVEN
DELANEY
DELAYED
DELAYER
DELBERT
DELEING
DELETED
DELETES
DELIBES
DELICTI
DELICTS
DELIGHT
DELILAH
DELIMIT
DELIRIA
DELISTS
DELIVER
DELTAIC
DELTOID
DELUDED
DELUDES
DELUGED
DELUGES
DELUISE
DELVERS
DELVING
DEMANDS
DEMEANS
DEMERIT
DEMEROL
DEMESNE
DEMETER
DEMIGOD
DEMILLE
DEMISED
DEMISES
DEMONIC
DEMOTED
DEMOTES
DEMPSEY
DEMURER
DENDRON
DENEUVE
DENIALS
DENIECE
DENIERS
DENIZEN
DENMARK
DENNEHY
DENOTED
DENOTES
DENSELY
DENSEST
DENSITY
DENTATE
DENTINE
DENTING
DENTIST
DENTURE
DENUDED
DENUDES
DENYING
DEODARS
DEPALMA
DEPARTS
DEPECHE
DEPENDS
DEPICTS
DEPLANE
DEPLETE
DEPLORE
DEPLOYS
DEPONED
DEPONES
DEPORTS
DEPOSAL
DEPOSED
DEPOSER
DEPOSES
DEPOSIT
DEPRAVE
DEPRESS
DEPRIVE
DEPUTED
DEPUTES
DERAILS
DERBIES
DERIDED
DERIDES
DERIVED
DERIVES
DERNIER
DERRICK
DERRING
DERVISH
DESALTS
DESCANT
DESCEND
DESCENT
DESERTS
DESERVE
DESIGNS
DESIRED
DESIREE
DESIRES
DESISTS
DESKSET
DESKTOP
DESMOND
DESOTOS
DESPAIR
DESPISE
DESPITE
DESPOIL
DESPOTS
DESSERT
DESTINE
DESTINY
DESTROY
DETAILS
DETAINS
DETECTS
DETENTE
DETESTS
DETOURS
DETRACT
DETRAIN
DETROIT
DEUTERO
DEVALUE
DEVEINS
DEVELOP
DEVIANT
DEVIATE
DEVICES
DEVILED
DEVILLE
DEVILRY
DEVIOUS
DEVISED
DEVISES
DEVOLVE
DEVOTED
DEVOTEE
DEVOTES
DEVOURS
DEVRIES
DEWCLAW
DEWDROP
DEWILDE
DEWLAPS
DEWLINE
DEXTRIN

D•E••••
DEEDING
DEEJAYS
DEEMING
DEEPEND
DEEPENS
DEEPEST
DEEPFAT
DEEPFRY
DEEPSEA
DEEPSET
DEEPSIX
DEERFLY
DIEDOFF
DIEDOUT
DIEDOWN
DIEHARD
DIESELS
DIESOFF
DIESOUT
DIETARY
DIETERS
DIETING
DOESKIN
DOEUVRE
DREADED
DREAMED
DREAMER
DREAMON
DREAMUP
DREDGED
DREDGER
DREDGES
DREIDEL
DREISER
DRESDEN
DRESSED
DRESSER
DRESSES
DRESSUP
DREWOUT
DREYFUS
DUEDATE
DUELERS
DUELING
DUELIST
DUENNAS
DWEEZIL
DWELLED
DWELLER

D••E•••
DANELAW
DARESAY
DARESTO
DATEDLY
DAZEDLY
DEBEERS
DECEITS
DECEIVE
DEFEATS
DEFECTS
DEFENCE
DEFENDS
DEFENSE
DEJECTS
DELEING
DELETED
DELETES
DEMEANS
DEMERIT
DEMEROL
DEMESNE
DEMETER
DENEUVE
DEPECHE
DEPENDS
DESERTS
DESERVE
DETECTS
DETENTE
DETESTS
DEVEINS
DEVELOP
DIDEROT
DIGESTS
DILEMMA
DINEDIN
DINEDON
DINESEN
DINESIN
DINESON
DINETTE
DIRECTS
DISEASE
DIVERGE
DIVERSE
DIVERTS
DIVESIN
DIVESTS
DOCENTS
DOGEARS
DOLEFUL
DOLEOUT
DONEFOR
DONEGAL
DOPEOUT
DOTEDON
DOTESON
DOVEBAR
DOVECOT
DOYENNE
DOZENTH
DOZEOFF
DRIEDUP
DRIESUP
DRSEUSS
DRYEYED
DUDEDUP
DUKEDOM
DUTEOUS
DWEEZIL

D•••E••
DAFTEST
DAGGERS
DAMPENS
DAMPERS
DAMPEST
DAMSELS
DANCERS
DANDERS
DANGERS
DANIELS
DANKEST
DANSEUR
DARKENS
DARKEST
DARLEEN
DARLENE
DARNERS
DARRELL
DARTERS
DASHERS
DAUBERS
DAYBEDS
DEADEND
DEADENS
DEADEYE
DEAFENS
DEAFEST
DEALERS
DEAREST
DEBEERS
DECREED
DECREES
DEEPEND
DEEPENS
DEEPEST
DEFLECT
DEFTEST
DEGREES
DEICERS
DEKLERK
DELBERT
DELVERS
DENIECE
DENIERS
DENNEHY
DENSELY
DENSEST
DEPLETE
DEPRESS
DESCEND
DESCENT
DESSERT
DEUTERO
DIADEMS
DIALECT
DIALERS
DIAPERS
DICIEST
DICKENS
DICKERS
DICKEYS
DIESELS
DIETERS
DIFFERS
DIGGERS
DIGRESS
DIMMERS
DIMMEST
DIMNESS
DINNERS
DIOCESE
DIOMEDE
DIPPERS
DISCERN
DISPELS
DISSECT
DISSENT
DISTEND
DITHERS
DITHERY
DOCKERS
DOCKETS
DODDERS
DODGERS
DOGLEGS
DOLMENS
DONKEYS
DOPIEST
DORMERS
DORSETT
DOSSERS
DOUREST
DOWNERS
DOWSERS
DRAPERS
DRAPERY
DRAWERS
DRIVEAT
DRIVEIN
DRIVELS
DRIVERS
DRIVEUP
DRONERS
DROVERS
DRYCELL
DRYNESS
DRYWELL
DUBBERS
DUBIETY
DUCHESS
DUDGEON
DUELERS
DUFFELS
DUFFERS
DULLEST
DUMBEST
DUNGEON
DUNKERS
DUODENA
DURRELL
DUSTERS

D••••E•
DABBLED
DABBLER
DABBLES
DADDIES
DAFFIER
DAHOMEY
DAILIES
DAIMLER
DAIRIES
DAISIES
DALLIED
DALLIER
DALLIES
DALTREY
DAMAGED
DAMAGES
DANDIER
DANDIES
DANDLED
DANDLES
DANGLED
DANGLER
DANGLES
DAPPLED
DAPPLES
DARLEEN
DATASET
DAUMIER
DAUNTED
DAWDLED
DAWDLER
DAWDLES
DAZZLED
DAZZLER
DAZZLES
DEADSEA
DEADSET
DEBAKEY
DEBASED
DEBASES
DEBATED
DEBATER
DEBATES
DEBITED
DEBONED
DEBONES
DEBRIEF
DEBUTED
DECADES
DECAYED
DECIBEL
DECIDED
DECIDES
DECKLES
DECODED
DECODER
DECODES
DECOYED
DECREED
DECREES
DECRIED
DECRIES
DEDUCED
DEDUCES
DEEPSEA
DEEPSET
DEFACED
DEFACES
DEFAMED
DEFAMES
DEFILED
DEFILER
DEFILES
DEFINED
DEFINES
DEFUSED
DEFUSES
DEGREES
DEIFIED
DEIFIES
DEIGNED
DEITIES
DEKOVEN
DELANEY
DELAYED
DELAYER
DELETED
DELETES
DELIBES
DELIVER
DELUDED
DELUDES
DELUGED
DELUGES
DEMETER
DEMISED
DEMISES
DEMOTED
DEMOTES
DEMPSEY
DEMURER
DENIZEN
DENOTED
DENOTES
DENUDED
DENUDES
DEPONED
DEPONES
DEPOSED
DEPOSER
DEPOSES
DEPUTED
DEPUTES
DERBIES
DERIDED
DERIDES
DERIVED
DERIVES
DERNIER
DESIRED
DESIREE
DESIRES
DESKSET
DEVICES
DEVILED
DEVISED
DEVISES
DEVOTED
DEVOTEE
DEVOTES
DEVRIES
DIARIES
DIBBLED
DIBBLES
DICKIES
DIDDLED
DIDDLES
DIDDLEY
DIDOVER
DILATED
DILATES
DILLIES
DILUTED
DILUTER
DILUTES

DIMPLED
DIMPLES
DINESEN
DINGIER
DINGLES
DINGOES
DINKIER
DINKIES
DIOPTER
DIPOLES
DIRTIED
DIRTIER
DIRTIES
DISCOED
DISOBEY
DISUSED
DITCHED
DITCHES
DITTIES
DITTOED
DIVIDED
DIVIDER
DIVIDES
DIVINED
DIVINER
DIVINES
DIVVIED
DIVVIES
DIZZIED
DIZZIER
DIZZIES
DOGCHEW
DOGGIES
DOGSLED
DOILIES
DOLLIED
DOLLIES
DOLORES
DONATED
DONATES
DOODLED
DOODLER
DOODLES
DOORMEN
DOOZIES
DOPPLER
DOSAGES
DOSSIER
DOTTIER
DOTTLES
DOUBLED
DOUBLES
DOUBLET
DOUBLEU
DOUBTED
DOUBTER
DOWAGER
DOWDIER
DOWNIER
DOWRIES
DRABBER
DRAFTED
DRAFTEE
DRAGGED
DRAGNET
DRAINED
DRAINER
DRATTED
DRAWLED
DREADED
DREAMED
DREAMER
DREDGED
DREDGER
DREDGES
DREIDEL
DREISER
DRESDEN
DRESSED
DRESSER
DRESSES
DRIBLET
DRIFTED
DRIFTER
DRILLED
DRILLER
DRINKER
DRIPPED
DROLLER
DROOLED
DROOLER
DROOPED
DROPLET
DROPPED
DROPPER
DROWNED
DROWSED
DROWSES
DRUBBED
DRUCKER
DRUDGED
DRUDGES
DRUGGED
DRUMMED
DRUMMER
DRYEYED
DUCHIES
DUCKIER
DUDDIES
DUMMIED
DUMMIES
DUMPIER
DUSKIER
DUSTIER
DWARFED
DWARVES
DWELLED
DWELLER

D•••••E

DARKAGE
DARLENE
DAYCARE
DAYTIME
DEADEYE
DEBACLE
DEBARGE
DECEIVE
DECLARE
DECLINE
DEFARGE
DEFENCE
DEFENSE
DEFLATE
DEGRADE
DEHISCE
DELUISE
DEMESNE
DEMILLE
DENEUVE
DENIECE
DENTATE
DENTINE
DENTURE
DEPECHE
DEPLANE
DEPLETE
DEPLORE
DEPRAVE
DEPRIVE
DESERVE
DESIREE
DESPISE
DESPITE
DESTINE
DETENTE
DEVALUE
DEVIATE
DEVILLE
DEVOLVE
DEVOTEE
DEWILDE
DEWLINE
DHURRIE
DICTATE
DIFFUSE
DINETTE
DIOCESE
DIOMEDE
DIOXIDE
DISABLE
DISEASE
DISLIKE
DISPOSE
DISPUTE
DISROBE
DIVERGE
DIVERSE
DIVORCE
DIVULGE
DOCKAGE
DOEUVRE
DOGFACE
DOGGONE
DONAHUE
DONJOSE
DOORDIE
DORMICE
DOYENNE
DRAFTEE
DRAYAGE
DRIBBLE
DRIZZLE
DRYHOLE
DUBUQUE
DUCTILE
DUEDATE
DURABLE
DURANCE
DURANTE
DWINDLE

•DE••••

ADELINE
ADENINE
ADEPTLY
IDEALLY
IDEATED
IDEATES
IDENTIC

•D•E•••

ADDEDIN
ADDEDON
ADDEDTO
ADDEDUP
ADDENDA
ADDENDS
ADHERED
ADHERES
ADRENAL
ADVENTS
ADVERBS
ADVERSE
ADVERTS
EDGEDIN
EDGEOUT
EDGESIN

•D••E••

ADDRESS
ADORERS
EDGIEST
ODDMENT
ODDNESS

•D•••E•

ADAPTED
ADAPTER
ADDUCED
ADDUCES
ADHERED
ADHERES
ADJURED
ADJURES
ADMIRED
ADMIRER
ADMIRES
ADMIXED
ADMIXES
ADOPTED
ADOPTEE
ADOPTER
ADORNED
ADVISED
ADVISER
ADVISES
EDASNER
EDIBLES
EDIFIED
EDIFIES
IDEATED
IDEATES
ODYSSEY
PDJAMES

•D••••E

ADAMITE
ADDABLE
ADELINE
ADENINE
ADIPOSE
ADJUDGE
ADOLPHE
ADOPTEE
ADULATE
ADVANCE
ADVERSE
EDIFICE
EDUCATE
IDOLIZE

••DE•••

ADDEDIN
ADDEDON
ADDEDTO
ADDEDUP
ADDENDA
ADDENDS
ALDENTE
ANDEANS
ARDENCY
BADEGGS
BEDECKS
BEDELIA
BEDEVIL
BEDEWED
BODEGAS
BODEREK
CADENCE
CADENZA
CADETTE
CODEINE
DIDEROT
DUDEDUP
ELDERLY
ENDEARS
ENDEMIC
FADEDIN
FADEINS
FADEOUT
FADESIN
FEDERAL
FIDELIO
GIDEONS
HIDEOUS
HIDEOUT
INDENTS
INDEPTH
INDEXED
INDEXES
JADEDLY
JADEITE
MADEFOR
MADEHAY
MADEIRA
MADEOFF
MADEOUT
MADEWAY
MEDEVAC
MIDEAST
MODELAS
MODELED
MODELER
MODELTS
MODERNS
MODESTO
MODESTY
MUDEELS
ORDEALS
ORDERED
ORDERER
ORDERLY
REDEALS
REDEALT
REDEEMS
REDEYES
RIDEOFF
RIDEOUT
RODENTS
RODEOFF
RODEOUT
SIDEARM
SIDEBAR
SIDEBET
SIDECAR
SIDEMAN
SIDEMEN
STDENIS
UNDERGO
WADESIN
WIDENED
YODELED
YODELER

••D•E••

ADDRESS
ANDREAS
ANDRESS
ANDREWS
BADGERS
BADNESS
BEDREST
BIDDERS
BUDGETS
CADGERS
CODGERS
CUDGELS
DODDERS
DODGERS
DUDGEON
ENDLESS
FIDGETS
FIDGETY
FODDERS
GADGETS
GADGETY
GODDESS
GODSEND
HEDGERS
INDWELL
JUDDERS
KIDDERS
KIDNEYS
LADDERS
LADLERS
LEDGERS
LIDLESS
LODGERS
MADDENS
MADDERS
MADDEST
MADNESS
MEDLEYS
MIDDENS
MIDGETS
MIDTERM
MIDWEEK
MIDWEST
MIDYEAR
MUDDERS
MUDEELS
MUDHENS
NODDERS
NUDGERS
ODDMENT
ODDNESS
OLDNESS
OLDNEWS
OLDWEST
PADDERS
PIDGEON
REDCELL
REDCENT
REDDEER
REDDENS
REDDEST
REDEEMS
REDHEAD
REDHEAT
REDMEAT
REDNESS
REDRESS
RODGERS
RUDDERS
SADDENS
SADDEST
SADNESS
TEDDERS
TIDIEST
UNDRESS
WIDGEON
WIDGETS

••D••E•

ABDOMEN
ADDUCED
ADDUCES
AEDILES
ANDOVER
AUDITED
BADDIES
BEDEWED
BEDIZEN
BIDDIES
BODEREK
BODICES
BUDDIES
BUDGIES
CADDIED
CADDIES
CADUCEI
CODDLED
CODDLER
CODDLES
CODICES
CUDDLED
CUDDLES
DADDIES
DEDUCED
DEDUCES
DIDDLED
DIDDLES
DIDDLEY
DIDOVER
DUDDIES
ECDYSES
ENDIVES
ENDOWED
ENDURED
ENDURES
ENDUSER
FIDDLED
FIDDLER
FIDDLES
FUDDLED
FUDDLES
GADSDEN
GIDDIER
GODFREY
HEDDLES
HUDDLED
HUDDLES
INDEXED
INDEXES
INDICES
INDITED
INDITES
INDUCED
INDUCER
INDUCES
IODATES
IODIDES
IODIZED
IODIZES
KIDDIES
LADDIES
MADAMEX
MADCHEN
MEDALED
MEDDLED
MEDDLER
MEDDLES
MIDDIES
MIDDLEC
MIDDLES
MIDWEEK
MODELED
MODELER
MODULES
MUDDIED
MUDDIER
MUDDIES
MUDDLED
MUDDLER
MUDDLES
MUDPIES
NODULES
OLDSTER
ORDERED
ORDERER
PADDIES
PADDLED
PADDLER
PADDLES
PEDALED
PEDDLED
PEDDLER
PEDDLES
PEDICEL
PODGIER
PUDDLED
PUDDLES
PUDGIER
RADAMES
RADDLED
RADDLES
RADICES
RADIOED
REDATED
REDATES
REDDEER
REDEYES
REDUCED
REDUCER
REDUCES
RIDDLED
RIDDLER
RIDDLES
RUDDIER
SADDLED
SADDLER
SADDLES
SEDATER
SEDUCED
SEDUCER
SEDUCES
SIDEBET
SIDEMEN
SUDSIER
TEDDIES
TODDIES
TODDLED
TODDLER
TODDLES
UNDATED
UPDATED
UPDATES
WADDLED
WADDLER
WADDLES
WEDGIES
WIDENED
WIDOWED
WIDOWER
YODELED
YODELER

••D•••E

ADDABLE
ALDENTE
ANDANTE
ARDMORE
AUDIBLE
BEDSIDE
BEDTIME
CADENCE
CADETTE
CODEINE
ENDGAME
ENDORSE
ENDWISE
ENDZONE
GODLIKE
HYDRATE
INDULGE
JADEITE
MEDIATE
MEDUSAE
MIDLIFE
MIDLINE
MIDRISE
MIDSIZE
MIDWIFE
MODISTE
OLDLINE
OLDTIME
PADRONE
PEDICLE
RADIATE
RADICLE
REDLINE
REDPINE
REDROSE
REDTAPE
REDWINE
TADPOLE
UNDRAPE

•••DE••

ABIDEBY
ACADEME
ACADEMY
AMADEUS
ANADEMS
ARIDEST
ARTDECO
BALDEST
BENDERS
BIDDERS
BIGDEAL
BINDERS
BINDERY
BIRDERS
BOLDEST
BORDERS
BURDENS
CALDERA
CANDELA
CARDERS
CINDERS
COLDEST
CONDEMN
CORDELL
CORDERO
CRUDELY
CRUDEST
DANDERS
DEADEND
DEADENS
DEADEYE
DIADEMS
DODDERS
DUODENA
EVADERS
EVIDENT
FEEDERS
FENDERS
FINDERS
FODDERS
FOLDERS
FONDEST
GANDERS
GARDENS
GAUDENS
GENDERS
GEODESY
GILDERS
GIRDERS
GLADEYE
GLIDERS
GODDESS
GOODEGG
GRADERS
HARDENS
HARDEST
HEADERS
HERDERS
HINDERS
HOLDERS
HOYDENS
JUDDERS
KIDDERS
KINDEST
LADDERS
LANDERS
LARDERS
LEADERS
LENDERS
LEWDEST
LINDENS
LOADERS
LOUDEST
MADDENS
MADDERS
MADDEST
MAIDENS
MANDELA
MENDERS
MIDDENS
MILDEST
MILDEWS
MILDEWY
MINDERS
MISDEAL
MISDEED
MOLDERS
MORDENT
MUDDERS
MURDERS
NEWDEAL
NODDERS
PADDERS
PANDECT
PANDERS
PENDENT
POLDERS
PONDERS
POWDERS
POWDERY
PRUDENT
PRUDERY
RAIDERS
RAWDEAL
READERS
REDDEER
REDDENS
REDDEST
RENDERS
ROEDEER
RONDEAU
RONDELS
RUDDERS
RUNDEEP
SADDENS
SADDEST
SANDERS
SEEDERS
SEIDELS
SENDERS
SLIDEIN
SLIDERS
SNIDELY
SNIDEST
SOLDERS
SPADERS
SPIDERS
SPIDERY
STUDENT
SUBDEBS
SUNDECK
SUNDERS
SUNDEWS
TANDEMS
TEDDERS
TENDERS
THEDEEP
TINDERS
TRADEIN
TRADEON
TRADERS
TRADEUP
TRIDENT
TRUDEAU
WANDERS
WARDENS
WARDERS
WEEDERS
WELDERS
WENDELL
WENDERS
WILDEST
WINDERS
WONDERS
YESDEAR
ZANDERS

•••D•E•

BADDIES
BANDIED
BANDIES
BAWDIER
BEADIER
BEADLES
BIDDIES
BIRDIED
BIRDIES
BIRDMEN
BLADDER
BONDMEN
BOODLES
BOWDLER
BRADLEE
BRADLEY
BRIDGED
BRIDGES
BRIDGET
BRIDLED
BRIDLES
BUDDIES
BUNDLED
BUNDLES
CADDIED
CADDIES
CANDIED
CANDIES
CANDLES
CODDLED
CODDLER
CODDLES
CRADLED
CRADLES
CUDDLED
CUDDLES
CURDLED
CURDLES
DADDIES
DANDIER
DANDIES
DANDLED
DANDLES
DAWDLED
DAWDLER
DAWDLES
DEADSEA
DEADSET
DIDDLED
DIDDLES
DIDDLEY
DOODLED
DOODLER
DOODLES
DOWDIER
DREDGED
DREDGER
DREDGES
DRUDGED
DRUDGES
DUDDIES
FIDDLED
FIDDLER
FIDDLES
FIEDLER
FLEDGED
FLEDGES
FONDLED
FONDLES
FONDUES
FOODWEB
FRIDGES
FUDDLED
FUDDLES
GARDNER
GAUDIER
GIDDIER
GIRDLED
GIRDLES
GLADDEN
GLADDER
GOODIES
GOODMEN
GRIDDED
GRIDDER
GRUDGED
GRUDGES
HANDIER
HANDLED
HANDLER
HANDLES
HANDSET
HARDIER
HARDSET
HEADIER
HEADMEN
HEADSET
HEDDLES
HUDDLED
HUDDLES
HUNDRED
HURDLED
HURDLER
HURDLES
ICEDTEA
KIDDIES
KINDLED
KINDLES
KINDRED
KLUDGES
LADDIES
LARDNER
LINDIED
LINDIES
LINDSEY
MANDREL
MEDDLED
MEDDLER
MEDDLES
MIDDIES
MIDDLEC
MIDDLES
MILDRED
MINDSET
MISDEED
MISDOES
MOLDIER
MOODIER
MORDRED
MUDDIED
MUDDIER
MUDDIES
MUDDLED
MUDDLER
MUDDLES
NEEDIER
NEEDLED
NEEDLES
NOODLES
ONADIET
OUTDOES
OUTDREW
PADDIES
PADDLED
PADDLER
PADDLES
PARDNER
PEDDLED
PEDDLER
PEDDLES
PERDIEM
PLEDGED
PLEDGEE
PLEDGER
PLEDGES
PLODDED
PLODDER
POODLES
PRODDED
PRODDER
PUDDLED

PUDDLES
RADDLED
RADDLES
RANDIER
READIED
READIER
READIES
REDDEER
REEDIER
RIDDLED
RIDDLER
RIDDLES
ROADBED
ROADIES
ROEDEER
ROWDIER
ROWDIES
RUDDIER
RUNDEEP
SADDLED
SADDLER
SADDLES
SANDIER
SANDMEN
SCUDDED
SEEDBED
SEEDIER
SHADIER
SHODDEN
SHUDDER
SKIDDED
SKIDDER
SLEDDED
SLEDDER
SLEDGES
SLUDGES
SMIDGEN
SMUDGED
SMUDGES
SOLDIER
STUDDED
STUDIED
STUDIES
SUBDUED
SUBDUER
SUBDUES
SUNDAES
TARDIER
TEDDIES
THEDEEP
THUDDED
TIEDYED
TIEDYES
TOADIED
TOADIES
TODDIES
TODDLED
TODDLER
TODDLES
TRODDEN
TRUDGED
TRUDGER
TRUDGES
WADDLED
WADDLER
WADDLES
WEEDIER
WINDIER
WOODIER
WOODIES
WORDIER
YARDMEN

•••D••E

ACADEME
AIRDATE
ALIDADE
ANODIZE
ANODYNE
BANDAGE
BELDAME
BOBDOLE
BONDAGE
BRADLEE
CANDICE
CANDIDE
CONDOLE
CONDONE
CONDUCE
CORDAGE
CORDATE
CORDITE
DEADEYE
DUEDATE
ERUDITE
FREDDIE
GLADEYE
GOODBYE
GOODJOE
GOODONE
GRIDDLE
INADAZE
JIMDINE
KILDARE
MANDATE
MISDATE
MISDONE
MONDALE
MUNDANE
ONADARE
ONADATE
OUTDONE
OXIDASE
OXIDIZE
PLEDGEE
PREDATE
PRODUCE
PRUDHOE
SARDINE
SKYDIVE
SWADDLE
TRADUCE
TWADDLE
TWIDDLE
VANDINE
VANDYKE
VERDURE
WILDONE
WORDONE
YARDAGE

••••DE•

ABRADED
ABRADES
ACCEDED
ACCEDER
ACCEDES
ALLUDED
ALLUDES
ALMADEN
AMENDED
APSIDES
ARCADES
ASUNDER
AUBADES
AVOIDED
AWARDED
AWARDEE
AWARDER
BEARDED
BESIDES
BETIDED
BETIDES
BLADDER
BLANDER
BLENDED
BLENDER
BLINDED
BLINDER
BLONDER
BLONDES
BLOODED
BLUNDER
BOARDED
BOARDER
BOLIDES
BOULDER
BOUNDED
BOUNDER
BRAIDED
BRAIDER
BRANDED
BRANDER
BREADED
BREEDER
BROADEN
BROADER
BROODED
BROODER
BUILDER
CHOWDER
CITADEL
CLOUDED
CLOWDER
CROWDED
DECADES
DECIDED
DECIDES
DECODED
DECODER
DECODES
DELUDED
DELUDES
DENUDED
DENUDES
DERIDED
DERIDES
DIVIDED
DIVIDER
DIVIDES
DREADED
DREIDEL
DRESDEN
EMENDED
EMENDER
ENCODED
ENCODER
ENCODES
EVANDER
FACADES
FIELDED
FIELDER
FLOODED
FOUNDED
FOUNDER
GADSDEN
GLADDEN
GLADDER
GOUNDER
GOURDES
GRANDEE
GRANDER
GRENDEL
GRIDDED
GRIDDER
GRINDER
GUARDED
GUILDER
HOARDED
HOARDER
HOUNDED
IMPEDED
IMPEDES
INCUDES
INFIDEL
INSIDER
INSIDES
INVADED
INVADER
INVADES
IODIDES
JOINDER
KNEADED
KNEADER
LAUNDER
LEANDER
LOURDES
MAUNDER
MEANDER
MOULDED
MOULDER
MOUNDED
NAIADES
ONORDER
PARADED
PARADES
PLEADED
PLEADER
PLODDED
PLODDER
PLUNDER
POMADED
POMADES
POUNDED
POUNDER
PRODDED
PRODDER
PROUDER
PYXIDES
RAPIDER
RECEDED
RECEDES
RECODED
RECODES
REMODEL
REORDER
RESIDED
RESIDES
ROLODEX
ROUNDED
ROUNDER
RUBYDEE
SCALDED
SCENDED
SCOLDED
SCOLDER
SCUDDED
SECEDED
SECEDER
SECEDES
SHODDEN
SHUDDER
SKIDDED
SKIDDER
SLANDER
SLEDDED
SLEDDER
SLENDER
SMOLDER
SOLIDER
SOUNDED
SOUNDER
SPANDEX
SPEEDED
SPEEDER
SPENDER
SPONDEE
STAIDER
STANDEE
STRIDER
STRIDES
STRUDEL
STUDDED
THUDDED
THUNDER
TIMIDER
TIRADES
TIREDER
TOORDER
TREADED
TREADER
TRENDED
TRIODES
TRODDEN
UNAIDED
UNENDED
UNLADES
UPENDED
VIVIDER
WEIRDER
WHAUDEN
WIELDED
WOUNDED
YIELDED

••••D•E

ABRIDGE
ADJUDGE
ARIADNE
ARLEDGE
AWARDEE
BLONDIE
BRINDLE
CICADAE
COMEDUE
DOORDIE
DWINDLE
FREDDIE
GRANDEE
GRIDDLE
HAIRDYE
JANEDOE
JOHNDOE
OVERDUE
PASTDUE
RESIDUE
RUBYDEE
RUSHDIE
SINEDIE
SPINDLE
SPONDEE
STANDEE
SWADDLE
SWINDLE
TREADLE
TRUNDLE
TWADDLE
TWIDDLE
WHEEDLE
WOULDBE

•••••DE

ALAMODE
ALIDADE
ALLENDE
ASTRIDE
BALLADE
BARCODE
BEDSIDE
BRIGADE
BROCADE
BROMIDE
CANDIDE
CARBIDE
CASCADE
CATHODE
CHARADE
COCKADE
COLLIDE
COLLUDE
COMMODE
COMRADE
CONCEDE
CONFIDE
CORRODE
COWHIDE
CRUSADE
DEGRADE
DEWILDE
DIOMEDE
DIOXIDE
EBBTIDE
ENGARDE
EPISODE
EXCLUDE
EXPLODE
EXTRUDE
FORBADE
GIRONDE
GRENADE
HAYRIDE
HEYJUDE
IMPLODE
INCLUDE
INTRUDE
JOYRIDE
LEETIDE
LIMEADE
LOWTIDE
MANMADE
NITRIDE
NUCLIDE
OBTRUDE
OCCLUDE
OFFSIDE
OUTSIDE
PEPTIDE
PERVADE
PRECEDE
PRELUDE
PRESIDE
PROVIDE
RAWHIDE
REGRADE
RETRADE
RIPTIDE
ROULADE
SEASIDE
SECLUDE
SUBSIDE
SULFIDE
TOPSIDE
TVGUIDE
UPGRADE
WAYSIDE
YAOUNDE
ZIPCODE

D•F••••

DAFFIER
DAFFILY
DAFTEST
DEFACED
DEFACES
DEFACTO
DEFAMED
DEFAMES
DEFARGE
DEFAULT
DEFEATS
DEFECTS
DEFENCE
DEFENDS
DEFENSE
DEFIANT
DEFICIT
DEFILED
DEFILER
DEFILES
DEFINED
DEFINES
DEFLATE
DEFLECT
DEFORMS
DEFRAUD
DEFRAYS
DEFROCK
DEFROST
DEFTEST
DEFUNCT
DEFUSED
DEFUSES
DEFYING
DIFFERS
DIFFUSE
DOFFING
DUFFELS
DUFFERS

D••F•••

DAFFIER
DAFFILY
DEAFENS
DEAFEST
DEIFIED
DEIFIES
DIFFERS
DIFFUSE
DOFFING
DOGFACE
DOGFISH
DRAFTED
DRAFTEE
DRIFTED
DRIFTER
DUFFELS
DUFFERS

D•••F••

DEEPFAT
DEEPFRY
DEERFLY
DOLEFUL
DONEFOR
DREYFUS
DUTIFUL
DWARFED

D••••F•

DASHOFF
DIEDOFF
DIESOFF
DIGNIFY
DISTAFF
DOZEOFF
DROPOFF
DUSTOFF

D•••••F

DASHOFF
DEBRIEF
DIEDOFF
DIESOFF
DISTAFF
DOZEOFF
DROPOFF
DUSTOFF

•D•F•••

EDIFICE
EDIFIED
EDIFIES

••DF•••

BIDFAIR
CODFISH
GODFREY
OLDFOGY
REDFINS
REDFIRS
REDFLAG
REDFORD

••D•F••

BODYFAT
MADEFOR

••D••F•

MADEOFF
MIDLIFE
MIDRIFF
MIDWIFE
NODSOFF
RIDEOFF
RODEOFF
RODOLFO
UPDRAFT

••D•••F

MADEOFF
MIDRIFF
NODSOFF
REDWOLF
RIDEOFF
RODEOFF

•••DF••

HANDFUL
HEEDFUL
LAIDFOR
MINDFUL
NEEDFUL
PAIDFOR
SANDFLY
SENDFOR

•••D•F•

ACIDIFY
DIEDOFF
HANDOFF
HEADOFF
HELDOFF
HOLDOFF
LAIDOFF
LEADOFF
MACDUFF
PAIDOFF
SENDOFF
SOLDOFF
TEEDOFF
TOLDOFF
WARDOFF

•••D••F

DIEDOFF
HANDOFF
HEADOFF
HELDOFF
HOLDOFF
LAIDOFF
LEADOFF
MACDUFF
PAIDOFF
SENDOFF
SHADOOF
SOLDOFF
TEEDOFF
TOLDOFF
WALDORF
WARDOFF

••••D•F

AHEADOF
HEARDOF
TIREDOF

D•G••••

DAGGERS
DAGWOOD
DEGAUSS
DEGRADE
DEGREES
DIGESTS
DIGGERS
DIGGING
DIGITAL
DIGNIFY
DIGNITY
DIGRAPH
DIGRESS
DIGSOUT
DOGCART
DOGCHEW
DOGCHOW
DOGDAYS
DOGEARS
DOGFACE
DOGFISH
DOGGIES
DOGGING
DOGGONE
DOGLEGS
DOGMATA
DOGSHOW
DOGSLED
DOGSTAR
DOGTAGS
DOGTROT
DOGWOOD
DUGONGS
DUGOUTS

D••G•••

DAGGERS
DANGERS
DANGLED
DANGLER
DANGLES
DEIGNED
DIAGRAM
DIDGOOD
DIGGERS
DIGGING
DINGBAT
DINGIER
DINGILY
DINGING
DINGLES
DINGOES
DISGUST
DODGERS
DODGING
DODGSON
DOGGIES
DOGGING
DOGGONE
DOUGHTY
DOUGLAS
DRAGGED
DRAGNET
DRAGONS
DRAGOON
DRAGOUT
DRAGSIN
DRAGSON
DRUGGED
DUDGEON
DUNGEON

D•••G••

DAMAGED
DAMAGES
DECAGON
DELIGHT
DELUGED
DELUGES
DEMIGOD
DESIGNS
DOINGIN
DOINGUP
DONEGAL
DOSAGES
DOWAGER
DRAGGED
DRAUGHT
DREDGED
DREDGER
DREDGES
DROUGHT
DRUDGED
DRUDGES
DRUGGED

D••••G•

DARKAGE
DEBARGE
DEFARGE
DIALOGS
DIVERGE
DIVULGE
DOCKAGE
DOGLEGS
DOGTAGS
DOMINGO
DRAYAGE
DUGONGS
DURANGO

D•••••G

DABBING
DAMMING
DAMNING
DAMPING
DANCING
DAPPING
DARLING
DARNING
DARTING
DASHING
DAUBING
DAWNING
DAYLONG
DEALING
DECALOG
DECKING
DEEDING
DEEMING
DEFYING
DEICING
DELEING
DELVING
DENTING
DENYING
DERRING
DIALING
DIETING
DIGGING
DIMMING
DINGING
DIPPING
DISHING
DISHRAG
DOCKING
DODGING
DOFFING
DOGGING
DOLLING
DONKING
DONNING
DOOMING
DOTTING
DOUSING
DOWNING
DOWSING
DRAPING
DRAWING
DRAYING
DRIVING
DRONING
DUBBING
DUCKING
DUCTING
DUELING
DULLING
DUMPING
DUNKING
DUNNING
DUSTING

•DG••••

EDGEDIN
EDGEOUT
EDGESIN
EDGIEST
EDGINGS

•D•G•••

ADAGIOS

•D•••G•

ADJUDGE
EDGINGS

•D••••G

ADDLING
ADORING
EDDYING
EDITING
EDUCING
RDLAING

••DG•••

BADGERS
BADGUYS
BUDGETS
BUDGIES
BUDGING
CADGERS
CADGING
CODGERS
CUDGELS
DIDGOOD
DODGERS
DODGING
DODGSON
DUDGEON
ENDGAME
FIDGETS
FIDGETY
FUDGING
GADGETS
GADGETY
HEDGERS
HEDGING
JUDGING
LEDGERS
LODGERS
LODGING
MIDGETS
NUDGERS
NUDGING
OLDGOLD
PIDGEON
PIDGINS
PODGIER
PUDGIER
REDGUMS
RIDGING
RIDGWAY
RODGERS
WEDGIES
WEDGING
WIDGEON
WIDGETS

••D•G••

BADEGGS
BODEGAS
INDIGOS

••D••G•

BADEGGS
BEDBUGS
ENDINGS
HIDALGO
INDULGE
OLDFOGY
REDDOGS
SIDINGS
TIDINGS
UNDERGO

••D•••G

ADDLING
BEDDING
BIDDING
BUDDING
BUDGING
CADGING
DODGING
EDDYING
ENDUING
FUDGING
GADDING
HEDGING
JUDGING
KIDDING
LADLING
LADYBUG
LODGING
MADDING
NODDING
NUDGING
PADDING
PUDDING
REDDING
REDFLAG
REDOING
REDWING
RIDDING
RIDGING
SIDLING
SODDING
SUDSING
TEDDING
TIDYING
UNDOING
UNDYING
WADDING
WEDDING
WEDGING

•••DG••

BRIDGED
BRIDGES
BRIDGET
DREDGED
DREDGER
DREDGES
DRUDGED
DRUDGES
FLEDGED
FLEDGES
FRIDGES
GRUDGED
GRUDGES
HANDGUN
KLUDGES
PLEDGED
PLEDGEE
PLEDGER
PLEDGES
SLEDGES
SLUDGES
SMIDGEN
SMUDGED
SMUDGES
TRUDGED
TRUDGER

TRUDGES

•••D•G•
BANDAGE
BONDAGE
CONDIGN
CORDAGE
GOODEGG
GUNDOGS
HOTDOGS
LAPDOGS
PRODIGY
PYEDOGS
REDDOGS
SEADOGS
SUNDOGS
TOPDOGS
TOYDOGS
VERDUGO
YARDAGE

•••D••G
ABIDING
BALDING
BANDING
BEADING
BEDDING
BENDING
BIDDING
BINDING
BIRDDOG
BIRDING
BONDING
BUDDING
CARDING
CHIDING
CORDING
CURDING
DEEDING
ELIDING
ELUDING
ERODING
EVADING
EXUDING
FEEDBAG
FEEDING
FENDING
FEUDING
FINDING
FOLDING
FORDING
FUNDING
GADDING
GELDING
GILDING
GIRDING
GLIDING
GOADING
GOLDBUG
GOLDING
GOODEGG
GRADING
GUIDING
HANDBAG
HANDING
HARDING
HEADING
HEEDING
HERDING
HOLDING
KIDDING
LANDING
LARDING
LAUDING
LEADING
LENDING
LOADING
LORDING
MADDING
MELDING
MENDING
MINDING
MOLDING
NEEDING
NODDING
PADDING
PENDING
PRIDING
PUDDING
RAIDING
READING
REDDING
REEDING
RENDING
RIDDING
ROADHOG
SANDBAG
SANDHOG
SANDING
SEEDING
SENDING
SHADING
SLEDDOG
SLIDING
SODDING
SPADING
TEDDING
TENDING
TRADING
VENDING
VOIDING
WADDING
WARDING
WEDDING
WEEDING
WELDING
WENDING
WILDING
WINDBAG
WINDING
WORDING

••••DG•
ABRIDGE
ADJUDGE
ARLEDGE

••••D•G
BIRDDOG
BULLDOG
CORNDOG
FIREDOG
HANGDOG
MOONDOG
SHINDIG
SHOWDOG
SLEDDOG

DH•••••
DHURRIE

D•H••••
DAHLIAS
DAHOMEY
DEHISCE
DEHORNS

D••H•••
DABHAND
DAPHNIS
DASHERS
DASHIKI
DASHING
DASHOFF
DIAHANN
DIEHARD
DISHING
DISHOUT
DISHPAN
DISHRAG
DITHERS
DITHERY
DRYHOLE
DUCHESS
DUCHIES

D•••H••
DAUPHIN
DITCHED
DITCHES
DOGCHEW
DOGCHOW
DOGSHOW
DOLPHIN
DONAHUE
DOUGHTY
DRACHMA

D••••H•
DEARTHS
DELIGHT
DENNEHY
DEPECHE
DOROTHY
DRAUGHT
DROUGHT

D•••••H
DAMPISH
DARKISH
DEBAUCH
DEBORAH
DEBOUCH
DELILAH
DERVISH
DIGRAPH
DIPTYCH
DOGFISH
DOLTISH
DOZENTH
DULLISH

•DH••••
ADHERED
ADHERES

•D•H•••
IDAHOAN

•D••H••
EDAPHIC

•D•••H•
ADOLPHE

••DH•••
MUDHENS
OLDHAND
REDHAIR
REDHATS
REDHEAD
REDHEAT
REDHOTS

••D•H••
BUDDHAS
GODTHAB
MADCHEN
MADEHAY
OLDCHAP

••D•••H
ALDRICH
CODFISH
FADDISH
GODUTCH
INDEPTH
INDUTCH
KADDISH
PADUCAH
REDDISH
RUDOLPH
YIDDISH

•••DH••
BUDDHAS
FORDHAM
HARDHAT
HARDHIT
PRUDHOE
ROADHOG
SANDHOG

•••D•H•
HOWDAHS
PURDAHS
WHYDAHS

•••D••H
FADDISH
KADDISH
KURDISH
MURDOCH
OBADIAH
PRUDISH
REDDISH
SWEDISH
YIDDISH

••••D•H
BREADTH
PLAYDOH

DI•••••
DIADEMS
DIAGRAM
DIAHANN
DIALECT
DIALERS
DIALING
DIALOGS
DIAMOND
DIAPERS
DIARIES
DIATOMS
DIBBLED
DIBBLES
DICIEST
DICKENS
DICKERS
DICKEYS
DICKIES
DICTATE
DICTION
DICTUMS
DIDACTS
DIDDLED
DIDDLES
DIDDLEY
DIDEROT
DIDGOOD
DIDOVER
DIEDOFF
DIEDOUT
DIEDOWN
DIEHARD
DIESELS
DIESOFF
DIESOUT
DIETARY
DIETERS
DIETING
DIFFERS
DIFFUSE
DIGESTS
DIGGERS
DIGGING
DIGITAL
DIGNIFY
DIGNITY
DIGRAPH
DIGRESS
DIGSOUT
DIKDIKS
DIKTATS
DILATED
DILATES
DILEMMA
DILLARD
DILLIES
DILUTED
DILUTER
DILUTES
DIMBULB
DIMITRI
DIMMERS
DIMMEST
DIMMING
DIMNESS
DIMOUTS
DIMPLED
DIMPLES
DIMWITS
DINEDIN
DINEDON
DINESEN
DINESIN
DINESON
DINETTE
DINGBAT
DINGIER
DINGILY
DINGING
DINGLES
DINGOES
DINKIER
DINKIES
DINMONT
DINNERS
DIOCESE
DIOMEDE
DIOPTER
DIORAMA
DIOXIDE
DIPLOID
DIPLOMA
DIPOLAR
DIPOLES
DIPPERS
DIPPING
DIPTYCH
DIRECTS
DIRNDLS
DIRTIED
DIRTIER
DIRTIES
DIRTILY
DISABLE
DISARMS
DISAVOW
DISBAND
DISBARS
DISCARD
DISCERN
DISCOED
DISCORD
DISCUSS
DISDAIN
DISEASE
DISGUST
DISHING
DISHOUT
DISHPAN
DISHRAG
DISJOIN
DISLIKE
DISMAYS
DISMISS
DISOBEY
DISOWNS
DISPELS
DISPLAY
DISPORT
DISPOSE
DISPUTE
DISROBE
DISRUPT
DISSECT
DISSENT
DISTAFF
DISTANT
DISTEND
DISTILL
DISTORT
DISTURB
DISUSED
DITCHED
DITCHES
DITHERS
DITHERY
DITTANY
DITTIES
DITTOED
DIURNAL
DIVERGE
DIVERSE
DIVERTS
DIVESIN
DIVESTS
DIVIDED
DIVIDER
DIVIDES
DIVINED
DIVINER
DIVINES
DIVISOR
DIVORCE
DIVULGE
DIVVIED
DIVVIES
DIZZIED
DIZZIER
DIZZIES
DIZZILY

D•I••••
DAILIES
DAIMLER
DAIRIES
DAISIES
DEICERS
DEICING
DEIFIED
DEIFIES
DEIGNED
DEITIES
DOILIES
DOINGIN
DOINGUP
DRIBBLE
DRIBLET
DRIEDUP
DRIESUP
DRIFTED
DRIFTER
DRILLED
DRILLER
DRINKER
DRIPDRY
DRIPPAN
DRIPPED
DRISTAN
DRIVEAT
DRIVEIN
DRIVELS
DRIVERS
DRIVEUP
DRIVING
DRIZZLE
DRIZZLY
DWINDLE

D••I•••
DANIELS
DAVINCI
DEBITED
DECIBEL
DECIDED
DECIDES
DECIMAL
DEFIANT
DEFICIT
DEFILED
DEFILER
DEFILES
DEFINED
DEFINES
DEHISCE
DELIBES
DELICTI
DELICTS
DELIGHT
DELILAH
DELIMIT
DELIRIA
DELISTS
DELIVER
DEMIGOD
DEMILLE
DEMISED
DEMISES
DENIALS
DENIECE
DENIERS
DENIZEN
DEPICTS
DERIDED
DERIDES
DERIVED
DERIVES
DESIGNS
DESIRED
DESIREE
DESIRES
DESISTS
DEVIANT
DEVIATE
DEVICES
DEVILED
DEVILLE
DEVILRY
DEVIOUS
DEVISED
DEVISES
DEWILDE
DICIEST
DIGITAL
DIMITRI
DIVIDED
DIVIDER
DIVIDES
DIVINED
DIVINER
DIVINES
DIVISOR
DOMINGO
DOMINOS
DOPIEST
DORITOS
DOSIDOS
DRAINED
DRAINER
DREIDEL
DREISER
DUBIETY
DUBIOUS
DUTIFUL

D•••I••
DABBING
DADAISM
DADAIST
DADDIES
DAFFIER
DAFFILY
DAHLIAS
DAILIES
DAIRIES
DAISIES
DALLIED
DALLIER
DALLIES
DAMMING
DAMNING
DAMPING
DAMPISH
DANCING
DANDIER
DANDIES
DAPPING
DARKISH
DARLING
DARNING
DARTING
DASHIKI
DASHING
DAUBING
DAUMIER
DAWKINS
DAWNING
DAYLILY
DAYSINN
DAYTIME
DEALING
DEBRIEF
DECEITS
DECEIVE
DECKING
DECLINE
DECRIED
DECRIES
DEEDING
DEEMING
DEFYING
DEICING
DEIFIED
DEIFIES
DEITIES
DELEING
DELUISE
DELVING
DENSITY
DENTINE
DENTING
DENTIST
DENYING
DEPRIVE
DERAILS
DERBIES
DERNIER
DERRICK
DERRING
DERVISH
DESPISE
DESPITE
DESTINE
DESTINY
DETAILS
DETAINS
DEVEINS
DEVRIES
DEWLINE
DIALING
DIARIES
DICKIES
DICTION
DIETING
DIGGING
DIGNIFY
DIGNITY
DIKDIKS
DILLIES
DIMMING
DIMWITS
DINGIER
DINGILY
DINGING
DINKIER
DINKIES
DIOXIDE
DIPPING
DIRTIED
DIRTIER
DIRTIES
DIRTILY
DISHING
DISLIKE
DISMISS
DISTILL
DITTIES
DIVVIED
DIVVIES
DIZZIED
DIZZIER
DIZZIES
DIZZILY
DOBBINS
DOCKING
DODGING
DOFFING
DOGFISH
DOGGIES
DOGGING
DOILIES
DOLLIED
DOLLIES
DOLLING
DOLTISH
DOMAINS
DONKING
DONNING
DOOMING
DOOZIES
DORMICE
DOSSIER
DOTTIER
DOTTING
DOUSING
DOWDIER
DOWDILY
DOWNIER
DOWNING
DOWRIES
DOWSING
DRAPING
DRAWING
DRAYING
DRIVING
DRONING
DROPINS
DUALITY
DUBBING
DUCHIES
DUCKIER
DUCKING
DUCTILE
DUCTING
DUDDIES
DUELING
DUELIST
DULLING
DULLISH
DUMMIED
DUMMIES
DUMPIER
DUMPING
DUNKING
DUNKIRK
DUNLINS
DUNNING
DUSKIER
DUSTIER
DUSTING

D••••I•
DAPHNIS
DAUPHIN
DAYTRIP
DEADAIR
DEALSIN
DEALTIN
DEARSIR
DECLAIM
DEEPSIX
DEFICIT
DELIMIT
DELIRIA
DELTAIC
DELTOID
DEMERIT
DEMONIC
DEPOSIT
DESPAIR
DESPOIL
DETRAIN
DETROIT
DEXTRIN
DHURRIE
DINEDIN
DINESIN
DIPLOID
DISDAIN
DISJOIN
DIVESIN
DOESKIN
DOINGIN
DOLPHIN
DOORDIE
DRAGSIN
DRASTIC
DRAWNIN
DRAWSIN
DRIVEIN
DROPSIN
DRUMLIN
DRYSUIT
DUCKPIN
DUKAKIS
DWEEZIL
DYNAMIC

D•••••I
DASHIKI
DAVINCI
DELICTI
DIMITRI

•DI••••
ADIPOSE
EDIBLES
EDIFICE
EDIFIED
EDIFIES
EDITING
EDITION
EDITORS
IDIAMIN
IDIOTIC

•D•I•••
ADDISON
ADMIRAL
ADMIRED
ADMIRER
ADMIRES
ADMIXED
ADMIXES
ADVISED
ADVISER
ADVISES
ADVISOR
EDGIEST
EDGINGS

•D••I••
ADAGIOS
ADAMITE
ADDLING
ADELINE
ADENINE
ADJOINS
ADORING
EDACITY
EDDYING
EDIFICE
EDIFIED
EDIFIES
EDITING
EDITION
EDUCING
IDOLIZE
RDLAING

•D•••I•
ADDEDIN
ADONAIS
EDAPHIC
EDGEDIN
EDGESIN
IDENTIC
IDIAMIN
IDIOTIC
IDYLLIC

••DI•••
ADDISON
AEDILES
ANDIRON
AUDIBLE
AUDIBLY
AUDITED
AUDITOR
BEDIZEN
BODICES
CEDILLA
CODICES
CODICIL
ENDINGS
ENDIVES
FADIMAN
INDIANA
INDIANS
INDICES
INDICIA
INDICTS
INDIGOS
INDITED
INDITES
IODIDES
IODIZED
IODIZES
KODIAKS
LADINOS
MADISON
MEDIANS
MEDIANT
MEDIATE
MEDICAL
MEDICOS
MEDIUMS
MODICUM
MODISTE
NUDISTS
OEDIPAL
OEDIPUS
ORDINAL
PEDICEL
PEDICLE
PODIUMS
RADIALS
RADIANS
RADIANT
RADIATE
RADICAL
RADICES
RADICLE
RADIOED
REDIALS
SIDINGS
TEDIOUS
TIDIEST
TIDINGS
ZODIACS

••D•I••
ADDLING
ALDRICH
BADDIES
BEDDING
BEDSIDE
BEDTIME
BIDDIES
BIDDING
BODKINS
BUDDIES
BUDDING
BUDGIES
BUDGING
CADDIED
CADDIES
CADGING
CADMIUM
CODEINE
CODFISH
DADAISM
DADAIST
DADDIES
DODGING
DUDDIES
EDDYING
ENDUING
ENDWISE
FADDISH
FADDISM
FADDIST
FADEINS
FUDGING
GADDING
GIDDIER
GIDDILY
GODLIKE
GODWITS
HADRIAN
HEDGING
JADEITE
JUDAISM
JUDGING
JUDOIST
KADDISH
KIDDIES
KIDDING
LADDIES
LADLING
LODGING
MADDING
MADEIRA
MADLIBS
MIDDIES
MIDLIFE
MIDLINE

MIDRIBS
MIDRIFF
MIDRISE
MIDSIZE
MIDWIFE
MUDDIED
MUDDIER
MUDDIES
MUDPIES
NODDING
NUDGING
NUDNIKS
OLDLINE
OLDNICK
OLDTIME
ORDAINS
PADDIES
PADDING
PIDGINS
PODGIER
PODRIDA
PUDDING
PUDGIER
REDBIRD
REDDING
REDDISH
REDFINS
REDFIRS
REDLINE
REDOING
REDPINE
REDWINE
REDWING
RIDDICK
RIDDING
RIDGING
RUDDIER
SIDLING
SODDING
SUDSIER
SUDSING
TEDDIES
TEDDING
TIDBITS
TIDYING
TODDIES
UNDOING
UNDYING
WADDING
WEDDING
WEDGIES
WEDGING
YIDDISH

••D••I•
ADDEDIN
ANDROID
ANDYKIM
BEDELIA
BEDEVIL
BEDOUIN
BIDFAIR
CODICIL
ECDYSIS
ENDEMIC
FADEDIN
FADESIN
FIDELIO
INDICIA
KIDSKIN
OLDMAID
REDHAIR
REDSKIN
SEDALIA
STDENIS
VIDALIA
WADESIN

••D•••I
CADUCEI
OLDUVAI
PADRONI

•••DI••
ABIDING
ACADIAN
ACIDIFY
ACIDITY
ANODIZE
ARIDITY
AVIDITY
BADDIES
BALDING
BANDIED
BANDIES
BANDING
BANDITO
BANDITS
BAWDIER
BAWDILY
BEADIER
BEADING
BEDDING
BENDING
BIDDIES
BIDDING
BINDING
BIRDIED
BIRDIES
BIRDING
BONDING
BUDDIES
BUDDING
CADDIED
CADDIES
CANDICE
CANDIDA
CANDIDE
CANDIDS
CANDIED
CANDIES
CARDING
CHIDING
COEDITS
CONDIGN
CORDIAL
CORDING
CORDITE
CREDITS
CRUDITY
CURDING
DADDIES
DANDIER
DANDIES
DEEDING
DIKDIKS
DOWDIER
DOWDILY
DUDDIES
ELIDING
ELUDING
ERODING
ERUDITE
EVADING
EXUDING
FADDISH
FADDISM
FADDIST
FEEDING
FENDING
FEUDING
FINDING
FOLDING
FORDING
FOSDICK
FUNDING
GADDING
GAUDIER
GAUDILY
GELDING
GIDDIER
GIDDILY
GILDING
GIRDING
GLIDING
GOADING
GOLDING
GOODIES
GORDIAN
GRADING
GUIDING
HANDIER
HANDILY
HANDING
HARDIER
HARDILY
HARDING
HEADIER
HEADILY
HEADING
HEEDING
HERDING
HOLDING
HOUDINI
IRIDIUM
JIMDINE
KADDISH
KIDDIES
KIDDING
KURDISH
LADDIES
LANDING
LARDING
LAUDING
LEADING
LEADINS
LENDING
LINDIED
LINDIES
LOADING
LORDING
MADDING
MELDING
MENDING
MIDDIES
MINDING
MISDIAL
MOLDIER
MOLDING
MOODIER
MOODILY
MUDDIED
MUDDIER
MUDDIES
NEEDIER
NEEDILY
NEEDING
NODDING
NORDICS
OBADIAH
ONADIET
OXIDIZE
PADDIES
PADDING
PANDITS
PAYDIRT
PENDING
PERDIEM
PHIDIAS
PREDICT
PRIDING
PRODIGY
PRUDISH
PUDDING
PUNDITS
RAIDING
RANDIER
READIED
READIER
READIES
READILY
READING
REDDING
REDDISH
REEDIER
REEDING
REEDITS
RENDING
RHODIUM
RIDDICK
RIDDING
ROADIES
ROWDIER
ROWDIES
ROWDILY
RUDDIER
SANDIER
SANDING
SARDINE
SEEDIER
SEEDILY
SEEDING
SENDING
SHADIER
SHADILY
SHADING
SKYDIVE
SLIDING
SODDING
SOLDIER
SPADING
STADIUM
STUDIED
STUDIES
STUDIOS
SUNDIAL
SWEDISH
TARDIER
TARDILY
TEDDIES
TEDDING
TENDING
TOADIED
TOADIES
TODDIES
TRADING
VANDINE
VENDING
VERDICT
VOIDING
WADDING
WARDING
WEDDING
WEEDIER
WEEDING
WELDING
WENDING
WILDING
WINDIER
WINDING
WOODIER
WOODIES
WORDIER
WORDILY
WORDING
YIDDISH

•••D•I•
ALADDIN
BALDRIC
BALDWIN
BANDAID
BOUDOIR
CONDUIT
DEADAIR
DISDAIN
FREDDIE
FREDRIC
GOODWIN
HANDSIN
HARDHIT
HEADPIN
HEADSIN
HENDRIX
LEADSIN
LORDJIM
MANDRIL
MAUDLIN
READMIT
READSIN
SENDSIN
SLIDEIN
TENDRIL
TRADEIN

•••D••I
HOUDINI

••••DI•
ADDEDIN
ALADDIN
AMRADIO
ARCADIA
BLONDIE
BORODIN
BOXEDIN
BUILDIN
CAVEDIN
CBRADIO
CLAUDIA
CLAUDIO
CLUEDIN
COMEDIC
DINEDIN
DOORDIE
EASEDIN
EDGEDIN
FADEDIN
FMRADIO
FREDDIE
HASIDIM
JURIDIC
KATYDID
KEYEDIN
LIVEDIN
MAULDIN
MELODIC
MOVEDIN
NOMADIC
OVERDID
PALADIN
PILEDIN
PLAUDIT
RAKEDIN
ROPEDIN
RUSHDIE
SALADIN
SHINDIG
SINEDIE
STANDIN
STOODIN
SYNODIC
TUNEDIN
WAVEDIN

••••D•I
HYUNDAI

•••••DI
BACARDI
COLLODI
EFFENDI
VIVALDI
VIVENDI

D•J••••
DEJECTS

D••J•••
DEEJAYS
DISJOIN
DONJONS
DONJOSE
DONJUAN

•DJ••••
ADJOINS
ADJOURN
ADJUDGE
ADJUNCT
ADJURED
ADJURES
ADJUSTS
PDJAMES

•D•J•••
ODDJOBS

••DJ•••
ODDJOBS

•••DJ••
GOODJOB
GOODJOE
LORDJIM

D•K••••
DAKOTAN
DAKOTAS
DEKLERK
DEKOVEN
DIKDIKS
DIKTATS
DUKAKIS
DUKEDOM
DYKSTRA

D••K•••
DANKEST
DARKAGE
DARKENS
DARKEST
DARKISH
DARKMAN
DAWKINS
DECKING
DECKLES
DECKOUT
DESKSET
DESKTOP
DICKENS
DICKERS
DICKEYS
DICKIES
DINKIER
DINKIES
DOCKAGE
DOCKERS
DOCKETS
DOCKING
DONKEYS
DONKING
DUCKIER
DUCKING
DUCKPIN
DUNKERS
DUNKING
DUNKIRK
DUSKIER

D•••K••
DEBAKEY
DOESKIN
DRINKER
DRUCKER
DUKAKIS

D••••K•
DAMASKS
DASHIKI
DEBARKS
DEBUNKS
DIKDIKS
DISLIKE
DYBBUKS

D•••••K
DAYBOOK
DEFROCK
DEKLERK
DENMARK
DERRICK
DRSPOCK
DRYDOCK
DUNKIRK

••DK•••
BODKINS

••D•K••
ANDYKIM
KIDSKIN
REDSKIN

••D••K•
BEDECKS
GODLIKE
KODIAKS
NUDNIKS
REDOAKS

••D•••K
BEDROCK
BODEREK
HADDOCK
MIDWEEK
MUDPACK
OLDNICK
PADDOCK
PADLOCK
REDBOOK
RIDDICK
SADSACK
TEDMACK
WEDLOCK
WIDMARK

•••D•K•
DIKDIKS
VANDYKE

•••D••K
BURDOCK
DRYDOCK
FOSDICK
HADDOCK
PADDOCK
RIDDICK
SUNDECK
VANDYCK

D•L••••
DALLIED
DALLIER
DALLIES
DALTREY
DELANEY
DELAYED
DELAYER
DELBERT
DELEING
DELETED
DELETES
DELIBES
DELICTI
DELICTS
DELIGHT
DELILAH
DELIMIT
DELIRIA
DELISTS
DELIVER
DELTAIC
DELTOID
DELUDED
DELUDES
DELUGED
DELUGES
DELUISE
DELVERS
DELVING
DILATED
DILATES
DILEMMA
DILLARD
DILLIES
DILUTED
DILUTER
DILUTES
DOLEFUL
DOLEOUT
DOLLARS
DOLLIED
DOLLIES
DOLLING
DOLLOPS
DOLLSUP
DOLMANS
DOLMENS
DOLORES
DOLPHIN
DOLTISH
DULLARD
DULLEST
DULLING
DULLISH

D••L•••
DAHLIAS
DAILIES
DALLIED
DALLIER
DALLIES
DARLEEN
DARLENE
DARLING
DAYLILY
DAYLONG
DEALERS
DEALING
DEALOUT
DEALSIN
DEALTIN
DECLAIM
DECLARE
DECLASS
DECLINE
DEFLATE
DEFLECT
DEKLERK
DEPLANE
DEPLETE
DEPLORE
DEPLOYS
DEWLAPS
DEWLINE
DIALECT
DIALERS
DIALING
DIALOGS
DILLARD
DILLIES
DIPLOID
DIPLOMA
DISLIKE
DOGLEGS
DOILIES
DOLLARS
DOLLIED
DOLLIES
DOLLING
DOLLOPS
DOLLSUP
DRILLED
DRILLER
DROLLER
DUALITY
DUELERS
DUELING
DUELIST
DULLARD
DULLEST
DULLING
DULLISH
DUNLINS
DWELLED
DWELLER

D•••L••
DABBLED
DABBLER
DABBLES
DAIMLER
DANDLED
DANDLES
DANELAW
DANGLED
DANGLER
DANGLES
DAPPLED
DAPPLES
DAWDLED
DAWDLER
DAWDLES
DAZZLED
DAZZLER
DAZZLES
DECALOG
DECKLES
DEDALUS
DEFILED
DEFILER
DEFILES
DELILAH
DEMILLE
DEPALMA
DESALTS
DEVALUE
DEVELOP
DEVILED
DEVILLE
DEVILRY
DEVOLVE
DEWCLAW
DEWILDE
DIBBLED
DIBBLES
DIDDLED
DIDDLES
DIDDLEY
DIMPLED
DIMPLES
DINGLES
DIPOLAR
DIPOLES
DISPLAY
DIVULGE
DOGSLED
DOODLED
DOODLER
DOODLES
DOPPLER
DOTTLES
DOUBLED
DOUBLES
DOUBLET
DOUBLEU
DOUGLAS
DRAWLED
DRIBLET
DRILLED
DRILLER
DROLLER
DROOLED
DROOLER
DROPLET
DRUMLIN
DWELLED
DWELLER

D••••L•
DACTYLS
DAFFILY
DAMSELS
DANIELS
DARRELL
DATEDLY
DAYLILY
DAZEDLY
DEBACLE
DECARLO
DEERFLY
DEFAULT
DEMILLE
DENIALS
DENSELY
DERAILS
DETAILS
DEVILLE
DIESELS
DIMBULB
DINGILY
DIRNDLS
DIRTILY
DISABLE
DISPELS
DISTILL
DIZZILY
DORSALS
DOSSALS
DOWDILY
DRACULA
DRIBBLE
DRIVELS
DRIZZLE
DRIZZLY
DRYCELL
DRYHOLE
DRYWALL
DRYWELL
DUCTILE
DUFFELS
DURABLE
DURABLY
DURRELL
DWINDLE

D•••••L
DARRELL
DECIBEL
DECIMAL
DEMEROL
DEPOSAL
DESPOIL
DIGITAL
DISTILL
DIURNAL
DOLEFUL
DONEGAL
DREIDEL
DRYCELL
DRYWALL
DRYWELL
DURRELL
DUTIFUL
DWEEZIL

•DL••••
RDLAING

•D•L•••
ADDLING
ADELINE
ADOLPHE
ADULATE
IDOLIZE
IDYLLIC
ODDLOTS

•D••L••
EDIBLES
IDEALLY
IDYLLIC

•D•••L•
ADDABLE
ADEPTLY
IDEALLY
ODDBALL

•D••••L
ADMIRAL
ADRENAL
ODDBALL

••DL•••
ADDLING
BEDLAMP
ENDLESS
GODLIKE
LADLERS
LADLING
LIDLESS
MADLIBS
MEDLEYS
MIDLAND
MIDLIFE
MIDLINE
ODDLOTS
OLDLINE
PADLOCK
PEDLARS
REDLINE
SIDLING
WEDLOCK

••D•L••
AEDILES
BEDELIA
CEDILLA
CODDLED
CODDLER
CODDLES
CUDDLED
CUDDLES
DEDALUS
DIDDLED
DIDDLES
DIDDLEY
ENDPLAY
FIDDLED
FIDDLER
FIDDLES
FIDELIO
FUDDLED
FUDDLES
HEDDLES
HIDALGO
HUDDLED
HUDDLES
INDULGE
MEDALED
MEDDLED
MEDDLER
MEDDLES
MEDULLA
MIDDLEC
MIDDLES
MODELAS
MODELED
MODELER
MODELTS
MODULAR
MODULES
MUDDLED
MUDDLER
MUDDLES
NODULAR
NODULES
PADDLED
PADDLER
PADDLES
PEDALED
PEDDLED
PEDDLER
PEDDLES
PUDDLED
PUDDLES
RADDLED
RADDLES
REDFLAG
RIDDLED
RIDDLER
RIDDLES
RODOLFO
RUDOLPH
SADDLED
SADDLER
SADDLES
SEDALIA
TODDLED
TODDLER
TODDLES
VIDALIA
WADDLED
WADDLER
WADDLES
YODELED
YODELER

••D••L•
ADDABLE
AUDIBLE
AUDIBLY
BADCOLD
BEDROLL
CEDILLA
CUDGELS
ELDERLY
GIDDILY
INDWELL
JADEDLY
MEDULLA
MUDEELS
ODDBALL
OLDGOLD
ORDEALS
ORDERLY
PEDICLE
RADIALS
RADICLE
REDCELL
REDEALS
REDEALT
REDIALS
REDPOLL
REDWOLF
TADPOLE

••D•••L
BEDEVIL
BEDROLL
CODICIL
FEDERAL
INDWELL
MEDICAL
ODDBALL
OEDIPAL
ORDINAL
PEDICEL
RADICAL
REDCELL
REDPOLL

•••DL••
BEADLES
BOODLES
BOWDLER
BRADLEE
BRADLEY
BRIDLED
BRIDLES
BUNDLED
BUNDLES
CANDLES
CODDLED
CODDLER
CODDLES
CRADLED
CRADLES
CUDDLED
CUDDLES
CURDLED
CURDLES
DANDLED
DANDLES
DAWDLED
DAWDLER
DAWDLES
DIDDLED
DIDDLES
DIDDLEY
DOODLED
DOODLER
DOODLES
FEEDLOT
FIDDLED
FIDDLER
FIDDLES
FIEDLER
FONDLED
FONDLES
FUDDLED
FUDDLES
GIRDLED
GIRDLES
HANDLED
HANDLER
HANDLES
HEDDLES
HOODLUM
HUDDLED
HUDDLES
HURDLED
HURDLER
HURDLES
KINDLED
KINDLES
LAIDLOW
MAUDLIN
MEDDLED
MEDDLER
MEDDLES
MIDDLEC
MIDDLES
MUDDLED
MUDDLER
MUDDLES
NEEDLED
NEEDLES
NOODLES
PADDLED
PADDLER
PADDLES
PEDDLED
PEDDLER
PEDDLES
POODLES
PUDDLED
PUDDLES
RADDLED
RADDLES
RIDDLED
RIDDLER
RIDDLES
SADDLED
SADDLER
SADDLES
SANDLOT
TODDLED
TODDLER
TODDLES
WADDLED
WADDLER
WADDLES
WOODLOT

•••D•L•
BAWDILY
BOBDOLE
BRIDALS
CANDELA
CONDOLE
CORDELL
CRUDELY
DOWDILY
GAUDILY
GIDDILY
GONDOLA
GOODALL
GRIDDLE
HANDILY
HARDILY
HEADILY
KENDALL
MANDALA
MANDELA
MONDALE
MOODILY
NEEDILY
RAGDOLL
RANDALL
READILY
RONDELS
ROWDILY
SANDALS
SANDFLY
SEEDILY
SEIDELS
SHADILY
SNIDELY
SWADDLE
TARDILY
TWADDLE
TWIDDLE
VANDALS
WENDELL
WORDILY

•••D••L
BIGDEAL
CORDELL
CORDIAL
GOODALL
GRADUAL
HANDFUL
HEEDFUL
KENDALL
MANDREL
MANDRIL
MINDFUL
MISDEAL
MISDIAL
NEEDFUL
NEWDEAL
RAGDOLL
RANDALL
RAWDEAL
SUNDIAL
TENDRIL
WENDELL

••••DL•
ACRIDLY
BLANDLY
BLINDLY
BRINDLE
BROADLY
DATEDLY
DAZEDLY
DIRNDLS
DWINDLE
FETIDLY
FIXEDLY
FLUIDLY
GRANDLY
GRIDDLE
HUMIDLY
JADEDLY
LIVIDLY
LUCIDLY
LURIDLY
NAKEDLY
PROUDLY
RAPIDLY
RIGIDLY
ROUNDLY
SOLIDLY
SOUNDLY
SPINDLE
SPINDLY
STAIDLY
SWADDLE
SWINDLE
TEPIDLY
THIRDLY
TIMIDLY
TIREDLY
TREADLE
TRUNDLE
TWADDLE
TWIDDLE
UNGODLY
VALIDLY
VAPIDLY
VEXEDLY
VIVIDLY
WEIRDLY
WHEEDLE
WORLDLY

••••D•L
BIMODAL
BIPEDAL
CITADEL
DREIDEL
GRENDEL
INFIDEL
OVOIDAL
REMODEL
SCANDAL
STRUDEL
SYNODAL

D•M••••
DAMAGED
DAMAGES
DAMASKS
DAMMING
DAMNING
DAMPENS
DAMPERS
DAMPEST
DAMPING
DAMPISH
DAMSELS
DAMSONS
DEMANDS
DEMEANS
DEMERIT
DEMEROL
DEMESNE
DEMETER
DEMIGOD
DEMILLE
DEMISED
DEMISES
DEMONIC
DEMOTED
DEMOTES
DEMPSEY
DEMURER
DIMBULB
DIMITRI
DIMMERS
DIMMEST
DIMMING
DIMNESS
DIMOUTS
DIMPLED
DIMPLES
DIMWITS
DOMAINS
DOMINGO
DOMINOS
DUMBEST
DUMDUMS
DUMMIED
DUMMIES
DUMMYUP
DUMPIER
DUMPING

D••M•••
DAIMLER
DAMMING
DAUMIER
DEEMING
DENMARK
DESMOND
DIAMOND
DIMMERS
DIMMEST
DIMMING
DINMONT
DIOMEDE
DISMAYS
DISMISS
DOGMATA
DOLMANS
DOLMENS
DOOMING
DORMANT
DORMERS
DORMICE
DRUMLIN
DRUMMED
DRUMMER
DRUMSUP
DUMMIED
DUMMIES
DUMMYUP

D•••M••
DAHOMEY
DARKMAN
DECAMPS
DECIMAL
DEFAMED
DEFAMES
DELIMIT
DILEMMA
DOORMAN
DOORMAT
DOORMEN
DREAMED
DREAMER
DREAMON
DREAMUP
DRUMMED
DRUMMER
DUSTMOP
DYNAMIC
DYNAMOS

D••••M•
DAYCAMP
DAYTIME
DEFORMS
DEPALMA
DIADEMS
DIATOMS
DICTUMS
DILEMMA
DIORAMA
DIPLOMA
DISARMS
DRACHMA
DUMDUMS

D•••••M
DADAISM
DAYROOM
DECLAIM
DECORUM
DIAGRAM
DUKEDOM

•DM••••
ADMIRAL
ADMIRED
ADMIRER
ADMIRES
ADMIXED
ADMIXES

•D•M•••
ADAMANT
ADAMITE
ADAMSON
ODDMENT

•D••M••
IDIAMIN
PDJAMES

••DM•••
ARDMORE
CADMIUM
ENDMOST
ODDMENT
OLDMAID
OLDMOON
REDMEAT
TEDMACK
WIDMARK

••D•M••
ABDOMEN
ENDEMIC
FADIMAN
MADAMEX
RADAMES
SIDEMAN
SIDEMEN

••D••M•
BEDLAMP
BEDTIME
ENDGAME
MEDIUMS
OLDTIME
PODIUMS
REDEEMS
REDGUMS

••D•••M
ANDYKIM
BEDROOM
CADMIUM
DADAISM
FADDISM
JUDAISM
MIDTERM
MODICUM
SIDEARM

•••DM••
BIRDMAN
BIRDMEN
BONDMAN
BONDMEN
FELDMAN
GOODMAN
GOODMEN
HEADMAN
HEADMEN
READMIT
ROADMAP
SANDMAN
SANDMEN
YARDMAN
YARDMEN

•••D•M•
ACADEME
ACADEMY
AIRDAMS
ANADEMS
BELDAME
BELDAMS
CONDEMN
DIADEMS
DUMDUMS
TANDEMS

•••D••M
EARDRUM
FADDISM
FORDHAM
HOODLUM
HUMDRUM
IRIDIUM
LORDJIM
PERDIEM
RHODIUM
STADIUM
YARDARM

••••DM•
GRANDMA

••••D•M
BOREDOM
CZARDOM
DUKEDOM
EARLDOM
FIEFDOM
FREEDOM
GRANDAM
HASIDIM
KINGDOM
MACADAM
MILLDAM
POTSDAM
SERFDOM
SHAHDOM
STARDOM

D•N••••
DANCERS
DANCING
DANDERS
DANDIER
DANDIES
DANDLED
DANDLES
DANELAW
DANGERS
DANGLED
DANGLER
DANGLES
DANIELS
DANKEST
DANSEUR
DENDRON
DENEUVE
DENIALS
DENIECE
DENIERS
DENIZEN
DENMARK
DENNEHY
DENOTED
DENOTES
DENSELY
DENSEST
DENSITY
DENTATE
DENTINE
DENTING
DENTIST
DENTURE
DENUDED
DENUDES
DENYING
DINEDIN
DINEDON
DINESEN
DINESIN
DINESON
DINETTE
DINGBAT
DINGIER
DINGILY
DINGING
DINGLES
DINGOES
DINKIER
DINKIES
DINMONT
DINNERS
DONAHUE
DONATED
DONATES
DONATOR
DONEFOR
DONEGAL
DONJONS
DONJOSE
DONJUAN
DONKEYS
DONKING
DONNING
DONOVAN
DUNAWAY
DUNGEON
DUNKERS
DUNKING
DUNKIRK
DUNLINS
DUNNING
DYNAMIC
DYNAMOS
DYNASTS
DYNASTY

D••N•••
DAMNING
DARNERS
DARNING
DAUNTED
DAWNING
DENNEHY
DERNIER
DIGNIFY
DIGNITY
DIMNESS
DINNERS
DIRNDLS
DOINGIN
DOINGUP
DONNING
DOWNBOW
DOWNERS
DOWNIER
DOWNING
DOWNPAT
DRINKER
DRONERS
DRONING
DRYNESS
DUENNAS
DUNNING
DWINDLE

D•••N••
DAPHNIS
DAVINCI
DEBONED
DEBONES
DEBUNKS
DECANTS
DEFENCE
DEFENDS
DEFENSE
DEFINED
DEFINES
DEFUNCT
DEIGNED
DELANEY
DEMANDS
DEMONIC
DEPENDS
DEPONED
DEPONES
DETENTE
DIURNAL
DIVINED
DIVINER
DIVINES
DOCENTS
DOMINGO
DOMINOS
DOYENNE
DOZENTH
DRAGNET
DRAINED
DRAINER
DRAWNIN
DRAWNON
DRAWNUP
DROWNED
DUENNAS
DUGONGS
DURANCE
DURANGO
DURANTE

D••••N•
DABBING
DABHAND
DAMMING
DAMNING
DAMPENS
DAMPING
DAMSONS
DANCING
DAPPING
DARKENS
DARLENE
DARLING
DARNING
DARTING
DASHING
DAUBING
DAWKINS
DAWNING
DAYLONG
DAYSINN
DAYTONA
DEACONS
DEADEND
DEADENS
DEAFENS
DEALING
DECKING
DECLINE
DEEDING
DEEMING
DEEPEND
DEEPENS
DEFIANT
DEFYING
DEHORNS
DEICING
DELEING
DELVING
DEMEANS
DEMESNE
DENTINE
DENTING
DENYING
DEPLANE
DERRING
DESCANT
DESCEND
DESCENT
DESIGNS
DESMOND
DESTINE
DESTINY
DETAINS
DEVEINS
DEVIANT
DEWLINE
DIAHANN
DIALING
DIAMOND
DICKENS
DIETING
DIGGING
DIMMING
DINGING
DINMONT
DIPPING
DISBAND
DISHING
DISOWNS
DISSENT
DISTANT
DISTEND
DITTANY
DOBBINS
DOCKING
DODGING
DOFFING
DOGGING
DOGGONE
DOLLING
DOLMANS
DOLMENS
DOMAINS
DONJONS
DONKING
DONNING
DOOMING
DORMANT
DOTTING
DOUSING
DOWNING
DOWSING
DOYENNE
DRAGONS
DRAPING
DRAWING
DRAYING
DRIVING
DRONING
DROPINS
DRYRUNS
DUBBING
DUCKING
DUCTING
DUELING
DULLING
DUMPING
DUNKING
DUNLINS
DUNNING
DUODENA
DUSTING

D•••••N
DAKOTAN
DARKMAN
DARLEEN
DAUPHIN
DAYSINN
DEADPAN
DEALSIN
DEALTIN
DECAGON
DEKOVEN
DENDRON
DENIZEN
DETRAIN
DEXTRIN
DIAHANN
DICTION
DIEDOWN
DINEDIN
DINEDON
DINESEN
DINESIN
DINESON
DISCERN
DISDAIN
DISHPAN
DISJOIN
DIVESIN
DODGSON
DOESKIN
DOINGIN
DOLPHIN
DONJUAN
DONOVAN
DOORMAN
DOORMEN
DOTEDON
DOTESON
DRAGOON
DRAGSIN
DRAGSON
DRAWNIN
DRAWNON
DRAWSIN
DRAWSON
DREAMON
DRESDEN
DRIPPAN
DRISTAN
DRIVEIN
DROPSIN
DRUMLIN
DUCKPIN
DUDGEON
DUNGEON
DUSTPAN

•D•N•••
ADENINE
ADONAIS
IDENTIC
ODDNESS

•D••N••
ADDENDA
ADDENDS
ADDONTO
ADJUNCT
ADORNED
ADRENAL
ADVANCE
ADVENTS
EDASNER
EDGINGS

•D•••N•
ADAMANT
ADDLING
ADELINE
ADENINE
ADJOINS
ADORING
EDDYING
EDITING
EDUCING
ODDMENT
RDLAING

•D••••N
ADAMSON
ADDEDIN
ADDEDON
ADDISON
ADJOURN
EDGEDIN
EDGESIN
EDITION
IDAHOAN
IDIAMIN

••DN•••
BADNESS
KIDNAPS
KIDNEYS
MADNESS
NUDNIKS
ODDNESS
OLDNESS
OLDNEWS
OLDNICK
REDNESS
SADNESS

••D•N••
ADDENDA
ADDENDS
ADDONTO
ALDENTE
ANDANTE
ARDENCY
CADENCE
CADENZA
ENDINGS
GODUNOV
INDENTS
LADINOS
MADONNA
ORDINAL
PEDANTS
REDANTS
RODENTS
SIDINGS
STDENIS
TIDINGS
VEDANTA
WIDENED

••D••N•
ADDLING
ANDEANS
BEDDING
BIDDING
BODKINS
BUDDING
BUDGING
CADGING
CODEINE
DODGING
EDDYING
ENDRUNS
ENDUING
ENDZONE
FADEINS
FUDGING
GADDING
GIDEONS
GODSEND
GODSONS
HEDGING
HYDRANT
INDIANA
INDIANS
JUDGING
KIDDING
LADLING
LODGING
MADDENS
MADDING
MADONNA
MADRONA
MEDIANS
MEDIANT
MIDDENS
MIDLAND
MIDLINE
MODERNS
MUDHENS
NODDING
NUDGING
ODDMENT
OLDHAND
OLDLINE
ORDAINS
PADDING
PADRONE
PADRONI
PIDGINS
PUDDING
RADIANS
RADIANT
REDCENT
REDDENS
REDDING
REDFINS
REDLINE
REDOING
REDOUND
REDPINE
REDWINE
REDWING
RIDDING
RIDGING
SADDENS
SIDLING
SODDING

SUDSING
TEDDING
TIDYING
UNDOING
UNDYING
WADDING
WEDDING
WEDGING

••D•••N
ABDOMEN
ADDEDIN
ADDEDON
ADDISON
ANDIRON
ANDSOON
AUDUBON
BEDDOWN
BEDIZEN
BEDOUIN
CADDOAN
DODGSON
DUDGEON
FADEDIN
FADESIN
FADIMAN
GADSDEN
HADRIAN
KIDSKIN
MADCHEN
MADISON
MIDTOWN
OLDMOON
PIDGEON
REDRAWN
REDSKIN
SIDEMAN
SIDEMEN
UNDRAWN
WADESIN
WIDGEON

•••DN••
GARDNER
LARDNER
PARDNER

•••D•N•
ABIDING
ANODYNE
BALDING
BANDANA
BANDING
BEADING
BEDDING
BENDING
BIDDING
BINDING
BIRDING
BONDING
BUDDING
BURDENS
CARDING
CHIDING
CONDONE
CORDING
CORDONS
CURDING
DEADEND
DEADENS
DEEDING
DUODENA
ELIDING
ELUDING
ERODING
EVADING
EVIDENT
EXUDING
FEEDING
FENDING
FEUDING
FINDING
FOLDING
FONDANT
FORDING
FUNDING
GADDING
GARDENS
GAUDENS
GELDING
GILDING
GIRDING
GLIDING
GOADING
GOLDING
GOODONE
GRADING
GUIDING
GUIDONS
HANDING
HARDENS
HARDING
HEADING
HEEDING
HERDING
HOLDING
HOUDINI
HOYDENS
JIMDINE
KIDDING
LANDING
LARDING
LARDONS
LAUDING
LEADING
LEADINS
LENDING
LINDENS
LOADING
LORDING
MADDENS
MADDING
MAIDENS
MANDANS
MELDING
MENDING
MIDDENS
MINDING
MISDONE
MOLDING
MORDANT
MORDENT
MUNDANE
NEEDING
NODDING
OUTDONE
OXIDANT
PADDING
PARDONS
PENDANT
PENDENT
PENDING
PRIDING
PRUDENT
PUDDING
RAIDING
READING
REDDENS
REDDING
REEDING
RENDING
RIDDING
SADDENS
SANDING
SARDINE
SEEDING
SENDING
SHADING
SLIDING
SODDING
SPADING
STUDENT
TEDDING
TENDING
TENDONS
TRADING
TRIDENT
VANDINE
VENDING
VERDANT
VOIDING
WADDING
WARDENS
WARDING
WEDDING
WEEDING
WELDING
WENDING
WILDING
WILDONE
WINDING
WORDING
WORDONE

•••D••N
ACADIAN
ALADDIN
BALDWIN
BEDDOWN
BIRDMAN
BIRDMEN
BOGDOWN
BONDMAN
BONDMEN
CADDOAN
CALDRON
CONDEMN
CONDIGN
CUTDOWN
DEADPAN
DENDRON
DIEDOWN
DISDAIN
FEEDSON
FELDMAN
GETDOWN
GLADDEN
GOLDWYN
GOODMAN
GOODMEN
GOODSON
GOODWIN
GORDIAN
GOTDOWN
HANDGUN
HANDSIN
HANDSON
HARDPAN
HARDWON
HEADMAN
HEADMEN
HEADPIN
HEADSIN
HOEDOWN
HOLDSON
LAYDOWN
LEADSIN
LEADSON
LETDOWN
LIEDOWN
LOWDOWN
MAUDLIN
MOWDOWN
PINDOWN
PREDAWN
PUTDOWN
READSIN
RUBDOWN
RUNDOWN
SANDMAN
SANDMEN
SATDOWN
SENDSIN
SETDOWN
SHODDEN
SITDOWN
SLIDEIN
SMIDGEN
SUNDOWN
TIEDOWN
TRADEIN
TRADEON
TRODDEN
YARDMAN
YARDMEN

••••DN•
ARIADNE
COULDNT
ECHIDNA
WOULDNT

••••D•N
ABANDON
ADDEDIN
ADDEDON
ALADDIN
ALMADEN
BORODIN
BOXEDIN
BRANDON
BRENDAN
BROADEN
BUILDIN
BUILDON
CAVEDIN
CELADON
CLUEDIN
DINEDIN
DINEDON
DOTEDON
DRESDEN
EASEDIN
EDGEDIN
EGGEDON
FADEDIN
FRIEDAN
GADSDEN
GLADDEN
GLUEDON
HALFDAN
JOURDAN
KEYEDIN
LANGDON
LIVEDIN
LIVEDON
MAULDIN
MOVEDIN
NEVADAN
ONANDON
PALADIN
PILEDIN
PILEDON
RAKEDIN
RAMADAN
REARDON
ROPEDIN
ROUNDON
RUANDAN
RWANDAN
SALADIN
SHELDON
SHODDEN
SNOWDON
SPIEDON
STANDIN
STANDON
STOODIN
TRIEDON
TRODDEN
TUNEDIN
UGANDAN
WAVEDIN
WHAUDEN

DO•••••
DOBBINS
DOCENTS
DOCKAGE
DOCKERS
DOCKETS
DOCKING
DOCTORS
DODDERS
DODGERS
DODGING
DODGSON
DOESKIN
DOEUVRE
DOFFING
DOGCART
DOGCHEW
DOGCHOW
DOGDAYS
DOGEARS
DOGFACE
DOGFISH
DOGGIES
DOGGING
DOGGONE
DOGLEGS
DOGMATA
DOGSHOW
DOGSLED
DOGSTAR
DOGTAGS
DOGTROT
DOGWOOD
DOILIES
DOINGIN
DOINGUP
DOLEFUL
DOLEOUT
DOLLARS
DOLLIED
DOLLIES
DOLLING
DOLLOPS
DOLLSUP
DOLMANS
DOLMENS
DOLORES
DOLPHIN
DOLTISH
DOMAINS
DOMINGO
DOMINOS
DONAHUE
DONATED
DONATES
DONATOR
DONEFOR
DONEGAL
DONJONS
DONJOSE
DONJUAN
DONKEYS
DONKING
DONNING
DONOVAN
DOODADS
DOODLED
DOODLER
DOODLES
DOOMING
DOORDIE
DOORMAN
DOORMAT
DOORMEN
DOORWAY
DOOZIES
DOPEOUT
DOPIEST
DOPPLER
DORITOS
DORMANT
DORMERS
DORMICE
DOROTHY
DORSALS
DORSETT
DOSAGES
DOSIDOS
DOSSALS
DOSSERS
DOSSIER
DOTEDON
DOTESON
DOTTIER
DOTTING
DOTTLES
DOUBLED
DOUBLES
DOUBLET
DOUBLEU
DOUBTED
DOUBTER
DOUGHTY
DOUGLAS
DOUREST
DOUSING
DOVEBAR
DOVECOT
DOWAGER
DOWDIER
DOWDILY
DOWNBOW
DOWNERS
DOWNIER
DOWNING
DOWNPAT
DOWRIES
DOWSERS
DOWSING
DOYENNE
DOZENTH
DOZEOFF

D•O••••
DEODARS
DIOCESE
DIOMEDE
DIOPTER
DIORAMA
DIOXIDE
DOODADS
DOODLED
DOODLER
DOODLES
DOOMING
DOORDIE
DOORMAN
DOORMAT
DOORMEN
DOORWAY
DOOZIES
DROLLER
DRONERS
DRONING
DROOLED
DROOLER
DROOPED
DROPINS
DROPLET
DROPOFF
DROPOUT
DROPPED
DROPPER
DROPSBY
DROPSIN
DROUGHT
DROVERS
DROWNED
DROWSED
DROWSES
DUODENA

D••O•••
DAHOMEY
DAKOTAN
DAKOTAS
DEBONED
DEBONES
DEBORAH
DEBOUCH
DECOCTS
DECODED
DECODER
DECODES
DECORUM
DECOYED
DEFORMS
DEHORNS
DEKOVEN
DEMONIC
DEMOTED
DEMOTES
DENOTED
DENOTES
DEPONED
DEPONES
DEPORTS
DEPOSAL
DEPOSED
DEPOSER
DEPOSES
DEPOSIT
DESOTOS
DETOURS
DEVOLVE
DEVOTED
DEVOTEE
DEVOTES
DEVOURS
DIDOVER
DIMOUTS
DIPOLAR
DIPOLES
DISOBEY
DISOWNS
DIVORCE
DOLORES
DONOVAN
DOROTHY
DROOLED
DROOLER
DROOPED
DUGONGS
DUGOUTS

D•••O••
DAGWOOD
DAMSONS
DASBOOT
DASHOFF
DAYBOOK
DAYLONG
DAYROOM
DAYTONA
DEACONS
DEALOUT
DEBTORS
DECKOUT
DEFROCK
DEFROST
DELTOID
DEPLORE
DEPLOYS
DESMOND
DESPOIL
DESPOTS
DETROIT
DEVIOUS
DIALOGS
DIAMOND
DIATOMS
DIDGOOD
DIEDOFF
DIEDOUT
DIEDOWN
DIESOFF
DIESOUT
DIGSOUT
DINGOES
DINMONT
DIPLOID
DIPLOMA
DISCOED
DISCORD
DISHOUT
DISJOIN
DISPORT
DISPOSE
DISROBE
DISTORT
DITTOED
DOCTORS
DOGGONE
DOGWOOD
DOLEOUT
DOLLOPS
DONJONS
DONJOSE
DOPEOUT
DOZEOFF
DRAGONS
DRAGOON
DRAGOUT
DRAWOUT
DREWOUT
DROPOFF
DROPOUT
DRSPOCK
DRYDOCK
DRYHOLE
DUBIOUS
DUSTOFF
DUTEOUS

D••••O•
DAGWOOD
DASBOOT
DAYBOOK
DAYROOM
DECAGON
DECALOG
DECAPOD
DEMEROL
DEMIGOD
DENDRON
DESKTOP
DESOTOS
DESTROY
DEVELOP
DEWDROP
DICTION
DIDEROT
DIDGOOD
DINEDON
DINESON
DISAVOW
DIVISOR
DODGSON
DOGCHOW
DOGSHOW
DOGTROT
DOGWOOD
DOMINOS
DONATOR
DONEFOR
DORITOS
DOSIDOS
DOTEDON
DOTESON
DOVECOT
DOWNBOW
DRAGOON
DRAGSON
DRAWNON
DRAWSON
DREAMON
DUDGEON
DUKEDOM
DUNGEON
DUSTMOP
DYNAMOS

D•••••O
DARESTO
DECARLO
DEFACTO
DEUTERO
DOMINGO
DURANGO

•DO••••
ADOLPHE
ADONAIS
ADOPTED
ADOPTEE
ADOPTER
ADORERS
ADORING
ADORNED
EDOUARD
IDOLIZE
ODOROUS

•D•O•••
ADDONTO
ADJOINS
ADJOURN
ADSORBS
IDIOTIC

•D••O••
ADIPOSE
EDGEOUT
EDITORS
IDAHOAN
ODDJOBS
ODDLOTS
ODOROUS

•D•••O•
ADAGIOS
ADAMSON
ADAPTOR
ADDEDON
ADDISON
ADVISOR
EDITION

•D••••O
ADDEDTO
ADDONTO
ADDUPTO

••DO•••
ABDOMEN
ADDONTO
ANDORRA
ANDOVER
ARDOURS
BEDOUIN
DIDOVER
ENDORSE
ENDOWED
FEDORAS
INDOORS
INDOUBT
JUDOIST
MADONNA
NODOUBT
OGDOADS
REDOAKS
REDOING
REDOUBT
REDOUND
RODOLFO
RUDOLPH
UNDOING
WIDOWED
WIDOWER

••D•O••
ANDROID
ANDSOON
ARDMORE
ARDUOUS
BADCOLD
BEDDOWN
BEDPOST
BEDROCK
BEDROLL
BEDROOM
CADDOAN
DIDGOOD
ENDMOST
ENDZONE
FADEOUT
GIDEONS
GODSONS
HADDOCK
HIDEOUS
HIDEOUT
HYDROUS
INDOORS
KEDROVA
MADEOFF
MADEOUT
MADRONA
MIDTOWN
NODSOFF
ODDJOBS
ODDLOTS
OLDFOGY
OLDGOLD
OLDMOON
PADDOCK
PADLOCK
PADRONE
PADRONI
RADIOED
REDBOOK
REDCOAT
REDDOGS
REDFORD
REDHOTS
REDPOLL
REDROSE
REDTOPS
REDWOLF
REDWOOD
RIDEOFF
RIDEOUT
RODEOFF
RODEOUT
TADPOLE
TEDIOUS
WEDLOCK

••D••O•
ADDEDON
ADDISON
ANDIRON
ANDSOON
AUDITOR
AUDUBON
BEDROOM
DIDEROT
DIDGOOD
DODGSON
DUDGEON
GODUNOV
INDIGOS
LADINOS
MADEFOR
MADISON
MEDICOS
OLDMOON
OLDPROS
PIDGEON
REDBOOK
REDSPOT
REDWOOD
SODAPOP
WIDGEON

••D•••O
ADDEDTO
ADDONTO
ADDUPTO
FIDELIO
HIDALGO
LEDUPTO
MODESTO
RODOLFO
UNDERGO

•••DO••
ACEDOUT
BEDDOWN
BOBDOLE
BOGDOWN
BOUDOIR
BOYDORR
BURDOCK
CADDOAN
CANDOUR
CARDOZO
CONDOLE
CONDONE
CONDORS
CORDOBA
CORDONS
CUTDOWN
DIEDOFF
DIEDOUT
DIEDOWN
DRYDOCK
EKEDOUT
FINDOUT
FOLDOUT
GETDOWN
GONDOLA
GOODONE
GOTDOWN
GUIDONS
GUNDOGS
HADDOCK
HANDOFF
HANDOUT
HEADOFF
HEADOUT
HELDOFF
HELDOUT
HOEDOWN
HOLDOFF
HOLDOUT
HOODOOS
HOTDOGS
ISADORA
LAIDOFF
LAIDOUT
LAPDOGS
LARDONS
LAYDOWN
LEADOFF
LEADOUT
LETDOWN
LIEDOWN
LOWDOWN
MEADOWS
MEADOWY
MENDOZA
MISDOES
MISDONE
MOWDOWN
MURDOCH
OUTDOES
OUTDONE
OUTDOOR
PADDOCK
PAIDOFF
PAIDOUT
PANDORA
PARDONS
PINDOWN
PUTDOWN
PYEDOGS
RAGDOLL
READOUT
REDDOGS
RUBDOWN
RUNDOWN
SATDOWN
SEADOGS
SENDOFF
SENDOUT
SETDOWN
SHADOOF
SHADOWS
SHADOWY
SITDOWN
SOLDOFF
SOLDOUT
SUNDOGS
SUNDOWN
TEEDOFF
TENDONS
TIEDOWN
TOLDOFF
TOPDOGS
TOYDOGS
VENDORS
WALDORF
WARDOFF
WEEDOUT
WILDONE
WINDOWS
WORDONE

•••D•O•
AIRDROP
BANDBOX
BIRDDOG
CALDRON
DENDRON
DEWDROP
EARDROP
FEEDLOT
FEEDSON
GOODJOB
GOODJOE
GOODSON
GUMDROP
HANDSON
HARDTOP

HARDWON
HOLDSON
HOODOOS
LAIDFOR
LAIDLOW
LEADSON
OUTDOOR
PAIDFOR
PRUDHOE
ROADHOG
SANDBOX
SANDHOG
SANDLOT
SEEDPOD
SENDFOR
SHADOOF
SKIDDOO
SKIDROW
SLEDDOG
STUDIOS
TRADEON
WINDROW
WINDSOR
WOODLOT
WOODROW

•••D••O
ARTDECO
BANDITO
CARDOZO
CORDERO
HOLDSTO
LEADSTO
SKIDDOO
TENDSTO
VERDUGO

••••DO•
ABANDON
ADDEDON
AHEADOF
ALBEDOS
BIRDDOG
BOREDOM
BRANDON
BUILDON
BULLDOG
CELADON
CORNDOG
CZARDOM
DINEDON
DOSIDOS
DOTEDON
DUKEDOM
EARLDOM
ECUADOR
EGGEDON
ESCUDOS
FIEFDOM
FIREDOG
FREEDOM
GLUEDON
HAIRDOS
HANGDOG
HEARDOF
HUMIDOR
JANEDOE
JOHNDOE
KINGDOM
LANGDON
LIBIDOS
LIVEDON
MALODOR
MATADOR
MIKADOS
MIRADOR
MOONDOG
ONANDON
PAPADOC
PARADOX
PERIDOT
PICADOR
PILEDON
PLAYDOH
REARDON
REREDOS
ROUNDON
SERFDOM
SHAHDOM
SHELDON
SHOWDOG
SKIDDOO
SLEDDOG
SNOWDON
SPIEDON
STANDON
STARDOM
TEREDOS
TIREDOF
TRIEDON
TUXEDOS
WEIRDOS
WYANDOT

••••D•O
ADDEDTO
AIMEDTO
AMRADIO
BOUNDTO
CBRADIO
CLAUDIO
FMRADIO
SKIDDOO
SOANDSO

•••••DO
ALFREDO
AVOCADO
BRAVADO
BUSHIDO
CRUZADO
GERALDO
MAKESDO
NOCANDO
ORLANDO
PLACIDO
RICARDO
TORNADO
TORPEDO

D•P••••
DAPHNIS
DAPPING
DAPPLED
DAPPLES
DEPALMA
DEPARTS
DEPECHE
DEPENDS
DEPICTS
DEPLANE
DEPLETE
DEPLORE
DEPLOYS
DEPONED
DEPONES
DEPORTS
DEPOSAL
DEPOSED
DEPOSER
DEPOSES
DEPOSIT
DEPRAVE
DEPRESS
DEPRIVE
DEPUTED
DEPUTES
DIPLOID
DIPLOMA
DIPOLAR
DIPOLES
DIPPERS
DIPPING
DIPTYCH
DOPEOUT
DOPIEST
DOPPLER

D••P•••
DAMPENS
DAMPERS
DAMPEST
DAMPING
DAMPISH
DAPPING
DAPPLED
DAPPLES
DAUPHIN
DEEPEND
DEEPENS
DEEPEST
DEEPFAT
DEEPFRY
DEEPSEA
DEEPSET
DEEPSIX
DEMPSEY
DESPAIR
DESPISE
DESPITE
DESPOIL
DESPOTS
DIAPERS
DIMPLED
DIMPLES
DIOPTER
DIPPERS
DIPPING
DISPELS
DISPLAY
DISPORT
DISPOSE
DISPUTE
DOLPHIN
DOPPLER
DRAPERS
DRAPERY
DRAPING
DRIPDRY
DRIPPAN
DRIPPED
DROPINS
DROPLET
DROPOFF
DROPOUT
DROPPED
DROPPER
DROPSBY
DROPSIN
DRSPOCK
DUMPIER
DUMPING

D•••P••
DEADPAN
DECAPOD
DISHPAN
DOWNPAT
DRIPPAN
DRIPPED
DROOPED
DROPPED
DROPPER
DUCKPIN
DUSTPAN

D••••P•
DECAMPS
DECRYPT
DEWLAPS
DIGRAPH
DISRUPT
DOLLOPS
DUSTUPS

D•••••P
DAYCAMP
DAYTRIP
DESKTOP
DEVELOP
DEWDROP
DOINGUP
DOLLSUP
DRAWNUP
DRAWSUP
DREAMUP
DRESSUP
DRIEDUP
DRIESUP
DRIVEUP
DRUMSUP
DUDEDUP
DUMMYUP
DUSTMOP

•D•P•••
ADAPTED
ADAPTER
ADAPTOR
ADEPTLY
ADIPOSE
ADOPTED
ADOPTEE
ADOPTER
EDAPHIC

•D••P••
ADDUPTO
ADOLPHE

•D••••P
ADDEDUP

••DP•••
BEDPOST
ENDPLAY
MUDPACK
MUDPIES
OLDPROS
REDPINE
REDPOLL
TADPOLE

••D•P••
ADDUPTO
INDEPTH
LEDUPTO
OEDIPAL
OEDIPUS
REDSPOT
SODAPOP

••D••P•
KIDNAPS
MADCAPS
REDCAPS
REDTAPE
REDTOPS
RUDOLPH
UNDRAPE

••D•••P
ADDEDUP
BEDLAMP
BUDDYUP
DUDEDUP
GIDDYAP
GIDDYUP
OLDCHAP
SODAPOP

•••DP••
DEADPAN
HARDPAN
HARDPUT
HEADPIN
SEEDPOD

•••D•P•
FOLDUPS
HOLDUPS
SENDUPS
WINDUPS

•••D••P
AIRDROP
BEADSUP
BINDSUP
BUDDYUP
DEWDROP
EARDROP
FOLDSUP
GIDDYAP
GIDDYUP
GUMDROP
HANDSUP
HARDTOP
HEADSUP
HOLDSUP
LEADSUP
ROADMAP
RUNDEEP
SENDSUP
THEDEEP
TRADEUP
WINDSUP

••••DP•
GRANDPA

••••D•P
ACTEDUP
ADDEDUP
ANTEDUP
BONEDUP
BOUNDUP
BOXEDUP
BUILDUP
DRIEDUP
DUDEDUP
EASEDUP
FIREDUP
FIXEDUP
HOLEDUP
HYPEDUP
KEYEDUP
LACEDUP
LINEDUP
MIXEDUP
OWNEDUP
PILEDUP
PIPEDUP
RAKEDUP
ROUNDUP
SAVEDUP
SEWEDUP
SIZEDUP
SPEEDUP
STANDUP
STOODUP
TONEDUP
TUNEDUP
TYPEDUP
WIPEDUP
WISEDUP
WOUNDUP

D•••Q••
DUBUQUE

••••DQ•
PSANDQS

DR•••••
DRABBER
DRACHMA
DRACULA
DRAFTED
DRAFTEE
DRAGGED
DRAGNET
DRAGONS
DRAGOON
DRAGOUT
DRAGSIN
DRAGSON
DRAINED
DRAINER
DRAPERS
DRAPERY
DRAPING
DRASTIC
DRATTED
DRAUGHT
DRAWBAR
DRAWERS
DRAWING
DRAWLED
DRAWNIN
DRAWNON
DRAWNUP
DRAWOUT
DRAWSIN
DRAWSON
DRAWSUP
DRAYAGE
DRAYING
DREADED
DREAMED
DREAMER
DREAMON
DREAMUP
DREDGED
DREDGER
DREDGES
DREIDEL
DREISER
DRESDEN
DRESSED
DRESSER
DRESSES
DRESSUP
DREWOUT
DREYFUS
DRIBBLE
DRIBLET
DRIEDUP
DRIESUP
DRIFTED
DRIFTER
DRILLED
DRILLER
DRINKER
DRIPDRY
DRIPPAN
DRIPPED
DRISTAN
DRIVEAT
DRIVEIN
DRIVELS
DRIVERS
DRIVEUP
DRIVING
DRIZZLE
DRIZZLY
DROLLER
DRONERS
DRONING
DROOLED
DROOLER
DROOPED
DROPINS
DROPLET
DROPOFF
DROPOUT
DROPPED
DROPPER
DROPSBY
DROPSIN
DROUGHT
DROVERS
DROWNED
DROWSED
DROWSES
DRSEUSS
DRSPOCK
DRUBBED
DRUCKER
DRUDGED
DRUDGES
DRUGGED
DRUMLIN
DRUMMED
DRUMMER
DRUMSUP
DRYCELL
DRYDOCK
DRYEYED
DRYHOLE
DRYNESS
DRYRUNS
DRYSUIT
DRYWALL
DRYWELL

D•R••••
DARESAY
DARESTO
DARKAGE
DARKENS
DARKEST
DARKISH
DARKMAN
DARLEEN
DARLENE
DARLING
DARNERS
DARNING
DARRELL
DARTERS
DARTING
DERAILS
DERBIES
DERIDED
DERIDES
DERIVED
DERIVES
DERNIER
DERRICK
DERRING
DERVISH
DIRECTS
DIRNDLS
DIRTIED
DIRTIER
DIRTIES
DIRTILY
DORITOS
DORMANT
DORMERS
DORMICE
DOROTHY
DORSALS
DORSETT
DURABLE
DURABLY
DURANCE
DURANGO
DURANTE
DURRELL

D••R•••
DAIRIES
DARRELL
DAYROOM
DEAREST
DEARSIR
DEARTHS
DEBRIEF
DECREED
DECREES
DECRIED
DECRIES
DECRYPT
DEERFLY
DEFRAUD
DEFRAYS
DEFROCK
DEFROST
DEGRADE
DEGREES
DEPRAVE
DEPRESS
DEPRIVE
DERRICK
DERRING
DETRACT
DETRAIN
DETROIT
DEVRIES
DHURRIE
DIARIES
DIGRAPH
DIGRESS
DIORAMA
DISROBE
DISRUPT
DIURNAL
DOORDIE
DOORMAN
DOORMAT
DOORMEN
DOORWAY
DOUREST
DOWRIES
DRYRUNS
DURRELL
DWARFED
DWARVES

D•••R••
DALTREY
DAYTRIP
DEBARGE
DEBARKS
DEBORAH
DECARLO
DECORUM
DEFARGE
DEFORMS
DEHORNS
DELIRIA
DEMERIT
DEMEROL
DEMURER
DENDRON
DEPARTS
DEPORTS
DESERTS
DESERVE
DESIRED
DESIREE
DESIRES
DESTROY
DEWDROP
DEXTRIN
DHURRIE
DIAGRAM
DIDEROT
DISARMS
DISHRAG
DIVERGE
DIVERSE
DIVERTS
DIVORCE
DOGTROT
DOLORES
DUBARRY

D••••R•
DAGGERS
DAMPERS
DANCERS
DANDERS
DANGERS
DARNERS
DARTERS
DASHERS
DASTARD
DAUBERS
DAYCARE
DEALERS
DEBEERS
DEBTORS
DECLARE
DEEPFRY
DEICERS
DEKLERK
DELBERT
DELVERS
DENIERS
DENMARK
DENTURE
DEODARS
DEPLORE
DESSERT
DETOURS
DEUTERO
DEVILRY
DEVOURS
DIALERS
DIAPERS
DICKERS
DIEHARD
DIETARY
DIETERS
DIFFERS
DIGGERS
DILLARD
DIMITRI
DIMMERS
DINNERS
DIPPERS
DISBARS
DISCARD
DISCERN
DISCORD
DISPORT
DISTORT
DISTURB
DITHERS
DITHERY
DOCKERS
DOCTORS
DODDERS
DODGERS
DOEUVRE
DOGCART
DOGEARS
DOLLARS
DORMERS
DOSSERS
DOWNERS
DOWSERS
DRAPERS
DRAPERY
DRAWERS
DRIPDRY
DRIVERS
DRONERS
DROVERS
DUBARRY
DUBBERS
DUELERS
DUFFERS
DULLARD
DUNKERS
DUNKIRK
DUSTERS
DYKSTRA

D•••••R
DABBLER
DAFFIER
DAIMLER
DALLIER
DANDIER
DANGLER
DANSEUR
DAUMIER
DAWDLER
DAYSTAR
DAZZLER
DEADAIR
DEARSIR
DEBATER
DECODER
DEFILER
DELAYER
DELIVER
DEMETER
DEMURER
DEPOSER
DERNIER
DESPAIR
DIDOVER
DILUTER
DINGIER
DINKIER
DIOPTER
DIPOLAR
DIRTIER
DIVIDER
DIVINER
DIVISOR
DIZZIER
DOGSTAR
DONATOR
DONEFOR
DOODLER
DOPPLER
DOSSIER
DOTTIER
DOUBTER
DOVEBAR
DOWAGER
DOWDIER
DOWNIER
DRABBER
DRAINER
DRAWBAR
DREAMER
DREDGER
DREISER
DRESSER
DRIFTER
DRILLER
DRINKER
DROLLER
DROOLER
DROPPER
DRUCKER
DRUMMER
DUCKIER
DUMPIER
DUSKIER
DUSTIER
DWELLER

•DR••••
ADRENAL

•D•R•••
ADDRESS
ADORERS
ADORING
ADORNED
ODOROUS

•D••R••
ADHERED
ADHERES
ADJURED
ADJURES
ADMIRAL
ADMIRED
ADMIRER
ADMIRES
ADSORBS
ADVERBS
ADVERSE
ADVERTS
EDWARDS
IDCARDS

•D•••R•
ADJOURN
ADORERS
EDITORS
EDOUARD

•D••••R
ADAPTER
ADAPTOR
ADMIRER
ADOPTER
ADVISER
ADVISOR
EDASNER

••DR•••
ADDRESS
ALDRICH
ANDREAS
ANDRESS
ANDREWS
ANDROID
BEDREST
BEDROCK
BEDROLL
BEDROOM
ENDRUNS
HADRIAN
HYDRANT
HYDRATE
HYDROUS
KEDROVA
MADRONA
MIDRIBS
MIDRIFF
MIDRISE
PADRONE
PADRONI
PODRIDA
REDRAWN
REDRAWS
REDRESS
REDROSE
UNDRAPE
UNDRAWN
UNDRESS
UPDRAFT

••D•R••
ANDIRON
ANDORRA
BODEREK
DIDEROT
ELDERLY
ENDORSE
ENDURED
ENDURES
FEDERAL
FEDORAS
GODFREY
MODERNS
OLDPROS
ORDERED
ORDERER
ORDERLY
UNDERGO

••D••R•
ANDORRA
ARDMORE
ARDOURS
BADGERS
BIDDERS
CADBURY
CADGERS
CODGERS
DODDERS
DODGERS
ENDEARS
FODDERS
GODDARD
HEDGERS
INDOORS
JUDDERS
KIDDERS
LADDERS
LADLERS
LEDGERS
LODGERS
MADDERS
MADEIRA
MIDTERM
MUDDERS
NODDERS
NUDGERS
PADDERS
PEDLARS
REDBIRD
REDFIRS
REDFORD
RODGERS
RUDDERS
RUDYARD
SIDEARM
SUDBURY
TEDDERS
WIDMARK

••D•••R
ANDOVER
AUDITOR
BIDFAIR
CODDLER
DIDOVER
ENDUSER
FIDDLER
GIDDIER
INDUCER
MADEFOR
MEDDLER
MIDYEAR
MODELER
MODULAR
MUDDIER
MUDDLER

NODULAR
OLDSTER
ORDERER
PADDLER
PEDDLER
PODGIER
PUDGIER
REDDEER
REDHAIR
REDSTAR
REDUCER
RIDDLER
RUDDIER
SADDLER
SEDATER
SEDUCER
SIDEBAR
SIDECAR
SUDSIER
TODDLER
WADDLER
WIDOWER
YODELER

•••DR••

AIRDROP
BALDRIC
CALDRON
DENDRON
DEWDROP
EARDROP
EARDRUM
FREDRIC
GUMDROP
HENDRIX
HUMDRUM
HUNDRED
KINDRED
MANDREL
MANDRIL
MILDRED
MORDRED
OUTDRAW
OUTDREW
SKIDROW
TENDRIL
TUNDRAS
WINDROW
WOODROW

•••D•R•

BENDERS
BIDDERS
BINDERS
BINDERY
BIRDERS
BORDERS
BOYDORR
CALDERA
CARDERS
CINDERS
CONDORS
CORDERO
DANDERS
DEODARS
DODDERS
EVADERS
FEEDERS
FENDERS
FINDERS
FODDERS
FOLDERS
GANDERS
GENDERS
GILDERS
GIRDERS
GLIDERS
GODDARD
GRADERS
HEADERS
HERDERS
HINDERS
HOLDERS
ISADORA
JUDDERS
KIDDERS
KILDARE
LADDERS
LANDERS
LARDERS
LEADERS
LENDERS
LOADERS
MADDERS
MENDERS
MINDERS
MOLDERS
MUDDERS
MURDERS
NODDERS
ONADARE
PADDERS
PANDERS
PANDORA
PAYDIRT
POLDERS
PONDERS
POWDERS
POWDERY
PRUDERY
RAIDERS
READERS
RENDERS
RUDDERS
SANDERS
SEEDERS
SENDERS
SLIDERS
SOLDERS
SPADERS
SPIDERS
SPIDERY
SUNDERS
TEDDERS
TENDERS
TINDERS
TRADERS
VENDORS
VERDURE
WALDORF
WANDERS
WARDERS
WEEDERS
WELDERS
WENDERS
WINDERS
WONDERS
WOODARD
YARDARM
ZANDERS

•••D••R

BAWDIER
BEADIER
BLADDER
BOUDOIR
BOWDLER
BOYDORR
CANDOUR
CHEDDAR
CODDLER
COLDWAR
DANDIER
DAWDLER
DEADAIR
DOODLER
DOWDIER
DREDGER
FIDDLER
FIEDLER
GARDNER
GAUDIER
GIDDIER
GLADDER
GOODBAR
GRIDDER
HANDCAR
HANDIER
HANDLER
HARDIER
HEADIER
HURDLER
LAIDFOR
LARDNER
MEDDLER
MOLDIER
MOODIER
MUDDIER
MUDDLER
NEEDIER
OUTDOOR
PADDLER
PAIDFOR
PARDNER
PEDDLER
PLEDGER
PLODDER
PRODDER
RANDIER
READIER
REDDEER
REEDIER
RIDDLER
ROEDEER
ROWDIER
RUDDIER
SADDLER
SANDBAR
SANDIER
SEEDIER
SENDFOR
SHADIER
SHUDDER
SKIDDER
SLEDDER
SOLDIER
SUBDUER
TARDIER
TODDLER
TRUDGER
WADDLER
WEEDIER
WINDIER
WINDSOR
WOODIER
WORDIER
YESDEAR

••••DR•

BLOWDRY
BONEDRY
DRIPDRY
FOUNDRY
LAUNDRY
PALEDRY
PHAEDRA
RUNSDRY

••••D•R

ACCEDER
ASUNDER
AWARDER
BLADDER
BLANDER
BLENDER
BLINDER
BLONDER
BLUNDER
BOARDER
BOULDER
BOUNDER
BRAIDER
BRANDER
BREEDER
BROADER
BROODER
BUILDER
CHEDDAR
CHOWDER
CLOWDER
DECODER
DIVIDER
ECUADOR
EMENDER
ENCODER
EVANDER
FIELDER
FOUNDER
GLADDER
GOUNDER
GRANDER
GRIDDER
GRINDER
GUILDER
HOARDER
HUMIDOR
INSIDER
INVADER
JOINDER
KNEADER
LAUNDER
LEANDER
MALODOR
MATADOR
MAUNDER
MEANDER
MIRADOR
MOULDER
ONORDER
PICADOR
PLEADER
PLODDER
PLUNDER
POUNDER
PRODDER
PROUDER
RAPIDER
REORDER
ROUNDER
SCOLDER
SECEDER
SHUDDER
SKIDDER
SLANDER
SLEDDER
SLENDER
SMOLDER
SOLIDER
SOUNDER
SPEEDER
SPENDER
STAIDER
STRIDER
THUNDER
TIMIDER
TIREDER
TOORDER
TREADER
VIVIDER
WEIRDER

D•S••••

DASBOOT
DASHERS
DASHIKI
DASHING
DASHOFF
DASTARD
DESALTS
DESCANT
DESCEND
DESCENT
DESERTS
DESERVE
DESIGNS
DESIRED
DESIREE
DESIRES
DESISTS
DESKSET
DESKTOP
DESMOND
DESOTOS
DESPAIR
DESPISE
DESPITE
DESPOIL
DESPOTS
DESSERT
DESTINE
DESTINY
DESTROY
DISABLE
DISARMS
DISAVOW
DISBAND
DISBARS
DISCARD
DISCERN
DISCOED
DISCORD
DISCUSS
DISDAIN
DISEASE
DISGUST
DISHING
DISHOUT
DISHPAN
DISHRAG
DISJOIN
DISLIKE
DISMAYS
DISMISS
DISOBEY
DISOWNS
DISPELS
DISPLAY
DISPORT
DISPOSE
DISPUTE
DISROBE
DISRUPT
DISSECT
DISSENT
DISTAFF
DISTANT
DISTEND
DISTILL
DISTORT
DISTURB
DISUSED
DOSAGES
DOSIDOS
DOSSALS
DOSSERS
DOSSIER
DRSEUSS
DRSPOCK
DUSKIER
DUSTERS
DUSTIER
DUSTING
DUSTMOP
DUSTOFF
DUSTPAN
DUSTUPS

D••S•••

DAISIES
DAMSELS
DAMSONS
DANSEUR
DAYSINN
DAYSTAR
DENSELY
DENSEST
DENSITY
DESSERT
DIESELS
DIESOFF
DIESOUT
DIGSOUT
DISSECT
DISSENT
DOESKIN
DOGSHOW
DOGSLED
DOGSTAR
DORSALS
DORSETT
DOSSALS
DOSSERS
DOSSIER
DOUSING
DOWSERS
DOWSING
DRASTIC
DRESDEN
DRESSED
DRESSER
DRESSES
DRESSUP
DRISTAN
DRYSUIT
DYKSTRA

D•••S••

DAMASKS
DARESAY
DARESTO
DATASET
DEADSEA
DEADSET
DEALSIN
DEARSIR
DEBASED
DEBASES
DEBUSSY
DEEPSEA
DEEPSET
DEEPSIX
DEFUSED
DEFUSES
DEHISCE
DELISTS
DEMESNE
DEMISED
DEMISES
DEMPSEY
DEPOSAL
DEPOSED
DEPOSER
DEPOSES
DEPOSIT
DESISTS
DESKSET
DETESTS
DEVISED
DEVISES
DIGESTS
DINESEN
DINESIN
DINESON
DISUSED
DIVESIN
DIVESTS
DIVISOR
DODGSON
DOLLSUP
DOTESON
DRAGSIN
DRAGSON
DRAWSIN
DRAWSON
DRAWSUP
DREISER
DRESSED
DRESSER
DRESSES
DRESSUP
DRIESUP
DROPSBY
DROPSIN
DROWSED
DROWSES
DRUMSUP
DYNASTS
DYNASTY

D••••S•

DADAISM
DADAIST
DAFTEST
DAMPEST
DAMPISH
DANKEST
DARKEST
DARKISH
DEAFEST
DEAREST
DEBUSSY
DECLASS
DEEPEST
DEFENSE
DEFROST
DEFTEST
DEGAUSS
DELUISE
DENSEST
DENTIST
DEPRESS
DERVISH
DESPISE
DICIEST
DIFFUSE
DIGRESS
DIMMEST
DIMNESS
DIOCESE
DISCUSS
DISEASE
DISGUST
DISMISS
DISPOSE
DIVERSE
DOGFISH
DOLTISH
DONJOSE
DOPIEST
DOUREST
DRSEUSS
DRYNESS
DUCHESS
DUELIST
DULLEST
DULLISH
DUMBEST

D•••••S

DABBLES
DACTYLS
DADDIES
DAGGERS
DAHLIAS
DAILIES
DAIRIES
DAISIES
DAKOTAS
DALLIES
DAMAGES
DAMASKS
DAMPENS
DAMPERS
DAMSELS
DAMSONS
DANCERS
DANDERS
DANDIES
DANDLES
DANGERS
DANGLES
DANIELS
DAPHNIS
DAPPLES
DARKENS
DARNERS
DARTERS
DASHERS
DAUBERS
DAWDLES
DAWKINS
DAYBEDS
DAZZLES
DEACONS
DEADENS
DEAFENS
DEALERS
DEARTHS
DEBARKS
DEBASES
DEBATES
DEBEERS
DEBONES
DEBTORS
DEBUNKS
DECADES
DECAMPS
DECANTS
DECEITS
DECIDES
DECKLES
DECLASS
DECOCTS
DECODES
DECREES
DECRIES
DEDALUS
DEDUCES
DEDUCTS
DEEJAYS
DEEPENS
DEFACES
DEFAMES
DEFEATS
DEFECTS
DEFENDS
DEFILES
DEFINES
DEFORMS
DEFRAYS
DEFUSES
DEGAUSS
DEGREES
DEHORNS
DEICERS
DEIFIES
DEITIES
DEJECTS
DELETES
DELIBES
DELICTS
DELISTS
DELUDES
DELUGES
DELVERS
DEMANDS
DEMEANS
DEMISES
DEMOTES
DENIALS
DENIERS
DENOTES
DENUDES
DEODARS
DEPARTS
DEPENDS
DEPICTS
DEPLOYS
DEPONES
DEPORTS
DEPOSES
DEPRESS
DEPUTES
DERAILS
DERBIES
DERIDES
DERIVES
DESALTS
DESERTS
DESIGNS
DESIRES
DESISTS
DESOTOS
DESPOTS
DETAILS
DETAINS
DETECTS
DETESTS
DETOURS
DEVEINS
DEVICES
DEVIOUS
DEVISES
DEVOTES
DEVOURS
DEVRIES
DEWLAPS
DIADEMS
DIALERS
DIALOGS
DIAPERS
DIARIES
DIATOMS
DIBBLES
DICKENS
DICKERS
DICKEYS
DICKIES
DICTUMS
DIDACTS
DIDDLES
DIESELS
DIETERS
DIFFERS
DIGESTS
DIGGERS
DIGRESS
DIKDIKS
DIKTATS
DILATES
DILLIES
DILUTES
DIMMERS
DIMNESS
DIMOUTS
DIMPLES
DIMWITS
DINGLES
DINGOES
DINKIES
DINNERS
DIPOLES
DIPPERS
DIRECTS
DIRNDLS
DIRTIES
DISARMS
DISBARS
DISCUSS
DISMAYS
DISMISS
DISOWNS
DISPELS
DITCHES
DITHERS
DITTIES
DIVERTS
DIVESTS
DIVIDES
DIVINES
DIVVIES
DIZZIES
DOBBINS
DOCENTS
DOCKERS
DOCKETS
DOCTORS
DODDERS
DODGERS
DOGDAYS
DOGEARS
DOGGIES
DOGLEGS
DOGTAGS
DOILIES
DOLLARS
DOLLIES
DOLLOPS
DOLMANS
DOLMENS
DOLORES
DOMAINS
DOMINOS
DONATES
DONJONS
DONKEYS
DOODADS
DOODLES
DOOZIES
DORITOS
DORMERS
DORSALS
DOSAGES
DOSIDOS
DOSSALS
DOSSERS
DOTTLES
DOUBLES
DOUGLAS
DOWNERS
DOWRIES
DOWSERS
DRAGONS
DRAPERS
DRAWERS
DREDGES
DRESSES
DREYFUS
DRIVELS
DRIVERS
DRONERS
DROPINS
DROVERS
DROWSES
DRSEUSS
DRUDGES
DRYNESS
DRYRUNS
DUBBERS
DUBIOUS
DUCHESS
DUCHIES
DUDDIES
DUELERS
DUENNAS
DUFFELS
DUFFERS
DUGONGS
DUGOUTS
DUKAKIS
DUMDUMS
DUMMIES
DUNKERS
DUNLINS
DUSTERS
DUSTUPS
DUTEOUS
DWARVES
DYBBUKS
DYNAMOS
DYNASTS

•DS••••

ADSORBS

•D•S•••

EDASNER
ODYSSEY

•D••S••

ADAMSON
ADDISON
ADJUSTS
ADVISED
ADVISER
ADVISES
ADVISOR
EDGESIN
ODYSSEY

•D•••S•

ADDRESS
ADIPOSE
ADVERSE
EDGIEST
ODDNESS

•D••••S

ADAGIOS
ADDENDS
ADDRESS
ADDUCES
ADDUCTS
ADHERES
ADJOINS
ADJURES
ADJUSTS
ADMIRES
ADMIXES
ADONAIS
ADORERS
ADSORBS
ADVENTS
ADVERBS
ADVERTS
ADVISES
EDGINGS
EDIBLES
EDIFIES
EDITORS
EDWARDS
IDCARDS
IDEATES
ODDJOBS
ODDLOTS
ODDNESS
ODOROUS
PDJAMES

••DS•••

ANDSOON
BEDSIDE
GADSDEN
GODSEND
GODSONS
KIDSKIN
MIDSIZE
NODSOFF
OLDSTER
REDSKIN
REDSPOT
REDSTAR
SADSACK
SUDSIER
SUDSING

••D•S••

ADDISON
DODGSON
ECDYSES
ECDYSIS
ENDUSER
FADESIN
MADISON
MEDUSAE
MEDUSAS
MODESTO
MODESTY
MODISTE
NUDISTS
WADESIN

••D••S•

ADDRESS
ANDRESS
BADNESS
BEDPOST
BEDREST
CODFISH
DADAISM
DADAIST
ENDLESS
ENDMOST
ENDORSE
ENDWISE
FADDISH
FADDISM
FADDIST
GODDESS
JUDAISM
JUDOIST
KADDISH
LIDLESS
MADDEST
MADNESS
MIDEAST
MIDRISE
MIDWEST
ODDNESS
OLDNESS
OLDWEST
REDDEST
REDDISH
REDNESS
REDRESS
REDROSE
SADDEST
SADNESS
TIDIEST
UNDRESS
YIDDISH

••D•••S

ABDUCTS
ADDENDS
ADDRESS
ADDUCES

ADDUCTS
AEDILES
ANDEANS
ANDREAS
ANDRESS
ANDREWS
ARDOURS
ARDUOUS
BADDIES
BADEGGS
BADGERS
BADGUYS
BADNESS
BEDAUBS
BEDBUGS
BEDECKS
BIDDERS
BIDDIES
BODEGAS
BODICES
BODKINS
BUDDHAS
BUDDIES
BUDGETS
BUDGIES
CADDIES
CADGERS
CODDLES
CODGERS
CODICES
CUDDLES
CUDGELS
DADDIES
DEDALUS
DEDUCES
DEDUCTS
DIDACTS
DIDDLES
DODDERS
DODGERS
DUDDIES
ECDYSES
ECDYSIS
ENDEARS
ENDINGS
ENDIVES
ENDLESS
ENDRUNS
ENDURES
ENDWAYS
FADEINS
FEDORAS
FIDDLES
FIDGETS
FODDERS
FUDDLES
GADGETS
GIDEONS
GODDESS
GODSONS
GODWITS
HEDDLES
HEDGERS
HIDEOUS
HUDDLES
HYDROUS
INDENTS
INDEXES
INDIANS
INDICES
INDICTS
INDIGOS
INDITES
INDOORS
INDUCES
INDUCTS
IODATES
IODIDES
IODIZES
JUDDERS
KIDDERS
KIDDIES
KIDNAPS
KIDNEYS
KODIAKS
LADDERS
LADDIES
LADINOS
LADLERS
LEDGERS
LIDLESS
LODGERS
MADCAPS
MADDENS
MADDERS
MADLIBS
MADNESS
MEDDLES
MEDIANS
MEDICOS
MEDIUMS
MEDLEYS
MEDUSAS
MIDDAYS
MIDDENS
MIDDIES
MIDDLES
MIDGETS
MIDRIBS
MIDWAYS
MODELAS
MODELTS
MODERNS
MODULES
MUDDERS
MUDDIES
MUDDLES
MUDEELS
MUDHENS
MUDPIES
NODDERS
NODULES
NUDGERS
NUDISTS
NUDNIKS
ODDJOBS
ODDLOTS
ODDNESS
OEDIPUS
OGDOADS
OLDDAYS
OLDNESS
OLDNEWS
OLDPROS
ORDAINS
ORDEALS
PADDERS
PADDIES
PADDLES
PEDANTS
PEDDLES
PEDLARS
PIDGINS
PODIUMS
PUDDLES
RADAMES
RADDLES
RADIALS
RADIANS
RADICES
REDACTS
REDANTS
REDATES
REDBUDS
REDCAPS
REDDENS
REDDOGS
REDEALS
REDEEMS
REDEYES
REDFINS
REDFIRS
REDGUMS
REDHATS
REDHOTS
REDIALS
REDNESS
REDOAKS
REDRAWS
REDRESS
REDTOPS
REDUCES
RIDDLES
RODENTS
RODGERS
RUDDERS
SADDENS
SADDLES
SADNESS
SEDUCES
SIDINGS
STDENIS
TEDDERS
TEDDIES
TEDIOUS
TIDBITS
TIDINGS
TODDIES
TODDLES
UNDRESS
UPDATES
WADDLES
WEDGIES
WIDGETS
ZODIACS

•••DS••

BANDSAW
BEADSUP
BINDSUP
DEADSEA
DEADSET
FEEDSON
FOLDSUP
GOODSON
HANDSAW
HANDSET
HANDSIN
HANDSON
HANDSUP
HARDSET
HEADSET
HEADSIN
HEADSUP
HOLDSON
HOLDSTO
HOLDSUP
LANDSAT
LEADSIN
LEADSON
LEADSTO
LEADSUP
LINDSAY
LINDSEY
MINDSET
READSIN
SENDSIN
SENDSUP
TENDSTO
WINDSOR
WINDSUP

•••D•S•

ARIDEST
BALDEST
BOLDEST
COLDEST
CRUDEST
FADDISH
FADDISM
FADDIST
FONDEST
GEODESY
GODDESS
HARDEST
KADDISH
KINDEST
KURDISH
LEWDEST
LOUDEST
MADDEST
MILDEST
OXIDASE
PRUDISH
REDDEST
REDDISH
SADDEST
SAWDUST
SNIDEST
SWEDISH
WILDEST
YIDDISH

•••D••S

AIRDAMS
AMADEUS
ANADEMS
AOUDADS
BADDIES
BANDIES
BANDITS
BEADLES
BELDAMS
BENDERS
BIDDERS
BIDDIES
BINDERS
BIRDERS
BIRDIES
BOODLES
BORDERS
BRIDALS
BRIDGES
BRIDLES
BUDDHAS
BUDDIES
BUNDLES
BURDENS
CADDIES
CANDIDS
CANDIES
CANDLES
CARDERS
CINDERS
CODDLES
COEDITS
CONDORS
CORDONS
CRADLES
CREDITS
CUDDLES
CURDLES
DADDIES
DANDERS
DANDIES
DANDLES
DAWDLES
DEADENS
DEODARS
DIADEMS
DIDDLES
DIKDIKS
DODDERS
DOGDAYS
DOODADS
DOODLES
DREDGES
DRUDGES
DUDDIES
DUMDUMS
EVADERS
FEEDERS
FENDERS
FIDDLES
FINDERS
FLEDGES
FODDERS
FOLDERS
FOLDUPS
FONDLES
FONDUES
FRIDAYS
FRIDGES
FUDDLES
GANDERS
GARDENS
GAUDENS
GENDERS
GILDERS
GIRDERS
GIRDLES
GLIDERS
GODDESS
GOODBYS
GOODIES
GRADERS
GRUDGES
GUIDONS
GUNDOGS
HANDLES
HARDENS
HEADERS
HEDDLES
HERDERS
HEYDAYS
HINDERS
HOLDERS
HOLDUPS
HOODOOS
HOTDOGS
HOWDAHS
HOYDENS
HUDDLES
HURDLES
JUDDERS
KIDDERS
KIDDIES
KINDLES
KLUDGES
LADDERS
LADDIES
LANDAUS
LANDERS
LAPDOGS
LARDERS
LARDONS
LEADERS
LEADINS
LENDERS
LINDENS
LINDIES
LOADERS
MADDENS
MADDERS
MAIDENS
MANDANS
MANDAYS
MAYDAYS
MEADOWS
MEDDLES
MENDERS
MIDDAYS
MIDDENS
MIDDIES
MIDDLES
MILDEWS
MINDERS
MISDOES
MOLDERS
MONDAYS
MUDDERS
MUDDIES
MUDDLES
MURDERS
NEEDLES
NODDERS
NOODLES
NORDICS
OLDDAYS
OUTDOES
PADDERS
PADDIES
PADDLES
PANDERS
PANDITS
PARDONS
PAYDAYS
PEDDLES
PHIDIAS
PLEDGES
POLDERS
PONDERS
POODLES
POWDERS
PUDDLES
PUNDITS
PURDAHS
PYEDOGS
RADDLES
RAIDERS
READERS
READIES
REDDENS
REDDOGS
REEDITS
RENDERS
RIDDLES
ROADIES
RONDELS
ROWDIES
RUDDERS
SADDENS
SADDLES
SANDALS
SANDERS
SEADOGS
SEEDERS
SEIDELS
SENDERS
SENDUPS
SHADOWS
SLEDGES
SLIDERS
SLUDGES
SMUDGES
SOLDERS
SPADERS
SPIDERS
STUDIES
STUDIOS
SUBDEBS
SUBDUES
SUNDAES
SUNDAYS
SUNDERS
SUNDEWS
SUNDOGS
TANDEMS
TEDDERS
TEDDIES
TENDERS
TENDONS
TIEDYES
TINDERS
TOADIES
TODDIES
TODDLES
TOPDOGS
TOYDOGS
TRADERS
TRUDGES
TUNDRAS
VANDALS
VENDORS
WADDLES
WANDERS
WARDENS
WARDERS
WEEDERS
WELDERS
WENDERS
WHYDAHS
WINDERS
WINDOWS
WINDUPS
WONDERS
WOODIES
ZANDERS

••••DS•

SOANDSO

••••D•S

ABRADES
ACCEDES
AGENDAS
ALBEDOS
ALLUDES
APSIDES
ARCADES
ARMADAS
AUBADES
BESIDES
BETIDES
BLONDES
BOLIDES
CICADAS
CZARDAS
DECADES
DECIDES
DECODES
DELUDES
DENUDES
DERIDES
DIRNDLS
DIVIDES
DOSIDOS
ENCODES
ESCUDOS
FACADES
GELADAS
GOURDES
HAIRDOS
IMPEDES
INCUDES
INSIDES
INVADES
IODIDES
LAMBDAS
LIBIDOS
LOURDES
MIKADOS
NAIADES
ONEIDAS
PAGODAS
PARADES
POMADES
POSADAS
PSANDQS
PYXIDES
RAMADAS
RECEDES
RECODES
REMUDAS
REREDOS
RESIDES
SECEDES
STRIDES
TEREDOS
TIRADES
TRIODES
TUXEDOS
UNLADES
WEIRDOS

•••••DS

ABOUNDS
ACARIDS
ACCORDS
ADDENDS
AFFORDS
ALMONDS
AOUDADS
APPENDS
ASCENDS
ATTENDS
AUGENDS
BALLADS
BEHOLDS
BRIARDS
BYROADS
BYWORDS
CALENDS
CANARDS
CANDIDS
COWARDS
CUSPIDS
DAYBEDS
DEFENDS
DEMANDS
DEPENDS
DOODADS
EDWARDS
ELAPIDS
ENFOLDS
ENGIRDS
ENNEADS
ERRANDS
EXCEEDS
EXPANDS
EXPENDS
EXTENDS
EYELIDS
FAGENDS
FLYRODS
FORBIDS
FRIENDS
GERUNDS
GROUNDS
HAZARDS
HEPTADS
HERALDS
HOTBEDS
HOTRODS
HOWARDS
HYBRIDS
IDCARDS
IMPENDS
INNARDS
INROADS
INTENDS
INWARDS
ISLANDS
ISOPODS
KEYPADS
KOBOLDS
LEGENDS
LIQUIDS
LIZARDS
MAENADS
MALTEDS
MARAUDS
METHODS
MILORDS
MYRIADS
NEREIDS
NIMRODS
OBTUNDS
OFFENDS
OGDOADS
ONWARDS
ORCHIDS
OSMONDS
OUTBIDS
OXFORDS
PEAPODS
PENTADS
PERIODS
PETARDS
PONGIDS
PREMEDS
RAMRODS
REBINDS
RECORDS
REDBUDS
REFUNDS
REGARDS
RELOADS
REMANDS
REMENDS
REMINDS
REMOLDS
REREADS
RESANDS
RESEEDS
RESENDS
RETARDS
REWARDS
REWELDS
REWINDS
REWORDS
RIBANDS
ROBARDS
ROLAIDS
SCREEDS
SEABEDS
SECONDS
SHIELDS
SHROUDS
SPREADS
STRANDS
SUNGODS
TABARDS
TAGENDS
TETRADS
THREADS
TIERODS
TOROIDS
TOWARDS
TRIPODS
UNBENDS
UNBINDS
UNFOLDS
UNGIRDS
UNHANDS
UNIPODS
UNLOADS
UNWINDS
UPHOLDS
UPLANDS
UPLOADS
UPWARDS
VESPIDS
WANTADS
WARGODS
WIZARDS

D•T••••

DATASET
DATEDLY
DETAILS
DETAINS
DETECTS
DETENTE
DETESTS
DETOURS
DETRACT
DETRAIN
DETROIT
DITCHED
DITCHES
DITHERS
DITHERY
DITTANY
DITTIES
DITTOED
DOTEDON
DOTESON
DOTTIER
DOTTING
DOTTLES
DUTEOUS
DUTIFUL

D••T•••

DACTYLS
DAFTEST
DALTREY
DARTERS
DARTING
DASTARD
DAYTIME
DAYTONA
DAYTRIP
DEBTORS
DEFTEST
DEITIES
DELTAIC
DELTOID
DENTATE
DENTINE
DENTING
DENTIST
DENTURE
DESTINE
DESTINY
DESTROY
DEUTERO
DEXTRIN
DIATOMS
DICTATE
DICTION
DICTUMS
DIETARY
DIETERS
DIETING
DIKTATS
DIPTYCH
DIRTIED
DIRTIER
DIRTIES
DIRTILY
DISTAFF
DISTANT
DISTEND
DISTILL
DISTORT
DISTURB
DITTANY
DITTIES
DITTOED
DOCTORS
DOGTAGS
DOGTROT
DOLTISH
DOTTIER
DOTTING
DOTTLES
DRATTED
DUCTILE
DUCTING
DUSTERS
DUSTIER
DUSTING
DUSTMOP
DUSTOFF
DUSTPAN
DUSTUPS

D•••T••

DAKOTAN
DAKOTAS
DAUNTED
DAYSTAR
DEALTIN
DEARTHS
DEBATED
DEBATER
DEBATES
DEBITED
DEBUTED
DELETED
DELETES
DEMETER
DEMOTED
DEMOTES
DENOTED
DENOTES
DEPUTED
DEPUTES
DESKTOP
DESOTOS
DEVOTED
DEVOTEE
DEVOTES
DIGITAL
DILATED
DILATES
DILUTED
DILUTER
DILUTES
DIMITRI
DINETTE
DIOPTER
DOGSTAR
DONATED
DONATES
DONATOR
DORITOS
DOROTHY
DOUBTED
DOUBTER
DRAFTED
DRAFTEE
DRASTIC
DRATTED
DRIFTED
DRIFTER
DRISTAN
DYKSTRA

D••••T•

DARESTO
DECANTS
DECEITS
DECOCTS
DEDUCTS
DEFACTO
DEFEATS
DEFECTS
DEFLATE
DEJECTS
DELICTI
DELICTS
DELISTS
DENSITY
DENTATE
DEPARTS
DEPICTS
DEPLETE
DEPORTS
DESALTS
DESERTS
DESISTS
DESPITE
DESPOTS
DETECTS
DETENTE
DETESTS
DEVIATE
DICTATE
DIDACTS
DIGESTS
DIGNITY
DIKTATS
DIMOUTS
DIMWITS
DINETTE
DIRECTS
DISPUTE
DIVERTS
DIVESTS
DOCENTS
DOCKETS
DOGMATA
DORSETT
DOUGHTY
DOZENTH
DUALITY
DUBIETY
DUEDATE
DUGOUTS
DURANTE
DYNASTS
DYNASTY

D•••••T

DADAIST
DAFTEST
DAMPEST
DANKEST
DARKEST
DASBOOT
DATASET
DEADSET
DEAFEST
DEALOUT
DEAREST
DECKOUT
DECRYPT
DEEPEST
DEEPFAT
DEEPSET
DEFAULT
DEFIANT
DEFICIT
DEFLECT
DEFROST
DEFTEST
DEFUNCT
DELBERT
DELIGHT
DELIMIT
DEMERIT
DENSEST
DENTIST
DEPOSIT
DESCANT
DESCENT
DESKSET
DESSERT
DETRACT
DETROIT
DEVIANT
DIALECT
DICIEST
DIDEROT
DIEDOUT
DIESOUT

DIGSOUT
DIMMEST
DINGBAT
DINMONT
DISGUST
DISHOUT
DISPORT
DISRUPT
DISSECT
DISSENT
DISTANT
DISTORT
DOGCART
DOGTROT
DOLEOUT
DOORMAT
DOPEOUT
DOPIEST
DORMANT
DORSETT
DOUBLET
DOUREST
DOVECOT
DOWNPAT
DRAGNET
DRAGOUT
DRAUGHT
DRAWOUT
DREWOUT
DRIBLET
DRIVEAT
DROPLET
DROPOUT
DROUGHT
DRYSUIT
DUELIST
DULLEST
DUMBEST

•D•T•••
EDITING
EDITION
EDITORS

•D••T••
ADAPTED
ADAPTER
ADAPTOR
ADEPTLY
ADOPTED
ADOPTEE
ADOPTER
IDEATED
IDEATES
IDENTIC
IDIOTIC

•D•••T•
ADAMITE
ADDEDTO
ADDONTO
ADDUCTS
ADDUPTO
ADJUSTS
ADULATE
ADVENTS
ADVERTS
EDACITY
EDUCATE
ODDLOTS

•D••••T
ADAMANT
ADJUNCT
EDGEOUT
EDGIEST
ODDMENT

••DT•••
BEDTIME
GODTHAB
MIDTERM
MIDTOWN
OLDTIME
REDTAPE
REDTOPS

••D•T••
AUDITED
AUDITOR
CADETTE
GODUTCH
INDITED
INDITES
INDUTCH
IODATES
OLDSTER
REDATED
REDATES
REDSTAR
SEDATER
UNDATED
UPDATED
UPDATES

••D••T•
ABDUCTS
ADDEDTO
ADDONTO
ADDUCTS
ADDUPTO
ALDENTE
ANDANTE
BUDGETS
CADETTE
DEDUCTS
DIDACTS
FIDGETS
FIDGETY
GADGETS
GADGETY
GODWITS
HYDRATE
INDENTS
INDEPTH
INDICTS
INDUCTS
JADEITE
LEDUPTO
MEDIATE
MIDGETS
MODELTS
MODESTO
MODESTY
MODISTE
NUDISTS
ODDLOTS
PEDANTS
RADIATE
REDACTS
REDANTS
REDHATS
REDHOTS
RODENTS
TIDBITS
VEDANTA
WIDGETS

••D•••T
BEDPOST
BEDREST
BODYFAT
DADAIST
DIDEROT
ENDMOST
FADDIST
FADEOUT
HIDEOUT
HYDRANT
INDOUBT
JUDOIST
MADDEST
MADEOUT
MEDIANT
MIDEAST
MIDWEST
NODOUBT
ODDMENT
OLDWEST
RADIANT
REDCENT
REDCOAT
REDDEST
REDEALT
REDHEAT
REDMEAT
REDOUBT
REDSPOT
RIDEOUT
RODEOUT
SADDEST
SIDEBET
TIDIEST
UPDRAFT

•••DT••
HARDTOP
ICEDTEA

•••D•T•
ACIDITY
AIRDATE
ARIDITY
AVIDITY
BANDITO
BANDITS
COEDITS
CORDATE
CORDITE
CREDITS
CRUDITY
DUEDATE
ERUDITE
HOLDSTO
LEADSTO
MANDATE
MISDATE
OFFDUTY
ONADATE
PANDITS
PREDATE
PUNDITS
RAWDATA
REEDITS
SEADUTY
TENDSTO

•••D••T
ACEDOUT
ARIDEST
BALDEST
BOLDEST
BRIDGET
COLDCUT
COLDEST
CONDUCT
CONDUIT
CRUDEST
DEADSET
DIEDOUT
EKEDOUT
EVIDENT
FADDIST
FEEDLOT
FINDOUT
FOLDOUT
FONDANT
FONDEST
HANDOUT
HANDSET
HARDEST
HARDHAT
HARDHIT
HARDPUT
HARDSET
HEADOUT
HEADSET
HELDOUT
HOLDOUT
KINDEST
LAIDOUT
LANDSAT
LEADOUT
LEWDEST
LOUDEST
MADDEST
MILDEST
MINDSET
MORDANT
MORDENT
ONADIET
OXIDANT
PAIDOUT
PANDECT
PAYDIRT
PENDANT
PENDENT
PREDICT
PRODUCT
PRUDENT
READMIT
READOUT
REDDEST
SADDEST
SANDLOT
SAWDUST
SENDOUT
SNIDEST
SOLDOUT
STUDENT
TRIDENT
VERDANT
VERDICT
VIADUCT
WEEDOUT
WILDCAT
WILDEST
WOODCUT
WOODLOT

••••DT•
ADDEDTO
AIMEDTO
BOUNDTO
BREADTH

••••D•T
AIMEDAT
COULDNT
PAWEDAT
PERIDOT
PLAUDIT
POKEDAT
WOULDNT
WYANDOT

•••••DT
SCHMIDT

DU•••••
DUALITY
DUBARRY
DUBBERS
DUBBING
DUBIETY
DUBIOUS
DUBUQUE
DUCHESS
DUCHIES
DUCKIER
DUCKING
DUCKPIN
DUCTILE
DUCTING
DUDDIES
DUDEDUP
DUDGEON
DUEDATE
DUELERS
DUELING
DUELIST
DUENNAS
DUFFELS
DUFFERS
DUGONGS
DUGOUTS
DUKAKIS
DUKEDOM
DULLARD
DULLEST
DULLING
DULLISH
DUMBEST
DUMDUMS
DUMMIED
DUMMIES
DUMMYUP
DUMPIER
DUMPING
DUNAWAY
DUNGEON
DUNKERS
DUNKING
DUNKIRK
DUNLINS
DUNNING
DUODENA
DURABLE
DURABLY
DURANCE
DURANGO
DURANTE
DURRELL
DUSKIER
DUSTERS
DUSTIER
DUSTING
DUSTMOP
DUSTOFF
DUSTPAN
DUSTUPS
DUTEOUS
DUTIFUL

D•U••••
DAUBERS
DAUBING
DAUMIER
DAUNTED
DAUPHIN
DEUTERO
DHURRIE
DIURNAL
DOUBLED
DOUBLES
DOUBLET
DOUBLEU
DOUBTED
DOUBTER
DOUGHTY
DOUGLAS
DOUREST
DOUSING
DRUBBED
DRUCKER
DRUDGED
DRUDGES
DRUGGED
DRUMLIN
DRUMMED
DRUMMER
DRUMSUP

D••U•••
DEBUNKS
DEBUSSY
DEBUTED
DEDUCED
DEDUCES
DEDUCTS
DEFUNCT
DEFUSED
DEFUSES
DELUDED
DELUDES
DELUGED
DELUGES
DELUISE
DEMURER
DENUDED
DENUDES
DEPUTED
DEPUTES
DILUTED
DILUTER
DILUTES
DISUSED
DIVULGE
DOEUVRE
DRAUGHT
DROUGHT
DUBUQUE

D•••U••
DEBAUCH
DEBOUCH
DEFAULT
DEGAUSS
DENEUVE
DENTURE
DETOURS
DEVOURS
DICTUMS
DIFFUSE
DIMBULB
DIMOUTS
DISCUSS
DISGUST
DISPUTE
DISRUPT
DISTURB
DONJUAN
DRACULA
DRSEUSS
DRYRUNS
DRYSUIT
DUGOUTS
DUMDUMS
DUSTUPS
DYBBUKS

D••••U•
DANSEUR
DEALOUT
DECKOUT
DECORUM
DEDALUS
DEFRAUD
DEVALUE
DEVIOUS
DIEDOUT
DIESOUT
DIGSOUT
DISHOUT
DOINGUP
DOLEFUL
DOLEOUT
DOLLSUP
DONAHUE
DOPEOUT
DRAGOUT
DRAWNUP
DRAWOUT
DRAWSUP
DREAMUP
DRESSUP
DREWOUT
DREYFUS
DRIEDUP
DRIESUP
DRIVEUP
DROPOUT
DRUMSUP
DUBIOUS
DUBUQUE
DUDEDUP
DUMMYUP
DUTEOUS
DUTIFUL

D•••••U
DOUBLEU

•DU••••
ADULATE
EDUCATE
EDUCING

•D•U•••
ADDUCED
ADDUCES
ADDUCTS
ADDUPTO
ADJUDGE
ADJUNCT
ADJURED
ADJURES
ADJUSTS
EDOUARD

•D••U••
ADJOURN

•D•••U•
ADDEDUP
EDGEOUT
ODOROUS

••DU•••
ABDUCTS
ADDUCED
ADDUCES
ADDUCTS
ADDUPTO
ARDUOUS
AUDUBON
CADUCEI
DEDUCED
DEDUCES
DEDUCTS
ENDUING
ENDURED
ENDURES
ENDUSER
GODUNOV
GODUTCH
INDUCED
INDUCER
INDUCES
INDUCTS
INDULGE
INDUTCH
LEDUPTO
MEDULLA
MEDUSAE
MEDUSAS
MODULAR
MODULES
NODULAR
NODULES
OLDUVAI
PADUCAH
REDUCED
REDUCER
REDUCES
SEDUCED
SEDUCER
SEDUCES

••D•U••
ARDOURS
BADGUYS
BEDAUBS
BEDBUGS
BEDOUIN
CADBURY
ENDRUNS
INDOUBT
MEDIUMS
NODOUBT
PODIUMS
REDBUDS
REDGUMS
REDOUBT
REDOUND
SUDBURY

••D••U•
ADDEDUP
ARDUOUS
BUDDYUP
CADMIUM
DEDALUS
DUDEDUP
FADEOUT
GIDDYUP
HIDEOUS
HIDEOUT
HYDROUS
LADYBUG
MADEOUT
MODICUM
OEDIPUS
RIDEOUT
RODEOUT
TEDIOUS

•••DU••
CONDUCE
CONDUCT
CONDUIT
DUMDUMS
FOLDUPS
FONDUES
GRADUAL
HOLDUPS
MACDUFF
OFFDUTY
PRODUCE
PRODUCT
SAWDUST
SEADUTY
SENDUPS
SUBDUED
SUBDUER
SUBDUES
TRADUCE
VERDUGO
VERDURE
VIADUCT
WINDUPS

•••D•U•
ACEDOUT
AMADEUS
BEADSUP
BINDSUP
BUDDYUP
CANDOUR
COLDCUT
DIEDOUT
EARDRUM
EKEDOUT
FINDOUT
FOLDOUT
FOLDSUP
GIDDYUP
GOLDBUG
HANDFUL
HANDGUN
HANDOUT
HANDSUP
HARDPUT
HEADOUT
HEADSUP
HEEDFUL
HELDOUT
HOLDOUT
HOLDSUP
HOODLUM
HUMDRUM
IRIDIUM
LAIDOUT
LANDAUS
LEADOUT
LEADSUP
MINDFUL
NEEDFUL
PAIDOUT
READOUT
RHODIUM
SENDOUT
SENDSUP
SOLDOUT
STADIUM
TRADEUP
WEEDOUT
WINDSUP
WOODCUT

•••D••U
RONDEAU
TRUDEAU

••••DU•
ACTEDUP
ADDEDUP
ANTEDUP
BONEDUP
BOUNDUP
BOXEDUP
BUILDUP
COMEDUE
DRIEDUP
DUDEDUP
EASEDUP
FIREDUP
FIXEDUP
HOLEDUP
HYPEDUP
KEYEDUP
LACEDUP
LINEDUP
MIXEDUP
OVERDUB
OVERDUE
OWNEDUP
PASTDUE
PILEDUP
PIPEDUP
RAKEDUP
RESIDUE
ROUNDUP
SAVEDUP
SEWEDUP
SIZEDUP
SPEEDUP
STANDUP
STOODUP
TONEDUP
TUNEDUP
TYPEDUP
WIPEDUP
WISEDUP
WOUNDUP

D•V••••
DAVINCI
DEVALUE
DEVEINS
DEVELOP
DEVIANT
DEVIATE
DEVICES
DEVILED
DEVILLE
DEVILRY
DEVIOUS
DEVISED
DEVISES
DEVOLVE
DEVOTED
DEVOTEE
DEVOTES
DEVOURS
DEVRIES
DIVERGE
DIVERSE
DIVERTS
DIVESIN
DIVESTS
DIVIDED
DIVIDER
DIVIDES
DIVINED
DIVINER
DIVINES
DIVISOR
DIVORCE
DIVULGE
DIVVIED
DIVVIES
DOVEBAR
DOVECOT

D••V•••
DELVERS
DELVING
DERVISH
DIVVIED
DIVVIES
DRIVEAT
DRIVEIN
DRIVELS
DRIVERS
DRIVEUP
DRIVING
DROVERS

D•••V••
DEKOVEN
DELIVER
DERIVED
DERIVES
DIDOVER
DISAVOW
DOEUVRE
DONOVAN
DWARVES

D••••V•
DECEIVE
DENEUVE
DEPRAVE
DEPRIVE
DESERVE
DEVOLVE

•DV••••
ADVANCE
ADVENTS
ADVERBS
ADVERSE
ADVERTS
ADVISED
ADVISER
ADVISES
ADVISOR

••D•V••
ANDOVER
BEDEVIL
DIDOVER
ENDIVES
MEDEVAC
OLDUVAI

••D••V•
KEDROVA

••D•••V
GODUNOV

•••D•V•
SKYDIVE

DW•••••
DWARFED
DWARVES
DWEEZIL
DWELLED
DWELLER
DWINDLE

D•W••••
DAWDLED
DAWDLER
DAWDLES
DAWKINS
DAWNING
DEWCLAW
DEWDROP
DEWILDE
DEWLAPS
DEWLINE
DOWAGER
DOWDIER
DOWDILY
DOWNBOW
DOWNERS
DOWNIER
DOWNING
DOWNPAT
DOWRIES
DOWSERS
DOWSING

D••W•••
DAGWOOD
DIMWITS
DOGWOOD
DRAWBAR
DRAWERS
DRAWING
DRAWLED
DRAWNIN
DRAWNON
DRAWNUP
DRAWOUT
DRAWSIN
DRAWSON
DRAWSUP
DREWOUT
DROWNED
DROWSED
DROWSES
DRYWALL
DRYWELL

D•••W••
DISOWNS
DOORWAY
DUNAWAY

D••••W•
DIEDOWN

D•••••W
DANELAW
DEWCLAW
DISAVOW
DOGCHEW
DOGCHOW
DOGSHOW
DOWNBOW

•DW••••
EDWARDS

••DW•••
ENDWAYS
ENDWISE
GODWITS
INDWELL
MIDWAYS
MIDWEEK
MIDWEST
MIDWIFE
OLDWEST
REDWINE
REDWING
REDWOLF
REDWOOD

••D•W••
BEDEWED
ENDOWED
MADEWAY
RIDGWAY
WIDOWED
WIDOWER

••D••W•
ANDREWS
BEDDOWN
MIDTOWN
OLDNEWS
REDRAWN
REDRAWS
UNDRAWN

•••DW••
BALDWIN
COLDWAR
FOODWEB
GOLDWYN
GOODWIN
HARDWON
HEADWAY
ROADWAY

•••D•W•
BEDDOWN
BOGDOWN
CUTDOWN
DIEDOWN
GETDOWN
GOTDOWN
HOEDOWN

LAYDOWN
LETDOWN
LIEDOWN
LOWDOWN
MEADOWS
MEADOWY
MILDEWS
MILDEWY
MOWDOWN
PINDOWN
PREDAWN
PUTDOWN
RUBDOWN
RUNDOWN
SATDOWN
SETDOWN
SHADOWS
SHADOWY
SITDOWN
SUNDEWS
SUNDOWN
TIEDOWN
WINDOWS

•••D••W

BANDSAW
HANDSAW
LAIDLOW
OUTDRAW
OUTDREW
SKIDROW
WINDROW
WOODROW

••••D•W

JACKDAW

D•X••••

DEXTRIN

D••X•••

DIOXIDE

D•••••X

DEEPSIX

•D••X••

ADMIXED
ADMIXES

••D•X••

INDEXED
INDEXES

••D•••X

MADAMEX

•••D••X

BANDBOX
HENDRIX
SANDBOX

••••D•X

BROADAX
PARADOX
ROLODEX
SPANDEX

DY•••••

DYBBUKS
DYKSTRA
DYNAMIC
DYNAMOS
DYNASTS
DYNASTY

D•Y••••

DAYBEDS
DAYBOOK
DAYCAMP
DAYCARE
DAYLILY
DAYLONG
DAYROOM
DAYSINN
DAYSTAR
DAYTIME
DAYTONA
DAYTRIP
DOYENNE
DRYCELL
DRYDOCK
DRYEYED
DRYHOLE
DRYNESS
DRYRUNS
DRYSUIT
DRYWALL
DRYWELL

D••Y•••

DEFYING
DENYING
DRAYAGE
DRAYING
DREYFUS

D•••Y••

DACTYLS
DECAYED
DECOYED
DECRYPT
DELAYED
DELAYER
DIPTYCH
DRYEYED
DUMMYUP

D••••Y•

DEADEYE
DEEJAYS
DEFRAYS
DEPLOYS
DICKEYS
DISMAYS
DOGDAYS
DONKEYS

D•••••Y

DAFFILY
DAHOMEY
DALTREY
DARESAY
DATEDLY
DAYLILY
DAZEDLY
DEBAKEY
DEBUSSY
DEEPFRY
DEERFLY
DELANEY
DEMPSEY
DENNEHY
DENSELY
DENSITY
DESTINY
DESTROY
DEVILRY
DIDDLEY
DIETARY
DIGNIFY
DIGNITY
DINGILY
DIRTILY
DISOBEY
DISPLAY
DITHERY
DITTANY
DIZZILY
DOORWAY
DOROTHY
DOUGHTY
DOWDILY
DRAPERY
DRIPDRY
DRIZZLY
DROPSBY
DUALITY
DUBARRY
DUBIETY
DUNAWAY
DURABLY
DYNASTY

•DY••••

IDYLLIC
ODYSSEY

•D•Y•••

EDDYING

•D••••Y

ADEPTLY
EDACITY
IDEALLY
ODYSSEY

••DY•••

ANDYKIM
BODYFAT
ECDYSES
ECDYSIS
EDDYING
LADYBUG
LADYDAY
MIDYEAR
RUDYARD
TIDYING
UNDYING

••D•Y••

BUDDYUP
GIDDYAP
GIDDYUP
REDEYES

••D••Y•

BADGUYS
ENDWAYS
KIDNEYS
MEDLEYS
MIDDAYS
MIDWAYS
OLDDAYS

••D•••Y

ARDENCY
AUDIBLY
CADBURY
DIDDLEY
ELDERLY
ENDPLAY
FIDGETY
GADGETY
GIDDILY
GODFREY
JADEDLY
LADYDAY
MADEHAY
MADEWAY
MODESTY
OLDFOGY
ORDERLY
RIDGWAY
SUDBURY

•••DY••

ANODYNE
BUDDYUP
GIDDYAP
GIDDYUP
TIEDYED
TIEDYES
VANDYCK
VANDYKE

•••D•Y•

DEADEYE
DOGDAYS
FRIDAYS
GLADEYE
GOLDWYN
GOODBYE
GOODBYS
HEYDAYS
MANDAYS
MAYDAYS
MIDDAYS
MONDAYS
OLDDAYS
PAYDAYS
SUNDAYS

•••D••Y

ABIDEBY
ACADEMY
ACIDIFY
ACIDITY
ARIDITY
AVIDITY
BAWDILY
BINDERY
BRADLEY
CRUDELY
CRUDITY
DIDDLEY
DOWDILY
GAUDILY
GEODESY
GIDDILY
HANDILY
HARDILY
HEADILY
HEADWAY
LINDSAY
LINDSEY
MEADOWY
MILDEWY
MOODILY
NEEDILY
OFFDUTY
POWDERY
PRODIGY
PRUDERY
READILY
ROADWAY
ROWDILY
SANDFLY
SEADUTY
SEEDILY
SHADILY
SHADOWY
SNIDELY
SPIDERY
TARDILY
WORDILY

••••DY•

HAIRDYE

••••D•Y

ACRIDLY
BLANDLY
BLINDLY
BLOWDRY
BONEDRY
BROADLY
BYANDBY
DATEDLY
DAZEDLY
DRIPDRY
FARADAY
FETIDLY
FIXEDLY
FLAGDAY
FLUIDLY
FOUNDRY
GRANDLY
HOLIDAY
HUMIDLY
JADEDLY
LADYDAY
LAUNDRY
LIVIDLY
LUCIDLY
LURIDLY
NAKEDLY
NAMEDAY
NEWSDAY
NOONDAY
PALEDRY
PROUDLY
RAPIDLY
RIGIDLY
ROUNDLY
RUNSDRY
SAMEDAY
SNOWDAY
SOLIDLY
SOMEDAY
SOUNDLY
SPINDLY
STAIDLY
STANDBY
STOODBY
TEPIDLY
THIRDLY
TIMIDLY
TIREDLY
TUESDAY
UNGODLY
VALIDLY
VAPIDLY
VEXEDLY
VIVIDLY
WEEKDAY
WEIRDLY
WORKDAY
WORLDLY

•••••DY

ALREADY
ANYBODY
CASSIDY
CUSTODY
KENNEDY
ORGANDY
ORMANDY
PEABODY
PERFIDY
PROSODY
RAGGEDY
SUBSIDY
THREADY
TRAGEDY
UNHANDY
UNREADY
WCHANDY

D•Z••••

DAZEDLY
DAZZLED
DAZZLER
DAZZLES
DIZZIED
DIZZIER
DIZZIES
DIZZILY
DOZENTH
DOZEOFF

D••Z•••

DAZZLED
DAZZLER
DAZZLES
DIZZIED
DIZZIER
DIZZIES
DIZZILY
DOOZIES
DRIZZLE
DRIZZLY

D•••Z••

DENIZEN
DRIZZLE
DRIZZLY
DWEEZIL

•D•••Z•

IDOLIZE

••DZ•••

ENDZONE

••D•Z••

BEDIZEN
IODIZED
IODIZES

••D••Z•

CADENZA
MIDSIZE

•••D•Z•

ANODIZE
CARDOZO
INADAZE
MENDOZA
OXIDIZE

EA•••••

EAGERER
EAGERLY
EAGLETS
EAGLING
EARACHE
EARDROP
EARDRUM
EARFLAP
EARFULS
EARHART
EARLDOM
EARLIER
EARLOBE
EARLOCK
EARLYON
EARMARK
EARMUFF
EARNERS
EARNEST
EARNING
EARPLUG
EARRING
EARSHOT
EARTHEN
EARTHLY
EARWIGS
EASEDIN
EASEDUP
EASEOFF
EASESIN
EASESUP
EASIEST
EASTEND
EASTERN
EASTERS
EASTMAN
EATABLE
EATAWAY
EATCROW
EATENAT
EATENUP
EATSOUT

E•A••••

EDACITY
EDAPHIC
EDASNER
EGALITE
ELAPIDS
ELAPSED
ELAPSES
ELASTIC
ELATERS
ELATING
ELATION
EMANATE
EMANUEL
ENABLED
ENABLES
ENACTED
ENACTOR
ENAMELS
ENAMORS
ENAMOUR
EPARCHS
EPAULET
ERASERS
ERASING
ERASMUS
ERASURE
ETAGERE
ETAMINE
EVACUEE
EVADERS
EVADING
EVANDER
EVANGEL
EVASION
EVASIVE
EXACTED
EXACTER
EXACTLY
EXACTOR
EXALTED
EXAMINE
EXAMPLE

E••A•••

EARACHE
EATABLE
EATAWAY
ECLAIRS
ECUADOR
EDWARDS
EFFACED
EFFACES
ELEANOR
EMBANKS
EMBARGO
EMBARKS
EMBASSY
EMPANEL
EMPATHY
ENCAGED
ENCAGES
ENCAMPS
ENCASED
ENCASES
ENGAGED
ENGAGES
ENGARDE
ENHANCE
ENLACED
ENLACES
ENLARGE
ENMASSE
ENRAGED
ENRAGES
ENTAILS
EQUABLE
EQUABLY
EQUALED
EQUALLY
EQUATED
EQUATES
EQUATOR
ERRANDS
ERRATIC
ERRATUM
ESCAPED
ESCAPEE
ESCAPES
ESCARPS
ESPANOL
ESSAYED
ESTATES
ETHANOL
EURASIA
EXHALED
EXHALES
EXHAUST
EXPANDS
EXPANSE
EXPARTE

E•••A••

EARHART
EARMARK
ECKHART
ECSTASY
EDOUARD
EDUCATE
EGGCASE
ELEGANT
ELEVATE
ELKHART
EMANATE
EMBRACE
EMERALD
EMIRATE
EMULATE
ENCHAIN
ENCHANT
ENCLAVE
ENDEARS
ENDGAME
ENDWAYS
ENGLAND
ENGRAFT
ENGRAMS
ENGRAVE
ENNEADS
ENPLANE
ENSLAVE
ENSNARE
ENSNARL
ENTRAIN
ENTRANT
ENTRAPS
ENWRAPS
ESPIALS
ESTRADA
ESTRAYS
ESTUARY
EXCLAIM
EXPIATE
EXPLAIN
EXTRACT
EYEBALL
EYEBANK
EYELASH
EYEWASH

E••••A•

EARFLAP
EASTMAN
EATAWAY
EATENAT
EGGHEAD
ELEGIAC
ELYSIAN
ENDPLAY
ENIGMAS
ENTREAT
EPIGRAM
ESCHEAT
ESPOSAS
ESTIVAL
ETERNAL
ETESIAN
ETHICAL
ETONIAN
EXURBAN

E•••••A

ECHIDNA
ELECTRA
ELEKTRA
EMERITA
EMPORIA
ENCOMIA
ERITREA
EROTICA
ESTONIA
ESTRADA
ETRURIA
EURASIA
EXOTICA
EXURBIA

•EA••••

BEACHED
BEACHES
BEACONS
BEADIER
BEADING
BEADLES
BEADSUP
BEAGLES
BEAKERS
BEAMIER
BEAMING
BEAMSUP
BEANBAG
BEANERY
BEANIES
BEANING
BEARCAT
BEARDED
BEARERS
BEARHUG
BEARING
BEARISH
BEAROFF
BEAROUT
BEARPAW
BEARSON
BEARSUP
BEASTIE
BEASTLY
BEATERS
BEATIFY
BEATING
BEATLES
BEATNIK
BEATOUT
BEATRIX
BEATSIT
BEATSUP
BEATTIE
BEAVERS
CEASING
DEACONS
DEADAIR
DEADEND
DEADENS
DEADEYE
DEADPAN
DEADSEA
DEADSET
DEAFENS
DEAFEST
DEALERS
DEALING
DEALOUT
DEALSIN
DEALTIN
DEAREST
DEARSIR
DEARTHS
FEARERS
FEARFUL
FEARING
FEASTED
FEATHER
FEATURE
GEARBOX
GEARING
GEARSTO
GEARSUP
HEADERS
HEADIER
HEADILY
HEADING
HEADMAN
HEADMEN
HEADOFF
HEADOUT
HEADPIN
HEADSET
HEADSIN
HEADSUP
HEADWAY
HEALALL
HEALERS
HEALING
HEALTHY
HEAPING
HEARDOF
HEARERS
HEARING
HEARKEN
HEAROUT
HEARSAY
HEARSOF
HEARTEN
HEARTHS
HEATERS
HEATHEN
HEATHER
HEATING
HEATSUP
HEATTER
HEAVEHO
HEAVENS
HEAVERS
HEAVETO
HEAVIER
HEAVIES
HEAVILY
HEAVING
JEALOUS
JEANARP
JEANLUC
JEANNIE
LEACHED
LEACHES
LEACOCK
LEADERS
LEADING
LEADINS
LEADOFF
LEADOUT
LEADSIN
LEADSON
LEADSTO
LEADSUP
LEAFIER
LEAFING
LEAFLET
LEAGUER
LEAGUES
LEAKAGE
LEAKERS
LEAKIER
LEAKING
LEANDER
LEANERS
LEANEST
LEANING
LEANSON
LEANTOS
LEAPERS
LEAPING
LEARJET
LEARNED
LEARNER
LEASERS
LEASHED
LEASHES
LEASING
LEATHER
LEAVENS
LEAVING
MEADOWS
MEADOWY
MEALIER
MEALIES
MEANDER
MEANEST
MEANIES
MEANING
MEASLES
MEASURE
MEATIER
NEAREST
NEARING
NEARYOU
NEATENS
NEATEST
PEABEAN
PEABODY
PEACHED
PEACHES
PEACOAT
PEACOCK
PEAFOWL
PEAHENS
PEAKING
PEALING
PEANUTS
PEAPODS
PEARLED
PEARSON
PEASANT
PEASOUP
PEATBOG
PEAVEYS
REACHED
REACHES
REACTED
REACTOR
REACTTO
READERS
READIED
READIER
READIES
READILY
READING
READMIT
READOUT
READSIN
REAFFIX
REAGENT
REAIRED
REALISM
REALIST
REALITY
REALIZE
REALTOR
REAMASS
REAMERS
REAMING
REAPERS
REAPING
REARDON
REAREND
REARERS
REARGUE
REARING
REARMED
REARSUP
REASONS
REAVAIL
SEABAGS
SEABASS
SEABEDS
SEABEES
SEABIRD
SEABORG
SEACOWS
SEADOGS
SEADUTY
SEAFANS
SEAFOOD
SEAGATE
SEAGIRT
SEAGRAM
SEAGULL
SEALABS
SEALANE
SEALANT
SEALEGS
SEALERS
SEALILY
SEALING
SEALION
SEALOFF
SEALSUP
SEAMIER
SEAMING
SEAMOSS
SEANCES
SEAPORT
SEARING
SEASALT
SEASICK
SEASIDE
SEASLUG
SEASONS
SEASTAR
SEATERS
SEATING
SEATTLE
SEAWALL
SEAWARD
SEAWAYS
SEAWEED
TEABAGS
TEABALL
TEACAKE
TEACART
TEACHER
TEACHES
TEACHIN
TEACUPS

TEALEAF
TEAMING
TEAMSUP
TEAPOTS
TEAPOYS
TEARFUL
TEARGAS
TEARIER
TEARILY
TEARING
TEAROFF
TEAROOM
TEAROSE
TEARSAT
TEARSUP
TEASELS
TEASERS
TEASETS
TEASHOP
TEASING
TEATIME
TEATRAY
WEAKENS
WEAKEST
WEAKISH
WEALTHY
WEANING
WEAPONS
WEARERS
WEARIED
WEARIER
WEARIES
WEARILY
WEARING
WEAROFF
WEAROUT
WEASELS
WEATHER
WEAVERS
WEAVING
YEAREND
YEARNED
YEARNER
YEARNTO
YEATEAM
ZEALAND
ZEALOTS
ZEALOUS

•E•A•••
AERATED
AERATES
AERATOR
BECALMS
BECAUSE
BEDAUBS
BEFALLS
BEHAVED
BEHAVES
BELABOR
BELAKUN
BELATED
BELAYED
BENATAR
BENAZIR
BERATED
BERATES
BETAKEN
BETAKES
BETAMAX
BETARAY
BEWAILS
CELADON
CERAMIC
CEZANNE
DEBACLE
DEBAKEY
DEBARGE
DEBARKS
DEBASED
DEBASES
DEBATED
DEBATER
DEBATES
DEBAUCH
DECADES
DECAGON
DECALOG
DECAMPS
DECANTS
DECAPOD
DECARLO
DECAYED
DEDALUS
DEFACED
DEFACES
DEFACTO
DEFAMED
DEFAMES
DEFARGE
DEFAULT
DEGAUSS
DELANEY
DELAYED
DELAYER
DEMANDS
DEPALMA
DEPARTS
DERAILS
DESALTS
DETAILS
DETAINS
DEVALUE
FEMALES
GELADAS
GELATIN
GELATIS
GERAINT
GERALDO
GETAWAY
HEPARIN
HEPATIC
HERALDS
HEXAGON
KERATIN
LEBANON
LEBARON
LECARRE
LEGALLY
LEGATEE
LEGATES
LEGATOS
LEHAVRE
LEPANTO
MEDALED
MELANGE
MELANIE
MELANIN
MENACED
MENACES
MENAGES
METATES
NEGATED
NEGATES
NEGATOR
NEPALIS
NEVADAN
NEWAGER
PEDALED
PEDANTS
PEGASUS
PELAGES
PELAGIC
PENALTY
PENANCE
PENATES
PETALED
PETARDS
REBASTE
REBATED
REBATES
RECALLS
RECANED
RECANES
RECANTS
RECASTS
REDACTS
REDANTS
REDATED
REDATES
REFACED
REFACES
REGAINS
REGALED
REGALES
REGALIA
REGALLY
REGARDS
REGATTA
REHANGS
RELACED
RELACES
RELAPSE
RELATED
RELATES
RELAXED
RELAXES
RELAYED
REMAILS
REMAINS
REMAKES
REMANDS
REMARKS
REMARRY
RENAILS
RENAMED
RENAMES
RENAULT
REPAINT
REPAIRS
REPAPER
REPASTE
REPASTS
REPAVED
REPAVES
RERAISE
RERATED
RERATES
RESALES
RESALTS
RESANDS
RETAILS
RETAINS
RETAKEN
RETAKES
RETAPED
RETAPES
RETARDS
RETAXED
RETAXES
REVALUE
REVAMPS
REWARDS
REWARMS
REWAXED
REWAXES
SECANTS
SEDALIA
SEDATER
SENATES
SENATOR
SERAPES
SERAPHS
SERAPIS
SESAMES
TELAVIV
TENABLE
TENABLY
TENACES
TENANCY
TENANTS
TERAPHS
TETANUS
VEDANTA
VERANDA
ZENANAS

•E••A••
AERIALS
BEDLAMP
BEEBALM
BEEFALO
BEGGARS
BELDAME
BELDAMS
BELFAST
BELLAMY
BELTANE
BEMOANS
BENEATH
BENGALI
BENGALS
BEREAVE
BERNARD
BETHANY
BETRAYS
CELLARS
CEMBALO
CENTAUR
CENTAVO
CEREALS
CERTAIN
DEADAIR
DECLAIM
DECLARE
DECLASS
DEEJAYS
DEFEATS
DEFIANT
DEFLATE
DEFRAUD
DEFRAYS
DEGRADE
DELTAIC
DEMEANS
DENIALS
DENMARK
DENTATE
DEODARS
DEPLANE
DEPRAVE
DESCANT
DESPAIR
DETRACT
DETRAIN
DEVIANT
DEVIATE
DEWLAPS
FERRARI
FERRARO
FERRATE
GEEGAWS
GENNARO
GERMANE
GERMANS
GERMANY
GESTALT
GESTATE
GETBACK
GEWGAWS
HEALALL
HEBRAIC
HECTARE
HEEHAWS
HENBANE
HENNAED
HEPCATS
HEPTADS
HERBAGE
HERBALS
HERMANN
HETMANS
HEYDAYS
JEANARP
JETWASH
KENDALL
KENYANS
KEYCARD
KEYPADS
LEAKAGE
LEEWARD
LENFANT
LEONARD
LEOPARD
LEOTARD
LESPAUL
MEDIANS
MEDIANT
MEDIATE
MENIALS
MERMAID
MESCALS
MESSAGE
MESSALA
METHANE
NECTARS
NEONATE
NESCAFE
NEWGATE
NEWHART
NEWMATH
NEWWAVE
PEASANT
PECCANT
PECCARY
PEDLARS
PEERAGE
PELTATE
PENDANT
PENNAME
PENNANT
PENNATE
PENPALS
PENTADS
PEONAGE
PEPPARD
PEPTALK
PERCALE
PERHAPS
PERTAIN
PERVADE
PETNAME
REAMASS
REAVAIL
RECHALK
RECLAIM
RECLAME
REDCAPS
REDEALS
REDEALT
REDHAIR
REDHATS
REDIALS
REDOAKS
REDRAWN
REDRAWS
REDTAPE
REENACT
REFRACT
REFRAIN
REFRAME
REGNANT
REGRADE
REHEALS
REHEARD
REHEARS
REHEATS
RELEARN
RELEASE
RELIANT
RELOADS
REMNANT
RENTALS
REPEALS
REPEATS
REPLACE
REPLANS
REPLANT
REPLATE
REPLAYS
REREADS
RESCALE
RESEALS
RESEATS
RESTAGE
RESTAIN
RESTAMP
RESTART
RESTATE
RETEACH
RETRACE
RETRACK
RETRACT
RETRADE
RETRAIN
REVEALS
REWEAVE
REWRAPS
REXCATS
REYNARD
SEABAGS
SEABASS
SEAFANS
SEAGATE
SEALABS
SEALANE
SEALANT
SEASALT
SEAWALL
SEAWARD
SEAWAYS
SEESAWS
SELVAGE
SENSATE
SERIALS
SERIATE
SERRATE
SERVALS
SERVANT
SETBACK
SETSAIL
SEXTANS
SEXTANT
TEABAGS
TEABALL
TEACAKE
TEACART
TEDMACK
TEENAGE
TELLALL
TERNARY
TERNATE
TERRACE
TERRAIN
TETRADS
VEEJAYS
VERBALS
VERDANT
WELFARE
WELLAND
WENTAPE
WETBARS
WETLAND
YESMAAM
ZEALAND
ZERMATT

•E•••A•
AEOLIAN
AEROBAT
BEANBAG
BEARCAT
BEARPAW
BEECHAM
BEESWAX
BELGIAN
BELLJAR
BELLMAN
BELTWAY
BENATAR
BENTHAM
BERGMAN
BESMEAR
BESPEAK
BESTIAL
BESTMAN
BETAMAX
BETARAY
CENTRAL
DEADPAN
DEBORAH
DECIMAL
DEEPFAT
DELILAH
DEPOSAL
DEWCLAW
FEDERAL
FEDORAS
FEEDBAG
FELDMAN
FEMORAL
FEYNMAN
GEISHAS
GELADAS
GENERAL
GENTIAN
GETAWAY
HEADMAN
HEADWAY
HEARSAY
HEELTAP
HEGIRAS
HELICAL
HELIPAD
HELLCAT
HELLMAN
HESHVAN
HESSIAN
JEERSAT
JERBOAS
JETBOAT
KEEPSAT
KEESHAN
KEROUAC
KETCHAM
LEERSAT
LEXICAL
MEDEVAC
MEDICAL
MEDUSAE
MEDUSAS
MEGRYAN
MENORAH
MESSIAH
MEXICAN
NEBULAE
NEBULAR
NEBULAS
NEUTRAL
NEVADAN
NEWDEAL
NEWSDAY
NEWSMAN
NEWYEAR
OEDIPAL
PEABEAN
PEACOAT
PECKSAT
PEEKSAT
PEERSAT
PELICAN
PELOTAS
PEMICAN
PERLMAN
PERSIAN
PERUSAL
PESETAS
REBEKAH
RECITAL
RECLEAN
REDCOAT
REDFLAG
REDHEAD
REDHEAT
REDMEAT
REDSTAR
REFUSAL
REGULAR
REMORAS
REMOVAL
REMUDAS
RENEWAL
REPOMAN
RETINAE
RETINAL
RETINAS
RETREAD
RETREAT
RETRIAL
REVIVAL
SEAGRAM
SEASTAR
SECULAR
SEMINAL
SEMINAR
SENECAS
SENEGAL
SENORAS
SENSUAL
SERBIAN
SEVERAL
TEALEAF
TEARGAS
TEARSAT
TEATRAY
TEHERAN
TELERAN
TELSTAR
TEMPLAR
TERTIAL
TESTBAN
TEXTUAL
VEGETAL
VENTRAL
VETERAN
WEEKDAY
WENTBAD
YEATEAM
YELLSAT
YEREVAN
YESDEAR
YESMAAM
ZENANAS
ZEUGMAS

•E••••A
BEDELIA
BEGONIA
BEGORRA
BELINDA
BERETTA
BERMUDA
CECILIA
CEDILLA
CELESTA
CEREBRA
DEADSEA
DEEPSEA
DELIRIA
DEPALMA
FELICIA
FELUCCA
GEORGIA
HERBTEA
JESSICA
KEDROVA
KENOSHA
LEMPIRA
LEONORA
LETITIA
MEDULLA
MELINDA
MELISSA
MENDOZA
MESSALA
MESSINA
PERGOLA
PERSONA
PETUNIA
REBECCA
REGALIA
REGATTA
REPLICA
RETSINA
SEDALIA
SEGOVIA
SEQUOIA
SESTINA
TEMPERA
TEMPURA
TEQUILA
TESSERA
VEDANTA
VENTURA
VERANDA
VERBENA
YESHIVA
ZENOBIA

••EA•••
AHEADOF
AREARUG
AREAWAY
AYEAYES
BLEAKER
BLEAKLY
BLEARED
BLEATED
BREADED
BREADTH
BREAKER
BREAKIN
BREAKUP
BREASTS
BREATHE
BREATHS
BREATHY
CHEAPEN
CHEAPER
CHEAPIE
CHEAPLY
CHEATED
CHEATER
CLEANED
CLEANER
CLEANLY
CLEANSE
CLEANUP
CLEARED
CLEARER
CLEARLY
CLEARUP
CLEAVED
CLEAVER
CLEAVES
CLEAVON
CREAKED
CREAMED
CREAMER
CREASED
CREASES
CREATED
CREATES
CREATOR
DREADED
DREAMED
DREAMER
DREAMON
DREAMUP
ELEANOR
FLEABAG
FREAKED
GLEAMED
GLEANED
GLEANER
GLEASON
GREASED
GREASER
GREASES
GREATER
GREATLY
GREAVES
ICEAGES
ICEAXES
IDEALLY
IDEATED
IDEATES
KNEADED
KNEADER
LIEABED
OCEANIA
OCEANIC
OCEANID
OCEANUS
OLEATES
PLEADED
PLEADER
PLEASED
PLEASER
PLEASES
PLEATED
PREACHY
PREAMPS
SHEARED
SHEARER
SHEATHE
SHEATHS
SHEAVED
SHEAVES
SMEARED
SNEAKED
SNEAKER
SNEAKIN
SPEAKER
SPEAKOF
SPEAKUP
SPEARED
STEALTH
STEAMED
STEAMER
SWEARAT
SWEARBY
SWEARER
SWEARIN
SWEARTO
SWEATED
SWEATER
THEATER
THEATRE
TREACLE
TREACLY
TREADED
TREADER
TREADLE
TREASON
TREATED
TWEAKED
UNEARTH
USEABLE
WHEATON
WREAKED
WREATHE
WREATHS

••E•A••
ABELARD
ABENAKI
ACETATE
AGESAGO
AVERAGE
BEEBALM
BEEFALO
CAESARS
COEVALS
CRETANS
CUEBALL
CUECARD
DEEJAYS
DIEHARD
DIETARY
DUEDATE
ELEGANT
ELEVATE
EMERALD
EYEBALL
EYEBANK
EYELASH
EYEWASH
GEEGAWS
GOESAPE
GRENADA
GRENADE
GUEVARA
HAEMATO
HEEHAWS
HOECAKE
ICEBAGS
ICECAPS
ICELAND
ICEPACK
IKEBANA
INEXACT
IRELAND
ITERANT
ITERATE
LEEWARD
MAENADS
OPENAIR
OPERAND
OPERATE
OREGANO
OVERACT
OVERAGE
OVERALL
OVERATE
OVERAWE
PEERAGE
PIEBALD
PIEPANS
PLENARY
PRECAST
PREDATE
PREDAWN
PREFABS
PREFACE
PRELATE
PREPAID
PREPARE
PREPAYS
PRESAGE
PRESALE
PRETAPE
PREVAIL
PREWASH
REENACT
SEESAWS
SHEBANG
SHEPARD
SMETANA
STEWARD
STEWART
TEENAGE
THEBABE
THERAPY
TIERACK
TIETACK
TOECAPS
TOENAIL
TOETAPS
TRENARY
TREPANS
VEEJAYS

••E••A•
AGENDAS
AREAWAY
AREOLAE
AREOLAR
AREOLAS
BEECHAM
BEESWAX
BOERWAR
BRENDAN
BRENNAN
CHEDDAR
CHEETAH
CHEMLAB
COEQUAL
CREWMAN
DEEPFAT
DUENNAS
ELEGIAC
ETERNAL
ETESIAN
FEEDBAG
FIESTAS
FLEABAG
FREEMAN
FREEWAY
FREITAG
FRENEAU
FRETSAW
GOESBAD
GRECIAN
HEELTAP
IBERIAN
ICEBOAT
JEERSAT
KEEPSAT
KEESHAN
KNEECAP
KNEEPAD
LEERSAT
ONEIDAS
OPENBAR
OVEREAT
OVERLAP
OVERLAY
OVERRAN
OVERSAW
PEEKSAT
PEERSAT
PREHEAT
PRELOAD
PRESOAK
QUETZAL
SHECRAB
SHEILAE
SHEILAH
SHEILAS

SHELLAC
SHERMAN
SHERPAS
SIENNAS
SIERRAS
SIESTAS
SNEERAT
SPECIAL
STELLAR
STERNAL
SWEARAT
THEREAT
THERMAL
TREERAT
TUESDAY
UNEQUAL
VIETNAM
WEEKDAY
WHEREAS
WHEREAT

••E•••A

ACEROLA
AMERICA
AMERIKA
CAESURA
CHELSEA
CREMONA
DEEPSEA
ELECTRA
ELEKTRA
EMERITA
FREESIA
GRENADA
GUEVARA
ICEDTEA
IKEBANA
INERTIA
OCEANIA
OLESTRA
OPENSEA
OVERSEA
PLECTRA
QUECHUA
SMETANA
SPECTRA
THERESA

•••EA••

ABREAST
ACREAGE
ALLEARS
ALREADY
ANDEANS
ANNEALS
APPEALS
APPEARS
APPEASE
ARREARS
ATHEART
ATLEAST
ATPEACE
AUREATE
BATEAUX
BENEATH
BEREAVE
BONEASH
BUREAUS
BYHEART
CAPEANN
CAVEART
CAVEATS
CEREALS
CUREALL
DEFEATS
DEMEANS
DISEASE
DOGEARS
ENDEARS
ENNEADS
FAREAST
FINEART
FIREANT
FIREARM
FOREARM
GATEAUX
IMPEACH
INPEACE
INSEAMS
KOREANS
LIMEADE
LINEAGE
LINEATE
MALEATE
MIDEAST
MILEAGE
ONLEAVE
ORDEALS
ORLEANS
OUTEATS
PAGEANT
POLEAXE
REDEALS
REDEALT
REHEALS
REHEARD
REHEARS
REHEATS
RELEARN
RELEASE
REPEALS
REPEATS
REREADS
RESEALS
RESEATS
RETEACH
REVEALS
REWEAVE
ROSEATE
SCREAKS
SCREAMS
SIDEARM
SPREADS
SQUEAKS
SQUEAKY
SQUEALS
STREAKS
STREAKY
STREAMS
TAKEAIM
THREADS
THREADY
THREATS
TINEARS
TONEARM
UNHEARD
UNLEARN
UNLEASH
UNREADY
UNSEALS
UNSEATS
UNWEAVE
UPBEATS

•••E•A•

ADRENAL
AIMEDAT
AMOEBAE
AMOEBAS
ARSENAL
ASSEGAI
AZTECAN
BASEMAN
BASEPAY
BATEMAN
BIKEWAY
BIPEDAL
BLUEJAY
BLUELAW
BODEGAS
CAMERAS
CASELAW
CATENAE
CAVEMAN
CHEETAH
CINEMAS
CINEMAX
COLEMAN
COMESAT
DANELAW
DARESAY
DONEGAL
DOVEBAR
EATENAT
FEDERAL
FIREMAN
FLIESAT
FOREMAN
FOREPAW
FORERAN
FORESAW
FREEMAN
FREEWAY
FRIEDAN
GAMELAW
GATEMAN
GATEWAY
GAVEWAY
GENERAL
GIVEWAY
HUMERAL
ILLEGAL
INGEMAR
JANEWAY
JUVENAL
KNEECAP
KNEEPAD
KUTENAI
LATERAL
LATERAN
LIBERAL
LIKEMAD
LINEMAN
LITERAL
LIVEOAK
MADEHAY
MADEWAY
MAKEHAY
MAKEPAR
MAKEWAY
MATEWAN
MEDEVAC
MINERAL
MODELAS
MULETAS
NAMEDAY
NAMETAG
NOSEBAG
NOSEGAY
NOTEPAD
NOVENAS
NUMERAL
PACECAR
PAWEDAT
PESETAS
PIKEMAN
PINESAP
PINETAR
POKEDAT
POKESAT
POLECAT
RACECAR
RACEWAY
RAREGAS
REBEKAH
RENEWAL
RICERAT
SAMEDAY
SCHEMAS
SCLERAS
SENECAS
SENEGAL
SEVERAL
SIDEBAR
SIDECAR
SIDEMAN
SNEERAT
SOLEDAD
SOMEDAY
SOMEWAY
TEHERAN
TELERAN
TIBETAN
TIMELAG
TIMEWAS
TOTEBAG
TREERAT
TUTELAR
VEGETAL
VETERAN
VINEGAR
WINEBAR
WINESAP
WIRETAP
WISEMAN
YEREVAN
ZAREBAS

•••E••A

ADDENDA
ALBERTA
ALGEBRA
ALGERIA
AMNESIA
ANAEMIA
ANTENNA
APHELIA
ARIETTA
ARMENIA
AUREOLA
BARETTA
BEDELIA
BERETTA
BIRETTA
BOHEMIA
CADENZA
CAMELIA
CAPELLA
CELESTA
CEREBRA
CORETTA
CULEBRA
DILEMMA
FREESIA
INTEGRA
LIBERIA
LORETTA
LOUELLA
MADEIRA
MAGENTA
MINEOLA
MINERVA
NIGERIA
NOVELLA
OPHELIA
OSCEOLA
PANETTA
PATELLA
PHAEDRA
POLENTA
RAVENNA
REBECCA
ROBERTA
ROSETTA
SIBERIA
SILESIA
VANESSA

••••EA•

ABOREAL
AIRHEAD
ALLHEAL
ANDREAS
ANTBEAR
ARAMEAN
AZALEAS
BAYLEAF
BESMEAR
BESPEAK
BIGDEAL
BIGHEAD
BOOLEAN
BOXSEAT
BUGBEAR
CARSEAT
CATHEAD
CHAPEAU
CHATEAU
CHILEAN
COCTEAU
CONCEAL
CONGEAL
CORNEAL
CORNEAS
COWPEAS
CRIMEAN
DRIVEAT
EGGHEAD
ENTREAT
ESCHEAT
FATHEAD
FIGLEAF
FLYLEAF
FORBEAR
FORREAL
FRENEAU
FURSEAL
GOAHEAD
GUINEAS
HIALEAH
HOTHEAD
HOTSEAT
INAHEAP
INSTEAD
JUGHEAD
LACTEAL
LAMBEAU
LIPREAD
LOWBEAM
LOWGEAR
LUNGEAT
MANYEAR
MARCEAU
MIDYEAR
MISDEAL
MISHEAR
MISLEAD
MISREAD
MRCLEAN
NEWDEAL
NEWYEAR
NOSWEAT
NOUVEAU
NUCLEAR
NUTMEAT
OAKLEAF
OATMEAL
OFFBEAT
OFFPEAK
OFFYEAR
ONATEAR
ORPHEAN
OUTWEAR
OVEREAT
PEABEAN
PHINEAS
PINHEAD
PLATEAU
PREHEAT
PROTEAN
RAMBEAU
RAWDEAL
RECLEAN
REDHEAD
REDHEAT
REDMEAT
RETREAD
RETREAT
RONDEAU
ROYBEAN
SNIPEAT
SOYBEAN
SPIREAS
STAREAT
SUBHEAD
SUNBEAM
SURREAL
SWOREAT
TABLEAU
TEALEAF
THEREAT
THOREAU
TONNEAU
TOWHEAD
TRUDEAU
UNCLEAN
UNCLEAR
VALJEAN
WATTEAU
WAXBEAN
WHEREAS
WHEREAT
YEATEAM
YESDEAR

••••E•A

ALAMEDA
CALDERA
CANDELA
CARNERA
CHIMERA
DUODENA
HYGIEIA
IPANEMA
MANDELA
NORIEGA
NOXZEMA
POMPEIA
PORSENA
RIGVEDA
RIVIERA
TAFFETA
TEMPERA
TESSERA
THERESA
VERBENA
VISCERA
WOOMERA

•••••EA

ARALSEA
AVONLEA
CHELSEA
COCHLEA
DEADSEA
DEEPSEA
ERITREA
GALATEA
HERBTEA
HIGHTEA
ICEDTEA
KARASEA
KILAUEA
OPENSEA
OVERSEA
PANACEA
ROSSSEA
SNOWPEA
SULUSEA
TRACHEA

EB•••••

EBBTIDE
EBONIES
EBONITE
EBWHITE

E•B••••

EBBTIDE
ELBOWED
EMBANKS
EMBARGO
EMBARKS
EMBASSY
EMBLEMS
EMBRACE
EMBROIL
EMBRYOS

E••B•••

EDIBLES
ENABLED
ENABLES
EYEBALL
EYEBANK
EYEBOLT
EYEBROW

E•••B••

EATABLE
ENNOBLE
ENROBED
ENROBES
ENTEBBE
EQUABLE
EQUABLY
EXHIBIT
EXURBAN
EXURBIA

E••••B•

EARLOBE
ENTEBBE

•EB••••

DEBACLE
DEBAKEY
DEBARGE
DEBARKS
DEBASED
DEBASES
DEBATED
DEBATER
DEBATES
DEBAUCH
DEBEERS
DEBITED
DEBONED
DEBONES
DEBORAH
DEBOUCH
DEBRIEF
DEBTORS
DEBUNKS
DEBUSSY
DEBUTED
FEBRILE
HEBRAIC
HEBREWS
LEBANON
LEBARON
NEBBISH
NEBULAE
NEBULAR
NEBULAS
PEBBLED
PEBBLES
REBASTE
REBATED
REBATES
REBECCA
REBEKAH
REBINDS
REBIRTH
REBLOOM
REBOILS
REBOLTS
REBOOTS
REBOUND
REBOZOS
REBUFFS
REBUILD
REBUILT
REBUKED
REBUKES
REBUSES
WEBBING
WEBFEET
WEBFOOT
WEBSITE
WEBSTER
WEBTOED
ZEBULON

•E•B•••

BEDBUGS
BEEBALM
BERBERS
CEMBALO
DELBERT
DERBIES
FEEBLER
GERBILS
GETBACK
HENBANE
HENBITS
HEPBURN
HERBAGE
HERBALS
HERBERT
HERBTEA
JEEBIES
JERBOAS
JETBOAT
KEEBLER
LEIBNIZ
MEMBERS
NEBBISH
NEWBORN
PEABEAN
PEABODY
PEBBLED
PEBBLES
REDBIRD
REDBOOK
REDBUDS
REUBENS
SEABAGS
SEABASS
SEABEDS
SEABEES
SEABIRD
SEABORG
SERBIAN
SETBACK
TEABAGS
TEABALL
TEMBLOR
TERBIUM
VERBALS
VERBENA
VERBOSE
WEBBING
WETBARS

•E••B••

AEROBAT
AEROBES
AEROBIC
BEANBAG
BELABOR
BELLBOY
BESTBOY
CELEBES
CELEBRE
CEREBRA
DECIBEL
DELIBES
FEEDBAG
GEARBOX
GEMSBOK
JEZEBEL
LEGIBLE
LEGIBLY
NEWSBOY
PEATBOG
SEEDBED
TENABLE
TENABLY
TESTBAN
WENTBAD
ZENOBIA

•E•••B•

BEDAUBS
BENUMBS
LETITBE
REDOUBT
RESORBS
REVERBS
SEALABS

•E••••B

KEYCLUB
PERTURB

••EB•••

BEEBALM
CUEBALL
EYEBALL
EYEBANK
EYEBOLT
EYEBROW
FEEBLER
ICEBAGS
ICEBERG
ICEBLUE
ICEBOAT
IKEBANA
JEEBIES
JOEBLOW
KEEBLER
NIEBUHR
PIEBALD
PREBEND
PUEBLOS
ROEBUCK
SHEBANG
THEBABE
THEBLOB
TREBLED
TREBLES

••E•B••

ACERBIC
ALEMBIC
FEEDBAG
FLEABAG
FREEBEE
FREEBIE
GOESBAD
LIEABED
OPENBAR
OVERBIG
OVERBUY
SEEDBED
SHERBET
STEUBEN
TREMBLE
TREMBLY
USEABLE

••E••B•

CHERUBS
ICECUBE
PREFABS
SWEARBY
THEBABE
THEREBY
WHEREBY

••E•••B

CHEMLAB
OVERDUB
SHECRAB
THEBLOB

•••EB••

ALGEBRA
AMOEBAE
AMOEBAS
AMOEBIC
BLUEBOY
CELEBES
CELEBRE
CEREBRA
CULEBRA
DOVEBAR
ENTEBBE
FIREBOX
FIREBUG
FREEBEE
FREEBIE
GAZEBOS
JEZEBEL
JUKEBOX
JUNEBUG
LOVEBUG
NOSEBAG
PAGEBOY
PHOEBES
PHOEBUS
RAREBIT
ROSEBUD
SHOEBOX
SIDEBAR
SIDEBET
TOTEBAG
WINEBAR
ZAREBAS

•••E•B•

ADVERBS
COMESBY
ENTEBBE
LAZENBY
MORESBY
REVERBS

•••E••B

NOSEJOB

••••EB•

ABIDEBY
BYTHEBY
COBWEBS
PLACEBO
SUBDEBS
SWOREBY
THEREBY
WHEREBY

••••E•B

POTHERB
PROVERB

•••••EB

FOODWEB

EC•••••

ECDYSES
ECDYSIS
ECHELON
ECHIDNA
ECHINUS
ECHOING
ECKHART
ECLAIRS
ECLIPSE
ECLOGUE
ECOLOGY
ECONOMY
ECSTASY
ECTYPES
ECUADOR

E•C••••

ENCAGED
ENCAGES
ENCAMPS
ENCASED
ENCASES
ENCHAIN
ENCHANT
ENCLAVE
ENCLOSE
ENCODED
ENCODER
ENCODES
ENCOMIA
ENCORES
ENCRUST
ENCRYPT
ESCAPED
ESCAPEE
ESCAPES
ESCARPS
ESCHEAT
ESCHEWS
ESCORTS
ESCROWS
ESCUDOS
ETCHERS
ETCHING
EUCHRED
EUCHRES
EXCEEDS
EXCEPTS
EXCERPT
EXCISED
EXCISES
EXCITED
EXCITES
EXCLAIM
EXCLUDE
EXCRETE
EXCUSED
EXCUSES

E••C•••

EATCROW
EDACITY
EDUCATE
EDUCING
EGGCASE
EGGCUPS
EJECTED
ELECTED
ELECTEE
ELECTOR
ELECTRA
ELECTRO
ELICITS
ENACTED
ENACTOR
EPICENE
EPICURE
ERECTED
ERECTER
ERECTLY
ERECTOR
ERICSON
ERUCTED
EVACUEE
EVICTED
EXACTED
EXACTER
EXACTLY
EXACTOR
EXECUTE
EYECUPS

E•••C••

EARACHE
EFFACED
EFFACES
EFFECTS
ENLACED
ENLACES
ENTICED
ENTICER
ENTICES
EPARCHS
ETHICAL
EUNUCHS
EVINCED
EVINCES
EXPECTS

E••••C•

EARLOCK
EDIFICE
EHRLICH
ELGRECO
EMBRACE
ENFORCE
ENHANCE
ENOUNCE
EROTICA
ESSENCE
ETHNICS
EXOTICA
EXOTICS
EXTINCT
EXTRACT

E•••••C

EDAPHIC
ELASTIC
ELEGIAC
ENDEMIC
ERISTIC
ERRATIC

•EC••••

BECALMS
BECAUSE
BECKETT
BECKONS
BECLOUD
BECOMES
CECILIA
DECADES
DECAGON
DECALOG
DECAMPS
DECANTS
DECAPOD
DECARLO
DECAYED

DECEITS
DECEIVE
DECIBEL
DECIDED
DECIDES
DECIMAL
DECKING
DECKLES
DECKOUT
DECLAIM
DECLARE
DECLASS
DECLINE
DECOCTS
DECODED
DECODER
DECODES
DECORUM
DECOYED
DECREED
DECREES
DECRIED
DECRIES
DECRYPT
GECKOES
HECKLED
HECKLER
HECKLES
HECTARE
HECTORS
LECARRE
LECTERN
LECTORS
LECTURE
NECKERS
NECKING
NECKTIE
NECTARS
PECCANT
PECCARY
PECKING
PECKISH
PECKSAT
PECTINS
RECALLS
RECANED
RECANES
RECANTS
RECASTS
RECEDED
RECEDES
RECEIPT
RECEIVE
RECENCY
RECHALK
RECHECK
RECHOSE
RECIPES
RECITAL
RECITED
RECITER
RECITES
RECKONS
RECLAIM
RECLAME
RECLEAN
RECLINE
RECLUSE
RECODED
RECODES
RECOILS
RECOLOR
RECORDS
RECORKS
RECOUNT
RECOUPS
RECOVER
RECROOM
RECROSS
RECRUIT
RECTIFY
RECTORS
RECTORY
RECUSED
RECUSES
RECYCLE
SECANTS
SECEDED
SECEDER
SECEDES
SECLUDE
SECONDS
SECRECY
SECRETE
SECRETS
SECTION
SECTORS
SECULAR
SECURED
SECURER
SECURES
TECHIES
VECTORS

•E•C•••

BEACHED
BEACHES
BEACONS
BEECHAM
BEECHER
BEECHES
BELCHED
BELCHES
BENCHED
BENCHES
DEACONS
DEICERS
DEICING
DESCANT
DESCEND
DESCENT
DEWCLAW
FENCERS
FENCING
FETCHED
FETCHES
HENCOOP
HEPCATS
HERCULE
KERCHOO
KETCHAM
KETCHES
KETCHUP
KEYCARD
KEYCLUB
LEACHED
LEACHES
LEACOCK
LEECHED
LEECHES
MENCKEN
MERCIES
MERCURY
MESCALS
NESCAFE
PEACHED
PEACHES
PEACOAT
PEACOCK
PECCANT
PECCARY
PENCILS
PERCALE
PERCENT
PERCHED
PERCHES
PETCOCK
REACHED
REACHES
REACTED
REACTOR
REACTTO
REDCAPS
REDCELL
REDCENT
REDCOAT
REOCCUR
RESCALE
RESCIND
RESCUED
RESCUER
RESCUES
REXCATS
SEACOWS
SEICHES
TEACAKE
TEACART
TEACHER
TEACHES
TEACHIN
TEACUPS
TEICHER
TERCELS
TERCETS
TETCHED
VETCHES
WELCHED
WELCHES
WELCOME
WENCHES
WETCELL

•E••C••

BEARCAT
BEDECKS
CEVICHE
DEBACLE
DECOCTS
DEDUCED
DEDUCES
DEDUCTS
DEFACED
DEFACES
DEFACTO
DEFECTS
DEFICIT
DEJECTS
DELICTI
DELICTS
DEPECHE
DEPICTS
DETECTS
DEVICES
FELICIA
FELUCCA
HELICAL
HELICES
HELICON
HELLCAT
JERICHO
LEXICAL
LEXICON
MEDICAL
MEDICOS
MENACED
MENACES
MEXICAN
PEDICEL
PEDICLE
PELICAN
PEMICAN
PENUCHE
REBECCA
RECYCLE
REDACTS
REDUCED
REDUCER
REDUCES
REFACED
REFACES
REJECTS
RELACED
RELACES
RELICTS
RELOCKS
REOCCUR
RESECTS
RETICLE
SEANCES
SEDUCED
SEDUCER
SEDUCES
SELECTS
SENECAS
TENACES
VEHICLE

•E•••C•

BEDROCK
BERNICE
BESEECH
BEWITCH
CELTICS
DEBAUCH
DEBOUCH
DEFENCE
DEFLECT
DEFROCK
DEFUNCT
DEHISCE
DENIECE
DERRICK
DETRACT
FELUCCA
FETLOCK
GETBACK
HEMLOCK
HENPECK
HEROICS
JESSICA
LEACOCK
LETTUCE
MENISCI
METRICS
NEGLECT
PEACOCK
PENANCE
PERFECT
PETCOCK
PETROCK
REBECCA
RECENCY
RECHECK
REELECT
REENACT
REFLECT
REFRACT
REGENCY
REJOICE
REPLACE
REPLICA
REPRICE
RESPECT
RESTOCK
RETEACH
RETOUCH
RETRACE
RETRACK
RETRACT
REVOICE
SEASICK
SECRECY
SELLECK
SERPICO
SERVICE
SETBACK
TEDMACK
TENANCY
TERENCE
TERRACE
VEENECK
VERDICT
WEDLOCK

•E••••C

AELFRIC
AEROBIC
CENTRIC
CERAMIC
DELTAIC
DEMONIC
GENERIC
GENETIC
HEBRAIC
HEPATIC
HERETIC
JEANLUC
KEROUAC
MEDEVAC
MEIOTIC
MELODIC
PELAGIC
SEISMIC
SELENIC
SEMITIC

••EC•••

ATECROW
BEECHAM
BEECHER
BEECHES
CHECHEN
CHECKED
CHECKER
CHECKIN
CHECKUP
CRECHES
CUECARD
EJECTED
ELECTED
ELECTEE
ELECTOR
ELECTRA
ELECTRO
ERECTED
ERECTER
ERECTLY
ERECTOR
EXECUTE
EYECUPS
FLECHES
FLECKED
FRECKLE
GRECIAN
HOECAKE
ICECAPS
ICECOLD
ICECUBE
IRECKON
LEECHED
LEECHES
PIECERS
PIECING
PLECTRA
PRECAST
PRECEDE
PRECEPT
PRECISE
PRECOOK
PRECOOL
QUECHUA
SHECRAB
SPECIAL
SPECIES
SPECIFY
SPECKLE
SPECTER
SPECTOR
SPECTRA
SPECTRE
TIECLIP
TOECAPS
WRECKED
WRECKER

••E•C••

ALENCON
AMERCED
AMERCES
APERCUS
COERCED
COERCES
CREWCUT
FIERCER
FLEECED
FLEECES
FRESCOS
KNEECAP
PIERCED
PIERCES
PREACHY
SKETCHY
SPENCER
STENCIL
TREACLE
TREACLY

••E••C•

AMERICA
CLERICS
CREVICE
ICEPACK
ICEPICK
INEXACT
NOETICS
OVERACT
POETICS
PREDICT
PREFACE
PREFECT
REELECT
REENACT
ROEBUCK
TIERACK
TIETACK
VEENECK

••E•••C

ACERBIC
ALEMBIC
ASEPTIC
ELEGIAC
FREDRIC
IDENTIC
LAENNEC
OCEANIC
SHELLAC
SKEPTIC

•••EC••

AFFECTS
ASPECTS
AZTECAN
BEDECKS
BISECTS
CAPECOD
DEFECTS
DEJECTS
DEPECHE
DETECTS
DIRECTS
DOVECOT
EFFECTS
EXPECTS
FLEECED
FLEECES
INFECTS
INJECTS
INSECTS
KNEECAP
KOPECKS
OBJECTS
PACECAR
POLECAT
RACECAR
REBECCA
REJECTS
RESECTS
SELECTS
SENECAS
SIDECAR
TIMECOP
UTRECHT
VOTECHS

•••E•C•

ABSENCE
ARDENCY
ATPEACE
BESEECH
CADENCE
COGENCY
DEFENCE
ESSENCE
FAIENCE
FLUENCY
ILIESCU
IMPEACH
INPEACE
IONESCO
LATENCY
LICENCE
OFFENCE
POTENCY
REBECCA
RECENCY
REGENCY
RETEACH
SCIENCE
SCREECH
SILENCE
SQUELCH
STRETCH
TERENCE
URGENCY
VALENCE
VANEYCK

•••E••C

AMOEBIC
ANGELIC
ARSENIC
ASCETIC
COMEDIC
ENDEMIC
GENERIC
GENETIC
HERETIC
HOMERIC
KINETIC
MALEFIC
MEDEVAC
MIMETIC
NUMERIC
PHRENIC
POLEMIC
SELENIC
TONELOC
TOTEMIC

••••EC•

ARTDECO
BESEECH
BOMBECK
BRUBECK
CALTECH
CANSECO
COLLECT
CONNECT
CORRECT
DEFLECT
DENIECE
DIALECT
DISSECT
ELGRECO
HENPECK
INFLECT
INSPECT
LOWNECK
LOWTECH
NEGLECT
PANDECT
PARSECS
PERFECT
PREFECT
PROJECT
PROTECT
RECHECK
REELECT
REFLECT
RESPECT
SCREECH
SECRECY
SELLECK
SUBJECT
SUNDECK
SUSPECT
TOLTECS
TRISECT
VEENECK
WOZZECK

••••E•C

NUCLEIC
POULENC

•••••EC

LAENNEC
LAUTREC
MIDDLEC
ZAPOTEC

ED•••••

EDACITY
EDAPHIC
EDASNER
EDDYING
EDGEDIN
EDGEOUT
EDGESIN
EDGIEST
EDGINGS
EDIBLES
EDIFICE
EDIFIED
EDIFIES
EDITING
EDITION
EDITORS
EDOUARD
EDUCATE
EDUCING
EDWARDS

E•D••••

ECDYSES
ECDYSIS
EDDYING
ELDERLY
ENDEARS
ENDEMIC
ENDGAME
ENDINGS
ENDIVES
ENDLESS
ENDMOST
ENDORSE
ENDOWED
ENDPLAY
ENDRUNS
ENDUING
ENDURED
ENDURES
ENDUSER
ENDWAYS
ENDWISE
ENDZONE

E••D•••

EARDROP
EARDRUM
EKEDOUT
ELIDING
ELUDING
ERODING
ERUDITE
EVADERS
EVADING
EVIDENT
EXUDING

E•••D••

EARLDOM
EASEDIN
EASEDUP
ECHIDNA
ECUADOR
EDGEDIN
EGGEDON
EMENDED
EMENDER
ENCODED
ENCODER
ENCODES
ESCUDOS
EVANDER

E••••D•

EBBTIDE
EDWARDS
EFFENDI
ELAPIDS
ENFOLDS
ENGARDE
ENGIRDS
ENNEADS
EPISODE
ERRANDS
ESTRADA
EXCEEDS
EXCLUDE
EXPANDS
EXPENDS
EXPLODE
EXTENDS
EXTRUDE
EYELIDS

E•••••D

EASTEND
EDIFIED
EDOUARD
EFFACED
EFFUSED
EGESTED
EGGHEAD
EJECTED
ELAPSED
ELBOWED
ELECTED
EMENDED
EMERALD
EMERGED
EMERSED
EMITTED
EMPTIED
ENABLED
ENACTED
ENCAGED
ENCASED
ENCODED
ENDOWED
ENDURED
ENGAGED
ENGLAND
ENGLUND
ENISLED
ENJOYED
ENLACED
ENRAGED
ENROBED
ENSILED
ENSURED
ENTERED
ENTICED
EQUALED
EQUATED
ERECTED
ERUCTED
ERUPTED
ESCAPED
ESSAYED
EUCHRED
EVERTED
EVICTED
EVINCED
EVOLVED
EVULSED
EXACTED
EXALTED
EXCISED
EXCITED
EXCUSED
EXERTED
EXHALED
EXISTED
EXPIRED
EXPOSED
EXPOUND
EXULTED

•ED••••

AEDILES
BEDAUBS
BEDBUGS
BEDDING
BEDDOWN
BEDECKS
BEDELIA
BEDEVIL
BEDEWED
BEDIZEN
BEDLAMP
BEDOUIN
BEDPOST
BEDREST
BEDROCK
BEDROLL
BEDROOM
BEDSIDE
BEDTIME
CEDILLA
DEDALUS
DEDUCED
DEDUCES
DEDUCTS
FEDERAL
FEDORAS
HEDDLES
HEDGERS
HEDGING
KEDROVA
LEDGERS
LEDUPTO
MEDALED
MEDDLED
MEDDLER
MEDDLES
MEDEVAC
MEDIANS
MEDIANT
MEDIATE
MEDICAL
MEDICOS
MEDIUMS
MEDLEYS
MEDULLA
MEDUSAE
MEDUSAS
OEDIPAL
OEDIPUS
PEDALED
PEDANTS
PEDDLED
PEDDLER
PEDDLES
PEDICEL
PEDICLE
PEDLARS
REDACTS
REDANTS
REDATED
REDATES
REDBIRD
REDBOOK
REDBUDS
REDCAPS
REDCELL
REDCENT
REDCOAT
REDDEER
REDDENS
REDDEST
REDDING
REDDISH
REDDOGS
REDEALS
REDEALT
REDEEMS
REDEYES
REDFINS
REDFIRS
REDFLAG
REDFORD
REDGUMS
REDHAIR
REDHATS
REDHEAD
REDHEAT
REDHOTS
REDIALS
REDLINE
REDMEAT
REDNESS
REDOAKS
REDOING
REDOUBT
REDOUND
REDPINE
REDPOLL
REDRAWN
REDRAWS
REDRESS
REDROSE
REDSKIN
REDSPOT
REDSTAR
REDTAPE
REDTOPS
REDUCED
REDUCER
REDUCES
REDWINE
REDWING
REDWOLF
REDWOOD
SEDALIA
SEDATER
SEDUCED
SEDUCER
SEDUCES
TEDDERS
TEDDIES
TEDDING
TEDIOUS
TEDMACK
VEDANTA
WEDDING
WEDGIES
WEDGING
WEDLOCK

•E•D•••

BEADIER
BEADING
BEADLES
BEADSUP
BEDDING
BEDDOWN
BELDAME
BELDAMS
BENDERS
BENDING
DEADAIR
DEADEND
DEADENS
DEADEYE
DEADPAN
DEADSEA
DEADSET
DEEDING
DENDRON
DEODARS
DEWDROP
FEEDBAG
FEEDERS
FEEDING
FEEDLOT
FEEDSON
FELDMAN
FENDERS
FENDING
FEUDING
GELDING
GENDERS
GEODESY
GETDOWN
HEADERS
HEADIER
HEADILY
HEADING
HEADMAN
HEADMEN
HEADOFF
HEADOUT
HEADPIN
HEADSET
HEADSIN
HEADSUP
HEADWAY
HEDDLES
HEEDFUL
HEEDING
HELDOFF
HELDOUT
HENDRIX
HERDERS
HERDING
HEYDAYS

KENDALL
LEADERS
LEADING
LEADINS
LEADOFF
LEADOUT
LEADSIN
LEADSON
LEADSTO
LEADSUP
LENDERS
LENDING
LETDOWN
LEWDEST
MEADOWS
MEADOWY
MEDDLED
MEDDLER
MEDDLES
MELDING
MENDERS
MENDING
MENDOZA
NEEDFUL
NEEDIER
NEEDILY
NEEDING
NEEDLED
NEEDLES
NEWDEAL
PEDDLED
PEDDLER
PEDDLES
PENDANT
PENDENT
PENDING
PERDIEM
READERS
READIED
READIER
READIES
READILY
READING
READMIT
READOUT
READSIN
REDDEER
REDDENS
REDDEST
REDDING
REDDISH
REDDOGS
REEDIER
REEDING
REEDITS
RENDERS
RENDING
SEADOGS
SEADUTY
SEEDBED
SEEDERS
SEEDIER
SEEDILY
SEEDING
SEEDPOD
SEIDELS
SENDERS
SENDFOR
SENDING
SENDOFF
SENDOUT
SENDSIN
SENDSUP
SENDUPS
SETDOWN
TEDDERS
TEDDIES
TEDDING
TEEDOFF
TENDERS
TENDING
TENDONS
TENDRIL
TENDSTO
VENDING
VENDORS
VERDANT
VERDICT
VERDUGO
VERDURE
WEDDING
WEEDERS
WEEDIER
WEEDING
WEEDOUT
WELDERS
WELDING
WENDELL
WENDERS
WENDING
YESDEAR

•E••D••

BEARDED
BESIDES
BETIDED
BETIDES
CELADON
DECADES
DECIDED
DECIDES
DECODED
DECODER
DECODES
DELUDED
DELUDES
DENUDED
DENUDES
DERIDED
DERIDES
FETIDLY
GELADAS
HEARDOF
KEYEDIN
KEYEDUP
LEANDER
MEANDER
MELODIC
NEVADAN
NEWSDAY
PERIDOT
REARDON
RECEDED
RECEDES
RECODED
RECODES
REMODEL
REMUDAS
REORDER
REREDOS
RESIDED
RESIDES
RESIDUE
SECEDED
SECEDER
SECEDES
SERFDOM
SEWEDUP
TEPIDLY
TEREDOS
VEXEDLY
WEEKDAY
WEIRDER
WEIRDLY
WEIRDOS

•E•••D•

BEDSIDE
BEHOLDS
BELINDA
BERMUDA
DEFENDS
DEGRADE
DEMANDS
DEPENDS
DEWILDE
GERALDO
GERUNDS
HEPTADS
HERALDS
HEYJUDE
KENNEDY
KEYPADS
LEETIDE
LEGENDS
MELINDA
METHODS
NEREIDS
PEABODY
PEAPODS
PENTADS
PEPTIDE
PERFIDY
PERIODS
PERVADE
PETARDS
REBINDS
RECORDS
REDBUDS
REFUNDS
REGARDS
REGRADE
RELOADS
REMANDS
REMENDS
REMINDS
REMOLDS
REREADS
RESANDS
RESEEDS
RESENDS
RETARDS
RETRADE
REWARDS
REWELDS
REWINDS
REWORDS
SEABEDS
SEASIDE
SECLUDE
SECONDS
TETRADS
VERANDA
VESPIDS

•E••••D

AERATED
BEACHED
BEARDED
BECLOUD
BEDEWED
BEHAVED
BELATED
BELAYED
BELCHED
BELLIED
BELOVED
BEMIRED
BEMUSED
BENCHED
BERATED
BERNARD
BERRIED
BERTHED
BETIDED
BEVELED
CENTRED
DEADEND
DEBASED
DEBATED
DEBITED
DEBONED
DEBUTED
DECAPOD
DECAYED
DECIDED
DECODED
DECOYED
DECREED
DECRIED
DEDUCED
DEEPEND
DEFACED
DEFAMED
DEFILED
DEFINED
DEFRAUD
DEFUSED
DEIFIED
DEIGNED
DELAYED
DELETED
DELTOID
DELUDED
DELUGED
DEMIGOD
DEMISED
DEMOTED
DENOTED
DENUDED
DEPONED
DEPOSED
DEPUTED
DERIDED
DERIVED
DESCEND
DESIRED
DESMOND
DEVILED
DEVISED
DEVOTED
FEASTED
FEIGNED
FEINTED
FERRIED
FETCHED
GENTLED
HECKLED
HEISTED
HELIPAD
HENNAED
HENREID
HEYWOOD
JELLIED
JEMMIED
JEWELED
KEYCARD
KEYWORD
LEACHED
LEARNED
LEASHED
LEECHED
LEEWARD
LEONARD
LEOPARD
LEOPOLD
LEOTARD
LEVELED
LEVERED
MEDALED
MEDDLED
MENACED
MERITED
MERMAID
METERED
NEEDLED
NEGATED
NEIGHED
NESTLED
NETTLED
PEACHED
PEARLED
PEBBLED
PEDALED
PEDDLED
PEOPLED
PEPPARD
PERCHED
PERUSED
PESTLED
PETALED
PETERED
REACHED
REACTED
READIED
REAIRED
REAREND
REARMED
REBATED
REBOUND
REBUILD
REBUKED
RECANED
RECEDED
RECITED
RECODED
RECUSED
REDATED
REDBIRD
REDFORD
REDHEAD
REDOUND
REDUCED
REDWOOD
REFACED
REFINED
REFRIED
REFUSED
REFUTED
REGALED
REGLUED
REHEARD
REHIRED
REIGNED
REINKED
REKEYED
RELACED
RELATED
RELAXED
RELAYED
RELINED
RELIVED
REMIXED
REMOVED
REMOWED
RENAMED
RENEGED
RENEWED
REOILED
REPAVED
REPINED
REPLIED
REPOSED
REPUTED
RERATED
RESCIND
RESCUED
RESIDED
RESILED
RESOLED
RESOUND
RESPOND
RESUMED
RETAPED
RETAXED
RETILED
RETIMED
RETIRED
RETOWED
RETREAD
RETRIED
RETUNED
RETYPED
REUPPED
REVELED
REVERED
REVILED
REVISED
REVIVED
REVOKED
REWAXED
REWIRED
REWOUND
REXREED
REYNARD
REZONED
SEABIRD
SEAFOOD
SEAWARD
SEAWEED
SECEDED
SECURED
SEDUCED
SEEDBED
SEEDPOD
SEESRED
SEETHED
SERRIED
SETTLED
SEVERED
TEETHED
TELEXED
TEMPTED
TENFOLD
TENONED
TENURED
TETCHED
WEARIED
WEBTOED
WEEKEND
WEIGHED
WELCHED
WELLAND
WELLFED
WENTBAD
WESTEND
WETLAND
YEAREND
YEARNED
ZEALAND

••ED•••

ACEDOUT
CHEDDAR
COEDITS
CREDITS
DEEDING
DIEDOFF
DIEDOUT
DIEDOWN
DREDGED
DREDGER
DREDGES
DUEDATE
EKEDOUT
FEEDBAG
FEEDERS
FEEDING
FEEDLOT
FEEDSON
FIEDLER
FLEDGED
FLEDGES
FREDDIE
FREDRIC
HEEDFUL
HEEDING
HOEDOWN
ICEDTEA
LIEDOWN
NEEDFUL
NEEDIER
NEEDILY
NEEDING
NEEDLED
NEEDLES
PLEDGED
PLEDGEE
PLEDGER
PLEDGES
PREDATE
PREDAWN
PREDICT
PYEDOGS
REEDIER
REEDING
REEDITS
ROEDEER
SEEDBED
SEEDERS
SEEDIER
SEEDILY
SEEDING
SEEDPOD
SLEDDED
SLEDDER
SLEDDOG
SLEDGES
SWEDISH
TEEDOFF
THEDEEP
TIEDOWN
TIEDYED
TIEDYES
WEEDERS
WEEDIER
WEEDING
WEEDOUT

••E•D••

AGENDAS
AHEADOF
AMENDED
BLENDED
BLENDER
BREADED
BREADTH
BREEDER
BRENDAN
CHEDDAR
DREADED
DREIDEL
DRESDEN
EMENDED
EMENDER
FIEFDOM
FIELDED
FIELDER
FREDDIE
FREEDOM
GRENDEL
KNEADED
KNEADER
ONEIDAS
OVERDID
OVERDUB
OVERDUE
PLEADED
PLEADER
SCENDED
SHELDON
SLEDDED
SLEDDER
SLEDDOG
SLENDER
SPEEDED
SPEEDER
SPEEDUP
SPENDER
TREADED
TREADER
TREADLE
TRENDED
TUESDAY
UNENDED
UPENDED
WEEKDAY
WHEEDLE
WIELDED
YIELDED

••E••D•

EYELIDS
GRENADA
GRENADE
LEETIDE
MAENADS
PRECEDE
PRELUDE
PREMEDS
PRESIDE
TIERODS

••E•••D

ABELARD
ABETTED
ALERTED
AMENDED
AMERCED
AMERIND
ANEROID
AVENGED
AVERRED
AVERTED
BLEARED
BLEATED
BLEEPED
BLENDED
BLESSED
BREADED
BREEZED
CHEATED
CHECKED
CHEEPED
CHEERED
CHEVIED
CLEANED
CLEARED
CLEAVED
CLERKED
COERCED
CREAKED
CREAMED
CREASED
CREATED
CREEPED
CRESTED
CUECARD
DEEPEND
DIEHARD
DREADED
DREAMED
DREDGED
DRESSED
DWELLED
EGESTED
EJECTED
ELECTED
EMENDED
EMERALD
EMERGED
EMERSED
ERECTED
EVERTED
EXERTED
FIELDED
FLECKED
FLEDGED
FLEECED
FLENSED
FLESHED
FREAKED
FRETTED
FUELROD
GIELGUD
GLEAMED
GLEANED
GOESBAD
GREASED
GREENED
GREETED
GUESSED
GUESTED
ICECOLD
ICELAND
IDEATED
IRELAND
KNEADED
KNEELED
KNEEPAD
KNELLED
LEECHED
LEEWARD
LIEABED
NEEDLED
OCEANID
ONEEYED
OPENEND
OPERAND
OVERDID
PIEBALD
PIERCED
PLEADED
PLEASED
PLEATED
PLEDGED
PREBEND
PREENED
PRELOAD
PREPAID
PRESSED
PRETEND
QUEERED
QUELLED
QUERIED
QUESTED
SCENDED
SCENTED
SEEDBED
SEEDPOD
SEESRED
SEETHED
SHEARED
SHEAVED
SHEERED
SHEETED
SHELLED
SHELVED
SHEPARD
SLEDDED
SLEEKED
SLEETED
SMEARED
SMELLED
SMELTED
SNEAKED
SNEERED
SNEEZED
SPEARED
SPEEDED
SPELLED
STEAMED
STEELED
STEEPED
STEERED
STEMMED
STEPPED
STEROID
STETTED
STEWARD
SWEATED
SWELLED
SWERVED
TEETHED
TIEDYED
TOEHOLD
TREADED
TREATED
TREBLED
TREKKED
TRENDED
TWEAKED
TWEETED
TWEEZED
UNENDED
UPENDED
WEEKEND
WHEELED
WHEEZED
WHELPED
WHETTED
WIELDED
WREAKED
WRECKED
WRESTED
YIELDED

•••ED••

ACCEDED
ACCEDER
ACCEDES
ACTEDUP
ADDEDIN
ADDEDON
ADDEDTO
ADDEDUP
AIMEDAT
AIMEDTO
ALBEDOS
ANTEDUP
ARLEDGE
BIPEDAL
BONEDRY
BONEDUP
BOREDOM
BOXEDIN
BOXEDUP
BREEDER
CAVEDIN
CLUEDIN
COMEDIC
COMEDUE
DATEDLY
DAZEDLY
DINEDIN
DINEDON
DOTEDON
DRIEDUP
DUDEDUP
DUKEDOM
EASEDIN
EASEDUP
EDGEDIN
EGGEDON
FADEDIN
FIREDOG
FIREDUP
FIXEDLY
FIXEDUP
FREEDOM
FRIEDAN
GLUEDON
HOLEDUP
HYPEDUP
IMPEDED
IMPEDES
JADEDLY
JANEDOE
KEYEDIN
KEYEDUP
LACEDUP
LINEDUP
LIVEDIN
LIVEDON
MIXEDUP
MOVEDIN
NAKEDLY
NAMEDAY
OWNEDUP
PALEDRY
PAWEDAT
PHAEDRA
PILEDIN
PILEDON
PILEDUP
PIPEDUP
POKEDAT
RAKEDIN
RAKEDUP
RECEDED
RECEDES
REREDOS
ROPEDIN
SAMEDAY
SAVEDUP
SECEDED
SECEDER
SECEDES
SEWEDUP
SINEDIE
SIZEDUP
SOLEDAD
SOMEDAY
SPEEDED
SPEEDER
SPEEDUP
SPIEDON
TEREDOS
TIREDER
TIREDLY
TIREDOF
TONEDUP
TRIEDON
TUNEDIN
TUNEDUP
TUXEDOS
TYPEDUP
VEXEDLY
WAVEDIN
WHEEDLE
WIPEDUP
WISEDUP

•••E•D•

ADDENDA
ADDENDS
ALLENDE
ALREADY
APPENDS
ASCENDS
ATTENDS
AUGENDS
CALENDS
DEFENDS
DEPENDS
EFFENDI
ENNEADS
EXCEEDS
EXPENDS
EXTENDS
FAGENDS
FRIENDS
IMPENDS
INTENDS
LEGENDS
LIMEADE
MAKESDO
NEREIDS
OFFENDS
REMENDS
REREADS
RESEEDS
RESENDS
REWELDS
SCREEDS
SHIELDS
SPREADS
TAGENDS
THREADS
THREADY
UNBENDS
UNREADY
VIVENDI

•••E••D

ACCEDED
ADHERED
ALLEGED
ALTERED
ANGERED
ANNELID
ANNEXED
BEDEWED
BEVELED
BLEEPED
BOGEYED
BOWERED
BREEZED
BRIEFED
BUGEYED
CAMEOED
CAPECOD
CAPERED
CATERED
CHEEPED
CHEERED
COHERED
COVERED
COVETED
COWERED
COZENED
CREEPED
DELETED
DRYEYED
ENTERED
FACETED
FLEECED
GAVELED
GREENED
GREETED
GRIEVED
HOMERED
HONEYED
HOVERED
IMPEDED
INDEXED
INHERED
JEWELED
KNEELED
KNEEPAD
LABELED
LAPELED
LAYERED
LEVELED
LEVERED
LIBELED
LIKEMAD
LIKENED

LIVENED
LOWERED
METERED
MITERED
MODELED
MONEYED
MOSEYED
NOTEPAD
OFFERED
ONEEYED
ORDERED
OSTEOID
PANELED
PAPERED
PETERED
POPEYED
POWERED
PREENED
QUEERED
QUIETED
RAVELED
RAVENED
RECEDED
REHEARD
REKEYED
RENEGED
RENEWED
REVELED
REVERED
RIPENED
RIVETED
ROSEBUD
ROSERED
SCHEMED
SCREWED
SECEDED
SEVERED
SHEERED
SHEETED
SLEEKED
SLEETED
SNEERED
SNEEZED
SOBERED
SOLEDAD
SPEEDED
SPIELED
STEELED
STEEPED
STEERED
STREWED
TAPERED
TELEXED
THIEVED
TOKENED
TOWELED
TOWERED
TWEETED
TWEEZED
UNHEARD
UNSEWED
USHERED
UTTERED
WAGERED
WAKENED
WATERED
WAVERED
WHEELED
WHEEZED
WIDENED
WINERED
WIZENED
YODELED

••••ED•

ALAMEDA
ALFREDO
CONCEDE
DAYBEDS
DIOMEDE
EXCEEDS
HOTBEDS
KENNEDY
MALTEDS
PRECEDE
PREMEDS
RAGGEDY
RESEEDS
RIGVEDA
SCREEDS
SEABEDS
TORPEDO
TRAGEDY

••••E•D

AIRHEAD
ANISEED
BACKEND
BARTEND
BIGBEND
BIGHEAD
BOOKEND
CATHEAD
COMMEND
CONREID
CONTEND
COWHERD
DEADEND
DECREED
DEEPEND
DESCEND
DISTEND
EASTEND
EGGHEAD
FATHEAD
FORFEND
GLACEED
GOAHEAD
GOATEED
GODSEND
HAYSEED
HENREID
HIGHEND
HOTHEAD
INBREED
INFIELD
INSTEAD
JUGHEAD
LINSEED
LIPREAD
LOUREED
MILLEND
MINUEND
MISDEED
MISLEAD
MISREAD
OPENEND
PINHEAD
PORTEND
PREBEND
PRETEND
PROCEED
RAGWEED
REAREND
REDHEAD
RETREAD
REXREED
SAUTEED
SEAWEED
STIPEND
SUBHEAD
SUBTEND
SUCCEED
SUSPEND
TAILEND
TOWHEAD
WEEKEND
WESTEND
YEAREND

•••••ED

ABASHED
ABETTED
ABJURED
ABLATED
ABORTED
ABRADED
ABUTTED
ACCEDED
ACCRUED
ACCUSED
ADAPTED
ADDUCED
ADHERED
ADJURED
ADMIRED
ADMIXED
ADOPTED
ADORNED
ADVISED
AERATED
AFFIXED
ALARMED
ALERTED
ALIGNED
ALLAYED
ALLEGED
ALLOWED
ALLOYED
ALLUDED
ALLURED
ALTERED
AMASSED
AMENDED
AMERCED
ANGERED
ANISEED
ANNEXED
ANNOYED
APPLIED
APPOSED
APRONED
ARBORED
ARMORED
AROUSED
ARRAYED
ARRIVED
ASHAMED
ASPIRED
ASSAYED
ASSUMED
ASSURED
ATTIRED
ATTUNED
AUDITED
AUGURED
AVAILED
AVENGED
AVERRED
AVERTED
AVIATED
AVOIDED
AVULSED
AWAITED
AWARDED
BABBLED
BAFFLED
BANDIED
BATCHED
BATIKED
BATTLED
BEACHED
BEARDED
BEDEWED
BEHAVED
BELATED
BELAYED
BELCHED
BELLIED
BELOVED
BEMIRED
BEMUSED
BENCHED
BERATED
BERRIED
BERTHED
BETIDED
BEVELED
BIASSED
BIGOTED
BIRCHED
BIRDIED
BIRTHED
BLABBED
BLACKED
BLANKED
BLASTED
BLATTED
BLEARED
BLEATED
BLEEPED
BLENDED
BLESSED
BLINDED
BLINKED
BLIPPED
BLITZED
BLOATED
BLOCKED
BLOODED
BLOOMED
BLOOPED
BLOTTED
BLOUSED
BLUFFED
BLUNTED
BLURRED
BLURTED
BLUSHED
BOARDED
BOASTED
BOBBLED
BOBSLED
BOGEYED
BOGGLED
BOOGIED
BOOSTED
BOTCHED
BOTTLED
BOUNCED
BOUNDED
BOWERED
BRAGGED
BRAIDED
BRAINED
BRAISED
BRANDED
BRAWLED
BREADED
BREEZED
BRICKED
BRIDGED
BRIDLED
BRIEFED
BRIMMED
BROILED
BRONZED
BROODED
BROOKED
BROWNED
BROWSED
BRUISED
BRUITED
BRUSHED
BUBBLED
BUCKLED
BUGEYED
BULLIED
BUMBLED
BUNCHED
BUNCOED
BUNDLED
BUNGLED
BUNKBED
BUNKOED
BURBLED
BURGLED
BUSTLED
BYLINED
CACKLED
CADDIED
CAJOLED
CAMEOED
CANDIED
CAPERED
CAROLED
CAROMED
CARRIED
CASTLED
CATERED
CAULKED
CAVILED
CENTRED
CHAINED
CHAIRED
CHALKED
CHAMPED
CHANCED
CHANGED
CHANTED
CHAPPED
CHARGED
CHARMED
CHARRED
CHARTED
CHATTED
CHEATED
CHECKED
CHEEPED
CHEERED
CHEVIED
CHILLED
CHINKED
CHINNED
CHIPPED
CHIRPED
CHOMPED
CHOPPED
CHUCKED
CHUGGED
CHUMMED
CHURNED
CINCHED
CIRCLED
CLACKED
CLAIMED
CLAMMED
CLAMPED
CLANGED
CLANKED
CLAPPED
CLASHED
CLASPED
CLASSED
CLEANED
CLEARED
CLEAVED
CLERKED
CLICKED
CLIMBED
CLINKED
CLIPPED
CLOAKED
CLOCKED
CLOGGED
CLOPPED
CLOTHED
CLOTTED
CLOUDED
CLOUTED
CLOWNED
CLUBBED
CLUCKED
CLUMPED
CLUNKED
COACHED
COASTED
COBBLED
CODDLED
COERCED
COHERED
COLORED
CONGAED
COOPTED
CORNFED
COUCHED
COUGHED
COUNTED
COUPLED
COURSED
COURTED
COVERED
COVETED
COWERED
COZENED
CRABBED
CRACKED
CRADLED
CRAFTED
CRAMMED
CRAMPED
CRANKED
CRASHED
CRAWLED
CREAKED
CREAMED
CREASED
CREATED
CREEPED
CRESTED
CRIBBED
CRICKED
CRIMPED
CRINGED
CRISPED
CROAKED
CROOKED
CROONED
CROPPED
CROSSED
CROWDED
CROWNED
CRUISED
CRUSHED
CRUSTED
CUDDLED
CURDLED
CURRIED
DABBLED
DALLIED
DAMAGED
DANDLED
DANGLED
DAPPLED
DAUNTED
DAWDLED
DAZZLED
DEBASED
DEBATED
DEBITED
DEBONED
DEBUTED
DECAYED
DECIDED
DECODED
DECOYED
DECREED
DECRIED
DEDUCED
DEFACED
DEFAMED
DEFILED
DEFINED
DEFUSED
DEIFIED
DEIGNED
DELAYED
DELETED
DELUDED
DELUGED
DEMISED
DEMOTED
DENOTED
DENUDED
DEPONED
DEPOSED
DEPUTED
DERIDED
DERIVED
DESIRED
DEVILED
DEVISED
DEVOTED
DIBBLED
DIDDLED
DILATED
DILUTED
DIMPLED
DIRTIED
DISCOED
DISUSED
DITCHED
DITTOED
DIVIDED
DIVINED
DIVVIED
DIZZIED
DOGSLED
DOLLIED
DONATED
DOODLED
DOUBLED
DOUBTED
DRAFTED
DRAGGED
DRAINED
DRATTED
DRAWLED
DREADED
DREAMED
DREDGED
DRESSED
DRIFTED
DRILLED
DRIPPED
DROOLED
DROOPED
DROPPED
DROWNED
DROWSED
DRUBBED
DRUDGED
DRUGGED
DRUMMED
DRYEYED
DUMMIED
DWARFED
DWELLED
EDIFIED
EFFACED
EFFUSED
EGESTED
EJECTED
ELAPSED
ELBOWED
ELECTED
EMENDED
EMERGED
EMERSED
EMITTED
EMPTIED
ENABLED
ENACTED
ENCAGED
ENCASED
ENCODED
ENDOWED
ENDURED
ENGAGED
ENISLED
ENJOYED
ENLACED
ENRAGED
ENROBED
ENSILED
ENSURED
ENTERED
ENTICED
EQUALED
EQUATED
ERECTED
ERUCTED
ERUPTED
ESCAPED
ESSAYED
EUCHRED
EVERTED
EVICTED
EVINCED
EVOLVED
EVULSED
EXACTED
EXALTED
EXCISED
EXCITED
EXCUSED
EXERTED
EXHALED
EXISTED
EXPIRED
EXPOSED
EXULTED
FACETED
FAGOTED
FAINTED
FANCIED
FAULTED
FAVORED
FEASTED
FEIGNED
FEINTED
FERRIED
FETCHED
FIDDLED
FIELDED
FIGURED
FILCHED
FIXATED
FIZZLED
FLAGGED
FLAILED
FLAMBED
FLANKED
FLAPPED
FLASHED
FLATBED
FLATTED
FLECKED
FLEDGED
FLEECED
FLENSED
FLESHED
FLICKED
FLIPPED
FLIRTED
FLITTED
FLOATED
FLOCKED
FLOGGED
FLOODED
FLOORED
FLOPPED
FLOSSED
FLOURED
FLOUTED
FLUBBED
FLUFFED
FLUNKED
FLUSHED
FOCUSED
FOISTED
FONDLED
FOOZLED
FORAGED
FOUNDED
FRANKED
FREAKED
FRETTED
FRILLED
FRINGED
FRISKED
FRITTED
FRIZZED
FROCKED
FRONTED
FROSTED
FROTHED
FROWNED
FRUITED
FUDDLED
FUMBLED
GABBLED
GAMBLED
GANGLED
GARAGED
GARBLED
GARGLED
GAVELED
GENTLED
GHOSTED
GIGGLED
GIRDLED
GLACEED
GLANCED
GLASSED
GLEAMED
GLEANED
GLINTED
GLITZED
GLOATED
GLOMMED
GLORIED
GLOSSED
GLUTTED
GNARLED
GNARRED
GNASHED
GOATEED
GOBBLED
GOGGLED
GRABBED
GRAFTED
GRAINED
GRANTED
GRAPHED
GRASPED
GRASSED
GREASED
GREENED
GREETED
GRIDDED
GRIEVED
GRILLED
GRINNED
GRIPPED
GRITTED
GROANED
GROOMED
GROOVED
GROSSED
GROUPED
GROUSED
GROUTED
GROWLED
GRUBBED
GRUDGED
GRUMPED
GRUNTED
GUARDED
GUESSED
GUESTED
GURGLED
GUSSIED
GUZZLED
GYRATED
HABITED
HAGGLED
HANDLED
HARRIED
HASSLED
HATCHED
HAUNTED
HAYSEED
HECKLED
HEISTED
HENNAED
HITCHED
HOARDED
HOBBLED
HOGTIED
HOISTED
HOMERED
HONEYED
HONORED
HOUNDED
HOVERED
HUDDLED
HULLOED
HUMBLED
HUMORED
HUNCHED
HUNDRED
HURDLED
HURRIED
HURTLED
HUSTLED
IDEATED
IGNITED
IGNORED
ILLBRED
ILLUSED
IMBIBED
IMBRUED
IMMIXED
IMMURED
IMPALED
IMPEDED
IMPLIED
IMPOSED
IMPUTED
INBREED
INCISED
INCITED
INDEXED
INDITED
INDUCED
INFUSED
INHALED
INHERED
INJURED
INSURED
INTONED
INVADED
INVITED
INVOKED
IODIZED
IONIZED
JANGLED
JAUNTED
JELLIED
JEMMIED
JEWELED
JIGGLED
JIMMIED
JINGLED
JOGGLED
JOINTED
JOISTED
JOLLIED
JOSTLED
JOUNCED
JOUSTED
JUGGLED
JUMBLED
KAYAKED
KIBBLED
KINDLED
KINDRED
KNEADED
KNEELED
KNELLED
KNITTED
KNOBBED
KNOCKED
KNOTTED
KNURLED
LABELED
LABORED
LAPELED
LASSOED
LATCHED
LAUGHED
LAYERED
LEACHED
LEARNED
LEASHED
LEECHED
LEVELED
LEVERED
LIAISED
LIBELED
LIEABED
LIGATED
LIGHTED
LIKENED
LIMITED
LINDIED
LINSEED
LIVENED
LOATHED
LOBBIED
LOCATED
LOUNGED
LOUREED
LOWBRED
LOWERED
LUNCHED
LURCHED
LUSTRED
LUXATED
MAITRED
MAJORED
MAMBOED
MANAGED
MANFRED
MANGLED
MANTLED
MARBLED
MARCHED
MARRIED
MATCHED
MATURED
MEDALED
MEDDLED
MENACED
MERITED
METERED
MILDRED
MINGLED
MINORED
MISCUED
MISDEED
MISUSED
MITERED
MIZZLED
MODELED
MONEYED
MOOCHED
MORDRED
MORPHED
MOSEYED
MOTORED
MOTTLED
MOULDED
MOULTED
MOUNDED
MOUNTED
MOUSSED
MOUTHED
MUDDIED
MUDDLED
MUFFLED
MULCHED
MULCTED
MUMBLED
MUNCHED
MUSCLED
MUTATED
MUZZLED
NATURED
NEEDLED
NEGATED
NEIGHED
NESTLED
NETTLED
NIBBLED
NIGGLED
NOTATED
NOTCHED
NOTICED
NUANCED
NUZZLED
OBLIGED
OFFERED
OMITTED
ONEEYED
OPPOSED
ORBITED
ORDERED
OSMOSED
PADDLED
PAINTED
PANELED
PAPERED
PARADED
PARCHED
PAROLED
PARRIED
PARTIED
PATCHED
PEACHED
PEARLED
PEBBLED
PEDALED
PEDDLED
PEOPLED
PERCHED
PERUSED
PESTLED
PETALED

PETERED
PHOTOED
PHRASED
PICKLED
PIERCED
PIFFLED
PILOTED
PINCHED
PIRATED
PITCHED
PIVOTED
PLAGUED
PLAITED
PLANKED
PLANNED
PLANTED
PLASHED
PLEADED
PLEASED
PLEATED
PLEDGED
PLINKED
PLODDED
PLOPPED
PLOTTED
PLUCKED
PLUGGED
PLUMBED
PLUMPED
PLUNGED
PLUNKED
POACHED
POINTED
POLICED
POLKAED
POMADED
POPEYED
POPPLED
POSITED
POUCHED
POUNCED
POUNDED
POWERED
PRAISED
PRANCED
PRANKED
PREENED
PRESSED
PRICKED
PRIMPED
PRINKED
PRINTED
PROCEED
PRODDED
PRONGED
PROOFED
PROPPED
PROWLED
PSALMED
PSYCHED
PUDDLED
PUNCHED
PURFLED
PURPLED
PURSUED
PUTTIED
PUZZLED
QUACKED
QUAFFED
QUAILED
QUASHED
QUEERED
QUELLED

QUERIED
QUESTED
QUIETED
QUILLED
QUILTED
QUIPPED
QUIZZED
RADDLED
RADIOED
RAFFLED
RAGWEED
RALLIED
RAMBLED
RANCHED
RANKLED
RASSLED
RATTLED
RAVAGED
RAVELED
RAVENED
RAZORED
REACHED
REACTED
READIED
REAIRED
REARMED
REBATED
REBUKED
RECANED
RECEDED
RECITED
RECODED
RECUSED
REDATED
REDUCED
REFACED
REFINED
REFRIED
REFUSED
REFUTED
REGALED
REGLUED
REHIRED
REIGNED
REINKED
REKEYED
RELACED
RELATED
RELAXED
RELAYED
RELINED
RELIVED
REMIXED
REMOVED
REMOWED
RENAMED
RENEGED
RENEWED
REOILED
REPAVED
REPINED
REPLIED
REPOSED
REPUTED
RERATED
RESCUED
RESIDED
RESILED
RESOLED
RESUMED
RETAPED
RETAXED
RETILED

RETIMED
RETIRED
RETOWED
RETRIED
RETUNED
RETYPED
REUPPED
REVELED
REVERED
REVILED
REVISED
REVIVED
REVOKED
REWAXED
REWIRED
REXREED
REZONED
RIDDLED
RIFFLED
RIGHTED
RIPENED
RIPPLED
RIVALED
RIVETED
ROACHED
ROADBED
ROASTED
ROOSTED
ROSERED
ROTATED
ROUGHED
ROUNDED
ROUSTED
RUFFLED
RUMBAED
RUMBLED
RUMORED
RUMPLED
RUSTLED
SADDLED
SAINTED
SALLIED
SALUTED
SAMBAED
SAMOYED
SAMPLED
SAUTEED
SAVAGED
SAVORED
SCALDED
SCALPED
SCAMMED
SCAMPED
SCANNED
SCANTED
SCARFED
SCARPED
SCARRED
SCATHED
SCATTED
SCENDED
SCENTED
SCHEMED
SCOFFED
SCOLDED
SCOOPED
SCOOTED
SCORNED
SCOURED
SCOUTED
SCOWLED
SCRAPED
SCREWED

SCUDDED
SCUFFED
SCULLED
SCYTHED
SEAWEED
SECEDED
SECURED
SEDUCED
SEEDBED
SEESRED
SEETHED
SERRIED
SETTLED
SEVERED
SHAFTED
SHAGGED
SHAMMED
SHANKED
SHARPED
SHEARED
SHEAVED
SHEERED
SHEETED
SHELLED
SHELVED
SHIFTED
SHILLED
SHINNED
SHIPPED
SHIRKED
SHIRRED
SHOCKED
SHOPPED
SHORTED
SHOUTED
SHUCKED
SHUNNED
SHUNTED
SHUSHED
SIGHTED
SINGLED
SIZZLED
SKIDDED
SKILLED
SKIMMED
SKIMPED
SKINNED
SKIPPED
SKIRLED
SKIRRED
SKIRTED
SKULKED
SKUNKED
SLABBED
SLACKED
SLAMMED
SLANTED
SLAPPED
SLASHED
SLATTED
SLEDDED
SLEEKED
SLEETED
SLICKED
SLIMMED
SLINKED
SLIPPED
SLOGGED
SLOPPED
SLOSHED
SLOTTED
SLUGGED
SLUICED

SLUMMED
SLUMPED
SLURPED
SLURRED
SMACKED
SMARTED
SMASHED
SMEARED
SMELLED
SMELTED
SMIRKED
SMUDGED
SNACKED
SNAFUED
SNAGGED
SNAPPED
SNARLED
SNEAKED
SNEERED
SNEEZED
SNIFFED
SNIPPED
SNOOPED
SNOOTED
SNOOZED
SNORTED
SNUBBED
SNUFFED
SOBERED
SOFABED
SOOTHED
SORTIED
SOUGHED
SOUNDED
SOURCED
SPALLED
SPANKED
SPANNED
SPARGED
SPARKED
SPARRED
SPATTED
SPAWNED
SPEARED
SPEEDED
SPELLED
SPIELED
SPILLED
SPLAYED
SPLICED
SPOILED
SPONGED
SPOOFED
SPOOKED
SPOOLED
SPOONED
SPORTED
SPOTTED
SPOUTED
SPRAYED
SPRUCED
SPURNED
SPURRED
SPURTED
SQUARED
SQUIRED
STABBED
STABLED
STACKED
STAFFED
STAGGED
STAINED
STALKED

STALLED
STAMPED
STAPLED
STARRED
STARTED
STARVED
STASHED
STEAMED
STEELED
STEEPED
STEERED
STEMMED
STEPPED
STETTED
STIFFED
STIFLED
STILLED
STILTED
STINTED
STIRRED
STOCKED
STOMPED
STOOPED
STOPPED
STORIED
STORMED
STRAFED
STRAYED
STREWED
STRIPED
STRIVED
STROKED
STUBBED
STUDDED
STUDIED
STUFFED
STUMPED
STUNNED
STUNTED
STYMIED
SUBDUED
SUCCEED
SUGARED
SULLIED
SUTURED
SWABBED
SWAMPED
SWAPPED
SWARMED
SWATHED
SWATTED
SWEATED
SWELLED
SWERVED
SWIGGED
SWILLED
SWIRLED
SWISHED
SWOONED
SWOOPED
SYNCHED
TACKLED
TAINTED
TALLIED
TALONED
TANGLED
TANGOED
TAPERED
TARRIED
TATTLED
TAUNTED
TEETHED
TELEXED

TEMPTED
TENONED
TENURED
TETCHED
THANKED
THIEVED
THINNED
THRIVED
THUDDED
THUMBED
THUMPED
TICKLED
TIEDYED
TINGLED
TINKLED
TIPPLED
TIPTOED
TOADIED
TOASTED
TODDLED
TOGGLED
TOKENED
TONGUED
TOOTHED
TOOTLED
TOPPLED
TORCHED
TOTALED
TOUCHED
TOUSLED
TOWELED
TOWERED
TRACKED
TRAILED
TRAINED
TRAMPED
TRAPPED
TRASHED
TRAWLED
TREADED
TREATED
TREBLED
TREKKED
TRENDED
TRICKED
TRIFLED
TRIGGED
TRILLED
TRIMMED
TRIPLED
TRIPPED
TROLLED
TROOPED
TROTHED
TROTTED
TRUCKED
TRUDGED
TRUMPED
TRUSSED
TRUSTED
TRYSTED
TUMBLED
TURTLED
TUSSLED
TUTORED
TWANGED
TWEAKED
TWEETED
TWEEZED
TWILLED
TWINBED
TWINGED
TWINNED

TWIRLED
TWISTED
TWITTED
UMPIRED
UNAIDED
UNAIMED
UNAIRED
UNARMED
UNASKED
UNBAKED
UNBOWED
UNBOXED
UNCAGED
UNCASED
UNDATED
UNENDED
UNFAZED
UNFIXED
UNGLUED
UNIFIED
UNLACED
UNLIKED
UNLINED
UNLOVED
UNMOVED
UNNAMED
UNOILED
UNPAVED
UNPILED
UNRATED
UNROBED
UNSATED
UNSEWED
UNTAMED
UNTAPED
UNTRIED
UNTUNED
UNYOKED
UNZONED
UPDATED
UPENDED
USHERED
USURPED
UTTERED
VACATED
VAULTED
VAUNTED
VISITED
VOUCHED
VOYAGED
WADDLED
WAFFLED
WAGERED
WAGGLED
WAISTED
WAKENED
WALTZED
WAMBLED
WANGLED
WARBLED
WATCHED
WATERED
WAVERED
WEARIED
WEBTOED
WEIGHED
WELCHED
WELLFED
WHACKED
WHAMMED
WHARFED
WHEELED
WHEEZED

WHELPED
WHETTED
WHIFFED
WHIPPED
WHIRLED
WHIRRED
WHISKED
WHIZZED
WHOMPED
WHOOPED
WHOPPED
WHORLED
WHUPPED
WIDENED
WIDOWED
WIELDED
WIGGLED
WIMPLED
WINCHED
WINERED
WIZENED
WOBBLED
WORRIED
WORSTED
WOUNDED
WRACKED
WRAPPED
WREAKED
WRECKED
WRESTED
WRITHED
WRONGED
YACHTED
YEARNED
YIELDED
YODELED

EE•••••

EELIEST
EELSKIN
EERIEST

E•E••••

EGESTED
EJECTED
EKEDOUT
EKESOUT
ELEANOR
ELECTED
ELECTEE
ELECTOR
ELECTRA
ELECTRO
ELEGANT
ELEGIAC
ELEGIES
ELEGIST
ELEISON
ELEKTRA
ELEMENT
ELEVATE
ELEVENS
EMENDED
EMENDER
EMERALD
EMERGED
EMERGES
EMERITA
EMERITI
EMERSED
EMERSON
ENEMIES
EPEEIST
EPERGNE
ERECTED
ERECTER
ERECTLY
ERECTOR
ERELONG
EREMITE
EREWHON
ETERNAL
ETESIAN
EVENEST
EVENING
EVENKIS
EVENOUT
EVENSUP
EVEREST
EVERETT
EVERTED
EXECUTE
EXEMPLI
EXEMPTS
EXERTED
EYEBALL
EYEBANK
EYEBOLT
EYEBROW
EYECUPS
EYEFULS
EYEHOLE
EYELASH
EYELETS
EYELIDS
EYESORE
EYEWASH
EZEKIEL

E••E•••

EAGERER
EAGERLY
EASEDIN
EASEDUP
EASEOFF
EASESIN
EASESUP
EATENAT
EATENUP
ECHELON
EDGEDIN
EDGEOUT
EDGESIN
EFFECTS
EFFENDI
EGGEDON
ELDERLY
EMPEROR
ENDEARS
ENDEMIC
ENNEADS
ENTEBBE
ENTENTE
ENTERED
ENVELOP
EPEEIST
EQUERRY
ERNESTO
ESSENCE
ESSENES
ESTEEMS
ESTELLE
ESTEVEZ
ETIENNE
EUGENIE
EUTERPE
EXCEEDS
EXCEPTS
EXCERPT
EXPECTS
EXPENDS
EXPENSE
EXPERTS
EXTENDS
EXTENTS

E•••E••

EAGLETS
EARNERS
EARNEST
EASIEST
EASTEND
EASTERN
EASTERS
EDGIEST
EELIEST
EERIEST
EGGHEAD
ELATERS
ELEMENT
ELEVENS
ELGRECO
ELOPERS
ELYSEES
EMBLEMS
EMINENT
EMOTERS
EMPRESS
ENAMELS
ENDLESS
ENTREAT
ENTREES
EPICENE
EPIGENE
EPSTEIN
ERASERS
ESCHEAT
ESCHEWS
ESTEEMS
ESTHETE
ETAGERE
ETCHERS
EVADERS
EVENEST
EVEREST
EVERETT
EVIDENT
EVILEST
EVILEYE
EVOKERS
EXCEEDS
EXCRETE
EXIGENT
EXPRESS
EXTREME
EXUPERY
EYELETS

E••••E•

EAGERER
EARLIER
EARTHEN
EBONIES
ECDYSES
ECTYPES
EDASNER
EDIBLES
EDIFIED
EDIFIES
EFFACED
EFFACES
EFFUSED
EFFUSES
EGESTED
EJECTED
ELAPSED
ELAPSES
ELBOWED
ELECTED
ELECTEE
ELEGIES
ELMTREE
ELYSEES
EMANUEL
EMENDED
EMENDER
EMERGED
EMERGES
EMERSED
EMIGRES
EMITTED
EMITTER
EMPANEL
EMPIRES
EMPOWER
EMPTIED
EMPTIER
EMPTIES
ENABLED
ENABLES
ENACTED
ENCAGED
ENCAGES
ENCASED
ENCASES
ENCODED
ENCODER
ENCODES
ENCORES
ENDIVES
ENDOWED
ENDURED
ENDURES
ENDUSER
ENEMIES
ENGAGED
ENGAGES
ENGINES
ENISLED
ENISLES
ENJOYED
ENLACED
ENLACES
ENLIVEN
ENRAGED
ENRAGES
ENROBED
ENROBES
ENSILED
ENSILES
ENSURED
ENSURES
ENTERED
ENTICED
ENTICER
ENTICES
ENTREES
ENTRIES
ENZYMES
EPAULET
EPITHET
EPOXIES
EQUALED
EQUATED
EQUATES
EQUINES
ERECTED
ERECTER
ERITREA
ERMINES
ERUCTED
ERUPTED
ESCAPED
ESCAPEE
ESCAPES
ESSAYED
ESSENES
ESTATES
ESTEVEZ
ETOILES
EUCHRED
EUCHRES
EVACUEE
EVANDER
EVANGEL
EVERTED
EVICTED
EVILLER
EVINCED
EVINCES
EVOLVED
EVOLVES
EVULSED
EVULSES
EXACTED
EXACTER
EXALTED
EXCISED
EXCISES
EXCITED
EXCITES
EXCUSED
EXCUSES
EXERTED
EXHALED
EXHALES
EXISTED
EXPIRED
EXPIRES
EXPOSED
EXPOSES
EXULTED
EXWIVES
EZEKIEL

E•••••E

EARACHE
EARLOBE
EATABLE
EBBTIDE
EBONITE
EBWHITE
ECLIPSE
ECLOGUE
EDIFICE
EDUCATE
EGALITE
EGGCASE
ELECTEE
ELEVATE
ELLIPSE
ELMTREE
ELUSIVE
EMANATE
EMBRACE

EMIRATE
EMOTIVE
EMULATE
ENCLAVE
ENCLOSE
ENDGAME
ENDORSE
ENDWISE
ENDZONE
ENFORCE
ENGARDE
ENGORGE
ENGRAVE
ENHANCE
ENLARGE
ENMASSE
ENNOBLE
ENOUNCE
ENPLANE
ENROUTE
ENSLAVE
ENSNARE
ENSUITE
ENTEBBE
ENTENTE
ENTHUSE
ENTITLE
ENTWINE
EPERGNE
EPICENE
EPICURE
EPIGENE
EPIGONE
EPISODE
EPISTLE
EPITOME
EQUABLE
ERASURE
EREMITE
EROSIVE
ERSKINE
ERUDITE
ESCAPEE
ESPOUSE
ESQUIRE
ESSENCE
ESTELLE
ESTHETE
ETAGERE
ETAMINE
ETIENNE
EUGENIE
EUTERPE
EVACUEE
EVASIVE
EVILEYE
EXAMINE
EXAMPLE
EXCLUDE
EXCRETE
EXECUTE
EXPANSE
EXPARTE
EXPENSE
EXPIATE
EXPLODE
EXPLORE
EXPUNGE
EXTREME
EXTRUDE
EYEHOLE
EYESORE

•EE••••

BEEBALM
BEECHAM
BEECHER
BEECHES
BEEFALO
BEEFIER
BEEFING
BEEFSUP
BEEGEES
BEEHIVE
BEELINE
BEEPERS
BEEPING
BEESWAX
BEETLES
BEETREE
DEEDING
DEEJAYS
DEEMING
DEEPEND
DEEPENS
DEEPEST
DEEPFAT
DEEPFRY
DEEPSEA
DEEPSET
DEEPSIX
DEERFLY
FEEBLER
FEEDBAG
FEEDERS
FEEDING
FEEDLOT
FEEDSON
FEELERS
FEELFOR
FEELIES
FEELING
FEELOUT
GEEGAWS
GEEWHIZ
GEEZERS
HEEDFUL
HEEDING
HEEHAWS
HEELERS
HEELING
HEELTAP
JEEBIES
JEERERS
JEERING
JEERSAT
KEEBLER
KEELING
KEENERS
KEENEST
KEENING
KEEPERS
KEEPING
KEEPOFF
KEEPSAT
KEEPSIN
KEEPSON
KEEPSTO
KEEPSUP
KEESHAN
LEECHED
LEECHES
LEERERS
LEERIER
LEERILY
LEERING
LEERSAT
LEETIDE
LEEWARD
MEEKEST
MEETING
NEEDFUL
NEEDIER
NEEDILY
NEEDING
NEEDLED
NEEDLES
PEEKING
PEEKOUT
PEEKSAT
PEELERS
PEELING
PEELOFF
PEEPERS
PEEPING
PEEPLES
PEERAGE
PEERESS
PEERING
PEEROUT
PEERSAT
PEERSIN
PEEVING
PEEVISH
PEEWEES
REEDIER
REEDING
REEDITS
REEFERS
REEFING
REEKING
REELECT
REELING
REELOFF
REELSIN
REENACT
REENTER
REENTRY
SEEDBED
SEEDERS
SEEDIER
SEEDILY
SEEDING
SEEDPOD
SEEHERE
SEEKERS
SEEKING
SEEKOUT
SEEMING
SEEPING
SEEPSIN
SEERESS
SEESAWS
SEESFIT
SEESOFF
SEESOUT
SEESRED
SEETHED
SEETHES
SEETOIT
TEEDOFF
TEEMING
TEENAGE
TEENERS
TEENIER
TEEPEES
TEESOFF
TEETERS
TEETHED
TEETHER
TEETHES
VEEJAYS
VEENECK
VEERING
WEEDERS
WEEDIER
WEEDING
WEEDOUT
WEEKDAY
WEEKEND
WEENIES
WEEPERS
WEEPIER
WEEPING
WEEVILS

•E•E•••

BEDECKS
BEDELIA
BEDEVIL
BEDEWED
BEHESTS
BENEATH
BENEFIT
BEREAVE
BERETTA
BESEECH
BESEEMS
BEVELED
BEVERLY
CELEBES
CELEBRE
CELESTA
CELESTE
CEMENTS
CEREALS
CEREBRA
DEBEERS
DECEITS
DECEIVE
DEFEATS
DEFECTS
DEFENCE
DEFENDS
DEFENSE
DEJECTS
DELEING
DELETED
DELETES
DEMEANS
DEMERIT
DEMEROL
DEMESNE
DEMETER
DENEUVE
DEPECHE
DEPENDS
DESERTS
DESERVE
DETECTS
DETENTE
DETESTS
DEVEINS
DEVELOP
FEDERAL
FENETRE
GENERAL
GENERIC
GENERIS
GENESEE
GENESES
GENESIS
GENETIC
GERENTS
GETEVEN
HERETIC
JEWELED
JEWELER
JEWELRY
JEZEBEL
KEYEDIN
KEYEDUP
LEGENDS
LEVELED
LEVELER
LEVELLY
LEVERED
LEVERET
MEDEVAC
MEMENTO
METEORS
METEOUT
METERED
NEMEROV
NEMESES
NEMESIS
NEREIDS
PESETAS
PETERED
REBECCA
REBEKAH
RECEDED
RECEDES
RECEIPT
RECEIVE
RECENCY
REDEALS
REDEALT
REDEEMS
REDEYES
REFEREE
REFERTO
REGENCY
REGENTS
REHEALS
REHEARD
REHEARS
REHEATS
REHEELS
REJECTS
REKEYED
RELEARN
RELEASE
RELENTS
REMELTS
REMENDS
RENEGED
RENEGER
RENEGES
RENEWAL
RENEWED
RENEWER
REPEALS
REPEATS
REPENTS
REREADS
REREDOS
RERENTS
RESEALS
RESEATS
RESECTS
RESEEDS
RESELLS
RESENDS
RESENTS
RESERVE
RETEACH
RETELLS
RETESTS
REVEALS
REVELED
REVELER
REVELRY
REVENGE
REVENUE
REVERBS
REVERED
REVERES
REVERIE
REVERSE
REVERTS
REWEAVE
REWELDS
SECEDED
SECEDER
SECEDES
SELECTS
SELENIC
SENECAS
SENEGAL
SERENER
SEVENTH
SEVENTY
SEVENUP
SEVERAL
SEVERED
SEVERER
SEWEDUP
TEHERAN
TELERAN
TELEXED
TELEXES
TEREDOS
TERENCE
VEGETAL
VENEERS
VETERAN
VEXEDLY
YEMENIS
YEREVAN

•E••E••

AERIEST
BEAKERS
BEANERY
BEARERS
BEATERS
BEAVERS
BECKETT
BEDREST
BEEGEES
BEEPERS
BELIEFS
BELIEVE
BENDERS
BENNETT
BENZENE
BEQUEST
BERBERS
BERGERE
BERNESE
BERSERK
BESEECH
BESEEMS
BESIEGE
BESMEAR
BESPEAK
BETHELS
BETTERS
BETWEEN
BEZIERS
CENSERS
CENTERS
CEPHEUS
DEADEND
DEADENS
DEADEYE
DEAFENS
DEAFEST
DEALERS
DEAREST
DEBEERS
DECREED
DECREES
DEEPEND
DEEPENS
DEEPEST
DEFLECT
DEFTEST
DEGREES
DEICERS
DEKLERK
DELBERT
DELVERS
DENIECE
DENIERS
DENNEHY
DENSELY
DENSEST
DEPLETE
DEPRESS
DESCEND
DESCENT
DESSERT
DEUTERO
EELIEST
EERIEST
FEARERS
FEEDERS
FEELERS
FELLERS
FENCERS
FENDERS
FERMENT
FERRETS
FERVENT
FESTERS
FETTERS
GEEZERS
GENDERS
GENOESE
GENTEEL
GEODESY
GETWELL
GEYSERS
HEADERS
HEALERS
HEARERS
HEATERS
HEAVEHO
HEAVENS
HEAVERS
HEAVETO
HEBREWS
HEDGERS
HEELERS
HEIFERS
HEIFETZ
HEIRESS
HELLENE
HELLERS
HELMETS
HELPERS
HEMMERS
HENNERY
HENPECK
HENREID
HERBERT
HERDERS
HERSELF
HEWLETT
JEERERS
JEFFERS
JENNETS
JERSEYS
JESTERS
KEENERS
KEENEST
KEEPERS
KEGLERS
KENNEDY
KENNELS
KENNETH
KERNELS
KEYWEST
LEADERS
LEAKERS
LEANERS
LEANEST
LEAPERS
LEASERS
LEAVENS
LECTERN
LEDGERS
LEERERS
LENDERS
LENIENT
LESSEES
LESSENS
LETTERS
LEVIERS
LEWDEST
MEANEST
MEDLEYS
MEEKEST
MEMBERS
MENDERS
MERGERS
METIERS
MEWLERS
NEAREST
NEATENS
NEATEST
NECKERS
NEGLECT
NEPHEWS
NESTEGG
NESTERS
NEWDEAL
NEWLEFT
NEWNESS
NEWYEAR
PEABEAN
PEAHENS
PEAVEYS
PEELERS
PEEPERS
PEERESS
PEEWEES
PELLETS
PELTERS
PENDENT
PENNERS
PENSEES
PEPPERS
PEPPERY
PERCENT
PERFECT
PERNELL
PERSEUS
PERTEST
PERVERT
PESTERS
PETRELS
PETTERS
PEUGEOT
READERS
REAGENT
REAMERS
REAPERS
REAREND
REARERS
RECHECK
RECLEAN
REDCELL
REDCENT
REDDEER
REDDENS
REDDEST
REDEEMS
REDHEAD
REDHEAT
REDMEAT
REDNESS
REDRESS
REEFERS
REELECT
REFLECT
REFRESH
REFUELS
REGRESS
REGRETS
REHEELS
RELIEFS
RELIEVE
RELIEVO
RELLENO
RENDERS
RENTERS
REOPENS
REPLETE
REPRESS
REQUEST
RESEEDS
RESPECT
RESTERS
RETREAD
RETREAT
REUBENS
REUTERS
REVIEWS
REXREED
SEABEDS
SEABEES
SEALEGS
SEALERS
SEATERS
SEAWEED
SECRECY
SECRETE
SECRETS
SEEDERS
SEEHERE
SEEKERS
SEERESS
SEGMENT
SEIDELS
SEINERS
SEIZERS
SELLECK
SELLERS
SENDERS
SENNETT
SEPTETS
SEQUELS
SERPENT
SERVERS
SERVEUP
SESTETS
SETTEES
SETTERS
SEXIEST
SEXTETS
TEALEAF
TEASELS
TEASERS
TEASETS
TEDDERS
TEENERS
TEEPEES
TEETERS
TELLERS
TEMPERA
TEMPERS
TEMPEST
TENDERS
TENNERS
TENSELY
TENSEST
TENSEUP
TENTERS
TERCELS
TERCETS
TERRENE
TERRETS
TERSELY
TERSEST
TESSERA
TESTEES
TESTERS
TETHERS
VEENECK
VELVETS
VELVETY
VENEERS
VENTERS
VERBENA
VERGERS
VERMEER
VERMEIL
VERVETS
VESPERS
VESSELS
VESTEES
VETOERS
WEAKENS
WEAKEST
WEARERS
WEASELS
WEAVERS
WEBFEET
WEEDERS
WEEKEND
WEEPERS
WELDERS
WELTERS
WENDELL
WENDERS
WESTEND
WESTERN
WETCELL
WETHERS
WETNESS
WETTEST
YEAREND
YEATEAM
YELPERS
YESDEAR
YEVGENY

•E•••E•

AEDILES
AERATED
AERATES
AEROBES
BEACHED
BEACHES
BEADIER
BEADLES
BEAGLES
BEAMIER
BEANIES
BEARDED
BEATLES
BECOMES
BEDEWED
BEDIZEN
BEECHER
BEECHES
BEEFIER
BEEGEES
BEETLES
BEETREE
BEHAVED
BEHAVES
BELATED
BELAYED
BELCHED
BELCHES
BELLIED
BELLIES
BELLMEN
BELOVED
BEMIRED
BEMIRES
BEMUSED
BEMUSES
BENCHED
BENCHES
BENTLEY
BENTSEN
BERATED
BERATES
BERNSEN
BERRIED
BERRIES
BERTHED
BESIDES
BESTMEN
BESTREW
BETAKEN
BETAKES
BETIDED
BETIDES
BETIMES
BETOKEN
BETWEEN
BEVELED
CELEBES
CENTRED
CENTRES
CERUMEN
DEADSEA
DEADSET
DEBAKEY
DEBASED
DEBASES
DEBATED
DEBATER
DEBATES
DEBITED
DEBONED
DEBONES
DEBRIEF
DEBUTED
DECADES
DECAYED
DECIBEL
DECIDED
DECIDES
DECKLES
DECODED
DECODER
DECODES
DECOYED
DECREED
DECREES
DECRIED
DECRIES
DEDUCED
DEDUCES
DEEPSEA
DEEPSET
DEFACED
DEFACES
DEFAMED
DEFAMES
DEFILED
DEFILER
DEFILES
DEFINED
DEFINES
DEFUSED
DEFUSES
DEGREES
DEIFIED
DEIFIES
DEIGNED
DEITIES
DEKOVEN
DELANEY
DELAYED
DELAYER
DELETED
DELETES
DELIBES
DELIVER
DELUDED
DELUDES
DELUGED
DELUGES
DEMETER
DEMISED
DEMISES
DEMOTED
DEMOTES
DEMPSEY
DEMURER
DENIZEN
DENOTED
DENOTES
DENUDED
DENUDES
DEPONED
DEPONES
DEPOSED
DEPOSER
DEPOSES
DEPUTED
DEPUTES
DERBIES
DERIDED
DERIDES
DERIVED
DERIVES
DERNIER
DESIRED
DESIREE
DESIRES
DESKSET
DEVICES
DEVILED
DEVISED
DEVISES
DEVOTED
DEVOTEE
DEVOTES
DEVRIES
FEASTED
FEATHER
FEEBLER
FEELIES
FEIFFER
FEIGNED
FEINTED
FELINES
FEMALES
FERRIED
FERRIES
FERULES
FETCHED
FETCHES
FETTLES
GECKOES
GENESEE
GENESES
GENTEEL
GENTLED
GENTLER
GENTLES
GEORGES
GESSOES
GETEVEN
GETOVER
GETSSET
HEADIER
HEADMEN
HEADSET
HEARKEN
HEARTEN
HEATHEN
HEATHER
HEATTER
HEAVIER
HEAVIES
HECKLED
HECKLER
HECKLES
HEDDLES
HEFTIER
HEISTED
HELICES
HELIXES
HEMSLEY
HENNAED
HERBTEA
HERSHEY
JEEBIES
JEFFREY

JELLIED
JELLIES
JEMMIED
JEMMIES
JENNIES
JERKIER
JETTIES
JEWELED
JEWELER
JEZEBEL
KEEBLER
KELPIES
KESTREL
KETCHES
KETONES
KETTLES
KEWPIES
LEACHED
LEACHES
LEAFIER
LEAFLET
LEAGUER
LEAGUES
LEAKIER
LEANDER
LEARJET
LEARNED
LEARNER
LEASHED
LEASHES
LEATHER
LEECHED
LEECHES
LEERIER
LEFTIES
LEGATEE
LEGATES
LEGGIER
LEGUMES
LEISTER
LESSEES
LETSSEE
LETTRES
LEVELED
LEVELER
LEVERED
LEVERET
LEVITES
MEALIER
MEALIES
MEANDER
MEANIES
MEASLES
MEATIER
MEDALED
MEDDLED
MEDDLER
MEDDLES
MEIOSES
MEISSEN
MEMOREX
MENACED
MENACES
MENAGES
MENCKEN
MERCIES
MERIMEE
MERITED
MERRIER
MESSIER
METATES
METERED
METOOER

METTLES
NEEDIER
NEEDLED
NEEDLES
NEGATED
NEGATES
NEIGHED
NEITHER
NEMESES
NERVIER
NESTLED
NESTLER
NESTLES
NETTLED
NETTLES
NEWAGER
NEWSIER
NEWSMEN
NEXUSES
OEUVRES
PEACHED
PEACHES
PEARLED
PEBBLED
PEBBLES
PEDALED
PEDDLED
PEDDLER
PEDDLES
PEDICEL
PEEPLES
PEEWEES
PELAGES
PENATES
PENNIES
PENSEES
PEONIES
PEOPLED
PEOPLES
PEPPIER
PERCHED
PERCHES
PERDIEM
PERIGEE
PERKIER
PERPLEX
PERRIER
PERUKES
PERUSED
PERUSER
PERUSES
PESKIER
PESTLED
PESTLES
PETALED
PETERED
PETITES
PETTIER
REACHED
REACHES
REACTED
READIED
READIER
READIES
REAIRED
REARMED
REBATED
REBATES
REBUKED
REBUKES
REBUSES
RECANED
RECANES

RECEDED
RECEDES
RECIPES
RECITED
RECITER
RECITES
RECODED
RECODES
RECOVER
RECUSED
RECUSES
REDATED
REDATES
REDDEER
REDEYES
REDUCED
REDUCER
REDUCES
REEDIER
REENTER
REFACED
REFACES
REFEREE
REFINED
REFINER
REFINES
REFIRES
REFRIED
REFRIES
REFUGEE
REFUGES
REFUSED
REFUSER
REFUSES
REFUTED
REFUTER
REFUTES
REGALED
REGALES
REGIMEN
REGIMES
REGLUED
REGLUES
REHIRED
REHIRES
REIGNED
REINKED
REKEYED
RELACED
RELACES
RELATED
RELATES
RELAXED
RELAXES
RELAYED
RELINED
RELINES
RELIVED
RELIVES
REMAKES
REMIXED
REMIXES
REMODEL
REMOTER
REMOTES
REMOVED
REMOVER
REMOVES
REMOWED
RENAMED
RENAMES
RENEGED
RENEGER

RENEGES
RENEWED
RENEWER
RENOTES
REOILED
REORDER
REPAPER
REPAVED
REPAVES
REPINED
REPINES
REPLIED
REPLIES
REPOSED
REPOSES
REPUTED
REPUTES
REQUIEM
RERATED
RERATES
RESALES
RESCUED
RESCUER
RESCUES
RESHOES
RESIDED
RESIDES
RESILED
RESILES
RESOLED
RESOLES
RESUMED
RESUMES
RETAKEN
RETAKES
RETAPED
RETAPES
RETAXED
RETAXES
RETILED
RETILES
RETIMED
RETIMES
RETIRED
RETIREE
RETIRES
RETOWED
RETRIED
RETRIES
RETUNED
RETUNES
RETYPED
RETYPES
REUPPED
REUTHER
REVELED
REVELER
REVERED
REVERES
REVILED
REVILES
REVISED
REVISER
REVISES
REVIVED
REVIVES
REVOKED
REVOKES
REWAXED
REWAXES
REWIRED
REWIRES
REWOVEN

REXREED
REZONED
REZONES
SEABEES
SEAMIER
SEANCES
SEAWEED
SECEDED
SECEDER
SECEDES
SECURED
SECURER
SECURES
SEDATER
SEDUCED
SEDUCER
SEDUCES
SEEDBED
SEEDIER
SEESRED
SEETHED
SEETHES
SEICHES
SELTZER
SEMITES
SENATES
SENORES
SERAPES
SERENER
SERRIED
SESAMES
SETTEES
SETTLED
SETTLER
SETTLES
SEVERED
SEVERER
TEACHER
TEACHES
TEARIER
TECHIES
TEDDIES
TEENIER
TEEPEES
TEETHED
TEETHER
TEETHES
TEICHER
TELEXED
TELEXES
TELLIES
TEMPLES
TEMPTED
TEMPTER
TENACES
TENNIEL
TENONED
TENURED
TENURES
TERRIER
TERRIES
TESTEES
TESTIER
TETCHED
VEGGIES
VERMEER
VERNIER
VESTEES
VETCHES
WEARIED
WEARIER
WEARIES
WEATHER

WEBFEET
WEBSTER
WEBTOED
WEDGIES
WEEDIER
WEENIES
WEEPIER
WEIGHED
WEIRDER
WELCHED
WELCHES
WELLFED
WELLSET
WENCHES
WERNHER
WERTHER
YEARNED
YEARNER
ZESTIER

•E••••E

BEASTIE
BEATTIE
BECAUSE
BEDSIDE
BEDTIME
BEEHIVE
BEELINE
BEETREE
BEGRIME
BEGUILE
BEGUINE
BEHOOVE
BELDAME
BELIEVE
BELTANE
BENZENE
BEREAVE
BERGERE
BERNESE
BERNICE
BESIEGE
BESPOKE
BEZIQUE
CELEBRE
CELESTE
CENSURE
CENTIME
CEVICHE
CEZANNE
DEADEYE
DEBACLE
DEBARGE
DECEIVE
DECLARE
DECLINE
DEFARGE
DEFENCE
DEFENSE
DEFLATE
DEGRADE
DEHISCE
DELUISE
DEMESNE
DEMILLE
DENEUVE
DENIECE
DENTATE
DENTINE
DENTURE
DEPECHE
DEPLANE
DEPLETE

DEPLORE
DEPRAVE
DEPRIVE
DESERVE
DESIREE
DESPISE
DESPITE
DESTINE
DETENTE
DEVALUE
DEVIATE
DEVILLE
DEVOLVE
DEVOTEE
DEWILDE
DEWLINE
FEATURE
FEBRILE
FENETRE
FERRATE
FERRITE
FERRULE
FERTILE
FESTIVE
GEFILTE
GEMLIKE
GENESEE
GENOESE
GENTILE
GENUINE
GERMANE
GESTATE
GESTURE
HECTARE
HELLENE
HELOISE
HEMLINE
HENBANE
HERBAGE
HERCULE
HEROINE
HEYJUDE
JEANNIE
KEYHOLE
KEYLIME
KEYNOTE
LEAKAGE
LECARRE
LECTURE
LEETIDE
LEGATEE
LEGIBLE
LEHAVRE
LEISURE
LEONINE
LETITBE
LETSSEE
LETTUCE
MEASURE
MEDIATE
MEDUSAE
MELANGE
MELANIE
MELROSE
MEMOIRE
MERIMEE
MESSAGE
METHANE
NEBULAE
NECKTIE
NEONATE
NEPTUNE
NESCAFE

NETSUKE
NEURONE
NEVILLE
NEWGATE
NEWWAVE
PEDICLE
PEERAGE
PELISSE
PELTATE
PENANCE
PENNAME
PENNATE
PENSIVE
PENUCHE
PEONAGE
PEPTIDE
PERCALE
PERFUME
PERIGEE
PERJURE
PERLITE
PERVADE
PETIOLE
PETNAME
REALIZE
REARGUE
REBASTE
RECEIVE
RECHOSE
RECLAME
RECLINE
RECLUSE
RECYCLE
REDLINE
REDPINE
REDROSE
REDTAPE
REDWINE
REFEREE
REFRAME
REFUGEE
REGRADE
REISSUE
REJOICE
RELAPSE
RELEASE
RELIEVE
REMORSE
REPASTE
REPLACE
REPLATE
REPLETE
REPRICE
REPRISE
REPROVE
REPTILE
REPULSE
REQUIRE
REQUITE
RERAISE
RERINSE
REROUTE
RESCALE
RESERVE
RESIDUE
RESOLVE
RESPIRE
RESPITE
RESTAGE
RESTATE
RESTIVE
RESTORE
RESTYLE

RESURGE
RETICLE
RETINAE
RETINUE
RETIREE
RETITLE
RETRACE
RETRADE
REUNITE
REVALUE
REVENGE
REVENUE
REVERIE
REVERSE
REVOICE
REVOLVE
REWEAVE
REWRITE
REWROTE
SEAGATE
SEALANE
SEASIDE
SEATTLE
SECLUDE
SECRETE
SEEHERE
SELVAGE
SENSATE
SERIATE
SERRATE
SERVICE
SERVILE
SESSILE
SETLINE
SEVIGNE
SEVILLE
TEACAKE
TEAROSE
TEATIME
TEENAGE
TEKTITE
TENABLE
TENSILE
TENSIVE
TERENCE
TERHUNE
TERMITE
TERNATE
TERRACE
TERRENE
TEXTILE
TEXTURE
VEHICLE
VENTURE
VERBOSE
VERDURE
VESTIGE
VESTURE
WEBSITE
WELCOME
WELFARE
WENTAPE

••EE•••

BLEEPED
BLEEPER
BREEDER
BREEZED
BREEZES
CHEEPED
CHEERED
CHEERIO
CHEERUP
CHEESES
CHEETAH
CHEETOS
CHEEVER
CREEPED
CREEPER
CREEPUP
DWEEZIL
EPEEIST
FLEECED
FLEECES
FLEEING
FLEETER
FLEETLY
FREEBEE
FREEBIE
FREEDOM
FREEING
FREEMAN
FREEMEN
FREESIA
FREEWAY
FREEZER
FREEZES
GLEEFUL
GREELEY
GREENED
GREENER
GREETED
GREETER
KLEENEX
KNEECAP
KNEEING
KNEELED
KNEELER
KNEEPAD
OKEEFFE
ONEEYED
PREEMIE
PREEMPT
PREENED
PREENER
QUEENLY
QUEERED
QUEERER
QUEERLY
SHEERED
SHEERER
SHEERLY
SHEETED
SKEETER
SKEEZIX
SLEEKED
SLEEKEN
SLEEKER
SLEEKLY
SLEEPER
SLEEPIN
SLEEPON
SLEETED
SLEEVES
SNEERAT
SNEERED
SNEERER
SNEEZED
SNEEZER
SNEEZES
SPEEDED
SPEEDER
SPEEDUP
STEELED
STEELER
STEELIE
STEEPED
STEEPEN
STEEPER
STEEPLE
STEEPLY
STEERED
STEERER
SWEEPER
SWEEPUP
SWEETEN
SWEETER
SWEETIE
SWEETLY
SWEETON
TREEING
TREERAT
TREETOP
TWEETED
TWEETER
TWEEZED
TWEEZES
WHEEDLE
WHEELED
WHEELER
WHEELIE
WHEEZED
WHEEZER
WHEEZES

••E•E••

AGELESS
AWELESS
BEEGEES
BEEPERS
BREVETS
BREWERS
BREWERY
CHEWERS
CLEMENS
CLEMENT
CRENELS
CREWELS
DEEPEND
DEEPENS
DEEPEST
DIESELS
DIETERS
DUELERS
ELEMENT
ELEVENS
EVENEST
EVEREST
EVERETT
EYELETS
FEEDERS
FEELERS
FRENEAU
FUELERS
GEEZERS
GREYEST
HEELERS
ICEBERG
ICELESS
JAEGERS
JEERERS
KEENERS
KEENEST
KEEPERS
LEERERS
LIENEES
MAEWEST
MEEKEST
OMELETS
ONENESS
ONESELF
OPENEND
OPENERS
OVEREAT
PEELERS
PEEPERS
PEERESS
PEEWEES
PIECERS
POETESS
PREBEND
PRECEDE
PRECEPT
PREFECT
PREFERS
PREHEAT
PREMEDS
PRESELL
PRESENT
PRESETS
PRETEEN
PRETEND
PRETEST
PRETEXT
PREVENT
QUEUERS
QUEUEUP
REEFERS
REELECT
ROEDEER
SCENERY
SEEDERS
SEEHERE
SEEKERS
SEERESS
SHEKELS
SKEWERS
STEREOS
STEVENS
STEWERS
TEENERS
TEEPEES
TEETERS
THEDEEP
THEREAT
THEREBY
THEREIN
THEREOF
THEREON
THERESA
THERETO
THESEUS
TIELESS
TOELESS
USELESS
VEENECK
VIEWERS
WEEDERS
WEEKEND
WEEPERS
WHEREAS
WHEREAT
WHEREBY
WHEREIN
WHEREOF
WHERETO
WIENERS

••E••E•

ABETTED
ALERTED
ALERTER
AMENDED
AMERCED
AMERCES
APERIES
ATELIER
AVENGED
AVENGER
AVENGES
AVENUES
AVERRED
AVERTED
AYEAYES
BEECHER
BEECHES
BEEFIER
BEEGEES
BEETLES
BEETREE
BLEAKER
BLEARED
BLEATED
BLEEPED
BLEEPER
BLENDED
BLENDER
BLESSED
BLESSES
BREADED
BREAKER
BREEDER
BREEZED
BREEZES
BRENNER
CHEAPEN
CHEAPER
CHEATED
CHEATER
CHECHEN
CHECKED
CHECKER
CHEEPED
CHEERED
CHEESES
CHEEVER
CHELSEA
CHENIER
CHEQUER
CHEQUES
CHESTER
CHEVIED
CHEVIES
CHEVRES
CHEWIER
CLEANED
CLEANER
CLEARED
CLEARER
CLEAVED
CLEAVER
CLEAVES
CLERKED
COERCED
COERCES
CREAKED
CREAMED
CREAMER
CREASED
CREASES
CREATED
CREATES
CRECHES
CREEPED
CREEPER

CREOLES
CRESSES
CRESTED
CREWMEN
DEEPSEA
DEEPSET
DREADED
DREAMED
DREAMER
DREDGED
DREDGER
DREDGES
DREIDEL
DREISER
DRESDEN
DRESSED
DRESSER
DRESSES
DWELLED
DWELLER
EGESTED
EJECTED
ELECTED
ELECTEE
ELEGIES
EMENDED
EMENDER
EMERGED
EMERGES
EMERSED
ENEMIES
ERECTED
ERECTER
EVERTED
EXERTED
EZEKIEL
FEEBLER
FEELIES
FIEDLER
FIELDED
FIELDER
FIERCER
FIERIER
FLECHES
FLECKED
FLEDGED
FLEDGES
FLEECED
FLEECES
FLEETER
FLENSED
FLENSES
FLESHED
FLESHES
FLEXNER
FREAKED
FREEBEE
FREEMEN
FREEZER
FREEZES
FRESHEN
FRESHER
FRESHET
FRETTED
GLEAMED
GLEANED
GLEANER
GREASED
GREASER
GREASES
GREATER
GREAVES
GREELEY

GREENED
GREENER
GREETED
GREETER
GRENDEL
GUESSED
GUESSER
GUESSES
GUESTED
ICEAGES
ICEAXES
ICEDTEA
ICEFREE
IDEATED
IDEATES
JEEBIES
KEEBLER
KLEENEX
KNEADED
KNEADER
KNEELED
KNEELER
KNELLED
KNESSET
LAENNEC
LAERTES
LEECHED
LEECHES
LEERIER
LIEABED
LIENEES
LIEOVER
LIERNES
LOESSER
LOESSES
NEEDIER
NEEDLED
NEEDLES
NIELSEN
OLEATES
ONEEYED
ONESTEP
OPENSEA
ORESTES
OVERSEA
OVERSEE
PEEPLES
PEEWEES
PIERCED
PIERCES
PIETIES
PLEADED
PLEADER
PLEASED
PLEASER
PLEASES
PLEATED
PLEDGED
PLEDGEE
PLEDGER
PLEDGES
PREENED
PREENER
PREMIER
PRESLEY
PRESSED
PRESSER
PRESSES
PRETEEN
PRETZEL
PREVIEW
QUEERED
QUEERER

QUELLED
QUERIED
QUERIES
QUESTED
REEDIER
REENTER
ROEDEER
SCENDED
SCENTED
SCEPTER
SEEDBED
SEEDIER
SEESRED
SEETHED
SEETHES
SHEARED
SHEARER
SHEAVED
SHEAVES
SHEERED
SHEERER
SHEETED
SHELLED
SHELLER
SHELLEY
SHELTER
SHELVED
SHELVES
SHERBET
SKEETER
SKELTER
SLEDDED
SLEDDER
SLEDGES
SLEEKED
SLEEKEN
SLEEKER
SLEEPER
SLEETED
SLEEVES
SLENDER
SMEARED
SMELLED
SMELTED
SMELTER
SNEAKED
SNEAKER
SNEERED
SNEERER
SNEEZED
SNEEZER
SNEEZES
SNELLEN
SPEAKER
SPEARED
SPECIES
SPECTER
SPEEDED
SPEEDER
SPELLED
SPELLER
SPENCER
SPENDER
SPENSER
STEAMED
STEAMER
STEELED
STEELER
STEEPED
STEEPEN
STEEPER
STEERED
STEERER

STEIGER
STEINEM
STEINER
STEMMED
STENGEL
STEPHEN
STEPPED
STEPPER
STEPPES
STERNER
STETTED
STEUBEN
SVELTER
SWEARER
SWEATED
SWEATER
SWEEPER
SWEETEN
SWEETER
SWELLED
SWELTER
SWERVED
SWERVES
TEENIER
TEEPEES
TEETHED
TEETHER
TEETHES
THEATER
THEDEEP
THEOREM
TIEDYED
TIEDYES
TIERNEY
TREADED
TREADER
TREATED
TREBLED
TREBLES
TREKKED
TREKKER
TRENDED
TRESSES
TSETSES
TWEAKED
TWEETED
TWEETER
TWEEZED
TWEEZES
TWELVES
UNENDED
UPENDED
WEEDIER
WEENIES
WEEPIER
WHEELED
WHEELER
WHEEZED
WHEEZER
WHEEZES
WHELPED
WHETHER
WHETTED
WIELDED
WIENIES
WREAKED
WRECKED
WRECKER
WRESTED
YIELDED
ZOELLER

••E•••E

ACEROSE
ACETATE
ACETONE
ADELINE
ADENINE
ALEWIFE
ANEMONE
APELIKE
AREOLAE
AVERAGE
AWESOME
BEEHIVE
BEELINE
BEETREE
BREATHE
CHEAPIE
CHEMISE
CLEANSE
CREVICE
DOEUVRE
DUEDATE
ELECTEE
ELEVATE
EPERGNE
EREMITE
EXECUTE
EYEHOLE
EYESORE
FRECKLE
FREDDIE
FREEBEE
FREEBIE
GOESAPE
GRENADE
HOECAKE
ICEBLUE
ICECUBE
ICEFLOE
ICEFREE
ITEMIZE
ITERATE
LEETIDE
MCENROE
OBELIZE
OKEEFFE
ONETIME
OPENTOE
OPERATE
OPEROSE
OVERAGE
OVERATE
OVERAWE
OVERDUE
OVERLIE
OVERSEE
OVERUSE
PEERAGE
PLEDGEE
PRECEDE
PRECISE
PREDATE
PREEMIE
PREFACE
PRELATE
PRELUDE
PREMISE
PREPARE
PREPPIE
PRESAGE
PRESALE
PRESIDE
PRESUME

PRETAPE
PUERILE
SCEPTRE
SEEHERE
SHEATHE
SHEILAE
SHELTIE
SPECKLE
SPECTRE
STEELIE
STEEPLE
STERILE
SWEETIE
TEENAGE
THEATRE
THEBABE
TIELINE
TOESHOE
TREACLE
TREADLE
TREKKIE
TREMBLE
TRESTLE
USEABLE
WHEEDLE
WHEELIE
WOEISME
WREATHE
WRESTLE

•••EE••

AFREETS
AGREETO
BALEENS
BESEECH
BESEEMS
CAREENS
CAREERS
DEBEERS
ESTEEMS
EXCEEDS
LATEENS
MUDEELS
NOSEEUM
PAPEETE
REDEEMS
REHEELS
RESEEDS
SCREECH
SCREEDS
SCREENS
SPLEENS
SQUEEZE
STREETS
THREERS
TUREENS
UNREELS
VENEERS

•••E•E•

ACCEDED
ACCEDER
ACCEDES
ACHENES
ADHERED
ADHERES
ALIENEE
ALKENES
ALLEGED
ALLEGER
ALLEGES
ALLELES
ALLEYES

ALTERED
ALTERER
AMMETER
AMPERES
ANGELES
ANGERED
ANNEXED
ANNEXES
APHESES
BASEMEN
BEDEWED
BEVELED
BIGEYES
BILEVEL
BIREMES
BLEEPED
BLEEPER
BODEREK
BOGEYED
BOWERED
BREEDER
BREEZED
BREEZES
BRIEFED
BRIEFER
BRUEGEL
BUGEYED
CAMEOED
CAPELET
CAPERED
CATERED
CATERER
CAVEMEN
CELEBES
CHEEPED
CHEERED
CHEESES
CHEEVER
COHERED
COHERES
COVERED
COVETED
COWERED
COZENED
CREEPED
CREEPER
CRUELER
DELETED
DELETES
DEMETER
DINESEN
DRYEYED
EAGERER
ENTERED
ESSENES
ESTEVEZ
FACETED
FIREMEN
FLEECED
FLEECES
FLEETER
FORELEG
FOREMEN
FORESEE
FOREVER
FREEBEE
FREEMEN
FREEZER
FREEZES
FRIEZES
GAMETES
GATELEG
GATEMEN

GAVELED
GENESEE
GENESES
GETEVEN
GORETEX
GOTEVEN
GREELEY
GREENED
GREENER
GREETED
GREETER
GRIEVED
GRIEVER
GRIEVES
HOMERED
HONEYED
HOVERED
HOVERER
HOWEVER
IMPEDED
IMPEDES
INDEXED
INDEXES
INHERED
INHERES
INTEGER
JEWELED
JEWELER
JEZEBEL
JIMENEZ
KLEENEX
KNEELED
KNEELER
KNIEVEL
LABELED
LABELER
LAPELED
LATEXES
LAYERED
LEVELED
LEVELER
LEVERED
LEVERET
LIBELED
LIBELER
LIFENET
LIKENED
LIKENEW
LINEMEN
LIVENED
LORELEI
LOWERED
MANEGES
METERED
MITERED
MODELED
MODELER
MONEYED
MOSEYED
NEMESES
NINEVEH
NUREYEV
OFFERED
OFFERER
OFTENER
ONEEYED
ORDERED
ORDERER
PANELED
PAPERED
PAPERER
PETERED
PHOEBES

PIKEMEN
POPEYED
POWERED
PREENED
PREENER
QUEERED
QUEERER
QUIETED
QUIETEN
QUIETER
RACEMES
RAMESES
RAVELED
RAVENED
RECEDED
RECEDES
REDEYES
REFEREE
REKEYED
RENEGED
RENEGER
RENEGES
RENEWED
RENEWER
REVELED
REVELER
REVERED
REVERES
RIBEYES
RIPENED
RIVETED
RIVETER
ROSERED
SCHEMED
SCHEMER
SCHEMES
SCREWED
SECEDED
SECEDER
SECEDES
SERENER
SEVERED
SEVERER
SHEERED
SHEERER
SHEETED
SIDEBET
SIDEMEN
SKEETER
SLEEKED
SLEEKEN
SLEEKER
SLEEPER
SLEETED
SLEEVES
SNEERED
SNEERER
SNEEZED
SNEEZER
SNEEZES
SOBERED
SOBERER
SPEEDED
SPEEDER
SPHERES
SPIEGEL
SPIELED
SPIELER
STEELED
STEELER
STEEPED
STEEPEN
STEEPER

STEERED
STEERER
STIEGEL
STPETER
STREWED
STREWER
SWEEPER
SWEETEN
SWEETER
TAKETEN
TAPERED
TELEXED
TELEXES
THIEVED
THIEVES
TIREDER
TOKENED
TOWELED
TOWERED
TWEETED
TWEETER
TWEEZED
TWEEZES
TYPESET
UNSEWED
USHERED
UTTERED
UTTERER
WAGERED
WAGERER
WAKENED
WAKENER
WATERED
WATERER
WAVELET
WAVERED
WAVERER
WHEELED
WHEELER
WHEEZED
WHEEZER
WHEEZES
WHOEVER
WIDENED
WINERED
WISEMEN
WIZENED
YODELED
YODELER

•••E••E

ABSENCE
ACREAGE
ADVERSE
ALDENTE
ALIENEE
ALLENDE
AMOEBAE
ANNETTE
APPEASE
ARLEDGE
ASPERSE
ATPEACE
AUREATE
AUREOLE
BABETTE
BEREAVE
BURETTE
CADENCE
CADETTE
CATENAE
CAYENNE
CELEBRE

CELESTE
CODEINE
COLETTE
COMEDUE
COTERIE
DECEIVE
DEFENCE
DEFENSE
DEMESNE
DENEUVE
DEPECHE
DESERVE
DETENTE
DINETTE
DISEASE
DIVERGE
DIVERSE
DOYENNE
ENTEBBE
ENTENTE
ESSENCE
ESTELLE
ETIENNE
EUGENIE
EUTERPE
EXPENSE
FABERGE
FAIENCE
FENETRE
FINESSE
FIRENZE
FORESEE
FREEBEE
FREEBIE
GAZELLE
GAZETTE
GENESEE
GISELLE
IMMENSE
IMMERSE
INCENSE
INGENUE
INPEACE
INTENSE
INTERSE
INVERSE
JADEITE
JANEDOE
LABELLE
LAVERNE
LAYETTE
LICENCE
LICENSE
LIMEADE
LINEAGE
LINEATE
LIVEONE
LOZENGE
LUCERNE
MAJESTE
MAJEURE
MALEATE
MILEAGE
MOSELLE
MUSETTE
NACELLE
NANETTE
NOVELLE
OBSERVE
OBVERSE
OFFENCE
OFFENSE
OKEEFFE

ONLEAVE
ORIENTE
ORNETTE
PALETTE
PAPEETE
PIPETTE
POLEAXE
PREEMIE
RECEIVE
REFEREE
RELEASE
RESERVE
REVENGE
REVENUE
REVERIE
REVERSE
REWEAVE
ROSEATE
ROSELLE
ROSETTE
ROZELLE
SCIENCE
SILENCE
SINEDIE
SOMEONE
SQUEEZE
STEELIE
STEEPLE
SUZETTE
SWEETIE
TAKEONE
TERENCE
TRIESTE
UNNERVE
UNWEAVE
VALENCE
VALERIE
WHEEDLE
WHEELIE
WYNETTE

••••EE•

ANISEED
APOGEES
BAILEES
BARKEEP
BEEGEES
BETWEEN
BIGFEET
BOOTEES
BUNGEES
BURGEES
CANTEEN
COFFEES
COLLEEN
COMPEER
COULEES
DARLEEN
DECREED
DECREES
DEGREES
ELYSEES
ENTREES
FIFTEEN
GENTEEL
GLACEED
GOATEED
GOATEES
HASBEEN
HAYSEED
INBREED
JAYCEES
JAYVEES

LESSEES
LIENEES
LINSEED
LISTEES
LOUREED
LOWHEEL
MAUREEN
MCQUEEN
MIDWEEK
MISDEED
MONKEES
MYNHEER
NANKEEN
PARSEES
PAWNEES
PEEWEES
PENSEES
PIONEER
PRETEEN
PROCEED
PUGREES
PUTTEES
RAGWEED
REDDEER
REXREED
ROEDEER
RUNDEEP
RUSHEES
SAUTEED
SCHMEER
SEABEES
SEAWEED
SETTEES
SIGNEES
SIXTEEN
SOIREES
SUCCEED
TARHEEL
TEEPEES
TESTEES
THEDEEP
TOFFEES
TOUPEES
TOWHEES
UMPTEEN
UPSWEEP
USSTEEL
VERMEER
VESTEES
WEBFEET
YANKEES

••••E•E

ABILENE
ACADEME
ACCRETE
ACHIEVE
ALLHERE
ARRIERE
ATHLETE
AUSTERE
BELIEVE
BENZENE
BERGERE
BERNESE
BESIEGE
BUCKEYE
BURMESE
CARRERE
CATSEYE
CHINESE
COCHERE
COLLEGE

COMPETE
CONCEDE
CONVENE
CORTEGE
DARLENE
DEADEYE
DENIECE
DEPLETE
DIOCESE
DIOMEDE
EPICENE
EPIGENE
ESTHETE
ETAGERE
EVILEYE
EXCRETE
EXTREME
FISHEYE
GENOESE
GLADEYE
GRUYERE
HAWKEYE
HELLENE
HITHERE
HYGIENE
IMOGENE
LUMIERE
MACHETE
MALTESE
MARLENE
MICHELE
MIOCENE
MOLIERE
NAIVETE
NOWHERE
OBSCENE
PAPEETE
PHONEME
PRECEDE
PROTEGE
RELIEVE
REPLETE
RIVIERE
SCALENE
SECRETE
SEEHERE
SHUTEYE
SIAMESE
SINCERE
SLOVENE
SOCKEYE
SOLFEGE
SOSUEME
SOTHERE
SQUEEZE
STYRENE
SUPREME
TANGERE
TERRENE
TOLUENE
TRAPEZE
TRIREME
UKULELE
WALLEYE

•••••EE
ADOPTEE
ALIENEE
ANNALEE
AURALEE
AWARDEE
BANSHEE
BEETREE

BOURREE
BRADLEE
DESIREE
DEVOTEE
DRAFTEE
ELECTEE
ELMTREE
ESCAPEE
EVACUEE
FIANCEE
FORESEE
FORFREE
FREEBEE
FRISBEE
GALILEE
GENESEE
GOLFTEE
GRANDEE
GRANTEE
GUMTREE
HOLYSEE
HONOREE
ICEFREE
JIMCHEE
JUBILEE
LEGATEE
LETSSEE
LOOKSEE
MANATEE
MARQUEE
MATINEE
MERIMEE
MUSTSEE
NOMINEE
OAKTREE
OVERSEE
PAROLEE
PERIGEE
PLEDGEE
PRITHEE
REFEREE
REFUGEE
RETIREE
RUBYDEE
SARALEE
SHAWNEE
SOIGNEE
SPONDEE
STANDEE
STANLEE
TAXFREE
TOYNBEE
TRAINEE
TROCHEE
TRUCKEE
TRUSTEE
UPATREE
WHOOPEE
YAHTZEE

EF•••••
EFFACED
EFFACES
EFFECTS
EFFENDI
EFFORTS
EFFUSED
EFFUSES

E•F••••
EFFACED
EFFACES
EFFECTS

EFFENDI
EFFORTS
EFFUSED
EFFUSES
ENFOLDS
ENFORCE

E••F•••
EARFLAP
EARFULS
EDIFICE
EDIFIED
EDIFIES
EYEFULS

E••••F•
EARMUFF
EASEOFF
ENGRAFT
ENGULFS

E•••••F
EARMUFF
EASEOFF

•EF••••
BEFALLS
BEFOULS
DEFACED
DEFACES
DEFACTO
DEFAMED
DEFAMES
DEFARGE
DEFAULT
DEFEATS
DEFECTS
DEFENCE
DEFENDS
DEFENSE
DEFIANT
DEFICIT
DEFILED
DEFILER
DEFILES
DEFINED
DEFINES
DEFLATE
DEFLECT
DEFORMS
DEFRAUD
DEFRAYS
DEFROCK
DEFROST
DEFTEST
DEFUNCT
DEFUSED
DEFUSES
DEFYING
GEFILTE
HEFTIER
HEFTILY
HEFTING
JEFFERS
JEFFREY
LEFTIES
LEFTIST
LEFTOFF
LEFTOUT
REFACED
REFACES
REFEREE
REFERTO

REFFING
REFILLS
REFILMS
REFINED
REFINER
REFINES
REFIRES
REFLECT
REFORMS
REFRACT
REFRAIN
REFRAME
REFRESH
REFRIED
REFRIES
REFUELS
REFUGEE
REFUGES
REFUNDS
REFUSAL
REFUSED
REFUSER
REFUSES
REFUTED
REFUTER
REFUTES

•E•F•••
AELFRIC
BEEFALO
BEEFIER
BEEFING
BEEFSUP
BELFAST
DEAFENS
DEAFEST
DEIFIED
DEIFIES
FEIFFER
HEIFERS
HEIFETZ
JEFFERS
JEFFREY
LEAFIER
LEAFING
LEAFLET
LENFANT
MENFOLK
PEAFOWL
PERFECT
PERFIDY
PERFORM
PERFUME
REAFFIX
REDFINS
REDFIRS
REDFLAG
REDFORD
REEFERS
REEFING
REFFING
SEAFANS
SEAFOOD
SELFISH
SERFDOM
TENFOLD
TENFOUR
WEBFEET
WEBFOOT
WELFARE

•E••F••
BENEFIT

DEEPFAT
DEEPFRY
DEERFLY
FEARFUL
FEELFOR
FEIFFER
FELLFOR
FELTFOR
HEEDFUL
HELPFUL
LETSFLY
NEEDFUL
REAFFIX
REBUFFS
RESTFUL
SEESFIT
SENDFOR
SENTFOR
TEARFUL
WELLFED
WENTFOR
ZESTFUL

•E•••F•
BEAROFF
BEATIFY
BEGSOFF
BELIEFS
CERTIFY
FELLOFF
GETSOFF
HEADOFF
HELDOFF
KEEPOFF
KEPTOFF
LEADOFF
LEFTOFF
LETSOFF
NESCAFE
NEWLEFT
PEELOFF
PETRIFY
REBUFFS
RECTIFY
REELOFF
RELIEFS
REUNIFY
SEALOFF
SEESOFF
SELLOFF
SENDOFF
SENTOFF
SETSOFF
TEAROFF
TEEDOFF
TEESOFF
TELLOFF
TERRIFY
TESTIFY
VERSIFY
WEAROFF
WELLOFF
WENTOFF

•E••••F
BEAROFF
BEGSOFF
BEOWULF
DEBRIEF
FELLOFF
GETSOFF
HEADOFF
HEARDOF

HEARSOF
HELDOFF
HERSELF
KEEPOFF
KEPTOFF
LEADOFF
LEFTOFF
LETSOFF
NETSURF
PEELOFF
REDWOLF
REELOFF
REPROOF
SEALOFF
SEESOFF
SELLOFF
SENDOFF
SENTOFF
SETSOFF
TEALEAF
TEAROFF
TEEDOFF
TEESOFF
TELLOFF
WEAROFF
WELLOFF
WENTOFF

••EF•••
BEEFALO
BEEFIER
BEEFING
BEEFSUP
EYEFULS
FIEFDOM
ICEFLOE
ICEFREE
PREFABS
PREFACE
PREFECT
PREFERS
REEFERS
REEFING
TREFOIL

••E•F••
BRERFOX
DEEPFAT
DEEPFRY
DEERFLY
DREYFUS
FEELFOR
FRETFUL
GLEEFUL
GOESFOR
HEEDFUL
NEEDFUL
OKEEFFE
OVERFLY
SEESFIT
TWELFTH

••E••F•
ALEWIFE
BLEWOFF
DIEDOFF
DIESOFF
GOESOFF
KEEPOFF
OKEEFFE
PEELOFF
REELOFF
SEESOFF

SHERIFF
SPECIFY
TEEDOFF
TEESOFF

••E•••F
AHEADOF
BLEWOFF
DIEDOFF
DIESOFF
GOESOFF
KEEPOFF
ONESELF
PEELOFF
REELOFF
SEESOFF
SHERIFF
SHEWOLF
SPEAKOF
TEEDOFF
TEESOFF
THEREOF
WHEREOF

•••EF••
BALEFUL
BANEFUL
BENEFIT
BLUEFIN
BLUEFLU
BLUEFOX
BRIEFED
BRIEFER
BRIEFLY
CAREFOR
CAREFUL
CHIEFLY
DOLEFUL
DONEFOR
FAKEFUR
FATEFUL
FIREFLY
GLEEFUL
HATEFUL
HOPEFUL
MADEFOR
MAKEFOR
MALEFIC
OKEEFFE
PAGEFUL
PINEFOR
PIPEFUL
POKEFUN
TUNEFUL
WAKEFUL

•••E•F•
BAKEOFF
BITEOFF
CAMEOFF
COMEOFF
DOZEOFF
EASEOFF
FACEOFF
FIREOFF
GAVEOFF
GIVEOFF
MADEOFF
MAKEOFF
OKEEFFE
RAKEOFF
RIDEOFF
RODEOFF

TAKEOFF
TIMEOFF
TOREOFF
WAVEOFF
WOREOFF

•••E••F
BAKEOFF
BITEOFF
CAMEOFF
COMEOFF
DOZEOFF
EASEOFF
FACEOFF
FIREOFF
GAVEOFF
GIVEOFF
MADEOFF
MAKEOFF
RAKEOFF
RIDEOFF
RODEOFF
TAKEOFF
TIMEOFF
TIREDOF
TOREOFF
WAVEOFF
WOREOFF

••••EF•
BELIEFS
FARLEFT
LIQUEFY
NEWLEFT
RELIEFS
STUPEFY

••••E•F
AWAREOF
BAYLEAF
FIGLEAF
FLYLEAF
HERSELF
HIMSELF
INAWEOF
NONSELF
OAKLEAF
ONESELF
OURSELF
SPOKEOF
TEALEAF
THEREOF
THYSELF
WHEREOF

•••••EF
DEBRIEF
INBRIEF

EG•••••
EGALITE
EGESTED
EGGCASE
EGGCUPS
EGGEDON
EGGHEAD
EGGNOGS
EGGROLL
EGOISTS
EGOTISM
EGOTIST
EGOTRIP

E•G••••
EAGERER
EAGERLY
EAGLETS
EAGLING
EDGEDIN
EDGEOUT
EDGESIN
EDGIEST
EDGINGS
EGGCASE
EGGCUPS
EGGEDON
EGGHEAD
EGGNOGS
EGGROLL
EIGHTHS
ELGRECO
ENGAGED
ENGAGES
ENGARDE
ENGINES
ENGIRDS
ENGLAND
ENGLISH
ENGLUND
ENGORGE
ENGRAFT
ENGRAMS
ENGRAVE
ENGROSS
ENGULFS
EUGENIE

E••G•••
ELEGANT
ELEGIAC
ELEGIES
ELEGIST
EMIGRES
ENDGAME
ENIGMAS
EPIGENE
EPIGONE
EPIGRAM
ETAGERE
EXIGENT

E•••G••
ECLOGUE
EMERGED
EMERGES
ENCAGED
ENCAGES
ENGAGED
ENGAGES
ENRAGED
ENRAGES
ENSIGNS
EPERGNE
EVANGEL

E••••G•
EARWIGS
ECOLOGY
EDGINGS
EGGNOGS
EMBARGO
ENDINGS
ENGORGE
ENLARGE
EPILOGS
EXPUNGE

E•••••G
EAGLING
EARNING
EARPLUG
EARRING
ECHOING
EDDYING
EDITING
EDUCING
ELATING
ELIDING
ELOPING
ELUDING
ELUTING
EMOTING
ENDUING
ENSUING
ENURING
ENVYING
ERASING
ERELONG
ERODING
ESPYING
ETCHING
EVADING
EVENING
EVOKING
EXILING
EXITING
EXUDING

•EG••••
BEGGARS
BEGGING
BEGONIA
BEGORRA
BEGRIME
BEGSOFF
BEGUILE
BEGUINE
DEGAUSS
DEGRADE
DEGREES
HEGIRAS
KEGLERS
LEGALLY
LEGATEE
LEGATES
LEGATOS
LEGENDS
LEGGIER
LEGGING
LEGHORN
LEGIBLE
LEGIBLY
LEGIONS
LEGISTS
LEGPULL
LEGROOM
LEGUMES
LEGWORK
MEGOHMS
MEGRIMS
MEGRYAN
NEGATED
NEGATES
NEGATOR
NEGLECT
PEGASUS
PEGGING
PEGTOPS
REGAINS
REGALED

REGALES
REGALIA
REGALLY
REGARDS
REGATTA
REGENCY
REGENTS
REGIMEN
REGIMES
REGIONS
REGLUED
REGLUES
REGNANT
REGRADE
REGRESS
REGRETS
REGROUP
REGULAR
REGULUS
SEGMENT
SEGOVIA
VEGETAL
VEGGIES
VEGGING

•E•G•••
BEAGLES
BEEGEES
BEGGARS
BEGGING
BELGIAN
BELGIUM
BENGALI
BENGALS
BERGERE
BERGMAN
BERGSON
DEIGNED
FEIGNED
GEEGAWS
GENGHIS
GEWGAWS
HEDGERS
HEDGING
HEIGHHO
HEIGHTS
JETGUNS
LEAGUER
LEAGUES
LEDGERS
LEGGIER
LEGGING
LENGTHS
LENGTHY
MERGERS
MERGING
NEIGHED
NEWGATE
PEGGING
PENGUIN
PERGOLA
PEUGEOT
REAGENT
REDGUMS
REIGNED
SEAGATE
SEAGIRT
SEAGRAM
SEAGULL
VEGGIES
VEGGING
VEIGHTS
VERGERS

VERGING
WEDGIES
WEDGING
WEIGHED
WEIGHIN
WEIGHTS
WEIGHTY
YEVGENY
ZEUGMAS

•E••G••
DECAGON
DELIGHT
DELUGED
DELUGES
DEMIGOD
DESIGNS
GEORGES
GEORGIA
HEXAGON
MENAGES
NEWAGER
PELAGES
PELAGIC
PERIGEE
REARGUE
REFUGEE
REFUGES
RELIGHT
RENEGED
RENEGER
RENEGES
REPUGNS
RESIGNS
SENEGAL
SEVIGNE
TEARGAS

•E•••G•
BEDBUGS
BELONGS
BESIEGE
DEBARGE
DEFARGE
GEOLOGY
HERBAGE
HEXSIGN
KELLOGG
LEAKAGE
MELANGE
MESSAGE
NESTEGG
PEERAGE
PEONAGE
REDDOGS
REHANGS
RESINGS
RESTAGE
RESURGE
REVENGE
SEABAGS
SEADOGS
SEALEGS
SELVAGE
TEABAGS
TEENAGE
VERDUGO
VERTIGO
VESTIGE

•E••••G
BEADING
BEAMING

BEANBAG
BEANING
BEARHUG
BEARING
BEATING
BEDDING
BEEFING
BEEPING
BEGGING
BEIJING
BELLING
BELTING
BELYING
BENDING
BESTING
BETTING
CEASING
CEILING
CENSING
DEALING
DECALOG
DECKING
DEEDING
DEEMING
DEFYING
DEICING
DELEING
DELVING
DENTING
DENYING
DERRING
FEARING
FEEDBAG
FEEDING
FEELING
FELLING
FENCING
FENDING
FEUDING
GEARING
GELDING
GELLING
GETTING
HEADING
HEALING
HEAPING
HEARING
HEATING
HEAVING
HEDGING
HEEDING
HEELING
HEFTING
HELMING
HELPING
HEMMING
HERDING
HERRING
JEERING
JELLING
JERKING
JESTING
JETTING
KEELING
KEENING
KEEPING
KELLOGG
KERNING
KEYRING
LEADING
LEAFING
LEAKING
LEANING

LEAPING
LEASING
LEAVING
LEERING
LEGGING
LEIPZIG
LEMMING
LENDING
LESSING
LETTING
LEVYING
MEANING
MEETING
MELDING
MELTING
MENDING
MEOWING
MERGING
MESHING
MESSING
MEWLING
NEARING
NECKING
NEEDING
NESTEGG
NESTING
NETTING
PEAKING
PEALING
PEATBOG
PECKING
PEEKING
PEELING
PEEPING
PEERING
PEEVING
PEGGING
PELTING
PENDING
PENNING
PEPPING
PERKING
PERMING
PETTING
READING
REAMING
REAPING
REARING
REDDING
REDFLAG
REDOING
REDWING
REEDING
REEFING
REEKING
REELING
REFFING
REINING
RELYING
RENDING
RENTING
RESTING
REVVING
SEABORG
SEALING
SEAMING
SEARING
SEASLUG
SEATING
SEEDING
SEEKING
SEEMING
SEEPING

SEINING
SEIZING
SELLING
SENDING
SENSING
SERLING
SERVING
SETTING
TEAMING
TEARING
TEASING
TEDDING
TEEMING
TELLING
TENDING
TENSING
TENTING
TERMING
TESTING
VEERING
VEGGING
VEILING
VEINING
VENDING
VENTING
VERGING
VESTING
VETOING
VETTING
WEANING
WEARING
WEAVING
WEBBING
WEDDING
WEDGING
WEEDING
WEEPING
WELDING
WELLING
WELTING
WENDING
WETTING
YELLING
YELPING
YESSING
ZEITUNG
ZEROING

••EG•••

BEEGEES
ELEGANT
ELEGIAC
ELEGIES
ELEGIST
GEEGAWS
GREGORY
JAEGERS
OREGANO

••E•G••

AVENGED
AVENGER
AVENGES
DREDGED
DREDGER
DREDGES
EMERGED
EMERGES
EPERGNE
FLEDGED
FLEDGES
FREIGHT
GIELGUD

ICEAGES
PLEDGED
PLEDGEE
PLEDGER
PLEDGES
SLEDGES
SLEIGHS
SLEIGHT
STEIGER
STENGEL

••E••G•

AGESAGO
AMERIGO
AVERAGE
ICEBAGS
OVERAGE
PEERAGE
PRESAGE
PYEDOGS
TEENAGE

••E•••G

AREARUG
BEEFING
BEEPING
BREWING
CHEWING
CREWING
DEEDING
DEEMING
DIETING
DUELING
ERELONG
EVENING
FEEDBAG
FEEDING
FEELING
FLEABAG
FLEEING
FLEMING
FLEXING
FREEING
FREITAG
FUELING
GREYING
HEEDING
HEELING
ICEBERG
JEERING
KEELING
KEENING
KEEPING
KNEEING
LEERING
MEETING
NEEDING
OBEYING
OPENING
OVERBIG
PEEKING
PEELING
PEEPING
PEERING
PEEVING
PFENNIG
PIECING
QUEUING
REEDING
REEFING
REEKING
REELING
SEEDING

SEEKING
SEEMING
SEEPING
SHEBANG
SKEWING
SLEDDOG
SPEWING
STEWING
TEEMING
TIERING
TREEING
VEERING
VIEWING
WEEDING
WEEPING

•••EG••

ALLEGED
ALLEGER
ALLEGES
ALLEGRO
ASSEGAI
BADEGGS
BODEGAS
BRUEGEL
DONEGAL
ILLEGAL
INTEGER
INTEGRA
MANEGES
NOSEGAY
OBREGON
RAREGAS
RENEGED
RENEGER
RENEGES
SENEGAL
SLOEGIN
SPIEGEL
STIEGEL
VINEGAR
WISEGUY
WOBEGON

•••E•G•

ACREAGE
ALLERGY
ARLEDGE
BADEGGS
DIVERGE
FABERGE
FOREIGN
INVEIGH
LINEAGE
LOZENGE
MILEAGE
RALEIGH
REVENGE
SYNERGY
UNDERGO

•••E••G

ANTEING
BLUEING
CLUEING
DELEING
FIREBUG
FIREDOG
FLEEING
FORELEG
FREEING
GATELEG
JUNEBUG

KNEEING
LOVEBUG
NAMETAG
NOSEBAG
SHOEING
TIMELAG
TOTEBAG
TREEING
TRUEING
YULELOG

••••EG•

BESIEGE
COLLEGE
CORTEGE
DOGLEGS
GOODEGG
MONTEGO
NESTEGG
NORIEGA
NUTMEGS
ONTHEGO
PROTEGE
SEALEGS
SOLFEGE
TUAREGS

••••E•G

GINSENG
GOODEGG
ICEBERG
NESTEGG

•••••EG

BOOTLEG
FORELEG
GATELEG

EH•••••

EHRLICH

E•H••••

ECHELON
ECHIDNA
ECHINUS
ECHOING
ENHANCE
ETHANOL
ETHICAL
ETHNICS
EXHALED
EXHALES
EXHAUST
EXHIBIT
EXHORTS

E••H•••

EARHART
EBWHITE
ECKHART
EGGHEAD
EIGHTHS
ELKHART
ENCHAIN
ENCHANT
ENTHUSE
ESCHEAT
ESCHEWS
ESTHETE
ETCHERS
ETCHING
EUCHRED
EUCHRES

EUPHONY
EYEHOLE

E•••H••

EARSHOT
EARTHEN
EARTHLY
EDAPHIC
EPITHET
EREWHON

E••••H•

EARACHE
EIGHTHS
EMPATHY
EOLITHS
EPARCHS
EUNUCHS

E•••••H

EHRLICH
ENGLISH
EYELASH
EYEWASH

•EH••••

BEHAVED
BEHAVES
BEHESTS
BEHOLDS
BEHOOVE
DEHISCE
DEHORNS
LEHAVRE
REHANGS
REHEALS
REHEARD
REHEARS
REHEATS
REHEELS
REHIRED
REHIRES
REHOOKS
TEHERAN
VEHICLE

•E•H•••

BEEHIVE
BETHANY
BETHELS
BETHINK
CEPHEUS
HEEHAWS
HESHVAN
KEYHOLE
LEGHORN
MENHIRS
MESHING
METHANE
METHODS
NEPHEWS
NEWHART
PEAHENS
PERHAPS
RECHALK
RECHECK
RECHOSE
REDHAIR
REDHATS
REDHEAD
REDHEAT
REDHOTS
RESHIPS

RESHOES
RESHOOT
RETHINK
SEEHERE
TECHIES
TERHUNE
TETHERS
WETHERS
YESHIVA
ZEPHYRS

•E••H••

BEACHED
BEACHES
BEARHUG
BEECHAM
BEECHER
BEECHES
BELCHED
BELCHES
BELLHOP
BENCHED
BENCHES
BENTHAM
BERTHED
FEATHER
FETCHED
FETCHES
GEEWHIZ
GEISHAS
GENGHIS
HEATHEN
HEATHER
HEIGHHO
HEIGHTS
HERSHEY
KEESHAN
KERCHOO
KETCHAM
KETCHES
KETCHUP
LEACHED
LEACHES
LEASHED
LEASHES
LEATHER
LEECHED
LEECHES
MEGOHMS
MEMPHIS
MENTHOL
MENUHIN
NEIGHED
NEITHER
PEACHED
PEACHES
PERCHED
PERCHES
REACHED
REACHES
REUTHER
SEETHED
SEETHES
SEICHES
TEACHER
TEACHES
TEACHIN
TEASHOP
TEETHED
TEETHER
TEETHES
TEICHER
TETCHED

VEIGHTS
VETCHES
WEATHER
WEIGHED
WEIGHIN
WEIGHTS
WEIGHTY
WELCHED
WELCHES
WENCHES
WERNHER
WERTHER

•E•••H•

BELUSHI
CERIPHS
CEVICHE
DEARTHS
DELIGHT
DENNEHY
DEPECHE
HEALTHY
HEARTHS
HEAVEHO
HEIGHHO
JERICHO
KENOSHA
LENGTHS
LENGTHY
LESOTHO
PENUCHE
RELIGHT
SERAPHS
TERAPHS
WEALTHY
ZENITHS

•E••••H

BEARISH
BENEATH
BESEECH
BETROTH
BEWITCH
DEBAUCH
DEBORAH
DEBOUCH
DELILAH
DERVISH
JETWASH
KENNETH
MENORAH
MESSIAH
NEBBISH
NEOLITH
NEWMATH
PECKISH
PEEVISH
PETTISH
REBEKAH
REBIRTH
REDDISH
REFRESH
RETEACH
RETOUCH
SELFISH
SEVENTH
WEAKISH

••EH•••

BEEHIVE
DIEHARD
EYEHOLE
HEEHAWS

JOEHILL
PREHEAT
SEEHERE
TOEHOLD

••E•H••

BEECHAM
BEECHER
BEECHES
CHECHEN
CHEKHOV
CRECHES
EREWHON
FLECHES
FLESHED
FLESHES
FRESHEN
FRESHER
FRESHET
FRESHLY
GEEWHIZ
ICESHOW
KEESHAN
LEECHED
LEECHES
ONESHOT
QUECHUA
SEETHED
SEETHES
STEPHEN
TEETHED
TEETHER
TEETHES
TOESHOE
WHETHER

••E••H•

BREATHE
BREATHS
BREATHY
FREIGHT
GUELPHS
NIEBUHR
PREACHY
SHEATHE
SHEATHS
SHEIKHS
SKETCHY
SLEIGHS
SLEIGHT
SLEUTHS
WREATHE
WREATHS

••E•••H

BLEMISH
BREADTH
CHEETAH
CHERISH
EYELASH
EYEWASH
FLEMISH
PEEVISH
PREWASH
SHEILAH
STEALTH
SWEDISH
TWELFTH
UNEARTH

•••EH••

BASEHIT
MADEHAY

MAKEHAY
SOMEHOW

•••E•H•

DEPECHE
UTRECHT
VOTECHS

•••E••H

BENEATH
BESEECH
BONEASH
CHEETAH
DOZENTH
IMPEACH
INDEPTH
INVEIGH
NINEVEH
OGREISH
RALEIGH
REBEKAH
RETEACH
SCREECH
SEVENTH
SQUELCH
STRETCH
UNLEASH

••••EH•

DENNEHY
HEAVEHO

••••E•H

BESEECH
CALTECH
HIALEAH
JAPHETH
KENNETH
LOWTECH
MACBETH
NCWYETH
REFRESH
SCREECH

•••••EH

NINEVEH

EI•••••

EIGHTHS

E•I••••

EDIBLES
EDIFICE
EDIFIED
EDIFIES
EDITING
EDITION
EDITORS
ELICITS
ELIDING
ELISION
ELITISM
ELITIST
ELIXIRS
EMIGRES
EMINENT
EMIRATE
EMITTED
EMITTER
ENIGMAS
ENISLED
ENISLES
EPICENE

EPICURE
EPIGENE
EPIGONE
EPIGRAM
EPILOGS
EPISODE
EPISTLE
EPITHET
EPITOME
ERICSON
ERISTIC
ERITREA
ETIENNE
EVICTED
EVIDENT
EVILEST
EVILEYE
EVILLER
EVINCED
EVINCES
EXIGENT
EXILING
EXISTED
EXITING

E••I•••

EASIEST
ECHIDNA
ECHINUS
ECLIPSE
EDGIEST
EDGINGS
EELIEST
EERIEST
EGOISTS
ELEISON
ELLIOTT
ELLIPSE
ELLISON
ELMISTI
EMPIRES
ENDINGS
ENDIVES
ENGINES
ENGIRDS
ENLISTS
ENLIVEN
ENSIGNS
ENSILED
ENSILES
ENTICED
ENTICER
ENTICES
ENTITLE
ENVIOUS
EOLITHS
EPSILON
EQUINES
EQUINOX
ERMINES
ESKIMOS
ESPIALS
ESTIVAL
ETHICAL
ETOILES
EXCISED
EXCISES
EXCITED
EXCITES
EXHIBIT
EXPIATE
EXPIRED
EXPIRES

EXTINCT
EXWIVES

E•••I••

EAGLING
EARLIER
EARNING
EARRING
EARWIGS
EBBTIDE
EBONIES
EBONITE
EBWHITE
ECHOING
ECLAIRS
EDACITY
EDDYING
EDIFICE
EDIFIED
EDIFIES
EDITING
EDITION
EDUCING
EGALITE
EGOTISM
EGOTIST
EHRLICH
ELAPIDS
ELATING
ELATION
ELEGIAC
ELEGIES
ELEGIST
ELICITS
ELIDING
ELISION
ELITISM
ELITIST
ELIXIRS
ELOPING
ELUDING
ELUSIVE
ELUTING
ELUTION
ELUVIUM
ELYSIAN
ELYSIUM
EMERITA
EMERITI
EMOTING
EMOTION
EMOTIVE
EMPTIED
EMPTIER
EMPTIES
EMPTILY
ENDUING
ENDWISE
ENEMIES
ENGLISH
ENJOINS
ENSUING
ENSUITE
ENTAILS
ENTRIES
ENTWINE
ENURING
ENVYING
EPEEIST
EPOXIES
ERASING
EREMITE
ERODING

EROSION
EROSIVE
EROTICA
ERSKINE
ERUDITE
ESPYING
ESQUIRE
ETAMINE
ETCHING
ETESIAN
ETHNICS
ETONIAN
EVADING
EVASION
EVASIVE
EVENING
EVOKING
EXAMINE
EXILING
EXITING
EXOTICA
EXOTICS
EXUDING
EYELIDS
EZEKIEL

E••••I•

EASEDIN
EASESIN
ECDYSIS
EDAPHIC
EDGEDIN
EDGESIN
EELSKIN
EGOTRIP
ELASTIC
EMBROIL
EMPORIA
ENCHAIN
ENCOMIA
ENDEMIC
ENTRAIN
EPSTEIN
ERISTIC
ERRATIC
ESTONIA
ESTORIL
ETRURIA
EUGENIE
EURASIA
EVENKIS
EXCLAIM
EXHIBIT
EXPLAIN
EXPLOIT
EXURBIA

E•••••I

EFFENDI
ELMISTI
EMERITI
EXEMPLI

•EI••••

BEIJING
CEILING
DEICERS
DEICING
DEIFIED
DEIFIES
DEIGNED
DEITIES
FEIFFER

FEIGNED
FEINTED
GEISHAS
HEIFERS
HEIFETZ
HEIGHHO
HEIGHTS
HEINOUS
HEIRESS
HEISTED
KEILLOR
LEIBNIZ
LEIPZIG
LEISTER
LEISURE
MEIOSES
MEIOSIS
MEIOTIC
MEISSEN
NEIGHED
NEITHER
REIGNED
REINING
REINKED
REINSIN
REISSUE
SEICHES
SEIDELS
SEINERS
SEINING
SEISMIC
SEIZERS
SEIZING
TEICHER
VEIGHTS
VEILING
VEINING
WEIGHED
WEIGHIN
WEIGHTS
WEIGHTY
WEIRDER
WEIRDLY
WEIRDOS
ZEITUNG

•E•I•••

AEDILES
AERIALS
AERIEST
BEDIZEN
BELIEFS
BELIEVE
BELINDA
BEMIRED
BEMIRES
BENISON
BESIDES
BESIEGE
BETIDED
BETIDES
BETIMES
BEWITCH
BEZIERS
BEZIQUE
CECILIA
CEDILLA
CERIPHS
CEVICHE
DEBITED
DECIBEL
DECIDED
DECIDES
DECIMAL
DEFIANT
DEFICIT
DEFILED
DEFILER
DEFILES
DEFINED
DEFINES
DEHISCE
DELIBES
DELICTI
DELICTS
DELIGHT
DELILAH
DELIMIT
DELIRIA
DELISTS
DELIVER
DEMIGOD
DEMILLE
DEMISED
DEMISES
DENIALS
DENIECE
DENIERS
DENIZEN
DEPICTS
DERIDED
DERIDES
DERIVED
DERIVES
DESIGNS
DESIRED
DESIREE
DESIRES
DESISTS
DEVIANT
DEVIATE
DEVICES
DEVILED
DEVILLE
DEVILRY
DEVIOUS
DEVISED
DEVISES
DEWILDE
EELIEST
EERIEST
FELICIA
FELINES
FETIDLY
GEFILTE
GERITOL
GETINTO
GETITON
HEGIRAS
HELICAL
HELICES
HELICON
HELIPAD
HELIXES
JERICHO
LEGIBLE
LEGIBLY
LEGIONS
LEGISTS
LENIENT
LETINON
LETITBE
LETITIA
LEVIERS
LEVITES
LEXICAL
LEXICON
MEDIANS
MEDIANT
MEDIATE
MEDICAL
MEDICOS
MEDIUMS
MELINDA
MELISSA
MENIALS
MENISCI
MERIMEE
MERINOS
MERITED
METIERS
MEXICAN
NEVILLE
OEDIPAL
OEDIPUS
PEDICEL
PEDICLE
PELICAN
PELISSE
PEMICAN
PERIDOT
PERIGEE
PERIODS
PETIOLE
PETITES
REAIRED
REBINDS
REBIRTH
RECIPES
RECITAL
RECITED
RECITER
RECITES
REDIALS
REFILLS
REFILMS
REFINED
REFINER
REFINES
REFIRES
REGIMEN
REGIMES
REGIONS
REHIRED
REHIRES
RELIANT
RELICTS
RELIEFS
RELIEVE
RELIEVO
RELIGHT
RELINED
RELINES
RELISTS
RELIVED
RELIVES
REMINDS
REMIXED
REMIXES
REOILED
REPINED
REPINES
RERINSE
RESIDED
RESIDES
RESIDUE
RESIGNS
RESILED
RESILES
RESINGS
RESISTS
RETICLE
RETILED
RETILES
RETIMED
RETIMES
RETINAE
RETINAL
RETINAS
RETINUE
RETIRED
RETIREE
RETIRES
RETITLE
REVIEWS
REVILED
REVILES
REVISED
REVISER
REVISES
REVISIT
REVIVAL
REVIVED
REVIVES
REWINDS
REWIRED
REWIRES
SEMINAL
SEMINAR
SEMIPRO
SEMITES
SEMITIC
SENIORS
SERIALS
SERIATE
SERIOUS
SETINTO
SEVIGNE
SEVILLE
SEXIEST
SEXISTS
TEDIOUS
TEPIDLY
VEHICLE
VENISON
ZENITHS

•E••I••

AEOLIAN
BEADIER
BEADING
BEAMIER
BEAMING
BEANIES
BEANING
BEARING
BEARISH
BEATIFY
BEATING
BEDDING
BEDSIDE
BEDTIME
BEEFIER
BEEFING
BEEHIVE
BEELINE
BEEPING
BEGGING
BEGRIME
BEGUILE
BEGUINE
BEIJING
BELGIAN
BELGIUM
BELLIED
BELLIES
BELLING
BELLINI
BELTING
BELYING
BENDING
BERLIOZ
BERLITZ
BERNICE
BERRIED
BERRIES
BESTIAL
BESTING
BESTIRS
BETHINK
BETTING
BETWIXT
BEWAILS
CEASING
CEILING
CELLINI
CELLIST
CELSIUS
CELTICS
CENSING
CENTIME
CENTIMO
CERTIFY
CESSION
DEALING
DEBRIEF
DECEITS
DECEIVE
DECKING
DECLINE
DECRIED
DECRIES
DEEDING
DEEMING
DEFYING
DEICING
DEIFIED
DEIFIES
DEITIES
DELEING
DELUISE
DELVING
DENSITY
DENTINE
DENTING
DENTIST
DENYING
DEPRIVE
DERAILS
DERBIES
DERNIER
DERRICK
DERRING
DERVISH
DESPISE
DESPITE
DESTINE
DESTINY
DETAILS
DETAINS
DEVEINS
DEVRIES
DEWLINE
FEARING
FEBRILE
FEEDING
FEELIES
FEELING
FELLING
FELLINI
FENCING
FENDING
FERMIUM
FERRIED
FERRIES
FERRITE
FERTILE
FESTIVE
FEUDING
GEARING
GELDING
GELLING
GEMLIKE
GENTIAN
GENTILE
GENUINE
GERAINT
GERBILS
GETTING
HEADIER
HEADILY
HEADING
HEALING
HEAPING
HEARING
HEATING
HEAVIER
HEAVIES
HEAVILY
HEAVING
HEDGING
HEEDING
HEELING
HEFTIER
HEFTILY
HEFTING
HELLION
HELMING
HELOISE
HELPING
HEMLINE
HEMMING
HENBITS
HERDING
HERMITS
HEROICS
HEROINE
HEROISM
HERRING
HERRIOT
HESSIAN
HEXSIGN
JEEBIES
JEERING
JELLIED
JELLIES
JELLING
JEMMIED
JEMMIES
JENNIES
JERKIER
JERKILY
JERKING
JERKINS
JESSICA
JESTING
JESUITS
JETTIES
JETTING
KEELING
KEENING
KEEPING
KELPIES
KERNING
KEWPIES
KEYLIME
KEYRING
LEADING
LEADINS
LEAFIER
LEAFING
LEAKIER
LEAKING
LEANING
LEAPING
LEASING
LEAVING
LEERIER
LEERILY
LEERING
LEETIDE
LEFTIES
LEFTIST
LEGGIER
LEGGING
LEMMING
LEMPIRA
LENDING
LENTILS
LEONINE
LESSING
LETTING
LEVYING
MEALIER
MEALIES
MEANIES
MEANING
MEATIER
MEETING
MEGRIMS
MELDING
MELTING
MEMOIRE
MEMOIRS
MENDING
MENHIRS
MENTION
MEOWING
MERCIES
MERGING
MERRIER
MERRILL
MERRILY
MESHING
MESSIAH
MESSIER
MESSILY
MESSINA
MESSING
MESTIZO
METRICS
MEWLING
NEARING
NEBBISH
NECKING
NEEDIER
NEEDILY
NEEDING
NEOLITH
NEREIDS
NERVIER
NERVILY
NESTING
NETTING
NEWSIER
PEAKING
PEALING
PECKING
PECKISH
PECTINS
PEEKING
PEELING
PEEPING
PEERING
PEEVING
PEEVISH
PEGGING
PELTING
PENCILS
PENDING
PENNIES
PENNING
PENSION
PENSIVE
PEONIES
PEPPIER
PEPPILY
PEPPING
PEPSINS
PEPTIDE
PERDIEM
PERFIDY
PERKIER
PERKILY
PERKING
PERKINS
PERLITE
PERMING
PERMITS
PERRIER
PERSIAN
PERSIST
PERSIUS
PESKIER
PESKILY
PETRIFY
PETTIER
PETTILY
PETTING
PETTISH
READIED
READIER
READIES
READILY
READING
REALISM
REALIST
REALITY
REALIZE
REAMING
REAPING
REARING
REBOILS
REBUILD
REBUILT
RECEIPT
RECEIVE
RECLINE
RECOILS
RECTIFY
REDBIRD
REDDING
REDDISH
REDFINS
REDFIRS
REDLINE
REDOING
REDPINE
REDWINE
REDWING
REEDIER
REEDING
REEDITS
REEFING
REEKING
REELING
REFFING
REFRIED
REFRIES
REGAINS
REINING
REJOICE
REJOINS
RELYING
REMAILS
REMAINS
RENAILS
RENDING
RENNINS
RENTING
REPAINT
REPAIRS
REPLICA
REPLIED
REPLIES
REPRICE
REPRINT
REPRISE
REPTILE
REQUIEM
REQUIRE
REQUITE
RERAISE
RESCIND
RESHIPS
RESPIRE
RESPITE
RESTING
RESTIVE
RETAILS
RETAINS
RETHINK
RETRIAL
RETRIED
RETRIES
RETRIMS
RETSINA
REUNIFY
REUNION
REUNITE
REVOICE
REVVING
REWRITE
SEABIRD
SEAGIRT
SEALILY
SEALING
SEALION
SEAMIER
SEAMING
SEARING
SEASICK
SEASIDE
SEATING
SECTION
SEEDIER
SEEDILY
SEEDING
SEEKING
SEEMING
SEEPING
SEINING
SEIZING
SELFISH
SELKIRK
SELLING
SENDING
SENSING
SEQUINS
SERBIAN
SERLING
SERPICO
SERRIED
SERVICE
SERVILE
SERVING
SESSILE
SESSION
SESTINA
SETLINE
SETTING
TEAMING
TEARIER
TEARILY
TEARING
TEASING
TEATIME
TECHIES
TEDDIES
TEDDING
TEEMING
TEENIER
TEKTITE
TELLIES
TELLING
TENDING
TENNIEL
TENPINS
TENSILE
TENSING
TENSION
TENSIVE
TENTING
TEQUILA
TERBIUM
TERMING
TERMINI
TERMITE
TERRIER
TERRIES
TERRIFY
TERTIAL
TESTIER
TESTIFY
TESTILY
TESTING
TEXTILE
VEERING
VEGGIES
VEGGING
VEILING
VEINING
VENDING
VENTING
VERDICT
VERGING
VERNIER
VERSIFY
VERSION
VERTIGO
VESPIDS
VESTIGE
VESTING
VETOING
VETTING
WEAKISH
WEANING
WEARIED
WEARIER
WEARIES
WEARILY
WEARING
WEAVING
WEBBING
WEBSITE
WEDDING
WEDGIES
WEDGING
WEEDIER
WEEDING
WEENIES
WEEPIER
WEEPING
WEEVILS
WELDING
WELKINS
WELLING
WELTING
WENDING
WESKITS
WETTING
YELLING
YELPING
YESHIVA
YESSING
ZEROING
ZESTIER

•E•••I•

AELFRIC
AEROBIC
BEASTIE
BEATNIK
BEATRIX
BEATSIT
BEATTIE
BEDELIA
BEDEVIL
BEDOUIN
BEGONIA
BENAZIR
BENEFIT
CECILIA
CENTRIC
CERAMIC
CERTAIN
DEADAIR
DEALSIN
DEALTIN
DEARSIR
DECLAIM
DEEPSIX
DEFICIT
DELIMIT
DELIRIA
DELTAIC
DELTOID
DEMERIT
DEMONIC
DEPOSIT
DESPAIR
DESPOIL
DETRAIN
DETROIT
DEXTRIN
EELSKIN
FELICIA
GEEWHIZ
GELATIN
GELATIS
GENERIC
GENERIS
GENESIS
GENETIC
GENGHIS
GEORGIA
HEADPIN
HEADSIN
HEBRAIC
HENDRIX
HENREID
HEPARIN
HEPATIC
HERETIC
JEANNIE
KEEPSIN
KERATIN
KEYEDIN
LEADSIN
LEIBNIZ
LEIPZIG
LETITIA
LETSLIP
MEIOSIS
MEIOTIC
MELANIE
MELANIN
MELODIC
MEMPHIS
MENUHIN
MERMAID
MESSKIT
NECKTIE
NEMESIS
NEPALIS
PEERSIN
PELAGIC
PENGUIN
PERTAIN
PETUNIA
READMIT
READSIN
REAFFIX
REAVAIL
RECLAIM
RECRUIT
REDHAIR
REDSKIN
REELSIN
REFRAIN
REGALIA
REINSIN
RESTAIN
RETRAIN
REVERIE
REVISIT
SEDALIA
SEEPSIN
SEESFIT
SEETOIT
SEGOVIA
SEISMIC
SELENIC
SEMITIC
SENDSIN
SEQUOIA
SERAPIS
SETSAIL
TEACHIN
TELAVIV
TENDRIL
TERRAIN
VERMEIL
WEIGHIN
WETSUIT
YELTSIN
YEMENIS
ZENOBIA

•E••••I

BELLINI
BELUSHI
BENGALI
CELLINI
DELICTI
FELLINI
FERRARI
MENISCI
MENOTTI
TERMINI

••EI•••

AGEISTS
DREIDEL
DREISER
ELEISON
FREIGHT
FREITAG
ONEIDAS
SHEIKHS
SHEILAE
SHEILAH
SHEILAS
SLEIGHS
SLEIGHT
STEIGER
STEINEM
STEINER
THEISTS
TIEINTO
WOEISME

••E•I••

ADELINE
ADENINE
ALEWIFE
AMENITY
AMERICA
AMERIGO
AMERIKA
AMERIND
APELIKE
APERIES
ATELIER
BEEFIER
BEEFING
BEEHIVE
BEELINE
BEEPING
BLEMISH
BLERIOT
BREVITY
BREWING
CHEMISE
CHEMIST
CHENIER
CHERISH
CHEVIED
CHEVIES

CHEVIOT
CHEWIER
CHEWING
CLERICS
COEDITS
COEXIST
CREDITS
CRETINS
CREVICE
CREWING
DEEDING
DEEMING
DIETING
DUELING
DUELIST
ELEGIAC
ELEGIES
ELEGIST
EMERITA
EMERITI
ENEMIES
EPEEIST
EREMITE
ETESIAN
EVENING
EYELIDS
EZEKIEL
FEEDING
FEELIES
FEELING
FIERIER
FIERILY
FLEEING
FLEMING
FLEMISH
FLEXING
FREEING
FUELING
GRECIAN
GREYING
HEEDING
HEELING
IBERIAN
ICEMILK
ICEPICK
ICERINK
ITEMIZE
JEEBIES
JEERING
JOEHILL
KEELING
KEENING
KEEPING
KNEEING
LEERIER
LEERILY
LEERING
LEETIDE
MEETING
NEEDIER
NEEDILY
NEEDING
NOETICS
OBELISK
OBELIZE
OBEYING
OLEMISS
ONETIME
OPENING
PEEKING
PEELING
PEEPING
PEERING
PEEVING
PEEVISH
PIECING
PIETIES
PIETINS
PIETISM
POETICS
PRECISE
PREDICT
PRELIMS
PREMIER
PREMISE
PREMIUM
PRESIDE
PREVIEW
PUERILE
QUERIED
QUERIES
QUEUING
REEDIER
REEDING
REEDITS
REEFING
REEKING
REELING
RHENIUM
SEEDIER
SEEDILY
SEEDING
SEEKING
SEEMING
SEEPING
SHERIFF
SKEWING
SPECIAL
SPECIES
SPECIFY
SPEWING
STEPINS
STERILE
STEWING
SWEDISH
TEEMING
TEENIER
TIELINE
TIEPINS
TIERING
TREEING
TREVINO
TSELIOT
VEERING
VIEWING
WEEDIER
WEEDING
WEENIES
WEEPIER
WEEPING
WEEVILS
WIENIES

••E••I•
ACERBIC
ALEMBIC
ANEROID
ASEPSIS
ASEPTIC
BREAKIN
BRESLIN
CHEAPIE
CHECKIN
CHEERIO
CHERVIL
DEEPSIX
DOESKIN
DWEEZIL
EVENKIS
FREDDIE
FREDRIC
FREEBIE
FREESIA
FUELOIL
GEEWHIZ
GHERKIN
GREMLIN
IDENTIC
INERTIA
KEEPSIN
KREMLIN
MUEZZIN
OBERLIN
OCEANIA
OCEANIC
OCEANID
OPENAIR
OPENPIT
OVERBIG
OVERDID
OVERLIE
PEERSIN
PFENNIG
PREEMIE
PREPAID
PREPPIE
PREVAIL
QUENTIN
REELSIN
SEEPSIN
SEESFIT
SEETOIT
SHELTIE
SHERWIN
SKEEZIX
SKEPTIC
SLEEPIN
SLEPTIN
SNEAKIN
STEELIE
STENCIL
STEPSIN
STEROID
SWEARIN
SWEETIE
THEREIN
THESPIS
TIECLIP
TOENAIL
TREFOIL
TREKKIE
TRELLIS
UTENSIL
WHEELIE
WHEREIN

••E•••I
ABENAKI
EMERITI
EXEMPLI
MAESTRI

•••EI••
ANTEING
ATHEISM
ATHEIST
BLUEING
CAVEINS
CLUEING
CODEINE
COHEIRS
DECEITS
DECEIVE
DELEING
DEVEINS
EPEEIST
FADEINS
FLEEING
FOREIGN
FREEING
INVEIGH
JADEITE
JANEIRO
KNEEING
LOVEINS
MADEIRA
NEREIDS
OGREISH
RALEIGH
RECEIPT
RECEIVE
SHOEING
TREEING
TRUEING
UNVEILS

•••E•I•
ADDEDIN
ALBENIZ
ALGERIA
AMNESIA
AMOEBIC
ANAEMIA
ANGELIC
ANNELID
APHELIA
ARMENIA
ARSENIC
ARSENIO
ARTEMIS
ASCETIC
BASEHIT
BEDELIA
BEDEVIL
BENEFIT
BLUEFIN
BOHEMIA
BOXEDIN
BOXESIN
CAKEMIX
CAMELIA
CAVEDIN
CAVESIN
CHEERIO
CLUEDIN
CLUESIN
COMEDIC
COMESIN
COTERIE
CSLEWIS
DEMERIT
DINEDIN
DINESIN
DIVESIN
DWEEZIL
EASEDIN
EASESIN
EDGEDIN
EDGESIN
ENDEMIC
EUGENIE
FADEDIN
FADESIN
FIDELIO
FIRELIT
FLIESIN
FREEBIE
FREESIA
GENERIC
GENERIS
GENESIS
GENETIC
GIVESIN
GONERIL
HAMELIN
HERETIC
HOMERIC
IMPERIL
INHERIT
INTERIM
JAVELIN
KEYEDIN
KINETIC
LIBERIA
LIVEDIN
LIVESIN
LOSESIT
MAKESIT
MALEFIC
MIMESIS
MIMETIC
MOVEDIN
MOVESIN
NEMESIS
NIGERIA
NUMERIC
OPHELIA
OSTEOID
PHOENIX
PHRENIC
PILEDIN
PILESIN
POLEMIC
PREEMIE
RAKEDIN
RAKESIN
RAMEKIN
RAREBIT
REVERIE
ROPEDIN
ROPESIN
ROSEOIL
SELENIC
SIBERIA
SILESIA
SINEDIE
SKEEZIX
SLEEPIN
SLOEGIN
STDENIS
STEELIE
SWEETIE
TAKEAIM
TAKENIN
TAKESIN
THREWIN
TOTEMIC
TUNEDIN
TUNESIN
VALERIE
VOTESIN
WADESIN
WAVEDIN
WAVESIN
WHEELIE
YEMENIS

•••E••I
ALVEOLI
ASSEGAI
BASENJI
CORELLI
EFFENDI
KUTENAI
LORELEI
SCHERZI
VIVENDI

••••EI•
ALAMEIN
ANAHEIM
BARGEIN
BROKEIN
CLOSEIN
CONCEIT
CONREID
DRIVEIN
EPSTEIN
FORFEIT
HENREID
HOLBEIN
HOWBEIT
HUSSEIN
HYGIEIA
MULLEIN
NUCLEIC
PHASEIN
POMPEIA
POMPEII
PROTEIN
SHAREIN
SLIDEIN
SURFEIT
SWOREIN
THEREIN
TRADEIN
VERMEIL
VILLEIN
WHEREIN
WRITEIN
WROTEIN

••••E•I
ALFIERI
ISRAELI
POMPEII
SALIERI
ZAMBEZI

•••••EI
CADUCEI
GALILEI
LORELEI
SHARPEI

EJ•••••
EJECTED

E•J••••
ENJOINS
ENJOYED

•EJ••••
DEJECTS
JEJUNUM
REJECTS
REJOICE
REJOINS

•E•J•••
BEIJING
DEEJAYS
HEYJUDE
PERJURE
PERJURY
VEEJAYS

•E••J••
BELLJAR
LEARJET

••EJ•••
DEEJAYS
VEEJAYS

••E•J••
OVERJOY

•••EJ••
BLUEJAY
NOSEJOB

•••E•J•
BASENJI

EK•••••
EKEDOUT
EKESOUT

E•K••••
ECKHART
ELKHART
ESKIMOS

E••K•••
ELEKTRA
ERSKINE
EVOKERS
EVOKING
EZEKIEL

E•••K••
EELSKIN
EVENKIS

E••••K•
EMBANKS
EMBARKS

E•••••K
EARLOCK
EARMARK
EYEBANK

•EK••••
DEKLERK
DEKOVEN
REKEYED
TEKTITE

•E•K•••
BEAKERS
BECKETT
BECKONS
DECKING
DECKLES
DECKOUT
DESKSET
DESKTOP
GECKOES
HECKLED
HECKLER
HECKLES
JERKIER
JERKILY
JERKING
JERKINS
LEAKAGE
LEAKERS
LEAKIER
LEAKING
MEEKEST
NECKERS
NECKING
NECKTIE
PEAKING
PECKING
PECKISH
PECKSAT
PEEKING
PEEKOUT
PEEKSAT
PERKIER
PERKILY
PERKING
PERKINS
PERKSUP
PESKIER
PESKILY
RECKONS
REEKING
SEEKERS
SEEKING
SEEKOUT
SELKIRK
WEAKENS
WEAKEST
WEAKISH
WEEKDAY
WEEKEND
WELKINS
WESKITS

•E••K••
BELAKUN
BETAKEN
BETAKES
BETOKEN
DEBAKEY
EELSKIN
HEARKEN
MENCKEN
MESSKIT
PERUKES
REBEKAH
REBUKED
REBUKES
REDSKIN
REINKED
REMAKES
RETAKEN
RETAKES
REVOKED
REVOKES

•E•••K•
BEDECKS
BESPOKE
DEBARKS
DEBUNKS
GEMLIKE
NETSUKE
RECORKS
REDOAKS
REHOOKS
RELOCKS
REMARKS
REWORKS
TEACAKE

•E••••K
BEATNIK
BEDROCK
BERSERK
BESPEAK
BETHINK
DEFROCK
DEKLERK
DENMARK
DERRICK
FETLOCK
GEMSBOK
GETBACK
HEMLOCK
HENPECK
LEACOCK
LEGWORK
MENFOLK
NETWORK
NEWLOOK
NEWYORK
PEACOCK
PEPTALK
PETCOCK
PETROCK
RECHALK
RECHECK
REDBOOK
RESTOCK
RETHINK
RETRACK
SEASICK
SELKIRK
SELLECK
SETBACK
TEDMACK
VEENECK
WEDLOCK

••EK•••
CHEKHOV
ELEKTRA
EZEKIEL
MEEKEST
PEEKING
PEEKOUT
PEEKSAT
REEKING
SEEKERS
SEEKING
SEEKOUT
SHEKELS
TREKKED
TREKKER
TREKKIE
WEEKDAY
WEEKEND

••E•K••
BLEAKER
BLEAKLY
BREAKER
BREAKIN
BREAKUP
CHECKED
CHECKER
CHECKIN
CHECKUP
CLERKED
CREAKED
DOESKIN
EVENKIS
FLECKED
FREAKED
FRECKLE
GHERKIN
IRECKON
SHEIKHS
SLEEKED
SLEEKEN
SLEEKER
SLEEKLY
SNEAKED
SNEAKER
SNEAKIN
SPEAKER
SPEAKOF
SPEAKUP
SPECKLE
TREKKED
TREKKER
TREKKIE
TWEAKED
WREAKED
WRECKED
WRECKER

••E••K•
ABENAKI
AMERIKA
APELIKE
GRETZKY
HOECAKE

••E•••K
EYEBANK
ICEMILK
ICEPACK
ICEPICK
ICERINK
OBELISK
PRECOOK
PRESOAK
ROEBUCK
SPELUNK
TIERACK
TIETACK
VEENECK

•••EK••
RAMEKIN
REBEKAH
SLEEKED
SLEEKEN
SLEEKER
SLEEKLY

•••E•K•
BEDECKS
BLUESKY
KOPECKS
SCREAKS
SQUEAKS
SQUEAKY
STREAKS
STREAKY

•••E••K
BODEREK
LIVEOAK
VANEYCK

••••EK•
SHRIEKS

••••E•K
BERSERK
BESPEAK
BOMBECK
BRUBECK
DEKLERK
HAUBERK
HENPECK
LOWNECK
MIDWEEK
OFFPEAK
RECHECK
SELLECK
SUNDECK
VEENECK
WOZZECK

•••••EK
BODEREK
JANACEK
KAISHEK
MIDWEEK
ZATOPEK

EL•••••
ELAPIDS
ELAPSED
ELAPSES
ELASTIC
ELATERS
ELATING
ELATION
ELBOWED
ELDERLY
ELEANOR
ELECTED
ELECTEE
ELECTOR
ELECTRA
ELECTRO
ELEGANT
ELEGIAC
ELEGIES
ELEGIST
ELEISON
ELEKTRA
ELEMENT
ELEVATE
ELEVENS
ELGRECO
ELICITS
ELIDING
ELISION
ELITISM
ELITIST
ELIXIRS
ELKHART
ELLIOTT
ELLIPSE
ELLISON
ELMISTI
ELMTREE
ELOPERS
ELOPING
ELUDING
ELUSIVE
ELUTING
ELUTION
ELUVIUM
ELYSEES
ELYSIAN
ELYSIUM

E•L••••
ECLAIRS
ECLIPSE
ECLOGUE
EELIEST
EELSKIN
ELLIOTT
ELLIPSE
ELLISON
ENLACED
ENLACES
ENLARGE
ENLISTS
ENLIVEN
EOLITHS

E••L•••
EAGLETS
EAGLING
EARLDOM
EARLIER
EARLOBE
EARLOCK
EARLYON
ECOLOGY
EGALITE
EHRLICH
EMBLEMS
EMPLOYS
EMULATE
ENCLAVE
ENCLOSE
ENDLESS
ENGLAND
ENGLISH
ENGLUND
ENPLANE
ENSLAVE
EPILOGS
ERELONG
EVILEST
EVILEYE
EVILLER
EVOLVED
EVOLVES
EVULSED
EVULSES
EXALTED
EXCLAIM
EXCLUDE
EXILING
EXPLAIN
EXPLODE
EXPLOIT
EXPLORE
EXULTED
EYELASH
EYELETS
EYELIDS

E•••L••
EARFLAP
EARPLUG
ECHELON
EDIBLES
EMMYLOU
ENABLED
ENABLES
ENDPLAY
ENFOLDS
ENGULFS
ENISLED
ENISLES
ENROLLS
ENSILED
ENSILES
ENVELOP
EPAULET
EPSILON
EQUALED
EQUALLY
ESTELLE
ETOILES
EVILLER
EXHALED
EXHALES

E••••L•
EAGERLY
EARFULS
EARTHLY
EATABLE
EGGROLL
ELDERLY
EMERALD
EMPTILY
ENAMELS
ENNOBLE
ENROLLS
ENSOULS
ENTAILS
ENTITLE
EPISTLE
EQUABLE
EQUABLY
EQUALLY
ERECTLY
ESPIALS
ESTELLE
EXACTLY
EXAMPLE
EXEMPLI
EYEBALL
EYEBOLT
EYEFULS
EYEHOLE

E•••••L
EGGROLL
EMANUEL
EMBROIL
EMPANEL
ENSNARL
ESPANOL
ESTIVAL
ESTORIL
ETERNAL
ETHANOL
ETHICAL
EVANGEL
EYEBALL
EZEKIEL

•EL••••
AELFRIC
BELABOR
BELAKUN
BELATED
BELAYED
BELCHED
BELCHES
BELDAME
BELDAMS

BELFAST
BELGIAN
BELGIUM
BELIEFS
BELIEVE
BELINDA
BELLAMY
BELLBOY
BELLHOP
BELLIED
BELLIES
BELLING
BELLINI
BELLJAR
BELLMAN
BELLMEN
BELLOWS
BELLYUP
BELMONT
BELONGS
BELOVED
BELTANE
BELTING
BELTWAY
BELUSHI
BELYING
CELADON
CELEBES
CELEBRE
CELESTA
CELESTE
CELLARS
CELLINI
CELLIST
CELSIUS
CELTICS
DELANEY
DELAYED
DELAYER
DELBERT
DELEING
DELETED
DELETES
DELIBES
DELICTI
DELICTS
DELIGHT
DELILAH
DELIMIT
DELIRIA
DELISTS
DELIVER
DELTAIC
DELTOID
DELUDED
DELUDES
DELUGED
DELUGES
DELUISE
DELVERS
DELVING
EELIEST
EELSKIN
FELDMAN
FELICIA
FELINES
FELLERS
FELLFOR
FELLING
FELLINI
FELLOFF
FELLOUT
FELLOWS
FELTFOR
FELTOUT
FELUCCA
GELADAS
GELATIN
GELATIS
GELDING
GELLING
HELDOFF
HELDOUT
HELICAL
HELICES
HELICON
HELIPAD
HELIXES
HELLCAT
HELLENE
HELLERS
HELLION
HELLMAN
HELMETS
HELMING
HELOISE
HELOTRY
HELPERS
HELPFUL
HELPING
HELPOUT
JELLIED
JELLIES
JELLING
KELLOGG
KELPIES
MELANGE
MELANIE
MELANIN
MELDING
MELINDA
MELISSA
MELLOWS
MELODIC
MELROSE
MELTING
NELSONS
PELAGES
PELAGIC
PELICAN
PELISSE
PELLETS
PELOTAS
PELTATE
PELTERS
PELTING
RELACED
RELACES
RELAPSE
RELATED
RELATES
RELAXED
RELAXES
RELAYED
RELEARN
RELEASE
RELENTS
RELIANT
RELICTS
RELIEFS
RELIEVE
RELIEVO
RELIGHT
RELINED
RELINES
RELISTS
RELIVED
RELIVES
RELLENO
RELOADS
RELOCKS
RELYING
SELECTS
SELENIC
SELFISH
SELKIRK
SELLECK
SELLERS
SELLING
SELLOFF
SELLOUT
SELTZER
SELVAGE
TELAVIV
TELERAN
TELEXED
TELEXES
TELLALL
TELLERS
TELLIES
TELLING
TELLOFF
TELLSON
TELSTAR
VELLUMS
VELOURS
VELVETS
VELVETY
WELCHED
WELCHES
WELCOME
WELDERS
WELDING
WELFARE
WELKINS
WELLAND
WELLFED
WELLING
WELLOFF
WELLRUN
WELLSET
WELLSUP
WELTERS
WELTING
YELLING
YELLOWS
YELLSAT
YELPERS
YELPING
YELTSIN

•E•L•••

AEOLIAN
BECLOUD
BEDLAMP
BEELINE
BELLAMY
BELLBOY
BELLHOP
BELLIED
BELLIES
BELLING
BELLINI
BELLJAR
BELLMAN
BELLMEN
BELLOWS
BELLYUP
BERLIOZ
BERLITZ
CEILING
CELLARS
CELLINI
CELLIST
DEALERS
DEALING
DEALOUT
DEALSIN
DEALTIN
DECLAIM
DECLARE
DECLASS
DECLINE
DEFLATE
DEFLECT
DEKLERK
DEPLANE
DEPLETE
DEPLORE
DEPLOYS
DEWLAPS
DEWLINE
FEELERS
FEELFOR
FEELIES
FEELING
FEELOUT
FELLERS
FELLFOR
FELLING
FELLINI
FELLOFF
FELLOUT
FELLOWS
FETLOCK
GELLING
GEMLIKE
GEOLOGY
GETLOST
HEALALL
HEALERS
HEALING
HEALTHY
HEELERS
HEELING
HEELTAP
HELLCAT
HELLENE
HELLERS
HELLION
HELLMAN
HEMLINE
HEMLOCK
HEWLETT
JEALOUS
JELLIED
JELLIES
JELLING
KEELING
KEGLERS
KEILLOR
KELLOGG
KEYLIME
MEALIER
MEALIES
MEDLEYS
MELLOWS
MERLOTS
MEWLERS
MEWLING
NEGLECT
NEOLITH
NEWLEFT
NEWLOOK
PEALING
PEDLARS
PEELERS
PEELING
PEELOFF
PELLETS
PEPLUMS
PERLITE
PERLMAN
REALISM
REALIST
REALITY
REALIZE
REALTOR
REBLOOM
RECLAIM
RECLAME
RECLEAN
RECLINE
RECLUSE
REDLINE
REELECT
REELING
REELOFF
REELSIN
REFLECT
REGLUED
REGLUES
RELLENO
REPLACE
REPLANS
REPLANT
REPLATE
REPLAYS
REPLETE
REPLICA
REPLIED
REPLIES
SEALABS
SEALANE
SEALANT
SEALEGS
SEALERS
SEALILY
SEALING
SEALION
SEALOFF
SEALSUP
SECLUDE
SELLECK
SELLERS
SELLING
SELLOFF
SELLOUT
SERLING
SETLINE
TEALEAF
TELLALL
TELLERS
TELLIES
TELLING
TELLOFF
TELLSON
VEILING
VELLUMS
WEALTHY
WEDLOCK
WELLAND
WELLFED
WELLING
WELLOFF
WELLRUN
WELLSET
WELLSUP
WETLAND
YELLING
YELLOWS
YELLSAT
ZEALAND
ZEALOTS
ZEALOUS

•E••L••

AEDILES
BEADLES
BEAGLES
BEATLES
BECALMS
BEDELIA
BEETLES
BEFALLS
BEHOLDS
BENTLEY
BEVELED
CECILIA
CEDILLA
DECALOG
DECKLES
DEDALUS
DEFILED
DEFILER
DEFILES
DELILAH
DEMILLE
DEPALMA
DESALTS
DEVALUE
DEVELOP
DEVILED
DEVILLE
DEVILRY
DEVOLVE
DEWCLAW
DEWILDE
FEEBLER
FEEDLOT
FEMALES
FERULES
FETTLES
GEFILTE
GENTLED
GENTLER
GENTLES
GERALDO
HECKLED
HECKLER
HECKLES
HEDDLES
HEMSLEY
HERALDS
JEANLUC
JEWELED
JEWELER
JEWELRY
KEEBLER
KEILLOR
KERPLOP
KETTLES
KEYCLUB
LEAFLET
LEGALLY
LETSLIP
LEVELED
LEVELER
LEVELLY
MEASLES
MEDALED
MEDDLED
MEDDLER
MEDDLES
MEDULLA
METTLES
NEBULAE
NEBULAR
NEBULAS
NEEDLED
NEEDLES
NEPALIS
NESTLED
NESTLER
NESTLES
NETTLED
NETTLES
NEVILLE
PEARLED
PEBBLED
PEBBLES
PEDALED
PEDDLED
PEDDLER
PEDDLES
PEEPLES
PENALTY
PENULTS
PEOPLED
PEOPLES
PERPLEX
PESTLED
PESTLES
PETALED
REBOLTS
RECALLS
RECOLOR
REDFLAG
REFILLS
REFILMS
REGALED
REGALES
REGALIA
REGALLY
REGULAR
REGULUS
REMELTS
REMOLDS
REOILED
REPOLLS
REPULSE
RESALES
RESALTS
RESELLS
RESILED
RESILES
RESOLED
RESOLES
RESOLVE
RESULTS
RETELLS
RETILED
RETILES
REVALUE
REVELED
REVELER
REVELRY
REVILED
REVILES
REVOLTS
REVOLVE
REWELDS
SEASLUG
SECULAR
SEDALIA
SETTLED
SETTLER
SETTLES
SEVILLE
TEMBLOR
TEMPLAR
TEMPLES
ZEBULON

•E•••L•

AERIALS
BEASTLY
BEDROLL
BEEBALM
BEEFALO
BEFALLS
BEFOULS
BEGUILE
BENGALI
BENGALS
BEOWULF
BERTOLT
BETHELS
BEVERLY
BEWAILS
CEDILLA
CEMBALO
CEREALS
DEBACLE
DECARLO
DEERFLY
DEFAULT
DEMILLE
DENIALS
DENSELY
DERAILS
DETAILS
DEVILLE
FEBRILE
FERRULE
FERTILE
FETIDLY
GENTILE
GERBILS
GESTALT
GETWELL
HEADILY
HEALALL
HEAVILY
HEFTILY
HERBALS
HERCULE
HERSELF
JERKILY
KENDALL
KENNELS
KERNELS
KEYHOLE
LEERILY
LEGALLY
LEGIBLE
LEGIBLY
LEGPULL
LENTILS
LEOPOLD
LETSFLY
LEVELLY
MEDULLA
MENFOLK
MENIALS
MERRILL
MERRILY
MESCALS
MESSALA
MESSILY
NEEDILY
NERVILY
NEVILLE
PEDICLE
PENCILS
PENPALS
PEPPILY
PEPTALK
PERCALE
PERGOLA
PERKILY
PERNELL
PESKILY
PETIOLE
PETRELS
PETTILY
READILY
REBOILS
REBUILD
REBUILT
RECALLS
RECHALK
RECOILS
RECYCLE
REDCELL
REDEALS
REDEALT
REDIALS
REDPOLL
REDWOLF
REFILLS
REFUELS
REGALLY
REHEALS
REHEELS
REMAILS
RENAILS
RENAULT
RENTALS
REPEALS
REPOLLS
REPTILE
RESCALE
RESEALS
RESELLS
RESTYLE
RETAILS
RETELLS
RETICLE
RETITLE
RETOOLS
REVEALS
SEAGULL
SEALILY
SEASALT
SEATTLE
SEAWALL
SEEDILY
SEIDELS
SEQUELS
SERIALS
SERVALS
SERVILE
SESSILE
SEVILLE
TEABALL
TEARILY
TEASELS
TELLALL
TENABLE
TENABLY
TENFOLD
TENSELY
TENSILE
TEPIDLY
TEQUILA
TERCELS
TERSELY
TESTILY
TEXTILE
VEHICLE
VERBALS
VESSELS
VEXEDLY
WEARILY
WEASELS
WEEVILS
WEIRDLY
WENDELL
WETCELL

•E••••L

AEROSOL
BEDEVIL
BEDROLL
BESTIAL
CENTRAL
DECIBEL
DECIMAL
DEMEROL
DEPOSAL
DESPOIL
FEARFUL
FEDERAL
FEMORAL
GENERAL
GENTEEL
GERITOL
GETWELL
HEALALL
HEEDFUL
HELICAL
HELPFUL
JEZEBEL
KENDALL
KESTREL
LEGPULL
LESPAUL
LEXICAL
MEDICAL
MENTHOL
MERRILL
NEEDFUL
NEUTRAL
NEWDEAL
OEDIPAL
PEAFOWL
PEDICEL
PERNELL
PERUSAL
REAVAIL
RECITAL
REDCELL
REDPOLL
REFUSAL
REMODEL
REMOVAL
RENEWAL
RESTFUL
RETINAL
RETRIAL
REVIVAL
SEAGULL
SEAWALL
SEMINAL
SENEGAL
SENSUAL
SETSAIL
SEVERAL
TEABALL
TEARFUL
TELLALL
TENDRIL
TENNIEL
TERTIAL
TEXTUAL
VEGETAL
VENTRAL
VERMEIL
WENDELL
WETCELL
ZESTFUL

••EL•••

ABELARD
ADELINE
AGELESS
APELIKE
ATELIER
AWELESS
BEELINE
CHELSEA
DUELERS
DUELING
DUELIST
DWELLED
DWELLER
ERELONG
EYELASH
EYELETS
EYELIDS
FEELERS
FEELFOR
FEELIES
FEELING
FEELOUT
FIELDED
FIELDER
FUELERS
FUELING
FUELOIL
FUELROD
GIELGUD
GUELPHS
HEELERS
HEELING
HEELTAP
ICELAND
ICELESS
IRELAND
KEELING
KNELLED
NIELSEN
OBELISK
OBELIZE
OCELOTS
OMELETS
PEELERS
PEELING
PEELOFF
PRELATE
PRELIMS
PRELOAD
PRELUDE
QUELLED
REELECT
REELING
REELOFF
REELSIN
SHELDON
SHELLAC
SHELLED
SHELLER
SHELLEY
SHELTER
SHELTIE
SHELTON
SHELVED
SHELVES
SKELTER
SKELTON
SMELLED
SMELTED
SMELTER
SNELLEN
SPELLED
SPELLER
SPELUNK
STELLAR
SVELTER
SWELLED
SWELLUP
SWELTER
SWELTRY
TIELESS
TIELINE
TOELESS
TOELOOP
TRELLIS
TSELIOT
TWELFTH
TWELVES
USELESS
WHELPED
WIELDED
YIELDED
ZOELLER

••E•L••

AREOLAE
AREOLAR
AREOLAS
BEETLES
BRESLIN
CHEMLAB
CREOLES
DWELLED
DWELLER
FEEBLER
FEEDLOT
FIEDLER
GREELEY
GREMLIN
ICEBLUE
ICEFLOE
IDEALLY
JOEBLOW
KEEBLER
KNEELED
KNEELER
KNELLED
KREMLIN
LIESLOW
NEEDLED
NEEDLES
OBERLIN
OVERLAP
OVERLAY
OVERLIE
PEEPLES
PRESLEY
PUEBLOS
QUELLED
SHEILAE
SHEILAH
SHEILAS
SHELLAC
SHELLED
SHELLER
SHELLEY
SMELLED
SNELLEN
SPELLED
SPELLER
STEALTH
STEELED
STEELER
STEELIE
STELLAR
SWELLED
SWELLUP
THEBLOB
TIECLIP
TREBLED
TREBLES
TRELLIS
WHEELED
WHEELER
WHEELIE
ZOELLER

••E••L•

ACEROLA
ADEPTLY
ALERTLY
BEEBALM
BEEFALO
BLEAKLY
CHEAPLY
CLEANLY
CLEARLY
COEVALS
CRENELS
CREWELS
CUEBALL
DEERFLY
DIESELS
EMERALD
ERECTLY
EXEMPLI
EYEBALL
EYEBOLT
EYEFULS
EYEHOLE
FIERILY
FLEETLY
FRECKLE
FRESHLY
GREATLY
ICECOLD
ICEMILK
IDEALLY
INEPTLY
INERTLY
JOEHILL
LEERILY
NEEDILY
ONESELF
OVERALL

OVERFLY
OVERTLY
PHENOLS
PIEBALD
PRESALE
PRESELL
PUERILE
QUEENLY
QUEERLY
SEEDILY
SHEERLY
SHEKELS
SHEWOLF
SLEEKLY
SPECKLE
STEEPLE
STEEPLY
STERILE
STERNLY
STEROLS
SWEETLY
TOEHOLD
TREACLE
TREACLY
TREADLE
TREMBLE
TREMBLY
TREMOLO
TRESTLE
USEABLE
WEEVILS
WHEEDLE
WRESTLE

••E•••L

CHERVIL
COEQUAL
CREOSOL
CUEBALL
DREIDEL
DWEEZIL
ETERNAL
EYEBALL
EZEKIEL
FRETFUL
FUELOIL
GLEEFUL
GRENDEL
HEEDFUL
JOEHILL
NEEDFUL
OVERALL
PRECOOL
PRESELL
PRETZEL
PREVAIL
QUETZAL
SPECIAL
STENCIL
STENGEL
STERNAL
THERMAL
TOENAIL
TREFOIL
UNEQUAL
UTENSIL

•••EL••

ALLELES
ANGELES
ANGELIC
ANGELOU
ANGELUS
ANNELID
APHELIA
BEDELIA
BEVELED
BIBELOT
BIGELOW
BLUELAW
CAMELIA
CAMELOT
CAPELET
CAPELLA
CASELAW
CORELLI
CRUELER
CRUELLY
DANELAW
DEVELOP
ECHELON
ENVELOP
ESTELLE
FIDELIO
FIRELIT
FORELEG
GAMELAW
GATELEG
GAVELED
GAZELLE
GISELLE
GREELEY
HAMELIN
HGWELLS
HOWELLS
JAVELIN
JEWELED
JEWELER
JEWELRY
KNEELED
KNEELER
LABELED
LABELER
LABELLE
LAPELED
LEVELED
LEVELER
LEVELLY
LIBELED
LIBELER
LORELEI
LOUELLA
MODELAS
MODELED
MODELER
MODELTS
MORELLO
MOSELLE
NACELLE
NOVELLA
NOVELLE
NOVELTY
OPHELIA
OTHELLO
PANELED
PATELLA
POMELOS
RAVELED
REMELTS
RESELLS
RETELLS
REVELED
REVELER
REVELRY
REWELDS
ROSELLE
ROZELLE
SHIELDS
SPIELED
SPIELER
SQUELCH
STEELED
STEELER
STEELIE
TIMELAG
TONELOC
TOWELED
TUPELOS
TUTELAR
UCCELLO
WAVELET
WHEELED
WHEELER
WHEELIE
YODELED
YODELER
YULELOG

•••E•L•

ALVEOLI
ANNEALS
APPEALS
AUREOLA
AUREOLE
BEVERLY
BLUEFLU
BRIEFLY
CAPELLA
CEREALS
CHIEFLY
CORELLI
CRUELLY
CUREALL
CUREALL
DATEDLY
DAZEDLY
EAGERLY
ELDERLY
ESTELLE
FIREFLY
FIXEDLY
FLEETLY
GAZELLE
GISELLE
HGWELLS
HOWELLS
JADEDLY
LABELLE
LEVELLY
LOUELLA
LOVERLY
MINEOLA
MISERLY
MORELLO
MOSELLE
MUDEELS
NACELLE
NAKEDLY
NOVELLA
NOVELLE
ORDEALS
ORDERLY
OSCEOLA
OTHELLO
PATELLA
QUEENLY
QUEERLY
QUIETLY
REDEALS
REDEALT
REHEALS
REHEELS
REPEALS
RESEALS
RESELLS
RETELLS
REVEALS
ROSELLE
ROZELLE
SHEERLY
SLEEKLY
SOBERLY
SQUEALS
STEEPLE
STEEPLY
SWEETLY
TIREDLY
UCCELLO
UNREELS
UNSEALS
UNVEILS
UTTERLY
VEXEDLY
WHEEDLE

•••E••L

ADRENAL
ARSENAL
BALEFUL
BANEFUL
BEDEVIL
BILEVEL
BIPEDAL
BRUEGEL
CAREFUL
CUREALL
DEMEROL
DOLEFUL
DONEGAL
DWEEZIL
FATEFUL
FEDERAL
GENERAL
GLEEFUL
GONERIL
HATEFUL
HOPEFUL
HUMERAL
ILLEGAL
IMPERIL
JEZEBEL
JUVENAL
KNIEVEL
LATERAL
LIBERAL
LITERAL
MINERAL
NUMERAL
PAGEFUL
PIPEFUL
RENEWAL
ROSEOIL
SENEGAL
SEVERAL
SPIEGEL
STIEGEL
TUNEFUL
TYLENOL
VEGETAL
WAKEFUL

••••EL•

ACUTELY
AGILELY
BARBELL
BARBELS
BARRELS
BETHELS
BOSWELL
BRAVELY
BUSHELS
CANCELS
CANDELA
CARRELS
CARTELS
CHAPELS
CHISELS
CLAVELL
CLOSELY
COMPELS
CORBELS
CORDELL
CORNELL
CORYELL
COWBELL
CRENELS
CREWELS
CRUDELY
CUDGELS
DAMSELS
DANIELS
DARRELL
DENSELY
DIESELS
DISPELS
DRIVELS
DRYCELL
DRYWELL
DUFFELS
DURRELL
ENAMELS
FALSELY
FALWELL
FANBELT
FUNNELS
GETWELL
GOSPELS
GOTWELL
GRAVELS
GRAVELY
GROVELS
GUNNELS
HERSELF
HIMSELF
HOSTELS
HUBBELL
INANELY
INDWELL
INFIELD
INKWELL
IRATELY
ISOHELS
ISRAELI
KENNELS
KERNELS
LAPBELT
LARGELY
LAURELS
LINTELS
LISTELS
LITHELY
LOOSELY
MANDELA
MANTELS
MARCELS
MARVELS
MAXWELL
MICHELE
MORSELS
MUDEELS
MUSSELS
NAIVELY
NICKELS
NONSELF
NOTWELL
OILWELL
ONESELF
OURSELF
OUTSELL
PARCELS
PARNELL
PASSELS
PASTELS
PERNELL
PETRELS
POMMELS
PRESELL
PROPELS
PUMMELS
PURCELL
RAPPELS
REDCELL
REFUELS
REHEELS
RONDELS
ROSWELL
RUNNELS
RUSSELL
SEIDELS
SEQUELS
SHAPELY
SHEKELS
SHOVELS
SITWELL
SNIDELY
SNIVELS
SORRELS
SPARELY
SPINELS
STATELY
STOKELY
SUAVELY
SUNBELT
SWIVELS
TANGELO
TARBELL
TASSELS
TEASELS
TENSELY
TERCELS
TERSELY
THYSELF
TINSELS
TRAVELS
TRITELY
TROWELS
TUNNELS
UKULELE
UNREELS
VAGUELY
VESSELS
WEASELS
WENDELL
WETCELL
WILHELM
WYCHELM

••••E•L

ABOREAL
ALLHEAL
BARBELL
BIGDEAL
BOSWELL
CLAVELL
CONCEAL
CONGEAL
CORDELL
CORNEAL
CORNELL
CORYELL
COWBELL
DARRELL
DRYCELL
DRYWELL
DURRELL
FALWELL
FORREAL
FURSEAL
GENTEEL
GETWELL
GOTWELL
HUBBELL
INDWELL
INKWELL
LACTEAL
LOWHEEL
MAXWELL
MISDEAL
NEWDEAL
NOTWELL
OATMEAL
OILWELL
OUTSELL
PARNELL
PASSEUL
PERNELL
PRESELL
PURCELL
RAWDEAL
REDCELL
ROSWELL
RUSSELL
SITWELL
SURREAL
TARBELL
TARHEEL
USSTEEL
VERMEIL
WENDELL
WETCELL

•••••EL

ANNABEL
APPAREL
BILEVEL
BRUEGEL
CALOMEL
CARAMEL
CARAVEL
CHANCEL
CHANNEL
CHATTEL
CHUNNEL
CITADEL
COLONEL
COUNSEL
COZUMEL
DECIBEL
DREIDEL
EMANUEL
EMPANEL
EVANGEL
EZEKIEL
FALAFEL
FLANNEL
GABRIEL
GAMBREL
GENTEEL
GRAPNEL
GRENDEL
IMPANEL
INFIDEL
ISHMAEL
JEZEBEL
KESTREL
KNIEVEL
LOWHEEL
MANDREL
MICHAEL
MONGREL
PEDICEL
PRETZEL
QUARREL
RAPHAEL
REMODEL
SANIBEL
SATCHEL
SCALPEL
SHRIVEL
SNORKEL
SPANIEL
SPIEGEL
STENGEL
STIEGEL
STRUDEL
SYNFUEL
TARHEEL
TENNIEL
TRAMMEL
TRAUBEL
TUMBREL
UNRAVEL
USSTEEL
WASTREL

EM•••••

EMANATE
EMANUEL
EMBANKS
EMBARGO
EMBARKS
EMBASSY
EMBLEMS
EMBRACE
EMBROIL
EMBRYOS
EMENDED
EMENDER
EMERALD
EMERGED
EMERGES
EMERITA
EMERITI
EMERSED
EMERSON
EMIGRES
EMINENT
EMIRATE
EMITTED
EMITTER
EMMYLOU
EMOTERS
EMOTING
EMOTION
EMOTIVE
EMPANEL
EMPATHY
EMPEROR
EMPIRES
EMPLOYS
EMPORIA
EMPOWER
EMPRESS
EMPTIED
EMPTIER
EMPTIES
EMPTILY
EMULATE

E•M••••

ELMISTI
ELMTREE
EMMYLOU
ENMASSE
ERMINES

E••M•••

EARMARK
EARMUFF
ELEMENT
ENAMELS
ENAMORS
ENAMOUR
ENDMOST
ENEMIES
EREMITE
ETAMINE
EXAMINE
EXAMPLE
EXEMPLI
EXEMPTS

E•••M••

EASTMAN
ENCAMPS
ENCOMIA
ENDEMIC
ENIGMAS
ENZYMES
ERASMUS
ESKIMOS

E••••M•

ECONOMY
EMBLEMS
ENDGAME
ENGRAMS
EPITOME
EPONYMS
ESTEEMS
EXTREME

E•••••M

EARDRUM
EARLDOM
EGOTISM
ELITISM
ELUVIUM
ELYSIUM
EPIGRAM
ERRATUM
EXCLAIM

•EM••••

BEMIRED
BEMIRES
BEMOANS
BEMUSED
BEMUSES
CEMBALO
CEMENTS
DEMANDS
DEMEANS
DEMERIT
DEMEROL
DEMESNE
DEMETER
DEMIGOD
DEMILLE
DEMISED
DEMISES
DEMONIC
DEMOTED
DEMOTES
DEMPSEY
DEMURER
FEMALES
FEMORAL
GEMLIKE
GEMSBOK
HEMLINE
HEMLOCK
HEMMERS
HEMMING
HEMSLEY
JEMMIED
JEMMIES
LEMMING
LEMPIRA
MEMBERS
MEMENTO
MEMOIRE
MEMOIRS
MEMOREX
MEMPHIS
NEMEROV
NEMESES
NEMESIS
PEMICAN
REMAILS
REMAINS
REMAKES
REMANDS
REMARKS
REMARRY
REMELTS
REMENDS
REMINDS
REMIXED
REMIXES
REMNANT
REMODEL
REMOLDS
REMORAS
REMORSE
REMOTER
REMOTES
REMOUNT
REMOVAL
REMOVED
REMOVER
REMOVES
REMOWED
REMUDAS
SEMINAL
SEMINAR
SEMIPRO
SEMITES
SEMITIC
TEMBLOR
TEMPERA
TEMPERS
TEMPEST
TEMPLAR
TEMPLES
TEMPTED
TEMPTER
TEMPURA
YEMENIS

•E•M•••

BEAMIER
BEAMING
BEAMSUP
BELMONT
BERMUDA
BESMEAR
DEEMING
DENMARK
DESMOND
FERMENT
FERMIUM
GERMANE
GERMANS
GERMANY
HELMETS
HELMING
HEMMERS
HEMMING
HERMANN
HERMITS
HETMANS
JEMMIED
JEMMIES
LEMMING
MERMAID
NEWMATH
NEWMOON
NEWMOWN
PERMING
PERMITS
REAMASS
REAMERS
REAMING
REDMEAT
SEAMIER
SEAMING
SEAMOSS
SEEMING
SEGMENT
SERMONS
SEYMOUR
TEAMING
TEAMSUP
TEDMACK
TEEMING
TERMING
TERMINI
TERMITE
VERMEER
VERMEIL
VERMONT
WETMOPS
YESMAAM
ZERMATT

•E••M••

BECOMES
BELLMAN
BELLMEN
BENUMBS
BERGMAN
BESTMAN
BESTMEN
BETAMAX
BETIMES
CERAMIC
CERUMEN
DECAMPS
DECIMAL
DEFAMED
DEFAMES
DELIMIT
FELDMAN
FEYNMAN
HEADMAN
HEADMEN
HELLMAN
LEGUMES
MERIMEE
NEWSMAN
NEWSMEN
PERLMAN
READMIT
REARMED
REGIMEN
REGIMES
RENAMED
RENAMES
REPOMAN
RESUMED
RESUMES
RETIMED
RETIMES
REVAMPS
SEISMIC
SESAMES
ZEUGMAS

•E•••M•

BECALMS
BEDLAMP
BEDTIME
BEGRIME
BELDAME
BELDAMS
BELLAMY
BESEEMS
CENTIME
CENTIMO
DEFORMS
DEPALMA
KEYLIME
MEDIUMS
MEGOHMS
MEGRIMS
PENNAME
PEPLUMS
PERFUME
PETNAME
RECLAME
REDEEMS
REDGUMS
REFILMS
REFORMS
REFRAME
RESTAMP
RETRIMS
REWARMS
TEATIME
VELLUMS
WELCOME

•E••••M

BEDROOM
BEEBALM
BEECHAM
BELGIUM
BENTHAM
DECLAIM
DECORUM
FERMIUM
HEROISM
JEJUNUM
KETCHAM
LEGROOM
PERDIEM
PERFORM
REALISM
REBLOOM
RECLAIM
RECROOM
REQUIEM
SEAGRAM
SERFDOM
TEAROOM
TERBIUM
YEATEAM
YESMAAM

••EM•••

ALEMBIC
ANEMONE
BLEMISH
CHEMISE
CHEMIST
CHEMLAB
CLEMENS
CLEMENT
CLEMSON
CREMONA
DEEMING
ELEMENT
ENEMIES
EREMITE
EXEMPLI
EXEMPTS
FLEMING
FLEMISH
FREMONT
GREMLIN
HAEMATO
ICEMILK
ITEMIZE
KREMLIN
OLEMISS
PREMEDS
PREMIER
PREMISE
PREMIUM
SEEMING
STEMMED
TEEMING
TREMBLE
TREMBLY
TREMOLO
TREMORS

••E•M••

CREAMED
CREAMER
CREWMAN
CREWMEN
DREAMED
DREAMER
DREAMON
DREAMUP
FREEMAN
FREEMEN
GLEAMED

PREAMPS
PREEMIE
PREEMPT
SHERMAN
STEAMED
STEAMER
STEMMED
THERMAL
THERMOS

••E••M•

AWESOME
FRENUMS
ONETIME
PHENOMS
PLENUMS
PRELIMS
PRESUME
WOEISME

••E•••M

BEEBALM
BEECHAM
CHETRUM
FIEFDOM
FREEDOM
OMENTUM
PIETISM
PREMIUM
RHENIUM
STEINEM
STERNUM
THEOREM
VIETNAM

•••EM••

ANAEMIA
ARTEMIS
ARTEMUS
ATTEMPT
BASEMAN
BASEMEN
BATEMAN
BIREMES
BOHEMIA
CAKEMIX
CAVEMAN
CAVEMEN
CINEMAS
CINEMAX
COLEMAN
DILEMMA
ENDEMIC
FIREMAN
FIREMEN
FOREMAN
FOREMEN
FREEMAN
FREEMEN
GATEMAN
GATEMEN
INGEMAR
LIKEMAD
LINEMAN
LINEMEN
PIKEMAN
PIKEMEN
POLEMIC
PREEMIE
PREEMPT
RACEMES
SCHEMAS
SCHEMED
SCHEMER
SCHEMES
SIDEMAN
SIDEMEN
TOTEMIC
UNKEMPT
UPTEMPO
WISEMAN
WISEMEN

•••E•M•

BESEEMS
DILEMMA
ESTEEMS
INSEAMS
LYCEUMS
MUSEUMS
PALERMO
REDEEMS
SCREAMS
STREAMS

•••E••M

ATHEISM
BOREDOM
DUKEDOM
FIREARM
FOREARM
FREEDOM
INTERIM
NOSEEUM
PINETUM
SIDEARM
TAKEAIM
TONEARM

••••EM•

ACADEME
ACADEMY
ALCHEMY
ANADEMS
ANTHEMS
BESEEMS
CONDEMN
CONTEMN
DIADEMS
EMBLEMS
ESTEEMS
EXTREME
IPANEMA
MAYHEMS
MOSLEMS
NOXZEMA
PHONEME
PTOLEMY
REDEEMS
SACHEMS
SANREMO
SOSUEME
SUPREME
SUPREMO
SYSTEMS
TANDEMS
TRIREME

••••E•M

ANAHEIM
LOWBEAM
MIDTERM
NOSEEUM
SUNBEAM
WILHELM
WYCHELM
YEATEAM

•••••EM

APOTHEM
HAARLEM
HOMINEM
PERDIEM
PROBLEM
REQUIEM
STEINEM
THEOREM

EN•••••

ENABLED
ENABLES
ENACTED
ENACTOR
ENAMELS
ENAMORS
ENAMOUR
ENCAGED
ENCAGES
ENCAMPS
ENCASED
ENCASES
ENCHAIN
ENCHANT
ENCLAVE
ENCLOSE
ENCODED
ENCODER
ENCODES
ENCOMIA
ENCORES
ENCRUST
ENCRYPT
ENDEARS
ENDEMIC
ENDGAME
ENDINGS
ENDIVES
ENDLESS
ENDMOST
ENDORSE
ENDOWED
ENDPLAY
ENDRUNS
ENDUING
ENDURED
ENDURES
ENDUSER
ENDWAYS
ENDWISE
ENDZONE
ENEMIES
ENFOLDS
ENFORCE
ENGAGED
ENGAGES
ENGARDE
ENGINES
ENGIRDS
ENGLAND
ENGLISH
ENGLUND
ENGORGE
ENGRAFT
ENGRAMS
ENGRAVE
ENGROSS
ENGULFS
ENHANCE
ENIGMAS
ENISLED
ENISLES
ENJOINS
ENJOYED
ENLACED
ENLACES
ENLARGE
ENLISTS
ENLIVEN
ENMASSE
ENNEADS
ENNOBLE
ENOUNCE
ENPLANE
ENRAGED
ENRAGES
ENROBED
ENROBES
ENROLLS
ENROOTS
ENROUTE
ENSIGNS
ENSILED
ENSILES
ENSLAVE
ENSNARE
ENSNARL
ENSOULS
ENSUING
ENSUITE
ENSURED
ENSURES
ENTAILS
ENTEBBE
ENTENTE
ENTERED
ENTHUSE
ENTICED
ENTICER
ENTICES
ENTITLE
ENTRAIN
ENTRANT
ENTRAPS
ENTREAT
ENTREES
ENTRIES
ENTROPY
ENTRUST
ENTWINE
ENURING
ENVELOP
ENVIOUS
ENVYING
ENWRAPS
ENZYMES

E•N••••

ENNEADS
ENNOBLE
ERNESTO
EUNUCHS

E••N•••

EARNERS
EARNEST
EARNING
EBONIES
EBONITE
ECONOMY
EGGNOGS
EMANATE
EMANUEL
EMENDED
EMENDER
EMINENT
ENSNARE
ENSNARL
EPONYMS
ETHNICS
ETONIAN
EVANDER
EVANGEL
EVENEST
EVENING
EVENKIS
EVENOUT
EVENSUP
EVINCED
EVINCES

E•••N••

EATENAT
EATENUP
ECHINUS
EDASNER
EDGINGS
EFFENDI
ELEANOR
EMBANKS
EMPANEL
ENDINGS
ENGINES
ENHANCE
ENOUNCE
ENTENTE
EQUINES
EQUINOX
ERMINES
ERRANDS
ESPANOL
ESSENCE
ESSENES
ESTONIA
ETERNAL
ETHANOL
ETIENNE
EUGENIE
EXPANDS
EXPANSE
EXPENDS
EXPENSE
EXPUNGE
EXTENDS
EXTENTS
EXTINCT

E••••N•

EAGLING
EARNING
EARRING
EASTEND
ECHIDNA
ECHOING
EDDYING
EDITING
EDUCING
ELATING
ELEGANT
ELEMENT
ELEVENS
ELIDING
ELOPING
ELUDING
ELUTING
EMINENT
EMOTING
ENCHANT
ENDRUNS
ENDUING
ENDZONE
ENGLAND
ENGLUND
ENJOINS
ENPLANE
ENSIGNS
ENSUING
ENTRANT
ENTWINE
ENURING
ENVYING
EPERGNE
EPICENE
EPIGENE
EPIGONE
ERASING
ERELONG
ERODING
ERSKINE
ESPYING
ETAMINE
ETCHING
ETIENNE
EUPHONY
EVADING
EVENING
EVIDENT
EVOKING
EXAMINE
EXIGENT
EXILING
EXITING
EXPOUND
EXUDING
EYEBANK

E•••••N

EARLYON
EARTHEN
EASEDIN
EASESIN
EASTERN
EASTMAN
ECHELON
EDGEDIN
EDGESIN
EDITION
EELSKIN
EGGEDON
ELATION
ELEISON
ELISION
ELLISON
ELUTION
ELYSIAN
EMERSON
EMOTION
ENCHAIN
ENLIVEN
ENTRAIN
EPSILON
EPSTEIN
EREWHON
ERICSON
EROSION
ETESIAN
ETONIAN
EVASION
EXPLAIN
EXURBAN

•EN••••

BENATAR
BENAZIR
BENCHED
BENCHES
BENDERS
BENDING
BENEATH
BENEFIT
BENGALI
BENGALS
BENISON
BENNETT
BENTHAM
BENTLEY
BENTSEN
BENUMBS
BENZENE
CENSERS
CENSING
CENSORS
CENSURE
CENTAUR
CENTAVO
CENTERS
CENTIME
CENTIMO
CENTRAL
CENTRED
CENTRES
CENTRIC
CENTURY
DENDRON
DENEUVE
DENIALS
DENIECE
DENIERS
DENIZEN
DENMARK
DENNEHY
DENOTED
DENOTES
DENSELY
DENSEST
DENSITY
DENTATE
DENTINE
DENTING
DENTIST
DENTURE
DENUDED
DENUDES
DENYING
FENCERS
FENCING
FENDERS
FENDING
FENETRE
GENDERS
GENERAL
GENERIC
GENERIS
GENESEE
GENESES
GENESIS
GENETIC
GENGHIS
GENNARO
GENOESE
GENTEEL
GENTIAN
GENTILE
GENTLED
GENTLER
GENTLES
GENUINE
HENBANE
HENBITS
HENCOOP
HENDRIX
HENNAED
HENNERY
HENPECK
HENREID
JENNETS
JENNIES
KENDALL
KENNEDY
KENNELS
KENNETH
KENOSHA
KENYANS
LENDERS
LENDING
LENFANT
LENGTHS
LENGTHY
LENIENT
LENTILS
MENACED
MENACES
MENAGES
MENCKEN
MENDERS
MENDING
MENDOZA
MENFOLK
MENHIRS
MENIALS
MENISCI
MENORAH
MENOTTI
MENTHOL
MENTION
MENTORS
MENUHIN
PENALTY
PENANCE
PENATES
PENCILS
PENDANT
PENDENT
PENDING
PENGUIN
PENNAME
PENNANT
PENNATE
PENNERS
PENNIES
PENNING
PENNONS
PENPALS
PENSEES
PENSION
PENSIVE
PENTADS
PENUCHE
PENULTS
RENAILS
RENAMED
RENAMES
RENAULT
RENDERS
RENDING
RENEGED
RENEGER
RENEGES
RENEWAL
RENEWED
RENEWER
RENNINS
RENOTES
RENTALS
RENTERS
RENTING
SENATES
SENATOR
SENDERS
SENDFOR
SENDING
SENDOFF
SENDOUT
SENDSIN
SENDSUP
SENDUPS
SENECAS
SENEGAL
SENIORS
SENNETT
SENORAS
SENORES
SENSATE
SENSING
SENSORS
SENSORY
SENSUAL
SENTFOR
SENTOFF
SENTOUT
TENABLE
TENABLY
TENACES
TENANCY
TENANTS
TENDERS
TENDING
TENDONS
TENDRIL
TENDSTO
TENFOLD
TENFOUR
TENNERS
TENNIEL
TENONED
TENPINS
TENSELY
TENSEST
TENSEUP
TENSILE
TENSING
TENSION
TENSIVE
TENSORS
TENSPOT
TENTERS
TENTING
TENUOUS
TENURED
TENURES
VENDING
VENDORS
VENEERS
VENISON
VENTERS
VENTING
VENTRAL
VENTURA
VENTURE
WENCHES
WENDELL
WENDERS
WENDING
WENTAPE
WENTBAD
WENTFOR
WENTOFF
WENTOUT
ZENANAS
ZENITHS
ZENOBIA

•E•N•••

BEANBAG
BEANERY
BEANIES
BEANING
BENNETT
BERNARD
BERNESE
BERNICE
BERNSEN
DENNEHY
DERNIER
FEINTED
FEYNMAN
GENNARO
HEINOUS
HENNAED
HENNERY
HEXNUTS
JEANARP
JEANLUC
JEANNIE
JENNETS
JENNIES
KEENERS
KEENEST
KEENING
KENNEDY
KENNELS
KENNETH
KERNELS
KERNING
KEYNOTE
LEANDER
LEANERS
LEANEST
LEANING
LEANSON
LEANTOS
LEONARD
LEONINE
LEONORA
MEANDER
MEANEST
MEANIES
MEANING
NEONATE
NEWNESS
PEANUTS
PENNAME
PENNANT
PENNATE
PENNERS
PENNIES
PENNING
PENNONS
PEONAGE
PEONIES
PERNELL
PETNAME
REDNESS
REENACT
REENTER
REENTRY
REGNANT
REINING
REINKED
REINSIN
REMNANT
RENNINS
REUNIFY
REUNION
REUNITE
REYNARD
SEANCES
SEINERS
SEINING
SENNETT
TEENAGE
TEENERS
TEENIER
TENNERS
TENNIEL
TERNARY
TERNATE
VEENECK
VEINING
VERNIER
WEANING
WEENIES
WERNHER
WETNESS

•E••N••

BEATNIK
BEGONIA
BELINDA
BELONGS
CEMENTS
CEZANNE
DEBONED
DEBONES
DEBUNKS
DECANTS
DEFENCE
DEFENDS
DEFENSE
DEFINED
DEFINES
DEFUNCT
DEIGNED
DELANEY
DEMANDS
DEMONIC
DEPENDS
DEPONED
DEPONES
DETENTE
FEIGNED
FELINES
GERENTS
GERUNDS
GETINTO
JEANNIE
JEJUNUM
KETONES
LEARNED
LEARNER
LEBANON
LEGENDS
LEIBNIZ
LEPANTO
LETINON
MELANGE
MELANIE
MELANIN
MELINDA
MEMENTO
MERINOS
PEDANTS
PENANCE
PETUNIA
REBINDS
RECANED
RECANES
RECANTS
RECENCY
REDANTS
REFINED
REFINER
REFINES
REFUNDS
REGENCY
REGENTS
REHANGS
REIGNED
RELENTS
RELINED
RELINES
REMANDS
REMENDS
REMINDS
REPENTS
REPINED
REPINES
RERENTS
RERINSE
RESANDS
RESENDS
RESENTS
RESINGS
RETINAE
RETINAL
RETINAS
RETINUE
RETUNED
RETUNES
REVENGE
REVENUE
REWINDS
REZONED
REZONES
SECANTS
SECONDS
SELENIC
SEMINAL
SEMINAR
SERENER
SETINTO
SEVENTH
SEVENTY
SEVENUP
TENANCY
TENANTS
TENONED
TERENCE
TETANUS
VEDANTA
VERANDA
YEARNED
YEARNER
YEARNTO
YEMENIS
ZENANAS

•E•••N•

BEACONS
BEADING
BEAMING
BEANING
BEARING
BEATING
BECKONS
BEDDING
BEEFING
BEELINE
BEEPING
BEGGING
BEGUINE
BEIJING
BELLING
BELLINI
BELMONT
BELTANE
BELTING
BELYING
BEMOANS
BENDING
BENZENE
BESTING
BETHANY
BETHINK
BETTING
CEASING
CEILING
CELLINI
CENSING
CEZANNE
DEACONS
DEADEND
DEADENS
DEAFENS
DEALING
DECKING
DECLINE
DEEDING
DEEMING
DEEPEND
DEEPENS
DEFIANT
DEFYING
DEHORNS
DEICING
DELEING
DELVING
DEMEANS
DEMESNE
DENTINE
DENTING
DENYING
DEPLANE
DERRING
DESCANT
DESCEND
DESCENT
DESIGNS
DESMOND
DESTINE
DESTINY
DETAINS
DEVEINS
DEVIANT
DEWLINE
FEARING
FEEDING
FEELING
FELLING
FELLINI

FENCING
FENDING
FERMENT
FERVENT
FEUDING
GEARING
GELDING
GELLING
GENUINE
GERAINT
GERMANE
GERMANS
GERMANY
GETTING
HEADING
HEALING
HEAPING
HEARING
HEATING
HEAVENS
HEAVING
HEDGING
HEEDING
HEELING
HEFTING
HELLENE
HELMING
HELPING
HEMLINE
HEMMING
HENBANE
HERDING
HERMANN
HEROINE
HERRING
HETMANS
JEERING
JELLING
JERKING
JERKINS
JESTING
JETGUNS
JETSONS
JETTING
KEELING
KEENING
KEEPING
KENYANS
KERNING
KEYRING
LEADING
LEADINS
LEAFING
LEAKING
LEANING
LEAPING
LEASING
LEAVENS
LEAVING
LEERING
LEGGING
LEGIONS
LEMMING
LENDING
LENFANT
LENIENT
LEONINE
LEPTONS
LESSENS
LESSING
LESSONS
LETTING
LEVYING
MEANING
MEDIANS
MEDIANT
MEETING
MELDING
MELTING
MENDING
MEOWING
MERGING
MESHING
MESSINA
MESSING
METHANE
MEWLING
NEARING
NEATENS
NECKING
NEEDING
NELSONS
NEPTUNE
NESTING
NETTING
NEURONE
NEURONS
NEWTONS
PEAHENS
PEAKING
PEALING
PEASANT
PECCANT
PECKING
PECTINS
PEEKING
PEELING
PEEPING
PEERING
PEEVING
PEGGING
PELTING
PENDANT
PENDENT
PENDING
PENNANT
PENNING
PENNONS
PEPPING
PEPSINS
PERCENT
PERKING
PERKINS
PERMING
PERSONA
PERSONS
PETTING
READING
REAGENT
REAMING
REAPING
REAREND
REARING
REASONS
REBOUND
RECKONS
RECLINE
RECOUNT
REDCENT
REDDENS
REDDING
REDFINS
REDLINE
REDOING
REDOUND
REDPINE
REDWINE
REDWING
REEDING
REEFING
REEKING
REELING
REFFING
REGAINS
REGIONS
REGNANT
REINING
REJOINS
RELIANT
RELLENO
RELYING
REMAINS
REMNANT
REMOUNT
RENDING
RENNINS
RENTING
REOPENS
REPAINT
REPLANS
REPLANT
REPRINT
REPUGNS
RESCIND
RESIGNS
RESOUND
RESPOND
RESTING
RETAINS
RETHINK
RETSINA
RETURNS
REUBENS
REVVING
REWOUND
SEAFANS
SEALANE
SEALANT
SEALING
SEAMING
SEARING
SEASONS
SEATING
SEEDING
SEEKING
SEEMING
SEEPING
SEGMENT
SEINING
SEIZING
SELLING
SENDING
SENSING
SEQUINS
SERLING
SERMONS
SERPENT
SERVANT
SERVING
SESTINA
SETLINE
SETTING
SEVIGNE
SEXTANS
SEXTANT
SEXTONS
TEAMING
TEARING
TEASING
TEDDING
TEEMING
TELLING
TENDING
TENDONS
TENPINS
TENSING
TENTING
TERHUNE
TERMING
TERMINI
TERRENE
TESTING
TEUTONS
VEERING
VEGGING
VEILING
VEINING
VENDING
VENTING
VERBENA
VERDANT
VERGING
VERMONT
VESTING
VETOING
VETTING
WEAKENS
WEANING
WEAPONS
WEARING
WEAVING
WEBBING
WEDDING
WEDGING
WEEDING
WEEKEND
WEEPING
WELDING
WELKINS
WELLAND
WELLING
WELTING
WENDING
WESTEND
WETLAND
WETTING
YEAREND
YELLING
YELPING
YESSING
YEVGENY
ZEALAND
ZEITUNG
ZEROING

•E••••N

AEOLIAN
BEARSON
BEDDOWN
BEDIZEN
BEDOUIN
BELAKUN
BELGIAN
BELLMAN
BELLMEN
BENISON
BENTSEN
BERGMAN
BERGSON
BERNSEN
BESTMAN
BESTMEN
BETAKEN
BETOKEN
BETWEEN
CELADON
CERTAIN
CERUMEN
CESSION
DEADPAN
DEALSIN
DEALTIN
DECAGON
DEKOVEN
DENDRON
DENIZEN
DETRAIN
DEXTRIN
EELSKIN
FEEDSON
FELDMAN
FESTOON
FEYNMAN
GELATIN
GENTIAN
GETDOWN
GETEVEN
GETITON
HEADMAN
HEADMEN
HEADPIN
HEADSIN
HEARKEN
HEARTEN
HEATHEN
HELICON
HELLION
HELLMAN
HEPARIN
HEPBURN
HERMANN
HESHVAN
HESSIAN
HEXAGON
HEXSIGN
KEEPSIN
KEEPSON
KEESHAN
KERATIN
KEYEDIN
LEADSIN
LEADSON
LEANSON
LEBANON
LEBARON
LECTERN
LEGHORN
LETDOWN
LETINON
LEXICON
MEGRYAN
MEISSEN
MELANIN
MENCKEN
MENTION
MENUHIN
MEXICAN
NEUTRON
NEVADAN
NEWBORN
NEWMOON
NEWMOWN
NEWSMAN
NEWSMEN
NEWTOWN
PEABEAN
PEARSON
PEERSIN
PELICAN
PEMICAN
PENGUIN
PENSION
PERLMAN
PERSIAN
PERTAIN
READSIN
REARDON
RECLEAN
REDRAWN
REDSKIN
REELSIN
REFRAIN
REGIMEN
REINSIN
RELEARN
REPOMAN
RESTAIN
RETAKEN
RETRAIN
REUNION
REWOVEN
SEALION
SECTION
SEEPSIN
SENDSIN
SERBIAN
SESSION
SETDOWN
SETUPON
TEACHIN
TEHERAN
TELERAN
TELLSON
TENSION
TERRAIN
TESTBAN
VENISON
VERSION
VETERAN
WEIGHIN
WELLRUN
WESTERN
YELTSIN
YEREVAN
ZEBULON

••EN•••

ABENAKI
ADENINE
AGENDAS
ALENCON
AMENDED
AMENITY
AVENGED
AVENGER
AVENGES
AVENUES
BIENTOT
BLENDED
BLENDER
BRENDAN
BRENNAN
BRENNER
CHENIER
CRENELS
DUENNAS
EMENDED
EMENDER
EVENEST
EVENING
EVENKIS
EVENOUT
EVENSUP
FLENSED
FLENSES
FRENEAU
FRENUMS
GRENADA
GRENADE
GRENDEL
IDENTIC
KEENERS
KEENEST
KEENING
LAENNEC
LIENEES
MAENADS
MCENROE
OMENTUM
ONENESS
OPENAIR
OPENBAR
OPENEND
OPENERS
OPENING
OPENPIT
OPENSEA
OPENSUP
OPENTOE
PFENNIG
PHENOLS
PHENOMS
PLENARY
PLENUMS
QUENTIN
REENACT
REENTER
REENTRY
RHENIUM
SCENDED
SCENERY
SCENTED
SIENNAS
SLENDER
SPENCER
SPENDER
SPENSER
STENCIL
STENGEL
STENTOR
TEENAGE
TEENERS
TEENIER
TOENAIL
TRENARY
TRENDED
TRENTON
UNENDED
UPENDED
UTENSIL
VEENECK
WEENIES
WIENERS
WIENIES

••E•N••

BRENNAN
BRENNER
CLEANED
CLEANER
CLEANLY
CLEANSE
CLEANUP
DUENNAS
ELEANOR
ETERNAL
FLEXNER
GLEANED
GLEANER
GREENED
GREENER
KLEENEX
LAENNEC
LIERNES
OCEANIA
OCEANIC
OCEANID
OCEANUS
PFENNIG
PREENED
PREENER
QUEENLY
SIENNAS
STEINEM
STEINER
STERNAL
STERNER
STERNLY
STERNUM
TIEINTO
TIERNEY
VIETNAM

••E••N•

ACETONE
ADELINE
ADENINE
AMERIND
ANEMONE
BEEFING
BEELINE
BEEPING
BRETONS
BREWING
CHEWING
CLEMENS
CLEMENT
CREMONA
CRETANS
CRETINS
CREWING
DEEDING
DEEMING
DEEPEND
DEEPENS
DIETING
DUELING
ELEGANT
ELEMENT
ELEVENS
EPERGNE
ERELONG
EVENING
EYEBANK
FEEDING
FEELING
FLEEING
FLEMING
FLEXING
FREEING
FREMONT
FUELING
GREYING
HEEDING
HEELING
ICELAND
ICERINK
IKEBANA
IRELAND
ITERANT
JEERING
KEELING
KEENING
KEEPING
KMESONS
KNEEING
LEERING
MEETING
NEEDING
OBEYING
OPENEND
OPENING
OPERAND
OREGANO
PEEKING
PEELING
PEEPING
PEERING
PEEVING
PIECING
PIEPANS
PIETINS
PREBEND
PRESENT
PRETEND
PREVENT
QUEUING
REEDING
REEFING
REEKING
REELING
SEEDING
SEEKING
SEEMING
SEEPING
SHEBANG
SKEWING
SMETANA
SPELUNK
SPEWING
STEPINS
STEVENS
STEWING
TEEMING
TIELINE
TIEPINS
TIERING
TREEING
TREPANS
TREVINO
VEERING
VIEWING
WEEDING
WEEKEND
WEEPING

••E•••N

ALENCON
BREAKIN
BRENDAN
BRENNAN
BRESLIN
BRESSON
CHEAPEN
CHECHEN
CHECKIN
CHEVRON
CLEAVON
CLEMSON
CREWMAN
CREWMEN
DIEDOWN
DOESKIN
DREAMON
DRESDEN
ELEISON
EMERSON
EREWHON
ETESIAN
FEEDSON
FREEMAN
FREEMEN
FRESHEN
GHERKIN
GLEASON
GRECIAN
GREMLIN
HOEDOWN
IBERIAN
IRECKON
KEEPSIN
KEEPSON
KEESHAN
KREMLIN
LIEDOWN
MUEZZIN
NIELSEN
OBERLIN
OVERRAN
OVERRUN
PEERSIN
PREDAWN
PRESSON
PRESTON
PRETEEN
PREYSON
QUENTIN
REELSIN
SEEPSIN
SHELDON
SHELTON
SHERMAN
SHERWIN
SKELTON
SLEEKEN
SLEEPIN
SLEEPON
SLEPTIN
SLEPTON
SNEAKIN
SNELLEN
STEEPEN
STEPHEN
STEPSIN
STEPSON
STETSON
STEUBEN
SWEARIN
SWEETEN
SWEETON
THEREIN
THEREON
TIEDOWN
TREASON
TRENTON
WHEATON
WHEREIN

•••EN••

ABSENCE
ABSENTS
ACCENTS
ACHENES
ADDENDA
ADDENDS
ADRENAL
ADVENTS
ALBENIZ
ALDENTE
ALIENEE
ALIENOR
ALKENES
ALLENDE
ANTENNA
APLENTY
APPENDS
ARDENCY
ARMENIA
ARSENAL
ARSENIC
ARSENIO
ASCENDS
ASCENTS
ASSENTS
ATTENDS
AUGENDS
BARENTS
BASENJI
CADENCE
CADENZA
CALENDS
CATENAE
CAYENNE
CEMENTS
CLIENTS
COGENCY
COZENED
DEFENCE
DEFENDS
DEFENSE
DEPENDS
DETENTE
DOCENTS
DOYENNE
DOZENTH
EATENAT
EATENUP
EFFENDI
ENTENTE
ESSENCE
ESSENES
ETIENNE
EUGENIE
EXPENDS
EXPENSE
EXTENDS
EXTENTS
FAGENDS
FAIENCE
FIRENZE
FLUENCY
FOMENTS
FRIENDS
GERENTS
GIVENTO
GREENED
GREENER
HAVENOT
IMMENSE
IMPENDS
INCENSE
INDENTS
INGENUE
INTENDS
INTENSE
INTENTS
INVENTS
JIMENEZ
JUVENAL
KLEENEX
KUTENAI
LAMENTS
LATENCY
LATENTS
LAZENBY
LEGENDS
LICENCE
LICENSE
LIFENET
LIKENED
LIKENEW
LIVENED
LORENZO
LOZENGE
MAGENTA
MEMENTO
MOMENTS
NOVENAS
OFFENCE
OFFENDS
OFFENSE
OFTENER
ORIENTE
ORIENTS
PARENTS
PATENTS
PHOENIX
PHRENIC
PIMENTO
PINENUT
POLENTA
POTENCY
PREENED
PREENER
QUEENLY
RAVENED
RAVENNA
RECENCY
REGENCY
REGENTS
RELENTS
REMENDS
REPENTS
RERENTS
RESENDS
RESENTS
REVENGE
REVENUE
RIPENED
RODENTS
SCIENCE
SELENIC
SERENER
SEVENTH
SEVENTY
SEVENUP
SILENCE
SILENTS
SIMENON
STDENIS
TAGENDS
TAKENIN
TAKENON
TALENTS
TERENCE
TOKENED
TYLENOL
UNBENDS
URGENCY
VALENCE
VIVENDI
WAKENED
WAKENER
WIDENED
WIZENED
WOKENUP
YEMENIS

•••E•N•

ANDEANS
ANTEING
ANTENNA
BALEENS
BLUEING
CAPEANN
CAREENS
CASERNS
CAVEINS
CAVERNS
CAYENNE
CLUEING
CODEINE
COMEONS
DELEING
DEMEANS
DEMESNE
DEVEINS
DOYENNE
ETIENNE
FADEINS
FIREANT
FLEEING
FREEING
GIDEONS
GOVERNS
INFERNO
INTERNS
KNEEING
KOREANS
LATEENS
LAVERNE
LIVEONE
LOVEINS
LUCERNE
MODERNS
ORLEANS
PAGEANT
PATERNO
PIGEONS
RAVENNA
SALERNO
SCREENS
SHOEING
SOMEONE
SPLEENS
TAKEONE
TAVERNS
TREEING
TRUEING
TUREENS
WYVERNS

•••E••N

ACHERON
ACHESON
ADDEDIN
ADDEDON
AILERON
AZTECAN

BASEMAN
BASEMEN
BATEMAN
BLUEFIN
BOXEDIN
BOXESIN
CAMERON
CAPEANN
CAVEDIN
CAVEMAN
CAVEMEN
CAVESIN
CLUEDIN
CLUESIN
COLEMAN
COMESIN
COMESON
DINEDIN
DINEDON
DINESEN
DINESIN
DINESON
DIVESIN
DOTEDON
DOTESON
EASEDIN
EASESIN
ECHELON
EDGEDIN
EDGESIN
EGGEDON
FADEDIN
FADESIN
FIREMAN
FIREMEN
FLIESIN
FOREIGN
FOREMAN
FOREMEN
FORERAN
FORERUN
FREEMAN
FREEMEN
FRIEDAN
GATEMAN
GATEMEN
GETEVEN
GIVESIN
GLUEDON
GOTEVEN
HAMELIN
HIRESON
HOMERUN
JAMESON
JAVELIN
KEYEDIN
LATERAN
LATERON
LINEMAN
LINEMEN
LIVEDIN
LIVEDON
LIVESIN
LIVESON
MATEWAN
MOVEDIN
MOVESIN
MUMESON
OBREGON
PHAETON
PIKEMAN
PIKEMEN
PILEDIN
PILEDON
PILESIN
PILESON
PIMESON
POKEFUN
QUIETEN
RAKEDIN
RAKESIN
RAMEKIN
RELEARN
ROBESON
ROPEDIN
ROPESIN
RULESON
SIDEMAN
SIDEMEN
SIMENON
SLEEKEN
SLEEPIN
SLEEPON
SLOEGIN
SPIEDON
SPIESON
STEEPEN
SWEETEN
SWEETON
TAKENIN
TAKENON
TAKESIN
TAKESON
TAKETEN
TEHERAN
TELERAN
THREWIN
TIBETAN
TRIEDON
TRIESON
TUNEDIN
TUNESIN
UNLEARN
VETERAN
VOTESIN
WADESIN
WAVEDIN
WAVESIN
WISEMAN
WISEMEN
WOBEGON
YEREVAN

••••EN•

ABILENE
AILMENT
ALIMENT
AMBIENT
ANCIENT
AUGMENT
AWAKENS
BACKEND
BALEENS
BARRENS
BARTEND
BATTENS
BENZENE
BIGBEND
BIOGENY
BOOKEND
BURDENS
CAREENS
CLEMENS
CLEMENT
COMMEND
COMMENT
CONSENT
CONTEND
CONTENT
CONVENE
CONVENT
COZZENS
CRAVENS
CURRENT
DAMPENS
DARKENS
DARLENE
DEADEND
DEADENS
DEAFENS
DEEPEND
DEEPENS
DESCEND
DESCENT
DICKENS
DISSENT
DISTEND
DOLMENS
DUODENA
EASTEND
ELEMENT
ELEVENS
EMINENT
EPICENE
EPIGENE
EVIDENT
EXIGENT
FASTENS
FATTENS
FERMENT
FERVENT
FIGMENT
FORFEND
FORRENT
FORWENT
FULGENT
GARDENS
GARMENT
GAUDENS
GINSENG
GODSEND
HAPPENS
HARDENS
HARKENS
HASTENS
HEAVENS
HELLENE
HIGHEND
HOYDENS
HYGIENE
HYPHENS
IMOGENE
JAYLENO
KITTENS
KOBLENZ
LAMBENT
LARCENY
LATEENS
LATTENS
LAURENT
LEAVENS
LENIENT
LESSENS
LICHENS
LINDENS
LISTENS
LOOSENS
MADDENS
MAIDENS
MARLENE
MARTENS
MIDDENS
MILLEND
MINUEND
MIOCENE
MITTENS
MIZZENS
MORDENT
MUDHENS
NASCENT
NEATENS
OBSCENE
ODDMENT
OPENEND
OPULENT
PARVENU
PATIENT
PATTENS
PAYMENT
PEAHENS
PENDENT
PERCENT
PICKENS
PIGMENT
PIGPENS
PLATENS
POLLENS
PORSENA
PORTEND
PORTENT
POULENC
PREBEND
PRESENT
PRETEND
PREVENT
PROGENY
PRUDENT
PUNGENT
PUPTENT
RAIMENT
REAGENT
REAREND
REDCENT
REDDENS
RELLENO
REOPENS
REUBENS
SADDENS
SALIENT
SAPIENS
SAPIENT
SARGENT
SCALENE
SCREENS
SEGMENT
SERPENT
SICKENS
SLOVENE
SLOVENS
SOFTENS
SOLVENT
SPLEENS
STAMENS
STEVENS
STIPEND
STUDENT
STYRENE
SUBTEND
SUSPEND
TAILEND
TANGENT
TAUTENS
TERRENE
TOLUENE
TORMENT
TORRENT
TRIDENT
TUREENS
UNGUENT
UNSPENT
USOPENS
VERBENA
VINCENT
VIOLENT
WARDENS
WARRENS
WEAKENS
WEEKEND
WESTEND
WHITENS
WOOLENS
WORSENS
YEAREND
YEVGENY

••••E•N

ACTAEON
ALAMEIN
ARAMEAN
BARGEIN
BETWEEN
BITTERN
BOOLEAN
BROKEIN
BURGEON
CANTEEN
CHILEAN
CISTERN
CLOSEIN
COLLEEN
CONCERN
CONDEMN
CONTEMN
CRIMEAN
DARLEEN
DISCERN
DRIVEIN
DUDGEON
DUNGEON
EASTERN
EPSTEIN
FIFTEEN
FONTEYN
GALLEON
HASBEEN
HOLBEIN
HUSSEIN
LANTERN
LECTERN
MAUREEN
MCQUEEN
MRCLEAN
MULLEIN
NANKEEN
NUCLEON
OAKFERN
ORPHEAN
PASTERN
PATTERN
PEABEAN
PHASEIN
PIDGEON
POSTERN
PRETEEN
PROTEAN
PROTEIN
RECLEAN
ROYBEAN
SHAREIN
SIXTEEN
SLIDEIN
SOTHERN
SOYBEAN
SURGEON
SWOREIN
THEREIN
THEREON
TINTERN
TRADEIN
TRADEON
UMPTEEN
UNCLEAN
VALJEAN
VILLEIN
WAXBEAN
WESTERN
WHEREIN
WIDGEON
WRITEIN
WROTEIN

•••••EN

ABDOMEN
ALBUMEN
ALMADEN
ANTIGEN
BASEMEN
BATSMEN
BEDIZEN
BELLMEN
BENTSEN
BERNSEN
BESTMEN
BETAKEN
BETOKEN
BETWEEN
BIRDMEN
BITUMEN
BLACKEN
BLITZEN
BOATMEN
BONDMEN
BRACKEN
BRITTEN
BROADEN
BULLPEN
BUSHMEN
CANTEEN
CAVEMEN
CERUMEN
CHAPMEN
CHASTEN
CHEAPEN
CHECHEN
CHICHEN
CHICKEN
CITIZEN
CITROEN
COARSEN
COLLEEN
CREWMEN
CRYOGEN
DARLEEN
DEKOVEN
DENIZEN
DINESEN
DOORMEN
DRESDEN
EARTHEN
ENLIVEN
FIFTEEN
FIREMEN
FLAGMEN
FLATTEN
FOOTMEN
FOREMEN
FREEMEN
FRESHEN
FROGMEN
GADSDEN
GATEMEN
GETEVEN
GLADDEN
GLISTEN
GOODMEN
GOTEVEN
HALOGEN
HANGMEN
HANGTEN
HARSHEN
HASBEEN
HEADMEN
HEARKEN
HEARTEN
HEATHEN
HOARSEN
HOBOKEN
IRONMEN
JANSSEN
JANTZEN
JAZZMEN
KINSMEN
KITCHEN
LIGHTEN
LINEMEN
MADCHEN
MALAREN
MANXMEN
MARCHEN
MAUREEN
MCQUEEN
MEISSEN
MENCKEN
MILKMEN
MOISTEN
MOORHEN
MUTAGEN
NANKEEN
NEWSMEN
NIELSEN
PAULSEN
PIKEMEN
PLAYPEN
PLOWMEN
POSTMEN
PRETEEN
PROPMEN
PUTAMEN
QUICKEN
QUIETEN
REGIMEN
RETAKEN
REWOVEN
RONTGEN
ROUGHEN
SAMISEN
SANDMEN
SARACEN
SARAZEN
SAYWHEN
SCRIVEN
SHARPEN
SHIPMEN
SHODDEN
SHORTEN
SHOWMEN
SIDEMEN
SIXTEEN
SLACKEN
SLEEKEN
SMARTEN
SMIDGEN
SMITTEN
SNELLEN
SNOWMEN
STASSEN
STEEPEN
STEPHEN
STEUBEN
STIFFEN
STOLLEN
STRIVEN
SWEETEN
SWOLLEN
TAKETEN
THICKEN
TIGHTEN
TOLKIEN
TOOKTEN
TOUGHEN
TRODDEN
UMPTEEN
UPRISEN
WHAUDEN
WISEMEN
WOLFMEN
WOOLLEN
WORKMEN
WRITTEN
YARDMEN

EO•••••

EOLITHS

E•O••••

EBONIES
EBONITE
ECOLOGY
ECONOMY
EDOUARD
EGOISTS
EGOTISM
EGOTIST
EGOTRIP
ELOPERS
ELOPING
EMOTERS
EMOTING
EMOTION
EMOTIVE
ENOUNCE
EPONYMS
EPOXIES
ERODING
EROSION
EROSIVE
EROTICA
ETOILES
ETONIAN
EVOKERS
EVOKING
EVOLVED
EVOLVES
EXOTICA
EXOTICS

E••O•••

ECHOING
ECLOGUE
EFFORTS
ELBOWED
EMPORIA
EMPOWER
ENCODED
ENCODER
ENCODES
ENCOMIA
ENCORES
ENDORSE
ENDOWED
ENFOLDS
ENFORCE
ENGORGE
ENJOINS
ENJOYED
ENNOBLE
ENROBED
ENROBES
ENROLLS
ENROOTS
ENROUTE
ENSOULS
ESCORTS
ESPOSAS
ESPOSOS
ESPOUSE
ESTONIA
ESTORIL
EXHORTS
EXPORTS
EXPOSED
EXPOSES
EXPOUND
EXTORTS

E•••O••

EARLOBE
EARLOCK
EASEOFF
EATSOUT
ECOLOGY
ECONOMY
EDGEOUT
EDITORS
EGGNOGS
EGGROLL
EKEDOUT
EKESOUT
ELLIOTT
EMBROIL
EMPLOYS
ENAMORS
ENAMOUR
ENCLOSE
ENDMOST
ENDZONE
ENGROSS
ENROOTS
ENTROPY
ENVIOUS
EPIGONE
EPILOGS
EPISODE
EPITOME
ERELONG
ESCROWS
EUPHONY
EVENOUT
EXPLODE
EXPLOIT
EXPLORE
EYEBOLT
EYEHOLE
EYESORE

E••••O•

EARDROP
EARLDOM
EARLYON
EARSHOT
EATCROW
ECHELON
ECUADOR
EDITION
EGGEDON
ELATION
ELEANOR
ELECTOR
ELEISON
ELISION
ELLISON
ELUTION
EMBRYOS
EMERSON
EMMYLOU
EMOTION
EMPEROR
ENACTOR
ENVELOP
EPSILON
EQUATOR
EQUINOX
ERECTOR
EREWHON
ERICSON
EROSION
ESCUDOS
ESKIMOS
ESPANOL
ESPOSOS
ETHANOL
EVASION
EXACTOR
EYEBROW

E•••••O

ELECTRO
ELGRECO
EMBARGO
ERNESTO

•EO••••

AEOLIAN
BEOWULF
DEODARS
GEODESY
GEOLOGY
GEORGES
GEORGIA
LEONARD
LEONINE
LEONORA
LEOPARD
LEOPOLD
LEOTARD
MEOWING
NEOLITH
NEONATE
PEONAGE
PEONIES
PEOPLED
PEOPLES
REOCCUR
REOILED
REOPENS
REORDER

•E•O•••

AEROBAT
AEROBES
AEROBIC
AEROSOL
BECOMES
BEDOUIN
BEFOULS
BEGONIA
BEGORRA
BEHOLDS
BEHOOVE
BELONGS
BELOVED
BEMOANS
BETOKEN
DEBONED
DEBONES
DEBORAH
DEBOUCH
DECOCTS
DECODED
DECODER
DECODES
DECORUM
DECOYED
DEFORMS
DEHORNS
DEKOVEN
DEMONIC
DEMOTED
DEMOTES
DENOTED
DENOTES
DEPONED
DEPONES
DEPORTS
DEPOSAL
DEPOSED
DEPOSER
DEPOSES
DEPOSIT
DESOTOS
DETOURS
DEVOLVE
DEVOTED
DEVOTEE
DEVOTES
DEVOURS
FEDORAS
FEMORAL
GENOESE
GETOVER
HELOISE
HELOTRY
HEROICS
HEROINE
HEROISM
KENOSHA
KEROUAC
KETONES
LESOTHO
MEGOHMS
MEIOSES
MEIOSIS
MEIOTIC
MELODIC
MEMOIRE
MEMOIRS
MEMOREX
MENORAH
MENOTTI
METOOER
PELOTAS
REBOILS
REBOLTS
REBOOTS
REBOUND
REBOZOS
RECODED
RECODES
RECOILS
RECOLOR
RECORDS
RECORKS
RECOUNT
RECOUPS
RECOVER
REDOAKS
REDOING
REDOUBT
REDOUND
REFORMS
REHOOKS
REJOICE
REJOINS
RELOADS
RELOCKS
REMODEL
REMOLDS
REMORAS
REMORSE
REMOTER
REMOTES
REMOUNT
REMOVAL
REMOVED
REMOVER
REMOVES
REMOWED
RENOTES
REPOLLS
REPOMAN
REPORTS
REPOSED
REPOSES
REROUTE
RESOLED
RESOLES
RESOLVE
RESORBS
RESORTS
RESOUND
RETOOLS
RETORTS
RETOUCH
RETOWED
REVOICE
REVOKED
REVOKES
REVOLTS
REVOLVE
REWORDS
REWORKS
REWOUND
REWOVEN
REZONED
REZONES
SECONDS
SEGOVIA
SENORAS
SENORES
TENONED
VELOURS
VETOERS
VETOING
ZENOBIA
ZEROING

•E••O••

BEACONS
BEAROFF
BEAROUT
BEATOUT
BECKONS
BECLOUD
BEDDOWN
BEDPOST
BEDROCK
BEDROLL
BEDROOM
BEGSOFF
BEHOOVE
BELLOWS
BELMONT
BERTOLT
BESPOKE
BESTOWS
BETROTH
BETTORS
CENSORS
DEACONS
DEALOUT
DEBTORS
DECKOUT
DEFROCK
DEFROST
DELTOID
DEPLORE
DEPLOYS
DESMOND
DESPOIL
DESPOTS
DETROIT
DEVIOUS
FEELOUT
FELLOFF
FELLOUT
FELLOWS
FELTOUT
FERROUS
FERVORS
FERVOUR
FESTOON
FETLOCK
GECKOES
GEOLOGY
GESSOES
GETDOWN
GETLOST
GETSOFF
GETSOUT
HEADOFF
HEADOUT
HEAROUT
HECTORS
HEINOUS
HELDOFF
HELDOUT
HELPOUT
HEMLOCK
HENCOOP

HEYWOOD
JEALOUS
JERBOAS
JETBOAT
JETPORT
JETSONS
KEDROVA
KEEPOFF
KELLOGG
KEPTOFF
KEPTOUT
KEYHOLE
KEYNOTE
KEYWORD
LEACOCK
LEADOFF
LEADOUT
LECTORS
LEFTOFF
LEFTOUT
LEGHORN
LEGIONS
LEGROOM
LEGWORK
LEONORA
LEOPOLD
LEPTONS
LESSONS
LESSORS
LETDOWN
LETSOFF
LETSOUT
MEADOWS
MEADOWY
MELLOWS
MELROSE
MENDOZA
MENFOLK
MENTORS
MERLOTS
METEORS
METEOUT
METHODS
METOOER
NELSONS
NERVOUS
NETWORK
NEURONE
NEURONS
NEWBORN
NEWLOOK
NEWMOON
NEWMOWN
NEWPORT
NEWTONS
NEWTOWN
NEWYORK
PEABODY
PEACOAT
PEACOCK
PEAFOWL
PEAPODS
PEASOUP
PEEKOUT
PEELOFF
PEEROUT
PEGTOPS
PENNONS
PEQUOTS
PERFORM
PERGOLA
PERIODS
PERSONA
PERSONS
PETCOCK
PETIOLE
PETROCK
PETROUS
READOUT
REASONS
REBLOOM
REBOOTS
RECHOSE
RECKONS
RECROOM
RECROSS
RECTORS
RECTORY
REDBOOK
REDCOAT
REDDOGS
REDFORD
REDHOTS
REDPOLL
REDROSE
REDTOPS
REDWOLF
REDWOOD
REELOFF
REGIONS
REGROUP
REHOOKS
REPROOF
REPROVE
RESHOES
RESHOOT
RESPOND
RESTOCK
RESTORE
RETOOLS
REWROTE
SEABORG
SEACOWS
SEADOGS
SEAFOOD
SEALOFF
SEAMOSS
SEAPORT
SEASONS
SECTORS
SEEKOUT
SEESOFF
SEESOUT
SEETOIT
SELLOFF
SELLOUT
SENDOFF
SENDOUT
SENIORS
SENSORS
SENSORY
SENTOFF
SENTOUT
SEQUOIA
SERIOUS
SERMONS
SETDOWN
SETSOFF
SETSOUT
SEXTONS
SEYMOUR
TEAPOTS
TEAPOYS
TEAROFF
TEAROOM
TEAROSE
TEDIOUS
TEEDOFF
TEESOFF
TELLOFF
TENDONS
TENFOLD
TENFOUR
TENSORS
TENUOUS
TERRORS
TESTOUT
TEUTONS
VECTORS
VENDORS
VERBOSE
VERMONT
WEAPONS
WEAROFF
WEAROUT
WEBFOOT
WEBTOED
WEDLOCK
WEEDOUT
WELCOME
WELLOFF
WENTOFF
WENTOUT
WETMOPS
YELLOWS
ZEALOTS
ZEALOUS

•E•••O•

AERATOR
AEROSOL
BEARSON
BEDROOM
BELABOR
BELLBOY
BELLHOP
BENISON
BERGSON
BERLIOZ
BESTBOY
CELADON
CESSION
DECAGON
DECALOG
DECAPOD
DEMEROL
DEMIGOD
DENDRON
DESKTOP
DESOTOS
DESTROY
DEVELOP
DEWDROP
FEEDLOT
FEEDSON
FEELFOR
FELLFOR
FELTFOR
FESTOON
GEARBOX
GEMSBOK
GERITOL
GETITON
HEARDOF
HEARSOF
HELICON
HELLION
HENCOOP
HERRIOT
HEXAGON
HEYWOOD
KEEPSON
KEILLOR
KERCHOO
KERPLOP
LEADSON
LEANSON
LEANTOS
LEBANON
LEBARON
LEGATOS
LEGROOM
LETINON
LEXICON
MEDICOS
MENTHOL
MENTION
MERINOS
NEARYOU
NEGATOR
NEMEROV
NEUTRON
NEWLOOK
NEWMOON
NEWSBOY
PEARSON
PEATBOG
PENSION
PERIDOT
PEUGEOT
REACTOR
REALTOR
REARDON
REBLOOM
REBOZOS
RECOLOR
RECROOM
REDBOOK
REDSPOT
REDWOOD
REPROOF
REREDOS
RESHOOT
REUNION
SEAFOOD
SEALION
SECTION
SEEDPOD
SENATOR
SENDFOR
SENTFOR
SERFDOM
SESSION
SETUPON
TEAROOM
TEASHOP
TELLSON
TEMBLOR
TENSION
TENSPOT
TEREDOS
VENISON
VERSION
WEBFOOT
WEIRDOS
WENTFOR
ZEBULON

•E••••O

BEEFALO
CEMBALO
CENTAVO
CENTIMO
DECARLO
DEFACTO
DEUTERO
FERRARO
GEARSTO
GENNARO
GERALDO
GETINTO
HEAVEHO
HEAVETO
HEIGHHO
JERICHO
KEEPSTO
KERCHOO
LEADSTO
LEDUPTO
LEPANTO
LESOTHO
MEMENTO
MESTIZO
REACTTO
REFERTO
RELIEVO
RELLENO
SEMIPRO
SERPICO
SETINTO
TENDSTO
VERDUGO
VERTIGO
YEARNTO

••EO•••

AREOLAE
AREOLAR
AREOLAS
CREOLES
CREOSOL
LIEOVER
THEOREM

••E•O••

ACEDOUT
ACEROLA
ACEROSE
ACESOUT
ACETONE
ANEMONE
ANEROID
AWESOME
BLEWOFF
BLEWOUT
BRETONS
CHEROOT
CHEWOUT
CREMONA
DIEDOFF
DIEDOUT
DIEDOWN
DIESOFF
DIESOUT
DREWOUT
EKEDOUT
EKESOUT
ERELONG
EVENOUT
EYEBOLT
EYEHOLE
EYESORE
FEELOUT
FLEXORS
FREMONT
FUELOIL
GOESOFF
GOESOUT
GREGORY
HOEDOWN
ICEBOAT
ICECOLD
KEEPOFF
KMESONS
LIEDOWN
OCELOTS
ONEROUS
OPEROSE
PEEKOUT
PEELOFF
PEEROUT
PHENOLS
PHENOMS
PLEXORS
PRECOOK
PRECOOL
PRELOAD
PRESOAK
PRESORT
PYEDOGS
REELOFF
RHETORS
SEEKOUT
SEESOFF
SEESOUT
SEETOIT
SHEWOLF
STEPOUT
STEROID
STEROLS
TEEDOFF
TEESOFF
THEROUX
TIEDOWN
TIERODS
TOEHOLD
TOELOOP
TREFOIL
TREMOLO
TREMORS
WEEDOUT

••E••O•

ABETTOR
AHEADOF
ALENCON
ATECROW
BIENTOT
BLERIOT
BRERFOX
BRESSON
CHEETOS
CHEKHOV
CHEROOT
CHEVIOT
CHEVRON
CLEAVON
CLEMSON
CREATOR
CREOSOL
DREAMON
ELEANOR
ELECTOR
ELEISON
EMERSON
ERECTOR
EREWHON
EYEBROW
FEEDLOT
FEEDSON
FEELFOR
FIEFDOM
FREEDOM
FRESCOS
FUELROD
GHETTOS
GLEASON
GOESFOR
ICEFLOE
ICESHOW
INERROR
IRECKON
JOEBLOW
KEEPSON
LIESLOW
MCENROE
ONESHOT
OPENTOE
OVERJOY
PIERROT
PRECOOK
PRECOOL
PRESSON
PRESTON
PRESTOS
PREYSON
PUEBLOS
SEEDPOD
SHELDON
SHELTON
SKELTON
SLEDDOG
SLEEPON
SLEPTON
SPEAKOF
SPECTOR
STENTOR
STEPSON
STEREOS
STETSON
SWEETON
THEBLOB
THEREOF
THEREON
THERMOS
TOELOOP
TOESHOE
TREASON
TREETOP
TRENTON
TSELIOT
WHEATON
WHEREOF

••E•••O

AGESAGO
AMERIGO
BEEFALO
CHEERIO
ELECTRO
HAEMATO
KEEPSTO
MAESTRO
OREGANO
SWEARTO
THERETO
TIEINTO
TREMOLO
TREVINO
WHERETO

•••EO••

ALVEOLI
AQUEOUS
AUREOLA
AUREOLE
BAKEOFF
BITEOFF
BOREOUT
CAMEOED
CAMEOFF
CAMEOUT
COMEOFF
COMEONS
COMEOUT
DOLEOUT
DOPEOUT
DOZEOFF
DUTEOUS
EASEOFF
EDGEOUT
FACEOFF
FADEOUT
FIREOFF
GASEOUS
GAVEOFF
GAVEOUT
GIDEONS
GIVEOFF
GIVEOUT
HIDEOUS
HIDEOUT
HOLEOUT
IGNEOUS
LIVEOAK
LIVEONE
LIVEOUT
LOSEOUT
MADEOFF
MADEOUT
MAKEOFF
MAKEOUT
METEORS
METEOUT
MINEOLA
MOVEOUT
NOSEOUT
OSCEOLA
OSTEOID
PIGEONS
PITEOUS
RAKEOFF
RIDEOFF
RIDEOUT
RODEOFF
RODEOUT
ROSEOIL
RULEOUT
SOMEONE
TAKEOFF
TAKEONE
TAKEOUT
TIMEOFF
TIMEOUT
TIREOUT
TOREOFF
TOREOUT
TUNEOUT
WAVEOFF
WIPEOUT
WOREOFF
WOREOUT

•••E•O•

ACHERON
ACHESON
ADDEDON
AILERON
ALBEDOS
ALIENOR
ANGELOU
BIBELOT
BIGELOW
BLUEBOY
BLUEFOX
BOLEROS
BOREDOM
CAMELOT
CAMERON
CAPECOD
CAREFOR
CHEETOS
COMESON
DEMEROL
DEVELOP
DIDEROT
DINEDON
DINESON
DONEFOR
DOTEDON
DOTESON
DOVECOT
DUKEDOM
ECHELON
EGGEDON
EMPEROR
ENVELOP
FIREBOX
FIREDOG
FREEDOM
GAZEBOS
GLUEDON
HAVENOT
HIRESON
JAMESON
JANEDOE
JUKEBOX
LATERON
LIVEDON
LIVESON
MADEFOR
MAKEFOR
MUMESON
NEMEROV
NOSEJOB
OBREGON
PAGEBOY
PHAETON
PILEDON
PILESON
PIMESON
PINEFOR
POMELOS
PRAETOR
REREDOS
ROBESON
ROPETOW
RULESON
SHOEBOX
SIMENON
SLEEPON
SOMEHOW
SPIEDON
SPIESON
SWEETON
TAKENON
TAKESON
TEREDOS
TIMECOP
TIREDOF
TONELOC
TONEROW
TOREROS
TREETOP
TRIEDON
TRIESON
TUPELOS
TUXEDOS
TYLENOL
VICEROY
WOBEGON
YULELOG

•••E••O

ADDEDTO
AGREETO
AIMEDTO
ALBERTO
ALLEGRO
ARSENIO
CHEERIO
COMESTO
DARESTO
ERNESTO
FIDELIO
GIVENTO
GIVESTO
INFERNO
INPETTO
IONESCO
JANEIRO
LORENZO
MAKESDO
MEMENTO
MODESTO
MORELLO
OTHELLO
PALERMO
PATERNO
PIMENTO
REFERTO
ROBERTO
SALERNO
SCHERZO
STRETTO
TAKESTO
UCCELLO
UMBERTO
UNDERGO
UPTEMPO

••••EO•

ACTAEON
AWAREOF
BURGEON
DUDGEON
DUNGEON
GALLEON
INAWEOF
NUCLEON
PEUGEOT
PIDGEON
SPOKEOF
STEREOS
SURGEON
THEREOF
THEREON
TRADEON
WHEREOF
WIDGEON

••••E•O

AGREETO
ALFREDO
ARTDECO
CANSECO
CORDERO
DEUTERO
ELGRECO
HEAVEHO
HEAVETO
JAYLENO
MAGNETO
MONTEGO
NONZERO
ONTHEGO
PLACEBO
RELIEVO
RELLENO
SANREMO
SUBZERO
SUPREMO
TANGELO
THERETO
TORPEDO
VAQUERO
WHERETO
WRITETO
WROTETO

•••••EO

GALILEO

EP•••••

EPARCHS
EPAULET
EPEEIST
EPERGNE
EPICENE
EPICURE
EPIGENE
EPIGONE
EPIGRAM
EPILOGS
EPISODE
EPISTLE
EPITHET
EPITOME
EPONYMS
EPOXIES
EPSILON
EPSTEIN

E•P••••

EMPANEL
EMPATHY
EMPEROR
EMPIRES
EMPLOYS
EMPORIA
EMPOWER
EMPRESS
EMPTIED
EMPTIER
EMPTIES
EMPTILY
ENPLANE
ESPANOL
ESPIALS
ESPOSAS
ESPOSOS
ESPOUSE
ESPYING
EUPHONY
EXPANDS
EXPANSE
EXPARTE
EXPECTS
EXPENDS
EXPENSE
EXPERTS
EXPIATE
EXPIRED
EXPIRES
EXPLAIN
EXPLODE
EXPLOIT
EXPLORE
EXPORTS
EXPOSED
EXPOSES
EXPOUND
EXPRESS
EXPUNGE

E••P•••

EARPLUG
EDAPHIC
ELAPIDS
ELAPSED
ELAPSES
ELOPERS
ELOPING
ENDPLAY
ERUPTED
EXUPERY

E•••P••

ECLIPSE
ECTYPES
ELLIPSE
ESCAPED
ESCAPEE
ESCAPES
EXAMPLE
EXCEPTS
EXEMPLI
EXEMPTS

E••••P•

EGGCUPS
ENCAMPS
ENCRYPT
ENTRAPS
ENTROPY
ENWRAPS
ESCARPS
EUTERPE
EXCERPT
EYECUPS

E•••••P

EARDROP
EARFLAP
EASEDUP
EASESUP
EATENUP
EGOTRIP
ENVELOP
EVENSUP

•EP••••

CEPHEUS
DEPALMA
DEPARTS
DEPECHE
DEPENDS
DEPICTS
DEPLANE
DEPLETE
DEPLORE
DEPLOYS
DEPONED
DEPONES
DEPORTS
DEPOSAL
DEPOSED
DEPOSER
DEPOSES
DEPOSIT
DEPRAVE
DEPRESS
DEPRIVE
DEPUTED
DEPUTES
HEPARIN
HEPATIC
HEPBURN
HEPCATS
HEPTADS
KEPTOFF
KEPTOUT
LEPANTO
LEPTONS
NEPALIS
NEPHEWS
NEPTUNE
PEPLUMS
PEPPARD
PEPPERS
PEPPERY
PEPPIER
PEPPILY
PEPPING
PEPSINS
PEPTALK
PEPTIDE
REPAINT
REPAIRS
REPAPER
REPASTE
REPASTS
REPAVED
REPAVES
REPEALS
REPEATS
REPENTS
REPINED
REPINES
REPLACE
REPLANS
REPLANT
REPLATE
REPLAYS
REPLETE
REPLICA
REPLIED
REPLIES
REPOLLS
REPOMAN
REPORTS
REPOSED
REPOSES
REPRESS
REPRICE
REPRINT
REPRISE
REPROOF

REPROVE
REPTILE
REPUGNS
REPULSE
REPUTED
REPUTES
SEPTETS
TEPIDLY
ZEPHYRS

•E•P•••

BEDPOST
BEEPERS
BEEPING
BESPEAK
BESPOKE
DEEPEND
DEEPENS
DEEPEST
DEEPFAT
DEEPFRY
DEEPSEA
DEEPSET
DEEPSIX
DEMPSEY
DESPAIR
DESPISE
DESPITE
DESPOIL
DESPOTS
HEAPING
HELPERS
HELPFUL
HELPING
HELPOUT
HENPECK
JETPORT
KEEPERS
KEEPING
KEEPOFF
KEEPSAT
KEEPSIN
KEEPSON
KEEPSTO
KEEPSUP
KELPIES
KERPLOP
KEWPIES
KEYPADS
LEAPERS
LEAPING
LEGPULL
LEIPZIG
LEMPIRA
LEOPARD
LEOPOLD
LESPAUL
MEMPHIS
NEWPORT
PEAPODS
PEEPERS
PEEPING
PEEPLES
PENPALS
PEOPLED
PEOPLES
PEPPARD
PEPPERS
PEPPERY
PEPPIER
PEPPILY
PEPPING
PERPLEX
REAPERS
REAPING
REDPINE
REDPOLL
REOPENS
RESPECT
RESPIRE
RESPITE
RESPOND
REUPPED
SEAPORT
SEEPING
SEEPSIN
SERPENT
SERPICO
TEAPOTS
TEAPOYS
TEEPEES
TEMPERA
TEMPERS
TEMPEST
TEMPLAR
TEMPLES
TEMPTED
TEMPTER
TEMPURA
TENPINS
VESPERS
VESPIDS
WEAPONS
WEEPERS
WEEPIER
WEEPING
YELPERS
YELPING

•E••P••

BEARPAW
CERIPHS
DEADPAN
DECAPOD
HEADPIN
HELIPAD
LEDUPTO
OEDIPAL
OEDIPUS
RECIPES
REDSPOT
RELAPSE
REPAPER
RETAPED
RETAPES
RETYPED
RETYPES
REUPPED
SEEDPOD
SEMIPRO
SERAPES
SERAPHS
SERAPIS
SETUPON
TENSPOT
TERAPHS

•E•••P•

DECAMPS
DECRYPT
DEWLAPS
PEGTOPS
PERHAPS
RECEIPT
RECOUPS
REDCAPS
REDTAPE
REDTOPS
RESHIPS
REVAMPS
REWRAPS
SENDUPS
TEACUPS
WENTAPE
WETMOPS

•E••••P

BEADSUP
BEAMSUP
BEARSUP
BEATSUP
BEDLAMP
BEEFSUP
BELLHOP
BELLYUP
DESKTOP
DEVELOP
DEWDROP
GEARSUP
HEADSUP
HEATSUP
HEELTAP
HENCOOP
JEANARP
KEEPSUP
KERPLOP
KETCHUP
KEYEDUP
LEADSUP
LETSLIP
PEASOUP
PERKSUP
REARSUP
REGROUP
RESTAMP
RESTSUP
SEALSUP
SENDSUP
SERVEUP
SEVENUP
SEWEDUP
TEAMSUP
TEARSUP
TEASHOP
TENSEUP
WELLSUP

••EP•••

ADEPTLY
ASEPSIS
ASEPTIC
BEEPERS
BEEPING
DEEPEND
DEEPENS
DEEPEST
DEEPFAT
DEEPFRY
DEEPSEA
DEEPSET
DEEPSIX
ICEPACK
ICEPICK
INEPTLY
KEEPERS
KEEPING
KEEPOFF
KEEPSAT
KEEPSIN
KEEPSON
KEEPSTO
KEEPSUP
PEEPERS
PEEPING
PEEPLES
PIEPANS
PREPAID
PREPARE
PREPAYS
PREPPIE
SCEPTER
SCEPTRE
SEEPING
SEEPSIN
SHEPARD
SKEPTIC
SLEPTIN
SLEPTON
STEPHEN
STEPINS
STEPOUT
STEPPED
STEPPER
STEPPES
STEPSIN
STEPSON
STEPSUP
STEPUPS
SWEPTUP
TEEPEES
TIEPINS
TREPANS
WEEPERS
WEEPIER
WEEPING

••E•P••

BLEEPED
BLEEPER
CHEAPEN
CHEAPER
CHEAPIE
CHEAPLY
CHEEPED
CREEPED
CREEPER
CREEPUP
EXEMPLI
EXEMPTS
GUELPHS
KNEEPAD
OPENPIT
PREPPIE
SEEDPOD
SHERPAS
SLEEPER
SLEEPIN
SLEEPON
STEEPED
STEEPEN
STEEPER
STEEPLE
STEEPLY
STEPPED
STEPPER
STEPPES
SWEEPER
SWEEPUP
THESPIS
WHELPED

••E••P•

EYECUPS
GOESAPE
ICECAPS
PREAMPS
PRECEPT
PREEMPT
PRETAPE
STEPUPS
THERAPY
TOECAPS
TOETAPS

••E•••P

BEEFSUP
BREAKUP
CHECKUP
CHEERUP
CHEWSUP
CLEANUP
CLEARUP
CREEPUP
DREAMUP
DRESSUP
EVENSUP
HEELTAP
KEEPSUP
KNEECAP
ONESTEP
OPENSUP
OVERLAP
QUEUEUP
SPEAKUP
SPEEDUP
STEPSUP
SWEEPUP
SWELLUP
SWEPTUP
THEDEEP
TIECLIP
TOELOOP
TREETOP

•••EP••

ACCEPTS
BASEPAY
BLEEPED
BLEEPER
CHEEPED
CREEPED
CREEPER
CREEPUP
EXCEPTS
FOREPAW
INCEPTS
INDEPTH
KNEEPAD
MAKEPAR
NOTEPAD
SLEEPER
SLEEPIN
SLEEPON
STEEPED
STEEPEN
STEEPER
STEEPLE
STEEPLY
SWEEPER
SWEEPUP

•••E•P•

ATTEMPT
EUTERPE
EXCERPT
GIVEUPS
LINEUPS
MAKEUPS
PILEUPS
PREEMPT
RECEIPT
TUNEUPS
UNKEMPT
UPTEMPO

•••E••P

ACTEDUP
ADDEDUP
ANTEDUP
ANTESUP
BONEDUP
BONESUP
BOXEDUP
BOXESUP
CHEERUP
COMESUP
COVERUP
CREEPUP
DEVELOP
DRIEDUP
DRIESUP
DUDEDUP
EASEDUP
EASESUP
EATENUP
ENVELOP
FIREDUP
FIRESUP
FIXEDUP
FIXESUP
GIVESUP
HOLEDUP
HOLESUP
HYPEDUP
KEYEDUP
KNEECAP
LACEDUP
LACESUP
LINEDUP
LINESUP
MAKESUP
MIXEDUP
MIXESUP
OWNEDUP
PILEDUP
PILESUP
PINESAP
PIPEDUP
PIPESUP
RAKEDUP
RAKESUP
SAVEDUP
SAVESUP
SCREWUP
SEVENUP
SEWEDUP
SIZEDUP
SIZESUP
SPEEDUP
SWEEPUP
TAKESUP
TIMECOP
TIMESUP
TONEDUP
TONESUP
TREETOP
TUNEDUP
TUNESUP
TYPEDUP
TYPESUP
WAKESUP
WINESAP
WIPEDUP
WIPESUP
WIRETAP
WISEDUP
WISESUP
WOKENUP

••••EP•

CONCEPT
FORCEPS
INSTEPS
PRECEPT
SCHLEPP
SCHLEPS
TRICEPS
UNSWEPT
UPSWEPT

••••E•P

ANTWERP
BARKEEP
BORNEUP
BRACEUP
BROKEUP
CHOKEUP
CLOSEUP
DRIVEUP
FLAREUP
FRAMEUP
INAHEAP
JUICEUP
LOUSEUP
PASTEUP
QUEUEUP
RAISEUP
RUNDEEP
SCAREUP
SCHLEPP
SERVEUP
SHAKEUP
SHAPEUP
SPICEUP
SPOKEUP
STOREUP
TENSEUP
THEDEEP
TRADEUP
UPSWEEP
WRITEUP
WROTEUP

•••••EP

BARKEEP
BOXSTEP
MISSTEP
ONESTEP
OUTSTEP
RUNDEEP
THEDEEP
TWOSTEP
UPSWEEP

EQ•••••

EQUABLE
EQUABLY
EQUALED
EQUALLY
EQUATED
EQUATES
EQUATOR
EQUERRY
EQUINES
EQUINOX

E•Q••••

ESQUIRE

•EQ••••

BEQUEST
PEQUOTS
REQUEST
REQUIEM
REQUIRE
REQUITE
SEQUELS
SEQUINS
SEQUOIA
TEQUILA

•E••Q••

BEZIQUE

••EQ•••

CHEQUER
CHEQUES
COEQUAL
UNEQUAL

••••EQ•

ONTHEQT

ER•••••

ERASERS
ERASING
ERASMUS
ERASURE
ERECTED
ERECTER
ERECTLY
ERECTOR
ERELONG
EREMITE
EREWHON
ERICSON
ERISTIC
ERITREA
ERMINES
ERNESTO
ERODING
EROSION
EROSIVE
EROTICA
ERRANDS
ERRATIC
ERRATUM
ERSKINE
ERUCTED
ERUDITE
ERUPTED

E•R••••

EARACHE
EARDROP
EARDRUM
EARFLAP
EARFULS
EARHART
EARLDOM
EARLIER
EARLOBE
EARLOCK
EARLYON
EARMARK
EARMUFF
EARNERS
EARNEST
EARNING
EARPLUG
EARRING
EARSHOT
EARTHEN
EARTHLY
EARWIGS
EERIEST
EHRLICH
ENRAGED
ENRAGES
ENROBED
ENROBES
ENROLLS
ENROOTS
ENROUTE
ERRANDS
ERRATIC
ERRATUM
ETRURIA
EURASIA

E••R•••

EARRING
EGGROLL
ELGRECO
EMBRACE
EMBROIL
EMBRYOS
EMERALD
EMERGED
EMERGES
EMERITA
EMERITI
EMERSED
EMERSON
EMIRATE
EMPRESS
ENCRUST
ENCRYPT
ENDRUNS
ENGRAFT
ENGRAMS
ENGRAVE
ENGROSS
ENTRAIN
ENTRANT
ENTRAPS
ENTREAT
ENTREES
ENTRIES
ENTROPY
ENTRUST
ENURING
ENWRAPS
EPARCHS
EPERGNE
ESCROWS
ESTRADA
ESTRAYS
ETERNAL
EVEREST
EVERETT
EVERTED
EXCRETE
EXERTED
EXPRESS
EXTRACT
EXTREME
EXTRUDE
EXURBAN
EXURBIA

E•••R••

EAGERER
EAGERLY
EARDROP
EARDRUM
EATCROW
EDWARDS
EFFORTS
EGOTRIP
ELDERLY
ELMTREE
EMBARGO
EMBARKS
EMIGRES
EMPEROR
EMPIRES
EMPORIA
ENCORES
ENDORSE
ENDURED
ENDURES
ENFORCE
ENGARDE
ENGIRDS
ENGORGE
ENLARGE
ENSURED
ENSURES
ENTERED
EPIGRAM
EQUERRY
ERITREA
ESCARPS
ESCORTS
ESTORIL
ETRURIA
EUCHRED
EUCHRES
EUTERPE
EXCERPT
EXHORTS
EXPARTE
EXPERTS
EXPIRED
EXPIRES
EXPORTS
EXTORTS
EYEBROW

E••••R•

EARHART
EARMARK
EARNERS
EASTERN
EASTERS
ECKHART
ECLAIRS
EDITORS
EDOUARD
ELATERS
ELECTRA
ELECTRO
ELEKTRA
ELIXIRS
ELKHART
ELOPERS
EMOTERS
ENAMORS
ENDEARS
ENSNARE
ENSNARL
EPICURE
EQUERRY
ERASERS
ERASURE
ESQUIRE
ESTUARY
ETAGERE
ETCHERS
EVADERS
EVOKERS
EXPLORE
EXUPERY
EYESORE

E•••••R

EAGERER
EARLIER
ECUADOR
EDASNER
ELEANOR
ELECTOR
EMENDER
EMITTER
EMPEROR
EMPOWER
EMPTIER
ENACTOR
ENAMOUR
ENCODER
ENDUSER
ENTICER
EQUATOR
ERECTER
ERECTOR
EVANDER
EVILLER
EXACTER
EXACTOR

•ER••••

AERATED
AERATES
AERATOR
AERIALS
AERIEST
AEROBAT
AEROBES
AEROBIC
AEROSOL
BERATED
BERATES
BERBERS
BEREAVE
BERETTA
BERGERE
BERGMAN
BERGSON
BERLIOZ
BERLITZ
BERMUDA
BERNARD
BERNESE
BERNICE
BERNSEN
BERRIED
BERRIES
BERSERK
BERTHED
BERTOLT
CERAMIC
CEREALS
CEREBRA
CERIPHS
CERTAIN
CERTIFY
CERUMEN
DERAILS
DERBIES
DERIDED
DERIDES
DERIVED
DERIVES
DERNIER
DERRICK
DERRING
DERVISH
EERIEST
FERMENT
FERMIUM
FERRARI
FERRARO
FERRATE
FERRETS
FERRIED
FERRIES
FERRITE
FERROUS
FERRULE
FERTILE
FERULES
FERVENT
FERVORS
FERVOUR
GERAINT
GERALDO
GERBILS
GERENTS
GERITOL
GERMANE
GERMANS
GERMANY
GERUNDS
HERALDS
HERBAGE
HERBALS
HERBERT
HERBTEA
HERCULE
HERDERS
HERDING
HERETIC
HERMANN
HERMITS
HEROICS
HEROINE
HEROISM
HERRING
HERRIOT
HERSELF
HERSHEY
JERBOAS
JERICHO
JERKIER
JERKILY
JERKING
JERKINS
JERSEYS
KERATIN
KERCHOO
KERNELS
KERNING
KEROUAC
KERPLOP
MERCIES
MERCURY
MERGERS
MERGING
MERIMEE
MERINOS
MERITED
MERLOTS
MERMAID
MERRIER
MERRILL
MERRILY
NEREIDS
NERVIER
NERVILY
NERVOUS
PERCALE
PERCENT
PERCHED
PERCHES
PERDIEM
PERFECT
PERFIDY
PERFORM
PERFUME
PERGOLA
PERHAPS
PERIDOT
PERIGEE
PERIODS
PERJURE
PERJURY
PERKIER
PERKILY
PERKING
PERKINS
PERKSUP
PERLITE
PERLMAN
PERMING
PERMITS
PERNELL
PERPLEX
PERRIER
PERSEUS
PERSIAN
PERSIST
PERSIUS
PERSONA
PERSONS
PERTAIN
PERTEST
PERTURB
PERUKES
PERUSAL
PERUSED
PERUSER
PERUSES
PERVADE
PERVERT
RERAISE
RERATED
RERATES
REREADS
REREDOS
RERENTS
RERINSE
REROUTE
SERAPES
SERAPHS
SERAPIS
SERBIAN
SERENER

SERFDOM
SERIALS
SERIATE
SERIOUS
SERLING
SERMONS
SERPENT
SERPICO
SERRATE
SERRIED
SERVALS
SERVANT
SERVERS
SERVEUP
SERVICE
SERVILE
SERVING
TERAPHS
TERBIUM
TERCELS
TERCETS
TEREDOS
TERENCE
TERHUNE
TERMING
TERMINI
TERMITE
TERNARY
TERNATE
TERRACE
TERRAIN
TERRENE
TERRETS
TERRIER
TERRIES
TERRIFY
TERRORS
TERSELY
TERSEST
TERTIAL
VERANDA
VERBALS
VERBENA
VERBOSE
VERDANT
VERDICT
VERDUGO
VERDURE
VERGERS
VERGING
VERMEER
VERMEIL
VERMONT
VERNIER
VERSIFY
VERSION
VERTIGO
VERVETS
WERNHER
WERTHER
YEREVAN
ZERMATT
ZEROING

•E•R•••

BEARCAT
BEARDED
BEARERS
BEARHUG
BEARING
BEARISH
BEAROFF
BEAROUT
BEARPAW
BEARSON
BEARSUP
BEDREST
BEDROCK
BEDROLL
BEDROOM
BEGRIME
BERRIED
BERRIES
BETRAYS
BETROTH
DEAREST
DEARSIR
DEARTHS
DEBRIEF
DECREED
DECREES
DECRIED
DECRIES
DECRYPT
DEERFLY
DEFRAUD
DEFRAYS
DEFROCK
DEFROST
DEGRADE
DEGREES
DEPRAVE
DEPRESS
DEPRIVE
DERRICK
DERRING
DETRACT
DETRAIN
DETROIT
DEVRIES
FEARERS
FEARFUL
FEARING
FEBRILE
FERRARI
FERRARO
FERRATE
FERRETS
FERRIED
FERRIES
FERRITE
FERROUS
FERRULE
GEARBOX
GEARING
GEARSTO
GEARSUP
GEORGES
GEORGIA
HEARDOF
HEARERS
HEARING
HEARKEN
HEAROUT
HEARSAY
HEARSOF
HEARTEN
HEARTHS
HEBRAIC
HEBREWS
HEIRESS
HENREID
HERRING
HERRIOT
JEERERS
JEERING
JEERSAT
KEDROVA
KEYRING
LEARJET
LEARNED
LEARNER
LEERERS
LEERIER
LEERILY
LEERING
LEERSAT
LEGROOM
MEGRIMS
MEGRYAN
MELROSE
MERRIER
MERRILL
MERRILY
METRICS
NEAREST
NEARING
NEARYOU
NEURONE
NEURONS
PEARLED
PEARSON
PEERAGE
PEERESS
PEERING
PEEROUT
PEERSAT
PEERSIN
PERRIER
PETRELS
PETRIFY
PETROCK
PETROUS
REARDON
REAREND
REARERS
REARGUE
REARING
REARMED
REARSUP
RECROOM
RECROSS
RECRUIT
REDRAWN
REDRAWS
REDRESS
REDROSE
REFRACT
REFRAIN
REFRAME
REFRESH
REFRIED
REFRIES
REGRADE
REGRESS
REGRETS
REGROUP
REORDER
REPRESS
REPRICE
REPRINT
REPRISE
REPROOF
REPROVE
RETRACE
RETRACK
RETRACT
RETRADE
RETRAIN
RETREAD
RETREAT
RETRIAL
RETRIED
RETRIES
RETRIMS
REWRAPS
REWRITE
REWROTE
REXREED
SEARING
SECRECY
SECRETE
SECRETS
SEERESS
SERRATE
SERRIED
TEARFUL
TEARGAS
TEARIER
TEARILY
TEARING
TEAROFF
TEAROOM
TEAROSE
TEARSAT
TEARSUP
TERRACE
TERRAIN
TERRENE
TERRETS
TERRIER
TERRIES
TERRIFY
TERRORS
TETRADS
VEERING
WEARERS
WEARIED
WEARIER
WEARIES
WEARILY
WEARING
WEAROFF
WEAROUT
WEIRDER
WEIRDLY
WEIRDOS
YEAREND
YEARNED
YEARNER
YEARNTO

•E••R••

AELFRIC
BEATRIX
BEETREE
BEGORRA
BEMIRED
BEMIRES
BESTREW
BETARAY
BEVERLY
CENTRAL
CENTRED
CENTRES
CENTRIC
DEBARGE
DEBARKS
DEBORAH
DECARLO
DECORUM
DEFARGE
DEFORMS
DEHORNS
DELIRIA
DEMERIT
DEMEROL
DEMURER
DENDRON
DEPARTS
DEPORTS
DESERTS
DESERVE
DESIRED
DESIREE
DESIRES
DESTROY
DEWDROP
DEXTRIN
FEDERAL
FEDORAS
FEMORAL
GENERAL
GENERIC
GENERIS
HEGIRAS
HENDRIX
HEPARIN
JEFFREY
KESTREL
LEBARON
LECARRE
LETTRES
LEVERED
LEVERET
MEMOREX
MENORAH
METERED
NEMEROV
NEUTRAL
NEUTRON
OEUVRES
PETARDS
PETERED
REAIRED
REBIRTH
RECORDS
RECORKS
REFEREE
REFERTO
REFIRES
REFORMS
REGARDS
REHIRED
REHIRES
REMARKS
REMARRY
REMORAS
REMORSE
REPORTS
RESERVE
RESORBS
RESORTS
RESURGE
RETARDS
RETIRED
RETIREE
RETIRES
RETORTS
RETURNS
REVERBS
REVERED
REVERES
REVERIE
REVERSE
REVERTS
REWARDS
REWARMS
REWIRED
REWIRES
REWORDS
REWORKS
SEAGRAM
SECURED
SECURER
SECURES
SEESRED
SENORAS
SENORES
SEVERAL
SEVERED
SEVERER
TEATRAY
TEHERAN
TELERAN
TENDRIL
TENURED
TENURES
VENTRAL
VETERAN
WELLRUN

•E•••R•

BEAKERS
BEANERY
BEARERS
BEATERS
BEAVERS
BEEPERS
BEGGARS
BEGORRA
BENDERS
BERBERS
BERGERE
BERNARD
BERSERK
BESTIRS
BETTERS
BETTORS
BEZIERS
CELEBRE
CELLARS
CENSERS
CENSORS
CENSURE
CENTERS
CENTURY
CEREBRA
DEALERS
DEBEERS
DEBTORS
DECLARE
DEEPFRY
DEICERS
DEKLERK
DELBERT
DELVERS
DENIERS
DENMARK
DENTURE
DEODARS
DEPLORE
DESSERT
DETOURS
DEUTERO
DEVILRY
DEVOURS
FEARERS
FEATURE
FEEDERS
FEELERS
FELLERS
FENCERS
FENDERS
FENETRE
FERRARI
FERRARO
FERVORS
FESTERS
FETTERS
GEEZERS
GENDERS
GENNARO
GESTURE
GEYSERS
HEADERS
HEALERS
HEARERS
HEATERS
HEAVERS
HECTARE
HECTORS
HEDGERS
HEELERS
HEIFERS
HELLERS
HELOTRY
HELPERS
HEMMERS
HENNERY
HEPBURN
HERBERT
HERDERS
JEANARP
JEERERS
JEFFERS
JESTERS
JETPORT
JEWELRY
KEENERS
KEEPERS
KEGLERS
KEYCARD
KEYWORD
LEADERS
LEAKERS
LEANERS
LEAPERS
LEASERS
LECARRE
LECTERN
LECTORS
LECTURE
LEDGERS
LEERERS
LEEWARD
LEGHORN
LEGWORK
LEHAVRE
LEISURE
LEMPIRA
LENDERS
LEONARD
LEONORA
LEOPARD
LEOTARD
LESSORS
LETTERS
LEVIERS
MEASURE
MEMBERS
MEMOIRE
MEMOIRS
MENDERS
MENHIRS
MENTORS
MERCURY
MERGERS
METEORS
METIERS
MEWLERS
NECKERS
NECTARS
NESTERS
NETSURF
NETWORK
NEWBORN
NEWHART
NEWPORT
NEWYORK
PECCARY
PEDLARS
PEELERS
PEEPERS
PELTERS
PENNERS
PEPPARD
PEPPERS
PEPPERY
PERFORM
PERJURE
PERJURY
PERTURB
PERVERT
PESTERS
PETTERS
READERS
REAMERS
REAPERS
REARERS
RECTORS
RECTORY
REDBIRD
REDFIRS
REDFORD
REEFERS
REENTRY
REHEARD
REHEARS
RELEARN
REMARRY
RENDERS
RENTERS
REPAIRS
REQUIRE
RESPIRE
RESTART
RESTERS
RESTORE
REUTERS
REVELRY
REYNARD
SEABIRD
SEABORG
SEAGIRT
SEALERS
SEAPORT
SEATERS
SEAWARD
SECTORS
SEEDERS
SEEHERE
SEEKERS
SEINERS
SEIZERS
SELKIRK
SELLERS
SEMIPRO
SENDERS
SENIORS
SENSORS
SENSORY
SERVERS
SETTERS
TEACART
TEASERS
TEDDERS
TEENERS
TEETERS
TELLERS
TEMPERA
TEMPERS
TEMPURA
TENDERS
TENNERS
TENSORS
TENTERS
TERNARY
TERRORS
TESSERA
TESTERS
TETHERS
TEXTURE
VECTORS
VELOURS
VENDORS
VENEERS
VENTERS
VENTURA
VENTURE
VERDURE
VERGERS
VESPERS
VESTURE
VETOERS
WEARERS
WEAVERS
WEEDERS
WEEPERS
WELDERS
WELFARE
WELTERS
WENDERS
WESTERN
WETBARS
WETHERS
YELPERS
ZEPHYRS

•E••••R

AERATOR
BEADIER
BEAMIER
BEECHER
BEEFIER
BELABOR
BELLJAR
BENATAR
BENAZIR
BESMEAR
CENTAUR
DEADAIR
DEARSIR
DEBATER
DECODER
DEFILER
DELAYER
DELIVER
DEMETER
DEMURER
DEPOSER
DERNIER
DESPAIR
FEATHER
FEEBLER
FEELFOR
FEIFFER
FELLFOR
FELTFOR
FERVOUR
GENTLER
GETOVER
HEADIER
HEATHER
HEATTER
HEAVIER
HECKLER
HEFTIER
JERKIER
JEWELER
KEEBLER
KEILLOR
LEAFIER
LEAGUER
LEAKIER
LEANDER
LEARNER
LEATHER
LEERIER
LEGGIER
LEISTER
LEVELER
MEALIER
MEANDER
MEATIER
MEDDLER
MERRIER
MESSIER
METOOER
NEBULAR
NEEDIER
NEGATOR
NEITHER
NERVIER
NESTLER
NEWAGER
NEWSIER
NEWYEAR
PEDDLER
PEPPIER
PERKIER
PERRIER
PERUSER
PESKIER
PETTIER
REACTOR
READIER
REALTOR
RECITER
RECOLOR
RECOVER
REDDEER
REDHAIR
REDSTAR
REDUCER
REEDIER
REENTER
REFINER
REFUSER
REFUTER
REGULAR
REMOTER
REMOVER
RENEGER
RENEWER
REOCCUR
REORDER
REPAPER
RESCUER
REUTHER
REVELER
REVISER
SEAMIER
SEASTAR
SECEDER
SECULAR
SECURER
SEDATER
SEDUCER
SEEDIER
SELTZER
SEMINAR
SENATOR
SENDFOR
SENTFOR
SERENER
SETTLER
SEVERER
SEYMOUR
TEACHER
TEARIER
TEENIER
TEETHER
TEICHER
TELSTAR
TEMBLOR
TEMPLAR
TEMPTER
TENFOUR
TERRIER
TESTIER
VERMEER
VERNIER
WEARIER
WEATHER
WEBSTER
WEEDIER
WEEPIER
WEIRDER
WENTFOR
WERNHER
WERTHER
YEARNER
YESDEAR
ZESTIER

••ER•••

ACERBIC
ACEROLA
ACEROSE
ALERTED
ALERTER
ALERTLY
AMERCED
AMERCES
AMERICA
AMERIGO
AMERIKA
AMERIND
ANEROID
APERCUS
APERIES
AVERAGE
AVERRED
AVERTED
BLERIOT
BOERWAR
BRERFOX
CHERISH
CHEROOT
CHERUBS
CHERVIL
CLERICS
CLERKED
COERCED
COERCES
DEERFLY
EMERALD
EMERGED
EMERGES
EMERITA
EMERITI
EMERSED
EMERSON
EPERGNE
ETERNAL
EVEREST
EVERETT
EVERTED
EXERTED
FIERCER
FIERIER
FIERILY
GHERKIN
IBERIAN
ICERINK
INERROR
INERTIA
INERTLY
ITERANT
ITERATE
JEERERS
JEERING
JEERSAT
LAERTES
LEERERS
LEERIER
LEERILY
LEERING
LEERSAT
LIERNES
OBERLIN
ONEROUS
OPERAND
OPERATE
OPEROSE
OVERACT
OVERAGE
OVERALL
OVERATE
OVERAWE
OVERBIG
OVERBUY
OVERDID
OVERDUB
OVERDUE
OVEREAT
OVERFLY
OVERJOY
OVERLAP
OVERLAY
OVERLIE
OVERRAN
OVERRUN
OVERSAW
OVERSEA
OVERSEE
OVERTLY
OVERUSE
PEERAGE
PEERESS
PEERING
PEEROUT
PEERSAT
PEERSIN
PIERCED
PIERCES
PIERROT
PUERILE
QUERIED
QUERIES
SEERESS
SHERBET
SHERIFF
SHERMAN
SHERPAS
SHERWIN
SIERRAS
STEREOS
STERILE
STERNAL
STERNER
STERNLY
STERNUM
STEROID
STEROLS
SWERVED
SWERVES
THERAPY
THEREAT
THEREBY
THEREIN
THEREOF
THEREON
THERESA
THERETO
THERMAL
THERMOS
THEROUX
TIERACK
TIERING
TIERNEY
TIERODS
VEERING
WHEREAS
WHEREAT
WHEREBY
WHEREIN
WHEREOF
WHERETO

••E•R••

AREARUG
ATECROW
AVERRED
BEETREE
BLEARED
CHEERED
CHEERIO
CHEERUP
CHETRUM
CHEVRES
CHEVRON
CLEARED
CLEARER
CLEARLY
CLEARUP
EYEBROW
FREDRIC

FUELROD
ICEFREE
INERROR
MCENROE
OVERRAN
OVERRUN
PIERROT
QUEERED
QUEERER
QUEERLY
SEESRED
SHEARED
SHEARER
SHECRAB
SHEERED
SHEERER
SHEERLY
SIERRAS
SMEARED
SNEERAT
SNEERED
SNEERER
SPEARED
STEERED
STEERER
SWEARAT
SWEARBY
SWEARER
SWEARIN
SWEARTO
THEOREM
TREERAT
UNEARTH

••E••R•

ABELARD
BEEPERS
BREWERS
BREWERY
CAESARS
CAESURA
CHEWERS
CUECARD
DEEPFRY
DIEHARD
DIETARY
DIETERS
DOEUVRE
DUELERS
ELECTRA
ELECTRO
ELEKTRA
EYESORE
FEEDERS
FEELERS
FLEXORS
FUELERS
GEEZERS
GREGORY
GUEVARA
HEELERS
ICEBERG
JAEGERS
JEERERS
KEENERS
KEEPERS
LEERERS
LEEWARD
MAESTRI
MAESTRO
OLESTRA
OPENERS
PEELERS
PEEPERS
PIECERS
PLECTRA
PLENARY
PLEXORS
PREFERS
PREPARE
PRESORT
QUEUERS
REEFERS
REENTRY
RHETORS
SCENERY
SCEPTRE
SEEDERS
SEEHERE
SEEKERS
SHEPARD
SKEWERS
SPECTRA
SPECTRE
STEWARD
STEWART
STEWERS
SWELTRY
TEENERS
TEETERS
THEATRE
TREMORS
TRENARY
VIEWERS
WEEDERS
WEEPERS
WIENERS

••E•••R

ABETTOR
ALERTER
AREOLAR
ATELIER
AVENGER
BEECHER
BEEFIER
BLEAKER
BLEEPER
BLENDER
BOERWAR
BREAKER
BREEDER
BRENNER
CHEAPER
CHEATER
CHECKER
CHEDDAR
CHEEVER
CHENIER
CHEQUER
CHESTER
CHEWIER
CLEANER
CLEARER
CLEAVER
CREAMER
CREATOR
CREEPER
DREAMER
DREDGER
DREISER
DRESSER
DWELLER
ELEANOR
ELECTOR
EMENDER
ERECTER
ERECTOR
FEEBLER
FEELFOR
FIEDLER
FIELDER
FIERCER
FIERIER
FLEETER
FLEXNER
FREEZER
FRESHER
GLEANER
GOESFOR
GREASER
GREATER
GREENER
GREETER
GUESSER
INERROR
KEEBLER
KNEADER
KNEELER
LEERIER
LIEOVER
LOESSER
NEEDIER
NIEBUHR
OPENAIR
OPENBAR
PLEADER
PLEASER
PLEDGER
PREENER
PREMIER
PRESSER
QUEERER
REEDIER
REENTER
ROEDEER
SCEPTER
SEEDIER
SHEARER
SHEERER
SHELLER
SHELTER
SKEETER
SKELTER
SLEDDER
SLEEKER
SLEEPER
SLENDER
SMELTER
SNEAKER
SNEERER
SNEEZER
SPEAKER
SPECTER
SPECTOR
SPEEDER
SPELLER
SPENCER
SPENDER
SPENSER
STEAMER
STEELER
STEEPER
STEERER
STEIGER
STEINER
STELLAR
STENTOR
STEPPER
STERNER
SVELTER
SWEARER
SWEATER
SWEEPER
SWEETER
SWELTER
TEENIER
TEETHER
THEATER
TREADER
TREKKER
TWEETER
WEEDIER
WEEPIER
WHEELER
WHEEZER
WHETHER
WRECKER
ZOELLER

•••ER••

ACHERON
ADHERED
ADHERES
ADVERBS
ADVERSE
ADVERTS
AILERON
ALBERTA
ALBERTO
ALGERIA
ALLERGY
ALTERED
ALTERER
AMHERST
AMPERES
ANGERED
ASPERSE
ASSERTS
BEVERLY
BODEREK
BOLEROS
BOWERED
CAMERAS
CAMERON
CAPERED
CASERNS
CATERED
CATERER
CAVERNS
CHEERED
CHEERIO
CHEERUP
COHERED
COHERES
COTERIE
COVERED
COVERUP
COWERED
DEMERIT
DEMEROL
DESERTS
DESERVE
DIDEROT
DIVERGE
DIVERSE
DIVERTS
EAGERER
EAGERLY
ELDERLY
EMPEROR
ENTERED
EQUERRY
EUTERPE
EXCERPT
EXPERTS
FABERGE
FEDERAL
FORERAN
FORERUN
GENERAL
GENERIC
GENERIS
GONERIL
GOVERNS
HOMERED
HOMERIC
HOMERUN
HOVERED
HOVERER
HUMERAL
HUMERUS
IMMERSE
IMPERIL
INFERNO
INHERED
INHERES
INHERIT
INSERTS
INTERIM
INTERNS
INTERSE
INVERSE
INVERTS
LATERAL
LATERAN
LATERON
LAVERNE
LAYERED
LEVERED
LEVERET
LIBERAL
LIBERIA
LIBERTY
LITERAL
LOVERLY
LOWERED
LUCERNE
METERED
MINERAL
MINERVA
MISERLY
MITERED
MODERNS
NEMEROV
NIGERIA
NUMERAL
NUMERIC
OBSERVE
OBVERSE
OBVERTS
OFFERED
OFFERER
ORDERED
ORDERER
ORDERLY
PALERMO
PAPERED
PAPERER
PATERNO
PETERED
POVERTY
POWERED
PUBERTY
QUEERED
QUEERER
QUEERLY
REFEREE
REFERTO
RESERVE
REVERBS
REVERED
REVERES
REVERIE
REVERSE
REVERTS
RICERAT
ROBERTA
ROBERTO
ROBERTS
ROSERED
SALERNO
SCHERZI
SCHERZO
SCLERAS
SEVERAL
SEVERED
SEVERER
SHEERED
SHEERER
SHEERLY
SIBERIA
SNEERAT
SNEERED
SNEERER
SOBERED
SOBERER
SOBERLY
SPHERES
STEERED
STEERER
SYNERGY
TAPERED
TAVERNS
TEHERAN
TELERAN
THIERRY
TONEROW
TOREROS
TOWERED
TREERAT
UMBERTO
UNDERGO
UNNERVE
USHERED
UTTERED
UTTERER
UTTERLY
VALERIE
VETERAN
VICEROY
WAGERED
WAGERER
WATERED
WATERER
WAVERED
WAVERER
WINERED
WYVERNS

•••E•R•

ALGEBRA
ALLEARS
ALLEGRO
APPEARS
ARREARS
ATHEART
AUTEURS
BONEDRY
BYHEART
CAREERS
CAVEART
CELEBRE
CEREBRA
COHEIRS
CULEBRA
DEBEERS
DOGEARS
ENDEARS
EQUERRY
FENETRE
FINEART
FIREARM
FOREARM
INTEGRA
JANEIRO
JEWELRY
MADEIRA
MAJEURE
METEORS
PALEDRY
PHAEDRA
POSEURS
REHEARD
REHEARS
RELEARN
REVELRY
SIDEARM
THIERRY
THREERS
TINEARS
TONEARM
UNHEARD
UNLEARN
VENEERS

•••E••R

ACCEDER
ALIENOR
ALLEGER
ALTERER
AMMETER
BLEEPER
BREEDER
BRIEFER
CAREFOR
CATERER
CHEEVER
CREEPER
CRUELER
DEMETER
DONEFOR
DOVEBAR
EAGERER
EMPEROR
FAKEFUR
FLEETER
FOREVER
FREEZER
GREENER
GREETER
GRIEVER
HOVERER
HOWEVER
INGEMAR
INTEGER
JEWELER
KNEELER
LABELER
LEVELER
LIBELER
MADEFOR
MAKEFOR
MAKEPAR
MODELER
OFFERER
OFTENER
ORDERER
PACECAR
PAPERER
PINEFOR
PINETAR
PRAETOR
PREENER
QUEERER
QUIETER
RACECAR
RENEGER
RENEWER
REVELER
RIVETER
SCHEMER
SECEDER
SERENER
SEVERER
SHEERER
SIDEBAR
SIDECAR
SKEETER
SLEEKER
SLEEPER
SNEERER
SNEEZER
SOBERER
SPEEDER
SPIELER
STEELER
STEEPER
STEERER
STPETER
STREWER
SWEEPER
SWEETER
TIREDER
TUTELAR
TWEETER
UTTERER
VINEGAR
WAGERER
WAKENER
WATERER
WAVERER
WHEELER
WHEEZER
WHOEVER
WINEBAR
YODELER

••••ER•

ABUSERS
ADORERS
ALFIERI
ALGIERS
ALLHERE
AMBLERS
ANGLERS
ANSWERS
ANTHERS
ANTLERS
ANTWERP
ARCHERS
ARCHERY
ARGUERS
ARRIERE
AUSTERE
AVOWERS
BACKERS
BADGERS
BAGGERS
BAILERS
BANKERS
BANNERS
BANTERS
BARBERS
BARKERS
BARTERS
BASTERS
BATHERS
BATTERS
BATTERY
BAWLERS
BEAKERS
BEANERY
BEARERS
BEATERS
BEAVERS
BEEPERS
BENDERS
BERBERS
BERGERE
BERSERK
BETTERS
BEZIERS
BICKERS
BIDDERS
BIGGERS
BINDERS
BINDERY
BIRDERS
BITTERN
BITTERS
BLAZERS
BLOWERS
BOATERS
BOBBERS
BOILERS
BOMBERS
BONKERS
BOOMERS
BOPPERS
BORDERS
BOTHERS
BOWLERS
BOWYERS
BRACERS
BRAVERY
BRAYERS
BREWERS
BREWERY
BRIBERY
BROKERS
BUFFERS
BUGLERS
BUMMERS
BUMPERS
BUNKERS
BURGERS
BURNERS
BUTLERS
BUTTERS
BUTTERY
BUZZERS
CABLERS
CADGERS
CAHIERS
CALDERA
CALLERS
CALVERT
CAMBERS
CAMPERS
CANKERS
CANNERS
CANNERY
CANTERS
CAPPERS
CARDERS
CAREERS
CARNERA
CARPERS
CARRERE
CARTERS
CARVERS
CASTERS
CENSERS
CENTERS
CHASERS
CHEWERS
CHIMERA
CHOKERS
CINDERS
CIPHERS
CISTERN
CLAWERS
CLOVERS
COALERS
COAXERS
COCHERE
CODGERS
COFFERS
COINERS
COLBERT
COMBERS
CONCERN
CONCERT
CONFERS
CONGERS
CONKERS
CONNERY
CONVERT
COOKERS
COOKERY
COOLERS
COOPERS
COPIERS
COPPERS
COPPERY
COPTERS
CORDERO
CORKERS
CORNERS
COTTERS
COWHERD
CRATERS
CRAVERS
CROWERS
CULVERT
CURLERS
CUTLERS
CUTLERY
CUTTERS
CYCLERS
CYPHERS
DAGGERS
DAMPERS
DANCERS
DANDERS
DANGERS
DARNERS
DARTERS
DASHERS
DAUBERS
DEALERS
DEBEERS
DEICERS
DEKLERK
DELBERT
DELVERS
DENIERS
DESSERT
DEUTERO
DIALERS
DIAPERS
DICKERS
DIETERS
DIFFERS
DIGGERS
DIMMERS
DINNERS
DIPPERS
DISCERN
DITHERS
DITHERY
DOCKERS
DODDERS
DODGERS
DORMERS
DOSSERS
DOWNERS
DOWSERS
DRAPERS
DRAPERY
DRAWERS
DRIVERS
DRONERS
DROVERS
DUBBERS
DUELERS
DUFFERS
DUNKERS
DUSTERS
EARNERS
EASTERN
EASTERS
ELATERS
ELOPERS
EMOTERS
ERASERS
ETAGERE
ETCHERS
EVADERS
EVOKERS
EXUPERY
FALTERS
FARMERS
FATHERS
FAWNERS
FEARERS
FEEDERS
FEELERS
FELLERS
FENCERS
FENDERS
FESTERS
FETTERS
FIBBERS
FILBERT
FILLERS
FILTERS
FINDERS
FINGERS
FISHERS
FISHERY
FITTERS
FLAKERS
FLOWERS
FLOWERY
FODDERS
FOGGERS
FOLDERS
FOLGERS
FOOLERY
FOOTERS
FOPPERY
FORCERS
FORGERS
FORGERY
FORKERS
FOSTERS
FOWLERS
FUELERS
GABBERS
GAFFERS
GAINERS
GAITERS
GALLERY
GANDERS
GARNERS
GARTERS
GASSERS
GATHERS
GAUGERS
GAWKERS
GEEZERS
GENDERS
GEYSERS
GIBBERS
GILBERT
GILDERS
GINGERS
GINGERY
GIRDERS
GLAZERS
GLIDERS
GLOWERS
GNAWERS
GOLFERS
GOMPERS
GOOBERS
GOPHERS
GOUGERS
GRADERS
GRATERS
GRAZERS
GRIPERS
GROCERS
GROCERY
GROWERS
GRUYERE
GUNNERS
GUNNERY
GUSHERS
GUTTERS
GYPPERS
HACKERS
HALTERS
HAMMERS
HAMPERS
HANGERS
HANKERS
HARPERS
HATTERS
HAUBERK
HAULERS
HAWKERS
HAWSERS
HEADERS
HEALERS
HEARERS
HEATERS
HEAVERS
HEDGERS
HEELERS
HEIFERS
HELLERS
HELPERS
HEMMERS
HENNERY
HERBERT
HERDERS
HINDERS
HISSERS
HITHERE
HITTERS
HOAXERS
HOLDERS
HOLLERS
HONKERS
HOOFERS
HOOTERS
HOPPERS
HOSIERS
HOSIERY
HOWLERS
HUGGERS
HULLERS
HUMMERS
HUNGERS
HUNKERS
HUNTERS
HURLERS
HUSKERS
ICEBERG
IMAGERS
IMAGERY
IRONERS
ISOMERS
ISSUERS
JABBERS
JAEGERS
JAILERS
JAMMERS
JASPERS
JEERERS
JEFFERS
JESTERS
JIGGERS
JIGGERY
JITTERS
JITTERY
JOBBERS
JOGGERS
JOINERS
JOINERY
JUDDERS
JUICERS
JUMPERS
JUNKERS
KAISERS
KEENERS
KEEPERS
KEGLERS
KICKERS
KIDDERS
KILLERS
KIPPERS
KISSERS
KNAVERY
KOSHERS
KRATERS

LAAGERS
LADDERS
LADLERS
LAGGERS
LAMBERT
LANCERS
LANDERS
LANTERN
LARDERS
LASHERS
LATHERS
LATHERY
LAWYERS
LEADERS
LEAKERS
LEANERS
LEAPERS
LEASERS
LECTERN
LEDGERS
LEERERS
LENDERS
LETTERS
LEVIERS
LIBBERS
LIFTERS
LIMBERS
LIMNERS
LINGERS
LINKERS
LITTERS
LOADERS
LOAFERS
LOANERS
LOBBERS
LOCKERS
LODGERS
LOGGERS
LOITERS
LOOKERS
LOOPERS
LOOTERS
LOPPERS
LOTTERY
LOUVERS
LUBBERS
LUGGERS
LUMBERS
LUMIERE
LUMPERS
LUNKERS
LUSTERS
MADDERS
MAILERS
MANGERS
MANNERS
MAPPERS
MARKERS
MASHERS
MASKERS
MASTERS
MASTERY
MATHERS
MATTERS
MEMBERS
MENDERS
MERGERS
METIERS
MEWLERS
MIDTERM
MILKERS
MILLERS
MINCERS

MINDERS
MINTERS
MISTERS
MOANERS
MOCKERS
MOCKERY
MOILERS
MOLDERS
MOLIERE
MOLTERS
MONGERS
MOPPERS
MOTHERS
MOUSERS
MUDDERS
MUGGERS
MULLERS
MUMMERS
MUMMERY
MURDERS
MUSHERS
MUSTERS
MUTTERS
MYSTERY
NABBERS
NAILERS
NAPPERS
NATTERS
NECKERS
NESTERS
NICKERS
NIPPERS
NODDERS
NONZERO
NOSHERS
NOWHERE
NUDGERS
NUMBERS
NUNNERY
NURSERS
NURSERY
NUTTERS
OAKFERN
ONAGERS
OPENERS
OPINERS
OSTLERS
OUSTERS
OYSTERS
PACKERS
PADDERS
PALTERS
PAMPERS
PANDERS
PANNERS
PANZERS
PARSERS
PASSERS
PASTERN
PATTERN
PATTERS
PAUPERS
PAWNERS
PEELERS
PEEPERS
PELTERS
PENNERS
PEPPERS
PEPPERY
PERVERT
PESTERS
PETTERS
PHASERS

PICKERS
PIECERS
PILFERS
PINCERS
PINNERS
PITTERS
PLACERS
PLANERS
PLATERS
PLAYERS
PLOVERS
PLOWERS
POLDERS
POLLERS
PONDERS
POPPERS
PORKERS
PORTERS
POSTERN
POSTERS
POTHERB
POTHERS
POTTERS
POTTERY
POURERS
POUTERS
POWDERS
POWDERY
PRATERS
PRAYERS
PREFERS
PRICERS
PRIMERS
PROBERS
PROSERS
PROVERB
PROVERS
PRUDERY
PRUNERS
PUCKERS
PUFFERS
PUFFERY
PUMPERS
PUNTERS
PURRERS
PURSERS
PUTTERS
QUAKERS
QUAVERS
QUAVERY
QUEUERS
QUIVERS
QUOTERS
RAFTERS
RAIDERS
RAILERS
RAISERS
RANGERS
RANKERS
RANTERS
RAPIERS
RAPPERS
RASHERS
RASPERS
RASTERS
RATTERS
READERS
REAMERS
REAPERS
REARERS
REEFERS
RENDERS
RENTERS

RESTERS
REUTERS
RHYMERS
RIFLERS
RIFLERY
RIGGERS
RINGERS
RIOTERS
RIPPERS
RISKERS
RIVIERA
RIVIERE
ROAMERS
ROARERS
ROBBERS
ROBBERY
ROCKERS
RODGERS
ROGUERY
ROLLERS
ROMPERS
ROOFERS
ROOKERY
ROOMERS
ROOTERS
ROSTERS
ROTTERS
ROUTERS
RUBBERS
RUBBERY
RUDDERS
RUINERS
RUNNERS
RUSHERS
RUTGERS
SACKERS
SALIERI
SALTERS
SALVERS
SANDERS
SAPPERS
SASSERS
SAUCERS
SAWYERS
SCALERS
SCARERS
SCENERY
SCORERS
SCOTERS
SEALERS
SEATERS
SEEDERS
SEEHERE
SEEKERS
SEINERS
SEIZERS
SELLERS
SENDERS
SERVERS
SETTERS
SHAKERS
SHAPERS
SHARERS
SHAVERS
SHINERS
SHIVERS
SHOVERS
SHOWERS
SHOWERY
SHUBERT
SIFTERS
SIGHERS
SIGNERS

SILVERS
SILVERY
SIMMERS
SIMPERS
SINCERE
SINGERS
SINKERS
SINNERS
SIPPERS
SISTERS
SITTERS
SKATERS
SKEWERS
SKIVERS
SLAVERS
SLAVERY
SLAYERS
SLICERS
SLIDERS
SLIVERS
SMILERS
SMOKERS
SNORERS
SOAKERS
SOAPERS
SOARERS
SOBBERS
SOLDERS
SOLVERS
SOONERS
SORCERY
SORTERS
SOTHERE
SOTHERN
SPACERS
SPADERS
SPIDERS
SPIDERY
SPIKERS
STAGERS
STARERS
STEWERS
STOKERS
STONERS
STORERS
STYLERS
SUBVERT
SUBZERO
SUCKERS
SUFFERS
SULKERS
SUMMERS
SUMMERY
SUNDERS
SUPPERS
SURFERS
SURGERY
SUTLERS
SWAYERS
SWIPERS
TACKERS
TALKERS
TAMPERS
TANGERE
TANKERS
TANNERS
TANNERY
TAPPERS
TASTERS
TATTERS
TEASERS
TEDDERS
TEENERS

TEETERS
TELLERS
TEMPERA
TEMPERS
TENDERS
TENNERS
TENTERS
TESSERA
TESTERS
TETHERS
THALERS
THREERS
TICKERS
TILLERS
TILTERS
TIMBERS
TINDERS
TINKERS
TINNERS
TINTERN
TINTERS
TIPPERS
TITHERS
TITTERS
TOILERS
TOOTERS
TOPPERS
TOSSERS
TOTTERS
TOTTERY
TOURERS
TOUTERS
TOWNERS
TRABERT
TRACERS
TRACERY
TRADERS
TRAVERS
TROWERS
TUCKERS
TUGGERS
TURNERS
TUSKERS
TWOFERS
ULSTERS
UNITERS
USURERS
VAMPERS
VAQUERO
VENEERS
VENTERS
VERGERS
VESPERS
VETOERS
VIEWERS
VISCERA
VIZIERS
WAGGERY
WAILERS
WAITERS
WAIVERS
WALKERS
WALTERS
WANDERS
WARDERS
WASHERS
WASTERS
WEARERS
WEAVERS
WEEDERS
WEEPERS
WELDERS
WELTERS

WENDERS
WESTERN
WETHERS
WHALERS
WHINERS
WICKERS
WIENERS
WINCERS
WINDERS
WINGERS
WINKERS
WINNERS
WINTERS
WINTERY
WISHERS
WITHERS
WONDERS
WOOFERS
WOOMERA
WORKERS
WRITERS
YAKKERS
YAMMERS
YAPPERS
YAWNERS
YAWPERS
YELPERS
YONKERS
YOWLERS
ZANDERS
ZAPPERS
ZINGERS
ZIPPERS
ZITHERS
ZONKERS

••••E•R

AMATEUR
ANTBEAR
BESMEAR
BUGBEAR
COMPEER
DANSEUR
FLANEUR
FORBEAR
HAUTEUR
LIQUEUR
LOWGEAR
MANYEAR
MASSEUR
MIDYEAR
MISHEAR
MYNHEER
NEWYEAR
NUCLEAR
OFFYEAR
ONATEAR
OUTWEAR
PASTEUR
PIONEER
REDDEER
ROEDEER
SCHMEER
UNCLEAR
VERMEER
YESDEAR

•••••ER

ACCEDER
ACCUSER
ADAPTER
ADMIRER
ADOPTER

ADVISER
ALARMER
ALERTER
ALIGNER
ALLAYER
ALLEGER
ALLOVER
ALTERER
ALUNSER
AMMETER
ANDOVER
ANGRIER
ANOTHER
ANTSIER
AQUIFER
AQUIVER
ARBITER
ARMORER
ARRIVER
ASPIRER
ASSAYER
ASUNDER
ATELIER
AVENGER
AWARDER
BAFFLER
BAGGIER
BALKIER
BALMIER
BARMIER
BARRIER
BATTIER
BATTLER
BAWDIER
BEADIER
BEAMIER
BEECHER
BEEFIER
BITTIER
BLABBER
BLACKER
BLADDER
BLANDER
BLANKER
BLASTER
BLATHER
BLEAKER
BLEEPER
BLENDER
BLINDER
BLINKER
BLISTER
BLITHER
BLOCKER
BLONDER
BLOOMER
BLOOPER
BLOTTER
BLOWIER
BLUBBER
BLUFFER
BLUNDER
BLUNTER
BLUSHER
BLUSTER
BOARDER
BOASTER
BOGGLER
BOLSTER
BONNIER
BOOSLER
BOOSTER
BOSSIER

BOTTLER
BOULDER
BOUNCER
BOUNDER
BOWDLER
BRAGGER
BRAIDER
BRANDER
BRASHER
BRAWLER
BRAZIER
BREAKER
BREEDER
BRENNER
BRIEFER
BRINGER
BRINIER
BRISKER
BROADER
BROILER
BROODER
BROTHER
BROWNER
BROWSER
BRUISER
BRYNNER
BUCKLER
BUGGIER
BUILDER
BULKIER
BUMBLER
BUMPIER
BUNGLER
BURGHER
BURLIER
BUSHIER
BUTCHER
CACKLER
CAJOLER
CALIBER
CALIPER
CAMPIER
CANNIER
CAROLER
CARRIER
CARTIER
CASHIER
CATCHER
CATERER
CATTIER
CAULKER
CAVILER
CHAMBER
CHAMFER
CHANGER
CHANTER
CHAPTER
CHARGER
CHARIER
CHARMER
CHARTER
CHASTER
CHATTER
CHAUCER
CHEAPER
CHEATER
CHECKER
CHEEVER
CHENIER
CHEQUER
CHESTER
CHEWIER
CHIGGER

CHILLER
CHIPPER
CHITTER
CHOICER
CHOOSER
CHOPPER
CHOWDER
CHUKKER
CLABBER
CLAIMER
CLAMBER
CLAMMER
CLAPPER
CLATTER
CLAVIER
CLAYIER
CLEANER
CLEARER
CLEAVER
CLIMBER
CLINKER
CLIPPER
CLOBBER
CLOCKER
CLOWDER
CLUNKER
CLUSTER
CLUTTER
CNTOWER
COARSER
COASTER
COBBLER
COCKIER
CODDLER
COLLIER
COLLYER
COMFIER
COMPEER
CONIFER
CONQUER
CORNIER
COSTNER
COULTER
COUNTER
COURIER
COURSER
CRABBER
CRACKER
CRAFTER
CRAMMER
CRASSER
CRAWLER
CRAZIER
CREAMER
CREEPER
CRIMPER
CRISPER
CRITTER
CROONER
CROPPER
CROSIER
CROSSER
CRUELER
CRUISER
CRULLER
CRUSHER
CURLIER
CURRIER
CURVIER
CUSHIER
CUSSLER
DABBLER
DAFFIER

DAIMLER
DALLIER
DANDIER
DANGLER
DAUMIER
DAWDLER
DAZZLER
DEBATER
DECODER
DEFILER
DELAYER
DELIVER
DEMETER
DEMURER
DEPOSER
DERNIER
DIDOVER
DILUTER
DINGIER
DINKIER
DIOPTER
DIRTIER
DIVIDER
DIVINER
DIZZIER
DOODLER
DOPPLER
DOSSIER
DOTTIER
DOUBTER
DOWAGER
DOWDIER
DOWNIER
DRABBER
DRAINER
DREAMER
DREDGER
DREISER
DRESSER
DRIFTER
DRILLER
DRINKER
DROLLER
DROOLER
DROPPER
DRUCKER
DRUMMER
DUCKIER
DUMPIER
DUSKIER
DUSTIER
DWELLER
EAGERER
EARLIER
EDASNER
EMENDER
EMITTER
EMPOWER
EMPTIER
ENCODER
ENDUSER
ENTICER
ERECTER
EVANDER
EVILLER
EXACTER
FAINTER
FANCIER
FARRIER
FARTHER
FEATHER
FEEBLER
FEIFFER

FICKLER
FIDDLER
FIEDLER
FIELDER
FIERCER
FIERIER
FIGHTER
FIGURER
FILCHER
FILMIER
FISCHER
FISHIER
FIZZIER
FLAKIER
FLANKER
FLAPPER
FLASHER
FLATTER
FLEETER
FLEXNER
FLICKER
FLIPPER
FLITTER
FLIVVER
FLOATER
FLUSTER
FLUTTER
FLYOVER
FNUMBER
FOAMIER
FOGGIER
FORAGER
FOREVER
FORSTER
FOUNDER
FOURIER
FRAILER
FRANKER
FRASIER
FRAZIER
FREEZER
FRESHER
FRITTER
FROWNER
FUMBLER
FUNKIER
FUNNIER
FURRIER
FURTHER
FUSSIER
FUSTIER
FUZZIER
GABBIER
GAGSTER
GAMBLER
GARDNER
GAUCHER
GAUDIER
GAUNTER
GAUZIER
GAWKIER
GENTLER
GETOVER
GIDDIER
GIGGLER
GLACIER
GLADDER
GLAZIER
GLEANER
GLIBBER
GLIMMER
GLITTER
GLUMMER

GOBBLER
GOOFIER
GOOPIER
GOTOVER
GOUNDER
GRABBER
GRAMMER
GRANDER
GRANGER
GREASER
GREATER
GREENER
GREETER
GRIDDER
GRIEVER
GRIFTER
GRIMIER
GRIMMER
GRINDER
GRINNER
GRIPPER
GROANER
GROLIER
GROOMER
GROSSER
GROUPER
GROUSER
GROWLER
GRUFFER
GUESSER
GUILDER
GUMMIER
GUNKIER
GUNTHER
GUSHIER
GUTSIER
GUZZLER
HAGGLER
HAIRIER
HAMSTER
HANDIER
HANDLER
HANOVER
HAPPIER
HARDIER
HARRIER
HARSHER
HASTIER
HATCHER
HEADIER
HEATHER
HEATTER
HEAVIER
HECKLER
HEFTIER
HILLIER
HIPSTER
HITCHER
HOARDER
HOARIER
HOARSER
HOLSTER
HONORER
HOOSIER
HOPOVER
HORSIER
HOSTLER
HOVERER
HOWEVER
HUFFIER
HUMBLER
HURDLER
HUSKIER

HUSTLER
IGNITER
IGNORER
IMPURER
INCITER
INDUCER
INHALER
INSIDER
INTEGER
INTONER
INVADER
INVOKER
IONIZER
ITCHIER
JANVIER
JAZZIER
JERKIER
JEWELER
JOINDER
JOLLIER
JOSTLER
JOUSTER
JUGGLER
JUICIER
JUMPIER
JUNIPER
JUNKIER
JUPITER
KAYAKER
KEEBLER
KINKIER
KNEADER
KNEELER
KNITTER
KNOCKER
KOOKIER
LABELER
LABORER
LACQUER
LALAKER
LANKIER
LARDNER
LASSOER
LAUGHER
LAUNDER
LAYOVER
LEAFIER
LEAGUER
LEAKIER
LEANDER
LEARNER
LEATHER
LEERIER
LEGGIER
LEISTER
LEVELER
LIBELER
LIEOVER
LIGHTER
LINTIER
LIPPIER
LITTLER
LOAMIER
LOBBYER
LOBSTER
LOCATER
LOESSER
LOFTIER
LOONIER
LOOPIER
LOUNGER
LOUSIER
LOWLIER

LUCIFER
LUCKIER
LUMPIER
LUNCHER
LUSTIER
MANAGER
MANGIER
MANLIER
MARCHER
MARINER
MATURER
MAUNDER
MAXBAER
MEALIER
MEANDER
MEATIER
MEDDLER
MERRIER
MESSIER
METOOER
MILKIER
MINGLER
MINIVER
MINTIER
MISTIER
MOBSTER
MODELER
MOISTER
MOLDIER
MONIKER
MONOMER
MONSTER
MOOCHER
MOODIER
MOSSIER
MOULDER
MOUSIER
MUDDIER
MUDDLER
MUFFLER
MUGGIER
MUMBLER
MUNCHER
MURKIER
MUSHIER
MUSTIER
MUZZIER
MYNHEER
NASTIER
NATTIER
NEEDIER
NEITHER
NERVIER
NESTLER
NEWAGER
NEWSIER
NIBBLER
NIFTIER
NIMBLER
NIPPIER
NOISIER
NONUSER
NORTHER
NUBBIER
NUTTIER
NUZZLER
OBTUSER
OCTOBER
OFFERER
OFFICER
OFTENER
OLDSTER
OLIVIER

ONORDER
ONPAPER
OPPOSER
ORBITER
ORDERER
PADDLER
PAINTER
PALAVER
PALMIER
PANNIER
PANTHER
PAPERER
PARDNER
PARTNER
PASTIER
PEDDLER
PEPPIER
PERKIER
PERRIER
PERUSER
PESKIER
PETTIER
PHILTER
PHONIER
PIASTER
PICKIER
PILSNER
PINCHER
PIONEER
PITCHER
PITHIER
PLAINER
PLANNER
PLANTER
PLASTER
PLATTER
PLEADER
PLEASER
PLEDGER
PLODDER
PLOTTER
PLUGGER
PLUMBER
PLUMMER
PLUMPER
PLUNDER
PLUNGER
PLUSHER
POACHER
PODGIER
POINTER
POITIER
POLITER
POLYMER
POPOVER
POUNCER
POUNDER
POUTIER
PRAISER
PRANCER
PREENER
PREMIER
PRESSER
PRICIER
PRIMMER
PRINTER
PRODDER
PROFFER
PROOFER
PROSIER
PROSPER
PROUDER
PROWLER

PSALTER
PUDGIER
PUFFIER
PUNCHER
PUNSTER
PURSUER
PUSHIER
PUTOVER
PUZZLER
QUAFFER
QUARTER
QUEERER
QUICKER
QUIETER
QUILTER
QUIPPER
QUITTER
RAFFLER
RAGGIER
RAINIER
RAMBLER
RANCHER
RANDIER
RANGIER
RANOVER
RAPIDER
RASPIER
RATTIER
RATTLER
READIER
RECITER
RECOVER
REDDEER
REDUCER
REEDIER
REENTER
REFINER
REFUSER
REFUTER
REMOTER
REMOVER
RENEGER
RENEWER
REORDER
REPAPER
RESCUER
REUTHER
REVELER
REVISER
RICHTER
RIDDLER
RIGHTER
RISKIER
RITZIER
RIVETER
ROASTER
ROCKIER
ROEDEER
ROISTER
ROOMIER
ROOSTER
ROTIFER
ROUGHER
ROUNDER
ROWDIER
RUDDIER
RUMMIER
RUNNIER
RUNOVER
RUNTIER
RUSTIER
RUSTLER
SADDLER

SAGGIER
SALTIER
SAMPLER
SANDIER
SAPPIER
SASSIER
SAUCIER
SAUNTER
SAVAGER
SAVVIER
SCALIER
SCALPER
SCAMPER
SCANNER
SCANTER
SCARCER
SCARIER
SCATTER
SCEPTER
SCHEMER
SCHMEER
SCOFFER
SCOLDER
SCOOPER
SCOOTER
SCOURER
SCOUTER
SCOWLER
SCRAPER
SCULLER
SCUPPER
SEAMIER
SECEDER
SECURER
SEDATER
SEDUCER
SEEDIER
SELTZER
SERENER
SETTLER
SEVERER
SHADIER
SHAFFER
SHAKIER
SHANTER
SHARPER
SHATNER
SHATTER
SHEARER
SHEERER
SHELLER
SHELTER
SHIMMER
SHINIER
SHIPPER
SHIRKER
SHOCKER
SHOOTER
SHOPPER
SHORTER
SHOUTER
SHOWIER
SHRINER
SHRIVER
SHUCKER
SHUDDER
SHUTTER
SHYSTER
SILKIER
SILLIER
SIMPLER
SKEETER
SKELTER

SKIDDER
SKIMMER
SKINNER
SKIPPER
SKITTER
SKULKER
SLACKER
SLAMMER
SLANDER
SLASHER
SLATHER
SLATIER
SLEDDER
SLEEKER
SLEEPER
SLENDER
SLICKER
SLIMIER
SLIMMER
SLINGER
SLIPPER
SLITHER
SLOBBER
SLUGGER
SLUMBER
SMACKER
SMALLER
SMARTER
SMASHER
SMATTER
SMELTER
SMOKIER
SMOLDER
SMOTHER
SMUGGER
SNACKER
SNAKIER
SNAPPER
SNEAKER
SNEERER
SNEEZER
SNICKER
SNIFFER
SNIFTER
SNIGGER
SNOOKER
SNOOPER
SNORTER
SNOWIER
SNUFFER
SNUGGER
SOAPIER
SOBERER
SOGGIER
SOLDIER
SOLIDER
SOOTHER
SOOTIER
SORRIER
SOUNDER
SOUPIER
SPACIER
SPANKER
SPANNER
SPARSER
SPATTER
SPEAKER
SPECTER
SPEEDER
SPELLER
SPENCER
SPENDER
SPENSER

SPICIER
SPIELER
SPIKIER
SPINIER
SPINNER
SPLICER
SPOILER
SPONGER
SPOOFER
SPOONER
SPOTTER
SPOUTER
SPRAYER
SPRUCER
SPURNER
SPUTTER
SQUARER
STABLER
STAFFER
STAGGER
STAGIER
STAIDER
STAINER
STALKER
STAMMER
STAPLER
STARKER
STARTER
STEAMER
STEELER
STEEPER
STEERER
STEIGER
STEINER
STEPPER
STERNER
STICKER
STIFFER
STILLER
STINGER
STINKER
STIRRER
STOLLER
STONIER
STOPPER
STOUTER
STPETER
STREWER
STRIDER
STRIKER
STRIPER
STRIVER
STUFFER
STUMPER
STUNNER
SUBDUER
SUBTLER
SUDSIER
SULKIER
SUNNIER
SUPPLER
SURLIER
SUTTNER
SVELTER
SWAGGER
SWANKER
SWAPPER
SWATTER
SWEARER
SWEATER
SWEEPER
SWEETER
SWELTER

SWIFTER
SWIMMER
SWINGER
SWITZER
TACKIER
TACKLER
TANAGER
TANGIER
TAPSTER
TARDIER
TARSIER
TASTIER
TATTIER
TATTLER
TAWNIER
TEACHER
TEARIER
TEENIER
TEETHER
TEICHER
TEMPTER
TERRIER
TESTIER
THEATER
THICKER
THINKER
THINNER
THITHER
THROWER
THUMPER
THUNDER
THURBER
TICKLER
TIGHTER
TIMIDER
TINNIER
TIPPLER
TIPSIER
TIPSTER
TIREDER
TOASTER
TODDLER
TOFFLER
TOORDER
TOUGHER
TRACKER
TRAILER
TRAINER
TRAPPER
TRAWLER
TREADER
TREKKER
TRICKER
TRIFLER
TRIGGER
TRIMMER
TRIPPER
TROOPER
TROTTER
TROUPER
TROUSER
TRUCKER
TRUDGER
TRYSTER
TUBBIER
TUMBLER
TWEETER
TWIRLER
TWISTER
TWITTER
UNCOVER
UNIFIER
UNWISER

UPRIVER
URBANER
USURPER
UTTERER
VAULTER
VAUNTER
VERMEER
VERNIER
VINTNER
VIVIDER
VOUCHER
VOYAGER
WACKIER
WADDLER
WAFFLER
WAGERER
WAGONER
WAKENER
WALTZER
WANGLER
WARBLER
WATCHER
WATERER
WAVERER
WEARIER
WEATHER
WEBSTER
WEEDIER
WEEPIER
WEIRDER
WERNHER
WERTHER
WHEELER
WHEEZER
WHETHER
WHIMPER
WHISKER
WHISPER
WHITHER
WHOEVER
WHOPPER
WIDOWER
WIGGLER
WINDIER
WINKLER
WISPIER
WITTIER
WOODIER
WOOLIER
WOOSTER
WOOZIER
WORDIER
WORMIER
WORRIER
WRAPPER
WRECKER
WRINGER
WRONGER
YEARNER
YODELER
YOUNGER
YUCKIER
YUMMIER
ZESTIER
ZINGIER
ZIPPIER
ZOELLER

ES•••••

ESCAPED
ESCAPEE
ESCAPES
ESCARPS
ESCHEAT
ESCHEWS
ESCORTS
ESCROWS
ESCUDOS
ESKIMOS
ESPANOL
ESPIALS
ESPOSAS
ESPOSOS
ESPOUSE
ESPYING
ESQUIRE
ESSAYED
ESSENCE
ESSENES
ESTATES
ESTEEMS
ESTELLE
ESTEVEZ
ESTHETE
ESTIVAL
ESTONIA
ESTORIL
ESTRADA
ESTRAYS
ESTUARY

E•S••••

EASEDIN
EASEDUP
EASEOFF
EASESIN
EASESUP
EASIEST
EASTEND
EASTERN
EASTERS
EASTMAN
ECSTASY
ENSIGNS
ENSILED
ENSILES
ENSLAVE
ENSNARE
ENSNARL
ENSOULS
ENSUING
ENSUITE
ENSURED
ENSURES
EPSILON
EPSTEIN
ERSKINE
ESSAYED
ESSENCE
ESSENES

E••S•••

EARSHOT
EATSOUT
EDASNER
EELSKIN
EGESTED
EKESOUT
ELASTIC
ELISION
ELUSIVE
ELYSEES
ELYSIAN
ELYSIUM
ENISLED
ENISLES
EPISODE
EPISTLE
ERASERS
ERASING
ERASMUS
ERASURE
ERISTIC
EROSION
EROSIVE
ETESIAN
EVASION
EVASIVE
EXISTED
EYESORE

E•••S••

EASESIN
EASESUP
ECDYSES
ECDYSIS
EDGESIN
EFFUSED
EFFUSES
EGOISTS
ELAPSED
ELAPSES
ELEISON
ELLISON
ELMISTI
EMBASSY
EMERSED
EMERSON
ENCASED
ENCASES
ENDUSER
ENLISTS
ENMASSE
ERICSON
ERNESTO
ESPOSAS
ESPOSOS
EURASIA
EVENSUP
EVULSED
EVULSES
EXCISED
EXCISES
EXCUSED
EXCUSES
EXPOSED
EXPOSES

E••••S•

EARNEST
EASIEST
ECLIPSE
ECSTASY
EDGIEST
EELIEST
EERIEST
EGGCASE
EGOTISM
EGOTIST
ELEGIST
ELITISM
ELITIST
ELLIPSE
EMBASSY
EMPRESS
ENCLOSE
ENCRUST
ENDLESS
ENDMOST
ENDORSE
ENDWISE
ENGLISH
ENGROSS
ENMASSE
ENTHUSE
ENTRUST
EPEEIST
ESPOUSE
EVENEST
EVEREST
EVILEST
EXHAUST
EXPANSE
EXPENSE
EXPRESS
EYELASH
EYEWASH

E•••••S

EAGLETS
EARFULS
EARNERS
EARWIGS
EASTERS
EBONIES
ECDYSES
ECDYSIS
ECHINUS
ECLAIRS
ECTYPES
EDGINGS
EDIBLES
EDIFIES
EDITORS
EDWARDS
EFFACES
EFFECTS
EFFORTS
EFFUSES
EGGCUPS
EGGNOGS
EGOISTS
EIGHTHS
ELAPIDS
ELAPSES
ELATERS
ELEGIES
ELEVENS
ELICITS
ELIXIRS
ELOPERS
ELYSEES
EMBANKS
EMBARKS
EMBLEMS
EMBRYOS
EMERGES
EMIGRES
EMOTERS
EMPIRES
EMPLOYS
EMPRESS
EMPTIES
ENABLES
ENAMELS
ENAMORS
ENCAGES
ENCAMPS
ENCASES
ENCODES
ENCORES
ENDEARS
ENDINGS
ENDIVES
ENDLESS
ENDRUNS
ENDURES
ENDWAYS
ENEMIES
ENFOLDS
ENGAGES
ENGINES
ENGIRDS
ENGRAMS
ENGROSS
ENGULFS
ENIGMAS
ENISLES
ENJOINS
ENLACES
ENLISTS
ENNEADS
ENRAGES
ENROBES
ENROLLS
ENROOTS
ENSIGNS
ENSILES
ENSOULS
ENSURES
ENTAILS
ENTICES
ENTRAPS
ENTREES
ENTRIES
ENVIOUS
ENWRAPS
ENZYMES
EOLITHS
EPARCHS
EPILOGS
EPONYMS
EPOXIES
EQUATES
EQUINES
ERASERS
ERASMUS
ERMINES
ERRANDS
ESCAPES
ESCARPS
ESCHEWS
ESCORTS
ESCROWS
ESCUDOS
ESKIMOS
ESPIALS
ESPOSAS
ESPOSOS
ESSENES
ESTATES
ESTEEMS
ESTRAYS
ETCHERS
ETHNICS
ETOILES
EUCHRES
EUNUCHS
EVADERS
EVENKIS
EVINCES
EVOKERS
EVOLVES
EVULSES
EXCEEDS

EXCEPTS
EXCISES
EXCITES
EXCUSES
EXEMPTS
EXHALES
EXHORTS
EXOTICS
EXPANDS
EXPECTS
EXPENDS
EXPERTS
EXPIRES
EXPORTS
EXPOSES
EXPRESS
EXTENDS
EXTENTS
EXTORTS
EXWIVES
EYECUPS
EYEFULS
EYELETS
EYELIDS

•ES••••

BESEECH
BESEEMS
BESIDES
BESIEGE
BESMEAR
BESPEAK
BESPOKE
BESTBOY
BESTIAL
BESTING
BESTIRS
BESTMAN
BESTMEN
BESTOWS
BESTREW
CESSION
DESALTS
DESCANT
DESCEND
DESCENT
DESERTS
DESERVE
DESIGNS
DESIRED
DESIREE
DESIRES
DESISTS
DESKSET
DESKTOP
DESMOND
DESOTOS
DESPAIR
DESPISE
DESPITE
DESPOIL
DESPOTS
DESSERT
DESTINE
DESTINY
DESTROY
FESTERS
FESTIVE
FESTOON
GESSOES
GESTALT
GESTATE
GESTURE
HESHVAN
HESSIAN
JESSICA
JESTERS
JESTING
JESUITS
KESTREL
LESOTHO
LESPAUL
LESSEES
LESSENS
LESSING
LESSONS
LESSORS
MESCALS
MESHING
MESSAGE
MESSALA
MESSIAH
MESSIER
MESSILY
MESSINA
MESSING
MESSKIT
MESTIZO
NESCAFE
NESTEGG
NESTERS
NESTING
NESTLED
NESTLER
NESTLES
PESETAS
PESKIER
PESKILY
PESTERS
PESTLED
PESTLES
RESALES
RESALTS
RESANDS
RESCALE
RESCIND
RESCUED
RESCUER
RESCUES
RESEALS
RESEATS
RESECTS
RESEEDS
RESELLS
RESENDS
RESENTS
RESERVE
RESHIPS
RESHOES
RESHOOT
RESIDED
RESIDES
RESIDUE
RESIGNS
RESILED
RESILES
RESINGS
RESISTS
RESOLED
RESOLES
RESOLVE
RESORBS
RESORTS
RESOUND
RESPECT
RESPIRE
RESPITE
RESPOND
RESTAGE
RESTAIN
RESTAMP
RESTART
RESTATE
RESTERS
RESTFUL
RESTING
RESTIVE
RESTOCK
RESTORE
RESTSUP
RESTYLE
RESULTS
RESUMED
RESUMES
RESURGE
SESAMES
SESSILE
SESSION
SESTETS
SESTINA
TESSERA
TESTBAN
TESTEES
TESTERS
TESTIER
TESTIFY
TESTILY
TESTING
TESTOUT
VESPERS
VESPIDS
VESSELS
VESTEES
VESTIGE
VESTING
VESTURE
WESKITS
WESTEND
WESTERN
YESDEAR
YESHIVA
YESMAAM
YESSING
ZESTFUL
ZESTIER

•E•S•••

BEASTIE
BEASTLY
BEDSIDE
BEESWAX
BEGSOFF
BERSERK
CEASING
CELSIUS
CENSERS
CENSING
CENSORS
CENSURE
CESSION
DENSELY
DENSEST
DENSITY
DESSERT
EELSKIN
FEASTED
GEISHAS
GEMSBOK
GESSOES
GETSOFF
GETSOUT
GETSSET
GEYSERS
HEISTED
HEMSLEY
HERSELF
HERSHEY
HESSIAN
HEXSIGN
JERSEYS
JESSICA
JETSONS
KEESHAN
LEASERS
LEASHED
LEASHES
LEASING
LEISTER
LEISURE
LESSEES
LESSENS
LESSING
LESSONS
LESSORS
LETSFLY
LETSLIP
LETSOFF
LETSOUT
LETSSEE
MEASLES
MEASURE
MEISSEN
MESSAGE
MESSALA
MESSIAH
MESSIER
MESSILY
MESSINA
MESSING
MESSKIT
NELSONS
NETSUKE
NETSURF
NEWSBOY
NEWSDAY
NEWSIER
NEWSMAN
NEWSMEN
PEASANT
PEASOUP
PENSEES
PENSION
PENSIVE
PEPSINS
PERSEUS
PERSIAN
PERSIST
PERSIUS
PERSONA
PERSONS
REASONS
REDSKIN
REDSPOT
REDSTAR
REISSUE
RETSINA
SEASALT
SEASICK
SEASIDE
SEASLUG
SEASONS
SEASTAR
SEESAWS
SEESFIT
SEESOFF
SEESOUT
SEESRED
SEISMIC
SENSATE
SENSING
SENSORS
SENSORY
SENSUAL
SESSILE
SESSION
SETSAIL
SETSOFF
SETSOUT
TEASELS
TEASERS
TEASETS
TEASHOP
TEASING
TEESOFF
TELSTAR
TENSELY
TENSEST
TENSEUP
TENSILE
TENSING
TENSION
TENSIVE
TENSORS
TENSPOT
TERSELY
TERSEST
TESSERA
VERSIFY
VERSION
VESSELS
WEASELS
WEBSITE
WEBSTER
WETSUIT
YESSING

•E••S••

AEROSOL
BEADSUP
BEAMSUP
BEARSON
BEARSUP
BEATSIT
BEATSUP
BEEFSUP
BEHESTS
BELUSHI
BEMUSED
BEMUSES
BENISON
BENTSEN
BERGSON
BERNSEN
CELESTA
CELESTE
DEADSEA
DEADSET
DEALSIN
DEARSIR
DEBASED
DEBASES
DEBUSSY
DEEPSEA
DEEPSET
DEEPSIX
DEFUSED
DEFUSES
DEHISCE
DELISTS
DEMESNE
DEMISED
DEMISES
DEMPSEY
DEPOSAL
DEPOSED
DEPOSER
DEPOSES
DEPOSIT
DESISTS
DESKSET
DETESTS
DEVISED
DEVISES
FEEDSON
GEARSTO
GEARSUP
GENESEE
GENESES
GENESIS
GETSSET
HEADSET
HEADSIN
HEADSUP
HEARSAY
HEARSOF
HEATSUP
JEERSAT
KEEPSAT
KEEPSIN
KEEPSON
KEEPSTO
KEEPSUP
KENOSHA
LEADSIN
LEADSON
LEADSTO
LEADSUP
LEANSON
LEERSAT
LEGISTS
LETSSEE
MEDUSAE
MEDUSAS
MEIOSES
MEIOSIS
MEISSEN
MELISSA
MENISCI
NEMESES
NEMESIS
NEXUSES
PEARSON
PECKSAT
PEEKSAT
PEERSAT
PEERSIN
PEGASUS
PELISSE
PERKSUP
PERUSAL
PERUSED
PERUSER
PERUSES
READSIN
REARSUP
REBASTE
REBUSES
RECASTS
RECUSED
RECUSES
REELSIN
REFUSAL
REFUSED
REFUSER
REFUSES
REINSIN
REISSUE
RELISTS
REPASTE
REPASTS
REPOSED
REPOSES
RESISTS
RESTSUP
RETESTS
REVISED
REVISER
REVISES
REVISIT
SEALSUP
SEEPSIN
SENDSIN
SENDSUP
SEXISTS
TEAMSUP
TEARSAT
TEARSUP
TELLSON
TENDSTO
VENISON
WELLSET
WELLSUP
YELLSAT
YELTSIN

•E•••S•

AERIEST
BEARISH
BECAUSE
BEDPOST
BEDREST
BELFAST
BEQUEST
BERNESE
CELLIST
DEAFEST
DEAREST
DEBUSSY
DECLASS
DEEPEST
DEFENSE
DEFROST
DEFTEST
DEGAUSS
DELUISE
DENSEST
DENTIST
DEPRESS
DERVISH
DESPISE
EELIEST
EERIEST
GENOESE
GEODESY
GETLOST
HEIRESS
HELOISE
HEROISM
JETWASH
KEENEST
KEYWEST
LEANEST
LEFTIST
LEWDEST
MEANEST
MEEKEST
MELISSA
MELROSE
NEAREST
NEATEST
NEBBISH
NEWNESS
PECKISH
PEERESS
PEEVISH
PELISSE
PERSIST
PERTEST
PETTISH
REALISM
REALIST
REAMASS
RECHOSE
RECLUSE
RECROSS
REDDEST
REDDISH
REDNESS
REDRESS
REDROSE
REFRESH
REGRESS
RELAPSE
RELEASE
REMORSE
REPRESS
REPRISE
REPULSE
REQUEST
RERAISE
RERINSE
REVERSE
SEABASS
SEAMOSS
SEERESS
SELFISH
SEXIEST
TEAROSE
TEMPEST
TENSEST
TERSEST
VERBOSE
WEAKEST
WEAKISH
WETNESS
WETTEST

•E••••S

AEDILES
AERATES
AERIALS
AEROBES
BEACHES
BEACONS
BEADLES
BEAGLES
BEAKERS
BEANIES
BEARERS
BEATERS
BEATLES
BEAVERS
BECALMS
BECKONS
BECOMES
BEDAUBS
BEDBUGS
BEDECKS
BEECHES
BEEGEES
BEEPERS
BEETLES
BEFALLS
BEFOULS
BEGGARS
BEHAVES
BEHESTS
BEHOLDS
BELCHES
BELDAMS
BELIEFS
BELLIES
BELLOWS
BELONGS
BEMIRES
BEMOANS
BEMUSES
BENCHES
BENDERS
BENGALS
BENUMBS
BERATES
BERBERS
BERRIES
BESEEMS
BESIDES
BESTIRS
BESTOWS
BETAKES
BETHELS
BETIDES
BETIMES
BETRAYS
BETTERS
BETTORS
BEWAILS
BEZIERS
CELEBES
CELLARS
CELSIUS
CELTICS
CEMENTS
CENSERS
CENSORS
CENTERS
CENTRES
CEPHEUS
CEREALS
CERIPHS
DEACONS
DEADENS
DEAFENS
DEALERS
DEARTHS
DEBARKS
DEBASES
DEBATES
DEBEERS
DEBONES
DEBTORS
DEBUNKS
DECADES
DECAMPS
DECANTS
DECEITS
DECIDES
DECKLES
DECLASS
DECOCTS
DECODES
DECREES
DECRIES
DEDALUS
DEDUCES
DEDUCTS
DEEJAYS
DEEPENS
DEFACES
DEFAMES
DEFEATS
DEFECTS
DEFENDS
DEFILES
DEFINES
DEFORMS
DEFRAYS
DEFUSES
DEGAUSS
DEGREES
DEHORNS
DEICERS
DEIFIES
DEITIES
DEJECTS
DELETES
DELIBES
DELICTS
DELISTS
DELUDES
DELUGES
DELVERS
DEMANDS
DEMEANS
DEMISES
DEMOTES
DENIALS
DENIERS
DENOTES
DENUDES
DEODARS
DEPARTS
DEPENDS
DEPICTS
DEPLOYS
DEPONES
DEPORTS
DEPOSES
DEPRESS
DEPUTES
DERAILS
DERBIES
DERIDES
DERIVES
DESALTS
DESERTS
DESIGNS
DESIRES
DESISTS
DESOTOS
DESPOTS
DETAILS
DETAINS
DETECTS
DETESTS
DETOURS
DEVEINS
DEVICES
DEVIOUS
DEVISES
DEVOTES
DEVOURS
DEVRIES
DEWLAPS
FEARERS
FEDORAS
FEEDERS
FEELERS
FEELIES
FELINES
FELLERS
FELLOWS
FEMALES
FENCERS
FENDERS
FERRETS
FERRIES
FERROUS
FERULES
FERVORS
FESTERS
FETCHES
FETTERS
FETTLES
GECKOES
GEEGAWS
GEEZERS
GEISHAS
GELADAS
GELATIS
GENDERS
GENERIS
GENESES
GENESIS
GENGHIS
GENTLES
GEORGES
GERBILS
GERENTS
GERMANS
GERUNDS
GESSOES
GEWGAWS
GEYSERS
HEADERS
HEALERS
HEARERS
HEARTHS
HEATERS
HEAVENS
HEAVERS
HEAVIES
HEBREWS
HECKLES
HECTORS
HEDDLES
HEDGERS
HEEHAWS
HEELERS
HEGIRAS
HEIFERS
HEIGHTS
HEINOUS
HEIRESS
HELICES
HELIXES
HELLERS
HELMETS
HELPERS
HEMMERS
HENBITS
HEPCATS
HEPTADS
HERALDS
HERBALS
HERDERS
HERMITS
HEROICS
HETMANS
HEXNUTS
HEYDAYS
JEALOUS
JEEBIES
JEERERS
JEFFERS
JELLIES
JEMMIES
JENNETS
JENNIES
JERBOAS
JERKINS
JERSEYS
JESTERS
JESUITS
JETGUNS
JETSONS
JETTIES
KEENERS
KEEPERS
KEGLERS
KELPIES
KENNELS
KENYANS
KERNELS
KETCHES
KETONES
KETTLES
KEWPIES
KEYPADS
LEACHES
LEADERS
LEADINS
LEAGUES
LEAKERS
LEANERS
LEANTOS
LEAPERS
LEASERS
LEASHES
LEAVENS
LECTORS
LEDGERS
LEECHES
LEERERS
LEFTIES
LEGATES
LEGATOS
LEGENDS
LEGIONS
LEGISTS
LEGUMES
LENDERS
LENGTHS
LENTILS
LEPTONS
LESSEES
LESSENS
LESSONS
LESSORS
LETTERS
LETTRES
LEVIERS
LEVITES
MEADOWS
MEALIES
MEANIES
MEASLES
MEDDLES
MEDIANS
MEDICOS
MEDIUMS
MEDLEYS
MEDUSAS
MEGOHMS
MEGRIMS
MEIOSES
MEIOSIS
MELLOWS
MEMBERS
MEMOIRS
MEMPHIS
MENACES
MENAGES
MENDERS
MENHIRS
MENIALS
MENTORS
MERCIES
MERGERS
MERINOS
MERLOTS
MESCALS
METATES
METEORS
METHODS
METIERS
METRICS
METTLES
MEWLERS
NEATENS
NEBULAS
NECKERS
NECTARS
NEEDLES
NEGATES
NELSONS
NEMESES
NEMESIS
NEPALIS
NEPHEWS
NEREIDS
NERVOUS
NESTERS
NESTLES
NETTLES
NEURONS
NEWNESS
NEWTONS
NEXUSES
OEDIPUS
OEUVRES
PEACHES
PEAHENS
PEANUTS
PEAPODS
PEAVEYS
PEBBLES
PECTINS
PEDANTS
PEDDLES
PEDLARS
PEELERS
PEEPERS
PEEPLES
PEERESS
PEEWEES
PEGASUS
PEGTOPS
PELAGES
PELLETS

PELOTAS
PELTERS
PENATES
PENCILS
PENNERS
PENNIES
PENNONS
PENPALS
PENSEES
PENTADS
PENULTS
PEONIES
PEOPLES
PEPLUMS
PEPPERS
PEPSINS
PEQUOTS
PERCHES
PERHAPS
PERIODS
PERKINS
PERMITS
PERSEUS
PERSIUS
PERSONS
PERUKES
PERUSES
PESETAS
PESTERS
PESTLES
PETARDS
PETITES
PETRELS
PETROUS
PETTERS
REACHES
READERS
READIES
REAMASS
REAMERS
REAPERS
REARERS
REASONS
REBATES
REBINDS
REBOILS
REBOLTS
REBOOTS
REBOZOS
REBUFFS
REBUKES
REBUSES
RECALLS
RECANES
RECANTS
RECASTS
RECEDES
RECIPES
RECITES
RECKONS
RECODES
RECOILS
RECORDS
RECORKS
RECOUPS
RECROSS
RECTORS
RECUSES
REDACTS
REDANTS
REDATES
REDBUDS
REDCAPS

REDDENS
REDDOGS
REDEALS
REDEEMS
REDEYES
REDFINS
REDFIRS
REDGUMS
REDHATS
REDHOTS
REDIALS
REDNESS
REDOAKS
REDRAWS
REDRESS
REDTOPS
REDUCES
REEDITS
REEFERS
REFACES
REFILLS
REFILMS
REFINES
REFIRES
REFORMS
REFRIES
REFUELS
REFUGES
REFUNDS
REFUSES
REFUTES
REGAINS
REGALES
REGARDS
REGENTS
REGIMES
REGIONS
REGLUES
REGRESS
REGRETS
REGULUS
REHANGS
REHEALS
REHEARS
REHEATS
REHEELS
REHIRES
REHOOKS
REJECTS
REJOINS
RELACES
RELATES
RELAXES
RELENTS
RELICTS
RELIEFS
RELINES
RELISTS
RELIVES
RELOADS
RELOCKS
REMAILS
REMAINS
REMAKES
REMANDS
REMARKS
REMELTS
REMENDS
REMINDS
REMIXES
REMOLDS
REMORAS
REMOTES

REMOVES
REMUDAS
RENAILS
RENAMES
RENDERS
RENEGES
RENNINS
RENOTES
RENTALS
RENTERS
REOPENS
REPAIRS
REPASTS
REPAVES
REPEALS
REPEATS
REPENTS
REPINES
REPLANS
REPLAYS
REPLIES
REPOLLS
REPORTS
REPOSES
REPRESS
REPUGNS
REPUTES
RERATES
REREADS
REREDOS
RERENTS
RESALES
RESALTS
RESANDS
RESCUES
RESEALS
RESEATS
RESECTS
RESEEDS
RESELLS
RESENDS
RESENTS
RESHIPS
RESHOES
RESIDES
RESIGNS
RESILES
RESINGS
RESISTS
RESOLES
RESORBS
RESORTS
RESTERS
RESULTS
RESUMES
RETAILS
RETAINS
RETAKES
RETAPES
RETARDS
RETAXES
RETELLS
RETESTS
RETILES
RETIMES
RETINAS
RETIRES
RETOOLS
RETORTS
RETRIES
RETRIMS
RETUNES
RETURNS

RETYPES
REUBENS
REUTERS
REVAMPS
REVEALS
REVERBS
REVERES
REVERTS
REVIEWS
REVILES
REVISES
REVIVES
REVOKES
REVOLTS
REWARDS
REWARMS
REWAXES
REWELDS
REWINDS
REWIRES
REWORDS
REWORKS
REWRAPS
REXCATS
REZONES
SEABAGS
SEABASS
SEABEDS
SEABEES
SEACOWS
SEADOGS
SEAFANS
SEALABS
SEALEGS
SEALERS
SEAMOSS
SEANCES
SEASONS
SEATERS
SEAWAYS
SECANTS
SECEDES
SECONDS
SECRETS
SECTORS
SECURES
SEDUCES
SEEDERS
SEEKERS
SEERESS
SEESAWS
SEETHES
SEICHES
SEIDELS
SEINERS
SEIZERS
SELECTS
SELLERS
SEMITES
SENATES
SENDERS
SENDUPS
SENECAS
SENIORS
SENORAS
SENORES
SENSORS
SEPTETS
SEQUELS
SEQUINS
SERAPES
SERAPHS
SERAPIS

SERIALS
SERIOUS
SERMONS
SERVALS
SERVERS
SESAMES
SESTETS
SETTEES
SETTERS
SETTLES
SEXISTS
SEXTANS
SEXTETS
SEXTONS
TEABAGS
TEACHES
TEACUPS
TEAPOTS
TEAPOYS
TEARGAS
TEASELS
TEASERS
TEASETS
TECHIES
TEDDERS
TEDDIES
TEDIOUS
TEENERS
TEEPEES
TEETERS
TEETHES
TELEXES
TELLERS
TELLIES
TEMPERS
TEMPLES
TENACES
TENANTS
TENDERS
TENDONS
TENNERS
TENPINS
TENSORS
TENTERS
TENUOUS
TENURES
TERAPHS
TERCELS
TERCETS
TEREDOS
TERRETS
TERRIES
TERRORS
TESTEES
TESTERS
TETANUS
TETHERS
TETRADS
TEUTONS
VECTORS
VEEJAYS
VEGGIES
VEIGHTS
VELLUMS
VELOURS
VELVETS
VENDORS
VENEERS
VENTERS
VERBALS
VERGERS
VERVETS
VESPERS

VESPIDS
VESSELS
VESTEES
VETCHES
VETOERS
WEAKENS
WEAPONS
WEARERS
WEARIES
WEASELS
WEAVERS
WEDGIES
WEEDERS
WEENIES
WEEPERS
WEEVILS
WEIGHTS
WEIRDOS
WELCHES
WELDERS
WELKINS
WELTERS
WENCHES
WENDERS
WESKITS
WETBARS
WETHERS
WETMOPS
WETNESS
YELLOWS
YELPERS
YEMENIS
ZEALOTS
ZEALOUS
ZENANAS
ZENITHS
ZEPHYRS
ZEUGMAS

••ES•••

ACESOUT
AGESAGO
AWESOME
BEESWAX
BLESSED
BLESSES
BRESLIN
BRESSON
CAESARS
CAESURA
CHESTER
CRESSES
CRESTED
DIESELS
DIESOFF
DIESOUT
DOESKIN
DRESDEN
DRESSED
DRESSER
DRESSES
DRESSUP
EGESTED
EKESOUT
ETESIAN
EYESORE
FIESTAS
FLESHED
FLESHES
FRESCOS
FRESHEN
FRESHER
FRESHET
FRESHLY
GOESAPE
GOESBAD
GOESFOR
GOESOFF
GOESOUT
GUESSED
GUESSER
GUESSES
GUESTED
ICESHOW
KEESHAN
KMESONS
KNESSET
LIESLOW
LOESSER
LOESSES
MAESTRI
MAESTRO
OLESTRA
ONESELF
ONESHOT
ONESTEP
ORESTES
PRESAGE
PRESALE
PRESELL
PRESENT
PRESETS
PRESIDE
PRESLEY
PRESOAK
PRESORT
PRESSED
PRESSER
PRESSES
PRESSON
PRESTON
PRESTOS
PRESUME
QUESTED
SEESAWS
SEESFIT
SEESOFF
SEESOUT
SEESRED
SIESTAS
TEESOFF
THESEUS
THESPIS
TOESHOE
TRESSES
TRESTLE
TUESDAY
WRESTED
WRESTLE

••E•S••

AGEISTS
ASEPSIS
BEEFSUP
BLESSED
BLESSES
BREASTS
BRESSON
CHEESES
CHELSEA
CHEWSUP
CLEMSON
CREASED
CREASES
CREOSOL
CRESSES
DEEPSEA
DEEPSET
DEEPSIX
DREISER
DRESSED
DRESSER
DRESSES
DRESSUP
ELEISON
EMERSED
EMERSON
EVENSUP
FEEDSON
FLENSED
FLENSES
FREESIA
FRETSAW
GLEASON
GREASED
GREASER
GREASES
GUESSED
GUESSER
GUESSES
JEERSAT
KEEPSAT
KEEPSIN
KEEPSON
KEEPSTO
KEEPSUP
KNESSET
LEERSAT
LOESSER
LOESSES
NIELSEN
OPENSEA
OPENSUP
OVERSAW
OVERSEA
OVERSEE
PEEKSAT
PEERSAT
PEERSIN
PLEASED
PLEASER
PLEASES
PRESSED
PRESSER
PRESSES
PRESSON
PREYSON
REELSIN
SEEPSIN
SPENSER
STEPSIN
STEPSON
STEPSUP
STETSON
THEISTS
TREASON
TRESSES
TSETSES
UTENSIL
WOEISME

••E•S•

ACEROSE
AGELESS
AWELESS
BLEMISH
CHEMISE
CHEMIST
CHERISH
CLEANSE
COEXIST
DEEPEST
DUELIST
ELEGIST
EPEEIST
EVENEST
EVEREST
EYELASH
EYEWASH
FLEMISH
GREYEST
ICELESS
KEENEST
MAEWEST
MEEKEST
OBELISK
OLEMISS
ONENESS
OPEROSE
OVERUSE
PEERESS
PEEVISH
PIETISM
POETESS
PRECAST
PRECISE
PREMISE
PRETEST
PREWASH
SEERESS
SWEDISH
THERESA
TIELESS
TOELESS
USELESS

••E•••S

AGEISTS
AGELESS
AGENDAS
AMERCES
APERCUS
APERIES
AREOLAS
ASEPSIS
AVENGES
AVENUES
AWELESS
AYEAYES
BEECHES
BEEGEES
BEEPERS
BEETLES
BLESSES
BREASTS
BREATHS
BREEZES
BRETONS
BREVETS
BREWERS
CAESARS
CHEESES
CHEETOS
CHEQUES
CHERUBS
CHEVIES
CHEVRES
CHEWERS
CLEAVES
CLEMENS
CLERICS
COEDITS
COERCES
COEVALS
CREASES
CREATES
CRECHES
CREDITS
CRENELS
CREOLES
CRESSES
CRETANS
CRETINS
CREWELS
DEEJAYS
DEEPENS
DIESELS
DIETERS
DREDGES
DRESSES
DREYFUS
DUELERS
DUENNAS
ELEGIES
ELEVENS
EMERGES
ENEMIES
EVENKIS
EXEMPTS
EYECUPS
EYEFULS
EYELETS
EYELIDS
FEEDERS
FEELERS
FEELIES
FIESTAS
FLECHES
FLEDGES
FLEECES
FLENSES
FLESHES
FLEXORS
FREEZES
FRENUMS
FRESCOS
FUELERS
GEEGAWS
GEEZERS
GHETTOS
GREASES
GREAVES
GUELPHS
GUESSES
HEEHAWS
HEELERS
ICEAGES
ICEAXES
ICEBAGS
ICECAPS
ICELESS
IDEATES
JAEGERS
JEEBIES
JEERERS
KEENERS
KEEPERS
KMESONS
LAERTES
LEECHES
LEERERS
LIENEES
LIERNES
LOESSES
MAENADS
NEEDLES
NOETICS
OCEANUS
OCELOTS
OLEATES
OLEMISS
OMELETS
ONEIDAS
ONENESS
ONEROUS
OPENERS
ORESTES
PEELERS
PEEPERS
PEEPLES
PEERESS
PEEWEES
PHENOLS
PHENOMS
PIECERS
PIEPANS
PIERCES
PIETIES
PIETINS
PLEASES
PLEDGES
PLENUMS
PLEXORS
POETESS
POETICS
PREAMPS
PREFABS
PREFERS
PRELIMS
PREMEDS
PREPAYS
PRESETS
PRESSES
PRESTOS
PUEBLOS
PYEDOGS
QUERIES
QUEUERS
REEDITS
REEFERS
RHETORS
SEEDERS
SEEKERS
SEERESS
SEESAWS
SEETHES
SHEATHS
SHEAVES
SHEIKHS
SHEILAS
SHEKELS
SHELVES
SHERPAS
SIENNAS
SIERRAS
SIESTAS
SKEWERS
SLEDGES
SLEEVES
SLEIGHS
SLEUTHS
SNEEZES
SPECIES
STEPINS
STEPPES
STEPUPS
STEREOS
STEROLS
STEVENS
STEWERS
SWERVES
TEENERS
TEEPEES
TEETERS
TEETHES
THEISTS
THERMOS
THESEUS
THESPIS
TIEDYES
TIELESS
TIEPINS
TIERODS
TOECAPS
TOELESS
TOETAPS
TREBLES
TRELLIS
TREMORS
TREPANS
TRESSES
TSETSES
TWEEZES
TWELVES
USELESS
VEEJAYS
VIEWERS
WEEDERS
WEENIES
WEEPERS
WEEVILS
WHEEZES
WHEREAS
WIENERS
WIENIES
WREATHS

•••ES••

ACHESON
AMNESIA
AMNESTY
ANTESUP
APHESES
ARRESTS
ATTESTS
BEHESTS
BLUESKY
BONESUP
BOXESIN
BOXESUP
CAVESIN
CELESTA
CELESTE
CHEESES
CLUESIN
COMESAT
COMESBY
COMESIN
COMESON
COMESTO
COMESUP
CROESUS
DARESAY
DARESTO
DEMESNE
DETESTS
DIGESTS
DINESEN
DINESIN
DINESON
DIVESIN
DIVESTS
DOTESON
DRIESUP
EASESIN
EASESUP
EDGESIN
ERNESTO
FADESIN
FINESSE
FIRESUP
FIXESUP
FLIESAT
FLIESIN
FORESAW
FORESEE
FORESTS
FREESIA
GENESEE
GENESES
GENESIS
GIVESIN
GIVESTO
GIVESUP
HIRESON
HOLESUP
HONESTY
ILIESCU
INFESTS
INGESTS
INVESTS
IONESCO
IQTESTS
JAMESON
LACESUP
LINESUP
LIVESIN
LIVESON
LOSESIT
MAJESTE
MAJESTY
MAKESDO
MAKESIT
MAKESUP
MIMESIS
MIXESUP
MODESTO
MODESTY
MOLESTS
MORESBY
MOVESIN
MUMESON
NEMESES
NEMESIS
PILESIN
PILESON
PILESUP
PIMESON
PINESAP
PIPESUP
POKESAT
PRIESTS
RAKESIN
RAKESUP
RAMESES
RETESTS
ROBESON
ROPESIN
RULESON
SAVESUP
SILESIA
SIZESUP
SPIESON
TAKESIN

TAKESON
TAKESTO
TAKESUP
TIMESUP
TONESUP
TRIESON
TRIESTE
TUNESIN
TUNESUP
TYPESET
TYPESUP
VANESSA
VOTESIN
WADESIN
WAKESUP
WAVESIN
WINESAP
WIPESUP
WISESUP

•••E•S•

ABREAST
ADVERSE
AMHERST
APPEASE
ASPERSE
ATHEISM
ATHEIST
ATLEAST
BONEASH
DEFENSE
DISEASE
DIVERSE
DRSEUSS
EPEEIST
EXPENSE
FAREAST
FINESSE
IMMENSE
IMMERSE
INCENSE
INTENSE
INTERSE
INVERSE
LICENSE
MIDEAST
OBVERSE
OFFENSE
OGREISH
RELEASE
REVERSE
UNLEASH
VANESSA

•••E••S

ABSENTS
ACCEDES
ACCENTS
ACCEPTS
ACHENES
ADDENDS
ADHERES
ADVENTS
ADVERBS
ADVERTS
AFFECTS
AFREETS
ALBEDOS
ALKENES
ALLEARS
ALLEGES
ALLELES
ALLEYES
AMOEBAS
AMPERES
ANDEANS
ANGELES
ANGELUS
ANNEALS
ANNEXES
APHESES
APPEALS
APPEARS
APPENDS
AQUEOUS
ARREARS
ARRESTS
ARTEMIS
ARTEMUS
ASCENDS
ASCENTS
ASPECTS
ASSENTS
ASSERTS
ATTENDS
ATTESTS
AUGENDS
AUTEURS
BADEGGS
BALEENS
BARENTS
BEDECKS
BEHESTS
BESEEMS
BIGEYES
BIREMES
BISECTS
BODEGAS
BOLEROS
BREEZES
BUREAUS
CALENDS
CAMERAS
CAREENS
CAREERS
CASERNS
CAVEATS
CAVEINS
CAVERNS
CELEBES
CEMENTS
CEREALS
CHEESES
CHEETOS
CINEMAS
CLIENTS
COHEIRS
COHERES
COMEONS
CROESUS
CSLEWIS
DEBEERS
DECEITS
DEFEATS
DEFECTS
DEFENDS
DEJECTS
DELETES
DEMEANS
DEPENDS
DESERTS
DETECTS
DETESTS
DEVEINS
DIGESTS
DIRECTS
DIVERTS
DIVESTS
DOCENTS
DOGEARS
DRSEUSS
DUTEOUS
EFFECTS
ENDEARS
ENNEADS
ESSENES
ESTEEMS
EXCEEDS
EXCEPTS
EXPECTS
EXPENDS
EXPERTS
EXTENDS
EXTENTS
FADEINS
FAGENDS
FLEECES
FOMENTS
FORESTS
FREEZES
FRIENDS
FRIEZES
GAMETES
GASEOUS
GAZEBOS
GENERIS
GENESES
GENESIS
GERENTS
GIDEONS
GIVEUPS
GOVERNS
GRIEVES
HGWELLS
HIDEOUS
HOWELLS
HUMERUS
IGNEOUS
IMPEDES
IMPENDS
IMPETUS
INCEPTS
INDENTS
INDEXES
INFECTS
INFESTS
INGESTS
INHERES
INJECTS
INSEAMS
INSECTS
INSERTS
INTENDS
INTENTS
INTERNS
INVENTS
INVERTS
INVESTS
IQTESTS
KOPECKS
KOREANS
LAMENTS
LATEENS
LATENTS
LATEXES
LEGENDS
LINEUPS
LOVEINS
LYCEUMS
MAKEUPS
MANEGES
METEORS
MIMESIS
MODELAS
MODELTS
MODERNS
MOLESTS
MOMENTS
MUDEELS
MULETAS
MUSEUMS
NEMESES
NEMESIS
NEREIDS
NOVENAS
OBJECTS
OBVERTS
OFFENDS
ORDEALS
ORIENTS
ORLEANS
OUTEATS
PARENTS
PATENTS
PESETAS
PHOEBES
PHOEBUS
PIGEONS
PILEUPS
PITEOUS
POMELOS
POSEURS
PRIESTS
RACEMES
RAMESES
RAREGAS
RECEDES
REDEALS
REDEEMS
REDEYES
REGENTS
REHEALS
REHEARS
REHEATS
REHEELS
REJECTS
RELENTS
REMELTS
REMENDS
RENEGES
REPEALS
REPEATS
REPENTS
REREADS
REREDOS
RERENTS
RESEALS
RESEATS
RESECTS
RESEEDS
RESELLS
RESENDS
RESENTS
RETELLS
RETESTS
REVEALS
REVERBS
REVERES
REVERTS
REWELDS
RIBEYES
ROBERTS
RODENTS
SCHEMAS
SCHEMES
SCLERAS
SCREAKS
SCREAMS
SCREEDS
SCREENS
SECEDES
SELECTS
SENECAS
SHIELDS
SILENTS
SLEEVES
SNEEZES
SPHERES
SPLEENS
SPREADS
SQUEAKS
SQUEALS
STDENIS
STREAKS
STREAMS
STREETS
TAGENDS
TALENTS
TAVERNS
TELEXES
TEREDOS
THIEVES
THREADS
THREATS
THREERS
TIMEWAS
TINEARS
TOREROS
TUNEUPS
TUPELOS
TUREENS
TUXEDOS
TWEEZES
UNBENDS
UNREELS
UNSEALS
UNSEATS
UNVEILS
UPBEATS
URTEXTS
VENEERS
VOTECHS
WHEEZES
WYVERNS
YEMENIS
ZAREBAS

••••ES•

ACHIEST
ACTRESS
ADDRESS
AERIEST
AGELESS
AGGRESS
AIMLESS
AIRIEST
AIRLESS
AMPLEST
ANAPEST
ANDRESS
APTNESS
ARIDEST
ARMLESS
ARMREST
ARTIEST
ARTLESS
ASHIEST
ASHLESS
AWELESS
BADNESS
BALDEST
BEDREST
BEQUEST
BERNESE
BIGGEST
BIGNESS
BOLDEST
BONIEST
BRAVEST
BURGESS
BURMESE
BUSIEST
CAGIEST
CALMEST
CAPLESS
CARLESS
CHINESE
CLOSEST
COLDEST
CONFESS
CONGEST
CONTEST
COOLEST
COYNESS
COZIEST
CRUDEST
CURTEST
CYPRESS
DAFTEST
DAMPEST
DANKEST
DARKEST
DEAFEST
DEAREST
DEEPEST
DEFTEST
DENSEST
DEPRESS
DICIEST
DIGRESS
DIMMEST
DIMNESS
DIOCESE
DOPIEST
DOUREST
DRYNESS
DUCHESS
DULLEST
DUMBEST
EARNEST
EASIEST
EDGIEST
EELIEST
EERIEST
EMPRESS
ENDLESS
EVENEST
EVEREST
EVILEST
EXPRESS
FAIREST
FALSEST
FARWEST
FASTEST
FATLESS
FATNESS
FATTEST
FIRMEST
FITNESS
FITTEST
FONDEST
FORREST
FOULEST
FOXIEST
FULLEST
FUNFEST
GABFEST
GAMIEST
GENOESE
GEODESY
GODDESS
GOOIEST
GORIEST
GRAVEST
GRAYEST
GREYEST
GUTLESS
HAPLESS
HARDEST
HARNESS
HARVEST
HATLESS
HAZIEST
HEIRESS
HIGHEST
HIPNESS
HIPPEST
HITLESS
HOLIEST
HOMIEST
HOSTESS
HOTNESS
HOTTEST
ICELESS
ICINESS
ICKIEST
IFFIEST
ILLNESS
IMPRESS
INAMESS
INANEST
INGRESS
INQUEST
IPCRESS
IRATEST
JAGLESS
JOYLESS
KEENEST
KEYWEST
KINDEST
LACIEST
LANKEST
LARGESS
LARGEST
LAWLESS
LAXNESS
LAZIEST
LEANEST
LEWDEST
LIDLESS
LIMIEST
LIMPEST
LIONESS
LITHEST
LOGIEST
LONGEST
LOOSEST
LOUDEST
LOWNESS
LUSHEST
MADDEST
MADNESS
MAEWEST
MALTESE
MEANEST
MEEKEST
MIDWEST
MILDEST
NEAREST
NEATEST
NEWNESS
NIGHEST
NOBLEST
NOSIEST
NUMBEST
OARLESS
ODDNESS
OILIEST
OLDNESS
OLDWEST
ONENESS
OPPRESS
PATNESS
PEERESS
PERTEST
PINIEST
PINKEST
PINLESS
POETESS
POKIEST
POOREST
POSHEST
POSSESS
PRETEST
PROCESS
PROFESS
PROTEST
PROWESS
PUNIEST
RACIEST
RANKEST
RASHEST
RAWNESS
REDDEST
REDNESS
REDRESS
REFRESH
REGRESS
REPRESS
REQUEST
RICHEST
SADDEST
SADNESS
SEERESS
SEXIEST
SHYNESS
SIAMESE
SICKEST
SLOWEST
SLYNESS
SNIDEST
SOFTEST
SOONEST
SOUREST
SPAREST
SPRIEST
SPRYEST
STALEST
SUAVEST
SUCCESS
SUGGEST
SUNLESS
TALLEST
TANNEST
TARTEST
TAUTEST
TEMPEST
TENSEST
TERSEST
THERESA
TIDIEST
TIELESS
TIGRESS
TINIEST
TOELESS
TONIEST
TRITEST
UGLIEST
UNBLEST
UNDRESS
USELESS
VAGUEST
VAINEST
VASTEST
WARIEST
WARMEST
WAVIEST
WAXIEST
WEAKEST
WETNESS
WETTEST
WHITEST
WILDEST
WILIEST
WIRIEST
WITLESS
WITNESS
WRYNESS
ZANIEST

••••E•S

ABUSERS
ACTRESS
ADDRESS
ADORERS
AFREETS
AGELESS
AGGRESS
AIGRETS
AIMLESS
AIRLESS
ALGIERS
AMADEUS
AMBLERS
AMULETS
ANADEMS
ANDREAS
ANDRESS
ANDREWS
ANGLERS
ANKLETS
ANSWERS
ANTAEUS
ANTHEMS
ANTHERS
ANTLERS
APOGEES
APTNESS
ARCHERS
ARGUERS
ARMLESS
ARMLETS
ARTLESS
ASHLESS
AUKLETS
AVOCETS
AVOWERS
AWAKENS
AWELESS
AZALEAS
BACKERS
BADGERS
BADNESS
BAGGERS
BAILEES
BAILERS
BAILEYS
BALEENS
BALLETS
BANKERS
BANNERS
BANTERS
BARBELS
BARBERS
BARKERS
BARLEYS
BARNEYS
BARRELS
BARRENS
BARTERS
BASKETS
BASSETS
BASTERS
BATHERS
BATTENS
BATTERS
BAWLERS
BEAKERS
BEARERS
BEATERS
BEAVERS
BEEGEES
BEEPERS
BELIEFS
BENDERS
BERBERS
BESEEMS
BETHELS
BETTERS
BEZIERS
BICKERS
BIDDERS
BIGGERS
BIGNESS
BILLETS
BINDERS
BIRDERS
BITTERS
BLAZERS
BLOWERS
BOATERS
BOBBERS
BOILERS
BOMBERS
BONKERS
BONNETS
BOOMERS
BOOTEES
BOPPERS
BORDERS
BOSKETS
BOTHERS
BOWLERS
BOWYERS
BRACERS
BRAYERS
BREVETS
BREWERS
BROKERS
BRUNETS
BUCKETS
BUDGETS
BUFFERS
BUFFETS
BUGLERS
BULLETS
BUMMERS
BUMPERS
BUNGEES
BUNKERS
BURDENS
BURGEES
BURGERS
BURGESS
BURNERS
BUSHELS
BUTLERS
BUTTERS
BUZZERS
CABLERS
CACHETS
CADGERS
CAHIERS
CALLERS
CAMBERS
CAMPERS
CANCELS
CANKERS
CANNERS
CANTERS
CAPLESS
CAPLETS
CAPPERS
CARDERS
CAREENS
CAREERS
CARLESS
CARNETS
CARPERS
CARPETS
CARRELS
CARTELS
CARTERS
CARVERS
CASHEWS
CASTERS
CENSERS
CENTERS
CEPHEUS
CHALETS
CHAPELS
CHASERS
CHEWERS
CHISELS
CHOKERS
CINDERS
CIPHERS
CLARETS
CLAWERS
CLEMENS
CLORETS
CLOSETS
CLOVERS
COALERS
COAXERS
COBWEBS
CODGERS
COFFEES
COFFERS
COINERS
COLLETS
COMBERS
COMPELS
CONFERS
CONFESS
CONGERS
CONKERS
CONVEYS
COOKERS
COOLERS
COOPERS
COPIERS
COPPERS
COPTERS
CORBELS
CORKERS
CORNEAS
CORNERS
CORNETS
CORSETS
COSSETS
COTTERS
COULEES
COWPEAS
COYNESS
COZZENS
CRATERS
CRAVENS
CRAVERS
CRENELS
CREWELS
CROWERS
CUDGELS
CURFEWS
CURLERS
CURLEWS
CURVETS
CUTLERS
CUTLETS
CUTTERS
CYCLERS
CYGNETS
CYPHERS
CYPRESS
DAGGERS
DAMPENS
DAMPERS
DAMSELS
DANCERS
DANDERS
DANGERS
DANIELS
DARKENS
DARNERS
DARTERS
DASHERS
DAUBERS
DAYBEDS
DEADENS
DEAFENS
DEALERS
DEBEERS
DECREES
DEEPENS
DEGREES
DEICERS
DELVERS
DENIERS
DEPRESS
DIADEMS
DIALERS
DIAPERS
DICKENS
DICKERS
DICKEYS
DIESELS
DIETERS
DIFFERS
DIGGERS
DIGRESS
DIMMERS
DIMNESS
DINNERS
DIPPERS
DISPELS
DITHERS
DOCKERS
DOCKETS
DODDERS
DODGERS
DOGLEGS
DOLMENS
DONKEYS
DORMERS
DOSSERS
DOWNERS
DOWSERS
DRAPERS
DRAWERS
DRIVELS
DRIVERS
DRONERS
DROVERS
DRYNESS
DUBBERS
DUCHESS
DUELERS
DUFFELS
DUFFERS
DUNKERS
DUSTERS
EAGLETS
EARNERS
EASTERS
ELATERS
ELEVENS
ELOPERS
ELYSEES
EMBLEMS
EMOTERS
EMPRESS
ENAMELS
ENDLESS
ENTREES
ERASERS
ESCHEWS
ESTEEMS
ETCHERS
EVADERS
EVOKERS
EXCEEDS
EXPRESS
EYELETS
FALTERS
FANJETS
FARMERS
FASTENS
FATHERS
FATLESS
FATNESS
FATTENS
FAUCETS
FAWNERS
FEARERS
FEEDERS
FEELERS
FELLERS
FENCERS
FENDERS

FERRETS
FESTERS
FETTERS
FIBBERS
FIDGETS
FILLERS
FILLETS
FILTERS
FINDERS
FINGERS
FISHERS
FITNESS
FITTERS
FLAKERS
FLORETS
FLOWERS
FLYNETS
FODDERS
FOGGERS
FOLDERS
FOLGERS
FOOTERS
FORCEPS
FORCERS
FORGERS
FORGETS
FORKERS
FOSTERS
FOWLERS
FUELERS
FUNNELS
GABBERS
GADGETS
GAFFERS
GAINERS
GAITERS
GALLEYS
GANDERS
GANNETS
GARDENS
GARNERS
GARNETS
GARRETS
GARTERS
GASJETS
GASKETS
GASSERS
GATHERS
GAUDENS
GAUGERS
GAWKERS
GEEZERS
GENDERS
GEYSERS
GIBBERS
GIBBETS
GIBLETS
GILDERS
GIMLETS
GINGERS
GIRDERS
GLAZERS
GLIDERS
GLOWERS
GNAWERS
GOATEES
GOBLETS
GODDESS
GOLFERS
GOMPERS
GOOBERS
GOPHERS
GORGETS

GOSPELS
GOUGERS
GRADERS
GRATERS
GRAVELS
GRAZERS
GRIPERS
GRIVETS
GROCERS
GROVELS
GROWERS
GUINEAS
GULLETS
GUNNELS
GUNNERS
GURNEYS
GUSHERS
GUSSETS
GUTLESS
GUTTERS
GYPPERS
HACKERS
HALTERS
HAMLETS
HAMMERS
HAMPERS
HANGERS
HANKERS
HAPLESS
HAPPENS
HARDENS
HARKENS
HARNESS
HARPERS
HASTENS
HATLESS
HATTERS
HAULERS
HAWKERS
HAWSERS
HEADERS
HEALERS
HEARERS
HEATERS
HEAVENS
HEAVERS
HEBREWS
HEDGERS
HEELERS
HEIFERS
HEIRESS
HELLERS
HELMETS
HELPERS
HEMMERS
HERDERS
HINDERS
HIPNESS
HISSERS
HITLESS
HITTERS
HOAXERS
HOLDERS
HOLLERS
HONKERS
HOOFERS
HOOTERS
HOPPERS
HORNETS
HOSIERS
HOSTELS
HOSTESS
HOTBEDS

HOTNESS
HOWLERS
HOYDENS
HUGGERS
HULLERS
HUMMERS
HUNGERS
HUNKERS
HUNTERS
HURLERS
HUSKERS
HYPHENS
ICELESS
ICINESS
ILLNESS
IMAGERS
IMARETS
IMPRESS
INAMESS
INGRESS
INSTEPS
IPCRESS
IRONERS
ISOHELS
ISOMERS
ISSUERS
JABBERS
JACKETS
JAEGERS
JAGLESS
JAILERS
JAMMERS
JASPERS
JAYCEES
JAYVEES
JEERERS
JEFFERS
JENNETS
JERSEYS
JESTERS
JIGGERS
JITNEYS
JITTERS
JOBBERS
JOCKEYS
JOGGERS
JOINERS
JOYLESS
JUDDERS
JUICERS
JUMPERS
JUNKERS
JUNKETS
KAISERS
KEENERS
KEEPERS
KEGLERS
KENNELS
KERNELS
KICKERS
KIDDERS
KIDNEYS
KILLERS
KIPPERS
KISSERS
KITTENS
KOSHERS
KRATERS
LAAGERS
LABRETS
LACKEYS
LADDERS
LADLERS

LAGGERS
LANCERS
LANCETS
LANDERS
LAPPETS
LARDERS
LARGESS
LASHERS
LATEENS
LATHERS
LATTENS
LAURELS
LAWLESS
LAWYERS
LAXNESS
LEADERS
LEAKERS
LEANERS
LEAPERS
LEASERS
LEAVENS
LEDGERS
LEERERS
LENDERS
LESSEES
LESSENS
LETTERS
LEVIERS
LIBBERS
LICHENS
LIDLESS
LIENEES
LIFTERS
LIMBERS
LIMNERS
LIMPETS
LINDENS
LINGERS
LINKERS
LINNETS
LINTELS
LIONESS
LIONETS
LISTEES
LISTELS
LISTENS
LITTERS
LOADERS
LOAFERS
LOANERS
LOBBERS
LOCKERS
LOCKETS
LODGERS
LOGGERS
LOITERS
LOOKERS
LOOPERS
LOOSENS
LOOTERS
LOPPERS
LOUVERS
LOWNESS
LUBBERS
LUGGERS
LUMBERS
LUMPERS
LUNKERS
LUSTERS
MADDENS
MADDERS
MADNESS
MAGNETS

MAGUEYS
MAIDENS
MAILERS
MALLETS
MALTEDS
MANGERS
MANNERS
MANTELS
MAPPERS
MARCELS
MARKERS
MARKETS
MARTENS
MARVELS
MASHERS
MASKERS
MASTERS
MATHERS
MATHEWS
MATTERS
MAYHEMS
MEDLEYS
MEMBERS
MENDERS
MERGERS
METIERS
MEWLERS
MIDDENS
MIDGETS
MILDEWS
MILIEUS
MILKERS
MILLERS
MILLETS
MINCERS
MINDERS
MINTERS
MINUETS
MISTERS
MITTENS
MIZZENS
MOANERS
MOCKERS
MOILERS
MOLDERS
MOLTERS
MONGERS
MONKEES
MONKEYS
MOPPERS
MOPPETS
MORSELS
MOSLEMS
MOTHERS
MOUSERS
MUDDERS
MUDEELS
MUDHENS
MUGGERS
MULLERS
MULLETS
MUMMERS
MUPPETS
MURDERS
MUSHERS
MUSKETS
MUSSELS
MUSTERS
MUTTERS
NABBERS
NAILERS
NAPPERS
NATTERS

NEATENS
NECKERS
NEPHEWS
NESTERS
NEWNESS
NICKELS
NICKERS
NIPPERS
NODDERS
NOSHERS
NUCLEUS
NUDGERS
NUGGETS
NUMBERS
NURSERS
NUTLETS
NUTMEGS
NUTTERS
OARLESS
ODDNESS
OFFSETS
OLDNESS
OLDNEWS
OMELETS
ONAGERS
ONENESS
OPENERS
OPINERS
OPPRESS
ORPHEUS
OSPREYS
OSTLERS
OUSTERS
OUTLETS
OUTSETS
OYSTERS
PACKERS
PACKETS
PADDERS
PALLETS
PALTERS
PAMPERS
PANDERS
PANNERS
PANZERS
PARCELS
PARGETS
PARLEYS
PARSECS
PARSEES
PARSERS
PASSELS
PASSERS
PASTELS
PATNESS
PATTENS
PATTERS
PAUPERS
PAWNEES
PAWNERS
PEAHENS
PEAVEYS
PEELERS
PEEPERS
PEERESS
PEEWEES
PELLETS
PELTERS
PENNERS
PENSEES
PEPPERS
PERSEUS
PESTERS

PETRELS
PETTERS
PHASERS
PHINEAS
PICKENS
PICKERS
PICKETS
PIECERS
PIGLETS
PIGPENS
PILFERS
PINCERS
PINLESS
PINNERS
PIOLETS
PIRAEUS
PITTERS
PLACERS
PLANERS
PLANETS
PLATENS
PLATERS
PLAYERS
PLOVERS
PLOWERS
POCKETS
POETESS
POLDERS
POLLENS
POLLERS
POMMELS
PONDERS
POPPERS
POPPETS
PORKERS
PORTERS
POSSESS
POSSETS
POSTERS
POTHERS
POTTERS
POURERS
POUTERS
POWDERS
PRATERS
PRAYERS
PREFERS
PREMEDS
PRESETS
PRICERS
PRIMERS
PRIVETS
PROBERS
PROCESS
PROFESS
PROPELS
PROSERS
PROTEUS
PROVERS
PROWESS
PRUNERS
PUCKERS
PUFFERS
PUGREES
PULLETS
PULLEYS
PUMMELS
PUMPERS
PUNTERS
PUPPETS
PURRERS
PURSERS
PURVEYS

PUTTEES
PUTTERS
QUAKERS
QUAVERS
QUEUERS
QUIVERS
QUOTERS
RABBETS
RACKETS
RAFTERS
RAIDERS
RAILERS
RAISERS
RAMJETS
RANGERS
RANKERS
RANTERS
RAPIERS
RAPPELS
RAPPERS
RASHERS
RASPERS
RASTERS
RATTERS
RAWNESS
READERS
REAMERS
REAPERS
REARERS
REDDENS
REDEEMS
REDNESS
REDRESS
REEFERS
REFUELS
REGRESS
REGRETS
REHEELS
RELIEFS
RENDERS
RENTERS
REOPENS
REPRESS
RESEEDS
RESTERS
REUBENS
REUTERS
REVIEWS
RHYMERS
RICKEYS
RIFLERS
RIGGERS
RILLETS
RINGERS
RIOTERS
RIPPERS
RISKERS
ROAMERS
ROARERS
ROBBERS
ROCKERS
ROCKETS
RODGERS
ROLLERS
ROMNEYS
ROMPERS
RONDELS
ROOFERS
ROOMERS
ROOTERS
ROSTERS
ROTTERS
ROUTERS

RUBBERS
RUDDERS
RUINERS
RUNLETS
RUNNELS
RUNNERS
RUSHEES
RUSHERS
RUSSETS
RUTGERS
SACHEMS
SACHETS
SACKERS
SADDENS
SADNESS
SALTERS
SALVERS
SANDERS
SAPIENS
SAPPERS
SASSERS
SAUCERS
SAWYERS
SCALERS
SCARERS
SCHLEPS
SCORERS
SCOTERS
SCREEDS
SCREENS
SEABEDS
SEABEES
SEALEGS
SEALERS
SEATERS
SECRETS
SEEDERS
SEEKERS
SEERESS
SEIDELS
SEINERS
SEIZERS
SELLERS
SENDERS
SEPTETS
SEQUELS
SERVERS
SESTETS
SETTEES
SETTERS
SEXTETS
SHAKERS
SHAPERS
SHARERS
SHAVERS
SHEKELS
SHINERS
SHIVERS
SHOVELS
SHOVERS
SHOWERS
SHRIEKS
SHYNESS
SICKENS
SIFTERS
SIGHERS
SIGNEES
SIGNERS
SIGNETS
SILVERS
SIMMERS
SIMPERS
SINGERS

SINKERS
SINNERS
SIPPERS
SIPPETS
SISTERS
SITTERS
SKATERS
SKEWERS
SKIVERS
SLAVERS
SLAYERS
SLICERS
SLIDERS
SLIVERS
SLOVENS
SLYNESS
SMILERS
SMOKERS
SNIVELS
SNORERS
SOAKERS
SOAPERS
SOARERS
SOBBERS
SOCKETS
SOFTENS
SOIREES
SOLDERS
SOLVERS
SONNETS
SOONERS
SORBETS
SORRELS
SORTERS
SOVIETS
SPACERS
SPADERS
SPIDERS
SPIKERS
SPINELS
SPINETS
SPIREAS
SPLEENS
STAGERS
STAMENS
STARERS
STARETS
STEREOS
STEVENS
STEWERS
STOKERS
STONERS
STORERS
STOREYS
STREETS
STYLERS
STYLETS
SUBDEBS
SUBLETS
SUBSETS
SUCCESS
SUCKERS
SUFFERS
SULKERS
SUMMERS
SUNDERS
SUNDEWS
SUNLESS
SUNSETS
SUPPERS
SURFERS
SURREYS
SURVEYS

SUTLERS
SWAYERS
SWIPERS
SWIVELS
SYSTEMS
TABLETS
TACKERS
TALKERS
TAMPERS
TANDEMS
TANKERS
TANNERS
TAPPERS
TAPPETS
TARGETS
TASSELS
TASTERS
TATTERS
TAUTENS
TEASELS
TEASERS
TEASETS
TEDDERS
TEENERS
TEEPEES
TEETERS
TELLERS
TEMPERS
TENDERS
TENNERS
TENTERS
TERCELS
TERCETS
TERRETS
TESTEES
TESTERS
TETHERS
THALERS
THESEUS
THREERS
TICKERS
TICKETS
TIELESS
TIGRESS
TILLERS
TILTERS
TIMBERS
TINDERS
TINKERS
TINNERS
TINSELS
TINTERS
TIPPERS
TIPPETS
TITHERS
TITTERS
TOELESS
TOFFEES
TOILERS
TOILETS
TOLTECS
TOOTERS
TOPPERS
TOSSERS
TOTTERS
TOUPEES
TOURERS
TOUTERS
TOWHEES
TOWNERS
TRACERS
TRADERS
TRAVELS

TRAVERS
TRICEPS
TRIVETS
TROWELS
TROWERS
TUAREGS
TUCKERS
TUFFETS
TUGGERS
TUNNELS
TUREENS
TURKEYS
TURNERS
TURRETS
TUSKERS
TWOFERS
ULSTERS
UNDRESS
UNITERS
UNREELS
USELESS
USOPENS
USURERS
VALLEYS
VAMPERS
VARLETS
VELVETS
VENEERS
VENTERS
VERGERS
VERVETS
VESPERS
VESSELS
VESTEES
VETOERS
VIEWERS
VIOLETS
VIZIERS
VOLLEYS
WAILERS
WAITERS
WAIVERS
WALKERS
WALLETS
WALTERS
WANDERS
WARDENS
WARDERS
WARRENS
WASHERS
WASTERS
WEAKENS
WEARERS
WEASELS
WEAVERS
WEEDERS
WEEPERS
WELDERS
WELTERS
WENDERS
WETHERS
WETNESS
WHALERS
WHEREAS
WHINERS
WHITENS
WICKERS
WICKETS
WIDGETS
WIENERS
WIGLETS
WINCERS
WINDERS

WINGERS
WINKERS
WINNERS
WINTERS
WISHERS
WITHERS
WITLESS
WITNESS
WONDERS
WOOFERS
WOOLENS
WORKERS
WORSENS
WRITERS
WRYNESS
YAKKERS
YAMMERS
YANKEES
YAPPERS
YAWNERS
YAWPERS
YELPERS
YONKERS
YOWLERS
ZANDERS
ZAPPERS
ZINGERS
ZIPPERS
ZITHERS
ZONKERS

•••••ES

ABASHES
ABJURES
ABLATES
ABRADES
ABYSSES
ACCEDES
ACCRUES
ACCUSES
ACHATES
ACHENES
ACTIVES
ADDUCES
ADHERES
ADJURES
ADMIRES
ADMIXES
ADVISES
AEDILES
AERATES
AEROBES
AFFINES
AFFIXES
AFRAMES
AGNATES
AITCHES
ALCOVES
ALIASES
ALKENES
ALLEGES
ALLELES
ALLEYES
ALLUDES
ALLURES
AMASSES
AMBRIES
AMERCES
AMPERES
AMPULES
ANGELES
ANNEXES
ANTARES

ANTIBES	BILLIES	CANDIES	CROSSES	DIVIDES	EXPIRES	GEORGES	HURDLES	JUJUBES	MANGOES	NOODLES	PIERCES	RATITES
APACHES	BINGOES	CANDLES	CRUISES	DIVINES	EXPOSES	GESSOES	HURRIES	JUMBLES	MANTLES	NOTATES	PIETIES	RATTLES
APERIES	BIRCHES	CANINES	CRUSHES	DIVVIES	EXWIVES	GIBLUES	HURTLES	JUNCOES	MARBLES	NOTCHES	PIFFLES	RAVAGES
APHESES	BIRDIES	CANTLES	CUBBIES	DIZZIES	FABARES	GIGGLES	HUSKIES	JUNGLES	MARCHES	NOTICES	PIGGIES	RAVINES
APOGEES	BIREMES	CARAFES	CUDDLES	DOGGIES	FACADES	GILLIES	HUSSIES	JUNKIES	MARINES	NOVICES	PINCHES	REACHES
APPLIES	BISQUES	CARGOES	CURATES	DOILIES	FAIRIES	GIPSIES	HUSTLES	KELPIES	MARQUES	NOZZLES	PINKIES	READIES
APPOSES	BLESSES	CARIBES	CURDLES	DOLLIES	FANCIES	GIRDLES	HUTCHES	KETCHES	MARRIES	NUANCES	PINONES	REBATES
APSIDES	BLITZES	CARNIES	CURRIES	DOLORES	FEELIES	GLANCES	HYRACES	KETONES	MARSHES	NUBBLES	PIRATES	REBUKES
ARCADES	BLONDES	CAROLES	DABBLES	DONATES	FELINES	GLASSES	HYRAXES	KETTLES	MASHIES	NUZZLES	PITCHES	REBUSES
ARCHIES	BLOUSES	CARRIES	DADDIES	DOODLES	FEMALES	GLITZES	ICEAGES	KEWPIES	MASQUES	OBLATES	PLAGUES	RECANES
ARGIVES	BLUSHES	CASTLES	DAILIES	DOOZIES	FERRIES	GLORIES	ICEAXES	KIBBLES	MATCHES	OBLIGES	PLAICES	RECEDES
ARGYLES	BMOVIES	CATCHES	DAIRIES	DOSAGES	FERULES	GLOSSES	ICICLES	KIDDIES	MATURES	OCTANES	PLAINES	RECIPES
AROUSES	BOBBIES	CAYUSES	DAISIES	DOTTLES	FETCHES	GNASHES	IDEATES	KILTIES	MEALIES	OCTAVES	PLAQUES	RECITES
ARRASES	BOBBLES	CELEBES	DALLIES	DOUBLES	FETTLES	GOALIES	IGNITES	KINDLES	MEANIES	OEUVRES	PLASHES	RECODES
ARRISES	BODICES	CENTRES	DAMAGES	DOWRIES	FIACRES	GOATEES	IGNORES	KIRTLES	MEASLES	OFFICES	PLEASES	RECUSES
ARRIVES	BOGGLES	CHAISES	DANDIES	DREDGES	FIANCES	GOBBLES	ILLUSES	KISHKES	MEDDLES	OLEATES	PLEDGES	REDATES
ASPIRES	BOLIDES	CHANCES	DANDLES	DRESSES	FICUSES	GOGGLES	IMAGOES	KITTIES	MEIOSES	OOCYTES	PLUNGES	REDEYES
ASSIZES	BOLUSES	CHANGES	DANGLES	DROWSES	FIDDLES	GOODIES	IMBIBES	KLUDGES	MENACES	OOLITES	PLUSHES	REDUCES
ASSUMES	BONGOES	CHARGES	DAPPLES	DRUDGES	FIFTIES	GOURDES	IMBRUES	KLUTZES	MENAGES	OPAQUES	PLUSSES	REFACES
ASSURES	BONUSES	CHARLES	DAWDLES	DUCHIES	FIGURES	GRAMMES	IMMIXES	KNISHES	MERCIES	OPIATES	POACHES	REFINES
ATHOMES	BOOBIES	CHASSES	DAZZLES	DUDDIES	FILCHES	GRANGES	IMMURES	KYLIKES	METATES	OPPOSES	POBOXES	REFIRES
ATLASES	BOODLES	CHEESES	DEBASES	DUMMIES	FILLIES	GRASSES	IMPALES	LADDIES	METTLES	ORACLES	POLICES	REFRIES
ATOMIES	BOOGIES	CHEQUES	DEBATES	DWARVES	FINALES	GRAVIES	IMPEDES	LAERTES	MIDDIES	ORANGES	POMADES	REFUGES
ATTIMES	BOOKIES	CHEVIES	DEBONES	EBONIES	FINCHES	GREASES	IMPLIES	LARCHES	MIDDLES	ORESTES	POOCHES	REFUSES
ATTIRES	BOONIES	CHEVRES	DECADES	ECDYSES	FIPPLES	GREAVES	IMPOSES	LASSIES	MINGLES	ORIOLES	POODLES	REFUTES
ATTUNES	BOOTEES	CHILIES	DECIDES	ECTYPES	FITCHES	GRIEVES	IMPUTES	LASSOES	MINUSES	ORPINES	POPPIES	REGALES
AUBADES	BOOTIES	CHOICES	DECKLES	EDIBLES	FIXATES	GRILLES	INCISES	LATCHES	MINUTES	OSCINES	POPPLES	REGIMES
AUNTIES	BORATES	CHOOSES	DECODES	EDIFIES	FIZZLES	GROOVES	INCITES	LATEXES	MIRAGES	OSMOSES	PORCHES	REGLUES
AUSSIES	BOTCHES	CHROMES	DECREES	EFFACES	FLAMBES	GROSSES	INCOMES	LATICES	MISCUES	OUTAGES	PORGIES	REHIRES
AVENGES	BOTTLES	CINCHES	DECRIES	EFFUSES	FLANGES	GROUSES	INCUDES	LEACHES	MISDOES	OUTDOES	POTAGES	RELACES
AVENUES	BOUNCES	CIRCLES	DEDUCES	ELAPSES	FLASHES	GRUDGES	INDEXES	LEAGUES	MISSIES	OUTGOES	POTPIES	RELATES
AVIATES	BOVINES	CIRQUES	DEFACES	ELEGIES	FLECHES	GUESSES	INDICES	LEASHES	MISUSES	PADDIES	POUCHES	RELAXES
AVULSES	BOWTIES	CIVVIES	DEFAMES	ELYSEES	FLEDGES	GUIMPES	INDITES	LEECHES	MITOSES	PADDLES	POUNCES	RELINES
AYEAYES	BRAISES	CLAQUES	DEFILES	EMERGES	FLEECES	GULCHES	INDUCES	LEFTIES	MIZZLES	PAIUTES	PRAISES	RELIVES
BABBLES	BRASSES	CLASHES	DEFINES	EMIGRES	FLENSES	GULLIES	INFUSES	LEGATES	MOBILES	PALACES	PRANCES	REMAKES
BADDIES	BRAVOES	CLASSES	DEFUSES	EMPIRES	FLESHES	GUNNIES	INHALES	LEGUMES	MODULES	PALATES	PRESSES	REMIXES
BAFFLES	BREEZES	CLAUSES	DEGREES	EMPTIES	FLOSSES	GUPPIES	INHERES	LESSEES	MOMMIES	PAMBIES	PRINCES	REMOTES
BAGGIES	BRIDGES	CLEAVES	DEIFIES	ENABLES	FLUSHES	GURGLES	INJOKES	LETTRES	MONKEES	PANSIES	PRIVIES	REMOVES
BAILEES	BRIDLES	CLICHES	DEITIES	ENCAGES	FOCSLES	GUSSIES	INJURES	LEVITES	MOOCHES	PARADES	PROXIES	RENAMES
BANDIES	BROGUES	CLIQUES	DELETES	ENCASES	FOCUSES	GUSTOES	INMATES	LIAISES	MORALES	PARCHES	PSYCHES	RENEGES
BANGLES	BRONZES	CLOCHES	DELIBES	ENCODES	FOIBLES	GUZZLES	INSIDES	LIENEES	MOSQUES	PAROLES	PUDDLES	RENOTES
BANJOES	BROWSES	CLOQUES	DELUDES	ENCORES	FOLLIES	GYPSIES	INSOLES	LIERNES	MOTIVES	PARRIES	PUGREES	REPAVES
BASQUES	BRUISES	CLOTHES	DELUGES	ENDIVES	FONDLES	GYRATES	INSURES	LIGATES	MOTTLES	PARSEES	PUMICES	REPINES
BATCHES	BRUSHES	COACHES	DEMISES	ENDURES	FONDUES	HACKIES	INTAKES	LIMOGES	MOTTOES	PARTIES	PUNCHES	REPLIES
BATTLES	BUBBLES	COBBLES	DEMOTES	ENEMIES	FOOZLES	HACKLES	INTONES	LINAGES	MOUSSES	PARURES	PUNKIES	REPOSES
BAUBLES	BUCKLES	COCKLES	DENOTES	ENGAGES	FORAGES	HAGGLES	INVADES	LINDIES	MRBONES	PATAKES	PUPPIES	REPUTES
BEACHES	BUCKOES	CODDLES	DENUDES	ENGINES	FORGOES	HALITES	INVITES	LINGOES	MUDDIES	PATCHES	PURFLES	RERATES
BEADLES	BUDDIES	CODICES	DEPONES	ENISLES	FORTIES	HAMITES	INVOKES	LISTEES	MUDDLES	PATSIES	PURPLES	RESALES
BEAGLES	BUDGIES	COERCES	DEPOSES	ENLACES	FRAISES	HANDLES	IODATES	LITOTES	MUDPIES	PATTIES	PURSUES	RESCUES
BEANIES	BUGGIES	COFFEES	DEPUTES	ENRAGES	FRANCES	HANKIES	IODIDES	LOACHES	MUFFLES	PAVANES	PUTTEES	RESHOES
BEATLES	BULLIES	COHERES	DERBIES	ENROBES	FRAPPES	HARPIES	IODIZES	LOATHES	MULCHES	PAWNEES	PUTTIES	RESIDES
BECOMES	BUMBLES	COLLIES	DERIDES	ENSILES	FREEZES	HARRIES	IONIZES	LOBBIES	MUMBLES	PDJAMES	PUZZLES	RESILES
BEECHES	BUNCHES	COLONES	DERIVES	ENSURES	FRIDGES	HASSLES	IRONIES	LOCALES	MUMMIES	PEACHES	PYGMIES	RESOLES
BEEGEES	BUNDLES	CONCHES	DESIRES	ENTICES	FRIEZES	HATCHES	IVORIES	LOCATES	MUNCHES	PEBBLES	PYRITES	RESUMES
BEETLES	BUNGEES	COOKIES	DEVICES	ENTREES	FRINGES	HEAVIES	JACQUES	LOESSES	MUSCLES	PEDDLES	PYXIDES	RETAKES
BEHAVES	BUNGLES	COOTIES	DEVISES	ENTRIES	FRIZZES	HECKLES	JANGLES	LOLLIES	MUTATES	PEEPLES	QUASHES	RETAPES
BELCHES	BUNNIES	COSINES	DEVOTES	ENZYMES	FUDDLES	HEDDLES	JAYCEES	LONGUES	MUZZLES	PEEWEES	QUERIES	RETAXES
BELLIES	BURBLES	COUCHES	DEVRIES	EPOXIES	FUMBLES	HELICES	JAYVEES	LOONIES	MYRTLES	PELAGES	QUICHES	RETILES
BEMIRES	BURGEES	COULEES	DIARIES	EQUATES	FUNGOES	HELIXES	JEEBIES	LORISES	NAIADES	PENATES	QUINCES	RETIMES
BEMUSES	BURGLES	COUPLES	DIBBLES	EQUINES	FUNNIES	HINNIES	JELLIES	LORRIES	NANNIES	PENNIES	QUIZZES	RETIRES
BENCHES	BUSBIES	COURSES	DICKIES	ERMINES	FURORES	HIPPIES	JEMMIES	LOTUSES	NATIVES	PENSEES	RABBLES	RETRIES
BERATES	BUSTLES	COWRIES	DIDDLES	ESCAPES	FUTURES	HITCHES	JENNIES	LOUNGES	NATURES	PEONIES	RACEMES	RETUNES
BERRIES	BYGONES	COYOTES	DILATES	ESSENES	GABBLES	HOAGIES	JETTIES	LOURDES	NEEDLES	PEOPLES	RADAMES	RETYPES
BESIDES	BYLINES	CRADLES	DILLIES	ESTATES	GAGGLES	HOBBIES	JIFFIES	LOUVRES	NEGATES	PERCHES	RADDLES	REVERES
BETAKES	CABBIES	CRASHES	DILUTES	ETOILES	GAMBLES	HOBBLES	JIGGLES	LUNCHES	NEMESES	PERUKES	RADICES	REVILES
BETIDES	CACKLES	CRAZIES	DIMPLES	EUCHRES	GAMETES	HOGTIES	JIMMIES	LUPINES	NESTLES	PERUSES	RAFFLES	REVISES
BETIMES	CADDIES	CREASES	DINGLES	EVINCES	GAMINES	HOLLIES	JINGLES	LURCHES	NETTLES	PESTLES	RALLIES	REVIVES
BIALIES	CAIQUES	CREATES	DINGOES	EVOLVES	GARAGES	HOMBRES	JINGOES	LUSTRES	NEXUSES	PETITES	RAMBLES	REVOKES
BIDDIES	CAJOLES	CRECHES	DINKIES	EVULSES	GARBLES	HOOPOES	JOGGLES	LUXATES	NIBBLES	PHLOXES	RAMESES	REWAXES
BIGEYES	CALYCES	CREOLES	DIPOLES	EXCISES	GARGLES	HUBBIES	JOLLIES	MAGPIES	NIGGLES	PHOEBES	RANCHES	REWIRES
BIGGIES	CALYXES	CRESSES	DIRTIES	EXCITES	GECKOES	HUDDLES	JOSTLES	MANAGES	NINNIES	PHONIES	RANKLES	REZONES
BIGTOES	CAMISES	CRINGES	DITCHES	EXCUSES	GENESES	HUMBLES	JOUNCES	MANEGES	NODULES	PHRASES	RAPINES	RIBEYES
BILBOES	CANAPES	CRONIES	DITTIES	EXHALES	GENTLES	HUNCHES	JUGGLES	MANGLES	NOGALES	PICKLES	RASSLES	RICKLES

RIDDLES
RIFFLES
RIPPLES
ROACHES
ROADIES
ROCKIES
ROOKIES
ROOMIES
ROTATES
ROWDIES
RUBBLES
RUFFLES
RUMBLES
RUMPLES
RUSHEES
RUSTLES
SABINES
SADDLES
SALLIES
SALUTES
SALVOES
SAMITES
SAMPLES
SASSIES
SATIRES
SAVAGES
SCARVES
SCATHES
SCHEMES
SCHMOES
SCONCES
SCRAPES
SCRIBES
SCURVES
SCYTHES
SEABEES
SEANCES
SECEDES
SECURES
SEDUCES
SEETHES
SEICHES
SEMITES
SENATES
SENORES
SERAPES
SESAMES
SETTEES
SETTLES
SHAKOES
SHEAVES
SHELVES
SHIITES
SHOPPES
SHRIKES
SHRINES
SHRIVES
SHUSHES
SICKLES
SIGNEES
SILLIES
SIMILES
SINGLES
SINUSES
SISSIES
SIXTIES
SIZZLES
SKOSHES
SLASHES
SLEDGES
SLEEVES
SLOSHES
SLUDGES
SLUICES
SLUSHES
SMASHES
SMOKIES
SMUDGES
SNEEZES
SNOOZES
SOFTIES
SOIREES
SOLACES
SOLUTES
SOOTHES
SORITES
SORTIES
SOURCES
SPARGES
SPECIES
SPHERES
SPITZES
SPLICES
SPLINES
SPONGES
SPOUSES
SPRITES
SPRUCES
SQUARES
SQUIRES
STABLES
STANCES
STAPLES
STARVES
STASHES
STATUES
STEPPES
STICHES
STIFLES
STOGIES
STOOGES
STORIES
STRAFES
STRIDES
STRIKES
STRIPES
STRIVES
STROBES
STROKES
STUDIES
STURGES
STYMIES
SUBDUES
SULKIES
SULLIES
SUNDAES
SUTURES
SWATHES
SWERVES
SWISHES
SYNCHES
TABBIES
TACKLES
TAFFIES
TAILLES
TALKIES
TALLIES
TALUSES
TAMALES
TANGLES
TANSIES
TARRIES
TATTLES
TEACHES
TECHIES
TEDDIES
TEEPEES
TEETHES
TELEXES
TELLIES
TEMPLES
TENACES
TENURES
TERRIES
TESTEES
THIEVES
THRIVES
THRONES
TICKLES
TIEDYES
TIMBRES
TINGLES
TINKLES
TIPPLES
TIPTOES
TIRADES
TISANES
TISSUES
TITTLES
TIZZIES
TOADIES
TODDIES
TODDLES
TOFFEES
TOGGLES
TONGUES
TOOTLES
TOPAZES
TOPPLES
TORCHES
TORQUES
TOUCHES
TOUPEES
TOUSLES
TOWHEES
TOWNIES
TRANCES
TRASHES
TREBLES
TRESSES
TRIFLES
TRIODES
TRIPLES
TRIUNES
TROCHES
TROUPES
TRUDGES
TRUSSES
TSETSES
TUMBLES
TUMMIES
TUNNIES
TURTLES
TUSSLES
TWEEZES
TWELVES
TWINGES
ULYSSES
UMPIRES
UNBOXES
UNCAGES
UNCASES
UNIFIES
UNITIES
UNLACES
UNLADES
UNMAKES
UNPILES
UNROBES
UNTUNES
UNYOKES
UPDATES
UPRISES
UPTAKES
VACATES
VALISES
VEGGIES
VESTEES
VETCHES
VIRTUES
VIRUSES
VISAGES
VITTLES
VOLUMES
VOUCHES
VOYAGES
WADDLES
WAFFLES
WAGGLES
WAHINES
WALTZES
WAMBLES
WANGLES
WARBLES
WATCHES
WATTLES
WEARIES
WEDGIES
WEENIES
WELCHES
WENCHES
WHARVES
WHEEZES
WHIZZES
WIENIES
WIGGLES
WILLIES
WIMPLES
WINCHES
WITCHES
WOBBLES
WOODIES
WOOLIES
WORRIES
WRITHES
YANKEES
YUPPIES
ZILCHES
ZOMBIES
ZOUAVES
ZYGOTES

ET•••••

ETAGERE
ETAMINE
ETCHERS
ETCHING
ETERNAL
ETESIAN
ETHANOL
ETHICAL
ETHNICS
ETIENNE
ETOILES
ETONIAN
ETRURIA

E•T••••

EATABLE
EATAWAY
EATCROW
EATENAT
EATENUP
EATSOUT
ECTYPES
ENTAILS
ENTEBBE
ENTENTE
ENTERED
ENTHUSE
ENTICED
ENTICER
ENTICES
ENTITLE
ENTRAIN
ENTRANT
ENTRAPS
ENTREAT
ENTREES
ENTRIES
ENTROPY
ENTRUST
ENTWINE
ESTATES
ESTEEMS
ESTELLE
ESTEVEZ
ESTHETE
ESTIVAL
ESTONIA
ESTORIL
ESTRADA
ESTRAYS
ESTUARY
EUTERPE
EXTENDS
EXTENTS
EXTINCT
EXTORTS
EXTRACT
EXTREME
EXTRUDE

E••T•••

EARTHEN
EARTHLY
EASTEND
EASTERN
EASTERS
EASTMAN
EBBTIDE
ECSTASY
EDITING
EDITION
EDITORS
EGOTISM
EGOTIST
EGOTRIP
ELATERS
ELATING
ELATION
ELITISM
ELITIST
ELMTREE
ELUTING
ELUTION
EMITTED
EMITTER
EMOTERS
EMOTING
EMOTION
EMOTIVE
EMPTIED
EMPTIER
EMPTIES
EMPTILY
EPITHET
EPITOME
EPSTEIN
ERITREA
EROTICA
EXITING
EXOTICA
EXOTICS

E•••T••

EGESTED
EIGHTHS
EJECTED
ELASTIC
ELECTED
ELECTEE
ELECTOR
ELECTRA
ELECTRO
ELEKTRA
EMITTED
EMITTER
EMPATHY
ENACTED
ENACTOR
ENTITLE
EOLITHS
EPISTLE
EQUATED
EQUATES
EQUATOR
ERECTED
ERECTER
ERECTLY
ERECTOR
ERISTIC
ERRATIC
ERRATUM
ERUCTED
ERUPTED
ESTATES
EVERTED
EVICTED
EXACTED
EXACTER
EXACTLY
EXACTOR
EXALTED
EXCITED
EXCITES
EXERTED
EXISTED
EXULTED

E••••T•

EAGLETS
EBONITE
EBWHITE
EDACITY
EDUCATE
EFFECTS
EFFORTS
EGALITE
EGOISTS
ELEVATE
ELICITS
ELLIOTT
ELMISTI
EMANATE
EMERITA
EMERITI
EMIRATE
EMULATE
ENLISTS
ENROOTS
ENROUTE
ENSUITE
ENTENTE
EREMITE
ERNESTO
ERUDITE
ESCORTS
ESTHETE
EVERETT
EXCEPTS
EXCRETE
EXECUTE
EXEMPTS
EXHORTS
EXPARTE
EXPECTS
EXPERTS
EXPIATE
EXPORTS
EXTENTS
EXTORTS
EYELETS

E•••••T

EARHART
EARNEST
EARSHOT
EASIEST
EATENAT
EATSOUT
ECKHART
EDGEOUT
EDGIEST
EELIEST
EERIEST
EGOTIST
EKEDOUT
EKESOUT
ELEGANT
ELEGIST
ELEMENT
ELITIST
ELKHART
ELLIOTT
EMINENT
ENCHANT
ENCRUST
ENCRYPT
ENDMOST
ENGRAFT
ENTRANT
ENTREAT
ENTRUST
EPAULET
EPEEIST
EPITHET
ESCHEAT
EVENEST
EVENOUT
EVEREST
EVERETT
EVIDENT
EVILEST
EXCERPT
EXHAUST
EXHIBIT
EXIGENT
EXPLOIT
EXTINCT
EXTRACT
EYEBOLT

•ET••••

BETAKEN
BETAKES
BETAMAX
BETARAY
BETHANY
BETHELS
BETHINK
BETIDED
BETIDES
BETIMES
BETOKEN
BETRAYS
BETROTH
BETTERS
BETTING
BETTORS
BETWEEN
BETWIXT
DETAILS
DETAINS
DETECTS
DETENTE
DETESTS
DETOURS
DETRACT
DETRAIN
DETROIT
FETCHED
FETCHES
FETIDLY
FETLOCK
FETTERS
FETTLES
GETAWAY
GETBACK
GETDOWN
GETEVEN
GETINTO
GETITON
GETLOST
GETOVER
GETSOFF
GETSOUT
GETSSET
GETTING
GETWELL
HETMANS
JETBOAT
JETGUNS
JETPORT
JETSONS
JETTIES
JETTING
JETWASH
KETCHAM
KETCHES
KETCHUP
KETONES
KETTLES
LETDOWN
LETINON
LETITBE
LETITIA
LETSFLY
LETSLIP
LETSOFF
LETSOUT
LETSSEE
LETTERS
LETTING
LETTRES
LETTUCE
METATES
METEORS
METEOUT
METERED
METHANE
METHODS
METIERS
METOOER
METRICS
METTLES
NETSUKE
NETSURF
NETTING
NETTLED
NETTLES
NETWORK
PETALED
PETARDS
PETCOCK
PETERED
PETIOLE
PETITES
PETNAME
PETRELS
PETRIFY
PETROCK
PETROUS
PETTERS
PETTIER
PETTILY
PETTING
PETTISH
PETUNIA
RETAILS
RETAINS
RETAKEN
RETAKES
RETAPED
RETAPES
RETARDS
RETAXED
RETAXES
RETEACH
RETELLS
RETESTS
RETHINK
RETICLE
RETILED
RETILES
RETIMED
RETIMES
RETINAE
RETINAL
RETINAS
RETINUE
RETIRED
RETIREE
RETIRES
RETITLE
RETOOLS
RETORTS
RETOUCH
RETOWED
RETRACE
RETRACK
RETRACT
RETRADE
RETRAIN
RETREAD
RETREAT
RETRIAL
RETRIED
RETRIES
RETRIMS
RETSINA
RETUNED
RETUNES
RETURNS
RETYPED
RETYPES
SETBACK
SETDOWN
SETINTO
SETLINE
SETSAIL
SETSOFF
SETSOUT
SETTEES
SETTERS
SETTING
SETTLED
SETTLER
SETTLES
SETUPON
TETANUS
TETCHED
TETHERS
TETRADS
VETCHES
VETERAN
VETOERS
VETOING
VETTING
WETBARS
WETCELL
WETHERS
WETLAND
WETMOPS
WETNESS
WETSUIT
WETTEST
WETTING

•E•T•••

BEATERS
BEATIFY
BEATING
BEATLES
BEATNIK
BEATOUT
BEATRIX
BEATSIT
BEATSUP
BEATTIE
BEDTIME
BEETLES
BEETREE
BELTANE
BELTING
BELTWAY
BENTHAM
BENTLEY
BENTSEN
BERTHED
BERTOLT
BESTBOY
BESTIAL
BESTING
BESTIRS
BESTMAN
BESTMEN
BESTOWS
BESTREW
BETTERS
BETTING
BETTORS
CELTICS
CENTAUR
CENTAVO
CENTERS
CENTIME
CENTIMO
CENTRAL
CENTRED
CENTRES
CENTRIC
CENTURY
CERTAIN
CERTIFY
DEBTORS
DEFTEST
DEITIES
DELTAIC
DELTOID
DENTATE
DENTINE
DENTING
DENTIST
DENTURE
DESTINE
DESTINY
DESTROY
DEUTERO
DEXTRIN
FEATHER
FEATURE
FELTFOR
FELTOUT
FERTILE
FESTERS
FESTIVE
FESTOON
FETTERS
FETTLES
GENTEEL
GENTIAN
GENTILE
GENTLED
GENTLER
GENTLES
GESTALT
GESTATE
GESTURE
GETTING
HEATERS
HEATHEN
HEATHER
HEATING
HEATSUP
HEATTER
HECTARE
HECTORS
HEFTIER
HEFTILY
HEFTING
HEPTADS
JESTERS
JESTING
JETTIES
JETTING
KEPTOFF
KEPTOUT
KESTREL
KETTLES
LEATHER
LECTERN
LECTORS
LECTURE
LEETIDE
LEFTIES
LEFTIST
LEFTOFF
LEFTOUT
LENTILS
LEOTARD
LEPTONS
LETTERS
LETTING
LETTRES
LETTUCE
MEATIER
MEETING
MELTING
MENTHOL
MENTION
MENTORS
MESTIZO
METTLES
NEATENS
NEATEST
NECTARS
NEITHER
NEPTUNE
NESTEGG
NESTERS
NESTING
NESTLED
NESTLER
NESTLES
NETTING
NETTLED
NETTLES
NEUTRAL
NEUTRON
NEWTONS
NEWTOWN
PEATBOG
PECTINS
PEGTOPS
PELTATE
PELTERS
PELTING
PENTADS
PEPTALK
PEPTIDE
PERTAIN
PERTEST
PERTURB
PESTERS
PESTLED
PESTLES
PETTERS
PETTIER
PETTILY
PETTING
PETTISH
RECTIFY
RECTORS
RECTORY
REDTAPE
REDTOPS
RENTALS
RENTERS
RENTING
REPTILE
RESTAGE
RESTAIN
RESTAMP
RESTART
RESTATE
RESTERS
RESTFUL
RESTING
RESTIVE
RESTOCK
RESTORE
RESTSUP
RESTYLE
REUTERS
REUTHER
SEATERS
SEATING
SEATTLE
SECTION
SECTORS
SEETHED
SEETHES
SEETOIT
SELTZER
SENTFOR
SENTOFF
SENTOUT
SEPTETS
SESTETS
SESTINA
SETTEES
SETTERS
SETTING
SETTLED
SETTLER
SETTLES
SEXTANS
SEXTANT
SEXTETS
SEXTONS
TEATIME
TEATRAY
TEETERS
TEETHED
TEETHER
TEETHES
TEKTITE
TENTERS
TENTING
TERTIAL
TESTBAN
TESTEES
TESTERS
TESTIER
TESTIFY
TESTILY
TESTING
TESTOUT
TEUTONS
TEXTILE
TEXTUAL
TEXTURE
VECTORS
VENTERS
VENTING
VENTRAL
VENTURA
VENTURE
VERTIGO
VESTEES
VESTIGE
VESTING
VESTURE
VETTING
WEATHER
WEBTOED
WELTERS
WELTING

WENTAPE
WENTBAD
WENTFOR
WENTOFF
WENTOUT
WERTHER
WESTEND
WESTERN
WETTEST
WETTING
YEATEAM
YELTSIN
ZEITUNG
ZESTFUL
ZESTIER

•E••T••
AERATED
AERATES
AERATOR
BEASTIE
BEASTLY
BEATTIE
BELATED
BENATAR
BERATED
BERATES
BERETTA
BEWITCH
DEALTIN
DEARTHS
DEBATED
DEBATER
DEBATES
DEBITED
DEBUTED
DELETED
DELETES
DEMETER
DEMOTED
DEMOTES
DENOTED
DENOTES
DEPUTED
DEPUTES
DESKTOP
DESOTOS
DEVOTED
DEVOTEE
DEVOTES
FEASTED
FEINTED
FENETRE
GELATIN
GELATIS
GENETIC
GERITOL
GETITON
HEALTHY
HEARTEN
HEARTHS
HEATTER
HEELTAP
HEISTED
HELOTRY
HEPATIC
HERBTEA
HERETIC
KERATIN
LEANTOS
LEGATEE
LEGATES
LEGATOS
LEISTER
LENGTHS
LENGTHY
LESOTHO
LETITBE
LETITIA
LEVITES
MEIOTIC
MENOTTI
MERITED
METATES
NECKTIE
NEGATED
NEGATES
NEGATOR
PELOTAS
PENATES
PESETAS
PETITES
REACTED
REACTOR
REACTTO
REALTOR
REBATED
REBATES
RECITAL
RECITED
RECITER
RECITES
REDATED
REDATES
REDSTAR
REENTER
REENTRY
REFUTED
REFUTER
REFUTES
REGATTA
RELATED
RELATES
REMOTER
REMOTES
RENOTES
REPUTED
REPUTES
RERATED
RERATES
RETITLE
SEASTAR
SEATTLE
SEDATER
SEMITES
SEMITIC
SENATES
SENATOR
TELSTAR
TEMPTED
TEMPTER
VEGETAL
WEALTHY
WEBSTER
ZENITHS

•E•••T•
BECKETT
BEHESTS
BENEATH
BENNETT
BERETTA
BERLITZ
BETROTH
CELESTA
CELESTE
CEMENTS
DECANTS
DECEITS
DECOCTS
DEDUCTS
DEFACTO
DEFEATS
DEFECTS
DEFLATE
DEJECTS
DELICTI
DELICTS
DELISTS
DENSITY
DENTATE
DEPARTS
DEPICTS
DEPLETE
DEPORTS
DESALTS
DESERTS
DESISTS
DESPITE
DESPOTS
DETECTS
DETENTE
DETESTS
DEVIATE
FERRATE
FERRETS
FERRITE
GEARSTO
GEFILTE
GERENTS
GESTATE
GETINTO
HEAVETO
HEIFETZ
HEIGHTS
HELMETS
HENBITS
HEPCATS
HERMITS
HEWLETT
HEXNUTS
JENNETS
JESUITS
KEEPSTO
KENNETH
KEYNOTE
LEADSTO
LEDUPTO
LEGISTS
LEPANTO
MEDIATE
MEMENTO
MENOTTI
MERLOTS
NEOLITH
NEONATE
NEWGATE
NEWMATH
PEANUTS
PEDANTS
PELLETS
PELTATE
PENALTY
PENNATE
PENULTS
PEQUOTS
PERLITE
PERMITS
REACTTO
REALITY
REBASTE
REBIRTH
REBOLTS
REBOOTS
RECANTS
RECASTS
REDACTS
REDANTS
REDHATS
REDHOTS
REEDITS
REFERTO
REGATTA
REGENTS
REGRETS
REHEATS
REJECTS
RELENTS
RELICTS
RELISTS
REMELTS
REPASTE
REPASTS
REPEATS
REPENTS
REPLATE
REPLETE
REPORTS
REQUITE
RERENTS
REROUTE
RESALTS
RESEATS
RESECTS
RESENTS
RESISTS
RESORTS
RESPITE
RESTATE
RESULTS
RETESTS
RETORTS
REUNITE
REVERTS
REVOLTS
REWRITE
REWROTE
REXCATS
SEADUTY
SEAGATE
SECANTS
SECRETE
SECRETS
SELECTS
SENNETT
SENSATE
SEPTETS
SERIATE
SERRATE
SESTETS
SETINTO
SEVENTH
SEVENTY
SEXISTS
SEXTETS
TEAPOTS
TEASETS
TEKTITE
TENANTS
TENDSTO
TERCETS
TERMITE
TERNATE
TERRETS
VEDANTA
VEIGHTS
VELVETS
VELVETY
VERVETS
WEBSITE
WEIGHTS
WEIGHTY
WESKITS
YEARNTO
ZEALOTS
ZERMATT

•E••••T
AERIEST
AEROBAT
BEARCAT
BEAROUT
BEATOUT
BEATSIT
BECKETT
BEDPOST
BEDREST
BELFAST
BELMONT
BENEFIT
BENNETT
BEQUEST
BERTOLT
BETWIXT
CELLIST
DEADSET
DEAFEST
DEALOUT
DEAREST
DECKOUT
DECRYPT
DEEPEST
DEEPFAT
DEEPSET
DEFAULT
DEFIANT
DEFICIT
DEFLECT
DEFROST
DEFTEST
DEFUNCT
DELBERT
DELIGHT
DELIMIT
DEMERIT
DENSEST
DENTIST
DEPOSIT
DESCANT
DESCENT
DESKSET
DESSERT
DETRACT
DETROIT
DEVIANT
EELIEST
EERIEST
FEEDLOT
FEELOUT
FELLOUT
FELTOUT
FERMENT
FERVENT
GERAINT
GESTALT
GETLOST
GETSOUT
GETSSET
HEADOUT
HEADSET
HEAROUT
HELDOUT
HELLCAT
HELPOUT
HERBERT
HERRIOT
HEWLETT
JEERSAT
JETBOAT
JETPORT
KEENEST
KEEPSAT
KEPTOUT
KEYWEST
LEADOUT
LEAFLET
LEANEST
LEARJET
LEERSAT
LEFTIST
LEFTOUT
LENFANT
LENIENT
LETSOUT
LEVERET
LEWDEST
MEANEST
MEDIANT
MEEKEST
MESSKIT
METEOUT
NEAREST
NEATEST
NEGLECT
NEWHART
NEWLEFT
NEWPORT
PEACOAT
PEASANT
PECCANT
PECKSAT
PEEKOUT
PEEKSAT
PEEROUT
PEERSAT
PENDANT
PENDENT
PENNANT
PERCENT
PERFECT
PERIDOT
PERSIST
PERTEST
PERVERT
PEUGEOT
READMIT
READOUT
REAGENT
REALIST
REBUILT
RECEIPT
RECOUNT
RECRUIT
REDCENT
REDCOAT
REDDEST
REDEALT
REDHEAT
REDMEAT
REDOUBT
REDSPOT
REELECT
REENACT
REFLECT
REFRACT
REGNANT
RELIANT
RELIGHT
REMNANT
REMOUNT
RENAULT
REPAINT
REPLANT
REPRINT
REQUEST
RESHOOT
RESPECT
RESTART
RETRACT
RETREAT
REVISIT
SEAGIRT
SEALANT
SEAPORT
SEASALT
SEEKOUT
SEESFIT
SEESOUT
SEETOIT
SEGMENT
SELLOUT
SENDOUT
SENNETT
SENTOUT
SERPENT
SERVANT
SETSOUT
SEXIEST
SEXTANT
TEACART
TEARSAT
TEMPEST
TENSEST
TENSPOT
TERSEST
TESTOUT
VERDANT
VERDICT
VERMONT
WEAKEST
WEAROUT
WEBFEET
WEBFOOT
WEEDOUT
WELLSET
WENTOUT
WETSUIT
WETTEST
YELLSAT
ZERMATT

••ET•••
ABETTED
ABETTOR
ACETATE
ACETONE
BEETLES
BEETREE
BRETONS
CHETRUM
CRETANS
CRETINS
DIETARY
DIETERS
DIETING
FRETFUL
FRETSAW
FRETTED
GHETTOS
GRETZKY
LEETIDE
MEETING
NOETICS
ONETIME
PIETIES
PIETINS
PIETISM
POETESS
POETICS
PRETAPE
PRETEEN
PRETEND
PRETEST
PRETEXT
PRETZEL
QUETZAL
RHETORS
SEETHED
SEETHES
SEETOIT
SKETCHY
SMETANA
STETSON
STETTED
TEETERS
TEETHED
TEETHER
TEETHES
TIETACK
TOETAPS
TSETSES
VIETNAM
WHETHER
WHETTED

••E•T••
ABETTED
ABETTOR
ADEPTLY
ALERTED
ALERTER
ALERTLY
ASEPTIC
AVERTED
BIENTOT
BLEATED
BREATHE
BREATHS
BREATHY
CHEATED
CHEATER
CHEETAH
CHEETOS
CHESTER
CREATED
CREATES
CREATOR
CRESTED
EGESTED
EJECTED
ELECTED
ELECTEE
ELECTOR
ELECTRA
ELECTRO
ELEKTRA
ERECTED
ERECTER
ERECTLY
ERECTOR
EVERTED
EXERTED
FIESTAS
FLEETER
FLEETLY
FREITAG
FRETTED
GHETTOS
GREATER
GREATLY
GREETED
GREETER
GUESTED
HEELTAP
ICEDTEA
IDEATED
IDEATES
IDENTIC
INEPTLY
INERTIA
INERTLY
LAERTES
MAESTRI
MAESTRO
OLEATES
OLESTRA
OMENTUM
ONESTEP
OPENTOE
ORESTES
OVERTLY
PLEATED
PLECTRA
PRESTON
PRESTOS
QUENTIN
QUESTED
REENTER
REENTRY
SCENTED
SCEPTER
SCEPTRE
SHEATHE
SHEATHS
SHEETED
SHELTER
SHELTIE
SHELTON
SIESTAS
SKEETER
SKELTER
SKELTON
SKEPTIC
SLEETED
SLEPTIN
SLEPTON
SLEUTHS
SMELTED
SMELTER
SPECTER
SPECTOR
SPECTRA
SPECTRE
STENTOR
STETTED
SVELTER
SWEATED
SWEATER
SWEETEN
SWEETER
SWEETIE
SWEETLY
SWEETON
SWELTER
SWELTRY
SWEPTUP
THEATER
THEATRE
TREATED
TREETOP
TRENTON
TRESTLE
TWEETED
TWEETER
WHEATON
WHETTED
WREATHE
WREATHS
WRESTED
WRESTLE

••E••T•
ACETATE
AGEISTS
AMENITY
BREADTH
BREASTS
BREVETS
BREVITY
COEDITS
CREDITS
DUEDATE
ELEVATE
EMERITA
EMERITI
EREMITE
EVERETT
EXECUTE
EXEMPTS
EYELETS
HAEMATO
ITERATE
KEEPSTO
OCELOTS
OMELETS
OPERATE
OVERATE
PREDATE
PRELATE
PRESETS
REEDITS
STEALTH
SWEARTO
THEISTS
THERETO
TIEINTO
TWELFTH
UNEARTH
WHERETO

••E•••T
ACEDOUT
ACESOUT
BIENTOT
BLERIOT
BLEWOUT
CHEMIST
CHEROOT
CHEVIOT
CHEWOUT
CLEMENT
COEXIST
CREWCUT
DEEPEST
DEEPFAT
DEEPSET
DIEDOUT
DIESOUT
DREWOUT
DUELIST
EKEDOUT
EKESOUT
ELEGANT
ELEGIST
ELEMENT
EPEEIST
EVENEST
EVENOUT
EVEREST
EVERETT
EYEBOLT
FEEDLOT
FEELOUT
FREIGHT
FREMONT
FRESHET
GOESOUT
GREYEST
ICEBOAT
INEXACT
ITERANT
JEERSAT
KEENEST
KEEPSAT
KNESSET
LEERSAT
MAEWEST
MEEKEST
ONESHOT
OPENPIT
OVERACT
OVEREAT
PEEKOUT
PEEKSAT
PEEROUT
PEERSAT
PIERROT
PRECAST
PRECEPT
PREDICT
PREEMPT
PREFECT
PREHEAT
PRESENT
PRESORT
PRETEST
PRETEXT
PREVENT
REELECT
REENACT
SEEKOUT
SEESFIT
SEESOUT
SEETOIT
SHERBET
SLEIGHT
SNEERAT
STEPOUT
STEWART
SWEARAT
THEREAT
TREERAT
TSELIOT
WEEDOUT
WHEREAT

•••ET••
AMMETER
ANNETTE
ARIETTA
ASCETIC
BABETTE
BARETTA
BERETTA
BIRETTA
BURETTE
CADETTE
CHEETAH
CHEETOS
COLETTE
CORETTA
COVETED
DELETED
DELETES
DEMETER
DINETTE
FACETED
FENETRE
FLEETER
FLEETLY
GAMETES
GAZETTE
GENETIC
GORETEX
GREETED
GREETER
HERETIC
IMPETUS
INPETTO
KINETIC
LAYETTE
LORETTA
MIMETIC
MULETAS
MUSETTE
NAMETAG
NANETTE
ORNETTE
PALETTE
PANETTA
PESETAS
PHAETON
PINETAR
PINETUM
PIPETTE
PRAETOR
QUIETED
QUIETEN
QUIETER
QUIETLY
RIVETED
RIVETER
ROPETOW
ROSETTA
ROSETTE
SHEETED
SKEETER
SLEETED
STPETER
STRETCH
STRETTO
SUZETTE
SWEETEN
SWEETER
SWEETIE
SWEETLY
SWEETON
TAKETEN
TIBETAN
TREETOP
TWEETED
TWEETER
VEGETAL
WIRETAP
WYNETTE

•••E•T•
ABSENTS
ACCENTS
ACCEPTS
ADDEDTO
ADVENTS
ADVERTS
AFFECTS
AFREETS
AGREETO
AIMEDTO
ALBERTA
ALBERTO
ALDENTE
AMNESTY
ANNETTE
APLENTY
ARIETTA
ARRESTS
ASCENTS
ASPECTS
ASSENTS
ASSERTS
ATTESTS
AUREATE
BABETTE
BARENTS
BARETTA
BEHESTS
BENEATH
BERETTA
BIRETTA
BISECTS
BURETTE
CADETTE
CAVEATS
CELESTA
CELESTE
CEMENTS
CLIENTS
COLETTE
COMESTO
CORETTA
DARESTO
DECEITS
DEFEATS
DEFECTS
DEJECTS
DESERTS
DETECTS
DETENTE
DETESTS
DIGESTS
DINETTE
DIRECTS
DIVERTS
DIVESTS
DOCENTS
DOZENTH
EFFECTS
ENTENTE
ERNESTO
EXCEPTS

EXPECTS
EXPERTS
EXTENTS
FOMENTS
FORESTS
GAZETTE
GERENTS
GIVENTO
GIVESTO
HONESTY
INCEPTS
INDENTS
INDEPTH
INFECTS
INFESTS
INGESTS
INJECTS
INPETTO
INSECTS
INSERTS
INTENTS
INVENTS
INVERTS
INVESTS
IQTESTS
JADEITE
LAMENTS
LATENTS
LAYETTE
LIBERTY
LINEATE
LORETTA
MAGENTA
MAJESTE
MAJESTY
MALEATE
MEMENTO
MODELTS
MODESTO
MODESTY
MOLESTS
MOMENTS
MUSETTE
NANETTE
NOVELTY
OBJECTS
OBVERTS
ORIENTE
ORIENTS
ORNETTE
OUTEATS
PALETTE
PANETTA
PAPEETE
PARENTS
PATENTS
PIMENTO
PIPETTE
POLENTA
POVERTY
PRIESTS
PUBERTY
REFERTO
REGENTS
REHEATS
REJECTS
RELENTS
REMELTS
REPEATS
REPENTS
RERENTS
RESEATS
RESECTS
RESENTS
RETESTS
REVERTS
ROBERTA
ROBERTO
ROBERTS
RODENTS
ROSEATE
ROSETTA
ROSETTE
SELECTS
SEVENTH
SEVENTY
SILENTS
STREETS
STRETTO
SUZETTE
TAKESTO
TALENTS
THREATS
TRIESTE
UMBERTO
UNSEATS
UPBEATS
URTEXTS
WYNETTE

•••E••T

ABREAST
AIMEDAT
AMHERST
ATHEART
ATHEIST
ATLEAST
ATTEMPT
BASEHIT
BENEFIT
BIBELOT
BOREOUT
BYHEART
CAMELOT
CAMEOUT
CAPELET
CAVEART
COMEOUT
COMESAT
DEMERIT
DIDEROT
DOLEOUT
DOPEOUT
DOVECOT
EATENAT
EDGEOUT
EPEEIST
EXCERPT
FADEOUT
FAREAST
FINEART
FIREANT
FIRELIT
FLIESAT
GAVEOUT
GIVEOUT
HAVENOT
HIDEOUT
HOLEOUT
INHERIT
LEVERET
LIFENET
LIVEOUT
LOSEOUT
LOSESIT
MADEOUT
MAKEOUT
MAKESIT
METEOUT
MIDEAST
MOVEOUT
NOSEOUT
PAGEANT
PAWEDAT
PINENUT
POKEDAT
POKESAT
POLECAT
PREEMPT
RAREBIT
RECEIPT
REDEALT
RICERAT
RIDEOUT
RODEOUT
RULEOUT
SIDEBET
SNEERAT
TAKEOUT
TIMEOUT
TIREOUT
TOREOUT
TREERAT
TUNEOUT
TYPESET
UNKEMPT
UTRECHT
WAVELET
WIPEOUT
WOREOUT

••••ET•

ACCRETE
AFREETS
AGREETO
AIGRETS
AMULETS
ANKLETS
ANXIETY
ARMLETS
ATHLETE
AUKLETS
AVOCETS
BALLETS
BARRETT
BASKETS
BASSETS
BECKETT
BENNETT
BILLETS
BONNETS
BOSKETS
BREVETS
BRUNETS
BUCKETS
BUDGETS
BUFFETS
BUFFETT
BULLETS
BURNETT
CABLETV
CACHETS
CAPLETS
CARNETS
CARPETS
CHALETS
CLARETS
CLORETS
CLOSETS
COLLETS
COMPETE
CORBETT
CORNETS
CORSETS
COSSETS
CURVETS
CUTLETS
CYGNETS
DEPLETE
DOCKETS
DORSETT
DUBIETY
EAGLETS
ESTHETE
EVERETT
EXCRETE
EYELETS
FANJETS
FAUCETS
FAWCETT
FERRETS
FIDGETS
FIDGETY
FILLETS
FLORETS
FLYNETS
FOLLETT
FORGETS
GADGETS
GADGETY
GANNETS
GANNETT
GARNETS
GARRETS
GARRETT
GASJETS
GASKETS
GIBBETS
GIBLETS
GIMLETS
GOBLETS
GORGETS
GOSSETT
GRIVETS
GULLETS
GUSSETS
HACKETT
HAMLETS
HAMMETT
HEAVETO
HEIFETZ
HELMETS
HEWLETT
HORNETS
IMARETS
IMPIETY
JACKETS
JAPHETH
JENNETS
JUNKETS
KENNETH
LABRETS
LANCETS
LAPPETS
LICKETY
LIMPETS
LINNETS
LIONETS
LOCKETS
MACBETH
MACHETE
MAGNETO
MAGNETS
MALLETS
MARKETS
MIDGETS
MILLETS
MILLETT
MINUETS
MOPPETS
MULLETS
MUPPETS
MUSKETS
NAIVETE
NCWYETH
NUGGETS
NUTLETS
OFFSETS
OMELETS
OUTLETS
OUTSETS
PACKETS
PALLETS
PAPEETE
PARGETS
PELLETS
PICKETS
PICKETT
PIGLETS
PIOLETS
PLANETS
POCKETS
POPPETS
POSSETS
PRESETS
PRIVETS
PUCKETT
PULLETS
PUPPETS
RABBETS
RACKETS
RAMJETS
REGRETS
REPLETE
RICKETY
RILLETS
ROCKETS
RUNLETS
RUSSETS
SACHETS
SATIETY
SECRETE
SECRETS
SENNETT
SEPTETS
SESTETS
SEXTETS
SIGNETS
SIPPETS
SOCIETY
SOCKETS
SONNETS
SORBETS
SOVIETS
SPINETS
STARETS
STREETS
STYLETS
SUBLETS
SUBSETS
SUNSETS
TABLETS
TAFFETA
TAPPETS
TARGETS
TEASETS
TERCETS
TERRETS
THERETO
TICKETS
TIPPETS
TOILETS
TRIVETS
TUFFETS
TURRETS
VARIETY
VARLETS
VELVETS
VELVETY
VERVETS
VIOLETS
WALLETS
WHERETO
WICKETS
WIDGETS
WIGLETS
WRITETO
WROTETO

••••E•T

ACHIEST
AERIEST
AILMENT
AIRIEST
ALIMENT
AMBIENT
AMPLEST
ANAPEST
ANCIENT
ARIDEST
ARMREST
ARTIEST
ASHIEST
AUGMENT
BALDEST
BARRETT
BECKETT
BEDREST
BENNETT
BEQUEST
BIGFEET
BIGGEST
BOLDEST
BONIEST
BOXSEAT
BRAVEST
BUFFETT
BURNETT
BUSIEST
CAGIEST
CALMEST
CALVERT
CARSEAT
CLEMENT
CLOSEST
COLBERT
COLDEST
COLLECT
COMMENT
CONCEIT
CONCEPT
CONCERT
CONGEST
CONNECT
CONSENT
CONTENT
CONTEST
CONTEXT
CONVENT
CONVERT
COOLEST
CORBETT
CORRECT
COZIEST
CRUDEST
CULVERT
CURRENT
CURTEST
DAFTEST
DAMPEST
DANKEST
DARKEST
DEAFEST
DEAREST
DEEPEST
DEFLECT
DEFTEST
DELBERT
DENSEST
DESCENT
DESSERT
DIALECT
DICIEST
DIMMEST
DISSECT
DISSENT
DOPIEST
DORSETT
DOUREST
DRIVEAT
DULLEST
DUMBEST
EARNEST
EASIEST
EDGIEST
EELIEST
EERIEST
ELEMENT
EMINENT
ENTREAT
ESCHEAT
EVENEST
EVEREST
EVERETT
EVIDENT
EVILEST
EXIGENT
FAIREST
FALSEST
FANBELT
FARLEFT
FARWEST
FASTEST
FATTEST
FAWCETT
FERMENT
FERVENT
FIGMENT
FILBERT
FIRMEST
FITTEST
FOLLETT
FONDEST
FORFEIT
FORRENT
FORREST
FORWENT
FOULEST
FOXIEST
FULGENT
FULLEST
FUNFEST
GABFEST
GAMIEST
GANNETT
GARMENT
GARRETT
GILBERT
GOOIEST
GORIEST
GOSSETT
GRAVEST
GRAYEST
GREYEST
HACKETT
HAMMETT
HARDEST
HARVEST
HAZIEST
HERBERT
HEWLETT
HIGHEST
HIPPEST
HOLIEST
HOMIEST
HOTSEAT
HOTTEST
HOWBEIT
ICKIEST
IFFIEST
INANEST
INFLECT
INQUEST
INSPECT
IRATEST
KEENEST
KEYWEST
KINDEST
LACIEST
LAMBENT
LAMBERT
LANKEST
LAPBELT
LARGEST
LAURENT
LAZIEST
LEANEST
LENIENT
LEWDEST
LIMIEST
LIMPEST
LITHEST
LOGIEST
LONGEST
LOOSEST
LOUDEST
LUNGEAT
LUSHEST
MADDEST
MAEWEST
MEANEST
MEEKEST
MIDWEST
MILDEST
MILLETT
MORDENT
NASCENT
NEAREST
NEATEST
NEGLECT
NEWLEFT
NIGHEST
NOBLEST
NOSIEST
NOSWEAT
NUMBEST
NUTMEAT
ODDMENT
OFFBEAT
OILIEST
OLDWEST
ONTHEQT
OPULENT
OVEREAT
PANDECT
PATIENT
PAYMENT
PENDENT
PERCENT
PERFECT
PERTEST
PERVERT
PEUGEOT
PICKETT
PIGMENT
PINIEST
PINKEST
POKIEST
POOREST
PORTENT
POSHEST
PRECEPT
PREFECT
PREHEAT
PRESENT
PRETEST
PRETEXT
PREVENT
PROJECT
PROTECT
PROTEST
PRUDENT
PUCKETT
PUNGENT
PUNIEST
PUPTENT
RACIEST
RAIMENT
RANKEST
RASHEST
REAGENT
REDCENT
REDDEST
REDHEAT
REDMEAT
REELECT
REFLECT
REQUEST
RESPECT
RETREAT
RICHEST
SADDEST
SALIENT
SAPIENT
SARGENT
SEGMENT
SENNETT
SERPENT
SEXIEST
SHUBERT
SICKEST
SLOWEST
SNIDEST
SNIPEAT
SOFTEST
SOLVENT
SOONEST
SOUREST
SPAREST
SPRIEST
SPRYEST
STALEST
STAREAT
STUDENT
SUAVEST
SUBJECT
SUBTEXT
SUBVERT
SUGGEST
SUNBELT
SURFEIT
SUSPECT
SWOREAT
TALLEST
TANGENT
TANNEST
TARTEST
TAUTEST
TEMPEST
TENSEST
TERSEST
THEREAT
TIDIEST
TINIEST
TONIEST
TORMENT
TORRENT
TRABERT
TRIDENT
TRISECT
TRITEST
UGLIEST
UNBLEST
UNGUENT
UNSPENT
UNSWEPT
UPSWEPT
VAGUEST
VAINEST
VASTEST
VINCENT
VIOLENT
WARIEST
WARMEST
WAVIEST
WAXIEST
WEAKEST
WEBFEET
WETTEST
WHEREAT
WHITEST
WILDEST
WILIEST
WIRIEST
ZANIEST

•••••ET

BANQUET
BARONET
BAYONET
BIGFEET
BLANKET
BOOKLET
BOUQUET
BRACKET
BRIDGET
BRIQUET
BRISKET
BULBLET
CABARET
CABINET
CALUMET
CAPELET
CAPULET
CHAPLET
CIRCLET
CORONET
COUPLET
CRICKET
CROCHET
CROQUET
CRUMPET
DATASET
DEADSET
DEEPSET
DESKSET
DOUBLET
DRAGNET
DRIBLET
DROPLET
EPAULET
EPITHET
FISHNET
FRESHET
GANTLET
GETSSET
GILLNET
GOURMET
GRILLET
GROMMET
HAIRNET
HANDSET
HARDSET
HARRIET
HATCHET
HEADSET
JACONET
JOLLIET
KNESSET
LEAFLET
LEARJET
LEVERET
LIFENET
MAIGRET
MARGRET
MINARET
MINDSET
MOONSET
NAILSET
ONADIET
PARAPET
PARQUET
PLACKET
PLAYLET
PLUMMET
PROPHET
PROPJET
QUARTET
QUINTET
QUONSET
RACQUET
RATCHET
RINGLET
RIVULET
ROOTLET
SCARLET
SHERBET
SIDEBET
SKILLET
SNIGLET
SNIPPET
STARLET
TABORET
THICKET
TRINKET
TRIPLET
TRIPPET
TRUMPET
TYPESET
WAVELET
WEBFEET
WELLSET
WHIPPET

EU•••••

EUCHRED
EUCHRES
EUGENIE
EUNUCHS
EUPHONY
EURASIA
EUTERPE

E•U••••

ECUADOR
EDUCATE
EDUCING
ELUDING
ELUSIVE
ELUTING
ELUTION
ELUVIUM
EMULATE
ENURING
EQUABLE
EQUABLY
EQUALED
EQUALLY
EQUATED
EQUATES
EQUATOR
EQUERRY
EQUINES
EQUINOX
ERUCTED
ERUDITE
ERUPTED
EVULSED
EVULSES
EXUDING
EXULTED
EXUPERY
EXURBAN
EXURBIA

E••U•••

EDOUARD
EFFUSED
EFFUSES
ENDUING
ENDURED
ENDURES
ENDUSER
ENGULFS
ENOUNCE
ENSUING
ENSUITE
ENSURED
ENSURES
EPAULET
ESCUDOS
ESQUIRE
ESTUARY
ETRURIA
EUNUCHS
EXCUSED
EXCUSES
EXPUNGE

E•••U••

EARFULS
EARMUFF
EGGCUPS
EMANUEL
ENCRUST
ENDRUNS
ENGLUND
ENROUTE
ENSOULS
ENTHUSE
ENTRUST
EPICURE
ERASURE
ESPOUSE
EVACUEE
EXCLUDE
EXECUTE
EXHAUST
EXPOUND
EXTRUDE
EYECUPS
EYEFULS

E••••U•

EARDRUM
EARPLUG
EASEDUP
EASESUP
EATENUP
EATSOUT
ECHINUS
ECLOGUE
EDGEOUT
EKEDOUT
EKESOUT
ELUVIUM
ELYSIUM
ENAMOUR
ENVIOUS
ERASMUS
ERRATUM
EVENOUT
EVENSUP

E•••••U

EMMYLOU

•EU••••

DEUTERO
FEUDING
NEURONE
NEURONS
NEUTRAL
NEUTRON
OEUVRES
PEUGEOT
REUBENS
REUNIFY
REUNION
REUNITE
REUPPED
REUTERS
REUTHER
TEUTONS
ZEUGMAS

•E•U•••

BEGUILE
BEGUINE

BELUSHI
BEMUSED
BEMUSES
BENUMBS
BEQUEST
CERUMEN
DEBUNKS
DEBUSSY
DEBUTED
DEDUCED
DEDUCES
DEDUCTS
DEFUNCT
DEFUSED
DEFUSES
DELUDED
DELUDES
DELUGED
DELUGES
DELUISE
DEMURER
DENUDED
DENUDES
DEPUTED
DEPUTES
FELUCCA
FERULES
GENUINE
GERUNDS
JEJUNUM
JESUITS
LEDUPTO
LEGUMES
MEDULLA
MEDUSAE
MEDUSAS
MENUHIN
NEBULAE
NEBULAR
NEBULAS
NEXUSES
PENUCHE
PENULTS
PEQUOTS
PERUKES
PERUSAL
PERUSED
PERUSER
PERUSES
PETUNIA
REBUFFS
REBUILD
REBUILT
REBUKED
REBUKES
REBUSES
RECUSED
RECUSES
REDUCED
REDUCER
REDUCES
REFUELS
REFUGEE
REFUGES
REFUNDS
REFUSAL
REFUSED
REFUSER
REFUSES
REFUTED
REFUTER
REFUTES
REGULAR
REGULUS
REMUDAS
REPUGNS
REPULSE
REPUTED
REPUTES
REQUEST
REQUIEM
REQUIRE
REQUITE
RESULTS
RESUMED
RESUMES
RESURGE
RETUNED
RETUNES
RETURNS
SECULAR
SECURED
SECURER
SECURES
SEDUCED
SEDUCER
SEDUCES
SEQUELS
SEQUINS
SEQUOIA
SETUPON
TENUOUS
TENURED
TENURES
TEQUILA
ZEBULON

•E••U••

BECAUSE
BEDAUBS
BEDBUGS
BEDOUIN
BEFOULS
BEOWULF
BERMUDA
CENSURE
CENTURY
DEBAUCH
DEBOUCH
DEFAULT
DEGAUSS
DENEUVE
DENTURE
DETOURS
DEVOURS
FEATURE
FERRULE
GESTURE
HEPBURN
HERCULE
HEXNUTS
HEYJUDE
JETGUNS
KEROUAC
LEAGUER
LEAGUES
LECTURE
LEGPULL
LEISURE
LETTUCE
MEASURE
MEDIUMS
MERCURY
NEPTUNE
NETSUKE
NETSURF
PEANUTS
PENGUIN
PEPLUMS
PERFUME
PERJURE
PERJURY
PERTURB
REBOUND
RECLUSE
RECOUNT
RECOUPS
RECRUIT
REDBUDS
REDGUMS
REDOUBT
REDOUND
REGLUED
REGLUES
REMOUNT
RENAULT
REROUTE
RESCUED
RESCUER
RESCUES
RESOUND
RETOUCH
REWOUND
SEADUTY
SEAGULL
SECLUDE
SENDUPS
SENSUAL
TEACUPS
TEMPURA
TERHUNE
TEXTUAL
TEXTURE
VELLUMS
VELOURS
VENTURA
VENTURE
VERDUGO
VERDURE
VESTURE
WETSUIT
ZEITUNG

•E•••U•

BEADSUP
BEAMSUP
BEARHUG
BEAROUT
BEARSUP
BEATOUT
BEATSUP
BECLOUD
BEEFSUP
BELAKUN
BELGIUM
BELLYUP
BEZIQUE
CELSIUS
CENTAUR
CEPHEUS
DEALOUT
DECKOUT
DECORUM
DEDALUS
DEFRAUD
DEVALUE
DEVIOUS
FEARFUL
FEELOUT
FELLOUT
FELTOUT
FERMIUM
FERROUS
FERVOUR
GEARSUP
GETSOUT
HEADOUT
HEADSUP
HEAROUT
HEATSUP
HEEDFUL
HEINOUS
HELDOUT
HELPFUL
HELPOUT
JEALOUS
JEANLUC
JEJUNUM
KEEPSUP
KEPTOUT
KETCHUP
KEYCLUB
KEYEDUP
LEADOUT
LEADSUP
LEFTOUT
LESPAUL
LETSOUT
METEOUT
NEEDFUL
NERVOUS
OEDIPUS
PEASOUP
PEEKOUT
PEEROUT
PEGASUS
PERKSUP
PERSEUS
PERSIUS
PETROUS
READOUT
REARGUE
REARSUP
REGROUP
REGULUS
REISSUE
REOCCUR
RESIDUE
RESTFUL
RESTSUP
RETINUE
REVALUE
REVENUE
SEALSUP
SEASLUG
SEEKOUT
SEESOUT
SELLOUT
SENDOUT
SENDSUP
SENTOUT
SERIOUS
SERVEUP
SETSOUT
SEVENUP
SEWEDUP
SEYMOUR
TEAMSUP
TEARFUL
TEARSUP
TEDIOUS
TENFOUR
TENSEUP
TENUOUS
TERBIUM
TESTOUT
TETANUS
WEAROUT
WEEDOUT
WELLRUN
WELLSUP
WENTOUT
ZEALOUS
ZESTFUL

•E••••U

NEARYOU

••EU•••

DOEUVRE
QUEUERS
QUEUEUP
QUEUING
SLEUTHS
STEUBEN

••E•U••

AVENUES
CAESURA
CHEQUER
CHEQUES
CHERUBS
COEQUAL
EXECUTE
EYECUPS
EYEFULS
FRENUMS
ICECUBE
NIEBUHR
OVERUSE
PLENUMS
PRELUDE
PRESUME
ROEBUCK
SPELUNK
STEPUPS
UNEQUAL

••E••U•

ACEDOUT
ACESOUT
APERCUS
AREARUG
BEEFSUP
BLEWOUT
BREAKUP
CHECKUP
CHEERUP
CHETRUM
CHEWOUT
CHEWSUP
CLEANUP
CLEARUP
CREEPUP
CREWCUT
DIEDOUT
DIESOUT
DREAMUP
DRESSUP
DREWOUT
DREYFUS
EKEDOUT
EKESOUT
EVENOUT
EVENSUP
FEELOUT
FRETFUL
GIELGUD
GLEEFUL
GOESOUT
HEEDFUL
ICEBLUE
KEEPSUP
NEEDFUL
OCEANUS
OMENTUM
ONEROUS
OPENSUP
OVERBUY
OVERDUB
OVERDUE
OVERRUN
PEEKOUT
PEEROUT
PREMIUM
QUECHUA
QUEUEUP
RHENIUM
SEEKOUT
SEESOUT
SPEAKUP
SPEEDUP
STEPOUT
STEPSUP
STERNUM
SWEEPUP
SWELLUP
SWEPTUP
THEROUX
THESEUS
WEEDOUT

••E•••U

FRENEAU

•••EU••

AUTEURS
DENEUVE
DRSEUSS
GIVEUPS
LINEUPS
LYCEUMS
MAJEURE
MAKEUPS
MUSEUMS
PILEUPS
POSEURS
TUNEUPS

•••E•U•

ACTEDUP
ADDEDUP
ANGELUS
ANTEDUP
ANTESUP
AQUEOUS
ARTEMUS
BALEFUL
BANEFUL
BATEAUX
BONEDUP
BONESUP
BOREOUT
BOXEDUP
BOXESUP
BUREAUS
CAMEOUT
CAREFUL
CHEERUP
COMEDUE
COMEOUT
COMESUP
COVERUP
CREEPUP
CROESUS
DOLEFUL
DOLEOUT
DOPEOUT
DRIEDUP
DRIESUP
DUDEDUP
DUTEOUS
EASEDUP
EASESUP
EATENUP
EDGEOUT
FADEOUT
FAKEFUR
FATEFUL
FIREBUG
FIREDUP
FIRESUP
FIXEDUP
FIXESUP
FORERUN
GASEOUS
GATEAUX
GAVEOUT
GIVEOUT
GIVESUP
GLEEFUL
HATEFUL
HIDEOUS
HIDEOUT
HOLEDUP
HOLEOUT
HOLESUP
HOMERUN
HOPEFUL
HUMERUS
HYPEDUP
IGNEOUS
IMPETUS
INGENUE
JUNEBUG
KEYEDUP
LACEDUP
LACESUP
LINEDUP
LINESUP
LIVEOUT
LOSEOUT
LOVEBUG
MADEOUT
MAKEOUT
MAKESUP
METEOUT
MIXEDUP
MIXESUP
MOVEOUT
NOSEEUM
NOSEOUT
OWNEDUP
PAGEFUL
PHOEBUS
PILEDUP
PILESUP
PINENUT
PINETUM
PIPEDUP
PIPEFUL
PIPESUP
PITEOUS
POKEFUN
RAKEDUP
RAKESUP
REVENUE
RIDEOUT
RODEOUT
ROSEBUD
RULEOUT
SAVEDUP
SAVESUP
SCREWUP
SEVENUP
SEWEDUP
SIZEDUP
SIZESUP
SPEEDUP
SWEEPUP
TAKEOUT
TAKESUP
TIMEOUT
TIMESUP
TIREOUT
TONEDUP
TONESUP
TOREOUT
TUNEDUP
TUNEFUL
TUNEOUT
TUNESUP
TYPEDUP
TYPESUP
WAKEFUL
WAKESUP
WIPEDUP
WIPEOUT
WIPESUP
WISEDUP
WISEGUY
WISESUP
WOKENUP
WOREOUT

•••E••U

ANGELOU
BLUEFLU
ILIESCU

••••EU•

AMADEUS
AMATEUR
ANTAEUS
BORNEUP
BRACEUP
BROKEUP
CEPHEUS
CHOKEUP
CLOSEUP
DANSEUR
DRIVEUP
FLANEUR
FLAREUP
FRAMEUP
HAUTEUR
JUICEUP
LIQUEUR
LOUSEUP
MASSEUR
MILIEUS
MILIEUX
MIMIEUX
MONTEUX
NOSEEUM
NUCLEUS
ORPHEUS
PASSEUL
PASTEUP
PASTEUR
PERSEUS
PIRAEUS
PROTEUS
QUEUEUP
RAISEUP
SCAREUP
SERVEUP
SHAKEUP
SHAPEUP
SPICEUP
SPOKEUP
STOREUP
TENSEUP
THESEUS
TRADEUP
WRITEUP
WROTEUP

••••E•U

CHAPEAU
CHATEAU
COCTEAU
FRENEAU
LAMBEAU
MARCEAU
NOUVEAU
PARVENU
PLATEAU
RAMBEAU
RONDEAU
TABLEAU
THOREAU
TONNEAU
TRUDEAU
WATTEAU

•••••EU

DOUBLEU
PURLIEU

EV•••••

EVACUEE
EVADERS
EVADING
EVANDER
EVANGEL
EVASION
EVASIVE
EVENEST
EVENING
EVENKIS
EVENOUT
EVENSUP
EVEREST
EVERETT
EVERTED
EVICTED
EVIDENT
EVILEST
EVILEYE
EVILLER
EVINCED
EVINCES
EVOKERS
EVOKING
EVOLVED
EVOLVES
EVULSED
EVULSES

E•V••••

ENVELOP
ENVIOUS
ENVYING

E••V•••

ELEVATE
ELEVENS
ELUVIUM

E•••V••

ENDIVES
ENLIVEN
ESTEVEZ
ESTIVAL
EVOLVED
EVOLVES
EXWIVES

E••••V•

ELUSIVE
EMOTIVE
ENCLAVE
ENGRAVE
ENSLAVE
EROSIVE
EVASIVE

•EV••••

BEVELED
BEVERLY
CEVICHE
DEVALUE
DEVEINS
DEVELOP
DEVIANT
DEVIATE
DEVICES
DEVILED
DEVILLE
DEVILRY
DEVIOUS
DEVISED
DEVISES
DEVOLVE
DEVOTED
DEVOTEE
DEVOTES
DEVOURS
DEVRIES
LEVELED
LEVELER
LEVELLY
LEVERED
LEVERET
LEVIERS
LEVITES
LEVYING
NEVADAN
NEVILLE
REVALUE
REVAMPS
REVEALS
REVELED
REVELER
REVELRY
REVENGE
REVENUE
REVERBS
REVERED
REVERES
REVERIE
REVERSE
REVERTS
REVIEWS
REVILED
REVILES
REVISED
REVISER
REVISES
REVISIT
REVIVAL
REVIVED
REVIVES
REVOICE
REVOKED
REVOKES
REVOLTS
REVOLVE
REVVING
SEVENTH
SEVENTY
SEVENUP
SEVERAL
SEVERED
SEVERER
SEVIGNE
SEVILLE
YEVGENY

•E•V•••

BEAVERS
DELVERS
DELVING
DERVISH
FERVENT
FERVORS
FERVOUR
HEAVEHO
HEAVENS
HEAVERS
HEAVETO
HEAVIER
HEAVIES
HEAVILY
HEAVING
LEAVENS
LEAVING
NERVIER
NERVILY
NERVOUS
OEUVRES
PEAVEYS
PEEVING
PEEVISH
PERVADE
PERVERT
REAVAIL
REVVING
SELVAGE
SERVALS
SERVANT
SERVERS
SERVEUP
SERVICE
SERVILE
SERVING
VELVETS
VELVETY
VERVETS
WEAVERS
WEAVING
WEEVILS

•E••V••

BEDEVIL
BEHAVED
BEHAVES
BELOVED
DEKOVEN
DELIVER
DERIVED
DERIVES
GETEVEN
GETOVER
HESHVAN
LEHAVRE
MEDEVAC
RECOVER
RELIVED
RELIVES
REMOVAL
REMOVED
REMOVER
REMOVES
REPAVED
REPAVES
REVIVAL
REVIVED
REVIVES
REWOVEN
SEGOVIA
TELAVIV
YEREVAN

•E•••V•

BEEHIVE
BEHOOVE
BELIEVE
BEREAVE
CENTAVO
DECEIVE
DENEUVE
DEPRAVE
DEPRIVE
DESERVE
DEVOLVE
FESTIVE
KEDROVA
NEWWAVE
PENSIVE
RECEIVE
RELIEVE
RELIEVO
REPROVE
RESERVE
RESOLVE
RESTIVE
REVOLVE
REWEAVE
TENSIVE
YESHIVA

•E••••V

NEMEROV
TELAVIV

••EV•••

BREVETS
BREVITY
CHEVIED
CHEVIES
CHEVIOT
CHEVRES
CHEVRON
COEVALS
CREVICE
ELEVATE
ELEVENS
GUEVARA
PEEVING
PEEVISH
PREVAIL
PREVENT
PREVIEW
STEVENS
TREVINO
WEEVILS

••E•V••

CHEEVER
CHERVIL
CLEAVED
CLEAVER
CLEAVES
CLEAVON
DOEUVRE
GREAVES
LIEOVER
SHEAVED
SHEAVES
SHELVED
SHELVES
SLEEVES
SWERVED
SWERVES
TWELVES

••E••V•

BEEHIVE

••E•••V

CHEKHOV

•••EV••

BEDEVIL
BILEVEL
CHEEVER
ESTEVEZ
FOREVER
GETEVEN
GOTEVEN
GRIEVED
GRIEVER
GRIEVES
HOWEVER
KNIEVEL
MEDEVAC
NINEVEH
SLEEVES
THIEVED
THIEVES
WHOEVER
YEREVAN

•••E•V•

BEREAVE
DECEIVE
DENEUVE
DESERVE
MINERVA
OBSERVE
ONLEAVE
RECEIVE
RESERVE
REWEAVE
UNNERVE
UNWEAVE

•••E••V
NEMEROV
NUREYEV

••••EV•
ACHIEVE
BELIEVE
RELIEVE
RELIEVO

••••E•V
CABLETV

•••••EV
NUREYEV

E•W••••
EBWHITE
EDWARDS
ENWRAPS
EXWIVES

E••W•••
EARWIGS
ENDWAYS
ENDWISE
ENTWINE
EREWHON
EYEWASH

E•••W••
EATAWAY
ELBOWED
EMPOWER
ENDOWED

E••••W•
ESCHEWS
ESCROWS

E•••••W
EATCROW
EYEBROW

•EW••••
BEWAILS
BEWITCH
DEWCLAW
DEWDROP
DEWILDE
DEWLAPS
DEWLINE
GEWGAWS
HEWLETT
JEWELED
JEWELER
JEWELRY
KEWPIES
LEWDEST
MEWLERS
MEWLING
NEWAGER
NEWBORN
NEWDEAL
NEWGATE
NEWHART
NEWLEFT
NEWLOOK
NEWMATH
NEWMOON
NEWMOWN
NEWNESS
NEWPORT
NEWSBOY
NEWSDAY
NEWSIER
NEWSMAN
NEWSMEN
NEWTONS
NEWTOWN
NEWWAVE
NEWYEAR
NEWYORK
REWARDS
REWARMS
REWAXED
REWAXES
REWEAVE
REWELDS
REWINDS
REWIRED
REWIRES
REWORDS
REWORKS
REWOUND
REWOVEN
REWRAPS
REWRITE
REWROTE
SEWEDUP

•E•W•••
BEOWULF
BETWEEN
BETWIXT
GEEWHIZ
GETWELL
HEYWOOD
JETWASH
KEYWEST
KEYWORD
LEEWARD
LEGWORK
MEOWING
NETWORK
NEWWAVE
PEEWEES
REDWINE
REDWING
REDWOLF
REDWOOD
SEAWALL
SEAWARD
SEAWAYS
SEAWEED

•E••W••
BEDEWED
BEESWAX
BELTWAY
GETAWAY
HEADWAY
REMOWED
RENEWAL
RENEWED
RENEWER
RETOWED

•E•••W•
BEDDOWN
BELLOWS
BESTOWS
FELLOWS
GEEGAWS
GETDOWN
GEWGAWS
HEBREWS
HEEHAWS
LETDOWN
MEADOWS
MEADOWY
MELLOWS
NEPHEWS
NEWMOWN
NEWTOWN
PEAFOWL
REDRAWN
REDRAWS
REVIEWS
SEACOWS
SEESAWS
SETDOWN
YELLOWS

•E••••W
BEARPAW
BESTREW
DEWCLAW

••EW•••
ALEWIFE
BLEWOFF
BLEWOUT
BREWERS
BREWERY
BREWING
CHEWERS
CHEWIER
CHEWING
CHEWOUT
CHEWSUP
CREWCUT
CREWELS
CREWING
CREWMAN
CREWMEN
DREWOUT
EREWHON
EYEWASH
GEEWHIZ
LEEWARD
MAEWEST
PEEWEES
PREWASH
SHEWOLF
SKEWERS
SKEWING
SPEWING
STEWARD
STEWART
STEWERS
STEWING
VIEWERS
VIEWING

••E•W••
AREAWAY
BEESWAX
BOERWAR
FREEWAY
SHERWIN

••E••W•
DIEDOWN
GEEGAWS
HEEHAWS
HOEDOWN
LIEDOWN
OVERAWE
PREDAWN
SEESAWS
TIEDOWN

••E•••W
ATECROW
EYEBROW
FRETSAW
ICESHOW
JOEBLOW
LIESLOW
OVERSAW
PREVIEW

•••EW••
BEDEWED
BIKEWAY
CSLEWIS
FREEWAY
GATEWAY
GAVEWAY
GIVEWAY
JANEWAY
MADEWAY
MAKEWAY
MATEWAN
RACEWAY
RENEWAL
RENEWED
RENEWER
SCREWED
SCREWUP
SOMEWAY
STREWED
STREWER
THREWIN
TIMEWAS
UNSEWED

•••E••W
BIGELOW
BLUELAW
CASELAW
DANELAW
FOREPAW
FORESAW
GAMELAW
LIKENEW
ROPETOW
SOMEHOW
TONEROW

••••EW•
ANDREWS
CASHEWS
CURFEWS
CURLEWS
ESCHEWS
HEBREWS
MATHEWS
MILDEWS
MILDEWY
NEPHEWS
OLDNEWS
REVIEWS
SUNDEWS

•••••EW
AIRCREW
BESTREW
DOGCHEW
INASTEW
LIKENEW
MATTHEW
OUTDREW
OUTGREW
PREVIEW
PURVIEW
UNSCREW

EX•••••
EXACTED
EXACTER
EXACTLY
EXACTOR
EXALTED
EXAMINE
EXAMPLE
EXCEEDS
EXCEPTS
EXCERPT
EXCISED
EXCISES
EXCITED
EXCITES
EXCLAIM
EXCLUDE
EXCRETE
EXCUSED
EXCUSES
EXECUTE
EXEMPLI
EXEMPTS
EXERTED
EXHALED
EXHALES
EXHAUST
EXHIBIT
EXHORTS
EXIGENT
EXILING
EXISTED
EXITING
EXOTICA
EXOTICS
EXPANDS
EXPANSE
EXPARTE
EXPECTS
EXPENDS
EXPENSE
EXPERTS
EXPIATE
EXPIRED
EXPIRES
EXPLAIN
EXPLODE
EXPLOIT
EXPLORE
EXPORTS
EXPOSED
EXPOSES
EXPOUND
EXPRESS
EXPUNGE
EXTENDS
EXTENTS
EXTINCT
EXTORTS
EXTRACT
EXTREME
EXTRUDE
EXUDING
EXULTED
EXUPERY
EXURBAN
EXURBIA
EXWIVES

E••X•••
ELIXIRS
EPOXIES

E•••••X
EQUINOX

•EX••••
DEXTRIN
HEXAGON
HEXNUTS
HEXSIGN
LEXICAL
LEXICON
MEXICAN
NEXUSES
REXCATS
REXREED
SEXIEST
SEXISTS
SEXTANS
SEXTANT
SEXTETS
SEXTONS
TEXTILE
TEXTUAL
TEXTURE
VEXEDLY

•E••X••
HELIXES
RELAXED
RELAXES
REMIXED
REMIXES
RETAXED
RETAXES
REWAXED
REWAXES
TELEXED
TELEXES

•E•••X•
BETWIXT

•E••••X
BEATRIX
BEESWAX
BETAMAX
DEEPSIX
GEARBOX
HENDRIX
MEMOREX
PERPLEX
REAFFIX

••EX•••
COEXIST
FLEXING
FLEXNER
FLEXORS
INEXACT
PLEXORS

••E•X••
ICEAXES

••E••X•
PRETEXT

••E•••X
BEESWAX
BRERFOX
DEEPSIX
KLEENEX
SKEEZIX
THEROUX

•••EX••
ANNEXED
ANNEXES
INDEXED
INDEXES
LATEXES
TELEXED
TELEXES
URTEXTS

•••E•X•
POLEAXE

•••E••X
BATEAUX
BLUEFOX
CAKEMIX
CINEMAX
FIREBOX
GATEAUX
GORETEX
JUKEBOX
KLEENEX
PHOENIX
SHOEBOX
SKEEZIX

••••EX•
CONTEXT
PRETEXT
SUBTEXT

••••E•X
MILIEUX
MIMIEUX
MONTEUX

•••••EX
COMPLEX
GORETEX
KLEENEX
MADAMEX
MEMOREX
NARTHEX
PERPLEX
ROLODEX
SIMPLEX
SPANDEX
TRIPLEX

EY•••••
EYEBALL
EYEBANK
EYEBOLT
EYEBROW
EYECUPS
EYEFULS
EYEHOLE
EYELASH
EYELETS
EYELIDS
EYESORE
EYEWASH

E•Y••••
ELYSEES
ELYSIAN
ELYSIUM

E••Y•••
ECDYSES
ECDYSIS
ECTYPES
EDDYING
EMMYLOU
ENVYING
ENZYMES
ESPYING

E•••Y••
EARLYON
EMBRYOS
ENCRYPT
ENJOYED
EPONYMS
ESSAYED

E••••Y•
EMPLOYS
ENDWAYS
ESTRAYS
EVILEYE

E•••••Y
EAGERLY
EARTHLY
EATAWAY
ECOLOGY
ECONOMY
ECSTASY
EDACITY
ELDERLY
EMBASSY
EMPATHY
EMPTILY
ENDPLAY
ENTROPY
EQUABLY
EQUALLY
EQUERRY
ERECTLY
ESTUARY
EUPHONY
EXACTLY
EXUPERY

•EY••••
FEYNMAN
GEYSERS
HEYDAYS
HEYJUDE
HEYWOOD
KEYCARD
KEYCLUB
KEYEDIN
KEYEDUP
KEYHOLE
KEYLIME
KEYNOTE
KEYPADS
KEYRING
KEYWEST
KEYWORD
REYNARD
SEYMOUR

•E•Y•••
BELYING
DEFYING
DENYING
KENYANS
LEVYING
NEWYEAR
NEWYORK
RECYCLE
RELYING
RETYPED
RETYPES

•E••Y••
BELAYED
BELLYUP
DECAYED
DECOYED
DECRYPT
DELAYED
DELAYER
MEGRYAN
NEARYOU
REDEYES
REKEYED
RELAYED
RESTYLE
ZEPHYRS

•E•••Y•
BETRAYS
DEADEYE
DEEJAYS
DEFRAYS
DEPLOYS
HEYDAYS
JERSEYS
MEDLEYS
PEAVEYS
REPLAYS
SEAWAYS
TEAPOYS
VEEJAYS

•E••••Y
BEANERY
BEASTLY
BEATIFY
BELLAMY
BELLBOY
BELTWAY
BENTLEY
BESTBOY
BETARAY
BETHANY
BEVERLY
CENTURY
CERTIFY
DEBAKEY
DEBUSSY
DEEPFRY
DEERFLY
DELANEY
DEMPSEY
DENNEHY
DENSELY
DENSITY
DESTINY
DESTROY
DEVILRY
FETIDLY
GEODESY
GEOLOGY
GERMANY
GETAWAY
HEADILY
HEADWAY
HEALTHY
HEARSAY
HEAVILY
HEFTILY
HELOTRY
HEMSLEY
HENNERY
HERSHEY
JEFFREY
JERKILY
JEWELRY
KENNEDY
LEERILY
LEGALLY
LEGIBLY
LENGTHY
LETSFLY
LEVELLY
MEADOWY
MERCURY
MERRILY
MESSILY
NEEDILY
NERVILY
NEWSBOY
NEWSDAY
PEABODY
PECCARY
PENALTY
PEPPERY
PEPPILY
PERFIDY
PERJURY
PERKILY
PESKILY
PETRIFY
PETTILY
READILY
REALITY
RECENCY
RECTIFY
RECTORY
REENTRY
REGALLY
REGENCY
REMARRY
REUNIFY
REVELRY
SEADUTY
SEALILY
SECRECY
SEEDILY
SENSORY
SEVENTY
TEARILY
TEATRAY
TENABLY
TENANCY
TENSELY
TEPIDLY
TERNARY
TERRIFY
TERSELY
TESTIFY
TESTILY
VELVETY
VERSIFY
VEXEDLY
WEALTHY
WEARILY
WEEKDAY
WEIGHTY
WEIRDLY
YEVGENY

••EY•••
DREYFUS
GREYEST
GREYING
OBEYING
PREYSON

••E•Y••
AYEAYES
ONEEYED
TIEDYED
TIEDYES

••E••Y•
DEEJAYS
PREPAYS
VEEJAYS

••E•••Y
ADEPTLY
ALERTLY
AMENITY
AREAWAY
BLEAKLY
BREATHY
BREVITY
BREWERY
CHEAPLY
CLEANLY
CLEARLY
DEEPFRY
DEERFLY
DIETARY
ERECTLY
FIERILY
FLEETLY
FREEWAY
FRESHLY
GREATLY
GREELEY
GREGORY
GRETZKY
IDEALLY
INEPTLY
INERTLY
LEERILY
NEEDILY
OVERBUY
OVERFLY
OVERJOY
OVERLAY
OVERTLY
PLENARY
PREACHY
PRESLEY
QUEENLY
QUEERLY
REENTRY
SCENERY
SEEDILY
SHEERLY
SHELLEY
SKETCHY
SLEEKLY
SPECIFY
STEEPLY
STERNLY
SWEARBY
SWEETLY
SWELTRY
THERAPY
THEREBY
TIERNEY
TREACLY
TREMBLY
TRENARY
TUESDAY
WEEKDAY
WHEREBY

•••EY••
ALLEYES
BIGEYES
BOGEYED
BUGEYED
DRYEYED
HONEYED
MONEYED
MOSEYED
NUREYEV
ONEEYED
POPEYED
REDEYES
REKEYED
RIBEYES
VANEYCK

•••E••Y
ALLERGY
ALREADY
AMNESTY
APLENTY
ARDENCY
BASEPAY
BEVERLY
BIKEWAY
BLUEBOY
BLUEJAY
BLUESKY
BONEDRY
BRIEFLY
CHIEFLY
COGENCY
COMESBY
CRUELLY
DARESAY
DATEDLY
DAZEDLY
EAGERLY
ELDERLY
EQUERRY
FIREFLY
FIXEDLY
FLEETLY
FLUENCY
FREEWAY
GATEWAY
GAVEWAY
GIVEWAY
GREELEY
HONESTY
JADEDLY
JANEWAY
JEWELRY
LATENCY
LAZENBY
LEVELLY
LIBERTY
LOVERLY
MADEHAY
MADEWAY
MAJESTY
MAKEHAY
MAKEWAY
MISERLY
MODESTY
MORESBY
NAKEDLY
NAMEDAY
NOSEGAY
NOVELTY
ORDERLY
PAGEBOY
PALEDRY
POTENCY
POVERTY
PUBERTY
QUEENLY
QUEERLY
QUIETLY
RACEWAY
RECENCY
REGENCY
REVELRY
SAMEDAY
SEVENTY
SHEERLY
SLEEKLY
SOBERLY
SOMEDAY
SOMEWAY
SQUEAKY
STEEPLY
STREAKY
SWEETLY
SYNERGY
THIERRY
THREADY
TIREDLY
UNREADY
URGENCY
UTTERLY
VEXEDLY
VICEROY
WISEGUY

••••EY•
BAILEYS
BARLEYS
BARNEYS
BUCKEYE
CATSEYE
CONVEYS
DEADEYE
DICKEYS
DONKEYS
EVILEYE
FISHEYE
FONTEYN
GALLEYS
GLADEYE
GURNEYS
HAWKEYE
JERSEYS
JITNEYS
JOCKEYS
KIDNEYS
LACKEYS
MAGUEYS
MEDLEYS
MONKEYS
OSPREYS
PARLEYS

PEAVEYS
PULLEYS
PURVEYS
RICKEYS
ROMNEYS
SHUTEYE
SOCKEYE
STOREYS
SURREYS
SURVEYS
TURKEYS
VALLEYS
VOLLEYS
WALLEYE

••••E•Y

ABIDEBY
ACADEMY
ACUTELY
AGILELY
ALCHEMY
ANXIETY
ARCHERY
BATTERY
BEANERY
BINDERY
BIOGENY
BRAVELY
BRAVERY
BREWERY
BRIBERY
BUTTERY
BYTHEBY
CANNERY
CLOSELY
CONNERY
COOKERY
COPPERY
CRUDELY
CUTLERY
DENNEHY
DENSELY
DITHERY
DRAPERY
DUBIETY
EXUPERY
FALSELY
FIDGETY
FISHERY
FLOWERY
FOOLERY
FOPPERY
FORGERY
GADGETY
GALLERY
GEODESY
GINGERY
GRAVELY
GROCERY
GUNNERY
HENNERY
HOSIERY
IMAGERY
IMPIETY
INANELY
IRATELY
JIGGERY
JITTERY
JOINERY
KENNEDY
KNAVERY
LARCENY
LARGELY
LATHERY
LICKETY
LIQUEFY
LITHELY
LOOSELY
LOTTERY
MASTERY
MILDEWY
MOCKERY
MUMMERY
MYSTERY
NAIVELY
NUNNERY
NURSERY
PEPPERY
POTTERY
POWDERY
PROGENY
PRUDERY
PTOLEMY
PUFFERY
QUAVERY
RAGGEDY
RICKETY
RIFLERY
ROBBERY
ROGUERY
ROOKERY
RUBBERY
SATIETY
SCENERY
SECRECY
SHAPELY
SHOWERY
SILVERY
SLAVERY
SNIDELY
SOCIETY
SORCERY
SPARELY
SPIDERY
STATELY
STOKELY
STUPEFY
SUAVELY
SUMMERY
SURGERY
SWOREBY
TANNERY
TENSELY
TERSELY
THEREBY
TOTTERY
TRACERY
TRAGEDY
TRITELY
VAGUELY
VARIETY
VELVETY
WAGGERY
WHEREBY
WINTERY
YEVGENY

•••••EY

BALONEY
BENTLEY
BLARNEY
BRADLEY
BUCKLEY
CHANTEY
CHARLEY
CHIMNEY
CHUTNEY
CLOONEY
COCKNEY
COMFREY
CURTSEY
DAHOMEY
DALTREY
DEBAKEY
DELANEY
DEMPSEY
DIDDLEY
DISOBEY
FRAWLEY
GODFREY
GREELEY
GRIFFEY
HACKNEY
HEMSLEY
HERSHEY
HUNTLEY
JEFFREY
JOFFREY
JOURNEY
LAMPREY
LANGLEY
LINDSEY
MAHONEY
MALMSEY
MURPHEY
ODYSSEY
PAISLEY
PALFREY
PALJOEY
PARSLEY
PASSKEY
PRESLEY
QUIGLEY
SHARKEY
SHELLEY
SHIRLEY
SOUTHEY
STANLEY
STOOKEY
TIERNEY
TOURNEY
TROLLEY
TURNKEY
WHISKEY
WHITNEY
WINFREY
WOOLSEY
WRIGLEY

EZ•••••

EZEKIEL

E•Z••••

ENZYMES

E••Z•••

ENDZONE

E•••••Z

ESTEVEZ

•EZ••••

BEZIERS
BEZIQUE
CEZANNE
JEZEBEL
REZONED
REZONES

•E•Z•••

BENZENE
GEEZERS
SEIZERS
SEIZING

•E••Z••

BEDIZEN
BENAZIR
DENIZEN
LEIPZIG
REBOZOS
SELTZER

•E•••Z•

MENDOZA
MESTIZO
REALIZE

•E••••Z

BERLIOZ
BERLITZ
GEEWHIZ
HEIFETZ
LEIBNIZ

••EZ•••

GEEZERS
MUEZZIN

••E•Z••

BREEZED
BREEZES
DWEEZIL
FREEZER
FREEZES
GRETZKY
MUEZZIN
PRETZEL
QUETZAL
SKEEZIX
SNEEZED
SNEEZER
SNEEZES
TWEEZED
TWEEZES
WHEEZED
WHEEZER
WHEEZES

••E••Z•

ITEMIZE
OBELIZE

••E•••Z

GEEWHIZ

•••EZ••

BREEZED
BREEZES
DWEEZIL
FREEZER
FREEZES
FRIEZES
SKEEZIX
SNEEZED
SNEEZER
SNEEZES
TWEEZED
TWEEZES
WHEEZED
WHEEZER
WHEEZES

•••E•Z•

CADENZA
FIRENZE
LORENZO
SCHERZI
SCHERZO
SQUEEZE

•••E••Z

ALBENIZ
ESTEVEZ
JIMENEZ

••••EZ•

SQUEEZE
TRAPEZE
ZAMBEZI

••••E•Z

HEIFETZ
KOBLENZ

•••••EZ

ALVAREZ
ESTEVEZ
JIMENEZ
LAISSEZ
MARQUEZ
NATCHEZ

FA•••••

FABARES
FABERGE
FABRICS
FACADES
FACEOFF
FACETED
FACIALS
FACINGS
FACTION
FACTORS
FACTORY
FACTUAL
FACULTY
FADDISH
FADDISM
FADDIST
FADEDIN
FADEINS
FADEOUT
FADESIN
FADIMAN
FAGENDS
FAGGING
FAGOTED
FAIENCE
FAILING
FAILURE
FAINTED
FAINTER
FAINTLY
FAIREST
FAIRIES
FAIRING
FAIROFF
FAIRSUP
FAIRWAY
FAJITAS
FAKEFUR
FALAFEL
FALCONS
FALLACY
FALLFOR
FALLGUY
FALLING
FALLOFF
FALLOUT
FALLOWS
FALLSIN
FALLSON
FALLSTO
FALSELY
FALSEST
FALSIFY
FALSITY
FALTERS
FALWELL
FAMULUS
FANATIC
FANBELT
FANCIED
FANCIER
FANCIES
FANCILY
FANFARE
FANIONS
FANJETS
FANMAIL
FANNING
FANSOUT
FANTAIL
FANTASY
FANZINE
FARADAY
FARAWAY
FAREAST
FARGONE
FARLEFT
FARMERS
FARMING
FARMOUT
FARRAGO
FARRIER
FARROWS
FARTHER
FARWEST
FASCIAS
FASCISM
FASCIST
FASHION
FASTENS
FASTEST
FASTING
FASTONE
FATBACK
FATCATS
FATCITY
FATEFUL
FATHEAD
FATHERS
FATHOMS
FATIGUE
FATLESS
FATNESS
FATTENS
FATTEST
FATUITY
FATUOUS
FAUCETS
FAULTED
FAUSTUS
FAUVISM
FAUVIST
FAUXPAS
FAVORED
FAVOURS
FAWCETT
FAWNERS
FAWNING
FAYWRAY

F•A••••

FEARERS
FEARFUL
FEARING
FEASTED
FEATHER
FEATURE
FIACRES
FIANCEE
FIANCES
FIASCOS
FLACCID
FLACONS
FLAGDAY
FLAGGED
FLAGMAN
FLAGMEN
FLAGONS
FLAILED
FLAKERS
FLAKIER
FLAKING
FLAMBED
FLAMBES
FLAMING
FLANEUR
FLANGES
FLANKED
FLANKER
FLANNEL
FLAPPED
FLAPPER
FLAREUP
FLARING
FLASHED
FLASHER
FLASHES
FLATBED
FLATCAR
FLATOUT
FLATTED
FLATTEN
FLATTER
FLATTOP
FLAUNTS
FLAVORS
FLAVOUR
FLAWING
FLAYING
FOALING
FOAMIER
FOAMING
FRACTAL
FRAGILE
FRAICHE
FRAILER
FRAILTY
FRAISES
FRAMEUP
FRAMING
FRANCES
FRANCIS
FRANKED
FRANKER
FRANKIE
FRANKLY
FRANKOZ
FRANTIC
FRAPPES
FRASIER
FRAUGHT
FRAWLEY
FRAYING
FRAZIER
FRAZZLE

F••A•••

FABARES
FACADES
FALAFEL
FANATIC
FARADAY
FARAWAY
FEMALES
FINAGLE
FINALES
FINALLY
FINANCE
FIXABLE
FIXATED
FIXATES
FLEABAG
FLOATED
FLOATER
FLYAWAY
FMRADIO
FORAGED
FORAGER
FORAGES
FREAKED
FRIABLE

F•••A••

FACIALS
FALLACY
FANFARE
FANMAIL
FANTAIL
FANTASY
FAREAST
FARRAGO
FATBACK
FATCATS
FERRARI
FERRARO
FERRATE
FIJIANS
FINEART
FINIALS
FINLAND
FIREANT
FIREARM
FLYBALL
FLYCAST
FLYPAST
FLYWAYS
FOGBANK
FOLIAGE
FOLIATE
FOLKART
FONDANT
FOOTAGE
FORBADE
FOREARM
FORGAVE
FORMALS
FORMATS
FORSAKE
FORSALE
FORWARD
FOULARD
FOXTAIL
FRIDAYS
FRIGATE
FROMAGE
FROWARD
FRYPANS
FUNFAIR
FURBALL
FURNACE

F••••A•

FACTUAL
FADIMAN
FAIRWAY
FAJITAS
FARADAY
FARAWAY
FASCIAS
FATHEAD
FAUXPAS
FAYWRAY
FEDERAL
FEDORAS
FEEDBAG
FELDMAN
FEMORAL
FEYNMAN
FIBULAE
FIBULAS
FIESTAS
FIGLEAF
FIREMAN
FLAGDAY
FLAGMAN
FLATCAR
FLEABAG
FLIESAT
FLOTSAM
FLUVIAL
FLYAWAY
FLYLEAF
FLYTRAP
FOOTMAN
FOOTPAD
FORBEAR
FORDHAM
FOREMAN
FOREPAW
FORERAN
FORESAW
FORREAL
FORTRAN
FRACTAL
FREEMAN
FREEWAY
FREITAG
FRENEAU
FRETSAW
FRIEDAN
FRISIAN
FROGMAN
FRONTAL
FROWNAT
FURSEAL
FUSTIAN

F•••••A

FELICIA
FELUCCA
FLORIDA
FONTINA
FORMICA
FORMOSA
FORMULA
FORTUNA
FREESIA
FUCHSIA

•FA••••

OFASORT

•F•A•••

AFFABLE
AFFABLY
AFFAIRE
AFFAIRS
AFRAMES
EFFACED
EFFACES

•F••A••

AFFRAYS
AFGHANI
AFGHANS
OFFBASE
OFFHAND
OFFRAMP

•F•••A•

AFRICAN
OFFBEAT
OFFLOAD
OFFPEAK
OFFROAD
OFFYEAR

••FA•••

AFFABLE
AFFABLY
AFFAIRE
AFFAIRS
ALFALFA
ASFARAS
ATFAULT
BEFALLS
DEFACED
DEFACES
DEFACTO
DEFAMED
DEFAMES
DEFARGE
DEFAULT
EFFACED
EFFACES
INFANCY
INFANTA
INFANTS
INFAVOR
LAFARGE
NOFAULT
REFACED
REFACES
SAFARIS
SOFABED
UNFAZED

••F•A••

AFFRAYS
BUFFALO
CAFTANS
DEFEATS
DEFIANT
DEFLATE
DEFRAUD
DEFRAYS
GUFFAWS
INFLAME
INFLATE
KAFTANS
OFFBASE
OFFHAND
OFFRAMP
REFRACT
REFRAIN
REFRAME
TIFFANY

••F••A•

ASFARAS
BIFOCAL
HOFBRAU
HOFFMAN
OFFBEAT
OFFLOAD
OFFPEAK
OFFROAD
OFFYEAR
REFUSAL
RUFFIAN
RUFIYAA

••F•••A

ALFALFA
INFANTA
RUFIYAA
TAFFETA

•••FA••

AIRFARE
ANTFARM
BEEFALO
BELFAST
BIDFAIR
BUFFALO
BUSFARE
CARFARE
CONFABS
DOGFACE
FANFARE
FUNFAIR
GUFFAWS
LENFANT
LOOFAHS
MAYFAIR
OUTFACE
PARFAIT
PITFALL
PREFABS
PREFACE
PROFANE
SEAFANS
SHOFARS
SULFATE
SURFACE
TIFFANY
WARFARE
WELFARE

•••F•A•

EARFLAP
HALFDAN
HALFWAY
HOFFMAN
REDFLAG
RUFFIAN
SNIFFAT
WOLFGAL
WOLFMAN
WOLFRAM

•••F••A

TAFFETA

••••FA•

BODYFAT
DEEPFAT
HALIFAX
INSOFAR
LATIFAH
SNIFFAT
THUSFAR

••••F•A

RATAFIA

•••••FA

ALFALFA
MUSTAFA

F•B••••

FABARES
FABERGE
FABRICS
FEBRILE
FIBBERS
FIBBING
FIBRILS
FIBROUS
FIBULAE
FIBULAS
FOBBING
FOBSOFF

F••B•••

FANBELT
FATBACK
FEEBLER
FIBBERS
FIBBING
FILBERT
FLUBBED
FLYBALL
FLYBOYS
FOBBING
FOGBANK
FOGBOWS
FOIBLES
FORBADE
FORBEAR
FORBIDS
FORBORE
FUMBLED
FUMBLER
FUMBLES
FURBALL
FURBISH

F•••B••

FEEDBAG
FIREBOX
FIREBUG
FIXABLE
FLAMBED
FLAMBES
FLATBED
FLEABAG
FLUBBED
FNUMBER
FREEBEE
FREEBIE
FRIABLE
FRISBEE

F•••••B

FOODWEB

•F•B•••

OFFBASE
OFFBEAT

•F••B••

AFFABLE
AFFABLY

••FB•••

HOFBRAU
OFFBASE
OFFBEAT

••F•B••

AFFABLE
AFFABLY
SOFABED

•••F•B•

CONFABS
PREFABS

F•C••••

FACADES
FACEOFF
FACETED
FACIALS
FACINGS
FACTION
FACTORS
FACTORY
FACTUAL
FACULTY
FICKLER
FICTION
FICTIVE
FICUSES
FOCSLES
FOCUSED
FOCUSES
FUCHSIA

F••C•••

FALCONS
FANCIED
FANCIER
FANCIES
FANCILY
FASCIAS
FASCISM
FASCIST
FATCATS
FATCITY
FAUCETS
FAWCETT
FENCERS
FENCING
FETCHED
FETCHES
FIACRES
FILCHED
FILCHER
FILCHES
FINCHES
FISCHER
FITCHES
FLACCID
FLACONS
FLECHES
FLECKED

FLICKED
FLICKER
FLOCKED
FLOCKTO
FLYCAST
FORCEPS
FORCERS
FORCING
FRACTAL
FRECKLE
FRICKIE
FROCKED
FRYCOOK
FULCRUM

F•••C••
FELICIA
FELUCCA
FIANCEE
FIANCES
FIASCOS
FIERCER
FINICKY
FLACCID
FLATCAR
FLEECED
FLEECES
FRAICHE
FRANCES
FRANCIS
FRESCOS

F••••C•
FABRICS
FAIENCE
FALLACY
FATBACK
FELUCCA
FETLOCK
FINANCE
FLOUNCE
FLUENCY
FORMICA
FOSDICK
FROLICS
FURNACE
FUSTICS

F•••••C
FANATIC
FRANTIC
FREDRIC

•F••C••
AFFECTS
AFRICAN
EFFACED
EFFACES
EFFECTS
OFFICER
OFFICES

•F•••C•
AFFLICT
OFFENCE

••F•C••
AFFECTS
BIFOCAL
DEFACED
DEFACES
DEFACTO
DEFECTS
DEFICIT
EFFACED
EFFACES
EFFECTS
INFECTS
INFOCUS
OFFICER
OFFICES
REFACED
REFACES

••F••C•
AFFLICT
BYFORCE
DEFENCE
DEFLECT
DEFROCK
DEFUNCT
ENFORCE
INFANCY
INFLECT
INFLICT
INFORCE
OFFENCE
REFLECT
REFRACT
SUFFICE
UNFROCK

•••F•C•
DOGFACE
EDIFICE
ORIFICE
OUTFACE
PERFECT
PREFACE
PREFECT
SUFFICE
SURFACE

•••F••C
AELFRIC
TRAFFIC

••••F•C
MALEFIC
OSSIFIC
PACIFIC
TRAFFIC

F•D••••
FADDISH
FADDISM
FADDIST
FADEDIN
FADEINS
FADEOUT
FADESIN
FADIMAN
FEDERAL
FEDORAS
FIDDLED
FIDDLER
FIDDLES
FIDELIO
FIDGETS
FIDGETY
FODDERS
FUDDLED
FUDDLES
FUDGING

F••D•••
FADDISH
FADDISM
FADDIST
FEEDBAG
FEEDERS
FEEDING
FEEDLOT
FEEDSON
FELDMAN
FENDERS
FENDING
FEUDING
FIDDLED
FIDDLER
FIDDLES
FIEDLER
FINDERS
FINDING
FINDOUT
FLEDGED
FLEDGES
FODDERS
FOLDERS
FOLDING
FOLDOUT
FOLDSUP
FOLDUPS
FONDANT
FONDEST
FONDLED
FONDLES
FONDUES
FOODWEB
FORDHAM
FORDING
FOSDICK
FREDDIE
FREDRIC
FRIDAYS
FRIDGES
FUDDLED
FUDDLES
FUNDING

F•••D••
FACADES
FADEDIN
FARADAY
FETIDLY
FIEFDOM
FIELDED
FIELDER
FIREDOG
FIREDUP
FIXEDLY
FIXEDUP
FLAGDAY
FLOODED
FLUIDLY
FMRADIO
FOUNDED
FOUNDER
FOUNDRY
FREDDIE
FREEDOM
FRIEDAN

F••••D•
FAGENDS
FLORIDA
FLYRODS
FORBADE
FORBIDS
FRIENDS

F•••••D
FACETED
FAGOTED
FAINTED
FANCIED
FATHEAD
FAULTED
FAVORED
FEASTED
FEIGNED
FEINTED
FERRIED
FETCHED
FIDDLED
FIELDED
FIGURED
FILCHED
FINLAND
FIXATED
FIZZLED
FLACCID
FLAGGED
FLAILED
FLAMBED
FLANKED
FLAPPED
FLASHED
FLATBED
FLATTED
FLECKED
FLEDGED
FLEECED
FLENSED
FLESHED
FLICKED
FLIPPED
FLIRTED
FLITTED
FLOATED
FLOCKED
FLOGGED
FLOODED
FLOORED
FLOPPED
FLOSSED
FLOURED
FLOUTED
FLUBBED
FLUFFED
FLUNKED
FLUSHED
FOCUSED
FOISTED
FONDLED
FOOTPAD
FOOZLED
FORAGED
FORFEND
FORGOOD
FORWARD
FOULARD
FOUNDED
FRANKED
FREAKED
FRETTED
FRILLED
FRINGED
FRISKED
FRITTED
FRIZZED
FROCKED
FRONTED
FROSTED
FROTHED
FROWARD
FROWNED
FRUITED
FUDDLED
FUELROD
FUMBLED

•F•D•••
OFFDUTY

•F•••D•
AFFORDS
EFFENDI
OFFENDS
OFFSIDE

•F••••D
AFFIXED
EFFACED
EFFUSED
OFFERED
OFFHAND
OFFLOAD
OFFROAD

••FD•••
OFFDUTY

••F•D••
INFIDEL

••F••D•
AFFORDS
ALFREDO
DEFENDS
EFFENDI
ENFOLDS
OFFENDS
OFFSIDE
OXFORDS
REFUNDS
UNFOLDS

••F•••D
AFFIXED
BAFFLED
DEFACED
DEFAMED
DEFILED
DEFINED
DEFRAUD
DEFUSED
EFFACED
EFFUSED
GIFFORD
INFIELD
INFUSED
MUFFLED
OFFERED
OFFHAND
OFFLOAD
OFFROAD
PIFFLED
RAFFLED
REFACED
REFINED
REFRIED
REFUSED
REFUTED
RIFFLED
RUFFLED
SOFABED
UNFAZED
UNFIXED
WAFFLED

•••FD••
FIEFDOM
HALFDAN
SERFDOM

•••F•D•
CONFIDE
PERFIDY
SULFIDE

•••F••D
ASHFORD
BAFFLED
BLUFFED
CRAFTED
DEIFIED
DRAFTED
DRIFTED
EDIFIED
FLUFFED
FORFEND
GIFFORD
GRAFTED
LANFORD
LAWFORD
MANFRED
MITFORD
MUFFLED
MUMFORD
PIFFLED
PURFLED
QUAFFED
RAFFLED
REDFORD
RIFFLED
RUFFLED
SANFORD
SCOFFED
SCUFFED
SEAFOOD
SHAFTED
SHIFTED
SIXFOLD
SNAFUED
SNIFFED
SNUFFED
STAFFED
STIFFED
STIFLED
STUFFED
TENFOLD
TRIFLED
TWOFOLD
UNIFIED
WAFFLED
WHIFFED
WILFORD
WILFRID

••••F•D
BLUFFED
BRIEFED
CORNFED
DWARFED
FLUFFED
PROOFED
QUAFFED
SCARFED
SCOFFED
SCUFFED
SNIFFED
SNUFFED
SPOOFED
STAFFED
STIFFED
STRAFED
STUFFED
WELLFED
WHARFED
WHIFFED

FE•••••
FEARERS
FEARFUL
FEARING
FEASTED
FEATHER
FEATURE
FEBRILE
FEDERAL
FEDORAS
FEEBLER
FEEDBAG
FEEDERS
FEEDING
FEEDLOT
FEEDSON
FEELERS
FEELFOR
FEELIES
FEELING
FEELOUT
FEIFFER
FEIGNED
FEINTED
FELDMAN
FELICIA
FELINES
FELLERS
FELLFOR
FELLING
FELLINI
FELLOFF
FELLOUT
FELLOWS
FELTFOR
FELTOUT
FELUCCA
FEMALES
FEMORAL
FENCERS
FENCING
FENDERS
FENDING
FENETRE
FERMENT
FERMIUM
FERRARI
FERRARO
FERRATE
FERRETS
FERRIED
FERRIES
FERRITE
FERROUS
FERRULE
FERTILE
FERULES
FERVENT
FERVORS
FERVOUR
FESTERS
FESTIVE
FESTOON
FETCHED
FETCHES
FETIDLY
FETLOCK
FETTERS
FETTLES
FEUDING
FEYNMAN

F•E••••
FEEBLER
FEEDBAG
FEEDERS
FEEDING
FEEDLOT
FEEDSON
FEELERS
FEELFOR
FEELIES
FEELING
FEELOUT
FIEDLER
FIEFDOM
FIELDED
FIELDER
FIERCER
FIERIER
FIERILY
FIESTAS
FLEABAG
FLECHES
FLECKED
FLEDGED
FLEDGES
FLEECED
FLEECES
FLEEING
FLEETER
FLEETLY
FLEMING
FLEMISH
FLENSED
FLENSES
FLESHED
FLESHES
FLEXING
FLEXNER
FLEXORS
FREAKED
FRECKLE
FREDDIE
FREDRIC
FREEBEE
FREEBIE
FREEDOM
FREEING
FREEMAN
FREEMEN
FREESIA
FREEWAY
FREEZER
FREEZES
FREIGHT
FREITAG
FREMONT
FRENEAU
FRENUMS
FRESCOS
FRESHEN
FRESHER
FRESHET
FRESHLY
FRETFUL
FRETSAW
FRETTED
FUELERS
FUELING
FUELOIL
FUELROD

F••E•••
FABERGE
FACEOFF
FACETED
FADEDIN
FADEINS
FADEOUT
FADESIN
FAGENDS
FAIENCE
FAKEFUR
FAREAST
FATEFUL
FEDERAL
FENETRE
FIDELIO
FINEART
FINESSE
FIREANT
FIREARM
FIREBOX
FIREBUG
FIREDOG
FIREDUP
FIREFLY
FIRELIT
FIREMAN
FIREMEN
FIRENZE
FIREOFF
FIRESUP
FIXEDLY
FIXEDUP
FIXESUP
FLEECED
FLEECES
FLEEING
FLEETER
FLEETLY
FLIESAT
FLIESIN
FLUENCY
FOMENTS
FOREARM
FOREIGN
FORELEG
FOREMAN
FOREMEN
FOREPAW
FORERAN
FORERUN
FORESAW
FORESEE
FORESTS
FOREVER
FREEBEE
FREEBIE
FREEDOM
FREEING
FREEMAN
FREEMEN
FREESIA
FREEWAY
FREEZER
FREEZES
FRIEDAN
FRIENDS
FRIEZES

F•••E••
FAIREST
FALSELY
FALSEST
FALTERS
FALWELL
FANBELT
FANJETS
FARLEFT
FARMERS
FARWEST
FASTENS
FASTEST
FATHEAD
FATHERS
FATLESS
FATNESS
FATTENS
FATTEST
FAUCETS
FAWCETT
FAWNERS
FEARERS
FEEDERS
FEELERS
FELLERS
FENCERS
FENDERS
FERMENT
FERRETS
FERVENT
FESTERS
FETTERS
FIBBERS
FIDGETS
FIDGETY
FIFTEEN
FIGLEAF
FIGMENT
FILBERT
FILLERS
FILLETS
FILTERS
FINDERS
FINGERS
FIRMEST
FISHERS
FISHERY
FISHEYE
FITNESS
FITTERS
FITTEST
FLAKERS
FLANEUR
FLAREUP
FLORETS
FLOWERS
FLOWERY
FLYLEAF
FLYNETS
FODDERS
FOGGERS
FOLDERS
FOLGERS
FOLLETT
FONDEST
FONTEYN
FOOLERY
FOOTERS
FOPPERY
FORBEAR
FORCEPS
FORCERS
FORFEIT
FORFEND
FORGERS
FORGERY
FORGETS
FORKERS
FORREAL
FORRENT
FORREST
FORWENT
FOSTERS
FOULEST
FOWLERS
FOXIEST
FRAMEUP
FRENEAU
FUELERS
FULGENT
FULLEST
FUNFEST
FUNNELS
FURSEAL

F••••E•
FABARES
FACADES
FACETED
FAGOTED
FAINTED
FAINTER
FAIRIES
FALAFEL
FANCIED
FANCIER
FANCIES
FARRIER
FARTHER
FAULTED
FAVORED
FEASTED
FEATHER
FEEBLER
FEELIES
FEIFFER
FEIGNED
FEINTED
FELINES
FEMALES
FERRIED
FERRIES
FERULES
FETCHED
FETCHES
FETTLES
FIACRES
FIANCEE
FIANCES
FICKLER
FICUSES
FIDDLED
FIDDLER
FIDDLES
FIEDLER
FIELDED
FIELDER
FIERCER
FIERIER
FIFTEEN
FIFTIES
FIGHTER
FIGURED
FIGURER
FIGURES
FILCHED
FILCHER
FILCHES
FILLIES
FILMIER
FINALES
FINCHES
FIPPLES
FIREMEN
FISCHER
FISHIER
FISHNET
FITCHES
FIXATED
FIXATES
FIZZIER
FIZZLED
FIZZLES
FLAGGED
FLAGMEN
FLAILED
FLAKIER
FLAMBED
FLAMBES
FLANGES
FLANKED
FLANKER
FLANNEL
FLAPPED
FLAPPER
FLASHED
FLASHER
FLASHES
FLATBED
FLATTED
FLATTEN
FLATTER
FLECHES
FLECKED
FLEDGED
FLEDGES
FLEECED
FLEECES
FLEETER
FLENSED
FLENSES
FLESHED
FLESHES
FLEXNER
FLICKED
FLICKER
FLIPPED
FLIPPER
FLIRTED
FLITTED
FLITTER
FLIVVER
FLOATED
FLOATER
FLOCKED
FLOGGED
FLOODED
FLOORED
FLOPPED
FLOSSED
FLOSSES
FLOURED
FLOUTED
FLUBBED
FLUFFED
FLUNKED
FLUSHED
FLUSHES
FLUSTER
FLUTTER
FLYOVER
FNUMBER
FOAMIER
FOCSLES
FOCUSED
FOCUSES
FOGGIER
FOIBLES
FOISTED
FOLLIES
FONDLED
FONDLES
FONDUES
FOODWEB
FOOTMEN
FOOZLED
FOOZLES
FORAGED
FORAGER
FORAGES
FORELEG
FOREMEN
FORESEE
FOREVER
FORFREE
FORGOES
FORSTER
FORTIES
FOUNDED
FOUNDER
FOURIER
FRAILER
FRAISES
FRANCES
FRANKED
FRANKER
FRAPPES
FRASIER
FRAWLEY
FRAZIER
FREAKED
FREEBEE
FREEMEN
FREEZER
FREEZES
FRESHEN
FRESHER
FRESHET
FRETTED
FRIDGES
FRIEZES
FRILLED
FRINGED
FRINGES
FRISBEE
FRISKED
FRITTED
FRITTER
FRIZZED
FRIZZES
FROCKED
FROGMEN
FRONTED

FROSTED
FROTHED
FROWNED
FROWNER
FRUITED
FUDDLED
FUDDLES
FUMBLED
FUMBLER
FUMBLES
FUNGOES
FUNKIER
FUNNIER
FUNNIES
FURORES
FURRIER
FURTHER
FUSSIER
FUSTIER
FUTURES
FUZZIER

F•••••E

FABERGE
FAIENCE
FAILURE
FANFARE
FANZINE
FARGONE
FASTONE
FATIGUE
FEATURE
FEBRILE
FENETRE
FERRATE
FERRITE
FERRULE
FERTILE
FESTIVE
FIANCEE
FIBULAE
FICTIVE
FINAGLE
FINANCE
FINESSE
FIRENZE
FISHEYE
FISSILE
FISSURE
FIXABLE
FIXTURE
FLOUNCE
FOLIAGE
FOLIATE
FOOTAGE
FOOTSIE
FORBADE
FORBORE
FORESEE
FORFREE
FORGAVE
FORGIVE
FORGONE
FORLIFE
FORSAKE
FORSALE
FORSURE
FORTUNE
FOXFIRE
FOXHOLE
FRAGILE
FRAICHE
FRANKIE
FRAZZLE
FRECKLE
FREDDIE
FREEBEE
FREEBIE
FRIABLE
FRICKIE
FRIGATE
FRISBEE
FRIZZLE
FROMAGE
FULSOME
FURNACE
FURTIVE

•FE••••

PFENNIG

•F•E•••

AFFECTS
AFREETS
EFFECTS
EFFENDI
OFFENCE
OFFENDS
OFFENSE
OFFERED
OFFERER
OFTENER

•F••E••

AFREETS
IFFIEST
OFFBEAT
OFFPEAK
OFFSETS
OFFYEAR

•F•••E•

AFFINES
AFFIXED
AFFIXES
AFRAMES
EFFACED
EFFACES
EFFUSED
EFFUSES
OFFERED
OFFERER
OFFICER
OFFICES
OFTENER

•F••••E

AFFABLE
AFFAIRE
IFSTONE
OFFBASE
OFFENCE
OFFENSE
OFFLINE
OFFSIDE
OFFSITE

••FE•••

AFFECTS
DEFEATS
DEFECTS
DEFENCE
DEFENDS
DEFENSE
EFFECTS
EFFENDI
INFECTS
INFERNO
INFESTS
LIFENET
OFFENCE
OFFENDS
OFFENSE
OFFERED
OFFERER
REFEREE
REFERTO

••F•E••

ALFIERI
ALFREDO
BUFFERS
BUFFETS
BUFFETT
COFFEES
COFFERS
DAFTEST
DEFLECT
DEFTEST
DIFFERS
DUFFELS
DUFFERS
FIFTEEN
GAFFERS
IFFIEST
INFIELD
INFLECT
JEFFERS
LIFTERS
OFFBEAT
OFFPEAK
OFFSETS
OFFYEAR
PUFFERS
PUFFERY
RAFTERS
REFLECT
REFRESH
REFUELS
RIFLERS
RIFLERY
SIFTERS
SOFTENS
SOFTEST
SUFFERS
TAFFETA
TOFFEES
TUFFETS

••F••E•

AFFINES
AFFIXED
AFFIXES
BAFFLED
BAFFLER
BAFFLES
COFFEES
DAFFIER
DEFACED
DEFACES
DEFAMED
DEFAMES
DEFILED
DEFILER
DEFILES
DEFINED
DEFINES
DEFUSED
DEFUSES
EFFACED
EFFACES
EFFUSED
EFFUSES
FIFTEEN
FIFTIES
HEFTIER
HUFFIER
INFIDEL
INFUSED
INFUSES
JEFFREY
JIFFIES
JOFFREY
LEFTIES
LIFENET
LOFTIER
MUFFLED
MUFFLER
MUFFLES
NIFTIER
OFFERED
OFFERER
OFFICER
OFFICES
PIFFLED
PIFFLES
PUFFIER
RAFFLED
RAFFLER
RAFFLES
REFACED
REFACES
REFEREE
REFINED
REFINER
REFINES
REFIRES
REFRIED
REFRIES
REFUGEE
REFUGES
REFUSED
REFUSER
REFUSES
REFUTED
REFUTER
REFUTES
RIFFLED
RIFFLES
RUFFLED
RUFFLES
SOFABED
SOFTIES
TAFFIES
TOFFEES
TOFFLER
UNFAZED
UNFIXED
WAFFLED
WAFFLER
WAFFLES

••F•••E

AFFABLE
AFFAIRE
BYFORCE
DEFARGE
DEFENCE
DEFENSE
DEFLATE
DIFFUSE
ENFORCE
GEFILTE
INFLAME
INFLATE
INFORCE
LAFARGE
LAFITTE
OFFBASE
OFFENCE
OFFENSE
OFFLINE
OFFSIDE
OFFSITE
REFEREE
REFRAME
REFUGEE
SUFFICE
SUFFUSE

•••FE••

BIGFEET
BUFFERS
BUFFETS
BUFFETT
COFFEES
COFFERS
CONFERS
CONFESS
CURFEWS
DEAFENS
DEAFEST
DIFFERS
DUFFELS
DUFFERS
FORFEIT
FORFEND
FUNFEST
GABFEST
GAFFERS
GOLFERS
HEIFERS
HEIFETZ
HOOFERS
JEFFERS
LOAFERS
OAKFERN
PERFECT
PILFERS
PREFECT
PREFERS
PROFESS
PUFFERS
PUFFERY
REEFERS
ROOFERS
SOLFEGE
SUFFERS
SURFEIT
SURFERS
TAFFETA
TOFFEES
TUFFETS
TWOFERS
WEBFEET
WOOFERS

•••F•E•

BAFFLED
BAFFLER
BAFFLES
BEEFIER
BIGFEET
BLUFFED
BLUFFER
COFFEES
COMFIER
COMFREY
CRAFTED
CRAFTER
DAFFIER
DEIFIED
DEIFIES
DRAFTED
DRAFTEE
DRIFTED
DRIFTER
EDIFIED
EDIFIES
FEIFFER
FLUFFED
FORFREE
GODFREY
GOLFTEE
GOOFIER
GRAFTED
GRIFFEY
GRIFTER
GRUFFER
HUFFIER
ICEFREE
JEFFREY
JIFFIES
JOFFREY
LEAFIER
LEAFLET
MANFRED
MUFFLED
MUFFLER
MUFFLES
PALFREY
PIFFLED
PIFFLES
PROFFER
PUFFIER
PURFLED
PURFLES
QUAFFED
QUAFFER
RAFFLED
RAFFLER
RAFFLES
RIFFLED
RIFFLES
RUFFLED
RUFFLES
SCOFFED
SCOFFER
SCUFFED
SHAFFER
SHAFTED
SHIFTED
SNAFUED
SNIFFED
SNIFFER
SNIFTER
SNUFFED
SNUFFER
STAFFED
STAFFER
STIFFED
STIFFEN
STIFFER
STIFLED
STIFLES
STUFFED
STUFFER
SWIFTER
SYNFUEL
TAFFIES
TAXFREE
TOFFEES
TOFFLER
TRIFLED
TRIFLER
TRIFLES
UNIFIED
UNIFIER
UNIFIES
WAFFLED
WAFFLER
WAFFLES
WEBFEET
WHIFFED
WINFREY
WOLFMEN

•••F••E

AIRFARE
BONFIRE
BUSFARE
CARFARE
CONFIDE
CONFINE
CONFUSE
CONFUTE
DIFFUSE
DOGFACE
DRAFTEE
EDIFICE
FANFARE
FORFREE
FOXFIRE
GOLFTEE
GUNFIRE
ICEFLOE
ICEFREE
MISFILE
MISFIRE
ORIFICE
OUTFACE
PERFUME
PREFACE
PROFANE
PROFILE
PROFUSE
SCUFFLE
SHUFFLE
SNAFFLE
SNIFFLE
SNUFFLE
SOLFEGE
SOUFFLE
SUFFICE
SUFFUSE
SULFATE
SULFIDE
SULFITE
SURFACE
TAXFREE
TRUFFLE
WARFARE
WELFARE

••••FE•

AQUIFER
BLUFFED
BLUFFER
BRIEFED
BRIEFER
CARAFES
CHAMFER
CONIFER
CORNFED
DWARFED
FALAFEL
FEIFFER
FLUFFED
GRIFFEY
GRUFFER
LUCIFER
PROFFER
PROOFED
PROOFER
QUAFFED
QUAFFER
ROTIFER
SCARFED
SCOFFED
SCOFFER
SCUFFED
SHAFFER
SNIFFED
SNIFFER
SNUFFED
SNUFFER
SPOOFED
SPOOFER
STAFFED
STAFFER
STIFFED
STIFFEN
STIFFER
STRAFED
STRAFES
STUFFED
STUFFER
WELLFED
WHARFED
WHIFFED

••••F•E

AGRAFFE
ALLOFME
GIRAFFE
OKEEFFE
SCUFFLE
SHUFFLE
SNAFFLE
SNIFFLE
SNUFFLE
SOUFFLE
TRUFFLE

•••••FE

AGRAFFE
ALEWIFE
FORLIFE
GIRAFFE
LOWLIFE
MIDLIFE
MIDWIFE
NESCAFE
OKEEFFE
SANTAFE

F•F••••

FIFTEEN
FIFTIES

F••F•••

FANFARE
FEIFFER
FIEFDOM
FLUFFED
FLYFISH
FORFEIT
FORFEND
FORFREE
FOXFIRE
FULFILL
FULFILS
FUNFAIR
FUNFEST

F•••F••

FAKEFUR
FALAFEL
FALLFOR
FATEFUL
FEARFUL
FEELFOR
FEIFFER
FELLFOR
FELTFOR
FIREFLY
FISHFRY
FISTFUL
FLUFFED
FORKFUL
FRETFUL

F••••F•

FACEOFF
FAIROFF
FALLOFF
FALSIFY
FARLEFT
FELLOFF
FIREOFF
FOBSOFF
FORLIFE
FORTIFY

F•••••F

FACEOFF
FAIROFF
FALLOFF
FELLOFF
FIGLEAF
FIREOFF
FLYLEAF
FOBSOFF

•FF••••

AFFABLE
AFFABLY
AFFAIRE
AFFAIRS
AFFECTS
AFFINES
AFFIRMS
AFFIXED
AFFIXES
AFFLICT
AFFORDS
AFFRAYS
AFFRONT
EFFACED
EFFACES
EFFECTS
EFFENDI
EFFORTS
EFFUSED
EFFUSES
IFFIEST
OFFBASE
OFFBEAT
OFFDUTY
OFFENCE
OFFENDS
OFFENSE
OFFERED
OFFERER
OFFHAND
OFFHOUR
OFFICER
OFFICES
OFFLINE
OFFLOAD
OFFPEAK
OFFRAMP
OFFROAD
OFFSETS
OFFSIDE
OFFSITE
OFFYEAR

••FF•••

BAFFLED
BAFFLER
BAFFLES
BUFFALO
BUFFERS
BUFFETS
BUFFETT
BUFFING
BUFFOON
COFFEES
COFFERS
CUFFING
DAFFIER
DAFFILY
DIFFERS
DIFFUSE
DOFFING
DUFFELS
DUFFERS
GAFFERS
GAFFING
GIFFORD
GUFFAWS
HOFFMAN
HUFFIER
HUFFILY
HUFFING
JEFFERS
JEFFREY
JIFFIES
JOFFREY
LUFFING
MIFFING
MUFFING
MUFFINS
MUFFLED
MUFFLER
MUFFLES
PIFFLED
PIFFLES
PUFFERS
PUFFERY
PUFFIER
PUFFILY
PUFFING
PUFFINS
RAFFISH
RAFFLED
RAFFLER
RAFFLES
REFFING
RIFFING
RIFFLED
RIFFLES
RUFFIAN
RUFFLED
RUFFLES
SAFFRON
SOFFITS
SUFFERS
SUFFICE
SUFFOLK
SUFFUSE
TAFFETA
TAFFIES
TIFFANY
TOFFEES
TOFFLER
TUFFETS
WAFFLED
WAFFLER
WAFFLES

••F••F•

ALFALFA
LEFTOFF
LIFTOFF

••F•••F

LEFTOFF
LIFTOFF

•••FF••

BLUFFED
BLUFFER
BLUFFLY
CHIFFON
FEIFFER
FLUFFED
GRIFFEY
GRIFFIN
GRIFFON
GRUFFER
GRUFFLY
PROFFER
QUAFFED
QUAFFER
REAFFIX
SCOFFED
SCOFFER
SCUFFED
SCUFFLE
SHAFFER
SHUFFLE
SNAFFLE
SNIFFAT
SNIFFED
SNIFFER
SNIFFLE
SNUFFED
SNUFFER
SNUFFLE
SOUFFLE
STAFFED
STAFFER
STIFFED
STIFFEN
STIFFER
STIFFLY
STUFFED
STUFFER
TRAFFIC
TRUFFLE
WHIFFED

•••F•F•

GOOFOFF

•••F••F

GOOFOFF

••••FF•

AGRAFFE
CUTOFFS
GIRAFFE
LAYOFFS
OKEEFFE
PAYOFFS
POPOFFS
REBUFFS
RIPOFFS
RUNOFFS
SCRUFFS
SCRUFFY
TARIFFS
TIPOFFS

•••••FF

BACKOFF
BAILIFF
BAKEOFF
BEAROFF
BEGSOFF
BITEOFF
BLEWOFF
BLOWOFF
BRANIFF
BUGSOFF
BUYSOFF
BUZZOFF
CALLOFF
CAMEOFF
CASTOFF
COMEOFF
CONNIFF
COOKOFF
CUTSOFF
DASHOFF
DIEDOFF
DIESOFF
DISTAFF
DOZEOFF
DROPOFF
DUSTOFF
EARMUFF
EASEOFF
FACEOFF
FAIROFF
FALLOFF
FELLOFF
FIREOFF
FOBSOFF
GAVEOFF
GETSOFF
GIVEOFF
GOESOFF
GOOFOFF
HANDOFF
HANGOFF
HAULOFF
HEADOFF
HELDOFF
HOLDOFF
HOPSOFF
JUMPOFF
KARLOFF
KEEPOFF
KEPTOFF
KICKOFF
KISSOFF
LAIDOFF
LAYSOFF
LEADOFF
LEFTOFF
LETSOFF
LIFTOFF
LOGSOFF
MACDUFF
MADEOFF
MAKEOFF
MARKOFF
MASTIFF
MIDRIFF
NODSOFF
PAIDOFF
PAIROFF
PALMOFF
PASSOFF
PAWNOFF
PAYSOFF
PEELOFF
PICKOFF
PLAYOFF
PONTIFF
POPSOFF
PULLOFF
PUSHOFF
PUTSOFF
RAKEOFF
REELOFF
RIDEOFF
RIPSOFF
RODEOFF
RUNSOFF
RUSHOFF
SEALOFF
SEESOFF
SELLOFF
SENDOFF
SENTOFF
SETSOFF
SHERIFF
SHOWOFF
SHUTOFF
SIGNOFF
SOLDOFF
SPINOFF
SPUNOFF
STOPOFF
TAILOFF
TAKEOFF
TEAROFF
TEEDOFF
TEESOFF
TELLOFF
TICKOFF
TIMEOFF
TIPSOFF
TOLDOFF
TOOKOFF
TOPSOFF
TOREOFF
TOSSOFF
TURNOFF
WARDOFF
WASHOFF
WAVEOFF
WEAROFF
WELLOFF
WENTOFF
WOREOFF

WORKOFF
WORNOFF

F•G••••
FAGENDS
FAGGING
FAGOTED
FIGHTER
FIGLEAF
FIGMENT
FIGURED
FIGURER
FIGURES
FOGBANK
FOGBOWS
FOGGERS
FOGGIER
FOGGING
FOGHORN
FOGYISH
FOGYISM

F••G•••
FAGGING
FARGONE
FEIGNED
FIDGETS
FIDGETY
FINGERS
FIZGIGS
FLAGDAY
FLAGGED
FLAGMAN
FLAGMEN
FLAGONS
FLIGHTS
FLIGHTY
FLOGGED
FOGGERS
FOGGIER
FOGGING
FOLGERS
FORGAVE
FORGERS
FORGERY
FORGETS
FORGING
FORGIVE
FORGOES
FORGONE
FORGOOD
FRAGILE
FRIGATE
FRIGHTS
FROGMAN
FROGMEN
FUDGING
FULGENT
FULGHUM
FUNGOES

F•••G••
FALLGUY
FATIGUE
FINAGLE
FLAGGED
FLANGES
FLEDGED
FLEDGES
FLOGGED
FORAGED
FORAGER
FORAGES
FRAUGHT
FREIGHT
FRIDGES
FRINGED
FRINGES

F••••G•
FABERGE
FACINGS
FARRAGO
FILINGS
FIRINGS
FIXINGS
FIZGIGS
FLYHIGH
FOLIAGE
FOOTAGE
FOREIGN
FROMAGE

F•••••G
FAGGING
FAILING
FAIRING
FALLING
FANNING
FARMING
FASTING
FAWNING
FEARING
FEEDBAG
FEEDING
FEELING
FELLING
FENCING
FENDING
FEUDING
FIBBING
FILLING
FILMING
FINDING
FINKING
FIREBUG
FIREDOG
FIRMING
FISHING
FITTING
FIZZING
FLAKING
FLAMING
FLARING
FLAWING
FLAYING
FLEABAG
FLEEING
FLEMING
FLEXING
FLOWING
FLUTING
FOALING
FOAMING
FOBBING
FOGGING
FOILING
FOLDING
FOOLING
FOOTING
FORCING
FORDING
FORELEG
FORGING
FORKING
FORMING
FOULING
FOWLING
FRAMING
FRAYING
FREEING
FREITAG
FUDGING
FUELING
FUNDING
FUNNING
FURLING
FURLONG
FURRING
FUSSING
FUZZING

•FG••••
AFGHANI
AFGHANS

•F••••G
PFENNIG

••F•G••
REFUGEE
REFUGES

••F••G•
DEFARGE
LAFARGE

••F•••G
BUFFING
CUFFING
DEFYING
DOFFING
GAFFING
HEFTING
HUFFING
LIFTING
LOFTING
LUFFING
MIFFING
MUFFING
PUFFING
RAFTING
REFFING
RIFFING
RIFLING
RIFTING
SIFTING
TUFTING
WAFTING

•••FG••
WOLFGAL

•••F•G•
OLDFOGY
SOLFEGE

•••F••G
BEEFING
BUFFING
CHAFING
COIFING
CUFFING
DOFFING
GAFFING
GOLFING
GOOFING
GULFING
HOOFING
HUFFING
KNIFING
LEAFING
LOAFING
LUFFING
MIFFING
MUFFING
PUFFING
REDFLAG
REEFING
REFFING
RIFFING
ROOFING
SURFING
WOLFING
WOOFING

F••H•••
FASHION
FATHEAD
FATHERS
FATHOMS
FIGHTER
FISHERS
FISHERY
FISHEYE
FISHFRY
FISHIER
FISHILY
FISHING
FISHNET
FISHOUT
FLYHIGH
FOGHORN
FOXHOLE
FUCHSIA

F•••H••
FARTHER
FEATHER
FETCHED
FETCHES
FILCHED
FILCHER
FILCHES
FINCHES
FISCHER
FITCHES
FLASHED
FLASHER
FLASHES
FLECHES
FLESHED
FLESHES
FLIGHTS
FLIGHTY
FLUSHED
FLUSHES
FORDHAM
FRESHEN
FRESHER
FRESHET
FRESHLY
FRIGHTS
FROTHED
FULGHUM
FURTHER

F••••H•
FOURTHS
FRAICHE
FRAUGHT
FREIGHT

F•••••H
FADDISH
FINNISH
FLEMISH
FLYFISH
FLYHIGH
FOGYISH
FOOLISH
FOPPISH
FORSYTH
FURBISH
FURNISH

•F•H•••
AFGHANI
AFGHANS
OFFHAND
OFFHOUR

••FH•••
OFFHAND
OFFHOUR

••F•••H
RAFFISH
REFRESH

•••F•H•
LOOFAHS

•••F••H
CATFISH
CODFISH
DOGFISH
FLYFISH
PANFISH
RAFFISH
SAWFISH
SELFISH
SUNFISH
WOLFISH

••••F•H
LATIFAH
TWELFTH

FI•••••
FIACRES
FIANCEE
FIANCES
FIASCOS
FIBBERS
FIBBING
FIBRILS
FIBROUS
FIBULAE
FIBULAS
FICKLER
FICTION
FICTIVE
FICUSES
FIDDLED
FIDDLER
FIDDLES
FIDELIO
FIDGETS
FIDGETY
FIEDLER
FIEFDOM
FIELDED
FIELDER
FIERCER
FIERIER
FIERILY
FIESTAS
FIFTEEN
FIFTIES
FIGHTER
FIGLEAF
FIGMENT
FIGURED
FIGURER
FIGURES
FIJIANS
FILBERT
FILCHED
FILCHER
FILCHES
FILINGS
FILLERS
FILLETS
FILLIES
FILLING
FILLINS
FILLIPS
FILLOUT
FILLSIN
FILLSUP
FILLUPS
FILMIER
FILMING
FILTERS
FINAGLE
FINALES
FINALLY
FINANCE
FINCHES
FINDERS
FINDING
FINDOUT
FINEART
FINESSE
FINGERS
FINIALS
FINICKY
FINKING
FINLAND
FINNISH
FIPPLES
FIREANT
FIREARM
FIREBOX
FIREBUG
FIREDOG
FIREDUP
FIREFLY
FIRELIT
FIREMAN
FIREMEN
FIRENZE
FIREOFF
FIRESUP
FIRINGS
FIRKINS
FIRMEST
FIRMING
FIRMSUP
FIRSTLY
FISCHER
FISHERS
FISHERY
FISHEYE
FISHFRY
FISHIER
FISHILY
FISHING
FISHNET
FISHOUT
FISSILE
FISSION
FISSURE
FISTFUL
FITCHES
FITNESS
FITTERS
FITTEST
FITTING
FIXABLE
FIXATED
FIXATES
FIXEDLY
FIXEDUP
FIXESUP
FIXINGS
FIXTURE
FIZGIGS
FIZZIER
FIZZING
FIZZLED
FIZZLES

F•I••••
FAIENCE
FAILING
FAILURE
FAINTED
FAINTER
FAINTLY
FAIREST
FAIRIES
FAIRING
FAIROFF
FAIRSUP
FAIRWAY
FEIFFER
FEIGNED
FEINTED
FLICKED
FLICKER
FLIESAT
FLIESIN
FLIGHTS
FLIGHTY
FLIPPED
FLIPPER
FLIPUPS
FLIRTED
FLITTED
FLITTER
FLIVVER
FOIBLES
FOILING
FOISTED
FRIABLE
FRICKIE
FRIDAYS
FRIDGES
FRIEDAN
FRIENDS
FRIEZES
FRIGATE
FRIGHTS
FRILLED
FRINGED
FRINGES
FRISBEE
FRISIAN
FRISKED
FRISSON
FRITTED
FRITTER
FRIZZED
FRIZZES
FRIZZLE

F••I•••
FACIALS
FACINGS
FADIMAN
FAJITAS
FANIONS
FATIGUE
FELICIA
FELINES
FETIDLY
FIJIANS
FILINGS
FINIALS
FINICKY
FIRINGS
FIXINGS
FLAILED
FLUIDLY
FOLIAGE
FOLIATE
FORINTS
FOXIEST
FRAICHE
FRAILER
FRAILTY
FRAISES
FREIGHT
FREITAG
FRUITED
FUJITSU
FURIOUS

F•••I••
FABRICS
FACTION
FADDISH
FADDISM
FADDIST
FADEINS
FAGGING
FAILING
FAIRIES
FAIRING
FALLING
FALSIFY
FALSITY
FANCIED
FANCIER
FANCIES
FANCILY
FANNING
FANZINE
FARMING
FARRIER
FASCIAS
FASCISM
FASCIST
FASHION
FASTING
FATCITY
FATUITY
FAUVISM
FAUVIST
FAWNING
FEARING
FEBRILE
FEEDING
FEELIES
FEELING
FELLING
FELLINI
FENCING
FENDING
FERMIUM
FERRIED
FERRIES
FERRITE
FERTILE
FESTIVE
FEUDING
FIBBING
FIBRILS
FICTION
FICTIVE
FIERIER
FIERILY
FIFTIES
FILLIES
FILLING
FILLINS
FILLIPS
FILMIER
FILMING
FINDING
FINKING
FINNISH
FIRKINS
FIRMING
FISHIER
FISHILY
FISHING
FISSILE
FISSION
FITTING
FIZGIGS
FIZZIER
FIZZING
FLAKIER
FLAKING
FLAMING
FLARING
FLAWING
FLAYING
FLEEING
FLEMING
FLEMISH
FLEXING
FLORIDA
FLORINS
FLORIST
FLOWING
FLUTING
FLUTIST
FLUVIAL
FLYFISH
FLYHIGH
FOALING
FOAMIER
FOAMING
FOBBING
FOGGIER
FOGGING
FOGYISH
FOGYISM
FOILING
FOLDING
FOLLIES
FONTINA
FOOLING
FOOLISH
FOOTING
FOPPISH
FORBIDS
FORCING
FORDING
FOREIGN
FORGING
FORGIVE
FORKING
FORLIFE
FORMICA
FORMING
FORTIES
FORTIFY
FOSDICK
FOSSILS
FOULING
FOURIER
FOWLING
FOXFIRE
FRAGILE
FRAMING
FRASIER
FRAYING
FRAZIER
FREEING
FRISIAN
FROLICS
FUDGING
FUELING
FULFILL
FULFILS
FUNDING
FUNKIER
FUNNIER
FUNNIES
FUNNILY
FUNNING
FURBISH
FURLING
FURNISH
FURRIER
FURRING
FURTIVE
FUSSIER
FUSSILY
FUSSING
FUSTIAN
FUSTICS
FUSTIER
FUSTILY
FUZZIER
FUZZILY
FUZZING

F••••I•
FADEDIN
FADESIN
FALLSIN
FANATIC
FANMAIL
FANTAIL
FELICIA
FIDELIO
FILLSIN
FIRELIT
FLACCID
FLIESIN
FMRADIO
FOOTSIE
FORFEIT
FOULTIP
FOXTAIL
FRANCIS
FRANKIE
FRANTIC
FREDDIE
FREDRIC
FREEBIE
FREESIA
FRICKIE
FUCHSIA
FUELOIL
FUNFAIR

F•••••I
FELLINI
FERRARI

•F•I•••
AFFINES
AFFIRMS
AFFIXED
AFFIXES
AFRICAN
IFFIEST
OFFICER
OFFICES

•F••I••
AFFAIRE
AFFAIRS
AFFLICT
OFFLINE
OFFSIDE
OFFSITE

•F•••I•
PFENNIG

•F••••I
AFGHANI
EFFENDI

••FI•••
AFFINES
AFFIRMS
AFFIXED
AFFIXES
ALFIERI
DEFIANT
DEFICIT
DEFILED
DEFILER
DEFILES
DEFINED
DEFINES
GEFILTE
IFFIEST
INFIDEL
INFIELD
LAFITTE
MAFIOSO
MRFIXIT
OFFICER
OFFICES
REFILLS
REFILMS
REFINED
REFINER
REFINES
REFIRES
RUFIYAA
UNFIXED

••F•I••
AFFAIRE
AFFAIRS
AFFLICT
BUFFING
CUFFING
DAFFIER
DAFFILY
DEFYING
DOFFING
FIFTIES
GAFFING
HAFNIUM
HEFTIER
HEFTILY
HEFTING
HUFFIER
HUFFILY
HUFFING
INFLICT
JIFFIES
LEFTIES
LEFTIST
LIFTING
LOFTIER
LOFTILY
LOFTING
LUFFING
MIFFING
MUFFING
MUFFINS
NIFTIER
NIFTILY
OFFLINE
OFFSIDE
OFFSITE
PUFFIER
PUFFILY
PUFFING
PUFFINS
RAFFISH
RAFTING
REFFING
REFRIED
REFRIES
RIFFING
RIFLING
RIFTING
RUFFIAN
SIFTING
SOFFITS
SOFTIES
SUFFICE
TAFFIES
TUFTING
WAFTING

••F••I•
DEFICIT
GOFORIT
MRFIXIT
REFRAIN
SAFARIS

••F•••I
ALFIERI
EFFENDI

•••FI••
ARTFILM
BEEFIER
BEEFING
BONFIRE
BOWFINS
BUFFING
CATFISH
CHAFING
CODFISH
COIFING
COMFIER
COMFITS
CONFIDE
CONFINE
CONFIRM
CUFFING
DAFFIER
DAFFILY
DEIFIED
DEIFIES
DOFFING
DOGFISH
EDIFICE
EDIFIED
EDIFIES
FLYFISH
FOXFIRE
FULFILL
FULFILS
GAFFING
GINFIZZ
GOLFING
GOOFIER
GOOFING
GULFING
GUNFIRE
HOOFING
HUFFIER
HUFFILY
HUFFING
JIFFIES
KNIFING
LEAFIER
LEAFING
LOAFING
LUFFING
MIFFING
MISFILE
MISFIRE
MISFITS
MUFFING
MUFFINS
ORIFICE
OUTFITS
PANFISH
PERFIDY
PROFILE
PROFITS
PUFFIER
PUFFILY
PUFFING
PUFFINS
RAFFISH
RATFINK
REDFINS
REDFIRS
REEFING
REFFING
RIFFING
ROOFING
RUFFIAN
SAWFISH
SELFISH
SOFFITS
SUFFICE
SULFIDE
SULFITE

SUNFISH
SURFING
TAFFIES
UNIFIED
UNIFIER
UNIFIES
WOLFING
WOLFISH
WOOFING

•••F•I•
AELFRIC
AIRFOIL
BIDFAIR
FORFEIT
FUNFAIR
GRIFFIN
HALFWIT
HOOFSIT
MAYFAIR
PARFAIT
REAFFIX
SURFEIT
TINFOIL
TRAFFIC
TREFOIL
WILFRID

••••FI•
BENEFIT
BLUEFIN
GRIFFIN
MALEFIC
OSSIFIC
OUTOFIT
PACIFIC
RATAFIA
REAFFIX
SEESFIT
TAILFIN
TRAFFIC

F•J••••
FAJITAS
FIJIANS
FUJITSU

F••J•••
FANJETS

F•K••••
FAKEFUR

F••K•••
FICKLER
FINKING
FIRKINS
FLAKERS
FLAKIER
FLAKING
FOLKART
FORKERS
FORKFUL
FORKING
FUNKIER

F•••K••
FLANKED
FLANKER
FLECKED
FLICKED
FLICKER
FLOCKED
FLOCKTO
FLUNKED
FRANKED
FRANKER
FRANKIE
FRANKLY
FRANKOZ
FREAKED
FRECKLE
FRICKIE
FRISKED
FROCKED

F••••K•
FINICKY
FORSAKE

F•••••K
FATBACK
FETLOCK
FOGBANK
FORSOOK
FOSDICK
FRYCOOK

•F••••K
OFFPEAK

••F•••K
DEFROCK
OFFPEAK
SUFFOLK
UNFROCK

•••F••K
HAYFORK
KINFOLK
MENFOLK
NORFOLK
RATFINK
SUFFOLK

FL•••••
FLACCID
FLACONS
FLAGDAY
FLAGGED
FLAGMAN
FLAGMEN
FLAGONS
FLAILED
FLAKERS
FLAKIER
FLAKING
FLAMBED
FLAMBES
FLAMING
FLANEUR
FLANGES
FLANKED
FLANKER
FLANNEL
FLAPPED
FLAPPER
FLAREUP
FLARING
FLASHED
FLASHER
FLASHES
FLATBED
FLATCAR
FLATOUT
FLATTED
FLATTEN
FLATTER
FLATTOP
FLAUNTS
FLAVORS
FLAVOUR
FLAWING
FLAYING
FLEABAG
FLECHES
FLECKED
FLEDGED
FLEDGES
FLEECED
FLEECES
FLEEING
FLEETER
FLEETLY
FLEMING
FLEMISH
FLENSED
FLENSES
FLESHED
FLESHES
FLEXING
FLEXNER
FLEXORS
FLICKED
FLICKER
FLIESAT
FLIESIN
FLIGHTS
FLIGHTY
FLIPPED
FLIPPER
FLIPUPS
FLIRTED
FLITTED
FLITTER
FLIVVER
FLOATED
FLOATER
FLOCKED
FLOCKTO
FLOGGED
FLOODED
FLOORED
FLOPPED
FLORETS
FLORIDA
FLORINS
FLORIST
FLOSSED
FLOSSES
FLOTSAM
FLOUNCE
FLOURED
FLOUTED
FLOWERS
FLOWERY
FLOWING
FLUBBED
FLUENCY
FLUFFED
FLUIDLY
FLUMMOX
FLUNKED
FLUSHED
FLUSHES
FLUSTER
FLUTING
FLUTIST
FLUTTER
FLUVIAL
FLYAWAY
FLYBALL
FLYBOYS
FLYCAST
FLYFISH
FLYHIGH
FLYLEAF
FLYNETS
FLYOVER
FLYPAST
FLYRODS
FLYTRAP
FLYWAYS

F•L••••
FALAFEL
FALCONS
FALLACY
FALLFOR
FALLGUY
FALLING
FALLOFF
FALLOUT
FALLOWS
FALLSIN
FALLSON
FALLSTO
FALSELY
FALSEST
FALSIFY
FALSITY
FALTERS
FALWELL
FELDMAN
FELICIA
FELINES
FELLERS
FELLFOR
FELLING
FELLINI
FELLOFF
FELLOUT
FELLOWS
FELTFOR
FELTOUT
FELUCCA
FILBERT
FILCHED
FILCHER
FILCHES
FILINGS
FILLERS
FILLETS
FILLIES
FILLING
FILLINS
FILLIPS
FILLOUT
FILLSIN
FILLSUP
FILLUPS
FILMIER
FILMING
FILTERS
FOLDERS
FOLDING
FOLDOUT
FOLDSUP
FOLDUPS
FOLGERS
FOLIAGE
FOLIATE
FOLKART
FOLLETT
FOLLIES
FOLLOWS
FULCRUM
FULFILL
FULFILS
FULGENT
FULGHUM
FULLEST
FULSOME

F••L•••
FAILING
FAILURE
FALLACY
FALLFOR
FALLGUY
FALLING
FALLOFF
FALLOUT
FALLOWS
FALLSIN
FALLSON
FALLSTO
FARLEFT
FATLESS
FAULTED
FEELERS
FEELFOR
FEELIES
FEELING
FEELOUT
FELLERS
FELLFOR
FELLING
FELLINI
FELLOFF
FELLOUT
FELLOWS
FETLOCK
FIELDED
FIELDER
FIGLEAF
FILLERS
FILLETS
FILLIES
FILLING
FILLINS
FILLIPS
FILLOUT
FILLSIN
FILLSUP
FILLUPS
FINLAND
FLYLEAF
FOALING
FOILING
FOLLETT
FOLLIES
FOLLOWS
FOOLERY
FOOLING
FOOLISH
FORLIFE
FORLORN
FOULARD
FOULEST
FOULING
FOULOUT
FOULSUP
FOULTIP
FOULUPS
FOWLERS
FOWLING
FRILLED
FROLICS
FUELERS
FUELING
FUELOIL
FUELROD
FULLEST
FURLING
FURLONG

F•••L••
FACULTY
FAMULUS
FEEBLER
FEEDLOT
FEMALES
FERULES
FETTLES
FIBULAE
FIBULAS
FICKLER
FIDDLED
FIDDLER
FIDDLES
FIDELIO
FIEDLER
FINALES
FINALLY
FIPPLES
FIRELIT
FIZZLED
FIZZLES
FLAILED
FOCSLES
FOIBLES
FONDLED
FONDLES
FOOZLED
FOOZLES
FORELEG
FRAILER
FRAILTY
FRAWLEY
FRILLED
FUDDLED
FUDDLES
FUMBLED
FUMBLER
FUMBLES

F••••L•
FACIALS
FAINTLY
FALSELY
FALWELL
FANBELT
FANCILY
FEBRILE
FERRULE
FERTILE
FETIDLY
FIBRILS
FIERILY
FINAGLE
FINALLY
FINIALS
FIREFLY
FIRSTLY
FISHILY
FISSILE
FIXABLE
FIXEDLY
FLEETLY
FLUIDLY
FLYBALL
FORMALS
FORMULA
FORSALE
FOSSILS
FOXHOLE
FRAGILE
FRANKLY
FRAZZLE
FRECKLE
FRESHLY
FRIABLE
FRIZZLE
FULFILL
FULFILS
FUNNELS
FUNNILY
FURBALL
FUSSILY
FUSTILY
FUZZILY

F•••••L
FACTUAL
FALAFEL
FALWELL
FANMAIL
FANTAIL
FATEFUL
FEARFUL
FEDERAL
FEMORAL
FISTFUL
FLANNEL
FLUVIAL
FLYBALL
FORKFUL
FORREAL
FOXTAIL
FRACTAL
FRETFUL
FRONTAL
FUELOIL
FULFILL
FURBALL
FURSEAL

•F•L•••
AFFLICT
OFFLINE
OFFLOAD

•F•••L•
AFFABLE
AFFABLY

••FL•••
AFFLICT
DEFLATE
DEFLECT
INFLAME
INFLATE
INFLECT
INFLICT
INFLOWS
OFFLINE
OFFLOAD
REFLECT
RIFLERS
RIFLERY
RIFLING

••F•L••
ALFALFA
AWFULLY
BAFFLED
BAFFLER
BAFFLES
BEFALLS
DEFILED
DEFILER
DEFILES
ENFOLDS
GEFILTE
MUFFLED
MUFFLER
MUFFLES
PIFFLED
PIFFLES
RAFFLED
RAFFLER
RAFFLES
REFILLS
REFILMS
RIFFLED
RIFFLES
RUFFLED
RUFFLES
TOFFLER
UNFOLDS
WAFFLED
WAFFLER
WAFFLES

••F••L•
AFFABLE
AFFABLY
ATFAULT
AWFULLY
BEFALLS
BEFOULS
BUFFALO
DAFFILY
DEFAULT
DUFFELS
HEFTILY
HUFFILY
INFIELD
LOFTILY
NIFTILY
NOFAULT
PUFFILY
REFILLS
REFUELS
SUFFOLK
UNFURLS

••F•••L
BIFOCAL
INFIDEL
REFUSAL

•••FL••
AIRFLOW
BAFFLED
BAFFLER
BAFFLES
EARFLAP
ICEFLOE
LEAFLET
MOUFLON
MUFFLED
MUFFLER
MUFFLES
OUTFLOW
PIFFLED
PIFFLES
PURFLED
PURFLES
RAFFLED
RAFFLER
RAFFLES
REDFLAG
RIFFLED
RIFFLES
RUFFLED
RUFFLES
STIFLED
STIFLES
TOFFLER
TRIFLED
TRIFLER
TRIFLES
WAFFLED
WAFFLER
WAFFLES

•••F•L•
ARMFULS
ARTFILM
BAGFULS
BEEFALO
BLUFFLY
BOXFULS
BUFFALO
CAPFULS
CARFULS
CUPFULS
DAFFILY
DUFFELS
EARFULS
EYEFULS
FULFILL
FULFILS
GRUFFLY
HUFFILY
JARFULS
JUGFULS
KINFOLK
LAPFULS
MENFOLK
MISFILE
NORFOLK
PITFALL
POTFULS
PROFILE
PUFFILY
SCUFFLE
SHUFFLE
SIXFOLD
SNAFFLE
SNIFFLE
SNUFFLE
SOUFFLE
STIFFLY
SUFFOLK
SWIFTLY
TENFOLD
TRUFFLE
TWOFOLD
VATFULS

•••F••L
AIRFOIL
FULFILL
PEAFOWL
PITFALL
SYNFUEL
TINFOIL
TOMFOOL
TREFOIL
WOLFGAL

••••FL•
ALOOFLY
BLOWFLY
BLUEFLU
BLUFFLY
BRIEFLY
CHIEFLY
DEERFLY
FIREFLY
GRUFFLY
LETSFLY
OVERFLY
SANDFLY
SCUFFLE
SHOOFLY
SHUFFLE
SNAFFLE
SNIFFLE
SNUFFLE
SOUFFLE
STIFFLY
TRUFFLE

••••F•L
BALEFUL
BANEFUL
BASHFUL
BOWLFUL
BRIMFUL
CAREFUL
DOLEFUL
DUTIFUL
FALAFEL
FATEFUL
FEARFUL
FISTFUL
FORKFUL
FRETFUL
GAINFUL
GLEEFUL
HANDFUL
HARMFUL
HATEFUL
HEEDFUL
HELPFUL
HOPEFUL
HURTFUL
LUSTFUL
MINDFUL
NEEDFUL
PAGEFUL
PAILFUL
PAINFUL
PIPEFUL
PITIFUL
PLAYFUL
RESTFUL
ROOMFUL
SACKFUL
SKILFUL
SOULFUL
TACTFUL
TANKFUL
TEARFUL
TRAYFUL
TUNEFUL
WAKEFUL
WILLFUL
WISHFUL
WISTFUL
ZESTFUL

FM•••••
FMRADIO

F•M••••
FAMULUS
FEMALES
FEMORAL
FOMENTS
FUMBLED
FUMBLER
FUMBLES

F••M•••
FANMAIL
FARMERS
FARMING
FARMOUT
FERMENT
FERMIUM
FIGMENT
FILMIER
FILMING
FIRMEST
FIRMING
FIRMSUP
FLAMBED
FLAMBES
FLAMING
FLEMING
FLEMISH
FLUMMOX
FNUMBER
FOAMIER
FOAMING
FORMALS
FORMATS
FORMICA
FORMING
FORMOSA
FORMULA
FRAMEUP
FRAMING
FREMONT
FROMAGE

F•••M••
FADIMAN
FELDMAN
FEYNMAN
FIREMAN
FIREMEN
FLAGMAN
FLAGMEN
FLUMMOX
FOOTMAN
FOOTMEN
FOREMAN
FOREMEN
FREEMAN
FREEMEN
FROGMAN
FROGMEN

F••••M•
FATHOMS
FRENUMS
FULSOME

F•••••M
FADDISM
FASCISM
FAUVISM
FERMIUM
FIEFDOM
FIREARM
FLOTSAM
FOGYISM
FORDHAM
FOREARM
FREEDOM
FULCRUM
FULGHUM

•F••M••
AFRAMES

•F•••M•
AFFIRMS
OFFRAMP

••F•M••
DEFAMED
DEFAMES
HOFFMAN

••F••M•
AFFIRMS
DEFORMS
INFLAME
INFORMS
OFFRAMP
REFILMS
REFORMS
REFRAME

••F•••M
HAFNIUM

•••FM••
HOFFMAN
WOLFMAN
WOLFMEN

•••F•M•
PERFUME

•••F••M
ANTFARM
ARTFILM
ARTFORM
CONFIRM
CONFORM
FIEFDOM
PERFORM
SERFDOM
UNIFORM
WOLFRAM

••••FM•
ALLOFME

FN•••••
FNUMBER

F•N••••
FANATIC
FANBELT
FANCIED
FANCIER
FANCIES
FANCILY
FANFARE
FANIONS
FANJETS
FANMAIL
FANNING
FANSOUT
FANTAIL
FANTASY
FANZINE
FENCERS
FENCING
FENDERS
FENDING
FENETRE
FINAGLE
FINALES
FINALLY
FINANCE
FINCHES
FINDERS
FINDING
FINDOUT
FINEART
FINESSE
FINGERS
FINIALS
FINICKY
FINKING
FINLAND
FINNISH
FONDANT
FONDEST
FONDLED
FONDLES
FONDUES
FONTEYN
FONTINA
FUNDING
FUNFAIR
FUNFEST
FUNGOES
FUNKIER
FUNNELS
FUNNIER
FUNNIES
FUNNILY
FUNNING

F••N•••
FAINTED
FAINTER
FAINTLY
FANNING
FATNESS
FAWNERS
FAWNING
FEINTED
FEYNMAN
FIANCEE
FIANCES
FINNISH
FITNESS
FLANEUR
FLANGES
FLANKED
FLANKER
FLANNEL
FLENSED
FLENSES
FLUNKED
FLYNETS
FOUNDED
FOUNDER

FOUNDRY
FRANCES
FRANCIS
FRANKED
FRANKER
FRANKIE
FRANKLY
FRANKOZ
FRANTIC
FRENEAU
FRENUMS
FRINGED
FRINGES
FRONTAL
FRONTED
FRONTON
FUNNELS
FUNNIER
FUNNIES
FUNNILY
FUNNING
FURNACE
FURNISH

F•••N••

FACINGS
FAGENDS
FAIENCE
FEIGNED
FELINES
FILINGS
FINANCE
FIRENZE
FIRINGS
FISHNET
FIXINGS
FLANNEL
FLAUNTS
FLEXNER
FLOUNCE
FLUENCY
FOMENTS
FORINTS
FRIENDS
FROWNAT
FROWNED
FROWNER

F••••N•

FADEINS
FAGGING
FAILING
FAIRING
FALCONS
FALLING
FANIONS
FANNING
FANZINE
FARGONE
FARMING
FASTENS
FASTING
FASTONE
FATTENS
FAWNING
FEARING
FEEDING
FEELING
FELLING
FELLINI
FENCING
FENDING
FERMENT
FERVENT
FEUDING
FIBBING
FIGMENT
FIJIANS
FILLING
FILLINS
FILMING
FINDING
FINKING
FINLAND
FIREANT
FIRKINS
FIRMING
FISHING
FITTING
FIZZING
FLACONS
FLAGONS
FLAKING
FLAMING
FLARING
FLAWING
FLAYING
FLEEING
FLEMING
FLEXING
FLORINS
FLOWING
FLUTING
FOALING
FOAMING
FOBBING
FOGBANK
FOGGING
FOILING
FOLDING
FONDANT
FONTINA
FOOLING
FOOTING
FORCING
FORDING
FORFEND
FORGING
FORGONE
FORKING
FORMING
FORRENT
FORTUNA
FORTUNE
FORWENT
FOULING
FOWLING
FRAMING
FRAYING
FREEING
FREMONT
FRYPANS
FUDGING
FUELING
FULGENT
FUNDING
FUNNING
FURLING
FURLONG
FURRING
FUSSING
FUZZING

F•••••N

FACTION
FADEDIN
FADESIN
FADIMAN
FALLSIN
FALLSON
FASHION
FEEDSON
FELDMAN
FESTOON
FEYNMAN
FICTION
FIFTEEN
FILLSIN
FIREMAN
FIREMEN
FISSION
FLAGMAN
FLAGMEN
FLATTEN
FLIESIN
FOGHORN
FONTEYN
FOOTMAN
FOOTMEN
FOREIGN
FOREMAN
FOREMEN
FORERAN
FORERUN
FORLORN
FORTRAN
FREEMAN
FREEMEN
FRESHEN
FRIEDAN
FRISIAN
FRISSON
FROGMAN
FROGMEN
FRONTON
FUSTIAN

•F•N•••

PFENNIG

•F••N••

AFFINES
EFFENDI
OFFENCE
OFFENDS
OFFENSE
OFTENER
PFENNIG

•F•••N•

AFFRONT
AFGHANI
AFGHANS
IFSTONE
OFFHAND
OFFLINE

•F••••N

AFRICAN

••FN•••

HAFNIUM

••F•N••

AFFINES
ALFONSO
DEFENCE
DEFENDS
DEFENSE
DEFINED
DEFINES
DEFUNCT
EFFENDI
INFANCY
INFANTA
INFANTS
LIFENET
OFFENCE
OFFENDS
OFFENSE
REFINED
REFINER
REFINES
REFUNDS

••F••N•

AFFRONT
BUFFING
CAFTANS
CUFFING
DEFIANT
DEFYING
DOFFING
GAFFING
HEFTING
HUFFING
INFERNO
INFRONT
KAFTANS
LIFTING
LOFTING
LUFFING
MIFFING
MUFFING
MUFFINS
OFFHAND
OFFLINE
PUFFING
PUFFINS
RAFTING
REFFING
RIFFING
RIFLING
RIFTING
SIFTING
SOFTENS
TIFFANY
TUFTING
UPFRONT
WAFTING

••F•••N

BUFFOON
FIFTEEN
HOFFMAN
REFRAIN
RUFFIAN
SAFFRON

•••FN••

ASOFNOW

•••F•N•

BEEFING
BOWFINS
BUFFING
CHAFING
COIFING
CONFINE
CUFFING
DEAFENS
DOFFING
FORFEND
GAFFING
GOLFING
GOOFING
GULFING
HOOFING
HUFFING
KNIFING
LEAFING
LENFANT
LOAFING
LUFFING
MIFFING
MUFFING
MUFFINS
PROFANE
PUFFING
PUFFINS
RATFINK
REDFINS
REEFING
REFFING
RIFFING
ROOFING
SEAFANS
SURFING
TIFFANY
WOLFING
WOOFING

•••F••N

BUFFOON
CHIFFON
CLIFTON
GRIFFIN
GRIFFON
HALFDAN
HOFFMAN
MOUFLON
OAKFERN
RUFFIAN
SAFFRON
STIFFEN
WOLFMAN
WOLFMEN

••••F•N

BLUEFIN
CHIFFON
GRIFFIN
GRIFFON
POKEFUN
STIFFEN
TAILFIN

FO•••••

FOALING
FOAMIER
FOAMING
FOBBING
FOBSOFF
FOCSLES
FOCUSED
FOCUSES
FODDERS
FOGBANK
FOGBOWS
FOGGERS
FOGGIER
FOGGING
FOGHORN
FOGYISH
FOGYISM
FOIBLES
FOILING
FOISTED
FOLDERS
FOLDING
FOLDOUT
FOLDSUP
FOLDUPS
FOLGERS
FOLIAGE
FOLIATE
FOLKART
FOLLETT
FOLLIES
FOLLOWS
FOMENTS
FONDANT
FONDEST
FONDLED
FONDLES
FONDUES
FONTEYN
FONTINA
FOODWEB
FOOLERY
FOOLING
FOOLISH
FOOTAGE
FOOTERS
FOOTING
FOOTMAN
FOOTMEN
FOOTPAD
FOOTSIE
FOOZLED
FOOZLES
FOPPERY
FOPPISH
FORAGED
FORAGER
FORAGES
FORBADE
FORBEAR
FORBIDS
FORBORE
FORCEPS
FORCERS
FORCING
FORDHAM
FORDING
FOREARM
FOREIGN
FORELEG
FOREMAN
FOREMEN
FOREPAW
FORERAN
FORERUN
FORESAW
FORESEE
FORESTS
FOREVER
FORFEIT
FORFEND
FORFREE
FORGAVE
FORGERS
FORGERY
FORGETS
FORGING
FORGIVE
FORGOES
FORGONE
FORGOOD
FORINTS
FORKERS
FORKFUL
FORKING
FORLIFE
FORLORN
FORMALS
FORMATS
FORMICA
FORMING
FORMOSA
FORMULA
FORREAL
FORRENT
FORREST
FORSAKE
FORSALE
FORSOOK
FORSTER
FORSURE
FORSYTH
FORTIES
FORTIFY
FORTRAN
FORTUNA
FORTUNE
FORWARD
FORWENT
FOSDICK
FOSSILS
FOSTERS
FOULARD
FOULEST
FOULING
FOULOUT
FOULSUP
FOULTIP
FOULUPS
FOUNDED
FOUNDER
FOUNDRY
FOURIER
FOURTHS
FOWLERS
FOWLING
FOXFIRE
FOXHOLE
FOXIEST
FOXTAIL
FOXTROT

F•O••••

FLOATED
FLOATER
FLOCKED
FLOCKTO
FLOGGED
FLOODED
FLOORED
FLOPPED
FLORETS
FLORIDA
FLORINS
FLORIST
FLOSSED
FLOSSES
FLOTSAM
FLOUNCE
FLOURED
FLOUTED
FLOWERS
FLOWERY
FLOWING
FOODWEB
FOOLERY
FOOLING
FOOLISH
FOOTAGE
FOOTERS
FOOTING
FOOTMAN
FOOTMEN
FOOTPAD
FOOTSIE
FOOZLED
FOOZLES
FROCKED
FROGMAN
FROGMEN
FROLICS
FROMAGE
FRONTAL
FRONTED
FRONTON
FROSTED
FROTHED
FROWARD
FROWNAT
FROWNED
FROWNER

F••O•••

FAGOTED
FAVORED
FAVOURS
FEDORAS
FEMORAL
FLOODED
FLOORED
FLYOVER
FURORES

F•••O••

FACEOFF
FACTORS
FACTORY
FADEOUT
FAIROFF
FALCONS
FALLOFF
FALLOUT
FALLOWS
FANIONS
FANSOUT
FARGONE
FARMOUT
FARROWS
FASTONE
FATHOMS
FATUOUS
FEELOUT
FELLOFF
FELLOUT
FELLOWS
FELTOUT
FERROUS
FERVORS
FERVOUR
FESTOON
FETLOCK
FIBROUS
FILLOUT
FINDOUT
FIREOFF
FISHOUT
FLACONS
FLAGONS
FLATOUT
FLAVORS
FLAVOUR
FLEXORS
FLYBOYS
FLYRODS
FOBSOFF
FOGBOWS
FOGHORN
FOLDOUT
FOLLOWS
FORBORE
FORGOES
FORGONE
FORGOOD
FORLORN
FORMOSA
FORSOOK
FOULOUT
FOXHOLE
FREMONT
FRYCOOK
FUELOIL
FULSOME
FUNGOES
FURIOUS
FURLONG
FURROWS

F••••O•

FACTION
FALLFOR
FALLSON
FASHION
FEEDLOT
FEEDSON
FEELFOR
FELLFOR
FELTFOR
FESTOON
FIASCOS
FICTION
FIEFDOM
FIREBOX
FIREDOG
FISSION
FLATTOP
FLUMMOX
FORGOOD
FORSOOK
FOXTROT
FRANKOZ
FREEDOM
FRESCOS
FRISSON
FRONTON
FRYCOOK
FUELROD
FUSSPOT

F•••••O

FALLSTO
FARRAGO
FERRARO
FIDELIO
FLOCKTO
FMRADIO

•F•O•••

AFFORDS
EFFORTS
OFSORTS

•F••O••

AFFRONT
IFSTONE
OFASORT
OFFHOUR
OFFLOAD
OFFROAD

••FO•••

AFFORDS
ALFONSO
BEFOULS
BIFOCAL
BYFORCE
DEFORMS
EFFORTS
ENFOLDS
ENFORCE
GOFORIT
INFOCUS
INFORCE
INFORMS
OXFORDS
REFORMS
UNFOLDS

••F•O••

AFFRONT
BUFFOON
DEFROCK
DEFROST
GIFFORD
INFLOWS
INFRONT
LEFTOFF
LEFTOUT
LIFTOFF
MAFIOSO
OFFHOUR
OFFLOAD
OFFROAD
SUFFOLK
UNFROCK
UPFRONT

••F••O•

BUFFOON
INFAVOR
SAFFRON
SOFTTOP

••F•••O

ALFONSO
ALFREDO
BUFFALO
DEFACTO
INFERNO
MAFIOSO
REFERTO

•••FO••

AIRFOIL
ARTFORM
ASHFORD
BALFOUR
BIGFOOT
BUFFOON
COMFORT
CONFORM
GIFFORD
GOOFOFF
HAYFORK
HOTFOOT
KINFOLK
LANFORD
LAWFORD
MENFOLK
MITFORD
MUMFORD
NORFOLK
OLDFOGY
PEAFOWL
PERFORM
REDFORD
SANFORD
SEAFOOD
SIXFOLD
SUFFOLK
TENFOLD
TENFOUR
TINFOIL
TOMFOOL
TREFOIL
TWOFOLD
UNIFORM
WEBFOOT
WILFORD

•••F•O•

AIRFLOW
ASOFNOW
BIGFOOT
BUFFOON
CHIFFON
CLIFTON
FIEFDOM
GRIFFON
HOTFOOT
ICEFLOE
MOUFLON
OUTFLOW
ROOFTOP
SAFFRON
SEAFOOD
SERFDOM
TOMFOOL
WEBFOOT

•••F••O

BEEFALO
BUFFALO
GOLFPRO

••••FO•

ASKSFOR
BLUEFOX
BRERFOX
CALLFOR
CAREFOR
CHIFFON
DONEFOR
FALLFOR
FEELFOR
FELLFOR
FELTFOR
GOESFOR
GOINFOR
GRIFFON
GUNSFOR
LAIDFOR
LAYSFOR
LOOKFOR
MADEFOR
MAKEFOR
PAIDFOR
PASSFOR
PAYSFOR
PINEFOR
PRAYFOR
ROOTFOR
SENDFOR
SENTFOR
SHOTFOR
WENTFOR
WHATFOR
WORKFOR

•••••FO

RODOLFO

F•P••••

FIPPLES
FOPPERY
FOPPISH

F••P•••

FIPPLES
FLAPPED
FLAPPER
FLIPPED
FLIPPER
FLIPUPS
FLOPPED
FLYPAST
FOPPERY
FOPPISH
FRAPPES
FRYPANS

F•••P••

FAUXPAS
FLAPPED
FLAPPER
FLIPPED
FLIPPER
FLOPPED
FOOTPAD
FOREPAW
FRAPPES
FUSSPOT

F••••P•

FILLIPS
FILLUPS
FLIPUPS
FOLDUPS
FORCEPS
FOULUPS

F•••••P

FAIRSUP
FILLSUP
FIREDUP
FIRESUP
FIRMSUP
FIXEDUP
FIXESUP
FLAREUP
FLATTOP
FLYTRAP
FOLDSUP
FOULSUP
FOULTIP
FRAMEUP

•F•P•••

OFFPEAK

•F••••P

OFFRAMP

••FP•••

OFFPEAK

••F•••P

LIFTSUP
OFFRAMP
SOFTTOP

•••FP••

GOLFPRO

•••F•P•

GOOFUPS

•••F••P

BEEFSUP
EARFLAP
GOOFSUP
ROOFTOP

FR•••••

FRACTAL
FRAGILE
FRAICHE
FRAILER
FRAILTY
FRAISES
FRAMEUP
FRAMING
FRANCES
FRANCIS
FRANKED
FRANKER
FRANKIE
FRANKLY
FRANKOZ
FRANTIC
FRAPPES
FRASIER
FRAUGHT
FRAWLEY
FRAYING
FRAZIER
FRAZZLE
FREAKED
FRECKLE
FREDDIE
FREDRIC
FREEBEE
FREEBIE
FREEDOM
FREEING
FREEMAN
FREEMEN
FREESIA
FREEWAY
FREEZER
FREEZES
FREIGHT
FREITAG
FREMONT
FRENEAU
FRENUMS
FRESCOS
FRESHEN
FRESHER
FRESHET
FRESHLY
FRETFUL
FRETSAW

FRETTED
FRIABLE
FRICKIE
FRIDAYS
FRIDGES
FRIEDAN
FRIENDS
FRIEZES
FRIGATE
FRIGHTS
FRILLED
FRINGED
FRINGES
FRISBEE
FRISIAN
FRISKED
FRISSON
FRITTED
FRITTER
FRIZZED
FRIZZES
FRIZZLE
FROCKED
FROGMAN
FROGMEN
FROLICS
FROMAGE
FRONTAL
FRONTED
FRONTON
FROSTED
FROTHED
FROWARD
FROWNAT
FROWNED
FROWNER
FRUITED
FRYCOOK
FRYPANS

F•R••••
FARADAY
FARAWAY
FAREAST
FARGONE
FARLEFT
FARMERS
FARMING
FARMOUT
FARRAGO
FARRIER
FARROWS
FARTHER
FARWEST
FERMENT
FERMIUM
FERRARI
FERRARO
FERRATE
FERRETS
FERRIED
FERRIES
FERRITE
FERROUS
FERRULE
FERTILE
FERULES
FERVENT
FERVORS
FERVOUR
FIREANT
FIREARM
FIREBOX
FIREBUG
FIREDOG
FIREDUP
FIREFLY
FIRELIT
FIREMAN
FIREMEN
FIRENZE
FIREOFF
FIRESUP
FIRINGS
FIRKINS
FIRMEST
FIRMING
FIRMSUP
FIRSTLY
FMRADIO
FORAGED
FORAGER
FORAGES
FORBADE
FORBEAR
FORBIDS
FORBORE
FORCEPS
FORCERS
FORCING
FORDHAM
FORDING
FOREARM
FOREIGN
FORELEG
FOREMAN
FOREMEN
FOREPAW
FORERAN
FORERUN
FORESAW
FORESEE
FORESTS
FOREVER
FORFEIT
FORFEND
FORFREE
FORGAVE
FORGERS
FORGERY
FORGETS
FORGING
FORGIVE
FORGOES
FORGONE
FORGOOD
FORINTS
FORKERS
FORKFUL
FORKING
FORLIFE
FORLORN
FORMALS
FORMATS
FORMICA
FORMING
FORMOSA
FORMULA
FORREAL
FORRENT
FORREST
FORSAKE
FORSALE
FORSOOK
FORSTER
FORSURE
FORSYTH
FORTIES
FORTIFY
FORTRAN
FORTUNA
FORTUNE
FORWARD
FORWENT
FURBALL
FURBISH
FURIOUS
FURLING
FURLONG
FURNACE
FURNISH
FURORES
FURRIER
FURRING
FURROWS
FURSEAL
FURTHER
FURTIVE

F••R•••
FABRICS
FAIREST
FAIRIES
FAIRING
FAIROFF
FAIRSUP
FAIRWAY
FARRAGO
FARRIER
FARROWS
FEARERS
FEARFUL
FEARING
FEBRILE
FERRARI
FERRARO
FERRATE
FERRETS
FERRIED
FERRIES
FERRITE
FERROUS
FERRULE
FIBRILS
FIBROUS
FIERCER
FIERIER
FIERILY
FLAREUP
FLARING
FLIRTED
FLORETS
FLORIDA
FLORINS
FLORIST
FLYRODS
FORREAL
FORRENT
FORREST
FOURIER
FOURTHS
FURRIER
FURRING
FURROWS

F•••R••
FABARES
FABERGE
FAVORED
FAYWRAY
FEDERAL
FEDORAS
FEMORAL
FIACRES
FIGURED
FIGURER
FIGURES
FLOORED
FLOURED
FLYTRAP
FORERAN
FORERUN
FORFREE
FORTRAN
FOXTROT
FREDRIC
FUELROD
FULCRUM
FURORES
FUTURES

F••••R•
FACTORS
FACTORY
FAILURE
FALTERS
FANFARE
FARMERS
FATHERS
FAVOURS
FAWNERS
FEARERS
FEATURE
FEEDERS
FEELERS
FELLERS
FENCERS
FENDERS
FENETRE
FERRARI
FERRARO
FERVORS
FESTERS
FETTERS
FIBBERS
FILBERT
FILLERS
FILTERS
FINDERS
FINEART
FINGERS
FIREARM
FISHERS
FISHERY
FISHFRY
FISSURE
FITTERS
FIXTURE
FLAKERS
FLAVORS
FLEXORS
FLOWERS
FLOWERY
FODDERS
FOGGERS
FOGHORN
FOLDERS
FOLGERS
FOLKART
FOOLERY
FOOTERS
FOPPERY
FORBORE
FORCERS
FOREARM
FORGERS
FORGERY
FORKERS
FORLORN
FORSURE
FORWARD
FOSTERS
FOULARD
FOUNDRY
FOWLERS
FOXFIRE
FROWARD
FUELERS

F•••••R
FAINTER
FAKEFUR
FALLFOR
FANCIER
FARRIER
FARTHER
FEATHER
FEEBLER
FEELFOR
FEIFFER
FELLFOR
FELTFOR
FERVOUR
FICKLER
FIDDLER
FIEDLER
FIELDER
FIERCER
FIERIER
FIGHTER
FIGURER
FILCHER
FILMIER
FISCHER
FISHIER
FIZZIER
FLAKIER
FLANEUR
FLANKER
FLAPPER
FLASHER
FLATCAR
FLATTER
FLAVOUR
FLEETER
FLEXNER
FLICKER
FLIPPER
FLITTER
FLIVVER
FLOATER
FLUSTER
FLUTTER
FLYOVER
FNUMBER
FOAMIER
FOGGIER
FORAGER
FORBEAR
FOREVER
FORSTER
FOUNDER
FOURIER
FRAILER
FRANKER
FRASIER
FRAZIER
FREEZER
FRESHER
FRITTER
FROWNER
FUMBLER
FUNFAIR
FUNKIER
FUNNIER
FURRIER
FURTHER
FUSSIER
FUSTIER
FUZZIER

•FR••••
AFRAMES
AFREETS
AFRICAN

•F•R•••
AFFRAYS
AFFRONT
OFFRAMP
OFFROAD

•F••R••
AFFIRMS
AFFORDS
EFFORTS
OFFERED
OFFERER
OFSORTS

•F•••R•
AFFAIRE
AFFAIRS
OFASORT

•F••••R
OFFERER
OFFHOUR
OFFICER
OFFYEAR
OFTENER

••FR•••
AFFRAYS
AFFRONT
ALFREDO
DEFRAUD
DEFRAYS
DEFROCK
DEFROST
INFRONT
OFFRAMP
OFFROAD
REFRACT
REFRAIN
REFRAME
REFRESH
REFRIED
REFRIES
UNFROCK
UPFRONT

••F•R••
AFFIRMS
AFFORDS
ASFARAS
BYFORCE
DEFARGE
DEFORMS
EFFORTS
ENFORCE
GOFORIT
HOFBRAU
INFERNO
INFORCE
INFORMS
JEFFREY
JOFFREY
LAFARGE
OFFERED
OFFERER
OXFORDS
REFEREE
REFERTO
REFIRES
REFORMS
SAFARIS
SAFFRON
UNFURLS

••F••R•
AFFAIRE
AFFAIRS
ALFIERI
BUFFERS
COFFERS
DIFFERS
DUFFERS
GAFFERS
GIFFORD
JEFFERS
LIFTERS
PUFFERS
PUFFERY
RAFTERS
RIFLERS
RIFLERY
SIFTERS
SUFFERS

••F•••R
BAFFLER
DAFFIER
DEFILER
HEFTIER
HUFFIER
INFAVOR
LOFTIER
MUFFLER
NIFTIER
OFFERER
OFFHOUR
OFFICER
OFFYEAR
PUFFIER
RAFFLER
REFINER
REFUSER
REFUTER
TOFFLER
WAFFLER

•••FR••
AELFRIC
COMFREY
FORFREE
GODFREY
ICEFREE
JEFFREY
JOFFREY
MANFRED
PALFREY
SAFFRON
TAXFREE
WILFRID
WINFREY
WOLFRAM

•••F•R•
AIRFARE
ANTFARM
ARTFORM
ASHFORD
BONFIRE
BUFFERS
BUSFARE
CARFARE
COFFERS
COMFORT
CONFERS
CONFIRM
CONFORM
DIFFERS
DUFFERS
FANFARE
FOXFIRE
GAFFERS
GIFFORD
GOLFERS
GOLFPRO
GUNFIRE
HAYFORK
HEIFERS
HOOFERS
JEFFERS
LANFORD
LAWFORD
LOAFERS
MISFIRE
MITFORD
MUMFORD
OAKFERN
PERFORM
PILFERS
PREFERS
PUFFERS
PUFFERY
REDFIRS
REDFORD
REEFERS
ROOFERS
SANFORD
SHOFARS
SUFFERS
SURFERS
TWOFERS
UNIFORM
WARFARE
WELFARE
WILFORD
WOOFERS

•••F••R
BAFFLER
BALFOUR
BEEFIER
BIDFAIR
BLUFFER
COMFIER
CRAFTER
DAFFIER
DRIFTER
FEIFFER
FUNFAIR
GOOFIER
GRIFTER
GRUFFER
HUFFIER
LEAFIER
MAYFAIR
MUFFLER
PROFFER
PUFFIER
QUAFFER
RAFFLER
SCOFFER
SHAFFER
SNIFFER
SNIFTER
SNUFFER
STAFFER
STIFFER
STUFFER
SWIFTER
TENFOUR
TOFFLER
TRIFLER
UNIFIER
WAFFLER

••••FR•
DEEPFRY
FISHFRY
STIRFRY

••••F•R
AQUIFER
ASKSFOR
BLUFFER
BRIEFER
CALLFOR
CAREFOR
CHAMFER
CONIFER
DONEFOR
FAKEFUR
FALLFOR
FEELFOR
FEIFFER
FELLFOR
FELTFOR
GOESFOR
GOINFOR
GRUFFER
GUNSFOR
INSOFAR
LAIDFOR
LAYSFOR
LOOKFOR
LUCIFER
MADEFOR
MAKEFOR
PAIDFOR
PASSFOR
PAYSFOR
PINEFOR
PRAYFOR
PROFFER
PROOFER
QUAFFER
ROOTFOR
ROTIFER
SCOFFER
SENDFOR
SENTFOR
SHAFFER
SHOTFOR
SNIFFER
SNUFFER
SPOOFER
STAFFER
STIFFER
STUFFER
THUSFAR
WENTFOR
WHATFOR
WORKFOR

F•S••••
FASCIAS
FASCISM
FASCIST
FASHION
FASTENS
FASTEST
FASTING
FASTONE
FESTERS
FESTIVE
FESTOON
FISCHER
FISHERS
FISHERY
FISHEYE
FISHFRY
FISHIER
FISHILY
FISHING
FISHNET
FISHOUT
FISSILE
FISSION
FISSURE
FISTFUL
FOSDICK
FOSSILS
FOSTERS
FUSSIER
FUSSILY
FUSSING
FUSSPOT
FUSTIAN
FUSTICS
FUSTIER
FUSTILY

F••S•••
FALSELY
FALSEST
FALSIFY
FALSITY
FANSOUT
FAUSTUS
FEASTED
FIASCOS
FIESTAS
FIRSTLY
FISSILE
FISSION
FISSURE
FLASHED
FLASHER
FLASHES
FLESHED
FLESHES
FLOSSED
FLOSSES
FLUSHED
FLUSHES
FLUSTER
FOBSOFF
FOCSLES
FOISTED
FORSAKE
FORSALE
FORSOOK
FORSTER
FORSURE
FORSYTH
FOSSILS
FRASIER
FRESCOS
FRESHEN
FRESHER
FRESHET
FRESHLY
FRISBEE
FRISIAN
FRISKED
FRISSON
FROSTED
FULSOME
FURSEAL
FUSSIER
FUSSILY
FUSSING
FUSSPOT

F•••S••
FADESIN
FAIRSUP
FALLSIN
FALLSON
FALLSTO
FEEDSON
FICUSES
FILLSIN
FILLSUP
FINESSE
FIRESUP
FIRMSUP
FIXESUP
FLENSED
FLENSES
FLIESAT
FLIESIN
FLOSSED
FLOSSES
FLOTSAM
FOCUSED
FOCUSES
FOLDSUP
FOOTSIE
FORESAW
FORESEE
FORESTS
FOULSUP
FRAISES
FREESIA
FRETSAW
FRISSON
FUCHSIA

F••••S•
FADDISH
FADDISM
FADDIST
FAIREST
FALSEST
FANTASY
FAREAST
FARWEST
FASCISM
FASCIST
FASTEST
FATLESS
FATNESS
FATTEST
FAUVISM
FAUVIST
FINESSE
FINNISH
FIRMEST
FITNESS
FITTEST
FLEMISH
FLORIST
FLUTIST
FLYCAST
FLYFISH
FLYPAST
FOGYISH
FOGYISM
FONDEST
FOOLISH
FOPPISH
FORMOSA
FORREST
FOULEST
FOXIEST
FUJITSU
FULLEST
FUNFEST
FURBISH
FURNISH

F•••••S
FABARES
FABRICS
FACADES
FACIALS
FACINGS
FACTORS
FADEINS
FAGENDS
FAIRIES
FAJITAS
FALCONS
FALLOWS
FALTERS
FAMULUS
FANCIES
FANIONS
FANJETS
FARMERS
FARROWS
FASCIAS
FASTENS
FATCATS
FATHERS
FATHOMS
FATLESS
FATNESS
FATTENS
FATUOUS
FAUCETS
FAUSTUS
FAUXPAS
FAVOURS
FAWNERS
FEARERS
FEDORAS
FEEDERS
FEELERS
FEELIES
FELINES
FELLERS
FELLOWS
FEMALES
FENCERS
FENDERS
FERRETS
FERRIES
FERROUS
FERULES
FERVORS
FESTERS
FETCHES
FETTERS
FETTLES
FIACRES
FIANCES
FIASCOS
FIBBERS
FIBRILS
FIBROUS
FIBULAS
FICUSES
FIDDLES
FIDGETS
FIESTAS
FIFTIES
FIGURES
FIJIANS
FILCHES
FILINGS
FILLERS
FILLETS
FILLIES
FILLINS
FILLIPS
FILLUPS
FILTERS
FINALES
FINCHES
FINDERS
FINGERS
FINIALS
FIPPLES
FIRINGS
FIRKINS
FISHERS
FITCHES
FITNESS
FITTERS
FIXATES
FIXINGS
FIZGIGS
FIZZLES
FLACONS
FLAGONS
FLAKERS
FLAMBES
FLANGES
FLASHES
FLAUNTS
FLAVORS
FLECHES
FLEDGES
FLEECES
FLENSES
FLESHES
FLEXORS
FLIGHTS
FLIPUPS
FLORETS
FLORINS
FLOSSES
FLOWERS

FLUSHES
FLYBOYS
FLYNETS
FLYRODS
FLYWAYS
FOCSLES
FOCUSES
FODDERS
FOGBOWS
FOGGERS
FOIBLES
FOLDERS
FOLDUPS
FOLGERS
FOLLIES
FOLLOWS
FOMENTS
FONDLES
FONDUES
FOOTERS
FOOZLES
FORAGES
FORBIDS
FORCEPS
FORCERS
FORESTS
FORGERS
FORGETS
FORGOES
FORINTS
FORKERS
FORMALS
FORMATS
FORTIES
FOSSILS
FOSTERS
FOULUPS
FOURTHS
FOWLERS
FRAISES
FRANCES
FRANCIS
FRAPPES
FREEZES
FRENUMS
FRESCOS
FRIDAYS
FRIDGES
FRIENDS
FRIEZES
FRIGHTS
FRINGES
FRIZZES
FROLICS
FRYPANS
FUDDLES
FUELERS
FULFILS
FUMBLES
FUNGOES
FUNNELS
FUNNIES
FURIOUS
FURORES
FURROWS
FUSTICS
FUTURES

•FS••••
IFSTONE
OFSORTS

•F•S•••
OFASORT
OFFSETS
OFFSIDE
OFFSITE

•F••S••
EFFUSED
EFFUSES

•F•••S•
IFFIEST
OFFBASE
OFFENSE

•F••••S
AFFAIRS
AFFECTS
AFFINES
AFFIRMS
AFFIXES
AFFORDS
AFFRAYS
AFGHANS
AFRAMES
AFREETS
EFFACES
EFFECTS
EFFORTS
EFFUSES
OFFENDS
OFFICES
OFFSETS
OFSORTS

••FS•••
OFFSETS
OFFSIDE
OFFSITE

••F•S••
DEFUSED
DEFUSES
EFFUSED
EFFUSES
INFESTS
INFUSED
INFUSES
LIFTSUP
REFUSAL
REFUSED
REFUSER
REFUSES

••F••S•
ALFONSO
DAFTEST
DEFENSE
DEFROST
DEFTEST
DIFFUSE
IFFIEST
LEFTIST
MAFIOSO
OFFBASE
OFFENSE
RAFFISH
REFRESH
SOFTEST
SUFFUSE

••F•••S
AFFAIRS
AFFECTS
AFFINES
AFFIRMS
AFFIXES
AFFORDS
AFFRAYS
ASFARAS
BAFFLES
BEFALLS
BEFOULS
BUFFERS
BUFFETS
CAFTANS
COFFEES
COFFERS
DEFACES
DEFAMES
DEFEATS
DEFECTS
DEFENDS
DEFILES
DEFINES
DEFORMS
DEFRAYS
DEFUSES
DIFFERS
DUFFELS
DUFFERS
EFFACES
EFFECTS
EFFORTS
EFFUSES
ENFOLDS
FIFTIES
GAFFERS
GUFFAWS
INFANTS
INFECTS
INFESTS
INFLOWS
INFOCUS
INFORMS
INFUSES
JEFFERS
JIFFIES
KAFTANS
LEFTIES
LIFTERS
MUFFINS
MUFFLES
OFFENDS
OFFICES
OFFSETS
OXFORDS
PIFFLES
PUFFERS
PUFFINS
RAFFLES
RAFTERS
REFACES
REFILLS
REFILMS
REFINES
REFIRES
REFORMS
REFRIES
REFUELS
REFUGES
REFUNDS
REFUSES
REFUTES
RIFFLES
RIFLERS
RUFFLES
SAFARIS
SIFTERS
SOFFITS
SOFTENS
SOFTIES
SUFFERS
TAFFIES
TOFFEES
TUFFETS
UNFOLDS
UNFURLS
WAFFLES

•••FS••
BEEFSUP
GOOFSUP
HOOFSIT

•••F•S•
BELFAST
CATFISH
CODFISH
CONFESS
CONFUSE
CRAFTSY
DEAFEST
DIFFUSE
DOGFISH
FLYFISH
FUNFEST
GABFEST
PANFISH
PROFESS
PROFUSE
RAFFISH
SAWFISH
SELFISH
SUFFUSE
SUNFISH
WOLFISH

•••F••S
ARMFULS
BAFFLES
BAGFULS
BOWFINS
BOXFULS
BUFFERS
BUFFETS
CAPFULS
CARFULS
COFFEES
COFFERS
COMFITS
CONFABS
CONFERS
CONFESS
CUPFULS
CURFEWS
DEAFENS
DEIFIES
DIFFERS
DUFFELS
DUFFERS
EARFULS
EDIFIES
EYEFULS
FULFILS
GAFFERS
GOLFERS
GOOFUPS
GUFFAWS
HEIFERS
HOOFERS
JARFULS
JEFFERS
JIFFIES
JUGFULS
LAPFULS
LOAFERS
LOOFAHS
MISFITS
MUFFINS
MUFFLES
OUTFITS
PIFFLES
PILFERS
POTFULS
PREFABS
PREFERS
PROFESS
PROFITS
PUFFERS
PUFFINS
PURFLES
RAFFLES
REDFINS
REDFIRS
REEFERS
RIFFLES
ROOFERS
RUFFLES
SEAFANS
SHOFARS
SOFFITS
STIFLES
SUFFERS
SURFERS
TAFFIES
TOFFEES
TRIFLES
TUFFETS
TWOFERS
UNIFIES
VATFULS
WAFFLES
WOOFERS

••••F•S
CARAFES
CUTOFFS
DREYFUS
LAYOFFS
PAYOFFS
POPOFFS
REBUFFS
RIPOFFS
RUNOFFS
SCRUFFS
SHRIFTS
STRAFES
TARIFFS
THRIFTS
TIPOFFS
UPLIFTS

•••••FS
BELIEFS
CUTOFFS
ENGULFS
LAYOFFS
MASSIFS
PAYOFFS
POPOFFS
REBUFFS
RELIEFS
RIPOFFS
RUNOFFS
SCRUFFS
TARIFFS
TIPOFFS

F•T••••
FATBACK
FATCATS
FATCITY
FATEFUL
FATHEAD
FATHERS
FATHOMS
FATIGUE
FATLESS
FATNESS
FATTENS
FATTEST
FATUITY
FATUOUS
FETCHED
FETCHES
FETIDLY
FETLOCK
FETTERS
FETTLES
FITCHES
FITNESS
FITTERS
FITTEST
FITTING
FUTURES

F••T•••
FACTION
FACTORS
FACTORY
FACTUAL
FALTERS
FANTAIL
FANTASY
FARTHER
FASTENS
FASTEST
FASTING
FASTONE
FATTENS
FATTEST
FEATHER
FEATURE
FELTFOR
FELTOUT
FERTILE
FESTERS
FESTIVE
FESTOON
FETTERS
FETTLES
FICTION
FICTIVE
FIFTEEN
FIFTIES
FILTERS
FISTFUL
FITTERS
FITTEST
FITTING
FIXTURE
FLATBED
FLATCAR
FLATOUT
FLATTED
FLATTEN
FLATTER
FLATTOP
FLITTED
FLITTER
FLOTSAM
FLUTING
FLUTIST
FLUTTER
FLYTRAP
FONTEYN
FONTINA
FOOTAGE
FOOTERS
FOOTING
FOOTMAN
FOOTMEN
FOOTPAD
FOOTSIE
FORTIES
FORTIFY
FORTRAN
FORTUNA
FORTUNE
FOSTERS
FOXTAIL
FOXTROT
FRETFUL
FRETSAW
FRETTED
FRITTED
FRITTER
FROTHED
FURTHER
FURTIVE
FUSTIAN
FUSTICS
FUSTIER
FUSTILY

F•••T••
FACETED
FAGOTED
FAINTED
FAINTER
FAINTLY
FAJITAS
FANATIC
FAULTED
FAUSTUS
FEASTED
FEINTED
FENETRE
FIESTAS
FIGHTER
FIRSTLY
FIXATED
FIXATES
FLATTED
FLATTEN
FLATTER
FLATTOP
FLEETER
FLEETLY
FLIRTED
FLITTED
FLITTER
FLOATED
FLOATER
FLOUTED
FLUSTER
FLUTTER
FOISTED
FORSTER
FOULTIP
FOURTHS
FRACTAL
FRANTIC
FREITAG
FRETTED
FRITTED
FRITTER
FRONTAL
FRONTED
FRONTON
FROSTED
FRUITED
FUJITSU

F••••T•
FACULTY
FALLSTO
FALSITY
FANJETS
FATCATS
FATCITY
FATUITY
FAUCETS
FAWCETT
FERRATE
FERRETS
FERRITE
FIDGETS
FIDGETY
FILLETS
FLAUNTS
FLIGHTS
FLIGHTY
FLOCKTO
FLORETS
FLYNETS
FOLIATE
FOLLETT
FOMENTS
FORESTS
FORGETS
FORINTS
FORMATS
FORSYTH
FRAILTY
FRIGATE
FRIGHTS

F•••••T
FADDIST
FADEOUT
FAIREST
FALLOUT
FALSEST
FANBELT
FANSOUT
FAREAST
FARLEFT
FARMOUT
FARWEST
FASCIST
FASTEST
FATTEST
FAUVIST
FAWCETT
FEEDLOT
FEELOUT
FELLOUT
FELTOUT
FERMENT
FERVENT
FIGMENT
FILBERT
FILLOUT
FINDOUT
FINEART
FIREANT
FIRELIT
FIRMEST
FISHNET
FISHOUT
FITTEST
FLATOUT
FLIESAT
FLORIST
FLUTIST
FLYCAST
FLYPAST
FOLDOUT
FOLKART
FOLLETT
FONDANT
FONDEST
FORFEIT
FORRENT
FORREST
FORWENT
FOULEST
FOULOUT
FOXIEST
FOXTROT
FRAUGHT
FREIGHT
FREMONT
FRESHET
FROWNAT
FULGENT
FULLEST
FUNFEST
FUSSPOT

•FT••••
OFTENER

•F•T•••
IFSTONE

•F•••T•
AFFECTS
AFREETS
EFFECTS
EFFORTS
OFFDUTY
OFFSETS
OFFSITE
OFSORTS

•F••••T
AFFLICT
AFFRONT
IFFIEST
OFASORT
OFFBEAT

••FT•••
CAFTANS
DAFTEST
DEFTEST
FIFTEEN
FIFTIES
HEFTIER
HEFTILY
HEFTING
KAFTANS
LEFTIES
LEFTIST
LEFTOFF
LEFTOUT
LIFTERS
LIFTING
LIFTOFF
LIFTSUP
LOFTIER
LOFTILY
LOFTING
NIFTIER
NIFTILY
RAFTERS
RAFTING
RIFTING
SIFTERS
SIFTING
SOFTENS
SOFTEST
SOFTIES
SOFTTOP
TUFTING
WAFTING

••F•T••
LAFITTE
REFUTED
REFUTER
REFUTES
SOFTTOP

••F••T•
AFFECTS
BUFFETS
BUFFETT
DEFACTO
DEFEATS
DEFECTS
DEFLATE
EFFECTS
EFFORTS
GEFILTE
INFANTA
INFANTS
INFECTS
INFESTS
INFLATE
LAFITTE
OFFDUTY
OFFSETS
OFFSITE
REFERTO
SOFFITS
TAFFETA
TUFFETS

••F•••T
AFFLICT
AFFRONT
ATFAULT
BUFFETT
DAFTEST
DEFAULT
DEFIANT
DEFICIT
DEFLECT
DEFROST
DEFTEST
DEFUNCT
GOFORIT
IFFIEST
INFLECT
INFLICT
INFRONT
LEFTIST
LEFTOUT
LIFENET
MRFIXIT
NOFAULT
OFFBEAT
REFLECT
REFRACT
SOFTEST
UPFRONT

•••FT••
CLIFTON
CRAFTED
CRAFTER
CRAFTSY
DRAFTED
DRAFTEE
DRIFTED
DRIFTER
GOLFTEE
GRAFTED
GRIFTER
ROOFTOP
SHAFTED
SHIFTED
SNIFTER
SWIFTER
SWIFTLY

•••F•T•
BUFFETS
BUFFETT
COMFITS
CONFUTE
HEIFETZ
MISFITS
OUTFITS
PROFITS
SOFFITS
SULFATE
SULFITE
TAFFETA
TUFFETS

•••F••T
BELFAST
BIGFEET
BIGFOOT
BUFFETT
COMFORT
DEAFEST
FORFEIT
FUNFEST
GABFEST
HALFWIT
HOOFSIT
HOTFOOT
LEAFLET
LENFANT
PARFAIT
PERFECT
PREFECT
SNIFFAT
SURFEIT
WEBFEET
WEBFOOT

••••FT•
SHRIFTS
THRIFTS
THRIFTY
TWELFTH
UPLIFTS

••••F•T
BENEFIT
BODYFAT
DEEPFAT
OUTOFIT
SEESFIT
SNIFFAT

•••••FT
AIRLIFT
ENGRAFT
FARLEFT
HAYLOFT
NEWLEFT
SKILIFT
UPDRAFT

FU•••••
FUCHSIA
FUDDLED
FUDDLES
FUDGING
FUELERS
FUELING
FUELOIL
FUELROD
FUJITSU
FULCRUM
FULFILL
FULFILS
FULGENT
FULGHUM
FULLEST
FULSOME
FUMBLED
FUMBLER
FUMBLES
FUNDING
FUNFAIR
FUNFEST
FUNGOES
FUNKIER
FUNNELS
FUNNIER
FUNNIES
FUNNILY
FUNNING
FURBALL
FURBISH
FURIOUS
FURLING
FURLONG
FURNACE
FURNISH
FURORES
FURRIER
FURRING
FURROWS
FURSEAL
FURTHER
FURTIVE
FUSSIER
FUSSILY
FUSSING
FUSSPOT
FUSTIAN
FUSTICS
FUSTIER
FUSTILY
FUTURES
FUZZIER
FUZZILY
FUZZING

F•U••••
FAUCETS
FAULTED
FAUSTUS
FAUVISM
FAUVIST
FAUXPAS
FEUDING
FLUBBED
FLUENCY
FLUFFED
FLUIDLY
FLUMMOX
FLUNKED
FLUSHED
FLUSHES
FLUSTER
FLUTING
FLUTIST
FLUTTER
FLUVIAL
FNUMBER
FOULARD
FOULEST
FOULING
FOULOUT
FOULSUP
FOULTIP
FOULUPS
FOUNDED
FOUNDER
FOUNDRY
FOURIER
FOURTHS
FRUITED

F••U•••
FACULTY
FAMULUS
FATUITY
FATUOUS
FELUCCA
FERULES
FIBULAE
FIBULAS
FICUSES
FIGURED
FIGURER
FIGURES
FLAUNTS
FLOUNCE
FLOURED
FLOUTED
FOCUSED
FOCUSES
FRAUGHT
FUTURES

F•••U••
FACTUAL
FAILURE
FAVOURS
FEATURE
FERRULE
FILLUPS
FISSURE
FIXTURE

FLIPUPS
FOLDUPS
FONDUES
FORMULA
FORSURE
FORTUNA
FORTUNE
FOULUPS
FRENUMS

F••••U•
FADEOUT
FAIRSUP
FAKEFUR
FALLGUY
FALLOUT
FAMULUS
FANSOUT
FARMOUT
FATEFUL
FATIGUE
FATUOUS
FAUSTUS
FEARFUL
FEELOUT
FELLOUT
FELTOUT
FERMIUM
FERROUS
FERVOUR
FIBROUS
FILLOUT
FILLSUP
FINDOUT
FIREBUG
FIREDUP
FIRESUP
FIRMSUP
FISHOUT
FISTFUL
FIXEDUP
FIXESUP
FLANEUR
FLAREUP
FLATOUT
FLAVOUR
FOLDOUT
FOLDSUP
FORERUN
FORKFUL
FOULOUT
FOULSUP
FRAMEUP
FRETFUL
FULCRUM
FULGHUM
FURIOUS

F•••••U
FRENEAU
FUJITSU

•F•U•••
EFFUSED
EFFUSES

•F••U••
OFFDUTY

•F•••U•
OFFHOUR

••FU•••
AWFULLY
DEFUNCT
DEFUSED
DEFUSES
EFFUSED
EFFUSES
INFUSED
INFUSES
REFUELS
REFUGEE
REFUGES
REFUNDS
REFUSAL
REFUSED
REFUSER
REFUSES
REFUTED
REFUTER
REFUTES
UNFURLS

••F•U••
ATFAULT
BEFOULS
DEFAULT
DIFFUSE
NOFAULT
OFFDUTY
SUFFUSE

••F••U•
DEFRAUD
HAFNIUM
INFOCUS
LEFTOUT
LIFTSUP
OFFHOUR

••F•••U
HOFBRAU

•••FU••
ARMFULS
BAGFULS
BOXFULS
CAPFULS
CARFULS
CONFUSE
CONFUTE
CUPFULS
DIFFUSE
EARFULS
EYEFULS
GOOFUPS
JARFULS
JUGFULS
LAPFULS
PERFUME
POTFULS
PROFUSE
SNAFUED
SUFFUSE
SYNFUEL
VATFULS

•••F•U•
BALFOUR
BEEFSUP
GOOFSUP
TENFOUR

••••FU•
BALEFUL
BANEFUL
BASHFUL
BOWLFUL
BRIMFUL
CAREFUL
DOLEFUL
DREYFUS
DUTIFUL
FAKEFUR
FATEFUL
FEARFUL
FISTFUL
FORKFUL
FRETFUL
GAINFUL
GLEEFUL
HANDFUL
HARMFUL
HATEFUL
HEEDFUL
HELPFUL
HOPEFUL
HURTFUL
LUSTFUL
MINDFUL
NEEDFUL
PAGEFUL
PAILFUL
PAINFUL
PIPEFUL
PITIFUL
PLAYFUL
POKEFUN
RESTFUL
ROOMFUL
SACKFUL
SKILFUL
SOULFUL
TACTFUL
TANKFUL
TEARFUL
TRAYFUL
TUNEFUL
WAKEFUL
WILLFUL
WISHFUL
WISTFUL
ZESTFUL

••••F•U
BLUEFLU

F•V••••
FAVORED
FAVOURS

F••V•••
FAUVISM
FAUVIST
FERVENT
FERVORS
FERVOUR
FLAVORS
FLAVOUR
FLIVVER
FLUVIAL

F•••V••
FLIVVER
FLYOVER
FOREVER

F••••V•
FESTIVE
FICTIVE
FORGAVE
FORGIVE
FURTIVE

••F•V••
INFAVOR

F•W••••
FAWCETT
FAWNERS
FAWNING
FOWLERS
FOWLING

F••W•••
FALWELL
FARWEST
FAYWRAY
FLAWING
FLOWERS
FLOWERY
FLOWING
FLYWAYS
FORWARD
FORWENT
FRAWLEY
FROWARD
FROWNAT
FROWNED
FROWNER

F•••W••
FAIRWAY
FARAWAY
FLYAWAY
FOODWEB
FREEWAY

F••••W•
FALLOWS
FARROWS
FELLOWS
FOGBOWS
FOLLOWS
FURROWS

F•••••W
FOREPAW
FORESAW
FRETSAW

••F••W•
GUFFAWS
INFLOWS

•••FW••
HALFWAY
HALFWIT

•••F•W•
CURFEWS
GUFFAWS
PEAFOWL

•••F••W
AIRFLOW
ASOFNOW
OUTFLOW

F•X••••
FIXABLE
FIXATED
FIXATES
FIXEDLY
FIXEDUP
FIXESUP
FIXINGS
FIXTURE
FOXFIRE
FOXHOLE
FOXIEST
FOXTAIL
FOXTROT

F••X•••
FAUXPAS
FLEXING
FLEXNER
FLEXORS

F•••••X
FIREBOX
FLUMMOX

•F••X••
AFFIXED
AFFIXES

••F•X••
AFFIXED
AFFIXES
MRFIXIT
UNFIXED

•••F••X
REAFFIX

••••F•X
BLUEFOX
BRERFOX
HALIFAX
REAFFIX

F•Y••••
FAYWRAY
FEYNMAN
FLYAWAY
FLYBALL
FLYBOYS
FLYCAST
FLYFISH
FLYHIGH
FLYLEAF
FLYNETS
FLYOVER
FLYPAST
FLYRODS
FLYTRAP
FLYWAYS
FRYCOOK
FRYPANS

F••Y•••
FLAYING
FOGYISH
FOGYISM
FRAYING

F•••Y••
FORSYTH

F••••Y•
FISHEYE
FLYBOYS
FLYWAYS
FONTEYN
FRIDAYS

F•••••Y
FACTORY
FACULTY
FAINTLY
FAIRWAY
FALLACY
FALLGUY
FALSELY
FALSIFY
FALSITY
FANCILY
FANTASY
FARADAY
FARAWAY
FATCITY
FATUITY
FAYWRAY
FETIDLY
FIDGETY
FIERILY
FINALLY
FINICKY
FIREFLY
FIRSTLY
FISHERY
FISHFRY
FISHILY
FIXEDLY
FLAGDAY
FLEETLY
FLIGHTY
FLOWERY
FLUENCY
FLUIDLY
FLYAWAY
FOOLERY
FOPPERY
FORGERY
FORTIFY
FOUNDRY
FRAILTY
FRANKLY
FRAWLEY
FREEWAY
FRESHLY
FUNNILY
FUSSILY
FUSTILY
FUZZILY

•F•Y•••
OFFYEAR

•F•••Y•
AFFRAYS

•F••••Y
AFFABLY
OFFDUTY

••FY•••
DEFYING
OFFYEAR

••F•Y••
RUFIYAA

••F••Y•
AFFRAYS
DEFRAYS

••F•••Y
AFFABLY
AWFULLY
DAFFILY
HEFTILY
HUFFILY
INFANCY
JEFFREY
JOFFREY
LOFTILY
NIFTILY
OFFDUTY
PUFFERY
PUFFILY
RIFLERY
TIFFANY

•••F••Y
BLUFFLY
COMFREY
CRAFTSY
DAFFILY
GODFREY
GRIFFEY
GRUFFLY
HALFWAY
HUFFILY
JEFFREY
JOFFREY
OLDFOGY
PALFREY
PERFIDY
PUFFERY
PUFFILY
STIFFLY
SWIFTLY
TIFFANY
WINFREY

••••F•Y
ALOOFLY
BLOWFLY
BLUFFLY
BRIEFLY
CHIEFLY
DEEPFRY
DEERFLY
FIREFLY
FISHFRY
GRIFFEY
GRUFFLY
LETSFLY
OVERFLY
SANDFLY
SCRUFFY
SHOOFLY
STIFFLY
STIRFRY
THRIFTY

•••••FY
ACIDIFY
AMPLIFY
BEATIFY
CALCIFY
CERTIFY
CLARIFY
DIGNIFY
FALSIFY
FORTIFY
GLORIFY
GRATIFY
HORRIFY
JUSTIFY
LIQUEFY
MAGNIFY
MOLLIFY
MORTIFY
MYSTIFY
NULLIFY
PETRIFY
QUALIFY
RECTIFY
REUNIFY
SALSIFY
SATISFY
SCARIFY
SCRUFFY
SIGNIFY
SPECIFY
STUPEFY
TERRIFY
TESTIFY
VERSIFY
VITRIFY

F•Z••••
FIZGIGS
FIZZIER
FIZZING
FIZZLED
FIZZLES
FUZZIER
FUZZILY
FUZZING

F••Z•••
FANZINE
FIZZIER
FIZZING
FIZZLED
FIZZLES
FOOZLED
FOOZLES
FRAZIER
FRAZZLE
FRIZZED
FRIZZES
FRIZZLE
FUZZIER
FUZZILY
FUZZING

F•••Z••
FRAZZLE
FREEZER
FREEZES
FRIEZES
FRIZZED
FRIZZES
FRIZZLE

F••••Z•
FIRENZE

F•••••Z
FRANKOZ

••F•Z••
UNFAZED

•••F•Z•
GINFIZZ

•••F••Z
GINFIZZ
HEIFETZ

GA•••••
GABBERS
GABBIER
GABBING
GABBLED
GABBLES
GABBROS
GABFEST
GABRIEL
GADDING
GADGETS
GADGETY
GADSDEN
GAFFERS
GAFFING
GAGARIN
GAGGING
GAGGLES
GAGLINE
GAGRULE
GAGSTER
GAINERS
GAINFUL
GAINING
GAINSAY
GAINSON
GAITERS
GAITING
GALAHAD
GALATEA
GALATIA
GALILEE
GALILEI
GALILEO
GALLANT
GALLEON
GALLERY
GALLEYS
GALLICO
GALLING
GALLIUM
GALLONS
GALLOPS
GALOOTS
GALUMPH
GALVANI
GAMBIAN
GAMBITS
GAMBLED
GAMBLER
GAMBLES
GAMBOLS
GAMBREL
GAMELAW
GAMETES
GAMIEST
GAMINES
GAMMONS
GANDERS
GANGING
GANGLED
GANGLIA
GANGSAW
GANGSTA
GANGSUP
GANGWAY
GANNETS
GANNETT
GANTLET
GAPPING
GARAGED
GARAGES
GARBAGE
GARBING
GARBLED
GARBLES
GARCONS
GARDENS
GARDNER
GARGLED
GARGLES
GARLAND
GARMENT
GARNERS
GARNETS
GARNISH
GARONNE
GARRETS
GARRETT
GARRICK
GARTERS
GASBAGS
GASCAPS
GASCONS
GASEOUS
GASHING
GASJETS
GASKETS
GASKINS
GASMAIN
GASOHOL
GASPING
GASPUMP
GASSERS
GASTRIC
GATEAUX
GATELEG
GATEMAN
GATEMEN
GATEWAY
GATHERS
GATLING
GAUCHER
GAUCHOS
GAUDENS
GAUDIER
GAUDILY
GAUGERS
GAUGING
GAUGUIN
GAUNTER
GAUNTLY
GAUTAMA
GAUZIER
GAUZILY
GAVELED
GAVEOFF
GAVEOUT
GAVEWAY
GAVIALS
GAVOTTE
GAWKERS
GAWKIER
GAWKING
GAYLORD
GAZEBOS
GAZELLE
GAZETTE
GAZZARA

G•A••••
GEARBOX
GEARING
GEARSTO
GEARSUP
GHASTLY
GIACOMO
GLACEED
GLACIAL
GLACIER
GLADDEN
GLADDER
GLADEYE
GLAMOUR
GLANCED
GLANCES
GLARING
GLASGOW
GLASSED
GLASSES
GLAZERS
GLAZIER
GLAZING
GNARLED
GNARRED
GNASHED
GNASHES
GNAWERS
GNAWING
GOABOUT
GOADING
GOAHEAD
GOALIES
GOALONG
GOATEED
GOATEES
GOATISH
GRABBAG
GRABBED
GRABBER
GRABSAT
GRACIAS
GRACILE
GRACING
GRACKLE
GRADERS
GRADING
GRADUAL
GRAFTED
GRAHAME
GRAHAMS
GRAINED
GRAMMAR
GRAMMER
GRAMMES
GRAMPUS
GRANADA
GRANARY
GRANDAM
GRANDEE
GRANDER
GRANDLY
GRANDMA
GRANDPA
GRANGER
GRANGES
GRANITE
GRANOLA
GRANTED
GRANTEE
GRANTOR
GRANULE
GRAPHED
GRAPHIC
GRAPNEL
GRAPPLE
GRASPED
GRASSED
GRASSES
GRATERS
GRATIFY
GRATING
GRAVELS
GRAVELY
GRAVEST
GRAVIES
GRAVING
GRAVITY
GRAVURE
GRAYEST
GRAYING
GRAYSON
GRAZERS
GRAZING
GUANACO
GUANINE
GUARANI
GUARDED
GUARGUM

G••A•••
GAGARIN
GALAHAD
GALATEA
GALATIA
GARAGED
GARAGES
GELADAS
GELATIN
GELATIS
GERAINT
GERALDO
GETAWAY
GIRAFFE
GIRASOL
GLEAMED
GLEANED
GLEANER
GLEASON
GLOATED
GOCARTS
GOKARTS
GOTAWAY
GOUACHE
GREASED
GREASER
GREASES
GREATER
GREATLY
GREAVES
GROANED
GROANER
GYRATED
GYRATES
GYRATOR

G•••A••
GALLANT
GALVANI
GARBAGE
GARLAND
GASBAGS
GASCAPS
GASMAIN
GATEAUX
GAUTAMA
GAVIALS
GAZZARA
GEEGAWS
GENNARO
GERMANE
GERMANS
GERMANY
GESTALT
GESTATE
GETBACK
GEWGAWS
GIMBALS
GIZZARD
GODDARD
GOESAPE
GOLIATH
GOODALL
GOSHAWK
GOTBACK
GOTLAND
GOULASH
GOURAMI
GRAHAME
GRAHAMS
GRANADA
GRANARY
GRENADA
GRENADE
GRIMACE
GUANACO
GUARANI
GUEVARA
GUFFAWS
GUITARS
GUMBALL
GUNWALE
GUSTAVE
GYMNAST

G••••A•
GAINSAY
GALAHAD
GAMBIAN
GAMELAW
GANGSAW
GANGWAY
GATEMAN
GATEWAY
GAVEWAY
GEISHAS
GELADAS
GENERAL
GENTIAN
GETAWAY
GIDDYAP
GILBLAS
GINGHAM
GIVEWAY
GLACIAL
GLORIAS
GLOSSAE
GLOTTAL
GOAHEAD
GODTHAB
GOESBAD
GOINGAT
GOODBAR
GOODMAN
GORDIAN
GOTAWAY
GOTCHAS
GRABBAG
GRABSAT

GRACIAS
GRADUAL
GRAMMAR
GRANDAM
GRECIAN
GRISHAM
GUINEAS
GUNBOAT
GUNPLAY
GURKHAS

G•••••A
GALATEA
GALATIA
GANGLIA
GANGSTA
GAUTAMA
GAZZARA
GEORGIA
GINGIVA
GONDOLA
GORILLA
GRANADA
GRANDMA
GRANDPA
GRANOLA
GRENADA
GUEVARA

•GA••••
AGAINST
AGAKHAN
AGASSIZ
EGALITE
UGANDAN

•G•A•••
AGNATES
AGRAFFE
IGUANAS
OGLALAS

•G••A••
AGESAGO
AGITATE
EGGCASE
OGDOADS

•G•••A•
AGAKHAN
AGENDAS
EGGHEAD
IGUANAS
OGLALAS
UGANDAN

•G••••A
AGRIPPA

••GA•••
BUGABOO
BUGALOO
DEGAUSS
ENGAGED
ENGAGES
ENGARDE
GAGARIN
HOGARTH
INGALLS
LEGALLY
LEGATEE
LEGATES
LEGATOS
LIGATED
LIGATES
MCGAVIN
MOGAMBO
NEGATED
NEGATES
NEGATOR
NOGALES
ORGANDY
ORGANIC
ORGANON
ORGANUM
ORGANZA
PEGASUS
REGAINS
REGALED
REGALES
REGALIA
REGALLY
REGARDS
REGATTA
SUGARED
TAGALOG

••G•A••
AFGHANI
AFGHANS
BAGGAGE
BEGGARS
BIGBAND
BIGBANG
BIGGAME
BIGNAME
COGNACS
COGNATE
DEGRADE
DIGRAPH
DOGCART
DOGDAYS
DOGEARS
DOGFACE
DOGMATA
DOGTAGS
EGGCASE
ENGLAND
ENGRAFT
ENGRAMS
ENGRAVE
FOGBANK
HAGGARD
HOGBACK
HOGWASH
INGRAIN
INGRATE
JAGUARS
JIGSAWS
JUGBAND
LAGGARD
LOGJAMS
LUGGAGE
MAGNATE
MAGYARS
MIGRANT
MIGRATE
NIGGARD
ONGUARD
PAGEANT
PIGTAIL
RAGLANS
REGNANT
REGRADE
SAGUARO
SIGNALS
TAGSALE
UPGRADE
VAGRANT
WAGTAIL
WIGWAGS
WIGWAMS
ZIGZAGS

••G••A•
ANGOLAN
ANGORAS
ANGULAR
AUGURAL
BAGHDAD
BIGDEAL
BIGHEAD
BUGBEAR
DIGITAL
DOGSTAR
EGGHEAD
FIGLEAF
HEGIRAS
HIGHHAT
HIGHWAY
INGEMAR
JUGHEAD
JUGULAR
LAGUNAS
LOGGIAS
LOGICAL
MAGICAL
MEGRYAN
PAGODAS
REGULAR
SAGINAW
TUGBOAT
VEGETAL

••G•••A
ALGEBRA
ALGERIA
AUGUSTA
BEGONIA
BEGORRA
DOGMATA
HIGHTEA
HYGIEIA
MAGENTA
NIGERIA
ORGANZA
REGALIA
REGATTA
RIGVEDA
SEGOVIA

•••GA••
ABIGAIL
BAGGAGE
BARGAIN
BEGGARS
BENGALI
BENGALS
BIGGAME
BRIGADE
BRIGAND
BROGANS
BULGARS
CALGARY
CHAGALL
COLGATE
CONGAED
CONGAME
COUGARS
ELEGANT
ENDGAME
FORGAVE
FRIGATE
GEEGAWS
GEWGAWS
HAGGARD
HANGARS
HUNGARY
LAGGARD
LONGAGO
LUGGAGE
MARGATE
MARGAUX
MARGAYS
MORGANA
MORGANS
NEWGATE
NIAGARA
NIGGARD
NOUGATS
OREGANO
ORIGAMI
SEAGATE
SLOGANS
TONGANS
VULGATE
WARGAME

•••G•A•
ANAGRAM
BELGIAN
BERGMAN
BINGHAM
BRIGHAM
BURGLAR
CONGEAL
DIAGRAM
DINGBAT
DOUGLAS
ELEGIAC
ENIGMAS
EPIGRAM
FLAGDAY
FLAGMAN
FROGMAN
GANGSAW
GANGWAY
GINGHAM
HANGMAN
KINGMAN
KINGRAT
KLUGMAN
LAUGHAT
LINGUAL
LOGGIAS
LOWGEAR
LUNGEAT
MACGRAW
MAUGHAM
PROGRAM
QUAGGAS
RIDGWAY
SEAGRAM
STIGMAS
STYGIAN
SYNGMAN
TRIGRAM
URUGUAY
VAUGHAN
VIRGOAN
ZEUGMAS

•••G••A
ARUGULA
GANGLIA
GANGSTA
GINGIVA
MORGANA
NIAGARA
PERGOLA
SANGRIA

••••GA•
AMALGAM
ASSEGAI
BODEGAS
CAYUGAS
COALGAS
DONEGAL
GOINGAT
ILLEGAL
JOHNGAY
NOSEGAY
QUAGGAS
RAREGAS
SENEGAL
STOPGAP
TEARGAS
TSONGAS
VINEGAR
WOLFGAL

••••G•A
ANTIGUA
BOLOGNA
GEORGIA
INTEGRA
LASAGNA
MANAGUA

•••••GA
NORIEGA
SYRINGA

G•B••••
GABBERS
GABBIER
GABBING
GABBLED
GABBLES
GABBROS
GABFEST
GABRIEL
GIBBERS
GIBBETS
GIBBONS
GIBBOUS
GIBLETS
GIBLUES
GOBBLED
GOBBLER
GOBBLES
GOBLETS
GOBLINS
GOBROKE

G••B•••
GABBERS
GABBIER
GABBING
GABBLED
GABBLES
GABBROS
GAMBIAN
GAMBITS
GAMBLED
GAMBLER
GAMBLES
GAMBOLS
GAMBREL
GARBAGE
GARBING
GARBLED
GARBLES
GASBAGS
GERBILS
GETBACK
GIBBERS
GIBBETS
GIBBONS
GIBBOUS
GILBERT
GILBLAS
GIMBALS
GLIBBER
GLOBULE
GOABOUT
GOBBLED
GOBBLER
GOBBLES
GOOBERS
GOTBACK
GRABBAG
GRABBED
GRABBER
GRABSAT
GRUBBED
GUMBALL
GUNBOAT

G•••B••
GAZEBOS
GEARBOX
GEMSBOK
GLIBBER
GOESBAD
GOLDBUG
GOODBAR
GOODBYE
GOODBYS
GRABBAG
GRABBED
GRABBER
GRUBBED
GRUMBLE

G••••B•
GOINGBY

G•••••B
GODTHAB
GOODJOB

•G••B••
IGNOBLE
IGNOBLY

••GB•••
BIGBAND
BIGBANG
BIGBEND
BIGBIRD
BIGBOYS
BUGBEAR
COGBURN
FOGBANK
FOGBOWS
HOGBACK
JUGBAND
LOGBOOK
TUGBOAT

••G•B••
ALGEBRA
BUGABOO
HIGHBOY
LEGIBLE
LEGIBLY
PAGEBOY

••G••B•
MOGAMBO

•••GB••
DINGBAT
LONGBOW

••••GB•
GOINGBY
SWINGBY

G•C••••
GECKOES
GOCARTS

G••C•••
GARCONS
GASCAPS
GASCONS
GAUCHER
GAUCHOS
GIACOMO
GLACEED
GLACIAL
GLACIER
GLUCOSE
GNOCCHI
GOTCHAS
GRACIAS
GRACILE
GRACING
GRACKLE
GRECIAN
GROCERS
GROCERY
GULCHES

G•••C••
GLANCED
GLANCES
GNOCCHI
GOUACHE
GROUCHO
GROUCHY

G••••C•
GALLICO
GARRICK
GETBACK
GIMMICK
GODUTCH
GOTBACK
GOTHICS
GRIMACE
GUANACO
GUNLOCK

G•••••C
GASTRIC
GENERIC
GENETIC
GNOSTIC
GRAPHIC

•G•C•••
EGGCASE
EGGCUPS

••GC•••
DOGCART
DOGCHEW
DOGCHOW
EGGCASE
EGGCUPS

••G•C••
LOGICAL
MAGICAL
NOGUCHI

••G••C•
COGENCY
COGNACS
DOGFACE
ELGRECO
HOGBACK
NEGLECT
REGENCY
URGENCY

••G•••C
ANGELIC
ORGANIC

•••G••C
ELEGIAC

••••G•C
ILLOGIC
PELAGIC
YOUNGMC

G•D••••
GADDING
GADGETS
GADGETY
GADSDEN
GIDDIER
GIDDILY
GIDDYAP
GIDDYUP
GIDEONS
GODDARD
GODDESS
GODFREY
GODLIKE
GODSEND
GODSONS
GODTHAB
GODUNOV
GODUTCH
GODWITS

G••D•••
GADDING
GANDERS
GARDENS
GARDNER
GAUDENS
GAUDIER
GAUDILY
GELDING
GENDERS
GEODESY
GETDOWN
GIDDIER
GIDDILY
GIDDYAP
GIDDYUP
GILDERS
GILDING
GIRDERS
GIRDING
GIRDLED
GIRDLES
GLADDEN
GLADDER
GLADEYE
GLIDERS
GLIDING
GOADING
GODDARD
GODDESS
GOLDBUG
GOLDING
GOLDWYN
GONDOLA
GOODALL
GOODBAR
GOODBYE
GOODBYS
GOODEGG
GOODIES
GOODJOB
GOODJOE
GOODMAN
GOODMEN
GOODONE
GOODSON
GOODWIN
GORDIAN
GOTDOWN
GRADERS
GRADING
GRADUAL
GRIDDED
GRIDDER
GRIDDLE
GRUDGED
GRUDGES
GUIDING
GUIDONS
GUMDROP
GUNDOGS

G•••D••
GADSDEN
GELADAS
GLADDEN
GLADDER
GLUEDON
GOUNDER
GOURDES
GRANDAM
GRANDEE
GRANDER
GRANDLY
GRANDMA
GRANDPA
GRENDEL
GRIDDED
GRIDDER
GRIDDLE
GRINDER
GUARDED
GUILDER

G••••D•
GERALDO
GERUNDS
GIRONDE
GRANADA
GRENADA
GRENADE
GROUNDS

G•••••D
GABBLED
GALAHAD
GAMBLED
GANGLED
GARAGED
GARBLED
GARGLED
GARLAND
GAVELED
GAYLORD
GENTLED
GHOSTED
GIELGUD
GIFFORD
GIGGLED
GIRDLED
GIZZARD
GLACEED
GLANCED
GLASSED
GLEAMED
GLEANED
GLINTED
GLITZED
GLOATED
GLOMMED
GLORIED
GLOSSED
GLUTTED
GNARLED
GNARRED
GNASHED
GOAHEAD
GOATEED
GOBBLED
GODDARD
GODSEND
GOESBAD
GOGGLED
GOROUND
GOTLAND
GRABBED
GRAFTED
GRAINED
GRANTED
GRAPHED
GRASPED
GRASSED
GREASED
GREENED
GREETED
GRIDDED
GRIEVED
GRILLED
GRINNED
GRIPPED
GRITTED
GROANED
GROOMED
GROOVED
GROSSED
GROUPED
GROUSED
GROUTED
GROWLED
GRUBBED
GRUDGED
GRUMPED
GRUNTED
GUARDED
GUESSED
GUESTED
GURGLED
GUSSIED
GUZZLED
GYRATED

•GD••••
OGDOADS

•G••D••
AGENDAS
EGGEDON
UGANDAN

•G•••D•
OGDOADS

•G••••D
AGROUND
EGESTED
EGGHEAD
IGNITED
IGNORED

••GD•••
BIGDEAL
BOGDOWN
DOGDAYS
RAGDOLL

••G•D••
BAGHDAD
EDGEDIN
EGGEDON
PAGODAS
RIGIDLY
UNGODLY

••G••D•
AUGENDS
DEGRADE
ENGARDE
ENGIRDS
FAGENDS
LEGENDS
ORGANDY
RAGGEDY
REGARDS
REGRADE
RIGVEDA
TAGENDS
TVGUIDE
UNGIRDS
UPGRADE

••G•••D
ANGERED
AUGURED
BAGHDAD
BAGNOLD
BIGBAND
BIGBEND
BIGBIRD
BIGHEAD
BIGOTED
BOGEYED
BOGGLED
BUGEYED
DAGWOOD
DOGSLED
DOGWOOD
EGGHEAD
ENGAGED
ENGLAND
ENGLUND
FAGOTED
FIGURED
GIGGLED
GOGGLED
HAGGARD
HAGGLED
HIGHEND
HOGTIED
HOGWILD
JIGGLED
JOGGLED
JUGBAND
JUGGLED
JUGHEAD
LAGGARD
LIGATED
LIGHTED
NEGATED
NIGGARD
NIGGLED
ONGUARD
RAGWEED
REGALED
REGLUED
RIGHTED
SIGHTED
SIGMUND
SUGARED
TOGGLED
UNGLUED
WAGERED
WAGGLED
WIGGLED

•••GD••
FLAGDAY
HANGDOG
KINGDOM
LANGDON

•••G•D•
BRIGADE
PONGIDS
RAGGEDY
SUNGODS
TRAGEDY
WARGODS

•••G••D
ALIGNED
BOGGLED
BOOGIED
BRAGGED
BRIGAND
BUNGLED
BURGLED
CHUGGED
CLOGGED
CONGAED
COUGHED
DANGLED
DEIGNED
DIDGOOD
DRAGGED
DRUGGED
FEIGNED
FLAGGED
FLOGGED
FORGOOD
GANGLED
GARGLED
GIGGLED
GOGGLED
GURGLED
HAGGARD
HAGGLED
JANGLED
JIGGLED
JINGLED
JOGGLED
JUGGLED
LAGGARD
LANGUID
LAUGHED
MANGLED
MINGLED
NEIGHED
NIGGARD
NIGGLED
OLDGOLD
PLAGUED
PLUGGED
REIGNED
ROUGHED
SHAGGED
SINGLED
SLOGGED
SLUGGED
SNAGGED
SOUGHED
STAGGED
SWIGGED
TANGLED
TANGOED
TINGLED
TOGGLED
TONGUED
TRIGGED
WAGGLED
WANGLED
WEIGHED
WIGGLED

••••G•D
ALLEGED
AVENGED
BRAGGED
BRIDGED
CHANGED
CHARGED
CHUGGED
CLANGED
CLOGGED
CRINGED
DAMAGED
DELUGED
DEMIGOD
DRAGGED
DREDGED
DRUDGED
DRUGGED
EMERGED
ENCAGED
ENGAGED
ENRAGED
FLAGGED

FLEDGED
FLOGGED
FORAGED
FRINGED
GARAGED
GIELGUD
GRUDGED
LOUNGED
MANAGED
OBLIGED
PLEDGED
PLUGGED
PLUNGED
PRONGED
RAVAGED
RENEGED
SAVAGED
SHAGGED
SLOGGED
SLUGGED
SMUDGED
SNAGGED
SPARGED
SPONGED
STAGGED
SWIGGED
TRIGGED
TRUDGED
TWANGED
TWINGED
UNCAGED
VOYAGED
WRONGED

GE•••••

GEARBOX
GEARING
GEARSTO
GEARSUP
GECKOES
GEEGAWS
GEEWHIZ
GEEZERS
GEFILTE
GEISHAS
GELADAS
GELATIN
GELATIS
GELDING
GELLING
GEMLIKE
GEMSBOK
GENDERS
GENERAL
GENERIC
GENERIS
GENESEE
GENESES
GENESIS
GENETIC
GENGHIS
GENNARO
GENOESE
GENTEEL
GENTIAN
GENTILE
GENTLED
GENTLER
GENTLES
GENUINE
GEODESY
GEOLOGY
GEORGES
GEORGIA
GERAINT
GERALDO
GERBILS
GERENTS
GERITOL
GERMANE
GERMANS
GERMANY
GERUNDS
GESSOES
GESTALT
GESTATE
GESTURE
GETAWAY
GETBACK
GETDOWN
GETEVEN
GETINTO
GETITON
GETLOST
GETOVER
GETSOFF
GETSOUT
GETSSET
GETTING
GETWELL
GEWGAWS
GEYSERS

G•E••••

GEEGAWS
GEEWHIZ
GEEZERS
GHERKIN
GHETTOS
GIELGUD
GLEAMED
GLEANED
GLEANER
GLEASON
GLEEFUL
GOESAPE
GOESBAD
GOESFOR
GOESOFF
GOESOUT
GREASED
GREASER
GREASES
GREATER
GREATLY
GREAVES
GRECIAN
GREELEY
GREENED
GREENER
GREETED
GREETER
GREGORY
GREMLIN
GRENADA
GRENADE
GRENDEL
GRETZKY
GREYEST
GREYING
GUELPHS
GUESSED
GUESSER
GUESSES
GUESTED
GUEVARA

G••E•••

GAMELAW
GAMETES
GASEOUS
GATEAUX
GATELEG
GATEMAN
GATEMEN
GATEWAY
GAVELED
GAVEOFF
GAVEOUT
GAVEWAY
GAZEBOS
GAZELLE
GAZETTE
GENERAL
GENERIC
GENERIS
GENESEE
GENESES
GENESIS
GENETIC
GERENTS
GETEVEN
GIDEONS
GISELLE
GIVENTO
GIVEOFF
GIVEOUT
GIVESIN
GIVESTO
GIVESUP
GIVEUPS
GIVEWAY
GLEEFUL
GLUEDON
GONERIL
GORETEX
GOTEVEN
GOVERNS
GREELEY
GREENED
GREENER
GREETED
GREETER
GRIEVED
GRIEVER
GRIEVES

G•••E••

GABBERS
GABFEST
GADGETS
GADGETY
GAFFERS
GAINERS
GAITERS
GALLEON
GALLERY
GALLEYS
GAMIEST
GANDERS
GANNETS
GANNETT
GARDENS
GARMENT
GARNERS
GARNETS
GARRETS
GARRETT
GARTERS
GASJETS
GASKETS
GASSERS
GATHERS
GAUDENS
GAUGERS
GAWKERS
GEEZERS
GENDERS
GENOESE
GENTEEL
GEODESY
GETWELL
GEYSERS
GIBBERS
GIBBETS
GIBLETS
GILBERT
GILDERS
GIMLETS
GINGERS
GINGERY
GINSENG
GIRDERS
GLACEED
GLADEYE
GLAZERS
GLIDERS
GLOWERS
GNAWERS
GOAHEAD
GOATEED
GOATEES
GOBLETS
GODDESS
GODSEND
GOLFERS
GOMPERS
GOOBERS
GOODEGG
GOOIEST
GOPHERS
GORGETS
GORIEST
GOSPELS
GOSSETT
GOTWELL
GOUGERS
GRADERS
GRATERS
GRAVELS
GRAVELY
GRAVEST
GRAYEST
GRAZERS
GREYEST
GRIPERS
GRIVETS
GROCERS
GROCERY
GROVELS
GROWERS
GRUYERE
GUINEAS
GULLETS
GUNNELS
GUNNERS
GUNNERY
GURNEYS
GUSHERS
GUSSETS
GUTLESS
GUTTERS
GYPPERS

G••••E•

GABBIER
GABBLED
GABBLES
GABRIEL
GADSDEN
GAGGLES
GAGSTER
GALATEA
GALILEE
GALILEI
GALILEO
GAMBLED
GAMBLER
GAMBLES
GAMBREL
GAMETES
GAMINES
GANGLED
GANTLET
GARAGED
GARAGES
GARBLED
GARBLES
GARDNER
GARGLED
GARGLES
GATELEG
GATEMEN
GAUCHER
GAUDIER
GAUNTER
GAUZIER
GAVELED
GAWKIER
GECKOES
GENESEE
GENESES
GENTEEL
GENTLED
GENTLER
GENTLES
GEORGES
GESSOES
GETEVEN
GETOVER
GETSSET
GHOSTED
GIBLUES
GIDDIER
GIGGLED
GIGGLER
GIGGLES
GILLIES
GILLNET
GIPSIES
GIRDLED
GIRDLES
GLACEED
GLACIER
GLADDEN
GLADDER
GLANCED
GLANCES
GLASSED
GLASSES
GLAZIER
GLEAMED
GLEANED
GLEANER
GLIBBER
GLIMMER
GLINTED
GLISTEN
GLITTER
GLITZED
GLITZES
GLOATED
GLOMMED
GLORIED
GLORIES
GLOSSED
GLOSSES
GLUMMER
GLUTTED
GNARLED
GNARRED
GNASHED
GNASHES
GOALIES
GOATEED
GOATEES
GOBBLED
GOBBLER
GOBBLES
GODFREY
GOGGLED
GOGGLES
GOLFTEE
GOODIES
GOODMEN
GOOFIER
GOOPIER
GORETEX
GOTEVEN
GOTOVER
GOUNDER
GOURDES
GOURMET
GRABBED
GRABBER
GRAFTED
GRAINED
GRAMMER
GRAMMES
GRANDEE
GRANDER
GRANGER
GRANGES
GRANTED
GRANTEE
GRAPHED
GRAPNEL
GRASPED
GRASSED
GRASSES
GRAVIES
GREASED
GREASER
GREASES
GREATER
GREAVES
GREELEY
GREENED
GREENER
GREETED
GREETER
GRENDEL
GRIDDED
GRIDDER
GRIEVED
GRIEVER
GRIEVES
GRIFFEY
GRIFTER
GRILLED
GRILLES
GRILLET
GRIMIER
GRIMMER
GRINDER
GRINNED
GRINNER
GRIPPED
GRIPPER
GRITTED
GROANED
GROANER
GROLIER
GROMMET
GROOMED
GROOMER
GROOVED
GROOVES
GROSSED
GROSSER
GROSSES
GROUPED
GROUPER
GROUSED
GROUSER
GROUSES
GROUTED
GROWLED
GROWLER
GRUBBED
GRUDGED
GRUDGES
GRUFFER
GRUMPED
GRUNTED
GUARDED
GUESSED
GUESSER
GUESSES
GUESTED
GUILDER
GUIMPES
GULCHES
GULLIES
GUMMIER
GUMTREE
GUNKIER
GUNNIES
GUNTHER
GUPPIES
GURGLED
GURGLES
GUSHIER
GUSSIED
GUSSIES
GUSTOES
GUTSIER
GUZZLED
GUZZLER
GUZZLES
GYPSIES
GYRATED
GYRATES

G•••••E

GAGLINE
GAGRULE
GALILEE
GARBAGE
GARONNE
GAVOTTE
GAZELLE
GAZETTE
GEFILTE
GEMLIKE
GENESEE
GENOESE
GENTILE
GENUINE
GERMANE
GESTATE
GESTURE
GILMORE
GIRAFFE
GIRONDE
GISELLE
GLADEYE
GLIMPSE
GLOBULE
GLOSSAE
GLUCOSE
GOBROKE
GODLIKE
GOESAPE
GOLFTEE
GOODBYE
GOODJOE
GOODONE
GOUACHE
GRACILE
GRACKLE
GRAHAME
GRANDEE
GRANITE
GRANTEE
GRANULE
GRAPPLE
GRAVURE
GRENADE
GRIDDLE
GRIMACE
GRISTLE
GRIZZLE
GROUPIE
GRUMBLE
GRUYERE
GUANINE
GUMSHOE
GUMTREE
GUNFIRE
GUNWALE
GUSTAVE
GUTHRIE
GYMSHOE

•GE••••

AGEISTS
AGELESS
AGENDAS
AGESAGO
EGESTED

•G•E•••

AGREETO
EGGEDON
HGWELLS
IGNEOUS
OGREISH

•G••E••

AGELESS
AGGRESS
AGILELY
AGREETO
EGGHEAD
UGLIEST

•G•••E•

AGNATES
EGESTED
IGNITED
IGNITER
IGNITES
IGNORED
IGNORER
IGNORES

•G••••E

AGITATE
AGONIZE
AGRAFFE
EGALITE
EGGCASE
IGNOBLE

••GE•••

ALGEBRA
ALGERIA
ANGELES
ANGELIC
ANGELOU
ANGELUS
ANGERED
AUGENDS
BIGELOW
BIGEYES
BOGEYED
BUGEYED
COGENCY
DIGESTS
DOGEARS
EAGERER
EAGERLY
EDGEDIN
EDGEOUT
EDGESIN
EGGEDON
EUGENIE
FAGENDS
INGEMAR
INGENUE
INGESTS
LEGENDS
MAGENTA
NIGERIA
PAGEANT
PAGEBOY
PAGEFUL
PIGEONS
REGENCY
REGENTS
TAGENDS
URGENCY
VEGETAL
WAGERED
WAGERER

••G•E••

AGGRESS
AIGRETS
ALGIERS
ANGLERS
ARGUERS
AUGMENT
BAGGERS
BIGBEND
BIGDEAL
BIGFEET
BIGGERS
BIGGEST
BIGHEAD
BIGNESS
BUGBEAR
BUGLERS
CAGIEST
CYGNETS
DAGGERS
DEGREES
DIGGERS
DIGRESS
DOGLEGS
EAGLETS
EDGIEST
EGGHEAD
ELGRECO
FIGLEAF
FIGMENT
FOGGERS
HIGHEND
HIGHEST
HUGGERS
HYGIEIA
HYGIENE
INGRESS
JAGLESS
JIGGERS
JIGGERY
JOGGERS
JUGHEAD
KEGLERS
LAGGERS
LOGGERS
LOGIEST
LUGGERS
MAGNETO
MAGNETS
MAGUEYS
MUGGERS
NEGLECT
NIGHEST
NUGGETS
PIGLETS
PIGMENT
PIGPENS
PUGREES
RAGGEDY
RAGWEED
REGRESS
REGRETS
RIGGERS
RIGVEDA
ROGUERY
SEGMENT
SIGHERS
SIGNEES
SIGNERS
SIGNETS
SUGGEST
TIGRESS
TUGGERS
UNGUENT
VAGUELY
VAGUEST
WAGGERY
WIGLETS

••G••E•

ANGELES
ANGERED
ANGRIER
ARGIVES
ARGYLES
AUGURED
BAGGIER
BAGGIES
BIGEYES
BIGFEET
BIGGIES
BIGOTED
BIGTOES
BOGEYED
BOGGLED
BOGGLER
BOGGLES
BUGEYED
BUGGIER
BUGGIES
BYGONES
DEGREES
DOGCHEW
DOGGIES
DOGSLED
EAGERER
ENGAGED
ENGAGES
ENGINES
FAGOTED
FIGHTER
FIGURED
FIGURER
FIGURES
FOGGIER
GAGGLES
GAGSTER
GIGGLED
GIGGLER
GIGGLES
GOGGLED
GOGGLES
HAGGLED
HAGGLER
HAGGLES
HIGHTEA
HOGTIED
HOGTIES
JIGGLED
JIGGLES
JOGGLED
JOGGLES
JUGGLED
JUGGLER
JUGGLES
LEGATEE
LEGATES
LEGGIER
LEGUMES
LIGATED
LIGATES
LIGHTED
LIGHTEN
LIGHTER
MAGPIES
MUGGIER
NEGATED
NEGATES
NIGGLED
NIGGLES
NOGALES
PIGGIES
PUGREES
PYGMIES
RAGGIER
RAGWEED
REGALED
REGALES
REGIMEN
REGIMES
REGLUED
REGLUES
RIGHTED
RIGHTER
SAGGIER
SIGHTED
SIGNEES
SOGGIER
SUGARED
TIGHTEN
TIGHTER
TOGGLED
TOGGLES
UNGLUED
VEGGIES
WAGERED
WAGERER
WAGGLED
WAGGLES
WAGONER
WIGGLED
WIGGLER
WIGGLES
ZYGOTES

••G•••E

ARGONNE
AUGUSTE
BAGGAGE
BAGPIPE
BEGRIME
BEGUILE
BEGUINE
BIGGAME
BIGNAME
BIGTIME
BOGHOLE
COGNATE
DEGRADE
DOGFACE
DOGGONE
EGGCASE
ENGARDE
ENGORGE
ENGRAVE
EUGENIE
GAGLINE
GAGRULE
HYGIENE
INGENUE
INGRATE
JUGWINE
LEGATEE
LEGIBLE
LIGNITE
LUGGAGE
MAGNATE
MCGUIRE
MIGRATE
NIGHTIE
PIGLIKE
PUGNOSE
RAGTIME
REGRADE
TAGLINE
TAGSALE
TVGUIDE
UPGRADE

•••GE••

APOGEES
BADGERS
BAGGERS
BARGEIN
BEEGEES
BERGERE
BIGGERS
BIGGEST
BIOGENY
BUDGETS
BUNGEES
BURGEES
BURGEON
BURGERS
BURGESS
CADGERS
CODGERS
CONGEAL
CONGERS
CONGEST
CUDGELS
DAGGERS
DANGERS
DIGGERS
DODGERS
DUDGEON
DUNGEON
EPIGENE
ETAGERE
EXIGENT
FIDGETS
FIDGETY
FINGERS
FOGGERS
FOLGERS
FORGERS
FORGERY
FORGETS
FULGENT
GADGETS
GADGETY
GAUGERS
GINGERS
GINGERY
GORGETS
GOUGERS
HANGERS
HEDGERS
HUGGERS
HUNGERS
IMAGERS
IMAGERY
IMOGENE
JAEGERS
JIGGERS
JIGGERY
JOGGERS
LAAGERS
LAGGERS
LARGELY
LARGESS
LARGEST
LEDGERS
LINGERS
LODGERS
LOGGERS
LONGEST
LOWGEAR
LUGGERS
LUNGEAT
MANGERS
MERGERS
MIDGETS
MONGERS
MUGGERS

NUDGERS
NUGGETS
ONAGERS
PARGETS
PEUGEOT
PIDGEON
PROGENY
PUNGENT
RAGGEDY
RANGERS
REAGENT
RIGGERS
RINGERS
RODGERS
RUTGERS
SARGENT
SINGERS
STAGERS
SUGGEST
SURGEON
SURGERY
TANGELO
TANGENT
TANGERE
TARGETS
TRAGEDY
TUGGERS
VERGERS
WAGGERY
WIDGEON
WIDGETS
WINGERS
YEVGENY
ZINGERS

•••G•E•

ALIGNED
ALIGNER
APOGEES
BAGGIER
BAGGIES
BANGLES
BEAGLES
BEEGEES
BIGGIES
BINGOES
BOGGLED
BOGGLER
BOGGLES
BONGOES
BOOGIED
BOOGIES
BRAGGED
BRAGGER
BROGUES
BUDGIES
BUGGIER
BUGGIES
BUNGEES
BUNGLED
BUNGLER
BUNGLES
BURGEES
BURGHER
BURGLED
BURGLES
CARGOES
CHIGGER
CHUGGED
CLOGGED
CONGAED
COUGHED
DANGLED
DANGLER
DANGLES
DEIGNED
DINGIER
DINGLES
DINGOES
DOGGIES
DRAGGED
DRAGNET
DRUGGED
ELEGIES
EMIGRES
FEIGNED
FLAGGED
FLAGMEN
FLOGGED
FOGGIER
FORGOES
FROGMEN
FUNGOES
GAGGLES
GANGLED
GARGLED
GARGLES
GIGGLED
GIGGLER
GIGGLES
GOGGLED
GOGGLES
GURGLED
GURGLES
HAGGLED
HAGGLER
HAGGLES
HANGMEN
HANGTEN
HOAGIES
IMAGOES
JANGLED
JANGLES
JIGGLED
JIGGLES
JINGLED
JINGLES
JINGOES
JOGGLED
JOGGLES
JUGGLED
JUGGLER
JUGGLES
JUNGLES
LANGLEY
LAUGHED
LAUGHER
LEAGUER
LEAGUES
LEGGIER
LINGOES
LONGUES
MAIGRET
MANGIER
MANGLED
MANGLES
MANGOES
MARGRET
MINGLED
MINGLER
MINGLES
MONGREL
MUGGIER
NEIGHED
NIGGLED
NIGGLES
OUTGOES
OUTGREW
PIGGIES
PLAGUED
PLAGUES
PLUGGED
PLUGGER
PODGIER
PORGIES
PUDGIER
QUIGLEY
RAGGIER
RANGIER
REIGNED
RINGLET
ROUGHED
ROUGHEN
ROUGHER
SAGGIER
SHAGGED
SINGLED
SINGLES
SLOGGED
SLUGGED
SLUGGER
SMUGGER
SNAGGED
SNIGGER
SNIGLET
SNUGGER
SOGGIER
SOIGNEE
SOUGHED
STAGGED
STAGGER
STAGIER
STOGIES
SWAGGER
SWIGGED
TANGIER
TANGLED
TANGLES
TANGOED
TINGLED
TINGLES
TOGGLED
TOGGLES
TONGUED
TONGUES
TOUGHEN
TOUGHER
TRIGGED
TRIGGER
VEGGIES
WAGGLED
WAGGLES
WANGLED
WANGLER
WANGLES
WEDGIES
WEIGHED
WIGGLED
WIGGLER
WIGGLES
WRIGLEY
ZINGIER

•••G••E

ALLGONE
BAGGAGE
BERGERE
BIGGAME
BRIGADE
COLGATE
CONGAME
DOGGONE
ENDGAME
EPIGENE
EPIGONE
ETAGERE
FARGONE
FORGAVE
FORGIVE
FORGONE
FRAGILE
FRIGATE
IMAGINE
IMOGENE
LUGGAGE
MARGATE
NEWGATE
SEAGATE
SMUGGLE
SNIGGLE
SNUGGLE
SOIGNEE
TANGERE
TOUGHIE
VIRGULE
VULGATE
WARGAME
WRIGGLE
YANGTZE

••••GE•

ALLEGED
ALLEGER
ALLEGES
ANTIGEN
AVENGED
AVENGER
AVENGES
BRAGGED
BRAGGER
BRIDGED
BRIDGES
BRIDGET
BRINGER
BRUEGEL
CHANGED
CHANGER
CHANGES
CHARGED
CHARGER
CHARGES
CHIGGER
CHUGGED
CLANGED
CLOGGED
CRINGED
CRINGES
CRYOGEN
DAMAGED
DAMAGES
DELUGED
DELUGES
DOSAGES
DOWAGER
DRAGGED
DREDGED
DREDGER
DREDGES
DRUDGED
DRUDGES
DRUGGED
EMERGED
EMERGES
ENCAGED
ENCAGES
ENGAGED
ENGAGES
ENRAGED
ENRAGES
EVANGEL
FLAGGED
FLANGES
FLEDGED
FLEDGES
FLOGGED
FORAGED
FORAGER
FORAGES
FRIDGES
FRINGED
FRINGES
GARAGED
GARAGES
GEORGES
GRANGER
GRANGES
GRUDGED
GRUDGES
HALOGEN
ICEAGES
INTEGER
KLUDGES
LIMOGES
LINAGES
LOUNGED
LOUNGER
LOUNGES
MANAGED
MANAGER
MANAGES
MANEGES
MENAGES
MIRAGES
MUTAGEN
NEWAGER
OBLIGED
OBLIGES
ORANGES
OUTAGES
PELAGES
PERIGEE
PLEDGED
PLEDGEE
PLEDGER
PLEDGES
PLUGGED
PLUGGER
PLUNGED
PLUNGER
PLUNGES
POTAGES
PRONGED
RAVAGED
RAVAGES
REFUGEE
REFUGES
RENEGED
RENEGER
RENEGES
RONTGEN
SAVAGED
SAVAGER
SAVAGES
SHAGGED
SLEDGES
SLINGER
SLOGGED
SLUDGES
SLUGGED
SLUGGER
SMIDGEN
SMUDGED
SMUDGES
SMUGGER
SNAGGED
SNIGGER
SNUGGER
SPARGED
SPARGES
SPIEGEL
SPONGED
SPONGER
SPONGES
STAGGED
STAGGER
STEIGER
STENGEL
STIEGEL
STINGER
STOOGES
STURGES
SWAGGER
SWIGGED
SWINGER
TANAGER
TRIGGED
TRIGGER
TRUDGED
TRUDGER
TRUDGES
TWANGED
TWINGED
TWINGES
UNCAGED
UNCAGES
VISAGES
VOYAGED
VOYAGER
VOYAGES
WRINGER
WRONGED
WRONGER
YOUNGER

••••G•E

ATINGLE
COLOGNE
ECLOGUE
EPERGNE
FATIGUE
FINAGLE
INVOGUE
KRINGLE
LASAGNE
PERIGEE
PIROGUE
PLEDGEE
REARGUE
REFUGEE
SEVIGNE
SHINGLE
SMUGGLE
SNIGGLE
SNUGGLE
SPANGLE
WRANGLE
WRIGGLE

•••••GE

ABRIDGE
ACREAGE
ADJUDGE
ARLEDGE
ARRANGE
ASSUAGE
ATLARGE
AVERAGE
BABBAGE
BAGGAGE
BANDAGE
BARRAGE
BESIEGE
BONDAGE
CABBAGE
CARTAGE
COINAGE
COLLAGE
COLLEGE
CORDAGE
CORKAGE
CORSAGE
CORTEGE
COTTAGE
COURAGE
DARKAGE
DEBARGE
DEFARGE
DIVERGE
DIVULGE
DOCKAGE
DRAYAGE
ENGORGE
ENLARGE
EXPUNGE
FABERGE
FOLIAGE
FOOTAGE
FROMAGE
GARBAGE
HAULAGE
HERBAGE
HOSTAGE
IMPINGE
INDULGE
IRONAGE
JAZZAGE
LAFARGE
LEAKAGE
LINEAGE
LINKAGE
LOZENGE
LUGGAGE
MASSAGE
MELANGE
MESSAGE
MILEAGE
MONTAGE
MOORAGE
MOULAGE
ONSTAGE
OUTRAGE
OVERAGE
PACKAGE
PANURGE
PASSAGE
PEERAGE
PEONAGE
PILLAGE
PLUMAGE
PORTAGE
POSTAGE
POTTAGE
PRESAGE
PROTEGE
RAMPAGE
RESTAGE
RESURGE
REVENGE
RIBCAGE
RUMMAGE
SALVAGE
SAUSAGE
SCOURGE
SCROOGE
SELVAGE
SINKAGE
SOLFEGE
SPLURGE
STORAGE
STRANGE
SYRINGE
TEENAGE
TILLAGE
TONNAGE
UMBRAGE
UPSTAGE
UPSURGE
VANTAGE
VESTIGE
VILLAGE
VINTAGE
VOLTAGE
WASTAGE
WATTAGE
YARDAGE

G•F••••

GAFFERS
GAFFING
GEFILTE
GIFFORD
GOFORIT
GUFFAWS

G••F•••

GABFEST
GAFFERS
GAFFING
GIFFORD
GINFIZZ
GODFREY
GOLFERS
GOLFING
GOLFPRO
GOLFTEE
GOOFIER
GOOFING
GOOFOFF
GOOFSUP
GOOFUPS
GRAFTED
GRIFFEY
GRIFFIN
GRIFFON
GRIFTER
GRUFFER
GRUFFLY
GUFFAWS
GULFING
GUNFIRE

G•••F••

GAINFUL
GIRAFFE
GLEEFUL
GOESFOR
GOINFOR
GRIFFEY
GRIFFIN
GRIFFON
GRUFFER
GRUFFLY
GUNSFOR

G••••F•

GAVEOFF
GETSOFF
GIRAFFE
GIVEOFF
GLORIFY
GOESOFF
GOOFOFF
GRATIFY

G•••••F

GAVEOFF
GETSOFF
GIVEOFF
GOESOFF
GOOFOFF

•G••F••

AGRAFFE

•G•••F•

AGRAFFE

••GF•••

BAGFULS
BIGFEET
BIGFOOT
DOGFACE
DOGFISH
JUGFULS

••G•F••

PAGEFUL

••G••F•

BEGSOFF
BUGSOFF
DIGNIFY
ENGRAFT
ENGULFS
LOGSOFF
MAGNIFY
SIGNIFY
SIGNOFF

••G•••F

BEGSOFF
BUGSOFF
FIGLEAF
LOGSOFF
SIGNOFF

•••G•F•

HANGOFF

•••G••F

HANGOFF

G•G••••

GAGARIN
GAGGING
GAGGLES
GAGLINE
GAGRULE
GAGSTER
GIGGLED
GIGGLER
GIGGLES
GIGOLOS
GOGGLED
GOGGLES

G••G•••

GADGETS
GADGETY
GAGGING
GAGGLES
GANGING
GANGLED
GANGLIA
GANGSAW
GANGSTA
GANGSUP
GANGWAY
GARGLED
GARGLES
GAUGERS
GAUGING
GAUGUIN
GEEGAWS
GENGHIS
GEWGAWS
GIGGLED
GIGGLER
GIGGLES
GINGERS
GINGERY
GINGHAM
GINGIVA
GOGGLED
GOGGLES
GONGING
GOOGOLS
GORGETS
GORGING
GORGONS
GOUGERS
GOUGING
GREGORY
GRIGRIS
GURGLED
GURGLES

G•••G••

GARAGED
GARAGES
GEORGES
GEORGIA
GIELGUD
GIORGIO
GLASGOW
GOINGAT
GOINGBY
GOINGIN
GOINGON
GOINGUP
GRANGER
GRANGES
GRUDGED
GRUDGES
GUARGUM

G••••G•

GARBAGE
GASBAGS
GEOLOGY
GOODEGG
GUNDOGS

G•••••G

GABBING
GADDING
GAFFING
GAGGING
GAINING
GAITING
GALLING
GANGING
GAPPING
GARBING
GASHING
GASPING
GATELEG
GATLING
GAUGING
GAWKING
GEARING
GELDING
GELLING
GETTING
GILDING
GILLING
GINNING
GINSENG
GIRDING
GLARING
GLAZING
GLIDING
GLOWING
GNAWING
GOADING
GOALONG
GOLDBUG
GOLDING
GOLFING
GONGING
GOODEGG
GOOFING
GOOSING
GORGING
GOSLING
GOUGING
GOWRONG
GRABBAG
GRACING
GRADING
GRATING
GRAVING
GRAYING
GRAZING
GREYING
GRIPING
GROPING
GROWING
GUIDING
GULFING
GULLING
GULPING
GUMMING
GUNNING
GUSHING
GUSTING
GUTTING
GYPPING

•GG••••

AGGRESS
EGGCASE
EGGCUPS
EGGEDON
EGGHEAD
EGGNOGS
EGGROLL

•G•••G•

AGESAGO
EGGNOGS

••GG•••

BAGGAGE
BAGGERS
BAGGIER
BAGGIES
BAGGILY
BAGGING
BEGGARS
BEGGING
BIGGAME
BIGGERS
BIGGEST
BIGGIES
BIGGUNS
BOGGING
BOGGLED
BOGGLER
BOGGLES
BUGGIER
BUGGIES
BUGGING
DAGGERS
DIGGERS
DIGGING
DOGGIES
DOGGING
DOGGONE
FAGGING
FOGGERS
FOGGIER
FOGGING
GAGGING
GAGGLES
GIGGLED
GIGGLER
GIGGLES
GOGGLED
GOGGLES
HAGGARD
HAGGLED
HAGGLER
HAGGLES
HIGGINS
HOGGING
HUGGERS
HUGGING
JAGGING
JIGGERS
JIGGERY
JIGGING
JIGGLED
JIGGLES
JOGGERS
JOGGING
JOGGLED
JOGGLES
JUGGLED
JUGGLER
JUGGLES
LAGGARD
LAGGERS
LAGGING
LEGGIER
LEGGING
LOGGERS
LOGGIAS
LOGGING
LOGGINS
LUGGAGE
LUGGERS
LUGGING
MUGGERS
MUGGIER
MUGGING
NAGGING
NIGGARD
NIGGLED
NIGGLES
NOGGINS
NUGGETS
PEGGING
PIGGIES
PIGGING
PIGGISH
RAGGEDY
RAGGIER
RAGGING
RIGGERS
RIGGING
SAGGIER
SAGGING
SOGGIER
SOGGILY
SUGGEST
TAGGING
TOGGING
TOGGLED
TOGGLES
TUGGERS
TUGGING
VEGGIES
VEGGING
WAGGERY
WAGGING
WAGGISH
WAGGLED
WAGGLES
WAGGONS
WIGGLED
WIGGLER
WIGGLES
ZAGGING
ZIGGING

••G•G••

ENGAGED
ENGAGES

••G••G•

BAGGAGE
BIGWIGS
DOGLEGS
DOGTAGS
DUGONGS
EDGINGS
EGGNOGS
ENGORGE
LUGGAGE
RAGRUGS
WIGWAGS
ZIGZAGS

••G•••G

ANGLING
ARGUING
BAGGING
BEGGING

BIGBANG
BOGGING
BUGGING
BUGLING
DIGGING
DOGGING
EAGLING
FAGGING
FOGGING
GAGGING
HOGGING
HUGGING
JAGGING
JIGGING
JOGGING
LAGGING
LEGGING
LOGGING
LUGGING
MUGGING
NAGGING
ONGOING
PEGGING
PIGGING
RAGGING
RIGGING
SAGGING
SIGHING
SIGNING
TAGALOG
TAGGING
TOGGING
TUGGING
VEGGING
WAGGING
ZAGGING
ZIGGING

•••GG••

BRAGGED
BRAGGER
CHIGGER
CHUGGED
CLOGGED
DRAGGED
DRUGGED
FLAGGED
FLOGGED
PLUGGED
PLUGGER
QUAGGAS
SHAGGED
SLOGGED
SLUGGED
SLUGGER
SMUGGER
SMUGGLE
SNAGGED
SNIGGER
SNIGGLE
SNUGGER
SNUGGLE
STAGGED
STAGGER
SWAGGER
SWIGGED
TRIGGED
TRIGGER
WRIGGLE
WRIGGLY

•••G•G•

BAGGAGE
FIZGIGS
LONGAGO
LUGGAGE
VANGOGH

•••G••G

BAGGING
BANGING
BARGING
BEGGING
BINGING
BOGGING
BONGING
BUDGING
BUGGING
BULGING
BUNGING
CADGING
DIGGING
DINGING
DODGING
DOGGING
FAGGING
FOGGING
FORGING
FUDGING
GAGGING
GANGING
GAUGING
GONGING
GORGING
GOUGING
HANGDOG
HANGING
HEDGING
HINGING
HOGGING
HUGGING
IMAGING
JAGGING
JIGGING
JOGGING
JUDGING
KINGING
LAGGING
LEGGING
LODGING
LOGGING
LONGING
LUGGING
LUNGING
MERGING
MUGGING
NAGGING
NUDGING
PEGGING
PIGGING
PINGING
PURGING
RAGGING
RANGING
RIDGING
RIGGING
RINGING
ROUGING
SAGGING
SINGING
STAGING
SURGING
TAGGING
TINGING
TOGGING
TUGGING
VEGGING
VERGING
WAGGING
WEDGING
WINGING
ZAGGING
ZIGGING
ZINGING

••••GG•

BADEGGS
SCRAGGY

•••••GG

GOODEGG
KELLOGG
NESTEGG

GH•••••

GHASTLY
GHERKIN
GHETTOS
GHOSTED
GHOSTLY

G••H•••

GASHING
GATHERS
GOAHEAD
GOPHERS
GOSHAWK
GOTHICS
GRAHAME
GRAHAMS
GUSHERS
GUSHIER
GUSHING
GUTHRIE

G•••H••

GALAHAD
GASOHOL
GAUCHER
GAUCHOS
GEEWHIZ
GEISHAS
GENGHIS
GINGHAM
GNASHED
GNASHES
GODTHAB
GOTCHAS
GRAPHED
GRAPHIC
GRISHAM
GRYPHON
GULCHES
GUMSHOE
GUNSHOT
GUNTHER
GURKHAS
GYMSHOE

G••••H•

GNOCCHI
GOUACHE
GROUCHO
GROUCHY
GROWTHS
GUELPHS

G•••••H

GALUMPH
GARNISH
GIRLISH
GOATISH
GODUTCH
GOLIATH
GOULASH

•G•H•••

EGGHEAD

•G••H••

AGAKHAN

•G••••H

OGREISH

••GH•••

AFGHANI
AFGHANS
BAGHDAD
BIGHEAD
BIGHORN
BOGHOLE
EGGHEAD
EIGHTHS
FIGHTER
FOGHORN
HIGHBOY
HIGHEND
HIGHEST
HIGHHAT
HIGHLOW
HIGHTEA
HIGHTOP
HIGHWAY
JUGHEAD
LEGHORN
LIGHTED
LIGHTEN
LIGHTER
LIGHTLY
LIGHTUP
MIGHTNT
NIGHEST
NIGHTIE
NIGHTLY
RIGHTED
RIGHTER
RIGHTLY
RIGHTON
SIGHERS
SIGHING
SIGHTED
SIGHTLY
TIGHTEN
TIGHTER
TIGHTLY
YOGHURT

••G•H••

BIGSHOT
DOGCHEW
DOGCHOW
DOGSHOW
HIGHHAT
MEGOHMS
MUGSHOT

••G••H•

BIGJOHN
EIGHTHS
NOGUCHI

••G•••H

DIGRAPH
DOGFISH
ENGLISH
FOGYISH
HOGARTH
HOGWASH
PIGGISH
ROGUISH
WAGGISH

•••GH••

ALIGHTS
BINGHAM
BLIGHTS
BRIGHAM
BULGHUR
BURGHER
COUGHED
COUGHUP
DOUGHTY
FLIGHTS
FLIGHTY
FRIGHTS
FULGHUM
GENGHIS
GINGHAM
HAUGHTY
HEIGHHO
HEIGHTS
KNIGHTS
LAUGHAT
LAUGHED
LAUGHER
LAUGHIN
MAUGHAM
NAUGHTS
NAUGHTY
NEIGHED
PLIGHTS
ROUGHED
ROUGHEN
ROUGHER
ROUGHIT
ROUGHLY
ROUGHUP
SLIGHTS
SORGHUM
SOUGHED
TOUGHEN
TOUGHER
TOUGHIE
TOUGHLY
VAUGHAN
VEIGHTS
WEIGHED
WEIGHIN
WEIGHTS
WEIGHTY
WRIGHTS

•••G•H•

HEIGHHO
LENGTHS
LENGTHY

•••G••H

LONGISH
PIGGISH
VANGOGH
WAGGISH

••••GH•

ALRIGHT
BROUGHT
DELIGHT
DRAUGHT
DROUGHT
FRAUGHT
FREIGHT
INSIGHT
MRRIGHT
ONSIGHT
PLOUGHS
RELIGHT
SLEIGHS
SLEIGHT
SLOUGHS
THOUGHT
TONIGHT
TROUGHS
UPRIGHT
UPTIGHT
WROUGHT

•••••GH

BOROUGH
FLYHIGH
INVEIGH
RALEIGH
SKYHIGH
THROUGH
VANGOGH

GI•••••

GIACOMO
GIBBERS
GIBBETS
GIBBONS
GIBBOUS
GIBLETS
GIBLUES
GIDDIER
GIDDILY
GIDDYAP
GIDDYUP
GIDEONS
GIELGUD
GIFFORD
GIGGLED
GIGGLER
GIGGLES
GIGOLOS
GILBERT
GILBLAS
GILDERS
GILDING
GILLIES
GILLING
GILLNET
GILMORE
GIMBALS
GIMLETS
GIMMICK
GINFIZZ
GINGERS
GINGERY
GINGHAM
GINGIVA
GINMILL
GINNING
GINSENG
GIORGIO
GIPSIES
GIRAFFE
GIRASOL
GIRDERS
GIRDING
GIRDLED
GIRDLES
GIRLISH
GIRONDE
GISELLE
GIVENTO
GIVEOFF
GIVEOUT
GIVESIN
GIVESTO
GIVESUP
GIVEUPS
GIVEWAY
GIZZARD

G•I••••

GAINERS
GAINFUL
GAINING
GAINSAY
GAINSON
GAITERS
GAITING
GEISHAS
GLIBBER
GLIDERS
GLIDING
GLIMMER
GLIMPSE
GLINTED
GLISTEN
GLITTER
GLITZED
GLITZES
GOINFOR
GOINGAT
GOINGBY
GOINGIN
GOINGON
GOINGUP
GRIDDED
GRIDDER
GRIDDLE
GRIEVED
GRIEVER
GRIEVES
GRIFFEY
GRIFFIN
GRIFFON
GRIFTER
GRIGRIS
GRILLED
GRILLES
GRILLET
GRIMACE
GRIMIER
GRIMMER
GRINDER
GRINNED
GRINNER
GRIPERS
GRIPING
GRIPPED
GRIPPER
GRISHAM
GRISSOM
GRISTLE
GRISTLY
GRITTED
GRIVETS
GRIZZLE
GRIZZLY
GUIDING
GUIDONS
GUILDER
GUIMPES
GUINEAS
GUITARS

G••I•••

GALILEE
GALILEI
GALILEO
GAMIEST
GAMINES
GAVIALS
GEFILTE
GERITOL
GETINTO
GETITON
GOLIATH
GOOIEST
GORIEST
GORILLA
GOTINTO
GRAINED

G•••I••

GABBIER
GABBING
GABRIEL
GADDING
GAFFING
GAGGING
GAGLINE
GAINING
GAITING
GALLICO
GALLING
GALLIUM
GAMBIAN
GAMBITS
GANGING
GAPPING
GARBING
GARNISH
GARRICK
GASHING
GASKINS
GASPING
GATLING
GAUDIER
GAUDILY
GAUGING
GAUZIER
GAUZILY
GAWKIER
GAWKING
GEARING
GELDING
GELLING
GEMLIKE
GENTIAN
GENTILE
GENUINE
GERAINT
GERBILS
GETTING
GIDDIER
GIDDILY
GILDING
GILLIES
GILLING
GIMMICK
GINFIZZ
GINGIVA
GINMILL
GINNING
GIPSIES
GIRDING
GIRLISH
GLACIAL
GLACIER
GLARING
GLAZIER
GLAZING
GLIDING
GLORIAS
GLORIED
GLORIES
GLORIFY
GLOWING
GNAWING
GOADING
GOALIES
GOATISH
GOBLINS
GODLIKE
GODWITS
GOLDING
GOLFING
GONGING
GOODIES
GOOFIER
GOOFING
GOOPIER
GOOSING
GORDIAN
GORGING
GOSLING
GOSSIPS
GOSSIPY
GOTHICS
GOUGING
GRACIAS
GRACILE
GRACING
GRADING
GRANITF
GRATIFY
GRATING
GRAVIES
GRAVING
GRAVITY
GRAYING
GRAZING
GRECIAN
GREYING
GRIMIER
GRIPING
GROLIER
GROPING
GROPIUS
GROWING
GRUNION
GUANINE
GUIDING
GULFING
GULLIES
GULLING
GULPING
GUMMIER
GUMMING
GUNFIRE
GUNKIER
GUNNIES
GUNNING
GUPPIES
GUSHIER
GUSHING
GUSSIED
GUSSIES
GUSTILY
GUSTING
GUTSIER
GUTSILY
GUTTING
GYPPING
GYPSIES

G••••I•

GAGARIN
GALATIA
GANGLIA
GASMAIN
GASTRIC
GAUGUIN
GEEWHIZ
GELATIN
GELATIS
GENERIC
GENERIS
GENESIS
GENETIC
GENGHIS
GEORGIA
GHERKIN
GIORGIO
GIVESIN
GLOTTIS
GNOSTIC
GOFORIT
GOINGIN
GONERIL
GOODWIN
GRAPHIC
GREMLIN
GRIFFIN
GRIGRIS
GROUPIE
GUTHRIE

G•••••I

GALILEI
GALVANI
GNOCCHI
GOURAMI
GUARANI

•GI••••

AGILELY
AGILITY
AGITATE

•G•I•••

AGAINST
AGEISTS
AGRIPPA
EGOISTS
IGNITED
IGNITER
IGNITES
UGLIEST

•G••I••

AGILITY
AGONIST
AGONIZE
EGALITE
EGOTISM
EGOTIST
OGREISH

•G•••I•

AGASSIZ
AGOUTIS
EGOTRIP

••GI•••

ALGIERS
ARGIVES
CAGIEST
DIGITAL
EDGIEST
EDGINGS
ENGINES
ENGIRDS
HEGIRAS
HYGIEIA
HYGIENE
LEGIBLE
LEGIBLY
LEGIONS
LEGISTS
LOGICAL
LOGIEST
MAGICAL
MAGINOT
PIGIRON
REGIMEN
REGIMES
REGIONS
RIGIDLY
SAGINAW
UNGIRDS

••G•I••

ANGLING
ANGRIER
ANGRILY
ARGUING
BAGGIER
BAGGIES
BAGGILY
BAGGING
BAGPIPE
BEGGING
BEGRIME
BEGUILE
BEGUINE
BIGBIRD
BIGGIES
BIGTIME
BIGWIGS
BOGGING
BUGGIER
BUGGIES
BUGGING
BUGLING
DIGGING
DIGNIFY
DIGNITY
DOGFISH
DOGGIES
DOGGING
EAGLING
ENGLISH
FAGGING
FOGGIER
FOGGING
FOGYISH
FOGYISM
GAGGING
GAGLINE
HIGGINS
HOGGING
HOGTIED
HOGTIES
HOGWILD
HUGGING
JAGGING
JIGGING
JOGGING
JUGWINE
LAGGING
LEGGIER
LEGGING
LIGNITE
LOGGIAS
LOGGING
LOGGINS
LUGGING
MAGNIFY
MAGPIES
MCGUIRE
MEGRIMS
MUGGIER
MUGGING
NAGGING
NOGGINS
ONGOING
PEGGING
PIGGIES
PIGGING
PIGGISH
PIGLIKE
PYGMIES
RAGGIER
RAGGING
RAGTIME
REGAINS
RIGGING
ROGUISH
SAGGIER
SAGGING
SIGHING
SIGNIFY
SIGNING
SOGGIER
SOGGILY
TAGGING
TAGLINE
TOGGING
TUGGING
TVGUIDE
VEGGIES
VEGGING
WAGGING
WAGGISH
ZAGGING
ZIGGING

••G••I•

ALGERIA
ANGELIC
BEGONIA
EDGEDIN
EDGESIN
EUGENIE
GAGARIN
HYGIEIA
INGRAIN
MCGAVIN
NIGERIA
NIGHTIE
ORGANIC
PIGSKIN
PIGTAIL
REGALIA
SEGOVIA
SIGNSIN
WAGTAIL

••G•••I

AFGHANI
NOGUCHI

•••GI••

ADAGIOS
BAGGIER
BAGGIES
BAGGILY
BAGGING
BANGING
BARGING
BEGGING
BELGIAN
BELGIUM
BIGGIES
BINGING
BOGGING
BONGING
BOOGIED
BOOGIES
BUDGIES
BUDGING
BUGGIER
BUGGIES
BUGGING
BULGING
BUNGING
CADGING
COWGIRL
DIGGING
DINGIER
DINGILY
DINGING
DODGING
DOGGIES
DOGGING
ELEGIAC
ELEGIES
ELEGIST
FAGGING
FIZGIGS
FOGGIER
FOGGING
FORGING
FORGIVE
FRAGILE
FUDGING
GAGGING
GANGING
GAUGING
GINGIVA
GONGING
GORGING
GOUGING
HANGING
HEDGING
HIGGINS
HINGING
HOAGIES
HOGGING
HUGGING
IMAGINE
IMAGING
JAGGING

JIGGING
JOGGING
JUDGING
KINGING
LAGGING
LEGGIER
LEGGING
LODGING
LOGGIAS
LOGGING
LOGGINS
LONGING
LONGISH
LUGGING
LUNGING
MANGIER
MARGINS
MERGING
MUGGIER
MUGGING
NAGGING
NOGGINS
NUDGING
ORIGINS
PEGGING
PIDGINS
PIGGIES
PIGGING
PIGGISH
PINGING
PODGIER
PONGIDS
PORGIES
PUDGIER
PURGING
RAGGIER
RAGGING
RANGIER
RANGING
RIDGING
RIGGING
RINGING
ROUGING
SAGGIER
SAGGING
SEAGIRT
SINGING
SOGGIER
SOGGILY
STAGIER
STAGILY
STAGING
STOGIES
STYGIAN
SURGING
TAGGING
TANGIER
TINGING
TOGGING
TUGGING
VEGGIES
VEGGING
VERGING
VIRGINS
WAGGING
WAGGISH
WEDGIES
WEDGING
WINGING
ZAGGING
ZIGGING
ZINGIER
ZINGING

•••G•I•

ABIGAIL
BARGAIN
BARGEIN
CHAGRIN
DRAGSIN
GANGLIA
GAUGUIN
GENGHIS
GRIGRIS
HANGSIN
KINGPIN
LANGUID
LAUGHIN
PENGUIN
PILGRIM
PLUGSIN
ROUGHIT
SANGRIA
TOUGHIE
TUNGOIL
WEIGHIN
WINGSIT
WINGTIP

•••G••I

BENGALI
ORIGAMI

••••GI•

BRINGIN
DOINGIN
GEORGIA
GIORGIO
GOINGIN
ICINGIN
ILLOGIC
KOSYGIN
PELAGIC
SLOEGIN
TLINGIT
TYINGIN

••••G•I

ASSEGAI
SHANGRI
ZWINGLI

G••J•••

GASJETS

G•••J••

GOODJOB
GOODJOE

••GJ•••

BIGJOHN
LOGJAMS

G•K••••

GOKARTS

G••K•••

GASKETS
GASKINS
GAWKERS
GAWKIER
GAWKING
GECKOES
GUNKIER
GURKHAS

G•••K••

GHERKIN
GRACKLE

G••••K•

GEMLIKE
GOBROKE
GODLIKE
GRETZKY
GROMYKO

G•••••K

GARRICK
GEMSBOK
GETBACK
GIMMICK
GOSHAWK
GOTBACK
GUNLOCK

•G•K•••

AGAKHAN

••G•K••

PIGSKIN

••G••K•

PIGLIKE

••G•••K

FOGBANK
HOGBACK
LEGWORK
LOGBOOK

•••GK••

BANGKOK

•••G••K

BANGKOK

GL•••••

GLACEED
GLACIAL
GLACIER
GLADDEN
GLADDER
GLADEYE
GLAMOUR
GLANCED
GLANCES
GLARING
GLASGOW
GLASSED
GLASSES
GLAZERS
GLAZIER
GLAZING
GLEAMED
GLEANED
GLEANER
GLEASON
GLEEFUL
GLIBBER
GLIDERS
GLIDING
GLIMMER
GLIMPSE
GLINTED
GLISTEN
GLITTER
GLITZED
GLITZES
GLOATED
GLOBULE
GLOMMED
GLORIAS
GLORIED
GLORIES
GLORIFY
GLOSSAE
GLOSSED
GLOSSES
GLOTTAL
GLOTTIS
GLOWERS
GLOWING
GLUCOSE
GLUEDON
GLUMMER
GLUTTED
GLUTTON

G•L••••

GALAHAD
GALATEA
GALATIA
GALILEE
GALILEI
GALILEO
GALLANT
GALLEON
GALLERY
GALLEYS
GALLICO
GALLING
GALLIUM
GALLONS
GALLOPS
GALOOTS
GALUMPH
GALVANI
GELADAS
GELATIN
GELATIS
GELDING
GELLING
GILBERT
GILBLAS
GILDERS
GILDING
GILLIES
GILLING
GILLNET
GILMORE
GOLDBUG
GOLDING
GOLDWYN
GOLFERS
GOLFING
GOLFPRO
GOLFTEE
GOLIATH
GULCHES
GULFING
GULLETS
GULLIES
GULLING
GULPING

G••L•••

GAGLINE
GALLANT
GALLEON
GALLERY
GALLEYS
GALLICO
GALLING
GALLIUM
GALLONS
GALLOPS
GARLAND
GATLING
GAYLORD
GELLING
GEMLIKE
GEOLOGY
GETLOST
GIBLETS
GIBLUES
GIELGUD
GILLIES
GILLING
GILLNET
GIMLETS
GIRLISH
GOALIES
GOALONG
GOBLETS
GOBLINS
GODLIKE
GOSLING
GOTLAND
GOULASH
GRILLED
GRILLES
GRILLET
GROLIER
GUELPHS
GUILDER
GULLETS
GULLIES
GULLING
GUNLOCK
GUTLESS

G•••L••

GABBLED
GABBLES
GAGGLES
GALILEE
GALILEI
GALILEO
GAMBLED
GAMBLER
GAMBLES
GAMELAW
GANGLED
GANGLIA
GANTLET
GARBLED
GARBLES
GARGLED
GARGLES
GATELEG
GAVELED
GAZELLE
GEFILTE
GENTLED
GENTLER
GENTLES
GERALDO
GIGGLED
GIGGLER
GIGGLES
GIGOLOS
GILBLAS
GIRDLED
GIRDLES
GISELLE
GNARLED
GOBBLED
GOBBLER
GOBBLES
GOGGLED
GOGGLES
GORILLA
GREELEY
GREMLIN
GRILLED
GRILLES
GRILLET
GROWLED
GROWLER
GUNPLAY
GURGLED
GURGLES
GUZZLED
GUZZLER
GUZZLES

G••••L•

GAGRULE
GAMBOLS
GAUDILY
GAUNTLY
GAUZILY
GAVIALS
GAZELLE
GENTILE
GERBILS
GESTALT
GETWELL
GHASTLY
GHOSTLY
GIDDILY
GIMBALS
GINMILL
GISELLE
GLOBULE
GONDOLA
GOODALL
GOOGOLS
GORILLA
GOSPELS
GOTWELL
GRACILE
GRACKLE
GRANDLY
GRANOLA
GRANULE
GRAPPLE
GRAVELS
GRAVELY
GREATLY
GRIDDLE
GRISTLE
GRISTLY
GRIZZLE
GRIZZLY
GROSSLY
GROVELS
GRUFFLY
GRUMBLE
GUMBALL
GUNMOLL
GUNNELS
GUNWALE
GUSTILY
GUTSILY

G•••••L

GABRIEL
GAINFUL
GAMBREL
GASOHOL
GENERAL
GENTEEL
GERITOL
GETWELL
GINMILL
GIRASOL
GLACIAL
GLEEFUL
GLOTTAL
GONERIL
GOODALL
GOTWELL
GRADUAL
GRAPNEL
GRENDEL
GUMBALL
GUNMOLL

•GL••••

OGLALAS
UGLIEST

•G•L•••

AGELESS
AGILELY
AGILITY
EGALITE

•G••L••

HGWELLS
OGLALAS

•G•••L•

AGILELY
EGGROLL
HGWELLS
IGNOBLE
IGNOBLY

•G••••L

EGGROLL

••GL•••

ANGLERS
ANGLING
BUGLERS
BUGLING
DOGLEGS
EAGLETS
EAGLING
ENGLAND
ENGLISH
ENGLUND
FIGLEAF
GAGLINE
JAGLESS
KEGLERS
NEGLECT
PIGLETS
PIGLIKE
RAGLANS
REGLUED
REGLUES
TAGLINE
UNGLUED
WIGLETS

••G•L••

ANGELES
ANGELIC
ANGELOU
ANGELUS
ANGOLAN
ANGULAR
ARGYLES
BIGELOW
BOGGLED
BOGGLER
BOGGLES
BUGALOO
DOGSLED
ENGULFS
GAGGLES
GIGGLED
GIGGLER
GIGGLES
GIGOLOS
GOGGLED
GOGGLES
HAGGLED
HAGGLER
HAGGLES
HIGHLOW
INGALLS
JIGGLED
JIGGLES
JOGGLED
JOGGLES
JUGGLED
JUGGLER
JUGGLES
JUGULAR
LEGALLY
NIGGLED
NIGGLES
NOGALES
REGALED
REGALES
REGALIA
REGALLY
REGULAR
REGULUS
TAGALOG
TOGGLED
TOGGLES
WAGGLED
WAGGLES
WIGGLED
WIGGLER
WIGGLES

••G••L•

ANGRILY
BAGFULS
BAGGILY
BAGNOLD
BEGUILE
BOGHOLE
EAGERLY
EGGROLL
HOGWILD
INGALLS
JUGFULS
LEGALLY
LEGIBLE
LEGIBLY
LEGPULL
LIGHTLY
NIGHTLY
RAGDOLL
REGALLY
RIGHTLY
RIGIDLY
SIGHTLY
SIGNALS
SOGGILY
TAGSALE
TIGHTLY
UNGODLY
VAGUELY

••G•••L

AUGURAL
BIGDEAL
DIGITAL
EGGROLL
LEGPULL
LOGICAL
MAGICAL
PAGEFUL
PIGTAIL
RAGDOLL
VEGETAL
WAGTAIL

•••GL••

BANGLES
BEAGLES
BOGGLED
BOGGLER
BOGGLES
BUNGLED
BUNGLER
BUNGLES
BURGLAR
BURGLED
BURGLES
DANGLED
DANGLER
DANGLES
DINGLES
DOUGLAS
GAGGLES
GANGLED
GANGLIA
GARGLED
GARGLES
GIGGLED
GIGGLER
GIGGLES
GOGGLED
GOGGLES
GURGLED
GURGLES
HAGGLED
HAGGLER
HAGGLES
JANGLED
JANGLES
JIGGLED
JIGGLES
JINGLED
JINGLES
JOGGLED
JOGGLES
JUGGLED
JUGGLER
JUGGLES
JUNGLES
LANGLEY
MANGLED
MANGLES
MINGLED
MINGLER
MINGLES
NIGGLED
NIGGLES
QUIGLEY
RINGLET
SINGLED
SINGLES
SNIGLET
TANGLED
TANGLES
TINGLED
TINGLES
TOGGLED
TOGGLES
WAGGLED
WAGGLES
WANGLED
WANGLER
WANGLES
WIGGLED
WIGGLER
WIGGLES
WRIGLEY

•••G•L•

ARUGULA
BAGGILY
BENGALI
BENGALS
CHAGALL
CUDGELS
DINGILY
FRAGILE
GOOGOLS
LARGELY
MONGOLS
OLDGOLD
PERGOLA
ROUGHLY
SEAGULL
SMUGGLE
SNIGGLE
SNUGGLE
SOGGILY
STAGILY
TANGELO
TOUGHLY
VIRGULE
WRIGGLE
WRIGGLY

•••G••L

ABIGAIL
CHAGALL
CONGEAL
COWGIRL
LINGUAL
MONGREL
SEAGULL
TUNGOIL

••••GL•

ATINGLE
FINAGLE
KRINGLE
SHINGLE
SMUGGLE
SNIGGLE
SNUGGLE
SPANGLE
SPANGLY
WRANGLE
WRIGGLE
WRIGGLY
WRONGLY
ZWINGLI

••••G•L

BRUEGEL
DONEGAL
EVANGEL
ILLEGAL
SENEGAL
SPIEGEL
STENGEL
STIEGEL
WOLFGAL

G•M••••

GAMBIAN
GAMBITS
GAMBLED
GAMBLER
GAMBLES
GAMBOLS
GAMBREL
GAMELAW
GAMETES
GAMIEST
GAMINES
GAMMONS
GEMLIKE
GEMSBOK
GIMBALS
GIMLETS
GIMMICK
GOMPERS
GUMBALL
GUMDROP
GUMMIER
GUMMING
GUMSHOE
GUMTREE
GYMNAST
GYMSHOE

G••M•••

GAMMONS
GARMENT
GASMAIN
GERMANE
GERMANS
GERMANY
GILMORE
GIMMICK
GINMILL
GLAMOUR
GLIMMER
GLIMPSE
GLOMMED
GLUMMER
GNOMONS
GRAMMAR
GRAMMER
GRAMMES
GRAMPUS
GREMLIN
GRIMACE
GRIMIER
GRIMMER
GROMMET
GROMYKO
GRUMBLE
GRUMPED
GUIMPES
GUMMIER
GUMMING
GUNMOLL

G•••M••

GALUMPH
GATEMAN
GATEMEN
GLEAMED
GLIMMER
GLOMMED
GLUMMER
GOODMAN
GOODMEN
GOURMET
GRAMMAR
GRAMMER
GRAMMES
GRIMMER
GROMMET
GROOMED
GROOMER

G••••M•

GASPUMP
GAUTAMA
GIACOMO
GOURAMI
GRAHAME
GRAHAMS
GRANDMA

G•••••M

GALLIUM
GINGHAM
GRANDAM
GRISHAM
GRISSOM
GUARGUM

•G••••M

EGOTISM

••GM•••

AUGMENT
DOGMATA
FIGMENT
PIGMENT
PYGMIES
RAGMOPS
SEGMENT
SIGMUND

••G•M••

INGEMAR
LEGUMES
MOGAMBO
REGIMEN
REGIMES

••G••M•

BEGRIME
BIGGAME
BIGNAME
BIGTIME
ENGRAMS
LOGJAMS
MAGNUMS
MEGOHMS
MEGRIMS
MUGWUMP
RAGTIME
WIGWAMS

••G•••M

FOGYISM
LEGROOM
ORGANUM

•••GM••

BERGMAN
ENIGMAS
FLAGMAN
FLAGMEN
FROGMAN
FROGMEN
HANGMAN
HANGMEN
KINGMAN
KLUGMAN
STIGMAS
SYNGMAN
ZEUGMAS

•••G•M•

BIGGAME
CONGAME
ENDGAME
ORIGAMI
REDGUMS
WARGAME

•••G••M

ANAGRAM
BELGIUM
BINGHAM
BRIGHAM
DIAGRAM
EPIGRAM
FULGHUM
GINGHAM
KINGDOM
MAUGHAM
PILGRIM
PROGRAM
SEAGRAM
SORGHUM
TRIGRAM

••••GM•

YOUNGMC

••••G•M

AMALGAM
GUARGUM

GN•••••

GNARLED
GNARRED
GNASHED
GNASHES
GNAWERS
GNAWING
GNOCCHI
GNOMONS
GNOSTIC

G•N••••

GANDERS
GANGING
GANGLED
GANGLIA
GANGSAW
GANGSTA
GANGSUP

GANGWAY
GANNETS
GANNETT
GANTLET
GENDERS
GENERAL
GENERIC
GENERIS
GENESEE
GENESES
GENESIS
GENETIC
GENGHIS
GENNARO
GENOESE
GENTEEL
GENTIAN
GENTILE
GENTLED
GENTLER
GENTLES
GENUINE
GINFIZZ
GINGERS
GINGERY
GINGHAM
GINGIVA
GINMILL
GINNING
GINSENG
GONDOLA
GONERIL
GONGING
GUNBOAT
GUNDOGS
GUNFIRE
GUNKIER
GUNLOCK
GUNMOLL
GUNNELS
GUNNERS
GUNNERY
GUNNIES
GUNNING
GUNPLAY
GUNSFOR
GUNSHOT
GUNTHER
GUNWALE

G••N•••

GAINERS
GAINFUL
GAINING
GAINSAY
GAINSON
GANNETS
GANNETT
GARNERS
GARNETS
GARNISH
GAUNTER
GAUNTLY
GENNARO
GINNING
GLANCED
GLANCES
GLINTED
GOINFOR
GOINGAT
GOINGBY
GOINGIN
GOINGON
GOINGUP
GOUNDER
GRANADA
GRANARY
GRANDAM
GRANDEE
GRANDER
GRANDLY
GRANDMA
GRANDPA
GRANGER
GRANGES
GRANITE
GRANOLA
GRANTED
GRANTEE
GRANTOR
GRANULE
GRENADA
GRENADE
GRENDEL
GRINDER
GRINNED
GRINNER
GRUNION
GRUNTED
GUANACO
GUANINE
GUINEAS
GUNNELS
GUNNERS
GUNNERY
GUNNIES
GUNNING
GURNEYS
GYMNAST

G•••N••

GAMINES
GARDNER
GARONNE
GERENTS
GERUNDS
GETINTO
GILLNET
GIRONDE
GIVENTO
GLEANED
GLEANER
GODUNOV
GOTINTO
GRAINED
GRAPNEL
GREENED
GREENER
GRINNED
GRINNER
GROANED
GROANER
GROUNDS
GROWNUP

G••••N•

GABBING
GADDING
GAFFING
GAGGING
GAGLINE
GAINING
GAITING
GALLANT
GALLING
GALLONS
GALVANI
GAMMONS
GANGING
GAPPING
GARBING
GARCONS
GARDENS
GARLAND
GARMENT
GARONNE
GASCONS
GASHING
GASKINS
GASPING
GATLING
GAUDENS
GAUGING
GAWKING
GEARING
GELDING
GELLING
GENUINE
GERAINT
GERMANE
GERMANS
GERMANY
GETTING
GIBBONS
GIDEONS
GILDING
GILLING
GINNING
GINSENG
GIRDING
GLARING
GLAZING
GLIDING
GLOWING
GNAWING
GNOMONS
GOADING
GOALONG
GOBLINS
GODSEND
GODSONS
GOLDING
GOLFING
GONGING
GOODONE
GOOFING
GOOSING
GORGING
GORGONS
GOROUND
GOSLING
GOTLAND
GOUGING
GOVERNS
GOWRONG
GRACING
GRADING
GRATING
GRAVING
GRAYING
GRAZING
GREYING
GRIPING
GROPING
GROWING
GUANINE
GUARANI
GUIDING
GUIDONS
GULFING
GULLING
GULPING
GUMMING
GUNNING
GUSHING
GUSTING
GUTTING
GYPPING

G•••••N

GADSDEN
GAGARIN
GAINSON
GALLEON
GAMBIAN
GASMAIN
GATEMAN
GATEMEN
GAUGUIN
GELATIN
GENTIAN
GETDOWN
GETEVEN
GETITON
GHERKIN
GIVESIN
GLADDEN
GLEASON
GLISTEN
GLUEDON
GLUTTON
GOINGIN
GOINGON
GOLDWYN
GOODMAN
GOODMEN
GOODSON
GOODWIN
GORDIAN
GOTDOWN
GOTEVEN
GRAYSON
GRECIAN
GREMLIN
GRIFFIN
GRIFFON
GROWSON
GRUNION
GRYPHON

•GN••••

AGNATES
IGNEOUS
IGNITED
IGNITER
IGNITES
IGNOBLE
IGNOBLY
IGNORED
IGNORER
IGNORES

•G•N•••

AGENDAS
AGONIST
AGONIZE
EGGNOGS
UGANDAN

•G••N••

AGAINST
IGUANAS

•G•••N•

AGROUND

•G••••N

AGAKHAN
EGGEDON
UGANDAN

••GN•••

BAGNOLD
BIGNAME
BIGNESS
COGNACS
COGNATE
CYGNETS
DIGNIFY
DIGNITY
EGGNOGS
LIGNITE
LUGNUTS
MAGNATE
MAGNETO
MAGNETS
MAGNIFY
MAGNUMS
PIGNUTS
PUGNOSE
REGNANT
SIGNALS
SIGNEES
SIGNERS
SIGNETS
SIGNIFY
SIGNING
SIGNOFF
SIGNOUT
SIGNSIN
SIGNSON
SIGNSUP

••G•N••

ARGONNE
AUGENDS
BEGONIA
BYGONES
COGENCY
DUGONGS
EDGINGS
ENGINES
EUGENIE
FAGENDS
INGENUE
LAGUNAS
LEGENDS
MAGENTA
MAGINOT
ORGANDY
ORGANIC
ORGANON
ORGANUM
ORGANZA
REGENCY
REGENTS
SAGINAW
TAGENDS
URGENCY
WAGONER

••G••N•

AFGHANI
AFGHANS
ANGLING
ARGONNE
ARGUING
AUGMENT
BAGGING
BEGGING
BEGUINE
BIGBAND
BIGBANG
BIGBEND
BIGGUNS
BOGGING
BUGGING
BUGLING
DIGGING
DOGGING
DOGGONE
EAGLING
ENGLAND
ENGLUND
FAGGING
FIGMENT
FOGBANK
FOGGING
GAGGING
GAGLINE
HIGGINS
HIGHEND
HOGGING
HUGGING
HYGIENE
JAGGING
JIGGING
JOGGING
JUGBAND
JUGWINE
LAGGING
LAGOONS
LEGGING
LEGIONS
LOGGING
LOGGINS
LUGGING
MIGHTNT
MIGRANT
MUGGING
NAGGING
NOGGINS
ONGOING
PAGEANT
PEGGING
PIGEONS
PIGGING
PIGMENT
PIGPENS
RAGGING
RAGLANS
REGAINS
REGIONS
REGNANT
RIGGING
SAGGING
SEGMENT
SIGHING
SIGMUND
SIGNING
TAGGING
TAGLINE
TOGGING
TUGGING
UNGUENT
VAGRANT
VEGGING
WAGGING
WAGGONS
ZAGGING
ZIGGING

••G•••N

ANGOLAN
BIGHORN
BIGJOHN
BOGDOWN
COGBURN
EDGEDIN
EDGESIN
EGGEDON
FOGHORN
GAGARIN
INGRAIN
INGROWN
LEGHORN
LIGHTEN
MCGAVIN
MEGRYAN
ORGANON
PIGIRON
PIGSKIN
REGIMEN
RIGHTON
SIGNSIN
SIGNSON
TIGHTEN

•••GN••

ALIGNED
ALIGNER
AVIGNON
CHIGNON
DEIGNED
DRAGNET
FEIGNED
REIGNED
SOIGNEE
WINGNUT

•••G•N•

AIRGUNS
ALLGONE
BAGGING
BANGING
BARGING
BEGGING
BIGGUNS
BINGING
BIOGENY
BOGGING
BONGING
BRIGAND
BROGANS
BUDGING
BUGGING
BULGING
BUNGING
CADGING
CAPGUNS
DIGGING
DINGING
DODGING
DOGGING
DOGGONE
DRAGONS
ELEGANT
EPIGENE
EPIGONE
EXIGENT
FAGGING
FARGONE
FLAGONS
FOGGING
FORGING
FORGONE
FUDGING
FULGENT
GAGGING
GANGING
GAUGING
GONGING
GORGING
GORGONS
GOUGING
HANGING
HEDGING
HIGGINS
HINGING
HOGGING
HUGGING
IMAGINE
IMAGING
IMOGENE
ISOGONS
JAGGING
JARGONS
JETGUNS
JIGGING
JOGGING
JUDGING
KINGING
LAGGING
LEGGING
LODGING
LOGGING
LOGGINS
LONGING
LUGGING
LUNGING
MARGINS
MERGING
MORGANA
MORGANS
MUGGING
NAGGING
NOGGINS
NUDGING
OREGANO
ORIGINS
OUTGUNS
PEGGING
PIDGINS
PIGGING
PINGING
POPGUNS
PROGENY
PUNGENT
PURGING
RAGGING
RANGING
RAYGUNS
REAGENT
RIDGING
RIGGING
RINGING
ROUGING
SAGGING
SARGENT
SHOGUNS
SINGING
SIXGUNS
SLOGANS
STAGING
SURGING
TAGGING
TANGENT
TINGING
TOGGING
TONGANS
TOPGUNS
TRIGONS
TUGGING
VEGGING
VERGING
VIRGINS
WAGGING
WAGGONS
WEDGING
WINGING
YEVGENY
ZAGGING
ZIGGING
ZINGING

•••G••N

AVIGNON
BARGAIN
BARGEIN
BELGIAN
BERGMAN
BERGSON
BURGEON
CHAGRIN
CHIGNON
DODGSON
DRAGOON
DRAGSIN
DRAGSON
DUDGEON
DUNGEON
FLAGMAN
FLAGMEN
FROGMAN
FROGMEN
GAUGUIN
HANGMAN
HANGMEN
HANGSIN
HANGSON
HANGTEN
KINGMAN
KINGPIN
KLUGMAN
LANGDON
LAUGHIN
LONGRUN
LONGTON
PENGUIN
PIDGEON
PLUGSIN
RANGOON
ROUGHEN
STYGIAN
SURGEON
SYNGMAN
TOUGHEN
VAUGHAN
VIRGOAN
WEIGHIN
WIDGEON

••••GN•

ASSIGNS
BOLOGNA
COLOGNE
COSIGNS
DESIGNS
ENSIGNS
EPERGNE
IMPUGNS
LASAGNA
LASAGNE
MALIGNS
OPPUGNS
REPUGNS
RESIGNS
SEVIGNE

••••G•N

ANTIGEN
BLOWGUN
BRINGIN
BRINGON
BURPGUN
CRYOGEN
DECAGON
DOINGIN
GOINGIN
GOINGON
HALOGEN
HANDGUN
HEXAGON
ICINGIN
KLINGON
KOSYGIN
MUTAGEN
NONAGON
OBREGON
OCTAGON
PARAGON
POLYGON
RONTGEN
SHOTGUN
SLOEGIN
SMIDGEN
STUNGUN
TYINGIN
WOBEGON
YOUNGUN

•••••GN

ARRAIGN
CONDIGN
CONSIGN
FOREIGN
HEXSIGN

GO•••••

GOABOUT
GOADING
GOAHEAD
GOALIES
GOALONG
GOATEED
GOATEES
GOATISH
GOBBLED
GOBBLER
GOBBLES
GOBLETS
GOBLINS
GOBROKE
GOCARTS
GODDARD
GODDESS
GODFREY
GODLIKE
GODSEND
GODSONS
GODTHAB
GODUNOV
GODUTCH
GODWITS
GOESAPE
GOESBAD
GOESFOR
GOESOFF
GOESOUT
GOFORIT
GOGGLED
GOGGLES
GOINFOR
GOINGAT
GOINGBY
GOINGIN
GOINGON
GOINGUP
GOKARTS
GOLDBUG
GOLDING
GOLDWYN
GOLFERS
GOLFING
GOLFPRO
GOLFTEE
GOLIATH
GOMPERS
GONDOLA
GONERIL
GONGING
GOOBERS
GOODALL
GOODBAR
GOODBYE
GOODBYS
GOODEGG
GOODIES
GOODJOB
GOODJOE
GOODMAN
GOODMEN
GOODONE
GOODSON
GOODWIN
GOOFIER
GOOFING
GOOFOFF
GOOFSUP
GOOFUPS
GOOGOLS
GOOIEST
GOOPIER
GOOSING
GOPHERS
GORDIAN
GORETEX
GORGETS
GORGING
GORGONS
GORIEST
GORILLA
GOROUND
GOSHAWK
GOSLING
GOSPELS
GOSSETT
GOSSIPS
GOSSIPY
GOTAWAY
GOTBACK
GOTCHAS
GOTDOWN
GOTEVEN
GOTHICS
GOTINTO
GOTLAND
GOTOPOT
GOTOVER
GOTWELL
GOUACHE
GOUGERS
GOUGING
GOULASH
GOUNDER
GOURAMI
GOURDES
GOURMET
GOVERNS
GOWRONG

G•O••••

GEODESY
GEOLOGY
GEORGES
GEORGIA
GHOSTED
GHOSTLY
GIORGIO
GLOATED
GLOBULE
GLOMMED
GLORIAS
GLORIED
GLORIES
GLORIFY
GLOSSAE
GLOSSED
GLOSSES
GLOTTAL
GLOTTIS
GLOWERS
GLOWING
GNOCCHI
GNOMONS
GNOSTIC
GOOBERS
GOODALL
GOODBAR
GOODBYE
GOODBYS
GOODEGG
GOODIES
GOODJOB
GOODJOE
GOODMAN
GOODMEN
GOODONE
GOODSON
GOODWIN
GOOFIER
GOOFING
GOOFOFF
GOOFSUP
GOOFUPS
GOOGOLS
GOOIEST
GOOPIER
GOOSING
GROANED
GROANER
GROCERS
GROCERY
GROLIER
GROMMET
GROMYKO
GROOMED
GROOMER
GROOVED
GROOVES
GROPING
GROPIUS
GROSSED
GROSSER
GROSSES
GROSSLY
GROTTOS
GROUCHO
GROUCHY
GROUNDS
GROUPED
GROUPER
GROUPIE
GROUSED
GROUSER
GROUSES
GROUTED
GROVELS
GROWERS
GROWING
GROWLED
GROWLER
GROWNUP
GROWSON
GROWSUP
GROWTHS

G••O•••

GALOOTS
GARONNE
GASOHOL
GAVOTTE
GENOESE
GETOVER
GIGOLOS
GIRONDE
GOFORIT
GOROUND
GOTOPOT
GOTOVER
GROOMED
GROOMER
GROOVED
GROOVES

G•••O••

GALLONS
GALLOPS
GALOOTS
GAMBOLS
GAMMONS
GARCONS
GASCONS
GASEOUS
GAVEOFF
GAVEOUT
GAYLORD
GECKOES
GEOLOGY
GESSOES
GETDOWN
GETLOST
GETSOFF
GETSOUT
GIACOMO
GIBBONS
GIBBOUS
GIDEONS
GIFFORD
GILMORE

GIVEOFF
GIVEOUT
GLAMOUR
GLUCOSE
GNOMONS
GOABOUT
GOALONG
GOBROKE
GODSONS
GOESOFF
GOESOUT
GONDOLA
GOODONE
GOOFOFF
GOOGOLS
GORGONS
GOTDOWN
GOWRONG
GRANOLA
GREGORY
GUIDONS
GUNBOAT
GUNDOGS
GUNLOCK
GUNMOLL
GUSTOES

G••••O•
GABBROS
GAINSON
GALLEON
GASOHOL
GAUCHOS
GAZEBOS
GEARBOX
GEMSBOK
GERITOL
GETITON
GHETTOS
GIGOLOS
GIRASOL
GLASGOW
GLEASON
GLUEDON
GLUTTON
GODUNOV
GOESFOR
GOINFOR
GOINGON
GOODJOB
GOODJOE
GOODSON
GOTOPOT
GRANTOR
GRAYSON
GRIFFON
GRISSOM
GROTTOS
GROWSON
GRUNION
GRYPHON
GUMDROP
GUMSHOE
GUNSFOR
GUNSHOT
GYMSHOE
GYRATOR

G•••••O
GALILEO
GALLICO
GEARSTO
GENNARO
GERALDO
GETINTO
GIACOMO
GIORGIO
GIVENTO
GIVESTO
GOLFPRO
GOTINTO
GROMYKO
GROUCHO
GUANACO

•GO••••
AGONIST
AGONIZE
AGOUTIS
EGOISTS
EGOTISM
EGOTIST
EGOTRIP

•G•O•••
AGROUND
IGNOBLE
IGNOBLY
IGNORED
IGNORER
IGNORES
OGDOADS

•G••O••
EGGNOGS
EGGROLL
IGNEOUS

•G•••O•
EGGEDON

•G••••O
AGESAGO
AGREETO

••GO•••
ANGOLAN
ANGORAS
ARGONNE
BEGONIA
BEGORRA
BIGOTED
BIGOTRY
BYGONES
DUGONGS
DUGOUTS
ENGORGE
FAGOTED
GIGOLOS
LAGOONS
MEGOHMS
ONGOING
PAGODAS
RAGOUTS
RIGOURS
SEGOVIA
UNGODLY
VIGOURS
WAGONER
ZYGOTES

••G•O••
BAGNOLD
BEGSOFF
BIGBOYS
BIGFOOT
BIGHORN
BIGJOHN
BIGTOES
BIGTOPS
BOGDOWN
BOGHOLE
BUGSOFF
BUGSOUT
DAGWOOD
DIGSOUT
DOGGONE
DOGWOOD
EDGEOUT
EGGNOGS
EGGROLL
ENGROSS
FOGBOWS
FOGHORN
INGROUP
INGROWN
LAGOONS
LEGHORN
LEGIONS
LEGROOM
LEGWORK
LOGBOOK
LOGSOFF
LOGSOUT
PEGTOPS
PIGEONS
PIGSOUT
PUGNOSE
RAGDOLL
RAGMOPS
RAGTOPS
REGIONS
REGROUP
SIGNOFF
SIGNOUT
TAGSOUT
TUGBOAT
WAGGONS
WIGSOUT

••G••O•
ANGELOU
BIGELOW
BIGFOOT
BIGSHOT
BUGABOO
BUGALOO
DAGWOOD
DOGCHOW
DOGSHOW
DOGTROT
DOGWOOD
EGGEDON
GIGOLOS
HIGHBOY
HIGHLOW
HIGHTOP
LEGATOS
LEGROOM
LOGBOOK
MAGINOT
MUGSHOT
NEGATOR
ORGANON
PAGEBOY
PIGIRON
RIGHTON
SIGNSON
TAGALOG

••G•••O
BUGABOO
BUGALOO
ELGRECO
MAGNETO
MOGAMBO
SAGUARO

•••GO••
ALLGONE
BINGOES
BONGOES
BURGOOS
CARGOES
DIDGOOD
DINGOES
DOGGONE
DRAGONS
DRAGOON
DRAGOUT
EPIGONE
FARGONE
FLAGONS
FORGOES
FORGONE
FORGOOD
FUNGOES
GOOGOLS
GORGONS
GREGORY
HANGOFF
HANGOUT
HUNGOUT
IMAGOES
ISOGONS
JARGONS
JINGOES
LINGOES
MANGOES
MONGOLS
OLDGOLD
OUTGOES
PERGOLA
RANGOON
RINGOUT
SANGOUT
SINGOUT
SPIGOTS
SUNGODS
TANGOED
TRIGONS
TUNGOIL
VANGOGH
VIRGOAN
WAGGONS
WARGODS

•••G•O•
ADAGIOS
AVIGNON
BANGKOK
BERGSON
BURGEON
BURGOOS
CHIGNON
DIDGOOD
DODGSON
DRAGOON
DRAGSON
DUDGEON
DUNGEON
FORGOOD
HANGDOG
HANGSON
KINGDOM
LANGDON
LANGUOR
LONGBOW
LONGTON
OUTGROW
PEUGEOT
PIDGEON
RANGOON
SURGEON
WIDGEON

•••G••O
HEIGHHO
LONGAGO
OREGANO
SINGSTO
TANGELO

••••GO•
BRINGON
CLANGOR
DECAGON
DEMIGOD
GLASGOW
GOINGON
HEXAGON
INDIGOS
KLINGON
LITHGOW
MRMAGOO
NONAGON
OBREGON
OCTAGON
PAPAGOS
PARAGON
POLYGON
VIRAGOS
WOBEGON

••••G•O
ALLEGRO
BRINGTO
CLINGTO
GIORGIO
LYINGTO
MRMAGOO
OWINGTO

•••••GO
AGESAGO
AMERIGO
CHICAGO
DOMINGO
DURANGO
EMBARGO
FARRAGO
HIDALGO
LONGAGO
LUMBAGO
MONTEGO
ONTHEGO
SAPSAGO
UNDERGO
VERDUGO
VERTIGO
ZHIVAGO

G•P••••
GAPPING
GIPSIES
GOPHERS
GUPPIES
GYPPERS
GYPPING
GYPSIES

G••P•••
GAPPING
GASPING
GASPUMP
GOMPERS
GOOPIER
GOSPELS
GRAPHED
GRAPHIC
GRAPNEL
GRAPPLE
GRIPERS
GRIPING
GRIPPED
GRIPPER
GROPING
GROPIUS
GRYPHON
GULPING
GUNPLAY
GUPPIES
GYPPERS
GYPPING

G•••P••
GLIMPSE
GOLFPRO
GOTOPOT
GRAMPUS
GRAPPLE
GRASPED
GRIPPED
GRIPPER
GROUPED
GROUPER
GROUPIE
GRUMPED
GUELPHS
GUIMPES

G••••P•
GALLOPS
GALUMPH
GASCAPS
GIVEUPS
GOESAPE
GOOFUPS
GOSSIPS
GOSSIPY
GRANDPA

G•••••P
GANGSUP
GASPUMP
GEARSUP
GIDDYAP
GIDDYUP
GIVESUP
GOINGUP
GOOFSUP
GROWNUP
GROWSUP
GUMDROP
GUSSYUP

•G••P••
AGRIPPA

•G•••P•
AGRIPPA
EGGCUPS

•G••••P
EGOTRIP

••GP•••
BAGPIPE
LEGPULL
MAGPIES
PIGPENS

••G••P•
BAGPIPE
BIGTOPS
DIGRAPH
EGGCUPS
PEGTOPS
RAGMOPS
RAGTOPS

••G•••P
HIGHTOP
INGROUP
LIGHTUP
MUGWUMP
REGROUP
SIGNSUP

•••GP••
KINGPIN

•••G•P•
HANGUPS

•••G••P
BANGSUP
CLOGSUP
COUGHUP
GANGSUP
HANGSUP
RINGSUP
ROUGHUP
WINGTIP

••••G•P
BRINGUP
DOINGUP
GOINGUP
STOPGAP
TYINGUP
USINGUP

GR•••••
GRABBAG
GRABBED
GRABBER
GRABSAT
GRACIAS
GRACILE
GRACING
GRACKLE
GRADERS
GRADING
GRADUAL
GRAFTED
GRAHAME
GRAHAMS
GRAINED
GRAMMAR
GRAMMER
GRAMMES
GRAMPUS
GRANADA
GRANARY
GRANDAM
GRANDEE
GRANDER
GRANDLY
GRANDMA
GRANDPA
GRANGER
GRANGES
GRANITE
GRANOLA
GRANTED
GRANTEE
GRANTOR
GRANULE
GRAPHED
GRAPHIC
GRAPNEL
GRAPPLE
GRASPED
GRASSED
GRASSES
GRATERS
GRATIFY
GRATING
GRAVELS
GRAVELY
GRAVEST
GRAVIES
GRAVING
GRAVITY
GRAVURE
GRAYEST
GRAYING
GRAYSON
GRAZERS
GRAZING
GREASED
GREASER
GREASES
GREATER
GREATLY
GREAVES
GRECIAN
GREELEY
GREENED
GREENER
GREETED
GREETER
GREGORY
GREMLIN
GRENADA
GRENADE
GRENDEL
GRETZKY
GREYEST
GREYING
GRIDDED
GRIDDER
GRIDDLE
GRIEVED
GRIEVER
GRIEVES
GRIFFEY
GRIFFIN
GRIFFON
GRIFTER
GRIGRIS
GRILLED
GRILLES
GRILLET
GRIMACE
GRIMIER
GRIMMER
GRINDER
GRINNED
GRINNER
GRIPERS
GRIPING
GRIPPED
GRIPPER
GRISHAM
GRISSOM
GRISTLE
GRISTLY
GRITTED
GRIVETS
GRIZZLE
GRIZZLY
GROANED
GROANER
GROCERS
GROCERY
GROLIER
GROMMET
GROMYKO
GROOMED
GROOMER
GROOVED
GROOVES
GROPING
GROPIUS
GROSSED
GROSSER
GROSSES
GROSSLY
GROTTOS
GROUCHO
GROUCHY
GROUNDS
GROUPED
GROUPER
GROUPIE
GROUSED
GROUSER
GROUSES
GROUTED
GROVELS
GROWERS
GROWING
GROWLED
GROWLER
GROWNUP
GROWSON
GROWSUP
GROWTHS
GRUBBED
GRUDGED
GRUDGES
GRUFFER
GRUFFLY
GRUMBLE
GRUMPED
GRUNION
GRUNTED
GRUYERE
GRYPHON

G•R••••
GARAGED
GARAGES
GARBAGE
GARBING
GARBLED
GARBLES
GARCONS
GARDENS
GARDNER
GARGLED
GARGLES
GARLAND
GARMENT
GARNERS
GARNETS
GARNISH
GARONNE
GARRETS
GARRETT
GARRICK
GARTERS
GERAINT
GERALDO
GERBILS
GERENTS
GERITOL
GERMANE
GERMANS
GERMANY
GERUNDS
GIRAFFE
GIRASOL
GIRDERS
GIRDING
GIRDLED
GIRDLES
GIRLISH
GIRONDE
GORDIAN
GORETEX
GORGETS
GORGING
GORGONS
GORIEST
GORILLA
GOROUND
GURGLED
GURGLES
GURKHAS
GURNEYS
GYRATED
GYRATES
GYRATOR

G••R•••
GABRIEL
GAGRULE
GARRETS
GARRETT
GARRICK
GEARBOX
GEARING
GEARSTO
GEARSUP
GEORGES
GEORGIA
GHERKIN
GIORGIO
GLARING
GLORIAS
GLORIED
GLORIES
GLORIFY
GNARLED
GNARRED
GOBROKE
GOURAMI
GOURDES
GOURMET
GOWRONG
GUARANI
GUARDED
GUARGUM

G•••R••
GABBROS
GAGARIN
GAMBREL
GASTRIC
GENERAL
GENERIC
GENERIS
GNARRED
GOCARTS
GODFREY
GOFORIT
GOKARTS
GONERIL
GOVERNS
GRIGRIS
GUMDROP
GUMTREE
GUTHRIE

G••••R•
GABBERS
GAFFERS
GAINERS
GAITERS
GALLERY
GANDERS
GARNERS
GARTERS
GASSERS
GATHERS
GAUGERS
GAWKERS
GAYLORD
GAZZARA
GEEZERS
GENDERS
GENNARO
GESTURE
GEYSERS
GIBBERS
GIFFORD
GILBERT
GILDERS
GILMORE
GINGERS
GINGERY
GIRDERS
GIZZARD
GLAZERS
GLIDERS
GLOWERS
GNAWERS
GODDARD
GOLFERS
GOLFPRO
GOMPERS
GOOBERS
GOPHERS
GOUGERS
GRADERS
GRANARY
GRATERS
GRAVURE
GRAZERS
GREGORY
GRIPERS
GROCERS
GROCERY
GROWERS
GRUYERE
GUEVARA
GUITARS
GUNFIRE
GUNNERS
GUNNERY
GUSHERS
GUTTERS
GYPPERS

G•••••R
GABBIER
GAGSTER
GAMBLER
GARDNER
GAUCHER
GAUDIER
GAUNTER
GAUZIER
GAWKIER
GENTLER
GETOVER
GIDDIER
GIGGLER
GLACIER
GLADDER
GLAMOUR
GLAZIER
GLEANER
GLIBBER
GLIMMER
GLITTER
GLUMMER
GOBBLER
GOESFOR
GOINFOR
GOODBAR
GOOFIER
GOOPIER
GOTOVER
GOUNDER
GRABBER
GRAMMAR
GRAMMER
GRANDER
GRANGER
GRANTOR
GREASER
GREATER
GREENER
GREETER
GRIDDER
GRIEVER
GRIFTER
GRIMIER
GRIMMER
GRINDER
GRINNER
GRIPPER
GROANER
GROLIER
GROOMER
GROSSER
GROUPER
GROUSER
GROWLER
GRUFFER
GUESSER
GUILDER
GUMMIER
GUNKIER
GUNSFOR
GUNTHER
GUSHIER
GUTSIER
GUZZLER
GYRATOR

•GR••••
AGRAFFE
AGREETO
AGRIPPA
AGROUND
OGREISH

•G•R•••
AGGRESS
EGGROLL

•G••R••
EGOTRIP
IGNORED
IGNORER
IGNORES

•G••••R
IGNITER
IGNORER

••GR•••
AGGRESS
AIGRETS
ANGRIER
ANGRILY
BEGRIME
DEGRADE
DEGREES
DIGRAPH
DIGRESS
EGGROLL
ELGRECO
ENGRAFT
ENGRAMS
ENGRAVE
ENGROSS
GAGRULE
INGRAIN
INGRATE
INGRESS
INGROUP
INGROWN
LEGROOM
MEGRIMS
MEGRYAN
MIGRANT
MIGRATE
PUGREES
RAGRUGS
REGRADE
REGRESS
REGRETS
REGROUP
TIGRESS
UPGRADE
VAGRANT

••G•R••
ALGERIA
ANGERED
ANGORAS
AUGURAL
AUGURED
BEGORRA

DOGTROT
EAGERER
EAGERLY
ENGARDE
ENGIRDS
ENGORGE
FIGURED
FIGURER
FIGURES
GAGARIN
HEGIRAS
HOGARTH
NIGERIA
PIGIRON
REGARDS
SUGARED
UNGIRDS
WAGERED
WAGERER
YOGURTS

••G••R•
ALGEBRA
ALGIERS
ANGLERS
ARGUERS
BAGGERS
BEGGARS
BEGORRA
BIGBIRD
BIGGERS
BIGHORN
BIGOTRY
BUGLERS
COGBURN
DAGGERS
DIGGERS
DOGCART
DOGEARS
FOGGERS
FOGHORN
HAGGARD
HUGGERS
JAGUARS
JIGGERS
JIGGERY
JOGGERS
KEGLERS
LAGGARD
LAGGERS
LEGHORN
LEGWORK
LOGGERS
LUGGERS
MAGYARS
MCGUIRE
MUGGERS
NIGGARD
ONGUARD
RIGGERS
RIGOURS
ROGUERY
SAGUARO
SIGHERS
SIGNERS
TUGGERS
VIGOURS
WAGGERY
YOGHURT

••G•••R
ANGRIER
ANGULAR
BAGGIER
BOGGLER
BUGBEAR
BUGGIER
DOGSTAR
EAGERER
FIGHTER
FIGURER
FOGGIER
GAGSTER
GIGGLER
HAGGLER
INGEMAR
JUGGLER
JUGULAR
LEGGIER
LIGHTER
MUGGIER
NEGATOR
RAGGIER
REGULAR
RIGHTER
SAGGIER
SOGGIER
TIGHTER
WAGERER
WAGONER
WIGGLER

•••GR••
ANAGRAM
CHAGRIN
DIAGRAM
EMIGRES
EPIGRAM
GRIGRIS
KINGRAT
LONGRUN
MACGRAW
MAIGRET
MARGRET
MONGREL
OUTGREW
OUTGROW
PILGRIM
PROGRAM
SANGRIA
SEAGRAM
TRIGRAM

•••G•R•
BADGERS
BAGGERS
BEGGARS
BERGERE
BIGGERS
BULGARS
BURGERS
CADGERS
CALGARY
CODGERS
CONGERS
COUGARS
COWGIRL
DAGGERS
DANGERS
DIGGERS
DODGERS
ETAGERE
FINGERS
FOGGERS
FOLGERS
FORGERS
FORGERY
GAUGERS
GINGERS
GINGERY
GOUGERS
GREGORY
HAGGARD
HANGARS
HANGERS
HEDGERS
HUGGERS
HUNGARY
HUNGERS
IMAGERS
IMAGERY
JAEGERS
JIGGERS
JIGGERY
JOGGERS
LAAGERS
LAGGARD
LAGGERS
LANGTRY
LANGURS
LEDGERS
LINGERS
LODGERS
LOGGERS
LUGGERS
MANGERS
MERGERS
MONGERS
MUGGERS
NIAGARA
NIGGARD
NUDGERS
ONAGERS
RANGERS
RIGGERS
RINGERS
RODGERS
RUTGERS
SEAGIRT
SINGERS
STAGERS
SURGERY
TANGERE
TUGGERS
VERGERS
WAGGERY
WINGERS
ZINGERS

•••G••R
ALIGNER
BAGGIER
BOGGLER
BRAGGER
BUGGIER
BULGHUR
BUNGLER
BURGHER
BURGLAR
CHIGGER
DANGLER
DINGIER
FOGGIER
GIGGLER
HAGGLER
JUGGLER
LANGUOR
LAUGHER
LEAGUER
LEGGIER
LOWGEAR
MANGIER
MINGLER
MUGGIER
PLUGGER
PODGIER
PUDGIER
RAGGIER
RANGIER
ROUGHER
SAGGIER
SLUGGER
SMUGGER
SNIGGER
SNUGGER
SOGGIER
STAGGER
STAGIER
SWAGGER
TANGIER
TOUGHER
TRIGGER
WANGLER
WIGGLER
ZINGIER

••••GR•
ALLEGRO
INTEGRA
SHANGRI

••••G•R
ALLEGER
AVENGER
BRAGGER
BRINGER
CHANGER
CHARGER
CHIGGER
CLANGOR
DOWAGER
DREDGER
FORAGER
GRANGER
INTEGER
LOUNGER
MANAGER
NEWAGER
PLEDGER
PLUGGER
PLUNGER
RENEGER
SAVAGER
SLINGER
SLUGGER
SMUGGER
SNIGGER
SNUGGER
SPONGER
STAGGER
STEIGER
STINGER
SWAGGER
SWINGER
TANAGER
TRIGGER
TRUDGER
VINEGAR
VOYAGER
WRINGER
WRONGER
YOUNGER

G•S••••
GASBAGS
GASCAPS
GASCONS
GASEOUS
GASHING
GASJETS
GASKETS
GASKINS
GASMAIN
GASOHOL
GASPING
GASPUMP
GASSERS
GASTRIC
GESSOES
GESTALT
GESTATE
GESTURE
GISELLE
GOSHAWK
GOSLING
GOSPELS
GOSSETT
GOSSIPS
GOSSIPY
GUSHERS
GUSHIER
GUSHING
GUSSETS
GUSSIED
GUSSIES
GUSSYUP
GUSTAVE
GUSTILY
GUSTING
GUSTOES

G••S•••
GADSDEN
GAGSTER
GASSERS
GEISHAS
GEMSBOK
GESSOES
GETSOFF
GETSOUT
GETSSET
GEYSERS
GHASTLY
GHOSTED
GHOSTLY
GINSENG
GIPSIES
GLASGOW
GLASSED
GLASSES
GLISTEN
GLOSSAE
GLOSSED
GLOSSES
GNASHED
GNASHES
GNOSTIC
GODSEND
GODSONS
GOESAPE
GOESBAD
GOESFOR
GOESOFF
GOESOUT
GOOSING
GOSSETT
GOSSIPS
GOSSIPY
GRASPED
GRASSED
GRASSES
GRISHAM
GRISSOM
GRISTLE
GRISTLY
GROSSED
GROSSER
GROSSES
GROSSLY
GUESSED
GUESSER
GUESSES
GUESTED
GUMSHOE
GUNSFOR
GUNSHOT
GUSSETS
GUSSIED
GUSSIES
GUSSYUP
GUTSIER
GUTSILY
GYMSHOE
GYPSIES

G•••S••
GAINSAY
GAINSON
GANGSAW
GANGSTA
GANGSUP
GEARSTO
GEARSUP
GENESEE
GENESES
GENESIS
GETSSET
GIRASOL
GIVESIN
GIVESTO
GIVESUP
GLASSED
GLASSES
GLEASON
GLOSSAE
GLOSSED
GLOSSES
GOODSON
GOOFSUP
GRABSAT
GRASSED
GRASSES
GRAYSON
GREASED
GREASER
GREASES
GRISSOM
GROSSED
GROSSER
GROSSES
GROSSLY
GROUSED
GROUSER
GROUSES
GROWSON
GROWSUP
GUESSED
GUESSER
GUESSES

G••••S•
GABFEST
GAMIEST
GARNISH
GENOESE
GEODESY
GETLOST
GIRLISH
GLIMPSE
GLUCOSE
GOATISH
GODDESS
GOOIEST
GORIEST
GOULASH
GRAVEST
GRAYEST
GREYEST
GUTLESS
GYMNAST

G•••••S
GABBERS
GABBLES
GABBROS
GADGETS
GAFFERS
GAGGLES
GAINERS
GAITERS
GALLEYS
GALLONS
GALLOPS
GALOOTS
GAMBITS
GAMBLES
GAMBOLS
GAMETES
GAMINES
GAMMONS
GANDERS
GANNETS
GARAGES
GARBLES
GARCONS
GARDENS
GARGLES
GARNERS
GARNETS
GARRETS
GARTERS
GASBAGS
GASCAPS
GASCONS
GASEOUS
GASJETS
GASKETS
GASKINS
GASSERS
GATHERS
GAUCHOS
GAUDENS
GAUGERS
GAVIALS
GAWKERS
GAZEBOS
GECKOES
GEEGAWS
GEEZERS
GEISHAS
GELADAS
GELATIS
GENDERS
GENERIS
GENESES
GENESIS
GENGHIS
GENTLES
GEORGES
GERBILS
GERENTS
GERMANS
GERUNDS
GESSOES
GEWGAWS
GEYSERS
GHETTOS
GIBBERS
GIBBETS
GIBBONS
GIBBOUS
GIBLETS
GIBLUES
GIDEONS
GIGGLES
GIGOLOS
GILBLAS
GILDERS
GILLIES
GIMBALS
GIMLETS
GINGERS
GIPSIES
GIRDERS
GIRDLES
GIVEUPS
GLANCES
GLASSES
GLAZERS
GLIDERS
GLITZES
GLORIAS
GLORIES
GLOSSES
GLOTTIS
GLOWERS
GNASHES
GNAWERS
GNOMONS
GOALIES
GOATEES
GOBBLES
GOBLETS
GOBLINS
GOCARTS
GODDESS
GODSONS
GODWITS
GOGGLES
GOKARTS
GOLFERS
GOMPERS
GOOBERS
GOODBYS
GOODIES
GOOFUPS
GOOGOLS
GOPHERS
GORGETS
GORGONS
GOSPELS
GOSSIPS
GOTCHAS
GOTHICS
GOUGERS
GOURDES
GOVERNS
GRACIAS
GRADERS
GRAHAMS
GRAMMES
GRAMPUS
GRANGES
GRASSES
GRATERS
GRAVELS
GRAVIES
GRAZERS
GREASES
GREAVES
GRIEVES
GRIGRIS
GRILLES
GRIPERS
GRIVETS
GROCERS
GROOVES
GROPIUS
GROSSES
GROTTOS
GROUNDS
GROUSES
GROVELS
GROWERS
GROWTHS
GRUDGES
GUELPHS
GUESSES
GUFFAWS
GUIDONS
GUIMPES
GUINEAS
GUITARS
GULCHES
GULLETS
GULLIES
GUNDOGS
GUNNELS
GUNNERS
GUNNIES
GUPPIES
GURGLES
GURKHAS
GURNEYS
GUSHERS
GUSSETS
GUSSIES
GUSTOES
GUTLESS
GUTTERS
GUZZLES
GYPPERS
GYPSIES
GYRATES

•G•S•••
AGASSIZ
AGESAGO
EGESTED

•G••S••
AGASSIZ
AGEISTS
EGOISTS

•G•••S•
AGAINST
AGELESS
AGGRESS
AGONIST
EGGCASE
EGOTISM
EGOTIST
OGREISH
UGLIEST

•G••••S
AGEISTS
AGELESS
AGENDAS
AGGRESS
AGNATES
AGOUTIS
EGGCUPS
EGGNOGS
EGOISTS
HGWELLS
IGNEOUS
IGNITES
IGNORES
IGUANAS
OGDOADS
OGLALAS

••GS•••
BEGSOFF
BIGSHOT
BUGSOFF
BUGSOUT
DIGSOUT
DOGSHOW
DOGSLED
DOGSTAR
GAGSTER
JIGSAWS
LOGSOFF
LOGSOUT
MUGSHOT
PIGSKIN
PIGSOUT
TAGSALE
TAGSOUT
WIGSOUT

••G•S••
AUGUSTA
AUGUSTE
DIGESTS
EDGESIN
INGESTS
LEGISTS
PEGASUS
SIGNSIN
SIGNSON
SIGNSUP

••G••S•
AGGRESS
BIGGEST
BIGNESS
CAGIEST
DEGAUSS
DIGRESS
DOGFISH
EDGIEST
EGGCASE
ENGLISH
ENGROSS
FOGYISH
FOGYISM
HIGHEST
HOGWASH
INGRESS
JAGLESS
LOGIEST
NIGHEST
PIGGISH
PUGNOSE
REGRESS
ROGUISH
SUGGEST
TIGRESS
VAGUEST
WAGGISH

••G•••S
AFGHANS
AGGRESS
AIGRETS
ALGIERS
ANGELES
ANGELUS
ANGLERS
ANGORAS
ARGIVES
ARGUERS
ARGYLES
AUGENDS
BAGFULS
BAGGERS
BAGGIES
BEGGARS
BIGBOYS
BIGEYES
BIGGERS
BIGGIES
BIGGUNS
BIGNESS
BIGTOES
BIGTOPS
BIGWIGS
BOGGLES
BUGGIES
BUGLERS
BYGONES
COGNACS
CYGNETS
DAGGERS
DEGAUSS
DEGREES
DIGESTS
DIGGERS
DIGRESS
DOGDAYS
DOGEARS
DOGGIES
DOGLEGS
DOGTAGS
DUGONGS
DUGOUTS
EAGLETS
EDGINGS
EGGCUPS
EGGNOGS
EIGHTHS
ENGAGES
ENGINES
ENGIRDS
ENGRAMS
ENGROSS
ENGULFS
FAGENDS
FIGURES
FOGBOWS
FOGGERS
GAGGLES
GIGGLES
GIGOLOS
GOGGLES
HAGGLES
HEGIRAS
HIGGINS
HOGTIES
HUGGERS
INGALLS
INGESTS
INGRESS
JAGLESS
JAGUARS
JIGGERS
JIGGLES
JIGSAWS
JOGGERS
JOGGLES
JUGFULS
JUGGLES
KEGLERS
LAGGERS
LAGOONS
LAGUNAS
LEGATES
LEGATOS
LEGENDS
LEGIONS
LEGISTS
LEGUMES
LIGATES
LOGGERS
LOGGIAS
LOGGINS
LOGJAMS
LUGGERS
LUGNUTS
MAGNETS
MAGNUMS
MAGPIES
MAGUEYS
MAGYARS
MEGOHMS
MEGRIMS
MUGGERS
NEGATES
NIGGLES
NOGALES
NOGGINS
NUGGETS
PAGODAS
PEGASUS
PEGTOPS
PIGEONS
PIGGIES
PIGLETS
PIGNUTS
PIGPENS
PUGREES
PYGMIES
RAGLANS
RAGMOPS
RAGOUTS
RAGRUGS
RAGTOPS
REGAINS
REGALES
REGARDS
REGENTS
REGIMES
REGIONS
REGLUES
REGRESS
REGRETS
REGULUS
RIGGERS
RIGOURS
SIGHERS
SIGNALS
SIGNEES
SIGNERS
SIGNETS
TAGENDS
TIGRESS
TOGGLES
TUGGERS
UNGIRDS
VEGGIES
VIGOURS
WAGGLES
WAGGONS
WIGGLES
WIGLETS
WIGWAGS
WIGWAMS
YOGURTS
ZIGZAGS
ZYGOTES

•••GS••
BANGSUP
BERGSON
CLOGSUP
DODGSON
DRAGSIN
DRAGSON
GANGSAW
GANGSTA
GANGSUP
HANGSIN
HANGSON
HANGSUP
PLUGSIN
RINGSUP
SINGSTO
WINGSIT

•••G•S•
BIGGEST
BURGESS
CONGEST
DISGUST
ELEGIST
LARGESS
LARGEST
LONGEST
LONGISH
PIGGISH
SUGGEST
WAGGISH

•••G••S
ADAGIOS
AIRGUNS
ALIGHTS
APOGEES
BADGERS
BADGUYS
BAGGERS
BAGGIES
BANGLES
BEAGLES
BEEGEES
BEGGARS
BENGALS

BIGGERS
BIGGIES
BIGGUNS
BINGOES
BLIGHTS
BOGGLES
BONGOES
BOOGIES
BROGANS
BROGUES
BUDGETS
BUDGIES
BUGGIES
BULGARS
BUNGEES
BUNGLES
BURGEES
BURGERS
BURGESS
BURGLES
BURGOOS
CADGERS
CAPGUNS
CARGOES
CODGERS
CONGERS
COUGARS
CUDGELS
DAGGERS
DANGERS
DANGLES
DIGGERS
DINGLES
DINGOES
DODGERS
DOGGIES
DOUGLAS
DRAGONS
ELEGIES
EMIGRES
ENIGMAS
FIDGETS
FINGERS
FIZGIGS
FLAGONS
FLIGHTS
FOGGERS
FOLGERS
FORGERS
FORGETS
FORGOES
FRIGHTS
FUNGOES
GADGETS
GAGGLES
GARGLES
GAUGERS
GEEGAWS
GENGHIS
GEWGAWS
GIGGLES
GINGERS
GOGGLES
GOOGOLS
GORGETS
GORGONS
GOUGERS
GRIGRIS
GURGLES
HAGGLES
HANGARS
HANGERS
HANGUPS

HEDGERS
HEIGHTS
HIGGINS
HOAGIES
HUGGERS
HUNGERS
IMAGERS
IMAGOES
ISOGONS
JAEGERS
JANGLES
JARGONS
JETGUNS
JIGGERS
JIGGLES
JINGLES
JINGOES
JOGGERS
JOGGLES
JUGGLES
JUNGLES
KNIGHTS
LAAGERS
LAGGERS
LANGURS
LARGESS
LEAGUES
LEDGERS
LENGTHS
LINGERS
LINGOES
LODGERS
LOGGERS
LOGGIAS
LOGGINS
LONGUES
LUGGERS
MANGERS
MANGLES
MANGOES
MARGAYS
MARGINS
MERGERS
MIDGETS
MINGLES
MONGERS
MONGOLS
MORGANS
MUGGERS
NAUGHTS
NIGGLES
NOGGINS
NOUGATS
NUDGERS
NUGGETS
ONAGERS
ORIGINS
OUTGOES
OUTGUNS
PARGETS
PIDGINS
PIGGIES
PLAGUES
PLIGHTS
PONGIDS
POPGUNS
PORGIES
QUAGGAS
RANGERS
RAYGUNS
REDGUMS
RIGGERS
RINGERS

RODGERS
RUTGERS
SHOGUNS
SINGERS
SINGLES
SIXGUNS
SLIGHTS
SLOGANS
SPIGOTS
STAGERS
STIGMAS
STOGIES
SUNGODS
TANGLES
TARGETS
TINGLES
TOGGLES
TONGANS
TONGUES
TOPGUNS
TRIGONS
TUGGERS
VEGGIES
VEIGHTS
VERGERS
VIRGINS
WAGGLES
WAGGONS
WANGLES
WARGODS
WEDGIES
WEIGHTS
WIDGETS
WIGGLES
WINGERS
WRIGHTS
ZEUGMAS
ZINGERS

••••GS•

AMONGST

••••G•S

ALLEGES
ASSIGNS
AVENGES
BADEGGS
BODEGAS
BRIDGES
CAYUGAS
CHANGES
CHARGES
COALGAS
COSIGNS
CRINGES
DAMAGES
DELUGES
DESIGNS
DOSAGES
DREDGES
DRUDGES
EMERGES
ENCAGES
ENGAGES
ENRAGES
ENSIGNS
FLANGES
FLEDGES
FORAGES
FRIDGES
FRINGES
GARAGES
GEORGES

GRANGES
GRUDGES
ICEAGES
IMPUGNS
INDIGOS
KLUDGES
LIMOGES
LINAGES
LOUNGES
MALIGNS
MANAGES
MANEGES
MENAGES
MIRAGES
OBLIGES
OPPUGNS
ORANGES
OUTAGES
PAPAGOS
PELAGES
PLEDGES
PLOUGHS
PLUNGES
POTAGES
QUAGGAS
RAREGAS
RAVAGES
REFUGES
RENEGES
REPUGNS
RESIGNS
SAVAGES
SLEDGES
SLEIGHS
SLOUGHS
SLUDGES
SMUDGES
SPARGES
SPONGES
STOOGES
STURGES
TEARGAS
TROUGHS
TRUDGES
TSONGAS
TWINGES
UNCAGES
VIRAGOS
VISAGES
VOYAGES

•••••GS

AIRBAGS
AIRINGS
ANALOGS
AWNINGS
BADEGGS
BARONGS
BEDBUGS
BELONGS
BIGWIGS
CASINGS
COMINGS
CYBORGS
DIALOGS
DOGLEGS
DOGTAGS
DUGONGS
EARWIGS
EDGINGS
EGGNOGS
ENDINGS
EPILOGS

FACINGS
FILINGS
FIRINGS
FIXINGS
FIZGIGS
GASBAGS
GUNDOGS
HAZINGS
HOTDOGS
HUMBUGS
ICEBAGS
INNINGS
KITBAGS
LACINGS
LAPDOGS
LININGS
LIVINGS
MAKINGS
NUTMEGS
OBLONGS
OILRIGS
OUTINGS
PARINGS
PHOTOGS
PILINGS
PIPINGS
PROLOGS
PYEDOGS
QUAHOGS
RAGRUGS
RATINGS
RAVINGS
REDDOGS
REHANGS
RESINGS
RISINGS
RULINGS
SARONGS
SAVINGS
SAWLOGS
SAYINGS
SEABAGS
SEADOGS
SEALEGS
SIDINGS
SIZINGS
SOWBUGS
SPRINGS
STALAGS
STRINGS
SUNDOGS
TAPINGS
TEABAGS
THRONGS
TIDINGS
TIMINGS
TOPDOGS
TOYDOGS
TUAREGS
UNCLOGS
UNPLUGS
UNSNAGS
VIKINGS
WIGWAGS
ZIGZAGS

G•T••••

GATEAUX
GATELEG
GATEMAN
GATEMEN
GATEWAY
GATHERS

GATLING
GETAWAY
GETBACK
GETDOWN
GETEVEN
GETINTO
GETITON
GETLOST
GETOVER
GETSOFF
GETSOUT
GETSSET
GETTING
GETWELL
GOTAWAY
GOTBACK
GOTCHAS
GOTDOWN
GOTEVEN
GOTHICS
GOTINTO
GOTLAND
GOTOPOT
GOTOVER
GOTWELL
GUTHRIE
GUTLESS
GUTSIER
GUTSILY
GUTTERS
GUTTING

G••T•••

GAITERS
GAITING
GANTLET
GARTERS
GASTRIC
GAUTAMA
GENTEEL
GENTIAN
GENTILE
GENTLED
GENTLER
GENTLES
GESTALT
GESTATE
GESTURE
GETTING
GHETTOS
GLITTER
GLITZED
GLITZES
GLOTTAL
GLOTTIS
GLUTTED
GLUTTON
GOATEED
GOATEES
GOATISH
GODTHAB
GRATERS
GRATIFY
GRATING
GRETZKY
GRITTED
GROTTOS
GUITARS
GUMTREE
GUNTHER
GUSTAVE
GUSTILY
GUSTING

GUSTOES
GUTTERS
GUTTING

G•••T••

GAGSTER
GALATEA
GALATIA
GAMETES
GAUNTER
GAUNTLY
GAVOTTE
GAZETTE
GELATIN
GELATIS
GENETIC
GERITOL
GETITON
GHASTLY
GHETTOS
GHOSTED
GHOSTLY
GLINTED
GLISTEN
GLITTER
GLOATED
GLOTTAL
GLOTTIS
GLUTTED
GLUTTON
GNOSTIC
GODUTCH
GOLFTEE
GORETEX
GRAFTED
GRANTED
GRANTEE
GRANTOR
GREATER
GREATLY
GREETED
GREETER
GRIFTER
GRISTLE
GRISTLY
GRITTED
GROTTOS
GROUTED
GROWTHS
GRUNTED
GUESTED
GYRATED
GYRATES
GYRATOR

G••••T•

GADGETS
GADGETY
GALOOTS
GAMBITS
GANGSTA
GANNETS
GANNETT
GARNETS
GARRETS
GARRETT
GASJETS
GASKETS
GAVOTTE
GAZETTE
GEARSTO
GEFILTE
GERENTS

GESTATE
GETINTO
GIBBETS
GIBLETS
GIMLETS
GIVENTO
GIVESTO
GOBLETS
GOCARTS
GODWITS
GOKARTS
GOLIATH
GORGETS
GOSSETT
GOTINTO
GRANITE
GRAVITY
GRIVETS
GULLETS
GUSSETS

G•••••T

GABFEST
GALLANT
GAMIEST
GANNETT
GANTLET
GARMENT
GARRETT
GAVEOUT
GERAINT
GESTALT
GETLOST
GETSOUT
GETSSET
GILBERT
GILLNET
GIVEOUT
GOABOUT
GOESOUT
GOFORIT
GOINGAT
GOOIEST
GORIEST
GOSSETT
GOTOPOT
GOURMET
GRABSAT
GRAVEST
GRAYEST
GREYEST
GRILLET
GROMMET
GUNBOAT
GUNSHOT
GYMNAST

•G•T•••

AGITATE
EGOTISM
EGOTIST
EGOTRIP

•G••T••

AGNATES
AGOUTIS
EGESTED
IGNITED
IGNITER
IGNITES

•G•••T•

AGEISTS

AGILITY
AGITATE
AGREETO
EGALITE
EGOISTS

•G••••T

AGAINST
AGONIST
EGOTIST
UGLIEST

••GT•••

BIGTIME
BIGTOES
BIGTOPS
DOGTAGS
DOGTROT
HOGTIED
HOGTIES
PEGTOPS
PIGTAIL
RAGTIME
RAGTOPS
WAGTAIL

••G•T••

BIGOTED
BIGOTRY
DIGITAL
DOGSTAR
EIGHTHS
FAGOTED
FIGHTER
GAGSTER
HIGHTEA
HIGHTOP
LEGATEE
LEGATES
LEGATOS
LIGATED
LIGATES
LIGHTED
LIGHTEN
LIGHTER
LIGHTLY
LIGHTUP
MIGHTNT
NEGATED
NEGATES
NEGATOR
NIGHTIE
NIGHTLY
REGATTA
RIGHTED
RIGHTER
RIGHTLY
RIGHTON
SIGHTED
SIGHTLY
TIGHTEN
TIGHTER
TIGHTLY
VEGETAL
ZYGOTES

••G••T•

AIGRETS
AUGUSTA
AUGUSTE
COGNATE
CYGNETS
DIGESTS

DIGNITY
DOGMATA
DUGOUTS
EAGLETS
HOGARTH
INGESTS
INGRATE
LEGISTS
LIGNITE
LUGNUTS
MAGENTA
MAGNATE
MAGNETO
MAGNETS
MIGRATE
NUGGETS
PIGLETS
PIGNUTS
RAGOUTS
REGATTA
REGENTS
REGRETS
SIGNETS
WIGLETS
YOGURTS

••G•••T

AUGMENT
BIGFEET
BIGFOOT
BIGGEST
BIGSHOT
BUGSOUT
CAGIEST
DIGSOUT
DOGCART
DOGTROT
EDGEOUT
EDGIEST
ENGRAFT
FIGMENT
HIGHEST
HIGHHAT
LOGIEST
LOGSOUT
MAGINOT
MIGHTNT
MIGRANT
MUGSHOT
NEGLECT
NIGHEST
PAGEANT
PIGMENT
PIGSOUT
REGNANT
SEGMENT
SIGNOUT
SUGGEST
TAGSOUT
TUGBOAT
UNGUENT
VAGRANT
VAGUEST
WIGSOUT
YOGHURT

•••GT••

HANGTEN
KINGTUT
LANGTRY
LENGTHS
LENGTHY
LONGTON

WINGTIP
YANGTZE

•••G•T•

ALIGHTS
BLIGHTS
BUDGETS
COLGATE
DOUGHTY
FIDGETS
FIDGETY
FLIGHTS
FLIGHTY
FORGETS
FRIGATE
FRIGHTS
GADGETS
GADGETY
GANGSTA
GORGETS
HAUGHTY
HEIGHTS
KNIGHTS
MARGATE
MIDGETS
NAUGHTS
NAUGHTY
NEWGATE
NOUGATS
NUGGETS
PARGETS
PLIGHTS
SEAGATE
SINGSTO
SLIGHTS
SPIGOTS
TARGETS
VEIGHTS
VULGATE
WEIGHTS
WEIGHTY
WIDGETS
WRIGHTS

•••G••T

BIGGEST
CONGEST
DINGBAT
DISGUST
DRAGNET
DRAGOUT
ELEGANT
ELEGIST
EXIGENT
FULGENT
HANGOUT
HUNGOUT
KINGRAT
KINGTUT
LARGEST
LAUGHAT
LONGEST
LUNGEAT
MAIGRET
MARGRET
PEUGEOT
PUNGENT
REAGENT
RINGLET
RINGOUT
ROUGHIT
SANGOUT
SARGENT

SEAGIRT
SINGOUT
SNIGLET
SUGGEST
TANGENT
WINGNUT
WINGSIT

••••GT•

BRINGTO
CLINGTO
LYINGTO
OWINGTO

••••G•T

ALRIGHT
AMONGST
BRIDGET
BROUGHT
DELIGHT
DRAUGHT
DROUGHT
FRAUGHT
FREIGHT
GOINGAT
INSIGHT
MRRIGHT
ONSIGHT
RELIGHT
SLEIGHT
THOUGHT
TLINGIT
TONIGHT
UPRIGHT
UPTIGHT
WROUGHT

GU•••••

GUANACO
GUANINE
GUARANI
GUARDED
GUARGUM
GUELPHS
GUESSED
GUESSER
GUESSES
GUESTED
GUEVARA
GUFFAWS
GUIDING
GUIDONS
GUILDER
GUIMPES
GUINEAS
GUITARS
GULCHES
GULFING
GULLETS
GULLIES
GULLING
GULPING
GUMBALL
GUMDROP
GUMMIER
GUMMING
GUMSHOE
GUMTREE
GUNBOAT
GUNDOGS
GUNFIRE
GUNKIER
GUNLOCK

GUNMOLL
GUNNELS
GUNNERS
GUNNERY
GUNNIES
GUNNING
GUNPLAY
GUNSFOR
GUNSHOT
GUNTHER
GUNWALE
GUPPIES
GURGLED
GURGLES
GURKHAS
GURNEYS
GUSHERS
GUSHIER
GUSHING
GUSSETS
GUSSIED
GUSSIES
GUSSYUP
GUSTAVE
GUSTILY
GUSTING
GUSTOES
GUTHRIE
GUTLESS
GUTSIER
GUTSILY
GUTTERS
GUTTING
GUZZLED
GUZZLER
GUZZLES

G•U••••

GAUCHER
GAUCHOS
GAUDENS
GAUDIER
GAUDILY
GAUGERS
GAUGING
GAUGUIN
GAUNTER
GAUNTLY
GAUTAMA
GAUZIER
GAUZILY
GLUCOSE
GLUEDON
GLUMMER
GLUTTED
GLUTTON
GOUACHE
GOUGERS
GOUGING
GOULASH
GOUNDER
GOURAMI
GOURDES
GOURMET
GRUBBED
GRUDGED
GRUDGES
GRUFFER
GRUFFLY
GRUMBLE
GRUMPED
GRUNION
GRUNTED

GRUYERE

G••U•••
GALUMPH
GENUINE
GERUNDS
GODUNOV
GODUTCH
GROUCHO
GROUCHY
GROUNDS
GROUPED
GROUPER
GROUPIE
GROUSED
GROUSER
GROUSES
GROUTED

G•••U••
GAGRULE
GASPUMP
GAUGUIN
GESTURE
GIBLUES
GIVEUPS
GLOBULE
GOOFUPS
GOROUND
GRADUAL
GRANULE
GRAVURE

G••••U•
GAINFUL
GALLIUM
GANGSUP
GASEOUS
GATEAUX
GAVEOUT
GEARSUP
GETSOUT
GIBBOUS
GIDDYUP
GIELGUD
GIVEOUT
GIVESUP
GLAMOUR
GLEEFUL
GOABOUT
GOESOUT
GOINGUP
GOLDBUG
GOOFSUP
GRAMPUS
GROPIUS
GROWNUP
GROWSUP
GUARGUM
GUSSYUP

•GU••••
IGUANAS

•G•U•••
AGOUTIS

•G••U••
AGROUND
EGGCUPS

•G•••U•
IGNEOUS

••GU•••
ANGULAR
ARGUERS
ARGUING
AUGURAL
AUGURED
AUGUSTA
AUGUSTE
BEGUILE
BEGUINE
ENGULFS
FIGURED
FIGURER
FIGURES
JAGUARS
JUGULAR
LAGUNAS
LEGUMES
MAGUEYS
MCGUIRE
NOGUCHI
ONGUARD
REGULAR
REGULUS
ROGUERY
ROGUISH
SAGUARO
TVGUIDE
UNGUENT
VAGUELY
VAGUEST
YOGURTS

••G•U••
BAGFULS
BIGGUNS
COGBURN
DEGAUSS
DUGOUTS
EGGCUPS
ENGLUND
GAGRULE
JUGFULS
LEGPULL
LUGNUTS
MAGNUMS
MUGWUMP
PIGNUTS
RAGOUTS
RAGRUGS
REGLUED
REGLUES
RIGOURS
SIGMUND
UNGLUED
VIGOURS
YOGHURT

••G••U•
ANGELUS
BUGSOUT
DIGSOUT
EDGEOUT
INGENUE
INGROUP
LIGHTUP
LOGSOUT
ORGANUM
PAGEFUL
PEGASUS
PIGSOUT
REGROUP
REGULUS
SIGNOUT
SIGNSUP
TAGSOUT
WIGSOUT

••G•••U
ANGELOU

•••GU••
AIRGUNS
ARUGULA
BADGUYS
BIGGUNS
BROGUES
CAPGUNS
DISGUST
GAUGUIN
HANGUPS
JETGUNS
LANGUID
LANGUOR
LANGURS
LEAGUER
LEAGUES
LINGUAL
LONGUES
OUTGUNS
PENGUIN
PLAGUED
PLAGUES
POPGUNS
RAYGUNS
REDGUMS
SEAGULL
SHOGUNS
SIXGUNS
TONGUED
TONGUES
TOPGUNS
URUGUAY
VIRGULE

•••G•U•
BANGSUP
BELGIUM
BULGHUR
CLOGSUP
COUGHUP
DRAGOUT
FULGHUM
GANGSUP
HANGOUT
HANGSUP
HUNGOUT
KINGTUT
LONGRUN
MARGAUX
RINGOUT
RINGSUP
ROUGHUP
SANGOUT
SINGOUT
SORGHUM
WINGNUT

••••GU•
ANTIGUA
BLOWGUN
BRINGUP
BURPGUN
DOINGUP
ECLOGUE
FALLGUY
FATIGUE
GIELGUD
GOINGUP
GUARGUM
HANDGUN
INVOGUE
MANAGUA
PIROGUE
REARGUE
SHOTGUN
STUNGUN
TYINGUP
USINGUP
WISEGUY
YOUNGUN

G•V••••
GAVELED
GAVEOFF
GAVEOUT
GAVEWAY
GAVIALS
GAVOTTE
GIVENTO
GIVEOFF
GIVEOUT
GIVESIN
GIVESTO
GIVESUP
GIVEUPS
GIVEWAY
GOVERNS

G••V•••
GALVANI
GRAVELS
GRAVELY
GRAVEST
GRAVIES
GRAVING
GRAVITY
GRAVURE
GRIVETS
GROVELS
GUEVARA

G•••V••
GETEVEN
GETOVER
GOTEVEN
GOTOVER
GREAVES
GRIEVED
GRIEVER
GRIEVES
GROOVED
GROOVES

G••••V•
GINGIVA
GUSTAVE

G•••••V
GODUNOV

••GV•••
RIGVEDA

••G•V••
ARGIVES
MCGAVIN
SEGOVIA

••G••V•
ENGRAVE

•••G•V•
FORGAVE
FORGIVE
GINGIVA

G•W••••
GAWKERS
GAWKIER
GAWKING
GEWGAWS
GOWRONG

G••W•••
GEEWHIZ
GETWELL
GLOWERS
GLOWING
GNAWERS
GNAWING
GODWITS
GOTWELL
GROWERS
GROWING
GROWLED
GROWLER
GROWNUP
GROWSON
GROWSUP
GROWTHS
GUNWALE

G•••W••
GANGWAY
GATEWAY
GAVEWAY
GETAWAY
GIVEWAY
GOLDWYN
GOODWIN
GOTAWAY

G••••W•
GEEGAWS
GETDOWN
GEWGAWS
GOSHAWK
GOTDOWN
GUFFAWS

G•••••W
GAMELAW
GANGSAW
GLASGOW

•GW••••
HGWELLS

••GW•••
BIGWIGS
DAGWOOD
DOGWOOD
HOGWASH
HOGWILD
JUGWINE
LEGWORK
MUGWUMP
RAGWEED
WIGWAGS
WIGWAMS

••G•W••
HIGHWAY

••G••W•
BOGDOWN
FOGBOWS
INGROWN
JIGSAWS

••G•••W
BIGELOW
DOGCHEW
DOGCHOW
DOGSHOW
HIGHLOW
SAGINAW

•••GW••
GANGWAY
RIDGWAY

•••G•W•
GEEGAWS
GEWGAWS

•••G••W
GANGSAW
LONGBOW
MACGRAW
OUTGREW
OUTGROW

••••G•W
GLASGOW
LITHGOW

G•••••X
GATEAUX
GEARBOX
GORETEX

•••G••X
MARGAUX

GY•••••
GYMNAST
GYMSHOE
GYPPERS
GYPPING
GYPSIES
GYRATED
GYRATES
GYRATOR

G•Y••••
GAYLORD
GEYSERS
GRYPHON

G••Y•••
GRAYEST
GRAYING
GRAYSON
GREYEST
GREYING
GRUYERE

G•••Y••
GIDDYAP
GIDDYUP
GROMYKO
GUSSYUP

G••••Y•
GALLEYS
GLADEYE
GOLDWYN
GOODBYE
GOODBYS
GURNEYS

G•••••Y
GADGETY
GAINSAY
GALLERY
GANGWAY
GATEWAY
GAUDILY
GAUNTLY
GAUZILY
GAVEWAY
GEODESY
GEOLOGY
GERMANY
GETAWAY
GHASTLY
GHOSTLY
GIDDILY
GINGERY
GIVEWAY
GLORIFY
GODFREY
GOINGBY
GOSSIPY
GOTAWAY
GRANARY
GRANDLY
GRATIFY
GRAVELY
GRAVITY
GREATLY
GREELEY
GREGORY
GRETZKY
GRIFFEY
GRISTLY
GRIZZLY
GROCERY
GROSSLY
GROUCHY
GRUFFLY
GUNNERY
GUNPLAY
GUSTILY
GUTSILY

•G••••Y
AGILELY
AGILITY
IGNOBLY

••GY•••
ARGYLES
FOGYISH
FOGYISM
MAGYARS

••G•Y••
BIGEYES
BOGEYED
BUGEYED
MEGRYAN

••G••Y•
BIGBOYS
DOGDAYS
MAGUEYS

••G•••Y
ANGRILY
BAGGILY
BIGOTRY
COGENCY
DIGNIFY
DIGNITY
EAGERLY
HIGHBOY
HIGHWAY
JIGGERY
LEGALLY
LEGIBLY
LIGHTLY
MAGNIFY
NIGHTLY
ORGANDY
PAGEBOY
RAGGEDY
REGALLY
REGENCY
RIGHTLY
RIGIDLY
ROGUERY
SIGHTLY
SIGNIFY
SOGGILY
TIGHTLY
UNGODLY
URGENCY
VAGUELY
WAGGERY

•••G•Y•
BADGUYS
MARGAYS

•••G••Y
BAGGILY
BIOGENY
CALGARY
DINGILY
DOUGHTY
FIDGETY
FLAGDAY
FLIGHTY
FORGERY
GADGETY
GANGWAY
GINGERY
GREGORY
HAUGHTY
HUNGARY
IMAGERY
JIGGERY
LANGLEY
LANGTRY
LARGELY
LENGTHY
NAUGHTY
PROGENY
QUIGLEY
RAGGEDY
RIDGWAY
ROUGHLY
SOGGILY
STAGILY
SURGERY
TOUGHLY
TRAGEDY
URUGUAY
WAGGERY
WEIGHTY
WRIGGLY
WRIGLEY
YEVGENY

••••G•Y
FALLGUY
GOINGBY
JOHNGAY
NOSEGAY
SCRAGGY
SPANGLY
SWINGBY
WISEGUY
WRIGGLY
WRONGLY

•••••GY
ALLERGY
ANALOGY
APOLOGY
BIOLOGY
ECOLOGY
GEOLOGY
LITURGY
OLDFOGY
PRODIGY
SCRAGGY
SPRINGY
STRINGY
SYNERGY
TRILOGY
ZOOLOGY
ZYMURGY

G•Z••••
GAZEBOS
GAZELLE
GAZETTE
GAZZARA
GIZZARD
GUZZLED
GUZZLER
GUZZLES

G••Z•••
GAUZIER
GAUZILY
GAZZARA
GEEZERS
GIZZARD
GLAZERS
GLAZIER
GLAZING
GRAZERS
GRAZING
GRIZZLE
GRIZZLY
GUZZLED
GUZZLER
GUZZLES

G•••Z••
GLITZED
GLITZES
GRETZKY
GRIZZLE
GRIZZLY

G••••Z•
GINFIZZ

G•••••Z
GEEWHIZ
GINFIZZ

•G•••Z•
AGONIZE

•G••••Z
AGASSIZ

••GZ•••
ZIGZAGS

••G••Z•
ORGANZA

•••G•Z•
YANGTZE

HA•••••
HAARLEM
HABITAT
HABITED
HABITUE
HACKERS
HACKETT
HACKIES
HACKING
HACKLES
HACKMAN
HACKNEY
HACKSAW
HADDOCK
HADRIAN
HAEMATO
HAFNIUM
HAGGARD
HAGGLED
HAGGLER
HAGGLES
HAHNIUM
HAILING
HAIRCUT
HAIRDOS
HAIRDYE
HAIRIER
HAIRNET
HAIRPIN
HAITIAN
HALCYON
HALFDAN
HALFWAY
HALFWIT
HALIBUT
HALIFAX
HALITES
HALLOWS
HALLWAY
HALOGEN
HALOING
HALSTON
HALTERS
HALTING
HALVING
HALYARD
HAMBURG
HAMELIN
HAMHOCK
HAMITES
HAMITIC
HAMITUP
HAMLETS
HAMMERS
HAMMETT
HAMMILY
HAMMING
HAMMOCK
HAMMOND
HAMPERS
HAMPTON
HAMSTER
HANCOCK
HANDBAG
HANDCAR
HANDFUL
HANDGUN
HANDIER
HANDILY
HANDING
HANDLED
HANDLER
HANDLES
HANDOFF
HANDOUT
HANDSAW
HANDSET
HANDSIN
HANDSON
HANDSUP
HANGARS
HANGDOG
HANGERS
HANGING
HANGMAN
HANGMEN
HANGOFF
HANGOUT
HANGSIN
HANGSON
HANGSUP
HANGTEN
HANGUPS
HANKERS
HANKIES
HANOVER
HANSARP
HANSOLO
HANSOMS
HANUKAH
HAPLESS
HAPPENS
HAPPIER
HAPPILY
HARBORS
HARBOUR
HARDENS
HARDEST
HARDHAT
HARDHIT
HARDIER
HARDILY
HARDING
HARDPAN
HARDPUT
HARDSET
HARDTOP
HARDWON
HARICOT
HARKENS
HARKING
HARMFUL
HARMING
HARMONY
HARNESS
HARPERS
HARPIES
HARPING
HARPIST
HARPOON
HARPSON
HARRIED
HARRIER
HARRIES
HARRIET
HARROWS
HARSHEN
HARSHER
HARSHLY
HARTMAN
HARVARD
HARVEST
HASBEEN
HASHING
HASIDIM
HASSLED
HASSLES
HASSOCK
HASTENS
HASTIER
HASTILY
HASTING
HATCHED
HATCHER
HATCHES
HATCHET
HATEFUL
HATLESS
HATPINS
HATRACK
HATTERS
HATTING
HAUBERK
HAUGHTY
HAULAGE
HAULERS
HAULING
HAULOFF
HAULSUP
HAUNTED
HAUTBOY
HAUTEUR
HAVARTI
HAVENOT
HAWHAWS
HAWKERS
HAWKEYE
HAWKING
HAWKINS
HAWKISH
HAWSERS
HAYFORK
HAYLOFT
HAYMOWS
HAYRACK
HAYRIDE
HAYSEED
HAYWARD
HAYWIRE
HAZARDS
HAZIEST
HAZINGS

H•A••••
HAARLEM
HEADERS
HEADIER
HEADILY
HEADING
HEADMAN
HEADMEN
HEADOFF
HEADOUT
HEADPIN
HEADSET
HEADSIN
HEADSUP
HEADWAY
HEALALL
HEALERS
HEALING
HEALTHY
HEAPING
HEARDOF
HEARERS
HEARING
HEARKEN
HEAROUT
HEARSAY
HEARSOF
HEARTEN
HEARTHS
HEATERS
HEATHEN
HEATHER
HEATING
HEATSUP
HEATTER
HEAVEHO
HEAVENS
HEAVERS
HEAVETO
HEAVIER
HEAVIES
HEAVILY
HEAVING
HIALEAH
HOAGIES
HOARDED
HOARDER
HOARIER
HOARSEN
HOARSER
HOAXERS
HOAXING
HYALINE

H••A•••
HAVARTI
HAZARDS
HEPARIN
HEPATIC
HERALDS
HEXAGON
HIBACHI
HIDALGO
HIJACKS
HILAIRE
HIRABLE
HITACHI
HOGARTH
HORATIO
HOSANNA
HOWARDS
HUMANLY
HYRACES
HYRAXES

H•••A••
HAEMATO
HAGGARD
HALYARD
HANGARS

HANSARP
HARVARD
HATRACK
HAULAGE
HAWHAWS
HAYRACK
HAYWARD
HEALALL
HEBRAIC
HECTARE
HEEHAWS
HENBANE
HENNAED
HEPCATS
HEPTADS
HERBAGE
HERBALS
HERMANN
HETMANS
HEYDAYS
HILLARY
HISPANO
HOBNAIL
HOECAKE
HOGBACK
HOGWASH
HOLLAND
HOLYARK
HOOHAHS
HOOKAHS
HOSTAGE
HOTCAKE
HOTCAPS
HOTCARS
HOTWARS
HOWDAHS
HUBBARD
HUBCAPS
HUNGARY
HURRAHS
HUSBAND
HUSHABY
HUSSARS
HUZZAHS
HYDRANT
HYDRATE
HYMNALS

H••••A•

HABITAT
HACKMAN
HACKSAW
HADRIAN
HAITIAN
HALFDAN
HALFWAY
HALIFAX
HALLWAY
HANDBAG
HANDCAR
HANDSAW
HANGMAN
HANUKAH
HARDHAT
HARDPAN
HARTMAN
HEADMAN
HEADWAY
HEARSAY
HEELTAP
HEGIRAS
HELICAL
HELIPAD
HELLCAT
HELLMAN
HESHVAN
HESSIAN
HIALEAH
HICKMAN
HIGHHAT
HIGHWAY
HINTSAT
HOFBRAU
HOFFMAN
HOLIDAY
HOLMOAK
HOLYWAR
HOOPLAS
HOOTSAT
HOTHEAD
HOTSEAT
HOUSMAN
HUMERAL
HYUNDAI

H•••••A

HERBTEA
HIGHTEA
HOSANNA
HYGIEIA

•HA••••

CHABLIS
CHACHAS
CHAFING
CHAGALL
CHAGRIN
CHAINED
CHAIRED
CHAISES
CHALETS
CHALICE
CHALKED
CHALKUP
CHALLIS
CHAMBER
CHAMFER
CHAMOIS
CHAMPED
CHANCED
CHANCEL
CHANCES
CHANGED
CHANGER
CHANGES
CHANNEL
CHANSON
CHANTED
CHANTER
CHANTEY
CHAOTIC
CHAPATI
CHAPEAU
CHAPELS
CHAPLET
CHAPLIN
CHAPMAN
CHAPMEN
CHAPPED
CHAPTER
CHARADE
CHARGED
CHARGER
CHARGES
CHARIER
CHARILY
CHARIOT
CHARITY
CHARLES
CHARLEY
CHARLIE
CHARMED
CHARMER
CHARMIN
CHARRED
CHARTED
CHARTER
CHASERS
CHASING
CHASSES
CHASSIS
CHASTEN
CHASTER
CHATEAU
CHATHAM
CHATSUP
CHATTED
CHATTEL
CHATTER
CHAUCER
GHASTLY
KHAYYAM
PHAEDRA
PHAETON
PHALANX
PHANTOM
PHARAOH
PHARYNX
PHASEIN
PHASERS
PHASING
SHACKLE
SHADIER
SHADILY
SHADING
SHADOOF
SHADOWS
SHADOWY
SHAFFER
SHAFTED
SHAGGED
SHAHDOM
SHAKERS
SHAKEUP
SHAKIER
SHAKILY
SHAKING
SHAKOES
SHALALA
SHALLOT
SHALLOW
SHALOMS
SHAMANS
SHAMBLE
SHAMING
SHAMMED
SHAMPOO
SHANANA
SHANGRI
SHANKAR
SHANKED
SHANNON
SHANTER
SHAPELY
SHAPERS
SHAPEUP
SHAPING
SHAPIRO
SHAREIN
SHARERS
SHARING
SHARKEY
SHARPED
SHARPEI
SHARPEN
SHARPER
SHARPLY
SHASTRI
SHATNER
SHATTER
SHAVERS
SHAVING
SHAWNEE
SHAWWAL
THALERS
THANKED
THATCHY
THATSIT
THAWING
WHACKED
WHALERS
WHALING
WHAMMED
WHARFED
WHARTON
WHARVES
WHATFOR
WHATNOT
WHAUDEN

•H•A•••

AHEADOF
CHEAPEN
CHEAPER
CHEAPIE
CHEAPLY
CHEATED
CHEATER
CHIANTI
PHRASAL
PHRASED
PHRASES
SHEARED
SHEARER
SHEATHE
SHEATHS
SHEAVED
SHEAVES
SHIATSU
THEATER
THEATRE
THRALLS
THWACKS
THWARTS
WHEATON

•H••A••

CHAGALL
CHAPATI
CHARADE
CHICAGO
CHICANA
CHICANO
CHORALE
CHORALS
OHIOANS
PHALANX
PHARAOH
RHUBARB
SHALALA
SHAMANS
SHANANA
SHEBANG
SHEPARD
SHOFARS
THEBABE
THERAPY
THINAIR
THREADS
THREADY
THREATS
THROATS
THROATY
WHYDAHS
ZHIVAGO

•H•••A•

CHACHAS
CHAPEAU
CHAPMAN
CHATEAU
CHATHAM
CHEDDAR
CHEETAH
CHEMLAB
CHILEAN
CHLORAL
CHOCTAW
CHOLLAS
CHUKKAS
KHAYYAM
PHIDIAS
PHINEAS
PHOBIAS
PHRASAL
RHUMBAS
SHANKAR
SHAWWAL
SHECRAB
SHEILAE
SHEILAH
SHEILAS
SHELLAC
SHERMAN
SHERPAS
SHIPMAN
SHOOTAT
SHOWMAN
THEREAT
THERMAL
THINMAN
THOREAU
THRUWAY
THURMAN
THUSFAR
WHEREAS
WHEREAT
WHIPSAW
WHITMAN

•H••••A

CHELSEA
CHICANA
CHIMERA
PHAEDRA
SHALALA
SHANANA
THERESA

••HA•••

ACHATES
AMHARIC
ASHAMED
ASHANTI
BAHAMAS
BEHAVED
BEHAVES
COHABIT
ENHANCE
ETHANOL
EXHALED
EXHALES
EXHAUST
ICHABOD
INHABIT
INHALED
INHALER
INHALES
INHASTE
ITHACAN
JOHANNA
LEHAVRE
MAHALIA
MAHARIS
MAHATMA
MOHAIRS
MOHAWKS
REHANGS
SAHARAN
SCHATZI
UNHANDS
UNHANDY
UNHAPPY
WCHANDY

••H•A••

ASHCANS
ASHLAND
ASHLARS
ASHRAMS
ATHEART
ATHWART
BAHRAIN
BYHEART
ISHMAEL
NAHUATL
PAHLAVI
REHEALS
REHEARD
REHEARS
REHEATS
SCHNAPS
UNHEARD

••H••A•

ASHTRAY
BAHAMAS
DAHLIAS
ETHICAL
INHUMAN
ITHACAN
JOHNGAY
JOHNJAY
KAHUNAS
MOHICAN
SAHARAN
SCHEMAS
SCHOLAR
TEHERAN

••H•••A

APHELIA
BOHEMIA
ECHIDNA
JOHANNA
MAHALIA
MAHATMA
OPHELIA
SCHIRRA

•••HA••

AFGHANI
AFGHANS
ALLHAIL
ALOHAOE
ARCHAIC
ASPHALT
BETHANY
BOKHARA
CATHAIR
COWHAND
CUSHAWS
DABHAND
DIAHANN
DIEHARD
EARHART
ECKHART
ELKHART
ENCHAIN
ENCHANT
GOSHAWK
GRAHAME
GRAHAMS
HAWHAWS
HEEHAWS
HOOHAHS
HUSHABY
INPHASE
INSHAPE
METHANE
MICHAEL
MIKHAIL
MILHAUD
MISHAPS
NEWHART
OFFHAND
OLDHAND
OMPHALI
ORCHARD
ORPHANS
PERHAPS
RAPHAEL
RECHALK
REDHAIR
REDHATS
RICHARD
SASHAYS
TINHATS
TOPHATS
UNCHAIN
UTAHANS
ZACHARY

•••H•A•

AIRHEAD
ALLHEAL
ANAHUAC
ARCHWAY
BAGHDAD
BATHMAT
BIGHEAD
BRAHMAN
BRAHMAS
BUSHMAN
CASHBAR
CATHEAD
COCHRAN
DISHPAN
DISHRAG
EGGHEAD
ESCHEAT
FATHEAD
GOAHEAD
HESHVAN
HIGHHAT
HIGHWAY
HOTHEAD
IDAHOAN
INAHEAP
JUGHEAD
MATHIAS
MISHEAR
MITHRAS
ORPHEAN
PATHWAY
PINHEAD
POOHBAH
PREHEAT
PYTHIAS
REDHEAD
REDHEAT
RICHMAN
SICHUAN
SUBHEAD
TOWHEAD
TUCHMAN
WASHRAG
YASHMAK

•••H••A

AMPHORA
BOKHARA
BOTHNIA
COCHLEA
FUCHSIA
HIGHTEA
KACHINA
MACHINA
NAPHTHA
TOSHIBA
WICHITA
YESHIVA

••••HA•

ABRAHAM
AGAKHAN
BALIHAI
BEECHAM
BENTHAM
BINGHAM
BRIGHAM
BUDDHAS
CAPSHAW
CHACHAS
CHATHAM
FORDHAM
GALAHAD
GEISHAS
GINGHAM
GODTHAB
GOTCHAS
GRISHAM
GURKHAS
HARDHAT
HIGHHAT
KEESHAN
KETCHAM
KWACHAS
LAUGHAT
MADEHAY
MAKEHAY
MARKHAM
MARSHAL
MATTHAU
MAUGHAM
MCLUHAN
NARWHAL
OLDCHAP
PANCHAX
PASCHAL
PINCHAS
RAINHAT
SILKHAT
SIOBHAN
VAUGHAN
XANTHAN
YITZHAK

••••H•A

CYNTHIA
DRACHMA
KRISHNA
QUECHUA
TRACHEA

•••••HA

ALYOSHA
KENOSHA
NAPHTHA
NATASHA
PIRANHA
RICKSHA
TABITHA

H•B••••

HABITAT
HABITED
HABITUE
HEBRAIC
HEBREWS
HIBACHI
HOBBIES
HOBBITS
HOBBLED
HOBBLES
HOBNAIL
HOBNOBS
HOBOING
HOBOKEN
HUBBARD
HUBBELL
HUBBIES
HUBBUBS
HUBCAPS
HYBRIDS

H••B•••

HAMBURG
HARBORS
HARBOUR
HASBEEN
HAUBERK
HENBANE
HENBITS
HEPBURN
HERBAGE
HERBALS
HERBERT
HERBTEA
HIPBONE
HIPBOOT
HOBBIES
HOBBITS
HOBBLED
HOBBLES
HOFBRAU
HOGBACK
HOLBEIN
HOMBRES
HOMBURG
HOTBEDS
HOWBEIT
HUBBARD
HUBBELL
HUBBIES
HUBBUBS
HUMBLED
HUMBLER
HUMBLES
HUMBUGS
HUSBAND

H•••B••

HALIBUT
HANDBAG
HAUTBOY
HIGHBOY
HIRABLE

H••••B•

HOBNOBS
HORNSBY
HOTTUBS
HUBBUBS
HUSHABY

•H•B•••

CHABLIS
PHOBIAS
PHOBICS
RHUBARB
SHEBANG
SHUBERT
THEBABE
THEBLOB

•H••B••

CHAMBER
PHILBIN
PHOEBES
PHOEBUS
RHOMBUS
RHUMBAS
SHAMBLE
SHERBET
SHOEBOX
SHOWBIZ
SHRUBBY
THIMBLE
THUMBED
THURBER

•H•••B•

CHERUBS
SHRUBBY
THEBABE
THEREBY
WHEREBY

•H••••B

CHEMLAB
RHUBARB
SHECRAB
THEBLOB

••HB•••

ASHBURY

••H•B••

COHABIT
EXHIBIT
ICHABOD
INHABIT
INHIBIT

•••HB••

CASHBAR
CASHBOX
HIGHBOY
POOHBAH

•••H•B•

BYTHEBY
HUSHABY
TOSHIBA

•••H••B

BATHTUB
POTHERB
WASHTUB

••••H•B

GODTHAB

H•C••••

HACKERS
HACKETT
HACKIES
HACKING
HACKLES
HACKMAN
HACKNEY
HACKSAW
HECKLED
HECKLER
HECKLES
HECTARE
HECTORS
HICCUPS
HICKMAN
HICKORY
HOCKING

H••C•••

HALCYON
HANCOCK
HATCHED
HATCHER
HATCHES
HATCHET
HENCOOP
HEPCATS
HERCULE
HICCUPS
HITCHED
HITCHER
HITCHES
HOECAKE
HONCHOS
HOTCAKE
HOTCAPS
HOTCARS
HOWCOME
HUBCAPS
HUNCHED
HUNCHES
HUTCHES

H•••C••

HAIRCUT
HANDCAR
HARICOT
HELICAL
HELICES
HELICON
HELLCAT
HIBACHI
HIJACKS
HITACHI
HOLYCOW
HOOTCHY
HYRACES

H••••C•

HADDOCK
HAMHOCK
HAMMOCK
HANCOCK
HASSOCK
HATRACK
HAYRACK
HEMLOCK
HENPECK
HEROICS
HILLOCK
HOGBACK
HOSPICE
HUMMOCK

H•••••C

HAMITIC
HEBRAIC
HEPATIC
HERETIC
HOMERIC

•H•C•••

CHACHAS
CHECHEN
CHECKED
CHECKER
CHECKIN
CHECKUP
CHICAGO
CHICANA
CHICANO
CHICHEN
CHICKEN
CHICORY
CHOCTAW
CHUCKED
CHUCKLE
SHACKLE
SHECRAB
SHOCKED
SHOCKER
SHUCKED
SHUCKER
THICKEN
THICKER
THICKET
THICKLY
WHACKED

•H••C••

CHANCED
CHANCEL
CHANCES
CHAUCER
CHOICER
CHOICES
SHTICKS
THATCHY
THWACKS

•H•••C•

CHALICE
EHRLICH
PHOBICS
PHONICS
PHYSICS
SHYLOCK
THINICE

•H••••C

CHAOTIC
CHRONIC
PHRENIC
SHELLAC

••HC•••

ASHCANS

••H•C••

ETHICAL
ITHACAN
MOHICAN
VEHICLE

••H••C•

DEHISCE
ENHANCE
ETHNICS
SCHLOCK
UNHITCH

••H•••C

AMHARIC

•••HC••

CASHCOW

•••H•C•

GOTHICS
HAMHOCK
RECHECK

•••H••C

ANAHUAC
ARCHAIC

••••H•C

EDAPHIC
GRAPHIC
POSTHOC
PSYCHIC
PYRRHIC
TROPHIC
XANTHIC

H•D••••

HADDOCK
HADRIAN
HEDDLES
HEDGERS
HEDGING
HIDALGO
HIDEOUS
HIDEOUT
HUDDLED
HUDDLES
HYDRANT
HYDRATE
HYDROUS

H••D•••

HADDOCK
HANDBAG

HANDCAR
HANDFUL
HANDGUN
HANDIER
HANDILY
HANDING
HANDLED
HANDLER
HANDLES
HANDOFF
HANDOUT
HANDSAW
HANDSET
HANDSIN
HANDSON
HANDSUP
HARDENS
HARDEST
HARDHAT
HARDHIT
HARDIER
HARDILY
HARDING
HARDPAN
HARDPUT
HARDSET
HARDTOP
HARDWON
HEADERS
HEADIER
HEADILY
HEADING
HEADMAN
HEADMEN
HEADOFF
HEADOUT
HEADPIN
HEADSET
HEADSIN
HEADSUP
HEADWAY
HEDDLES
HEEDFUL
HEEDING
HELDOFF
HELDOUT
HENDRIX
HERDERS
HERDING
HEYDAYS
HINDERS
HOEDOWN
HOLDERS
HOLDING
HOLDOFF
HOLDOUT
HOLDSON
HOLDSTO
HOLDSUP
HOLDUPS
HOODLUM
HOODOOS
HOTDOGS
HOUDINI
HOWDAHS
HOYDENS
HUDDLED
HUDDLES
HUMDRUM
HUNDRED
HURDLED
HURDLER
HURDLES

H•••D••
HAIRDOS
HAIRDYE
HALFDAN
HANGDOG
HASIDIM
HEARDOF
HOARDED
HOARDER
HOLEDUP
HOLIDAY
HOUNDED
HUMIDLY
HUMIDOR
HYPEDUP
HYUNDAI

H••••D•
HAYRIDE
HAZARDS
HEPTADS
HERALDS
HEYJUDE
HOTBEDS
HOTRODS
HOWARDS
HYBRIDS

H•••••D
HABITED
HAGGARD
HAGGLED
HALYARD
HAMMOND
HANDLED
HARRIED
HARVARD
HASSLED
HATCHED
HAUNTED
HAYSEED
HAYWARD
HECKLED
HEISTED
HELIPAD
HENNAED
HENREID
HEYWOOD
HIGHEND
HITCHED
HOARDED
HOBBLED
HOGTIED
HOGWILD
HOISTED
HOLLAND
HOMERED
HOMINID
HONEYED
HONORED
HOTHEAD
HOUNDED
HOVERED
HUBBARD
HUDDLED
HULLOED
HUMBLED
HUMORED
HUNCHED
HUNDRED
HURDLED
HURRIED
HURTLED
HUSBAND
HUSTLED

•H•D•••
CHEDDAR
CHIDING
PHIDIAS
RHODIUM
SHADIER
SHADILY
SHADING
SHADOOF
SHADOWS
SHADOWY
SHODDEN
SHUDDER
THEDEEP
THUDDED
WHYDAHS

•H••D••
AHEADOF
CHEDDAR
CHOWDER
PHAEDRA
SHAHDOM
SHELDON
SHINDIG
SHODDEN
SHOWDOG
SHUDDER
THIRDLY
THUDDED
THUNDER
WHAUDEN
WHEEDLE

•H•••D•
CHARADE
SHIELDS
SHROUDS
THREADS
THREADY

•H••••D
CHAINED
CHAIRED
CHALKED
CHAMPED
CHANCED
CHANGED
CHANTED
CHAPPED
CHARGED
CHARMED
CHARRED
CHARTED
CHATTED
CHEATED
CHECKED
CHEEPED
CHEERED
CHEVIED
CHILLED
CHINKED
CHINNED
CHIPPED
CHIRPED
CHOMPED
CHOPPED
CHUCKED
CHUGGED
CHUMMED
CHURNED
GHOSTED
PHOTOED
PHRASED
SHAFTED
SHAGGED
SHAMMED
SHANKED
SHARPED
SHEARED
SHEAVED
SHEERED
SHEETED
SHELLED
SHELVED
SHEPARD
SHIFTED
SHILLED
SHINNED
SHIPPED
SHIRKED
SHIRRED
SHOCKED
SHOPPED
SHORTED
SHOUTED
SHUCKED
SHUNNED
SHUNTED
SHUSHED
THANKED
THIEVED
THINNED
THRIVED
THUDDED
THUMBED
THUMPED
WHACKED
WHAMMED
WHARFED
WHEELED
WHEEZED
WHELPED
WHETTED
WHIFFED
WHIPPED
WHIRLED
WHIRRED
WHISKED
WHIZKID
WHIZZED
WHOMPED
WHOOPED
WHOPPED
WHORLED
WHUPPED

••H•D••
ECHIDNA
JOHNDOE

••H••D•
BEHOLDS
SCHMIDT
UNHANDS
UNHANDY
UPHOLDS
WCHANDY

••H•••D
ADHERED
ASHAMED
ASHFORD
ASHLAND
BEHAVED
COHERED
EXHALED
ICHABOD
INHALED
INHERED
REHEARD
REHIRED
SCHEMED
UNHEARD
USHERED

•••HD••
BAGHDAD
RUSHDIE
SHAHDOM

•••H•D•
BUSHIDO
CATHODE
COWHIDE
METHODS
ORCHIDS
RAWHIDE

•••H••D
AIRHEAD
BAGHDAD
BIGHEAD
BOYHOOD
CATHEAD
COWHAND
COWHERD
DABHAND
DIEHARD
EGGHEAD
EUCHRED
FATHEAD
GOAHEAD
HIGHEND
HOTHEAD
JUGHEAD
LIGHTED
MANHOOD
MILHAUD
OFFHAND
OLDHAND
ORCHARD
PINHEAD
REDHEAD
RICHARD
RIGHTED
SIGHTED
SUBHEAD
TOEHOLD
TOWHEAD
YACHTED

••••H•D
ABASHED
BATCHED
BEACHED
BELCHED
BENCHED
BERTHED
BIRCHED
BIRTHED
BLUSHED
BOTCHED
BRUSHED
BUNCHED
CINCHED
CLASHED
CLOTHED
COACHED
COUCHED
COUGHED
CRASHED
CRUSHED
DITCHED
FETCHED
FILCHED
FLASHED
FLESHED
FLUSHED
FROTHED
GALAHAD
GNASHED
GRAPHED
HATCHED
HITCHED
HUNCHED
LATCHED
LAUGHED
LEACHED
LEASHED
LEECHED
LOATHED
LUNCHED
LURCHED
MARCHED
MATCHED
MOOCHED
MORPHED
MOUTHED
MULCHED
MUNCHED
NEIGHED
NOTCHED
PARCHED
PATCHED
PEACHED
PERCHED
PINCHED
PITCHED
PLASHED
POACHED
POUCHED
PSYCHED
PUNCHED
QUASHED
RANCHED
REACHED
ROACHED
ROUGHED
SCATHED
SCYTHED
SEETHED
SHUSHED
SLASHED
SLOSHED
SMASHED
SOOTHED
SOUGHED
STASHED
SWATHED
SWISHED
SYNCHED
TEETHED
TETCHED
TOOTHED
TORCHED
TOUCHED
TRASHED
TROTHED
VOUCHED
WATCHED
WEIGHED
WELCHED
WINCHED
WRITHED

HE•••••
HEADERS
HEADIER
HEADILY
HEADING
HEADMAN
HEADMEN
HEADOFF
HEADOUT
HEADPIN
HEADSET
HEADSIN
HEADSUP
HEADWAY
HEALALL
HEALERS
HEALING
HEALTHY
HEAPING
HEARDOF
HEARERS
HEARING
HEARKEN
HEAROUT
HEARSAY
HEARSOF
HEARTEN
HEARTHS
HEATERS
HEATHEN
HEATHER
HEATING
HEATSUP
HEATTER
HEAVEHO
HEAVENS
HEAVERS
HEAVETO
HEAVIER
HEAVIES
HEAVILY
HEAVING
HEBRAIC
HEBREWS
HECKLED
HECKLER
HECKLES
HECTARE
HECTORS
HEDDLES
HEDGERS
HEDGING
HEEDFUL
HEEDING
HEEHAWS
HEELERS
HEELING
HEELTAP
HEFTIER
HEFTILY
HEFTING
HEGIRAS
HEIFERS
HEIFETZ
HEIGHHO
HEIGHTS
HEINOUS
HEIRESS
HEISTED
HELDOFF
HELDOUT
HELICAL
HELICES
HELICON
HELIPAD
HELIXES
HELLCAT
HELLENE
HELLERS
HELLION
HELLMAN
HELMETS
HELMING
HELOISE
HELOTRY
HELPERS
HELPFUL
HELPING
HELPOUT
HEMLINE
HEMLOCK
HEMMERS
HEMMING
HEMSLEY
HENBANE
HENBITS
HENCOOP
HENDRIX
HENNAED
HENNERY
HENPECK
HENREID
HEPARIN
HEPATIC
HEPBURN
HEPCATS
HEPTADS
HERALDS
HERBAGE
HERBALS
HERBERT
HERBTEA
HERCULE
HERDERS
HERDING
HERETIC
HERMANN
HERMITS
HEROICS
HEROINE
HEROISM
HERRING
HERRIOT
HERSELF
HERSHEY
HESHVAN
HESSIAN
HETMANS
HEWLETT
HEXAGON
HEXNUTS
HEXSIGN
HEYDAYS
HEYJUDE
HEYWOOD

H•E••••
HAEMATO
HEEDFUL
HEEDING
HEEHAWS
HEELERS
HEELING
HEELTAP
HOECAKE
HOEDOWN

H••E•••
HAMELIN
HATEFUL
HAVENOT
HERETIC
HGWELLS
HIDEOUS
HIDEOUT
HIRESON
HOLEDUP
HOLEOUT
HOLESUP
HOMERED
HOMERIC
HOMERUN
HONESTY
HONEYED
HOPEFUL
HOVERED
HOVERER
HOWELLS
HOWEVER
HUMERAL
HUMERUS
HYPEDUP

H•••E••
HACKERS
HACKETT
HALTERS
HAMLETS
HAMMERS
HAMMETT
HAMPERS
HANGERS
HANKERS
HAPLESS
HAPPENS
HARDENS
HARDEST
HARKENS
HARNESS
HARPERS
HARVEST
HASBEEN
HASTENS
HATLESS
HATTERS
HAUBERK
HAULERS
HAUTEUR
HAWKERS
HAWKEYE
HAWSERS
HAYSEED
HAZIEST
HEADERS
HEALERS
HEARERS
HEATERS
HEAVEHO
HEAVENS
HEAVERS
HEAVETO
HEBREWS
HEDGERS
HEELERS
HEIFERS
HEIFETZ
HEIRESS
HELLENE
HELLERS
HELMETS
HELPERS
HEMMERS
HENNERY
HENPECK
HENREID
HERBERT
HERDERS
HERSELF
HEWLETT
HIALEAH
HIGHEND
HIGHEST
HIMSELF
HINDERS
HIPNESS
HIPPEST
HISSERS
HITHERE
HITLESS
HITTERS
HOAXERS
HOLBEIN
HOLDERS
HOLIEST
HOLLERS
HOMIEST
HONKERS
HOOFERS
HOOTERS
HOPPERS
HORNETS
HOSIERS
HOSIERY
HOSTELS
HOSTESS
HOTBEDS
HOTHEAD
HOTNESS
HOTSEAT
HOTTEST
HOWBEIT
HOWLERS
HOYDENS
HUBBELL
HUGGERS
HULLERS
HUMMERS
HUNGERS
HUNKERS
HUNTERS
HURLERS
HUSKERS
HUSSEIN
HYGIEIA
HYGIENE
HYPHENS

H••••E•
HAARLEM
HABITED
HACKIES
HACKLES
HACKNEY
HAGGLED
HAGGLER
HAGGLES
HAIRIER
HAIRNET
HALITES
HALOGEN
HAMITES
HAMSTER
HANDIER
HANDLED
HANDLER
HANDLES
HANDSET
HANGMEN
HANGTEN
HANKIES
HANOVER
HAPPIER
HARDIER
HARDSET
HARPIES
HARRIED
HARRIER
HARRIES
HARRIET
HARSHEN
HARSHER
HASBEEN
HASSLED
HASSLES
HASTIER
HATCHED
HATCHER
HATCHES
HATCHET
HAUNTED
HAYSEED
HEADIER
HEADMEN
HEADSET
HEARKEN
HEARTEN
HEATHEN
HEATHER
HEATTER
HEAVIER
HEAVIES
HECKLED
HECKLER
HECKLES
HEDDLES
HEFTIER
HEISTED
HELICES
HELIXES
HEMSLEY
HENNAED
HERBTEA
HERSHEY
HIGHTEA
HILLIER
HINNIES
HIPPIES
HIPSTER
HITCHED
HITCHER
HITCHES
HOAGIES
HOARDED
HOARDER
HOARIER
HOARSEN
HOARSER
HOBBIES
HOBBLED
HOBBLES
HOBOKEN
HOGTIED
HOGTIES
HOISTED
HOLLIES
HOLSTER
HOLYSEE
HOMBRES
HOMERED
HOMINEM
HONEYED
HONORED
HONOREE
HONORER
HOOPOES
HOOSIER
HOPOVER
HORSIER
HOSTLER
HOUNDED
HOVERED
HOVERER
HOWEVER
HUBBIES
HUDDLED
HUDDLES
HUFFIER
HULLOED
HUMBLED
HUMBLER
HUMBLES
HUMORED
HUNCHED
HUNCHES
HUNDRED
HUNTLEY
HURDLED
HURDLER
HURDLES
HURRIED
HURRIES
HURTLED
HURTLES
HUSKIER
HUSKIES
HUSSIES
HUSTLED
HUSTLER
HUSTLES
HUTCHES
HYRACES
HYRAXES

H•••••E
HABITUE
HAIRDYE
HAULAGE
HAWKEYE
HAYRIDE
HAYWIRE
HECTARE
HELLENE
HELOISE
HEMLINE
HENBANE
HERBAGE
HERCULE
HEROINE
HEYJUDE
HILAIRE
HIPBONE
HIRABLE
HIRSUTE
HITHERE
HITTITE
HOECAKE
HOLYOKE
HOLYSEE
HONOREE
HORMONE
HOSPICE
HOSTAGE
HOSTILE
HOTCAKE
HOTLINE
HOTWIRE
HOWCOME
HYALINE
HYDRATE
HYGIENE

•HE••••
AHEADOF
CHEAPEN
CHEAPER
CHEAPIE
CHEAPLY
CHEATED
CHEATER
CHECHEN
CHECKED
CHECKER
CHECKIN
CHECKUP
CHEDDAR
CHEEPED
CHEERED
CHEERIO
CHEERUP
CHEESES
CHEETAH
CHEETOS
CHEEVER
CHEKHOV
CHELSEA
CHEMISE
CHEMIST
CHEMLAB
CHENIER
CHEQUER
CHEQUES
CHERISH
CHEROOT
CHERUBS
CHERVIL
CHESTER
CHETRUM
CHEVIED
CHEVIES
CHEVIOT
CHEVRES
CHEVRON
CHEWERS
CHEWIER
CHEWING
CHEWOUT
CHEWSUP
GHERKIN
GHETTOS
PHENOLS
PHENOMS
RHENIUM
RHETORS
SHEARED

SHEARER
SHEATHE
SHEATHS
SHEAVED
SHEAVES
SHEBANG
SHECRAB
SHEERED
SHEERER
SHEERLY
SHEETED
SHEIKHS
SHEILAE
SHEILAH
SHEILAS
SHEKELS
SHELDON
SHELLAC
SHELLED
SHELLER
SHELLEY
SHELTER
SHELTIE
SHELTON
SHELVED
SHELVES
SHEPARD
SHERBET
SHERIFF
SHERMAN
SHERPAS
SHERWIN
SHEWOLF
THEATER
THEATRE
THEBABE
THEBLOB
THEDEEP
THEISTS
THEOREM
THERAPY
THEREAT
THEREBY
THEREIN
THEREOF
THEREON
THERESA
THERETO
THERMAL
THERMOS
THEROUX
THESEUS
THESPIS
WHEATON
WHEEDLE
WHEELED
WHEELER
WHEELIE
WHEEZED
WHEEZER
WHEEZES
WHELPED
WHEREAS
WHEREAT
WHEREBY
WHEREIN
WHEREOF
WHERETO
WHETHER
WHETTED

•H•E•••

CHEEPED
CHEERED
CHEERIO
CHEERUP
CHEESES
CHEETAH
CHEETOS
CHEEVER
CHIEFLY
PHAEDRA
PHAETON
PHOEBES
PHOEBUS
PHOENIX
PHRENIC
SHEERED
SHEERER
SHEERLY
SHEETED
SHIELDS
SHOEBOX
SHOEING
THIERRY
THIEVED
THIEVES
THREADS
THREADY
THREATS
THREERS
THREWIN
WHEEDLE
WHEELED
WHEELER
WHEELIE
WHEEZED
WHEEZER
WHEEZES
WHOEVER

•H••E••

CHALETS
CHAPEAU
CHAPELS
CHASERS
CHATEAU
CHEWERS
CHILEAN
CHIMERA
CHINESE
CHISELS
CHOKERS
CHOKEUP
PHASEIN
PHASERS
PHINEAS
PHONEME
RHYMERS
SHAKERS
SHAKEUP
SHAPELY
SHAPERS
SHAPEUP
SHAREIN
SHARERS
SHAVERS
SHEKELS
SHINERS
SHIVERS
SHOVELS
SHOVERS
SHOWERS
SHOWERY
SHRIEKS
SHUBERT
SHUTEYE
SHYNESS
THALERS
THEDEEP
THEREAT
THEREBY
THEREIN
THEREOF
THEREON
THERESA
THERETO
THESEUS
THOREAU
THREERS
THYSELF
WHALERS
WHEREAS
WHEREAT
WHEREBY
WHEREIN
WHEREOF
WHERETO
WHINERS
WHITENS
WHITEST

•H•••E•

CHAINED
CHAIRED
CHAISES
CHALKED
CHAMBER
CHAMFER
CHAMPED
CHANCED
CHANCEL
CHANCES
CHANGED
CHANGER
CHANGES
CHANNEL
CHANTED
CHANTER
CHANTEY
CHAPLET
CHAPMEN
CHAPPED
CHAPTER
CHARGED
CHARGER
CHARGES
CHARIER
CHARLES
CHARLEY
CHARMED
CHARMER
CHARRED
CHARTED
CHARTER
CHASSES
CHASTEN
CHASTER
CHATTED
CHATTEL
CHATTER
CHAUCER
CHEAPEN
CHEAPER
CHEATED
CHEATER
CHECHEN
CHECKED
CHECKER
CHEEPED
CHEERED
CHEESES
CHEEVER
CHELSEA
CHENIER
CHEQUER
CHEQUES
CHESTER
CHEVIED
CHEVIES
CHEVRES
CHEWIER
CHICHEN
CHICKEN
CHIGGER
CHILIES
CHILLED
CHILLER
CHIMNEY
CHINKED
CHINNED
CHIPPED
CHIPPER
CHIRPED
CHITTER
CHOICER
CHOICES
CHOMPED
CHOOSER
CHOOSES
CHOPPED
CHOPPER
CHOWDER
CHROMES
CHUCKED
CHUGGED
CHUKKER
CHUMMED
CHUNNEL
CHURNED
CHUTNEY
GHOSTED
PHILTER
PHLOXES
PHOEBES
PHONIER
PHONIES
PHOTOED
PHRASED
PHRASES
SHADIER
SHAFFER
SHAFTED
SHAGGED
SHAKIER
SHAKOES
SHAMMED
SHANKED
SHANTER
SHARKEY
SHARPED
SHARPEI
SHARPEN
SHARPER
SHATNER
SHATTER
SHAWNEE
SHEARED
SHEARER
SHEAVED
SHEAVES
SHEERED
SHEERER
SHEETED
SHELLED
SHELLER
SHELLEY
SHELTER
SHELVED
SHELVES
SHERBET
SHIFTED
SHIITES
SHILLED
SHIMMER
SHINIER
SHINNED
SHIPMEN
SHIPPED
SHIPPER
SHIRKED
SHIRKER
SHIRLEY
SHIRRED
SHOCKED
SHOCKER
SHODDEN
SHOOTER
SHOPPED
SHOPPER
SHOPPES
SHORTED
SHORTEN
SHORTER
SHOUTED
SHOUTER
SHOWIER
SHOWMEN
SHRIKES
SHRINER
SHRINES
SHRIVEL
SHRIVER
SHRIVES
SHUCKED
SHUCKER
SHUDDER
SHUNNED
SHUNTED
SHUSHED
SHUSHES
SHUTTER
SHYSTER
THANKED
THEATER
THEDEEP
THEOREM
THICKEN
THICKER
THICKET
THIEVED
THIEVES
THINKER
THINNED
THINNER
THITHER
THRIVED
THRIVES
THRONES
THROWER
THUDDED
THUMBED
THUMPED
THUMPER
THUNDER
THURBER
WHACKED
WHAMMED
WHARFED
WHARVES
WHAUDEN
WHEELED
WHEELER
WHEEZED
WHEEZER
WHEEZES
WHELPED
WHETHER
WHETTED
WHIFFED
WHIMPER
WHIPPED
WHIPPET
WHIRLED
WHIRRED
WHISKED
WHISKER
WHISKEY
WHISPER
WHITHER
WHITNEY
WHIZZED
WHIZZES
WHOEVER
WHOMPED
WHOOPED
WHOOPEE
WHOPPED
WHOPPER
WHORLED
WHUPPED

•H••••E

CHALICE
CHARADE
CHARLIE
CHEAPIE
CHEMISE
CHINESE
CHORALE
CHORINE
CHORTLE
CHUCKLE
DHURRIE
PHILTRE
PHONEME
RHIZOME
SHACKLE
SHAMBLE
SHAWNEE
SHEATHE
SHEILAE
SHELTIE
SHINGLE
SHUFFLE
SHUTEYE
SHUTTLE
THEATRE
THEBABE
THIMBLE
THINICE
THISTLE
WHEEDLE
WHEELIE
WHISTLE
WHITTLE
WHOOPEE

••HE•••

ACHENES
ACHERON
ACHESON
ADHERED
ADHERES
AMHERST
APHELIA
APHESES
ATHEART
ATHEISM
ATHEIST
BEHESTS
BOHEMIA
BYHEART
COHEIRS
COHERED
COHERES
ECHELON
INHERED
INHERES
INHERIT
OPHELIA
OTHELLO
REHEALS
REHEARD
REHEARS
REHEATS
REHEELS
SCHEMAS
SCHEMED
SCHEMER
SCHEMES
SCHERZI
SCHERZO
SPHERES
TEHERAN
UNHEARD
USHERED

••H•E••

ACHIEST
ACHIEVE
ASHIEST
ASHLESS
ATHLETE
CAHIERS
REHEELS
SCHLEPP
SCHLEPS
SCHMEER

••H••E•

ACHATES
ACHENES
ADHERED
ADHERES
APHESES
ASHAMED
ATHOMES
BEHAVED
BEHAVES
COHERED
COHERES
DAHOMEY
EXHALED
EXHALES
INHALED
INHALER
INHALES
INHERED
INHERES
ISHMAEL
MAHONEY
REHIRED
REHIRES
SCHEMED
SCHEMER
SCHEMES
SCHMEER
SCHMOES
SPHERES
USHERED
WAHINES
YAHTZEE

••H•••E

ACHIEVE
ATHLETE
BEHOOVE
DEHISCE
ENHANCE
INHASTE
INHOUSE
JOHNDOE
JOHNNIE
LEHAVRE
UNHORSE
VEHICLE
YAHTZEE

•••HE••

AIRHEAD
ALCHEMY
ALLHEAL
ALLHERE
ANAHEIM
ANTHEMS
ANTHERS
ARCHERS
ARCHERY
BATHERS
BETHELS
BIGHEAD
BOTHERS
BUSHELS
BYTHEBY
CACHETS
CASHEWS
CATHEAD
CEPHEUS
CIPHERS
COCHERE
COWHERD
CYPHERS
DASHERS
DITHERS
DITHERY
DUCHESS
EGGHEAD
ESCHEAT
ESCHEWS
ESTHETE
ETCHERS
FATHEAD
FATHERS
FISHERS
FISHERY
FISHEYE
GATHERS
GOAHEAD
GOPHERS
GUSHERS
HIGHEND
HIGHEST
HITHERE
HOTHEAD
HYPHENS
INAHEAP
ISOHELS
JAPHETH
JUGHEAD
KOSHERS
LASHERS
LATHERS
LATHERY
LICHENS
LITHELY
LITHEST
LOWHEEL
LUSHEST
MACHETE
MASHERS
MATHERS
MATHEWS
MAYHEMS
MICHELE
MISHEAR
MOTHERS
MUDHENS
MUSHERS
MYNHEER
NEPHEWS
NIGHEST
NOSHERS
NOWHERE
ONTHEGO
ONTHEQT
ORPHEAN
ORPHEUS
PEAHENS
PINHEAD
POSHEST
POTHERB
POTHERS
PREHEAT
RASHERS
RASHEST
RECHECK
REDHEAD
REDHEAT
RICHEST
RUSHEES
RUSHERS
SACHEMS
SACHETS
SEEHERE
SIGHERS
SOTHERE
SOTHERN
SUBHEAD
TARHEEL
TETHERS
TITHERS
TOWHEAD
TOWHEES
WASHERS
WETHERS
WILHELM
WISHERS
WITHERS
WYCHELM
ZITHERS

•••H•E•

ARCHIES
BUSHIER
BUSHMEN
CASHIER
COCHLEA
CUSHIER
DUCHIES
EUCHRED
EUCHRES
FIGHTER
FISHIER
FISHNET
GUSHIER
HIGHTEA
ITCHIER
KISHKES
LIGHTED
LIGHTEN
LIGHTER
LOWHEEL
MASHIES
MICHAEL
MUSHIER
MYNHEER
PITHIER
PUSHIER
RAPHAEL
RESHOES
RICHTER
RIGHTED
RIGHTER
RUSHEES
SIGHTED
TARHEEL
TECHIES
TIGHTEN
TIGHTER
TOWHEES
YACHTED

•••H••E

AIRHOLE
ALLHERE
ALOHAOE
ARCHIVE
ARMHOLE
BEEHIVE
BOBHOPE
BOGHOLE
CATHODE
COCHERE
COCHISE
COWHIDE
DRYHOLE
EBWHITE
ENTHUSE
ESTHETE
EYEHOLE
FISHEYE
FOXHOLE
GRAHAME
GUTHRIE
HITHERE
INPHASE
INSHAPE
KEYHOLE
MACHETE
MACHINE
MANHOLE
METHANE
MICHELE
NIGHTIE
NOTHOME
NOWHERE
ONSHORE
PINHOLE
POTHOLE
RATHOLE
RAWHIDE
RECHOSE
RUNHOME
RUSHDIE
SEEHERE
SOTHERE
TERHUNE

••••HE•

ABASHED
ABASHES
AITCHES
ANOTHER
APACHES
APOTHEM
BANSHEE
BATCHED
BATCHES
BEACHED
BEACHES
BEECHER
BEECHES
BELCHED
BELCHES
BENCHED
BENCHES
BERTHED
BIRCHED
BIRCHES
BIRTHED
BLATHER
BLITHER
BLUSHED
BLUSHER
BLUSHES
BOTCHED
BOTCHES
BRASHER
BROTHER
BRUSHED
BRUSHES
BUNCHED
BUNCHES
BURGHER
BUTCHER
CATCHER
CATCHES
CHECHEN
CHICHEN
CINCHED
CINCHES
CLASHED
CLASHES
CLICHES
CLOCHES
CLOTHED
CLOTHES
COACHED
COACHES
CONCHES
COUCHED
COUCHES
COUGHED
CRASHED
CRASHES
CRECHES
CROCHET
CRUSHED
CRUSHER
CRUSHES
DITCHED
DITCHES
DOGCHEW
EARTHEN
EPITHET
FARTHER
FEATHER
FETCHED
FETCHES
FILCHED
FILCHER
FILCHES
FINCHES
FISCHER
FITCHES
FLASHED
FLASHER
FLASHES
FLECHES
FLESHED
FLESHES
FLUSHED
FLUSHES
FRESHEN
FRESHER
FRESHET
FROTHED
FURTHER
GAUCHER
GNASHED
GNASHES
GRAPHED
GULCHES
GUNTHER
HARSHEN
HARSHER
HATCHED
HATCHER
HATCHES
HATCHET
HEATHEN
HEATHER
HERSHEY
HITCHED
HITCHER
HITCHES
HUNCHED
HUNCHES
HUTCHES
JIMCHEE
KAISHEK
KETCHES
KITCHEN
KNISHES
LARCHES
LATCHED
LATCHES
LAUGHED
LAUGHER
LEACHED
LEACHES
LEASHED
LEASHES
LEATHER
LEECHED
LEECHES
LOACHES
LOATHED
LOATHES
LUNCHED
LUNCHER
LUNCHES
LURCHED
LURCHES
MADCHEN
MARCHED
MARCHEN
MARCHER
MARCHES
MARSHES
MATCHED
MATCHES
MATTHEW
MOOCHED
MOOCHER
MOOCHES
MOORHEN
MORPHED
MOUTHED
MULCHED
MULCHES
MUNCHED
MUNCHER
MUNCHES
MURPHEY
NARTHEX
NATCHEZ
NEIGHED
NEITHER
NORTHER
NOTCHED
NOTCHES
PANTHER
PARCHED
PARCHES
PATCHED
PATCHES
PEACHED
PEACHES
PERCHED
PERCHES
PINCHED
PINCHER
PINCHES
PITCHED
PITCHER
PITCHES
PLASHED
PLASHES
PLUSHER
PLUSHES
POACHED
POACHER
POACHES
POOCHES
PORCHES
POUCHED
POUCHES
PRITHEE
PROPHET
PSYCHED
PSYCHES
PUNCHED
PUNCHER
PUNCHES
QUASHED
QUASHES
QUICHES
RANCHED
RANCHER
RANCHES
RATCHET
REACHED
REACHES
REUTHER
ROACHED
ROACHES
ROUGHED

ROUGHEN
ROUGHER
SATCHEL
SAYWHEN
SCATHED
SCATHES
SCYTHED
SCYTHES
SEETHED
SEETHES
SEICHES
SHUSHED
SHUSHES
SKOSHES
SLASHED
SLASHER
SLASHES
SLATHER
SLITHER
SLOSHED
SLOSHES
SLUSHES
SMASHED
SMASHER
SMASHES
SMOTHER
SOOTHED
SOOTHER
SOOTHES
SOUGHED
SOUTHEY
STASHED
STASHES
STEPHEN
STICHES
SWATHED
SWATHES
SWISHED
SWISHES
SYNCHED
SYNCHES
TEACHER
TEACHES
TEETHED
TEETHER
TEETHES
TEICHER
TETCHED
THITHER
TOOTHED
TORCHED
TORCHES
TOUCHED
TOUCHES
TOUGHEN
TOUGHER
TRACHEA
TRASHED
TRASHES
TROCHEE
TROCHES
TROTHED
VETCHES
VOUCHED
VOUCHER
VOUCHES
WATCHED
WATCHER
WATCHES
WEATHER
WEIGHED
WELCHED
WELCHES
WENCHES
WERNHER
WERTHER
WHETHER
WHITHER
WINCHED
WINCHES
WITCHES
WRITHED
WRITHES
ZILCHES

••••H•E

ARACHNE
BACKHOE
BANSHEE
DONAHUE
GUMSHOE
GYMSHOE
IVANHOE
JIMCHEE
PRITHEE
PRUDHOE
RITCHIE
TOESHOE
TOUGHIE
TROCHEE

•••••HE

ADOLPHE
ATTACHE
BLANCHE
BREATHE
BRIOCHE
CEVICHE
DEPECHE
EARACHE
FRAICHE
GOUACHE
LAROCHE
PANACHE
PENUCHE
PORSCHE
SHEATHE
STROPHE
WREATHE

H•F••••

HAFNIUM
HEFTIER
HEFTILY
HEFTING
HOFBRAU
HOFFMAN
HUFFIER
HUFFILY
HUFFING

H••F•••

HALFDAN
HALFWAY
HALFWIT
HAYFORK
HEIFERS
HEIFETZ
HOFFMAN
HOOFERS
HOOFING
HOOFSIT
HOTFOOT
HUFFIER
HUFFILY
HUFFING

H•••F••

HALIFAX
HANDFUL
HARMFUL
HATEFUL
HEEDFUL
HELPFUL
HOPEFUL
HURTFUL

H••••F•

HANDOFF
HANGOFF
HAULOFF
HAYLOFT
HEADOFF
HELDOFF
HOLDOFF
HOPSOFF
HORRIFY

H•••••F

HANDOFF
HANGOFF
HAULOFF
HEADOFF
HEARDOF
HEARSOF
HELDOFF
HERSELF
HIMSELF
HIPROOF
HOLDOFF
HOPSOFF

•H•F•••

CHAFING
CHIFFON
SHAFFER
SHAFTED
SHIFTED
SHOFARS
SHUFFLE
WHIFFED

•H••F••

CHAMFER
CHIEFLY
CHIFFON
SHAFFER
SHOOFLY
SHOTFOR
SHRIFTS
SHUFFLE
THRIFTS
THRIFTY
THUSFAR
WHARFED
WHATFOR
WHIFFED

•H•••F•

SHERIFF
SHOWOFF
SHUTOFF

•H••••F

AHEADOF
SHADOOF
SHERIFF
SHEWOLF
SHORTOF
SHOWOFF
SHUTOFF
THEREOF
THINKOF
THYSELF
WHEREOF

••HF•••

ASHFORD

•••HF••

BASHFUL
FISHFRY
WISHFUL

•••H•F•

DASHOFF
PUSHOFF
RUSHOFF
WASHOFF

•••H••F

DASHOFF
PUSHOFF
RUSHOFF
WASHOFF

HG•••••

HGWELLS

H•G••••

HAGGARD
HAGGLED
HAGGLER
HAGGLES
HEGIRAS
HIGGINS
HIGHBOY
HIGHEND
HIGHEST
HIGHHAT
HIGHLOW
HIGHTEA
HIGHTOP
HIGHWAY
HOGARTH
HOGBACK
HOGGING
HOGTIED
HOGTIES
HOGWASH
HOGWILD
HUGGERS
HUGGING
HYGIEIA
HYGIENE

H••G•••

HAGGARD
HAGGLED
HAGGLER
HAGGLES
HANGARS
HANGDOG
HANGERS
HANGING
HANGMAN
HANGMEN
HANGOFF
HANGOUT
HANGSIN
HANGSON
HANGSUP
HANGTEN
HANGUPS
HAUGHTY
HEDGERS
HEDGING
HEIGHHO
HEIGHTS
HIGGINS
HINGING
HOAGIES
HOGGING
HUGGERS
HUGGING
HUNGARY
HUNGERS
HUNGOUT

H•••G••

HALOGEN
HANDGUN
HEXAGON

H••••G•

HAULAGE
HAZINGS
HERBAGE
HEXSIGN
HIDALGO
HOSTAGE
HOTDOGS
HUMBUGS

H•••••G

HACKING
HAILING
HALOING
HALTING
HALVING
HAMBURG
HAMMING
HANDBAG
HANDING
HANGDOG
HANGING
HARDING
HARKING
HARMING
HARPING
HASHING
HASTING
HATTING
HAULING
HAWKING
HEADING
HEALING
HEAPING
HEARING
HEATING
HEAVING
HEDGING
HEEDING
HEELING
HEFTING
HELMING
HELPING
HEMMING
HERDING
HERRING
HILLING
HINGING
HINTING
HISSING
HITTING
HOAXING
HOBOING
HOCKING
HOGGING
HOLDING
HOMBURG
HONKING
HOOFING
HOOKING
HOOPING
HOOTING
HOPPING
HORNING
HORSING
HOSTING
HOUSING
HOWLING
HUFFING
HUGGING
HULKING
HULLING
HUMMING
HUNTING
HURLING
HURTING
HUSHING
HUSKING
HYPOING

•H•G•••

CHAGALL
CHAGRIN
CHIGGER
CHIGNON
CHUGGED
SHAGGED
SHOGUNS

•H••G••

CHANGED
CHANGER
CHANGES
CHARGED
CHARGER
CHARGES
CHIGGER
CHUGGED
SHAGGED
SHANGRI
SHINGLE
SHOTGUN
THOUGHT

•H•••G•

CHICAGO
PHOTOGS
THRONGS
THROUGH
ZHIVAGO

•H••••G

CHAFING
CHASING
CHEWING
CHIDING
CHIMING
PHASING
PHONING
RHYMING
SHADING
SHAKING
SHAMING
SHAPING
SHARING
SHAVING
SHEBANG
SHINDIG
SHINING
SHOEING
SHOOING
SHORING
SHOVING
SHOWDOG
SHOWING
THAWING
WHALING
WHILING
WHINING
WHITING

••H•G••

JOHNGAY

••H••G•

REHANGS

••H•••G

ACHTUNG
ECHOING

•••HG••

LITHGOW

•••H•G•

FLYHIGH
ONTHEGO
QUAHOGS
SKYHIGH

•••H••G

ARCHING
BASHING
BATHING
BUSHHOG
BUSHING
BUSHPIG
CACHING
CASHING
DASHING
DISHING
DISHRAG
ETCHING
FISHING
GASHING
GUSHING
HASHING
HUSHING
INCHING
ITCHING
JOSHING
LASHING
LATHING
MASHING
MESHING
MUSHING
NOSHING
NOTHING
PITHING
PUSHING
RUCHING
RUSHING
SIGHING
TITHING
WASHING
WASHRAG
WISHING

••••H•G

BEARHUG
BUSHHOG
ROADHOG
SANDHOG
WARTHOG

HH•••••

HHMUNRO

H•H••••

HAHNIUM

H••H•••

HAMHOCK
HASHING
HAWHAWS
HEEHAWS
HESHVAN
HIGHBOY
HIGHEND
HIGHEST
HIGHHAT
HIGHLOW
HIGHTEA
HIGHTOP
HIGHWAY
HITHERE
HOOHAHS
HOTHEAD
HUSHABY
HUSHING
HYPHENS

H•••H••

HARDHAT
HARDHIT
HARSHEN
HARSHER
HARSHLY
HATCHED
HATCHER
HATCHES
HATCHET
HAUGHTY
HEATHEN
HEATHER
HEIGHHO
HEIGHTS
HERSHEY
HIGHHAT
HITCHED
HITCHER
HITCHES
HONCHOS
HOTSHOT
HUNCHED
HUNCHES
HUTCHES

H••••H•

HEALTHY
HEARTHS
HEAVEHO
HEIGHHO
HIBACHI
HITACHI
HOOHAHS
HOOKAHS
HOOTCHY
HOWDAHS
HURRAHS
HUZZAHS

H•••••H

HANUKAH
HAWKISH
HIALEAH
HOGARTH
HOGWASH

•H•H•••

SHAHDOM
SHIHTZU

•H••H••

CHACHAS
CHATHAM
CHECHEN
CHEKHOV
CHICHEN
RHYTHMS
SHUSHED
SHUSHES
THITHER
WHETHER
WHITHER

•H•••H•

SHEATHE
SHEATHS
SHEIKHS
THATCHY
THOUGHT
WHOSWHO
WHYDAHS

•H••••H

CHEETAH
CHERISH
EHRLICH
PHARAOH
SHEILAH
THROUGH
WHITISH

••H•••H

OSHKOSH
UNHITCH

•••HH••

BUSHHOG
HIGHHAT

•••H•H•

EIGHTHS
HOOHAHS
NAPHTHA

•••H••H

FLYHIGH
JAPHETH
POOHBAH
SKYHIGH

••••HH•

HEIGHHO

HI•••••

HIALEAH
HIBACHI
HICCUPS
HICKMAN
HICKORY
HIDALGO
HIDEOUS
HIDEOUT
HIGGINS
HIGHBOY
HIGHEND
HIGHEST
HIGHHAT
HIGHLOW
HIGHTEA
HIGHTOP
HIGHWAY
HIJACKS
HIJINKS
HILAIRE
HILLARY
HILLIER
HILLING
HILLOCK
HILLTOP
HIMSELF
HINDERS
HINGING
HINNIES
HINTING
HINTSAT
HIPBONE
HIPBOOT
HIPNESS
HIPPEST
HIPPIES
HIPROOF
HIPSTER
HIRABLE
HIRESON
HIRSUTE
HISPANO
HISSERS
HISSING
HISTORY
HITACHI
HITCHED
HITCHER
HITCHES
HITHERE
HITLESS
HITLIST
HITTERS
HITTING
HITTITE

H•I••••

HAILING
HAIRCUT
HAIRDOS
HAIRDYE
HAIRIER
HAIRNET
HAIRPIN
HAITIAN
HEIFERS
HEIFETZ
HEIGHHO
HEIGHTS
HEINOUS
HEIRESS
HEISTED
HOISTED

H••I•••

HABITAT
HABITED
HABITUE
HALIBUT
HALIFAX
HALITES
HAMITES
HAMITIC
HAMITUP
HARICOT
HASIDIM
HAZIEST
HAZINGS
HEGIRAS
HELICAL
HELICES
HELICON
HELIPAD
HELIXES
HIJINKS
HOLIDAY
HOLIEST
HOMIEST
HOMINEM
HOMINID
HORIZON
HOSIERS
HOSIERY
HUMIDLY
HUMIDOR
HYGIEIA
HYGIENE

H•••I••

HACKIES
HACKING
HADRIAN
HAFNIUM
HAHNIUM
HAILING
HAIRIER
HAITIAN
HALOING
HALTING
HALVING
HAMMILY
HAMMING
HANDIER
HANDILY
HANDING
HANGING
HANKIES
HAPPIER
HAPPILY
HARDIER
HARDILY
HARDING
HARKING
HARMING
HARPIES
HARPING
HARPIST
HARRIED
HARRIER
HARRIES
HARRIET
HASHING
HASTIER
HASTILY
HASTING
HATPINS
HATTING
HAULING
HAWKING
HAWKINS
HAWKISH
HAYRIDE
HAYWIRE
HEADIER
HEADILY
HEADING
HEALING
HEAPING
HEARING
HEATING
HEAVIER
HEAVIES
HEAVILY
HEAVING
HEDGING
HEEDING
HEELING
HEFTIER
HEFTILY
HEFTING
HELLION
HELMING
HELOISE
HELPING
HEMLINE
HEMMING
HENBITS
HERDING
HERMITS
HEROICS
HEROINE
HEROISM
HERRING
HERRIOT
HESSIAN
HEXSIGN
HIGGINS
HILAIRE
HILLIER
HILLING
HINGING
HINNIES
HINTING
HIPPIES
HISSING
HITLIST
HITTING
HITTITE
HOAGIES
HOARIER
HOAXING
HOBBIES
HOBBITS
HOBOING
HOCKING
HOGGING
HOGTIED
HOGTIES
HOGWILD
HOLDING
HOLLIES
HOLMIUM
HONKING
HOOFING
HOOKING
HOOPING
HOOSIER
HOOTING
HOPKINS
HOPPING
HORNING
HORNIST
HORRIFY
HORSIER
HORSING
HOSKINS
HOSPICE
HOSTILE
HOSTING
HOTLINE
HOTLIPS
HOTTIPS
HOTWIRE
HOUDINI
HOUSING
HOWLING
HUBBIES
HUFFIER
HUFFILY
HUFFING
HUGGING
HULKING
HULLING
HUMMING
HUNTING
HURLING
HURRIED
HURRIES
HURTING
HUSHING
HUSKIER
HUSKIES
HUSKILY
HUSKING
HUSSIES
HYALINE
HYBRIDS
HYPOING

H••••I•

HAIRPIN
HALFWIT
HAMELIN
HAMITIC
HANDSIN
HANGSIN
HARDHIT
HASIDIM
HEADPIN
HEADSIN
HEBRAIC
HENDRIX
HENREID
HEPARIN
HEPATIC
HERETIC
HOBNAIL
HOLBEIN
HOMERIC
HOMINID
HOOFSIT
HOPTOIT
HORATIO
HOWBEIT
HUSSEIN
HYGIEIA

H•••••I

HAVARTI
HIBACHI
HITACHI
HOUDINI
HYUNDAI

•HI••••

CHIANTI
CHICAGO
CHICANA
CHICANO
CHICHEN

CHICKEN
CHICORY
CHIDING
CHIEFLY
CHIFFON
CHIGGER
CHIGNON
CHILEAN
CHILIES
CHILLED
CHILLER
CHIMERA
CHIMING
CHIMNEY
CHINESE
CHINKED
CHINNED
CHINOOK
CHINTZY
CHINUPS
CHIPPED
CHIPPER
CHIPSIN
CHIRPED
CHISELS
CHITTER
OHIOANS
PHIDIAS
PHILBIN
PHILLIP
PHILTER
PHILTRE
PHINEAS
RHIZOME
SHIATSU
SHIELDS
SHIFTED
SHIHTZU
SHIITES
SHILLED
SHIMMER
SHINDIG
SHINERS
SHINGLE
SHINIER
SHINING
SHINNED
SHIPMAN
SHIPMEN
SHIPOUT
SHIPPED
SHIPPER
SHIRKED
SHIRKER
SHIRLEY
SHIRRED
SHIVERS
THICKEN
THICKER
THICKET
THICKLY
THIERRY
THIEVED
THIEVES
THIMBLE
THINAIR
THINICE
THINKER
THINKOF
THINKUP
THINMAN
THINNED
THINNER
THIRDLY
THIRSTS
THIRSTY
THISTLE
THITHER
WHIFFED
WHILING
WHIMPER
WHINERS
WHINING
WHIPPED
WHIPPET
WHIPSAW
WHIPSUP
WHIRLED
WHIRRED
WHISKED
WHISKER
WHISKEY
WHISPER
WHISTLE
WHITENS
WHITEST
WHITHER
WHITING
WHITISH
WHITMAN
WHITNEY
WHITTLE
WHIZKID
WHIZZED
WHIZZES
ZHIVAGO

•H•I•••

CHAINED
CHAIRED
CHAISES
CHOICER
CHOICES
CHRISMS
CHRISTI
CHRISTO
CHRISTY
SHEIKHS
SHEILAE
SHEILAH
SHEILAS
SHIITES
SHRIEKS
SHRIFTS
SHRIKES
SHRILLS
SHRILLY
SHRIMPS
SHRINER
SHRINES
SHRINKS
SHRIVEL
SHRIVER
SHRIVES
SHTICKS
THEISTS
THRIFTS
THRIFTY
THRILLS
THRIVED
THRIVES

•H••I••

CHAFING
CHALICE
CHARIER
CHARILY
CHARIOT
CHARITY
CHASING
CHEMISE
CHEMIST
CHENIER
CHERISH
CHEVIED
CHEVIES
CHEVIOT
CHEWIER
CHEWING
CHIDING
CHILIES
CHIMING
CHORINE
CHORIZO
EHRLICH
PHASING
PHIDIAS
PHOBIAS
PHOBICS
PHONICS
PHONIER
PHONIES
PHONILY
PHONING
PHYSICS
RHENIUM
RHODIUM
RHYMING
SHADIER
SHADILY
SHADING
SHAKIER
SHAKILY
SHAKING
SHAMING
SHAPING
SHAPIRO
SHARING
SHAVING
SHERIFF
SHINIER
SHINING
SHOEING
SHOOING
SHOOINS
SHORING
SHOVING
SHOWIER
SHOWILY
SHOWING
THAWING
THINICE
THORIUM
THULIUM
WHALING
WHILING
WHINING
WHITING
WHITISH

•H•••I•

CHABLIS
CHAGRIN
CHALLIS
CHAMOIS
CHAOTIC
CHAPLIN
CHARLIE
CHARMIN
CHASSIS
CHEAPIE
CHECKIN
CHEERIO
CHERVIL
CHIPSIN
CHRONIC
DHURRIE
GHERKIN
PHASEIN
PHILBIN
PHILLIP
PHOENIX
PHRENIC
PHYLLIS
SHAREIN
SHELTIE
SHERWIN
SHINDIG
SHOWBIZ
SHOWNIN
SHOWSIN
SHUTSIN
THATSIT
THEREIN
THESPIS
THINAIR
THREWIN
THROWIN
WHEELIE
WHEREIN
WHIZKID

•H••••I

CHAPATI
CHIANTI
CHRISTI
SHANGRI
SHARPEI
SHASTRI

••HI•••

ACHIEST
ACHIEVE
ASHIEST
ATHIRST
CAHIERS
DEHISCE
ECHIDNA
ECHINUS
ETHICAL
EXHIBIT
INHIBIT
MOHICAN
REHIRED
REHIRES
SCHIRRA
SCHISMS
TSHIRTS
UNHITCH
VEHICLE
WAHINES

••H•I••

ATHEISM
ATHEIST
COHEIRS
DAHLIAS
ECHOING
ETHNICS
HAHNIUM
MOHAIRS
SCHMIDT
SCHWINN

••H••I•

AMHARIC
APHELIA
BAHRAIN
BOHEMIA
COHABIT
EXHIBIT
INHABIT
INHERIT
INHIBIT
JOHNNIE
MAHALIA
MAHARIS
OPHELIA

••H•••I

ASHANTI
PAHLAVI
SCHATZI
SCHERZI

•••HI••

AKIHITO
ANTHILL
ARCHIES
ARCHING
ARCHIVE
BASHING
BATHING
BEEHIVE
BETHINK
BUSHIDO
BUSHIER
BUSHING
CACHING
CASHIER
CASHING
COCHISE
COWHIDE
CUSHIER
CUSHION
DASHIKI
DASHING
DISHING
DUCHIES
EBWHITE
ETCHING
FASHION
FISHIER
FISHILY
FISHING
FLYHIGH
GASHING
GOTHICS
GUSHIER
GUSHING
HASHING
HUSHING
INCHING
ITCHIER
ITCHING
JOEHILL
JOSHING
KACHINA
LASHING
LATHING
LITHIUM
MACHINA
MACHINE
MASHIES
MASHING
MATHIAS
MENHIRS
MESHING
MISHITS
MRCHIPS
MUSHIER
MUSHILY
MUSHING
MUZHIKS
NOBHILL
NOSHING
NOTHING
ORCHIDS
OUTHITS
PACHISI
PITHIER
PITHILY
PITHING
PUSHIER
PUSHILY
PUSHING
PYTHIAS
RAWHIDE
RESHIPS
RETHINK
RUCHING
RUSHING
SAMHILL
SASHIMI
SIGHING
SIKHISM
SKYHIGH
SOPHISM
SOPHIST
SWAHILI
TECHIES
TITHING
TOSHIBA
URCHINS
WASHING
WICHITA
WISHING
YESHIVA

•••H•I•

ALLHAIL
ANAHEIM
ARCHAIC
BATHOIL
BOTHNIA
BRAHMIN
BUSHPIG
CATHAIR
DAPHNIS
ENCHAIN
FUCHSIA
GUTHRIE
KASHMIR
MIKHAIL
NIGHTIE
PUSHKIN
PUSHPIN
REDHAIR
RUSHDIE
UNCHAIN

•••H••I

AFGHANI
DASHIKI
OMPHALI
PACHISI
SASHIMI
SWAHILI

••••HI•

AIRSHIP
BASEHIT
CYNTHIA
DAUPHIN
DOLPHIN
EDAPHIC
GEEWHIZ
GENGHIS
GRAPHIC
HARDHIT
JOACHIM
KINSHIP
LAUGHIN
LITCHIS
MEMPHIS
MENUHIN
PITCHIN
PSYCHIC
PUNCHIN
PYRRHIC
RITCHIE
ROUGHIT
TEACHIN
TOUGHIE
TROPHIC
WARSHIP
WATCHIT
WEIGHIN
WORSHIP
XANTHIC

••••H•I

BALIHAI
BOLSHOI

•••••HI

ACANTHI
BELUSHI
BRONCHI
GNOCCHI
HIBACHI
HITACHI
KARACHI
MALACHI
NOGUCHI

H•J••••

HIJACKS
HIJINKS

H••J•••

HEYJUDE

••H•J••

JOHNJAY

H••K•••

HACKERS
HACKETT
HACKIES
HACKING
HACKLES
HACKMAN
HACKNEY
HACKSAW
HANKERS
HANKIES
HARKENS
HARKING
HAWKERS
HAWKEYE
HAWKING
HAWKINS
HAWKISH
HECKLED
HECKLER
HECKLES
HICKMAN
HICKORY
HOCKING
HONKERS
HONKING
HOOKAHS
HOOKING
HOOKSUP
HOOKUPS
HOPKINS
HOSKINS
HULKING
HUNKERS
HUSKERS
HUSKIER
HUSKIES
HUSKILY
HUSKING

H•••K••

HANUKAH
HEARKEN
HOBOKEN

H••••K•

HIJACKS
HIJINKS
HOECAKE
HOLYOKE
HOTCAKE

H•••••K

HADDOCK
HAMHOCK
HAMMOCK
HANCOCK
HASSOCK
HATRACK
HAUBERK
HAYFORK
HAYRACK
HEMLOCK
HENPECK
HILLOCK
HOGBACK
HOLMOAK
HOLYARK
HUMMOCK

•H•K•••

CHEKHOV
CHOKERS
CHOKEUP
CHUKKAS
CHUKKER
SHAKERS
SHAKEUP
SHAKIER
SHAKILY
SHAKING
SHAKOES
SHEKELS

•H••K••

CHALKED
CHALKUP
CHECKED
CHECKER
CHECKIN
CHECKUP
CHICKEN
CHINKED
CHUCKED
CHUCKLE
CHUKKAS
CHUKKER
GHERKIN
SHACKLE
SHANKAR
SHANKED
SHARKEY
SHEIKHS
SHIRKED
SHIRKER
SHOCKED
SHOCKER
SHOOKUP
SHRIKES
SHUCKED
SHUCKER
THANKED
THICKEN
THICKER
THICKET
THICKLY
THINKER
THINKOF
THINKUP
WHACKED
WHISKED
WHISKER
WHISKEY
WHIZKID

•H•••K•

CHOMSKY
SHRIEKS
SHRINKS
SHTICKS
THWACKS

•H••••K

CHINOOK
SHYLOCK

••HK•••

OSHKOSH

••H••K•

MOHAWKS
REHOOKS
UNHOOKS

••H•••K

OKHOTSK
SCHLOCK

•••HK••

KISHKES
PUSHKIN

•••H•K•

DASHIKI
MUZHIKS

•••H••K

BETHINK
GOSHAWK
HAMHOCK
POTHOOK
RECHALK
RECHECK
RETHINK
SKYHOOK
YASHMAK

••••H•K

KAISHEK
YITZHAK

H•L••••

HALCYON
HALFDAN
HALFWAY
HALFWIT
HALIBUT
HALIFAX
HALITES
HALLOWS
HALLWAY
HALOGEN
HALOING
HALSTON
HALTERS
HALTING
HALVING
HALYARD
HELDOFF
HELDOUT
HELICAL
HELICES
HELICON
HELIPAD
HELIXES
HELLCAT
HELLENE
HELLERS
HELLION
HELLMAN
HELMETS
HELMING
HELOISE
HELOTRY
HELPERS
HELPFUL
HELPING
HELPOUT
HILAIRE
HILLARY
HILLIER
HILLING
HILLOCK
HILLTOP
HOLBEIN
HOLDERS
HOLDING
HOLDOFF
HOLDOUT
HOLDSON
HOLDSTO
HOLDSUP
HOLDUPS
HOLEDUP
HOLEOUT
HOLESUP
HOLIDAY
HOLIEST
HOLLAND
HOLLERS
HOLLIES
HOLLOWS
HOLMIUM
HOLMOAK
HOLSTER
HOLYARK
HOLYCOW
HOLYOKE
HOLYSEE
HOLYWAR
HULKING
HULLERS
HULLING
HULLOED

H••L•••

HAILING
HALLOWS
HALLWAY
HAMLETS
HAPLESS
HATLESS
HAULAGE
HAULERS
HAULING
HAULOFF
HAULSUP
HAYLOFT
HEALALL
HEALERS
HEALING
HEALTHY
HEELERS
HEELING
HEELTAP
HELLCAT
HELLENE
HELLERS
HELLION
HELLMAN
HEMLINE
HEMLOCK
HEWLETT
HIALEAH
HILLARY
HILLIER
HILLING
HILLOCK
HILLTOP
HITLESS
HITLIST
HOLLAND
HOLLERS
HOLLIES
HOLLOWS
HOTLINE
HOTLIPS
HOWLERS
HOWLING
HULLERS
HULLING
HULLOED
HURLERS
HURLING
HYALINE

H•••L••

HAARLEM
HACKLES
HAGGLED
HAGGLER
HAGGLES
HAMELIN
HANDLED
HANDLER
HANDLES
HASSLED
HASSLES
HECKLED
HECKLER
HECKLES
HEDDLES
HEMSLEY
HERALDS
HGWELLS
HIDALGO
HIGHLOW
HOBBLED
HOBBLES
HOODLUM
HOOPLAS
HOSTLER
HOWELLS
HUDDLED
HUDDLES
HUMBLED
HUMBLER
HUMBLES
HUNTLEY
HURDLED
HURDLER
HURDLES
HURTLED
HURTLES
HUSTLED
HUSTLER
HUSTLES

H••••L•

HAMMILY
HANDILY
HANSOLO
HAPPILY
HARDILY
HARSHLY
HASTILY
HEADILY
HEALALL
HEAVILY
HEFTILY
HERBALS
HERCULE
HERSELF
HGWELLS
HIMSELF
HIRABLE
HOGWILD
HOSTELS
HOSTILE
HOWELLS
HUBBELL
HUFFILY
HUMANLY
HUMIDLY
HUSKILY
HYMNALS

H•••••L

HANDFUL
HARMFUL
HATEFUL
HEALALL
HEEDFUL
HELICAL
HELPFUL
HOBNAIL
HOOTOWL
HOPEFUL
HUBBELL
HUMERAL
HURTFUL

•HL••••

CHLORAL
PHLOXES

•H•L•••

CHALETS
CHALICE
CHALKED
CHALKUP
CHALLIS
CHELSEA
CHILEAN
CHILIES
CHILLED
CHILLER
CHOLLAS
EHRLICH
PHALANX
PHILBIN
PHILLIP
PHILTER
PHILTRE
PHYLLIS
SHALALA
SHALLOT
SHALLOW
SHALOMS
SHELDON
SHELLAC
SHELLED
SHELLER
SHELLEY
SHELTER
SHELTIE
SHELTON
SHELVED
SHELVES
SHILLED
SHYLOCK
THALERS
THULIUM
WHALERS
WHALING
WHELPED
WHILING

•H••L••

CHABLIS
CHALLIS
CHAPLET
CHAPLIN
CHARLES
CHARLEY
CHARLIE
CHEMLAB
CHILLED
CHILLER
CHOLLAS
PHILLIP
PHYLLIS
SHALLOT
SHALLOW
SHEILAE
SHEILAH
SHEILAS
SHELLAC
SHELLED
SHELLER
SHELLEY
SHIELDS
SHILLED
SHIRLEY
SHRILLS

SHRILLY
THEBLOB
THRALLS
THRILLS
WHEELED
WHEELER
WHEELIE
WHIRLED
WHORLED

•H•••L•
CHAGALL
CHAPELS
CHARILY
CHEAPLY
CHIEFLY
CHISELS
CHORALE
CHORALS
CHORTLE
CHUCKLE
GHASTLY
GHOSTLY
PHENOLS
PHONILY
SHACKLE
SHADILY
SHAKILY
SHALALA
SHAMBLE
SHAPELY
SHARPLY
SHEERLY
SHEKELS
SHEWOLF
SHINGLE
SHOOFLY
SHORTLY
SHOVELS
SHOWILY
SHRILLS
SHRILLY
SHUFFLE
SHUTTLE
THICKLY
THIMBLE
THIRDLY
THISTLE
THRALLS
THRILLS
THYSELF
WHEEDLE
WHISTLE
WHITTLE

•H••••L
CHAGALL
CHANCEL
CHANNEL
CHATTEL
CHERVIL
CHLORAL
CHUNNEL
PHRASAL
SHAWWAL
SHRIVEL
THERMAL

••HL•••
ASHLAND
ASHLARS
ASHLESS
ATHLETE
DAHLIAS
PAHLAVI
SCHLEPP
SCHLEPS
SCHLOCK

••H•L••
APHELIA
BEHOLDS
ECHELON
EXHALED
EXHALES
INHALED
INHALER
INHALES
MAHALIA
OPHELIA
OTHELLO
SCHOLAR
UPHOLDS

••H••L•
OTHELLO
REHEALS
REHEELS
SCHOOLS
VEHICLE

••H•••L
ETHANOL
ETHICAL
ISHMAEL
NAHUATL

•••HL••
COCHLEA
HIGHLOW

•••H•L•
AIRHOLE
ANTHILL
ARMHOLE
ASPHALT
BETHELS
BOGHOLE
BUSHELS
DRYHOLE
EYEHOLE
FISHILY
FOXHOLE
ISOHELS
JOEHILL
KEYHOLE
LIGHTLY
LITHELY
MANHOLE
MICHELE
MUSHILY
NICHOLS
NIGHTLY
NOBHILL
OMPHALI
PINHOLE
PITHILY
POTHOLE
PUSHILY
RATHOLE
RECHALK
RIGHTLY
SAMHILL
SIGHTLY
SWAHILI
TIGHTLY
TOEHOLD
WILHELM
WYCHELM

•••H••L
ALLHAIL
ALLHEAL
ANTHILL
BASHFUL
BATHOIL
JOEHILL
LOWHEEL
MICHAEL
MIKHAIL
NOBHILL
RAPHAEL
SAMHILL
TARHEEL
WISHFUL

••••HL•
APISHLY
BRASHLY
EARTHLY
FRESHLY
HARSHLY
MONTHLY
PLUSHLY
ROUGHLY
TOUGHLY

••••H•L
ALCOHOL
GASOHOL
MARSHAL
MENTHOL
NARWHAL
PASCHAL
SATCHEL

H•M••••
HAMBURG
HAMELIN
HAMHOCK
HAMITES
HAMITIC
HAMITUP
HAMLETS
HAMMERS
HAMMETT
HAMMILY
HAMMING
HAMMOCK
HAMMOND
HAMPERS
HAMPTON
HAMSTER
HEMLINE
HEMLOCK
HEMMERS
HEMMING
HEMSLEY
HHMUNRO
HIMSELF
HOMBRES
HOMBURG
HOMERED
HOMERIC
HOMERUN
HOMIEST
HOMINEM
HOMINID
HOMONYM
HUMANLY
HUMBLED
HUMBLER
HUMBLES
HUMBUGS
HUMDRUM
HUMERAL
HUMERUS
HUMIDLY
HUMIDOR
HUMMERS
HUMMING
HUMMOCK
HUMORED
HUMOURS
HYMNALS

H••M•••
HAEMATO
HAMMERS
HAMMETT
HAMMILY
HAMMING
HAMMOCK
HAMMOND
HARMFUL
HARMING
HARMONY
HAYMOWS
HELMETS
HELMING
HEMMERS
HEMMING
HERMANN
HERMITS
HETMANS
HOLMIUM
HOLMOAK
HORMONE
HUMMERS
HUMMING
HUMMOCK

H•••M••
HACKMAN
HANGMAN
HANGMEN
HARTMAN
HEADMAN
HEADMEN
HELLMAN
HICKMAN
HOFFMAN
HOUSMAN

H••••M•
HANSOMS
HOWCOME

H•••••M
HAARLEM
HAFNIUM
HAHNIUM
HASIDIM
HEROISM
HOLMIUM
HOMINEM
HOMONYM
HOODLUM
HUMDRUM

•HM••••
HHMUNRO

•H•M•••
CHAMBER
CHAMFER
CHAMOIS
CHAMPED
CHEMISE
CHEMIST
CHEMLAB
CHIMERA
CHIMING
CHIMNEY
CHOMPED
CHOMSKY
CHUMMED
RHOMBUS
RHUMBAS
RHYMERS
RHYMING
SHAMANS
SHAMBLE
SHAMING
SHAMMED
SHAMPOO
SHIMMER
THIMBLE
THOMSON
THUMBED
THUMPED
THUMPER
WHAMMED
WHIMPER
WHOMPED

•H••M••
CHAPMAN
CHAPMEN
CHARMED
CHARMER
CHARMIN
CHROMES
CHUMMED
SHAMMED
SHERMAN
SHIMMER
SHIPMAN
SHIPMEN
SHOWMAN
SHOWMEN
SHRIMPS
THERMAL
THERMOS
THINMAN
THURMAN
WHAMMED
WHITMAN

•H•••M•
CHRISMS
PHENOMS
PHONEME
RHIZOME
RHYTHMS
SHALOMS

•H••••M
CHATHAM
CHETRUM
KHAYYAM
PHANTOM
RHENIUM
RHODIUM
SHAHDOM
THEOREM
THORIUM
THULIUM

••HM•••
ISHMAEL
SCHMEER
SCHMIDT
SCHMOES
SCHMOOS

••H•M••
ASHAMED
ATHOMES
BAHAMAS
BOHEMIA
DAHOMEY
INHUMAN
SCHEMAS
SCHEMED
SCHEMER
SCHEMES

••H••M•
ASHRAMS
MAHATMA
SCHISMS

••H•••M
ATHEISM
HAHNIUM

•••HM••
BATHMAT
BRAHMAN
BRAHMAS
BRAHMIN
BUSHMAN
BUSHMEN
ISTHMUS
KASHMIR
RICHMAN
TUCHMAN
YASHMAK

•••H•M•
ALCHEMY
ANTHEMS
FATHOMS
GRAHAME
GRAHAMS
MAYHEMS
NOTHOME
RUNHOME
SACHEMS
SASHIMI

•••H••M
ANAHEIM
LITHIUM
SHAHDOM
SIKHISM
SOPHISM
WILHELM
WYCHELM

••••HM•
DRACHMA
MEGOHMS
RHYTHMS
SATCHMO

••••H•M
ABRAHAM
APOTHEM
BEECHAM
BENTHAM
BINGHAM
BRIGHAM
CHATHAM
FORDHAM
FULGHUM
GINGHAM
GRISHAM
JOACHIM
KETCHAM
MARKHAM
MAUGHAM
MITCHUM
SORGHUM

H•N••••
HANCOCK
HANDBAG
HANDCAR
HANDFUL
HANDGUN
HANDIER
HANDILY
HANDING
HANDLED
HANDLER
HANDLES
HANDOFF
HANDOUT
HANDSAW
HANDSET
HANDSIN
HANDSON
HANDSUP
HANGARS
HANGDOG
HANGERS
HANGING
HANGMAN
HANGMEN
HANGOFF
HANGOUT
HANGSIN
HANGSON
HANGSUP
HANGTEN
HANGUPS
HANKERS
HANKIES
HANOVER
HANSARP
HANSOLO
HANSOMS
HANUKAH
HENBANE
HENBITS
HENCOOP
HENDRIX
HENNAED
HENNERY
HENPECK
HENREID
HINDERS
HINGING
HINNIES
HINTING
HINTSAT
HONCHOS
HONESTY
HONEYED
HONKERS
HONKING
HONORED
HONOREE
HONORER
HONOURS
HUNCHED
HUNCHES
HUNDRED
HUNGARY
HUNGERS
HUNGOUT
HUNKERS
HUNTERS
HUNTING
HUNTLEY

H••N•••
HAFNIUM
HAHNIUM
HARNESS
HAUNTED
HEINOUS
HENNAED
HENNERY
HEXNUTS
HINNIES
HIPNESS
HOBNAIL
HOBNOBS
HORNETS
HORNING
HORNIST
HORNSBY
HOTNESS
HOUNDED
HYMNALS
HYUNDAI

H•••N••
HACKNEY
HAIRNET
HAVENOT
HAZINGS
HHMUNRO
HIJINKS
HOMINEM
HOMINID
HOMONYM
HOSANNA
HUMANLY

H••••N•
HACKING
HAILING
HALOING
HALTING
HALVING
HAMMING
HAMMOND
HANDING
HANGING
HAPPENS
HARDENS
HARDING
HARKENS
HARKING
HARMING
HARMONY
HARPING
HASHING
HASTENS
HASTING
HATPINS
HATTING
HAULING
HAWKING
HAWKINS
HEADING
HEALING
HEAPING
HEARING
HEATING
HEAVENS
HEAVING
HEDGING
HEEDING
HEELING
HEFTING
HELLENE
HELMING
HELPING
HEMLINE
HEMMING
HENBANE
HERDING
HERMANN
HEROINE
HERRING
HETMANS
HIGGINS
HIGHEND
HILLING
HINGING
HINTING
HIPBONE
HISPANO
HISSING
HITTING
HOAXING
HOBOING
HOCKING
HOGGING
HOLDING
HOLLAND
HONKING
HOOFING
HOOKING
HOOPING
HOOTING
HOPKINS
HOPPING
HORMONE
HORNING
HORSING
HOSANNA
HOSKINS
HOSTING
HOTLINE
HOUDINI
HOUSING
HOWLING
HOYDENS
HUFFING
HUGGING
HULKING
HULLING
HUMMING
HUNTING
HURLING
HURTING
HUSBAND
HUSHING
HUSKING
HYALINE
HYDRANT
HYGIENE
HYPHENS
HYPOING

H•••••N
HACKMAN
HADRIAN
HAIRPIN
HAITIAN
HALCYON
HALFDAN
HALOGEN
HALSTON
HAMELIN
HAMPTON
HANDGUN
HANDSIN
HANDSON
HANGMAN
HANGMEN
HANGSIN
HANGSON
HANGTEN
HARDPAN
HARDWON
HARPOON
HARPSON
HARSHEN
HARTMAN
HASBEEN
HEADMAN
HEADMEN
HEADPIN
HEADSIN
HEARKEN
HEARTEN
HEATHEN
HELICON
HELLION
HELLMAN
HEPARIN
HEPBURN
HERMANN
HESHVAN
HESSIAN
HEXAGON
HEXSIGN
HICKMAN
HIRESON
HOARSEN
HOBOKEN
HOEDOWN
HOFFMAN
HOLBEIN
HOLDSON
HOMERUN
HORIZON
HOUSMAN
HOUSTON
HUSSEIN

•H•N•••
CHANCED
CHANCEL
CHANCES
CHANGED
CHANGER
CHANGES
CHANNEL
CHANSON
CHANTED
CHANTER
CHANTEY
CHENIER
CHINESE
CHINKED
CHINNED
CHINOOK
CHINTZY
CHINUPS
CHUNNEL
PHANTOM
PHENOLS
PHENOMS
PHINEAS
PHONEME
PHONICS
PHONIER
PHONIES
PHONILY
PHONING
RHENIUM
SHANANA
SHANGRI
SHANKAR
SHANKED
SHANNON
SHANTER
SHINDIG
SHINERS
SHINGLE
SHINIER
SHINING
SHINNED
SHUNNED
SHUNTED
SHYNESS
THANKED
THINAIR
THINICE
THINKER
THINKOF
THINKUP
THINMAN
THINNED
THINNER
THUNDER
WHINERS
WHINING

•H••N••
CHAINED
CHANNEL
CHIANTI
CHIGNON
CHIMNEY
CHINNED
CHRONIC
CHUNNEL
CHURNED
CHUTNEY
HHMUNRO
PHOENIX
PHRENIC
SHANNON
SHATNER
SHAWNEE
SHINNED
SHOWNIN
SHRINER
SHRINES
SHRINKS
SHUNNED
THINNED
THINNER
THRONES
THRONGS
WHATNOT
WHITNEY

•H•••N•
CHAFING
CHASING
CHEWING
CHICANA
CHICANO
CHIDING
CHIMING
CHORINE
OHIOANS
PHALANX
PHARYNX
PHASING
PHONING
PHOTONS
RHYMING
SHADING
SHAKING
SHAMANS
SHAMING
SHANANA
SHAPING
SHARING
SHAVING
SHEBANG
SHINING
SHOEING
SHOGUNS
SHOOING
SHOOINS
SHORING
SHOVING
SHOWING
THAWING
WHALING
WHILING
WHINING
WHITENS
WHITING

•H••••N
CHAGRIN
CHANSON
CHAPLIN
CHAPMAN
CHAPMEN
CHARMIN
CHASTEN
CHEAPEN
CHECHEN
CHECKIN
CHEVRON
CHICHEN
CHICKEN
CHIFFON
CHIGNON
CHILEAN
CHIPSIN
GHERKIN
PHAETON
PHASEIN
PHILBIN
SHANNON
SHAREIN
SHARPEN
SHELDON
SHELTON
SHERMAN
SHERWIN
SHIPMAN
SHIPMEN
SHODDEN
SHORTEN
SHOTGUN
SHOWMAN
SHOWMEN
SHOWNIN
SHOWSIN
SHUTSIN
THEREIN
THEREON
THICKEN
THINMAN
THOMSON
THREWIN
THROWIN
THURMAN
WHARTON
WHAUDEN
WHEATON
WHEREIN
WHITMAN

••HN•••
ETHNICS
HAHNIUM
JOHNDOE
JOHNGAY
JOHNJAY
JOHNNIE
JOHNSON
SCHNAPS

••H•N••
ACHENES
ASHANTI
ECHINUS
ENHANCE
ETHANOL
JOHANNA
JOHNNIE
KAHUNAS
MAHONEY
REHANGS
UNHANDS
UNHANDY
WAHINES
WCHANDY

••H••N•
ACHTUNG
ASHCANS
ASHLAND
DEHORNS
ECHIDNA
ECHOING
JOHANNA
SCHWINN

••H•••N
ACHERON
ACHESON
BAHRAIN
ECHELON
INHUMAN
ITHACAN
JOHNSON
MOHICAN
SAHARAN
SCHWINN
TEHERAN

•••HN••
BOTHNIA
DAPHNIS
FISHNET

•••H•N•
AFGHANI
AFGHANS
ANTHONY
ARCHING
ARCHONS
BASHING
BATHING
BETHANY
BETHINK
BUSHING
CACHING
CASHING
COWHAND
DABHAND
DASHING
DIAHANN
DISHING
ENCHANT
ETCHING
EUPHONY
FISHING
GASHING
GUSHING
HASHING
HIGHEND
HUSHING
HYPHENS
INCHING
ITCHING
JOBHUNT
JOSHING
KACHINA
LASHING
LATHING
LICHENS
MACHINA
MACHINE
MANHUNT
MASHING
MESHING
METHANE
MIGHTNT
MUDHENS
MUSHING
NOSHING
NOTHING
OFFHAND
OLDHAND
ORPHANS
PEAHENS
PITHING
PUSHING
PYTHONS
RETHINK
RUCHING
RUSHING
SIGHING
SIPHONS
TERHUNE
TITHING
URCHINS
UTAHANS
WASHING
WISHING

•••H••N
BIGHORN
BRAHMAN
BRAHMIN
BUSHMAN
BUSHMEN
CALHOUN
COCHRAN
CUSHION
DIAHANN
DISHPAN
ENCHAIN
FASHION
FOGHORN
HESHVAN
IDAHOAN
INKHORN
KATHRYN
LEGHORN
LIGHTEN
ORPHEAN
PUSHKIN
PUSHPIN
RICHMAN
RIGHTON
SAXHORN
SICHUAN
SOTHERN
TIGHTEN
TINHORN
TUCHMAN
TYPHOON
UNCHAIN
UNSHORN

••••HN•
ARACHNE
KRISHNA
STJOHNS

••••H•N
AGAKHAN
CATCHON
CHECHEN
CHICHEN
DAUPHIN
DOLPHIN
EARTHEN
EREWHON
FRESHEN
GRYPHON
HARSHEN
HEATHEN
KEESHAN
KITCHEN
LAUGHIN
MADCHEN
MARCHEN
MARCHON
MCLUHAN
MCMAHON
MENUHIN
MOORHEN
PITCHIN
PUNCHIN
PYNCHON
ROUGHEN
SAYWHEN
SIOBHAN
STEPHEN
TEACHIN
TOUCHON
TOUGHEN
VAUGHAN
WEIGHIN
XANTHAN

•••••HN
BIGJOHN

HO•••••
HOAGIES
HOARDED
HOARDER
HOARIER
HOARSEN
HOARSER
HOAXERS
HOAXING
HOBBIES
HOBBITS
HOBBLED
HOBBLES
HOBNAIL
HOBNOBS
HOBOING
HOBOKEN
HOCKING
HOECAKE
HOEDOWN
HOFBRAU
HOFFMAN
HOGARTH
HOGBACK
HOGGING
HOGTIED
HOGTIES
HOGWASH
HOGWILD
HOISTED
HOLBEIN
HOLDERS
HOLDING
HOLDOFF
HOLDOUT
HOLDSON
HOLDSTO
HOLDSUP
HOLDUPS
HOLEDUP
HOLEOUT
HOLESUP
HOLIDAY
HOLIEST
HOLLAND
HOLLERS
HOLLIES
HOLLOWS
HOLMIUM
HOLMOAK
HOLSTER
HOLYARK
HOLYCOW
HOLYOKE
HOLYSEE
HOLYWAR
HOMBRES
HOMBURG
HOMERED
HOMERIC
HOMERUN
HOMIEST
HOMINEM
HOMINID
HOMONYM
HONCHOS
HONESTY
HONEYED
HONKERS
HONKING
HONORED
HONOREE
HONORER
HONOURS
HOODLUM
HOODOOS
HOOFERS
HOOFING
HOOFSIT
HOOHAHS
HOOKAHS
HOOKING
HOOKSUP
HOOKUPS
HOOPING
HOOPLAS
HOOPOES
HOOSIER
HOOTCHY
HOOTERS
HOOTING
HOOTOWL
HOOTSAT
HOPEFUL
HOPKINS
HOPOVER
HOPPERS
HOPPING
HOPSOFF
HOPTOIT
HORATIO
HORIZON
HORMONE
HORNETS
HORNING
HORNIST
HORNSBY
HORRIFY
HORRORS
HORSIER
HORSING
HOSANNA
HOSIERS
HOSIERY
HOSKINS
HOSPICE
HOSTAGE
HOSTELS
HOSTESS
HOSTILE
HOSTING
HOSTLER
HOTBEDS
HOTCAKE
HOTCAPS
HOTCARS
HOTDOGS
HOTFOOT
HOTHEAD
HOTLINE
HOTLIPS
HOTNESS
HOTPOTS
HOTRODS
HOTSEAT
HOTSHOT
HOTSPOT
HOTSPUR
HOTTEST
HOTTIPS
HOTTUBS
HOTWARS
HOTWIRE
HOUDINI
HOUNDED
HOUSING
HOUSMAN
HOUSTON
HOVERED
HOVERER
HOWARDS
HOWBEIT
HOWCOME
HOWDAHS
HOWELLS
HOWEVER
HOWLERS
HOWLING
HOYDENS

H•O••••
HOODLUM
HOODOOS
HOOFERS
HOOFING
HOOFSIT
HOOHAHS
HOOKAHS
HOOKING
HOOKSUP
HOOKUPS
HOOPING
HOOPLAS
HOOPOES
HOOSIER
HOOTCHY
HOOTERS
HOOTING
HOOTOWL
HOOTSAT

H••O•••
HALOGEN
HALOING
HANOVER
HELOISE
HELOTRY
HEROICS
HEROINE
HEROISM
HOBOING
HOBOKEN
HOMONYM
HONORED
HONOREE
HONORER
HONOURS
HOPOVER
HUMORED
HUMOURS
HYPOING

H•••O••
HADDOCK
HALLOWS
HAMHOCK
HAMMOCK
HAMMOND
HANCOCK
HANDOFF
HANDOUT
HANGOFF
HANGOUT
HANSOLO
HANSOMS
HARBORS
HARBOUR
HARMONY
HARPOON
HARROWS
HASSOCK
HAULOFF
HAYFORK
HAYLOFT
HAYMOWS
HEADOFF
HEADOUT
HEAROUT
HECTORS
HEINOUS
HELDOFF
HELDOUT
HELPOUT
HEMLOCK
HENCOOP
HEYWOOD
HICKORY
HIDEOUS
HIDEOUT
HILLOCK
HIPBONE
HIPBOOT
HIPROOF
HISTORY
HOBNOBS
HOEDOWN
HOLDOFF
HOLDOUT
HOLEOUT
HOLLOWS
HOLMOAK
HOLYOKE
HOODOOS
HOOPOES
HOOTOWL
HOPSOFF
HOPTOIT
HORMONE
HORRORS
HOTDOGS
HOTFOOT
HOTPOTS
HOTRODS
HOWCOME
HULLOED
HUMMOCK
HUNGOUT
HYDROUS
HYSSOPS

H••••O•
HAIRDOS
HALCYON
HALSTON
HAMPTON
HANDSON
HANGDOG
HANGSON
HARDTOP
HARDWON
HARICOT
HARPOON
HARPSON
HAUTBOY
HAVENOT
HEARDOF
HEARSOF
HELICON
HELLION
HENCOOP
HERRIOT
HEXAGON
HEYWOOD
HIGHBOY
HIGHLOW
HIGHTOP
HILLTOP
HIPBOOT
HIPROOF
HIRESON
HOLDSON
HOLYCOW
HONCHOS
HOODOOS
HORIZON
HOTFOOT
HOTSHOT
HOTSPOT
HOUSTON
HUMIDOR

H•••••O
HAEMATO
HANSOLO
HEAVEHO
HEAVETO
HEIGHHO
HHMUNRO
HIDALGO
HISPANO
HOLDSTO
HORATIO

•HO••••
CHOCTAW
CHOICER
CHOICES
CHOKERS
CHOKEUP
CHOLLAS
CHOMPED
CHOMSKY
CHOOSER
CHOOSES
CHOPPED
CHOPPER
CHORALE
CHORALS
CHORINE
CHORIZO
CHORTLE
CHOWDER
GHOSTED
GHOSTLY
PHOBIAS
PHOBICS
PHOEBES
PHOEBUS
PHOENIX
PHONEME
PHONICS
PHONIER
PHONIES
PHONILY
PHONING
PHOTOED
PHOTOGS
PHOTONS
PHOTOOP
RHODIUM
RHOMBUS
SHOCKED
SHOCKER
SHODDEN
SHOEBOX
SHOEING
SHOFARS
SHOGUNS
SHOOFLY
SHOOING
SHOOINS
SHOOKUP
SHOOTAT
SHOOTER
SHOOTUP
SHOPPED
SHOPPER
SHOPPES
SHORING
SHORTED
SHORTEN
SHORTER
SHORTLY
SHORTOF
SHOTFOR
SHOTGUN
SHOTPUT
SHOUTED
SHOUTER
SHOVELS
SHOVERS
SHOVING
SHOWBIZ
SHOWDOG
SHOWERS
SHOWERY
SHOWIER
SHOWILY
SHOWING
SHOWMAN
SHOWMEN
SHOWNIN
SHOWOFF
SHOWSIN
SHOWSUP
THOMSON
THOREAU
THORIUM
THOUGHT
WHOEVER
WHOMPED
WHOOPED
WHOOPEE
WHOPPED
WHOPPER
WHORLED
WHOSWHO

•H•O•••
CHAOTIC
CHLORAL
CHOOSER
CHOOSES
CHROMES
CHRONIC
OHIOANS
PHLOXES
SHOOFLY
SHOOING
SHOOINS
SHOOKUP
SHOOTAT
SHOOTER
SHOOTUP
SHROUDS
THEOREM
THROATS
THROATY
THRONES
THRONGS
THROUGH
THROWER
THROWIN
WHOOPED
WHOOPEE

•H••O••
CHAMOIS
CHEROOT
CHEWOUT
CHICORY
CHINOOK
PHENOLS
PHENOMS
PHOTOED
PHOTOGS
PHOTONS
PHOTOOP
RHETORS
RHIZOME
SHADOOF
SHADOWS
SHADOWY
SHAKOES
SHALOMS
SHEWOLF
SHIPOUT
SHOWOFF
SHUTOFF
SHUTOUT
SHYLOCK
THEROUX

•H•••O•
AHEADOF
CHANSON
CHARIOT
CHEETOS
CHEKHOV
CHEROOT
CHEVIOT
CHEVRON
CHIFFON
CHIGNON
CHINOOK
GHETTOS
PHAETON
PHANTOM
PHARAOH
PHOTOOP
SHADOOF
SHAHDOM
SHALLOT
SHALLOW
SHAMPOO
SHANNON
SHELDON
SHELTON
SHOEBOX
SHORTOF
SHOTFOR
SHOWDOG
THEBLOB
THEREOF
THEREON
THERMOS
THINKOF
THOMSON
WHARTON
WHATFOR
WHATNOT
WHEATON
WHEREOF

•H••••O
CHEERIO
CHICAGO
CHICANO
CHORIZO
CHRISTO
HHMUNRO
SHAMPOO
SHAPIRO
THERETO
WHERETO
WHOSWHO
ZHIVAGO

••HO•••
ATHOMES
BEHOLDS
BEHOOVE
CAHOOTS
COHORTS
COHOSTS
DAHOMEY
DEHORNS
ECHOING
EXHORTS
INHOUSE
MAHONEY
MAHOUTS
OKHOTSK
REHOOKS
SCHOLAR
SCHOOLS
UNHOOKS
UNHORSE
UPHOLDS

••H•O••
ASHFORD
BEHOOVE
CAHOOTS
OSHKOSH
REHOOKS
SCHLOCK
SCHMOES
SCHMOOS
SCHOOLS
UNHOOKS

••H••O•
ACHERON
ACHESON
ECHELON
ETHANOL
ICHABOD
JOHNDOE
JOHNSON
SCHMOOS

••H•••O
OTHELLO
SCHERZO

•••HO••
AIRHOLE
AMPHORA
ANCHORS
ANCHOVY
ANTHONY
ARCHONS
ARMHOLE
AUTHORS
BARHOPS
BATHOIL
BIGHORN
BISHOPS
BOBHOPE
BOGHOLE
BOOHOOS
BOYHOOD
CACHOUS
CALHOUN
CARHOPS
CASHOUT
CATHODE
DASHOFF
DISHOUT
DRYHOLE
EUPHONY
EYEHOLE
FATHOMS
FISHOUT
FOGHORN
FOXHOLE
HAMHOCK
IDAHOAN
INKHORN
INSHORT
JOBHOPS
KEYHOLE
LEGHORN
MANHOLE
MANHOOD
MANHOUR
METHODS
NICHOLS
NOSHOWS
NOTHOME
OFFHOUR
ONSHORE
PINHOLE
POTHOLE
POTHOOK
PUSHOFF
PYTHONS
QUAHOGS
RATHOLE
RECHOSE
REDHOTS
RESHOES
RESHOOT
RUNHOME
RUSHOFF
SAXHORN
SIPHONS
SKYHOOK
TINHORN
TOEHOLD
TVSHOWS
TYPHOON
UNSHORN
UPSHOTS
WASHOFF
WASHOUT
WITHOUT

•••H•O•
ALOHAOE
BOOHOOS
BOYHOOD
BUSHHOG
CASHBOX
CASHCOW
CUSHION
FASHION
HIGHBOY
HIGHLOW
HIGHTOP
LITHGOW
MANHOOD
POTHOOK
RESHOOT
RIGHTON
SHAHDOM
SKYHOOK
TYPHOON

•••H••O
AKIHITO
BUSHIDO
ONTHEGO

••••HO•
AIRSHOW
ALCOHOL
BACKHOE
BELLHOP
BIGSHOT
BOKCHOY
BOLSHOI
BUSHHOG
CAMPHOR
CATCHON
CHEKHOV
DOGCHOW
DOGSHOW
EARSHOT
EREWHON
GASOHOL
GAUCHOS
GRYPHON
GUMSHOE
GUNSHOT
GYMSHOE
HONCHOS
HOTSHOT
ICESHOW
IVANHOE
KERCHOO
KNOWHOW
MARCHON
MARKHOR
MCMAHON
MENTHOL
MUGSHOT
NAVAHOS
ONESHOT
PONCHOS
PORTHOS
POSTHOC
POTSHOT
PRUDHOE
PYNCHON
RANCHOS
RIMSHOT
ROADHOG
SALCHOW
SANDHOG
SOMEHOW
TEASHOP
TOESHOE
TOUCHON
TOYSHOP
USOSHOW
WARTHOG

••••H•O
HEIGHHO
KERCHOO
SATCHMO

•••••HO
ARAPAHO
GROUCHO
HEAVEHO
HEIGHHO
JERICHO
LESOTHO
ORNITHO
TALLYHO
WHOSWHO

H•P••••
HAPLESS
HAPPENS
HAPPIER
HAPPILY
HEPARIN
HEPATIC
HEPBURN
HEPCATS
HEPTADS
HIPBONE
HIPBOOT
HIPNESS
HIPPEST
HIPPIES
HIPROOF
HIPSTER
HOPEFUL
HOPKINS
HOPOVER
HOPPERS
HOPPING
HOPSOFF
HOPTOIT
HYPEDUP
HYPHENS
HYPOING

H••P•••
HAMPERS
HAMPTON
HAPPENS
HAPPIER
HAPPILY
HARPERS
HARPIES
HARPING
HARPIST
HARPOON
HARPSON
HATPINS
HEAPING
HELPERS
HELPFUL
HELPING
HELPOUT
HENPECK
HIPPEST
HIPPIES
HISPANO
HOOPING
HOOPLAS
HOOPOES

HOPPERS
HOPPING
HOSPICE
HOTPOTS

H•••P••

HAIRPIN
HARDPAN
HARDPUT
HEADPIN
HELIPAD
HOTSPOT
HOTSPUR

H••••P•

HANGUPS
HICCUPS
HOLDUPS
HOOKUPS
HOTCAPS
HOTLIPS
HOTTIPS
HUBCAPS
HYSSOPS

H•••••P

HAMITUP
HANDSUP
HANGSUP
HANSARP
HARDTOP
HAULSUP
HEADSUP
HEATSUP
HEELTAP
HENCOOP
HIGHTOP
HILLTOP
HOLDSUP
HOLEDUP
HOLESUP
HOOKSUP
HYPEDUP

•H•P•••

CHAPATI
CHAPEAU
CHAPELS
CHAPLET
CHAPLIN
CHAPMAN
CHAPMEN
CHAPPED
CHAPTER
CHIPPED
CHIPPER
CHIPSIN
CHOPPED
CHOPPER
SHAPELY
SHAPERS
SHAPEUP
SHAPING
SHAPIRO
SHEPARD
SHIPMAN
SHIPMEN
SHIPOUT
SHIPPED
SHIPPER
SHOPPED
SHOPPER
SHOPPES
WHIPPED
WHIPPET
WHIPSAW
WHIPSUP
WHOPPED
WHOPPER
WHUPPED

•H••P••

CHAMPED
CHAPPED
CHEAPEN
CHEAPER
CHEAPIE
CHEAPLY
CHEEPED
CHIPPED
CHIPPER
CHIRPED
CHOMPED
CHOPPED
CHOPPER
SHAMPOO
SHARPED
SHARPEI
SHARPEN
SHARPER
SHARPLY
SHERPAS
SHIPPED
SHIPPER
SHOPPED
SHOPPER
SHOPPES
SHOTPUT
THESPIS
THUMPED
THUMPER
WHELPED
WHIMPER
WHIPPED
WHIPPET
WHISPER
WHOMPED
WHOOPED
WHOOPEE
WHOPPED
WHOPPER
WHUPPED

•H•••P•

CHINUPS
SHRIMPS
THERAPY

•H••••P

CHALKUP
CHATSUP
CHECKUP
CHEERUP
CHEWSUP
CHOKEUP
PHILLIP
PHOTOOP
SHAKEUP
SHAPEUP
SHOOKUP
SHOOTUP
SHOWSUP
SHUTSUP
THEDEEP
THINKUP
WHIPSUP

••H•P••

UNHAPPY

••H••P•

SCHLEPP
SCHLEPS
SCHNAPS
UNHAPPY

••H•••P

SCHLEPP

•••HP••

BUSHPIG
DISHPAN
PUSHPIN

•••H•P•

BARHOPS
BISHOPS
BOBHOPE
CARHOPS
INSHAPE
JOBHOPS
LASHUPS
MISHAPS
MRCHIPS
PERHAPS
PUSHUPS
RESHIPS

•••H••P

HIGHTOP
INAHEAP
LIGHTUP

••••H•P

AIRSHIP
BELLHOP
BRUSHUP
CATCHUP
COUGHUP
KETCHUP
KINSHIP
MATCHUP
OLDCHAP
PATCHUP
PSYCHUP
PUNCHUP
ROUGHUP
SMASHUP
TEASHOP
TOUCHUP
TOYSHOP
WARSHIP
WORSHIP

•H•Q•••

CHEQUER
CHEQUES

•••H•Q•

ONTHEQT

H•R••••

HARBORS
HARBOUR
HARDENS
HARDEST
HARDHAT
HARDHIT
HARDIER
HARDILY
HARDING
HARDPAN
HARDPUT
HARDSET
HARDTOP
HARDWON
HARICOT
HARKENS
HARKING
HARMFUL
HARMING
HARMONY
HARNESS
HARPERS
HARPIES
HARPING
HARPIST
HARPOON
HARPSON
HARRIED
HARRIER
HARRIES
HARRIET
HARROWS
HARSHEN
HARSHER
HARSHLY
HARTMAN
HARVARD
HARVEST
HERALDS
HERBAGE
HERBALS
HERBERT
HERBTEA
HERCULE
HERDERS
HERDING
HERETIC
HERMANN
HERMITS
HEROICS
HEROINE
HEROISM
HERRING
HERRIOT
HERSELF
HERSHEY
HIRABLE
HIRESON
HIRSUTE
HORATIO
HORIZON
HORMONE
HORNETS
HORNING
HORNIST
HORNSBY
HORRIFY
HORRORS
HORSIER
HORSING
HURDLED
HURDLER
HURDLES
HURLERS
HURLING
HURRAHS
HURRIED
HURRIES
HURTFUL
HURTING
HURTLED
HURTLES
HYRACES
HYRAXES

H••R•••

HAARLEM
HADRIAN
HAIRCUT
HAIRDOS
HAIRDYE
HAIRIER
HAIRNET
HAIRPIN
HARRIED
HARRIER
HARRIES
HARRIET
HARROWS
HATRACK
HAYRACK
HAYRIDE
HEARDOF
HEARERS
HEARING
HEARKEN
HEAROUT
HEARSAY
HEARSOF
HEARTEN
HEARTHS
HEBRAIC
HEBREWS
HEIRESS
HENREID
HERRING
HERRIOT
HIPROOF
HOARDED
HOARDER
HOARIER
HOARSEN
HOARSER
HORRIFY
HORRORS
HOTRODS
HURRAHS
HURRIED
HURRIES
HYBRIDS
HYDRANT
HYDRATE
HYDROUS

H•••R••

HAVARTI
HAZARDS
HEGIRAS
HENDRIX
HEPARIN
HOFBRAU
HOGARTH
HOMBRES
HOMERED
HOMERIC
HOMERUN
HONORED
HONOREE
HONORER
HOVERED
HOVERER
HOWARDS
HUMDRUM
HUMERAL
HUMERUS
HUMORED
HUNDRED

H••••R•

HACKERS
HAGGARD
HALTERS
HALYARD
HAMBURG
HAMMERS
HAMPERS
HANGARS
HANGERS
HANKERS
HANSARP
HARBORS
HARPERS
HARVARD
HATTERS
HAUBERK
HAULERS
HAWKERS
HAWSERS
HAYFORK
HAYWARD
HAYWIRE
HEADERS
HEALERS
HEARERS
HEATERS
HEAVERS
HECTARE
HECTORS
HEDGERS
HEELERS
HEIFERS
HELLERS
HELOTRY
HELPERS
HEMMERS
HENNERY
HEPBURN
HERBERT
HERDERS
HHMUNRO
HICKORY
HILAIRE
HILLARY
HINDERS
HISSERS
HISTORY
HITHERE
HITTERS
HOAXERS
HOLDERS
HOLLERS
HOLYARK
HOMBURG
HONKERS
HONOURS
HOOFERS
HOOTERS
HOPPERS
HORRORS
HOSIERS
HOSIERY
HOTCARS
HOTWARS
HOTWIRE
HOWLERS
HUBBARD
HUGGERS
HULLERS
HUMMERS
HUMOURS
HUNGARY
HUNGERS
HUNKERS
HUNTERS
HURLERS
HUSKERS
HUSSARS

H•••••R

HAGGLER
HAIRIER
HAMSTER
HANDCAR
HANDIER
HANDLER
HANOVER
HAPPIER
HARBOUR
HARDIER
HARRIER
HARSHER
HASTIER
HATCHER
HAUTEUR
HEADIER
HEATHER
HEATTER
HEAVIER
HECKLER
HEFTIER
HILLIER
HIPSTER
HITCHER
HOARDER
HOARIER
HOARSER
HOLSTER
HOLYWAR
HONORER
HOOSIER
HOPOVER
HORSIER
HOSTLER
HOTSPUR
HOVERER
HOWEVER
HUFFIER
HUMBLER
HUMIDOR
HURDLER
HUSKIER
HUSTLER

•HR••••

CHRISMS
CHRISTI
CHRISTO
CHRISTY
CHROMES
CHRONIC
EHRLICH
PHRASAL
PHRASED
PHRASES
PHRENIC
SHRIEKS
SHRIFTS
SHRIKES
SHRILLS
SHRILLY
SHRIMPS
SHRINER
SHRINES
SHRINKS
SHRIVEL
SHRIVER
SHRIVES
SHROUDS
SHRUBBY
THRALLS
THREADS
THREADY
THREATS
THREERS
THREWIN
THRIFTS
THRIFTY
THRILLS
THRIVED
THRIVES
THROATS
THROATY
THRONES
THRONGS
THROUGH
THROWER
THROWIN
THRUSTS
THRUWAY

•H•R•••

CHARADE
CHARGED
CHARGER
CHARGES
CHARIER
CHARILY
CHARIOT
CHARITY
CHARLES
CHARLEY
CHARLIE
CHARMED
CHARMER
CHARMIN
CHARRED
CHARTED
CHARTER
CHERISH
CHEROOT
CHERUBS
CHERVIL
CHIRPED
CHORALE
CHORALS
CHORINE
CHORIZO
CHORTLE
CHURNED
DHURRIE
GHERKIN
PHARAOH
PHARYNX
SHAREIN
SHARERS
SHARING
SHARKEY
SHARPED
SHARPEI
SHARPEN
SHARPER
SHARPLY
SHERBET
SHERIFF
SHERMAN
SHERPAS
SHERWIN
SHIRKED
SHIRKER
SHIRLEY
SHIRRED
SHORING
SHORTED
SHORTEN
SHORTER
SHORTLY
SHORTOF
THERAPY
THEREAT
THEREBY
THEREIN
THEREOF
THEREON
THERESA
THERETO
THERMAL
THERMOS
THEROUX
THIRDLY
THIRSTS
THIRSTY
THOREAU
THORIUM
THURBER
THURMAN
WHARFED
WHARTON
WHARVES
WHEREAS
WHEREAT
WHEREBY
WHEREIN
WHEREOF
WHERETO
WHIRLED
WHIRRED
WHORLED

•H••R••

CHAGRIN
CHAIRED
CHARRED
CHEERED
CHEERIO
CHEERUP
CHETRUM
CHEVRES
CHEVRON
CHLORAL
DHURRIE
SHEARED
SHEARER
SHECRAB
SHEERED
SHEERER
SHEERLY
SHIRRED
THEOREM
THIERRY
THWARTS
WHIRRED

•H•••R•

CHASERS
CHEWERS
CHICORY
CHIMERA
CHOKERS
HHMUNRO
PHAEDRA
PHASERS
PHILTRE
RHETORS
RHUBARB
RHYMERS
SHAKERS
SHANGRI
SHAPERS
SHAPIRO
SHARERS
SHASTRI
SHAVERS
SHEPARD
SHINERS
SHIVERS
SHOFARS
SHOVERS
SHOWERS
SHOWERY
SHUBERT
THALERS
THEATRE
THIERRY
THREERS
WHALERS
WHINERS

•H••••R

CHAMBER
CHAMFER
CHANGER
CHANTER
CHAPTER
CHARGER
CHARIER
CHARMER
CHARTER
CHASTER
CHATTER
CHAUCER
CHEAPER
CHEATER
CHECKER
CHEDDAR
CHEEVER
CHENIER
CHEQUER
CHESTER
CHEWIER
CHIGGER
CHILLER
CHIPPER
CHITTER
CHOICER
CHOOSER
CHOPPER
CHOWDER
CHUKKER
PHILTER
PHONIER
SHADIER
SHAFFER
SHAKIER
SHANKAR
SHANTER
SHARPER
SHATNER
SHATTER
SHEARER
SHEERER
SHELLER
SHELTER
SHIMMER
SHINIER
SHIPPER
SHIRKER
SHOCKER
SHOOTER
SHOPPER
SHORTER
SHOTFOR
SHOUTER
SHOWIER
SHRINER
SHRIVER
SHUCKER
SHUDDER
SHUTTER
SHYSTER
THEATER
THICKER
THINAIR
THINKER
THINNER
THITHER
THROWER
THUMPER
THUNDER
THURBER
THUSFAR
WHATFOR
WHEELER
WHEEZER
WHETHER
WHIMPER
WHISKER
WHISPER
WHITHER
WHOEVER
WHOPPER

••HR•••

ASHRAMS
BAHRAIN

••H•R••

ACHERON
ADHERED
ADHERES
AMHARIC
AMHERST
ASHTRAY
ATHIRST
COHERED
COHERES
COHORTS
DEHORNS
EXHORTS
INHERED
INHERES
INHERIT
MAHARIS
REHIRED
REHIRES
SAHARAN
SCHERZI
SCHERZO
SCHIRRA
SPHERES
TEHERAN
TSHIRTS
UNHORSE
USHERED

••H••R•

ASHBURY
ASHFORD
ASHLARS
ATHEART
ATHWART
BYHEART
CAHIERS
COHEIRS
LEHAVRE
MOHAIRS
REHEARD
REHEARS
SCHIRRA
UNHEARD

••H•••R

INHALER
SCHEMER
SCHMEER
SCHOLAR

•••HR••

COCHRAN
DISHRAG
EUCHRED
EUCHRES
GUTHRIE
KATHRYN
MITHRAS
WASHRAG

•••H•R•

ALLHERE
AMPHORA
ANCHORS
ANTHERS
ARCHERS
ARCHERY
AUTHORS
BATHERS
BIGHORN
BOKHARA
BOTHERS
CIPHERS
COCHERE
COWHERD
CYPHERS
DASHERS
DIEHARD
DITHERS
DITHERY
EARHART
ECKHART
ELKHART
ETCHERS
FATHERS
FISHERS
FISHERY
FISHFRY
FOGHORN
GATHERS
GOPHERS
GUSHERS
HITHERE
INKHORN
INSHORT
KOSHERS
LASHERS
LATHERS
LATHERY
LEGHORN
MASHERS
MATHERS
MENHIRS
MOTHERS
MUSHERS
NEWHART
NOSHERS
NOWHERE
ONSHORE
ORCHARD
POTHERB
POTHERS
RASHERS
RICHARD
RUSHERS
SAXHORN
SEEHERE
SIGHERS
SOTHERE
SOTHERN
TETHERS
TINHORN
TITHERS
UNSHORN
WASHERS
WETHERS
WISHERS
WITHERS
YOGHURT
ZACHARY
ZEPHYRS
ZITHERS

•••H••R

BUSHIER
CASHBAR
CASHIER
CATHAIR
CUSHIER
FIGHTER
FISHIER
GUSHIER
ITCHIER
KASHMIR
LIGHTER
MANHOUR
MISHEAR
MUSHIER
MYNHEER
OFFHOUR
PITHIER
PUSHIER
REDHAIR
RICHTER
RIGHTER
TIGHTER

••••H•R

ANOTHER
BEECHER
BLATHER
BLITHER
BLUSHER
BRASHER
BROTHER
BULGHUR
BURGHER
BUTCHER
CAMPHOR
CATCHER
CRUSHER
FARTHER

FEATHER
FILCHER
FISCHER
FLASHER
FRESHER
FURTHER
GAUCHER
GUNTHER
HARSHER
HATCHER
HEATHER
HITCHER
LAUGHER
LEATHER
LUNCHER
MARCHER
MARKHOR
MOOCHER
MUNCHER
NEITHER
NORTHER
PANTHER
PINCHER
PITCHER
PLUSHER
POACHER
PUNCHER
RANCHER
REUTHER
ROUGHER
SLASHER
SLATHER
SLITHER
SMASHER
SMOTHER
SOOTHER
SULPHUR
TEACHER
TEETHER
TEICHER
THITHER
TOUGHER
VOUCHER
WATCHER
WEATHER
WERNHER
WERTHER
WHETHER
WHITHER

•••••HR
NIEBUHR

H•S••••
HASBEEN
HASHING
HASIDIM
HASSLED
HASSLES
HASSOCK
HASTENS
HASTIER
HASTILY
HASTING
HESHVAN
HESSIAN
HISPANO
HISSERS
HISSING
HISTORY
HOSANNA
HOSIERS
HOSIERY
HOSKINS
HOSPICE
HOSTAGE
HOSTELS
HOSTESS
HOSTILE
HOSTING
HOSTLER
HUSBAND
HUSHABY
HUSHING
HUSKERS
HUSKIER
HUSKIES
HUSKILY
HUSKING
HUSSARS
HUSSEIN
HUSSIES
HUSTLED
HUSTLER
HUSTLES
HYSSOPS

H••S•••
HALSTON
HAMSTER
HANSARP
HANSOLO
HANSOMS
HARSHEN
HARSHER
HARSHLY
HASSLED
HASSLES
HASSOCK
HAWSERS
HAYSEED
HEISTED
HEMSLEY
HERSELF
HERSHEY
HESSIAN
HEXSIGN
HIMSELF
HIPSTER
HIRSUTE
HISSERS
HISSING
HOISTED
HOLSTER
HOOSIER
HOPSOFF
HORSIER
HORSING
HOTSEAT
HOTSHOT
HOTSPOT
HOTSPUR
HOUSING
HOUSMAN
HOUSTON
HUSSARS
HUSSEIN
HUSSIES
HYSSOPS

H•••S••
HACKSAW
HANDSAW
HANDSET
HANDSIN
HANDSON
HANDSUP
HANGSIN
HANGSON
HANGSUP
HARDSET
HARPSON
HAULSUP
HEADSET
HEADSIN
HEADSUP
HEARSAY
HEARSOF
HEATSUP
HINTSAT
HIRESON
HOARSEN
HOARSER
HOLDSON
HOLDSTO
HOLDSUP
HOLESUP
HOLYSEE
HONESTY
HOOFSIT
HOOKSUP
HOOTSAT
HORNSBY

H••••S•
HAPLESS
HARDEST
HARNESS
HARPIST
HARVEST
HATLESS
HAWKISH
HAZIEST
HEIRESS
HELOISE
HEROISM
HIGHEST
HIPNESS
HIPPEST
HITLESS
HITLIST
HOGWASH
HOLIEST
HOMIEST
HORNIST
HOSTESS
HOTNESS
HOTTEST

H•••••S
HACKERS
HACKIES
HACKLES
HAGGLES
HAIRDOS
HALITES
HALLOWS
HALTERS
HAMITES
HAMLETS
HAMMERS
HAMPERS
HANDLES
HANGARS
HANGERS
HANGUPS
HANKERS
HANKIES
HANSOMS
HAPLESS
HAPPENS
HARBORS
HARDENS
HARKENS
HARNESS
HARPERS
HARPIES
HARRIES
HARROWS
HASSLES
HASTENS
HATCHES
HATLESS
HATPINS
HATTERS
HAULERS
HAWHAWS
HAWKERS
HAWKINS
HAWSERS
HAYMOWS
HAZARDS
HAZINGS
HEADERS
HEALERS
HEARERS
HEARTHS
HEATERS
HEAVENS
HEAVERS
HEAVIES
HEBREWS
HECKLES
HECTORS
HEDDLES
HEDGERS
HEEHAWS
HEELERS
HEGIRAS
HEIFERS
HEIGHTS
HEINOUS
HEIRESS
HELICES
HELIXES
HELLERS
HELMETS
HELPERS
HEMMERS
HENBITS
HEPCATS
HEPTADS
HERALDS
HERBALS
HERDERS
HERMITS
HEROICS
HETMANS
HEXNUTS
HEYDAYS
HGWELLS
HICCUPS
HIDEOUS
HIGGINS
HIJACKS
HIJINKS
HINDERS
HINNIES
HIPNESS
HIPPIES
HISSERS
HITCHES
HITLESS
HITTERS
HOAGIES
HOAXERS
HOBBIES
HOBBITS
HOBBLES
HOBNOBS
HOGTIES
HOLDERS
HOLDUPS
HOLLERS
HOLLIES
HOLLOWS
HOMBRES
HONCHOS
HONKERS
HONOURS
HOODOOS
HOOFERS
HOOHAHS
HOOKAHS
HOOKUPS
HOOPLAS
HOOPOES
HOOTERS
HOPKINS
HOPPERS
HORNETS
HORRORS
HOSIERS
HOSKINS
HOSTELS
HOSTESS
HOTBEDS
HOTCAPS
HOTCARS
HOTDOGS
HOTLIPS
HOTNESS
HOTPOTS
HOTRODS
HOTTIPS
HOTTUBS
HOTWARS
HOWARDS
HOWDAHS
HOWELLS
HOWLERS
HOYDENS
HUBBIES
HUBBUBS
HUBCAPS
HUDDLES
HUGGERS
HULLERS
HUMBLES
HUMBUGS
HUMERUS
HUMMERS
HUMOURS
HUNCHES
HUNGERS
HUNKERS
HUNTERS
HURDLES
HURLERS
HURRAHS
HURRIES
HURTLES
HUSKERS
HUSKIES
HUSSARS
HUSSIES
HUSTLES
HUTCHES
HUZZAHS
HYBRIDS
HYDROUS
HYMNALS
HYPHENS
HYRACES
HYRAXES
HYSSOPS

•H•S•••
CHASERS
CHASING
CHASSES
CHASSIS
CHASTEN
CHASTER
CHESTER
CHISELS
GHASTLY
GHOSTED
GHOSTLY
PHASEIN
PHASERS
PHASING
PHYSICS
SHASTRI
SHUSHED
SHUSHES
SHYSTER
THESEUS
THESPIS
THISTLE
THUSFAR
THYSELF
WHISKED
WHISKER
WHISKEY
WHISPER
WHISTLE
WHOSWHO

•H••S••
CHAISES
CHANSON
CHASSES
CHASSIS
CHATSUP
CHEESES
CHELSEA
CHEWSUP
CHIPSIN
CHOMSKY
CHOOSER
CHOOSES
CHRISMS
CHRISTI
CHRISTO
CHRISTY
PHRASAL
PHRASED
PHRASES
SHOWSIN
SHOWSUP
SHUTSIN
SHUTSUP
THATSIT
THEISTS
THIRSTS
THIRSTY
THOMSON
THRUSTS
WHIPSAW
WHIPSUP

•H•••S•
CHEMISE
CHEMIST
CHERISH
CHINESE
SHIATSU
SHYNESS
THERESA
WHITEST
WHITISH

•H••••S
CHABLIS
CHACHAS
CHAISES
CHALETS
CHALLIS
CHAMOIS
CHANCES
CHANGES
CHAPELS
CHARGES
CHARLES
CHASERS
CHASSES
CHASSIS
CHEESES
CHEETOS
CHEQUES
CHERUBS
CHEVIES
CHEVRES
CHEWERS
CHILIES
CHINUPS
CHISELS
CHOICES
CHOKERS
CHOLLAS
CHOOSES
CHORALS
CHRISMS
CHROMES
CHUKKAS
GHETTOS
OHIOANS
PHASERS
PHENOLS
PHENOMS
PHIDIAS
PHINEAS
PHLOXES
PHOBIAS
PHOBICS
PHOEBES
PHOEBUS
PHONICS
PHONIES
PHOTOGS
PHOTONS
PHRASES
PHYLLIS
PHYSICS
RHETORS
RHOMBUS
RHUMBAS
RHYMERS
RHYTHMS
SHADOWS
SHAKERS
SHAKOES
SHALOMS
SHAMANS
SHAPERS
SHARERS
SHAVERS
SHEATHS
SHEAVES
SHEIKHS
SHEILAS
SHEKELS
SHELVES
SHERPAS
SHIELDS
SHIITES
SHINERS
SHIVERS
SHOFARS
SHOGUNS
SHOOINS
SHOPPES
SHOVELS
SHOVERS
SHOWERS
SHRIEKS
SHRIFTS
SHRIKES
SHRILLS
SHRIMPS
SHRINES
SHRINKS
SHRIVES
SHROUDS
SHTICKS
SHUSHES
SHYNESS
THALERS
THEISTS
THERMOS
THESEUS
THESPIS
THIEVES
THIRSTS
THRALLS
THREADS
THREATS
THREERS
THRIFTS
THRILLS
THRIVES
THROATS
THRONES
THRONGS
THRUSTS
THWACKS
THWARTS
WHALERS
WHARVES
WHEEZES
WHEREAS
WHINERS
WHITENS
WHIZZES
WHYDAHS

••H•S••
ACHESON
APHESES
BEHESTS
COHOSTS
DEHISCE
INHASTE
JOHNSON
SCHISMS

••H••S•
ACHIEST
AMHERST
ASHIEST
ASHLESS
ATHEISM
ATHEIST
ATHIRST
EXHAUST
INHOUSE
OKHOTSK
OSHKOSH
UNHORSE

••H•••S
ACHATES
ACHENES
ADHERES
APHESES
ASHCANS
ASHLARS
ASHLESS
ASHRAMS
ATHOMES
BAHAMAS
BEHAVES
BEHESTS
BEHOLDS
CAHIERS
CAHOOTS
COHEIRS
COHERES
COHORTS
COHOSTS
DAHLIAS
DEHORNS
ECHINUS
ETHNICS
EXHALES
EXHORTS
INHALES
INHERES
KAHUNAS
MAHARIS
MAHOUTS
MOHAIRS
MOHAWKS
REHANGS
REHEALS
REHEARS
REHEATS
REHEELS
REHIRES
REHOOKS
SCHEMAS
SCHEMES
SCHISMS
SCHLEPS
SCHMOES
SCHMOOS
SCHNAPS
SCHOOLS
SPHERES
TSHIRTS
UNHANDS
UNHOOKS
UPHOLDS
WAHINES

•••HS••
FUCHSIA

•••H•S•
COCHISE
DUCHESS
ENTHUSE
HIGHEST
INPHASE
LITHEST
LUSHEST
NIGHEST
PACHISI
POSHEST
RASHEST
RECHOSE
RICHEST
SIKHISM
SOPHISM
SOPHIST

•••H••S
AFGHANS
ANCHORS
ANTHEMS
ANTHERS
ARCHERS
ARCHIES
ARCHONS
AUTHORS
BARHOPS
BATHERS
BETHELS
BISHOPS
BOOHOOS
BOTHERS
BRAHMAS
BUSHELS
CACHETS
CACHOUS
CARHOPS
CASHEWS
CEPHEUS
CIPHERS
CUSHAWS
CYPHERS
DAPHNIS
DASHERS
DITHERS
DUCHESS
DUCHIES
EIGHTHS
ESCHEWS
ETCHERS
EUCHRES
FATHERS
FATHOMS
FISHERS
GATHERS
GOPHERS
GOTHICS
GRAHAMS
GUSHERS
HAWHAWS
HEEHAWS
HOOHAHS
HYPHENS
ISOHELS
ISTHMUS
JOBHOPS
KISHKES
KOSHERS
LASHERS
LASHUPS
LATHERS
LICHENS
MASHERS
MASHIES
MATHERS
MATHEWS
MATHIAS
MAYHEMS
MENHIRS
METHODS
MISHAPS
MISHITS
MITHRAS
MOTHERS
MRCHIPS
MUDHENS
MUSHERS
MUZHIKS
NEPHEWS
NICHOLS
NOSHERS
NOSHOWS
ORCHIDS
ORPHANS
ORPHEUS
OUTHITS
PEAHENS
PERHAPS
POTHERS
PUSHUPS
PYTHIAS
PYTHONS
QUAHOGS
RASHERS
REDHATS
REDHOTS
RESHIPS
RESHOES
RUSHEES
RUSHERS
SACHEMS
SACHETS
SASHAYS
SIGHERS
SIPHONS
TECHIES
TETHERS
TINHATS
TITHERS
TOPHATS
TOWHEES
TVSHOWS
UPSHOTS
URCHINS
UTAHANS
WASHERS
WETHERS
WISHERS
WITHERS
ZEPHYRS
ZITHERS

••••H•S
ABASHES
AITCHES
ALIGHTS
APACHES
BACCHUS
BATCHES
BEACHES
BEECHES
BELCHES
BENCHES
BIRCHES
BLIGHTS
BLUSHES
BOTCHES
BRUSHES
BUDDHAS
BUNCHES
CATCHES
CHACHAS
CINCHES
CLASHES
CLICHES
CLOCHES
CLOTHES
COACHES
CONCHES
COUCHES
CRASHES
CRECHES
CRUSHES
DITCHES
FETCHES
FILCHES
FINCHES
FITCHES
FLASHES
FLECHES
FLESHES
FLIGHTS
FLUSHES
FRIGHTS
GAUCHOS
GEISHAS
GENGHIS
GNASHES
GOTCHAS
GULCHES
GURKHAS
HATCHES
HEIGHTS
HITCHES
HONCHOS
HUNCHES
HUTCHES
KETCHES
KNIGHTS
KNISHES
KWACHAS
LARCHES
LATCHES
LEACHES
LEASHES
LEECHES
LITCHIS
LOACHES
LOATHES
LUNCHES
LURCHES
MALTHUS
MARCHES
MARSHES
MATCHES
MEGOHMS
MEMPHIS
MOOCHES
MULCHES
MUNCHES
NAUGHTS
NAVAHOS
NOTCHES
PARCHES
PATCHES
PEACHES
PERCHES
PINCHAS
PINCHES
PITCHES
PLASHES
PLIGHTS
PLUSHES
POACHES
PONCHOS
POOCHES
PORCHES
PORTHOS
POUCHES
PSYCHES
PUNCHES
PYRRHUS
QUASHES
QUICHES
RANCHES
RANCHOS
REACHES
RHYTHMS
ROACHES
SCATHES
SCYTHES
SEETHES
SEICHES
SHUSHES
SKOSHES
SLASHES
SLIGHTS
SLOSHES
SLUSHES
SMASHES
SOOTHES
STASHES
STICHES
STJOHNS
SWATHES
SWISHES
SYNCHES
TEACHES
TEETHES
TORCHES
TOUCHES
TRASHES
TROCHES
VEIGHTS
VETCHES
VOUCHES
WATCHES
WEIGHTS
WELCHES
WENCHES
WINCHES
WITCHES
WRIGHTS
WRITHES
ZILCHES

•••••HS
AUROCHS
BREATHS
BYPATHS
CALIPHS
CERIPHS
DEARTHS
EIGHTHS
EOLITHS
EPARCHS
EUNUCHS
FOURTHS

GROWTHS
GUELPHS
HEARTHS
HOOHAHS
HOOKAHS
HOWDAHS
HURRAHS
HUZZAHS
IOMOTHS
KAZAKHS
LENGTHS
LOOFAHS
MATZOHS
MULLAHS
OOLITHS
OOMPAHS
PARAPHS
PARIAHS
PLINTHS
PLOUGHS
PUNKAHS
PURDAHS
RUPIAHS
SERAPHS
SHEATHS
SHEIKHS
SLEIGHS
SLEUTHS
SLOUGHS
SMOOTHS
TERAPHS
TROUGHS
VOTECHS
WHYDAHS
WRAITHS
WREATHS
ZENITHS

H•T••••
HATCHED
HATCHER
HATCHES
HATCHET
HATEFUL
HATLESS
HATPINS
HATRACK
HATTERS
HATTING
HETMANS
HITACHI
HITCHED
HITCHER
HITCHES
HITHERE
HITLESS
HITLIST
HITTERS
HITTING
HITTITE
HOTBEDS
HOTCAKE
HOTCAPS
HOTCARS
HOTDOGS
HOTFOOT
HOTHEAD
HOTLINE
HOTLIPS
HOTNESS
HOTPOTS
HOTRODS
HOTSEAT
HOTSHOT
HOTSPOT
HOTSPUR
HOTTEST
HOTTIPS
HOTTUBS
HOTWARS
HOTWIRE
HUTCHES

H••T•••
HAITIAN
HALTERS
HALTING
HARTMAN
HASTENS
HASTIER
HASTILY
HASTING
HATTERS
HATTING
HAUTBOY
HAUTEUR
HEATERS
HEATHEN
HEATHER
HEATING
HEATSUP
HEATTER
HECTARE
HECTORS
HEFTIER
HEFTILY
HEFTING
HEPTADS
HINTING
HINTSAT
HISTORY
HITTERS
HITTING
HITTITE
HOGTIED
HOGTIES
HOOTCHY
HOOTERS
HOOTING
HOOTOWL
HOOTSAT
HOPTOIT
HOSTAGE
HOSTELS
HOSTESS
HOSTILE
HOSTING
HOSTLER
HOTTEST
HOTTIPS
HOTTUBS
HUNTERS
HUNTING
HUNTLEY
HURTFUL
HURTING
HURTLED
HURTLES
HUSTLED
HUSTLER
HUSTLES

H•••T••
HABITAT
HABITED
HABITUE
HALITES
HALSTON
HAMITES
HAMITIC
HAMITUP
HAMPTON
HAMSTER
HANGTEN
HARDTOP
HAUNTED
HEALTHY
HEARTEN
HEARTHS
HEATTER
HEELTAP
HEISTED
HELOTRY
HEPATIC
HERBTEA
HERETIC
HIGHTEA
HIGHTOP
HILLTOP
HIPSTER
HOISTED
HOLSTER
HORATIO
HOUSTON

H••••T•
HACKETT
HAEMATO
HAMLETS
HAMMETT
HAUGHTY
HAVARTI
HEAVETO
HEIFETZ
HEIGHTS
HELMETS
HENBITS
HEPCATS
HERMITS
HEWLETT
HEXNUTS
HIRSUTE
HITTITE
HOBBITS
HOGARTH
HOLDSTO
HONESTY
HORNETS
HOTPOTS
HYDRATE

H•••••T
HABITAT
HACKETT
HAIRCUT
HAIRNET
HALFWIT
HALIBUT
HAMMETT
HANDOUT
HANDSET
HANGOUT
HARDEST
HARDHAT
HARDHIT
HARDPUT
HARDSET
HARICOT
HARPIST
HARRIET
HARVEST
HATCHET
HAVENOT
HAYLOFT
HAZIEST
HEADOUT
HEADSET
HEAROUT
HELDOUT
HELLCAT
HELPOUT
HERBERT
HERRIOT
HEWLETT
HIDEOUT
HIGHEST
HIGHHAT
HINTSAT
HIPBOOT
HIPPEST
HITLIST
HOLDOUT
HOLEOUT
HOLIEST
HOMIEST
HOOFSIT
HOOTSAT
HOPTOIT
HORNIST
HOTFOOT
HOTSEAT
HOTSHOT
HOTSPOT
HOTTEST
HOWBEIT
HUNGOUT
HYDRANT

•HT••••
SHTICKS

•H•T•••
CHATEAU
CHATHAM
CHATSUP
CHATTED
CHATTEL
CHATTER
CHETRUM
CHITTER
CHUTNEY
GHETTOS
PHOTOED
PHOTOGS
PHOTONS
PHOTOOP
RHETORS
RHYTHMS
SHATNER
SHATTER
SHOTFOR
SHOTGUN
SHOTPUT
SHUTEYE
SHUTOFF
SHUTOUT
SHUTSIN
SHUTSUP
SHUTTER
SHUTTLE
THATCHY
THATSIT
THITHER
WHATFOR
WHATNOT
WHETHER
WHETTED
WHITENS
WHITEST
WHITHER
WHITING
WHITISH
WHITMAN
WHITNEY
WHITTLE

•H••T••
CHANTED
CHANTER
CHANTEY
CHAOTIC
CHAPTER
CHARTED
CHARTER
CHASTEN
CHASTER
CHATTED
CHATTEL
CHATTER
CHEATED
CHEATER
CHEETAH
CHEETOS
CHESTER
CHINTZY
CHITTER
CHOCTAW
CHORTLE
GHASTLY
GHETTOS
GHOSTED
GHOSTLY
PHAETON
PHANTOM
PHILTER
PHILTRE
SHAFTED
SHANTER
SHASTRI
SHATTER
SHEATHE
SHEATHS
SHEETED
SHELTER
SHELTIE
SHELTON
SHIATSU
SHIFTED
SHIHTZU
SHIITES
SHOOTAT
SHOOTER
SHOOTUP
SHORTED
SHORTEN
SHORTER
SHORTLY
SHORTOF
SHOUTED
SHOUTER
SHUNTED
SHUTTER
SHUTTLE
SHYSTER
THEATER
THEATRE
THISTLE
WHARTON
WHEATON
WHETTED
WHISTLE
WHITTLE

•H•••T•
CHALETS
CHAPATI
CHARITY
CHIANTI
CHRISTI
CHRISTO
CHRISTY
SHRIFTS
THEISTS
THERETO
THIRSTS
THIRSTY
THREATS
THRIFTS
THRIFTY
THROATS
THROATY
THRUSTS
THWARTS
WHERETO

•H••••T
CHAPLET
CHARIOT
CHEMIST
CHEROOT
CHEVIOT
CHEWOUT
SHALLOT
SHERBET
SHIPOUT
SHOOTAT
SHOTPUT
SHUBERT
SHUTOUT
THATSIT
THEREAT
THICKET
THOUGHT
WHATNOT
WHEREAT
WHIPPET
WHITEST

••HT•••
ACHTUNG
ASHTRAY
YAHTZEE

••H•T••
ACHATES
MAHATMA
OKHOTSK
SCHATZI
UNHITCH

••H••T•
ASHANTI
ATHLETE
BEHESTS
CAHOOTS
COHORTS
COHOSTS
EXHORTS
INHASTE
MAHOUTS
NAHUATL
REHEATS
TSHIRTS

••H•••T
ACHIEST
AMHERST
ASHIEST
ATHEART
ATHEIST
ATHIRST
ATHWART
BYHEART
COHABIT
EXHAUST
EXHIBIT
INHABIT
INHERIT
INHIBIT
SCHMIDT

•••HT••
BATHTUB
EIGHTHS
FIGHTER
HIGHTEA
HIGHTOP
LIGHTED
LIGHTEN
LIGHTER
LIGHTLY
LIGHTUP
MIGHTNT
NAPHTHA
NIGHTIE
NIGHTLY
RICHTER
RIGHTED
RIGHTER
RIGHTLY
RIGHTON
SHIHTZU
SIGHTED
SIGHTLY
TIGHTEN
TIGHTER
TIGHTLY
WASHTUB
YACHTED

•••H•T•
AKIHITO
CACHETS
EBWHITE
ESTHETE
JAPHETH
MACHETE
MISHITS
OUTHITS
REDHATS
REDHOTS
SACHETS
TINHATS
TOPHATS
UPSHOTS
WICHITA

•••H••T
ASPHALT
BATHMAT
CASHOUT
DISHOUT
EARHART
ECKHART
ELKHART
ENCHANT
ESCHEAT
FISHNET
FISHOUT
HIGHEST
HIGHHAT
INSHORT
JOBHUNT
LITHEST
LUSHEST
MANHUNT
MIGHTNT
NEWHART
NIGHEST
ONTHEQT
POSHEST
PREHEAT
RASHEST
REDHEAT
RESHOOT
RICHEST
SOPHIST
WASHOUT
WITHOUT
YOGHURT

••••HT•
ALIGHTS
BLIGHTS
DOUGHTY
FLIGHTS
FLIGHTY
FRIGHTS
HAUGHTY
HEIGHTS
KNIGHTS
NAUGHTS
NAUGHTY
PLIGHTS
SLIGHTS
VEIGHTS
WEIGHTS
WEIGHTY
WRIGHTS

••••H•T
BASEHIT
BIGSHOT
CROCHET
EARSHOT
EPITHET
FRESHET
GUNSHOT
HARDHAT
HARDHIT
HATCHET
HIGHHAT
HOTSHOT
LAUGHAT
MUGSHOT
ONESHOT
POTSHOT
PROPHET
RAINHAT
RATCHET
RIMSHOT
ROUGHIT
SILKHAT
WATCHIT

•••••HT
ALRIGHT
BORSCHT
BROUGHT
DELIGHT
DRAUGHT
DROUGHT
FRAUGHT
FREIGHT
INSIGHT
MRRIGHT
ONSIGHT
RELIGHT
SLEIGHT
THOUGHT
TONIGHT
UPRIGHT
UPTIGHT
UTRECHT
WROUGHT

HU•••••
HUBBARD
HUBBELL
HUBBIES
HUBBUBS
HUBCAPS
HUDDLED
HUDDLES
HUFFIER
HUFFILY
HUFFING
HUGGERS
HUGGING
HULKING
HULLERS
HULLING
HULLOED
HUMANLY
HUMBLED
HUMBLER
HUMBLES
HUMBUGS
HUMDRUM
HUMERAL
HUMERUS
HUMIDLY
HUMIDOR
HUMMERS
HUMMING
HUMMOCK
HUMORED
HUMOURS
HUNCHED
HUNCHES
HUNDRED
HUNGARY
HUNGERS
HUNGOUT
HUNKERS
HUNTERS
HUNTING
HUNTLEY
HURDLED
HURDLER
HURDLES
HURLERS
HURLING
HURRAHS
HURRIED
HURRIES
HURTFUL
HURTING
HURTLED
HURTLES
HUSBAND
HUSHABY
HUSHING
HUSKERS
HUSKIER
HUSKIES
HUSKILY
HUSKING
HUSSARS
HUSSEIN
HUSSIES
HUSTLED
HUSTLER
HUSTLES
HUTCHES
HUZZAHS

H•U••••
HAUBERK
HAUGHTY
HAULAGE
HAULERS
HAULING
HAULOFF
HAULSUP
HAUNTED
HAUTBOY
HAUTEUR
HOUDINI
HOUNDED
HOUSING
HOUSMAN
HOUSTON
HYUNDAI

H••U•••
HANUKAH
HHMUNRO

H•••U••
HAMBURG
HANGUPS
HEPBURN
HERCULE
HEXNUTS
HEYJUDE
HICCUPS
HIRSUTE
HOLDUPS
HOMBURG
HONOURS
HOOKUPS
HOTTUBS
HUBBUBS
HUMBUGS
HUMOURS

H••••U•
HABITUE
HAFNIUM
HAHNIUM
HAIRCUT
HALIBUT
HAMITUP
HANDFUL
HANDGUN
HANDOUT
HANDSUP
HANGOUT
HANGSUP
HARBOUR
HARDPUT
HARMFUL
HATEFUL
HAULSUP
HAUTEUR
HEADOUT
HEADSUP
HEAROUT
HEATSUP
HEEDFUL
HEINOUS
HELDOUT
HELPFUL
HELPOUT
HIDEOUS
HIDEOUT
HOLDOUT
HOLDSUP
HOLEDUP
HOLEOUT
HOLESUP
HOLMIUM
HOMERUN
HOODLUM
HOOKSUP
HOPEFUL
HOTSPUR
HUMDRUM
HUMERUS
HUNGOUT
HURTFUL
HYDROUS
HYPEDUP

H•••••U
HOFBRAU

•HU••••
CHUCKED
CHUCKLE
CHUGGED
CHUKKAS
CHUKKER
CHUMMED
CHUNNEL
CHURNED
CHUTNEY
DHURRIE
RHUBARB
RHUMBAS
SHUBERT
SHUCKED
SHUCKER
SHUDDER
SHUFFLE
SHUNNED
SHUNTED
SHUSHED
SHUSHES
SHUTEYE
SHUTOFF
SHUTOUT
SHUTSIN
SHUTSUP
SHUTTER
SHUTTLE
THUDDED
THULIUM
THUMBED
THUMPED
THUMPER
THUNDER
THURBER
THURMAN
THUSFAR
WHUPPED

•H•U•••
CHAUCER
HHMUNRO
SHOUTED
SHOUTER
SHRUBBY
THOUGHT
THRUSTS
THRUWAY
WHAUDEN

•H••U••
CHEQUER
CHEQUES
CHERUBS
CHINUPS
SHOGUNS
SHROUDS
THROUGH

•H•••U•
CHALKUP
CHATSUP
CHECKUP
CHEERUP
CHETRUM
CHEWOUT
CHEWSUP
CHOKEUP
PHOEBUS
RHENIUM
RHODIUM
RHOMBUS
SHAKEUP
SHAPEUP
SHIPOUT
SHOOKUP
SHOOTUP
SHOTGUN
SHOTPUT
SHOWSUP
SHUTOUT
SHUTSUP
THEROUX
THESEUS
THINKUP
THORIUM
THULIUM
WHIPSUP

•H••••U
CHAPEAU
CHATEAU
SHIATSU
SHIHTZU
THOREAU

••HU•••
INHUMAN
KAHUNAS
NAHUATL

••H•U••
ACHTUNG
ASHBURY
EXHAUST
INHOUSE
MAHOUTS

••H••U•
ECHINUS
HAHNIUM

•••HU••
ANAHUAC
ENTHUSE
JOBHUNT
LASHUPS
MANHUNT
PUSHUPS
SICHUAN
TERHUNE
YOGHURT

•••H•U•
BASHFUL
BATHTUB
CACHOUS
CALHOUN
CASHOUT
CEPHEUS
DISHOUT
FISHOUT
ISTHMUS
LIGHTUP
LITHIUM
MANHOUR
MILHAUD
OFFHOUR
ORPHEUS
WASHOUT
WASHTUB
WISHFUL
WITHOUT

•••H••U
SHIHTZU

••••HU•
BACCHUS
BEARHUG
BRUSHUP
BULGHUR
CATCHUP
COUGHUP
DONAHUE
FULGHUM
KETCHUP
MALTHUS
MATCHUP
MITCHUM
PATCHUP
PSYCHUP
PUNCHUP
PYRRHUS
QUECHUA
ROUGHUP
SMASHUP
SORGHUM
SULPHUR
TOUCHUP

•••••HU
MATTHAU

H•V••••
HAVARTI
HAVENOT
HOVERED
HOVERER

H••V•••
HALVING
HARVARD
HARVEST
HEAVEHO
HEAVENS
HEAVERS
HEAVETO
HEAVIER
HEAVIES
HEAVILY
HEAVING

H•••V••
HANOVER
HESHVAN
HOPOVER
HOWEVER

•H•V•••
CHEVIED
CHEVIES
CHEVIOT
CHEVRES
CHEVRON
SHAVERS
SHAVING
SHIVERS
SHOVELS
SHOVERS
SHOVING
ZHIVAGO

•H••V••
CHEEVER
CHERVIL
SHEAVED
SHEAVES
SHELVED
SHELVES
SHRIVEL
SHRIVER
SHRIVES
THIEVED
THIEVES
THRIVED
THRIVES
WHARVES
WHOEVER

•H••••V
CHEKHOV

••H•V••
BEHAVED
BEHAVES
LEHAVRE

••H••V•
ACHIEVE
BEHOOVE
PAHLAVI

•••HV••
HESHVAN

•••H•V•
ANCHOVY
ARCHIVE
BEEHIVE
YESHIVA

••••H•V
CHEKHOV

H•W••••
HAWHAWS
HAWKERS
HAWKEYE
HAWKING
HAWKINS
HAWKISH
HAWSERS
HEWLETT
HGWELLS
HOWARDS
HOWBEIT
HOWCOME
HOWDAHS
HOWELLS
HOWEVER
HOWLERS
HOWLING

H••W•••
HAYWARD
HAYWIRE
HEYWOOD
HOGWASH
HOGWILD
HOTWARS
HOTWIRE

H•••W••
HALFWAY
HALFWIT
HALLWAY
HARDWON
HEADWAY
HIGHWAY
HOLYWAR

H••••W•
HALLOWS
HARROWS
HAWHAWS
HAYMOWS
HEBREWS
HEEHAWS
HOEDOWN
HOLLOWS
HOOTOWL

H•••••W
HACKSAW
HANDSAW
HIGHLOW
HOLYCOW

•HW••••
THWACKS
THWARTS

•H•W•••
CHEWERS
CHEWIER
CHEWING
CHEWOUT
CHEWSUP
CHOWDER
SHAWNEE
SHAWWAL
SHEWOLF
SHOWBIZ
SHOWDOG
SHOWERS
SHOWERY
SHOWIER
SHOWILY
SHOWING
SHOWMAN
SHOWMEN
SHOWNIN
SHOWOFF
SHOWSIN
SHOWSUP
THAWING

•H••W••
SHAWWAL
SHERWIN
THREWIN
THROWER
THROWIN
THRUWAY
WHOSWHO

•H•••W•
SHADOWS
SHADOWY

•H••••W
CHOCTAW
SHALLOW
WHIPSAW

••HW•••
ATHWART
SCHWINN

••H•W••
MOHAWKS

•••HW••
ARCHWAY
HIGHWAY
PATHWAY

•••H•W•
CASHEWS
CUSHAWS
ESCHEWS
GOSHAWK
HAWHAWS
HEEHAWS
MATHEWS
NEPHEWS
NOSHOWS
TVSHOWS

•••H••W
CASHCOW
HIGHLOW
LITHGOW

••••H•W
AIRSHOW
CAPSHAW
DOGCHEW
DOGCHOW
DOGSHOW
ICESHOW
KNOWHOW
MATTHEW
SALCHOW
SOMEHOW
USOSHOW

H•X••••
HEXAGON
HEXNUTS
HEXSIGN

H••X•••
HOAXERS
HOAXING

H•••X••
HELIXES
HYRAXES

H•••••X
HALIFAX
HENDRIX

•H••X••
PHLOXES

•H••••X
PHALANX
PHARYNX
PHOENIX
SHOEBOX
THEROUX

•••H••X
CASHBOX

••••H•X
NARTHEX
PANCHAX

HY•••••
HYALINE
HYBRIDS
HYDRANT
HYDRATE
HYDROUS
HYGIEIA
HYGIENE
HYMNALS
HYPEDUP
HYPHENS
HYPOING
HYRACES
HYRAXES
HYSSOPS
HYUNDAI

H•Y••••
HAYFORK
HAYLOFT
HAYMOWS
HAYRACK
HAYRIDE
HAYSEED
HAYWARD
HAYWIRE
HEYDAYS
HEYJUDE
HEYWOOD
HOYDENS

H••Y•••
HALYARD
HOLYARK
HOLYCOW
HOLYOKE
HOLYSEE
HOLYWAR

H•••Y••
HALCYON
HONEYED

H••••Y•
HAIRDYE
HAWKEYE
HEYDAYS
HOMONYM

H•••••Y
HACKNEY
HALFWAY
HALLWAY
HAMMILY
HANDILY
HAPPILY
HARDILY
HARMONY
HARSHLY
HASTILY
HAUGHTY
HAUTBOY
HEADILY
HEADWAY
HEALTHY
HEARSAY
HEAVILY
HEFTILY
HELOTRY
HEMSLEY
HENNERY
HERSHEY
HICKORY
HIGHBOY
HIGHWAY
HILLARY
HISTORY
HOLIDAY
HONESTY
HOOTCHY
HORNSBY
HORRIFY
HOSIERY
HUFFILY
HUMANLY
HUMIDLY
HUNGARY
HUNTLEY
HUSHABY
HUSKILY

•HY••••
PHYLLIS
PHYSICS
RHYMERS
RHYMING
RHYTHMS
SHYLOCK
SHYNESS
SHYSTER
THYSELF
WHYDAHS

•H•Y•••
KHAYYAM

•H••Y••
KHAYYAM
PHARYNX

•H•••Y•
SHUTEYE

•H••••Y
CHANTEY
CHARILY
CHARITY
CHARLEY
CHEAPLY
CHICORY
CHIEFLY
CHIMNEY
CHINTZY
CHOMSKY
CHRISTY
CHUTNEY
GHASTLY
GHOSTLY
PHONILY
SHADILY
SHADOWY
SHAKILY
SHAPELY
SHARKEY
SHARPLY
SHEERLY
SHELLEY
SHIRLEY
SHOOFLY
SHORTLY
SHOWERY
SHOWILY
SHRILLY
SHRUBBY
THATCHY
THERAPY
THEREBY
THICKLY
THIERRY
THIRDLY
THIRSTY
THREADY
THRIFTY
THROATY
THRUWAY
WHEREBY
WHISKEY
WHITNEY

••H•••Y
ASHBURY
ASHTRAY
DAHOMEY
JOHNGAY
JOHNJAY
MAHONEY
UNHANDY
UNHAPPY
WCHANDY

•••HY••
ZEPHYRS

•••H•Y•
FISHEYE
KATHRYN
SASHAYS

•••H••Y
ALCHEMY
ANCHOVY
ANTHONY
ARCHERY
ARCHWAY
BETHANY
BYTHEBY
DITHERY
EUPHONY
FISHERY
FISHFRY
FISHILY
HIGHBOY
HIGHWAY
HUSHABY
LATHERY
LIGHTLY
LITHELY
MUSHILY
NIGHTLY
PATHWAY
PITHILY
PUSHILY
RIGHTLY
SIGHTLY
TIGHTLY
ZACHARY

••••H•Y
APISHLY
BOKCHOY
BRASHLY
DOUGHTY
EARTHLY
FLIGHTY
FRESHLY
HARSHLY
HAUGHTY
HERSHEY
MADEHAY
MAKEHAY
MONTHLY
MURPHEY
NAUGHTY
PLUSHLY
ROUGHLY
SOUTHEY
TOUGHLY
WEIGHTY

•••••HY
ANARCHY
ATROPHY
BLOTCHY
BREATHY
CRUNCHY
DENNEHY
DOROTHY
EMPATHY
GROUCHY
HEALTHY
HOOTCHY
KITSCHY
KOOTCHY
LENGTHY
PAUNCHY
PREACHY
SKETCHY
SLOUCHY
SPLASHY
SQUISHY
STARCHY
SWARTHY
THATCHY
TIMOTHY
TWITCHY
WEALTHY

H•Z••••
HAZARDS
HAZIEST
HAZINGS
HUZZAHS

H••Z•••
HUZZAHS

H•••Z••
HORIZON

H•••••Z
HEIFETZ

•H•Z•••
RHIZOME
WHIZKID
WHIZZED
WHIZZES

•H••Z••
WHEEZED
WHEEZER
WHEEZES
WHIZZED
WHIZZES

•H•••Z•
CHINTZY
CHORIZO
SHIHTZU

•H••••Z
SHOWBIZ

••H•Z••
YAHTZEE

••H••Z•
SCHATZI
SCHERZI
SCHERZO

•••H•Z•
SHIHTZU

••••H•Z
GEEWHIZ
NATCHEZ

IA•••••
IACOCCA

I•A••••
IDAHOAN
IMAGERS
IMAGERY
IMAGINE
IMAGING
IMAGOES
IMAMATE
IMARETS
INADAZE
INAHEAP
INAMESS
INANELY
INANEST
INAPTLY
INARUSH
INASNIT
INASPIN
INASPOT
INASTEW
INAWEOF
INAWORD
IPANEMA
IRANIAN
IRATELY
IRATEST
ISADORA
ITALIAN
ITALICS
IVANHOE

I••A•••
ICEAGES
ICEAXES
ICHABOD
IDCARDS
IDEALLY
IDEATED
IDEATES
IDIAMIN
IGUANAS
IMPACTS
IMPAIRS
IMPALAS
IMPALED
IMPALES
IMPANEL
IMPARTS
IMPASSE
IMPASTO
INCANTS
INFANCY
INFANTA
INFANTS
INFAVOR
INGALLS
INHABIT
INHALED
INHALER
INHALES
INHASTE
INMATES
INNARDS
INTAKES
INVACUO
INVADED
INVADER
INVADES
INVALID
INWARDS
IODATES
ISLAMIC
ISLANDS
ISRAELI
ITHACAN

I•••A••
IBNSAUD
ICEBAGS
ICECAPS
ICELAND
ICEPACK
IKEBANA
IMAMATE
IMITATE
IMPEACH
IMPLANT
INADAZE
INBOARD
INDIANA
INDIANS
INEXACT
INFLAME
INFLATE
INGRAIN
INGRATE
INPEACE
INPHASE
INPLACE
INROADS
INSCAPE
INSEAMS
INSHAPE
INSPANS
INSTALL
INSTANT
INSTATE
IRELAND
IRONAGE
ISHMAEL
ISOBARS
ISOLATE
ITERANT
ITERATE

I••••A•
IBERIAN
ICEBOAT
IDAHOAN
IGUANAS
ILLEGAL
IMMORAL
IMPALAS
INAHEAP
INGEMAR
INHUMAN
INITIAL
INKYCAP
INNOWAY
INSOFAR
INSTEAD
INSULAR
IRANIAN
IRONMAN
ITALIAN
ITHACAN

I•••••A
IACOCCA
ICEDTEA
IKEBANA
INDIANA
INDICIA
INERTIA
INFANTA
INOCULA
INTEGRA
IPANEMA
ISADORA
IWOJIMA

•IA••••
BIALIES
BIASING
BIASSED
DIADEMS
DIAGRAM
DIAHANN
DIALECT
DIALERS
DIALING
DIALOGS
DIAMOND
DIAPERS
DIARIES
DIATOMS
FIACRES
FIANCEE
FIANCES
FIASCOS
GIACOMO
HIALEAH
LIAISED
LIAISES
LIAISON
MIAMIAN
MIASMAS
MIASMIC
NIAGARA
PIANISM
PIANIST
PIASTER
PIASTRE
PIAZZAS
SIAMESE
VIADUCT

•I•A•••
BIVALVE
BIZARRE
CICADAE
CICADAS
CITABLE
CITADEL
DIDACTS
DILATED
DILATES
DISABLE
DISARMS
DISAVOW
FINAGLE
FINALES
FINALLY
FINANCE
FIXABLE
FIXATED
FIXATES
GIRAFFE
GIRASOL
HIBACHI
HIDALGO
HIJACKS
HILAIRE
HIRABLE
HITACHI
JICAMAS
KILAUEA
KIWANIS
LIEABED
LIGATED
LIGATES
LIKABLE
LINAGES
LIVABLE
LIZARDS
MIKADOS
MINABLE
MINARET
MIRACLE
MIRADOR
MIRAGES
MIRAMAR
MIRAMAX
MIRANDA
MISALLY
MIXABLE
PICADOR
PICANTE
PICAROS
PICASSO
PINATAS
PIRAEUS
PIRANHA
PIRATED
PIRATES
PIRATIC
PITAPAT
PIZARRO
RIBANDS
RICARDO
RIVALED
RIVALRY
SINATRA
SIZABLE
SIZABLY
TIRADES
TISANES
TITANIA
TITANIC
VIDALIA
VIRAGOS
VISAGES
VISAVIS
VITALLY
VITAMIN
VIVALDI
WIZARDS

•I••A••
AIRBAGS
AIRBALL
AIRBASE
AIRDAMS
AIRDATE
AIRFARE
AIRLANE
AIRMAIL
AIRMASS
AIRRAID
AIRSACS
AIRTAXI
AIRWAVE
AIRWAYS
BIDFAIR
BIGBAND
BIGBANG
BIGGAME
BIGNAME
BIOMASS
BIPLANE
BITMAPS
BITPART
CILIATE
CINZANO
CITRATE
DIAHANN
DICTATE
DIEHARD
DIETARY
DIGRAPH
DIKTATS
DILLARD
DIORAMA
DISBAND
DISBARS
DISCARD
DISDAIN
DISEASE
DISMAYS
DISTAFF
DISTANT
DITTANY
FIJIANS
FINEART
FINIALS
FINLAND
FIREANT
FIREARM
GIMBALS
GIZZARD
HILLARY
HISPANO
JIGSAWS
JIMJAMS
KIDNAPS
KILDARE
KIMBALL
KIRMANS
KITBAGS
LIBRARY
LIBYANS
LIMEADE
LINEAGE
LINEATE
LINKAGE
LIPBALM
MICHAEL
MICMACS
MIDDAYS
MIDEAST
MIDLAND
MIDWAYS
MIGRANT
MIGRATE
MIKHAIL
MILEAGE
MILHAUD
MILLAND
MILLARD
MINOANS
MISCALL
MISCAST
MISDATE
MISHAPS
MISLAID
MISLAYS
MISMATE
MISNAME
MISSALS
MISTAKE
NIAGARA
NIGGARD
NIRVANA
NITRATE
NITTANY
OILCAKE
OILCANS
OILLAMP
OILPANS
PICCARD
PICKAXE
PIEBALD
PIEPANS
PIGTAIL
PILLAGE
PILLARS
PINBALL
PINNACE
PINNATE
PINOAKS
PINTAIL
PINWALE
PIQUANT
PITFALL
PITSAWS
PIZZAZZ

QINTARS
RIBCAGE
RICHARD
RIMBAUD
RIOTACT
RIPRAPS
RIPSAWS
RITUALS
SIDEARM
SIGNALS
SIMIANS
SINKAGE
SIOUANS
SITUATE
SIXPACK
TICTACS
TIERACK
TIETACK
TIFFANY
TIJUANA
TILLAGE
TIMBALE
TIMBALS
TINCANS
TINEARS
TINHATS
TITRATE
VIBRANT
VIBRATE
VIBRATO
VILLAGE
VILLAIN
VINTAGE
VIOLATE
VISUALS
VITIATE
WIDMARK
WIGWAGS
WIGWAMS
WILLARD
ZIGZAGS

•I•••A•

AIMEDAT
AIRBOAT
AIRHEAD
AIRPLAY
BIFOCAL
BIGDEAL
BIGHEAD
BIKEWAY
BIMODAL
BINGHAM
BIPEDAL
BIPOLAR
BIRDMAN
BIVOUAC
CICADAE
CICADAS
CINEMAS
CINEMAX
DIAGRAM
DIGITAL
DINGBAT
DIPOLAR
DISHPAN
DISHRAG
DISPLAY
DIURNAL
FIBULAE
FIBULAS
FIESTAS
FIGLEAF
FIREMAN
GIDDYAP
GILBLAS
GINGHAM
GIVEWAY
HIALEAH
HICKMAN
HIGHHAT
HIGHWAY
HINTSAT
JICAMAS
JILLIAN
KINGMAN
KINGRAT
KINSMAN
LIBERAL
LIKEMAD
LILLIAN
LILYPAD
LINBIAO
LINDSAY
LINEMAN
LINGUAL
LIPREAD
LITERAL
LIVEOAK
MIAMIAN
MIASMAS
MIDYEAR
MILKMAN
MILLDAM
MIMOSAS
MINERAL
MINICAM
MINIMAL
MINIVAN
MIRAMAR
MIRAMAX
MISDEAL
MISDIAL
MISHEAR
MISLEAD
MISPLAY
MISREAD
MISTRAL
MITHRAS
MITZVAH
NICOLAS
NIKOLAI
PIAZZAS
PICKSAT
PIKEMAN
PINATAS
PINCHAS
PINESAP
PINETAR
PINHEAD
PITAPAT
PITTMAN
PIVOTAL
RICERAT
RICHMAN
RIDGWAY
SICHUAN
SICKBAY
SICKPAY
SIDEBAR
SIDECAR
SIDEMAN
SIENNAS
SIERRAS
SIESTAS
SILICAS
SILKHAT
SIMILAR
SIOBHAN
TIBETAN
TIMELAG
TIMEWAS
TINSTAR
TITULAR
VICTUAL
VICUNAS
VIETNAM
VINEGAR
VIRGOAN
VIRTUAL
VIZSLAS
WILDCAT
WILLIAM
WINDBAG
WINEBAR
WINESAP
WINKSAT
WIRETAP
WISEMAN
YITZHAK
ZINNIAS

•I••••A

BIRETTA
CIBORIA
DILEMMA
DIORAMA
DIPLOMA
GINGIVA
HIGHTEA
KILAUEA
LIBERIA
MILITIA
MINEOLA
MINERVA
MINOLTA
MINORCA
MINUTIA
MIRANDA
NIAGARA
NICOSIA
NIGERIA
NIRVANA
PIRANHA
RICKSHA
RICOTTA
RIGVEDA
RIORITA
RIVIERA
SIBERIA
SILESIA
SINATRA
TIJUANA
TITANIA
VIDALIA
VISCERA
VISTULA
WICHITA

••IA•••

ALIASES
AMIABLE
AMIABLY
ARIADNE
ASIATIC
AVIANCA
AVIATED
AVIATES
AVIATOR
AXIALLY
BRIARDS
CHIANTI
FRIABLE
IDIAMIN
JAIALAI
NAIADES
OPIATES
PLIABLE
PLIABLY
PLIANCY
SHIATSU

••I•A••

ABIGAIL
AGITATE
ALIBABA
ALIDADE
ANIMALS
ANIMATE
ANIMATO
ARIKARA
BOITANO
BRIDALS
BRIGADE
BRIGAND
BRITAIN
CAIMANS
CHICAGO
CHICANA
CHICANO
CLIMATE
CLIPART
COINAGE
CUIRASS
EMIRATE
FRIDAYS
FRIGATE
GRIMACE
GUITARS
IMITATE
MAITAIS
OHIOANS
OKINAWA
ORIGAMI
OXIDANT
OXIDASE
PAISANO
PRIMACY
PRIMARY
PRIMATE
PRIVACY
PRIVATE
SKIMASK
SPINACH
SPIRALS
SPIRANT
TAIPANS
THINAIR
UNITARY
ZHIVAGO

••I••A•

ARISTAE
ARISTAS
AXILLAE
BLINKAT
BRIGHAM
BRILLAT
CHILEAN
CRIMEAN
DRIPPAN
DRISTAN
DRIVEAT
ENIGMAS
EPIGRAM
FAIRWAY
FLIESAT
FRIEDAN
FRISIAN
GAINSAY
GEISHAS
GOINGAT
GRISHAM
GUINEAS
HAITIAN
INITIAL
JAIALAI
MAILBAG
OJIBWAS
OJIBWAY
PHIDIAS
PHINEAS
QUINOAS
RAILSAT
RAILWAY
RAINHAT
RAINMAN
SHIPMAN
SNIFFAT
SNIPEAT
SPIREAS
STIGMAS
THINMAN
TRIGRAM
TRISTAN
TRIVIAL
WHIPSAW
WHITMAN

••I•••A

ALIBABA
ARIETTA
ARIKARA
ARIZONA
AVIANCA
CHICANA
CHIMERA
ERITREA
KRISHNA
OKINAWA
SPINOZA

•••IA••

AERIALS
ANTIART
CILIATE
DEFIANT
DENIALS
DEVIANT
DEVIATE
ESPIALS
EXPIATE
FACIALS
FIJIANS
FINIALS
FOLIAGE
FOLIATE
GAVIALS
GOLIATH
INDIANA
INDIANS
JULIANA
KODIAKS
LABIALS
LABIATE
LARIATS
LUCIANO
MANIACS
MARIANA
MEDIANS
MEDIANT
MEDIATE
MENIALS
MYRIADS
NUBIANS
OBVIATE
PARIAHS
PONIARD
RADIALS
RADIANS
RADIANT
RADIATE
REDIALS
RELIANT
RUPIAHS
SATIATE
SERIALS
SERIATE
SIMIANS
SOCIALS
STRIATE
SYRIANS
TATIANA
TOPIARY
UNCIALS
VALIANT
VARIANT
VITIATE
ZODIACS

•••I•A•

ADMIRAL
AFRICAN
ANTIWAR
AQUINAS
ARNICAS
ARRIVAL
ARTISAN
BALIHAI
BKLIBAN
BOLIVAR
CALIBAN
CAPITAL
CAPITAN
CARINAS
COMICAL
CONICAL
CYNICAL
DECIMAL
DELILAH
DIGITAL
ESTIVAL
ETHICAL
FADIMAN
FAJITAS
FREITAG
HABITAT
HALIFAX
HEGIRAS
HELICAL
HELIPAD
HOLIDAY
LAMINAE
LAMINAL
LAMINAR
LAMINAS
LATIFAH
LATINAS
LEXICAL
LOGICAL
LYRICAL
MAGICAL
MARINAS
MARITAL
MAXIMAL
MEDICAL
MEXICAN
MINICAM
MINIMAL
MINIVAN
MOHICAN
MUSICAL
NOMINAL
OEDIPAL
ONEIDAS
OPTICAL
OPTIMAL
ORBITAL
ORDINAL
OVOIDAL
PATINAS
PELICAN
PEMICAN
PURITAN
RADICAL
RARITAN
RECITAL
RETINAE
RETINAL
RETINAS
REVIVAL
RUFIYAA
SAGINAW
SEMINAL
SEMINAR
SHEILAE
SHEILAH
SHEILAS
SILICAS
SIMILAR
STOICAL
SURINAM
TAXICAB
TAXIWAY
TOPICAL
TROIKAS
TYPICAL
VATICAN

•••I••A

AGRIPPA
ANTIGUA
BATISTA
BELINDA
BOLIVIA
CARIOCA
CECILIA
CEDILLA
DELIRIA
ECHIDNA
FELICIA
GORILLA
HYGIEIA
INDIANA
INDICIA
JULIANA
LAVINIA
LETITIA
MARIANA
MARIMBA
MATILDA
MAXILLA
MELINDA
MELISSA
MILITIA
NAMIBIA
NORIEGA
PAPILLA
RIVIERA
RUFIYAA
SCHIRRA
SYRINGA
TABITHA
TAPIOCA
TATIANA
TUNISIA
VANILLA

••••IA•

ACACIAS
ACADIAN
AEOLIAN
ANANIAS
ARABIAN
ASOCIAL
BELGIAN
BESTIAL
CASPIAN
CASSIAS
COAXIAL
CORDIAL
CRANIAL
CRUCIAL
DAHLIAS
ELEGIAC
ELYSIAN
ETESIAN
ETONIAN
FASCIAS
FLUVIAL
FRISIAN
FUSTIAN
GAMBIAN
GENTIAN
GLACIAL
GLORIAS
GORDIAN
GRACIAS
GRECIAN
HADRIAN
HAITIAN
HESSIAN
IBERIAN
INITIAL
IRANIAN
ITALIAN
JILLIAN
LAOTIAN
LATVIAN
LILLIAN
LINBIAO
LOGGIAS
MARTIAL
MARTIAN
MATHIAS
MESSIAH
MIAMIAN
MISDIAL
NUPTIAL
NUTRIAS
OBADIAH
ONTRIAL
OXONIAN
PARTIAL
PERSIAN
PHIDIAS
PHOBIAS
PLUVIAL
PONTIAC
PYTHIAS
RETRIAL
RUFFIAN
RUSSIAN
SAURIAN
SERBIAN
SPATIAL
SPECIAL
STYGIAN
STYRIAN
SUNDIAL
TERTIAL
TRIVIAL
TRUCIAL
UMBRIAN
UTOPIAN
UTOPIAS
UXORIAL
WILLIAM
WOZNIAK
ZAMBIAN
ZINNIAS
ZOYSIAS

••••I•A

AMERICA
AMERIKA
BOBVILA
BURKINA
CANDIDA
CANTINA
CORRIDA
CORSICA
CZARINA
EMERITA
EROTICA
EXOTICA
FLORIDA
FONTINA
FORMICA
GINGIVA
IWOJIMA
JAMAICA
JESSICA
KACHINA
LEMPIRA
MACHINA
MADEIRA
MARTINA
MESSINA
OCARINA
PAPRIKA
PARTITA
PASTINA
PAULINA
PODRIDA
REPLICA
RETSINA
RIORITA
SABRINA
SESTINA
STAMINA
TEQUILA
TOSHIBA
TSARINA
TZARINA
WICHITA
YESHIVA

•••••IA

ALBANIA
ALGERIA
ALLUVIA
AMMONIA
AMNESIA
ANAEMIA
ANOSMIA
ANTONIA
APHELIA
AQUARIA
ARCADIA
ARMENIA
ASSYRIA
ASTORIA
AUSTRIA
BAVARIA
BEDELIA
BEGONIA
BOHEMIA
BOLIVIA
BOTHNIA
CAMELIA
CARAMIA
CECILIA
CIBORIA
CLAUDIA
CROATIA
CYNTHIA
DELIRIA
EMPORIA
ENCOMIA
ESTONIA
ETRURIA
EURASIA
EXURBIA
FELICIA
FREESIA
FUCHSIA
GALATIA
GANGLIA
GEORGIA
HYGIEIA
INDICIA
INERTIA
LAVINIA
LETITIA
LIBERIA
MAHALIA
MILITIA
MINUTIA
MORAVIA
NAMIBIA
NATALIA
NICOSIA
NIGERIA
OCEANIA
OCTAVIA
OLYMPIA
OPHELIA
PETUNIA
POMPEIA
PRUSSIA
RATAFIA
REGALIA
ROMANIA
SAMARIA
SANGRIA
SEDALIA
SEGOVIA
SEQUOIA
SIBERIA
SILESIA
SOLARIA
SOMALIA
STLUCIA
TALARIA
TITANIA
TUNISIA
VIDALIA
ZENOBIA

IB•••••

IBERIAN
IBNSAUD

I•B••••

IMBIBED
IMBIBES
IMBRUED
IMBRUES
IMBUING
INBLOOM
INBOARD
INBOUND
INBREED
INBRIEF

I••B•••

ICEBAGS
ICEBERG
ICEBLUE
ICEBOAT
IKEBANA
ILLBRED
INKBLOT
ISOBARS

I•••B••

ICHABOD
IGNOBLE
IGNOBLY
IMBIBED
IMBIBES
INHABIT
INHIBIT
INORBIT

I••••B•

ICECUBE
INDOUBT

•IB••••

BIBELOT
CIBORIA
DIBBLED
DIBBLES
FIBBERS
FIBBING
FIBRILS
FIBROUS
FIBULAE
FIBULAS
GIBBERS
GIBBETS
GIBBONS
GIBBOUS
GIBLETS
GIBLUES
HIBACHI
JIBBOOM
KIBBLED
KIBBLES
KIBBUTZ
LIBBERS
LIBBING
LIBELED
LIBELER
LIBERAL
LIBERIA
LIBERTY
LIBIDOS
LIBRARY
LIBYANS
NIBBLED
NIBBLER
NIBBLES
NIBLICK
RIBANDS
RIBBING
RIBBONS
RIBCAGE
RIBEYES
SIBERIA
SIBLING
TIBETAN
VIBRANT
VIBRATE
VIBRATO

•I•B•••

AIRBAGS
AIRBALL
AIRBASE
AIRBOAT
BIGBAND
BIGBANG
BIGBEND
BIGBIRD
BIGBOYS
BILBOES
DIBBLED
DIBBLES
DIMBULB
DISBAND
DISBARS
FIBBERS
FIBBING
FILBERT
GIBBERS
GIBBETS
GIBBONS
GIBBOUS
GILBERT
GILBLAS
GIMBALS
HIPBONE
HIPBOOT
JIBBOOM
KIBBLED
KIBBLES
KIBBUTZ
KIMBALL
KITBAGS
LIBBERS
LIBBING
LIMBERS
LIMBING
LINBIAO
LIPBALM
NIBBLED
NIBBLER
NIBBLES
NIEBUHR
NIMBLER
NIOBIUM
PIEBALD
PINBALL
PITBOSS
PITBULL
RIBBING
RIBBONS
RIMBAUD
SIOBHAN
TIDBITS
TIMBALE
TIMBALS
TIMBERS
TIMBRES
TITBITS

•I••B••

CITABLE
DINGBAT
DISABLE
DISOBEY
FIREBOX
FIREBUG
FIXABLE
HIGHBOY
HIRABLE
LIEABED
LIKABLE
LIVABLE
MINABLE
MINIBUS
MIXABLE
PILLBOX
PILLBUG
RISIBLE
SICKBAY
SIDEBAR
SIDEBET
SIZABLE
SIZABLY
VISIBLE
VISIBLY
WINDBAG
WINEBAR

•I•••B•

DISROBE
MICROBE
MIDRIBS
RIOLOBO

•I••••B

DIMBULB
DISTURB
LIONCUB

••IB•••

ALIBABA
AMIBLUE
BRIBERY
BRIBING
CLIBURN
CRIBBED
CUIBONO
DRIBBLE
DRIBLET
EDIBLES
FOIBLES
GLIBBER
LEIBNIZ
OJIBWAS
OJIBWAY
QUIBBLE
SKIBOOT
TRIBUNE
TRIBUTE

••I•B••
AMIABLE AMIABLY CLIMBED CLIMBER CRIBBED DRIBBLE FRIABLE FRISBEE GLIBBER MAILBAG MAILBOX PHILBIN PLIABLE PLIABLY QUIBBLE RAINBOW THIMBLE TWINBED

••I••B•
ABIDEBY ALIBABA GOINGBY NAIROBI SWINGBY

•••IB••
ANTIBES AUDIBLE AUDIBLY BKLIBAN CALIBAN CALIBER CALIBRE CARIBES CARIBOU DECIBEL DELIBES EXHIBIT HALIBUT IMBIBED IMBIBES INHIBIT LEGIBLE LEGIBLY MINIBUS NAMIBIA OMNIBUS PARIBUS RISIBLE SANIBEL SCRIBES VISIBLE VISIBLY

•••I•B•
LETITBE MARIMBA

•••I••B
TAXICAB

••••IB•
ASCRIBE MADLIBS MIDRIBS TOSHIBA

IC•••••
ICEAGES ICEAXES ICEBAGS ICEBERG ICEBLUE ICEBOAT ICECAPS ICECOLD ICECUBE ICEDTEA ICEFLOE ICEFREE ICELAND ICELESS ICEMILK ICEPACK ICEPICK ICERINK ICESHOW ICHABOD ICICLES ICINESS ICINGIN ICKIEST

I•C••••
IACOCCA IDCARDS INCANTS INCENSE INCEPTS INCHING INCIPIT INCISED INCISES INCISOR INCITED INCITER INCITES INCIVIL INCLINE INCLOSE INCLUDE INCOMES INCUDES IPCRESS ITCHIER ITCHING

I••C•••
ICECAPS ICECOLD ICECUBE ICICLES INOCULA INSCAPE IRECKON

I•••C••
IACOCCA ILLICIT IMPACTS INDICES INDICIA INDICTS INDUCED INDUCER INDUCES INDUCTS INFECTS INFOCUS INJECTS INKYCAP INSECTS INVACUO ITHACAN

I••••C•
IACOCCA ICEPACK ICEPICK ILIESCU IMPEACH INDUTCH INEXACT INFANCY INFLECT INFLICT INFORCE INPEACE INPLACE INSPECT INSTOCK INVOICE IONESCO IPSWICH ITALICS

I•••••C
IDENTIC IDIOTIC IDYLLIC ILLOGIC ISLAMIC

•IC••••
BICKERS BICOLOR BICYCLE CICADAE CICADAS DICIEST DICKENS DICKERS DICKEYS DICKIES DICTATE DICTION DICTUMS FICKLER FICTION FICTIVE FICUSES HICCUPS HICKMAN HICKORY JICAMAS KICKERS KICKING KICKOFF KICKOUT KICKSIN KICKSUP KICKUPS LICENCE LICENSE LICHENS LICITLY LICKETY LICKING MICHAEL MICHELE MICMACS MICROBE MICRONS NICCOLO NICHOLS NICKELS NICKERS NICKING NICOLAS NICOSIA PICADOR PICANTE PICAROS PICASSO PICCARD PICCOLO PICKAXE PICKENS PICKERS PICKETS PICKETT PICKIER PICKING PICKLED PICKLES PICKOFF PICKOUT PICKSAT PICKSON PICKSUP PICKUPS PICNICS PICTURE RICARDO RICERAT RICHARD RICHEST RICHMAN RICHTER RICKETY RICKEYS RICKLES RICKSHA RICOTTA SICCING SICHUAN SICKBAY SICKENS SICKEST SICKLES SICKOUT SICKPAY TICKERS TICKETS TICKING TICKLED TICKLER TICKLES TICKOFF TICTACS VICEROY VICIOUS VICTIMS VICTORS VICTORY VICTUAL VICUNAS WICHITA WICKERS WICKETS WICKIUP

•I•C•••
AIRCOOL AIRCREW AITCHES BIRCHED BIRCHES BISCUIT CINCHED CINCHES CIRCLED CIRCLES CIRCLET CIRCUIT CIRCUSY DIOCESE DISCARD DISCERN DISCOED DISCORD DISCUSS DITCHED DITCHES FIACRES FILCHED FILCHER FILCHES FINCHES FISCHER FITCHES GIACOMO HICCUPS HITCHED HITCHER HITCHES JIMCHEE KITCHEN LINCOLN LITCHIS MINCERS MINCING MIOCENE MISCALL MISCAST MISCUED MISCUES MITCHUM NICCOLO OILCAKE OILCANS PICCARD PICCOLO PIECERS PIECING PINCERS PINCHAS PINCHED PINCHER PINCHES PINCURL PISCINE PISCOPO PITCHED PITCHER PITCHES PITCHIN RIBCAGE RIPCORD RITCHIE SICCING SINCERE SITCOMS TIECLIP TINCANS VINCENT VISCERA VISCOUS WINCERS WINCHED WINCHES WINCING WITCHES ZILCHES ZIPCODE ZIRCONS

•I••C••
BICYCLE BIFOCAL BISECTS DIDACTS DIRECTS FIANCEE FIANCES FIASCOS FIERCER FINICKY HIBACHI HIJACKS HITACHI KITSCHY LIONCUB MILKCOW MIMICRY MINICAM MIRACLE PIERCED PIERCES PINOCLE SIDECAR SILICAS SILICON SIROCCO TIMECOP WILDCAT

•I•••C•
AIRLOCK AIRSACS AIRSOCK BIONICS DIALECT DIPTYCH DISSECT DIVORCE FINANCE GIMMICK HILLOCK LICENCE MICMACS MINORCA NIBLICK NITPICK PICNICS PIMLICO PINNACE RIDDICK RIOTACT SILENCE SIROCCO SIXPACK TICTACS TIERACK TIETACK TITMICE VIADUCT

•I••••C
BIVOUAC KINETIC LIPSYNC MIASMIC MIDDLEC MIMETIC MITOTIC PIRATIC TITANIC

••IC•••
BRICKED CHICAGO CHICANA CHICANO CHICHEN CHICKEN CHICORY CLICHES CLICKED CRICKED CRICKET DEICERS DEICING ELICITS EPICENE EPICURE ERICSON EVICTED FLICKED FLICKER FRICKIE ICICLES JUICERS JUICEUP JUICIER JUICILY JUICING OMICRON PRICERS PRICIER PRICING PRICKED PRICKLE PRICKLY QUICHES QUICKEN QUICKER QUICKIE QUICKLY SEICHES SLICERS SLICING SLICKED SLICKER SLICKLY SNICKER SPICEUP SPICIER SPICING STICHES STICKER STICKTO STICKUP TEICHER THICKEN THICKER THICKET THICKLY TRICEPS TRICKED TRICKER TRICKLE TRICORN TRICOTS UNICORN VOICING

••I•C••
BRIOCHE EVINCED EVINCES HAIRCUT PRINCES QUINCES TWITCHY

••I••C•
AVIANCA CLINICS CRITICS EDIFICE FAIENCE GRIMACE ILIESCU ORIFICE ORINOCO PLIANCY PRIMACY PRIVACY SCIENCE SPINACH THINICE TRISECT

••I•••C
ASIATIC ERISTIC IDIOTIC MEIOTIC SEISMIC

•••IC••
AFRICAN APRICOT ARNICAS ARTICLE ATTICUS AURICLE BODICES CALICOS CEVICHE CHOICER CHOICES CODICES CODICIL COMICAL CONICAL CUBICLE CUTICLE CYNICAL DEFICIT DELICTI DELICTS DEPICTS DEVICES ENTICED ENTICER ENTICES ETHICAL FELICIA FINICKY FRAICHE HARICOT HELICAL HELICES HELICON ILLICIT INDICES INDICIA INDICTS JERICHO LATICES LEXICAL LEXICON LOGICAL LYRICAL MAGICAL MEDICAL MEDICOS MEXICAN MIMICRY MINICAM MODICUM MOHICAN MUSICAL NOTICED NOTICES NOVICES OFFICER OFFICES OPTICAL OSSICLE PANICKY PANICLE PEDICEL PEDICLE PELICAN PEMICAN PLAICES POLICED POLICES PUMICES RADICAL RADICES RADICLE RELICTS RETICLE RUBICON SHTICKS SILICAS SILICON SLUICED SLUICES SOLICIT SPLICED SPLICER SPLICES STOICAL TAXICAB TOPICAL TUNICLE TYPICAL UPTICKS VATICAN VEHICLE

•••I•C•
ANTIOCH BEWITCH CARIOCA DAVINCI DEHISCE DENIECE EXTINCT JALISCO MANIACS MENISCI NABISCO SQUINCH TAPIOCA UNHITCH ZODIACS

•••I••C
ACTINIC HAMITIC JURIDIC OSSIFIC PACIFIC POLITIC SATIRIC SEMITIC

••••IC•
AFFLICT ALDRICH AMERICA AUSPICE AVARICE BERNICE BIONICS CANDICE CAPRICE CARRICK CELTICS CHALICE CLARICE CLERICS CLINICS CONNICK CONVICT COPPICE CORNICE CORSICA COWLICK CREVICE CRITICS DERRICK DORMICE EDIFICE EHRLICH EROTICA ETHNICS EXOTICA EXOTICS FABRICS FORMICA FOSDICK FROLICS FUSTICS GALLICO GARRICK GIMMICK GOTHICS HEROICS HOSPICE ICEPICK INFLICT INVOICE IPSWICH ITALICS JAMAICA JESSICA JUSTICE KUBRICK LATTICE MASTICS MAURICE METRICS MOSAICS MYSTICS NIBLICK NITPICK NOETICS NORDICS OLDNICK ORIFICE OSTRICH PACKICE PATRICE PATRICK PHOBICS PHONICS PHYSICS PICNICS PIMLICO POETICS PORTICO PREDICT PUBLICS REJOICE REPLICA REPRICE REVOICE RIDDICK ROLLICK RUBRICS RUSTICS SEASICK SERPICO SERVICE STATICE STATICS SUFFICE TACTICS TAMPICO THINICE TITMICE TOPKICK TROPICS UNSTICK VERDICT WARWICK

••••I•C
ELEGIAC PONTIAC

•••••IC
ACERBIC ACRYLIC ACTINIC AELFRIC AEROBIC ALEMBIC AMHARIC AMOEBIC ANGELIC ANOSMIC AQUATIC ARAMAIC ARCHAIC ARSENIC ASCETIC ASEPTIC ASIATIC BALDRIC BUCOLIC CALORIC CAMBRIC CANONIC CAUSTIC CENTRIC CERAMIC CHAOTIC CHRONIC CLASSIC COMEDIC CRYPTIC DELTAIC DEMONIC DRASTIC DYNAMIC EDAPHIC ELASTIC ENDEMIC ERISTIC ERRATIC FANATIC FRANTIC FREDRIC GASTRIC GENERIC GENETIC GNOSTIC GRAPHIC HAMITIC HEBRAIC HEPATIC HERETIC HOMERIC IDENTIC IDIOTIC IDYLLIC ILLOGIC ISLAMIC JURIDIC KINETIC LACONIC LUNATIC MALEFIC MANTRIC MASONIC MEIOTIC MELODIC MIASMIC MIMETIC MITOTIC NOMADIC NUCLEIC NUMERIC OCEANIC OLYMPIC ORGANIC OSMOTIC OSSIFIC PACIFIC PELAGIC PHRENIC PIRATIC PLASTIC POLEMIC POLITIC PROSAIC PSYCHIC PYRRHIC ROBOTIC SATIRIC SEISMIC SELENIC SEMITIC SKEPTIC SOMATIC STANNIC STYPTIC SYNODIC TITANIC TOTEMIC TRAFFIC TROPHIC VOCALIC VOLTAIC XANTHIC

ID•••••
IDAHOAN IDCARDS IDEALLY IDEATED IDEATES IDENTIC IDIAMIN IDIOTIC IDOLIZE IDYLLIC

I•D••••
INDENTS INDEPTH INDEXED INDEXES INDIANA INDIANS INDICES INDICIA INDICTS INDIGOS INDITED INDITES INDOORS INDOUBT INDUCED INDUCER INDUCES INDUCTS INDULGE INDUTCH INDWELL IODATES IODIDES IODIZED IODIZES

I••D•••
ICEDTEA INADAZE IRIDIUM ISADORA

I•••D••
IMPEDED IMPEDES INCUDES INFIDEL INSIDER INSIDES INVADED INVADER INVADES IODIDES

I••••D•
IDCARDS IMPENDS IMPLODE INCLUDE INNARDS INROADS INTENDS INTRUDE INWARDS ISLANDS ISOPODS

I•••••D
IBNSAUD ICECOLD

ICELAND
ICHABOD
IDEATED
IGNITED
IGNORED
ILLBRED
ILLUSED
ILLWIND
IMBIBED
IMBRUED
IMMIXED
IMMURED
IMPALED
IMPEDED
IMPLIED
IMPOSED
IMPOUND
IMPUTED
INAWORD
INBOARD
INBOUND
INBREED
INCISED
INCITED
INDEXED
INDITED
INDUCED
INFIELD
INFUSED
INHALED
INHERED
INJURED
INSIPID
INSTEAD
INSURED
INTONED
INVADED
INVALID
INVITED
INVOKED
IODIZED
IONIZED
IRELAND

•ID••••

BIDDERS
BIDDIES
BIDDING
BIDFAIR
DIDACTS
DIDDLED
DIDDLES
DIDDLEY
DIDEROT
DIDGOOD
DIDOVER
FIDDLED
FIDDLER
FIDDLES
FIDELIO
FIDGETS
FIDGETY
GIDDIER
GIDDILY
GIDDYAP
GIDDYUP
GIDEONS
HIDALGO
HIDEOUS
HIDEOUT
KIDDERS
KIDDIES
KIDDING
KIDNAPS
KIDNEYS
KIDSKIN
LIDLESS
MIDDAYS
MIDDENS
MIDDIES
MIDDLEC
MIDDLES
MIDEAST
MIDGETS
MIDLAND
MIDLIFE
MIDLINE
MIDRIBS
MIDRIFF
MIDRISE
MIDSIZE
MIDTERM
MIDTOWN
MIDWAYS
MIDWEEK
MIDWEST
MIDWIFE
MIDYEAR
PIDGEON
PIDGINS
RIDDICK
RIDDING
RIDDLED
RIDDLER
RIDDLES
RIDEOFF
RIDEOUT
RIDGING
RIDGWAY
SIDEARM
SIDEBAR
SIDEBET
SIDECAR
SIDEMAN
SIDEMEN
SIDINGS
SIDLING
TIDBITS
TIDIEST
TIDINGS
TIDYING
VIDALIA
WIDENED
WIDGEON
WIDGETS
WIDMARK
WIDOWED
WIDOWER
YIDDISH

•I•D•••

AIRDAMS
AIRDATE
AIRDROP
BIDDERS
BIDDIES
BIDDING
BIGDEAL
BINDERS
BINDERY
BINDING
BINDSUP
BIRDDOG
BIRDERS
BIRDIED
BIRDIES
BIRDING
BIRDMAN
BIRDMEN
CINDERS
DIADEMS
DIDDLED
DIDDLES
DIDDLEY
DIEDOFF
DIEDOUT
DIEDOWN
DIKDIKS
DISDAIN
FIDDLED
FIDDLER
FIDDLES
FIEDLER
FINDERS
FINDING
FINDOUT
GIDDIER
GIDDILY
GIDDYAP
GIDDYUP
GILDERS
GILDING
GIRDERS
GIRDING
GIRDLED
GIRDLES
HINDERS
JIMDINE
KIDDERS
KIDDIES
KIDDING
KILDARE
KINDEST
KINDLED
KINDLES
KINDRED
LIEDOWN
LINDENS
LINDIED
LINDIES
LINDSAY
LINDSEY
MIDDAYS
MIDDENS
MIDDIES
MIDDLEC
MIDDLES
MILDEST
MILDEWS
MILDEWY
MILDRED
MINDERS
MINDFUL
MINDING
MINDSET
MISDATE
MISDEAL
MISDEED
MISDIAL
MISDOES
MISDONE
PINDOWN
RIDDICK
RIDDING
RIDDLED
RIDDLER
RIDDLES
SITDOWN
TIEDOWN
TIEDYED
TIEDYES
TINDERS
VIADUCT
WILDCAT
WILDEST
WILDING
WILDONE
WINDBAG
WINDERS
WINDIER
WINDING
WINDOWS
WINDROW
WINDSOR
WINDSUP
WINDUPS
YIDDISH

•I••D••

AIMEDAT
AIMEDTO
BIMODAL
BIPEDAL
BIRDDOG
CICADAE
CICADAS
CITADEL
DINEDIN
DINEDON
DIRNDLS
DIVIDED
DIVIDER
DIVIDES
FIEFDOM
FIELDED
FIELDER
FIREDOG
FIREDUP
FIXEDLY
FIXEDUP
KINGDOM
LIBIDOS
LINEDUP
LIVEDIN
LIVEDON
LIVIDLY
MIKADOS
MILLDAM
MIRADOR
MIXEDUP
PICADOR
PILEDIN
PILEDON
PILEDUP
PIPEDUP
RIGIDLY
SINEDIE
SIZEDUP
TIMIDER
TIMIDLY
TIRADES
TIREDER
TIREDLY
TIREDOF
VIVIDER
VIVIDLY
WIELDED
WIPEDUP
WISEDUP
YIELDED

•I•••D•

DIOMEDE
DIOXIDE
GIRONDE
LIMEADE
LIQUIDS
LIZARDS
MILORDS
MIRANDA
NIMRODS
NITRIDE
RIBANDS
RICARDO
RIGVEDA
RIPTIDE
TIERODS
VIVALDI
VIVENDI
WIZARDS
ZIPCODE

•I••••D

AIRHEAD
AIRRAID
BIASSED
BIGBAND
BIGBEND
BIGBIRD
BIGHEAD
BIGOTED
BIRCHED
BIRDIED
BIRTHED
CINCHED
CIRCLED
DIAMOND
DIBBLED
DIDDLED
DIDGOOD
DIEHARD
DILATED
DILLARD
DILUTED
DIMPLED
DIPLOID
DIRTIED
DISBAND
DISCARD
DISCOED
DISCORD
DISTEND
DISUSED
DITCHED
DITTOED
DIVIDED
DIVINED
DIVVIED
DIZZIED
FIDDLED
FIELDED
FIGURED
FILCHED
FINLAND
FIXATED
FIZZLED
GIELGUD
GIFFORD
GIGGLED
GIRDLED
GIZZARD
HIGHEND
HITCHED
JIGGLED
JIMMIED
JINGLED
KIBBLED
KINDLED
KINDRED
LIAISED
LIBELED
LIEABED
LIGATED
LIGHTED
LIKEMAD
LIKENED
LILYPAD
LIMITED
LINDIED
LINSEED
LIPREAD
LIVENED
MIDLAND
MILDRED
MILHAUD
MILLAND
MILLARD
MILLEND
MINGLED
MINORED
MINUEND
MISCUED
MISDEED
MISLAID
MISLEAD
MISREAD
MISUSED
MISWORD
MITERED
MITFORD
MIZZLED
NIBBLED
NIGGARD
NIGGLED
PICCARD
PICKLED
PIEBALD
PIERCED
PIFFLED
PILOTED
PINCHED
PINHEAD
PIRATED
PITCHED
PIVOTED
RICHARD
RIDDLED
RIFFLED
RIGHTED
RIMBAUD
RIPCORD
RIPENED
RIPPLED
RIVALED
RIVETED
SIGHTED
SIGMUND
SINGLED
SIXFOLD
SIZZLED
TICKLED
TIEDYED
TINGLED
TINKLED
TIPPLED
TIPTOED
VISITED
WIDENED
WIDOWED
WIELDED
WIGGLED
WILFORD
WILFRID
WILLARD
WIMPLED
WINCHED
WINERED
WIZENED
YIELDED

••ID•••

ABIDEBY
ABIDING
ACIDIFY
ACIDITY
ALIDADE
ARIDEST
ARIDITY
AVIDITY
BRIDALS
BRIDGED
BRIDGES
BRIDGET
BRIDLED
BRIDLES
CHIDING
ELIDING
EVIDENT
FRIDAYS
FRIDGES
GLIDERS
GLIDING
GRIDDED
GRIDDER
GRIDDLE
GUIDING
GUIDONS
IRIDIUM
LAIDFOR
LAIDLOW
LAIDOFF
LAIDOUT
MAIDENS
OXIDANT
OXIDASE
OXIDIZE
PAIDFOR
PAIDOFF
PAIDOUT
PHIDIAS
PRIDING
RAIDERS
RAIDING
SEIDELS
SKIDDED
SKIDDER
SKIDDOO
SKIDROW
SLIDEIN
SLIDERS
SLIDING
SMIDGEN
SNIDELY
SNIDEST
SPIDERS
SPIDERY
TRIDENT
TWIDDLE
VOIDING

••I•D••

ARIADNE
BLINDED
BLINDER
BLINDLY
BRINDLE
BUILDER
BUILDIN
BUILDON
BUILDUP
DRIEDUP
DRIPDRY
DWINDLE
FRIEDAN
GRIDDED
GRIDDER
GRIDDLE
GRINDER
GUILDER
HAIRDOS
HAIRDYE
JOINDER
NAIADES
SHINDIG
SKIDDED
SKIDDER
SKIDDOO
SPIEDON
SPINDLE
SPINDLY
SWINDLE
THIRDLY
TRIEDON
TRIODES
TWIDDLE
WEIRDER
WEIRDLY
WEIRDOS

••I••D•

ALIDADE
BRIARDS
BRIGADE
EPISODE
FRIENDS
SHIELDS
TRIPODS
UNIPODS

••I•••D

ALIGNED
ANISEED
AVIATED
BLINDED
BLINKED
BLIPPED
BLITZED
BRICKED
BRIDGED
BRIDLED
BRIEFED
BRIGAND
BRIMMED
CHILLED
CHINKED
CHINNED
CHIPPED
CHIRPED
CLICKED
CLIMBED
CLINKED
CLIPPED
CRIBBED
CRICKED
CRIMPED
CRINGED
CRINOID
CRISPED
DEIFIED
DEIGNED
DRIFTED
DRILLED
DRIPPED
EDIFIED
EMITTED
ENISLED
EVICTED
EVINCED
EXISTED
FAINTED
FEIGNED
FEINTED
FLICKED
FLIPPED
FLIRTED
FLITTED
FOISTED
FRILLED
FRINGED
FRISKED
FRITTED
FRIZZED
GLINTED
GLITZED
GRIDDED
GRIEVED
GRILLED
GRINNED
GRIPPED
GRITTED
HEISTED
HOISTED
JOINTED
JOISTED
KNITTED
MAITRED
NEIGHED
OMITTED
PAINTED
PLINKED
POINTED
PRICKED
PRIMPED
PRINKED
PRINTED
QUIETED
QUILLED
QUILTED
QUIPPED
QUIZZED
REIGNED
REINKED
SAINTED
SHIFTED
SHILLED
SHINNED
SHIPPED
SHIRKED
SHIRRED
SKIDDED
SKILLED
SKIMMED
SKIMPED
SKINNED
SKIPPED
SKIRLED
SKIRRED
SKIRTED
SLICKED
SLIMMED
SLINKED
SLIPPED
SMIRKED
SNIFFED
SNIPPED
SPIELED
SPILLED
STIFFED
STIFLED
STILLED
STILTED
STINTED
STIPEND
STIRRED
SWIGGED
SWILLED
SWIRLED
SWISHED
TAILEND
TAINTED
THIEVED
THINNED
TRICKED
TRIFLED
TRIGGED
TRILLED
TRIMMED
TRIPLED
TRIPPED
TWILLED
TWINBED
TWINGED
TWINNED
TWIRLED
TWISTED
TWITTED
UNIFIED
WAISTED
WEIGHED
WHIFFED
WHIPPED
WHIRLED
WHIRRED
WHISKED
WHIZKID
WHIZZED
WRITHED

•••ID••

ABRIDGE
ACRIDLY
APSIDES
AVOIDED
BESIDES
BETIDED
BETIDES
BOLIDES
BRAIDED
BRAIDER
DECIDED
DECIDES
DERIDED
DERIDES
DIVIDED
DIVIDER
DIVIDES
DOSIDOS
DREIDEL
ECHIDNA
FETIDLY
FLUIDLY
HASIDIM
HOLIDAY
HUMIDLY
HUMIDOR
INFIDEL
INSIDER
INSIDES
IODIDES
JURIDIC
LIBIDOS
LIVIDLY
LUCIDLY
LURIDLY
ONEIDAS
OVOIDAL
PERIDOT
PYXIDES
RAPIDER
RAPIDLY
RESIDED
RESIDES
RESIDUE
RIGIDLY
SOLIDER
SOLIDLY
STAIDER
STAIDLY
STRIDER
STRIDES
TEPIDLY
TIMIDER
TIMIDLY
UNAIDED
VALIDLY
VAPIDLY
VIVIDER
VIVIDLY

•••I•D•

BELINDA
DEWILDE
ENGIRDS
MATILDA
MELINDA
MYRIADS
PERIODS
REBINDS
REMINDS
REWINDS
UNBINDS
UNGIRDS
UNWINDS

•••I••D

ADMIRED
ADMIXED
ADVISED
AFFIXED
ARRIVED
ASPIRED
ATTIRED
AUDITED
AVAILED
AVOIDED
AWAITED
BATIKED
BEMIRED
BETIDED
BRAIDED
BRAINED
BRAISED
BROILED
BRUISED
BRUITED
BYLINED
CAVILED
CHAINED
CHAIRED
CLAIMED
CRUISED
DEBITED
DECIDED
DEFILED
DEFINED
DEMIGOD
DEMISED
DERIDED
DERIVED
DESIRED
DEVILED
DEVISED
DIVIDED
DIVINED
DRAINED
ENSILED
ENTICED
EXCISED
EXCITED
EXPIRED
FLAILED
FRUITED
GRAINED
HABITED
HELIPAD
HOMINID
IGNITED
IMBIBED
IMMIXED
INCISED
INCITED
INDITED
INFIELD
INSIPID
INVITED
IODIZED
IONIZED
LIAISED
LIMITED
MERITED
NOTICED
OBLIGED
ORBITED
PLAITED
POLICED
PONIARD
POSITED
PRAISED
QUAILED
RADIOED
REAIRED
RECITED
REFINED
REHIRED
RELINED
RELIVED
REMIXED
REOILED
REPINED
RESIDED
RESILED
RETILED
RETIMED
RETIRED
REVILED
REVISED
REVIVED
REWIRED
SLUICED
SPLICED
SPOILED
SQUIRED
STAINED
STRIPED
STRIVED
THRIVED
TRAILED
TRAINED
UMPIRED
UNAIDED
UNAIMED
UNAIRED
UNFIXED
UNLIKED
UNLINED
UNOILED
UNPILED
VISITED

••••ID•

ACARIDS
ASTRIDE
BEDSIDE
BROMIDE
BUSHIDO
CANDIDA
CANDIDE
CANDIDS
CARBIDE
CASSIDY
COLLIDE
CONFIDE
CORRIDA
COWHIDE
CUSPIDS
DIOXIDE
EBBTIDE
ELAPIDS
EYELIDS
FLORIDA
FORBIDS
HAYRIDE
HYBRIDS
JOYRIDE
LEETIDE
LIQUIDS
LOWTIDE
NEREIDS
NITRIDE
NUCLIDE
OFFSIDE
ORCHIDS
OUTBIDS
OUTSIDE
PEPTIDE
PERFIDY
PLACIDO
PODRIDA
PONGIDS
PRESIDE
PROVIDE
RAWHIDE
RIPTIDE
ROLAIDS
SCHMIDT
SEASIDE
SUBSIDE
SUBSIDY

SULFIDE
TOPSIDE
TOROIDS
TVGUIDE
VESPIDS
WAYSIDE

••••I•D

AMERIND
APPLIED
BANDIED
BELLIED
BERRIED
BIGBIRD
BIRDIED
BOOGIED
BULLIED
CADDIED
CANDIED
CARRIED
CATBIRD
CHEVIED
COWBIRD
CURRIED
DALLIED
DECRIED
DEIFIED
DIRTIED
DIVVIED
DIZZIED
DOLLIED
DUMMIED
EDIFIED
EMPTIED
FANCIED
FERRIED
GLORIED
GUSSIED
HARRIED
HOGTIED
HOGWILD
HURRIED
ILLWIND
IMPLIED
JAYBIRD
JELLIED
JEMMIED
JIMMIED
JOLLIED
LINDIED
LOBBIED
MANKIND
MARRIED
MUDDIED
PARRIED
PARTIED
PUTTIED
QUERIED
RALLIED
READIED
REBUILD
REDBIRD
REFRIED
REPLIED
RESCIND
RETRIED
SALLIED
SEABIRD
SERRIED
SORTIED
STORIED
STUDIED
STYMIED
SULLIED
TALLIED
TARRIED
TOADIED
UNIFIED
UNTRIED
WEARIED
WORRIED

•••••ID

AIRRAID
ANDROID
ANEROID
ANNELID
ANTACID
BANDAID
BARMAID
CAROTID
COLLOID
CONREID
CRINOID
DELTOID
DIPLOID
FLACCID
HENREID
HOMINID
INSIPID
INVALID
KATYDID
KOOLAID
LANGUID
LOWPAID
MASTOID
MERMAID
MISLAID
NAYSAID
NONSKID
OCEANID
OLDMAID
OSTEOID
OUTLAID
OVERDID
PREPAID
PYRAMID
SQUALID
STEROID
SUNMAID
TABLOID
UPBRAID
WAYLAID
WHIZKID
WILFRID

I•E••••

IBERIAN
ICEAGES
ICEAXES
ICEBAGS
ICEBERG
ICEBLUE
ICEBOAT
ICECAPS
ICECOLD
ICECUBE
ICEDTEA
ICEFLOE
ICEFREE
ICELAND
ICELESS
ICEMILK
ICEPACK
ICEPICK
ICERINK
ICESHOW
IDEALLY
IDEATED
IDEATES
IDENTIC
IKEBANA
INEPTLY
INERROR
INERTIA
INERTLY
INEXACT
IRECKON
IRELAND
ITEMIZE
ITERANT
ITERATE

I••E•••

IGNEOUS
ILIESCU
ILLEGAL
IMMENSE
IMMERSE
IMPEACH
IMPEDED
IMPEDES
IMPENDS
IMPERIL
IMPETUS
INCENSE
INCEPTS
INDENTS
INDEPTH
INDEXED
INDEXES
INFECTS
INFERNO
INFESTS
INGEMAR
INGENUE
INGESTS
INHERED
INHERES
INHERIT
INJECTS
INPEACE
INPETTO
INSEAMS
INSECTS
INSERTS
INTEGER
INTEGRA
INTENDS
INTENSE
INTENTS
INTERIM
INTERNS
INTERSE
INVEIGH
INVENTS
INVERSE
INVERTS
INVESTS
IONESCO
IQTESTS

I•••E••

ICEBERG
ICELESS
ICINESS
ICKIEST
IFFIEST
ILLNESS
IMAGERS
IMAGERY
IMARETS
IMOGENE
IMPIETY
IMPRESS
INAHEAP
INAMESS
INANELY
INANEST
INAWEOF
INBREED
INDWELL
INFIELD
INFLECT
INGRESS
INKWELL
INQUEST
INSPECT
INSTEAD
INSTEPS
IPANEMA
IPCRESS
IRATELY
IRATEST
IRONERS
ISOHELS
ISOMERS
ISRAELI
ISSUERS

I••••E•

ICEAGES
ICEAXES
ICEDTEA
ICEFREE
ICICLES
IDEATED
IDEATES
IGNITED
IGNITER
IGNITES
IGNORED
IGNORER
IGNORES
ILLBRED
ILLUSED
ILLUSES
IMAGOES
IMBIBED
IMBIBES
IMBRUED
IMBRUES
IMMIXED
IMMIXES
IMMURED
IMMURES
IMPALED
IMPALES
IMPANEL
IMPEDED
IMPEDES
IMPLIED
IMPLIES
IMPOSED
IMPOSES
IMPURER
IMPUTED
IMPUTES
INASTEW
INBREED
INBRIEF
INCISED
INCISES
INCITED
INCITER
INCITES
INCOMES
INCUDES
INDEXED
INDEXES
INDICES
INDITED
INDITES
INDUCED
INDUCER
INDUCES
INFIDEL
INFUSED
INFUSES
INHALED
INHALER
INHALES
INHERED
INHERES
INJOKES
INJURED
INJURES
INMATES
INSIDER
INSIDES
INSOLES
INSURED
INSURES
INTAKES
INTEGER
INTONED
INTONER
INTONES
INVADED
INVADER
INVADES
INVITED
INVITES
INVOKED
INVOKER
INVOKES
IODATES
IODIDES
IODIZED
IODIZES
IONIZED
IONIZER
IONIZES
IRONIES
IRONMEN
ISHMAEL
ITCHIER
IVORIES

I•••••E

ICEBLUE
ICECUBE
ICEFLOE
ICEFREE
IDOLIZE
IFSTONE
IGNOBLE
IMAGINE
IMAMATE
IMITATE
IMMENSE
IMMERSE
IMOGENE
IMPASSE
IMPINGE
IMPLODE
IMPLORE
IMPROVE
IMPULSE
INADAZE
INCENSE
INCLINE
INCLOSE
INCLUDE
INDULGE
INFLAME
INFLATE
INFORCE
INGENUE
INGRATE
INHASTE
INHOUSE
INPEACE
INPHASE
INPLACE
INQUIRE
INSCAPE
INSHAPE
INSPIRE
INSTATE
INSTORE
INSTYLE
INTENSE
INTERSE
INTRUDE
INUTILE
INVERSE
INVOGUE
INVOICE
INVOLVE
IRKSOME
IRONAGE
IRONORE
ISOLATE
ISOTOPE
ITEMIZE
ITERATE
IVANHOE

•IE••••

BIENTOT
DIEDOFF
DIEDOUT
DIEDOWN
DIEHARD
DIESELS
DIESOFF
DIESOUT
DIETARY
DIETERS
DIETING
FIEDLER
FIEFDOM
FIELDED
FIELDER
FIERCER
FIERIER
FIERILY
FIESTAS
GIELGUD
LIEABED
LIEDOWN
LIENEES
LIEOVER
LIERNES
LIESLOW
NIEBUHR
NIELSEN
PIEBALD
PIECERS
PIECING
PIEPANS
PIERCED
PIERCES
PIERROT
PIETIES
PIETINS
PIETISM
SIENNAS
SIERRAS
SIESTAS
TIECLIP
TIEDOWN
TIEDYED
TIEDYES
TIEINTO
TIELESS
TIELINE
TIEPINS
TIERACK
TIERING
TIERNEY
TIERODS
TIETACK
VIETNAM
VIEWERS
VIEWING
WIELDED
WIENERS
WIENIES
YIELDED

•I•E•••

AILERON
AIMEDAT
AIMEDTO
BIBELOT
BIGELOW
BIGEYES
BIKEWAY
BILEVEL
BIPEDAL
BIREMES
BIRETTA
BISECTS
BITEOFF
CINEMAS
CINEMAX
DIDEROT
DIGESTS
DILEMMA
DINEDIN
DINEDON
DINESEN
DINESIN
DINESON
DINETTE
DIRECTS
DISEASE
DIVERGE
DIVERSE
DIVERTS
DIVESIN
DIVESTS
FIDELIO
FINEART
FINESSE
FIREANT
FIREARM
FIREBOX
FIREBUG
FIREDOG
FIREDUP
FIREFLY
FIRELIT
FIREMAN
FIREMEN
FIRENZE
FIREOFF
FIRESUP
FIXEDLY
FIXEDUP
FIXESUP
GIDEONS
GISELLE
GIVENTO
GIVEOFF
GIVEOUT
GIVESIN
GIVESTO
GIVESUP
GIVEUPS
GIVEWAY
HIDEOUS
HIDEOUT
HIRESON
JIMENEZ
KINETIC
LIBELED
LIBELER
LIBERAL
LIBERIA
LIBERTY
LICENCE
LICENSE
LIFENET
LIKEMAD
LIKENED
LIKENEW
LIMEADE
LINEAGE
LINEATE
LINEDUP
LINEMAN
LINEMEN
LINESUP
LINEUPS
LITERAL
LIVEDIN
LIVEDON
LIVENED
LIVEOAK
LIVEONE
LIVEOUT
LIVESIN
LIVESON
MIDEAST
MILEAGE
MIMESIS
MIMETIC
MINEOLA
MINERAL
MINERVA
MISERLY
MITERED
MIXEDUP
MIXESUP
NIGERIA
NINEVEH
PIGEONS
PIKEMAN
PIKEMEN
PILEDIN
PILEDON
PILEDUP
PILESIN
PILESON
PILESUP
PILEUPS
PIMENTO
PIMESON
PINEFOR
PINENUT
PINESAP
PINETAR
PINETUM
PIPEDUP
PIPEFUL
PIPESUP
PIPETTE
PITEOUS
RIBEYES
RICERAT
RIDEOFF
RIDEOUT
RIPENED
RIVETED
RIVETER
SIBERIA
SIDEARM
SIDEBAR
SIDEBET
SIDECAR
SIDEMAN
SIDEMEN
SILENCE
SILENTS
SILESIA
SIMENON
SINEDIE
SIZEDUP
SIZESUP
TIBETAN
TIMECOP
TIMELAG
TIMEOFF
TIMEOUT
TIMESUP
TIMEWAS
TINEARS
TIREDER
TIREDLY
TIREDOF
TIREOUT
VICEROY
VINEGAR
VIVENDI
WIDENED
WINEBAR
WINERED
WINESAP
WIPEDUP
WIPEOUT
WIPESUP
WIRETAP
WISEDUP
WISEGUY
WISEMAN
WISEMEN
WISESUP
WIZENED

•I••E••

AIGRETS
AILMENT
AIMLESS
AIRHEAD
AIRIEST
AIRLESS
BICKERS
BIDDERS
BIGBEND
BIGDEAL
BIGFEET
BIGGERS
BIGGEST
BIGHEAD
BIGNESS
BILLETS
BINDERS
BINDERY
BIOGENY
BIRDERS
BITTERN
BITTERS
CINDERS
CIPHERS
CISTERN
DIADEMS
DIALECT
DIALERS
DIAPERS
DICIEST
DICKENS
DICKERS
DICKEYS
DIESELS
DIETERS
DIFFERS
DIGGERS
DIGRESS
DIMMERS
DIMMEST
DIMNESS
DINNERS
DIOCESE
DIOMEDE
DIPPERS
DISCERN
DISPELS
DISSECT
DISSENT
DISTEND
DITHERS
DITHERY
FIBBERS
FIDGETS
FIDGETY
FIFTEEN
FIGLEAF
FIGMENT
FILBERT
FILLERS
FILLETS
FILTERS
FINDERS
FINGERS
FIRMEST
FISHERS
FISHERY
FISHEYE
FITNESS
FITTERS
FITTEST
GIBBERS
GIBBETS
GIBLETS
GILBERT
GILDERS
GIMLETS
GINGERS
GINGERY
GINSENG
GIRDERS
HIALEAH
HIGHEND
HIGHEST
HIMSELF
HINDERS
HIPNESS
HIPPEST
HISSERS
HITHERE
HITLESS
HITTERS
JIGGERS
JIGGERY
JITNEYS
JITTERS
JITTERY
KICKERS
KIDDERS
KIDNEYS
KILLERS
KINDEST
KIPPERS
KISSERS
KITTENS
LIBBERS
LICHENS
LICKETY
LIDLESS
LIENEES
LIFTERS
LIMBERS
LIMIEST
LIMNERS
LIMPEST
LIMPETS
LINDENS
LINGERS
LINKERS
LINNETS
LINSEED
LINTELS
LIONESS
LIONETS
LIPREAD
LIQUEFY
LIQUEUR
LISTEES
LISTELS
LISTENS
LITHELY
LITHEST
LITTERS
MICHELE
MIDDENS
MIDGETS
MIDTERM
MIDWEEK
MIDWEST
MIDYEAR
MILDEST
MILDEWS
MILDEWY
MILIEUS
MILIEUX
MILKERS
MILLEND
MILLERS
MILLETS
MILLETT
MIMIEUX
MINCERS
MINDERS
MINTERS
MINUEND
MINUETS
MIOCENE
MISDEAL
MISDEED
MISHEAR
MISLEAD
MISREAD
MISTERS
MITTENS
MIZZENS
NICKELS
NICKERS
NIGHEST
NIPPERS
OILIEST
OILWELL
PICKENS
PICKERS
PICKETS
PICKETT
PIDGEON
PIECERS
PIGLETS
PIGMENT
PIGPENS
PILFERS
PINCERS
PINHEAD
PINIEST
PINKEST
PINLESS
PINNERS
PIOLETS
PIONEER
PIRAEUS
PITTERS
RICHEST
RICKETY
RICKEYS
RIFLERS
RIFLERY
RIGGERS
RIGVEDA
RILLETS
RINGERS
RIOTERS
RIPPERS
RISKERS
RIVIERA
RIVIERE
SIAMESE
SICKENS
SICKEST
SIFTERS
SIGHERS
SIGNEES
SIGNERS
SIGNETS
SILVERS
SILVERY
SIMMERS
SIMPERS
SINCERE
SINGERS
SINKERS
SINNERS
SIPPERS
SIPPETS
SISTERS
SITTERS
SITWELL
SIXTEEN
TICKERS
TICKETS
TIDIEST
TIELESS
TIGRESS
TILLERS
TILTERS
TIMBERS
TINDERS
TINIEST
TINKERS
TINNERS
TINSELS
TINTERN
TINTERS
TIPPERS
TIPPETS
TITHERS
TITTERS
VIEWERS
VILLEIN
VINCENT
VIOLENT
VIOLETS
VISCERA
VIZIERS
WICKERS
WICKETS
WIDGEON
WIDGETS
WIENERS
WIGLETS
WILDEST
WILHELM
WILIEST
WINCERS
WINDERS
WINGERS
WINKERS
WINNERS
WINTERS
WINTERY
WIRIEST
WISHERS
WITHERS
WITLESS
WITNESS
ZINGERS
ZIPPERS
ZITHERS

•I•••E•

AIRCREW
AITCHES
BIALIES
BIASSED
BIDDIES
BIGEYES
BIGFEET
BIGGIES
BIGOTED
BIGTOES
BILBOES
BILEVEL
BILLIES
BINGOES
BIRCHED
BIRCHES
BIRDIED

BIRDIES
BIRDMEN
BIREMES
BIRTHED
BISQUES
BITTIER
BITUMEN
CINCHED
CINCHES
CIRCLED
CIRCLES
CIRCLET
CIRQUES
CITADEL
CITIZEN
CITROEN
CIVVIES
DIARIES
DIBBLED
DIBBLES
DICKIES
DIDDLED
DIDDLES
DIDDLEY
DIDOVER
DILATED
DILATES
DILLIES
DILUTED
DILUTER
DILUTES
DIMPLED
DIMPLES
DINESEN
DINGIER
DINGLES
DINGOES
DINKIER
DINKIES
DIOPTER
DIPOLES
DIRTIED
DIRTIER
DIRTIES
DISCOED
DISOBEY
DISUSED
DITCHED
DITCHES
DITTIES
DITTOED
DIVIDED
DIVIDER
DIVIDES
DIVINED
DIVINER
DIVINES
DIVVIED
DIVVIES
DIZZIED
DIZZIER
DIZZIES
FIACRES
FIANCEE
FIANCES
FICKLER
FICUSES
FIDDLED
FIDDLER
FIDDLES
FIEDLER
FIELDED
FIELDER

FIERCER
FIERIER
FIFTEEN
FIFTIES
FIGHTER
FIGURED
FIGURER
FIGURES
FILCHED
FILCHER
FILCHES
FILLIES
FILMIER
FINALES
FINCHES
FIPPLES
FIREMEN
FISCHER
FISHIER
FISHNET
FITCHES
FIXATED
FIXATES
FIZZIER
FIZZLED
FIZZLES
GIBLUES
GIDDIER
GIGGLED
GIGGLER
GIGGLES
GILLIES
GILLNET
GIPSIES
GIRDLED
GIRDLES
HIGHTEA
HILLIER
HINNIES
HIPPIES
HIPSTER
HITCHED
HITCHER
HITCHES
JIFFIES
JIGGLED
JIGGLES
JIMCHEE
JIMENEZ
JIMMIED
JIMMIES
JINGLED
JINGLES
JINGOES
KIBBLED
KIBBLES
KIDDIES
KILAUEA
KILTIES
KINDLED
KINDLES
KINDRED
KINKIER
KINSMEN
KIRTLES
KISHKES
KITCHEN
KITTIES
LIAISED
LIAISES
LIBELED
LIBELER
LIEABED

LIENEES
LIEOVER
LIERNES
LIFENET
LIGATED
LIGATES
LIGHTED
LIGHTEN
LIGHTER
LIKENED
LIKENEW
LIMITED
LIMOGES
LINAGES
LINDIED
LINDIES
LINDSEY
LINEMEN
LINGOES
LINSEED
LINTIER
LIPPIER
LISTEES
LITOTES
LITTLER
LIVENED
MICHAEL
MIDDIES
MIDDLEC
MIDDLES
MIDWEEK
MILDRED
MILKIER
MILKMEN
MINARET
MINDSET
MINGLED
MINGLER
MINGLES
MINIVER
MINORED
MINTIER
MINUSES
MINUTES
MIRAGES
MISCUED
MISCUES
MISDEED
MISDOES
MISSIES
MISSTEP
MISTIER
MISUSED
MISUSES
MITERED
MITOSES
MIZZLED
MIZZLES
NIBBLED
NIBBLER
NIBBLES
NIELSEN
NIFTIER
NIGGLED
NIGGLES
NIMBLER
NINEVEH
NINNIES
NIPPIER
PIASTER
PICKIER
PICKLED
PICKLES

PIERCED
PIERCES
PIETIES
PIFFLED
PIFFLES
PIGGIES
PIKEMEN
PILOTED
PILSNER
PINCHED
PINCHER
PINCHES
PINKIES
PINONES
PIONEER
PIRATED
PIRATES
PITCHED
PITCHER
PITCHES
PITHIER
PIVOTED
RIBEYES
RICHTER
RICKLES
RIDDLED
RIDDLER
RIDDLES
RIFFLED
RIFFLES
RIGHTED
RIGHTER
RINGLET
RIPENED
RIPPLED
RIPPLES
RISKIER
RITZIER
RIVALED
RIVETED
RIVETER
RIVULET
SICKLES
SIDEBET
SIDEMEN
SIGHTED
SIGNEES
SILKIER
SILLIER
SILLIES
SIMILES
SIMPLER
SIMPLEX
SINGLED
SINGLES
SINUSES
SISSIES
SIXTEEN
SIXTIES
SIZZLED
SIZZLES
TICKLED
TICKLER
TICKLES
TIEDYED
TIEDYES
TIERNEY
TIGHTEN
TIGHTER
TIMBRES
TIMIDER
TINGLED
TINGLES

TINKLED
TINKLES
TINNIER
TIPPLED
TIPPLER
TIPPLES
TIPSIER
TIPSTER
TIPTOED
TIPTOES
TIRADES
TIREDER
TISANES
TISSUES
TITTLES
TIZZIES
VINTNER
VIRTUES
VIRUSES
VISAGES
VISITED
VITTLES
VIVIDER
WIDENED
WIDOWED
WIDOWER
WIELDED
WIENIES
WIGGLED
WIGGLER
WIGGLES
WILLIES
WIMPLED
WIMPLES
WINCHED
WINCHES
WINDIER
WINERED
WINFREY
WINKLER
WISEMEN
WISPIER
WITCHES
WITTIER
WIZENED
YIELDED
ZILCHES
ZINGIER
ZIPPIER

•I••••E

AIRBASE
AIRDATE
AIRFARE
AIRHOLE
AIRLANE
AIRLINE
AIRMILE
AIRTIME
AIRWAVE
BICYCLE
BIGGAME
BIGNAME
BIGTIME
BIPLANE
BIVALVE
BIZARRE
CICADAE
CILIATE
CITABLE
CITRATE
CITRINE
DICTATE

DIFFUSE
DINETTE
DIOCESE
DIOMEDE
DIOXIDE
DISABLE
DISEASE
DISLIKE
DISPOSE
DISPUTE
DISROBE
DIVERGE
DIVERSE
DIVORCE
DIVULGE
FIANCEE
FIBULAE
FICTIVE
FINAGLE
FINANCE
FINESSE
FIRENZE
FISHEYE
FISSILE
FISSURE
FIXABLE
FIXTURE
GILMORE
GIRAFFE
GIRONDE
GISELLE
HILAIRE
HIPBONE
HIRABLE
HIRSUTE
HITHERE
HITTITE
JIMCHEE
JIMDINE
KILDARE
KIRSTIE
LICENCE
LICENSE
LIGNITE
LIKABLE
LIMEADE
LINEAGE
LINEATE
LINKAGE
LIONIZE
LISSOME
LIVABLE
LIVEONE
MICHELE
MICROBE
MIDLIFE
MIDLINE
MIDRISE
MIDSIZE
MIDWIFE
MIGRATE
MILEAGE
MINABLE
MIOCENE
MIRACLE
MISDATE
MISDONE
MISFILE
MISFIRE
MISMATE
MISNAME
MISRULE
MISSILE

MISSIVE
MISTAKE
MISTYPE
MIXABLE
MIXTURE
NIGHTIE
NITRATE
NITRIDE
NITRITE
OILCAKE
PIASTRE
PICANTE
PICKAXE
PICTURE
PIGLIKE
PILLAGE
PINHOLE
PINNACE
PINNATE
PINOCLE
PINWALE
PIPETTE
PIROGUE
PISCINE
PISMIRE
PISTOLE
RIBCAGE
RIPOSTE
RIPTIDE
RISIBLE
RISSOLE
RITCHIE
RIVIERE
SIAMESE
SILENCE
SINCERE
SINEDIE
SINKAGE
SISTINE
SITUATE
SIZABLE
TIELINE
TILLAGE
TIMBALE
TINTYPE
TITMICE
TITRATE
VIBRATE
VILLAGE
VINTAGE
VIOLATE
VIRGULE
VISIBLE
VITIATE
WILDONE
WILLKIE
WINSOME
ZIPCODE

••IE•••

ALIENEE
ALIENOR
ARIETTA
BRIEFED
BRIEFER
BRIEFLY
CHIEFLY
CLIENTS
DRIEDUP
DRIESUP
ETIENNE
FAIENCE
FLIESAT

FLIESIN
FRIEDAN
FRIENDS
FRIEZES
GRIEVED
GRIEVER
GRIEVES
ILIESCU
KNIEVEL
ORIENTE
ORIENTS
PRIESTS
QUIETED
QUIETEN
QUIETER
QUIETLY
SCIENCE
SHIELDS
SPIEDON
SPIEGEL
SPIELED
SPIELER
SPIESON
STIEGEL
THIERRY
THIEVED
THIEVES
TRIEDON
TRIESON
TRIESTE

••I•E••

ABIDEBY
ABILENE
AGILELY
ALIMENT
ANISEED
ARIDEST
BAILEES
BAILERS
BAILEYS
BOILERS
BRIBERY
CHILEAN
CHIMERA
CHINESE
CHISELS
COINERS
CRIMEAN
DEICERS
DRIVEAT
DRIVEIN
DRIVELS
DRIVERS
DRIVEUP
EMINENT
EPICENE
EPIGENE
EVIDENT
EVILEST
EVILEYE
EXIGENT
FAIREST
GAINERS
GAITERS
GLIDERS
GRIPERS
GRIVETS
GUINEAS
HEIFERS
HEIFETZ
HEIRESS
ICINESS

JAILERS
JOINERS
JOINERY
JUICERS
JUICEUP
KAISERS
LOITERS
MAIDENS
MAILERS
MOILERS
NAILERS
NAIVELY
NAIVETE
OPINERS
PHINEAS
PRICERS
PRIMERS
PRIVETS
QUIVERS
RAIDERS
RAILERS
RAIMENT
RAISERS
RAISEUP
RUINERS
SEIDELS
SEINERS
SEIZERS
SHINERS
SHIVERS
SKIVERS
SLICERS
SLIDEIN
SLIDERS
SLIVERS
SMILERS
SNIDELY
SNIDEST
SNIPEAT
SNIVELS
SOIREES
SPICEUP
SPIDERS
SPIDERY
SPIKERS
SPINELS
SPINETS
SPIREAS
STIPEND
SWIPERS
SWIVELS
TAILEND
TOILERS
TOILETS
TRICEPS
TRIDENT
TRIREME
TRISECT
TRITELY
TRITEST
TRIVETS
UNITERS
VAINEST
WAILERS
WAITERS
WAIVERS
WHINERS
WHITENS
WHITEST
WRITEIN
WRITERS
WRITETO
WRITEUP

••I••E•

ALIASES
ALIENEE
ALIGNED
ALIGNER
ANISEED
AVIATED
AVIATES
BAILEES
BLINDED
BLINDER
BLINKED
BLINKER
BLIPPED
BLISTER
BLITHER
BLITZED
BLITZEN
BLITZES
BRICKED
BRIDGED
BRIDGES
BRIDGET
BRIDLED
BRIDLES
BRIEFED
BRIEFER
BRIMMED
BRINGER
BRINIER
BRIQUET
BRISKER
BRISKET
BRITTEN
BUILDER
CAIQUES
CHICHEN
CHICKEN
CHIGGER
CHILIES
CHILLED
CHILLER
CHIMNEY
CHINKED
CHINNED
CHIPPED
CHIPPER
CHIRPED
CHITTER
CLICHES
CLICKED
CLIMBED
CLIMBER
CLINKED
CLINKER
CLIPPED
CLIPPER
CLIQUES
CRIBBED
CRICKED
CRICKET
CRIMPED
CRIMPER
CRINGED
CRINGES
CRISPED
CRISPER
CRITTER
DAILIES
DAIMLER
DAIRIES
DAISIES
DEIFIED

DEIFIES
DEIGNED
DEITIES
DOILIES
DRIBLET
DRIFTED
DRIFTER
DRILLED
DRILLER
DRINKER
DRIPPED
EDIBLES
EDIFIED
EDIFIES
EMIGRES
EMITTED
EMITTER
ENISLED
ENISLES
EPITHET
ERITREA
EVICTED
EVILLER
EVINCED
EVINCES
EXISTED
FAINTED
FAINTER
FAIRIES
FEIFFER
FEIGNED
FEINTED
FLICKED
FLICKER
FLIPPED
FLIPPER
FLIRTED
FLITTED
FLITTER
FLIVVER
FOIBLES
FOISTED
FRIDGES
FRIEZES
FRILLED
FRINGED
FRINGES
FRISBEE
FRISKED
FRITTED
FRITTER
FRIZZED
FRIZZES
GLIBBER
GLIMMER
GLINTED
GLISTEN
GLITTER
GLITZED
GLITZES
GRIDDED
GRIDDER
GRIEVED
GRIEVER
GRIEVES
GRIFFEY
GRIFTER
GRILLED
GRILLES
GRILLET
GRIMIER
GRIMMER
GRINDER

GRINNED
GRINNER
GRIPPED
GRIPPER
GRITTED
GUILDER
GUIMPES
HAIRIER
HAIRNET
HEISTED
HOISTED
ICICLES
JOINDER
JOINTED
JOISTED
JUICIER
KAISHEK
KNIEVEL
KNISHES
KNITTED
KNITTER
LAISSEZ
LEISTER
MAIGRET
MAITRED
MEIOSES
MEISSEN
MOISTEN
MOISTER
NAIADES
NAILSET
NEIGHED
NEITHER
NOISIER
OLIVIER
OMITTED
OPIATES
ORIOLES
PAINTED
PAINTER
PAISLEY
PAIUTES
PHILTER
PLINKED
POINTED
POINTER
POITIER
PRICIER
PRICKED
PRIMMER
PRIMPED
PRINCES
PRINKED
PRINTED
PRINTER
PRITHEE
PRIVIES
QUICHES
QUICKEN
QUICKER
QUIETED
QUIETEN
QUIETER
QUIGLEY
QUILLED
QUILTED
QUILTER
QUINCES
QUINTET
QUIPPED
QUIPPER
QUITTER
QUIZZED

QUIZZES
RAINIER
REIGNED
REINKED
ROISTER
SAINTED
SEICHES
SHIFTED
SHIITES
SHILLED
SHIMMER
SHINIER
SHINNED
SHIPMEN
SHIPPED
SHIPPER
SHIRKED
SHIRKER
SHIRLEY
SHIRRED
SKIDDED
SKIDDER
SKILLED
SKILLET
SKIMMED
SKIMMER
SKIMPED
SKINNED
SKINNER
SKIPPED
SKIPPER
SKIRLED
SKIRRED
SKIRTED
SKITTER
SLICKED
SLICKER
SLIMIER
SLIMMED
SLIMMER
SLINGER
SLINKED
SLIPPED
SLIPPER
SLITHER
SMIDGEN
SMIRKED
SMITTEN
SNICKER
SNIFFED
SNIFFER
SNIFTER
SNIGGER
SNIGLET
SNIPPED
SNIPPET
SOIGNEE
SOIREES
SPICIER
SPIEGEL
SPIELED
SPIELER
SPIKIER
SPILLED
SPINIER
SPINNER
SPITZES
STICHES
STICKER
STIEGEL
STIFFED
STIFFEN
STIFFER

STIFLED
STIFLES
STILLED
STILLER
STILTED
STINGER
STINKER
STINTED
STIRRED
STIRRER
SWIFTER
SWIGGED
SWILLED
SWIMMER
SWINGER
SWIRLED
SWISHED
SWISHES
SWITZER
TAILLES
TAINTED
TEICHER
THICKEN
THICKER
THICKET
THIEVED
THIEVES
THINKER
THINNED
THINNER
THITHER
TRICKED
TRICKER
TRIFLED
TRIFLER
TRIFLES
TRIGGED
TRIGGER
TRILLED
TRIMMED
TRIMMER
TRINKET
TRIODES
TRIPLED
TRIPLES
TRIPLET
TRIPLEX
TRIPPED
TRIPPER
TRIPPET
TRIUNES
TWILLED
TWINBED
TWINGED
TWINGES
TWINNED
TWIRLED
TWIRLER
TWISTED
TWISTER
TWITTED
TWITTER
UNIFIED
UNIFIER
UNIFIES
UNITIES
WAISTED
WEIGHED
WEIRDER
WHIFFED
WHIMPER
WHIPPED
WHIPPET
WHIRLED
WHIRRED
WHISKED
WHISKER
WHISKEY
WHISPER
WHITHER
WHITNEY
WHIZZED
WHIZZES
WRIGLEY
WRINGER
WRITHED
WRITHES
WRITTEN

••I•••E

ABILENE
ADIPOSE
AGITATE
ALIDADE
ALIENEE
AMIABLE
AMIBLUE
ANILINE
ANIMATE
ARIADNE
ARISTAE
ASININE
ATINGLE
ATISSUE
AXILLAE
BRIGADE
BRINDLE
BRIOCHE
BRISTLE
BRITTLE
CHINESE
CLIMATE
COINAGE
CRINKLE
CUISINE
DRIBBLE
DRIZZLE
DWINDLE
EDIFICE
EMIRATE
EPICENE
EPICURE
EPIGENE
EPIGONE
EPISODE
EPISTLE
EPITOME
ETIENNE
EVILEYE
FAIENCE
FAILURE
FRIABLE
FRICKIE
FRIGATE
FRISBEE
FRIZZLE
GLIMPSE
GRIDDLE
GRIMACE
GRISTLE
GRIZZLE
HAIRDYE
IMITATE
KRINGLE
LEISURE
NAIVETE
NOISOME
OLIVINE
ORIENTE
ORIFICE
OXIDASE
OXIDIZE
PHILTRE
PLIABLE
PRICKLE
PRIMATE
PRITHEE
PRIVATE
QUIBBLE
QUICKIE
QUININE
QUINQUE
QUIVIVE
QUIXOTE
REISSUE
RHIZOME
SCIENCE
SHINGLE
SKIPOLE
SKITTLE
SNIFFLE
SNIGGLE
SOIGNEE
SPINDLE
STIPPLE
SWINDLE
SWIZZLE
THIMBLE
THINICE
THISTLE
TRIBUNE
TRIBUTE
TRICKLE
TRIESTE
TRIREME
TRITONE
TWIDDLE
TWINKLE
UNITIVE
UTILIZE
WHISTLE
WHITTLE
WRIGGLE
WRINKLE

•••IE••

ACHIEST
ACHIEVE
AERIEST
AIRIEST
ALFIERI
ALGIERS
AMBIENT
ANCIENT
ANXIETY
ARRIERE
ARTIEST
ASHIEST
BELIEFS
BELIEVE
BESIEGE
BEZIERS
BONIEST
BUSIEST
CAGIEST
CAHIERS
COPIERS
COZIEST
DANIELS
DENIECE
DENIERS
DICIEST
DOPIEST
DUBIETY
EASIEST
EDGIEST
EELIEST
EERIEST
FOXIEST
GAMIEST
GOOIEST
GORIEST
HAZIEST
HOLIEST
HOMIEST
HOSIERS
HOSIERY
HYGIEIA
HYGIENE
ICKIEST
IFFIEST
IMPIETY
INFIELD
LACIEST
LAZIEST
LENIENT
LEVIERS
LIMIEST
LOGIEST
LUMIERE
METIERS
MILIEUS
MILIEUX
MIMIEUX
MOLIERE
NORIEGA
NOSIEST
OILIEST
PATIENT
PINIEST
POKIEST
PUNIEST
RACIEST
RAPIERS
RELIEFS
RELIEVE
RELIEVO
REVIEWS
RIVIERA
RIVIERE
SALIENT
SALIERI
SAPIENS
SAPIENT
SATIETY
SEXIEST
SHRIEKS
SOCIETY
SOVIETS
SPRIEST
TIDIEST
TINIEST
TONIEST
UGLIEST
VARIETY
VIZIERS
WARIEST
WAVIEST
WAXIEST
WILIEST
WIRIEST
ZANIEST

•••I•E•

ACTIVES
ADMIRED
ADMIRER
ADMIRES
ADMIXED
ADMIXES
ADVISED
ADVISER
ADVISES
AEDILES
AFFINES
AFFIXED
AFFIXES
ANTIBES
ANTIGEN
APSIDES
AQUIFER
AQUIVER
ARBITER
ARGIVES
ARRISES
ARRIVED
ARRIVER
ARRIVES
ASPIRED
ASPIRER
ASPIRES
ASSIZES
ATTIMES
ATTIRED
ATTIRES
AUDITED
AVAILED
AVOIDED
AWAITED
BATIKED
BEDIZEN
BEMIRED
BEMIRES
BESIDES
BETIDED
BETIDES
BETIMES
BODICES
BOLIDES
BOVINES
BRAIDED
BRAIDER
BRAINED
BRAISED
BRAISES
BROILED
BROILER
BRUISED
BRUISER
BRUISES
BRUITED
BYLINED
BYLINES
CABINET
CALIBER
CALIPER
CAMISES
CANINES
CARIBES
CAVILED
CAVILER
CHAINED
CHAIRED
CHAISES
CHOICER
CHOICES
CITIZEN
CLAIMED
CLAIMER
CODICES
CONIFER
COSINES
CRUISED
CRUISER
CRUISES
DEBITED
DECIBEL
DECIDED
DECIDES
DEFILED
DEFILER
DEFILES
DEFINED
DEFINES
DELIBES
DELIVER
DEMISED
DEMISES
DENIZEN
DERIDED
DERIDES
DERIVED
DERIVES
DESIRED
DESIREE
DESIRES
DEVICES
DEVILED
DEVISED
DEVISES
DIVIDED
DIVIDER
DIVIDES
DIVINED
DIVINER
DIVINES
DRAINED
DRAINER
DREIDEL
DREISER
EMPIRES
ENDIVES
ENGINES
ENLIVEN
ENSILED
ENSILES
ENTICED
ENTICER
ENTICES
EQUINES
ERMINES
ETOILES
EXCISED
EXCISES
EXCITED
EXCITES
EXPIRED
EXPIRES
EXWIVES
FELINES
FLAILED
FRAILER
FRAISES
FRUITED
GALILEE
GALILEI
GALILEO
GAMINES
GRAINED
HABITED
HALITES
HAMITES
HELICES
HELIXES
HOMINEM
IGNITED
IGNITER
IGNITES
IMBIBED
IMBIBES
IMMIXED
IMMIXES
INCISED
INCISES
INCITED
INCITER
INCITES
INDICES
INDITED
INDITES
INFIDEL
INSIDER
INSIDES
INVITED
INVITES
IODIDES
IODIZED
IODIZES
IONIZED
IONIZER
IONIZES
JUBILEE
JUNIPER
JUPITER
KYLIKES
LATICES
LEVITES
LIAISED
LIAISES
LIMITED
LORISES
LUCIFER
LUPINES
MARINER
MARINES
MATINEE
MERIMEE
MERITED
MINIVER
MOBILES
MONIKER
MOTIVES
NATIVES
NOMINEE
NOTICED
NOTICES
NOVICES
OBLIGED
OBLIGES
OFFICER
OFFICES
OOLITES
ORBITED
ORBITER
ORPINES
OSCINES
PEDICEL
PERIGEE
PETITES
PLAICES
PLAINER
PLAINES
PLAITED
POLICED
POLICES
POLITER
POSITED
PRAISED
PRAISER
PRAISES
PUMICES
PYRITES
PYXIDES
QUAILED
RADICES
RADIOED
RAPIDER
RAPINES
RATITES
RAVINES
REAIRED
RECIPES
RECITED
RECITER
RECITES
REFINED
REFINER
REFINES
REFIRES
REGIMEN
REGIMES
REHIRED
REHIRES
RELINED
RELINES
RELIVED
RELIVES
REMIXED
REMIXES
REOILED
REPINED
REPINES
RESIDED
RESIDES
RESILED
RESILES
RETILED
RETILES
RETIMED
RETIMES
RETIRED
RETIREE
RETIRES
REVILED
REVILES
REVISED
REVISER
REVISES
REVIVED
REVIVES
REWIRED
REWIRES
ROTIFER
SABINES
SAMISEN
SAMITES
SANIBEL
SATIRES
SCRIBES
SCRIVEN
SEMITES
SHIITES
SHRIKES
SHRINER
SHRINES
SHRIVEL
SHRIVER
SHRIVES
SIMILES
SLUICED
SLUICES
SOLIDER
SORITES
SPLICED
SPLICER
SPLICES
SPLINES
SPOILED
SPOILER
SPRITES
SQUIRED
SQUIRES
STAIDER
STAINED
STAINER
STEIGER
STEINEM
STEINER
STRIDER
STRIDES
STRIKER
STRIKES
STRIPED
STRIPER
STRIPES
STRIVED
STRIVEN
STRIVER
STRIVES
THRIVED
THRIVES
TIMIDER
TRAILED
TRAILER
TRAINED
TRAINEE
TRAINER
UMPIRED
UMPIRES
UNAIDED
UNAIMED
UNAIRED
UNFIXED
UNLIKED
UNLINED
UNOILED
UNPILED
UNPILES
UNWISER
UPRISEN
UPRISES
UPRIVER
VALISES
VISITED
VIVIDER
WAHINES

•••I••E

AAMILNE
ABRIDGE
ACHIEVE
ANTIQUE
ARRIERE
ARTICLE
ARTISTE
AUDIBLE
AURICLE
BATISTE
BELIEVE
BESIEGE
BEZIQUE
BRAILLE
CALIBRE
CAMILLE
CEVICHE
CILIATE
COMIQUE
CUBICLE
CUTICLE
DEHISCE
DEMILLE
DENIECE
DESIREE
DEVIATE
DEVILLE
DEWILDE
ECLIPSE
ELLIPSE
ENTITLE
EXPIATE
FATIGUE
FOLIAGE
FOLIATE
FRAICHE
GALILEE
GEFILTE
HABITUE
HYGIENE
IMPINGE
JUBILEE
LABIATE
LAFITTE
LALIQUE
LAMINAE
LEGIBLE
LETITBE
LUCILLE
LUMIERE
MANIPLE
MATINEE
MATISSE
MEDIATE
MERIMEE
MODISTE
MOLIERE
MONIQUE
NEVILLE
NOMINEE
OBLIQUE
OBVIATE
ORVILLE
OSSICLE
PANICLE
PEDICLE
PELISSE
PERIGEE
PETIOLE
PRAIRIE
RADIATE
RADICLE
RELIEVE
RERINSE
RESIDUE
RETICLE
RETINAE
RETINUE
RETIREE
RETITLE
RISIBLE
RIVIERE
SATIATE
SERIATE
SEVIGNE
SEVILLE
SHEILAE
STRIATE
SYRINGE
TRAINEE
TRAIPSE
TUNICLE
VEHICLE
VISIBLE
VITIATE
WOEISME

••••IE•

AMBRIES
ANGRIER
ANTSIER
APERIES
APPLIED
APPLIES
ARCHIES
ATELIER
ATOMIES
AUNTIES
AUSSIES
BADDIES
BAGGIER
BAGGIES
BALKIER
BALMIER
BANDIED
BANDIES
BARMIER
BARRIER
BATTIER
BAWDIER
BEADIER
BEAMIER
BEANIES
BEEFIER
BELLIED
BELLIES
BERRIED
BERRIES
BIALIES
BIDDIES
BIGGIES
BILLIES
BIRDIED
BIRDIES
BITTIER
BLOWIER
BMOVIES
BOBBIES
BONNIER
BOOBIES
BOOGIED
BOOGIES
BOOKIES
BOONIES
BOOTIES
BOSSIER
BOWTIES
BRAZIER
BRINIER
BUDDIES
BUDGIES
BUGGIER
BUGGIES
BULKIER
BULLIED
BULLIES
BUMPIER
BUNNIES
BURLIER
BUSBIES
BUSHIER
CABBIES
CADDIED
CADDIES
CAMPIER
CANDIED
CANDIES
CANNIER
CARNIES
CARRIED
CARRIER
CARRIES
CARTIER
CASHIER
CATTIER
CHARIER
CHENIER
CHEVIED
CHEVIES
CHEWIER
CHILIES
CIVVIES
CLAVIER
CLAYIER
COCKIER
COLLIER
COLLIES
COMFIER
COOKIES
COOTIES
CORNIER
COURIER
COWRIES
CRAZIER
CRAZIES
CRONIES
CROSIER
CUBBIES
CURLIER
CURRIED
CURRIER
CURRIES
CURVIER
CUSHIER
DADDIES
DAFFIER
DAILIES
DAIRIES
DAISIES
DALLIED
DALLIER
DALLIES
DANDIER
DANDIES
DAUMIER
DEBRIEF
DECRIED
DECRIES
DEIFIED
DEIFIES
DEITIES
DERBIES
DERNIER
DEVRIES
DIARIES
DICKIES
DILLIES
DINGIER
DINKIER
DINKIES
DIRTIED
DIRTIER
DIRTIES
DITTIES
DIVVIED
DIVVIES
DIZZIED
DIZZIER
DIZZIES
DOGGIES
DOILIES
DOLLIED
DOLLIES
DOOZIES
DOSSIER
DOTTIER
DOWDIER
DOWNIER
DOWRIES
DUCHIES
DUCKIER
DUDDIES
DUMMIED
DUMMIES
DUMPIER
DUSKIER
DUSTIER
EARLIER
EBONIES
EDIFIED
EDIFIES
ELEGIES
EMPTIED
EMPTIER
EMPTIES
ENEMIES
ENTRIES
EPOXIES
EZEKIEL
FAIRIES
FANCIED
FANCIER
FANCIES
FARRIER
FEELIES
FERRIED
FERRIES
FIERIER
FIFTIES
FILLIES
FILMIER
FISHIER
FIZZIER
FLAKIER
FOAMIER
FOGGIER
FOLLIES
FORTIES
FOURIER
FRASIER
FRAZIER
FUNKIER
FUNNIER
FUNNIES
FURRIER
FUSSIER
FUSTIER
FUZZIER
GABBIER
GABRIEL
GAUDIER
GAUZIER

GAWKIER
GIDDIER
GILLIES
GIPSIES
GLACIER
GLAZIER
GLORIED
GLORIES
GOALIES
GOODIES
GOOFIER
GOOPIER
GRAVIES
GRIMIER
GROLIER
GULLIES
GUMMIER
GUNKIER
GUNNIES
GUPPIES
GUSHIER
GUSSIED
GUSSIES
GUTSIER
GYPSIES
HACKIES
HAIRIER
HANDIER
HANKIES
HAPPIER
HARDIER
HARPIES
HARRIED
HARRIER
HARRIES
HARRIET
HASTIER
HEADIER
HEAVIER
HEAVIES
HEFTIER
HILLIER
HINNIES
HIPPIES
HOAGIES
HOARIER
HOBBIES
HOGTIED
HOGTIES
HOLLIES
HOOSIER
HORSIER
HUBBIES
HUFFIER
HURRIED
HURRIES
HUSKIER
HUSKIES
HUSSIES
IMPLIED
IMPLIES
INBRIEF
IRONIES
ITCHIER
IVORIES
JANVIER
JAZZIER
JEEBIES
JELLIED
JELLIES
JEMMIED
JEMMIES
JENNIES
JERKIER
JETTIES
JIFFIES
JIMMIED
JIMMIES
JOLLIED
JOLLIER
JOLLIES
JOLLIET
JUICIER
JUMPIER
JUNKIER
JUNKIES
KELPIES
KEWPIES
KIDDIES
KILTIES
KINKIER
KITTIES
KOOKIER
LADDIES
LANKIER
LASSIES
LEAFIER
LEAKIER
LEERIER
LEFTIES
LEGGIER
LINDIED
LINDIES
LINTIER
LIPPIER
LOAMIER
LOBBIED
LOBBIES
LOFTIER
LOLLIES
LOONIER
LOONIES
LOOPIER
LORRIES
LOUSIER
LOWLIER
LUCKIER
LUMPIER
LUSTIER
MAGPIES
MANGIER
MANLIER
MARRIED
MARRIES
MASHIES
MEALIER
MEALIES
MEANIES
MEATIER
MERCIES
MERRIER
MESSIER
MIDDIES
MILKIER
MINTIER
MISSIES
MISTIER
MOLDIER
MOMMIES
MOODIER
MOSSIER
MOUSIER
MUDDIED
MUDDIER
MUDDIES
MUDPIES
MUGGIER
MUMMIES
MURKIER
MUSHIER
MUSTIER
MUZZIER
NANNIES
NASTIER
NATTIER
NEEDIER
NERVIER
NEWSIER
NIFTIER
NINNIES
NIPPIER
NOISIER
NUBBIER
NUTTIER
OLIVIER
ONADIET
PADDIES
PALMIER
PAMBIES
PANNIER
PANSIES
PARRIED
PARRIES
PARTIED
PARTIES
PASTIER
PATSIES
PATTIES
PENNIES
PEONIES
PEPPIER
PERDIEM
PERKIER
PERRIER
PESKIER
PETTIER
PHONIER
PHONIES
PICKIER
PIETIES
PIGGIES
PINKIES
PITHIER
PODGIER
POITIER
POPPIES
PORGIES
POTPIES
POUTIER
PREMIER
PREVIEW
PRICIER
PRIVIES
PROSIER
PROXIES
PUDGIER
PUFFIER
PUNKIES
PUPPIES
PURLIEU
PURVIEW
PUSHIER
PUTTIED
PUTTIES
PYGMIES
QUERIED
QUERIES
RAGGIER
RAINIER
RALLIED
RALLIES
RANDIER
RANGIER
RASPIER
RATTIER
READIED
READIER
READIES
REEDIER
REFRIED
REFRIES
REPLIED
REPLIES
REQUIEM
RETRIED
RETRIES
RISKIER
RITZIER
ROADIES
ROCKIER
ROCKIES
ROOKIES
ROOMIER
ROOMIES
ROWDIER
ROWDIES
RUDDIER
RUMMIER
RUNNIER
RUNTIER
RUSTIER
SAGGIER
SALLIED
SALLIES
SALTIER
SANDIER
SAPPIER
SASSIER
SASSIES
SAUCIER
SAVVIER
SCALIER
SCARIER
SEAMIER
SEEDIER
SERRIED
SHADIER
SHAKIER
SHINIER
SHOWIER
SILKIER
SILLIER
SILLIES
SISSIES
SIXTIES
SLATIER
SLIMIER
SMOKIER
SMOKIES
SNAKIER
SNOWIER
SOAPIER
SOFTIES
SOGGIER
SOLDIER
SOOTIER
SORRIER
SORTIED
SORTIES
SOUPIER
SPACIER
SPANIEL
SPECIES
SPICIER
SPIKIER
SPINIER
STAGIER
STOGIES
STONIER
STORIED
STORIES
STUDIED
STUDIES
STYMIED
STYMIES
SUDSIER
SULKIER
SULKIES
SULLIED
SULLIES
SUNNIER
SURLIER
TABBIES
TACKIER
TAFFIES
TALKIES
TALLIED
TALLIES
TANGIER
TANSIES
TARDIER
TARRIED
TARRIES
TARSIER
TASTIER
TATTIER
TAWNIER
TEARIER
TECHIES
TEDDIES
TEENIER
TELLIES
TENNIEL
TERRIER
TERRIES
TESTIER
TINNIER
TIPSIER
TIZZIES
TOADIED
TOADIES
TODDIES
TOLKIEN
TOWNIES
TUBBIER
TUMMIES
TUNNIES
UNIFIED
UNIFIER
UNIFIES
UNITIES
UNTRIED
VEGGIES
VERNIER
WACKIER
WEARIED
WEARIER
WEARIES
WEDGIES
WEEDIER
WEENIES
WEEPIER
WIENIES
WILLIES
WINDIER
WISPIER
WITTIER
WOODIER
WOODIES
WOOLIER
WOOLIES
WOOZIER
WORDIER
WORMIER
WORRIED
WORRIER
WORRIES
YUCKIER
YUMMIER
YUPPIES
ZESTIER
ZINGIER
ZIPPIER
ZOMBIES

•••••I•E

ABUSIVE
ACONITE
ACQUIRE
ADAMITE
ADELINE
ADENINE
AFFAIRE
AGONIZE
AIRLINE
AIRMILE
AIRTIME
ALEWIFE
ALLTIME
AMATIVE
ANILINE
ANODIZE
ANTOINE
ANYTIME
APATITE
APELIKE
APPRISE
APPRIZE
ARCHIVE
ARCSINE
ARMOIRE
ASCRIBE
ASININE
ASTAIRE
ASTRIDE
ATOMIZE
ATTRITE
AUSPICE
AVARICE
AZURITE
BAGPIPE
BAPTIZE
BAUXITE
BEDSIDE
BEDTIME
BEEHIVE
BEELINE
BEGRIME
BEGUILE
BEGUINE
BERNICE
BIGTIME
BONFIRE
BOWLINE
BOXKITE
BROMIDE
BROMINE
BUSLINE
BUYTIME
CALCITE
CANDICE
CANDIDE
CAPRICE
CAPSIZE
CAPTIVE
CARBIDE
CARBINE
CARMINE
CASTILE
CATLIKE
CENTIME
CHALICE
CHEMISE
CHORINE
CITRINE
CLARICE
COCHISE
CODEINE
COLLIDE
COMBINE
COMPILE
CONCISE
CONFIDE
CONFINE
CONNIVE
COPPICE
CORDITE
CORNICE
COWHIDE
CREVICE
CUISINE
CURSIVE
CUTTIME
DAYTIME
DECEIVE
DECLINE
DELUISE
DENTINE
DEPRIVE
DESPISE
DESPITE
DESTINE
DEWLINE
DIOXIDE
DISLIKE
DORMICE
DUCTILE
EBBTIDE
EBONITE
EBWHITE
EDIFICE
EGALITE
ELUSIVE
EMOTIVE
ENDWISE
ENSUITE
ENTWINE
EREMITE
EROSIVE
ERSKINE
ERUDITE
ESQUIRE
ETAMINE
EVASIVE
EXAMINE
FANZINE
FEBRILE
FERRITE
FERTILE
FESTIVE
FICTIVE
FISSILE
FORGIVE
FORLIFE
FOXFIRE
FRAGILE
FURTIVE
GAGLINE
GEMLIKE
GENTILE
GENUINE
GODLIKE
GRACILE
GRANITE
GUANINE
GUNFIRE
HAYRIDE
HAYWIRE
HELOISE
HEMLINE
HEROINE
HILAIRE
HITTITE
HOSPICE
HOSTILE
HOTLINE
HOTWIRE
HYALINE
IDOLIZE
IMAGINE
INCLINE
INQUIRE
INSPIRE
INUTILE
INVOICE
ITEMIZE
JADEITE
JASMINE
JAWLINE
JIMDINE
JOYRIDE
JUGWINE
JUSTICE
JUSTINE
KEYLIME
LARAINE
LATTICE
LEETIDE
LEONINE
LIGNITE
LIONIZE
LOWLIFE
LOWRISE
LOWTIDE
MACHINE
MALAISE
MASSIVE
MAURICE
MAYTIME
MAYWINE
MCGUIRE
MCSWINE
MEMOIRE
MIDLIFE
MIDLINE
MIDRISE
MIDSIZE
MIDWIFE
MISFILE
MISFIRE
MISSILE
MISSIVE
MORAINE
MORTISE
NAPTIME
NITRIDE
NITRITE
NUCLIDE
OBELIZE
OFFLINE
OFFSIDE
OFFSITE
OLDLINE
OLDTIME
OLIVINE
ONETIME
OPALINE
ORIFICE
OUTLINE
OUTLIVE
OUTSIDE
OUTSIZE
OWLLIKE
OXIDIZE
PACKICE
PANPIPE
PARTITE
PASSIVE
PASTIME
PATRICE
PAULINE
PENSIVE
PEPTIDE
PERLITE
PIGLIKE
PISCINE
PISMIRE
PLOSIVE
PONTINE
PORCINE
PRALINE
PRECISE
PREMISE
PRESIDE
PROFILE
PROMISE
PROVIDE
PUERILE
QUININE
QUIVIVE
RAGTIME
RATLINE
RAWHIDE
REALIZE
RECEIVE
RECLINE
REDLINE
REDPINE
REDWINE
REJOICE
REPRICE
REPRISE
REPTILE
REQUIRE
REQUITE
RERAISE
RESPIRE
RESPITE
RESTIVE
REUNITE
REVOICE
REWRITE
RIPTIDE
ROMAINE
ROUTINE
SALTINE
SARDINE
SEASIDE
SERVICE
SERVILE
SESSILE
SETLINE
SISTINE
SKYDIVE
SKYLINE
STABILE
STATICE
STERILE
STYLIZE
SUBLIME
SUBSIDE
SUFFICE
SULFIDE
SULFITE
SUNRISE
SURMISE
SURVIVE
TACTILE
TAGLINE
TANLINE
TAURINE
TEATIME
TEKTITE
TENSILE
TENSIVE
TERMITE
TEXTILE
THINICE
TIELINE
TITMICE
TONTINE
TOPSIDE
TURBINE
TVGUIDE
TWOTIME
UKRAINE
UNALIKE
UNITIVE
UPRAISE
URANITE
UTILIZE
VACCINE
VAMPIRE
VANDINE
VESTIGE
VULPINE
WARLIKE
WARTIME
WAYSIDE
WEBSITE

••••••IE

BEASTIE
BEATTIE
BLONDIE
BOLOTIE
BRASSIE
BROWNIE
CALORIE
CAPAPIE
CHARLIE
CHEAPIE
COTERIE
CRAPPIE
DHURRIE
DOORDIE
EUGENIE
FOOTSIE
FRANKIE
FREDDIE
FREEBIE
FRICKIE
GROUPIE
GUTHRIE
JEANNIE
JOHNNIE
KIRSTIE
LARAMIE
MELANIE
MOUNTIE
NATALIE
NECKTIE
NIGHTIE
OVERLIE
PORKPIE
PRAIRIE
PREEMIE
PREPPIE
QUICKIE
REVERIE
RITCHIE
ROSALIE
RUSHDIE
SCOTTIE
SHELTIE
SINEDIE
STEELIE
STOOLIE
SWEETIE
SWOOSIE
TOOTSIE
TOUGHIE
TREKKIE
VALERIE
WHEELIE
WILLKIE

IF•••••

IFFIEST
IFSTONE

I•F••••

IFFIEST
INFANCY
INFANTA
INFANTS
INFAVOR
INFECTS
INFERNO
INFESTS
INFIDEL
INFIELD
INFLAME
INFLATE
INFLECT
INFLICT
INFLOWS
INFOCUS
INFORCE
INFORMS
INFRONT
INFUSED
INFUSES

I••F•••

ICEFLOE
ICEFREE

I•••F••

INSOFAR

I•••••F

INAWEOF
INBRIEF

•IF••••

BIFOCAL
DIFFERS
DIFFUSE
FIFTEEN
FIFTIES
GIFFORD
JIFFIES
LIFENET
LIFTERS
LIFTING
LIFTOFF
LIFTSUP
MIFFING
NIFTIER
NIFTILY
PIFFLED
PIFFLES
RIFFING
RIFFLED
RIFFLES
RIFLERS
RIFLERY
RIFLING
RIFTING
SIFTERS
SIFTING
TIFFANY

•I•F•••

AIRFARE
AIRFLOW
AIRFOIL
BIDFAIR
BIGFEET
BIGFOOT
DIFFERS
DIFFUSE
FIEFDOM
GIFFORD
GINFIZZ
JIFFIES
KINFOLK
MIFFING
MISFILE
MISFIRE
MISFITS
MITFORD
PIFFLED
PIFFLES
PILFERS
PITFALL
RIFFING
RIFFLED
RIFFLES
SIXFOLD
TIFFANY
TINFOIL
WILFORD
WILFRID
WINFREY

•I••F••

FIREFLY
FISHFRY
FISTFUL
GIRAFFE
MINDFUL
PINEFOR
PIPEFUL
PITIFUL
RIPOFFS
TIPOFFS
WILLFUL
WISHFUL
WISTFUL

•I•••F•

AIRLIFT
BITEOFF
DIEDOFF
DIESOFF
DIGNIFY
DISTAFF
FIREOFF
GIRAFFE
GIVEOFF
KICKOFF
KISSOFF
LIFTOFF
LIQUEFY
MIDLIFE
MIDRIFF
MIDWIFE
PICKOFF
RIDEOFF
RIPOFFS
RIPSOFF
SIGNIFY
SIGNOFF
TICKOFF
TIMEOFF
TIPOFFS
TIPSOFF
VITRIFY

•I••••F

AIRWOLF
BITEOFF
DIEDOFF
DIESOFF
DISTAFF
FIGLEAF
FIREOFF
GIVEOFF
HIMSELF
HIPROOF
KICKOFF
KISSOFF
LIFTOFF
MIDRIFF
PICKOFF
RIDEOFF
RIPSOFF
SIGNOFF
TICKOFF
TIMEOFF
TIPSOFF
TIREDOF

••IF•••

CHIFFON
CLIFTON
COIFING
DEIFIED
DEIFIES
DRIFTED
DRIFTER
EDIFICE
EDIFIED
EDIFIES
FEIFFER
GRIFFEY
GRIFFIN

GRIFFON
GRIFTER
HEIFERS
HEIFETZ
KNIFING
ORIFICE
SHIFTED
SNIFFAT
SNIFFED
SNIFFER
SNIFFLE
SNIFTER
STIFFED
STIFFEN
STIFFER
STIFFLY
STIFLED
STIFLES
SWIFTER
SWIFTLY
TRIFLED
TRIFLER
TRIFLES
UNIFIED
UNIFIER
UNIFIES
UNIFORM
WHIFFED

••I•F••
BRIEFED
BRIEFER
BRIEFLY
BRIMFUL
CHIEFLY
CHIFFON
FEIFFER
GAINFUL
GOINFOR
GRIFFEY
GRIFFIN
GRIFFON
LAIDFOR
PAIDFOR
PAILFUL
PAINFUL
SKILFUL
SNIFFAT
SNIFFED
SNIFFER
SNIFFLE
STIFFED
STIFFEN
STIFFER
STIFFLY
STIRFRY
TAILFIN
WHIFFED

••I••F•
ACIDIFY
BAILIFF
FAIROFF
LAIDOFF
PAIDOFF
PAIROFF
SKILIFT
SPINOFF
TAILOFF

••I•••F
BAILIFF
FAIROFF
LAIDOFF
PAIDOFF
PAIROFF
SPINOFF
TAILOFF
THINKOF

•••IF••
AQUIFER
CONIFER
DUTIFUL
HALIFAX
LATIFAH
LUCIFER
OSSIFIC
PACIFIC
PITIFUL
ROTIFER
SHRIFTS
TARIFFS
THRIFTS
THRIFTY
UPLIFTS

•••I•F•
BELIEFS
RELIEFS
SATISFY
TARIFFS

••••IF•
ACIDIFY
AIRLIFT
ALEWIFE
AMPLIFY
BAILIFF
BEATIFY
BRANIFF
CALCIFY
CERTIFY
CLARIFY
CONNIFF
DIGNIFY
FALSIFY
FORLIFE
FORTIFY
GLORIFY
GRATIFY
HORRIFY
JUSTIFY
LOWLIFE
MAGNIFY
MASSIFS
MASTIFF
MIDLIFE
MIDRIFF
MIDWIFE
MOLLIFY
MORTIFY
MYSTIFY
NULLIFY
PETRIFY
PONTIFF
QUALIFY
RECTIFY
REUNIFY
SALSIFY
SCARIFY
SHERIFF
SIGNIFY
SKILIFT
SPECIFY
TERRIFY
TESTIFY
VERSIFY
VITRIFY

••••I•F
BAILIFF
BRANIFF
CONNIFF
DEBRIEF
INBRIEF
MASTIFF
MIDRIFF
PONTIFF
SHERIFF

IG•••••
IGNEOUS
IGNITED
IGNITER
IGNITES
IGNOBLE
IGNOBLY
IGNORED
IGNORER
IGNORES
IGUANAS

I•G••••
INGALLS
INGEMAR
INGENUE
INGESTS
INGRAIN
INGRATE
INGRESS
INGROUP
INGROWN

I••G•••
IMAGERS
IMAGERY
IMAGINE
IMAGING
IMAGOES
IMOGENE
ISOGONS

I•••G••
ICEAGES
ICINGIN
ILLEGAL
ILLOGIC
IMPUGNS
INDIGOS
INSIGHT
INTEGER
INTEGRA
INVOGUE

I••••G•
ICEBAGS
IMPINGE
INDULGE
INNINGS
INVEIGH
IRONAGE

I•••••G
ICEBERG
IMAGING
IMBUING
INCHING
INKLING
INURING
IRONING
ISSUING
ITCHING

•IG••••
AIGRETS
BIGBAND
BIGBANG
BIGBEND
BIGBIRD
BIGBOYS
BIGDEAL
BIGELOW
BIGEYES
BIGFEET
BIGFOOT
BIGGAME
BIGGERS
BIGGEST
BIGGIES
BIGGUNS
BIGHEAD
BIGHORN
BIGJOHN
BIGNAME
BIGNESS
BIGOTED
BIGOTRY
BIGSHOT
BIGTIME
BIGTOES
BIGTOPS
BIGWIGS
DIGESTS
DIGGERS
DIGGING
DIGITAL
DIGNIFY
DIGNITY
DIGRAPH
DIGRESS
DIGSOUT
EIGHTHS
FIGHTER
FIGLEAF
FIGMENT
FIGURED
FIGURER
FIGURES
GIGGLED
GIGGLER
GIGGLES
GIGOLOS
HIGGINS
HIGHBOY
HIGHEND
HIGHEST
HIGHHAT
HIGHLOW
HIGHTEA
HIGHTOP
HIGHWAY
JIGGERS
JIGGERY
JIGGING
JIGGLED
JIGGLES
JIGSAWS
LIGATED
LIGATES
LIGHTED
LIGHTEN
LIGHTER
LIGHTLY
LIGHTUP
LIGNITE
MIGHTNT
MIGRANT
MIGRATE
NIGERIA
NIGGARD
NIGGLED
NIGGLES
NIGHEST
NIGHTIE
NIGHTLY
PIGEONS
PIGGIES
PIGGING
PIGGISH
PIGIRON
PIGLETS
PIGLIKE
PIGMENT
PIGNUTS
PIGPENS
PIGSKIN
PIGSOUT
PIGTAIL
RIGGERS
RIGGING
RIGHTED
RIGHTER
RIGHTLY
RIGHTON
RIGIDLY
RIGOURS
RIGVEDA
SIGHERS
SIGHING
SIGHTED
SIGHTLY
SIGMUND
SIGNALS
SIGNEES
SIGNERS
SIGNETS
SIGNIFY
SIGNING
SIGNOFF
SIGNOUT
SIGNSIN
SIGNSON
SIGNSUP
TIGHTEN
TIGHTER
TIGHTLY
TIGRESS
VIGOURS
WIGGLED
WIGGLER
WIGGLES
WIGLETS
WIGSOUT
WIGWAGS
WIGWAMS
ZIGGING
ZIGZAGS

•I•G•••
AIRGUNS
BIGGAME
BIGGERS
BIGGEST
BIGGIES
BIGGUNS
BINGHAM
BINGING
BINGOES
BIOGENY
DIAGRAM
DIDGOOD
DIGGERS
DIGGING
DINGBAT
DINGIER
DINGILY
DINGING
DINGLES
DINGOES
DISGUST
FIDGETS
FIDGETY
FINGERS
FIZGIGS
GIGGLED
GIGGLER
GIGGLES
GINGERS
GINGERY
GINGHAM
GINGIVA
HIGGINS
HINGING
JIGGERS
JIGGERY
JIGGING
JIGGLED
JIGGLES
JINGLED
JINGLES
JINGOES
KINGDOM
KINGING
KINGMAN
KINGPIN
KINGRAT
KINGTUT
LINGERS
LINGOES
LINGUAL
MIDGETS
MINGLED
MINGLER
MINGLES
NIAGARA
NIGGARD
NIGGLED
NIGGLES
PIDGEON
PIDGINS
PIGGIES
PIGGING
PIGGISH
PILGRIM
PINGING
RIDGING
RIDGWAY
RIGGERS
RIGGING
RINGERS
RINGING
RINGLET
RINGOUT
RINGSUP
SINGERS
SINGING
SINGLED
SINGLES
SINGOUT
SINGSTO
SIXGUNS
TINGING
TINGLED
TINGLES
VIRGINS
VIRGOAN
VIRGULE
WIDGEON
WIDGETS
WIGGLED
WIGGLER
WIGGLES
WINGERS
WINGING
WINGNUT
WINGSIT
WINGTIP
ZIGGING
ZINGERS
ZINGIER
ZINGING

•I••G••
FINAGLE
GIELGUD
GIORGIO
LIMOGES
LINAGES
LITHGOW
MIRAGES
PIROGUE
VINEGAR
VIRAGOS
VISAGES
WISEGUY

•I•••G•
AIRBAGS
AIRINGS
BIGWIGS
BIOLOGY
DIALOGS
DIVERGE
DIVULGE
FILINGS
FIRINGS
FIXINGS
FIZGIGS
HIDALGO
KITBAGS
LINEAGE
LININGS
LINKAGE
LITURGY
LIVINGS
MILEAGE
OILRIGS
PILINGS
PILLAGE
PIPINGS
RIBCAGE
RISINGS
SIDINGS
SINKAGE
SIZINGS
TIDINGS
TILLAGE
TIMINGS
VIKINGS
VILLAGE
VINTAGE
WIGWAGS
ZIGZAGS

•I••••G
BIASING
BIDDING
BIGBANG
BILKING
BILLING
BINDING
BINGING
BINNING
BIRDDOG
BIRDING
BIRLING
BITTING
DIALING
DIETING
DIGGING
DIMMING
DINGING
DIPPING
DISHING
DISHRAG
FIBBING
FILLING
FILMING
FINDING
FINKING
FIREBUG
FIREDOG
FIRMING
FISHING
FITTING
FIZZING
GILDING
GILLING
GINNING
GINSENG
GIRDING
HILLING
HINGING
HINTING
HISSING
HITTING
JIGGING
JILTING
JINKING
JINXING
KICKING
KIDDING
KILLING
KILTING
KINGING
KINKING
KIPLING
KISSING
LIBBING
LICKING
LIFTING
LILTING
LIMBING
LIMNING
LIMPING
LINKING
LIPPING
LISPING
LISTING
MIFFING
MILKING
MILLING
MINCING
MINDING
MINTING
MISSING
MISTING
MITRING
NICKING
NIPPING
OINKING
PICKING
PIECING
PIGGING
PILLBUG
PILLING
PINGING
PINKING
PINNING
PIQUING
PITHING
PITTING
PITYING
RIBBING
RIDDING
RIDGING
RIFFING
RIFLING
RIFTING
RIGGING
RIMMING
RINGING
RINSING
RIOTING
RIPPING
RISKING
SIBLING
SICCING
SIDLING
SIFTING
SIGHING
SIGNING
SILOING
SILTING
SINGING
SINKING
SIPPING
SITTING
TICKING
TIDYING
TIERING
TILLING
TILTING
TIMELAG
TINGING
TINTING
TIPPING
TITHING
TITLING
VIEWING
WILDING
WILLING
WILTING
WINCING
WINDBAG
WINDING
WINGING
WINKING
WINNING
WISHING
WISPING
WITTING
YIPPING
ZIGGING
ZINGING
ZIPPING

••IG•••
ABIGAIL
ALIGHTS
ALIGNED
ALIGNER
AVIGNON
BLIGHTS
BRIGADE
BRIGAND
BRIGHAM
CHIGGER
CHIGNON
DEIGNED
EMIGRES
ENIGMAS
EPIGENE
EPIGONE
EPIGRAM
EXIGENT
FEIGNED
FLIGHTS
FLIGHTY
FRIGATE
FRIGHTS
GRIGRIS
HEIGHHO
HEIGHTS
KNIGHTS
MAIGRET
NEIGHED
ORIGAMI
ORIGINS
PLIGHTS
QUIGLEY
REIGNED
SLIGHTS
SNIGGER
SNIGGLE
SNIGLET
SOIGNEE
SPIGOTS
STIGMAS
SWIGGED
TRIGGED
TRIGGER
TRIGONS
TRIGRAM
VEIGHTS
WEIGHED
WEIGHIN
WEIGHTS
WEIGHTY
WRIGGLE
WRIGGLY
WRIGHTS
WRIGLEY

••I•G••
ATINGLE
BRIDGED
BRIDGES
BRIDGET
BRINGER
BRINGIN
BRINGON
BRINGTO
BRINGUP
CHIGGER
CLINGTO
CRINGED
CRINGES
DOINGIN
DOINGUP
FRIDGES
FRINGED
FRINGES
GOINGAT
GOINGBY
GOINGIN
GOINGON
GOINGUP
ICINGIN
KLINGON
KRINGLE
LYINGTO
OWINGTO
SHINGLE
SLINGER
SMIDGEN
SNIGGER
SNIGGLE
SPIEGEL
STIEGEL
STINGER
SWIGGED
SWINGBY
SWINGER
TLINGIT
TRIGGED
TRIGGER
TWINGED
TWINGES
TYINGIN
TYINGUP
USINGUP
WRIGGLE
WRIGGLY
WRINGER
ZWINGLI

••I••G•
CHICAGO
COINAGE
EPILOGS
TRILOGY
ZHIVAGO

••I•••G
ABIDING
ARISING
BAILING
BAITING
BEIJING
BOILING
BRIBING
BRINING
CEILING
CHIDING
CHIMING
COIFING
COILING
COINING
DEICING
DRIVING
EDITING
ELIDING
EXILING
EXITING
FAILING
FAIRING
FOILING
GAINING
GAITING
GLIDING
GRIPING
GUIDING
HAILING
JAILING
JOINING
JUICING
KNIFING
LEIPZIG
MAILBAG
MAILING
MOILING
NAILING
NOISING
OPINING
PAIRING
POISING
PRICING
PRIDING
PRIMING
PRIZING
RAIDING
RAILING
RAINING
RAISING
REINING
ROILING
RUINING
SAILING
SEINING
SEIZING
SHINDIG
SHINING
SLICING
SLIDING
SMILING
SMITING
SNIPING
SOILING
SPICING
SPIKING
SPITING
SUITING
SWIPING
TAILING
TOILING
TWINING
UNITING
VEILING
VEINING
VOICING
VOIDING
WAILING
WAITING
WAIVING
WHILING
WHINING
WHITING
WRITING
ZEITUNG

•••IG••
ALRIGHT
ANTIGEN
ANTIGUA
ASSIGNS
COSIGNS
DELIGHT
DEMIGOD
DESIGNS
ENSIGNS
FATIGUE
FREIGHT
INDIGOS
INSIGHT
MALIGNS
MRRIGHT
OBLIGED
OBLIGES
ONSIGHT
PERIGEE
RELIGHT
RESIGNS
SEVIGNE
SLEIGHS
SLEIGHT
STEIGER
TONIGHT
UPRIGHT
UPTIGHT

•••I•G•
ABRIDGE
AIRINGS
AWNINGS
BESIEGE
CASINGS
COMINGS
DOMINGO
EDGINGS
ENDINGS
FACINGS
FILINGS
FIRINGS
FIXINGS
FOLIAGE
HAZINGS
IMPINGE
INNINGS
LACINGS
LININGS
LIVINGS
MAKINGS
NORIEGA
OUTINGS
PARINGS
PILINGS
PIPINGS
RATINGS
RAVINGS
RESINGS
RISINGS
RULINGS
SAVINGS
SAYINGS
SIDINGS
SIZINGS
SPRINGS
SPRINGY
STRINGS
STRINGY
SYRINGA
SYRINGE
TAPINGS
TIDINGS
TIMINGS
VIKINGS

•••I••G
ANTILOG
FREITAG
TAXIING
WYSIWYG

••••IG•
AMERIGO
ARRAIGN
BIGWIGS
CONDIGN

CONSIGN
EARWIGS
FIZGIGS
FLYHIGH
FOREIGN
HEXSIGN
INVEIGH
OILRIGS
PRODIGY
RALEIGH
SKYHIGH
VERTIGO
VESTIGE

••••I•G

ABASING
ABATING
ABIDING
ABUSING
ADDLING
ADORING
ALAKING
ALLYING
AMAZING
AMBLING
AMUSING
ANGLING
ANTEING
ARCHING
ARGUING
ARISING
ATONING
AVOWING
AWAKING
BABYING
BACKING
BAGGING
BAILING
BAITING
BALDING
BALKING
BANDING
BANGING
BANKING
BANNING
BARBING
BARGING
BARKING
BARRING
BASHING
BASKING
BASTING
BATHING
BATTING
BATWING
BAWLING
BEADING
BEAMING
BEANING
BEARING
BEATING
BEDDING
BEEFING
BEEPING
BEGGING
BEIJING
BELLING
BELTING
BELYING
BENDING
BESTING
BETTING
BIASING
BIDDING
BILKING
BILLING
BINDING
BINGING
BINNING
BIRDING
BIRLING
BITTING
BLAMING
BLARING
BLAZING
BLOWING
BLUEING
BOATING
BOBBING
BOGGING
BOILING
BOLTING
BOMBING
BONDING
BONGING
BOOKING
BOOMING
BOOTING
BOPPING
BOSSING
BOWLING
BRACING
BRAKING
BRAVING
BRAYING
BRAZING
BREWING
BRIBING
BRINING
BUCKING
BUDDING
BUDGING
BUFFING
BUGGING
BUGLING
BULGING
BULKING
BULLING
BUMMING
BUMPING
BUNGING
BUNKING
BUNTING
BUOYING
BURLING
BURNING
BURPING
BURYING
BUSHING
BUSSING
BUSTING
BUSYING
BUTTING
BUZZING
CABLING
CACHING
CADGING
CALKING
CALLING
CALMING
CALVING
CAMPING
CANNING
CANTING
CAPPING
CARDING
CARPING
CARTING
CARVING
CASHING
CASTING
CATTING
CAUSING
CEASING
CEILING
CENSING
CHAFING
CHASING
CHEWING
CHIDING
CHIMING
CLAWING
CLONING
CLOSING
CLOYING
CLUEING
COATING
COAXING
COCKING
COIFING
COILING
COINING
COMBING
CONKING
CONNING
COOKING
COOLING
COOPING
COPPING
COPYING
CORDING
CORKING
CORNING
COSTING
COWLING
COZYING
CRANING
CRATING
CRAVING
CRAZING
CREWING
CROWING
CUFFING
CULLING
CUNNING
CUPPING
CURBING
CURDING
CURLING
CURSING
CURVING
CUSSING
CUTTING
CYCLING
DABBING
DAMMING
DAMNING
DAMPING
DANCING
DAPPING
DARLING
DARNING
DARTING
DASHING
DAUBING
DAWNING
DEALING
DECKING
DEEDING
DEEMING
DEFYING
DEICING
DELEING
DELVING
DENTING
DENYING
DERRING
DIALING
DIETING
DIGGING
DIMMING
DINGING
DIPPING
DISHING
DOCKING
DODGING
DOFFING
DOGGING
DOLLING
DONKING
DONNING
DOOMING
DOTTING
DOUSING
DOWNING
DOWSING
DRAPING
DRAWING
DRAYING
DRIVING
DRONING
DUBBING
DUCKING
DUCTING
DUELING
DULLING
DUMPING
DUNKING
DUNNING
DUSTING
EAGLING
EARNING
EARRING
ECHOING
EDDYING
EDITING
EDUCING
ELATING
ELIDING
ELOPING
ELUDING
ELUTING
EMOTING
ENDUING
ENSUING
ENURING
ENVYING
ERASING
ERODING
ESPYING
ETCHING
EVADING
EVENING
EVOKING
EXILING
EXITING
EXUDING
FAGGING
FAILING
FAIRING
FALLING
FANNING
FARMING
FASTING
FAWNING
FEARING
FEEDING
FEELING
FELLING
FENCING
FENDING
FEUDING
FIBBING
FILLING
FILMING
FINDING
FINKING
FIRMING
FISHING
FITTING
FIZZING
FLAKING
FLAMING
FLARING
FLAWING
FLAYING
FLEEING
FLEMING
FLEXING
FLOWING
FLUTING
FOALING
FOAMING
FOBBING
FOGGING
FOILING
FOLDING
FOOLING
FOOTING
FORCING
FORDING
FORGING
FORKING
FORMING
FOULING
FOWLING
FRAMING
FRAYING
FREEING
FUDGING
FUELING
FUNDING
FUNNING
FURLING
FURRING
FUSSING
FUZZING
GABBING
GADDING
GAFFING
GAGGING
GAINING
GAITING
GALLING
GANGING
GAPPING
GARBING
GASHING
GASPING
GATLING
GAUGING
GAWKING
GEARING
GELDING
GELLING
GETTING
GILDING
GILLING
GINNING
GIRDING
GLARING
GLAZING
GLIDING
GLOWING
GNAWING
GOADING
GOLDING
GOLFING
GONGING
GOOFING
GOOSING
GORGING
GOSLING
GOUGING
GRACING
GRADING
GRATING
GRAVING
GRAYING
GRAZING
GREYING
GRIPING
GROPING
GROWING
GUIDING
GULFING
GULLING
GULPING
GUMMING
GUNNING
GUSHING
GUSTING
GUTTING
GYPPING
HACKING
HAILING
HALOING
HALTING
HALVING
HAMMING
HANDING
HANGING
HARDING
HARKING
HARMING
HARPING
HASHING
HASTING
HATTING
HAULING
HAWKING
HEADING
HEALING
HEAPING
HEARING
HEATING
HEAVING
HEDGING
HEEDING
HEELING
HEFTING
HELMING
HELPING
HEMMING
HERDING
HERRING
HILLING
HINGING
HINTING
HISSING
HITTING
HOAXING
HOBOING
HOCKING
HOGGING
HOLDING
HONKING
HOOFING
HOOKING
HOOPING
HOOTING
HOPPING
HORNING
HORSING
HOSTING
HOUSING
HOWLING
HUFFING
HUGGING
HULKING
HULLING
HUMMING
HUNTING
HURLING
HURTING
HUSHING
HUSKING
HYPOING
IMAGING
IMBUING
INCHING
INKLING
INURING
IRONING
ISSUING
ITCHING
JABBING
JACKING
JAGGING
JAILING
JAMMING
JARRING
JAZZING
JEERING
JELLING
JERKING
JESTING
JETTING
JIGGING
JILTING
JINKING
JINXING
JOBBING
JOGGING
JOINING
JOLTING
JOSHING
JOTTING
JUDGING
JUICING
JUMPING
JUNKING
JURYING
JUTTING
KAYOING
KEELING
KEENING
KEEPING
KERNING
KEYRING
KICKING
KIDDING
KILLING
KILTING
KINGING
KINKING
KIPLING
KISSING
KNEEING
KNIFING
KNOWING
LACKING
LADLING
LAGGING
LAMMING
LANDING
LANSING
LAPPING
LAPSING
LAPWING
LARDING
LASHING
LASTING
LATHING
LAUDING
LEADING
LEAFING
LEAKING
LEANING
LEAPING
LEASING
LEAVING
LEERING
LEGGING
LEMMING
LENDING
LESSING
LETTING
LEVYING
LIBBING
LICKING
LIFTING
LILTING
LIMBING
LIMNING
LIMPING
LINKING
LIPPING
LISPING
LISTING
LOADING
LOAFING
LOAMING
LOANING
LOBBING
LOCKING
LODGING
LOFTING
LOGGING
LOLLING
LONGING
LOOKING
LOOMING
LOOPING
LOOSING
LOOTING
LOPPING
LORDING
LOTTING
LOUSING
LUCKING
LUFFING
LUGGING
LULLING
LUMPING
LUNGING
LURKING
LUSTING
MADDING
MAILING
MALTING
MANNING
MAPPING
MARKING
MARRING
MASHING
MASKING
MASSING
MATTING
MAULING
MEANING
MEETING
MELDING
MELTING
MENDING
MEOWING
MERGING
MESHING
MESSING
MEWLING
MIFFING
MILKING
MILLING
MINCING
MINDING
MINTING
MISSING
MISTING
MITRING
MOANING
MOBBING
MOCKING
MOILING
MOLDING
MOLTING
MOONING
MOORING
MOPPING
MORNING
MOSSING
MOUSING
MUCKING
MUFFING
MUGGING
MULLING
MUSHING
MUSSING
NABBING
NAGGING
NAILING
NAPPING
NEARING
NECKING
NEEDING
NESTING
NETTING
NICKING
NIPPING
NODDING
NOISING
NOOSING
NOSHING
NOTHING
NUDGING
NULLING
NUMBING
NURSING
NUTTING
OBEYING
OINKING
OKAYING
ONGOING
OPENING
OPINING
ORATING
OUSTING
PACKING
PADDING
PAIRING
PALLING
PALMING
PANNING
PANTING
PARKING
PARRING
PARSING
PARTING
PASSING
PASTING
PATTING
PAULING
PAUSING
PAWNING
PEAKING
PEALING
PECKING
PEEKING
PEELING
PEEPING
PEERING
PEEVING
PEGGING
PELTING
PENDING
PENNING
PEPPING
PERKING
PERMING
PETTING
PHASING
PHONING
PICKING
PIECING
PIGGING
PILLING
PINGING
PINKING
PINNING
PIQUING
PITHING
PITTING
PITYING
PLACING
PLANING
PLATING
PLAYING
PLOWING
PLUMING
POISING
POLLING
PONYING
POOLING
POOPING
POPPING
POSTING
POTTING
POURING
POUTING
PRATING
PRAYING
PRICING
PRIDING
PRIMING
PRIZING
PROBING
PROSING
PROVING
PRUNING
PUDDING
PUFFING
PULLING
PULSING
PUMPING
PUNNING
PUNTING
PURGING
PURLING
PURRING
PURSING
PUSHING
PUTTING
QUAKING
QUEUING
QUOTING
RACKING
RAFTING
RAGGING
RAIDING
RAILING
RAINING
RAISING
RAMMING
RANGING
RANKING
RANTING
RAPPING
RASPING
RATTING
RAZZING
RDLAING
READING
REAMING
REAPING
REARING
REDDING
REDOING
REDWING
REEDING
REEFING
REEKING
REELING
REFFING
REINING
RELYING
RENDING
RENTING
RESTING
REVVING
RHYMING
RIBBING
RIDDING
RIDGING
RIFFING
RIFLING
RIFTING
RIGGING
RIMMING
RINGING
RINSING
RIOTING
RIPPING
RISKING
ROAMING
ROARING
ROBBING
ROCKING
ROILING
ROLLING
ROMPING
ROOFING
ROOKING
ROOMING
ROOTING
ROTTING
ROUGING
ROUSING
ROUTING
RUBBING
RUCHING
RUCKING
RUINING
RUNNING
RUSHING
RUSTING
SACKING
SAGGING
SAILING
SALTING
SALVING
SANDING
SAPLING
SAPPING
SASSING
SCALING
SCARING
SCOPING
SCORING
SEALING
SEAMING
SEARING
SEATING
SEEDING
SEEKING
SEEMING
SEEPING
SEINING
SEIZING
SELLING
SENDING
SENSING
SERLING
SERVING
SETTING
SHADING
SHAKING
SHAMING
SHAPING
SHARING
SHAVING
SHINING
SHOEING
SHOOING
SHORING
SHOVING
SHOWING
SIBLING
SICCING
SIDLING
SIFTING
SIGHING
SIGNING
SILOING
SILTING
SINGING
SINKING
SIPPING
SITTING
SKATING
SKEWING
SLAKING
SLATING
SLAVING
SLICING
SLIDING
SLOPING
SLOWING
SMILING
SMITING
SMOKING
SNAKING
SNARING
SNIPING
SNORING
SNOWING
SOAKING
SOAPING
SOARING
SOBBING
SOCKING
SODDING
SOILING
SOLOING
SOLVING
SOPPING
SORTING
SOURING
SPACING
SPADING
SPARING
SPAYING
SPEWING
SPICING
SPIKING
SPITING
SPOKING
SPUMING
STAGING
STAKING
STARING
STATING
STAVING
STAYING
STEWING
STOKING
STONING
STORING
STOWING
STYLING
SUBBING
SUCKING
SUDSING
SUITING
SULKING
SUMMING
SUNNING
SUPPING
SURFING
SURGING
SUSSING
SWAYING
SWIPING
SYNCING
TABBING
TABLING
TACKING
TAGGING
TAILING
TALKING
TAMPING

TANKING
TANNING
TAPPING
TARRING
TASKING
TASTING
TATTING
TAXIING
TEAMING
TEARING
TEASING
TEDDING
TEEMING
TELLING
TENDING
TENSING
TENTING
TERMING
TESTING
THAWING
TICKING
TIDYING
TIERING
TILLING
TILTING
TINGING
TINTING
TIPPING
TITHING
TITLING
TOGGING
TOILING
TOLLING
TOOLING
TOOTING
TOPPING
TOSSING
TOTTING
TOURING
TOUTING
TRACING
TRADING
TREEING
TRUEING
TUCKING
TUFTING
TUGGING
TURNING
TWINING
UNDOING
UNDYING
UNITING
UNTYING
UPSWING
VALUING
VAMPING
VARYING
VEERING
VEGGING
VEILING
VEINING
VENDING
VENTING
VERGING
VESTING
VETOING
VETTING
VIEWING
VOICING
VOIDING
WADDING
WAFTING
WAGGING
WAILING
WAITING
WAIVING
WALKING
WALLING
WANTING
WARDING
WARMING
WARNING
WARPING
WARRING
WASHING
WASTING
WAXWING
WEANING
WEARING
WEAVING
WEBBING
WEDDING
WEDGING
WEEDING
WEEPING
WELDING
WELLING
WELTING
WENDING
WETTING
WHALING
WHILING
WHINING
WHITING
WILDING
WILLING
WILTING
WINCING
WINDING
WINGING
WINKING
WINNING
WISHING
WISPING
WITTING
WOLFING
WOOFING
WORDING
WORKING
WRITING
WYOMING
XRATING
XRAYING
YAKKING
YANKING
YAPPING
YARNING
YAWNING
YELLING
YELPING
YESSING
YIPPING
YOWLING
YOYOING
ZAGGING
ZAPPING
ZEROING
ZIGGING
ZINGING
ZIPPING
ZONKING
ZOOMING

•••••IG

BUSHPIG
JURYRIG
LEIPZIG
OVERBIG
PFENNIG
SHINDIG
TALKBIG

I•H••••

ICHABOD
INHABIT
INHALED
INHALER
INHALES
INHASTE
INHERED
INHERES
INHERIT
INHIBIT
INHOUSE
INHUMAN
ISHMAEL
ITHACAN

I••H•••

IDAHOAN
INAHEAP
INCHING
INKHORN
INPHASE
INSHAPE
INSHORT
ISOHELS
ISTHMUS
ITCHIER
ITCHING

I•••H••

ICESHOW
IVANHOE

I••••H•

INSIGHT
IOMOTHS

I•••••H

IMPEACH
INARUSH
INDEPTH
INDUTCH
INTRUTH
INVEIGH
IPSWICH

•I•H•••

AIRHEAD
AIRHOLE
BIGHEAD
BIGHORN
BISHOPS
CIPHERS
DIAHANN
DIEHARD
DISHING
DISHOUT
DISHPAN
DISHRAG
DITHERS
DITHERY
EIGHTHS
FIGHTER
FISHERS
FISHERY
FISHEYE
FISHFRY
FISHIER
FISHILY
FISHING
FISHNET
FISHOUT
HIGHBOY
HIGHEND
HIGHEST
HIGHHAT
HIGHLOW
HIGHTEA
HIGHTOP
HIGHWAY
HITHERE
KISHKES
LICHENS
LIGHTED
LIGHTEN
LIGHTER
LIGHTLY
LIGHTUP
LITHELY
LITHEST
LITHGOW
LITHIUM
MICHAEL
MICHELE
MIGHTNT
MIKHAIL
MILHAUD
MISHAPS
MISHEAR
MISHITS
MITHRAS
NICHOLS
NIGHEST
NIGHTIE
NIGHTLY
PINHEAD
PINHOLE
PITHIER
PITHILY
PITHING
RICHARD
RICHEST
RICHMAN
RICHTER
RIGHTED
RIGHTER
RIGHTLY
RIGHTON
SICHUAN
SIGHERS
SIGHING
SIGHTED
SIGHTLY
SIKHISM
SIPHONS
TIGHTEN
TIGHTER
TIGHTLY
TINHATS
TINHORN
TITHERS
TITHING
WICHITA
WILHELM
WISHERS
WISHFUL
WISHING
WITHERS
WITHOUT
ZITHERS

•I••H••

AIRSHIP
AIRSHOW
AITCHES
BIGSHOT
BINGHAM
BIRCHED
BIRCHES
BIRTHED
CINCHED
CINCHES
DITCHED
DITCHES
FILCHED
FILCHER
FILCHES
FINCHES
FISCHER
FITCHES
GINGHAM
HIGHHAT
HITCHED
HITCHER
HITCHES
JIMCHEE
KINSHIP
KITCHEN
LITCHIS
MITCHUM
PINCHAS
PINCHED
PINCHER
PINCHES
PITCHED
PITCHER
PITCHES
PITCHIN
RIMSHOT
RITCHIE
SILKHAT
SIOBHAN
WINCHED
WINCHES
WITCHES
YITZHAK
ZILCHES

•I•••H•

BIGJOHN
EIGHTHS
HIBACHI
HITACHI
KITSCHY
NIEBUHR
PIRANHA
RICKSHA
TIMOTHY

•I••••H

BISMUTH
DIGRAPH
DIPTYCH
FINNISH
GIRLISH
HIALEAH
MISSISH
MITZVAH
NINEVEH
PIGGISH
PINKISH
PIXYISH
YIDDISH

••IH•••

AKIHITO
SHIHTZU

••I•H••

ALIGHTS
APISHLY
BLIGHTS
BLITHER
BRIGHAM
CHICHEN
CLICHES
EPITHET
FLIGHTS
FLIGHTY
FRIGHTS
GEISHAS
GRISHAM
HEIGHHO
HEIGHTS
KAISHEK
KNIGHTS
KNISHES
KRISHNA
NEIGHED
NEITHER
PLIGHTS
PRITHEE
QUICHES
RAINHAT
SEICHES
SLIGHTS
SLITHER
STICHES
SWISHED
SWISHES
TEICHER
THITHER
VEIGHTS
WEIGHED
WEIGHIN
WEIGHTS
WEIGHTY
WHITHER
WRIGHTS
WRITHED
WRITHES

••I••H•

BRIOCHE
HEIGHHO
PLINTHS
TWITCHY

••I•••H

AZIMUTH
BRITISH
SPINACH
TRIUMPH
WHITISH

•••IH••

BALIHAI

•••I•H•

ALRIGHT
CALIPHS
CERIPHS
CEVICHE
DELIGHT
EOLITHS
FRAICHE
FREIGHT
INSIGHT
JERICHO
MRRIGHT
ONSIGHT
OOLITHS
ORNITHO
PARIAHS
RELIGHT
RUPIAHS
SHEIKHS
SLEIGHS
SLEIGHT
SQUISHY
TABITHA
TONIGHT
UPRIGHT
UPTIGHT
WRAITHS
ZENITHS

•••I••H

ANTIOCH
BEWITCH
CORINTH
DELILAH
GOLIATH
LATIFAH
REBIRTH
SHEILAH
SQUINCH
UNHITCH

••••I•H

ABOLISH
ALDRICH
ANOUILH
BABYISH
BEARISH
BLEMISH
BOOKISH
BOORISH
BRITISH
BRUTISH
BULLISH
BURNISH
CATFISH
CATTISH
CHERISH
CODFISH
COLTISH
CORNISH
CULTISH
DAMPISH
DARKISH
DERVISH
DOGFISH
DOLTISH
DULLISH
EHRLICH
ENGLISH
FADDISH
FINNISH
FLEMISH
FLYFISH
FLYHIGH
FOGYISH
FOOLISH
FOPPISH
FURBISH
FURNISH
GARNISH
GIRLISH
GOATISH
HAWKISH
INVEIGH
IPSWICH
KADDISH
KNAVISH
KURDISH
LONGISH
MANNISH
MAWKISH
MESSIAH
MISSISH
MONKISH
MOORISH
NEBBISH
NEOLITH
NOURISH
OBADIAH
OGREISH
OSTRICH
PANFISH
PECKISH
PEEVISH
PETTISH
PIGGISH
PINKISH
PIXYISH
PRUDISH
PUBLISH
PUCKISH
RAFFISH
RALEIGH
REDDISH
ROGUISH
RUBBISH
RUNWITH
SAWFISH
SELFISH
SKYHIGH
SLAVISH
SOPWITH
SOURISH
SPANISH
STYLISH
SUNFISH
SWEDISH
TALLISH
TANNISH
TARNISH
TURKISH
VARNISH
WAGGISH
WARMISH
WASPISH
WEAKISH
WHITISH
WOLFISH
YIDDISH

I•I••••

ICICLES
ICINESS
ICINGIN
IDIAMIN
IDIOTIC
ILIESCU
IMITATE
INITIAL
IRIDIUM
IRISOUT

I••I•••

ICKIEST
IFFIEST
IGNITED
IGNITER
IGNITES
ILLICIT
IMBIBED
IMBIBES
IMMIXED
IMMIXES
IMPIETY
IMPINGE
IMPIOUS
INCIPIT
INCISED
INCISES
INCISOR
INCITED
INCITER
INCITES
INCIVIL
INDIANA
INDIANS
INDICES
INDICIA
INDICTS
INDIGOS
INDITED
INDITES
INFIDEL
INFIELD
INHIBIT
INNINGS
INSIDER
INSIDES
INSIGHT
INSIPID
INSISTS
INVITED
INVITES
INVITRO
IODIDES
IODIZED
IODIZES
IONIZED
IONIZER
IONIZES

I•••I••

IBERIAN
ICEMILK
ICEPICK
ICERINK
IDOLIZE
ILLWILL
ILLWIND
IMAGINE
IMAGING
IMBUING
IMPAIRS
IMPLIED
IMPLIES
IMPRINT
INBRIEF
INCHING
INCLINE
INFLICT
INITIAL
INKLING
INPOINT
INPRINT
INQUIRE
INQUIRY
INSPIRE
INSTILL
INSTILS
INTUITS
INURING
INUTILE
INVEIGH
INVOICE
IPSWICH
IRANIAN
IRIDIUM
IRONIES
IRONING
ISSUING
ITALIAN
ITALICS
ITCHIER
ITCHING
ITEMIZE
IVORIES
IWOJIMA

I••••I•

ICINGIN
IDENTIC
IDIAMIN
IDIOTIC
IDYLLIC
ILLICIT
ILLOGIC
IMPERIL
INASNIT
INASPIN
INCIPIT
INCIVIL
INDICIA
INERTIA
INGRAIN
INHABIT
INHERIT
INHIBIT
INORBIT
INSIPID
INSULIN
INTERIM
INTROIT
INVALID
ISLAMIC

I•••••I

ISRAELI

•I•I•••

AIRIEST
AIRINGS
BIKINIS
BILIOUS
CILIATE
CITIZEN
CIVILLY
DICIEST
DIGITAL
DIMITRI
DIVIDED
DIVIDER
DIVIDES
DIVINED
DIVINER
DIVINES
DIVISOR
FIJIANS
FILINGS
FINIALS
FINICKY
FIRINGS
FIXINGS
HIJINKS
LIAISED
LIAISES
LIAISON
LIBIDOS
LICITLY
LIMIEST
LIMITED
LININGS
LITINTO
LIVIDLY
LIVINGS
MILIEUS
MILIEUX
MILITIA
MIMICRY
MIMIEUX
MINIBUS
MINICAM
MINIMAL
MINIMUM
MINIONS
MINIVAN
MINIVER
MIXITUP
OILIEST
PIGIRON
PILINGS
PINIEST
PINIONS
PIPINGS
PITIFUL
RIGIDLY
RIPINTO
RISIBLE
RISINGS
RIVIERA
RIVIERE
SIDINGS
SILICAS
SILICON
SIMIANS
SIMILAR
SIMILES
SIZINGS
TIDIEST
TIDINGS
TIEINTO
TIMIDER
TIMIDLY
TIMINGS
TINIEST
VICIOUS
VIKINGS
VISIBLE
VISIBLY
VISIONS
VISITED
VISITOR
VITIATE
VIVIDER
VIVIDLY
VIZIERS
WILIEST
WIRIEST

•I••I••

AIRLIFT
AIRLINE
AIRMILE
AIRTIME
BIALIES
BIASING
BIDDIES
BIDDING
BIGBIRD
BIGGIES
BIGTIME
BIGWIGS
BILKING
BILLIES
BILLING
BILLION
BINDING
BINGING
BINNING
BIONICS
BIRDIED
BIRDIES
BIRDING
BIRLING
BITTIER
BITTING
CITRINE
CIVVIES
DIALING
DIARIES
DICKIES
DICTION
DIETING
DIGGING
DIGNIFY
DIGNITY
DIKDIKS
DILLIES
DIMMING
DIMWITS
DINGIER
DINGILY
DINGING
DINKIER
DINKIES
DIOXIDE
DIPPING
DIRTIED
DIRTIER
DIRTIES
DIRTILY
DISHING
DISLIKE
DISMISS
DISTILL
DITTIES
DIVVIED
DIVVIES
DIZZIED
DIZZIER
DIZZIES
DIZZILY
FIBBING
FIBRILS
FICTION
FICTIVE
FIERIER
FIERILY
FIFTIES
FILLIES
FILLING
FILLINS
FILLIPS
FILMIER
FILMING
FINDING
FINKING
FINNISH
FIRKINS
FIRMING
FISHIER
FISHILY
FISHING
FISSILE
FISSION
FITTING
FIZGIGS
FIZZIER
FIZZING
GIDDIER
GIDDILY
GILDING
GILLIES
GILLING
GIMMICK
GINFIZZ
GINGIVA
GINMILL
GINNING
GIPSIES
GIRDING
GIRLISH
HIGGINS
HILAIRE
HILLIER
HILLING
HINGING
HINNIES
HINTING
HIPPIES
HISSING
HITLIST
HITTING
HITTITE
JIFFIES
JIGGING
JILLIAN
JILLION
JILTING
JIMDINE
JIMMIED
JIMMIES
JINKING
JINXING
KICKING
KIDDIES
KIDDING
KILLING
KILTIES
KILTING
KINGING
KINKIER
KINKING
KIPLING
KISSING
KITTIES
LIBBING
LICKING
LIFTING
LIGNITE
LILLIAN
LILTING
LIMBING
LIMNING
LIMPING
LINBIAO
LINDIED
LINDIES
LINKING
LINTIER
LIONIZE

LIPPIER
LIPPING
LIQUIDS
LISPING
LISTING
LITHIUM
MIAMIAN
MIDDIES
MIDLIFE
MIDLINE
MIDRIBS
MIDRIFF
MIDRISE
MIDSIZE
MIDWIFE
MIFFING
MILKIER
MILKING
MILLING
MILLION
MINCING
MINDING
MINTIER
MINTING
MISDIAL
MISFILE
MISFIRE
MISFITS
MISHITS
MISSIES
MISSILE
MISSING
MISSION
MISSISH
MISSIVE
MISTIER
MISTILY
MISTING
MITRING
NIBLICK
NICKING
NIFTIER
NIFTILY
NINNIES
NIOBIUM
NIPPIER
NIPPING
NITPICK
NITRIDE
NITRITE
NITWITS
OILRIGS
OINKING
PIANISM
PIANIST
PICKIER
PICKING
PICNICS
PIDGINS
PIECING
PIETIES
PIETINS
PIETISM
PIGGIES
PIGGING
PIGGISH
PIGLIKE
PILLING
PILLION
PIMLICO
PINGING
PINKIES
PINKING

PINKISH
PINNING
PIPKINS
PIPPINS
PIQUING
PISCINE
PISMIRE
PISTILS
PITHIER
PITHILY
PITHING
PITTING
PITYING
PIXYISH
RIBBING
RIDDICK
RIDDING
RIDGING
RIFFING
RIFLING
RIFTING
RIGGING
RIMMING
RINGING
RINSING
RIORITA
RIOTING
RIPPING
RIPTIDE
RISKIER
RISKING
RITZIER
SIBLING
SICCING
SIDLING
SIFTING
SIGHING
SIGNIFY
SIGNING
SIKHISM
SILKIER
SILKILY
SILLIER
SILLIES
SILOING
SILTING
SINGING
SINKING
SIPPING
SISKINS
SISSIES
SISTINE
SITTING
SIXTIES
TICKING
TIDBITS
TIDYING
TIELINE
TIEPINS
TIERING
TILLING
TILTING
TIMMINS
TINGING
TINNIER
TINNILY
TINTING
TIPPING
TIPSIER
TIPSILY
TITBITS
TITHING
TITLING

TITLIST
TITMICE
TIZZIES
VICTIMS
VIEWING
VIOLINS
VIOLIST
VIRGINS
VITRIFY
VITRIOL
WICHITA
WICKIUP
WIENIES
WILDING
WILLIAM
WILLIES
WILLING
WILTING
WINCING
WINDIER
WINDING
WINGING
WINKING
WINNING
WISHING
WISPIER
WISPILY
WISPING
WITTIER
WITTILY
WITTING
YIDDISH
YIPPING
ZIGGING
ZILLION
ZINGIER
ZINGING
ZINNIAS
ZIPPIER
ZIPPING

•I•••I•

AIRFOIL
AIRMAIL
AIRRAID
AIRSHIP
BIDFAIR
BIKINIS
BISCUIT
CIBORIA
CIRCUIT
DINEDIN
DINESIN
DIPLOID
DISDAIN
DISJOIN
DIVESIN
FIDELIO
FILLSIN
FIRELIT
GIORGIO
GIVESIN
KICKSIN
KIDSKIN
KINETIC
KINGPIN
KINSHIP
KIRSTIE
KIWANIS
LIBERIA
LITCHIS
LIVEDIN
LIVESIN
MIASMIC
MIKHAIL
MILITIA
MIMESIS
MIMETIC
MINUTIA
MISLAID
MITOSIS
MITOTIC
NICOSIA
NIGERIA
NIGHTIE
OILSKIN
PIGSKIN
PIGTAIL
PILEDIN
PILESIN
PILGRIM
PINTAIL
PIRATIC
PITCHIN
RITCHIE
SIBERIA
SIGNSIN
SILESIA
SINEDIE
SINKSIN
SIRLOIN
TIECLIP
TINFOIL
TINYTIM
TIOMKIN
TITANIA
TITANIC
VIDALIA
VILLAIN
VILLEIN
VISAVIS
VITAMIN
WILFRID
WILLKIE
WINGSIT
WINGTIP

•I••••I

AIRTAXI
DIMITRI
HIBACHI
HITACHI
NIKOLAI
VIVALDI
VIVENDI

••II•••

SHIITES

••I•I••

ABIDING
ABILITY
ACIDIFY
ACIDITY
AGILITY
AKIHITO
ANILINE
ANIMISM
ANIMIST
ARIDITY
ARISING
ASININE
AVIDITY
BAILIFF
BAILING
BAITING
BEIJING
BOILING
BRIBING
BRINIER
BRINING
BRITISH
CEILING
CHIDING
CHILIES
CHIMING
CLINICS
COIFING
COILING
COINING
CRITICS
CUISINE
DAILIES
DAIRIES
DAISIES
DEICING
DEIFIED
DEIFIES
DEITIES
DOILIES
DRIVING
EDIFICE
EDIFIED
EDIFIES
EDITING
EDITION
ELICITS
ELIDING
ELISION
ELITISM
ELITIST
ELIXIRS
EXILING
EXITING
FAILING
FAIRIES
FAIRING
FOILING
FRISIAN
GAINING
GAITING
GLIDING
GRIMIER
GRIPING
GUIDING
HAILING
HAIRIER
HAITIAN
INITIAL
IRIDIUM
JAILING
JOINING
JUICIER
JUICILY
JUICING
KNIFING
MAILING
MOILING
NAILING
NOISIER
NOISILY
NOISING
OLIVIER
OLIVINE
OPINING
OPINION
ORIFICE
ORIGINS
OXIDIZE
PAIRING
PHIDIAS
POISING
POITIER
PRICIER
PRICING
PRIDING
PRIMING
PRIVIES
PRIZING
QUININE
QUIVIVE
RAIDING
RAILING
RAINIER
RAINING
RAISING
RAISINS
REINING
ROILING
RUINING
SAILING
SEINING
SEIZING
SHINIER
SHINING
SKILIFT
SLICING
SLIDING
SLIMIER
SMILING
SMITING
SNIPING
SOILING
SPICIER
SPICING
SPIKIER
SPIKING
SPINIER
SPIRITO
SPIRITS
SPITING
SUITING
SWIPING
TAILING
TBILISI
THINICE
TOILING
TRINITY
TRITIUM
TRIVIAL
TUITION
TWINING
UNIFIED
UNIFIER
UNIFIES
UNITIES
UNITING
UNITIVE
UTILITY
UTILIZE
VEILING
VEINING
VOICING
VOIDING
WAIKIKI
WAILING
WAITING
WAIVING
WHILING
WHINING
WHITING
WHITISH
WRITING

••I••I•

ABIGAIL
ASIATIC
BRINGIN
BRITAIN
BUILDIN
BUILTIN
CHIPSIN
CRINOID
CRISPIN
DOINGIN
DRIVEIN
ERISTIC
FLIESIN
FRICKIE
GOINGIN
GRIFFIN
GRIGRIS
HAIRPIN
ICINGIN
IDIAMIN
IDIOTIC
JOINSIN
LEIBNIZ
LEIPZIG
MAITAIS
MEIOSIS
MEIOTIC
PHILBIN
PHILLIP
QUICKIE
REINSIN
SEISMIC
SHINDIG
SKISUIT
SLIDEIN
SLIMJIM
STIRSIN
TAILFIN
THINAIR
TLINGIT
TRILLIN
TYINGIN
WEIGHIN
WHIZKID
WRITEIN

••I•••I

CHIANTI
JAIALAI
NAIROBI
ORIGAMI
STIMULI
TBILISI
TRIPOLI
WAIKIKI
ZWINGLI

•••II••

TAXIING

•••I•I•

ACTINIC
ASPIRIN
BIKINIS
BOLIVIA
CECILIA
CODICIL
DEFICIT
DELIMIT
DELIRIA
EXHIBIT
FELICIA
HAMITIC
HASIDIM
HOMINID
HYGIEIA
ILLICIT
INCIPIT
INCIVIL
INDICIA
INHIBIT
INSIPID
JURIDIC
LAVINIA
LETITIA
MILITIA
MRFIXIT
NAMIBIA
OSSIFIC
PACIFIC
POLITIC
PRAIRIE
REVISIT
RUBITIN
SATIRIC
SEMITIC
SOLICIT
TUNISIA
UNCIVIL
WAPITIS

•••I••I

ALFIERI
APRIORI
BACILLI
BALIHAI
CHRISTI
DAVINCI
DELICTI
DIMITRI
ELMISTI
GALILEI
MENISCI
RAVIOLI
SALIERI
VANILLI

••••I•I

BELLINI
CASSINI
CELLINI
DASHIKI
EMERITI
FELLINI
HOUDINI
KONTIKI
KUWAITI
MANCINI
MARTINI
PACHISI
PUCCINI
ROSSINI
SANTINI
SASHIMI
SWAHILI
TBILISI
TERMINI
WAIKIKI

•••••II

POMPEII
ROCKYII

I•J••••

INJECTS
INJOKES
INJURED
INJURES

I••J•••

IWOJIMA

•IJ••••

FIJIANS
HIJACKS
HIJINKS
TIJUANA

•I•J•••

BIGJOHN
DISJOIN
JIMJAMS

•I••J••

KILLJOY

••IJ•••

BEIJING
SKIJUMP

••I•J••

SLIMJIM

IK•••••

IKEBANA

I•K••••

ICKIEST
INKBLOT
INKHORN
INKLING
INKSPOT
INKWELL
INKYCAP
IRKSOME

I•••K••

INJOKES
INTAKES
INVOKED
INVOKER
INVOKES
IRECKON

I•••••K

ICEMILK
ICEPACK
ICEPICK
ICERINK
INSTOCK

•IK••••

BIKEWAY
BIKINIS
DIKDIKS
DIKTATS
KIKUYUS
LIKABLE
LIKEMAD
LIKENED
LIKENEW
MIKADOS
MIKHAIL
NIKOLAI
PIKEMAN
PIKEMEN
SIKHISM
VIKINGS

•I•K•••

BICKERS
BILKING
DICKENS
DICKERS
DICKEYS
DICKIES
DINKIER
DINKIES
FICKLER
FINKING
FIRKINS
HICKMAN
HICKORY
JINKING
KICKERS
KICKING
KICKOFF
KICKOUT
KICKSIN
KICKSUP
KICKUPS
KINKIER
KINKING
LICKETY
LICKING
LINKAGE
LINKERS
LINKING
LINKUPS
MILKCOW
MILKERS
MILKIER
MILKING
MILKMAN
MILKMEN
MILKRUN
MILKSOP
NICKELS
NICKERS
NICKING
OINKING
PICKAXE
PICKENS
PICKERS
PICKETS
PICKETT
PICKIER
PICKING
PICKLED
PICKLES
PICKOFF
PICKOUT
PICKSAT
PICKSON
PICKSUP
PICKUPS
PINKEST
PINKIES
PINKING
PINKISH
PIPKINS
RICKETY
RICKEYS
RICKLES
RICKSHA
RISKERS
RISKIER
RISKING
SICKBAY
SICKENS
SICKEST
SICKLES
SICKOUT
SICKPAY
SILKHAT
SILKIER
SILKILY
SINKAGE
SINKERS
SINKING
SINKSIN
SISKINS
TICKERS
TICKETS
TICKING
TICKLED
TICKLER
TICKLES
TICKOFF
TINKERS
TINKLED
TINKLES
WICKERS
WICKETS
WICKIUP
WINKERS
WINKING
WINKLER
WINKOUT
WINKSAT

•I••K••

KIDSKIN
KISHKES
OILSKIN
PIGSKIN
TIOMKIN
WILLKIE

•I•••K•

DIKDIKS
DISLIKE
FINICKY
HIJACKS
HIJINKS
MISTAKE
OILCAKE
PIGLIKE
PINOAKS

•I••••K

AIRLOCK
AIRSOCK
GIMMICK
HILLOCK
KINFOLK
LIVEOAK
MIDWEEK
MISTOOK
NIBLICK
NITPICK
RIDDICK
SIXPACK
TIERACK
TIETACK
TINWORK
WIDMARK
YITZHAK

••IK•••

ARIKARA
SPIKERS
SPIKIER
SPIKING
WAIKIKI

••I•K••

BLINKAT
BLINKED
BLINKER
BRICKED
BRISKER
BRISKET
BRISKLY
CHICKEN
CHINKED
CLICKED
CLINKED
CLINKER
CRICKED
CRICKET
CRINKLE
CRINKLY
DRINKER
FLICKED
FLICKER
FRICKIE
FRISKED
PLINKED
PRICKED
PRICKLE
PRICKLY
PRINKED
QUICKEN
QUICKER
QUICKIE
QUICKLY
REINKED
SHIRKED
SHIRKER
SLICKED
SLICKER
SLICKLY
SLINKED
SMIRKED
SNICKER
STICKER
STICKTO
STICKUP
STINKER
THICKEN
THICKER
THICKET
THICKLY
THINKER
THINKOF
THINKUP
TRICKED
TRICKER
TRICKLE
TRINKET
TWINKLE
TWINKLY
WHISKED
WHISKER
WHISKEY
WHIZKID
WRINKLE
WRINKLY

••I••K•

WAIKIKI

••I•••K

CHINOOK
KAISHEK
SKIMASK

•••IK••

BATIKED
KYLIKES
MONIKER
SHEIKHS
SHRIKES
STRIKER
STRIKES
TROIKAS
UNLIKED

•••I•K•

FINICKY
HIJINKS
KODIAKS
PANICKY
SHRIEKS
SHRINKS
SHTICKS
UNKINKS
UNLINKS
UPLINKS
UPTICKS

••••IK•

AMERIKA
APELIKE
CATLIKE
DASHIKI
DIKDIKS
DISLIKE
GEMLIKE
GODLIKE
KONTIKI
MUZHIKS
NUDNIKS
OWLLIKE
PAPRIKA
PIGLIKE
SUSLIKS
UNALIKE
WAIKIKI
WARLIKE

••••I•K

BETHINK
CARRICK
CONNICK
COWLICK
DERRICK
DUNKIRK
FOSDICK
GARRICK
GIMMICK
ICEMILK
ICEPICK
ICERINK
KUBRICK
NIBLICK
NITPICK
OBELISK
OLDNICK
PATRICK
RATFINK
RAWSILK
RETHINK
RIDDICK
ROLLICK
SEASICK
SELKIRK

TOPKICK
UNSTICK
WARWICK
WOZNIAK

•••••IK
BEATNIK
SPUTNIK

IL•••••
ILIESCU
ILLBRED
ILLEGAL
ILLICIT
ILLNESS
ILLOGIC
ILLUSED
ILLUSES
ILLWILL
ILLWIND

I•L••••
ILLBRED
ILLEGAL
ILLICIT
ILLNESS
ILLOGIC
ILLUSED
ILLUSES
ILLWILL
ILLWIND
ISLAMIC
ISLANDS

I••L•••
ICELAND
ICELESS
IDOLIZE
IDYLLIC
IMPLANT
IMPLIED
IMPLIES
IMPLODE
IMPLORE
INBLOOM
INCLINE
INCLOSE
INCLUDE
INFLAME
INFLATE
INFLECT
INFLICT
INFLOWS
INKLING
INPLACE
IRELAND
ISOLATE
ITALIAN
ITALICS

I•••L••
ICEBLUE
ICEFLOE
ICICLES
IDEALLY
IDYLLIC
IMPALAS
IMPALED
IMPALES
IMPULSE
INDULGE
INGALLS
INHALED
INHALER
INHALES
INKBLOT
INSOLES
INSULAR
INSULIN
INSULTS
INVALID
INVOLVE

I••••L•
ICECOLD
ICEMILK
IDEALLY
IGNOBLE
IGNOBLY
ILLWILL
INANELY
INAPTLY
INDWELL
INEPTLY
INERTLY
INFIELD
INGALLS
INKWELL
INOCULA
INSTALL
INSTILL
INSTILS
INSTYLE
INUTILE
IRATELY
ISOHELS
ISRAELI

I•••••L
ILLEGAL
ILLWILL
IMMORAL
IMPANEL
IMPERIL
INCIVIL
INDWELL
INFIDEL
INITIAL
INKWELL
INSTALL
INSTILL
ISHMAEL

•IL••••
AILERON
AILMENT
BILBOES
BILEVEL
BILIOUS
BILKING
BILLETS
BILLIES
BILLING
BILLION
BILLOWS
BILLOWY
CILIATE
DILATED
DILATES
DILEMMA
DILLARD
DILLIES
DILUTED
DILUTER
DILUTES
FILBERT
FILCHED
FILCHER
FILCHES
FILINGS
FILLERS
FILLETS
FILLIES
FILLING
FILLINS
FILLIPS
FILLOUT
FILLSIN
FILLSUP
FILLUPS
FILMIER
FILMING
FILTERS
GILBERT
GILBLAS
GILDERS
GILDING
GILLIES
GILLING
GILLNET
GILMORE
HILAIRE
HILLARY
HILLIER
HILLING
HILLOCK
HILLTOP
JILLIAN
JILLION
JILTING
KILAUEA
KILDARE
KILLERS
KILLING
KILLJOY
KILOTON
KILTIES
KILTING
LILLIAN
LILTING
LILYPAD
MILDEST
MILDEWS
MILDEWY
MILDRED
MILEAGE
MILHAUD
MILIEUS
MILIEUX
MILITIA
MILKCOW
MILKERS
MILKIER
MILKING
MILKMAN
MILKMEN
MILKRUN
MILKSOP
MILLAND
MILLARD
MILLDAM
MILLEND
MILLERS
MILLETS
MILLETT
MILLING
MILLION
MILLRUN
MILORDS
NILSSON
OILCAKE
OILCANS
OILIEST
OILLAMP
OILPANS
OILRIGS
OILSKIN
OILWELL
PILEDIN
PILEDON
PILEDUP
PILESIN
PILESON
PILESUP
PILEUPS
PILFERS
PILGRIM
PILINGS
PILLAGE
PILLARS
PILLBOX
PILLBUG
PILLING
PILLION
PILLORY
PILLOWS
PILLOWY
PILOTED
PILSNER
RILLETS
SILENCE
SILENTS
SILESIA
SILICAS
SILICON
SILKHAT
SILKIER
SILKILY
SILLIER
SILLIES
SILOING
SILTING
SILVERS
SILVERY
TILLAGE
TILLERS
TILLING
TILTERS
TILTING
VILLAGE
VILLAIN
VILLEIN
WILDCAT
WILDEST
WILDING
WILDONE
WILFORD
WILFRID
WILHELM
WILIEST
WILLARD
WILLFUL
WILLIAM
WILLIES
WILLING
WILLKIE
WILLOWS
WILLOWY
WILLSON
WILTING
ZILCHES
ZILLION

•I•L•••
AIMLESS
AIRLANE
AIRLESS
AIRLIFT
AIRLINE
AIRLOCK
BIALIES
BILLETS
BILLIES
BILLING
BILLION
BILLOWS
BILLOWY
BIOLOGY
BIPLANE
BIRLING
DIALECT
DIALERS
DIALING
DIALOGS
DILLARD
DILLIES
DIPLOID
DIPLOMA
DISLIKE
FIELDED
FIELDER
FIGLEAF
FILLERS
FILLETS
FILLIES
FILLING
FILLINS
FILLIPS
FILLOUT
FILLSIN
FILLSUP
FILLUPS
FINLAND
GIBLETS
GIBLUES
GIELGUD
GILLIES
GILLING
GILLNET
GIMLETS
GIRLISH
HIALEAH
HILLARY
HILLIER
HILLING
HILLOCK
HILLTOP
HITLESS
HITLIST
JILLIAN
JILLION
KILLERS
KILLING
KILLJOY
KIPLING
LIDLESS
LILLIAN
MIDLAND
MIDLIFE
MIDLINE
MILLAND
MILLARD
MILLDAM
MILLEND
MILLERS
MILLETS
MILLETT
MILLING
MILLION
MILLRUN
MISLAID
MISLAYS
MISLEAD
NIBLICK
NIELSEN
OILLAMP
PIGLETS
PIGLIKE
PILLAGE
PILLARS
PILLBOX
PILLBUG
PILLING
PILLION
PILLORY
PILLOWS
PILLOWY
PIMLICO
PINLESS
PIOLETS
RIFLERS
RIFLERY
RIFLING
RILLETS
RIOLOBO
SIBLING
SIDLING
SILLIER
SILLIES
SIRLOIN
TIELESS
TIELINE
TILLAGE
TILLERS
TILLING
TITLING
TITLIST
VILLAGE
VILLAIN
VILLEIN
VIOLATE
VIOLENT
VIOLETS
VIOLINS
VIOLIST
WIELDED
WIGLETS
WILLARD
WILLFUL
WILLIAM
WILLIES
WILLING
WILLKIE
WILLOWS
WILLOWY
WILLSON
WITLESS
YIELDED
ZILLION

•I••L••
AIRFLOW
AIRPLAY
BIBELOT
BICOLOR
BIGELOW
BIPOLAR
BIVALVE
CIRCLED
CIRCLES
CIRCLET
CIVILLY
DIBBLED
DIBBLES
DIDDLED
DIDDLES
DIDDLEY
DIMPLED
DIMPLES
DINGLES
DIPOLAR
DIPOLES
DISPLAY
DIVULGE
FIBULAE
FIBULAS
FICKLER
FIDDLED
FIDDLER
FIDDLES
FIDELIO
FIEDLER
FINALES
FINALLY
FIPPLES
FIRELIT
FIZZLED
FIZZLES
GIGGLED
GIGGLER
GIGGLES
GIGOLOS
GILBLAS
GIRDLED
GIRDLES
GISELLE
HIDALGO
HIGHLOW
JIGGLED
JIGGLES
JINGLED
JINGLES
KIBBLED
KIBBLES
KINDLED
KINDLES
KIRTLES
LIBELED
LIBELER
LIESLOW
LITTLER
MIDDLEC
MIDDLES
MINGLED
MINGLER
MINGLES
MINOLTA
MISALLY
MISPLAY
MIZZLED
MIZZLES
NIBBLED
NIBBLER
NIBBLES
NICOLAS
NIGGLED
NIGGLES
NIKOLAI
NIMBLER
PICKLED
PICKLES
PIFFLED
PIFFLES
RICKLES
RIDDLED
RIDDLER
RIDDLES
RIFFLED
RIFFLES
RINGLET
RIPPLED
RIPPLES
RIVALED
RIVALRY
RIVULET
SICKLES
SIMILAR
SIMILES
SIMPLER
SIMPLEX
SINGLED
SINGLES
SIZZLED
SIZZLES
TICKLED
TICKLER
TICKLES
TIECLIP
TIMELAG
TINGLED
TINGLES
TINKLED
TINKLES
TIPPLED
TIPPLER
TIPPLES
TITTLES
TITULAR
VIDALIA
VITALLY
VITTLES
VIVALDI
VIZSLAS
WIGGLED
WIGGLER
WIGGLES
WIMPLED
WIMPLES
WINKLER
WINSLOW

•I•••L•
AIRBALL
AIRHOLE
AIRMILE
AIRWOLF
BICYCLE
CITABLE
CIVILLY
DIESELS
DIMBULB
DINGILY
DIRNDLS
DIRTILY
DISABLE
DISPELS
DISTILL
DIZZILY
FIBRILS
FIERILY
FINAGLE
FINALLY
FINIALS
FIREFLY
FIRSTLY
FISHILY
FISSILE
FIXABLE
FIXEDLY
GIDDILY
GIMBALS
GINMILL
GISELLE
HIMSELF
HIRABLE
KIMBALL
KINFOLK
LICITLY
LIGHTLY
LIKABLE
LINCOLN
LINTELS
LIPBALM
LISTELS
LITHELY
LIVABLE
LIVIDLY
MICHELE
MINABLE
MINEOLA
MIRACLE
MISALLY
MISCALL
MISERLY
MISFILE
MISRULE
MISSALS
MISSILE
MISTILY
MIXABLE
NICCOLO
NICHOLS
NICKELS
NIFTILY
NIGHTLY
OILWELL
PICCOLO
PIEBALD
PINBALL
PINHOLE
PINOCLE
PINWALE
PIOUSLY
PISTILS
PISTOLE
PISTOLS
PITBULL
PITFALL
PITHILY
RIGHTLY
RIGIDLY
RISIBLE
RISSOLE
RITUALS
SIGHTLY
SIGNALS
SILKILY
SITWELL
SIXFOLD
SIZABLE
SIZABLY
TIGHTLY
TIMBALE
TIMBALS
TIMIDLY
TINNILY
TINSELS
TIPSILY
TIREDLY
VIRGULE
VISIBLE
VISIBLY
VISTULA
VISUALS
VITALLY
VIVIDLY
WILHELM
WISPILY
WITTILY

•I••••L
AIRBALL
AIRCOOL
AIRFOIL
AIRMAIL
BIFOCAL
BIGDEAL
BILEVEL
BIMODAL
BIPEDAL
CITADEL
DIGITAL
DISTILL
DIURNAL
FISTFUL
GINMILL
GIRASOL
KIMBALL
LIBERAL
LINGUAL
LITERAL
MICHAEL
MIKHAIL
MINDFUL
MINERAL
MINIMAL
MISCALL
MISDEAL
MISDIAL
MISTRAL
OILWELL
PIGTAIL
PINBALL
PINCURL
PINTAIL
PIPEFUL
PITBULL
PITFALL
PITIFUL
PIVOTAL
SITWELL
TINFOIL
VICTUAL
VIRTUAL
VITRIOL
WILLFUL
WISHFUL
WISTFUL

••IL•••
ABILENE
ABILITY
AGILELY
AGILITY
ANILINE
AXILLAE
BAILEES
BAILERS
BAILEYS
BAILIFF
BAILING
BAILORS
BAILOUT
BOILERS
BOILING
BRILLAT
BUILDER
BUILDIN
BUILDON
BUILDUP
BUILTIN
BUILTON
BUILTUP
CEILING
CHILEAN
CHILIES
CHILLED
CHILLER
COILING
COILSUP
DAILIES
DOILIES
DRILLED
DRILLER
EPILOGS
EVILEST
EVILEYE
EVILLER
EXILING
FAILING
FAILURE
FOILING
FRILLED
GRILLED
GRILLES
GRILLET
GUILDER
HAILING
JAILERS
JAILING
KEILLOR
MAILBAG
MAILBOX
MAILERS
MAILING
MAILLOT
MOILERS
MOILING
NAILERS
NAILING
NAILSET
PAILFUL
PAILOUS
PHILBIN
PHILLIP
PHILTER
PHILTRE
QUILLED
QUILTED
QUILTER
RAILERS
RAILING
RAILSAT
RAILWAY
ROILING
SAILING
SAILORS
SHILLED
SKILFUL
SKILIFT
SKILLED
SKILLET
SMILERS
SMILING
SOILING
SPILLED
STILLED
STILLER
STILTED
STILTON
SWILLED
TAILEND
TAILFIN
TAILING
TAILLES
TAILOFF
TAILORS
TBILISI
TOILERS
TOILETS
TOILING
TRILLED
TRILLIN
TRILOGY
TWILLED
UTILITY
UTILIZE
VEILING
WAILERS
WAILING
WHILING

••I•L••
AMIBLUE
AXIALLY
AXILLAE
BRIDLED
BRIDLES
BRILLAT
CHILLED
CHILLER
DAIMLER
DRIBLET
DRILLED
DRILLER
EDIBLES
ENISLED
ENISLES
EVILLER
FOIBLES
FRILLED
GRILLED
GRILLES
GRILLET
ICICLES
JAIALAI
KEILLOR
LAIDLOW
MAILLOT
ORIOLES
PAISLEY
PHILLIP
QUIGLEY
QUILLED
SHIELDS
SHILLED
SHIRLEY
SKILLED
SKILLET
SKIRLED
SNIGLET
SPIELED
SPIELER
SPILLED
STIFLED
STIFLES
STILLED
STILLER
SWILLED
SWIRLED
TAILLES
TRIFLED
TRIFLER
TRIFLES
TRILLED
TRILLIN
TRIPLED
TRIPLES
TRIPLET
TRIPLEX
TWILLED
TWIRLED
TWIRLER
WHIRLED
WRIGLEY

••I••L•
AGILELY
AMIABLE
AMIABLY
ANIMALS
APISHLY
ATINGLE
AXIALLY
BLINDLY
BRIDALS
BRIEFLY
BRINDLE
BRISKLY
BRISTLE
BRISTLY
BRITTLE
CHIEFLY
CHISELS
CRINKLE
CRINKLY
CRISPLY
DRIBBLE
DRIVELS
DRIZZLE
DRIZZLY
DWINDLE
EPISTLE
FAINTLY
FRIABLE
FRIZZLE
GRIDDLE
GRISTLE
GRISTLY
GRIZZLE
GRIZZLY
JOINTLY
JUICILY
KRINGLE
MOISTLY
NAIVELY
NOISILY
PLIABLE
PLIABLY
PRICKLE
PRICKLY
QUIBBLE
QUICKLY
QUIETLY
SAINTLY
SEIDELS
SHINGLE
SKIPOLE
SKITTLE
SLICKLY

SNIDELY
SNIFFLE
SNIGGLE
SNIVELS
SPINDLE
SPINDLY
SPINELS
SPIRALS
STIFFLY
STIMULI
STIPPLE
SWIFTLY
SWINDLE
SWIVELS
SWIZZLE
THICKLY
THIMBLE
THIRDLY
THISTLE
TRICKLE
TRIPOLI
TRITELY
TWIDDLE
TWINKLE
TWINKLY
WEIRDLY
WHISTLE
WHITTLE
WRIGGLE
WRIGGLY
WRINKLE
WRINKLY
ZWINGLI

••I•••L
ABIGAIL
BRIMFUL
BRISTOL
GAINFUL
INITIAL
KNIEVEL
PAILFUL
PAINFUL
SKILFUL
SPIEGEL
STIEGEL
TRIVIAL

•••IL••
AAMILNE
AEDILES
ANTILOG
AVAILED
BACILLI
BRAILLE
BROILED
BROILER
CAMILLE
CAVILED
CAVILER
CECILIA
CEDILLA
CIVILLY
COPILOT
DEFILED
DEFILER
DEFILES
DELILAH
DEMILLE
DEVILED
DEVILLE
DEVILRY
DEWILDE
ENSILED
ENSILES
EPSILON
ETOILES
FLAILED
FRAILER
FRAILTY
GALILEE
GALILEI
GALILEO
GEFILTE
GORILLA
JUBILEE
LUCILLE
MANILOW
MARILYN
MATILDA
MAXILLA
MOBILES
MURILLO
NEVILLE
ORVILLE
PAPILLA
QUAILED
REFILLS
REFILMS
REOILED
RESILED
RESILES
RETILED
RETILES
REVILED
REVILES
SEVILLE
SHEILAE
SHEILAH
SHEILAS
SHRILLS
SHRILLY
SIMILAR
SIMILES
SPOILED
SPOILER
THRILLS
TRAILED
TRAILER
TROILUS
UNOILED
UNPILED
UNPILES
UPSILON
UTRILLO
VANILLA
VANILLI

•••I•L•
ACRIDLY
AERIALS
ARTICLE
AUDIBLE
AUDIBLY
AURICLE
BACILLI
BRAILLE
CAMILLE
CEDILLA
CIVILLY
CUBICLE
CUTICLE
DANIELS
DEMILLE
DENIALS
DEVILLE
ENTITLE
ESPIALS
FACIALS
FETIDLY
FINIALS
FLUIDLY
GAVIALS
GORILLA
HUMIDLY
INFIELD
LABIALS
LEGIBLE
LEGIBLY
LICITLY
LIVIDLY
LUCIDLY
LUCILLE
LURIDLY
MANIPLE
MAXILLA
MENIALS
MURILLO
NEVILLE
ORVILLE
OSSICLE
PANICLE
PAPILLA
PEDICLE
PETIOLE
PLAINLY
RADIALS
RADICLE
RAPIDLY
RAVIOLI
REDIALS
REFILLS
RETICLE
RETITLE
RIGIDLY
RISIBLE
SERIALS
SEVILLE
SHRILLS
SHRILLY
SOCIALS
SOLIDLY
STAIDLY
TACITLY
TEPIDLY
THRILLS
TIMIDLY
TUNICLE
UNCIALS
UTRILLO
VALIDLY
VANILLA
VANILLI
VAPIDLY
VEHICLE
VISIBLE
VISIBLY
VIVIDLY

•••I••L
ADMIRAL
ARRIVAL
CAPITAL
CAPITOL
CLAIROL
CODICIL
COMICAL
CONICAL
CYNICAL
DECIBEL
DECIMAL
DIGITAL
DREIDEL
DUTIFUL
ESTIVAL
ETHICAL
GERITOL
HELICAL
INCIVIL
INFIDEL
LAMINAL
LEXICAL
LOGICAL
LYRICAL
MAGICAL
MARITAL
MAXIMAL
MEDICAL
MINIMAL
MUSICAL
NOMINAL
OEDIPAL
OPTICAL
OPTIMAL
ORBITAL
ORDINAL
OVOIDAL
PEDICEL
PITIFUL
RADICAL
RECITAL
RETINAL
REVIVAL
SANIBEL
SEMINAL
SHRIVEL
STOICAL
TOPICAL
TYPICAL
UNCIVIL

••••IL•
AIRMILE
ANGRILY
ANOUILH
ANTHILL
ARTFILM
ASSAILS
BAGGILY
BAWDILY
BEGUILE
BEWAILS
BOBVILA
BONNILY
BOSSILY
CANNILY
CASTILE
CATTILY
CHARILY
COCKILY
COMPILE
CORNILY
CRAZILY
DAFFILY
DAYLILY
DERAILS
DETAILS
DINGILY
DIRTILY
DISTILL
DIZZILY
DOWDILY
DUCTILE
EMPTILY
ENTAILS
FANCILY
FEBRILE
FERTILE
FIBRILS
FIERILY
FISHILY
FISSILE
FOSSILS
FRAGILE
FULFILL
FULFILS
FUNNILY
FUSSILY
FUSTILY
FUZZILY
GAUDILY
GAUZILY
GENTILE
GERBILS
GIDDILY
GINMILL
GRACILE
GUSTILY
GUTSILY
HAMMILY
HANDILY
HAPPILY
HARDILY
HASTILY
HEADILY
HEAVILY
HEFTILY
HOGWILD
HOSTILE
HUFFILY
HUSKILY
ICEMILK
ILLWILL
INSTILL
INSTILS
INUTILE
JAZZILY
JERKILY
JOEHILL
JOLLILY
JUICILY
LANKILY
LEERILY
LENTILS
LOFTILY
LOUSILY
LUCKILY
LUSTILY
MERRILL
MERRILY
MESSILY
MISFILE
MISSILE
MISTILY
MOODILY
MURKILY
MUSHILY
MUSTILY
MUZZILY
NASTILY
NATTILY
NEEDILY
NERVILY
NIFTILY
NOBHILL
NOISILY
NUTTILY
PENCILS
PEPPILY
PERKILY
PESKILY
PETTILY
PHONILY
PISTILS
PITHILY
PROFILE
PROSILY
PUERILE
PUFFILY
PUSHILY
RAWSILK
READILY
REBOILS
REBUILD
REBUILT
RECOILS
REMAILS
RENAILS
REPTILE
RETAILS
ROWDILY
RUSTILY
SALTILY
SAMHILL
SASSILY
SAUCILY
SAVVILY
SAWMILL
SCARILY
SEALILY
SEEDILY
SERVILE
SESSILE
SHADILY
SHAKILY
SHOWILY
SILKILY
SOGGILY
STABILE
STAGILY
STERILE
STONILY
SULKILY
SUNNILY
SURLILY
SWAHILI
TACKILY
TACTILE
TARDILY
TASTILY
TEARILY
TENSILE
TEQUILA
TESTILY
TEXTILE
TINNILY
TIPSILY
TONSILS
UNCOILS
UNVEILS
WACKILY
WAYBILL
WEARILY
WEEVILS
WISPILY
WITTILY
WOOZILY
WORDILY

••••I•L
ANTHILL
ASOCIAL
BESTIAL
COAXIAL
CORDIAL
COWGIRL
CRANIAL
CRUCIAL
DISTILL
EZEKIEL
FLUVIAL
FULFILL
GABRIEL
GINMILL
GLACIAL
ILLWILL
INITIAL
INSTILL
JOEHILL
MARTIAL
MERRILL
MISDIAL
NOBHILL
NUPTIAL
ONTRIAL
PARTIAL
PLUVIAL
RETRIAL
SAMHILL
SAWMILL
SPANIEL
SPATIAL
SPECIAL
SUNDIAL
TENNIEL
TERTIAL
TRIVIAL
TRUCIAL
UXORIAL
VITRIOL
WAYBILL

•••••IL
ABIGAIL
AIRFOIL
AIRMAIL
ALLHAIL
BATHOIL
BEDEVIL
BOBTAIL
CATTAIL
CHERVIL
COALOIL
CODICIL
CORNOIL
COUNCIL
CURTAIL
DESPOIL
DWEEZIL
EMBROIL
ESTORIL
FANMAIL
FANTAIL
FOXTAIL
FUELOIL
GONERIL
HOBNAIL
IMPERIL
INCIVIL
JONQUIL
LAMPOIL
MANDRIL
MIKHAIL
NOSTRIL
PALMOIL
PARBOIL
PIGTAIL
PINTAIL
PREVAIL
RATTAIL
REAVAIL
ROSEOIL
SETSAIL
STENCIL
SUBSOIL
TENDRIL
TINFOIL
TOENAIL
TOPSAIL
TOPSOIL
TRAVAIL
TREFOIL
TUNGOIL
TURMOIL
UNCIVIL
UTENSIL
VERMEIL
WAGTAIL
WASSAIL

IM•••••
IMAGERS
IMAGERY
IMAGINE
IMAGING
IMAGOES
IMAMATE
IMARETS
IMBIBED
IMBIBES
IMBRUED
IMBRUES
IMBUING
IMITATE
IMMENSE
IMMERSE
IMMIXED
IMMIXES
IMMORAL
IMMURED
IMMURES
IMOGENE
IMPACTS
IMPAIRS
IMPALAS
IMPALED
IMPALES
IMPANEL
IMPARTS
IMPASSE
IMPASTO
IMPEACH
IMPEDED
IMPEDES
IMPENDS
IMPERIL
IMPETUS
IMPIETY
IMPINGE
IMPIOUS
IMPLANT
IMPLIED
IMPLIES
IMPLODE
IMPLORE
IMPORTS
IMPOSED
IMPOSES
IMPOSTS
IMPOUND
IMPRESS
IMPRINT
IMPROVE
IMPUGNS
IMPULSE
IMPURER
IMPUTED
IMPUTES
IMSORRY

I•M••••
IMMENSE
IMMERSE
IMMIXED
IMMIXES
IMMORAL
IMMURED
IMMURES
INMATES
IOMOTHS

I••M•••
ICEMILK
IMAMATE
INAMESS
ISHMAEL
ISOMERS
ITEMIZE

I•••M••
IDIAMIN
INCOMES
INGEMAR
INHUMAN
IRONMAN
IRONMEN
ISLAMIC
ISTHMUS

I••••M•
INFLAME
INFORMS
INSEAMS
IPANEMA
IRKSOME
IWOJIMA

I•••••M
INBLOOM
INTERIM
IRIDIUM

•IM••••
AIMEDAT
AIMEDTO
AIMLESS
BIMODAL
DIMBULB
DIMITRI
DIMMERS
DIMMEST
DIMMING
DIMNESS
DIMOUTS
DIMPLED
DIMPLES
DIMWITS
GIMBALS
GIMLETS
GIMMICK
HIMSELF
JIMCHEE
JIMDINE
JIMENEZ
JIMJAMS
JIMMIED
JIMMIES
JIMRYUN
KIMBALL
KIMONOS
LIMBERS
LIMBING
LIMEADE
LIMIEST
LIMITED
LIMNERS
LIMNING
LIMOGES
LIMPEST
LIMPETS
LIMPING
LIMPOPO
MIMESIS
MIMETIC
MIMICRY
MIMIEUX
MIMOSAS
NIMBLER
NIMRODS
PIMENTO
PIMESON
PIMLICO
RIMBAUD
RIMMING
RIMSHOT
SIMENON
SIMIANS
SIMILAR
SIMILES
SIMMERS
SIMMONS
SIMPERS
SIMPLER
SIMPLEX
SIMPSON
TIMBALE
TIMBALS
TIMBERS
TIMBRES
TIMECOP
TIMELAG
TIMEOFF
TIMEOUT
TIMESUP
TIMEWAS
TIMIDER
TIMIDLY
TIMINGS
TIMMINS
TIMOTHY
WIMPLED
WIMPLES

•I•M•••
AILMENT
AIRMAIL
AIRMASS
AIRMILE
BIOMASS
BISMUTH
BITMAPS
DIAMOND
DIMMERS
DIMMEST
DIMMING
DINMONT
DIOMEDE
DISMAYS
DISMISS
FIGMENT
FILMIER
FILMING
FIRMEST
FIRMING
FIRMSUP
GILMORE
GIMMICK
GINMILL
JIMMIED
JIMMIES
KIRMANS
MIAMIAN
MICMACS
MISMATE
PIGMENT
PISMIRE
RIMMING
SIAMESE
SIGMUND
SIMMERS
SIMMONS
TIMMINS
TIOMKIN
TITMICE
WIDMARK

•I••M••
BIRDMAN
BIRDMEN
BIREMES
BITUMEN
CINEMAS
CINEMAX
DILEMMA
FIREMAN
FIREMEN
HICKMAN
JICAMAS
KINGMAN
KINSMAN
KINSMEN
LIKEMAD
LINEMAN
LINEMEN
MIASMAS
MIASMIC
MILKMAN
MILKMEN
MINIMAL
MINIMUM
MIRAMAR
MIRAMAX
PIKEMAN
PIKEMEN
PITTMAN
RICHMAN
SIDEMAN
SIDEMEN
VITAMIN
WISEMAN
WISEMEN

•I•••M•
AIRDAMS
AIRPUMP
AIRTIME
BIGGAME
BIGNAME
BIGTIME
DIADEMS
DIATOMS
DICTUMS
DILEMMA
DIORAMA
DIPLOMA
DISARMS
GIACOMO
JIMJAMS
LISSOME
MISNAME
OILLAMP
SITCOMS
VICTIMS
WIGWAMS
WINSOME

•I••••M
BINGHAM
DIAGRAM
FIEFDOM
FIREARM
GINGHAM
JIBBOOM
KINGDOM
LIPBALM
LITHIUM
MIDTERM
MILLDAM
MINICAM
MINIMUM
MITCHUM
NIOBIUM
PIANISM
PIETISM
PILGRIM
PINETUM
SIDEARM
SIKHISM
SISTRUM
TINYTIM
VIETNAM
WILHELM
WILLIAM

••IM•••
ALIMENT
ALIMONY
ANIMALS
ANIMATE
ANIMATO
ANIMISM
ANIMIST
AZIMUTH
BRIMFUL
BRIMMED
CAIMANS
CHIMERA
CHIMING
CHIMNEY
CLIMATE
CLIMBED
CLIMBER
CRIMEAN
CRIMPED
CRIMPER
CRIMSON
DAIMLER
GLIMMER
GLIMPSE
GRIMACE
GRIMIER
GRIMMER
GUIMPES
PRIMACY
PRIMARY
PRIMATE
PRIMERS
PRIMING
PRIMMER
PRIMPED
RAIMENT
SHIMMER
SKIMASK
SKIMMED
SKIMMER
SKIMPED
SLIMIER
SLIMJIM
SLIMMED
SLIMMER
STIMULI
SWIMMER
THIMBLE
TRIMMED
TRIMMER
WHIMPER

••I•M••
BRIMMED
ENIGMAS
GLIMMER
GRIMMER
IDIAMIN
PRIMMER
RAINMAN
SEISMIC
SHIMMER
SHIPMAN
SHIPMEN
SKIMMED
SKIMMER
SLIMMED
SLIMMER
STIGMAS
SWIMMER
THINMAN
TRIMMED
TRIMMER
TRIUMPH
WHITMAN

••I••M•
EPITOME
NOISOME
ORIGAMI
RHIZOME
SKIJUMP
TRIREME

••I•••M
ANIMISM
BRIGHAM
ELITISM
EPIGRAM
GRISHAM
GRISSOM
IRIDIUM
SLIMJIM
TRIGRAM
TRITIUM

UNIFORM

•••IM••
ATTIMES
BETIMES
CLAIMED
CLAIMER
DECIMAL
DELIMIT
ESKIMOS
FADIMAN
MARIMBA
MAXIMAL
MAXIMUM
MAXIMUS
MERIMEE
MINIMAL
MINIMUM
OPTIMAL
OPTIMUM
REGIMEN
REGIMES
RETIMED
RETIMES
SCRIMPS
SCRIMPY
SHRIMPS
UNAIMED

•••I•M•
AFFIRMS
ATRIUMS
CHRISMS
MEDIUMS
PODIUMS
REFILMS
SCHISMS
SQUIRMS
SQUIRMY
TRUISMS
WOEISME

•••I••M
HASIDIM
HOMINEM
MAXIMUM
MINICAM
MINIMUM
MODICUM
OPTIMUM
STEINEM
SURINAM

••••IM•
AIRTIME
ALLTIME
ANYTIME
BEDTIME
BEGRIME
BIGTIME
BUYTIME
CENTIME
CENTIMO
CUTTIME
DAYTIME
IWOJIMA
KEYLIME
MAYTIME
MEGRIMS
MUSLIMS
NAPTIME
OLDTIME
ONETIME
PASTIME
PRELIMS
PROXIMO
RAGTIME
RETRIMS
SASHIMI
SUBLIME
TEATIME
TWOTIME
VICTIMS
WARTIME

••••I•M
ANIMISM
ARTFILM
ATAVISM
ATHEISM
BAPTISM
BELGIUM
CADMIUM
CALCIUM
CAMBIUM
CONFIRM
CRANIUM
CULTISM
CZARISM
DADAISM
EGOTISM
ELITISM
ELUVIUM
ELYSIUM
FADDISM
FASCISM
FAUVISM
FERMIUM
FOGYISM
GALLIUM
HAFNIUM
HAHNIUM
HEROISM
HOLMIUM
IRIDIUM
JUDAISM
LAMAISM
LITHIUM
MARXISM
NATRIUM
NIOBIUM
PALLIUM
PERDIEM
PIANISM
PIETISM
PREMIUM
REALISM
REQUIEM
RHENIUM
RHODIUM
SIKHISM
SOPHISM
STADIUM
TERBIUM
THORIUM
THULIUM
TORYISM
TOURISM
TRITIUM
TROPISM
URANIUM
WILLIAM
YTTRIUM

•••••IM
ACCLAIM
ANAHEIM
ANDYKIM
DECLAIM
EXCLAIM
HASIDIM
INTERIM
JOACHIM
LORDJIM
PILGRIM
RECLAIM
SLIMJIM
TAKEAIM
TINYTIM

IN•••••
INADAZE
INAHEAP
INAMESS
INANELY
INANEST
INAPTLY
INARUSH
INASNIT
INASPIN
INASPOT
INASTEW
INAWEOF
INAWORD
INBLOOM
INBOARD
INBOUND
INBREED
INBRIEF
INCANTS
INCENSE
INCEPTS
INCHING
INCIPIT
INCISED
INCISES
INCISOR
INCITED
INCITER
INCITES
INCIVIL
INCLINE
INCLOSE
INCLUDE
INCOMES
INCUDES
INDENTS
INDEPTH
INDEXED
INDEXES
INDIANA
INDIANS
INDICES
INDICIA
INDICTS
INDIGOS
INDITED
INDITES
INDOORS
INDOUBT
INDUCED
INDUCER
INDUCES
INDUCTS
INDULGE
INDUTCH
INDWELL
INEPTLY
INERROR
INERTIA
INERTLY
INEXACT
INFANCY
INFANTA
INFANTS
INFAVOR
INFECTS
INFERNO
INFESTS
INFIDEL
INFIELD
INFLAME
INFLATE
INFLECT
INFLICT
INFLOWS
INFOCUS
INFORCE
INFORMS
INFRONT
INFUSED
INFUSES
INGALLS
INGEMAR
INGENUE
INGESTS
INGRAIN
INGRATE
INGRESS
INGROUP
INGROWN
INHABIT
INHALED
INHALER
INHALES
INHASTE
INHERED
INHERES
INHERIT
INHIBIT
INHOUSE
INHUMAN
INITIAL
INJECTS
INJOKES
INJURED
INJURES
INKBLOT
INKHORN
INKLING
INKSPOT
INKWELL
INKYCAP
INMATES
INNARDS
INNINGS
INNOWAY
INOCULA
INORBIT
INPEACE
INPETTO
INPHASE
INPLACE
INPOINT
INPRINT
INQUEST
INQUIRE
INQUIRY
INROADS
INSCAPE
INSEAMS
INSECTS
INSERTS
INSHAPE
INSHORT
INSIDER
INSIDES
INSIGHT
INSIPID
INSISTS
INSOFAR
INSOLES
INSPANS
INSPECT
INSPIRE
INSPOTS
INSTALL
INSTANT
INSTATE
INSTEAD
INSTEPS
INSTILL
INSTILS
INSTOCK
INSTORE
INSTYLE
INSULAR
INSULIN
INSULTS
INSURED
INSURES
INTAKES
INTEGER
INTEGRA
INTENDS
INTENSE
INTENTS
INTERIM
INTERNS
INTERSE
INTONED
INTONER
INTONES
INTROIT
INTRUDE
INTRUST
INTRUTH
INTUITS
INURING
INUTILE
INVACUO
INVADED
INVADER
INVADES
INVALID
INVEIGH
INVENTS
INVERSE
INVERTS
INVESTS
INVITED
INVITES
INVITRO
INVOGUE
INVOICE
INVOKED
INVOKER
INVOKES
INVOLVE
INWARDS

I•N••••
IBNSAUD
IGNEOUS
IGNITED
IGNITER
IGNITES
IGNOBLE
IGNOBLY
IGNORED
IGNORER
IGNORES
INNARDS
INNINGS
INNOWAY
IONESCO
IONIZED
IONIZER
IONIZES

I••N•••
ICINESS
ICINGIN
IDENTIC
ILLNESS
INANELY
INANEST
IPANEMA
IRANIAN
IRONAGE
IRONERS
IRONIES
IRONING
IRONMAN
IRONMEN
IRONORE
IRONOUT
IVANHOE

I•••N••
IGUANAS
IMMENSE
IMPANEL
IMPENDS
IMPINGE
INASNIT
INCANTS
INCENSE
INDENTS
INFANCY
INFANTA
INFANTS
INGENUE
INNINGS
INTENDS
INTENSE
INTENTS
INTONED
INTONER
INTONES
INVENTS
ISLANDS

I••••N•
ICELAND
ICERINK
IFSTONE
IKEBANA
ILLWIND
IMAGINE
IMAGING
IMBUING
IMOGENE
IMPLANT
IMPOUND
IMPRINT
IMPUGNS
INBOUND
INCHING
INCLINE
INDIANA
INDIANS
INFERNO
INFRONT
INKLING
INPOINT
INPRINT
INSPANS
INSTANT
INTERNS
INURING
IRELAND
IRONING
ISOGONS
ISSUING
ITCHING
ITERANT

I•••••N
IBERIAN
ICINGIN
IDAHOAN
IDIAMIN
INASPIN
INGRAIN
INGROWN
INHUMAN
INKHORN
INSULIN
IRANIAN
IRECKON
IRONMAN
IRONMEN
ITALIAN
ITHACAN

•IN••••
BINDERS
BINDERY
BINDING
BINDSUP
BINGHAM
BINGING
BINGOES
BINNING
CINCHED
CINCHES
CINDERS
CINEMAS
CINEMAX
CINZANO
DINEDIN
DINEDON
DINESEN
DINESIN
DINESON
DINETTE
DINGBAT
DINGIER
DINGILY
DINGING
DINGLES
DINGOES
DINKIER
DINKIES
DINMONT
DINNERS
FINAGLE
FINALES
FINALLY
FINANCE
FINCHES
FINDERS
FINDING
FINDOUT
FINEART
FINESSE
FINGERS
FINIALS
FINICKY
FINKING
FINLAND
FINNISH
GINFIZZ
GINGERS
GINGERY
GINGHAM
GINGIVA
GINMILL
GINNING
GINSENG
HINDERS
HINGING
HINNIES
HINTING
HINTSAT
JINGLED
JINGLES
JINGOES
JINKING
JINXING
KINDEST
KINDLED
KINDLES
KINDRED
KINETIC
KINFOLK
KINGDOM
KINGING
KINGMAN
KINGPIN
KINGRAT
KINGTUT
KINKIER
KINKING
KINSHIP
KINSMAN
KINSMEN
LINAGES
LINBIAO
LINCOLN
LINDENS
LINDIED
LINDIES
LINDSAY
LINDSEY
LINEAGE
LINEATE
LINEDUP
LINEMAN
LINEMEN
LINESUP
LINEUPS
LINGERS
LINGOES
LINGUAL
LININGS
LINKAGE
LINKERS
LINKING
LINKUPS
LINNETS
LINSEED
LINTELS
LINTIER
MINABLE
MINARET
MINCERS
MINCING
MINDERS
MINDFUL
MINDING
MINDSET
MINEOLA
MINERAL
MINERVA
MINGLED
MINGLER
MINGLES
MINIBUS
MINICAM
MINIMAL
MINIMUM
MINIONS
MINIVAN
MINIVER
MINNOWS
MINOANS
MINOLTA
MINORCA
MINORED
MINTERS
MINTIER
MINTING
MINUEND
MINUETS
MINUSES
MINUTES
MINUTIA
NINEVEH
NINNIES
OINKING
PINATAS
PINBALL
PINCERS
PINCHAS
PINCHED
PINCHER
PINCHES
PINCURL
PINDOWN
PINEFOR
PINENUT
PINESAP
PINETAR
PINETUM
PINGING
PINHEAD
PINHOLE
PINIEST
PINIONS
PINKEST
PINKIES
PINKING
PINKISH
PINLESS
PINNACE
PINNATE
PINNERS
PINNING
PINOAKS
PINOCLE
PINONES
PINTAIL
PINWALE
QINTARS
RINGERS
RINGING
RINGLET
RINGOUT
RINGSUP
RINSING
SINATRA
SINCERE
SINEDIE
SINGERS
SINGING
SINGLED
SINGLES
SINGOUT
SINGSTO
SINKAGE
SINKERS
SINKING
SINKSIN
SINNERS
SINUOUS
SINUSES
TINCANS
TINDERS
TINEARS
TINFOIL
TINGING
TINGLED
TINGLES
TINHATS
TINHORN
TINIEST
TINKERS
TINKLED
TINKLES
TINNERS
TINNIER
TINNILY
TINSELS
TINSTAR
TINTERN
TINTERS
TINTING
TINTYPE
TINWORK
TINYTIM
VINCENT
VINEGAR
VINTAGE
VINTNER
WINCERS
WINCHED
WINCHES
WINCING
WINDBAG
WINDERS
WINDIER
WINDING
WINDOWS
WINDROW
WINDSOR
WINDSUP
WINDUPS
WINEBAR
WINERED
WINESAP
WINFREY
WINGERS
WINGING
WINGNUT
WINGSIT
WINGTIP
WINKERS
WINKING
WINKLER
WINKOUT
WINKSAT
WINNERS
WINNING
WINNOWS
WINSLOW
WINSOME
WINSOUT
WINSTON
WINTERS
WINTERY
ZINGERS
ZINGIER
ZINGING
ZINNIAS

•I•N•••
BIENTOT
BIGNAME
BIGNESS
BINNING
BIONICS
DIGNIFY
DIGNITY
DIMNESS
DINNERS
DIRNDLS
FIANCEE
FIANCES
FINNISH
FITNESS
GINNING
HINNIES
HIPNESS
JITNEYS
KIDNAPS
KIDNEYS
LIENEES
LIGNITE
LIMNERS
LIMNING
LINNETS
LIONCUB
LIONESS
LIONETS
LIONIZE
MINNOWS
MISNAME
NINNIES
PIANISM
PIANIST
PICNICS
PIGNUTS
PINNACE
PINNATE
PINNERS
PINNING
PIONEER
SIENNAS
SIGNALS
SIGNEES
SIGNERS
SIGNETS
SIGNIFY
SIGNING
SIGNOFF
SIGNOUT
SIGNSIN
SIGNSON
SIGNSUP
SINNERS
TINNERS
TINNIER
TINNILY
WIENERS
WIENIES
WINNERS
WINNING
WINNOWS
WITNESS
ZINNIAS

•I••N••
AIRINGS
BIKINIS
DIURNAL
DIVINED
DIVINER
DIVINES
FILINGS
FINANCE
FIRENZE
FIRINGS
FISHNET
FIXINGS
GILLNET
GIRONDE
GIVENTO
HIJINKS
JIMENEZ
KIMONOS
KIWANIS
LICENCE
LICENSE
LIERNES
LIFENET
LIKENED
LIKENEW
LININGS
LITINTO
LIVENED
LIVINGS
MIRANDA
PICANTE
PILINGS
PILSNER
PIMENTO
PINENUT
PINONES
PIPINGS
PIRANHA
RIBANDS
RIPENED
RIPINTO
RISINGS
SIDINGS
SIENNAS
SILENCE
SILENTS
SIMENON
SIZINGS
TIDINGS
TIEINTO
TIERNEY
TIMINGS
TISANES
TITANIA
TITANIC
VICUNAS
VIETNAM
VIKINGS
VINTNER
VIVENDI
WIDENED
WINGNUT
WIZENED

•I•••N•
AILMENT
AIRGUNS
AIRLANE
AIRLINE
BIASING
BIDDING
BIGBAND
BIGBANG
BIGBEND
BIGGUNS
BILKING
BILLING
BINDING
BINGING
BINNING
BIOGENY
BIPLANE
BIRDING
BIRLING
BITTING
CINZANO
CITRINE
CITRONS
DIAHANN
DIALING
DIAMOND
DICKENS
DIETING
DIGGING
DIMMING
DINGING
DINMONT
DIPPING
DISBAND
DISHING
DISOWNS
DISSENT
DISTANT
DISTEND
DITTANY
FIBBING
FIGMENT
FIJIANS
FILLING
FILLINS
FILMING
FINDING
FINKING
FINLAND
FIREANT
FIRKINS
FIRMING
FISHING
FITTING
FIZZING
GIBBONS
GIDEONS
GILDING
GILLING
GINNING
GINSENG
GIRDING
HIGGINS
HIGHEND
HILLING
HINGING
HINTING
HIPBONE
HISPANO
HISSING

HITTING
JIGGING
JILTING
JIMDINE
JINKING
JINXING
KICKING
KIDDING
KILLING
KILTING
KINGING
KINKING
KIPLING
KIRMANS
KISSING
KITTENS
LIBBING
LIBYANS
LICHENS
LICKING
LIFTING
LILTING
LIMBING
LIMNING
LIMPING
LINDENS
LINKING
LIPPING
LIPSYNC
LISPING
LISTENS
LISTING
LIVEONE
MICRONS
MIDDENS
MIDLAND
MIDLINE
MIFFING
MIGHTNT
MIGRANT
MILKING
MILLAND
MILLEND
MILLING
MINCING
MINDING
MINIONS
MINOANS
MINTING
MINUEND
MIOCENE
MISDONE
MISSING
MISTING
MITRING
MITTENS
MIZZENS
NICKING
NIPPING
NIRVANA
NITTANY
OILCANS
OILPANS
OINKING
PICKENS
PICKING
PIDGINS
PIECING
PIEPANS
PIETINS
PIGEONS
PIGGING
PIGMENT

PIGPENS
PILLING
PINGING
PINIONS
PINKING
PINNING
PIPKINS
PIPPINS
PIQUANT
PIQUING
PISCINE
PISTONS
PITHING
PITTING
PITYING
RIBBING
RIBBONS
RIDDING
RIDGING
RIFFING
RIFLING
RIFTING
RIGGING
RIMMING
RINGING
RINSING
RIOTING
RIPPING
RISKING
SIBLING
SICCING
SICKENS
SIDLING
SIFTING
SIGHING
SIGMUND
SIGNING
SILOING
SILTING
SIMIANS
SIMMONS
SINGING
SINKING
SIOUANS
SIPHONS
SIPPING
SISKINS
SISTINE
SITTING
SIXGUNS
TICKING
TIDYING
TIELINE
TIEPINS
TIERING
TIFFANY
TIJUANA
TILLING
TILTING
TIMMINS
TINCANS
TINGING
TINTING
TIPPING
TITHING
TITLING
VIBRANT
VIEWING
VINCENT
VIOLENT
VIOLINS
VIRGINS
VISIONS

WILDING
WILDONE
WILLING
WILTING
WINCING
WINDING
WINGING
WINKING
WINNING
WISHING
WISPING
WITTING
YIPPING
ZIGGING
ZINGING
ZIPPING
ZIRCONS

•I••••N

AILERON
BIGHORN
BIGJOHN
BILLION
BIRDMAN
BIRDMEN
BITTERN
BITUMEN
CISTERN
CITIZEN
CITROEN
DIAHANN
DICTION
DIEDOWN
DINEDIN
DINEDON
DINESEN
DINESIN
DINESON
DISCERN
DISDAIN
DISHPAN
DISJOIN
DIVESIN
FICTION
FIFTEEN
FILLSIN
FIREMAN
FIREMEN
FISSION
GIVESIN
HICKMAN
HIRESON
JILLIAN
JILLION
JIMRYUN
KICKSIN
KIDSKIN
KILOTON
KINGMAN
KINGPIN
KINSMAN
KINSMEN
KITCHEN
LIAISON
LIEDOWN
LIGHTEN
LILLIAN
LINCOLN
LINEMAN
LINEMEN
LIVEDIN
LIVEDON
LIVESIN

LIVESON
MIAMIAN
MIDTOWN
MILKMAN
MILKMEN
MILKRUN
MILLION
MILLRUN
MINIVAN
MISSION
NIELSEN
NILSSON
OILSKIN
PICKSON
PIDGEON
PIGIRON
PIGSKIN
PIKEMAN
PIKEMEN
PILEDIN
PILEDON
PILESIN
PILESON
PILLION
PIMESON
PINDOWN
PITCHIN
PITTMAN
RICHMAN
RIGHTON
RIPTORN
SICHUAN
SIDEMAN
SIDEMEN
SIGNSIN
SIGNSON
SILICON
SIMENON
SIMPSON
SINKSIN
SIOBHAN
SIRLOIN
SITDOWN
SIXTEEN
TIBETAN
TIEDOWN
TIGHTEN
TINHORN
TINTERN
TIOMKIN
VILLAIN
VILLEIN
VIRGOAN
VITAMIN
WIDGEON
WILLSON
WINSTON
WISEMAN
WISEMEN
ZILLION

••IN•••

ASININE
ATINGLE
BLINDED
BLINDER
BLINDLY
BLINKAT
BLINKED
BLINKER
BRINDLE
BRINGER
BRINGIN

BRINGON
BRINGTO
BRINGUP
BRINIER
BRINING
CHINESE
CHINKED
CHINNED
CHINOOK
CHINTZY
CHINUPS
CLINGTO
CLINICS
CLINKED
CLINKER
CLINTON
COINAGE
COINERS
COINING
CRINGED
CRINGES
CRINKLE
CRINKLY
CRINOID
DOINGIN
DOINGUP
DRINKER
DWINDLE
EMINENT
EVINCED
EVINCES
FAINTED
FAINTER
FAINTLY
FEINTED
FRINGED
FRINGES
GAINERS
GAINFUL
GAINING
GAINSAY
GAINSON
GLINTED
GOINFOR
GOINGAT
GOINGBY
GOINGIN
GOINGON
GOINGUP
GRINDER
GRINNED
GRINNER
GUINEAS
HEINOUS
ICINESS
ICINGIN
JOINDER
JOINERS
JOINERY
JOINING
JOINSIN
JOINSUP
JOINTED
JOINTLY
KLINGON
KRINGLE
LYINGTO
MAINTOP
OKINAWA
OMINOUS
OPINERS
OPINING
OPINION

ORINOCO
OWINGTO
PAINFUL
PAINTED
PAINTER
PHINEAS
PLINKED
PLINTHS
POINTED
POINTER
POINTTO
PRINCES
PRINKED
PRINTED
PRINTER
QUINCES
QUININE
QUINOAS
QUINQUE
QUINTET
RAINBOW
RAINHAT
RAINIER
RAINING
RAINMAN
RAINOUT
REINING
REINKED
REINSIN
RUINERS
RUINING
RUINOUS
SAINTED
SAINTLY
SEINERS
SEINING
SHINDIG
SHINERS
SHINGLE
SHINIER
SHINING
SHINNED
SKINNED
SKINNER
SLINGER
SLINKED
SPINACH
SPINDLE
SPINDLY
SPINELS
SPINETS
SPINIER
SPINNER
SPINOFF
SPINOUT
SPINOZA
STINGER
STINKER
STINTED
SWINDLE
SWINGBY
SWINGER
TAINTED
THINAIR
THINICE
THINKER
THINKOF
THINKUP
THINMAN
THINNED
THINNER
TLINGIT
TRINITY

TRINKET
TWINBED
TWINGED
TWINGES
TWINING
TWINKLE
TWINKLY
TWINNED
TYINGIN
TYINGUP
USINGUP
VAINEST
VEINING
WHINERS
WHINING
WRINGER
WRINKLE
WRINKLY
ZWINGLI

••I•N••

ALIENEE
ALIENOR
ALIGNED
ALIGNER
AVIANCA
AVIGNON
CHIANTI
CHIGNON
CHIMNEY
CHINNED
CLIENTS
DEIGNED
ETIENNE
FAIENCE
FEIGNED
FRIENDS
GRINNED
GRINNER
HAIRNET
LEIBNIZ
ORIENTE
ORIENTS
PLIANCY
REIGNED
SCIENCE
SHINNED
SKINNED
SKINNER
SOIGNEE
SPINNER
THINNED
THINNER
TRIUNES
TWINNED
WHITNEY

••I••N•

ABIDING
ABILENE
ALIMENT
ALIMONY
ANILINE
ARIADNE
ARISING
ARIZONA
ASININE
BAILING
BAITING
BEIJING
BOILING
BOITANO
BRIBING

BRIGAND
BRINING
BRITONS
CAIMANS
CEILING
CHICANA
CHICANO
CHIDING
CHIMING
CLIPONS
COIFING
COILING
COINING
CUIBONO
CUISINE
DEICING
DRIVING
EDITING
ELIDING
EMINENT
EPICENE
EPIGENE
EPIGONE
ETIENNE
EVIDENT
EXIGENT
EXILING
EXITING
FAILING
FAIRING
FOILING
GAINING
GAITING
GLIDING
GRIPING
GUIDING
GUIDONS
HAILING
JAILING
JOINING
JUICING
KNIFING
KRISHNA
MAIDENS
MAILING
MOILING
NAILING
NOISING
OHIOANS
OLIVINE
OPINING
ORIGINS
ORISONS
OXIDANT
PAIRING
PAISANO
POISING
POISONS
PRICING
PRIDING
PRIMING
PRISONS
PRIZING
QUININE
RAIDING
RAILING
RAIMENT
RAINING
RAISING
RAISINS
REINING
ROILING
RUINING

SAILING
SEINING
SEIZING
SHINING
SKIRUNS
SLICING
SLIDING
SLIPONS
SMILING
SMITING
SNIPING
SOILING
SPICING
SPIKING
SPIRANT
SPITING
STIPEND
SUITING
SWIPING
TAILEND
TAILING
TAIPANS
TOILING
TRIBUNE
TRIDENT
TRIGONS
TRITONE
TRITONS
TWINING
UNISONS
UNITING
VEILING
VEINING
VOICING
VOIDING
WAILING
WAITING
WAIVING
WHILING
WHINING
WHITENS
WHITING
WRITING
ZEITUNG

••I•••N

AVIGNON
BLITZEN
BRINGIN
BRINGON
BRITAIN
BRITTEN
BRITTON
BUILDIN
BUILDON
BUILTIN
BUILTON
CAISSON
CHICHEN
CHICKEN
CHIFFON
CHIGNON
CHILEAN
CHIPSIN
CLIBURN
CLIFTON
CLINTON
CRIMEAN
CRIMSON
CRISPIN
DOINGIN
DRIPPAN
DRISTAN

DRIVEIN
EDITION
ELISION
ERICSON
FLIESIN
FRIEDAN
FRISIAN
FRISSON
GAINSON
GLISTEN
GOINGIN
GOINGON
GRIFFIN
GRIFFON
HAIRPIN
HAITIAN
ICINGIN
IDIAMIN
JOINSIN
KLINGON
MEISSEN
MOISTEN
OMICRON
OPINION
PHILBIN
POISSON
QUICKEN
QUIETEN
RAINMAN
REINSIN
SHIPMAN
SHIPMEN
SLIDEIN
SMIDGEN
SMITTEN
SPIEDON
SPIESON
STIFFEN
STILTON
STIRSIN
TAILFIN
THICKEN
THINMAN
TRICORN
TRIEDON
TRIESON
TRILLIN
TRISTAN
TUITION
TYINGIN
UNICORN
WAITSON
WEIGHIN
WHITMAN
WRITEIN
WRITTEN

•••IN••

ACTINIC
AFFINES
AGAINST
AIRINGS
ALBINOS
ANOINTS
AQUINAS
AWNINGS
BELINDA
BIKINIS
BOVINES
BRAINED
BYLINED
BYLINES
CABINET

CANINES
CARINAS
CASINGS
CASINOS
CHAINED
COMINGS
CORINTH
COSINES
CUTINTO
DAVINCI
DEFINED
DEFINES
DIVINED
DIVINER
DIVINES
DOMINGO
DOMINOS
DRAINED
DRAINER
ECHINUS
EDGINGS
ENDINGS
ENGINES
EQUINES
EQUINOX
ERMINES
EXTINCT
FACINGS
FELINES
FILINGS
FIRINGS
FIXINGS
FORINTS
GAMINES
GETINTO
GOTINTO
GRAINED
HAZINGS
HIJINKS
HOMINEM
HOMINID
IMPINGE
INNINGS
JACINTO
LACINGS
LADINOS
LAMINAE
LAMINAL
LAMINAR
LAMINAS
LATINAS
LATINOS
LAVINIA
LAYINTO
LETINON
LININGS
LITINTO
LIVINGS
LUPINES
MAGINOT
MAKINGS
MARINAS
MARINER
MARINES
MATINEE
MELINDA
MERINOS
NOMINAL
NOMINEE
ORDINAL
ORPINES
OSCINES
OUTINGS

PARINGS
PATINAS
PILINGS
PIPINGS
PLAINER
PLAINES
PLAINLY
PLAINTS
PRYINTO
RANINTO
RAPINES
RATINGS
RAVINES
RAVINGS
REBINDS
REFINED
REFINER
REFINES
RELINED
RELINES
REMINDS
REPINED
REPINES
RERINSE
RESINGS
RETINAE
RETINAL
RETINAS
RETINUE
REWINDS
RIPINTO
RISINGS
RULINGS
RUNINTO
SABINES
SAGINAW
SAVINGS
SAYINGS
SEMINAL
SEMINAR
SETINTO
SHRINER
SHRINES
SHRINKS
SIDINGS
SIZINGS
SPLINES
SPLINTS
SPRINGS
SPRINGY
SPRINTS
SQUINCH
SQUINTS
SQUINTY
STAINED
STAINER
STEINEM
STEINER
STRINGS
STRINGY
SURINAM
SYRINGA
SYRINGE
TAPINGS
TIDINGS
TIEINTO
TIMINGS
TRAINED
TRAINEE
TRAINER
UNBINDS
UNKINKS
UNLINED

UNLINKS
UNWINDS
UPLINKS
USTINOV
VIKINGS
WAHINES

•••I•N•

AAMILNE
ACTIONS
AMBIENT
AMNIONS
ANCIENT
ASSIGNS
BUNIONS
CATIONS
COSIGNS
DEFIANT
DESIGNS
DEVIANT
ECHIDNA
ENSIGNS
FANIONS
FIJIANS
HYGIENE
INDIANA
INDIANS
JULIANA
LEGIONS
LENIENT
LOTIONS
LUCIANO
MALIGNS
MARIANA
MEDIANS
MEDIANT
MINIONS
MOTIONS
NATIONS
NOTIONS
NUBIANS
OPTIONS
PATIENT
PINIONS
POTIONS
RADIANS
RADIANT
RATIONS
REGIONS
RELIANT
RESIGNS
SALIENT
SAPIENS
SAPIENT
SEVIGNE
SIMIANS
SYRIANS
TATIANA
TAXIING
VALIANT
VARIANT
VISIONS

•••I••N

ADDISON
AFRICAN
ALLISON
ANDIRON
ANTIGEN
ARTISAN
ASPIRIN
BEDIZEN
BENISON

BKLIBAN
CALIBAN
CAPITAN
CITIZEN
DENIZEN
ELEISON
ELLISON
ENLIVEN
EPSILON
FADIMAN
GETITON
HELICON
HORIZON
LETINON
LEXICON
LIAISON
MADISON
MARILYN
MEXICAN
MINIVAN
MOHICAN
ORBISON
PELICAN
PEMICAN
PIGIRON
PURITAN
RARITAN
REGIMEN
RUBICON
RUBITIN
SAMISEN
SCRIVEN
SILICON
STRIVEN
UPRISEN
UPSILON
VATICAN
VENISON

••••IN•

ABASING
ABATING
ABIDING
ABUSING
ADDLING
ADELINE
ADENINE
ADJOINS
ADORING
AIRLINE
ALAKING
ALLYING
AMAZING
AMBLING
AMERIND
AMUSING
ANGLING
ANILINE
ANTEING
ANTOINE
APPOINT
ARCHING
ARCSINE
ARGUING
ARISING
ASININE
ATONING
ATTAINS
AVOWING
AWAKING
BABYING
BACKING
BAGGING

BAILING
BAITING
BALDING
BALKING
BAMBINO
BANDING
BANGING
BANKING
BANNING
BARBING
BARGING
BARKING
BARRING
BASHING
BASKING
BASTING
BATHING
BATTING
BATWING
BAWLING
BEADING
BEAMING
BEANING
BEARING
BEATING
BEDDING
BEEFING
BEELINE
BEEPING
BEGGING
BEGUINE
BEIJING
BELLING
BELLINI
BELTING
BELYING
BENDING
BESTING
BETHINK
BETTING
BIASING
BIDDING
BILKING
BILLING
BINDING
BINGING
BINNING
BIRDING
BIRLING
BITTING
BLAMING
BLARING
BLAZING
BLOWING
BLUEING
BOATING
BOBBING
BOBBINS
BODKINS
BOGGING
BOILING
BOLTING
BOMBING
BONDING
BONGING
BOOKING
BOOMING
BOOTING
BOPPING
BOSSING
BOWFINS
BOWLINE
BOWLING

BRACING
BRAKING
BRAVING
BRAYING
BRAZING
BREWING
BRIBING
BRINING
BROMINE
BUCKING
BUDDING
BUDGING
BUFFING
BUGGING
BUGLING
BULGING
BULKING
BULLING
BUMMING
BUMPING
BUNGING
BUNKING
BUNTING
BUOYING
BURKINA
BURLING
BURNING
BURPING
BURYING
BUSHING
BUSKINS
BUSLINE
BUSSING
BUSTING
BUSYING
BUTTING
BUZZING
CABLING
CACHING
CADGING
CALKING
CALKINS
CALLING
CALLINS
CALMING
CALVING
CAMPING
CANNING
CANTINA
CANTING
CAPPING
CARBINE
CARDING
CARMINE
CARPING
CARTING
CARVING
CASHING
CASSINI
CASTING
CATKINS
CATTING
CAUSING
CAVEINS
CEASING
CEILING
CELLINI
CENSING
CHAFING
CHASING
CHEWING
CHIDING
CHIMING

CHORINE
CITRINE
CLAWING
CLONING
CLOSING
CLOYING
CLUEING
COATING
COAXING
COCKING
CODEINE
COIFING
COILING
COINING
COLLINS
COMBINE
COMBING
CONFINE
CONKING
CONNING
COOKING
COOLING
COOPING
COPPING
COPYING
CORDING
CORKING
CORNING
COSTING
COUSINS
COWLING
COZYING
CRANING
CRATING
CRAVING
CRAZING
CRETINS
CREWING
CROWING
CUFFING
CUISINE
CULLING
CUNNING
CUPPING
CURBING
CURDING
CURLING
CURSING
CURVING
CUSSING
CUTTING
CYCLING
CZARINA
DABBING
DAMMING
DAMNING
DAMPING
DANCING
DAPPING
DARLING
DARNING
DARTING
DASHING
DAUBING
DAWKINS
DAWNING
DAYSINN
DEALING
DECKING
DECLINE
DEEDING
DEEMING
DEFYING

DEICING
DELEING
DELVING
DENTINE
DENTING
DENYING
DERRING
DESTINE
DESTINY
DETAINS
DEVEINS
DEWLINE
DIALING
DIETING
DIGGING
DIMMING
DINGING
DIPPING
DISHING
DOBBINS
DOCKING
DODGING
DOFFING
DOGGING
DOLLING
DOMAINS
DONKING
DONNING
DOOMING
DOTTING
DOUSING
DOWNING
DOWSING
DRAPING
DRAWING
DRAYING
DRIVING
DRONING
DROPINS
DUBBING
DUCKING
DUCTING
DUELING
DULLING
DUMPING
DUNKING
DUNLINS
DUNNING
DUSTING
EAGLING
EARNING
EARRING
ECHOING
EDDYING
EDITING
EDUCING
ELATING
ELIDING
ELOPING
ELUDING
ELUTING
EMOTING
ENDUING
ENJOINS
ENSUING
ENTWINE
ENURING
ENVYING
ERASING
ERODING
ERSKINE
ESPYING
ETAMINE

ETCHING
EVADING
EVENING
EVOKING
EXAMINE
EXILING
EXITING
EXUDING
FADEINS
FAGGING
FAILING
FAIRING
FALLING
FANNING
FANZINE
FARMING
FASTING
FAWNING
FEARING
FEEDING
FEELING
FELLING
FELLINI
FENCING
FENDING
FEUDING
FIBBING
FILLING
FILLINS
FILMING
FINDING
FINKING
FIRKINS
FIRMING
FISHING
FITTING
FIZZING
FLAKING
FLAMING
FLARING
FLAWING
FLAYING
FLEEING
FLEMING
FLEXING
FLORINS
FLOWING
FLUTING
FOALING
FOAMING
FOBBING
FOGGING
FOILING
FOLDING
FONTINA
FOOLING
FOOTING
FORCING
FORDING
FORGING
FORKING
FORMING
FOULING
FOWLING
FRAMING
FRAYING
FREEING
FUDGING
FUELING
FUNDING
FUNNING
FURLING
FURRING

FUSSING
FUZZING
GABBING
GADDING
GAFFING
GAGGING
GAGLINE
GAINING
GAITING
GALLING
GANGING
GAPPING
GARBING
GASHING
GASKINS
GASPING
GATLING
GAUGING
GAWKING
GEARING
GELDING
GELLING
GENUINE
GERAINT
GETTING
GILDING
GILLING
GINNING
GIRDING
GLARING
GLAZING
GLIDING
GLOWING
GNAWING
GOADING
GOBLINS
GOLDING
GOLFING
GONGING
GOOFING
GOOSING
GORGING
GOSLING
GOUGING
GRACING
GRADING
GRATING
GRAVING
GRAYING
GRAZING
GREYING
GRIPING
GROPING
GROWING
GUANINE
GUIDING
GULFING
GULLING
GULPING
GUMMING
GUNNING
GUSHING
GUSTING
GUTTING
GYPPING
HACKING
HAILING
HALOING
HALTING
HALVING
HAMMING
HANDING
HANGING

HARDING
HARKING
HARMING
HARPING
HASHING
HASTING
HATPINS
HATTING
HAULING
HAWKING
HAWKINS
HEADING
HEALING
HEAPING
HEARING
HEATING
HEAVING
HEDGING
HEEDING
HEELING
HEFTING
HELMING
HELPING
HEMLINE
HEMMING
HERDING
HEROINE
HERRING
HIGGINS
HILLING
HINGING
HINTING
HISSING
HITTING
HOAXING
HOBOING
HOCKING
HOGGING
HOLDING
HONKING
HOOFING
HOOKING
HOOPING
HOOTING
HOPKINS
HOPPING
HORNING
HORSING
HOSKINS
HOSTING
HOTLINE
HOUDINI
HOUSING
HOWLING
HUFFING
HUGGING
HULKING
HULLING
HUMMING
HUNTING
HURLING
HURTING
HUSHING
HUSKING
HYALINE
HYPOING
ICERINK
ILLWIND
IMAGINE
IMAGING
IMBUING
IMPRINT
INCHING

INCLINE
INKLING
INPOINT
INPRINT
INURING
IRONING
ISSUING
ITCHING
JABBING
JACKING
JAGGING
JAILING
JAMMING
JARRING
JASMINE
JAWLINE
JAZZING
JEERING
JELLING
JERKING
JERKINS
JESTING
JETTING
JIGGING
JILTING
JIMDINE
JINKING
JINXING
JOBBING
JOGGING
JOINING
JOLTING
JOSHING
JOTTING
JUDGING
JUGWINE
JUICING
JUMPING
JUNKING
JURYING
JUSTINE
JUTTING
KACHINA
KAYOING
KEELING
KEENING
KEEPING
KERNING
KEYRING
KICKING
KIDDING
KILLING
KILTING
KINGING
KINKING
KIPLING
KISSING
KNEEING
KNIFING
KNOWING
LACKING
LADLING
LAGGING
LAMMING
LANDING
LANSING
LAPPING
LAPSING
LAPWING
LARAINE
LARDING
LASHING
LASTING

LATHING
LAUDING
LEADING
LEADINS
LEAFING
LEAKING
LEANING
LEAPING
LEASING
LEAVING
LEERING
LEGGING
LEMMING
LENDING
LEONINE
LESSING
LETTING
LEVYING
LIBBING
LICKING
LIFTING
LILTING
LIMBING
LIMNING
LIMPING
LINKING
LIPPING
LISPING
LISTING
LOADING
LOAFING
LOAMING
LOANING
LOBBING
LOCKING
LOCKINS
LODGING
LOFTING
LOGGING
LOGGINS
LOLLING
LONGING
LOOKING
LOOMING
LOOPING
LOOSING
LOOTING
LOPPING
LORDING
LOTTING
LOUSING
LOVEINS
LUCKING
LUFFING
LUGGING
LULLING
LUMPING
LUNGING
LURKING
LUSTING
MACHINA
MACHINE
MADDING
MAILING
MALTING
MANCINI
MANKIND
MANNING
MAPPING
MARGINS
MARKING
MARLINS
MARRING

MARTINA
MARTINI
MARTINO
MARTINS
MASHING
MASKING
MASSING
MATTING
MAULING
MAYWINE
MCSWINE
MEANING
MEETING
MELDING
MELTING
MENDING
MEOWING
MERGING
MESHING
MESSINA
MESSING
MEWLING
MIDLINE
MIFFING
MILKING
MILLING
MINCING
MINDING
MINTING
MISSING
MISTING
MITRING
MOANING
MOBBING
MOCKING
MOILING
MOLDING
MOLTING
MOONING
MOORING
MOPPING
MORAINE
MORNING
MOSSING
MOUSING
MUCKING
MUFFING
MUFFINS
MUGGING
MULLING
MUNTINS
MUSHING
MUSLINS
MUSSING
NABBING
NAGGING
NAILING
NAPKINS
NAPPING
NEARING
NECKING
NEEDING
NESTING
NETTING
NICKING
NIPPING
NODDING
NOGGINS
NOISING
NOOSING
NOSHING
NOTHING
NUBBINS

NUDGING
NULLING
NUMBING
NURSING
NUTTING
OBEYING
OBTAINS
OCARINA
OFFLINE
OINKING
OKAYING
OLDLINE
OLIVINE
ONGOING
OPALINE
OPENING
OPINING
ORATING
ORDAINS
ORIGINS
OUSTING
OUTLINE
PACKING
PADDING
PAIRING
PALLING
PALMING
PANNING
PANTING
PARKING
PARRING
PARSING
PARTING
PASSING
PASTINA
PASTING
PATTING
PAULINA
PAULINE
PAULING
PAUSING
PAWNING
PEAKING
PEALING
PECKING
PECTINS
PEEKING
PEELING
PEEPING
PEERING
PEEVING
PEGGING
PELTING
PENDING
PENNING
PEPPING
PEPSINS
PERKING
PERKINS
PERMING
PETTING
PHASING
PHONING
PICKING
PIDGINS
PIECING
PIETINS
PIGGING
PILLING
PINGING
PINKING
PINNING
PIPKINS

PIPPINS
PIQUING
PISCINE
PITHING
PITTING
PITYING
PLACING
PLANING
PLATING
PLAYING
PLOWING
PLUMING
POISING
POLLING
PONTINE
PONYING
POOLING
POOPING
POPLINS
POPPING
POPPINS
PORCINE
POSTING
POTTING
POURING
POUTING
PRALINE
PRATING
PRAYING
PRICING
PRIDING
PRIMING
PRIZING
PROBING
PROSING
PROVING
PRUNING
PUCCINI
PUDDING
PUFFING
PUFFINS
PULLING
PULSING
PUMPING
PUNNING
PUNTING
PURGING
PURLING
PURLINS
PURRING
PURSING
PUSHING
PUTTING
QUAKING
QUEUING
QUININE
QUOTING
RACKING
RAFTING
RAGGING
RAIDING
RAILING
RAINING
RAISING
RAISINS
RAMMING
RANGING
RANKING
RANTING
RAPPING
RASPING
RATFINK
RATLINE

RATTING
RAZZING
RDLAING
READING
REAMING
REAPING
REARING
RECLINE
REDDING
REDFINS
REDLINE
REDOING
REDPINE
REDWINE
REDWING
REEDING
REEFING
REEKING
REELING
REFFING
REGAINS
REINING
REJOINS
RELYING
REMAINS
RENDING
RENNINS
RENTING
REPAINT
REPRINT
RESCIND
RESTING
RETAINS
RETHINK
RETSINA
REVVING
RHYMING
RIBBING
RIDDING
RIDGING
RIFFING
RIFLING
RIFTING
RIGGING
RIMMING
RINGING
RINSING
RIOTING
RIPPING
RISKING
ROAMING
ROARING
ROBBING
ROBBINS
ROCKING
ROILING
ROLLING
ROLLINS
ROMAINE
ROMPING
ROOFING
ROOKING
ROOMING
ROOTING
ROSSINI
ROTTING
ROUGING
ROUSING
ROUTINE
ROUTING
RUBBING
RUCHING
RUCKING
RUINING
RUNNING
RUSHING
RUSTING
SABRINA
SACKING
SAGGING
SAILING
SALTINE
SALTING
SALVING
SANDING
SANTINI
SAPLING
SAPPING
SARDINE
SASSING
SCALING
SCARING
SCHWINN
SCOPING
SCORING
SEALING
SEAMING
SEARING
SEATING
SEEDING
SEEKING
SEEMING
SEEPING
SEINING
SEIZING
SELLING
SENDING
SENSING
SEQUINS
SERLING
SERVING
SESTINA
SETLINE
SETTING
SHADING
SHAKING
SHAMING
SHAPING
SHARING
SHAVING
SHINING
SHOEING
SHOOING
SHOOINS
SHORING
SHOVING
SHOWING
SIBLING
SICCING
SIDLING
SIFTING
SIGHING
SIGNING
SILOING
SILTING
SINGING
SINKING
SIPPING
SISKINS
SISTINE
SITTING
SKATING
SKEWING
SKYLINE
SLAKING
SLATING
SLAVING
SLICING
SLIDING
SLOPING
SLOWING
SMILING
SMITING
SMOKING
SNAKING
SNARING
SNIPING
SNORING
SNOWING
SOAKING
SOAPING
SOARING
SOBBING
SOCKING
SODDING
SOILING
SOLOING
SOLVING
SOPPING
SORTING
SOURING
SPACING
SPADING
SPARING
SPAVINS
SPAYING
SPEWING
SPICING
SPIKING
SPITING
SPOKING
SPRAINS
SPUMING
STAGING
STAKING
STAMINA
STARING
STATING
STAVING
STAYING
STEPINS
STEWING
STOKING
STONING
STORING
STOWING
STRAINS
STYLING
SUBBING
SUCKING
SUDSING
SUITING
SULKING
SUMMING
SUNNING
SUPPING
SURFING
SURGING
SUSSING
SWAYING
SWIPING
SYNCING
TABBING
TABLING
TACKING
TAGGING
TAGLINE
TAILING
TALKING
TAMPING
TANKING
TANLINE
TANNING
TANNINS
TAPPING
TARRING
TASKING
TASTING
TATTING
TAURINE
TAXIING
TEAMING
TEARING
TEASING
TEDDING
TEEMING
TELLING
TENDING
TENPINS
TENSING
TENTING
TERMING
TERMINI
TESTING
THAWING
TICKING
TIDYING
TIELINE
TIEPINS
TIERING
TILLING
TILTING
TIMMINS
TINGING
TINTING
TIPPING
TITHING
TITLING
TOCSINS
TOGGING
TOILING
TOLLING
TONTINE
TOOLING
TOOTING
TOPPING
TOSSING
TOTTING
TOURING
TOUTING
TRACING
TRADING
TREEING
TREVINO
TRUEING
TSARINA
TUCKING
TUFTING
TUGGING
TURBINE
TURNING
TWINING
TZARINA
UKRAINE
UNDOING
UNDYING
UNITING
UNTYING
UPSWING
URCHINS
VACCINE
VALUING
VAMPING
VANDINE
VARMINT
VARYING
VEERING
VEGGING
VEILING
VEINING
VENDING
VENTING
VERGING
VESTING
VETOING
VETTING
VIEWING
VIOLINS
VIRGINS
VOICING
VOIDING
VULPINE
WADDING
WAFTING
WAGGING
WAILING
WAITING
WAIVING
WALKING
WALKINS
WALLING
WANTING
WARDING
WARMING
WARNING
WARPING
WARRING
WASHING
WASTING
WAXWING
WEANING
WEARING
WEAVING
WEBBING
WEDDING
WEDGING
WEEDING
WEEPING
WELDING
WELKINS
WELLING
WELTING
WENDING
WETTING
WHALING
WHILING
WHINING
WHITING
WILDING
WILLING
WILTING
WINCING
WINDING
WINGING
WINKING
WINNING
WISHING
WISPING
WITTING
WOLFING
WOOFING
WORDING
WORKING
WRITING
WYOMING
XRATING
XRAYING
YAKKING
YANKING
YAPPING
YARNING
YAWNING
YELLING
YELPING
YESSING
YIPPING
YOWLING
YOYOING
ZAGGING
ZAPPING
ZEROING
ZIGGING
ZINGING
ZIPPING
ZONKING
ZOOMING

••••I•N

ACADIAN
AEOLIAN
ANTLION
ARABIAN
ARRAIGN
AUCTION
BASTION
BELGIAN
BILLION
BULLION
CAMPION
CAPTION
CARRION
CASPIAN
CAUTION
CESSION
CLARION
CONDIGN
CONSIGN
CUSHION
DAYSINN
DICTION
EDITION
ELATION
ELISION
ELUTION
ELYSIAN
EMOTION
EROSION
ETESIAN
ETONIAN
EVASION
FACTION
FASHION
FICTION
FISSION
FOREIGN
FRISIAN
FUSTIAN
GAMBIAN
GENTIAN
GORDIAN
GRECIAN
GRUNION
HADRIAN
HAITIAN
HELLION
HESSIAN
HEXSIGN
IBERIAN
IRANIAN
ITALIAN
JILLIAN
JILLION
KRATION
LAOTIAN
LATVIAN
LILLIAN
MANSION
MARMION
MARTIAN
MENTION
MIAMIAN
MILLION
MISSION
MULLION
OPINION
ORATION
OVATION
OXONIAN
PASSION
PENSION
PERSIAN
PILLION
PLOSION
PORTION
REUNION
RUCTION
RUFFIAN
RUSSIAN
SAURIAN
SCHWINN
SEALION
SECTION
SERBIAN
SESSION
STATION
STYGIAN
STYRIAN
SUASION
SUCTION
TENSION
TOLKIEN
TORSION
TUITION
UMBRIAN
UNCTION
UTOPIAN
VERSION
ZAMBIAN
ZILLION

•••••IN

ABSTAIN
ADDEDIN
ALADDIN
ALAMEIN
ALBUMIN
ANTONIN
ASPIRIN
BACKSIN
BAHRAIN
BALDWIN
BARGAIN
BARGEIN
BEDOUIN
BLOWSIN
BLUEFIN
BORODIN
BOXEDIN
BOXESIN
BRAHMIN
BREAKIN
BRESLIN
BRINGIN
BRITAIN
BROKEIN
BUILDIN
BUILTIN
BUMPKIN
BUTTSIN
CALLSIN
CAPTAIN
CAVEDIN
CAVESIN
CERTAIN
CHAGRIN
CHAPLIN
CHARMIN
CHECKIN
CHIPSIN
CLOCKIN
CLOSEIN
CLUEDIN
CLUESIN
COALBIN
COMESIN
CONJOIN
CONTAIN
COSTAIN
CRISPIN
CURTAIN
DAUPHIN
DEALSIN
DEALTIN
DETRAIN
DEXTRIN
DINEDIN
DINESIN
DISDAIN
DISJOIN
DIVESIN
DOESKIN
DOINGIN
DOLPHIN
DRAGSIN
DRAWNIN
DRAWSIN
DRIVEIN
DROPSIN
DRUMLIN
DUCKPIN
EASEDIN
EASESIN
EDGEDIN
EDGESIN
EELSKIN
ENCHAIN
ENTRAIN
EPSTEIN
EXPLAIN
FADEDIN
FADESIN
FALLSIN
FILLSIN
FLIESIN
GAGARIN
GASMAIN
GAUGUIN
GELATIN
GHERKIN
GIVESIN
GOINGIN
GOODWIN
GREMLIN
GRIFFIN
HAIRPIN
HAMELIN
HANDSIN
HANGSIN
HEADPIN
HEADSIN
HEPARIN
HOLBEIN
HUSSEIN
ICINGIN
IDIAMIN
INASPIN
INGRAIN
INSULIN
JACOBIN
JAVELIN
JOAQUIN
JOINSIN
JUMPSIN
KEEPSIN
KERATIN
KEYEDIN
KICKSIN
KIDSKIN
KINGPIN
KOSYGIN
KREMLIN
KTOSLIN
LANOLIN
LAUGHIN
LEADSIN
LIVEDIN
LIVESIN
LOOKSIN
MAUDLIN
MAULDIN
MAYALIN
MCGAVIN
MELANIN
MENUHIN
MOVEDIN
MOVESIN
MUEZZIN
MULLEIN
OBERLIN
OILSKIN
PALADIN
PEERSIN
PENGUIN
PERTAIN
PHASEIN
PHILBIN
PIGSKIN
PILEDIN
PILESIN
PITCHIN
PLUGSIN
POURSIN
PROTEIN
PUMPKIN
PUNCHIN
PURLOIN
PUSHKIN
PUSHPIN
QUENTIN
RAKEDIN
RAKESIN
RAMEKIN
READSIN
REDSKIN
REELSIN
REFRAIN
REINSIN
RESTAIN
RETRAIN
ROPEDIN
ROPESIN
RUBITIN
SALADIN
SAVARIN
SEEPSIN
SENDSIN
SHAREIN
SHERWIN
SHOWNIN
SHOWSIN
SHUTSIN
SIGNSIN
SINKSIN
SIRLOIN
SLATKIN
SLEEPIN
SLEPTIN
SLIDEIN
SLOEGIN
SNEAKIN
SNOWSIN
SOCKSIN
STANDIN
STEPSIN
STIRSIN
STOODIN
STOPSIN
SUBJOIN
SUCKSIN
SUSTAIN
SWEARIN
SWOREIN
TAILFIN
TAKENIN
TAKESIN
TAMARIN
TEACHIN
TERRAIN
THEREIN
THREWIN
THROWIN
TIOMKIN
TRADEIN
TRILLIN
TUCKSIN
TUNEDIN
TUNESIN
TURNSIN
TYINGIN
UNCHAIN
VILLAIN
VILLEIN
VITAMIN
VOTESIN
WADESIN
WANTSIN
WAVEDIN
WAVESIN
WEIGHIN
WHEREIN
WORKSIN
WRITEIN
WROTEIN
YELTSIN
ZOOMSIN

IO•••••

IODATES
IODIDES
IODIZED
IODIZES
IOMOTHS
IONESCO
IONIZED
IONIZER
IONIZES

I•O••••

IDOLIZE
IMOGENE
INOCULA
INORBIT
IRONAGE
IRONERS
IRONIES
IRONING
IRONMAN
IRONMEN
IRONORE
IRONOUT
ISOBARS
ISOGONS
ISOHELS
ISOLATE
ISOMERS
ISOPODS
ISOTOPE
IVORIES
IWOJIMA

I••O•••

IACOCCA
IDIOTIC
IGNOBLE
IGNOBLY
IGNORED
IGNORER
IGNORES
ILLOGIC
IMMORAL
IMPORTS
IMPOSED
IMPOSES
IMPOSTS
IMPOUND
IMSORRY
INBOARD
INBOUND
INCOMES
INDOORS
INDOUBT
INFOCUS
INFORCE
INFORMS
INHOUSE
INJOKES
INNOWAY
INPOINT
INROADS
INSOFAR
INSOLES
INTONED
INTONER
INTONES
INVOGUE
INVOICE
INVOKED
INVOKER
INVOKES
INVOLVE
IOMOTHS

I•••O••

ICEBOAT
ICECOLD
IDAHOAN
IFSTONE
IGNEOUS
IMAGOES
IMPIOUS
IMPLODE
IMPLORE
IMPROVE
INAWORD
INBLOOM
INCLOSE
INDOORS
INFLOWS
INFRONT
INGROUP
INGROWN
INKHORN
INSHORT
INSPOTS
INSTOCK
INSTORE
INTROIT
IRISOUT
IRKSOME
IRONORE
IRONOUT
ISADORA
ISOGONS
ISOPODS
ISOTOPE

I••••O•

ICEFLOE
ICESHOW
ICHABOD
INASPOT
INAWEOF
INBLOOM
INCISOR
INDIGOS
INERROR
INFAVOR
INKBLOT
INKSPOT
IRECKON
IVANHOE

I•••••O

IMPASTO
INFERNO
INPETTO
INVACUO
INVITRO
IONESCO

•IO••••

BIOGENY
BIOLOGY
BIOMASS
BIONICS
DIOCESE
DIOMEDE
DIOPTER
DIORAMA
DIOXIDE
GIORGIO
LIONCUB
LIONESS
LIONETS
LIONIZE
MIOCENE
NIOBIUM
PIOLETS
PIONEER
PIOUSLY
RIOLOBO
RIORITA
RIOTACT
RIOTERS
RIOTING
RIOTOUS
SIOBHAN
SIOUANS
TIOMKIN
VIOLATE
VIOLENT
VIOLETS
VIOLINS
VIOLIST

•I•O•••

BICOLOR
BIFOCAL
BIGOTED
BIGOTRY
BIMODAL
BIPOLAR
BIVOUAC
CIBORIA
DIDOVER
DIMOUTS
DIPOLAR
DIPOLES
DISOBEY
DISOWNS
DIVORCE
GIGOLOS
GIRONDE
KILOTON
KIMONOS
LIEOVER
LIMOGES
LITOTES
MILORDS
MIMOSAS
MINOANS
MINOLTA
MINORCA
MINORED
MITOSES
MITOSIS
MITOTIC
NICOLAS
NICOSIA
NIKOLAI
PILOTED
PINOAKS
PINOCLE
PINONES
PIROGUE
PIVOTAL
PIVOTED
RICOTTA
RIGOURS
RIPOFFS
RIPOSTE
RISOTTO
SILOING
SIROCCO
TIMOTHY
TIPOFFS
VIGOURS
WIDOWED

WIDOWER

•I••O••

AIRBOAT
AIRCOOL
AIRFOIL
AIRHOLE
AIRLOCK
AIRPORT
AIRSOCK
AIRSOUT
AIRWOLF
BIGBOYS
BIGFOOT
BIGHORN
BIGJOHN
BIGTOES
BIGTOPS
BILBOES
BILIOUS
BILLOWS
BILLOWY
BINGOES
BIOLOGY
BISHOPS
BITEOFF
CITROEN
CITRONS
DIALOGS
DIAMOND
DIATOMS
DIDGOOD
DIEDOFF
DIEDOUT
DIEDOWN
DIESOFF
DIESOUT
DIGSOUT
DINGOES
DINMONT
DIPLOID
DIPLOMA
DISCOED
DISCORD
DISHOUT
DISJOIN
DISPORT
DISPOSE
DISROBE
DISTORT
DITTOED
FIBROUS
FILLOUT
FINDOUT
FIREOFF
FISHOUT
GIACOMO
GIBBONS
GIBBOUS
GIDEONS
GIFFORD
GILMORE
GIVEOFF
GIVEOUT
HICKORY
HIDEOUS
HIDEOUT
HILLOCK
HIPBONE
HIPBOOT
HIPROOF
HISTORY
JIBBOOM
JINGOES
KICKOFF
KICKOUT
KINFOLK
KISSOFF
LIEDOWN
LIFTOFF
LIMPOPO
LINCOLN
LINGOES
LIQUORS
LISSOME
LIVEOAK
LIVEONE
LIVEOUT
MICROBE
MICRONS
MIDTOWN
MINEOLA
MINIONS
MINNOWS
MIRRORS
MISDOES
MISDONE
MISSOUT
MISTOOK
MISWORD
MITFORD
NICCOLO
NICHOLS
NIMRODS
NITROUS
PICCOLO
PICKOFF
PICKOUT
PIGEONS
PIGSOUT
PILLORY
PILLOWS
PILLOWY
PINDOWN
PINHOLE
PINIONS
PISCOPO
PISTOLE
PISTOLS
PISTONS
PITBOSS
PITEOUS
RIBBONS
RIDEOFF
RIDEOUT
RINGOUT
RIOLOBO
RIOTOUS
RIPCORD
RIPSOFF
RIPTORN
RISSOLE
SICKOUT
SIGNOFF
SIGNOUT
SIMMONS
SINGOUT
SINUOUS
SIPHONS
SIRLOIN
SITCOMS
SITDOWN
SITSOUT
SIXFOLD
TICKOFF
TIEDOWN
TIERODS
TIMEOFF
TIMEOUT
TINFOIL
TINHORN
TINWORK
TIPSOFF
TIPTOED
TIPTOES
TIPTOPS
TIREOUT
VICIOUS
VICTORS
VICTORY
VIRGOAN
VISCOUS
VISIONS
WIGSOUT
WILDONE
WILFORD
WILLOWS
WILLOWY
WINDOWS
WINKOUT
WINNOWS
WINSOME
WINSOUT
WIPEOUT
WITHOUT
ZIPCODE
ZIRCONS

•I•••O•

AILERON
AIRCOOL
AIRDROP
AIRFLOW
AIRSHOW
BIBELOT
BICOLOR
BIENTOT
BIGELOW
BIGFOOT
BIGSHOT
BILLION
BIRDDOG
BISTROS
DICTION
DIDEROT
DIDGOOD
DINEDON
DINESON
DISAVOW
DIVISOR
FIASCOS
FICTION
FIEFDOM
FIREBOX
FIREDOG
FISSION
GIGOLOS
GIRASOL
HIGHBOY
HIGHLOW
HIGHTOP
HILLTOP
HIPBOOT
HIPROOF
HIRESON
JIBBOOM
JILLION
KILLJOY
KILOTON
KIMONOS
KINGDOM
LIAISON
LIBIDOS
LIESLOW
LITHGOW
LIVEDON
LIVESON
MIKADOS
MILKCOW
MILKSOP
MILLION
MIRADOR
MISSION
MISTOOK
NILSSON
PICADOR
PICAROS
PICKSON
PIDGEON
PIERROT
PIGIRON
PILEDON
PILESON
PILLBOX
PILLION
PIMESON
PINEFOR
PITSTOP
RIGHTON
RIMSHOT
SIGNSON
SILICON
SIMENON
SIMPSON
TIMECOP
TIREDOF
VICEROY
VIRAGOS
VISITOR
VITRIOL
WIDGEON
WILLSON
WINDROW
WINDSOR
WINSLOW
WINSTON
ZILLION

•I••••O

AIMEDTO
CINZANO
FIDELIO
GIACOMO
GIORGIO
GIVENTO
GIVESTO
HIDALGO
HISPANO
LIMPOPO
LINBIAO
LITINTO
NICCOLO
PICASSO
PICCOLO
PIMENTO
PIMLICO
PISCOPO
PIZARRO
RICARDO
RIOLOBO
RIPINTO
RISOTTO
SINGSTO
SIROCCO
TIEINTO
VIBRATO

••IO•••

ARIOSOS
ARIOSTO
BRIOCHE
IDIOTIC
MEIOSES
MEIOSIS
MEIOTIC
OHIOANS
ORIOLES
PRIORTO
TRIODES

••I•O••

ADIPOSE
ALIMONY
ARIZONA
BAILORS
BAILOUT
BRITONS
CHICORY
CHINOOK
CLIPONS
CRINOID
CUIBONO
EDITORS
EPIGONE
EPILOGS
EPISODE
EPITOME
FAIROFF
GUIDONS
HEINOUS
IRISOUT
LAIDOFF
LAIDOUT
NAIROBI
NOISOME
OMINOUS
ORINOCO
ORISONS
PAIDOFF
PAIDOUT
PAILOUS
PAIROFF
POISONS
PRISONS
QUINOAS
QUIXOTE
RAINOUT
RHIZOME
RUINOUS
SAILORS
SHIPOUT
SKIBOOT
SKIPOLE
SKIPOUT
SKITOWS
SLIPONS
SLIPOUT
SPIGOTS
SPINOFF
SPINOUT
SPINOZA
SUITORS
TAILOFF
TAILORS
TRICORN
TRICOTS
TRIGONS
TRILOGY
TRIPODS
TRIPOLI
TRITONE
TRITONS
UNICORN
UNIFORM
UNIPODS
UNISONS
WAITOUT

••I••O•

ALIENOR
ARIOSOS
ARISTOS
AVIATOR
AVIGNON
BRINGON
BRISTOL
BRITTON
BUILDON
BUILTON
CAISSON
CHIFFON
CHIGNON
CHINOOK
CLIFTON
CLINTON
CRIMSON
EDITION
ELISION
ERICSON
FRISSON
GAINSON
GOINFOR
GOINGON
GRIFFON
GRISSOM
HAIRDOS
KEILLOR
KLINGON
LAIDFOR
LAIDLOW
MAILBOX
MAILLOT
MAINTOP
OMICRON
OPINION
PAIDFOR
POISSON
RAINBOW
SCISSOR
SKIBOOT
SKIDDOO
SKIDROW
SPIEDON
SPIESON
STILTON
THINKOF
TRIEDON
TRIESON
TUITION
WAITSON
WEIRDOS

••I•••O

AKIHITO
ANIMATO
ARIOSTO
BOITANO
BRINGTO
CHICAGO
CHICANO
CLINGTO
CUIBONO
HEIGHHO
LYINGTO
ORINOCO
OWINGTO
PAISANO
POINTTO
PRIORTO
SKIDDOO
SPIRITO
STICKTO
WRITETO
ZHIVAGO

•••IO••

ACTIONS
AMNIONS
ANTIOCH
ANXIOUS
APRIORI
BILIOUS
BUNIONS
CARIOCA
CATIONS
COPIOUS
CURIOUS
DEVIOUS
DUBIOUS
ENVIOUS
FANIONS
FURIOUS
IMPIOUS
JUNIORS
LEGIONS
LOTIONS
MAFIOSO
MINIONS
MOTIONS
NATIONS
NOTIONS
NOXIOUS
OBVIOUS
OPTIONS
PAVIOUR
PERIODS
PETIOLE
PINIONS
POTIONS
RADIOED
RATIONS
RAVIOLI
REGIONS
SAVIORS
SENIORS
SERIOUS
TAPIOCA
TEDIOUS
VARIOUS
VICIOUS
VISIONS

•••I•O•

ADDISON
ADVISOR
ALBINOS
ALLISON
ANDIRON
ANTILOG
APRICOT
AUDITOR
BENISON
BONITOS
CALICOS
CAPITOL
CARIBOU
CASINOS
CLAIROL
COPILOT
DEMIGOD
DIVISOR
DOMINOS
DORITOS
DOSIDOS
ELEISON
ELLISON
EPSILON
EQUINOX
ESKIMOS
GERITOL
GETITON
HARICOT
HELICON
HORIZON
HUMIDOR
INCISOR
INDIGOS
JANITOR
LADINOS
LATINOS
LETINON
LEXICON
LIAISON
LIBIDOS
MADISON
MAGINOT
MANILOW
MANITOU
MEDICOS
MERINOS
MONITOR
ORBISON
PERIDOT
PIGIRON
RUBICON
SILICON
TRAITOR
UPSILON
USTINOV
VENISON
VISITOR

•••I••O

CHRISTO
CUTINTO
DOMINGO
GALILEO
GETINTO
GOTINTO
INVITRO
JACINTO
JALISCO
JERICHO
LAYINTO
LITINTO
LUCIANO
MAFIOSO
MURILLO
NABISCO
ORNITHO
PRYINTO
PUTITTO
RANINTO
RELIEVO
RIPINTO
RUNINTO
SEMIPRO
SETINTO
TIEINTO
UTRILLO

••••IO•

ADAGIOS
ANTLION
AUCTION
BARRIOS
BASTION
BERLIOZ
BILLION
BLERIOT
BULLION
CAMPION
CAPTION
CARRION
CAUTION
CESSION
CHARIOT
CHEVIOT
CLARION
CUSHION
CYPRIOT
DICTION
EDITION
ELATION
ELISION
ELUTION
EMOTION
EROSION
EVASION
FACTION
FASHION
FICTION
FISSION
GRUNION
HELLION
HERRIOT
JILLION
KRATION
MANSION
MARMION
MENTION
MILLION
MISSION
MULLION
NUNCIOS
OPINION
ORATION
OVATION
PASSION
PATRIOT
PENSION
PILLION
PLOSION
PORTION
RANRIOT
REUNION
RUCTION
RUNRIOT
SEALION
SECTION
SESSION
STATION
STUDIOS
SUASION
SUCTION
TENSION
TORSION
TSELIOT
TUITION
UNCTION
VERSION
VITRIOL
WARRIOR
ZILLION

••••I•O

AKIHITO
AMERIGO
BAMBINO
BANDITO
BURRITO
BUSHIDO
CENTIMO
CHORIZO
GALLICO
JANEIRO
LINBIAO
MARTINO
MESTIZO
PIMLICO
PLACIDO
PORTICO
PROVISO
PROXIMO
SERPICO
SHAPIRO
SPIRITO
TAMPICO
TREVINO
VERTIGO

•••••IO

AMRADIO
ANTONIO
ARSENIO
CBRADIO
CHEERIO
CLAUDIO
CONBRIO
FIDELIO
FMRADIO
GIORGIO
HORATIO
ONTARIO
SCORPIO

IP•••••

IPANEMA
IPCRESS
IPSWICH

I•P••••

IMPACTS
IMPAIRS
IMPALAS
IMPALED
IMPALES
IMPANEL
IMPARTS
IMPASSE
IMPASTO
IMPEACH
IMPEDED
IMPEDES
IMPENDS
IMPERIL
IMPETUS
IMPIETY
IMPINGE
IMPIOUS
IMPLANT
IMPLIED
IMPLIES
IMPLODE
IMPLORE
IMPORTS
IMPOSED
IMPOSES
IMPOSTS
IMPOUND
IMPRESS
IMPRINT
IMPROVE
IMPUGNS
IMPULSE
IMPURER
IMPUTED
IMPUTES
INPEACE
INPETTO
INPHASE
INPLACE
INPOINT
INPRINT

I••P•••

ICEPACK
ICEPICK
INAPTLY
INEPTLY
INSPANS
INSPECT
INSPIRE
INSPOTS
ISOPODS

I•••P••

INASPIN
INASPOT
INCEPTS
INCIPIT
INDEPTH
INKSPOT
INSIPID
IRRUPTS

I••••P•

ICECAPS
INSCAPE
INSHAPE
INSTEPS
ISOTOPE

I•••••P

INAHEAP
INGROUP
INKYCAP

•IP••••

BIPEDAL
BIPLANE
BIPOLAR
CIPHERS
DIPLOID
DIPLOMA
DIPOLAR
DIPOLES
DIPPERS
DIPPING
DIPTYCH
FIPPLES
GIPSIES
HIPBONE
HIPBOOT
HIPNESS
HIPPEST
HIPPIES
HIPROOF
HIPSTER
KIPLING
KIPPERS
LIPBALM
LIPPIER
LIPPING
LIPREAD
LIPSYNC
NIPPERS
NIPPIER
NIPPING
PIPEDUP
PIPEFUL
PIPESUP
PIPETTE
PIPINGS
PIPKINS
PIPPINS
RIPCORD
RIPENED
RIPINTO
RIPOFFS
RIPOSTE
RIPPERS
RIPPING
RIPPLED
RIPPLES
RIPRAPS
RIPSAWS
RIPSOFF
RIPTIDE
RIPTORN
SIPHONS
SIPPERS
SIPPETS
SIPPING
TIPOFFS
TIPPERS
TIPPETS
TIPPING
TIPPLED
TIPPLER
TIPPLES
TIPSIER
TIPSILY
TIPSOFF
TIPSTER
TIPTOED
TIPTOES
TIPTOPS
WIPEDUP
WIPEOUT
WIPESUP
YIPPING
ZIPCODE
ZIPPERS
ZIPPIER
ZIPPING

•I•P•••

AIRPLAY
AIRPORT
AIRPUMP
BITPART
DIAPERS
DIMPLED
DIMPLES
DIOPTER
DIPPERS
DIPPING
DISPELS
DISPLAY
DISPORT
DISPOSE
DISPUTE
FIPPLES
HIPPEST
HIPPIES
HISPANO
KIPPERS
LIMPEST
LIMPETS
LIMPING
LIMPOPO
LIPPIER
LIPPING
LISPING
MISPLAY
NIPPERS
NIPPIER
NIPPING
NITPICK
OILPANS
PIEPANS
PIGPENS
PIPPINS
RIPPERS
RIPPING
RIPPLED
RIPPLES
SIMPERS
SIMPLER
SIMPLEX
SIMPSON
SIPPERS
SIPPETS
SIPPING
SIXPACK
TIEPINS
TIPPERS
TIPPETS
TIPPING
TIPPLED
TIPPLER
TIPPLES
WIMPLED
WIMPLES
WISPIER
WISPILY
WISPING
YIPPING
ZIPPERS
ZIPPIER
ZIPPING

•I••P••

DISHPAN
KINGPIN
LILYPAD
PITAPAT
SICKPAY

•I•••P•

BIGTOPS
BISHOPS
BITMAPS
DIGRAPH
DISRUPT
FILLIPS
FILLUPS

GIVEUPS
HICCUPS
KICKUPS
KIDNAPS
LIMPOPO
LINEUPS
LINKUPS
MISHAPS
MISTYPE
PICKUPS
PILEUPS
PISCOPO
RIPRAPS
TINTYPE
TIPTOPS
WINDUPS

•I••••P
AIRDROP
AIRPUMP
AIRSHIP
BINDSUP
FILLSUP
FIREDUP
FIRESUP
FIRMSUP
FIXEDUP
FIXESUP
GIDDYAP
GIDDYUP
GIVESUP
HIGHTOP
HILLTOP
KICKSUP
KINSHIP
LIFTSUP
LIGHTUP
LINEDUP
LINESUP
MILKSOP
MISSTEP
MIXEDUP
MIXESUP
MIXITUP
OILLAMP
PICKSUP
PILEDUP
PILESUP
PINESAP
PIPEDUP
PIPESUP
PITSTOP
RINGSUP
SIGNSUP
SIZEDUP
SIZESUP
TIECLIP
TIMECOP
TIMESUP
WICKIUP
WINDSUP
WINESAP
WINGTIP
WIPEDUP
WIPESUP
WIRETAP
WISEDUP
WISESUP

••IP•••
ADIPOSE
BLIPPED
CHIPPED
CHIPPER
CHIPSIN
CLIPART
CLIPONS
CLIPPED
CLIPPER
DRIPDRY
DRIPPAN
DRIPPED
FLIPPED
FLIPPER
FLIPUPS
GRIPERS
GRIPING
GRIPPED
GRIPPER
LEIPZIG
QUIPPED
QUIPPER
SHIPMAN
SHIPMEN
SHIPOUT
SHIPPED
SHIPPER
SKIPOLE
SKIPOUT
SKIPPED
SKIPPER
SLIPONS
SLIPOUT
SLIPPED
SLIPPER
SLIPSUP
SLIPUPS
SNIPEAT
SNIPING
SNIPPED
SNIPPET
STIPEND
STIPPLE
SWIPERS
SWIPING
TAIPANS
TRIPLED
TRIPLES
TRIPLET
TRIPLEX
TRIPODS
TRIPOLI
TRIPPED
TRIPPER
TRIPPET
TRIPSUP
UNIPODS
WHIPPED
WHIPPET
WHIPSAW
WHIPSUP

••I•P••
BLIPPED
CHIPPED
CHIPPER
CHIRPED
CLIPPED
CLIPPER
CRIMPED
CRIMPER
CRISPED
CRISPER
CRISPIN
CRISPLY
CRISPUS
DRIPPAN
DRIPPED
FLIPPED
FLIPPER
GLIMPSE
GRIPPED
GRIPPER
GUIMPES
HAIRPIN
PRIMPED
QUIPPED
QUIPPER
SHIPPED
SHIPPER
SKIMPED
SKIPPED
SKIPPER
SLIPPED
SLIPPER
SNIPPED
SNIPPET
STIPPLE
TRIPPED
TRIPPER
TRIPPET
WHIMPER
WHIPPED
WHIPPET
WHISPER

••I••P•
CHINUPS
FLIPUPS
SLIPUPS
TRICEPS
TRIUMPH

••I•••P
BRINGUP
BUILDUP
BUILTUP
COILSUP
DOINGUP
DRIEDUP
DRIESUP
DRIVEUP
FAIRSUP
GOINGUP
JOINSUP
JUICEUP
MAINTOP
PAIRSUP
PHILLIP
RAISEUP
SKIJUMP
SLIPSUP
SPICEUP
STICKUP
STIRRUP
STIRSUP
SUITSUP
THINKUP
TRIPSUP
TYINGUP
USINGUP
WAITSUP
WHIPSUP
WRITEUP

•••IP••
AGRIPPA
CALIPER
CALIPHS
CERIPHS
ECLIPSE
ELLIPSE
HELIPAD
INCIPIT
INSIPID
JUNIPER
MANIPLE
OCCIPUT
OEDIPAL
OEDIPUS
RECIPES
SCRIPPS
SCRIPTS
SEMIPRO
STRIPED
STRIPER
STRIPES
TRAIPSE

•••I•P•
AGRIPPA
SCRIMPS
SCRIMPY
SCRIPPS
SHRIMPS

•••I••P
HAMITUP
MIXITUP
SPLITUP

••••IP•
BAGPIPE
CATNIPS
FILLIPS
GOSSIPS
GOSSIPY
HOTLIPS
HOTTIPS
MRCHIPS
PANPIPE
RECEIPT
RESHIPS
TURNIPS

••••I•P
RYKRISP
WICKIUP

•••••IP
AIRSHIP
COWSLIP
DAYTRIP
EGOTRIP
FOULTIP
KINSHIP
LETSLIP
NONSLIP
PARSNIP
PHILLIP
TIECLIP
WARSHIP
WINGTIP
WORSHIP

IQ•••••
IQTESTS

I•Q••••
INQUEST
INQUIRE
INQUIRY

•IQ••••
LIQUEFY
LIQUEUR
LIQUIDS
LIQUORS
PIQUANT
PIQUING

•I•Q•••
BISQUES
CIRQUES

••IQ•••
BRIQUET
CAIQUES
CLIQUES

••I•Q••
QUINQUE

•••IQ••
ANTIQUE
BEZIQUE
COMIQUE
LALIQUE
MONIQUE
OBLIQUE

IR•••••
IRANIAN
IRATELY
IRATEST
IRECKON
IRELAND
IRIDIUM
IRISOUT
IRKSOME
IRONAGE
IRONERS
IRONIES
IRONING
IRONMAN
IRONMEN
IRONORE
IRONOUT
IRRUPTS

I•R••••
INROADS
IRRUPTS
ISRAELI

I••R•••
IBERIAN
ICERINK
IMARETS
IMBRUED
IMBRUES
IMPRESS
IMPRINT
IMPROVE
INARUSH
INBREED
INBRIEF
INERROR
INERTIA
INERTLY
INFRONT
INGRAIN
INGRATE
INGRESS
INGROUP
INGROWN
INORBIT
INPRINT
INTROIT
INTRUDE
INTRUST
INTRUTH
INURING
IPCRESS
ITERANT
ITERATE
IVORIES

I•••R••
ICEFREE
IDCARDS
IGNORED
IGNORER
IGNORES
ILLBRED
IMMERSE
IMMORAL
IMMURED
IMMURES
IMPARTS
IMPERIL
IMPORTS
IMPURER
IMSORRY
INERROR
INFERNO
INFORCE
INFORMS
INHERED
INHERES
INHERIT
INJURED
INJURES
INNARDS
INSERTS
INSURED
INSURES
INTERIM
INTERNS
INTERSE
INVERSE
INVERTS
INWARDS

I••••R•
ICEBERG
IMAGERS
IMAGERY
IMPAIRS
IMPLORE
IMSORRY
INAWORD
INBOARD
INDOORS
INKHORN
INQUIRE
INQUIRY
INSHORT
INSPIRE
INSTORE
INTEGRA
INVITRO
IRONERS
IRONORE
ISADORA
ISOBARS
ISOMERS
ISSUERS

I•••••R
IGNITER
IGNORER
IMPURER
INCISOR
INCITER
INDUCER
INERROR
INFAVOR
INGEMAR
INHALER
INSIDER
INSOFAR
INSULAR
INTEGER
INTONER
INVADER
INVOKER
IONIZER
ITCHIER

•IR••••
AIRBAGS
AIRBALL
AIRBASE
AIRBOAT
AIRCOOL
AIRCREW
AIRDAMS
AIRDATE
AIRDROP
AIRFARE
AIRFLOW
AIRFOIL
AIRGUNS
AIRHEAD
AIRHOLE
AIRIEST
AIRINGS
AIRLANE
AIRLESS
AIRLIFT
AIRLINE
AIRLOCK
AIRMAIL
AIRMASS
AIRMILE
AIRPLAY
AIRPORT
AIRPUMP
AIRRAID
AIRSACS
AIRSHIP
AIRSHOW
AIRSOCK
AIRSOUT
AIRTAXI
AIRTIME
AIRWAVE
AIRWAYS
AIRWOLF
BIRCHED
BIRCHES
BIRDDOG
BIRDERS
BIRDIED
BIRDIES
BIRDING
BIRDMAN
BIRDMEN
BIREMES
BIRETTA
BIRLING
BIRTHED
CIRCLED
CIRCLES
CIRCLET
CIRCUIT
CIRCUSY
CIRQUES
DIRECTS
DIRNDLS
DIRTIED
DIRTIER
DIRTIES
DIRTILY
FIREANT
FIREARM
FIREBOX
FIREBUG
FIREDOG
FIREDUP
FIREFLY
FIRELIT
FIREMAN
FIREMEN
FIRENZE
FIREOFF
FIRESUP
FIRINGS
FIRKINS
FIRMEST
FIRMING
FIRMSUP
FIRSTLY
GIRAFFE
GIRASOL
GIRDERS
GIRDING
GIRDLED
GIRDLES
GIRLISH
GIRONDE
HIRABLE
HIRESON
HIRSUTE
KIRMANS
KIRSTIE
KIRTLES
MIRACLE
MIRADOR
MIRAGES
MIRAMAR
MIRAMAX
MIRANDA
MIRRORS
NIRVANA
PIRAEUS
PIRANHA
PIRATED
PIRATES
PIRATIC
PIROGUE
SIRLOIN
SIROCCO
TIRADES
TIREDER
TIREDLY
TIREDOF
TIREOUT
VIRAGOS
VIRGINS
VIRGOAN
VIRGULE
VIRTUAL
VIRTUES
VIRUSES
WIRETAP
WIRIEST
ZIRCONS

•I•R•••
AIGRETS
AIRRAID
CITRATE
CITRINE
CITROEN
CITRONS
DIARIES
DIGRAPH
DIGRESS
DIORAMA
DISROBE
DISRUPT
DIURNAL
FIBRILS
FIBROUS
FIERCER
FIERIER
FIERILY
GIORGIO
HIPROOF
JIMRYUN
LIBRARY
LIERNES
LIPREAD
MICROBE
MICRONS
MIDRIBS
MIDRIFF
MIDRISE
MIGRANT
MIGRATE
MIRRORS
MISREAD
MISRULE
MITRING
NIMRODS
NITRATE
NITRIDE
NITRITE
NITROUS
OILRIGS
PIERCED
PIERCES
PIERROT
RIORITA
RIPRAPS
SIERRAS
TIERACK
TIERING
TIERNEY
TIERODS
TIGRESS
TITRATE
VIBRANT
VIBRATE
VIBRATO
VITRIFY
VITRIOL

•I••R••
AILERON
AIRCREW
AIRDROP
BISTROS
BIZARRE
CIBORIA
DIAGRAM
DIDEROT
DISARMS
DISHRAG
DIVERGE
DIVERSE
DIVERTS
DIVORCE
FIACRES
FIGURED
FIGURER
FIGURES
KINDRED
KINGRAT
LIBERAL
LIBERIA
LIBERTY
LITERAL
LITURGY
LIZARDS
MILDRED
MILKRUN
MILLRUN
MILORDS
MINARET
MINERAL
MINERVA
MINORCA
MINORED
MISERLY
MISTRAL
MITERED
MITHRAS
NIGERIA
PICAROS
PIERROT
PIGIRON
PILGRIM
PIZARRO
RICARDO
RICERAT
SIBERIA
SIERRAS
SISTRUM
TIMBRES
VICEROY
WILFRID
WINDROW
WINERED
WINFREY
WIZARDS

•I•••R•
AIRFARE
AIRPORT
BICKERS
BIDDERS
BIGBIRD
BIGGERS
BIGHORN
BIGOTRY
BINDERS
BINDERY
BIRDERS
BITPART
BITTERN
BITTERS
BIZARRE
CINDERS
CIPHERS
CISTERN
DIALERS
DIAPERS
DICKERS
DIEHARD
DIETARY
DIETERS
DIFFERS
DIGGERS
DILLARD
DIMITRI
DIMMERS
DINNERS
DIPPERS
DISBARS
DISCARD
DISCERN
DISCORD
DISPORT
DISTORT
DISTURB
DITHERS
DITHERY
FIBBERS
FILBERT
FILLERS
FILTERS
FINDERS
FINEART
FINGERS
FIREARM
FISHERS
FISHERY
FISHFRY
FISSURE
FITTERS
FIXTURE
GIBBERS
GIFFORD
GILBERT
GILDERS
GILMORE
GINGERS
GINGERY
GIRDERS
GIZZARD
HICKORY
HILAIRE
HILLARY
HINDERS
HISSERS
HISTORY
HITHERE
HITTERS
JIGGERS
JIGGERY
JITTERS
JITTERY
KICKERS
KIDDERS
KILDARE
KILLERS
KIPPERS
KISSERS
LIBBERS
LIBRARY
LIFTERS
LIMBERS
LIMNERS
LINGERS
LINKERS
LIQUORS
LITTERS
MIDTERM
MILKERS
MILLARD
MILLERS
MIMICRY
MINCERS
MINDERS
MINTERS
MIRRORS
MISFIRE
MISTERS
MISWORD
MITFORD
MIXTURE
NIAGARA
NICKERS
NIGGARD
NIPPERS
PIASTRE
PICCARD
PICKERS
PICTURE
PIECERS
PILFERS
PILLARS
PILLORY
PINCERS
PINCURL
PINNERS
PISMIRE
PITTERS
PIZARRO
QINTARS
RICHARD
RIFLERS
RIFLERY
RIGGERS
RIGOURS
RINGERS
RIOTERS
RIPCORD
RIPPERS
RIPTORN
RISKERS
RIVALRY
RIVIERA
RIVIERE
SIDEARM
SIFTERS
SIGHERS
SIGNERS
SILVERS
SILVERY
SIMMERS
SIMPERS
SINATRA
SINCERE
SINGERS
SINKERS
SINNERS
SIPPERS
SISTERS
SITTERS
TICKERS
TILLERS
TILTERS
TIMBERS
TINDERS
TINEARS
TINHORN
TINKERS
TINNERS
TINTERN
TINTERS
TINWORK
TIPPERS
TITHERS
TITTERS
VICTORS
VICTORY
VIEWERS
VIGOURS
VISCERA
VIZIERS
WICKERS
WIDMARK
WIENERS
WILFORD
WILLARD
WINCERS
WINDERS
WINGERS
WINKERS
WINNERS
WINTERS
WINTERY
WISHERS
WITHERS
ZINGERS
ZIPPERS
ZITHERS

•I••••R
BICOLOR
BIDFAIR
BIPOLAR
BITTIER
DIDOVER
DILUTER
DINGIER
DINKIER
DIOPTER
DIPOLAR
DIRTIER
DIVIDER
DIVINER
DIVISOR
DIZZIER
FICKLER
FIDDLER
FIEDLER
FIELDER
FIERCER
FIERIER
FIGHTER
FIGURER
FILCHER
FILMIER
FISCHER
FISHIER
FIZZIER
GIDDIER
GIGGLER
HILLIER
HIPSTER
HITCHER
KINKIER
LIBELER
LIEOVER
LIGHTER
LINTIER
LIPPIER
LIQUEUR
LITTLER
MIDYEAR
MILKIER
MINGLER
MINIVER
MINTIER
MIRADOR

MIRAMAR
MISHEAR
MISTIER
NIBBLER
NIEBUHR
NIFTIER
NIMBLER
NIPPIER
PIASTER
PICADOR
PICKIER
PILSNER
PINCHER
PINEFOR
PINETAR
PIONEER
PITCHER
PITHIER
RICHTER
RIDDLER
RIGHTER
RISKIER
RITZIER
RIVETER
SIDEBAR
SIDECAR
SILKIER
SILLIER
SIMILAR
SIMPLER
TICKLER
TIGHTER
TIMIDER
TINNIER
TINSTAR
TIPPLER
TIPSIER
TIPSTER
TIREDER
TITULAR
VINEGAR
VINTNER
VISITOR
VIVIDER
WIDOWER
WIGGLER
WINDIER
WINDSOR
WINEBAR
WINKLER
WISPIER
WITTIER
ZINGIER
ZIPPIER

••IR•••

CHIRPED
CUIRASS
DAIRIES
EMIRATE
FAIREST
FAIRIES
FAIRING
FAIROFF
FAIRSUP
FAIRWAY
FLIRTED
HAIRCUT
HAIRDOS
HAIRDYE
HAIRIER
HAIRNET
HAIRPIN
HEIRESS
NAIROBI
PAIRING
PAIROFF
PAIRSUP
SHIRKED
SHIRKER
SHIRLEY
SHIRRED
SKIRLED
SKIRRED
SKIRTED
SKIRUNS
SMIRKED
SOIREES
SPIRALS
SPIRANT
SPIREAS
SPIRITO
SPIRITS
STIRFRY
STIRRED
STIRRER
STIRRUP
STIRSIN
STIRSUP
SWIRLED
THIRDLY
THIRSTS
THIRSTY
TRIREME
TWIRLED
TWIRLER
WEIRDER
WEIRDLY
WEIRDOS
WHIRLED
WHIRRED

••I•R••

BRIARDS
EMIGRES
EPIGRAM
ERITREA
GRIGRIS
MAIGRET
MAITRED
OMICRON
PRIORTO
SHIRRED
SKIDROW
SKIRRED
STIRRED
STIRRER
STIRRUP
THIERRY
TRIGRAM
WHIRRED

••I••R•

ARIKARA
BAILERS
BAILORS
BOILERS
BRIBERY
CHICORY
CHIMERA
CLIBURN
CLIPART
COINERS
DEICERS
DRIPDRY
DRIVERS
EDITORS
ELIXIRS
EPICURE
FAILURE
GAINERS
GAITERS
GLIDERS
GRIPERS
GUITARS
HEIFERS
JAILERS
JOINERS
JOINERY
JUICERS
KAISERS
LEISURE
LOITERS
MAILERS
MOILERS
NAILERS
OPINERS
PHILTRE
PRICERS
PRIMARY
PRIMERS
QUIVERS
RAIDERS
RAILERS
RAISERS
RUINERS
SAILORS
SEINERS
SEIZERS
SHINERS
SHIVERS
SKIVERS
SLICERS
SLIDERS
SLIVERS
SMILERS
SPIDERS
SPIDERY
SPIKERS
STIRFRY
SUITORS
SWIPERS
TAILORS
THIERRY
TOILERS
TRICORN
UNICORN
UNIFORM
UNITARY
UNITERS
WAILERS
WAITERS
WAIVERS
WHINERS
WRITERS

••I•••R

ALIENOR
ALIGNER
AVIATOR
BLINDER
BLINKER
BLISTER
BLITHER
BRIEFER
BRINGER
BRINIER
BRISKER
BUILDER
CHIGGER
CHILLER
CHIPPER
CHITTER
CLIMBER
CLINKER
CLIPPER
CRIMPER
CRISPER
CRITTER
DAIMLER
DRIFTER
DRILLER
DRINKER
EMITTER
EVILLER
FAINTER
FEIFFER
FLICKER
FLIPPER
FLITTER
FLIVVER
FRITTER
GLIBBER
GLIMMER
GLITTER
GOINFOR
GRIDDER
GRIEVER
GRIFTER
GRIMIER
GRIMMER
GRINDER
GRINNER
GRIPPER
GUILDER
HAIRIER
JOINDER
JUICIER
KEILLOR
KNITTER
LAIDFOR
LEISTER
MOISTER
NEITHER
NOISIER
OLIVIER
PAIDFOR
PAINTER
PHILTER
POINTER
POITIER
PRICIER
PRIMMER
PRINTER
QUICKER
QUIETER
QUILTER
QUIPPER
QUITTER
RAINIER
ROISTER
SCISSOR
SHIMMER
SHINIER
SHIPPER
SHIRKER
SKIDDER
SKIMMER
SKINNER
SKIPPER
SKITTER
SLICKER
SLIMIER
SLIMMER
SLINGER
SLIPPER
SLITHER
SNICKER
SNIFFER
SNIFTER
SNIGGER
SPICIER
SPIELER
SPIKIER
SPINIER
SPINNER
STICKER
STIFFER
STILLER
STINGER
STINKER
STIRRER
SWIFTER
SWIMMER
SWINGER
SWITZER
TEICHER
THICKER
THINAIR
THINKER
THINNER
THITHER
TRICKER
TRIFLER
TRIGGER
TRIMMER
TRIPPER
TWIRLER
TWISTER
TWITTER
UNIFIER
WEIRDER
WHIMPER
WHISKER
WHISPER
WHITHER
WRINGER

•••IR••

ADMIRAL
ADMIRED
ADMIRER
ADMIRES
AFFIRMS
ANDIRON
ASPIRED
ASPIRER
ASPIRES
ASPIRIN
ATHIRST
ATTIRED
ATTIRES
BEMIRED
BEMIRES
CHAIRED
CLAIROL
DELIRIA
DESIRED
DESIREE
DESIRES
EMPIRES
ENGIRDS
EXPIRED
EXPIRES
HEGIRAS
JABIRUS
PIGIRON
PRAIRIE
REAIRED
REBIRTH
REFIRES
REHIRED
REHIRES
RETIRED
RETIREE
RETIRES
REWIRED
REWIRES
SATIRES
SATIRIC
SCHIRRA
SQUIRED
SQUIRES
SQUIRMS
SQUIRMY
SQUIRTS
TSHIRTS
UMPIRED
UMPIRES
UNAIRED
UNGIRDS

•••I•R•

ALFIERI
ALGIERS
ANTIART
APRIORI
ARRIERE
BEZIERS
CAHIERS
CALIBRE
COPIERS
DENIERS
DEVILRY
DIMITRI
HOSIERS
HOSIERY
INVITRO
JUNIORS
LEVIERS
LUMIERE
METIERS
MIMICRY
MOLIERE
PONIARD
RAPIERS
RIVIERA
RIVIERE
SALIERI
SAVIORS
SCHIRRA
SEMIPRO
SENIORS
TOPIARY
VIZIERS

•••I••R

ADMIRER
ADVISER
ADVISOR
ANTIWAR
AQUIFER
AQUIVER
ARBITER
ARRIVER
ASPIRER
AUDITOR
BOLIVAR
BRAIDER
BROILER
BRUISER
CALIBER
CALIPER
CAVILER
CHOICER
CLAIMER
CONIFER
CRUISER
DEFILER
DELIVER
DIVIDER
DIVINER
DIVISOR
DRAINER
DREISER
ENTICER
FRAILER
HUMIDOR
IGNITER
INCISOR
INCITER
INSIDER
IONIZER
JANITOR
JUNIPER
JUPITER
LAMINAR
LUCIFER
MARINER
MINIVER
MONIKER
MONITOR
OFFICER
ORBITER
PAVIOUR
PLAINER
POLITER
PRAISER
RAPIDER
RECITER
REFINER
REVISER
ROTIFER
SEMINAR
SHRINER
SHRIVER
SIMILAR
SOLIDER
SPLICER
SPOILER
STAIDER
STAINER
STEIGER
STEINER
STRIDER
STRIKER
STRIPER
STRIVER
TIMIDER
TRAILER
TRAINER
TRAITOR
UNWISER
UPRIVER
VISITOR
VIVIDER

••••IR•

ACQUIRE
AFFAIRE
AFFAIRS
ARMOIRE
ASTAIRE
BESTIRS
BIGBIRD
BONFIRE
CATBIRD
COHEIRS
CONFIRM
COWBIRD
COWGIRL
DUNKIRK
ECLAIRS
ELIXIRS
ESQUIRE
FOXFIRE
GUNFIRE
HAYWIRE
HILAIRE
HOTWIRE
IMPAIRS
INQUIRE
INQUIRY
INSPIRE
JANEIRO
JAYBIRD
LEMPIRA
MADEIRA
MCGUIRE
MEMOIRE
MEMOIRS
MENHIRS
MISFIRE
MOHAIRS
PAYDIRT
PISMIRE
REDBIRD
REDFIRS
REPAIRS
REQUIRE
RESPIRE
SANTIRS
SEABIRD
SEAGIRT
SELKIRK
SHAPIRO
VAMPIRE

••••I•R

ANGRIER
ANTSIER
ATELIER
BAGGIER
BALKIER
BALMIER
BARMIER
BARRIER
BATTIER
BAWDIER
BEADIER
BEAMIER
BEEFIER
BITTIER
BLOWIER
BONNIER
BOSSIER
BRAZIER
BRINIER
BUGGIER
BULKIER
BUMPIER
BURLIER
BUSHIER
CAMPIER
CANNIER
CARRIER
CARTIER
CASHIER
CATTIER
CHARIER
CHENIER
CHEWIER
CLAVIER
CLAYIER
COCKIER
COLLIER
COMFIER
CORNIER
COURIER
CRAZIER
CROSIER
CURLIER
CURRIER
CURVIER
CUSHIER
DAFFIER
DALLIER
DANDIER
DAUMIER
DERNIER
DINGIER
DINKIER
DIRTIER
DIZZIER
DOSSIER
DOTTIER
DOWDIER
DOWNIER
DUCKIER
DUMPIER
DUSKIER
DUSTIER
EARLIER
EMPTIER
FANCIER
FARRIER
FIERIER
FILMIER
FISHIER
FIZZIER
FLAKIER
FOAMIER
FOGGIER
FOURIER
FRASIER
FRAZIER
FUNKIER
FUNNIER
FURRIER
FUSSIER
FUSTIER
FUZZIER
GABBIER
GAUDIER
GAUZIER
GAWKIER
GIDDIER
GLACIER
GLAZIER
GOOFIER
GOOPIER
GRIMIER
GROLIER
GUMMIER
GUNKIER
GUSHIER
GUTSIER
HAIRIER
HANDIER
HAPPIER
HARDIER
HARRIER
HASTIER
HEADIER
HEAVIER
HEFTIER
HILLIER
HOARIER
HOOSIER
HORSIER
HUFFIER
HUSKIER
ITCHIER
JANVIER
JAZZIER
JERKIER
JOLLIER
JUICIER
JUMPIER
JUNKIER
KINKIER
KOOKIER
LANKIER
LEAFIER
LEAKIER
LEERIER
LEGGIER
LINTIER
LIPPIER
LOAMIER
LOFTIER
LOONIER
LOOPIER
LOUSIER
LOWLIER
LUCKIER
LUMPIER
LUSTIER
MANGIER
MANLIER
MEALIER
MEATIER
MERRIER
MESSIER
MILKIER
MINTIER
MISTIER
MOLDIER
MOODIER
MOSSIER
MOUSIER
MUDDIER
MUGGIER
MURKIER
MUSHIER
MUSTIER
MUZZIER
NASTIER
NATTIER
NEEDIER
NERVIER
NEWSIER
NIFTIER
NIPPIER
NOISIER
NUBBIER
NUTTIER
OLIVIER
PALMIER
PANNIER
PASTIER
PEPPIER
PERKIER
PERRIER
PESKIER
PETTIER
PHONIER
PICKIER
PITHIER
PODGIER
POITIER
POUTIER
PREMIER
PRICIER
PROSIER
PUDGIER
PUFFIER
PUSHIER
RAGGIER
RAINIER
RANDIER
RANGIER
RASPIER
RATTIER
READIER
REEDIER
RISKIER
RITZIER
ROCKIER
ROOMIER
ROWDIER
RUDDIER
RUMMIER
RUNNIER
RUNTIER
RUSTIER
SAGGIER
SALTIER
SANDIER
SAPPIER
SASSIER
SAUCIER
SAVVIER
SCALIER
SCARIER
SEAMIER
SEEDIER
SHADIER
SHAKIER
SHINIER
SHOWIER
SILKIER
SILLIER
SLATIER
SLIMIER
SMOKIER
SNAKIER
SNOWIER
SOAPIER
SOGGIER
SOLDIER
SOOTIER
SORRIER
SOUPIER
SPACIER
SPICIER
SPIKIER
SPINIER
STAGIER
STONIER
SUDSIER
SULKIER
SUNNIER
SURLIER
TACKIER
TANGIER
TARDIER
TARSIER
TASTIER
TATTIER
TAWNIER
TEARIER
TEENIER
TERRIER
TESTIER
TINNIER
TIPSIER
TUBBIER
UNIFIER
VERNIER
WACKIER
WARRIOR
WEARIER
WEEDIER
WEEPIER
WINDIER
WISPIER
WITTIER
WOODIER
WOOLIER
WOOZIER
WORDIER
WORMIER
WORRIER
YUCKIER
YUMMIER
ZESTIER
ZINGIER
ZIPPIER

•••••IR

BENAZIR
BIDFAIR
BONSOIR
BOUDOIR
CATHAIR
CORSAIR
DEADAIR
DEARSIR
DESPAIR
FUNFAIR
KASHMIR
MAYFAIR
OPENAIR
REDHAIR
THINAIR

IS•••••

ISADORA
ISHMAEL
ISLAMIC
ISLANDS
ISOBARS
ISOGONS
ISOHELS
ISOLATE
ISOMERS
ISOPODS
ISOTOPE
ISRAELI
ISSUERS
ISSUING
ISTHMUS

I•S••••

IFSTONE
IMSORRY
INSCAPE
INSEAMS
INSECTS
INSERTS
INSHAPE
INSHORT
INSIDER
INSIDES
INSIGHT
INSIPID
INSISTS
INSOFAR
INSOLES
INSPANS
INSPECT
INSPIRE
INSPOTS
INSTALL
INSTANT
INSTATE
INSTEAD
INSTEPS
INSTILL
INSTILS
INSTOCK
INSTORE
INSTYLE
INSULAR
INSULIN
INSULTS
INSURED
INSURES
IPSWICH
ISSUERS
ISSUING

I••S•••

IBNSAUD
ICESHOW
INASNIT
INASPIN
INASPOT
INASTEW
INKSPOT
IRISOUT
IRKSOME

I•••S••

ILIESCU
ILLUSED
ILLUSES
IMPASSE
IMPASTO
IMPOSED
IMPOSES
IMPOSTS
INCISED
INCISES
INCISOR
INFESTS
INFUSED
INFUSES
INGESTS
INHASTE
INSISTS
INVESTS
IONESCO
IQTESTS

I••••S•

ICELESS
ICINESS

ICKIEST
IFFIEST
ILLNESS
IMMENSE
IMMERSE
IMPASSE
IMPRESS
IMPULSE
INAMESS
INANEST
INARUSH
INCENSE
INCLOSE
INGRESS
INHOUSE
INPHASE
INQUEST
INTENSE
INTERSE
INTRUST
INVERSE
IPCRESS
IRATEST

I•••••S

ICEAGES
ICEAXES
ICEBAGS
ICECAPS
ICELESS
ICICLES
ICINESS
IDCARDS
IDEATES
IGNEOUS
IGNITES
IGNORES
IGUANAS
ILLNESS
ILLUSES
IMAGERS
IMAGOES
IMARETS
IMBIBES
IMBRUES
IMMIXES
IMMURES
IMPACTS
IMPAIRS
IMPALAS
IMPALES
IMPARTS
IMPEDES
IMPENDS
IMPETUS
IMPIOUS
IMPLIES
IMPORTS
IMPOSES
IMPOSTS
IMPRESS
IMPUGNS
IMPUTES
INAMESS
INCANTS
INCEPTS
INCISES
INCITES
INCOMES
INCUDES
INDENTS
INDEXES
INDIANS
INDICES
INDICTS
INDIGOS
INDITES
INDOORS
INDUCES
INDUCTS
INFANTS
INFECTS
INFESTS
INFLOWS
INFOCUS
INFORMS
INFUSES
INGALLS
INGESTS
INGRESS
INHALES
INHERES
INJECTS
INJOKES
INJURES
INMATES
INNARDS
INNINGS
INROADS
INSEAMS
INSECTS
INSERTS
INSIDES
INSISTS
INSOLES
INSPANS
INSPOTS
INSTEPS
INSTILS
INSULTS
INSURES
INTAKES
INTENDS
INTENTS
INTERNS
INTONES
INTUITS
INVADES
INVENTS
INVERTS
INVESTS
INVITES
INVOKES
INWARDS
IODATES
IODIDES
IODIZES
IOMOTHS
IONIZES
IPCRESS
IQTESTS
IRONERS
IRONIES
IRRUPTS
ISLANDS
ISOBARS
ISOGONS
ISOHELS
ISOMERS
ISOPODS
ISSUERS
ISTHMUS
ITALICS
IVORIES

•IS••••

BISCUIT
BISECTS
BISHOPS
BISMUTH
BISQUES
BISTROS
CISTERN
DISABLE
DISARMS
DISAVOW
DISBAND
DISBARS
DISCARD
DISCERN
DISCOED
DISCORD
DISCUSS
DISDAIN
DISEASE
DISGUST
DISHING
DISHOUT
DISHPAN
DISHRAG
DISJOIN
DISLIKE
DISMAYS
DISMISS
DISOBEY
DISOWNS
DISPELS
DISPLAY
DISPORT
DISPOSE
DISPUTE
DISROBE
DISRUPT
DISSECT
DISSENT
DISTAFF
DISTANT
DISTEND
DISTILL
DISTORT
DISTURB
DISUSED
FISCHER
FISHERS
FISHERY
FISHEYE
FISHFRY
FISHIER
FISHILY
FISHING
FISHNET
FISHOUT
FISSILE
FISSION
FISSURE
FISTFUL
GISELLE
HISPANO
HISSERS
HISSING
HISTORY
KISHKES
KISSERS
KISSING
KISSOFF
LISPING
LISSOME
LISTEES
LISTELS
LISTENS
LISTING
MISALLY
MISCALL
MISCAST
MISCUED
MISCUES
MISDATE
MISDEAL
MISDEED
MISDIAL
MISDOES
MISDONE
MISERLY
MISFILE
MISFIRE
MISFITS
MISHAPS
MISHEAR
MISHITS
MISLAID
MISLAYS
MISLEAD
MISMATE
MISNAME
MISPLAY
MISREAD
MISRULE
MISSALS
MISSIES
MISSILE
MISSING
MISSION
MISSISH
MISSIVE
MISSOUT
MISSTEP
MISTAKE
MISTERS
MISTIER
MISTILY
MISTING
MISTOOK
MISTRAL
MISTYPE
MISUSED
MISUSES
MISWORD
PISCINE
PISCOPO
PISMIRE
PISTILS
PISTOLE
PISTOLS
PISTONS
RISIBLE
RISINGS
RISKERS
RISKIER
RISKING
RISOTTO
RISSOLE
SISKINS
SISSIES
SISTERS
SISTINE
SISTRUM
TISANES
TISSUES
VISAGES
VISAVIS
VISCERA
VISCOUS
VISIBLE
VISIBLY
VISIONS
VISITED
VISITOR
VISTULA
VISUALS
WISEDUP
WISEGUY
WISEMAN
WISEMEN
WISESUP
WISHERS
WISHFUL
WISHING
WISPIER
WISPILY
WISPING
WISTFUL

•I•S•••

AIRSACS
AIRSHIP
AIRSHOW
AIRSOCK
AIRSOUT
BIASING
BIASSED
BIGSHOT
DIESELS
DIESOFF
DIESOUT
DIGSOUT
DISSECT
DISSENT
FIASCOS
FIESTAS
FIRSTLY
FISSILE
FISSION
FISSURE
GINSENG
GIPSIES
HIMSELF
HIPSTER
HIRSUTE
HISSERS
HISSING
JIGSAWS
KIDSKIN
KINSHIP
KINSMAN
KINSMEN
KIRSTIE
KISSERS
KISSING
KISSOFF
KITSCHY
LIESLOW
LINSEED
LIPSYNC
LISSOME
MIASMAS
MIASMIC
MIDSIZE
MISSALS
MISSIES
MISSILE
MISSING
MISSION
MISSISH
MISSIVE
MISSOUT
MISSTEP
NILSSON
OILSKIN
PIASTER
PIASTRE
PIGSKIN
PIGSOUT
PILSNER
PITSAWS
PITSTOP
RIMSHOT
RINSING
RIPSAWS
RIPSOFF
RISSOLE
SIESTAS
SISSIES
SITSOUT
TINSELS
TINSTAR
TIPSIER
TIPSILY
TIPSOFF
TIPSTER
TISSUES
VIZSLAS
WIGSOUT
WINSLOW
WINSOME
WINSOUT
WINSTON

•I••S••

BIASSED
BINDSUP
DIGESTS
DINESEN
DINESIN
DINESON
DISUSED
DIVESIN
DIVESTS
DIVISOR
FICUSES
FILLSIN
FILLSUP
FINESSE
FIRESUP
FIRMSUP
FIXESUP
GIRASOL
GIVESIN
GIVESTO
GIVESUP
HINTSAT
HIRESON
KICKSIN
KICKSUP
LIAISED
LIAISES
LIAISON
LIFTSUP
LINDSAY
LINDSEY
LINESUP
LIVESIN
LIVESON
MILKSOP
MIMESIS
MIMOSAS
MINDSET
MINUSES
MISUSED
MISUSES
MITOSES
MITOSIS
MIXESUP
NICOSIA
NIELSEN
NILSSON
PICASSO
PICKSAT
PICKSON
PICKSUP
PILESIN
PILESON
PILESUP
PIMESON
PINESAP
PIOUSLY
PIPESUP
RICKSHA
RINGSUP
RIPOSTE
SIGNSIN
SIGNSON
SIGNSUP
SILESIA
SIMPSON
SINGSTO
SINKSIN
SINUSES
SIZESUP
TIMESUP
VIRUSES
WILLSON
WINDSOR
WINDSUP
WINESAP
WINGSIT
WINKSAT
WIPESUP
WISESUP

•I•••S•

AIMLESS
AIRBASE
AIRIEST
AIRLESS
AIRMASS
BIGGEST
BIGNESS
BIOMASS
CIRCUSY
DICIEST
DIFFUSE
DIGRESS
DIMMEST
DIMNESS
DIOCESE
DISCUSS
DISEASE
DISGUST
DISMISS
DISPOSE
DIVERSE
FINESSE
FINNISH
FIRMEST
FITNESS
FITTEST
GIRLISH
HIGHEST
HIPNESS
HIPPEST
HITLESS
HITLIST
KINDEST
LICENSE
LIDLESS
LIMIEST
LIMPEST
LIONESS
LITHEST
MIDEAST
MIDRISE
MIDWEST
MILDEST
MISCAST
MISSISH
NIGHEST
OILIEST
PIANISM
PIANIST
PICASSO
PIETISM
PIGGISH
PINIEST
PINKEST
PINKISH
PINLESS
PITBOSS
PIXYISH
RICHEST
SIAMESE
SICKEST
SIKHISM
TIDIEST
TIELESS
TIGRESS
TINIEST
TITLIST
VIOLIST
WILDEST
WILIEST
WIRIEST
WITLESS
WITNESS
YIDDISH

•I••••S

AIGRETS
AIMLESS
AIRBAGS
AIRDAMS
AIRGUNS
AIRINGS
AIRLESS
AIRMASS
AIRSACS
AIRWAYS
AITCHES
BIALIES
BICKERS
BIDDERS
BIDDIES
BIGBOYS
BIGEYES
BIGGERS
BIGGIES
BIGGUNS
BIGNESS
BIGTOES
BIGTOPS
BIGWIGS
BIKINIS
BILBOES
BILIOUS
BILLETS
BILLIES
BILLOWS
BINDERS
BINGOES
BIOMASS
BIONICS
BIRCHES
BIRDERS
BIRDIES
BIREMES
BISECTS
BISHOPS
BISQUES
BISTROS
BITMAPS
BITTERS
CICADAS
CINCHES
CINDERS
CINEMAS
CIPHERS
CIRCLES
CIRQUES
CITRONS
CIVVIES
DIADEMS
DIALERS
DIALOGS
DIAPERS
DIARIES
DIATOMS
DIBBLES
DICKENS
DICKERS
DICKEYS
DICKIES
DICTUMS
DIDACTS
DIDDLES
DIESELS
DIETERS
DIFFERS
DIGESTS
DIGGERS
DIGRESS
DIKDIKS
DIKTATS
DILATES
DILLIES
DILUTES
DIMMERS
DIMNESS
DIMOUTS
DIMPLES
DIMWITS
DINGLES
DINGOES
DINKIES
DINNERS
DIPOLES
DIPPERS
DIRECTS
DIRNDLS
DIRTIES
DISARMS
DISBARS
DISCUSS
DISMAYS
DISMISS
DISOWNS
DISPELS
DITCHES
DITHERS
DITTIES
DIVERTS
DIVESTS
DIVIDES
DIVINES
DIVVIES
DIZZIES
EIGHTHS
FIACRES
FIANCES
FIASCOS
FIBBERS
FIBRILS
FIBROUS
FIBULAS
FICUSES
FIDDLES
FIDGETS
FIESTAS
FIFTIES
FIGURES
FIJIANS
FILCHES
FILINGS
FILLERS
FILLETS
FILLIES
FILLINS
FILLIPS
FILLUPS
FILTERS
FINALES
FINCHES
FINDERS
FINGERS
FINIALS
FIPPLES
FIRINGS
FIRKINS
FISHERS
FITCHES
FITNESS
FITTERS
FIXATES
FIXINGS
FIZGIGS
FIZZLES
GIBBERS
GIBBETS
GIBBONS
GIBBOUS
GIBLETS
GIBLUES
GIDEONS
GIGGLES
GIGOLOS
GILBLAS
GILDERS
GILLIES
GIMBALS
GIMLETS
GINGERS
GIPSIES
GIRDERS
GIRDLES
GIVEUPS
HICCUPS
HIDEOUS
HIGGINS
HIJACKS
HIJINKS
HINDERS
HINNIES
HIPNESS
HIPPIES
HISSERS
HITCHES
HITLESS
HITTERS
JICAMAS
JIFFIES
JIGGERS
JIGGLES
JIGSAWS
JIMJAMS
JIMMIES
JINGLES
JINGOES
JITNEYS
JITTERS
KIBBLES
KICKERS
KICKUPS
KIDDERS
KIDDIES
KIDNAPS
KIDNEYS
KIKUYUS
KILLERS
KILTIES
KIMONOS
KINDLES
KIPPERS
KIRMANS
KIRTLES
KISHKES
KISSERS
KITBAGS
KITTENS
KITTIES
KIWANIS
LIAISES
LIBBERS
LIBIDOS
LIBYANS
LICHENS
LIDLESS
LIENEES
LIERNES
LIFTERS
LIGATES
LIMBERS
LIMNERS
LIMOGES
LIMPETS
LINAGES
LINDENS
LINDIES
LINEUPS
LINGERS
LINGOES
LININGS
LINKERS
LINKUPS
LINNETS
LINTELS
LIONESS
LIONETS
LIQUIDS
LIQUORS
LISTEES
LISTELS
LISTENS
LITCHIS
LITOTES
LITTERS
LIVINGS
LIZARDS
MIASMAS
MICMACS
MICRONS
MIDDAYS
MIDDENS
MIDDIES
MIDDLES
MIDGETS
MIDRIBS
MIDWAYS
MIKADOS
MILDEWS
MILIEUS
MILKERS
MILLERS
MILLETS
MILORDS
MIMESIS
MIMOSAS
MINCERS
MINDERS
MINGLES
MINIBUS
MINIONS
MINNOWS
MINOANS
MINTERS
MINUETS
MINUSES
MINUTES
MIRAGES
MIRRORS
MISCUES
MISDOES
MISFITS
MISHAPS
MISHITS
MISLAYS
MISSALS
MISSIES
MISTERS
MISUSES
MITHRAS
MITOSES
MITOSIS
MITTENS
MIZZENS
MIZZLES
NIBBLES
NICHOLS
NICKELS
NICKERS
NICOLAS
NIGGLES
NIMRODS
NINNIES
NIPPERS
NITROUS
NITWITS
OILCANS
OILPANS
OILRIGS
PIAZZAS
PICAROS
PICKENS
PICKERS
PICKETS
PICKLES
PICKUPS
PICNICS
PIDGINS
PIECERS
PIEPANS
PIERCES
PIETIES
PIETINS
PIFFLES
PIGEONS
PIGGIES
PIGLETS
PIGNUTS
PIGPENS
PILEUPS
PILFERS
PILINGS
PILLARS
PILLOWS
PINATAS
PINCERS
PINCHAS
PINCHES
PINIONS
PINKIES
PINLESS
PINNERS
PINOAKS
PINONES
PIOLETS
PIPINGS
PIPKINS
PIPPINS
PIRAEUS
PIRATES
PISTILS
PISTOLS
PISTONS
PITBOSS
PITCHES
PITEOUS
PITSAWS
PITTERS
QINTARS
RIBANDS
RIBBONS
RIBEYES
RICKEYS
RICKLES
RIDDLES
RIFFLES
RIFLERS
RIGGERS
RIGOURS
RILLETS
RINGERS
RIOTERS
RIOTOUS
RIPOFFS
RIPPERS
RIPPLES
RIPRAPS
RIPSAWS
RISINGS
RISKERS
RITUALS
SICKENS
SICKLES
SIDINGS
SIENNAS
SIERRAS
SIESTAS
SIFTERS
SIGHERS
SIGNALS

SIGNEES
SIGNERS
SIGNETS
SILENTS
SILICAS
SILLIES
SILVERS
SIMIANS
SIMILES
SIMMERS
SIMMONS
SIMPERS
SINGERS
SINGLES
SINKERS
SINNERS
SINUOUS
SINUSES
SIOUANS
SIPHONS
SIPPERS
SIPPETS
SISKINS
SISSIES
SISTERS
SITCOMS
SITTERS
SIXGUNS
SIXTIES
SIZINGS
SIZZLES
TICKERS
TICKETS
TICKLES
TICTACS
TIDBITS
TIDINGS
TIEDYES
TIELESS
TIEPINS
TIERODS
TIGRESS
TILLERS
TILTERS
TIMBALS
TIMBERS
TIMBRES
TIMEWAS
TIMINGS
TIMMINS
TINCANS
TINDERS
TINEARS
TINGLES
TINHATS
TINKERS
TINKLES
TINNERS
TINSELS
TINTERS
TIPOFFS
TIPPERS
TIPPETS
TIPPLES
TIPTOES
TIPTOPS
TIRADES
TISANES
TISSUES
TITBITS
TITHERS
TITTERS
TITTLES

TIZZIES
VICIOUS
VICTIMS
VICTORS
VICUNAS
VIEWERS
VIGOURS
VIKINGS
VIOLETS
VIOLINS
VIRAGOS
VIRGINS
VIRTUES
VIRUSES
VISAGES
VISAVIS
VISCOUS
VISIONS
VISUALS
VITTLES
VIZIERS
VIZSLAS
WICKERS
WICKETS
WIDGETS
WIENERS
WIENIES
WIGGLES
WIGLETS
WIGWAGS
WIGWAMS
WILLIES
WILLOWS
WIMPLES
WINCERS
WINCHES
WINDERS
WINDOWS
WINDUPS
WINGERS
WINKERS
WINNERS
WINNOWS
WINTERS
WISHERS
WITCHES
WITHERS
WITLESS
WITNESS
WIZARDS
ZIGZAGS
ZILCHES
ZINGERS
ZINNIAS
ZIPPERS
ZIRCONS
ZITHERS

••IS•••

ANISEED
APISHLY
ARISING
ARISTAE
ARISTAS
ARISTOS
ATISSUE
BLISTER
BRISKER
BRISKET
BRISKLY
BRISTLE
BRISTLY
BRISTOL

CAISSON
CHISELS
CRISPED
CRISPER
CRISPIN
CRISPLY
CRISPUS
CUISINE
DAISIES
DRISTAN
ELISION
ENISLED
ENISLES
EPISODE
EPISTLE
ERISTIC
EXISTED
FOISTED
FRISBEE
FRISIAN
FRISKED
FRISSON
GEISHAS
GLISTEN
GRISHAM
GRISSOM
GRISTLE
GRISTLY
HEISTED
HOISTED
IRISOUT
JOISTED
KAISERS
KAISHEK
KNISHES
KRISHNA
LAISSEZ
LEISTER
LEISURE
MEISSEN
MOISTEN
MOISTER
MOISTLY
NOISIER
NOISILY
NOISING
NOISOME
ORISONS
PAISANO
PAISLEY
POISING
POISONS
POISSON
PRISONS
RAISERS
RAISEUP
RAISING
RAISINS
REISSUE
ROISTER
SCISSOR
SEISMIC
SKISUIT
SWISHED
SWISHES
THISTLE
TRISECT
TRISTAN
TWISTED
TWISTER
UNISONS
WAISTED
WHISKED

WHISKER
WHISKEY
WHISPER
WHISTLE

••I•S••

ALIASES
ARIOSOS
ARIOSTO
ATISSUE
CAISSON
CHIPSIN
COILSUP
CRIMSON
DRIESUP
ERICSON
FAIRSUP
FLIESAT
FLIESIN
FRISSON
GAINSAY
GAINSON
GRISSOM
ILIESCU
JOINSIN
JOINSUP
LAISSEZ
MEIOSES
MEIOSIS
MEISSEN
NAILSET
PAIRSUP
POISSON
PRIESTS
RAILSAT
REINSIN
REISSUE
SCISSOR
SLIPSUP
SPIESON
STIRSIN
STIRSUP
SUITSUP
THIRSTS
THIRSTY
TRIESON
TRIESTE
TRIPSUP
WAITSON
WAITSUP
WHIPSAW
WHIPSUP

••I••S•

ADIPOSE
ANIMISM
ANIMIST
ARIDEST
BRITISH
CHINESE
CUIRASS
ELITISM
ELITIST
EVILEST
FAIREST
GLIMPSE
HEIRESS
ICINESS
OXIDASE
SHIATSU
SKIMASK
SNIDEST
TBILISI

TRITEST
VAINEST
WHITEST
WHITISH

••I•••S

ALIASES
ALIGHTS
ANIMALS
ARIOSOS
ARISTAS
ARISTOS
AVIATES
BAILEES
BAILERS
BAILEYS
BAILORS
BLIGHTS
BLITZES
BOILERS
BRIARDS
BRIDALS
BRIDGES
BRIDLES
BRITONS
CAIMANS
CAIQUES
CHILIES
CHINUPS
CHISELS
CLICHES
CLIENTS
CLINICS
CLIPONS
CLIQUES
COINERS
CRINGES
CRISPUS
CRITICS
CUIRASS
DAILIES
DAIRIES
DAISIES
DEICERS
DEIFIES
DEITIES
DOILIES
DRIVELS
DRIVERS
EDIBLES
EDIFIES
EDITORS
ELICITS
ELIXIRS
EMIGRES
ENIGMAS
ENISLES
EPILOGS
EVINCES
FAIRIES
FLIGHTS
FLIPUPS
FOIBLES
FRIDAYS
FRIDGES
FRIENDS
FRIEZES
FRIGHTS
FRINGES
FRIZZES
GAINERS
GAITERS
GEISHAS

GLIDERS
GLITZES
GRIEVES
GRIGRIS
GRILLES
GRIPERS
GRIVETS
GUIDONS
GUIMPES
GUINEAS
GUITARS
HAIRDOS
HEIFERS
HEIGHTS
HEINOUS
HEIRESS
ICICLES
ICINESS
JAILERS
JOINERS
JUICERS
KAISERS
KNIGHTS
KNISHES
LOITERS
MAIDENS
MAILERS
MAITAIS
MEIOSES
MEIOSIS
MOILERS
NAIADES
NAILERS
OHIOANS
OJIBWAS
OMINOUS
OPIATES
OPINERS
ORIENTS
ORIGINS
ORIOLES
ORISONS
PAILOUS
PAIUTES
PHIDIAS
PHINEAS
PLIGHTS
PLINTHS
POISONS
PRICERS
PRIESTS
PRIMERS
PRINCES
PRISONS
PRIVETS
PRIVIES
QUICHES
QUINCES
QUINOAS
QUIVERS
QUIZZES
RAIDERS
RAILERS
RAISERS
RAISINS
RUINERS
RUINOUS
SAILORS
SEICHES
SEIDELS
SEINERS
SEIZERS
SHIELDS

SHIITES
SHINERS
SHIVERS
SKIRUNS
SKITOWS
SKIVERS
SLICERS
SLIDERS
SLIGHTS
SLIPONS
SLIPUPS
SLIVERS
SMILERS
SNIVELS
SOIREES
SPIDERS
SPIGOTS
SPIKERS
SPINELS
SPINETS
SPIRALS
SPIREAS
SPIRITS
SPITZES
STICHES
STIFLES
STIGMAS
SUITORS
SWIPERS
SWISHES
SWIVELS
TAILLES
TAILORS
TAIPANS
THIEVES
THIRSTS
TOILERS
TOILETS
TRICEPS
TRICOTS
TRIFLES
TRIGONS
TRIODES
TRIPLES
TRIPODS
TRITONS
TRIUNES
TRIVETS
TWINGES
UNIFIES
UNIPODS
UNISONS
UNITERS
UNITIES
VEIGHTS
WAILERS
WAITERS
WAIVERS
WEIGHTS
WEIRDOS
WHINERS
WHITENS
WHIZZES
WRIGHTS
WRITERS
WRITHES

•••IS••

ADDISON
ADVISED
ADVISER
ADVISES
ADVISOR

AGEISTS
ALLISON
AORISTS
ARRISES
ARTISAN
ARTISTE
ARTISTS
ASSISTS
BATISTA
BATISTE
BENISON
BRAISED
BRAISES
BRUISED
BRUISER
BRUISES
CAMISES
CHAISES
CHRISMS
CHRISTI
CHRISTO
CHRISTY
CRUISED
CRUISER
CRUISES
CUBISTS
DEHISCE
DELISTS
DEMISED
DEMISES
DESISTS
DEVISED
DEVISES
DIVISOR
DREISER
EGOISTS
ELEISON
ELLISON
ELMISTI
ENLISTS
EXCISED
EXCISES
FRAISES
INCISED
INCISES
INCISOR
INSISTS
JALISCO
JURISTS
LEGISTS
LIAISED
LIAISES
LIAISON
LORISES
LUTISTS
LYRISTS
MADISON
MAOISTS
MATISSE
MELISSA
MENISCI
MODISTE
NABISCO
NUDISTS
OBOISTS
ORBISON
PELISSE
PRAISED
PRAISER
PRAISES
PURISTS
RELISTS
RESISTS

REVISED
REVISER
REVISES
REVISIT
SAMISEN
SATISFY
SCHISMS
SEXISTS
SQUISHY
TAOISTS
THEISTS
TRUISMS
TUBISTS
TUNISIA
TYPISTS
UNWISER
UPRISEN
UPRISES
VALISES
VENISON
WOEISME

•••I•S•

ACHIEST
AERIEST
AGAINST
AIRIEST
ARTIEST
ASHIEST
ATHIRST
BONIEST
BUSIEST
CAGIEST
COZIEST
DICIEST
DOPIEST
EASIEST
ECLIPSE
EDGIEST
EELIEST
EERIEST
ELLIPSE
FOXIEST
FUJITSU
GAMIEST
GOOIEST
GORIEST
HAZIEST
HOLIEST
HOMIEST
ICKIEST
IFFIEST
JUJITSU
LACIEST
LAZIEST
LIMIEST
LOGIEST
MAFIOSO
MATISSE
MELISSA
NOSIEST
OILIEST
PELISSE
PINIEST
POKIEST
PUNIEST
RACIEST
RERINSE
SEXIEST
SPRIEST
TIDIEST
TINIEST
TONIEST

TRAIPSE
UGLIEST
WARIEST
WAVIEST
WAXIEST
WILIEST
WIRIEST
ZANIEST

•••I••S

ACTIONS
ACTIVES
ADMIRES
ADMIXES
ADVISES
AEDILES
AERIALS
AFFINES
AFFIRMS
AFFIXES
AGEISTS
AIRINGS
ALBINOS
ALGIERS
AMNIONS
ANOINTS
ANTIBES
ANXIOUS
AORISTS
APSIDES
AQUINAS
ARGIVES
ARNICAS
ARRISES
ARRIVES
ARTISTS
ASPIRES
ASSIGNS
ASSISTS
ASSIZES
ATRIUMS
ATTICUS
ATTIMES
ATTIRES
AWNINGS
BELIEFS
BEMIRES
BESIDES
BETIDES
BETIMES
BEZIERS
BIKINIS
BILIOUS
BODICES
BOLIDES
BONITOS
BOVINES
BRAISES
BRUISES
BUNIONS
BYLINES
CAHIERS
CALICOS
CALIPHS
CAMISES
CANINES
CARIBES
CARINAS
CASINGS
CASINOS
CATIONS
CERIPHS
CHAISES

CHOICES
CHRISMS
CODICES
COMINGS
COPIERS
COPIOUS
COSIGNS
COSINES
CRUISES
CUBISTS
CURIOUS
DANIELS
DECIDES
DEFILES
DEFINES
DELIBES
DELICTS
DELISTS
DEMISES
DENIALS
DENIERS
DEPICTS
DERIDES
DERIVES
DESIGNS
DESIRES
DESISTS
DEVICES
DEVIOUS
DEVISES
DIVIDES
DIVINES
DOMINOS
DORITOS
DOSIDOS
DUBIOUS
ECHINUS
EDGINGS
EGOISTS
EMPIRES
ENDINGS
ENDIVES
ENGINES
ENGIRDS
ENLISTS
ENSIGNS
ENSILES
ENTICES
ENVIOUS
EOLITHS
EQUINES
ERMINES
ESKIMOS
ESPIALS
ETOILES
EXCISES
EXCITES
EXPIRES
EXWIVES
FACIALS
FACINGS
FAJITAS
FANIONS
FELINES
FIJIANS
FILINGS
FINIALS
FIRINGS
FIXINGS
FORINTS
FRAISES
FURIOUS
GAMINES

GAVIALS
HALITES
HAMITES
HAZINGS
HEGIRAS
HELICES
HELIXES
HIJINKS
HOSIERS
IGNITES
IMBIBES
IMMIXES
IMPIOUS
INCISES
INCITES
INDIANS
INDICES
INDICTS
INDIGOS
INDITES
INNINGS
INSIDES
INSISTS
INVITES
IODIDES
IODIZES
IONIZES
JABIRUS
JUNIORS
JURISTS
KODIAKS
KYLIKES
LABIALS
LACINGS
LADINOS
LAMINAS
LARIATS
LATICES
LATINAS
LATINOS
LEGIONS
LEGISTS
LEVIERS
LEVITES
LIAISES
LIBIDOS
LININGS
LIVINGS
LORISES
LOTIONS
LUPINES
LUTISTS
LYRISTS
MAKINGS
MALIGNS
MANIACS
MAOISTS
MARINAS
MARINES
MAXIMUS
MEDIANS
MEDICOS
MEDIUMS
MENIALS
MERINOS
METIERS
MILIEUS
MINIBUS
MINIONS
MOBILES
MOTIONS
MOTIVES
MYRIADS

NATIONS
NATIVES
NOTICES
NOTIONS
NOVICES
NOXIOUS
NUBIANS
NUDISTS
OBLIGES
OBOISTS
OBVIOUS
OEDIPUS
OFFICES
OMNIBUS
ONEIDAS
OOLITES
OOLITHS
OPTIONS
ORPINES
OSCINES
OUTINGS
PARIAHS
PARIBUS
PARINGS
PATINAS
PERIODS
PETITES
PILINGS
PINIONS
PIPINGS
PLAICES
PLAINES
PLAINTS
PODIUMS
POLICES
POTIONS
PRAISES
PUMICES
PURISTS
PYRITES
PYXIDES
RADIALS
RADIANS
RADICES
RAPIERS
RAPINES
RATINGS
RATIONS
RATITES
RAVINES
RAVINGS
REBINDS
RECIPES
RECITES
REDIALS
REFILLS
REFILMS
REFINES
REFIRES
REGIMES
REGIONS
REHIRES
RELICTS
RELIEFS
RELINES
RELISTS
RELIVES
REMINDS
REMIXES
REPINES
RESIDES
RESIGNS
RESILES

RESINGS
RESISTS
RETILES
RETIMES
RETINAS
RETIRES
REVIEWS
REVILES
REVISES
REVIVES
REWINDS
REWIRES
RISINGS
RULINGS
RUPIAHS
SABINES
SAMITES
SAPIENS
SATIRES
SAVINGS
SAVIORS
SAYINGS
SCHISMS
SCRIBES
SCRIMPS
SCRIPPS
SCRIPTS
SEMITES
SENIORS
SERIALS
SERIOUS
SEXISTS
SHEIKHS
SHEILAS
SHIITES
SHRIEKS
SHRIFTS
SHRIKES
SHRILLS
SHRIMPS
SHRINES
SHRINKS
SHRIVES
SHTICKS
SIDINGS
SILICAS
SIMIANS
SIMILES
SIZINGS
SLEIGHS
SLUICES
SOCIALS
SORITES
SOVIETS
SPLICES
SPLINES
SPLINTS
SPRINGS
SPRINTS
SPRITES
SQUINTS
SQUIRES
SQUIRMS
SQUIRTS
STKITTS
STRIDES
STRIKES
STRINGS
STRIPES
STRIVES
SYRIANS
TACITUS
TAOISTS
TAPINGS
TARIFFS
TEDIOUS
THEISTS
THRIFTS
THRILLS
THRIVES
TIDINGS
TIMINGS
TROIKAS
TROILUS
TRUISMS
TSHIRTS
TUBISTS
TYPISTS
UMPIRES
UNBINDS
UNCIALS
UNGIRDS
UNKINKS
UNLINKS
UNPILES
UNWINDS
UPLIFTS
UPLINKS
UPRISES
UPTICKS
VALISES
VARIOUS
VICIOUS
VIKINGS
VISIONS
VIZIERS
WAHINES
WAPITIS
WRAITHS
ZENITHS
ZODIACS

••••IS•

ABOLISH
AGONIST
ANIMISM
ANIMIST
APPRISE
ATAVISM
ATAVIST
ATHEISM
ATHEIST
BABYISH
BAPTISM
BAPTIST
BASSIST
BEARISH
BLEMISH
BOOKISH
BOORISH
BRITISH
BRUTISH
BULLISH
BURNISH
CATFISH
CATTISH
CELLIST
CHEMISE
CHEMIST
CHERISH
COCHISE
CODFISH
COEXIST
COLTISH
CONCISE
CONSIST
COPYIST
CORNISH
CULTISH
CULTISM
CULTIST
CYCLIST
CZARISM
CZARIST
DADAISM
DADAIST
DAMPISH
DARKISH
DELUISE
DENTIST
DERVISH
DESPISE
DISMISS
DOGFISH
DOLTISH
DUELIST
DULLISH
EGOTISM
EGOTIST
ELEGIST
ELITISM
ELITIST
ENDWISE
ENGLISH
EPEEIST
FADDISH
FADDISM
FADDIST
FASCISM
FASCIST
FAUVISM
FAUVIST
FINNISH
FLEMISH
FLORIST
FLUTIST
FLYFISH
FOGYISH
FOGYISM
FOOLISH
FOPPISH
FURBISH
FURNISH
GARNISH
GIRLISH
GOATISH
HARPIST
HAWKISH
HELOISE
HEROISM
HITLIST
HORNIST
JUDAISM
JUDOIST
KADDISH
KNAVISH
KURDISH
LAMAISM
LAMAIST
LEFTIST
LONGISH
LOWRISE
MALAISE
MANNISH
MARXISM
MAWKISH
MIDRISE
MISSISH
MONKISH
MOORISH
MORTISE
NEBBISH
NOURISH
OBELISK
OCULIST
OGREISH
OLEMISS
PACHISI
PALMIST
PANFISH
PAULIST
PECKISH
PEEVISH
PERSIST
PETTISH
PIANISM
PIANIST
PIETISM
PIGGISH
PINKISH
PIXYISH
POLOIST
PRECISE
PREMISE
PROMISE
PROTIST
PROVISO
PRUDISH
PUBLISH
PUCKISH
RAFFISH
REALISM
REALIST
REDDISH
REPRISE
RERAISE
ROGUISH
RUBBISH
RYKRISP
SAWFISH
SELFISH
SIKHISM
SLAVISH
SOLOIST
SOPHISM
SOPHIST
SOURISH
SPANISH
STATIST
STYLISH
STYLIST
SUBSIST
SUNFISH
SUNKIST
SUNRISE
SURMISE
SWEDISH
TALLISH
TANNISH
TARNISH
TBILISI
TITLIST
TORYISM
TOURISM
TOURIST
TROPISM
TSARIST
TUBAIST
TURKISH
UNTWIST
UPRAISE
VARNISH
VIOLIST
WAGGISH
WARMISH
WASPISH
WEAKISH
WHITISH
WOLFISH
YIDDISH

••••I•S

ACACIAS
ACARIDS
ACQUITS
ADAGIOS
ADJOINS
AFFAIRS
AMBRIES
ANANIAS
APERIES
APPLIES
ARCHIES
ARMPITS
ASSAILS
ATOMIES
ATTAINS
ATTRITS
AUNTIES
AUSSIES
BADDIES
BAGGIES
BANDIES
BANDITS
BARRIOS
BEANIES
BELLIES
BERRIES
BESTIRS
BEWAILS
BIALIES
BIDDIES
BIGGIES
BIGWIGS
BILLIES
BIONICS
BIRDIES
BMOVIES
BOBBIES
BOBBINS
BODKINS
BOOBIES
BOOGIES
BOOKIES
BOONIES
BOOTIES
BOWFINS
BOWTIES
BUDDIES
BUDGIES
BUGGIES
BULLIES
BUNNIES
BUSBIES
BUSKINS
CABBIES
CADDIES
CALKINS
CALLINS
CANDIDS
CANDIES
CARNIES
CARRIES
CASSIAS
CASSIUS
CATKINS
CATNIPS
CAVEINS
CELSIUS
CELTICS
CHEVIES
CHILIES
CIVVIES
CLERICS
CLINICS
COEDITS
COHEIRS
COLLIES
COLLINS
COMFITS
COMMITS
COOKIES
COOTIES
COUSINS
COWRIES
CRAZIES
CREDITS
CRETINS
CRITICS
CRONIES
CUBBIES
CURRIES
CUSPIDS
DADDIES
DAHLIAS
DAILIES
DAIRIES
DAISIES
DALLIES
DANDIES
DAWKINS
DECEITS
DECRIES
DEIFIES
DEITIES
DERAILS
DERBIES
DETAILS
DETAINS
DEVEINS
DEVRIES
DIARIES
DICKIES
DIKDIKS
DILLIES
DIMWITS
DINKIES
DIRTIES
DISMISS
DITTIES
DIVVIES
DIZZIES
DOBBINS
DOGGIES
DOILIES
DOLLIES
DOMAINS
DOOZIES
DOWRIES
DROPINS
DUCHIES
DUDDIES
DUMMIES
DUNLINS
EARWIGS
EBONIES
ECLAIRS
EDIFIES
ELAPIDS
ELEGIES
ELICITS
ELIXIRS
EMPTIES
ENEMIES
ENJOINS
ENTAILS
ENTRIES
EPOXIES
ETHNICS
EXOTICS
EYELIDS
FABRICS
FADEINS
FAIRIES
FANCIES
FASCIAS
FEELIES
FERRIES
FIBRILS
FIFTIES
FILLIES
FILLINS
FILLIPS
FIRKINS
FIZGIGS
FLORINS
FOLLIES
FORBIDS
FORTIES
FOSSILS
FROLICS
FULFILS
FUNNIES
FUSTICS
GAMBITS
GASKINS
GERBILS
GILLIES
GIPSIES
GLORIAS
GLORIES
GOALIES
GOBLINS
GODWITS
GOODIES
GOSSIPS
GOTHICS
GRACIAS
GRAVIES
GROPIUS
GULLIES
GUNNIES
GUPPIES
GUSSIES
GYPSIES
HACKIES
HANKIES
HARPIES
HARRIES
HATPINS
HAWKINS
HEAVIES
HENBITS
HERMITS
HEROICS
HIGGINS
HINNIES
HIPPIES
HOAGIES
HOBBIES
HOBBITS
HOGTIES
HOLLIES
HOPKINS
HOSKINS
HOTLIPS
HOTTIPS
HUBBIES
HURRIES
HUSKIES
HUSSIES
HYBRIDS
IMPAIRS
IMPLIES
INSTILS
INTUITS
IRONIES
ITALICS
IVORIES
JEEBIES
JELLIES
JEMMIES
JENNIES
JERKINS
JESUITS
JETTIES
JIFFIES
JIMMIES
JOLLIES
JUNKIES
KELPIES
KEWPIES
KIDDIES
KILTIES
KITTIES
LADDIES
LASSIES
LEADINS
LEFTIES
LENTILS
LINDIES
LIQUIDS
LOBBIES
LOCKINS
LOGGIAS
LOGGINS
LOLLIES
LOONIES
LORRIES
LOVEINS
MADLIBS
MAGPIES
MARGINS
MARLINS
MARRIES
MARTINS
MASHIES
MASSIFS
MASTICS
MATHIAS
MEALIES
MEANIES
MEGRIMS
MEMOIRS
MENHIRS
MERCIES
METRICS
MIDDIES
MIDRIBS
MISFITS
MISHITS
MISSIES
MOHAIRS
MOMMIES
MOSAICS
MRCHIPS
MUDDIES
MUDPIES
MUFFINS
MUMMIES
MUNTINS
MUSLIMS
MUSLINS
MUZHIKS
MYSTICS
NANNIES
NAPKINS
NEREIDS
NINNIES
NITWITS
NOETICS
NOGGINS
NORDICS
NUBBINS
NUDNIKS
NUNCIOS
NUTRIAS
OBTAINS
OILRIGS
OLEMISS
ORCHIDS
ORDAINS
ORIGINS
OUTBIDS
OUTFITS
OUTHITS
OUTWITS
PADDIES
PAMBIES
PANDITS
PANSIES
PARRIES
PARTIES
PATSIES
PATTIES
PECTINS
PENCILS
PENNIES
PEONIES
PEPSINS
PERKINS
PERMITS
PERSIUS
PHIDIAS
PHOBIAS
PHOBICS
PHONICS
PHONIES
PHYSICS
PICNICS
PIDGINS
PIETIES
PIETINS
PIGGIES
PINKIES
PIPKINS
PIPPINS
PISTILS
POETICS
PONGIDS
PONTIUS
POPLINS
POPPIES
POPPINS
PORGIES
POTPIES
PRELIMS
PRIVIES
PROFITS
PROXIES
PUBLICS
PUFFINS
PULPITS
PUNDITS
PUNKIES
PUPPIES
PURLINS
PUTTIES
PYGMIES
PYTHIAS
QUERIES
RABBITS
RAISINS
RALLIES
READIES
REBOILS
RECOILS
REDFINS
REDFIRS
REEDITS
REFRIES
REGAINS
REJOINS
REMAILS
REMAINS
RENAILS
RENNINS
REPAIRS
REPLIES
RESHIPS
RETAILS
RETAINS
RETRIES
RETRIMS
ROADIES
ROBBINS
ROCKIES
ROLAIDS
ROLLINS
ROOKIES
ROOMIES
ROWDIES
RUBRICS
RUSTICS
SALLIES
SANTIRS
SASSIES
SEQUINS
SHOOINS
SILLIES
SISKINS
SISSIES
SIXTIES
SMOKIES
SOFFITS
SOFTIES
SORTIES
SPAVINS
SPECIES
SPIRITS
SPRAINS
STATICS
STEPINS
STOGIES
STORIES
STRAINS
STRAITS
STUDIES
STUDIOS
STYMIES
SUBMITS
SULKIES
SULLIES
SUMMITS
SUSLIKS
TABBIES
TACTICS
TAFFIES
TALKIES
TALLIES
TANNINS
TANSIES
TARPITS
TARRIES
TECHIES
TEDDIES
TELLIES
TENPINS
TERRIES
TIDBITS
TIEPINS
TIMMINS
TITBITS
TIZZIES
TOADIES
TOCSINS
TODDIES
TOMTITS
TONSILS
TOROIDS
TOWNIES
TROPICS
TUMMIES
TUNNIES
TURNIPS
TWOBITS
UNCOILS
UNIFIES
UNITIES
UNKNITS
UNVEILS
URCHINS
UTOPIAS
VEGGIES
VESPIDS
VICTIMS
VIOLINS
VIRGINS
WALKINS
WEARIES
WEDGIES
WEENIES
WEEVILS
WELKINS
WESKITS
WIENIES
WILLIES
WOODIES
WOOLIES
WORRIES
YUPPIES
ZINNIAS
ZOMBIES
ZOYSIAS

•••••IS

ABNAKIS
ADONAIS
AGOUTIS
ALKALIS
ARTEMIS
ASEPSIS
BIKINIS
BORZOIS
CHABLIS
CHALLIS
CHAMOIS
CHASSIS
CSLEWIS
DAPHNIS
DUKAKIS
ECDYSIS
EVENKIS
FRANCIS
GELATIS
GENERIS
GENESIS
GENGHIS
GLOTTIS
GRIGRIS
KABUKIS
KIWANIS
LITCHIS
MAHARIS
MAITAIS
MARQUIS
MAUROIS
MEIOSIS
MEMPHIS
MIMESIS
MITOSIS
MORANIS
MUTATIS
NEMESIS
NEPALIS
NOKOMIS
ONASSIS
OSMOSIS
PHYLLIS
POLARIS
SAFARIS
SALAMIS
SALUKIS
SANLUIS
SERAPIS
SOMALIS
STDENIS
STLOUIS
TATAMIS
THESPIS
TRAVOIS
TRELLIS
VISAVIS
WAPITIS
YEMENIS

IT•••••

ITALIAN
ITALICS
ITCHIER
ITCHING
ITEMIZE
ITERANT
ITERATE
ITHACAN

I•T••••

INTAKES
INTEGER
INTEGRA
INTENDS
INTENSE
INTENTS
INTERIM
INTERNS
INTERSE
INTONED
INTONER
INTONES
INTROIT
INTRUDE
INTRUST
INTRUTH
INTUITS
IQTESTS
ISTHMUS

I••T•••

IFSTONE
IMITATE
INITIAL
INSTALL
INSTANT
INSTATE
INSTEAD
INSTEPS
INSTILL
INSTILS
INSTOCK
INSTORE
INSTYLE
INUTILE
IRATELY
IRATEST
ISOTOPE

I•••T••

ICEDTEA
IDEATED
IDEATES
IDENTIC
IDIOTIC
IGNITED
IGNITER
IGNITES
IMPETUS
IMPUTED
IMPUTES
INAPTLY
INASTEW
INCITED
INCITER
INCITES
INDITED
INDITES
INDUTCH
INEPTLY
INERTIA
INERTLY
INMATES
INPETTO
INVITED
INVITES
INVITRO
IODATES
IOMOTHS

I••••T•

IMAMATE
IMARETS
IMITATE
IMPACTS
IMPARTS
IMPASTO
IMPIETY
IMPORTS
IMPOSTS
INCANTS
INCEPTS

INDENTS
INDEPTH
INDICTS
INDUCTS
INFANTA
INFANTS
INFECTS
INFESTS
INFLATE
INGESTS
INGRATE
INHASTE
INJECTS
INPETTO
INSECTS
INSERTS
INSISTS
INSPOTS
INSTATE
INSULTS
INTENTS
INTRUTH
INTUITS
INVENTS
INVERTS
INVESTS
IQTESTS
IRRUPTS
ISOLATE
ITERATE

I•••••T

ICEBOAT
ICKIEST
IFFIEST
ILLICIT
IMPLANT
IMPRINT
INANEST
INASNIT
INASPOT
INCIPIT
INDOUBT
INEXACT
INFLECT
INFLICT
INFRONT
INHABIT
INHERIT
INHIBIT
INKBLOT
INKSPOT
INORBIT
INPOINT
INPRINT
INQUEST
INSHORT
INSIGHT
INSPECT
INSTANT
INTROIT
INTRUST
IRATEST
IRISOUT
IRONOUT
ITERANT

•IT••••

AITCHES
BITEOFF
BITMAPS
BITPART
BITTERN
BITTERS
BITTIER
BITTING
BITUMEN
CITABLE
CITADEL
CITIZEN
CITRATE
CITRINE
CITROEN
CITRONS
DITCHED
DITCHES
DITHERS
DITHERY
DITTANY
DITTIES
DITTOED
FITCHES
FITNESS
FITTERS
FITTEST
FITTING
HITACHI
HITCHED
HITCHER
HITCHES
HITHERE
HITLESS
HITLIST
HITTERS
HITTING
HITTITE
JITNEYS
JITTERS
JITTERY
KITBAGS
KITCHEN
KITSCHY
KITTENS
KITTIES
LITCHIS
LITERAL
LITHELY
LITHEST
LITHGOW
LITHIUM
LITINTO
LITOTES
LITTERS
LITTLER
LITURGY
MITCHUM
MITERED
MITFORD
MITHRAS
MITOSES
MITOSIS
MITOTIC
MITRING
MITTENS
MITZVAH
NITPICK
NITRATE
NITRIDE
NITRITE
NITROUS
NITTANY
NITWITS
PITAPAT
PITBOSS
PITBULL
PITCHED
PITCHER
PITCHES
PITCHIN
PITEOUS
PITFALL
PITHIER
PITHILY
PITHING
PITIFUL
PITSAWS
PITSTOP
PITTERS
PITTING
PITTMAN
PITYING
RITCHIE
RITUALS
RITZIER
SITCOMS
SITDOWN
SITSOUT
SITTERS
SITTING
SITUATE
SITWELL
TITANIA
TITANIC
TITBITS
TITHERS
TITHING
TITLING
TITLIST
TITMICE
TITRATE
TITTERS
TITTLES
TITULAR
VITALLY
VITAMIN
VITIATE
VITRIFY
VITRIOL
VITTLES
WITCHES
WITHERS
WITHOUT
WITLESS
WITNESS
WITTIER
WITTILY
WITTING
YITZHAK
ZITHERS

•I•T•••

AIRTAXI
AIRTIME
BIGTIME
BIGTOES
BIGTOPS
BIRTHED
BISTROS
BITTERN
BITTERS
BITTIER
BITTING
CISTERN
DIATOMS
DICTATE
DICTION
DICTUMS
DIETARY
DIETERS
DIETING
DIKTATS
DIPTYCH
DIRTIED
DIRTIER
DIRTIES
DIRTILY
DISTAFF
DISTANT
DISTEND
DISTILL
DISTORT
DISTURB
DITTANY
DITTIES
DITTOED
FICTION
FICTIVE
FIFTEEN
FIFTIES
FILTERS
FISTFUL
FITTERS
FITTEST
FITTING
FIXTURE
HINTING
HINTSAT
HISTORY
HITTERS
HITTING
HITTITE
JILTING
JITTERS
JITTERY
KILTIES
KILTING
KIRTLES
KITTENS
KITTIES
LIFTERS
LIFTING
LIFTOFF
LIFTSUP
LILTING
LINTELS
LINTIER
LISTEES
LISTELS
LISTENS
LISTING
LITTERS
LITTLER
MIDTERM
MIDTOWN
MINTERS
MINTIER
MINTING
MISTAKE
MISTERS
MISTIER
MISTILY
MISTING
MISTOOK
MISTRAL
MISTYPE
MITTENS
MIXTURE
NIFTIER
NIFTILY
NITTANY
PICTURE
PIETIES
PIETINS
PIETISM
PIGTAIL
PINTAIL
PISTILS
PISTOLE
PISTOLS
PISTONS
PITTERS
PITTING
PITTMAN
QINTARS
RIFTING
RIOTACT
RIOTERS
RIOTING
RIOTOUS
RIPTIDE
RIPTORN
SIFTERS
SIFTING
SILTING
SISTERS
SISTINE
SISTRUM
SITTERS
SITTING
SIXTEEN
SIXTIES
TICTACS
TIETACK
TILTERS
TILTING
TINTERN
TINTERS
TINTING
TINTYPE
TIPTOED
TIPTOES
TIPTOPS
TITTERS
TITTLES
VICTIMS
VICTORS
VICTORY
VICTUAL
VIETNAM
VINTAGE
VINTNER
VIRTUAL
VIRTUES
VISTULA
VITTLES
WILTING
WINTERS
WINTERY
WISTFUL
WITTIER
WITTILY
WITTING

•I••T••

BIENTOT
BIGOTED
BIGOTRY
BIRETTA
DIGITAL
DILATED
DILATES
DILUTED
DILUTER
DILUTES
DIMITRI
DINETTE
DIOPTER
EIGHTHS
FIESTAS
FIGHTER
FIRSTLY
FIXATED
FIXATES
HIGHTEA
HIGHTOP
HILLTOP
HIPSTER
KILOTON
KINETIC
KINGTUT
KIRSTIE
LICITLY
LIGATED
LIGATES
LIGHTED
LIGHTEN
LIGHTER
LIGHTLY
LIGHTUP
LIMITED
LITOTES
MIGHTNT
MILITIA
MIMETIC
MINUTES
MINUTIA
MISSTEP
MITOTIC
MIXITUP
NIGHTIE
NIGHTLY
PIASTER
PIASTRE
PILOTED
PINATAS
PINETAR
PINETUM
PIPETTE
PIRATED
PIRATES
PIRATIC
PITSTOP
PIVOTAL
PIVOTED
RICHTER
RICOTTA
RIGHTED
RIGHTER
RIGHTLY
RIGHTON
RISOTTO
RIVETED
RIVETER
SIESTAS
SIGHTED
SIGHTLY
SINATRA
TIBETAN
TIGHTEN
TIGHTER
TIGHTLY
TIMOTHY
TINSTAR
TINYTIM
TIPSTER
VISITED
VISITOR
WINGTIP
WINSTON
WIRETAP

•I•••T•

AIGRETS
AIMEDTO
AIRDATE
BILLETS
BIRETTA
BISECTS
BISMUTH
CILIATE
CITRATE
DICTATE
DIDACTS
DIGESTS
DIGNITY
DIKTATS
DIMOUTS
DIMWITS
DINETTE
DIRECTS
DISPUTE
DIVERTS
DIVESTS
FIDGETS
FIDGETY
FILLETS
GIBBETS
GIBLETS
GIMLETS
GIVENTO
GIVESTO
HIRSUTE
HITTITE
KIBBUTZ
LIBERTY
LICKETY
LIGNITE
LIMPETS
LINEATE
LINNETS
LIONETS
LITINTO
MIDGETS
MIGRATE
MILLETS
MILLETT
MINOLTA
MINUETS
MISDATE
MISFITS
MISHITS
MISMATE
NITRATE
NITRITE
NITWITS
PICANTE
PICKETS
PICKETT
PIGLETS
PIGNUTS
PIMENTO
PINNATE
PIOLETS
PIPETTE
RICKETY
RICOTTA
RILLETS
RIORITA
RIPINTO
RIPOSTE
RISOTTO
SIGNETS
SILENTS
SINGSTO
SIPPETS
SITUATE
TICKETS
TIDBITS
TIEINTO
TINHATS
TIPPETS
TITBITS
TITRATE
VIBRATE
VIBRATO
VIOLATE
VIOLETS
VITIATE
WICHITA
WICKETS
WIDGETS
WIGLETS

•I••••T

AILMENT
AIMEDAT
AIRBOAT
AIRIEST
AIRLIFT
AIRPORT
AIRSOUT
BIBELOT
BIENTOT
BIGFEET
BIGFOOT
BIGGEST
BIGSHOT
BISCUIT
BITPART
CIRCLET
CIRCUIT
DIALECT
DICIEST
DIDEROT
DIEDOUT
DIESOUT
DIGSOUT
DIMMEST
DINGBAT
DINMONT
DISGUST
DISHOUT
DISPORT
DISRUPT
DISSECT
DISSENT
DISTANT
DISTORT
FIGMENT
FILBERT
FILLOUT
FINDOUT
FINEART
FIREANT
FIRELIT
FIRMEST
FISHNET
FISHOUT
FITTEST
GILBERT
GILLNET
GIVEOUT
HIDEOUT
HIGHEST
HIGHHAT
HINTSAT
HIPBOOT
HIPPEST
HITLIST
KICKOUT
KINDEST
KINGRAT
KINGTUT
LIFENET
LIMIEST
LIMPEST
LITHEST
LIVEOUT
MIDEAST
MIDWEST
MIGHTNT
MIGRANT
MILDEST
MILLETT
MINARET
MINDSET
MISCAST
MISSOUT
NIGHEST
OILIEST
PIANIST
PICKETT
PICKOUT
PICKSAT
PIERROT
PIGMENT
PIGSOUT
PINENUT
PINIEST
PINKEST
PIQUANT
PITAPAT
RICERAT
RICHEST
RIDEOUT
RIMSHOT
RINGLET
RINGOUT
RIOTACT
RIVULET
SICKEST
SICKOUT
SIDEBET
SIGNOUT
SILKHAT
SINGOUT
SITSOUT
TIDIEST
TIMEOUT
TINIEST
TIREOUT
TITLIST
VIADUCT
VIBRANT
VINCENT
VIOLENT
VIOLIST
WIGSOUT
WILDCAT
WILDEST
WILIEST
WINGNUT
WINGSIT
WINKOUT
WINKSAT
WINSOUT
WIPEOUT
WIRIEST
WITHOUT

••IT•••

AGITATE
BAITING
BLITHER
BLITZED
BLITZEN
BLITZES
BOITANO
BRITAIN
BRITISH
BRITONS
BRITTEN
BRITTLE
BRITTON
CHITTER
CRITICS
CRITTER
DEITIES
EDITING
EDITION
EDITORS
ELITISM
ELITIST
EMITTED
EMITTER
EPITHET
EPITOME
ERITREA
EXITING
FLITTED
FLITTER
FRITTED
FRITTER
GAITERS
GAITING
GLITTER
GLITZED
GLITZES
GRITTED
GUITARS
HAITIAN
IMITATE
INITIAL
KNITTED
KNITTER
LOITERS
MAITAIS
MAITRED
NEITHER
OMITTED
POITIER
PRITHEE
QUITTER
SKITOWS
SKITTER
SKITTLE
SLITHER
SMITING
SMITTEN
SPITING
SPITZES
SUITING
SUITORS
SUITSUP
SWITZER
THITHER
TRITELY
TRITEST
TRITIUM
TRITONE
TRITONS
TUITION
TWITCHY
TWITTED
TWITTER
UNITARY
UNITERS
UNITIES
UNITING
UNITIVE
WAITERS
WAITING
WAITOUT
WAITSON
WAITSUP
WHITENS
WHITEST
WHITHER
WHITING
WHITISH
WHITMAN
WHITNEY
WHITTLE
WRITEIN
WRITERS
WRITETO
WRITEUP
WRITHED
WRITHES
WRITING
WRITTEN
ZEITUNG

••I•T••

ARIETTA
ARISTAE
ARISTAS
ARISTOS
ASIATIC
AVIATED
AVIATES
AVIATOR
BLISTER
BRISTLE
BRISTLY
BRISTOL
BRITTEN
BRITTLE
BRITTON
BUILTIN
BUILTON
BUILTUP
CHINTZY
CHITTER
CLIFTON
CLINTON
CRITTER
DRIFTED
DRIFTER
DRISTAN
EMITTED
EMITTER
EPISTLE
ERISTIC
EVICTED
EXISTED
FAINTED
FAINTER
FAINTLY
FEINTED
FLIRTED
FLITTED
FLITTER
FOISTED
FRITTED
FRITTER
GLINTED
GLISTEN
GLITTER
GRIFTER
GRISTLE
GRISTLY
GRITTED
HEISTED
HOISTED
IDIOTIC
JOINTED
JOINTLY
JOISTED
KNITTED
KNITTER
LEISTER
MAINTOP
MEIOTIC
MOISTEN
MOISTER
MOISTLY
OMITTED
OPIATES
PAINTED
PAINTER
PAIUTES
PHILTER
PHILTRE
PLINTHS
POINTED
POINTER
POINTTO
PRINTED
PRINTER
QUIETED
QUIETEN
QUIETER
QUIETLY
QUILTED
QUILTER
QUINTET
QUITTER
ROISTER
SAINTED
SAINTLY
SHIATSU
SHIFTED
SHIHTZU
SHIITES
SKIRTED
SKITTER
SKITTLE
SMITTEN
SNIFTER
STILTED
STILTON
STINTED
SWIFTER
SWIFTLY
TAINTED
THISTLE
TRISTAN
TWISTED
TWISTER
TWITTED
TWITTER
WAISTED
WHISTLE
WHITTLE
WRITTEN

••I••T•

ABILITY
ACIDITY
AGILITY
AGITATE
AKIHITO
ALIGHTS
ANIMATE
ANIMATO
ARIDITY
ARIETTA
ARIOSTO
AVIDITY
AZIMUTH
BLIGHTS
BRINGTO
CHIANTI
CLIENTS
CLIMATE
CLINGTO
ELICITS
EMIRATE
FLIGHTS
FLIGHTY
FRIGATE
FRIGHTS
GRIVETS
HEIFETZ
HEIGHTS
IMITATE
KNIGHTS
LYINGTO
NAIVETE
ORIENTE
ORIENTS
OWINGTO
PLIGHTS
POINTTO
PRIESTS
PRIMATE
PRIORTO
PRIVATE
PRIVETS
QUIXOTE
SLIGHTS
SPIGOTS
SPINETS
SPIRITO
SPIRITS
STICKTO
THIRSTS
THIRSTY
TOILETS
TRIBUTE
TRICOTS
TRIESTE
TRINITY
TRIVETS
UTILITY
VEIGHTS
WEIGHTS
WEIGHTY
WRIGHTS
WRITETO

••I•••T

ALIMENT
ANIMIST
ARIDEST
BAILOUT
BLINKAT
BRIDGET
BRILLAT

BRIQUET
BRISKET
CLIPART
CRICKET
DRIBLET
DRIVEAT
ELITIST
EMINENT
EPITHET
EVIDENT
EVILEST
EXIGENT
FAIREST
FLIESAT
GOINGAT
GRILLET
HAIRCUT
HAIRNET
IRISOUT
LAIDOUT
MAIGRET
MAILLOT
NAILSET
OXIDANT
PAIDOUT
QUINTET
RAILSAT
RAIMENT
RAINHAT
RAINOUT
SHIPOUT
SKIBOOT
SKILIFT
SKILLET
SKIPOUT
SKISUIT
SLIPOUT
SNIDEST
SNIFFAT
SNIGLET
SNIPEAT
SNIPPET
SPINOUT
SPIRANT
THICKET
TLINGIT
TRIDENT
TRINKET
TRIPLET
TRIPPET
TRISECT
TRITEST
VAINEST
WAITOUT
WHIPPET
WHITEST

•••IT••

ARBITER
AUDITED
AUDITOR
AWAITED
BEWITCH
BONITOS
BRUITED
CAPITAL
CAPITAN
CAPITOL
DEBITED
DIGITAL
DIMITRI
DORITOS
ENTITLE
EOLITHS
EXCITED
EXCITES
FAJITAS
FREITAG
FRUITED
FUJITSU
GERITOL
GETITON
HABITAT
HABITED
HABITUE
HALITES
HAMITES
HAMITIC
HAMITUP
IGNITED
IGNITER
IGNITES
INCITED
INCITER
INCITES
INDITED
INDITES
INVITED
INVITES
INVITRO
JANITOR
JUJITSU
JUPITER
LAFITTE
LETITBE
LETITIA
LEVITES
LICITLY
LIMITED
MANITOU
MARITAL
MERITED
MILITIA
MIXITUP
MONITOR
OOLITES
OOLITHS
ORBITAL
ORBITED
ORBITER
ORNITHO
PETITES
PLAITED
POLITER
POLITIC
POSITED
PURITAN
PUTITTO
PYRITES
RARITAN
RATITES
RECITAL
RECITED
RECITER
RECITES
RETITLE
RUBITIN
SAMITES
SEMITES
SEMITIC
SHIITES
SORITES
SPLITUP
SPRITES
STKITTS
TABITHA
TACITLY
TACITUS
TRAITOR
UNHITCH
VISITED
VISITOR
WAPITIS
WRAITHS
ZENITHS

•••I•T•

AGEISTS
ANOINTS
ANXIETY
AORISTS
ARTISTE
ARTISTS
ASSISTS
BATISTA
BATISTE
CHRISTI
CHRISTO
CHRISTY
CILIATE
CORINTH
CUBISTS
CUTINTO
DELICTI
DELICTS
DELISTS
DEPICTS
DESISTS
DEVIATE
DUBIETY
EGOISTS
ELLIOTT
ELMISTI
ENLISTS
EXPIATE
FOLIATE
FORINTS
FRAILTY
GEFILTE
GETINTO
GOLIATH
GOTINTO
IMPIETY
INDICTS
INSISTS
JACINTO
JURISTS
LABIATE
LAFITTE
LARIATS
LAYINTO
LEGISTS
LITINTO
LUTISTS
LYRISTS
MAOISTS
MEDIATE
MODISTE
NUDISTS
OBOISTS
OBVIATE
PLAINTS
PRYINTO
PURISTS
PUTITTO
RADIATE
RANINTO
REBIRTH
RELICTS
RELISTS
RESISTS
RIPINTO
RUNINTO
SATIATE
SATIETY
SCRIPTS
SERIATE
SETINTO
SEXISTS
SHRIFTS
SOCIETY
SOVIETS
SPLINTS
SPRINTS
SQUINTS
SQUINTY
SQUIRTS
STKITTS
STRIATE
TAOISTS
THEISTS
THRIFTS
THRIFTY
TIEINTO
TSHIRTS
TUBISTS
TYPISTS
UPLIFTS
VARIETY
VITIATE

•••I••T

ACHIEST
AERIEST
AGAINST
AIRIEST
ALRIGHT
AMBIENT
ANCIENT
ANTIART
APRICOT
ARTIEST
ASHIEST
ATHIRST
BONIEST
BUSIEST
CABINET
CAGIEST
COPILOT
COZIEST
DEFIANT
DEFICIT
DELIGHT
DELIMIT
DEVIANT
DICIEST
DOPIEST
EASIEST
EDGIEST
EELIEST
EERIEST
ELLIOTT
EXHIBIT
EXTINCT
FOXIEST
FREIGHT
GAMIEST
GOOIEST
GORIEST
HABITAT
HALIBUT
HARICOT
HAZIEST
HOLIEST
HOMIEST
ICKIEST
IFFIEST
ILLICIT
INCIPIT
INHIBIT
INSIGHT
LACIEST
LAZIEST
LENIENT
LIMIEST
LOGIEST
MAGINOT
MEDIANT
MRFIXIT
MRRIGHT
NOSIEST
OCCIPUT
OILIEST
ONSIGHT
PATIENT
PERIDOT
PINIEST
POKIEST
PUNIEST
RACIEST
RADIANT
RELIANT
RELIGHT
REVISIT
SALIENT
SAPIENT
SEXIEST
SLEIGHT
SOLICIT
SPRIEST
TIDIEST
TINIEST
TONIEST
TONIGHT
UGLIEST
UPRIGHT
UPTIGHT
VALIANT
VARIANT
WARIEST
WAVIEST
WAXIEST
WILIEST
WIRIEST
ZANIEST

••••IT•

ABILITY
ACIDITY
ACONITE
ACQUITS
ADAMITE
AGILITY
AKIHITO
AMENITY
ANNUITY
APATITE
ARIDITY
ARMPITS
ATTRITE
ATTRITS
AVIDITY
AZURITE
BABBITT
BANDITO
BANDITS
BAUXITE
BAYCITY
BERLITZ
BOXKITE
BREVITY
BULLITT
BURRITO
CALCITE
CHARITY
CLARITY
COEDITS
COMFITS
COMMITS
CORDITE
CREDITS
CRUDITY
DECEITS
DENSITY
DESPITE
DIGNITY
DIMWITS
DUALITY
EBONITE
EBWHITE
EDACITY
EGALITE
ELICITS
EMERITA
EMERITI
ENSUITE
EREMITE
ERUDITE
FALSITY
FATCITY
FATUITY
FERRITE
GAMBITS
GODWITS
GRANITE
GRAVITY
HENBITS
HERMITS
HITTITE
HOBBITS
INTUITS
JADEITE
JESUITS
JOLLITY
KUWAITI
LIGNITE
MISFITS
MISHITS
NEOLITH
NITRITE
NITWITS
OFFSITE
OPACITY
OUTFITS
OUTHITS
OUTWITS
PANDITS
PARTITA
PARTITE
PAUCITY
PERLITE
PERMITS
PROBITY
PROFITS
PULPITS
PUNDITS
QUALITY
RABBITS
RABBITT
REALITY
REEDITS
REQUITE
RESPITE
REUNITE
REWRITE
RIORITA
RUNWITH
SOFFITS
SOPWITH
SPIRITO
SPIRITS
STRAITS
SUAVITY
SUBMITS
SULFITE
SUMMITS
SUNCITY
TARPITS
TEKTITE
TERMITE
TIDBITS
TITBITS
TOMTITS
TRINITY
TWOBITS
UNKNITS
URANITE
UTILITY
VACUITY
VARSITY
WEBSITE
WESKITS
WICHITA

••••I•T

AFFLICT
AGONIST
AIRLIFT
ANIMIST
APPOINT
ATAVIST
ATHEIST
BABBITT
BAPTIST
BASSIST
BETWIXT
BLERIOT
BULLITT
CELLIST
CHARIOT
CHEMIST
CHEVIOT
COEXIST
CONSIST
CONVICT
COPYIST
CULTIST
CYCLIST
CYPRIOT
CZARIST
DADAIST
DENTIST
DUELIST
EGOTIST
ELEGIST
ELITIST
EPEEIST
FADDIST
FASCIST
FAUVIST
FLORIST
FLUTIST
GERAINT
HARPIST
HARRIET
HERRIOT
HITLIST
HORNIST
IMPRINT
INFLICT
INPOINT
INPRINT
JOLLIET
JUDOIST
LAMAIST
LEFTIST
OCULIST
ONADIET
PALMIST
PATRIOT
PAULIST
PAYDIRT
PERSIST
PIANIST
POLOIST
PREDICT
PROTIST
RABBITT
RANRIOT
REALIST
REBUILT
RECEIPT
REPAINT
REPRINT
RUNRIOT
SCHMIDT
SEAGIRT
SKILIFT
SOLOIST
SOPHIST
STATIST
STYLIST
SUBSIST
SUNKIST
TITLIST
TOURIST
TSARIST
TSELIOT
TUBAIST
UNTWIST
VARMINT
VERDICT
VIOLIST

•••••IT

AQUAVIT
BABYSIT
BACKBIT
BACKLIT
BASEHIT
BEATSIT
BENEFIT
BISCUIT
BLOWSIT
CIRCUIT
COCKPIT
COHABIT
CONCEIT
CONDUIT
COOLSIT
CULPRIT
DEFICIT
DELIMIT
DEMERIT
DEPOSIT
DETROIT
DRYSUIT
EXHIBIT
EXPLOIT
FIRELIT
FORFEIT
GOFORIT
HALFWIT
HARDHIT
HOOFSIT
HOPTOIT
HOWBEIT
ILLICIT
INASNIT
INCIPIT
INHABIT
INHERIT
INHIBIT
INORBIT
INTROIT
LAWSUIT
LOSESIT
MAKESIT
MANUMIT
MESSKIT
MOONLIT
MRFIXIT
NOTABIT
OPENPIT
OUTOFIT
PARFAIT
PLAUDIT
PURSUIT
RAREBIT
READMIT
RECRUIT
REVISIT
ROUGHIT
SEESFIT
SEETOIT
SKISUIT
SOLICIT
SPOTLIT
STARLIT
SUBUNIT
SURFEIT
THATSIT
TLINGIT
TRANSIT
WATCHIT
WETSUIT
WINGSIT
YOPLAIT

I•U••••

IGUANAS
INURING
INUTILE

I••U•••

ILLUSED
ILLUSES
IMBUING
IMMURED
IMMURES
IMPUGNS
IMPULSE
IMPURER
IMPUTED
IMPUTES
INCUDES
INDUCED
INDUCER
INDUCES
INDUCTS
INDULGE
INDUTCH
INFUSED
INFUSES
INHUMAN
INJURED
INJURES
INQUEST
INQUIRE
INQUIRY
INSULAR
INSULIN
INSULTS
INSURED
INSURES
INTUITS
IRRUPTS
ISSUERS
ISSUING

I•••U••

ICECUBE
IMBRUED
IMBRUES
IMPOUND
INARUSH
INBOUND
INCLUDE
INDOUBT
INHOUSE
INOCULA
INTRUDE
INTRUST
INTRUTH

I••••U•

IBNSAUD
ICEBLUE
IGNEOUS
IMPETUS
IMPIOUS
INFOCUS
INGENUE
INGROUP
INVACUO
INVOGUE
IRIDIUM
IRISOUT
IRONOUT
ISTHMUS

I•••••U

ILIESCU

•IU••••

DIURNAL

•I•U•••

BITUMEN
DILUTED
DILUTER
DILUTES
DISUSED
DIVULGE
FIBULAE
FIBULAS
FICUSES
FIGURED
FIGURER
FIGURES
KIKUYUS
LIQUEFY
LIQUEUR
LIQUIDS
LIQUORS
LITURGY
MINUEND
MINUETS
MINUSES
MINUTES
MINUTIA
MISUSED
MISUSES
PIOUSLY
PIQUANT
PIQUING
RITUALS
RIVULET
SINUOUS
SINUSES
SIOUANS
SITUATE
TIJUANA
TITULAR
VICUNAS
VIRUSES
VISUALS

•I••U••

AIRGUNS
AIRPUMP
BIGGUNS
BISCUIT
BISMUTH
BISQUES
BIVOUAC
CIRCUIT
CIRCUSY
CIRQUES
DICTUMS
DIFFUSE
DIMBULB
DIMOUTS
DISCUSS
DISGUST
DISPUTE
DISRUPT
DISTURB
FILLUPS
FISSURE
FIXTURE
GIBLUES
GIVEUPS
HICCUPS
HIRSUTE
KIBBUTZ
KICKUPS
KILAUEA
LINEUPS
LINGUAL
LINKUPS
MISCUED
MISCUES
MISRULE
MIXTURE
NIEBUHR
PICKUPS
PICTURE
PIGNUTS
PILEUPS
PINCURL
PITBULL
RIGOURS
SICHUAN
SIGMUND
SIXGUNS
TISSUES
VIADUCT
VICTUAL
VIGOURS
VIRGULE
VIRTUAL
VIRTUES
VISTULA
WINDUPS

•I•••U•

AIRSOUT
BILIOUS
BINDSUP
DIEDOUT
DIESOUT
DIGSOUT
DISHOUT
FIBROUS
FILLOUT
FILLSUP
FINDOUT
FIREBUG
FIREDUP
FIRESUP
FIRMSUP
FISHOUT
FISTFUL
FIXEDUP
FIXESUP
GIBBOUS
GIDDYUP
GIELGUD
GIVEOUT
GIVESUP
HIDEOUS
HIDEOUT
JIMRYUN
KICKOUT
KICKSUP
KIKUYUS
KINGTUT
LIFTSUP
LIGHTUP
LINEDUP
LINESUP
LIONCUB
LIQUEUR
LITHIUM
LIVEOUT
MILHAUD
MILIEUS
MILIEUX
MILKRUN
MILLRUN
MIMIEUX
MINDFUL
MINIBUS
MINIMUM
MISSOUT
MITCHUM
MIXEDUP
MIXESUP
MIXITUP
NIOBIUM
NITROUS
PICKOUT
PICKSUP
PIGSOUT
PILEDUP
PILESUP
PILLBUG
PINENUT
PINETUM
PIPEDUP
PIPEFUL
PIPESUP
PIRAEUS
PIROGUE
PITEOUS
PITIFUL
RIDEOUT
RIMBAUD
RINGOUT
RINGSUP
RIOTOUS
SICKOUT
SIGNOUT
SIGNSUP
SINGOUT
SINUOUS
SISTRUM
SITSOUT
SIZEDUP
SIZESUP
TIMEOUT
TIMESUP
TIREOUT
VICIOUS
VISCOUS
WICKIUP
WIGSOUT
WILLFUL
WINDSUP
WINGNUT
WINKOUT
WINSOUT
WIPEDUP
WIPEOUT
WIPESUP
WISEDUP
WISEGUY
WISESUP
WISHFUL
WISTFUL
WITHOUT

••IU•••

PAIUTES
TRIUMPH
TRIUNES

••I•U••

AZIMUTH
BRIQUET
CAIQUES
CHINUPS
CLIBURN
CLIQUES
EPICURE
FAILURE
FLIPUPS
LEISURE
SKIJUMP
SKIRUNS
SKISUIT
SLIPUPS
STIMULI
TRIBUNE
TRIBUTE
ZEITUNG

••I••U•
AMIBLUE
ATISSUE
BAILOUT
BRIMFUL
BRINGUP
BUILDUP
BUILTUP
COILSUP
CRISPUS
DOINGUP
DRIEDUP
DRIESUP
DRIVEUP
FAIRSUP
GAINFUL
GOINGUP
HAIRCUT
HEINOUS
IRIDIUM
IRISOUT
JOINSUP
JUICEUP
LAIDOUT
OMINOUS
PAIDOUT
PAILFUL
PAILOUS
PAINFUL
PAIRSUP
QUINQUE
RAINOUT
RAISEUP
REISSUE
RUINOUS
SHIPOUT
SKILFUL
SKIPOUT
SLIPOUT
SLIPSUP
SPICEUP
SPINOUT
STICKUP
STIRRUP
STIRSUP
SUITSUP
THINKUP
TRIPSUP
TRITIUM
TYINGUP
USINGUP
WAITOUT
WAITSUP
WHIPSUP
WRITEUP

••I•••U
ILIESCU
SHIATSU
SHIHTZU

•••IU••
ATRIUMS
MEDIUMS
PODIUMS

•••I•U•
ANTIGUA
ANTIQUE
ANXIOUS
ATTICUS
BEZIQUE
BILIOUS
COMIQUE
COPIOUS
CURIOUS
DEVIOUS
DUBIOUS
DUTIFUL
ECHINUS
ENVIOUS
FATIGUE
FURIOUS
HABITUE
HALIBUT
HAMITUP
IMPIOUS
JABIRUS
LALIQUE
MAXIMUM
MAXIMUS
MILIEUS
MILIEUX
MIMIEUX
MINIBUS
MINIMUM
MIXITUP
MODICUM
MONIQUE
NOXIOUS
OBLIQUE
OBVIOUS
OCCIPUT
OEDIPUS
OMNIBUS
OPTIMUM
PARIBUS
PAVIOUR
PITIFUL
RESIDUE
RETINUE
SERIOUS
SPLITUP
TACITUS
TEDIOUS
TROILUS
VARIOUS
VICIOUS

•••I••U
CARIBOU
FUJITSU
JUJITSU
MANITOU

••••IU•
BELGIUM
CADMIUM
CALCIUM
CAMBIUM
CASSIUS
CELSIUS
CRANIUM
ELUVIUM
ELYSIUM
FERMIUM
GALLIUM
GROPIUS
HAFNIUM
HAHNIUM
HOLMIUM
IRIDIUM
LITHIUM
NATRIUM
NIOBIUM
PALLIUM
PERSIUS
PONTIUS
PREMIUM
RHENIUM
RHODIUM
STADIUM
TERBIUM
THORIUM
THULIUM
TRITIUM
URANIUM
WICKIUP
YTTRIUM

••••I•U
PURLIEU

IV•••••
IVANHOE
IVORIES

I•V••••
INVACUO
INVADED
INVADER
INVADES
INVALID
INVEIGH
INVENTS
INVERSE
INVERTS
INVESTS
INVITED
INVITES
INVITRO
INVOGUE
INVOICE
INVOKED
INVOKER
INVOKES
INVOLVE

I•••V••
INCIVIL
INFAVOR

I••••V•
IMPROVE
INVOLVE

•IV••••
BIVALVE
BIVOUAC
CIVILLY
CIVVIES
DIVERGE
DIVERSE
DIVERTS
DIVESIN
DIVESTS
DIVIDED
DIVIDER
DIVIDES
DIVINED
DIVINER
DIVINES
DIVISOR
DIVORCE
DIVULGE
DIVVIED
DIVVIES
GIVENTO
GIVEOFF
GIVEOUT
GIVESIN
GIVESTO
GIVESUP
GIVEUPS
GIVEWAY
LIVABLE
LIVEDIN
LIVEDON
LIVENED
LIVEOAK
LIVEONE
LIVEOUT
LIVESIN
LIVESON
LIVIDLY
LIVINGS
PIVOTAL
PIVOTED
RIVALED
RIVALRY
RIVETED
RIVETER
RIVIERA
RIVIERE
RIVULET
VIVALDI
VIVENDI
VIVIDER
VIVIDLY

•I•V•••
CIVVIES
DIVVIED
DIVVIES
NIRVANA
RIGVEDA
SILVERS
SILVERY

•I••V••
BILEVEL
DIDOVER
DISAVOW
LIEOVER
MINIVAN
MINIVER
MITZVAH
NINEVEH
VISAVIS

•I•••V•
AIRWAVE
BIVALVE
FICTIVE
GINGIVA
MINERVA
MISSIVE

••IV•••
DRIVEAT
DRIVEIN
DRIVELS
DRIVERS
DRIVEUP
DRIVING
FLIVVER
GRIVETS
NAIVELY
NAIVETE
OLIVIER
OLIVINE
PRIVACY
PRIVATE
PRIVETS
PRIVIES
QUIVERS
QUIVIVE
SHIVERS
SKIVERS
SLIVERS
SNIVELS
SWIVELS
TRIVETS
TRIVIAL
WAIVERS
WAIVING
ZHIVAGO

••I•V••
FLIVVER
GRIEVED
GRIEVER
GRIEVES
KNIEVEL
THIEVED
THIEVES

••I••V•
QUIVIVE
UNITIVE

•••IV••
ACTIVES
AQUIVER
ARGIVES
ARRIVAL
ARRIVED
ARRIVER
ARRIVES
BOLIVAR
BOLIVIA
DELIVER
DERIVED
DERIVES
ENDIVES
ENLIVEN
ESTIVAL
EXWIVES
INCIVIL
MINIVAN
MINIVER
MOTIVES
NATIVES
RELIVED
RELIVES
REVIVAL
REVIVED
REVIVES
SCRIVEN
SHRIVEL
SHRIVER
SHRIVES
STRIVED
STRIVEN
STRIVER
STRIVES
THRIVED
THRIVES
UNCIVIL
UPRIVER

•••I•V•
ACHIEVE
BELIEVE
RELIEVE
RELIEVO

•••I••V
USTINOV

••••IV•
ABUSIVE
AMATIVE
ARCHIVE
BEEHIVE
CAPTIVE
CONNIVE
CURSIVE
DECEIVE
DEPRIVE
ELUSIVE
EMOTIVE
EROSIVE
EVASIVE
FESTIVE
FICTIVE
FORGIVE
FURTIVE
GINGIVA
MASSIVE
MISSIVE
OUTLIVE
PASSIVE
PENSIVE
PLOSIVE
QUIVIVE
RECEIVE
RESTIVE
SKYDIVE
SURVIVE
TENSIVE
UNITIVE
YESHIVA

•••••IV
ROCKYIV
TELAVIV

IW•••••
IWOJIMA

I•W••••
INWARDS

I••W•••
ILLWILL
ILLWIND
INAWEOF
INAWORD
INDWELL
INKWELL
IPSWICH

I•••W••
INNOWAY

I••••W•
INFLOWS
INGROWN

I•••••W
ICESHOW
INASTEW

•IW••••
KIWANIS

•I•W•••
AIRWAVE
AIRWAYS
AIRWOLF
BIGWIGS
DIMWITS
MIDWAYS
MIDWEEK
MIDWEST
MIDWIFE
MISWORD
NITWITS
OILWELL
PINWALE
SITWELL
TINWORK
VIEWERS
VIEWING
WIGWAGS
WIGWAMS

•I••W••
BIKEWAY
DISOWNS
GIVEWAY
HIGHWAY
RIDGWAY
TIMEWAS
WIDOWED
WIDOWER

•I•••W•
BILLOWS
BILLOWY
DIEDOWN
JIGSAWS
LIEDOWN
MIDTOWN
MILDEWS
MILDEWY
MINNOWS
PILLOWS
PILLOWY
PINDOWN
PITSAWS
RIPSAWS
SITDOWN
TIEDOWN
WILLOWS
WILLOWY
WINDOWS
WINNOWS

•I••••W
AIRCREW
AIRFLOW
AIRSHOW
BIGELOW
DISAVOW
HIGHLOW
LIESLOW
LIKENEW
LITHGOW
MILKCOW
WINDROW
WINSLOW

••I•W••
FAIRWAY
OJIBWAS
OJIBWAY
RAILWAY

••I••W•
OKINAWA
SKITOWS

••I•••W
LAIDLOW
RAINBOW
SKIDROW
WHIPSAW

•••IW••
ANTIWAR
TAXIWAY
WYSIWYG

•••I•W•
REVIEWS

•••I••W
MANILOW
SAGINAW

••••I•W
PREVIEW
PURVIEW

I••X•••
INEXACT

I•••X••
ICEAXES
IMMIXED
IMMIXES
INDEXED
INDEXES

•IX••••
FIXABLE
FIXATED
FIXATES
FIXEDLY
FIXEDUP
FIXESUP
FIXINGS
FIXTURE
MIXABLE
MIXEDUP
MIXESUP
MIXITUP
MIXTURE
PIXYISH
SIXFOLD
SIXGUNS
SIXPACK
SIXTEEN
SIXTIES

•I•X•••
DIOXIDE
JINXING

•I•••X•
AIRTAXI
PICKAXE

•I••••X
CINEMAX
FIREBOX
MILIEUX
MIMIEUX
MIRAMAX
PILLBOX
SIMPLEX

••IX•••
ELIXIRS
QUIXOTE

••I•••X
MAILBOX
TRIPLEX

•••IX••
ADMIXED
ADMIXES
AFFIXED
AFFIXES
HELIXES
IMMIXED
IMMIXES
MRFIXIT
REMIXED
REMIXES
UNFIXED

•••I••X
EQUINOX
HALIFAX
MILIEUX
MIMIEUX

••••IX•
BETWIXT

•••••IX
BEATRIX
CAKEMIX
DEEPSIX
HENDRIX
PHOENIX
REAFFIX
SKEEZIX
STCROIX

I•Y••••
IDYLLIC

I••Y•••
INKYCAP

I•••Y••
INSTYLE

I•••••Y
IDEALLY
IGNOBLY
IMAGERY
IMPIETY
IMSORRY
INANELY
INAPTLY
INEPTLY
INERTLY
INFANCY
INNOWAY
INQUIRY
IRATELY

•I•Y•••
BICYCLE
LIBYANS
LILYPAD
MIDYEAR
PITYING
PIXYISH
TIDYING
TINYTIM

•I••Y••
BIGEYES
DIPTYCH
GIDDYAP
GIDDYUP
JIMRYUN
KIKUYUS
LIPSYNC
MISTYPE
RIBEYES
TIEDYED
TIEDYES
TINTYPE

•I•••Y•
AIRWAYS
BIGBOYS
DICKEYS
DISMAYS
FISHEYE
JITNEYS
KIDNEYS
MIDDAYS
MIDWAYS
MISLAYS
RICKEYS

•I••••Y
AIRPLAY
BIGOTRY
BIKEWAY
BILLOWY
BINDERY
BIOGENY
BIOLOGY
CIRCUSY
CIVILLY
DIDDLEY
DIETARY
DIGNIFY
DIGNITY
DINGILY
DIRTILY
DISOBEY
DISPLAY
DITHERY
DITTANY
DIZZILY
FIDGETY
FIERILY
FINALLY
FINICKY
FIREFLY
FIRSTLY
FISHERY
FISHFRY
FISHILY
FIXEDLY
GIDDILY
GINGERY
GIVEWAY
HICKORY
HIGHBOY
HIGHWAY
HILLARY
HISTORY
JIGGERY
JITTERY
KILLJOY
KITSCHY
LIBERTY
LIBRARY
LICITLY
LICKETY
LIGHTLY
LINDSAY
LINDSEY
LIQUEFY
LITHELY
LITURGY
LIVIDLY
MILDEWY
MIMICRY
MISALLY
MISERLY
MISPLAY
MISTILY
NIFTILY
NIGHTLY
NITTANY
PILLORY
PILLOWY
PIOUSLY
PITHILY
RICKETY
RIDGWAY
RIFLERY
RIGHTLY
RIGIDLY
RIVALRY
SICKBAY
SICKPAY
SIGHTLY
SIGNIFY
SILKILY
SILVERY
SIZABLY
TIERNEY
TIFFANY
TIGHTLY
TIMIDLY
TIMOTHY
TINNILY
TIPSILY
TIREDLY
VICEROY
VICTORY
VISIBLY
VITALLY
VITRIFY
VIVIDLY
WILLOWY
WINFREY
WINTERY
WISEGUY
WISPILY
WITTILY

••I••Y•
BAILEYS
EVILEYE
FRIDAYS
HAIRDYE

••I•••Y
ABIDEBY
ABILITY
ACIDIFY
ACIDITY
AGILELY
AGILITY
ALIMONY
AMIABLY
APISHLY
ARIDITY
AVIDITY
AXIALLY
BLINDLY
BRIBERY
BRIEFLY
BRISKLY
BRISTLY
CHICORY
CHIEFLY
CHIMNEY
CHINTZY
CRINKLY
CRISPLY
DRIPDRY
DRIZZLY
FAINTLY
FAIRWAY
FLIGHTY
GAINSAY
GOINGBY
GRIFFEY
GRISTLY
GRIZZLY
JOINERY
JOINTLY
JUICILY
MOISTLY
NAIVELY
NOISILY
OJIBWAY
PAISLEY
PLIABLY
PLIANCY
PRICKLY
PRIMACY
PRIMARY
PRIVACY
QUICKLY
QUIETLY
QUIGLEY
RAILWAY
SAINTLY
SHIRLEY
SLICKLY
SNIDELY
SPIDERY
SPINDLY
STIFFLY
STIRFRY
SWIFTLY
SWINGBY
THICKLY
THIERRY
THIRDLY
THIRSTY
TRILOGY
TRINITY
TRITELY
TWINKLY
TWITCHY
UNITARY
UTILITY
WEIGHTY
WEIRDLY
WHISKEY
WHITNEY
WRIGGLY
WRIGLEY
WRINKLY

•••IY••
RUFIYAA

•••I•Y•
MARILYN
WYSIWYG

•••I••Y
ACRIDLY
ANXIETY
AUDIBLY
CHRISTY
CIVILLY
DEVILRY
DUBIETY
FETIDLY
FINICKY
FLUIDLY
FRAILTY
HOLIDAY
HOSIERY
HUMIDLY
IMPIETY
LEGIBLY
LICITLY
LIVIDLY
LUCIDLY
LURIDLY
MIMICRY
PANICKY
PLAINLY
RAPIDLY
RIGIDLY
SATIETY
SATISFY
SCRIMPY
SHRILLY
SOCIETY
SOLIDLY
SPRINGY
SQUINTY
SQUIRMY
SQUISHY
STAIDLY
STRINGY
TACITLY
TAXIWAY
TEPIDLY
THRIFTY
TIMIDLY
TOPIARY
VALIDLY
VAPIDLY
VARIETY
VISIBLY
VIVIDLY

••••I•Y
ABILITY
ACIDIFY
ACIDITY
AGILITY
AMENITY
AMPLIFY
ANGRILY
ANNUITY
ARIDITY
AVIDITY
BAGGILY
BAWDILY
BAYCITY
BEATIFY
BONNILY
BOSSILY
BREVITY
CALCIFY

CANNILY
CASSIDY
CATTILY
CERTIFY
CHARILY
CHARITY
CLARIFY
CLARITY
COCKILY
CORNILY
CRAZILY
CRUDITY
DAFFILY
DAYLILY
DENSITY
DESTINY
DIGNIFY
DIGNITY
DINGILY
DIRTILY
DIZZILY
DOWDILY
DUALITY
EDACITY
EMPTILY
FALSIFY
FALSITY
FANCILY
FATCITY
FATUITY
FIERILY
FISHILY
FORTIFY
FUNNILY
FUSSILY
FUSTILY
FUZZILY
GAUDILY
GAUZILY
GIDDILY
GLORIFY
GOSSIPY
GRATIFY
GRAVITY
GUSTILY
GUTSILY
HAMMILY
HANDILY
HAPPILY
HARDILY
HASTILY
HEADILY
HEAVILY
HEFTILY
HORRIFY
HUFFILY
HUSKILY
INQUIRY
JAZZILY
JERKILY
JOLLILY
JOLLITY
JUICILY
JUSTIFY
LANKILY
LEERILY
LOFTILY
LOUSILY
LUCKILY
LUSTILY
MAGNIFY
MERRILY
MESSILY
MISTILY
MOLLIFY
MOODILY
MORTIFY
MURKILY
MUSHILY
MUSTILY
MUZZILY
MYSTIFY
NASTILY
NATTILY
NEEDILY
NERVILY
NIFTILY
NOISILY
NULLIFY
NUTTILY
OPACITY
PAUCITY
PEPPILY
PERFIDY
PERKILY
PESKILY
PETRIFY
PETTILY
PHONILY
PITHILY
PROBITY
PRODIGY
PROSILY
PUFFILY
PUSHILY
QUALIFY
QUALITY
READILY
REALITY
RECTIFY
REUNIFY
ROWDILY
RUSTILY
SALSIFY
SALTILY
SASSILY
SAUCILY
SAVVILY
SCARIFY
SCARILY
SEALILY
SEEDILY
SHADILY
SHAKILY
SHOWILY
SIGNIFY
SILKILY
SOGGILY
SPECIFY
STAGILY
STONILY
SUAVITY
SUBSIDY
SULKILY
SUNCITY
SUNNILY
SURLILY
TACKILY
TARDILY
TASTILY
TEARILY
TERRIFY
TESTIFY
TESTILY
TINNILY
TIPSILY
TRINITY
UTILITY
VACUITY
VARSITY
VERSIFY
VITRIFY
WACKILY
WEARILY
WISPILY
WITTILY
WOOZILY
WORDILY

I•••Z••
IODIZED
IODIZES
IONIZED
IONIZER
IONIZES

I••••Z•
IDOLIZE
INADAZE
ITEMIZE

•IZ••••
BIZARRE
DIZZIED
DIZZIER
DIZZIES
DIZZILY
FIZGIGS
FIZZIER
FIZZING
FIZZLED
FIZZLES
GIZZARD
LIZARDS
MIZZENS
MIZZLED
MIZZLES
PIZARRO
PIZZAZZ
SIZABLE
SIZABLY
SIZEDUP
SIZESUP
SIZINGS
SIZZLED
SIZZLES
TIZZIES
VIZIERS
VIZSLAS
WIZARDS
WIZENED

•I•Z•••
CINZANO
DIZZIED
DIZZIER
DIZZIES
DIZZILY
FIZZIER
FIZZING
FIZZLED
FIZZLES
GIZZARD
MITZVAH
MIZZENS
MIZZLED
MIZZLES
PIAZZAS
PIZZAZZ
RITZIER
SIZZLED
SIZZLES
TIZZIES
YITZHAK
ZIGZAGS

•I••Z••
CITIZEN
PIAZZAS

•I•••Z•
FIRENZE
GINFIZZ
LIONIZE
MIDSIZE
PIZZAZZ

•I••••Z
GINFIZZ
JIMENEZ
KIBBUTZ
PIZZAZZ

••IZ•••
ARIZONA
DRIZZLE
DRIZZLY
FRIZZED
FRIZZES
FRIZZLE
GRIZZLE
GRIZZLY
PRIZING
QUIZZED
QUIZZES
RHIZOME
SEIZERS
SEIZING
SWIZZLE
WHIZKID
WHIZZED
WHIZZES

••I•Z••
BLITZED
BLITZEN
BLITZES
DRIZZLE
DRIZZLY
FRIEZES
FRIZZED
FRIZZES
FRIZZLE
GLITZED
GLITZES
GRIZZLE
GRIZZLY
LEIPZIG
QUIZZED
QUIZZES
SPITZES
SWITZER
SWIZZLE
WHIZZED
WHIZZES

••I••Z•
CHINTZY
OXIDIZE
SHIHTZU
SPINOZA
UTILIZE

••I•••Z
HEIFETZ
LAISSEZ
LEIBNIZ

•••IZ••
ASSIZES
BEDIZEN
CITIZEN
DENIZEN
HORIZON
IODIZED
IODIZES
IONIZED
IONIZER
IONIZES

••••IZ•
AGONIZE
ANODIZE
APPRIZE
ATOMIZE
BAPTIZE
CAPSIZE
CHORIZO
GINFIZZ
IDOLIZE
ITEMIZE
LIONIZE
MESTIZO
MIDSIZE
OBELIZE
OUTSIZE
OXIDIZE
REALIZE
STYLIZE
UTILIZE

••••I•Z
BERLIOZ
BERLITZ
GINFIZZ

•••••IZ
AGASSIZ
ALBENIZ
GEEWHIZ
LEIBNIZ
SHOWBIZ

JA•••••
JABBERS
JABBING
JABIRUS
JACANAS
JACCUSE
JACINTO
JACKALS
JACKASS
JACKDAW
JACKETS
JACKING
JACKPOT
JACKSON
JACKSUP
JACKTAR
JACOBIN
JACONET
JACQUES
JACUZZI
JADEDLY
JADEITE
JAEGERS
JAGGING
JAGLESS
JAGUARS
JAIALAI
JAILERS
JAILING
JAKARTA
JALISCO
JAMAICA
JAMESON
JAMMERS
JAMMING
JAMPACK
JANACEK
JANEDOE
JANEIRO
JANEWAY
JANGLED
JANGLES
JANITOR
JANSSEN
JANTZEN
JANUARY
JANVIER
JAPHETH
JARFULS
JARGONS
JARRING
JASMINE
JASPERS
JAUNTED
JAVAMAN
JAVELIN
JAWBONE
JAWLINE
JAYBIRD
JAYCEES
JAYLENO
JAYVEES
JAYWALK
JAZZAGE
JAZZIER
JAZZILY
JAZZING
JAZZMAN
JAZZMEN

J•A••••
JEALOUS
JEANARP
JEANLUC
JEANNIE
JOACHIM
JOAQUIN

J••A•••
JACANAS
JAIALAI
JAKARTA
JAMAICA
JANACEK
JAVAMAN
JICAMAS
JOCASTA
JOHANNA
JUDAISM
JUMANJI

J•••A••
JACKALS
JACKASS
JAGUARS
JAMPACK
JANUARY
JAYWALK
JAZZAGE
JEANARP
JETWASH
JIGSAWS
JIMJAMS
JOBBANK
JUGBAND
JULIANA
JUNKART
JUTLAND

J••••A•
JACANAS
JACKDAW
JACKTAR
JAIALAI
JANEWAY
JAVAMAN
JAZZMAN
JEERSAT
JERBOAS
JETBOAT
JICAMAS
JILLIAN
JOCULAR
JOHNGAY
JOHNJAY
JOURDAN
JOURNAL
JUGHEAD
JUGULAR
JUMPSAT
JUNKMAN
JUVENAL

J•••••A
JAKARTA
JAMAICA
JESSICA
JOCASTA
JOHANNA
JULIANA

•J•••A•
OJIBWAS
OJIBWAY

••JA•••
HIJACKS
PAJAMAS
PDJAMES
PYJAMAS

••J•A••
FIJIANS
TIJUANA

••J••A•
FAJITAS
PAJAMAS
PYJAMAS

••J•••A
LAJOLLA
MAJORCA
TIJUANA

•••JA••
DEEJAYS
JIMJAMS
LOGJAMS
PUNJABI
SKYJACK
TROJANS
VEEJAYS

•••J•A•
DONJUAN
SANJUAN
VALJEAN

•••J••A
IWOJIMA

••••JA•
BELLJAR
BLUEJAY
CULTJAM
JOHNJAY
KARAJAN

J•B••••
JABBERS
JABBING
JABIRUS
JIBBOOM
JOBBANK
JOBBERS
JOBBING
JOBHOPS
JOBHUNT
JOBLOTS
JUBILEE

J••B•••
JABBERS
JABBING
JAWBONE
JAYBIRD
JEEBIES
JERBOAS
JETBOAT
JIBBOOM
JOBBANK
JOBBERS
JOBBING
JOEBLOW
JUGBAND
JUMBLED
JUMBLES

J•••B••
JACOBIN
JEZEBEL
JUJUBES
JUKEBOX
JUNEBUG

•J•B•••
OJIBWAS
OJIBWAY

••J•B••
JUJUBES

•••J•B•
CONJOBS
ODDJOBS
PUNJABI

••••J•B
GOODJOB
NOSEJOB
SNOWJOB

J•C••••
JACANAS
JACCUSE
JACINTO
JACKALS
JACKASS
JACKDAW
JACKETS
JACKING
JACKPOT
JACKSON
JACKSUP
JACKTAR
JACOBIN
JACONET
JACQUES
JACUZZI
JICAMAS
JOCASTA
JOCKEYS
JOCULAR

J••C•••
JACCUSE
JAYCEES
JIMCHEE
JOACHIM
JUICERS
JUICEUP
JUICIER
JUICILY
JUICING
JUNCOES

J•••C••
JANACEK
JERICHO
JOUNCED
JOUNCES
JUMPCUT

J••••C•
JALISCO
JAMAICA
JAMPACK
JESSICA
JUSTICE

J•••••C
JEANLUC
JURIDIC

•J•C•••
EJECTED

••J•C••
DEJECTS
HIJACKS
INJECTS
OBJECTS
REJECTS

••J••C•
ADJUNCT
MAJORCA
REJOICE

•••J•C•
PROJECT
SKYJACK
SUBJECT

J•D••••
JADEDLY
JADEITE
JUDAISM
JUDDERS
JUDGING
JUDOIST

J••D•••
JIMDINE
JUDDERS

J•••D••
JACKDAW
JADEDLY
JANEDOE
JOHNDOE
JOINDER
JOURDAN
JURIDIC

J••••D•
JOYRIDE

J•••••D
JANGLED
JAUNTED
JAYBIRD
JELLIED
JEMMIED
JEWELED
JIGGLED
JIMMIED
JINGLED
JOGGLED
JOINTED
JOISTED
JOLLIED
JOSTLED
JOUNCED
JOUSTED
JUGBAND
JUGGLED
JUGHEAD
JUMBLED
JUTLAND

•J••••D
EJECTED

••J•D••
ADJUDGE

••J•••D
ABJURED
ADJURED
CAJOLED
ENJOYED
INJURED
MAJORED

•••J•D•
HEYJUDE

JE•••••
JEALOUS
JEANARP
JEANLUC
JEANNIE
JEEBIES
JEERERS
JEERING
JEERSAT
JEFFERS
JEFFREY
JEJUNUM
JELLIED
JELLIES
JELLING
JEMMIED
JEMMIES
JENNETS
JENNIES
JERBOAS
JERICHO
JERKIER
JERKILY
JERKING
JERKINS
JERSEYS
JESSICA
JESTERS
JESTING
JESUITS
JETBOAT
JETGUNS
JETPORT
JETSONS
JETTIES
JETTING
JETWASH
JEWELED
JEWELER
JEWELRY
JEZEBEL

J•E••••
JAEGERS
JEEBIES
JEERERS
JEERING
JEERSAT
JOEBLOW
JOEHILL

J••E•••
JADEDLY
JADEITE
JAMESON
JANEDOE
JANEIRO
JANEWAY
JAVELIN
JEWELED
JEWELER
JEWELRY
JEZEBEL
JIMENEZ
JUKEBOX
JUNEBUG
JUVENAL

J•••E••
JABBERS
JACKETS
JAEGERS
JAGLESS
JAILERS
JAMMERS
JAPHETH
JASPERS
JAYCEES
JAYLENO
JAYVEES
JEERERS
JEFFERS
JENNETS
JERSEYS
JESTERS
JIGGERS
JIGGERY
JITNEYS
JITTERS
JITTERY
JOBBERS
JOCKEYS
JOGGERS
JOINERS
JOINERY
JOYLESS
JUDDERS
JUGHEAD
JUICERS
JUICEUP
JUMPERS
JUNKERS
JUNKETS

J••••E•
JACONET
JACQUES
JANACEK
JANGLED
JANGLES
JANSSEN
JANTZEN
JANVIER
JAUNTED
JAYCEES
JAYVEES
JAZZIER
JAZZMEN
JEEBIES
JEFFREY
JELLIED
JELLIES
JEMMIED
JEMMIES
JENNIES
JERKIER
JETTIES
JEWELED
JEWELER
JEZEBEL
JIFFIES
JIGGLED
JIGGLES
JIMCHEE
JIMENEZ
JIMMIED
JIMMIES
JINGLED
JINGLES
JINGOES
JOFFREY
JOGGLED
JOGGLES
JOINDER
JOINTED
JOISTED
JOLLIED
JOLLIER
JOLLIES
JOLLIET
JOSTLED
JOSTLER
JOSTLES
JOUNCED
JOUNCES
JOURNEY
JOUSTED
JOUSTER
JUBILEE
JUGGLED
JUGGLER
JUGGLES
JUICIER
JUJUBES
JUMBLED
JUMBLES
JUMPIER
JUNCOES
JUNGLES
JUNIPER
JUNKIER
JUNKIES
JUPITER

J•••••E
JACCUSE
JADEITE
JANEDOE
JASMINE
JAWBONE
JAWLINE
JAZZAGE
JEANNIE
JIMCHEE
JIMDINE
JOHNDOE
JOHNNIE
JOYRIDE
JUBILEE
JUGWINE
JUSTICE
JUSTINE

•JE••••
EJECTED

•J•••E•
EJECTED

••JE•••
DEJECTS
INJECTS
MAJESTE
MAJESTY
MAJEURE
OBJECTS
REJECTS

••J••E•
ABJURED
ABJURES
ADJURED
ADJURES
CAJOLED
CAJOLER
CAJOLES
ENJOYED
INJOKES
INJURED
INJURES
JUJUBES
MAJORED
PDJAMES

••J•••E
ADJUDGE
MAJESTE
MAJEURE

REJOICE

•••JE••
FANJETS
GASJETS
PROJECT
RAMJETS
SUBJECT
VALJEAN

•••J•E•
BANJOES
PALJOEY

•••J••E
CONJURE
DONJOSE
HEYJUDE
PERJURE
SANJOSE

••••JE•
LEARJET
PROPJET

••••J•E
GOODJOE

J•F••••
JEFFERS
JEFFREY
JIFFIES
JOFFREY

J••F•••
JARFULS
JEFFERS
JEFFREY
JIFFIES
JOFFREY
JUGFULS

J••••F•
JUMPOFF
JUSTIFY

J•••••F
JUMPOFF

J•G••••
JAGGING
JAGLESS
JAGUARS
JIGGERS
JIGGERY
JIGGING
JIGGLED
JIGGLES
JIGSAWS
JOGGERS
JOGGING
JOGGLED
JOGGLES
JUGBAND
JUGFULS
JUGGLED
JUGGLER
JUGGLES
JUGHEAD
JUGULAR
JUGWINE

J••G•••
JAEGERS
JAGGING
JANGLED
JANGLES
JARGONS
JETGUNS
JIGGERS
JIGGERY
JIGGING
JIGGLED
JIGGLES
JINGLED
JINGLES
JINGOES
JOGGERS
JOGGING
JOGGLED
JOGGLES
JUDGING
JUGGLED
JUGGLER
JUGGLES
JUNGLES

J•••G••
JOHNGAY

J••••G•
JAZZAGE

J•••••G
JABBING
JACKING
JAGGING
JAILING
JAMMING
JARRING
JAZZING
JEERING
JELLING
JERKING
JESTING
JETTING
JIGGING
JILTING
JINKING
JINXING
JOBBING
JOGGING
JOINING
JOLTING
JOSHING
JOTTING
JUDGING
JUICING
JUMPING
JUNEBUG
JUNKING
JURYING
JURYRIG
JUTTING

••J••G•
ADJUDGE

•••J••G
BEIJING

J•H••••
JOHANNA
JOHNDOE
JOHNGAY
JOHNJAY
JOHNNIE
JOHNSON

J••H•••
JAPHETH
JOBHOPS
JOBHUNT
JOEHILL
JOSHING
JUGHEAD

J•••H••
JIMCHEE
JOACHIM

J••••H•
JERICHO

J•••••H
JAPHETH
JETWASH

••J•H••
STJOHNS

•••J•H•
BIGJOHN

JI•••••
JIBBOOM
JICAMAS
JIFFIES
JIGGERS
JIGGERY
JIGGING
JIGGLED
JIGGLES
JIGSAWS
JILLIAN
JILLION
JILTING
JIMCHEE
JIMDINE
JIMENEZ
JIMJAMS
JIMMIED
JIMMIES
JIMRYUN
JINGLED
JINGLES
JINGOES
JINKING
JINXING
JITNEYS
JITTERS
JITTERY

J•I••••
JAIALAI
JAILERS
JAILING
JOINDER
JOINERS
JOINERY
JOINING
JOINSIN
JOINSUP
JOINTED
JOINTLY
JOISTED
JUICERS
JUICEUP
JUICIER
JUICILY
JUICING

J••I•••
JABIRUS
JACINTO
JALISCO
JANITOR
JERICHO
JUBILEE
JUJITSU
JULIANA
JUNIORS
JUNIPER
JUPITER
JURIDIC
JURISTS

J•••I••
JABBING
JACKING
JADEITE
JAGGING
JAILING
JAMAICA
JAMMING
JANEIRO
JANVIER
JARRING
JASMINE
JAWLINE
JAYBIRD
JAZZIER
JAZZILY
JAZZING
JEEBIES
JEERING
JELLIED
JELLIES
JELLING
JEMMIED
JEMMIES
JENNIES
JERKIER
JERKILY
JERKING
JERKINS
JESSICA
JESTING
JESUITS
JETTIES
JETTING
JIFFIES
JIGGING
JILLIAN
JILLION
JILTING
JIMDINE
JIMMIED
JIMMIES
JINKING
JINXING
JOBBING
JOEHILL
JOGGING
JOINING
JOLLIED
JOLLIER
JOLLIES
JOLLIET
JOLLILY
JOLLITY
JOLTING
JOSHING
JOTTING
JOYRIDE
JUDAISM
JUDGING
JUDOIST
JUGWINE
JUICIER
JUICILY
JUICING
JUMPIER
JUMPING
JUNKIER
JUNKIES
JUNKING
JURYING
JUSTICE
JUSTIFY
JUSTINE
JUTTING

J••••I•
JACOBIN
JAVELIN
JEANNIE
JOACHIM
JOAQUIN
JOHNNIE
JOINSIN
JONQUIL
JUMPSIN
JURIDIC
JURYRIG

J•••••I
JACUZZI
JAIALAI
JUMANJI

•JI••••
OJIBWAS
OJIBWAY

••JI•••
FAJITAS
FIJIANS
FUJITSU
HIJINKS
JUJITSU

••J•I••
ADJOINS
ENJOINS
REJOICE
REJOINS

•••JI••
BEIJING
IWOJIMA

•••J•I•
CONJOIN
DISJOIN
SUBJOIN

•••J••I
BONJOVI
PUNJABI

••••JI•
LORDJIM
SLIMJIM

•••••JI
BASENJI
JUMANJI

J•J••••
JEJUNUM
JUJITSU
JUJUBES

J••J•••
JIMJAMS

J•••J••
JOHNJAY

J••••J•
JUMANJI

J•K••••
JAKARTA
JUKEBOX

J••K•••
JACKALS
JACKASS
JACKDAW
JACKETS
JACKING
JACKPOT
JACKSON
JACKSUP
JACKTAR
JERKIER
JERKILY
JERKING
JERKINS
JINKING
JOCKEYS
JUNKART
JUNKERS
JUNKETS
JUNKIER
JUNKIES
JUNKING
JUNKMAN

J•••••K
JAMPACK
JANACEK
JAYWALK
JOBBANK

••J•K••
INJOKES

••J••K•
HIJACKS
HIJINKS

•••J••K
SKYJACK

J•L••••
JALISCO
JELLIED
JELLIES
JELLING
JILLIAN
JILLION
JILTING
JOLLIED
JOLLIER
JOLLIES
JOLLIET
JOLLILY
JOLLITY
JOLTING
JULIANA

J••L•••
JAGLESS
JAILERS
JAILING
JAWLINE
JAYLENO
JEALOUS
JELLIED
JELLIES
JELLING
JILLIAN
JILLION
JOBLOTS
JOLLIED
JOLLIER
JOLLIES
JOLLIET
JOLLILY
JOLLITY
JOYLESS
JUTLAND

J•••L••
JAIALAI
JANGLED
JANGLES
JAVELIN
JEANLUC
JEWELED
JEWELER
JEWELRY
JIGGLED
JIGGLES
JINGLED
JINGLES
JOCULAR
JOEBLOW
JOGGLED
JOGGLES
JOSTLED
JOSTLER
JOSTLES
JUBILEE
JUGGLED
JUGGLER
JUGGLES
JUGULAR
JUMBLED
JUMBLES
JUNGLES

J••••L•
JACKALS
JADEDLY
JARFULS
JAYWALK
JAZZILY
JERKILY
JOEHILL
JOINTLY
JOLLILY
JUGFULS
JUICILY

J•••••L
JEZEBEL
JOEHILL
JONQUIL
JOURNAL
JUVENAL

••J•L••
CAJOLED
CAJOLER
CAJOLES

••J••L•
LAJOLLA

J•M••••
JAMAICA
JAMESON
JAMMERS
JAMMING
JAMPACK
JEMMIED
JEMMIES
JIMCHEE
JIMDINE
JIMENEZ
JIMJAMS
JIMMIED
JIMMIES
JIMRYUN
JUMANJI
JUMBLED
JUMBLES
JUMPCUT
JUMPERS
JUMPIER
JUMPING
JUMPOFF
JUMPSAT
JUMPSIN
JUMPSON
JUMPSUP

J••M•••
JAMMERS
JAMMING
JASMINE
JEMMIED
JEMMIES
JIMMIED
JIMMIES

J•••M••
JAVAMAN
JAZZMAN
JAZZMEN
JICAMAS
JUNKMAN

J••••M•
JIMJAMS

J•••••M
JEJUNUM
JIBBOOM
JOACHIM
JUDAISM

••J•M••
PAJAMAS
PDJAMES
PYJAMAS

••J•••M
JEJUNUM

•••J•M•
IWOJIMA
JIMJAMS
LOGJAMS
OUTJUMP
SKIJUMP

••••J•M
CULTJAM
LORDJIM
SLIMJIM

J•N••••
JANACEK
JANEDOE
JANEIRO
JANEWAY
JANGLED
JANGLES
JANITOR
JANSSEN
JANTZEN
JANUARY
JANVIER
JENNETS
JENNIES
JINGLED
JINGLES
JINGOES
JINKING
JINXING
JONQUIL
JUNCOES
JUNEBUG
JUNGLES
JUNIORS
JUNIPER
JUNKART
JUNKERS
JUNKETS
JUNKIER
JUNKIES
JUNKING
JUNKMAN

J••N•••
JAUNTED
JEANARP
JEANLUC
JEANNIE
JENNETS
JENNIES
JITNEYS
JOHNDOE
JOHNGAY
JOHNJAY
JOHNNIE
JOHNSON
JOINDER
JOINERS
JOINERY
JOINING
JOINSIN
JOINSUP
JOINTED
JOINTLY
JOUNCED
JOUNCES

J•••N••
JACANAS
JACINTO
JACONET
JEANNIE
JEJUNUM
JIMENEZ
JOHANNA
JOHNNIE
JOURNAL
JOURNEY
JUMANJI
JUSTNOW
JUVENAL

J••••N•
JABBING
JACKING
JAGGING
JAILING
JAMMING
JARGONS
JARRING
JASMINE
JAWBONE
JAWLINE
JAYLENO
JAZZING
JEERING
JELLING
JERKING
JERKINS
JESTING
JETGUNS
JETSONS
JETTING
JIGGING
JILTING
JIMDINE
JINKING
JINXING
JOBBANK
JOBBING
JOBHUNT
JOGGING
JOHANNA
JOINING
JOLTING
JOSHING
JOTTING
JUDGING
JUGBAND
JUGWINE
JUICING
JULIANA
JUMPING
JUNKING
JURYING
JUSTINE
JUTLAND
JUTTING

J•••••N
JACKSON
JACOBIN
JAMESON
JANSSEN
JANTZEN
JAVAMAN
JAVELIN
JAZZMAN
JAZZMEN
JILLIAN
JILLION
JIMRYUN
JOAQUIN
JOHNSON
JOINSIN
JOURDAN
JUMPSIN
JUMPSON
JUNKMAN

••J•N••
ADJUNCT
HIJINKS
JEJUNUM

••J••N•
ADJOINS
ENJOINS
FIJIANS
REJOINS
STJOHNS
TIJUANA

••J•••N
ADJOURN
SOJOURN

•••J•N•
BEIJING
DONJONS
TROJANS

•••J••N
BIGJOHN
CONJOIN
DISJOIN
DONJUAN
SANJUAN
SUBJOIN
VALJEAN

••••J•N
KARAJAN

JO•••••
JOACHIM
JOAQUIN
JOBBANK
JOBBERS
JOBBING
JOBHOPS
JOBHUNT
JOBLOTS
JOCASTA
JOCKEYS
JOCULAR
JOEBLOW
JOEHILL
JOFFREY
JOGGERS
JOGGING
JOGGLED
JOGGLES
JOHANNA
JOHNDOE
JOHNGAY
JOHNJAY
JOHNNIE
JOHNSON
JOINDER
JOINERS
JOINERY
JOINING
JOINSIN
JOINSUP
JOINTED
JOINTLY
JOISTED
JOLLIED
JOLLIER
JOLLIES
JOLLIET
JOLLILY
JOLLITY
JOLTING
JONQUIL
JOSHING
JOSTLED
JOSTLER
JOSTLES
JOTTING
JOUNCED
JOUNCES
JOURDAN
JOURNAL
JOURNEY
JOUSTED
JOUSTER
JOYLESS
JOYRIDE

J••O•••
JACOBIN
JACONET
JUDOIST

J•••O••
JARGONS
JAWBONE
JEALOUS
JERBOAS
JETBOAT
JETPORT
JETSONS
JIBBOOM
JINGOES
JOBHOPS
JOBLOTS
JUMPOFF
JUNCOES
JUNIORS

J••••O•
JACKPOT
JACKSON
JAMESON
JANEDOE
JANITOR
JIBBOOM
JILLION
JOEBLOW
JOHNDOE
JOHNSON
JUKEBOX
JUMPSON
JUSTNOW

J•••••O
JACINTO
JALISCO
JANEIRO
JAYLENO
JERICHO

••JO•••
ADJOINS
ADJOURN
CAJOLED
CAJOLER
CAJOLES
ENJOINS
ENJOYED
INJOKES
LAJOLLA
MAJORCA
MAJORED
REJOICE
REJOINS
SOJOURN
STJOHNS

•••JO••
BANJOES
BIGJOHN
BONJOUR
BONJOVI
CONJOBS
CONJOIN
DISJOIN
DONJONS
DONJOSE
ODDJOBS
PALJOEY
SANJOSE
SUBJOIN

••••JO•
GOODJOB
GOODJOE
KILLJOY
NAVAJOS
NOSEJOB
OVERJOY
SNOWJOB

J•P••••
JAPHETH
JUPITER

J••P•••
JAMPACK
JASPERS
JETPORT
JUMPCUT
JUMPERS
JUMPIER
JUMPING
JUMPOFF
JUMPSAT
JUMPSIN
JUMPSON
JUMPSUP

J•••P••
JACKPOT
JUNIPER

J••••P•
JOBHOPS

J•••••P
JACKSUP
JEANARP
JOINSUP
JUICEUP
JUMPSUP

•••J••P
OUTJUMP
SKIJUMP

J••Q•••
JACQUES

JOAQUIN
JONQUIL

J•R••••
JARFULS
JARGONS
JARRING
JERBOAS
JERICHO
JERKIER
JERKILY
JERKING
JERKINS
JERSEYS
JURIDIC
JURISTS
JURYING
JURYRIG

J••R•••
JARRING
JEERERS
JEERING
JEERSAT
JIMRYUN
JOURDAN
JOURNAL
JOURNEY
JOYRIDE

J•••R••
JABIRUS
JAKARTA
JEFFREY
JOFFREY
JURYRIG

J••••R•
JABBERS
JAEGERS
JAGUARS
JAILERS
JAMMERS
JANEIRO
JANUARY
JASPERS
JAYBIRD
JEANARP
JEERERS
JEFFERS
JESTERS
JETPORT
JEWELRY
JIGGERS
JIGGERY
JITTERS
JITTERY
JOBBERS
JOGGERS
JOINERS
JOINERY
JUDDERS
JUICERS
JUMPERS
JUNIORS
JUNKART
JUNKERS

J•••••R
JACKTAR
JANITOR
JANVIER
JAZZIER
JERKIER
JEWELER
JOCULAR
JOINDER
JOLLIER
JOSTLER
JOUSTER
JUGGLER
JUGULAR
JUICIER
JUMPIER
JUNIPER
JUNKIER
JUPITER

••J•R••
ABJURED
ABJURES
ADJURED
ADJURES
INJURED
INJURES
MAJORCA
MAJORED

••J••R•
ADJOURN
MAJEURE
SOJOURN

••J•••R
CAJOLER

•••J•R•
CONJURE
PERJURE
PERJURY

•••J••R
BONJOUR

••••J•R
BELLJAR

J•S••••
JASMINE
JASPERS
JESSICA
JESTERS
JESTING
JESUITS
JOSHING
JOSTLED
JOSTLER
JOSTLES
JUSTICE
JUSTIFY
JUSTINE
JUSTNOW

J••S•••
JANSSEN
JERSEYS
JESSICA
JETSONS
JIGSAWS
JOISTED
JOUSTED
JOUSTER

J•••S••
JACKSON
JACKSUP
JALISCO
JAMESON
JANSSEN
JEERSAT
JOCASTA
JOHNSON
JOINSIN
JOINSUP
JUMPSAT
JUMPSIN
JUMPSON
JUMPSUP
JURISTS

J••••S•
JACCUSE
JACKASS
JAGLESS
JETWASH
JOYLESS
JUDAISM
JUDOIST
JUJITSU

J•••••S
JABBERS
JABIRUS
JACANAS
JACKALS
JACKASS
JACKETS
JACQUES
JAEGERS
JAGLESS
JAGUARS
JAILERS
JAMMERS
JANGLES
JARFULS
JARGONS
JASPERS
JAYCEES
JAYVEES
JEALOUS
JEEBIES
JEERERS
JEFFERS
JELLIES
JEMMIES
JENNETS
JENNIES
JERBOAS
JERKINS
JERSEYS
JESTERS
JESUITS
JETGUNS
JETSONS
JETTIES
JICAMAS
JIFFIES
JIGGERS
JIGGLES
JIGSAWS
JIMJAMS
JIMMIES
JINGLES
JINGOES
JITNEYS
JITTERS
JOBBERS
JOBHOPS
JOBLOTS
JOCKEYS
JOGGERS
JOGGLES
JOINERS
JOLLIES
JOSTLES
JOUNCES
JOYLESS
JUDDERS
JUGFULS
JUGGLES
JUICERS
JUJUBES
JUMBLES
JUMPERS
JUNCOES
JUNGLES
JUNIORS
JUNKERS
JUNKETS
JUNKIES
JURISTS

•J••••S
OJIBWAS

••J•S••
ADJUSTS
MAJESTE
MAJESTY

••J••S•
FUJITSU
JUJITSU

••J•••S
ABJURES
ADJOINS
ADJURES
ADJUSTS
CAJOLES
DEJECTS
ENJOINS
FAJITAS
FIJIANS
HIJACKS
HIJINKS
INJECTS
INJOKES
INJURES
JUJUBES
OBJECTS
PAJAMAS
PDJAMES
PYJAMAS
REJECTS
REJOINS
STJOHNS

•••J•S•
DONJOSE
SANJOSE

•••J••S
BANJOES
CONJOBS
DEEJAYS
DONJONS
FANJETS
GASJETS
LOGJAMS
ODDJOBS
RAMJETS
TROJANS
VEEJAYS

••••J•S
NAVAJOS

J•T••••
JETBOAT
JETGUNS
JETPORT
JETSONS
JETTIES
JETTING
JETWASH
JITNEYS
JITTERS
JITTERY
JOTTING
JUTLAND
JUTTING

J••T•••
JANTZEN
JESTERS
JESTING
JETTIES
JETTING
JILTING
JITTERS
JITTERY
JOLTING
JOSTLED
JOSTLER
JOSTLES
JOTTING
JUSTICE
JUSTIFY
JUSTINE
JUSTNOW
JUTTING

J•••T••
JACKTAR
JANITOR
JAUNTED
JOINTED
JOINTLY
JOISTED
JOUSTED
JOUSTER
JUJITSU
JUPITER

J••••T•
JACINTO
JACKETS
JADEITE
JAKARTA
JAPHETH
JENNETS
JESUITS
JOBLOTS
JOCASTA
JOLLITY
JUNKETS
JURISTS

J•••••T
JACKPOT
JACONET
JEERSAT
JETBOAT
JETPORT
JOBHUNT
JOLLIET
JUDOIST
JUMPCUT
JUMPSAT
JUNKART

•J••T••
EJECTED

••J•T••
FAJITAS
FUJITSU
JUJITSU

••J••T•
ADJUSTS
DEJECTS
INJECTS
MAJESTE
MAJESTY
OBJECTS
REJECTS

••J•••T
ADJUNCT

•••J•T•
FANJETS
GASJETS
RAMJETS

•••J••T
PROJECT
SUBJECT

••••J•T
LEARJET
PROPJET

JU•••••
JUBILEE
JUDAISM
JUDDERS
JUDGING
JUDOIST
JUGBAND
JUGFULS
JUGGLED
JUGGLER
JUGGLES
JUGHEAD
JUGULAR
JUGWINE
JUICERS
JUICEUP
JUICIER
JUICILY
JUICING
JUJITSU
JUJUBES
JUKEBOX
JULIANA
JUMANJI
JUMBLED
JUMBLES
JUMPCUT
JUMPERS
JUMPIER
JUMPING
JUMPOFF
JUMPSAT
JUMPSIN
JUMPSON
JUMPSUP
JUNCOES
JUNEBUG
JUNGLES
JUNIORS
JUNIPER
JUNKART
JUNKERS
JUNKETS
JUNKIER
JUNKIES
JUNKING
JUNKMAN
JUPITER
JURIDIC
JURISTS
JURYING
JURYRIG
JUSTICE
JUSTIFY
JUSTINE
JUSTNOW
JUTLAND
JUTTING
JUVENAL

J•U••••
JAUNTED
JOUNCED
JOUNCES
JOURDAN
JOURNAL
JOURNEY
JOUSTED
JOUSTER

J••U•••
JACUZZI
JAGUARS
JANUARY
JEJUNUM
JESUITS
JOCULAR
JUGULAR
JUJUBES

J•••U••
JACCUSE
JACQUES
JARFULS
JETGUNS
JOAQUIN
JOBHUNT
JONQUIL
JUGFULS

J••••U•
JABIRUS
JACKSUP
JEALOUS
JEANLUC
JEJUNUM
JIMRYUN
JOINSUP
JUICEUP
JUMPCUT
JUMPSUP
JUNEBUG

J•••••U
JUJITSU

••JU•••
ABJURED
ABJURES
ADJUDGE
ADJUNCT
ADJURED
ADJURES
ADJUSTS
INJURED
INJURES
JEJUNUM
JUJUBES
TIJUANA

••J•U••
ADJOURN
MAJEURE
SOJOURN

••J••U•
JEJUNUM

••J•••U
FUJITSU
JUJITSU

•••JU••
CONJURE
DONJUAN
HEYJUDE
OUTJUMP
PERJURE
PERJURY
SANJUAN
SKIJUMP

•••J•U•
BONJOUR

J•V••••
JAVAMAN
JAVELIN
JUVENAL

J••V•••
JANVIER
JAYVEES

•••J•V•
BONJOVI

J•W••••
JAWBONE
JAWLINE
JEWELED
JEWELER
JEWELRY

J••W•••
JAYWALK
JETWASH
JUGWINE

J•••W••
JANEWAY

J••••W•
JIGSAWS

J•••••W
JACKDAW
JOEBLOW
JUSTNOW

•J••W••
OJIBWAS
OJIBWAY

J••X•••
JINXING

J•••••X
JUKEBOX

J•Y••••
JAYBIRD
JAYCEES
JAYLENO
JAYVEES
JAYWALK
JOYLESS
JOYRIDE

J••Y•••
JURYING
JURYRIG

J•••Y••
JIMRYUN

J••••Y•
JERSEYS
JITNEYS
JOCKEYS

J•••••Y
JADEDLY
JANEWAY
JANUARY
JAZZILY
JEFFREY
JERKILY
JEWELRY
JIGGERY
JITTERY
JOFFREY
JOHNGAY
JOHNJAY
JOINERY
JOINTLY
JOLLILY
JOLLITY
JOURNEY
JUICILY
JUSTIFY

•J••••Y
OJIBWAY

••J•Y••
ENJOYED

••J•••Y
MAJESTY

•••J•Y•
DEEJAYS
VEEJAYS

•••J••Y
PALJOEY
PERJURY

••••J•Y
BLUEJAY
JOHNJAY
KILLJOY
OVERJOY

J•Z••••
JAZZAGE
JAZZIER
JAZZILY
JAZZING
JAZZMAN
JAZZMEN
JEZEBEL

J••Z•••
JAZZAGE
JAZZIER
JAZZILY
JAZZING
JAZZMAN
JAZZMEN

J•••Z••
JACUZZI
JANTZEN

J••••Z•
JACUZZI

J•••••Z
JIMENEZ

KA•••••
KABUKIS
KACHINA
KADDISH
KAFTANS
KAHUNAS
KAISERS
KAISHEK
KAMPALA
KANAKAS
KANSANS
KARACHI
KARAJAN
KARAKUL
KARAKUM
KARAOKE
KARASEA
KARLOFF
KAROLYI
KASHMIR
KATHRYN
KATYDID
KAYAKED
KAYAKER
KAYOING
KAZAKHS

K•A••••
KHAYYAM
KLAMATH
KLATSCH
KLAXONS
KNAVERY
KNAVISH
KRATERS
KRATION
KWACHAS
KWANZAS

K••A•••
KANAKAS
KARACHI
KARAJAN
KARAKUL
KARAKUM
KARAOKE
KARASEA
KAYAKED
KAYAKER
KAZAKHS
KERATIN
KILAUEA
KIWANIS
KNEADED
KNEADER
KOLACKY
KOMATSU
KUWAITI

K•••A••
KAFTANS
KAMPALA
KANSANS
KENDALL
KENYANS
KEYCARD
KEYPADS
KIDNAPS
KILDARE
KIMBALL
KIRMANS
KITBAGS
KKKKATY
KLAMATH
KODIAKS
KOOLAID
KOREANS

K••••A•
KAHUNAS
KANAKAS
KARAJAN
KEEPSAT
KEESHAN
KEROUAC
KETCHAM
KHAYYAM
KINGMAN
KINGRAT
KINSMAN
KLUGMAN
KNEECAP
KNEEPAD
KORUNAS
KUMQUAT
KUTENAI
KWACHAS
KWANZAS

K•••••A
KACHINA
KAMPALA
KARASEA
KEDROVA
KENOSHA
KILAUEA
KRISHNA

•KA••••
OKAYING
SKATERS
SKATING

•K•A•••
UKRAINE

•K••A••
IKEBANA
KKKKATY
OKINAWA
SKIMASK
SKYCAPS
SKYJACK
SKYLARK
SKYWARD
SKYWAYS

•K•••A•
BKLIBAN

•K••••A
IKEBANA
OKINAWA

••KA•••
ACKACKS
ALKALIS
ASKANCE
DUKAKIS
GOKARTS
JAKARTA
LIKABLE
MIKADOS
SUKARNO

••K•A••
AWKWARD
BAKLAVA
BOKHARA
DIKTATS
ECKHART
ELKHART
KKKKATY
MIKHAIL
OAKLAND
OAKLAWN
TAKEAIM

••K••A•
BIKEWAY
DAKOTAN
DAKOTAS
INKYCAP
LAKOTAS
LIKEMAD
MAKEHAY
MAKEPAR
MAKEWAY
NIKOLAI
OAKLEAF
PIKEMAN
POKEDAT
POKESAT

••K•••A
BAKLAVA
BOKHARA
DYKSTRA
JAKARTA

•••KA••
ARIKARA
BALKANS
COCKADE
CORKAGE
DARKAGE
DOCKAGE
FOLKART
HOOKAHS
JACKALS
JACKASS
JUNKART
KKKKATY
LEAKAGE
LINKAGE
PACKAGE
PACKARD
PICKAXE
POLKAED
PUNKAHS
SINKAGE
SPOKANE
TANKARD
TOPKAPI

•••K•A•
AGAKHAN
BACKBAY
BARKSAT
BUCKRAM
BUCKSAW
CHUKKAS
DARKMAN
GURKHAS
HACKMAN
HACKSAW
HICKMAN
JACKDAW
JACKTAR
JUNKMAN
LOOKSAT
MARKHAM
MARKKAA
MILKMAN
MUSKRAT
PACKRAT
PARKWAY
PECKSAT
PEEKSAT
PICKSAT
QUOKKAS
SICKBAY
SICKPAY
SILKHAT
TALKSAT
WALKMAN
WALKWAY
WEEKDAY
WINKSAT
WORKDAY
WORKMAN

•••K••A
ARIKARA
BURKINA
ELEKTRA
MARKKAA
MARKOVA
RICKSHA

••••KA•
ALASKAN
BLINKAT
CHUKKAS
HANUKAH
KANAKAS
MARKKAA
MARYKAY
MOLOKAI
QUOKKAS
REBEKAH
SHANKAR

TROIKAS

••••K•A
MARKKAA

•••••KA
AMERIKA
BAZOOKA
MAZURKA
PALOOKA
PAPRIKA

K•B••••
KABUKIS
KIBBLED
KIBBLES
KIBBUTZ
KOBLENZ
KOBOLDS
KUBRICK

K••B•••
KEEBLER
KIBBLED
KIBBLES
KIBBUTZ
KIMBALL
KITBAGS
KNOBBED

K•••B••
KNOBBED

K•••••B
KEYCLUB

•K•B•••
IKEBANA
SKIBOOT
SKYBLUE

•K••B••
BKLIBAN

••KB•••
INKBLOT

••K•B••
JUKEBOX
LIKABLE

•••KB••
BACKBAY
BACKBIT
BUNKBED
LOCKBOX
SICKBAY
TALKBIG

•••K••B
BACKRUB

K•C••••
KACHINA
KICKERS
KICKING
KICKOFF
KICKOUT
KICKSIN
KICKSUP
KICKUPS

K••C•••
KERCHOO
KETCHAM
KETCHES
KETCHUP
KEYCARD
KEYCLUB
KITCHEN
KNOCKED
KNOCKER
KNUCKLE
KWACHAS

K•••C••
KARACHI
KITSCHY
KNEECAP
KOLACKY
KOOTCHY
KOPECKS

K••••C•
KLATSCH
KUBRICK

K•••••C
KEROUAC
KINETIC

•K•C•••
SKYCAPS

•K••C••
SKETCHY

•K•••C•
SKYJACK

•K••••C
SKEPTIC

••KC•••
BOKCHOY

••K•C••
ACKACKS
INKYCAP

••K••C•
ASKANCE

•••KC••
MILKCOW

•••K•C•
PACKICE
TOPKICK

•••K••C
RAYKROC

K•D••••
KADDISH
KEDROVA
KIDDERS
KIDDIES
KIDDING
KIDNAPS
KIDNEYS
KIDSKIN
KODIAKS

K••D•••
KADDISH
KENDALL
KIDDERS
KIDDIES
KIDDING
KILDARE
KINDEST
KINDLED
KINDLES
KINDRED
KLUDGES
KURDISH

K•••D••
KATYDID
KEYEDIN
KEYEDUP
KINGDOM
KNEADED
KNEADER

K••••D•
KENNEDY
KEYPADS
KOBOLDS

K•••••D
KATYDID
KAYAKED
KEYCARD
KEYWORD
KIBBLED
KINDLED
KINDRED
KNEADED
KNEELED
KNEEPAD
KNELLED
KNITTED
KNOBBED
KNOCKED
KNOTTED
KNURLED
KOOLAID

•K•D•••
EKEDOUT
SKIDDED
SKIDDER
SKIDDOO
SKIDROW
SKYDIVE

•K••D••
SKIDDED
SKIDDER
SKIDDOO

•K••••D
SKIDDED
SKILLED
SKIMMED
SKIMPED
SKINNED
SKIPPED
SKIRLED
SKIRRED
SKIRTED
SKULKED
SKUNKED
SKYWARD

••KD•••
DIKDIKS

••K•D••
DUKEDOM
MIKADOS
NAKEDLY
POKEDAT
RAKEDIN
RAKEDUP

••K••D•
MAKESDO

••K•••D
AWKWARD
AYKROYD
LIKEMAD
LIKENED
OAKLAND
REKEYED
TOKENED
WAKENED

•••KD••
JACKDAW
WEEKDAY
WORKDAY

•••K•D•
COCKADE

•••K••D
BACKEND
BOOKEND
BUCKLED
BUNKBED
BUNKOED
CACKLED
HECKLED
MANKIND
PACKARD
PICKLED
POLKAED
RANKLED
TACKLED
TANKARD
TICKLED
TINKLED
TREKKED
WEEKEND

••••K•D
BATIKED
BLACKED
BLANKED
BLINKED
BLOCKED
BRICKED
BROOKED
CAULKED
CHALKED
CHECKED
CHINKED
CHUCKED
CLACKED
CLANKED
CLERKED
CLICKED
CLINKED
CLOAKED
CLOCKED
CLUCKED
CLUNKED
CRACKED
CRANKED
CREAKED
CRICKED
CROAKED
CROOKED
FLANKED
FLECKED
FLICKED
FLOCKED
FLUNKED
FRANKED
FREAKED
FRISKED
FROCKED
INVOKED
KAYAKED
KNOCKED
NONSKID
PLANKED
PLINKED
PLUCKED
PLUNKED
PRANKED
PRICKED
PRINKED
QUACKED
REBUKED
REINKED
REVOKED
SHANKED
SHIRKED
SHOCKED
SHUCKED
SKULKED
SKUNKED
SLACKED
SLEEKED
SLICKED
SLINKED
SMACKED
SMIRKED
SNACKED
SNEAKED
SPANKED
SPARKED
SPOOKED
STACKED
STALKED
STOCKED
STROKED
THANKED
TRACKED
TREKKED
TRICKED
TRUCKED
TWEAKED
UNASKED
UNBAKED
UNLIKED
UNYOKED
WHACKED
WHISKED
WHIZKID
WRACKED
WREAKED
WRECKED

KE•••••
KEDROVA
KEEBLER
KEELING
KEENERS
KEENEST
KEENING
KEEPERS
KEEPING
KEEPOFF
KEEPSAT
KEEPSIN
KEEPSON
KEEPSTO
KEEPSUP
KEESHAN
KEGLERS
KEILLOR
KELLOGG
KELPIES
KENDALL
KENNEDY
KENNELS
KENNETH
KENOSHA
KENYANS
KEPTOFF
KEPTOUT
KERATIN
KERCHOO
KERNELS
KERNING
KEROUAC
KERPLOP
KESTREL
KETCHAM
KETCHES
KETCHUP
KETONES
KETTLES
KEWPIES
KEYCARD
KEYCLUB
KEYEDIN
KEYEDUP
KEYHOLE
KEYLIME
KEYNOTE
KEYPADS
KEYRING
KEYWEST
KEYWORD

K•E••••
KEEBLER
KEELING
KEENERS
KEENEST
KEENING
KEEPERS
KEEPING
KEEPOFF
KEEPSAT
KEEPSIN
KEEPSON
KEEPSTO
KEEPSUP
KEESHAN
KLEENEX
KMESONS
KNEADED
KNEADER
KNEECAP
KNEEING
KNEELED
KNEELER
KNEEPAD
KNELLED
KNESSET
KREMLIN

K••E•••
KEYEDIN
KEYEDUP
KINETIC
KLEENEX
KNEECAP
KNEEING
KNEELED
KNEELER
KNEEPAD
KNIEVEL
KOPECKS
KOREANS
KUTENAI

K•••E••
KAISERS
KEENERS
KEENEST
KEEPERS
KEGLERS
KENNEDY
KENNELS
KENNETH
KERNELS
KEYWEST
KICKERS
KIDDERS
KIDNEYS
KILLERS
KINDEST
KIPPERS
KISSERS
KITTENS
KNAVERY
KOBLENZ
KOSHERS
KRATERS

K••••E•
KAISHEK
KARASEA
KAYAKED
KAYAKER
KEEBLER
KELPIES
KESTREL
KETCHES
KETONES
KETTLES
KEWPIES
KIBBLED
KIBBLES
KIDDIES
KILAUEA
KILTIES
KINDLED
KINDLES
KINDRED
KINKIER
KINSMEN
KIRTLES
KISHKES
KITCHEN
KITTIES
KLEENEX
KLUDGES
KLUTZES
KNEADED
KNEADER
KNEELED
KNEELER
KNELLED
KNESSET
KNIEVEL
KNISHES
KNITTED
KNITTER
KNOBBED
KNOCKED
KNOCKER
KNOTTED
KNURLED
KOOKIER
KYLIKES

K•••••E
KARAOKE
KEYHOLE
KEYLIME
KEYNOTE
KILDARE
KIRSTIE
KNUCKLE
KRINGLE

•KE••••
EKEDOUT
EKESOUT
IKEBANA
OKEEFFE
SKEETER
SKEEZIX
SKELTER
SKELTON
SKEPTIC
SKETCHY
SKEWERS
SKEWING

•K•E•••
OKEEFFE
SKEETER
SKEEZIX

•K••E••
SKATERS
SKEWERS
SKIVERS
UKULELE

•K•••E•
SKEETER
SKELTER
SKIDDED
SKIDDER
SKILLED
SKILLET
SKIMMED
SKIMMER
SKIMPED
SKINNED
SKINNER
SKIPPED
SKIPPER
SKIRLED
SKIRRED
SKIRTED
SKITTER
SKOSHES
SKULKED
SKULKER
SKUNKED

•K••••E
OKEEFFE
SKIPOLE
SKITTLE
SKYBLUE
SKYDIVE
SKYLINE
UKRAINE
UKULELE

••KE•••
ALKENES
BAKEOFF
BIKEWAY
CAKEMIX
DUKEDOM
FAKEFUR
JUKEBOX
LIKEMAD
LIKENED
LIKENEW
MAKEFOR
MAKEHAY
MAKEOFF
MAKEOUT
MAKEPAR
MAKESDO
MAKESIT
MAKESUP
MAKEUPS
MAKEWAY
NAKEDLY
PIKEMAN
PIKEMEN
POKEDAT
POKEFUN
POKESAT
RAKEDIN
RAKEDUP
RAKEOFF
RAKESIN
RAKESUP
REKEYED
TAKEAIM
TAKENIN
TAKENON
TAKEOFF
TAKEONE
TAKEOUT
TAKESIN
TAKESON
TAKESTO
TAKESUP
TAKETEN
TOKENED
UNKEMPT
WAKEFUL
WAKENED
WAKENER
WAKESUP
WOKENUP

••K•E••
ANKLETS
AUKLETS
DEKLERK
ICKIEST
INKWELL
OAKFERN
OAKLEAF
POKIEST
YAKKERS

••K••E•
ALKENES
DEKOVEN
LIKENED
LIKENEW
OAKTREE
PIKEMEN
REKEYED
TAKETEN
TOKENED
WAKENED
WAKENER

••K•••E
ASKANCE
IRKSOME
LIKABLE
OAKTREE
TAKEONE
TEKTITE

•••KE••
AWAKENS
BACKEND
BACKERS
BANKERS
BARKEEP
BARKERS
BASKETS
BEAKERS
BECKETT
BICKERS
BONKERS
BOOKEND
BOSKETS
BROKEIN
BROKERS
BROKEUP
BUCKETS
BUCKEYE
BUNKERS
CANKERS
CHOKERS
CHOKEUP
CONKERS
COOKERS
COOKERY
CORKERS
DANKEST
DARKENS
DARKEST
DICKENS
DICKERS
DICKEYS
DOCKERS
DOCKETS
DONKEYS
DUNKERS
EVOKERS
FLAKERS
FORKERS
GASKETS
GAWKERS
HACKERS
HACKETT
HANKERS
HARKENS
HAWKERS
HAWKEYE
HONKERS
HUNKERS
HUSKERS
JACKETS
JOCKEYS
JUNKERS
JUNKETS
KICKERS
LACKEYS
LANKEST
LEAKERS
LICKETY
LINKERS
LOCKERS
LOCKETS
LOOKERS
LUNKERS
MARKERS
MARKETS
MASKERS
MEEKEST
MILKERS
MOCKERS
MOCKERY
MONKEES
MONKEYS
MUSKETS
NANKEEN
NECKERS
NICKELS
NICKERS
PACKERS
PACKETS
PICKENS
PICKERS
PICKETS
PICKETT
PINKEST
POCKETS
PORKERS
PUCKERS
PUCKETT
QUAKERS
RACKETS
RANKERS
RANKEST
RICKETY
RICKEYS
RISKERS
ROCKERS
ROCKETS
ROOKERY
SACKERS
SEEKERS
SHAKERS
SHAKEUP
SHEKELS
SICKENS
SICKEST
SINKERS
SMOKERS
SOAKERS
SOCKETS
SOCKEYE
SPIKERS
SPOKEOF
SPOKEUP
STOKELY
STOKERS
SUCKERS
SULKERS
TACKERS
TALKERS
TANKERS
TICKERS
TICKETS
TINKERS
TUCKERS
TURKEYS
TUSKERS
WALKERS
WEAKENS
WEAKEST
WEEKEND
WICKERS
WICKETS
WINKERS
WORKERS
YAKKERS
YANKEES
YONKERS
ZONKERS

•••K•E•
BALKIER
BARKEEP
BOOKIES
BOOKLET
BUCKLED
BUCKLER
BUCKLES
BUCKLEY
BUCKOES
BULKIER
BUNKBED
BUNKOED
CACKLED
CACKLER
CACKLES
CHUKKER
COCKIER
COCKLES
COCKNEY
COOKIES
DECKLES
DESKSET
DICKIES
DINKIER
DINKIES
DUCKIER
DUSKIER
EZEKIEL
FICKLER
FLAKIER
FUNKIER
GAWKIER
GECKOES
GUNKIER
HACKIES
HACKLES
HACKNEY
HANKIES
HECKLED
HECKLER
HECKLES
HUSKIER
HUSKIES
JERKIER
JUNKIER
JUNKIES
KINKIER
KOOKIER
LANKIER
LEAKIER
LOOKSEE
LUCKIER
MILKIER
MILKMEN
MONKEES
MURKIER
NANKEEN
PERKIER
PESKIER
PICKIER
PICKLED
PICKLES
PINKIES
POLKAED
PUNKIES
RANKLED
RANKLES
RICKLES
RISKIER
ROCKIER
ROCKIES
ROOKIES
SHAKIER
SHAKOES
SICKLES
SILKIER
SMOKIER
SMOKIES
SNAKIER
SPIKIER
SULKIER
SULKIES
TACKIER
TACKLED
TACKLER
TACKLES
TALKIES
TICKLED
TICKLER
TICKLES
TINKLED
TINKLES
TOLKIEN
TOOKTEN
TREKKED
TREKKER
WACKIER
WINKLER
WORKMEN
YANKEES
YUCKIER

•••K••E
BACKHOE
BOXKITE
BUCKEYE
COCKADE
CORKAGE
DARKAGE
DOCKAGE
ERSKINE
HAWKEYE
LEAKAGE
LINKAGE
LOOKSEE
NECKTIE
PACKAGE
PACKICE
PICKAXE
PORKPIE
SINKAGE
SOCKEYE
SPOKANE
TREKKIE

••••KE•
BATIKED

BETAKEN
BETAKES
BETOKEN
BLACKED
BLACKEN
BLACKER
BLANKED
BLANKER
BLANKET
BLEAKER
BLINKED
BLINKER
BLOCKED
BLOCKER
BRACKEN
BRACKET
BREAKER
BRICKED
BRISKER
BRISKET
BROOKED
CAULKED
CAULKER
CHALKED
CHECKED
CHECKER
CHICKEN
CHINKED
CHUCKED
CHUKKER
CLACKED
CLANKED
CLERKED
CLICKED
CLINKED
CLINKER
CLOAKED
CLOCKED
CLOCKER
CLUCKED
CLUNKED
CLUNKER
CRACKED
CRACKER
CRANKED
CREAKED
CRICKED
CRICKET
CROAKED
CROOKED
DEBAKEY
DRINKER
DRUCKER
FLANKED
FLANKER
FLECKED
FLICKED
FLICKER
FLOCKED
FLUNKED
FRANKED
FRANKER
FREAKED
FRISKED
FROCKED
HEARKEN
HOBOKEN
INJOKES
INTAKES
INVOKED
INVOKER
INVOKES
KAYAKED
KAYAKER
KISHKES
KNOCKED
KNOCKER
KYLIKES
LALAKER
MENCKEN
MONIKER
PASSKEY
PATAKES
PERUKES
PLACKET
PLANKED
PLINKED
PLUCKED
PLUNKED
PRANKED
PRICKED
PRINKED
QUACKED
QUICKEN
QUICKER
REBUKED
REBUKES
REINKED
REMAKES
RETAKEN
RETAKES
REVOKED
REVOKES
SHANKED
SHARKEY
SHIRKED
SHIRKER
SHOCKED
SHOCKER
SHRIKES
SHUCKED
SHUCKER
SKULKED
SKULKER
SKUNKED
SLACKED
SLACKEN
SLACKER
SLEEKED
SLEEKEN
SLEEKER
SLICKED
SLICKER
SLINKED
SMACKED
SMACKER
SMIRKED
SNACKED
SNACKER
SNEAKED
SNEAKER
SNICKER
SNOOKER
SNORKEL
SPANKED
SPANKER
SPARKED
SPEAKER
SPOOKED
STACKED
STALKED
STALKER
STARKER
STICKER
STINKER
STOCKED
STOOKEY
STRIKER
STRIKES
STROKED
STROKES
SWANKER
THANKED
THICKEN
THICKER
THICKET
THINKER
TRACKED
TRACKER
TREKKED
TREKKER
TRICKED
TRICKER
TRINKET
TRUCKED
TRUCKEE
TRUCKER
TURNKEY
TWEAKED
UNASKED
UNBAKED
UNLIKED
UNMAKES
UNYOKED
UNYOKES
UPTAKES
WHACKED
WHISKED
WHISKER
WHISKEY
WRACKED
WREAKED
WRECKED
WRECKER

••••K•E
CHUCKLE
CRACKLE
CRINKLE
FRANKIE
FRECKLE
FRICKIE
GRACKLE
KNUCKLE
PRICKLE
QUICKIE
SHACKLE
SPACKLE
SPARKLE
SPECKLE
TREKKIE
TRICKLE
TRUCKEE
TRUCKLE
TWINKLE
WILLKIE
WRINKLE

•••••KE
APELIKE
ATSTAKE
BESPOKE
CATLIKE
CONVOKE
COWPOKE
CUPCAKE
DISLIKE
FORSAKE
GEMLIKE
GOBROKE
GODLIKE
HOECAKE
HOLYOKE
HOTCAKE
KARAOKE
MISTAKE
NETSUKE
OILCAKE
OROURKE
OUTTAKE
OWLLIKE
PANCAKE
PARTAKE
PIGLIKE
PROVOKE
ROANOKE
TEACAKE
UNALIKE
VANDYKE
WARLIKE

K•F••••
KAFTANS

K••F•••
KINFOLK
KNIFING

K••••F•
KARLOFF
KEEPOFF
KEPTOFF
KICKOFF
KISSOFF

K•••••F
KARLOFF
KEEPOFF
KEPTOFF
KICKOFF
KISSOFF

•K••F••
OKEEFFE
SKILFUL

•K•••F•
OKEEFFE
SKILIFT

••KF•••
OAKFERN

••K•F••
ASKSFOR
FAKEFUR
MAKEFOR
POKEFUN
WAKEFUL

••K••F•
BAKEOFF
MAKEOFF
RAKEOFF
TAKEOFF

••K•••F
BAKEOFF
MAKEOFF
OAKLEAF
RAKEOFF
TAKEOFF

•••KF••
FORKFUL
LOOKFOR
SACKFUL
TANKFUL
WORKFOR

•••K•F•
BACKOFF
COOKOFF
KICKOFF
MARKOFF
PICKOFF
TICKOFF
TOOKOFF
WORKOFF

•••K••F
BACKOFF
COOKOFF
KICKOFF
MARKOFF
PICKOFF
SPOKEOF
TICKOFF
TOOKOFF
WORKOFF

••••K•F
SPEAKOF
THINKOF

K•G••••
KEGLERS

K••G•••
KINGDOM
KINGING
KINGMAN
KINGPIN
KINGRAT
KINGTUT
KLUGMAN
KNIGHTS

K•••G••
KLINGON
KLUDGES
KOSYGIN
KRINGLE

K••••G•
KELLOGG
KITBAGS

K•••••G
KAYOING
KEELING
KEENING
KEEPING
KELLOGG
KERNING
KEYRING
KICKING
KIDDING
KILLING
KILTING
KINGING
KINKING
KIPLING
KISSING
KNEEING
KNIFING
KNOWING

•K•••G•
SKYHIGH

•K••••G
OKAYING
SKATING
SKEWING

••K••G•
MAKINGS
VIKINGS

••K•••G
INKLING
YAKKING

•••K•G•
CORKAGE
DARKAGE
DOCKAGE
LEAKAGE
LINKAGE
PACKAGE
SINKAGE

•••K••G
ALAKING
AWAKING
BACKING
BACKLOG
BALKING
BANKING
BARKING
BASKING
BILKING
BOOKING
BRAKING
BUCKING
BULKING
BUNKING
CALKING
COCKING
CONKING
COOKING
CORKING
DECKING
DOCKING
DONKING
DUCKING
DUNKING
EVOKING
FINKING
FLAKING
FORKING
GAWKING
HACKING
HARKING
HAWKING
HOCKING
HONKING
HOOKING
HULKING
HUSKING
JACKING
JERKING
JINKING
JUNKING
KICKING
KINKING
LACKING
LEAKING
LICKING
LINKING
LOCKING
LOOKING
LUCKING
LURKING
MARKING
MASKING
MILKING
MOCKING
MUCKING
NECKING
NICKING
OINKING
PACKING
PARKING
PEAKING
PECKING
PEEKING
PERKING
PICKING
PINKING
QUAKING
RACKING
RANKING
REEKING
RISKING
ROCKING
ROOKING
RUCKING
SACKING
SEEKING
SHAKING
SINKING
SLAKING
SMOKING
SNAKING
SOAKING
SOCKING
SPIKING
SPOKING
STAKING
STOKING
SUCKING
SULKING
TACKING
TALKBIG
TALKING
TANKING
TASKING
TICKING
TUCKING
WALKING
WINKING
WORKING
YAKKING
YANKING
ZONKING

KH•••••
KHAYYAM

K•H••••
KAHUNAS

K••H•••
KACHINA
KASHMIR
KATHRYN
KEYHOLE
KISHKES
KOSHERS

K•••H••
KAISHEK
KEESHAN
KERCHOO
KETCHAM
KETCHES
KETCHUP
KINSHIP
KITCHEN
KNIGHTS
KNISHES
KNOWHOW
KRISHNA
KWACHAS

K••••H•
KARACHI
KAZAKHS
KENOSHA
KITSCHY
KOOTCHY

K•••••H
KADDISH
KENNETH
KLAMATH
KLATSCH
KNAVISH
KURDISH

•KH••••
OKHOTSK

•K•H•••
AKIHITO
SKYHIGH
SKYHOOK

•K••H••
SKOSHES

•K•••H•
SKETCHY

•K••••H
SKYHIGH

••KH•••
BOKHARA
ECKHART
ELKHART
INKHORN
MIKHAIL
SIKHISM

••K•H••
BOKCHOY
MAKEHAY

•••KH••
AGAKHAN
BACKHOE
CHEKHOV
GURKHAS
MARKHAM
MARKHOR
SILKHAT

•••K•H•
HOOKAHS
PUNKAHS
RICKSHA

•••K••H
BOOKISH
DARKISH
HAWKISH
MAWKISH
MONKISH
OSHKOSH
PECKISH
PINKISH
PUCKISH
TURKISH
WEAKISH

••••KH•
KAZAKHS
SHEIKHS

••••K•H
HANUKAH
REBEKAH

KI•••••
KIBBLED
KIBBLES
KIBBUTZ
KICKERS
KICKING
KICKOFF
KICKOUT
KICKSIN
KICKSUP
KICKUPS
KIDDERS
KIDDIES
KIDDING
KIDNAPS
KIDNEYS
KIDSKIN
KIKUYUS
KILAUEA
KILDARE
KILLERS
KILLING
KILLJOY
KILOTON
KILTIES
KILTING
KIMBALL
KIMONOS
KINDEST
KINDLED
KINDLES
KINDRED
KINETIC
KINFOLK
KINGDOM
KINGING
KINGMAN
KINGPIN
KINGRAT
KINGTUT
KINKIER
KINKING
KINSHIP
KINSMAN
KINSMEN
KIPLING
KIPPERS
KIRMANS
KIRSTIE
KIRTLES
KISHKES
KISSERS
KISSING
KISSOFF
KITBAGS
KITCHEN
KITSCHY
KITTENS
KITTIES
KIWANIS

K•I••••
KAISERS
KAISHEK
KEILLOR
KLINGON
KNIEVEL
KNIFING
KNIGHTS
KNISHES
KNITTED
KNITTER
KRINGLE
KRISHNA

K••I•••
KODIAKS
KYLIKES

K•••I••
KACHINA
KADDISH
KAYOING
KEELING
KEENING
KEEPING
KELPIES
KERNING
KEWPIES
KEYLIME
KEYRING
KICKING
KIDDIES
KIDDING
KILLING
KILTIES
KILTING
KINGING
KINKIER
KINKING
KIPLING
KISSING
KITTIES
KNAVISH
KNEEING
KNIFING
KNOWING
KONTIKI
KOOKIER
KRATION
KUBRICK
KURDISH
KUWAITI

K••••I•
KABUKIS
KASHMIR
KATYDID
KEEPSIN
KERATIN
KEYEDIN
KICKSIN
KIDSKIN
KINETIC
KINGPIN
KINSHIP
KIRSTIE
KIWANIS
KOOLAID
KOSYGIN
KREMLIN
KTOSLIN

K•••••I
KARACHI
KAROLYI
KONTIKI
KUTENAI
KUWAITI

•KI••••
AKIHITO
OKINAWA
SKIBOOT
SKIDDED
SKIDDER
SKIDDOO
SKIDROW
SKIJUMP
SKILFUL
SKILIFT
SKILLED
SKILLET
SKIMASK
SKIMMED
SKIMMER
SKIMPED
SKINNED
SKINNER
SKIPOLE
SKIPOUT
SKIPPED
SKIPPER
SKIRLED
SKIRRED
SKIRTED
SKIRUNS
SKISUIT
SKITOWS
SKITTER
SKITTLE
SKIVERS

•K•I•••
BKLIBAN

•K••I••
AKIHITO
OKAYING
SKATING
SKEWING
SKILIFT
SKYDIVE
SKYHIGH
SKYLINE
UKRAINE

•K•••I•
SKEEZIX
SKEPTIC
SKISUIT

••KI•••
BIKINIS
ESKIMOS
ICKIEST
MAKINGS
POKIEST
STKITTS
UNKINKS
VIKINGS

••K•I••
DIKDIKS
INKLING
RYKRISP
SIKHISM
TEKTITE
UNKNITS
YAKKING

••K••I•
ALKALIS
BIKINIS
CAKEMIX
DUKAKIS
MAKESIT
MIKHAIL
NOKOMIS
RAKEDIN
RAKESIN
TAKEAIM
TAKENIN
TAKESIN

••K•••I
NIKOLAI

•••KI••
ALAKING
AWAKING
BACKING
BALKIER
BALKING
BANKING
BARKING
BASKING
BILKING
BODKINS
BOOKIES
BOOKING
BOOKISH
BOXKITE
BRAKING
BUCKING
BULKIER
BULKING
BUNKING
BURKINA
BUSKINS
CALKING
CALKINS
CATKINS
COCKIER
COCKILY
COCKING
CONKING
COOKIES
COOKING
CORKING
DARKISH
DAWKINS
DECKING
DICKIES
DINKIER
DINKIES
DOCKING
DONKING
DUCKIER
DUCKING
DUNKING
DUNKIRK
DUSKIER
ERSKINE
EVOKING
EZEKIEL
FINKING
FIRKINS
FLAKIER
FLAKING
FORKING
FUNKIER
GASKINS
GAWKIER
GAWKING
GUNKIER
HACKIES
HACKING
HANKIES
HARKING
HAWKING
HAWKINS
HAWKISH
HOCKING
HONKING
HOOKING
HOPKINS
HOSKINS
HULKING
HUSKIER
HUSKIES
HUSKILY
HUSKING
JACKING
JERKIER
JERKILY
JERKING
JERKINS
JINKING
JUNKIER
JUNKIES
JUNKING
KICKING
KINKIER
KINKING
KOOKIER
LACKING
LANKIER
LANKILY
LEAKIER
LEAKING
LICKING
LINKING
LOCKING
LOCKINS
LOOKING
LUCKIER
LUCKILY
LUCKING
LURKING
MANKIND
MARKING
MASKING
MAWKISH
MILKIER
MILKING
MOCKING
MONKISH
MUCKING
MURKIER
MURKILY
NAPKINS
NECKING
NICKING

OINKING
PACKICE
PACKING
PARKING
PEAKING
PECKING
PECKISH
PEEKING
PERKIER
PERKILY
PERKING
PERKINS
PESKIER
PESKILY
PICKIER
PICKING
PINKIES
PINKING
PINKISH
PIPKINS
PUCKISH
PUNKIES
QUAKING
RACKING
RANKING
REEKING
RISKIER
RISKING
ROCKIER
ROCKIES
ROCKING
ROOKIES
ROOKING
RUCKING
SACKING
SEEKING
SELKIRK
SHAKIER
SHAKILY
SHAKING
SILKIER
SILKILY
SINKING
SISKINS
SLAKING
SMOKIER
SMOKIES
SMOKING
SNAKIER
SNAKING
SOAKING
SOCKING
SPIKIER
SPIKING
SPOKING
STAKING
STOKING
SUCKING
SULKIER
SULKIES
SULKILY
SULKING
SUNKIST
TACKIER
TACKILY
TACKING
TALKIES
TALKING
TANKING
TASKING
TICKING
TOLKIEN
TOPKICK
TUCKING
TURKISH
WACKIER
WACKILY
WAIKIKI
WALKING
WALKINS
WEAKISH
WELKINS
WESKITS
WICKIUP
WINKING
WORKING
YAKKING
YANKING
YUCKIER
ZONKING

•••K•I•
BACKBIT
BACKLIT
BACKSIN
BROKEIN
COCKPIT
DUCKPIN
KICKSIN
LOOKSIN
NECKTIE
PORKPIE
ROCKYII
ROCKYIV
SINKSIN
SOCKSIN
SUCKSIN
TALKBIG
TREKKIE
TUCKSIN
WORKSIN

•••K••I
ROCKYII
TOPKAPI
WAIKIKI

••••KI•
ABNAKIS
ANDYKIM
BREAKIN
BUMPKIN
CHECKIN
CLOCKIN
DOESKIN
DUKAKIS
EELSKIN
EVENKIS
FRANKIE
FRICKIE
GHERKIN
KABUKIS
KIDSKIN
MESSKIT
NONSKID
OILSKIN
PIGSKIN
PUMPKIN
PUSHKIN
QUICKIE
RAMEKIN
REDSKIN
SALUKIS
SLATKIN
SNEAKIN
TIOMKIN
TREKKIE
WHIZKID
WILLKIE

••••K•I
MOLOKAI

•••••KI
ABENAKI
DASHIKI
KONTIKI
PULASKI
WAIKIKI

K•••J••
KARAJAN
KILLJOY

•K•J•••
SKIJUMP
SKYJACK

KK•••••
KKKKATY

K•K••••
KIKUYUS
KKKKATY

K••K•••
KICKERS
KICKING
KICKOFF
KICKOUT
KICKSIN
KICKSUP
KICKUPS
KINKIER
KINKING
KKKKATY
KOOKIER

K•••K••
KABUKIS
KANAKAS
KARAKUL
KARAKUM
KAYAKED
KAYAKER
KAZAKHS
KIDSKIN
KISHKES
KNOCKED
KNOCKER
KNUCKLE
KYLIKES

K••••K•
KARAOKE
KODIAKS
KOLACKY
KONTIKI
KOPECKS

K•••••K
KAISHEK
KINFOLK
KUBRICK

•KK••••
KKKKATY

•K•K•••
KKKKATY

•K••K••
SKULKED
SKULKER
SKUNKED

•K••••K
OKHOTSK
SKIMASK
SKYHOOK
SKYJACK
SKYLARK

••KK•••
KKKKATY
YAKKERS
YAKKING

••K•K••
DUKAKIS

••K••K•
ACKACKS
DIKDIKS
MUKLUKS
UNKINKS

••K•••K
DEKLERK
YAKUTSK

•••KK••
CHUKKAS
CHUKKER
MARKKAA
QUOKKAS
TREKKED
TREKKER
TREKKIE

•••K•K•
WAIKIKI

•••K••K
DUNKIRK
SELKIRK
TOPKICK

••••K•K
BANGKOK

KL•••••
KLAMATH
KLATSCH
KLAXONS
KLEENEX
KLINGON
KLUDGES
KLUGMAN
KLUTZES

K•L••••
KELLOGG
KELPIES
KILAUEA
KILDARE
KILLERS
KILLING
KILLJOY
KILOTON
KILTIES
KILTING
KOLACKY
KYLIKES

K••L•••
KARLOFF
KEELING
KEGLERS
KEILLOR
KELLOGG
KEYLIME
KILLERS
KILLING
KILLJOY
KIPLING
KNELLED
KOBLENZ
KOOLAID
KOWLOON

K•••L••
KAROLYI
KEEBLER
KEILLOR
KERPLOP
KETTLES
KEYCLUB
KIBBLED
KIBBLES
KINDLED
KINDLES
KIRTLES
KNEELED
KNEELER
KNELLED
KNURLED
KOBOLDS
KREMLIN
KTOSLIN

K••••L•
KAMPALA
KENDALL
KENNELS
KERNELS
KEYHOLE
KIMBALL
KINFOLK
KNUCKLE
KRINGLE

K•••••L
KARAKUL
KENDALL
KESTREL
KIMBALL
KNIEVEL

•KL••••
BKLIBAN

•K•L•••
SKELTER
SKELTON
SKILFUL
SKILIFT
SKILLED
SKILLET
SKULKED
SKULKER
SKYLARK
SKYLINE
UKULELE

•K••L••
SKILLED
SKILLET
SKIRLED
SKYBLUE

•K•••L•
SKIPOLE
SKITTLE
UKULELE

•K••••L
SKILFUL

••KL•••
ANKLETS
AUKLETS
BAKLAVA
DEKLERK
INKLING
MUKLUKS
OAKLAND
OAKLAWN
OAKLEAF

••K•L••
ALKALIS
INKBLOT
NIKOLAI

••K••L•
INKWELL
LIKABLE
NAKEDLY

••K•••L
INKWELL
MIKHAIL
WAKEFUL

•••KL••
BACKLIT
BACKLOG
BOOKLET
BUCKLED
BUCKLER
BUCKLES
BUCKLEY
CACKLED
CACKLER
CACKLES
COCKLES
DECKLES
FICKLER
HACKLES
HECKLED
HECKLER
HECKLES
PICKLED
PICKLES
RANKLED
RANKLES
RICKLES
SICKLES
TACKLED
TACKLER
TACKLES
TICKLED
TICKLER
TICKLES
TINKLED
TINKLES
WINKLER

•••K•L•
COCKILY
HUSKILY
JACKALS
JERKILY
LANKILY
LUCKILY
MURKILY
NICKELS
PERKILY
PESKILY
SHAKILY
SHEKELS
SILKILY
STOKELY
SULKILY
TACKILY
WACKILY

•••K••L
EZEKIEL
FORKFUL
SACKFUL
TANKFUL

••••KL•
BLACKLY
BLANKLY
BLEAKLY
BRISKLY
CHUCKLE
CRACKLE
CRINKLE
CRINKLY
FRANKLY
FRECKLE
GRACKLE
KNUCKLE
PRICKLE
PRICKLY
QUICKLY
SHACKLE
SLEEKLY
SLICKLY
SPACKLE
SPARKLE
SPECKLE
STARKLY
THICKLY
TRICKLE
TRUCKLE
TWINKLE
TWINKLY
WRINKLE
WRINKLY

••••K•L
KARAKUL
SNORKEL

KM•••••
KMESONS

K•M••••
KAMPALA
KIMBALL
KIMONOS
KOMATSU
KUMQUAT

K••M•••
KIRMANS
KLAMATH
KREMLIN

K•••M••
KASHMIR
KINGMAN
KINSMAN
KINSMEN
KLUGMAN

K••••M•
KEYLIME

K•••••M
KARAKUM
KETCHAM
KHAYYAM
KINGDOM

•K•M•••
SKIMASK
SKIMMED
SKIMMER
SKIMPED

•K••M••
SKIMMED
SKIMMER

•K•••M•
SKIJUMP

••KM•••
OAKMOSS

••K•M••
CAKEMIX
ESKIMOS
LIKEMAD
NOKOMIS
PIKEMAN
PIKEMEN
UNKEMPT

••K••M•
IRKSOME

••K•••M
DUKEDOM
SIKHISM
TAKEAIM

•••KM••
DARKMAN
HACKMAN
HICKMAN
JUNKMAN
MILKMAN
MILKMEN
WALKMAN
WORKMAN
WORKMEN

•••K••M
BUCKRAM
MARKHAM

••••K•M
ANDYKIM
KARAKUM

KN•••••
KNAVERY
KNAVISH
KNEADED
KNEADER
KNEECAP
KNEEING
KNEELED
KNEELER
KNEEPAD
KNELLED
KNESSET
KNIEVEL
KNIFING
KNIGHTS
KNISHES
KNITTED
KNITTER
KNOBBED
KNOCKED
KNOCKER
KNOSSOS
KNOTTED
KNOWHOW
KNOWING
KNUCKLE
KNURLED

K•N••••
KANAKAS
KANSANS
KENDALL
KENNEDY
KENNELS
KENNETH
KENOSHA
KENYANS
KINDEST
KINDLED
KINDLES
KINDRED
KINETIC
KINFOLK
KINGDOM
KINGING
KINGMAN
KINGPIN
KINGRAT
KINGTUT
KINKIER
KINKING
KINSHIP
KINSMAN
KINSMEN
KONTIKI

K••N•••
KEENERS
KEENEST
KEENING
KENNEDY
KENNELS
KENNETH
KERNELS
KERNING
KEYNOTE
KIDNAPS
KIDNEYS
KLINGON
KRINGLE
KWANZAS

K•••N••
KAHUNAS
KETONES
KIMONOS
KIWANIS
KLEENEX
KORUNAS
KUTENAI

K••••N•
KACHINA
KAFTANS
KANSANS
KAYOING
KEELING
KEENING
KEEPING
KENYANS
KERNING
KEYRING
KICKING
KIDDING
KILLING
KILTING
KINGING
KINKING
KIPLING
KIRMANS
KISSING
KITTENS
KLAXONS
KMESONS
KNEEING
KNIFING
KNOWING
KOBLENZ
KOREANS
KRISHNA

K•••••N
KARAJAN
KATHRYN
KEEPSIN
KEEPSON
KEESHAN
KERATIN
KEYEDIN
KICKSIN
KIDSKIN
KILOTON
KINGMAN
KINGPIN
KINSMAN
KINSMEN
KITCHEN
KLINGON
KLUGMAN
KOSYGIN
KOWLOON
KRATION
KREMLIN
KRYPTON
KTOSLIN

•K•N•••
OKINAWA
SKINNED
SKINNER
SKUNKED

•K••N••
SKINNED
SKINNER

•K•••N•
IKEBANA
OKAYING
SKATING
SKEWING
SKIRUNS
SKYLINE
UKRAINE

•K••••N
BKLIBAN
SKELTON

••KN•••
UNKNITS
UNKNOTS
UNKNOWN

••K•N••
ALKENES
ASKANCE
BIKINIS
LIKENED
LIKENEW
MAKINGS
TAKENIN
TAKENON
TOKENED
UNKINKS
VIKINGS
WAKENED
WAKENER
WOKENUP

••K••N•
INKLING
OAKLAND
SUKARNO
TAKEONE
YAKKING
YOKOONO

••K•••N
DAKOTAN
DEKOVEN
INKHORN
OAKFERN
OAKLAWN
PIKEMAN
PIKEMEN
POKEFUN
RAKEDIN
RAKESIN
TAKENIN
TAKENON
TAKESIN
TAKESON
TAKETEN
UNKNOWN

•••KN••
BOWKNOT
COCKNEY
HACKNEY
LOCKNUT
TOPKNOT
YOUKNOW

•••K•N•
ALAKING
AWAKENS
AWAKING
BACKEND
BACKING
BALKANS
BALKING
BANKING
BARKING
BASKING
BECKONS
BILKING
BODKINS
BOOKEND
BOOKING
BRAKING
BUCKING
BULKING
BUNKING
BURKINA
BUSKINS
CALKING
CALKINS
CATKINS
COCKING
CONKING
COOKING
CORKING
DARKENS
DAWKINS
DECKING
DICKENS
DOCKING
DONKING
DUCKING
DUNKING
ERSKINE
EVOKING
FINKING
FIRKINS
FLAKING
FORKING
GASKINS
GAWKING
HACKING
HARKENS
HARKING
HAWKING
HAWKINS
HOCKING
HONKING
HOOKING
HOPKINS
HOSKINS
HULKING
HUSKING
JACKING
JERKING
JERKINS
JINKING
JUNKING
KICKING
KINKING
LACKING
LEAKING
LICKING
LINKING
LOCKING
LOCKINS
LOOKING
LUCKING
LURKING
MANKIND
MARKING
MASKING
MILKING
MOCKING
MUCKING
NAPKINS
NECKING
NICKING
OINKING
PACKING
PARKING
PEAKING
PECKING
PEEKING
PERKING
PERKINS
PICKENS
PICKING
PINKING
PIPKINS
QUAKING
RACKING
RANKING
RECKONS
REEKING
RISKING
ROCKING
ROOKING
RUCKING
SACKING
SEEKING
SHAKING
SICKENS
SINKING
SISKINS
SLAKING
SMOKING
SNAKING
SOAKING
SOCKING
SPIKING
SPOKANE
SPOKING
STAKING
STOKING
SUCKING
SULKING
TACKING
TALKING
TANKING
TASKING
TICKING
TUCKING
WALKING
WALKINS
WALKONS
WEAKENS
WEEKEND
WELKINS
WINKING
WORKING
YAKKING
YANKING
ZONKING

•••K••N
AGAKHAN
BACKSIN
BANKSON
BROKEIN
DARKMAN
DUCKPIN
HACKMAN
HICKMAN
JACKSON
JUNKMAN
KICKSIN
LOOKSIN
LOOKSON
MILKMAN

MILKMEN
MILKRUN
NANKEEN
PICKSON
SINKSIN
SOCKSIN
SUCKSIN
TACKSON
TOLKIEN
TOOKTEN
TUCKSIN
WALKMAN
WORKMAN
WORKMEN
WORKSIN
WORKSON
YANKTON

••••K•N
ALASKAN
BELAKUN
BETAKEN
BETOKEN
BLACKEN
BRACKEN
BREAKIN
BUMPKIN
CHECKIN
CHICKEN
CLOCKIN
DOESKIN
EELSKIN
GHERKIN
HEARKEN
HOBOKEN
IRECKON
KIDSKIN
MENCKEN
OILSKIN
PIGSKIN
PUMPKIN
PUSHKIN
QUICKEN
RAMEKIN
REDSKIN
RETAKEN
SLACKEN
SLATKIN
SLEEKEN
SNEAKIN
THICKEN
TIOMKIN

KO•••••
KOBLENZ
KOBOLDS
KODIAKS
KOLACKY
KOMATSU
KONTIKI
KOOKIER
KOOLAID
KOOTCHY
KOPECKS
KOREANS
KORUNAS
KOSHERS
KOSYGIN
KOWLOON
KOWTOWS

K•O•••••
KNOBBED
KNOCKED
KNOCKER
KNOSSOS
KNOTTED
KNOWHOW
KNOWING
KOOKIER
KOOLAID
KOOTCHY
KTOSLIN

K••O•••
KAROLYI
KAYOING
KENOSHA
KEROUAC
KETONES
KILOTON
KIMONOS
KOBOLDS

K•••O••
KARAOKE
KARLOFF
KEDROVA
KEEPOFF
KELLOGG
KEPTOFF
KEPTOUT
KEYHOLE
KEYNOTE
KEYWORD
KICKOFF
KICKOUT
KINFOLK
KISSOFF
KLAXONS
KMESONS
KOWLOON
KOWTOWS

K••••O•
KEEPSON
KEILLOR
KERCHOO
KERPLOP
KILLJOY
KILOTON
KIMONOS
KINGDOM
KLINGON
KNOSSOS
KNOWHOW
KOWLOON
KRATION
KRYPTON

K•••••O
KEEPSTO
KERCHOO

•KO••••
SKOSHES

•K•O•••
OKHOTSK

•K••O••
EKEDOUT
EKESOUT
SKIBOOT
SKIPOLE
SKIPOUT
SKITOWS
SKYHOOK

•K•••O•
SKELTON
SKIBOOT
SKIDDOO
SKIDROW
SKYHOOK

•K••••O
AKIHITO
SKIDDOO

••KO•••
DAKOTAN
DAKOTAS
DEKOVEN
LAKOTAS
NIKOLAI
NOKOMIS
YOKOONO

••K•O••
ASKSOUT
AYKROYD
BAKEOFF
INKHORN
IRKSOME
MAKEOFF
MAKEOUT
OAKMOSS
RAKEOFF
TAKEOFF
TAKEONE
TAKEOUT
UNKNOTS
UNKNOWN
YOKOONO

••K••O•
ASKSFOR
BOKCHOY
DUKEDOM
ESKIMOS
INKBLOT
INKSPOT
JUKEBOX
MAKEFOR
MIKADOS
TAKENON
TAKESON

••K•••O
MAKESDO
SUKARNO
TAKESTO
YOKOONO

•••KO••
BACKOFF
BACKOUT
BECKONS
BUCKOES
BUNKOED
CONKOUT
COOKOFF
COOKOUT
CUCKOOS
DECKOUT
GECKOES
HICKORY
KICKOFF
KICKOUT
LOCKOUT
LOOKOUT
LUCKOUT
MARKOFF
MARKOVA
OSHKOSH
PEEKOUT
PICKOFF
PICKOUT
RECKONS
SACKOUT
SEEKOUT
SHAKOES
SICKOUT
TALKOUT
TICKOFF
TOOKOFF
TOOKOUT
WALKONS
WALKOUT
WINKOUT
WORKOFF
WORKOUT
ZONKOUT

•••K•O•
BACKHOE
BACKLOG
BANKSON
BOWKNOT
CHEKHOV
CUCKOOS
DESKTOP
JACKPOT
JACKSON
LOCKBOX
LOOKFOR
LOOKSON
MARKHOR
MILKCOW
MILKSOP
PICKSON
RAYKROC
SPOKEOF
TACKSON
TANKTOP
TOPKNOT
WORKFOR
WORKSON
YANKTON
YOUKNOW

•••K••O
LOOKSTO
TALKSTO

••••KO•
BANGKOK
FRANKOZ
IRECKON
NABOKOV
SPEAKOF
THINKOF

••••K•O
FLOCKTO
STICKTO
STUCKTO

•••••KO
GROMYKO

K•P••••
KEPTOFF
KEPTOUT
KIPLING
KIPPERS
KOPECKS

K••P•••
KAMPALA
KEEPERS
KEEPING
KEEPOFF
KEEPSAT
KEEPSIN
KEEPSON
KEEPSTO
KEEPSUP
KELPIES
KERPLOP
KEWPIES
KEYPADS
KIPPERS
KRYPTON

K•••P••
KINGPIN
KNEEPAD

K••••P•
KICKUPS
KIDNAPS

K•••••P
KEEPSUP
KERPLOP
KETCHUP
KEYEDUP
KICKSUP
KINSHIP
KNEECAP

•K•P•••
SKEPTIC
SKIPOLE
SKIPOUT
SKIPPED
SKIPPER

•K••P••
SKIMPED
SKIPPED
SKIPPER

•K•••P•
SKYCAPS

•K••••P
SKIJUMP

••K•P••
INKSPOT
MAKEPAR

••K••P•
MAKEUPS
UNKEMPT

••K•••P
INKYCAP
MAKESUP
RAKEDUP
RAKESUP
RYKRISP
TAKESUP
WAKESUP
WOKENUP

•••KP••
COCKPIT
DUCKPIN
JACKPOT
PORKPIE
SICKPAY

•••K•P•
BACKUPS
HOOKUPS
KICKUPS
LINKUPS
LOCKUPS
LOOKUPS
MARKUPS
MOCKUPS
PICKUPS
TOPKAPI
WALKUPS
WORKUPS

•••K••P
BACKSUP
BARKEEP
BROKEUP
BUCKSUP
CHOKEUP
COOKSUP
DESKTOP
HOOKSUP
JACKSUP
KICKSUP
LOCKSUP
LOOKSUP
MARKSUP
MILKSOP
MUCKSUP
PACKSUP
PERKSUP
PICKSUP
RACKSUP
SHAKEUP
SOAKSUP
SPOKEUP
TALKSUP
TANKSUP
TANKTOP
WICKIUP
WORKSUP

••••K•P
BREAKUP
CHALKUP
CHECKUP
CRACKUP
CRANKUP
SHOOKUP
SPEAKUP
STACKUP
STICKUP
STOCKUP
STUCKUP
THINKUP

K••Q•••
KUMQUAT

KR•••••
KRATERS
KRATION
KREMLIN
KRINGLE
KRISHNA
KRYPTON

K•R••••
KARACHI
KARAJAN
KARAKUL
KARAKUM
KARAOKE
KARASEA
KARLOFF
KAROLYI
KERATIN
KERCHOO
KERNELS
KERNING
KEROUAC
KERPLOP
KIRMANS
KIRSTIE
KIRTLES
KOREANS
KORUNAS
KURDISH

K••R•••
KEDROVA
KEYRING
KNURLED
KUBRICK

K•••R••
KATHRYN
KESTREL
KINDRED
KINGRAT

K••••R•
KAISERS
KEENERS
KEEPERS
KEGLERS
KEYCARD
KEYWORD
KICKERS
KIDDERS
KILDARE
KILLERS
KIPPERS
KISSERS
KNAVERY
KOSHERS
KRATERS

K•••••R
KASHMIR
KAYAKER
KEEBLER
KEILLOR
KINKIER
KNEADER
KNEELER
KNITTER
KNOCKER
KOOKIER

•KR••••
UKRAINE

•K•R•••
SKIRLED
SKIRRED
SKIRTED
SKIRUNS

•K••R••
SKIDROW
SKIRRED

•K•••R•
SKATERS
SKEWERS
SKIVERS
SKYLARK
SKYWARD

•K••••R
SKEETER
SKELTER
SKIDDER
SKIMMER
SKINNER
SKIPPER
SKITTER
SKULKER

••KR•••
AYKROYD
RYKRISP

••K•R••
GOKARTS
JAKARTA
OAKTREE
SUKARNO

••K••R•
AWKWARD
BOKHARA
DEKLERK
DYKSTRA
ECKHART
ELKHART
INKHORN
OAKFERN
YAKKERS

••K•••R
ASKSFOR
FAKEFUR
MAKEFOR
MAKEPAR
WAKENER

•••KR••
BACKRUB
BUCKRAM
MILKRUN
MUSKRAT
PACKRAT
RAYKROC

•••K•R•
ARIKARA
BACKERS
BANKERS
BARKERS
BEAKERS
BICKERS
BONKERS
BROKERS
BUNKERS
CANKERS
CHOKERS
CONKERS
COOKERS
COOKERY
CORKERS
DICKERS
DOCKERS
DUNKERS
DUNKIRK
ELEKTRA
EVOKERS
FLAKERS
FOLKART
FORKERS
GAWKERS
HACKERS
HANKERS
HAWKERS
HICKORY
HONKERS
HUNKERS
HUSKERS
JUNKART
JUNKERS
KICKERS
LEAKERS
LINKERS
LOCKERS
LOOKERS
LUNKERS
MARKERS
MASKERS
MILKERS
MOCKERS
MOCKERY
NECKERS
NICKERS
PACKARD
PACKERS
PICKERS
PORKERS
PUCKERS
QUAKERS
RANKERS
RISKERS
ROCKERS
ROOKERY
SACKERS
SEEKERS
SELKIRK
SHAKERS
SINKERS
SMOKERS
SOAKERS
SPIKERS
STOKERS
SUCKERS
SULKERS
TACKERS
TALKERS
TANKARD
TANKERS
TICKERS
TINKERS
TUCKERS
TUSKERS
WALKERS
WICKERS
WINKERS
WORKERS
YAKKERS
YONKERS
ZONKERS

•••K••R
BALKIER
BUCKLER
BULKIER
CACKLER
CHUKKER
COCKIER
DINKIER
DUCKIER
DUSKIER
FICKLER
FLAKIER
FUNKIER
GAWKIER
GUNKIER
HECKLER
HUSKIER
JACKTAR
JERKIER
JUNKIER
KINKIER
KOOKIER
LANKIER
LEAKIER
LOOKFOR
LUCKIER
MARKHOR
MILKIER
MURKIER
PERKIER
PESKIER
PICKIER
RISKIER
ROCKIER
SHAKIER
SILKIER
SMOKIER
SNAKIER
SPIKIER
SULKIER
TACKIER
TACKLER
TICKLER
TREKKER
WACKIER
WINKLER
WORKFOR
YUCKIER

••••KR•
CONAKRY

••••K•R
BLACKER
BLANKER
BLEAKER
BLINKER
BLOCKER
BREAKER
BRISKER
CAULKER
CHECKER
CHUKKER
CLINKER
CLOCKER
CLUNKER
CRACKER
DRINKER
DRUCKER
FLANKER
FLICKER
FRANKER
INVOKER
KAYAKER
KNOCKER
LALAKER
MONIKER
QUICKER
SHANKAR
SHIRKER
SHOCKER
SHUCKER
SKULKER
SLACKER
SLEEKER
SLICKER
SMACKER
SNACKER
SNEAKER
SNICKER
SNOOKER
SPANKER
SPEAKER
STALKER
STARKER
STICKER
STINKER
STRIKER
SWANKER
THICKER
THINKER
TRACKER
TREKKER
TRICKER
TRUCKER
WHISKER
WRECKER

•••••KR
ABUBAKR

K•S••••
KASHMIR
KESTREL
KISHKES
KISSERS
KISSING
KISSOFF
KOSHERS
KOSYGIN

K••S•••
KAISERS
KAISHEK
KANSANS
KEESHAN
KIDSKIN
KINSHIP
KINSMAN
KINSMEN
KIRSTIE
KISSERS
KISSING
KISSOFF
KITSCHY
KMESONS
KNESSET
KNISHES
KNOSSOS
KRISHNA
KTOSLIN

K•••S••
KARASEA
KEEPSAT
KEEPSIN
KEEPSON
KEEPSTO
KEEPSUP
KENOSHA
KICKSIN
KICKSUP
KLATSCH
KNESSET
KNOSSOS

K••••S•
KADDISH
KEENEST
KEYWEST
KINDEST
KNAVISH
KOMATSU
KURDISH

K•••••S
KABUKIS
KAFTANS
KAHUNAS
KAISERS
KANAKAS
KANSANS
KAZAKHS
KEENERS
KEEPERS
KEGLERS
KELPIES
KENNELS
KENYANS
KERNELS
KETCHES
KETONES
KETTLES
KEWPIES
KEYPADS
KIBBLES
KICKERS
KICKUPS
KIDDERS
KIDDIES
KIDNAPS
KIDNEYS
KIKUYUS
KILLERS
KILTIES
KIMONOS
KINDLES
KIPPERS
KIRMANS
KIRTLES
KISHKES
KISSERS
KITBAGS
KITTENS
KITTIES
KIWANIS
KLAXONS
KLUDGES
KLUTZES
KMESONS
KNIGHTS
KNISHES
KNOSSOS
KOBOLDS
KODIAKS
KOPECKS
KOREANS
KORUNAS
KOSHERS
KOWTOWS
KRATERS
KWACHAS
KWANZAS
KYLIKES

•K•S•••
EKESOUT
SKISUIT
SKOSHES

•K•••S•
OKHOTSK
SKIMASK

•K••••S
SKATERS
SKEWERS
SKIRUNS
SKITOWS
SKIVERS
SKOSHES
SKYCAPS
SKYWAYS

••KS•••
ASKSFOR
ASKSOUT
DYKSTRA
INKSPOT
IRKSOME

••K•S••
MAKESDO
MAKESIT
MAKESUP
POKESAT
RAKESIN
RAKESUP
TAKESIN
TAKESON
TAKESTO
TAKESUP
WAKESUP

••K••S•
ICKIEST
OAKMOSS
POKIEST
RYKRISP
SIKHISM
YAKUTSK

••K•••S
ACKACKS
ALKALIS
ALKENES
ANKLETS
AUKLETS
BIKINIS
DAKOTAS
DIKDIKS
DIKTATS
DUKAKIS
ESKIMOS
GOKARTS
KIKUYUS
LAKOTAS
MAKEUPS
MAKINGS
MIKADOS

MUKLUKS
NOKOMIS
OAKMOSS
STKITTS
UNKINKS
UNKNITS
UNKNOTS
VIKINGS
YAKKERS

•••KS••

BACKSIN
BACKSUP
BANKSON
BARKSAT
BUCKSAW
BUCKSUP
COOKSUP
DESKSET
HACKSAW
HOOKSUP
JACKSON
JACKSUP
KICKSIN
KICKSUP
LOCKSUP
LOOKSAT
LOOKSEE
LOOKSIN
LOOKSON
LOOKSTO
LOOKSUP
MARKSUP
MILKSOP
MUCKSUP
PACKSUP
PECKSAT
PEEKSAT
PERKSUP
PICKSAT
PICKSON
PICKSUP
RACKSUP
RICKSHA
SINKSIN
SOAKSUP
SOCKSIN
SUCKSIN
TACKSON
TALKSAT
TALKSTO
TALKSUP
TANKSUP
TUCKSIN
WINKSAT
WORKSIN
WORKSON
WORKSUP

•••K•S•

BOOKISH
DANKEST
DARKEST
DARKISH
HAWKISH
JACKASS
LANKEST
MAWKISH
MEEKEST
MONKISH
OSHKOSH
PECKISH
PINKEST
PINKISH
PUCKISH
RANKEST
SICKEST
SUNKIST
TURKISH
WEAKEST
WEAKISH

•••K••S

AWAKENS
BACKERS
BACKUPS
BALKANS
BANKERS
BARKERS
BASKETS
BEAKERS
BECKONS
BICKERS
BODKINS
BONKERS
BOOKIES
BOSKETS
BROKERS
BUCKETS
BUCKLES
BUCKOES
BUNKERS
BUSKINS
CACKLES
CALKINS
CANKERS
CATKINS
CHOKERS
CHUKKAS
COCKLES
CONKERS
COOKERS
COOKIES
CORKERS
CUCKOOS
DARKENS
DAWKINS
DECKLES
DICKENS
DICKERS
DICKEYS
DICKIES
DINKIES
DOCKERS
DOCKETS
DONKEYS
DUNKERS
EVOKERS
FIRKINS
FLAKERS
FORKERS
GASKETS
GASKINS
GAWKERS
GECKOES
GURKHAS
HACKERS
HACKIES
HACKLES
HANKERS
HANKIES
HARKENS
HAWKERS
HAWKINS
HECKLES
HONKERS
HOOKAHS
HOOKUPS
HOPKINS
HOSKINS
HUNKERS
HUSKERS
HUSKIES
JACKALS
JACKASS
JACKETS
JERKINS
JOCKEYS
JUNKERS
JUNKETS
JUNKIES
KICKERS
KICKUPS
LACKEYS
LEAKERS
LINKERS
LINKUPS
LOCKERS
LOCKETS
LOCKINS
LOCKUPS
LOOKERS
LOOKUPS
LUNKERS
MARKERS
MARKETS
MARKUPS
MASKERS
MILKERS
MOCKERS
MOCKUPS
MONKEES
MONKEYS
MUSKETS
NAPKINS
NECKERS
NICKELS
NICKERS
PACKERS
PACKETS
PERKINS
PICKENS
PICKERS
PICKETS
PICKLES
PICKUPS
PINKIES
PIPKINS
POCKETS
PORKERS
PUCKERS
PUNKAHS
PUNKIES
QUAKERS
QUOKKAS
RACKETS
RANKERS
RANKLES
RECKONS
RICKEYS
RICKLES
RISKERS
ROCKERS
ROCKETS
ROCKIES
ROOKIES
SACKERS
SEEKERS
SHAKERS
SHAKOES
SHEKELS
SICKENS
SICKLES
SINKERS
SISKINS
SMOKERS
SMOKIES
SOAKERS
SOCKETS
SPIKERS
STOKERS
SUCKERS
SULKERS
SULKIES
TACKERS
TACKLES
TALKERS
TALKIES
TANKERS
TICKERS
TICKETS
TICKLES
TINKERS
TINKLES
TUCKERS
TURKEYS
TUSKERS
WALKERS
WALKINS
WALKONS
WALKUPS
WEAKENS
WELKINS
WESKITS
WICKERS
WICKETS
WINKERS
WORKERS
WORKUPS
YAKKERS
YANKEES
YONKERS
ZONKERS

••••K•S

ABNAKIS
BETAKES
CHUKKAS
DUKAKIS
EVENKIS
INJOKES
INTAKES
INVOKES
KABUKIS
KANAKAS
KAZAKHS
KISHKES
KYLIKES
PATAKES
PERUKES
QUOKKAS
REBUKES
REMAKES
RETAKES
REVOKES
SALUKIS
SHEIKHS
SHRIKES
STRIKES
STROKES
TROIKAS
UNMAKES
UNYOKES
UPTAKES

•••••KS

ACKACKS
ANORAKS
ARAWAKS
ATTACKS
ATTUCKS
BEDECKS
BUROAKS
DAMASKS
DEBARKS
DEBUNKS
DIKDIKS
DYBBUKS
EMBANKS
EMBARKS
HIJACKS
HIJINKS
KODIAKS
KOPECKS
MOHAWKS
MUKLUKS
MUZHIKS
NUDNIKS
PINOAKS
RECORKS
REDOAKS
REHOOKS
RELOCKS
REMARKS
REWORKS
SCREAKS
SHRIEKS
SHRINKS
SHTICKS
SLOVAKS
SQUAWKS
SQUEAKS
STREAKS
SUSLIKS
TANOAKS
THWACKS
UNCORKS
UNHOOKS
UNKINKS
UNLINKS
UNLOCKS
UNMASKS
UNPACKS
UNTACKS
UPLINKS
UPTICKS

KT•••••

KTOSLIN

K•T••••

KATHRYN
KATYDID
KETCHAM
KETCHES
KETCHUP
KETONES
KETTLES
KITBAGS
KITCHEN
KITSCHY
KITTENS
KITTIES
KUTENAI

K••T•••

KAFTANS
KEPTOFF
KEPTOUT
KESTREL
KETTLES
KILTIES
KILTING
KIRTLES
KITTENS
KITTIES
KLATSCH
KLUTZES
KNITTED
KNITTER
KNOTTED
KONTIKI
KOOTCHY
KOWTOWS
KRATERS
KRATION

K•••T••

KERATIN
KILOTON
KINETIC
KINGTUT
KIRSTIE
KNITTED
KNITTER
KNOTTED
KOMATSU
KRYPTON

K••••T•

KEEPSTO
KENNETH
KEYNOTE
KIBBUTZ
KKKKATY
KLAMATH
KNIGHTS
KUWAITI

K•••••T

KEENEST
KEEPSAT
KEPTOUT
KEYWEST
KICKOUT
KINDEST
KINGRAT
KINGTUT
KNESSET
KUMQUAT

•K•T•••

SKATERS
SKATING
SKETCHY
SKITOWS
SKITTER
SKITTLE

•K••T••

OKHOTSK
SKEETER
SKELTER
SKELTON
SKEPTIC
SKIRTED
SKITTER
SKITTLE

•K•••T•

AKIHITO
KKKKATY

•K••••T

EKEDOUT
EKESOUT
SKIBOOT
SKILIFT
SKILLET
SKIPOUT
SKISUIT

••KT•••

DIKTATS
OAKTREE
TEKTITE

••K•T••

DAKOTAN
DAKOTAS
DYKSTRA
LAKOTAS
STKITTS
TAKETEN
YAKUTSK

••K••T•

ANKLETS
AUKLETS
DIKTATS
GOKARTS
JAKARTA
KKKKATY
STKITTS
TAKESTO
TEKTITE
UNKNITS
UNKNOTS

••K•••T

ASKSOUT
ECKHART
ELKHART
ICKIEST
INKBLOT
INKSPOT
MAKEOUT
MAKESIT
POKEDAT
POKESAT
POKIEST
TAKEOUT
UNKEMPT

•••KT••

DESKTOP
ELEKTRA
JACKTAR
NECKTIE
TANKTOP
TOOKTEN
YANKTON

•••K•T•

BASKETS
BECKETT
BOSKETS
BOXKITE
BUCKETS
DOCKETS
GASKETS
HACKETT
JACKETS
JUNKETS
KKKKATY
LICKETY
LOCKETS
LOOKSTO
MARKETS
MUSKETS
PACKETS
PICKETS
PICKETT
POCKETS
PUCKETT
RACKETS
RICKETY
ROCKETS
SOCKETS
TALKSTO
TICKETS
WESKITS
WICKETS

•••K••T

BACKBIT
BACKLIT
BACKOUT
BARKSAT
BECKETT
BOOKLET
BOWKNOT
COCKPIT
CONKOUT
COOKOUT
DANKEST
DARKEST
DECKOUT
DESKSET
FOLKART
HACKETT
JACKPOT
JUNKART
KICKOUT
LANKEST
LOCKNUT
LOCKOUT
LOOKOUT
LOOKSAT
LUCKOUT
MEEKEST
MUSKRAT
PACKRAT
PECKSAT
PEEKOUT
PEEKSAT
PICKETT
PICKOUT
PICKSAT
PINKEST
PUCKETT
RANKEST
SACKOUT
SEEKOUT
SICKEST
SICKOUT
SILKHAT
SUNKIST
TALKOUT
TALKSAT
TOOKOUT
TOPKNOT
WALKOUT
WEAKEST
WINKOUT
WINKSAT
WORKOUT
ZONKOUT

••••KT•

FLOCKTO
STICKTO
STUCKTO

••••K•T

BLANKET
BLINKAT
BRACKET
BRISKET
CRICKET
MESSKIT
PLACKET
THICKET
TRINKET

KU•••••

KUBRICK
KUMQUAT
KURDISH
KUTENAI
KUWAITI

K•U••••

KLUDGES
KLUGMAN
KLUTZES
KNUCKLE
KNURLED

K••U•••

KABUKIS
KAHUNAS
KIKUYUS
KORUNAS

K•••U••

KEROUAC
KIBBUTZ
KICKUPS
KILAUEA
KUMQUAT

K••••U•

KARAKUL
KARAKUM
KEEPSUP
KEPTOUT
KETCHUP
KEYCLUB
KEYEDUP
KICKOUT
KICKSUP
KIKUYUS
KINGTUT

K•••••U

KOMATSU

•KU••••

SKULKED
SKULKER
SKUNKED
UKULELE

•K••U••

SKIJUMP
SKIRUNS
SKISUIT

•K•••U•

EKEDOUT
EKESOUT
SKILFUL
SKIPOUT
SKYBLUE

••KU•••

KIKUYUS
YAKUTSK

••K•U••

MAKEUPS
MUKLUKS

••K••U•

ASKSOUT
FAKEFUR
KIKUYUS
MAKEOUT
MAKESUP
POKEFUN
RAKEDUP
RAKESUP
TAKEOUT
TAKESUP
WAKEFUL
WAKESUP
WOKENUP

•••KU••

BACKUPS
HOOKUPS
KICKUPS
LINKUPS
LOCKUPS
LOOKUPS
MARKUPS
MOCKUPS
PICKUPS
WALKUPS
WORKUPS

•••K•U•

BACKOUT
BACKRUB
BACKSUP
BROKEUP
BUCKSUP
CHOKEUP
CONKOUT
COOKOUT
COOKSUP
DECKOUT
FORKFUL
HOOKSUP
JACKSUP
KICKOUT
KICKSUP
LOCKNUT
LOCKOUT
LOCKSUP
LOOKOUT
LOOKSUP
LUCKOUT
MARKSUP
MILKRUN
MUCKSUP
PACKSUP
PEEKOUT
PERKSUP
PICKOUT
PICKSUP
RACKSUP
SACKFUL
SACKOUT
SEEKOUT
SHAKEUP
SICKOUT
SOAKSUP
SPOKEUP
TALKOUT
TALKSUP
TANKFUL
TANKSUP
TOOKOUT
WALKOUT
WICKIUP
WINKOUT
WORKOUT
WORKSUP
ZONKOUT

••••KU•

BELAKUN
BREAKUP
CHALKUP
CHECKUP
CRACKUP
CRANKUP
KARAKUL
KARAKUM
SHOOKUP
SPEAKUP
STACKUP
STICKUP
STOCKUP
STUCKUP
THINKUP

K••V•••

KNAVERY
KNAVISH

K•••V••

KNIEVEL

K••••V•

KEDROVA

•K•V•••

SKIVERS

•K•••V•

SKYDIVE

••K•V••

DEKOVEN

••K••V•

BAKLAVA

•••K•V•

MARKOVA

•••K••V

CHEKHOV
ROCKYIV

••••K•V

NABOKOV

KW•••••

KWACHAS
KWANZAS

K•W••••

KEWPIES
KIWANIS
KOWLOON
KOWTOWS
KUWAITI

K••W•••

KEYWEST
KEYWORD
KNOWHOW
KNOWING

K••••W•

KOWTOWS

K•••••W

KNOWHOW

•K•W•••

SKEWERS
SKEWING
SKYWARD
SKYWAYS

•K•••W•

OKINAWA
SKITOWS

•K••••W

SKIDROW

••KW•••

AWKWARD
INKWELL

••K•W••

BIKEWAY
MAKEWAY

••K••W•

OAKLAWN
UNKNOWN

••K•••W

LIKENEW

•••KW••

PARKWAY
WALKWAY

•••K••W

BUCKSAW
HACKSAW
JACKDAW
MILKCOW
YOUKNOW

K••X•••

KLAXONS

K•••••X

KLEENEX

•K••••X

SKEEZIX

••K•••X

CAKEMIX
JUKEBOX

•••K•X•

PICKAXE

•••K••X

LOCKBOX

KY•••••

KYLIKES

K•Y••••

KAYAKED
KAYAKER
KAYOING
KEYCARD
KEYCLUB
KEYEDIN
KEYEDUP
KEYHOLE
KEYLIME
KEYNOTE
KEYPADS
KEYRING
KEYWEST
KEYWORD
KRYPTON

K••Y•••

KATYDID
KENYANS
KHAYYAM
KOSYGIN

K•••Y••

KHAYYAM
KIKUYUS

K••••Y•

KAROLYI
KATHRYN
KIDNEYS

K•••••Y

KENNEDY
KILLJOY
KITSCHY
KKKKATY
KNAVERY
KOLACKY
KOOTCHY

•KY••••

SKYBLUE
SKYCAPS
SKYDIVE
SKYHIGH
SKYHOOK
SKYJACK
SKYLARK
SKYLINE
SKYWARD
SKYWAYS

•K•Y•••

OKAYING

•K•••Y•

SKYWAYS

•K••••Y

KKKKATY
SKETCHY

••KY•••

INKYCAP

••K•Y••
KIKUYUS
REKEYED

••K••Y•
AYKROYD

••K•••Y
BIKEWAY
BOKCHOY
KKKKATY
MAKEHAY
MAKEWAY
NAKEDLY

•••KY••
ROCKYII
ROCKYIV

•••K•Y•
BUCKEYE
DICKEYS
DONKEYS
HAWKEYE
JOCKEYS
LACKEYS
MONKEYS
RICKEYS
SOCKEYE
TURKEYS

•••K••Y
BACKBAY
BUCKLEY
COCKILY
COCKNEY
COOKERY
HACKNEY
HICKORY
HUSKILY
JERKILY
KKKKATY
LANKILY
LICKETY
LUCKILY
MOCKERY
MURKILY
PARKWAY
PERKILY
PESKILY
RICKETY
ROOKERY
SHAKILY
SICKBAY
SICKPAY
SILKILY
STOKELY
SULKILY
TACKILY
WACKILY
WALKWAY
WEEKDAY
WORKDAY

••••K•Y
BLACKLY
BLANKLY
BLEAKLY
BRISKLY
CONAKRY
CRINKLY
DEBAKEY
FRANKLY
MARYKAY
PASSKEY
PRICKLY
QUICKLY
SHARKEY
SLEEKLY
SLICKLY
STARKLY
STOOKEY
THICKLY
TURNKEY
TWINKLY
WHISKEY
WRINKLY

•••••KY
BLUESKY
CHOMSKY
FINICKY
GRETZKY
KOLACKY
PANICKY
SPASSKY
SQUEAKY
STREAKY
TROTSKY
UNLUCKY
VRONSKY

K•Z••••
KAZAKHS

K•••Z••
KLUTZES
KWANZAS

K•••••Z
KIBBUTZ
KOBLENZ

•K••Z••
SKEEZIX

••••K•Z
FRANKOZ

LA•••••
LAAGERS
LABAMBA
LABCOAT
LABELED
LABELER
LABELLE
LABIALS
LABIATE
LABORED
LABORER
LABOURS
LABRETS
LACEDUP
LACESUP
LACIEST
LACINGS
LACKEYS
LACKING
LACONIC
LACOSTE
LACQUER
LACTASE
LACTATE
LACTEAL
LACTOSE
LACUNAE
LACUNAL
LACUNAS
LADDERS
LADDIES
LADINOS
LADLERS
LADLING
LADYBUG
LADYDAY
LAENNEC
LAERTES
LAFARGE
LAFITTE
LAGGARD
LAGGERS
LAGGING
LAGOONS
LAGUNAS
LAIDFOR
LAIDLOW
LAIDOFF
LAIDOUT
LAISSEZ
LAJOLLA
LAKOTAS
LALAKER
LALANNE
LALIQUE
LAMAISM
LAMAIST
LAMARCK
LAMBADA
LAMBDAS
LAMBEAU
LAMBENT
LAMBERT
LAMENTS
LAMINAE
LAMINAL
LAMINAR
LAMINAS
LAMMING
LAMOTTA
LAMPOIL
LAMPOON
LAMPREY
LANCERS
LANCETS
LANDAUS
LANDERS
LANDING
LANDSAT
LANFORD
LANGDON
LANGLEY
LANGTRY
LANGUID
LANGUOR
LANGURS
LANKEST
LANKIER
LANKILY
LANOLIN
LANSING
LANTANA
LANTERN
LANYARD
LAOCOON
LAOTIAN
LAPALMA
LAPBELT
LAPDOGS
LAPELED
LAPFULS
LAPLACE
LAPLAND
LAPLATA
LAPORTE
LAPPETS
LAPPING
LAPROBE
LAPSING
LAPTOPS
LAPWING
LARAINE
LARAMIE
LARCENY
LARCHES
LARDERS
LARDING
LARDNER
LARDONS
LARGELY
LARGESS
LARGEST
LARIATS
LAROCHE
LARRUPS
LASAGNA
LASAGNE
LASALLE
LASCALA
LASCAUX
LASHERS
LASHING
LASHUPS
LASORDA
LASSIES
LASSOED
LASSOER
LASSOES
LASTING
LASTORY
LATCHED
LATCHES
LATEENS
LATENCY
LATENTS
LATERAL
LATERAN
LATERON
LATEXES
LATHERS
LATHERY
LATHING
LATICES
LATIFAH
LATINAS
LATINOS
LATTENS
LATTICE
LATVIAN
LAUDING
LAUGHAT
LAUGHED
LAUGHER
LAUGHIN
LAUNDER
LAUNDRY
LAURELS
LAURENT
LAUTREC
LAVALSE
LAVERNE
LAVINIA
LAWFORD
LAWLESS
LAWSUIT
LAWYERS
LAXNESS
LAYAWAY
LAYDOWN
LAYERED
LAYETTE
LAYINTO
LAYOFFS
LAYOUTS
LAYOVER
LAYSFOR
LAYSLOW
LAYSOFF
LAYSOUT
LAZARUS
LAZENBY
LAZIEST

L•A••••
LAAGERS
LEACHED
LEACHES
LEACOCK
LEADERS
LEADING
LEADINS
LEADOFF
LEADOUT
LEADSIN
LEADSON
LEADSTO
LEADSUP
LEAFIER
LEAFING
LEAFLET
LEAGUER
LEAGUES
LEAKAGE
LEAKERS
LEAKIER
LEAKING
LEANDER
LEANERS
LEANEST
LEANING
LEANSON
LEANTOS
LEAPERS
LEAPING
LEARJET
LEARNED
LEARNER
LEASERS
LEASHED
LEASHES
LEASING
LEATHER
LEAVENS
LEAVING
LIAISED
LIAISES
LIAISON
LOACHES
LOADERS
LOADING
LOAFERS
LOAFING
LOAMIER
LOAMING
LOANERS
LOANING
LOATHED
LOATHES

L••A•••
LABAMBA
LAFARGE
LALAKER
LALANNE
LAMAISM
LAMAIST
LAMARCK
LAPALMA
LARAINE
LARAMIE
LASAGNA
LASAGNE
LASALLE
LAVALSE
LAYAWAY
LAZARUS
LEBANON
LEBARON
LECARRE
LEGALLY
LEGATEE
LEGATES
LEGATOS
LEHAVRE
LEPANTO
LIEABED
LIGATED
LIGATES
LIKABLE
LINAGES
LIVABLE
LIZARDS
LOCALES
LOCALLY
LOCATED
LOCATER
LOCATES
LOCATOR
LOVABLE
LOYALLY
LOYALTY
LUNATIC
LUXATED
LUXATES

L•••A••
LABIALS
LABIATE
LACTASE
LACTATE
LAGGARD
LAMBADA
LANDAUS
LANTANA
LANYARD
LAPLACE
LAPLAND
LAPLATA
LARIATS
LASCALA
LASCAUX
LEAKAGE
LEEWARD
LENFANT
LEONARD
LEOPARD
LEOTARD
LESPAUL
LIBRARY
LIBYANS
LIMEADE
LINEAGE
LINEATE
LINKAGE
LIPBALM
LOGJAMS
LOMBARD
LONGAGO
LOOFAHS
LOQUATS
LOWBALL
LOWLAND
LOWPAID
LUCIANO
LUGGAGE
LULLABY
LUMBAGO
LUMBARS

L••••A•
LABCOAT
LACTEAL
LACUNAE
LACUNAL
LACUNAS
LADYDAY
LAGUNAS
LAKOTAS
LAMBDAS
LAMBEAU
LAMINAE
LAMINAL
LAMINAR
LAMINAS
LANDSAT
LAOTIAN
LATERAL
LATERAN
LATIFAH
LATINAS
LATVIAN
LAUGHAT
LAYAWAY
LEERSAT
LEXICAL
LIBERAL
LIKEMAD
LILLIAN
LILYPAD
LINBIAO
LINDSAY
LINEMAN
LINGUAL
LIPREAD
LITERAL
LIVEOAK
LOGGIAS
LOGICAL
LOOKSAT
LOWBEAM
LOWGEAR
LOWROAD
LUNGEAT
LYRICAL

L•••••A
LABAMBA
LAJOLLA
LAMBADA
LAMOTTA
LANTANA
LAPALMA
LAPLATA
LASAGNA
LASCALA
LASORDA
LAVINIA
LEMPIRA
LEONORA
LETITIA
LIBERIA
LORETTA
LOUELLA

•LA••••
ALABAMA
ALADDIN
ALAKING
ALAMEDA
ALAMEIN
ALAMODE
ALARCON
ALARMED
ALARMER
ALARUMS
ALASKAN
BLABBED
BLABBER
BLACKED
BLACKEN
BLACKER
BLACKLY
BLADDER
BLAMING
BLANCHE
BLANDER
BLANDLY
BLANKED
BLANKER
BLANKET
BLANKLY
BLARING
BLARNEY
BLASTED
BLASTER
BLATANT
BLATHER
BLATTED
BLAZERS
BLAZING
BLAZONS
CLABBER
CLACKED
CLAIMED
CLAIMER
CLAIROL
CLAMBER
CLAMMED
CLAMMER
CLAMORS
CLAMPED
CLAMSUP
CLANGED
CLANGOR
CLANKED
CLAPPED
CLAPPER
CLAPTON
CLAQUES
CLARETS
CLARICE
CLARIFY
CLARION
CLARITY
CLASHED
CLASHES
CLASPED
CLASSED
CLASSES
CLASSIC
CLATTER
CLAUDIA
CLAUDIO
CLAUSES
CLAVELL
CLAVIER
CLAWERS
CLAWING
CLAYIER
CLAYTON
ELAPIDS
ELAPSED
ELAPSES
ELASTIC
ELATERS
ELATING
ELATION
FLACCID
FLACONS
FLAGDAY
FLAGGED
FLAGMAN
FLAGMEN
FLAGONS
FLAILED
FLAKERS
FLAKIER
FLAKING
FLAMBED
FLAMBES
FLAMING
FLANEUR
FLANGES
FLANKED
FLANKER
FLANNEL
FLAPPED
FLAPPER
FLAREUP
FLARING
FLASHED
FLASHER
FLASHES
FLATBED
FLATCAR
FLATOUT
FLATTED
FLATTEN
FLATTER
FLATTOP
FLAUNTS
FLAVORS
FLAVOUR
FLAWING
FLAYING
GLACEED
GLACIAL
GLACIER
GLADDEN
GLADDER
GLADEYE
GLAMOUR
GLANCED
GLANCES
GLARING
GLASGOW
GLASSED
GLASSES
GLAZERS
GLAZIER
GLAZING
KLAMATH
KLATSCH
KLAXONS
PLACARD
PLACATE
PLACEBO
PLACERS
PLACIDO
PLACING
PLACKET
PLAGUED
PLAGUES
PLAICES
PLAINER
PLAINES
PLAINLY
PLAINTS
PLAITED
PLANERS
PLANETS
PLANING
PLANKED
PLANNED
PLANNER
PLANSON
PLANTAR
PLANTED
PLANTER
PLAQUES
PLASHED
PLASHES
PLASMAS
PLASTER
PLASTIC
PLATEAU
PLATENS
PLATERS
PLATING
PLATOON
PLATTER
PLATYPI
PLAUDIT
PLAUTUS
PLAYACT
PLAYBOY
PLAYDOH
PLAYERS
PLAYFUL
PLAYING
PLAYLET
PLAYOFF
PLAYOUT
PLAYPEN
PLAYSAT
PLAYSON
PLAYSUP
SLABBED
SLACKED
SLACKEN
SLACKER
SLAKING
SLALOMS
SLAMMED
SLAMMER
SLANDER
SLANTED
SLAPPED
SLASHED
SLASHER
SLASHES
SLATHER
SLATIER
SLATING
SLATKIN
SLATTED
SLAVERS
SLAVERY
SLAVING
SLAVISH
SLAYERS
SLAYTON
ULALUME
ULANOVA

•L•A•••
ALBANIA
ALCAZAR
ALFALFA
ALIASES
ALKALIS
ALLAYED
ALLAYER
ALMAATA
ALMADEN
ALMANAC
ALPACAS
ALVAREZ
BLEAKER
BLEAKLY
BLEARED
BLEATED
BLOATED
CLEANED
CLEANER
CLEANLY
CLEANSE
CLEANUP
CLEARED
CLEARER
CLEARLY
CLEARUP
CLEAVED
CLEAVER
CLEAVES
CLEAVON
CLOAKED
ELEANOR
FLEABAG
FLOATED
FLOATER
FLYAWAY
GLEAMED
GLEANED
GLEANER
GLEASON
GLOATED
OLEATES
PLEADED
PLEADER
PLEASED
PLEASER
PLEASES
PLEATED
PLIABLE
PLIABLY
PLIANCY
ULYANOV

•L••A••
ALABAMA
ALIBABA
ALIDADE
ALLEARS
ALLHAIL
ALMAATA
ALOHAOE
ALREADY
BLATANT
CLIMATE
CLIPART
ELEGANT
ELEVATE
ELKHART
FLYBALL
FLYCAST
FLYPAST
FLYWAYS
KLAMATH
OLDDAYS
OLDHAND
OLDMAID
PLACARD
PLACATE
PLAYACT
PLENARY
PLUMAGE
PLURALS
SLOGANS
SLOVAKS
ULLMANN
ULULANT
ULULATE

•L•••A•
ALASKAN
ALCAZAR
ALLHEAL
ALLSTAR
ALMANAC
ALPACAS
ALSORAN
ALTOSAX
ALUMNAE
ALUMNAL
BLINKAT
BLUEJAY
BLUELAW
CLUBCAR
ELEGIAC
ELYSIAN
FLAGDAY
FLAGMAN
FLATCAR
FLEABAG
FLIESAT
FLOTSAM
FLUVIAL
FLYAWAY
FLYLEAF
FLYTRAP
GLACIAL
GLORIAS
GLOSSAE
GLOTTAL
ILLEGAL
KLUGMAN
OLDCHAP
OLDUVAI
PLANTAR
PLASMAS
PLATEAU
PLAYSAT
PLOWMAN
PLUVIAL
SLOTCAR

•L••••A
ALABAMA
ALAMEDA
ALBANIA
ALBERTA
ALFALFA
ALGEBRA
ALGERIA
ALIBABA
ALLUVIA
ALMAATA
ALTOONA
ALYOSHA
CLAUDIA
ELECTRA
ELEKTRA
FLORIDA
OLESTRA
OLYMPIA
PLECTRA
ULANOVA

••LA•••
ABLATED
ABLATES
ABLAUTS
ALLAYED
ALLAYER
ATLANTA
ATLARGE
ATLASES
ATLATLS
BALANCE
BALATON
BELABOR
BELAKUN
BELATED
BELAYED
CCLAMPS
CELADON
DELANEY
DELAYED
DELAYER
DILATED
DILATES
ECLAIRS
ENLACED
ENLACES
ENLARGE
FALAFEL
GALAHAD
GALATEA
GALATIA
GELADAS
GELATIN
GELATIS
HILAIRE
ISLAMIC
ISLANDS
KILAUEA
KOLACKY
LALAKER
LALANNE
MALABAR
MALACCA
MALACHI
MALAISE
MALAMUD
MALAREN
MALAYAN
MELANGE
MELANIE
MELANIN

OBLASTS
OBLATES
OGLALAS
ORLANDO
PALACES
PALADIN
PALANCE
PALATAL
PALATES
PALAVER
PALAZZI
PALAZZO
PELAGES
PELAGIC
POLARIS
PULASKI
RDLAING
RELACED
RELACES
RELAPSE
RELATED
RELATES
RELAXED
RELAXES
RELAYED
ROLAIDS
SALAAMS
SALABLE
SALADIN
SALAMIS
SALAZAR
SOLACES
SOLARIA
SPLASHY
SPLAYED
TALARIA
TELAVIV
UMLAUTS
UNLACED
UNLACES
UNLADES
UNLATCH
UPLANDS
VALANCE

••L•A••

ALLEARS
ALLHAIL
ATLEAST
BALKANS
BALLADE
BALLADS
BALLARD
BALLAST
BALSAMS
BELDAME
BELDAMS
BELFAST
BELLAMY
BELTANE
BULGARS
BULWARK
CALGARY
CALPACS
CALVARY
CELLARS
CILIATE
COLGATE
COLLAGE
COLLARD
COLLARS
COLLATE
DELTAIC
DILLARD
DOLLARS
DOLMANS
DULLARD
FALLACY
FOLIAGE
FOLIATE
FOLKART
GALLANT
GALVANI
GOLIATH
HALYARD
HILLARY
HOLLAND
HOLYARK
JULIANA
KILDARE
LULLABY
MALEATE
MALLARD
MALRAUX
MILEAGE
MILHAUD
MILLAND
MILLARD
MULLAHS
OILCAKE
OILCANS
OILLAMP
OILPANS
ONLEAVE
ORLEANS
PALMATE
PELTATE
PILLAGE
PILLARS
POLEAXE
POLKAED
PULSARS
PULSATE
RELEARN
RELEASE
RELIANT
RELOADS
ROLVAAG
SALAAMS
SALVAGE
SELVAGE
SULFATE
SULTANA
SULTANS
SYLLABI
SYLVANS
TELLALL
TILLAGE
TULSANS
ULLMANN
UNLEARN
UNLEASH
UNLOADS
UPLOADS
VALIANT
VALUATE
VILLAGE
VILLAIN
VOLCANO
VOLTAGE
VOLTAIC
VULCANS
VULGATE
WALLABY
WALLACE
WALLACH
WALMART
WELFARE
WELLAND
WILLARD

••L••A•

ALLHEAL
ALLSTAR
BALBOAS
BALIHAI
BELGIAN
BELLJAR
BELLMAN
BELTWAY
BKLIBAN
BOLIVAR
CALIBAN
CHLORAL
COLDWAR
COLEMAN
CULTJAM
DELILAH
FELDMAN
GALAHAD
GELADAS
GILBLAS
HALFDAN
HALFWAY
HALIFAX
HALLWAY
HELICAL
HELIPAD
HELLCAT
HELLMAN
HOLIDAY
HOLMOAK
HOLYWAR
ILLEGAL
JILLIAN
LILLIAN
LILYPAD
MALABAR
MALAYAN
MCLUHAN
MILKMAN
MILLDAM
MOLOKAI
MULETAS
OGLALAS
PALATAL
PALOMAR
PELICAN
PELOTAS
POLECAT
POLLTAX
PULLMAN
PULLTAB
ROLLBAR
ROLVAAG
SALAZAR
SCLERAS
SILICAS
SILKHAT
SOLEDAD
TALKSAT
TELERAN
TELSTAR
TOLLWAY
VALJEAN
WALKMAN
WALKWAY
WILDCAT
WILLIAM
WOLFGAL
WOLFMAN
WOLFRAM
YELLSAT

••L•••A

ALLUVIA
ATLANTA
BELINDA
BOLIVIA
BOLOGNA
CALDERA
CELESTA
COLONNA
CULEBRA
DELIRIA
DILEMMA
FELICIA
FELUCCA
GALATEA
GALATIA
JULIANA
KILAUEA
MALACCA
MELINDA
MELISSA
MILITIA
PALOOKA
POLENTA
SALSODA
SILESIA
SOLARIA
STLUCIA
SULTANA
SULUSEA
TALARIA

•••LA••

ABELARD
ACCLAIM
ADULATE
AIRLANE
AMYLASE
APPLAUD
ARCLAMP
ASHLAND
ASHLARS
BAKLAVA
BALLADE
BALLADS
BALLARD
BALLAST
BEDLAMP
BELLAMY
BIPLANE
BURLAPS
BYPLAYS
CELLARS
COLLAGE
COLLARD
COLLARS
COLLATE
COOLANT
COPLAND
CUTLASS
DECLAIM
DECLARE
DECLASS
DEFLATE
DEPLANE
DEWLAPS
DILLARD
DOLLARS
DULLARD
EMULATE
ENCLAVE
ENGLAND
ENPLANE
ENSLAVE
EXCLAIM
EXPLAIN
EYELASH
FALLACY
FINLAND
FOULARD
GALLANT
GARLAND
GOTLAND
GOULASH
HAULAGE
HEALALL
HILLARY
HOLLAND
ICELAND
IMPLANT
INFLAME
INFLATE
INPLACE
IRELAND
ISOLATE
JUTLAND
KOOLAID
LAPLACE
LAPLAND
LAPLATA
LOWLAND
LULLABY
MALLARD
MIDLAND
MILLAND
MILLARD
MISLAID
MISLAYS
MOULAGE
MULLAHS
OAKLAND
OAKLAWN
OILLAMP
OUTLAID
OUTLAND
OUTLAST
OUTLAWS
OUTLAYS
PAHLAVI
PARLAYS
PEDLARS
PHALANX
PILLAGE
PILLARS
POPLARS
PRELATE
RAGLANS
RANLATE
RECLAIM
RECLAME
REPLACE
REPLANS
REPLANT
REPLATE
REPLAYS
ROULADE
RUNLAPS
SCALARS
SEALABS
SEALANE
SEALANT
SHALALA
SKYLARK
STALAGS
SUNLAMP
SYLLABI
TELLALL
TILLAGE
TOYLAND
TRALALA
ULULANT
ULULATE
UNCLASP
VILLAGE
VILLAIN
VIOLATE
WALLABY
WALLACE
WALLACH
WAYLAID
WAYLAYS
WELLAND
WETLAND
WILLARD
YOPLAIT
ZEALAND

•••L•A•

AEOLIAN
AMALGAM
ARMLOAD
AXILLAE
AZALEAS
BAYLEAF
BELLJAR
BELLMAN
BOOLEAN
BRILLAT
CARLOAD
CHILEAN
CHOLLAS
COALCAR
COALGAS
COALTAR
DAHLIAS
FIGLEAF
FLYLEAF
HALLWAY
HEELTAP
HELLCAT
HELLMAN
HIALEAH
ITALIAN
JILLIAN
LILLIAN
MAILBAG
MILLDAM
MISLEAD
MRCLEAN
NUCLEAR
OAKLEAF
OFFLOAD
PAYLOAD
PERLMAN
POLLTAX
PRELOAD
PULLMAN
PULLTAB
RAILSAT
RAILWAY
RECLEAN
ROLLBAR
SHELLAC
STELLAR
TABLEAU
TEALEAF
TOLLWAY
UNCLEAN
UNCLEAR
UNCLOAK
WILLIAM
YELLSAT

•••L••A

ARALSEA
BAKLAVA
CHELSEA
DIPLOMA
LAPLATA
PAULINA
PAVLOVA
REPLICA
SHALALA
TRALALA

••••LA•

AIRPLAY
ANGOLAN
ANGULAR
ANNULAR
AREOLAE
AREOLAR
AREOLAS
ASTOLAT
AXILLAE
BIPOLAR
BLUELAW
BRILLAT
BURGLAR
CABALAS
CASELAW
CATALAN
CHEMLAB
CHOLLAS
CUPOLAS
DANELAW
DELILAH
DEWCLAW
DIPOLAR
DISPLAY
DOUGLAS
EARFLAP
ENDPLAY
FIBULAE
FIBULAS
GAMELAW
GILBLAS
GUNPLAY
HOOPLAS
IMPALAS
INSULAR
JAIALAI
JOCULAR
JUGULAR
MACULAE
MISPLAY
MODELAS
MODULAR
NEBULAE
NEBULAR
NEBULAS
NICOLAS
NIKOLAI
NODULAR
OGLALAS
ORTOLAN
OUTPLAY
OVERLAP
OVERLAY
PAYOLAS
POPULAR
REDFLAG
REGULAR
ROMULAN
SAVALAS
SCHOLAR
SECULAR
SHEILAE
SHEILAH
SHEILAS
SHELLAC
SIMILAR
STELLAR
TABULAR
TEMPLAR
TIMELAG
TITULAR
TUBULAR
TUTELAR
VIZSLAS

••••L•A

ALFALFA
APHELIA
AVONLEA
BEDELIA
CAMELIA
CAPELLA
CATALPA
CECILIA
CEDILLA
COCHLEA
COROLLA
DEPALMA
GANGLIA
GORILLA
LAJOLLA
LAPALMA
LOUELLA
MAHALIA
MATILDA
MAXILLA
MEDULLA
MINOLTA
NATALIA
NOVELLA
OPHELIA
PAPILLA
PATELLA
REGALIA
SEDALIA
SOMALIA
VANILLA
VIDALIA

•••••LA

ACEROLA
AMAPOLA
ARUGULA
AUREOLA
BOBVILA
CANDELA
CAPELLA
CEDILLA
COPPOLA
COROLLA
CRAYOLA
DRACULA
FORMULA
GONDOLA
GORILLA
GRANOLA
INOCULA
KAMPALA
LAJOLLA
LASCALA
LOUELLA
MANDALA
MANDELA
MARSALA
MAXILLA
MEDULLA
MESSALA
MINEOLA
NOVELLA
OSCEOLA
PAPILLA
PATELLA
PERGOLA
PORTOLA
SCAPULA
SHALALA
SPATULA
TAMBALA
TEQUILA
TRALALA
UPPSALA
VANILLA
VISTULA

L•B••••

LABAMBA
LABCOAT
LABELED
LABELER
LABELLE
LABIALS
LABIATE
LABORED
LABORER
LABOURS
LABRETS
LEBANON
LEBARON
LIBBERS
LIBBING
LIBELED
LIBELER
LIBERAL
LIBERIA
LIBERTY
LIBIDOS
LIBRARY
LIBYANS
LOBBERS
LOBBIED
LOBBIES
LOBBING
LOBBYER
LOBSTER
LUBBERS
LUBBOCK

L••B•••

LAMBADA
LAMBDAS
LAMBEAU
LAMBENT
LAMBERT
LAPBELT
LEIBNIZ
LIBBERS
LIBBING
LIMBERS
LIMBING
LINBIAO
LIPBALM
LOBBERS
LOBBIED
LOBBIES
LOBBING
LOBBYER
LOGBOOK
LOMBARD
LOWBALL
LOWBEAM
LOWBLOW
LOWBORN
LOWBOYS
LOWBRED
LOWBROW
LUBBERS
LUBBOCK
LUMBAGO
LUMBARS
LUMBERS

L•••B••

LADYBUG
LEGIBLE
LEGIBLY
LIEABED
LIKABLE
LIVABLE
LOCKBOX
LONGBOW
LOVABLE
LOVEBUG

L••••B•

LABAMBA
LAPROBE
LAZENBY
LETITBE
LULLABY

L•••••B

LIONCUB

•LB••••

ALBANIA
ALBEDOS
ALBENIZ
ALBERTA
ALBERTO
ALBINOS
ALBUMEN
ALBUMIN
ELBOWED

•L•B•••

ALABAMA
ALIBABA
BLABBED
BLABBER
BLUBBER
CLABBER
CLIBURN
CLOBBER
CLUBBED
CLUBCAR
FLUBBED
FLYBALL
FLYBOYS
GLIBBER
GLOBULE
ILLBRED
SLABBED
SLOBBER

•L••B••

ALEMBIC
ALGEBRA
BLABBED
BLABBER
BLUBBER
BLUEBOY
CLABBER
CLAMBER
CLIMBED
CLIMBER
CLOBBER
CLUBBED
FLAMBED
FLAMBES
FLATBED
FLEABAG
FLUBBED
GLIBBER
PLAYBOY
PLIABLE
PLIABLY
PLOWBOY
PLUMBED
PLUMBER
SLABBED
SLOBBER
SLUMBER

•L•••B•

ALIBABA
PLACEBO

••LB•••

BALBOAS
BILBOES
BULBLET
BULBOUS
BULBULS
COLBERT
DELBERT
FILBERT
GILBERT
GILBLAS
HOLBEIN
ILLBRED

••L•B••

BALLBOY
BELABOR
BELLBOY
BKLIBAN
CALIBAN
CALIBER
CALIBRE
CALLBOX
CELEBES
CELEBRE
COLOBUS
CULEBRA
DELIBES
GOLDBUG
HALIBUT
MALABAR
PILLBOX
PILLBUG
ROLLBAR
SALABLE
SALTBOX
SOLUBLE
TALKBIG
VOLUBLE
VOLUBLY

••L••B•

COLUMBO
LULLABY
SYLLABI
WALLABY

••L•••B

PULLTAB

•••LB••

BALLBOY
BELLBOY
CALLBOX
COALBIN
MAILBAG
MAILBOX
PHILBIN
PILLBOX
PILLBUG
ROLLBAR
TOOLBOX

•••L•B•

EARLOBE
LULLABY
MADLIBS
RIOLOBO
SEALABS
SYLLABI
WALLABY
WOULDBE

•••L••B

COULOMB
PULLTAB

••••L•B

CHEMLAB
KEYCLUB
THEBLOB

•••••LB

DIMBULB

L•C••••

LACEDUP
LACESUP
LACIEST
LACINGS
LACKEYS
LACKING
LACONIC
LACOSTE
LACQUER
LACTASE
LACTATE
LACTEAL
LACTOSE
LACUNAE
LACUNAL
LACUNAS
LECARRE
LECTERN
LECTORS
LECTURE
LICENCE
LICENSE
LICHENS
LICITLY
LICKETY
LICKING
LLCOOLJ
LOCALES
LOCALLY
LOCATED
LOCATER
LOCATES
LOCATOR
LOCKBOX
LOCKERS
LOCKETS
LOCKING
LOCKINS
LOCKNUT
LOCKOUT
LOCKSUP
LOCKUPS
LOCUSTS
LUCERNE
LUCIANO
LUCIDLY
LUCIFER
LUCILLE
LUCKIER
LUCKILY
LUCKING
LUCKOUT
LYCEUMS

L••C•••

LABCOAT
LANCERS
LANCETS
LAOCOON
LARCENY
LARCHES
LASCALA
LASCAUX
LATCHED
LATCHES
LEACHED
LEACHES
LEACOCK
LEECHED
LEECHES
LINCOLN
LITCHIS
LOACHES
LUNCHED
LUNCHER
LUNCHES
LURCHED
LURCHES

L•••C••

LAROCHE
LATICES
LEXICAL
LEXICON
LIONCUB
LOGICAL
LYRICAL

L••••C•

LAMARCK
LAPLACE
LATENCY
LATTICE
LEACOCK
LETTUCE
LICENCE

LOWNECK
LOWTECH
LUBBOCK

L•••••C
LACONIC
LAENNEC
LAUTREC
LIPSYNC
LUNATIC

•LC••••
ALCAZAR
ALCHEMY
ALCOHOL
ALCOVES
LLCOOLJ

•L•C•••
BLACKED
BLACKEN
BLACKER
BLACKLY
BLOCKED
BLOCKER
CLACKED
CLICHES
CLICKED
CLOCHES
CLOCKED
CLOCKER
CLOCKIN
CLUCKED
ELECTED
ELECTEE
ELECTOR
ELECTRA
ELECTRO
ELICITS
FLACCID
FLACONS
FLECHES
FLECKED
FLICKED
FLICKER
FLOCKED
FLOCKTO
FLYCAST
GLACEED
GLACIAL
GLACIER
GLUCOSE
OLDCHAP
PLACARD
PLACATE
PLACEBO
PLACERS
PLACIDO
PLACING
PLACKET
PLECTRA
PLUCKED
SLACKED
SLACKEN
SLACKER
SLICERS
SLICING
SLICKED
SLICKER
SLICKLY

•L•C••
ALARCON
ALENCON
ALPACAS
BLANCHE
BLOTCHY
CLUBCAR
FLACCID
FLATCAR
FLEECED
FLEECES
GLANCED
GLANCES
ILLICIT
PLAICES
SLOTCAR
SLOUCHY
SLUICED
SLUICES

•L•••C•
ALDRICH
CLARICE
CLERICS
CLINICS
ELGRECO
FLOUNCE
FLUENCY
ILIESCU
KLATSCH
OLDNICK
PLAYACT
PLIANCY

•L••••C
ALEMBIC
ALMANAC
CLASSIC
ELASTIC
ELEGIAC
ILLOGIC
OLYMPIC
PLASTIC

••LC•••
BALCONY
BELCHED
BELCHES
CALCIFY
CALCITE
CALCIUM
FALCONS
FILCHED
FILCHER
FILCHES
FULCRUM
GULCHES
HALCYON
MALCOLM
MULCHED
MULCHES
MULCTED
OILCAKE
OILCANS
SALCHOW
VOLCANO
VULCANS
WALCOTT
WELCHED
WELCHES
WELCOME
ZILCHES

••L•C••
CALICOS
CALYCES
COLDCUT
DELICTI
DELICTS
ENLACED
ENLACES
FELICIA
FELUCCA
HELICAL
HELICES
HELICON
HELLCAT
HOLYCOW
ILLICIT
KOLACKY
MALACCA
MALACHI
MILKCOW
PALACES
PELICAN
POLECAT
POLICED
POLICES
RELACED
RELACES
RELICTS
RELOCKS
SELECTS
SILICAS
SILICON
SOLACES
SOLICIT
SPLICED
SPLICER
SPLICES
STLUCIA
UNLACED
UNLACES
UNLOCKS
UNLUCKY
WILDCAT

••L••C•
BALANCE
BULLOCK
CALPACS
CALTECH
CELTICS
COLLECT
FALLACY
FELUCCA
GALLICO
HILLOCK
JALISCO
MALACCA
PALANCE
POLLOCK
ROLLICK
SELLECK
SILENCE
SPLOTCH
TOLTECS
UNLATCH
VALANCE
VALENCE
WALLACE
WALLACH

••L•••C
AELFRIC
BALDRIC
CALORIC
DELTAIC
ILLOGIC
ISLAMIC
MALEFIC
MELODIC
PELAGIC
POLEMIC
POLITIC
SELENIC
VOLTAIC

•••LC••
COALCAR
HELLCAT

•••L•C•
AFFLICT
AIRLOCK
ARMLOCK
BULLOCK
CHALICE
COLLECT
COWLICK
DEFLECT
DIALECT
EARLOCK
EHRLICH
FALLACY
FETLOCK
FROLICS
GALLICO
GUNLOCK
HEMLOCK
HILLOCK
INFLECT
INFLICT
INPLACE
ITALICS
LAPLACE
MATLOCK
NEGLECT
NIBLICK
OARLOCK
PADLOCK
PIMLICO
POLLOCK
POTLUCK
PUBLICS
REELECT
REFLECT
REPLACE
REPLICA
ROLLICK
SCHLOCK
SELLECK
SHYLOCK
WALLACE
WALLACH
WARLOCK
WEDLOCK

•••L••C
IDYLLIC
NUCLEIC
POULENC
SHELLAC

••••LC•
SQUELCH

••••L•C
ACRYLIC
ANGELIC
BUCOLIC
IDYLLIC
JEANLUC
MIDDLEC
SHELLAC
TONELOC
VOCALIC

L•D••••
LADDERS
LADDIES
LADINOS
LADLERS
LADLING
LADYBUG
LADYDAY
LEDGERS
LEDUPTO
LIDLESS
LODGERS
LODGING

L••D•••
LADDERS
LADDIES
LAIDFOR
LAIDLOW
LAIDOFF
LAIDOUT
LANDAUS
LANDERS
LANDING
LANDSAT
LAPDOGS
LARDERS
LARDING
LARDNER
LARDONS
LAUDING
LAYDOWN
LEADERS
LEADING
LEADINS
LEADOFF
LEADOUT
LEADSIN
LEADSON
LEADSTO
LEADSUP
LENDERS
LENDING
LETDOWN
LEWDEST
LIEDOWN
LINDENS
LINDIED
LINDIES
LINDSAY
LINDSEY
LOADERS
LOADING
LORDING
LORDJIM
LOUDEST
LOWDOWN

L•••D••
LACEDUP
LADYDAY
LAMBDAS
LANGDON
LAUNDER
LAUNDRY
LEANDER
LIBIDOS
LINEDUP
LIVEDIN
LIVEDON
LIVIDLY
LOURDES
LUCIDLY
LURIDLY

L••••D•
LAMBADA
LASORDA
LEETIDE
LEGENDS
LIMEADE
LIQUIDS
LIZARDS
LOWTIDE

L•••••D
LABELED
LABORED
LAGGARD
LANFORD
LANGUID
LANYARD
LAPELED
LAPLAND
LASSOED
LATCHED
LAUGHED
LAWFORD
LAYERED
LEACHED
LEARNED
LEASHED
LEECHED
LEEWARD
LEONARD
LEOPARD
LEOPOLD
LEOTARD
LEVELED
LEVERED
LIAISED
LIBELED
LIEABED
LIGATED
LIGHTED
LIKEMAD
LIKENED
LILYPAD
LIMITED
LINDIED
LINSEED
LIPREAD
LIVENED
LOATHED
LOBBIED
LOCATED
LOMBARD
LOUNGED
LOUREED
LOWBRED
LOWERED
LOWLAND
LOWPAID
LOWROAD
LUNCHED
LURCHED
LUSTRED
LUXATED

•LD••••
ALDENTE
ALDRICH
ELDERLY
OLDCHAP
OLDDAYS
OLDFOGY
OLDGOLD
OLDHAND
OLDLINE
OLDMAID
OLDMOON
OLDNESS
OLDNEWS
OLDNICK
OLDPROS
OLDSTER
OLDTIME
OLDUVAI
OLDWEST

•L•D•••
ALADDIN
ALIDADE
BLADDER
ELIDING
ELUDING
FLEDGED
FLEDGES
GLADDEN
GLADDER
GLADEYE
GLIDERS
GLIDING
KLUDGES
OLDDAYS
PLEDGED
PLEDGEE
PLEDGER
PLEDGES
PLODDED
PLODDER
SLEDDED
SLEDDER
SLEDDOG
SLEDGES
SLIDEIN
SLIDERS
SLIDING
SLUDGES

•L••D••
ALADDIN
ALBEDOS
ALLUDED
ALLUDES
ALMADEN
BLADDER
BLANDER
BLANDLY
BLENDED
BLENDER
BLINDED
BLINDER
BLINDLY
BLONDER
BLONDES
BLONDIE
BLOODED
BLOWDRY
BLUNDER
CLAUDIA
CLAUDIO
CLOUDED
CLOWDER
CLUEDIN
FLAGDAY
FLOODED
FLUIDLY
GLADDEN
GLADDER
GLUEDON
PLAUDIT
PLAYDOH
PLEADED
PLEADER
PLODDED
PLODDER
PLUNDER
SLANDER
SLEDDED
SLEDDER
SLEDDOG
SLENDER

•L•••D•
ALAMEDA
ALAMODE
ALFREDO
ALIDADE
ALLENDE
ALMONDS
ALREADY
ELAPIDS
FLORIDA
FLYRODS
PLACIDO

•L••••D
ALARMED
ALERTED
ALIGNED
ALLAYED
ALLEGED
ALLOWED
ALLOYED
ALLTOLD
ALLUDED
ALLURED
ALTERED
BLABBED
BLACKED
BLANKED
BLASTED
BLATTED
BLEARED
BLEATED
BLEEPED
BLENDED
BLESSED
BLINDED
BLINKED
BLIPPED
BLITZED
BLOATED
BLOCKED
BLOODED
BLOOMED
BLOOPED
BLOTTED
BLOUSED
BLUFFED
BLUNTED
BLURRED
BLURTED
BLUSHED
CLACKED
CLAIMED
CLAMMED
CLAMPED
CLANGED
CLANKED
CLAPPED
CLASHED
CLASPED
CLASSED
CLEANED
CLEARED
CLEAVED
CLERKED
CLICKED
CLIMBED
CLINKED
CLIPPED
CLOAKED
CLOCKED
CLOGGED
CLOPPED
CLOTHED
CLOTTED
CLOUDED
CLOUTED
CLOWNED
CLUBBED
CLUCKED
CLUMPED
CLUNKED
ELAPSED
ELBOWED
ELECTED
FLACCID
FLAGGED
FLAILED
FLAMBED
FLANKED
FLAPPED
FLASHED
FLATBED
FLATTED
FLECKED
FLEDGED
FLEECED
FLENSED
FLESHED
FLICKED
FLIPPED
FLIRTED
FLITTED
FLOATED
FLOCKED
FLOGGED
FLOODED
FLOORED
FLOPPED
FLOSSED
FLOURED
FLOUTED
FLUBBED
FLUFFED
FLUNKED
FLUSHED
GLACEED
GLANCED
GLASSED
GLEAMED
GLEANED
GLINTED
GLITZED
GLOATED
GLOMMED
GLORIED
GLOSSED
GLUTTED
ILLBRED
ILLUSED
ILLWIND
OLDGOLD
OLDHAND
OLDMAID
PLACARD
PLAGUED
PLAITED
PLANKED
PLANNED
PLANTED
PLASHED
PLEADED
PLEASED
PLEATED
PLEDGED
PLINKED
PLODDED
PLOPPED
PLOTTED
PLUCKED
PLUGGED
PLUMBED
PLUMPED
PLUNGED
PLUNKED
PLYWOOD
SLABBED
SLACKED
SLAMMED
SLANTED
SLAPPED
SLASHED
SLATTED
SLEDDED
SLEEKED
SLEETED
SLICKED
SLIMMED
SLINKED
SLIPPED
SLOGGED
SLOPPED
SLOSHED
SLOTTED
SLUGGED
SLUICED
SLUMMED
SLUMPED
SLURPED
SLURRED

••LD•••
BALDEST
BALDING
BALDRIC
BALDWIN
BELDAME
BELDAMS
BOLDEST
CALDERA
CALDRON
COLDCUT
COLDEST
COLDWAR
FELDMAN
FOLDERS
FOLDING
FOLDOUT
FOLDSUP
FOLDUPS
GELDING
GILDERS
GILDING
GOLDBUG
GOLDING
GOLDWYN
HELDOFF
HELDOUT
HOLDERS
HOLDING
HOLDOFF
HOLDOUT
HOLDSON
HOLDSTO
HOLDSUP
HOLDUPS
KILDARE
MELDING
MILDEST
MILDEWS
MILDEWY
MILDRED
MOLDERS
MOLDIER
MOLDING
POLDERS
SOLDERS
SOLDIER
SOLDOFF
SOLDOUT
TOLDOFF
WALDORF
WELDERS
WELDING
WILDCAT
WILDEST
WILDING
WILDONE

••L•D••
ALLUDED
ALLUDES
ARLEDGE
BOLIDES
BULLDOG
CELADON
DELUDED
DELUDES
GELADAS
HALFDAN
HOLEDUP
HOLIDAY
MALODOR
MELODIC
MILLDAM
PALADIN
PALEDRY
PILEDIN
PILEDON
PILEDUP
ROLODEX
SALADIN
SOLEDAD
SOLIDER
SOLIDLY
UNLADES
VALIDLY

••L••D•
ALLENDE
BALLADE
BALLADS
BELINDA
CALENDS
COLLIDE
COLLODI
COLLUDE
ISLANDS
MALTEDS
MELINDA
MILORDS
ORLANDO
RELOADS
ROLAIDS
SALSODA
SULFIDE
UNLOADS
UPLANDS
UPLOADS

••L•••D
ABLATED
ALLAYED
ALLEGED
ALLOWED
ALLOYED
ALLTOLD
ALLUDED
ALLURED
BALLARD
BELATED
BELAYED
BELCHED
BELLIED
BELOVED
BULLIED
BYLINED
COLLARD
COLLOID
COLORED
DALLIED
DELAYED
DELETED
DELTOID
DELUDED
DELUGED
DILATED
DILLARD
DILUTED
DOLLIED
DULLARD
ENLACED
FILCHED
GALAHAD
HALYARD
HELIPAD
HOLLAND
HULLOED
ILLBRED
ILLUSED
ILLWIND
JELLIED
JOLLIED
LILYPAD
MALAMUD
MALLARD
MILDRED
MILHAUD
MILLAND
MILLARD
MILLEND
MULCHED
MULCTED
OBLIGED
PILOTED
POLICED
POLKAED
RALLIED
RELACED
RELATED
RELAXED
RELAYED
RELINED
RELIVED
SALLIED
SALUTED
SOLEDAD
SPLAYED
SPLICED
SULLIED
TALLIED
TALONED
TELEXED
UNLACED
UNLIKED
UNLINED
UNLOVED
WALTZED
WELCHED
WELLAND
WELLFED
WILFORD
WILFRID
WILLARD

•••LD••
BOULDER
BUILDER
BUILDIN
BUILDON
BUILDUP
BULLDOG
COULDNT
EARLDOM
FIELDED
FIELDER
GUILDER
MAULDIN
MILLDAM
MOULDED
MOULDER
SCALDED
SCOLDED
SCOLDER
SHELDON
SMOLDER
WIELDED
WORLDLY
WOULDBE
WOULDNT
YIELDED

•••L•D•
BALLADE
BALLADS
COLLIDE
COLLODI
COLLUDE
EXCLUDE
EXPLODE
EYELIDS
IMPLODE
INCLUDE
NUCLIDE
OCCLUDE
PRELUDE

ROULADE
SECLUDE

•••L••D

ABELARD
APPLAUD
APPLIED
ARMLOAD
ASHLAND
AVULSED
BALLARD
BECLOUD
BELLIED
BULLIED
CARLOAD
CAULKED
CHALKED
CHILLED
COLLARD
COLLOID
COPLAND
DALLIED
DILLARD
DIPLOID
DOLLIED
DRILLED
DULLARD
DWELLED
ENGLAND
ENGLUND
EVOLVED
EVULSED
EXALTED
EXULTED
FAULTED
FIELDED
FINLAND
FOULARD
FRILLED
FUELROD
GARLAND
GAYLORD
GIELGUD
GOTLAND
GRILLED
HOLLAND
HULLOED
ICELAND
IMPLIED
IRELAND
JELLIED
JOLLIED
JUTLAND
KNELLED
KOOLAID
LAPLAND
LOWLAND
MALLARD
MIDLAND
MILLAND
MILLARD
MILLEND
MISLAID
MISLEAD
MOULDED
MOULTED
OAKLAND
OFFLOAD
OUTLAID
OUTLAND
OUTLOUD
OXBLOOD
PAYLOAD
PRELOAD
PSALMED
QUELLED
QUILLED
QUILTED
RALLIED
REGLUED
REPLIED
SALLIED
SCALDED
SCALPED
SCOLDED
SCULLED
SHELLED
SHELVED
SHILLED
SKILLED
SKULKED
SMELLED
SMELTED
SPALLED
SPELLED
SPILLED
STALKED
STALLED
STILLED
STILTED
SULLIED
SWELLED
SWILLED
TABLOID
TAILEND
TALLIED
TOYLAND
TRILLED
TROLLED
TWILLED
UNGLUED
VAULTED
WARLORD
WAYLAID
WELLAND
WELLFED
WETLAND
WHELPED
WIELDED
WILLARD
YIELDED
ZEALAND

••••LD•

BEHOLDS
DEWILDE
ENFOLDS
GERALDO
HERALDS
KOBOLDS
MATILDA
REMOLDS
REWELDS
SHIELDS
UNFOLDS
UPHOLDS
VIVALDI

••••L•D

ANNELID
AVAILED
BABBLED
BAFFLED
BATTLED
BEVELED
BOBBLED
BOBSLED
BOGGLED
BOTTLED
BRAWLED
BRIDLED
BROILED
BUBBLED
BUCKLED
BUMBLED
BUNDLED
BUNGLED
BURBLED
BURGLED
BUSTLED
CACKLED
CAJOLED
CAROLED
CASTLED
CAVILED
CHILLED
CIRCLED
COBBLED
CODDLED
COUPLED
CRADLED
CRAWLED
CUDDLED
CURDLED
DABBLED
DANDLED
DANGLED
DAPPLED
DAWDLED
DAZZLED
DEFILED
DEVILED
DIBBLED
DIDDLED
DIMPLED
DOGSLED
DOODLED
DOUBLED
DRAWLED
DRILLED
DROOLED
DWELLED
ENABLED
ENISLED
ENSILED
EQUALED
EXHALED
FIDDLED
FIZZLED
FLAILED
FONDLED
FOOZLED
FRILLED
FUDDLED
FUMBLED
GABBLED
GAMBLED
GANGLED
GARBLED
GARGLED
GAVELED
GENTLED
GIGGLED
GIRDLED
GNARLED
GOBBLED
GOGGLED
GRILLED
GROWLED
GURGLED
GUZZLED
HAGGLED
HANDLED
HASSLED
HECKLED
HOBBLED
HUDDLED
HUMBLED
HURDLED
HURTLED
HUSTLED
IMPALED
INHALED
INVALID
JANGLED
JEWELED
JIGGLED
JINGLED
JOGGLED
JOSTLED
JUGGLED
JUMBLED
KIBBLED
KINDLED
KNEELED
KNELLED
KNURLED
LABELED
LAPELED
LEVELED
LIBELED
MANGLED
MANTLED
MARBLED
MEDALED
MEDDLED
MINGLED
MIZZLED
MODELED
MOTTLED
MUDDLED
MUFFLED
MUMBLED
MUSCLED
MUZZLED
NEEDLED
NESTLED
NETTLED
NIBBLED
NIGGLED
NUZZLED
PADDLED
PANELED
PAROLED
PEARLED
PEBBLED
PEDALED
PEDDLED
PEOPLED
PESTLED
PETALED
PICKLED
PIFFLED
POPPLED
PROWLED
PUDDLED
PURFLED
PURPLED
PUZZLED
QUAILED
QUELLED
QUILLED
RADDLED
RAFFLED
RAMBLED
RANKLED
RASSLED
RATTLED
RAVELED
REGALED
REOILED
RESILED
RESOLED
RETILED
REVELED
REVILED
RIDDLED
RIFFLED
RIPPLED
RIVALED
RUFFLED
RUMBLED
RUMPLED
RUSTLED
SADDLED
SAMPLED
SCOWLED
SCULLED
SETTLED
SHELLED
SHILLED
SINGLED
SIZZLED
SKILLED
SKIRLED
SMELLED
SNARLED
SPALLED
SPELLED
SPIELED
SPILLED
SPOILED
SPOOLED
SQUALID
STABLED
STALLED
STAPLED
STEELED
STIFLED
STILLED
SWELLED
SWILLED
SWIRLED
TACKLED
TANGLED
TATTLED
TICKLED
TINGLED
TINKLED
TIPPLED
TODDLED
TOGGLED
TOOTLED
TOPPLED
TOTALED
TOUSLED
TOWELED
TRAILED
TRAWLED
TREBLED
TRIFLED
TRILLED
TRIPLED
TROLLED
TUMBLED
TURTLED
TUSSLED
TWILLED
TWIRLED
UNOILED
UNPILED
WADDLED
WAFFLED
WAGGLED
WAMBLED
WANGLED
WARBLED
WHEELED
WHIRLED
WHORLED
WIGGLED
WIMPLED
WOBBLED
YODELED

•••••LD

ALLTOLD
BADCOLD
BAGNOLD
EMERALD
HOGWILD
ICECOLD
INFIELD
LEOPOLD
OLDGOLD
OUTSOLD
PIEBALD
REBUILD
SIXFOLD
TENFOLD
TOEHOLD
TWOFOLD

LE•••••

LEACHED
LEACHES
LEACOCK
LEADERS
LEADING
LEADINS
LEADOFF
LEADOUT
LEADSIN
LEADSON
LEADSTO
LEADSUP
LEAFIER
LEAFING
LEAFLET
LEAGUER
LEAGUES
LEAKAGE
LEAKERS
LEAKIER
LEAKING
LEANDER
LEANERS
LEANEST
LEANING
LEANSON
LEANTOS
LEAPERS
LEAPING
LEARJET
LEARNED
LEARNER
LEASERS
LEASHED
LEASHES
LEASING
LEATHER
LEAVENS
LEAVING
LEBANON
LEBARON
LECARRE
LECTERN
LECTORS
LECTURE
LEDGERS
LEDUPTO
LEECHED
LEECHES
LEERERS
LEERIER
LEERILY
LEERING
LEERSAT
LEETIDE
LEEWARD
LEFTIES
LEFTIST
LEFTOFF
LEFTOUT
LEGALLY
LEGATEE
LEGATES
LEGATOS
LEGENDS
LEGGIER
LEGGING
LEGHORN
LEGIBLE
LEGIBLY
LEGIONS
LEGISTS
LEGPULL
LEGROOM
LEGUMES
LEGWORK
LEHAVRE
LEIBNIZ
LEIPZIG
LEISTER
LEISURE
LEMMING
LEMPIRA
LENDERS
LENDING
LENFANT
LENGTHS
LENGTHY
LENIENT
LENTILS
LEONARD
LEONINE
LEONORA
LEOPARD
LEOPOLD
LEOTARD
LEPANTO
LEPTONS
LESOTHO
LESPAUL
LESSEES
LESSENS
LESSING
LESSONS
LESSORS
LETDOWN
LETINON
LETITBE
LETITIA
LETSFLY
LETSLIP
LETSOFF
LETSOUT
LETSSEE
LETTERS
LETTING
LETTRES
LETTUCE
LEVELED
LEVELER
LEVELLY
LEVERED
LEVERET
LEVIERS
LEVITES
LEVYING
LEWDEST
LEXICAL
LEXICON

L•E••••

LAENNEC
LAERTES
LEECHED
LEECHES
LEERERS
LEERIER
LEERILY
LEERING
LEERSAT
LEETIDE
LEEWARD
LIEABED
LIEDOWN
LIENEES
LIEOVER
LIERNES
LIESLOW
LOESSER
LOESSES

L••E•••

LABELED
LABELER
LABELLE
LACEDUP
LACESUP
LAMENTS
LAPELED
LATEENS
LATENCY
LATENTS
LATERAL
LATERAN
LATERON
LATEXES
LAVERNE
LAYERED
LAYETTE
LAZENBY
LEGENDS
LEVELED
LEVELER
LEVELLY
LEVERED
LEVERET
LIBELED
LIBELER
LIBERAL
LIBERIA
LIBERTY
LICENCE
LICENSE
LIFENET
LIKEMAD
LIKENED
LIKENEW
LIMEADE
LINEAGE
LINEATE
LINEDUP
LINEMAN
LINEMEN
LINESUP
LINEUPS
LITERAL
LIVEDIN
LIVEDON
LIVENED
LIVEOAK
LIVEONE
LIVEOUT
LIVESIN
LIVESON
LORELEI
LORENZO
LORETTA
LOSEOUT
LOSESIT
LOUELLA
LOVEBUG
LOVEINS
LOVERLY
LOWERED
LOZENGE
LUCERNE
LYCEUMS

L•••E••

LAAGERS
LABRETS
LACIEST
LACKEYS
LACTEAL
LADDERS
LADLERS
LAGGERS
LAMBEAU
LAMBENT
LAMBERT
LANCERS
LANCETS
LANDERS
LANKEST
LANTERN
LAPBELT
LAPPETS
LARCENY
LARDERS
LARGELY
LARGESS
LARGEST
LASHERS
LATEENS
LATHERS
LATHERY
LATTENS
LAURELS
LAURENT
LAWLESS
LAWYERS
LAXNESS
LAZIEST
LEADERS
LEAKERS
LEANERS
LEANEST
LEAPERS
LEASERS
LEAVENS
LECTERN
LEDGERS
LEERERS
LENDERS
LENIENT
LESSEES
LESSENS
LETTERS
LEVIERS
LEWDEST
LIBBERS
LICHENS
LICKETY
LIDLESS
LIENEES
LIFTERS
LIMBERS
LIMIEST
LIMNERS
LIMPEST
LIMPETS
LINDENS
LINGERS
LINKERS
LINNETS
LINSEED
LINTELS
LIONESS
LIONETS
LIPREAD
LIQUEFY
LIQUEUR
LISTEES
LISTELS
LISTENS
LITHELY
LITHEST
LITTERS
LOADERS
LOAFERS
LOANERS
LOBBERS
LOCKERS
LOCKETS
LODGERS
LOGGERS
LOGIEST
LOITERS
LONGEST
LOOKERS
LOOPERS
LOOSELY
LOOSENS
LOOSEST
LOOTERS
LOPPERS
LOTTERY
LOUDEST
LOUREED
LOUSEUP
LOUVERS
LOWBEAM
LOWGEAR
LOWHEEL
LOWNECK
LOWNESS
LOWTECH
LUBBERS
LUGGERS
LUMBERS
LUMIERE
LUMPERS
LUNGEAT
LUNKERS
LUSHEST
LUSTERS

L••••E•

LABELED
LABELER
LABORED
LABORER
LACQUER
LADDIES
LAENNEC
LAERTES
LAISSEZ
LALAKER
LAMPREY
LANGLEY
LANKIER
LAPELED
LARCHES
LARDNER
LASSIES
LASSOED
LASSOER
LASSOES
LATCHED
LATCHES
LATEXES
LATICES
LAUGHED
LAUGHER
LAUNDER
LAUTREC
LAYERED
LAYOVER
LEACHED
LEACHES
LEAFIER
LEAFLET
LEAGUER
LEAGUES
LEAKIER
LEANDER
LEARJET
LEARNED
LEARNER
LEASHED
LEASHES
LEATHER
LEECHED
LEECHES
LEERIER
LEFTIES
LEGATEE
LEGATES
LEGGIER
LEGUMES
LEISTER
LESSEES
LETSSEE
LETTRES
LEVELED
LEVELER
LEVERED
LEVERET
LEVITES
LIAISED
LIAISES
LIBELED
LIBELER
LIEABED
LIENEES
LIEOVER
LIERNES
LIFENET
LIGATED
LIGATES
LIGHTED
LIGHTEN
LIGHTER
LIKENED
LIKENEW
LIMITED
LIMOGES
LINAGES
LINDIED
LINDIES
LINDSEY
LINEMEN
LINGOES
LINSEED
LINTIER
LIPPIER
LISTEES
LITOTES
LITTLER
LIVENED
LOACHES
LOAMIER
LOATHED
LOATHES
LOBBIED
LOBBIES
LOBBYER
LOBSTER
LOCALES
LOCATED
LOCATER
LOCATES
LOESSER
LOESSES
LOFTIER
LOLLIES
LONGUES
LOOKSEE
LOONIER
LOONIES
LOOPIER
LORELEI
LORISES
LORRIES
LOTUSES
LOUNGED
LOUNGER
LOUNGES
LOURDES
LOUREED
LOUSIER
LOUVRES
LOWBRED
LOWERED
LOWHEEL
LOWLIER
LUCIFER
LUCKIER
LUMPIER
LUNCHED
LUNCHER
LUNCHES
LUPINES
LURCHED
LURCHES
LUSTIER
LUSTRED
LUSTRES
LUXATED
LUXATES

L•••••E

LABELLE
LABIATE
LACOSTE
LACTASE
LACTATE
LACTOSE
LACUNAE
LAFARGE
LAFITTE
LALANNE
LALIQUE
LAMINAE
LAPLACE
LAPORTE
LAPROBE
LARAINE
LARAMIE
LAROCHE
LASAGNE
LASALLE
LATTICE
LAVALSE
LAVERNE
LAYETTE
LEAKAGE
LECARRE
LECTURE
LEETIDE
LEGATEE
LEGIBLE
LEHAVRE
LEISURE
LEONINE
LETITBE
LETSSEE
LETTUCE
LICENCE
LICENSE
LIGNITE
LIKABLE
LIMEADE
LINEAGE
LINEATE
LINKAGE
LIONIZE
LISSOME
LIVABLE
LIVEONE
LOOKSEE
LOVABLE
LOWLIFE
LOWRISE
LOWTIDE
LOZENGE
LUCERNE
LUCILLE
LUGGAGE
LUMIERE

•LE••••

ALEMBIC
ALENCON
ALERTED

ALERTER
ALERTLY
ALEWIFE
BLEAKER
BLEAKLY
BLEARED
BLEATED
BLEEPED
BLEEPER
BLEMISH
BLENDED
BLENDER
BLERIOT
BLESSED
BLESSES
BLEWOFF
BLEWOUT
CLEANED
CLEANER
CLEANLY
CLEANSE
CLEANUP
CLEARED
CLEARER
CLEARLY
CLEARUP
CLEAVED
CLEAVER
CLEAVES
CLEAVON
CLEMENS
CLEMENT
CLEMSON
CLERICS
CLERKED
ELEANOR
ELECTED
ELECTEE
ELECTOR
ELECTRA
ELECTRO
ELEGANT
ELEGIAC
ELEGIES
ELEGIST
ELEISON
ELEKTRA
ELEMENT
ELEVATE
ELEVENS
FLEABAG
FLECHES
FLECKED
FLEDGED
FLEDGES
FLEECED
FLEECES
FLEEING
FLEETER
FLEETLY
FLEMING
FLEMISH
FLENSED
FLENSES
FLESHED
FLESHES
FLEXING
FLEXNER
FLEXORS
GLEAMED
GLEANED
GLEANER
GLEASON
GLEEFUL
KLEENEX
OLEATES
OLEMISS
OLESTRA
PLEADED
PLEADER
PLEASED
PLEASER
PLEASES
PLEATED
PLECTRA
PLEDGED
PLEDGEE
PLEDGER
PLEDGES
PLENARY
PLENUMS
PLEXORS
SLEDDED
SLEDDER
SLEDDOG
SLEDGES
SLEEKED
SLEEKEN
SLEEKER
SLEEKLY
SLEEPER
SLEEPIN
SLEEPON
SLEETED
SLEEVES
SLEIGHS
SLEIGHT
SLENDER
SLEPTIN
SLEPTON
SLEUTHS

•L•E•••

ALBEDOS
ALBENIZ
ALBERTA
ALBERTO
ALDENTE
ALGEBRA
ALGERIA
ALIENEE
ALIENOR
ALKENES
ALLEARS
ALLEGED
ALLEGER
ALLEGES
ALLEGRO
ALLELES
ALLENDE
ALLERGY
ALLEYES
ALREADY
ALTERED
ALTERER
ALVEOLI
BLEEPED
BLEEPER
BLUEBOY
BLUEFIN
BLUEFLU
BLUEFOX
BLUEING
BLUEJAY
BLUELAW
BLUESKY
CLIENTS
CLUEDIN
CLUEING
CLUESIN
ELDERLY
FLEECED
FLEECES
FLEEING
FLEETER
FLEETLY
FLIESAT
FLIESIN
FLUENCY
GLEEFUL
GLUEDON
ILIESCU
ILLEGAL
KLEENEX
SLEEKED
SLEEKEN
SLEEKER
SLEEKLY
SLEEPER
SLEEPIN
SLEEPON
SLEETED
SLEEVES
SLOEGIN

•L••E••

ALAMEDA
ALAMEIN
ALCHEMY
ALFIERI
ALFREDO
ALGIERS
ALIMENT
ALLHEAL
ALLHERE
BLAZERS
BLOWERS
CLARETS
CLAVELL
CLAWERS
CLEMENS
CLEMENT
CLORETS
CLOSEIN
CLOSELY
CLOSEST
CLOSETS
CLOSEUP
CLOVERS
ELATERS
ELEMENT
ELEVENS
ELGRECO
ELOPERS
ELYSEES
FLAKERS
FLANEUR
FLAREUP
FLORETS
FLOWERS
FLOWERY
FLYLEAF
FLYNETS
GLACEED
GLADEYE
GLAZERS
GLIDERS
GLOWERS
ILLNESS
OLDNESS
OLDNEWS
OLDWEST
PLACEBO
PLACERS
PLANERS
PLANETS
PLATEAU
PLATENS
PLATERS
PLAYERS
PLOVERS
PLOWERS
SLAVERS
SLAVERY
SLAYERS
SLICERS
SLIDEIN
SLIDERS
SLIVERS
SLOVENE
SLOVENS
SLOWEST
SLYNESS
ULSTERS

•L•••E•

ALARMED
ALARMER
ALBUMEN
ALCOVES
ALERTED
ALERTER
ALIASES
ALIENEE
ALIGNED
ALIGNER
ALKENES
ALLAYED
ALLAYER
ALLEGED
ALLEGER
ALLEGES
ALLELES
ALLEYES
ALLOVER
ALLOWED
ALLOYED
ALLUDED
ALLUDES
ALLURED
ALLURES
ALMADEN
ALTERED
ALTERER
ALUNSER
ALVAREZ
BLABBED
BLABBER
BLACKED
BLACKEN
BLACKER
BLADDER
BLANDER
BLANKED
BLANKER
BLANKET
BLARNEY
BLASTED
BLASTER
BLATHER
BLATTED
BLEAKER
BLEARED
BLEATED
BLEEPED
BLEEPER
BLENDED
BLENDER
BLESSED
BLESSES
BLINDED
BLINDER
BLINKED
BLINKER
BLIPPED
BLISTER
BLITHER
BLITZED
BLITZEN
BLITZES
BLOATED
BLOCKED
BLOCKER
BLONDER
BLONDES
BLOODED
BLOOMED
BLOOMER
BLOOPED
BLOOPER
BLOTTED
BLOTTER
BLOUSED
BLOUSES
BLOWIER
BLUBBER
BLUFFED
BLUFFER
BLUNDER
BLUNTED
BLUNTER
BLURRED
BLURTED
BLUSHED
BLUSHER
BLUSHES
BLUSTER
CLABBER
CLACKED
CLAIMED
CLAIMER
CLAMBER
CLAMMED
CLAMMER
CLAMPED
CLANGED
CLANKED
CLAPPED
CLAPPER
CLAQUES
CLASHED
CLASHES
CLASPED
CLASSED
CLASSES
CLATTER
CLAUSES
CLAVIER
CLAYIER
CLEANED
CLEANER
CLEARED
CLEARER
CLEAVED
CLEAVER
CLEAVES
CLERKED
CLICHES
CLICKED
CLIMBED
CLIMBER
CLINKED
CLINKER
CLIPPED
CLIPPER
CLIQUES
CLOAKED
CLOBBER
CLOCHES
CLOCKED
CLOCKER
CLOGGED
CLOONEY
CLOPPED
CLOQUES
CLOTHED
CLOTHES
CLOTTED
CLOUDED
CLOUTED
CLOWDER
CLOWNED
CLUBBED
CLUCKED
CLUMPED
CLUNKED
CLUNKER
CLUSTER
CLUTTER
ELAPSED
ELAPSES
ELBOWED
ELECTED
ELECTEE
ELEGIES
ELMTREE
ELYSEES
FLAGGED
FLAGMEN
FLAILED
FLAKIER
FLAMBED
FLAMBES
FLANGES
FLANKED
FLANKER
FLANNEL
FLAPPED
FLAPPER
FLASHED
FLASHER
FLASHES
FLATBED
FLATTED
FLATTEN
FLATTER
FLECHES
FLECKED
FLEDGED
FLEDGES
FLEECED
FLEECES
FLEETER
FLENSED
FLENSES
FLESHED
FLESHES
FLEXNER
FLICKED
FLICKER
FLIPPED
FLIPPER
FLIRTED
FLITTED
FLITTER
FLIVVER
FLOATED
FLOATER
FLOCKED
FLOGGED
FLOODED
FLOORED
FLOPPED
FLOSSED
FLOSSES
FLOURED
FLOUTED
FLUBBED
FLUFFED
FLUNKED
FLUSHED
FLUSHES
FLUSTER
FLUTTER
FLYOVER
GLACEED
GLACIER
GLADDEN
GLADDER
GLANCED
GLANCES
GLASSED
GLASSES
GLAZIER
GLEAMED
GLEANED
GLEANER
GLIBBER
GLIMMER
GLINTED
GLISTEN
GLITTER
GLITZED
GLITZES
GLOATED
GLOMMED
GLORIED
GLORIES
GLOSSED
GLOSSES
GLUMMER
GLUTTED
ILLBRED
ILLUSED
ILLUSES
KLEENEX
KLUDGES
KLUTZES
OLDSTER
OLEATES
OLIVIER
PLACKET
PLAGUED
PLAGUES
PLAICES
PLAINER
PLAINES
PLAITED
PLANKED
PLANNED
PLANNER
PLANTED
PLANTER
PLAQUES
PLASHED
PLASHES
PLASTER
PLATTER
PLAYLET
PLAYPEN
PLEADED
PLEADER
PLEASED
PLEASER
PLEASES
PLEATED
PLEDGED
PLEDGEE
PLEDGER
PLEDGES
PLINKED
PLODDED
PLODDER
PLOPPED
PLOTTED
PLOTTER
PLOWMEN
PLUCKED
PLUGGED
PLUGGER
PLUMBED
PLUMBER
PLUMMER
PLUMMET
PLUMPED
PLUMPER
PLUNDER
PLUNGED
PLUNGER
PLUNGES
PLUNKED
PLUSHER
PLUSHES
PLUSSES
SLABBED
SLACKED
SLACKEN
SLACKER
SLAMMED
SLAMMER
SLANDER
SLANTED
SLAPPED
SLASHED
SLASHER
SLASHES
SLATHER
SLATIER
SLATTED
SLEDDED
SLEDDER
SLEDGES
SLEEKED
SLEEKEN
SLEEKER
SLEEPER
SLEETED
SLEEVES
SLENDER
SLICKED
SLICKER
SLIMIER
SLIMMED
SLIMMER
SLINGER
SLINKED
SLIPPED
SLIPPER
SLITHER
SLOBBER
SLOGGED
SLOPPED
SLOSHED
SLOSHES
SLOTTED
SLUDGES
SLUGGED
SLUGGER
SLUICED
SLUICES
SLUMBER
SLUMMED
SLUMPED
SLURPED
SLURRED
SLUSHES
ULYSSES

•L••••E

ALAMODE
ALDENTE
ALEWIFE
ALIDADE
ALIENEE
ALLENDE
ALLGONE
ALLHERE
ALLOFME
ALLTIME
ALOHAOE
ALUMNAE
BLANCHE
BLONDIE
CLARICE
CLEANSE
CLIMATE
CLOSURE
CLOTURE
ELECTEE
ELEVATE
ELLIPSE
ELMTREE
ELUSIVE
FLOUNCE
GLADEYE
GLIMPSE
GLOBULE
GLOSSAE
GLUCOSE
OLDLINE
OLDTIME
OLIVINE
PLACATE
PLEDGEE
PLIABLE
PLOSIVE
PLUMAGE
SLOVENE
ULALUME
ULULATE

••LE•••

AILERON
ALLEARS
ALLEGED
ALLEGER
ALLEGES
ALLEGRO
ALLELES
ALLENDE
ALLERGY
ALLEYES
APLENTY
ARLEDGE
ATLEAST
BALEENS
BALEFUL
BILEVEL
BOLEROS
CALENDS
CELEBES
CELEBRE
CELESTA
CELESTE
COLEMAN
COLETTE
CSLEWIS
CULEBRA
DELEING
DELETED
DELETES
DILEMMA
DOLEFUL
DOLEOUT
HOLEDUP
HOLEOUT
HOLESUP
ILLEGAL
MALEATE
MALEFIC
MILEAGE
MOLESTS
MULETAS
ONLEAVE
ORLEANS
PALEDRY
PALERMO
PALETTE
PILEDIN
PILEDON
PILEDUP
PILESIN
PILESON
PILESUP
PILEUPS
POLEAXE
POLECAT
POLEMIC
POLENTA
RALEIGH
RELEARN
RELEASE
RELENTS
RULEOUT
RULESON
SALERNO
SCLERAS
SELECTS
SELENIC
SILENCE
SILENTS
SILESIA
SOLEDAD
SPLEENS
TALENTS
TELERAN
TELEXED
TELEXES
TYLENOL
UNLEARN
UNLEASH
VALENCE
VALERIE
YULELOG

••L•E••

AILMENT
ALLHEAL
ALLHERE
BALDEST
BALEENS
BALLETS
BELIEFS
BELIEVE
BILLETS
BOLDEST
BULLETS
CALDERA
CALLERS
CALMEST
CALTECH
CALVERT
COLBERT
COLDEST
COLLECT
COLLEEN
COLLEGE
COLLETS
CULVERT
DELBERT
DELVERS
DOLMENS
DULLEST
EELIEST
FALSELY
FALSEST
FALTERS
FALWELL
FELLERS
FILBERT
FILLERS
FILLETS
FILTERS
FOLDERS
FOLGERS
FOLLETT
FULGENT
FULLEST
GALLEON
GALLERY
GALLEYS
GILBERT
GILDERS
GOLFERS
GULLETS
HALTERS
HELLENE
HELLERS
HELMETS
HELPERS
HOLBEIN
HOLDERS
HOLIEST
HOLLERS
HULLERS
ILLNESS
KILLERS
MALLETS
MALTEDS
MALTESE
MILDEST
MILDEWS
MILDEWY
MILIEUS
MILIEUX
MILKERS
MILLEND
MILLERS
MILLETS
MILLETT
MOLDERS
MOLIERE
MOLTERS
MULLEIN
MULLERS
MULLETS
OILIEST
OILWELL
PALLETS
PALTERS
PELLETS
PELTERS
PILFERS
POLDERS
POLLENS
POLLERS
PULLETS
PULLEYS
RELIEFS
RELIEVE
RELIEVO
RELLENO
RILLETS
ROLLERS
SALIENT
SALIERI
SALTERS
SALVERS
SELLECK
SELLERS
SILVERS
SILVERY
SOLDERS
SOLFEGE
SOLVENT
SOLVERS
SPLEENS
SULKERS
TALKERS
TALLEST
TELLERS
TILLERS
TILTERS
TOLTECS
TOLUENE
UGLIEST
VALJEAN
VALLEYS
VELVETS
VELVETY
VILLEIN
VOLLEYS
WALKERS
WALLETS
WALLEYE
WALTERS
WELDERS
WELTERS
WILDEST
WILHELM
WILIEST
YELPERS

••L••E•

ABLATED
ABLATES
ALLAYED
ALLAYER
ALLEGED
ALLEGER
ALLEGES
ALLELES
ALLEYES
ALLOVER
ALLOWED
ALLOYED
ALLUDED
ALLUDES
ALLURED
ALLURES
ATLASES
BALKIER
BALMIER
BALONEY
BELATED
BELAYED
BELCHED
BELCHES
BELLIED
BELLIES
BELLMEN
BELOVED
BILBOES
BILEVEL
BILLIES
BOLIDES
BOLSTER
BOLUSES
BULBLET
BULKIER
BULLIED
BULLIES
BULLPEN
BYLINED
BYLINES
CALIBER
CALIPER
CALOMEL
CALUMET
CALYCES
CALYXES
CELEBES
COLLEEN
COLLIER
COLLIES
COLLYER
COLONEL
COLONES
COLORED
DALLIED
DALLIER
DALLIES
DALTREY
DELANEY
DELAYED
DELAYER
DELETED
DELETES
DELIBES
DELIVER
DELUDED
DELUDES
DELUGED
DELUGES
DILATED
DILATES
DILLIES
DILUTED
DILUTER

DILUTES
DOLLIED
DOLLIES
DOLORES
ENLACED
ENLACES
ENLIVEN
FALAFEL
FELINES
FILCHED
FILCHER
FILCHES
FILLIES
FILMIER
FOLLIES
GALATEA
GALILEE
GALILEI
GALILEO
GILLIES
GILLNET
GOLFTEE
GULCHES
GULLIES
HALITES
HALOGEN
HELICES
HELIXES
HILLIER
HOLLIES
HOLSTER
HOLYSEE
HULLOED
ILLBRED
ILLUSED
ILLUSES
JELLIED
JELLIES
JOLLIED
JOLLIER
JOLLIES
JOLLIET
KELPIES
KILAUEA
KILTIES
KYLIKES
LALAKER
LOLLIES
MALAREN
MALMSEY
MILDRED
MILKIER
MILKMEN
MOLDIER
MULCHED
MULCHES
MULCTED
OBLATES
OBLIGED
OBLIGES
OOLITES
PALACES
PALATES
PALAVER
PALFREY
PALJOEY
PALMIER
PELAGES
PHLOXES
PILOTED
PILSNER
POLICED
POLICES
POLITER
POLKAED
POLYMER
RALLIED
RALLIES
RELACED
RELACES
RELATED
RELATES
RELAXED
RELAXES
RELAYED
RELINED
RELINES
RELIVED
RELIVES
ROLODEX
SALLIED
SALLIES
SALTIER
SALUTED
SALUTES
SALVOES
SELTZER
SILKIER
SILLIER
SILLIES
SOLACES
SOLDIER
SOLIDER
SOLUTES
SPLAYED
SPLICED
SPLICER
SPLICES
SPLINES
SULKIER
SULKIES
SULLIED
SULLIES
SULUSEA
TALKIES
TALLIED
TALLIES
TALONED
TALUSES
TELEXED
TELEXES
TELLIES
TOLKIEN
UNLACED
UNLACES
UNLADES
UNLIKED
UNLINED
UNLOVED
VALISES
VOLUMES
WALTZED
WALTZER
WALTZES
WELCHED
WELCHES
WELLFED
WELLSET
WILLIES
WOLFMEN
ZILCHES

••L•••E

ALLENDE
ALLGONE
ALLHERE
ALLOFME
ALLTIME
ARLEDGE
ATLARGE
AXLROSE
BALANCE
BALLADE
BELDAME
BELIEVE
BELTANE
BOLOTIE
CALCITE
CALIBRE
CALORIE
CALZONE
CELEBRE
CELESTE
CILIATE
COLETTE
COLGATE
COLLAGE
COLLATE
COLLEGE
COLLIDE
COLLUDE
COLOGNE
CULOTTE
CULTURE
DELUISE
ECLIPSE
ECLOGUE
ELLIPSE
ENLARGE
FOLIAGE
FOLIATE
FULSOME
GALILEE
GILMORE
GOLFTEE
HELLENE
HELOISE
HILAIRE
HOLYOKE
HOLYSEE
KILDARE
LALANNE
LALIQUE
MALAISE
MALEATE
MALTESE
MALTOSE
MELANGE
MELANIE
MELROSE
MILEAGE
MOLIERE
OBLIQUE
OILCAKE
ONLEAVE
OWLLIKE
PALANCE
PALETTE
PALMATE
PELISSE
PELTATE
PILLAGE
POLEAXE
POLLUTE
PULSATE
RELAPSE
RELEASE
RELIEVE
SALABLE
SALTINE
SALVAGE
SELVAGE
SILENCE
SOLFEGE
SOLUBLE
SPLURGE
SULFATE
SULFIDE
SULFITE
TILLAGE
TOLUENE
UNLOOSE
VALANCE
VALENCE
VALERIE
VALUATE
VILLAGE
VOLPONE
VOLTAGE
VOLUBLE
VULGATE
VULPINE
VULTURE
WALLACE
WALLEYE
WALPOLE
WELCOME
WELFARE
WILDONE
WILLKIE

•••LE••

ABILENE
AGELESS
AGILELY
AIMLESS
AIRLESS
AMBLERS
AMPLEST
AMULETS
ANGLERS
ANKLETS
ANTLERS
ARMLESS
ARMLETS
ARTLESS
ASHLESS
ATHLETE
AUKLETS
AWELESS
AZALEAS
BAILEES
BAILERS
BAILEYS
BALLETS
BARLEYS
BAWLERS
BAYLEAF
BILLETS
BOILERS
BOOLEAN
BOWLERS
BUGLERS
BULLETS
BUTLERS
CABLERS
CABLETV
CALLERS
CAPLESS
CAPLETS
CARLESS
CHALETS
CHILEAN
COALERS
COLLECT
COLLEEN
COLLEGE
COLLETS
COOLERS
COOLEST
COULEES
CURLERS
CURLEWS
CUTLERS
CUTLERY
CUTLETS
CYCLERS
DARLEEN
DARLENE
DEALERS
DEFLECT
DEKLERK
DEPLETE
DIALECT
DIALERS
DOGLEGS
DUELERS
DULLEST
EAGLETS
EMBLEMS
ENDLESS
EVILEST
EVILEYE
EYELETS
FARLEFT
FATLESS
FEELERS
FELLERS
FIGLEAF
FILLERS
FILLETS
FLYLEAF
FOLLETT
FOOLERY
FOULEST
FOWLERS
FUELERS
FULLEST
GALLEON
GALLERY
GALLEYS
GIBLETS
GIMLETS
GOBLETS
GULLETS
GUTLESS
HAMLETS
HAPLESS
HATLESS
HAULERS
HEALERS
HEELERS
HELLENE
HELLERS
HEWLETT
HIALEAH
HITLESS
HOLLERS
HOWLERS
HULLERS
HURLERS
ICELESS
INFLECT
JAGLESS
JAILERS
JAYLENO
JOYLESS
KEGLERS
KILLERS
KOBLENZ
LADLERS
LAWLESS
LIDLESS
MAILERS
MALLETS
MARLENE
MEDLEYS
MEWLERS
MILLEND
MILLERS
MILLETS
MILLETT
MISLEAD
MOILERS
MOSLEMS
MRCLEAN
MULLEIN
MULLERS
MULLETS
NAILERS
NEGLECT
NEWLEFT
NOBLEST
NUCLEAR
NUCLEIC
NUCLEON
NUCLEUS
NUTLETS
OAKLEAF
OARLESS
OMELETS
OPULENT
OSTLERS
OUTLETS
PALLETS
PARLEYS
PEELERS
PELLETS
PIGLETS
PINLESS
PIOLETS
POLLENS
POLLERS
POULENC
PTOLEMY
PULLETS
PULLEYS
RAILERS
RECLEAN
REELECT
REFLECT
RELLENO
REPLETE
RIFLERS
RIFLERY
RILLETS
ROLLERS
RUNLETS
SCALENE
SCALERS
SCHLEPP
SCHLEPS
SEALEGS
SEALERS
SELLECK
SELLERS
SMILERS
STALEST
STYLERS
STYLETS
SUBLETS
SUNLESS
SUTLERS
TABLEAU
TABLETS
TAILEND
TALLEST
TEALEAF
TELLERS
THALERS
TIELESS
TILLERS
TOELESS
TOILERS
TOILETS
UKULELE
UNBLEST
UNCLEAN
UNCLEAR
USELESS
VALLEYS
VARLETS
VILLEIN
VIOLENT
VIOLETS
VOLLEYS
WAILERS
WALLETS
WALLEYE
WHALERS
WIGLETS
WITLESS
WOOLENS
YOWLERS

•••L•E•

APPLIED
APPLIES
ARALSEA
ATELIER
AVULSED
AVULSES
BAILEES
BELLIED
BELLIES
BELLMEN
BIALIES
BILLIES
BOULDER
BUILDER
BULLIED
BULLIES
BULLPEN
BURLIER
CAULKED
CAULKER
CHALKED
CHELSEA
CHILIES
CHILLED
CHILLER
COLLEEN
COLLIER
COLLIES
COLLYER
COULEES
COULTER
CRULLER
CURLIER
DAILIES
DALLIED
DALLIER
DALLIES
DARLEEN
DILLIES
DOILIES
DOLLIED
DOLLIES
DRILLED
DRILLER
DROLLER
DWELLED
DWELLER
EARLIER
EVILLER
EVOLVED
EVOLVES
EVULSED
EVULSES
EXALTED
EXULTED
FAULTED
FEELIES
FIELDED
FIELDER
FILLIES
FOLLIES
FRILLED
GIBLUES
GILLIES
GILLNET
GOALIES
GRILLED
GRILLES
GRILLET
GROLIER
GUILDER
GULLIES
HILLIER
HOLLIES
HULLOED
IMPLIED
IMPLIES
JELLIED
JELLIES
JOLLIED
JOLLIER
JOLLIES
JOLLIET
KNELLED
LOLLIES
LOWLIER
MANLIER
MEALIER
MEALIES
MOULDED
MOULDER
MOULTED
NAILSET
NIELSEN
PAULSEN
PHILTER
PSALMED
PSALTER
PURLIEU
QUELLED
QUILLED
QUILTED
QUILTER
RALLIED
RALLIES
REGLUED
REGLUES
REPLIED
REPLIES
SALLIED
SALLIES
SCALDED
SCALIER
SCALPED
SCALPEL
SCALPER
SCOLDED
SCOLDER
SCULLED
SCULLER
SHELLED
SHELLER
SHELLEY
SHELTER
SHELVED
SHELVES
SHILLED
SILLIER
SILLIES
SKELTER
SKILLED
SKILLET
SKULKED
SKULKER
SMALLER
SMELLED
SMELTED
SMELTER
SMOLDER
SNELLEN
SPALLED
SPELLED
SPELLER
SPILLED
STALKED
STALKER
STALLED
STILLED
STILLER
STILTED
STOLLEN
STOLLER
SULLIED
SULLIES
SURLIER
SVELTER
SWELLED
SWELTER
SWILLED
SWOLLEN
TAILLES
TALLIED
TALLIES
TELLIES
TRILLED
TROLLED
TROLLEY
TWELVES
TWILLED
UNGLUED
VAULTED
VAULTER
WELLFED
WELLSET
WHELPED
WIELDED
WILLIES
WOOLIER
WOOLIES
WOOLLEN
WOOLSEY
YIELDED
ZOELLER

•••L••E

ABALONE
ABILENE
ACOLYTE
ADELINE
ADOLPHE
ADULATE
AIRLANE
AIRLINE
AMYLASE
ANALYSE
ANALYZE
ANILINE
APELIKE
ATHLETE
AXILLAE
BALLADE
BEELINE
BIPLANE
BOWLINE
BUSLINE
CARLYLE
CATLIKE
CHALICE
COLLAGE
COLLATE
COLLEGE
COLLIDE
COLLUDE
CYCLONE
DARLENE
DECLARE
DECLINE
DEFLATE
DEPLANE
DEPLETE
DEPLORE
DEWLINE
DISLIKE
EARLOBE
EGALITE
EMULATE
ENCLAVE
ENCLOSE
ENPLANE
ENSLAVE
EVILEYE
EXCLUDE
EXPLODE
EXPLORE
FAILURE
FORLIFE
GAGLINE
GEMLIKE
GODLIKE
HAULAGE
HELLENE
HEMLINE
HOTLINE
HYALINE
IDOLIZE
IMPLODE
IMPLORE
INCLINE
INCLOSE
INCLUDE
INFLAME
INFLATE
INPLACE
ISOLATE
JAWLINE
KEYLIME
LAPLACE
LOWLIFE
MARLENE
MARLOWE
MIDLIFE
MIDLINE
MOULAGE
NUCLIDE
OBELIZE
OCCLUDE
OFFLINE
OLDLINE
OPALINE
OUTLINE
OUTLIVE
OWLLIKE
PAULINE
PERLITE
PHILTRE
PIGLIKE
PILLAGE
POLLUTE
PRALINE
PRELATE
PRELUDE
RANLATE
RATLINE
REALIZE
RECLAME
RECLINE
RECLUSE
REDLINE
REPLACE
REPLATE
REPLETE
ROBLOWE
ROULADE
SCALENE
SEALANE
SECLUDE
SETLINE
SHELTIE
SKYLINE
STYLIZE
SUBLIME
TAGLINE
TANLINE
TIELINE
TILLAGE
UKULELE
ULALUME
ULULATE
UNALIKE
UNCLOSE
UPCLOSE
UTILIZE
VILLAGE
VIOLATE
WALLACE
WALLEYE
WARLIKE
WILLKIE
WOULDBE

••••LE•

AEDILES
ALLELES
AMPULES
ANGELES
ANNALEE
ARGYLES
AURALEE
AVAILED
AVONLEA
BABBLED
BABBLES
BAFFLED
BAFFLER
BAFFLES
BANGLES
BATTLED
BATTLER
BATTLES
BAUBLES
BEADLES
BEAGLES
BEATLES
BEETLES
BENTLEY
BEVELED
BOBBLED
BOBBLES
BOBSLED
BOGGLED
BOGGLER
BOGGLES
BOODLES
BOOKLET
BOOSLER
BOOTLEG
BOTTLED
BOTTLER
BOTTLES
BOWDLER
BRADLEE
BRADLEY
BRAWLED
BRAWLER
BRIDLED
BRIDLES
BROILED
BROILER
BUBBLED
BUBBLES
BUCKLED
BUCKLER
BUCKLES
BUCKLEY
BULBLET
BUMBLED
BUMBLER
BUMBLES
BUNDLED
BUNDLES
BUNGLED
BUNGLER
BUNGLES
BURBLED
BURBLES
BURGLED
BURGLES
BUSTLED
BUSTLES
CACKLED
CACKLER
CACKLES
CAJOLED
CAJOLER
CAJOLES
CANDLES
CANTLES
CAPELET
CAPULET
CAROLED
CAROLER
CAROLES
CASTLED
CASTLES
CAVILED
CAVILER
CHAPLET
CHARLES
CHARLEY
CHILLED
CHILLER
CIRCLED
CIRCLES
CIRCLET
COBBLED
COBBLER
COBBLES
COCHLEA
COCKLES
CODDLED
CODDLER
CODDLES
COMPLEX
COUPLED
COUPLES
COUPLET
CRADLED
CRADLES
CRAWLED
CRAWLER
CREOLES
CRUELER
CRULLER
CUDDLED
CUDDLES
CURDLED
CURDLES
CUSSLER
DABBLED
DABBLER
DABBLES
DAIMLER
DANDLED
DANDLES
DANGLED
DANGLER
DANGLES
DAPPLED
DAPPLES
DAWDLED
DAWDLER
DAWDLES
DAZZLED
DAZZLER
DAZZLES
DECKLES
DEFILED
DEFILER
DEFILES
DEVILED
DIBBLED
DIBBLES
DIDDLED
DIDDLES
DIDDLEY
DIMPLED
DIMPLES
DINGLES
DIPOLES
DOGSLED
DOODLED
DOODLER
DOODLES

DOPPLER
DOTTLES
DOUBLED
DOUBLES
DOUBLET
DOUBLEU
DRAWLED
DRIBLET
DRILLED
DRILLER
DROLLER
DROOLED
DROOLER
DROPLET
DWELLED
DWELLER
EDIBLES
ENABLED
ENABLES
ENISLED
ENISLES
ENSILED
ENSILES
EPAULET
EQUALED
ETOILES
EVILLER
EXHALED
EXHALES
FEEBLER
FEMALES
FERULES
FETTLES
FICKLER
FIDDLED
FIDDLER
FIDDLES
FIEDLER
FINALES
FIPPLES
FIZZLED
FIZZLES
FLAILED
FOCSLES
FOIBLES
FONDLED
FONDLES
FOOZLED
FOOZLES
FORELEG
FRAILER
FRAWLEY
FRILLED
FUDDLED
FUDDLES
FUMBLED
FUMBLER
FUMBLES
GABBLED
GABBLES
GAGGLES
GALILEE
GALILEI
GALILEO
GAMBLED
GAMBLER
GAMBLES
GANGLED
GANTLET
GARBLED
GARBLES
GARGLED
GARGLES

GATELEG
GAVELED
GENTLED
GENTLER
GENTLES
GIGGLED
GIGGLER
GIGGLES
GIRDLED
GIRDLES
GNARLED
GOBBLED
GOBBLER
GOBBLES
GOGGLED
GOGGLES
GREELEY
GRILLED
GRILLES
GRILLET
GROWLED
GROWLER
GURGLED
GURGLES
GUZZLED
GUZZLER
GUZZLES
HAARLEM
HACKLES
HAGGLED
HAGGLER
HAGGLES
HANDLED
HANDLER
HANDLES
HASSLED
HASSLES
HECKLED
HECKLER
HECKLES
HEDDLES
HEMSLEY
HOBBLED
HOBBLES
HOSTLER
HUDDLED
HUDDLES
HUMBLED
HUMBLER
HUMBLES
HUNTLEY
HURDLED
HURDLER
HURDLES
HURTLED
HURTLES
HUSTLED
HUSTLER
HUSTLES
ICICLES
IMPALED
IMPALES
INHALED
INHALER
INHALES
INSOLES
JANGLED
JANGLES
JEWELED
JEWELER
JIGGLED
JIGGLES
JINGLED

JINGLES
JOGGLED
JOGGLES
JOSTLED
JOSTLER
JOSTLES
JUBILEE
JUGGLED
JUGGLER
JUGGLES
JUMBLED
JUMBLES
JUNGLES
KEEBLER
KETTLES
KIBBLED
KIBBLES
KINDLED
KINDLES
KIRTLES
KNEELED
KNEELER
KNELLED
KNURLED
LABELED
LABELER
LANGLEY
LAPELED
LEAFLET
LEVELED
LEVELER
LIBELED
LIBELER
LITTLER
LOCALES
LORELEI
MANGLED
MANGLES
MANTLED
MANTLES
MARBLED
MARBLES
MEASLES
MEDALED
MEDDLED
MEDDLER
MEDDLES
METTLES
MIDDLEC
MIDDLES
MINGLED
MINGLER
MINGLES
MIZZLED
MIZZLES
MOBILES
MODELED
MODELER
MODULES
MORALES
MOTTLED
MOTTLES
MUDDLED
MUDDLER
MUDDLES
MUFFLED
MUFFLER
MUFFLES
MUMBLED
MUMBLER
MUMBLES
MUSCLED
MUSCLES

MUZZLED
MUZZLES
MYRTLES
NEEDLED
NEEDLES
NESTLED
NESTLER
NESTLES
NETTLED
NETTLES
NIBBLED
NIBBLER
NIBBLES
NIGGLED
NIGGLES
NIMBLER
NODULES
NOGALES
NOODLES
NOZZLES
NUBBLES
NUZZLED
NUZZLER
NUZZLES
ORACLES
ORIOLES
PADDLED
PADDLER
PADDLES
PAISLEY
PANELED
PAROLED
PAROLEE
PAROLES
PARSLEY
PEARLED
PEBBLED
PEBBLES
PEDALED
PEDDLED
PEDDLER
PEDDLES
PEEPLES
PEOPLED
PEOPLES
PERPLEX
PESTLED
PESTLES
PETALED
PICKLED
PICKLES
PIFFLED
PIFFLES
PLAYLET
POODLES
POPPLED
POPPLES
PRESLEY
PROBLEM
PROWLED
PROWLER
PUDDLED
PUDDLES
PURFLED
PURFLES
PURPLED
PURPLES
PUZZLED
PUZZLER
PUZZLES
QUAILED
QUELLED
QUIGLEY

QUILLED
RABBLES
RADDLED
RADDLES
RAFFLED
RAFFLER
RAFFLES
RAMBLED
RAMBLER
RAMBLES
RANKLED
RANKLES
RASSLED
RASSLES
RATTLED
RATTLER
RATTLES
RAVELED
REGALED
REGALES
REOILED
RESALES
RESILED
RESILES
RESOLED
RESOLES
RETILED
RETILES
REVELED
REVELER
REVILED
REVILES
RICKLES
RIDDLED
RIDDLER
RIDDLES
RIFFLED
RIFFLES
RINGLET
RIPPLED
RIPPLES
RIVALED
RIVULET
ROOTLET
RUBBLES
RUFFLED
RUFFLES
RUMBLED
RUMBLES
RUMPLED
RUMPLES
RUSTLED
RUSTLER
RUSTLES
SADDLED
SADDLER
SADDLES
SAMPLED
SAMPLER
SAMPLES
SARALEE
SCARLET
SCOWLED
SCOWLER
SCULLED
SCULLER
SETTLED
SETTLER
SETTLES
SHELLED
SHELLER
SHELLEY
SHILLED

SHIRLEY
SICKLES
SIMILES
SIMPLER
SIMPLEX
SINGLED
SINGLES
SIZZLED
SIZZLES
SKILLED
SKILLET
SKIRLED
SMALLER
SMELLED
SNARLED
SNELLEN
SNIGLET
SPALLED
SPELLED
SPELLER
SPIELED
SPIELER
SPILLED
SPOILED
SPOILER
SPOOLED
STABLED
STABLER
STABLES
STALLED
STANLEE
STANLEY
STAPLED
STAPLER
STAPLES
STARLET
STEELED
STEELER
STIFLED
STIFLES
STILLED
STILLER
STOLLEN
STOLLER
SUBTLER
SUPPLER
SWELLED
SWILLED
SWIRLED
SWOLLEN
TACKLED
TACKLER
TACKLES
TAILLES
TAMALES
TANGLED
TANGLES
TATTLED
TATTLER
TATTLES
TEMPLES
TICKLED
TICKLER
TICKLES
TINGLED
TINGLES
TINKLED
TINKLES
TIPPLED
TIPPLER
TIPPLES
TITTLES
TODDLED

TODDLER
TODDLES
TOFFLER
TOGGLED
TOGGLES
TOOTLED
TOOTLES
TOPPLED
TOPPLES
TOTALED
TOUSLED
TOUSLES
TOWELED
TRAILED
TRAILER
TRAWLED
TRAWLER
TREBLED
TREBLES
TRIFLED
TRIFLER
TRIFLES
TRILLED
TRIPLED
TRIPLES
TRIPLET
TRIPLEX
TROLLED
TROLLEY
TUMBLED
TUMBLER
TUMBLES
TURTLED
TURTLES
TUSSLED
TUSSLES
TWILLED
TWIRLED
TWIRLER
UNOILED
UNPILED
UNPILES
VITTLES
WADDLED
WADDLER
WADDLES
WAFFLED
WAFFLER
WAFFLES
WAGGLED
WAGGLES
WAMBLED
WAMBLES
WANGLED
WANGLER
WANGLES
WARBLED
WARBLER
WARBLES
WATTLES
WAVELET
WHEELED
WHEELER
WHIRLED
WHORLED
WIGGLED
WIGGLER
WIGGLES
WIMPLED
WIMPLES
WINKLER
WOBBLED
WOBBLES

WOOLLEN
WRIGLEY
YODELED
YODELER
ZOELLER

••••L•E

AAMILNE
ABSOLVE
AMIBLUE
ANNALEE
AREOLAE
AURALEE
AXILLAE
BIVALVE
BRADLEE
BRAILLE
CAMILLE
CHARLIE
DEMILLE
DEVALUE
DEVILLE
DEVOLVE
DEWILDE
DIVULGE
ESTELLE
FIBULAE
GALILEE
GAZELLE
GEFILTE
GISELLE
ICEBLUE
ICEFLOE
IMPULSE
INDULGE
INVOLVE
JUBILEE
LABELLE
LASALLE
LAVALSE
LUCILLE
MACULAE
MOSELLE
NACELLE
NATALIE
NEBULAE
NEVILLE
NOVELLE
ORVILLE
OVERLIE
PAROLEE
REPULSE
RESOLVE
REVALUE
REVOLVE
ROSALIE
ROSELLE
ROZELLE
SARALEE
SEVILLE
SHEILAE
SKYBLUE
STANLEE
STEELIE
STOOLIE
WHEELIE

•••••LE

ACTABLE
ADDABLE
AFFABLE
AIRHOLE
AIRMILE
AMIABLE
AMPOULE
ANATOLE
APOSTLE
ARMHOLE
ARTICLE
ATINGLE
AUDIBLE
AUREOLE
AURICLE
BEGUILE
BICYCLE
BOBDOLE
BOGHOLE
BRAILLE
BRAMBLE
BRINDLE
BRISTLE
BRITTLE
BUYABLE
CAMILLE
CAPABLE
CAPSULE
CARLYLE
CASTILE
CHORALE
CHORTLE
CHUCKLE
CITABLE
COMPILE
CONDOLE
CONSOLE
CRACKLE
CRINKLE
CRUMBLE
CRUMPLE
CUBICLE
CUTICLE
DEBACLE
DEMILLE
DEVILLE
DISABLE
DRIBBLE
DRIZZLE
DRYHOLE
DUCTILE
DURABLE
DWINDLE
EATABLE
ENNOBLE
ENTITLE
EPISTLE
EQUABLE
ESTELLE
EXAMPLE
EYEHOLE
FEBRILE
FERRULE
FERTILE
FINAGLE
FISSILE
FIXABLE
FORSALE
FOXHOLE
FRAGILE
FRAZZLE
FRECKLE
FRIABLE
FRIZZLE
GAGRULE
GAZELLE
GENTILE
GISELLE

GLOBULE
GRACILE
GRACKLE
GRANULE
GRAPPLE
GRIDDLE
GRISTLE
GRIZZLE
GRUMBLE
GUNWALE
HERCULE
HIRABLE
HOSTILE
IGNOBLE
INSTYLE
INUTILE
KEYHOLE
KNUCKLE
KRINGLE
LABELLE
LASALLE
LEGIBLE
LIKABLE
LIVABLE
LOVABLE
LUCILLE
MANACLE
MANHOLE
MANIPLE
MAYPOLE
MICHELE
MINABLE
MIRACLE
MISFILE
MISRULE
MISSILE
MIXABLE
MONDALE
MONOCLE
MOSELLE
MOVABLE
MUTABLE
NACELLE
NEVILLE
NOTABLE
NOVELLE
OCTUPLE
ORVILLE
OSSICLE
PANICLE
PARABLE
PAYABLE
PEDICLE
PERCALE
PETIOLE
PINHOLE
PINOCLE
PINWALE
PISTOLE
PLIABLE
POTABLE
POTHOLE
PRATTLE
PRESALE
PRICKLE
PROFILE
PUERILE
QUIBBLE
RADICLE
RATABLE
RATHOLE
RECYCLE
REPTILE

RESCALE
RESTYLE
RETICLE
RETITLE
RISIBLE
RISSOLE
ROSELLE
ROZELLE
RUMPOLE
SALABLE
SAVABLE
SCRUPLE
SCUFFLE
SCUTTLE
SEATTLE
SERVILE
SESSILE
SEVILLE
SHACKLE
SHAMBLE
SHINGLE
SHUFFLE
SHUTTLE
SIZABLE
SKIPOLE
SKITTLE
SMUGGLE
SNAFFLE
SNIFFLE
SNIGGLE
SNUFFLE
SNUGGLE
SOLUBLE
SOUFFLE
SPACKLE
SPANGLE
SPARKLE
SPECKLE
SPINDLE
STABILE
STARTLE
STEEPLE
STERILE
STIPPLE
STUBBLE
STUMBLE
SWADDLE
SWINDLE
SWIZZLE
SYSTOLE
TACTILE
TADPOLE
TAGSALE
TAMABLE
TAXABLE
TENABLE
TENSILE
TEXTILE
THIMBLE
THISTLE
TIMBALE
TOSCALE
TRAMPLE
TREACLE
TREADLE
TREMBLE
TRESTLE
TRICKLE
TROUBLE
TRUCKLE
TRUFFLE
TRUNDLE
TUNICLE

TWADDLE
TWIDDLE
TWINKLE
UKULELE
UPSCALE
USEABLE
VACUOLE
VEHICLE
VIRGULE
VISIBLE
VOLUBLE
WALPOLE
WHEEDLE
WHISTLE
WHITTLE
WRANGLE
WRESTLE
WRIGGLE
WRINKLE

L•F••••

LAFARGE
LAFITTE
LEFTIES
LEFTIST
LEFTOFF
LEFTOUT
LIFENET
LIFTERS
LIFTING
LIFTOFF
LIFTSUP
LOFTIER
LOFTILY
LOFTING
LUFFING

L••F•••

LANFORD
LAPFULS
LAWFORD
LEAFIER
LEAFING
LEAFLET
LENFANT
LOAFERS
LOAFING
LOOFAHS
LUFFING

L•••F••

LAIDFOR
LATIFAH
LAYOFFS
LAYSFOR
LETSFLY
LOOKFOR
LUCIFER
LUSTFUL

L••••F•

LAIDOFF
LAYOFFS
LAYSOFF
LEADOFF
LEFTOFF
LETSOFF
LIFTOFF
LIQUEFY
LOGSOFF
LOWLIFE

L•••••F

LAIDOFF
LAYSOFF
LEADOFF
LEFTOFF
LETSOFF
LIFTOFF
LOGSOFF

•LF••••

ALFALFA
ALFIERI
ALFONSO
ALFREDO

•L•F•••

BLUFFED
BLUFFER
BLUFFLY
CLIFTON
FLUFFED
FLYFISH
OLDFOGY

•L••F••

ALLOFME
ALOOFLY
BLOWFLY
BLUEFIN
BLUEFLU
BLUEFOX
BLUFFED
BLUFFER
BLUFFLY
FLUFFED
GLEEFUL
PLAYFUL

•L•••F•

ALEWIFE
ALFALFA
BLEWOFF
BLOWOFF
CLARIFY
GLORIFY
PLAYOFF

•L••••F

BLEWOFF
BLOWOFF
FLYLEAF
PLAYOFF

••LF•••

AELFRIC
BALFOUR
BELFAST
FULFILL
FULFILS
GOLFERS
GOLFING
GOLFPRO
GOLFTEE
GULFING
HALFDAN
HALFWAY
HALFWIT
PALFREY
PILFERS
SELFISH
SOLFEGE
SULFATE
SULFIDE

SULFITE
WELFARE
WILFORD
WILFRID
WOLFGAL
WOLFING
WOLFISH
WOLFMAN
WOLFMEN
WOLFRAM

••L•F••

ALLOFME
BALEFUL
CALLFOR
DOLEFUL
FALAFEL
FALLFOR
FELLFOR
FELTFOR
HALIFAX
HELPFUL
MALEFIC
UPLIFTS
WELLFED
WILLFUL

••L••F•

BELIEFS
CALCIFY
CALLOFF
FALLOFF
FALSIFY
FELLOFF
HELDOFF
HOLDOFF
MOLLIFY
NULLIFY
PALMOFF
PULLOFF
RELIEFS
SALSIFY
SELLOFF
SOLDOFF
TELLOFF
TOLDOFF
WELLOFF

••L•••F

CALLOFF
FALLOFF
FELLOFF
HELDOFF
HOLDOFF
PALMOFF
PULLOFF
SELLOFF
SOLDOFF
TELLOFF
TOLDOFF
WALDORF
WELLOFF

•••LF••

BOWLFUL
CALLFOR
FALLFOR
FEELFOR
FELLFOR
PAILFUL
SKILFUL
SOULFUL
TAILFIN
TWELFTH
WELLFED
WILLFUL

•••L•F•

AIRLIFT
AMPLIFY
BAILIFF
CALLOFF
FALLOFF
FARLEFT
FELLOFF
FORLIFE
HAULOFF
HAYLOFT
KARLOFF
LOWLIFE
MIDLIFE
MOLLIFY
NEWLEFT
NULLIFY
PEELOFF
PULLOFF
QUALIFY
REELOFF
SEALOFF
SELLOFF
SKILIFT
TAILOFF
TELLOFF
WELLOFF

•••L••F

BAILIFF
BAYLEAF
CALLOFF
FALLOFF
FELLOFF
FIGLEAF
FLYLEAF
HAULOFF
KARLOFF
OAKLEAF
PEELOFF
PULLOFF
REELOFF
SEALOFF
SELLOFF
TAILOFF
TEALEAF
TELLOFF
WELLOFF

••••LF•

ALFALFA
ENGULFS
RODOLFO

•••••LF

AIRWOLF
BEOWULF
CRYWOLF
HERSELF
HIMSELF
NONSELF
ONESELF
OURSELF
REDWOLF
SHEWOLF
THYSELF

L•G••••

LAGGARD
LAGGERS
LAGGING
LAGOONS
LAGUNAS
LEGALLY
LEGATEE
LEGATES
LEGATOS
LEGENDS
LEGGIER
LEGGING
LEGHORN
LEGIBLE
LEGIBLY
LEGIONS
LEGISTS
LEGPULL
LEGROOM
LEGUMES
LEGWORK
LIGATED
LIGATES
LIGHTED
LIGHTEN
LIGHTER
LIGHTLY
LIGHTUP
LIGNITE
LOGBOOK
LOGGERS
LOGGIAS
LOGGING
LOGGINS
LOGICAL
LOGIEST
LOGJAMS
LOGSOFF
LOGSOUT
LUGGAGE
LUGGERS
LUGGING
LUGNUTS

L••G•••

LAAGERS
LAGGARD
LAGGERS
LAGGING
LANGDON
LANGLEY
LANGTRY
LANGUID
LANGUOR
LANGURS
LARGELY
LARGESS
LARGEST
LAUGHAT
LAUGHED
LAUGHER
LAUGHIN
LEAGUER
LEAGUES
LEDGERS
LEGGIER
LEGGING
LENGTHS
LENGTHY
LINGERS
LINGOES
LINGUAL
LODGERS
LODGING
LOGGERS
LOGGIAS
LOGGING
LOGGINS
LONGAGO
LONGBOW
LONGEST
LONGING
LONGISH
LONGRUN
LONGTON
LONGUES
LOWGEAR
LUGGAGE
LUGGERS
LUGGING
LUNGEAT
LUNGING

L•••G••

LASAGNA
LASAGNE
LIMOGES
LINAGES
LITHGOW
LOUNGED
LOUNGER
LOUNGES
LYINGTO

L••••G•

LACINGS
LAFARGE
LAPDOGS
LEAKAGE
LINEAGE
LININGS
LINKAGE
LITURGY
LIVINGS
LONGAGO
LOZENGE
LUGGAGE
LUMBAGO

L•••••G

LACKING
LADLING
LADYBUG
LAGGING
LAMMING
LANDING
LANSING
LAPPING
LAPSING
LAPWING
LARDING
LASHING
LASTING
LATHING
LAUDING
LEADING
LEAFING
LEAKING
LEANING
LEAPING
LEASING
LEAVING
LEERING
LEGGING
LEIPZIG
LEMMING
LENDING
LESSING
LETTING
LEVYING
LIBBING
LICKING
LIFTING
LILTING
LIMBING
LIMNING
LIMPING
LINKING
LIPPING
LISPING
LISTING
LOADING
LOAFING
LOAMING
LOANING
LOBBING
LOCKING
LODGING
LOFTING
LOGGING
LOLLING
LONGING
LOOKING
LOOMING
LOOPING
LOOSING
LOOTING
LOPPING
LORDING
LOTTING
LOUSING
LOVEBUG
LUCKING
LUFFING
LUGGING
LULLING
LUMPING
LUNGING
LURKING
LUSTING

•LG••••

ALGEBRA
ALGERIA
ALGIERS
ELGRECO

•L•G•••

ALIGHTS
ALIGNED
ALIGNER
ALLGONE
BLIGHTS
CLOGGED
CLOGSUP
ELEGANT
ELEGIAC
ELEGIES
ELEGIST
FLAGDAY
FLAGGED
FLAGMAN
FLAGMEN
FLAGONS
FLIGHTS
FLIGHTY
FLOGGED
KLUGMAN
OLDGOLD
PLAGUED
PLAGUES
PLIGHTS
PLUGGED
PLUGGER
PLUGSIN
SLIGHTS
SLOGANS
SLOGGED
SLUGGED
SLUGGER

•L••G••

ALLEGED
ALLEGER
ALLEGES
ALLEGRO
ALRIGHT
BLOWGUN
CLANGED
CLANGOR
CLINGTO
CLOGGED
FLAGGED
FLANGES
FLEDGED
FLEDGES
FLOGGED
GLASGOW
ILLEGAL
ILLOGIC
KLINGON
KLUDGES
PLEDGED
PLEDGEE
PLEDGER
PLEDGES
PLOUGHS
PLUGGED
PLUGGER
PLUNGED
PLUNGER
PLUNGES
SLEDGES
SLEIGHS
SLEIGHT
SLINGER
SLOEGIN
SLOGGED
SLOUGHS
SLUDGES
SLUGGED
SLUGGER
TLINGIT

•L•••G•

ALLERGY
FLYHIGH
OLDFOGY
PLUMAGE

•L••••G

ALAKING
ALLYING
BLAMING
BLARING
BLAZING
BLOWING
BLUEING
CLAWING
CLONING
CLOSING
CLOYING
CLUEING
ELATING
ELIDING
ELOPING
ELUDING
ELUTING
FLAKING
FLAMING
FLARING
FLAWING
FLAYING
FLEABAG
FLEEING
FLEMING
FLEXING
FLOWING
FLUTING
GLARING
GLAZING
GLIDING
GLOWING
PLACING
PLANING
PLATING
PLAYING
PLOWING
PLUMING
SLAKING
SLATING
SLAVING
SLEDDOG
SLICING
SLIDING
SLOPING
SLOWING

••LG•••

ALLGONE
BELGIAN
BELGIUM
BULGARS
BULGHUR
BULGING
CALGARY
COLGATE
FOLGERS
FULGENT
FULGHUM
PILGRIM
VULGATE

••L•G••

ALLEGED
ALLEGER
ALLEGES
ALLEGRO
BOLOGNA
COLOGNE
DELIGHT
DELUGED
DELUGES
ECLOGUE
FALLGUY
HALOGEN
ILLEGAL
ILLOGIC
MALIGNS
OBLIGED
OBLIGES
PELAGES
PELAGIC
POLYGON
RELIGHT
WOLFGAL

••L••G•

ALLERGY
ARLEDGE
ATLARGE
BELONGS
COLLAGE
COLLEGE
ENLARGE
FILINGS
FOLIAGE
KELLOGG
MELANGE
MILEAGE
OBLONGS
OILRIGS
PILINGS
PILLAGE
RALEIGH
RULINGS
SALVAGE
SELVAGE
SOLFEGE
SPLURGE
TILLAGE
VILLAGE
VOLTAGE

••L•••G

ALLYING
BALDING
BALKING
BELLING
BELTING
BELYING
BILKING
BILLING
BOLTING
BULGING
BULKING
BULLDOG
BULLING
CALKING
CALLING
CALMING
CALVING
CULLING
DELEING
DELVING
DOLLING
DULLING
FALLING
FELLING
FILLING
FILMING
FOLDING
GALLING
GELDING
GELLING
GILDING
GILLING
GOLDBUG
GOLDING
GOLFING
GULFING
GULLING
GULPING
HALOING
HALTING
HALVING
HELMING
HELPING
HILLING
HOLDING
HULKING
HULLING
JELLING
JILTING
JOLTING
KELLOGG
KILLING
KILTING
LILTING
LOLLING
LULLING
MALTING
MELDING
MELTING
MILKING
MILLING
MOLDING
MOLTING
MULLING
NULLING
PALLING
PALMING
PELTING
PILLBUG
PILLING
POLLING
PULLING
PULSING
RDLAING
RELYING
ROLLING
ROLVAAG
SALTING
SALVING
SELLING
SILOING
SILTING
SOLOING
SOLVING
SULKING
TALKBIG
TALKING
TELLING
TILLING
TILTING
TOLLING
VALUING
WALKING
WALLING
WELDING
WELLING
WELTING
WILDING
WILLING
WILTING
WOLFING
YELLING
YELPING
YULELOG

•••LG••

AMALGAM
COALGAS
FALLGUY
GIELGUD

•••L•G•

ANALOGS
ANALOGY
APOLOGY
BIOLOGY
COLLAGE
COLLEGE
DIALOGS
DOGLEGS
ECOLOGY
EPILOGS
GEOLOGY
HAULAGE
KELLOGG
MOULAGE
PILLAGE
PROLOGS
SAWLOGS
SEALEGS
STALAGS
TILLAGE
TRILOGY
UNCLOGS
UNPLUGS
VILLAGE
ZOOLOGY

•••L••G

ADDLING
AMBLING
ANGLING
BAILING
BAWLING
BELLING
BILLING
BIRLING
BOILING
BOWLING
BUGLING
BULLDOG
BULLING
BURLING
CABLING
CALLING
CEILING
COILING
COOLING
COWLING
CULLING
CURLING
CYCLING
DARLING
DAYLONG
DEALING
DIALING
DOLLING
DUELING
DULLING
EAGLING
ERELONG
EXILING
FAILING
FALLING
FEELING
FELLING
FILLING
FOALING
FOILING
FOOLING
FOULING
FOWLING
FUELING
FURLING
FURLONG
GALLING
GATLING
GELLING
GILLING
GOALONG
GOSLING
GULLING
HAILING
HAULING
HEALING
HEELING
HILLING
HOWLING
HULLING
HURLING
INKLING
JAILING
JELLING
KEELING
KELLOGG
KILLING
KIPLING
LADLING
LOLLING
LULLING
MAILBAG
MAILING
MAULING
MEWLING
MILLING
MOILING
MULLING
NAILING
NULLING
PALLING
PAULING
PEALING
PEELING
PILLBUG
PILLING
POLLING
POOLING
PROLONG
PULLING
PURLING
RAILING
REELING
RIFLING
ROILING
ROLLING
SAILING
SAPLING
SCALING
SEALING
SELLING
SERLING
SIBLING
SIDLING
SMILING
SOILING
STYLING
TABLING
TAILING
TELLING
TILLING
TITLING
TOILING
TOLLING
TOOLING
VEILING
WAILING
WALLING
WELLING
WHALING
WHILING
WILLING
YELLING
YOWLING

••••LG•

DIVULGE
HIDALGO
INDULGE

••••L•G

ANTILOG
BACKLOG
BOOTLEG
CATALOG
DECALOG
EARPLUG
FORELEG
GATELEG
MONOLOG
REDFLAG
SEASLUG
TAGALOG
TIMELAG
YULELOG

L•H••••

LEHAVRE

L••H•••

LASHERS
LASHING
LASHUPS
LATHERS
LATHERY
LATHING
LEGHORN
LICHENS
LIGHTED
LIGHTEN
LIGHTER
LIGHTLY
LIGHTUP
LITHELY
LITHEST
LITHGOW
LITHIUM
LOWHEEL
LUSHEST

L•••H••

LARCHES
LATCHED
LATCHES
LAUGHAT
LAUGHED
LAUGHER
LAUGHIN
LEACHED
LEACHES
LEASHED
LEASHES
LEATHER
LEECHED
LEECHES
LITCHIS
LOACHES
LOATHED
LOATHES
LUNCHED
LUNCHER
LUNCHES
LURCHED
LURCHES

L••••H•

LAROCHE
LENGTHS
LENGTHY
LESOTHO
LOOFAHS

L•••••H

LATIFAH
LONGISH
LOWTECH

•L•H•••

ALCHEMY
ALLHAIL
ALLHEAL
ALLHERE
ALOHAOE
ELKHART
FLYHIGH
OLDHAND

•L••H••

ALCOHOL
ALIGHTS
BLATHER
BLIGHTS
BLITHER
BLUSHED
BLUSHER
BLUSHES
CLASHED
CLASHES
CLICHES
CLOCHES
CLOTHED
CLOTHES
FLASHED
FLASHER
FLASHES
FLECHES
FLESHED
FLESHES
FLIGHTS
FLIGHTY
FLUSHED
FLUSHES
OLDCHAP
PLASHED
PLASHES
PLIGHTS
PLUSHER
PLUSHES
PLUSHLY
SLASHED
SLASHER
SLASHES
SLATHER
SLIGHTS
SLITHER
SLOSHED
SLOSHES
SLUSHES

•L•••H•

ALRIGHT
ALYOSHA
BLANCHE
BLOTCHY
PLINTHS
PLOUGHS
SLEIGHS
SLEIGHT
SLEUTHS
SLOUCHY
SLOUGHS

•L••••H
ALDRICH
ALWORTH
BLEMISH
FLEMISH
FLYFISH
FLYHIGH
KLAMATH
KLATSCH
PLAYDOH
SLAVISH

••LH•••
ALLHAIL
ALLHEAL
ALLHERE
CALHOUN
MILHAUD
WILHELM

••L•H••
BALIHAI
BELCHED
BELCHES
BELLHOP
BOLSHOI
BULGHUR
DOLPHIN
FILCHED
FILCHER
FILCHES
FULGHUM
GALAHAD
GULCHES
MALTHUS
MCLUHAN
MULCHED
MULCHES
SALCHOW
SILKHAT
SULPHUR
WELCHED
WELCHES
ZILCHES

••L••H•
BELUSHI
CALIPHS
DELIGHT
EOLITHS
MALACHI
MULLAHS
OOLITHS
RELIGHT
SPLASHY
TALLYHO

••L•••H
BULLISH
BULRUSH
CALTECH
COLTISH
CULTISH
DELILAH
DOLTISH
DULLISH
GALUMPH
GOLIATH
RALEIGH
SELFISH
SPLOTCH
TALLISH
UNLATCH
UNLEASH
WALLACH
WOLFISH

•••LH••
BELLHOP

•••L•H•
ADOLPHE
GUELPHS
HEALTHY
MULLAHS
TALLYHO
WEALTHY

•••L••H
ABOLISH
BULLISH
DULLISH
EHRLICH
ENGLISH
EYELASH
FOOLISH
GIRLISH
GOULASH
HIALEAH
NEOLITH
PUBLISH
STYLISH
TALLISH
TWELFTH
WALLACH

••••L•H
DELILAH
RUDOLPH
SHEILAH
SQUELCH
STEALTH

•••••LH
ANOUILH

LI•••••
LIAISED
LIAISES
LIAISON
LIBBERS
LIBBING
LIBELED
LIBELER
LIBERAL
LIBERIA
LIBERTY
LIBIDOS
LIBRARY
LIBYANS
LICENCE
LICENSE
LICHENS
LICITLY
LICKETY
LICKING
LIDLESS
LIEABED
LIEDOWN
LIENEES
LIEOVER
LIERNES
LIESLOW
LIFENET
LIFTERS
LIFTING
LIFTOFF
LIFTSUP
LIGATED
LIGATES
LIGHTED
LIGHTEN
LIGHTER
LIGHTLY
LIGHTUP
LIGNITE
LIKABLE
LIKEMAD
LIKENED
LIKENEW
LILLIAN
LILTING
LILYPAD
LIMBERS
LIMBING
LIMEADE
LIMIEST
LIMITED
LIMNERS
LIMNING
LIMOGES
LIMPEST
LIMPETS
LIMPING
LIMPOPO
LINAGES
LINBIAO
LINCOLN
LINDENS
LINDIED
LINDIES
LINDSAY
LINDSEY
LINEAGE
LINEATE
LINEDUP
LINEMAN
LINEMEN
LINESUP
LINEUPS
LINGERS
LINGOES
LINGUAL
LININGS
LINKAGE
LINKERS
LINKING
LINKUPS
LINNETS
LINSEED
LINTELS
LINTIER
LIONCUB
LIONESS
LIONETS
LIONIZE
LIPBALM
LIPPIER
LIPPING
LIPREAD
LIPSYNC
LIQUEFY
LIQUEUR
LIQUIDS
LIQUORS
LISPING
LISSOME
LISTEES
LISTELS
LISTENS
LISTING
LITCHIS
LITERAL
LITHELY
LITHEST
LITHGOW
LITHIUM
LITINTO
LITOTES
LITTERS
LITTLER
LITURGY
LIVABLE
LIVEDIN
LIVEDON
LIVENED
LIVEOAK
LIVEONE
LIVEOUT
LIVESIN
LIVESON
LIVIDLY
LIVINGS
LIZARDS

L•I••••
LAIDFOR
LAIDLOW
LAIDOFF
LAIDOUT
LAISSEZ
LEIBNIZ
LEIPZIG
LEISTER
LEISURE
LOITERS
LYINGTO

L••I•••
LABIALS
LABIATE
LACIEST
LACINGS
LADINOS
LAFITTE
LALIQUE
LAMINAE
LAMINAL
LAMINAR
LAMINAS
LARIATS
LATICES
LATIFAH
LATINAS
LATINOS
LAVINIA
LAYINTO
LAZIEST
LEGIBLE
LEGIBLY
LEGIONS
LEGISTS
LENIENT
LETINON
LETITBE
LETITIA
LEVIERS
LEVITES
LEXICAL
LEXICON
LIAISED
LIAISES
LIAISON
LIBIDOS
LICITLY
LIMIEST
LIMITED
LININGS
LITINTO
LIVIDLY
LIVINGS
LOGICAL
LOGIEST
LORISES
LOTIONS
LUCIANO
LUCIDLY
LUCIFER
LUCILLE
LUMIERE
LUPINES
LURIDLY
LUTISTS
LYRICAL
LYRISTS

L•••I••
LACKING
LADDIES
LADLING
LAGGING
LAMAISM
LAMAIST
LAMMING
LANDING
LANKIER
LANKILY
LANSING
LAOTIAN
LAPPING
LAPSING
LAPWING
LARAINE
LARDING
LASHING
LASSIES
LASTING
LATHING
LATTICE
LATVIAN
LAUDING
LEADING
LEADINS
LEAFIER
LEAFING
LEAKIER
LEAKING
LEANING
LEAPING
LEASING
LEAVING
LEERIER
LEERILY
LEERING
LEETIDE
LEFTIES
LEFTIST
LEGGIER
LEGGING
LEMMING
LEMPIRA
LENDING
LENTILS
LEONINE
LESSING
LETTING
LEVYING
LIBBING
LICKING
LIFTING
LIGNITE
LILLIAN
LILTING
LIMBING
LIMNING
LIMPING
LINBIAO
LINDIED
LINDIES
LINKING
LINTIER
LIONIZE
LIPPIER
LIPPING
LIQUIDS
LISPING
LISTING
LITHIUM
LOADING
LOAFING
LOAMIER
LOAMING
LOANING
LOBBIED
LOBBIES
LOBBING
LOCKING
LOCKINS
LODGING
LOFTIER
LOFTILY
LOFTING
LOGGIAS
LOGGING
LOGGINS
LOLLIES
LOLLING
LONGING
LONGISH
LOOKING
LOOMING
LOONIER
LOONIES
LOOPIER
LOOPING
LOOSING
LOOTING
LOPPING
LORDING
LORRIES
LOTTING
LOUSIER
LOUSILY
LOUSING
LOVEINS
LOWLIER
LOWLIFE
LOWRISE
LOWTIDE
LUCKIER
LUCKILY
LUCKING
LUFFING
LUGGING
LULLING
LUMPIER
LUMPING
LUNGING
LURKING
LUSTIER
LUSTILY
LUSTING

L••••I•
LACONIC
LAMPOIL
LANGUID
LANOLIN
LARAMIE
LAUGHIN
LAVINIA
LAWSUIT
LEADSIN
LEIBNIZ
LEIPZIG
LETITIA
LETSLIP
LIBERIA
LITCHIS
LIVEDIN
LIVESIN
LOOKSIN
LORDJIM
LOSESIT
LOWPAID
LUNATIC

L•••••I
LORELEI

•LI••••
ALIASES
ALIBABA
ALIDADE
ALIENEE
ALIENOR
ALIGHTS
ALIGNED
ALIGNER
ALIMENT
ALIMONY
BLIGHTS
BLINDED
BLINDER
BLINDLY
BLINKAT
BLINKED
BLINKER
BLIPPED
BLISTER
BLITHER
BLITZED
BLITZEN
BLITZES
CLIBURN
CLICHES
CLICKED
CLIENTS
CLIFTON
CLIMATE
CLIMBED
CLIMBER
CLINGTO
CLINICS
CLINKED
CLINKER
CLINTON
CLIPART
CLIPONS
CLIPPED
CLIPPER
CLIQUES
ELICITS
ELIDING
ELISION
ELITISM
ELITIST
ELIXIRS
FLICKED
FLICKER
FLIESAT
FLIESIN
FLIGHTS
FLIGHTY
FLIPPED
FLIPPER
FLIPUPS
FLIRTED
FLITTED
FLITTER
FLIVVER
GLIBBER
GLIDERS
GLIDING
GLIMMER
GLIMPSE
GLINTED
GLISTEN
GLITTER
GLITZED
GLITZES
ILIESCU
KLINGON
OLIVIER
OLIVINE
PLIABLE
PLIABLY
PLIANCY
PLIGHTS
PLINKED
PLINTHS
SLICERS
SLICING
SLICKED
SLICKER
SLICKLY
SLIDEIN
SLIDERS
SLIDING
SLIGHTS
SLIMIER
SLIMJIM
SLIMMED
SLIMMER
SLINGER
SLINKED
SLIPONS
SLIPOUT
SLIPPED
SLIPPER
SLIPSUP
SLIPUPS
SLITHER
SLIVERS
TLINGIT

•L•I•••
ALBINOS
ALFIERI
ALGIERS
ALLISON
ALRIGHT
CLAIMED
CLAIMER
CLAIROL
ELEISON
ELLIOTT
ELLIPSE
ELLISON
ELMISTI
FLAILED
FLUIDLY
ILLICIT
PLAICES
PLAINER
PLAINES
PLAINLY
PLAINTS
PLAITED
SLEIGHS
SLEIGHT
SLUICED
SLUICES

•L••I••
ALAKING
ALDRICH
ALEWIFE
ALLTIME
ALLYING
BLAMING
BLARING
BLAZING
BLEMISH
BLERIOT
BLOWIER
BLOWING
BLUEING
CLARICE
CLARIFY
CLARION
CLARITY
CLAVIER
CLAWING
CLAYIER
CLERICS
CLINICS
CLONING
CLOSING
CLOYING
CLUEING
ELAPIDS
ELATING
ELATION
ELEGIAC
ELEGIES
ELEGIST
ELICITS
ELIDING
ELISION
ELITISM
ELITIST
ELIXIRS
ELOPING
ELUDING
ELUSIVE
ELUTING
ELUTION
ELUVIUM
ELYSIAN
ELYSIUM
FLAKIER
FLAKING
FLAMING
FLARING
FLAWING
FLAYING
FLEEING
FLEMING
FLEMISH
FLEXING
FLORIDA
FLORINS
FLORIST
FLOWING
FLUTING
FLUTIST
FLUVIAL
FLYFISH
FLYHIGH
GLACIAL
GLACIER
GLARING
GLAZIER
GLAZING
GLIDING
GLORIAS
GLORIED
GLORIES
GLORIFY
GLOWING
ILLWILL
ILLWIND
OLDLINE
OLDNICK
OLDTIME
OLEMISS
OLIVIER
OLIVINE
PLACIDO
PLACING
PLANING
PLATING
PLAYING
PLOSION
PLOSIVE
PLOWING
PLUMING
PLUVIAL
SLAKING
SLATIER
SLATING
SLAVING
SLAVISH
SLICING
SLIDING
SLIMIER
SLOPING
SLOWING

•L•••I•
ALADDIN
ALAMEIN
ALBANIA
ALBENIZ
ALBUMIN
ALEMBIC
ALGERIA
ALKALIS
ALLHAIL
ALLUVIA
BLONDIE
BLOWSIN
BLOWSIT
BLUEFIN
CLASSIC
CLAUDIA
CLAUDIO
CLOCKIN
CLOSEIN
CLUEDIN
CLUESIN
ELASTIC
FLACCID
FLIESIN
GLOTTIS
ILLICIT
ILLOGIC
OLDMAID
OLYMPIA
OLYMPIC
PLASTIC
PLAUDIT
PLUGSIN
SLATKIN
SLEEPIN
SLEPTIN
SLIDEIN
SLIMJIM
SLOEGIN
TLINGIT

•L••••I
ALFIERI
ALVEOLI
ELMISTI
OLDUVAI
PLATYPI

••LI•••
ALLISON
BALIHAI
BELIEFS
BELIEVE
BELINDA
BILIOUS
BKLIBAN
BOLIDES
BOLIVAR
BOLIVIA
BYLINED
BYLINES
CALIBAN
CALIBER
CALIBRE
CALICOS
CALIPER
CALIPHS
CILIATE
DELIBES
DELICTI
DELICTS
DELIGHT
DELILAH
DELIMIT
DELIRIA
DELISTS
DELIVER
ECLIPSE
EELIEST
ELLIOTT
ELLIPSE
ELLISON
ENLISTS
ENLIVEN
EOLITHS
FELICIA
FELINES
FILINGS
FOLIAGE
FOLIATE
GALILEE
GALILEI
GALILEO
GOLIATH
HALIBUT
HALIFAX
HALITES
HELICAL
HELICES
HELICON
HELIPAD
HELIXES
HOLIDAY
HOLIEST
ILLICIT
JALISCO
JULIANA
KYLIKES
LALIQUE
MALIGNS
MELINDA
MELISSA
MILIEUS
MILIEUX
MILITIA
MOLIERE
OBLIGED
OBLIGES
OBLIQUE
OILIEST
OOLITES
OOLITHS
PELICAN
PELISSE
PILINGS
POLICED
POLICES
POLITER
POLITIC
RELIANT
RELICTS
RELIEFS
RELIEVE
RELIEVO
RELIGHT
RELINED
RELINES
RELISTS
RELIVED
RELIVES
RULINGS
SALIENT
SALIERI
SILICAS
SILICON
SOLICIT
SOLIDER
SOLIDLY
SPLICED
SPLICER
SPLICES
SPLINES
SPLINTS
SPLITUP
UGLIEST
UNLIKED
UNLINED
UNLINKS
UPLIFTS
UPLINKS
VALIANT
VALIDLY
VALISES
WILIEST

••L•I••
ALLTIME
ALLYING
BALDING
BALKIER
BALKING
BALMIER
BELGIAN
BELGIUM
BELLIED
BELLIES
BELLING
BELLINI
BELTING
BELYING
BILKING
BILLIES
BILLING
BILLION
BOLTING
BULGING
BULKIER
BULKING
BULLIED
BULLIES
BULLING
BULLION
BULLISH
BULLITT
CALCIFY
CALCITE
CALCIUM
CALKING
CALKINS
CALLING
CALLINS
CALMING
CALVING
CELLINI
CELLIST
CELSIUS
CELTICS
COLLIDE
COLLIER
COLLIES
COLLINS
COLTISH
CULLING
CULTISH
CULTISM
CULTIST
DALLIED
DALLIER
DALLIES
DELEING
DELUISE
DELVING
DILLIES
DOLLIED
DOLLIES
DOLLING
DOLTISH
DULLING
DULLISH
ECLAIRS
FALLING
FALSIFY
FALSITY
FELLING
FELLINI
FILLIES
FILLING
FILLINS

FILLIPS
FILMIER
FILMING
FOLDING
FOLLIES
FULFILL
FULFILS
GALLICO
GALLING
GALLIUM
GELDING
GELLING
GILDING
GILLIES
GILLING
GOLDING
GOLFING
GULFING
GULLIES
GULLING
GULPING
HALOING
HALTING
HALVING
HELLION
HELMING
HELOISE
HELPING
HILAIRE
HILLIER
HILLING
HOLDING
HOLLIES
HOLMIUM
HULKING
HULLING
ILLWILL
ILLWIND
JELLIED
JELLIES
JELLING
JILLIAN
JILLION
JILTING
JOLLIED
JOLLIER
JOLLIES
JOLLIET
JOLLILY
JOLLITY
JOLTING
KELPIES
KILLING
KILTIES
KILTING
LILLIAN
LILTING
LOLLIES
LOLLING
LULLING
MALAISE
MALTING
MELDING
MELTING
MILKIER
MILKING
MILLING
MILLION
MOLDIER
MOLDING
MOLLIFY
MOLTING
MULLING
MULLION
NULLIFY
NULLING
OILRIGS
OWLLIKE
PALLING
PALLIUM
PALMIER
PALMING
PALMIST
PELTING
PILLING
PILLION
POLLING
POLOIST
PULLING
PULPITS
PULSING
RALEIGH
RALLIED
RALLIES
RDLAING
RELYING
ROLAIDS
ROLLICK
ROLLING
ROLLINS
SALLIED
SALLIES
SALSIFY
SALTIER
SALTILY
SALTINE
SALTING
SALVING
SELFISH
SELKIRK
SELLING
SILKIER
SILKILY
SILLIER
SILLIES
SILOING
SILTING
SOLDIER
SOLOING
SOLOIST
SOLVING
SULFIDE
SULFITE
SULKIER
SULKIES
SULKILY
SULKING
SULLIED
SULLIES
TALKIES
TALKING
TALLIED
TALLIES
TALLISH
TELLIES
TELLING
TILLING
TILTING
TOLKIEN
TOLLING
VALUING
VULPINE
WALKING
WALKINS
WALLING
WELDING
WELKINS
WELLING
WELTING
WILDING
WILLIAM
WILLIES
WILLING
WILTING
WOLFING
WOLFISH
YELLING
YELPING
ZILLION

••L••I•
AELFRIC
ALLHAIL
ALLUVIA
BALDRIC
BALDWIN
BOLIVIA
BOLOTIE
CALLSIN
CALORIC
CALORIE
COLLOID
CSLEWIS
CULPRIT
DELIMIT
DELIRIA
DELTAIC
DELTOID
DOLPHIN
EELSKIN
FALLSIN
FELICIA
FILLSIN
GALATIA
GELATIN
GELATIS
HALFWIT
HOLBEIN
ILLICIT
ILLOGIC
ISLAMIC
MALEFIC
MELANIE
MELANIN
MELODIC
MILITIA
MULLEIN
OILSKIN
PALADIN
PALMOIL
PELAGIC
PILEDIN
PILESIN
PILGRIM
POLARIS
POLEMIC
POLITIC
SALADIN
SALAMIS
SALUKIS
SELENIC
SILESIA
SOLARIA
SOLICIT
STLOUIS
STLUCIA
TALARIA
TALKBIG
TELAVIV
VALERIE
VILLAIN
VILLEIN
VOLTAIC
WILFRID
WILLKIE
YELTSIN

••L•••I
BALIHAI
BELLINI
BELUSHI
BOLSHOI
CELLINI
COLLODI
COLOSSI
DELICTI
FELLINI
GALILEI
GALVANI
MALACHI
MOLOKAI
PALAZZI
PULASKI
SALIERI
SYLLABI
TOLSTOI

•••LI••
ABILITY
ABOLISH
ADDLING
ADELINE
AEOLIAN
AFFLICT
AGILITY
AIRLIFT
AIRLINE
AMBLING
AMPLIFY
ANGLING
ANILINE
ANTLION
APELIKE
APPLIED
APPLIES
ATELIER
BAILIFF
BAILING
BAWLING
BEELINE
BELLIED
BELLIES
BELLING
BELLINI
BERLIOZ
BERLITZ
BIALIES
BILLIES
BILLING
BILLION
BIRLING
BOILING
BOWLINE
BOWLING
BUGLING
BULLIED
BULLIES
BULLING
BULLION
BULLISH
BULLITT
BURLIER
BURLING
BUSLINE
CABLING
CALLING
CALLINS
CATLIKE
CEILING
CELLINI
CELLIST
CHALICE
CHILIES
COILING
COLLIDE
COLLIER
COLLIES
COLLINS
COOLING
COWLICK
COWLING
CULLING
CURLIER
CURLING
CYCLING
CYCLIST
DAHLIAS
DAILIES
DALLIED
DALLIER
DALLIES
DARLING
DAYLILY
DEALING
DECLINE
DEWLINE
DIALING
DILLIES
DISLIKE
DOILIES
DOLLIED
DOLLIES
DOLLING
DUALITY
DUELING
DUELIST
DULLING
DULLISH
DUNLINS
EAGLING
EARLIER
EGALITE
EHRLICH
ENGLISH
EXILING
EYELIDS
FAILING
FALLING
FEELIES
FEELING
FELLING
FELLINI
FILLIES
FILLING
FILLINS
FILLIPS
FOALING
FOILING
FOLLIES
FOOLING
FOOLISH
FORLIFE
FOULING
FOWLING
FROLICS
FUELING
FURLING
GAGLINE
GALLICO
GALLING
GALLIUM
GATLING
GELLING
GEMLIKE
GILLIES
GILLING
GIRLISH
GOALIES
GOBLINS
GODLIKE
GOSLING
GROLIER
GULLIES
GULLING
HAILING
HAULING
HEALING
HEELING
HELLION
HEMLINE
HILLIER
HILLING
HITLIST
HOLLIES
HOTLINE
HOTLIPS
HOWLING
HULLING
HURLING
HYALINE
IDOLIZE
IMPLIED
IMPLIES
INCLINE
INFLICT
INKLING
ITALIAN
ITALICS
JAILING
JAWLINE
JELLIED
JELLIES
JELLING
JILLIAN
JILLION
JOLLIED
JOLLIER
JOLLIES
JOLLIET
JOLLILY
JOLLITY
KEELING
KEYLIME
KILLING
KIPLING
LADLING
LILLIAN
LOLLIES
LOLLING
LOWLIER
LOWLIFE
LULLING
MADLIBS
MAILING
MANLIER
MARLINS
MAULING
MEALIER
MEALIES
MEWLING
MIDLIFE
MIDLINE
MILLING
MILLION
MOILING
MOLLIFY
MULLING
MULLION
MUSLIMS
MUSLINS
NAILING
NEOLITH
NIBLICK
NUCLIDE
NULLIFY
NULLING
OBELISK
OBELIZE
OCULIST
OFFLINE
OLDLINE
OPALINE
OUTLINE
OUTLIVE
OWLLIKE
PALLING
PALLIUM
PAULINA
PAULINE
PAULING
PAULIST
PEALING
PEELING
PERLITE
PIGLIKE
PILLING
PILLION
PIMLICO
POLLING
POOLING
POPLINS
PRALINE
PRELIMS
PUBLICS
PUBLISH
PULLING
PURLIEU
PURLING
PURLINS
QUALIFY
QUALITY
RAILING
RALLIED
RALLIES
RATLINE
REALISM
REALIST
REALITY
REALIZE
RECLINE
REDLINE
REELING
REPLICA
REPLIED
REPLIES
RIFLING
ROILING
ROLLICK
ROLLING
ROLLINS
SAILING
SALLIED
SALLIES
SAPLING
SCALIER
SCALING
SEALILY
SEALING
SEALION
SELLING
SERLING
SETLINE
SIBLING
SIDLING
SILLIER
SILLIES
SKILIFT
SKYLINE
SMILING
SOILING
STYLING
STYLISH
STYLIST
STYLIZE
SUBLIME
SULLIED
SULLIES
SURLIER
SURLILY
SUSLIKS
TABLING
TAGLINE
TAILING
TALLIED
TALLIES
TALLISH
TANLINE
TBILISI
TELLIES
TELLING
THULIUM
TIELINE
TILLING
TITLING
TITLIST
TOILING
TOLLING
TOOLING
TSELIOT
UNALIKE
UTILITY
UTILIZE
VEILING
VIOLINS
VIOLIST
WAILING
WALLING
WARLIKE
WELLING
WHALING
WHILING
WILLIAM
WILLIES
WILLING
WOOLIER
WOOLIES
YELLING
YOWLING
ZILLION

•••L•I•
ACCLAIM
BUILDIN
BUILTIN
CALLSIN
CHALLIS
COALBIN
COALOIL
COLLOID
COOLSIT
DEALSIN
DEALTIN
DECLAIM
DIPLOID
EXCLAIM
EXPLAIN
EXPLOIT
FALLSIN
FILLSIN
FOULTIP
FUELOIL
IDYLLIC
KOOLAID
MAULDIN
MISLAID
MULLEIN
NUCLEIC
OUTLAID
PHILBIN
PHILLIP
PHYLLIS
PURLOIN
RECLAIM
REELSIN
SANLUIS
SHELTIE
SIRLOIN
TABLOID
TAILFIN
TRELLIS
TRILLIN
VILLAIN
VILLEIN
WAYLAID
WILLKIE
YOPLAIT

•••L••I
BELLINI
CELLINI
COLLODI
FELLINI
PAHLAVI
SYLLABI
TBILISI

••••LI•
ACRYLIC
ALKALIS
ANGELIC
ANNELID
APHELIA
BACKLIT
BEDELIA
BRESLIN
BUCOLIC
CAMELIA
CECILIA
CHABLIS
CHALLIS
CHAPLIN
CHARLIE
COWSLIP
DRUMLIN
FIDELIO
FIRELIT
GANGLIA
GREMLIN
HAMELIN
IDYLLIC
INSULIN
INVALID
JAVELIN
KREMLIN
KTOSLIN
LANOLIN
LETSLIP
MAHALIA
MAUDLIN
MAYALIN
MOONLIT
NATALIA
NATALIE
NEPALIS
NONSLIP
OBERLIN
OPHELIA
OVERLIE
PHILLIP
PHYLLIS
REGALIA
ROSALIE
SEDALIA
SOMALIA
SOMALIS
SPOTLIT
SQUALID
STARLIT
STEELIE
STOOLIE
TIECLIP
TRELLIS
TRILLIN
VIDALIA
VOCALIC
WHEELIE

••••L•I
BACILLI
CORELLI
GALILEI
JAIALAI
KAROLYI
LORELEI
NIKOLAI
VANILLI
VIVALDI

•••••LI
ALVEOLI
BACILLI
BENGALI
CANNOLI
CORELLI
EXEMPLI
ISRAELI
OMPHALI
RAVIOLI
STIMULI
SWAHILI
TRIPOLI
VANILLI
ZWINGLI

L•J••••
LAJOLLA

L••J•••
LOGJAMS

L•••J••
LEARJET
LORDJIM

L•••••J
LLCOOLJ

•L••J••
BLUEJAY
SLIMJIM

•L••••J
LLCOOLJ

••LJ•••
PALJOEY
VALJEAN

••L•J••
BELLJAR
CULTJAM
KILLJOY

•••LJ••
BELLJAR
KILLJOY

•••••LJ
LLCOOLJ

L•K••••
LAKOTAS
LIKABLE
LIKEMAD
LIKENED
LIKENEW

L••K•••
LACKEYS
LACKING
LANKEST
LANKIER
LANKILY
LEAKAGE
LEAKERS
LEAKIER
LEAKING
LICKETY
LICKING
LINKAGE
LINKERS
LINKING
LINKUPS
LOCKBOX
LOCKERS
LOCKETS
LOCKING
LOCKINS
LOCKNUT
LOCKOUT
LOCKSUP
LOCKUPS
LOOKERS
LOOKFOR
LOOKING
LOOKOUT
LOOKSAT
LOOKSEE
LOOKSIN
LOOKSON
LOOKSTO
LOOKSUP
LOOKUPS
LUCKIER
LUCKILY
LUCKING
LUCKOUT
LUNKERS
LURKING

L•••K••
LALAKER

L•••••K
LAMARCK
LEACOCK
LEGWORK
LIVEOAK
LOGBOOK
LOWNECK
LUBBOCK

•LK••••
ALKALIS
ALKENES
ELKHART

•L•K•••
ALAKING
ELEKTRA
FLAKERS
FLAKIER
FLAKING
SLAKING

•L••K••
ALASKAN
BLACKED
BLACKEN
BLACKER
BLACKLY
BLANKED
BLANKER
BLANKET
BLANKLY
BLEAKER
BLEAKLY
BLINKAT
BLINKED
BLINKER
BLOCKED
BLOCKER
CLACKED
CLANKED
CLERKED
CLICKED
CLINKED
CLINKER
CLOAKED
CLOCKED
CLOCKER
CLOCKIN
CLUCKED
CLUNKED
CLUNKER
FLANKED
FLANKER
FLECKED
FLICKED
FLICKER
FLOCKED
FLOCKTO
FLUNKED
PLACKET
PLANKED
PLINKED
PLUCKED
PLUNKED
SLACKED
SLACKEN
SLACKER
SLATKIN
SLEEKED
SLEEKEN
SLEEKER
SLEEKLY
SLICKED
SLICKER
SLICKLY
SLINKED

•L•••K•
BLUESKY
SLOVAKS

•L••••K
OLDNICK

••LK•••
BALKANS
BALKIER
BALKING
BILKING
BULKIER
BULKING
CALKING
CALKINS
FOLKART
HULKING
MILKCOW
MILKERS
MILKIER
MILKING
MILKMAN
MILKMEN
MILKRUN
MILKSOP
POLKAED
SELKIRK
SILKHAT
SILKIER
SILKILY
SULKERS
SULKIER
SULKIES
SULKILY
SULKING
TALKBIG
TALKERS
TALKIES
TALKING
TALKOUT
TALKSAT
TALKSTO
TALKSUP
TOLKIEN
WALKERS
WALKING
WALKINS
WALKMAN
WALKONS
WALKOUT
WALKUPS
WALKWAY
WELKINS

••L•K••
BELAKUN
EELSKIN

KYLIKES
LALAKER
MOLOKAI
OILSKIN
SALUKIS
UNLIKED
WILLKIE

••L••K•
HOLYOKE
KOLACKY
OILCAKE
OWLLIKE
PALOOKA
PULASKI
RELOCKS
UNLINKS
UNLOCKS
UNLUCKY
UPLINKS

••L•••K
BULLOCK
BULWARK
HILLOCK
HOLMOAK
HOLYARK
MOLLUSK
POLLOCK
ROLLICK
SELKIRK
SELLECK

•••LK••
CAULKED
CAULKER
CHALKED
CHALKUP
SKULKED
SKULKER
STALKED
STALKER
WILLKIE

•••L•K•
APELIKE
CATLIKE
DISLIKE
GEMLIKE
GODLIKE
MUKLUKS
OWLLIKE
PIGLIKE
SUSLIKS
UNALIKE
WARLIKE

•••L••K
AIRLOCK
ARMLOCK
BULLOCK
COWLICK
DEKLERK
EARLOCK
FETLOCK
GUNLOCK
HEMLOCK
HILLOCK
MATLOCK
MOLLUSK
NEWLOOK
NIBLICK
OARLOCK
OBELISK
OUTLOOK
PADLOCK
POLLOCK
POTLUCK
ROLLICK
SCHLOCK
SELLECK
SHYLOCK
SKYLARK
SPELUNK
UNCLOAK
WARLOCK
WEDLOCK

•••••LK
CATWALK
ICEMILK
JAYWALK
KINFOLK
MENFOLK
NORFOLK
OUTTALK
PEPTALK
RAWSILK
RECHALK
SUFFOLK

LL•••••
LLCOOLJ

L•L••••
LALAKER
LALANNE
LALIQUE
LILLIAN
LILTING
LILYPAD
LOLLIES
LOLLING
LULLABY
LULLING

L••L•••
LADLERS
LADLING
LAPLACE
LAPLAND
LAPLATA
LAWLESS
LIDLESS
LILLIAN
LOLLIES
LOLLING
LOWLAND
LOWLIER
LOWLIFE
LULLABY
LULLING

L•••L••
LABELED
LABELER
LABELLE
LAIDLOW
LAJOLLA
LANGLEY
LANOLIN
LAPALMA
LAPELED
LASALLE
LAVALSE
LAYSLOW
LEAFLET
LEGALLY
LETSLIP
LEVELED
LEVELER
LEVELLY
LIBELED
LIBELER
LIESLOW
LITTLER
LOCALES
LOCALLY
LORELEI
LOUELLA
LOWBLOW
LOYALLY
LOYALTY
LUCILLE

L••••L•
LABELLE
LABIALS
LAJOLLA
LANKILY
LAPBELT
LAPFULS
LARGELY
LASALLE
LASCALA
LAURELS
LEERILY
LEGALLY
LEGIBLE
LEGIBLY
LEGPULL
LENTILS
LEOPOLD
LETSFLY
LEVELLY
LICITLY
LIGHTLY
LIKABLE
LINCOLN
LINTELS
LIPBALM
LISTELS
LITHELY
LIVABLE
LIVIDLY
LLCOOLJ
LOCALLY
LOFTILY
LOOSELY
LOUELLA
LOUSILY
LOVABLE
LOVERLY
LOWBALL
LOYALLY
LUCIDLY
LUCILLE
LUCKILY
LURIDLY
LUSTILY

L•••••L
LACTEAL
LACUNAL
LAMINAL
LAMPOIL
LATERAL
LEGPULL
LESPAUL
LEXICAL
LIBERAL
LINGUAL
LITERAL
LOGICAL
LOWBALL
LOWHEEL
LUSTFUL
LYRICAL

•LL••••
ALLAYED
ALLAYER
ALLEARS
ALLEGED
ALLEGER
ALLEGES
ALLEGRO
ALLELES
ALLENDE
ALLERGY
ALLEYES
ALLGONE
ALLHAIL
ALLHEAL
ALLHERE
ALLISON
ALLOFME
ALLOVER
ALLOWED
ALLOYED
ALLSTAR
ALLSTON
ALLTIME
ALLTOLD
ALLUDED
ALLUDES
ALLURED
ALLURES
ALLUVIA
ALLYING
ALLYSON
ELLIOTT
ELLIPSE
ELLISON
ILLBRED
ILLEGAL
ILLICIT
ILLNESS
ILLOGIC
ILLUSED
ILLUSES
ILLWILL
ILLWIND
ULLMANN

•L•L•••
FLYLEAF
OLDLINE
SLALOMS
ULALUME
ULULANT
ULULATE

•L••L••
ALFALFA
ALKALIS
ALLELES
BLUELAW
FLAILED
PLAYLET

•L•••L•
ALERTLY
ALLTOLD
ALOOFLY
ALVEOLI
BLACKLY
BLANDLY
BLANKLY
BLEAKLY
BLINDLY
BLOWFLY
BLUEFLU
BLUFFLY
BLUNTLY
CLAVELL
CLEANLY
CLEARLY
CLOSELY
ELDERLY
FLEETLY
FLUIDLY
FLYBALL
GLOBULE
ILLWILL
LLCOOLJ
OLDGOLD
PLAINLY
PLIABLE
PLIABLY
PLURALS
PLUSHLY
SLEEKLY
SLICKLY

•L••••L
ALCOHOL
ALLHAIL
ALLHEAL
ALUMNAL
CLAIROL
CLAVELL
FLANNEL
FLUVIAL
FLYBALL
GLACIAL
GLEEFUL
GLOTTAL
ILLEGAL
ILLWILL
PLAYFUL
PLUVIAL

••LL•••
BALLADE
BALLADS
BALLARD
BALLAST
BALLBOY
BALLETS
BALLOON
BALLOTS
BALLSUP
BELLAMY
BELLBOY
BELLHOP
BELLIED
BELLIES
BELLING
BELLINI
BELLJAR
BELLMAN
BELLMEN
BELLOWS
BELLYUP
BILLETS
BILLIES
BILLING
BILLION
BILLOWS
BILLOWY
BULLDOG
BULLETS
BULLIED
BULLIES
BULLING
BULLION
BULLISH
BULLITT
BULLOCK
BULLPEN
BULLRUN
CALLBOX
CALLERS
CALLFOR
CALLING
CALLINS
CALLOFF
CALLOUS
CALLOUT
CALLSIN
CALLSON
CALLSUP
CELLARS
CELLINI
CELLIST
COLLAGE
COLLARD
COLLARS
COLLATE
COLLECT
COLLEEN
COLLEGE
COLLETS
COLLIDE
COLLIER
COLLIES
COLLINS
COLLODI
COLLOID
COLLOPS
COLLUDE
COLLYER
CULLING
DALLIED
DALLIER
DALLIES
DILLARD
DILLIES
DOLLARS
DOLLIED
DOLLIES
DOLLING
DOLLOPS
DOLLSUP
DULLARD
DULLEST
DULLING
DULLISH
FALLACY
FALLFOR
FALLGUY
FALLING
FALLOFF
FALLOUT
FALLOWS
FALLSIN
FALLSON
FALLSTO
FELLERS
FELLFOR
FELLING
FELLINI
FELLOFF
FELLOUT
FELLOWS
FILLERS
FILLETS
FILLIES
FILLING
FILLINS
FILLIPS
FILLOUT
FILLSIN
FILLSUP
FILLUPS
FOLLETT
FOLLIES
FOLLOWS
FULLEST
GALLANT
GALLEON
GALLERY
GALLEYS
GALLICO
GALLING
GALLIUM
GALLONS
GALLOPS
GELLING
GILLIES
GILLING
GILLNET
GULLETS
GULLIES
GULLING
HALLOWS
HALLWAY
HELLCAT
HELLENE
HELLERS
HELLION
HELLMAN
HILLARY
HILLIER
HILLING
HILLOCK
HILLTOP
HOLLAND
HOLLERS
HOLLIES
HOLLOWS
HULLERS
HULLING
HULLOED
JELLIED
JELLIES
JELLING
JILLIAN
JILLION
JOLLIED
JOLLIER
JOLLIES
JOLLIET
JOLLILY
JOLLITY
KELLOGG
KILLERS
KILLING
KILLJOY
LILLIAN
LOLLIES
LOLLING
LULLABY
LULLING
MALLARD
MALLETS
MALLOWS
MELLOWS
MILLAND
MILLARD
MILLDAM
MILLEND
MILLERS
MILLETS
MILLETT
MILLING
MILLION
MILLRUN
MOLLIFY
MOLLUSK
MULLAHS
MULLEIN
MULLERS
MULLETS
MULLING
MULLION
NULLIFY
NULLING
OILLAMP
OWLLIKE
PALLETS
PALLING
PALLIUM
PELLETS
PILLAGE
PILLARS
PILLBOX
PILLBUG
PILLING
PILLION
PILLORY
PILLOWS
PILLOWY
POLLENS
POLLERS
POLLING
POLLOCK
POLLTAX
POLLUTE
PULLETS
PULLEYS
PULLING
PULLMAN
PULLOFF
PULLONS
PULLOUT
PULLSUP
PULLTAB
PULLUPS
RALLIED
RALLIES
RALLYTO
RELLENO
RILLETS
ROLLBAR
ROLLERS
ROLLICK
ROLLING
ROLLINS
ROLLOUT
ROLLSUP
ROLLTOP
SALLIED
SALLIES
SELLECK
SELLERS
SELLING
SELLOFF
SELLOUT
SILLIER
SILLIES
SULLIED
SULLIES
SYLLABI
TALLEST
TALLIED
TALLIES
TALLISH
TALLOWS
TALLYHO
TALLYUP
TELLALL
TELLERS
TELLIES
TELLING
TELLOFF
TELLSON
TILLAGE
TILLERS
TILLING
TOLLING
TOLLWAY
VALLEYS
VELLUMS
VILLAGE
VILLAIN
VILLEIN
VOLLEYS
WALLABY
WALLACE
WALLACH
WALLETS
WALLEYE
WALLING
WALLOON
WALLOPS
WALLOWS
WALLSUP
WELLAND
WELLFED
WELLING
WELLOFF
WELLRUN
WELLSET
WELLSUP
WILLARD
WILLFUL
WILLIAM
WILLIES
WILLING
WILLKIE
WILLOWS
WILLOWY
WILLSON
YELLING
YELLOWS
YELLSAT
ZILLION

••L•L••
ALLELES
BULBLET
DELILAH
GALILEE
GALILEI
GALILEO
GILBLAS
OGLALAS
YULELOG

••L••L•
ALLTOLD
ATLATLS
BULBULS
FALSELY
FALWELL
FULFILL
FULFILS
ILLWILL
JOLLILY
MALCOLM
OILWELL
SALABLE
SALTILY
SILKILY
SOLIDLY
SOLUBLE
SULKILY
TELLALL
VALIDLY
VOLUBLE
VOLUBLY
WALPOLE
WILHELM

••L•••L
ALLHAIL
ALLHEAL
BALEFUL
BILEVEL
CALOMEL
CHLORAL
COLONEL
DOLEFUL
FALAFEL
FALWELL
FULFILL
HELICAL
HELPFUL
ILLEGAL
ILLWILL
OILWELL
PALATAL
PALMOIL
TELLALL
TYLENOL
WILLFUL
WOLFGAL

•••LL••
AXILLAE
BRILLAT
CHALLIS
CHILLED
CHILLER
CHOLLAS
CRULLER
DRILLED
DRILLER
DROLLER
DWELLED
DWELLER
EVILLER
FRILLED
GRILLED
GRILLES
GRILLET
IDYLLIC
KEILLOR
KNELLED
MAILLOT
PHILLIP
PHYLLIS
QUELLED
QUILLED
SCALLOP
SCULLED
SCULLER
SHALLOT
SHALLOW
SHELLAC
SHELLED
SHELLER
SHELLEY
SHILLED
SKILLED
SKILLET
SMALLER
SMELLED
SNELLEN
SPALLED
SPELLED
SPELLER
SPILLED
STALLED
STELLAR
STILLED
STILLER
STOLLEN
STOLLER
SWALLOW
SWELLED
SWELLUP
SWILLED
SWOLLEN
TAILLES
TRELLIS
TRILLED
TRILLIN
TROLLED
TROLLEY
TWILLED
WOOLLEN
ZOELLER

•••L•L•
AGILELY
CARLYLE
DAYLILY
HEALALL
JOLLILY
SEALILY
SHALALA
SURLILY
TELLALL
TRALALA
UKULELE
WORLDLY

•••L••L
AXOLOTL
BOWLFUL
COALOIL
FUELOIL
HEALALL
PAILFUL
SCALPEL
SKILFUL
SOULFUL
TELLALL
WILLFUL

••••LL•
APPALLS
AURALLY
AWFULLY
AXIALLY
BACILLI
BANALLY
BASALLY
BEFALLS
BRAILLE
CAMILLE
CAPELLA
CEDILLA
CIVILLY
CORELLI
COROLLA
CRUELLY
DEMILLE
DEVILLE
ENROLLS
EQUALLY
ESTELLE
FINALLY
GAZELLE
GISELLE
GORILLA
HGWELLS
HOWELLS
IDEALLY
INGALLS
LABELLE
LAJOLLA
LASALLE
LEGALLY
LEVELLY
LOCALLY
LOUELLA
LOYALLY
LUCILLE
MAXILLA
MCCALLS
MEDULLA
MISALLY
MORALLY
MORELLO
MOSELLE
MURILLO
NACELLE
NASALLY
NEVILLE
NOVELLA
NOVELLE
ORVILLE
OTHELLO
PAPILLA
PATELLA
RECALLS
REFILLS
REGALLY
REPOLLS
RESELLS
RETELLS
ROSELLE
ROYALLY
ROZELLE
SCROLLS
SEVILLE
SHRILLS
SHRILLY
SQUALLS
STROLLS
THRALLS
THRILLS
TONALLY
TOTALLY
UCCELLO
UNROLLS
USUALLY
UTRILLO
VANILLA
VANILLI
VITALLY
VOCALLY
ZONALLY

•••••LL
AIRBALL
ANTHILL
BARBELL
BEDROLL
BOSWELL
CARROLL
CATCALL
CHAGALL
CLAVELL
CORDELL
CORNELL
CORYELL
COWBELL
CUEBALL
CUREALL
DARRELL
DISTILL
DRYCELL
DRYWALL
DRYWELL
DURRELL
EGGROLL
EYEBALL
FALWELL
FLYBALL
FULFILL
FURBALL
GETWELL
GINMILL
GOODALL
GOTWELL
GUMBALL
GUNMOLL
HEALALL
HUBBELL
ILLWILL
INDWELL
INKWELL
INSTALL
INSTILL
JOEHILL
KENDALL
KIMBALL
LEGPULL
LOWBALL
MAXWELL
MERRILL
MISCALL
NOBHILL
NOTWELL
ODDBALL
OILWELL
ONAROLL
OUTSELL
OVERALL
PARNELL
PERNELL
PINBALL
PITBULL

PITFALL
PRESELL
PURCELL
RAGDOLL
RANDALL
REDCELL
REDPOLL
ROSWELL
RUSSELL
SAMHILL
SAWMILL
SEAGULL
SEAWALL
SITWELL
TARBELL
TEABALL
TELLALL
TOOTALL
WAYBILL
WENDELL
WETCELL

L•M••••

LAMAISM
LAMAIST
LAMARCK
LAMBADA
LAMBDAS
LAMBEAU
LAMBENT
LAMBERT
LAMENTS
LAMINAE
LAMINAL
LAMINAR
LAMINAS
LAMMING
LAMOTTA
LAMPOIL
LAMPOON
LAMPREY
LEMMING
LEMPIRA
LIMBERS
LIMBING
LIMEADE
LIMIEST
LIMITED
LIMNERS
LIMNING
LIMOGES
LIMPEST
LIMPETS
LIMPING
LIMPOPO
LOMBARD
LUMBAGO
LUMBARS
LUMBERS
LUMIERE
LUMPERS
LUMPIER
LUMPING
LUMPSUM

L••M•••

LAMMING
LEMMING
LOAMIER
LOAMING
LOOMING

L•••M••

LABAMBA
LARAMIE
LEGUMES
LIKEMAD
LINEMAN
LINEMEN

L••••M•

LAPALMA
LISSOME
LOGJAMS
LYCEUMS

L•••••M

LAMAISM
LEGROOM
LIPBALM
LITHIUM
LORDJIM
LOWBEAM
LUMPSUM

•LM••••

ALMAATA
ALMADEN
ALMANAC
ALMONDS
ELMISTI
ELMTREE

•L•M•••

ALAMEDA
ALAMEIN
ALAMODE
ALEMBIC
ALIMENT
ALIMONY
ALUMNAE
ALUMNAL
ALUMNUS
BLAMING
BLEMISH
CLAMBER
CLAMMED
CLAMMER
CLAMORS
CLAMPED
CLAMSUP
CLEMENS
CLEMENT
CLEMSON
CLIMATE
CLIMBED
CLIMBER
CLUMPED
ELEMENT
FLAMBED
FLAMBES
FLAMING
FLEMING
FLEMISH
FLUMMOX
GLAMOUR
GLIMMER
GLIMPSE
GLOMMED
GLUMMER
KLAMATH
OLDMAID
OLDMOON
OLEMISS
OLYMPIA
OLYMPIC
OLYMPUS
PLUMAGE
PLUMBED
PLUMBER
PLUMING
PLUMMER
PLUMMET
PLUMPED
PLUMPER
SLAMMED
SLAMMER
SLIMIER
SLIMJIM
SLIMMED
SLIMMER
SLUMBER
SLUMMED
SLUMPED
ULLMANN

•L••M••

ALARMED
ALARMER
ALBUMEN
ALBUMIN
BLOOMED
BLOOMER
CLAIMED
CLAIMER
CLAMMED
CLAMMER
FLAGMAN
FLAGMEN
FLUMMOX
GLEAMED
GLIMMER
GLOMMED
GLUMMER
KLUGMAN
PLASMAS
PLOWMAN
PLOWMEN
PLUMMER
PLUMMET
SLAMMED
SLAMMER
SLIMMED
SLIMMER
SLUMMED

•L•••M•

ALABAMA
ALARUMS
ALCHEMY
ALLOFME
ALLTIME
OLDTIME
PLENUMS
SLALOMS
ULALUME

•L••••M

ALYSSUM
BLOSSOM
ELITISM
ELUVIUM
ELYSIUM
FLOTSAM
SLIMJIM

••LM•••

AILMENT
BALMIER
BELMONT
CALMEST
CALMING
DOLMANS
DOLMENS
FILMIER
FILMING
GILMORE
HELMETS
HELMING
HOLMIUM
HOLMOAK
MALMSEY
PALMATE
PALMIER
PALMING
PALMIST
PALMOFF
PALMOIL
SALMONS
ULLMANN
WALMART

••L•M••

BELLMAN
BELLMEN
CALOMEL
CALUMET
CALUMNY
CCLAMPS
COLEMAN
COLUMBO
COLUMNS
DELIMIT
DILEMMA
FELDMAN
GALUMPH
HELLMAN
ISLAMIC
MALAMUD
MILKMAN
MILKMEN
PALOMAR
POLEMIC
POLYMER
PULLMAN
SALAMIS
SOLOMON
VOLUMES
WALKMAN
WOLFMAN
WOLFMEN

••L••M•

ALLOFME
ALLTIME
BALSAMS
BELDAME
BELDAMS
BELLAMY
DILEMMA
FULSOME
OILLAMP
PALERMO
SALAAMS
VELLUMS
WELCOME

••L•••M

BELGIUM
CALCIUM
CULTISM
CULTJAM
FULCRUM
FULGHUM
GALLIUM
HOLMIUM
MALCOLM
MILLDAM
PALLIUM
PILGRIM
WILHELM
WILLIAM
WOLFRAM

•••LM••

BELLMAN
BELLMEN
HELLMAN
PERLMAN
PSALMED
PULLMAN

•••L•M•

ARCLAMP
ASYLUMS
BEDLAMP
BELLAMY
COULOMB
DIPLOMA
EMBLEMS
INFLAME
KEYLIME
MOSLEMS
MUSLIMS
OILLAMP
PABLUMS
PEPLUMS
PRELIMS
PTOLEMY
RECLAME
SHALOMS
SLALOMS
SUBLIME
SUNLAMP
ULALUME
VELLUMS

•••L••M

ACCLAIM
AMALGAM
DECLAIM
EARLDOM
EXCLAIM
GALLIUM
INBLOOM
MILLDAM
PALLIUM
REALISM
REBLOOM
RECLAIM
THULIUM
WILLIAM

••••LM•

BECALMS
DEPALMA
LAPALMA
REFILMS

••••L•M

ABSALOM
HAARLEM
HOODLUM
PABULUM
PROBLEM

•••••LM

ARTFILM
BEEBALM
LIPBALM
MALCOLM
WILHELM
WYCHELM

L•N••••

LANCERS
LANCETS
LANDAUS
LANDERS
LANDING
LANDSAT
LANFORD
LANGDON
LANGLEY
LANGTRY
LANGUID
LANGUOR
LANGURS
LANKEST
LANKIER
LANKILY
LANOLIN
LANSING
LANTANA
LANTERN
LANYARD
LENDERS
LENDING
LENFANT
LENGTHS
LENGTHY
LENIENT
LENTILS
LINAGES
LINBIAO
LINCOLN
LINDENS
LINDIED
LINDIES
LINDSAY
LINDSEY
LINEAGE
LINEATE
LINEDUP
LINEMAN
LINEMEN
LINESUP
LINEUPS
LINGERS
LINGOES
LINGUAL
LININGS
LINKAGE
LINKERS
LINKING
LINKUPS
LINNETS
LINSEED
LINTELS
LINTIER
LONGAGO
LONGBOW
LONGEST
LONGING
LONGISH
LONGRUN
LONGTON
LONGUES
LONNROT
LUNATIC
LUNCHED
LUNCHER
LUNCHES
LUNGEAT
LUNGING
LUNKERS

L••N•••

LAENNEC
LAUNDER
LAUNDRY
LAXNESS
LEANDER
LEANERS
LEANEST
LEANING
LEANSON
LEANTOS
LEONARD
LEONINE
LEONORA
LIENEES
LIGNITE
LIMNERS
LIMNING
LINNETS
LIONCUB
LIONESS
LIONETS
LIONIZE
LOANERS
LOANING
LONNROT
LOONIER
LOONIES
LOUNGED
LOUNGER
LOUNGES
LOWNECK
LOWNESS
LUGNUTS
LYINGTO

L•••N••

LACINGS
LACONIC
LACUNAE
LACUNAL
LACUNAS
LADINOS
LAENNEC
LAGUNAS
LALANNE
LAMENTS
LAMINAE
LAMINAL
LAMINAR
LAMINAS
LARDNER
LATENCY
LATENTS
LATINAS
LATINOS
LAVINIA
LAYINTO
LAZENBY
LEARNED
LEARNER
LEBANON
LEGENDS
LEIBNIZ
LEPANTO
LETINON
LICENCE
LICENSE
LIERNES
LIFENET
LIKENED
LIKENEW
LININGS
LITINTO
LIVENED
LIVINGS
LOCKNUT
LORENZO
LOZENGE
LUPINES

L••••N•

LACKING
LADLING
LAGGING
LAGOONS
LALANNE
LAMBENT
LAMMING
LANDING
LANSING
LANTANA
LAPLAND
LAPPING
LAPSING
LAPWING
LARAINE
LARCENY
LARDING
LARDONS
LASAGNA
LASAGNE
LASHING
LASTING
LATEENS
LATHING
LATTENS
LAUDING
LAURENT
LAVERNE
LEADING
LEADINS
LEAFING
LEAKING
LEANING
LEAPING
LEASING
LEAVENS
LEAVING
LEERING
LEGGING
LEGIONS
LEMMING
LENDING
LENFANT
LENIENT
LEONINE
LEPTONS
LESSENS
LESSING
LESSONS
LETTING
LEVYING
LIBBING
LIBYANS
LICHENS
LICKING
LIFTING
LILTING
LIMBING
LIMNING
LIMPING
LINDENS
LINKING
LIPPING
LIPSYNC
LISPING
LISTENS
LISTING
LIVEONE
LOADING
LOAFING
LOAMING
LOANING
LOBBING
LOCKING
LOCKINS
LODGING
LOFTING
LOGGING
LOGGINS
LOLLING
LONGING
LOOKING
LOOMING
LOOPING
LOOSENS
LOOSING
LOOTING
LOPPING
LORDING
LOTIONS
LOTTING
LOUSING
LOVEINS
LOWLAND
LUCERNE
LUCIANO
LUCKING
LUFFING
LUGGING
LULLING
LUMPING
LUNGING
LURKING
LUSTING

L•••••N

LAMPOON
LANGDON
LANOLIN
LANTERN
LAOCOON
LAOTIAN
LATERAN
LATERON
LATVIAN
LAUGHIN
LAYDOWN
LEADSIN
LEADSON
LEANSON
LEBANON
LEBARON
LECTERN
LEGHORN
LETDOWN
LETINON
LEXICON
LIAISON
LIEDOWN
LIGHTEN
LILLIAN
LINCOLN
LINEMAN
LINEMEN
LIVEDIN
LIVEDON
LIVESIN
LIVESON
LONGRUN
LONGTON
LOOKSIN
LOOKSON
LOWBORN
LOWDOWN

•L•N•••

ALENCON
ALUNSER
BLANCHE
BLANDER
BLANDLY
BLANKED
BLANKER
BLANKET
BLANKLY
BLENDED
BLENDER
BLINDED
BLINDER
BLINDLY
BLINKAT
BLINKED
BLINKER
BLONDER
BLONDES
BLONDIE
BLUNDER
BLUNTED
BLUNTER
BLUNTLY
CLANGED
CLANGOR
CLANKED
CLINGTO
CLINICS
CLINKED
CLINKER
CLINTON
CLONING
CLUNKED
CLUNKER
FLANEUR
FLANGES
FLANKED
FLANKER
FLANNEL
FLENSED
FLENSES
FLUNKED
FLYNETS
GLANCED
GLANCES
GLINTED
ILLNESS
KLINGON
OLDNESS
OLDNEWS
OLDNICK
PLANERS
PLANETS
PLANING
PLANKED
PLANNED
PLANNER
PLANSON
PLANTAR
PLANTED
PLANTER
PLENARY
PLENUMS
PLINKED
PLINTHS
PLUNDER
PLUNGED
PLUNGER
PLUNGES
PLUNKED
SLANDER
SLANTED
SLENDER
SLINGER
SLINKED
SLYNESS
TLINGIT
ULANOVA

•L••N••

ALBANIA
ALBENIZ
ALBINOS
ALDENTE
ALFONSO
ALIENEE
ALIENOR
ALIGNED
ALIGNER
ALKENES
ALLENDE
ALMANAC
ALMONDS
ALUMNAE
ALUMNAL
ALUMNUS
BLARNEY
BLOWNUP
CLEANED
CLEANER
CLEANLY
CLEANSE
CLEANUP
CLIENTS
CLOONEY
CLOWNED
ELEANOR
FLANNEL
FLAUNTS
FLEXNER
FLOUNCE
FLUENCY
GLEANED
GLEANER
KLEENEX
PLAINER
PLAINES
PLAINLY
PLAINTS
PLANNED
PLANNER
PLIANCY
ULYANOV

•L•••N•

ALAKING
ALIMENT
ALIMONY
ALLGONE
ALLYING
ALTOONA
BLAMING
BLARING
BLATANT
BLAZING
BLAZONS
BLOWING
BLUEING
CLAWING
CLEMENS
CLEMENT
CLIPONS
CLONING
CLOSING
CLOYING
CLUEING
ELATING
ELEGANT
ELEMENT
ELEVENS
ELIDING
ELOPING
ELUDING
ELUTING
FLACONS
FLAGONS
FLAKING
FLAMING
FLARING
FLAWING
FLAYING
FLEEING
FLEMING
FLEXING
FLORINS
FLOWING
FLUTING
GLARING
GLAZING
GLIDING
GLOWING
ILLWIND
KLAXONS
OLDHAND
OLDLINE
OLIVINE
PLACING
PLANING
PLATENS
PLATING
PLAYING
PLOWING
PLUMING
SLAKING
SLATING
SLAVING
SLICING
SLIDING
SLIPONS
SLOGANS
SLOPING
SLOVENE
SLOVENS
SLOWING
ULLMANN
ULULANT

•L••••N

ALADDIN
ALAMEIN
ALARCON
ALASKAN
ALBUMEN
ALBUMIN
ALENCON
ALLISON
ALLSTON
ALLYSON
ALMADEN
ALSORAN
BLACKEN
BLITZEN
BLOUSON
BLOWGUN
BLOWSIN
BLUEFIN
CLAPTON
CLARION
CLAYTON
CLEAVON
CLEMSON
CLIBURN
CLIFTON
CLINTON
CLOCKIN
CLOSEIN
CLUEDIN
CLUESIN
ELATION
ELEISON
ELISION
ELLISON
ELUTION
ELYSIAN
FLAGMAN
FLAGMEN
FLATTEN
FLIESIN
GLADDEN
GLEASON
GLISTEN
GLUEDON
GLUTTON
KLINGON
KLUGMAN
OLDMOON
PLANSON
PLATOON
PLAYPEN
PLAYSON
PLOSION
PLOWMAN
PLOWMEN
PLUGSIN
SLACKEN
SLATKIN
SLAYTON
SLEEKEN
SLEEPIN
SLEEPON
SLEPTIN
SLEPTON
SLIDEIN
SLOEGIN
ULLMANN

••LN•••

ILLNESS
WALNUTS

••L•N••

ALLENDE

APLENTY
ATLANTA
BALANCE
BALONEY
BELINDA
BELONGS
BYLINED
BYLINES
CALENDS
COLONEL
COLONES
COLONNA
DELANEY
FELINES
FILINGS
GILLNET
ISLANDS
LALANNE
MELANGE
MELANIE
MELANIN
MELINDA
OBLONGS
ORLANDO
PALANCE
PILINGS
PILSNER
POLENTA
RELENTS
RELINED
RELINES
RULINGS
SELENIC
SILENCE
SILENTS
SPLINES
SPLINTS
TALENTS
TALONED
TYLENOL
UNLINED
UNLINKS
UPLANDS
UPLINKS
VALANCE
VALENCE

••L••N•

AILMENT
ALLGONE
ALLYING
BALCONY
BALDING
BALEENS
BALKANS
BALKING
BELLING
BELLINI
BELMONT
BELTANE
BELTING
BELYING
BILKING
BILLING
BOLOGNA
BOLTING
BULGING
BULKING
BULLING
CALKING
CALKINS
CALLING
CALLINS
CALMING
CALUMNY
CALVING
CALZONE
CELLINI
COLLINS
COLOGNE
COLONNA
COLUMNS
CULLING
DELEING
DELVING
DOLLING
DOLMANS
DOLMENS
DULLING
FALCONS
FALLING
FELLING
FELLINI
FILLING
FILLINS
FILMING
FOLDING
FULGENT
GALLANT
GALLING
GALLONS
GALVANI
GELDING
GELLING
GILDING
GILLING
GOLDING
GOLFING
GULFING
GULLING
GULPING
HALOING
HALTING
HALVING
HELLENE
HELMING
HELPING
HILLING
HOLDING
HOLLAND
HULKING
HULLING
ILLWIND
JELLING
JILTING
JOLTING
JULIANA
KILLING
KILTING
LALANNE
LILTING
LOLLING
LULLING
MALIGNS
MALTING
MELDING
MELTING
MILKING
MILLAND
MILLEND
MILLING
MOLDING
MOLTING
MULLING
NELSONS
NULLING
OILCANS
OILPANS
ORLEANS
PALLING
PALMING
PELTING
PILLING
POLLENS
POLLING
PULLING
PULLONS
PULSING
RDLAING
RELIANT
RELLENO
RELYING
ROLLING
ROLLINS
SALERNO
SALIENT
SALMONS
SALOONS
SALTINE
SALTING
SALVING
SELLING
SILOING
SILTING
SOLOING
SOLVENT
SOLVING
SPLEENS
SULKING
SULTANA
SULTANS
SYLVANS
TALKING
TELLING
TILLING
TILTING
TOLLING
TOLUENE
TULSANS
ULLMANN
VALIANT
VALUING
VOLCANO
VOLPONE
VULCANS
VULPINE
WALKING
WALKINS
WALKONS
WALLING
WELDING
WELKINS
WELLAND
WELLING
WELTING
WILDING
WILDONE
WILLING
WILTING
WOLFING
YELLING
YELPING

••L•••N

AILERON
ALLISON
ALLSTON
ALLYSON
BALATON
BALDWIN
BALLOON
BELAKUN
BELGIAN
BELLMAN
BELLMEN
BILLION
BKLIBAN
BULLION
BULLPEN
BULLRUN
CALDRON
CALHOUN
CALIBAN
CALLSIN
CALLSON
CELADON
COLEMAN
COLLEEN
DOLPHIN
EELSKIN
ELLISON
ENLIVEN
FALLSIN
FALLSON
FELDMAN
FILLSIN
GALLEON
GELATIN
GOLDWYN
HALCYON
HALFDAN
HALOGEN
HALSTON
HELICON
HELLION
HELLMAN
HOLBEIN
HOLDSON
JILLIAN
JILLION
KILOTON
LILLIAN
MALAREN
MALAYAN
MCLUHAN
MELANIN
MILKMAN
MILKMEN
MILKRUN
MILLION
MILLRUN
MULLEIN
MULLION
NILSSON
OILSKIN
PALADIN
PELICAN
PILEDIN
PILEDON
PILESIN
PILESON
PILLION
POLYGON
PULLMAN
RALSTON
RELEARN
RULESON
SALADIN
SILICON
SOLOMON
TELERAN
TELLSON
TOLKIEN
ULLMANN
UNLEARN
VALJEAN
VILLAIN
VILLEIN
WALKMAN
WALLOON
WELLRUN
WILLSON
WOLFMAN
WOLFMEN
YELTSIN
ZILLION

•••LN••

GILLNET

•••L•N•

ABALONE
ABILENE
ADDLING
ADELINE
AIRLANE
AIRLINE
AMBLING
ANGLING
ANILINE
ASHLAND
BAILING
BAWLING
BEELINE
BELLING
BELLINI
BILLING
BIPLANE
BIRLING
BOILING
BOWLINE
BOWLING
BUGLING
BULLING
BURLING
BUSLINE
CABLING
CALLING
CALLINS
CEILING
CELLINI
COILING
COLLINS
COOLANT
COOLING
COPLAND
COULDNT
COWLING
CULLING
CURLING
CYCLING
CYCLONE
DARLENE
DARLING
DAYLONG
DEALING
DECLINE
DEPLANE
DEWLINE
DIALING
DOLLING
DUELING
DULLING
DUNLINS
EAGLING
ENGLAND
ENGLUND
ENPLANE
ERELONG
EXILING
FAILING
FALLING
FEELING
FELLING
FELLINI
FILLING
FILLINS
FINLAND
FOALING
FOILING
FOOLING
FOULING
FOWLING
FUELING
FURLING
FURLONG
GAGLINE
GALLANT
GALLING
GALLONS
GARLAND
GATLING
GELLING
GILLING
GOALONG
GOBLINS
GOSLING
GOTLAND
GULLING
HAILING
HAULING
HEALING
HEELING
HELLENE
HEMLINE
HILLING
HOLLAND
HOTLINE
HOWLING
HULLING
HURLING
HYALINE
ICELAND
IMPLANT
INCLINE
INKLING
IRELAND
JAILING
JAWLINE
JAYLENO
JELLING
JUTLAND
KEELING
KILLING
KIPLING
KOBLENZ
LADLING
LAPLAND
LOLLING
LOWLAND
LULLING
MAILING
MARLENE
MARLINS
MAULING
MEWLING
MIDLAND
MIDLINE
MILLAND
MILLEND
MILLING
MOILING
MULLING
MUSLINS
NAILING
NULLING
OAKLAND
OFFLINE
OLDLINE
OPALINE
OPULENT
OUTLAND
OUTLINE
PALLING
PAULINA
PAULINE
PAULING
PEALING
PEELING
PHALANX
PILLING
POLLENS
POLLING
POOLING
POPLINS
POULENC
PRALINE
PROLONG
PULLING
PULLONS
PURLING
PURLINS
RAGLANS
RAILING
RATLINE
RECLINE
REDLINE
REELING
RELLENO
REPLANS
REPLANT
RIFLING
ROILING
ROLLING
ROLLINS
SAILING
SAPLING
SCALENE
SCALING
SEALANE
SEALANT
SEALING
SELLING
SERLING
SETLINE
SIBLING
SIDLING
SKYLINE
SMILING
SOILING
SPELUNK
STOLONS
STYLING
TABLING
TAGLINE
TAILEND
TAILING
TANLINE
TELLING
TIELINE
TILLING
TITLING
TOILING
TOLLING
TOOLING
TOYLAND
ULULANT
VEILING
VIOLENT
VIOLINS
WAILING
WALLING
WELLAND
WELLING
WETLAND
WHALING
WHILING
WILLING
WOOLENS
WOULDNT
YELLING
YOWLING
ZEALAND

•••L••N

AEOLIAN
ANTLION
BALLOON
BELLMAN
BELLMEN
BILLION
BOOLEAN
BUILDIN
BUILDON
BUILTIN
BUILTON
BULLION
BULLPEN
BULLRUN
CALLSIN
CALLSON
CARLSON
CARLTON
CHILEAN
COALBIN
COLLEEN
DARLEEN
DEALSIN
DEALTIN
EARLYON
EXPLAIN
FALLSIN
FALLSON
FILLSIN
FORLORN
GALLEON
HELLION
HELLMAN
ITALIAN
JILLIAN
JILLION
KOWLOON
LILLIAN
MAULDIN
MILLION
MILLRUN
MRCLEAN
MULLEIN
MULLION
NIELSEN
NUCLEON
OAKLAWN
PAULSEN
PERLMAN
PHILBIN
PILLION
PULLMAN
PURLOIN
RECLEAN
REELSIN
SEALION
SHELDON
SHELTON
SIRLOIN
SKELTON
SNELLEN
STILTON
STOLLEN
SWOLLEN
TAILFIN
TELLSON
TRILLIN
UNCLEAN
VILLAIN
VILLEIN
WALLOON
WELLRUN
WILLSON
WOOLLEN
ZILLION

••••LN•

AAMILNE

••••L•N

ANGOLAN
BABYLON
BRESLIN
CAROLYN
CATALAN
CHAPLIN
DRUMLIN
ECHELON
EPSILON
GREMLIN
HAMELIN
INSULIN
JAVELIN
KREMLIN
KTOSLIN
LANOLIN
MARILYN
MAUDLIN
MAYALIN
MOUFLON
OBERLIN
ORTOLAN
ROMULAN
SNELLEN
STOLLEN
SWOLLEN
TRILLIN
UPSILON
WOOLLEN
ZEBULON

•••••LN

LINCOLN

LO•••••

LOACHES
LOADERS
LOADING
LOAFERS
LOAFING
LOAMIER
LOAMING
LOANERS
LOANING
LOATHED
LOATHES
LOBBERS
LOBBIED
LOBBIES
LOBBING
LOBBYER
LOBSTER
LOCALES
LOCALLY
LOCATED
LOCATER
LOCATES
LOCATOR
LOCKBOX
LOCKERS
LOCKETS
LOCKING
LOCKINS
LOCKNUT
LOCKOUT
LOCKSUP
LOCKUPS
LOCUSTS
LODGERS
LODGING
LOESSER
LOESSES
LOFTIER
LOFTILY
LOFTING
LOGBOOK
LOGGERS
LOGGIAS
LOGGING
LOGGINS
LOGICAL
LOGIEST
LOGJAMS
LOGSOFF
LOGSOUT
LOITERS
LOLLIES
LOLLING
LOMBARD
LONGAGO
LONGBOW
LONGEST
LONGING
LONGISH
LONGRUN
LONGTON
LONGUES
LONNROT
LOOFAHS
LOOKERS
LOOKFOR
LOOKING
LOOKOUT
LOOKSAT
LOOKSEE
LOOKSIN
LOOKSON
LOOKSTO
LOOKSUP
LOOKUPS
LOOMING
LOONIER
LOONIES
LOOPERS
LOOPIER
LOOPING
LOOSELY
LOOSENS
LOOSEST
LOOSING
LOOTERS
LOOTING
LOPPERS
LOPPING
LOQUATS
LORDING
LORDJIM
LORELEI
LORENZO
LORETTA
LORISES
LORRIES
LOSEOUT
LOSESIT
LOSTOUT
LOTIONS
LOTTERY
LOTTING
LOTUSES
LOUDEST
LOUELLA
LOUNGED
LOUNGER
LOUNGES
LOURDES
LOUREED
LOUSEUP
LOUSIER
LOUSILY
LOUSING
LOUVERS
LOUVRES
LOVABLE
LOVEBUG
LOVEINS
LOVERLY
LOWBALL
LOWBEAM
LOWBLOW
LOWBORN
LOWBOYS
LOWBRED
LOWBROW
LOWDOWN
LOWERED
LOWGEAR
LOWHEEL
LOWLAND
LOWLIER
LOWLIFE
LOWNECK
LOWNESS
LOWPAID
LOWRISE
LOWROAD
LOWTECH
LOWTIDE
LOYALLY
LOYALTY
LOZENGE

L•O••••

LAOCOON
LAOTIAN
LEONARD
LEONINE
LEONORA
LEOPARD
LEOPOLD
LEOTARD
LIONCUB
LIONESS
LIONETS
LIONIZE
LOOFAHS
LOOKERS
LOOKFOR
LOOKING
LOOKOUT
LOOKSAT
LOOKSEE
LOOKSIN
LOOKSON
LOOKSTO
LOOKSUP
LOOKUPS
LOOMING
LOONIER
LOONIES
LOOPERS
LOOPIER
LOOPING
LOOSELY
LOOSENS
LOOSEST
LOOSING
LOOTERS
LOOTING

L••O•••

LABORED
LABORER
LABOURS
LACONIC
LACOSTE
LAGOONS
LAJOLLA
LAKOTAS
LAMOTTA
LANOLIN
LAPORTE
LAROCHE
LASORDA
LAYOFFS
LAYOUTS
LAYOVER
LESOTHO
LIEOVER
LIMOGES
LITOTES
LLCOOLJ

L•••O••

LABCOAT
LACTOSE
LAGOONS
LAIDOFF
LAIDOUT
LAMPOIL
LAMPOON
LANFORD
LAOCOON
LAPDOGS
LAPROBE
LAPTOPS
LARDONS
LASSOED
LASSOER
LASSOES
LASTORY
LAWFORD
LAYDOWN
LAYSOFF
LAYSOUT
LEACOCK
LEADOFF
LEADOUT
LECTORS
LEFTOFF
LEFTOUT
LEGHORN
LEGIONS
LEGROOM
LEGWORK
LEONORA
LEOPOLD
LEPTONS
LESSONS
LESSORS
LETDOWN
LETSOFF
LETSOUT
LIEDOWN
LIFTOFF
LIMPOPO
LINCOLN
LINGOES
LIQUORS
LISSOME
LIVEOAK
LIVEONE
LIVEOUT
LLCOOLJ
LOCKOUT
LOGBOOK
LOGSOFF
LOGSOUT
LOOKOUT
LOSEOUT
LOSTOUT
LOTIONS
LOWBORN
LOWBOYS
LOWDOWN
LOWROAD
LUBBOCK
LUCKOUT

L••••O•

LADINOS
LAIDFOR
LAIDLOW
LAMPOON
LANGDON
LANGUOR
LAOCOON
LATERON
LATINOS
LAYSFOR
LAYSLOW
LEADSON
LEANSON
LEANTOS
LEBANON
LEBARON
LEGATOS
LEGROOM
LETINON
LEXICON
LIAISON
LIBIDOS
LIESLOW
LITHGOW
LIVEDON

LIVESON
LOCATOR
LOCKBOX
LOGBOOK
LONGBOW
LONGTON
LONNROT
LOOKFOR
LOOKSON
LOWBLOW
LOWBROW

L•••••O
LAYINTO
LEADSTO
LEDUPTO
LEPANTO
LESOTHO
LIMPOPO
LINBIAO
LITINTO
LONGAGO
LOOKSTO
LORENZO
LUCIANO
LUMBAGO
LYINGTO

•LO••••
ALOHAOE
ALOOFLY
BLOATED
BLOCKED
BLOCKER
BLONDER
BLONDES
BLONDIE
BLOODED
BLOOMED
BLOOMER
BLOOPED
BLOOPER
BLOSSOM
BLOTCHY
BLOTOUT
BLOTTED
BLOTTER
BLOUSED
BLOUSES
BLOUSON
BLOWDRY
BLOWERS
BLOWFLY
BLOWGUN
BLOWIER
BLOWING
BLOWNUP
BLOWOFF
BLOWOUT
BLOWSIN
BLOWSIT
BLOWSUP
BLOWUPS
CLOAKED
CLOBBER
CLOCHES
CLOCKED
CLOCKER
CLOCKIN
CLOGGED
CLOGSUP
CLONING
CLOONEY
CLOPPED
CLOQUES
CLORETS
CLOSEIN
CLOSELY
CLOSEST
CLOSETS
CLOSEUP
CLOSING
CLOSURE
CLOTHED
CLOTHES
CLOTTED
CLOTURE
CLOUDED
CLOUTED
CLOVERS
CLOWDER
CLOWNED
CLOYING
ELOPERS
ELOPING
FLOATED
FLOATER
FLOCKED
FLOCKTO
FLOGGED
FLOODED
FLOORED
FLOPPED
FLORETS
FLORIDA
FLORINS
FLORIST
FLOSSED
FLOSSES
FLOTSAM
FLOUNCE
FLOURED
FLOUTED
FLOWERS
FLOWERY
FLOWING
GLOATED
GLOBULE
GLOMMED
GLORIAS
GLORIED
GLORIES
GLORIFY
GLOSSAE
GLOSSED
GLOSSES
GLOTTAL
GLOTTIS
GLOWERS
GLOWING
OLOROSO
PLODDED
PLODDER
PLOPPED
PLOSION
PLOSIVE
PLOTTED
PLOTTER
PLOUGHS
PLOVERS
PLOWBOY
PLOWERS
PLOWING
PLOWMAN
PLOWMEN
SLOBBER
SLOEGIN
SLOGANS
SLOGGED
SLOPING
SLOPPED
SLOSHED
SLOSHES
SLOTCAR
SLOTTED
SLOUCHY
SLOUGHS
SLOVAKS
SLOVENE
SLOVENS
SLOWEST
SLOWING
SLOWSUP

•L•O•••
ALCOHOL
ALCOVES
ALFONSO
ALLOFME
ALLOVER
ALLOWED
ALLOYED
ALMONDS
ALOOFLY
ALSORAN
ALTOONA
ALTOSAX
ALWORTH
ALYOSHA
BLOODED
BLOOMED
BLOOMER
BLOOPED
BLOOPER
CLOONEY
ELBOWED
FLOODED
FLOORED
FLYOVER
ILLOGIC
LLCOOLJ

•L••O••
ALAMODE
ALIMONY
ALLGONE
ALLTOLD
ALTOONA
ALVEOLI
BLAZONS
BLEWOFF
BLEWOUT
BLOTOUT
BLOWOFF
BLOWOUT
CLAMORS
CLIPONS
ELLIOTT
FLACONS
FLAGONS
FLATOUT
FLAVORS
FLAVOUR
FLEXORS
FLYBOYS
FLYRODS
GLAMOUR
GLUCOSE
KLAXONS
LLCOOLJ
OLDFOGY
OLDGOLD
OLDMOON
OLOROSO
PLATOON
PLAYOFF
PLAYOUT
PLEXORS
PLYWOOD
SLALOMS
SLIPONS
SLIPOUT
ULANOVA

•L•••O•
ALARCON
ALBEDOS
ALBINOS
ALCOHOL
ALENCON
ALIENOR
ALLISON
ALLSTON
ALLYSON
ALOHAOE
BLERIOT
BLOSSOM
BLOUSON
BLUEBOY
BLUEFOX
CLAIROL
CLANGOR
CLAPTON
CLARION
CLAYTON
CLEAVON
CLEMSON
CLIFTON
CLINTON
ELATION
ELEANOR
ELECTOR
ELEISON
ELISION
ELLISON
ELUTION
FLATTOP
FLUMMOX
GLASGOW
GLEASON
GLUEDON
GLUTTON
KLINGON
OLDMOON
OLDPROS
PLANSON
PLATOON
PLAYBOY
PLAYDOH
PLAYSON
PLOSION
PLOWBOY
PLYWOOD
SLAYTON
SLEDDOG
SLEEPON
SLEPTON
ULYANOV

•L••••O
ALBERTO
ALFONSO
ALFREDO
ALLEGRO
CLAUDIO
CLINGTO
ELECTRO
ELGRECO
FLOCKTO
OLOROSO
PLACEBO
PLACIDO

••LO•••
ALLOFME
ALLOVER
ALLOWED
ALLOYED
BALONEY
BELONGS
BELOVED
BOLOGNA
BOLOTIE
CALOMEL
CALORIC
CALORIE
CHLORAL
COLOBUS
COLOGNE
COLONEL
COLONES
COLONNA
COLORED
COLOSSI
COLOURS
CULOTTE
DOLORES
ECLOGUE
GALOOTS
HALOGEN
HALOING
HELOISE
HELOTRY
ILLOGIC
KILOTON
MALODOR
MELODIC
MILORDS
MOLOKAI
MOLOTOV
OBLONGS
OBLOQUY
PALOMAR
PALOOKA
PELOTAS
PHLOXES
PILOTED
POLOIST
RELOADS
RELOCKS
ROLODEX
SALOONS
SILOING
SOLOING
SOLOIST
SOLOMON
SPLOTCH
STLOUIS
TALONED
UNLOADS
UNLOCKS
UNLOOSE
UNLOVED
UPLOADS
VALOURS
VELOURS

••L•O••
ALLGONE
ALLTOLD
AXLROSE
BALBOAS
BALCONY
BALFOUR
BALLOON
BALLOTS
BELLOWS
BELMONT
BILBOES
BILIOUS
BILLOWS
BILLOWY
BULBOUS
BULLOCK
CALHOUN
CALLOFF
CALLOUS
CALLOUT
CALZONE
COLLODI
COLLOID
COLLOPS
DELTOID
DOLEOUT
DOLLOPS
ELLIOTT
FALCONS
FALLOFF
FALLOUT
FALLOWS
FELLOFF
FELLOUT
FELLOWS
FELTOUT
FILLOUT
FOLDOUT
FOLLOWS
FULSOME
GALLONS
GALLOPS
GALOOTS
GILMORE
HALLOWS
HELDOFF
HELDOUT
HELPOUT
HILLOCK
HOLDOFF
HOLDOUT
HOLEOUT
HOLLOWS
HOLMOAK
HOLYOKE
HULLOED
KELLOGG
MALCOLM
MALLOWS
MALTOSE
MELLOWS
MELROSE
NELSONS
PALJOEY
PALMOFF
PALMOIL
PALOOKA
PILLORY
PILLOWS
PILLOWY
POLLOCK
PULLOFF
PULLONS
PULLOUT
ROLLOUT
RULEOUT
SALMONS
SALOONS
SALSODA
SALVOES
SELLOFF
SELLOUT
SOLDOFF
SOLDOUT
TALKOUT
TALLOWS
TELLOFF
TOLDOFF
UNLOOSE
VOLPONE
WALCOTT
WALDORF
WALKONS
WALKOUT
WALLOON
WALLOPS
WALLOWS
WALPOLE
WELCOME
WELLOFF
WILDONE
WILFORD
WILLOWS
WILLOWY
YELLOWS

••L••O•
AILERON
ALLISON
ALLSTON
ALLYSON
BALATON
BALLBOY
BALLOON
BELABOR
BELLBOY
BELLHOP
BILLION
BOLEROS
BOLSHOI
BULLDOG
BULLION
CALDRON
CALICOS
CALLBOX
CALLFOR
CALLSON
CELADON
ELLISON
FALLFOR
FALLSON
FELLFOR
FELTFOR
GALLEON
HALCYON
HALSTON
HELICON
HELLION
HILLTOP
HOLDSON
HOLYCOW
JILLION
KILLJOY
KILOTON
MALODOR
MILKCOW
MILKSOP
MILLION
MOLOTOV
MULLION
NILSSON
ONLYYOU
PILEDON
PILESON
PILLBOX
PILLION
POLYGON
RALSTON
ROLLTOP
RULESON
SALCHOW
SALTBOX
SILICON
SOLOMON
TELLSON
TOLSTOI
TOLSTOY
TYLENOL
WALLOON
WILLSON
YULELOG
ZILLION

••L•••O
ALLEGRO
CALYPSO
COLUMBO
FALLSTO
GALILEO
GALLICO
GOLFPRO
HOLDSTO
JALISCO
ORLANDO
PALAZZO
PALERMO
RALLYTO
RELIEVO
RELLENO
SALERNO
TALKSTO
TALLYHO
VOLCANO

•••LO••
ABALONE
AIRLOCK
ANALOGS
ANALOGY
APOLOGY
ARMLOAD
ARMLOCK
ATALOSS
AXOLOTL
BAILORS
BAILOUT
BALLOON
BALLOTS
BAWLOUT
BECLOUD
BELLOWS
BILLOWS
BILLOWY
BIOLOGY
BULLOCK
CALLOFF
CALLOUS
CALLOUT
CARLOAD
COALOIL
COLLODI
COLLOID
COLLOPS
COULOMB
CYCLONE
CYCLOPS
DAYLONG
DEALOUT
DEPLORE
DEPLOYS
DIALOGS
DIPLOID
DIPLOMA
DOLLOPS
EARLOBE
EARLOCK
ECOLOGY
EMPLOYS
ENCLOSE
EPILOGS
ERELONG
EXPLODE
EXPLOIT
EXPLORE
FALLOFF
FALLOUT
FALLOWS
FEELOUT
FELLOFF
FELLOUT
FELLOWS
FETLOCK
FILLOUT
FOLLOWS
FORLORN
FOULOUT
FUELOIL
FURLONG
GALLONS
GALLOPS
GAYLORD
GEOLOGY
GETLOST
GOALONG
GUNLOCK
HALLOWS
HAULOFF
HAYLOFT
HEMLOCK
HILLOCK
HOLLOWS
HULLOED
IMPLODE
IMPLORE
INBLOOM
INCLOSE
INFLOWS
JEALOUS
JOBLOTS
KARLOFF
KELLOGG
KOWLOON
MALLOWS
MARLOWE
MATLOCK
MELLOWS
MERLOTS
NEWLOOK
OARLOCK
OCELOTS
ODDLOTS
OFFLOAD
OUTLOOK
OUTLOUD
OXBLOOD
PADLOCK
PAILOUS
PARLORS
PARLOUR
PARLOUS
PAVLOVA
PAYLOAD
PEELOFF
PILLORY
PILLOWS
PILLOWY
POLLOCK
PRELOAD
PROLOGS
PROLONG
PULLOFF
PULLONS
PULLOUT
PURLOIN
REBLOOM
REELOFF
RIOLOBO
ROBLOWE
ROLLOUT
SAILORS
SAWLOGS
SCHLOCK
SEALOFF
SELLOFF
SELLOUT
SHALOMS
SHYLOCK
SIRLOIN
SLALOMS
STOLONS
TABLOID
TAILOFF
TAILORS
TALLOWS
TELLOFF
TOELOOP
TRILOGY
UNCLOAK
UNCLOGS
UNCLOSE
UPCLOSE
WALLOON
WALLOPS
WALLOWS
WARLOCK
WARLORD
WEDLOCK
WELLOFF
WILLOWS
WILLOWY
YELLOWS
ZEALOTS
ZEALOUS
ZOOLOGY

•••L•O•
ANTLION
BALLBOY
BALLOON
BELLBOY
BELLHOP
BERLIOZ
BILLION
BUILDON
BUILTON
BULLDOG
BULLION
CALLBOX
CALLFOR
CALLSON
CARLSON
CARLTON
EARLDOM
EARLYON
FALLFOR
FALLSON
FEELFOR
FELLFOR
FUELROD
GALLEON
HELLION
HILLTOP
INBLOOM
JILLION
KEILLOR
KILLJOY
KOWLOON
MAILBOX
MAILLOT
MILLION
MULLION
NEWLOOK
NUCLEON
OUTLOOK
OXBLOOD
PILLBOX
PILLION
REALTOR
REBLOOM
ROLLTOP
SCALLOP
SEALION
SHALLOT
SHALLOW
SHELDON
SHELTON
SKELTON
SMALTOS
STILTON
SWALLOW
TELLSON
TOELOOP
TOOLBOX
TSELIOT
WALLOON
WILLSON
ZILLION

•••L••O
FALLSTO
GALLICO
JAYLENO
PIMLICO
RALLYTO
RELLENO
RIOLOBO
TALLYHO

••••LO•
ABSALOM
AIRFLOW
ANGELOU
ANTILOG
BABYLON
BACKLOG
BIBELOT
BICOLOR
BIGELOW
BUGALOO
CAMELOT
CATALOG
COPILOT
DECALOG
DEVELOP
ECHELON
EMMYLOU
ENVELOP
EPSILON
FEEDLOT
GIGOLOS
HIGHLOW
ICEFLOE
INKBLOT
JOEBLOW
KEILLOR
KERPLOP
LAIDLOW
LAYSLOW
LIESLOW
LOWBLOW
MAILLOT
MANILOW
MARYLOU
MONOLOG
MOUFLON
OUTFLOW
POMELOS
PUEBLOS
RECOLOR
SANDLOT
SCALLOP
SHALLOT
SHALLOW
SQUALOR
SUBPLOT
SWALLOW
TAGALOG
TEMBLOR
THEBLOB
TONELOC
TUPELOS
UPSILON
WINSLOW
WOODLOT
YULELOG
ZEBULON

••••L•O
BUGALOO
FIDELIO
GALILEO
GERALDO
HIDALGO
MORELLO
MURILLO
OTHELLO
RODOLFO
UCCELLO
UTRILLO

•••••LO
BEEFALO
BUFFALO
CEMBALO
DECARLO
HANSOLO
MORELLO
MURILLO
NICCOLO
OTHELLO
PICCOLO
TANGELO
TREMOLO
UCCELLO
UTRILLO

L•P••••
LAPALMA
LAPBELT
LAPDOGS
LAPELED
LAPFULS
LAPLACE
LAPLAND
LAPLATA
LAPORTE
LAPPETS
LAPPING
LAPROBE
LAPSING
LAPTOPS
LAPWING
LEPANTO
LEPTONS
LIPBALM
LIPPIER
LIPPING
LIPREAD
LIPSYNC
LOPPERS
LOPPING
LUPINES

L••P•••
LAMPOIL
LAMPOON
LAMPREY
LAPPETS
LAPPING
LEAPERS
LEAPING
LEGPULL
LEIPZIG
LEMPIRA
LEOPARD
LEOPOLD
LESPAUL
LIMPEST
LIMPETS
LIMPING
LIMPOPO
LIPPIER
LIPPING
LISPING
LOOPERS
LOOPIER
LOOPING
LOPPERS
LOPPING
LOWPAID
LUMPERS
LUMPIER
LUMPING
LUMPSUM

L•••P••
LEDUPTO
LILYPAD

L••••P•
LAPTOPS

LARRUPS
LASHUPS
LIMPOPO
LINEUPS
LINKUPS
LOCKUPS
LOOKUPS

L•••••P

LACEDUP
LACESUP
LEADSUP
LETSLIP
LIFTSUP
LIGHTUP
LINEDUP
LINESUP
LOCKSUP
LOOKSUP
LOUSEUP

•LP••••

ALPACAS

•L•P•••

BLIPPED
CLAPPED
CLAPPER
CLAPTON
CLIPART
CLIPONS
CLIPPED
CLIPPER
CLOPPED
ELAPIDS
ELAPSED
ELAPSES
ELOPERS
ELOPING
FLAPPED
FLAPPER
FLIPPED
FLIPPER
FLIPUPS
FLOPPED
FLYPAST
OLDPROS
PLOPPED
SLAPPED
SLEPTIN
SLEPTON
SLIPONS
SLIPOUT
SLIPPED
SLIPPER
SLIPSUP
SLIPUPS
SLOPING
SLOPPED

•L••P••

BLEEPED
BLEEPER
BLIPPED
BLOOPED
BLOOPER
CLAMPED
CLAPPED
CLAPPER
CLASPED
CLIPPED
CLIPPER
CLOPPED
CLUMPED
ELLIPSE
FLAPPED
FLAPPER
FLIPPED
FLIPPER
FLOPPED
GLIMPSE
OLYMPIA
OLYMPIC
OLYMPUS
PLAYPEN
PLOPPED
PLUMPED
PLUMPER
SLAPPED
SLEEPER
SLEEPIN
SLEEPON
SLIPPED
SLIPPER
SLOPPED
SLUMPED
SLURPED

•L•••P•

BLOWUPS
FLIPUPS
PLATYPI
SLIPUPS

•L••••P

BLOWNUP
BLOWSUP
CLAMSUP
CLEANUP
CLEARUP
CLOGSUP
CLOSEUP
FLAREUP
FLATTOP
FLYTRAP
OLDCHAP
PLAYSUP
SLIPSUP
SLOWSUP

••LP•••

CALPACS
CULPRIT
DOLPHIN
GULPING
HELPERS
HELPFUL
HELPING
HELPOUT
KELPIES
OILPANS
PULPITS
SULPHUR
VOLPONE
VULPINE
WALPOLE
YELPERS
YELPING

••L•P••

BULLPEN
CALIPER
CALIPHS
CALYPSO
ECLIPSE
ELLIPSE
GOLFPRO
HELIPAD
LILYPAD
RELAPSE

••L••P•

CCLAMPS
COLLOPS
DOLLOPS
FILLIPS
FILLUPS
FOLDUPS
GALLOPS
GALUMPH
HOLDUPS
PILEUPS
PULLUPS
WALKUPS
WALLOPS

••L•••P

BALLSUP
BELLHOP
BELLYUP
CALLSUP
DOLLSUP
FILLSUP
FOLDSUP
HILLTOP
HOLDSUP
HOLEDUP
HOLESUP
MILKSOP
OILLAMP
PILEDUP
PILESUP
PULLSUP
ROLLSUP
ROLLTOP
SPLITUP
TALKSUP
TALLYUP
WALLSUP
WELLSUP

•••LP••

ADOLPHE
BULLPEN
GUELPHS
SCALPED
SCALPEL
SCALPER
SCULPTS
WHELPED

•••L•P•

BURLAPS
COLLOPS
CYCLOPS
DEWLAPS
DOLLOPS
FILLIPS
FILLUPS
FOULUPS
GALLOPS
HOTLIPS
PULLUPS
RUNLAPS
SCHLEPP
SCHLEPS
WALLOPS

•••L••P

ARCLAMP
BALLSUP
BEDLAMP
BELLHOP
BELLYUP
BUILDUP
BUILTUP
CALLSUP
CHALKUP
COILSUP
CURLSUP
DOLLSUP
FILLSUP
FOULSUP
FOULTIP
HAULSUP
HEELTAP
HILLTOP
OILLAMP
PHILLIP
PULLSUP
ROLLSUP
ROLLTOP
SCALLOP
SCHLEPP
SEALSUP
SUNLAMP
SWELLUP
TALLYUP
TOELOOP
TOOLSUP
UNCLASP
WALLSUP
WELLSUP

••••LP•

CATALPA
RUDOLPH

••••L•P

COWSLIP
DEVELOP
EARFLAP
ENVELOP
KERPLOP
LETSLIP
NONSLIP
OVERLAP
PHILLIP
SCALLOP
SWELLUP
TIECLIP

L•Q••••

LIQUEFY
LIQUEUR
LIQUIDS
LIQUORS
LOQUATS

L••Q•••

LACQUER

L•••Q••

LALIQUE

•L•Q•••

CLAQUES
CLIQUES
CLOQUES
PLAQUES

••L•Q••

LALIQUE
OBLIQUE
OBLOQUY

L•R••••

LARAINE
LARAMIE
LARCENY
LARCHES
LARDERS
LARDING
LARDNER
LARDONS
LARGELY
LARGESS
LARGEST
LARIATS
LAROCHE
LARRUPS
LORDING
LORDJIM
LORELEI
LORENZO
LORETTA
LORISES
LORRIES
LURCHED
LURCHES
LURIDLY
LURKING
LYRICAL
LYRISTS

L••R•••

LABRETS
LAERTES
LAPROBE
LARRUPS
LAURELS
LAURENT
LEARJET
LEARNED
LEARNER
LEERERS
LEERIER
LEERILY
LEERING
LEERSAT
LEGROOM
LIBRARY
LIERNES
LIPREAD
LORRIES
LOURDES
LOUREED
LOWRISE
LOWROAD

L•••R••

LABORED
LABORER
LAFARGE
LAMARCK
LAMPREY
LAPORTE
LASORDA
LATERAL
LATERAN
LATERON
LAUTREC
LAVERNE
LAYERED
LAZARUS
LEBARON
LECARRE
LETTRES
LEVERED
LEVERET
LIBERAL
LIBERIA
LIBERTY
LITERAL
LITURGY
LIZARDS
LONGRUN
LONNROT
LOUVRES
LOVERLY
LOWBRED
LOWBROW
LOWERED
LUCERNE
LUSTRED
LUSTRES

L••••R•

LAAGERS
LABOURS
LADDERS
LADLERS
LAGGARD
LAGGERS
LAMBERT
LANCERS
LANDERS
LANFORD
LANGTRY
LANGURS
LANTERN
LANYARD
LARDERS
LASHERS
LASTORY
LATHERS
LATHERY
LAUNDRY
LAWFORD
LAWYERS
LEADERS
LEAKERS
LEANERS
LEAPERS
LEASERS
LECARRE
LECTERN
LECTORS
LECTURE
LEDGERS
LEERERS
LEEWARD
LEGHORN
LEGWORK
LEHAVRE
LEISURE
LEMPIRA
LENDERS
LEONARD
LEONORA
LEOPARD
LEOTARD
LESSORS
LETTERS
LEVIERS
LIBBERS
LIBRARY
LIFTERS
LIMBERS
LIMNERS
LINGERS
LINKERS
LIQUORS
LITTERS
LOADERS
LOAFERS
LOANERS
LOBBERS
LOCKERS
LODGERS
LOGGERS
LOITERS
LOMBARD
LOOKERS
LOOPERS
LOOTERS
LOPPERS
LOTTERY
LOUVERS
LOWBORN
LUBBERS
LUGGERS
LUMBARS
LUMBERS
LUMIERE
LUMPERS
LUNKERS
LUSTERS

L•••••R

LABELER
LABORER
LACQUER
LAIDFOR
LALAKER
LAMINAR
LANGUOR
LANKIER
LARDNER
LASSOER
LAUGHER
LAUNDER
LAYOVER
LAYSFOR
LEAFIER
LEAGUER
LEAKIER
LEANDER
LEARNER
LEATHER
LEERIER
LEGGIER
LEISTER
LEVELER
LIBELER
LIEOVER
LIGHTER
LINTIER
LIPPIER
LIQUEUR
LITTLER
LOAMIER
LOBBYER
LOBSTER
LOCATER
LOCATOR
LOESSER
LOFTIER
LOOKFOR
LOONIER
LOOPIER
LOUNGER
LOUSIER
LOWGEAR
LOWLIER
LUCIFER
LUCKIER
LUMPIER
LUNCHER
LUSTIER

•LR••••

ALREADY
ALRIGHT

•L•R•••

ALARCON
ALARMED
ALARMER
ALARUMS
ALDRICH
ALERTED
ALERTER
ALERTLY
ALFREDO
BLARING
BLARNEY
BLERIOT
BLURRED
BLURTED
CLARETS
CLARICE
CLARIFY
CLARION
CLARITY
CLERICS
CLERKED
CLORETS
ELGRECO
FLAREUP
FLARING
FLIRTED
FLORETS
FLORIDA
FLORINS
FLORIST
FLYRODS
GLARING
GLORIAS
GLORIED
GLORIES
GLORIFY
OLOROSO
PLURALS
SLURPED
SLURRED

•L••R••

ALBERTA
ALBERTO
ALGERIA
ALLERGY
ALLURED
ALLURES
ALSORAN
ALTERED
ALTERER
ALVAREZ
ALWORTH
BLEARED
BLURRED
CLAIROL
CLEARED
CLEARER
CLEARLY
CLEARUP
ELDERLY
ELMTREE
FLOORED
FLOURED
FLYTRAP
ILLBRED
OLDPROS
SLURRED

•L•••R•

ALFIERI
ALGEBRA
ALGIERS
ALLEARS
ALLEGRO
ALLHERE
BLAZERS
BLOWDRY
BLOWERS
CLAMORS
CLAWERS
CLIBURN
CLIPART
CLOSURE
CLOTURE
CLOVERS
ELATERS
ELECTRA
ELECTRO
ELEKTRA
ELIXIRS
ELKHART
ELOPERS
FLAKERS
FLAVORS
FLEXORS
FLOWERS
FLOWERY
GLAZERS
GLIDERS
GLOWERS
OLESTRA
PLACARD
PLACERS
PLANERS
PLATERS
PLAYERS
PLECTRA
PLENARY
PLEXORS
PLOVERS
PLOWERS
SLAVERS
SLAVERY
SLAYERS
SLICERS
SLIDERS
SLIVERS
ULSTERS

•L••••R

ALARMER
ALCAZAR
ALERTER
ALIENOR
ALIGNER
ALLAYER
ALLEGER
ALLOVER
ALLSTAR
ALTERER
ALUNSER
BLABBER
BLACKER
BLADDER
BLANDER
BLANKER
BLASTER
BLATHER
BLEAKER
BLEEPER
BLENDER
BLINDER
BLINKER
BLISTER
BLITHER
BLOCKER
BLONDER
BLOOMER
BLOOPER
BLOTTER
BLOWIER
BLUBBER
BLUFFER
BLUNDER
BLUNTER
BLUSHER
BLUSTER
CLABBER
CLAIMER
CLAMBER
CLAMMER
CLANGOR
CLAPPER
CLATTER
CLAVIER
CLAYIER
CLEANER
CLEARER
CLEAVER
CLIMBER
CLINKER
CLIPPER
CLOBBER
CLOCKER
CLOWDER
CLUBCAR
CLUNKER
CLUSTER
CLUTTER
ELEANOR
ELECTOR
FLAKIER
FLANEUR
FLANKER
FLAPPER
FLASHER
FLATCAR
FLATTER
FLAVOUR
FLEETER
FLEXNER
FLICKER
FLIPPER
FLITTER
FLIVVER
FLOATER
FLUSTER
FLUTTER
FLYOVER
GLACIER
GLADDER
GLAMOUR
GLAZIER
GLEANER
GLIBBER
GLIMMER
GLITTER
GLUMMER
OLDSTER
OLIVIER
PLAINER
PLANNER
PLANTAR
PLANTER
PLASTER
PLATTER
PLEADER
PLEASER
PLEDGER
PLODDER
PLOTTER
PLUGGER
PLUMBER
PLUMMER
PLUMPER
PLUNDER
PLUNGER
PLUSHER
SLACKER
SLAMMER
SLANDER
SLASHER
SLATHER
SLATIER
SLEDDER
SLEEKER
SLEEPER
SLENDER
SLICKER
SLIMIER
SLIMMER
SLINGER
SLIPPER
SLITHER
SLOBBER
SLOTCAR
SLUGGER
SLUMBER

••LR•••

AXLROSE
BULRUSH
MALRAUX
MELROSE
OILRIGS

••L•R••

AELFRIC
AILERON
ALLERGY
ALLURED
ALLURES
ATLARGE
BALDRIC
BOLEROS
BULLRUN
CALDRON
CALORIC
CALORIE
CHLORAL
COLORED
CULPRIT
DALTREY
DELIRIA
DOLORES
ENLARGE
FULCRUM
ILLBRED
MALAREN
MILDRED
MILKRUN
MILLRUN
MILORDS
PALERMO
PALFREY
PILGRIM
POLARIS
SALERNO
SCLERAS
SOLARIA
SPLURGE
TALARIA
TELERAN
VALERIE
WELLRUN
WILFRID
WOLFRAM

••L••R•

ALLEARS
ALLEGRO
ALLHERE
BALLARD
BULGARS
BULWARK
CALDERA
CALGARY
CALIBRE
CALLERS
CALVARY
CALVERT
CELEBRE
CELLARS
COLBERT
COLLARD
COLLARS
COLOURS
CULEBRA
CULTURE
CULVERT
DELBERT
DELVERS
DILLARD
DOLLARS
DULLARD
ECLAIRS
FALTERS
FELLERS
FILBERT
FILLERS
FILTERS
FOLDERS
FOLGERS
FOLKART
GALLERY
GILBERT
GILDERS
GILMORE
GOLFERS
GOLFPRO
HALTERS
HALYARD
HELLERS
HELOTRY
HELPERS
HILAIRE
HILLARY
HOLDERS
HOLLERS
HOLYARK
HULLERS
KILDARE
KILLERS
MALLARD
MILKERS
MILLARD
MILLERS
MOLDERS
MOLIERE
MOLTERS
MULLERS
PALEDRY
PALTERS
PELTERS
PILFERS
PILLARS
PILLORY
POLDERS
POLLERS
PULSARS
RELEARN
ROLLERS
SALIERI
SALTERS
SALVERS
SELKIRK
SELLERS
SILVERS
SILVERY
SOLDERS
SOLVERS
SULKERS
TALKERS
TELLERS
TILLERS
TILTERS
UNLEARN
VALOURS
VELOURS
VULTURE
WALDORF
WALKERS
WALMART
WALTERS
WELDERS
WELFARE
WELTERS
WILFORD
WILLARD
YELPERS

••L•••R

ALLAYER
ALLEGER
ALLOVER
ALLSTAR
BALFOUR
BALKIER
BALMIER
BELABOR
BELLJAR
BOLIVAR
BOLSTER
BULGHUR
BULKIER
CALIBER
CALIPER
CALLFOR
COLDWAR
COLLIER
COLLYER

DALLIER
DELAYER
DELIVER
DILUTER
FALLFOR
FELLFOR
FELTFOR
FILCHER
FILMIER
HILLIER
HOLSTER
HOLYWAR
JOLLIER
LALAKER
MALABAR
MALODOR
MILKIER
MOLDIER
PALAVER
PALMIER
PALOMAR
PILSNER
POLITER
POLYMER
ROLLBAR
SALAZAR
SALTIER
SELTZER
SILKIER
SILLIER
SOLDIER
SOLIDER
SPLICER
SULKIER
SULPHUR
TELSTAR
WALTZER

•••LR••

BULLRUN
FUELROD
MILLRUN
WELLRUN

•••L•R•

ABELARD
AMBLERS
ANGLERS
ANTLERS
ASHLARS
BAILERS
BAILORS
BALLARD
BAWLERS
BOILERS
BOWLERS
BUGLERS
BUTLERS
CABLERS
CALLERS
CELLARS
COALERS
COLLARD
COLLARS
COOLERS
CURLERS
CUTLERS
CUTLERY
CYCLERS
DEALERS
DECLARE
DEKLERK
DEPLORE
DIALERS
DILLARD
DOLLARS
DUELERS
DULLARD
EXPLORE
FAILURE
FEELERS
FELLERS
FILLERS
FOOLERY
FORLORN
FOULARD
FOWLERS
FUELERS
GALLERY
GAYLORD
HAULERS
HEALERS
HEELERS
HELLERS
HILLARY
HOLLERS
HOWLERS
HULLERS
HURLERS
IMPLORE
JAILERS
KEGLERS
KILLERS
LADLERS
MAILERS
MALLARD
MEWLERS
MILLARD
MILLERS
MOILERS
MULLERS
NAILERS
OSTLERS
PARLORS
PEDLARS
PEELERS
PHILTRE
PILLARS
PILLORY
POLLERS
POPLARS
POULTRY
RAILERS
RIFLERS
RIFLERY
ROLLERS
SAILORS
SCALARS
SCALERS
SEALERS
SELLERS
SKYLARK
SMILERS
STYLERS
SUTLERS
SWELTRY
TAILORS
TELLERS
THALERS
TILLERS
TOILERS
WAILERS
WARLORD
WHALERS
WILLARD
YOWLERS

•••L••R

ATELIER
BELLJAR
BOULDER
BUILDER
BURLIER
CALLFOR
CAULKER
CHILLER
COALCAR
COALTAR
COLLIER
COLLYER
COULTER
CRULLER
CURLIER
DALLIER
DRILLER
DROLLER
DWELLER
EARLIER
EVILLER
FALLFOR
FEELFOR
FELLFOR
FIELDER
GROLIER
GUILDER
HILLIER
JOLLIER
KEILLOR
LOWLIER
MANLIER
MEALIER
MOULDER
NUCLEAR
PARLOUR
PHILTER
PSALTER
QUILTER
REALTOR
ROLLBAR
SCALIER
SCALPER
SCOLDER
SCULLER
SHELLER
SHELTER
SILLIER
SKELTER
SKULKER
SMALLER
SMELTER
SMOLDER
SPELLER
STALKER
STELLAR
STILLER
STOLLER
SURLIER
SVELTER
SWELTER
UNCLEAR
VAULTER
WOOLIER
ZOELLER

••••LR•

CAVALRY
DEVILRY
JEWELRY
REVELRY
RIVALRY

••••L•R

ANGULAR
ANNULAR
AREOLAR
BAFFLER
BATTLER
BICOLOR
BIPOLAR
BOGGLER
BOOSLER
BOTTLER
BOWDLER
BRAWLER
BROILER
BUCKLER
BUMBLER
BUNGLER
BURGLAR
CACKLER
CAJOLER
CAROLER
CAVILER
CHILLER
COBBLER
CODDLER
CRAWLER
CRUELER
CRULLER
CUSSLER
DABBLER
DAIMLER
DANGLER
DAWDLER
DAZZLER
DEFILER
DIPOLAR
DOODLER
DOPPLER
DRILLER
DROLLER
DROOLER
DWELLER
EVILLER
FEEBLER
FICKLER
FIDDLER
FIEDLER
FRAILER
FUMBLER
GAMBLER
GENTLER
GIGGLER
GOBBLER
GROWLER
GUZZLER
HAGGLER
HANDLER
HECKLER
HOSTLER
HUMBLER
HURDLER
HUSTLER
INHALER
INSULAR
JEWELER
JOCULAR
JOSTLER
JUGGLER
JUGULAR
KEEBLER
KEILLOR
KNEELER
LABELER
LEVELER
LIBELER
LITTLER
MEDDLER
MINGLER
MODELER
MODULAR
MUDDLER
MUFFLER
MUMBLER
NEBULAR
NESTLER
NIBBLER
NIMBLER
NODULAR
NUZZLER
PADDLER
PEDDLER
POPULAR
PROWLER
PUZZLER
RAFFLER
RAMBLER
RATTLER
RECOLOR
REGULAR
REVELER
RIDDLER
RUSTLER
SADDLER
SAMPLER
SCHOLAR
SCOWLER
SCULLER
SECULAR
SETTLER
SHELLER
SIMILAR
SIMPLER
SMALLER
SPELLER
SPIELER
SPOILER
SQUALOR
STABLER
STAPLER
STEELER
STELLAR
STILLER
STOLLER
SUBTLER
SUPPLER
TABULAR
TACKLER
TATTLER
TEMBLOR
TEMPLAR
TICKLER
TIPPLER
TITULAR
TODDLER
TOFFLER
TRAILER
TRAWLER
TRIFLER
TUBULAR
TUMBLER
TUTELAR
TWIRLER
WADDLER
WAFFLER
WANGLER
WARBLER
WHEELER
WIGGLER
WINKLER
YODELER
ZOELLER

L•S••••

LASAGNA
LASAGNE
LASALLE
LASCALA
LASCAUX
LASHERS
LASHING
LASHUPS
LASORDA
LASSIES
LASSOED
LASSOER
LASSOES
LASTING
LASTORY
LESOTHO
LESPAUL
LESSEES
LESSENS
LESSING
LESSONS
LESSORS
LISPING
LISSOME
LISTEES
LISTELS
LISTENS
LISTING
LOSEOUT
LOSESIT
LOSTOUT
LUSHEST
LUSTERS
LUSTFUL
LUSTIER
LUSTILY
LUSTING
LUSTRED
LUSTRES

L••S•••

LAISSEZ
LANSING
LAPSING
LASSIES
LASSOED
LASSOER
LASSOES
LAWSUIT
LAYSFOR
LAYSLOW
LAYSOFF
LAYSOUT
LEASERS
LEASHED
LEASHES
LEASING
LEISTER
LEISURE
LESSEES
LESSENS
LESSING
LESSONS
LESSORS
LETSFLY
LETSLIP
LETSOFF
LETSOUT
LETSSEE
LIESLOW
LINSEED
LIPSYNC
LISSOME
LOBSTER
LOESSER
LOESSES
LOGSOFF
LOGSOUT
LOOSELY
LOOSENS
LOOSEST
LOOSING
LOUSEUP
LOUSIER
LOUSILY
LOUSING

L•••S••

LACESUP
LACOSTE
LAISSEZ
LANDSAT
LEADSIN
LEADSON
LEADSTO
LEADSUP
LEANSON
LEERSAT
LEGISTS
LETSSEE
LIAISED
LIAISES
LIAISON
LIFTSUP
LINDSAY
LINDSEY
LINESUP
LIVESIN
LIVESON
LOCKSUP
LOCUSTS
LOESSER
LOESSES
LOOKSAT
LOOKSEE
LOOKSIN
LOOKSON
LOOKSTO
LOOKSUP
LORISES
LOSESIT
LOTUSES
LUMPSUM
LUTISTS
LYRISTS

L••••S•

LACIEST
LACTASE
LACTOSE
LAMAISM
LAMAIST
LANKEST
LARGESS
LARGEST
LAVALSE
LAWLESS
LAXNESS
LAZIEST
LEANEST
LEFTIST
LEWDEST
LICENSE
LIDLESS
LIMIEST
LIMPEST
LIONESS
LITHEST
LOGIEST
LONGEST
LONGISH
LOOSEST
LOUDEST
LOWNESS
LOWRISE
LUSHEST

L•••••S

LAAGERS
LABIALS
LABOURS
LABRETS
LACINGS
LACKEYS
LACUNAS
LADDERS
LADDIES
LADINOS
LADLERS
LAERTES
LAGGERS
LAGOONS
LAGUNAS
LAKOTAS
LAMBDAS
LAMENTS
LAMINAS
LANCERS
LANCETS
LANDAUS
LANDERS
LANGURS
LAPDOGS
LAPFULS
LAPPETS
LAPTOPS
LARCHES
LARDERS
LARDONS
LARGESS
LARIATS
LARRUPS
LASHERS
LASHUPS
LASSIES
LASSOES
LATCHES
LATEENS
LATENTS
LATEXES
LATHERS
LATICES
LATINAS
LATINOS
LATTENS
LAURELS
LAWLESS
LAWYERS
LAXNESS
LAYOFFS
LAYOUTS
LAZARUS
LEACHES
LEADERS
LEADINS
LEAGUES
LEAKERS
LEANERS
LEANTOS
LEAPERS
LEASERS
LEASHES
LEAVENS
LECTORS
LEDGERS
LEECHES
LEERERS
LEFTIES
LEGATES
LEGATOS
LEGENDS
LEGIONS
LEGISTS
LEGUMES
LENDERS
LENGTHS
LENTILS
LEPTONS
LESSEES
LESSENS
LESSONS
LESSORS
LETTERS
LETTRES
LEVIERS
LEVITES
LIAISES
LIBBERS
LIBIDOS
LIBYANS
LICHENS
LIDLESS
LIENEES
LIERNES
LIFTERS
LIGATES
LIMBERS
LIMNERS
LIMOGES
LIMPETS
LINAGES
LINDENS
LINDIES
LINEUPS
LINGERS
LINGOES
LININGS
LINKERS
LINKUPS
LINNETS
LINTELS
LIONESS
LIONETS
LIQUIDS
LIQUORS
LISTEES
LISTELS
LISTENS
LITCHIS
LITOTES
LITTERS
LIVINGS
LIZARDS
LOACHES
LOADERS
LOAFERS
LOANERS
LOATHES
LOBBERS
LOBBIES
LOCALES
LOCATES
LOCKERS
LOCKETS
LOCKINS
LOCKUPS
LOCUSTS
LODGERS
LOESSES
LOGGERS
LOGGIAS
LOGGINS
LOGJAMS
LOITERS
LOLLIES
LONGUES
LOOFAHS
LOOKERS
LOOKUPS
LOONIES
LOOPERS
LOOSENS
LOOTERS
LOPPERS
LOQUATS
LORISES
LORRIES
LOTIONS
LOTUSES
LOUNGES
LOURDES
LOUVERS
LOUVRES
LOVEINS
LOWBOYS
LOWNESS
LUBBERS
LUGGERS
LUGNUTS
LUMBARS
LUMBERS
LUMPERS
LUNCHES
LUNKERS
LUPINES
LURCHES
LUSTERS
LUSTRES
LUTISTS
LUXATES
LYCEUMS
LYRISTS

•LS••••

ALSORAN
ULSTERS

•L•S•••

ALASKAN
ALLSTAR
ALLSTON
ALYSSUM
BLASTED
BLASTER
BLESSED
BLESSES
BLISTER
BLOSSOM
BLUSHED
BLUSHER
BLUSHES
BLUSTER
CLASHED
CLASHES
CLASPED
CLASSED
CLASSES
CLASSIC
CLOSEIN
CLOSELY
CLOSEST
CLOSETS
CLOSEUP
CLOSING
CLOSURE
CLUSTER
ELASTIC
ELISION
ELUSIVE
ELYSEES
ELYSIAN
ELYSIUM
FLASHED
FLASHER
FLASHES
FLESHED
FLESHES
FLOSSED
FLOSSES
FLUSHED
FLUSHES
FLUSTER
GLASGOW
GLASSED
GLASSES
GLISTEN
GLOSSAE
GLOSSED
GLOSSES
OLDSTER
OLESTRA
PLASHED
PLASHES
PLASMAS
PLASTER
PLASTIC
PLOSION
PLOSIVE
PLUSHER
PLUSHES
PLUSHLY
PLUSSES
SLASHED
SLASHER
SLASHES
SLOSHED
SLOSHES
SLUSHES
ULYSSES

•L••S••

ALIASES
ALLISON
ALLYSON
ALTOSAX
ALUNSER
ALYOSHA
ALYSSUM
BLESSED
BLESSES
BLOSSOM
BLOUSED
BLOUSES
BLOUSON
BLOWSIN
BLOWSIT
BLOWSUP
BLUESKY
CLAMSUP
CLASSED
CLASSES
CLASSIC
CLAUSES
CLEMSON
CLOGSUP
CLUESIN
ELAPSED
ELAPSES
ELEISON
ELLISON
ELMISTI
FLENSED
FLENSES
FLIESAT
FLIESIN
FLOSSED
FLOSSES
FLOTSAM
GLASSED
GLASSES
GLEASON
GLOSSAE
GLOSSED
GLOSSES
ILIESCU
ILLUSED
ILLUSES
KLATSCH
PLANSON
PLAYSAT
PLAYSON
PLAYSUP
PLEASED
PLEASER
PLEASES
PLUGSIN
PLUSSES
SLIPSUP
SLOWSUP
ULYSSES

•L•••S•

ALFONSO
BLEMISH
CLEANSE
CLOSEST
ELEGIST
ELITISM
ELITIST
ELLIPSE
FLEMISH
FLORIST
FLUTIST
FLYCAST
FLYFISH
FLYPAST
GLIMPSE
GLUCOSE
ILLNESS
OLDNESS
OLDWEST
OLEMISS
OLOROSO
SLAVISH
SLOWEST
SLYNESS

•L••••S

ALARUMS
ALBEDOS
ALBINOS
ALCOVES
ALGIERS
ALIASES
ALIGHTS
ALKALIS
ALKENES
ALLEARS
ALLEGES
ALLELES
ALLEYES
ALLUDES
ALLURES
ALMONDS
ALPACAS
ALUMNUS
BLAZERS
BLAZONS
BLESSES
BLIGHTS
BLITZES
BLONDES
BLOUSES
BLOWERS
BLOWUPS
BLUSHES
CLAMORS
CLAQUES
CLARETS
CLASHES
CLASSES
CLAUSES
CLAWERS
CLEAVES
CLEMENS
CLERICS
CLICHES
CLIENTS
CLINICS
CLIPONS
CLIQUES
CLOCHES
CLOQUES
CLORETS
CLOSETS
CLOTHES
CLOVERS
ELAPIDS
ELAPSES
ELATERS
ELEGIES
ELEVENS
ELICITS
ELIXIRS
ELOPERS
ELYSEES
FLACONS
FLAGONS
FLAKERS
FLAMBES
FLANGES
FLASHES
FLAUNTS
FLAVORS
FLECHES
FLEDGES
FLEECES

FLENSES
FLESHES
FLEXORS
FLIGHTS
FLIPUPS
FLORETS
FLORINS
FLOSSES
FLOWERS
FLUSHES
FLYBOYS
FLYNETS
FLYRODS
FLYWAYS
GLANCES
GLASSES
GLAZERS
GLIDERS
GLITZES
GLORIAS
GLORIES
GLOSSES
GLOTTIS
GLOWERS
ILLNESS
ILLUSES
KLAXONS
KLUDGES
KLUTZES
OLDDAYS
OLDNESS
OLDNEWS
OLDPROS
OLEATES
OLEMISS
OLYMPUS
PLACERS
PLAGUES
PLAICES
PLAINES
PLAINTS
PLANERS
PLANETS
PLAQUES
PLASHES
PLASMAS
PLATENS
PLATERS
PLAUTUS
PLAYERS
PLEASES
PLEDGES
PLENUMS
PLEXORS
PLIGHTS
PLINTHS
PLOUGHS
PLOVERS
PLOWERS
PLUNGES
PLURALS
PLUSHES
PLUSSES
SLALOMS
SLASHES
SLAVERS
SLAYERS
SLEDGES
SLEEVES
SLEIGHS
SLEUTHS
SLICERS
SLIDERS
SLIGHTS
SLIPONS
SLIPUPS
SLIVERS
SLOGANS
SLOSHES
SLOUGHS
SLOVAKS
SLOVENS
SLUDGES
SLUICES
SLUSHES
SLYNESS
ULSTERS
ULYSSES

••LS•••

ALLSTAR
ALLSTON
BALSAMS
BOLSHOI
BOLSTER
CELSIUS
EELSKIN
FALSELY
FALSEST
FALSIFY
FALSITY
FULSOME
HALSTON
HOLSTER
NELSONS
NILSSON
OILSKIN
PILSNER
PULSARS
PULSATE
PULSING
RALSTON
SALSIFY
SALSODA
TELSTAR
TOLSTOI
TOLSTOY
TULSANS

••L•S••

ALLISON
ALLYSON
ATLASES
BALLSUP
BELUSHI
BOLUSES
CALLSIN
CALLSON
CALLSUP
CELESTA
CELESTE
COLOSSI
DELISTS
DOLLSUP
ELLISON
ENLISTS
FALLSIN
FALLSON
FALLSTO
FILLSIN
FILLSUP
FOLDSUP
HOLDSON
HOLDSTO
HOLDSUP
HOLESUP
HOLYSEE
ILLUSED
ILLUSES
JALISCO
MALMSEY
MELISSA
MILKSOP
MOLESTS
NILSSON
OBLASTS
PELISSE
PILESIN
PILESON
PILESUP
PULASKI
PULLSUP
RELISTS
ROLLSUP
RULESON
SILESIA
SPLASHY
SULUSEA
TALKSAT
TALKSTO
TALKSUP
TALUSES
TELLSON
VALISES
WALLSUP
WELLSET
WELLSUP
WILLSON
YELLSAT
YELTSIN

••L••S•

ATLEAST
AXLROSE
BALDEST
BALLAST
BELFAST
BOLDEST
BULLISH
BULRUSH
CALMEST
CALYPSO
CELLIST
COLDEST
COLOSSI
COLTISH
CULTISH
CULTISM
CULTIST
DELUISE
DOLTISH
DULLEST
DULLISH
ECLIPSE
EELIEST
ELLIPSE
FALSEST
FULLEST
HELOISE
HOLIEST
ILLNESS
MALAISE
MALTESE
MALTOSE
MELISSA
MELROSE
MILDEST
MOLLUSK
OILIEST
PALMIST
PELISSE
POLOIST
RELAPSE
RELEASE
SELFISH
SOLOIST
TALLEST
TALLISH
UGLIEST
UNLEASH
UNLOOSE
WILDEST
WILIEST
WOLFISH

••L•••S

ABLATES
ABLAUTS
ALLEARS
ALLEGES
ALLELES
ALLEYES
ALLUDES
ALLURES
ATLASES
ATLATLS
BALBOAS
BALEENS
BALKANS
BALLADS
BALLETS
BALLOTS
BALSAMS
BELCHES
BELDAMS
BELIEFS
BELLIES
BELLOWS
BELONGS
BILBOES
BILIOUS
BILLETS
BILLIES
BILLOWS
BOLEROS
BOLIDES
BOLUSES
BULBOUS
BULBULS
BULGARS
BULLETS
BULLIES
BYLINES
CALENDS
CALICOS
CALIPHS
CALKINS
CALLERS
CALLINS
CALLOUS
CALPACS
CALYCES
CALYXES
CCLAMPS
CELEBES
CELLARS
CELSIUS
CELTICS
COLLARS
COLLETS
COLLIES
COLLINS
COLLOPS
COLOBUS
COLONES
COLOURS
COLUMNS
CSLEWIS
DALLIES
DELETES
DELIBES
DELICTS
DELISTS
DELUDES
DELUGES
DELVERS
DILATES
DILLIES
DILUTES
DOLLARS
DOLLIES
DOLLOPS
DOLMANS
DOLMENS
DOLORES
ECLAIRS
ENLACES
ENLISTS
EOLITHS
FALCONS
FALLOWS
FALTERS
FELINES
FELLERS
FELLOWS
FILCHES
FILINGS
FILLERS
FILLETS
FILLIES
FILLINS
FILLIPS
FILLUPS
FILTERS
FOLDERS
FOLDUPS
FOLGERS
FOLLIES
FOLLOWS
FULFILS
GALLEYS
GALLONS
GALLOPS
GALOOTS
GELADAS
GELATIS
GILBLAS
GILDERS
GILLIES
GOLFERS
GULCHES
GULLETS
GULLIES
HALITES
HALLOWS
HALTERS
HELICES
HELIXES
HELLERS
HELMETS
HELPERS
HOLDERS
HOLDUPS
HOLLERS
HOLLIES
HOLLOWS
HULLERS
ILLNESS
ILLUSES
ISLANDS
JELLIES
JOLLIES
KELPIES
KILLERS
KILTIES
KYLIKES
LOLLIES
MALIGNS
MALLETS
MALLOWS
MALTEDS
MALTHUS
MELLOWS
MILDEWS
MILIEUS
MILKERS
MILLERS
MILLETS
MILORDS
MOLDERS
MOLESTS
MOLTERS
MULCHES
MULETAS
MULLAHS
MULLERS
MULLETS
NELSONS
OBLASTS
OBLATES
OBLIGES
OBLONGS
OGLALAS
OILCANS
OILPANS
OILRIGS
OOLITES
OOLITHS
ORLEANS
PALACES
PALATES
PALLETS
PALTERS
PELAGES
PELLETS
PELOTAS
PELTERS
PHLOXES
PILEUPS
PILFERS
PILINGS
PILLARS
PILLOWS
POLARIS
POLDERS
POLICES
POLLENS
POLLERS
PULLETS
PULLEYS
PULLONS
PULLUPS
PULPITS
PULSARS
RALLIES
RELACES
RELATES
RELAXES
RELENTS
RELICTS
RELIEFS
RELINES
RELISTS
RELIVES
RELOADS
RELOCKS
RILLETS
ROLAIDS
ROLLERS
ROLLINS
RULINGS
SALAAMS
SALAMIS
SALLIES
SALMONS
SALOONS
SALTERS
SALUKIS
SALUTES
SALVERS
SALVOES
SCLERAS
SELECTS
SELLERS
SILENTS
SILICAS
SILLIES
SILVERS
SOLACES
SOLDERS
SOLUTES
SOLVERS
SPLEENS
SPLICES
SPLINES
SPLINTS
STLOUIS
SULKERS
SULKIES
SULLIES
SULTANS
SYLVANS
TALENTS
TALKERS
TALKIES
TALLIES
TALLOWS
TALUSES
TELEXES
TELLERS
TELLIES
TILLERS
TILTERS
TOLTECS
TULSANS
UMLAUTS
UNLACES
UNLADES
UNLINKS
UNLOADS
UNLOCKS
UPLANDS
UPLIFTS
UPLINKS
UPLOADS
VALISES
VALLEYS
VALOURS
VELLUMS
VELOURS
VELVETS
VOLLEYS
VOLUMES
VULCANS
WALKERS
WALKINS
WALKONS
WALKUPS
WALLETS
WALLOPS
WALLOWS
WALNUTS
WALTERS
WALTZES
WELCHES
WELDERS
WELKINS
WELTERS
WILLIES
WILLOWS
YELLOWS
YELPERS
ZILCHES

•••LS••

ARALSEA
AVULSED
AVULSES
BALLSUP
CALLSIN
CALLSON
CALLSUP
CARLSON
CHELSEA
COILSUP
COOLSIT
CURLSUP
DEALSIN
DOLLSUP
EVULSED
EVULSES
FALLSIN
FALLSON
FALLSTO
FILLSIN
FILLSUP
FOULSUP
HAULSUP
NAILSET
NIELSEN
PAULSEN
PULLSUP
RAILSAT
REELSIN
ROLLSUP
SEALSUP
TELLSON
TOOLSUP
WALLSUP
WELLSET
WELLSUP
WILLSON
WOOLSEY
YELLSAT

•••L•S•

ABOLISH
AGELESS
AIMLESS
AIRLESS
AMPLEST
AMYLASE
ANALYSE
ANALYST
ARMLESS
ARTLESS
ASHLESS
ATALOSS
AWELESS
BALLAST
BULLISH
CAPLESS
CARLESS
CELLIST
COOLEST
CUTLASS
CYCLIST
DECLASS
DUELIST
DULLEST
DULLISH
ENCLOSE
ENDLESS
ENGLISH
EVILEST
EYELASH
FATLESS
FOOLISH
FOULEST
FULLEST
GETLOST
GIRLISH
GOULASH
GUTLESS
HAPLESS
HATLESS
HITLESS
HITLIST
ICELESS
INCLOSE
JAGLESS
JOYLESS
LAWLESS
LIDLESS
MOLLUSK
NOBLEST
OARLESS
OBELISK
OCULIST
OUTLAST
PAULIST
PINLESS
PUBLISH
REALISM
REALIST
RECLUSE
STALEST
STYLISH
STYLIST
SUNLESS
TALLEST
TALLISH
TBILISI
TIELESS
TITLIST
TOELESS
UNBLEST
UNCLASP
UNCLOSE
UPCLOSE
USELESS
VIOLIST
WITLESS

•••L••S

AGELESS
AIMLESS
AIRLESS
AMBLERS
AMULETS
ANALOGS
ANGLERS
ANKLETS
ANTLERS
APPLIES
ARMLESS
ARMLETS
ARTLESS
ASHLARS
ASHLESS
ASYLUMS
ATALOSS
AUKLETS
AVULSES
AWELESS
AZALEAS
BAILEES
BAILERS
BAILEYS
BAILORS
BALLADS
BALLETS
BALLOTS
BARLEYS
BAWLERS
BELLIES
BELLOWS
BIALIES
BILLETS
BILLIES
BILLOWS
BOILERS
BOWLERS
BUGLERS
BULLETS
BULLIES
BURLAPS
BUTLERS
BYPLAYS
CABLERS
CALLERS
CALLINS
CALLOUS
CAPLESS
CAPLETS
CARLESS
CELLARS
CHALETS
CHALLIS
CHILIES
CHOLLAS
COALERS
COALGAS
COLLARS
COLLETS
COLLIES
COLLINS
COLLOPS
COOLERS
COULEES
CURLERS
CURLEWS
CUTLASS
CUTLERS
CUTLETS
CYCLERS
CYCLOPS
DAHLIAS
DAILIES
DALLIES
DEALERS
DECLASS
DEPLOYS
DEWLAPS
DIALERS
DIALOGS
DILLIES
DOGLEGS
DOILIES
DOLLARS
DOLLIES
DOLLOPS
DUELERS
DUNLINS
EAGLETS
EMBLEMS
EMPLOYS
ENDLESS
EPILOGS
EVOLVES
EVULSES
EYELETS
EYELIDS
FALLOWS
FATLESS
FEELERS
FEELIES
FELLERS
FELLOWS
FILLERS
FILLETS
FILLIES
FILLINS
FILLIPS
FILLUPS
FOLLIES
FOLLOWS
FOULUPS
FOWLERS
FROLICS
FUELERS
GALLEYS
GALLONS
GALLOPS
GIBLETS
GIBLUES
GILLIES
GIMLETS
GOALIES
GOBLETS
GOBLINS
GRILLES
GUELPHS
GULLETS
GULLIES
GUTLESS
HALLOWS
HAMLETS
HAPLESS
HATLESS
HAULERS
HEALERS
HEELERS
HELLERS
HITLESS
HOLLERS
HOLLIES
HOLLOWS
HOTLIPS
HOWLERS
HULLERS
HURLERS
ICELESS
IMPLIES
INFLOWS
ITALICS
JAGLESS
JAILERS
JEALOUS
JELLIES
JOBLOTS
JOLLIES
JOYLESS
KEGLERS
KILLERS
LADLERS
LAWLESS
LIDLESS
LOLLIES
MADLIBS
MAILERS
MALLETS
MALLOWS
MARLINS
MEALIES
MEDLEYS
MELLOWS
MERLOTS
MEWLERS
MILLERS
MILLETS
MISLAYS
MOILERS
MOSLEMS
MUKLUKS
MULLAHS
MULLERS
MULLETS
MUSLIMS
MUSLINS
NAILERS
NUCLEUS
NUTLETS
OARLESS
OCELOTS
ODDLOTS
OMELETS
OSTLERS
OUTLAWS
OUTLAYS
OUTLETS
PABLUMS
PAILOUS
PALLETS
PARLAYS
PARLEYS
PARLORS
PARLOUS
PEDLARS
PEELERS
PELLETS
PEPLUMS
PHYLLIS
PIGLETS
PILLARS
PILLOWS
PINLESS
PIOLETS
POLLENS
POLLERS
POPLARS
POPLINS
PRELIMS
PROLOGS
PUBLICS
PULLETS
PULLEYS
PULLONS
PULLUPS
PURLINS
RAGLANS
RAILERS
RALLIES
REGLUES
REPLANS
REPLAYS
REPLIES
RIFLERS
RILLETS
ROLLERS
ROLLINS
RUNLAPS
RUNLETS
SAILORS
SALLIES
SANLUIS
SAWLOGS
SCALARS
SCALERS
SCHLEPS
SCULPTS
SEALABS
SEALEGS
SEALERS
SELLERS
SHALOMS
SHELVES
SILLIES
SLALOMS
SMALTOS
SMILERS
STALAGS
STOLONS
STYLERS
STYLETS
SUBLETS
SULLIES
SUNLESS
SUSLIKS
SUTLERS
TABLETS
TAILLES
TAILORS
TALLIES
TALLOWS
TELLERS
TELLIES
THALERS
TIELESS
TILLERS
TOELESS
TOILERS
TOILETS
TRELLIS
TWELVES
UNCLOGS
UNPLUGS
USELESS
VALLEYS
VARLETS
VELLUMS
VIOLETS
VIOLINS
VOLLEYS
WAILERS
WALLETS
WALLOPS
WALLOWS
WAYLAYS

WHALERS
WIGLETS
WILLIES
WILLOWS
WITLESS
WOOLENS
WOOLIES
YELLOWS
YOWLERS
ZEALOTS
ZEALOUS

••••LS•

IMPULSE
LAVALSE
REPULSE

••••L•S

AEDILES
ALKALIS
ALLELES
AMPULES
ANGELES
ANGELUS
ANNULUS
APPALLS
AREOLAS
ARGYLES
BABBLES
BAFFLES
BANGLES
BASALTS
BATTLES
BAUBLES
BEADLES
BEAGLES
BEATLES
BECALMS
BEETLES
BEFALLS
BEHOLDS
BOBBLES
BOGGLES
BOODLES
BOTTLES
BRIDLES
BUBBLES
BUCKLES
BUMBLES
BUNDLES
BUNGLES
BURBLES
BURGLES
BUSTLES
CABALAS
CACKLES
CAJOLES
CANDLES
CANTLES
CAROLES
CAROLUS
CASTLES
CHABLIS
CHALLIS
CHARLES
CHOLLAS
CIRCLES
COBBLES
COCKLES
CODDLES
COUPLES
CRADLES
CREOLES
CUDDLES
CUMULUS
CUPOLAS
CURDLES
DABBLES
DANDLES
DANGLES
DAPPLES
DAWDLES
DAZZLES
DECKLES
DEDALUS
DEFILES
DESALTS
DIBBLES
DIDDLES
DIMPLES
DINGLES
DIPOLES
DOODLES
DOTTLES
DOUBLES
DOUGLAS
EDIBLES
ENABLES
ENFOLDS
ENGULFS
ENISLES
ENROLLS
ENSILES
ETOILES
EXHALES
FAMULUS
FEMALES
FERULES
FETTLES
FIBULAS
FIDDLES
FINALES
FIPPLES
FIZZLES
FOCSLES
FOIBLES
FONDLES
FOOZLES
FUDDLES
FUMBLES
GABBLES
GAGGLES
GAMBLES
GARBLES
GARGLES
GENTLES
GIGGLES
GIGOLOS
GILBLAS
GIRDLES
GOBBLES
GOGGLES
GRILLES
GURGLES
GUZZLES
HACKLES
HAGGLES
HANDLES
HASSLES
HECKLES
HEDDLES
HERALDS
HGWELLS
HOBBLES
HOOPLAS
HOWELLS
HUDDLES
HUMBLES
HURDLES
HURTLES
HUSTLES
ICICLES
IMPALAS
IMPALES
INGALLS
INHALES
INSOLES
INSULTS
JANGLES
JIGGLES
JINGLES
JOGGLES
JOSTLES
JUGGLES
JUMBLES
JUNGLES
KETTLES
KIBBLES
KINDLES
KIRTLES
KOBOLDS
LOCALES
MANGLES
MANTLES
MARBLES
MCCALLS
MEASLES
MEDDLES
METTLES
MIDDLES
MINGLES
MIZZLES
MOBILES
MODELAS
MODELTS
MODULES
MORALES
MOTTLES
MUDDLES
MUFFLES
MUMBLES
MUSCLES
MUZZLES
MYRTLES
NEBULAS
NEEDLES
NEPALIS
NESTLES
NETTLES
NIBBLES
NICOLAS
NIGGLES
NODULES
NOGALES
NONPLUS
NOODLES
NOZZLES
NUBBLES
NUZZLES
OCCULTS
OGLALAS
ORACLES
ORIOLES
ORMOLUS
PADDLES
PAROLES
PAYOLAS
PEBBLES
PEDDLES
PEEPLES
PENULTS
PEOPLES
PESTLES
PHYLLIS
PICKLES
PIFFLES
POMELOS
POODLES
POPPLES
PUDDLES
PUEBLOS
PURFLES
PURPLES
PUZZLES
RABBLES
RADDLES
RAFFLES
RAMBLES
RANKLES
RASSLES
RATTLES
REBOLTS
RECALLS
REFILLS
REFILMS
REGALES
REGULUS
REMELTS
REMOLDS
REPOLLS
RESALES
RESALTS
RESELLS
RESILES
RESOLES
RESULTS
RETELLS
RETILES
REVILES
REVOLTS
REWELDS
RICKLES
RIDDLES
RIFFLES
RIPPLES
ROMULUS
RUBBLES
RUFFLES
RUMBLES
RUMPLES
RUSTLES
SADDLES
SAMPLES
SAVALAS
SCROLLS
SETTLES
SHEILAS
SHIELDS
SHRILLS
SICKLES
SIMILES
SINGLES
SIZZLES
SOMALIS
SQUALLS
STABLES
STAPLES
STIFLES
STROLLS
SURPLUS
TACKLES
TAILLES
TAMALES
TANGLES
TATTLES
TEMPLES
THRALLS
THRILLS
TICKLES
TINGLES
TINKLES
TIPPLES
TITTLES
TODDLES
TOGGLES
TOOTLES
TOPPLES
TOUSLES
TREBLES
TRELLIS
TRIFLES
TRIPLES
TROILUS
TUMBLES
TUMULTS
TUMULUS
TUPELOS
TURTLES
TUSSLES
UNBOLTS
UNFOLDS
UNPILES
UNROLLS
UPHOLDS
VITTLES
VIZSLAS
WADDLES
WAFFLES
WAGGLES
WAMBLES
WANGLES
WARBLES
WATTLES
WIGGLES
WIMPLES
WOBBLES

•••••LS

AERIALS
ANIMALS
ANNEALS
ANNUALS
APPALLS
APPEALS
ARMFULS
ASSAILS
ATLATLS
AVOWALS
BAGFULS
BARBELS
BARRELS
BEFALLS
BEFOULS
BENGALS
BETHELS
BEWAILS
BOXFULS
BRIDALS
BULBULS
BUSHELS
CANCELS
CAPFULS
CARFULS
CARPALS
CARRELS
CARTELS
CASUALS
CEREALS
CHAPELS
CHISELS
CHORALS
COEVALS
COMPELS
CONSULS
CORBELS
CORRALS
CRENELS
CREWELS
CUDGELS
CUPFULS
CYMBALS
DACTYLS
DAMSELS
DANIELS
DENIALS
DERAILS
DETAILS
DIESELS
DIRNDLS
DISPELS
DORSALS
DOSSALS
DRIVELS
DUFFELS
EARFULS
ENAMELS
ENROLLS
ENSOULS
ENTAILS
ESPIALS
EYEFULS
FACIALS
FIBRILS
FINIALS
FORMALS
FOSSILS
FULFILS
FUNNELS
GAMBOLS
GAVIALS
GERBILS
GIMBALS
GOOGOLS
GOSPELS
GRAVELS
GROVELS
GUNNELS
HERBALS
HGWELLS
HOSTELS
HOWELLS
HYMNALS
INGALLS
INSTILS
ISOHELS
JACKALS
JARFULS
JUGFULS
KENNELS
KERNELS
LABIALS
LAPFULS
LAURELS
LENTILS
LINTELS
LISTELS
MAMMALS
MANTELS
MANUALS
MARCELS
MARVELS
MCCALLS
MENIALS
MESCALS
MISSALS
MONGOLS
MORSELS
MORTALS
MUDEELS
MUSSELS
MUTUALS
NARWALS
NICHOLS
NICKELS
NORMALS
ORDEALS
PARCELS
PASSELS
PASTELS
PATROLS
PENCILS
PENPALS
PETRELS
PHENOLS
PISTILS
PISTOLS
PLURALS
POMMELS
PORTALS
POTFULS
PROPELS
PUMMELS
RADIALS
RAPPELS
RASCALS
REBOILS
RECALLS
RECOILS
REDEALS
REDIALS
REFILLS
REFUELS
REHEALS
REHEELS
REMAILS
RENAILS
RENTALS
REPEALS
REPOLLS
RESEALS
RESELLS
RETAILS
RETELLS
RETOOLS
REVEALS
RITUALS
RONDELS
RUNNELS
SANDALS
SCHOOLS
SCRAWLS
SCROLLS
SEIDELS
SEQUELS
SERIALS
SERVALS
SHEKELS
SHOVELS
SHRILLS
SIGNALS
SNIVELS
SOCIALS
SORRELS
SPINELS
SPIRALS
SPRAWLS
SQUALLS
SQUEALS
STEROLS
STROLLS
SWIVELS
SYMBOLS
TARSALS
TASSELS
TEASELS
TERCELS
THRALLS
THRILLS
TIMBALS
TINSELS
TONSILS
TRAVELS
TROWELS
TUNNELS
UNCIALS
UNCOILS
UNCURLS
UNFURLS
UNREELS
UNROLLS
UNSEALS
UNVEILS
VANDALS
VASSALS
VATFULS
VERBALS
VESSELS
VISUALS
WEASELS
WEEVILS

L•T••••

LATCHED
LATCHES
LATEENS
LATENCY
LATENTS
LATERAL
LATERAN
LATERON
LATEXES
LATHERS
LATHERY
LATHING
LATICES
LATIFAH
LATINAS
LATINOS
LATTENS
LATTICE
LATVIAN
LETDOWN
LETINON
LETITBE
LETITIA
LETSFLY
LETSLIP
LETSOFF
LETSOUT
LETSSEE
LETTERS
LETTING
LETTRES
LETTUCE
LITCHIS
LITERAL
LITHELY
LITHEST
LITHGOW
LITHIUM
LITINTO
LITOTES
LITTERS
LITTLER
LITURGY
LOTIONS
LOTTERY
LOTTING
LOTUSES
LUTISTS

L••T•••

LACTASE
LACTATE
LACTEAL
LACTOSE
LANTANA
LANTERN
LAOTIAN
LAPTOPS
LASTING
LASTORY
LATTENS
LATTICE
LAUTREC
LEATHER
LECTERN
LECTORS
LECTURE
LEETIDE
LEFTIES
LEFTIST
LEFTOFF
LEFTOUT
LENTILS
LEOTARD
LEPTONS
LETTERS
LETTING
LETTRES
LETTUCE
LIFTERS
LIFTING
LIFTOFF
LIFTSUP
LILTING
LINTELS
LINTIER
LISTEES
LISTELS
LISTENS
LISTING
LITTERS
LITTLER
LOATHED
LOATHES
LOFTIER
LOFTILY
LOFTING
LOITERS
LOOTERS
LOOTING
LOSTOUT
LOTTERY
LOTTING
LOWTECH
LOWTIDE
LUSTERS
LUSTFUL
LUSTIER
LUSTILY
LUSTING
LUSTRED
LUSTRES

L•••T••

LAERTES
LAFITTE
LAKOTAS
LAMOTTA
LANGTRY
LAYETTE
LEANTOS
LEGATEE
LEGATES
LEGATOS
LEISTER
LENGTHS
LENGTHY
LESOTHO
LETITBE
LETITIA
LEVITES
LICITLY
LIGATED
LIGATES
LIGHTED
LIGHTEN
LIGHTER
LIGHTLY
LIGHTUP
LIMITED
LITOTES
LOBSTER
LOCATED
LOCATER
LOCATES
LOCATOR
LONGTON
LORETTA
LUNATIC
LUXATED
LUXATES

L••••T•

LABIATE
LABRETS
LACOSTE
LACTATE
LAFITTE
LAMENTS
LAMOTTA
LANCETS
LAPLATA
LAPORTE
LAPPETS
LARIATS
LATENTS
LAYETTE
LAYINTO
LAYOUTS
LEADSTO
LEDUPTO
LEGISTS
LEPANTO
LIBERTY
LICKETY
LIGNITE
LIMPETS
LINEATE
LINNETS
LIONETS
LITINTO
LOCKETS
LOCUSTS
LOOKSTO
LOQUATS
LORETTA
LOYALTY
LUGNUTS
LUTISTS
LYINGTO
LYRISTS

L•••••T

LABCOAT
LACIEST
LAIDOUT
LAMAIST
LAMBENT
LAMBERT
LANDSAT
LANKEST
LAPBELT
LARGEST
LAUGHAT
LAURENT
LAWSUIT
LAYSOUT
LAZIEST
LEADOUT
LEAFLET
LEANEST
LEARJET
LEERSAT
LEFTIST
LEFTOUT
LENFANT
LENIENT
LETSOUT
LEVERET
LEWDEST
LIFENET
LIMIEST
LIMPEST
LITHEST
LIVEOUT
LOCKNUT
LOCKOUT
LOGIEST
LOGSOUT
LONGEST
LONNROT
LOOKOUT
LOOKSAT
LOOSEST
LOSEOUT
LOSESIT
LOSTOUT
LOUDEST
LUCKOUT
LUNGEAT
LUSHEST

•LT••••

ALTERED
ALTERER
ALTOONA
ALTOSAX

•L•T•••

ALLTIME
ALLTOLD
BLATANT
BLATHER
BLATTED
BLITHER
BLITZED
BLITZEN
BLITZES
BLOTCHY
BLOTOUT
BLOTTED
BLOTTER
CLATTER
CLOTHED
CLOTHES
CLOTTED
CLOTURE
CLUTTER
ELATERS
ELATING
ELATION
ELITISM
ELITIST
ELMTREE
ELUTING
ELUTION
FLATBED
FLATCAR
FLATOUT
FLATTED
FLATTEN
FLATTER
FLATTOP
FLITTED
FLITTER
FLOTSAM
FLUTING
FLUTIST
FLUTTER
FLYTRAP
GLITTER
GLITZED
GLITZES
GLOTTAL
GLOTTIS
GLUTTED
GLUTTON
KLATSCH
KLUTZES
OLDTIME
PLATEAU
PLATENS
PLATERS
PLATING
PLATOON
PLATTER
PLATYPI
PLOTTED
PLOTTER
SLATHER
SLATIER
SLATING
SLATKIN
SLATTED
SLITHER
SLOTCAR
SLOTTED
ULSTERS

•L••T••

ALERTED
ALERTER
ALERTLY
ALLSTAR
ALLSTON
BLASTED
BLASTER
BLATTED
BLEATED
BLISTER
BLOATED
BLOTTED
BLOTTER
BLUNTED
BLUNTER
BLUNTLY
BLURTED
BLUSTER
CLAPTON
CLATTER
CLAYTON
CLIFTON
CLINTON
CLOTTED
CLOUTED
CLUSTER
CLUTTER
ELASTIC
ELECTED
ELECTEE
ELECTOR
ELECTRA
ELECTRO
ELEKTRA
FLATTED
FLATTEN
FLATTER
FLATTOP
FLEETER
FLEETLY
FLIRTED
FLITTED
FLITTER
FLOATED
FLOATER
FLOUTED
FLUSTER
FLUTTER
GLINTED
GLISTEN
GLITTER
GLOATED
GLOTTAL
GLOTTIS
GLUTTED
GLUTTON
OLDSTER
OLEATES
OLESTRA
PLAITED
PLANTAR
PLANTED
PLANTER
PLASTER
PLASTIC
PLATTER
PLAUTUS
PLEATED
PLECTRA
PLINTHS
PLOTTED
PLOTTER
SLANTED
SLATTED
SLAYTON
SLEETED
SLEPTIN

SLEPTON
SLEUTHS
SLOTTED

•L•••T•

ALBERTA
ALBERTO
ALDENTE
ALIGHTS
ALMAATA
ALWORTH
BLIGHTS
CLARETS
CLARITY
CLIENTS
CLIMATE
CLINGTO
CLORETS
CLOSETS
ELEVATE
ELICITS
ELLIOTT
ELMISTI
FLAUNTS
FLIGHTS
FLIGHTY
FLOCKTO
FLORETS
FLYNETS
KLAMATH
PLACATE
PLAINTS
PLANETS
PLIGHTS
SLIGHTS
ULULATE

•L••••T

ALIMENT
ALRIGHT
BLANKET
BLATANT
BLERIOT
BLEWOUT
BLINKAT
BLOTOUT
BLOWOUT
BLOWSIT
CLEMENT
CLIPART
CLOSEST
ELEGANT
ELEGIST
ELEMENT
ELITIST
ELKHART
ELLIOTT
FLATOUT
FLIESAT
FLORIST
FLUTIST
FLYCAST
FLYPAST
ILLICIT
OLDWEST
PLACKET
PLAUDIT
PLAYACT
PLAYLET
PLAYOUT
PLAYSAT
PLUMMET
SLEIGHT
SLIPOUT
SLOWEST
TLINGIT
ULULANT

••LT•••

ALLTIME
ALLTOLD
BELTANE
BELTING
BELTWAY
BOLTING
CALTECH
CELTICS
COLTISH
CULTISH
CULTISM
CULTIST
CULTJAM
CULTURE
DALTREY
DELTAIC
DELTOID
DOLTISH
FALTERS
FELTFOR
FELTOUT
FILTERS
HALTERS
HALTING
JILTING
JOLTING
KILTIES
KILTING
LILTING
MALTEDS
MALTESE
MALTHUS
MALTING
MALTOSE
MELTING
MOLTERS
MOLTING
PALTERS
PELTATE
PELTERS
PELTING
SALTBOX
SALTERS
SALTIER
SALTILY
SALTINE
SALTING
SELTZER
SILTING
SULTANA
SULTANS
TILTERS
TILTING
TOLTECS
VOLTAGE
VOLTAIC
VULTURE
WALTERS
WALTZED
WALTZER
WALTZES
WELTERS
WELTING
WILTING
YELTSIN

••L•T••

ABLATED
ABLATES
ALLSTAR
ALLSTON
ATLATLS
BALATON
BELATED
BOLOTIE
BOLSTER
COLETTE
CULOTTE
DELETED
DELETES
DILATED
DILATES
DILUTED
DILUTER
DILUTES
EOLITHS
GALATEA
GALATIA
GELATIN
GELATIS
GOLFTEE
HALITES
HALSTON
HELOTRY
HILLTOP
HOLSTER
KILOTON
MILITIA
MOLOTOV
MULCTED
MULETAS
OBLATES
OOLITES
OOLITHS
PALATAL
PALATES
PALETTE
PELOTAS
PILOTED
POLITER
POLITIC
POLLTAX
PULLTAB
RALSTON
RELATED
RELATES
ROLLTOP
SALUTED
SALUTES
SOLUTES
SPLITUP
SPLOTCH
TELSTAR
TOLSTOI
TOLSTOY
UNLATCH

••L••T•

ABLAUTS
APLENTY
ATLANTA
BALLETS
BALLOTS
BILLETS
BULLETS
BULLITT
CALCITE
CELESTA
CELESTE
CILIATE
COLETTE
COLGATE
COLLATE
COLLETS
CULOTTE
DELICTI
DELICTS
DELISTS
ELLIOTT
ENLISTS
FALLSTO
FALSITY
FILLETS
FOLIATE
FOLLETT
GALOOTS
GOLIATH
GULLETS
HELMETS
HOLDSTO
JOLLITY
MALEATE
MALLETS
MILLETS
MILLETT
MOLESTS
MULLETS
OBLASTS
PALETTE
PALLETS
PALMATE
PELLETS
PELTATE
POLENTA
POLLUTE
PULLETS
PULPITS
PULSATE
RALLYTO
RELENTS
RELICTS
RELISTS
RILLETS
SELECTS
SILENTS
SPLINTS
SULFATE
SULFITE
TALENTS
TALKSTO
UMLAUTS
UPLIFTS
VALUATE
VELVETS
VELVETY
VULGATE
WALCOTT
WALLETS
WALNUTS

••L•••T

AILMENT
ATLEAST
BALDEST
BALLAST
BELFAST
BELMONT
BOLDEST
BULBLET
BULLITT
CALLOUT
CALMEST
CALUMET
CALVERT
CELLIST
COLBERT
COLDCUT
COLDEST
COLLECT
CULPRIT
CULTIST
CULVERT
DELBERT
DELIGHT
DELIMIT
DOLEOUT
DULLEST
EELIEST
ELLIOTT
FALLOUT
FALSEST
FELLOUT
FELTOUT
FILBERT
FILLOUT
FOLDOUT
FOLKART
FOLLETT
FULGENT
FULLEST
GALLANT
GILBERT
GILLNET
HALFWIT
HALIBUT
HELDOUT
HELLCAT
HELPOUT
HOLDOUT
HOLEOUT
HOLIEST
ILLICIT
JOLLIET
MILDEST
MILLETT
OILIEST
PALMIST
POLECAT
POLOIST
PULLOUT
RELIANT
RELIGHT
ROLLOUT
RULEOUT
SALIENT
SELLOUT
SILKHAT
SOLDOUT
SOLICIT
SOLOIST
SOLVENT
TALKOUT
TALKSAT
TALLEST
UGLIEST
VALIANT
WALCOTT
WALKOUT
WALMART
WELLSET
WILDCAT
WILDEST
WILIEST
YELLSAT

•••LT••

BUILTIN
BUILTON
BUILTUP
CARLTON
COALTAR
COULTER
DEALTIN
EXALTED
EXULTED
FAULTED
FOULTIP
HEALTHY
HEELTAP
HILLTOP
MOULTED
PHILTER
PHILTRE
POLLTAX
POULTRY
PSALTER
PULLTAB
QUILTED
QUILTER
REALTOR
ROLLTOP
SHELTER
SHELTIE
SHELTON
SKELTER
SKELTON
SMALTOS
SMELTED
SMELTER
STILTED
STILTON
SVELTER
SWELTER
SWELTRY
VAULTED
VAULTER
WEALTHY

•••L•T•

ABILITY
ACOLYTE
ADULATE
AGILITY
AMULETS
ANKLETS
ARMLETS
ATHLETE
AUKLETS
AXOLOTL
BALLETS
BALLOTS
BERLITZ
BILLETS
BULLETS
BULLITT
CABLETV
CAPLETS
CHALETS
COLLATE
COLLETS
CUTLETS
DEFLATE
DEPLETE
DUALITY
EAGLETS
EGALITE
EMULATE
EYELETS
FALLSTO
FILLETS
FOLLETT
GIBLETS
GIMLETS
GOBLETS
GULLETS
HAMLETS
HEWLETT
INFLATE
ISOLATE
JOBLOTS
JOLLITY
LAPLATA
MALLETS
MERLOTS
MILLETS
MILLETT
MULLETS
NEOLITH
NUTLETS
OCELOTS
ODDLOTS
OMELETS
OUTLETS
PALLETS
PELLETS
PERLITE
PIGLETS
PIOLETS
POLLUTE
PRELATE
PULLETS
QUALITY
RALLYTO
RANLATE
REALITY
REPLATE
REPLETE
RILLETS
RUNLETS
SCULPTS
STYLETS
SUBLETS
TABLETS
TOILETS
TWELFTH
ULULATE
UTILITY
VARLETS
VIOLATE
VIOLETS
WALLETS
WIGLETS
ZEALOTS

•••L••T

AFFLICT
AIRLIFT
AMPLEST
ANALYST
BAILOUT
BALLAST
BAWLOUT
BRILLAT
BULLITT
CALLOUT
CELLIST
COLLECT
COOLANT
COOLEST
COOLSIT
COULDNT
CYCLIST
DEALOUT
DEFLECT
DIALECT
DUELIST
DULLEST
EVILEST
EXPLOIT
FALLOUT
FARLEFT
FEELOUT
FELLOUT
FILLOUT
FOLLETT
FOULEST
FOULOUT
FULLEST
GALLANT
GETLOST
GILLNET
GRILLET
HAYLOFT
HELLCAT
HEWLETT
HITLIST
IMPLANT
INFLECT
INFLICT
JOLLIET
MAILLOT
MILLETT
NAILSET
NEGLECT
NEWLEFT
NOBLEST
OCULIST
OPULENT
OUTLAST
PAULIST
PULLOUT
RAILSAT
REALIST
REELECT
REFLECT
REPLANT
ROLLOUT
SEALANT
SELLOUT
SHALLOT
SKILIFT
SKILLET
STALEST
STYLIST
TALLEST
TITLIST
TSELIOT
ULULANT
UNBLEST
VIOLENT
VIOLIST
WELLSET
WOULDNT
YELLSAT
YOPLAIT

••••LT•

BASALTS
DESALTS
FACULTY
FRAILTY
GEFILTE
INSULTS
LOYALTY
MINOLTA
MODELTS
NOVELTY
OCCULTS
PENALTY
PENULTS
REBOLTS
REMELTS
RESALTS
RESULTS
REVOLTS
ROYALTY
STEALTH
TUMULTS
UNBOLTS

••••L•T

ABSOLUT
ASTOLAT
BACKLIT
BIBELOT
BOOKLET
BRILLAT
BULBLET
CAMELOT
CAPELET
CAPULET
CHAPLET
CIRCLET
COPILOT
COUPLET
DOUBLET
DRIBLET
DROPLET
EPAULET
FEEDLOT
FIRELIT
GANTLET
GRILLET
INKBLOT
LEAFLET
MAILLOT
MOONLIT
PLAYLET
RINGLET
RIVULET
ROOTLET
SANDLOT
SCARLET
SHALLOT
SKILLET
SNIGLET
SPOTLIT
STARLET
STARLIT
SUBPLOT
TRIPLET
WAVELET
WOODLOT

•••••LT

ASPHALT
ASSAULT
ATFAULT
BERTOLT
CONSULT
DEFAULT
EYEBOLT
FANBELT
GESTALT
LAPBELT
NOFAULT
REBUILT
REDEALT
RENAULT
SEASALT
SUNBELT

LU•••••

LUBBERS
LUBBOCK
LUCERNE
LUCIANO
LUCIDLY
LUCIFER
LUCILLE
LUCKIER
LUCKILY
LUCKING
LUCKOUT
LUFFING
LUGGAGE
LUGGERS
LUGGING
LUGNUTS
LULLABY
LULLING
LUMBAGO
LUMBARS
LUMBERS
LUMIERE
LUMPERS
LUMPIER
LUMPING
LUMPSUM
LUNATIC
LUNCHED
LUNCHER
LUNCHES
LUNGEAT
LUNGING
LUNKERS
LUPINES
LURCHED
LURCHES
LURIDLY
LURKING
LUSHEST
LUSTERS
LUSTFUL
LUSTIER
LUSTILY
LUSTING
LUSTRED
LUSTRES
LUTISTS
LUXATED
LUXATES

L•U••••

LAUDING
LAUGHAT
LAUGHED
LAUGHER
LAUGHIN
LAUNDER
LAUNDRY
LAURELS
LAURENT
LAUTREC
LOUDEST
LOUELLA
LOUNGED
LOUNGER
LOUNGES
LOURDES
LOUREED
LOUSEUP
LOUSIER
LOUSILY
LOUSING
LOUVERS
LOUVRES

L••U•••

LACUNAE
LACUNAL
LACUNAS
LAGUNAS
LEDUPTO
LEGUMES
LIQUEFY
LIQUEUR
LIQUIDS
LIQUORS
LITURGY
LOCUSTS
LOQUATS
LOTUSES

L•••U••

LABOURS
LACQUER
LANGUID
LANGUOR
LANGURS
LAPFULS
LARRUPS
LASHUPS
LAWSUIT
LAYOUTS
LEAGUER
LEAGUES
LECTURE
LEGPULL
LEISURE
LETTUCE
LINEUPS
LINGUAL
LINKUPS
LOCKUPS
LONGUES
LOOKUPS
LUGNUTS
LYCEUMS

L••••U•

LACEDUP
LACESUP
LADYBUG
LAIDOUT
LALIQUE
LANDAUS
LASCAUX
LAYSOUT
LAZARUS
LEADOUT
LEADSUP
LEFTOUT
LESPAUL
LETSOUT
LIFTSUP
LIGHTUP
LINEDUP
LINESUP
LIONCUB
LIQUEUR
LITHIUM
LIVEOUT
LOCKNUT
LOCKOUT
LOCKSUP
LOGSOUT
LONGRUN
LOOKOUT
LOOKSUP
LOSEOUT
LOSTOUT
LOUSEUP
LOVEBUG
LUCKOUT
LUMPSUM
LUSTFUL

L•••••U

LAMBEAU

•LU••••

ALUMNAE
ALUMNAL
ALUMNUS
ALUNSER
BLUBBER
BLUEBOY
BLUEFIN
BLUEFLU
BLUEFOX
BLUEING
BLUEJAY
BLUELAW
BLUESKY
BLUFFED
BLUFFER
BLUFFLY
BLUNDER
BLUNTED
BLUNTER
BLUNTLY
BLURRED
BLURTED
BLUSHED
BLUSHER
BLUSHES
BLUSTER
CLUBBED
CLUBCAR
CLUCKED
CLUEDIN
CLUEING
CLUESIN
CLUMPED
CLUNKED
CLUNKER
CLUSTER
CLUTTER
ELUDING
ELUSIVE
ELUTING
ELUTION
ELUVIUM
FLUBBED
FLUENCY
FLUFFED
FLUIDLY
FLUMMOX
FLUNKED
FLUSHED
FLUSHES
FLUSTER
FLUTING
FLUTIST
FLUTTER
FLUVIAL
GLUCOSE
GLUEDON
GLUMMER
GLUTTED
GLUTTON
KLUDGES
KLUGMAN
KLUTZES
PLUCKED
PLUGGED
PLUGGER
PLUGSIN
PLUMAGE
PLUMBED
PLUMBER
PLUMING
PLUMMER
PLUMMET
PLUMPED
PLUMPER
PLUNDER
PLUNGED
PLUNGER
PLUNGES
PLUNKED
PLURALS
PLUSHER
PLUSHES
PLUSHLY
PLUSSES
PLUVIAL
SLUDGES
SLUGGED
SLUGGER
SLUICED
SLUICES
SLUMBER
SLUMMED
SLUMPED
SLURPED
SLURRED
SLUSHES
ULULANT
ULULATE

•L•U•••

ALBUMEN
ALBUMIN
ALLUDED
ALLUDES
ALLURED
ALLURES
ALLUVIA
BLOUSED
BLOUSES
BLOUSON
CLAUDIA
CLAUDIO
CLAUSES
CLOUDED
CLOUTED
FLAUNTS
FLOUNCE
FLOURED
FLOUTED
ILLUSED
ILLUSES
OLDUVAI
PLAUDIT
PLAUTUS
PLOUGHS
SLEUTHS

SLOUCHY
SLOUGHS

•L••U••
ALARUMS
BLOWUPS
CLAQUES
CLIBURN
CLIQUES
CLOQUES
CLOSURE
CLOTURE
FLIPUPS
GLOBULE
PLAGUED
PLAGUES
PLAQUES
PLENUMS
SLIPUPS
ULALUME

•L•••U•
ALUMNUS
ALYSSUM
BLEWOUT
BLOTOUT
BLOWGUN
BLOWNUP
BLOWOUT
BLOWSUP
CLAMSUP
CLEANUP
CLEARUP
CLOGSUP
CLOSEUP
ELUVIUM
ELYSIUM
FLANEUR
FLAREUP
FLATOUT
FLAVOUR
GLAMOUR
GLEEFUL
OLYMPUS
PLAUTUS
PLAYFUL
PLAYOUT
PLAYSUP
SLIPOUT
SLIPSUP
SLOWSUP

•L••••U
BLUEFLU
ILIESCU
PLATEAU

••LU•••
ALLUDED
ALLUDES
ALLURED
ALLURES
ALLUVIA
BELUSHI
BOLUSES
CALUMET
CALUMNY
COLUMBO
COLUMNS
DELUDED
DELUDES
DELUGED
DELUGES
DELUISE
DILUTED
DILUTER
DILUTES
FELUCCA
GALUMPH
ILLUSED
ILLUSES
MCLUHAN
SALUKIS
SALUTED
SALUTES
SOLUBLE
SOLUTES
SPLURGE
STLUCIA
SULUSEA
TALUSES
TOLUENE
UNLUCKY
VALUATE
VALUING
VOLUBLE
VOLUBLY
VOLUMES

••L•U••
ABLAUTS
BULBULS
BULRUSH
COLLUDE
COLOURS
CULTURE
FILLUPS
FOLDUPS
HOLDUPS
KILAUEA
MOLLUSK
PILEUPS
POLLUTE
PULLUPS
STLOUIS
UMLAUTS
VALOURS
VELLUMS
VELOURS
VULTURE
WALKUPS
WALNUTS

••L••U•
BALEFUL
BALFOUR
BALLSUP
BELAKUN
BELGIUM
BELLYUP
BILIOUS
BULBOUS
BULGHUR
BULLRUN
CALCIUM
CALHOUN
CALLOUS
CALLOUT
CALLSUP
CELSIUS
COLDCUT
COLOBUS
DOLEFUL
DOLEOUT
DOLLSUP
ECLOGUE
FALLGUY
FALLOUT
FELLOUT
FELTOUT
FILLOUT
FILLSUP
FOLDOUT
FOLDSUP
FULCRUM
FULGHUM
GALLIUM
GOLDBUG
HALIBUT
HELDOUT
HELPFUL
HELPOUT
HOLDOUT
HOLDSUP
HOLEDUP
HOLEOUT
HOLESUP
HOLMIUM
LALIQUE
MALAMUD
MALRAUX
MALTHUS
MILHAUD
MILIEUS
MILIEUX
MILKRUN
MILLRUN
OBLIQUE
OBLOQUY
PALLIUM
PILEDUP
PILESUP
PILLBUG
PULLOUT
PULLSUP
ROLLOUT
ROLLSUP
RULEOUT
SELLOUT
SOLDOUT
SPLITUP
SULPHUR
TALKOUT
TALKSUP
TALLYUP
WALKOUT
WALLSUP
WELLRUN
WELLSUP
WILLFUL

••L•••U
ONLYYOU

•••LU••
ASYLUMS
COLLUDE
ENGLUND
EXCLUDE
FAILURE
FILLUPS
FOULUPS
GIBLUES
INCLUDE
MOLLUSK
MUKLUKS
OCCLUDE
PABLUMS
PEPLUMS
POLLUTE
POTLUCK
PRELUDE
PULLUPS
RECLUSE
REGLUED
REGLUES
SANLUIS
SECLUDE
SPELUNK
ULALUME
UNGLUED
UNPLUGS
VELLUMS

•••L•U•
APPLAUD
BAILOUT
BALLSUP
BAWLOUT
BECLOUD
BELLYUP
BOWLFUL
BUILDUP
BUILTUP
BULLRUN
CALLOUS
CALLOUT
CALLSUP
CHALKUP
COILSUP
CURLSUP
DEALOUT
DOLLSUP
FALLGUY
FALLOUT
FEELOUT
FELLOUT
FILLOUT
FILLSUP
FOULOUT
FOULSUP
GALLIUM
GIELGUD
HAULSUP
JEALOUS
MILLRUN
NUCLEUS
OUTLOUD
PAILFUL
PAILOUS
PALLIUM
PARLOUR
PARLOUS
PILLBUG
PULLOUT
PULLSUP
ROLLOUT
ROLLSUP
SEALSUP
SELLOUT
SKILFUL
SOULFUL
SWELLUP
TALLYUP
THULIUM
TOOLSUP
WALLSUP
WELLRUN
WELLSUP
WILLFUL
ZEALOUS

•••L••U
PURLIEU
TABLEAU

••••LU•
ABSOLUT
AMIBLUE
ANGELUS
ANNULUS
CAROLUS
CUMULUS
DEDALUS
DEVALUE
EARPLUG
FAMULUS
HOODLUM
ICEBLUE
JEANLUC
KEYCLUB
NONPLUS
ORMOLUS
PABULUM
REGULUS
REVALUE
ROMULUS
SEASLUG
SKYBLUE
SURPLUS
SWELLUP
TROILUS
TUMULUS

••••L•U
ANGELOU
DOUBLEU
EMMYLOU
MARYLOU

•••••LU
BLUEFLU

L•V••••
LAVALSE
LAVERNE
LAVINIA
LEVELED
LEVELER
LEVELLY
LEVERED
LEVERET
LEVIERS
LEVITES
LEVYING
LIVABLE
LIVEDIN
LIVEDON
LIVENED
LIVEOAK
LIVEONE
LIVEOUT
LIVESIN
LIVESON
LIVIDLY
LIVINGS
LOVABLE
LOVEBUG
LOVEINS
LOVERLY

L••V•••
LATVIAN
LEAVENS
LEAVING
LOUVERS
LOUVRES

L•••V••
LAYOVER
LEHAVRE
LIEOVER

•LV••••
ALVAREZ
ALVEOLI

•L•V•••
CLAVELL
CLAVIER
CLOVERS
ELEVATE
ELEVENS
ELUVIUM
FLAVORS
FLAVOUR
FLIVVER
FLUVIAL
OLIVIER
OLIVINE
PLOVERS
PLUVIAL
SLAVERS
SLAVERY
SLAVING
SLAVISH
SLIVERS
SLOVAKS
SLOVENE
SLOVENS

•L••V••
ALCOVES
ALLOVER
ALLUVIA
CLEAVED
CLEAVER
CLEAVES
CLEAVON
FLIVVER
FLYOVER
OLDUVAI
SLEEVES

•L•••V•
ELUSIVE
PLOSIVE
ULANOVA

•L••••V
ULYANOV

••LV•••
CALVARY
CALVERT
CALVING
CULVERT
DELVERS
DELVING
GALVANI
HALVING
ROLVAAG
SALVAGE
SALVERS
SALVING
SALVOES
SELVAGE
SILVERS
SILVERY
SOLVENT
SOLVERS
SOLVING
SYLVANS
VELVETS
VELVETY

••L•V••
ALLOVER
ALLUVIA
BELOVED
BILEVEL
BOLIVAR
BOLIVIA
DELIVER
ENLIVEN
PALAVER
RELIVED
RELIVES
TELAVIV
UNLOVED

••L••V•
BELIEVE
ONLEAVE
RELIEVE
RELIEVO

••L•••V
MOLOTOV
TELAVIV

•••LV••
EVOLVED
EVOLVES
SHELVED
SHELVES
TWELVES

•••L•V•
BAKLAVA
ENCLAVE
ENSLAVE
OUTLIVE
PAHLAVI
PAVLOVA

•••L••V
CABLETV

••••LV•
ABSOLVE
BIVALVE
DEVOLVE
INVOLVE
RESOLVE
REVOLVE

L•W••••
LAWFORD
LAWLESS
LAWSUIT
LAWYERS
LEWDEST
LOWBALL
LOWBEAM
LOWBLOW
LOWBORN
LOWBOYS
LOWBRED
LOWBROW
LOWDOWN
LOWERED
LOWGEAR
LOWHEEL
LOWLAND
LOWLIER
LOWLIFE
LOWNECK
LOWNESS
LOWPAID
LOWRISE
LOWROAD
LOWTECH
LOWTIDE

L••W•••
LAPWING
LEEWARD
LEGWORK

L•••W••
LAYAWAY

L••••W•
LAYDOWN
LETDOWN
LIEDOWN
LOWDOWN

L•••••W
LAIDLOW
LAYSLOW
LIESLOW
LIKENEW
LITHGOW
LONGBOW
LOWBLOW
LOWBROW

•LW••••
ALWORTH

•L•W•••
ALEWIFE
BLEWOFF
BLEWOUT
BLOWDRY
BLOWERS
BLOWFLY
BLOWGUN
BLOWIER
BLOWING
BLOWNUP
BLOWOFF
BLOWOUT
BLOWSIN
BLOWSIT
BLOWSUP
BLOWUPS
CLAWERS
CLAWING
CLOWDER
CLOWNED
FLAWING
FLOWERS
FLOWERY
FLOWING
FLYWAYS
GLOWERS
GLOWING
ILLWILL
ILLWIND
OLDWEST
PLOWBOY
PLOWERS
PLOWING
PLOWMAN
PLOWMEN
PLYWOOD
SLOWEST
SLOWING
SLOWSUP

•L••W••
ALLOWED
ELBOWED
FLYAWAY

•L•••W•
OLDNEWS

•L••••W
BLUELAW
GLASGOW

••LW•••
BULWARK
FALWELL
ILLWILL
ILLWIND
OILWELL

••L•W••
ALLOWED
BALDWIN
BELTWAY
COLDWAR
CSLEWIS
GOLDWYN
HALFWAY
HALFWIT
HALLWAY
HOLYWAR
TOLLWAY
WALKWAY

••L••W•
BELLOWS
BILLOWS
BILLOWY
FALLOWS
FELLOWS
FOLLOWS
HALLOWS
HOLLOWS
MALLOWS
MELLOWS
MILDEWS
MILDEWY
PILLOWS
PILLOWY
TALLOWS
WALLOWS
WILLOWS
WILLOWY
YELLOWS

••L•••W
HOLYCOW
MILKCOW
SALCHOW

•••LW••
HALLWAY
RAILWAY
TOLLWAY

•••L•W•
BELLOWS
BILLOWS
BILLOWY
CURLEWS
FALLOWS
FELLOWS
FOLLOWS
HALLOWS
HOLLOWS
INFLOWS
MALLOWS
MARLOWE
MELLOWS
OAKLAWN
OUTLAWS
PILLOWS
PILLOWY
ROBLOWE
TALLOWS
WALLOWS
WILLOWS
WILLOWY
YELLOWS

•••L••W
SHALLOW
SWALLOW

••••L•W
AIRFLOW
BIGELOW
BLUELAW
CASELAW
DANELAW
DEWCLAW
GAMELAW
HIGHLOW
JOEBLOW
LAIDLOW
LAYSLOW
LIESLOW
LOWBLOW
MANILOW
OUTFLOW
SHALLOW
SWALLOW
WINSLOW

L•X••••
LAXNESS
LEXICAL
LEXICON
LUXATED
LUXATES

L•••X••
LATEXES

L•••••X
LASCAUX
LOCKBOX

•L•X•••
ELIXIRS
FLEXING
FLEXNER
FLEXORS
KLAXONS
PLEXORS

•L••••X
ALTOSAX
BLUEFOX
FLUMMOX
KLEENEX

••L•X••
CALYXES
HELIXES
PHLOXES
RELAXED
RELAXES
TELEXED
TELEXES

••L••X•
POLEAXE

••L•••X
CALLBOX
HALIFAX
MALRAUX
MILIEUX
PILLBOX
POLLTAX
ROLODEX
SALTBOX

•••L••X
CALLBOX
MAILBOX
PHALANX
PILLBOX
POLLTAX
TOOLBOX

••••L•X
COMPLEX
PERPLEX
SIMPLEX
TRIPLEX

LY•••••
LYCEUMS
LYINGTO
LYRICAL
LYRISTS

L•Y••••
LAYAWAY
LAYDOWN
LAYERED
LAYETTE
LAYINTO
LAYOFFS
LAYOUTS
LAYOVER
LAYSFOR
LAYSLOW
LAYSOFF
LAYSOUT
LOYALLY
LOYALTY

L••Y•••
LADYBUG
LADYDAY
LANYARD
LAWYERS
LEVYING
LIBYANS
LILYPAD

L•••Y••
LIPSYNC
LOBBYER

L••••Y•
LACKEYS
LOWBOYS

L•••••Y
LADYDAY
LAMPREY
LANGLEY
LANGTRY
LANKILY
LARCENY
LARGELY
LASTORY
LATENCY
LATHERY
LAUNDRY
LAYAWAY
LAZENBY
LEERILY
LEGALLY
LEGIBLY
LENGTHY
LETSFLY
LEVELLY
LIBERTY
LIBRARY
LICITLY
LICKETY
LIGHTLY
LINDSAY
LINDSEY
LIQUEFY
LITHELY
LITURGY
LIVIDLY
LOCALLY
LOFTILY
LOOSELY
LOTTERY
LOUSILY
LOVERLY
LOYALLY
LOYALTY
LUCIDLY
LUCKILY
LULLABY
LURIDLY
LUSTILY

•LY••••
ALYOSHA
ALYSSUM
ELYSEES
ELYSIAN
ELYSIUM
FLYAWAY
FLYBALL
FLYBOYS
FLYCAST
FLYFISH
FLYHIGH
FLYLEAF
FLYNETS
FLYOVER
FLYPAST
FLYRODS
FLYTRAP
FLYWAYS
OLYMPIA
OLYMPIC
OLYMPUS
PLYWOOD
SLYNESS
ULYANOV
ULYSSES

•L•Y•••
ALLYING
ALLYSON
CLAYIER
CLAYTON
CLOYING
FLAYING
PLAYACT
PLAYBOY
PLAYDOH
PLAYERS
PLAYFUL
PLAYING
PLAYLET
PLAYOFF
PLAYOUT
PLAYPEN
PLAYSAT
PLAYSON
PLAYSUP
SLAYERS
SLAYTON

•L••Y••
ALLAYED
ALLAYER
ALLEYES
ALLOYED
PLATYPI

•L•••Y•
FLYBOYS
FLYWAYS
GLADEYE
OLDDAYS

•L••••Y
ALCHEMY
ALERTLY
ALIMONY
ALLERGY
ALOOFLY
ALREADY
BLACKLY
BLANDLY
BLANKLY
BLARNEY
BLEAKLY
BLINDLY
BLOTCHY
BLOWDRY
BLOWFLY
BLUEBOY
BLUEJAY
BLUESKY
BLUFFLY
BLUNTLY
CLARIFY
CLARITY
CLEANLY
CLEARLY
CLOONEY
CLOSELY
ELDERLY
FLAGDAY
FLEETLY
FLIGHTY
FLOWERY

FLUENCY
FLUIDLY
FLYAWAY
GLORIFY
OLDFOGY
PLAINLY
PLAYBOY
PLENARY
PLIABLY
PLIANCY
PLOWBOY
PLUSHLY
SLAVERY
SLEEKLY
SLICKLY
SLOUCHY

••LY•••
ALLYING
ALLYSON
BELYING
CALYCES
CALYPSO
CALYXES
HALYARD
HOLYARK
HOLYCOW
HOLYOKE
HOLYSEE
HOLYWAR
LILYPAD
ONLYYOU
POLYGON
POLYMER
RELYING

••L•Y••
ALLAYED
ALLAYER
ALLEYES
ALLOYED
BELAYED
BELLYUP
COLLYER
DELAYED
DELAYER
HALCYON
MALAYAN
ONLYYOU
RALLYTO
RELAYED
SPLAYED
TALLYHO
TALLYUP

••L••Y•
GALLEYS
GOLDWYN
PULLEYS
VALLEYS
VOLLEYS
WALLEYE

••L•••Y
ALLERGY
APLENTY
BALCONY
BALLBOY
BALONEY
BELLAMY
BELLBOY
BELTWAY
BILLOWY
CALCIFY
CALGARY
CALUMNY
CALVARY
DALTREY
DELANEY
FALLACY
FALLGUY
FALSELY
FALSIFY
FALSITY
GALLERY
HALFWAY
HALLWAY
HELOTRY
HILLARY
HOLIDAY
JOLLILY
JOLLITY
KILLJOY
KOLACKY
LULLABY
MALMSEY
MILDEWY
MOLLIFY
NULLIFY
OBLOQUY
PALEDRY
PALFREY
PALJOEY
PILLORY
PILLOWY
SALSIFY
SALTILY
SILKILY
SILVERY
SOLIDLY
SPLASHY
SULKILY
TOLLWAY
TOLSTOY
UNLUCKY
VALIDLY
VELVETY
VOLUBLY
WALKWAY
WALLABY
WILLOWY

•••LY••
ACOLYTE
ANALYSE
ANALYST
ANALYZE
BELLYUP
CARLYLE
COLLYER
EARLYON
RALLYTO
TALLYHO
TALLYUP

•••L•Y•
BAILEYS
BARLEYS
BYPLAYS
DEPLOYS
EMPLOYS
EVILEYE
GALLEYS
MEDLEYS
MISLAYS
OUTLAYS
PARLAYS
PARLEYS
PULLEYS
REPLAYS
VALLEYS
VOLLEYS
WALLEYE
WAYLAYS

•••L••Y
ABILITY
AGILELY
AGILITY
AMPLIFY
ANALOGY
APOLOGY
BALLBOY
BELLAMY
BELLBOY
BILLOWY
BIOLOGY
CUTLERY
DAYLILY
DUALITY
ECOLOGY
FALLACY
FALLGUY
FOOLERY
GALLERY
GEOLOGY
HALLWAY
HEALTHY
HILLARY
JOLLILY
JOLLITY
KILLJOY
LULLABY
MOLLIFY
NULLIFY
PILLORY
PILLOWY
POULTRY
PTOLEMY
QUALIFY
QUALITY
RAILWAY
REALITY
RIFLERY
SEALILY
SHELLEY
SURLILY
SWELTRY
TOLLWAY
TRILOGY
TROLLEY
UTILITY
WALLABY
WEALTHY
WILLOWY
WOOLSEY
WORLDLY
ZOOLOGY

••••LY•
CAROLYN
KAROLYI
MARILYN

••••L•Y
AIRPLAY
AURALLY
AWFULLY
AXIALLY
BANALLY
BASALLY
BENTLEY
BRADLEY
BUCKLEY
CAVALRY
CHARLEY
CIVILLY
CRUELLY
DEVILRY
DIDDLEY
DISPLAY
ENDPLAY
EQUALLY
FACULTY
FINALLY
FRAILTY
FRAWLEY
GREELEY
GUNPLAY
HEMSLEY
HUNTLEY
IDEALLY
JEWELRY
LANGLEY
LEGALLY
LEVELLY
LOCALLY
LOYALLY
LOYALTY
MISALLY
MISPLAY
MORALLY
NASALLY
NOVELTY
OUTPLAY
OVERLAY
PAISLEY
PARSLEY
PENALTY
PRESLEY
QUIGLEY
REGALLY
REVELRY
RIVALRY
ROYALLY
ROYALTY
SHELLEY
SHIRLEY
SHRILLY
STANLEY
TONALLY
TOTALLY
TROLLEY
USUALLY
VITALLY
VOCALLY
WRIGLEY
ZONALLY

•••••LY
ACRIDLY
ACUTELY
ADEPTLY
AFFABLY
AGILELY
ALERTLY
ALOOFLY
AMIABLY
ANGRILY
ANOMALY
APISHLY
AUDIBLY
AURALLY
AWFULLY
AXIALLY
BAGGILY
BANALLY
BASALLY
BAWDILY
BEASTLY
BEVERLY
BLACKLY
BLANDLY
BLANKLY
BLEAKLY
BLINDLY
BLOWFLY
BLUFFLY
BLUNTLY
BONNILY
BOSSILY
BRAMBLY
BRASHLY
BRAVELY
BRIEFLY
BRISKLY
BRISTLY
BROADLY
CANNILY
CAPABLY
CATTILY
CHARILY
CHEAPLY
CHIEFLY
CIVILLY
CLEANLY
CLEARLY
CLOSELY
COCKILY
CORNILY
COURTLY
CRASSLY
CRAZILY
CRINKLY
CRISPLY
CROSSLY
CRUDELY
CRUELLY
CRUMBLY
CRUMPLY
DAFFILY
DATEDLY
DAYLILY
DAZEDLY
DEERFLY
DENSELY
DINGILY
DIRTILY
DIZZILY
DOWDILY
DRIZZLY
DURABLY
EAGERLY
EARTHLY
ELDERLY
EMPTILY
EQUABLY
EQUALLY
ERECTLY
EXACTLY
FAINTLY
FALSELY
FANCILY
FETIDLY
FIERILY
FINALLY
FIREFLY
FIRSTLY
FISHILY
FIXEDLY
FLEETLY
FLUIDLY
FRANKLY
FRESHLY
FUNNILY
FUSSILY
FUSTILY
FUZZILY
GAUDILY
GAUNTLY
GAUZILY
GHASTLY
GHOSTLY
GIDDILY
GRANDLY
GRAVELY
GREATLY
GRISTLY
GRIZZLY
GROSSLY
GRUFFLY
GUSTILY
GUTSILY
HAMMILY
HANDILY
HAPPILY
HARDILY
HARSHLY
HASTILY
HEADILY
HEAVILY
HEFTILY
HUFFILY
HUMANLY
HUMIDLY
HUSKILY
IDEALLY
IGNOBLY
INANELY
INAPTLY
INEPTLY
INERTLY
IRATELY
JADEDLY
JAZZILY
JERKILY
JOINTLY
JOLLILY
JUICILY
LANKILY
LARGELY
LEERILY
LEGALLY
LEGIBLY
LETSFLY
LEVELLY
LICITLY
LIGHTLY
LITHELY
LIVIDLY
LOCALLY
LOFTILY
LOOSELY
LOUSILY
LOVERLY
LOYALLY
LUCIDLY
LUCKILY
LURIDLY
LUSTILY
MERRILY
MESSILY
MISALLY
MISERLY
MISTILY
MOISTLY
MONTHLY
MOODILY
MORALLY
MURKILY
MUSHILY
MUSTILY
MUTABLY
MUZZILY
NAIVELY
NAKEDLY
NASALLY
NASTILY
NATTILY
NEEDILY
NERVILY
NIFTILY
NIGHTLY
NOISILY
NOTABLY
NUTTILY
ORDERLY
OVERFLY
OVERTLY
PANOPLY
PEPPILY
PERKILY
PESKILY
PETTILY
PHONILY
PIOUSLY
PITHILY
PLAINLY
PLIABLY
PLUSHLY
PRICKLY
PROSILY
PROUDLY
PUFFILY
PUSHILY
QUEENLY
QUEERLY
QUICKLY
QUIETLY
RAPIDLY
READILY
REGALLY
RIGHTLY
RIGIDLY
ROUGHLY
ROUNDLY
ROWDILY
ROYALLY
RUSTILY
SAINTLY
SALTILY
SANDFLY
SASSILY
SAUCILY
SAVVILY
SCANTLY
SCARILY
SCRAWLY
SEALILY
SEEDILY
SHADILY
SHAKILY
SHAPELY
SHARPLY
SHEERLY
SHOOFLY
SHORTLY
SHOWILY
SHRILLY
SIGHTLY
SILKILY
SIZABLY
SLEEKLY
SLICKLY
SMARTLY
SNIDELY
SOBERLY
SOGGILY
SOLIDLY
SOUNDLY
SPANGLY
SPARELY
SPINDLY
STAGILY
STAIDLY
STARKLY
STATELY
STEEPLY
STERNLY
STIFFLY
STOKELY
STONILY
STOUTLY
STUBBLY
SUAVELY
SULKILY
SUNNILY
SURLILY
SWEETLY
SWIFTLY
TACITLY
TACKILY
TARDILY
TASTILY
TEARILY
TENABLY
TENSELY
TEPIDLY
TERSELY
TESTILY
THICKLY
THIRDLY
TIGHTLY
TIMIDLY
TINNILY
TIPSILY
TIREDLY
TONALLY
TOTALLY
TOUGHLY
TREACLY
TREMBLY
TRITELY
TWINKLY
UNGODLY
USUALLY
UTTERLY
VAGUELY
VALIDLY
VAPIDLY
VEXEDLY
VISIBLY
VITALLY
VIVIDLY
VOCALLY
VOLUBLY
WACKILY
WEARILY
WEIRDLY
WISPILY
WITTILY
WOMANLY
WOOZILY
WORDILY
WORLDLY
WRIGGLY
WRINKLY
WRONGLY
ZONALLY

L•Z••••
LAZARUS
LAZENBY
LAZIEST
LIZARDS
LOZENGE

L•••Z••
LEIPZIG

L••••Z•
LIONIZE
LORENZO

L•••••Z
LAISSEZ
LEIBNIZ

•L•Z•••
BLAZERS
BLAZING
BLAZONS
GLAZERS
GLAZIER
GLAZING

•L••Z••
ALCAZAR
BLITZED
BLITZEN
BLITZES
GLITZED
GLITZES
KLUTZES

•L••••Z
ALBENIZ
ALVAREZ

••LZ•••
CALZONE

••L•Z••
PALAZZI
PALAZZO
SALAZAR
SELTZER
WALTZED
WALTZER
WALTZES

••L••Z•
PALAZZI
PALAZZO

•••L•Z•
ANALYZE
IDOLIZE
OBELIZE
REALIZE
STYLIZE
UTILIZE

•••L••Z
BERLIOZ
BERLITZ
KOBLENZ

MA•••••
MACABRE
MACADAM
MACAQUE
MACBETH
MACDUFF
MACGRAW
MACHETE
MACHINA
MACHINE
MACRAME
MACRONS
MACULAE
MADAMEX
MADCAPS
MADCHEN
MADDENS
MADDERS
MADDEST
MADDING
MADEFOR
MADEHAY
MADEIRA
MADEOFF
MADEOUT
MADEWAY
MADISON
MADLIBS
MADNESS
MADONNA
MADRONA
MAENADS
MAESTRI
MAESTRO
MAEWEST
MAFIOSO
MAGENTA
MAGICAL
MAGINOT
MAGNATE
MAGNETO
MAGNETS
MAGNIFY
MAGNUMS
MAGPIES
MAGUEYS
MAGYARS
MAHALIA
MAHARIS
MAHATMA
MAHONEY
MAHOUTS
MAIDENS
MAIGRET
MAILBAG
MAILBOX
MAILERS
MAILING
MAILLOT
MAINTOP
MAITAIS
MAITRED
MAJESTE
MAJESTY
MAJEURE
MAJORCA
MAJORED
MAKEFOR
MAKEHAY
MAKEOFF
MAKEOUT
MAKEPAR
MAKESDO
MAKESIT
MAKESUP
MAKEUPS
MAKEWAY
MAKINGS
MALABAR
MALACCA
MALACHI
MALAISE
MALAMUD
MALAREN
MALAYAN
MALCOLM
MALEATE
MALEFIC
MALIGNS
MALLARD
MALLETS
MALLOWS
MALMSEY
MALODOR
MALRAUX
MALTEDS
MALTESE
MALTHUS
MALTING
MALTOSE
MAMBOED
MAMMALS
MAMMOTH
MANACLE
MANAGED
MANAGER
MANAGES
MANAGUA
MANANAS
MANATEE
MANCINI
MANDALA
MANDANS
MANDATE
MANDAYS
MANDELA
MANDREL
MANDRIL
MANEGES
MANFRED
MANGERS
MANGIER
MANGLED
MANGLES
MANGOES
MANHOLE
MANHOOD
MANHOUR
MANHUNT
MANIACS
MANILOW
MANIPLE
MANITOU
MANKIND
MANLIER
MANMADE
MANNERS
MANNING
MANNISH
MANOWAR
MANSARD
MANSION
MANTELS
MANTLED
MANTLES
MANTRAP
MANTRAS
MANTRIC
MANUALS
MANUMIT
MANXCAT
MANXMAN
MANXMEN
MANYEAR
MAOISTS
MAPPERS
MAPPING
MARABOU
MARACAS
MARAUDS
MARBLED
MARBLES
MARCEAU
MARCELS
MARCHED
MARCHEN
MARCHER
MARCHES
MARCHON
MARCONI
MARGATE
MARGAUX
MARGAYS
MARGINS
MARGRET
MARIANA
MARILYN
MARIMBA
MARINAS
MARINER
MARINES
MARITAL
MARKERS
MARKETS
MARKHAM
MARKHOR
MARKING
MARKKAA
MARKOFF
MARKOVA
MARKSUP
MARKUPS
MARLENE
MARLINS
MARLOWE
MARMARA
MARMION
MARMOTS
MAROONS
MARQUEE
MARQUES
MARQUEZ
MARQUIS
MARRIED
MARRIES
MARRING
MARROWS
MARRYME
MARSALA
MARSHAL
MARSHES
MARTENS
MARTIAL
MARTIAN
MARTINA
MARTINI
MARTINO
MARTINS
MARTYRS
MARVELS
MARXISM
MARYANN
MARYKAY
MARYLOU
MASCARA
MASCOTS
MASHERS
MASHIES
MASHING
MASKERS
MASKING
MASONIC
MASONRY
MASQUES
MASSAGE
MASSEUR
MASSIFS
MASSING
MASSIVE
MASTABA
MASTERS
MASTERY
MASTICS
MASTIFF
MASTOID
MATADOR
MATCHED
MATCHES
MATCHUP
MATEWAN
MATHERS
MATHEWS
MATHIAS
MATILDA
MATINEE
MATISSE
MATLOCK
MATRONS
MATTERS
MATTHAU
MATTHEW
MATTING
MATTOCK
MATURED
MATURER
MATURES
MATZOHS
MAUDLIN
MAUGHAM
MAULDIN
MAULING
MAUNDER
MAUREEN
MAURICE
MAUROIS
MAWKISH
MAXBAER
MAXBORN
MAXILLA
MAXIMAL
MAXIMUM

MAXIMUS
MAXWELL
MAYALIN
MAYDAYS
MAYFAIR
MAYHEMS
MAYNARD
MAYORAL
MAYPOLE
MAYTIME
MAYWINE
MAZURKA

M•A••••
MBABANE
MEADOWS
MEADOWY
MEALIER
MEALIES
MEANDER
MEANEST
MEANIES
MEANING
MEASLES
MEASURE
MEATIER
MIAMIAN
MIASMAS
MIASMIC
MOANERS
MOANING
MUAMMAR
MYANMAR

M••A•••
MACABRE
MACADAM
MACAQUE
MADAMEX
MAHALIA
MAHARIS
MAHATMA
MALABAR
MALACCA
MALACHI
MALAISE
MALAMUD
MALAREN
MALAYAN
MANACLE
MANAGED
MANAGER
MANAGES
MANAGUA
MANANAS
MANATEE
MARABOU
MARACAS
MARAUDS
MATADOR
MAYALIN
MCCALLS
MCGAVIN
MCMAHON
MEDALED
MELANGE
MELANIE
MELANIN
MENACED
MENACES
MENAGES
METATES
MIKADOS
MINABLE
MINARET
MIRACLE
MIRADOR
MIRAGES
MIRAMAR
MIRAMAX
MIRANDA
MISALLY
MIXABLE
MOGAMBO
MOHAIRS
MOHAWKS
MONARCH
MORAINE
MORALES
MORALLY
MORANIS
MORAVIA
MOSAICS
MOVABLE
MRMAGOO
MUBARAK
MUTABLE
MUTABLY
MUTAGEN
MUTANTS
MUTATED
MUTATES
MUTATIS
MYMAMMY

M•••A••
MACRAME
MADCAPS
MAENADS
MAGNATE
MAGYARS
MAITAIS
MALEATE
MALLARD
MALRAUX
MAMMALS
MANDALA
MANDANS
MANDATE
MANDAYS
MANIACS
MANMADE
MANSARD
MANUALS
MARGATE
MARGAUX
MARGAYS
MARIANA
MARMARA
MARSALA
MARYANN
MASCARA
MASSAGE
MASTABA
MAXBAER
MAYDAYS
MAYFAIR
MAYNARD
MBABANE
MEDIANS
MEDIANT
MEDIATE
MENIALS
MERMAID
MESCALS
MESSAGE
MESSALA
METHANE
MICHAEL
MICMACS
MIDDAYS
MIDEAST
MIDLAND
MIDWAYS
MIGRANT
MIGRATE
MIKHAIL
MILEAGE
MILHAUD
MILLAND
MILLARD
MINOANS
MISCALL
MISCAST
MISDATE
MISHAPS
MISLAID
MISLAYS
MISMATE
MISNAME
MISSALS
MISTAKE
MOBCAPS
MOMBASA
MONDALE
MONDAYS
MONTAGE
MONTANA
MONTAND
MONTANE
MOORAGE
MORDANT
MORGANA
MORGANS
MORTALS
MORTARS
MOULAGE
MUDPACK
MULLAHS
MUNDANE
MUSCATS
MUSTAFA
MUSTANG
MUSTARD
MUTUALS
MYRIADS

M••••A•
MACADAM
MACGRAW
MACULAE
MADEHAY
MADEWAY
MAGICAL
MAILBAG
MAKEHAY
MAKEPAR
MAKEWAY
MALABAR
MALAYAN
MANANAS
MANOWAR
MANTRAP
MANTRAS
MANXCAT
MANXMAN
MANYEAR
MARACAS
MARCEAU
MARINAS
MARITAL
MARKHAM
MARKKAA
MARSHAL
MARTIAL
MARTIAN
MARYKAY
MATEWAN
MATHIAS
MATTHAU
MAUGHAM
MAXIMAL
MAYORAL
MCLUHAN
MEDEVAC
MEDICAL
MEDUSAE
MEDUSAS
MEGRYAN
MENORAH
MESSIAH
MEXICAN
MIAMIAN
MIASMAS
MIDYEAR
MILKMAN
MILLDAM
MIMOSAS
MINERAL
MINICAM
MINIMAL
MINIVAN
MIRAMAR
MIRAMAX
MISDEAL
MISDIAL
MISHEAR
MISLEAD
MISPLAY
MISREAD
MISTRAL
MITHRAS
MITZVAH
MODELAS
MODULAR
MOHICAN
MOLOKAI
MRCLEAN
MUAMMAR
MUBARAK
MULETAS
MUSICAL
MUSKRAT
MYANMAR

M•••••A
MACHINA
MADEIRA
MADONNA
MADRONA
MAGENTA
MAHALIA
MAHATMA
MAJORCA
MALACCA
MANAGUA
MANDALA
MANDELA
MARIANA
MARIMBA
MARKKAA
MARKOVA
MARMARA
MARSALA
MARTINA
MASCARA
MASTABA
MATILDA
MAXILLA
MAZURKA
MEDULLA
MELINDA
MELISSA
MENDOZA
MESSALA
MESSINA
MILITIA
MINEOLA
MINERVA
MINOLTA
MINORCA
MINUTIA
MIRANDA
MOMBASA
MONTANA
MONTOYA
MORAVIA
MORGANA
MUSTAFA

•MA••••
AMADEUS
AMALGAM
AMAPOLA
AMASSED
AMASSES
AMATEUR
AMATIVE
AMATORY
AMAZING
AMAZONS
EMANATE
EMANUEL
IMAGERS
IMAGERY
IMAGINE
IMAGING
IMAGOES
IMAMATE
IMARETS
SMACKED
SMACKER
SMALLER
SMALTOS
SMARTED
SMARTEN
SMARTER
SMARTLY
SMASHED
SMASHER
SMASHES
SMASHUP
SMATTER

•M•A•••
AMHARIC
AMIABLE
AMIABLY
AMRADIO
EMBANKS
EMBARGO
EMBARKS
EMBASSY
EMPANEL
EMPATHY
FMRADIO
IMPACTS
IMPAIRS
IMPALAS
IMPALED
IMPALES
IMPANEL
IMPARTS
IMPASSE
IMPASTO
SMEARED
UMLAUTS

•M••A••
AMYLASE
EMANATE
EMBRACE
EMERALD
EMIRATE
EMULATE
IMAMATE
IMITATE
IMPEACH
IMPLANT
OMPHALI
SMETANA
UMBRAGE

•M•••A•
AMALGAM
AMOEBAE
AMOEBAS
AMSCRAY
IMMORAL
IMPALAS
UMBRIAN

•M••••A
AMAPOLA
AMERICA
AMERIKA
AMMONIA
AMNESIA
AMPHORA
EMERITA
EMPORIA
SMETANA

••MA•••
ALMAATA
ALMADEN
ALMANAC
ARMADAS
DAMAGED
DAMAGES
DAMASKS
DEMANDS
DOMAINS
ENMASSE
FEMALES
HUMANLY
INMATES
JAMAICA
JUMANJI
KOMATSU
LAMAISM
LAMAIST
LAMARCK
MCMAHON
MRMAGOO
MYMAMMY
NOMADIC
ORMANDY
POMADED
POMADES
RAMADAN
RAMADAS
REMAILS
REMAINS
REMAKES
REMANDS
REMARKS
REMARRY
ROMAINE
ROMANCE
ROMANIA
ROMANOV
ROMANSH
SAMARIA
SOMALIA
SOMALIS
SOMATIC
SUMATRA
TAMABLE
TAMALES
TAMARIN
UNMAKES
UNMASKS
WOMANLY

••M•A••
ALMAATA
ARMBAND
ARMYANT
BEMOANS
BOMBARD
BOMBAST
CAMPARI
CEMBALO
COMBATS
COMMAND
COMPACT
COMPANY
COMPARE
COMPASS
COMRADE
CYMBALS
DEMEANS
GIMBALS
GUMBALL
GYMNAST
HYMNALS
JAMPACK
JIMJAMS
KAMPALA
KIMBALL
LAMBADA
LIMEADE
LOMBARD
LUMBAGO
LUMBARS
MAMMALS
MOMBASA
NUMBATS
OOMPAHS
POMPANO
RAMPAGE
RAMPANT
RAMPART
REMNANT
RIMBAUD
RUMBAED
RUMMAGE
SAMBAED
SAMBARS
SAMOANS
SAMPANS
SAMSARA
SIMIANS
SUMMARY
TAMBALA
TAMMANY
TAMTAMS
TIMBALE
TIMBALS
TOMCATS
TYMPANA
TYMPANI
WOMBATS

••M••A•
ADMIRAL
AIMEDAT
ALMANAC
ARMADAS
ARMLOAD
BIMODAL
CAMERAS
COMESAT
COMICAL
FEMORAL
GAMBIAN
GAMELAW
HUMERAL
IMMORAL
JUMPSAT
KUMQUAT
LAMBDAS
LAMBEAU
LAMINAE
LAMINAL
LAMINAR
LAMINAS
MIMOSAS
NAMEDAY
NAMETAG
NOMINAL
NUMERAL
PEMICAN
RAMADAN
RAMADAS
RAMBEAU
REMORAS
REMOVAL
REMUDAS
ROMULAN
SAMEDAY
SAMOVAR
SAMPRAS
SAMURAI
SEMINAL
SEMINAR
SIMILAR
SOMEDAY
SOMEWAY
TEMPLAR
TIMELAG
TIMEWAS
ZAMBIAN

••M•••A
ALMAATA
AMMONIA
ARMENIA
CAMELIA
JAMAICA
KAMPALA
LAMBADA
LAMOTTA
LEMPIRA
MOMBASA
NAMIBIA
POMPEIA
ROMANIA
SAMARIA
SAMSARA
SOMALIA
SUMATRA
TAMBALA
TEMPERA
TEMPURA
TYMPANA

•••MA••
ADAMANT
AIRMAIL
AIRMASS
ANIMALS
ANIMATE
ANIMATO
ANOMALY
ARAMAIC
ATAMANS
BARMAID
BIOMASS
BITMAPS
BROMATE
CAIMANS
CLIMATE
COMMAND
DENMARK
DISMAYS
DOGMATA
DOLMANS
DORMANT
EARMARK
FANMAIL
FORMALS
FORMATS
FROMAGE
GASMAIN
GERMANE
GERMANS
GERMANY
GRIMACE
HAEMATO
HERMANN
HETMANS
IMAMATE
ISHMAEL
KIRMANS
KLAMATH
MAMMALS
MANMADE
MARMARA
MERMAID
MICMACS
MISMATE
NEWMATH
NORMALS
NORMAND
NORMANS
OLDMAID
PALMATE
PLUMAGE
PRIMACY
PRIMARY
PRIMATE
REAMASS
RUMMAGE
SHAMANS
SKIMASK
STOMACH
STOMATA
SUMMARY
SUNMAID
TAMMANY
TARMACS
TEDMACK
TOPMAST
ULLMANN
WALMART
WIDMARK
YESMAAM
YOUMANS
ZERMATT

•••M•A•
ALUMNAE
ALUMNAL
ARAMEAN
BESMEAR
CHEMLAB
CRIMEAN
GRAMMAR
HOLMOAK
MIAMIAN
MUAMMAR
NUTMEAT
OATMEAL
REDMEAT
RHUMBAS
TRAMCAR
TRAMPAS
YESMAAM

•••M••A
ALAMEDA
BERMUDA
CHIMERA
CREMONA
DOGMATA
FORMICA
FORMOSA
FORMULA
MARMARA
OLYMPIA
OXYMORA
STAMINA
STOMATA
WOOMERA

••••MA•
ABYSMAL
AUTOMAT
BAHAMAS
BASEMAN
BATEMAN
BATHMAT
BATSMAN
BELLMAN
BERGMAN
BESTMAN
BETAMAX
BIRDMAN
BOATMAN
BONDMAN
BRAHMAN
BRAHMAS
BUSHMAN
CAVEMAN
CHAPMAN
CINEMAS
CINEMAX
COLEMAN
CREWMAN
DARKMAN
DECIMAL
DOORMAN
DOORMAT
EASTMAN
ENIGMAS
FADIMAN
FELDMAN
FEYNMAN
FIREMAN
FLAGMAN
FOOTMAN
FOREMAN
FREEMAN
FROGMAN
GATEMAN
GOODMAN
GRAMMAR
HACKMAN
HANGMAN
HARTMAN
HEADMAN
HELLMAN
HICKMAN
HOFFMAN
HOUSMAN
INGEMAR
INHUMAN
IRONMAN
JAVAMAN
JAZZMAN
JICAMAS
JUNKMAN
KINGMAN
KINSMAN
KLUGMAN
LIKEMAD
LINEMAN
MANXMAN
MAXIMAL
MIASMAS
MILKMAN
MINIMAL
MIRAMAR
MIRAMAX
MUAMMAR
MYANMAR
NEWSMAN
OPTIMAL
OTTOMAN
PAJAMAS
PALOMAR
PANAMAS
PERLMAN
PIKEMAN
PITTMAN
PLASMAS
PLOWMAN
POSTMAN
POTOMAC
PROPMAN
PULLMAN
PYJAMAS
RAINMAN
REPOMAN
RICHMAN
ROADMAP
SANDMAN
SCHEMAS
SHERMAN
SHIPMAN
SHOWMAN
SIDEMAN
SNOWMAN
STARMAN
STARMAP
STIGMAS
SYNGMAN
THERMAL
THINMAN
THURMAN
TRAUMAS
TUCHMAN
WALKMAN
WHITMAN
WISEMAN
WOLFMAN
WORKMAN
YARDMAN
YASHMAK
ZEUGMAS

••••M•A
ANAEMIA
ANOSMIA
BOHEMIA
CARAMBA
CARAMIA
DILEMMA
ENCOMIA
LABAMBA
MARIMBA

•••••MA
ALABAMA
ATACAMA
DEPALMA
DILEMMA
DIORAMA
DIPLOMA
DRACHMA
GAUTAMA
GRANDMA
IPANEMA
IWOJIMA
LAPALMA
MAHATMA
NOXZEMA
SATSUMA

MB•••••
MBABANE

M•B••••
MOBBING
MOBCAPS
MOBILES
MOBSTER
MRBONES
MUBARAK

M••B•••
MACBETH
MAMBOED
MARBLED
MARBLES
MAXBAER
MAXBORN
MBABANE
MEMBERS
MOBBING
MOMBASA
MUMBLED
MUMBLER
MUMBLES

M•••B••
MACABRE
MAILBAG
MAILBOX
MALABAR
MARABOU
MINABLE
MINIBUS
MIXABLE
MOVABLE
MUTABLE
MUTABLY

M••••B•
MADLIBS
MARIMBA
MASTABA
MICROBE
MIDRIBS
MOGAMBO
MORESBY

•MB••••
AMBIENT
AMBLERS
AMBLING
AMBRIES
AMBROSE
EMBANKS
EMBARGO
EMBARKS
EMBASSY
EMBLEMS
EMBRACE
EMBROIL
EMBRYOS
IMBIBED
IMBIBES
IMBRUED
IMBRUES
IMBUING
UMBERTO
UMBRAGE
UMBRIAN

•M•B•••
AMIBLUE

•M••B••
AMIABLE
AMIABLY
AMOEBAE
AMOEBAS
AMOEBIC
IMBIBED
IMBIBES
OMNIBUS

••MB•••
ARMBAND
BAMBINO
BAMBOOS
BOMBARD
BOMBAST
BOMBECK
BOMBERS
BOMBING
BUMBLED
BUMBLER
BUMBLES
CAMBERS
CAMBIUM
CAMBRIC

CEMBALO
COMBATS
COMBERS
COMBINE
COMBING
COMBUST
CYMBALS
DIMBULB
DUMBEST
FUMBLED
FUMBLER
FUMBLES
GAMBIAN
GAMBITS
GAMBLED
GAMBLER
GAMBLES
GAMBOLS
GAMBREL
GIMBALS
GUMBALL
HAMBURG
HOMBRES
HOMBURG
HUMBLED
HUMBLER
HUMBLES
HUMBUGS
JUMBLED
JUMBLES
KIMBALL
LAMBADA
LAMBDAS
LAMBEAU
LAMBENT
LAMBERT
LIMBERS
LIMBING
LOMBARD
LUMBAGO
LUMBARS
LUMBERS
MAMBOED
MEMBERS
MOMBASA
MUMBLED
MUMBLER
MUMBLES
NIMBLER
NUMBATS
NUMBERS
NUMBEST
NUMBING
PAMBIES
RAMBEAU
RAMBLED
RAMBLER
RAMBLES
RIMBAUD
RUMBAED
RUMBLED
RUMBLES
SAMBAED
SAMBARS
SYMBOLS
TAMBALA
TAMBOUR
TEMBLOR
TIMBALE
TIMBALS
TIMBERS
TIMBRES
TOMBOYS
TUMBLED
TUMBLER
TUMBLES
TUMBREL
WAMBLED
WAMBLES
WOMBATS
ZAMBEZI
ZAMBIAN
ZOMBIES

••M•B••
GEMSBOK
NAMIBIA
TAMABLE

••M••B•
COMESBY

••M•••B
DIMBULB

•••MB••
ALEMBIC
BOOMBOX
BRAMBLE
BRAMBLY
CHAMBER
CLAMBER
CLIMBED
CLIMBER
CRUMBLE
CRUMBLY
FLAMBED
FLAMBES
FNUMBER
GRUMBLE
PLUMBED
PLUMBER
RHOMBUS
RHUMBAS
SHAMBLE
SLUMBER
STUMBLE
THIMBLE
THUMBED
TREMBLE
TREMBLY

•••M••B
CHEMLAB

••••MB•
BENUMBS
CARAMBA
COLUMBO
LABAMBA
MARIMBA
MOGAMBO

•••••MB
COULOMB
COXCOMB
SUCCUMB

MC•••••
MCCALLS
MCENROE
MCGAVIN
MCGUIRE
MCLUHAN
MCMAHON
MCQUEEN
MCSWINE

M•C••••
MACABRE
MACADAM
MACAQUE
MACBETH
MACDUFF
MACGRAW
MACHETE
MACHINA
MACHINE
MACRAME
MACRONS
MACULAE
MCCALLS
MICHAEL
MICHELE
MICMACS
MICROBE
MICRONS
MOCKERS
MOCKERY
MOCKING
MOCKUPS
MRCHIPS
MRCLEAN
MUCKING
MUCKSUP

M••C•••
MADCAPS
MADCHEN
MALCOLM
MANCINI
MARCEAU
MARCELS
MARCHED
MARCHEN
MARCHER
MARCHES
MARCHON
MARCONI
MASCARA
MASCOTS
MATCHED
MATCHES
MATCHUP
MENCKEN
MERCIES
MERCURY
MESCALS
MINCERS
MINCING
MIOCENE
MISCALL
MISCAST
MISCUED
MISCUES
MITCHUM
MOBCAPS
MOOCHED
MOOCHER
MOOCHES
MULCHED
MULCHES
MULCTED
MUNCHED
MUNCHER
MUNCHES
MUSCATS
MUSCLED
MUSCLES
MUSCOVY

M•••C••
MAGICAL
MALACCA
MALACHI
MANACLE
MANXCAT
MARACAS
MEDICAL
MEDICOS
MENACED
MENACES
MEXICAN
MILKCOW
MIMICRY
MINICAM
MIRACLE
MODICUM
MOHICAN
MONOCLE
MONOCOT
MOROCCO
MUSICAL

M••••C•
MAJORCA
MALACCA
MANIACS
MASTICS
MATLOCK
MATTOCK
MAURICE
MENISCI
METRICS
MICMACS
MINORCA
MONARCH
MOROCCO
MOSAICS
MRSPOCK
MUDPACK
MURDOCH
MYSTICS

M•••••C
MALEFIC
MANTRIC
MASONIC
MEDEVAC
MEIOTIC
MELODIC
MIASMIC
MIDDLEC
MIMETIC
MITOTIC

•M•C•••
AMSCRAY
OMICRON
SMACKED
SMACKER

•M••C••
AMERCED
AMERCES
IMPACTS

•M•••C•
AMERICA
EMBRACE
IMPEACH

•M••••C
AMHARIC
AMOEBIC

••MC•••
JIMCHEE
TOMCATS

••M•C••
COMICAL
JUMPCUT
MIMICRY
PEMICAN
PUMICES
TIMECOP

••M••C•
ARMLOCK
BOMBECK
COMPACT
GIMMICK
HAMHOCK
HAMMOCK
HEMLOCK
HUMMOCK
JAMAICA
JAMPACK
LAMARCK
PIMLICO
ROMANCE
TAMPICO

••M•••C
ALMANAC
CAMBRIC
COMEDIC
DEMONIC
HAMITIC
HOMERIC
MIMETIC
NOMADIC
NUMERIC
OSMOTIC
SEMITIC
SOMATIC

•••MC••
TRAMCAR

•••M•C•
DORMICE
FORMICA
GIMMICK
GRIMACE
HAMMOCK
HUMMOCK
MICMACS
PRIMACY
STOMACH
TARMACS
TEDMACK
TITMICE

•••M••C
ALEMBIC
ARAMAIC
OLYMPIC

••••M•C
ANOSMIC
CERAMIC
DYNAMIC
ENDEMIC
ISLAMIC
MIASMIC
POLEMIC
POTOMAC
SEISMIC
TOTEMIC

•••••MC
YOUNGMC

M•D••••
MADAMEX
MADCAPS
MADCHEN
MADDENS
MADDERS
MADDEST
MADDING
MADEFOR
MADEHAY
MADEIRA
MADEOFF
MADEOUT
MADEWAY
MADISON
MADLIBS
MADNESS
MADONNA
MADRONA
MEDALED
MEDDLED
MEDDLER
MEDDLES
MEDEVAC
MEDIANS
MEDIANT
MEDIATE
MEDICAL
MEDICOS
MEDIUMS
MEDLEYS
MEDULLA
MEDUSAE
MEDUSAS
MIDDAYS
MIDDENS
MIDDIES
MIDDLEC
MIDDLES
MIDEAST
MIDGETS
MIDLAND
MIDLIFE
MIDLINE
MIDRIBS
MIDRIFF
MIDRISE
MIDSIZE
MIDTERM
MIDTOWN
MIDWAYS
MIDWEEK
MIDWEST
MIDWIFE
MIDYEAR
MODELAS
MODELED
MODELER
MODELTS
MODERNS
MODESTO
MODESTY
MODICUM
MODISTE
MODULAR
MODULES
MUDDERS
MUDDIED
MUDDIER
MUDDIES
MUDDLED
MUDDLER
MUDDLES
MUDEELS
MUDHENS
MUDPACK
MUDPIES

M••D•••
MACDUFF
MADDENS
MADDERS
MADDEST
MADDING
MAIDENS
MANDALA
MANDANS
MANDATE
MANDAYS
MANDELA
MANDREL
MANDRIL
MAUDLIN
MAYDAYS
MEADOWS
MEADOWY
MEDDLED
MEDDLER
MEDDLES
MELDING
MENDERS
MENDING
MENDOZA
MIDDAYS
MIDDENS
MIDDIES
MIDDLEC
MIDDLES
MILDEST
MILDEWS
MILDEWY
MILDRED
MINDERS
MINDFUL
MINDING
MINDSET
MISDATE
MISDEAL
MISDEED
MISDIAL
MISDOES
MISDONE
MOLDERS
MOLDIER
MOLDING
MONDALE
MONDAYS
MOODIER
MOODILY
MORDANT
MORDENT
MORDRED
MOWDOWN
MUDDERS
MUDDIED
MUDDIER
MUDDIES
MUDDLED
MUDDLER
MUDDLES
MUNDANE
MURDERS
MURDOCH

M•••D••
MACADAM
MALODOR
MATADOR
MAULDIN
MAUNDER
MEANDER
MELODIC
MIKADOS
MILLDAM
MIRADOR
MIXEDUP
MOONDOG
MOULDED
MOULDER
MOUNDED
MOVEDIN

M••••D•
MAENADS
MAKESDO
MALTEDS
MANMADE
MARAUDS
MATILDA
MELINDA
METHODS
MILORDS
MIRANDA
MYRIADS

M•••••D
MAITRED
MAJORED
MALAMUD
MALLARD
MAMBOED
MANAGED
MANFRED
MANGLED
MANHOOD
MANKIND
MANSARD
MANTLED
MARBLED
MARCHED
MARRIED
MASTOID
MATCHED
MATURED
MAYNARD
MEDALED
MEDDLED
MENACED
MERITED
MERMAID
METERED
MIDLAND
MILDRED
MILHAUD
MILLAND
MILLARD
MILLEND
MINGLED
MINORED
MINUEND
MISCUED
MISDEED
MISLAID
MISLEAD
MISREAD
MISUSED
MISWORD
MITERED
MITFORD
MIZZLED
MODELED
MONEYED
MONTAND
MOOCHED
MORDRED
MORPHED
MOSEYED
MOTORED
MOTTLED
MOULDED
MOULTED
MOUNDED
MOUNTED
MOUSSED
MOUTHED
MUDDIED
MUDDLED
MUFFLED
MULCHED
MULCTED
MUMBLED
MUMFORD
MUNCHED
MUSCLED
MUSTARD
MUTATED
MUZZLED

•M•D•••
AMADEUS
SMIDGEN
SMUDGED
SMUDGES

•M••D••
AMENDED
AMRADIO
EMENDED
EMENDER
FMRADIO
IMPEDED
IMPEDES
SMOLDER

•M•••D•
IMPENDS
IMPLODE

•M••••D
AMASSED
AMENDED
AMERCED
AMERIND
EMENDED
EMERALD
EMERGED
EMERSED
EMITTED
EMPTIED
IMBIBED
IMBRUED
IMMIXED
IMMURED
IMPALED
IMPEDED
IMPLIED
IMPOSED
IMPOUND
IMPUTED
OMITTED
SMACKED
SMARTED
SMASHED
SMEARED
SMELLED
SMELTED
SMIRKED
SMUDGED
UMPIRED

••MD•••
DUMDUMS
GUMDROP
HUMDRUM
JIMDINE

••M•D••
AIMEDAT
AIMEDTO
ALMADEN
ARMADAS
BIMODAL
COMEDIC
COMEDUE
HUMIDLY
HUMIDOR
LAMBDAS
NAMEDAY
NOMADIC
POMADED
POMADES
RAMADAN
RAMADAS
REMODEL
REMUDAS
SAMEDAY
SOMEDAY
TIMIDER
TIMIDLY

••M••D•
ALMONDS
COMMODE
COMRADE
DEMANDS
LAMBADA
LIMEADE
NIMRODS
ORMANDY
OSMONDS
RAMRODS
REMANDS
REMENDS
REMINDS
REMOLDS

••M•••D
ADMIRED
ADMIXED
ARMBAND
ARMLOAD
ARMORED
BEMIRED
BEMUSED
BOMBARD
BUMBLED
CAMEOED
COMMAND
COMMEND
DAMAGED
DEMIGOD
DEMISED
DEMOTED
DIMPLED
DUMMIED
FUMBLED
GAMBLED
HAMMOND
HOMERED
HOMINID
HUMBLED
HUMORED
IMMIXED
IMMURED
JEMMIED
JIMMIED
JUMBLED
LIMITED
LOMBARD
MAMBOED
MUMBLED
MUMFORD
OSMOSED
POMADED
RAMBLED
REMIXED
REMOVED
REMOWED
RIMBAUD
RUMBAED
RUMBLED
RUMORED
RUMPLED
SAMBAED
SAMOYED
SAMPLED
TEMPTED
TUMBLED
UNMOVED
WAMBLED
WIMPLED

•••M•D•
ALAMEDA
ALAMODE
BERMUDA
BROMIDE
COMMODE
DIOMEDE
MANMADE
PREMEDS
SCHMIDT

•••M••D
BARMAID
BRIMMED
CHAMPED
CHOMPED
CHUMMED
CLAMMED
CLAMPED
CLIMBED
CLUMPED
COMMAND
COMMEND
CRAMMED
CRAMPED
CRIMPED
DESMOND
DIAMOND
DRUMMED
DUMMIED
FLAMBED
GLOMMED
GRUMPED
HAMMOND
JEMMIED
JIMMIED
MERMAID
NORMAND
OLDMAID
PLUMBED
PLUMPED
PRIMPED
RAYMOND
SCAMMED
SCAMPED
SHAMMED
SIGMUND
SKIMMED
SKIMPED
SLAMMED
SLIMMED
SLUMMED
SLUMPED
STAMPED
STEMMED
STOMPED
STUMPED
STYMIED
SUNMAID
SWAMPED
THUMBED
THUMPED
TRAMPED
TRIMMED
TRUMPED
WHAMMED
WHOMPED

••••M•D
ALARMED
ASHAMED
ASSUMED
BLOOMED
BRIMMED
CAROMED
CHARMED
CHUMMED
CLAIMED
CLAMMED
CRAMMED
CREAMED
DEFAMED
DREAMED
DRUMMED
GLEAMED
GLOMMED
GROOMED
LIKEMAD
MALAMUD
PSALMED
PYRAMID
REARMED
RENAMED
RESUMED
RETIMED
SCAMMED
SCHEMED
SHAMMED
SKIMMED
SLAMMED
SLIMMED
SLUMMED
STEAMED
STEMMED
STORMED
SWARMED
TRIMMED
UNAIMED
UNARMED
UNNAMED
UNTAMED
WHAMMED

ME•••••
MEADOWS
MEADOWY
MEALIER
MEALIES
MEANDER
MEANEST
MEANIES
MEANING
MEASLES
MEASURE
MEATIER
MEDALED
MEDDLED
MEDDLER
MEDDLES
MEDEVAC
MEDIANS
MEDIANT
MEDIATE
MEDICAL
MEDICOS
MEDIUMS
MEDLEYS
MEDULLA
MEDUSAE
MEDUSAS
MEEKEST
MEETING
MEGOHMS
MEGRIMS
MEGRYAN
MEIOSES
MEIOSIS
MEIOTIC
MEISSEN
MELANGE
MELANIE
MELANIN
MELDING
MELINDA
MELISSA
MELLOWS
MELODIC
MELROSE
MELTING
MEMBERS
MEMENTO
MEMOIRE
MEMOIRS
MEMOREX
MEMPHIS
MENACED
MENACES
MENAGES
MENCKEN
MENDERS
MENDING
MENDOZA

MENFOLK
MENHIRS
MENIALS
MENISCI
MENORAH
MENOTTI
MENTHOL
MENTION
MENTORS
MENUHIN
MEOWING
MERCIES
MERCURY
MERGERS
MERGING
MERIMEE
MERINOS
MERITED
MERLOTS
MERMAID
MERRIER
MERRILL
MERRILY
MESCALS
MESHING
MESSAGE
MESSALA
MESSIAH
MESSIER
MESSILY
MESSINA
MESSING
MESSKIT
MESTIZO
METATES
METEORS
METEOUT
METERED
METHANE
METHODS
METIERS
METOOER
METRICS
METTLES
MEWLERS
MEWLING
MEXICAN

M•E••••

MAENADS
MAESTRI
MAESTRO
MAEWEST
MCENROE
MEEKEST
MEETING
MUEZZIN

M••E•••

MADEFOR
MADEHAY
MADEIRA
MADEOFF
MADEOUT
MADEWAY
MAGENTA
MAJESTE
MAJESTY
MAJEURE
MAKEFOR
MAKEHAY
MAKEOFF
MAKEOUT
MAKEPAR
MAKESDO
MAKESIT
MAKESUP
MAKEUPS
MAKEWAY
MALEATE
MALEFIC
MANEGES
MATEWAN
MEDEVAC
MEMENTO
METEORS
METEOUT
METERED
MIDEAST
MILEAGE
MIMESIS
MIMETIC
MINEOLA
MINERAL
MINERVA
MISERLY
MITERED
MIXEDUP
MIXESUP
MODELAS
MODELED
MODELER
MODELTS
MODERNS
MODESTO
MODESTY
MOLESTS
MOMENTS
MONEYED
MORELLO
MORESBY
MOSELLE
MOSEYED
MOVEDIN
MOVEOUT
MOVESIN
MUDEELS
MULETAS
MUMESON
MUSETTE
MUSEUMS

M•••E••

MACBETH
MACHETE
MADDENS
MADDERS
MADDEST
MADNESS
MAEWEST
MAGNETO
MAGNETS
MAGUEYS
MAIDENS
MAILERS
MALLETS
MALTEDS
MALTESE
MANDELA
MANGERS
MANNERS
MANTELS
MANYEAR
MAPPERS
MARCEAU
MARCELS
MARKERS
MARKETS
MARLENE
MARTENS
MARVELS
MASHERS
MASKERS
MASSEUR
MASTERS
MASTERY
MATHERS
MATHEWS
MATTERS
MAUREEN
MAXWELL
MAYHEMS
MCQUEEN
MEANEST
MEDLEYS
MEEKEST
MEMBERS
MENDERS
MERGERS
METIERS
MEWLERS
MICHELE
MIDDENS
MIDGETS
MIDTERM
MIDWEEK
MIDWEST
MIDYEAR
MILDEST
MILDEWS
MILDEWY
MILIEUS
MILIEUX
MILKERS
MILLEND
MILLERS
MILLETS
MILLETT
MIMIEUX
MINCERS
MINDERS
MINTERS
MINUEND
MINUETS
MIOCENE
MISDEAL
MISDEED
MISHEAR
MISLEAD
MISREAD
MISTERS
MITTENS
MIZZENS
MOANERS
MOCKERS
MOCKERY
MOILERS
MOLDERS
MOLIERE
MOLTERS
MONGERS
MONKEES
MONKEYS
MONTEGO
MONTEUX
MOPPERS
MOPPETS
MORDENT
MORSELS
MOSLEMS
MOTHERS
MOUSERS
MRCLEAN
MUDDERS
MUDEELS
MUDHENS
MUGGERS
MULLEIN
MULLERS
MULLETS
MUMMERS
MUMMERY
MUPPETS
MURDERS
MUSHERS
MUSKETS
MUSSELS
MUSTERS
MUTTERS
MYNHEER
MYSTERY

M••••E•

MADAMEX
MADCHEN
MAGPIES
MAHONEY
MAIGRET
MAITRED
MAJORED
MALAREN
MALMSEY
MAMBOED
MANAGED
MANAGER
MANAGES
MANATEE
MANDREL
MANEGES
MANFRED
MANGIER
MANGLED
MANGLES
MANGOES
MANLIER
MANTLED
MANTLES
MANXMEN
MARBLED
MARBLES
MARCHED
MARCHEN
MARCHER
MARCHES
MARGRET
MARINER
MARINES
MARQUEE
MARQUES
MARQUEZ
MARRIED
MARRIES
MARSHES
MASHIES
MASQUES
MATCHED
MATCHES
MATINEE
MATTHEW
MATURED
MATURER
MATURES
MAUNDER
MAUREEN
MAXBAER
MCQUEEN
MEALIER
MEALIES
MEANDER
MEANIES
MEASLES
MEATIER
MEDALED
MEDDLED
MEDDLER
MEDDLES
MEIOSES
MEISSEN
MEMOREX
MENACED
MENACES
MENAGES
MENCKEN
MERCIES
MERIMEE
MERITED
MERRIER
MESSIER
METATES
METERED
METOOER
METTLES
MICHAEL
MIDDIES
MIDDLEC
MIDDLES
MIDWEEK
MILDRED
MILKIER
MILKMEN
MINARET
MINDSET
MINGLED
MINGLER
MINGLES
MINIVER
MINORED
MINTIER
MINUSES
MINUTES
MIRAGES
MISCUED
MISCUES
MISDEED
MISDOES
MISSIES
MISSTEP
MISTIER
MISUSED
MISUSES
MITERED
MITOSES
MIZZLED
MIZZLES
MOBILES
MOBSTER
MODELED
MODELER
MODULES
MOISTEN
MOISTER
MOLDIER
MOMMIES
MONEYED
MONGREL
MONIKER
MONKEES
MONOMER
MONSTER
MOOCHED
MOOCHER
MOOCHES
MOODIER
MOONSET
MOORHEN
MORALES
MORDRED
MORPHED
MOSEYED
MOSQUES
MOSSIER
MOTIVES
MOTORED
MOTTLED
MOTTLES
MOTTOES
MOULDED
MOULDER
MOULTED
MOUNDED
MOUNTED
MOUSIER
MOUSSED
MOUSSES
MOUTHED
MRBONES
MUDDIED
MUDDIER
MUDDIES
MUDDLED
MUDDLER
MUDDLES
MUDPIES
MUFFLED
MUFFLER
MUFFLES
MUGGIER
MULCHED
MULCHES
MULCTED
MUMBLED
MUMBLER
MUMBLES
MUMMIES
MUNCHED
MUNCHER
MUNCHES
MURKIER
MURPHEY
MUSCLED
MUSCLES
MUSHIER
MUSTIER
MUSTSEE
MUTAGEN
MUTATED
MUTATES
MUZZIER
MUZZLED
MUZZLES
MYNHEER
MYRTLES

M•••••E

MACABRE
MACAQUE
MACHETE
MACHINE
MACRAME
MACULAE
MAGNATE
MAJESTE
MAJEURE
MALAISE
MALEATE
MALTESE
MALTOSE
MANACLE
MANATEE
MANDATE
MANHOLE
MANIPLE
MANMADE
MARGATE
MARLENE
MARLOWE
MARQUEE
MARRYME
MASSAGE
MASSIVE
MATINEE
MATISSE
MAURICE
MAYPOLE
MAYTIME
MAYWINE
MBABANE
MCENROE
MCGUIRE
MCSWINE
MEASURE
MEDIATE
MEDUSAE
MELANGE
MELANIE
MELROSE
MEMOIRE
MERIMEE
MESSAGE
METHANE
MICHELE
MICROBE
MIDLIFE
MIDLINE
MIDRISE
MIDSIZE
MIDWIFE
MIGRATE
MILEAGE
MINABLE
MIOCENE
MIRACLE
MISDATE
MISDONE
MISFILE
MISFIRE
MISMATE
MISNAME
MISRULE
MISSILE
MISSIVE
MISTAKE
MISTYPE
MIXABLE
MIXTURE
MODISTE
MOLIERE
MONDALE
MONIQUE
MONOCLE
MONTAGE
MONTANE
MOORAGE
MORAINE
MORTISE
MOSELLE
MOULAGE
MOUNTIE
MOVABLE
MUNDANE
MUSETTE
MUSTSEE
MUTABLE

•ME••••

AMENDED
AMENITY
AMERCED
AMERCES
AMERICA
AMERIGO
AMERIKA
AMERIND
EMENDED
EMENDER
EMERALD
EMERGED
EMERGES
EMERITA
EMERITI
EMERSED
EMERSON
KMESONS
OMELETS
OMENTUM
SMEARED
SMELLED
SMELTED
SMELTER
SMETANA

•M•E•••

AMHERST
AMMETER
AMNESIA
AMNESTY
AMOEBAE
AMOEBAS
AMOEBIC
AMPERES
EMPEROR
IMMENSE
IMMERSE
IMPEACH
IMPEDED
IMPEDES
IMPENDS
IMPERIL
IMPETUS
UMBERTO

•M••E••

AMADEUS
AMATEUR
AMBIENT
AMBLERS
AMPLEST
AMULETS
EMBLEMS
EMINENT
EMOTERS
EMPRESS
IMAGERS
IMAGERY
IMARETS
IMOGENE
IMPIETY
IMPRESS
OMELETS
SMILERS
SMOKERS
UMPTEEN

•M•••E•

AMASSED
AMASSES
AMBRIES
AMENDED
AMERCED
AMERCES
AMMETER
AMPERES
AMPULES
BMOVIES
EMANUEL
EMENDED
EMENDER
EMERGED
EMERGES
EMERSED
EMIGRES
EMITTED
EMITTER
EMPANEL
EMPIRES
EMPOWER
EMPTIED
EMPTIER
EMPTIES
IMAGOES
IMBIBED
IMBIBES
IMBRUED
IMBRUES
IMMIXED
IMMIXES
IMMURED
IMMURES
IMPALED
IMPALES
IMPANEL
IMPEDED
IMPEDES
IMPLIED
IMPLIES
IMPOSED
IMPOSES
IMPURER
IMPUTED
IMPUTES
OMITTED
SMACKED
SMACKER
SMALLER
SMARTED
SMARTEN
SMARTER
SMASHED
SMASHER
SMASHES
SMATTER
SMEARED
SMELLED
SMELTED
SMELTER
SMIDGEN
SMIRKED
SMITTEN
SMOKIER
SMOKIES
SMOLDER
SMOTHER
SMUDGED
SMUDGES
SMUGGER
UMPIRED
UMPIRES
UMPTEEN

•M••••E

AMATIVE
AMBROSE
AMIABLE
AMIBLUE
AMOEBAE
AMPOULE
AMYLASE
EMANATE
EMBRACE
EMIRATE
EMOTIVE
EMULATE
IMAGINE
IMAMATE
IMITATE
IMMENSE
IMMERSE
IMOGENE
IMPASSE
IMPINGE
IMPLODE
IMPLORE
IMPROVE
IMPULSE
SMUGGLE
UMBRAGE

••ME•••

AIMEDAT
AIMEDTO
AMMETER
ARMENIA
CAMELIA
CAMELOT
CAMEOED
CAMEOFF
CAMEOUT
CAMERAS
CAMERON
CEMENTS
COMEDIC
COMEDUE
COMEOFF
COMEONS
COMEOUT
COMESAT
COMESBY
COMESIN
COMESON
COMESTO
COMESUP
DEMEANS
DEMERIT
DEMEROL
DEMESNE
DEMETER
FOMENTS
GAMELAW
GAMETES
HAMELIN
HOMERED
HOMERIC
HOMERUN
HUMERAL
HUMERUS
IMMENSE
IMMERSE
JAMESON
JIMENEZ
LAMENTS
LIMEADE
MEMENTO
MIMESIS
MIMETIC
MOMENTS
MUMESON
NAMEDAY
NAMETAG
NEMEROV
NEMESES
NEMESIS
NUMERAL
NUMERIC
PIMENTO
PIMESON
POMELOS
RAMEKIN
RAMESES
REMELTS
REMENDS
SAMEDAY
SIMENON
SOMEDAY
SOMEHOW
SOMEONE
SOMEWAY
TIMECOP
TIMELAG
TIMEOFF
TIMEOUT
TIMESUP
TIMEWAS
YEMENIS

••M•E••

AIMLESS
ARMLESS
ARMLETS
ARMREST
BOMBECK
BOMBERS
BUMMERS
BUMPERS
CAMBERS
CAMPERS
COMBERS
COMMEND
COMMENT
COMPEER
COMPELS
COMPETE
DAMPENS
DAMPERS
DAMPEST
DAMSELS
DIMMERS
DIMMEST
DIMNESS
DUMBEST
GAMIEST
GIMLETS
GOMPERS
HAMLETS
HAMMERS
HAMMETT
HAMPERS
HEMMERS
HIMSELF
HOMIEST
HUMMERS
JAMMERS
JUMPERS
LAMBEAU
LAMBENT
LAMBERT
LIMBERS
LIMIEST
LIMNERS
LIMPEST
LIMPETS
LUMBERS
LUMIERE
LUMPERS
MEMBERS
MIMIEUX
MUMMERS
MUMMERY
NUMBERS
NUMBEST
PAMPERS
POMMELS
POMPEIA
POMPEII
PUMMELS
PUMPERS
RAMBEAU
RAMJETS
ROMNEYS
ROMPERS
SIMMERS
SIMPERS
SUMMERS
SUMMERY
TAMPERS
TEMPERA
TEMPERS
TEMPEST
TIMBERS
VAMPERS
YAMMERS
ZAMBEZI

••M••E•

ADMIRED
ADMIRER
ADMIRES
ADMIXED
ADMIXES
ALMADEN
AMMETER
ARMORED
ARMORER
BEMIRED
BEMIRES
BEMUSED
BEMUSES
BUMBLED
BUMBLER
BUMBLES
BUMPIER
CAMEOED
CAMISES
CAMPIER
COMFIER
COMFREY
COMPEER
COMPLEX
DAMAGED
DAMAGES
DEMETER
DEMISED
DEMISES
DEMOTED
DEMOTES
DEMPSEY
DEMURER
DIMPLED
DIMPLES
DUMMIED
DUMMIES
DUMPIER
ELMTREE
ERMINES
FEMALES
FUMBLED
FUMBLER
FUMBLES
GAMBLED
GAMBLER
GAMBLES
GAMBREL
GAMETES
GAMINES
GUMMIER
GUMTREE
HAMITES
HAMSTER
HEMSLEY
HOMBRES
HOMERED
HOMINEM
HUMBLED
HUMBLER
HUMBLES
HUMORED
IMMIXED
IMMIXES
IMMURED
IMMURES
INMATES
JEMMIED
JEMMIES
JIMCHEE
JIMENEZ
JIMMIED
JIMMIES
JUMBLED
JUMBLES
JUMPIER
LAMPREY
LIMITED
LIMOGES
LUMPIER
MAMBOED
MEMOREX
MOMMIES
MUMBLED
MUMBLER
MUMBLES
MUMMIES
NEMESES
NIMBLER
NOMINEE
OSMOSED
OSMOSES
PAMBIES
POMADED
POMADES
PUMICES

RAMBLED
RAMBLER
RAMBLES
RAMESES
REMAKES
REMIXED
REMIXES
REMODEL
REMOTER
REMOTES
REMOVED
REMOVER
REMOVES
REMOWED
RUMBAED
RUMBLED
RUMBLES
RUMMIER
RUMORED
RUMPLED
RUMPLES
SAMBAED
SAMISEN
SAMITES
SAMOYED
SAMPLED
SAMPLER
SAMPLES
SEMITES
SIMILES
SIMPLER
SIMPLEX
TAMALES
TEMPLES
TEMPTED
TEMPTER
TIMBRES
TIMIDER
TUMBLED
TUMBLER
TUMBLES
TUMBREL
TUMMIES
UNMAKES
UNMOVED
WAMBLED
WAMBLES
WIMPLED
WIMPLES
YUMMIER
ZOMBIES

••M•••E

AAMILNE
ARMHOLE
ARMOIRE
CAMILLE
COMBINE
COMEDUE
COMIQUE
COMMODE
COMMOVE
COMMUNE
COMMUTE
COMPARE
COMPETE
COMPILE
COMPOSE
COMPOTE
COMPUTE
COMRADE
DEMESNE
DEMILLE
ELMTREE
ENMASSE
GEMLIKE
GUMSHOE
GUMTREE
GYMSHOE
HEMLINE
IMMENSE
IMMERSE
JIMCHEE
JIMDINE
LAMINAE
LIMEADE
LUMIERE
MEMOIRE
NOMINEE
RAMPAGE
REMORSE
ROMAINE
ROMANCE
RUMMAGE
RUMPOLE
SOMEONE
TAMABLE
TIMBALE
VAMOOSE
VAMPIRE

•••ME••

AILMENT
ALAMEDA
ALAMEIN
ALIMENT
ARAMEAN
AUGMENT
BESMEAR
BOOMERS
BUMMERS
BURMESE
CALMEST
CHIMERA
CLEMENS
CLEMENT
COMMEND
COMMENT
CRIMEAN
DIMMERS
DIMMEST
DIOMEDE
DOLMENS
DORMERS
ELEMENT
ENAMELS
FARMERS
FERMENT
FIGMENT
FIRMEST
FRAMEUP
GARMENT
HAMMERS
HAMMETT
HELMETS
HEMMERS
HUMMERS
INAMESS
ISOMERS
JAMMERS
MUMMERS
MUMMERY
NUTMEAT
NUTMEGS
OATMEAL
ODDMENT
PAYMENT
PIGMENT
POMMELS
PREMEDS
PRIMERS
PUMMELS
RAIMENT
REAMERS
REDMEAT
RHYMERS
ROAMERS
ROOMERS
SCHMEER
SEGMENT
SIAMESE
SIMMERS
STAMENS
SUMMERS
SUMMERY
TORMENT
VERMEER
VERMEIL
WARMEST
WOOMERA
YAMMERS

•••M•E•

ATOMIES
BALMIER
BARMIER
BEAMIER
BRIMMED
CHAMBER
CHAMFER
CHAMPED
CHIMNEY
CHOMPED
CHUMMED
CLAMBER
CLAMMED
CLAMMER
CLAMPED
CLIMBED
CLIMBER
CLUMPED
CRAMMED
CRAMMER
CRAMPED
CRIMPED
CRIMPER
CRUMPET
DAIMLER
DAUMIER
DRUMMED
DRUMMER
DUMMIED
DUMMIES
ENEMIES
FILMIER
FLAMBED
FLAMBES
FNUMBER
FOAMIER
GLIMMER
GLOMMED
GLUMMER
GRAMMER
GRAMMES
GRIMIER
GRIMMER
GROMMET
GRUMPED
GUIMPES
GUMMIER
ISHMAEL
JEMMIED
JEMMIES
JIMMIED
JIMMIES
LOAMIER
MALMSEY
MOMMIES
MUMMIES
PALMIER
PLUMBED
PLUMBER
PLUMMER
PLUMMET
PLUMPED
PLUMPER
PREMIER
PRIMMER
PRIMPED
PYGMIES
ROOMIER
ROOMIES
RUMMIER
SCAMMED
SCAMPED
SCAMPER
SCHMEER
SCHMOES
SEAMIER
SHAMMED
SHIMMER
SKIMMED
SKIMMER
SKIMPED
SLAMMED
SLAMMER
SLIMIER
SLIMMED
SLIMMER
SLUMBER
SLUMMED
SLUMPED
STAMMER
STAMPED
STEMMED
STOMPED
STUMPED
STUMPER
STYMIED
STYMIES
SWAMPED
SWIMMER
THUMBED
THUMPED
THUMPER
TRAMMEL
TRAMPED
TRIMMED
TRIMMER
TRUMPED
TRUMPET
TUMMIES
VERMEER
WHAMMED
WHIMPER
WHOMPED
WORMIER
YUMMIER

•••M••E

ADAMITE
AIRMILE
ALAMODE
ALUMNAE
ANEMONE
ANIMATE
ANYMORE
ARDMORE
ATOMIZE
BRAMBLE
BROMATE
BROMIDE
BROMINE
BURMESE
CARMINE
CHEMISE
CLIMATE
COMMODE
COMMOVE
COMMUNE
COMMUTE
CRUMBLE
CRUMPLE
DIOMEDE
DORMICE
EREMITE
ETAMINE
EXAMINE
EXAMPLE
FROMAGE
GERMANE
GILMORE
GLIMPSE
GRIMACE
GRUMBLE
HORMONE
IMAMATE
ITEMIZE
JASMINE
MANMADE
MISMATE
PALMATE
PISMIRE
PLUMAGE
PREMISE
PRIMATE
PROMISE
PROMOTE
RUMMAGE
SHAMBLE
SIAMESE
SPUMONE
STUMBLE
SURMISE
TERMITE
THIMBLE
TITMICE
TRAMPLE
TREMBLE

••••ME•

ABDOMEN
AFRAMES
ALARMED
ALARMER
ALBUMEN
ASHAMED
ASSUMED
ASSUMES
ATHOMES
ATTIMES
BASEMEN
BATSMEN
BECOMES
BELLMEN
BESTMEN
BETIMES
BIRDMEN
BIREMES
BITUMEN
BLOOMED
BLOOMER
BOATMEN
BONDMEN
BRIMMED
BUSHMEN
CALOMEL
CALUMET
CARAMEL
CAROMED
CAVEMEN
CERUMEN
CHAPMEN
CHARMED
CHARMER
CHROMES
CHUMMED
CLAIMED
CLAIMER
CLAMMED
CLAMMER
COZUMEL
CRAMMED
CRAMMER
CREAMED
CREAMER
CREWMEN
DAHOMEY
DEFAMED
DEFAMES
DOORMEN
DREAMED
DREAMER
DRUMMED
DRUMMER
ENZYMES
FIREMEN
FLAGMEN
FOOTMEN
FOREMEN
FREEMEN
FROGMEN
GATEMEN
GLEAMED
GLIMMER
GLOMMED
GLUMMER
GOODMEN
GOURMET
GRAMMER
GRAMMES
GRIMMER
GROMMET
GROOMED
GROOMER
HANGMEN
HEADMEN
INCOMES
IRONMEN
JAZZMEN
KINSMEN
LEGUMES
LINEMEN
MADAMEX
MANXMEN
MERIMEE
MILKMEN
MONOMER
NEWSMEN
PDJAMES
PIKEMEN
PLOWMEN
PLUMMER
PLUMMET
POLYMER
POSTMEN
PRIMMER
PROPMEN
PSALMED
PUTAMEN
RACEMES
RADAMES
REARMED
REGIMEN
REGIMES
RENAMED
RENAMES
RESUMED
RESUMES
RETIMED
RETIMES
SANDMEN
SCAMMED
SCHEMED
SCHEMER
SCHEMES
SESAMES
SHAMMED
SHIMMER
SHIPMEN
SHOWMEN
SIDEMEN
SKIMMED
SKIMMER
SLAMMED
SLAMMER
SLIMMED
SLIMMER
SLUMMED
SNOWMEN
STAMMER
STEAMED
STEAMER
STEMMED
STORMED
SWARMED
SWIMMER
TRAMMEL
TRIMMED
TRIMMER
UNAIMED
UNARMED
UNNAMED
UNTAMED
VOLUMES
WHAMMED
WISEMEN
WOLFMEN
WORKMEN
YARDMEN

••••M•E

LARAMIE
MERIMEE
PREEMIE

•••••ME

ACADEME
AIRTIME
ALLOFME
ALLTIME
ANYTIME
AWESOME
BEDTIME
BEGRIME
BELDAME
BIGGAME
BIGNAME
BIGTIME
BUYTIME
CENTIME
CONGAME
CONSUME
COSTUME
CUTTIME
DAYTIME
ENDGAME
EPITOME
EXTREME
FULSOME
GRAHAME
HOWCOME
INFLAME
IRKSOME
KEYLIME
LISSOME
MACRAME
MARRYME
MAYTIME
MISNAME
NAPTIME
NOISOME
NOTHOME
OLDTIME
ONETIME
OUTCOME
PASTIME
PENNAME
PERFUME
PETNAME
PHONEME
PRESUME
RAGTIME
RECLAME
REFRAME
RHIZOME
RUNHOME
SAOTOME
SOSUEME
SUBLIME
SUBSUME
SUPREME
SURNAME
TEATIME
TRIREME
TWOSOME
TWOTIME
ULALUME
WARGAME
WARTIME
WELCOME
WINSOME
WOEISME

M•F••••

MAFIOSO
MIFFING
MRFIXIT
MUFFING
MUFFINS
MUFFLED
MUFFLER
MUFFLES

M••F•••

MANFRED
MAYFAIR
MENFOLK
MIFFING
MISFILE
MISFIRE
MISFITS
MITFORD
MOUFLON
MUFFING
MUFFINS
MUFFLED
MUFFLER
MUFFLES
MUMFORD

M•••F••

MADEFOR
MAKEFOR
MALEFIC
MINDFUL

M••••F•

MACDUFF
MADEOFF
MAGNIFY
MAKEOFF
MARKOFF
MASSIFS
MASTIFF
MIDLIFE
MIDRIFF
MIDWIFE
MOLLIFY
MORTIFY
MUSTAFA
MYSTIFY

M•••••F

MACDUFF
MADEOFF
MAKEOFF
MARKOFF
MASTIFF
MIDRIFF

•M•••F•

AMPLIFY

••MF•••

ARMFULS
COMFIER
COMFITS
COMFORT
COMFREY
MUMFORD
TOMFOOL

••M••F•

CAMEOFF
COMEOFF
JUMPOFF
TIMEOFF

••M•••F

CAMEOFF
COMEOFF
HIMSELF
JUMPOFF
TIMEOFF

•••MF••

BRIMFUL
CHAMFER
HARMFUL
ROOMFUL

•••M•F•

EARMUFF
PALMOFF

•••M••F

EARMUFF
PALMOFF

M•G••••

MAGENTA
MAGICAL
MAGINOT
MAGNATE
MAGNETO
MAGNETS
MAGNIFY
MAGNUMS
MAGPIES
MAGUEYS
MAGYARS
MCGAVIN
MCGUIRE
MEGOHMS
MEGRIMS
MEGRYAN
MIGHTNT
MIGRANT
MIGRATE
MOGAMBO
MUGGERS
MUGGIER
MUGGING
MUGSHOT
MUGWUMP

M••G•••

MACGRAW
MAIGRET
MANGERS
MANGIER
MANGLED
MANGLES
MANGOES
MARGATE
MARGAUX
MARGAYS
MARGINS
MARGRET
MAUGHAM
MERGERS
MERGING
MIDGETS
MINGLED
MINGLER
MINGLES
MONGERS
MONGOLS
MONGREL
MORGANA
MORGANS
MUGGERS
MUGGIER
MUGGING

M•••G••

MALIGNS
MANAGED
MANAGER
MANAGES
MANAGUA
MANEGES
MENAGES
MIRAGES
MRMAGOO
MRRIGHT
MUTAGEN

M••••G•

MAKINGS
MASSAGE
MELANGE
MESSAGE
MILEAGE
MONTAGE
MONTEGO
MOORAGE
MOULAGE

M•••••G

MADDING
MAILBAG
MAILING
MALTING
MANNING
MAPPING
MARKING
MARRING
MASHING
MASKING
MASSING
MATTING
MAULING
MEANING
MEETING
MELDING
MELTING
MENDING
MEOWING
MERGING
MESHING
MESSING
MEWLING
MIFFING
MILKING
MILLING
MINCING
MINDING
MINTING
MISSING
MISTING
MITRING
MOANING
MOBBING
MOCKING
MOILING
MOLDING
MOLTING
MONOLOG
MOONDOG
MOONING
MOORING
MOPPING
MORNING
MOSSING
MOUSING
MUCKING
MUFFING
MUGGING
MULLING
MUSHING
MUSSING
MUSTANG

•M•G•••

EMIGRES
IMAGERS
IMAGERY
IMAGINE
IMAGING
IMAGOES
IMOGENE
SMUGGER
SMUGGLE

•M••G••

AMALGAM
AMONGST
EMERGED
EMERGES
IMPUGNS
SMIDGEN
SMUDGED
SMUDGES
SMUGGER
SMUGGLE

•M•••G•

AMERIGO
EMBARGO
IMPINGE
UMBRAGE

•M••••G

AMAZING
AMBLING
AMUSING
EMOTING
IMAGING
IMBUING
SMILING
SMITING
SMOKING

••M•G••

DAMAGED
DAMAGES
DEMIGOD
LIMOGES
MRMAGOO

••M••G•

COMINGS
DOMINGO
HUMBUGS
LUMBAGO
RAMPAGE
RUMMAGE
TIMINGS
ZYMURGY

••M•••G

BOMBING
BUMMING
BUMPING
CAMPING
COMBING
DAMMING
DAMNING
DAMPING
DIMMING
DUMPING
GUMMING
HAMBURG
HAMMING
HEMMING
HOMBURG
HUMMING
JAMMING
JUMPING
LAMMING
LEMMING
LIMBING
LIMNING
LIMPING
LUMPING
NAMETAG
NUMBING
PUMPING
RAMMING
RIMMING
ROMPING
SAMSUNG
SUMMING
TAMPING
TIMELAG
VAMPING

•••M•G•

FROMAGE
NUTMEGS
PLUMAGE
RUMMAGE

•••M••G

BEAMING
BLAMING
BOOMING
BUMMING
CALMING
CHIMING
DAMMING
DEEMING
DIMMING
DOOMING
FARMING
FILMING
FIRMING
FLAMING
FLEMING
FOAMING
FORMING
FRAMING
GUMMING
HAMMING
HARMING
HELMING
HEMMING
HUMMING
JAMMING
LAMMING
LEMMING
LOAMING
LOOMING
PALMING
PERMING
PLUMING
PRIMING
RAMMING
REAMING
RHYMING
RIMMING
ROAMING
ROOMING
SEAMING
SEEMING
SHAMING

SPUMING
SUMMING
TEAMING
TEEMING
TERMING
WARMING
WYOMING
ZOOMING

M•H••••

MAHALIA
MAHARIS
MAHATMA
MAHONEY
MAHOUTS
MOHAIRS
MOHAWKS
MOHICAN

M••H•••

MACHETE
MACHINA
MACHINE
MANHOLE
MANHOOD
MANHOUR
MANHUNT
MASHERS
MASHIES
MASHING
MATHERS
MATHEWS
MATHIAS
MAYHEMS
MENHIRS
MESHING
METHANE
METHODS
MICHAEL
MICHELE
MIGHTNT
MIKHAIL
MILHAUD
MISHAPS
MISHEAR
MISHITS
MITHRAS
MOTHERS
MRCHIPS
MUDHENS
MUSHERS
MUSHIER
MUSHILY
MUSHING
MUZHIKS
MYNHEER

M•••H••

MADCHEN
MADEHAY
MAKEHAY
MALTHUS
MARCHED
MARCHEN
MARCHER
MARCHES
MARCHON
MARKHAM
MARKHOR
MARSHAL
MARSHES
MATCHED
MATCHES
MATCHUP
MATTHAU
MATTHEW
MAUGHAM
MCLUHAN
MCMAHON
MEGOHMS
MEMPHIS
MENTHOL
MENUHIN
MITCHUM
MONTHLY
MOOCHED
MOOCHER
MOOCHES
MOORHEN
MORPHED
MOUTHED
MUGSHOT
MULCHED
MULCHES
MUNCHED
MUNCHER
MUNCHES
MURPHEY

M••••H•

MALACHI
MATZOHS
MRRIGHT
MULLAHS

M•••••H

MACBETH
MAMMOTH
MANNISH
MAWKISH
MENORAH
MESSIAH
MISSISH
MITZVAH
MONARCH
MONKISH
MOORISH
MURDOCH

•MH••••

AMHARIC
AMHERST

•M•H•••

AMPHORA
OMPHALI

•M••H••

SMASHED
SMASHER
SMASHES
SMASHUP
SMOTHER

•M•••H•

EMPATHY
SMOOTHS

•M••••H

IMPEACH

••MH•••

ARMHOLE
HAMHOCK
SAMHILL

••M•H••

CAMPHOR
GUMSHOE
GYMSHOE
JIMCHEE
MCMAHON
MEMPHIS
RIMSHOT
SOMEHOW

••M••H•

IOMOTHS
OOMPAHS
TIMOTHY

••M•••H

DAMPISH
MAMMOTH
ROMANSH

•••M••H

AZIMUTH
BISMUTH
BLEMISH
FLEMISH
KLAMATH
MAMMOTH
NEWMATH
STOMACH
WARMISH

••••M•H

GALUMPH
TRIUMPH

MI•••••

MIAMIAN
MIASMAS
MIASMIC
MICHAEL
MICHELE
MICMACS
MICROBE
MICRONS
MIDDAYS
MIDDENS
MIDDIES
MIDDLEC
MIDDLES
MIDEAST
MIDGETS
MIDLAND
MIDLIFE
MIDLINE
MIDRIBS
MIDRIFF
MIDRISE
MIDSIZE
MIDTERM
MIDTOWN
MIDWAYS
MIDWEEK
MIDWEST
MIDWIFE
MIDYEAR
MIFFING
MIGHTNT
MIGRANT
MIGRATE
MIKADOS
MIKHAIL
MILDEST
MILDEWS
MILDEWY
MILDRED
MILEAGE
MILHAUD
MILIEUS
MILIEUX
MILITIA
MILKCOW
MILKERS
MILKIER
MILKING
MILKMAN
MILKMEN
MILKRUN
MILKSOP
MILLAND
MILLARD
MILLDAM
MILLEND
MILLERS
MILLETS
MILLETT
MILLING
MILLION
MILLRUN
MILORDS
MIMESIS
MIMETIC
MIMICRY
MIMIEUX
MIMOSAS
MINABLE
MINARET
MINCERS
MINCING
MINDERS
MINDFUL
MINDING
MINDSET
MINEOLA
MINERAL
MINERVA
MINGLED
MINGLER
MINGLES
MINIBUS
MINICAM
MINIMAL
MINIMUM
MINIONS
MINIVAN
MINIVER
MINNOWS
MINOANS
MINOLTA
MINORCA
MINORED
MINTERS
MINTIER
MINTING
MINUEND
MINUETS
MINUSES
MINUTES
MINUTIA
MIOCENE
MIRACLE
MIRADOR
MIRAGES
MIRAMAR
MIRAMAX
MIRANDA
MIRRORS
MISALLY
MISCALL
MISCAST
MISCUED
MISCUES
MISDATE
MISDEAL
MISDEED
MISDIAL
MISDOES
MISDONE
MISERLY
MISFILE
MISFIRE
MISFITS
MISHAPS
MISHEAR
MISHITS
MISLAID
MISLAYS
MISLEAD
MISMATE
MISNAME
MISPLAY
MISREAD
MISRULE
MISSALS
MISSIES
MISSILE
MISSING
MISSION
MISSISH
MISSIVE
MISSOUT
MISSTEP
MISTAKE
MISTERS
MISTIER
MISTILY
MISTING
MISTOOK
MISTRAL
MISTYPE
MISUSED
MISUSES
MISWORD
MITCHUM
MITERED
MITFORD
MITHRAS
MITOSES
MITOSIS
MITOTIC
MITRING
MITTENS
MITZVAH
MIXABLE
MIXEDUP
MIXESUP
MIXITUP
MIXTURE
MIZZENS
MIZZLED
MIZZLES

M•I••••

MAIDENS
MAIGRET
MAILBAG
MAILBOX
MAILERS
MAILING
MAILLOT
MAINTOP
MAITAIS
MAITRED
MEIOSES
MEIOSIS
MEIOTIC
MEISSEN
MOILERS
MOILING
MOISTEN
MOISTER
MOISTLY

M••I•••

MADISON
MAFIOSO
MAGICAL
MAGINOT
MAKINGS
MALIGNS
MANIACS
MANILOW
MANIPLE
MANITOU
MAOISTS
MARIANA
MARILYN
MARIMBA
MARINAS
MARINER
MARINES
MARITAL
MATILDA
MATINEE
MATISSE
MAXILLA
MAXIMAL
MAXIMUM
MAXIMUS
MEDIANS
MEDIANT
MEDIATE
MEDICAL
MEDICOS
MEDIUMS
MELINDA
MELISSA
MENIALS
MENISCI
MERIMEE
MERINOS
MERITED
METIERS
MEXICAN
MILIEUS
MILIEUX
MILITIA
MIMICRY
MIMIEUX
MINIBUS
MINICAM
MINIMAL
MINIMUM
MINIONS
MINIVAN
MINIVER
MIXITUP
MOBILES
MODICUM
MODISTE
MOHICAN
MOLIERE
MONIKER
MONIQUE
MONITOR
MOTIONS
MOTIVES
MRFIXIT
MRRIGHT
MURILLO
MUSICAL
MYRIADS

M•••I••

MACHINA
MACHINE
MADDING
MADEIRA
MADLIBS
MAGNIFY
MAGPIES
MAILING
MALAISE
MALTING
MANCINI
MANGIER
MANKIND
MANLIER
MANNING
MANNISH
MANSION
MAPPING
MARGINS
MARKING
MARLINS
MARMION
MARRIED
MARRIES
MARRING
MARTIAL
MARTIAN
MARTINA
MARTINI
MARTINO
MARTINS
MARXISM
MASHIES
MASHING
MASKING
MASSIFS
MASSING
MASSIVE
MASTICS
MASTIFF
MATHIAS
MATTING
MAULING
MAURICE
MAWKISH
MAYTIME
MAYWINE
MCGUIRE
MCSWINE
MEALIER
MEALIES
MEANIES
MEANING
MEATIER
MEETING
MEGRIMS
MELDING
MELTING
MEMOIRE
MEMOIRS
MENDING
MENHIRS
MENTION
MEOWING
MERCIES
MERGING
MERRIER
MERRILL
MERRILY
MESHING
MESSIAH
MESSIER
MESSILY
MESSINA
MESSING
MESTIZO
METRICS
MEWLING
MIAMIAN
MIDDIES
MIDLIFE
MIDLINE
MIDRIBS
MIDRIFF
MIDRISE
MIDSIZE
MIDWIFE
MIFFING
MILKIER
MILKING
MILLING
MILLION
MINCING
MINDING
MINTIER
MINTING
MISDIAL
MISFILE
MISFIRE
MISFITS
MISHITS
MISSIES
MISSILE
MISSING
MISSION
MISSISH
MISSIVE
MISTIER
MISTILY
MISTING
MITRING
MOANING
MOBBING
MOCKING
MOHAIRS
MOILING
MOLDIER
MOLDING
MOLLIFY
MOLTING
MOMMIES
MONKISH
MOODIER
MOODILY
MOONING
MOORING
MOORISH
MOPPING
MORAINE
MORNING
MORTIFY
MORTISE
MOSAICS
MOSSIER
MOSSING
MOUSIER
MOUSING
MRCHIPS
MUCKING
MUDDIED
MUDDIER
MUDDIES
MUDPIES
MUFFING
MUFFINS
MUGGIER
MUGGING
MULLING
MULLION
MUMMIES
MUNTINS
MURKIER
MURKILY
MUSHIER
MUSHILY
MUSHING
MUSLIMS
MUSLINS
MUSSING
MUSTIER
MUSTILY
MUZHIKS
MUZZIER
MUZZILY
MYSTICS
MYSTIFY

M••••I•

MAHALIA
MAHARIS
MAITAIS
MAKESIT
MALEFIC
MANDRIL
MANTRIC
MANUMIT
MARQUIS
MASONIC
MASTOID
MAUDLIN
MAULDIN
MAUROIS
MAYALIN
MAYFAIR
MCGAVIN
MEIOSIS
MEIOTIC
MELANIE
MELANIN
MELODIC
MEMPHIS
MENUHIN
MERMAID
MESSKIT
MIASMIC
MIKHAIL
MILITIA
MIMESIS
MIMETIC
MINUTIA
MISLAID
MITOSIS
MITOTIC
MOONLIT
MORANIS
MORAVIA
MOUNTIE
MOVEDIN
MOVESIN
MRFIXIT
MUEZZIN
MULLEIN
MUTATIS

M•••••I

MAESTRI
MALACHI
MANCINI
MARCONI
MARTINI
MENISCI
MENOTTI
MOLOKAI

•MI••••

AMIABLE
AMIABLY
AMIBLUE
EMIGRES
EMINENT
EMIRATE
EMITTED
EMITTER
IMITATE
OMICRON
OMINOUS
OMITTED
SMIDGEN
SMILERS
SMILING
SMIRKED
SMITING
SMITTEN

•M•I•••

AMBIENT
AMNIONS
EMPIRES
IMBIBED
IMBIBES
IMMIXED
IMMIXES
IMPIETY
IMPINGE
IMPIOUS
OMNIBUS
UMPIRED
UMPIRES

•M••I••

AMATIVE
AMAZING
AMBLING
AMBRIES
AMENITY
AMERICA
AMERIGO
AMERIKA
AMERIND
AMPLIFY
AMUSING
BMOVIES
EMERITA
EMERITI
EMOTING
EMOTION
EMOTIVE
EMPTIED
EMPTIER
EMPTIES
EMPTILY
IMAGINE
IMAGING
IMBUING
IMPAIRS
IMPLIED
IMPLIES
IMPRINT
SMILING
SMITING
SMOKIER
SMOKIES
SMOKING
UMBRIAN

•M•••I•

AMHARIC
AMMONIA
AMNESIA
AMOEBIC
AMRADIO
EMBROIL
EMPORIA
FMRADIO
IMPERIL

•M••••I

EMERITI
OMPHALI

••MI•••

AAMILNE
ADMIRAL
ADMIRED
ADMIRER
ADMIRES
ADMIXED
ADMIXES
BEMIRED
BEMIRES
CAMILLE
CAMISES
COMICAL
COMINGS
COMIQUE
DEMIGOD
DEMILLE
DEMISED
DEMISES
DIMITRI
DOMINGO
DOMINOS
ELMISTI
ERMINES
GAMIEST
GAMINES
HAMITES
HAMITIC
HAMITUP
HOMIEST
HOMINEM
HOMINID
HUMIDLY
HUMIDOR
IMMIXED
IMMIXES
LAMINAE
LAMINAL
LAMINAR
LAMINAS
LIMIEST
LIMITED
LUMIERE
MIMICRY
MIMIEUX
NAMIBIA
NOMINAL
NOMINEE
PEMICAN
PUMICES
REMINDS
REMIXED
REMIXES
SAMISEN
SAMITES
SEMINAL
SEMINAR
SEMIPRO
SEMITES
SEMITIC
SIMIANS
SIMILAR
SIMILES
TIMIDER
TIMIDLY
TIMINGS

••M•I••

ARMOIRE
ARMPITS
BAMBINO
BOMBING
BUMMING
BUMPIER
BUMPING
CAMBIUM
CAMPIER
CAMPING
CAMPION
COMBINE
COMBING
COMFIER
COMFITS
COMMITS
COMPILE
DAMMING
DAMNING
DAMPING
DAMPISH
DIMMING
DIMWITS
DOMAINS
DUMMIED
DUMMIES
DUMPIER
DUMPING
GAMBIAN
GAMBITS
GEMLIKE
GIMMICK
GUMMIER
GUMMING
HAMMILY
HAMMING
HEMLINE
HEMMING
HUMMING
JAMAICA
JAMMING
JEMMIED
JEMMIES
JIMDINE
JIMMIED
JIMMIES
JUMPIER
JUMPING
LAMAISM
LAMAIST
LAMMING
LEMMING
LEMPIRA
LIMBING
LIMNING
LIMPING
LUMPIER
LUMPING
MEMOIRE
MEMOIRS
MOMMIES
MUMMIES
NUMBING
PAMBIES
PIMLICO
PUMPING
RAMMING
REMAILS
REMAINS
RIMMING
ROMAINE
ROMPING
RUMMIER
SAMHILL
SUMMING
SUMMITS
TAMPICO
TAMPING
TIMMINS
TOMTITS
TUMMIES
VAMPING
VAMPIRE
YUMMIER
ZAMBIAN
ZOMBIES

••M••I•

AMMONIA
ARMENIA
BUMPKIN
CAMBRIC
CAMELIA
COMEDIC
COMESIN
DEMERIT
DEMONIC
HAMELIN
HAMITIC
HOMERIC
HOMINID
JUMPSIN
LAMPOIL
MEMPHIS
MIMESIS
MIMETIC
NAMIBIA
NEMESIS
NOMADIC
NUMERIC
OSMOSIS
OSMOTIC
POMPEIA
POMPEII
PUMPKIN
RAMEKIN
ROMANIA
SAMARIA
SEMITIC
SOMALIA
SOMALIS
SOMATIC

TAMARIN
YEMENIS

••M•••I
CAMPARI
DIMITRI
ELMISTI
JUMANJI
POMPEII
SAMURAI
TYMPANI
ZAMBEZI

•••MI••
ADAMITE
AIRMILE
ANIMISM
ANIMIST
ATOMIES
ATOMIZE
BALMIER
BARMIER
BEAMIER
BEAMING
BLAMING
BLEMISH
BOOMING
BROMIDE
BROMINE
BUMMING
CADMIUM
CALMING
CARMINE
CHEMISE
CHEMIST
CHIMING
COMMITS
DAMMING
DAUMIER
DEEMING
DIMMING
DISMISS
DOOMING
DORMICE
DUMMIED
DUMMIES
ENEMIES
EREMITE
ETAMINE
EXAMINE
FARMING
FERMIUM
FILMIER
FILMING
FIRMING
FLAMING
FLEMING
FLEMISH
FOAMIER
FOAMING
FORMICA
FORMING
FRAMING
GIMMICK
GINMILL
GRIMIER
GUMMIER
GUMMING
HAMMILY
HAMMING
HARMING
HELMING
HEMMING
HERMITS
HOLMIUM
HUMMING
ICEMILK
ITEMIZE
JAMMING
JASMINE
JEMMIED
JEMMIES
JIMMIED
JIMMIES
LAMMING
LEMMING
LOAMIER
LOAMING
LOOMING
MARMION
MIAMIAN
MOMMIES
MUMMIES
OLEMISS
PALMIER
PALMING
PALMIST
PERMING
PERMITS
PISMIRE
PLUMING
PREMIER
PREMISE
PREMIUM
PRIMING
PROMISE
PYGMIES
RAMMING
REAMING
RHYMING
RIMMING
ROAMING
ROOMIER
ROOMIES
ROOMING
RUMMIER
SAWMILL
SCHMIDT
SEAMIER
SEAMING
SEEMING
SHAMING
SLIMIER
SPUMING
STAMINA
STYMIED
STYMIES
SUBMITS
SUMMING
SUMMITS
SURMISE
TEAMING
TEEMING
TERMING
TERMINI
TERMITE
TIMMINS
TITMICE
TUMMIES
VARMINT
WARMING
WARMISH
WORMIER
WYOMING
YUMMIER
ZOOMING

•••M•I•
AIRMAIL
ALAMEIN
ALEMBIC
ARAMAIC
BARMAID
CHAMOIS
DRUMLIN
FANMAIL
GASMAIN
GREMLIN
KREMLIN
MERMAID
OLDMAID
OLYMPIA
OLYMPIC
PALMOIL
SLIMJIM
SUNMAID
TIOMKIN
TURMOIL
VERMEIL
ZOOMSIN

•••M••I
EXEMPLI
SPUMONI
STIMULI
TERMINI

••••MI•
ALBUMIN
ANAEMIA
ANOSMIA
ANOSMIC
ARTEMIS
BOHEMIA
BRAHMIN
CAKEMIX
CARAMIA
CERAMIC
CHARMIN
DELIMIT
DYNAMIC
ENCOMIA
ENDEMIC
IDIAMIN
ISLAMIC
KASHMIR
LARAMIE
MANUMIT
MIASMIC
NOKOMIS
POLEMIC
PREEMIE
PYRAMID
READMIT
SALAMIS
SEISMIC
TATAMIS
TOTEMIC
VITAMIN

•••••MI
GOURAMI
ORIGAMI
SASHIMI
TSUNAMI

M•J••••
MAJESTE
MAJESTY
MAJEURE
MAJORCA
MAJORED

••MJ•••
JIMJAMS
RAMJETS

••M••J•
JUMANJI

•••MJ••
SLIMJIM

M•K••••
MAKEFOR
MAKEHAY
MAKEOFF
MAKEOUT
MAKEPAR
MAKESDO
MAKESIT
MAKESUP
MAKEUPS
MAKEWAY
MAKINGS
MIKADOS
MIKHAIL
MUKLUKS

M••K•••
MANKIND
MARKERS
MARKETS
MARKHAM
MARKHOR
MARKING
MARKKAA
MARKOFF
MARKOVA
MARKSUP
MARKUPS
MASKERS
MASKING
MAWKISH
MEEKEST
MILKCOW
MILKERS
MILKIER
MILKING
MILKMAN
MILKMEN
MILKRUN
MILKSOP
MOCKERS
MOCKERY
MOCKING
MOCKUPS
MONKEES
MONKEYS
MONKISH
MUCKING
MUCKSUP
MURKIER
MURKILY
MUSKETS
MUSKRAT

M•••K••
MARKKAA
MARYKAY
MENCKEN
MESSKIT
MOLOKAI
MONIKER

M••••K•
MAZURKA
MISTAKE
MOHAWKS
MUKLUKS
MUZHIKS

M•••••K
MATLOCK
MATTOCK
MENFOLK
MIDWEEK
MISTOOK
MOLLUSK
MRSPOCK
MUBARAK
MUDPACK

•M•K•••
SMOKERS
SMOKIER
SMOKIES
SMOKING

•M••K••
SMACKED
SMACKER
SMIRKED

•M•••K•
AMERIKA
EMBANKS
EMBARKS

••M•K••
BUMPKIN
PUMPKIN
RAMEKIN
REMAKES
UNMAKES

••M••K•
DAMASKS
GEMLIKE
REMARKS
UNMASKS

••M•••K
ARMLOCK
BOMBECK
GEMSBOK
GIMMICK
HAMHOCK
HAMMOCK
HEMLOCK
HUMMOCK
JAMPACK
LAMARCK

•••MK••
TIOMKIN

•••M•K•
CHOMSKY
GROMYKO

•••M••K
DENMARK
EARMARK
GIMMICK
HAMMOCK
HOLMOAK
HUMMOCK
ICEMILK
SKIMASK
TEDMACK
WIDMARK

••••M•K
RUNAMOK
YASHMAK

M•L••••
MALABAR
MALACCA
MALACHI
MALAISE
MALAMUD
MALAREN
MALAYAN
MALCOLM
MALEATE
MALEFIC
MALIGNS
MALLARD
MALLETS
MALLOWS
MALMSEY
MALODOR
MALRAUX
MALTEDS
MALTESE
MALTHUS
MALTING
MALTOSE
MCLUHAN
MELANGE
MELANIE
MELANIN
MELDING
MELINDA
MELISSA
MELLOWS
MELODIC
MELROSE
MELTING
MILDEST
MILDEWS
MILDEWY
MILDRED
MILEAGE
MILHAUD
MILIEUS
MILIEUX
MILITIA
MILKCOW
MILKERS
MILKIER
MILKING
MILKMAN
MILKMEN
MILKRUN
MILKSOP
MILLAND
MILLARD
MILLDAM
MILLEND
MILLERS
MILLETS
MILLETT
MILLING
MILLION
MILLRUN
MILORDS
MOLDERS
MOLDIER
MOLDING
MOLESTS
MOLIERE
MOLLIFY
MOLLUSK
MOLOKAI
MOLOTOV
MOLTERS
MOLTING
MULCHED
MULCHES
MULCTED
MULETAS
MULLAHS
MULLEIN
MULLERS
MULLETS
MULLING
MULLION

M••L•••
MADLIBS
MAILBAG
MAILBOX
MAILERS
MAILING
MAILLOT
MALLARD
MALLETS
MALLOWS
MANLIER
MARLENE
MARLINS
MARLOWE
MATLOCK
MAULDIN
MAULING
MEALIER
MEALIES
MEDLEYS
MELLOWS
MERLOTS
MEWLERS
MEWLING
MIDLAND
MIDLIFE
MIDLINE
MILLAND
MILLARD
MILLDAM
MILLEND
MILLERS
MILLETS
MILLETT
MILLING
MILLION
MILLRUN
MISLAID
MISLAYS
MISLEAD
MOILERS
MOILING
MOLLIFY
MOLLUSK
MOSLEMS
MOULAGE
MOULDED
MOULDER
MOULTED
MRCLEAN
MUKLUKS
MULLAHS
MULLEIN
MULLERS
MULLETS
MULLING
MULLION
MUSLIMS
MUSLINS

M•••L••
MACULAE
MAHALIA
MAILLOT
MANGLED
MANGLES
MANILOW
MANTLED
MANTLES
MARBLED
MARBLES
MARILYN
MARYLOU
MATILDA
MAUDLIN
MAXILLA
MAYALIN
MCCALLS
MEASLES
MEDALED
MEDDLED
MEDDLER
MEDDLES
MEDULLA
METTLES
MIDDLEC
MIDDLES
MINGLED
MINGLER
MINGLES
MINOLTA
MISALLY
MISPLAY
MIZZLED
MIZZLES
MOBILES
MODELAS
MODELED
MODELER
MODELTS
MODULAR
MODULES
MONOLOG
MOONLIT
MORALES
MORALLY
MORELLO
MOSELLE
MOTTLED
MOTTLES
MOUFLON
MUDDLED
MUDDLER
MUDDLES
MUFFLED
MUFFLER
MUFFLES
MUMBLED
MUMBLER
MUMBLES
MURILLO
MUSCLED
MUSCLES
MUZZLED
MUZZLES
MYRTLES

M••••L•
MALCOLM
MAMMALS
MANACLE
MANDALA
MANDELA
MANHOLE
MANIPLE
MANTELS
MANUALS
MARCELS
MARSALA
MARVELS
MAXILLA
MAXWELL
MAYPOLE
MCCALLS
MEDULLA
MENFOLK
MENIALS
MERRILL
MERRILY
MESCALS
MESSALA
MESSILY
MICHELE
MINABLE
MINEOLA
MIRACLE
MISALLY
MISCALL
MISERLY
MISFILE
MISRULE
MISSALS
MISSILE
MISTILY
MIXABLE
MOISTLY
MONDALE
MONGOLS
MONOCLE
MONTHLY
MOODILY
MORALLY
MORELLO
MORSELS
MORTALS
MOSELLE
MOVABLE
MUDEELS
MURILLO
MURKILY
MUSHILY
MUSSELS
MUSTILY
MUTABLE
MUTABLY
MUTUALS
MUZZILY

M•••••L
MAGICAL
MANDREL
MANDRIL
MARITAL
MARSHAL
MARTIAL
MAXIMAL
MAXWELL
MAYORAL
MEDICAL
MENTHOL
MERRILL
MICHAEL
MIKHAIL
MINDFUL
MINERAL
MINIMAL
MISCALL
MISDEAL
MISDIAL
MISTRAL
MONGREL
MUSICAL

•ML••••
UMLAUTS

•M•L•••
AMALGAM
AMBLERS
AMBLING
AMPLEST
AMPLIFY
AMULETS
AMYLASE
EMBLEMS
EMPLOYS
EMULATE
IMPLANT
IMPLIED
IMPLIES
IMPLODE
IMPLORE
OMELETS
SMALLER
SMALTOS
SMELLED
SMELTED
SMELTER
SMILERS
SMILING
SMOLDER

•M••L••
AMIBLUE
AMPULES
EMMYLOU
IMPALAS
IMPALED
IMPALES
IMPULSE
SMALLER
SMELLED

•M•••L•
AMAPOLA
AMIABLE
AMIABLY
AMPOULE
EMERALD
EMPTILY
OMPHALI
SMARTLY
SMUGGLE

•M••••L
EMANUEL
EMBROIL
EMPANEL
IMMORAL
IMPANEL
IMPERIL

••ML•••
AIMLESS
ARMLESS
ARMLETS
ARMLOAD
ARMLOCK
GEMLIKE
GIMLETS
HAMLETS
HEMLINE
HEMLOCK
PIMLICO

••M•L••
AAMILNE
BUMBLED
BUMBLER
BUMBLES
CAMELIA
CAMELOT
CAMILLE
COMPLEX
CUMULUS
DEMILLE
DIMPLED
DIMPLES
EMMYLOU
FAMULUS
FEMALES
FUMBLED
FUMBLER
FUMBLES
GAMBLED
GAMBLER
GAMBLES
GAMELAW
HAMELIN
HEMSLEY
HUMBLED
HUMBLER
HUMBLES
JUMBLED
JUMBLES
MUMBLED
MUMBLER
MUMBLES
NIMBLER
ORMOLUS
POMELOS
RAMBLED
RAMBLER
RAMBLES
REMELTS
REMOLDS
ROMULAN
ROMULUS
RUMBLED
RUMBLES
RUMPLED
RUMPLES
SAMPLED
SAMPLER
SAMPLES
SIMILAR
SIMILES
SIMPLER
SIMPLEX
SOMALIA
SOMALIS
TAMALES
TEMBLOR
TEMPLAR
TEMPLES
TIMELAG
TUMBLED
TUMBLER
TUMBLES
TUMULTS
TUMULUS
WAMBLED
WAMBLES
WIMPLED
WIMPLES

••M••L•
ARMFULS
ARMHOLE
CAMILLE
CEMBALO
COMPELS
COMPILE
CYMBALS
DAMSELS
DEMILLE
DIMBULB
GAMBOLS
GIMBALS
GUMBALL
HAMMILY
HIMSELF
HUMANLY
HUMIDLY
HYMNALS
KAMPALA
KIMBALL
MAMMALS
POMMELS
PUMMELS
REMAILS
RUMPOLE
SAMHILL
SYMBOLS
TAMABLE
TAMBALA
TIMBALE
TIMBALS
TIMIDLY
WOMANLY

••M•••L
ADMIRAL
BIMODAL
COMICAL
DEMEROL
FEMORAL
GAMBREL
GUMBALL
HUMERAL
IMMORAL
KIMBALL
LAMINAL
LAMPOIL
NOMINAL
NUMERAL
REMODEL
REMOVAL
SAMHILL
SEMINAL
TOMFOOL
TUMBREL

•••ML••
CHEMLAB
DAIMLER
DRUMLIN
GREMLIN
KREMLIN

•••M•L•
AIRMILE
ANIMALS
ANOMALY
BRAMBLE
BRAMBLY
CRUMBLE
CRUMBLY
CRUMPLE
CRUMPLY
ENAMELS
EXAMPLE
EXEMPLI
FORMALS
FORMULA
GINMILL
GRUMBLE
GUNMOLL
HAMMILY
ICEMILK
MAMMALS
NORMALS
POMMELS
PUMMELS
SAWMILL
SHAMBLE
STIMULI
STUMBLE
THIMBLE
TRAMPLE
TREMBLE
TREMBLY
TREMOLO

•••M••L
AIRMAIL
ALUMNAL
BRIMFUL
FANMAIL
GINMILL
GUNMOLL
HARMFUL
ISHMAEL
OATMEAL
PALMOIL
ROOMFUL
SAWMILL
TRAMMEL
TURMOIL
VERMEIL

••••M•L
ABYSMAL
CALOMEL
CARAMEL
COZUMEL
DECIMAL
MAXIMAL
MINIMAL
OPTIMAL
THERMAL
TRAMMEL

M•M••••
MAMBOED
MAMMALS
MAMMOTH
MCMAHON
MEMBERS

MEMENTO
MEMOIRE
MEMOIRS
MEMOREX
MEMPHIS
MIMESIS
MIMETIC
MIMICRY
MIMIEUX
MIMOSAS
MOMBASA
MOMENTS
MOMMIES
MRMAGOO
MUMBLED
MUMBLER
MUMBLES
MUMESON
MUMFORD
MUMMERS
MUMMERY
MUMMIES
MYMAMMY

M••M•••
MALMSEY
MAMMALS
MAMMOTH
MANMADE
MARMARA
MARMION
MARMOTS
MERMAID
MIAMIAN
MICMACS
MISMATE
MOMMIES
MORMONS
MUAMMAR
MUMMERS
MUMMERY
MUMMIES
MURMURS
MUUMUUS

M•••M••
MADAMEX
MALAMUD
MANUMIT
MANXMAN
MANXMEN
MARIMBA
MAXIMAL
MAXIMUM
MAXIMUS
MERIMEE
MIASMAS
MIASMIC
MILKMAN
MILKMEN
MINIMAL
MINIMUM
MIRAMAR
MIRAMAX
MOGAMBO
MONOMER
MUAMMAR
MYANMAR
MYMAMMY

M••••M•
MACRAME
MAGNUMS
MAHATMA
MARRYME
MAYHEMS
MAYTIME
MEDIUMS
MEGOHMS
MEGRIMS
MISNAME
MOSLEMS
MUGWUMP
MUSEUMS
MUSLIMS
MYMAMMY

M•••••M
MACADAM
MALCOLM
MARKHAM
MARXISM
MAUGHAM
MAXIMUM
MIDTERM
MILLDAM
MINICAM
MINIMUM
MITCHUM
MODICUM

•MM••••
AMMETER
AMMONIA
EMMYLOU
IMMENSE
IMMERSE
IMMIXED
IMMIXES
IMMORAL
IMMURED
IMMURES

•M•M•••
IMAMATE

•M•••M•
EMBLEMS

•M••••M
AMALGAM
OMENTUM

••MM•••
BUMMERS
BUMMING
COMMAND
COMMEND
COMMENT
COMMITS
COMMODE
COMMONS
COMMOVE
COMMUNE
COMMUTE
DAMMING
DIMMERS
DIMMEST
DIMMING
DUMMIED
DUMMIES
DUMMYUP
GAMMONS
GIMMICK
GUMMIER
GUMMING
HAMMERS
HAMMETT
HAMMILY
HAMMING
HAMMOCK
HAMMOND
HEMMERS
HEMMING
HUMMERS
HUMMING
HUMMOCK
JAMMERS
JAMMING
JEMMIED
JEMMIES
JIMMIED
JIMMIES
LAMMING
LEMMING
MAMMALS
MAMMOTH
MOMMIES
MUMMERS
MUMMERY
MUMMIES
POMMELS
PUMMELS
RAMMING
RIMMING
RUMMAGE
RUMMIER
SIMMERS
SIMMONS
SUMMARY
SUMMERS
SUMMERY
SUMMING
SUMMITS
SUMMONS
TAMMANY
TIMMINS
TUMMIES
YAMMERS
YUMMIER

••M•M••
MYMAMMY

••M••M•
DUMDUMS
JIMJAMS
MYMAMMY
POMPOMS
TAMTAMS
TOMTOMS

••M•••M
CAMBIUM
HOMINEM
HOMONYM
HUMDRUM
LAMAISM
LUMPSUM
SYMPTOM

•••MM••
BRIMMED
CHUMMED
CLAMMED
CLAMMER
CRAMMED
CRAMMER
DRUMMED
DRUMMER
FLUMMOX
GLIMMER
GLOMMED
GLUMMER
GRAMMAR
GRAMMER
GRAMMES
GRIMMER
GROMMET
MUAMMAR
PLUMMER
PLUMMET
PRIMMER
SCAMMED
SHAMMED
SHIMMER
SKIMMED
SKIMMER
SLAMMED
SLAMMER
SLIMMED
SLIMMER
SLUMMED
STAMMER
STEMMED
SWIMMER
TRAMMEL
TRIMMED
TRIMMER
WHAMMED

•••M••M
ANIMISM
CADMIUM
FERMIUM
HOLMIUM
PREMIUM
SLIMJIM
YESMAAM

••••MM•
DILEMMA
MYMAMMY

••••M•M
MAXIMUM
MINIMUM
OPTIMUM

M•N••••
MANACLE
MANAGED
MANAGER
MANAGES
MANAGUA
MANANAS
MANATEE
MANCINI
MANDALA
MANDANS
MANDATE
MANDAYS
MANDELA
MANDREL
MANDRIL
MANEGES
MANFRED
MANGERS
MANGIER
MANGLED
MANGLES
MANGOES
MANHOLE
MANHOOD
MANHOUR
MANHUNT
MANIACS
MANILOW
MANIPLE
MANITOU
MANKIND
MANLIER
MANMADE
MANNERS
MANNING
MANNISH
MANOWAR
MANSARD
MANSION
MANTELS
MANTLED
MANTLES
MANTRAP
MANTRAS
MANTRIC
MANUALS
MANUMIT
MANXCAT
MANXMAN
MANXMEN
MANYEAR
MENACED
MENACES
MENAGES
MENCKEN
MENDERS
MENDING
MENDOZA
MENFOLK
MENHIRS
MENIALS
MENISCI
MENORAH
MENOTTI
MENTHOL
MENTION
MENTORS
MENUHIN
MINABLE
MINARET
MINCERS
MINCING
MINDERS
MINDFUL
MINDING
MINDSET
MINEOLA
MINERAL
MINERVA
MINGLED
MINGLER
MINGLES
MINIBUS
MINICAM
MINIMAL
MINIMUM
MINIONS
MINIVAN
MINIVER
MINNOWS
MINOANS
MINOLTA
MINORCA
MINORED
MINTERS
MINTIER
MINTING
MINUEND
MINUETS
MINUSES
MINUTES
MINUTIA
MONARCH
MONDALE
MONDAYS
MONEYED
MONGERS
MONGOLS
MONGREL
MONIKER
MONIQUE
MONITOR
MONKEES
MONKEYS
MONKISH
MONOCLE
MONOCOT
MONOLOG
MONOMER
MONSOON
MONSTER
MONTAGE
MONTANA
MONTAND
MONTANE
MONTEGO
MONTEUX
MONTHLY
MONTOYA
MUNCHED
MUNCHER
MUNCHES
MUNDANE
MUNTINS
MYNHEER

M••N•••
MADNESS
MAENADS
MAGNATE
MAGNETO
MAGNETS
MAGNIFY
MAGNUMS
MAINTOP
MANNERS
MANNING
MANNISH
MAUNDER
MAYNARD
MCENROE
MEANDER
MEANEST
MEANIES
MEANING
MINNOWS
MISNAME
MOANERS
MOANING
MOONDOG
MOONING
MOONLIT
MOONSET
MORNING
MOUNDED
MOUNTED
MOUNTIE
MYANMAR

M•••N••
MADONNA
MAGENTA
MAGINOT
MAHONEY
MAKINGS
MANANAS
MARINAS
MARINER
MARINES
MASONIC
MASONRY
MATINEE
MELANGE
MELANIE
MELANIN
MELINDA
MEMENTO
MERINOS
MIRANDA
MOMENTS
MORANIS
MRBONES
MUTANTS

M••••N•
MACHINA
MACHINE
MACRONS
MADDENS
MADDING
MADONNA
MADRONA
MAIDENS
MAILING
MALIGNS
MALTING
MANCINI
MANDANS
MANHUNT
MANKIND
MANNING
MAPPING
MARCONI
MARGINS
MARIANA
MARKING
MARLENE
MARLINS
MAROONS
MARRING
MARTENS
MARTINA
MARTINI
MARTINO
MARTINS
MARYANN
MASHING
MASKING
MASSING
MATRONS
MATTING
MAULING
MAYWINE
MBABANE
MCSWINE
MEANING
MEDIANS
MEDIANT
MEETING
MELDING
MELTING
MENDING
MEOWING
MERGING
MESHING
MESSINA
MESSING
METHANE
MEWLING
MICRONS
MIDDENS
MIDLAND
MIDLINE
MIFFING
MIGHTNT
MIGRANT
MILKING
MILLAND
MILLEND
MILLING
MINCING
MINDING
MINIONS
MINOANS
MINTING
MINUEND
MIOCENE
MISDONE
MISSING
MISTING
MITRING
MITTENS
MIZZENS
MOANING
MOBBING
MOCKING
MODERNS
MOILING
MOLDING
MOLTING
MONTANA
MONTAND
MONTANE
MOONING
MOORING
MOPPING
MORAINE
MORDANT
MORDENT
MORGANA
MORGANS
MORMONS
MORNING
MOSSING
MOTIONS
MOUSING
MOUTONS
MUCKING
MUDHENS
MUFFING
MUFFINS
MUGGING
MULLING
MUNDANE
MUNTINS
MUSHING
MUSLINS
MUSSING
MUSTANG
MUTTONS

M•••••N
MADCHEN
MADISON
MALAREN
MALAYAN
MANSION
MANXMAN
MANXMEN
MARCHEN
MARCHON
MARILYN
MARMION
MARTIAN
MARYANN
MATEWAN
MAUDLIN
MAULDIN
MAUREEN
MAXBORN
MAYALIN
MCGAVIN
MCLUHAN
MCMAHON
MCQUEEN
MEGRYAN
MEISSEN
MELANIN
MENCKEN
MENTION
MENUHIN
MEXICAN
MIAMIAN
MIDTOWN
MILKMAN
MILKMEN
MILKRUN
MILLION
MILLRUN
MINIVAN
MISSION
MOHICAN
MOISTEN
MONSOON
MOORHEN
MOUFLON
MOVEDIN
MOVESIN
MOWDOWN
MRCLEAN
MUEZZIN
MULLEIN
MULLION
MUMESON
MUTAGEN

•MN••••
AMNESIA
AMNESTY
AMNIONS
OMNIBUS

•M•N•••
AMENDED
AMENITY
AMONGST
EMANATE
EMANUEL
EMENDED
EMENDER
EMINENT
OMENTUM
OMINOUS

•M••N••
AMMONIA
AMOUNTS
EMBANKS
EMPANEL
IMMENSE
IMPANEL
IMPENDS
IMPINGE

•M•••N•
AMAZING
AMAZONS
AMBIENT
AMBLING
AMERIND
AMNIONS
AMUSING
EMINENT
EMOTING
IMAGINE
IMAGING
IMBUING
IMOGENE
IMPLANT
IMPOUND
IMPRINT
IMPUGNS
KMESONS
SMETANA
SMILING
SMITING
SMOKING

•M••••N
EMERSON
EMOTION
OMICRON
SMARTEN
SMIDGEN
SMITTEN
UMBRIAN
UMPTEEN

••MN•••
DAMNING
DIMNESS
GYMNAST
HYMNALS
LIMNERS
LIMNING
REMNANT
ROMNEYS
SAMNUNN

••M•N••
ALMANAC
ALMONDS
AMMONIA
ARMENIA
CEMENTS
COMINGS
DEMANDS
DEMONIC
DOMINGO
DOMINOS
ERMINES
FOMENTS
GAMINES
HHMUNRO
HOMINEM
HOMINID
HOMONYM
HUMANLY
IMMENSE
JIMENEZ
JUMANJI
KIMONOS
LAMENTS
LAMINAE
LAMINAL
LAMINAR
LAMINAS
MEMENTO
MOMENTS
NOMINAL
NOMINEE
ORMANDY
OSMONDS
PIMENTO
REMANDS
REMENDS
REMINDS
ROMANCE
ROMANIA
ROMANOV
ROMANSH
SEMINAL
SEMINAR
SIMENON
TIMINGS
WOMANLY
YEMENIS

••M••N•
AAMILNE
ARMBAND
ARMYANT
BAMBINO
BEMOANS
BOMBING
BUMMING
BUMPING
CAMPING
COMBINE
COMBING
COMEONS
COMMAND
COMMEND
COMMENT
COMMONS
COMMUNE
COMPANY
DAMMING
DAMNING
DAMPENS
DAMPING
DAMSONS
DEMEANS
DEMESNE
DIMMING
DOMAINS
DUMPING
GAMMONS
GUMMING
HAMMING
HAMMOND
HEMLINE
HEMMING
HUMMING
JAMMING
JIMDINE
JUMPING
LAMBENT
LAMMING
LEMMING
LIMBING
LIMNING
LIMPING
LUMPING
NUMBING
POMPANO
POMPONS
PUMPING
RAMMING
RAMPANT
REMAINS
REMNANT
REMOUNT
RIMMING
ROMAINE
ROMPING
SAMNUNN
SAMOANS
SAMPANS
SAMSUNG
SIMIANS
SIMMONS
SOMEONE
SUMMING
SUMMONS
TAMMANY
TAMPING
TIMMINS
TYMPANA
TYMPANI
VAMPING

••M•••N
ALMADEN
BUMPKIN
CAMERON
CAMPION
COMESIN
COMESON
GAMBIAN
HAMELIN
HAMPTON
HOMERUN
JAMESON
JIMRYUN
JUMPSIN
JUMPSON
LAMPOON
MCMAHON
MUMESON
PEMICAN
PIMESON
PUMPKIN
RAMADAN
RAMEKIN
ROMULAN
SAMISEN
SAMNUNN
SAMPSON
SIMENON
SIMPSON
TAMARIN
ZAMBIAN

•••MN••
ALUMNAE
ALUMNAL
ALUMNUS
CHIMNEY

•••M•N•
ADAMANT
AILMENT
ALIMENT
ALIMONY
ANEMONE
ATAMANS
AUGMENT
BEAMING
BELMONT
BLAMING
BOOMING
BROMINE
BUMMING
CAIMANS
CALMING
CARMINE
CHIMING
CLEMENS
CLEMENT
COMMAND
COMMEND
COMMENT
COMMONS
COMMUNE
CREMONA
DAMMING
DEEMING
DESMOND
DIAMOND
DIMMING
DINMONT
DOLMANS
DOLMENS
DOOMING
DORMANT
ELEMENT
ETAMINE
EXAMINE
FARMING
FERMENT
FIGMENT
FILMING
FIRMING
FLAMING
FLEMING
FOAMING
FORMING
FRAMING
FREMONT
GAMMONS
GARMENT
GERMANE
GERMANS
GERMANY
GNOMONS
GUMMING
HAMMING
HAMMOND
HARMING
HARMONY
HELMING
HEMMING
HERMANN
HETMANS
HORMONE
HUMMING
JAMMING
JASMINE
KIRMANS
LAMMING
LEMMING
LOAMING
LOOMING
MORMONS
NORMAND
NORMANS
ODDMENT
PALMING
PAYMENT

PERMING
PIGMENT
PLUMING
PRIMING
RAIMENT
RAMMING
RAYMOND
REAMING
RHYMING
RIMMING
ROAMING
ROOMING
SALMONS
SEAMING
SEEMING
SEGMENT
SERMONS
SHAMANS
SHAMING
SIGMUND
SIMMONS
SPUMING
SPUMONE
SPUMONI
STAMENS
STAMINA
SUMMING
SUMMONS
TAMMANY
TEAMING
TEEMING
TERMING
TERMINI
TIMMINS
TORMENT
ULLMANN
VARMINT
VERMONT
WARMING
WYOMING
YOUMANS
ZOOMING

•••M••N
ADAMSON
ALAMEIN
ARAMEAN
CLEMSON
CRAMPON
CRIMEAN
CRIMSON
DRUMLIN
GASMAIN
GREMLIN
HERMANN
KREMLIN
MARMION
MIAMIAN
NEWMOON
NEWMOWN
OLDMOON
THOMSON
TIOMKIN
ULLMANN
ZOOMSIN

••••MN•
AUTUMNS
CALUMNY
COLUMNS

••••M•N
ABDOMEN
ALBUMEN
ALBUMIN
BASEMAN
BASEMEN
BATEMAN
BATSMAN
BATSMEN
BELLMAN
BELLMEN
BERGMAN
BESTMAN
BESTMEN
BIRDMAN
BIRDMEN
BITUMEN
BOATMAN
BOATMEN
BONDMAN
BONDMEN
BRAHMAN
BRAHMIN
BUSHMAN
BUSHMEN
CAVEMAN
CAVEMEN
CERUMEN
CHAPMAN
CHAPMEN
CHARMIN
COLEMAN
CREWMAN
CREWMEN
DARKMAN
DOORMAN
DOORMEN
DREAMON
EASTMAN
FADIMAN
FELDMAN
FEYNMAN
FIREMAN
FIREMEN
FLAGMAN
FLAGMEN
FOOTMAN
FOOTMEN
FOREMAN
FOREMEN
FREEMAN
FREEMEN
FROGMAN
FROGMEN
GATEMAN
GATEMEN
GOODMAN
GOODMEN
HACKMAN
HANGMAN
HANGMEN
HARTMAN
HEADMAN
HEADMEN
HELLMAN
HICKMAN
HOFFMAN
HOUSMAN
IDIAMIN
INHUMAN
IRONMAN
IRONMEN
JAVAMAN
JAZZMAN
JAZZMEN
JUNKMAN
KINGMAN
KINSMAN
KINSMEN
KLUGMAN
LINEMAN
LINEMEN
MANXMAN
MANXMEN
MILKMAN
MILKMEN
NEWSMAN
NEWSMEN
OTTOMAN
PERLMAN
PIKEMAN
PIKEMEN
PITTMAN
PLOWMAN
PLOWMEN
POSTMAN
POSTMEN
PROPMAN
PROPMEN
PULLMAN
PUTAMEN
RAINMAN
REGIMEN
REPOMAN
RICHMAN
SANDMAN
SANDMEN
SHERMAN
SHIPMAN
SHIPMEN
SHOWMAN
SHOWMEN
SIDEMAN
SIDEMEN
SNOWMAN
SNOWMEN
SOLOMON
STARMAN
SYNGMAN
THINMAN
THURMAN
TUCHMAN
VITAMIN
WALKMAN
WHITMAN
WISEMAN
WISEMEN
WOLFMAN
WOLFMEN
WORKMAN
WORKMEN
YARDMAN
YARDMEN

•••••MN
CONDEMN
CONTEMN

MO•••••
MOANERS
MOANING
MOBBING
MOBCAPS
MOBILES
MOBSTER
MOCKERS
MOCKERY
MOCKING
MOCKUPS
MODELAS
MODELED
MODELER
MODELTS
MODERNS
MODESTO
MODESTY
MODICUM
MODISTE
MODULAR
MODULES
MOGAMBO
MOHAIRS
MOHAWKS
MOHICAN
MOILERS
MOILING
MOISTEN
MOISTER
MOISTLY
MOLDERS
MOLDIER
MOLDING
MOLESTS
MOLIERE
MOLLIFY
MOLLUSK
MOLOKAI
MOLOTOV
MOLTERS
MOLTING
MOMBASA
MOMENTS
MOMMIES
MONARCH
MONDALE
MONDAYS
MONEYED
MONGERS
MONGOLS
MONGREL
MONIKER
MONIQUE
MONITOR
MONKEES
MONKEYS
MONKISH
MONOCLE
MONOCOT
MONOLOG
MONOMER
MONSOON
MONSTER
MONTAGE
MONTANA
MONTAND
MONTANE
MONTEGO
MONTEUX
MONTHLY
MONTOYA
MOOCHED
MOOCHER
MOOCHES
MOODIER
MOODILY
MOONDOG
MOONING
MOONLIT
MOONSET
MOORAGE
MOORHEN
MOORING
MOORISH
MOPPERS
MOPPETS
MOPPING
MORAINE
MORALES
MORALLY
MORANIS
MORAVIA
MORDANT
MORDENT
MORDRED
MORELLO
MORESBY
MORGANA
MORGANS
MORMONS
MORNING
MOROCCO
MORPHED
MORROWS
MORSELS
MORTALS
MORTARS
MORTIFY
MORTISE
MOSAICS
MOSELLE
MOSEYED
MOSLEMS
MOSQUES
MOSSIER
MOSSING
MOTHERS
MOTIONS
MOTIVES
MOTORED
MOTTLED
MOTTLES
MOTTOES
MOUFLON
MOULAGE
MOULDED
MOULDER
MOULTED
MOUNDED
MOUNTED
MOUNTIE
MOUSERS
MOUSIER
MOUSING
MOUSSED
MOUSSES
MOUTHED
MOUTONS
MOVABLE
MOVEDIN
MOVEOUT
MOVESIN
MOWDOWN

M•O••••
MAOISTS
MEOWING
MIOCENE
MOOCHED
MOOCHER
MOOCHES
MOODIER
MOODILY
MOONDOG
MOONING
MOONLIT
MOONSET
MOORAGE
MOORHEN
MOORING
MOORISH

M••O•••
MADONNA
MAHONEY
MAHOUTS
MAJORCA
MAJORED
MALODOR
MANOWAR
MAROONS
MASONIC
MASONRY
MAYORAL
MEGOHMS
MEIOSES
MEIOSIS
MEIOTIC
MELODIC
MEMOIRE
MEMOIRS
MEMOREX
MENORAH
MENOTTI
METOOER
MILORDS
MIMOSAS
MINOANS
MINOLTA
MINORCA
MINORED
MITOSES
MITOSIS
MITOTIC
MOLOKAI
MOLOTOV
MONOCLE
MONOCOT
MONOLOG
MONOMER
MOROCCO
MOTORED
MRBONES

M•••O••
MACRONS
MADEOFF
MADEOUT
MADRONA
MAFIOSO
MAKEOFF
MAKEOUT
MALCOLM
MALLOWS
MALTOSE
MAMBOED
MAMMOTH
MANGOES
MANHOLE
MANHOOD
MANHOUR
MARCONI
MARKOFF
MARKOVA
MARLOWE
MARMOTS
MAROONS
MARROWS
MASCOTS
MASTOID
MATLOCK
MATRONS
MATTOCK
MATZOHS
MAUROIS
MAXBORN
MAYPOLE
MEADOWS
MEADOWY
MELLOWS
MELROSE
MENDOZA
MENFOLK
MENTORS
MERLOTS
METEORS
METEOUT
METHODS
METOOER
MICROBE
MICRONS
MIDTOWN
MINEOLA
MINIONS
MINNOWS
MIRRORS
MISDOES
MISDONE
MISSOUT
MISTOOK
MISWORD
MITFORD
MONGOLS
MONSOON
MONTOYA
MORMONS
MORROWS
MOTIONS
MOTTOES
MOUTONS
MOVEOUT
MOWDOWN
MRSPOCK
MUMFORD
MURDOCH
MUSCOVY
MUTTONS

M••••O•
MADEFOR
MADISON
MAGINOT
MAILBOX
MAILLOT
MAINTOP
MAKEFOR
MALODOR
MANHOOD
MANILOW
MANITOU
MANSION
MARABOU
MARCHON
MARKHOR
MARMION
MARYLOU
MATADOR
MCENROE
MCMAHON
MEDICOS
MENTHOL
MENTION
MERINOS
MIKADOS
MILKCOW
MILKSOP
MILLION
MIRADOR
MISSION
MISTOOK
MOLOTOV
MONITOR
MONOCOT
MONOLOG
MONSOON
MOONDOG
MOUFLON
MRMAGOO
MUGSHOT
MULLION
MUMESON

M•••••O
MAESTRO
MAFIOSO
MAGNETO
MAKESDO
MARTINO
MEMENTO
MESTIZO
MODESTO
MOGAMBO
MONTEGO
MORELLO
MOROCCO
MRMAGOO
MURILLO

•MO••••
AMOEBAE
AMOEBAS
AMOEBIC
AMONGST
AMOROUS
AMOUNTS
BMOVIES
EMOTERS
EMOTING
EMOTION
EMOTIVE
IMOGENE
SMOKERS
SMOKIER
SMOKIES
SMOKING
SMOLDER
SMOOTHS
SMOTHER

•M•O•••
AMMONIA
AMPOULE
EMPORIA
EMPOWER
IMMORAL
IMPORTS
IMPOSED
IMPOSES
IMPOSTS
IMPOUND
IMSORRY
SMOOTHS

•M••O••
AMAPOLA
AMATORY
AMAZONS
AMBROSE
AMNIONS
AMOROUS
AMPHORA
EMBROIL
EMPLOYS
IMAGOES
IMPIOUS
IMPLODE
IMPLORE
IMPROVE
KMESONS
OMINOUS

•M•••O•
EMBRYOS
EMERSON
EMMYLOU
EMOTION
EMPEROR
OMICRON
SMALTOS

•M••••O
AMERIGO
AMRADIO
EMBARGO
FMRADIO
IMPASTO
UMBERTO

••MO•••
ALMONDS
AMMONIA
ARMOIRE
ARMORED
ARMORER
ARMOURS
BEMOANS
BIMODAL
COMOROS
DEMONIC
DEMOTED
DEMOTES
DIMOUTS
FEMORAL
HOMONYM
HUMORED
HUMOURS
IMMORAL
IOMOTHS
KIMONOS
LAMOTTA
LIMOGES
MEMOIRE
MEMOIRS
MEMOREX
MIMOSAS
ORMOLUS
OSMONDS
OSMOSED
OSMOSES
OSMOSIS
OSMOTIC
REMODEL
REMOLDS
REMORAS
REMORSE
REMOTER
REMOTES
REMOUNT
REMOVAL
REMOVED
REMOVER
REMOVES
REMOWED
RUMORED
RUMOURS
SAMOANS
SAMOVAR
SAMOYED
TIMOTHY
UNMOVED
VAMOOSE

••M•O••
ARMHOLE
ARMLOAD
ARMLOCK
BAMBOOS
BUMSOUT
CAMEOED
CAMEOFF
CAMEOUT
CAMPOUT
COMEOFF
COMEONS
COMEOUT
COMFORT
COMMODE
COMMONS
COMMOVE
COMPORT
COMPOSE
COMPOST
COMPOTE
DAMSONS
GAMBOLS
GAMMONS
HAMHOCK
HAMMOCK
HAMMOND
HEMLOCK
HUMMOCK
JUMPOFF
LAMPOIL
LAMPOON
LIMPOPO
MAMBOED
MAMMOTH
MUMFORD
NIMRODS
POMPOMS
POMPONS
POMPOUS
RAMRODS
RUMPOLE
SIMMONS
SOMEONE
SUMMONS
SYMBOLS
TAMBOUR
TIMEOFF
TIMEOUT
TOMBOYS
TOMFOOL
TOMTOMS
VAMOOSE

••M••O•
BAMBOOS
CAMELOT
CAMERON
CAMPHOR
CAMPION
COMESON
COMOROS
DEMEROL
DEMIGOD
DOMINOS
EMMYLOU
GEMSBOK
GUMDROP
GUMSHOE
GYMSHOE
HAMPTON
HUMIDOR
JAMESON
JUMPSON
KIMONOS
LAMPOON
MCMAHON
MRMAGOO
MUMESON
NEMEROV
PIMESON
POMELOS
RIMSHOT
ROMANOV
SAMPSON
SIMENON
SIMPSON
SOMEHOW
SYMPTOM
TEMBLOR
TIMECOP
TOMFOOL

••M•••O
AIMEDTO
BAMBINO
CEMBALO
COMESTO
DOMINGO
HHMUNRO
LIMPOPO
LUMBAGO
MEMENTO
MRMAGOO
PIMENTO
PIMLICO
POMPANO
SEMIPRO
TAMPICO

•••MO••
ALAMODE
ALIMONY
ANEMONE
ANYMORE
ARDMORE
BELMONT
CHAMOIS
CLAMORS
COMMODE
COMMONS
COMMOVE
CREMONA
DESMOND
DIAMOND
DINMONT
ENAMORS
ENAMOUR
ENDMOST
FARMOUT
FORMOSA
FREMONT
GAMMONS
GILMORE
GLAMOUR
GNOMONS
GUNMOLL
HAMMOCK
HAMMOND
HARMONY
HAYMOWS
HOLMOAK
HORMONE
HUMMOCK
MAMMOTH
MARMOTS
MORMONS
NEWMOON
NEWMOWN
OAKMOSS
OLDMOON
OXYMORA
PALMOFF
PALMOIL
PROMOTE
RAGMOPS
RAYMOND
SALMONS
SCHMOES
SCHMOOS
SEAMOSS
SERMONS
SEYMOUR
SIMMONS
SPUMONE
SPUMONI
SUMMONS
TOPMOST
TREMOLO
TREMORS
TURMOIL
VERMONT
WETMOPS

•••M•O•
ADAMSON
BOOMBOX
CLEMSON
CRAMPON
CRIMSON
FLUMMOX
MARMION
NEWMOON
OLDMOON
SCHMOOS
SHAMPOO
THOMSON

•••M••O
ANIMATO
GROMYKO
HAEMATO
SHAMPOO
TREMOLO

••••MO•
DREAMON
DUSTMOP
DYNAMOS
ESKIMOS
FLUMMOX
RUNAMOK
SOLOMON
THERMOS

••••M•O
COLUMBO
MOGAMBO
UPTEMPO

•••••MO
CENTIMO
GIACOMO
PALERMO
PROXIMO
SANREMO
SATCHMO
SUPREMO

M•P••••
MAPPERS
MAPPING
MOPPERS
MOPPETS
MOPPING
MUPPETS

M••P•••
MAGPIES
MAPPERS
MAPPING
MAYPOLE
MEMPHIS
MISPLAY
MOPPERS
MOPPETS
MOPPING
MORPHED
MRSPOCK
MUDPACK
MUDPIES
MUPPETS
MURPHEY

M•••P••
MAKEPAR
MANIPLE

M••••P•
MADCAPS
MAKEUPS
MARKUPS
MISHAPS
MISTYPE
MOBCAPS
MOCKUPS
MRCHIPS

M•••••P
MAINTOP
MAKESUP
MANTRAP
MARKSUP
MATCHUP
MILKSOP
MISSTEP
MIXEDUP
MIXESUP
MIXITUP
MUCKSUP
MUGWUMP

•MP••••
AMPERES
AMPHORA
AMPLEST

AMPLIFY
AMPOULE
AMPULES
EMPANEL
EMPATHY
EMPEROR
EMPIRES
EMPLOYS
EMPORIA
EMPOWER
EMPRESS
EMPTIED
EMPTIER
EMPTIES
EMPTILY
IMPACTS
IMPAIRS
IMPALAS
IMPALED
IMPALES
IMPANEL
IMPARTS
IMPASSE
IMPASTO
IMPEACH
IMPEDED
IMPEDES
IMPENDS
IMPERIL
IMPETUS
IMPIETY
IMPINGE
IMPIOUS
IMPLANT
IMPLIED
IMPLIES
IMPLODE
IMPLORE
IMPORTS
IMPOSED
IMPOSES
IMPOSTS
IMPOUND
IMPRESS
IMPRINT
IMPROVE
IMPUGNS
IMPULSE
IMPURER
IMPUTED
IMPUTES
OMPHALI
UMPIRED
UMPIRES
UMPTEEN

•M•P•••
AMAPOLA

•M••••P
SMASHUP

••MP•••
ARMPITS
BUMPERS
BUMPIER
BUMPING
BUMPKIN
BUMPSUP
CAMPARI
CAMPERS
CAMPHOR
CAMPIER
CAMPING
CAMPION
CAMPOUT
COMPACT
COMPANY
COMPARE
COMPASS
COMPEER
COMPELS
COMPETE
COMPILE
COMPLEX
COMPORT
COMPOSE
COMPOST
COMPOTE
COMPUTE
DAMPENS
DAMPERS
DAMPEST
DAMPING
DAMPISH
DEMPSEY
DIMPLED
DIMPLES
DUMPIER
DUMPING
GOMPERS
HAMPERS
HAMPTON
JAMPACK
JUMPCUT
JUMPERS
JUMPIER
JUMPING
JUMPOFF
JUMPSAT
JUMPSIN
JUMPSON
JUMPSUP
KAMPALA
LAMPOIL
LAMPOON
LAMPREY
LEMPIRA
LIMPEST
LIMPETS
LIMPING
LIMPOPO
LUMPERS
LUMPIER
LUMPING
LUMPSUM
MEMPHIS
OOMPAHS
PAMPERS
POMPANO
POMPEIA
POMPEII
POMPOMS
POMPONS
POMPOUS
PUMPERS
PUMPING
PUMPKIN
PUMPSUP
RAMPAGE
RAMPANT
RAMPART
ROMPERS
ROMPING
RUMPLED
RUMPLES
RUMPOLE
SAMPANS
SAMPLED
SAMPLER
SAMPLES
SAMPRAS
SAMPSON
SIMPERS
SIMPLER
SIMPLEX
SIMPSON
SYMPTOM
TAMPERS
TAMPICO
TAMPING
TEMPERA
TEMPERS
TEMPEST
TEMPLAR
TEMPLES
TEMPTED
TEMPTER
TEMPURA
TYMPANA
TYMPANI
VAMPERS
VAMPING
VAMPIRE
WIMPLED
WIMPLES

••M•P••
SEMIPRO

••M••P•
LIMPOPO

••M•••P
BUMPSUP
COMESUP
DUMMYUP
GUMDROP
HAMITUP
JUMPSUP
PUMPSUP
TIMECOP
TIMESUP

•••MP••
CHAMPED
CHOMPED
CLAMPED
CLUMPED
CRAMPED
CRAMPON
CRIMPED
CRIMPER
CRUMPET
CRUMPLE
CRUMPLY
EXAMPLE
EXEMPLI
EXEMPTS
GLIMPSE
GRAMPUS
GRUMPED
GUIMPES
OLYMPIA
OLYMPIC
OLYMPUS
PLUMPED
PLUMPER
PRIMPED
PROMPTS
SCAMPED
SCAMPER
SHAMPOO
SKIMPED
SLUMPED
STAMPED
STOMPED
STUMPED
STUMPER
SWAMPED
THUMPED
THUMPER
TRAMPAS
TRAMPED
TRAMPLE
TRUMPED
TRUMPET
TRUMPUP
WHIMPER
WHOMPED

•••M•P•
BITMAPS
RAGMOPS
WARMUPS
WETMOPS

•••M••P
BEAMSUP
CLAMSUP
DRUMSUP
DUMMYUP
FIRMSUP
FRAMEUP
TEAMSUP
TRUMPUP
WARMSUP

••••MP•
ATTEMPT
CCLAMPS
DECAMPS
ENCAMPS
GALUMPH
PREAMPS
PREEMPT
REVAMPS
SCRIMPS
SCRIMPY
SHRIMPS
TRIUMPH
UNKEMPT
UPTEMPO

••••M•P
DREAMUP
DUSTMOP
ROADMAP
STARMAP

•••••MP
AIRPUMP
ARCLAMP
BEDLAMP
DAYCAMP
GASPUMP
MUGWUMP
NOTRUMP
OFFRAMP
OILLAMP
OUTJUMP
RESTAMP
SKIJUMP
SUNLAMP

M•Q••••
MCQUEEN

M••Q•••
MARQUEE
MARQUES
MARQUEZ
MARQUIS
MASQUES
MOSQUES

M•••Q••
MACAQUE
MONIQUE

••MQ•••
KUMQUAT

••M•Q••
COMIQUE

MR•••••
MRBONES
MRCHIPS
MRCLEAN
MRFIXIT
MRMAGOO
MRRIGHT
MRSPOCK

M•R••••
MARABOU
MARACAS
MARAUDS
MARBLED
MARBLES
MARCEAU
MARCELS
MARCHED
MARCHEN
MARCHER
MARCHES
MARCHON
MARCONI
MARGATE
MARGAUX
MARGAYS
MARGINS
MARGRET
MARIANA
MARILYN
MARIMBA
MARINAS
MARINER
MARINES
MARITAL
MARKERS
MARKETS
MARKHAM
MARKHOR
MARKING
MARKKAA
MARKOFF
MARKOVA
MARKSUP
MARKUPS
MARLENE
MARLINS
MARLOWE
MARMARA
MARMION
MARMOTS
MAROONS
MARQUEE
MARQUES
MARQUEZ
MARQUIS
MARRIED
MARRIES
MARRING
MARROWS
MARRYME
MARSALA
MARSHAL
MARSHES
MARTENS
MARTIAL
MARTIAN
MARTINA
MARTINI
MARTINO
MARTINS
MARTYRS
MARVELS
MARXISM
MARYANN
MARYKAY
MARYLOU
MERCIES
MERCURY
MERGERS
MERGING
MERIMEE
MERINOS
MERITED
MERLOTS
MERMAID
MERRIER
MERRILL
MERRILY
MIRACLE
MIRADOR
MIRAGES
MIRAMAR
MIRAMAX
MIRANDA
MIRRORS
MORAINE
MORALES
MORALLY
MORANIS
MORAVIA
MORDANT
MORDENT
MORDRED
MORELLO
MORESBY
MORGANA
MORGANS
MORMONS
MORNING
MOROCCO
MORPHED
MORROWS
MORSELS
MORTALS
MORTARS
MORTIFY
MORTISE
MRRIGHT
MURDERS
MURDOCH
MURILLO
MURKIER
MURKILY
MURMURS
MURPHEY
MYRIADS
MYRTLES

M••R•••
MACRAME
MACRONS
MADRONA
MALRAUX
MARRIED
MARRIES
MARRING
MARROWS
MARRYME
MATRONS
MAUREEN
MAURICE
MAUROIS
MEGRIMS
MEGRYAN
MELROSE
MERRIER
MERRILL
MERRILY
METRICS
MICROBE
MICRONS
MIDRIBS
MIDRIFF
MIDRISE
MIGRANT
MIGRATE
MIRRORS
MISREAD
MISRULE
MITRING
MOORAGE
MOORHEN
MOORING
MOORISH
MORROWS

M•••R••
MACGRAW
MAHARIS
MAIGRET
MAITRED
MAJORCA
MAJORED
MALAREN
MANDREL
MANDRIL
MANFRED
MANTRAP
MANTRAS
MANTRIC
MARGRET
MATURED
MATURER
MATURES
MAYORAL
MAZURKA
MCENROE
MEMOREX
MENORAH
METERED
MILDRED
MILKRUN
MILLRUN
MILORDS
MINARET
MINERAL
MINERVA
MINORCA
MINORED
MISERLY
MISTRAL
MITERED
MITHRAS
MODERNS
MONARCH
MONGREL
MORDRED
MOTORED
MUBARAK
MUSKRAT

M••••R•
MACABRE
MADDERS
MADEIRA
MAESTRI
MAESTRO
MAGYARS
MAILERS
MAJEURE
MALLARD
MANGERS
MANNERS
MANSARD
MAPPERS
MARKERS
MARMARA
MARTYRS
MASCARA
MASHERS
MASKERS
MASONRY
MASTERS
MASTERY
MATHERS
MATTERS
MAXBORN
MAYNARD
MCGUIRE
MEASURE
MEMBERS
MEMOIRE
MEMOIRS
MENDERS
MENHIRS
MENTORS
MERCURY
MERGERS
METEORS
METIERS
MEWLERS
MIDTERM
MILKERS
MILLARD
MILLERS
MIMICRY
MINCERS
MINDERS
MINTERS
MIRRORS
MISFIRE
MISTERS
MISWORD
MITFORD
MIXTURE
MOANERS
MOCKERS
MOCKERY
MOHAIRS
MOILERS
MOLDERS
MOLIERE
MOLTERS
MONGERS
MOPPERS
MORTARS
MOTHERS
MOUSERS
MUDDERS
MUGGERS
MULLERS
MUMFORD
MUMMERS
MUMMERY
MURDERS
MURMURS
MUSHERS
MUSTARD
MUSTERS
MUTTERS
MYSTERY

M•••••R
MADEFOR
MAKEFOR
MAKEPAR
MALABAR
MALODOR
MANAGER
MANGIER
MANHOUR
MANLIER
MANOWAR
MANYEAR
MARCHER
MARINER
MARKHOR
MASSEUR
MATADOR
MATURER
MAUNDER
MAXBAER
MAYFAIR
MEALIER
MEANDER
MEATIER
MEDDLER
MERRIER
MESSIER
METOOER
MIDYEAR
MILKIER
MINGLER
MINIVER
MINTIER
MIRADOR
MIRAMAR
MISHEAR
MISTIER
MOBSTER
MODELER
MODULAR
MOISTER
MOLDIER
MONIKER
MONITOR
MONOMER
MONSTER
MOOCHER
MOODIER
MOSSIER
MOULDER
MOUSIER
MUAMMAR
MUDDIER
MUDDLER
MUFFLER
MUGGIER
MUMBLER
MUNCHER
MURKIER
MUSHIER
MUSTIER
MUZZIER
MYANMAR
MYNHEER

•MR••••
AMRADIO
FMRADIO

•M•R•••
AMBRIES
AMBROSE
AMERCED
AMERCES
AMERICA
AMERIGO
AMERIKA
AMERIND
AMOROUS
EMBRACE
EMBROIL
EMBRYOS
EMERALD
EMERGED
EMERGES
EMERITA
EMERITI
EMERSED
EMERSON
EMIRATE
EMPRESS
IMARETS
IMBRUED
IMBRUES
IMPRESS
IMPRINT
IMPROVE
SMARTED
SMARTEN
SMARTER
SMARTLY
SMIRKED
UMBRAGE
UMBRIAN

•M••R••
AMHARIC
AMHERST
AMPERES
AMSCRAY
EMBARGO
EMBARKS
EMIGRES
EMPEROR
EMPIRES
EMPORIA
IMMERSE
IMMORAL
IMMURED
IMMURES
IMPARTS
IMPERIL
IMPORTS
IMPURER
IMSORRY
OMICRON
SMEARED
UMBERTO
UMPIRED
UMPIRES

•M•••R•
AMATORY
AMBLERS
AMPHORA
EMOTERS
IMAGERS
IMAGERY
IMPAIRS
IMPLORE
IMSORRY
SMILERS
SMOKERS

•M••••R
AMATEUR
AMMETER
EMENDER
EMITTER
EMPEROR
EMPOWER
EMPTIER
IMPURER
SMACKER
SMALLER
SMARTER
SMASHER
SMATTER
SMELTER
SMOKIER
SMOLDER
SMOTHER
SMUGGER

••MR•••
ARMREST
COMRADE
JIMRYUN
NIMRODS
RAMRODS

••M•R••
ADMIRAL
ADMIRED
ADMIRER
ADMIRES
ARMORED
ARMORER
BEMIRED
BEMIRES
CAMBRIC
CAMERAS
CAMERON
COMFREY
COMOROS
DEMERIT
DEMEROL
DEMURER
ELMTREE
FEMORAL
GAMBREL
GUMDROP
GUMTREE
HOMBRES
HOMERED
HOMERIC
HOMERUN
HUMDRUM
HUMERAL
HUMERUS
HUMORED
IMMERSE
IMMORAL
IMMURED
IMMURES
LAMARCK
LAMPREY
MEMOREX
NEMEROV
NUMERAL
NUMERIC
REMARKS
REMARRY
REMORAS
REMORSE
RUMORED
SAMARIA
SAMPRAS
SAMURAI
TAMARIN
TIMBRES
TUMBREL
ZYMURGY

••M••R•
ARMOIRE
ARMOURS
BOMBARD
BOMBERS
BUMMERS
BUMPERS
CAMBERS
CAMPARI
CAMPERS
COMBERS
COMFORT
COMPARE
COMPORT
DAMPERS
DIMITRI
DIMMERS
GOMPERS
HAMBURG
HAMMERS
HAMPERS
HEMMERS
HHMUNRO
HOMBURG
HUMMERS
HUMOURS
JAMMERS
JUMPERS
LAMBERT
LEMPIRA
LIMBERS
LIMNERS
LOMBARD
LUMBARS
LUMBERS
LUMIERE
LUMPERS
MEMBERS
MEMOIRE
MEMOIRS
MIMICRY
MUMFORD
MUMMERS
MUMMERY
NUMBERS
PAMPERS
PUMPERS
RAMPART
REMARRY
ROMPERS
RUMOURS
SAMBARS
SAMSARA
SEMIPRO
SIMMERS
SIMPERS
SUMATRA
SUMMARY
SUMMERS
SUMMERY
TAMPERS
TEMPERA
TEMPERS
TEMPURA
TIMBERS
VAMPERS
VAMPIRE
YAMMERS

••M•••R
ADMIRER
AMMETER
ARMORER
BUMBLER
BUMPIER
CAMPHOR
CAMPIER
COMFIER
COMPEER
DEMETER
DEMURER
DUMPIER
FUMBLER
GAMBLER
GUMMIER
HAMSTER
HUMBLER
HUMIDOR
JUMPIER
LAMINAR
LUMPIER
MUMBLER
NIMBLER
RAMBLER
REMOTER
REMOVER
RUMMIER
SAMOVAR
SAMPLER
SEMINAR
SIMILAR
SIMPLER
TAMBOUR
TEMBLOR
TEMPLAR
TEMPTER
TIMIDER
TUMBLER
YUMMIER

•••M•R•
ANYMORE
ARDMORE
BOOMERS
BUMMERS
CHIMERA

CLAMORS
DENMARK
DIMMERS
DORMERS
EARMARK
ENAMORS
FARMERS
GILMORE
HAMMERS
HEMMERS
HUMMERS
ISOMERS
JAMMERS
MARMARA
MUMMERS
MUMMERY
MURMURS
OXYMORA
PISMIRE
PRIMARY
PRIMERS
REAMERS
RHYMERS
ROAMERS
ROOMERS
SIMMERS
SUMMARY
SUMMERS
SUMMERY
TREMORS
WALMART
WIDMARK
WOOMERA
YAMMERS

•••M••R

BALMIER
BARMIER
BEAMIER
BESMEAR
CHAMBER
CHAMFER
CLAMBER
CLAMMER
CLIMBER
CRAMMER
CRIMPER
DAIMLER
DAUMIER
DRUMMER
ENAMOUR
FILMIER
FNUMBER
FOAMIER
GLAMOUR
GLIMMER
GLUMMER
GRAMMAR
GRAMMER
GRIMIER
GRIMMER
GUMMIER
LOAMIER
MUAMMAR
PALMIER
PLUMBER
PLUMMER
PLUMPER
PREMIER
PRIMMER
ROOMIER
RUMMIER
SCAMPER
SCHMEER
SEAMIER
SEYMOUR
SHIMMER
SKIMMER
SLAMMER
SLIMIER
SLIMMER
SLUMBER
STAMMER
STUMPER
SWIMMER
THUMPER
TRAMCAR
TRIMMER
VERMEER
WHIMPER
WORMIER
YUMMIER

••••M•R

ALARMER
BLOOMER
CHARMER
CLAIMER
CLAMMER
CRAMMER
CREAMER
DREAMER
DRUMMER
GLIMMER
GLUMMER
GRAMMAR
GRAMMER
GRIMMER
GROOMER
INGEMAR
KASHMIR
MIRAMAR
MONOMER
MUAMMAR
MYANMAR
PALOMAR
PLUMMER
POLYMER
PRIMMER
SCHEMER
SHIMMER
SKIMMER
SLAMMER
SLIMMER
STAMMER
STEAMER
SWIMMER
TRIMMER

M•S••••

MASCARA
MASCOTS
MASHERS
MASHIES
MASHING
MASKERS
MASKING
MASONIC
MASONRY
MASQUES
MASSAGE
MASSEUR
MASSIFS
MASSING
MASSIVE
MASTABA
MASTERS
MASTERY
MASTICS
MASTIFF
MASTOID
MCSWINE
MESCALS
MESHING
MESSAGE
MESSALA
MESSIAH
MESSIER
MESSILY
MESSINA
MESSING
MESSKIT
MESTIZO
MISALLY
MISCALL
MISCAST
MISCUED
MISCUES
MISDATE
MISDEAL
MISDEED
MISDIAL
MISDOES
MISDONE
MISERLY
MISFILE
MISFIRE
MISFITS
MISHAPS
MISHEAR
MISHITS
MISLAID
MISLAYS
MISLEAD
MISMATE
MISNAME
MISPLAY
MISREAD
MISRULE
MISSALS
MISSIES
MISSILE
MISSING
MISSION
MISSISH
MISSIVE
MISSOUT
MISSTEP
MISTAKE
MISTERS
MISTIER
MISTILY
MISTING
MISTOOK
MISTRAL
MISTYPE
MISUSED
MISUSES
MISWORD
MOSAICS
MOSELLE
MOSEYED
MOSLEMS
MOSQUES
MOSSIER
MOSSING
MRSPOCK
MUSCATS
MUSCLED
MUSCLES
MUSCOVY
MUSETTE
MUSEUMS
MUSHERS
MUSHIER
MUSHILY
MUSHING
MUSICAL
MUSKETS
MUSKRAT
MUSLIMS
MUSLINS
MUSSELS
MUSSING
MUSTAFA
MUSTANG
MUSTARD
MUSTERS
MUSTIER
MUSTILY
MUSTSEE
MYSTERY
MYSTICS
MYSTIFY

M••S•••

MAESTRI
MAESTRO
MANSARD
MANSION
MARSALA
MARSHAL
MARSHES
MASSAGE
MASSEUR
MASSIFS
MASSING
MASSIVE
MEASLES
MEASURE
MEISSEN
MESSAGE
MESSALA
MESSIAH
MESSIER
MESSILY
MESSINA
MESSING
MESSKIT
MIASMAS
MIASMIC
MIDSIZE
MISSALS
MISSIES
MISSILE
MISSING
MISSION
MISSISH
MISSIVE
MISSOUT
MISSTEP
MOBSTER
MOISTEN
MOISTER
MOISTLY
MONSOON
MONSTER
MORSELS
MOSSIER
MOSSING
MOUSERS
MOUSIER
MOUSING
MOUSSED
MOUSSES
MUGSHOT
MUSSELS
MUSSING

M•••S••

MADISON
MAJESTE
MAJESTY
MAKESDO
MAKESIT
MAKESUP
MALMSEY
MAOISTS
MARKSUP
MATISSE
MEDUSAE
MEDUSAS
MEIOSES
MEIOSIS
MEISSEN
MELISSA
MENISCI
MILKSOP
MIMESIS
MIMOSAS
MINDSET
MINUSES
MISUSED
MISUSES
MITOSES
MITOSIS
MIXESUP
MODESTO
MODESTY
MODISTE
MOLESTS
MOONSET
MORESBY
MOUSSED
MOUSSES
MOVESIN
MUCKSUP
MUMESON
MUSTSEE

M••••S•

MADDEST
MADNESS
MAEWEST
MAFIOSO
MALAISE
MALTESE
MALTOSE
MANNISH
MARXISM
MATISSE
MAWKISH
MEANEST
MEEKEST
MELISSA
MELROSE
MIDEAST
MIDRISE
MIDWEST
MILDEST
MISCAST
MISSISH
MOLLUSK
MOMBASA
MONKISH
MOORISH
MORTISE

M•••••S

MACRONS
MADCAPS
MADDENS
MADDERS
MADLIBS
MADNESS
MAENADS
MAGNETS
MAGNUMS
MAGPIES
MAGUEYS
MAGYARS
MAHARIS
MAHOUTS
MAIDENS
MAILERS
MAITAIS
MAKEUPS
MAKINGS
MALIGNS
MALLETS
MALLOWS
MALTEDS
MALTHUS
MAMMALS
MANAGES
MANANAS
MANDANS
MANDAYS
MANEGES
MANGERS
MANGLES
MANGOES
MANIACS
MANNERS
MANTELS
MANTLES
MANTRAS
MANUALS
MAOISTS
MAPPERS
MARACAS
MARAUDS
MARBLES
MARCELS
MARCHES
MARGAYS
MARGINS
MARINAS
MARINES
MARKERS
MARKETS
MARKUPS
MARLINS
MARMOTS
MAROONS
MARQUES
MARQUIS
MARRIES
MARROWS
MARSHES
MARTENS
MARTINS
MARTYRS
MARVELS
MASCOTS
MASHERS
MASHIES
MASKERS
MASQUES
MASSIFS
MASTERS
MASTICS
MATCHES
MATHERS
MATHEWS
MATHIAS
MATRONS
MATTERS
MATURES
MATZOHS
MAUROIS
MAXIMUS
MAYDAYS
MAYHEMS
MCCALLS
MEADOWS
MEALIES
MEANIES
MEASLES
MEDDLES
MEDIANS
MEDICOS
MEDIUMS
MEDLEYS
MEDUSAS
MEGOHMS
MEGRIMS
MEIOSES
MEIOSIS
MELLOWS
MEMBERS
MEMOIRS
MEMPHIS
MENACES
MENAGES
MENDERS
MENHIRS
MENIALS
MENTORS
MERCIES
MERGERS
MERINOS
MERLOTS
MESCALS
METATES
METEORS
METHODS
METIERS
METRICS
METTLES
MEWLERS
MIASMAS
MICMACS
MICRONS
MIDDAYS
MIDDENS
MIDDIES
MIDDLES
MIDGETS
MIDRIBS
MIDWAYS
MIKADOS
MILDEWS
MILIEUS
MILKERS
MILLERS
MILLETS
MILORDS
MIMESIS
MIMOSAS
MINCERS
MINDERS
MINGLES
MINIBUS
MINIONS
MINNOWS
MINOANS
MINTERS
MINUETS
MINUSES
MINUTES
MIRAGES
MIRRORS
MISCUES
MISDOES
MISFITS
MISHAPS
MISHITS
MISLAYS
MISSALS
MISSIES
MISTERS
MISUSES
MITHRAS
MITOSES
MITOSIS
MITTENS
MIZZENS
MIZZLES
MOANERS
MOBCAPS
MOBILES
MOCKERS
MOCKUPS
MODELAS
MODELTS
MODERNS
MODULES
MOHAIRS
MOHAWKS
MOILERS
MOLDERS
MOLESTS
MOLTERS
MOMENTS
MOMMIES
MONDAYS
MONGERS
MONGOLS
MONKEES
MONKEYS
MOOCHES
MOPPERS
MOPPETS
MORALES
MORANIS
MORGANS
MORMONS
MORROWS
MORSELS
MORTALS
MORTARS
MOSAICS
MOSLEMS
MOSQUES
MOTHERS
MOTIONS
MOTIVES
MOTTLES
MOTTOES
MOUSERS
MOUSSES
MOUTONS
MRBONES
MRCHIPS
MUDDERS
MUDDIES
MUDDLES
MUDEELS
MUDHENS
MUDPIES
MUFFINS
MUFFLES
MUGGERS
MUKLUKS
MULCHES
MULETAS
MULLAHS
MULLERS
MULLETS
MUMBLES
MUMMERS
MUMMIES
MUNCHES
MUNTINS
MUPPETS
MURDERS
MURMURS
MUSCATS
MUSCLES
MUSEUMS
MUSHERS
MUSKETS
MUSLIMS
MUSLINS
MUSSELS
MUSTERS
MUTANTS
MUTATES
MUTATIS
MUTTERS
MUTTONS
MUTUALS
MUUMUUS
MUZHIKS
MUZZLES
MYRIADS
MYRTLES
MYSTICS

•MS••••

AMSCRAY
IMSORRY

•M•S•••

AMASSED
AMASSES
AMUSING
KMESONS
SMASHED
SMASHER
SMASHES
SMASHUP

•M••S••

AMASSED
AMASSES
AMNESIA
AMNESTY
EMBASSY
EMERSED
EMERSON
IMPASSE
IMPASTO
IMPOSED
IMPOSES
IMPOSTS

•M•••S•

AMBROSE
AMHERST
AMONGST
AMPLEST
AMYLASE
EMBASSY
EMPRESS
IMMENSE
IMMERSE
IMPASSE
IMPRESS
IMPULSE

•M••••S

AMADEUS
AMASSES
AMAZONS
AMBLERS
AMBRIES
AMERCES
AMNIONS
AMOEBAS
AMOROUS
AMOUNTS
AMPERES
AMPULES
AMULETS
BMOVIES
EMBANKS
EMBARKS
EMBLEMS
EMBRYOS
EMERGES
EMIGRES
EMOTERS
EMPIRES
EMPLOYS
EMPRESS
EMPTIES
IMAGERS
IMAGOES
IMARETS
IMBIBES
IMBRUES
IMMIXES
IMMURES
IMPACTS
IMPAIRS
IMPALAS
IMPALES
IMPARTS
IMPEDES
IMPENDS
IMPETUS
IMPIOUS
IMPLIES
IMPORTS
IMPOSES
IMPOSTS
IMPRESS
IMPUGNS
IMPUTES
KMESONS
OMELETS
OMINOUS
OMNIBUS
SMALTOS
SMASHES
SMILERS
SMOKERS
SMOKIES
SMOOTHS
SMUDGES
UMLAUTS
UMPIRES

••MS•••

BUMSOUT
DAMSELS
DAMSONS
GEMSBOK
GUMSHOE
GYMSHOE
HAMSTER
HEMSLEY
HIMSELF
RIMSHOT
SAMSARA
SAMSUNG

••M•S••

BEMUSED
BEMUSES
BUMPSUP
CAMISES
COMESAT
COMESBY
COMESIN
COMESON
COMESTO
COMESUP
DAMASKS
DEMESNE
DEMISED
DEMISES
DEMPSEY
ELMISTI
ENMASSE
JAMESON
JUMPSAT
JUMPSIN
JUMPSON
JUMPSUP
LUMPSUM
MIMESIS
MIMOSAS
MUMESON
NEMESES
NEMESIS
OSMOSED
OSMOSES
OSMOSIS
PIMESON
PUMPSUP
RAMESES
SAMISEN
SAMPSON
SIMPSON
TIMESUP
UNMASKS

••M••S•

AIMLESS
ARMLESS
ARMREST
BOMBAST
COMBUST
COMPASS
COMPOSE
COMPOST
DAMPEST
DAMPISH
DIMMEST
DIMNESS
DUMBEST
ENMASSE
GAMIEST
GYMNAST
HOMIEST
IMMENSE
IMMERSE
KOMATSU
LAMAISM
LAMAIST
LIMIEST
LIMPEST
MOMBASA
NUMBEST
REMORSE
ROMANSH
TEMPEST
VAMOOSE

••M•••S

ADMIRES
ADMIXES
AIMLESS
ALMONDS
ARMADAS
ARMFULS
ARMLESS
ARMLETS
ARMOURS
ARMPITS
BAMBOOS
BEMIRES
BEMOANS
BEMUSES
BOMBERS
BUMBLES
BUMMERS
BUMPERS
CAMBERS
CAMERAS
CAMISES
CAMPERS
CEMENTS
COMBATS
COMBERS
COMEONS
COMFITS
COMINGS
COMMITS
COMMONS
COMOROS
COMPASS
COMPELS
CUMULUS
CYMBALS
DAMAGES
DAMASKS
DAMPENS
DAMPERS
DAMSELS
DAMSONS
DEMANDS
DEMEANS
DEMISES
DEMOTES
DIMMERS
DIMNESS
DIMOUTS
DIMPLES
DIMWITS
DOMAINS
DOMINOS
DUMDUMS
DUMMIES
ERMINES
FAMULUS
FEMALES
FOMENTS
FUMBLES
GAMBITS
GAMBLES
GAMBOLS
GAMETES
GAMINES
GAMMONS
GIMBALS
GIMLETS
GOMPERS
HAMITES
HAMLETS
HAMMERS
HAMPERS
HEMMERS
HOMBRES
HUMBLES
HUMBUGS
HUMERUS
HUMMERS
HUMOURS
HYMNALS
IMMIXES
IMMURES
INMATES
IOMOTHS
JAMMERS
JEMMIES
JIMJAMS
JIMMIES
JUMBLES
JUMPERS
KIMONOS
LAMBDAS
LAMENTS
LAMINAS
LIMBERS
LIMNERS
LIMOGES
LIMPETS
LUMBARS
LUMBERS
LUMPERS
MAMMALS
MEMBERS
MEMOIRS
MEMPHIS
MIMESIS
MIMOSAS
MOMENTS
MOMMIES
MUMBLES
MUMMERS
MUMMIES
NEMESES
NEMESIS
NIMRODS
NUMBATS
NUMBERS
OOMPAHS
ORMOLUS
OSMONDS
OSMOSES
OSMOSIS
PAMBIES
PAMPERS
POMADES
POMELOS
POMMELS

POMPOMS
POMPONS
POMPOUS
PUMICES
PUMMELS
PUMPERS
RAMADAS
RAMBLES
RAMESES
RAMJETS
RAMRODS
REMAILS
REMAINS
REMAKES
REMANDS
REMARKS
REMELTS
REMENDS
REMINDS
REMIXES
REMOLDS
REMORAS
REMOTES
REMOVES
REMUDAS
ROMNEYS
ROMPERS
ROMULUS
RUMBLES
RUMOURS
RUMPLES
SAMBARS
SAMITES
SAMOANS
SAMPANS
SAMPLES
SAMPRAS
SEMITES
SIMIANS
SIMILES
SIMMERS
SIMMONS
SIMPERS
SOMALIS
SUMMERS
SUMMITS
SUMMONS
SYMBOLS
TAMALES
TAMPERS
TAMTAMS
TEMPERS
TEMPLES
TIMBALS
TIMBERS
TIMBRES
TIMEWAS
TIMINGS
TIMMINS
TOMBOYS
TOMCATS
TOMTITS
TOMTOMS
TUMBLES
TUMMIES
TUMULTS
TUMULUS
UNMAKES
UNMASKS
VAMPERS
WAMBLES
WIMPLES
WOMBATS
YAMMERS
YEMENIS
ZOMBIES

•••MS••

ADAMSON
BEAMSUP
CHOMSKY
CLAMSUP
CLEMSON
CRIMSON
DRUMSUP
FIRMSUP
MALMSEY
TEAMSUP
THOMSON
WARMSUP
ZOOMSIN

•••M•S•

AIRMASS
ANIMISM
ANIMIST
BIOMASS
BLEMISH
BURMESE
CALMEST
CHEMISE
CHEMIST
DIMMEST
DISMISS
ENDMOST
FIRMEST
FLEMISH
FORMOSA
GLIMPSE
INAMESS
OAKMOSS
OLEMISS
PALMIST
PREMISE
PROMISE
REAMASS
SEAMOSS
SIAMESE
SKIMASK
SURMISE
TOPMAST
TOPMOST
WARMEST
WARMISH

•••M••S

AIRMASS
ALUMNUS
ANIMALS
ATAMANS
ATOMIES
BIOMASS
BITMAPS
BOOMERS
BUMMERS
CAIMANS
CHAMOIS
CLAMORS
CLEMENS
COMMITS
COMMONS
DIMMERS
DISMAYS
DISMISS
DOLMANS
DOLMENS
DORMERS
DUMMIES
ENAMELS
ENAMORS
ENEMIES
EXEMPTS
FARMERS
FLAMBES
FORMALS
FORMATS
GAMMONS
GERMANS
GNOMONS
GRAMMES
GRAMPUS
GUIMPES
HAMMERS
HAYMOWS
HELMETS
HEMMERS
HERMITS
HETMANS
HUMMERS
INAMESS
ISOMERS
JAMMERS
JEMMIES
JIMMIES
KIRMANS
MAMMALS
MARMOTS
MICMACS
MOMMIES
MORMONS
MUMMERS
MUMMIES
MURMURS
MUUMUUS
NORMALS
NORMANS
NUTMEGS
OAKMOSS
OLEMISS
OLYMPUS
PERMITS
POMMELS
PREMEDS
PRIMERS
PROMPTS
PUMMELS
PYGMIES
RAGMOPS
REAMASS
REAMERS
RHOMBUS
RHUMBAS
RHYMERS
ROAMERS
ROOMERS
ROOMIES
SALMONS
SCHMOES
SCHMOOS
SEAMOSS
SERMONS
SHAMANS
SIMMERS
SIMMONS
STAMENS
STYMIES
SUBMITS
SUMMERS
SUMMITS
SUMMONS
TARMACS
TIMMINS
TRAMPAS
TREMORS
TUMMIES
WARMUPS
WETMOPS
YAMMERS
YOUMANS

••••M•S

AFRAMES
ARTEMIS
ARTEMUS
ASSUMES
ATHOMES
ATTIMES
AUTUMNS
BAHAMAS
BECOMES
BENUMBS
BETIMES
BIREMES
BRAHMAS
CCLAMPS
CHROMES
CINEMAS
COLUMNS
DECAMPS
DEFAMES
DYNAMOS
ENCAMPS
ENIGMAS
ENZYMES
ERASMUS
ESKIMOS
GRAMMES
INCOMES
ISTHMUS
JICAMAS
LEGUMES
MAXIMUS
MIASMAS
NOKOMIS
PAJAMAS
PANAMAS
PDJAMES
PLASMAS
PREAMPS
PYJAMAS
PYRAMUS
RACEMES
RADAMES
REGIMES
RENAMES
RESUMES
RETIMES
REVAMPS
SALAMIS
SCHEMAS
SCHEMES
SCRIMPS
SESAMES
SHRIMPS
STIGMAS
TATAMIS
THERMOS
TRAUMAS
VOLUMES
ZEUGMAS

•••••MS

AFFIRMS
AIRDAMS
ALARUMS
ANADEMS
ANONYMS
ANTHEMS
ASHRAMS
ASYLUMS
ATRIUMS
BALSAMS
BANTAMS
BECALMS
BELDAMS
BESEEMS
BOTTOMS
CHRISMS
CUSTOMS
DEFORMS
DIADEMS
DIATOMS
DICTUMS
DISARMS
DUMDUMS
EMBLEMS
ENGRAMS
EPONYMS
ESTEEMS
FATHOMS
FRENUMS
GRAHAMS
HANSOMS
INFORMS
INSEAMS
JIMJAMS
LOGJAMS
LYCEUMS
MAGNUMS
MAYHEMS
MEDIUMS
MEGOHMS
MEGRIMS
MOSLEMS
MUSEUMS
MUSLIMS
NONCOMS
PABLUMS
PEPLUMS
PHENOMS
PLENUMS
PODIUMS
POMPOMS
POSSUMS
PRELIMS
QUORUMS
RANSOMS
REDEEMS
REDGUMS
REFILMS
REFORMS
RETRIMS
REWARMS
RHYTHMS
SACHEMS
SALAAMS
SCHISMS
SCREAMS
SHALOMS
SITCOMS
SLALOMS
SQUIRMS
STREAMS
SYSTEMS
TAMTAMS
TANDEMS
TOMTOMS
TRUISMS
VACUUMS
VELLUMS
VICTIMS
WIGWAMS

M•T••••

MATADOR
MATCHED
MATCHES
MATCHUP
MATEWAN
MATHERS
MATHEWS
MATHIAS
MATILDA
MATINEE
MATISSE
MATLOCK
MATRONS
MATTERS
MATTHAU
MATTHEW
MATTING
MATTOCK
MATURED
MATURER
MATURES
MATZOHS
METATES
METEORS
METEOUT
METERED
METHANE
METHODS
METIERS
METOOER
METRICS
METTLES
MITCHUM
MITERED
MITFORD
MITHRAS
MITOSES
MITOSIS
MITOTIC
MITRING
MITTENS
MITZVAH
MOTHERS
MOTIONS
MOTIVES
MOTORED
MOTTLED
MOTTLES
MOTTOES
MUTABLE
MUTABLY
MUTAGEN
MUTANTS
MUTATED
MUTATES
MUTATIS
MUTTERS
MUTTONS
MUTUALS

M••T•••

MAITAIS
MAITRED
MALTEDS
MALTESE
MALTHUS
MALTING
MALTOSE
MANTELS
MANTLED
MANTLES
MANTRAP
MANTRAS
MANTRIC
MARTENS
MARTIAL
MARTIAN
MARTINA
MARTINI
MARTINO
MARTINS
MARTYRS
MASTABA
MASTERS
MASTERY
MASTICS
MASTIFF
MASTOID
MATTERS
MATTHAU
MATTHEW
MATTING
MATTOCK
MAYTIME
MEATIER
MEETING
MELTING
MENTHOL
MENTION
MENTORS
MESTIZO
METTLES
MIDTERM
MIDTOWN
MINTERS
MINTIER
MINTING
MISTAKE
MISTERS
MISTIER
MISTILY
MISTING
MISTOOK
MISTRAL
MISTYPE
MITTENS
MIXTURE
MOLTERS
MOLTING
MONTAGE
MONTANA
MONTAND
MONTANE
MONTEGO
MONTEUX
MONTHLY
MONTOYA
MORTALS
MORTARS
MORTIFY
MORTISE
MOTTLED
MOTTLES
MOTTOES
MOUTHED
MOUTONS
MUNTINS
MUSTAFA
MUSTANG
MUSTARD
MUSTERS
MUSTIER
MUSTILY
MUSTSEE
MUTTERS
MUTTONS
MYRTLES
MYSTERY
MYSTICS
MYSTIFY

M•••T••

MAESTRI
MAESTRO
MAHATMA
MAINTOP
MANATEE
MANITOU
MARITAL
MEIOTIC
MENOTTI
MERITED
METATES
MIGHTNT
MILITIA
MIMETIC
MINUTES
MINUTIA
MISSTEP
MITOTIC
MIXITUP
MOBSTER
MOISTEN
MOISTER
MOISTLY
MOLOTOV
MONITOR
MONSTER
MOULTED
MOUNTED
MOUNTIE
MULCTED
MULETAS
MUSETTE
MUTATED
MUTATES
MUTATIS

M••••T•

MACBETH
MACHETE
MAGENTA
MAGNATE
MAGNETO
MAGNETS
MAHOUTS
MAJESTE
MAJESTY
MALEATE
MALLETS
MAMMOTH
MANDATE
MAOISTS
MARGATE
MARKETS
MARMOTS
MASCOTS
MEDIATE
MEMENTO
MENOTTI
MERLOTS
MIDGETS
MIGRATE
MILLETS
MILLETT
MINOLTA
MINUETS
MISDATE
MISFITS
MISHITS
MISMATE
MODELTS
MODESTO
MODESTY
MODISTE
MOLESTS
MOMENTS
MOPPETS
MULLETS
MUPPETS
MUSCATS
MUSETTE
MUSKETS
MUTANTS

M•••••T

MADDEST
MADEOUT
MAEWEST
MAGINOT
MAIGRET
MAILLOT
MAKEOUT
MAKESIT
MANHUNT
MANUMIT
MANXCAT
MARGRET
MEANEST
MEDIANT
MEEKEST
MESSKIT
METEOUT
MIDEAST
MIDWEST
MIGHTNT
MIGRANT
MILDEST
MILLETT
MINARET
MINDSET
MISCAST
MISSOUT
MONOCOT
MOONLIT
MOONSET
MORDANT
MORDENT
MOVEOUT
MRFIXIT
MRRIGHT
MUGSHOT
MUSKRAT

•M•T•••

AMATEUR
AMATIVE
AMATORY
EMITTED
EMITTER
EMOTERS
EMOTING
EMOTION
EMOTIVE
EMPTIED
EMPTIER
EMPTIES
EMPTILY
IMITATE
OMITTED
SMATTER
SMETANA
SMITING
SMITTEN
SMOTHER
UMPTEEN

•M••T••

AMMETER
EMITTED
EMITTER
EMPATHY
IMPETUS
IMPUTED
IMPUTES
OMENTUM
OMITTED
SMALTOS
SMARTED
SMARTEN
SMARTER
SMARTLY
SMATTER
SMELTED
SMELTER
SMITTEN
SMOOTHS

•M•••T•

AMENITY
AMNESTY
AMOUNTS
AMULETS
EMANATE
EMERITA
EMERITI
EMIRATE
EMULATE
IMAMATE
IMARETS
IMITATE
IMPACTS
IMPARTS
IMPASTO
IMPIETY
IMPORTS
IMPOSTS
OMELETS
UMBERTO
UMLAUTS

•M••••T

AMBIENT
AMHERST
AMONGST
AMPLEST
EMINENT
IMPLANT
IMPRINT

••MT•••

ELMTREE
GUMTREE
TAMTAMS
TOMTITS
TOMTOMS

••M•T••

AMMETER
DEMETER
DEMOTED
DEMOTES
DIMITRI
GAMETES
HAMITES
HAMITIC
HAMITUP
HAMPTON
HAMSTER
INMATES
IOMOTHS
KOMATSU
LAMOTTA
LIMITED
MIMETIC
NAMETAG
OSMOTIC
REMOTER
REMOTES
SAMITES
SEMITES
SEMITIC
SOMATIC
SUMATRA
SYMPTOM
TEMPTED
TEMPTER
TIMOTHY

••M••T•

AIMEDTO
ALMAATA
ARMLETS
ARMPITS
CEMENTS
COMBATS
COMESTO
COMFITS
COMMITS
COMMUTE
COMPETE
COMPOTE
COMPUTE
DIMOUTS
DIMWITS
ELMISTI
FOMENTS
GAMBITS
GIMLETS
HAMLETS
HAMMETT
LAMENTS
LAMOTTA
LIMPETS
MAMMOTH
MEMENTO
MOMENTS
NUMBATS
PIMENTO
RAMJETS
REMELTS
SUMMITS
TOMCATS
TOMTITS
TUMULTS
WOMBATS

••M•••T

AIMEDAT
ARMREST
ARMYANT
BOMBAST
BUMSOUT
CAMELOT
CAMEOUT
CAMPOUT
COMBUST
COMEOUT
COMESAT
COMFORT
COMMENT
COMPACT
COMPORT
COMPOST
DAMPEST
DEMERIT
DIMMEST
DUMBEST
GAMIEST
GYMNAST
HAMMETT
HOMIEST
JUMPCUT
JUMPSAT
KUMQUAT
LAMAIST
LAMBENT
LAMBERT
LIMIEST
LIMPEST
NUMBEST
RAMPANT
RAMPART
REMNANT
REMOUNT
RIMSHOT
TEMPEST
TIMEOUT

•••M•T•

ADAMITE
ANIMATE
ANIMATO
AZIMUTH
BISMUTH
BROMATE
CLIMATE
COMMITS
COMMUTE
DOGMATA
EREMITE
EXEMPTS
FORMATS
HAEMATO
HAMMETT
HELMETS
HERMITS
IMAMATE
KLAMATH
MAMMOTH
MARMOTS
MISMATE
NEWMATH
PALMATE
PERMITS
PRIMATE
PROMOTE
PROMPTS
STOMATA
SUBMITS
SUMMITS
TERMITE
ZERMATT

•••M••T

ADAMANT
AILMENT
ALIMENT
ANIMIST
AUGMENT
BELMONT
CALMEST
CHEMIST
CLEMENT
COMMENT
CRUMPET
DIMMEST
DINMONT
DORMANT
ELEMENT
ENDMOST
FARMOUT
FERMENT
FIGMENT
FIRMEST
FREMONT
GARMENT
GROMMET
HAMMETT
NUTMEAT
ODDMENT
PALMIST
PAYMENT
PIGMENT
PLUMMET
RAIMENT
REDMEAT
SCHMIDT
SEGMENT
TOPMAST
TOPMOST
TORMENT
TRUMPET
VARMINT
VERMONT
WALMART
WARMEST
ZERMATT

••••M•T

ATTEMPT
AUTOMAT
BATHMAT
CALUMET
DELIMIT
DOORMAT
GOURMET
GROMMET
MANUMIT
PLUMMET
PREEMPT
READMIT
UNKEMPT

MU•••••

MUAMMAR
MUBARAK
MUCKING
MUCKSUP
MUDDERS
MUDDIED
MUDDIER
MUDDIES

MUDDLED
MUDDLER
MUDDLES
MUDEELS
MUDHENS
MUDPACK
MUDPIES
MUEZZIN
MUFFING
MUFFINS
MUFFLED
MUFFLER
MUFFLES
MUGGERS
MUGGIER
MUGGING
MUGSHOT
MUGWUMP
MUKLUKS
MULCHED
MULCHES
MULCTED
MULETAS
MULLAHS
MULLEIN
MULLERS
MULLETS
MULLING
MULLION
MUMBLED
MUMBLER
MUMBLES
MUMESON
MUMFORD
MUMMERS
MUMMERY
MUMMIES
MUNCHED
MUNCHER
MUNCHES
MUNDANE
MUNTINS
MUPPETS
MURDERS
MURDOCH
MURILLO
MURKIER
MURKILY
MURMURS
MURPHEY
MUSCATS
MUSCLED
MUSCLES
MUSCOVY
MUSETTE
MUSEUMS
MUSHERS
MUSHIER
MUSHILY
MUSHING
MUSICAL
MUSKETS
MUSKRAT
MUSLIMS
MUSLINS
MUSSELS
MUSSING
MUSTAFA
MUSTANG
MUSTARD
MUSTERS
MUSTIER
MUSTILY

MUSTSEE
MUTABLE
MUTABLY
MUTAGEN
MUTANTS
MUTATED
MUTATES
MUTATIS
MUTTERS
MUTTONS
MUTUALS
MUUMUUS
MUZHIKS
MUZZIER
MUZZILY
MUZZLED
MUZZLES

M•U••••
MAUDLIN
MAUGHAM
MAULDIN
MAULING
MAUNDER
MAUREEN
MAURICE
MAUROIS
MOUFLON
MOULAGE
MOULDED
MOULDER
MOULTED
MOUNDED
MOUNTED
MOUNTIE
MOUSERS
MOUSIER
MOUSING
MOUSSED
MOUSSES
MOUTHED
MOUTONS
MUUMUUS

M••U•••
MACULAE
MAGUEYS
MANUALS
MANUMIT
MATURED
MATURER
MATURES
MAZURKA
MCGUIRE
MCLUHAN
MCQUEEN
MEDULLA
MEDUSAE
MEDUSAS
MENUHIN
MINUEND
MINUETS
MINUSES
MINUTES
MINUTIA
MISUSED
MISUSES
MODULAR
MODULES
MUTUALS

M•••U••
MACDUFF

MAGNUMS
MAHOUTS
MAJEURE
MAKEUPS
MANHUNT
MARAUDS
MARKUPS
MARQUEE
MARQUES
MARQUEZ
MARQUIS
MASQUES
MEASURE
MEDIUMS
MERCURY
MISCUED
MISCUES
MISRULE
MIXTURE
MOCKUPS
MOLLUSK
MOSQUES
MUGWUMP
MUKLUKS
MURMURS
MUSEUMS
MUUMUUS

M••••U•
MACAQUE
MADEOUT
MAKEOUT
MAKESUP
MALAMUD
MALRAUX
MALTHUS
MANAGUA
MANHOUR
MARGAUX
MARKSUP
MASSEUR
MATCHUP
MAXIMUM
MAXIMUS
METEOUT
MILHAUD
MILIEUS
MILIEUX
MILKRUN
MILLRUN
MIMIEUX
MINDFUL
MINIBUS
MINIMUM
MISSOUT
MITCHUM
MIXEDUP
MIXESUP
MIXITUP
MODICUM
MONIQUE
MONTEUX
MOVEOUT
MUCKSUP
MUUMUUS

M•••••U
MANITOU
MARABOU
MARCEAU
MARYLOU
MATTHAU

•MU••••
AMULETS
AMUSING
EMULATE
SMUDGED
SMUDGES
SMUGGER
SMUGGLE

•M•U•••
AMOUNTS
AMPULES
IMBUING
IMMURED
IMMURES
IMPUGNS
IMPULSE
IMPURER
IMPUTED
IMPUTES

•M••U••
AMPOULE
EMANUEL
IMBRUED
IMBRUES
IMPOUND
UMLAUTS

•M•••U•
AMADEUS
AMATEUR
AMIBLUE
AMOROUS
IMPETUS
IMPIOUS
OMENTUM
OMINOUS
OMNIBUS
SMASHUP

•M••••U
EMMYLOU

••MU•••
BEMUSED
BEMUSES
CUMULUS
DEMURER
FAMULUS
HHMUNRO
IMMURED
IMMURES
REMUDAS
ROMULAN
ROMULUS
SAMURAI
TUMULTS
TUMULUS
ZYMURGY

••M•U••
ARMFULS
ARMOURS
COMBUST
COMMUNE
COMMUTE
COMPUTE
DIMBULB
DIMOUTS
DUMDUMS
HAMBURG
HOMBURG

HUMBUGS
HUMOURS
KUMQUAT
REMOUNT
RUMOURS
SAMNUNN
SAMSUNG
TEMPURA

••M••U•
BUMPSUP
BUMSOUT
CAMBIUM
CAMEOUT
CAMPOUT
COMEDUE
COMEOUT
COMESUP
COMIQUE
CUMULUS
DUMMYUP
FAMULUS
HAMITUP
HOMERUN
HUMDRUM
HUMERUS
JIMRYUN
JUMPCUT
JUMPSUP
LUMPSUM
MIMIEUX
ORMOLUS
POMPOUS
PUMPSUP
RIMBAUD
ROMULUS
TAMBOUR
TIMEOUT
TIMESUP
TUMULUS

••M•••U
EMMYLOU
KOMATSU
LAMBEAU
RAMBEAU

•••MU••
AZIMUTH
BERMUDA
BISMUTH
COMMUNE
COMMUTE
EARMUFF
FORMULA
MURMURS
MUUMUUS
SIGMUND
STIMULI
WARMUPS

•••M•U•
ALUMNUS
BEAMSUP
BRIMFUL
CADMIUM
CLAMSUP
DRUMSUP
DUMMYUP
ENAMOUR
FARMOUT
FERMIUM
FIRMSUP

FRAMEUP
GLAMOUR
GRAMPUS
HARMFUL
HOLMIUM
MUUMUUS
OLYMPUS
PREMIUM
RHOMBUS
ROOMFUL
SEYMOUR
TEAMSUP
TRUMPUP
WARMSUP

••••MU•
ARTEMUS
DREAMUP
ERASMUS
ISTHMUS
MALAMUD
MAXIMUM
MAXIMUS
MINIMUM
OPTIMUM
PYRAMUS

M•V••••
MOVABLE
MOVEDIN
MOVEOUT
MOVESIN

M••V•••
MARVELS

M•••V••
MCGAVIN
MEDEVAC
MINIVAN
MINIVER
MITZVAH
MORAVIA
MOTIVES

M••••V•
MARKOVA
MASSIVE
MINERVA
MISSIVE
MUSCOVY

M•••••V
MOLOTOV

•M•V•••
BMOVIES

•M•••V•
AMATIVE
EMOTIVE
IMPROVE

••M•V••
REMOVAL
REMOVED
REMOVER
REMOVES
SAMOVAR
UNMOVED

••M••V•
COMMOVE

••M•••V
NEMEROV
ROMANOV

•••M•V•
COMMOVE

M•W••••
MAWKISH
MEWLERS
MEWLING
MOWDOWN

M••W•••
MAEWEST
MAXWELL
MAYWINE
MCSWINE
MEOWING
MIDWAYS
MIDWEEK
MIDWEST
MIDWIFE
MISWORD
MUGWUMP

M•••W••
MADEWAY
MAKEWAY
MANOWAR
MATEWAN
MOHAWKS

M••••W•
MALLOWS
MARLOWE
MARROWS
MATHEWS
MEADOWS
MEADOWY
MELLOWS
MIDTOWN
MILDEWS
MILDEWY
MINNOWS
MORROWS
MOWDOWN

M•••••W
MACGRAW
MANILOW
MATTHEW
MILKCOW

•M••W••
EMPOWER

••MW•••
DIMWITS

••M•W••
REMOWED
SOMEWAY
TIMEWAS

••M•••W
GAMELAW
SOMEHOW

•••M•W•
HAYMOWS
NEWMOWN

M•X••••
MAXBAER
MAXBORN
MAXILLA
MAXIMAL
MAXIMUM
MAXIMUS
MAXWELL
MEXICAN
MIXABLE
MIXEDUP
MIXESUP
MIXITUP
MIXTURE

M••X•••
MANXCAT
MANXMAN
MANXMEN
MARXISM

M•••X••
MRFIXIT

M•••••X
MADAMEX
MAILBOX
MALRAUX
MARGAUX
MEMOREX
MILIEUX
MIMIEUX
MIRAMAX
MONTEUX

•M••X••
IMMIXED
IMMIXES

••M•X••
ADMIXED
ADMIXES
IMMIXED
IMMIXES
REMIXED
REMIXES

••M•••X
COMPLEX
MEMOREX
MIMIEUX
SIMPLEX

•••M••X
BOOMBOX
FLUMMOX

••••M•X
BETAMAX
CAKEMIX
CINEMAX
FLUMMOX
MADAMEX
MIRAMAX

MY•••••
MYANMAR
MYMAMMY
MYNHEER
MYRIADS
MYRTLES
MYSTERY
MYSTICS

MYSTIFY

M•Y••••
MAYALIN
MAYDAYS
MAYFAIR
MAYHEMS
MAYNARD
MAYORAL
MAYPOLE
MAYTIME
MAYWINE

M••Y•••
MAGYARS
MANYEAR
MARYANN
MARYKAY
MARYLOU
MIDYEAR

M•••Y••
MALAYAN
MARRYME
MARTYRS
MEGRYAN
MISTYPE
MONEYED
MOSEYED

M••••Y•
MAGUEYS
MANDAYS
MARGAYS
MARILYN
MAYDAYS
MEDLEYS
MIDDAYS
MIDWAYS
MISLAYS
MONDAYS
MONKEYS
MONTOYA

M•••••Y
MADEHAY
MADEWAY
MAGNIFY
MAHONEY
MAJESTY
MAKEHAY
MAKEWAY
MALMSEY
MARYKAY
MASONRY
MASTERY
MEADOWY
MERCURY
MERRILY
MESSILY
MILDEWY
MIMICRY
MISALLY
MISERLY
MISPLAY
MISTILY
MOCKERY
MODESTY
MOISTLY
MOLLIFY
MONTHLY
MOODILY
MORALLY

MORESBY
MORTIFY
MUMMERY
MURKILY
MURPHEY
MUSCOVY
MUSHILY
MUSTILY
MUTABLY
MUZZILY
MYMAMMY
MYSTERY
MYSTIFY

•MY••••
AMYLASE

•M•Y•••
EMMYLOU

•M••Y••
EMBRYOS

•M•••Y•
EMPLOYS

•M••••Y
AMATORY
AMENITY
AMIABLY
AMNESTY
AMPLIFY
AMSCRAY
EMBASSY
EMPATHY
EMPTILY
IMAGERY
IMPIETY
IMSORRY
SMARTLY

••MY•••
ARMYANT
EMMYLOU

••M•Y••
DUMMYUP
JIMRYUN
SAMOYED

••M••Y•
HOMONYM
ROMNEYS
TOMBOYS

••M•••Y
COMESBY
COMFREY
COMPANY
DEMPSEY
HAMMILY
HEMSLEY
HUMANLY
HUMIDLY
LAMPREY
MIMICRY
MUMMERY
MYMAMMY
NAMEDAY
ORMANDY
REMARRY
SAMEDAY
SOMEDAY

SOMEWAY
SUMMARY
SUMMERY
TAMMANY
TIMIDLY
TIMOTHY
WOMANLY
ZYMURGY

•••MY••
DUMMYUP
GROMYKO

•••M•Y•
DISMAYS

•••M••Y
ALIMONY
ANOMALY
BRAMBLY
CHIMNEY
CHOMSKY
CRUMBLY
CRUMPLY
GERMANY
HAMMILY
HARMONY
MALMSEY
MUMMERY
PRIMACY
PRIMARY
SUMMARY
SUMMERY
TAMMANY
TREMBLY

••••M•Y
CALUMNY
DAHOMEY
MYMAMMY
SCRIMPY

•••••MY
ACADEMY
ALCHEMY
ANATOMY
BELLAMY
ECONOMY
MYMAMMY
PTOLEMY
SQUIRMY

M•Z••••
MAZURKA
MIZZENS
MIZZLED
MIZZLES
MUZHIKS
MUZZIER
MUZZILY
MUZZLED
MUZZLES

M••Z•••
MATZOHS
MITZVAH
MIZZENS
MIZZLED
MIZZLES
MUEZZIN
MUZZIER
MUZZILY
MUZZLED

MUZZLES

M•••Z••
MUEZZIN

M••••Z•
MENDOZA
MESTIZO
MIDSIZE

M•••••Z
MARQUEZ

•M•Z•••
AMAZING
AMAZONS

••M••Z•
ZAMBEZI

••M•••Z
JIMENEZ

•••M•Z•
ATOMIZE
ITEMIZE

NA•••••
NABBERS
NABBING
NABISCO
NABOKOV
NACELLE
NAGGING
NAHUATL
NAIADES
NAILERS
NAILING
NAILSET
NAIROBI
NAIVELY
NAIVETE
NAKEDLY
NAMEDAY
NAMETAG
NAMIBIA
NANETTE
NANKEEN
NANNIES
NAPHTHA
NAPKINS
NAPPERS
NAPPING
NAPTIME
NARRATE
NARROWS
NARTHEX
NARWALS
NARWHAL
NASALLY
NASCENT
NASTASE
NASTIER
NASTILY
NATALIA
NATALIE
NATASHA
NATCHEZ
NATIONS
NATIVES
NATRIUM
NATTERS
NATTIER

NATTILY
NATURAL
NATURED
NATURES
NAUGHTS
NAUGHTY
NAVAHOS
NAVAJOS
NAVARRE
NAYSAID
NAYSAYS

N•A••••
NEAREST
NEARING
NEARYOU
NEATENS
NEATEST
NIAGARA
NUANCED
NUANCES

N••A•••
NAIADES
NASALLY
NATALIA
NATALIE
NATASHA
NAVAHOS
NAVAJOS
NAVARRE
NEGATED
NEGATES
NEGATOR
NEPALIS
NEVADAN
NEWAGER
NOCANDO
NOFAULT
NOGALES
NOMADIC
NONAGON
NOTABIT
NOTABLE
NOTABLY
NOTATED
NOTATES
NOVARRO

N•••A••
NAHUATL
NARRATE
NARWALS
NASTASE
NAYSAID
NAYSAYS
NECTARS
NEONATE
NESCAFE
NEWGATE
NEWHART
NEWMATH
NEWWAVE
NIAGARA
NIGGARD
NIRVANA
NITRATE
NITTANY
NORMALS
NORMAND
NORMANS
NOUGATS
NUBIANS

NUMBATS

N••••A•

NAMEDAY
NAMETAG
NARWHAL
NATURAL
NEBULAE
NEBULAR
NEBULAS
NEUTRAL
NEVADAN
NEWDEAL
NEWSDAY
NEWSMAN
NEWYEAR
NICOLAS
NIKOLAI
NODULAR
NOMINAL
NOONDAY
NOSEBAG
NOSEGAY
NOSWEAT
NOTEPAD
NOUVEAU
NOVENAS
NUCLEAR
NUMERAL
NUPTIAL
NUTMEAT
NUTRIAS

N•••••A

NAMIBIA
NAPHTHA
NATALIA
NATASHA
NIAGARA
NICOSIA
NIGERIA
NIRVANA
NORIEGA
NOVELLA
NOXZEMA

•NA••••

ANADEMS
ANAEMIA
ANAGRAM
ANAHEIM
ANAHUAC
ANALOGS
ANALOGY
ANALYSE
ANALYST
ANALYZE
ANANIAS
ANAPEST
ANARCHY
ANASAZI
ANATOLE
ANATOMY
ENABLED
ENABLES
ENACTED
ENACTOR
ENAMELS
ENAMORS
ENAMOUR
GNARLED
GNARRED
GNASHED
GNASHES
GNAWERS
GNAWING
INADAZE
INAHEAP
INAMESS
INANELY
INANEST
INAPTLY
INARUSH
INASNIT
INASPIN
INASPOT
INASTEW
INAWEOF
INAWORD
KNAVERY
KNAVISH
ONADARE
ONADATE
ONADIET
ONAGERS
ONANDON
ONAROLL
ONASSIS
ONATEAR
SNACKED
SNACKER
SNAFFLE
SNAFUED
SNAGGED
SNAKIER
SNAKING
SNAPONS
SNAPPED
SNAPPER
SNAPSAT
SNAPSTO
SNAPSUP
SNARING
SNARLED
UNAIDED
UNAIMED
UNAIRED
UNALIKE
UNARMED
UNASKED
UNAVOCE
UNAWARE

•N•A•••

ANDANTE
ANNABEL
ANNALEE
ANNATTO
ANTACID
ANTAEUS
ANTARES
ENCAGED
ENCAGES
ENCAMPS
ENCASED
ENCASES
ENGAGED
ENGAGES
ENGARDE
ENHANCE
ENLACED
ENLACES
ENLARGE
ENMASSE
ENRAGED
ENRAGES
ENTAILS
INCANTS
INFANCY
INFANTA
INFANTS
INFAVOR
INGALLS
INHABIT
INHALED
INHALER
INHALES
INHASTE
INMATES
INNARDS
INTAKES
INVACUO
INVADED
INVADER
INVADES
INVALID
INWARDS
KNEADED
KNEADER
ONPAPER
ONTARIO
ONWARDS
SNEAKED
SNEAKER
SNEAKIN
UNBAKED
UNCAGED
UNCAGES
UNCANNY
UNCASED
UNCASES
UNDATED
UNEARTH
UNFAZED
UNHANDS
UNHANDY
UNHAPPY
UNLACED
UNLACES
UNLADES
UNLATCH
UNMAKES
UNMASKS
UNNAMED
UNPACKS
UNPAVED
UNRATED
UNRAVEL
UNSATED
UNTACKS
UNTAMED
UNTAPED

•N••A••

ANASAZI
ANDEANS
ANIMALS
ANIMATE
ANIMATO
ANNEALS
ANNUALS
ANOMALY
ANORAKS
ANSPACH
ANTFARM
ANTIART
ENCHAIN
ENCHANT
ENCLAVE
ENDEARS
ENDGAME
ENDWAYS
ENGLAND
ENGRAFT
ENGRAMS
ENGRAVE
ENNEADS
ENPLANE
ENSLAVE
ENSNARE
ENSNARL
ENTRAIN
ENTRANT
ENTRAPS
ENWRAPS
INADAZE
INBOARD
INDIANA
INDIANS
INEXACT
INFLAME
INFLATE
INGRAIN
INGRATE
INPEACE
INPHASE
INPLACE
INROADS
INSCAPE
INSEAMS
INSHAPE
INSPANS
INSTALL
INSTANT
INSTATE
ONADARE
ONADATE
ONBOARD
ONGUARD
ONLEAVE
ONSTAGE
SNOCATS
UNAWARE
UNCHAIN
UNCIALS
UNCLASP
UNCRATE
UNDRAPE
UNDRAWN
UNHEARD
UNITARY
UNLEARN
UNLEASH
UNLOADS
UNREADY
UNSEALS
UNSEATS
UNSNAGS
UNSNAPS
UNSNARL
UNSTACK
UNTRAPS
UNWEAVE
UNWRAPS

•N•••A•

ANAGRAM
ANAHUAC
ANANIAS
ANDREAS
ANGOLAN
ANGORAS
ANGULAR
ANNULAR
ANTBEAR
ANTIWAR
ENDPLAY
ENIGMAS
ENTREAT
INAHEAP
INGEMAR
INHUMAN
INITIAL
INKYCAP
INNOWAY
INSOFAR
INSTEAD
INSULAR
KNEECAP
KNEEPAD
ONATEAR
ONEIDAS
ONTRIAL
SNAPSAT
SNEERAT
SNIFFAT
SNIPEAT
SNOWCAP
SNOWDAY
SNOWMAN
UNCLEAN
UNCLEAR
UNCLOAK
UNEQUAL
UNSTRAP
UNUSUAL

•N••••A

ANAEMIA
ANDORRA
ANOSMIA
ANTENNA
ANTIGUA
ANTONIA
ENCOMIA
INDIANA
INDICIA
INERTIA
INFANTA
INOCULA
INTEGRA
SNOWPEA

••NA•••

ABNAKIS
AGNATES
ANNABEL
ANNALEE
ANNATTO
BANALLY
BANANAS
BENATAR
BENAZIR
BONANZA
CANAPES
CANARDS
CANASTA
CONAKRY
DONAHUE
DONATED
DONATES
DONATOR
DUNAWAY
DYNAMIC
DYNAMOS
DYNASTS
DYNASTY
FANATIC
FINAGLE
FINALES
FINALLY
FINANCE
INNARDS
JANACEK
KANAKAS
LINAGES
LUNATIC
MANACLE
MANAGED
MANAGER
MANAGES
MANAGUA
MANANAS
MANATEE
MENACED
MENACES
MENAGES
MINABLE
MINARET
MONARCH
NONAGON
PANACEA
PANACHE
PANAMAS
PENALTY
PENANCE
PENATES
PINATAS
RANAWAY
RENAILS
RENAMED
RENAMES
RENAULT
RUNAMOK
RUNAWAY
SENATES
SENATOR
SINATRA
SONATAS
SYNAPSE
TANAGER
TENABLE
TENABLY
TENACES
TENANCY
TENANTS
TONALLY
UNNAMED
ZENANAS
ZONALLY

••N•A••

ANNEALS
ANNUALS
AYNRAND
BANDAGE
BANDAID
BANDANA
BANTAMS
BANYANS
BENEATH
BENGALI
BENGALS
BONDAGE
BONEASH
CANCANS
CANTATA
CANVASS
CENTAUR
CENTAVO
CINZANO
CONCAVE
CONFABS
CONGAED
CONGAME
CONRACK
CONTACT
CONTAIN
DENIALS
DENMARK
DENTATE
ENNEADS
FANFARE
FANMAIL
FANTAIL
FANTASY
FINEART
FINIALS
FINLAND
FONDANT
FUNFAIR
GENNARO
GUNWALE
HANGARS
HANSARP
HENBANE
HENNAED
HUNGARY
IBNSAUD
JANUARY
JUNKART
KANSANS
KENDALL
KENYANS
LANDAUS
LANTANA
LANYARD
LENFANT
LINEAGE
LINEATE
LINKAGE
LONGAGO
MANDALA
MANDANS
MANDATE
MANDAYS
MANIACS
MANMADE
MANSARD
MANUALS
MENIALS
MINOANS
MONDALE
MONDAYS
MONTAGE
MONTANA
MONTAND
MONTANE
MUNDANE
PANCAKE
PENDANT
PENNAME
PENNANT
PENNATE
PENPALS
PENTADS
PINBALL
PINNACE
PINNATE
PINOAKS
PINTAIL
PINWALE
PONIARD
PUNJABI
PUNKAHS
QINTARS
RANDALL
RANLATE
RANSACK
RENTALS
RUNBACK
RUNLAPS
RUNWAYS
SANDALS
SANTAFE
SANTANA
SENSATE
SINKAGE
SUNBATH
SUNDAES
SUNDAYS
SUNLAMP
SUNMAID
SUNRAYS
SUNTANS
TANKARD
TANOAKS
TANTARA
TINCANS
TINEARS
TINHATS
TONEARM
TONGANS
TONNAGE
VANDALS
VANTAGE
VANZANT
VINTAGE
WANNABE
WANTADS
WENTAPE

••N••A•

ANNULAR
ARNICAS
BANANAS
BANDSAW
BENATAR
BENTHAM
BINGHAM
BONDMAN
CENTRAL
CINEMAS
CINEMAX
CONCEAL
CONGEAL
CONICAL
CONTRAS
CYNICAL
DANELAW
DINGBAT
DONEGAL
DONJUAN
DONOVAN
DUNAWAY
GANGSAW
GANGWAY
GENERAL
GENTIAN
GINGHAM
GUNBOAT
GUNPLAY
HANDBAG
HANDCAR
HANDSAW
HANGMAN
HANUKAH
HINTSAT
INNOWAY
JANEWAY
JUNKMAN
KANAKAS
KINGMAN
KINGRAT
KINSMAN
LANDSAT
LINBIAO
LINDSAY
LINEMAN
LINGUAL
LUNGEAT
MANANAS
MANOWAR
MANTRAP
MANTRAS
MANXCAT
MANXMAN
MANYEAR
MENORAH
MINERAL
MINICAM
MINIMAL
MINIVAN
PANAMAS
PANCHAX
PINATAS
PINCHAS
PINESAP
PINETAR
PINHEAD
PONTIAC
RANAWAY
RENEWAL
RONDEAU
RUNAWAY
SANDBAG
SANDBAR
SANDMAN
SANJUAN
SENECAS
SENEGAL
SENORAS
SENSUAL
SONATAS
SUNBEAM
SUNDIAL
SYNGMAN
SYNODAL
TINSTAR
TONNEAU
TUNDRAS
VENTRAL
VINEGAR
WENTBAD
WINDBAG
WINEBAR
WINESAP
WINKSAT
XANTHAN
ZENANAS
ZINNIAS

••N•••A

AMNESIA
BANDANA
BONANZA
CANASTA
CANDELA
CANDIDA
CANTATA
CANTINA
CYNTHIA
FONTINA
GANGLIA
GANGSTA
GINGIVA
GONDOLA
KENOSHA
LANTANA
MANAGUA
MANDALA
MANDELA
MENDOZA
MINEOLA
MINERVA
MINOLTA
MINORCA
MINUTIA
MONTANA
MONTOYA
PANACEA
PANDORA
PANETTA
SANGRIA
SANTANA
SINATRA
TANTARA
TUNISIA
VANESSA
VANILLA
VENTURA
WYNONNA
ZENOBIA

•••NA••

ABENAKI
ADONAIS
BARNARD
BERNARD
BIGNAME
CATNAPS
COGNACS
COGNATE
COINAGE
EMANATE
ENSNARE
ENSNARL
FURNACE
GENNARO
GRANADA
GRANARY
GRENADA
GRENADE
GUANACO
GYMNAST
HENNAED
HOBNAIL
HYMNALS
IRONAGE
JEANARP
KIDNAPS
LEONARD
MAENADS
MAGNATE
MAYNARD
MISNAME
NEONATE
OCANADA
OKINAWA
OPENAIR
PENNAME
PENNANT
PENNATE
PEONAGE
PETNAME
PINNACE
PINNATE
PLENARY
REENACT
REGNANT
REMNANT
REYNARD
SCHNAPS
SHANANA
SIGNALS
SPINACH
SURNAME
TEENAGE
TERNARY
TERNATE
THINAIR
TOENAIL
TONNAGE
TORNADO
TRENARY
TSUNAMI
UNSNAGS
UNSNAPS
UNSNARL
WANNABE

•••N•A•

AGENDAS
ANANIAS
BEANBAG
BLINKAT
BRENDAN
BRENNAN
COONCAT
CORNEAL
CORNEAS
CRANIAL
DOWNPAT
DUENNAS
ETONIAN
FEYNMAN
FRENEAU
FRONTAL
GAINSAY
GOINGAT
GRANDAM
GUINEAS
HYUNDAI
IRANIAN
IRONMAN
JOHNGAY
JOHNJAY
KWANZAS
MYANMAR
NOONDAY
OPENBAR
OXONIAN
PHINEAS
PLANTAR
QUINOAS
RAINHAT
RAINMAN
RUANDAN
RWANDAN
SCANDAL
SHANKAR
SIENNAS
STANZAS
THINMAN
TONNEAU
TSONGAS
UGANDAN
WOZNIAK
ZINNIAS

•••N••A

AVONLEA
CARNERA
GRANADA
GRANDMA
GRANDPA
GRANOLA
GRENADA
IPANEMA
LEONORA
OCANADA
OKINAWA
OPENSEA
SHANANA
SPINOZA
ULANOVA

••••NA•

ADRENAL
ALMANAC
ALUMNAE
ALUMNAL
AQUINAS
ARSENAL
BANANAS
BRENNAN
BROSNAN
CABANAS
CARINAS
CATENAE
CORONAE
CORONAS
DIURNAL
DUENNAS
EATENAT
ETERNAL
FROWNAT
IGUANAS
JACANAS
JOURNAL
JUVENAL
KAHUNAS
KORUNAS
KUTENAI
LACUNAE
LACUNAL
LACUNAS
LAGUNAS
LAMINAE
LAMINAL
LAMINAR
LAMINAS
LATINAS
MANANAS
MARINAS
NOMINAL
NOVENAS
ORDINAL
PATINAS
RETINAE
RETINAL
RETINAS
SAGINAW
SARANAC
SEMINAL
SEMINAR
SIENNAS
STERNAL
SURINAM
VICUNAS
VIETNAM
ZENANAS

••••N•A

ADDENDA
ALBANIA
AMMONIA
ANTENNA
ANTONIA
ARMENIA
ATLANTA
AVIANCA
BEGONIA
BELINDA
BONANZA
BOTHNIA
CADENZA
COLONNA
ESTONIA
HOSANNA
INFANTA
JOHANNA
LAVINIA
MADONNA
MAGENTA
MELINDA
MIRANDA
OCEANIA
ORGANZA
PETUNIA
PIRANHA
POLENTA
RAVENNA
ROMANIA
ROSANNA
ROTUNDA
SAVANNA
SUSANNA
SYRINGA
TITANIA
VEDANTA
VERANDA
WYNONNA

•••••NA

ALTOONA
ANTENNA
ARIZONA
BANDANA
BOLOGNA
BURKINA
CANTINA
CHICANA
COLONNA
CREMONA
CZARINA
DAYTONA
DUODENA
ECHIDNA
FONTINA
FORTUNA
HOSANNA
IKEBANA
INDIANA
JOHANNA
JULIANA
KACHINA
KRISHNA
LANTANA

LASAGNA
MACHINA
MADONNA
MADRONA
MARIANA
MARTINA
MESSINA
MONTANA
MORGANA
NIRVANA
OCARINA
PASTINA
PAULINA
PERSONA
PORSENA
RAVENNA
RETSINA
ROSANNA
SABRINA
SANTANA
SAVANNA
SESTINA
SHANANA
SMETANA
STAMINA
SULTANA
SUSANNA
TARZANA
TATIANA
TIJUANA
TSARINA
TYMPANA
TZARINA
VERBENA
WYNONNA

N•B••••
NABBERS
NABBING
NABISCO
NABOKOV
NEBBISH
NEBULAE
NEBULAR
NEBULAS
NIBBLED
NIBBLER
NIBBLES
NIBLICK
NOBHILL
NOBLEST
NUBBIER
NUBBINS
NUBBLES
NUBIANS

N••B•••
NABBERS
NABBING
NEBBISH
NEWBORN
NIBBLED
NIBBLER
NIBBLES
NIEBUHR
NIMBLER
NIOBIUM
NUBBIER
NUBBINS
NUBBLES
NUMBATS
NUMBERS
NUMBEST
NUMBING

N•••B••
NAMIBIA
NEWSBOY
NOSEBAG
NOTABIT
NOTABLE
NOTABLY

N••••B•
NAIROBI
NODOUBT

N•••••B
NOSEJOB

•NB••••
INBLOOM
INBOARD
INBOUND
INBREED
INBRIEF
ONBOARD
UNBAKED
UNBENDS
UNBINDS
UNBLEST
UNBOLTS
UNBOUND
UNBOWED
UNBOXED
UNBOXES

•N•B•••
ANTBEAR
ANYBODY
ENABLED
ENABLES
INKBLOT
KNOBBED
SNUBBED

•N••B••
ANNABEL
ANTIBES
ENNOBLE
ENROBED
ENROBES
ENTEBBE
FNUMBER
INHABIT
INHIBIT
INORBIT
KNOBBED
SNUBBED
UNROBED
UNROBES

•N•••B•
ENTEBBE
INDOUBT

•N••••B
SNOWJOB

••NB•••
BONBONS
CONBRIO
FANBELT
GUNBOAT
HENBANE
HENBITS
LINBIAO
PINBALL
RUNBACK
SANBORN
SUNBATH
SUNBEAM
SUNBELT
SUNBURN

••N•B••
ANNABEL
BANDBOX
BUNKBED
DINGBAT
ENNOBLE
HANDBAG
IGNOBLE
IGNOBLY
JUNEBUG
LONGBOW
MINABLE
MINIBUS
OMNIBUS
SANDBAG
SANDBAR
SANDBOX
SANIBEL
TENABLE
TENABLY
WENTBAD
WINDBAG
WINEBAR
ZENOBIA

••N••B•
BENUMBS
CONFABS
CONJOBS
PUNJABI
WANNABE

•••NB••
BEANBAG
DOWNBOW
OPENBAR
RAINBOW
TOYNBEE
TWINBED

•••N•B•
BYANDBY
GOINGBY
HOBNOBS
HORNSBY
STANDBY
SWINGBY
WANNABE

•••N••B
CORNCOB
LIONCUB

••••NB•
LAZENBY

NC•••••
NCWYETH

N•C••••
NACELLE
NECKERS
NECKING
NECKTIE
NECTARS
NICCOLO
NICHOLS
NICKELS
NICKERS
NICKING
NICOLAS
NICOSIA
NOCANDO
NOCTURN
NOCUOUS
NUCLEAR
NUCLEIC
NUCLEON
NUCLEUS
NUCLIDE

N••C•••
NASCENT
NATCHEZ
NESCAFE
NICCOLO
NONCOMS
NOTCHED
NOTCHES
NUNCIOS

N•••C••
NOGUCHI
NOTICED
NOTICES
NOVICES
NUANCED
NUANCES

N••••C•
NABISCO
NEGLECT
NIBLICK
NITPICK
NOETICS
NORDICS

N•••••C
NOMADIC
NUCLEIC
NUMERIC

•NC••••
ANCHORS
ANCHOVY
ANCIENT
ENCAGED
ENCAGES
ENCAMPS
ENCASED
ENCASES
ENCHAIN
ENCHANT
ENCLAVE
ENCLOSE
ENCODED
ENCODER
ENCODES
ENCOMIA
ENCORES
ENCRUST
ENCRYPT
INCANTS
INCENSE
INCEPTS
INCHING
INCIPIT
INCISED
INCISES
INCISOR
INCITED
INCITER
INCITES
INCIVIL
INCLINE
INCLOSE
INCLUDE
INCOMES
INCUDES
UNCAGED
UNCAGES
UNCANNY
UNCASED
UNCASES
UNCHAIN
UNCIALS
UNCIVIL
UNCLASP
UNCLEAN
UNCLEAR
UNCLOAK
UNCLOGS
UNCLOSE
UNCOILS
UNCORKS
UNCOUTH
UNCOVER
UNCRATE
UNCTION
UNCURLS

•N•C•••
ANTCOWS
ENACTED
ENACTOR
GNOCCHI
INOCULA
INSCAPE
KNOCKED
KNOCKER
KNUCKLE
SNACKED
SNACKER
SNICKER
SNOCATS
SNOCONE
UNICORN
UNSCREW

•N••C••
ANARCHY
ANTACID
ENLACED
ENLACES
ENTICED
ENTICER
ENTICES
GNOCCHI
INDICES
INDICIA
INDICTS
INDUCED
INDUCER
INDUCES
INDUCTS
INFECTS
INFOCUS
INJECTS
INKYCAP
INSECTS
INVACUO
KNEECAP
SNOWCAP
UNLACED
UNLACES
UNLOCKS
UNLUCKY
UNPACKS
UNTACKS

•N•••C•
ANSPACH
ANTIOCH
ENFORCE
ENHANCE
ENOUNCE
INDUTCH
INEXACT
INFANCY
INFLECT
INFLICT
INFORCE
INPEACE
INPLACE
INSPECT
INSTOCK
INVOICE
UNAVOCE
UNFROCK
UNHITCH
UNLATCH
UNSTACK
UNSTICK
UNSTUCK

•N••••C
ANAHUAC
ANGELIC
ANOSMIC
ENDEMIC
GNOSTIC

••NC•••
BENCHED
BENCHES
BUNCHED
BUNCHES
BUNCOED
CANCANS
CANCELS
CINCHED
CINCHES
CONCAVE
CONCEAL
CONCEDE
CONCEIT
CONCEPT
CONCERN
CONCERT
CONCHES
CONCISE
CONCOCT
CONCORD
CONCURS
DANCERS
DANCING
FANCIED
FANCIER
FANCIES
FANCILY
FENCERS
FENCING
FINCHES
HANCOCK
HENCOOP
HONCHOS
HUNCHED
HUNCHES
JUNCOES
LANCERS
LANCETS
LINCOLN
LUNCHED
LUNCHER
LUNCHES
MANCINI
MENCKEN
MINCERS
MINCING
MUNCHED
MUNCHER
MUNCHES
NONCOMS
NUNCIOS
PANCAKE
PANCHAX
PENCILS
PINCERS
PINCHAS
PINCHED
PINCHER
PINCHES
PINCURL
PONCHOS
PUNCHED
PUNCHER
PUNCHES
PUNCHIN
PUNCHUP
PYNCHON
RANCHED
RANCHER
RANCHES
RANCHOS
RANCOUR
SANCTUM
SINCERE
SUNCITY
SYNCHED
SYNCHES
SYNCING
TINCANS
VINCENT
WENCHES
WINCERS
WINCHED
WINCHES
WINCING

••N•C••
ARNICAS
CONICAL
CYNICAL
EUNUCHS
FINICKY
HANDCAR
JANACEK
MANACLE
MANXCAT
MENACED
MENACES
MINICAM
MONOCLE
MONOCOT
PANACEA
PANACHE
PANICKY
PANICLE
PENUCHE
PINOCLE
SENECAS
TENACES
TUNICLE
VANOCUR

••N••C•
BANNOCK
CANDICE
CANSECO
CONCOCT
CONDUCE
CONDUCT
CONNECT
CONNICK
CONRACK
CONTACT
CONVICT
DENIECE
FINANCE
GUNLOCK
HANCOCK
HENPECK
IONESCO
MANIACS
MENISCI
MINORCA
MONARCH
PANDECT
PENANCE
PINNACE
RANSACK
RUNBACK
SUNDECK
TENANCY
VANDYCK
VANEYCK

••N•••C
CANONIC
CENTRIC
DYNAMIC
FANATIC
GENERIC
GENETIC
KINETIC
LUNATIC
MANTRIC
PONTIAC
SYNODIC
TONELOC
XANTHIC

•••NC••
ALENCON
BLANCHE
BOUNCED
BOUNCER
BOUNCES
BRONCHI
BRONCOS
CHANCED
CHANCEL
CHANCES
COONCAT
CORNCOB
COUNCIL
CRUNCHY
EVINCED
EVINCES
FIANCEE
FIANCES
FRANCES
FRANCIS
GLANCED
GLANCES
JOUNCED
JOUNCES
LIONCUB
NUANCED
NUANCES
PAUNCHY
POUNCED
POUNCER
POUNCES
PRANCED
PRANCER
PRANCES
PRINCES
QUINCES
SCONCES
SEANCES
SPENCER
STANCES
STENCIL
TRANCES

•••N•C•
BANNOCK
BERNICE
BIONICS
CLINICS
COGNACS
CONNECT
CONNICK
CORNICE
ETHNICS
FURNACE
GUANACO
LOWNECK
OLDNICK
ORINOCO
PHONICS
PICNICS
PINNACE
REENACT
SPINACH
THINICE
VEENECK

•••N••C
FRANTIC
IDENTIC
JEANLUC
LAENNEC
STANNIC
YOUNGMC

••••NC•
ABSENCE
ADJUNCT
ADVANCE
ARDENCY
ASKANCE
AVIANCA
BALANCE
CADENCE
COGENCY
DAVINCI
DEFENCE
DEFUNCT
DURANCE
ENHANCE
ENOUNCE
ESSENCE
EXTINCT
FAIENCE
FINANCE
FLOUNCE
FLUENCY
INFANCY
LATENCY
LICENCE
OFFENCE
PALANCE
PENANCE
PLIANCY
POTENCY
RECENCY
REGENCY
ROMANCE
SCIENCE
SCRUNCH
SILENCE
SQUINCH
STAUNCH
TENANCY
TERENCE
TROUNCE
TRUANCY
URGENCY
VACANCY
VALANCE
VALENCE

••••N•C
ACTINIC
ALMANAC
ARSENIC
CANONIC
CHRONIC
DEMONIC
LACONIC
LAENNEC
MASONIC
OCEANIC
ORGANIC
PHRENIC
SARANAC
SELENIC
STANNIC
TITANIC

•••••NC
LIPSYNC
POULENC

N•D••••
NODDERS
NODDING
NODOUBT
NODSOFF
NODULAR
NODULES
NUDGERS
NUDGING
NUDISTS
NUDNIKS

N••D•••
NEEDFUL
NEEDIER
NEEDILY
NEEDING
NEEDLED
NEEDLES
NEWDEAL
NODDERS
NODDING
NOODLES
NORDICS

N•••D••
NAIADES
NAKEDLY
NAMEDAY
NEVADAN
NEWSDAY
NOMADIC
NOONDAY

N••••D•
NEREIDS
NIMRODS
NITRIDE
NOCANDO
NUCLIDE

N•••••D
NATURED
NAYSAID
NEEDLED
NEGATED
NEIGHED
NESTLED
NETTLED
NIBBLED
NIGGARD
NIGGLED
NONSKID
NORMAND
NOTATED
NOTCHED
NOTEPAD
NOTICED
NUANCED
NUZZLED

•ND••••
ANDANTE
ANDEANS
ANDIRON
ANDORRA
ANDOVER
ANDREAS
ANDRESS
ANDREWS
ANDROID
ANDSOON
ANDYKIM
ENDEARS
ENDEMIC
ENDGAME
ENDINGS
ENDIVES
ENDLESS
ENDMOST
ENDORSE
ENDOWED
ENDPLAY
ENDRUNS
ENDUING
ENDURED
ENDURES
ENDUSER
ENDWAYS
ENDWISE
ENDZONE
INDENTS
INDEPTH
INDEXED
INDEXES
INDIANA
INDIANS
INDICES
INDICIA
INDICTS
INDIGOS
INDITED
INDITES
INDOORS
INDOUBT
INDUCED
INDUCER
INDUCES
INDUCTS
INDULGE
INDUTCH
INDWELL
UNDATED
UNDERGO
UNDOING
UNDRAPE
UNDRAWN
UNDRESS
UNDYING

•N•D•••
ANADEMS
ANODIZE
ANODYNE
INADAZE
ONADARE
ONADATE
ONADIET
SNIDELY
SNIDEST

•N••D••
ANTEDUP
ENCODED
ENCODER
ENCODES
INCUDES
INFIDEL
INSIDER
INSIDES
INVADED
INVADER
INVADES
KNEADED
KNEADER
ONANDON
ONEIDAS
ONORDER
SNOWDAY
SNOWDON
UNAIDED
UNENDED
UNGODLY
UNLADES

•N•••D•
ANYBODY
ENFOLDS
ENGARDE
ENGIRDS
ENNEADS
INCLUDE
INNARDS
INROADS
INTENDS
INTRUDE
INWARDS
ONWARDS
UNBENDS
UNBINDS
UNFOLDS
UNGIRDS
UNHANDS
UNHANDY
UNIPODS
UNLOADS
UNREADY
UNWINDS

•N••••D
ANDROID
ANEROID
ANGERED
ANISEED
ANNELID
ANNEXED
ANNOYED
ANTACID
ENABLED
ENACTED
ENCAGED
ENCASED
ENCODED
ENDOWED
ENDURED
ENGAGED
ENGLAND
ENGLUND
ENISLED
ENJOYED
ENLACED
ENRAGED
ENROBED
ENSILED
ENSURED
ENTERED
ENTICED
GNARLED
GNARRED
GNASHED
INAWORD
INBOARD
INBOUND
INBREED
INCISED
INCITED
INDEXED
INDITED
INDUCED
INFIELD
INFUSED
INHALED
INHERED
INJURED
INSIPID
INSTEAD
INSURED
INTONED
INVADED
INVALID
INVITED
INVOKED
KNEADED
KNEELED
KNEEPAD
KNELLED
KNITTED
KNOBBED

KNOCKED
KNOTTED
KNURLED
ONBOARD
ONEEYED
ONGUARD
SNACKED
SNAFUED
SNAGGED
SNAPPED
SNARLED
SNEAKED
SNEERED
SNEEZED
SNIFFED
SNIPPED
SNOOPED
SNOOTED
SNOOZED
SNORTED
SNUBBED
SNUFFED
UNAIDED
UNAIMED
UNAIRED
UNARMED
UNASKED
UNBAKED
UNBOUND
UNBOWED
UNBOXED
UNCAGED
UNCASED
UNDATED
UNENDED
UNFAZED
UNFIXED
UNGLUED
UNHEARD
UNIFIED
UNLACED
UNLIKED
UNLINED
UNLOVED
UNMOVED
UNNAMED
UNOILED
UNPAVED
UNPILED
UNRATED
UNROBED
UNSATED
UNSEWED
UNSOUND
UNTAMED
UNTAPED
UNTRIED
UNTUNED
UNWOUND
UNYOKED
UNZONED

••ND•••

BANDAGE
BANDAID
BANDANA
BANDBOX
BANDIED
BANDIES
BANDING
BANDITO
BANDITS
BANDSAW
BENDERS
BENDING
BINDERS
BINDERY
BINDING
BINDSUP
BONDAGE
BONDING
BONDMAN
BONDMEN
BUNDLED
BUNDLES
CANDELA
CANDICE
CANDIDA
CANDIDE
CANDIDS
CANDIED
CANDIES
CANDLES
CANDOUR
CINDERS
CONDEMN
CONDIGN
CONDOLE
CONDONE
CONDORS
CONDUCE
CONDUCT
CONDUIT
DANDERS
DANDIER
DANDIES
DANDLED
DANDLES
DENDRON
FENDERS
FENDING
FINDERS
FINDING
FINDOUT
FONDANT
FONDEST
FONDLED
FONDLES
FONDUES
FUNDING
GANDERS
GENDERS
GONDOLA
GUNDOGS
HANDBAG
HANDCAR
HANDFUL
HANDGUN
HANDIER
HANDILY
HANDING
HANDLED
HANDLER
HANDLES
HANDOFF
HANDOUT
HANDSAW
HANDSET
HANDSIN
HANDSON
HANDSUP
HENDRIX
HINDERS
HUNDRED
KENDALL
KINDEST
KINDLED
KINDLES
KINDRED
LANDAUS
LANDERS
LANDING
LANDSAT
LENDERS
LENDING
LINDENS
LINDIED
LINDIES
LINDSAY
LINDSEY
MANDALA
MANDANS
MANDATE
MANDAYS
MANDELA
MANDREL
MANDRIL
MENDERS
MENDING
MENDOZA
MINDERS
MINDFUL
MINDING
MINDSET
MONDALE
MONDAYS
MUNDANE
PANDECT
PANDERS
PANDITS
PANDORA
PENDANT
PENDENT
PENDING
PINDOWN
PONDERS
PUNDITS
RANDALL
RANDIER
RENDERS
RENDING
RONDEAU
RONDELS
RUNDEEP
RUNDOWN
SANDALS
SANDBAG
SANDBAR
SANDBOX
SANDERS
SANDFLY
SANDHOG
SANDIER
SANDING
SANDLOT
SANDMAN
SANDMEN
SENDERS
SENDFOR
SENDING
SENDOFF
SENDOUT
SENDSIN
SENDSUP
SENDUPS
SUNDAES
SUNDAYS
SUNDECK
SUNDERS
SUNDEWS
SUNDIAL
SUNDOGS
SUNDOWN
TANDEMS
TENDERS
TENDING
TENDONS
TENDRIL
TENDSTO
TINDERS
TUNDRAS
VANDALS
VANDINE
VANDYCK
VANDYKE
VENDING
VENDORS
WANDERS
WENDELL
WENDERS
WENDING
WINDBAG
WINDERS
WINDIER
WINDING
WINDOWS
WINDROW
WINDSOR
WINDSUP
WINDUPS
WONDERS
ZANDERS

••N•D••

BONEDRY
BONEDUP
DENUDED
DENUDES
DINEDIN
DINEDON
HANGDOG
JANEDOE
KINGDOM
LANGDON
LINEDUP
OWNEDUP
RUNSDRY
SINEDIE
SYNODAL
SYNODIC
TONEDUP
TUNEDIN
TUNEDUP

••N••D•

CANARDS
CANDIDA
CANDIDE
CANDIDS
CONCEDE
CONFIDE
ENNEADS
INNARDS
KENNEDY
MANMADE
PENTADS
PONGIDS
SUNGODS
WANTADS

••N•••D

ANNELID
ANNEXED
ANNOYED
AYNRAND
BANDAID
BANDIED
BENCHED
BUNCHED
BUNCOED
BUNDLED
BUNGLED
BUNKBED
BUNKOED
CANDIED
CENTRED
CINCHED
CONCORD
CONGAED
CONREID
CONTEND
DANDLED
DANGLED
DENOTED
DENUDED
DONATED
FANCIED
FINLAND
FONDLED
GANGLED
GENTLED
HANDLED
HENNAED
HENREID
HONEYED
HONORED
HUNCHED
HUNDRED
IBNSAUD
IGNITED
IGNORED
IONIZED
JANGLED
JINGLED
KINDLED
KINDRED
LANFORD
LANGUID
LANYARD
LINDIED
LINSEED
LUNCHED
MANAGED
MANFRED
MANGLED
MANHOOD
MANKIND
MANSARD
MANTLED
MENACED
MINGLED
MINORED
MINUEND
MONEYED
MONTAND
MUNCHED
NONSKID
PANELED
PINCHED
PINHEAD
PONIARD
PUNCHED
RANCHED
RANKLED
RENAMED
RENEGED
RENEWED
SANFORD
SINGLED
SUNMAID
SYNCHED
TANGLED
TANGOED
TANKARD
TENFOLD
TENONED
TENURED
TINGLED
TINKLED
TONGUED
UNNAMED
WANGLED
WENTBAD
WINCHED
WINERED

•••ND••

ABANDON
AGENDAS
AMENDED
ASUNDER
BLANDER
BLANDLY
BLENDED
BLENDER
BLINDED
BLINDER
BLINDLY
BLONDER
BLONDES
BLONDIE
BLUNDER
BOUNDED
BOUNDER
BOUNDTO
BOUNDUP
BRANDED
BRANDER
BRANDON
BRENDAN
BRINDLE
BYANDBY
CORNDOG
DIRNDLS
DWINDLE
EMENDED
EMENDER
EVANDER
FOUNDED
FOUNDER
FOUNDRY
GOUNDER
GRANDAM
GRANDEE
GRANDER
GRANDLY
GRANDMA
GRANDPA
GRENDEL
GRINDER
HOUNDED
HYUNDAI
JOHNDOE
JOINDER
LAUNDER
LAUNDRY
LEANDER
MAUNDER
MEANDER
MOONDOG
MOUNDED
NOONDAY
ONANDON
PLUNDER
POUNDED
POUNDER
PSANDQS
ROUNDED
ROUNDER
ROUNDLY
ROUNDON
ROUNDUP
RUANDAN
RWANDAN
SCANDAL
SCENDED
SHINDIG
SLANDER
SLENDER
SOANDSO
SOUNDED
SOUNDER
SOUNDLY
SPANDEX
SPENDER
SPINDLE
SPINDLY
SPONDEE
STANDBY
STANDEE
STANDIN
STANDON
STANDUP
SWINDLE
THUNDER
TRENDED
TRUNDLE
UGANDAN
UNENDED
UPENDED
WOUNDED
WOUNDUP
WYANDOT

•••N•D•

GRANADA
GRENADA
GRENADE
KENNEDY
MAENADS
OCANADA
TORNADO

•••N••D

AMENDED
AVENGED
BAGNOLD
BARNARD
BERNARD
BLANKED
BLENDED
BLINDED
BLINKED
BLUNTED
BOUNCED
BOUNDED
BRANDED
BRONZED
CHANCED
CHANGED
CHANTED
CHINKED
CHINNED
CLANGED
CLANKED
CLINKED
CLUNKED
CORNFED
COUNTED
CRANKED
CRINGED
CRINOID
DAUNTED
EMENDED
EVINCED
FAINTED
FEINTED
FLANKED
FLENSED
FLUNKED
FOUNDED
FRANKED
FRINGED
FRONTED
GLANCED
GLINTED
GRANTED
GRINNED
GRUNTED
HAUNTED
HENNAED
HOUNDED
JAUNTED
JOINTED
JOUNCED
LEONARD
LOUNGED
MAYNARD
MOUNDED
MOUNTED
NUANCED
OPENEND
PAINTED
PLANKED
PLANNED
PLANTED
PLINKED
PLUNGED
PLUNKED
POINTED
POUNCED
POUNDED
PRANCED
PRANKED
PRINKED
PRINTED
PRONGED
REINKED
REYNARD
ROUNDED
SAINTED
SCANNED
SCANTED
SCENDED
SCENTED
SHANKED
SHINNED
SHUNNED
SHUNTED
SKINNED
SKUNKED
SLANTED
SLINKED
SOUNDED
SPANKED
SPANNED
SPONGED
STINTED
STUNNED
STUNTED
TAINTED
TAUNTED
THANKED
THINNED
TRENDED
TWANGED
TWINBED
TWINGED
TWINNED
UNENDED
UPENDED
VAUNTED
WOUNDED
WRONGED

••••ND•

ABOUNDS
ADDENDA
ADDENDS
ALLENDE
ALMONDS
APPENDS
ASCENDS
ATTENDS
AUGENDS
BELINDA
CALENDS
DEFENDS
DEMANDS
DEPENDS
EFFENDI
ERRANDS
EXPANDS
EXPENDS
EXTENDS
FAGENDS
FRIENDS
GERUNDS
GIRONDE
GROUNDS
IMPENDS
INTENDS
ISLANDS
LEGENDS
MELINDA
MIRANDA
NOCANDO
OBTUNDS
OFFENDS
ORGANDY
ORLANDO
ORMANDY
OSMONDS
REBINDS
REFUNDS
REMANDS
REMENDS
REMINDS
RESANDS
RESENDS
REWINDS
RIBANDS
ROTUNDA
SECONDS
STRANDS
TAGENDS
UNBENDS
UNBINDS
UNHANDS
UNHANDY
UNWINDS
UPLANDS
VERANDA
VIVENDI
WCHANDY
YAOUNDE

••••N•D

ADORNED
ALIGNED
APRONED
ATTUNED
BRAINED
BROWNED
BYLINED
CHAINED
CHINNED
CHURNED
CLEANED
CLOWNED
COZENED
CROONED
CROWNED
DEBONED
DEFINED
DEIGNED
DEPONED
DIVINED
DRAINED
DROWNED
FEIGNED
FROWNED
GLEANED
GRAINED
GREENED
GRINNED
GROANED
HOMINID
INTONED
LEARNED
LIKENED
LIVENED
OCEANID
PLANNED
PREENED
RAVENED
RECANED
REFINED
REIGNED
RELINED
REPINED
RETUNED
REZONED
RIPENED
SCANNED
SCORNED
SHINNED
SHUNNED
SKINNED
SPANNED
SPAWNED
SPOONED
SPURNED
STAINED
STUNNED
SWOONED
TALONED
TENONED
THINNED
TOKENED
TRAINED
TWINNED
UNLINED
UNTUNED
UNZONED
WAKENED
WIDENED
WIZENED
YEARNED

•••••ND

ABSCOND
AGROUND
AMERIND
ARMBAND
ASHLAND
ASTOUND
AYNRAND
BACKEND
BARTEND
BIGBAND
BIGBEND
BOOKEND
BRIGAND
COMMAND
COMMEND
CONTEND
COPLAND
COWHAND
DABHAND
DEADEND
DEEPEND
DESCEND
DESMOND
DIAMOND
DISBAND
DISTEND
EASTEND
ENGLAND
ENGLUND
EXPOUND
FINLAND
FORFEND
GARLAND
GODSEND
GOROUND
GOTLAND
HAMMOND
HIGHEND
HOLLAND
HUSBAND
ICELAND
ILLWIND
IMPOUND
INBOUND
IRELAND
JUGBAND
JUTLAND
LAPLAND
LOWLAND
MANKIND
MIDLAND
MILLAND
MILLEND
MINUEND
MONTAND
NORMAND
OAKLAND
OFFHAND
OLDHAND
OPENEND
OPERAND
OROTUND
OUTLAND
PORTEND
PREBEND
PRETEND
RAYMOND
REAREND
REBOUND
REDOUND
RESCIND
RESOUND
RESPOND
REWOUND
ROSTAND
SIGMUND
STIPEND
SUBTEND
SUSPEND
TAILEND
TOYLAND
UNBOUND
UNSOUND
UNWOUND
WEEKEND
WELLAND
WESTEND
WETLAND
YEAREND
ZEALAND

NE•••••

NEAREST
NEARING
NEARYOU
NEATENS
NEATEST
NEBBISH
NEBULAE
NEBULAR
NEBULAS
NECKERS
NECKING
NECKTIE
NECTARS
NEEDFUL
NEEDIER
NEEDILY
NEEDING
NEEDLED
NEEDLES
NEGATED
NEGATES
NEGATOR
NEGLECT
NEIGHED
NEITHER
NELSONS
NEMEROV
NEMESES
NEMESIS
NEOLITH
NEONATE
NEPALIS
NEPHEWS
NEPTUNE
NEREIDS
NERVIER
NERVILY
NERVOUS
NESCAFE
NESTEGG
NESTERS
NESTING
NESTLED
NESTLER
NESTLES
NETSUKE
NETSURF
NETTING
NETTLED
NETTLES
NETWORK
NEURONE
NEURONS
NEUTRAL
NEUTRON
NEVADAN
NEVILLE
NEWAGER
NEWBORN
NEWDEAL
NEWGATE
NEWHART
NEWLEFT
NEWLOOK
NEWMATH
NEWMOON
NEWMOWN
NEWNESS
NEWPORT
NEWSBOY
NEWSDAY
NEWSIER
NEWSMAN
NEWSMEN
NEWTONS
NEWTOWN
NEWWAVE
NEWYEAR
NEWYORK
NEXUSES

N•E••••

NEEDFUL
NEEDIER
NEEDILY
NEEDING
NEEDLED
NEEDLES
NIEBUHR
NIELSEN
NOETICS

N••E•••

NACELLE
NAKEDLY
NAMEDAY
NAMETAG
NANETTE
NEMEROV
NEMESES
NEMESIS
NEREIDS
NIGERIA
NINEVEH
NOSEBAG
NOSEEUM
NOSEGAY
NOSEJOB
NOSEOUT
NOTEPAD
NOVELLA
NOVELLE
NOVELTY
NOVENAS
NUMERAL
NUMERIC

NUREYEV

N•••E••

NABBERS
NAILERS
NAIVELY
NAIVETE
NANKEEN
NAPPERS
NASCENT
NATTERS
NCWYETH
NEAREST
NEATENS
NEATEST
NECKERS
NEGLECT
NEPHEWS
NESTEGG
NESTERS
NEWDEAL
NEWLEFT
NEWNESS
NEWYEAR
NICKELS
NICKERS
NIGHEST
NIPPERS
NOBLEST
NODDERS
NONSELF
NONZERO
NORIEGA
NOSEEUM
NOSHERS
NOSIEST
NOSWEAT
NOTWELL
NOUVEAU
NOWHERE
NOXZEMA
NUCLEAR
NUCLEIC
NUCLEON
NUCLEUS
NUDGERS
NUGGETS
NUMBERS
NUMBEST
NUNNERY
NURSERS
NURSERY
NUTLETS
NUTMEAT
NUTMEGS
NUTTERS

N••••E•

NAIADES
NAILSET
NANKEEN
NANNIES
NARTHEX
NASTIER
NATCHEZ
NATIVES
NATTIER
NATURED
NATURES
NEEDIER
NEEDLED
NEEDLES
NEGATED
NEGATES
NEIGHED
NEITHER
NEMESES
NERVIER
NESTLED
NESTLER
NESTLES
NETTLED
NETTLES
NEWAGER
NEWSIER
NEWSMEN
NEXUSES
NIBBLED
NIBBLER
NIBBLES
NIELSEN
NIFTIER
NIGGLED
NIGGLES
NIMBLER
NINEVEH
NINNIES
NIPPIER
NODULES
NOGALES
NOISIER
NOMINEE
NONUSER
NOODLES
NORTHER
NOTATED
NOTATES
NOTCHED
NOTCHES
NOTICED
NOTICES
NOVICES
NOZZLES
NUANCED
NUANCES
NUBBIER
NUBBLES
NUREYEV
NUTTIER
NUZZLED
NUZZLER
NUZZLES

N•••••E

NACELLE
NAIVETE
NANETTE
NAPTIME
NARRATE
NASTASE
NATALIE
NAVARRE
NEBULAE
NECKTIE
NEONATE
NEPTUNE
NESCAFE
NETSUKE
NEURONE
NEVILLE
NEWGATE
NEWWAVE
NIGHTIE
NITRATE
NITRIDE
NITRITE
NOISOME
NOMINEE
NOTABLE
NOTHOME
NOTSURE
NOTTRUE
NOVELLE
NOWHERE
NUCLIDE
NURTURE

•NE••••

ANEMONE
ANEROID
ENEMIES
INEPTLY
INERROR
INERTIA
INERTLY
INEXACT
KNEADED
KNEADER
KNEECAP
KNEEING
KNEELED
KNEELER
KNEEPAD
KNELLED
KNESSET
ONEEYED
ONEIDAS
ONENESS
ONEROUS
ONESELF
ONESHOT
ONESTEP
ONETIME
SNEAKED
SNEAKER
SNEAKIN
SNEERAT
SNEERED
SNEERER
SNEEZED
SNEEZER
SNEEZES
SNELLEN
UNEARTH
UNENDED
UNEQUAL

•N•E•••

ANAEMIA
ANDEANS
ANGELES
ANGELIC
ANGELOU
ANGELUS
ANGERED
ANNEALS
ANNELID
ANNETTE
ANNEXED
ANNEXES
ANTEDUP
ANTEING
ANTENNA
ANTESUP
ENDEARS
ENDEMIC
ENNEADS
ENTEBBE
ENTENTE
ENTERED
ENVELOP
INCENSE
INCEPTS
INDENTS
INDEPTH
INDEXED
INDEXES
INFECTS
INFERNO
INFESTS
INGEMAR
INGENUE
INGESTS
INHERED
INHERES
INHERIT
INJECTS
INPEACE
INPETTO
INSEAMS
INSECTS
INSERTS
INTEGER
INTEGRA
INTENDS
INTENSE
INTENTS
INTERIM
INTERNS
INTERSE
INVEIGH
INVENTS
INVERSE
INVERTS
INVESTS
KNEECAP
KNEEING
KNEELED
KNEELER
KNEEPAD
KNIEVEL
ONEEYED
ONLEAVE
SNEERAT
SNEERED
SNEERER
SNEEZED
SNEEZER
SNEEZES
UNBENDS
UNDERGO
UNHEARD
UNKEMPT
UNLEARN
UNLEASH
UNNERVE
UNREADY
UNREELS
UNSEALS
UNSEATS
UNSEWED
UNVEILS
UNWEAVE

•N••E••

ANADEMS
ANAHEIM
ANAPEST
ANCIENT
ANDREAS
ANDRESS
ANDREWS
ANGLERS
ANISEED
ANKLETS
ANSWERS
ANTAEUS
ANTBEAR
ANTHEMS
ANTHERS
ANTLERS
ANTWERP
ANXIETY
ENAMELS
ENDLESS
ENTREAT
ENTREES
GNAWERS
INAHEAP
INAMESS
INANELY
INANEST
INAWEOF
INBREED
INDWELL
INFIELD
INFLECT
INGRESS
INKWELL
INQUEST
INSPECT
INSTEAD
INSTEPS
KNAVERY
ONAGERS
ONATEAR
ONENESS
ONESELF
ONTHEGO
ONTHEQT
SNIDELY
SNIDEST
SNIPEAT
SNIVELS
SNORERS
UNBLEST
UNCLEAN
UNCLEAR
UNDRESS
UNGUENT
UNITERS
UNREELS
UNSPENT
UNSWEPT

•N•••E•

ANDOVER
ANGELES
ANGERED
ANGRIER
ANISEED
ANNABEL
ANNALEE
ANNEXED
ANNEXES
ANNOYED
ANOTHER
ANTARES
ANTIBES
ANTIGEN
ANTSIER
CNTOWER
ENABLED
ENABLES
ENACTED
ENCAGED
ENCAGES
ENCASED
ENCASES
ENCODED
ENCODER
ENCODES
ENCORES
ENDIVES
ENDOWED
ENDURED
ENDURES
ENDUSER
ENEMIES
ENGAGED
ENGAGES
ENGINES
ENISLED
ENISLES
ENJOYED
ENLACED
ENLACES
ENLIVEN
ENRAGED
ENRAGES
ENROBED
ENROBES
ENSILED
ENSILES
ENSURED
ENSURES
ENTERED
ENTICED
ENTICER
ENTICES
ENTREES
ENTRIES
ENZYMES
FNUMBER
GNARLED
GNARRED
GNASHED
GNASHES
INASTEW
INBREED
INBRIEF
INCISED
INCISES
INCITED
INCITER
INCITES
INCOMES
INCUDES
INDEXED
INDEXES
INDICES
INDITED
INDITES
INDUCED
INDUCER
INDUCES
INFIDEL
INFUSED
INFUSES
INHALED
INHALER
INHALES
INHERED
INHERES
INJOKES
INJURED
INJURES
INMATES
INSIDER
INSIDES
INSOLES
INSURED
INSURES
INTAKES
INTEGER
INTONED
INTONER
INTONES
INVADED
INVADER
INVADES
INVITED
INVITES
INVOKED
INVOKER
INVOKES
KNEADED
KNEADER
KNEELED
KNEELER
KNELLED
KNESSET
KNIEVEL
KNISHES
KNITTED
KNITTER
KNOBBED
KNOCKED
KNOCKER
KNOTTED
KNURLED
ONADIET
ONEEYED
ONESTEP
ONORDER
ONPAPER
SNACKED
SNACKER
SNAFUED
SNAGGED
SNAKIER
SNAPPED
SNAPPER
SNARLED
SNEAKED
SNEAKER
SNEERED
SNEERER
SNEEZED
SNEEZER
SNEEZES
SNELLEN
SNICKER
SNIFFED
SNIFFER
SNIFTER
SNIGGER
SNIGLET
SNIPPED
SNIPPET
SNOOKER
SNOOPED
SNOOPER
SNOOTED
SNOOZED
SNOOZES
SNORKEL
SNORTED
SNORTER
SNOWIER
SNOWMEN
SNOWPEA
SNUBBED
SNUFFED
SNUFFER
SNUGGER
UNAIDED
UNAIMED
UNAIRED
UNARMED
UNASKED
UNBAKED
UNBOWED
UNBOXED
UNBOXES
UNCAGED
UNCAGES
UNCASED
UNCASES
UNCOVER
UNDATED
UNENDED
UNFAZED
UNFIXED
UNGLUED
UNIFIED
UNIFIER
UNIFIES
UNITIES
UNLACED
UNLACES
UNLADES
UNLIKED
UNLINED
UNLOVED
UNMAKES
UNMOVED
UNNAMED
UNOILED
UNPAVED
UNPILED
UNPILES
UNRATED
UNRAVEL
UNROBED
UNROBES
UNSATED
UNSCREW
UNSEWED
UNTAMED
UNTAPED
UNTRIED
UNTUNED
UNTUNES
UNWISER
UNYOKED
UNYOKES
UNZONED

•N••••E

ANALYSE
ANALYZE
ANATOLE
ANDANTE
ANEMONE
ANILINE
ANIMATE
ANNALEE
ANNETTE
ANODIZE
ANODYNE
ANTIQUE
ANTOINE
ANYMORE
ANYTIME
ENCLAVE
ENCLOSE
ENDGAME
ENDORSE
ENDWISE
ENDZONE
ENFORCE
ENGARDE
ENGORGE
ENGRAVE
ENHANCE
ENLARGE
ENMASSE
ENNOBLE
ENOUNCE
ENPLANE
ENROUTE
ENSLAVE
ENSNARE
ENSUITE
ENTEBBE
ENTENTE
ENTHUSE
ENTITLE
ENTWINE
INADAZE
INCENSE
INCLINE
INCLOSE
INCLUDE
INDULGE
INFLAME
INFLATE
INFORCE
INGENUE
INGRATE
INHASTE
INHOUSE
INPEACE
INPHASE
INPLACE
INQUIRE
INSCAPE
INSHAPE
INSPIRE
INSTATE
INSTORE
INSTYLE
INTENSE
INTERSE
INTRUDE
INUTILE
INVERSE
INVOGUE
INVOICE
INVOLVE
KNUCKLE
ONADARE
ONADATE
ONETIME
ONLEAVE
ONSHORE
ONSTAGE
SNAFFLE
SNIFFLE
SNIGGLE
SNOCONE
SNUFFLE
SNUGGLE
UNALIKE
UNAVOCE
UNAWARE
UNCLOSE
UNCRATE
UNDRAPE
UNHORSE
UNITIVE
UNLOOSE
UNNERVE
UNQUOTE
UNWEAVE

••NE•••

AMNESIA
AMNESTY
ANNEALS
ANNELID
ANNETTE
ANNEXED
ANNEXES
BANEFUL
BENEATH
BENEFIT
BONEASH
BONEDRY
BONEDUP
BONESUP
CINEMAS
CINEMAX
DANELAW
DENEUVE
DINEDIN
DINEDON
DINESEN
DINESIN
DINESON
DINETTE
DONEFOR
DONEGAL
ENNEADS
ERNESTO
FENETRE
FINEART
FINESSE
GENERAL
GENERIC
GENERIS
GENESEE
GENESES
GENESIS
GENETIC
GONERIL
HONESTY
HONEYED
IGNEOUS
IONESCO
JANEDOE
JANEIRO
JANEWAY
JUNEBUG
KINETIC
LINEAGE
LINEATE
LINEDUP
LINEMAN
LINEMEN
LINESUP
LINEUPS
MANEGES
MINEOLA
MINERAL
MINERVA
MONEYED
NANETTE
NINEVEH
ORNETTE
OWNEDUP
PANELED
PANETTA
PINEFOR
PINENUT
PINESAP
PINETAR
PINETUM
RENEGED
RENEGER
RENEGES
RENEWAL
RENEWED
RENEWER
SENECAS
SENEGAL
SINEDIE
SYNERGY
TINEARS
TONEARM
TONEDUP
TONELOC
TONEROW
TONESUP
TUNEDIN
TUNEDUP
TUNEFUL
TUNEOUT
TUNESIN
TUNESUP
TUNEUPS
UNNERVE
VANESSA
VANEYCK
VENEERS
VINEGAR
WINEBAR
WINERED
WINESAP
WYNETTE

••N•E••

BANKERS
BANNERS
BANTERS
BENDERS
BENNETT
BENZENE
BINDERS
BINDERY
BONIEST
BONKERS
BONNETS
BUNGEES
BUNKERS
CANCELS
CANDELA
CANKERS
CANNERS
CANNERY
CANSECO
CANTEEN
CANTERS
CENSERS
CENTERS
CINDERS
CONCEAL
CONCEDE
CONCEIT
CONCEPT
CONCERN
CONCERT
CONDEMN
CONFERS
CONFESS
CONGEAL
CONGERS
CONGEST
CONKERS
CONNECT
CONNERY
CONREID
CONSENT
CONTEMN
CONTEND
CONTENT
CONTEST
CONTEXT
CONVENE
CONVENT
CONVERT
CONVEYS
DANCERS
DANDERS
DANGERS
DANIELS
DANKEST
DANSEUR
DENIECE
DENIERS
DENNEHY
DENSELY
DENSEST
DINNERS
DONKEYS
DUNGEON
DUNKERS
FANBELT
FANJETS
FENCERS
FENDERS
FINDERS
FINGERS
FONDEST
FONTEYN
FUNFEST
FUNNELS
GANDERS
GANNETS
GANNETT
GENDERS
GENOESE
GENTEEL
GINGERS
GINGERY
GINSENG
GUNNELS
GUNNERS
GUNNERY
HANGERS
HANKERS
HENNERY
HENPECK
HENREID
HINDERS
HONKERS
HUNGERS
HUNKERS
HUNTERS
JENNETS
JUNKERS
JUNKETS
KENNEDY
KENNELS
KENNETH
KINDEST
LANCERS
LANCETS
LANDERS
LANKEST
LANTERN
LENDERS
LENIENT
LINDENS
LINGERS
LINKERS
LINNETS
LINSEED
LINTELS
LONGEST
LUNGEAT
LUNKERS
MANDELA
MANGERS
MANNERS
MANTELS
MANYEAR
MENDERS
MINCERS
MINDERS
MINTERS
MINUEND
MINUETS
MONGERS
MONKEES
MONKEYS
MONTEGO
MONTEUX
MYNHEER
NANKEEN
NONSELF
NONZERO
NUNNERY
PANDECT
PANDERS
PANNERS
PANZERS
PENDENT
PENNERS
PENSEES
PINCERS
PINHEAD
PINIEST
PINKEST
PINLESS
PINNERS
PONDERS
PUNGENT
PUNIEST
PUNTERS
RANGERS
RANKERS
RANKEST
RANTERS
RENDERS
RENTERS
RINGERS
RONDEAU
RONDELS
RUNDEEP
RUNLETS
RUNNELS
RUNNERS
SANDERS
SANREMO
SENDERS
SENNETT
SINCERE

SINGERS
SINKERS
SINNERS
SONNETS
SUNBEAM
SUNBELT
SUNDECK
SUNDERS
SUNDEWS
SUNLESS
SUNSETS
TANDEMS
TANGELO
TANGENT
TANGERE
TANKERS
TANNERS
TANNERY
TANNEST
TENDERS
TENNERS
TENSELY
TENSEST
TENSEUP
TENTERS
TINDERS
TINIEST
TINKERS
TINNERS
TINSELS
TINTERN
TINTERS
TONIEST
TONNEAU
TUNNELS
VENEERS
VENTERS
VINCENT
WANDERS
WENDELL
WENDERS
WINCERS
WINDERS
WINGERS
WINKERS
WINNERS
WINTERS
WINTERY
WONDERS
YANKEES
YONKERS
ZANDERS
ZANIEST
ZINGERS
ZONKERS

••N••E•

AGNATES
ANNABEL
ANNALEE
ANNEXED
ANNEXES
ANNOYED
AUNTIES
BANDIED
BANDIES
BANGLES
BANJOES
BANQUET
BANSHEE
BENCHED
BENCHES
BENTLEY
BENTSEN
BINGOES
BONDMEN
BONGOES
BONNIER
BONUSES
BUNCHED
BUNCHES
BUNCOED
BUNDLED
BUNDLES
BUNGEES
BUNGLED
BUNGLER
BUNGLES
BUNKBED
BUNKOED
BUNNIES
CANAPES
CANDIED
CANDIES
CANDLES
CANINES
CANNIER
CANTEEN
CANTLES
CENTRED
CENTRES
CINCHED
CINCHES
CONCHES
CONGAED
CONIFER
CONQUER
DANDIER
DANDIES
DANDLED
DANDLES
DANGLED
DANGLER
DANGLES
DENIZEN
DENOTED
DENOTES
DENUDED
DENUDES
DINESEN
DINGIER
DINGLES
DINGOES
DINKIER
DINKIES
DONATED
DONATES
FANCIED
FANCIER
FANCIES
FINALES
FINCHES
FONDLED
FONDLES
FONDUES
FUNGOES
FUNKIER
FUNNIER
FUNNIES
GANGLED
GANTLET
GENESEE
GENESES
GENTEEL
GENTLED
GENTLER
GENTLES
GUNKIER
GUNNIES
GUNTHER
HANDIER
HANDLED
HANDLER
HANDLES
HANDSET
HANGMEN
HANGTEN
HANKIES
HANOVER
HENNAED
HINNIES
HONEYED
HONORED
HONOREE
HONORER
HUNCHED
HUNCHES
HUNDRED
HUNTLEY
IGNITED
IGNITER
IGNITES
IGNORED
IGNORER
IGNORES
IONIZED
IONIZER
IONIZES
JANACEK
JANGLED
JANGLES
JANSSEN
JANTZEN
JANVIER
JENNIES
JINGLED
JINGLES
JINGOES
JUNCOES
JUNGLES
JUNIPER
JUNKIER
JUNKIES
KINDLED
KINDLES
KINDRED
KINKIER
KINSMEN
LANGLEY
LANKIER
LINAGES
LINDIED
LINDIES
LINDSEY
LINEMEN
LINGOES
LINSEED
LINTIER
LONGUES
LUNCHED
LUNCHER
LUNCHES
MANAGED
MANAGER
MANAGES
MANATEE
MANDREL
MANEGES
MANFRED
MANGIER
MANGLED
MANGLES
MANGOES
MANLIER
MANTLED
MANTLES
MANXMEN
MENACED
MENACES
MENAGES
MENCKEN
MINARET
MINDSET
MINGLED
MINGLER
MINGLES
MINIVER
MINORED
MINTIER
MINUSES
MINUTES
MONEYED
MONGREL
MONIKER
MONKEES
MONOMER
MONSTER
MUNCHED
MUNCHER
MUNCHES
MYNHEER
NANKEEN
NANNIES
NINEVEH
NINNIES
NONUSER
PANACEA
PANELED
PANNIER
PANSIES
PANTHER
PENATES
PENNIES
PENSEES
PINCHED
PINCHER
PINCHES
PINKIES
PINONES
PUNCHED
PUNCHER
PUNCHES
PUNKIES
PUNSTER
RANCHED
RANCHER
RANCHES
RANDIER
RANGIER
RANKLED
RANKLES
RANOVER
RENAMED
RENAMES
RENEGED
RENEGER
RENEGES
RENEWED
RENEWER
RENOTES
RINGLET
RONTGEN
RUNDEEP
RUNNIER
RUNOVER
RUNTIER
SANDIER
SANDMEN
SANIBEL
SENATES
SENORES
SINGLED
SINGLES
SINUSES
SUNDAES
SUNNIER
SYNCHED
SYNCHES
SYNFUEL
TANAGER
TANGIER
TANGLED
TANGLES
TANGOED
TANSIES
TENACES
TENNIEL
TENONED
TENURED
TENURES
TINGLED
TINGLES
TINKLED
TINKLES
TINNIER
TONGUED
TONGUES
TUNNIES
UNNAMED
VINTNER
WANGLED
WANGLER
WANGLES
WENCHES
WINCHED
WINCHES
WINDIER
WINERED
WINFREY
WINKLER
YANKEES
ZINGIER

••N•••E

ANNALEE
ANNETTE
BANDAGE
BANSHEE
BENZENE
BONDAGE
BONFIRE
CANDICE
CANDIDE
CANZONE
CENSURE
CENTIME
CONCAVE
CONCEDE
CONCISE
CONDOLE
CONDONE
CONDUCE
CONFIDE
CONFINE
CONFUSE
CONFUTE
CONGAME
CONJURE
CONNIVE
CONNOTE
CONSOLE
CONSUME
CONTUSE
CONVENE
CONVOKE
DENEUVE
DENIECE
DENTATE
DENTINE
DENTURE
DINETTE
DONAHUE
DONJOSE
ENNOBLE
FANFARE
FANZINE
FENETRE
FINAGLE
FINANCE
FINESSE
GENESEE
GENOESE
GENTILE
GENUINE
GUNFIRE
GUNWALE
HENBANE
HONOREE
IGNOBLE
JANEDOE
LINEAGE
LINEATE
LINKAGE
MANACLE
MANATEE
MANDATE
MANHOLE
MANIPLE
MANMADE
MINABLE
MONDALE
MONIQUE
MONOCLE
MONTAGE
MONTANE
MUNDANE
NANETTE
ORNETTE
PANACHE
PANCAKE
PANICLE
PANPIPE
PANURGE
PENANCE
PENNAME
PENNATE
PENSIVE
PENUCHE
PINHOLE
PINNACE
PINNATE
PINOCLE
PINWALE
PONTINE
RANLATE
RUNHOME
SANJOSE
SANTAFE
SENSATE
SINCERE
SINEDIE
SINKAGE
SUNRISE
SYNAPSE
TANGERE
TANLINE
TENABLE
TENSILE
TENSIVE
TINTYPE
TONNAGE
TONSURE
TONTINE
TUNICLE
UNNERVE
VANDINE
VANDYKE
VANTAGE
VENTURE
VINTAGE
WANNABE
WENTAPE
WINSOME
WYNETTE
YANGTZE

•••NE••

APTNESS
BADNESS
BANNERS
BARNEYS
BEANERY
BENNETT
BERNESE
BIGNESS
BONNETS
BORNEUP
BRUNETS
BURNERS
BURNETT
CANNERS
CANNERY
CARNERA
CARNETS
CHINESE
COINERS
CONNECT
CONNERY
CORNEAL
CORNEAS
CORNELL
CORNERS
CORNETS
COYNESS
CRENELS
CYGNETS
DARNERS
DENNEHY
DIMNESS
DINNERS
DOWNERS
DRONERS
DRYNESS
EARNERS
EARNEST
EMINENT
EVENEST
FATNESS
FAWNERS
FITNESS
FLANEUR
FLYNETS
FRENEAU
FUNNELS
GAINERS
GANNETS
GANNETT
GARNERS
GARNETS
GUINEAS
GUNNELS
GUNNERS
GUNNERY
GURNEYS
HARNESS
HENNERY
HIPNESS
HORNETS
HOTNESS
ICINESS
ILLNESS
INANELY
INANEST
IPANEMA
IRONERS
JENNETS
JITNEYS
JOINERS
JOINERY
KEENERS
KEENEST
KENNEDY
KENNELS
KENNETH
KERNELS
KIDNEYS
LAXNESS
LEANERS
LEANEST
LIENEES
LIMNERS
LINNETS
LIONESS
LIONETS
LOANERS
LOWNECK
LOWNESS
MADNESS
MAGNETO
MAGNETS
MANNERS
MEANEST
MOANERS
NEWNESS
NUNNERY
ODDNESS
OLDNESS
OLDNEWS
ONENESS
OPENEND
OPENERS
OPINERS
PANNERS
PARNELL
PATNESS
PAWNEES
PAWNERS
PENNERS
PERNELL
PHINEAS
PHONEME
PINNERS
PIONEER
PLANERS
PLANETS
PRUNERS
RAWNESS
REDNESS
ROMNEYS
RUINERS
RUNNELS
RUNNERS
SADNESS
SCENERY
SEINERS
SENNETT
SHINERS
SHYNESS
SIGNEES
SIGNERS
SIGNETS
SINNERS
SLYNESS
SONNETS
SOONERS
SOONEST
SPINELS
SPINETS
STONERS
TANNERS
TANNERY
TANNEST
TEENERS
TENNERS
TINNERS
TONNEAU
TOWNERS
TUNNELS
TURNERS
VAINEST
VEENECK
WETNESS
WHINERS
WIENERS
WINNERS
WITNESS
WRYNESS
YAWNERS

•••N•E•

ALUNSER
AMENDED
ASUNDER
AVENGED
AVENGER
AVENGES
AVENUES
AVONLEA
BEANIES
BERNSEN
BLANDER
BLANKED
BLANKER
BLANKET
BLENDED
BLENDER
BLINDED
BLINDER
BLINKED
BLINKER
BLONDER
BLONDES
BLUNDER
BLUNTED
BLUNTER
BONNIER
BOONIES
BOUNCED
BOUNCER
BOUNCES
BOUNDED
BOUNDER
BRANDED
BRANDER
BRENNER
BRINGER
BRINIER
BRONZED
BRONZES
BRYNNER
BUNNIES
CANNIER
CARNIES
CHANCED
CHANCEL
CHANCES
CHANGED
CHANGER
CHANGES
CHANNEL
CHANTED
CHANTER
CHANTEY
CHENIER
CHINKED
CHINNED
CHUNNEL
CLANGED
CLANKED
CLINKED
CLINKER
CLUNKED
CLUNKER
CORNFED
CORNIER
COUNSEL
COUNTED
COUNTER
CRANKED
CRINGED
CRINGES
CRONIES
DAUNTED
DERNIER
DOWNIER
DRINKER
EBONIES
EMANUEL
EMENDED
EMENDER
EVANDER
EVANGEL
EVINCED
EVINCES
FAINTED
FAINTER
FEINTED
FIANCEE
FIANCES
FLANGES
FLANKED
FLANKER
FLANNEL
FLENSED
FLENSES
FLUNKED
FOUNDED
FOUNDER
FRANCES
FRANKED
FRANKER
FRINGED
FRINGES
FRONTED
FUNNIER
FUNNIES
GAUNTER
GLANCED
GLANCES
GLINTED
GOUNDER
GRANDEE
GRANDER
GRANGER
GRANGES
GRANTED
GRANTEE
GRENDEL
GRINDER
GRINNED
GRINNER
GRUNTED
GUNNIES
HAUNTED
HENNAED
HINNIES
HOUNDED
IRONIES
IRONMEN
JAUNTED
JENNIES
JOINDER
JOINTED
JOUNCED
JOUNCES
LAENNEC
LAUNDER
LEANDER
LIENEES
LOONIER
LOONIES
LOUNGED
LOUNGER
LOUNGES
MAUNDER
MEANDER
MEANIES
MOONSET
MOUNDED
MOUNTED
NANNIES
NINNIES
NUANCED
NUANCES
OPENSEA
ORANGES
PAINTED
PAINTER
PANNIER
PAWNEES
PENNIES
PEONIES
PHONIER
PHONIES
PIONEER
PLANKED
PLANNED
PLANNER
PLANTED
PLANTER
PLINKED
PLUNDER
PLUNGED
PLUNGER
PLUNGES
PLUNKED
POINTED
POINTER
POUNCED
POUNCER
POUNCES
POUNDED
POUNDER
PRANCED
PRANCER
PRANCES
PRANKED
PRINCES
PRINKED
PRINTED
PRINTER
PRONGED
QUINCES
QUINTET
QUONSET
RAINIER
REENTER
REINKED
ROUNDED
ROUNDER
RUNNIER
SAINTED
SAUNTER
SCANNED
SCANNER
SCANTED
SCANTER
SCENDED
SCENTED
SCONCES
SEANCES
SHANKED
SHANTER
SHINIER
SHINNED
SHUNNED
SHUNTED
SIGNEES
SKINNED
SKINNER
SKUNKED
SLANDER
SLANTED
SLENDER
SLINGER
SLINKED
SOUNDED
SOUNDER
SPANDEX
SPANIEL
SPANKED
SPANKER
SPANNED
SPANNER
SPENCER
SPENDER
SPENSER
SPINIER
SPINNER
SPONDEE
SPONGED
SPONGER
SPONGES
STANCES
STANDEE
STANLEE
STANLEY
STENGEL
STINGER
STINKER
STINTED
STONIER
STUNNED
STUNNER
STUNTED
SUNNIER
SWANKER
SWINGER
TAINTED
TAUNTED
TAWNIER
TEENIER
TENNIEL
THANKED
THINKER
THINNED
THINNER
THUNDER
TINNIER
TOWNIES
TOYNBEE
TRANCES
TRENDED
TRINKET
TUNNIES
TURNKEY
TWANGED
TWINBED
TWINGED
TWINGES
TWINNED
UNENDED
UPENDED
VAUNTED
VAUNTER
VERNIER
WEENIES
WERNHER
WIENIES
WOUNDED
WRINGER
WRONGED
WRONGER
YOUNGER

•••N••E

ACONITE
ADENINE
AGONIZE
ASININE
ATINGLE
BERNESE
BERNICE
BIGNAME
BLANCHE
BLONDIE
BRINDLE
BYANOSE
CHINESE
COGNATE
COINAGE
CONNIVE
CONNOTE
CORNICE
CRINKLE
DWINDLE
EBONITE
EMANATE
ENSNARE

FIANCEE
FRANKIE
FURNACE
GRANDEE
GRANITE
GRANTEE
GRANULE
GRENADE
GUANINE
IRONAGE
IRONORE
IVANHOE
JEANNIE
JOHNDOE
JOHNNIE
KEYNOTE
KRINGLE
LEONINE
LIGNITE
LIONIZE
MAGNATE
MCENROE
MISNAME
MOUNTIE
NEONATE
OPENTOE
PENNAME
PENNATE
PEONAGE
PETNAME
PHONEME
PINNACE
PINNATE
PUGNOSE
QUININE
QUINQUE
REUNITE
ROANOKE
SHINGLE
SPANGLE
SPINDLE
SPONDEE
STANDEE
STANLEE
SURNAME
SWINDLE
TEENAGE
TERNATE
THINICE
TONNAGE
TOYNBEE
TRUNDLE
TWINKLE
URANITE
WANNABE
WRANGLE
WRINKLE

••••NE•
ACHENES
ADORNED
AFFINES
ALIENEE
ALIGNED
ALIGNER
ALKENES
APRONED
ATTUNED
ATTUNES
BALONEY
BARONET
BAYONET
BLARNEY
BOVINES
BRAINED
BRENNER
BROWNED
BROWNER
BRYNNER
BYGONES
BYLINED
BYLINES
CABINET
CANINES
CHAINED
CHANNEL
CHIMNEY
CHINNED
CHUNNEL
CHURNED
CHUTNEY
CLEANED
CLEANER
CLOONEY
CLOWNED
COCKNEY
COLONEL
COLONES
CORONET
COSINES
COSTNER
COZENED
CROONED
CROONER
CROWNED
DEBONED
DEBONES
DEFINED
DEFINES
DEIGNED
DELANEY
DEPONED
DEPONES
DIVINED
DIVINER
DIVINES
DRAGNET
DRAINED
DRAINER
DROWNED
EDASNER
EMPANEL
ENGINES
EQUINES
ERMINES
ESSENES
FEIGNED
FELINES
FISHNET
FLANNEL
FLEXNER
FROWNED
FROWNER
GAMINES
GARDNER
GILLNET
GLEANED
GLEANER
GRAINED
GRAPNEL
GREENED
GREENER
GRINNED
GRINNER
GROANED
GROANER
HACKNEY
HAIRNET
HOMINEM
IMPANEL
INTONED
INTONER
INTONES
JACONET
JIMENEZ
JOURNEY
KETONES
KLEENEX
LAENNEC
LARDNER
LEARNED
LEARNER
LIERNES
LIFENET
LIKENED
LIKENEW
LIVENED
LUPINES
MAHONEY
MARINER
MARINES
MATINEE
MRBONES
NOMINEE
OCTANES
OFTENER
ORPINES
OSCINES
PARDNER
PARTNER
PAVANES
PILSNER
PINONES
PLAINER
PLAINES
PLANNED
PLANNER
PREENED
PREENER
RAPINES
RAVENED
RAVINES
RECANED
RECANES
REFINED
REFINER
REFINES
REIGNED
RELINED
RELINES
REPINED
REPINES
RETUNED
RETUNES
REZONED
REZONES
RIPENED
SABINES
SCANNED
SCANNER
SCORNED
SERENER
SHATNER
SHAWNEE
SHINNED
SHRINER
SHRINES
SHUNNED
SKINNED
SKINNER
SOIGNEE
SPANNED
SPANNER
SPAWNED
SPINNER
SPLINES
SPOONED
SPOONER
SPURNED
SPURNER
STAINED
STAINER
STEINEM
STEINER
STERNER
STUNNED
STUNNER
SUTTNER
SWOONED
TALONED
TENONED
THINNED
THINNER
THRONES
TIERNEY
TISANES
TOKENED
TOURNEY
TRAINED
TRAINEE
TRAINER
TRIUNES
TWINNED
UNLINED
UNTUNED
UNTUNES
UNZONED
URBANER
VINTNER
WAGONER
WAHINES
WAKENED
WAKENER
WHITNEY
WIDENED
WIZENED
YEARNED
YEARNER

••••N•E
ABSENCE
ADVANCE
ALDENTE
ALIENEE
ALLENDE
ALUMNAE
ANDANTE
ARGONNE
ARRANGE
ASKANCE
BALANCE
BROWNIE
CADENCE
CATENAE
CAYENNE
CEZANNE
CLEANSE
CORONAE
DEFENCE
DEFENSE
DETENTE
DOYENNE
DURANCE
DURANTE
ENHANCE
ENOUNCE
ENTENTE
ESSENCE
ETIENNE
EUGENIE
EXPANSE
EXPENSE
EXPUNGE
FAIENCE
FINANCE
FIRENZE
FLOUNCE
GARONNE
GIRONDE
IMMENSE
IMPINGE
INCENSE
INGENUE
INTENSE
JEANNIE
JOHNNIE
LACUNAE
LALANNE
LAMINAE
LICENCE
LICENSE
LOZENGE
MATINEE
MELANGE
MELANIE
NOMINEE
OFFENCE
OFFENSE
ORIENTE
PALANCE
PENANCE
PICANTE
RERINSE
RETINAE
RETINUE
REVENGE
REVENUE
ROMANCE
ROSANNE
ROXANNE
SCIENCE
SHAWNEE
SILENCE
SOIGNEE
STRANGE
SUSANNE
SUZANNE
SYRINGE
TERENCE
TRAINEE
TROUNCE
VALANCE
VALENCE
YAOUNDE

•••••NE
AAMILNE
ABALONE
ABILENE
ACETONE
ADELINE
ADENINE
AIRLANE
AIRLINE
ALLGONE
ANEMONE
ANILINE
ANODYNE
ANTOINE
ARACHNE
ARCSINE
ARGONNE
ARIADNE
ASININE
BEELINE
BEGUINE
BELTANE
BENZENE
BIPLANE
BOWLINE
BROMINE
BUSLINE
CALZONE
CANZONE
CARBINE
CARMINE
CAYENNE
CEZANNE
CHORINE
CITRINE
CODEINE
COLOGNE
COMBINE
COMMUNE
CONDONE
CONFINE
CONVENE
CUISINE
CYCLONE
DARLENE
DECLINE
DEMESNE
DENTINE
DEPLANE
DESTINE
DEWLINE
DOGGONE
DOYENNE
ENDZONE
ENPLANE
ENTWINE
EPERGNE
EPICENE
EPIGENE
EPIGONE
ERSKINE
ETAMINE
ETIENNE
EXAMINE
FANZINE
FARGONE
FASTONE
FORGONE
FORTUNE
GAGLINE
GARONNE
GENUINE
GERMANE
GOODONE
GUANINE
HELLENE
HEMLINE
HENBANE
HEROINE
HIPBONE
HORMONE
HOTLINE
HYALINE
HYGIENE
IFSTONE
IMAGINE
IMOGENE
INCLINE
JASMINE
JAWBONE
JAWLINE
JIMDINE
JUGWINE
JUSTINE
LALANNE
LARAINE
LASAGNE
LAVERNE
LEONINE
LIVEONE
LUCERNE
MACHINE
MARLENE
MAYWINE
MBABANE
MCSWINE
METHANE
MIDLINE
MIOCENE
MISDONE
MONTANE
MORAINE
MUNDANE
NEPTUNE
NEURONE
OBSCENE
OFFLINE
OLDLINE
OLIVINE
OPALINE
OSBORNE
OUTDONE
OUTLINE
PADRONE
PAULINE
PISCINE
PONTINE
PORCINE
PRALINE
PROFANE
PROPANE
QUININE
RATLINE
RECLINE
REDLINE
REDPINE
REDWINE
ROMAINE
ROSANNE
ROUTINE
ROXANNE
SALTINE
SARDINE
SCALENE
SEALANE
SETLINE
SEVIGNE
SISTINE
SKYLINE
SLOVENE
SNOCONE
SOMEONE
SOUTANE
SPOKANE
SPUMONE
STYRENE
SUSANNE
SUZANNE
TAGLINE
TAKEONE
TANLINE
TAURINE
TERHUNE
TERRENE
TIELINE
TOLUENE
TONTINE
TRIBUNE
TRITONE
TURBINE
TWOTONE
UKRAINE
UPBORNE
VACCINE
VANDINE
VOLPONE
VULPINE
WILDONE
WORDONE

N•F••••
NIFTIER
NIFTILY
NOFAULT

N••F•••
NORFOLK

N•••F••
NEEDFUL

N••••F•
NESCAFE
NEWLEFT
NODSOFF
NULLIFY

N•••••F
NETSURF
NODSOFF
NONSELF

•NF••••
ENFOLDS
ENFORCE
INFANCY
INFANTA
INFANTS
INFAVOR
INFECTS
INFERNO
INFESTS
INFIDEL
INFIELD
INFLAME
INFLATE
INFLECT
INFLICT
INFLOWS
INFOCUS
INFORCE
INFORMS
INFRONT
INFUSED
INFUSES
UNFAZED
UNFIXED
UNFOLDS
UNFROCK
UNFURLS

•N•F•••
ANTFARM
KNIFING
SNAFFLE
SNAFUED
SNIFFAT
SNIFFED
SNIFFER
SNIFFLE
SNIFTER
SNUFFED
SNUFFER
SNUFFLE
UNIFIED
UNIFIER
UNIFIES
UNIFORM

•N••F••
INSOFAR
SNAFFLE
SNIFFAT
SNIFFED
SNIFFER
SNIFFLE
SNUFFED
SNUFFER
SNUFFLE

•N•••F•
ENGRAFT
ENGULFS

•N••••F
INAWEOF
INBRIEF
ONESELF
ONTOPOF

••NF•••
BONFIRE
CONFABS
CONFERS
CONFESS
CONFIDE
CONFINE
CONFIRM
CONFORM
CONFUSE
CONFUTE
FANFARE
FUNFAIR
FUNFEST
GINFIZZ
GUNFIRE
KINFOLK
LANFORD
LENFANT
MANFRED
MENFOLK
PANFISH
SANFORD
SUNFISH
SYNFUEL
TENFOLD
TENFOUR
TINFOIL
WINFREY

••N•F••
BANEFUL
BENEFIT
CONIFER
DONEFOR
GUNSFOR
HANDFUL
MINDFUL
PINEFOR
RUNOFFS
SANDFLY
SENDFOR
SENTFOR
TANKFUL
TUNEFUL
WENTFOR

••N••F•
CONNIFF
HANDOFF
HANGOFF
PONTIFF
RUNOFFS
RUNSOFF
SANTAFE
SENDOFF
SENTOFF
WENTOFF

••N•••F
CONNIFF
HANDOFF
HANGOFF
NONSELF
PONTIFF
RUNSOFF
SENDOFF
SENTOFF
SUNROOF
WENTOFF

•••NF••
CORNFED
GAINFUL
GOINFOR
PAINFUL

•••N•F•
BRANIFF
CONNIFF
DIGNIFY
MAGNIFY
PAWNOFF
REUNIFY
SIGNIFY
SIGNOFF
SPINOFF
SPUNOFF
TURNOFF
WORNOFF

•••N••F
BRANIFF
CONNIFF
PAWNOFF
SIGNOFF
SPINOFF
SPUNOFF
THINKOF
TURNOFF
WORNOFF

••••N•F
BARANOF

N•G••••
NAGGING
NEGATED
NEGATES
NEGATOR
NEGLECT
NIGERIA
NIGGARD
NIGGLED
NIGGLES
NIGHEST
NIGHTIE
NIGHTLY
NOGALES
NOGGINS
NOGUCHI
NUGGETS

N••G•••
NAGGING
NAUGHTS
NAUGHTY
NEIGHED
NEWGATE
NIAGARA
NIGGARD
NIGGLED
NIGGLES
NOGGINS
NOUGATS
NUDGERS
NUDGING
NUGGETS

N•••G••
NEWAGER
NONAGON
NOSEGAY

N••••G•
NESTEGG
NORIEGA
NUTMEGS

N•••••G
NABBING
NAGGING
NAILING
NAMETAG
NAPPING
NEARING
NECKING
NEEDING
NESTEGG
NESTING
NETTING
NICKING
NIPPING
NODDING
NOISING
NOOSING
NOSEBAG
NOSHING
NOTHING
NUDGING
NULLING
NUMBING
NURSING
NUTTING

•NG••••
ANGELES
ANGELIC
ANGELOU
ANGELUS
ANGERED
ANGLERS
ANGLING
ANGOLAN
ANGORAS
ANGRIER
ANGRILY
ANGULAR
ENGAGED
ENGAGES
ENGARDE
ENGINES
ENGIRDS
ENGLAND
ENGLISH
ENGLUND
ENGORGE
ENGRAFT
ENGRAMS
ENGRAVE
ENGROSS
ENGULFS
INGALLS
INGEMAR
INGENUE
INGESTS
INGRAIN
INGRATE
INGRESS
INGROUP
INGROWN
ONGOING
ONGUARD
UNGIRDS
UNGLUED
UNGODLY
UNGUENT

•N•G•••
ANAGRAM
ENDGAME
ENIGMAS
KNIGHTS
ONAGERS
SNAGGED
SNIGGER
SNIGGLE
SNIGLET
SNUGGER
SNUGGLE

•N••G••
ANTIGEN
ANTIGUA
ENCAGED
ENCAGES
ENGAGED
ENGAGES
ENRAGED
ENRAGES
ENSIGNS
INDIGOS
INSIGHT
INTEGER
INTEGRA
INVOGUE
ONSIGHT
SNAGGED
SNIGGER
SNIGGLE
SNUGGER
SNUGGLE
UNCAGED
UNCAGES

•N•••G•
ANALOGS
ANALOGY
ENDINGS
ENGORGE
ENLARGE
INDULGE
INNINGS
INVEIGH
ONSTAGE
ONTHEGO
UNCLOGS
UNDERGO
UNPLUGS
UNSNAGS

•N••••G
ANGLING
ANTEING
ANTILOG
ENDUING
ENSUING
ENURING
ENVYING
GNAWING
INCHING
INKLING
INURING
KNEEING
KNIFING
KNOWING
ONGOING
SNAKING
SNARING
SNIPING
SNORING
SNOWING
UNDOING
UNDYING
UNITING
UNTYING

••NG•••
BANGING
BANGKOK
BANGLES
BANGSUP
BENGALI
BENGALS
BINGHAM
BINGING
BINGOES
BONGING
BONGOES
BUNGEES
BUNGING
BUNGLED
BUNGLER
BUNGLES
CONGAED
CONGAME
CONGEAL
CONGERS
CONGEST
DANGERS
DANGLED
DANGLER
DANGLES
DINGBAT

DINGIER
DINGILY
DINGING
DINGLES
DINGOES
DUNGEON
FINGERS
FUNGOES
GANGING
GANGLED
GANGLIA
GANGSAW
GANGSTA
GANGSUP
GANGWAY
GENGHIS
GINGERS
GINGERY
GINGHAM
GINGIVA
GONGING
HANGARS
HANGDOG
HANGERS
HANGING
HANGMAN
HANGMEN
HANGOFF
HANGOUT
HANGSIN
HANGSON
HANGSUP
HANGTEN
HANGUPS
HINGING
HUNGARY
HUNGERS
HUNGOUT
JANGLED
JANGLES
JINGLED
JINGLES
JINGOES
JUNGLES
KINGDOM
KINGING
KINGMAN
KINGPIN
KINGRAT
KINGTUT
LANGDON
LANGLEY
LANGTRY
LANGUID
LANGUOR
LANGURS
LENGTHS
LENGTHY
LINGERS
LINGOES
LINGUAL
LONGAGO
LONGBOW
LONGEST
LONGING
LONGISH
LONGRUN
LONGTON
LONGUES
LUNGEAT
LUNGING
MANGERS
MANGIER
MANGLED
MANGLES
MANGOES
MINGLED
MINGLER
MINGLES
MONGERS
MONGOLS
MONGREL
PENGUIN
PINGING
PONGIDS
PUNGENT
RANGERS
RANGIER
RANGING
RANGOON
RINGERS
RINGING
RINGLET
RINGOUT
RINGSUP
SANGOUT
SANGRIA
SINGERS
SINGING
SINGLED
SINGLES
SINGOUT
SINGSTO
SUNGODS
SYNGMAN
TANGELO
TANGENT
TANGERE
TANGIER
TANGLED
TANGLES
TANGOED
TINGING
TINGLED
TINGLES
TONGANS
TONGUED
TONGUES
TUNGOIL
VANGOGH
WANGLED
WANGLER
WANGLES
WINGERS
WINGING
WINGNUT
WINGSIT
WINGTIP
YANGTZE
ZINGERS
ZINGIER
ZINGING

••N•G••

DONEGAL
FINAGLE
HANDGUN
LINAGES
MANAGED
MANAGER
MANAGES
MANAGUA
MANEGES
MENAGES
NONAGON
RENEGED
RENEGER
RENEGES
RONTGEN
SENEGAL
TANAGER
TONIGHT
VINEGAR

••N••G•

AWNINGS
BANDAGE
BONDAGE
CONDIGN
CONSIGN
GUNDOGS
INNINGS
LINEAGE
LININGS
LINKAGE
LONGAGO
MONTAGE
MONTEGO
PANURGE
SINKAGE
SUNDOGS
SYNERGY
TONNAGE
VANGOGH
VANTAGE
VINTAGE

••N•••G

BANDING
BANGING
BANKING
BANNING
BENDING
BINDING
BINGING
BINNING
BONDING
BONGING
BUNGING
BUNKING
BUNTING
CANNING
CANTING
CENSING
CONKING
CONNING
CUNNING
DANCING
DENTING
DENYING
DINGING
DONKING
DONNING
DUNKING
DUNNING
FANNING
FENCING
FENDING
FINDING
FINKING
FUNDING
FUNNING
GANGING
GINNING
GINSENG
GONGING
GUNNING
HANDBAG
HANDING
HANGDOG
HANGING
HINGING
HINTING
HONKING
HUNTING
JINKING
JINXING
JUNEBUG
JUNKING
KINGING
KINKING
LANDING
LANSING
LENDING
LINKING
LONGING
LUNGING
MANNING
MENDING
MINCING
MINDING
MINTING
MONOLOG
OINKING
PANNING
PANTING
PENDING
PENNING
PINGING
PINKING
PINNING
PONYING
PUNNING
PUNTING
RANGING
RANKING
RANTING
RENDING
RENTING
RINGING
RINSING
RUNNING
SANDBAG
SANDHOG
SANDING
SENDING
SENSING
SINGING
SINKING
SUNNING
SYNCING
TANKING
TANNING
TENDING
TENSING
TENTING
TINGING
TINTING
VENDING
VENTING
WANTING
WENDING
WINCING
WINDBAG
WINDING
WINGING
WINKING
WINNING
YANKING
ZINGING
ZONKING

•••NG••

AMONGST
ATINGLE
AVENGED
AVENGER
AVENGES
BRINGER
BRINGIN
BRINGON
BRINGTO
BRINGUP
CHANGED
CHANGER
CHANGES
CLANGED
CLANGOR
CLINGTO
CRINGED
CRINGES
DOINGIN
DOINGUP
EVANGEL
FLANGES
FRINGED
FRINGES
GOINGAT
GOINGBY
GOINGIN
GOINGON
GOINGUP
GRANGER
GRANGES
ICINGIN
JOHNGAY
KLINGON
KRINGLE
LOUNGED
LOUNGER
LOUNGES
LYINGTO
ORANGES
OWINGTO
PLUNGED
PLUNGER
PLUNGES
PRONGED
SHANGRI
SHINGLE
SLINGER
SPANGLE
SPANGLY
SPONGED
SPONGER
SPONGES
STENGEL
STINGER
STUNGUN
SWINGBY
SWINGER
TLINGIT
TSONGAS
TWANGED
TWINGED
TWINGES
TYINGIN
TYINGUP
USINGUP
WRANGLE
WRINGER
WRONGED
WRONGER
WRONGLY
YOUNGER
YOUNGMC
YOUNGUN
ZWINGLI

•••N•G•

COINAGE
EGGNOGS
IRONAGE
PEONAGE
TEENAGE
TONNAGE
UNSNAGS

•••N••G

ATONING
BANNING
BEANBAG
BEANING
BINNING
BRINING
BURNING
CANNING
CLONING
COINING
CONNING
CORNDOG
CORNING
CRANING
CUNNING
DAMNING
DARNING
DAWNING
DONNING
DOWNING
DRONING
DUNNING
EARNING
EVENING
FANNING
FAWNING
FUNNING
GAINING
GINNING
GUNNING
HORNING
IRONING
JOINING
KEENING
KERNING
LEANING
LIMNING
LOANING
MANNING
MEANING
MOANING
MOONDOG
MOONING
MORNING
OPENING
OPINING
PANNING
PAWNING
PENNING
PFENNIG
PHONING
PINNING
PLANING
PRUNING
PUNNING
RAINING
REINING
RUINING
RUNNING
SEINING
SHINDIG
SHINING
SIGNING
STONING
SUNNING
TANNING
TURNING
TWINING
VEINING
WARNING
WEANING
WHINING
WINNING
YARNING
YAWNING

••••NG•

AIRINGS
ARRANGE
AWNINGS
BARONGS
BELONGS
CASINGS
COMINGS
DOMINGO
DUGONGS
DURANGO
EDGINGS
ENDINGS
EXPUNGE
FACINGS
FILINGS
FIRINGS
FIXINGS
HAZINGS
IMPINGE
INNINGS
LACINGS
LININGS
LIVINGS
LOZENGE
MAKINGS
MELANGE
OBLONGS
OUTINGS
PARINGS
PILINGS
PIPINGS
RATINGS
RAVINGS
REHANGS
RESINGS
REVENGE
RISINGS
RULINGS
SARONGS
SAVINGS
SAYINGS
SIDINGS
SIZINGS
SPRINGS
SPRINGY
STRANGE
STRINGS
STRINGY
SYRINGA
SYRINGE
TAPINGS
THRONGS
TIDINGS
TIMINGS
VIKINGS

••••N•G

PFENNIG

•••••NG

ABASING
ABATING
ABIDING
ABUSING
ACHTUNG
ADDLING
ADORING
ALAKING
ALLYING
AMAZING
AMBLING
AMUSING
ANGLING
ANTEING
ARCHING
ARGUING
ARISING
ARTSONG
ATONING
AVOWING
AWAKING
BABYING
BACKING
BAGGING
BAILING
BAITING
BALDING
BALKING
BANDING
BANGING
BANKING
BANNING
BARBING
BARGING
BARKING
BARRING
BASHING
BASKING
BASTING
BATHING
BATTING
BATWING
BAWLING
BEADING
BEAMING
BEANING
BEARING
BEATING
BEDDING
BEEFING
BEEPING
BEGGING
BEIJING
BELLING
BELTING
BELYING
BENDING
BESTING
BETTING
BIASING
BIDDING
BIGBANG
BILKING
BILLING
BINDING
BINGING
BINNING
BIRDING
BIRLING
BITTING
BLAMING
BLARING
BLAZING
BLOWING
BLUEING
BOATING
BOBBING
BOGGING
BOILING
BOLTING
BOMBING
BONDING
BONGING
BOOKING
BOOMING
BOOTING
BOPPING
BOSSING
BOWLING
BRACING
BRAKING
BRAVING
BRAYING
BRAZING
BREWING
BRIBING
BRINING
BUCKING
BUDDING
BUDGING
BUFFING
BUGGING
BUGLING
BULGING
BULKING
BULLING
BUMMING
BUMPING
BUNGING
BUNKING
BUNTING
BUOYING
BURLING
BURNING
BURPING
BURYING
BUSHING
BUSSING
BUSTING
BUSYING
BUTTING
BUZZING
CABLING
CACHING
CADGING
CALKING
CALLING
CALMING
CALVING
CAMPING
CANNING
CANTING
CAPPING
CARDING
CARPING
CARTING
CARVING
CASHING
CASTING
CATTING
CAUSING
CEASING
CEILING
CENSING
CHAFING
CHASING
CHEWING
CHIDING
CHIMING
CLAWING
CLONING
CLOSING
CLOYING
CLUEING
COATING
COAXING
COCKING
COIFING
COILING
COINING
COMBING
CONKING
CONNING
COOKING
COOLING
COOPING
COPPING
COPYING
CORDING
CORKING
CORNING
COSTING
COWLING
COZYING
CRANING
CRATING
CRAVING
CRAZING
CREWING
CROWING
CUFFING
CULLING
CUNNING
CUPPING
CURBING
CURDING
CURLING
CURSING
CURVING
CUSSING
CUTTING
CYCLING
CYYOUNG
DABBING
DAMMING
DAMNING
DAMPING
DANCING
DAPPING
DARLING
DARNING
DARTING
DASHING
DAUBING
DAWNING
DAYLONG
DEALING
DECKING
DEEDING
DEEMING
DEFYING
DEICING
DELEING
DELVING
DENTING
DENYING
DERRING
DIALING
DIETING
DIGGING
DIMMING
DINGING
DIPPING
DISHING
DOCKING
DODGING
DOFFING
DOGGING
DOLLING
DONKING
DONNING
DOOMING
DOTTING
DOUSING
DOWNING
DOWSING
DRAPING
DRAWING
DRAYING
DRIVING
DRONING
DUBBING
DUCKING
DUCTING
DUELING
DULLING
DUMPING
DUNKING
DUNNING
DUSTING
EAGLING
EARNING
EARRING
ECHOING
EDDYING
EDITING
EDUCING
ELATING
ELIDING
ELOPING
ELUDING
ELUTING
EMOTING
ENDUING
ENSUING
ENURING
ENVYING
ERASING
ERELONG
ERODING
ESPYING
ETCHING
EVADING
EVENING
EVOKING
EXILING
EXITING
EXUDING
FAGGING
FAILING
FAIRING
FALLING
FANNING
FARMING
FASTING
FAWNING
FEARING
FEEDING
FEELING
FELLING
FENCING
FENDING
FEUDING
FIBBING
FILLING
FILMING
FINDING
FINKING
FIRMING
FISHING
FITTING
FIZZING
FLAKING
FLAMING
FLARING
FLAWING
FLAYING
FLEEING
FLEMING
FLEXING
FLOWING
FLUTING
FOALING
FOAMING
FOBBING
FOGGING
FOILING
FOLDING
FOOLING
FOOTING
FORCING
FORDING
FORGING
FORKING
FORMING
FOULING
FOWLING
FRAMING
FRAYING
FREEING
FUDGING
FUELING
FUNDING
FUNNING
FURLING
FURLONG
FURRING
FUSSING
FUZZING
GABBING
GADDING
GAFFING
GAGGING
GAINING
GAITING
GALLING
GANGING
GAPPING
GARBING
GASHING
GASPING
GATLING
GAUGING
GAWKING
GEARING
GELDING
GELLING
GETTING
GILDING
GILLING
GINNING
GINSENG
GIRDING
GLARING
GLAZING
GLIDING
GLOWING
GNAWING
GOADING
GOALONG
GOLDING
GOLFING
GONGING
GOOFING
GOOSING
GORGING
GOSLING
GOUGING
GOWRONG
GRACING
GRADING
GRATING
GRAVING
GRAYING
GRAZING
GREYING
GRIPING
GROPING
GROWING
GUIDING
GULFING
GULLING
GULPING
GUMMING
GUNNING
GUSHING
GUSTING
GUTTING
GYPPING
HACKING
HAILING
HALOING
HALTING
HALVING
HAMMING
HANDING
HANGING
HARDING
HARKING
HARMING
HARPING
HASHING
HASTING
HATTING
HAULING
HAWKING
HEADING
HEALING
HEAPING
HEARING
HEATING
HEAVING
HEDGING
HEEDING
HEELING
HEFTING
HELMING
HELPING
HEMMING
HERDING
HERRING
HILLING
HINGING
HINTING

HISSING
HITTING
HOAXING
HOBOING
HOCKING
HOGGING
HOLDING
HONKING
HOOFING
HOOKING
HOOPING
HOOTING
HOPPING
HORNING
HORSING
HOSTING
HOUSING
HOWLING
HUFFING
HUGGING
HULKING
HULLING
HUMMING
HUNTING
HURLING
HURTING
HUSHING
HUSKING
HYPOING
IMAGING
IMBUING
INCHING
INKLING
INURING
IRONING
ISSUING
ITCHING
JABBING
JACKING
JAGGING
JAILING
JAMMING
JARRING
JAZZING
JEERING
JELLING
JERKING
JESTING
JETTING
JIGGING
JILTING
JINKING
JINXING
JOBBING
JOGGING
JOINING
JOLTING
JOSHING
JOTTING
JUDGING
JUICING
JUMPING
JUNKING
JURYING
JUTTING
KAYOING
KEELING
KEENING
KEEPING
KERNING
KEYRING
KICKING
KIDDING

KILLING
KILTING
KINGING
KINKING
KIPLING
KISSING
KNEEING
KNIFING
KNOWING
LACKING
LADLING
LAGGING
LAMMING
LANDING
LANSING
LAPPING
LAPSING
LAPWING
LARDING
LASHING
LASTING
LATHING
LAUDING
LEADING
LEAFING
LEAKING
LEANING
LEAPING
LEASING
LEAVING
LEERING
LEGGING
LEMMING
LENDING
LESSING
LETTING
LEVYING
LIBBING
LICKING
LIFTING
LILTING
LIMBING
LIMNING
LIMPING
LINKING
LIPPING
LISPING
LISTING
LOADING
LOAFING
LOAMING
LOANING
LOBBING
LOCKING
LODGING
LOFTING
LOGGING
LOLLING
LONGING
LOOKING
LOOMING
LOOPING
LOOSING
LOOTING
LOPPING
LORDING
LOTTING
LOUSING
LUCKING
LUFFING
LUGGING
LULLING
LUMPING

LUNGING
LURKING
LUSTING
MADDING
MAILING
MALTING
MANNING
MAPPING
MARKING
MARRING
MASHING
MASKING
MASSING
MATTING
MAULING
MEANING
MEETING
MELDING
MELTING
MENDING
MEOWING
MERGING
MESHING
MESSING
MEWLING
MIFFING
MILKING
MILLING
MINCING
MINDING
MINTING
MISSING
MISTING
MITRING
MOANING
MOBBING
MOCKING
MOILING
MOLDING
MOLTING
MOONING
MOORING
MOPPING
MORNING
MOSSING
MOUSING
MUCKING
MUFFING
MUGGING
MULLING
MUSHING
MUSSING
MUSTANG
NABBING
NAGGING
NAILING
NAPPING
NEARING
NECKING
NEEDING
NESTING
NETTING
NICKING
NIPPING
NODDING
NOISING
NOOSING
NOSHING
NOTHING
NUDGING
NULLING
NUMBING
NURSING

NUTTING
OBEYING
OINKING
OKAYING
ONGOING
OPENING
OPINING
ORATING
OUSTING
PACKING
PADDING
PAIRING
PALLING
PALMING
PANNING
PANTING
PARKING
PARRING
PARSING
PARTING
PASSING
PASTING
PATTING
PAULING
PAUSING
PAWNING
PEAKING
PEALING
PECKING
PEEKING
PEELING
PEEPING
PEERING
PEEVING
PEGGING
PELTING
PENDING
PENNING
PEPPING
PERKING
PERMING
PETTING
PHASING
PHONING
PICKING
PIECING
PIGGING
PILLING
PINGING
PINKING
PINNING
PIQUING
PITHING
PITTING
PITYING
PLACING
PLANING
PLATING
PLAYING
PLOWING
PLUMING
POISING
POLLING
PONYING
POOLING
POOPING
POPPING
POSTING
POTTING
POURING
POUTING
PRATING
PRAYING

PRICING
PRIDING
PRIMING
PRIZING
PROBING
PROLONG
PROSING
PROVING
PRUNING
PUDDING
PUFFING
PULLING
PULSING
PUMPING
PUNNING
PUNTING
PURGING
PURLING
PURRING
PURSING
PUSHING
PUTTING
QUAKING
QUEUING
QUOTING
RACKING
RAFTING
RAGGING
RAIDING
RAILING
RAINING
RAISING
RAMMING
RANGING
RANKING
RANTING
RAPPING
RASPING
RATTING
RAZZING
RDLAING
READING
REAMING
REAPING
REARING
REDDING
REDOING
REDWING
REEDING
REEFING
REEKING
REELING
REFFING
REINING
RELYING
RENDING
RENTING
RESTING
REVVING
RHYMING
RIBBING
RIDDING
RIDGING
RIFFING
RIFLING
RIFTING
RIGGING
RIMMING
RINGING
RINSING
RIOTING
RIPPING
RISKING

ROAMING
ROARING
ROBBING
ROCKING
ROILING
ROLLING
ROMPING
ROOFING
ROOKING
ROOMING
ROOTING
ROTTING
ROUGING
ROUSING
ROUTING
RUBBING
RUCHING
RUCKING
RUINING
RUNNING
RUSHING
RUSTING
SACKING
SAGGING
SAILING
SALTING
SALVING
SAMSUNG
SANDING
SAPLING
SAPPING
SASSING
SCALING
SCARING
SCOPING
SCORING
SEALING
SEAMING
SEARING
SEATING
SEEDING
SEEKING
SEEMING
SEEPING
SEINING
SEIZING
SELLING
SENDING
SENSING
SERLING
SERVING
SETTING
SHADING
SHAKING
SHAMING
SHAPING
SHARING
SHAVING
SHEBANG
SHINING
SHOEING
SHOOING
SHORING
SHOVING
SHOWING
SIBLING
SICCING
SIDLING
SIFTING
SIGHING
SIGNING
SILOING
SILTING

SINGING
SINKING
SIPPING
SITTING
SKATING
SKEWING
SLAKING
SLATING
SLAVING
SLICING
SLIDING
SLOPING
SLOWING
SMILING
SMITING
SMOKING
SNAKING
SNARING
SNIPING
SNORING
SNOWING
SOAKING
SOAPING
SOARING
SOBBING
SOCKING
SODDING
SOILING
SOLOING
SOLVING
SOPPING
SORTING
SOURING
SPACING
SPADING
SPARING
SPAYING
SPEWING
SPICING
SPIKING
SPITING
SPOKING
SPUMING
STAGING
STAKING
STARING
STATING
STAVING
STAYING
STEWING
STOKING
STONING
STORING
STOWING
STYLING
SUBBING
SUCKING
SUDSING
SUITING
SULKING
SUMMING
SUNNING
SUPPING
SURFING
SURGING
SUSSING
SWAYING
SWIPING
SYNCING
TABBING
TABLING
TACKING
TAGGING

TAILING
TALKING
TAMPING
TANKING
TANNING
TAPPING
TARRING
TASKING
TASTING
TATTING
TAXIING
TEAMING
TEARING
TEASING
TEDDING
TEEMING
TELLING
TENDING
TENSING
TENTING
TERMING
TESTING
THAWING
TICKING
TIDYING
TIERING
TILLING
TILTING
TINGING
TINTING
TIPPING
TITHING
TITLING
TOGGING
TOILING
TOLLING
TOOLING
TOOTING
TOPPING
TOSSING
TOTTING
TOURING
TOUTING
TRACING
TRADING
TREEING
TRUEING
TUCKING
TUFTING
TUGGING
TURNING
TWINING
UNDOING
UNDYING
UNITING
UNTYING
UPSWING
VALUING
VAMPING
VARYING
VEERING
VEGGING
VEILING
VEINING
VENDING
VENTING
VERGING
VESTING
VETOING
VETTING
VIEWING
VOICING
VOIDING

WADDING
WAFTING
WAGGING
WAILING
WAITING
WAIVING
WALKING
WALLING
WANTING
WARDING
WARMING
WARNING
WARPING
WARRING
WASHING
WASTING
WAXWING
WEANING
WEARING
WEAVING
WEBBING
WEDDING
WEDGING
WEEDING
WEEPING
WELDING
WELLING
WELTING
WENDING
WETTING
WHALING
WHILING
WHINING
WHITING
WILDING
WILLING
WILTING
WINCING
WINDING
WINGING
WINKING
WINNING
WISHING
WISPING
WITTING
WOLFING
WOOFING
WORDING
WORKING
WRITING
WYOMING
XRATING
XRAYING
YAKKING
YANKING
YAPPING
YARNING
YAWNING
YELLING
YELPING
YESSING
YIPPING
YOWLING
YOYOING
ZAGGING
ZAPPING
ZEITUNG
ZEROING
ZIGGING
ZINGING
ZIPPING
ZONKING
ZOOMING

N•H••••
NAHUATL

N••H•••
NAPHTHA
NEPHEWS
NEWHART
NICHOLS
NIGHEST
NIGHTIE
NIGHTLY
NOBHILL
NOSHERS
NOSHING
NOSHOWS
NOTHING
NOTHOME
NOWHERE

N•••H••
NARTHEX
NARWHAL
NATCHEZ
NAUGHTS
NAUGHTY
NAVAHOS
NEIGHED
NEITHER
NORTHER
NOTCHED
NOTCHES

N••••H•
NAPHTHA
NATASHA
NIEBUHR
NOGUCHI

N•••••H
NCWYETH
NEBBISH
NEOLITH
NEWMATH
NINEVEH
NOURISH

•NH••••
ENHANCE
INHABIT
INHALED
INHALER
INHALES
INHASTE
INHERED
INHERES
INHERIT
INHIBIT
INHOUSE
INHUMAN
UNHANDS
UNHANDY
UNHAPPY
UNHEARD
UNHITCH
UNHOOKS
UNHORSE

•N•H•••
ANAHEIM
ANAHUAC
ANCHORS
ANCHOVY
ANTHEMS
ANTHERS
ANTHILL
ANTHONY
ENCHAIN
ENCHANT
ENTHUSE
INAHEAP
INCHING
INKHORN
INPHASE
INSHAPE
INSHORT
ONSHORE
ONTHEGO
ONTHEQT
UNCHAIN
UNSHORN

•N••H••
ANOTHER
GNASHED
GNASHES
KNIGHTS
KNISHES
KNOWHOW
ONESHOT

•N•••H•
ANARCHY
GNOCCHI
INSIGHT
ONSIGHT

•N••••H
ANOUILH
ANSPACH
ANTIOCH
ENGLISH
INARUSH
INDEPTH
INDUTCH
INTRUTH
INVEIGH
KNAVISH
UNCOUTH
UNEARTH
UNHITCH
UNLATCH
UNLEASH
UNTRUTH

••NH•••
MANHOLE
MANHOOD
MANHOUR
MANHUNT
MENHIRS
MYNHEER
PINHEAD
PINHOLE
RUNHOME
TINHATS
TINHORN

••N•H••
BANSHEE
BENCHED
BENCHES
BENTHAM
BINGHAM
BUNCHED
BUNCHES
CINCHED
CINCHES
CONCHES
CYNTHIA
DONAHUE
FINCHES
GENGHIS
GINGHAM
GUNSHOT
GUNTHER
HONCHOS
HUNCHED
HUNCHES
KINSHIP
LUNCHED
LUNCHER
LUNCHES
MENTHOL
MENUHIN
MONTHLY
MUNCHED
MUNCHER
MUNCHES
PANCHAX
PANTHER
PINCHAS
PINCHED
PINCHER
PINCHES
PONCHOS
PUNCHED
PUNCHER
PUNCHES
PUNCHIN
PUNCHUP
PYNCHON
RANCHED
RANCHER
RANCHES
RANCHOS
SANDHOG
SYNCHED
SYNCHES
WENCHES
WINCHED
WINCHES
XANTHAN
XANTHIC

••N••H•
DENNEHY
EUNUCHS
KENOSHA
LENGTHS
LENGTHY
ORNITHO
PANACHE
PENUCHE
PUNKAHS
TONIGHT
ZENITHS

••N•••H
BENEATH
BONEASH
FINNISH
HANUKAH
KENNETH
LONGISH
MANNISH
MENORAH
MONARCH
MONKISH
NINEVEH
PANFISH
PINKISH
RUNWITH
SUNBATH
SUNFISH
TANNISH
VANGOGH

•••NH••
IVANHOE
RAINHAT
WERNHER

•••N•H•
ACANTHI
BLANCHE
BRONCHI
CRUNCHY
DENNEHY
PAUNCHY
PLINTHS

•••N••H
BURNISH
CORNISH
FINNISH
FURNISH
GARNISH
KENNETH
MANNISH
SPANISH
SPINACH
TANNISH
TARNISH
VARNISH

••••NH•
PIRANHA

••••N•H
CORINTH
DOZENTH
ROMANSH
SCRUNCH
SEVENTH
SQUINCH
STAUNCH

NI•••••
NIAGARA
NIBBLED
NIBBLER
NIBBLES
NIBLICK
NICCOLO
NICHOLS
NICKELS
NICKERS
NICKING
NICOLAS
NICOSIA
NIEBUHR
NIELSEN
NIFTIER
NIFTILY
NIGERIA
NIGGARD
NIGGLED
NIGGLES
NIGHEST
NIGHTIE
NIGHTLY
NIKOLAI

NILSSON
NIMBLER
NIMRODS
NINEVEH
NINNIES
NIOBIUM
NIPPERS
NIPPIER
NIPPING
NIRVANA
NITPICK
NITRATE
NITRIDE
NITRITE
NITROUS
NITTANY
NITWITS

N•I••••

NAIADES
NAILERS
NAILING
NAILSET
NAIROBI
NAIVELY
NAIVETE
NEIGHED
NEITHER
NOISIER
NOISILY
NOISING
NOISOME

N••I•••

NABISCO
NAMIBIA
NATIONS
NATIVES
NEVILLE
NOMINAL
NOMINEE
NORIEGA
NOSIEST
NOTICED
NOTICES
NOTIONS
NOVICES
NOXIOUS
NUBIANS
NUDISTS

N•••I••

NABBING
NAGGING
NAILING
NANNIES
NAPKINS
NAPPING
NAPTIME
NASTIER
NASTILY
NATRIUM
NATTIER
NATTILY
NEARING
NEBBISH
NECKING
NEEDIER
NEEDILY
NEEDING
NEOLITH
NEREIDS
NERVIER
NERVILY
NESTING
NETTING
NEWSIER
NIBLICK
NICKING
NIFTIER
NIFTILY
NINNIES
NIOBIUM
NIPPIER
NIPPING
NITPICK
NITRIDE
NITRITE
NITWITS
NOBHILL
NODDING
NOETICS
NOGGINS
NOISIER
NOISILY
NOISING
NOOSING
NORDICS
NOSHING
NOTHING
NOURISH
NUBBIER
NUBBINS
NUCLIDE
NUDGING
NUDNIKS
NULLIFY
NULLING
NUMBING
NUNCIOS
NUPTIAL
NURSING
NUTRIAS
NUTTIER
NUTTILY
NUTTING

N••••I•

NAMIBIA
NATALIA
NATALIE
NAYSAID
NECKTIE
NEMESIS
NEPALIS
NICOSIA
NIGERIA
NIGHTIE
NOKOMIS
NOMADIC
NONSKID
NONSLIP
NOSTRIL
NOTABIT
NUCLEIC
NUMERIC

N•••••I

NAIROBI
NIKOLAI
NOGUCHI

•NI••••

ANILINE
ANIMALS
ANIMATE
ANIMATO
ANIMISM
ANIMIST
ANISEED
ENIGMAS
ENISLED
ENISLES
INITIAL
KNIEVEL
KNIFING
KNIGHTS
KNISHES
KNITTED
KNITTER
SNICKER
SNIDELY
SNIDEST
SNIFFAT
SNIFFED
SNIFFER
SNIFFLE
SNIFTER
SNIGGER
SNIGGLE
SNIGLET
SNIPEAT
SNIPING
SNIPPED
SNIPPET
SNIVELS
UNICORN
UNIFIED
UNIFIER
UNIFIES
UNIFORM
UNIPODS
UNISONS
UNITARY
UNITERS
UNITIES
UNITING
UNITIVE

•N•I•••

ANCIENT
ANDIRON
ANOINTS
ANTIART
ANTIBES
ANTIGEN
ANTIGUA
ANTILOG
ANTIOCH
ANTIQUE
ANTIWAR
ANXIETY
ANXIOUS
ENDINGS
ENDIVES
ENGINES
ENGIRDS
ENLISTS
ENLIVEN
ENSIGNS
ENSILED
ENSILES
ENTICED
ENTICER
ENTICES
ENTITLE
ENVIOUS
INCIPIT
INCISED
INCISES
INCISOR
INCITED
INCITER
INCITES
INCIVIL
INDIANA
INDIANS
INDICES
INDICIA
INDICTS
INDIGOS
INDITED
INDITES
INFIDEL
INFIELD
INHIBIT
INNINGS
INSIDER
INSIDES
INSIGHT
INSIPID
INSISTS
INVITED
INVITES
INVITRO
ONEIDAS
ONSIGHT
UNAIDED
UNAIMED
UNAIRED
UNBINDS
UNCIALS
UNCIVIL
UNFIXED
UNGIRDS
UNHITCH
UNKINKS
UNLIKED
UNLINED
UNLINKS
UNOILED
UNPILED
UNPILES
UNWINDS
UNWISER

•N••I••

ANANIAS
ANGLING
ANGRIER
ANGRILY
ANILINE
ANIMISM
ANIMIST
ANNUITY
ANODIZE
ANOUILH
ANTEING
ANTHILL
ANTLION
ANTOINE
ANTSIER
ANYTIME
ENDUING
ENDWISE
ENEMIES
ENGLISH
ENJOINS
ENSUING
ENSUITE
ENTAILS
ENTRIES
ENTWINE
ENURING
ENVYING
GNAWING
INBRIEF
INCHING
INCLINE
INFLICT
INITIAL
INKLING
INPOINT
INPRINT
INQUIRE
INQUIRY
INSPIRE
INSTILL
INSTILS
INTUITS
INURING
INUTILE
INVEIGH
INVOICE
KNAVISH
KNEEING
KNIFING
KNOWING
ONADIET
ONETIME
ONGOING
ONTRIAL
SNAKIER
SNAKING
SNARING
SNIPING
SNORING
SNOWIER
SNOWING
UNALIKE
UNCOILS
UNCTION
UNDOING
UNDYING
UNIFIED
UNIFIER
UNIFIES
UNITIES
UNITING
UNITIVE
UNKNITS
UNSTICK
UNTRIED
UNTWIST
UNTYING
UNVEILS

•N•••I•

ANAEMIA
ANAHEIM
ANDROID
ANDYKIM
ANEROID
ANGELIC
ANNELID
ANOSMIA
ANOSMIC
ANTACID
ANTONIA
ANTONIN
ANTONIO
ENCHAIN
ENCOMIA
ENDEMIC
ENTRAIN
GNOSTIC
INASNIT
INASPIN
INCIPIT
INCIVIL
INDICIA
INERTIA
INGRAIN
INHABIT
INHERIT
INHIBIT
INORBIT
INSIPID
INSULIN
INTERIM
INTROIT
INVALID
ONASSIS
ONTARIO
SNEAKIN
SNOWSIN
UNCHAIN
UNCIVIL

•N••••I

ANASAZI
GNOCCHI

••NI•••

AMNIONS
ARNICAS
AWNINGS
BENISON
BONIEST
BONITOS
BUNIONS
CANINES
CONICAL
CONIFER
CYNICAL
DANIELS
DENIALS
DENIECE
DENIERS
DENIZEN
FANIONS
FINIALS
FINICKY
IGNITED
IGNITER
IGNITES
INNINGS
IONIZED
IONIZER
IONIZES
JANITOR
JUNIORS
JUNIPER
LENIENT
LININGS
MANIACS
MANILOW
MANIPLE
MANITOU
MENIALS
MENISCI
MINIBUS
MINICAM
MINIMAL
MINIMUM
MINIONS
MINIVAN
MINIVER
MONIKER
MONIQUE
MONITOR
OMNIBUS
ORNITHO
PANICKY
PANICLE
PINIEST
PINIONS
PONIARD
PUNIEST
RANINTO
RUNINTO
SANIBEL
SENIORS
TINIEST
TONIEST
TONIGHT
TUNICLE
TUNISIA
VANILLA
VANILLI
VENISON
ZANIEST
ZENITHS

••N•I••

ANNUITY
AUNTIES
BANDIED
BANDIES
BANDING
BANDITO
BANDITS
BANGING
BANKING
BANNING
BENDING
BINDING
BINGING
BINNING
BONDING
BONFIRE
BONGING
BONNIER
BONNILY
BUNGING
BUNKING
BUNNIES
BUNTING
CANDICE
CANDIDA
CANDIDE
CANDIDS
CANDIED
CANDIES
CANNIER
CANNILY
CANNING
CANTINA
CANTING
CENSING
CENTIME
CENTIMO
CONCISE
CONDIGN
CONFIDE
CONFINE
CONFIRM
CONKING
CONNICK
CONNIFF
CONNING
CONNIVE
CONSIGN
CONSIST
CONVICT
CUNNING
DANCING
DANDIER
DANDIES
DENSITY
DENTINE
DENTING
DENTIST
DENYING
DINGIER
DINGILY
DINGING
DINKIER
DINKIES
DONKING
DONNING
DUNKING
DUNKIRK
DUNLINS
DUNNING
FANCIED
FANCIER
FANCIES
FANCILY
FANNING
FANZINE
FENCING
FENDING
FINDING
FINKING
FINNISH
FONTINA
FUNDING
FUNKIER
FUNNIER
FUNNIES
FUNNILY
FUNNING
GANGING
GENTIAN
GENTILE
GENUINE
GINFIZZ
GINGIVA
GINMILL
GINNING
GONGING
GUNFIRE
GUNKIER
GUNNIES
GUNNING
HANDIER
HANDILY
HANDING
HANGING
HANKIES
HENBITS
HINGING
HINNIES
HINTING
HONKING
HUNTING
JANEIRO
JANVIER
JENNIES
JINKING
JINXING
JUNKIER
JUNKIES
JUNKING
KINGING
KINKIER
KINKING
KONTIKI
LANDING
LANKIER
LANKILY
LANSING
LENDING
LENTILS
LINBIAO
LINDIED
LINDIES
LINKING
LINTIER
LONGING
LONGISH
LUNGING
MANCINI
MANGIER
MANKIND
MANLIER
MANNING
MANNISH
MANSION
MENDING
MENHIRS
MENTION
MINCING
MINDING
MINTIER
MINTING
MONKISH
MUNTINS
NANNIES
NINNIES
NUNCIOS
OINKING
PANDITS
PANFISH
PANNIER
PANNING
PANPIPE
PANSIES
PANTING
PENCILS
PENDING
PENNIES
PENNING
PENSION
PENSIVE
PINGING
PINKIES
PINKING
PINKISH
PINNING
PONGIDS
PONTIAC
PONTIFF
PONTINE
PONTIUS
PONYING
PUNDITS
PUNKIES
PUNNING
PUNTING
RANDIER
RANGIER
RANGING
RANKING
RANRIOT
RANTING
RENAILS
RENDING
RENNINS
RENTING
RINGING
RINSING
RUNNIER
RUNNING
RUNRIOT
RUNTIER
RUNWITH
SANDIER
SANDING
SANTINI
SANTIRS
SENDING
SENSING
SINGING
SINKING
SUNCITY
SUNDIAL
SUNFISH
SUNKIST
SUNNIER
SUNNILY
SUNNING
SUNRISE
SYNCING
TANGIER
TANKING
TANLINE
TANNING
TANNINS
TANNISH
TANSIES
TENDING
TENNIEL
TENPINS
TENSILE
TENSING
TENSION
TENSIVE
TENTING
TINGING
TINNIER
TINNILY
TINTING
TONSILS
TONTINE
TUNNIES
VANDINE
VENDING
VENTING
WANTING
WENDING
WINCING
WINDIER
WINDING
WINGING
WINKING
WINNING
YANKING
ZINGIER
ZINGING
ZINNIAS
ZONKING

••N••I•

ABNAKIS
AMNESIA
ANNELID
BANDAID
BENAZIR
BENEFIT
BONSOIR
CANONIC
CENTRIC
CONBRIO
CONCEIT
CONDUIT
CONJOIN
CONREID
CONTAIN
CYNTHIA
DINEDIN
DINESIN
DYNAMIC
FANATIC
FANMAIL
FANTAIL
FUNFAIR
GANGLIA
GENERIC
GENERIS
GENESIS
GENETIC
GENGHIS
GONERIL
HANDSIN
HANGSIN
HENDRIX
HENREID
JONQUIL
KINETIC
KINGPIN
KINSHIP
LANGUID
LANOLIN
LUNATIC
MANDRIL
MANTRIC
MANUMIT
MENUHIN
MINUTIA
NONSKID
NONSLIP
PENGUIN
PINTAIL
PUNCHIN
SANGRIA
SANLUIS
SENDSIN
SINEDIE
SINKSIN
SUNMAID
SYNODIC
TENDRIL
TINFOIL
TINYTIM
TUNEDIN
TUNESIN
TUNGOIL
TUNISIA
WANTSIN
WINGSIT
WINGTIP
XANTHIC
ZENOBIA

••N•••I

BENGALI
BONJOVI
CANNOLI
KONTIKI
MANCINI
MENISCI
MENOTTI
PUNJABI
SANTINI
VANILLI

•••NI••

ACONITE
ADENINE
AGONIST
AGONIZE
AMENITY
ANANIAS
ASININE
ATONING
BANNING
BEANIES
BEANING
BERNICE
BINNING
BIONICS
BONNIER
BONNILY
BOONIES
BRANIFF
BRINIER
BRINING
BUNNIES
BURNING
BURNISH
CANNIER
CANNILY
CANNING
CARNIES
CATNIPS
CHENIER
CLINICS
CLONING
COINING
CONNICK
CONNIFF
CONNING
CONNIVE
CORNICE
CORNIER
CORNILY
CORNING
CORNISH
CRANIAL
CRANING
CRANIUM
CRONIES
CUNNING
DAMNING
DARNING
DAWNING
DERNIER
DIGNIFY
DIGNITY
DONNING
DOWNIER
DOWNING
DRONING
DUNNING
EARNING
EBONIES
EBONITE
ETHNICS
ETONIAN
EVENING
FANNING
FAWNING
FINNISH
FUNNIER
FUNNIES
FUNNILY
FUNNING
FURNISH
GAINING
GARNISH
GINNING
GRANITE
GRUNION
GUANINE
GUNNIES
GUNNING
HAFNIUM
HAHNIUM
HINNIES
HORNING
HORNIST
IRANIAN
IRONIES
IRONING
JENNIES
JOINING
KEENING
KERNING
LEANING
LEONINE
LIGNITE
LIMNING
LIONIZE
LOANING
LOONIER
LOONIES
MAGNIFY
MANNING
MANNISH
MEANIES
MEANING
MOANING
MOONING
MORNING
NANNIES
NINNIES
NUDNIKS
OLDNICK
OPENING
OPINING
OPINION
OXONIAN
PANNIER
PANNING
PAWNING
PENNIES
PENNING
PEONIES
PHONICS
PHONIER
PHONIES
PHONILY
PHONING
PIANISM
PIANIST
PICNICS
PINNING
PLANING
PRUNING
PUNNING
QUININE
RAINIER
RAINING
REINING
RENNINS
REUNIFY
REUNION

REUNITE
RHENIUM
RUINING
RUNNIER
RUNNING
SEINING
SHINIER
SHINING
SIGNIFY
SIGNING
SPANIEL
SPANISH
SPINIER
STONIER
STONILY
STONING
SUNNIER
SUNNILY
SUNNING
TANNING
TANNINS
TANNISH
TARNISH
TAWNIER
TEENIER
TENNIEL
THINICE
TINNIER
TINNILY
TOWNIES
TRINITY
TUNNIES
TURNING
TURNIPS
TWINING
UNKNITS
URANITE
URANIUM
VARNISH
VEINING
VERNIER
WARNING
WEANING
WEENIES
WHINING
WIENIES
WINNING
WOZNIAK
YARNING
YAWNING
ZINNIAS

•••N•I•
ADONAIS
BLONDIE
BRINGIN
CORNOIL
COUNCIL
CRINOID
DOINGIN
EVENKIS
FRANCIS
FRANKIE
FRANTIC
GOINGIN
HOBNAIL
ICINGIN
IDENTIC
JEANNIE
JOHNNIE
JOINSIN
MOONLIT
MOUNTIE
OPENAIR
OPENPIT
PFENNIG
QUENTIN
REINSIN
SHINDIG
SIGNSIN
STANDIN
STANNIC
STENCIL
THINAIR
TLINGIT
TOENAIL
TRANSIT
TURNSIN
TYINGIN
UTENSIL

•••N••I
ABENAKI
ACANTHI
BRONCHI
CANNOLI
HYUNDAI
SHANGRI
TSUNAMI
ZWINGLI

••••NI•
ACTINIC
ALBANIA
ALBENIZ
AMMONIA
ANTONIA
ANTONIN
ANTONIO
ARMENIA
ARSENIC
ARSENIO
BEATNIK
BEGONIA
BIKINIS
BOTHNIA
BROWNIE
CANONIC
CHRONIC
DAPHNIS
DEMONIC
DRAWNIN
ESTONIA
EUGENIE
HOMINID
INASNIT
JEANNIE
JOHNNIE
KIWANIS
LACONIC
LAVINIA
LEIBNIZ
MASONIC
MELANIE
MELANIN
MORANIS
OCEANIA
OCEANIC
OCEANID
ORGANIC
PARSNIP
PETUNIA
PFENNIG
PHOENIX
PHRENIC
ROMANIA
SELENIC
SHOWNIN
SPUTNIK
STANNIC
STDENIS
SUBUNIT
TAKENIN
TITANIA
TITANIC
YEMENIS

••••N•I
ASHANTI
BASENJI
CHIANTI
DAVINCI
EFFENDI
JUMANJI
KUTENAI
RAPANUI
VIVENDI

•••••NI
AFGHANI
BELLINI
CASSINI
CELLINI
FELLINI
GALVANI
GUARANI
HOUDINI
MANCINI
MARCONI
MARTINI
PADRONI
PUCCINI
ROSSINI
SANTINI
SPUMONI
TERMINI
TORTONI
TYMPANI

N•••J••
NAVAJOS
NOSEJOB

•NJ••••
ENJOINS
ENJOYED
INJECTS
INJOKES
INJURED
INJURES

•N••J••
SNOWJOB

••NJ•••
BANJOES
BONJOUR
BONJOVI
CONJOBS
CONJOIN
CONJURE
DONJONS
DONJOSE
DONJUAN
FANJETS
PUNJABI
SANJOSE
SANJUAN

•••NJ••
JOHNJAY

••••NJ•
BASENJI
JUMANJI

N•K••••
NAKEDLY
NIKOLAI
NOKOMIS

N••K•••
NANKEEN
NAPKINS
NECKERS
NECKING
NECKTIE
NICKELS
NICKERS
NICKING

N•••K••
NABOKOV
NONSKID

N••••K•
NETSUKE
NUDNIKS

N•••••K
NETWORK
NEWLOOK
NEWYORK
NIBLICK
NITPICK
NORFOLK

•NK••••
ANKLETS
INKBLOT
INKHORN
INKLING
INKSPOT
INKWELL
INKYCAP
UNKEMPT
UNKINKS
UNKNITS
UNKNOTS
UNKNOWN

•N•K•••
SNAKIER
SNAKING

•N••K••
ANDYKIM
INJOKES
INTAKES
INVOKED
INVOKER
INVOKES
KNOCKED
KNOCKER
KNUCKLE
SNACKED
SNACKER
SNEAKED
SNEAKER
SNEAKIN
SNICKER
SNOOKER
SNORKEL
UNASKED
UNBAKED
UNLIKED
UNMAKES
UNYOKED
UNYOKES

•N•••K•
ANORAKS
UNALIKE
UNCORKS
UNHOOKS
UNKINKS
UNLINKS
UNLOCKS
UNLUCKY
UNMASKS
UNPACKS
UNTACKS

•N••••K
INSTOCK
UNCLOAK
UNFROCK
UNSTACK
UNSTICK
UNSTUCK

••NK•••
BANKERS
BANKING
BANKSON
BONKERS
BUNKBED
BUNKERS
BUNKING
BUNKOED
CANKERS
CONKERS
CONKING
CONKOUT
DANKEST
DINKIER
DINKIES
DONKEYS
DONKING
DUNKERS
DUNKING
DUNKIRK
FINKING
FUNKIER
GUNKIER
HANKERS
HANKIES
HONKERS
HONKING
HUNKERS
JINKING
JUNKART
JUNKERS
JUNKETS
JUNKIER
JUNKIES
JUNKING
JUNKMAN
KINKIER
KINKING
LANKEST
LANKIER
LANKILY
LINKAGE
LINKERS
LINKING
LINKUPS
LUNKERS
MANKIND
MONKEES
MONKEYS
MONKISH
NANKEEN
OINKING
PINKEST
PINKIES
PINKING
PINKISH
PUNKAHS
PUNKIES
RANKERS
RANKEST
RANKING
RANKLED
RANKLES
SINKAGE
SINKERS
SINKING
SINKSIN
SUNKIST
TANKARD
TANKERS
TANKFUL
TANKING
TANKSUP
TANKTOP
TINKERS
TINKLED
TINKLES
WINKERS
WINKING
WINKLER
WINKOUT
WINKSAT
YANKEES
YANKING
YANKTON
YONKERS
ZONKERS
ZONKING
ZONKOUT

••N•K••
ABNAKIS
BANGKOK
CONAKRY
HANUKAH
KANAKAS
MENCKEN
MONIKER
NONSKID

••N••K•
CONVOKE
FINICKY
KONTIKI
PANCAKE
PANICKY
PINOAKS
TANOAKS
VANDYKE

••N•••K
BANGKOK
BANNOCK
CONNICK
CONRACK
DENMARK
DUNKIRK
GUNLOCK
HANCOCK
HENPECK
JANACEK
KINFOLK
MENFOLK
RANSACK
RUNAMOK
RUNBACK
SUNDECK
TINWORK
VANDYCK
VANEYCK

•••NK••
BLANKED
BLANKER
BLANKET
BLANKLY
BLINKAT
BLINKED
BLINKER
CHINKED
CLANKED
CLINKED
CLINKER
CLUNKED
CLUNKER
CRANKED
CRANKUP
CRINKLE
CRINKLY
DRINKER
EVENKIS
FLANKED
FLANKER
FLUNKED
FRANKED
FRANKER
FRANKIE
FRANKLY
FRANKOZ
PLANKED
PLINKED
PLUNKED
PRANKED
PRINKED
REINKED
SHANKAR
SHANKED
SKUNKED
SLINKED
SPANKED
SPANKER
STINKER
SWANKER
THANKED
THINKER
THINKOF
THINKUP
TRINKET
TURNKEY
TWINKLE
TWINKLY
WRINKLE
WRINKLY

•••N•K•
ABENAKI
NUDNIKS
ROANOKE
VRONSKY

•••N••K
BANNOCK
CHINOOK
CONNICK
LOWNECK
OLDNICK
VEENECK
WOZNIAK

••••NK•
DEBUNKS
EMBANKS
HIJINKS
SHRINKS
UNKINKS
UNLINKS
UPLINKS

••••N•K
BEATNIK
SPUTNIK

•••••NK
BETHINK
BURBANK
EYEBANK
FOGBANK
ICERINK
JOBBANK
OUTRANK
RATFINK
RETHINK
SPELUNK

N•L••••
NELSONS
NILSSON
NULLIFY
NULLING

N••L•••
NAILERS
NAILING
NAILSET
NEGLECT
NEOLITH
NEWLEFT
NEWLOOK
NIBLICK
NIELSEN
NOBLEST
NUCLEAR
NUCLEIC
NUCLEON
NUCLEUS
NUCLIDE
NULLIFY
NULLING
NUTLETS

N•••L••
NACELLE
NASALLY
NATALIA
NATALIE
NEBULAE
NEBULAR
NEBULAS
NEEDLED
NEEDLES
NEPALIS
NESTLED
NESTLER
NESTLES
NETTLED
NETTLES
NEVILLE
NIBBLED
NIBBLER
NIBBLES
NICOLAS
NIGGLED
NIGGLES
NIKOLAI
NIMBLER
NODULAR
NODULES
NOGALES
NONPLUS
NONSLIP
NOODLES
NOVELLA
NOVELLE
NOVELTY
NOZZLES
NUBBLES
NUZZLED
NUZZLER
NUZZLES

N••••L•
NACELLE
NAIVELY
NAKEDLY
NARWALS
NASALLY
NASTILY
NATTILY
NEEDILY
NERVILY
NEVILLE
NICCOLO
NICHOLS
NICKELS
NIFTILY
NIGHTLY
NOBHILL
NOFAULT
NOISILY
NONSELF
NORFOLK
NORMALS
NOTABLE
NOTABLY
NOTWELL
NOVELLA
NOVELLE
NUTTILY

N•••••L
NAHUATL
NARWHAL
NATURAL
NEEDFUL
NEUTRAL
NEWDEAL
NOBHILL
NOMINAL
NOSTRIL
NOTWELL
NUMERAL
NUPTIAL

•NL••••
ENLACED
ENLACES
ENLARGE
ENLISTS
ENLIVEN
ONLEAVE
ONLYYOU
UNLACED
UNLACES
UNLADES
UNLATCH
UNLEARN
UNLEASH
UNLIKED
UNLINED
UNLINKS
UNLOADS
UNLOCKS
UNLOOSE
UNLOVED
UNLUCKY

•N•L•••
ANALOGS
ANALOGY
ANALYSE
ANALYST
ANALYZE
ANGLERS
ANGLING
ANILINE
ANKLETS
ANTLERS
ANTLION
ENCLAVE
ENCLOSE
ENDLESS
ENGLAND
ENGLISH
ENGLUND
ENPLANE
ENSLAVE
INBLOOM
INCLINE
INCLOSE
INCLUDE
INFLAME
INFLATE
INFLECT
INFLICT
INFLOWS
INKLING
INPLACE
KNELLED
SNELLEN
UNALIKE
UNBLEST
UNCLASP
UNCLEAN
UNCLEAR
UNCLOAK
UNCLOGS
UNCLOSE
UNGLUED
UNPLUGS

•N••L••
ANGELES
ANGELIC
ANGELOU
ANGELUS
ANGOLAN
ANGULAR
ANNALEE
ANNELID
ANNULAR
ANNULUS
ANTILOG
ENABLED
ENABLES
ENDPLAY
ENFOLDS
ENGULFS
ENISLED
ENISLES
ENROLLS
ENSILED
ENSILES
ENVELOP
GNARLED
INDULGE
INGALLS
INHALED
INHALER
INHALES
INKBLOT
INSOLES
INSULAR
INSULIN
INSULTS
INVALID
INVOLVE
KNEELED
KNEELER
KNELLED
KNURLED
SNARLED
SNELLEN
SNIGLET
UNBOLTS
UNFOLDS
UNOILED
UNPILED
UNPILES
UNROLLS

•N•••L•
ANATOLE
ANGRILY
ANIMALS
ANNEALS
ANNUALS
ANOMALY
ANOUILH
ANTHILL
ENAMELS
ENNOBLE
ENROLLS
ENSOULS
ENTAILS
ENTITLE
INANELY
INAPTLY
INDWELL
INEPTLY
INERTLY
INFIELD
INGALLS
INKWELL
INOCULA
INSTALL
INSTILL
INSTILS
INSTYLE
INUTILE
KNUCKLE
ONAROLL
ONESELF
SNAFFLE
SNIDELY
SNIFFLE
SNIGGLE
SNIVELS
SNUFFLE
SNUGGLE
UNCIALS
UNCOILS
UNCURLS
UNFURLS
UNGODLY
UNREELS
UNROLLS
UNSEALS
UNVEILS

•N••••L
ANNABEL
ANTHILL
ENSNARL
INCIVIL
INDWELL
INFIDEL
INITIAL
INKWELL
INSTALL
INSTILL
KNIEVEL
ONAROLL
ONTRIAL
SNORKEL
UNCIVIL
UNEQUAL
UNRAVEL
UNSNARL
UNUSUAL

••NL•••
DUNLINS
FINLAND
GUNLOCK
MANLIER
PINLESS
RANLATE
RUNLAPS
RUNLETS
SANLUIS
SUNLAMP
SUNLESS
TANLINE

••N•L••
ANNALEE
ANNELID
ANNULAR
ANNULUS
BANALLY
BANGLES
BENTLEY
BUNDLED
BUNDLES
BUNGLED
BUNGLER
BUNGLES
CANDLES
CANTLES
DANDLED
DANDLES
DANELAW
DANGLED
DANGLER
DANGLES
DINGLES
FINALES
FINALLY
FONDLED
FONDLES
GANGLED
GANGLIA
GANTLET
GENTLED
GENTLER
GENTLES
GUNPLAY
HANDLED
HANDLER
HANDLES
HUNTLEY
JANGLED
JANGLES
JINGLED
JINGLES
JUNGLES
KINDLED
KINDLES
LANGLEY
LANOLIN
MANGLED
MANGLES
MANILOW
MANTLED
MANTLES
MINGLED
MINGLER
MINGLES
MINOLTA
MONOLOG
NONPLUS
NONSLIP
PANELED
PENALTY
PENULTS
RANKLED
RANKLES
RINGLET
SANDLOT
SINGLED
SINGLES
TANGLED
TANGLES
TINGLED
TINGLES
TINKLED
TINKLES
TONALLY
TONELOC
VANILLA
VANILLI
WANGLED
WANGLER
WANGLES
WINKLER
WINSLOW
ZONALLY

••N••L•
ANNEALS
ANNUALS
BANALLY
BENGALI
BENGALS
BONNILY
CANCELS
CANDELA
CANNILY

CANNOLI
CONDOLE
CONSOLE
CONSULS
CONSULT
DANIELS
DENIALS
DENSELY
DINGILY
ENNOBLE
FANBELT
FANCILY
FINAGLE
FINALLY
FINIALS
FUNNELS
FUNNILY
GENTILE
GINMILL
GONDOLA
GUNMOLL
GUNNELS
GUNWALE
HANDILY
HANSOLO
IGNOBLE
IGNOBLY
KENDALL
KENNELS
KINFOLK
LANKILY
LENTILS
LINCOLN
LINTELS
MANACLE
MANDALA
MANDELA
MANHOLE
MANIPLE
MANTELS
MANUALS
MENFOLK
MENIALS
MINABLE
MINEOLA
MONDALE
MONGOLS
MONOCLE
MONTHLY
NONSELF
PANICLE
PANOPLY
PENCILS
PENPALS
PINBALL
PINHOLE
PINOCLE
PINWALE
RANDALL
RENAILS
RENAULT
RENTALS
RONDELS
RUNNELS
SANDALS
SANDFLY
SUNBELT
SUNNILY
TANGELO
TENABLE
TENABLY
TENFOLD
TENSELY
TENSILE
TINNILY
TINSELS
TONALLY
TONSILS
TUNICLE
TUNNELS
VANDALS
VANILLA
VANILLI
WENDELL
ZONALLY

••N•••L

ANNABEL
BANEFUL
CENTRAL
CONCEAL
CONGEAL
CONICAL
CONTROL
CYNICAL
DONEGAL
FANMAIL
FANTAIL
GENERAL
GENTEEL
GINMILL
GONERIL
GUNMOLL
HANDFUL
JONQUIL
KENDALL
LINGUAL
MANDREL
MANDRIL
MENTHOL
MINDFUL
MINERAL
MINIMAL
MONGREL
PINBALL
PINCURL
PINTAIL
RANDALL
RENEWAL
SANIBEL
SENEGAL
SENSUAL
SUNDIAL
SYNFUEL
SYNODAL
TANKFUL
TENDRIL
TENNIEL
TINFOIL
TUNEFUL
TUNGOIL
VANPOOL
VENTRAL
WENDELL

•••NL••

AVONLEA
JEANLUC
MOONLIT
STANLEE
STANLEY

•••N•L•

ATINGLE
BAGNOLD
BLANDLY
BLANKLY
BLINDLY
BLUNTLY
BONNILY
BRINDLE
CANNILY
CANNOLI
CORNELL
CORNILY
CRENELS
CRINKLE
CRINKLY
DIRNDLS
DWINDLE
FAINTLY
FRANKLY
FUNNELS
FUNNILY
GAUNTLY
GRANDLY
GRANOLA
GRANULE
GUNNELS
HYMNALS
INANELY
JOINTLY
KENNELS
KERNELS
KRINGLE
PARNELL
PERNELL
PHENOLS
PHONILY
ROUNDLY
RUNNELS
SAINTLY
SCANTLY
SHINGLE
SIGNALS
SOUNDLY
SPANGLE
SPANGLY
SPINDLE
SPINDLY
SPINELS
STONILY
SUNNILY
SWINDLE
TINNILY
TRUNDLE
TUNNELS
TWINKLE
TWINKLY
WRANGLE
WRINKLE
WRINKLY
WRONGLY
ZWINGLI

•••N••L

BARNOWL
CHANCEL
CHANNEL
CHUNNEL
CORNEAL
CORNELL
CORNOIL
COUNCIL
COUNSEL
CRANIAL
EMANUEL
ENSNARL
EVANGEL
FLANNEL
FRONTAL
GAINFUL
GRENDEL
HOBNAIL
PAINFUL
PARNELL
PERNELL
SCANDAL
SPANIEL
STENCIL
STENGEL
TENNIEL
TOENAIL
UNSNARL
UTENSIL

••••NL•

CLEANLY
HUMANLY
PLAINLY
QUEENLY
STERNLY
WOMANLY

••••N•L

ADRENAL
ALUMNAL
ARSENAL
CHANNEL
CHUNNEL
COLONEL
DIURNAL
EMPANEL
ESPANOL
ETERNAL
ETHANOL
FLANNEL
GRAPNEL
IMPANEL
JOURNAL
JUVENAL
LACUNAL
LAMINAL
NOMINAL
ORDINAL
RETINAL
SEMINAL
STERNAL
TYLENOL

N•M••••

NAMEDAY
NAMETAG
NAMIBIA
NEMEROV
NEMESES
NEMESIS
NIMBLER
NIMRODS
NOMADIC
NOMINAL
NOMINEE
NUMBATS
NUMBERS
NUMBEST
NUMBING
NUMERAL
NUMERIC

N••M•••

NEWMATH
NEWMOON
NEWMOWN
NORMALS
NORMAND
NORMANS
NUTMEAT
NUTMEGS

N•••M••

NEWSMAN
NEWSMEN
NOKOMIS

N••••M•

NAPTIME
NOISOME
NONCOMS
NOTHOME
NOTRUMP
NOXZEMA

N•••••M

NATRIUM
NIOBIUM
NOSEEUM
NOSTRUM

•NM••••

ENMASSE
INMATES
UNMAKES
UNMASKS
UNMOVED

•N•M•••

ANEMONE
ANIMALS
ANIMATE
ANIMATO
ANIMISM
ANIMIST
ANOMALY
ANYMORE
ENAMELS
ENAMORS
ENAMOUR
ENDMOST
ENEMIES
FNUMBER
GNOMONS
INAMESS

•N••M••

ANAEMIA
ANOSMIA
ANOSMIC
ENCAMPS
ENCOMIA
ENDEMIC
ENIGMAS
ENZYMES
INCOMES
INGEMAR
INHUMAN
SNOWMAN
SNOWMEN
UNAIMED
UNARMED
UNKEMPT
UNNAMED
UNTAMED

•N•••M•

ANADEMS
ANATOMY
ANONYMS
ANTHEMS
ANYTIME
ENDGAME
ENGRAMS
INFLAME
INFORMS
INSEAMS
ONETIME

•N••••M

ANAGRAM
ANAHEIM
ANDYKIM
ANIMISM
ANTFARM
ANTONYM
INBLOOM
INTERIM
UNIFORM

••NM•••

DENMARK
DINMONT
FANMAIL
GINMILL
GUNMOLL
MANMADE
SUNMAID

••N•M••

BENUMBS
BONDMAN
BONDMEN
CINEMAS
CINEMAX
DYNAMIC
DYNAMOS
HANGMAN
HANGMEN
JUNKMAN
KINGMAN
KINSMAN
KINSMEN
LINEMAN
LINEMEN
MANUMIT
MANXMAN
MANXMEN
MINIMAL
MINIMUM
MONOMER
PANAMAS
RENAMED
RENAMES
RUNAMOK
SANDMAN
SANDMEN
SYNGMAN
UNNAMED

••N••M•

BANTAMS
CENTIME
CENTIMO
CONDEMN
CONGAME
CONSUME
CONTEMN
HANSOMS
NONCOMS
PENNAME
RANSOMS
RUNHOME
SANREMO
SUNLAMP
TANDEMS
WINSOME

••N•••M

BENTHAM
BINGHAM
CONFIRM
CONFORM
GINGHAM
KINGDOM
MINICAM
MINIMUM
PINETUM
SANCTUM
SUNBEAM
SUNROOM
SYNONYM
TANTRUM
TINYTIM
TONEARM

•••NM••

FEYNMAN
IRONMAN
IRONMEN
MYANMAR
RAINMAN
THINMAN

•••N•M•

ANONYMS
BIGNAME
ECONOMY
EPONYMS
FRENUMS
GRANDMA
IPANEMA
MAGNUMS
MISNAME
PENNAME
PETNAME
PHENOMS
PHONEME
PLENUMS
SURNAME
TSUNAMI
YOUNGMC

•••N••M

CRANIUM
GRANDAM
HAFNIUM
HAHNIUM
OMENTUM
PHANTOM
PIANISM
QUANTUM
RHENIUM
TRANSOM
URANIUM

••••N•M

ACRONYM
ANTONYM
HOMINEM
HOMONYM
JEJUNUM
ORGANUM
STEINEM
STERNUM
SURINAM
SYNONYM
VIETNAM

N•N••••

NANETTE
NANKEEN
NANNIES
NINEVEH
NINNIES
NONAGON
NONCOMS
NONPLUS
NONSELF
NONSKID
NONSLIP
NONSTOP
NONUSER
NONZERO
NUNCIOS
NUNNERY

N••N•••

NANNIES
NEONATE
NEWNESS
NINNIES
NOONDAY
NUANCED
NUANCES
NUDNIKS
NUNNERY

N•••N••

NOCANDO
NOMINAL
NOMINEE
NOVENAS

N••••N•

NABBING
NAGGING
NAILING
NAPKINS
NAPPING
NASCENT
NATIONS
NEARING
NEATENS
NECKING
NEEDING
NELSONS
NEPTUNE
NESTING
NETTING
NEURONE
NEURONS
NEWTONS
NICKING
NIPPING
NIRVANA
NITTANY
NODDING
NOGGINS
NOISING
NOOSING
NORMAND
NORMANS
NOSHING
NOTHING
NOTIONS
NUBBINS
NUBIANS
NUDGING
NULLING
NUMBING
NURSING
NUTTING

N•••••N

NANKEEN
NEUTRON
NEVADAN
NEWBORN
NEWMOON
NEWMOWN
NEWSMAN
NEWSMEN
NEWTOWN
NIELSEN
NILSSON
NOCTURN
NONAGON
NUCLEON

•NN••••

ANNABEL
ANNALEE
ANNATTO
ANNEALS
ANNELID
ANNETTE
ANNEXED
ANNEXES
ANNOYED
ANNUALS
ANNUITY
ANNULAR
ANNULUS
ENNEADS
ENNOBLE
INNARDS
INNINGS
INNOWAY
UNNAMED
UNNERVE

•N•N•••

ANANIAS
ANONYMS
ENSNARE
ENSNARL
INANELY
INANEST
ONANDON
ONENESS
UNENDED
UNKNITS
UNKNOTS
UNKNOWN
UNSNAGS
UNSNAPS
UNSNARL

•N••N••

ANDANTE
ANOINTS
ANTENNA
ANTONIA
ANTONIN
ANTONIO
ANTONYM
ENDINGS
ENGINES
ENHANCE
ENOUNCE
ENTENTE
INASNIT
INCANTS
INCENSE
INDENTS
INFANCY
INFANTA
INFANTS
INGENUE
INNINGS
INTENDS
INTENSE
INTENTS
INTONED
INTONER
INTONES
INVENTS
UNBENDS
UNBINDS
UNCANNY
UNHANDS
UNHANDY
UNKINKS
UNLINED
UNLINKS
UNTUNED
UNTUNES
UNWINDS
UNZONED

•N•••N•

ANCIENT
ANDEANS
ANEMONE
ANGLING
ANILINE
ANODYNE
ANTEING
ANTENNA
ANTHONY
ANTOINE
ENCHANT
ENDRUNS
ENDUING
ENDZONE
ENGLAND
ENGLUND
ENJOINS
ENPLANE
ENSIGNS
ENSUING
ENTRANT
ENTWINE
ENURING
ENVYING
GNAWING
GNOMONS
INBOUND
INCHING
INCLINE
INDIANA
INDIANS
INFERNO
INFRONT
INKLING
INPOINT
INPRINT
INSPANS
INSTANT
INTERNS
INURING
KNEEING
KNIFING
KNOWING
ONGOING
SNAKING
SNAPONS
SNARING
SNIPING
SNOCONE
SNORING
SNOWING
UNBOUND
UNCANNY
UNDOING
UNDYING
UNGUENT
UNISONS
UNITING
UNSOUND
UNSPENT
UNTYING
UNWOUND

•N••••N

ANDIRON
ANDSOON
ANGOLAN
ANTIGEN
ANTLION
ANTONIN
ENCHAIN
ENLIVEN
ENTRAIN
INASPIN
INGRAIN
INGROWN
INHUMAN
INKHORN
INSULIN
ONANDON
SNEAKIN
SNELLEN
SNOWDON
SNOWMAN
SNOWMEN
SNOWSIN
UNCHAIN
UNCLEAN
UNCTION
UNDRAWN
UNICORN
UNKNOWN
UNLEARN
UNSHORN

••NN•••

BANNERS
BANNING
BANNOCK
BENNETT
BINNING
BONNETS
BONNIER
BONNILY
BUNNIES
CANNERS
CANNERY
CANNIER
CANNILY
CANNING
CANNOLI
CANNONS
CONNECT
CONNERY
CONNICK
CONNIFF
CONNING
CONNIVE
CONNORS
CONNOTE
CUNNING
DENNEHY
DINNERS
DONNING
DUNNING
FANNING
FINNISH
FUNNELS
FUNNIER
FUNNIES
FUNNILY
FUNNING
GANNETS
GANNETT
GENNARO
GINNING
GUNNELS
GUNNERS
GUNNERY
GUNNIES
GUNNING
HENNAED
HENNERY
HINNIES
JENNETS
JENNIES
KENNEDY
KENNELS
KENNETH
LINNETS
LONNROT
MANNERS
MANNING
MANNISH
MINNOWS
NANNIES
NINNIES
NUNNERY
PANNERS
PANNIER
PANNING
PENNAME
PENNANT
PENNATE
PENNERS
PENNIES
PENNING
PENNONS
PINNACE
PINNATE
PINNERS
PINNING
PUNNING
RENNINS
RUNNELS
RUNNERS
RUNNIER
RUNNING
SENNETT
SINNERS
SONNETS
SUNNIER
SUNNILY
SUNNING
TANNERS
TANNERY
TANNEST
TANNING
TANNINS
TANNISH
TENNERS
TENNIEL
TINNERS
TINNIER
TINNILY
TONNAGE
TONNEAU
TUNNELS
TUNNIES
WANNABE
WINNERS
WINNING
WINNOWS
ZINNIAS

••N•N••

AWNINGS
BANANAS
BONANZA
CANINES
CANONIC
FINANCE
INNINGS
LININGS
MANANAS
PENANCE
PINENUT
PINONES
RANINTO
RUNINTO
SYNONYM
TENANCY
TENANTS
TENONED
VINTNER
WINGNUT
WYNONNA
ZENANAS

••N••N•

AMNIONS
AYNRAND
BANDANA
BANDING
BANGING
BANKING
BANNING
BANYANS
BENDING
BENZENE
BINDING
BINGING
BINNING
BONBONS
BONDING
BONGING
BUNGING
BUNIONS
BUNKING
BUNTING
CANCANS
CANNING
CANNONS
CANTINA
CANTING
CANTONS
CANYONS
CANZONE
CENSING
CINZANO

CONDONE
CONFINE
CONKING
CONNING
CONSENT
CONTEND
CONTENT
CONVENE
CONVENT
CUNNING
DANCING
DENTINE
DENTING
DENYING
DINGING
DINMONT
DONJONS
DONKING
DONNING
DUNKING
DUNLINS
DUNNING
FANIONS
FANNING
FANZINE
FENCING
FENDING
FINDING
FINKING
FINLAND
FONDANT
FONTINA
FUNDING
FUNNING
GANGING
GENUINE
GINNING
GINSENG
GONGING
GUNNING
HANDING
HANGING
HENBANE
HINGING
HINTING
HONKING
HUNTING
JINKING
JINXING
JUNKING
KANSANS
KENYANS
KINGING
KINKING
LANDING
LANSING
LANTANA
LENDING
LENFANT
LENIENT
LINDENS
LINKING
LONGING
LUNGING
MANCINI
MANDANS
MANHUNT
MANKIND
MANNING
MENDING
MINCING
MINDING
MINIONS
MINOANS
MINTING
MINUEND
MONTANA
MONTAND
MONTANE
MUNDANE
MUNTINS
OINKING
PANNING
PANTING
PENDANT
PENDENT
PENDING
PENNANT
PENNING
PENNONS
PINGING
PINIONS
PINKING
PINNING
PONTINE
PONYING
PUNGENT
PUNNING
PUNTING
RANGING
RANKING
RANTING
RENDING
RENNINS
RENTING
RINGING
RINSING
RUNNING
SANDING
SANTANA
SANTINI
SENDING
SENSING
SINGING
SINKING
SUNNING
SUNTANS
SYNCING
TANGENT
TANKING
TANLINE
TANNING
TANNINS
TENDING
TENDONS
TENPINS
TENSING
TENTING
TINCANS
TINGING
TINTING
TONGANS
TONTINE
VANDINE
VANZANT
VENDING
VENTING
VINCENT
WANTING
WENDING
WINCING
WINDING
WINGING
WINKING
WINNING
WONTONS
WYNONNA
YANKING
ZINGING
ZONKING

••N•••N

BANKSON
BENISON
BENTSEN
BONDMAN
BONDMEN
CANTEEN
CONCERN
CONDEMN
CONDIGN
CONJOIN
CONSIGN
CONTAIN
CONTEMN
DENDRON
DENIZEN
DINEDIN
DINEDON
DINESEN
DINESIN
DINESON
DONJUAN
DONOVAN
DUNGEON
FONTEYN
GENTIAN
HANDGUN
HANDSIN
HANDSON
HANGMAN
HANGMEN
HANGSIN
HANGSON
HANGTEN
JANSSEN
JANTZEN
JUNKMAN
KINGMAN
KINGPIN
KINSMAN
KINSMEN
LANGDON
LANOLIN
LANTERN
LINCOLN
LINEMAN
LINEMEN
LONGRUN
LONGTON
MANSION
MANXMAN
MANXMEN
MENCKEN
MENTION
MENUHIN
MINIVAN
MONSOON
NANKEEN
NONAGON
PENGUIN
PENSION
PINDOWN
PONTOON
PUNCHIN
PYNCHON
RANGOON
RONTGEN
RUNDOWN
SANBORN
SANDMAN
SANDMEN
SANJUAN
SENDSIN
SINKSIN
SUNBURN
SUNDOWN
SYNGMAN
TENSION
TINHORN
TINTERN
TUNEDIN
TUNESIN
VENISON
WANTSIN
WINSTON
XANTHAN
YANKTON

•••NN••

BRENNAN
BRENNER
BRYNNER
CHANNEL
CHINNED
CHUNNEL
DUENNAS
FLANNEL
GRINNED
GRINNER
JEANNIE
JOHNNIE
LAENNEC
OCONNOR
PFENNIG
PLANNED
PLANNER
SCANNED
SCANNER
SHANNON
SHINNED
SHUNNED
SIENNAS
SKINNED
SKINNER
SPANNED
SPANNER
SPINNER
STANNIC
STUNNED
STUNNER
THINNED
THINNER
TWINNED

•••N•N•

ADENINE
ASININE
ATONING
BANNING
BEANING
BINNING
BRINING
BURNING
CANNING
CANNONS
CLONING
COINING
CONNING
CORNING
CRANING
CUNNING
DAMNING
DARNING
DAWNING
DONNING
DOWNING
DRONING
DUNNING
EARNING
EMINENT
EVENING
FANNING
FAWNING
FUNNING
GAINING
GINNING
GUANINE
GUNNING
HORNING
IRONING
JOINING
KEENING
KERNING
LEANING
LEONINE
LIMNING
LOANING
MANNING
MEANING
MOANING
MOONING
MORNING
OPENEND
OPENING
OPINING
PANNING
PAWNING
PENNANT
PENNING
PENNONS
PHONING
PINNING
PLANING
PRUNING
PUNNING
QUININE
RAINING
REGNANT
REINING
REMNANT
RENNINS
RUINING
RUNNING
SAMNUNN
SEINING
SHANANA
SHINING
SIGNING
STONING
SUNNING
TANNING
TANNINS
TURNING
TWINING
VEINING
WARNING
WEANING
WHINING
WINNING
YARNING
YAWNING

•••N••N

ABANDON
ALENCON
BERNSEN
BRANDON
BRANSON
BRENDAN
BRENNAN
BRINGIN
BRINGON
BRONSON
CHANSON
CLINTON
COUNTON
DOINGIN
ETONIAN
FEYNMAN
FRONTON
GAINSON
GOINGIN
GOINGON
GRUNION
ICINGIN
IRANIAN
IRONMAN
IRONMEN
JOHNSON
JOINSIN
KLINGON
LEANSON
ONANDON
OPINION
OXONIAN
PLANSON
PRONOUN
QUENTIN
RAINMAN
REINSIN
REUNION
ROUNDON
RUANDAN
RWANDAN
SAMNUNN
SHANNON
SIGNSIN
SIGNSON
STANDIN
STANDON
STANTON
STUNGUN
SWANSON
THINMAN
TRENTON
TURNSIN
TURNSON
TYINGIN
UGANDAN
UNKNOWN
YOUNGUN

••••NN•

ANTENNA
ARGONNE
CAYENNE
CEZANNE
COLONNA
DOYENNE
ETIENNE
GARONNE
HOSANNA
JOHANNA
LALANNE
MADONNA
RAVENNA
ROSANNA
ROSANNE
ROXANNE
SAVANNA
SUSANNA
SUSANNE
SUZANNE
TYRANNY
UNCANNY
WYNONNA

••••N•N

ANTONIN
AVIGNON
BRENNAN
BROSNAN
CHIGNON
DRAWNIN
DRAWNON
LEBANON
LETINON
MELANIN
ORGANON
SHANNON
SHOWNIN
SIMENON
TAKENIN
TAKENON

•••••NN

CAPEANN
DAYSINN
DIAHANN
HERMANN
MARYANN
SAMNUNN
SCHWINN
ULLMANN

NO•••••

NOBHILL
NOBLEST
NOCANDO
NOCTURN
NOCUOUS
NODDERS
NODDING
NODOUBT
NODSOFF
NODULAR
NODULES
NOETICS
NOFAULT
NOGALES
NOGGINS
NOGUCHI
NOISIER
NOISILY
NOISING
NOISOME
NOKOMIS
NOMADIC
NOMINAL
NOMINEE
NONAGON
NONCOMS
NONPLUS
NONSELF
NONSKID
NONSLIP
NONSTOP
NONUSER
NONZERO
NOODLES
NOONDAY
NOOSING
NORDICS
NORFOLK
NORIEGA
NORMALS
NORMAND
NORMANS
NORTHER
NOSEBAG
NOSEEUM
NOSEGAY
NOSEJOB
NOSEOUT
NOSHERS
NOSHING
NOSHOWS
NOSIEST
NOSTRIL
NOSTRUM
NOSWEAT
NOTABIT
NOTABLE
NOTABLY
NOTATED
NOTATES
NOTCHED
NOTCHES
NOTEPAD
NOTHING
NOTHOME
NOTICED
NOTICES
NOTIONS
NOTRUMP
NOTSURE
NOTTRUE
NOTWELL
NOUGATS
NOURISH
NOUVEAU
NOVARRO
NOVELLA
NOVELLE
NOVELTY
NOVENAS
NOVICES
NOWHERE
NOXIOUS
NOXZEMA
NOZZLES

N•O••••

NEOLITH
NEONATE
NIOBIUM
NOODLES
NOONDAY
NOOSING

N••O•••

NABOKOV
NICOLAS
NICOSIA
NIKOLAI
NODOUBT
NOKOMIS

N•••O••

NAIROBI
NARROWS
NATIONS
NELSONS
NERVOUS
NETWORK
NEURONE
NEURONS
NEWBORN
NEWLOOK
NEWMOON
NEWMOWN
NEWPORT
NEWTONS
NEWTOWN
NEWYORK
NICCOLO
NICHOLS
NIMRODS
NITROUS
NOCUOUS
NODSOFF
NOISOME
NONCOMS
NORFOLK
NOSEOUT
NOSHOWS
NOTHOME
NOTIONS
NOXIOUS

N••••O•

NABOKOV
NAVAHOS
NAVAJOS
NEARYOU
NEGATOR
NEMEROV
NEUTRON
NEWLOOK
NEWMOON
NEWSBOY
NILSSON
NONAGON
NONSTOP
NOSEJOB
NUCLEON
NUNCIOS

N•••••O

NABISCO
NICCOLO
NOCANDO
NONZERO
NOVARRO

•NO••••

ANODIZE
ANODYNE
ANOINTS
ANOMALY
ANONYMS
ANORAKS
ANOSMIA
ANOSMIC
ANOTHER
ANOUILH
ENOUNCE
GNOCCHI
GNOMONS
GNOSTIC
INOCULA
INORBIT
KNOBBED
KNOCKED
KNOCKER
KNOSSOS
KNOTTED
KNOWHOW
KNOWING
ONORDER
SNOCATS
SNOCONE
SNOOKER
SNOOPED
SNOOPER
SNOOTED
SNOOZED
SNOOZES
SNORERS
SNORING
SNORKEL
SNORTED
SNORTER
SNOWCAP
SNOWDAY
SNOWDON
SNOWIER
SNOWING
SNOWJOB
SNOWMAN
SNOWMEN
SNOWPEA
SNOWSIN
UNOILED

•N•O•••

ANDORRA
ANDOVER
ANGOLAN
ANGORAS
ANNOYED
ANTOINE
ANTONIA
ANTONIN
ANTONIO
ANTONYM
CNTOWER
ENCODED
ENCODER
ENCODES
ENCOMIA
ENCORES
ENDORSE
ENDOWED
ENFOLDS
ENFORCE
ENGORGE
ENJOINS
ENJOYED
ENNOBLE
ENROBED
ENROBES
ENROLLS
ENROOTS
ENROUTE
ENSOULS
INBOARD
INBOUND
INCOMES
INDOORS
INDOUBT
INFOCUS
INFORCE
INFORMS
INHOUSE
INJOKES
INNOWAY
INPOINT
INROADS
INSOFAR
INSOLES
INTONED
INTONER
INTONES
INVOGUE
INVOICE
INVOKED
INVOKER
INVOKES
INVOLVE
ONBOARD
ONGOING
ONTOPOF
SNOOKER
SNOOPED
SNOOPER
SNOOTED
SNOOZED
SNOOZES
UNBOLTS
UNBOUND
UNBOWED
UNBOXED
UNBOXES
UNCOILS
UNCORKS
UNCOUTH
UNCOVER
UNDOING
UNFOLDS
UNGODLY
UNHOOKS
UNHORSE
UNLOADS
UNLOCKS
UNLOOSE
UNLOVED
UNMOVED
UNROBED
UNROBES
UNROLLS
UNSOUND
UNWOUND
UNYOKED
UNYOKES
UNZONED

•N••O••

ANALOGS
ANALOGY
ANATOLE
ANATOMY
ANCHORS
ANCHOVY
ANDROID
ANDSOON
ANEMONE
ANEROID
ANTCOWS
ANTHONY
ANTIOCH
ANXIOUS
ANYBODY
ANYMORE
ENAMORS
ENAMOUR
ENCLOSE
ENDMOST
ENDZONE
ENGROSS
ENROOTS
ENTROPY
ENVIOUS
GNOMONS
INAWORD
INBLOOM
INCLOSE
INDOORS
INFLOWS
INFRONT
INGROUP
INGROWN
INKHORN
INSHORT
INSPOTS
INSTOCK
INSTORE
INTROIT
ONAROLL
ONEROUS
ONSHORE
SNAPONS
SNOCONE
UNAVOCE
UNCLOAK
UNCLOGS
UNCLOSE
UNFROCK
UNHOOKS
UNICORN
UNIFORM
UNIPODS
UNISONS
UNKNOTS
UNKNOWN
UNLOOSE
UNQUOTE
UNSHORN
UNSTOPS

•N•••O•

ANDIRON
ANDSOON
ANGELOU
ANTILOG
ANTLION
ENACTOR
ENVELOP
INASPOT
INAWEOF
INBLOOM
INCISOR
INDIGOS
INERROR
INFAVOR
INKBLOT
INKSPOT
KNOSSOS
KNOWHOW
ONANDON
ONESHOT
ONLYYOU
ONTOPOF
SNOWDON
SNOWJOB
UNCTION

•N••••O

ANIMATO
ANNATTO
ANTONIO
INFERNO
INPETTO
INVACUO
INVITRO
ONTARIO
ONTHEGO
SNAPSTO
UNDERGO

••NO•••

ANNOYED
CANONIC
CANOPUS
DENOTED
DENOTES
DONOVAN
ENNOBLE
GENOESE
HANOVER
HONORED
HONOREE
HONORER
HONOURS
IGNOBLE
IGNOBLY
IGNORED
IGNORER
IGNORES
INNOWAY
KENOSHA
LANOLIN
MANOWAR
MENORAH
MENOTTI
MINOANS
MINOLTA
MINORCA
MINORED
MONOCLE
MONOCOT
MONOLOG
MONOMER
PANOPLY
PINOAKS
PINOCLE
PINONES
RANOVER
RENOTES
RUNOFFS
RUNOVER
SENORAS
SENORES
SYNODAL
SYNODIC
SYNONYM
TANOAKS
TENONED
VANOCUR
WYNONNA
ZENOBIA

••N•O••

AMNIONS
BANJOES
BANNOCK
BINGOES
BONBONS
BONGOES
BONJOUR
BONJOVI
BONSOIR
BUNCOED
BUNIONS
BUNKOED
CANDOUR
CANNOLI
CANNONS

CANTONS
CANTORS
CANYONS
CANZONE
CENSORS
CONCOCT
CONCORD
CONDOLE
CONDONE
CONDORS
CONFORM
CONJOBS
CONJOIN
CONKOUT
CONNORS
CONNOTE
CONSOLE
CONSORT
CONTORT
CONTOUR
CONVOKE
CONVOYS
DINGOES
DINMONT
DONJONS
DONJOSE
FANIONS
FANSOUT
FINDOUT
FUNGOES
GONDOLA
GUNBOAT
GUNDOGS
GUNLOCK
GUNMOLL
HANCOCK
HANDOFF
HANDOUT
HANGOFF
HANGOUT
HANSOLO
HANSOMS
HENCOOP
HUNGOUT
IGNEOUS
JINGOES
JUNCOES
JUNIORS
KINFOLK
LANFORD
LINCOLN
LINGOES
MANGOES
MANHOLE
MANHOOD
MANHOUR
MENDOZA
MENFOLK
MENTORS
MINEOLA
MINIONS
MINNOWS
MONGOLS
MONSOON
MONTOYA
NONCOMS
PANDORA
PANSOUT
PENNONS
PINDOWN
PINHOLE
PINIONS
PONTOON
RANCOUR
RANGOON
RANSOMS
RINGOUT
RUNDOWN
RUNHOME
RUNSOFF
RUNSOUT
SANBORN
SANFORD
SANGOUT
SANJOSE
SENDOFF
SENDOUT
SENIORS
SENSORS
SENSORY
SENTOFF
SENTOUT
SINGOUT
SINUOUS
SUNDOGS
SUNDOWN
SUNGODS
SUNROOF
SUNROOM
TANGOED
TENDONS
TENFOLD
TENFOUR
TENSORS
TENUOUS
TINFOIL
TINHORN
TINWORK
TUNEOUT
TUNGOIL
VANGOGH
VANPOOL
VENDORS
WANTOUT
WENTOFF
WENTOUT
WINDOWS
WINKOUT
WINNOWS
WINSOME
WINSOUT
WONTONS
ZONKOUT

••N••O•

BANDBOX
BANGKOK
BANKSON
BENISON
BONITOS
CONTROL
DENDRON
DINEDON
DINESON
DONATOR
DONEFOR
DUNGEON
DYNAMOS
GUNSFOR
GUNSHOT
HANDSON
HANGDOG
HANGSON
HENCOOP
HONCHOS
JANEDOE
JANITOR
KINGDOM
LANGDON
LANGUOR
LONGBOW
LONGTON
LONNROT
MANHOOD
MANILOW
MANITOU
MANSION
MENTHOL
MENTION
MONITOR
MONOCOT
MONOLOG
MONSOON
NONAGON
NONSTOP
NUNCIOS
PENSION
PINEFOR
PONCHOS
PONTOON
PYNCHON
RANCHOS
RANGOON
RANRIOT
RUNAMOK
RUNRIOT
SANDBOX
SANDHOG
SANDLOT
SENATOR
SENDFOR
SENTFOR
SUNROOF
SUNROOM
SUNSPOT
TANKTOP
TENSION
TENSPOT
TONELOC
TONEROW
VANPOOL
VENISON
WENTFOR
WINDROW
WINDSOR
WINSLOW
WINSTON
YANKTON

••N•••O

ANNATTO
BANDITO
CANSECO
CENTAVO
CENTIMO
CINZANO
CONBRIO
ERNESTO
GENNARO
HANSOLO
IONESCO
JANEIRO
LINBIAO
LONGAGO
MONTEGO
NONZERO
ORNITHO
RANINTO
RUNINTO
SANREMO
SINGSTO
TANGELO
TENDSTO
WANTSTO

•••NO••

BAGNOLD
BANNOCK
BARNOWL
BURNOUT
BYANOSE
CANNOLI
CANNONS
CHINOOK
CONNORS
CONNOTE
CORNOIL
CRINOID
ECONOMY
EGGNOGS
EVENOUT
GRANOLA
HEINOUS
HOBNOBS
IRONORE
IRONOUT
KEYNOTE
LEONORA
MINNOWS
OMINOUS
ORINOCO
OZONOUS
PAWNOFF
PENNONS
PHENOLS
PHENOMS
PRONOUN
PUGNOSE
QUINOAS
RAINOUT
ROANOKE
RUINOUS
SIGNOFF
SIGNOUT
SPINOFF
SPINOUT
SPINOZA
SPUNOFF
SPUNOUT
TORNOUT
TURNOFF
TURNOUT
ULANOVA
UNKNOTS
UNKNOWN
WINNOWS
WORNOFF
WORNOUT

•••N•O•

ABANDON
ALENCON
BIENTOT
BRANDON
BRANSON
BRINGON
BRONCOS
BRONSON
CHANSON
CHINOOK
CLANGOR
CLINTON
CORNCOB
CORNDOG
CORNROW
COUNTON
DOWNBOW
FRANKOZ
FRONTON
GAINSON
GOINFOR
GOINGON
GRANTOR
GRUNION
IVANHOE
JOHNDOE
JOHNSON
KLINGON
LEANSON
LEANTOS
LONNROT
MAINTOP
MCENROE
MOONDOG
OCONNOR
ONANDON
OPENTOE
OPINION
PHANTOM
PLANSON
RAINBOW
REUNION
ROUNDON
SHANNON
SIGNSON
SPONSOR
STANDON
STANTON
STENTOR
SWANSON
THINKOF
TRANSOM
TRENTON
TURNSON
WYANDOT

•••N••O

BOUNDTO
BRINGTO
CLINGTO
GENNARO
GUANACO
LYINGTO
MAGNETO
ORINOCO
OWINGTO
POINTTO
SOANDSO
TORNADO
TURNSTO

••••NO•

ALBINOS
ALIENOR
ASOFNOW
AVIGNON
BARANOF
BOWKNOT
CASINOS
CHIGNON
DOMINOS
DRAWNON
ELEANOR
EQUINOX
ESPANOL
ETHANOL
GODUNOV
HAVENOT
JUSTNOW
KIMONOS
LADINOS
LATINOS
LEBANON
LETINON
MAGINOT
MERINOS
OCONNOR
ORGANON
POCONOS
ROMANOV
SHANNON
SIMENON
TAKENON
TOPKNOT
TYLENOL
ULYANOV
UPTONOW
USTINOV
WHATNOT
YOUKNOW

••••N•O

ADDONTO
ALFONSO
ANTONIO
ARSENIO
CUTINTO
DOMINGO
DURANGO
GETINTO
GIVENTO
GOTINTO
HHMUNRO
JACINTO
LAYINTO
LEPANTO
LITINTO
LORENZO
MEMENTO
NOCANDO
ORLANDO
OTRANTO
PIMENTO
PRYINTO
RANINTO
RIPINTO
RUNINTO
SETINTO
SQUANTO
TARANTO
TIEINTO
TORONTO
YEARNTO

•••••NO

BAMBINO
BOITANO
CHICANO
CINZANO
CUIBONO
HISPANO
INFERNO
JAYLENO
LUCIANO
MARTINO
OREGANO
PAISANO
PATERNO
POMPANO
PROBONO
RELLENO
SALERNO
SOPRANO
SUKARNO
TREVINO
VOLCANO
YOKOONO

N•P••••

NAPHTHA
NAPKINS
NAPPERS
NAPPING
NAPTIME
NEPALIS
NEPHEWS
NEPTUNE
NIPPERS
NIPPIER
NIPPING
NUPTIAL

N••P•••

NAPPERS
NAPPING
NEWPORT
NIPPERS
NIPPIER
NIPPING
NITPICK
NONPLUS

N•••P••

NOTEPAD

N•••••P

NONSLIP
NONSTOP
NOTRUMP

•NP••••

ENPLANE
INPEACE
INPETTO
INPHASE
INPLACE
INPOINT
INPRINT
ONPAPER
UNPACKS
UNPAVED
UNPILED
UNPILES
UNPLUGS

•N•P•••

ANAPEST
ANSPACH
ENDPLAY
INAPTLY
INEPTLY
INSPANS
INSPECT
INSPIRE
INSPOTS
SNAPONS
SNAPPED
SNAPPER
SNAPSAT
SNAPSTO
SNAPSUP
SNIPEAT
SNIPING
SNIPPED
SNIPPET
UNIPODS
UNSPENT

•N••P••

INASPIN
INASPOT
INCEPTS
INCIPIT
INDEPTH
INKSPOT
INSIPID
KNEEPAD
ONPAPER
ONTOPOF
SNAPPED
SNAPPER
SNIPPED
SNIPPET
SNOOPED
SNOOPER
SNOWPEA
UNHAPPY
UNTAPED

•N•••P•

ENCAMPS
ENCRYPT
ENTRAPS
ENTROPY
ENWRAPS
INSCAPE
INSHAPE
INSTEPS
UNDRAPE
UNHAPPY
UNKEMPT
UNSNAPS
UNSTOPS
UNSWEPT
UNTRAPS
UNWRAPS

•N••••P

ANTEDUP
ANTESUP
ANTWERP
ENVELOP
INAHEAP
INGROUP
INKYCAP
KNEECAP
ONESTEP
SNAPSUP
SNOWCAP
UNCLASP
UNSTRAP

••NP•••

GUNPLAY
HENPECK
NONPLUS
PANPIPE
PENPALS
TENPINS
VANPOOL

••N•P••

CANAPES
CANOPUS
JUNIPER
KINGPIN
MANIPLE
PANOPLY
SUNSPOT
SYNAPSE
TENSPOT

••N••P•

CONCEPT
HANGUPS
LINEUPS
LINKUPS
PANPIPE
RUNLAPS
SENDUPS
TINTYPE
TUNEUPS
WENTAPE
WINDUPS

••N•••P

BANGSUP
BINDSUP
BONEDUP
BONESUP
GANGSUP
HANDSUP
HANGSUP
HANSARP
HENCOOP
KINSHIP
LINEDUP
LINESUP
MANTRAP
NONSLIP
NONSTOP
OWNEDUP
PINESAP
PUNCHUP
RINGSUP
RUNDEEP
SENDSUP
SUNLAMP
TANKSUP
TANKTOP
TENSEUP
TONEDUP
TONESUP
TUNEDUP
TUNESUP
WINDSUP
WINESAP
WINGTIP

•••NP••

DOWNPAT
OPENPIT

•••N•P•

CATNAPS
CATNIPS
CHINUPS
GRANDPA
KIDNAPS
SCHNAPS
TURNIPS
UNSNAPS

•••N••P

BORNEUP
BOUNDUP
BRINGUP
BURNSUP
BURNTUP
CRANKUP
DOINGUP
EVENSUP
GOINGUP
JEANARP
JOINSUP
MAINTOP
OPENSUP
ROUNDUP
SIGNSUP
STANDUP
THINKUP
TURNSUP
TYINGUP
USINGUP
WOUNDUP

••••N•P

BLOWNUP
CLEANUP
DRAWNUP
EATENUP
GROWNUP
PARSNIP
SEVENUP
WOKENUP

•NQ••••

INQUEST
INQUIRE
INQUIRY
UNQUOTE

•N•Q•••

UNEQUAL

•N••Q••

ANTIQUE

•N•••Q•

ONTHEQT

••NQ•••

BANQUET
CONQUER
JONQUIL

••N•Q••

MONIQUE

•••NQ••

QUINQUE

•••N•Q•

PSANDQS

N•R••••

NARRATE
NARROWS
NARTHEX
NARWALS
NARWHAL
NEREIDS
NERVIER
NERVILY
NERVOUS
NIRVANA
NORDICS
NORFOLK
NORIEGA
NORMALS
NORMAND
NORMANS
NORTHER
NUREYEV
NURSERS
NURSERY
NURSING
NURTURE

N••R•••

NAIROBI
NARRATE
NARROWS
NATRIUM
NEAREST
NEARING
NEARYOU
NEURONE
NEURONS
NIMRODS
NITRATE
NITRIDE
NITRITE
NITROUS
NOTRUMP
NOURISH
NUTRIAS

N•••R••

NATURAL
NATURED
NATURES
NAVARRE
NEMEROV
NEUTRAL
NEUTRON
NIGERIA
NOSTRIL
NOSTRUM
NOTTRUE
NOVARRO
NUMERAL
NUMERIC

N••••R•

NABBERS
NAILERS
NAPPERS
NATTERS
NAVARRE
NECKERS
NECTARS
NESTERS
NETSURF
NETWORK
NEWBORN
NEWHART
NEWPORT
NEWYORK
NIAGARA
NICKERS
NIGGARD
NIPPERS
NOCTURN
NODDERS
NONZERO
NOSHERS
NOTSURE
NOVARRO
NOWHERE
NUDGERS
NUMBERS
NUNNERY
NURSERS
NURSERY
NURTURE
NUTTERS

N•••••R

NASTIER
NATTIER
NEBULAR
NEEDIER
NEGATOR
NEITHER
NERVIER
NESTLER
NEWAGER
NEWSIER
NEWYEAR
NIBBLER
NIEBUHR
NIFTIER
NIMBLER
NIPPIER
NODULAR
NOISIER
NONUSER
NORTHER
NUBBIER
NUCLEAR
NUTTIER
NUZZLER

•NR••••

ENRAGED
ENRAGES
ENROBED
ENROBES
ENROLLS
ENROOTS
ENROUTE
INROADS
UNRATED
UNRAVEL
UNREADY
UNREELS
UNROBED
UNROBES
UNROLLS

•N•R•••

ANARCHY
ANDREAS
ANDRESS
ANDREWS
ANDROID
ANEROID
ANGRIER
ANGRILY
ANORAKS
ENCRUST
ENCRYPT
ENDRUNS
ENGRAFT
ENGRAMS
ENGRAVE
ENGROSS
ENTRAIN
ENTRANT
ENTRAPS
ENTREAT
ENTREES
ENTRIES
ENTROPY
ENTRUST
ENURING
ENWRAPS
GNARLED
GNARRED
INARUSH
INBREED
INBRIEF
INERROR
INERTIA
INERTLY
INFRONT
INGRAIN
INGRATE
INGRESS
INGROUP
INGROWN
INORBIT
INPRINT
INTROIT
INTRUDE
INTRUST
INTRUTH
INURING
KNURLED
ONAROLL
ONEROUS
ONORDER
ONTRIAL
SNARING
SNARLED
SNORERS
SNORING
SNORKEL
SNORTED
SNORTER
UNARMED
UNCRATE
UNDRAPE
UNDRAWN
UNDRESS
UNFROCK
UNTRAPS
UNTRIED
UNTRUTH
UNWRAPS

•N••R••

ANAGRAM
ANDIRON
ANDORRA
ANGERED
ANGORAS
ANTARES
ENCORES
ENDORSE
ENDURED
ENDURES
ENFORCE
ENGARDE
ENGIRDS
ENGORGE
ENLARGE
ENSURED
ENSURES
ENTERED
GNARRED
INERROR
INFERNO
INFORCE
INFORMS
INHERED
INHERES
INHERIT

INJURED
INJURES
INNARDS
INSERTS
INSURED
INSURES
INTERIM
INTERNS
INTERSE
INVERSE
INVERTS
INWARDS
ONTARIO
ONWARDS
SNEERAT
SNEERED
SNEERER
UNAIRED
UNCORKS
UNCURLS
UNDERGO
UNEARTH
UNFURLS
UNGIRDS
UNHORSE
UNNERVE
UNSCREW
UNSTRAP

•N•••R•

ANCHORS
ANDORRA
ANGLERS
ANSWERS
ANTFARM
ANTHERS
ANTIART
ANTLERS
ANTWERP
ANYMORE
ENAMORS
ENDEARS
ENSNARE
ENSNARL
GNAWERS
INAWORD
INBOARD
INDOORS
INKHORN
INQUIRE
INQUIRY
INSHORT
INSPIRE
INSTORE
INTEGRA
INVITRO
KNAVERY
ONADARE
ONAGERS
ONBOARD
ONGUARD
ONSHORE
SNORERS
UNAWARE
UNHEARD
UNICORN
UNIFORM
UNITARY
UNITERS
UNLEARN
UNSHORN
UNSNARL

•N••••R

ANDOVER
ANGRIER
ANGULAR
ANNULAR
ANOTHER
ANTBEAR
ANTIWAR
ANTSIER
CNTOWER
ENACTOR
ENAMOUR
ENCODER
ENDUSER
ENTICER
FNUMBER
INCISOR
INCITER
INDUCER
INERROR
INFAVOR
INGEMAR
INHALER
INSIDER
INSOFAR
INSULAR
INTEGER
INTONER
INVADER
INVOKER
KNEADER
KNEELER
KNITTER
KNOCKER
ONATEAR
ONORDER
ONPAPER
SNACKER
SNAKIER
SNAPPER
SNEAKER
SNEERER
SNEEZER
SNICKER
SNIFFER
SNIFTER
SNIGGER
SNOOKER
SNOOPER
SNORTER
SNOWIER
SNUFFER
SNUGGER
UNCLEAR
UNCOVER
UNIFIER
UNWISER

••NR•••

AYNRAND
CONRACK
CONREID
HENREID
RANRIOT
RUNRIOT
SANREMO
SUNRAYS
SUNRISE
SUNROOF
SUNROOM

••N•R••

CANARDS
CENTRAL
CENTRED
CENTRES
CENTRIC
CONBRIO
CONTRAS
CONTROL
DENDRON
GENERAL
GENERIC
GENERIS
GONERIL
HENDRIX
HONORED
HONOREE
HONORER
HUNDRED
IGNORED
IGNORER
IGNORES
INNARDS
KINDRED
KINGRAT
LONGRUN
LONNROT
MANDREL
MANDRIL
MANFRED
MANTRAP
MANTRAS
MANTRIC
MENORAH
MINARET
MINERAL
MINERVA
MINORCA
MINORED
MONARCH
MONGREL
PANURGE
SANGRIA
SENORAS
SENORES
SYNERGY
TANTRUM
TENDRIL
TENURED
TENURES
TONEROW
TUNDRAS
UNNERVE
VENTRAL
WINDROW
WINERED
WINFREY

••N••R•

BANKERS
BANNERS
BANTERS
BENDERS
BINDERS
BINDERY
BONEDRY
BONFIRE
BONKERS
BUNKERS
CANKERS
CANNERS
CANNERY
CANTERS
CANTORS
CENSERS
CENSORS
CENSURE
CENTERS
CENTURY
CINDERS
CONAKRY
CONCERN
CONCERT
CONCORD
CONCURS
CONDORS
CONFERS
CONFIRM
CONFORM
CONGERS
CONJURE
CONKERS
CONNERY
CONNORS
CONSORT
CONTORT
CONVERT
DANCERS
DANDERS
DANGERS
DENIERS
DENMARK
DENTURE
DINNERS
DUNKERS
DUNKIRK
FANFARE
FENCERS
FENDERS
FENETRE
FINDERS
FINEART
FINGERS
GANDERS
GENDERS
GENNARO
GINGERS
GINGERY
GUNFIRE
GUNNERS
GUNNERY
HANGARS
HANGERS
HANKERS
HANSARP
HENNERY
HINDERS
HONKERS
HONOURS
HUNGARY
HUNGERS
HUNKERS
HUNTERS
JANEIRO
JANUARY
JUNIORS
JUNKART
JUNKERS
LANCERS
LANDERS
LANFORD
LANGTRY
LANGURS
LANTERN
LANYARD
LENDERS
LINGERS
LINKERS
LUNKERS
MANGERS
MANNERS
MANSARD
MENDERS
MENHIRS
MENTORS
MINCERS
MINDERS
MINTERS
MONGERS
NONZERO
NUNNERY
PANDERS
PANDORA
PANNERS
PANZERS
PENNERS
PINCERS
PINCURL
PINNERS
PONDERS
PONIARD
PUNTERS
QINTARS
RANGERS
RANKERS
RANTERS
RENDERS
RENTERS
RINGERS
RUNNERS
RUNSDRY
SANBORN
SANDERS
SANFORD
SANTIRS
SENDERS
SENIORS
SENSORS
SENSORY
SINATRA
SINCERE
SINGERS
SINKERS
SINNERS
SUNBURN
SUNDERS
TANGERE
TANKARD
TANKERS
TANNERS
TANNERY
TANTARA
TENDERS
TENNERS
TENSORS
TENTERS
TINDERS
TINEARS
TINHORN
TINKERS
TINNERS
TINTERN
TINTERS
TINWORK
TONEARM
TONSURE
VENDORS
VENEERS
VENTERS
VENTURA
VENTURE
WANDERS
WENDERS
WINCERS
WINDERS
WINGERS
WINKERS
WINNERS
WINTERS
WINTERY
WONDERS
YONKERS
ZANDERS
ZINGERS
ZONKERS

••N•••R

ANNULAR
BENATAR
BENAZIR
BONJOUR
BONNIER
BONSOIR
BUNGLER
CANDOUR
CANNIER
CENTAUR
CONIFER
CONQUER
CONTOUR
DANDIER
DANGLER
DANSEUR
DINGIER
DINKIER
DONATOR
DONEFOR
FANCIER
FUNFAIR
FUNKIER
FUNNIER
GENTLER
GUNKIER
GUNSFOR
GUNTHER
HANDCAR
HANDIER
HANDLER
HANOVER
HONORER
IGNITER
IGNORER
IONIZER
JANITOR
JANVIER
JUNIPER
JUNKIER
KINKIER
LANGUOR
LANKIER
LINTIER
LUNCHER
MANAGER
MANGIER
MANHOUR
MANLIER
MANOWAR
MANYEAR
MINGLER
MINIVER
MINTIER
MONIKER
MONITOR
MONOMER
MONSTER
MUNCHER
MYNHEER
NONUSER
PANNIER
PANTHER
PINCHER
PINEFOR
PINETAR
PUNCHER
PUNSTER
RANCHER
RANCOUR
RANDIER
RANGIER
RANOVER
RENEGER
RENEWER
RUNNIER
RUNOVER
RUNTIER
SANDBAR
SANDIER
SENATOR
SENDFOR
SENTFOR
SUNNIER
TANAGER
TANGIER
TENFOUR
TINNIER
TINSTAR
VANOCUR
VINEGAR
VINTNER
WANGLER
WENTFOR
WINDIER
WINDSOR
WINEBAR
WINKLER
ZINGIER

•••NR••

CORNROW
LONNROT
MCENROE

•••N•R•

BANNERS
BARNARD
BEANERY
BERNARD
BURNERS
CANNERS
CANNERY
CARNERA
COINERS
CONNERY
CONNORS
CORNERS
COUNTRY
DARNERS
DINNERS
DOWNERS
DRONERS
EARNERS
ENSNARE
ENSNARL
FAWNERS
FOUNDRY
GAINERS
GARNERS
GENNARO
GRANARY
GUNNERS
GUNNERY
HENNERY
IRONERS
IRONORE
JEANARP
JOINERS
JOINERY
KEENERS
LAUNDRY
LEANERS
LEONARD
LEONORA
LIMNERS
LOANERS
MANNERS
MAYNARD
MOANERS
NUNNERY
OPENERS
OPINERS
PANNERS
PAWNERS
PENNERS
PINNERS
PLANERS
PLENARY
PRUNERS
REENTRY
REYNARD
RUINERS
RUNNERS
SCENERY
SEINERS
SHANGRI
SHINERS
SIGNERS
SINNERS
SOONERS
STONERS
TANNERS
TANNERY
TEENERS
TENNERS
TERNARY
TINNERS
TOWNERS
TRENARY
TURNERS
UNSNARL
WHINERS
WIENERS
WINNERS
YAWNERS

•••N••R

ALUNSER
ASUNDER
AVENGER
BLANDER
BLANKER
BLENDER
BLINDER
BLINKER
BLONDER
BLUNDER
BLUNTER
BONNIER
BOUNCER
BOUNDER
BRANDER
BRENNER
BRINGER
BRINIER
BRYNNER
CANNIER
CHANGER
CHANTER
CHENIER
CLANGOR
CLINKER
CLUNKER
CORNIER
COUNTER
DERNIER
DOWNIER
DRINKER
EMENDER
EVANDER
FAINTER
FLANEUR
FLANKER
FOUNDER
FRANKER
FUNNIER
GAUNTER
GOINFOR
GOUNDER
GRANDER
GRANGER
GRANTOR
GRINDER
GRINNER
JOINDER
LAUNDER
LEANDER
LOONIER
LOUNGER
MAUNDER
MEANDER
MYANMAR
OCONNOR
OPENAIR
OPENBAR
PAINTER
PANNIER
PHONIER
PIONEER
PLANNER
PLANTAR
PLANTER
PLUNDER
PLUNGER
POINTER
POUNCER
POUNDER
PRANCER
PRINTER
RAINIER
REENTER
ROUNDER
RUNNIER
SAUNTER
SCANNER
SCANTER
SHANKAR
SHANTER
SHINIER
SKINNER
SLANDER
SLENDER
SLINGER
SOUNDER
SPANKER
SPANNER
SPENCER
SPENDER
SPENSER
SPINIER
SPINNER
SPONGER
SPONSOR
STENTOR
STINGER
STINKER
STONIER
STUNNER
SUNNIER
SWANKER
SWINGER
TAWNIER
TEENIER
THINAIR
THINKER
THINNER
THUNDER
TINNIER
VAUNTER
VERNIER
WERNHER
WRINGER
WRONGER
YOUNGER

••••NR•

HHMUNRO
MASONRY

••••N•R

ALIENOR
ALIGNER
BRENNER
BROWNER
BRYNNER
CLEANER
COSTNER
CROONER
DIVINER
DRAINER
EDASNER
ELEANOR
FLEXNER
FROWNER
GARDNER
GLEANER
GREENER
GRINNER
GROANER
INTONER
LAMINAR
LARDNER
LEARNER
MARINER
OCONNOR
OFTENER
PARDNER
PARTNER
PILSNER
PLAINER
PLANNER
PREENER
REFINER
SCANNER
SEMINAR
SERENER
SHATNER
SHRINER
SKINNER
SPANNER
SPINNER
SPOONER
SPURNER
STAINER
STEINER
STERNER
STUNNER
SUTTNER
THINNER
TRAINER
URBANER
VINTNER
WAGONER
WAKENER
YEARNER

N•S••••

NASALLY
NASCENT
NASTASE
NASTIER
NASTILY
NESCAFE
NESTEGG
NESTERS
NESTING
NESTLED
NESTLER
NESTLES
NOSEBAG
NOSEEUM
NOSEGAY
NOSEJOB
NOSEOUT
NOSHERS
NOSHING
NOSHOWS
NOSIEST
NOSTRIL
NOSTRUM
NOSWEAT

N••S•••

NAYSAID
NAYSAYS
NELSONS
NETSUKE
NETSURF
NEWSBOY
NEWSDAY
NEWSIER
NEWSMAN
NEWSMEN
NILSSON
NODSOFF
NOISIER
NOISILY
NOISING
NOISOME
NONSELF
NONSKID
NONSLIP
NONSTOP
NOOSING
NOTSURE
NURSERS
NURSERY
NURSING

N•••S••

NABISCO
NAILSET
NATASHA
NEMESES
NEMESIS
NEXUSES
NICOSIA
NIELSEN
NILSSON
NONUSER
NUDISTS

N••••S•

NASTASE
NEAREST
NEATEST
NEBBISH
NEWNESS
NIGHEST
NOBLEST
NOSIEST
NOURISH
NUMBEST

N•••••S

NABBERS
NAIADES
NAILERS
NANNIES
NAPKINS
NAPPERS
NARROWS
NARWALS
NATIONS
NATIVES
NATTERS
NATURES
NAUGHTS
NAVAHOS
NAVAJOS
NAYSAYS
NEATENS
NEBULAS
NECKERS
NECTARS
NEEDLES
NEGATES
NELSONS
NEMESES
NEMESIS
NEPALIS
NEPHEWS
NEREIDS
NERVOUS
NESTERS
NESTLES
NETTLES
NEURONS
NEWNESS
NEWTONS
NEXUSES
NIBBLES
NICHOLS
NICKELS
NICKERS
NICOLAS
NIGGLES
NIMRODS
NINNIES
NIPPERS
NITROUS
NITWITS
NOCUOUS
NODDERS
NODULES
NOETICS
NOGALES
NOGGINS
NOKOMIS
NONCOMS
NONPLUS
NOODLES
NORDICS
NORMALS
NORMANS
NOSHERS
NOSHOWS
NOTATES
NOTCHES
NOTICES
NOTIONS
NOUGATS
NOVENAS
NOVICES
NOXIOUS
NOZZLES
NUANCES
NUBBINS
NUBBLES
NUBIANS
NUCLEUS
NUDGERS
NUDISTS
NUDNIKS
NUGGETS
NUMBATS
NUMBERS
NUNCIOS
NURSERS
NUTLETS
NUTMEGS
NUTRIAS
NUTTERS
NUZZLES

•NS••••

ANSPACH
ANSWERS
ENSIGNS
ENSILED
ENSILES
ENSLAVE
ENSNARE
ENSNARL
ENSOULS
ENSUING
ENSUITE
ENSURED
ENSURES
INSCAPE
INSEAMS
INSECTS
INSERTS
INSHAPE
INSHORT
INSIDER
INSIDES
INSIGHT
INSIPID
INSISTS
INSOFAR
INSOLES
INSPANS
INSPECT
INSPIRE
INSPOTS
INSTALL

INSTANT
INSTATE
INSTEAD
INSTEPS
INSTILL
INSTILS
INSTOCK
INSTORE
INSTYLE
INSULAR
INSULIN
INSULTS
INSURED
INSURES
ONSHORE
ONSIGHT
ONSTAGE
UNSATED
UNSCREW
UNSEALS
UNSEATS
UNSEWED
UNSHORN
UNSNAGS
UNSNAPS
UNSNARL
UNSOUND
UNSPENT
UNSTACK
UNSTICK
UNSTOPS
UNSTRAP
UNSTUCK
UNSWEPT

•N•S•••

ANASAZI
ANDSOON
ANISEED
ANOSMIA
ANOSMIC
ANTSIER
ENISLED
ENISLES
GNASHED
GNASHES
GNOSTIC
INASNIT
INASPIN
INASPOT
INASTEW
INKSPOT
KNESSET
KNISHES
KNOSSOS
ONASSIS
ONESELF
ONESHOT
ONESTEP
UNASKED
UNISONS
UNUSUAL

•N••S••

ANTESUP
ENCASED
ENCASES
ENDUSER
ENLISTS
ENMASSE
INCISED
INCISES
INCISOR
INFESTS
INFUSED
INFUSES
INGESTS
INHASTE
INSISTS
INVESTS
KNESSET
KNOSSOS
ONASSIS
SNAPSAT
SNAPSTO
SNAPSUP
SNOWSIN
UNCASED
UNCASES
UNMASKS
UNWISER

•N•••S•

ANALYSE
ANALYST
ANAPEST
ANDRESS
ANIMISM
ANIMIST
ENCLOSE
ENCRUST
ENDLESS
ENDMOST
ENDORSE
ENDWISE
ENGLISH
ENGROSS
ENMASSE
ENTHUSE
ENTRUST
INAMESS
INANEST
INARUSH
INCENSE
INCLOSE
INGRESS
INHOUSE
INPHASE
INQUEST
INTENSE
INTERSE
INTRUST
INVERSE
KNAVISH
ONENESS
SNIDEST
UNBLEST
UNCLASP
UNCLOSE
UNDRESS
UNHORSE
UNLEASH
UNLOOSE
UNTWIST

•N••••S

ANADEMS
ANALOGS
ANANIAS
ANCHORS
ANDEANS
ANDREAS
ANDRESS
ANDREWS
ANGELES
ANGELUS
ANGLERS
ANGORAS
ANIMALS
ANKLETS
ANNEALS
ANNEXES
ANNUALS
ANNULUS
ANOINTS
ANONYMS
ANORAKS
ANSWERS
ANTAEUS
ANTARES
ANTCOWS
ANTHEMS
ANTHERS
ANTIBES
ANTLERS
ANXIOUS
ENABLES
ENAMELS
ENAMORS
ENCAGES
ENCAMPS
ENCASES
ENCODES
ENCORES
ENDEARS
ENDINGS
ENDIVES
ENDLESS
ENDRUNS
ENDURES
ENDWAYS
ENEMIES
ENFOLDS
ENGAGES
ENGINES
ENGIRDS
ENGRAMS
ENGROSS
ENGULFS
ENIGMAS
ENISLES
ENJOINS
ENLACES
ENLISTS
ENNEADS
ENRAGES
ENROBES
ENROLLS
ENROOTS
ENSIGNS
ENSILES
ENSOULS
ENSURES
ENTAILS
ENTICES
ENTRAPS
ENTREES
ENTRIES
ENVIOUS
ENWRAPS
ENZYMES
GNASHES
GNAWERS
GNOMONS
INAMESS
INCANTS
INCEPTS
INCISES
INCITES
INCOMES
INCUDES
INDENTS
INDEXES
INDIANS
INDICES
INDICTS
INDIGOS
INDITES
INDOORS
INDUCES
INDUCTS
INFANTS
INFECTS
INFESTS
INFLOWS
INFOCUS
INFORMS
INFUSES
INGALLS
INGESTS
INGRESS
INHALES
INHERES
INJECTS
INJOKES
INJURES
INMATES
INNARDS
INNINGS
INROADS
INSEAMS
INSECTS
INSERTS
INSIDES
INSISTS
INSOLES
INSPANS
INSPOTS
INSTEPS
INSTILS
INSULTS
INSURES
INTAKES
INTENDS
INTENTS
INTERNS
INTONES
INTUITS
INVADES
INVENTS
INVERTS
INVESTS
INVITES
INVOKES
INWARDS
KNIGHTS
KNISHES
KNOSSOS
ONAGERS
ONASSIS
ONEIDAS
ONENESS
ONEROUS
ONWARDS
SNAPONS
SNEEZES
SNIVELS
SNOCATS
SNOOZES
SNORERS
UNBENDS
UNBINDS
UNBOLTS
UNBOXES
UNCAGES
UNCASES
UNCIALS
UNCLOGS
UNCOILS
UNCORKS
UNCURLS
UNDRESS
UNFOLDS
UNFURLS
UNGIRDS
UNHANDS
UNHOOKS
UNIFIES
UNIPODS
UNISONS
UNITERS
UNITIES
UNKINKS
UNKNITS
UNKNOTS
UNLACES
UNLADES
UNLINKS
UNLOADS
UNLOCKS
UNMAKES
UNMASKS
UNPACKS
UNPILES
UNPLUGS
UNREELS
UNROBES
UNROLLS
UNSEALS
UNSEATS
UNSNAGS
UNSNAPS
UNSTOPS
UNTACKS
UNTRAPS
UNTUNES
UNVEILS
UNWINDS
UNWRAPS
UNYOKES

••NS•••

BANSHEE
BONSOIR
CANSECO
CENSERS
CENSING
CENSORS
CENSURE
CONSENT
CONSIGN
CONSIST
CONSOLE
CONSORT
CONSULS
CONSULT
CONSUME
DANSEUR
DENSELY
DENSEST
DENSITY
FANSOUT
GINSENG
GUNSFOR
GUNSHOT
HANSARP
HANSOLO
HANSOMS
IBNSAUD
JANSSEN
KANSANS
KINSHIP
KINSMAN
KINSMEN
LANSING
LINSEED
MANSARD
MANSION
MONSOON
MONSTER
NONSELF
NONSKID
NONSLIP
NONSTOP
PANSIES
PANSOUT
PENSEES
PENSION
PENSIVE
PUNSTER
RANSACK
RANSOMS
RINSING
RUNSDRY
RUNSOFF
RUNSOUT
SENSATE
SENSING
SENSORS
SENSORY
SENSUAL
SUNSETS
SUNSPOT
TANSIES
TENSELY
TENSEST
TENSEUP
TENSILE
TENSING
TENSION
TENSIVE
TENSORS
TENSPOT
TINSELS
TINSTAR
TONSILS
TONSURE
WINSLOW
WINSOME
WINSOUT
WINSTON

••N•S••

AMNESIA
AMNESTY
BANDSAW
BANGSUP
BANKSON
BENISON
BENTSEN
BINDSUP
BONESUP
BONUSES
CANASTA
DINESEN
DINESIN
DINESON
DYNASTS
DYNASTY
ERNESTO
FINESSE
GANGSAW
GANGSTA
GANGSUP
GENESEE
GENESES
GENESIS
HANDSAW
HANDSET
HANDSIN
HANDSON
HANDSUP
HANGSIN
HANGSON
HANGSUP
HINTSAT
HONESTY
IONESCO
JANSSEN
KENOSHA
LANDSAT
LINDSAY
LINDSEY
LINESUP
MENISCI
MINDSET
MINUSES
NONUSER
PINESAP
RINGSUP
SENDSIN
SENDSUP
SINGSTO
SINKSIN
SINUSES
TANKSUP
TENDSTO
TONESUP
TUNESIN
TUNESUP
TUNISIA
VANESSA
VENISON
WANTSIN
WANTSTO
WINDSOR
WINDSUP
WINESAP
WINGSIT
WINKSAT

••N••S•

BONEASH
BONIEST
CANVASS
CONCISE
CONFESS
CONFUSE
CONGEST
CONSIST
CONTEST
CONTUSE
DANKEST
DENSEST
DENTIST
DONJOSE
FANTASY
FINESSE
FINNISH
FONDEST
FUNFEST
GENOESE
KINDEST
LANKEST
LONGEST
LONGISH
MANNISH
MONKISH
PANFISH
PINIEST
PINKEST
PINKISH
PINLESS
PUNIEST
RANKEST
SANJOSE
SUNFISH
SUNKIST
SUNLESS
SUNRISE
SYNAPSE
TANNEST
TANNISH
TENSEST
TINIEST
TONIEST
VANESSA
ZANIEST

••N•••S

ABNAKIS
AGNATES
AMNIONS
ANNEALS
ANNEXES
ANNUALS
ANNULUS
ARNICAS
AUNTIES
AWNINGS
BANANAS
BANDIES
BANDITS
BANGLES
BANJOES
BANKERS
BANNERS
BANTAMS
BANTERS
BANYANS
BENCHES
BENDERS
BENGALS
BENUMBS
BINDERS
BINGOES
BONBONS
BONGOES
BONITOS
BONKERS
BONNETS
BONUSES
BUNCHES
BUNDLES
BUNGEES
BUNGLES
BUNIONS
BUNKERS
BUNNIES
CANAPES
CANARDS
CANCANS
CANCELS
CANDIDS
CANDIES
CANDLES
CANINES
CANKERS
CANNERS
CANNONS
CANOPUS
CANTERS
CANTLES
CANTONS
CANTORS
CANVASS
CANYONS
CENSERS
CENSORS
CENTERS
CENTRES
CINCHES
CINDERS
CINEMAS
CONCHES
CONCURS
CONDORS
CONFABS
CONFERS
CONFESS
CONGERS
CONJOBS
CONKERS
CONNORS
CONSULS
CONTRAS
CONVEYS
CONVOYS
DANCERS
DANDERS
DANDIES
DANDLES
DANGERS
DANGLES
DANIELS
DENIALS
DENIERS
DENOTES
DENUDES
DINGLES
DINGOES
DINKIES
DINNERS
DONATES
DONJONS
DONKEYS
DUNKERS
DUNLINS
DYNAMOS
DYNASTS
ENNEADS
EUNUCHS
FANCIES
FANIONS
FANJETS
FENCERS
FENDERS
FINALES
FINCHES
FINDERS
FINGERS
FINIALS
FONDLES
FONDUES
FUNGOES
FUNNELS
FUNNIES
GANDERS
GANNETS
GENDERS
GENERIS
GENESES
GENESIS
GENGHIS
GENTLES
GINGERS
GUNDOGS
GUNNELS
GUNNERS
GUNNIES
HANDLES
HANGARS
HANGERS
HANGUPS
HANKERS
HANKIES
HANSOMS
HENBITS
HINDERS
HINNIES
HONCHOS
HONKERS
HONOURS
HUNCHES
HUNGERS
HUNKERS
HUNTERS
IGNEOUS
IGNITES
IGNORES
INNARDS
INNINGS
IONIZES
JANGLES
JENNETS
JENNIES
JINGLES
JINGOES
JUNCOES
JUNGLES
JUNIORS
JUNKERS
JUNKETS
JUNKIES
KANAKAS
KANSANS
KENNELS
KENYANS
KINDLES
LANCERS
LANCETS
LANDAUS
LANDERS
LANGURS
LENDERS
LENGTHS
LENTILS
LINAGES
LINDENS
LINDIES
LINEUPS
LINGERS
LINGOES
LININGS
LINKERS
LINKUPS
LINNETS
LINTELS
LONGUES
LUNCHES
LUNKERS
MANAGES
MANANAS
MANDANS
MANDAYS
MANEGES
MANGERS
MANGLES
MANGOES
MANIACS
MANNERS
MANTELS
MANTLES
MANTRAS
MANUALS
MENACES
MENAGES
MENDERS
MENHIRS
MENIALS
MENTORS
MINCERS
MINDERS
MINGLES
MINIBUS
MINIONS
MINNOWS
MINOANS
MINTERS
MINUETS
MINUSES
MINUTES
MONDAYS
MONGERS
MONGOLS
MONKEES
MONKEYS
MUNCHES
MUNTINS
NANNIES
NINNIES
NONCOMS
NONPLUS
NUNCIOS
OMNIBUS
PANAMAS
PANDERS
PANDITS
PANNERS
PANSIES
PANZERS
PENATES
PENCILS
PENNERS
PENNIES
PENNONS
PENPALS
PENSEES
PENTADS
PENULTS
PINATAS
PINCERS
PINCHAS
PINCHES
PINIONS
PINKIES
PINLESS
PINNERS
PINOAKS
PINONES
PONCHOS
PONDERS
PONGIDS
PONTIUS
PUNCHES
PUNDITS
PUNKAHS
PUNKIES
PUNTERS
QINTARS
RANCHES
RANCHOS
RANGERS
RANKERS
RANKLES
RANSOMS
RANTERS
RENAILS
RENAMES
RENDERS
RENEGES
RENNINS
RENOTES
RENTALS
RENTERS
RINGERS
RONDELS
RUNLAPS
RUNLETS
RUNNELS
RUNNERS
RUNOFFS
RUNWAYS
SANDALS
SANDERS
SANLUIS
SANTIRS
SENATES
SENDERS
SENDUPS
SENECAS
SENIORS
SENORAS
SENORES
SENSORS
SINGERS
SINGLES
SINKERS
SINNERS
SINUOUS
SINUSES
SONATAS
SONNETS
SUNDAES
SUNDAYS
SUNDERS
SUNDEWS
SUNDOGS
SUNGODS
SUNLESS
SUNRAYS
SUNSETS
SUNTANS
SYNCHES
TANDEMS
TANGLES
TANKERS
TANNERS
TANNINS
TANOAKS
TANSIES
TENACES
TENANTS
TENDERS
TENDONS
TENNERS
TENPINS
TENSORS
TENTERS
TENUOUS
TENURES
TINCANS
TINDERS
TINEARS
TINGLES
TINHATS
TINKERS
TINKLES
TINNERS
TINSELS
TINTERS
TONGANS
TONGUES
TONSILS
TUNDRAS
TUNEUPS
TUNNELS
TUNNIES
VANDALS
VENDORS
VENEERS
VENTERS
WANDERS
WANGLES
WANTADS
WENCHES
WENDERS
WINCERS
WINCHES
WINDERS
WINDOWS
WINDUPS
WINGERS
WINKERS
WINNERS
WINNOWS
WINTERS
WONDERS
WONTONS
YANKEES
YONKERS
ZANDERS
ZENANAS
ZENITHS
ZINGERS
ZINNIAS
ZONKERS

•••NS••

ALUNSER
BERNSEN
BRANSON
BRONSON
BURNSUP
CHANSON
COUNSEL
EVENSUP
FLENSED
FLENSES
GAINSAY
GAINSON
HORNSBY
JOHNSON
JOINSIN
JOINSUP
LEANSON
MOONSET
OPENSEA
OPENSUP

PLANSON
QUONSET
REINSIN
SIGNSIN
SIGNSON
SIGNSUP
SPENSER
SPONSOR
SWANSON
TRANSIT
TRANSOM
TURNSIN
TURNSON
TURNSTO
TURNSUP
UTENSIL
VRONSKY

•••N•S•

AGONIST
AMONGST
APTNESS
BADNESS
BERNESE
BIGNESS
BURNISH
BYANOSE
CHINESE
CORNISH
COYNESS
DIMNESS
DRYNESS
EARNEST
EVENEST
FATNESS
FINNISH
FITNESS
FURNISH
GARNISH
GYMNAST
HARNESS
HIPNESS
HORNIST
HOTNESS
ICINESS
ILLNESS
INANEST
KEENEST
LAXNESS
LEANEST
LIONESS
LOWNESS
MADNESS
MANNISH
MEANEST
NEWNESS
ODDNESS
OLDNESS
ONENESS
PATNESS
PIANISM
PIANIST
PUGNOSE
RAWNESS
REDNESS
SADNESS
SHYNESS
SLYNESS
SOANDSO
SOONEST
SPANISH
TANNEST
TANNISH
TARNISH
VAINEST
VARNISH
WETNESS
WITNESS
WRYNESS

•••N••S

ADONAIS
AGENDAS
ANANIAS
ANONYMS
APTNESS
AVENGES
AVENUES
BADNESS
BANNERS
BARNEYS
BEANIES
BIGNESS
BIONICS
BLONDES
BONNETS
BOONIES
BOUNCES
BRONCOS
BRONZES
BRUNETS
BUNNIES
BURNERS
CANNERS
CANNONS
CAPNUTS
CARNETS
CARNIES
CATNAPS
CATNIPS
CHANCES
CHANGES
CHINUPS
CLINICS
COGNACS
COINERS
CONNORS
CORNEAS
CORNERS
CORNETS
COYNESS
CRENELS
CRINGES
CRONIES
CYGNETS
DARNERS
DIMNESS
DINNERS
DIRNDLS
DOWNERS
DRONERS
DRYNESS
DUENNAS
EARNERS
EBONIES
EGGNOGS
EPONYMS
ETHNICS
EVENKIS
EVINCES
FATNESS
FAWNERS
FIANCES
FITNESS
FLANGES
FLENSES
FLYNETS
FRANCES
FRANCIS
FRENUMS
FRINGES
FUNNELS
FUNNIES
GAINERS
GANNETS
GARNERS
GARNETS
GLANCES
GRANGES
GUINEAS
GUNNELS
GUNNERS
GUNNIES
GURNEYS
HARNESS
HEINOUS
HEXNUTS
HINNIES
HIPNESS
HOBNOBS
HORNETS
HOTNESS
HYMNALS
ICINESS
ILLNESS
IRONERS
IRONIES
JENNETS
JENNIES
JITNEYS
JOINERS
JOUNCES
KEENERS
KENNELS
KERNELS
KIDNAPS
KIDNEYS
KWANZAS
LAXNESS
LEANERS
LEANTOS
LIENEES
LIMNERS
LINNETS
LIONESS
LIONETS
LOANERS
LOONIES
LOUNGES
LOWNESS
LUGNUTS
MADNESS
MAENADS
MAGNETS
MAGNUMS
MANNERS
MEANIES
MINNOWS
MOANERS
NANNIES
NEWNESS
NINNIES
NUANCES
NUDNIKS
ODDNESS
OLDNESS
OLDNEWS
OMINOUS
ONENESS
OPENERS
OPINERS
ORANGES
OZONOUS
PANNERS
PATNESS
PAWNEES
PAWNERS
PEANUTS
PENNERS
PENNIES
PENNONS
PEONIES
PHENOLS
PHENOMS
PHINEAS
PHONICS
PHONIES
PICNICS
PIGNUTS
PINNERS
PLANERS
PLANETS
PLENUMS
PLINTHS
PLUNGES
POUNCES
PRANCES
PRINCES
PRUNERS
PSANDQS
QUINCES
QUINOAS
RAWNESS
REDNESS
RENNINS
ROMNEYS
RUINERS
RUINOUS
RUNNELS
RUNNERS
SADNESS
SCHNAPS
SCONCES
SEANCES
SEINERS
SHINERS
SHYNESS
SIENNAS
SIGNALS
SIGNEES
SIGNERS
SIGNETS
SINNERS
SLYNESS
SONNETS
SOONERS
SPINELS
SPINETS
SPONGES
STANCES
STANZAS
STONERS
TANNERS
TANNINS
TEENERS
TENNERS
TINNERS
TOWNERS
TOWNIES
TRANCES
TSONGAS
TUNNELS
TUNNIES
TURNERS
TURNIPS
TWINGES
UNKNITS
UNKNOTS
UNSNAGS
UNSNAPS
WALNUTS
WEENIES
WETNESS
WHINERS
WIENERS
WIENIES
WINNERS
WINNOWS
WITNESS
WRYNESS
YAWNERS
ZINNIAS

••••NS•

AGAINST
ALFONSO
CLEANSE
DEFENSE
EXPANSE
EXPENSE
IMMENSE
INCENSE
INTENSE
LICENSE
OFFENSE
RERINSE
ROMANSH

••••N•S

ABOUNDS
ABSENTS
ACCENTS
ACHENES
ADDENDS
ADVENTS
AFFINES
AIRINGS
ALBINOS
ALKENES
ALMONDS
ALUMNUS
AMOUNTS
ANOINTS
APPENDS
AQUINAS
ASCENDS
ASCENTS
ASSENTS
ATTENDS
ATTUNES
AUGENDS
AWNINGS
BANANAS
BARENTS
BARONGS
BELONGS
BIKINIS
BOVINES
BYGONES
BYLINES
CABANAS
CALENDS
CANINES
CARINAS
CASINGS
CASINOS
CEMENTS
CLIENTS
COLONES
COMINGS
CORONAS
COSINES
DAPHNIS
DEBONES
DEBUNKS
DECANTS
DEFENDS
DEFINES
DEMANDS
DEPENDS
DEPONES
DIVINES
DOCENTS
DOMINOS
DUENNAS
DUGONGS
ECHINUS
EDGINGS
EMBANKS
ENDINGS
ENGINES
EQUINES
ERMINES
ERRANDS
ESSENES
EXPANDS
EXPENDS
EXTENDS
EXTENTS
FACINGS
FAGENDS
FELINES
FILINGS
FIRINGS
FIXINGS
FLAUNTS
FOMENTS
FORINTS
FRIENDS
GAMINES
GERENTS
GERUNDS
GROUNDS
HAZINGS
HIJINKS
IGUANAS
IMPENDS
INCANTS
INDENTS
INFANTS
INNINGS
INTENDS
INTENTS
INTONES
INVENTS
ISLANDS
JACANAS
KAHUNAS
KETONES
KIMONOS
KIWANIS
KORUNAS
LACINGS
LACUNAS
LADINOS
LAGUNAS
LAMENTS
LAMINAS
LATENTS
LATINAS
LATINOS
LEGENDS
LIERNES
LININGS
LIVINGS
LUPINES
MAKINGS
MANANAS
MARINAS
MARINES
MERINOS
MOMENTS
MORANIS
MRBONES
MUTANTS
NOVENAS
OBLONGS
OBTUNDS
OCEANUS
OCTANES
OCTANTS
OFFENDS
ORIENTS
ORPINES
OSCINES
OSMONDS
OUTINGS
PARENTS
PARINGS
PATENTS
PATINAS
PAVANES
PEDANTS
PILINGS
PINONES
PIPINGS
PLAINES
PLAINTS
POCONOS
RAPINES
RATINGS
RAVINES
RAVINGS
REBINDS
RECANES
RECANTS
REDANTS
REFINES
REFUNDS
REGENTS
REHANGS
RELENTS
RELINES
REMANDS
REMENDS
REMINDS
REPENTS
REPINES
RERENTS
RESANDS
RESENDS
RESENTS
RESINGS
RETINAS
RETUNES
REWINDS
REZONES
RIBANDS
RISINGS
RODENTS
RULINGS
SABINES
SARONGS
SAVANTS
SAVINGS
SAYINGS
SECANTS
SECONDS
SHRINES
SHRINKS
SIDINGS
SIENNAS
SILENTS
SIZINGS
SPLINES
SPLINTS
SPRINGS
SPRINTS
SQUINTS
STDENIS
STRANDS
STRINGS
TAGENDS
TALENTS
TAPINGS
TENANTS
TETANUS
THRONES
THRONGS
TIDINGS
TIMINGS
TISANES
TRIUNES
TRUANTS
TYRANTS
UNBENDS
UNBINDS
UNHANDS
UNKINKS
UNLINKS
UNTUNES
UNWINDS
UPLANDS
UPLINKS
VICUNAS
VIKINGS
WAHINES
YEMENIS
ZENANAS

•••••NS

ACTIONS
ADJOINS
AFGHANS
AIRGUNS
AMAZONS
AMNIONS
ANDEANS
ARCHONS
ASHCANS
ASSIGNS
ATAMANS
ATTAINS
AUBURNS
AUTUMNS
AWAKENS
BABOONS
BALEENS
BALKANS
BANYANS
BARRENS
BARYONS
BATTENS
BEACONS
BECKONS
BEMOANS
BIGGUNS
BLAZONS
BOBBINS
BODKINS
BONBONS
BOWFINS
BRETONS
BRITONS
BROGANS
BUNIONS
BURDENS
BUSKINS
BUTTONS
BYTURNS
CAFTANS
CAIMANS
CALKINS
CALLINS
CANCANS
CANNONS
CANTONS
CANYONS
CAPGUNS
CARBONS
CAREENS
CARTONS
CASERNS
CATIONS
CATKINS
CAVEINS
CAVERNS
CITRONS
CLEMENS
CLIPONS
COCOONS
COLLINS
COLUMNS
COMEONS
COMMONS
CORDONS
COSIGNS
COTTONS
COUPONS
COUSINS
COZZENS
CRAVENS
CRAYONS
CRETANS
CRETINS
DAMPENS
DAMSONS
DARKENS
DAWKINS
DEACONS
DEADENS
DEAFENS
DEEPENS
DEHORNS
DEMEANS
DESIGNS
DETAINS
DEVEINS
DICKENS
DISOWNS
DOBBINS
DOLMANS
DOLMENS
DOMAINS
DONJONS
DRAGONS
DROPINS
DRYRUNS
DUNLINS
ELEVENS
ENDRUNS
ENJOINS
ENSIGNS
FADEINS
FALCONS
FANIONS
FASTENS
FATTENS
FIJIANS
FILLINS
FIRKINS
FLACONS
FLAGONS
FLORINS
FRYPANS
GALLONS
GAMMONS
GARCONS
GARDENS
GASCONS
GASKINS
GAUDENS
GERMANS
GIBBONS
GIDEONS
GNOMONS
GOBLINS
GODSONS
GORGONS
GOVERNS
GUIDONS
HAPPENS
HARDENS
HARKENS
HASTENS
HATPINS
HAWKINS
HEAVENS
HETMANS
HIGGINS
HOPKINS
HOSKINS
HOYDENS
HYPHENS
IMPUGNS
INDIANS
INSPANS
INTERNS
ISOGONS
JARGONS
JERKINS
JETGUNS
JETSONS
KAFTANS
KANSANS
KENYANS
KIRMANS
KITTENS
KLAXONS
KMESONS
KOREANS
LAGOONS
LARDONS
LATEENS
LATTENS
LEADINS
LEAVENS
LEGIONS
LEPTONS
LESSENS
LESSONS
LIBYANS
LICHENS
LINDENS
LISTENS
LOCKINS
LOGGINS
LOOSENS
LOTIONS
LOVEINS
MACRONS
MADDENS
MAIDENS
MALIGNS
MANDANS
MARGINS
MARLINS
MAROONS
MARTENS
MARTINS
MATRONS
MEDIANS
MICRONS
MIDDENS
MINIONS
MINOANS
MITTENS
MIZZENS
MODERNS
MORGANS
MORMONS
MOTIONS
MOUTONS
MUDHENS
MUFFINS
MUNTINS
MUSLINS
MUTTONS
NAPKINS
NATIONS
NEATENS
NELSONS
NEURONS
NEWTONS
NOGGINS
NORMANS
NOTIONS
NUBBINS
NUBIANS
OBTAINS
OHIOANS
OILCANS
OILPANS
OPPUGNS
OPTIONS
ORDAINS
ORIGINS
ORISONS
ORLEANS
ORPHANS
OUTGUNS
OUTRUNS
PAPUANS
PARDONS
PARSONS
PATRONS
PATTENS
PEAHENS
PECTINS
PENNONS
PEPSINS
PERKINS
PERSONS
PHOTONS
PICKENS
PIDGINS
PIEPANS
PIETINS
PIGEONS
PIGPENS
PINIONS
PIPKINS
PIPPINS
PISTONS
PLATENS
POISONS
POLLENS
POMPONS
POPGUNS
POPLINS
POPPINS
POTIONS
PRISONS
PROTONS
PUFFINS
PULLONS
PURLINS
PYTHONS
RADIANS
RAGLANS
RAISINS
RATIONS
RATTANS
RAYGUNS
REASONS
RECKONS
REDDENS
REDFINS
REGAINS
REGIONS
REJOINS
REMAINS
RENNINS
REOPENS
REPLANS
REPUGNS
RESIGNS
RETAINS
RETURNS
REUBENS
RIBBONS
ROBBINS
ROLLINS
SADDENS
SALMONS
SALOONS
SAMOANS
SAMPANS
SAPIENS
SCREENS
SEAFANS
SEASONS
SEQUINS
SERMONS
SEXTANS
SEXTONS
SHAMANS
SHOGUNS
SHOOINS
SICKENS
SIMIANS
SIMMONS
SIOUANS
SIPHONS
SISKINS
SIXGUNS
SKIRUNS
SLIPONS
SLOGANS
SLOVENS
SNAPONS
SOFTENS
SPAVINS
SPLEENS
SPRAINS
STAMENS
STEPINS
STEVENS
STJOHNS
STOLONS
STRAINS
SUBORNS
SULTANS
SUMMONS
SUNTANS
SYLVANS
SYRIANS
TAIPANS
TANNINS
TARPONS
TARTANS
TAUTENS
TAVERNS
TENDONS
TENPINS
TEUTONS
TIEPINS
TIMMINS
TINCANS
TOCSINS
TONGANS
TOPGUNS
TOUCANS
TREPANS
TRIGONS
TRITONS
TROJANS
TULSANS
TURBANS
TUREENS
TYCOONS
UNISONS
UPTURNS
URCHINS
USOPENS
UTAHANS
VIOLINS
VIRGINS
VISIONS
VULCANS
WAGGONS
WALKINS
WALKONS
WARDENS
WARRENS
WEAKENS
WEAPONS
WELKINS
WHITENS
WONTONS
WOOLENS
WORSENS
WYVERNS
YAUPONS
YOUMANS
ZIRCONS

N•T••••

NATALIA

NATALIE
NATASHA
NATCHEZ
NATIONS
NATIVES
NATRIUM
NATTERS
NATTIER
NATTILY
NATURAL
NATURED
NATURES
NETSUKE
NETSURF
NETTING
NETTLED
NETTLES
NETWORK
NITPICK
NITRATE
NITRIDE
NITRITE
NITROUS
NITTANY
NITWITS
NOTABIT
NOTABLE
NOTABLY
NOTATED
NOTATES
NOTCHED
NOTCHES
NOTEPAD
NOTHING
NOTHOME
NOTICED
NOTICES
NOTIONS
NOTRUMP
NOTSURE
NOTTRUE
NOTWELL
NUTLETS
NUTMEAT
NUTMEGS
NUTRIAS
NUTTERS
NUTTIER
NUTTILY
NUTTING

N••T•••

NAPTIME
NARTHEX
NASTASE
NASTIER
NASTILY
NATTERS
NATTIER
NATTILY
NEATENS
NEATEST
NECTARS
NEITHER
NEPTUNE
NESTEGG
NESTERS
NESTING
NESTLED
NESTLER
NESTLES
NETTING
NETTLED
NETTLES
NEUTRAL
NEUTRON
NEWTONS
NEWTOWN
NIFTIER
NIFTILY
NITTANY
NOCTURN
NOETICS
NORTHER
NOSTRIL
NOSTRUM
NOTTRUE
NUPTIAL
NURTURE
NUTTERS
NUTTIER
NUTTILY
NUTTING

N•••T••

NAMETAG
NANETTE
NAPHTHA
NECKTIE
NEGATED
NEGATES
NEGATOR
NIGHTIE
NIGHTLY
NONSTOP
NOTATED
NOTATES

N••••T•

NAHUATL
NAIVETE
NANETTE
NARRATE
NAUGHTS
NAUGHTY
NCWYETH
NEOLITH
NEONATE
NEWGATE
NEWMATH
NITRATE
NITRITE
NITWITS
NOUGATS
NOVELTY
NUDISTS
NUGGETS
NUMBATS
NUTLETS

N•••••T

NAILSET
NASCENT
NEAREST
NEATEST
NEGLECT
NEWHART
NEWLEFT
NEWPORT
NIGHEST
NOBLEST
NODOUBT
NOFAULT
NOSEOUT
NOSIEST
NOSWEAT
NOTABIT
NUMBEST
NUTMEAT

•NT••••

ANTACID
ANTAEUS
ANTARES
ANTBEAR
ANTCOWS
ANTEDUP
ANTEING
ANTENNA
ANTESUP
ANTFARM
ANTHEMS
ANTHERS
ANTHILL
ANTHONY
ANTIART
ANTIBES
ANTIGEN
ANTIGUA
ANTILOG
ANTIOCH
ANTIQUE
ANTIWAR
ANTLERS
ANTLION
ANTOINE
ANTONIA
ANTONIN
ANTONIO
ANTONYM
ANTSIER
ANTWERP
CNTOWER
ENTAILS
ENTEBBE
ENTENTE
ENTERED
ENTHUSE
ENTICED
ENTICER
ENTICES
ENTITLE
ENTRAIN
ENTRANT
ENTRAPS
ENTREAT
ENTREES
ENTRIES
ENTROPY
ENTRUST
ENTWINE
INTAKES
INTEGER
INTEGRA
INTENDS
INTENSE
INTENTS
INTERIM
INTERNS
INTERSE
INTONED
INTONER
INTONES
INTROIT
INTRUDE
INTRUST
INTRUTH
INTUITS
ONTARIO
ONTHEGO
ONTHEQT
ONTOPOF
ONTRIAL
UNTACKS
UNTAMED
UNTAPED
UNTRAPS
UNTRIED
UNTRUTH
UNTUNED
UNTUNES
UNTWIST
UNTYING

•N•T•••

ANATOLE
ANATOMY
ANOTHER
ANYTIME
INITIAL
INSTALL
INSTANT
INSTATE
INSTEAD
INSTEPS
INSTILL
INSTILS
INSTOCK
INSTORE
INSTYLE
INUTILE
KNITTED
KNITTER
KNOTTED
ONATEAR
ONETIME
ONSTAGE
UNCTION
UNITARY
UNITERS
UNITIES
UNITING
UNITIVE
UNSTACK
UNSTICK
UNSTOPS
UNSTRAP
UNSTUCK

•N••T••

ANNATTO
ANNETTE
ENACTED
ENACTOR
ENTITLE
GNOSTIC
INAPTLY
INASTEW
INCITED
INCITER
INCITES
INDITED
INDITES
INDUTCH
INEPTLY
INERTIA
INERTLY
INMATES
INPETTO
INVITED
INVITES
INVITRO
KNITTED
KNITTER
KNOTTED
ONESTEP
SNIFTER
SNOOTED
SNORTED
SNORTER
UNDATED
UNHITCH
UNLATCH
UNRATED
UNSATED

•N•••T•

ANDANTE
ANIMATE
ANIMATO
ANKLETS
ANNATTO
ANNETTE
ANNUITY
ANOINTS
ANXIETY
ENLISTS
ENROOTS
ENROUTE
ENSUITE
ENTENTE
INCANTS
INCEPTS
INDENTS
INDEPTH
INDICTS
INDUCTS
INFANTA
INFANTS
INFECTS
INFESTS
INFLATE
INGESTS
INGRATE
INHASTE
INJECTS
INPETTO
INSECTS
INSERTS
INSISTS
INSPOTS
INSTATE
INSULTS
INTENTS
INTRUTH
INTUITS
INVENTS
INVERTS
INVESTS
KNIGHTS
ONADATE
SNAPSTO
SNOCATS
UNBOLTS
UNCOUTH
UNCRATE
UNEARTH
UNKNITS
UNKNOTS
UNQUOTE
UNSEATS
UNTRUTH

•N••••T

ANALYST
ANAPEST
ANCIENT
ANIMIST
ANTIART
ENCHANT
ENCRUST
ENCRYPT
ENDMOST
ENGRAFT
ENTRANT
ENTREAT
ENTRUST
INANEST
INASNIT
INASPOT
INCIPIT
INDOUBT
INEXACT
INFLECT
INFLICT
INFRONT
INHABIT
INHERIT
INHIBIT
INKBLOT
INKSPOT
INORBIT
INPOINT
INPRINT
INQUEST
INSHORT
INSIGHT
INSPECT
INSTANT
INTROIT
INTRUST
KNESSET
ONADIET
ONESHOT
ONSIGHT
ONTHEQT
SNAPSAT
SNEERAT
SNIDEST
SNIFFAT
SNIGLET
SNIPEAT
SNIPPET
UNBLEST
UNGUENT
UNKEMPT
UNSPENT
UNSWEPT
UNTWIST

••NT•••

AUNTIES
BANTAMS
BANTERS
BENTHAM
BENTLEY
BENTSEN
BUNTING
CANTATA
CANTEEN
CANTERS
CANTINA
CANTING
CANTLES
CANTONS
CANTORS
CENTAUR
CENTAVO
CENTERS
CENTIME
CENTIMO
CENTRAL
CENTRED
CENTRES
CENTRIC
CENTURY
CONTACT
CONTAIN
CONTEMN
CONTEND
CONTENT
CONTEST
CONTEXT
CONTORT
CONTOUR
CONTRAS
CONTROL
CONTUSE
CYNTHIA
DENTATE
DENTINE
DENTING
DENTIST
DENTURE
FANTAIL
FANTASY
FONTEYN
FONTINA
GANTLET
GENTEEL
GENTIAN
GENTILE
GENTLED
GENTLER
GENTLES
GUNTHER
HINTING
HINTSAT
HUNTERS
HUNTING
HUNTLEY
JANTZEN
KONTIKI
LANTANA
LANTERN
LENTILS
LINTELS
LINTIER
MANTELS
MANTLED
MANTLES
MANTRAP
MANTRAS
MANTRIC
MENTHOL
MENTION
MENTORS
MINTERS
MINTIER
MINTING
MONTAGE
MONTANA
MONTAND
MONTANE
MONTEGO
MONTEUX
MONTHLY
MONTOYA
MUNTINS
PANTHER
PANTING
PENTADS
PINTAIL
PONTIAC
PONTIFF
PONTINE
PONTIUS
PONTOON
PUNTERS
PUNTING
QINTARS
RANTERS
RANTING
RENTALS
RENTERS
RENTING
RONTGEN
RUNTIER
SANTAFE
SANTANA
SANTINI
SANTIRS
SENTFOR
SENTOFF
SENTOUT
SUNTANS
TANTARA
TANTRUM
TENTERS
TENTING
TINTERN
TINTERS
TINTING
TINTYPE
TONTINE
VANTAGE
VENTERS
VENTING
VENTRAL
VENTURA
VENTURE
VINTAGE
VINTNER
WANTADS
WANTING
WANTOUT
WANTSIN
WANTSTO
WENTAPE
WENTBAD
WENTFOR
WENTOFF
WENTOUT
WINTERS
WINTERY
WONTONS
XANTHAN
XANTHIC

••N•T••

AGNATES
ANNATTO
ANNETTE
BENATAR
BONITOS
DENOTED
DENOTES
DINETTE
DONATED
DONATES
DONATOR
FANATIC
FENETRE
GENETIC
HANGTEN
IGNITED
IGNITER
IGNITES
JANITOR
KINETIC
KINGTUT
LANGTRY
LENGTHS
LENGTHY
LONGTON
LUNATIC
MANATEE
MANITOU
MENOTTI
MINUTES
MINUTIA
MONITOR
MONSTER
NANETTE
NONSTOP
ORNETTE
ORNITHO
PANETTA
PENATES
PINATAS
PINETAR
PINETUM
PUNSTER
RENOTES
SANCTUM
SENATES
SENATOR
SINATRA
SONATAS
TANKTOP
TINSTAR
TINYTIM
WINGTIP
WINSTON
WYNETTE
YANGTZE
YANKTON
ZENITHS

••N••T•

AMNESTY
ANNATTO
ANNETTE
ANNUITY
BANDITO
BANDITS
BENEATH
BENNETT
BONNETS
CANASTA
CANTATA
CONFUTE
CONNOTE
DENSITY
DENTATE
DINETTE
DYNASTS
DYNASTY
ERNESTO
FANJETS
GANGSTA
GANNETS
GANNETT
HENBITS
HONESTY
JENNETS
JUNKETS
KENNETH
LANCETS
LINEATE
LINNETS
MANDATE
MENOTTI
MINOLTA
MINUETS
NANETTE
ORNETTE
PANDITS
PANETTA
PENALTY
PENNATE
PENULTS
PINNATE
PUNDITS
RANINTO
RANLATE
RUNINTO
RUNLETS
RUNWITH
SENNETT
SENSATE
SINGSTO
SONNETS
SUNBATH
SUNCITY
SUNSETS
TENANTS
TENDSTO
TINHATS
WANTSTO
WYNETTE

••N•••T

BANQUET
BENEFIT
BENNETT
BONIEST
CONCEIT
CONCEPT
CONCERT
CONCOCT
CONDUCT
CONDUIT
CONGEST
CONKOUT
CONNECT
CONSENT
CONSIST
CONSORT
CONSULT
CONTACT
CONTENT
CONTEST
CONTEXT
CONTORT
CONVENT
CONVERT
CONVICT
DANKEST
DENSEST
DENTIST
DINGBAT
DINMONT
FANBELT
FANSOUT
FINDOUT
FINEART
FONDANT
FONDEST
FUNFEST
GANNETT
GANTLET
GUNBOAT
GUNSHOT
HANDOUT
HANDSET
HANGOUT
HINTSAT
HUNGOUT
JUNKART
KINDEST
KINGRAT
KINGTUT
LANDSAT
LANKEST
LENFANT
LENIENT
LONGEST
LONNROT
LUNGEAT
MANHUNT
MANUMIT
MANXCAT
MINARET
MINDSET
MONOCOT
PANDECT
PANSOUT
PENDANT
PENDENT
PENNANT
PINENUT
PINIEST
PINKEST
PUNGENT
PUNIEST
RANKEST
RANRIOT
RENAULT
RINGLET
RINGOUT
RUNRIOT
RUNSOUT
SANDLOT
SANGOUT
SENDOUT
SENNETT
SENTOUT
SINGOUT
SUNBELT
SUNKIST
SUNSPOT
TANGENT
TANNEST
TENSEST
TENSPOT
TINIEST
TONIEST
TONIGHT
TUNEOUT
VANZANT
VINCENT
WANTOUT
WENTOUT
WINGNUT
WINGSIT
WINKOUT
WINKSAT
WINSOUT
ZANIEST
ZONKOUT

•••NT••

ACANTHI
BIENTOT
BLUNTED
BLUNTER
BLUNTLY
BURNTUP
CHANTED
CHANTER
CHANTEY
CHINTZY
CLINTON
COUNTED
COUNTER
COUNTON
COUNTRY
DAUNTED
FAINTED
FAINTER
FAINTLY
FEINTED
FRANTIC
FRONTAL
FRONTED
FRONTON
GAUNTER
GAUNTLY
GLINTED
GRANTED
GRANTEE
GRANTOR
GRUNTED
HAUNTED
IDENTIC
JAUNTED
JOINTED
JOINTLY
LEANTOS
MAINTOP
MOUNTED
MOUNTIE
OMENTUM
OPENTOE
PAINTED
PAINTER
PHANTOM
PLANTAR
PLANTED
PLANTER
PLINTHS
POINTED
POINTER
POINTTO
PRINTED
PRINTER
QUANTUM
QUENTIN
QUINTET
REENTER
REENTRY
SAINTED
SAINTLY
SAUNTER
SCANTED
SCANTER
SCANTLY
SCENTED
SHANTER
SHUNTED
SLANTED
STANTON
STENTOR
STINTED
STUNTED
TAINTED
TAUNTED
TRENTON
VAUNTED
VAUNTER

•••N•T•

ACONITE
AMENITY
BENNETT
BONNETS
BOUNDTO
BRINGTO
BRUNETS
BURNETT
CAPNUTS
CARNETS
CLINGTO
COGNATE
CONNOTE
CORNETS
CYGNETS
DIGNITY
EBONITE
EMANATE
FLYNETS
GANNETS
GANNETT
GARNETS
GRANITE
HEXNUTS
HORNETS
JENNETS
KENNETH
KEYNOTE
LIGNITE
LINNETS
LIONETS
LUGNUTS
LYINGTO
MAGNATE
MAGNETO
MAGNETS
NEONATE
OWINGTO
PEANUTS
PENNATE
PIGNUTS
PINNATE
PLANETS
POINTTO
REUNITE
SENNETT
SIGNETS
SONNETS
SPINETS
TERNATE
TRINITY
TURNSTO
UNKNITS
UNKNOTS
URANITE
WALNUTS

•••N••T

AGONIST
AMONGST
BENNETT
BIENTOT
BLANKET
BLINKAT
BURNETT

BURNOUT
CONNECT
COONCAT
DOWNPAT
EARNEST
EMINENT
EVENEST
EVENOUT
GANNETT
GOINGAT
GYMNAST
HORNIST
INANEST
IRONOUT
KEENEST
LEANEST
LONNROT
MEANEST
MOONLIT
MOONSET
OPENPIT
PENNANT
PIANIST
QUINTET
QUONSET
RAINHAT
RAINOUT
REENACT
REGNANT
REMNANT
SENNETT
SIGNOUT
SOONEST
SPINOUT
SPUNOUT
TANNEST
TLINGIT
TORNOUT
TRANSIT
TRINKET
TURNOUT
VAINEST
WORNOUT
WYANDOT

••••NT•
ABSENTS
ACCENTS
ADDONTO
ADVENTS
ALDENTE
AMOUNTS
ANDANTE
ANOINTS
APLENTY
ASCENTS
ASHANTI
ASSENTS
ATLANTA
BARENTS
CEMENTS
CHIANTI
CLIENTS
CORINTH
CUTINTO
DECANTS
DETENTE
DOCENTS
DOZENTH
DURANTE
ENTENTE
EXTENTS
FLAUNTS
FOMENTS
FORINTS
GERENTS
GETINTO
GIVENTO
GOTINTO
INCANTS
INDENTS
INFANTA
INFANTS
INTENTS
INVENTS
JACINTO
LAMENTS
LATENTS
LAYINTO
LEPANTO
LITINTO
MAGENTA
MEMENTO
MOMENTS
MUTANTS
OCTANTS
ORIENTE
ORIENTS
OTRANTO
PARENTS
PATENTS
PEDANTS
PICANTE
PIMENTO
PLAINTS
POLENTA
PRYINTO
RANINTO
RECANTS
REDANTS
REGENTS
RELENTS
REPENTS
RERENTS
RESENTS
RIPINTO
RODENTS
RUNINTO
SAVANTS
SECANTS
SETINTO
SEVENTH
SEVENTY
SILENTS
SPLINTS
SPRINTS
SQUANTO
SQUINTS
SQUINTY
TALENTS
TARANTO
TENANTS
TIEINTO
TORONTO
TRUANTS
TYRANTS
VEDANTA
YEARNTO

••••N•T
ADJUNCT
AGAINST
BARONET
BAYONET
BOWKNOT
CABINET
COCONUT
CORONET
DEFUNCT
DRAGNET
EATENAT
EXTINCT
FISHNET
FROWNAT
GILLNET
HAIRNET
HAVENOT
INASNIT
JACONET
LIFENET
LOCKNUT
MAGINOT
PINENUT
SUBUNIT
TOPKNOT
WHATNOT
WINGNUT

•••••NT
ACCOUNT
ADAMANT
AFFRONT
AILMENT
ALIMENT
AMBIENT
ANCIENT
APPOINT
ARMYANT
AUGMENT
BELMONT
BLATANT
BUOYANT
CLEMENT
COMMENT
CONSENT
CONTENT
CONVENT
COOLANT
COULDNT
COURANT
CURRANT
CURRENT
DEFIANT
DESCANT
DESCENT
DEVIANT
DINMONT
DISSENT
DISTANT
DORMANT
ELEGANT
ELEMENT
EMINENT
ENCHANT
ENTRANT
EVIDENT
EXIGENT
FERMENT
FERVENT
FIGMENT
FIREANT
FONDANT
FORRENT
FORWENT
FREMONT
FULGENT
GALLANT
GARMENT
GERAINT
HYDRANT
IMPLANT
IMPRINT
INFRONT
INPOINT
INPRINT
INSTANT
ITERANT
JOBHUNT
LAMBENT
LAURENT
LENFANT
LENIENT
MANHUNT
MEDIANT
MIGHTNT
MIGRANT
MORDANT
MORDENT
NASCENT
ODDMENT
OPULENT
OXIDANT
PAGEANT
PASSANT
PATIENT
PAYMENT
PEASANT
PECCANT
PENDANT
PENDENT
PENNANT
PERCENT
PIGMENT
PIQUANT
PORTENT
PRESENT
PREVENT
PRUDENT
PUNGENT
PUPTENT
RADIANT
RAIMENT
RAMPANT
REAGENT
RECOUNT
REDCENT
REGNANT
RELIANT
REMNANT
REMOUNT
REPAINT
REPLANT
REPRINT
SALIENT
SAPIENT
SARGENT
SEALANT
SEGMENT
SERPENT
SERVANT
SEXTANT
SOLVENT
SPIRANT
STUDENT
TANGENT
TORMENT
TORRENT
TRIDENT
ULULANT
UNGUENT
UNSPENT
UPFRONT
VAGRANT
VALIANT
VANZANT
VARIANT
VARMINT
VERDANT
VERMONT
VIBRANT
VINCENT
VIOLENT
WARRANT
WOULDNT

NU•••••
NUANCED
NUANCES
NUBBIER
NUBBINS
NUBBLES
NUBIANS
NUCLEAR
NUCLEIC
NUCLEON
NUCLEUS
NUCLIDE
NUDGERS
NUDGING
NUDISTS
NUDNIKS
NUGGETS
NULLIFY
NULLING
NUMBATS
NUMBERS
NUMBEST
NUMBING
NUMERAL
NUMERIC
NUNCIOS
NUNNERY
NUPTIAL
NUREYEV
NURSERS
NURSERY
NURSING
NURTURE
NUTLETS
NUTMEAT
NUTMEGS
NUTRIAS
NUTTERS
NUTTIER
NUTTILY
NUTTING
NUZZLED
NUZZLER
NUZZLES

N•U••••
NAUGHTS
NAUGHTY
NEURONE
NEURONS
NEUTRAL
NEUTRON
NOUGATS
NOURISH
NOUVEAU

N••U•••
NAHUATL
NATURAL
NATURED
NATURES
NEBULAE
NEBULAR
NEBULAS
NEXUSES
NOCUOUS
NODULAR
NODULES
NOGUCHI
NONUSER

N•••U••
NEPTUNE
NETSUKE
NETSURF
NIEBUHR
NOCTURN
NODOUBT
NOFAULT
NOTRUMP
NOTSURE
NURTURE

N••••U•
NATRIUM
NEEDFUL
NERVOUS
NIOBIUM
NITROUS
NOCUOUS
NONPLUS
NOSEEUM
NOSEOUT
NOSTRUM
NOTTRUE
NOXIOUS
NUCLEUS

N•••••U
NEARYOU
NOUVEAU

•NU••••
ENURING
FNUMBER
INURING
INUTILE
KNUCKLE
KNURLED
SNUBBED
SNUFFED
SNUFFER
SNUFFLE
SNUGGER
SNUGGLE
UNUSUAL

•N•U•••
ANGULAR
ANNUALS
ANNUITY
ANNULAR
ANNULUS
ANOUILH
ENDUING
ENDURED
ENDURES
ENDUSER
ENGULFS
ENOUNCE
ENSUING
ENSUITE
ENSURED
ENSURES
INCUDES
INDUCED
INDUCER
INDUCES
INDUCTS
INDULGE
INDUTCH
INFUSED
INFUSES
INHUMAN
INJURED
INJURES
INQUEST
INQUIRE
INQUIRY
INSULAR
INSULIN
INSULTS
INSURED
INSURES
INTUITS
ONGUARD
UNCURLS
UNFURLS
UNGUENT
UNLUCKY
UNQUOTE
UNTUNED
UNTUNES

•N••U••
ANAHUAC
ENCRUST
ENDRUNS
ENGLUND
ENROUTE
ENSOULS
ENTHUSE
ENTRUST
INARUSH
INBOUND
INCLUDE
INDOUBT
INHOUSE
INOCULA
INTRUDE
INTRUST
INTRUTH
SNAFUED
UNBOUND
UNCOUTH
UNEQUAL
UNGLUED
UNPLUGS
UNSOUND
UNSTUCK
UNTRUTH
UNUSUAL
UNWOUND

•N•••U•
ANGELUS
ANNULUS
ANTAEUS
ANTEDUP
ANTESUP
ANTIGUA
ANTIQUE
ANXIOUS
ENAMOUR
ENVIOUS
INFOCUS
INGENUE
INGROUP
INVACUO
INVOGUE
ONEROUS
SNAPSUP

•N••••U
ANGELOU
ONLYYOU

••NU•••
ANNUALS
ANNUITY
ANNULAR
ANNULUS
BENUMBS
BONUSES
DENUDED
DENUDES
EUNUCHS
GENUINE
HANUKAH
JANUARY
MANUALS
MANUMIT
MENUHIN
MINUEND
MINUETS
MINUSES
MINUTES
MINUTIA
NONUSER
PANURGE
PENUCHE
PENULTS
SINUOUS
SINUSES
TENUOUS
TENURED
TENURES

••N•U••
BANQUET
CENSURE
CENTURY
CONCURS
CONDUCE
CONDUCT
CONDUIT
CONFUSE
CONFUTE
CONJURE
CONQUER
CONSULS
CONSULT
CONSUME
CONTUSE
DENEUVE
DENTURE
DONJUAN
FONDUES
HANGUPS
HONOURS
JONQUIL
LANGUID
LANGUOR
LANGURS
LINEUPS
LINGUAL
LINKUPS
LONGUES
MANHUNT
PENGUIN
PINCURL
RENAULT
SANJUAN
SANLUIS
SENDUPS
SENSUAL
SUNBURN
SYNFUEL
TONGUED
TONGUES
TONSURE
TUNEUPS
VENTURA
VENTURE
WINDUPS

••N••U•
ANNULUS
BANEFUL
BANGSUP
BINDSUP
BONEDUP
BONESUP
BONJOUR
CANDOUR
CANOPUS
CENTAUR
CONKOUT
CONTOUR
DANSEUR
DONAHUE
FANSOUT
FINDOUT
GANGSUP
HANDFUL
HANDGUN
HANDOUT
HANDSUP
HANGOUT
HANGSUP
HUNGOUT
IBNSAUD
IGNEOUS
JUNEBUG
KINGTUT
LANDAUS
LINEDUP
LINESUP
LONGRUN
MANAGUA
MANHOUR
MINDFUL
MINIBUS
MINIMUM
MONIQUE
MONTEUX
NONPLUS
OMNIBUS
OWNEDUP
PANSOUT
PINENUT
PINETUM
PONTIUS
PUNCHUP
RANCOUR
RINGOUT
RINGSUP
RUNSOUT
SANCTUM
SANGOUT
SENDOUT
SENDSUP
SENTOUT
SINGOUT
SINUOUS
TANKFUL
TANKSUP
TANTRUM
TENFOUR
TENSEUP
TENUOUS
TONEDUP
TONESUP
TUNEDUP
TUNEFUL
TUNEOUT
TUNESUP
VANOCUR
WANTOUT
WENTOUT
WINDSUP
WINGNUT
WINKOUT
WINSOUT
ZONKOUT

••N•••U
MANITOU
RONDEAU
TONNEAU

•••NU••
AVENUES
CAPNUTS
CHINUPS
EMANUEL
FRENUMS
GRANULE
HEXNUTS
LUGNUTS
MAGNUMS
PEANUTS
PIGNUTS
PLENUMS
SAMNUNN
WALNUTS

•••N•U•
BORNEUP
BOUNDUP
BRINGUP
BURNOUT
BURNSUP
BURNTUP
CRANIUM
CRANKUP
DOINGUP
EVENOUT
EVENSUP
FLANEUR
GAINFUL
GOINGUP
HAFNIUM
HAHNIUM
HEINOUS
IRONOUT
JEANLUC
JOINSUP
LIONCUB
OMENTUM
OMINOUS
OPENSUP
OZONOUS
PAINFUL
PRONOUN
QUANTUM
QUINQUE
RAINOUT
RHENIUM
ROUNDUP
RUINOUS
SIGNOUT
SIGNSUP
SPINOUT
SPUNOUT
STANDUP
STUNGUN
THINKUP
TORNOUT
TURNOUT
TURNSUP
TYINGUP
URANIUM
USINGUP
WORNOUT
WOUNDUP
YOUNGUN

•••N••U
FRENEAU
TONNEAU

••••NU•
ALUMNUS
BLOWNUP
CLEANUP
COCONUT
DRAWNUP
EATENUP
ECHINUS
GROWNUP
INGENUE
JEJUNUM
LOCKNUT
OCEANUS
ORGANUM
PINENUT
RAPANUI
RETINUE
REVENUE
SEVENUP
STERNUM
TETANUS
WINGNUT
WOKENUP

•••••NU
PARVENU

N•V••••
NAVAHOS
NAVAJOS
NAVARRE
NEVADAN
NEVILLE
NOVARRO
NOVELLA
NOVELLE
NOVELTY
NOVENAS
NOVICES

N••V•••
NAIVELY
NAIVETE
NERVIER
NERVILY
NERVOUS
NIRVANA
NOUVEAU

N•••V••
NATIVES
NINEVEH

N••••V•
NEWWAVE

N•••••V
NABOKOV
NEMEROV
NUREYEV

•NV••••
ENVELOP
ENVIOUS
ENVYING
INVACUO
INVADED
INVADER
INVADES
INVALID
INVEIGH
INVENTS
INVERSE
INVERTS
INVESTS
INVITED
INVITES
INVITRO
INVOGUE
INVOICE
INVOKED
INVOKER
INVOKES
INVOLVE
UNVEILS

•N•V•••
KNAVERY
KNAVISH
SNIVELS
UNAVOCE

•N••V••
ANDOVER
ENDIVES
ENLIVEN
INCIVIL
INFAVOR
KNIEVEL
UNCIVIL
UNCOVER
UNLOVED
UNMOVED
UNPAVED
UNRAVEL

•N•••V•
ANCHOVY
ENCLAVE
ENGRAVE
ENSLAVE
INVOLVE
ONLEAVE
UNITIVE
UNNERVE
UNWEAVE

••NV•••
CANVASS
CONVENE
CONVENT
CONVERT
CONVEYS
CONVICT
CONVOKE
CONVOYS
JANVIER

••N•V••
DONOVAN
HANOVER
MINIVAN
MINIVER
NINEVEH
RANOVER
RUNOVER

••N••V•
BONJOVI
CENTAVO
CONCAVE
CONNIVE
DENEUVE
GINGIVA
MINERVA
PENSIVE
TENSIVE
UNNERVE

•••N•V•
CONNIVE
ULANOVA

••••N•V
GODUNOV
ROMANOV
ULYANOV
USTINOV

N•W••••
NCWYETH
NEWAGER
NEWBORN
NEWDEAL
NEWGATE
NEWHART
NEWLEFT
NEWLOOK
NEWMATH
NEWMOON
NEWMOWN
NEWNESS
NEWPORT
NEWSBOY
NEWSDAY
NEWSIER
NEWSMAN
NEWSMEN
NEWTONS
NEWTOWN
NEWWAVE
NEWYEAR
NEWYORK
NOWHERE

N••W•••
NARWALS
NARWHAL
NETWORK
NEWWAVE
NITWITS
NOSWEAT

NOTWELL

N••••W•
NARROWS
NEPHEWS
NEWMOWN
NEWTOWN
NOSHOWS

•NW••••
ENWRAPS
INWARDS
ONWARDS
UNWEAVE
UNWINDS
UNWISER
UNWOUND
UNWRAPS

•N•W•••
ANSWERS
ANTWERP
ENDWAYS
ENDWISE
ENTWINE
GNAWERS
GNAWING
INAWEOF
INAWORD
INDWELL
INKWELL
KNOWHOW
KNOWING
SNOWCAP
SNOWDAY
SNOWDON
SNOWIER
SNOWING
SNOWJOB
SNOWMAN
SNOWMEN
SNOWPEA
SNOWSIN
UNAWARE
UNSWEPT
UNTWIST

•N••W••
ANTIWAR
CNTOWER
ENDOWED
INNOWAY
UNBOWED
UNSEWED

•N•••W•
ANDREWS
ANTCOWS
INFLOWS
INGROWN
UNDRAWN
UNKNOWN

•N••••W
INASTEW
KNOWHOW
UNSCREW

••NW•••
GUNWALE
PINWALE
RUNWAYS
RUNWITH
TINWORK

••N•W••
DUNAWAY
GANGWAY
INNOWAY
JANEWAY
MANOWAR
RANAWAY
RENEWAL
RENEWED
RENEWER
RUNAWAY

••N••W•
MINNOWS
PINDOWN
RUNDOWN
SUNDEWS
SUNDOWN
WINDOWS
WINNOWS

••N•••W
BANDSAW
DANELAW
GANGSAW
HANDSAW
LONGBOW
MANILOW
TONEROW
WINDROW
WINSLOW

•••N•W•
BARNOWL
MINNOWS
OKINAWA
OLDNEWS
UNKNOWN
WINNOWS

•••N••W
CORNROW
DOWNBOW
RAINBOW

••••N•W
ASOFNOW
JUSTNOW
LIKENEW
SAGINAW
UPTONOW
YOUKNOW

N•X••••
NEXUSES
NOXIOUS
NOXZEMA

N•••••X
NARTHEX

•NX••••
ANXIETY
ANXIOUS

•N•X•••
INEXACT

•N••X••
ANNEXED
ANNEXES
INDEXED
INDEXES
UNBOXED
UNBOXES
UNFIXED

••NX•••
JINXING
MANXCAT
MANXMAN
MANXMEN

••N•X••
ANNEXED
ANNEXES

••N••X•
CONTEXT

••N•••X
BANDBOX
CINEMAX
HENDRIX
MONTEUX
PANCHAX
SANDBOX

•••N••X
SPANDEX

••••N•X
EQUINOX
KLEENEX
PHOENIX

•••••NX
PHALANX
PHARYNX

N•Y••••
NAYSAID
NAYSAYS

N••Y•••
NCWYETH
NEWYEAR
NEWYORK

N•••Y••
NEARYOU
NUREYEV

N••••Y•
NAYSAYS

N•••••Y
NAIVELY
NAKEDLY
NAMEDAY
NASALLY
NASTILY
NATTILY
NAUGHTY
NEEDILY
NERVILY
NEWSBOY
NEWSDAY
NIFTILY
NIGHTLY
NITTANY
NOISILY
NOONDAY
NOSEGAY
NOTABLY
NOVELTY
NULLIFY
NUNNERY
NURSERY
NUTTILY

•NY••••
ANYBODY
ANYMORE
ANYTIME
UNYOKED
UNYOKES

•N•Y•••
ANDYKIM
ENVYING
ENZYMES
INKYCAP
ONLYYOU
UNDYING
UNTYING

•N••Y••
ANALYSE
ANALYST
ANALYZE
ANNOYED
ANODYNE
ANONYMS
ENCRYPT
ENJOYED
INSTYLE
ONEEYED
ONLYYOU

•N•••Y•
ANTONYM
ENDWAYS

•N••••Y
ANALOGY
ANARCHY
ANATOMY
ANCHOVY
ANGRILY
ANNUITY
ANOMALY
ANTHONY
ANXIETY
ANYBODY
ENDPLAY
ENTROPY
INANELY
INAPTLY
INEPTLY
INERTLY
INFANCY
INNOWAY
INQUIRY
KNAVERY
SNIDELY
SNOWDAY
UNCANNY
UNGODLY
UNHANDY
UNHAPPY
UNITARY
UNLUCKY
UNREADY

••NY•••
BANYANS
CANYONS
DENYING
KENYANS
LANYARD
MANYEAR
PONYING
TINYTIM

••N•Y••
ANNOYED
HONEYED
MONEYED
TINTYPE
VANDYCK
VANDYKE
VANEYCK

••N••Y•
CONVEYS
CONVOYS
DONKEYS
FONTEYN
MANDAYS
MONDAYS
MONKEYS
MONTOYA
RUNWAYS
SUNDAYS
SUNRAYS
SYNONYM

••N•••Y
AMNESTY
ANNUITY
BANALLY
BENTLEY
BINDERY
BONEDRY
BONNILY
CANNERY
CANNILY
CENTURY
CONAKRY
CONNERY
DENNEHY
DENSELY
DENSITY
DINGILY
DUNAWAY
DYNASTY
FANCILY
FANTASY
FINALLY
FINICKY
FUNNILY
GANGWAY
GINGERY
GUNNERY
GUNPLAY
HANDILY
HENNERY
HONESTY
HUNGARY
HUNTLEY
IGNOBLY
INNOWAY
JANEWAY
JANUARY
KENNEDY
LANGLEY
LANGTRY
LANKILY
LENGTHY
LINDSAY
LINDSEY
MONTHLY
NUNNERY
PANICKY
PANOPLY
PENALTY
RANAWAY
RUNAWAY
RUNSDRY
SANDFLY
SENSORY
SUNCITY
SUNNILY
SYNERGY
TANNERY
TENABLY
TENANCY
TENSELY
TINNILY
TONALLY
WINFREY
WINTERY
ZONALLY

•••NY••
ANONYMS
EPONYMS

•••N•Y•
BARNEYS
GURNEYS
JITNEYS
KIDNEYS
ROMNEYS

•••N••Y
AMENITY
BEANERY
BLANDLY
BLANKLY
BLINDLY
BLUNTLY
BONNILY
BYANDBY
CANNERY
CANNILY
CHANTEY
CHINTZY
CONNERY
CORNILY
COUNTRY
CRINKLY
CRUNCHY
DENNEHY
DIGNIFY
DIGNITY
ECONOMY
FAINTLY
FOUNDRY
FRANKLY
FUNNILY
GAINSAY
GAUNTLY
GOINGBY
GRANARY
GRANDLY
GUNNERY
HENNERY
HORNSBY
INANELY
JOHNGAY
JOHNJAY
JOINERY
JOINTLY
KENNEDY
LAUNDRY
MAGNIFY
NOONDAY
NUNNERY
PAUNCHY
PHONILY
PLENARY
REENTRY
REUNIFY
ROUNDLY
SAINTLY
SCANTLY
SCENERY
SIGNIFY
SOUNDLY
SPANGLY
SPINDLY
STANDBY
STANLEY
STONILY
SUNNILY
SWINGBY
TANNERY
TERNARY
TINNILY
TRENARY
TRINITY
TURNKEY
TWINKLY
VRONSKY
WRINKLY
WRONGLY

••••NY•
ACRONYM
ANTONYM
HOMONYM
SYNONYM

••••N•Y
APLENTY
ARDENCY
BALONEY
BLARNEY
CHIMNEY
CHUTNEY
CLEANLY
CLOONEY
COCKNEY
COGENCY
DELANEY
FLUENCY
HACKNEY
HUMANLY
INFANCY
JOURNEY
LATENCY
LAZENBY
MAHONEY
MASONRY
ORGANDY
ORMANDY
PLAINLY
PLIANCY
POTENCY
QUEENLY
RECENCY
REGENCY
SEVENTY
SPRINGY
SQUINTY
STERNLY
STRINGY
TENANCY
TIERNEY
TOURNEY
TRUANCY
TYRANNY
UNCANNY
UNHANDY
URGENCY
VACANCY
WCHANDY
WHITNEY
WOMANLY

•••••NY
ALIMONY
ANTHONY
BALCONY
BETHANY
BIOGENY
CALUMNY
COMPANY
COTTONY
DESTINY
DITTANY
EUPHONY
GERMANY
HARMONY
LARCENY
NITTANY
PROGENY
SCRAWNY
TAMMANY
TIFFANY
TUSCANY
TYRANNY
UNCANNY
YEVGENY

N•Z••••
NOZZLES
NUZZLED
NUZZLER
NUZZLES

N••Z•••
NONZERO
NOXZEMA
NOZZLES
NUZZLED
NUZZLER
NUZZLES

N•••••Z
NATCHEZ

•NZ••••
ENZYMES
UNZONED

•N•Z•••
ENDZONE

•N••Z••
SNEEZED
SNEEZER
SNEEZES
SNOOZED
SNOOZES
UNFAZED

•N•••Z•
ANALYZE
ANASAZI
ANODIZE
INADAZE

••NZ•••
BENZENE
CANZONE
CINZANO
FANZINE
NONZERO
PANZERS
VANZANT

••N•Z••
BENAZIR
DENIZEN
IONIZED
IONIZER
IONIZES
JANTZEN

••N••Z•
BONANZA
GINFIZZ
MENDOZA
YANGTZE

••N•••Z
GINFIZZ

•••NZ••
BRONZED
BRONZES
KWANZAS
STANZAS

•••N•Z•
AGONIZE
CHINTZY
LIONIZE
SPINOZA

•••N••Z
FRANKOZ

••••NZ•
BONANZA
CADENZA
FIRENZE
LORENZO
ORGANZA

••••N•Z
ALBENIZ
JIMENEZ
LEIBNIZ

•••••NZ
KOBLENZ

OA•••••
OAKFERN
OAKLAND
OAKLAWN
OAKLEAF
OAKMOSS
OAKTREE
OARLESS
OARLOCK
OATMEAL

O•A••••
OBADIAH
OCANADA
OCARINA
OFASORT
OKAYING
ONADARE
ONADATE
ONADIET
ONAGERS
ONANDON
ONAROLL
ONASSIS
ONATEAR
OPACITY
OPALINE
OPAQUES
ORACLES
ORANGES
ORATING
ORATION
ORATORS
ORATORY
OVATION

O••A•••
OBLASTS
OBLATES
OBTAINS
OCEANIA
OCEANIC
OCEANID
OCEANUS
OCTAGON
OCTANES
OCTANTS
OCTAVES
OCTAVIA
OCTAVOS
OGLALAS
OLEATES
ONPAPER
ONTARIO
ONWARDS
OPIATES
ORDAINS
ORGANDY
ORGANIC
ORGANON
ORGANUM
ORGANZA
ORLANDO
ORMANDY
OTRANTO
OTTAWAS
OUTACTS
OUTAGES
OXCARTS

O•••A••
OAKLAND
OAKLAWN
OBVIATE
OCANADA
ODDBALL
OFFBASE
OFFHAND
OFFRAMP
OGDOADS
OHIOANS
OILCAKE
OILCANS
OILLAMP
OILPANS
OKINAWA
OLDDAYS
OLDHAND
OLDMAID
OMPHALI
ONADARE
ONADATE
ONBOARD
ONGUARD
ONLEAVE
ONSTAGE
OOMPAHS
OPENAIR
OPERAND
OPERATE
ORCHARD
ORDEALS
OREGANO
ORIGAMI
ORLEANS
ORPHANS
OUTBACK
OUTCAST
OUTEATS
OUTFACE
OUTLAID
OUTLAND
OUTLAST
OUTLAWS
OUTLAYS
OUTPACE
OUTRACE
OUTRAGE
OUTRANK
OUTTAKE
OUTTALK
OUTWARD
OVERACT
OVERAGE
OVERALL
OVERATE
OVERAWE
OXIDANT
OXIDASE

O••••A•
OAKLEAF
OATMEAL
OBADIAH
OEDIPAL
OFFBEAT
OFFLOAD
OFFPEAK
OFFROAD
OFFYEAR
OGLALAS
OJIBWAS
OJIBWAY
OLDCHAP
OLDUVAI
ONATEAR
ONEIDAS
ONTRIAL
OPENBAR
OPTICAL
OPTIMAL
ORBITAL
ORDINAL
ORPHEAN
ORTOLAN
OTTAWAS
OTTOMAN
OUTDRAW
OUTPLAY
OUTWEAR
OVEREAT
OVERLAP
OVERLAY
OVERRAN
OVERSAW
OVOIDAL
OXONIAN

O•••••A
OCANADA
OCARINA
OCEANIA
OCTAVIA
OKINAWA
OLESTRA
OLYMPIA
OPENSEA
OPHELIA
ORGANZA
OSCEOLA
OVERSEA
OXYMORA

•OA••••
BOARDED
BOARDER
BOASTED
BOASTER
BOATERS
BOATING
BOATMAN
BOATMEN
COACHED
COACHES
COALBIN
COALCAR
COALERS
COALGAS
COALOIL
COALTAR
COARSEN
COARSER
COASTAL
COASTED
COASTER
COATING
COAXERS
COAXIAL
COAXING
FOALING
FOAMIER
FOAMING
GOABOUT
GOADING
GOAHEAD
GOALIES
GOALONG
GOATEED
GOATEES
GOATISH
HOAGIES
HOARDED
HOARDER
HOARIER
HOARSEN
HOARSER
HOAXERS
HOAXING
JOACHIM
JOAQUIN
LOACHES
LOADERS
LOADING
LOAFERS
LOAFING
LOAMIER
LOAMING
LOANERS
LOANING
LOATHED
LOATHES
MOANERS
MOANING
POACHED
POACHER
POACHES
ROACHED
ROACHES
ROADBED
ROADHOG
ROADIES
ROADMAP
ROADWAY
ROAMERS
ROAMING
ROANOKE
ROARERS
ROARING
ROASTED
ROASTER
SOAKERS
SOAKING
SOAKSUP
SOANDSO
SOAPBOX
SOAPERS
SOAPIER
SOAPING
SOARERS
SOARING
TOADIED
TOADIES
TOASTED
TOASTER

•O•A•••
BONANZA
BORATES
COHABIT
CONAKRY
CORAZON
COWARDS
DOMAINS
DONAHUE
DONATED
DONATES
DONATOR
DOSAGES
DOWAGER
FORAGED
FORAGER
FORAGES
GOCARTS
GOKARTS
GOTAWAY
GOUACHE
HOGARTH
HORATIO
HOSANNA
HOWARDS
IODATES
JOCASTA
JOHANNA

KOLACKY
KOMATSU
LOCALES
LOCALLY
LOCATED
LOCATER
LOCATES
LOCATOR
LOVABLE
LOYALLY
LOYALTY
MOGAMBO
MOHAIRS
MOHAWKS
MONARCH
MORAINE
MORALES
MORALLY
MORANIS
MORAVIA
MOSAICS
MOVABLE
NOCANDO
NOFAULT
NOGALES
NOMADIC
NONAGON
NOTABIT
NOTABLE
NOTABLY
NOTATED
NOTATES
NOVARRO
POLARIS
POMADED
POMADES
POSADAS
POTABLE
POTAGES
ROBARDS
ROLAIDS
ROMAINE
ROMANCE
ROMANIA
ROMANOV
ROMANSH
ROSALIE
ROSANNA
ROSANNE
ROTATED
ROTATES
ROTATOR
ROXANNE
ROYALLY
ROYALTY
SODAPOP
SOFABED
SOLACES
SOLARIA
SOMALIA
SOMALIS
SOMATIC
SONATAS
TOBACCO
TONALLY
TOPAZES
TOTALED
TOTALLY
TOWARDS
TOWAWAY
VOCALIC
VOCALLY
VOYAGED
VOYAGER
VOYAGES
WOMANLY
ZONALLY
ZOUAVES

•O••A••

AOUDADS
BOBCATS
BOBTAIL
BOITANO
BOKHARA
BOMBARD
BOMBAST
BONDAGE
BONEASH
BOWSAWS
BOXCARS
COCKADE
COEVALS
COGNACS
COGNATE
COINAGE
COLGATE
COLLAGE
COLLARD
COLLARS
COLLATE
COMBATS
COMMAND
COMPACT
COMPANY
COMPARE
COMPASS
COMRADE
CONCAVE
CONFABS
CONGAED
CONGAME
CONRACK
CONTACT
CONTAIN
COOLANT
COPLAND
CORDAGE
CORDATE
CORKAGE
CORRALS
CORSAGE
CORSAIR
COSSACK
COSTAIN
COSTARS
COTTAGE
COUGARS
COURAGE
COURANT
COWHAND
DOCKAGE
DOGCART
DOGDAYS
DOGEARS
DOGFACE
DOGMATA
DOGTAGS
DOLLARS
DOLMANS
DOODADS
DORMANT
DORSALS
DOSSALS
FOGBANK
FOLIAGE
FOLIATE
FOLKART
FONDANT
FOOTAGE
FORBADE
FOREARM
FORGAVE
FORMALS
FORMATS
FORSAKE
FORSALE
FORWARD
FOULARD
FOXTAIL
GODDARD
GOESAPE
GOLIATH
GOODALL
GOSHAWK
GOTBACK
GOTLAND
GOULASH
GOURAMI
HOBNAIL
HOECAKE
HOGBACK
HOGWASH
HOLLAND
HOLYARK
HOOHAHS
HOOKAHS
HOSTAGE
HOTCAKE
HOTCAPS
HOTCARS
HOTWARS
HOWDAHS
JOBBANK
KODIAKS
KOOLAID
KOREANS
LOGJAMS
LOMBARD
LONGAGO
LOOFAHS
LOQUATS
LOWBALL
LOWLAND
LOWPAID
MOBCAPS
MOMBASA
MONDALE
MONDAYS
MONTAGE
MONTANA
MONTAND
MONTANE
MOORAGE
MORDANT
MORGANA
MORGANS
MORTALS
MORTARS
MOULAGE
NORMALS
NORMAND
NORMANS
NOUGATS
OOMPAHS
POLEAXE
POLKAED
POMPANO
PONIARD
POPLARS
POPTART
PORTAGE
PORTALS
POSTAGE
POTTAGE
ROLVAAG
ROSEATE
ROSTAND
ROULADE
SOCIALS
SOPRANO
SORBATE
SOUTANE
TOCCATA
TOECAPS
TOENAIL
TOETAPS
TOMCATS
TONEARM
TONGANS
TONNAGE
TOOTALL
TOPHATS
TOPIARY
TOPKAPI
TOPMAST
TOPSAIL
TORNADO
TOSCALE
TOSPARE
TOSTADA
TOUCANS
TOURACO
TOWCARS
TOWPATH
TOYLAND
VOLCANO
VOLTAGE
VOLTAIC
WOMBATS
WOODARD
YOPLAIT
YOUMANS
ZODIACS

•O•••A•

BOATMAN
BODEGAS
BODYFAT
BOERWAR
BOLIVAR
BONDMAN
BOOLEAN
BOXSEAT
COALCAR
COALGAS
COALTAR
COASTAL
COAXIAL
COCHRAN
COCTEAU
COEQUAL
COLDWAR
COLEMAN
COMESAT
COMICAL
CONCEAL
CONGEAL
CONICAL
CONTRAS
COONCAT
COPYCAT
CORDIAL
CORNEAL
CORNEAS
CORONAE
CORONAS
COWPEAS
DOGSTAR
DONEGAL
DONJUAN
DONOVAN
DOORMAN
DOORMAT
DOORWAY
DOUGLAS
DOVEBAR
DOWNPAT
FOOTMAN
FOOTPAD
FORBEAR
FORDHAM
FOREMAN
FOREPAW
FORERAN
FORESAW
FORREAL
FORTRAN
GOAHEAD
GODTHAB
GOESBAD
GOINGAT
GOODBAR
GOODMAN
GORDIAN
GOTAWAY
GOTCHAS
HOFBRAU
HOFFMAN
HOLIDAY
HOLMOAK
HOLYWAR
HOOPLAS
HOOTSAT
HOTHEAD
HOTSEAT
HOUSMAN
JOCULAR
JOHNGAY
JOHNJAY
JOURDAN
JOURNAL
KORUNAS
LOGGIAS
LOGICAL
LOOKSAT
LOWBEAM
LOWGEAR
LOWROAD
MODELAS
MODULAR
MOHICAN
MOLOKAI
NODULAR
NOMINAL
NOONDAY
NOSEBAG
NOSEGAY
NOSWEAT
NOTEPAD
NOUVEAU
NOVENAS
POKEDAT
POKESAT
POLECAT
POLLTAX
PONTIAC
POOHBAH
POPULAR
PORTRAY
POSADAS
POSTMAN
POSTWAR
POTOMAC
POTSDAM
ROADMAP
ROADWAY
ROLLBAR
ROLVAAG
ROMULAN
RONDEAU
RORQUAL
ROWBOAT
ROYBEAN
SOLEDAD
SOMEDAY
SOMEWAY
SONATAS
SORORAL
SOYBEAN
TOLLWAY
TONNEAU
TOPCOAT
TOPICAL
TOTEBAG
TOWAWAY
TOWHEAD
WOLFGAL
WOLFMAN
WOLFRAM
WORKDAY
WORKMAN
WOZNIAK
ZOYSIAS

•O••••A

BOBVILA
BOHEMIA
BOKHARA
BOLIVIA
BOLOGNA
BONANZA
BOTHNIA
COCHLEA
COLONNA
COPPOLA
CORDOBA
CORETTA
COROLLA
CORRIDA
CORSICA
DOGMATA
FONTINA
FORMICA
FORMOSA
FORMULA
FORTUNA
GONDOLA
GORILLA
HOSANNA
JOCASTA
JOHANNA
LORETTA
LOUELLA
MOMBASA
MONTANA
MONTOYA
MORAVIA
MORGANA
NORIEGA
NOVELLA
NOXZEMA
PODRIDA
POLENTA
POMPEIA
PORSENA
PORTOLA
ROBERTA
ROBUSTA
ROMANIA
ROSANNA
ROSETTA
ROSSSEA
ROTUNDA
SOLARIA
SOMALIA
TOCCATA
TOSHIBA
TOSTADA
WOOMERA

••OA•••

BLOATED
BROADAX
BROADEN
BROADER
BROADLY
CLOAKED
CROAKED
CROATIA
FLOATED
FLOATER
GLOATED
GROANED
GROANER

••O•A••

ADONAIS
ALOHAOE
ANOMALY
ANORAKS
AVOCADO
AVOWALS
BAOBABS
BIOMASS
BROCADE
BROGANS
BROMATE
BUOYANT
CHORALE
CHORALS
COOLANT
DEODARS
DIORAMA
DOODADS
EDOUARD
FOOTAGE
FROMAGE
FROWARD
GOODALL
HOOHAHS
HOOKAHS
IRONAGE
ISOBARS
ISOLATE
KOOLAID
LEONARD
LEOPARD
LEOTARD
LOOFAHS
MOORAGE
NEONATE
PEONAGE
PROBATE
PROFANE
PROPANE
PRORATA
PRORATE
PROSAIC
RIOTACT
SHOFARS
SIOUANS
SLOGANS
SLOVAKS
SNOCATS
SPOKANE
STOMACH
STOMATA
STORAGE
TOOTALL
TROCARS
TROJANS
TWOBASE
VIOLATE
WOODARD

••O••A•

ABOREAL
AEOLIAN
AMOEBAE
AMOEBAS
AROUSAL
ASOCIAL
BOOLEAN
BROADAX
BROSNAN
CHOCTAW
CHOLLAS
COONCAT
CROWBAR
DOORMAN
DOORMAT
DOORWAY
ETONIAN
FLOTSAM
FOOTMAN
FOOTPAD
FROGMAN
FRONTAL
FROWNAT
GLORIAS
GLOSSAE
GLOTTAL
GOODBAR
GOODMAN
HOOPLAS
HOOTSAT
IRONMAN
LAOTIAN
LOOKSAT
NOONDAY
OVOIDAL
OXONIAN
PHOBIAS
PLOWMAN
POOHBAH
PROGRAM
PROPMAN
PROTEAN
QUOKKAS
SHOOTAT
SHOWMAN
SIOBHAN
SLOTCAR
SNOWCAP
SNOWDAY
SNOWMAN
SPORRAN
SPOUSAL
STOICAL
STOPGAP
SWOREAT
THOREAU
TROIKAS
TSONGAS
TWOSTAR
UTOPIAN
UTOPIAS
UXORIAL

••O•••A

ANOSMIA
AVONLEA
CROATIA
DIORAMA
DUODENA
EROTICA
EXOTICA
FLORIDA
GEORGIA
INOCULA
IWOJIMA
LEONORA
PRORATA
RIORITA
SNOWPEA
STOMATA
WOOMERA

•••OA••

BEMOANS
BUROAKS
BYROADS
INBOARD
INROADS
MINOANS
OGDOADS
OHIOANS
ONBOARD
PINOAKS
PTBOATS
REDOAKS
RELOADS
SAMOANS
TANOAKS
THROATS
THROATY
UNLOADS
UPLOADS
UPROARS

•••O•A•

ACROBAT
AEROBAT
ALSORAN
ALTOSAX
ANGOLAN
ANGORAS
AREOLAE
AREOLAR
AREOLAS
ARROBAS
ASTOLAT
AURORAE
AURORAL
AURORAS
AUTOMAT
BIFOCAL
BIMODAL
BIPOLAR
BIVOUAC
CHLORAL
CORONAE
CORONAS
CUPOLAS
DAKOTAN
DAKOTAS
DEBORAH
DEPOSAL
DIPOLAR
DONOVAN
ESPOSAS
FEDORAS
FEMORAL
IMMORAL
INNOWAY
INSOFAR
KEROUAC
LAKOTAS
MANOWAR
MAYORAL
MENORAH
MIMOSAS
MOLOKAI
NICOLAS
NIKOLAI
ORTOLAN
OTTOMAN
PAGODAS
PALOMAR
PAYOLAS
PELOTAS
PIVOTAL
POTOMAC
RAYOVAC
REMORAS
REMOVAL
REPOMAN
SAMOVAR
SAROYAN
SCHOLAR
SENORAS
SHOOTAT
SORORAL
SYNODAL
UPTOPAR

•••O••A

ALTOONA
ALYOSHA
AMMONIA
ANDORRA
ANTONIA
ASTORIA
BAZOOKA
BEGONIA
BEGORRA
BOLOGNA
CIBORIA
COLONNA
COROLLA
EMPORIA
ENCOMIA
ESTONIA
IACOCCA
KENOSHA
LAJOLLA
LAMOTTA
LASORDA
MADONNA
MAJORCA
MINOLTA
MINORCA
NICOSIA
PALOOKA
RICOTTA
SEGOVIA
WYNONNA
ZENOBIA

••••OA•

AIRBOAT
ARMLOAD
BALBOAS
BARSOAP
CADDOAN
CARCOAT
CARLOAD
CATBOAT
GUNBOAT
HOLMOAK
ICEBOAT
IDAHOAN
JERBOAS
JETBOAT
LABCOAT
LIVEOAK
LOWROAD
OFFLOAD
OFFROAD
PAYLOAD
PEACOAT
PRELOAD
PRESOAK
QUINOAS
REDCOAT
ROWBOAT
SURCOAT
TOPCOAT
TUGBOAT
UNCLOAK
VIRGOAN

••••O•A

ACEROLA
ALTOONA
AMAPOLA
AMPHORA
ARIZONA
AUREOLA
BAZOOKA
CARIOCA
COPPOLA
CORDOBA
CRAYOLA
CREMONA
DAYTONA
DIPLOMA
FORMOSA
GONDOLA
GRANOLA
ISADORA
KEDROVA
LEONORA
MADRONA
MARKOVA
MENDOZA
MINEOLA
MONTOYA
OSCEOLA
OXYMORA
PALOOKA
PANDORA
PAVLOVA
PERGOLA
PERSONA
PORTOLA
SALSODA
SEQUOIA
SPINOZA
SUBROSA
TAPIOCA
ULANOVA

OB•••••

OBADIAH
OBELISK
OBELIZE
OBERLIN
OBEYING
OBJECTS
OBLASTS
OBLATES
OBLIGED
OBLIGES
OBLIQUE
OBLONGS
OBLOQUY
OBOISTS
OBREGON
OBSCENE
OBSCURE
OBSERVE
OBTAINS
OBTRUDE
OBTUNDS
OBTUSER
OBVERSE
OBVERTS
OBVIATE
OBVIOUS

O•B••••

ONBOARD
ORBISON
ORBITAL
ORBITED
ORBITER
OSBORNE
OXBLOOD

O••B•••

ODDBALL
OFFBASE
OFFBEAT
OJIBWAS
OJIBWAY
OUTBACK
OUTBIDS

O•••B••

OCTOBER
OMNIBUS
OPENBAR
OVERBIG
OVERBUY

O••••B•

ODDJOBS

O•••••B

OVERDUB

•OB••••

BOBBERS
BOBBIES
BOBBING
BOBBINS
BOBBLED
BOBBLES
BOBCATS
BOBDOLE
BOBHOPE
BOBSLED
BOBTAIL
BOBVILA
COBBLED
COBBLER
COBBLES
COBWEBS
DOBBINS
FOBBING
FOBSOFF
GOBBLED
GOBBLER
GOBBLES
GOBLETS
GOBLINS
GOBROKE
HOBBIES
HOBBITS
HOBBLED
HOBBLES
HOBNAIL
HOBNOBS
HOBOING
HOBOKEN
JOBBANK
JOBBERS
JOBBING
JOBHOPS
JOBHUNT
JOBLOTS
KOBLENZ
KOBOLDS
LOBBERS
LOBBIED
LOBBIES
LOBBING
LOBBYER
LOBSTER
MOBBING
MOBCAPS
MOBILES
MOBSTER
NOBHILL
NOBLEST
POBOXES
ROBARDS
ROBBERS
ROBBERY
ROBBING
ROBBINS
ROBERTA
ROBERTO
ROBERTS
ROBESON
ROBLOWE
ROBOCOP
ROBOTIC
ROBROYS
ROBUSTA
SOBBERS
SOBBING
SOBERED
SOBERER
SOBERLY
TOBACCO
WOBBLED

WOBBLES
WOBEGON

•O•B•••
BOBBERS
BOBBIES
BOBBING
BOBBINS
BOBBLED
BOBBLES
BOMBARD
BOMBAST
BOMBECK
BOMBERS
BOMBING
BONBONS
BOOBIES
BOOBOOS
COBBLED
COBBLER
COBBLES
COGBURN
COLBERT
COMBATS
COMBERS
COMBINE
COMBING
COMBUST
CONBRIO
CORBELS
CORBETT
COWBELL
COWBIRD
COWBOYS
DOBBINS
DOUBLED
DOUBLES
DOUBLET
DOUBLEU
DOUBTED
DOUBTER
FOBBING
FOGBANK
FOGBOWS
FOIBLES
FORBADE
FORBEAR
FORBIDS
FORBORE
GOABOUT
GOBBLED
GOBBLER
GOBBLES
GOOBERS
GOTBACK
HOBBIES
HOBBITS
HOBBLED
HOBBLES
HOFBRAU
HOGBACK
HOLBEIN
HOMBRES
HOMBURG
HOTBEDS
HOWBEIT
JOBBANK
JOBBERS
JOBBING
JOEBLOW
LOBBERS
LOBBIED
LOBBIES
LOBBING
LOBBYER
LOGBOOK
LOMBARD
LOWBALL
LOWBEAM
LOWBLOW
LOWBORN
LOWBOYS
LOWBRED
LOWBROW
MOBBING
MOMBASA
ROBBERS
ROBBERY
ROBBING
ROBBINS
ROEBUCK
ROWBOAT
ROYBEAN
SOBBERS
SOBBING
SORBATE
SORBETS
SOWBUGS
SOYBEAN
TOMBOYS
WOBBLED
WOBBLES
WOMBATS
ZOMBIES

•O••B••
BOOMBOX
BOURBON
COALBIN
COHABIT
COLOBUS
COPYBOY
DOVEBAR
DOWNBOW
GOESBAD
GOLDBUG
GOODBAR
GOODBYE
GOODBYS
LOCKBOX
LONGBOW
LOVABLE
LOVEBUG
MOVABLE
NOSEBAG
NOTABIT
NOTABLE
NOTABLY
POOHBAH
POORBOX
POORBOY
POSTBOX
POTABLE
ROADBED
ROLLBAR
ROSEBUD
SOAPBOX
SOFABED
SOLUBLE
TOOLBOX
TOTEBAG
TOYNBEE
VOLUBLE
VOLUBLY

•O•••B•
COBWEBS
COLUMBO
COMESBY
CONFABS
CONJOBS
CORDOBA
GOINGBY
HOBNOBS
HORNSBY
HOTTUBS
MOGAMBO
MORESBY
NODOUBT
TOSHIBA
WOULDBE

•O••••B
CORNCOB
COULOMB
COXCOMB
FOODWEB
GODTHAB
GOODJOB
NOSEJOB
POTHERB

••OB•••
BAOBABS
BOOBIES
BOOBOOS
CLOBBER
GLOBULE
GOOBERS
ISOBARS
KNOBBED
NIOBIUM
PHOBIAS
PHOBICS
PROBATE
PROBERS
PROBING
PROBITY
PROBLEM
PROBONO
SIOBHAN
SLOBBER
TWOBASE
TWOBITS

••O•B••
AMOEBAE
AMOEBAS
AMOEBIC
BOOMBOX
CLOBBER
CROWBAR
GOODBAR
GOODBYE
GOODBYS
INORBIT
KNOBBED
PHOEBES
PHOEBUS
PLOWBOY
POOHBAH
POORBOX
POORBOY
RHOMBUS
SHOEBOX
SHOWBIZ
SLOBBER
TOOLBOX
TROUBLE

••O••B•
BAOBABS
DROPSBY
RIOLOBO
STOODBY
SWOREBY

••O•••B
FOODWEB
GOODJOB
LIONCUB
PROVERB
SNOWJOB

•••OB••
ACROBAT
AEROBAT
AEROBES
AEROBIC
ARROBAS
COLOBUS
DISOBEY
ENNOBLE
ENROBED
ENROBES
IGNOBLE
IGNOBLY
JACOBIN
OCTOBER
STROBES
UNROBED
UNROBES
ZENOBIA

•••O•B•
ABSORBS
ADSORBS
INDOUBT
NODOUBT
REDOUBT
RESORBS
STOODBY

••••OB•
CONJOBS
CORDOBA
DISROBE
EARLOBE
HOBNOBS
LAPROBE
MICROBE
NAIROBI
ODDJOBS
RIOLOBO

••••O•B
COULOMB
COXCOMB

•••••OB
CORNCOB
GOODJOB
NOSEJOB
SNOWJOB
THEBLOB

OC•••••
OCANADA
OCARINA
OCCIPUT
OCCLUDE
OCCULTS
OCEANIA
OCEANIC
OCEANID
OCEANUS
OCELOTS
OCONNOR
OCTAGON
OCTANES
OCTANTS
OCTAVES
OCTAVIA
OCTAVOS
OCTOBER
OCTOPOD
OCTOPUS
OCTUPLE
OCULIST

O•C••••
OCCIPUT
OCCLUDE
OCCULTS
OOCYTES
ORCHARD
ORCHIDS
OSCEOLA
OSCINES
OXCARTS

O••C•••
OBSCENE
OBSCURE
OILCAKE
OILCANS
OLDCHAP
OMICRON
OPACITY
ORACLES
OUTCAST
OUTCOME
OUTCROP

O•••C••
OBJECTS
OFFICER
OFFICES
OPTICAL
OSSICLE
OUTACTS

O••••C•
OARLOCK
OFFENCE
OLDNICK
ORIFICE
ORINOCO
OSTRICH
OUTBACK
OUTFACE
OUTPACE
OUTRACE
OVERACT

O•••••C
OCEANIC
OLYMPIC
ORGANIC
OSMOTIC
OSSIFIC

•OC••••
COCHERE
COCHISE
COCHLEA
COCHRAN
COCKADE
COCKIER
COCKILY
COCKING
COCKLES
COCKNEY
COCKPIT
COCONUT
COCOONS
COCTEAU
DOCENTS
DOCKAGE
DOCKERS
DOCKETS
DOCKING
DOCTORS
FOCSLES
FOCUSED
FOCUSES
GOCARTS
HOCKING
JOCASTA
JOCKEYS
JOCULAR
LOCALES
LOCALLY
LOCATED
LOCATER
LOCATES
LOCATOR
LOCKBOX
LOCKERS
LOCKETS
LOCKING
LOCKINS
LOCKNUT
LOCKOUT
LOCKSUP
LOCKUPS
LOCUSTS
MOCKERS
MOCKERY
MOCKING
MOCKUPS
NOCANDO
NOCTURN
NOCUOUS
OOCYTES
POCKETS
POCONOS
ROCKERS
ROCKETS
ROCKIER
ROCKIES
ROCKING
ROCKYII
ROCKYIV
SOCIALS
SOCIETY
SOCKETS
SOCKEYE
SOCKING
SOCKSIN
TOCCATA
TOCSINS
VOCALIC
VOCALLY

•O•C•••
BOBCATS
BOKCHOY
BOTCHED
BOTCHES
BOXCARS
BOYCOTT
COACHED
COACHES
CONCAVE
CONCEAL
CONCEDE
CONCEIT
CONCEPT
CONCERN
CONCERT
CONCHES
CONCISE
CONCOCT
CONCORD
CONCURS
COUCHED
COUCHES
COXCOMB
DOGCART
DOGCHEW
DOGCHOW
FORCEPS
FORCERS
FORCING
GOTCHAS
HOECAKE
HONCHOS
HOTCAKE
HOTCAPS
HOTCARS
HOWCOME
JOACHIM
LOACHES
MOBCAPS
MOOCHED
MOOCHER
MOOCHES
NONCOMS
NOTCHED
NOTCHES
POACHED
POACHER
POACHES
PONCHOS
POOCHES
POPCORN
PORCHES
PORCINE
POUCHED
POUCHES
ROACHED
ROACHES
SORCERY
TOCCATA
TOECAPS
TOMCATS
TOPCOAT
TORCHED
TORCHES
TOSCALE
TOUCANS
TOUCHED
TOUCHES
TOUCHON
TOUCHUP
TOWCARS
VOICING
VOLCANO
VOUCHED
VOUCHER
VOUCHES

•O••C••
BODICES
BORSCHT
BOUNCED
BOUNCER
BOUNCES
COALCAR
CODICES
CODICIL
COERCED
COERCES
COLDCUT
COMICAL
CONICAL
COONCAT
COPYCAT
CORNCOB
COUNCIL
DOVECOT
GOUACHE
HOLYCOW
HOOTCHY
JOUNCED
JOUNCES
KOLACKY
KOOTCHY
KOPECKS
LOGICAL
MODICUM
MOHICAN
MONOCLE
MONOCOT
MOROCCO
NOGUCHI
NOTICED
NOTICES
NOVICES
POLECAT
POLICED
POLICES
PORSCHE
POUNCED
POUNCER
POUNCES
ROBOCOP
SOLACES
SOLICIT
SOUPCON
SOURCED
SOURCES
TOBACCO
TOPICAL
VOTECHS
WOODCUT

•O•••C•
BOMBECK
COGENCY
COGNACS
COLLECT
COMPACT
CONCOCT
CONDUCE
CONDUCT
CONNECT
CONNICK
CONRACK
CONTACT
CONVICT
COPPICE
CORNICE
CORRECT
CORSICA
COSSACK
COWLICK
DOGFACE
DORMICE
FORMICA
FOSDICK
GODUTCH
GOTBACK
GOTHICS
HOGBACK
HOSPICE
IONESCO
LOWNECK
LOWTECH
MONARCH
MOROCCO
MOSAICS
NOETICS
NORDICS
POETICS
POLLOCK
PORTICO
POTENCY
POTLUCK
ROEBUCK
ROLLICK
ROMANCE
TOBACCO
TOLTECS
TOPKICK
TOURACO
WOZZECK
ZODIACS

•O••••C
COMEDIC
HOMERIC
NOMADIC
POLEMIC
POLITIC
PONTIAC
POSTHOC
POTOMAC
POULENC
ROBOTIC
SOMATIC
TONELOC
TOTEMIC
VOCALIC
VOLTAIC
YOUNGMC

••OC•••
APOCOPE
ASOCIAL
AVOCADO
AVOCETS
BLOCKED
BLOCKER
BROCADE
CHOCTAW
CLOCHES
CLOCKED
CLOCKER
CLOCKIN
CROCHET
DIOCESE
FLOCKED
FLOCKTO
FROCKED
GNOCCHI
GROCERS
GROCERY
INOCULA
KNOCKED
KNOCKER
LAOCOON
MIOCENE
MOOCHED
MOOCHER
MOOCHES
POOCHES
PROCEED
PROCESS
PROCTOR
PROCURE
PROCYON
REOCCUR
SHOCKED
SHOCKER
SNOCATS
SNOCONE
STOCKED
STOCKUP
TROCARS
TROCHEE
TROCHES

••O•C••
BLOTCHY
BRONCHI
BRONCOS
CHOICER
CHOICES
COONCAT
GNOCCHI
GROUCHO
GROUCHY
HOOTCHY
KOOTCHY
LIONCUB
REOCCUR
SCONCES
SLOTCAR
SLOUCHY
SNOWCAP
STOICAL
WOODCUT

••O••C•
BIONICS
ENOUNCE
EROTICA
EXOTICA
EXOTICS
FLOUNCE
FROLICS
PHOBICS
PHONICS
PRODUCE
PRODUCT
PROJECT
PROTECT
RIOTACT
STOMACH
TROPICS
TROUNCE

••O•••C
AMOEBIC
ANOSMIC
GNOSTIC
PROSAIC
TROPHIC

•••OC••
AUROCHS
BIFOCAL
BRIOCHE
DECOCTS
IACOCCA
INFOCUS
LAROCHE
MONOCLE
MONOCOT
MOROCCO
PINOCLE
RELOCKS
ROBOCOP
SIROCCO
UNLOCKS
VANOCUR

•••O•C•
BYFORCE
DEBOUCH
DIVORCE
ENFORCE
HEROICS
IACOCCA
INFORCE
INVOICE
MAJORCA
MINORCA
MOROCCO
REJOICE
RETOUCH
REVOICE
SIROCCO
SPLOTCH

•••O••C
AEROBIC
BIVOUAC
BUCOLIC
CALORIC
CANONIC
CHAOTIC
CHRONIC
DEMONIC
IDIOTIC
ILLOGIC
KEROUAC
LACONIC
MASONIC
MEIOTIC
MELODIC
MITOTIC
OSMOTIC
POTOMAC
RAYOVAC
ROBOTIC
SYNODIC
ZAPOTEC

••••OC•
AIRLOCK
AIRSOCK
ANTIOCH
ARMLOCK
BANNOCK
BEDROCK
BULLOCK
BURDOCK
CARIOCA
CASSOCK
CONCOCT
DEFROCK
DRSPOCK
DRYDOCK
EARLOCK
FETLOCK
GUNLOCK
HADDOCK
HAMHOCK
HAMMOCK
HANCOCK
HASSOCK
HEMLOCK
HILLOCK
HUMMOCK
INSTOCK
LEACOCK
LUBBOCK
MATLOCK
MATTOCK
MRSPOCK
MURDOCH
OARLOCK
ORINOCO
PADDOCK
PADLOCK
PEACOCK
PETCOCK
PETROCK
POLLOCK
RESTOCK
SCHLOCK
SHYLOCK
TAPIOCA
TUSSOCK
UNAVOCE
UNFROCK
WARLOCK
WEDLOCK

•••••OC
PAPADOC
POSTHOC
RAYKROC
TONELOC

OD•••••
ODDBALL
ODDJOBS
ODDLOTS
ODDMENT
ODDNESS
ODOROUS
ODYSSEY

O•D••••
ODDBALL
ODDJOBS
ODDLOTS
ODDMENT
ODDNESS
OEDIPAL
OEDIPUS
OGDOADS
OLDCHAP
OLDDAYS
OLDFOGY
OLDGOLD
OLDHAND
OLDLINE
OLDMAID
OLDMOON
OLDNESS
OLDNEWS
OLDNICK
OLDPROS
OLDSTER
OLDTIME
OLDUVAI
OLDWEST
ORDAINS
ORDEALS
ORDERED
ORDERER
ORDERLY
ORDINAL

O••D•••
OBADIAH
OFFDUTY
OLDDAYS
ONADARE
ONADATE
ONADIET
OUTDOES
OUTDONE
OUTDOOR
OUTDRAW
OUTDREW
OXIDANT
OXIDASE
OXIDIZE

O•••D••
ONANDON
ONEIDAS
ONORDER
OVERDID
OVERDUB
OVERDUE
OVOIDAL
OWNEDUP

O••••D•
OBTRUDE
OBTUNDS
OCANADA
OCCLUDE
OFFENDS
OFFSIDE
OGDOADS
ONWARDS
ORCHIDS
ORGANDY
ORLANDO
ORMANDY
OSMONDS
OUTBIDS
OUTSIDE
OXFORDS

O•••••D
OAKLAND
OBLIGED
OCEANID
OCTOPOD
OFFERED
OFFHAND
OFFLOAD
OFFROAD
OLDGOLD
OLDHAND
OLDMAID
OMITTED
ONBOARD
ONEEYED

ONGUARD
OPENEND
OPERAND
OPPOSED
ORBITED
ORCHARD
ORDERED
OROTUND
OSMOSED
OSTEOID
OUTLAID
OUTLAND
OUTLOUD
OUTSOLD
OUTWARD
OVERDID
OXBLOOD

•OD••••
BODEGAS
BODEREK
BODICES
BODKINS
BODYFAT
CODDLED
CODDLER
CODDLES
CODEINE
CODFISH
CODGERS
CODICES
CODICIL
DODDERS
DODGERS
DODGING
DODGSON
FODDERS
GODDARD
GODDESS
GODFREY
GODLIKE
GODSEND
GODSONS
GODTHAB
GODUNOV
GODUTCH
GODWITS
IODATES
IODIDES
IODIZED
IODIZES
KODIAKS
LODGERS
LODGING
MODELAS
MODELED
MODELER
MODELTS
MODERNS
MODESTO
MODESTY
MODICUM
MODISTE
MODULAR
MODULES
NODDERS
NODDING
NODOUBT
NODSOFF
NODULAR
NODULES
PODGIER
PODIUMS
PODRIDA
RODENTS
RODEOFF
RODEOUT
RODGERS
RODOLFO
SODAPOP
SODDING
TODDIES
TODDLED
TODDLER
TODDLES
YODELED
YODELER
ZODIACS

•O•D•••
AOUDADS
BOBDOLE
BOGDOWN
BOLDEST
BONDAGE
BONDING
BONDMAN
BONDMEN
BOODLES
BORDERS
BOUDOIR
BOWDLER
BOYDORR
CODDLED
CODDLER
CODDLES
COEDITS
COLDCUT
COLDEST
COLDWAR
CONDEMN
CONDIGN
CONDOLE
CONDONE
CONDORS
CONDUCE
CONDUCT
CONDUIT
CORDAGE
CORDATE
CORDELL
CORDERO
CORDIAL
CORDING
CORDITE
CORDOBA
CORDONS
DODDERS
DOGDAYS
DOODADS
DOODLED
DOODLER
DOODLES
DOWDIER
DOWDILY
FODDERS
FOLDERS
FOLDING
FOLDOUT
FOLDSUP
FOLDUPS
FONDANT
FONDEST
FONDLED
FONDLES
FONDUES
FOODWEB
FORDHAM
FORDING
FOSDICK
GOADING
GODDARD
GODDESS
GOLDBUG
GOLDING
GOLDWYN
GONDOLA
GOODALL
GOODBAR
GOODBYE
GOODBYS
GOODEGG
GOODIES
GOODJOB
GOODJOE
GOODMAN
GOODMEN
GOODONE
GOODSON
GOODWIN
GORDIAN
GOTDOWN
HOEDOWN
HOLDERS
HOLDING
HOLDOFF
HOLDOUT
HOLDSON
HOLDSTO
HOLDSUP
HOLDUPS
HOODLUM
HOODOOS
HOTDOGS
HOUDINI
HOWDAHS
HOYDENS
LOADERS
LOADING
LORDING
LORDJIM
LOUDEST
LOWDOWN
MOLDERS
MOLDIER
MOLDING
MONDALE
MONDAYS
MOODIER
MOODILY
MORDANT
MORDENT
MORDRED
MOWDOWN
NODDERS
NODDING
NOODLES
NORDICS
POLDERS
PONDERS
POODLES
POWDERS
POWDERY
ROADBED
ROADHOG
ROADIES
ROADMAP
ROADWAY
ROEDEER
RONDEAU
RONDELS
ROWDIER
ROWDIES
ROWDILY
SODDING
SOLDERS
SOLDIER
SOLDOFF
SOLDOUT
TOADIED
TOADIES
TODDIES
TODDLED
TODDLER
TODDLES
TOLDOFF
TOPDOGS
TOYDOGS
VOIDING
WONDERS
WOODARD
WOODCUT
WOODIER
WOODIES
WOODLOT
WOODROW
WORDIER
WORDILY
WORDING
WORDONE

•O••D••
BOARDED
BOARDER
BOLIDES
BONEDRY
BONEDUP
BOREDOM
BORODIN
BOULDER
BOUNDED
BOUNDER
BOUNDTO
BOUNDUP
BOXEDIN
BOXEDUP
COMEDIC
COMEDUE
CORNDOG
COULDNT
DOORDIE
DOSIDOS
DOTEDON
FOUNDED
FOUNDER
FOUNDRY
GOUNDER
GOURDES
HOARDED
HOARDER
HOLEDUP
HOLIDAY
HOUNDED
IODIDES
JOHNDOE
JOINDER
JOURDAN
LOURDES
MOONDOG
MOULDED
MOULDER
MOUNDED
MOVEDIN
NOMADIC
NOONDAY
POKEDAT
POMADED
POMADES
POSADAS
POTSDAM
POUNDED
POUNDER
ROLODEX
ROPEDIN
ROUNDED
ROUNDER
ROUNDLY
ROUNDON
ROUNDUP
SOANDSO
SOLEDAD
SOLIDER
SOLIDLY
SOMEDAY
SOUNDED
SOUNDER
SOUNDLY
TONEDUP
TOORDER
WORKDAY
WORLDLY
WOULDBE
WOULDNT
WOUNDED
WOUNDUP

•O•••D•
AOUDADS
COCKADE
COLLIDE
COLLODI
COLLUDE
COMMODE
COMRADE
CONCEDE
CONFIDE
CORRIDA
CORRODE
COWARDS
COWHIDE
DOODADS
FORBADE
FORBIDS
HOTBEDS
HOTRODS
HOWARDS
JOYRIDE
KOBOLDS
LOWTIDE
NOCANDO
PODRIDA
PONGIDS
ROBARDS
ROLAIDS
ROTUNDA
ROULADE
TOPSIDE
TORNADO
TOROIDS
TORPEDO
TOSTADA
TOWARDS

•O••••D
BOARDED
BOASTED
BOBBLED
BOBSLED
BOGEYED
BOGGLED
BOMBARD
BOOGIED
BOOKEND
BOOSTED
BOTCHED
BOTTLED
BOUNCED
BOUNDED
BOWERED
BOXWOOD
BOYHOOD
COACHED
COASTED
COBBLED
CODDLED
COERCED
COHERED
COLLARD
COLLOID
COLORED
COMMAND
COMMEND
CONCORD
CONGAED
CONREID
CONTEND
COOPTED
COPLAND
CORNFED
COUCHED
COUGHED
COUNTED
COUPLED
COURSED
COURTED
COVERED
COVETED
COWBIRD
COWERED
COWHAND
COWHERD
COZENED
DOGSLED
DOGWOOD
DOLLIED
DONATED
DOODLED
DOUBLED
DOUBTED
FOCUSED
FOISTED
FONDLED
FOOTPAD
FOOZLED
FORAGED
FORFEND
FORGOOD
FORWARD
FOULARD
FOUNDED
GOAHEAD
GOATEED
GOBBLED
GODDARD
GODSEND
GOESBAD
GOGGLED
GOROUND
GOTLAND
HOARDED
HOBBLED
HOGTIED
HOGWILD
HOISTED
HOLLAND
HOMERED
HOMINID
HONEYED
HONORED
HOTHEAD
HOUNDED
HOVERED
IODIZED
IONIZED
JOGGLED
JOINTED
JOISTED
JOLLIED
JOSTLED
JOUNCED
JOUSTED
KOOLAID
LOATHED
LOBBIED
LOCATED
LOMBARD
LOUNGED
LOUREED
LOWBRED
LOWERED
LOWLAND
LOWPAID
LOWROAD
MODELED
MONEYED
MONTAND
MOOCHED
MORDRED
MORPHED
MOSEYED
MOTORED
MOTTLED
MOULDED
MOULTED
MOUNDED
MOUNTED
MOUSSED
MOUTHED
NONSKID
NORMAND
NOTATED
NOTCHED
NOTEPAD
NOTICED
POACHED
POINTED
POLICED
POLKAED
POMADED
PONIARD
POPEYED
POPPLED
PORTEND
POSITED
POUCHED
POUNCED
POUNDED
POWERED
ROACHED
ROADBED
ROASTED
ROOSTED
ROSEBUD
ROSERED
ROSTAND
ROTATED
ROUGHED
ROUNDED
ROUSTED
SOBERED
SOFABED
SOLEDAD
SOOTHED
SORTIED
SOUGHED
SOUNDED
SOURCED
TOADIED
TOASTED
TODDLED
TOEHOLD
TOGGLED
TOKENED
TONGUED
TOOTHED
TOOTLED
TOPPLED
TORCHED
TOTALED
TOUCHED
TOUSLED
TOWELED
TOWERED
TOWHEAD
TOYLAND
VOUCHED
VOYAGED
WOBBLED
WOODARD
WORRIED
WORSTED
WOUNDED
YODELED

••OD•••
ANODIZE
ANODYNE
BOODLES
DEODARS
DOODADS
DOODLED
DOODLER
DOODLES
DUODENA
ERODING
FOODWEB
GEODESY
GOODALL
GOODBAR
GOODBYE
GOODBYS
GOODEGG
GOODIES
GOODJOB
GOODJOE
GOODMAN
GOODMEN
GOODONE
GOODSON
GOODWIN
HOODLUM
HOODOOS
MOODIER
MOODILY
NOODLES
PLODDED
PLODDER
POODLES
PRODDED
PRODDER
PRODIGY
PRODUCE
PRODUCT
RHODIUM
SHODDEN
TRODDEN
WOODARD
WOODCUT
WOODIER
WOODIES
WOODLOT
WOODROW

••O•D••
AVOIDED
BLONDER
BLONDES
BLONDIE
BLOODED
BLOWDRY
BROADAX
BROADEN
BROADER
BROADLY
BROODED
BROODER
CHOWDER
CLOUDED
CLOWDER
CROWDED
DOORDIE
FLOODED
MOONDOG
NOONDAY
ONORDER
OVOIDAL
PLODDED
PLODDER
PRODDED
PRODDER
PROUDER
PROUDLY
REORDER
SCOLDED
SCOLDER
SHODDEN
SHOWDOG
SMOLDER
SNOWDAY
SNOWDON
SPONDEE
STOODBY
STOODIN
STOODUP
TOORDER
TRODDEN

••O••D•
ABOUNDS
AVOCADO
BROCADE
BROMIDE
DIOMEDE
DIOXIDE
DOODADS
FLORIDA
GROUNDS
ISOPODS
PROSODY
PROVIDE
YAOUNDE

••O•••D
ABORTED
ADOPTED
ADORNED
AROUSED
AVOIDED
BLOATED
BLOCKED
BLOODED
BLOOMED
BLOOPED
BLOTTED
BLOUSED
BOOGIED
BOOKEND
BOOSTED
BROILED
BRONZED
BROODED
BROOKED
BROWNED
BROWSED
CHOMPED
CHOPPED
CLOAKED
CLOCKED
CLOGGED
CLOPPED
CLOTHED
CLOTTED
CLOUDED
CLOUTED
CLOWNED
COOPTED
CROAKED
CROOKED
CROONED
CROPPED
CROSSED
CROWDED
CROWNED
DOODLED
DROOLED
DROOPED
DROPPED
DROWNED
DROWSED
EDOUARD
EVOLVED
FLOATED
FLOCKED
FLOGGED
FLOODED
FLOORED
FLOPPED
FLOSSED
FLOURED
FLOUTED
FOOTPAD
FOOZLED
FROCKED
FRONTED
FROSTED
FROTHED
FROWARD
FROWNED
GHOSTED
GLOATED
GLOMMED
GLORIED
GLOSSED
GROANED
GROOMED
GROOVED
GROSSED
GROUPED
GROUSED
GROUTED
GROWLED
KNOBBED
KNOCKED
KNOTTED
KOOLAID
LEONARD
LEOPARD
LEOPOLD
LEOTARD
MOOCHED
OROTUND
PEOPLED
PHOTOED
PLODDED
PLOPPED
PLOTTED
PROCEED
PRODDED
PRONGED
PROOFED
PROPPED
PROWLED
REOILED
ROOSTED
SCOFFED
SCOLDED
SCOOPED
SCOOTED
SCORNED
SCOURED
SCOUTED
SCOWLED
SHOCKED
SHOPPED
SHORTED
SHOUTED
SLOGGED
SLOPPED
SLOSHED
SLOTTED
SNOOPED
SNOOTED
SNOOZED
SNORTED
SOOTHED
SPOILED
SPONGED
SPOOFED
SPOOKED
SPOOLED
SPOONED
SPORTED
SPOTTED
SPOUTED
STOCKED
STOMPED
STOOPED
STOPPED
STORIED
STORMED
SWOONED
SWOOPED
TOOTHED
TOOTLED
TROLLED
TROOPED
TROTHED
TROTTED
TWOFOLD
UNOILED
WHOMPED
WHOOPED
WHOPPED
WHORLED
WOODARD
WRONGED

•••OD••
BIMODAL
BLOODED
BORODIN
BROODED
BROODER
DECODED
DECODER
DECODES
ENCODED
ENCODER
ENCODES
FLOODED
MALODOR
MELODIC
PAGODAS
RECODED
RECODES
REMODEL
ROLODEX
STOODBY
STOODIN
STOODUP
SYNODAL
SYNODIC
TRIODES
UNGODLY

•••O•D•
ACCORDS
AFFORDS
ALMONDS
BEHOLDS
BYROADS
BYWORDS
ENFOLDS
GIRONDE
INROADS
KOBOLDS
LASORDA
MILORDS
OGDOADS
OSMONDS
OXFORDS
RECORDS
RELOADS
REMOLDS
REWORDS
SECONDS
SHROUDS
TOROIDS
UNFOLDS
UNLOADS
UPHOLDS
UPLOADS

•••O••D
AGROUND
ALLOWED
ALLOYED
ANNOYED
APPOSED
APRONED
ARBORED
ARMORED
ASTOUND
BELOVED
BIGOTED
BLOODED
BLOOMED
BLOOPED
BROODED
BROOKED
CAJOLED
CAROLED
CAROMED
CAROTID
COLORED
CROOKED
CROONED
DEBONED
DECODED
DECOYED
DEMOTED
DENOTED
DEPONED
DEPOSED
DEVOTED
DROOLED
DROOPED
ELBOWED
ENCODED
ENDOWED
ENJOYED
ENROBED
EXPOSED
EXPOUND
FAGOTED
FAVORED
FLOODED
FLOORED
GOROUND
GROOMED
GROOVED
HONORED
HUMORED
IGNORED
IMPOSED
IMPOUND
INBOARD
INBOUND
INTONED
INVOKED
LABORED
MAJORED
MINORED
MOTORED
OCTOPOD
ONBOARD
OPPOSED
OSMOSED
PAROLED
PILOTED
PIVOTED
PROOFED
RAZORED
REBOUND
RECODED
REDOUND
REMOVED
REMOWED
REPOSED

RESOLED
RESOUND
RETOWED
REVOKED
REWOUND
REZONED
RUMORED
SAMOYED
SAVORED
SCOOPED
SCOOTED
SNOOPED
SNOOTED
SNOOZED
SPOOFED
SPOOKED
SPOOLED
SPOONED
STOOPED
STROKED
SWOONED
SWOOPED
TALONED
TENONED
TROOPED
TUTORED
UNBOUND
UNBOWED
UNBOXED
UNLOVED
UNMOVED
UNROBED
UNSOUND
UNWOUND
UNYOKED
UNZONED
WHOOPED
WIDOWED

••••OD•

ALAMODE
ANYBODY
BARCODE
CATHODE
COLLODI
COMMODE
CORRODE
CUSTODY
EPISODE
EXPLODE
FLYRODS
HOTRODS
IMPLODE
ISOPODS
METHODS
NIMRODS
PEABODY
PEAPODS
PERIODS
PROSODY
RAMRODS
SALSODA
SUNGODS
TIERODS
TRIPODS
UNIPODS
WARGODS
ZIPCODE

••••O•D

ABSCOND
ALLTOLD
ANDROID
ANEROID
ARMLOAD
ASHFORD
AYKROYD
BADCOLD
BAGNOLD
BECLOUD
BOXWOOD
BOYHOOD
BUNCOED
BUNKOED
CAMEOED
CARLOAD
COLLOID
CONCORD
CRINOID
DAGWOOD
DELTOID
DESMOND
DIAMOND
DIDGOOD
DIPLOID
DISCOED
DISCORD
DITTOED
DOGWOOD
FORGOOD
GAYLORD
GIFFORD
HAMMOND
HEYWOOD
HULLOED
ICECOLD
INAWORD
KEYWORD
LANFORD
LASSOED
LAWFORD
LEOPOLD
LOWROAD
MAMBOED
MANHOOD
MASTOID
MISWORD
MITFORD
MUMFORD
OFFLOAD
OFFROAD
OLDGOLD
OSTEOID
OUTLOUD
OUTSOLD
OXBLOOD
PAYLOAD
PHOTOED
PLYWOOD
PRELOAD
RADIOED
RAYMOND
REDFORD
REDWOOD
RESPOND
RIPCORD
SANFORD
SAWWOOD
SEAFOOD
SIXFOLD
STEROID
TABLOID
TANGOED
TENFOLD
TIPTOED
TOEHOLD
TWOFOLD
WARLORD
WEBTOED
WILFORD

•••••OD

BOXWOOD
BOYHOOD
CAPECOD
DAGWOOD
DECAPOD
DEMIGOD
DIDGOOD
DOGWOOD
FORGOOD
FUELROD
HEYWOOD
ICHABOD
MANHOOD
OCTOPOD
OXBLOOD
PLYWOOD
REDWOOD
SAWWOOD
SEAFOOD
SEEDPOD

OE•••••

OEDIPAL
OEDIPUS
OEUVRES

O•E••••

OBELISK
OBELIZE
OBERLIN
OBEYING
OCEANIA
OCEANIC
OCEANID
OCEANUS
OCELOTS
OKEEFFE
OLEATES
OLEMISS
OLESTRA
OMELETS
OMENTUM
ONEEYED
ONEIDAS
ONENESS
ONEROUS
ONESELF
ONESHOT
ONESTEP
ONETIME
OPENAIR
OPENBAR
OPENEND
OPENERS
OPENING
OPENPIT
OPENSEA
OPENSUP
OPENTOE
OPERAND
OPERATE
OPEROSE
OREGANO
ORESTES
OVERACT
OVERAGE
OVERALL
OVERATE
OVERAWE
OVERBIG
OVERBUY
OVERDID
OVERDUB
OVERDUE
OVEREAT
OVERFLY
OVERJOY
OVERLAP
OVERLAY
OVERLIE
OVERRAN
OVERRUN
OVERSAW
OVERSEA
OVERSEE
OVERTLY
OVERUSE

O••E•••

OBJECTS
OBREGON
OBSERVE
OBVERSE
OBVERTS
OFFENCE
OFFENDS
OFFENSE
OFFERED
OFFERER
OFTENER
OGREISH
OKEEFFE
ONEEYED
ONLEAVE
OPHELIA
ORDEALS
ORDERED
ORDERER
ORDERLY
ORIENTE
ORIENTS
ORLEANS
ORNETTE
OSCEOLA
OSTEOID
OTHELLO
OUTEATS
OWNEDUP

O•••E••

OAKFERN
OAKLEAF
OARLESS
OATMEAL
OBSCENE
ODDMENT
ODDNESS
OFFBEAT
OFFPEAK
OFFSETS
OFFYEAR
OILIEST
OILWELL
OLDNESS
OLDNEWS
OLDWEST
OMELETS
ONAGERS
ONATEAR
ONENESS
ONESELF
ONTHEGO
ONTHEQT
OPENEND
OPENERS
OPINERS
OPPRESS
OPULENT
ORPHEAN
ORPHEUS
OSPREYS
OSTLERS
OURSELF
OUSTERS
OUTLETS
OUTSELL
OUTSETS
OUTWEAR
OVEREAT
OYSTERS

O••••E•

OAKTREE
OBLATES
OBLIGED
OBLIGES
OBTUSER
OCTANES
OCTAVES
OCTOBER
ODYSSEY
OEUVRES
OFFERED
OFFERER
OFFICER
OFFICES
OFTENER
OLDSTER
OLEATES
OLIVIER
OMITTED
ONADIET
ONEEYED
ONESTEP
ONORDER
ONPAPER
OOCYTES
OOLITES
OPAQUES
OPENSEA
OPIATES
OPPOSED
OPPOSER
OPPOSES
ORACLES
ORANGES
ORBITED
ORBITER
ORDERED
ORDERER
ORESTES
ORIOLES
ORPINES
OSCINES
OSMOSED
OSMOSES
OUTAGES
OUTDOES
OUTDREW
OUTGOES
OUTGREW
OUTSTEP
OVERSEA
OVERSEE

O•••••E

OAKTREE
OBELIZE
OBLIQUE
OBSCENE
OBSCURE
OBSERVE
OBTRUDE
OBVERSE
OBVIATE
OCCLUDE
OCTUPLE
OFFBASE
OFFENCE
OFFENSE
OFFLINE
OFFSIDE
OFFSITE
OILCAKE
OKEEFFE
OLDLINE
OLDTIME
OLIVINE
ONADARE
ONADATE
ONETIME
ONLEAVE
ONSHORE
ONSTAGE
OPALINE
OPENTOE
OPERATE
OPEROSE
ORIENTE
ORIFICE
ORNETTE
OROURKE
ORVILLE
OSBORNE
OSSICLE
OUTCOME
OUTDONE
OUTFACE
OUTLINE
OUTLIVE
OUTPACE
OUTRACE
OUTRAGE
OUTSIDE
OUTSIZE
OUTTAKE
OUTVOTE
OUTWORE
OVERAGE
OVERATE
OVERAWE
OVERDUE
OVERLIE
OVERSEE
OVERUSE
OWLLIKE
OXIDASE
OXIDIZE

•OE••••

BOERWAR
COEDITS
COEQUAL
COERCED
COERCES
COEVALS
COEXIST
DOESKIN
DOEUVRE
GOESAPE
GOESBAD
GOESFOR
GOESOFF
GOESOUT
HOECAKE
HOEDOWN
JOEBLOW
JOEHILL
LOESSER
LOESSES
NOETICS
POETESS
POETICS
ROEBUCK
ROEDEER
TOECAPS
TOEHOLD
TOELESS
TOELOOP
TOENAIL
TOESHOE
TOETAPS
WOEISME
ZOELLER

•O•E•••

BODEGAS
BODEREK
BOGEYED
BOHEMIA
BOLEROS
BONEASH
BONEDRY
BONEDUP
BONESUP
BOREDOM
BOREOUT
BOWERED
BOXEDIN
BOXEDUP
BOXESIN
BOXESUP
CODEINE
COGENCY
COHEIRS
COHERED
COHERES
COLEMAN
COLETTE
COMEDIC
COMEDUE
COMEOFF
COMEONS
COMEOUT
COMESAT
COMESBY
COMESIN
COMESON
COMESTO
COMESUP
CORELLI
CORETTA
COTERIE
COVERED
COVERUP
COVETED
COWERED
COZENED
DOCENTS
DOGEARS
DOLEFUL
DOLEOUT
DONEFOR
DONEGAL
DOPEOUT
DOTEDON
DOTESON
DOVEBAR
DOVECOT
DOYENNE
DOZENTH
DOZEOFF
FOMENTS
FOREARM
FOREIGN
FORELEG
FOREMAN
FOREMEN
FOREPAW
FORERAN
FORERUN
FORESAW
FORESEE
FORESTS
FOREVER
GONERIL
GORETEX
GOTEVEN
GOVERNS
HOLEDUP
HOLEOUT
HOLESUP
HOMERED
HOMERIC
HOMERUN
HONESTY
HONEYED
HOPEFUL
HOVERED
HOVERER
HOWELLS
HOWEVER
IONESCO
KOPECKS
KOREANS
LORELEI
LORENZO
LORETTA
LOSEOUT
LOSESIT
LOUELLA
LOVEBUG
LOVEINS
LOVERLY
LOWERED
LOZENGE
MODELAS
MODELED
MODELER
MODELTS
MODERNS
MODESTO
MODESTY
MOLESTS
MOMENTS
MONEYED
MORELLO
MORESBY
MOSELLE
MOSEYED
MOVEDIN
MOVEOUT
MOVESIN
NOSEBAG
NOSEEUM
NOSEGAY
NOSEJOB
NOSEOUT
NOTEPAD
NOVELLA
NOVELLE
NOVELTY
NOVENAS
POKEDAT
POKEFUN
POKESAT
POLEAXE
POLECAT
POLEMIC
POLENTA
POMELOS
POPEYED
POSEURS
POTENCY
POVERTY
POWERED
ROBERTA
ROBERTO
ROBERTS
ROBESON
RODENTS
RODEOFF
RODEOUT
ROPEDIN
ROPESIN
ROPETOW
ROSEATE
ROSEBUD
ROSELLE
ROSEOIL
ROSERED
ROSETTA
ROSETTE
ROZELLE
SOBERED
SOBERER
SOBERLY
SOLEDAD
SOMEDAY
SOMEHOW
SOMEONE
SOMEWAY
TOKENED
TONEARM
TONEDUP
TONELOC
TONEROW
TONESUP
TOREOFF
TOREOUT
TOREROS
TOTEBAG
TOTEMIC
TOWELED
TOWERED
VOTECHS
VOTESIN
WOBEGON
WOKENUP
WOREOFF
WOREOUT
YODELED
YODELER

•O••E••

BOATERS
BOBBERS
BOILERS
BOLDEST
BOMBECK
BOMBERS
BONIEST
BONKERS
BONNETS
BOOKEND
BOOLEAN
BOOMERS
BOOTEES
BOPPERS
BORDERS
BORNEUP
BOSKETS
BOSWELL
BOTHERS
BOWLERS
BOWYERS
BOXSEAT
COALERS
COAXERS
COBWEBS
COCHERE
COCTEAU
CODGERS
COFFEES
COFFERS
COINERS
COLBERT
COLDEST
COLLECT
COLLEEN
COLLEGE
COLLETS
COMBERS
COMMEND
COMMENT
COMPEER
COMPELS
COMPETE
CONCEAL
CONCEDE
CONCEIT
CONCEPT
CONCERN
CONCERT
CONDEMN
CONFERS
CONFESS
CONGEAL
CONGERS
CONGEST
CONKERS
CONNECT
CONNERY
CONREID
CONSENT
CONTEMN
CONTEND
CONTENT
CONTEST
CONTEXT
CONVENE
CONVENT
CONVERT
CONVEYS
COOKERS
COOKERY
COOLERS
COOLEST
COOPERS
COPIERS
COPPERS
COPPERY
COPTERS
CORBELS
CORBETT
CORDELL
CORDERO
CORKERS
CORNEAL
CORNEAS
CORNELL
CORNERS
CORNETS
CORRECT
CORSETS
CORTEGE
CORYELL
COSSETS
COTTERS
COULEES
COWBELL
COWHERD
COWPEAS
COYNESS
COZIEST
COZZENS
DOCKERS
DOCKETS
DODDERS
DODGERS
DOGLEGS
DOLMENS
DONKEYS
DOPIEST
DORMERS
DORSETT
DOSSERS
DOUREST
DOWNERS
DOWSERS
FODDERS
FOGGERS
FOLDERS
FOLGERS
FOLLETT
FONDEST
FONTEYN
FOOLERY
FOOTERS
FOPPERY
FORBEAR
FORCEPS
FORCERS
FORFEIT
FORFEND
FORGERS
FORGERY
FORGETS
FORKERS
FORREAL
FORRENT
FORREST
FORWENT
FOSTERS
FOULEST
FOWLERS
FOXIEST
GOAHEAD
GOATEED
GOATEES
GOBLETS
GODDESS
GODSEND
GOLFERS
GOMPERS
GOOBERS
GOODEGG
GOOIEST
GOPHERS
GORGETS
GORIEST
GOSPELS
GOSSETT
GOTWELL
GOUGERS
HOAXERS
HOLBEIN
HOLDERS
HOLIEST
HOLLERS
HOMIEST
HONKERS
HOOFERS
HOOTERS
HOPPERS
HORNETS
HOSIERS
HOSIERY
HOSTELS
HOSTESS
HOTBEDS
HOTHEAD
HOTNESS
HOTSEAT
HOTTEST
HOWBEIT
HOWLERS
HOYDENS
JOBBERS
JOCKEYS
JOGGERS
JOINERS
JOINERY
JOYLESS
KOBLENZ
KOSHERS
LOADERS
LOAFERS
LOANERS
LOBBERS
LOCKERS
LOCKETS
LODGERS
LOGGERS
LOGIEST
LOITERS
LONGEST
LOOKERS
LOOPERS
LOOSELY
LOOSENS
LOOSEST
LOOTERS
LOPPERS
LOTTERY
LOUDEST
LOUREED
LOUSEUP
LOUVERS
LOWBEAM
LOWGEAR
LOWHEEL
LOWNECK
LOWNESS
LOWTECH
MOANERS
MOCKERS
MOCKERY
MOILERS
MOLDERS
MOLIERE
MOLTERS
MONGERS
MONKEES
MONKEYS
MONTEGO
MONTEUX
MOPPERS
MOPPETS
MORDENT
MORSELS
MOSLEMS
MOTHERS
MOUSERS
NOBLEST
NODDERS
NONSELF
NONZERO
NORIEGA
NOSEEUM
NOSHERS
NOSIEST
NOSWEAT
NOTWELL
NOUVEAU
NOWHERE
NOXZEMA
POCKETS
POETESS
POKIEST
POLDERS
POLLENS
POLLERS
POMMELS
POMPEIA
POMPEII
PONDERS
POOREST
POPPERS
POPPETS
PORKERS
PORSENA
PORTEND
PORTENT
PORTERS
POSHEST
POSSESS
POSSETS
POSTERN
POSTERS
POTHERB
POTHERS
POTTERS
POTTERY
POULENC
POURERS
POUTERS
POWDERS
POWDERY
ROAMERS
ROARERS
ROBBERS
ROBBERY
ROCKERS
ROCKETS
RODGERS

ROEDEER
ROGUERY
ROLLERS
ROMNEYS
ROMPERS
RONDEAU
RONDELS
ROOFERS
ROOKERY
ROOMERS
ROOTERS
ROSTERS
ROSWELL
ROTTERS
ROUTERS
ROYBEAN
SOAKERS
SOAPERS
SOARERS
SOBBERS
SOCIETY
SOCKETS
SOCKEYE
SOFTENS
SOFTEST
SOIREES
SOLDERS
SOLFEGE
SOLVENT
SOLVERS
SONNETS
SOONERS
SOONEST
SORBETS
SORCERY
SORRELS
SORTERS
SOSUEME
SOTHERE
SOTHERN
SOUREST
SOVIETS
SOYBEAN
TOELESS
TOFFEES
TOILERS
TOILETS
TOLTECS
TOLUENE
TONIEST
TONNEAU
TOOTERS
TOPPERS
TORMENT
TORPEDO
TORRENT
TOSSERS
TOTTERS
TOTTERY
TOUPEES
TOURERS
TOUTERS
TOWHEAD
TOWHEES
TOWNERS
VOLLEYS
WONDERS
WOOFERS
WOOLENS
WOOMERA
WORKERS
WORSENS
WOZZECK
YONKERS
YOWLERS
ZONKERS

•O•••E•

BOARDED
BOARDER
BOASTED
BOASTER
BOATMEN
BOBBIES
BOBBLED
BOBBLES
BOBSLED
BODEREK
BODICES
BOGEYED
BOGGLED
BOGGLER
BOGGLES
BOLIDES
BOLSTER
BOLUSES
BONDMEN
BONGOES
BONNIER
BONUSES
BOOBIES
BOODLES
BOOGIED
BOOGIES
BOOKIES
BOOKLET
BOONIES
BOOSLER
BOOSTED
BOOSTER
BOOTEES
BOOTIES
BOOTLEG
BORATES
BOSSIER
BOTCHED
BOTCHES
BOTTLED
BOTTLER
BOTTLES
BOULDER
BOUNCED
BOUNCER
BOUNCES
BOUNDED
BOUNDER
BOUQUET
BOURREE
BOVINES
BOWDLER
BOWERED
BOWTIES
BOXSTEP
COACHED
COACHES
COARSEN
COARSER
COASTED
COASTER
COBBLED
COBBLER
COBBLES
COCHLEA
COCKIER
COCKLES
COCKNEY
CODDLED
CODDLER
CODDLES
CODICES
COERCED
COERCES
COFFEES
COHERED
COHERES
COLLEEN
COLLIER
COLLIES
COLLYER
COLONEL
COLONES
COLORED
COMFIER
COMFREY
COMPEER
COMPLEX
CONCHES
CONGAED
CONIFER
CONQUER
COOKIES
COOPTED
COOTIES
CORNFED
CORNIER
CORONET
COSINES
COSTNER
COUCHED
COUCHES
COUGHED
COULEES
COULTER
COUNSEL
COUNTED
COUNTER
COUPLED
COUPLES
COUPLET
COURIER
COURSED
COURSER
COURSES
COURTED
COVERED
COVETED
COWERED
COWRIES
COYOTES
COZENED
COZUMEL
DOGCHEW
DOGGIES
DOGSLED
DOILIES
DOLLIED
DOLLIES
DOLORES
DONATED
DONATES
DOODLED
DOODLER
DOODLES
DOORMEN
DOOZIES
DOPPLER
DOSAGES
DOSSIER
DOTTIER
DOTTLES
DOUBLED
DOUBLES
DOUBLET
DOUBLEU
DOUBTED
DOUBTER
DOWAGER
DOWDIER
DOWNIER
DOWRIES
FOAMIER
FOCSLES
FOCUSED
FOCUSES
FOGGIER
FOIBLES
FOISTED
FOLLIES
FONDLED
FONDLES
FONDUES
FOODWEB
FOOTMEN
FOOZLED
FOOZLES
FORAGED
FORAGER
FORAGES
FORELEG
FOREMEN
FORESEE
FOREVER
FORFREE
FORGOES
FORSTER
FORTIES
FOUNDED
FOUNDER
FOURIER
GOALIES
GOATEED
GOATEES
GOBBLED
GOBBLER
GOBBLES
GODFREY
GOGGLED
GOGGLES
GOLFTEE
GOODIES
GOODMEN
GOOFIER
GOOPIER
GORETEX
GOTEVEN
GOTOVER
GOUNDER
GOURDES
GOURMET
HOAGIES
HOARDED
HOARDER
HOARIER
HOARSEN
HOARSER
HOBBIES
HOBBLED
HOBBLES
HOBOKEN
HOGTIED
HOGTIES
HOISTED
HOLLIES
HOLSTER
HOLYSEE
HOMBRES
HOMERED
HOMINEM
HONEYED
HONORED
HONOREE
HONORER
HOOPOES
HOOSIER
HOPOVER
HORSIER
HOSTLER
HOUNDED
HOVERED
HOVERER
HOWEVER
IODATES
IODIDES
IODIZED
IODIZES
IONIZED
IONIZER
IONIZES
JOFFREY
JOGGLED
JOGGLES
JOINDER
JOINTED
JOISTED
JOLLIED
JOLLIER
JOLLIES
JOLLIET
JOSTLED
JOSTLER
JOSTLES
JOUNCED
JOUNCES
JOURNEY
JOUSTED
JOUSTER
KOOKIER
LOACHES
LOAMIER
LOATHED
LOATHES
LOBBIED
LOBBIES
LOBBYER
LOBSTER
LOCALES
LOCATED
LOCATER
LOCATES
LOESSER
LOESSES
LOFTIER
LOLLIES
LONGUES
LOOKSEE
LOONIER
LOONIES
LOOPIER
LORELEI
LORISES
LORRIES
LOTUSES
LOUNGED
LOUNGER
LOUNGES
LOURDES
LOUREED
LOUSIER
LOUVRES
LOWBRED
LOWERED
LOWHEEL
LOWLIER
MOBILES
MOBSTER
MODELED
MODELER
MODULES
MOISTEN
MOISTER
MOLDIER
MOMMIES
MONEYED
MONGREL
MONIKER
MONKEES
MONOMER
MONSTER
MOOCHED
MOOCHER
MOOCHES
MOODIER
MOONSET
MOORHEN
MORALES
MORDRED
MORPHED
MOSEYED
MOSQUES
MOSSIER
MOTIVES
MOTORED
MOTTLED
MOTTLES
MOTTOES
MOULDED
MOULDER
MOULTED
MOUNDED
MOUNTED
MOUSIER
MOUSSED
MOUSSES
MOUTHED
NODULES
NOGALES
NOISIER
NOMINEE
NONUSER
NOODLES
NORTHER
NOTATED
NOTATES
NOTCHED
NOTCHES
NOTICED
NOTICES
NOVICES
NOZZLES
OOCYTES
OOLITES
POACHED
POACHER
POACHES
POBOXES
PODGIER
POINTED
POINTER
POITIER
POLICED
POLICES
POLITER
POLKAED
POLYMER
POMADED
POMADES
POOCHES
POODLES
POPEYED
POPOVER
POPPIES
POPPLED
POPPLES
PORCHES
PORGIES
POSITED
POSTMEN
POTAGES
POTPIES
POUCHED
POUCHES
POUNCED
POUNCER
POUNCES
POUNDED
POUNDER
POUTIER
POWERED
ROACHED
ROACHES
ROADBED
ROADIES
ROASTED
ROASTER
ROCKIER
ROCKIES
ROEDEER
ROISTER
ROLODEX
RONTGEN
ROOKIES
ROOMIER
ROOMIES
ROOSTED
ROOSTER
ROOTLET
ROSERED
ROSSSEA
ROTATED
ROTATES
ROTIFER
ROUGHED
ROUGHEN
ROUGHER
ROUNDED
ROUNDER
ROUSTED
ROWDIER
ROWDIES
SOAPIER
SOBERED
SOBERER
SOFABED
SOFTIES
SOGGIER
SOIGNEE
SOIREES
SOLACES
SOLDIER
SOLIDER
SOLUTES
SOOTHED
SOOTHER
SOOTHES
SOOTIER
SORITES
SORRIER
SORTIED
SORTIES
SOUGHED
SOUNDED
SOUNDER
SOUPIER
SOURCED
SOURCES
SOUTHEY
TOADIED
TOADIES
TOASTED
TOASTER
TODDIES
TODDLED
TODDLER
TODDLES
TOFFEES
TOFFLER
TOGGLED
TOGGLES
TOKENED
TOLKIEN
TONGUED
TONGUES
TOOKTEN
TOORDER
TOOTHED
TOOTLED
TOOTLES
TOPAZES
TOPPLED
TOPPLES
TORCHED
TORCHES
TORQUES
TOTALED
TOUCHED
TOUCHES
TOUGHEN
TOUGHER
TOUPEES
TOURNEY
TOUSLED
TOUSLES
TOWELED
TOWERED
TOWHEES
TOWNIES
TOYNBEE
VOLUMES
VOUCHED
VOUCHER
VOUCHES
VOYAGED
VOYAGER
VOYAGES
WOBBLED
WOBBLES
WOLFMEN
WOODIER
WOODIES
WOOLIER
WOOLIES
WOOLLEN
WOOLSEY
WOOSTER
WOOZIER
WORDIER
WORKMEN
WORMIER
WORRIED
WORRIER
WORRIES
WORSTED
WOUNDED
YODELED
YODELER
YOUNGER
ZOELLER
ZOMBIES
ZOUAVES

•O••••E

BOBDOLE
BOBHOPE
BOGHOLE
BOLOTIE
BONDAGE
BONFIRE
BOURREE
BOWLINE
BOXKITE
COCHERE
COCHISE
COCKADE
CODEINE
COGNATE
COINAGE
COLETTE
COLGATE
COLLAGE
COLLATE
COLLEGE
COLLIDE
COLLUDE
COLOGNE
COMBINE
COMEDUE
COMIQUE
COMMODE
COMMOVE
COMMUNE
COMMUTE
COMPARE
COMPETE
COMPILE
COMPOSE
COMPOTE
COMPUTE
COMRADE
CONCAVE
CONCEDE
CONCISE
CONDOLE
CONDONE
CONDUCE
CONFIDE
CONFINE
CONFUSE
CONFUTE
CONGAME
CONJURE
CONNIVE
CONNOTE
CONSOLE
CONSUME
CONTUSE
CONVENE
CONVOKE
COPPICE
CORDAGE
CORDATE
CORDITE
CORKAGE
CORNICE
CORONAE
CORRODE
CORSAGE
CORTEGE
COSTUME
COTERIE
COTTAGE
COURAGE
COUTURE
COWHIDE
COWPOKE
DOCKAGE
DOEUVRE
DOGFACE
DOGGONE
DONAHUE
DONJOSE
DOORDIE
DORMICE
DOYENNE
FOLIAGE
FOLIATE
FOOTAGE
FOOTSIE
FORBADE
FORBORE
FORESEE
FORFREE
FORGAVE
FORGIVE
FORGONE
FORLIFE
FORSAKE
FORSALE
FORSURE
FORTUNE
FOXFIRE
FOXHOLE
GOBROKE
GODLIKE
GOESAPE
GOLFTEE
GOODBYE
GOODJOE
GOODONE
GOUACHE
HOECAKE
HOLYOKE
HOLYSEE
HONOREE
HORMONE
HOSPICE
HOSTAGE
HOSTILE
HOTCAKE
HOTLINE
HOTWIRE
HOWCOME
JOHNDOE
JOHNNIE
JOYRIDE
LOOKSEE
LOVABLE
LOWLIFE
LOWRISE
LOWTIDE
LOZENGE
MODISTE
MOLIERE
MONDALE
MONIQUE
MONOCLE
MONTAGE
MONTANE
MOORAGE
MORAINE
MORTISE
MOSELLE
MOULAGE
MOUNTIE
MOVABLE
NOISOME
NOMINEE
NOTABLE
NOTHOME
NOTSURE
NOTTRUE
NOVELLE
NOWHERE
POLEAXE
POLLUTE
PONTINE
PORCINE
PORKPIE
PORSCHE
PORTAGE
POSTAGE
POSTURE
POTABLE
POTHOLE
POTTAGE
ROANOKE
ROBLOWE
ROMAINE
ROMANCE
ROSALIE
ROSANNE
ROSEATE
ROSELLE
ROSETTE
ROULADE
ROUTINE
ROXANNE
ROZELLE
SOCKEYE
SOIGNEE
SOLFEGE
SOLUBLE
SOMEONE
SORBATE
SOSUEME
SOTHERE
SOUFFLE
SOUTANE
TOESHOE
TOLUENE
TONNAGE
TONSURE
TONTINE
TOOTSIE
TOPSIDE
TOSCALE
TOSPARE
TOUGHIE
TOWROPE
TOYNBEE
VOLPONE
VOLTAGE
VOLUBLE
WOEISME
WORDONE
WOULDBE

••OE•••

AMOEBAE
AMOEBAS
AMOEBIC
CROESUS
PHOEBES
PHOEBUS
PHOENIX
SHOEBOX
SHOEING
SLOEGIN
WHOEVER

••O•E••

ABOREAL
ADORERS
APOGEES
AVOCETS
AVOWERS
BIOGENY
BLOWERS
BOOKEND
BOOLEAN
BOOMERS
BOOTEES
BROKEIN
BROKERS
BROKEUP
CHOKERS
CHOKEUP
CLORETS
CLOSEIN
CLOSELY
CLOSEST
CLOSETS
CLOSEUP
CLOVERS
COOKERS
COOKERY
COOLERS
COOLEST
COOPERS
CROWERS
DIOCESE
DIOMEDE
DRONERS
DROVERS
DUODENA
ELOPERS
EMOTERS
EVOKERS
FLORETS
FLOWERS
FLOWERY
FOOLERY
FOOTERS
GEODESY
GLOWERS
GOOBERS
GOODEGG
GOOIEST
GROCERS
GROCERY
GROVELS
GROWERS
HOOFERS
HOOTERS
IMOGENE
IRONERS
ISOHELS
ISOMERS
LIONESS
LIONETS
LOOKERS
LOOPERS
LOOSELY
LOOSENS
LOOSEST
LOOTERS
MIOCENE
PHONEME
PIOLETS
PIONEER
PLOVERS
PLOWERS
POOREST
PROBERS
PROCEED
PROCESS
PROFESS
PROGENY
PROJECT
PROPELS
PROSERS
PROTEAN
PROTECT
PROTEGE
PROTEIN
PROTEST
PROTEUS
PROVERB
PROVERS
PROWESS
PTOLEMY
QUOTERS
REOPENS
RIOTERS
ROOFERS
ROOKERY
ROOMERS
ROOTERS
SCORERS
SCOTERS
SHOVELS
SHOVERS
SHOWERS
SHOWERY
SLOVENE
SLOVENS
SLOWEST
SMOKERS
SNORERS
SOONERS
SOONEST
SPOKEOF
SPOKEUP
STOKELY
STOKERS
STONERS
STORERS
STOREUP
STOREYS
SWOREAT
SWOREBY
SWOREIN
THOREAU
TOOTERS
TROWELS
TROWERS
TWOFERS
USOPENS
VIOLENT
VIOLETS

WOOFERS
WOOLENS
WOOMERA
WROTEIN
WROTETO
WROTEUP

••O••E•

ABORTED
ADOPTED
ADOPTEE
ADOPTER
ADORNED
ANOTHER
APOGEES
APOTHEM
AROUSED
AROUSES
ATOMIES
AVOIDED
AVONLEA
BLOATED
BLOCKED
BLOCKER
BLONDER
BLONDES
BLOODED
BLOOMED
BLOOMER
BLOOPED
BLOOPER
BLOTTED
BLOTTER
BLOUSED
BLOUSES
BLOWIER
BMOVIES
BOOBIES
BOODLES
BOOGIED
BOOGIES
BOOKIES
BOOKLET
BOONIES
BOOSLER
BOOSTED
BOOSTER
BOOTEES
BOOTIES
BOOTLEG
BROADEN
BROADER
BROGUES
BROILED
BROILER
BRONZED
BRONZES
BROODED
BROODER
BROOKED
BROTHER
BROWNED
BROWNER
BROWSED
BROWSER
BROWSES
CHOICER
CHOICES
CHOMPED
CHOOSER
CHOOSES
CHOPPED
CHOPPER
CHOWDER
CLOAKED
CLOBBER
CLOCHES
CLOCKED
CLOCKER
CLOGGED
CLOONEY
CLOPPED
CLOQUES
CLOTHED
CLOTHES
CLOTTED
CLOUDED
CLOUTED
CLOWDER
CLOWNED
COOKIES
COOPTED
COOTIES
CROAKED
CROCHET
CRONIES
CROOKED
CROONED
CROONER
CROPPED
CROPPER
CROQUET
CROSIER
CROSSED
CROSSER
CROSSES
CROWDED
CROWNED
DIOPTER
DOODLED
DOODLER
DOODLES
DOORMEN
DOOZIES
DROLLER
DROOLED
DROOLER
DROOPED
DROPLET
DROPPED
DROPPER
DROWNED
DROWSED
DROWSES
EBONIES
EPOXIES
ETOILES
EVOLVED
EVOLVES
FLOATED
FLOATER
FLOCKED
FLOGGED
FLOODED
FLOORED
FLOPPED
FLOSSED
FLOSSES
FLOURED
FLOUTED
FOODWEB
FOOTMEN
FOOZLED
FOOZLES
FROCKED
FROGMEN
FRONTED
FROSTED
FROTHED
FROWNED
FROWNER
GEORGES
GHOSTED
GLOATED
GLOMMED
GLORIED
GLORIES
GLOSSED
GLOSSES
GOODIES
GOODMEN
GOOFIER
GOOPIER
GROANED
GROANER
GROLIER
GROMMET
GROOMED
GROOMER
GROOVED
GROOVES
GROSSED
GROSSER
GROSSES
GROUPED
GROUPER
GROUSED
GROUSER
GROUSES
GROUTED
GROWLED
GROWLER
HOOPOES
HOOSIER
IRONIES
IRONMEN
IVORIES
KNOBBED
KNOCKED
KNOCKER
KNOTTED
KOOKIER
LOOKSEE
LOONIER
LOONIES
LOOPIER
MOOCHED
MOOCHER
MOOCHES
MOODIER
MOONSET
MOORHEN
NOODLES
ONORDER
PEONIES
PEOPLED
PEOPLES
PHOEBES
PHONIER
PHONIES
PHOTOED
PIONEER
PLODDED
PLODDER
PLOPPED
PLOTTED
PLOTTER
PLOWMEN
POOCHES
POODLES
PROBLEM
PROCEED
PRODDED
PRODDER
PROFFER
PRONGED
PROOFED
PROOFER
PROPHET
PROPJET
PROPMEN
PROPPED
PROSIER
PROSPER
PROUDER
PROWLED
PROWLER
PROXIES
QUONSET
REOILED
REORDER
ROOKIES
ROOMIER
ROOMIES
ROOSTED
ROOSTER
ROOTLET
SCOFFED
SCOFFER
SCOLDED
SCOLDER
SCONCES
SCOOPED
SCOOPER
SCOOTED
SCOOTER
SCORNED
SCOURED
SCOURER
SCOUTED
SCOUTER
SCOWLED
SCOWLER
SHOCKED
SHOCKER
SHODDEN
SHOOTER
SHOPPED
SHOPPER
SHOPPES
SHORTED
SHORTEN
SHORTER
SHOUTED
SHOUTER
SHOWIER
SHOWMEN
SKOSHES
SLOBBER
SLOGGED
SLOPPED
SLOSHED
SLOSHES
SLOTTED
SMOKIER
SMOKIES
SMOLDER
SMOTHER
SNOOKER
SNOOPED
SNOOPER
SNOOTED
SNOOZED
SNOOZES
SNORKEL
SNORTED
SNORTER
SNOWIER
SNOWMEN
SNOWPEA
SOOTHED
SOOTHER
SOOTHES
SOOTIER
SPOILED
SPOILER
SPONDEE
SPONGED
SPONGER
SPONGES
SPOOFED
SPOOFER
SPOOKED
SPOOLED
SPOONED
SPOONER
SPORTED
SPOTTED
SPOTTER
SPOUSES
SPOUTED
SPOUTER
STOCKED
STOGIES
STOLLEN
STOLLER
STOMPED
STONIER
STOOGES
STOOKEY
STOOPED
STOPPED
STOPPER
STORIED
STORIES
STORMED
STOUTER
SWOLLEN
SWOONED
SWOOPED
TOOKTEN
TOORDER
TOOTHED
TOOTLED
TOOTLES
TROCHEE
TROCHES
TRODDEN
TROLLED
TROLLEY
TROOPED
TROOPER
TROTHED
TROTTED
TROTTER
TROUPER
TROUPES
TROUSER
TWOSTEP
UNOILED
WHOEVER
WHOMPED
WHOOPED
WHOOPEE
WHOPPED
WHOPPER
WHORLED
WOODIER
WOODIES
WOOLIER
WOOLIES
WOOLLEN
WOOLSEY
WOOSTER
WOOZIER
WRONGED
WRONGER

••O•••E

ACOLYTE
ACONITE
ADOLPHE
ADOPTEE
AGONIZE
ALOHAOE
AMOEBAE
ANODIZE
ANODYNE
APOCOPE
APOSTLE
ATOMIZE
BLONDIE
BROCADE
BROMATE
BROMIDE
BROMINE
BROWNIE
CHORALE
CHORINE
CHORTLE
CLOSURE
CLOTURE
DIOCESE
DIOMEDE
DIOXIDE
DOORDIE
EBONITE
EMOTIVE
ENOUNCE
EROSIVE
FLOUNCE
FOOTAGE
FOOTSIE
FROMAGE
GLOBULE
GLOSSAE
GOODBYE
GOODJOE
GOODONE
GROUPIE
IDOLIZE
IMOGENE
IRONAGE
IRONORE
ISOLATE
ISOTOPE
LEONINE
LIONIZE
LOOKSEE
MIOCENE
MOORAGE
NEONATE
OROURKE
PEONAGE
PHONEME
PLOSIVE
PROBATE
PROCURE
PRODUCE
PROFANE
PROFILE
PROFUSE
PROMISE
PROMOTE
PROPANE
PROPOSE
PRORATE
PROTEGE
PROVIDE
PROVOKE
SAOTOME
SCOTTIE
SCOURGE
SLOVENE
SNOCONE
SPOKANE
SPONDEE
STOOLIE
STORAGE
SWOOSIE
TOOTSIE
TROCHEE
TROUBLE
TROUNCE
TWOBASE
TWOSOME
TWOTIME
TWOTONE
VIOLATE
WHOOPEE
YAOUNDE

•••OE••

GENOESE
VETOERS

•••O•E•

ABDOMEN
AEROBES
ALCOVES
ALLOVER
ALLOWED
ALLOYED
ANDOVER
ANNOYED
APPOSED
APPOSES
APRONED
ARBORED
ARMORED
ARMORER
ATHOMES
BALONEY
BARONET
BAYONET
BECOMES
BELOVED
BETOKEN
BIGOTED
BLOODED
BLOOMED
BLOOMER
BLOOPED
BLOOPER
BROODED
BROODER
BROOKED
BYGONES
CAJOLED
CAJOLER
CAJOLES
CALOMEL
CAROLED
CAROLER
CAROLES
CAROMED
CHOOSER
CHOOSES
CHROMES
CLOONEY
CNTOWER
COLONEL
COLONES
COLORED
CORONET
COYOTES
CREOLES
CROOKED
CROONED
CROONER
CRYOGEN
DAHOMEY
DEBONED
DEBONES
DECODED
DECODER
DECODES
DECOYED
DEKOVEN
DEMOTED
DEMOTES
DENOTED
DENOTES
DEPONED
DEPONES
DEPOSED
DEPOSER
DEPOSES
DEVOTED
DEVOTEE
DEVOTES
DIDOVER
DIPOLES
DISOBEY
DOLORES
DROOLED
DROOLER
DROOPED
ELBOWED
EMPOWER
ENCODED
ENCODER
ENCODES
ENCORES
ENDOWED
ENJOYED
ENROBED
ENROBES
EXPOSED
EXPOSES
FAGOTED
FAVORED
FLOODED
FLOORED
FLYOVER
FURORES
GETOVER
GOTOVER
GROOMED
GROOMER
GROOVED
GROOVES
HALOGEN
HANOVER
HOBOKEN
HONORED
HONOREE
HONORER
HOPOVER
HUMORED
IGNORED
IGNORER
IGNORES
IMPOSED
IMPOSES
INCOMES
INJOKES
INSOLES
INTONED
INTONER
INTONES
INVOKED
INVOKER
INVOKES
JACONET
KETONES
LABORED
LABORER
LAYOVER
LIEOVER
LIMOGES
LITOTES
MAHONEY
MAJORED
MEIOSES
MEMOREX
METOOER
MINORED
MITOSES
MONOMER
MOTORED
MRBONES
OCTOBER
OPPOSED
OPPOSER
OPPOSES
ORIOLES
OSMOSED
OSMOSES
PAROLED
PAROLEE
PAROLES
PHLOXES
PILOTED
PINONES
PIVOTED
POBOXES
POPOVER
PROOFED
PROOFER
PUTOVER
RANOVER
RAZORED
RECODED
RECODES
RECOVER
REMODEL
REMOTER
REMOTES
REMOVED
REMOVER
REMOVES
REMOWED
RENOTES
REPOSED
REPOSES
RESOLED
RESOLES
RETOWED
REVOKED
REVOKES
REWOVEN
REZONED
REZONES
ROLODEX
RUMORED
RUNOVER
SAMOYED
SAVORED
SCOOPED
SCOOPER
SCOOTED
SCOOTER
SENORES
SHOOTER
SNOOKER
SNOOPED
SNOOPER
SNOOTED
SNOOZED
SNOOZES
SPOOFED
SPOOFER
SPOOKED
SPOOLED
SPOONED
SPOONER
STOOGES
STOOKEY
STOOPED
STROBES
STROKED
STROKES
SWOONED
SWOOPED
TABORET
TALONED
TENONED
THEOREM
THRONES
THROWER
TRIODES
TROOPED
TROOPER
TUTORED
UNBOWED
UNBOXED
UNBOXES
UNCOVER
UNLOVED
UNMOVED
UNROBED
UNROBES
UNYOKED
UNYOKES
UNZONED
WAGONER
WHOOPED
WHOOPEE
WIDOWED
WIDOWER
ZAPOTEC
ZATOPEK
ZYGOTES

•••O••E

ABSOLVE
ALLOFME
AMPOULE
ANTOINE
AREOLAE
ARGONNE
ARMOIRE
AURORAE
BAROQUE
BEHOOVE
BOLOTIE
BRIOCHE
BYFORCE
CABOOSE
CALORIE
CAROUSE
COLOGNE
CORONAE
CULOTTE
DEVOLVE
DEVOTEE
DIVORCE
ECLOGUE
ENDORSE
ENFORCE
ENGORGE
ENNOBLE
ENROUTE
ESPOUSE
GARONNE
GAVOTTE
GENOESE
GIRONDE
HELOISE
HEROINE
HONOREE
IGNOBLE
INFORCE
INHOUSE
INVOGUE
INVOICE
INVOLVE
LACOSTE
LAPORTE
LAROCHE
MEMOIRE
MONOCLE
OSBORNE
PAPOOSE
PAROLEE
PINOCLE
PIROGUE
REJOICE
REMORSE
REROUTE
RESOLVE
REVOICE
REVOLVE
RIPOSTE
SCROOGE
STOOLIE
STROPHE
SWOOSIE
UNHORSE
UNLOOSE
UPBORNE
VAMOOSE
WHOOPEE

••••OE•

BANJOES
BIGTOES
BILBOES
BINGOES
BONGOES
BRAVOES
BUCKOES
BUNCOED
BUNKOED
CAMEOED
CARGOES
CITROEN
DINGOES
DISCOED
DITTOED
FORGOES
FUNGOES
GECKOES
GESSOES
GUSTOES
HOOPOES
HULLOED
IMAGOES
JINGOES
JUNCOES
LASSOED
LASSOER
LASSOES
LINGOES
MAMBOED
MANGOES
METOOER
MISDOES
MOTTOES
OUTDOES
OUTGOES
PALJOEY
PHOTOED
RADIOED
RESHOES
SALVOES
SCHMOES
SHAKOES
TANGOED
TIPTOED
TIPTOES
WEBTOED

••••O•E

ABALONE
ACEROSE
ACETONE
ADIPOSE
AIRHOLE
ALAMODE
ALLGONE
AMBROSE
ANATOLE
ANEMONE
ANYMORE
APOCOPE
APPROVE
ARDMORE
ARMHOLE
AUREOLE
AWESOME
AXLROSE
BARCODE
BEHOOVE
BESPOKE
BOBDOLE
BOBHOPE
BOGHOLE
BYANOSE
CABOOSE
CALZONE
CANZONE
CATHODE
COMMODE
COMMOVE
COMPOSE
COMPOTE
CONDOLE
CONDONE
CONNOTE
CONSOLE
CONVOKE
CORRODE
COWPOKE
CYCLONE
DEPLORE
DISPOSE
DISROBE
DOGGONE
DONJOSE
DRYHOLE
EARLOBE
ENCLOSE
ENDZONE
EPIGONE
EPISODE
EPITOME
EXPLODE
EXPLORE
EYEHOLE
EYESORE
FARGONE
FASTONE
FORBORE
FORGONE
FOXHOLE
FULSOME
GILMORE
GLUCOSE
GOBROKE
GOODONE
HIPBONE
HOLYOKE
HORMONE
HOWCOME
IFSTONE
IMPLODE
IMPLORE
IMPROVE
INCLOSE
INSTORE
IRKSOME
IRONORE
ISOTOPE
JAWBONE
KARAOKE
KEYHOLE
KEYNOTE
LACTOSE
LAPROBE
LISSOME
LIVEONE
MALTOSE
MANHOLE
MARLOWE
MAYPOLE
MELROSE
MICROBE
MISDONE
NEURONE
NOISOME
NOTHOME
ONSHORE
OPEROSE
OUTCOME
OUTDONE
OUTVOTE
OUTWORE

PADRONE
PAPOOSE
PETIOLE
PINHOLE
PISTOLE
POTHOLE
PROMOTE
PROPOSE
PROVOKE
PUGNOSE
PURPOSE
QUIXOTE
RATHOLE
RECHOSE
REDROSE
REPROVE
RESTORE
REWROTE
RHIZOME
RISSOLE
ROANOKE
ROBLOWE
RUMPOLE
RUNHOME
SANJOSE
SAOTOME
SCROOGE
SKIPOLE
SNOCONE
SOMEONE
SPUMONE
SUCROSE
SUPPOSE
SYSTOLE
TADPOLE
TAKEONE
TEAROSE
TOWROPE
TRITONE
TWOSOME
TWOTONE
UNAVOCE
UNCLOSE
UNLOOSE
UNQUOTE
UPCLOSE
VACUOLE
VAMOOSE
VERBOSE
VOLPONE
WALPOLE
WELCOME
WILDONE
WINSOME
WORDONE
ZIPCODE

••••••OE

ALOHAOE
BACKHOE
GOODJOE
GUMSHOE
GYMSHOE
ICEFLOE
IVANHOE
JANEDOE
JOHNDOE
MCENROE
OPENTOE
PRUDHOE
TOESHOE

OF•••••

OFASORT
OFFBASE
OFFBEAT
OFFDUTY
OFFENCE
OFFENDS
OFFENSE
OFFERED
OFFERER
OFFHAND
OFFHOUR
OFFICER
OFFICES
OFFLINE
OFFLOAD
OFFPEAK
OFFRAMP
OFFROAD
OFFSETS
OFFSIDE
OFFSITE
OFFYEAR
OFSORTS
OFTENER

O•F••••

OFFBASE
OFFBEAT
OFFDUTY
OFFENCE
OFFENDS
OFFENSE
OFFERED
OFFERER
OFFHAND
OFFHOUR
OFFICER
OFFICES
OFFLINE
OFFLOAD
OFFPEAK
OFFRAMP
OFFROAD
OFFSETS
OFFSIDE
OFFSITE
OFFYEAR
OXFORDS

O••F•••

OAKFERN
OLDFOGY
ORIFICE
OUTFACE
OUTFITS
OUTFLOW

O•••F••

OKEEFFE
OSSIFIC
OUTOFIT
OVERFLY

O••••F•

OKEEFFE

O•••••F

OAKLEAF
ONESELF
ONTOPOF
OURSELF

•OF••••

COFFEES
COFFERS
DOFFING
GOFORIT
HOFBRAU
HOFFMAN
JOFFREY
LOFTIER
LOFTILY
LOFTING
NOFAULT
SOFABED
SOFFITS
SOFTENS
SOFTEST
SOFTIES
SOFTTOP
TOFFEES
TOFFLER

•O•F•••

BONFIRE
BOWFINS
BOXFULS
CODFISH
COFFEES
COFFERS
COIFING
COMFIER
COMFITS
COMFORT
COMFREY
CONFABS
CONFERS
CONFESS
CONFIDE
CONFINE
CONFIRM
CONFORM
CONFUSE
CONFUTE
DOFFING
DOGFACE
DOGFISH
FORFEIT
FORFEND
FORFREE
FOXFIRE
GODFREY
GOLFERS
GOLFING
GOLFPRO
GOLFTEE
GOOFIER
GOOFING
GOOFOFF
GOOFSUP
GOOFUPS
HOFFMAN
HOOFERS
HOOFING
HOOFSIT
HOTFOOT
JOFFREY
LOAFERS
LOAFING
LOOFAHS
MOUFLON
NORFOLK
POTFULS
ROOFERS
ROOFING
ROOFTOP
SOFFITS
SOLFEGE
SOUFFLE
TOFFEES
TOFFLER
TOMFOOL
WOLFGAL
WOLFING
WOLFISH
WOLFMAN
WOLFMEN
WOLFRAM
WOOFERS
WOOFING

•O••F••

BODYFAT
BOWLFUL
CONIFER
CORNFED
DOLEFUL
DONEFOR
FORKFUL
GOESFOR
GOINFOR
HOPEFUL
LOOKFOR
POKEFUN
POPOFFS
ROOMFUL
ROOTFOR
ROTIFER
SOUFFLE
SOULFUL
WORKFOR

•O•••F•

COMEOFF
CONNIFF
COOKOFF
DOZEOFF
FOBSOFF
FORLIFE
FORTIFY
GOESOFF
GOOFOFF
HOLDOFF
HOPSOFF
HORRIFY
LOGSOFF
LOWLIFE
MOLLIFY
MORTIFY
NODSOFF
PONTIFF
POPOFFS
POPSOFF
RODEOFF
RODOLFO
SOLDOFF
TOLDOFF
TOOKOFF
TOPSOFF
TOREOFF
TOSSOFF
WOREOFF
WORKOFF
WORNOFF

•O••••F

COMEOFF
CONNIFF
COOKOFF
DOZEOFF
FOBSOFF
GOESOFF
GOOFOFF
HOLDOFF
HOPSOFF
LOGSOFF
NODSOFF
NONSELF
PONTIFF
POPSOFF
RODEOFF
SOLDOFF
TOLDOFF
TOOKOFF
TOPSOFF
TOREOFF
TOSSOFF
WOREOFF
WORKOFF
WORNOFF

••OF•••

ASOFNOW
GOOFIER
GOOFING
GOOFOFF
GOOFSUP
GOOFUPS
HOOFERS
HOOFING
HOOFSIT
LOOFAHS
PROFANE
PROFESS
PROFFER
PROFILE
PROFITS
PROFUSE
ROOFERS
ROOFING
ROOFTOP
SCOFFED
SCOFFER
SHOFARS
TWOFERS
TWOFOLD
WOOFERS
WOOFING

••O•F••

ALOOFLY
BLOWFLY
LOOKFOR
PROFFER
PROOFED
PROOFER
ROOMFUL
ROOTFOR
SCOFFED
SCOFFER
SHOOFLY
SHOTFOR
SPOOFED
SPOOFER

••O••F•

BLOWOFF
COOKOFF
DROPOFF
GLORIFY
GOOFOFF
SHOWOFF
STOPOFF
TOOKOFF

••O•••F

BEOWULF
BLOWOFF
COOKOFF
DROPOFF
GOOFOFF
SHORTOF
SHOWOFF
SPOKEOF
STOPOFF
TOOKOFF

•••OF••

ALLOFME
ALOOFLY
CUTOFFS
INSOFAR
LAYOFFS
OUTOFIT
PAYOFFS
POPOFFS
PROOFED
PROOFER
RIPOFFS
RUNOFFS
SHOOFLY
SPOOFED
SPOOFER
TIPOFFS

•••O•F•

CUTOFFS
LAYOFFS
PAYOFFS
POPOFFS
RIPOFFS
RODOLFO
RUNOFFS
TIPOFFS

•••O••F

ONTOPOF

••••OF•

BACKOFF
BAKEOFF
BEAROFF
BEGSOFF
BITEOFF
BLEWOFF
BLOWOFF
BUGSOFF
BUYSOFF
BUZZOFF
CALLOFF
CAMEOFF
CASTOFF
COMEOFF
COOKOFF
CUTSOFF
DASHOFF
DIEDOFF
DIESOFF
DOZEOFF
DROPOFF
DUSTOFF
EASEOFF
FACEOFF
FAIROFF
FALLOFF
FELLOFF
FIREOFF
FOBSOFF
GAVEOFF
GETSOFF
GIVEOFF
GOESOFF
GOOFOFF
HANDOFF
HANGOFF
HAULOFF
HAYLOFT
HEADOFF
HELDOFF
HOLDOFF
HOPSOFF
JUMPOFF
KARLOFF
KEEPOFF
KEPTOFF
KICKOFF
KISSOFF
LAIDOFF
LAYSOFF
LEADOFF
LEFTOFF
LETSOFF
LIFTOFF
LOGSOFF
MADEOFF
MAKEOFF
MARKOFF
NODSOFF
PAIDOFF
PAIROFF
PALMOFF
PASSOFF
PAWNOFF
PAYSOFF
PEELOFF
PICKOFF
PLAYOFF
POPSOFF
PULLOFF
PUSHOFF
PUTSOFF
RAKEOFF
REELOFF
RIDEOFF
RIPSOFF
RODEOFF
RUNSOFF
RUSHOFF
SEALOFF
SEESOFF
SELLOFF
SENDOFF
SENTOFF
SETSOFF
SHOWOFF
SHUTOFF
SIGNOFF
SOLDOFF
SPINOFF
SPUNOFF
STOPOFF
TAILOFF
TAKEOFF
TEAROFF
TEEDOFF
TEESOFF
TELLOFF
TICKOFF
TIMEOFF
TIPSOFF
TOLDOFF
TOOKOFF
TOPSOFF
TOREOFF
TOSSOFF
TURNOFF
WARDOFF
WASHOFF
WAVEOFF
WEAROFF
WELLOFF
WENTOFF
WOREOFF
WORKOFF
WORNOFF

••••O•F

AIRWOLF
BACKOFF
BAKEOFF
BEAROFF
BEGSOFF
BITEOFF
BLEWOFF
BLOWOFF
BUGSOFF
BUYSOFF
BUZZOFF
CALLOFF
CAMEOFF
CASTOFF
COMEOFF
COOKOFF
CRYWOLF
CUTSOFF
DASHOFF
DIEDOFF
DIESOFF
DOZEOFF
DROPOFF
DUSTOFF
EASEOFF
FACEOFF
FAIROFF
FALLOFF
FELLOFF
FIREOFF
FOBSOFF
GAVEOFF
GETSOFF
GIVEOFF
GOESOFF
GOOFOFF
HANDOFF
HANGOFF
HAULOFF
HEADOFF
HELDOFF
HIPROOF
HOLDOFF
HOPSOFF
JUMPOFF
KARLOFF
KEEPOFF
KEPTOFF
KICKOFF
KISSOFF
LAIDOFF
LAYSOFF
LEADOFF
LEFTOFF
LETSOFF
LIFTOFF
LOGSOFF
MADEOFF
MAKEOFF
MARKOFF
NODSOFF
PAIDOFF
PAIROFF
PALMOFF
PASSOFF
PAWNOFF
PAYSOFF
PEELOFF
PICKOFF
PLAYOFF
POPSOFF
PULLOFF
PUSHOFF
PUTSOFF
RAKEOFF
REDWOLF
REELOFF
REPROOF
RIDEOFF
RIPSOFF
RODEOFF
RUNSOFF
RUSHOFF
SEALOFF
SEESOFF
SELLOFF
SENDOFF
SENTOFF
SETSOFF
SHADOOF
SHEWOLF
SHOWOFF
SHUTOFF
SIGNOFF
SOLDOFF
SPINOFF
SPUNOFF
STOPOFF
SUNROOF
TAILOFF
TAKEOFF
TEAROFF
TEEDOFF
TEESOFF
TELLOFF
TICKOFF
TIMEOFF
TIPSOFF
TOLDOFF
TOOKOFF
TOPSOFF
TOREOFF
TOSSOFF
TURNOFF
WALDORF
WARDOFF
WASHOFF
WAVEOFF
WEAROFF
WELLOFF
WENTOFF
WOREOFF
WORKOFF
WORNOFF

•••••OF

AHEADOF
AWAREOF
BARANOF
BYWAYOF
HEARDOF
HEARSOF
HIPROOF
INAWEOF
ONTOPOF
REPROOF
SHADOOF
SHORTOF
SPEAKOF
SPOKEOF
SUNROOF
THEREOF
THINKOF
TIREDOF
WHEREOF

OG•••••

OGDOADS
OGLALAS
OGREISH

O•G••••

ONGOING
ONGUARD
ORGANDY
ORGANIC
ORGANON
ORGANUM
ORGANZA

O••G•••

OLDGOLD
ONAGERS
OREGANO
ORIGAMI
ORIGINS
OUTGOES
OUTGREW
OUTGROW
OUTGUNS

O•••G••

OBLIGED
OBLIGES
OBREGON
OCTAGON
ONSIGHT
OPPUGNS
ORANGES
OUTAGES
OWINGTO

O••••G•

OBLONGS
OILRIGS
OLDFOGY
ONSTAGE
ONTHEGO
OUTINGS
OUTRAGE
OVERAGE

O•••••G

OBEYING
OINKING
OKAYING
ONGOING
OPENING
OPINING
ORATING
OUSTING
OVERBIG

•OG••••

BOGDOWN
BOGEYED
BOGGING
BOGGLED
BOGGLER
BOGGLES
BOGHOLE
COGBURN
COGENCY
COGNACS
COGNATE
DOGCART
DOGCHEW
DOGCHOW
DOGDAYS
DOGEARS
DOGFACE
DOGFISH
DOGGIES
DOGGING
DOGGONE
DOGLEGS
DOGMATA
DOGSHOW
DOGSLED
DOGSTAR
DOGTAGS
DOGTROT
DOGWOOD
FOGBANK
FOGBOWS
FOGGERS
FOGGIER
FOGGING
FOGHORN
FOGYISH
FOGYISM
GOGGLED
GOGGLES
HOGARTH
HOGBACK
HOGGING
HOGTIED
HOGTIES
HOGWASH
HOGWILD
JOGGERS
JOGGING
JOGGLED
JOGGLES
LOGBOOK
LOGGERS
LOGGIAS
LOGGING
LOGGINS
LOGICAL
LOGIEST
LOGJAMS
LOGSOFF
LOGSOUT
MOGAMBO
NOGALES
NOGGINS
NOGUCHI
ROGUERY
ROGUISH
SOGGIER
SOGGILY
TOGGING
TOGGLED
TOGGLES
YOGHURT
YOGURTS

•O•G•••

BOGGING
BOGGLED
BOGGLER
BOGGLES
BONGING
BONGOES
BOOGIED
BOOGIES
CODGERS
COLGATE
CONGAED
CONGAME
CONGEAL
CONGERS
CONGEST
COUGARS
COUGHED
COUGHUP
COWGIRL
DODGERS
DODGING
DODGSON
DOGGIES
DOGGING
DOGGONE
DOUGHTY
DOUGLAS
FOGGERS
FOGGIER
FOGGING
FOLGERS
FORGAVE
FORGERS
FORGERY
FORGETS
FORGING
FORGIVE
FORGOES
FORGONE
FORGOOD
GOGGLED
GOGGLES
GONGING
GOOGOLS
GORGETS
GORGING
GORGONS
GOUGERS
GOUGING
HOAGIES
HOGGING
JOGGERS
JOGGING
JOGGLED
JOGGLES
LODGERS
LODGING
LOGGERS
LOGGIAS
LOGGING
LOGGINS
LONGAGO
LONGBOW
LONGEST
LONGING
LONGISH
LONGRUN
LONGTON
LONGUES
LOWGEAR
MONGERS
MONGOLS
MONGREL
MORGANA
MORGANS
NOGGINS
NOUGATS
PODGIER
PONGIDS
POPGUNS
PORGIES
RODGERS
ROUGHED
ROUGHEN
ROUGHER
ROUGHIT
ROUGHLY
ROUGHUP
ROUGING
SOGGIER
SOGGILY
SOIGNEE
SORGHUM
SOUGHED
TOGGING
TOGGLED
TOGGLES
TONGANS
TONGUED
TONGUES
TOPGUNS
TOUGHEN
TOUGHER
TOUGHIE
TOUGHLY

•O••G••

BODEGAS
BOLOGNA
COALGAS
COLOGNE
COSIGNS
DOINGIN
DOINGUP
DONEGAL
DOSAGES
DOWAGER
FORAGED
FORAGER
FORAGES
GOINGAT
GOINGBY
GOINGIN
GOINGON
GOINGUP
JOHNGAY
KOSYGIN
LOUNGED
LOUNGER
LOUNGES
NONAGON
NOSEGAY
POLYGON
POTAGES
RONTGEN
TONIGHT
VOYAGED
VOYAGER

VOYAGES
WOBEGON
WOLFGAL
YOUNGER
YOUNGMC
YOUNGUN

•O•••G•

BONDAGE
BOROUGH
COINAGE
COLLAGE
COLLEGE
COMINGS
CONDIGN
CONSIGN
CORDAGE
CORKAGE
CORSAGE
CORTEGE
COTTAGE
COURAGE
DOCKAGE
DOGLEGS
DOGTAGS
DOMINGO
FOLIAGE
FOOTAGE
FOREIGN
GOODEGG
HOSTAGE
HOTDOGS
LONGAGO
LOZENGE
MONTAGE
MONTEGO
MOORAGE
MOULAGE
NORIEGA
PORTAGE
POSTAGE
POTTAGE
SOLFEGE
SOWBUGS
TONNAGE
TOPDOGS
TOYDOGS
VOLTAGE
ZOOLOGY

•O••••G

BOATING
BOBBING
BOGGING
BOILING
BOLTING
BOMBING
BONDING
BONGING
BOOKING
BOOMING
BOOTING
BOOTLEG
BOPPING
BOSSING
BOWLING
COATING
COAXING
COCKING
COIFING
COILING
COINING
COMBING
CONKING
CONNING
COOKING
COOLING
COOPING
COPPING
COPYING
CORDING
CORKING
CORNDOG
CORNING
COSTING
COWLING
COZYING
DOCKING
DODGING
DOFFING
DOGGING
DOLLING
DONKING
DONNING
DOOMING
DOTTING
DOUSING
DOWNING
DOWSING
FOALING
FOAMING
FOBBING
FOGGING
FOILING
FOLDING
FOOLING
FOOTING
FORCING
FORDING
FORELEG
FORGING
FORKING
FORMING
FOULING
FOWLING
GOADING
GOALONG
GOLDBUG
GOLDING
GOLFING
GONGING
GOODEGG
GOOFING
GOOSING
GORGING
GOSLING
GOUGING
GOWRONG
HOAXING
HOBOING
HOCKING
HOGGING
HOLDING
HOMBURG
HONKING
HOOFING
HOOKING
HOOPING
HOOTING
HOPPING
HORNING
HORSING
HOSTING
HOUSING
HOWLING
JOBBING
JOGGING
JOINING
JOLTING
JOSHING
JOTTING
LOADING
LOAFING
LOAMING
LOANING
LOBBING
LOCKING
LODGING
LOFTING
LOGGING
LOLLING
LONGING
LOOKING
LOOMING
LOOPING
LOOSING
LOOTING
LOPPING
LORDING
LOTTING
LOUSING
LOVEBUG
MOANING
MOBBING
MOCKING
MOILING
MOLDING
MOLTING
MONOLOG
MOONDOG
MOONING
MOORING
MOPPING
MORNING
MOSSING
MOUSING
NODDING
NOISING
NOOSING
NOSEBAG
NOSHING
NOTHING
POISING
POLLING
PONYING
POOLING
POOPING
POPPING
POSTING
POTTING
POURING
POUTING
ROADHOG
ROAMING
ROARING
ROBBING
ROCKING
ROILING
ROLLING
ROLVAAG
ROMPING
ROOFING
ROOKING
ROOMING
ROOTING
ROTTING
ROUGING
ROUSING
ROUTING
SOAKING
SOAPING
SOARING
SOBBING
SOCKING
SODDING
SOILING
SOLOING
SOLVING
SOPPING
SORTING
SOURING
TOGGING
TOILING
TOLLING
TOOLING
TOOTING
TOPPING
TOSSING
TOTEBAG
TOTTING
TOURING
TOUTING
VOICING
VOIDING
WOLFING
WOOFING
WORDING
WORKING
YOWLING
YOYOING
ZONKING
ZOOMING

••OG•••

APOGEES
BIOGENY
BOOGIED
BOOGIES
BROGANS
BROGUES
CLOGGED
CLOGSUP
FLOGGED
FROGMAN
FROGMEN
GOOGOLS
IMOGENE
ISOGONS
PROGENY
PROGRAM
SHOGUNS
SLOGANS
SLOGGED
STOGIES

••O•G••

AMONGST
BLOWGUN
BROUGHT
CLOGGED
DROUGHT
FLOGGED
GEORGES
GEORGIA
GIORGIO
PLOUGHS
PRONGED
SHOTGUN
SLOEGIN
SLOGGED
SLOUGHS
SPONGED
SPONGER
SPONGES
STOOGES
STOPGAP
THOUGHT
TROUGHS
TSONGAS
WRONGED
WRONGER
WRONGLY
WROUGHT

••O••G•

APOLOGY
BIOLOGY
ECOLOGY
FOOTAGE
FROMAGE
GEOLOGY
GOODEGG
IRONAGE
MOORAGE
PEONAGE
PHOTOGS
PRODIGY
PROLOGS
PROTEGE
SCOURGE
STORAGE
ZOOLOGY

••O•••G

ADORING
ATONING
AVOWING
BLOWING
BOOKING
BOOMING
BOOTING
BOOTLEG
BUOYING
CLONING
CLOSING
CLOYING
COOKING
COOLING
COOPING
CROWING
DOOMING
DRONING
ELOPING
EMOTING
ERODING
EVOKING
FLOWING
FOOLING
FOOTING
GLOWING
GOODEGG
GOOFING
GOOSING
GROPING
GROWING
HOOFING
HOOKING
HOOPING
HOOTING
IRONING
KNOWING
LOOKING
LOOMING
LOOPING
LOOSING
LOOTING
MEOWING
MOONDOG
MOONING
MOORING
NOOSING
PHONING
PLOWING
POOLING
POOPING
PROBING
PROLONG
PROSING
PROVING
QUOTING
RIOTING
ROOFING
ROOKING
ROOMING
ROOTING
SCOPING
SCORING
SHOEING
SHOOING
SHORING
SHOVING
SHOWDOG
SHOWING
SLOPING
SLOWING
SMOKING
SNORING
SNOWING
SPOKING
STOKING
STONING
STORING
STOWING
TOOLING
TOOTING
WOOFING
WYOMING
ZOOMING

•••OG••

BOLOGNA
COLOGNE
CRYOGEN
ECLOGUE
HALOGEN
ILLOGIC
INVOGUE
LIMOGES
PIROGUE
STOOGES

•••O•G•

BARONGS
BELONGS
BOROUGH
CYBORGS
DUGONGS
ENGORGE
OBLONGS
SARONGS
SCROOGE
THRONGS
THROUGH

•••O••G

CYYOUNG
ECHOING
HALOING
HOBOING
HYPOING
KAYOING
MONOLOG
ONGOING
REDOING
SHOOING
SILOING
SOLOING
UNDOING
VETOING
YOYOING
ZEROING

••••OG•

ANALOGS
ANALOGY
APOLOGY
BIOLOGY
DIALOGS
ECOLOGY
EGGNOGS
EPILOGS
GEOLOGY
GUNDOGS
HOTDOGS
KELLOGG
LAPDOGS
OLDFOGY
PHOTOGS
PROLOGS
PYEDOGS
QUAHOGS
REDDOGS
SAWLOGS
SCROOGE
SEADOGS
SUNDOGS
TOPDOGS
TOYDOGS
TRILOGY
UNCLOGS
VANGOGH
ZOOLOGY

••••O•G

ARTSONG
DAYLONG
ERELONG
FURLONG
GOALONG
GOWRONG
KELLOGG
PROLONG
SEABORG

•••••OG

ANTILOG
BACKLOG
BIRDDOG
BULLDOG
BUSHHOG
CATALOG
CORNDOG
DECALOG
FIREDOG
HANGDOG
MONOLOG
MOONDOG
PEATBOG
ROADHOG
SANDHOG
SHOWDOG
SLEDDOG
TAGALOG
WARTHOG
YULELOG

OH•••••

OHIOANS

O•H••••

OKHOTSK
OPHELIA
OSHKOSH
OTHELLO

O••H•••

OFFHAND
OFFHOUR
OLDHAND
OMPHALI
ONSHORE
ONTHEGO
ONTHEQT
ORCHARD
ORCHIDS
ORPHANS
ORPHEAN
ORPHEUS
OUTHITS

O•••H••

OLDCHAP
ONESHOT

O••••H•

ONSIGHT
OOLITHS
OOMPAHS
ORNITHO

O•••••H

OBADIAH
OGREISH
OSHKOSH
OSTRICH

•OH••••

BOHEMIA
COHABIT
COHEIRS
COHERED
COHERES
COHORTS
COHOSTS
JOHANNA
JOHNDOE
JOHNGAY
JOHNJAY
JOHNNIE
JOHNSON
MOHAIRS
MOHAWKS
MOHICAN

•O•H•••

BOBHOPE
BOGHOLE
BOKHARA
BOOHOOS
BOTHERS
BOTHNIA
BOYHOOD
COCHERE
COCHISE
COCHLEA
COCHRAN
COWHAND
COWHERD
COWHIDE
FOGHORN
FOXHOLE
GOAHEAD
GOPHERS
GOSHAWK
GOTHICS
HOOHAHS
HOTHEAD
JOBHOPS
JOBHUNT
JOEHILL
JOSHING
KOSHERS
LOWHEEL
MOTHERS
NOBHILL
NOSHERS
NOSHING
NOSHOWS
NOTHING
NOTHOME
NOWHERE
POOHBAH
POSHEST
POTHERB
POTHERS
POTHOLE
POTHOOK
SOPHISM
SOPHIST
SOTHERE
SOTHERN
TOEHOLD
TOPHATS
TOSHIBA
TOWHEAD
TOWHEES
YOGHURT

•O••H••

BOKCHOY
BOLSHOI
BOTCHED
BOTCHES
COACHED
COACHES
CONCHES
COUCHED
COUCHES
COUGHED
COUGHUP
DOGCHEW
DOGCHOW
DOGSHOW
DOLPHIN
DONAHUE
DOUGHTY
FORDHAM
GODTHAB
GOTCHAS
HONCHOS
HOTSHOT
JOACHIM
LOACHES
LOATHED
LOATHES
MONTHLY
MOOCHED
MOOCHER
MOOCHES
MOORHEN
MORPHED
MOUTHED
NORTHER
NOTCHED
NOTCHES
POACHED
POACHER
POACHES
PONCHOS
POOCHES
PORCHES
PORTHOS
POSTHOC
POTSHOT
POUCHED
POUCHES
ROACHED
ROACHES
ROADHOG
ROUGHED
ROUGHEN
ROUGHER
ROUGHIT
ROUGHLY
ROUGHUP
SOMEHOW
SOOTHED
SOOTHER
SOOTHES
SORGHUM
SOUGHED
SOUTHEY
TOESHOE
TOOTHED
TORCHED
TORCHES
TOUCHED
TOUCHES
TOUCHON
TOUCHUP
TOUGHEN
TOUGHER
TOUGHIE
TOUGHLY
TOYSHOP
VOUCHED
VOUCHER
VOUCHES
WORSHIP

•O•••H•

BORSCHT
DOROTHY
EOLITHS
FOURTHS
GOUACHE
HOOHAHS
HOOKAHS
HOOTCHY
HOWDAHS
IOMOTHS
KOOTCHY
LOOFAHS
NOGUCHI
OOLITHS
OOMPAHS
PORSCHE
TONIGHT
VOTECHS

•O••••H

BONEASH
BOOKISH
BOORISH
BOROUGH
CODFISH
COLTISH
CORINTH
CORNISH
DOGFISH
DOLTISH
DOZENTH
FOGYISH
FOOLISH
FOPPISH
FORSYTH
GOATISH
GODUTCH
GOLIATH
GOULASH
HOGARTH
HOGWASH
LONGISH
LOWTECH
MONARCH
MONKISH
MOORISH
NOURISH
POOHBAH
ROGUISH
ROMANSH
SOPWITH
SOURISH
TOWPATH
WOLFISH

••OH•••

ALOHAOE
BOOHOOS
HOOHAHS
ISOHELS
POOHBAH

••O•H••

ANOTHER
APOTHEM
BROTHER
CLOCHES
CLOTHED
CLOTHES
CROCHET
FROTHED
KNOWHOW
MOOCHED
MOOCHER
MOOCHES
MOORHEN
POOCHES
PROPHET
SIOBHAN
SKOSHES
SLOSHED
SLOSHES
SMOTHER
SOOTHED
SOOTHER
SOOTHES
TOOTHED
TROCHEE
TROCHES
TROPHIC
TROTHED
USOSHOW

••O••H•

ADOLPHE
BLOTCHY
BRONCHI
BROUGHT
DROUGHT
GNOCCHI
GROUCHO
GROUCHY
GROWTHS
HOOHAHS
HOOKAHS
HOOTCHY
KOOTCHY
LOOFAHS
PLOUGHS
SLOUCHY
SLOUGHS
SMOOTHS
THOUGHT
TROUGHS
WHOSWHO
WROUGHT

••O•••H

ABOLISH
ANOUILH
BOOKISH
BOORISH
FOOLISH
MOORISH
NEOLITH
POOHBAH
STOMACH

•••OH••

ALCOHOL
GASOHOL
MEGOHMS
STJOHNS

•••O•H•

ALYOSHA
ATROPHY
AUROCHS
BRIOCHE
DOROTHY
IOMOTHS
KENOSHA
LAROCHE
LESOTHO
SMOOTHS
STROPHE
TIMOTHY

•••O••H

ALWORTH
BOROUGH
DEBORAH
DEBOUCH
MENORAH
RETOUCH
RUDOLPH
SPLOTCH
THROUGH
UNCOUTH

••••OH•

BIGJOHN
MATZOHS

••••O•H

ANTIOCH
BETROTH
MAMMOTH
MURDOCH
OSHKOSH
VANGOGH

•••••OH

PHARAOH
PLAYDOH

OI•••••

OILCAKE
OILCANS
OILIEST
OILLAMP
OILPANS
OILRIGS
OILSKIN
OILWELL
OINKING

O•I••••

OHIOANS
OJIBWAS
OJIBWAY
OKINAWA
OLIVIER
OLIVINE
OMICRON
OMINOUS
OMITTED
OPIATES
OPINERS
OPINING
OPINION
ORIENTE
ORIENTS
ORIFICE
ORIGAMI
ORIGINS
ORINOCO
ORIOLES
ORISONS
OWINGTO
OXIDANT
OXIDASE
OXIDIZE

O••I•••

OBLIGED
OBLIGES
OBLIQUE
OBOISTS
OBVIATE
OBVIOUS
OCCIPUT
OEDIPAL
OEDIPUS
OFFICER
OFFICES
OILIEST
OMNIBUS
ONEIDAS
ONSIGHT
OOLITES
OOLITHS
OPTICAL
OPTIMAL
OPTIMUM
OPTIONS
ORBISON
ORBITAL
ORBITED

ORBITER
ORDINAL
ORNITHO
ORPINES
ORVILLE
OSCINES
OSSICLE
OSSIFIC
OUTINGS
OVOIDAL

O•••I••

OBADIAH
OBELISK
OBELIZE
OBEYING
OBTAINS
OCARINA
OCULIST
OFFLINE
OFFSIDE
OFFSITE
OGREISH
OILRIGS
OINKING
OKAYING
OLDLINE
OLDNICK
OLDTIME
OLEMISS
OLIVIER
OLIVINE
ONADIET
ONETIME
ONGOING
ONTRIAL
OPACITY
OPALINE
OPENING
OPINING
OPINION
ORATING
ORATION
ORCHIDS
ORDAINS
ORIFICE
ORIGINS
OSTRICH
OUSTING
OUTBIDS
OUTFITS
OUTHITS
OUTLINE
OUTLIVE
OUTSIDE
OUTSIZE
OUTWITS
OVATION
OWLLIKE
OXIDIZE
OXONIAN

O••••I•

OBERLIN
OCEANIA
OCEANIC
OCEANID
OCTAVIA
OILSKIN
OLDMAID
OLYMPIA
OLYMPIC
ONASSIS
ONTARIO
OPENAIR
OPENPIT
OPHELIA
ORGANIC
OSMOSIS
OSMOTIC
OSSIFIC
OSTEOID
OUTLAID
OUTOFIT
OVERBIG
OVERDID
OVERLIE

O•••••I

OLDUVAI
OMPHALI
ORIGAMI

•OI••••

BOILERS
BOILING
BOITANO
COIFING
COILING
COILSUP
COINAGE
COINERS
COINING
DOILIES
DOINGIN
DOINGUP
FOIBLES
FOILING
FOISTED
GOINFOR
GOINGAT
GOINGBY
GOINGIN
GOINGON
GOINGUP
HOISTED
JOINDER
JOINERS
JOINERY
JOINING
JOINSIN
JOINSUP
JOINTED
JOINTLY
JOISTED
LOITERS
MOILERS
MOILING
MOISTEN
MOISTER
MOISTLY
NOISIER
NOISILY
NOISING
NOISOME
POINTED
POINTER
POINTTO
POISING
POISONS
POISSON
POITIER
ROILING
ROISTER
SOIGNEE
SOILING
SOIREES
TOILERS
TOILETS
TOILING
VOICING
VOIDING

•O•I•••

AORISTS
BODICES
BOLIDES
BOLIVAR
BOLIVIA
BONIEST
BONITOS
BOVINES
CODICES
CODICIL
COMICAL
COMINGS
COMIQUE
CONICAL
CONIFER
COPIERS
COPILOT
COPIOUS
CORINTH
COSIGNS
COSINES
COZIEST
DOMINGO
DOMINOS
DOPIEST
DORITOS
DOSIDOS
EOLITHS
FOLIAGE
FOLIATE
FORINTS
FOXIEST
GOLIATH
GOOIEST
GORIEST
GORILLA
GOTINTO
HOLIDAY
HOLIEST
HOMIEST
HOMINEM
HOMINID
HORIZON
HOSIERS
HOSIERY
IODIDES
IODIZED
IODIZES
IONIZED
IONIZER
IONIZES
KODIAKS
LOGICAL
LOGIEST
LORISES
LOTIONS
MOBILES
MODICUM
MODISTE
MOHICAN
MOLIERE
MONIKER
MONIQUE
MONITOR
MOTIONS
MOTIVES
NOMINAL
NOMINEE
NORIEGA
NOSIEST
NOTICED
NOTICES
NOTIONS
NOVICES
NOXIOUS
OOLITES
OOLITHS
PODIUMS
POKIEST
POLICED
POLICES
POLITER
POLITIC
PONIARD
POSITED
POTIONS
ROTIFER
SOCIALS
SOCIETY
SOLICIT
SOLIDER
SOLIDLY
SORITES
SOVIETS
TONIEST
TONIGHT
TOPIARY
TOPICAL
WOEISME
ZODIACS

•O••I••

BOATING
BOBBIES
BOBBING
BOBBINS
BOBVILA
BODKINS
BOGGING
BOILING
BOLTING
BOMBING
BONDING
BONFIRE
BONGING
BONNIER
BONNILY
BOOBIES
BOOGIED
BOOGIES
BOOKIES
BOOKING
BOOKISH
BOOMING
BOONIES
BOORISH
BOOTIES
BOOTING
BOPPING
BOSSIER
BOSSILY
BOSSING
BOWFINS
BOWLINE
BOWLING
BOWTIES
BOXKITE
COATING
COAXIAL
COAXING
COCHISE
COCKIER
COCKILY
COCKING
CODEINE
CODFISH
COEDITS
COEXIST
COHEIRS
COIFING
COILING
COINING
COLLIDE
COLLIER
COLLIES
COLLINS
COLTISH
COMBINE
COMBING
COMFIER
COMFITS
COMMITS
COMPILE
CONCISE
CONDIGN
CONFIDE
CONFINE
CONFIRM
CONKING
CONNICK
CONNIFF
CONNING
CONNIVE
CONSIGN
CONSIST
CONVICT
COOKIES
COOKING
COOLING
COOPING
COOTIES
COPPICE
COPPING
COPYING
COPYIST
CORDIAL
CORDING
CORDITE
CORKING
CORNICE
CORNIER
CORNILY
CORNING
CORNISH
CORRIDA
CORSICA
COSTING
COURIER
COUSINS
COWBIRD
COWGIRL
COWHIDE
COWLICK
COWLING
COWRIES
COZYING
DOBBINS
DOCKING
DODGING
DOFFING
DOGFISH
DOGGIES
DOGGING
DOILIES
DOLLIED
DOLLIES
DOLLING
DOLTISH
DOMAINS
DONKING
DONNING
DOOMING
DOOZIES
DORMICE
DOSSIER
DOTTIER
DOTTING
DOUSING
DOWDIER
DOWDILY
DOWNIER
DOWNING
DOWRIES
DOWSING
FOALING
FOAMIER
FOAMING
FOBBING
FOGGIER
FOGGING
FOGYISH
FOGYISM
FOILING
FOLDING
FOLLIES
FONTINA
FOOLING
FOOLISH
FOOTING
FOPPISH
FORBIDS
FORCING
FORDING
FOREIGN
FORGING
FORGIVE
FORKING
FORLIFE
FORMICA
FORMING
FORTIES
FORTIFY
FOSDICK
FOSSILS
FOULING
FOURIER
FOWLING
FOXFIRE
GOADING
GOALIES
GOATISH
GOBLINS
GODLIKE
GODWITS
GOLDING
GOLFING
GONGING
GOODIES
GOOFIER
GOOFING
GOOPIER
GOOSING
GORDIAN
GORGING
GOSLING
GOSSIPS
GOSSIPY
GOTHICS
GOUGING
HOAGIES
HOARIER
HOAXING
HOBBIES
HOBBITS
HOBOING
HOCKING
HOGGING
HOGTIED
HOGTIES
HOGWILD
HOLDING
HOLLIES
HOLMIUM
HONKING
HOOFING
HOOKING
HOOPING
HOOSIER
HOOTING
HOPKINS
HOPPING
HORNING
HORNIST
HORRIFY
HORSIER
HORSING
HOSKINS
HOSPICE
HOSTILE
HOSTING
HOTLINE
HOTLIPS
HOTTIPS
HOTWIRE
HOUDINI
HOUSING
HOWLING
JOBBING
JOEHILL
JOGGING
JOINING
JOLLIED
JOLLIER
JOLLIES
JOLLIET
JOLLILY
JOLLITY
JOLTING
JOSHING
JOTTING
JOYRIDE
KONTIKI
KOOKIER
LOADING
LOAFING
LOAMIER
LOAMING
LOANING
LOBBIED
LOBBIES
LOBBING
LOCKING
LOCKINS
LODGING
LOFTIER
LOFTILY
LOFTING
LOGGIAS
LOGGING
LOGGINS
LOLLIES
LOLLING
LONGING
LONGISH
LOOKING
LOOMING
LOONIER
LOONIES
LOOPIER
LOOPING
LOOSING
LOOTING
LOPPING
LORDING
LORRIES
LOTTING
LOUSIER
LOUSILY
LOUSING
LOVEINS
LOWLIER
LOWLIFE
LOWRISE
LOWTIDE
MOANING
MOBBING
MOCKING
MOHAIRS
MOILING
MOLDIER
MOLDING
MOLLIFY
MOLTING
MOMMIES
MONKISH
MOODIER
MOODILY
MOONING
MOORING
MOORISH
MOPPING
MORAINE
MORNING
MORTIFY
MORTISE
MOSAICS
MOSSIER
MOSSING
MOUSIER
MOUSING
NOBHILL
NODDING
NOETICS
NOGGINS
NOISIER
NOISILY
NOISING
NOOSING
NORDICS
NOSHING
NOTHING
NOURISH
PODGIER
PODRIDA
POETICS
POISING
POITIER
POLLING
POLOIST
PONGIDS
PONTIAC
PONTIFF
PONTINE
PONTIUS
PONYING
POOLING
POOPING
POPLINS
POPPIES
POPPING
POPPINS
PORCINE
PORGIES
PORTICO
PORTION
POSTING
POTPIES
POTTING
POURING
POUTIER
POUTING
ROADIES
ROAMING
ROARING
ROBBING
ROBBINS
ROCKIER
ROCKIES
ROCKING
ROGUISH
ROILING
ROLAIDS
ROLLICK
ROLLING
ROLLINS
ROMAINE
ROMPING
ROOFING
ROOKIES
ROOKING
ROOMIER
ROOMIES
ROOMING
ROOTING
ROSSINI
ROTTING
ROUGING
ROUSING
ROUTINE
ROUTING
ROWDIER
ROWDIES
ROWDILY
SOAKING
SOAPIER
SOAPING
SOARING
SOBBING
SOCKING
SODDING
SOFFITS
SOFTIES
SOGGIER
SOGGILY
SOILING
SOLDIER
SOLOING
SOLOIST
SOLVING
SOOTIER
SOPHISM
SOPHIST
SOPPING
SOPWITH
SORRIER
SORTIED
SORTIES
SORTING
SOUPIER
SOURING
SOURISH
TOADIED
TOADIES
TOCSINS
TODDIES
TOGGING
TOILING
TOLKIEN
TOLLING
TOMTITS
TONSILS
TONTINE
TOOLING
TOOTING
TOPKICK
TOPPING
TOPSIDE
TOROIDS
TORSION
TORYISM
TOSHIBA
TOSSING
TOTTING
TOURING
TOURISM
TOURIST
TOUTING
TOWNIES
VOICING
VOIDING
WOLFING
WOLFISH
WOODIER
WOODIES
WOOFING
WOOLIER
WOOLIES
WOOZIER
WOOZILY
WORDIER
WORDILY
WORDING
WORKING
WORMIER
WORRIED
WORRIER
WORRIES
WOZNIAK
YOWLING
YOYOING
ZOMBIES
ZONKING
ZOOMING
ZOYSIAS

•O•••I•

BOBTAIL
BOHEMIA
BOLIVIA
BOLOTIE
BONSOIR
BORODIN
BORZOIS
BOTHNIA
BOUDOIR
BOXEDIN
BOXESIN
COALBIN
COALOIL
COCKPIT
CODICIL
COHABIT
COLLOID
COMEDIC
COMESIN
CONBRIO
CONCEIT
CONDUIT
CONJOIN
CONREID
CONTAIN
COOLSIT
CORNOIL
CORSAIR
COSTAIN
COTERIE
COUNCIL
COWSLIP
DOESKIN
DOINGIN
DOLPHIN
DOORDIE
FOOTSIE
FORFEIT
FOULTIP
FOXTAIL
GOFORIT
GOINGIN
GONERIL
GOODWIN
HOBNAIL
HOLBEIN
HOMERIC
HOMINID
HOOFSIT
HOPTOIT
HORATIO
HOWBEIT
JOACHIM
JOAQUIN
JOHNNIE
JOINSIN
JONQUIL
KOOLAID
KOSYGIN
LOOKSIN
LORDJIM
LOSESIT
LOWPAID
MOONLIT
MORANIS
MORAVIA
MOUNTIE
MOVEDIN
MOVESIN
NOKOMIS
NOMADIC
NONSKID
NONSLIP
NOSTRIL
NOTABIT
POLARIS
POLEMIC
POLITIC
POMPEIA
POMPEII
PORKPIE
POURSIN
ROBOTIC
ROCKYII
ROCKYIV
ROMANIA
ROPEDIN
ROPESIN
ROSALIE
ROSEOIL
ROUGHIT
SOCKSIN
SOLARIA
SOLICIT
SOMALIA
SOMALIS
SOMATIC
TOENAIL
TOOTSIE
TOPSAIL
TOPSOIL
TOTEMIC
TOUGHIE
VOCALIC
VOLTAIC
VOTESIN
WORKSIN
WORSHIP
YOPLAIT
ZOOMSIN

•O••••I

BOLSHOI
BONJOVI
COLLODI
COLOSSI
CORELLI
GOURAMI
HOUDINI
KONTIKI
LORELEI
MOLOKAI
NOGUCHI
POMPEII
ROCKYII
ROSSINI
TOLSTOI
TOPKAPI
TORTONI

••OI•••

ANOINTS
AVOIDED
BROILED
BROILER
CHOICER
CHOICES
EGOISTS
ETOILES
GOOIEST
MAOISTS
OBOISTS
OVOIDAL
REOILED
SPOILED
SPOILER
STOICAL
TAOISTS
TROIKAS
TROILUS
UNOILED

••O•I••

ABOLISH
ACONITE
ADORING
AEOLIAN
AGONIST
AGONIZE
ANODIZE
ANOUILH
ASOCIAL
ATOMIES
ATOMIZE
ATONING
AVOWING
BIONICS
BLOWIER
BLOWING
BMOVIES
BOOBIES
BOOGIED
BOOGIES
BOOKIES
BOOKING
BOOKISH
BOOMING
BOONIES
BOORISH
BOOTIES
BOOTING
BROMIDE
BROMINE
BUOYING
CHORINE
CHORIZO
CLONING
CLOSING
CLOYING
COOKIES
COOKING
COOLING
COOPING
COOTIES
CRONIES
CROSIER
CROWING
DIOXIDE
DOOMING
DOOZIES
DRONING
DROPINS
EBONIES
EBONITE
EGOTISM
EGOTIST
ELOPING
EMOTING
EMOTION
EMOTIVE
EPOXIES
ERODING
EROSION
EROSIVE
EROTICA
ETONIAN
EVOKING
EXOTICA
EXOTICS
FLORIDA
FLORINS
FLORIST
FLOWING
FOOLING
FOOLISH
FOOTING
FROLICS
GLORIAS
GLORIED

GLORIES
GLORIFY
GLOWING
GOODIES
GOOFIER
GOOFING
GOOPIER
GOOSING
GROLIER
GROPING
GROPIUS
GROWING
HOOFING
HOOKING
HOOPING
HOOSIER
HOOTING
IDOLIZE
IRONIES
IRONING
IVORIES
IWOJIMA
KNOWING
KOOKIER
LAOTIAN
LEONINE
LIONIZE
LOOKING
LOOMING
LOONIER
LOONIES
LOOPIER
LOOPING
LOOSING
LOOTING
MEOWING
MOODIER
MOODILY
MOONING
MOORING
MOORISH
NEOLITH
NIOBIUM
NOOSING
OXONIAN
PEONIES
PHOBIAS
PHOBICS
PHONICS
PHONIER
PHONIES
PHONILY
PHONING
PLOSION
PLOSIVE
PLOWING
POOLING
POOPING
PROBING
PROBITY
PRODIGY
PROFILE
PROFITS
PROMISE
PROSIER
PROSILY
PROSING
PROTIST
PROVIDE
PROVING
PROVISO
PROXIES
PROXIMO
QUOTING
RHODIUM
RIORITA
RIOTING
ROOFING
ROOKIES
ROOKING
ROOMIER
ROOMIES
ROOMING
ROOTING
SCOPING
SCORING
SHOEING
SHOOING
SHOOINS
SHORING
SHOVING
SHOWIER
SHOWILY
SHOWING
SLOPING
SLOWING
SMOKIER
SMOKIES
SMOKING
SNORING
SNOWIER
SNOWING
SOOTIER
SPOKING
STOGIES
STOKING
STONIER
STONILY
STONING
STORIED
STORIES
STORING
STOWING
THORIUM
TOOLING
TOOTING
TROPICS
TROPISM
TWOBITS
TWOTIME
UTOPIAN
UTOPIAS
UXORIAL
VIOLINS
VIOLIST
WOODIER
WOODIES
WOOFING
WOOLIER
WOOLIES
WOOZIER
WOOZILY
WYOMING
ZOOMING

••O••I•

ADONAIS
AGOUTIS
AMOEBIC
ANOSMIA
ANOSMIC
BLONDIE
BLOWSIN
BLOWSIT
BROKEIN
BROWNIE
CLOCKIN
CLOSEIN
COOLSIT
CROATIA
DOORDIE
DROPSIN
EGOTRIP
FOOTSIE
GEORGIA
GIORGIO
GLOTTIS
GNOSTIC
GOODWIN
GROUPIE
HOOFSIT
INORBIT
KOOLAID
KTOSLIN
LOOKSIN
MOONLIT
PHOENIX
PROSAIC
PROTEIN
SCORPIO
SCOTTIE
SHOWBIZ
SHOWNIN
SHOWSIN
SLOEGIN
SNOWSIN
SPOTLIT
STOODIN
STOOLIE
STOPSIN
SWOOSIE
SWOREIN
TIOMKIN
TOOTSIE
TROPHIC
WROTEIN
ZOOMSIN

••O•••I

BRONCHI
GNOCCHI

•••OI••

ADJOINS
ANTOINE
APPOINT
ARMOIRE
ECHOING
ENJOINS
HALOING
HELOISE
HEROICS
HEROINE
HEROISM
HOBOING
HYPOING
INPOINT
INVOICE
JUDOIST
KAYOING
MEMOIRE
MEMOIRS
ONGOING
POLOIST
REBOILS
RECOILS
REDOING
REJOICE
REJOINS
REVOICE
SHOOING
SHOOINS
SILOING
SOLOING
SOLOIST
TOROIDS
UNCOILS
UNDOING
VETOING
YOYOING
ZEROING

•••O•I•

AEROBIC
AMMONIA
ANTONIA
ANTONIN
ANTONIO
ASTORIA
BEDOUIN
BEGONIA
BOLOTIE
BORODIN
BUCOLIC
CALORIC
CALORIE
CANONIC
CAROTID
CHAOTIC
CHRONIC
CIBORIA
DEMONIC
DEPOSIT
EMPORIA
ENCOMIA
ESTONIA
ESTORIL
GOFORIT
IDIOTIC
ILLOGIC
JACOBIN
LACONIC
LANOLIN
MASONIC
MEIOSIS
MEIOTIC
MELODIC
MITOSIS
MITOTIC
NICOSIA
NOKOMIS
OSMOSIS
OSMOTIC
OUTOFIT
ROBOTIC
SEGOVIA
STLOUIS
STOODIN
STOOLIE
SWOOSIE
SYNODIC
THROWIN
ZENOBIA

•••O••I

COLOSSI
KAROLYI
MENOTTI
MOLOKAI
NIKOLAI

••••OI•

AIRFOIL
ANDROID
ANEROID
BATHOIL
BONSOIR
BORZOIS
BOUDOIR
CHAMOIS
COALOIL
COLLOID
CONJOIN
CORNOIL
CRINOID
DELTOID
DESPOIL
DETROIT
DIPLOID
DISJOIN
EMBROIL
EXPLOIT
FUELOIL
HOPTOIT
INTROIT
LAMPOIL
MASTOID
MAUROIS
OSTEOID
PALMOIL
PARBOIL
PURLOIN
ROSEOIL
SEETOIT
SEQUOIA
SIRLOIN
STCROIX
STEROID
SUBJOIN
SUBSOIL
TABLOID
TINFOIL
TOPSOIL
TRAVOIS
TREFOIL
TUNGOIL
TURMOIL

••••O•I

ALVEOLI
APRIORI
BONJOVI
CANNOLI
COLLODI
MARCONI
NAIROBI
PADRONI
RAVIOLI
SPUMONI
TORTONI
TRIPOLI

•••••OI

BOLSHOI
TOLSTOI

OJ•••••

OJIBWAS
OJIBWAY

O•J••••

OBJECTS

O••J•••

ODDJOBS
OUTJUMP

O•••J••

OVERJOY

•OJ••••

SOJOURN

•O•J•••

BONJOUR
BONJOVI
CONJOBS
CONJOIN
CONJURE
DONJONS
DONJOSE
DONJUAN
LOGJAMS

•O••J••

GOODJOB
GOODJOE
JOHNJAY
LORDJIM
NOSEJOB

••OJ•••

IWOJIMA
PROJECT
TROJANS

••O•J••

GOODJOB
GOODJOE
PROPJET
SNOWJOB

•••O••J

LLCOOLJ

••••O•J

LLCOOLJ

OK•••••

OKAYING
OKEEFFE
OKHOTSK
OKINAWA

O•K••••

OAKFERN
OAKLAND
OAKLAWN
OAKLEAF
OAKMOSS
OAKTREE

O••K•••

OINKING
OSHKOSH

O•••K••

OILSKIN

O••••K•

OILCAKE
OROURKE
OUTTAKE
OWLLIKE

O•••••K

OARLOCK
OBELISK
OFFPEAK
OKHOTSK
OLDNICK
OUTBACK
OUTLOOK
OUTRANK
OUTTALK
OUTWORK

•OK••••

BOKCHOY
BOKHARA
GOKARTS
NOKOMIS
POKEDAT
POKEFUN
POKESAT
POKIEST
TOKENED
WOKENUP
YOKOONO

•O•K•••

BODKINS
BONKERS
BOOKEND
BOOKIES
BOOKING
BOOKISH
BOOKLET
BOSKETS
BOWKNOT
BOXKITE
COCKADE
COCKIER
COCKILY
COCKING
COCKLES
COCKNEY
COCKPIT
CONKERS
CONKING
CONKOUT
COOKERS
COOKERY
COOKIES
COOKING
COOKOFF
COOKOUT
COOKSUP
CORKAGE
CORKERS
CORKING
DOCKAGE
DOCKERS
DOCKETS
DOCKING
DONKEYS
DONKING
FOLKART
FORKERS
FORKFUL
FORKING
HOCKING
HONKERS
HONKING
HOOKAHS
HOOKING
HOOKSUP
HOOKUPS
HOPKINS
HOSKINS
JOCKEYS
KOOKIER
LOCKBOX
LOCKERS
LOCKETS
LOCKING
LOCKINS
LOCKNUT
LOCKOUT
LOCKSUP
LOCKUPS
LOOKERS
LOOKFOR
LOOKING
LOOKOUT
LOOKSAT
LOOKSEE
LOOKSIN
LOOKSON
LOOKSTO
LOOKSUP
LOOKUPS
MOCKERS
MOCKERY
MOCKING
MOCKUPS
MONKEES
MONKEYS
MONKISH
POCKETS
POLKAED
PORKERS
PORKPIE
ROCKERS
ROCKETS
ROCKIER
ROCKIES
ROCKING
ROCKYII
ROCKYIV
ROOKERY
ROOKIES
ROOKING
SOAKERS
SOAKING
SOAKSUP
SOCKETS
SOCKEYE
SOCKING
SOCKSIN
TOLKIEN
TOOKOFF
TOOKOUT
TOOKTEN
TOPKAPI
TOPKICK
TOPKNOT
WORKDAY
WORKERS
WORKFOR
WORKING
WORKMAN
WORKMEN
WORKOFF
WORKOUT
WORKSIN
WORKSON
WORKSUP
WORKUPS
YONKERS
YOUKNOW
ZONKERS
ZONKING
ZONKOUT

•O••K••

CONAKRY
DOESKIN
HOBOKEN
MOLOKAI
MONIKER
NONSKID

•O•••K•

CONVOKE
COWPOKE
FORSAKE
GOBROKE
GODLIKE
HOECAKE
HOLYOKE
HOTCAKE
KODIAKS
KOLACKY
KONTIKI
KOPECKS
MOHAWKS
ROANOKE

•O••••K

BODEREK
BOMBECK
CONNICK
CONRACK
COSSACK
COWLICK
FOGBANK
FORSOOK
FOSDICK
GOSHAWK
GOTBACK
HOGBACK
HOLMOAK
HOLYARK
JOBBANK
LOGBOOK
LOWNECK
MOLLUSK
NORFOLK
POLLOCK
POTHOOK
POTLUCK
ROEBUCK
ROLLICK
TOPKICK
WOZNIAK
WOZZECK

••OK•••

BOOKEND
BOOKIES
BOOKING
BOOKISH
BOOKLET
BROKEIN
BROKERS
BROKEUP
CHOKERS
CHOKEUP
COOKERS
COOKERY
COOKIES
COOKING
COOKOFF
COOKOUT
COOKSUP
EVOKERS
EVOKING
HOOKAHS
HOOKING
HOOKSUP
HOOKUPS
KOOKIER
LOOKERS
LOOKFOR
LOOKING
LOOKOUT
LOOKSAT
LOOKSEE
LOOKSIN
LOOKSON
LOOKSTO
LOOKSUP
LOOKUPS
QUOKKAS
ROOKERY
ROOKIES
ROOKING
SMOKERS
SMOKIER
SMOKIES
SMOKING
SPOKANE
SPOKEOF
SPOKEUP
SPOKING
STOKELY
STOKERS
STOKING
TOOKOFF
TOOKOUT
TOOKTEN

••O•K••

BLOCKED
BLOCKER
BROOKED
CLOAKED
CLOCKED
CLOCKER
CLOCKIN
CROAKED
CROOKED
FLOCKED
FLOCKTO
FROCKED
KNOCKED
KNOCKER
QUOKKAS
SHOCKED
SHOCKER
SHOOKUP
SNOOKER
SNORKEL
SPOOKED
STOCKED
STOCKUP
STOOKEY
TIOMKIN
TROIKAS

••O••K•

ANORAKS
CHOMSKY
GROMYKO
OROURKE
PROVOKE
SLOVAKS
TROTSKY
VRONSKY

•••OK••

BETOKEN
BROOKED
CROOKED
HOBOKEN
INJOKES
INVOKED
INVOKER
INVOKES
MOLOKAI
NABOKOV
REVOKED
REVOKES
SHOOKUP
SNOOKER
SPOOKED
STOOKEY
STROKED
STROKES
UNYOKED
UNYOKES

•••O•K•

BAZOOKA
BUROAKS
PALOOKA
PINOAKS
RECORKS
REDOAKS
REHOOKS
RELOCKS
REWORKS
TANOAKS
UNCORKS
UNHOOKS
UNLOCKS

•••O••K

OKHOTSK
ZATOPEK

••••OK•

BAZOOKA
BESPOKE
CONVOKE
COWPOKE
GOBROKE
HOLYOKE
KARAOKE
PALOOKA
PROVOKE
REHOOKS
ROANOKE
UNHOOKS

••••O•K

AIRLOCK
AIRSOCK
ARMLOCK
ARTWORK
BANNOCK
BEDROCK
BULLOCK
BURDOCK
CASSOCK
CHINOOK
DAYBOOK
DEFROCK
DRSPOCK
DRYDOCK
EARLOCK
FETLOCK
FORSOOK
FRYCOOK
GUNLOCK
HADDOCK
HAMHOCK
HAMMOCK
HANCOCK
HASSOCK
HAYFORK
HEMLOCK
HILLOCK
HOLMOAK
HUMMOCK
INSTOCK
KINFOLK
LEACOCK
LEGWORK
LIVEOAK
LOGBOOK
LUBBOCK
MATLOCK
MATTOCK
MENFOLK
MISTOOK
MRSPOCK
NETWORK
NEWLOOK
NEWYORK
NORFOLK
OARLOCK
OUTLOOK
OUTWORK
PADDOCK
PADLOCK
PARTOOK
PEACOCK
PETCOCK
PETROCK
POLLOCK
POTHOOK
PRECOOK
PRESOAK
REDBOOK
RESTOCK
SCHLOCK
SHYLOCK
SKYHOOK
SUFFOLK
TINWORK
TUSSOCK
UNCLOAK
UNFROCK
WARLOCK
WAXWORK
WEDLOCK

•••••OK

BANGKOK
CHINOOK
DAYBOOK
FORSOOK
FRYCOOK
GEMSBOK
LOGBOOK
MISTOOK
NEWLOOK
OUTLOOK
PARTOOK
POTHOOK
PRECOOK
REDBOOK
RUNAMOK
SKYHOOK

OL•••••

OLDCHAP
OLDDAYS
OLDFOGY
OLDGOLD
OLDHAND
OLDLINE
OLDMAID
OLDMOON
OLDNESS
OLDNEWS
OLDNICK
OLDPROS
OLDSTER
OLDTIME
OLDUVAI
OLDWEST
OLEATES
OLEMISS
OLESTRA
OLIVIER
OLIVINE
OLOROSO
OLYMPIA
OLYMPIC
OLYMPUS

O•L••••

OBLASTS
OBLATES
OBLIGED
OBLIGES
OBLIQUE
OBLONGS
OBLOQUY
OGLALAS
OILCAKE
OILCANS
OILIEST
OILLAMP
OILPANS
OILRIGS
OILSKIN
OILWELL
ONLEAVE
ONLYYOU
OOLITES
OOLITHS
ORLANDO
ORLEANS
OWLLIKE

O••L•••

OAKLAND
OAKLAWN
OAKLEAF
OARLESS
OARLOCK
OBELISK
OBELIZE
OCCLUDE
OCELOTS
OCULIST
ODDLOTS
OFFLINE
OFFLOAD
OILLAMP
OLDLINE
OMELETS

OPALINE
OPULENT
OSTLERS
OUTLAID
OUTLAND
OUTLAST
OUTLAWS
OUTLAYS
OUTLETS
OUTLINE
OUTLIVE
OUTLOOK
OUTLOUD
OWLLIKE
OXBLOOD

O•••L••

OBERLIN
OCCULTS
OGLALAS
OPHELIA
ORACLES
ORIOLES
ORMOLUS
ORTOLAN
ORVILLE
OTHELLO
OUTFLOW
OUTPLAY
OVERLAP
OVERLAY
OVERLIE

O••••L•

OCTUPLE
ODDBALL
OILWELL
OLDGOLD
OMPHALI
ONAROLL
ONESELF
ORDEALS
ORDERLY
ORVILLE
OSCEOLA
OSSICLE
OTHELLO
OURSELF
OUTSELL
OUTSOLD
OUTTALK
OVERALL
OVERFLY
OVERTLY

O•••••L

OATMEAL
ODDBALL
OEDIPAL
OILWELL
ONAROLL
ONTRIAL
OPTICAL
OPTIMAL
ORBITAL
ORDINAL
OUTSELL
OVERALL
OVOIDAL

•OL••••

BOLDEST
BOLEROS
BOLIDES
BOLIVAR
BOLIVIA
BOLOGNA
BOLOTIE
BOLSHOI
BOLSTER
BOLTING
BOLUSES
COLBERT
COLDCUT
COLDEST
COLDWAR
COLEMAN
COLETTE
COLGATE
COLLAGE
COLLARD
COLLARS
COLLATE
COLLECT
COLLEEN
COLLEGE
COLLETS
COLLIDE
COLLIER
COLLIES
COLLINS
COLLODI
COLLOID
COLLOPS
COLLUDE
COLLYER
COLOBUS
COLOGNE
COLONEL
COLONES
COLONNA
COLORED
COLOSSI
COLOURS
COLTISH
COLUMBO
COLUMNS
DOLEFUL
DOLEOUT
DOLLARS
DOLLIED
DOLLIES
DOLLING
DOLLOPS
DOLLSUP
DOLMANS
DOLMENS
DOLORES
DOLPHIN
DOLTISH
EOLITHS
FOLDERS
FOLDING
FOLDOUT
FOLDSUP
FOLDUPS
FOLGERS
FOLIAGE
FOLIATE
FOLKART
FOLLETT
FOLLIES
FOLLOWS
GOLDBUG
GOLDING
GOLDWYN
GOLFERS
GOLFING
GOLFPRO
GOLFTEE
GOLIATH
HOLBEIN
HOLDERS
HOLDING
HOLDOFF
HOLDOUT
HOLDSON
HOLDSTO
HOLDSUP
HOLDUPS
HOLEDUP
HOLEOUT
HOLESUP
HOLIDAY
HOLIEST
HOLLAND
HOLLERS
HOLLIES
HOLLOWS
HOLMIUM
HOLMOAK
HOLSTER
HOLYARK
HOLYCOW
HOLYOKE
HOLYSEE
HOLYWAR
JOLLIED
JOLLIER
JOLLIES
JOLLIET
JOLLILY
JOLLITY
JOLTING
KOLACKY
LOLLIES
LOLLING
MOLDERS
MOLDIER
MOLDING
MOLESTS
MOLIERE
MOLLIFY
MOLLUSK
MOLOKAI
MOLOTOV
MOLTERS
MOLTING
OOLITES
OOLITHS
POLARIS
POLDERS
POLEAXE
POLECAT
POLEMIC
POLENTA
POLICED
POLICES
POLITER
POLITIC
POLKAED
POLLENS
POLLERS
POLLING
POLLOCK
POLLTAX
POLLUTE
POLOIST
POLYGON
POLYMER
ROLAIDS
ROLLBAR
ROLLERS
ROLLICK
ROLLING
ROLLINS
ROLLOUT
ROLLSUP
ROLLTOP
ROLODEX
ROLVAAG
SOLACES
SOLARIA
SOLDERS
SOLDIER
SOLDOFF
SOLDOUT
SOLEDAD
SOLFEGE
SOLICIT
SOLIDER
SOLIDLY
SOLOING
SOLOIST
SOLOMON
SOLUBLE
SOLUTES
SOLVENT
SOLVERS
SOLVING
TOLDOFF
TOLKIEN
TOLLING
TOLLWAY
TOLSTOI
TOLSTOY
TOLTECS
TOLUENE
VOLCANO
VOLLEYS
VOLPONE
VOLTAGE
VOLTAIC
VOLUBLE
VOLUBLY
VOLUMES
WOLFGAL
WOLFING
WOLFISH
WOLFMAN
WOLFMEN
WOLFRAM

•O•L•••

BOILERS
BOILING
BOOLEAN
BOULDER
BOWLERS
BOWLFUL
BOWLINE
BOWLING
COALBIN
COALCAR
COALERS
COALGAS
COALOIL
COALTAR
COILING
COILSUP
COLLAGE
COLLARD
COLLARS
COLLATE
COLLECT
COLLEEN
COLLEGE
COLLETS
COLLIDE
COLLIER
COLLIES
COLLINS
COLLODI
COLLOID
COLLOPS
COLLUDE
COLLYER
COOLANT
COOLERS
COOLEST
COOLING
COOLSIT
COPLAND
COULDNT
COULEES
COULOMB
COULTER
COWLICK
COWLING
DOGLEGS
DOILIES
DOLLARS
DOLLIED
DOLLIES
DOLLING
DOLLOPS
DOLLSUP
FOALING
FOILING
FOLLETT
FOLLIES
FOLLOWS
FOOLERY
FOOLING
FOOLISH
FORLIFE
FORLORN
FOULARD
FOULEST
FOULING
FOULOUT
FOULSUP
FOULTIP
FOULUPS
FOWLERS
FOWLING
GOALIES
GOALONG
GOBLETS
GOBLINS
GODLIKE
GOSLING
GOTLAND
GOULASH
HOLLAND
HOLLERS
HOLLIES
HOLLOWS
HOTLINE
HOTLIPS
HOWLERS
HOWLING
JOBLOTS
JOLLIED
JOLLIER
JOLLIES
JOLLIET
JOLLILY
JOLLITY
JOYLESS
KOBLENZ
KOOLAID
KOWLOON
LOLLIES
LOLLING
LOWLAND
LOWLIER
LOWLIFE
MOILERS
MOILING
MOLLIFY
MOLLUSK
MOSLEMS
MOULAGE
MOULDED
MOULDER
MOULTED
NOBLEST
POLLENS
POLLERS
POLLING
POLLOCK
POLLTAX
POLLUTE
POOLING
POPLARS
POPLINS
POTLUCK
POULENC
POULTRY
ROBLOWE
ROILING
ROLLBAR
ROLLERS
ROLLICK
ROLLING
ROLLINS
ROLLOUT
ROLLSUP
ROLLTOP
ROULADE
SOILING
SOULFUL
TOELESS
TOELOOP
TOILERS
TOILETS
TOILING
TOLLING
TOLLWAY
TOOLBOX
TOOLING
TOOLSUP
TOYLAND
VOLLEYS
WOOLENS
WOOLIER
WOOLIES
WOOLLEN
WOOLSEY
WORLDLY
WOULDBE
WOULDNT
YOPLAIT
YOWLERS
YOWLING
ZOELLER
ZOOLOGY

•O••L••

BOBBLED
BOBBLES
BOBSLED
BOGGLED
BOGGLER
BOGGLES
BOODLES
BOOKLET
BOOSLER
BOOTLEG
BOTTLED
BOTTLER
BOTTLES
BOWDLER
COBBLED
COBBLER
COBBLES
COCHLEA
COCKLES
CODDLED
CODDLER
CODDLES
COMPLEX
COPILOT
CORELLI
COROLLA
COUPLED
COUPLES
COUPLET
COWSLIP
DOGSLED
DOODLED
DOODLER
DOODLES
DOPPLER
DOTTLES
DOUBLED
DOUBLES
DOUBLET
DOUBLEU
DOUGLAS
FOCSLES
FOIBLES
FONDLED
FONDLES
FOOZLED
FOOZLES
FORELEG
GOBBLED
GOBBLER
GOBBLES
GOGGLED
GOGGLES
GORILLA
HOBBLED
HOBBLES
HOODLUM
HOOPLAS
HOSTLER
HOWELLS
JOCULAR
JOEBLOW
JOGGLED
JOGGLES
JOSTLED
JOSTLER
JOSTLES
KOBOLDS
LOCALES
LOCALLY
LORELEI
LOUELLA
LOWBLOW
LOYALLY
LOYALTY
MOBILES
MODELAS
MODELED
MODELER
MODELTS
MODULAR
MODULES
MONOLOG
MOONLIT
MORALES
MORALLY
MORELLO
MOSELLE
MOTTLED
MOTTLES
MOUFLON
NODULAR
NODULES
NOGALES
NONPLUS
NONSLIP
NOODLES
NOVELLA
NOVELLE
NOVELTY
NOZZLES
POMELOS
POODLES
POPPLED
POPPLES
POPULAR
RODOLFO
ROMULAN
ROMULUS
ROOTLET
ROSALIE
ROSELLE
ROYALLY
ROYALTY
ROZELLE
SOMALIA
SOMALIS
TODDLED
TODDLER
TODDLES
TOFFLER
TOGGLED
TOGGLES
TONALLY
TONELOC
TOOTLED
TOOTLES
TOPPLED
TOPPLES
TOTALED
TOTALLY
TOUSLED
TOUSLES
TOWELED
VOCALIC
VOCALLY
WOBBLED
WOBBLES
WOODLOT
WOOLLEN
YODELED
YODELER
ZOELLER
ZONALLY

•O•••L•

BOBDOLE
BOBVILA
BOGHOLE
BONNILY
BOSSILY
BOSWELL
BOXFULS
COCKILY
COEVALS
COMPELS
COMPILE
CONDOLE
CONSOLE
CONSULS
CONSULT
COPPOLA
CORBELS
CORDELL
CORELLI
CORNELL
CORNILY
COROLLA
CORRALS
CORYELL
COURTLY
COWBELL
DORSALS
DOSSALS
DOWDILY
FORMALS
FORMULA
FORSALE
FOSSILS
FOXHOLE
GONDOLA
GOODALL
GOOGOLS
GORILLA
GOSPELS
GOTWELL
HOGWILD
HOSTELS
HOSTILE
HOWELLS
JOEHILL
JOINTLY
JOLLILY
LOCALLY
LOFTILY
LOOSELY
LOUELLA
LOUSILY
LOVABLE
LOVERLY
LOWBALL
LOYALLY
MOISTLY
MONDALE
MONGOLS
MONOCLE
MONTHLY
MOODILY
MORALLY
MORELLO
MORSELS
MORTALS
MOSELLE
MOVABLE
NOBHILL
NOFAULT
NOISILY
NONSELF
NORFOLK
NORMALS
NOTABLE
NOTABLY
NOTWELL
NOVELLA
NOVELLE
POMMELS
PORTALS
PORTOLA
POTABLE
POTFULS
POTHOLE
RONDELS
ROSELLE
ROSWELL
ROUGHLY
ROUNDLY
ROWDILY
ROYALLY
ROZELLE
SOBERLY
SOCIALS
SOGGILY
SOLIDLY
SOLUBLE
SORRELS
SOUFFLE
SOUNDLY
TOEHOLD
TONALLY
TONSILS
TOOTALL
TOSCALE
TOTALLY
TOUGHLY
VOCALLY
VOLUBLE
VOLUBLY
WOMANLY
WOOZILY
WORDILY
WORLDLY
ZONALLY

•O••••L

BOBTAIL
BOSWELL
BOWLFUL
COALOIL
COASTAL
COAXIAL
CODICIL
COEQUAL
COLONEL
COMICAL
CONCEAL
CONGEAL
CONICAL
CONTROL
CORDELL
CORDIAL
CORNEAL
CORNELL
CORNOIL
CORYELL
COUNCIL
COUNSEL
COWBELL
COWGIRL
COZUMEL
DOLEFUL
DONEGAL
FORKFUL
FORREAL
FOXTAIL
GONERIL
GOODALL
GOTWELL
HOBNAIL
HOOTOWL
HOPEFUL
JOEHILL
JONQUIL
JOURNAL
LOGICAL
LOWBALL
LOWHEEL
MONGREL
NOBHILL
NOMINAL
NOSTRIL
NOTWELL
ROOMFUL
RORQUAL
ROSEOIL
ROSWELL
SORORAL
SOULFUL
TOENAIL
TOMFOOL
TOOTALL
TOPICAL
TOPSAIL
TOPSOIL
WOLFGAL

••OL•••

ABOLISH
ACOLYTE
ADOLPHE
AEOLIAN
APOLOGY
AXOLOTL
BIOLOGY
BOOLEAN
CHOLLAS
COOLANT
COOLERS
COOLEST
COOLING
COOLSIT
DROLLER
ECOLOGY
EVOLVED
EVOLVES
FOOLERY
FOOLING
FOOLISH
FROLICS
GEOLOGY
GROLIER
IDOLIZE
ISOLATE
KOOLAID
NEOLITH
PIOLETS
POOLING
PROLOGS
PROLONG
PTOLEMY
RIOLOBO
SCOLDED
SCOLDER
SMOLDER
STOLLEN
STOLLER
STOLONS
SWOLLEN
TOOLBOX
TOOLING
TOOLSUP
TROLLED
TROLLEY
VIOLATE
VIOLENT
VIOLETS
VIOLINS
VIOLIST
WOOLENS
WOOLIER
WOOLIES
WOOLLEN
WOOLSEY
ZOOLOGY

••O•L••

AVONLEA
BOODLES
BOOKLET
BOOSLER
BOOTLEG
BROILED
BROILER
CHOLLAS
DOODLED
DOODLER
DOODLES
DROLLER
DROOLED
DROOLER
DROPLET
ETOILES
FOOZLED
FOOZLES
GROWLED
GROWLER
HOODLUM
HOOPLAS
KTOSLIN
MOONLIT
NOODLES
PEOPLED
PEOPLES
POODLES
PROBLEM
PROWLED
PROWLER
REOILED
ROOTLET
SCOWLED
SCOWLER
SPOILED
SPOILER
SPOOLED
SPOTLIT
STOLLEN
STOLLER
STOOLIE
SWOLLEN
TOOTLED
TOOTLES
TROILUS
TROLLED
TROLLEY
UNOILED
WHORLED
WOODLOT
WOOLLEN

••O••L•

ALOOFLY
ANOMALY
ANOUILH
APOSTLE
AVOWALS
BEOWULF
BLOWFLY
BROADLY
CHORALE
CHORALS
CHORTLE
CLOSELY
CROSSLY
GHOSTLY
GLOBULE
GOODALL
GOOGOLS
GROSSLY
GROVELS
INOCULA
ISOHELS
LEOPOLD
LOOSELY
MOODILY
PHONILY
PIOUSLY
PROFILE
PROPELS
PROSILY
PROUDLY
SHOOFLY
SHORTLY
SHOVELS
SHOWILY
STOKELY
STONILY
STOUTLY
TOOTALL
TROUBLE
TROWELS
TWOFOLD
WOOZILY
WRONGLY

••O•••L

ABOREAL
AROUSAL
ASOCIAL
AXOLOTL
FRONTAL
GLOTTAL
GOODALL
HOOTOWL
OVOIDAL
ROOMFUL
SNORKEL
SPOUSAL
STOICAL
TOOTALL
UXORIAL

•••OL••

ABSOLUT
ABSOLVE
ANGOLAN
AREOLAE
AREOLAR
AREOLAS
ASTOLAT
BEHOLDS
BICOLOR
BIPOLAR

BUCOLIC
CAJOLED
CAJOLER
CAJOLES
CAROLED
CAROLER
CAROLES
CAROLUS
CAROLYN
COROLLA
CREOLES
CUPOLAS
DEVOLVE
DIPOLAR
DIPOLES
DROOLED
DROOLER
ENFOLDS
ENROLLS
GIGOLOS
INSOLES
INVOLVE
KAROLYI
KOBOLDS
LAJOLLA
LANOLIN
MINOLTA
MONOLOG
NICOLAS
NIKOLAI
ORIOLES
ORMOLUS
ORTOLAN
PAROLED
PAROLEE
PAROLES
PAYOLAS
REBOLTS
RECOLOR
REMOLDS
REPOLLS
RESOLED
RESOLES
RESOLVE
REVOLTS
REVOLVE
RODOLFO
RUDOLPH
SCHOLAR
SCROLLS
SPOOLED
STOOLIE
STROLLS
UNBOLTS
UNFOLDS
UNROLLS
UPHOLDS

•••O•L•

ALOOFLY
AMPOULE
BEFOULS
COROLLA
ENNOBLE
ENROLLS
ENSOULS
IGNOBLE
IGNOBLY
LAJOLLA
LLCOOLJ
MONOCLE
PANOPLY
PINOCLE
REBOILS
RECOILS
REPOLLS
RETOOLS
SCHOOLS
SCROLLS
SHOOFLY
STROLLS
UNCOILS
UNGODLY
UNROLLS

•••O••L

AEROSOL
ALCOHOL
AURORAL
BIFOCAL
BIMODAL
CALOMEL
CHLORAL
COLONEL
CREOSOL
DEPOSAL
ESTORIL
FEMORAL
GASOHOL
IMMORAL
MAYORAL
PIVOTAL
REMODEL
REMOVAL
SORORAL
SYNODAL

••••OL•

ACEROLA
AIRHOLE
AIRWOLF
ALLTOLD
ALVEOLI
AMAPOLA
ANATOLE
ARMHOLE
AUREOLA
AUREOLE
BADCOLD
BAGNOLD
BEDROLL
BERTOLT
BOBDOLE
BOGHOLE
CANNOLI
CARROLL
CONDOLE
CONSOLE
COPPOLA
CRAYOLA
CRYWOLF
DRYHOLE
EGGROLL
EYEBOLT
EYEHOLE
FOXHOLE
GAMBOLS
GONDOLA
GOOGOLS
GRANOLA
GUNMOLL
HANSOLO
ICECOLD
KEYHOLE
KINFOLK
LEOPOLD
LINCOLN
LLCOOLJ
MALCOLM
MANHOLE
MAYPOLE
MENFOLK
MINEOLA
MONGOLS
NICCOLO
NICHOLS
NORFOLK
OLDGOLD
ONAROLL
OSCEOLA
OUTSOLD
PATROLS
PAYROLL
PERGOLA
PETIOLE
PHENOLS
PICCOLO
PINHOLE
PISTOLE
PISTOLS
PORTOLA
POTHOLE
RAGDOLL
RATHOLE
RAVIOLI
REDPOLL
REDWOLF
RETOOLS
RISSOLE
RUMPOLE
SCHOOLS
SHEWOLF
SIXFOLD
SKIPOLE
STEROLS
SUFFOLK
SYMBOLS
SYSTOLE
TADPOLE
TENFOLD
TOEHOLD
TREMOLO
TRIPOLI
TWOFOLD
VACUOLE
WALPOLE

••••O•L

AIRCOOL
AIRFOIL
AXOLOTL
BARNOWL
BATHOIL
BEDROLL
CARPOOL
CARROLL
COALOIL
CORNOIL
DESPOIL
EGGROLL
EMBROIL
FUELOIL
GUNMOLL
HOOTOWL
LAMPOIL
ONAROLL
PALMOIL
PARBOIL
PAYROLL
PEAFOWL
PRECOOL
RAGDOLL
REDPOLL
ROSEOIL
SUBSOIL
TINFOIL
TOMFOOL
TOPSOIL
TREFOIL
TUNGOIL
TURMOIL
VANPOOL

•••••OL

AEROSOL
AIRCOOL
ALCOHOL
BRISTOL
CAPITOL
CARPOOL
CLAIROL
CONTROL
CREOSOL
DEMEROL
ESPANOL
ETHANOL
GASOHOL
GERITOL
GIRASOL
MENTHOL
PARASOL
PRECOOL
TOMFOOL
TYLENOL
VANPOOL
VITRIOL

OM•••••

OMELETS
OMENTUM
OMICRON
OMINOUS
OMITTED
OMNIBUS
OMPHALI

O•M••••

OOMPAHS
ORMANDY
ORMOLUS
OSMONDS
OSMOSED
OSMOSES
OSMOSIS
OSMOTIC

O••M•••

OAKMOSS
OATMEAL
ODDMENT
OLDMAID
OLDMOON
OLEMISS
OLYMPIA
OLYMPIC
OLYMPUS
OXYMORA

O•••M••

OPTIMAL
OPTIMUM
OTTOMAN

O••••M•

OFFRAMP
OILLAMP
OLDTIME
ONETIME
ORIGAMI
OUTCOME
OUTJUMP

O•••••M

OMENTUM
OPOSSUM
OPTIMUM
ORGANUM

•OM••••

BOMBARD
BOMBAST
BOMBECK
BOMBERS
BOMBING
COMBATS
COMBERS
COMBINE
COMBING
COMBUST
COMEDIC
COMEDUE
COMEOFF
COMEONS
COMEOUT
COMESAT
COMESBY
COMESIN
COMESON
COMESTO
COMESUP
COMFIER
COMFITS
COMFORT
COMFREY
COMICAL
COMINGS
COMIQUE
COMMAND
COMMEND
COMMENT
COMMITS
COMMODE
COMMONS
COMMOVE
COMMUNE
COMMUTE
COMOROS
COMPACT
COMPANY
COMPARE
COMPASS
COMPEER
COMPELS
COMPETE
COMPILE
COMPLEX
COMPORT
COMPOSE
COMPOST
COMPOTE
COMPUTE
COMRADE
DOMAINS
DOMINGO
DOMINOS
FOMENTS
GOMPERS
HOMBRES
HOMBURG
HOMERED
HOMERIC
HOMERUN
HOMIEST
HOMINEM
HOMINID
HOMONYM
IOMOTHS
KOMATSU
LOMBARD
MOMBASA
MOMENTS
MOMMIES
NOMADIC
NOMINAL
NOMINEE
OOMPAHS
POMADED
POMADES
POMELOS
POMMELS
POMPANO
POMPEIA
POMPEII
POMPOMS
POMPONS
POMPOUS
ROMAINE
ROMANCE
ROMANIA
ROMANOV
ROMANSH
ROMNEYS
ROMPERS
ROMPING
ROMULAN
ROMULUS
SOMALIA
SOMALIS
SOMATIC
SOMEDAY
SOMEHOW
SOMEONE
SOMEWAY
TOMBOYS
TOMCATS
TOMFOOL
TOMTITS
TOMTOMS
WOMANLY
WOMBATS
ZOMBIES

•O•M•••

BOOMBOX
BOOMERS
BOOMING
COMMAND
COMMEND
COMMENT
COMMITS
COMMODE
COMMONS
COMMOVE
COMMUNE
COMMUTE
DOGMATA
DOLMANS
DOLMENS
DOOMING
DORMANT
DORMERS
DORMICE
FOAMIER
FOAMING
FORMALS
FORMATS
FORMICA
FORMING
FORMOSA
FORMULA
HOLMIUM
HOLMOAK
HORMONE
LOAMIER
LOAMING
LOOMING
MOMMIES
MORMONS
NORMALS
NORMAND
NORMANS
POMMELS
ROAMERS
ROAMING
ROOMERS
ROOMFUL
ROOMIER
ROOMIES
ROOMING
TOPMAST
TOPMOST
TORMENT
WOOMERA
WORMIER
YOUMANS
ZOOMING
ZOOMSIN

•O••M••

BOATMAN
BOATMEN
BOHEMIA
BONDMAN
BONDMEN
COLEMAN
COLUMBO
COLUMNS
COZUMEL
DOORMAN
DOORMAT
DOORMEN
FOOTMAN
FOOTMEN
FOREMAN
FOREMEN
GOODMAN
GOODMEN
GOURMET
HOFFMAN
HOUSMAN
MOGAMBO
MONOMER
NOKOMIS
POLEMIC
POLYMER
POSTMAN
POSTMEN
POTOMAC
ROADMAP
SOLOMON
TOTEMIC
VOLUMES
WOLFMAN
WOLFMEN
WORKMAN
WORKMEN

•O•••M•

BOTTOMS
CONDEMN
CONGAME
CONSUME
CONTEMN
COSTUME
COULOMB
COXCOMB
GOURAMI
HOWCOME
LOGJAMS
MOSLEMS
NOISOME
NONCOMS
NOTHOME
NOTRUMP
NOXZEMA
PODIUMS
POMPOMS
POSSUMS
SOSUEME
TOMTOMS
WOEISME
YOUNGMC

•O••••M

BOREDOM
CONFIRM
CONFORM
FOGYISM
FORDHAM
FOREARM
HOLMIUM
HOMINEM
HOMONYM
HOODLUM
JOACHIM
LORDJIM
LOWBEAM
MODICUM
NOSEEUM
NOSTRUM
POTSDAM
ROSTRUM
SOPHISM
SORGHUM
TONEARM
TORYISM
TOURISM
WOLFRAM

••OM•••

ANOMALY
ATOMIES
ATOMIZE
BIOMASS
BOOMBOX
BOOMERS
BOOMING
BROMATE
BROMIDE
BROMINE
CHOMPED
CHOMSKY
DIOMEDE
DOOMING
FROMAGE
GLOMMED
GNOMONS
GROMMET
GROMYKO
ISOMERS
LOOMING
PROMISE
PROMOTE
PROMPTS
RHOMBUS
ROOMERS
ROOMFUL
ROOMIER
ROOMIES
ROOMING
STOMACH
STOMATA
STOMPED
THOMSON
TIOMKIN
WHOMPED
WOOMERA
WYOMING
ZOOMING
ZOOMSIN

••O•M••

ANOSMIA
ANOSMIC
BLOOMED
BLOOMER
DOORMAN
DOORMAT
DOORMEN
FOOTMAN
FOOTMEN
FROGMAN
FROGMEN
GLOMMED
GOODMAN
GOODMEN
GROMMET
GROOMED
GROOMER
IRONMAN
IRONMEN
PLOWMAN
PLOWMEN
PROPMAN
PROPMEN
SHOWMAN
SHOWMEN
SNOWMAN
SNOWMEN
STORMED

••O••M•

ANONYMS
DIORAMA
ECONOMY
EPONYMS
IWOJIMA
PHONEME
PROXIMO
PTOLEMY
QUORUMS
SAOTOME
TWOSOME
TWOTIME

••O•••M

APOTHEM
BLOSSOM
EGOTISM
FLOTSAM
HOODLUM
NIOBIUM
OPOSSUM
PROBLEM
PROGRAM
RHODIUM
THORIUM
TROPISM

•••OM••

ABDOMEN
ATHOMES
AUTOMAT
BECOMES
BLOOMED
BLOOMER
CALOMEL
CAROMED
CHROMES
DAHOMEY
ENCOMIA
GROOMED
GROOMER
INCOMES
MONOMER
NOKOMIS
OTTOMAN
PALOMAR
POTOMAC
REPOMAN
SOLOMON

•••O•M•

ALLOFME
DEFORMS
INFORMS
MEGOHMS
REFORMS

•••O••M

ACRONYM
ANTONYM
DECORUM
HEROISM
HOMONYM
SYNONYM
THEOREM

••••OM•

ANATOMY
AWESOME
BOTTOMS
COULOMB
COXCOMB
CUSTOMS
DIATOMS
DIPLOMA
ECONOMY
EPITOME
FATHOMS
FULSOME
GIACOMO
HANSOMS
HOWCOME
IRKSOME
LISSOME
NOISOME
NONCOMS
NOTHOME
OUTCOME
PHENOMS
POMPOMS
RANSOMS
RHIZOME
RUNHOME
SAOTOME
SHALOMS
SITCOMS
SLALOMS
TOMTOMS
TWOSOME
WELCOME
WINSOME

••••O•M

ARTFORM
BARROOM
BEDROOM
CONFORM
DAYROOM
INBLOOM
JIBBOOM
LEGROOM
MALCOLM
PERFORM
REBLOOM
RECROOM
SUNROOM
TAPROOM
TEAROOM
UNIFORM

•••••OM

ABSALOM
BARROOM
BEDROOM
BLOSSOM
BOREDOM
CZARDOM
DAYROOM
DUKEDOM
EARLDOM
FIEFDOM
FREEDOM
GRISSOM
INBLOOM
JIBBOOM
KINGDOM
LEGROOM
PHANTOM
REBLOOM
RECROOM
SERFDOM
SHAHDOM
STARDOM
SUNROOM
SYMPTOM
TAPROOM
TEAROOM
TRANSOM

ON•••••

ONADARE
ONADATE
ONADIET
ONAGERS
ONANDON
ONAROLL
ONASSIS
ONATEAR
ONBOARD
ONEEYED
ONEIDAS
ONENESS
ONEROUS
ONESELF
ONESHOT
ONESTEP
ONETIME
ONGOING
ONGUARD
ONLEAVE
ONLYYOU
ONORDER
ONPAPER
ONSHORE
ONSIGHT
ONSTAGE
ONTARIO
ONTHEGO
ONTHEQT
ONTOPOF
ONTRIAL
ONWARDS

O•N••••

OINKING
OMNIBUS
ORNETTE
ORNITHO
OWNEDUP

O••N•••

OCANADA
OCONNOR
ODDNESS
OKINAWA
OLDNESS
OLDNEWS
OLDNICK
OMENTUM
OMINOUS
ONANDON
ONENESS
OPENAIR
OPENBAR
OPENEND
OPENERS
OPENING
OPENPIT
OPENSEA
OPENSUP
OPENTOE
OPINERS
OPINING
OPINION
ORANGES
ORINOCO
OWINGTO
OXONIAN
OZONOUS

O•••N••

OBLONGS
OBTUNDS
OCEANIA
OCEANIC
OCEANID
OCEANUS
OCONNOR
OCTANES
OCTANTS
OFFENCE
OFFENDS
OFFENSE
OFTENER
ORDINAL
ORGANDY
ORGANIC
ORGANON
ORGANUM
ORGANZA
ORIENTE
ORIENTS
ORLANDO
ORMANDY
ORPINES
OSCINES
OSMONDS
OTRANTO
OUTINGS

O••••N•

OAKLAND
OBEYING
OBSCENE
OBTAINS
OCARINA
ODDMENT
OFFHAND
OFFLINE
OHIOANS
OILCANS
OILPANS
OINKING
OKAYING
OLDHAND
OLDLINE
OLIVINE
ONGOING
OPALINE
OPENEND
OPENING
OPERAND
OPINING
OPPUGNS
OPTIONS
OPULENT
ORATING
ORDAINS
OREGANO
ORIGINS
ORISONS
ORLEANS
OROTUND
ORPHANS
OSBORNE
OUSTING
OUTDONE
OUTGUNS
OUTLAND
OUTLINE
OUTRANK
OUTRUNS
OXIDANT

O•••••N

OAKFERN
OAKLAWN
OBERLIN
OBREGON
OCTAGON
OILSKIN
OLDMOON
OMICRON
ONANDON
OPINION
ORATION
ORBISON
ORGANON

ORPHEAN
ORTOLAN
OTTOMAN
OURTOWN
OUTWORN
OVATION
OVERRAN
OVERRUN
OXONIAN

•ON•••

BONANZA
BONBONS
BONDAGE
BONDING
BONDMAN
BONDMEN
BONEASH
BONEDRY
BONEDUP
BONESUP
BONFIRE
BONGING
BONGOES
BONIEST
BONITOS
BONJOUR
BONJOVI
BONKERS
BONNETS
BONNIER
BONNILY
BONSOIR
BONUSES
CONAKRY
CONBRIO
CONCAVE
CONCEAL
CONCEDE
CONCEIT
CONCEPT
CONCERN
CONCERT
CONCHES
CONCISE
CONCOCT
CONCORD
CONCURS
CONDEMN
CONDIGN
CONDOLE
CONDONE
CONDORS
CONDUCE
CONDUCT
CONDUIT
CONFABS
CONFERS
CONFESS
CONFIDE
CONFINE
CONFIRM
CONFORM
CONFUSE
CONFUTE
CONGAED
CONGAME
CONGEAL
CONGERS
CONGEST
CONICAL
CONIFER
CONJOBS
CONJOIN
CONJURE
CONKERS
CONKING
CONKOUT
CONNECT
CONNERY
CONNICK
CONNIFF
CONNING
CONNIVE
CONNORS
CONNOTE
CONQUER
CONRACK
CONREID
CONSENT
CONSIGN
CONSIST
CONSOLE
CONSORT
CONSULS
CONSULT
CONSUME
CONTACT
CONTAIN
CONTEMN
CONTEND
CONTENT
CONTEST
CONTEXT
CONTORT
CONTOUR
CONTRAS
CONTROL
CONTUSE
CONVENE
CONVENT
CONVERT
CONVEYS
CONVICT
CONVOKE
CONVOYS
DONAHUE
DONATED
DONATES
DONATOR
DONEFOR
DONEGAL
DONJONS
DONJOSE
DONJUAN
DONKEYS
DONKING
DONNING
DONOVAN
FONDANT
FONDEST
FONDLED
FONDLES
FONDUES
FONTEYN
FONTINA
GONDOLA
GONERIL
GONGING
HONCHOS
HONESTY
HONEYED
HONKERS
HONKING
HONORED
HONOREE
HONORER
HONOURS
IONESCO
IONIZED
IONIZER
IONIZES
JONQUIL
KONTIKI
LONGAGO
LONGBOW
LONGEST
LONGING
LONGISH
LONGRUN
LONGTON
LONGUES
LONNROT
MONARCH
MONDALE
MONDAYS
MONEYED
MONGERS
MONGOLS
MONGREL
MONIKER
MONIQUE
MONITOR
MONKEES
MONKEYS
MONKISH
MONOCLE
MONOCOT
MONOLOG
MONOMER
MONSOON
MONSTER
MONTAGE
MONTANA
MONTAND
MONTANE
MONTEGO
MONTEUX
MONTHLY
MONTOYA
NONAGON
NONCOMS
NONPLUS
NONSELF
NONSKID
NONSLIP
NONSTOP
NONUSER
NONZERO
PONCHOS
PONDERS
PONGIDS
PONIARD
PONTIAC
PONTIFF
PONTINE
PONTIUS
PONTOON
PONYING
RONDEAU
RONDELS
RONTGEN
SONATAS
SONNETS
TONALLY
TONEARM
TONEDUP
TONELOC
TONEROW
TONESUP
TONGANS
TONGUED
TONGUES
TONIEST
TONIGHT
TONNAGE
TONNEAU
TONSILS
TONSURE
TONTINE
WONDERS
WONTONS
YONKERS
ZONALLY
ZONKERS
ZONKING
ZONKOUT

•O•N•••

BONNETS
BONNIER
BONNILY
BOONIES
BORNEUP
BOUNCED
BOUNCER
BOUNCES
BOUNDED
BOUNDER
BOUNDTO
BOUNDUP
COGNACS
COGNATE
COINAGE
COINERS
COINING
CONNECT
CONNERY
CONNICK
CONNIFF
CONNING
CONNIVE
CONNORS
CONNOTE
COONCAT
CORNCOB
CORNDOG
CORNEAL
CORNEAS
CORNELL
CORNERS
CORNETS
CORNFED
CORNICE
CORNIER
CORNILY
CORNING
CORNISH
CORNOIL
CORNROW
COUNCIL
COUNSEL
COUNTED
COUNTER
COUNTON
COUNTRY
COYNESS
DOINGIN
DOINGUP
DONNING
DOWNBOW
DOWNERS
DOWNIER
DOWNING
DOWNPAT
FOUNDED
FOUNDER
FOUNDRY
GOINFOR
GOINGAT
GOINGBY
GOINGIN
GOINGON
GOINGUP
GOUNDER
HOBNAIL
HOBNOBS
HORNETS
HORNING
HORNIST
HORNSBY
HOTNESS
HOUNDED
JOHNDOE
JOHNGAY
JOHNJAY
JOHNNIE
JOHNSON
JOINDER
JOINERS
JOINERY
JOINING
JOINSIN
JOINSUP
JOINTED
JOINTLY
JOUNCED
JOUNCES
LOANERS
LOANING
LONNROT
LOONIER
LOONIES
LOUNGED
LOUNGER
LOUNGES
LOWNECK
LOWNESS
MOANERS
MOANING
MOONDOG
MOONING
MOONLIT
MOONSET
MORNING
MOUNDED
MOUNTED
MOUNTIE
NOONDAY
POINTED
POINTER
POINTTO
POUNCED
POUNCER
POUNCES
POUNDED
POUNDER
ROANOKE
ROMNEYS
ROUNDED
ROUNDER
ROUNDLY
ROUNDON
ROUNDUP
SOANDSO
SONNETS
SOONERS
SOONEST
SOUNDED
SOUNDER
SOUNDLY
TOENAIL
TONNAGE
TONNEAU
TORNADO
TORNOUT
TOWNERS
TOWNIES
TOYNBEE
WORNOFF
WORNOUT
WOUNDED
WOUNDUP
WOZNIAK
YOUNGER
YOUNGMC
YOUNGUN

•O••N••

BONANZA
BOTHNIA
BOVINES
BOWKNOT
COCKNEY
COCONUT
COGENCY
COLONEL
COLONES
COLONNA
COMINGS
CORINTH
CORONAE
CORONAS
CORONET
COSINES
COSTNER
COZENED
DOCENTS
DOMINGO
DOMINOS
DOYENNE
DOZENTH
FOMENTS
FORINTS
GODUNOV
GOTINTO
HOMINEM
HOMINID
HOMONYM
HOSANNA
JOHANNA
JOHNNIE
JOURNAL
JOURNEY
KORUNAS
LOCKNUT
LORENZO
LOZENGE
MOMENTS
MORANIS
NOCANDO
NOMINAL
NOMINEE
NOVENAS
POCONOS
POLENTA
POTENCY
RODENTS
ROMANCE
ROMANIA
ROMANOV
ROMANSH
ROSANNA
ROSANNE
ROTUNDA
ROXANNE
SOIGNEE
TOKENED
TOPKNOT
TORONTO
TOURNEY
WOKENUP
WOMANLY
YOUKNOW

•O•••N•

BOATING
BOBBING
BOBBINS
BODKINS
BOGGING
BOILING
BOITANO
BOLOGNA
BOLTING
BOMBING
BONBONS
BONDING
BONGING
BOOKEND
BOOKING
BOOMING
BOOTING
BOPPING
BOSSING
BOWFINS
BOWLINE
BOWLING
COATING
COAXING
COCKING
COCOONS
CODEINE
COIFING
COILING
COINING
COLLINS
COLOGNE
COLONNA
COLUMNS
COMBINE
COMBING
COMEONS
COMMAND
COMMEND
COMMENT
COMMONS
COMMUNE
COMPANY
CONDONE
CONFINE
CONKING
CONNING
CONSENT
CONTEND
CONTENT
CONVENE
CONVENT
COOKING
COOLANT
COOLING
COOPING
COPLAND
COPPING
COPYING
CORDING
CORDONS
CORKING
CORNING
COSIGNS
COSTING
COTTONS
COTTONY
COULDNT
COUPONS
COURANT
COUSINS
COWHAND
COWLING
COZYING
COZZENS
DOBBINS
DOCKING
DODGING
DOFFING
DOGGING
DOGGONE
DOLLING
DOLMANS
DOLMENS
DOMAINS
DONJONS
DONKING
DONNING
DOOMING
DORMANT
DOTTING
DOUSING
DOWNING
DOWSING
DOYENNE
FOALING
FOAMING
FOBBING
FOGBANK
FOGGING
FOILING
FOLDING
FONDANT
FONTINA
FOOLING
FOOTING
FORCING
FORDING
FORFEND
FORGING
FORGONE
FORKING
FORMING
FORRENT
FORTUNA
FORTUNE
FORWENT
FOULING
FOWLING
GOADING
GOALONG
GOBLINS
GODSEND
GODSONS
GOLDING
GOLFING
GONGING
GOODONE
GOOFING
GOOSING
GORGING
GORGONS
GOROUND
GOSLING
GOTLAND
GOUGING
GOVERNS
GOWRONG
HOAXING
HOBOING
HOCKING
HOGGING
HOLDING
HOLLAND
HONKING
HOOFING
HOOKING
HOOPING
HOOTING
HOPKINS
HOPPING
HORMONE
HORNING
HORSING
HOSANNA
HOSKINS
HOSTING
HOTLINE
HOUDINI
HOUSING
HOWLING
HOYDENS
JOBBANK
JOBBING
JOBHUNT
JOGGING
JOHANNA
JOINING
JOLTING
JOSHING
JOTTING
KOBLENZ
KOREANS
LOADING
LOAFING
LOAMING
LOANING
LOBBING
LOCKING
LOCKINS
LODGING
LOFTING
LOGGING
LOGGINS
LOLLING
LONGING
LOOKING
LOOMING
LOOPING
LOOSENS
LOOSING
LOOTING
LOPPING
LORDING
LOTIONS
LOTTING
LOUSING
LOVEINS
LOWLAND
MOANING
MOBBING
MOCKING
MODERNS
MOILING
MOLDING
MOLTING
MONTANA
MONTAND
MONTANE
MOONING
MOORING
MOPPING
MORAINE
MORDANT
MORDENT
MORGANA
MORGANS
MORMONS
MORNING
MOSSING
MOTIONS
MOUSING
MOUTONS
NODDING
NOGGINS
NOISING
NOOSING
NORMAND
NORMANS
NOSHING
NOTHING
NOTIONS
POISING
POISONS
POLLENS
POLLING
POMPANO
POMPONS
PONTINE
PONYING
POOLING
POOPING
POPGUNS
POPLINS
POPPING
POPPINS
PORCINE
PORSENA
PORTEND
PORTENT
POSTING
POTIONS
POTTING
POULENC
POURING
POUTING
ROAMING
ROARING
ROBBING
ROBBINS
ROCKING
ROILING
ROLLING
ROLLINS
ROMAINE
ROMPING
ROOFING
ROOKING
ROOMING
ROOTING
ROSANNA
ROSANNE
ROSSINI
ROSTAND
ROTTING
ROUGING
ROUSING
ROUTINE
ROUTING
ROXANNE
SOAKING
SOAPING
SOARING
SOBBING
SOCKING
SODDING
SOFTENS
SOILING
SOLOING
SOLVENT
SOLVING
SOMEONE
SOPPING
SOPRANO
SORTING
SOURING
SOUTANE
TOCSINS
TOGGING
TOILING
TOLLING
TOLUENE
TONGANS
TONTINE
TOOLING
TOOTING
TOPGUNS
TOPPING
TORMENT
TORRENT
TORTONI
TOSSING
TOTTING
TOUCANS
TOURING
TOUTING
TOYLAND
VOICING
VOIDING
VOLCANO
VOLPONE
WOLFING
WONTONS
WOOFING
WOOLENS
WORDING
WORDONE
WORKING
WORSENS
WOULDNT
YOKOONO
YOUMANS
YOWLING
YOYOING
ZONKING
ZOOMING

•O••••N

BOATMAN
BOATMEN
BOGDOWN
BONDMAN
BONDMEN
BOOLEAN
BORODIN
BOURBON
BOXEDIN
BOXESIN
COALBIN
COARSEN
COCHRAN
COGBURN
COLEMAN
COLLEEN
COMESIN
COMESON
CONCERN
CONDEMN
CONDIGN
CONJOIN
CONSIGN
CONTAIN
CONTEMN
CORAZON
COSTAIN
COUNTON
COWTOWN
DODGSON
DOESKIN
DOINGIN
DOLPHIN
DONJUAN
DONOVAN
DOORMAN
DOORMEN
DOTEDON
DOTESON
FOGHORN
FONTEYN
FOOTMAN
FOOTMEN
FOREIGN
FOREMAN
FOREMEN
FORERAN
FORERUN
FORLORN
FORTRAN
GOINGIN
GOINGON
GOLDWYN
GOODMAN
GOODMEN
GOODSON
GOODWIN
GORDIAN
GOTDOWN
GOTEVEN
HOARSEN
HOBOKEN
HOEDOWN
HOFFMAN
HOLBEIN
HOLDSON
HOMERUN
HORIZON
HOUSMAN
HOUSTON
JOAQUIN
JOHNSON
JOINSIN
JOURDAN
KOSYGIN
KOWLOON
LONGRUN
LONGTON
LOOKSIN
LOOKSON
LOWBORN
LOWDOWN
MOHICAN
MOISTEN
MONSOON
MOORHEN
MOUFLON
MOVEDIN
MOVESIN
MOWDOWN
NOCTURN
NONAGON
POISSON
POKEFUN
POLYGON
PONTOON
POPCORN
PORTION
POSTERN
POSTMAN
POSTMEN
POURSIN
ROBESON
ROMULAN
RONTGEN
ROPEDIN
ROPESIN
ROUGHEN
ROUNDON
ROYBEAN
SOCKSIN
SOJOURN
SOLOMON
SOTHERN
SOUPCON
SOYBEAN
TOLKIEN
TOOKTEN
TORSION
TOUCHON
TOUGHEN
VOTESIN
WOBEGON
WOLFMAN
WOLFMEN
WOOLLEN
WORKMAN
WORKMEN
WORKSIN
WORKSON
YOUNGUN
ZOOMSIN

••ON•••

ACONITE
ADONAIS
AGONIST
AGONIZE
AMONGST
ANONYMS
ATONING
AVONLEA
BIONICS
BLONDER
BLONDES
BLONDIE
BOONIES
BRONCHI
BRONCOS
BRONSON
BRONZED
BRONZES
CLONING
COONCAT
CRONIES

DRONERS
DRONING
EBONIES
EBONITE
ECONOMY
EPONYMS
ETONIAN
FRONTAL
FRONTED
FRONTON
IRONAGE
IRONERS
IRONIES
IRONING
IRONMAN
IRONMEN
IRONORE
IRONOUT
LEONARD
LEONINE
LEONORA
LIONCUB
LIONESS
LIONETS
LIONIZE
LOONIER
LOONIES
MOONDOG
MOONING
MOONLIT
MOONSET
NEONATE
NOONDAY
OCONNOR
OXONIAN
OZONOUS
PEONAGE
PEONIES
PHONEME
PHONICS
PHONIER
PHONIES
PHONILY
PHONING
PIONEER
PRONGED
PRONOUN
QUONSET
SCONCES
SOONERS
SOONEST
SPONDEE
SPONGED
SPONGER
SPONGES
SPONSOR
STONERS
STONIER
STONILY
STONING
TSONGAS
VRONSKY
WRONGED
WRONGER
WRONGLY

••O•N••

ABOUNDS
ADORNED
AMOUNTS
ANOINTS
ASOFNOW
BLOWNUP
BROSNAN
BROWNED
BROWNER
BROWNIE
CLOONEY
CLOWNED
CROONED
CROONER
CROWNED
DROWNED
ENOUNCE
FLOUNCE
FROWNAT
FROWNED
FROWNER
GROANED
GROANER
GROUNDS
GROWNUP
OCONNOR
PHOENIX
SCORNED
SHOWNIN
SPOONED
SPOONER
SWOONED
TROUNCE
YAOUNDE

••O••N•

ADORING
ANODYNE
ATONING
AVOWING
BIOGENY
BLOWING
BOOKEND
BOOKING
BOOMING
BOOTING
BROGANS
BROMINE
BUOYANT
BUOYING
CHORINE
CLONING
CLOSING
CLOYING
COOKING
COOLANT
COOLING
COOPING
CROWING
DOOMING
DRONING
DROPINS
DUODENA
ELOPING
EMOTING
ERODING
EVOKING
FLORINS
FLOWING
FOOLING
FOOTING
GLOWING
GNOMONS
GOODONE
GOOFING
GOOSING
GROPING
GROWING
HOOFING
HOOKING
HOOPING
HOOTING
IMOGENE
IRONING
ISOGONS
KNOWING
LEONINE
LOOKING
LOOMING
LOOPING
LOOSENS
LOOSING
LOOTING
MEOWING
MIOCENE
MOONING
MOORING
NOOSING
OROTUND
PHONING
PHOTONS
PLOWING
POOLING
POOPING
PROBING
PROBONO
PROFANE
PROGENY
PROLONG
PROPANE
PROSING
PROTONS
PROVING
QUOTING
REOPENS
RIOTING
ROOFING
ROOKING
ROOMING
ROOTING
SCOPING
SCORING
SHOEING
SHOGUNS
SHOOING
SHOOINS
SHORING
SHOVING
SHOWING
SIOUANS
SLOGANS
SLOPING
SLOVENE
SLOVENS
SLOWING
SMOKING
SNOCONE
SNORING
SNOWING
SPOKANE
SPOKING
STOKING
STOLONS
STONING
STORING
STOWING
TOOLING
TOOTING
TROJANS
TWOTONE
USOPENS
VIOLENT
VIOLINS
WOOFING
WOOLENS
WYOMING
ZOOMING

••O•••N

AEOLIAN
BLOUSON
BLOWGUN
BLOWSIN
BOOLEAN
BROADEN
BROKEIN
BRONSON
BROSNAN
CLOCKIN
CLOSEIN
CROUTON
DOORMAN
DOORMEN
DROPSIN
EMOTION
EROSION
ETONIAN
FOOTMAN
FOOTMEN
FROGMAN
FROGMEN
FRONTON
GOODMAN
GOODMEN
GOODSON
GOODWIN
GROWSON
IRONMAN
IRONMEN
KTOSLIN
LAOCOON
LAOTIAN
LOOKSIN
LOOKSON
MOORHEN
OXONIAN
PLOSION
PLOWMAN
PLOWMEN
PROCYON
PRONOUN
PROPMAN
PROPMEN
PROTEAN
PROTEIN
SHODDEN
SHORTEN
SHOTGUN
SHOWMAN
SHOWMEN
SHOWNIN
SHOWSIN
SIOBHAN
SLOEGIN
SNOWDON
SNOWMAN
SNOWMEN
SNOWSIN
SPORRAN
STOLLEN
STOODIN
STOPSIN
SWOLLEN
SWOREIN
THOMSON
TIOMKIN
TOOKTEN
TRODDEN
UTOPIAN
WOOLLEN
WROTEIN
ZOOMSIN

•••ON••

ACRONYM
ADDONTO
ALFONSO
ALMONDS
AMMONIA
ANTONIA
ANTONIN
ANTONIO
ANTONYM
APRONED
ARGONNE
BALONEY
BARONET
BARONGS
BAYONET
BEGONIA
BELONGS
BYGONES
CANONIC
CHRONIC
CLOONEY
COCONUT
COLONEL
COLONES
COLONNA
CORONAE
CORONAS
CORONET
CROONED
CROONER
DEBONED
DEBONES
DEMONIC
DEPONED
DEPONES
DUGONGS
ESTONIA
GARONNE
GIRONDE
HOMONYM
INTONED
INTONER
INTONES
JACONET
KETONES
KIMONOS
LACONIC
MADONNA
MAHONEY
MASONIC
MASONRY
MRBONES
OBLONGS
OSMONDS
PINONES
POCONOS
REZONED
REZONES
SARONGS
SECONDS
SPOONED
SPOONER
SWOONED
SYNONYM
TALONED
TENONED
THRONES
THRONGS
TORONTO
UNZONED
UPTONOW
WAGONER
WYNONNA

•••O•N•

ACCOUNT
ADJOINS
AGROUND
ALTOONA
ANTOINE
APPOINT
ARGONNE
ASTOUND
BABOONS
BEMOANS
BOLOGNA
COCOONS
COLOGNE
COLONNA
CYYOUNG
DEHORNS
DISOWNS
ECHOING
ENJOINS
EXPOUND
GARONNE
GOROUND
HALOING
HEROINE
HOBOING
HYPOING
IMPOUND
INBOUND
INPOINT
KAYOING
LAGOONS
MADONNA
MAROONS
MINOANS
OHIOANS
ONGOING
OSBORNE
REBOUND
RECOUNT
REDOING
REDOUND
REJOINS
REMOUNT
RESOUND
REWOUND
SALOONS
SAMOANS
SHOOING
SHOOINS
SILOING
SOLOING
STJOHNS
SUBORNS
TYCOONS
UNBOUND
UNDOING
UNSOUND
UNWOUND
UPBORNE
VETOING
WYNONNA
YOKOONO
YOYOING
ZEROING

•••O••N

ABDOMEN
ADJOURN
ALSORAN
ANGOLAN
ANTONIN
BEDOUIN
BETOKEN
BORODIN
CAROLYN
CRYOGEN
DAKOTAN
DEKOVEN
DONOVAN
HALOGEN
HOBOKEN
JACOBIN
KILOTON
LANOLIN
ORTOLAN
OTTOMAN
REPOMAN
REWOVEN
SAROYAN
SOJOURN
SOLOMON
STOODIN
THROWIN

••••ON•

ABALONE
ABSCOND
ACETONE
ACTIONS
AFFRONT
ALIMONY
ALLGONE
ALTOONA
AMAZONS
AMNIONS
ANEMONE
ANTHONY
ARCHONS
ARIZONA
ARTSONG
BABOONS
BALCONY
BARYONS
BEACONS
BECKONS
BELMONT
BLAZONS
BONBONS
BRETONS
BRITONS
BUNIONS
BUTTONS
CALZONE
CANNONS
CANTONS
CANYONS
CANZONE
CARBONS
CARTONS
CATIONS
CITRONS
CLIPONS
COCOONS
COMEONS
COMMONS
CONDONE
CORDONS
COTTONS
COTTONY
COUPONS
CRAYONS
CREMONA
CUIBONO
CYCLONE
DAMSONS
DAYLONG
DAYTONA
DEACONS
DESMOND
DIAMOND
DINMONT
DOGGONE
DONJONS
DRAGONS
ENDZONE
EPIGONE
ERELONG
EUPHONY
FALCONS
FANIONS
FARGONE
FASTONE
FLACONS
FLAGONS
FORGONE
FREMONT
FURLONG
GALLONS
GAMMONS
GARCONS
GASCONS
GIBBONS
GIDEONS
GNOMONS
GOALONG
GODSONS
GOODONE
GORGONS
GOWRONG
GUIDONS
HAMMOND
HARMONY
HIPBONE
HORMONE
IFSTONE
INFRONT
ISOGONS
JARGONS
JAWBONE
JETSONS
KLAXONS
KMESONS
LAGOONS
LARDONS
LEGIONS
LEPTONS
LESSONS
LIVEONE
LOTIONS
MACRONS
MADRONA
MARCONI
MAROONS
MATRONS
MICRONS
MINIONS
MISDONE
MORMONS
MOTIONS
MOUTONS
MUTTONS
NATIONS
NELSONS
NEURONE
NEURONS
NEWTONS
NOTIONS
OPTIONS
ORISONS
OUTDONE
PADRONE
PADRONI
PARDONS
PARSONS
PATRONS
PENNONS
PERSONA
PERSONS
PHOTONS
PIGEONS
PINIONS
PISTONS
POISONS
POMPONS
POTIONS
PRISONS
PROBONO
PROLONG
PROTONS
PULLONS
PYTHONS
RATIONS
RAYMOND
REASONS
RECKONS
REGIONS
RESPOND
RIBBONS
SALMONS
SALOONS
SEASONS
SERMONS
SEXTONS
SIMMONS
SIPHONS
SLIPONS
SNAPONS
SNOCONE
SOMEONE
SPUMONE
SPUMONI
STOLONS
SUMMONS
TAKEONE
TARPONS
TENDONS
TEUTONS
TORTONI
TRIGONS
TRITONE
TRITONS
TWOTONE
TYCOONS
UNISONS
UPFRONT
VERMONT
VISIONS
VOLPONE
WAGGONS
WALKONS
WEAPONS
WILDONE
WONTONS
WORDONE
YAUPONS
YOKOONO
ZIRCONS

••••O•N

ANDSOON
BALLOON
BASSOON
BEDDOWN
BIGHORN
BIGJOHN
BOGDOWN
BUFFOON
CADDOAN
CALHOUN
CARTOON
CITROEN
CONJOIN
COWTOWN
CUTDOWN
DIEDOWN
DISJOIN
DRAGOON
FESTOON
FOGHORN
FORLORN
GETDOWN
GOTDOWN
HARPOON
HOEDOWN
IDAHOAN
INGROWN
INKHORN
KOWLOON
LAMPOON
LAOCOON
LAYDOWN
LEGHORN
LETDOWN
LIEDOWN
LINCOLN
LOWBORN
LOWDOWN
MAXBORN
MIDTOWN
MONSOON
MOWDOWN
NEWBORN
NEWMOON
NEWMOWN
NEWTOWN
OLDMOON
OURTOWN
OUTWORN
PATROON
PINDOWN
PLATOON
PONTOON
POPCORN
PRONOUN
PURLOIN
PUTDOWN
RACCOON
RANGOON
RIPTORN
RUBDOWN
RUNDOWN
SANBORN
SASSOON
SATDOWN
SAXHORN
SETDOWN
SIRLOIN
SITDOWN
SUBJOIN
SUNDOWN
TIEDOWN
TINHORN
TRICORN
TYPHOON
UNICORN
UNKNOWN
UNSHORN
VIRGOAN
WALLOON
WAYWORN

•••••ON

ABANDON
ACHERON
ACHESON
ACTAEON
ACTUPON
ADAMSON
ADDEDON
ADDISON
AILERON
ALARCON
ALENCON
ALLISON
ALLSTON
ALLYSON
ANDIRON
ANDSOON
ANTLION
AUCTION
AUDUBON
AVIGNON
BABYLON
BALATON
BALLOON
BANKSON
BASSOON
BASTION
BEARSON
BENISON
BERGSON
BILLION
BLOUSON
BOURBON
BRANDON
BRANSON
BRAXTON
BRESSON
BRINGON
BRITTON
BRONSON
BUFFOON
BUILDON
BUILTON
BULLION
BURGEON
CAISSON
CALDRON
CALLSON
CAMERON
CAMPION
CAPTION
CARLSON
CARLTON
CARRION
CARRYON
CARTOON
CATCHON
CAUTION
CELADON
CESSION
CHANSON
CHEVRON
CHIFFON
CHIGNON
CLAPTON
CLARION
CLAYTON
CLEAVON
CLEMSON
CLIFTON
CLINTON
COMESON
CORAZON
COUNTON
CRAMPON
CRIMSON
CROUTON
CUSHION
DECAGON
DENDRON
DICTION
DINEDON
DINESON
DODGSON
DOTEDON
DOTESON
DRAGOON
DRAGSON
DRAWNON
DRAWSON
DREAMON
DUDGEON
DUNGEON
EARLYON
ECHELON
EDITION
EGGEDON
ELATION
ELEISON
ELISION
ELLISON
ELUTION
EMERSON
EMOTION
EPSILON
EREWHON
ERICSON
EROSION
EVASION
FACTION
FALLSON
FASHION
FEEDSON
FESTOON
FICTION
FISSION
FRISSON
FRONTON
GAINSON
GALLEON
GETITON
GLEASON
GLUEDON
GLUTTON
GOINGON
GOODSON
GRAYSON
GRIFFON
GROWSON
GRUNION
GRYPHON
HALCYON
HALSTON
HAMPTON
HANDSON
HANGSON
HARDWON
HARPOON
HARPSON
HELICON
HELLION
HEXAGON
HIRESON
HOLDSON
HORIZON
HOUSTON
IRECKON
JACKSON
JAMESON
JILLION
JOHNSON
JUMPSON
KEEPSON
KILOTON
KLINGON
KOWLOON
KRATION
KRYPTON
LAMPOON
LANGDON
LAOCOON
LATERON
LEADSON
LEANSON
LEBANON
LEBARON
LETINON
LEXICON
LIAISON
LIVEDON
LIVESON
LONGTON
LOOKSON
MADISON
MANSION
MARCHON
MARMION
MCMAHON
MENTION
MILLION
MISSION
MONSOON
MOUFLON
MULLION
MUMESON
NEUTRON
NEWMOON
NILSSON
NONAGON
NUCLEON
OBREGON
OCTAGON
OLDMOON
OMICRON
ONANDON
OPINION
ORATION
ORBISON
ORGANON
OVATION
PARAGON
PASSION

PATROON
PEARSON
PENSION
PHAETON
PICKSON
PIDGEON
PIGIRON
PILEDON
PILESON
PILLION
PIMESON
PLANSON
PLATOON
PLAYSON
PLOSION
POISSON
POLYGON
PONTOON
PORTION
PRESSON
PRESTON
PREYSON
PROCYON
PUTUPON
PYNCHON
RACCOON
RALSTON
RANGOON
REARDON
REUNION
RIGHTON
ROBESON
ROUNDON
RUBICON
RUCTION
RULESON
SAFFRON
SAMPSON
SASSOON
SEALION
SECTION
SESSION
SETUPON
SHANNON
SHELDON
SHELTON
SIGNSON
SILICON
SIMENON
SIMPSON
SKELTON
SLAYTON
SLEEPON
SLEPTON
SNOWDON
SOLOMON
SOUPCON
SPIEDON
SPIESON
SPURSON
STANDON
STANTON
STATION
STEPSON
STETSON
STILTON
SUASION
SUCTION
SURGEON
SWANSON
SWEETON
TACKSON
TAKENON

TAKESON
TELLSON
TENSION
THEREON
THOMSON
TORSION
TOUCHON
TRADEON
TREASON
TRENTON
TRIEDON
TRIESON
TUITION
TURNSON
TYPHOON
UNCTION
UPSILON
VENISON
VERSION
WAITSON
WALLOON
WHARTON
WHEATON
WIDGEON
WILLSON
WINSTON
WOBEGON
WORKSON
YANKTON
ZEBULON
ZILLION

00•••••
OOCYTES
OOLITES
OOLITHS
OOMPAHS

0•0••••
OBOISTS
OCONNOR
ODOROUS
OLOROSO
ONORDER
OPOSSUM
OROTUND
OROURKE
OVOIDAL
OXONIAN
OZONOUS

0••0•••
OBLONGS
OBLOQUY
OCTOBER
OCTOPOD
OCTOPUS
OFSORTS
OGDOADS
OHIOANS
OKHOTSK
ONBOARD
ONGOING
ONTOPOF
OPPOSED
OPPOSER
OPPOSES
ORIOLES
ORMOLUS
ORTOLAN
OSBORNE
OSMONDS
OSMOSED

OSMOSES
OSMOSIS
OSMOTIC
OTTOMAN
OUTOFIT
OXFORDS

0•••0••
OAKMOSS
OARLOCK
OBVIOUS
OCELOTS
ODDJOBS
ODDLOTS
ODOROUS
OFASORT
OFFHOUR
OFFLOAD
OFFROAD
OLDFOGY
OLDGOLD
OLDMOON
OLOROSO
OMINOUS
ONAROLL
ONEROUS
ONSHORE
OPEROSE
OPTIONS
OPTSOUT
ORATORS
ORATORY
ORINOCO
ORISONS
OSCEOLA
OSHKOSH
OSTEOID
OURTOWN
OUTCOME
OUTDOES
OUTDONE
OUTDOOR
OUTGOES
OUTLOOK
OUTLOUD
OUTPOST
OUTSOLD
OUTVOTE
OUTWORE
OUTWORK
OUTWORN
OXBLOOD
OXYMORA
OZONOUS

0••••0•
OBREGON
OCONNOR
OCTAGON
OCTAVOS
OCTOPOD
OLDMOON
OLDPROS
OMICRON
ONANDON
ONESHOT
ONLYYOU
ONTOPOF
OPENTOE
OPINION
ORATION
ORBISON
ORGANON

OUTCROP
OUTDOOR
OUTFLOW
OUTGROW
OUTLOOK
OVATION
OVERJOY
OXBLOOD

0•••••0
OLOROSO
ONTARIO
ONTHEGO
OREGANO
ORINOCO
ORLANDO
ORNITHO
OTHELLO
OTRANTO
OWINGTO

•00••••
BOOBIES
BOOBOOS
BOODLES
BOOGIED
BOOGIES
BOOHOOS
BOOKEND
BOOKIES
BOOKING
BOOKISH
BOOKLET
BOOLEAN
BOOMBOX
BOOMERS
BOOMING
BOONIES
BOORISH
BOOSLER
BOOSTED
BOOSTER
BOOSTUP
BOOTEES
BOOTIES
BOOTING
BOOTLEG
BOOTOUT
BOOTSUP
COOKERS
COOKERY
COOKIES
COOKING
COOKOFF
COOKOUT
COOKSUP
COOLANT
COOLERS
COOLEST
COOLING
COOLSIT
COONCAT
COOPERS
COOPING
COOPSUP
COOPTED
COOTIES
DOODADS
DOODLED
DOODLER
DOODLES
DOOMING
DOORDIE

DOORMAN
DOORMAT
DOORMEN
DOORWAY
DOOZIES
FOODWEB
FOOLERY
FOOLING
FOOLISH
FOOTAGE
FOOTERS
FOOTING
FOOTMAN
FOOTMEN
FOOTPAD
FOOTSIE
FOOZLED
FOOZLES
GOOBERS
GOODALL
GOODBAR
GOODBYE
GOODBYS
GOODEGG
GOODIES
GOODJOB
GOODJOE
GOODMAN
GOODMEN
GOODONE
GOODSON
GOODWIN
GOOFIER
GOOFING
GOOFOFF
GOOFSUP
GOOFUPS
GOOGOLS
GOOIEST
GOOPIER
GOOSING
HOODLUM
HOODOOS
HOOFERS
HOOFING
HOOFSIT
HOOHAHS
HOOKAHS
HOOKING
HOOKSUP
HOOKUPS
HOOPING
HOOPLAS
HOOPOES
HOOSIER
HOOTCHY
HOOTERS
HOOTING
HOOTOWL
HOOTSAT
KOOKIER
KOOLAID
KOOTCHY
LOOFAHS
LOOKERS
LOOKFOR
LOOKING
LOOKOUT
LOOKSAT
LOOKSEE
LOOKSIN
LOOKSON
LOOKSTO

LOOKSUP
LOOKUPS
LOOMING
LOONIER
LOONIES
LOOPERS
LOOPIER
LOOPING
LOOSELY
LOOSENS
LOOSEST
LOOSING
LOOTERS
LOOTING
MOOCHED
MOOCHER
MOOCHES
MOODIER
MOODILY
MOONDOG
MOONING
MOONLIT
MOONSET
MOORAGE
MOORHEN
MOORING
MOORISH
NOODLES
NOONDAY
NOOSING
POOCHES
POODLES
POOHBAH
POOLING
POOPING
POOPOUT
POORBOX
POORBOY
POOREST
ROOFERS
ROOFING
ROOFTOP
ROOKERY
ROOKIES
ROOKING
ROOMERS
ROOMFUL
ROOMIER
ROOMIES
ROOMING
ROOSTED
ROOSTER
ROOTERS
ROOTFOR
ROOTING
ROOTLET
ROOTOUT
SOONERS
SOONEST
SOOTHED
SOOTHER
SOOTHES
SOOTIER
TOOKOFF
TOOKOUT
TOOKTEN
TOOLBOX
TOOLING
TOOLSUP
TOORDER
TOOTALL
TOOTERS
TOOTHED

TOOTING
TOOTLED
TOOTLES
TOOTSIE
WOODARD
WOODCUT
WOODIER
WOODIES
WOODLOT
WOODROW
WOOFERS
WOOFING
WOOLENS
WOOLIER
WOOLIES
WOOLLEN
WOOLSEY
WOOMERA
WOOSTER
WOOZIER
WOOZILY
ZOOLOGY
ZOOMING
ZOOMSIN

•0•0•••
BOLOGNA
BOLOTIE
BORODIN
BOROUGH
COCONUT
COCOONS
COHORTS
COHOSTS
COLOBUS
COLOGNE
COLONEL
COLONES
COLONNA
COLORED
COLOSSI
COLOURS
COMOROS
COPOUTS
COROLLA
CORONAE
CORONAS
CORONET
COYOTES
DOLORES
DONOVAN
DOROTHY
GOFORIT
GOROUND
GOTOPOT
GOTOVER
HOBOING
HOBOKEN
HOMONYM
HONORED
HONOREE
HONORER
HONOURS
HOPOVER
IOMOTHS
KOBOLDS
MOLOKAI
MOLOTOV
MONOCLE
MONOCOT
MONOLOG
MONOMER
MOROCCO

MOTORED
NODOUBT
NOKOMIS
POBOXES
POCONOS
POLOIST
POPOFFS
POPOVER
POTOMAC
ROBOCOP
ROBOTIC
RODOLFO
ROLODEX
SOJOURN
SOLOING
SOLOIST
SOLOMON
SORORAL
TOROIDS
TORONTO
YOKOONO
YOYOING

•0••0••
BOBDOLE
BOBHOPE
BOGDOWN
BOGHOLE
BONBONS
BONGOES
BONJOUR
BONJOVI
BONSOIR
BOOBOOS
BOOHOOS
BOOTOUT
BOREOUT
BORROWS
BORZOIS
BOTTOMS
BOUDOIR
BOWSOUT
BOWWOWS
BOXTOPS
BOXWOOD
BOYCOTT
BOYDORR
BOYHOOD
COALOIL
COCOONS
COLLODI
COLLOID
COLLOPS
COMEOFF
COMEONS
COMEOUT
COMFORT
COMMODE
COMMONS
COMMOVE
COMPORT
COMPOSE
COMPOST
COMPOTE
CONCOCT
CONCORD
CONDOLE
CONDONE
CONDORS
CONFORM
CONJOBS
CONJOIN
CONKOUT

CONNORS
CONNOTE
CONSOLE
CONSORT
CONTORT
CONTOUR
CONVOKE
CONVOYS
COOKOFF
COOKOUT
COPIOUS
COPPOLA
COPSOUT
CORDOBA
CORDONS
CORNOIL
CORRODE
COTTONS
COTTONY
COULOMB
COUPONS
COWBOYS
COWPOKE
COWTOWN
COXCOMB
DOCTORS
DOGGONE
DOGWOOD
DOLEOUT
DOLLOPS
DONJONS
DONJOSE
DOPEOUT
DOZEOFF
FOBSOFF
FOGBOWS
FOGHORN
FOLDOUT
FOLLOWS
FORBORE
FORGOES
FORGONE
FORGOOD
FORLORN
FORMOSA
FORSOOK
FOULOUT
FOXHOLE
GOABOUT
GOALONG
GOBROKE
GODSONS
GOESOFF
GOESOUT
GONDOLA
GOODONE
GOOFOFF
GOOGOLS
GORGONS
GOTDOWN
GOWRONG
HOBNOBS
HOEDOWN
HOLDOFF
HOLDOUT
HOLEOUT
HOLLOWS
HOLMOAK
HOLYOKE
HOODOOS
HOOPOES
HOOTOWL
HOPSOFF

HOPTOIT
HORMONE
HORRORS
HOTDOGS
HOTFOOT
HOTPOTS
HOTRODS
HOWCOME
JOBHOPS
JOBLOTS
KOWLOON
KOWTOWS
LOCKOUT
LOGBOOK
LOGSOFF
LOGSOUT
LOOKOUT
LOSEOUT
LOSTOUT
LOTIONS
LOWBORN
LOWBOYS
LOWDOWN
LOWROAD
MONGOLS
MONSOON
MONTOYA
MORMONS
MORROWS
MOTIONS
MOTTOES
MOUTONS
MOVEOUT
MOWDOWN
NOCUOUS
NODSOFF
NOISOME
NONCOMS
NORFOLK
NOSEOUT
NOSHOWS
NOTHOME
NOTIONS
NOXIOUS
POISONS
POLLOCK
POMPOMS
POMPONS
POMPOUS
PONTOON
POOPOUT
POPCORN
POPSOFF
POPSOUT
POPTOPS
PORTOLA
POTHOLE
POTHOOK
POTIONS
POUROUT
POWWOWS
ROANOKE
ROBLOWE
ROBROYS
RODEOFF
RODEOUT
ROLLOUT
ROOTOUT
ROSEOIL
ROWBOAT
SOLDOFF
SOLDOUT
SOMEONE

SORROWS
TOEHOLD
TOELOOP
TOLDOFF
TOMBOYS
TOMFOOL
TOMTOMS
TOOKOFF
TOOKOUT
TOPCOAT
TOPDOGS
TOPMOST
TOPSOFF
TOPSOIL
TOPSOUT
TOREOFF
TOREOUT
TORNOUT
TORTONI
TOSSOFF
TOSSOUT
TOWROPE
TOYDOGS
VOLPONE
WONTONS
WORDONE
WOREOFF
WOREOUT
WORKOFF
WORKOUT
WORNOFF
WORNOUT
YOKOONO
ZONKOUT
ZOOLOGY

•0•••0•
BOKCHOY
BOLEROS
BOLSHOI
BONITOS
BOOBOOS
BOOHOOS
BOOMBOX
BOREDOM
BOURBON
BOUTROS
BOWKNOT
BOXWOOD
BOYHOOD
COMESON
COMOROS
CONTROL
COPILOT
COPYBOY
CORAZON
CORNCOB
CORNDOG
CORNROW
COUNTON
DODGSON
DOGCHOW
DOGSHOW
DOGTROT
DOGWOOD
DOMINOS
DONATOR
DONEFOR
DORITOS
DOSIDOS
DOTEDON
DOTESON
DOVECOT

DOWNBOW
FORGOOD
FORSOOK
FOXTROT
GODUNOV
GOESFOR
GOINFOR
GOINGON
GOODJOB
GOODJOE
GOODSON
GOTOPOT
HOLDSON
HOLYCOW
HONCHOS
HOODOOS
HORIZON
HOTFOOT
HOTSHOT
HOTSPOT
HOUSTON
JOEBLOW
JOHNDOE
JOHNSON
KOWLOON
LOCATOR
LOCKBOX
LOGBOOK
LONGBOW
LONGTON
LONNROT
LOOKFOR
LOOKSON
LOWBLOW
LOWBROW
MOLOTOV
MONITOR
MONOCOT
MONOLOG
MONSOON
MOONDOG
MOUFLON
NONAGON
NONSTOP
NOSEJOB
POCONOS
POISSON
POLYGON
POMELOS
PONCHOS
PONTOON
POORBOX
POORBOY
PORTHOS
PORTION
POSTBOX
POSTHOC
POTHOOK
POTSHOT
ROADHOG
ROBESON
ROBOCOP
ROLLTOP
ROMANOV
ROOFTOP
ROOTFOR
ROPETOW
ROTATOR
ROUNDON
SOAPBOX
SODAPOP
SOFTTOP
SOLOMON

SOMEHOW
SOUPCON
TOELOOP
TOESHOE
TOLSTOI
TOLSTOY
TOMFOOL
TONELOC
TONEROW
TOOLBOX
TOPKNOT
TOREROS
TORSION
TOUCHON
TOYSHOP
WOBEGON
WOODLOT
WOODROW
WORKFOR
WORKSON
YOUKNOW

•0••••0
BOITANO
BOUNDTO
COLUMBO
COMESTO
CONBRIO
CORDERO
DOMINGO
GOLFPRO
GOTINTO
HOLDSTO
HORATIO
IONESCO
LONGAGO
LOOKSTO
LORENZO
MODESTO
MOGAMBO
MONTEGO
MORELLO
MOROCCO
NOCANDO
NONZERO
NOVARRO
POINTTO
POMPANO
PORTICO
ROBERTO
RODOLFO
SOANDSO
SOPRANO
TOBACCO
TORNADO
TORONTO
TORPEDO
TOURACO
VOLCANO
YOKOONO

••00•••
ALOOFLY
BLOODED
BLOOMED
BLOOMER
BLOOPED
BLOOPER
BROODED
BROODER
BROOKED
CHOOSER
CHOOSES

CLOONEY
CROOKED
CROONED
CROONER
DROOLED
DROOLER
DROOPED
FLOODED
FLOORED
GROOMED
GROOMER
GROOVED
GROOVES
PROOFED
PROOFER
SCOOPED
SCOOPER
SCOOTED
SCOOTER
SHOOFLY
SHOOING
SHOOINS
SHOOKUP
SHOOTAT
SHOOTER
SHOOTUP
SMOOTHS
SNOOKER
SNOOPED
SNOOPER
SNOOTED
SNOOZED
SNOOZES
SPOOFED
SPOOFER
SPOOKED
SPOOLED
SPOONED
SPOONER
STOODBY
STOODIN
STOODUP
STOOGES
STOOKEY
STOOLIE
STOOPED
STOOPTO
SWOONED
SWOOPED
SWOOSIE
TROOPED
TROOPER
WHOOPED
WHOOPEE

••O•O••

AMOROUS
APOCOPE
APOLOGY
AXOLOTL
BIOLOGY
BLOTOUT
BLOWOFF
BLOWOUT
BOOBOOS
BOOHOOS
BOOTOUT
COOKOFF
COOKOUT
DROPOFF
DROPOUT
ECOLOGY
ECONOMY
GEOLOGY
GNOMONS
GOODONE
GOOFOFF
GOOGOLS
HOODOOS
HOOPOES
HOOTOWL
IRONORE
IRONOUT
ISOGONS
ISOPODS
ISOTOPE
LAOCOON
LEONORA
LEOPOLD
LOOKOUT
ODOROUS
OLOROSO
OZONOUS
PHOTOED
PHOTOGS
PHOTONS
PHOTOOP
POOPOUT
PROBONO
PROLOGS
PROLONG
PROMOTE
PRONOUN
PROPOSE
PROSODY
PROTONS
PROVOKE
PROVOST
RIOLOBO
RIOTOUS
ROOTOUT
SAOTOME
SHOWOFF
SNOCONE
STOLONS
STOPOFF
TOOKOFF
TOOKOUT
TROTOUT
TWOFOLD
TWOSOME
TWOTONE
ZOOLOGY

••O••O•

ALOHAOE
ASOFNOW
BLOSSOM
BLOUSON
BOOBOOS
BOOHOOS
BOOMBOX
BRONCOS
BRONSON
CROUTON
EMOTION
EROSION
FRONTON
GOODJOB
GOODJOE
GOODSON
GROTTOS
GROWSON
HOODOOS
KNOSSOS
KNOWHOW
LAOCOON
LOOKFOR
LOOKSON
MOONDOG
OCONNOR
PHOTOOP
PLOSION
PLOWBOY
POORBOX
POORBOY
PROCTOR
PROCYON
ROOFTOP
ROOTFOR
SHOEBOX
SHORTOF
SHOTFOR
SHOWDOG
SNOWDON
SNOWJOB
SPOKEOF
SPONSOR
THOMSON
TOOLBOX
USOSHOW
WOODLOT
WOODROW

••O•••O

AVOCADO
CHORIZO
FLOCKTO
GIORGIO
GROMYKO
GROUCHO
LOOKSTO
OLOROSO
PROBONO
PROVISO
PROXIMO
RIOLOBO
SCORPIO
STOOPTO
WHOSWHO
WROTETO

•••OO••

ALTOONA
BABOONS
BAZOOKA
BEHOOVE
CABOOSE
CAHOOTS
COCOONS
ENROOTS
GALOOTS
INDOORS
LAGOONS
LLCOOLJ
MAROONS
METOOER
PALOOKA
PAPOOSE
REBOOTS
REHOOKS
RETOOLS
SALOONS
SCHOOLS
SCROOGE
TYCOONS
UNHOOKS
UNLOOSE
UPROOTS
VAMOOSE
YOKOONO

•••O•O•

AEROSOL
ALCOHOL
APROPOS
ARIOSOS
ARROYOS
BICOLOR
COMOROS
CREOSOL
DESOTOS
ESPOSOS
GASOHOL
GIGOLOS
GOTOPOT
KILOTON
KIMONOS
MALODOR
MOLOTOV
MONOCOT
MONOLOG
NABOKOV
OCTOPOD
ONTOPOF
POCONOS
REBOZOS
RECOLOR
ROBOCOP
SOLOMON
UPTONOW

•••O••O

ADDONTO
ALFONSO
ANTONIO
ARIOSTO
LESOTHO
MOROCCO
PRIORTO
RISOTTO
RODOLFO
SIROCCO
STOOPTO
TORONTO
YOKOONO

••••OO•

AIRCOOL
ANDSOON
BALLOON
BAMBOOS
BARROOM
BASSOON
BEDROOM
BIGFOOT
BOOBOOS
BOOHOOS
BOXWOOD
BOYHOOD
BUFFOON
BURGOOS
CARPOOL
CARTOON
CHEROOT
CHINOOK
CUCKOOS
DAGWOOD
DASBOOT
DAYBOOK
DAYROOM
DIDGOOD
DOGWOOD
DRAGOON
FESTOON
FORGOOD
FORSOOK
FRYCOOK
HARPOON
HENCOOP
HEYWOOD
HIPBOOT
HIPROOF
HOODOOS
HOTFOOT
INBLOOM
JIBBOOM
KOWLOON
LAMPOON
LAOCOON
LEGROOM
LOGBOOK
MANHOOD
MISTOOK
MONSOON
NEWLOOK
NEWMOON
OLDMOON
OUTDOOR
OUTLOOK
OXBLOOD
PARTOOK
PATROON
PHOTOOP
PLATOON
PLYWOOD
PONTOON
POTHOOK
PRECOOK
PRECOOL
RACCOON
RANGOON
REBLOOM
RECROOM
REDBOOK
REDWOOD
REPROOF
RESHOOT
SASSOON
SAWWOOD
SCHMOOS
SEAFOOD
SHADOOF
SKIBOOT
SKYHOOK
SUNROOF
SUNROOM
TAPROOM
TAPROOT
TATTOOS
TEAROOM
TOELOOP
TOMFOOL
TYPHOON
VANPOOL
WALLOON
WEBFOOT

••••O•O

CARDOZO
CUIBONO
GIACOMO
HANSOLO
LIMPOPO
MAFIOSO
NICCOLO
OLOROSO
ORINOCO
PICCOLO
PISCOPO
PROBONO
RIOLOBO
SAPPORO
TREMOLO
YOKOONO

•••••OO

BUGABOO
BUGALOO
KERCHOO
MRMAGOO
SHAMPOO
SKIDDOO

OP•••••

OPACITY
OPALINE
OPAQUES
OPENAIR
OPENBAR
OPENEND
OPENERS
OPENING
OPENPIT
OPENSEA
OPENSUP
OPENTOE
OPERAND
OPERATE
OPEROSE
OPHELIA
OPIATES
OPINERS
OPINING
OPINION
OPOSSUM
OPPOSED
OPPOSER
OPPOSES
OPPRESS
OPPUGNS
OPTICAL
OPTIMAL
OPTIMUM
OPTIONS
OPTSOUT
OPULENT

O•P••••

OMPHALI
ONPAPER
OPPOSED
OPPOSER
OPPOSES
OPPRESS
OPPUGNS
ORPHANS
ORPHEAN
ORPHEUS
ORPINES
OSPREYS

O••P•••

OFFPEAK
OILPANS
OLDPROS
OOMPAHS
OUTPACE
OUTPLAY
OUTPOST
OUTPUTS

O•••P••

OCCIPUT
OCTOPOD
OCTOPUS
OCTUPLE
OEDIPAL
OEDIPUS
OLYMPIA
OLYMPIC
OLYMPUS
ONPAPER
ONTOPOF
OPENPIT

O•••••P

OFFRAMP
OILLAMP
OLDCHAP
ONESTEP
OPENSUP
OUTCROP
OUTJUMP
OUTSTEP
OVERLAP
OWNEDUP

•OP••••

BOPPERS
BOPPING
COPIERS
COPILOT
COPIOUS
COPLAND
COPOUTS
COPPERS
COPPERY
COPPICE
COPPING
COPPOLA
COPSOUT
COPTERS
COPYBOY
COPYCAT
COPYING
COPYIST
DOPEOUT
DOPIEST
DOPPLER
FOPPERY
FOPPISH
GOPHERS
HOPEFUL
HOPKINS
HOPOVER
HOPPERS
HOPPING
HOPSOFF
HOPTOIT
KOPECKS
LOPPERS
LOPPING
MOPPERS
MOPPETS
MOPPING
POPCORN
POPEYED
POPGUNS
POPLARS
POPLINS
POPOFFS
POPOVER
POPPERS
POPPETS
POPPIES
POPPING
POPPINS
POPPLED
POPPLES
POPSOFF
POPSOUT
POPTART
POPTOPS
POPULAR
ROPEDIN
ROPESIN
ROPETOW
SOPHISM
SOPHIST
SOPPING
SOPRANO
SOPWITH
TOPAZES
TOPCOAT
TOPDOGS
TOPGUNS
TOPHATS
TOPIARY
TOPICAL
TOPKAPI
TOPKICK
TOPKNOT
TOPMAST
TOPMOST
TOPPERS
TOPPING
TOPPLED
TOPPLES
TOPSAIL
TOPSIDE
TOPSOFF
TOPSOIL
TOPSOUT
YOPLAIT

•O•P•••

BOPPERS
BOPPING
COMPACT
COMPANY
COMPARE
COMPASS
COMPEER
COMPELS
COMPETE
COMPILE
COMPLEX
COMPORT
COMPOSE
COMPOST
COMPOTE
COMPUTE
COOPERS
COOPING
COOPSUP
COOPTED
COPPERS
COPPERY
COPPICE
COPPING
COPPOLA
COUPLED
COUPLES
COUPLET
COUPONS
COWPEAS
COWPOKE
DOLPHIN
DOPPLER
FOPPERY
FOPPISH
GOMPERS
GOOPIER
GOSPELS
HOOPING
HOOPLAS
HOOPOES
HOPPERS
HOPPING
HOSPICE
HOTPOTS
LOOPERS
LOOPIER
LOOPING
LOPPERS
LOPPING
LOWPAID
MOPPERS
MOPPETS
MOPPING
MORPHED
NONPLUS
OOMPAHS
POMPANO
POMPEIA
POMPEII
POMPOMS
POMPONS
POMPOUS
POOPING
POOPOUT
POPPERS
POPPETS
POPPIES
POPPING
POPPINS
POPPLED
POPPLES
POTPIES
ROMPERS
ROMPING
SOAPBOX
SOAPERS
SOAPIER
SOAPING
SOPPING
SOUPCON
SOUPIER
SOUPSUP
TOPPERS
TOPPING
TOPPLED
TOPPLES
TORPEDO
TOSPARE
TOUPEES
TOWPATH
VOLPONE

•O••P••

COCKPIT
DOWNPAT
FOOTPAD
FOREPAW
GOLFPRO
GOTOPOT
HOTSPOT
HOTSPUR
NOTEPAD
PORKPIE
SODAPOP

•O•••P•

BOBHOPE
BOXTOPS
COLLOPS
CONCEPT
CORRUPT
DOLLOPS
FOLDUPS
FORCEPS
FOULUPS
GOESAPE
GOOFUPS
GOSSIPS
GOSSIPY
HOLDUPS
HOOKUPS
HOTCAPS
HOTLIPS
HOTTIPS
JOBHOPS
LOCKUPS
LOOKUPS
MOBCAPS
MOCKUPS
POPTOPS
TOECAPS
TOETAPS
TOPKAPI
TOSSUPS
TOWROPE
WORKUPS

•O••••P

BONEDUP
BONESUP
BOOSTUP
BOOTSUP
BORNEUP
BOUNDUP
BOXEDUP
BOXESUP
BOXSTEP
COILSUP
COMESUP
COOKSUP
COOPSUP
COUGHUP
COVERUP
COWSLIP
DOINGUP
DOLLSUP
FOLDSUP
FOULSUP
FOULTIP
GOINGUP
GOOFSUP
HOLDSUP
HOLEDUP
HOLESUP
HOOKSUP
JOINSUP
LOCKSUP
LOOKSUP
LOUSEUP
NONSLIP
NONSTOP
NOTRUMP
ROADMAP
ROBOCOP
ROLLSUP
ROLLTOP
ROOFTOP
ROUGHUP
ROUNDUP
SOAKSUP
SODAPOP
SOFTTOP
SOUPSUP
TOELOOP
TONEDUP
TONESUP
TOOLSUP
TOUCHUP
TOYSHOP
WOKENUP
WORKSUP
WORSHIP
WOUNDUP

••OP•••

ADOPTED
ADOPTEE
ADOPTER
CHOPPED
CHOPPER
CLOPPED
COOPERS
COOPING
COOPSUP
COOPTED
CROPPED
CROPPER
CROPSUP
DIOPTER
DROPINS
DROPLET
DROPOFF
DROPOUT
DROPPED
DROPPER
DROPSBY
DROPSIN
ELOPERS
ELOPING
FLOPPED
GOOPIER
GROPING
GROPIUS
HOOPING
HOOPLAS
HOOPOES
ISOPODS
LEOPARD
LEOPOLD
LOOPERS
LOOPIER
LOOPING
PEOPLED
PEOPLES
PLOPPED
POOPING
POOPOUT
PROPANE
PROPELS
PROPHET
PROPJET
PROPMAN
PROPMEN
PROPOSE
PROPPED
PROPSUP
REOPENS
SCOPING
SHOPPED
SHOPPER
SHOPPES
SLOPING
SLOPPED
STOPGAP
STOPOFF
STOPPED
STOPPER
STOPSIN
STOPSUP
TROPHIC
TROPICS
TROPISM
USOPENS
UTOPIAN
UTOPIAS
WHOPPED
WHOPPER

••O•P••

ADOLPHE
BLOOPED
BLOOPER
CHOMPED
CHOPPED
CHOPPER
CLOPPED
CROPPED
CROPPER
DROOPED
DROPPED
DROPPER
FLOPPED
FOOTPAD
GROUPED
GROUPER
GROUPIE
PLOPPED
PROMPTS
PROPPED
PROSPER
SCOOPED
SCOOPER
SCORPIO
SHOPPED
SHOPPER
SHOPPES
SHOTPUT
SLOPPED
SNOOPED
SNOOPER
SNOWPEA
STOMPED
STOOPED
STOOPTO
STOPPED
STOPPER
SWOOPED
TROOPED
TROOPER
TROUPER
TROUPES
WHOMPED
WHOOPED
WHOOPEE
WHOPPED
WHOPPER

••O••P•

APOCOPE
BLOWUPS
GOOFUPS
HOOKUPS
ISOTOPE
LOOKUPS

••O•••P

BLOWNUP
BLOWSUP
BOOSTUP
BOOTSUP
BROKEUP
BUOYSUP
CHOKEUP
CLOGSUP
CLOSEUP
COOKSUP
COOPSUP
CROPSUP
CROSSUP
EGOTRIP
GOOFSUP
GROWNUP
GROWSUP
HOOKSUP
LOOKSUP
PHOTOOP
PROPSUP
ROOFTOP
SHOOKUP
SHOOTUP
SHOWSUP
SLOWSUP
SNOWCAP
SPOKEUP
STOCKUP
STOODUP
STOPGAP
STOPSUP
STOREUP
TOOLSUP
TWOSTEP
WROTEUP

•••OP••

APROPOS
ATROPHY
BLOOPED
BLOOPER
CANOPUS
DROOPED
GOTOPOT
OCTOPOD
OCTOPUS
ONTOPOF
PANOPLY
SCOOPED
SCOOPER
SNOOPED
SNOOPER
STOOPED
STOOPTO
STROPHE
SWOOPED
TROOPED
TROOPER
UPTOPAR
WHOOPED
WHOOPEE
ZATOPEK

•••O•P•
RECOUPS
RUDOLPH

•••O••P
ROBOCOP
SHOOKUP
SHOOTUP
STOODUP

••••OP•
APOCOPE
BARHOPS
BIGTOPS
BISHOPS
BOBHOPE
BOXTOPS
CARHOPS
COLLOPS
CYCLOPS
DOLLOPS
ENTROPY
GALLOPS
HYSSOPS
ISOTOPE
JOBHOPS
LAPTOPS
LIMPOPO
PEGTOPS
PISCOPO
POPTOPS
RAGMOPS
RAGTOPS
REDTOPS
TIPTOPS
TOWROPE
UNSTOPS
WALLOPS
WETMOPS

••••O•P
BARSOAP
HENCOOP
INGROUP
PEASOUP
PHOTOOP
REGROUP
TOELOOP

•••••OP
AIRDROP
BELLHOP
BUSSTOP
DESKTOP
DEVELOP
DEWDROP
DUSTMOP
EARDROP
ENVELOP
FLATTOP
GUMDROP
HARDTOP
HENCOOP
HIGHTOP
HILLTOP
KERPLOP
MAINTOP
MILKSOP
NONSTOP
OUTCROP
PHOTOOP
PITSTOP
ROBOCOP
ROLLTOP
ROOFTOP
SCALLOP
SODAPOP
SOFTTOP
TANKTOP
TEASHOP
TIMECOP
TOELOOP
TOYSHOP
TREETOP

O••Q•••
OPAQUES

O•••Q••
OBLIQUE
OBLOQUY

O••••Q•
ONTHEQT

•OQ••••
LOQUATS

•O•Q•••
BOUQUET
COEQUAL
CONQUER
JOAQUIN
JONQUIL
MOSQUES
RORQUAL
TORQUES

•O••Q••
COMIQUE
MONIQUE

••OQ•••
CLOQUES
CROQUET

•••OQ••
BAROQUE
OBLOQUY

OR•••••
ORACLES
ORANGES
ORATING
ORATION
ORATORS
ORATORY
ORBISON
ORBITAL
ORBITED
ORBITER
ORCHARD
ORCHIDS
ORDAINS
ORDEALS
ORDERED
ORDERER
ORDERLY
ORDINAL
OREGANO
ORESTES
ORGANDY
ORGANIC
ORGANON
ORGANUM
ORGANZA
ORIENTE
ORIENTS
ORIFICE
ORIGAMI
ORIGINS
ORINOCO
ORIOLES
ORISONS
ORLANDO
ORLEANS
ORMANDY
ORMOLUS
ORNETTE
ORNITHO
OROTUND
OROURKE
ORPHANS
ORPHEAN
ORPHEUS
ORPINES
ORTOLAN
ORVILLE

O•R••••
OARLESS
OARLOCK
OBREGON
OGREISH
OTRANTO
OURSELF
OURTOWN

O••R•••
OBERLIN
OBTRUDE
OCARINA
ODOROUS
OFFRAMP
OFFROAD
OILRIGS
OLOROSO
ONAROLL
ONEROUS
ONORDER
ONTRIAL
OPERAND
OPERATE
OPEROSE
OPPRESS
OSPREYS
OSTRICH
OUTRACE
OUTRAGE
OUTRANK
OUTRUNS
OVERACT
OVERAGE
OVERALL
OVERATE
OVERAWE
OVERBIG
OVERBUY
OVERDID
OVERDUB
OVERDUE
OVEREAT
OVERFLY
OVERJOY
OVERLAP
OVERLAY
OVERLIE
OVERRAN
OVERRUN
OVERSAW
OVERSEA
OVERSEE
OVERTLY
OVERUSE

O•••R••
OAKTREE
OBSERVE
OBVERSE
OBVERTS
OEUVRES
OFFERED
OFFERER
OFSORTS
OLDPROS
OMICRON
ONTARIO
ONWARDS
ORDERED
ORDERER
ORDERLY
OROURKE
OSBORNE
OUTCROP
OUTDRAW
OUTDREW
OUTGREW
OUTGROW
OVERRAN
OVERRUN
OXCARTS
OXFORDS

O••••R•
OAKFERN
OBSCURE
OFASORT
OLESTRA
ONADARE
ONAGERS
ONBOARD
ONGUARD
ONSHORE
OPENERS
OPINERS
ORATORS
ORATORY
ORCHARD
OSTLERS
OUSTERS
OUTWARD
OUTWORE
OUTWORK
OUTWORN
OXYMORA
OYSTERS

O•••••R
OBTUSER
OCONNOR
OCTOBER
OFFERER
OFFHOUR
OFFICER
OFFYEAR
OFTENER
OLDSTER
OLIVIER
ONATEAR
ONORDER
ONPAPER
OPENAIR
OPENBAR
OPPOSER
ORBITER
ORDERER
OUTDOOR
OUTWEAR

•OR••••
AORISTS
BORATES
BORDERS
BOREDOM
BOREOUT
BORNEUP
BORODIN
BOROUGH
BORROWS
BORSCHT
BORZOIS
CORAZON
CORBELS
CORBETT
CORDAGE
CORDATE
CORDELL
CORDERO
CORDIAL
CORDING
CORDITE
CORDOBA
CORDONS
CORELLI
CORETTA
CORINTH
CORKAGE
CORKERS
CORKING
CORNCOB
CORNDOG
CORNEAL
CORNEAS
CORNELL
CORNERS
CORNETS
CORNFED
CORNICE
CORNIER
CORNILY
CORNING
CORNISH
CORNOIL
CORNROW
COROLLA
CORONAE
CORONAS
CORONET
CORRALS
CORRECT
CORRIDA
CORRODE
CORRUPT
CORSAGE
CORSAIR
CORSETS
CORSICA
CORTEGE
CORYELL
DORITOS
DORMANT
DORMERS
DORMICE
DOROTHY
DORSALS
DORSETT
FORAGED
FORAGER
FORAGES
FORBADE
FORBEAR
FORBIDS
FORBORE
FORCEPS
FORCERS
FORCING
FORDHAM
FORDING
FOREARM
FOREIGN
FORELEG
FOREMAN
FOREMEN
FOREPAW
FORERAN
FORERUN
FORESAW
FORESEE
FORESTS
FOREVER
FORFEIT
FORFEND
FORFREE
FORGAVE
FORGERS
FORGERY
FORGETS
FORGING
FORGIVE
FORGOES
FORGONE
FORGOOD
FORINTS
FORKERS
FORKFUL
FORKING
FORLIFE
FORLORN
FORMALS
FORMATS
FORMICA
FORMING
FORMOSA
FORMULA
FORREAL
FORRENT
FORREST
FORSAKE
FORSALE
FORSOOK
FORSTER
FORSURE
FORSYTH
FORTIES
FORTIFY
FORTRAN
FORTUNA
FORTUNE
FORWARD
FORWENT
GORDIAN
GORETEX
GORGETS
GORGING
GORGONS
GORIEST
GORILLA
GOROUND
HORATIO
HORIZON
HORMONE
HORNETS
HORNING
HORNIST
HORNSBY
HORRIFY
HORRORS
HORSIER
HORSING
KOREANS
KORUNAS
LORDING
LORDJIM
LORELEI
LORENZO
LORETTA
LORISES
LORRIES
MORAINE
MORALES
MORALLY
MORANIS
MORAVIA
MORDANT
MORDENT
MORDRED
MORELLO
MORESBY
MORGANA
MORGANS
MORMONS
MORNING
MOROCCO
MORPHED
MORROWS
MORSELS
MORTALS
MORTARS
MORTIFY
MORTISE
NORDICS
NORFOLK
NORIEGA
NORMALS
NORMAND
NORMANS
NORTHER
PORCHES
PORCINE
PORGIES
PORKERS
PORKPIE
PORSCHE
PORSENA
PORTAGE
PORTALS
PORTEND
PORTENT
PORTERS
PORTHOS
PORTICO
PORTION
PORTOLA
PORTRAY
RORQUAL
SORBATE
SORBETS
SORCERY
SORGHUM
SORITES
SORORAL
SORRELS
SORRIER
SORROWS
SORTERS
SORTIED
SORTIES
SORTING
TORCHED
TORCHES
TOREOFF
TOREOUT
TOREROS
TORMENT
TORNADO
TORNOUT
TOROIDS
TORONTO
TORPEDO
TORQUES
TORRENT
TORSION
TORTONI
TORYISM
WORDIER
WORDILY
WORDING
WORDONE
WOREOFF
WOREOUT
WORKDAY
WORKERS
WORKFOR
WORKING
WORKMAN
WORKMEN
WORKOFF
WORKOUT
WORKSIN
WORKSON
WORKSUP
WORKUPS
WORLDLY
WORMIER
WORNOFF
WORNOUT
WORRIED
WORRIER
WORRIES
WORSENS
WORSHIP
WORSTED

•O•R•••
BOARDED
BOARDER
BOERWAR
BOORISH
BORROWS
BOURBON
BOURREE
COARSEN
COARSER
COERCED
COERCES
COMRADE
CONRACK
CONREID
CORRALS
CORRECT
CORRIDA
CORRODE
CORRUPT
COURAGE
COURANT
COURIER
COURSED
COURSER
COURSES
COURTED
COURTLY
COWRIES
DOORDIE
DOORMAN
DOORMAT
DOORMEN
DOORWAY
DOUREST
DOWRIES
FORREAL
FORRENT
FORREST
FOURIER
FOURTHS
GOBROKE
GOURAMI
GOURDES
GOURMET
GOWRONG
HOARDED
HOARDER
HOARIER
HOARSEN
HOARSER
HORRIFY
HORRORS
HOTRODS
JOURDAN
JOURNAL
JOURNEY
JOYRIDE
LORRIES
LOURDES
LOUREED
LOWRISE
LOWROAD
MOORAGE
MOORHEN
MOORING
MOORISH
MORROWS
NOTRUMP
NOURISH
PODRIDA
POORBOX
POORBOY
POOREST
POURERS
POURING
POUROUT
POURSIN
ROARERS
ROARING
ROBROYS
SOARERS
SOARING
SOIREES
SOPRANO
SORRELS
SORRIER
SORROWS
SOURCED
SOURCES
SOUREST
SOURING
SOURISH
TOORDER
TORRENT
TOURACO
TOURERS
TOURING
TOURISM
TOURIST
TOURNEY
TOWROPE
WORRIED
WORRIER
WORRIES

•O••R••
BODEREK
BOLEROS
BOURREE
BOUTROS
BOWERED
COCHRAN
COHERED
COHERES
COHORTS
COLORED
COMFREY
COMOROS
CONBRIO
CONTRAS
CONTROL
CORNROW
COTERIE
COVERED
COVERUP
COWARDS
COWERED
DOGTROT
DOLORES
FORERAN
FORERUN
FORFREE
FORTRAN
FOXTROT
GOCARTS
GODFREY
GOFORIT
GOKARTS
GONERIL
GOVERNS
HOFBRAU
HOGARTH
HOMBRES
HOMERED
HOMERIC
HOMERUN
HONORED
HONOREE
HONORER
HOVERED
HOVERER
HOWARDS
JOFFREY
LONGRUN
LONNROT
LOUVRES
LOVERLY
LOWBRED
LOWBROW
LOWERED
MODERNS
MONARCH
MONGREL
MORDRED
MOTORED
NOSTRIL
NOSTRUM
NOTTRUE
NOVARRO
POLARIS
PORTRAY
POVERTY
POWERED
ROBARDS
ROBERTA
ROBERTO
ROBERTS
ROSERED
ROSTRUM
SOBERED
SOBERER
SOBERLY
SOLARIA
SORORAL
TONEROW
TOREROS
TOWARDS
TOWERED
WOLFRAM
WOODROW
YOGURTS

•O•••R•
BOATERS
BOBBERS
BOILERS
BOKHARA
BOMBARD
BOMBERS
BONEDRY
BONFIRE
BONKERS
BOOMERS
BOPPERS
BORDERS
BOTHERS
BOWLERS
BOWYERS
BOXCARS
BOYDORR
COALERS
COAXERS
COCHERE
CODGERS
COFFERS
COGBURN
COHEIRS
COINERS
COLBERT
COLLARD
COLLARS
COLOURS
COMBERS
COMFORT
COMPARE
COMPORT
CONAKRY
CONCERN
CONCERT
CONCORD
CONCURS
CONDORS
CONFERS
CONFIRM
CONFORM
CONGERS
CONJURE
CONKERS
CONNERY
CONNORS
CONSORT
CONTORT
CONVERT
COOKERS
COOKERY
COOLERS
COOPERS
COPIERS
COPPERS
COPPERY
COPTERS
CORDERO
CORKERS
CORNERS
COSTARS
COTTERS
COUGARS
COUNTRY
COUTURE
COWBIRD
COWGIRL
COWHERD
DOCKERS
DOCTORS
DODDERS
DODGERS
DOEUVRE
DOGCART
DOGEARS
DOLLARS
DORMERS
DOSSERS
DOWNERS
DOWSERS
FODDERS
FOGGERS
FOGHORN
FOLDERS
FOLGERS
FOLKART
FOOLERY
FOOTERS
FOPPERY
FORBORE
FORCERS
FOREARM
FORGERS
FORGERY
FORKERS
FORLORN
FORSURE
FORWARD
FOSTERS
FOULARD
FOUNDRY
FOWLERS
FOXFIRE
GODDARD
GOLFERS
GOLFPRO
GOMPERS
GOOBERS
GOPHERS
GOUGERS
HOAXERS
HOLDERS
HOLLERS
HOLYARK
HOMBURG
HONKERS
HONOURS
HOOFERS
HOOTERS
HOPPERS
HORRORS
HOSIERS
HOSIERY
HOTCARS
HOTWARS
HOTWIRE
HOWLERS
JOBBERS
JOGGERS
JOINERS
JOINERY
KOSHERS
LOADERS
LOAFERS
LOANERS
LOBBERS
LOCKERS
LODGERS
LOGGERS
LOITERS
LOMBARD
LOOKERS
LOOPERS
LOOTERS
LOPPERS
LOTTERY
LOUVERS
LOWBORN
MOANERS
MOCKERS
MOCKERY
MOHAIRS
MOILERS
MOLDERS
MOLIERE
MOLTERS
MONGERS
MOPPERS
MORTARS
MOTHERS
MOUSERS
NOCTURN
NODDERS
NONZERO
NOSHERS
NOTSURE
NOVARRO
NOWHERE
POLDERS
POLLERS
PONDERS
PONIARD
POPCORN
POPLARS
POPPERS
POPTART
PORKERS
PORTERS
POSEURS
POSTERN
POSTERS
POSTURE
POTHERB
POTHERS
POTTERS
POTTERY
POULTRY
POURERS
POUTERS
POWDERS
POWDERY

ROAMERS
ROARERS
ROBBERS
ROBBERY
ROCKERS
RODGERS
ROGUERY
ROLLERS
ROMPERS
ROOFERS
ROOKERY
ROOMERS
ROOTERS
ROSTERS
ROTTERS
ROUTERS
SOAKERS
SOAPERS
SOARERS
SOBBERS
SOJOURN
SOLDERS
SOLVERS
SOONERS
SORCERY
SORTERS
SOTHERE
SOTHERN
TOILERS
TONEARM
TONSURE
TOOTERS
TOPIARY
TOPPERS
TOSPARE
TOSSERS
TOTTERS
TOTTERY
TOURERS
TOUTERS
TOWCARS
TOWNERS
WONDERS
WOODARD
WOOFERS
WOOMERA
WORKERS
YOGHURT
YONKERS
YOWLERS
ZONKERS

•O••••R

BOARDER
BOASTER
BOERWAR
BOGGLER
BOLIVAR
BOLSTER
BONJOUR
BONNIER
BONSOIR
BOOSLER
BOOSTER
BOSSIER
BOTTLER
BOUDOIR
BOULDER
BOUNCER
BOUNDER
BOWDLER
BOYDORR
COALCAR
COALTAR
COARSER
COASTER
COBBLER
COCKIER
CODDLER
COLDWAR
COLLIER
COLLYER
COMFIER
COMPEER
CONIFER
CONQUER
CONTOUR
CORNIER
CORSAIR
COSTNER
COULTER
COUNTER
COURIER
COURSER
DOGSTAR
DONATOR
DONEFOR
DOODLER
DOPPLER
DOSSIER
DOTTIER
DOUBTER
DOVEBAR
DOWAGER
DOWDIER
DOWNIER
FOAMIER
FOGGIER
FORAGER
FORBEAR
FOREVER
FORSTER
FOUNDER
FOURIER
GOBBLER
GOESFOR
GOINFOR
GOODBAR
GOOFIER
GOOPIER
GOTOVER
GOUNDER
HOARDER
HOARIER
HOARSER
HOLSTER
HOLYWAR
HONORER
HOOSIER
HOPOVER
HORSIER
HOSTLER
HOTSPUR
HOVERER
HOWEVER
IONIZER
JOCULAR
JOINDER
JOLLIER
JOSTLER
JOUSTER
KOOKIER
LOAMIER
LOBBYER
LOBSTER
LOCATER
LOCATOR
LOESSER
LOFTIER
LOOKFOR
LOONIER
LOOPIER
LOUNGER
LOUSIER
LOWGEAR
LOWLIER
MOBSTER
MODELER
MODULAR
MOISTER
MOLDIER
MONIKER
MONITOR
MONOMER
MONSTER
MOOCHER
MOODIER
MOSSIER
MOULDER
MOUSIER
NODULAR
NOISIER
NONUSER
NORTHER
POACHER
PODGIER
POINTER
POITIER
POLITER
POLYMER
POPOVER
POPULAR
POSTWAR
POUNCER
POUNDER
POUTIER
ROASTER
ROCKIER
ROEDEER
ROISTER
ROLLBAR
ROOMIER
ROOSTER
ROOTFOR
ROTATOR
ROTIFER
ROUGHER
ROUNDER
ROWDIER
SOAPIER
SOBERER
SOGGIER
SOLDIER
SOLIDER
SOOTHER
SOOTIER
SORRIER
SOUNDER
SOUPIER
TOASTER
TODDLER
TOFFLER
TOORDER
TOUGHER
VOUCHER
VOYAGER
WOODIER
WOOLIER
WOOSTER
WOOZIER
WORDIER
WORKFOR
WORMIER
WORRIER
YODELER
YOUNGER
ZOELLER

••OR•••

ABOREAL
ABORTED
ADORERS
ADORING
ADORNED
AMOROUS
ANORAKS
BOORISH
CHORALE
CHORALS
CHORINE
CHORIZO
CHORTLE
CLORETS
DIORAMA
DOORDIE
DOORMAN
DOORMAT
DOORMEN
DOORWAY
FLORETS
FLORIDA
FLORINS
FLORIST
GEORGES
GEORGIA
GIORGIO
GLORIAS
GLORIED
GLORIES
GLORIFY
INORBIT
IVORIES
MOORAGE
MOORHEN
MOORING
MOORISH
ODOROUS
OLOROSO
ONORDER
POORBOX
POORBOY
POOREST
PRORATA
PRORATE
QUORUMS
REORDER
RIORITA
SCORERS
SCORING
SCORNED
SCORPIO
SHORING
SHORTED
SHORTEN
SHORTER
SHORTLY
SHORTOF
SNORERS
SNORING
SNORKEL
SNORTED
SNORTER
SPORRAN
SPORTED
STORAGE
STORERS
STOREUP
STOREYS
STORIED
STORIES
STORING
STORMED
SWOREAT
SWOREBY
SWOREIN
THOREAU
THORIUM
TOORDER
UXORIAL
WHORLED

••O•R••

EGOTRIP
FLOORED
FLOURED
OROURKE
PROGRAM
SCOURED
SCOURER
SCOURGE
SPORRAN
WOODROW

••O••R•

ADORERS
AVOWERS
BLOWDRY
BLOWERS
BOOMERS
BROKERS
CHOKERS
CLOSURE
CLOTURE
CLOVERS
COOKERS
COOKERY
COOLERS
COOPERS
CROWERS
DEODARS
DRONERS
DROVERS
EDOUARD
ELOPERS
EMOTERS
EVOKERS
FLOWERS
FLOWERY
FOOLERY
FOOTERS
FROWARD
GLOWERS
GOOBERS
GROCERS
GROCERY
GROWERS
HOOFERS
HOOTERS
IRONERS
IRONORE
ISOBARS
ISOMERS
LEONARD
LEONORA
LEOPARD
LEOTARD
LOOKERS
LOOPERS
LOOTERS
PLOVERS
PLOWERS
PROBERS
PROCURE
PROSERS
PROVERB
PROVERS
QUOTERS
RIOTERS
ROOFERS
ROOKERY
ROOMERS
ROOTERS
SCORERS
SCOTERS
SHOFARS
SHOVERS
SHOWERS
SHOWERY
SMOKERS
SNORERS
SOONERS
STOKERS
STONERS
STORERS
TOOTERS
TROCARS
TROWERS
TWOFERS
WOODARD
WOOFERS
WOOMERA

••O•••R

ADOPTER
ANOTHER
BLOCKER
BLONDER
BLOOMER
BLOOPER
BLOTTER
BLOWIER
BOOSLER
BOOSTER
BROADER
BROILER
BROODER
BROTHER
BROWNER
BROWSER
CHOICER
CHOOSER
CHOPPER
CHOWDER
CLOBBER
CLOCKER
CLOWDER
CROONER
CROPPER
CROSIER
CROSSER
CROWBAR
DIOPTER
DOODLER
DROLLER
DROOLER
DROPPER
FLOATER
FROWNER
GOODBAR
GOOFIER
GOOPIER
GROANER
GROLIER
GROOMER
GROSSER
GROUPER
GROUSER
GROWLER
HOOSIER
KNOCKER
KOOKIER
LOOKFOR
LOONIER
LOOPIER
MOOCHER
MOODIER
OCONNOR
ONORDER
PHONIER
PIONEER
PLODDER
PLOTTER
PROCTOR
PRODDER
PROFFER
PROOFER
PROSIER
PROSPER
PROUDER
PROWLER
REOCCUR
REORDER
ROOMIER
ROOSTER
ROOTFOR
SCOFFER
SCOLDER
SCOOPER
SCOOTER
SCOURER
SCOUTER
SCOWLER
SHOCKER
SHOOTER
SHOPPER
SHORTER
SHOTFOR
SHOUTER
SHOWIER
SLOBBER
SLOTCAR
SMOKIER
SMOLDER
SMOTHER
SNOOKER
SNOOPER
SNORTER
SNOWIER
SOOTHER
SOOTIER
SPOILER
SPONGER
SPONSOR
SPOOFER
SPOONER
SPOTTER
SPOUTER
STOLLER
STONIER
STOPPER
STOUTER
TOORDER
TROOPER
TROTTER
TROUPER
TROUSER
TWOSTAR
WHOEVER
WHOPPER
WOODIER
WOOLIER
WOOSTER
WOOZIER
WRONGER

•••OR••

ABSORBS
ACCORDS
ADSORBS
AFFORDS
ALSORAN
ALWORTH
ANDORRA
ANGORAS
ARBORED
ARMORED
ARMORER
ASSORTS
ASTORIA
ATWORST
AURORAE
AURORAL
AURORAS
BEGORRA
BYFORCE
BYWORDS
CALORIC
CALORIE
CAVORTS
CHLORAL
CIBORIA
COHORTS
COLORED
COMOROS
CYBORGS
DEBORAH
DECORUM
DEFORMS
DEHORNS
DEPORTS
DIVORCE
DOLORES
EFFORTS
EMPORIA
ENCORES
ENDORSE
ENFORCE
ENGORGE
ESCORTS
ESTORIL
EXHORTS
EXPORTS
EXTORTS
FAVORED
FEDORAS
FEMORAL
FLOORED
FURORES
GOFORIT
HONORED
HONOREE
HONORER
HUMORED
IGNORED
IGNORER
IGNORES
IMMORAL
IMPORTS
IMSORRY
INFORCE
INFORMS
LABORED
LABORER
LAPORTE
LASORDA
MAJORCA
MAJORED
MAYORAL
MEMOREX
MENORAH
MILORDS
MINORCA
MINORED
MOTORED
OFSORTS
OSBORNE
OXFORDS
PRIORTO
RAZORED
RECORDS
RECORKS
REFORMS
REMORAS
REMORSE
REPORTS
RESORBS
RESORTS
RETORTS
REWORDS
REWORKS
RUMORED
SAVORED
SENORAS
SENORES
SORORAL
SUBORNS
TABORET
THEOREM
TUTORED
UNCORKS
UNHORSE
UPBORNE

•••O•R•

ADJOURN
ANDORRA
ARBOURS
ARDOURS
ARMOIRE
ARMOURS
BEGORRA
BIGOTRY
COLOURS
DETOURS
DEVOURS
FAVOURS
HELOTRY
HONOURS
HUMOURS
IMSORRY
INBOARD
INDOORS
LABOURS
MASONRY
MEMOIRE
MEMOIRS
ONBOARD
RIGOURS
RUMOURS
SAVOURS
SAVOURY
SOJOURN
UPROARS
VALOURS
VAPOURS
VELOURS
VETOERS
VIGOURS

•••O••R

ALLOVER
ANDOVER
AREOLAR
ARMORER
BICOLOR
BIPOLAR
BLOOMER
BLOOPER
BROODER
CAJOLER
CAROLER
CHOOSER
CNTOWER
CROONER
DECODER
DEPOSER
DIDOVER
DIPOLAR
DROOLER
EMPOWER
ENCODER
FLYOVER
GETOVER
GOTOVER
GROOMER
HANOVER
HONORER
HOPOVER
IGNORER
INSOFAR
INTONER
INVOKER
LABORER
LAYOVER
LIEOVER
MALODOR
MANOWAR
METOOER
MONOMER
OCTOBER
OPPOSER
PALOMAR
POPOVER
PROOFER
PUTOVER
RANOVER
RECOLOR
RECOVER
REMOTER
REMOVER
RUNOVER
SAMOVAR
SCHOLAR
SCOOPER
SCOOTER
SHOOTER
SNOOKER
SNOOPER
SPOOFER
SPOONER
THROWER
TROOPER
UNCOVER
UPTOPAR
VANOCUR
WAGONER
WIDOWER

••••OR•

AIRPORT
AMATORY
AMPHORA
ANCHORS
ANYMORE
APRIORI
ARDMORE
ARTFORM
ARTWORK
ASHFORD
AUTHORS
BAILORS
BETTORS
BIGHORN
BOYDORR
CANTORS
CAPTORS
CARPORT
CENSORS
CHICORY
CLAMORS
COMFORT
COMPORT
CONCORD
CONDORS
CONFORM
CONNORS
CONSORT
CONTORT
CURSORS
CURSORY
DEBTORS
DEPLORE
DISCORD
DISPORT
DISTORT
DOCTORS
EDITORS
ENAMORS
EXPLORE
EYESORE
FACTORS
FACTORY
FERVORS
FLAVORS
FLEXORS
FOGHORN
FORBORE
FORLORN
GAYLORD
GIFFORD
GILMORE
GREGORY
HARBORS
HAYFORK
HECTORS
HICKORY
HISTORY
HORRORS
IMPLORE
INAWORD
INDOORS
INKHORN
INSHORT
INSTORE
IRONORE
ISADORA
JETPORT
JUNIORS
KEYWORD
LANFORD
LASTORY
LAWFORD
LECTORS
LEGHORN
LEGWORK
LEONORA
LESSORS
LIQUORS
LOWBORN
MAXBORN
MENTORS
METEORS
MIRRORS
MISWORD
MITFORD
MUMFORD
NETWORK
NEWBORN
NEWPORT
NEWYORK
OFASORT
ONSHORE
ORATORS
ORATORY
OUTWORE
OUTWORK
OUTWORN
OXYMORA
PANDORA
PARLORS
PASTORS
PERFORM
PILLORY
PLEXORS
POPCORN
PRESORT
PURPORT
RAPPORT
RAPTORS
RECTORS
RECTORY
REDFORD
RESTORE
RHETORS
RIPCORD
RIPTORN
SAILORS
SANBORN
SANFORD
SAPPORO
SAVIORS
SAXHORN
SEABORG
SEAPORT
SECTORS
SENIORS
SENSORS
SENSORY
STATORS
STUPORS
SUCCORS
SUITORS
SUPPORT
TAILORS
TENSORS
TERRORS
TINHORN
TINWORK
TREMORS
TRICORN
UNICORN
UNIFORM
UNSHORN
VECTORS
VENDORS
VICTORS
VICTORY
WALDORF
WARLORD
WAXWORK
WAYWORN
WILFORD

••••O•R

BALFOUR
BONJOUR
BONSOIR
BOUDOIR
BOYDORR
CANDOUR
CONTOUR
ENAMOUR
FERVOUR
FLAVOUR
GLAMOUR
HARBOUR
LASSOER
MANHOUR
METOOER
OFFHOUR
OUTDOOR
PARLOUR
PAVIOUR
RANCOUR
SEYMOUR
SUCCOUR
TAMBOUR
TENFOUR

•••••OR

ABETTOR
ADAPTOR
ADVISOR
AERATOR
ALIENOR
ASKSFOR
AUDITOR
AVIATOR
BELABOR
BICOLOR
CALLFOR
CAMPHOR
CAREFOR
CLANGOR
CREATOR
CURATOR
DIVISOR
DONATOR
DONEFOR
ECUADOR
ELEANOR
ELECTOR
EMPEROR
ENACTOR
EQUATOR
ERECTOR
EXACTOR
FALLFOR
FEELFOR

FELLFOR
FELTFOR
GOESFOR
GOINFOR
GRANTOR
GUNSFOR
GYRATOR
HUMIDOR
INCISOR
INERROR
INFAVOR
JANITOR
KEILLOR
LAIDFOR
LANGUOR
LAYSFOR
LOCATOR
LOOKFOR
MADEFOR
MAKEFOR
MALODOR
MARKHOR
MATADOR
MIRADOR
MONITOR
NEGATOR
OCONNOR
OUTDOOR
PAIDFOR
PASSFOR
PAYSFOR
PICADOR
PINEFOR
PRAETOR
PRAYFOR
PROCTOR
REACTOR
REALTOR
RECOLOR
ROOTFOR
ROTATOR
SCISSOR
SENATOR
SENDFOR
SENTFOR
SHOTFOR
SPECTOR
SPONSOR
SQUALOR
STENTOR
TEMBLOR
TRACTOR
TRAITOR
VISITOR
WARRIOR
WENTFOR
WHATFOR
WINDSOR
WORKFOR

OS•••••
OSBORNE
OSCEOLA
OSCINES
OSHKOSH
OSMONDS
OSMOSED
OSMOSES
OSMOSIS
OSMOTIC
OSPREYS
OSSICLE
OSSIFIC
OSTEOID
OSTLERS
OSTRICH

O•S••••
OBSCENE
OBSCURE
OBSERVE
OFSORTS
ONSHORE
ONSIGHT
ONSTAGE
OSSICLE
OSSIFIC
OUSTERS
OUSTING
OYSTERS

O••S•••
ODYSSEY
OFASORT
OFFSETS
OFFSIDE
OFFSITE
OILSKIN
OLDSTER
OLESTRA
ONASSIS
ONESELF
ONESHOT
ONESTEP
OPOSSUM
OPTSOUT
ORESTES
ORISONS
OURSELF
OUTSELL
OUTSETS
OUTSIDE
OUTSIZE
OUTSOLD
OUTSTEP

O•••S••
OBLASTS
OBOISTS
OBTUSER
ODYSSEY
ONASSIS
OPENSEA
OPENSUP
OPOSSUM
OPPOSED
OPPOSER
OPPOSES
ORBISON
OSMOSED
OSMOSES
OSMOSIS
OVERSAW
OVERSEA
OVERSEE

O••••S•
OAKMOSS
OARLESS
OBELISK
OBVERSE
OCULIST
ODDNESS
OFFBASE
OFFENSE
OGREISH
OILIEST
OKHOTSK
OLDNESS
OLDWEST
OLEMISS
OLOROSO
ONENESS
OPEROSE
OPPRESS
OSHKOSH
OUTCAST
OUTLAST
OUTPOST
OVERUSE
OXIDASE

O•••••S
OAKMOSS
OARLESS
OBJECTS
OBLASTS
OBLATES
OBLIGES
OBLONGS
OBOISTS
OBTAINS
OBTUNDS
OBVERTS
OBVIOUS
OCCULTS
OCEANUS
OCELOTS
OCTANES
OCTANTS
OCTAVES
OCTAVOS
OCTOPUS
ODDJOBS
ODDLOTS
ODDNESS
ODOROUS
OEDIPUS
OEUVRES
OFFENDS
OFFICES
OFFSETS
OFSORTS
OGDOADS
OGLALAS
OHIOANS
OILCANS
OILPANS
OILRIGS
OJIBWAS
OLDDAYS
OLDNESS
OLDNEWS
OLDPROS
OLEATES
OLEMISS
OLYMPUS
OMELETS
OMINOUS
OMNIBUS
ONAGERS
ONASSIS
ONEIDAS
ONENESS
ONEROUS
ONWARDS
OOCYTES
OOLITES
OOLITHS
OOMPAHS
OPAQUES
OPENERS
OPIATES
OPINERS
OPPOSES
OPPRESS
OPPUGNS
OPTIONS
ORACLES
ORANGES
ORATORS
ORCHIDS
ORDAINS
ORDEALS
ORESTES
ORIENTS
ORIGINS
ORIOLES
ORISONS
ORLEANS
ORMOLUS
ORPHANS
ORPHEUS
ORPINES
OSCINES
OSMONDS
OSMOSES
OSMOSIS
OSPREYS
OSTLERS
OTTAWAS
OUSTERS
OUTACTS
OUTAGES
OUTBIDS
OUTDOES
OUTEATS
OUTFITS
OUTGOES
OUTGUNS
OUTHITS
OUTINGS
OUTLAWS
OUTLAYS
OUTLETS
OUTPUTS
OUTRUNS
OUTSETS
OUTWITS
OXCARTS
OXFORDS
OYSTERS
OZONOUS

•OS••••
BOSKETS
BOSSIER
BOSSILY
BOSSING
BOSWELL
COSIGNS
COSINES
COSSACK
COSSETS
COSTAIN
COSTARS
COSTING
COSTNER
COSTUME
DOSAGES
DOSIDOS
DOSSALS
DOSSERS
DOSSIER
FOSDICK
FOSSILS
FOSTERS
GOSHAWK
GOSLING
GOSPELS
GOSSETT
GOSSIPS
GOSSIPY
HOSANNA
HOSIERS
HOSIERY
HOSKINS
HOSPICE
HOSTAGE
HOSTELS
HOSTESS
HOSTILE
HOSTING
HOSTLER
JOSHING
JOSTLED
JOSTLER
JOSTLES
KOSHERS
KOSYGIN
LOSEOUT
LOSESIT
LOSTOUT
MOSAICS
MOSELLE
MOSEYED
MOSLEMS
MOSQUES
MOSSIER
MOSSING
NOSEBAG
NOSEEUM
NOSEGAY
NOSEJOB
NOSEOUT
NOSHERS
NOSHING
NOSHOWS
NOSIEST
NOSTRIL
NOSTRUM
NOSWEAT
POSADAS
POSEURS
POSHEST
POSITED
POSSESS
POSSETS
POSSUMS
POSTAGE
POSTBOX
POSTERN
POSTERS
POSTHOC
POSTING
POSTMAN
POSTMEN
POSTURE
POSTWAR
ROSALIE
ROSANNA
ROSANNE
ROSEATE
ROSEBUD
ROSELLE
ROSEOIL
ROSERED
ROSETTA
ROSETTE
ROSSINI
ROSSSEA
ROSTAND
ROSTERS
ROSTRUM
ROSWELL
SOSUEME
TOSCALE
TOSHIBA
TOSPARE
TOSSERS
TOSSING
TOSSOFF
TOSSOUT
TOSSUPS
TOSTADA

•O•S•••
BOASTED
BOASTER
BOBSLED
BOLSHOI
BOLSTER
BONSOIR
BOOSLER
BOOSTED
BOOSTER
BOOSTUP
BORSCHT
BOSSIER
BOSSILY
BOSSING
BOWSAWS
BOWSOUT
BOXSEAT
BOXSTEP
COASTAL
COASTED
COASTER
CONSENT
CONSIGN
CONSIST
CONSOLE
CONSORT
CONSULS
CONSULT
CONSUME
COPSOUT
CORSAGE
CORSAIR
CORSETS
CORSICA
COSSACK
COSSETS
COUSINS
COWSLIP
DOESKIN
DOGSHOW
DOGSLED
DOGSTAR
DORSALS
DORSETT
DOSSALS
DOSSERS
DOSSIER
DOUSING
DOWSERS
DOWSING
FOBSOFF
FOCSLES
FOISTED
FORSAKE
FORSALE
FORSOOK
FORSTER
FORSURE
FORSYTH
FOSSILS
GODSEND
GODSONS
GOESAPE
GOESBAD
GOESFOR
GOESOFF
GOESOUT
GOOSING
GOSSETT
GOSSIPS
GOSSIPY
HOISTED
HOLSTER
HOOSIER
HOPSOFF
HORSIER
HORSING
HOTSEAT
HOTSHOT
HOTSPOT
HOTSPUR
HOUSING
HOUSMAN
HOUSTON
JOISTED
JOUSTED
JOUSTER
LOBSTER
LOESSER
LOESSES
LOGSOFF
LOGSOUT
LOOSELY
LOOSENS
LOOSEST
LOOSING
LOUSEUP
LOUSIER
LOUSILY
LOUSING
MOBSTER
MOISTEN
MOISTER
MOISTLY
MONSOON
MONSTER
MORSELS
MOSSIER
MOSSING
MOUSERS
MOUSIER
MOUSING
MOUSSED
MOUSSES
NODSOFF
NOISIER
NOISILY
NOISING
NOISOME
NONSELF
NONSKID
NONSLIP
NONSTOP
NOOSING
NOTSURE
POISING
POISONS
POISSON
POPSOFF
POPSOUT
PORSCHE
PORSENA
POSSESS
POSSETS
POSSUMS
POTSDAM
POTSHOT
ROASTED
ROASTER
ROISTER
ROOSTED
ROOSTER
ROSSINI
ROSSSEA
ROUSING
ROUSTED
TOASTED
TOASTER
TOCSINS
TOESHOE
TOLSTOI
TOLSTOY
TONSILS
TONSURE
TOPSAIL
TOPSIDE
TOPSOFF
TOPSOIL
TOPSOUT
TORSION
TOSSERS
TOSSING
TOSSOFF
TOSSOUT
TOSSUPS
TOUSLED
TOUSLES
TOYSHOP
WOOSTER
WORSENS
WORSHIP
WORSTED
ZOYSIAS

•O••S••
AORISTS
BOLUSES
BONESUP
BONUSES
BOOTSUP
BOXESIN
BOXESUP
COARSEN
COARSER
COHOSTS
COILSUP
COLOSSI
COMESAT
COMESBY
COMESIN
COMESON
COMESTO
COMESUP
COOKSUP
COOLSIT
COOPSUP
COUNSEL
COURSED
COURSER
COURSES
DODGSON
DOLLSUP
DOTESON
FOCUSED
FOCUSES
FOLDSUP
FOOTSIE
FORESAW
FORESEE
FORESTS
FOULSUP
GOODSON
GOOFSUP
HOARSEN
HOARSER
HOLDSON
HOLDSTO
HOLDSUP
HOLESUP
HOLYSEE
HONESTY
HOOFSIT
HOOKSUP
HOOTSAT
HORNSBY
IONESCO
JOCASTA
JOHNSON
JOINSIN
JOINSUP
LOCKSUP
LOCUSTS
LOESSER
LOESSES
LOOKSAT
LOOKSEE
LOOKSIN
LOOKSON
LOOKSTO
LOOKSUP
LORISES
LOSESIT
LOTUSES
MODESTO
MODESTY
MODISTE
MOLESTS
MOONSET
MORESBY
MOUSSED
MOUSSES
MOVESIN
NONUSER
POISSON
POKESAT
POURSIN
ROBESON
ROBUSTA
ROLLSUP
ROPESIN
ROSSSEA
SOAKSUP
SOCKSIN
SOUPSUP
TONESUP
TOOLSUP
TOOTSIE
VOTESIN
WOEISME
WOOLSEY
WORKSIN
WORKSON
WORKSUP
ZOOMSIN

•O•••S•
BOLDEST
BOMBAST
BONEASH
BONIEST
BOOKISH
BOORISH
COCHISE
CODFISH
COEXIST
COLDEST
COLOSSI
COLTISH
COMBUST
COMPASS
COMPOSE
COMPOST
CONCISE
CONFESS
CONFUSE
CONGEST
CONSIST
CONTEST
CONTUSE
COOLEST
COPYIST
CORNISH
COYNESS
COZIEST
DOGFISH
DOLTISH
DONJOSE
DOPIEST
DOUREST
FOGYISH
FOGYISM
FONDEST
FOOLISH
FOPPISH
FORMOSA
FORREST
FOULEST
FOXIEST
GOATISH
GODDESS
GOOIEST
GORIEST
GOULASH
HOGWASH
HOLIEST
HOMIEST
HORNIST
HOSTESS
HOTNESS
HOTTEST
JOYLESS
KOMATSU
LOGIEST
LONGEST
LONGISH
LOOSEST
LOUDEST
LOWNESS
LOWRISE
MOLLUSK
MOMBASA
MONKISH
MOORISH
MORTISE
NOBLEST
NOSIEST
NOURISH
POETESS
POKIEST
POLOIST
POOREST
POSHEST
POSSESS
ROGUISH
ROMANSH
SOANDSO
SOFTEST
SOLOIST
SOONEST
SOPHISM
SOPHIST
SOUREST
SOURISH
TOELESS
TONIEST
TOPMAST
TOPMOST
TORYISM
TOURISM
TOURIST
WOLFISH

•O••••S
AORISTS
AOUDADS
BOATERS
BOBBERS
BOBBIES
BOBBINS
BOBBLES
BOBCATS
BODEGAS
BODICES
BODKINS
BOGGLES
BOILERS
BOLEROS
BOLIDES
BOLUSES
BOMBERS
BONBONS
BONGOES
BONITOS
BONKERS
BONNETS
BONUSES
BOOBIES
BOOBOOS
BOODLES
BOOGIES
BOOHOOS
BOOKIES
BOOMERS
BOONIES
BOOTEES
BOOTIES
BOPPERS
BORATES
BORDERS
BORROWS
BORZOIS
BOSKETS
BOTCHES
BOTHERS
BOTTLES
BOTTOMS
BOUNCES
BOUTROS
BOVINES
BOWFINS
BOWLERS
BOWSAWS
BOWTIES
BOWWOWS
BOWYERS
BOXCARS
BOXFULS
BOXTOPS
COACHES
COALERS
COALGAS
COAXERS
COBBLES
COBWEBS
COCKLES
COCOONS
CODDLES
CODGERS
CODICES
COEDITS
COERCES
COEVALS
COFFEES
COFFERS
COGNACS
COHEIRS
COHERES
COHORTS
COHOSTS
COINERS
COLLARS
COLLETS
COLLIES
COLLINS
COLLOPS
COLOBUS
COLONES
COLOURS
COLUMNS
COMBATS
COMBERS
COMEONS
COMFITS
COMINGS
COMMITS
COMMONS
COMOROS
COMPASS
COMPELS
CONCHES
CONCURS
CONDORS
CONFABS
CONFERS
CONFESS
CONGERS
CONJOBS
CONKERS
CONNORS
CONSULS
CONTRAS
CONVEYS
CONVOYS
COOKERS
COOKIES
COOLERS
COOPERS
COOTIES
COPIERS
COPIOUS
COPOUTS
COPPERS
COPTERS
CORBELS
CORDONS
CORKERS
CORNEAS
CORNERS
CORNETS
CORONAS
CORRALS
CORSETS
COSIGNS
COSINES
COSSETS
COSTARS
COTTERS
COTTONS
COUCHES
COUGARS
COULEES
COUPLES
COUPONS
COURSES
COUSINS
COWARDS
COWBOYS
COWPEAS
COWRIES
COYNESS
COYOTES
COZZENS
DOBBINS
DOCENTS
DOCKERS
DOCKETS
DOCTORS
DODDERS
DODGERS
DOGDAYS
DOGEARS
DOGGIES
DOGLEGS
DOGTAGS
DOILIES
DOLLARS
DOLLIES
DOLLOPS
DOLMANS
DOLMENS
DOLORES
DOMAINS
DOMINOS
DONATES
DONJONS
DONKEYS
DOODADS
DOODLES
DOOZIES
DORITOS
DORMERS
DORSALS
DOSAGES
DOSIDOS
DOSSALS
DOSSERS
DOTTLES
DOUBLES
DOUGLAS
DOWNERS
DOWRIES
DOWSERS

EOLITHS
FOCSLES
FOCUSES
FODDERS
FOGBOWS
FOGGERS
FOIBLES
FOLDERS
FOLDUPS
FOLGERS
FOLLIES
FOLLOWS
FOMENTS
FONDLES
FONDUES
FOOTERS
FOOZLES
FORAGES
FORBIDS
FORCEPS
FORCERS
FORESTS
FORGERS
FORGETS
FORGOES
FORINTS
FORKERS
FORMALS
FORMATS
FORTIES
FOSSILS
FOSTERS
FOULUPS
FOURTHS
FOWLERS
GOALIES
GOATEES
GOBBLES
GOBLETS
GOBLINS
GOCARTS
GODDESS
GODSONS
GODWITS
GOGGLES
GOKARTS
GOLFERS
GOMPERS
GOOBERS
GOODBYS
GOODIES
GOOFUPS
GOOGOLS
GOPHERS
GORGETS
GORGONS
GOSPELS
GOSSIPS
GOTCHAS
GOTHICS
GOUGERS
GOURDES
GOVERNS
HOAGIES
HOAXERS
HOBBIES
HOBBITS
HOBBLES
HOBNOBS
HOGTIES
HOLDERS
HOLDUPS
HOLLERS
HOLLIES
HOLLOWS
HOMBRES
HONCHOS
HONKERS
HONOURS
HOODOOS
HOOFERS
HOOHAHS
HOOKAHS
HOOKUPS
HOOPLAS
HOOPOES
HOOTERS
HOPKINS
HOPPERS
HORNETS
HORRORS
HOSIERS
HOSKINS
HOSTELS
HOSTESS
HOTBEDS
HOTCAPS
HOTCARS
HOTDOGS
HOTLIPS
HOTNESS
HOTPOTS
HOTRODS
HOTTIPS
HOTTUBS
HOTWARS
HOWARDS
HOWDAHS
HOWELLS
HOWLERS
HOYDENS
IODATES
IODIDES
IODIZES
IOMOTHS
IONIZES
JOBBERS
JOBHOPS
JOBLOTS
JOCKEYS
JOGGERS
JOGGLES
JOINERS
JOLLIES
JOSTLES
JOUNCES
JOYLESS
KOBOLDS
KODIAKS
KOPECKS
KOREANS
KORUNAS
KOSHERS
KOWTOWS
LOACHES
LOADERS
LOAFERS
LOANERS
LOATHES
LOBBERS
LOBBIES
LOCALES
LOCATES
LOCKERS
LOCKETS
LOCKINS
LOCKUPS
LOCUSTS
LODGERS
LOESSES
LOGGERS
LOGGIAS
LOGGINS
LOGJAMS
LOITERS
LOLLIES
LONGUES
LOOFAHS
LOOKERS
LOOKUPS
LOONIES
LOOPERS
LOOSENS
LOOTERS
LOPPERS
LOQUATS
LORISES
LORRIES
LOTIONS
LOTUSES
LOUNGES
LOURDES
LOUVERS
LOUVRES
LOVEINS
LOWBOYS
LOWNESS
MOANERS
MOBCAPS
MOBILES
MOCKERS
MOCKUPS
MODELAS
MODELTS
MODERNS
MODULES
MOHAIRS
MOHAWKS
MOILERS
MOLDERS
MOLESTS
MOLTERS
MOMENTS
MOMMIES
MONDAYS
MONGERS
MONGOLS
MONKEES
MONKEYS
MOOCHES
MOPPERS
MOPPETS
MORALES
MORANIS
MORGANS
MORMONS
MORROWS
MORSELS
MORTALS
MORTARS
MOSAICS
MOSLEMS
MOSQUES
MOTHERS
MOTIONS
MOTIVES
MOTTLES
MOTTOES
MOUSERS
MOUSSES
MOUTONS
NOCUOUS
NODDERS
NODULES
NOETICS
NOGALES
NOGGINS
NOKOMIS
NONCOMS
NONPLUS
NOODLES
NORDICS
NORMALS
NORMANS
NOSHERS
NOSHOWS
NOTATES
NOTCHES
NOTICES
NOTIONS
NOUGATS
NOVENAS
NOVICES
NOXIOUS
NOZZLES
OOCYTES
OOLITES
OOLITHS
OOMPAHS
POACHES
POBOXES
POCKETS
POCONOS
PODIUMS
POETESS
POETICS
POISONS
POLARIS
POLDERS
POLICES
POLLENS
POLLERS
POMADES
POMELOS
POMMELS
POMPOMS
POMPONS
POMPOUS
PONCHOS
PONDERS
PONGIDS
PONTIUS
POOCHES
POODLES
POPGUNS
POPLARS
POPLINS
POPOFFS
POPPERS
POPPETS
POPPIES
POPPINS
POPPLES
POPTOPS
PORCHES
PORGIES
PORKERS
PORTALS
PORTERS
PORTHOS
POSADAS
POSEURS
POSSESS
POSSETS
POSSUMS
POSTERS
POTAGES
POTFULS
POTHERS
POTIONS
POTPIES
POTTERS
POUCHES
POUNCES
POURERS
POUTERS
POWDERS
POWWOWS
ROACHES
ROADIES
ROAMERS
ROARERS
ROBARDS
ROBBERS
ROBBINS
ROBERTS
ROBROYS
ROCKERS
ROCKETS
ROCKIES
RODENTS
RODGERS
ROLAIDS
ROLLERS
ROLLINS
ROMNEYS
ROMPERS
ROMULUS
RONDELS
ROOFERS
ROOKIES
ROOMERS
ROOMIES
ROOTERS
ROSTERS
ROTATES
ROTTERS
ROUTERS
ROWDIES
SOAKERS
SOAPERS
SOARERS
SOBBERS
SOCIALS
SOCKETS
SOFFITS
SOFTENS
SOFTIES
SOIREES
SOLACES
SOLDERS
SOLUTES
SOLVERS
SOMALIS
SONATAS
SONNETS
SOONERS
SOOTHES
SORBETS
SORITES
SORRELS
SORROWS
SORTERS
SORTIES
SOURCES
SOVIETS
SOWBUGS
TOADIES
TOCSINS
TODDIES
TODDLES
TOECAPS
TOELESS
TOETAPS
TOFFEES
TOGGLES
TOILERS
TOILETS
TOLTECS
TOMBOYS
TOMCATS
TOMTITS
TOMTOMS
TONGANS
TONGUES
TONSILS
TOOTERS
TOOTLES
TOPAZES
TOPDOGS
TOPGUNS
TOPHATS
TOPPERS
TOPPLES
TORCHES
TOREROS
TOROIDS
TORQUES
TOSSERS
TOSSUPS
TOTTERS
TOUCANS
TOUCHES
TOUPEES
TOURERS
TOUSLES
TOUTERS
TOWARDS
TOWCARS
TOWHEES
TOWNERS
TOWNIES
TOYDOGS
VOLLEYS
VOLUMES
VOTECHS
VOUCHES
VOYAGES
WOBBLES
WOMBATS
WONDERS
WONTONS
WOODIES
WOOFERS
WOOLENS
WOOLIES
WORKERS
WORKUPS
WORRIES
WORSENS
YOGURTS
YONKERS
YOUMANS
YOWLERS
ZODIACS
ZOMBIES
ZONKERS
ZOUAVES
ZOYSIAS

••OS•••

ANOSMIA
ANOSMIC
APOSTLE
BLOSSOM
BOOSLER
BOOSTED
BOOSTER
BOOSTUP
BROSNAN
CLOSEIN
CLOSELY
CLOSEST
CLOSETS
CLOSEUP
CLOSING
CLOSURE
CROSIER
CROSSED
CROSSER
CROSSES
CROSSLY
CROSSUP
EROSION
EROSIVE
FLOSSED
FLOSSES
FROSTED
GHOSTED
GHOSTLY
GLOSSAE
GLOSSED
GLOSSES
GNOSTIC
GOOSING
GROSSED
GROSSER
GROSSES
GROSSLY
HOOSIER
KNOSSOS
KTOSLIN
LOOSELY
LOOSENS
LOOSEST
LOOSING
NOOSING
OPOSSUM
PLOSION
PLOSIVE
PROSAIC
PROSERS
PROSIER
PROSILY
PROSING
PROSODY
PROSPER
ROOSTED
ROOSTER
SKOSHES
SLOSHED
SLOSHES
TWOSOME
TWOSTAR
TWOSTEP
USOSHOW
WHOSWHO
WOOSTER

••O•S••

AROUSAL
AROUSED
AROUSES
BLOSSOM
BLOUSED
BLOUSES
BLOUSON
BLOWSIN
BLOWSIT
BLOWSUP
BOOTSUP
BRONSON
BROWSED
BROWSER
BROWSES
BUOYSUP
CHOMSKY
CHOOSER
CHOOSES
CLOGSUP
COOKSUP
COOLSIT
COOPSUP
CROESUS
CROPSUP
CROSSED
CROSSER
CROSSES
CROSSLY
CROSSUP
DROPSBY
DROPSIN
DROWSED
DROWSES
EGOISTS
FLOSSED
FLOSSES
FLOTSAM
FOOTSIE
GLOSSAE
GLOSSED
GLOSSES
GOODSON
GOOFSUP
GROSSED
GROSSER
GROSSES
GROSSLY
GROUSED
GROUSER
GROUSES
GROWSON
GROWSUP
HOOFSIT
HOOKSUP
HOOTSAT
KNOSSOS
LOOKSAT
LOOKSEE
LOOKSIN
LOOKSON
LOOKSTO
LOOKSUP
MAOISTS
MOONSET
OBOISTS
OPOSSUM
PIOUSLY
PROPSUP
QUONSET
SHOWSIN
SHOWSUP
SLOWSUP
SNOWSIN
SPONSOR
SPOUSAL
SPOUSES
STOPSIN
STOPSUP
SWOOSIE
TAOISTS
THOMSON
TOOLSUP
TOOTSIE
TROTSKY
TROUSER
VRONSKY
WOOLSEY
ZOOMSIN

••O••S•

ABOLISH
AGONIST
AMONGST
BIOMASS
BOOKISH
BOORISH
CLOSEST
COOLEST
DIOCESE
EGOTISM
EGOTIST
FLORIST
FOOLISH
GEODESY
GOOIEST
LIONESS
LOOSEST
MOORISH
OLOROSO
POOREST
PROCESS
PROFESS
PROFUSE
PROMISE
PROPOSE
PROTEST
PROTIST
PROVISO
PROVOST
PROWESS
SLOWEST
SOONEST
TROPISM
TWOBASE
VIOLIST

••O•••S

ABOUNDS
ADONAIS
ADORERS
AGOUTIS
AMOEBAS
AMOROUS
AMOUNTS
ANOINTS
ANONYMS
ANORAKS
APOGEES
AROUSES
ATOMIES
AVOCETS
AVOWALS
AVOWERS
BAOBABS
BIOMASS
BIONICS
BLONDES
BLOUSES
BLOWERS
BLOWUPS
BMOVIES
BOOBIES
BOOBOOS
BOODLES
BOOGIES
BOOHOOS
BOOKIES
BOOMERS
BOONIES
BOOTEES
BOOTIES
BROGANS
BROGUES
BROKERS
BRONCOS
BRONZES
BROWSES
CHOICES
CHOKERS
CHOLLAS
CHOOSES
CHORALS
CLOCHES
CLOQUES
CLORETS
CLOSETS
CLOTHES
CLOVERS
COOKERS
COOKIES
COOLERS
COOPERS
COOTIES
CROESUS
CRONIES
CROSSES
CROWERS
DEODARS
DOODADS
DOODLES
DOOZIES
DRONERS
DROPINS
DROVERS
DROWSES
EBONIES
EGOISTS
ELOPERS
EMOTERS
EPONYMS
EPOXIES
ETOILES
EVOKERS
EVOLVES
EXOTICS
FLORETS
FLORINS
FLOSSES
FLOWERS
FOOTERS
FOOZLES
FROLICS
GEORGES
GLORIAS
GLORIES
GLOSSES
GLOTTIS
GLOWERS
GNOMONS
GOOBERS
GOODBYS
GOODIES
GOOFUPS
GOOGOLS
GROCERS
GROOVES
GROPIUS
GROSSES
GROTTOS
GROUNDS
GROUSES
GROVELS
GROWERS
GROWTHS
HOODOOS
HOOFERS
HOOHAHS
HOOKAHS
HOOKUPS
HOOPLAS
HOOPOES
HOOTERS
IRONERS
IRONIES
ISOBARS
ISOGONS
ISOHELS
ISOMERS
ISOPODS
IVORIES
KNOSSOS
LIONESS
LIONETS
LOOFAHS
LOOKERS
LOOKUPS
LOONIES
LOOPERS
LOOSENS
LOOTERS
MAOISTS
MOOCHES
NOODLES
OBOISTS
ODOROUS
OZONOUS
PEONIES
PEOPLES
PHOBIAS
PHOBICS
PHOEBES
PHOEBUS
PHONICS
PHONIES
PHOTOGS
PHOTONS
PIOLETS
PLOUGHS
PLOVERS
PLOWERS
POOCHES
POODLES
PROBERS
PROCESS
PROFESS
PROFITS
PROLOGS
PROMPTS
PROPELS
PROSERS
PROTEUS
PROTONS
PROVERS
PROWESS
PROXIES
QUOKKAS
QUORUMS
QUOTERS
REOPENS
RHOMBUS
RIOTERS
RIOTOUS
ROOFERS
ROOKIES
ROOMERS
ROOMIES
ROOTERS
SCONCES
SCORERS
SCOTERS
SHOFARS
SHOGUNS
SHOOINS
SHOPPES
SHOVELS
SHOVERS
SHOWERS
SIOUANS
SKOSHES
SLOGANS
SLOSHES
SLOUGHS
SLOVAKS
SLOVENS
SMOKERS
SMOKIES
SMOOTHS
SNOCATS
SNOOZES
SNORERS
SOONERS
SOOTHES
SPONGES
SPOUSES
STOGIES
STOKERS
STOLONS
STONERS
STOOGES
STORERS
STOREYS
STORIES
TAOISTS
TOOTERS
TOOTLES
TROCARS
TROCHES
TROIKAS
TROILUS
TROJANS
TROPICS
TROUGHS
TROUPES
TROWELS
TROWERS
TSONGAS
TWOBITS
TWOFERS
USOPENS
UTOPIAS
VIOLETS
VIOLINS
WOODIES
WOOFERS
WOOLENS
WOOLIES

•••OS••

ACCOSTS
AEROSOL
ALTOSAX
ALYOSHA
APPOSED
APPOSES
ARIOSOS
ARIOSTO
CHOOSER
CHOOSES
COHOSTS
COLOSSI
CREOSOL
DEPOSAL
DEPOSED
DEPOSER
DEPOSES
DEPOSIT
ESPOSAS
ESPOSOS
EXPOSED
EXPOSES
IMPOSED
IMPOSES
IMPOSTS
KENOSHA
LACOSTE
MEIOSES
MEIOSIS
MIMOSAS
MITOSES
MITOSIS
NICOSIA
OPPOSED
OPPOSER
OPPOSES
OSMOSED
OSMOSES
OSMOSIS
REPOSED
REPOSES
RIPOSTE
SWOOSIE

•••O•S•

ALFONSO
ATWORST
CABOOSE
CAROUSE
COLOSSI
ENDORSE
ESPOUSE
GENOESE
HELOISE
HEROISM
INHOUSE
JUDOIST
OKHOTSK
PAPOOSE
POLOIST
REMORSE
SOLOIST
UNHORSE
UNLOOSE
VAMOOSE

•••O••S

ABSORBS
ACCORDS
ACCOSTS

ADJOINS
ADSORBS
AEROBES
AFFORDS
ALCOVES
ALMONDS
ANGORAS
APPOSES
APROPOS
ARBOURS
ARDOURS
AREOLAS
ARIOSOS
ARMOURS
ARROBAS
ARROYOS
ASSORTS
ATHOMES
AUROCHS
AURORAS
BABOONS
BARONGS
BECOMES
BEFOULS
BEHOLDS
BELONGS
BEMOANS
BUROAKS
BUYOUTS
BYGONES
BYROADS
BYWORDS
CAHOOTS
CAJOLES
CANOPUS
CAROLES
CAROLUS
CAVORTS
CHOOSES
CHROMES
COCOONS
COHORTS
COHOSTS
COLOBUS
COLONES
COLOURS
COMOROS
COPOUTS
CORONAS
COYOTES
CREOLES
CUPOLAS
CUTOFFS
CUTOUTS
CYBORGS
DAKOTAS
DEBONES
DECOCTS
DECODES
DEFORMS
DEHORNS
DEMOTES
DENOTES
DEPONES
DEPORTS
DEPOSES
DESOTOS
DETOURS
DEVOTES
DEVOURS
DIMOUTS
DIPOLES
DISOWNS
DOLORES
DUGONGS
DUGOUTS
EFFORTS
ENCODES
ENCORES
ENFOLDS
ENJOINS
ENROBES
ENROLLS
ENROOTS
ENSOULS
ESCORTS
ESPOSAS
ESPOSOS
EXHORTS
EXPORTS
EXPOSES
EXTORTS
FAVOURS
FEDORAS
FURORES
GALOOTS
GIGOLOS
GROOVES
HEROICS
HONOURS
HUMOURS
IGNORES
IMPORTS
IMPOSES
IMPOSTS
INCOMES
INDOORS
INFOCUS
INFORMS
INJOKES
INROADS
INSOLES
INTONES
INVOKES
IOMOTHS
KETONES
KIMONOS
KOBOLDS
LABOURS
LAGOONS
LAKOTAS
LAYOFFS
LAYOUTS
LIMOGES
LITOTES
MAHOUTS
MAROONS
MEGOHMS
MEIOSES
MEIOSIS
MEMOIRS
MILORDS
MIMOSAS
MINOANS
MITOSES
MITOSIS
MRBONES
NICOLAS
NOKOMIS
OBLONGS
OCTOPUS
OFSORTS
OGDOADS
OHIOANS
OPPOSES
ORIOLES
ORMOLUS
OSMONDS
OSMOSES
OSMOSIS
OXFORDS
PAGODAS
PAROLES
PAYOFFS
PAYOLAS
PAYOUTS
PELOTAS
PHLOXES
PINOAKS
PINONES
POBOXES
POCONOS
POPOFFS
PTBOATS
PUTOUTS
RAGOUTS
REBOILS
REBOLTS
REBOOTS
REBOZOS
RECODES
RECOILS
RECORDS
RECORKS
RECOUPS
REDOAKS
REFORMS
REHOOKS
REJOINS
RELOADS
RELOCKS
REMOLDS
REMORAS
REMOTES
REMOVES
RENOTES
REPOLLS
REPORTS
REPOSES
RESOLES
RESORBS
RESORTS
RETOOLS
RETORTS
REVOKES
REVOLTS
REWORDS
REWORKS
REZONES
RIGOURS
RIPOFFS
RUMOURS
RUNOFFS
SALOONS
SAMOANS
SARONGS
SAVOURS
SCHOOLS
SCROLLS
SECONDS
SENORAS
SENORES
SHOOINS
SHROUDS
SMOOTHS
SNOOZES
SPROUTS
STJOHNS
STLOUIS
STOOGES
STROBES
STROKES
STROLLS
SUBORNS
TANOAKS
THROATS
THRONES
THRONGS
TIPOFFS
TOROIDS
TRIODES
TRYOUTS
TYCOONS
UNBOLTS
UNBOXES
UNCOILS
UNCORKS
UNFOLDS
UNHOOKS
UNLOADS
UNLOCKS
UNROBES
UNROLLS
UNYOKES
UPHOLDS
UPLOADS
UPROARS
UPROOTS
VALOURS
VAPOURS
VELOURS
VETOERS
VIGOURS
ZYGOTES

••••OS•

ACEROSE
ADIPOSE
AMBROSE
ATALOSS
AXLROSE
BEDPOST
BYANOSE
CABOOSE
COMPOSE
COMPOST
DEFROST
DISPOSE
DONJOSE
ENCLOSE
ENDMOST
ENGROSS
FORMOSA
GETLOST
GLUCOSE
INCLOSE
LACTOSE
MAFIOSO
MALTOSE
MELROSE
OAKMOSS
OLOROSO
OPEROSE
OSHKOSH
OUTPOST
PAPOOSE
PITBOSS
PROPOSE
PROVOST
PUGNOSE
PURPOSE
RECHOSE
RECROSS
REDROSE
SANJOSE
SEAMOSS
SUBROSA
SUCROSE
SUPPOSE
TEAROSE
TOPMOST
UNCLOSE
UNLOOSE
UPCLOSE
VAMOOSE
VERBOSE

••••O•S

ACTIONS
AMAZONS
AMNIONS
AMOROUS
ANALOGS
ANCHORS
ANTCOWS
ANXIOUS
AQUEOUS
ARCHONS
ARDUOUS
ATALOSS
AUTHORS
BABOONS
BAILORS
BALBOAS
BALLOTS
BAMBOOS
BANJOES
BARHOPS
BARROWS
BARYONS
BATBOYS
BEACONS
BECKONS
BELLOWS
BESTOWS
BETTORS
BIGBOYS
BIGTOES
BIGTOPS
BILBOES
BILIOUS
BILLOWS
BINGOES
BISHOPS
BLAZONS
BONBONS
BONGOES
BOOBOOS
BOOHOOS
BORROWS
BORZOIS
BOTTOMS
BOWWOWS
BOXTOPS
BRAVOES
BRETONS
BRITONS
BUCKOES
BULBOUS
BUNIONS
BURBOTS
BURGOOS
BURROWS
BUSBOYS
BUTTONS
CACHOUS
CAHOOTS
CALLOUS
CANNONS
CANTONS
CANTORS
CANYONS
CAPTORS
CARBONS
CARBOYS
CARGOES
CARHOPS
CARROTS
CARTONS
CATIONS
CENSORS
CHAMOIS
CITRONS
CLAMORS
CLIPONS
COCOONS
COLLOPS
COMEONS
COMMONS
CONDORS
CONJOBS
CONNORS
CONVOYS
COPIOUS
CORDONS
COTTONS
COUPONS
COWBOYS
CRAYONS
CUCKOOS
CURIOUS
CURSORS
CUSTOMS
CYCLOPS
DAMSONS
DEACONS
DEBTORS
DEPLOYS
DESPOTS
DEVIOUS
DIALOGS
DIATOMS
DINGOES
DOCTORS
DOLLOPS
DONJONS
DRAGONS
DUBIOUS
DUTEOUS
EDITORS
EGGNOGS
EMPLOYS
ENAMORS
ENGROSS
ENROOTS
ENVIOUS
EPILOGS
ESCROWS
FACTORS
FALCONS
FALLOWS
FANIONS
FARROWS
FATHOMS
FATUOUS
FELLOWS
FERROUS
FERVORS
FIBROUS
FLACONS
FLAGONS
FLAVORS
FLEXORS
FLYBOYS
FLYRODS
FOGBOWS
FOLLOWS
FORGOES
FUNGOES
FURIOUS
FURROWS
GALLONS
GALLOPS
GALOOTS
GAMBOLS
GAMMONS
GARCONS
GASCONS
GASEOUS
GECKOES
GESSOES
GIBBONS
GIBBOUS
GIDEONS
GNOMONS
GODSONS
GOOGOLS
GORGONS
GUIDONS
GUNDOGS
GUSTOES
HALLOWS
HANSOMS
HARBORS
HARROWS
HAYMOWS
HECTORS
HEINOUS
HIDEOUS
HOBNOBS
HOLLOWS
HOODOOS
HOOPOES
HORRORS
HOTDOGS
HOTPOTS
HOTRODS
HYDROUS
HYSSOPS
IGNEOUS
IMAGOES
IMPIOUS
INDOORS
INFLOWS
INSPOTS
ISOGONS
ISOPODS
JARGONS
JEALOUS
JERBOAS
JETSONS
JINGOES
JOBHOPS
JOBLOTS
JUNCOES
JUNIORS
KLAXONS
KMESONS
KOWTOWS
LAGOONS
LAPDOGS
LAPTOPS
LARDONS
LASSOES
LECTORS
LEGIONS
LEPTONS
LESSONS
LESSORS
LINGOES
LIQUORS
LOTIONS
LOWBOYS
MACRONS
MALLOWS
MANGOES
MARMOTS
MAROONS
MARROWS
MASCOTS
MATRONS
MATZOHS
MAUROIS
MEADOWS
MELLOWS
MENTORS
MERLOTS
METEORS
METHODS
MICRONS
MINIONS
MINNOWS
MIRRORS
MISDOES
MONGOLS
MORMONS
MORROWS
MOTIONS
MOTTOES
MOUTONS
MUTTONS
NARROWS
NATIONS
NELSONS
NERVOUS
NEURONS
NEWTONS
NICHOLS
NIMRODS
NITROUS
NOCUOUS
NONCOMS
NOSHOWS
NOTIONS
NOXIOUS
OAKMOSS
OBVIOUS
OCELOTS
ODDJOBS
ODDLOTS
ODOROUS
OMINOUS
ONEROUS
OPTIONS
ORATORS
ORISONS
OUTDOES
OUTGOES
OZONOUS
PAILOUS
PARDONS
PARLORS
PARLOUS
PARROTS
PARSONS
PASTORS
PATROLS
PATRONS
PEAPODS
PEGTOPS
PENNONS
PEQUOTS
PERIODS
PERSONS
PETROUS
PHENOLS
PHENOMS
PHOTOGS
PHOTONS
PIGEONS
PILLOWS
PINIONS
PISTOLS
PISTONS
PITBOSS
PITEOUS
PLEXORS
POISONS
POMPOMS
POMPONS
POMPOUS
POPTOPS
POTIONS
POWWOWS
PRISONS
PROLOGS
PROTONS
PULLONS
PYEDOGS
PYTHONS
QUAHOGS
QUINOAS
RAGMOPS
RAGTOPS
RAMRODS
RANSOMS
RAPTORS
RATIONS
RAUCOUS
REASONS
REBOOTS
RECKONS
RECROSS
RECTORS
REDDOGS
REDHOTS
REDTOPS
REGIONS
REHOOKS
RESHOES
RETOOLS
RHETORS
RIBBONS
RIOTOUS
ROBROYS
RUINOUS
SAILORS
SALMONS
SALOONS
SALVOES
SAVIORS
SAWLOGS
SCHMOES
SCHMOOS
SCHOOLS
SEACOWS
SEADOGS
SEAMOSS
SEASONS
SECTORS
SENIORS
SENSORS
SERIOUS
SERMONS
SEXTONS
SHADOWS
SHAKOES
SHALOMS
SIMMONS
SINUOUS
SIPHONS
SITCOMS
SKITOWS
SLALOMS
SLIPONS
SNAPONS
SORROWS
SPIGOTS
STATORS
STEROLS
STOLONS
STUPORS
SUCCORS
SUITORS
SUMMONS
SUNDOGS
SUNGODS
SYMBOLS
TAILORS
TALLOWS
TARPONS
TATTOOS
TEAPOTS
TEAPOYS
TEDIOUS
TENDONS
TENSORS
TENUOUS
TERRORS
TEUTONS
TIERODS
TIPTOES
TIPTOPS
TOMBOYS
TOMTOMS
TOPDOGS
TOYDOGS
TRAVOIS
TREMORS
TRICOTS
TRIGONS
TRIPODS
TRITONS
TURBOTS
TVSHOWS
TYCOONS
UNCLOGS
UNHOOKS
UNIPODS
UNISONS
UNKNOTS
UNSTOPS
UPROOTS
UPSHOTS
VACUOUS
VARIOUS
VECTORS
VENDORS
VICIOUS
VICTORS
VISCOUS
VISIONS
WAGGONS
WALKONS
WALLOPS
WALLOWS
WARGODS
WEAPONS
WETMOPS
WILLOWS
WINDOWS
WINNOWS
WONTONS
YARROWS
YAUPONS
YELLOWS
ZEALOTS
ZEALOUS
ZIRCONS

•••••OS

ADAGIOS
ALBEDOS
ALBINOS
APROPOS
ARIOSOS
ARISTOS
ARROYOS
BAMBOOS
BARRIOS
BISTROS
BOLEROS
BONITOS
BOOBOOS
BOOHOOS
BOUTROS
BRONCOS
BURGOOS
CALICOS
CASINOS
CHEETOS
COMOROS
CRYPTOS
CUCKOOS
DESOTOS
DOMINOS
DORITOS
DOSIDOS
DYNAMOS
EMBRYOS
ESCUDOS
ESKIMOS
ESPOSOS
FIASCOS
FRESCOS
GABBROS
GAUCHOS
GAZEBOS
GHETTOS
GIGOLOS
GROTTOS
HAIRDOS
HONCHOS
HOODOOS
INDIGOS
KIMONOS
KNOSSOS
LADINOS
LATINOS
LEANTOS
LEGATOS
LIBIDOS
MEDICOS
MERINOS
MIKADOS
NAVAHOS
NAVAJOS
NUNCIOS
OCTAVOS
OLDPROS
PAPAGOS
PICAROS
POCONOS
POMELOS
PONCHOS
PORTHOS
PRESTOS
PUEBLOS
QUARTOS
RANCHOS
REBOZOS
REREDOS
SCHMOOS
SMALTOS
STEREOS
STUCCOS
STUDIOS
TATTOOS
TEREDOS
THERMOS
TOREROS
TUPELOS
TUXEDOS
VIRAGOS
WEIRDOS

OT•••••

OTHELLO
OTRANTO
OTTAWAS
OTTOMAN

O•T••••

OATMEAL
OBTAINS
OBTRUDE
OBTUNDS
OBTUSER
OCTAGON
OCTANES
OCTANTS
OCTAVES
OCTAVIA
OCTAVOS
OCTOBER
OCTOPOD
OCTOPUS
OCTUPLE
OFTENER
ONTARIO
ONTHEGO
ONTHEQT
ONTOPOF
ONTRIAL
OPTICAL
OPTIMAL
OPTIMUM
OPTIONS
OPTSOUT
ORTOLAN
OSTEOID
OSTLERS
OSTRICH
OTTAWAS
OTTOMAN
OUTACTS
OUTAGES
OUTBACK
OUTBIDS
OUTCAST
OUTCOME
OUTCROP
OUTDOES
OUTDONE
OUTDOOR
OUTDRAW
OUTDREW
OUTEATS
OUTFACE
OUTFITS
OUTFLOW
OUTGOES
OUTGREW
OUTGROW
OUTGUNS
OUTHITS
OUTINGS
OUTJUMP
OUTLAID
OUTLAND
OUTLAST
OUTLAWS
OUTLAYS
OUTLETS
OUTLINE
OUTLIVE
OUTLOOK
OUTLOUD
OUTOFIT
OUTPACE
OUTPLAY
OUTPOST
OUTPUTS
OUTRACE
OUTRAGE
OUTRANK
OUTRUNS
OUTSELL
OUTSETS
OUTSIDE
OUTSIZE
OUTSOLD
OUTSTEP
OUTTAKE
OUTTALK
OUTVOTE
OUTWARD
OUTWEAR
OUTWITS
OUTWORE
OUTWORK
OUTWORN

O••T•••

OAKTREE
OLDTIME
OMITTED
ONATEAR
ONETIME
ONSTAGE
ORATING
ORATION
ORATORS
ORATORY
OROTUND
OURTOWN
OUSTERS
OUSTING
OUTTAKE

OUTTALK
OVATION
OYSTERS

O•••T••

OBLATES
OKHOTSK
OLDSTER
OLEATES
OLESTRA
OMENTUM
OMITTED
ONESTEP
OOCYTES
OOLITES
OOLITHS
OPENTOE
OPIATES
ORBITAL
ORBITED
ORBITER
ORESTES
ORNETTE
ORNITHO
OSMOTIC
OUTSTEP
OVERTLY

O••••T•

OBJECTS
OBLASTS
OBOISTS
OBVERTS
OBVIATE
OCCULTS
OCELOTS
OCTANTS
ODDLOTS
OFFDUTY
OFFSETS
OFFSITE
OFSORTS
OMELETS
ONADATE
OPACITY
OPERATE
ORIENTE
ORIENTS
ORNETTE
OTRANTO
OUTACTS
OUTEATS
OUTFITS
OUTHITS
OUTLETS
OUTPUTS
OUTSETS
OUTVOTE
OUTWITS
OVERATE
OWINGTO
OXCARTS

O•••••T

OCCIPUT
OCULIST
ODDMENT
OFASORT
OFFBEAT
OILIEST
OLDWEST
ONADIET
ONESHOT
ONSIGHT
ONTHEQT
OPENPIT
OPTSOUT
OPULENT
OUTCAST
OUTLAST
OUTOFIT
OUTPOST
OVERACT
OVEREAT
OXIDANT

•OT••••

BOTCHED
BOTCHES
BOTHERS
BOTHNIA
BOTTLED
BOTTLER
BOTTLES
BOTTOMS
COTERIE
COTTAGE
COTTERS
COTTONS
COTTONY
DOTEDON
DOTESON
DOTTIER
DOTTING
DOTTLES
GOTAWAY
GOTBACK
GOTCHAS
GOTDOWN
GOTEVEN
GOTHICS
GOTINTO
GOTLAND
GOTOPOT
GOTOVER
GOTWELL
HOTBEDS
HOTCAKE
HOTCAPS
HOTCARS
HOTDOGS
HOTFOOT
HOTHEAD
HOTLINE
HOTLIPS
HOTNESS
HOTPOTS
HOTRODS
HOTSEAT
HOTSHOT
HOTSPOT
HOTSPUR
HOTTEST
HOTTIPS
HOTTUBS
HOTWARS
HOTWIRE
JOTTING
LOTIONS
LOTTERY
LOTTING
LOTUSES
MOTHERS
MOTIONS
MOTIVES
MOTORED
MOTTLED
MOTTLES
MOTTOES
NOTABIT
NOTABLE
NOTABLY
NOTATED
NOTATES
NOTCHED
NOTCHES
NOTEPAD
NOTHING
NOTHOME
NOTICED
NOTICES
NOTIONS
NOTRUMP
NOTSURE
NOTTRUE
NOTWELL
POTABLE
POTAGES
POTENCY
POTFULS
POTHERB
POTHERS
POTHOLE
POTHOOK
POTIONS
POTLUCK
POTOMAC
POTPIES
POTSDAM
POTSHOT
POTTAGE
POTTERS
POTTERY
POTTING
ROTATED
ROTATES
ROTATOR
ROTIFER
ROTTERS
ROTTING
ROTUNDA
SOTHERE
SOTHERN
TOTALED
TOTALLY
TOTEBAG
TOTEMIC
TOTTERS
TOTTERY
TOTTING
VOTECHS
VOTESIN

•O•T•••

BOATERS
BOATING
BOATMAN
BOATMEN
BOBTAIL
BOITANO
BOLTING
BOOTEES
BOOTIES
BOOTING
BOOTLEG
BOOTOUT
BOOTSUP
BOTTLED
BOTTLER
BOTTLES
BOTTOMS
BOUTROS
BOWTIES
BOXTOPS
COATING
COCTEAU
COLTISH
CONTACT
CONTAIN
CONTEMN
CONTEND
CONTENT
CONTEST
CONTEXT
CONTORT
CONTOUR
CONTRAS
CONTROL
CONTUSE
COOTIES
COPTERS
CORTEGE
COSTAIN
COSTARS
COSTING
COSTNER
COSTUME
COTTAGE
COTTERS
COTTONS
COTTONY
COUTURE
COWTOWN
DOCTORS
DOGTAGS
DOGTROT
DOLTISH
DOTTIER
DOTTING
DOTTLES
FONTEYN
FONTINA
FOOTAGE
FOOTERS
FOOTING
FOOTMAN
FOOTMEN
FOOTPAD
FOOTSIE
FORTIES
FORTIFY
FORTRAN
FORTUNA
FORTUNE
FOSTERS
FOXTAIL
FOXTROT
GOATEED
GOATEES
GOATISH
GODTHAB
HOGTIED
HOGTIES
HOOTCHY
HOOTERS
HOOTING
HOOTOWL
HOOTSAT
HOPTOIT
HOSTAGE
HOSTELS
HOSTESS
HOSTILE
HOSTING
HOSTLER
HOTTEST
HOTTIPS
HOTTUBS
JOLTING
JOSTLED
JOSTLER
JOSTLES
JOTTING
KONTIKI
KOOTCHY
KOWTOWS
LOATHED
LOATHES
LOFTIER
LOFTILY
LOFTING
LOITERS
LOOTERS
LOOTING
LOSTOUT
LOTTERY
LOTTING
LOWTECH
LOWTIDE
MOLTERS
MOLTING
MONTAGE
MONTANA
MONTAND
MONTANE
MONTEGO
MONTEUX
MONTHLY
MONTOYA
MORTALS
MORTARS
MORTIFY
MORTISE
MOTTLED
MOTTLES
MOTTOES
MOUTHED
MOUTONS
NOCTURN
NOETICS
NORTHER
NOSTRIL
NOSTRUM
NOTTRUE
POETESS
POETICS
POITIER
PONTIAC
PONTIFF
PONTINE
PONTIUS
PONTOON
POPTART
POPTOPS
PORTAGE
PORTALS
PORTEND
PORTENT
PORTERS
PORTHOS
PORTICO
PORTION
PORTOLA
PORTRAY
POSTAGE
POSTBOX
POSTERN
POSTERS
POSTHOC
POSTING
POSTMAN
POSTMEN
POSTURE
POSTWAR
POTTAGE
POTTERS
POTTERY
POTTING
POUTERS
POUTIER
POUTING
RONTGEN
ROOTERS
ROOTFOR
ROOTING
ROOTLET
ROOTOUT
ROSTAND
ROSTERS
ROSTRUM
ROTTERS
ROTTING
ROUTERS
ROUTINE
ROUTING
SOFTENS
SOFTEST
SOFTIES
SOFTTOP
SOOTHED
SOOTHER
SOOTHES
SOOTIER
SORTERS
SORTIED
SORTIES
SORTING
SOUTANE
SOUTHEY
TOETAPS
TOLTECS
TOMTITS
TOMTOMS
TONTINE
TOOTALL
TOOTERS
TOOTHED
TOOTING
TOOTLED
TOOTLES
TOOTSIE
TORTONI
TOSTADA
TOTTERS
TOTTERY
TOTTING
TOUTERS
TOUTING
VOLTAGE
VOLTAIC
WONTONS

•O••T••

BOASTED
BOASTER
BOLOTIE
BOLSTER
BONITOS
BOOSTED
BOOSTER
BOOSTUP
BORATES
BOXSTEP
COALTAR
COASTAL
COASTED
COASTER
COLETTE
COOPTED
CORETTA
COULTER
COUNTED
COUNTER
COUNTON
COUNTRY
COURTED
COURTLY
COVETED
COYOTES
DOGSTAR
DONATED
DONATES
DONATOR
DORITOS
DOROTHY
DOUBTED
DOUBTER
EOLITHS
FOISTED
FORSTER
FOULTIP
FOURTHS
GODUTCH
GOLFTEE
GORETEX
HOISTED
HOLSTER
HORATIO
HOUSTON
IODATES
IOMOTHS
JOINTED
JOINTLY
JOISTED
JOUSTED
JOUSTER
KOMATSU
LOBSTER
LOCATED
LOCATER
LOCATES
LOCATOR
LONGTON
LORETTA
MOBSTER
MOISTEN
MOISTER
MOISTLY
MOLOTOV
MONITOR
MONSTER
MOULTED
MOUNTED
MOUNTIE
NONSTOP
NOTATED
NOTATES
OOCYTES
OOLITES
OOLITHS
POINTED
POINTER
POINTTO
POLITER
POLITIC
POLLTAX
POSITED
POULTRY
ROASTED
ROASTER
ROBOTIC
ROISTER
ROLLTOP
ROOFTOP
ROOSTED
ROOSTER
ROPETOW
ROSETTA
ROSETTE
ROTATED
ROTATES
ROTATOR
ROUSTED
SOFTTOP
SOLUTES
SOMATIC
SONATAS
SORITES
TOASTED
TOASTER
TOLSTOI
TOLSTOY
TOOKTEN
WOOSTER
WORSTED

•O•••T•

AORISTS
BOBCATS
BONNETS
BOSKETS
BOUNDTO
BOXKITE
BOYCOTT
COEDITS
COGNATE
COHORTS
COHOSTS
COLETTE
COLGATE
COLLATE
COLLETS
COMBATS
COMESTO
COMFITS
COMMITS
COMMUTE
COMPETE
COMPOTE
COMPUTE
CONFUTE
CONNOTE
COPOUTS
CORBETT
CORDATE
CORDITE
CORETTA
CORINTH
CORNETS
CORSETS
COSSETS
DOCENTS
DOCKETS
DOGMATA
DORSETT
DOUGHTY
DOZENTH
FOLIATE
FOLLETT
FOMENTS
FORESTS
FORGETS
FORINTS
FORMATS
FORSYTH
GOBLETS
GOCARTS
GODWITS
GOKARTS
GOLIATH
GORGETS
GOSSETT
GOTINTO
HOBBITS
HOGARTH
HOLDSTO
HONESTY
HORNETS
HOTPOTS
JOBLOTS
JOCASTA
JOLLITY
LOCKETS
LOCUSTS
LOOKSTO
LOQUATS
LORETTA
LOYALTY
MODELTS
MODESTO
MODESTY
MODISTE
MOLESTS
MOMENTS
MOPPETS
NOUGATS
NOVELTY
POCKETS
POINTTO
POLENTA
POLLUTE
POPPETS
POSSETS
POVERTY
ROBERTA
ROBERTO
ROBERTS
ROBUSTA
ROCKETS
RODENTS
ROSEATE
ROSETTA
ROSETTE
ROYALTY
SOCIETY
SOCKETS
SOFFITS
SONNETS
SOPWITH
SORBATE
SORBETS
SOVIETS
TOCCATA
TOILETS
TOMCATS
TOMTITS
TOPHATS
TORONTO
TOWPATH
WOMBATS
YOGURTS

•O••••T

BODYFAT
BOLDEST
BOMBAST
BONIEST
BOOKLET
BOOTOUT
BOREOUT
BORSCHT
BOUQUET
BOWKNOT
BOWSOUT
BOXSEAT
BOYCOTT
COCKPIT
COCONUT
COEXIST
COHABIT
COLBERT
COLDCUT
COLDEST
COLLECT
COMBUST
COMEOUT
COMESAT
COMFORT
COMMENT
COMPACT
COMPORT
COMPOST
CONCEIT
CONCEPT
CONCERT
CONCOCT
CONDUCT
CONDUIT
CONGEST
CONKOUT
CONNECT
CONSENT
CONSIST
CONSORT
CONSULT
CONTACT
CONTENT
CONTEST
CONTEXT
CONTORT
CONVENT
CONVERT
CONVICT
COOKOUT
COOLANT
COOLEST
COOLSIT
COONCAT
COPILOT
COPSOUT
COPYCAT
COPYIST
CORBETT
CORONET
CORRECT
CORRUPT
COULDNT
COUPLET
COURANT
COZIEST
DOGCART
DOGTROT
DOLEOUT
DOORMAT
DOPEOUT
DOPIEST
DORMANT
DORSETT
DOUBLET
DOUREST
DOVECOT
DOWNPAT
FOLDOUT
FOLKART
FOLLETT
FONDANT
FONDEST
FORFEIT
FORRENT
FORREST
FORWENT
FOULEST
FOULOUT
FOXIEST
FOXTROT
GOABOUT
GOESOUT
GOFORIT
GOINGAT
GOOIEST
GORIEST
GOSSETT
GOTOPOT
GOURMET
HOLDOUT
HOLEOUT
HOLIEST
HOMIEST
HOOFSIT
HOOTSAT
HOPTOIT
HORNIST
HOTFOOT
HOTSEAT
HOTSHOT
HOTSPOT
HOTTEST
HOWBEIT
JOBHUNT
JOLLIET
LOCKNUT
LOCKOUT
LOGIEST
LOGSOUT
LONGEST
LONNROT
LOOKOUT
LOOKSAT
LOOSEST
LOSEOUT
LOSESIT
LOSTOUT
LOUDEST
MONOCOT
MOONLIT
MOONSET
MORDANT
MORDENT
MOVEOUT
NOBLEST
NODOUBT
NOFAULT
NOSEOUT
NOSIEST
NOSWEAT
NOTABIT
POKEDAT
POKESAT
POKIEST
POLECAT
POLOIST
POOPOUT
POOREST
POPSOUT
POPTART
PORTENT
POSHEST
POTSHOT
POUROUT
RODEOUT
ROLLOUT
ROOTLET
ROOTOUT
ROUGHIT
ROWBOAT
SOFTEST
SOLDOUT
SOLICIT
SOLOIST
SOLVENT
SOONEST
SOPHIST
SOUREST
TONIEST
TONIGHT
TOOKOUT
TOPCOAT
TOPKNOT
TOPMAST
TOPMOST
TOPSOUT
TOREOUT
TORMENT
TORNOUT
TORRENT
TOSSOUT
TOURIST
WOODCUT
WOODLOT
WOREOUT
WORKOUT
WORNOUT
WOULDNT
YOGHURT
YOPLAIT
ZONKOUT

••OT•••

ANOTHER
APOTHEM
BLOTCHY
BLOTOUT
BLOTTED
BLOTTER
BOOTEES
BOOTIES
BOOTING
BOOTLEG
BOOTOUT
BOOTSUP
BROTHER
CLOTHED
CLOTHES
CLOTTED
CLOTURE
COOTIES
EGOTISM
EGOTIST
EGOTRIP
EMOTERS
EMOTING
EMOTION
EMOTIVE
EROTICA
EXOTICA
EXOTICS
FLOTSAM
FOOTAGE
FOOTERS
FOOTING
FOOTMAN
FOOTMEN
FOOTPAD
FOOTSIE
FROTHED
GLOTTAL
GLOTTIS
GROTTOS
HOOTCHY
HOOTERS
HOOTING
HOOTOWL
HOOTSAT
ISOTOPE
KNOTTED
KOOTCHY
LAOTIAN
LEOTARD
LOOTERS
LOOTING
OROTUND
PHOTOED
PHOTOGS
PHOTONS
PHOTOOP
PLOTTED
PLOTTER
PROTEAN
PROTECT
PROTEGE
PROTEIN
PROTEST
PROTEUS
PROTIST
PROTONS
QUOTERS
QUOTING
RIOTACT
RIOTERS
RIOTING
RIOTOUS
ROOTERS
ROOTFOR
ROOTING
ROOTLET
ROOTOUT
SAOTOME
SCOTERS
SCOTTIE
SHOTFOR
SHOTGUN
SHOTPUT
SLOTCAR
SLOTTED
SMOTHER
SOOTHED
SOOTHER
SOOTHES
SOOTIER

SPOTLIT
SPOTTED
SPOTTER
TOOTALL
TOOTERS
TOOTHED
TOOTING
TOOTLED
TOOTLES
TOOTSIE
TROTHED
TROTOUT
TROTSKY
TROTTED
TROTTER
TWOTIME
TWOTONE
WROTEIN
WROTETO
WROTEUP

••O•T••

ABORTED
ADOPTED
ADOPTEE
ADOPTER
AGOUTIS
APOSTLE
BLOATED
BLOTTED
BLOTTER
BOOSTED
BOOSTER
BOOSTUP
CHOCTAW
CHORTLE
CLOTTED
CLOUTED
COOPTED
CROATIA
CROUTON
DIOPTER
FLOATED
FLOATER
FLOUTED
FRONTAL
FRONTED
FRONTON
FROSTED
GHOSTED
GHOSTLY
GLOATED
GLOTTAL
GLOTTIS
GNOSTIC
GROTTOS
GROUTED
GROWTHS
KNOTTED
PLOTTED
PLOTTER
PROCTOR
ROOFTOP
ROOSTED
ROOSTER
SCOOTED
SCOOTER
SCOTTIE
SCOUTED
SCOUTER
SHOOTAT
SHOOTER
SHOOTUP
SHORTED
SHORTEN
SHORTER
SHORTLY
SHORTOF
SHOUTED
SHOUTER
SLOTTED
SMOOTHS
SNOOTED
SNORTED
SNORTER
SPORTED
SPOTTED
SPOTTER
SPOUTED
SPOUTER
STOUTER
STOUTLY
TOOKTEN
TROTTED
TROTTER
TWOSTAR
TWOSTEP
WOOSTER

••O••T•

ACOLYTE
ACONITE
AMOUNTS
ANOINTS
AVOCETS
AXOLOTL
BROMATE
CLORETS
CLOSETS
EBONITE
EGOISTS
FLOCKTO
FLORETS
ISOLATE
LIONETS
LOOKSTO
MAOISTS
NEOLITH
NEONATE
OBOISTS
PIOLETS
PROBATE
PROBITY
PROFITS
PROMOTE
PROMPTS
PRORATA
PRORATE
RIORITA
SNOCATS
STOMATA
STOOPTO
TAOISTS
TWOBITS
VIOLATE
VIOLETS
WROTETO

••O•••T

AGONIST
AMONGST
BLOTOUT
BLOWOUT
BLOWSIT
BOOKLET
BOOTOUT
BROUGHT
BUOYANT
CLOSEST
COOKOUT
COOLANT
COOLEST
COOLSIT
COONCAT
CROCHET
CROQUET
DOORMAT
DROPLET
DROPOUT
DROUGHT
EGOTIST
FLORIST
FROWNAT
GOOIEST
GROMMET
HOOFSIT
HOOTSAT
INORBIT
IRONOUT
LOOKOUT
LOOKSAT
LOOSEST
MOONLIT
MOONSET
POOPOUT
POOREST
PRODUCT
PROJECT
PROPHET
PROPJET
PROTECT
PROTEST
PROTIST
PROVOST
QUONSET
RIOTACT
ROOTLET
ROOTOUT
SHOOTAT
SHOTPUT
SLOWEST
SOONEST
SPOTLIT
SWOREAT
THOUGHT
TOOKOUT
TROTOUT
VIOLENT
VIOLIST
WOODCUT
WOODLOT
WROUGHT

•••OT••

BIGOTED
BIGOTRY
BOLOTIE
CAROTID
CHAOTIC
COYOTES
CULOTTE
DAKOTAN
DAKOTAS
DEMOTED
DEMOTES
DENOTED
DENOTES
DESOTOS
DEVOTED
DEVOTEE
DEVOTES
DOROTHY
FAGOTED
GAVOTTE
HELOTRY
IDIOTIC
IOMOTHS
KILOTON
LAKOTAS
LAMOTTA
LESOTHO
LITOTES
MEIOTIC
MENOTTI
MITOTIC
MOLOTOV
OKHOTSK
OSMOTIC
PELOTAS
PILOTED
PIVOTAL
PIVOTED
REMOTER
REMOTES
RENOTES
RICOTTA
RISOTTO
ROBOTIC
SCOOTED
SCOOTER
SHOOTAT
SHOOTER
SHOOTUP
SMOOTHS
SNOOTED
SPLOTCH
TIMOTHY
ZAPOTEC
ZYGOTES

•••O•T•

ACCOSTS
ADDONTO
ALWORTH
ARIOSTO
ASSORTS
BUYOUTS
CAHOOTS
CAVORTS
COHORTS
COHOSTS
COPOUTS
CULOTTE
CUTOUTS
DECOCTS
DEPORTS
DIMOUTS
DUGOUTS
EFFORTS
ENROOTS
ENROUTE
ESCORTS
EXHORTS
EXPORTS
EXTORTS
GALOOTS
GAVOTTE
IMPORTS
IMPOSTS
LACOSTE
LAMOTTA
LAPORTE
LAYOUTS
MAHOUTS
MENOTTI
MINOLTA
OFSORTS
PAYOUTS
PRIORTO
PTBOATS
PUTOUTS
RAGOUTS
REBOLTS
REBOOTS
REPORTS
REROUTE
RESORTS
RETORTS
REVOLTS
RICOTTA
RIPOSTE
RISOTTO
SPROUTS
STOOPTO
THROATS
THROATY
TORONTO
TRYOUTS
UNBOLTS
UNCOUTH
UPROOTS

•••O••T

ABSOLUT
ACCOUNT
ACROBAT
AEROBAT
APPOINT
ASTOLAT
ATWORST
AUTOMAT
BARONET
BAYONET
COCONUT
CORONET
DEPOSIT
GOFORIT
GOTOPOT
INDOUBT
INPOINT
JACONET
JUDOIST
MONOCOT
NODOUBT
OUTOFIT
POLOIST
RECOUNT
REDOUBT
REMOUNT
SHOOTAT
SOLOIST
TABORET

••••OT•

AXOLOTL
BALLOTS
BETROTH
BOYCOTT
BURBOTS
CAHOOTS
CARROTS
COMPOTE
CONNOTE
DESPOTS
ELLIOTT
ENROOTS
GALOOTS
HOTPOTS
INSPOTS
JOBLOTS
KEYNOTE
MAMMOTH
MARMOTS
MASCOTS
MERLOTS
OCELOTS
ODDLOTS
OUTVOTE
PARROTS
PEQUOTS
PROMOTE
QUIXOTE
REBOOTS
REDHOTS
REWROTE
SPIGOTS
TEAPOTS
TRICOTS
TURBOTS
UNKNOTS
UNQUOTE
UPROOTS
UPSHOTS
WALCOTT
ZEALOTS

••••O•T

ACEDOUT
ACESOUT
ACTSOUT
AFFRONT
AIRBOAT
AIRPORT
AIRSOUT
ASKSOUT
BACKOUT
BAILOUT
BAWLOUT
BEAROUT
BEATOUT
BEDPOST
BELMONT
BERTOLT
BIGFOOT
BLEWOUT
BLOTOUT
BLOWOUT
BOOTOUT
BOREOUT
BOWSOUT
BOYCOTT
BUGSOUT
BUMSOUT
BURNOUT
BUSTOUT
BUTTOUT
BUYSOUT
CALLOUT
CAMEOUT
CAMPOUT
CARCOAT
CARPORT
CASHOUT
CASTOUT
CATBOAT
CHEROOT
CHEWOUT
COMEOUT
COMFORT
COMPORT
COMPOST
CONCOCT
CONKOUT
CONSORT
CONTORT
COOKOUT
COPSOUT
CUTSOUT
DASBOOT
DEALOUT
DECKOUT
DEFROST
DETROIT
DIEDOUT
DIESOUT
DIGSOUT
DINMONT
DISHOUT
DISPORT
DISTORT
DOLEOUT
DOPEOUT
DRAGOUT
DRAWOUT
DREWOUT
DROPOUT
EATSOUT
EDGEOUT
EKEDOUT
EKESOUT
ELLIOTT
ENDMOST
EVENOUT
EXPLOIT
EYEBOLT
FADEOUT
FALLOUT
FANSOUT
FARMOUT
FEELOUT
FELLOUT
FELTOUT
FILLOUT
FINDOUT
FISHOUT
FLATOUT
FOLDOUT
FOULOUT
FREMONT
GAVEOUT
GETLOST
GETSOUT
GIVEOUT
GOABOUT
GOESOUT
GUNBOAT
HANDOUT
HANGOUT
HAYLOFT
HEADOUT
HEAROUT
HELDOUT
HELPOUT
HIDEOUT
HIPBOOT
HOLDOUT
HOLEOUT
HOPTOIT
HOTFOOT
HUNGOUT
ICEBOAT
INFRONT
INSHORT
INTROIT
IRISOUT
IRONOUT
JETBOAT
JETPORT
KEPTOUT
KICKOUT
LABCOAT
LAIDOUT
LAYSOUT
LEADOUT
LEFTOUT
LETSOUT
LIVEOUT
LOCKOUT
LOGSOUT
LOOKOUT
LOSEOUT
LOSTOUT
LUCKOUT
MADEOUT
MAKEOUT
METEOUT
MISSOUT
MOVEOUT
NEWPORT
NOSEOUT
OFASORT
OPTSOUT
OUTPOST
PAIDOUT
PANSOUT
PARTOUT
PASSOUT
PAYSOUT
PEACOAT
PEEKOUT
PEEROUT
PICKOUT
PIGSOUT
PLAYOUT
POOPOUT
POPSOUT
POUROUT
PRESORT
PROVOST
PULLOUT
PURPORT
PUTSOUT
RAINOUT
RAPPORT
READOUT
REDCOAT
RESHOOT
RIDEOUT
RINGOUT
RODEOUT
ROLLOUT
ROOTOUT
ROWBOAT
RUBSOUT
RULEOUT
RUNSOUT
SACKOUT
SANGOUT
SEAPORT
SEEKOUT
SEESOUT
SEETOIT
SELLOUT
SENDOUT
SENTOUT
SETSOUT
SHIPOUT
SHUTOUT
SICKOUT
SIGNOUT
SINGOUT
SITSOUT
SKIBOOT
SKIPOUT
SLIPOUT
SOLDOUT
SPINOUT
SPUNOUT
STEPOUT
SUPPORT
SURCOAT
TAGSOUT
TAKEOUT
TALKOUT
TAPROOT
TAPSOUT
TESTOUT
TIMEOUT
TIREOUT
TOOKOUT
TOPCOAT
TOPMOST
TOPSOUT
TOREOUT
TORNOUT
TOSSOUT
TROTOUT
TUGBOAT
TUNEOUT
TURNOUT
UPFRONT
VERMONT
WAITOUT
WALCOTT
WALKOUT
WANTOUT
WASHOUT
WEAROUT
WEBFOOT
WEEDOUT
WENTOUT
WIGSOUT
WINKOUT
WINSOUT
WIPEOUT
WITHOUT
WOREOUT
WORKOUT
WORNOUT
ZONKOUT

•••••OT

APRICOT
BIBELOT
BIENTOT
BIGFOOT
BIGSHOT
BLERIOT
BOWKNOT
CAMELOT
CHARIOT
CHEROOT
CHEVIOT
COPILOT
CYPRIOT
DASBOOT
DIDEROT
DOGTROT
DOVECOT
EARSHOT
FEEDLOT
FOXTROT
FUSSPOT
GOTOPOT
GUNSHOT
HARICOT
HAVENOT
HERRIOT
HIPBOOT
HOTFOOT
HOTSHOT
HOTSPOT
INASPOT
INKBLOT
INKSPOT
JACKPOT
LONNROT
MAGINOT
MAILLOT
MONOCOT
MUGSHOT
ONESHOT
PATRIOT
PERIDOT
PEUGEOT
PIERROT
POTSHOT
RANRIOT
REDSPOT
RESHOOT
RIMSHOT
RUNRIOT
SANDLOT
SHALLOT
SKIBOOT
SUBPLOT
SUNSPOT
TAPROOT
TENSPOT
TOPKNOT
TSELIOT
WEBFOOT
WHATNOT
WOODLOT
WYANDOT

OU•••••

OURSELF
OURTOWN
OUSTERS
OUSTING
OUTACTS
OUTAGES
OUTBACK
OUTBIDS
OUTCAST
OUTCOME
OUTCROP
OUTDOES
OUTDONE
OUTDOOR
OUTDRAW
OUTDREW
OUTEATS
OUTFACE
OUTFITS
OUTFLOW
OUTGOES
OUTGREW
OUTGROW
OUTGUNS
OUTHITS
OUTINGS
OUTJUMP
OUTLAID
OUTLAND
OUTLAST
OUTLAWS
OUTLAYS
OUTLETS
OUTLINE
OUTLIVE
OUTLOOK
OUTLOUD
OUTOFIT
OUTPACE
OUTPLAY
OUTPOST
OUTPUTS
OUTRACE
OUTRAGE
OUTRANK
OUTRUNS
OUTSELL
OUTSETS
OUTSIDE
OUTSIZE
OUTSOLD
OUTSTEP
OUTTAKE
OUTTALK
OUTVOTE
OUTWARD
OUTWEAR
OUTWITS
OUTWORE
OUTWORK
OUTWORN

O•U••••

OCULIST
OEUVRES
OPULENT

O••U•••

OBTUNDS
OBTUSER
OCCULTS
OCTUPLE
OLDUVAI
ONGUARD
OPPUGNS
OROURKE

O•••U••

OBSCURE
OBTRUDE
OCCLUDE
OFFDUTY
OPAQUES
OROTUND
OUTGUNS
OUTJUMP
OUTPUTS
OUTRUNS
OVERUSE

O••••U•

OBLIQUE
OBLOQUY
OBVIOUS
OCCIPUT
OCEANUS
OCTOPUS
ODOROUS
OEDIPUS
OFFHOUR
OLYMPUS
OMENTUM
OMINOUS
OMNIBUS
ONEROUS
OPENSUP
OPOSSUM
OPTIMUM
OPTSOUT
ORGANUM
ORMOLUS
ORPHEUS
OUTLOUD
OVERBUY
OVERDUB
OVERDUE
OVERRUN
OWNEDUP
OZONOUS

O•••••U

ONLYYOU

•OU••••

AOUDADS
BOUDOIR
BOULDER
BOUNCED
BOUNCER
BOUNCES
BOUNDED
BOUNDER
BOUNDTO
BOUNDUP
BOUQUET
BOURBON
BOURREE
BOUTROS
COUCHED
COUCHES
COUGARS
COUGHED
COUGHUP
COULDNT
COULEES
COULOMB
COULTER
COUNCIL
COUNSEL
COUNTED
COUNTER
COUNTON
COUNTRY
COUPLED
COUPLES
COUPLET
COUPONS
COURAGE
COURANT
COURIER
COURSED
COURSER
COURSES
COURTED
COURTLY
COUSINS
COUTURE
DOUBLED
DOUBLES
DOUBLET
DOUBLEU
DOUBTED
DOUBTER
DOUGHTY
DOUGLAS
DOUREST
DOUSING
FOULARD
FOULEST
FOULING
FOULOUT
FOULSUP
FOULTIP
FOULUPS
FOUNDED
FOUNDER
FOUNDRY
FOURIER
FOURTHS
GOUACHE
GOUGERS
GOUGING
GOULASH
GOUNDER
GOURAMI
GOURDES
GOURMET
HOUDINI
HOUNDED
HOUSING
HOUSMAN
HOUSTON
JOUNCED
JOUNCES
JOURDAN
JOURNAL
JOURNEY
JOUSTED
JOUSTER
LOUDEST
LOUELLA
LOUNGED
LOUNGER
LOUNGES
LOURDES
LOUREED
LOUSEUP
LOUSIER
LOUSILY
LOUSING
LOUVERS
LOUVRES
MOUFLON
MOULAGE
MOULDED
MOULDER
MOULTED
MOUNDED
MOUNTED
MOUNTIE
MOUSERS
MOUSIER
MOUSING
MOUSSED
MOUSSES
MOUTHED
MOUTONS
NOUGATS
NOURISH
NOUVEAU
POUCHED
POUCHES

POULENC
POULTRY
POUNCED
POUNCER
POUNCES
POUNDED
POUNDER
POURERS
POURING
POUROUT
POURSIN
POUTERS
POUTIER
POUTING
ROUGHED
ROUGHEN
ROUGHER
ROUGHIT
ROUGHLY
ROUGHUP
ROUGING
ROULADE
ROUNDED
ROUNDER
ROUNDLY
ROUNDON
ROUNDUP
ROUSING
ROUSTED
ROUTERS
ROUTINE
ROUTING
SOUFFLE
SOUGHED
SOULFUL
SOUNDED
SOUNDER
SOUNDLY
SOUPCON
SOUPIER
SOUPSUP
SOURCED
SOURCES
SOUREST
SOURING
SOURISH
SOUTANE
SOUTHEY
TOUCANS
TOUCHED
TOUCHES
TOUCHON
TOUCHUP
TOUGHEN
TOUGHER
TOUGHIE
TOUGHLY
TOUPEES
TOURACO
TOURERS
TOURING
TOURISM
TOURIST
TOURNEY
TOUSLED
TOUSLES
TOUTERS
TOUTING
VOUCHED
VOUCHER
VOUCHES
WOULDBE
WOULDNT
WOUNDED
WOUNDUP
YOUKNOW
YOUMANS
YOUNGER
YOUNGMC
YOUNGUN
ZOUAVES

•O•U•••

BOLUSES
BONUSES
COLUMBO
COLUMNS
COZUMEL
DOEUVRE
FOCUSED
FOCUSES
GODUNOV
GODUTCH
JOCULAR
KORUNAS
LOCUSTS
LOQUATS
LOTUSES
MODULAR
MODULES
NOCUOUS
NODULAR
NODULES
NOGUCHI
NONUSER
POPULAR
ROBUSTA
ROGUERY
ROGUISH
ROMULAN
ROMULUS
ROTUNDA
SOLUBLE
SOLUTES
SOSUEME
TOLUENE
VOLUBLE
VOLUBLY
VOLUMES
YOGURTS

•O••U••

BOROUGH
BOUQUET
BOXFULS
COEQUAL
COGBURN
COLLUDE
COLOURS
COMBUST
COMMUNE
COMMUTE
COMPUTE
CONCURS
CONDUCE
CONDUCT
CONDUIT
CONFUSE
CONFUTE
CONJURE
CONQUER
CONSULS
CONSULT
CONSUME
CONTUSE
COPOUTS
CORRUPT
COSTUME
COUTURE
DONJUAN
FOLDUPS
FONDUES
FORMULA
FORSURE
FORTUNA
FORTUNE
FOULUPS
GOOFUPS
GOROUND
HOLDUPS
HOMBURG
HONOURS
HOOKUPS
HOTTUBS
JOAQUIN
JOBHUNT
JONQUIL
LOCKUPS
LONGUES
LOOKUPS
MOCKUPS
MOLLUSK
MOSQUES
NOCTURN
NODOUBT
NOFAULT
NOTRUMP
NOTSURE
PODIUMS
POLLUTE
POPGUNS
POSEURS
POSSUMS
POSTURE
POTFULS
POTLUCK
ROEBUCK
RORQUAL
SOJOURN
SOWBUGS
TONGUED
TONGUES
TONSURE
TOPGUNS
TORQUES
TOSSUPS
WORKUPS
YOGHURT

•O•••U•

BONEDUP
BONESUP
BONJOUR
BOOSTUP
BOOTOUT
BOOTSUP
BOREOUT
BORNEUP
BOUNDUP
BOWLFUL
BOWSOUT
BOXEDUP
BOXESUP
COCONUT
COILSUP
COLDCUT
COLOBUS
COMEDUE
COMEOUT
COMESUP
COMIQUE
CONKOUT
CONTOUR
COOKOUT
COOKSUP
COOPSUP
COPIOUS
COPSOUT
COUGHUP
COVERUP
DOINGUP
DOLEFUL
DOLEOUT
DOLLSUP
DONAHUE
DOPEOUT
FOLDOUT
FOLDSUP
FORERUN
FORKFUL
FOULOUT
FOULSUP
GOABOUT
GOESOUT
GOINGUP
GOLDBUG
GOOFSUP
HOLDOUT
HOLDSUP
HOLEDUP
HOLEOUT
HOLESUP
HOLMIUM
HOMERUN
HOODLUM
HOOKSUP
HOPEFUL
HOTSPUR
JOINSUP
LOCKNUT
LOCKOUT
LOCKSUP
LOGSOUT
LONGRUN
LOOKOUT
LOOKSUP
LOSEOUT
LOSTOUT
LOUSEUP
LOVEBUG
MODICUM
MONIQUE
MONTEUX
MOVEOUT
NOCUOUS
NONPLUS
NOSEEUM
NOSEOUT
NOSTRUM
NOTTRUE
NOXIOUS
POKEFUN
POMPOUS
PONTIUS
POOPOUT
POPSOUT
POUROUT
RODEOUT
ROLLOUT
ROLLSUP
ROMULUS
ROOMFUL
ROOTOUT
ROSEBUD
ROSTRUM
ROUGHUP
ROUNDUP
SOAKSUP
SOLDOUT
SORGHUM
SOULFUL
SOUPSUP
TONEDUP
TONESUP
TOOKOUT
TOOLSUP
TOPSOUT
TOREOUT
TORNOUT
TOSSOUT
TOUCHUP
WOKENUP
WOODCUT
WOREOUT
WORKOUT
WORKSUP
WORNOUT
WOUNDUP
YOUNGUN
ZONKOUT

•O••••U

COCTEAU
DOUBLEU
HOFBRAU
KOMATSU
NOUVEAU
RONDEAU
TONNEAU

••OU•••

ABOUNDS
AGOUTIS
AMOUNTS
ANOUILH
AROUSAL
AROUSED
AROUSES
BLOUSED
BLOUSES
BLOUSON
BROUGHT
CLOUDED
CLOUTED
CROUTON
DROUGHT
EDOUARD
ENOUNCE
FLOUNCE
FLOURED
FLOUTED
GROUCHO
GROUCHY
GROUNDS
GROUPED
GROUPER
GROUPIE
GROUSED
GROUSER
GROUSES
GROUTED
OROURKE
PIOUSLY
PLOUGHS
PROUDER
PROUDLY
SCOURED
SCOURER
SCOURGE
SCOUTED
SCOUTER
SHOUTED
SHOUTER
SIOUANS
SLOUCHY
SLOUGHS
SPOUSAL
SPOUSES
SPOUTED
SPOUTER
STOUTER
STOUTLY
THOUGHT
TROUBLE
TROUGHS
TROUNCE
TROUPER
TROUPES
TROUSER
WROUGHT
YAOUNDE

••O•U••

BEOWULF
BLOWUPS
BROGUES
CLOQUES
CLOSURE
CLOTURE
CROQUET
GLOBULE
GOOFUPS
HOOKUPS
INOCULA
LOOKUPS
OROTUND
PROCURE
PRODUCE
PRODUCT
PROFUSE
QUORUMS
SHOGUNS

••O••U•

AMOROUS
BLOTOUT
BLOWGUN
BLOWNUP
BLOWOUT
BLOWSUP
BOOSTUP
BOOTOUT
BOOTSUP
BROKEUP
BUOYSUP
CHOKEUP
CLOGSUP
CLOSEUP
COOKOUT
COOKSUP
COOPSUP
CROESUS
CROPSUP
CROSSUP
DROPOUT
GOOFSUP
GROPIUS
GROWNUP
GROWSUP
HOODLUM
HOOKSUP
IRONOUT
LIONCUB
LOOKOUT
LOOKSUP
NIOBIUM
ODOROUS
OPOSSUM
OZONOUS
PHOEBUS
POOPOUT
PRONOUN
PROPSUP
PROTEUS
REOCCUR
RHODIUM
RHOMBUS
RIOTOUS
ROOMFUL
ROOTOUT
SHOOKUP
SHOOTUP
SHOTGUN
SHOTPUT
SHOWSUP
SLOWSUP
SPOKEUP
STOCKUP
STOODUP
STOPSUP
STOREUP
THORIUM
TOOKOUT
TOOLSUP
TROILUS
TROTOUT
WOODCUT
WROTEUP

••O•••U

THOREAU

•••OU••

ACCOUNT
ADJOURN
AGROUND
AMPOULE
ARBOURS
ARDOURS
ARMOURS
ASTOUND
BEDOUIN
BEFOULS
BIVOUAC
BOROUGH
BUYOUTS
CAROUSE
COLOURS
COPOUTS
CUTOUTS
CYYOUNG
DEBOUCH
DETOURS
DEVOURS
DIMOUTS
DUGOUTS
ENROUTE
ENSOULS
ESPOUSE
EXPOUND
FAVOURS
GOROUND
HONOURS
HUMOURS
IMPOUND
INBOUND
INDOUBT
INHOUSE
KEROUAC
LABOURS
LAYOUTS
MAHOUTS
NODOUBT
PAYOUTS
PUTOUTS
RAGOUTS
REBOUND
RECOUNT
RECOUPS
REDOUBT
REDOUND
REMOUNT
REROUTE
RESOUND
RETOUCH
REWOUND
RIGOURS
RUMOURS
SAVOURS
SAVOURY
SHROUDS
SOJOURN
SPROUTS
STLOUIS
THROUGH
TRYOUTS
UNBOUND
UNCOUTH
UNSOUND
UNWOUND
VALOURS
VAPOURS
VELOURS
VIGOURS

•••O•U•

ABSOLUT
BAROQUE
CANOPUS
CAROLUS
COCONUT
COLOBUS
DECORUM
ECLOGUE
INFOCUS
INVOGUE
OBLOQUY
OCTOPUS
ORMOLUS
PIROGUE
SHOOKUP
SHOOTUP
STOODUP
VANOCUR

••••OU•

ACEDOUT
ACESOUT
ACTSOUT
AIRSOUT
AMOROUS
ANXIOUS
AQUEOUS
ARDUOUS
ASKSOUT
BACKOUT
BAILOUT
BALFOUR
BAWLOUT
BEAROUT
BEATOUT
BECLOUD
BILIOUS
BLEWOUT
BLOTOUT
BLOWOUT
BONJOUR
BOOTOUT
BOREOUT
BOWSOUT
BUGSOUT
BULBOUS
BUMSOUT
BURNOUT
BUSTOUT
BUTTOUT
BUYSOUT
CACHOUS
CALHOUN
CALLOUS
CALLOUT
CAMEOUT
CAMPOUT
CANDOUR
CASHOUT
CASTOUT
CHEWOUT
COMEOUT
CONKOUT
CONTOUR
COOKOUT
COPIOUS
COPSOUT
CURIOUS
CUTSOUT
DEALOUT
DECKOUT
DEVIOUS
DIEDOUT
DIESOUT
DIGSOUT
DISHOUT
DOLEOUT
DOPEOUT
DRAGOUT
DRAWOUT
DREWOUT
DROPOUT
DUBIOUS
DUTEOUS
EATSOUT
EDGEOUT
EKEDOUT
EKESOUT
ENAMOUR
ENVIOUS
EVENOUT
FADEOUT
FALLOUT
FANSOUT
FARMOUT
FATUOUS
FEELOUT
FELLOUT
FELTOUT
FERROUS
FERVOUR
FIBROUS
FILLOUT
FINDOUT
FISHOUT
FLATOUT
FLAVOUR
FOLDOUT
FOULOUT
FURIOUS
GASEOUS
GAVEOUT
GETSOUT
GIBBOUS
GIVEOUT
GLAMOUR
GOABOUT
GOESOUT
HANDOUT
HANGOUT
HARBOUR
HEADOUT
HEAROUT
HEINOUS
HELDOUT
HELPOUT
HIDEOUS
HIDEOUT
HOLDOUT
HOLEOUT
HUNGOUT
HYDROUS
IGNEOUS
IMPIOUS
INGROUP
IRISOUT
IRONOUT
JEALOUS
KEPTOUT
KICKOUT
LAIDOUT
LAYSOUT
LEADOUT
LEFTOUT
LETSOUT
LIVEOUT
LOCKOUT
LOGSOUT
LOOKOUT
LOSEOUT
LOSTOUT
LUCKOUT
MADEOUT
MAKEOUT
MANHOUR
METEOUT
MISSOUT
MOVEOUT
NERVOUS
NITROUS
NOCUOUS
NOSEOUT
NOXIOUS
OBVIOUS
ODOROUS
OFFHOUR
OMINOUS
ONEROUS
OPTSOUT
OUTLOUD
OZONOUS
PAIDOUT
PAILOUS
PANSOUT
PARLOUR
PARLOUS
PARTOUT
PASSOUT
PAVIOUR
PAYSOUT
PEASOUP
PEEKOUT
PEEROUT
PETROUS
PICKOUT
PIGSOUT
PITEOUS
PLAYOUT
POMPOUS
POOPOUT
POPSOUT
POUROUT
PRONOUN
PULLOUT
PUTSOUT
RAINOUT
RANCOUR
RAUCOUS
READOUT
REGROUP
RIDEOUT
RINGOUT
RIOTOUS
RODEOUT
ROLLOUT
ROOTOUT
RUBSOUT
RUINOUS
RULEOUT
RUNSOUT
SACKOUT
SANGOUT
SEEKOUT
SEESOUT
SELLOUT
SENDOUT
SENTOUT
SERIOUS
SETSOUT
SEYMOUR
SHIPOUT
SHUTOUT
SICKOUT
SIGNOUT
SINGOUT
SINUOUS
SITSOUT
SKIPOUT
SLIPOUT
SOLDOUT
SPINOUT
SPUNOUT
STEPOUT
SUCCOUR
TAGSOUT
TAKEOUT
TALKOUT
TAMBOUR
TAPSOUT
TEDIOUS
TENFOUR
TENUOUS
TESTOUT
THEROUX
TIMEOUT
TIREOUT
TOOKOUT
TOPSOUT
TOREOUT
TORNOUT
TOSSOUT
TROTOUT
TUNEOUT
TURNOUT
VACUOUS
VARIOUS
VICIOUS
VISCOUS
WAITOUT
WALKOUT
WANTOUT
WASHOUT
WEAROUT
WEEDOUT
WENTOUT
WIGSOUT
WINKOUT
WINSOUT
WIPEOUT
WITHOUT
WOREOUT
WORKOUT
WORNOUT
ZEALOUS
ZONKOUT

•••••OU

ANGELOU
CARIBOU
EMMYLOU
MANITOU
MARABOU
MARYLOU
NEARYOU
ONLYYOU

OV•••••

OVATION
OVERACT
OVERAGE
OVERALL
OVERATE
OVERAWE
OVERBIG
OVERBUY
OVERDID
OVERDUB
OVERDUE
OVEREAT
OVERFLY
OVERJOY
OVERLAP
OVERLAY
OVERLIE
OVERRAN
OVERRUN
OVERSAW
OVERSEA
OVERSEE
OVERTLY
OVERUSE
OVOIDAL

O•V••••

OBVERSE
OBVERTS
OBVIATE
OBVIOUS
ORVILLE

O••V•••

OEUVRES
OLIVIER
OLIVINE
OUTVOTE

O•••V••

OCTAVES
OCTAVIA
OCTAVOS
OLDUVAI

O••••V•

OBSERVE
ONLEAVE
OUTLIVE

•OV••••

BOVINES
COVERED
COVERUP
COVETED
DOVEBAR
DOVECOT
GOVERNS
HOVERED
HOVERER
LOVABLE
LOVEBUG
LOVEINS
LOVERLY
MOVABLE
MOVEDIN
MOVEOUT
MOVESIN
NOVARRO
NOVELLA
NOVELLE
NOVELTY
NOVENAS
NOVICES
POVERTY
SOVIETS

•O•V•••

BOBVILA
COEVALS
CONVENE
CONVENT
CONVERT
CONVEYS
CONVICT
CONVOKE
CONVOYS
LOUVERS
LOUVRES
NOUVEAU
ROLVAAG
SOLVENT
SOLVERS
SOLVING

•O••V••

BOLIVAR
BOLIVIA
DOEUVRE
DONOVAN
FOREVER
GOTEVEN
GOTOVER
HOPOVER
HOWEVER
MORAVIA

MOTIVES
POPOVER
ZOUAVES

•O•••V•
BONJOVI
COMMOVE
CONCAVE
CONNIVE
FORGAVE
FORGIVE

•O••••V
GODUNOV
MOLOTOV
ROCKYIV
ROMANOV

••OV•••
BMOVIES
CLOVERS
DROVERS
GROVELS
PLOVERS
PROVERB
PROVERS
PROVIDE
PROVING
PROVISO
PROVOKE
PROVOST
SHOVELS
SHOVERS
SHOVING
SLOVAKS
SLOVENE
SLOVENS

••O•V••
EVOLVED
EVOLVES
GROOVED
GROOVES
WHOEVER

••O••V•
EMOTIVE
EROSIVE
PLOSIVE

•••OV••
ALCOVES
ALLOVER
ANDOVER
BELOVED
DEKOVEN
DIDOVER
DONOVAN
FLYOVER
GETOVER
GOTOVER
GROOVED
GROOVES
HANOVER
HOPOVER
LAYOVER
LIEOVER
POPOVER
PUTOVER
RANOVER
RAYOVAC
RECOVER
REMOVAL
REMOVED
REMOVER
REMOVES
REWOVEN
RUNOVER
SAMOVAR
SEGOVIA
UNCOVER
UNLOVED
UNMOVED

•••O•V•
ABSOLVE
BEHOOVE
DEVOLVE
INVOLVE
RESOLVE
REVOLVE

•••O••V
MOLOTOV
NABOKOV

••••OV•
ANCHOVY
APPROVE
BEHOOVE
BONJOVI
COMMOVE
IMPROVE
KEDROVA
MARKOVA
MUSCOVY
PAVLOVA
REPROVE
ULANOVA

•••••OV
CHEKHOV
GODUNOV
MOLOTOV
NABOKOV
NEMEROV
ROMANOV
ULYANOV
USTINOV

OW•••••
OWINGTO
OWLLIKE
OWNEDUP

O•W••••
ONWARDS

O••W•••
OILWELL
OLDWEST
OUTWARD
OUTWEAR
OUTWITS
OUTWORE
OUTWORK
OUTWORN

O•••W••
OJIBWAS
OJIBWAY
OTTAWAS

O••••W•
OAKLAWN
OKINAWA
OLDNEWS
OURTOWN
OUTLAWS
OVERAWE

O•••••W
OUTDRAW
OUTDREW
OUTFLOW
OUTGREW
OUTGROW
OVERSAW

•OW••••
BOWDLER
BOWERED
BOWFINS
BOWKNOT
BOWLERS
BOWLFUL
BOWLINE
BOWLING
BOWSAWS
BOWSOUT
BOWTIES
BOWWOWS
BOWYERS
COWARDS
COWBELL
COWBIRD
COWBOYS
COWERED
COWGIRL
COWHAND
COWHERD
COWHIDE
COWLICK
COWLING
COWPEAS
COWPOKE
COWRIES
COWSLIP
COWTOWN
DOWAGER
DOWDIER
DOWDILY
DOWNBOW
DOWNERS
DOWNIER
DOWNING
DOWNPAT
DOWRIES
DOWSERS
DOWSING
FOWLERS
FOWLING
GOWRONG
HOWARDS
HOWBEIT
HOWCOME
HOWDAHS
HOWELLS
HOWEVER
HOWLERS
HOWLING
KOWLOON
KOWTOWS
LOWBALL
LOWBEAM
LOWBLOW
LOWBORN
LOWBOYS
LOWBRED
LOWBROW
LOWDOWN
LOWERED
LOWGEAR
LOWHEEL
LOWLAND
LOWLIER
LOWLIFE
LOWNECK
LOWNESS
LOWPAID
LOWRISE
LOWROAD
LOWTECH
LOWTIDE
MOWDOWN
NOWHERE
POWDERS
POWDERY
POWERED
POWWOWS
ROWBOAT
ROWDIER
ROWDIES
ROWDILY
SOWBUGS
TOWARDS
TOWAWAY
TOWCARS
TOWELED
TOWERED
TOWHEAD
TOWHEES
TOWNERS
TOWNIES
TOWPATH
TOWROPE
YOWLERS
YOWLING

•O•W•••
BOSWELL
BOWWOWS
BOXWOOD
COBWEBS
DOGWOOD
FORWARD
FORWENT
GODWITS
GOTWELL
HOGWASH
HOGWILD
HOTWARS
HOTWIRE
NOSWEAT
NOTWELL
POWWOWS
ROSWELL
SOPWITH

•O••W••
BOERWAR
COLDWAR
DOORWAY
FOODWEB
GOLDWYN
GOODWIN
GOTAWAY
HOLYWAR
MOHAWKS
POSTWAR
ROADWAY
SOMEWAY
TOLLWAY
TOWAWAY

•O•••W•
BOGDOWN
BORROWS
BOWSAWS
BOWWOWS
COWTOWN
FOGBOWS
FOLLOWS
GOSHAWK
GOTDOWN
HOEDOWN
HOLLOWS
HOOTOWL
KOWTOWS
LOWDOWN
MORROWS
MOWDOWN
NOSHOWS
POWWOWS
ROBLOWE
SORROWS

•O••••W
CORNROW
DOGCHEW
DOGCHOW
DOGSHOW
DOWNBOW
FOREPAW
FORESAW
HOLYCOW
JOEBLOW
LONGBOW
LOWBLOW
LOWBROW
ROPETOW
SOMEHOW
TONEROW
WOODROW
YOUKNOW

••OW•••
AVOWALS
AVOWERS
AVOWING
BEOWULF
BLOWDRY
BLOWERS
BLOWFLY
BLOWGUN
BLOWIER
BLOWING
BLOWNUP
BLOWOFF
BLOWOUT
BLOWSIN
BLOWSIT
BLOWSUP
BLOWUPS
BROWNED
BROWNER
BROWNIE
BROWSED
BROWSER
BROWSES
CHOWDER
CLOWDER
CLOWNED
CROWBAR
CROWDED
CROWERS
CROWING
CROWNED
DROWNED
DROWSED
DROWSES
FLOWERS
FLOWERY
FLOWING
FROWARD
FROWNAT
FROWNED
FROWNER
GLOWERS
GLOWING
GROWERS
GROWING
GROWLED
GROWLER
GROWNUP
GROWSON
GROWSUP
GROWTHS
KNOWHOW
KNOWING
MEOWING
PLOWBOY
PLOWERS
PLOWING
PLOWMAN
PLOWMEN
PROWESS
PROWLED
PROWLER
SCOWLED
SCOWLER
SHOWBIZ
SHOWDOG
SHOWERS
SHOWERY
SHOWIER
SHOWILY
SHOWING
SHOWMAN
SHOWMEN
SHOWNIN
SHOWOFF
SHOWSIN
SHOWSUP
SLOWEST
SLOWING
SLOWSUP
SNOWCAP
SNOWDAY
SNOWDON
SNOWIER
SNOWING
SNOWJOB
SNOWMAN
SNOWMEN
SNOWPEA
SNOWSIN
STOWING
TROWELS
TROWERS

••O•W••
DOORWAY
FOODWEB
GOODWIN
WHOSWHO

••O••W•
HOOTOWL

••O•••W
ASOFNOW
CHOCTAW
KNOWHOW
USOSHOW
WOODROW

•••OW••
ALLOWED
CNTOWER
DISOWNS
ELBOWED
EMPOWER
ENDOWED
INNOWAY
MANOWAR
REMOWED
RETOWED
THROWER
THROWIN
UNBOWED
WIDOWED
WIDOWER

•••O••W
UPTONOW

••••OW•
ANTCOWS
BARNOWL
BARROWS
BEDDOWN
BELLOWS
BESTOWS
BILLOWS
BILLOWY
BOGDOWN
BORROWS
BOWWOWS
BURROWS
COWTOWN
CUTDOWN
DIEDOWN
ESCROWS
FALLOWS
FARROWS
FELLOWS
FOGBOWS
FOLLOWS
FURROWS
GETDOWN
GOTDOWN
HALLOWS
HARROWS
HAYMOWS
HOEDOWN
HOLLOWS
HOOTOWL
INFLOWS
INGROWN
KOWTOWS
LAYDOWN
LETDOWN
LIEDOWN
LOWDOWN
MALLOWS
MARLOWE
MARROWS
MEADOWS
MEADOWY
MELLOWS
MIDTOWN
MINNOWS
MORROWS
MOWDOWN
NARROWS
NEWMOWN
NEWTOWN
NOSHOWS
OURTOWN
PEAFOWL
PILLOWS
PILLOWY
PINDOWN
POWWOWS
PUTDOWN
ROBLOWE
RUBDOWN
RUNDOWN
SATDOWN
SEACOWS
SETDOWN
SHADOWS
SHADOWY
SITDOWN
SKITOWS
SORROWS
SUNDOWN
TALLOWS
TIEDOWN
TVSHOWS
UNKNOWN
WALLOWS
WILLOWS
WILLOWY
WINDOWS
WINNOWS
YARROWS
YELLOWS

•••••OW
AIRFLOW
AIRSHOW
ASOFNOW
ATECROW
BIGELOW
CASHCOW
CORNROW
DISAVOW
DOGCHOW
DOGSHOW
DOWNBOW
EATCROW
EYEBROW
GLASGOW
HIGHLOW
HOLYCOW
ICESHOW
JOEBLOW
JUSTNOW
KNOWHOW
LAIDLOW
LAYSLOW
LIESLOW
LITHGOW
LONGBOW
LOWBLOW
LOWBROW
MANILOW
MILKCOW
OUTFLOW
OUTGROW
RAINBOW
ROPETOW
SALCHOW
SHALLOW
SKIDROW
SOMEHOW
SPARROW
SWALLOW
TONEROW
UPTONOW
USOSHOW
WINDROW
WINSLOW
WOODROW
YOUKNOW

OX•••••
OXBLOOD
OXCARTS
OXFORDS
OXIDANT
OXIDASE
OXIDIZE
OXONIAN
OXYMORA

•OX••••
BOXCARS
BOXEDIN
BOXEDUP
BOXESIN
BOXESUP
BOXFULS
BOXKITE
BOXSEAT
BOXSTEP
BOXTOPS
BOXWOOD
COXCOMB
FOXFIRE
FOXHOLE
FOXIEST
FOXTAIL
FOXTROT
NOXIOUS
NOXZEMA
ROXANNE

•O•X•••
COAXERS
COAXIAL
COAXING
COEXIST
HOAXERS
HOAXING

•O••X••
POBOXES

•O•••X•
CONTEXT
POLEAXE

•O••••X
BOOMBOX
COMPLEX
GORETEX
LOCKBOX
MONTEUX
POLLTAX
POORBOX
POSTBOX
ROLODEX
SOAPBOX
TOOLBOX

••OX•••
DIOXIDE
EPOXIES
PROXIES
PROXIMO

••O•••X
BOOMBOX
BROADAX
PHOENIX
POORBOX
SHOEBOX
TOOLBOX

•••OX••
PHLOXES
POBOXES
UNBOXED
UNBOXES

•••O••X
ALTOSAX
MEMOREX
ROLODEX

••••O•X
STCROIX
THEROUX

•••••OX
BANDBOX
BLUEFOX
BOOMBOX
BRERFOX
CALLBOX
CASHBOX
EQUINOX
FIREBOX
FLUMMOX
GEARBOX
JUKEBOX
LOCKBOX
MAILBOX
PARADOX
PILLBOX
POORBOX
POSTBOX
SALTBOX
SANDBOX
SHOEBOX
SOAPBOX
TOOLBOX

OY•••••
OYSTERS

O•Y••••
ODYSSEY
OLYMPIA
OLYMPIC
OLYMPUS
OXYMORA

O••Y•••
OBEYING
OFFYEAR
OKAYING
ONLYYOU
OOCYTES

O•••Y••
ONEEYED
ONLYYOU

O••••Y•
OLDDAYS
OSPREYS
OUTLAYS

O•••••Y
OBLOQUY
ODYSSEY
OFFDUTY
OJIBWAY
OLDFOGY
OPACITY
ORATORY
ORDERLY
ORGANDY
ORMANDY
OUTPLAY
OVERBUY
OVERFLY
OVERJOY
OVERLAY
OVERTLY

•OY••••
BOYCOTT
BOYDORR
BOYHOOD
COYNESS
COYOTES
DOYENNE
HOYDENS
JOYLESS
JOYRIDE
LOYALLY
LOYALTY
ROYALLY
ROYALTY
ROYBEAN
SOYBEAN
TOYDOGS
TOYLAND
TOYNBEE
TOYSHOP
VOYAGED
VOYAGER
VOYAGES
YOYOING
ZOYSIAS

•O•Y•••
BODYFAT
BOWYERS
COPYBOY
COPYCAT
COPYING
COPYIST
CORYELL
COZYING
FOGYISH
FOGYISM
HOLYARK
HOLYCOW
HOLYOKE
HOLYSEE
HOLYWAR
KOSYGIN
OOCYTES
POLYGON
POLYMER
PONYING
TORYISM

•O••Y••
BOGEYED
COLLYER
FORSYTH
HONEYED
LOBBYER
MONEYED
MOSEYED
POPEYED
ROCKYII
ROCKYIV

•O•••Y•
CONVEYS
CONVOYS
COWBOYS
DOGDAYS
DONKEYS
FONTEYN
GOLDWYN
GOODBYE
GOODBYS
HOMONYM
JOCKEYS
LOWBOYS
MONDAYS
MONKEYS
MONTOYA
ROBROYS
ROMNEYS
SOCKEYE
TOMBOYS
VOLLEYS

•O••••Y
BOKCHOY
BONEDRY
BONNILY
BOSSILY
COCKILY
COCKNEY
COGENCY
COMESBY
COMFREY
COMPANY
CONAKRY
CONNERY
COOKERY
COPPERY
COPYBOY
CORNILY
COTTONY
COUNTRY
COURTLY
DOORWAY
DOROTHY
DOUGHTY
DOWDILY
FOOLERY
FOPPERY
FORGERY
FORTIFY
FOUNDRY
GODFREY
GOINGBY
GOSSIPY
GOTAWAY
HOLIDAY
HONESTY
HOOTCHY
HORNSBY
HORRIFY
HOSIERY
JOFFREY
JOHNGAY
JOHNJAY
JOINERY
JOINTLY
JOLLILY
JOLLITY
JOURNEY
KOLACKY
KOOTCHY
LOCALLY
LOFTILY
LOOSELY
LOTTERY
LOUSILY
LOVERLY
LOYALLY
LOYALTY
MOCKERY
MODESTY
MOISTLY
MOLLIFY
MONTHLY
MOODILY
MORALLY
MORESBY
MORTIFY
NOISILY
NOONDAY
NOSEGAY
NOTABLY
NOVELTY
POORBOY
PORTRAY
POTENCY
POTTERY
POULTRY
POVERTY
POWDERY
ROADWAY
ROBBERY
ROGUERY
ROOKERY
ROUGHLY
ROUNDLY
ROWDILY
ROYALLY
ROYALTY
SOBERLY
SOCIETY
SOGGILY
SOLIDLY
SOMEDAY
SOMEWAY
SORCERY
SOUNDLY
SOUTHEY
TOLLWAY
TOLSTOY
TONALLY
TOPIARY
TOTALLY
TOTTERY
TOUGHLY
TOURNEY
TOWAWAY
VOCALLY
VOLUBLY
WOMANLY
WOOLSEY

WOOZILY
WORDILY
WORKDAY
WORLDLY
ZONALLY
ZOOLOGY

••OY•••
BUOYANT
BUOYING
BUOYSUP
CLOYING

••O•Y••
ACOLYTE
ANODYNE
ANONYMS
EPONYMS
GROMYKO
PROCYON

••O••Y•
GOODBYE
GOODBYS
STOREYS

••O•••Y
ALOOFLY
ANOMALY
APOLOGY
BIOGENY
BIOLOGY
BLOTCHY
BLOWDRY
BLOWFLY
BROADLY
CHOMSKY
CLOONEY
CLOSELY
COOKERY
CROSSLY
DOORWAY
DROPSBY
ECOLOGY
ECONOMY
FLOWERY
FOOLERY
GEODESY
GEOLOGY
GHOSTLY
GLORIFY
GROCERY
GROSSLY
GROUCHY
HOOTCHY
KOOTCHY
LOOSELY
MOODILY
NOONDAY
PHONILY
PIOUSLY
PLOWBOY
POORBOY
PROBITY
PRODIGY
PROGENY
PROSILY
PROSODY
PROUDLY
PTOLEMY
ROOKERY
SHOOFLY
SHORTLY
SHOWERY
SHOWILY
SLOUCHY
SNOWDAY
STOKELY
STONILY
STOODBY
STOOKEY
STOUTLY
SWOREBY
TROLLEY
TROTSKY
VRONSKY
WOOLSEY
WOOZILY
WRONGLY
ZOOLOGY

•••OY••
ALLOYED
ANNOYED
ARROYOS
DECOYED
ENJOYED
SAMOYED
SAROYAN

•••O•Y•
ACRONYM
ANTONYM
CAROLYN
HOMONYM
KAROLYI
SYNONYM

•••O••Y
ALOOFLY
ATROPHY
BALONEY
BIGOTRY
CLOONEY
DAHOMEY
DISOBEY
DOROTHY
HELOTRY
IGNOBLY
IMSORRY
INNOWAY
MAHONEY
MASONRY
OBLOQUY
PANOPLY
SAVOURY
SHOOFLY
STOODBY
STOOKEY
THROATY
TIMOTHY
UNGODLY

••••OY•
AYKROYD
BATBOYS
BIGBOYS
BUSBOYS
CARBOYS
CONVOYS
COWBOYS
DEPLOYS
EMPLOYS
FLYBOYS
LOWBOYS
MONTOYA
ROBROYS
TEAPOYS
TOMBOYS

••••O•Y
ALIMONY
AMATORY
ANALOGY
ANATOMY
ANCHOVY
ANTHONY
ANYBODY
APOLOGY
BALCONY
BILLOWY
BIOLOGY
CHICORY
COTTONY
CURSORY
CUSTODY
ECOLOGY
ECONOMY
ENTROPY
EUPHONY
FACTORY
GEOLOGY
GREGORY
HARMONY
HICKORY
HISTORY
LASTORY
MEADOWY
MUSCOVY
OLDFOGY
ORATORY
PALJOEY
PEABODY
PILLORY
PILLOWY
PROSODY
RECTORY
SENSORY
SHADOWY
TRILOGY
VICTORY
WILLOWY
ZOOLOGY

•••••OY
BALLBOY
BELLBOY
BESTBOY
BLUEBOY
BOKCHOY
COPYBOY
DESTROY
HAUTBOY
HIGHBOY
KILLJOY
NEWSBOY
OVERJOY
PAGEBOY
PLAYBOY
PLOWBOY
POORBOY
TOLSTOY
VICEROY

OZ•••••
OZONOUS

O••••Z•
OBELIZE
ORGANZA
OUTSIZE
OXIDIZE

•OZ••••
COZENED
COZIEST
COZUMEL
COZYING
COZZENS
DOZENTH
DOZEOFF
LOZENGE
NOZZLES
ROZELLE
WOZNIAK
WOZZECK

•O•Z•••
BORZOIS
COZZENS
DOOZIES
FOOZLED
FOOZLES
NONZERO
NOXZEMA
NOZZLES
WOOZIER
WOOZILY
WOZZECK

•O••Z••
CORAZON
HORIZON
IODIZED
IODIZES
IONIZED
IONIZER
IONIZES
TOPAZES

•O•••Z•
BONANZA
LORENZO

•O••••Z
KOBLENZ

••OZ•••
DOOZIES
FOOZLED
FOOZLES
WOOZIER
WOOZILY

••O•Z••
BRONZED
BRONZES
SNOOZED
SNOOZES

••O••Z•
AGONIZE
ANODIZE
ATOMIZE
CHORIZO
IDOLIZE
LIONIZE

••O•••Z
SHOWBIZ

•••OZ••
REBOZOS
SNOOZED
SNOOZES

••••OZ•
CARDOZO
MENDOZA
SPINOZA

•••••OZ
BERLIOZ
FRANKOZ

PA•••••
PABLUMS
PABULUM
PACECAR
PACHISI
PACIFIC
PACKAGE
PACKARD
PACKERS
PACKETS
PACKICE
PACKING
PACKRAT
PACKSUP
PADDERS
PADDIES
PADDING
PADDLED
PADDLER
PADDLES
PADDOCK
PADLOCK
PADRONE
PADRONI
PADUCAH
PAGEANT
PAGEBOY
PAGEFUL
PAGODAS
PAHLAVI
PAIDFOR
PAIDOFF
PAIDOUT
PAILFUL
PAILOUS
PAINFUL
PAINTED
PAINTER
PAIRING
PAIROFF
PAIRSUP
PAISANO
PAISLEY
PAIUTES
PAJAMAS
PALACES
PALADIN
PALANCE
PALATAL
PALATES
PALAVER
PALAZZI
PALAZZO
PALEDRY
PALERMO
PALETTE
PALFREY
PALJOEY
PALLETS
PALLING
PALLIUM
PALMATE
PALMIER
PALMING
PALMIST
PALMOFF
PALMOIL
PALOMAR
PALOOKA
PALTERS
PAMBIES
PAMPERS
PANACEA
PANACHE
PANAMAS
PANCAKE
PANCHAX
PANDECT
PANDERS
PANDITS
PANDORA
PANELED
PANETTA
PANFISH
PANICKY
PANICLE
PANNERS
PANNIER
PANNING
PANOPLY
PANPIPE
PANSIES
PANSOUT
PANTHER
PANTING
PANURGE
PANZERS
PAPADOC
PAPAGOS
PAPAYAS
PAPEETE
PAPERED
PAPERER
PAPILLA
PAPOOSE
PAPRIKA
PAPUANS
PAPYRUS
PARABLE
PARADED
PARADES
PARADOX
PARAGON
PARAPET
PARAPHS
PARASOL
PARBOIL
PARCELS
PARCHED
PARCHES
PARDNER
PARDONS
PARENTS
PARFAIT
PARGETS
PARIAHS
PARIBUS
PARINGS
PARKING
PARKWAY
PARLAYS
PARLEYS
PARLORS
PARLOUR
PARLOUS
PARNELL
PAROLED
PAROLEE
PAROLES
PARQUET
PARRIED
PARRIES
PARRING
PARROTS
PARSECS
PARSEES
PARSERS
PARSING
PARSLEY
PARSNIP
PARSONS
PARTAKE
PARTIAL
PARTIED
PARTIES
PARTING
PARTITA
PARTITE
PARTNER
PARTOOK
PARTOUT
PARTWAY
PARURES
PARVENU
PASCHAL
PASSAGE
PASSANT
PASSELS
PASSERS
PASSEUL
PASSFOR
PASSING
PASSION
PASSIVE
PASSKEY
PASSOFF
PASSOUT
PASTDUE
PASTELS
PASTERN
PASTEUP
PASTEUR
PASTIER
PASTIME
PASTINA
PASTING
PASTORS
PASTURE
PATAKES
PATCHED
PATCHES
PATCHUP
PATELLA
PATENTS
PATERNO
PATHWAY
PATIENT
PATINAS
PATNESS
PATRICE
PATRICK
PATRIOT
PATROLS
PATRONS
PATROON
PATSIES
PATTENS
PATTERN
PATTERS
PATTIES
PATTING
PAUCITY
PAULINA
PAULINE
PAULING
PAULIST
PAULSEN
PAUNCHY
PAUPERS
PAUSING
PAVANES
PAVIOUR
PAVLOVA
PAWEDAT
PAWNEES
PAWNERS
PAWNING
PAWNOFF
PAWPAWS
PAYABLE
PAYCASH
PAYDAYS
PAYDIRT
PAYLOAD
PAYMENT
PAYOFFS
PAYOLAS
PAYOUTS
PAYROLL
PAYSFOR
PAYSOFF
PAYSOUT

P•A••••
PEABEAN
PEABODY
PEACHED
PEACHES
PEACOAT
PEACOCK
PEAFOWL
PEAHENS
PEAKING
PEALING
PEANUTS
PEAPODS
PEARLED
PEARSON
PEASANT
PEASOUP
PEATBOG
PEAVEYS
PHAEDRA
PHAETON
PHALANX
PHANTOM
PHARAOH
PHARYNX
PHASEIN
PHASERS
PHASING
PIANISM
PIANIST
PIASTER
PIASTRE
PIAZZAS
PLACARD
PLACATE
PLACEBO
PLACERS
PLACIDO
PLACING
PLACKET
PLAGUED
PLAGUES
PLAICES
PLAINER
PLAINES
PLAINLY
PLAINTS
PLAITED
PLANERS
PLANETS
PLANING
PLANKED
PLANNED
PLANNER
PLANSON
PLANTAR
PLANTED
PLANTER
PLAQUES
PLASHED
PLASHES
PLASMAS
PLASTER
PLASTIC
PLATEAU
PLATENS
PLATERS
PLATING
PLATOON
PLATTER
PLATYPI
PLAUDIT
PLAUTUS
PLAYACT
PLAYBOY
PLAYDOH
PLAYERS
PLAYFUL
PLAYING
PLAYLET
PLAYOFF
PLAYOUT
PLAYPEN
PLAYSAT
PLAYSON
PLAYSUP
POACHED
POACHER
POACHES
PRAETOR
PRAIRIE
PRAISED
PRAISER
PRAISES
PRALINE
PRANCED
PRANCER
PRANCES
PRANKED
PRATERS
PRATING
PRATTLE
PRAYERS
PRAYFOR
PRAYING
PRAYSTO
PSALMED
PSALTER
PSANDQS

P••A•••
PAJAMAS
PALACES
PALADIN
PALANCE
PALATAL
PALATES
PALAVER
PALAZZI
PALAZZO
PANACEA
PANACHE
PANAMAS
PAPADOC
PAPAGOS
PAPAYAS
PARABLE
PARADED
PARADES
PARADOX
PARAGON
PARAPET
PARAPHS
PARASOL
PATAKES
PAVANES
PAYABLE
PDJAMES
PEDALED
PEDANTS
PEGASUS
PELAGES
PELAGIC
PENALTY
PENANCE
PENATES
PETALED
PETARDS
PHRASAL
PHRASED
PHRASES
PICADOR
PICANTE
PICAROS
PICASSO
PINATAS
PIRAEUS
PIRANHA
PIRATED
PIRATES
PIRATIC
PITAPAT
PIZARRO
PLEADED
PLEADER
PLEASED
PLEASER
PLEASES
PLEATED
PLIABLE
PLIABLY
PLIANCY
POLARIS
POMADED
POMADES
POSADAS
POTABLE
POTAGES
PREACHY
PREAMPS
PULASKI
PUTAMEN
PUTAWAY
PYJAMAS
PYRAMID
PYRAMUS

P•••A••
PACKAGE
PACKARD
PAGEANT
PAHLAVI
PAISANO
PALMATE
PANCAKE
PAPUANS
PARFAIT
PARIAHS
PARLAYS
PARTAKE
PASSAGE
PASSANT
PAWPAWS
PAYCASH
PAYDAYS
PEASANT
PECCANT
PECCARY
PEDLARS
PEERAGE
PELTATE
PENDANT
PENNAME
PENNANT
PENNATE
PENPALS
PENTADS
PEONAGE
PEPPARD
PEPTALK
PERCALE
PERHAPS
PERTAIN
PERVADE
PETNAME
PHALANX
PHARAOH
PICCARD
PICKAXE
PIEBALD
PIEPANS
PIGTAIL
PILLAGE
PILLARS
PINBALL
PINNACE
PINNATE
PINOAKS
PINTAIL
PINWALE
PIQUANT
PITFALL
PITSAWS
PIZZAZZ
PLACARD
PLACATE
PLAYACT
PLENARY
PLUMAGE
PLURALS
POLEAXE
POLKAED
POMPANO
PONIARD
POPLARS
POPTART
PORTAGE
PORTALS
POSTAGE
POTTAGE
PRECAST
PREDATE
PREDAWN
PREFABS
PREFACE
PRELATE
PREPAID
PREPARE
PREPAYS
PRESAGE
PRESALE
PRETAPE
PREVAIL
PREWASH
PRIMACY
PRIMARY
PRIMATE
PRIVACY
PRIVATE
PROBATE
PROFANE
PROPANE
PRORATA
PRORATE
PROSAIC
PTBOATS
PULSARS
PULSATE
PUNJABI
PUNKAHS
PURDAHS

P••••A•
PACECAR
PACKRAT
PADUCAH
PAGODAS
PAJAMAS
PALATAL
PALOMAR
PANAMAS
PANCHAX
PAPAYAS
PARKWAY
PARTIAL
PARTWAY
PASCHAL
PATHWAY
PATINAS
PAWEDAT
PAYLOAD
PAYOLAS
PEABEAN
PEACOAT
PECKSAT
PEEKSAT
PEERSAT
PELICAN
PELOTAS
PEMICAN
PERLMAN
PERSIAN
PERUSAL
PESETAS
PHIDIAS
PHINEAS
PHOBIAS
PHRASAL
PIAZZAS
PICKSAT
PIKEMAN
PINATAS
PINCHAS
PINESAP
PINETAR
PINHEAD
PITAPAT
PITTMAN
PIVOTAL
PLANTAR
PLASMAS
PLATEAU
PLAYSAT
PLOWMAN
PLUVIAL
POKEDAT
POKESAT
POLECAT
POLLTAX
PONTIAC
POOHBAH
POPULAR
PORTRAY
POSADAS
POSTMAN
POSTWAR
POTOMAC
POTSDAM
PREHEAT
PRELOAD
PRESOAK
PROGRAM
PROPMAN
PROTEAN
PULLMAN
PULLTAB
PURITAN
PUTAWAY
PYJAMAS
PYTHIAS

P•••••A
PALOOKA
PANACEA
PANDORA
PANETTA
PAPILLA
PAPRIKA
PARTITA
PASTINA
PATELLA
PAULINA
PAVLOVA
PERGOLA
PERSONA
PETUNIA
PHAEDRA
PIRANHA
PLECTRA
PODRIDA
POLENTA
POMPEIA
PORSENA
PORTOLA
PRORATA
PRUSSIA

•PA••••
APACHES
APATITE

EPARCHS
EPAULET
IPANEMA
OPACITY
OPALINE
OPAQUES
SPACERS
SPACIER
SPACING
SPACKLE
SPADERS
SPADING
SPALLED
SPANDEX
SPANGLE
SPANGLY
SPANIEL
SPANISH
SPANKED
SPANKER
SPANNED
SPANNER
SPARELY
SPAREST
SPARGED
SPARGES
SPARING
SPARKED
SPARKLE
SPARRED
SPARROW
SPARSER
SPARTAN
SPASSKY
SPATIAL
SPATTED
SPATTER
SPATULA
SPAVINS
SPAWNED
SPAYING
UPATREE

•P•A•••
APPALLS
APPAREL
OPIATES
SPEAKER
SPEAKOF
SPEAKUP
SPEARED
SPLASHY
SPLAYED
SPRAINS
SPRAWLS
SPRAYED
SPRAYER
UPDATED
UPDATES
UPLANDS
UPRAISE
UPTAKES
UPWARDS

•P••A••
APPEALS
APPEARS
APPEASE
APPLAUD
OPENAIR
OPERAND
OPERATE
SPINACH
SPIRALS
SPIRANT
SPOKANE
SPREADS
UPBEATS
UPBRAID
UPDRAFT
UPGRADE
UPLOADS
UPPSALA
UPROARS
UPSCALE
UPSTAGE
UPSTART
UPSTATE

•P•••A•
EPIGRAM
OPENBAR
OPTICAL
OPTIMAL
SPARTAN
SPATIAL
SPECIAL
SPIREAS
SPORRAN
SPOUSAL
UPTOPAR

•P••••A
APHELIA
IPANEMA
OPENSEA
OPHELIA
SPATULA
SPECTRA
SPINOZA
UPPSALA

••PA•••
ALPACAS
APPALLS
APPAREL
BYPATHS
CAPABLE
CAPABLY
CAPAPIE
DEPALMA
DEPARTS
EMPANEL
EMPATHY
ESPANOL
EXPANDS
EXPANSE
EXPARTE
HEPARIN
HEPATIC
IMPACTS
IMPAIRS
IMPALAS
IMPALED
IMPALES
IMPANEL
IMPARTS
IMPASSE
IMPASTO
LAPALMA
LEPANTO
NEPALIS
ONPAPER
PAPADOC
PAPAGOS
PAPAYAS
RAPANUI
REPAINT
REPAIRS
REPAPER
REPASTE
REPASTS
REPAVED
REPAVES
TOPAZES
UNPACKS
UNPAVED

••P•A••
APPEALS
APPEARS
APPEASE
APPLAUD
ASPHALT
ATPEACE
BIPLANE
BYPLAYS
CAPEANN
CAPTAIN
COPLAND
CUPCAKE
DEPLANE
DEPRAVE
ENPLANE
ESPIALS
EXPIATE
EXPLAIN
HEPCATS
HEPTADS
IMPEACH
IMPLANT
INPEACE
INPHASE
INPLACE
LAPLACE
LAPLAND
LAPLATA
LIPBALM
OMPHALI
ORPHANS
PAPUANS
PEPPARD
PEPTALK
POPLARS
POPTART
RAPHAEL
REPEALS
REPEATS
REPLACE
REPLANS
REPLANT
REPLATE
REPLAYS
RIPRAPS
RIPSAWS
RUPIAHS
SAPSAGO
SOPRANO
TOPHATS
TOPIARY
TOPKAPI
TOPMAST
TOPSAIL
UPPSALA
YOPLAIT

••P••A•
ALPACAS
BIPEDAL
BIPOLAR
CAPITAL
CAPITAN
CAPSHAW
CAPSTAN
COPYCAT
CUPOLAS
DEPOSAL
DIPOLAR
ESPOSAS
IMPALAS
LIPREAD
NUPTIAL
ORPHEAN
PAPAYAS
POPULAR
REPOMAN
TOPCOAT
TOPICAL
TYPICAL

••P•••A
AMPHORA
CAPELLA
COPPOLA
DEPALMA
DIPLOMA
EMPORIA
LAPALMA
LAPLATA
NAPHTHA
PAPILLA
PAPRIKA
REPLICA
TAPIOCA
UPPSALA

•••PA••
ANSPACH
ARAPAHO
BITPART
CALPACS
CAMPARI
CARPALS
CHAPATI
CLIPART
COMPACT
COMPANY
COMPARE
COMPASS
DESPAIR
FLYPAST
FRYPANS
HISPANO
ICEPACK
INSPANS
JAMPACK
KAMPALA
KEYPADS
LEOPARD
LESPAUL
LOWPAID
MUDPACK
OILPANS
OOMPAHS
OUTPACE
PAWPAWS
PENPALS
PEPPARD
PIEPANS
POMPANO
PREPAID
PREPARE
PREPAYS
PROPANE
RAMPAGE
RAMPANT
RAMPART
RATPACK
SAMPANS
SHEPARD
SIXPACK
SURPASS
TAIPANS
TOSPARE
TOWPATH
TREPANS
TYMPANA
TYMPANI
WARPATH

•••P•A•
AIRPLAY
BESPEAK
CASPIAN
CHAPEAU
CHAPMAN
COWPEAS
DEEPFAT
DISPLAY
DRIPPAN
ENDPLAY
GUNPLAY
HOOPLAS
JUMPSAT
KEEPSAT
MISPLAY
OFFPEAK
OUTPLAY
PROPMAN
SAMPRAS
SHIPMAN
SNAPSAT
SNIPEAT
STOPGAP
TEMPLAR
UTOPIAN
UTOPIAS
WHIPSAW

•••P••A
AMAPOLA
COPPOLA
DEEPSEA
KAMPALA
LEMPIRA
POMPEIA
SCAPULA
TEMPERA
TEMPURA
TYMPANA

••••PA•
BASEPAY
BEARPAW
CATSPAW
DEADPAN
DISHPAN
DOWNPAT
DRIPPAN
DUSTPAN
FAUXPAS
FOOTPAD
FOREPAW
HARDPAN
HELIPAD
KNEEPAD
LILYPAD
MAKEPAR
NOTEPAD
OEDIPAL
PITAPAT
SHERPAS
SICKPAY
TRAMPAS
UPTOPAR

••••P•A
AGRIPPA
OLYMPIA
SNOWPEA

•••••PA
AGRIPPA
CATALPA
GRANDPA

P•B••••
PABLUMS
PABULUM
PEBBLED
PEBBLES
POBOXES
PTBOATS
PUBERTY
PUBLICS
PUBLISH

P••B•••
PAMBIES
PARBOIL
PEABEAN
PEABODY
PEBBLED
PEBBLES
PHOBIAS
PHOBICS
PIEBALD
PINBALL
PITBOSS
PITBULL
PREBEND
PROBATE
PROBERS
PROBING
PROBITY
PROBLEM
PROBONO
PUEBLOS

P•••B••
PAGEBOY
PARABLE
PARIBUS
PAYABLE
PEATBOG
PHILBIN
PHOEBES
PHOEBUS
PILLBOX
PILLBUG
PLAYBOY
PLIABLE
PLIABLY
PLOWBOY
PLUMBED
PLUMBER
POOHBAH
POORBOX
POORBOY
POSTBOX
POTABLE

P••••B•
PLACEBO
PREFABS
PUNJABI

P•••••B
PERTURB
POTHERB
PROVERB
PULLTAB

•PB••••
UPBEATS
UPBORNE
UPBRAID

•P••B••
OPENBAR

••PB•••
HEPBURN
HIPBONE
HIPBOOT
LAPBELT
LIPBALM

••P•B••
CAPABLE
CAPABLY
COPYBOY

••P••B•
LAPROBE

•••PB••
SOAPBOX

•••P•B•
DROPSBY

P•C••••
PACECAR
PACHISI
PACIFIC
PACKAGE
PACKARD
PACKERS
PACKETS
PACKICE
PACKING
PACKRAT
PACKSUP
PECCANT
PECCARY
PECKING
PECKISH
PECKSAT
PECTINS
PICADOR
PICANTE
PICAROS
PICASSO
PICCARD
PICCOLO
PICKAXE
PICKENS
PICKERS
PICKETS
PICKETT
PICKIER
PICKING
PICKLED
PICKLES
PICKOFF
PICKOUT
PICKSAT
PICKSON
PICKSUP
PICKUPS
PICNICS
PICTURE
POCKETS
POCONOS
PUCCINI
PUCKERS
PUCKETT
PUCKISH

P••C•••
PANCAKE
PANCHAX
PARCELS
PARCHED
PARCHES
PASCHAL
PATCHED
PATCHES
PATCHUP
PAUCITY
PAYCASH
PEACHED
PEACHES
PEACOAT
PEACOCK
PECCANT
PECCARY
PENCILS
PERCALE
PERCENT
PERCHED
PERCHES
PETCOCK
PICCARD
PICCOLO
PIECERS
PIECING
PINCERS
PINCHAS
PINCHED
PINCHER
PINCHES
PINCURL
PISCINE
PISCOPO
PITCHED
PITCHER
PITCHES
PITCHIN
PLACARD
PLACATE
PLACEBO
PLACERS
PLACIDO
PLACING
PLACKET
PLECTRA
PLUCKED
POACHED
POACHER
POACHES
PONCHOS
POOCHES
POPCORN
PORCHES
PORCINE
POUCHED
POUCHES
PRECAST
PRECEDE
PRECEPT
PRECISE
PRECOOK
PRECOOL
PRICERS
PRICIER
PRICING
PRICKED
PRICKLE
PRICKLY
PROCEED
PROCESS
PROCTOR
PROCURE
PROCYON
PSYCHED
PSYCHES
PSYCHIC
PSYCHUP
PUCCINI
PUNCHED
PUNCHER
PUNCHES
PUNCHIN
PUNCHUP
PURCELL
PYNCHON

P•••C••
PACECAR
PADUCAH
PALACES
PANACEA
PANACHE
PANICKY
PANICLE
PAUNCHY
PEDICEL
PEDICLE
PELICAN
PEMICAN
PENUCHE
PIERCED
PIERCES
PINOCLE
PLAICES
POLECAT
POLICED
POLICES
PORSCHE
POUNCED
POUNCER
POUNCES
PRANCED
PRANCER
PRANCES
PREACHY
PRINCES
PUMICES

P••••C•
PACKICE
PADDOCK
PADLOCK
PALANCE
PANDECT
PARSECS
PATRICE
PATRICK
PEACOCK
PENANCE
PERFECT
PETCOCK
PETROCK
PHOBICS
PHONICS
PHYSICS
PICNICS
PIMLICO
PINNACE
PLAYACT
PLIANCY
POETICS
POLLOCK
PORTICO
POTENCY
POTLUCK
PREDICT
PREFACE
PREFECT
PRIMACY
PRIVACY
PRODUCE
PRODUCT
PROJECT
PROTECT
PUBLICS

P•••••C
PACIFIC
PAPADOC
PELAGIC
PHRENIC
PIRATIC
PLASTIC
POLEMIC
POLITIC
PONTIAC
POSTHOC
POTOMAC
POULENC
PROSAIC
PSYCHIC
PYRRHIC

•PC••••
IPCRESS
UPCLOSE

•P•C•••
APACHES
APOCOPE
EPICENE
EPICURE
OPACITY
SPACERS
SPACIER
SPACING
SPACKLE
SPECIAL
SPECIES
SPECIFY
SPECKLE
SPECTER
SPECTOR
SPECTRA
SPECTRE
SPICEUP
SPICIER
SPICING
UPSCALE

•P••C••
APERCUS
APRICOT
EPARCHS
OPTICAL
SPENCER
SPLICED
SPLICER
SPLICES
SPRUCED
SPRUCER
SPRUCES
UPTICKS

•P•••C•
IPSWICH
SPINACH
SPLOTCH

••PC•••
CUPCAKE
HEPCATS
POPCORN
RIPCORD
TOPCOAT
ZIPCODE

••P•C••
ALPACAS
ASPECTS
CAPECOD
COPYCAT
DEPECHE
DEPICTS
EXPECTS
IMPACTS
KOPECKS
TOPICAL
TYPICAL
UNPACKS

••P••C•
ATPEACE
CAPRICE
COPPICE
DIPTYCH
IMPEACH
INPEACE
INPLACE
LAPLACE
REPLACE
REPLICA
REPRICE
TAPIOCA
TOPKICK

••P•••C
HEPATIC
LIPSYNC
PAPADOC
ZAPOTEC

•••PC••
JUMPCUT
SOUPCON

•••P•C•
ANSPACH
AUSPICE
CALPACS
COMPACT
COPPICE
DRSPOCK
HENPECK
HOSPICE
ICEPACK
ICEPICK
INSPECT
JAMPACK
MRSPOCK
MUDPACK
NITPICK
OUTPACE
RATPACK
RESPECT
SERPICO
SIXPACK
SUSPECT
TAMPICO
TROPICS

•••P••C
ASEPTIC
CRYPTIC
EDAPHIC
GRAPHIC
SKEPTIC
STYPTIC
TROPHIC

••••P•C
OLYMPIC

PD•••••
PDJAMES

P•D••••
PADDERS
PADDIES
PADDING
PADDLED
PADDLER
PADDLES
PADDOCK
PADLOCK
PADRONE
PADRONI
PADUCAH
PEDALED
PEDANTS
PEDDLED
PEDDLER
PEDDLES
PEDICEL
PEDICLE
PEDLARS
PIDGEON
PIDGINS
PODGIER
PODIUMS
PODRIDA
PUDDING
PUDDLED
PUDDLES
PUDGIER

P••D•••
PADDERS
PADDIES
PADDING
PADDLED
PADDLER
PADDLES
PADDOCK
PAIDFOR
PAIDOFF
PAIDOUT
PANDECT
PANDERS
PANDITS
PANDORA
PARDNER
PARDONS
PAYDAYS
PAYDIRT
PEDDLED
PEDDLER
PEDDLES
PENDANT
PENDENT
PENDING
PERDIEM
PHIDIAS
PINDOWN
PLEDGED
PLEDGEE
PLEDGER
PLEDGES
PLODDED
PLODDER
POLDERS
PONDERS
POODLES
POWDERS
POWDERY
PREDATE
PREDAWN
PREDICT
PRIDING
PRODDED
PRODDER
PRODIGY
PRODUCE
PRODUCT
PRUDENT
PRUDERY
PRUDHOE
PRUDISH
PUDDING
PUDDLED
PUDDLES
PUNDITS
PURDAHS
PUTDOWN
PYEDOGS

P•••D••
PAGODAS
PALADIN
PALEDRY
PAPADOC
PARADED
PARADES
PARADOX
PASTDUE
PAWEDAT
PERIDOT
PHAEDRA
PICADOR
PILEDIN
PILEDON
PILEDUP
PIPEDUP
PLAUDIT
PLAYDOH
PLEADED

PLEADER
PLODDED
PLODDER
PLUNDER
POKEDAT
POMADED
POMADES
POSADAS
POTSDAM
POUNDED
POUNDER
PRODDED
PRODDER
PROUDER
PROUDLY
PSANDQS
PYXIDES

P••••D•

PEABODY
PEAPODS
PENTADS
PEPTIDE
PERFIDY
PERIODS
PERVADE
PETARDS
PLACIDO
PODRIDA
PONGIDS
PRECEDE
PRELUDE
PREMEDS
PRESIDE
PROSODY
PROVIDE

P•••••D

PACKARD
PADDLED
PAINTED
PANELED
PAPERED
PARADED
PARCHED
PAROLED
PARRIED
PARTIED
PATCHED
PAYLOAD
PEACHED
PEARLED
PEBBLED
PEDALED
PEDDLED
PEOPLED
PEPPARD
PERCHED
PERUSED
PESTLED
PETALED
PETERED
PHOTOED
PHRASED
PICCARD
PICKLED
PIEBALD
PIERCED
PIFFLED
PILOTED
PINCHED
PINHEAD
PIRATED
PITCHED
PIVOTED
PLACARD
PLAGUED
PLAITED
PLANKED
PLANNED
PLANTED
PLASHED
PLEADED
PLEASED
PLEATED
PLEDGED
PLINKED
PLODDED
PLOPPED
PLOTTED
PLUCKED
PLUGGED
PLUMBED
PLUMPED
PLUNGED
PLUNKED
PLYWOOD
POACHED
POINTED
POLICED
POLKAED
POMADED
PONIARD
POPEYED
POPPLED
PORTEND
POSITED
POUCHED
POUNCED
POUNDED
POWERED
PRAISED
PRANCED
PRANKED
PREBEND
PREENED
PRELOAD
PREPAID
PRESSED
PRETEND
PRICKED
PRIMPED
PRINKED
PRINTED
PROCEED
PRODDED
PRONGED
PROOFED
PROPPED
PROWLED
PSALMED
PSYCHED
PUDDLED
PUNCHED
PURFLED
PURPLED
PURSUED
PUTTIED
PUZZLED
PYRAMID

•PD••••

UPDATED
UPDATES
UPDRAFT

•P•D•••

SPADERS
SPADING
SPIDERS
SPIDERY

•P••D••

APSIDES
SPANDEX
SPEEDED
SPEEDER
SPEEDUP
SPENDER
SPIEDON
SPINDLE
SPINDLY
SPONDEE
UPENDED

•P•••D•

APPENDS
EPISODE
SPREADS
UPGRADE
UPHOLDS
UPLANDS
UPLOADS
UPWARDS

•P••••D

APPLAUD
APPLIED
APPOSED
APRONED
OPENEND
OPERAND
OPPOSED
SPALLED
SPANKED
SPANNED
SPARGED
SPARKED
SPARRED
SPATTED
SPAWNED
SPEARED
SPEEDED
SPELLED
SPIELED
SPILLED
SPLAYED
SPLICED
SPOILED
SPONGED
SPOOFED
SPOOKED
SPOOLED
SPOONED
SPORTED
SPOTTED
SPOUTED
SPRAYED
SPRUCED
SPURNED
SPURRED
SPURTED
UPBRAID
UPDATED
UPENDED

••PD•••

LAPDOGS
TOPDOGS

••P•D••

BIPEDAL
HYPEDUP
IMPEDED
IMPEDES
PAPADOC
PIPEDUP
RAPIDER
RAPIDLY
ROPEDIN
TEPIDLY
TYPEDUP
VAPIDLY
WIPEDUP

••P••D•

APPENDS
DEPENDS
EXPANDS
EXPENDS
EXPLODE
HEPTADS
IMPENDS
IMPLODE
PEPTIDE
RIPTIDE
TOPSIDE
ZIPCODE

••P•••D

APPLAUD
APPLIED
APPOSED
ASPIRED
CAPECOD
CAPERED
COPLAND
DAPPLED
DEPONED
DEPOSED
DEPUTED
DIPLOID
EMPTIED
EXPIRED
EXPOSED
EXPOUND
IMPALED
IMPEDED
IMPLIED
IMPOSED
IMPOUND
IMPUTED
LAPELED
LAPLAND
LIPREAD
OPPOSED
PAPERED
PEPPARD
POPEYED
POPPLED
REPAVED
REPINED
REPLIED
REPOSED
REPUTED
RIPCORD
RIPENED
RIPPLED
TAPERED
TIPPLED
TIPTOED
TOPPLED
UMPIRED
UNPAVED
UNPILED

•••PD••

DRIPDRY

•••P•D•

CUSPIDS
ELAPIDS
ISOPODS
KEYPADS
PEAPODS
TORPEDO
TRIPODS
UNIPODS
VESPIDS

•••P••D

ADAPTED
ADOPTED
BLIPPED
CHAPPED
CHIPPED
CHOPPED
CLAPPED
CLIPPED
CLOPPED
COOPTED
COUPLED
CROPPED
DAPPLED
DEEPEND
DIMPLED
DRIPPED
DROPPED
ELAPSED
ERUPTED
FLAPPED
FLIPPED
FLOPPED
GRAPHED
GRIPPED
LEOPARD
LEOPOLD
LOWPAID
MORPHED
PEOPLED
PEPPARD
PLOPPED
POPPLED
PREPAID
PROPPED
PURPLED
QUIPPED
RESPOND
REUPPED
RIPPLED
RUMPLED
SAMPLED
SHEPARD
SHIPPED
SHOPPED
SKIPPED
SLAPPED
SLIPPED
SLOPPED
SNAPPED
SNIPPED
STAPLED
STEPPED
STIPEND
STOPPED
SUSPEND
SWAPPED
TEMPTED
TIPPLED
TOPPLED
TRAPPED
TRIPLED
TRIPPED
WHIPPED
WHOPPED
WHUPPED
WIMPLED
WRAPPED

••••P•D

BLEEPED
BLIPPED
BLOOPED
CHAMPED
CHAPPED
CHEEPED
CHIPPED
CHIRPED
CHOMPED
CHOPPED
CLAMPED
CLAPPED
CLASPED
CLIPPED
CLOPPED
CLUMPED
CRAMPED
CREEPED
CRIMPED
CRISPED
CROPPED
DECAPOD
DRIPPED
DROOPED
DROPPED
ESCAPED
FLAPPED
FLIPPED
FLOPPED
FOOTPAD
GRASPED
GRIPPED
GROUPED
GRUMPED
HELIPAD
INSIPID
KNEEPAD
LILYPAD
NOTEPAD
OCTOPOD
PLOPPED
PLUMPED
PRIMPED
PROPPED
QUIPPED
RETAPED
RETYPED
REUPPED
SCALPED
SCAMPED
SCARPED
SCOOPED
SCRAPED
SEEDPOD
SHARPED
SHIPPED
SHOPPED
SKIMPED
SKIPPED
SLAPPED
SLIPPED
SLOPPED
SLUMPED
SLURPED
SNAPPED
SNIPPED
SNOOPED
STAMPED
STEEPED
STEPPED
STOMPED
STOOPED
STOPPED
STRIPED
STUMPED
SWAMPED
SWAPPED
SWOOPED
THUMPED
TRAMPED
TRAPPED
TRIPPED
TROOPED
TRUMPED
UNTAPED
USURPED
WHELPED
WHIPPED
WHOMPED
WHOOPED
WHOPPED
WHUPPED
WRAPPED

PE•••••

PEABEAN
PEABODY
PEACHED
PEACHES
PEACOAT
PEACOCK
PEAFOWL
PEAHENS
PEAKING
PEALING
PEANUTS
PEAPODS
PEARLED
PEARSON
PEASANT
PEASOUP
PEATBOG
PEAVEYS
PEBBLED
PEBBLES
PECCANT
PECCARY
PECKING
PECKISH
PECKSAT
PECTINS
PEDALED
PEDANTS
PEDDLED
PEDDLER
PEDDLES
PEDICEL
PEDICLE
PEDLARS
PEEKING
PEEKOUT
PEEKSAT
PEELERS
PEELING
PEELOFF
PEEPERS
PEEPING
PEEPLES
PEERAGE
PEERESS
PEERING
PEEROUT
PEERSAT
PEERSIN
PEEVING
PEEVISH
PEEWEES
PEGASUS
PEGGING
PEGTOPS
PELAGES
PELAGIC
PELICAN
PELISSE
PELLETS
PELOTAS
PELTATE
PELTERS
PELTING
PEMICAN
PENALTY
PENANCE
PENATES
PENCILS
PENDANT
PENDENT
PENDING
PENGUIN
PENNAME
PENNANT
PENNATE
PENNERS
PENNIES
PENNING
PENNONS
PENPALS
PENSEES
PENSION
PENSIVE
PENTADS
PENUCHE
PENULTS
PEONAGE
PEONIES
PEOPLED
PEOPLES
PEPLUMS
PEPPARD
PEPPERS
PEPPERY
PEPPIER
PEPPILY
PEPPING
PEPSINS
PEPTALK
PEPTIDE
PEQUOTS
PERCALE
PERCENT
PERCHED
PERCHES
PERDIEM
PERFECT
PERFIDY
PERFORM
PERFUME
PERGOLA
PERHAPS
PERIDOT
PERIGEE
PERIODS
PERJURE
PERJURY
PERKIER
PERKILY
PERKING
PERKINS
PERKSUP
PERLITE
PERLMAN
PERMING
PERMITS
PERNELL
PERPLEX
PERRIER
PERSEUS
PERSIAN
PERSIST
PERSIUS
PERSONA
PERSONS
PERTAIN
PERTEST
PERTURB
PERUKES
PERUSAL
PERUSED
PERUSER
PERUSES
PERVADE
PERVERT
PESETAS
PESKIER
PESKILY
PESTERS
PESTLED
PESTLES
PETALED
PETARDS
PETCOCK
PETERED
PETIOLE
PETITES
PETNAME
PETRELS
PETRIFY
PETROCK
PETROUS
PETTERS
PETTIER
PETTILY
PETTING
PETTISH
PETUNIA
PEUGEOT

P•E••••

PEEKING
PEEKOUT
PEEKSAT
PEELERS
PEELING
PEELOFF
PEEPERS
PEEPING
PEEPLES
PEERAGE
PEERESS
PEERING
PEEROUT
PEERSAT
PEERSIN
PEEVING
PEEVISH
PEEWEES
PFENNIG
PHENOLS
PHENOMS
PIEBALD
PIECERS
PIECING
PIEPANS
PIERCED
PIERCES
PIERROT
PIETIES
PIETINS
PIETISM
PLEADED
PLEADER
PLEASED
PLEASER
PLEASES
PLEATED
PLECTRA
PLEDGED
PLEDGEE
PLEDGER
PLEDGES
PLENARY
PLENUMS
PLEXORS
POETESS
POETICS
PREACHY
PREAMPS
PREBEND
PRECAST
PRECEDE
PRECEPT
PRECISE
PRECOOK
PRECOOL
PREDATE
PREDAWN
PREDICT
PREEMIE
PREEMPT
PREENED
PREENER
PREFABS
PREFACE
PREFECT
PREFERS
PREHEAT
PRELATE
PRELIMS
PRELOAD
PRELUDE
PREMEDS
PREMIER
PREMISE
PREMIUM
PREPAID
PREPARE
PREPAYS
PREPPIE
PRESAGE
PRESALE
PRESELL
PRESENT
PRESETS
PRESIDE
PRESLEY
PRESOAK
PRESORT
PRESSED
PRESSER
PRESSES
PRESSON
PRESTON
PRESTOS
PRESUME
PRETAPE
PRETEEN
PRETEND
PRETEST
PRETEXT
PRETZEL
PREVAIL
PREVENT
PREVIEW
PREWASH
PREYSON
PUEBLOS
PUERILE
PYEDOGS

P••E•••

PACECAR
PAGEANT
PAGEBOY
PAGEFUL
PALEDRY
PALERMO
PALETTE
PANELED
PANETTA
PAPEETE
PAPERED
PAPERER
PARENTS
PATELLA
PATENTS
PATERNO
PAWEDAT
PESETAS
PETERED
PHAEDRA
PHAETON
PHOEBES
PHOEBUS
PHOENIX
PHRENIC
PIGEONS
PIKEMAN
PIKEMEN
PILEDIN
PILEDON
PILEDUP
PILESIN
PILESON
PILESUP
PILEUPS
PIMENTO
PIMESON
PINEFOR
PINENUT
PINESAP
PINETAR
PINETUM
PIPEDUP
PIPEFUL
PIPESUP
PIPETTE
PITEOUS
POKEDAT
POKEFUN
POKESAT
POLEAXE
POLECAT
POLEMIC
POLENTA
POMELOS
POPEYED
POSEURS
POTENCY
POVERTY
POWERED
PRAETOR
PREEMIE
PREEMPT
PREENED
PREENER
PRIESTS
PUBERTY

P•••E••

PACKERS
PACKETS
PADDERS
PALLETS
PALTERS
PAMPERS
PANDECT
PANDERS
PANNERS
PANZERS
PAPEETE
PARCELS
PARGETS
PARLEYS
PARNELL
PARSECS
PARSEES
PARSERS
PARVENU
PASSELS
PASSERS
PASSEUL
PASTELS
PASTERN
PASTEUP
PASTEUR
PATIENT
PATNESS
PATTENS
PATTERN
PATTERS
PAUPERS
PAWNEES
PAWNERS
PAYMENT
PEABEAN
PEAHENS
PEAVEYS
PEELERS
PEEPERS
PEERESS
PEEWEES
PELLETS
PELTERS
PENDENT
PENNERS
PENSEES
PEPPERS
PEPPERY
PERCENT
PERFECT
PERNELL
PERSEUS
PERTEST
PERVERT
PESTERS
PETRELS
PETTERS
PEUGEOT
PHASEIN
PHASERS
PHINEAS
PHONEME
PICKENS
PICKERS
PICKETS
PICKETT
PIDGEON
PIECERS
PIGLETS
PIGMENT
PIGPENS
PILFERS
PINCERS
PINHEAD
PINIEST
PINKEST
PINLESS
PINNERS
PIOLETS
PIONEER
PIRAEUS
PITTERS
PLACEBO
PLACERS
PLANERS
PLANETS
PLATEAU
PLATENS
PLATERS
PLAYERS
PLOVERS
PLOWERS
POCKETS
POETESS
POKIEST
POLDERS
POLLENS
POLLERS
POMMELS
POMPEIA
POMPEII
PONDERS
POOREST
POPPERS
POPPETS
PORKERS
PORSENA
PORTEND
PORTENT
PORTERS
POSHEST
POSSESS
POSSETS
POSTERN
POSTERS
POTHERB
POTHERS
POTTERS
POTTERY
POULENC
POURERS

POUTERS
POWDERS
POWDERY
PRATERS
PRAYERS
PREBEND
PRECEDE
PRECEPT
PREFECT
PREFERS
PREHEAT
PREMEDS
PRESELL
PRESENT
PRESETS
PRETEEN
PRETEND
PRETEST
PRETEXT
PREVENT
PRICERS
PRIMERS
PRIVETS
PROBERS
PROCEED
PROCESS
PROFESS
PROGENY
PROJECT
PROPELS
PROSERS
PROTEAN
PROTECT
PROTEGE
PROTEIN
PROTEST
PROTEUS
PROVERB
PROVERS
PROWESS
PRUDENT
PRUDERY
PRUNERS
PTOLEMY
PUCKERS
PUCKETT
PUFFERS
PUFFERY
PUGREES
PULLETS
PULLEYS
PUMMELS
PUMPERS
PUNGENT
PUNIEST
PUNTERS
PUPPETS
PUPTENT
PURCELL
PURRERS
PURSERS
PURVEYS
PUTTEES
PUTTERS

P••••E•

PADDIES
PADDLED
PADDLER
PADDLES
PAINTED
PAINTER
PAISLEY
PAIUTES
PALACES
PALATES
PALAVER
PALFREY
PALJOEY
PALMIER
PAMBIES
PANACEA
PANELED
PANNIER
PANSIES
PANTHER
PAPERED
PAPERER
PARADED
PARADES
PARAPET
PARCHED
PARCHES
PARDNER
PAROLED
PAROLEE
PAROLES
PARQUET
PARRIED
PARRIES
PARSEES
PARSLEY
PARTIED
PARTIES
PARTNER
PARURES
PASSKEY
PASTIER
PATAKES
PATCHED
PATCHES
PATSIES
PATTIES
PAULSEN
PAVANES
PAWNEES
PDJAMES
PEACHED
PEACHES
PEARLED
PEBBLED
PEBBLES
PEDALED
PEDDLED
PEDDLER
PEDDLES
PEDICEL
PEEPLES
PEEWEES
PELAGES
PENATES
PENNIES
PENSEES
PEONIES
PEOPLED
PEOPLES
PEPPIER
PERCHED
PERCHES
PERDIEM
PERIGEE
PERKIER
PERPLEX
PERRIER
PERUKES
PERUSED
PERUSER
PERUSES
PESKIER
PESTLED
PESTLES
PETALED
PETERED
PETITES
PETTIER
PHILTER
PHLOXES
PHOEBES
PHONIER
PHONIES
PHOTOED
PHRASED
PHRASES
PIASTER
PICKIER
PICKLED
PICKLES
PIERCED
PIERCES
PIETIES
PIFFLED
PIFFLES
PIGGIES
PIKEMEN
PILOTED
PILSNER
PINCHED
PINCHER
PINCHES
PINKIES
PINONES
PIONEER
PIRATED
PIRATES
PITCHED
PITCHER
PITCHES
PITHIER
PIVOTED
PLACKET
PLAGUED
PLAGUES
PLAICES
PLAINER
PLAINES
PLAITED
PLANKED
PLANNED
PLANNER
PLANTED
PLANTER
PLAQUES
PLASHED
PLASHES
PLASTER
PLATTER
PLAYLET
PLAYPEN
PLEADED
PLEADER
PLEASED
PLEASER
PLEASES
PLEATED
PLEDGED
PLEDGEE
PLEDGER
PLEDGES
PLINKED
PLODDED
PLODDER
PLOPPED
PLOTTED
PLOTTER
PLOWMEN
PLUCKED
PLUGGED
PLUGGER
PLUMBED
PLUMBER
PLUMMER
PLUMMET
PLUMPED
PLUMPER
PLUNDER
PLUNGED
PLUNGER
PLUNGES
PLUNKED
PLUSHER
PLUSHES
PLUSSES
POACHED
POACHER
POACHES
POBOXES
PODGIER
POINTED
POINTER
POITIER
POLICED
POLICES
POLITER
POLKAED
POLYMER
POMADED
POMADES
POOCHES
POODLES
POPEYED
POPOVER
POPPIES
POPPLED
POPPLES
PORCHES
PORGIES
POSITED
POSTMEN
POTAGES
POTPIES
POUCHED
POUCHES
POUNCED
POUNCER
POUNCES
POUNDED
POUNDER
POUTIER
POWERED
PRAISED
PRAISER
PRAISES
PRANCED
PRANCER
PRANCES
PRANKED
PREENED
PREENER
PREMIER
PRESLEY
PRESSED
PRESSER
PRESSES
PRETEEN
PRETZEL
PREVIEW
PRICIER
PRICKED
PRIMMER
PRIMPED
PRINCES
PRINKED
PRINTED
PRINTER
PRITHEE
PRIVIES
PROBLEM
PROCEED
PRODDED
PRODDER
PROFFER
PRONGED
PROOFED
PROOFER
PROPHET
PROPJET
PROPMEN
PROPPED
PROSIER
PROSPER
PROUDER
PROWLED
PROWLER
PROXIES
PSALMED
PSALTER
PSYCHED
PSYCHES
PUDDLED
PUDDLES
PUDGIER
PUFFIER
PUGREES
PUMICES
PUNCHED
PUNCHER
PUNCHES
PUNKIES
PUNSTER
PUPPIES
PURFLED
PURFLES
PURLIEU
PURPLED
PURPLES
PURSUED
PURSUER
PURSUES
PURVIEW
PUSHIER
PUTAMEN
PUTOVER
PUTTEES
PUTTIED
PUTTIES
PUZZLED
PUZZLER
PUZZLES
PYGMIES
PYRITES
PYXIDES

P•••••E

PACKAGE
PACKICE
PADRONE
PALANCE
PALETTE
PALMATE
PANACHE
PANCAKE
PANICLE
PANPIPE
PANURGE
PAPEETE
PAPOOSE
PARABLE
PAROLEE
PARTAKE
PARTITE
PASSAGE
PASSIVE
PASTDUE
PASTIME
PASTURE
PATRICE
PAULINE
PAYABLE
PEDICLE
PEERAGE
PELISSE
PELTATE
PENANCE
PENNAME
PENNATE
PENSIVE
PENUCHE
PEONAGE
PEPTIDE
PERCALE
PERFUME
PERIGEE
PERJURE
PERLITE
PERVADE
PETIOLE
PETNAME
PHILTRE
PHONEME
PIASTRE
PICANTE
PICKAXE
PICTURE
PIGLIKE
PILLAGE
PINHOLE
PINNACE
PINNATE
PINOCLE
PINWALE
PIPETTE
PIROGUE
PISCINE
PISMIRE
PISTOLE
PLACATE
PLEDGEE
PLIABLE
PLOSIVE
PLUMAGE
POLEAXE
POLLUTE
PONTINE
PORCINE
PORKPIE
PORSCHE
PORTAGE
POSTAGE
POSTURE
POTABLE
POTHOLE
POTTAGE
PRAIRIE
PRALINE
PRATTLE
PRECEDE
PRECISE
PREDATE
PREEMIE
PREFACE
PRELATE
PRELUDE
PREMISE
PREPARE
PREPPIE
PRESAGE
PRESALE
PRESIDE
PRESUME
PRETAPE
PRICKLE
PRIMATE
PRITHEE
PRIVATE
PROBATE
PROCURE
PRODUCE
PROFANE
PROFILE
PROFUSE
PROMISE
PROMOTE
PROPANE
PROPOSE
PRORATE
PROTEGE
PROVIDE
PROVOKE
PRUDHOE
PUERILE
PUGNOSE
PULSATE
PURPOSE

•PE••••

APELIKE
APERCUS
APERIES
EPEEIST
EPERGNE
OPENAIR
OPENBAR
OPENEND
OPENERS
OPENING
OPENPIT
OPENSEA
OPENSUP
OPENTOE
OPERAND
OPERATE
OPEROSE
SPEAKER
SPEAKOF
SPEAKUP
SPEARED
SPECIAL
SPECIES
SPECIFY
SPECKLE
SPECTER
SPECTOR
SPECTRA
SPECTRE
SPEEDED
SPEEDER
SPEEDUP
SPELLED
SPELLER
SPELUNK
SPENCER
SPENDER
SPENSER
SPEWING
UPENDED

•P•E•••

APHELIA
APHESES
APLENTY
APPEALS
APPEARS
APPEASE
APPENDS
EPEEIST
OPHELIA
SPEEDED
SPEEDER
SPEEDUP
SPHERES
SPIEDON
SPIEGEL
SPIELED
SPIELER
SPIESON
SPLEENS
SPREADS
UPBEATS
UPTEMPO

•P••E••

APOGEES
APTNESS
EPICENE
EPIGENE
EPSTEIN
IPANEMA
IPCRESS
OPENEND
OPENERS
OPINERS
OPPRESS
OPULENT
SPACERS
SPADERS
SPARELY
SPAREST
SPICEUP
SPIDERS
SPIDERY
SPIKERS
SPINELS
SPINETS
SPIREAS
SPLEENS
SPOKEOF
SPOKEUP
SPRIEST
SPRYEST
UPSWEEP
UPSWEPT

•P•••E•

APACHES
APERIES
APHESES
APOGEES
APOTHEM
APPAREL
APPLIED
APPLIES
APPOSED
APPOSES
APRONED
APSIDES
EPAULET
EPITHET
EPOXIES
OPAQUES
OPENSEA
OPIATES
OPPOSED
OPPOSER
OPPOSES
SPACIER
SPALLED
SPANDEX
SPANIEL
SPANKED
SPANKER
SPANNED
SPANNER
SPARGED
SPARGES
SPARKED
SPARRED
SPARSER
SPATTED
SPATTER
SPAWNED
SPEAKER
SPEARED
SPECIES
SPECTER
SPEEDED
SPEEDER
SPELLED
SPELLER
SPENCER
SPENDER
SPENSER
SPHERES
SPICIER
SPIEGEL
SPIELED
SPIELER
SPIKIER
SPILLED
SPINIER
SPINNER
SPITZES
SPLAYED
SPLICED
SPLICER
SPLICES
SPLINES
SPOILED
SPOILER
SPONDEE
SPONGED
SPONGER
SPONGES
SPOOFED
SPOOFER
SPOOKED
SPOOLED
SPOONED
SPOONER
SPORTED
SPOTTED
SPOTTER
SPOUSES
SPOUTED
SPOUTER
SPRAYED
SPRAYER
SPRITES
SPRUCED
SPRUCER
SPRUCES
SPURNED
SPURNER
SPURRED
SPURTED
SPUTTER
UPATREE
UPDATED
UPDATES
UPENDED
UPRISEN
UPRISES
UPRIVER
UPSWEEP
UPTAKES

•P••••E

APATITE
APELIKE
APOCOPE
APOSTLE
APPEASE
APPRISE
APPRIZE
APPROVE
EPERGNE
EPICENE
EPICURE
EPIGENE
EPIGONE
EPISODE
EPISTLE
EPITOME
OPALINE
OPENTOE
OPERATE
OPEROSE
SPACKLE
SPANGLE
SPARKLE
SPECKLE
SPECTRE
SPINDLE
SPLURGE
SPOKANE
SPONDEE
SPUMONE
UPATREE
UPBORNE
UPCLOSE
UPGRADE
UPRAISE
UPSCALE
UPSTAGE
UPSTATE
UPSURGE

••PE•••

AMPERES
APPEALS
APPEARS
APPEASE
APPENDS
ASPECTS
ASPERSE
ATPEACE
BIPEDAL
CAPEANN
CAPECOD
CAPELET
CAPELLA
CAPERED
DEPECHE
DEPENDS
DOPEOUT
EMPEROR
EXPECTS
EXPENDS
EXPENSE
EXPERTS
HOPEFUL
HYPEDUP
IMPEACH
IMPEDED
IMPEDES
IMPENDS
IMPERIL
IMPETUS
INPEACE
INPETTO
KOPECKS
LAPELED
PAPEETE
PAPERED
PAPERER
PIPEDUP
PIPEFUL
PIPESUP
PIPETTE
POPEYED
REPEALS
REPEATS
REPENTS
RIPENED
ROPEDIN
ROPESIN
ROPETOW
STPETER
TAPERED
TUPELOS
TYPEDUP
TYPESET
TYPESUP
WIPEDUP
WIPEOUT
WIPESUP

••P•E••

AMPLEST
BOPPERS
CAPLESS
CAPLETS
CAPPERS
CEPHEUS
CIPHERS
COPIERS
COPPERS
COPPERY
COPTERS
CYPHERS
CYPRESS
DEPLETE
DEPRESS
DIPPERS
DOPIEST
EMPRESS
EXPRESS
FOPPERY
GOPHERS
GYPPERS
HAPLESS
HAPPENS
HIPNESS
HIPPEST
HOPPERS
HYPHENS
IMPIETY
IMPRESS
JAPHETH
KIPPERS
LAPBELT
LAPPETS
LIPREAD
LOPPERS
MAPPERS
MOPPERS
MOPPETS
MUPPETS
NAPPERS
NEPHEWS
NIPPERS
OPPRESS
ORPHEAN
ORPHEUS
OSPREYS
PAPEETE
PEPPERS
PEPPERY
POPPERS
POPPETS
PUPPETS
PUPTENT
RAPIERS
RAPPELS
RAPPERS
REPLETE
REPRESS
RIPPERS
SAPIENS
SAPIENT
SAPPERS
SEPTETS
SIPPERS
SIPPETS
SUPPERS
SUPREME
SUPREMO
TAPPERS
TAPPETS
TIPPERS
TIPPETS
TOPPERS
UMPTEEN
YAPPERS
ZAPPERS
ZIPPERS

••P••E•

AMPERES
AMPULES
APPAREL
APPLIED
APPLIES
APPOSED
APPOSES
ASPIRED
ASPIRER
ASPIRES
CAPELET
CAPERED
CAPULET
DAPPLED
DAPPLES
DEPONED
DEPONES
DEPOSED
DEPOSER
DEPOSES
DEPUTED
DEPUTES
DIPOLES
DOPPLER
EMPANEL
EMPIRES
EMPOWER
EMPTIED
EMPTIER
EMPTIES
EXPIRED
EXPIRES
EXPOSED
EXPOSES
FIPPLES
GIPSIES
GUPPIES
GYPSIES
HAPPIER
HIPPIES
HIPSTER
HOPOVER
IMPALED
IMPALES
IMPANEL
IMPEDED
IMPEDES
IMPLIED
IMPLIES
IMPOSED
IMPOSES
IMPURER
IMPUTED
IMPUTES
JUPITER
LAPELED
LIPPIER
LUPINES
NIPPIER
ONPAPER
OPPOSED
OPPOSER
OPPOSES
ORPINES
PAPERED
PAPERER
PEPPIER
POPEYED
POPOVER
POPPIES
POPPLED
POPPLES
PUPPIES
RAPHAEL
RAPIDER
RAPINES
REPAPER
REPAVED
REPAVES
REPINED
REPINES
REPLIED

REPLIES
REPOSED
REPOSES
REPUTED
REPUTES
RIPENED
RIPPLED
RIPPLES
SAPPIER
STPETER
SUPPLER
TAPERED
TAPSTER
TIPPLED
TIPPLER
TIPPLES
TIPSIER
TIPSTER
TIPTOED
TIPTOES
TOPAZES
TOPPLED
TOPPLES
TYPESET
UMPIRED
UMPIRES
UMPTEEN
UNPAVED
UNPILED
UNPILES
YUPPIES
ZAPOTEC
ZIPPIER

••P•••E

AMPOULE
APPEASE
APPRISE
APPRIZE
APPROVE
ASPERSE
ATPEACE
BAPTIZE
BIPLANE
CAPABLE
CAPAPIE
CAPRICE
CAPSIZE
CAPSULE
CAPTIVE
CAPTURE
COPPICE
CUPCAKE
DEPECHE
DEPLANE
DEPLETE
DEPLORE
DEPRAVE
DEPRIVE
ENPLANE
ESPOUSE
EXPANSE
EXPARTE
EXPENSE
EXPIATE
EXPLODE
EXPLORE
EXPUNGE
HIPBONE
IMPASSE
IMPINGE
IMPLODE
IMPLORE
IMPROVE
IMPULSE
INPEACE
INPHASE
INPLACE
LAPLACE
LAPORTE
LAPROBE
NAPTIME
NEPTUNE
PAPEETE
PAPOOSE
PEPTIDE
PIPETTE
RAPTURE
REPASTE
REPLACE
REPLATE
REPLETE
REPRICE
REPRISE
REPROVE
REPTILE
REPULSE
RIPOSTE
RIPTIDE
RUPTURE
SUPPOSE
SUPREME
TOPSIDE
ZIPCODE

•••PE••

ANAPEST
BEEPERS
BESPEAK
BOPPERS
BUMPERS
CAMPERS
CAPPERS
CARPERS
CARPETS
CHAPEAU
CHAPELS
COMPEER
COMPELS
COMPETE
COOPERS
COPPERS
COPPERY
COWPEAS
DAMPENS
DAMPERS
DAMPEST
DEEPEND
DEEPENS
DEEPEST
DIAPERS
DIPPERS
DISPELS
DRAPERS
DRAPERY
ELOPERS
EXUPERY
FOPPERY
GOMPERS
GOSPELS
GRIPERS
GYPPERS
HAMPERS
HAPPENS
HARPERS
HELPERS
HENPECK
HIPPEST
HOPPERS
INSPECT
JASPERS
JUMPERS
KEEPERS
KIPPERS
LAPPETS
LEAPERS
LIMPEST
LIMPETS
LOOPERS
LOPPERS
LUMPERS
MAPPERS
MOPPERS
MOPPETS
MUPPETS
NAPPERS
NIPPERS
OFFPEAK
PAMPERS
PAUPERS
PEEPERS
PEPPERS
PEPPERY
PIGPENS
POMPEIA
POMPEII
POPPERS
POPPETS
PROPELS
PUMPERS
PUPPETS
RAPPELS
RAPPERS
RASPERS
REAPERS
REOPENS
RESPECT
RIPPERS
ROMPERS
SAPPERS
SERPENT
SHAPELY
SHAPERS
SHAPEUP
SIMPERS
SIPPERS
SIPPETS
SNIPEAT
SOAPERS
STIPEND
STUPEFY
SUPPERS
SUSPECT
SUSPEND
SWIPERS
TAMPERS
TAPPERS
TAPPETS
TEEPEES
TEMPERA
TEMPERS
TEMPEST
TIPPERS
TIPPETS
TOPPERS
TORPEDO
TOUPEES
TRAPEZE
UNSPENT
USOPENS
VAMPERS
VESPERS
WEEPERS
YAPPERS
YAWPERS
YELPERS
ZAPPERS
ZIPPERS

•••P•E•

ADAPTED
ADAPTER
ADOPTED
ADOPTEE
ADOPTER
BLIPPED
BUMPIER
CAMPIER
CHAPLET
CHAPMEN
CHAPPED
CHAPTER
CHIPPED
CHIPPER
CHOPPED
CHOPPER
CLAPPED
CLAPPER
CLIPPED
CLIPPER
CLOPPED
COMPEER
COMPLEX
COOPTED
COUPLED
COUPLES
COUPLET
CROPPED
CROPPER
DAPPLED
DAPPLES
DEEPSEA
DEEPSET
DEMPSEY
DIMPLED
DIMPLES
DIOPTER
DOPPLER
DRIPPED
DROPLET
DROPPED
DROPPER
DUMPIER
ELAPSED
ELAPSES
ERUPTED
FIPPLES
FLAPPED
FLAPPER
FLIPPED
FLIPPER
FLOPPED
FRAPPES
GOOPIER
GRAPHED
GRAPNEL
GRIPPED
GRIPPER
GUPPIES
HAPPIER
HARPIES
HIPPIES
HOOPOES
JUMPIER
KELPIES
KEWPIES
LAMPREY
LIPPIER
LOOPIER
LUMPIER
MAGPIES
MORPHED
MUDPIES
MURPHEY
NIPPIER
PEEPLES
PEOPLED
PEOPLES
PEPPIER
PERPLEX
PLOPPED
POPPIES
POPPLED
POPPLES
POTPIES
PROPHET
PROPJET
PROPMEN
PROPPED
PUPPIES
PURPLED
PURPLES
QUIPPED
QUIPPER
RASPIER
REUPPED
RIPPLED
RIPPLES
RUMPLED
RUMPLES
SAMPLED
SAMPLER
SAMPLES
SAPPIER
SCEPTER
SCUPPER
SHIPMEN
SHIPPED
SHIPPER
SHOPPED
SHOPPER
SHOPPES
SIMPLER
SIMPLEX
SKIPPED
SKIPPER
SLAPPED
SLIPPED
SLIPPER
SLOPPED
SNAPPED
SNAPPER
SNIPPED
SNIPPET
SOAPIER
SOUPIER
STAPLED
STAPLER
STAPLES
STEPHEN
STEPPED
STEPPER
STEPPES
STOPPED
STOPPER
SUPPLER
SWAPPED
SWAPPER
TEEPEES
TEMPLES
TEMPTED
TEMPTER
TIPPLED
TIPPLER
TIPPLES
TOPPLED
TOPPLES
TOUPEES
TRAPPED
TRAPPER
TRIPLED
TRIPLES
TRIPLET
TRIPLEX
TRIPPED
TRIPPER
TRIPPET
WEEPIER
WHIPPED
WHIPPET
WHOPPED
WHOPPER
WHUPPED
WIMPLED
WIMPLES
WISPIER
WRAPPED
WRAPPER
YUPPIES
ZIPPIER

•••P••E

ADIPOSE
ADOPTEE
AUSPICE
BAGPIPE
BESPOKE
COMPARE
COMPETE
COMPILE
COMPOSE
COMPOTE
COMPUTE
COPPICE
COWPOKE
CRAPPIE
DESPISE
DESPITE
DISPOSE
DISPUTE
GRAPPLE
HOSPICE
INSPIRE
MAYPOLE
OUTPACE
PANPIPE
PREPARE
PREPPIE
PROPANE
PROPOSE
PURPOSE
RAMPAGE
REDPINE
RESPIRE
RESPITE
RUMPOLE
SCEPTRE
SKIPOLE
STIPPLE
SUPPOSE
TADPOLE
TOSPARE
TRAPEZE
VAMPIRE
VOLPONE
VULPINE
WALPOLE

••••PE•

BLEEPED
BLEEPER
BLIPPED
BLOOPED
BLOOPER
BULLPEN
CALIPER
CANAPES
CHAMPED
CHAPPED
CHEAPEN
CHEAPER
CHEEPED
CHIPPED
CHIPPER
CHIRPED
CHOMPED
CHOPPED
CHOPPER
CLAMPED
CLAPPED
CLAPPER
CLASPED
CLIPPED
CLIPPER
CLOPPED
CLUMPED
CRAMPED
CREEPED
CREEPER
CRIMPED
CRIMPER
CRISPED
CRISPER
CROPPED
CROPPER
CRUMPET
DRIPPED
DROOPED
DROPPED
DROPPER
ECTYPES
ESCAPED
ESCAPEE
ESCAPES
FLAPPED
FLAPPER
FLIPPED
FLIPPER
FLOPPED
FRAPPES
GRASPED
GRIPPED
GRIPPER
GROUPED
GROUPER
GRUMPED
GUIMPES
JUNIPER
ONPAPER
PARAPET
PLAYPEN
PLOPPED
PLUMPED
PLUMPER
PRIMPED
PROPPED
PROSPER
QUIPPED
QUIPPER
RECIPES
REPAPER
RETAPED
RETAPES
RETYPED
RETYPES
REUPPED
SCALPED
SCALPEL
SCALPER
SCAMPED
SCAMPER
SCARPED
SCOOPED
SCOOPER
SCRAPED
SCRAPER
SCRAPES
SCUPPER
SERAPES
SHARPED
SHARPEI
SHARPEN
SHARPER
SHIPPED
SHIPPER
SHOPPED
SHOPPER
SHOPPES
SKIMPED
SKIPPED
SKIPPER
SLAPPED
SLEEPER
SLIPPED
SLIPPER
SLOPPED
SLUMPED
SLURPED
SNAPPED
SNAPPER
SNIPPED
SNIPPET
SNOOPED
SNOOPER
SNOWPEA
STAMPED
STEEPED
STEEPEN
STEEPER
STEPPED
STEPPER
STEPPES
STOMPED
STOOPED
STOPPED
STOPPER
STRIPED
STRIPER
STRIPES
STUMPED
STUMPER
SWAMPED
SWAPPED
SWAPPER
SWEEPER
SWOOPED
THUMPED
THUMPER
TRAMPED
TRAPPED
TRAPPER
TRIPPED
TRIPPER
TRIPPET
TROOPED
TROOPER
TROUPER
TROUPES
TRUMPED
TRUMPET
UNTAPED
USURPED
USURPER
WHELPED
WHIMPER
WHIPPED
WHIPPET
WHISPER
WHOMPED
WHOOPED
WHOOPEE
WHOPPED
WHOPPER
WHUPPED
WRAPPED
WRAPPER
ZATOPEK

••••P•E

ADOLPHE
CAPAPIE
CHEAPIE
CRAPPIE
CRUMPLE
ECLIPSE
ELLIPSE
ESCAPEE
EXAMPLE
GLIMPSE
GRAPPLE
GROUPIE
MANIPLE
OCTUPLE
PORKPIE
PREPPIE
RELAPSE
SCRUPLE
STEEPLE
STIPPLE
STROPHE
SYNAPSE
TRAIPSE
TRAMPLE
WHOOPEE

•••••PE

APOCOPE
BAGPIPE
BOBHOPE
EUTERPE
GOESAPE
INSCAPE
INSHAPE
ISOTOPE
MISTYPE
PANPIPE
PRETAPE
REDTAPE
TINTYPE
TOWROPE
UNDRAPE
WENTAPE

PF•••••

PFENNIG

P•F••••

PIFFLED
PIFFLES
PUFFERS
PUFFERY
PUFFIER
PUFFILY
PUFFING
PUFFINS

P••F•••

PALFREY
PANFISH
PARFAIT
PEAFOWL
PERFECT
PERFIDY
PERFORM
PERFUME
PIFFLED
PIFFLES
PILFERS
PITFALL
POTFULS
PREFABS
PREFACE
PREFECT
PREFERS
PROFANE
PROFESS
PROFFER
PROFILE
PROFITS
PROFUSE
PUFFERS
PUFFERY
PUFFIER
PUFFILY
PUFFING
PUFFINS
PURFLED
PURFLES

P•••F••

PACIFIC
PAGEFUL
PAIDFOR
PAILFUL
PAINFUL
PASSFOR
PAYOFFS
PAYSFOR
PINEFOR
PIPEFUL
PITIFUL
PLAYFUL
POKEFUN
POPOFFS
PRAYFOR
PROFFER
PROOFED
PROOFER

P••••F•

PAIDOFF
PAIROFF
PALMOFF
PASSOFF
PAWNOFF
PAYOFFS
PAYSOFF
PEELOFF
PETRIFY
PICKOFF
PLAYOFF
PONTIFF
POPOFFS
POPSOFF
PULLOFF
PUSHOFF
PUTSOFF

P•••••F

PAIDOFF
PAIROFF
PALMOFF
PASSOFF
PAWNOFF
PAYSOFF
PEELOFF
PICKOFF
PLAYOFF
PONTIFF
POPSOFF
PULLOFF
PUSHOFF
PUTSOFF

•PF••••

UPFRONT

•P••F••

SPOOFED
SPOOFER
UPLIFTS

•P•••F•

SPECIFY
SPINOFF
SPUNOFF
UPDRAFT

•P••••F

SPEAKOF
SPINOFF
SPOKEOF
SPUNOFF

••PF•••

CAPFULS
CUPFULS
LAPFULS

••P•F••

HOPEFUL
PIPEFUL
POPOFFS
RIPOFFS
TIPOFFS

••P••F•

AMPLIFY
HOPSOFF
KEPTOFF
POPOFFS
POPSOFF
RIPOFFS
RIPSOFF
TIPOFFS
TIPSOFF
TOPSOFF

••P•••F

HIPROOF
HOPSOFF
KEPTOFF
POPSOFF
REPROOF
RIPSOFF
TIPSOFF
TOPSOFF

•••PF••

DEEPFAT
DEEPFRY
HELPFUL

•••P•F•

DROPOFF
JUMPOFF
KEEPOFF
STOPOFF
STUPEFY

•••P••F

DROPOFF
JUMPOFF
KEEPOFF
STOPOFF

••••P•F

ONTOPOF

P•G••••

PAGEANT
PAGEBOY
PAGEFUL
PAGODAS
PEGASUS
PEGGING
PEGTOPS
PIGEONS
PIGGIES
PIGGING
PIGGISH
PIGIRON
PIGLETS
PIGLIKE
PIGMENT
PIGNUTS
PIGPENS
PIGSKIN
PIGSOUT
PIGTAIL
PUGNOSE
PUGREES
PYGMIES

P••G•••

PARGETS
PEGGING
PENGUIN
PERGOLA
PEUGEOT
PIDGEON
PIDGINS
PIGGIES
PIGGING
PIGGISH
PILGRIM
PINGING
PLAGUED
PLAGUES
PLIGHTS
PLUGGED
PLUGGER
PLUGSIN
PODGIER
PONGIDS
POPGUNS
PORGIES
PROGENY
PROGRAM
PUDGIER
PUNGENT
PURGING

P•••G••

PAPAGOS
PARAGON
PELAGES
PELAGIC
PERIGEE
PIROGUE
PLEDGED
PLEDGEE
PLEDGER
PLEDGES
PLOUGHS
PLUGGED
PLUGGER
PLUNGED
PLUNGER
PLUNGES
POLYGON
POTAGES
PRONGED

P••••G•

PACKAGE
PANURGE
PARINGS
PASSAGE
PEERAGE
PEONAGE
PHOTOGS
PILINGS
PILLAGE
PIPINGS
PLUMAGE
PORTAGE
POSTAGE
POTTAGE
PRESAGE
PRODIGY
PROLOGS
PROTEGE
PYEDOGS

P•••••G

PACKING
PADDING
PAIRING
PALLING
PALMING
PANNING
PANTING
PARKING
PARRING
PARSING
PARTING
PASSING

PASTING
PATTING
PAULING
PAUSING
PAWNING
PEAKING
PEALING
PEATBOG
PECKING
PEEKING
PEELING
PEEPING
PEERING
PEEVING
PEGGING
PELTING
PENDING
PENNING
PEPPING
PERKING
PERMING
PETTING
PFENNIG
PHASING
PHONING
PICKING
PIECING
PIGGING
PILLBUG
PILLING
PINGING
PINKING
PINNING
PIQUING
PITHING
PITTING
PITYING
PLACING
PLANING
PLATING
PLAYING
PLOWING
PLUMING
POISING
POLLING
PONYING
POOLING
POOPING
POPPING
POSTING
POTTING
POURING
POUTING
PRATING
PRAYING
PRICING
PRIDING
PRIMING
PRIZING
PROBING
PROLONG
PROSING
PROVING
PRUNING
PUDDING
PUFFING
PULLING
PULSING
PUMPING
PUNNING
PUNTING
PURGING
PURLING
PURRING
PURSING
PUSHING
PUTTING

•PG••••
UPGRADE

•P•G•••
APOGEES
EPIGENE
EPIGONE
EPIGRAM
SPIGOTS

•P•G••
EPERGNE
OPPUGNS
SPANGLE
SPANGLY
SPARGED
SPARGES
SPIEGEL
SPONGED
SPONGER
SPONGES
UPRIGHT
UPTIGHT

•P•••G•
APOLOGY
EPILOGS
SPLURGE
SPRINGS
SPRINGY
UPSTAGE
UPSURGE

•P••••G
OPENING
OPINING
SPACING
SPADING
SPARING
SPAYING
SPEWING
SPICING
SPIKING
SPITING
SPOKING
SPUMING
UPSWING

••PG•••
CAPGUNS
POPGUNS
TOPGUNS

••P•G••
IMPUGNS
OPPUGNS
PAPAGOS
REPUGNS

••P••G•
EXPUNGE
IMPINGE
LAPDOGS
PIPINGS
SAPSAGO
TAPINGS
TOPDOGS
UNPLUGS

••P•••G
BOPPING
CAPPING
COPPING
COPYING
CUPPING
DAPPING
DIPPING
ESPYING
GAPPING
GYPPING
HOPPING
HYPOING
KIPLING
LAPPING
LAPSING
LAPWING
LIPPING
LOPPING
MAPPING
MOPPING
NAPPING
NIPPING
PEPPING
POPPING
RAPPING
RIPPING
SAPLING
SAPPING
SIPPING
SOPPING
SUPPING
TAPPING
TIPPING
TOPPING
YAPPING
YIPPING
ZAPPING
ZIPPING

•••PG••
BURPGUN
STOPGAP

•••P•G•
RAMPAGE

•••P••G
BEEPING
BOPPING
BUMPING
BURPING
CAMPING
CAPPING
CARPING
COOPING
COPPING
CUPPING
DAMPING
DAPPING
DIPPING
DRAPING
DUMPING
EARPLUG
ELOPING
GAPPING
GASPING
GRIPING
GROPING
GULPING
GYPPING
HARPING
HEAPING
HELPING
HOOPING
HOPPING
JUMPING
KEEPING
LAPPING
LEAPING
LEIPZIG
LIMPING
LIPPING
LISPING
LOOPING
LOPPING
LUMPING
MAPPING
MOPPING
NAPPING
NIPPING
PEEPING
PEPPING
POOPING
POPPING
PUMPING
RAPPING
RASPING
REAPING
RIPPING
ROMPING
SAPPING
SCOPING
SEEPING
SHAPING
SIPPING
SLOPING
SNIPING
SOAPING
SOPPING
SUPPING
SWIPING
TAMPING
TAPPING
TIPPING
TOPPING
VAMPING
WARPING
WEEPING
WISPING
YAPPING
YELPING
YIPPING
ZAPPING
ZIPPING

••••P•G
BUSHPIG

PH•••••
PHAEDRA
PHAETON
PHALANX
PHANTOM
PHARAOH
PHARYNX
PHASEIN
PHASERS
PHASING
PHENOLS
PHENOMS
PHIDIAS
PHILBIN
PHILLIP
PHILTER
PHILTRE
PHINEAS
PHLOXES
PHOBIAS
PHOBICS
PHOEBES
PHOEBUS
PHOENIX
PHONEME
PHONICS
PHONIER
PHONIES
PHONILY
PHONING
PHOTOED
PHOTOGS
PHOTONS
PHOTOOP
PHRASAL
PHRASED
PHRASES
PHRENIC
PHYLLIS
PHYSICS

P•H••••
PAHLAVI

P••H•••
PACHISI
PATHWAY
PEAHENS
PERHAPS
PINHEAD
PINHOLE
PITHIER
PITHILY
PITHING
POOHBAH
POSHEST
POTHERB
POTHERS
POTHOLE
POTHOOK
PREHEAT
PUSHIER
PUSHILY
PUSHING
PUSHKIN
PUSHOFF
PUSHPIN
PUSHUPS
PYTHIAS
PYTHONS

P•••H••
PANCHAX
PANTHER
PARCHED
PARCHES
PASCHAL
PATCHED
PATCHES
PATCHUP
PEACHED
PEACHES
PERCHED
PERCHES
PINCHAS
PINCHED
PINCHER
PINCHES
PITCHED
PITCHER
PITCHES
PITCHIN
PLASHED
PLASHES
PLIGHTS
PLUSHER
PLUSHES
PLUSHLY
POACHED
POACHER
POACHES
PONCHOS
POOCHES
PORCHES
PORTHOS
POSTHOC
POTSHOT
POUCHED
POUCHES
PRITHEE
PROPHET
PRUDHOE
PSYCHED
PSYCHES
PSYCHIC
PSYCHUP
PUNCHED
PUNCHER
PUNCHES
PUNCHIN
PUNCHUP
PYNCHON
PYRRHIC
PYRRHUS

P••••H•
PANACHE
PARAPHS
PARIAHS
PAUNCHY
PENUCHE
PIRANHA
PLINTHS
PLOUGHS
PORSCHE
PREACHY
PUNKAHS
PURDAHS

P•••••H
PADUCAH
PANFISH
PAYCASH
PECKISH
PEEVISH
PETTISH
PHARAOH
PIGGISH
PINKISH
PIXYISH
PLAYDOH
POOHBAH
PREWASH
PRUDISH
PUBLISH
PUCKISH

•PH••••
APHELIA
APHESES
OPHELIA
SPHERES
UPHOLDS

•P•H•••
UPSHOTS

•P••H••
APACHES
APISHLY
APOTHEM
EPITHET

•P•••H•
EPARCHS
SPLASHY
UPRIGHT
UPTIGHT

•P••••H
IPSWICH
SPANISH
SPINACH
SPLOTCH

••PH•••
AMPHORA
ASPHALT
CEPHEUS
CIPHERS
CYPHERS
DAPHNIS
EUPHONY
GOPHERS
HYPHENS
INPHASE
JAPHETH
NAPHTHA
NEPHEWS
OMPHALI
ORPHANS
ORPHEAN
ORPHEUS
RAPHAEL
SIPHONS
SOPHISM
SOPHIST
TOPHATS
TYPHOON
ZEPHYRS

••P•H••
CAPSHAW

••P••H•
BYPATHS
DEPECHE
EMPATHY
NAPHTHA
RUPIAHS

••P•••H
DIPTYCH
FOPPISH
IMPEACH
JAPHETH
SOPWITH

•••PH••
CAMPHOR
DAUPHIN
DOLPHIN
EDAPHIC
GRAPHED
GRAPHIC
GRYPHON
MEMPHIS
MORPHED
MURPHEY
PROPHET
STEPHEN
SULPHUR
TROPHIC

•••P•H•
ARAPAHO
OOMPAHS

•••P••H
ANSPACH
DAMPISH
FOPPISH
TOWPATH
WARPATH
WASPISH

••••PH•
ADOLPHE
ATROPHY
CALIPHS
CERIPHS
GUELPHS
PARAPHS
SERAPHS
STROPHE
TERAPHS

••••P•H
INDEPTH

•••••PH
DIGRAPH
GALUMPH
RUDOLPH
TRIUMPH

PI•••••
PIANISM
PIANIST
PIASTER
PIASTRE
PIAZZAS
PICADOR
PICANTE
PICAROS
PICASSO
PICCARD
PICCOLO
PICKAXE
PICKENS
PICKERS
PICKETS
PICKETT
PICKIER
PICKING
PICKLED
PICKLES
PICKOFF
PICKOUT
PICKSAT
PICKSON
PICKSUP
PICKUPS
PICNICS
PICTURE
PIDGEON
PIDGINS
PIEBALD
PIECERS
PIECING
PIEPANS
PIERCED
PIERCES
PIERROT
PIETIES
PIETINS
PIETISM
PIFFLED
PIFFLES
PIGEONS
PIGGIES
PIGGING
PIGGISH
PIGIRON
PIGLETS
PIGLIKE
PIGMENT
PIGNUTS
PIGPENS
PIGSKIN
PIGSOUT
PIGTAIL
PIKEMAN
PIKEMEN
PILEDIN
PILEDON
PILEDUP
PILESIN
PILESON
PILESUP
PILEUPS
PILFERS
PILGRIM
PILINGS
PILLAGE
PILLARS
PILLBOX
PILLBUG
PILLING
PILLION
PILLORY
PILLOWS
PILLOWY
PILOTED
PILSNER
PIMENTO
PIMESON
PIMLICO
PINATAS
PINBALL
PINCERS
PINCHAS
PINCHED
PINCHER
PINCHES
PINCURL
PINDOWN
PINEFOR
PINENUT
PINESAP
PINETAR
PINETUM
PINGING
PINHEAD
PINHOLE
PINIEST
PINIONS
PINKEST
PINKIES
PINKING
PINKISH
PINLESS
PINNACE
PINNATE
PINNERS
PINNING
PINOAKS
PINOCLE
PINONES
PINTAIL
PINWALE
PIOLETS
PIONEER
PIOUSLY
PIPEDUP
PIPEFUL
PIPESUP
PIPETTE
PIPINGS
PIPKINS
PIPPINS
PIQUANT
PIQUING
PIRAEUS
PIRANHA
PIRATED
PIRATES
PIRATIC
PIROGUE
PISCINE
PISCOPO
PISMIRE
PISTILS
PISTOLE
PISTOLS
PISTONS
PITAPAT
PITBOSS
PITBULL
PITCHED
PITCHER
PITCHES
PITCHIN
PITEOUS
PITFALL
PITHIER
PITHILY
PITHING
PITIFUL
PITSAWS
PITSTOP
PITTERS
PITTING
PITTMAN
PITYING
PIVOTAL
PIVOTED
PIXYISH
PIZARRO
PIZZAZZ

P•I••••
PAIDFOR
PAIDOFF
PAIDOUT
PAILFUL
PAILOUS
PAINFUL
PAINTED
PAINTER
PAIRING
PAIROFF
PAIRSUP
PAISANO
PAISLEY
PAIUTES
PHIDIAS
PHILBIN
PHILLIP
PHILTER
PHILTRE
PHINEAS
PLIABLE
PLIABLY
PLIANCY
PLIGHTS
PLINKED
PLINTHS
POINTED
POINTER
POINTTO
POISING
POISONS
POISSON
POITIER
PRICERS
PRICIER
PRICING
PRICKED
PRICKLE
PRICKLY
PRIDING
PRIESTS
PRIMACY
PRIMARY
PRIMATE
PRIMERS
PRIMING
PRIMMER
PRIMPED
PRINCES
PRINKED
PRINTED
PRINTER
PRIORTO
PRISONS
PRITHEE
PRIVACY
PRIVATE
PRIVETS
PRIVIES
PRIZING

P••I•••
PACIFIC
PANICKY
PANICLE
PAPILLA
PARIAHS
PARIBUS
PARINGS
PATIENT
PATINAS
PAVIOUR
PEDICEL
PEDICLE
PELICAN
PELISSE
PEMICAN
PERIDOT
PERIGEE
PERIODS
PETIOLE
PETITES
PIGIRON
PILINGS
PINIEST
PINIONS
PIPINGS
PITIFUL
PLAICES
PLAINER
PLAINES
PLAINLY
PLAINTS
PLAITED
PODIUMS
POKIEST
POLICED
POLICES
POLITER
POLITIC
PONIARD
POSITED
POTIONS
PRAIRIE
PRAISED
PRAISER
PRAISES
PRYINTO
PUMICES
PUNIEST
PURISTS
PURITAN
PUTITTO
PYRITES
PYXIDES

P•••I••
PACHISI
PACKICE
PACKING
PADDIES
PADDING
PAIRING
PALLING
PALLIUM
PALMIER
PALMING
PALMIST
PAMBIES
PANDITS
PANFISH
PANNIER
PANNING
PANPIPE
PANSIES
PANTING
PAPRIKA
PARKING
PARRIED
PARRIES
PARRING
PARSING
PARTIAL
PARTIED
PARTIES
PARTING
PARTITA
PARTITE
PASSING
PASSION
PASSIVE
PASTIER
PASTIME
PASTINA
PASTING
PATRICE
PATRICK
PATRIOT
PATSIES
PATTIES
PATTING
PAUCITY
PAULINA
PAULINE
PAULING
PAULIST
PAUSING
PAWNING
PAYDIRT
PEAKING
PEALING
PECKING
PECKISH
PECTINS
PEEKING
PEELING
PEEPING
PEERING
PEEVING
PEEVISH
PEGGING
PELTING
PENCILS
PENDING
PENNIES
PENNING
PENSION
PENSIVE
PEONIES
PEPPIER
PEPPILY
PEPPING
PEPSINS
PEPTIDE
PERDIEM
PERFIDY
PERKIER
PERKILY
PERKING
PERKINS
PERLITE
PERMING
PERMITS
PERRIER
PERSIAN
PERSIST
PERSIUS
PESKIER
PESKILY
PETRIFY
PETTIER
PETTILY
PETTING
PETTISH
PHASING
PHIDIAS
PHOBIAS
PHOBICS
PHONICS
PHONIER
PHONIES
PHONILY
PHONING
PHYSICS
PIANISM
PIANIST
PICKIER
PICKING
PICNICS
PIDGINS
PIECING
PIETIES
PIETINS

PIETISM
PIGGIES
PIGGING
PIGGISH
PIGLIKE
PILLING
PILLION
PIMLICO
PINGING
PINKIES
PINKING
PINKISH
PINNING
PIPKINS
PIPPINS
PIQUING
PISCINE
PISMIRE
PISTILS
PITHIER
PITHILY
PITHING
PITTING
PITYING
PIXYISH
PLACIDO
PLACING
PLANING
PLATING
PLAYING
PLOSION
PLOSIVE
PLOWING
PLUMING
PLUVIAL
PODGIER
PODRIDA
POETICS
POISING
POITIER
POLLING
POLOIST
PONGIDS
PONTIAC
PONTIFF
PONTINE
PONTIUS
PONYING
POOLING
POOPING
POPLINS
POPPIES
POPPING
POPPINS
PORCINE
PORGIES
PORTICO
PORTION
POSTING
POTPIES
POTTING
POURING
POUTIER
POUTING
PRALINE
PRATING
PRAYING
PRECISE
PREDICT
PRELIMS
PREMIER
PREMISE
PREMIUM
PRESIDE
PREVIEW
PRICIER
PRICING
PRIDING
PRIMING
PRIVIES
PRIZING
PROBING
PROBITY
PRODIGY
PROFILE
PROFITS
PROMISE
PROSIER
PROSILY
PROSING
PROTIST
PROVIDE
PROVING
PROVISO
PROXIES
PROXIMO
PRUDISH
PRUNING
PUBLICS
PUBLISH
PUCCINI
PUCKISH
PUDDING
PUDGIER
PUERILE
PUFFIER
PUFFILY
PUFFING
PUFFINS
PULLING
PULPITS
PULSING
PUMPING
PUNDITS
PUNKIES
PUNNING
PUNTING
PUPPIES
PURGING
PURLIEU
PURLING
PURLINS
PURRING
PURSING
PURVIEW
PUSHIER
PUSHILY
PUSHING
PUTTIED
PUTTIES
PUTTING
PYGMIES
PYTHIAS

P••••I•

PACIFIC
PALADIN
PALMOIL
PARBOIL
PARFAIT
PARSNIP
PEERSIN
PELAGIC
PENGUIN
PERTAIN
PETUNIA
PFENNIG
PHASEIN
PHILBIN
PHILLIP
PHOENIX
PHRENIC
PHYLLIS
PIGSKIN
PIGTAIL
PILEDIN
PILESIN
PILGRIM
PINTAIL
PIRATIC
PITCHIN
PLASTIC
PLAUDIT
PLUGSIN
POLARIS
POLEMIC
POLITIC
POMPEIA
POMPEII
PORKPIE
POURSIN
PRAIRIE
PREEMIE
PREPAID
PREPPIE
PREVAIL
PROSAIC
PROTEIN
PRUSSIA
PSYCHIC
PUMPKIN
PUNCHIN
PURLOIN
PURSUIT
PUSHKIN
PUSHPIN
PYRAMID
PYRRHIC

P•••••I

PACHISI
PADRONI
PAHLAVI
PALAZZI
PLATYPI
POMPEII
PUCCINI
PULASKI
PUNJABI

•PI••••

APISHLY
EPICENE
EPICURE
EPIGENE
EPIGONE
EPIGRAM
EPILOGS
EPISODE
EPISTLE
EPITHET
EPITOME
OPIATES
OPINERS
OPINING
OPINION
SPICEUP
SPICIER
SPICING
SPIDERS
SPIDERY
SPIEDON
SPIEGEL
SPIELED
SPIELER
SPIESON
SPIGOTS
SPIKERS
SPIKIER
SPIKING
SPILLED
SPINACH
SPINDLE
SPINDLY
SPINELS
SPINETS
SPINIER
SPINNER
SPINOFF
SPINOUT
SPINOZA
SPIRALS
SPIRANT
SPIREAS
SPIRITO
SPIRITS
SPITING
SPITZES

•P•I•••

APRICOT
APRIORI
APSIDES
EPSILON
OPTICAL
OPTIMAL
OPTIMUM
OPTIONS
SPLICED
SPLICER
SPLICES
SPLINES
SPLINTS
SPLITUP
SPOILED
SPOILER
SPRIEST
SPRINGS
SPRINGY
SPRINTS
SPRITES
UPLIFTS
UPLINKS
UPRIGHT
UPRISEN
UPRISES
UPRIVER
UPSILON
UPTICKS
UPTIGHT

•P••I••

APATITE
APELIKE
APERIES
APPLIED
APPLIES
APPOINT
APPRISE
APPRIZE
EPEEIST
EPOXIES
IPSWICH
OPACITY
OPALINE
OPENING
OPINING
OPINION
SPACIER
SPACING
SPADING
SPANIEL
SPANISH
SPARING
SPATIAL
SPAVINS
SPAYING
SPECIAL
SPECIES
SPECIFY
SPEWING
SPICIER
SPICING
SPIKIER
SPIKING
SPINIER
SPIRITO
SPIRITS
SPITING
SPOKING
SPRAINS
SPUMING
UPRAISE
UPSWING

•P•••I•

APHELIA
EPSTEIN
OPENAIR
OPENPIT
OPHELIA
SPOTLIT
SPUTNIK
UPBRAID

•P••••I

APRIORI
SPUMONI

••PI•••

ASPIRED
ASPIRER
ASPIRES
ASPIRIN
CAPITAL
CAPITAN
CAPITOL
COPIERS
COPILOT
COPIOUS
DEPICTS
DOPIEST
EMPIRES
ESPIALS
EXPIATE
EXPIRED
EXPIRES
IMPIETY
IMPINGE
IMPIOUS
JUPITER
LUPINES
ORPINES
PAPILLA
PIPINGS
RAPIDER
RAPIDLY
RAPIERS
RAPINES
REPINED
REPINES
RIPINTO
RUPIAHS
SAPIENS
SAPIENT
TAPINGS
TAPIOCA
TEPIDLY
TOPIARY
TOPICAL
TYPICAL
TYPISTS
UMPIRED
UMPIRES
UNPILED
UNPILES
VAPIDLY
WAPITIS

••P•I••

AMPLIFY
APPLIED
APPLIES
APPOINT
APPRISE
APPRIZE
BAPTISM
BAPTIST
BAPTIZE
BOPPING
CAPPING
CAPRICE
CAPSIZE
CAPTION
CAPTIVE
COPPICE
COPPING
COPYING
COPYIST
CUPPING
CYPRIOT
DAPPING
DEPRIVE
DIPPING
EMPTIED
EMPTIER
EMPTIES
EMPTILY
ESPYING
FOPPISH
GAPPING
GIPSIES
GUPPIES
GYPPING
GYPSIES
HAPPIER
HAPPILY
HIPPIES
HOPKINS
HOPPING
HYPOING
IMPAIRS
IMPLIED
IMPLIES
IMPRINT
INPOINT
INPRINT
KIPLING
LAPPING
LAPSING
LAPWING
LIPPIER
LIPPING
LOPPING
MAPPING
MOPPING
NAPKINS
NAPPING
NAPTIME
NIPPIER
NIPPING
NUPTIAL
PAPRIKA
PEPPIER
PEPPILY
PEPPING
PEPSINS
PEPTIDE
PIPKINS
PIPPINS
POPLINS
POPPIES
POPPING
POPPINS
PUPPIES
RAPPING
REPAINT
REPAIRS
REPLICA
REPLIED
REPLIES
REPRICE
REPRINT
REPRISE
REPTILE
RIPPING
RIPTIDE
SAPLING
SAPPIER
SAPPING
SIPPING
SOPHISM
SOPHIST
SOPPING
SOPWITH
SUPPING
TAPPING
TIPPING
TIPSIER
TIPSILY
TOPKICK
TOPPING
TOPSIDE
YAPPING
YIPPING
YUPPIES
ZAPPING
ZIPPIER
ZIPPING

••P••I•

ASPIRIN
CAPAPIE
CAPTAIN
DAPHNIS
DEPOSIT
DIPLOID
EMPORIA
EXPLAIN
EXPLOIT
HEPARIN
HEPATIC
HOPTOIT
IMPERIL
NEPALIS
ROPEDIN
ROPESIN
TOPSAIL
TOPSOIL
WAPITIS
YOPLAIT

••P•••I

OMPHALI
RAPANUI
TOPKAPI

•••PI••

ARMPITS
AUSPICE
BAGPIPE
BEEPING
BOPPING
BUMPIER
BUMPING
BURPING
CAMPIER
CAMPING
CAMPION
CAPPING
CARPING
CASPIAN
COMPILE
COOPING
COPPICE
COPPING
CUPPING
CUSPIDS
DAMPING
DAMPISH
DAPPING
DESPISE
DESPITE
DIPPING
DRAPING
DROPINS
DUMPIER
DUMPING
ELAPIDS
ELOPING
FOPPISH
GAPPING
GASPING
GOOPIER
GRIPING
GROPING
GROPIUS
GULPING
GUPPIES
GYPPING
HAPPIER
HAPPILY
HARPIES
HARPING
HARPIST
HATPINS
HEAPING
HELPING
HIPPIES
HOOPING
HOPPING
HOSPICE
ICEPICK
INSPIRE
JUMPIER
JUMPING
KEEPING
KELPIES
KEWPIES
LAPPING
LEAPING
LEMPIRA
LIMPING
LIPPIER
LIPPING
LISPING
LOOPIER
LOOPING
LOPPING
LUMPIER
LUMPING
MAGPIES
MAPPING
MOPPING
MUDPIES
NAPPING
NIPPIER
NIPPING
NITPICK
PANPIPE
PEEPING
PEPPIER
PEPPILY
PEPPING
PIPPINS
POOPING
POPPIES
POPPING
POPPINS
POTPIES
PULPITS
PUMPING
PUPPIES
RAPPING
RASPIER
RASPING
REAPING
REDPINE
RESPIRE
RESPITE
RIPPING
ROMPING
SAPPIER
SAPPING
SCOPING
SEEPING
SERPICO
SHAPING
SHAPIRO
SIPPING
SLOPING
SNIPING
SOAPIER
SOAPING
SOPPING
SOUPIER
STEPINS
SUPPING
SWIPING
TAMPICO
TAMPING
TAPPING
TARPITS
TENPINS
TIEPINS
TIPPING
TOPPING
TROPICS
TROPISM
UTOPIAN
UTOPIAS
VAMPING
VAMPIRE
VESPIDS
VULPINE
WARPING
WASPISH
WEEPIER
WEEPING
WISPIER
WISPILY
WISPING
YAPPING
YELPING
YIPPING
YUPPIES
ZAPPING
ZIPPIER
ZIPPING

•••P•I•

ASEPSIS
ASEPTIC
BUMPKIN
CHAPLIN
CHIPSIN
CRAPPIE
CRYPTIC
CULPRIT
DAUPHIN
DEEPSIX
DESPAIR
DESPOIL
DOLPHIN
DROPSIN
EDAPHIC
GRAPHIC
JUMPSIN
KEEPSIN
LAMPOIL
LEIPZIG
LOWPAID
MEMPHIS
POMPEIA
POMPEII
PREPAID
PREPPIE
PUMPKIN
SEEPSIN
SKEPTIC
SLEPTIN
STEPSIN
STOPSIN
STYPTIC
TROPHIC

•••P••I

CAMPARI
CHAPATI
POMPEII
TRIPOLI
TYMPANI

••••PI•

BUSHPIG
CAPAPIE
CHEAPIE
COCKPIT
CRAPPIE
CRISPIN
DUCKPIN
GROUPIE
HAIRPIN
HEADPIN
INASPIN
INCIPIT
INSIPID
KINGPIN
OLYMPIA
OLYMPIC
OPENPIT
PORKPIE
PREPPIE
PUSHPIN
SCORPIO
SERAPIS
SLEEPIN
THESPIS

••••P•I

EXEMPLI
SHARPEI

•••••PI

PLATYPI
TOPKAPI

P•J••••

PAJAMAS
PDJAMES
PYJAMAS

P••J•••

PALJOEY
PERJURE
PERJURY
PROJECT
PUNJABI

P•••J••

PROPJET

•••PJ••

PROPJET

P•K••••

PIKEMAN
PIKEMEN
POKEDAT
POKEFUN
POKESAT
POKIEST

P••K•••

PACKAGE
PACKARD
PACKERS
PACKETS
PACKICE
PACKING
PACKRAT
PACKSUP
PARKING
PARKWAY
PEAKING
PECKING
PECKISH
PECKSAT
PEEKING
PEEKOUT
PEEKSAT
PERKIER
PERKILY
PERKING
PERKINS
PERKSUP
PESKIER
PESKILY
PICKAXE
PICKENS
PICKERS
PICKETS
PICKETT
PICKIER
PICKING
PICKLED
PICKLES
PICKOFF
PICKOUT
PICKSAT
PICKSON
PICKSUP
PICKUPS
PINKEST
PINKIES
PINKING
PINKISH
PIPKINS
POCKETS
POLKAED
PORKERS
PORKPIE
PUCKERS
PUCKETT
PUCKISH
PUNKAHS
PUNKIES

P•••K••

PASSKEY
PATAKES
PERUKES
PIGSKIN
PLACKET
PLANKED
PLINKED
PLUCKED
PLUNKED
PRANKED
PRICKED
PRICKLE
PRICKLY
PRINKED
PUMPKIN
PUSHKIN

P••••K•

PALOOKA
PANCAKE
PANICKY
PAPRIKA
PARTAKE
PIGLIKE
PINOAKS
PROVOKE
PULASKI

P•••••K

PADDOCK
PADLOCK
PARTOOK
PATRICK
PEACOCK
PEPTALK
PETCOCK
PETROCK
POLLOCK
POTHOOK
POTLUCK
PRECOOK
PRESOAK

•P•K•••

SPIKERS
SPIKIER
SPIKING
SPOKANE
SPOKEOF
SPOKEUP
SPOKING

•P••K••

SPACKLE
SPANKED
SPANKER
SPARKED
SPARKLE
SPEAKER
SPEAKOF
SPEAKUP
SPECKLE
SPOOKED
UPTAKES

•P•••K•

APELIKE
SPASSKY
UPLINKS
UPTICKS

•P••••K

SPELUNK
SPUTNIK

••PK•••

HOPKINS
NAPKINS
PIPKINS
TOPKAPI
TOPKICK
TOPKNOT

••P••K•

CUPCAKE
KOPECKS
PAPRIKA
UNPACKS

••P•••K

PEPTALK
TOPKICK

•••PK••

BUMPKIN
PUMPKIN

•••P•K•

BESPOKE
COWPOKE

•••P••K

BESPEAK
DRSPOCK
HENPECK
ICEPACK
ICEPICK
JAMPACK
MRSPOCK
MUDPACK

NITPICK
OFFPEAK
RATPACK
SIXPACK

••••P•K
ZATOPEK

PL•••••
PLACARD
PLACATE
PLACEBO
PLACERS
PLACIDO
PLACING
PLACKET
PLAGUED
PLAGUES
PLAICES
PLAINER
PLAINES
PLAINLY
PLAINTS
PLAITED
PLANERS
PLANETS
PLANING
PLANKED
PLANNED
PLANNER
PLANSON
PLANTAR
PLANTED
PLANTER
PLAQUES
PLASHED
PLASHES
PLASMAS
PLASTER
PLASTIC
PLATEAU
PLATENS
PLATERS
PLATING
PLATOON
PLATTER
PLATYPI
PLAUDIT
PLAUTUS
PLAYACT
PLAYBOY
PLAYDOH
PLAYERS
PLAYFUL
PLAYING
PLAYLET
PLAYOFF
PLAYOUT
PLAYPEN
PLAYSAT
PLAYSON
PLAYSUP
PLEADED
PLEADER
PLEASED
PLEASER
PLEASES
PLEATED
PLECTRA
PLEDGED
PLEDGEE
PLEDGER
PLEDGES
PLENARY
PLENUMS
PLEXORS
PLIABLE
PLIABLY
PLIANCY
PLIGHTS
PLINKED
PLINTHS
PLODDED
PLODDER
PLOPPED
PLOSION
PLOSIVE
PLOTTED
PLOTTER
PLOUGHS
PLOVERS
PLOWBOY
PLOWERS
PLOWING
PLOWMAN
PLOWMEN
PLUCKED
PLUGGED
PLUGGER
PLUGSIN
PLUMAGE
PLUMBED
PLUMBER
PLUMING
PLUMMER
PLUMMET
PLUMPED
PLUMPER
PLUNDER
PLUNGED
PLUNGER
PLUNGES
PLUNKED
PLURALS
PLUSHER
PLUSHES
PLUSHLY
PLUSSES
PLUVIAL
PLYWOOD

P•L••••
PALACES
PALADIN
PALANCE
PALATAL
PALATES
PALAVER
PALAZZI
PALAZZO
PALEDRY
PALERMO
PALETTE
PALFREY
PALJOEY
PALLETS
PALLING
PALLIUM
PALMATE
PALMIER
PALMING
PALMIST
PALMOFF
PALMOIL
PALOMAR
PALOOKA
PALTERS
PELAGES
PELAGIC
PELICAN
PELISSE
PELLETS
PELOTAS
PELTATE
PELTERS
PELTING
PHLOXES
PILEDIN
PILEDON
PILEDUP
PILESIN
PILESON
PILESUP
PILEUPS
PILFERS
PILGRIM
PILINGS
PILLAGE
PILLARS
PILLBOX
PILLBUG
PILLING
PILLION
PILLORY
PILLOWS
PILLOWY
PILOTED
PILSNER
POLARIS
POLDERS
POLEAXE
POLECAT
POLEMIC
POLENTA
POLICED
POLICES
POLITER
POLITIC
POLKAED
POLLENS
POLLERS
POLLING
POLLOCK
POLLTAX
POLLUTE
POLOIST
POLYGON
POLYMER
PULASKI
PULLETS
PULLEYS
PULLING
PULLMAN
PULLOFF
PULLONS
PULLOUT
PULLSUP
PULLTAB
PULLUPS
PULPITS
PULSARS
PULSATE
PULSING

P••L•••
PABLUMS
PADLOCK
PAHLAVI
PAILFUL
PAILOUS
PALLETS
PALLING
PALLIUM
PARLAYS
PARLEYS
PARLORS
PARLOUR
PARLOUS
PAULINA
PAULINE
PAULING
PAULIST
PAULSEN
PAVLOVA
PAYLOAD
PEALING
PEDLARS
PEELERS
PEELING
PEELOFF
PELLETS
PEPLUMS
PERLITE
PERLMAN
PHALANX
PHILBIN
PHILLIP
PHILTER
PHILTRE
PHYLLIS
PIGLETS
PIGLIKE
PILLAGE
PILLARS
PILLBOX
PILLBUG
PILLING
PILLION
PILLORY
PILLOWS
PILLOWY
PIMLICO
PINLESS
PIOLETS
POLLENS
POLLERS
POLLING
POLLOCK
POLLTAX
POLLUTE
POOLING
POPLARS
POPLINS
POTLUCK
POULENC
POULTRY
PRALINE
PRELATE
PRELIMS
PRELOAD
PRELUDE
PROLOGS
PROLONG
PSALMED
PSALTER
PTOLEMY
PUBLICS
PUBLISH
PULLETS
PULLEYS
PULLING
PULLMAN
PULLOFF
PULLONS
PULLOUT
PULLSUP
PULLTAB
PULLUPS
PURLIEU
PURLING
PURLINS
PURLOIN

P•••L••
PABULUM
PADDLED
PADDLER
PADDLES
PAISLEY
PANELED
PAPILLA
PAROLED
PAROLEE
PAROLES
PARSLEY
PATELLA
PAYOLAS
PEARLED
PEBBLED
PEBBLES
PEDALED
PEDDLED
PEDDLER
PEDDLES
PEEPLES
PENALTY
PENULTS
PEOPLED
PEOPLES
PERPLEX
PESTLED
PESTLES
PETALED
PHILLIP
PHYLLIS
PICKLED
PICKLES
PIFFLED
PIFFLES
PLAYLET
POMELOS
POODLES
POPPLED
POPPLES
POPULAR
PRESLEY
PROBLEM
PROWLED
PROWLER
PUDDLED
PUDDLES
PUEBLOS
PURFLED
PURFLES
PURPLED
PURPLES
PUZZLED
PUZZLER
PUZZLES

P••••L•
PANICLE
PANOPLY
PAPILLA
PARABLE
PARCELS
PARNELL
PASSELS
PASTELS
PATELLA
PATROLS
PAYABLE
PAYROLL
PEDICLE
PENCILS
PENPALS
PEPPILY
PEPTALK
PERCALE
PERGOLA
PERKILY
PERNELL
PESKILY
PETIOLE
PETRELS
PETTILY
PHENOLS
PHONILY
PICCOLO
PIEBALD
PINBALL
PINHOLE
PINOCLE
PINWALE
PIOUSLY
PISTILS
PISTOLE
PISTOLS
PITBULL
PITFALL
PITHILY
PLAINLY
PLIABLE
PLIABLY
PLURALS
PLUSHLY
POMMELS
PORTALS
PORTOLA
POTABLE
POTFULS
POTHOLE
PRATTLE
PRESALE
PRESELL
PRICKLE
PRICKLY
PROFILE
PROPELS
PROSILY
PROUDLY
PUERILE
PUFFILY
PUMMELS
PURCELL
PUSHILY

P•••••L
PAGEFUL
PAILFUL
PAINFUL
PALATAL
PALMOIL
PARASOL
PARBOIL
PARNELL
PARTIAL
PASCHAL
PASSEUL
PAYROLL
PEAFOWL
PEDICEL
PERNELL
PERUSAL
PHRASAL
PIGTAIL
PINBALL
PINCURL
PINTAIL
PIPEFUL
PITBULL
PITFALL
PITIFUL
PIVOTAL
PLAYFUL
PLUVIAL
PRECOOL
PRESELL
PRETZEL
PREVAIL
PURCELL

•PL••••
APLENTY
SPLASHY
SPLAYED
SPLEENS
SPLICED
SPLICER
SPLICES
SPLINES
SPLINTS
SPLITUP
SPLOTCH
SPLURGE
UPLANDS
UPLIFTS
UPLINKS
UPLOADS

•P•L•••
APELIKE
APOLOGY
APPLAUD
APPLIED
APPLIES
EPILOGS
OPALINE
OPULENT
SPALLED
SPELLED
SPELLER
SPELUNK
SPILLED
UPCLOSE

•P••L••
APHELIA
APPALLS
EPAULET
EPSILON
OPHELIA
SPALLED
SPELLED
SPELLER
SPIELED
SPIELER
SPILLED
SPOILED
SPOILER
SPOOLED
SPOTLIT
UPHOLDS
UPSILON

•P•••L•
APISHLY
APOSTLE
APPALLS
APPEALS
EPISTLE
SPACKLE
SPANGLE
SPANGLY
SPARELY
SPARKLE
SPATULA
SPECKLE
SPINDLE
SPINDLY
SPINELS
SPIRALS
SPRAWLS
UPPSALA
UPSCALE

•P••••L
APPAREL
OPTICAL
OPTIMAL
SPANIEL
SPATIAL
SPECIAL
SPIEGEL
SPOUSAL

••PL•••
AMPLEST
AMPLIFY
APPLAUD
APPLIED
APPLIES
BIPLANE
BYPLAYS
CAPLESS
CAPLETS
COPLAND
DEPLANE
DEPLETE
DEPLORE
DEPLOYS
DIPLOID
DIPLOMA
EMPLOYS
ENPLANE
EXPLAIN
EXPLODE
EXPLOIT
EXPLORE
HAPLESS
IMPLANT
IMPLIED
IMPLIES
IMPLODE
IMPLORE
INPLACE
KIPLING
LAPLACE
LAPLAND
LAPLATA
PEPLUMS
POPLARS
POPLINS
REPLACE
REPLANS
REPLANT
REPLATE
REPLAYS
REPLETE
REPLICA
REPLIED
REPLIES
SAPLING
UNPLUGS
YOPLAIT

••P•L••
AMPULES
APPALLS
BIPOLAR
CAPELET
CAPELLA
CAPULET
COPILOT
CUPOLAS
DAPPLED
DAPPLES
DEPALMA
DIPOLAR
DIPOLES
DOPPLER
FIPPLES
IMPALAS
IMPALED
IMPALES
IMPULSE
LAPALMA
LAPELED
NEPALIS
PAPILLA
POPPLED
POPPLES
POPULAR
REPOLLS
REPULSE
RIPPLED
RIPPLES
SUPPLER
TIPPLED
TIPPLER
TIPPLES
TOPPLED
TOPPLES
TUPELOS
UNPILED
UNPILES

••P••L•
AMPOULE
APPALLS
APPEALS
ASPHALT
CAPABLE
CAPABLY
CAPELLA
CAPFULS
CAPSULE
COPPOLA
CUPFULS
EMPTILY
ESPIALS
HAPPILY
LAPBELT
LAPFULS
LIPBALM
OMPHALI
PAPILLA
PEPPILY
PEPTALK
RAPIDLY
RAPPELS
REPEALS
REPOLLS
REPTILE
TEPIDLY
TIPSILY
UPPSALA
VAPIDLY

••P•••L
APPAREL
BIPEDAL
CAPITAL
CAPITOL
DEPOSAL
EMPANEL
ESPANOL
HOPEFUL
IMPANEL
IMPERIL
NUPTIAL
PIPEFUL
RAPHAEL
TOPICAL
TOPSAIL
TOPSOIL
TYPICAL

•••PL••
AIRPLAY
CHAPLET
CHAPLIN
COMPLEX
COUPLED
COUPLES
COUPLET
DAPPLED
DAPPLES
DIMPLED
DIMPLES
DISPLAY
DOPPLER
DROPLET
EARPLUG
ENDPLAY
FIPPLES
GUNPLAY
HOOPLAS
KERPLOP
MISPLAY
NONPLUS
OUTPLAY
PEEPLES
PEOPLED
PEOPLES
PERPLEX
POPPLED
POPPLES
PURPLED
PURPLES
RIPPLED
RIPPLES
RUMPLED
RUMPLES
SAMPLED
SAMPLER
SAMPLES
SIMPLER
SIMPLEX
STAPLED
STAPLER
STAPLES
SUBPLOT
SUPPLER
SURPLUS
TEMPLAR
TEMPLES
TIPPLED
TIPPLER
TIPPLES
TOPPLED
TOPPLES
TRIPLED
TRIPLES
TRIPLET
TRIPLEX
WIMPLED
WIMPLES

•••P•L•
ADEPTLY
AMAPOLA
CARPALS
CHAPELS
COMPELS
COMPILE
COPPOLA
DISPELS
GOSPELS
GRAPPLE
HAPPILY
INAPTLY
INEPTLY
KAMPALA
LEGPULL
LEOPOLD
MAYPOLE
PENPALS
PEPPILY
PROPELS
RAPPELS
REDPOLL
RUMPOLE
SCAPULA
SHAPELY
SKIPOLE
STIPPLE
TADPOLE
TRIPOLI
WALPOLE
WISPILY

•••P••L
CARPOOL
DESPOIL
GRAPNEL
HELPFUL
LAMPOIL
LEGPULL
LESPAUL
REDPOLL
VANPOOL

••••PL•
CHEAPLY
CRISPLY
CRUMPLE
CRUMPLY
EXAMPLE
EXEMPLI
GRAPPLE
MANIPLE
OCTUPLE
PANOPLY
SCRUPLE
SHARPLY
STEEPLE
STEEPLY
STIPPLE
TRAMPLE

••••P•L
OEDIPAL
SCALPEL

P•M••••
PAMBIES
PAMPERS
PEMICAN
PIMENTO
PIMESON
PIMLICO
POMADED
POMADES
POMELOS
POMMELS
POMPANO
POMPEIA
POMPEII
POMPOMS
POMPONS
POMPOUS
PUMICES
PUMMELS
PUMPERS
PUMPING
PUMPKIN
PUMPSUP

P••M•••
PALMATE
PALMIER
PALMING
PALMIST
PALMOFF
PALMOIL
PAYMENT
PERMING
PERMITS
PIGMENT
PISMIRE
PLUMAGE
PLUMBED
PLUMBER
PLUMING
PLUMMER
PLUMMET
PLUMPED
PLUMPER
POMMELS
PREMEDS
PREMIER
PREMISE
PREMIUM
PRIMACY
PRIMARY
PRIMATE
PRIMERS
PRIMING
PRIMMER
PRIMPED
PROMISE
PROMOTE
PROMPTS
PUMMELS
PYGMIES

P•••M••
PAJAMAS
PALOMAR
PANAMAS
PDJAMES
PERLMAN
PIKEMAN
PIKEMEN
PITTMAN
PLASMAS
PLOWMAN
PLOWMEN
PLUMMER
PLUMMET
POLEMIC
POLYMER
POSTMAN
POSTMEN
POTOMAC
PREAMPS
PREEMIE
PREEMPT
PRIMMER
PROPMAN
PROPMEN
PSALMED
PULLMAN
PUTAMEN
PYJAMAS
PYRAMID
PYRAMUS

P••••M•
PABLUMS
PALERMO
PASTIME
PENNAME
PEPLUMS
PERFUME
PETNAME
PHENOMS
PHONEME
PLENUMS
PODIUMS
POMPOMS
POSSUMS
PRELIMS
PRESUME
PROXIMO
PTOLEMY

P•••••M
PABULUM
PALLIUM
PERDIEM
PERFORM
PHANTOM
PIANISM
PIETISM
PILGRIM
PINETUM
POTSDAM
PREMIUM
PROBLEM
PROGRAM

•P•M•••
SPUMING
SPUMONE
SPUMONI

•P••M••
OPTIMAL

OPTIMUM
UPTEMPO

•P•••M•
EPITOME
EPONYMS
IPANEMA

•P••••M
APOTHEM
EPIGRAM
OPOSSUM
OPTIMUM

••PM•••
TOPMAST
TOPMOST

••P•M••
REPOMAN

••P••M•
DEPALMA
DIPLOMA
LAPALMA
NAPTIME
PEPLUMS
SUPREME
SUPREMO

••P•••M
BAPTISM
LIPBALM
SOPHISM
TAPROOM

•••PM••
CHAPMAN
CHAPMEN
PROPMAN
PROPMEN
SHIPMAN
SHIPMEN

•••P•M•
AIRPUMP
GASPUMP
POMPOMS

•••P••M
LUMPSUM
SYMPTOM
TROPISM

P•N••••
PANACEA
PANACHE
PANAMAS
PANCAKE
PANCHAX
PANDECT
PANDERS
PANDITS
PANDORA
PANELED
PANETTA
PANFISH
PANICKY
PANICLE
PANNERS
PANNIER
PANNING
PANOPLY
PANPIPE
PANSIES
PANSOUT
PANTHER
PANTING
PANURGE
PANZERS
PENALTY
PENANCE
PENATES
PENCILS
PENDANT
PENDENT
PENDING
PENGUIN
PENNAME
PENNANT
PENNATE
PENNERS
PENNIES
PENNING
PENNONS
PENPALS
PENSEES
PENSION
PENSIVE
PENTADS
PENUCHE
PENULTS
PINATAS
PINBALL
PINCERS
PINCHAS
PINCHED
PINCHER
PINCHES
PINCURL
PINDOWN
PINEFOR
PINENUT
PINESAP
PINETAR
PINETUM
PINGING
PINHEAD
PINHOLE
PINIEST
PINIONS
PINKEST
PINKIES
PINKING
PINKISH
PINLESS
PINNACE
PINNATE
PINNERS
PINNING
PINOAKS
PINOCLE
PINONES
PINTAIL
PINWALE
PONCHOS
PONDERS
PONGIDS
PONIARD
PONTIAC
PONTIFF
PONTINE
PONTIUS
PONTOON
PONYING
PUNCHED
PUNCHER
PUNCHES
PUNCHIN
PUNCHUP
PUNDITS
PUNGENT
PUNIEST
PUNJABI
PUNKAHS
PUNKIES
PUNNING
PUNSTER
PUNTERS
PUNTING
PYNCHON

P••N•••
PAINFUL
PAINTED
PAINTER
PANNERS
PANNIER
PANNING
PARNELL
PATNESS
PAUNCHY
PAWNEES
PAWNERS
PAWNING
PAWNOFF
PEANUTS
PENNAME
PENNANT
PENNATE
PENNERS
PENNIES
PENNING
PENNONS
PEONAGE
PEONIES
PERNELL
PETNAME
PFENNIG
PHANTOM
PHENOLS
PHENOMS
PHINEAS
PHONEME
PHONICS
PHONIER
PHONIES
PHONILY
PHONING
PIANISM
PIANIST
PICNICS
PIGNUTS
PINNACE
PINNATE
PINNERS
PINNING
PIONEER
PLANERS
PLANETS
PLANING
PLANKED
PLANNED
PLANNER
PLANSON
PLANTAR
PLANTED
PLANTER
PLENARY
PLENUMS
PLINKED
PLINTHS
PLUNDER
PLUNGED
PLUNGER
PLUNGES
PLUNKED
POINTED
POINTER
POINTTO
POUNCED
POUNCER
POUNCES
POUNDED
POUNDER
PRANCED
PRANCER
PRANCES
PRANKED
PRINCES
PRINKED
PRINTED
PRINTER
PRONGED
PRONOUN
PRUNERS
PRUNING
PSANDQS
PUGNOSE
PUNNING

P•••N••
PALANCE
PARDNER
PARENTS
PARINGS
PARSNIP
PARTNER
PATENTS
PATINAS
PAVANES
PEDANTS
PENANCE
PETUNIA
PFENNIG
PHOENIX
PHRENIC
PICANTE
PILINGS
PILSNER
PIMENTO
PINENUT
PINONES
PIPINGS
PIRANHA
PLAINER
PLAINES
PLAINLY
PLAINTS
PLANNED
PLANNER
PLIANCY
POCONOS
POLENTA
POTENCY
PREENED
PREENER
PRYINTO

P••••N•
PACKING
PADDING
PADRONE
PADRONI
PAGEANT
PAIRING
PAISANO
PALLING
PALMING
PANNING
PANTING
PAPUANS
PARDONS
PARKING
PARRING
PARSING
PARSONS
PARTING
PARVENU
PASSANT
PASSING
PASTINA
PASTING
PATERNO
PATIENT
PATRONS
PATTENS
PATTING
PAULINA
PAULINE
PAULING
PAUSING
PAWNING
PAYMENT
PEAHENS
PEAKING
PEALING
PEASANT
PECCANT
PECKING
PECTINS
PEEKING
PEELING
PEEPING
PEERING
PEEVING
PEGGING
PELTING
PENDANT
PENDENT
PENDING
PENNANT
PENNING
PENNONS
PEPPING
PEPSINS
PERCENT
PERKING
PERKINS
PERMING
PERSONA
PERSONS
PETTING
PHALANX
PHARYNX
PHASING
PHONING
PHOTONS
PICKENS
PICKING
PIDGINS
PIECING
PIEPANS
PIETINS
PIGEONS
PIGGING
PIGMENT
PIGPENS
PILLING
PINGING
PINIONS
PINKING
PINNING
PIPKINS
PIPPINS
PIQUANT
PIQUING
PISCINE
PISTONS
PITHING
PITTING
PITYING
PLACING
PLANING
PLATENS
PLATING
PLAYING
PLOWING
PLUMING
POISING
POISONS
POLLENS
POLLING
POMPANO
POMPONS
PONTINE
PONYING
POOLING
POOPING
POPGUNS
POPLINS
POPPING
POPPINS
PORCINE
PORSENA
PORTEND
PORTENT
POSTING
POTIONS
POTTING
POULENC
POURING
POUTING
PRALINE
PRATING
PRAYING
PREBEND
PRESENT
PRETEND
PREVENT
PRICING
PRIDING
PRIMING
PRISONS
PRIZING
PROBING
PROBONO
PROFANE
PROGENY
PROLONG
PROPANE
PROSING
PROTONS
PROVING
PRUDENT
PRUNING
PUCCINI
PUDDING
PUFFING
PUFFINS
PULLING
PULLONS
PULSING
PUMPING
PUNGENT
PUNNING
PUNTING
PUPTENT
PURGING
PURLING
PURLINS
PURRING
PURSING
PUSHING
PUTTING
PYTHONS

P•••••N
PALADIN
PARAGON
PASSION
PASTERN
PATROON
PATTERN
PAULSEN
PEABEAN
PEARSON
PEERSIN
PELICAN
PEMICAN
PENGUIN
PENSION
PERLMAN
PERSIAN
PERTAIN
PHAETON
PHASEIN
PHILBIN
PICKSON
PIDGEON
PIGIRON
PIGSKIN
PIKEMAN
PIKEMEN
PILEDIN
PILEDON
PILESIN
PILESON
PILLION
PIMESON
PINDOWN
PITCHIN
PITTMAN
PLANSON
PLATOON
PLAYPEN
PLAYSON
PLOSION
PLOWMAN
PLOWMEN
PLUGSIN
POISSON
POKEFUN
POLYGON
PONTOON
POPCORN
PORTION
POSTERN
POSTMAN
POSTMEN
POURSIN
PREDAWN
PRESSON
PRESTON
PRETEEN
PREYSON
PROCYON
PRONOUN
PROPMAN
PROPMEN
PROTEAN
PROTEIN
PULLMAN
PUMPKIN
PUNCHIN
PURITAN
PURLOIN
PUSHKIN
PUSHPIN
PUTAMEN
PUTDOWN
PUTUPON
PYNCHON

•P•N•••
APTNESS
EPONYMS
IPANEMA
OPENAIR
OPENBAR
OPENEND
OPENERS
OPENING
OPENPIT
OPENSEA
OPENSUP
OPENTOE
OPINERS
OPINING
OPINION
SPANDEX
SPANGLE
SPANGLY
SPANIEL
SPANISH
SPANKED
SPANKER
SPANNED
SPANNER
SPENCER
SPENDER
SPENSER
SPINACH
SPINDLE
SPINDLY
SPINELS
SPINETS
SPINIER
SPINNER
SPINOFF
SPINOUT
SPINOZA
SPONDEE
SPONGED
SPONGER
SPONGES
SPONSOR
SPUNOFF
SPUNOUT
UPENDED

•P••N••
APLENTY
APPENDS
APRONED
SPANNED
SPANNER
SPAWNED
SPINNER
SPLINES
SPLINTS
SPOONED
SPOONER
SPRINGS
SPRINGY
SPRINTS
SPURNED
SPURNER
SPUTNIK
UPLANDS
UPLINKS
UPTONOW

•P•••N•
APPOINT
EPERGNE
EPICENE
EPIGENE
EPIGONE
OPALINE
OPENEND
OPENING
OPERAND
OPINING
OPPUGNS
OPTIONS
OPULENT
SPACING
SPADING
SPARING
SPAVINS
SPAYING
SPELUNK
SPEWING
SPICING
SPIKING
SPIRANT
SPITING
SPLEENS
SPOKANE
SPOKING
SPRAINS
SPUMING
SPUMONE
SPUMONI
UPBORNE
UPFRONT
UPSWING
UPTURNS

•P••••N
EPSILON
EPSTEIN
OPINION
SPARTAN
SPIEDON
SPIESON
SPORRAN
SPURSON
UPRISEN
UPSILON

••PN•••
CAPNUTS
HIPNESS

••P•N••
APPENDS
DAPHNIS
DEPENDS
DEPONED
DEPONES
EMPANEL
ESPANOL
EXPANDS
EXPANSE
EXPENDS
EXPENSE
EXPUNGE
IMPANEL
IMPENDS
IMPINGE
LEPANTO
LUPINES
ORPINES
PIPINGS
RAPANUI
RAPINES
REPENTS
REPINED
REPINES
RIPENED
RIPINTO
TAPINGS
TOPKNOT

••P••N•
APPOINT
BIPLANE
BOPPING
CAPEANN
CAPGUNS
CAPPING
COPLAND
COPPING
COPYING
CUPPING
DAPPING
DEPLANE
DIPPING
ENPLANE
ESPYING
EUPHONY
EXPOUND
GAPPING
GYPPING
HAPPENS
HIPBONE
HOPKINS
HOPPING
HYPHENS
HYPOING
IMPLANT
IMPOUND
IMPRINT
IMPUGNS
INPOINT
INPRINT
KIPLING
LAPLAND
LAPPING
LAPSING
LAPWING
LEPTONS
LIPPING
LIPSYNC
LOPPING
MAPPING
MOPPING
NAPKINS
NAPPING
NEPTUNE
NIPPING
OPPUGNS
ORPHANS
PAPUANS
PEPPING
PEPSINS
PIPKINS
PIPPINS
POPGUNS
POPLINS
POPPING
POPPINS
PUPTENT
RAPPING
REPAINT
REPLANS
REPLANT
REPRINT
REPUGNS
RIPPING
SAPIENS
SAPIENT
SAPLING
SAPPING
SIPHONS
SIPPING
SOPPING
SOPRANO
SUPPING
TAPPING
TIPPING
TOPGUNS
TOPPING
YAPPING
YIPPING
ZAPPING
ZIPPING

••P•••N
ASPIRIN
CAPEANN
CAPITAN
CAPSTAN
CAPTAIN
CAPTION
EXPLAIN
HEPARIN
HEPBURN
ORPHEAN
POPCORN
REPOMAN
RIPTORN
ROPEDIN
ROPESIN
TYPHOON
UMPTEEN

•••PN••
GRAPNEL

•••P•N•
BEEPING
BOPPING
BUMPING
BURPING
CAMPING
CAPPING
CARPING
CLIPONS
COMPANY
COOPING
COPPING
COUPONS
CUPPING
DAMPENS
DAMPING
DAPPING
DEEPEND
DEEPENS
DIPPING
DRAPING
DROPINS
DUMPING
ELOPING
FRYPANS
GAPPING
GASPING
GRIPING
GROPING
GULPING
GYPPING
HAPPENS
HARPING
HATPINS
HEAPING
HELPING
HISPANO
HOOPING
HOPPING
INSPANS
JUMPING
KEEPING
LAPPING
LEAPING
LIMPING
LIPPING
LISPING
LOOPING
LOPPING
LUMPING
MAPPING
MOPPING
NAPPING
NIPPING
OILPANS
PEEPING
PEPPING
PIEPANS
PIGPENS
PIPPINS
POMPANO
POMPONS
POOPING
POPPING
POPPINS
PROPANE
PUMPING
RAMPANT
RAPPING
RASPING
REAPING
REDPINE
REOPENS
RESPOND
RIPPING
ROMPING
SAMPANS
SAPPING
SCOPING
SEEPING
SERPENT
SHAPING
SIPPING
SLIPONS
SLOPING
SNAPONS
SNIPING
SOAPING
SOPPING
STEPINS
STIPEND
SUPPING
SUSPEND
SWIPING
TAIPANS
TAMPING
TAPPING
TARPONS
TENPINS
TIEPINS
TIPPING
TOPPING
TREPANS
TYMPANA
TYMPANI
UNSPENT
USOPENS
VAMPING
VOLPONE
VULPINE
WARPING
WEAPONS
WEEPING
WISPING
YAPPING
YAUPONS
YELPING
YIPPING
ZAPPING
ZIPPING

•••P••N
BUMPKIN
BURPGUN
CAMPION
CASPIAN
CHAPLIN
CHAPMAN
CHAPMEN
CHIPSIN
CLAPTON
DAUPHIN
DOLPHIN
DRIPPAN
DROPSIN
GRYPHON
HAMPTON
HARPOON
HARPSON
JUMPSIN
JUMPSON
KEEPSIN
KEEPSON
KRYPTON
LAMPOON
PROPMAN
PROPMEN
PUMPKIN
SAMPSON
SEEPSIN
SHIPMAN
SHIPMEN
SIMPSON
SLEPTIN
SLEPTON
SOUPCON

STEPHEN
STEPSIN
STEPSON
STOPSIN
UTOPIAN

••••P•N

ACTUPON
BULLPEN
CHEAPEN
CRAMPON
CRISPIN
DEADPAN
DISHPAN
DRIPPAN
DUCKPIN
DUSTPAN
HAIRPIN
HARDPAN
HEADPIN
INASPIN
KINGPIN
PLAYPEN
PUSHPIN
PUTUPON
SETUPON
SHARPEN
SLEEPIN
SLEEPON
STEEPEN

PO•••••

POACHED
POACHER
POACHES
POBOXES
POCKETS
POCONOS
PODGIER
PODIUMS
PODRIDA
POETESS
POETICS
POINTED
POINTER
POINTTO
POISING
POISONS
POISSON
POITIER
POKEDAT
POKEFUN
POKESAT
POKIEST
POLARIS
POLDERS
POLEAXE
POLECAT
POLEMIC
POLENTA
POLICED
POLICES
POLITER
POLITIC
POLKAED
POLLENS
POLLERS
POLLING
POLLOCK
POLLTAX
POLLUTE
POLOIST
POLYGON
POLYMER
POMADED
POMADES
POMELOS
POMMELS
POMPANO
POMPEIA
POMPEII
POMPOMS
POMPONS
POMPOUS
PONCHOS
PONDERS
PONGIDS
PONIARD
PONTIAC
PONTIFF
PONTINE
PONTIUS
PONTOON
PONYING
POOCHES
POODLES
POOHBAH
POOLING
POOPING
POOPOUT
POORBOX
POORBOY
POOREST
POPCORN
POPEYED
POPGUNS
POPLARS
POPLINS
POPOFFS
POPOVER
POPPERS
POPPETS
POPPIES
POPPING
POPPINS
POPPLED
POPPLES
POPSOFF
POPSOUT
POPTART
POPTOPS
POPULAR
PORCHES
PORCINE
PORGIES
PORKERS
PORKPIE
PORSCHE
PORSENA
PORTAGE
PORTALS
PORTEND
PORTENT
PORTERS
PORTHOS
PORTICO
PORTION
PORTOLA
PORTRAY
POSADAS
POSEURS
POSHEST
POSITED
POSSESS
POSSETS
POSSUMS
POSTAGE
POSTBOX
POSTERN
POSTERS
POSTHOC
POSTING
POSTMAN
POSTMEN
POSTURE
POSTWAR
POTABLE
POTAGES
POTENCY
POTFULS
POTHERB
POTHERS
POTHOLE
POTHOOK
POTIONS
POTLUCK
POTOMAC
POTPIES
POTSDAM
POTSHOT
POTTAGE
POTTERS
POTTERY
POTTING
POUCHED
POUCHES
POULENC
POULTRY
POUNCED
POUNCER
POUNCES
POUNDED
POUNDER
POURERS
POURING
POUROUT
POURSIN
POUTERS
POUTIER
POUTING
POVERTY
POWDERS
POWDERY
POWERED
POWWOWS

P•O••••

PEONAGE
PEONIES
PEOPLED
PEOPLES
PHOBIAS
PHOBICS
PHOEBES
PHOEBUS
PHOENIX
PHONEME
PHONICS
PHONIER
PHONIES
PHONILY
PHONING
PHOTOED
PHOTOGS
PHOTONS
PHOTOOP
PIOLETS
PIONEER
PIOUSLY
PLODDED
PLODDER
PLOPPED
PLOSION
PLOSIVE
PLOTTED
PLOTTER
PLOUGHS
PLOVERS
PLOWBOY
PLOWERS
PLOWING
PLOWMAN
PLOWMEN
POOCHES
POODLES
POOHBAH
POOLING
POOPING
POOPOUT
POORBOX
POORBOY
POOREST
PROBATE
PROBERS
PROBING
PROBITY
PROBLEM
PROBONO
PROCEED
PROCESS
PROCTOR
PROCURE
PROCYON
PRODDED
PRODDER
PRODIGY
PRODUCE
PRODUCT
PROFANE
PROFESS
PROFFER
PROFILE
PROFITS
PROFUSE
PROGENY
PROGRAM
PROJECT
PROLOGS
PROLONG
PROMISE
PROMOTE
PROMPTS
PRONGED
PRONOUN
PROOFED
PROOFER
PROPANE
PROPELS
PROPHET
PROPJET
PROPMAN
PROPMEN
PROPOSE
PROPPED
PROPSUP
PRORATA
PRORATE
PROSAIC
PROSERS
PROSIER
PROSILY
PROSING
PROSODY
PROSPER
PROTEAN
PROTECT
PROTEGE
PROTEIN
PROTEST
PROTEUS
PROTIST
PROTONS
PROUDER
PROUDLY
PROVERB
PROVERS
PROVIDE
PROVING
PROVISO
PROVOKE
PROVOST
PROWESS
PROWLED
PROWLER
PROXIES
PROXIMO
PTOLEMY

P••O•••

PAGODAS
PALOMAR
PALOOKA
PANOPLY
PAPOOSE
PAROLED
PAROLEE
PAROLES
PAYOFFS
PAYOLAS
PAYOUTS
PELOTAS
PHLOXES
PILOTED
PINOAKS
PINOCLE
PINONES
PIROGUE
PIVOTAL
PIVOTED
POBOXES
POCONOS
POLOIST
POPOFFS
POPOVER
POTOMAC
PRIORTO
PROOFED
PROOFER
PTBOATS
PUTOUTS
PUTOVER

P•••O••

PADDOCK
PADLOCK
PADRONE
PADRONI
PAIDOFF
PAIDOUT
PAILOUS
PAIROFF
PALJOEY
PALMOFF
PALMOIL
PALOOKA
PANDORA
PANSOUT
PAPOOSE
PARBOIL
PARDONS
PARLORS
PARLOUR
PARLOUS
PARROTS
PARSONS
PARTOOK
PARTOUT
PASSOFF
PASSOUT
PASTORS
PATROLS
PATRONS
PATROON
PAVIOUR
PAVLOVA
PAWNOFF
PAYLOAD
PAYROLL
PAYSOFF
PAYSOUT
PEABODY
PEACOAT
PEACOCK
PEAFOWL
PEAPODS
PEASOUP
PEEKOUT
PEELOFF
PEEROUT
PEGTOPS
PENNONS
PEQUOTS
PERFORM
PERGOLA
PERIODS
PERSONA
PERSONS
PETCOCK
PETIOLE
PETROCK
PETROUS
PHENOLS
PHENOMS
PHOTOED
PHOTOGS
PHOTONS
PHOTOOP
PICCOLO
PICKOFF
PICKOUT
PIGEONS
PIGSOUT
PILLORY
PILLOWS
PILLOWY
PINDOWN
PINHOLE
PINIONS
PISCOPO
PISTOLE
PISTOLS
PISTONS
PITBOSS
PITEOUS
PLATOON
PLAYOFF
PLAYOUT
PLEXORS
PLYWOOD
POISONS
POLLOCK
POMPOMS
POMPONS
POMPOUS
PONTOON
POOPOUT
POPCORN
POPSOFF
POPSOUT
POPTOPS
PORTOLA
POTHOLE
POTHOOK
POTIONS
POUROUT
POWWOWS
PRECOOK
PRECOOL
PRELOAD
PRESOAK
PRESORT
PRISONS
PROBONO
PROLOGS
PROLONG
PROMOTE
PRONOUN
PROPOSE
PROSODY
PROTONS
PROVOKE
PROVOST
PUGNOSE
PULLOFF
PULLONS
PULLOUT
PURLOIN
PURPORT
PURPOSE
PUSHOFF
PUTDOWN
PUTSOFF
PUTSOUT
PYEDOGS
PYTHONS

P••••O•

PAGEBOY
PAIDFOR
PAPADOC
PAPAGOS
PARADOX
PARAGON
PARASOL
PARTOOK
PASSFOR
PASSION
PATRIOT
PATROON
PAYSFOR
PEARSON
PEATBOG
PENSION
PERIDOT
PEUGEOT
PHAETON
PHANTOM
PHARAOH
PHOTOOP
PICADOR
PICAROS
PICKSON
PIDGEON
PIERROT
PIGIRON
PILEDON
PILESON
PILLBOX
PILLION
PIMESON
PINEFOR
PITSTOP
PLANSON
PLATOON
PLAYBOY
PLAYDOH
PLAYSON
PLOSION
PLOWBOY
PLYWOOD
POCONOS
POISSON
POLYGON
POMELOS
PONCHOS
PONTOON
POORBOX
POORBOY
PORTHOS
PORTION
POSTBOX
POSTHOC
POTHOOK
POTSHOT
PRAETOR
PRAYFOR
PRECOOK
PRECOOL
PRESSON
PRESTON
PRESTOS
PREYSON
PROCTOR
PROCYON
PRUDHOE
PUEBLOS
PUTUPON
PYNCHON

P•••••O

PAISANO
PALAZZO
PALERMO
PATERNO
PICASSO
PICCOLO
PIMENTO
PIMLICO
PISCOPO
PIZARRO
PLACEBO
PLACIDO
POINTTO
POMPANO
PORTICO
PRAYSTO
PRIORTO
PROBONO
PROVISO
PROXIMO
PRYINTO
PUTITTO

•PO••••

APOCOPE
APOGEES
APOLOGY
APOSTLE
APOTHEM
EPONYMS
EPOXIES
OPOSSUM
SPOILED
SPOILER
SPOKANE
SPOKEOF
SPOKEUP
SPOKING
SPONDEE
SPONGED
SPONGER
SPONGES
SPONSOR
SPOOFED
SPOOFER
SPOOKED
SPOOLED
SPOONED
SPOONER
SPORRAN
SPORTED
SPOTLIT
SPOTTED
SPOTTER
SPOUSAL
SPOUSES
SPOUTED
SPOUTER

•P•O•••

APPOINT
APPOSED
APPOSES
APRONED
APROPOS
OPPOSED
OPPOSER
OPPOSES
SPLOTCH
SPOOFED
SPOOFER
SPOOKED
SPOOLED
SPOONED
SPOONER
SPROUTS
UPBORNE
UPHOLDS
UPLOADS
UPROARS
UPROOTS
UPTONOW
UPTOPAR

•P••O••

APOCOPE
APOLOGY
APPROVE
APRIORI
EPIGONE
EPILOGS
EPISODE
EPITOME
OPEROSE
OPTIONS
OPTSOUT
SPIGOTS
SPINOFF
SPINOUT
SPINOZA
SPUMONE
SPUMONI
SPUNOFF
SPUNOUT
UPCLOSE
UPFRONT
UPROOTS
UPSHOTS

•P•••O•

APRICOT
APROPOS
EPSILON
OPENTOE
OPINION
SPARROW
SPEAKOF
SPECTOR
SPIEDON
SPIESON
SPOKEOF
SPONSOR
SPURSON
UPSILON
UPTONOW

•P••••O

SPIRITO
UPTEMPO

••PO•••

AMPOULE
APPOINT
APPOSED
APPOSES
BIPOLAR
COPOUTS
CUPOLAS
DEPONED
DEPONES
DEPORTS
DEPOSAL
DEPOSED
DEPOSER
DEPOSES
DEPOSIT
DIPOLAR
DIPOLES
EMPORIA
EMPOWER
ESPOSAS
ESPOSOS
ESPOUSE
EXPORTS
EXPOSED
EXPOSES
EXPOUND
HOPOVER
HYPOING
IMPORTS
IMPOSED
IMPOSES
IMPOSTS
IMPOUND
INPOINT
LAPORTE
OPPOSED
OPPOSER
OPPOSES
PAPOOSE
POPOFFS
POPOVER
REPOLLS
REPOMAN
REPORTS
REPOSED
REPOSES
RIPOFFS
RIPOSTE
TIPOFFS
VAPOURS
ZAPOTEC

••P•O••

AMPHORA
APPROVE
CAPTORS
COPIOUS
COPPOLA
COPSOUT
DEPLORE
DEPLOYS
DIPLOID
DIPLOMA
DOPEOUT
EMPLOYS
EUPHONY
EXPLODE
EXPLOIT
EXPLORE
HIPBONE
HIPBOOT
HIPROOF
HOPSOFF
HOPTOIT
IMPIOUS
IMPLODE
IMPLORE
IMPROVE
KEPTOFF
KEPTOUT
LAPDOGS
LAPROBE
LAPTOPS
LEPTONS
PAPOOSE
POPCORN
POPSOFF
POPSOUT
POPTOPS
RAPPORT
RAPTORS
REPROOF
REPROVE
RIPCORD
RIPSOFF
RIPTORN
SAPPORO
SIPHONS
SUPPORT
SUPPOSE
TAPIOCA
TAPROOM
TAPROOT
TAPSOUT
TIPSOFF
TIPTOED
TIPTOES
TIPTOPS
TOPCOAT
TOPDOGS
TOPMOST
TOPSOFF
TOPSOIL
TOPSOUT
TYPHOON
WIPEOUT
ZIPCODE

••P••O•

CAPECOD
CAPITOL
CAPTION
COPILOT
COPYBOY
CYPRIOT
EMPEROR
ESPANOL
ESPOSOS
HIPBOOT
HIPROOF
PAPADOC
PAPAGOS
REPROOF
ROPETOW
TAPROOM
TAPROOT
TOPKNOT
TUPELOS
TYPHOON

••P•••O

IMPASTO
INPETTO
LEPANTO
RIPINTO
SAPPORO
SAPSAGO
SOPRANO
SUPREMO

•••PO••

ADIPOSE
AIRPORT
AMAPOLA
BEDPOST
BESPOKE
CAMPOUT
CARPOOL
CARPORT
CLIPONS
COMPORT
COMPOSE
COMPOST
COMPOTE
COPPOLA
COUPONS
COWPOKE
DESPOIL
DESPOTS
DISPORT
DISPOSE
DROPOFF
DROPOUT
DRSPOCK
HARPOON
HELPOUT
HOOPOES
HOTPOTS
INSPOTS
ISOPODS
JETPORT
JUMPOFF
KEEPOFF
LAMPOIL
LAMPOON
LEOPOLD
LIMPOPO
MAYPOLE
MRSPOCK
NEWPORT
OUTPOST
PEAPODS
POMPOMS
POMPONS
POMPOUS
POOPOUT
PROPOSE
PURPORT
PURPOSE
RAPPORT
REDPOLL
RESPOND
RUMPOLE
SAPPORO
SEAPORT
SHIPOUT
SKIPOLE
SKIPOUT
SLIPONS
SLIPOUT
SNAPONS
STEPOUT
STOPOFF
STUPORS
SUPPORT
SUPPOSE
TADPOLE
TARPONS
TEAPOTS
TEAPOYS
TRIPODS
TRIPOLI
UNIPODS
VANPOOL
VOLPONE
WALPOLE
WEAPONS
YAUPONS

•••P•O•

ADAPTOR
CAMPHOR
CAMPION
CARPOOL
CLAPTON
CRYPTOS
GRYPHON
HAMPTON
HARPOON
HARPSON
JUMPSON
KEEPSON
KERPLOP
KRYPTON
LAMPOON
OLDPROS
SAMPSON
SIMPSON
SLEPTON
SOAPBOX
SOUPCON
STEPSON
SUBPLOT
SYMPTOM
VANPOOL

•••P••O
ARAPAHO
HISPANO
KEEPSTO
LIMPOPO
POMPANO
SAPPORO
SERPICO
SHAPIRO
SNAPSTO
TAMPICO
TORPEDO

••••PO•
ACTUPON
APROPOS
CRAMPON
DECAPOD
FUSSPOT
GOTOPOT
HOTSPOT
INASPOT
INKSPOT
JACKPOT
OCTOPOD
ONTOPOF
PUTUPON
REDSPOT
SEEDPOD
SETUPON
SHAMPOO
SLEEPON
SODAPOP
SUNSPOT
TENSPOT

••••P•O
ADDUPTO
CALYPSO
GOLFPRO
LEDUPTO
SCORPIO
SEMIPRO
SHAMPOO
STOOPTO

•••••PO
LIMPOPO
PISCOPO
UPTEMPO

P•P••••
PAPADOC
PAPAGOS
PAPAYAS
PAPEETE
PAPERED
PAPERER
PAPILLA
PAPOOSE
PAPRIKA
PAPUANS
PAPYRUS
PEPLUMS
PEPPARD
PEPPERS
PEPPERY
PEPPIER
PEPPILY
PEPPING
PEPSINS
PEPTALK
PEPTIDE
PIPEDUP
PIPEFUL
PIPESUP
PIPETTE
PIPINGS
PIPKINS
PIPPINS
POPCORN
POPEYED
POPGUNS
POPLARS
POPLINS
POPOFFS
POPOVER
POPPERS
POPPETS
POPPIES
POPPING
POPPINS
POPPLED
POPPLES
POPSOFF
POPSOUT
POPTART
POPTOPS
POPULAR
PUPPETS
PUPPIES
PUPTENT

P••P•••
PAMPERS
PANPIPE
PAUPERS
PAWPAWS
PEAPODS
PEEPERS
PEEPING
PEEPLES
PENPALS
PEOPLED
PEOPLES
PEPPARD
PEPPERS
PEPPERY
PEPPIER
PEPPILY
PEPPING
PERPLEX
PIEPANS
PIGPENS
PIPPINS
PLOPPED
POMPANO
POMPEIA
POMPEII
POMPOMS
POMPONS
POMPOUS
POOPING
POOPOUT
POPPERS
POPPETS
POPPIES
POPPING
POPPINS
POPPLED
POPPLES
POTPIES
PREPAID
PREPARE
PREPAYS
PREPPIE
PROPANE
PROPELS
PROPHET
PROPJET
PROPMAN
PROPMEN
PROPOSE
PROPPED
PROPSUP
PULPITS
PUMPERS
PUMPING
PUMPKIN
PUMPSUP
PUPPETS
PUPPIES
PURPLED
PURPLES
PURPORT
PURPOSE

P•••P••
PANOPLY
PARAPET
PARAPHS
PITAPAT
PLAYPEN
PLOPPED
PLUMPED
PLUMPER
PORKPiE
PREPPIE
PRIMPED
PROMPTS
PROPPED
PROSPER
PUSHPIN
PUTUPON

P••••P•
PANPIPE
PEGTOPS
PERHAPS
PICKUPS
PILEUPS
PISCOPO
PLATYPI
POPTOPS
PREAMPS
PRECEPT
PREEMPT
PRETAPE
PULLUPS
PUSHUPS

P•••••P
PACKSUP
PAIRSUP
PARSNIP
PASTEUP
PATCHUP
PEASOUP
PERKSUP
PHILLIP
PHOTOOP
PICKSUP
PILEDUP
PILESUP
PINESAP
PIPEDUP
PIPESUP
PITSTOP
PLAYSUP
PROPSUP
PSYCHUP
PULLSUP
PUMPSUP
PUNCHUP

•PP••••
APPALLS
APPAREL
APPEALS
APPEARS
APPEASE
APPENDS
APPLAUD
APPLIED
APPLIES
APPOINT
APPOSED
APPOSES
APPRISE
APPRIZE
APPROVE
OPPOSED
OPPOSER
OPPOSES
OPPRESS
OPPUGNS
UPPSALA

•P••P••
APROPOS
OPENPIT
UPTOPAR

•P•••P•
APOCOPE
UPSWEPT
UPTEMPO

•P••••P
OPENSUP
SPEAKUP
SPEEDUP
SPICEUP
SPLITUP
SPOKEUP
UPSWEEP

••PP•••
BOPPERS
BOPPING
CAPPERS
CAPPING
COPPERS
COPPERY
COPPICE
COPPING
COPPOLA
CUPPING
DAPPING
DAPPLED
DAPPLES
DIPPERS
DIPPING
DOPPLER
FIPPLES
FOPPERY
FOPPISH
GAPPING
GUPPIES
GYPPERS
GYPPING
HAPPENS
HAPPIER
HAPPILY
HIPPEST
HIPPIES
HOPPERS
HOPPING
KIPPERS
LAPPETS
LAPPING
LIPPIER
LIPPING
LOPPERS
LOPPING
MAPPERS
MAPPING
MOPPERS
MOPPETS
MOPPING
MUPPETS
NAPPERS
NAPPING
NIPPERS
NIPPIER
NIPPING
PEPPARD
PEPPERS
PEPPERY
PEPPIER
PEPPILY
PEPPING
PIPPINS
POPPERS
POPPETS
POPPIES
POPPING
POPPINS
POPPLED
POPPLES
PUPPETS
PUPPIES
RAPPELS
RAPPERS
RAPPING
RAPPORT
RIPPERS
RIPPING
RIPPLED
RIPPLES
SAPPERS
SAPPIER
SAPPING
SAPPORO
SIPPERS
SIPPETS
SIPPING
SOPPING
SUPPERS
SUPPING
SUPPLER
SUPPORT
SUPPOSE
TAPPERS
TAPPETS
TAPPING
TIPPERS
TIPPETS
TIPPING
TIPPLED
TIPPLER
TIPPLES
TOPPERS
TOPPING
TOPPLED
TOPPLES
YAPPERS
YAPPING
YIPPING
YUPPIES
ZAPPERS
ZAPPING
ZIPPERS
ZIPPIER
ZIPPING

••P•P••
CAPAPIE
ONPAPER
REPAPER

••P••P•
LAPTOPS
POPTOPS
RIPRAPS
TIPTOPS
TOPKAPI

••P•••P
HYPEDUP
PIPEDUP
PIPESUP
TYPEDUP
TYPESUP
WIPEDUP
WIPESUP

•••PP••
BLIPPED
CHAPPED
CHIPPED
CHIPPER
CHOPPED
CHOPPER
CLAPPED
CLAPPER
CLIPPED
CLIPPER
CLOPPED
CRAPPIE
CROPPED
CROPPER
DRIPPAN
DRIPPED
DROPPED
DROPPER
FLAPPED
FLAPPER
FLIPPED
FLIPPER
FLOPPED
FRAPPES
GRAPPLE
GRIPPED
GRIPPER
PLOPPED
PREPPIE
PROPPED
QUIPPED
QUIPPER
REUPPED
SCUPPER
SHIPPED
SHIPPER
SHOPPED
SHOPPER
SHOPPES
SKIPPED
SKIPPER
SLAPPED
SLIPPED
SLIPPER
SLOPPED
SNAPPED
SNAPPER
SNIPPED
SNIPPET
STEPPED
STEPPER
STEPPES
STIPPLE
STOPPED
STOPPER
SWAPPED
SWAPPER
TRAPPED
TRAPPER
TRIPPED
TRIPPER
TRIPPET
WHIPPED
WHIPPET
WHOPPED
WHOPPER
WHUPPED
WRAPPED
WRAPPER

•••P•P•
BAGPIPE
FLIPUPS
LIMPOPO
PANPIPE
SLIPUPS
STEPUPS
WRAPUPS

•••P••P
AIRPUMP
BUMPSUP
COOPSUP
CROPSUP
GASPUMP
JUMPSUP
KEEPSUP
KERPLOP
PROPSUP
PUMPSUP
SHAPEUP
SLIPSUP
SNAPSUP
SOUPSUP
STEPSUP
STOPGAP
STOPSUP
SWEPTUP
TRIPSUP
WHIPSUP
WRAPSUP

••••PP•
AGRIPPA
SCRAPPY
SCRIPPS
UNHAPPY

••••P•P
CREEPUP
SODAPOP
SWEEPUP
TRUMPUP

•••••PP
SCHLEPP

P•Q••••
PEQUOTS
PIQUANT
PIQUING

P••Q•••
PARQUET
PLAQUES

P••••Q•
PSANDQS

•P•Q•••
OPAQUES

PR•••••
PRAETOR
PRAIRIE
PRAISED
PRAISER
PRAISES
PRALINE
PRANCED
PRANCER
PRANCES
PRANKED
PRATERS
PRATING
PRATTLE
PRAYERS
PRAYFOR
PRAYING
PRAYSTO
PREACHY
PREAMPS
PREBEND
PRECAST
PRECEDE
PRECEPT
PRECISE
PRECOOK
PRECOOL
PREDATE
PREDAWN
PREDICT
PREEMIE
PREEMPT
PREENED
PREENER
PREFABS
PREFACE
PREFECT
PREFERS
PREHEAT
PRELATE
PRELIMS
PRELOAD
PRELUDE
PREMEDS
PREMIER
PREMISE
PREMIUM
PREPAID
PREPARE
PREPAYS
PREPPIE
PRESAGE
PRESALE
PRESELL
PRESENT
PRESETS
PRESIDE
PRESLEY
PRESOAK
PRESORT
PRESSED
PRESSER
PRESSES
PRESSON
PRESTON
PRESTOS
PRESUME
PRETAPE
PRETEEN
PRETEND
PRETEST
PRETEXT
PRETZEL
PREVAIL
PREVENT
PREVIEW
PREWASH
PREYSON
PRICERS
PRICIER
PRICING
PRICKED
PRICKLE
PRICKLY
PRIDING
PRIESTS
PRIMACY
PRIMARY
PRIMATE
PRIMERS
PRIMING
PRIMMER
PRIMPED
PRINCES
PRINKED
PRINTED
PRINTER
PRIORTO
PRISONS
PRITHEE
PRIVACY
PRIVATE
PRIVETS
PRIVIES
PRIZING
PROBATE
PROBERS
PROBING
PROBITY
PROBLEM
PROBONO
PROCEED
PROCESS
PROCTOR
PROCURE
PROCYON
PRODDED
PRODDER
PRODIGY
PRODUCE
PRODUCT
PROFANE
PROFESS
PROFFER
PROFILE
PROFITS
PROFUSE
PROGENY
PROGRAM
PROJECT
PROLOGS
PROLONG
PROMISE
PROMOTE
PROMPTS
PRONGED
PRONOUN
PROOFED
PROOFER
PROPANE
PROPELS
PROPHET
PROPJET
PROPMAN
PROPMEN
PROPOSE
PROPPED
PROPSUP
PRORATA
PRORATE
PROSAIC
PROSERS
PROSIER
PROSILY
PROSING
PROSODY
PROSPER
PROTEAN
PROTECT
PROTEGE
PROTEIN
PROTEST
PROTEUS
PROTIST
PROTONS
PROUDER
PROUDLY
PROVERB
PROVERS
PROVIDE
PROVING
PROVISO
PROVOKE
PROVOST
PROWESS
PROWLED
PROWLER
PROXIES
PROXIMO
PRUDENT
PRUDERY
PRUDHOE
PRUDISH
PRUNERS
PRUNING
PRUSSIA
PRYINTO

P•R••••
PARABLE
PARADED
PARADES
PARADOX
PARAGON
PARAPET
PARAPHS
PARASOL
PARBOIL
PARCELS
PARCHED
PARCHES
PARDNER
PARDONS
PARENTS
PARFAIT
PARGETS
PARIAHS
PARIBUS
PARINGS
PARKING
PARKWAY
PARLAYS
PARLEYS
PARLORS
PARLOUR
PARLOUS
PARNELL
PAROLED
PAROLEE
PAROLES
PARQUET
PARRIED
PARRIES
PARRING
PARROTS
PARSECS
PARSEES
PARSERS
PARSING
PARSLEY
PARSNIP
PARSONS
PARTAKE
PARTIAL
PARTIED
PARTIES
PARTING
PARTITA
PARTITE
PARTNER
PARTOOK
PARTOUT
PARTWAY
PARURES
PARVENU
PERCALE
PERCENT
PERCHED
PERCHES
PERDIEM
PERFECT
PERFIDY
PERFORM
PERFUME
PERGOLA
PERHAPS
PERIDOT
PERIGEE
PERIODS
PERJURE
PERJURY
PERKIER
PERKILY
PERKING
PERKINS
PERKSUP
PERLITE
PERLMAN
PERMING
PERMITS
PERNELL
PERPLEX
PERRIER
PERSEUS
PERSIAN
PERSIST
PERSIUS
PERSONA
PERSONS
PERTAIN
PERTEST
PERTURB
PERUKES
PERUSAL
PERUSED
PERUSER
PERUSES
PERVADE
PERVERT
PHRASAL
PHRASED
PHRASES
PHRENIC
PIRAEUS
PIRANHA
PIRATED
PIRATES
PIRATIC
PIROGUE
PORCHES
PORCINE
PORGIES
PORKERS
PORKPIE
PORSCHE
PORSENA
PORTAGE
PORTALS
PORTEND
PORTENT
PORTERS
PORTHOS
PORTICO
PORTION
PORTOLA
PORTRAY
PURCELL
PURDAHS
PURFLED
PURFLES
PURGING
PURISTS
PURITAN
PURLIEU
PURLING
PURLINS
PURLOIN
PURPLED
PURPLES
PURPORT
PURPOSE
PURRERS
PURRING
PURSERS
PURSING
PURSUED
PURSUER
PURSUES
PURSUIT
PURVEYS
PURVIEW
PYRAMID
PYRAMUS
PYRITES
PYRRHIC
PYRRHUS

P••R•••
PADRONE
PADRONI
PAIRING
PAIROFF
PAIRSUP
PAPRIKA
PARRIED
PARRIES
PARRING
PARROTS
PATRICE
PATRICK
PATRIOT
PATROLS
PATRONS
PATROON
PAYROLL
PEARLED
PEARSON
PEERAGE
PEERESS
PEERING
PEEROUT
PEERSAT
PEERSIN
PERRIER
PETRELS
PETRIFY
PETROCK
PETROUS
PHARAOH
PHARYNX
PIERCED
PIERCES
PIERROT
PLURALS
PODRIDA
POORBOX
POORBOY
POOREST
POURERS
POURING
POUROUT
POURSIN
PRORATA
PRORATE
PUERILE
PUGREES
PURRERS
PURRING
PYRRHIC
PYRRHUS

P•••R••
PACKRAT
PALERMO
PALFREY
PANURGE
PAPERED
PAPERER
PAPYRUS
PARURES
PATERNO
PETARDS
PETERED
PICAROS
PIERROT
PIGIRON
PILGRIM
PIZARRO
POLARIS
PORTRAY

POVERTY
POWERED
PRAIRIE
PRIORTO
PROGRAM
PUBERTY

P••••R•

PACKARD
PACKERS
PADDERS
PALEDRY
PALTERS
PAMPERS
PANDERS
PANDORA
PANNERS
PANZERS
PARLORS
PARSERS
PASSERS
PASTERN
PASTORS
PASTURE
PATTERN
PATTERS
PAUPERS
PAWNERS
PAYDIRT
PECCARY
PEDLARS
PEELERS
PEEPERS
PELTERS
PENNERS
PEPPARD
PEPPERS
PEPPERY
PERFORM
PERJURE
PERJURY
PERTURB
PERVERT
PESTERS
PETTERS
PHAEDRA
PHASERS
PHILTRE
PIASTRE
PICCARD
PICKERS
PICTURE
PIECERS
PILFERS
PILLARS
PILLORY
PINCERS
PINCURL
PINNERS
PISMIRE
PITTERS
PIZARRO
PLACARD
PLACERS
PLANERS
PLATERS
PLAYERS
PLECTRA
PLENARY
PLEXORS
PLOVERS
PLOWERS
POLDERS
POLLERS
PONDERS
PONIARD
POPCORN
POPLARS
POPPERS
POPTART
PORKERS
PORTERS
POSEURS
POSTERN
POSTERS
POSTURE
POTHERB
POTHERS
POTTERS
POTTERY
POULTRY
POURERS
POUTERS
POWDERS
POWDERY
PRATERS
PRAYERS
PREFERS
PREPARE
PRESORT
PRICERS
PRIMARY
PRIMERS
PROBERS
PROCURE
PROSERS
PROVERB
PROVERS
PRUDERY
PRUNERS
PUCKERS
PUFFERS
PUFFERY
PULSARS
PUMPERS
PUNTERS
PURPORT
PURRERS
PURSERS
PUTTERS

P•••••R

PACECAR
PADDLER
PAIDFOR
PAINTER
PALAVER
PALMIER
PALOMAR
PANNIER
PANTHER
PAPERER
PARDNER
PARLOUR
PARTNER
PASSFOR
PASTEUR
PASTIER
PAVIOUR
PAYSFOR
PEDDLER
PEPPIER
PERKIER
PERRIER
PERUSER
PESKIER
PETTIER
PHILTER
PHONIER
PIASTER
PICADOR
PICKIER
PILSNER
PINCHER
PINEFOR
PINETAR
PIONEER
PITCHER
PITHIER
PLAINER
PLANNER
PLANTAR
PLANTER
PLASTER
PLATTER
PLEADER
PLEASER
PLEDGER
PLODDER
PLOTTER
PLUGGER
PLUMBER
PLUMMER
PLUMPER
PLUNDER
PLUNGER
PLUSHER
POACHER
PODGIER
POINTER
POITIER
POLITER
POLYMER
POPOVER
POPULAR
POSTWAR
POUNCER
POUNDER
POUTIER
PRAETOR
PRAISER
PRANCER
PRAYFOR
PREENER
PREMIER
PRESSER
PRICIER
PRIMMER
PRINTER
PROCTOR
PRODDER
PROFFER
PROOFER
PROSIER
PROSPER
PROUDER
PROWLER
PSALTER
PUDGIER
PUFFIER
PUNCHER
PUNSTER
PURSUER
PUSHIER
PUTOVER
PUZZLER

•PR••••

APRICOT
APRIORI
APRONED
APROPOS
SPRAINS
SPRAWLS
SPRAYED
SPRAYER
SPREADS
SPRIEST
SPRINGS
SPRINGY
SPRINTS
SPRITES
SPROUTS
SPRUCED
SPRUCER
SPRUCES
SPRYEST
UPRAISE
UPRIGHT
UPRISEN
UPRISES
UPRIVER
UPROARS
UPROOTS

•P•R•••

APERCUS
APERIES
APPRISE
APPRIZE
APPROVE
EPARCHS
EPERGNE
IPCRESS
OPERAND
OPERATE
OPEROSE
OPPRESS
SPARELY
SPAREST
SPARGED
SPARGES
SPARING
SPARKED
SPARKLE
SPARRED
SPARROW
SPARSER
SPARTAN
SPIRALS
SPIRANT
SPIREAS
SPIRITO
SPIRITS
SPORRAN
SPORTED
SPURNED
SPURNER
SPURRED
SPURSON
SPURTED
UPBRAID
UPDRAFT
UPFRONT
UPGRADE

•P••R••

APPAREL
EPIGRAM
SPARRED
SPARROW
SPEARED
SPHERES
SPLURGE
SPORRAN
SPURRED
UPATREE
UPBORNE
UPSURGE
UPTURNS
UPWARDS

•P•••R•

APPEARS
APRIORI
EPICURE
OPENERS
OPINERS
SPACERS
SPADERS
SPECTRA
SPECTRE
SPIDERS
SPIDERY
SPIKERS
UPROARS
UPSTART

•P••••R

OPENAIR
OPENBAR
OPPOSER
SPACIER
SPANKER
SPANNER
SPARSER
SPATTER
SPEAKER
SPECTER
SPECTOR
SPEEDER
SPELLER
SPENCER
SPENDER
SPENSER
SPICIER
SPIELER
SPIKIER
SPINIER
SPINNER
SPLICER
SPOILER
SPONGER
SPONSOR
SPOOFER
SPOONER
SPOTTER
SPOUTER
SPRAYER
SPRUCER
SPURNER
SPUTTER
UPRIVER
UPTOPAR

••PR•••

APPRISE
APPRIZE
APPROVE
CAPRICE
CYPRESS
CYPRIOT
DEPRAVE
DEPRESS
DEPRIVE
EMPRESS
EXPRESS
HIPROOF
IMPRESS
IMPRINT
IMPROVE
INPRINT
LAPROBE
LIPREAD
OPPRESS
OSPREYS
PAPRIKA
REPRESS
REPRICE
REPRINT
REPRISE
REPROOF
REPROVE
RIPRAPS
SOPRANO
SUPREME
SUPREMO
TAPROOM
TAPROOT

••P•R••

AMPERES
APPAREL
ASPERSE
ASPIRED
ASPIRER
ASPIRES
ASPIRIN
CAPERED
DEPARTS
DEPORTS
EMPEROR
EMPIRES
EMPORIA
EXPARTE
EXPERTS
EXPIRED
EXPIRES
EXPORTS
HEPARIN
IMPARTS
IMPERIL
IMPORTS
IMPURER
LAPORTE
PAPERED
PAPERER
PAPYRUS
REPORTS
TAPERED
UMPIRED
UMPIRES

••P••R•

AMPHORA
APPEARS
BOPPERS
CAPPERS
CAPTORS
CAPTURE
CIPHERS
COPIERS
COPPERS
COPPERY
COPTERS
CYPHERS
DEPLORE
DIPPERS
EXPLORE
FOPPERY
GOPHERS
GYPPERS
HEPBURN
HOPPERS
IMPAIRS
IMPLORE
KIPPERS
LOPPERS
MAPPERS
MOPPERS
NAPPERS
NIPPERS
PEPPARD
PEPPERS
PEPPERY
POPCORN
POPLARS
POPPERS
POPTART
RAPIERS
RAPPERS
RAPPORT
RAPTORS
RAPTURE
REPAIRS
RIPCORD
RIPPERS
RIPTORN
RUPTURE
SAPPERS
SAPPORO
SIPPERS
SUPPERS
SUPPORT
TAPPERS
TIPPERS
TOPIARY
TOPPERS
VAPOURS
YAPPERS
ZAPPERS
ZEPHYRS
ZIPPERS

••P•••R

ASPIRER
BIPOLAR
DEPOSER
DIPOLAR
DOPPLER
EMPEROR
EMPOWER
EMPTIER
HAPPIER
HIPSTER
HOPOVER
IMPURER
JUPITER
LIPPIER
NIPPIER
ONPAPER
OPPOSER
PAPERER
PEPPIER
POPOVER
POPULAR
RAPIDER
REPAPER
SAPPIER
STPETER
SUPPLER
TAPSTER
TIPPLER
TIPSIER
TIPSTER
ZIPPIER

•••PR••

CULPRIT
LAMPREY
OLDPROS
SAMPRAS

•••P•R•

AIRPORT
BEEPERS
BITPART
BOPPERS
BUMPERS
CAMPARI
CAMPERS
CAPPERS
CARPERS
CARPORT
CLIPART
COMPARE
COMPORT
COOPERS
COPPERS
COPPERY
DAMPERS
DEEPFRY
DIAPERS
DIPPERS
DISPORT
DRAPERS
DRAPERY
DRIPDRY
ELOPERS
EXUPERY
FOPPERY
GOMPERS
GRIPERS
GYPPERS
HAMPERS
HARPERS
HELPERS
HOPPERS
INSPIRE
JASPERS
JETPORT
JUMPERS
KEEPERS
KIPPERS
LEAPERS
LEMPIRA
LEOPARD
LOOPERS
LOPPERS
LUMPERS
MAPPERS
MOPPERS
NAPPERS
NEWPORT
NIPPERS
PAMPERS
PAUPERS
PEEPERS
PEPPARD
PEPPERS
PEPPERY
POPPERS
PREPARE
PUMPERS
PURPORT
RAMPART
RAPPERS
RAPPORT
RASPERS
REAPERS
RESPIRE
RIPPERS
ROMPERS
SAPPERS
SAPPORO
SCEPTRE
SEAPORT
SHAPERS
SHAPIRO
SHEPARD
SIMPERS
SIPPERS
SOAPERS
STUPORS
SUPPERS
SUPPORT
SWIPERS
TAMPERS
TAPPERS
TEMPERA
TEMPERS
TEMPURA
TIPPERS
TOPPERS
TOSPARE
VAMPERS
VAMPIRE
VESPERS
WEEPERS
YAPPERS
YAWPERS
YELPERS
ZAPPERS
ZIPPERS

•••P••R

ADAPTER
ADAPTOR
ADOPTER
BUMPIER
CAMPHOR
CAMPIER
CHAPTER
CHIPPER
CHOPPER
CLAPPER
CLIPPER
COMPEER
CROPPER
DESPAIR
DIOPTER
DOPPLER
DROPPER
DUMPIER
FLAPPER
FLIPPER
GOOPIER
GRIPPER
HAPPIER
JUMPIER
LIPPIER
LOOPIER
LUMPIER
NIPPIER
PEPPIER
QUIPPER
RASPIER
SAMPLER
SAPPIER
SCEPTER
SCUPPER
SHIPPER
SHOPPER
SIMPLER
SKIPPER
SLIPPER
SNAPPER
SOAPIER
SOUPIER
STAPLER
STEPPER
STOPPER
SULPHUR
SUPPLER
SWAPPER
TEMPLAR
TEMPTER
TIPPLER
TRAPPER
TRIPPER
WEEPIER
WHOPPER
WISPIER
WRAPPER
ZIPPIER

••••PR•

GOLFPRO
SEMIPRO

••••P•R

BLEEPER
BLOOPER
CALIPER
CHEAPER
CHIPPER
CHOPPER
CLAPPER
CLIPPER
CREEPER
CRIMPER
CRISPER
CROPPER
DROPPER
FLAPPER
FLIPPER
GRIPPER
GROUPER
HOTSPUR
JUNIPER
MAKEPAR
ONPAPER
PLUMPER
PROSPER
QUIPPER
REPAPER
SCALPER
SCAMPER
SCOOPER
SCRAPER
SCUPPER
SHARPER
SHIPPER
SHOPPER
SKIPPER
SLEEPER
SLIPPER
SNAPPER
SNOOPER
STEEPER
STEPPER
STOPPER
STRIPER
STUMPER
SWAPPER
SWEEPER
THUMPER
TRAPPER
TRIPPER
TROOPER
TROUPER
UPTOPAR
USURPER
WHIMPER
WHISPER
WHOPPER
WRAPPER

PS•••••

PSALMED
PSALTER
PSANDQS
PSYCHED
PSYCHES
PSYCHIC
PSYCHUP

P•S••••

PASCHAL
PASSAGE
PASSANT
PASSELS
PASSERS
PASSEUL
PASSFOR
PASSING
PASSION
PASSIVE
PASSKEY
PASSOFF
PASSOUT
PASTDUE
PASTELS
PASTERN
PASTEUP
PASTEUR
PASTIER
PASTIME
PASTINA
PASTING
PASTORS
PASTURE
PESETAS
PESKIER
PESKILY
PESTERS
PESTLED
PESTLES
PISCINE
PISCOPO
PISMIRE
PISTILS
PISTOLE
PISTOLS
PISTONS
POSADAS
POSEURS
POSHEST
POSITED
POSSESS
POSSETS
POSSUMS
POSTAGE
POSTBOX
POSTERN
POSTERS
POSTHOC
POSTING
POSTMAN
POSTMEN
POSTURE
POSTWAR
PUSHIER
PUSHILY
PUSHING
PUSHKIN
PUSHOFF
PUSHPIN
PUSHUPS

P••S•••

PAISANO
PAISLEY
PANSIES
PANSOUT
PARSECS
PARSEES
PARSERS
PARSING
PARSLEY
PARSNIP
PARSONS
PASSAGE
PASSANT
PASSELS
PASSERS
PASSEUL
PASSFOR
PASSING
PASSION
PASSIVE
PASSKEY
PASSOFF
PASSOUT
PATSIES
PAUSING
PAYSFOR
PAYSOFF
PAYSOUT
PEASANT
PEASOUP
PENSEES
PENSION
PENSIVE
PEPSINS
PERSEUS
PERSIAN
PERSIST
PERSIUS
PERSONA
PERSONS
PHASEIN
PHASERS
PHASING
PHYSICS
PIASTER
PIASTRE
PIGSKIN
PIGSOUT
PILSNER
PITSAWS
PITSTOP
PLASHED
PLASHES
PLASMAS
PLASTER
PLASTIC
PLOSION
PLOSIVE
PLUSHER
PLUSHES
PLUSHLY
PLUSSES
POISING
POISONS
POISSON
POPSOFF
POPSOUT
PORSCHE
PORSENA
POSSESS
POSSETS
POSSUMS
POTSDAM
POTSHOT
PRESAGE
PRESALE
PRESELL
PRESENT
PRESETS
PRESIDE
PRESLEY
PRESOAK
PRESORT
PRESSED
PRESSER
PRESSES
PRESSON
PRESTON
PRESTOS
PRESUME
PRISONS
PROSAIC
PROSERS
PROSIER
PROSILY
PROSING
PROSODY
PROSPER
PRUSSIA
PULSARS
PULSATE
PULSING
PUNSTER
PURSERS
PURSING
PURSUED
PURSUER
PURSUES
PURSUIT
PUTSOFF
PUTSOUT

P•••S••

PACKSUP
PAIRSUP
PARASOL
PAULSEN
PEARSON
PECKSAT
PEEKSAT
PEERSAT
PEERSIN
PEGASUS
PELISSE
PERKSUP
PERUSAL
PERUSED
PERUSER

PERUSES
PHRASAL
PHRASED
PHRASES
PICASSO
PICKSAT
PICKSON
PICKSUP
PILESIN
PILESON
PILESUP
PIMESON
PINESAP
PIOUSLY
PIPESUP
PLANSON
PLAYSAT
PLAYSON
PLAYSUP
PLEASED
PLEASER
PLEASES
PLUGSIN
PLUSSES
POISSON
POKESAT
POURSIN
PRAISED
PRAISER
PRAISES
PRAYSTO
PRESSED
PRESSER
PRESSES
PRESSON
PREYSON
PRIESTS
PROPSUP
PRUSSIA
PULASKI
PULLSUP
PUMPSUP
PURISTS

P••••S•

PACHISI
PALMIST
PANFISH
PAPOOSE
PATNESS
PAULIST
PAYCASH
PECKISH
PEERESS
PEEVISH
PELISSE
PERSIST
PERTEST
PETTISH
PIANISM
PIANIST
PICASSO
PIETISM
PIGGISH
PINIEST
PINKEST
PINKISH
PINLESS
PITBOSS
PIXYISH
POETESS
POKIEST
POLOIST
POOREST
POSHEST
POSSESS
PRECAST
PRECISE
PREMISE
PRETEST
PREWASH
PROCESS
PROFESS
PROFUSE
PROMISE
PROPOSE
PROTEST
PROTIST
PROVISO
PROVOST
PROWESS
PRUDISH
PUBLISH
PUCKISH
PUGNOSE
PUNIEST
PURPOSE

P•••••S

PABLUMS
PACKERS
PACKETS
PADDERS
PADDIES
PADDLES
PAGODAS
PAILOUS
PAIUTES
PAJAMAS
PALACES
PALATES
PALLETS
PALTERS
PAMBIES
PAMPERS
PANAMAS
PANDERS
PANDITS
PANNERS
PANSIES
PANZERS
PAPAGOS
PAPAYAS
PAPUANS
PAPYRUS
PARADES
PARAPHS
PARCELS
PARCHES
PARDONS
PARENTS
PARGETS
PARIAHS
PARIBUS
PARINGS
PARLAYS
PARLEYS
PARLORS
PARLOUS
PAROLES
PARRIES
PARROTS
PARSECS
PARSEES
PARSERS
PARSONS
PARTIES
PARURES
PASSELS
PASSERS
PASTELS
PASTORS
PATAKES
PATCHES
PATENTS
PATINAS
PATNESS
PATROLS
PATRONS
PATSIES
PATTENS
PATTERS
PATTIES
PAUPERS
PAVANES
PAWNEES
PAWNERS
PAWPAWS
PAYDAYS
PAYOFFS
PAYOLAS
PAYOUTS
PDJAMES
PEACHES
PEAHENS
PEANUTS
PEAPODS
PEAVEYS
PEBBLES
PECTINS
PEDANTS
PEDDLES
PEDLARS
PEELERS
PEEPERS
PEEPLES
PEERESS
PEEWEES
PEGASUS
PEGTOPS
PELAGES
PELLETS
PELOTAS
PELTERS
PENATES
PENCILS
PENNERS
PENNIES
PENNONS
PENPALS
PENSEES
PENTADS
PENULTS
PEONIES
PEOPLES
PEPLUMS
PEPPERS
PEPSINS
PEQUOTS
PERCHES
PERHAPS
PERIODS
PERKINS
PERMITS
PERSEUS
PERSIUS
PERSONS
PERUKES
PERUSES
PESETAS
PESTERS
PESTLES
PETARDS
PETITES
PETRELS
PETROUS
PETTERS
PHASERS
PHENOLS
PHENOMS
PHIDIAS
PHINEAS
PHLOXES
PHOBIAS
PHOBICS
PHOEBES
PHOEBUS
PHONICS
PHONIES
PHOTOGS
PHOTONS
PHRASES
PHYLLIS
PHYSICS
PIAZZAS
PICAROS
PICKENS
PICKERS
PICKETS
PICKLES
PICKUPS
PICNICS
PIDGINS
PIECERS
PIEPANS
PIERCES
PIETIES
PIETINS
PIFFLES
PIGEONS
PIGGIES
PIGLETS
PIGNUTS
PIGPENS
PILEUPS
PILFERS
PILINGS
PILLARS
PILLOWS
PINATAS
PINCERS
PINCHAS
PINCHES
PINIONS
PINKIES
PINLESS
PINNERS
PINOAKS
PINONES
PIOLETS
PIPINGS
PIPKINS
PIPPINS
PIRAEUS
PIRATES
PISTILS
PISTOLS
PISTONS
PITBOSS
PITCHES
PITEOUS
PITSAWS
PITTERS
PLACERS
PLAGUES
PLAICES
PLAINES
PLAINTS
PLANERS
PLANETS
PLAQUES
PLASHES
PLASMAS
PLATENS
PLATERS
PLAUTUS
PLAYERS
PLEASES
PLEDGES
PLENUMS
PLEXORS
PLIGHTS
PLINTHS
PLOUGHS
PLOVERS
PLOWERS
PLUNGES
PLURALS
PLUSHES
PLUSSES
POACHES
POBOXES
POCKETS
POCONOS
PODIUMS
POETESS
POETICS
POISONS
POLARIS
POLDERS
POLICES
POLLENS
POLLERS
POMADES
POMELOS
POMMELS
POMPOMS
POMPONS
POMPOUS
PONCHOS
PONDERS
PONGIDS
PONTIUS
POOCHES
POODLES
POPGUNS
POPLARS
POPLINS
POPOFFS
POPPERS
POPPETS
POPPIES
POPPINS
POPPLES
POPTOPS
PORCHES
PORGIES
PORKERS
PORTALS
PORTERS
PORTHOS
POSADAS
POSEURS
POSSESS
POSSETS
POSSUMS
POSTERS
POTAGES
POTFULS
POTHERS
POTIONS
POTPIES
POTTERS
POUCHES
POUNCES
POURERS
POUTERS
POWDERS
POWWOWS
PRAISES
PRANCES
PRATERS
PRAYERS
PREAMPS
PREFABS
PREFERS
PRELIMS
PREMEDS
PREPAYS
PRESETS
PRESSES
PRESTOS
PRICERS
PRIESTS
PRIMERS
PRINCES
PRISONS
PRIVETS
PRIVIES
PROBERS
PROCESS
PROFESS
PROFITS
PROLOGS
PROMPTS
PROPELS
PROSERS
PROTEUS
PROTONS
PROVERS
PROWESS
PROXIES
PRUNERS
PSANDQS
PSYCHES
PTBOATS
PUBLICS
PUCKERS
PUDDLES
PUEBLOS
PUFFERS
PUFFINS
PUGREES
PULLETS
PULLEYS
PULLONS
PULLUPS
PULPITS
PULSARS
PUMICES
PUMMELS
PUMPERS
PUNCHES
PUNDITS
PUNKAHS
PUNKIES
PUNTERS
PUPPETS
PUPPIES
PURDAHS
PURFLES
PURISTS
PURLINS
PURPLES
PURRERS
PURSERS
PURSUES
PURVEYS
PUSHUPS
PUTOUTS
PUTTEES
PUTTERS
PUTTIES
PUZZLES
PYEDOGS
PYGMIES
PYJAMAS
PYRAMUS
PYRITES
PYRRHUS
PYTHIAS
PYTHONS
PYXIDES

•PS••••

APSIDES
EPSILON
EPSTEIN
IPSWICH
UPSCALE
UPSHOTS
UPSILON
UPSTAGE
UPSTART
UPSTATE
UPSURGE
UPSWEEP
UPSWEPT
UPSWING

•P•S•••

APISHLY
APOSTLE
EPISODE
EPISTLE
OPOSSUM
OPTSOUT
SPASSKY
UPPSALA

•P••S••

APHESES
APPOSED
APPOSES
OPENSEA
OPENSUP
OPOSSUM
OPPOSED
OPPOSER
OPPOSES
SPARSER
SPASSKY
SPENSER
SPIESON
SPLASHY
SPONSOR
SPOUSAL
SPOUSES
SPURSON
UPRISEN
UPRISES

•P•••S•

APPEASE
APPRISE
APTNESS
EPEEIST
IPCRESS
OPEROSE
OPPRESS
SPANISH
SPAREST
SPRIEST
SPRYEST
UPCLOSE
UPRAISE

•P••••S

APACHES
APERCUS
APERIES
APHESES
APOGEES
APPALLS
APPEALS
APPEARS
APPENDS
APPLIES
APPOSES
APROPOS
APSIDES
APTNESS
EPARCHS
EPILOGS
EPONYMS
EPOXIES
IPCRESS
OPAQUES
OPENERS
OPIATES
OPINERS
OPPOSES
OPPRESS
OPPUGNS
OPTIONS
SPACERS
SPADERS
SPARGES
SPAVINS
SPECIES
SPHERES
SPIDERS
SPIGOTS
SPIKERS
SPINELS
SPINETS
SPIRALS
SPIREAS
SPIRITS
SPITZES
SPLEENS
SPLICES
SPLINES
SPLINTS
SPONGES
SPOUSES
SPRAINS
SPRAWLS
SPREADS
SPRINGS
SPRINTS
SPRITES
SPROUTS
SPRUCES
UPBEATS
UPDATES
UPHOLDS
UPLANDS
UPLIFTS
UPLINKS
UPLOADS
UPRISES
UPROARS
UPROOTS
UPSHOTS
UPTAKES
UPTICKS
UPTURNS
UPWARDS

••PS•••

CAPSHAW
CAPSIZE
CAPSTAN
CAPSULE
COPSOUT
GIPSIES
GYPSIES
HIPSTER
HOPSOFF
LAPSING
LIPSYNC
PEPSINS
POPSOFF
POPSOUT
RIPSAWS
RIPSOFF
SAPSAGO
TAPSOUT
TAPSTER
TIPSIER
TIPSILY
TIPSOFF
TIPSTER
TOPSAIL
TOPSIDE
TOPSOFF
TOPSOIL
TOPSOUT
UPPSALA

••P•S••

APPOSED
APPOSES
DEPOSAL
DEPOSED
DEPOSER
DEPOSES
DEPOSIT
ESPOSAS
ESPOSOS
EXPOSED
EXPOSES
IMPASSE
IMPASTO
IMPOSED
IMPOSES
IMPOSTS
OPPOSED
OPPOSER
OPPOSES
PIPESUP
REPASTE
REPASTS
REPOSED
REPOSES
RIPOSTE
ROPESIN
TYPESET
TYPESUP
TYPISTS
WIPESUP

••P••S•

AMPLEST
APPEASE
APPRISE
ASPERSE
BAPTISM
BAPTIST
CAPLESS
COPYIST
CYPRESS
DEPRESS
DOPIEST
EMPRESS
ESPOUSE
EXPANSE
EXPENSE
EXPRESS
FOPPISH
HAPLESS
HIPNESS
HIPPEST
IMPASSE
IMPRESS
IMPULSE
INPHASE
OPPRESS
PAPOOSE
REPRESS
REPRISE
REPULSE
SOPHISM
SOPHIST
SUPPOSE
TOPMAST
TOPMOST

••P•••S

ALPACAS
AMPERES
AMPULES
APPALLS
APPEALS
APPEARS
APPENDS
APPLIES
APPOSES
ASPECTS
ASPIRES
BOPPERS
BYPATHS
BYPLAYS
CAPFULS
CAPGUNS
CAPLESS
CAPLETS
CAPNUTS
CAPPERS
CAPTORS
CEPHEUS
CIPHERS
COPIERS
COPIOUS
COPOUTS
COPPERS
COPTERS
CUPFULS
CUPOLAS
CYPHERS
CYPRESS
DAPHNIS
DAPPLES
DEPARTS
DEPENDS
DEPICTS
DEPLOYS
DEPONES
DEPORTS
DEPOSES
DEPRESS
DEPUTES
DIPOLES
DIPPERS
EMPIRES
EMPLOYS
EMPRESS
EMPTIES
ESPIALS
ESPOSAS
ESPOSOS
EXPANDS
EXPECTS
EXPENDS
EXPERTS
EXPIRES
EXPORTS
EXPOSES
EXPRESS
FIPPLES
GIPSIES
GOPHERS
GUPPIES
GYPPERS
GYPSIES
HAPLESS
HAPPENS
HEPCATS
HEPTADS
HIPNESS
HIPPIES
HOPKINS
HOPPERS
HYPHENS
IMPACTS
IMPAIRS
IMPALAS
IMPALES
IMPARTS
IMPEDES
IMPENDS
IMPETUS
IMPIOUS
IMPLIES
IMPORTS
IMPOSES
IMPOSTS
IMPRESS
IMPUGNS
IMPUTES
KIPPERS
KOPECKS
LAPDOGS
LAPFULS
LAPPETS
LAPTOPS
LEPTONS
LOPPERS
LUPINES
MAPPERS
MOPPERS
MOPPETS
MUPPETS
NAPKINS
NAPPERS
NEPALIS
NEPHEWS
NIPPERS
OPPOSES
OPPRESS
OPPUGNS
ORPHANS
ORPHEUS
ORPINES
OSPREYS
PAPAGOS
PAPAYAS
PAPUANS
PAPYRUS
PEPLUMS
PEPPERS
PEPSINS
PIPINGS
PIPKINS
PIPPINS
POPGUNS
POPLARS
POPLINS
POPOFFS
POPPERS
POPPETS
POPPIES
POPPINS
POPPLES
POPTOPS
PUPPETS
PUPPIES
RAPIERS
RAPINES
RAPPELS
RAPPERS
RAPTORS
REPAIRS
REPASTS
REPAVES
REPEALS
REPEATS
REPENTS
REPINES
REPLANS
REPLAYS
REPLIES
REPOLLS
REPORTS
REPOSES
REPRESS
REPUGNS
REPUTES
RIPOFFS
RIPPERS
RIPPLES
RIPRAPS
RIPSAWS
RUPIAHS
SAPIENS
SAPPERS
SEPTETS
SIPHONS
SIPPERS
SIPPETS
SUPPERS
TAPINGS
TAPPERS
TAPPETS
TIPOFFS
TIPPERS
TIPPETS
TIPPLES
TIPTOES
TIPTOPS
TOPAZES
TOPDOGS
TOPGUNS
TOPHATS
TOPPERS
TOPPLES
TUPELOS
TYPISTS
UMPIRES
UNPACKS
UNPILES
UNPLUGS
VAPOURS
WAPITIS
YAPPERS
YUPPIES
ZAPPERS
ZEPHYRS
ZIPPERS

•••PS••

ASEPSIS
BUMPSUP
CHIPSIN
COOPSUP
CROPSUP
DEEPSEA
DEEPSET
DEEPSIX
DEMPSEY
DROPSBY
DROPSIN
ELAPSED
ELAPSES
HARPSON
JUMPSAT
JUMPSIN
JUMPSON
JUMPSUP
KEEPSAT
KEEPSIN
KEEPSON
KEEPSTO
KEEPSUP
LUMPSUM
PROPSUP
PUMPSUP
SAMPSON
SEEPSIN
SIMPSON
SLIPSUP
SNAPSAT
SNAPSTO
SNAPSUP
SOUPSUP
STEPSIN
STEPSON
STEPSUP
STOPSIN
STOPSUP
TRIPSUP
WHIPSAW
WHIPSUP
WRAPSUP

•••P•S•

ADIPOSE
ANAPEST
BEDPOST

COMPASS
COMPOSE
COMPOST
DAMPEST
DAMPISH
DEEPEST
DESPISE
DISPOSE
FLYPAST
FOPPISH
HARPIST
HIPPEST
LIMPEST
OUTPOST
PROPOSE
PURPOSE
SUPPOSE
SURPASS
TEMPEST
TROPISM
WASPISH

•••P••S

ARMPITS
ASEPSIS
BEEPERS
BOPPERS
BUMPERS
CALPACS
CAMPERS
CAPPERS
CARPALS
CARPERS
CARPETS
CHAPELS
CLIPONS
COMPASS
COMPELS
COOPERS
COPPERS
COUPLES
COUPONS
COWPEAS
CRYPTOS
CUSPIDS
DAMPENS
DAMPERS
DAPPLES
DEEPENS
DESPOTS
DIAPERS
DIMPLES
DIPPERS
DISPELS
DRAPERS
DROPINS
ELAPIDS
ELAPSES
ELOPERS
FIPPLES
FLIPUPS
FRAPPES
FRYPANS
GOMPERS
GOSPELS
GRIPERS
GROPIUS
GUPPIES
GYPPERS
HAMPERS
HAPPENS
HARPERS
HARPIES
HATPINS
HELPERS
HIPPIES
HOOPLAS
HOOPOES
HOPPERS
HOTPOTS
INSPANS
INSPOTS
ISOPODS
JASPERS
JUMPERS
KEEPERS
KELPIES
KEWPIES
KEYPADS
KIPPERS
LAPPETS
LEAPERS
LIMPETS
LOOPERS
LOPPERS
LUMPERS
MAGPIES
MAPPERS
MEMPHIS
MOPPERS
MOPPETS
MUDPIES
MUPPETS
NAPPERS
NIPPERS
NONPLUS
OILPANS
OLDPROS
OOMPAHS
OUTPUTS
PAMPERS
PAUPERS
PAWPAWS
PEAPODS
PEEPERS
PEEPLES
PENPALS
PEOPLES
PEPPERS
PIEPANS
PIGPENS
PIPPINS
POMPOMS
POMPONS
POMPOUS
POPPERS
POPPETS
POPPIES
POPPINS
POPPLES
POTPIES
PREPAYS
PROPELS
PULPITS
PUMPERS
PUPPETS
PUPPIES
PURPLES
RAPPELS
RAPPERS
RASPERS
REAPERS
REOPENS
RIPPERS
RIPPLES
ROMPERS
RUMPLES
SAMPANS
SAMPLES
SAMPRAS
SAPPERS
SHAPERS
SHOPPES
SIMPERS
SIPPERS
SIPPETS
SLIPONS
SLIPUPS
SNAPONS
SOAPERS
STAPLES
STEPINS
STEPPES
STEPUPS
STUPORS
SUPPERS
SURPASS
SURPLUS
SWIPERS
TAIPANS
TAMPERS
TAPPERS
TAPPETS
TARPITS
TARPONS
TEAPOTS
TEAPOYS
TEEPEES
TEMPERS
TEMPLES
TENPINS
TIEPINS
TIPPERS
TIPPETS
TIPPLES
TOPPERS
TOPPLES
TOUPEES
TREPANS
TRIPLES
TRIPODS
TROPICS
UNIPODS
USOPENS
UTOPIAS
VAMPERS
VESPERS
VESPIDS
WEAPONS
WEEPERS
WIMPLES
WRAPUPS
YAPPERS
YAUPONS
YAWPERS
YELPERS
YUPPIES
ZAPPERS
ZIPPERS

••••PS•

CALYPSO
ECLIPSE
ELLIPSE
GLIMPSE
RELAPSE
SYNAPSE
TRAIPSE

••••P•S

ACCEPTS
APROPOS
CALIPHS
CANAPES
CANOPUS
CERIPHS
CRISPUS
ECTYPES
ESCAPES
EXCEPTS
EXEMPTS
FAUXPAS
FRAPPES
GRAMPUS
GUELPHS
GUIMPES
INCEPTS
IRRUPTS
OCTOPUS
OEDIPUS
OLYMPUS
PARAPHS
PROMPTS
RECIPES
RETAPES
RETYPES
SCRAPES
SCRIPPS
SCRIPTS
SCULPTS
SERAPES
SERAPHS
SERAPIS
SHERPAS
SHOPPES
STEPPES
STRIPES
TERAPHS
THESPIS
TRAMPAS
TROUPES

•••••PS

BACKUPS
BARHOPS
BIGTOPS
BISHOPS
BITMAPS
BLOWUPS
BOXTOPS
BURLAPS
CARHOPS
CATNAPS
CATNIPS
CCLAMPS
CHINUPS
COLLOPS
CYCLOPS
DECAMPS
DEWLAPS
DOLLOPS
DUSTUPS
EGGCUPS
ENCAMPS
ENTRAPS
ENWRAPS
ESCARPS
EYECUPS
FILLIPS
FILLUPS
FLIPUPS
FOLDUPS
FORCEPS
FOULUPS
GALLOPS
GASCAPS
GIVEUPS
GOOFUPS
GOSSIPS
HANGUPS
HICCUPS
HOLDUPS
HOOKUPS
HOTCAPS
HOTLIPS
HOTTIPS
HUBCAPS
HYSSOPS
ICECAPS
INSTEPS
JOBHOPS
KICKUPS
KIDNAPS
LAPTOPS
LARRUPS
LASHUPS
LINEUPS
LINKUPS
LOCKUPS
LOOKUPS
MADCAPS
MAKEUPS
MARKUPS
MISHAPS
MOBCAPS
MOCKUPS
MRCHIPS
PEGTOPS
PERHAPS
PICKUPS
PILEUPS
POPTOPS
PREAMPS
PULLUPS
PUSHUPS
RAGMOPS
RAGTOPS
RECOUPS
REDCAPS
REDTOPS
RESHIPS
REVAMPS
REWRAPS
RIPRAPS
RUNLAPS
SATRAPS
SCHLEPS
SCHNAPS
SCRIMPS
SCRIPPS
SENDUPS
SHRIMPS
SKYCAPS
SLIPUPS
STEPUPS
TEACUPS
TIPTOPS
TOECAPS
TOETAPS
TOSSUPS
TRICEPS
TUNEUPS
TURNIPS
UNSNAPS
UNSTOPS
UNTRAPS
UNWRAPS
WALKUPS
WALLOPS
WARMUPS
WETMOPS
WINDUPS
WORKUPS
WRAPUPS

PT•••••

PTBOATS
PTOLEMY

P•T••••

PATAKES
PATCHED
PATCHES
PATCHUP
PATELLA
PATENTS
PATERNO
PATHWAY
PATIENT
PATINAS
PATNESS
PATRICE
PATRICK
PATRIOT
PATROLS
PATRONS
PATROON
PATSIES
PATTENS
PATTERN
PATTERS
PATTIES
PATTING
PETALED
PETARDS
PETCOCK
PETERED
PETIOLE
PETITES
PETNAME
PETRELS
PETRIFY
PETROCK
PETROUS
PETTERS
PETTIER
PETTILY
PETTING
PETTISH
PETUNIA
PITAPAT
PITBOSS
PITBULL
PITCHED
PITCHER
PITCHES
PITCHIN
PITEOUS
PITFALL
PITHIER
PITHILY
PITHING
PITIFUL
PITSAWS
PITSTOP
PITTERS
PITTING
PITTMAN
PITYING
POTABLE
POTAGES
POTENCY
POTFULS
POTHERB
POTHERS
POTHOLE
POTHOOK
POTIONS
POTLUCK
POTOMAC
POTPIES
POTSDAM
POTSHOT
POTTAGE
POTTERS
POTTERY
POTTING
PUTAMEN
PUTAWAY
PUTDOWN
PUTITTO
PUTOUTS
PUTOVER
PUTSOFF
PUTSOUT
PUTTEES
PUTTERS
PUTTIED
PUTTIES
PUTTING
PUTUPON
PYTHIAS
PYTHONS

P••T•••

PALTERS
PANTHER
PANTING
PARTAKE
PARTIAL
PARTIED
PARTIES
PARTING
PARTITA
PARTITE
PARTNER
PARTOOK
PARTOUT
PARTWAY
PASTDUE
PASTELS
PASTERN
PASTEUP
PASTEUR
PASTIER
PASTIME
PASTINA
PASTING
PASTORS
PASTURE
PATTENS
PATTERN
PATTERS
PATTIES
PATTING
PEATBOG
PECTINS
PEGTOPS
PELTATE
PELTERS
PELTING
PENTADS
PEPTALK
PEPTIDE
PERTAIN
PERTEST
PERTURB
PESTERS
PESTLED
PESTLES
PETTERS
PETTIER
PETTILY
PETTING
PETTISH
PHOTOED
PHOTOGS
PHOTONS
PHOTOOP
PICTURE
PIETIES
PIETINS
PIETISM
PIGTAIL
PINTAIL
PISTILS
PISTOLE
PISTOLS
PISTONS
PITTERS
PITTING
PITTMAN
PLATEAU
PLATENS
PLATERS
PLATING
PLATOON
PLATTER
PLATYPI
PLOTTED
PLOTTER
POETESS
POETICS
POITIER
PONTIAC
PONTIFF
PONTINE
PONTIUS
PONTOON
POPTART
POPTOPS
PORTAGE
PORTALS
PORTEND
PORTENT
PORTERS
PORTHOS
PORTICO
PORTION
PORTOLA
PORTRAY
POSTAGE
POSTBOX
POSTERN
POSTERS
POSTHOC
POSTING
POSTMAN
POSTMEN
POSTURE
POSTWAR
POTTAGE
POTTERS
POTTERY
POTTING
POUTERS
POUTIER
POUTING
PRATERS
PRATING
PRATTLE
PRETAPE
PRETEEN
PRETEND
PRETEST
PRETEXT
PRETZEL
PRITHEE
PROTEAN
PROTECT
PROTEGE
PROTEIN
PROTEST
PROTEUS
PROTIST
PROTONS
PUNTERS
PUNTING
PUPTENT
PUTTEES
PUTTERS
PUTTIED
PUTTIES
PUTTING

P•••T••

PAINTED
PAINTER
PAIUTES
PALATAL
PALATES
PALETTE
PANETTA
PELOTAS
PENATES
PESETAS
PETITES
PHAETON
PHANTOM
PHILTER
PHILTRE
PIASTER
PIASTRE
PILOTED
PINATAS
PINETAR
PINETUM
PIPETTE
PIRATED
PIRATES
PIRATIC
PITSTOP
PIVOTAL
PIVOTED
PLAITED
PLANTAR
PLANTED
PLANTER
PLASTER
PLASTIC
PLATTER
PLAUTUS
PLEATED
PLECTRA
PLINTHS
PLOTTED
PLOTTER
POINTED
POINTER
POINTTO
POLITER
POLITIC
POLLTAX
POSITED
POULTRY
PRAETOR
PRATTLE
PRESTON
PRESTOS
PRINTED
PRINTER
PROCTOR
PSALTER
PULLTAB
PUNSTER
PURITAN
PUTITTO
PYRITES

P••••T•

PACKETS
PALETTE
PALLETS
PALMATE
PANDITS
PANETTA
PAPEETE
PARENTS
PARGETS
PARROTS
PARTITA
PARTITE
PATENTS
PAUCITY
PAYOUTS
PEANUTS
PEDANTS
PELLETS
PELTATE
PENALTY
PENNATE
PENULTS
PEQUOTS
PERLITE
PERMITS
PICANTE
PICKETS
PICKETT
PIGLETS
PIGNUTS
PIMENTO
PINNATE
PIOLETS
PIPETTE
PLACATE
PLAINTS
PLANETS
PLIGHTS
POCKETS
POINTTO
POLENTA
POLLUTE
POPPETS
POSSETS
POVERTY
PRAYSTO
PREDATE
PRELATE
PRESETS
PRIESTS
PRIMATE
PRIORTO
PRIVATE
PRIVETS
PROBATE
PROBITY
PROFITS
PROMOTE
PROMPTS
PRORATA
PRORATE
PRYINTO
PTBOATS
PUBERTY
PUCKETT
PULLETS
PULPITS
PULSATE
PUNDITS
PUPPETS
PURISTS
PUTITTO
PUTOUTS

P•••••T

PACKRAT
PAGEANT
PAIDOUT
PALMIST
PANDECT
PANSOUT
PARAPET
PARFAIT
PARQUET
PARTOUT
PASSANT
PASSOUT
PATIENT
PATRIOT
PAULIST
PAWEDAT
PAYDIRT
PAYMENT
PAYSOUT
PEACOAT
PEASANT
PECCANT
PECKSAT
PEEKOUT
PEEKSAT
PEEROUT
PEERSAT
PENDANT
PENDENT
PENNANT
PERCENT
PERFECT
PERIDOT
PERSIST
PERTEST
PERVERT
PEUGEOT
PIANIST
PICKETT
PICKOUT
PICKSAT
PIERROT
PIGMENT
PIGSOUT
PINENUT
PINIEST
PINKEST
PIQUANT
PITAPAT
PLACKET
PLAUDIT
PLAYACT
PLAYLET
PLAYOUT
PLAYSAT
PLUMMET
POKEDAT
POKESAT
POKIEST
POLECAT
POLOIST
POOPOUT
POOREST
POPSOUT
POPTART
PORTENT
POSHEST
POTSHOT
POUROUT
PRECAST
PRECEPT
PREDICT
PREEMPT
PREFECT
PREHEAT
PRESENT
PRESORT
PRETEST
PRETEXT
PREVENT
PRODUCT
PROJECT
PROPHET
PROPJET
PROTECT
PROTEST
PROTIST
PROVOST
PRUDENT
PUCKETT
PULLOUT
PUNGENT
PUNIEST
PUPTENT
PURPORT
PURSUIT
PUTSOUT

•PT••••

APTNESS
OPTICAL
OPTIMAL
OPTIMUM
OPTIONS
OPTSOUT
UPTAKES
UPTEMPO
UPTICKS
UPTIGHT
UPTONOW
UPTOPAR
UPTURNS

•P•T•••

APATITE
APOTHEM
EPITHET
EPITOME
EPSTEIN
SPATIAL
SPATTED
SPATTER
SPATULA
SPITING
SPITZES
SPOTLIT
SPOTTED
SPOTTER
SPUTNIK
SPUTTER
UPATREE
UPSTAGE
UPSTART
UPSTATE

•P••T••

APOSTLE
EPISTLE
OPENTOE
OPIATES
SPARTAN
SPATTED
SPATTER
SPECTER
SPECTOR
SPECTRA
SPECTRE
SPLITUP
SPLOTCH
SPORTED
SPOTTED
SPOTTER
SPOUTED
SPOUTER
SPRITES
SPURTED
SPUTTER
UPDATED
UPDATES

•P•••T•

APATITE
APLENTY
OPACITY
OPERATE
SPIGOTS
SPINETS
SPIRITO
SPIRITS
SPLINTS
SPRINTS
SPROUTS
UPBEATS
UPLIFTS
UPROOTS
UPSHOTS
UPSTATE

•P••••T

APPOINT
APRICOT
EPAULET
EPEEIST
EPITHET
OPENPIT
OPTSOUT
OPULENT
SPAREST
SPINOUT
SPIRANT
SPOTLIT
SPRIEST
SPRYEST
SPUNOUT

UPDRAFT
UPFRONT
UPRIGHT
UPSTART
UPSWEPT
UPTIGHT

••PT•••
BAPTISM
BAPTIST
BAPTIZE
CAPTAIN
CAPTION
CAPTIVE
CAPTORS
CAPTURE
COPTERS
DIPTYCH
EMPTIED
EMPTIER
EMPTIES
EMPTILY
HEPTADS
HOPTOIT
KEPTOFF
KEPTOUT
LAPTOPS
LEPTONS
NAPTIME
NEPTUNE
NUPTIAL
PEPTALK
PEPTIDE
POPTART
POPTOPS
PUPTENT
RAPTORS
RAPTURE
REPTILE
RIPTIDE
RIPTORN
RUPTURE
SEPTETS
TIPTOED
TIPTOES
TIPTOPS
UMPTEEN

••P•T••
BYPATHS
CAPITAL
CAPITAN
CAPITOL
CAPSTAN
DEPUTED
DEPUTES
EMPATHY
HEPATIC
HIPSTER
IMPETUS
IMPUTED
IMPUTES
INPETTO
JUPITER
NAPHTHA
PIPETTE
REPUTED
REPUTES
ROPETOW
STPETER
TAPSTER
TIPSTER
WAPITIS
ZAPOTEC

••P••T•
ASPECTS
CAPLETS
CAPNUTS
COPOUTS
DEPARTS
DEPICTS
DEPLETE
DEPORTS
EXPARTE
EXPECTS
EXPERTS
EXPIATE
EXPORTS
HEPCATS
IMPACTS
IMPARTS
IMPASTO
IMPIETY
IMPORTS
IMPOSTS
INPETTO
JAPHETH
LAPLATA
LAPORTE
LAPPETS
LEPANTO
MOPPETS
MUPPETS
PAPEETE
PIPETTE
POPPETS
PUPPETS
REPASTE
REPASTS
REPEATS
REPENTS
REPLATE
REPLETE
REPORTS
RIPINTO
RIPOSTE
SEPTETS
SIPPETS
SOPWITH
TAPPETS
TIPPETS
TOPHATS
TYPISTS

••P•••T
AMPLEST
APPOINT
ASPHALT
BAPTIST
CAPELET
CAPULET
COPILOT
COPSOUT
COPYCAT
COPYIST
CYPRIOT
DEPOSIT
DOPEOUT
DOPIEST
EXPLOIT
HIPBOOT
HIPPEST
HOPTOIT
IMPLANT
IMPRINT
INPOINT
INPRINT
KEPTOUT
LAPBELT
POPSOUT
POPTART
PUPTENT
RAPPORT
REPAINT
REPLANT
REPRINT
SAPIENT
SOPHIST
SUPPORT
TAPROOT
TAPSOUT
TOPCOAT
TOPKNOT
TOPMAST
TOPMOST
TOPSOUT
TYPESET
WIPEOUT
YOPLAIT

•••PT••
ADAPTED
ADAPTER
ADAPTOR
ADEPTLY
ADOPTED
ADOPTEE
ADOPTER
ASEPTIC
CHAPTER
CLAPTON
COOPTED
CRYPTIC
CRYPTOS
DIOPTER
ERUPTED
HAMPTON
INAPTLY
INEPTLY
KRYPTON
SCEPTER
SCEPTRE
SKEPTIC
SLEPTIN
SLEPTON
STYPTIC
SWEPTUP
SYMPTOM
TEMPTED
TEMPTER

•••P•T•
ARMPITS
CARPETS
CHAPATI
COMPETE
COMPOTE
COMPUTE
DESPITE
DESPOTS
DISPUTE
HOTPOTS
INSPOTS
KEEPSTO
LAPPETS
LIMPETS
MOPPETS
MUPPETS
OUTPUTS
POPPETS
PULPITS
PUPPETS
RESPITE
SIPPETS
SNAPSTO
TAPPETS
TARPITS
TEAPOTS
TIPPETS
TOWPATH
WARPATH

•••P••T
AIRPORT
ANAPEST
BEDPOST
BITPART
CAMPOUT
CARPORT
CHAPLET
CLIPART
COMPACT
COMPORT
COMPOST
COUPLET
CULPRIT
DAMPEST
DEEPEST
DEEPFAT
DEEPSET
DISPORT
DROPLET
DROPOUT
FLYPAST
HARPIST
HELPOUT
HIPPEST
INSPECT
JETPORT
JUMPCUT
JUMPSAT
KEEPSAT
LIMPEST
NEWPORT
OUTPOST
POOPOUT
PROPHET
PROPJET
PURPORT
RAMPANT
RAMPART
RAPPORT
RESPECT
SEAPORT
SERPENT
SHIPOUT
SKIPOUT
SLIPOUT
SNAPSAT
SNIPEAT
SNIPPET
STEPOUT
SUBPLOT
SUPPORT
SUSPECT
TEMPEST
TRIPLET
TRIPPET
UNSPENT
WHIPPET

••••PT•
ACCEPTS
ADDUPTO
EXCEPTS
EXEMPTS
INCEPTS
INDEPTH
IRRUPTS
LEDUPTO
PROMPTS
SCRIPTS
SCULPTS
STOOPTO

••••P•T
COCKPIT
CRUMPET
DOWNPAT
FUSSPOT
GOTOPOT
HARDPUT
HOTSPOT
INASPOT
INCIPIT
INKSPOT
JACKPOT
OCCIPUT
OPENPIT
PARAPET
PITAPAT
REDSPOT
SHOTPUT
SNIPPET
STAYPUT
SUNSPOT
TENSPOT
TRIPPET
TRUMPET
WHIPPET

•••••PT
ATTEMPT
CONCEPT
CORRUPT
DECRYPT
DISRUPT
ENCRYPT
EXCERPT
PRECEPT
PREEMPT
RECEIPT
UNKEMPT
UNSWEPT
UPSWEPT

PU•••••
PUBERTY
PUBLICS
PUBLISH
PUCCINI
PUCKERS
PUCKETT
PUCKISH
PUDDING
PUDDLED
PUDDLES
PUDGIER
PUEBLOS
PUERILE
PUFFERS
PUFFERY
PUFFIER
PUFFILY
PUFFING
PUFFINS
PUGNOSE
PUGREES
PULASKI
PULLETS
PULLEYS
PULLING
PULLMAN
PULLOFF
PULLONS
PULLOUT
PULLSUP
PULLTAB
PULLUPS
PULPITS
PULSARS
PULSATE
PULSING
PUMICES
PUMMELS
PUMPERS
PUMPING
PUMPKIN
PUMPSUP
PUNCHED
PUNCHER
PUNCHES
PUNCHIN
PUNCHUP
PUNDITS
PUNGENT
PUNIEST
PUNJABI
PUNKAHS
PUNKIES
PUNNING
PUNSTER
PUNTERS
PUNTING
PUPPETS
PUPPIES
PUPTENT
PURCELL
PURDAHS
PURFLED
PURFLES
PURGING
PURISTS
PURITAN
PURLIEU
PURLING
PURLINS
PURLOIN
PURPLED
PURPLES
PURPORT
PURPOSE
PURRERS
PURRING
PURSERS
PURSING
PURSUED
PURSUER
PURSUES
PURSUIT
PURVEYS
PURVIEW
PUSHIER
PUSHILY
PUSHING
PUSHKIN
PUSHOFF
PUSHPIN
PUSHUPS
PUTAMEN
PUTAWAY
PUTDOWN
PUTITTO
PUTOUTS
PUTOVER
PUTSOFF
PUTSOUT
PUTTEES
PUTTERS
PUTTIED
PUTTIES
PUTTING
PUTUPON
PUZZLED
PUZZLER
PUZZLES

P•U••••
PAUCITY
PAULINA
PAULINE
PAULING
PAULIST
PAULSEN
PAUNCHY
PAUPERS
PAUSING
PEUGEOT
PLUCKED
PLUGGED
PLUGGER
PLUGSIN
PLUMAGE
PLUMBED
PLUMBER
PLUMING
PLUMMER
PLUMMET
PLUMPED
PLUMPER
PLUNDER
PLUNGED
PLUNGER
PLUNGES
PLUNKED
PLURALS
PLUSHER
PLUSHES
PLUSHLY
PLUSSES
PLUVIAL
POUCHED
POUCHES
POULENC
POULTRY
POUNCED
POUNCER
POUNCES
POUNDED
POUNDER
POURERS
POURING
POUROUT
POURSIN
POUTERS
POUTIER
POUTING
PRUDENT
PRUDERY
PRUDHOE
PRUDISH
PRUNERS
PRUNING
PRUSSIA

P••U•••
PABULUM
PADUCAH
PAIUTES
PANURGE
PAPUANS
PARURES
PENUCHE
PENULTS
PEQUOTS
PERUKES
PERUSAL
PERUSED
PERUSER
PERUSES
PETUNIA
PIOUSLY
PIQUANT
PIQUING
PLAUDIT
PLAUTUS
PLOUGHS
POPULAR
PROUDER
PROUDLY
PUTUPON

P•••U••
PABLUMS
PARQUET
PASTURE
PAYOUTS
PEANUTS
PENGUIN
PEPLUMS
PERFUME
PERJURE
PERJURY
PERTURB
PICKUPS
PICTURE
PIGNUTS
PILEUPS
PINCURL
PITBULL
PLAGUED
PLAGUES
PLAQUES
PLENUMS
PODIUMS
POLLUTE
POPGUNS
POSEURS
POSSUMS
POSTURE
POTFULS
POTLUCK
PRELUDE
PRESUME
PROCURE
PRODUCE
PRODUCT
PROFUSE
PULLUPS
PURSUED
PURSUER
PURSUES
PURSUIT
PUSHUPS
PUTOUTS

P••••U•
PABULUM
PACKSUP
PAGEFUL
PAIDOUT
PAILFUL
PAILOUS
PAINFUL
PAIRSUP
PALLIUM
PANSOUT
PAPYRUS
PARIBUS
PARLOUR
PARLOUS
PARTOUT
PASSEUL
PASSOUT
PASTDUE
PASTEUP
PASTEUR
PATCHUP
PAVIOUR
PAYSOUT
PEASOUP
PEEKOUT
PEEROUT
PEGASUS
PERKSUP
PERSEUS
PERSIUS
PETROUS
PHOEBUS
PICKOUT
PICKSUP
PIGSOUT
PILEDUP
PILESUP
PILLBUG
PINENUT
PINETUM
PIPEDUP
PIPEFUL
PIPESUP
PIRAEUS
PIROGUE
PITEOUS
PITIFUL
PLAUTUS
PLAYFUL
PLAYOUT
PLAYSUP
POKEFUN
POMPOUS
PONTIUS
POOPOUT
POPSOUT
POUROUT
PREMIUM
PRONOUN
PROPSUP
PROTEUS
PSYCHUP
PULLOUT
PULLSUP
PUMPSUP
PUNCHUP
PUTSOUT
PYRAMUS
PYRRHUS

P•••••U
PARVENU
PLATEAU
PURLIEU

•PU••••
OPULENT
SPUMING
SPUMONE
SPUMONI
SPUNOFF
SPUNOUT
SPURNED
SPURNER
SPURRED
SPURSON
SPURTED
SPUTNIK
SPUTTER

•P•U•••
EPAULET
OPPUGNS
SPLURGE
SPOUSAL
SPOUSES
SPOUTED
SPOUTER
SPRUCED
SPRUCER
SPRUCES
UPSURGE
UPTURNS

•P••U••
EPICURE
OPAQUES
SPATULA
SPELUNK
SPROUTS

•P•••U•
APERCUS
APPLAUD
OPENSUP
OPOSSUM
OPTIMUM
OPTSOUT
SPEAKUP
SPEEDUP
SPICEUP
SPINOUT
SPLITUP
SPOKEUP
SPUNOUT

••PU•••
AMPULES
CAPULET
DEPUTED
DEPUTES
EXPUNGE
IMPUGNS
IMPULSE
IMPURER
IMPUTED
IMPUTES
OPPUGNS
PAPUANS
POPULAR
REPUGNS
REPULSE
REPUTED
REPUTES

••P•U••
AMPOULE
CAPFULS
CAPGUNS
CAPNUTS
CAPSULE
CAPTURE
COPOUTS
CUPFULS
ESPOUSE
EXPOUND
HEPBURN
IMPOUND
LAPFULS
NEPTUNE
PEPLUMS
POPGUNS
RAPTURE
RUPTURE
TOPGUNS
UNPLUGS
VAPOURS

••P••U•
APPLAUD
CEPHEUS
COPIOUS
COPSOUT
DOPEOUT
HOPEFUL
HYPEDUP
IMPETUS
IMPIOUS
KEPTOUT
ORPHEUS
PAPYRUS
PIPEDUP
PIPEFUL
PIPESUP
POPSOUT
RAPANUI
TAPSOUT
TOPSOUT
TYPEDUP
TYPESUP
WIPEDUP
WIPEOUT
WIPESUP

•••PU••
AIRPUMP
COMPUTE
DISPUTE
FLIPUPS
GASPUMP
LEGPULL
OUTPUTS
SCAPULA
SLIPUPS
STEPUPS
TEMPURA
WRAPUPS

•••P•U•
BUMPSUP
BURPGUN
CAMPOUT
COOPSUP
CROPSUP
DROPOUT
EARPLUG
GROPIUS
HELPFUL
HELPOUT
JUMPCUT
JUMPSUP
KEEPSUP
LESPAUL
LUMPSUM
NONPLUS
POMPOUS
POOPOUT
PROPSUP
PUMPSUP
SHAPEUP
SHIPOUT
SKIPOUT
SLIPOUT
SLIPSUP
SNAPSUP
SOUPSUP
STEPOUT
STEPSUP
STOPSUP
SULPHUR
SURPLUS
SWEPTUP
TRIPSUP
WHIPSUP
WRAPSUP

•••P••U
CHAPEAU

••••PU•
CANOPUS
CREEPUP
CRISPUS
GRAMPUS
HARDPUT
HOTSPUR
OCCIPUT
OCTOPUS
OEDIPUS
OLYMPUS
SHOTPUT
STAYPUT
SWEEPUP
TRUMPUP

P•V••••
PAVANES
PAVIOUR
PAVLOVA
PIVOTAL
PIVOTED
POVERTY

P••V•••
PARVENU
PEAVEYS
PEEVING
PEEVISH
PERVADE
PERVERT
PLOVERS
PLUVIAL
PREVAIL
PREVENT
PREVIEW
PRIVACY
PRIVATE
PRIVETS
PRIVIES
PROVERB
PROVERS
PROVIDE
PROVING
PROVISO
PROVOKE
PROVOST
PURVEYS
PURVIEW

P•••V••
PALAVER
POPOVER
PUTOVER

P••••V•
PAHLAVI
PASSIVE
PAVLOVA
PENSIVE
PLOSIVE

•P•V•••
SPAVINS

•P••V••
UPRIVER

•P•••V•
APPROVE

••P•V••
HOPOVER
POPOVER
REPAVED
REPAVES
UNPAVED

••P••V•
APPROVE
CAPTIVE
DEPRAVE
DEPRIVE
IMPROVE
REPROVE

P•W••••
PAWEDAT
PAWNEES
PAWNERS
PAWNING
PAWNOFF
PAWPAWS
POWDERS
POWDERY
POWERED
POWWOWS

P••W•••
PEEWEES
PINWALE
PLOWBOY
PLOWERS
PLOWING
PLOWMAN
PLOWMEN
PLYWOOD
POWWOWS
PREWASH
PROWESS
PROWLED
PROWLER

P•••W••
PARKWAY
PARTWAY
PATHWAY
POSTWAR
PUTAWAY

P••••W•
PAWPAWS
PEAFOWL
PILLOWS
PILLOWY
PINDOWN
PITSAWS
POWWOWS
PREDAWN
PUTDOWN

P•••••W
PREVIEW
PURVIEW

•PW••••
UPWARDS

•P•W•••
IPSWICH
SPAWNED
SPEWING
UPSWEEP
UPSWEPT
UPSWING

•P••W••
SPRAWLS

•P••••W
SPARROW
UPTONOW

••PW•••
LAPWING
SOPWITH

••P•W••
EMPOWER

••P••W•
NEPHEWS
RIPSAWS

••P•••W
CAPSHAW
ROPETOW

•••P•W•
PAWPAWS

•••P••W
WHIPSAW

••••P•W
BEARPAW
CATSPAW
FOREPAW

P•X••••
PIXYISH
PYXIDES

P••X•••
PLEXORS
PROXIES
PROXIMO

P•••X••
PHLOXES
POBOXES

P••••X•
PICKAXE
POLEAXE
PRETEXT

P•••••X
PANCHAX
PARADOX
PERPLEX
PHALANX
PHARYNX
PHOENIX
PILLBOX
POLLTAX
POORBOX
POSTBOX

•P•X•••
EPOXIES

•P••••X
SPANDEX

•••P••X
COMPLEX
DEEPSIX
PERPLEX
SIMPLEX
SOAPBOX
TRIPLEX

PY•••••
PYEDOGS
PYGMIES
PYJAMAS
PYNCHON
PYRAMID
PYRAMUS
PYRITES
PYRRHIC
PYRRHUS
PYTHIAS
PYTHONS
PYXIDES

P•Y••••
PAYABLE
PAYCASH
PAYDAYS
PAYDIRT
PAYLOAD
PAYMENT
PAYOFFS
PAYOLAS
PAYOUTS
PAYROLL
PAYSFOR
PAYSOFF
PAYSOUT
PHYLLIS
PHYSICS
PLYWOOD
PRYINTO
PSYCHED
PSYCHES
PSYCHIC
PSYCHUP

P••Y•••
PAPYRUS
PITYING
PIXYISH
PLAYACT
PLAYBOY
PLAYDOH
PLAYERS
PLAYFUL
PLAYING
PLAYLET
PLAYOFF
PLAYOUT
PLAYPEN
PLAYSAT
PLAYSON
PLAYSUP
POLYGON
POLYMER
PONYING
PRAYERS
PRAYFOR
PRAYING
PRAYSTO
PREYSON

P•••Y••
PAPAYAS
PHARYNX
PLATYPI
POPEYED
PROCYON

P••••Y•
PARLAYS
PARLEYS
PAYDAYS
PEAVEYS
PREPAYS
PULLEYS
PURVEYS

P•••••Y
PAGEBOY
PAISLEY
PALEDRY
PALFREY
PALJOEY
PANICKY
PANOPLY
PARKWAY
PARSLEY
PARTWAY
PASSKEY
PATHWAY
PAUCITY
PAUNCHY
PEABODY
PECCARY
PENALTY
PEPPERY
PEPPILY
PERFIDY
PERJURY
PERKILY
PESKILY
PETRIFY
PETTILY
PHONILY
PILLORY
PILLOWY
PIOUSLY
PITHILY
PLAINLY
PLAYBOY
PLENARY
PLIABLY
PLIANCY
PLOWBOY
PLUSHLY
POORBOY
PORTRAY
POTENCY
POTTERY
POULTRY
POVERTY
POWDERY
PREACHY
PRESLEY
PRICKLY
PRIMACY
PRIMARY
PRIVACY
PROBITY
PRODIGY
PROGENY
PROSILY
PROSODY
PROUDLY
PRUDERY
PTOLEMY
PUBERTY
PUFFERY
PUFFILY
PUSHILY
PUTAWAY

•P•Y•••
SPAYING
SPRYEST

•P••Y••
EPONYMS
SPLAYED
SPRAYED
SPRAYER

•P••••Y
APISHLY
APLENTY
APOLOGY
OPACITY
SPANGLY
SPARELY
SPASSKY
SPECIFY
SPIDERY
SPINDLY
SPLASHY
SPRINGY

••PY•••
COPYBOY
COPYCAT
COPYING
COPYIST
ESPYING
PAPYRUS

••P•Y••
DIPTYCH
LIPSYNC
PAPAYAS
POPEYED
ZEPHYRS

••P••Y•
BYPLAYS
DEPLOYS
EMPLOYS
OSPREYS
REPLAYS

••P•••Y
AMPLIFY
CAPABLY
COPPERY
COPYBOY
EMPATHY
EMPTILY
EUPHONY
FOPPERY
HAPPILY
IMPIETY
PEPPERY
PEPPILY
RAPIDLY
TEPIDLY
TIPSILY
TOPIARY
VAPIDLY

•••P•Y•
PREPAYS
TEAPOYS

•••P••Y
ADEPTLY
AIRPLAY
COMPANY
COPPERY
DEEPFRY
DEMPSEY
DISPLAY
DRAPERY
DRIPDRY
DROPSBY
ENDPLAY
EXUPERY
FOPPERY
GUNPLAY
HAPPILY
INAPTLY
INEPTLY
LAMPREY
MISPLAY
MURPHEY
OUTPLAY
PEPPERY
PEPPILY
SHAPELY
STUPEFY
WISPILY

••••P•Y
ATROPHY
BASEPAY
CHEAPLY
CRISPLY
CRUMPLY
PANOPLY
SCRAPPY
SHARPLY
SICKPAY
STEEPLY
UNHAPPY

•••••PY
ENTROPY
GOSSIPY
SCRAPPY
SCRIMPY
THERAPY
UNHAPPY

P•Z••••
PIZARRO
PIZZAZZ
PUZZLED
PUZZLER
PUZZLES

P••Z•••
PANZERS
PIAZZAS
PIZZAZZ
PRIZING
PUZZLED
PUZZLER
PUZZLES

P•••Z••
PALAZZI
PALAZZO
PIAZZAS
PRETZEL

P••••Z•
PALAZZI
PALAZZO
PIZZAZZ

P•••••Z
PIZZAZZ

•P••Z••
SPITZES

•P•••Z•
APPRIZE
SPINOZA

••P•Z••
TOPAZES

••P••Z•
APPRIZE
BAPTIZE
CAPSIZE

•••PZ••
LEIPZIG

•••P•Z•
TRAPEZE

Q•A••••
QUACKED
QUAFFED
QUAFFER
QUAGGAS
QUAHOGS
QUAILED
QUAKERS
QUAKING
QUALIFY
QUALITY
QUANTUM
QUARREL
QUARTER
QUARTET
QUARTOS
QUASARS
QUASHED
QUASHES
QUAVERS
QUAVERY

Q•••A••
QINTARS
QUASARS

Q••••A•
QUAGGAS
QUETZAL
QUINOAS
QUOKKAS

Q•••••A
QUECHUA

•Q•A•••
AQUARIA
AQUATIC
AQUAVIT
EQUABLE
EQUABLY
EQUALED
EQUALLY
EQUATED
EQUATES
EQUATOR
SQUALID
SQUALLS
SQUALOR
SQUANTO
SQUARED
SQUARER
SQUARES
SQUAWKS

•Q••A••
SQUEAKS
SQUEAKY
SQUEALS

•Q•••A•
AQUINAS

•Q••••A
AQUARIA

••Q•A••
LOQUATS
PIQUANT
TSQUARE

••Q•••A
SEQUOIA
TEQUILA

•••Q•A•
COEQUAL
KUMQUAT
RORQUAL
UNEQUAL

Q••B•••
QUIBBLE

Q•••B••
QUIBBLE

•Q••B••
EQUABLE
EQUABLY

Q••C•••
QUACKED
QUECHUA
QUICHES
QUICKEN
QUICKER
QUICKIE
QUICKLY

Q•••C••
QUINCES

•Q•••C•
SQUELCH
SQUINCH

•Q••••C
AQUATIC

Q•••••D
QUACKED
QUAFFED
QUAILED
QUASHED
QUEERED
QUELLED
QUERIED
QUESTED
QUIETED
QUILLED
QUILTED
QUIPPED
QUIZZED

•Q••••D
EQUALED
EQUATED
SQUALID
SQUARED
SQUIRED

••Q••D•
LIQUIDS

Q•E••••
QUECHUA
QUEENLY
QUEERED
QUEERER
QUEERLY
QUELLED
QUENTIN
QUERIED
QUERIES
QUESTED
QUETZAL
QUEUERS
QUEUEUP
QUEUING

Q••E•••
QUEENLY
QUEERED
QUEERER
QUEERLY
QUIETED
QUIETEN
QUIETER
QUIETLY

Q•••E••
QUAKERS
QUAVERS
QUAVERY
QUEUERS
QUEUEUP
QUIVERS
QUOTERS

Q••••E•
QUACKED
QUAFFED
QUAFFER
QUAILED
QUARREL
QUARTER
QUARTET
QUASHED
QUASHES
QUEERED
QUEERER
QUELLED
QUERIED
QUERIES
QUESTED
QUICHES
QUICKEN
QUICKER
QUIETED
QUIETEN
QUIETER
QUIGLEY
QUILLED
QUILTED
QUILTER
QUINCES
QUINTET
QUIPPED
QUIPPER
QUITTER
QUIZZED
QUIZZES
QUONSET

Q•••••E
QUIBBLE
QUICKIE
QUININE
QUINQUE
QUIVIVE
QUIXOTE

•Q•E•••
AQUEOUS
EQUERRY
IQTESTS
SQUEAKS
SQUEAKY
SQUEALS
SQUEEZE
SQUELCH

•Q••E••
SQUEEZE

•Q•••E•
AQUIFER
AQUIVER
EQUALED
EQUATED
EQUATES
EQUINES
SQUARED
SQUARER
SQUARES
SQUIRED
SQUIRES

•Q••••E
EQUABLE
SQUEEZE

••Q•E••
BEQUEST
INQUEST
LIQUEFY
LIQUEUR
MCQUEEN
REQUEST
SEQUELS
VAQUERO

••Q••E•
MCQUEEN
REQUIEM

••Q•••E
ACQUIRE
ESQUIRE
INQUIRE
REQUIRE
REQUITE
TSQUARE
UNQUOTE

•••Q•E•
BANQUET
BASQUES
BISQUES
BOUQUET
BRIQUET
CAIQUES
CHEQUER
CHEQUES
CIRQUES
CLAQUES
CLIQUES
CLOQUES
CONQUER
CROQUET
JACQUES
LACQUER
MARQUEE
MARQUES
MARQUEZ
MASQUES
MOSQUES
OPAQUES
PARQUET
PLAQUES
RACQUET
TORQUES

•••Q••E
MARQUEE

••••Q•E
ANTIQUE
BAROQUE
BEZIQUE
BRUSQUE
COMIQUE
DUBUQUE
LALIQUE
MACAQUE
MONIQUE
OBLIQUE
QUINQUE

Q••F•••
QUAFFED
QUAFFER

Q•••F••
QUAFFED
QUAFFER

Q••••F•
QUALIFY

•Q••F••
AQUIFER

••Q•F••
LIQUEFY

Q••G•••
QUAGGAS
QUIGLEY

Q•••G••
QUAGGAS

Q••••G•
QUAHOGS

Q•••••G
QUAKING
QUEUING
QUOTING

••Q•••G
PIQUING

Q••H•••
QUAHOGS

Q•••H••
QUASHED
QUASHES
QUECHUA
QUICHES

•Q•••H•
SQUISHY

•Q••••H
SQUELCH
SQUINCH

QI•••••
QINTARS

Q•I••••
QUIBBLE
QUICHES
QUICKEN
QUICKER
QUICKIE
QUICKLY
QUIETED
QUIETEN
QUIETER
QUIETLY
QUIGLEY
QUILLED
QUILTED
QUILTER
QUINCES
QUININE
QUINOAS
QUINQUE
QUINTET
QUIPPED
QUIPPER
QUITTER
QUIVERS
QUIVIVE
QUIXOTE
QUIZZED
QUIZZES

Q••I•••
QUAILED

Q•••I••
QUAKING
QUALIFY
QUALITY
QUERIED
QUERIES
QUEUING
QUININE
QUIVIVE
QUOTING

Q••••I•
QUENTIN
QUICKIE

•Q•I•••
AQUIFER
AQUINAS
AQUIVER
EQUINES
EQUINOX
SQUINCH
SQUINTS
SQUINTY
SQUIRED
SQUIRES
SQUIRMS
SQUIRMY
SQUIRTS
SQUISHY

•Q•••I•
AQUARIA
AQUATIC
AQUAVIT
SQUALID

••Q•I••
ACQUIRE
ACQUITS
ESQUIRE
INQUIRE
INQUIRY
LIQUIDS
PIQUING
REQUIEM
REQUIRE
REQUITE
SEQUINS
TEQUILA

••Q••I•
SEQUOIA

•••Q•I•
JOAQUIN
JONQUIL
MARQUIS

Q••K•••
QUAKERS
QUAKING
QUOKKAS

Q•••K••
QUACKED
QUICKEN
QUICKER
QUICKIE
QUICKLY
QUOKKAS

•Q•••K•
SQUAWKS
SQUEAKS
SQUEAKY

Q••L•••
QUALIFY
QUALITY
QUELLED
QUILLED
QUILTED
QUILTER

Q•••L••
QUAILED
QUELLED
QUIGLEY
QUILLED

Q••••L•
QUEENLY
QUEERLY
QUIBBLE
QUICKLY
QUIETLY

Q•••••L
QUARREL
QUETZAL

•Q••L••
EQUALED
EQUALLY
SQUALID
SQUALLS
SQUALOR
SQUELCH

•Q•••L•
EQUABLE
EQUABLY
EQUALLY
SQUALLS
SQUEALS

••Q••L•
SEQUELS
TEQUILA

•••Q••L
COEQUAL
JONQUIL
RORQUAL
UNEQUAL

Q••••M•
QUORUMS

Q•••••M
QUANTUM

•Q•••M•
SQUIRMS
SQUIRMY

••Q•••M
REQUIEM

Q•N••••
QINTARS

Q••N•••
QUANTUM
QUENTIN
QUINCES
QUININE
QUINOAS
QUINQUE
QUINTET
QUONSET

Q•••N••
QUEENLY

Q••••N•
QUAKING
QUEUING
QUININE
QUOTING

Q•••••N
QUENTIN
QUICKEN
QUIETEN

•Q••N••
AQUINAS
EQUINES
EQUINOX
SQUANTO
SQUINCH
SQUINTS
SQUINTY

••Q••N•
PIQUANT
PIQUING
SEQUINS

••Q•••N
MCQUEEN

•••Q••N
JOAQUIN

Q•O••••
QUOKKAS
QUONSET
QUORUMS
QUOTERS
QUOTING

Q•••O••
QUAHOGS
QUINOAS
QUIXOTE

Q••••O•
QUARTOS

•Q••O••
AQUEOUS

•Q•••O•
EQUATOR
EQUINOX
SQUALOR

•Q••••O
SQUANTO

••Q•O••
LIQUORS
PEQUOTS
SEQUOIA
UNQUOTE

••Q•••O
VAQUERO

Q••P•••
QUIPPED
QUIPPER

Q•••P••
QUIPPED
QUIPPER

Q•••••P
QUEUEUP

Q•••Q••
QUINQUE

Q••R•••
QUARREL
QUARTER
QUARTET
QUARTOS
QUERIED
QUERIES
QUORUMS

Q•••R••
QUARREL
QUEERED
QUEERER
QUEERLY

Q••••R•
QINTARS
QUAKERS
QUASARS
QUAVERS
QUAVERY
QUEUERS
QUIVERS
QUOTERS

Q•••••R
QUAFFER
QUARTER
QUEERER
QUICKER
QUIETER
QUILTER
QUIPPER
QUITTER

•Q••R••
AQUARIA
EQUERRY
SQUARED
SQUARER
SQUARES
SQUIRED
SQUIRES
SQUIRMS
SQUIRMY
SQUIRTS

•Q•••R•
EQUERRY

•Q••••R
AQUIFER
AQUIVER
EQUATOR
SQUALOR
SQUARER

••Q••R•
ACQUIRE
ESQUIRE
INQUIRE
INQUIRY
LIQUORS
REQUIRE
TSQUARE
VAQUERO

••Q•••R
LIQUEUR

•••Q••R
CHEQUER
CONQUER
LACQUER

Q••S•••
QUASARS
QUASHED
QUASHES
QUESTED

Q•••S••
QUONSET

Q•••••S
QINTARS
QUAGGAS
QUAHOGS
QUAKERS
QUARTOS
QUASARS
QUASHES
QUAVERS
QUERIES
QUEUERS
QUICHES
QUINCES
QUINOAS
QUIVERS
QUIZZES
QUOKKAS
QUORUMS
QUOTERS

•Q••S••
IQTESTS
SQUISHY

•Q••••S
AQUEOUS
AQUINAS
EQUATES
EQUINES
IQTESTS
SQUALLS
SQUARES
SQUAWKS
SQUEAKS
SQUEALS
SQUINTS
SQUIRES
SQUIRMS
SQUIRTS

••Q••S•
BEQUEST
INQUEST
REQUEST

••Q•••S
ACQUITS
LIQUIDS
LIQUORS
LOQUATS
PEQUOTS
SEQUELS
SEQUINS

•••Q••S
BASQUES
BISQUES
CAIQUES
CHEQUES
CIRQUES
CLAQUES
CLIQUES
CLOQUES
JACQUES
MARQUES
MARQUIS
MASQUES
MOSQUES
OPAQUES
PLAQUES
TORQUES

•••••QS
PSANDQS

Q••T•••
QINTARS
QUETZAL
QUITTER
QUOTERS
QUOTING

Q•••T••
QUANTUM
QUARTER
QUARTET
QUARTOS
QUENTIN
QUESTED
QUIETED
QUIETEN
QUIETER
QUIETLY
QUILTED
QUILTER
QUINTET
QUITTER

Q••••T•
QUALITY
QUIXOTE

Q•••••T
QUARTET
QUINTET
QUONSET

•QT••••
IQTESTS

•Q••T••
AQUATIC
EQUATED
EQUATES
EQUATOR

•Q•••T•
IQTESTS
SQUANTO
SQUINTS
SQUINTY
SQUIRTS

•Q••••T
AQUAVIT

••Q••T•
ACQUITS
LOQUATS
PEQUOTS
REQUITE
UNQUOTE

••Q•••T
BEQUEST
INQUEST
PIQUANT
REQUEST

•••Q••T
BANQUET
BOUQUET
BRIQUET
CROQUET
KUMQUAT
PARQUET
RACQUET

•••••QT
ONTHEQT

QU•••••
QUACKED
QUAFFED
QUAFFER
QUAGGAS
QUAHOGS
QUAILED
QUAKERS
QUAKING
QUALIFY
QUALITY
QUANTUM
QUARREL
QUARTER
QUARTET
QUARTOS
QUASARS
QUASHED
QUASHES
QUAVERS
QUAVERY
QUECHUA
QUEENLY
QUEERED
QUEERER
QUEERLY
QUELLED
QUENTIN
QUERIED
QUERIES
QUESTED
QUETZAL
QUEUERS
QUEUEUP
QUEUING
QUIBBLE
QUICHES
QUICKEN
QUICKER
QUICKIE
QUICKLY
QUIETED
QUIETEN
QUIETER
QUIETLY
QUIGLEY
QUILLED
QUILTED
QUILTER
QUINCES
QUININE
QUINOAS
QUINQUE
QUINTET
QUIPPED
QUIPPER
QUITTER
QUIVERS
QUIVIVE
QUIXOTE
QUIZZED
QUIZZES
QUOKKAS
QUONSET
QUORUMS
QUOTERS
QUOTING

Q••U•••
QUEUERS
QUEUEUP
QUEUING

Q•••U••
QUORUMS

Q••••U•
QUANTUM
QUECHUA
QUEUEUP
QUINQUE

•QU••••
AQUARIA
AQUATIC
AQUAVIT
AQUEOUS
AQUIFER
AQUINAS
AQUIVER
EQUABLE
EQUABLY
EQUALED
EQUALLY
EQUATED
EQUATES
EQUATOR
EQUERRY
EQUINES
EQUINOX
SQUALID
SQUALLS
SQUALOR
SQUANTO
SQUARED
SQUARER
SQUARES
SQUAWKS
SQUEAKS
SQUEAKY
SQUEALS
SQUEEZE
SQUELCH
SQUINCH
SQUINTS
SQUINTY
SQUIRED
SQUIRES
SQUIRMS
SQUIRMY
SQUIRTS
SQUISHY

•Q•••U•
AQUEOUS

••QU•••
ACQUIRE
ACQUITS
BEQUEST
ESQUIRE
INQUEST
INQUIRE
INQUIRY
LIQUEFY
LIQUEUR
LIQUIDS
LIQUORS
LOQUATS
MCQUEEN
PEQUOTS
PIQUANT
PIQUING
REQUEST
REQUIEM
REQUIRE
REQUITE
SEQUELS
SEQUINS
SEQUOIA
TEQUILA
TSQUARE
UNQUOTE
VAQUERO

••Q••U•
LIQUEUR

•••QU••
BANQUET
BASQUES
BISQUES
BOUQUET
BRIQUET
CAIQUES
CHEQUER
CHEQUES
CIRQUES
CLAQUES
CLIQUES
CLOQUES
COEQUAL
CONQUER
CROQUET
JACQUES
JOAQUIN
JONQUIL
KUMQUAT
LACQUER
MARQUEE
MARQUES
MARQUEZ
MARQUIS
MASQUES
MOSQUES
OPAQUES
PARQUET
PLAQUES
RACQUET
RORQUAL
TORQUES
UNEQUAL

••••QU•
ANTIQUE
BAROQUE
BEZIQUE
BRUSQUE
COMIQUE
DUBUQUE
LALIQUE
MACAQUE
MONIQUE
OBLIQUE
OBLOQUY
QUINQUE

Q••V•••
QUAVERS
QUAVERY
QUIVERS
QUIVIVE

Q••••V•
QUIVIVE

•Q••V••
AQUAVIT
AQUIVER

•Q••W••
SQUAWKS

Q••X•••
QUIXOTE

•Q••••X
EQUINOX

Q•••••Y
QUALIFY
QUALITY
QUAVERY
QUEENLY
QUEERLY
QUICKLY
QUIETLY
QUIGLEY

•Q••••Y
EQUABLY
EQUALLY
EQUERRY
SQUEAKY
SQUINTY
SQUIRMY
SQUISHY

••Q•••Y
INQUIRY
LIQUEFY

••••Q•Y
OBLOQUY

Q••Z•••
QUIZZED
QUIZZES

Q•••Z••
QUETZAL
QUIZZED
QUIZZES

•Q•••Z•
SQUEEZE

•••Q••Z
MARQUEZ

RA•••••
RABBETS
RABBITS
RABBITT
RABBLES
RACCOON
RACECAR
RACEMES
RACEWAY
RACIEST
RACKETS
RACKING
RACKSUP
RACQUET
RADAMES
RADDLED
RADDLES
RADIALS
RADIANS
RADIANT
RADIATE
RADICAL
RADICES
RADICLE
RADIOED
RAFFISH
RAFFLED
RAFFLER
RAFFLES
RAFTERS
RAFTING
RAGDOLL
RAGGEDY
RAGGIER
RAGGING
RAGLANS
RAGMOPS
RAGOUTS
RAGRUGS
RAGTIME
RAGTOPS
RAGWEED
RAIDERS
RAIDING
RAILERS
RAILING
RAILSAT
RAILWAY
RAIMENT
RAINBOW
RAINHAT
RAINIER
RAINING
RAINMAN
RAINOUT
RAISERS
RAISEUP
RAISING
RAISINS
RAKEDIN
RAKEDUP
RAKEOFF
RAKESIN
RAKESUP
RALEIGH
RALLIED
RALLIES
RALLYTO
RALSTON
RAMADAN
RAMADAS
RAMBEAU
RAMBLED
RAMBLER
RAMBLES
RAMEKIN
RAMESES
RAMJETS
RAMMING
RAMPAGE
RAMPANT
RAMPART
RAMRODS
RANAWAY
RANCHED
RANCHER
RANCHES
RANCHOS
RANCOUR
RANDALL
RANDIER
RANGERS
RANGIER
RANGING
RANGOON
RANINTO
RANKERS
RANKEST
RANKING
RANKLED
RANKLES
RANLATE
RANOVER
RANRIOT
RANSACK
RANSOMS
RANTERS
RANTING
RAPANUI
RAPHAEL
RAPIDER
RAPIDLY
RAPIERS
RAPINES
RAPPELS
RAPPERS
RAPPING
RAPPORT
RAPTORS
RAPTURE
RAREBIT
RAREGAS
RARITAN
RASCALS
RASHERS
RASHEST
RASPERS
RASPIER
RASPING
RASSLED
RASSLES
RASTERS
RATABLE
RATAFIA
RATATAT
RATCHET
RATFINK
RATHOLE
RATINGS
RATIONS
RATITES
RATLINE
RATPACK
RATRACE
RATTAIL
RATTANS
RATTERS
RATTIER
RATTING
RATTLED
RATTLER
RATTLES
RATTRAP
RAUCOUS
RAVAGED
RAVAGES
RAVELED
RAVENED
RAVENNA
RAVINES
RAVINGS
RAVIOLI
RAWDATA
RAWDEAL
RAWHIDE
RAWNESS
RAWSILK
RAYBURN
RAYGUNS
RAYKROC
RAYMOND
RAYOVAC
RAZORED
RAZZING

R•A••••
REACHED
REACHES
REACTED
REACTOR
REACTTO
READERS
READIED
READIER
READIES
READILY
READING
READMIT
READOUT
READSIN
REAFFIX
REAGENT
REAIRED
REALISM
REALIST
REALITY
REALIZE
REALTOR
REAMASS
REAMERS
REAMING
REAPERS
REAPING
REARDON
REAREND
REARERS
REARGUE
REARING
REARMED
REARSUP
REASONS
REAVAIL
ROACHED
ROACHES
ROADBED
ROADHOG
ROADIES
ROADMAP
ROADWAY
ROAMERS
ROAMING
ROANOKE
ROARERS
ROARING
ROASTED
ROASTER
RUANDAN
RWANDAN

R••A•••
RADAMES
RAMADAN
RAMADAS
RANAWAY
RAPANUI
RATABLE
RATAFIA
RATATAT
RAVAGED
RAVAGES
RDLAING
REBASTE
REBATED
REBATES
RECALLS
RECANED
RECANES
RECANTS
RECASTS
REDACTS
REDANTS
REDATED
REDATES
REFACED
REFACES
REGAINS
REGALED
REGALES
REGALIA
REGALLY
REGARDS
REGATTA
REHANGS
RELACED
RELACES
RELAPSE
RELATED
RELATES
RELAXED
RELAXES
RELAYED
REMAILS
REMAINS
REMAKES
REMANDS
REMARKS
REMARRY
RENAILS
RENAMED
RENAMES
RENAULT
REPAINT
REPAIRS
REPAPER
REPASTE
REPASTS
REPAVED
REPAVES
RERAISE
RERATED
RERATES
RESALES
RESALTS
RESANDS
RETAILS
RETAINS
RETAKEN
RETAKES
RETAPED
RETAPES
RETARDS
RETAXED
RETAXES
REVALUE
REVAMPS
REWARDS
REWARMS
REWAXED
REWAXES
RIBANDS
RICARDO
RIVALED
RIVALRY
ROBARDS
ROLAIDS
ROMAINE
ROMANCE
ROMANIA
ROMANOV
ROMANSH
ROSALIE
ROSANNA
ROSANNE
ROTATED
ROTATES
ROTATOR
ROXANNE
ROYALLY
ROYALTY
RUNAMOK
RUNAWAY

R•••A••
RADIALS
RADIANS
RADIANT
RADIATE
RAGLANS

RAMPAGE
RAMPANT
RAMPART
RANDALL
RANLATE
RANSACK
RAPHAEL
RASCALS
RATPACK
RATRACE
RATTAIL
RATTANS
RAWDATA
REAMASS
REAVAIL
RECHALK
RECLAIM
RECLAME
REDCAPS
REDEALS
REDEALT
REDHAIR
REDHATS
REDIALS
REDOAKS
REDRAWN
REDRAWS
REDTAPE
REENACT
REFRACT
REFRAIN
REFRAME
REGNANT
REGRADE
REHEALS
REHEARD
REHEARS
REHEATS
RELEARN
RELEASE
RELIANT
RELOADS
REMNANT
RENTALS
REPEALS
REPEATS
REPLACE
REPLANS
REPLANT
REPLATE
REPLAYS
REREADS
RESCALE
RESEALS
RESEATS
RESTAGE
RESTAIN
RESTAMP
RESTART
RESTATE
RETEACH
RETRACE
RETRACK
RETRACT
RETRADE
RETRAIN
REVEALS
REWEAVE
REWRAPS
REXCATS
REYNARD
RHUBARB
RIBCAGE
RICHARD
RIMBAUD
RIOTACT
RIPRAPS
RIPSAWS
RITUALS
ROLVAAG
ROSEATE
ROSTAND
ROULADE
RUDYARD
RUMBAED
RUMMAGE
RUNBACK
RUNLAPS
RUNWAYS
RUPIAHS

R••••A•

RACECAR
RACEWAY
RADICAL
RAILSAT
RAILWAY
RAINHAT
RAINMAN
RAMADAN
RAMADAS
RAMBEAU
RANAWAY
RAREGAS
RARITAN
RATATAT
RATTRAP
RAWDEAL
RAYOVAC
REBEKAH
RECITAL
RECLEAN
REDCOAT
REDFLAG
REDHEAD
REDHEAT
REDMEAT
REDSTAR
REFUSAL
REGULAR
REMORAS
REMOVAL
REMUDAS
RENEWAL
REPOMAN
RETINAE
RETINAL
RETINAS
RETREAD
RETREAT
RETRIAL
REVIVAL
RHUMBAS
RICERAT
RICHMAN
RIDGWAY
ROADMAP
ROADWAY
ROLLBAR
ROLVAAG
ROMULAN
RONDEAU
RORQUAL
ROWBOAT
ROYBEAN
RUANDAN
RUFFIAN
RUFIYAA
RUNAWAY
RUSSIAN
RWANDAN

R•••••A

RATAFIA
RAVENNA
RAWDATA
REBECCA
REGALIA
REGATTA
REPLICA
RETSINA
RICKSHA
RICOTTA
RIGVEDA
RIORITA
RIVIERA
ROBERTA
ROBUSTA
ROMANIA
ROSANNA
ROSETTA
ROSSSEA
ROTUNDA
RUFIYAA

•RA••••

ARABIAN
ARACHNE
ARALSEA
ARAMAIC
ARAMEAN
ARAPAHO
ARAWAKS
BRACERS
BRACEUP
BRACING
BRACKEN
BRACKET
BRADLEE
BRADLEY
BRAGGED
BRAGGER
BRAHMAN
BRAHMAS
BRAHMIN
BRAIDED
BRAIDER
BRAILLE
BRAINED
BRAISED
BRAISES
BRAKING
BRAMBLE
BRAMBLY
BRANDED
BRANDER
BRANDON
BRANIFF
BRANSON
BRASHER
BRASHLY
BRASSES
BRASSIE
BRAVADO
BRAVELY
BRAVERY
BRAVEST
BRAVING
BRAVOES
BRAVURA
BRAWLED
BRAWLER
BRAXTON
BRAYERS
BRAYING
BRAZIER
BRAZING
CRABBED
CRABBER
CRACKED
CRACKER
CRACKLE
CRACKUP
CRADLED
CRADLES
CRAFTED
CRAFTER
CRAFTSY
CRAMMED
CRAMMER
CRAMPED
CRAMPON
CRANIAL
CRANING
CRANIUM
CRANKED
CRANKUP
CRAPPIE
CRASHED
CRASHES
CRASSER
CRASSLY
CRASSUS
CRATERS
CRATING
CRAVATS
CRAVENS
CRAVERS
CRAVING
CRAWDAD
CRAWLED
CRAWLER
CRAYOLA
CRAYONS
CRAZIER
CRAZIES
CRAZILY
CRAZING
DRABBER
DRACHMA
DRACULA
DRAFTED
DRAFTEE
DRAGGED
DRAGNET
DRAGONS
DRAGOON
DRAGOUT
DRAGSIN
DRAGSON
DRAINED
DRAINER
DRAPERS
DRAPERY
DRAPING
DRASTIC
DRATTED
DRAUGHT
DRAWBAR
DRAWERS
DRAWING
DRAWLED
DRAWNIN
DRAWNON
DRAWNUP
DRAWOUT
DRAWSIN
DRAWSON
DRAWSUP
DRAYAGE
DRAYING
ERASERS
ERASING
ERASMUS
ERASURE
FRACTAL
FRAGILE
FRAICHE
FRAILER
FRAILTY
FRAISES
FRAMEUP
FRAMING
FRANCES
FRANCIS
FRANKED
FRANKER
FRANKIE
FRANKLY
FRANKOZ
FRANTIC
FRAPPES
FRASIER
FRAUGHT
FRAWLEY
FRAYING
FRAZIER
FRAZZLE
GRABBAG
GRABBED
GRABBER
GRABSAT
GRACIAS
GRACILE
GRACING
GRACKLE
GRADERS
GRADING
GRADUAL
GRAFTED
GRAHAME
GRAHAMS
GRAINED
GRAMMAR
GRAMMER
GRAMMES
GRAMPUS
GRANADA
GRANARY
GRANDAM
GRANDEE
GRANDER
GRANDLY
GRANDMA
GRANDPA
GRANGER
GRANGES
GRANITE
GRANOLA
GRANTED
GRANTEE
GRANTOR
GRANULE
GRAPHED
GRAPHIC
GRAPNEL
GRAPPLE
GRASPED
GRASSED
GRASSES
GRATERS
GRATIFY
GRATING
GRAVELS
GRAVELY
GRAVEST
GRAVIES
GRAVING
GRAVITY
GRAVURE
GRAYEST
GRAYING
GRAYSON
GRAZERS
GRAZING
IRANIAN
IRATELY
IRATEST
KRATERS
KRATION
ORACLES
ORANGES
ORATING
ORATION
ORATORS
ORATORY
PRAETOR
PRAIRIE
PRAISED
PRAISER
PRAISES
PRALINE
PRANCED
PRANCER
PRANCES
PRANKED
PRATERS
PRATING
PRATTLE
PRAYERS
PRAYFOR
PRAYING
PRAYSTO
TRABERT
TRACERS
TRACERY
TRACHEA
TRACING
TRACKED
TRACKER
TRACTOR
TRADEIN
TRADEON
TRADERS
TRADEUP
TRADING
TRADUCE
TRAFFIC
TRAGEDY
TRAILED
TRAILER
TRAINED
TRAINEE
TRAINER
TRAIPSE
TRAITOR
TRALALA
TRAMCAR
TRAMMEL
TRAMPAS
TRAMPED
TRAMPLE
TRANCES
TRANSIT
TRANSOM
TRAPEZE
TRAPPED
TRAPPER
TRASHED
TRASHES
TRAUBEL
TRAUMAS
TRAVAIL
TRAVELS
TRAVERS
TRAVOIS
TRAWLED
TRAWLER
TRAYFUL
URANITE
URANIUM
WRACKED
WRAITHS
WRANGLE
WRAPPED
WRAPPER
WRAPSUP
WRAPUPS
XRATING
XRAYING

•R•A•••

ARCADES
ARCADIA
AREARUG
AREAWAY
ARIADNE
ARMADAS
ARRAIGN
ARRANGE
ARRASES
ARRAYED
BREADED
BREADTH
BREAKER
BREAKIN
BREAKUP
BREASTS
BREATHE
BREATHS
BREATHY
BRIARDS
BROADAX
BROADEN
BROADER
BROADLY
CREAKED
CREAMED
CREAMER
CREASED
CREASES
CREATED
CREATES
CREATOR
CROAKED
CROATIA
DREADED
DREAMED
DREAMER
DREAMON
DREAMUP
ERRANDS
ERRATIC
ERRATUM
FREAKED
FRIABLE
GREASED
GREASER
GREASES
GREATER
GREATLY
GREAVES
GROANED
GROANER
MRMAGOO
ORDAINS
ORGANDY
ORGANIC
ORGANON
ORGANUM
ORGANZA
ORLANDO
ORMANDY
PREACHY
PREAMPS
TREACLE
TREACLY
TREADED
TREADER
TREADLE
TREASON
TREATED
TRUANCY
TRUANTS
URBANER
WREAKED
WREATHE
WREATHS

•R••A••

ARAMAIC
ARAPAHO
ARAWAKS
ARCHAIC
ARCLAMP
ARIKARA
ARMBAND
ARMYANT
ARREARS
ARTWARE
BRAVADO
BRIDALS
BRIGADE
BRIGAND
BRITAIN
BROCADE
BROGANS
BROMATE
CRAVATS
CRETANS
CRUSADE
CRUZADO
CRYBABY
DRAYAGE
DRYWALL
FRIDAYS
FRIGATE
FROMAGE
FROWARD
FRYPANS
GRAHAME
GRAHAMS
GRANADA
GRANARY
GRENADA
GRENADE
GRIMACE
IRELAND
IRONAGE
ORCHARD
ORDEALS
OREGANO
ORIGAMI
ORLEANS
ORPHANS
PRECAST
PREDATE
PREDAWN
PREFABS
PREFACE
PRELATE
PREPAID
PREPARE
PREPAYS
PRESAGE
PRESALE
PRETAPE
PREVAIL
PREWASH
PRIMACY
PRIMARY
PRIMATE
PRIVACY
PRIVATE
PROBATE
PROFANE
PROPANE
PRORATA
PRORATE
PROSAIC
TRALALA
TRAVAIL
TRENARY
TREPANS
TROCARS
TROJANS

•R•••A•

ARABIAN
ARAMEAN
ARCHWAY
AREAWAY
AREOLAE
AREOLAR
AREOLAS
ARISTAE
ARISTAS
ARMADAS
ARMLOAD
ARNICAS
AROUSAL
ARRIVAL
ARROBAS
ARSENAL
ARTISAN
BRAHMAN
BRAHMAS
BRENDAN
BRENNAN
BRIGHAM
BRILLAT
BROADAX
BROSNAN
CRANIAL
CRAWDAD
CREWMAN
CRIMEAN
CROWBAR
CRUCIAL
CRYSTAL
DRAWBAR
DRIPPAN
DRISTAN
DRIVEAT
FRACTAL
FREEMAN
FREEWAY
FREITAG
FRENEAU
FRETSAW
FRIEDAN
FRISIAN
FROGMAN
FRONTAL
FROWNAT
GRABBAG
GRABSAT
GRACIAS
GRADUAL
GRAMMAR
GRANDAM
GRECIAN
GRISHAM
IRANIAN
IRONMAN
MRCLEAN
ORBITAL
ORDINAL
ORPHEAN
ORTOLAN
PREHEAT
PRELOAD
PRESOAK
PROGRAM
PROPMAN
PROTEAN
TRAMCAR
TRAMPAS
TRAUMAS
TREERAT
TRIGRAM
TRISTAN
TRIVIAL
TROIKAS
TRUCIAL
TRUDEAU
URUGUAY

•R••••A

ARALSEA
ARCADIA
ARIETTA
ARIKARA
ARIZONA
ARMENIA
ARUGULA
BRAVURA
CRAYOLA
CREMONA
CROATIA
DRACHMA
DRACULA
ERITREA
EROTICA
FREESIA
GRANADA
GRANDMA
GRANDPA
GRANOLA
GRENADA
KRISHNA
ORGANZA
PRORATA
PRUSSIA
TRACHEA
TRALALA

••RA•••

ABRADED
ABRADES
ABRAHAM
AERATED
AERATES
AERATOR
AFRAMES
AGRAFFE
AMRADIO
ARRAIGN
ARRANGE
ARRASES
ARRAYED
AURALEE
AURALLY
BARANOF
BERATED
BERATES
BORATES
CARACAL
CARACAS
CARAFES
CARAMBA
CARAMEL
CARAMIA
CARAVAN
CARAVEL
CARAWAY
CBRADIO
CERAMIC
CORAZON
CURACAO
CURATES
CURATOR
DERAILS
DURABLE
DURABLY
DURANCE
DURANGO
DURANTE
EARACHE
ENRAGED
ENRAGES
ERRANDS
ERRATIC
ERRATUM
EURASIA
FARADAY
FARAWAY
FMRADIO
FORAGED
FORAGER
FORAGES
GARAGED
GARAGES
GERAINT
GERALDO
GIRAFFE
GIRASOL
GYRATED
GYRATES
GYRATOR
HERALDS
HIRABLE
HORATIO
HYRACES
HYRAXES
ISRAELI
KARACHI
KARAJAN
KARAKUL
KARAKUM
KARAOKE
KARASEA
KERATIN
LARAINE
LARAMIE
MARABOU
MARACAS
MARAUDS
MIRACLE
MIRADOR
MIRAGES
MIRAMAR
MIRAMAX
MIRANDA
MORAINE
MORALES
MORALLY
MORANIS
MORAVIA
OTRANTO
PARABLE
PARADED
PARADES
PARADOX
PARAGON
PARAPET
PARAPHS
PARASOL
PHRASAL
PHRASED
PHRASES
PIRAEUS
PIRANHA
PIRATED
PIRATES
PIRATIC
PYRAMID
PYRAMUS
RERAISE
RERATED
RERATES
SARACEN
SARALEE
SARANAC
SARAWAK
SARAZEN
SCRAGGY
SCRAPED
SCRAPER
SCRAPES
SCRAPPY
SCRATCH
SCRAWLS
SCRAWLY
SCRAWNY
SERAPES
SERAPHS
SERAPIS
SPRAINS
SPRAWLS
SPRAYED
SPRAYER
STRAFED
STRAFES
STRAINS
STRAITS
STRANDS
STRANGE
STRASSE
STRATUM
STRATUS
STRAUSS
STRAYED
TARANTO
TERAPHS
THRALLS
TIRADES
TYRANNY
TYRANTS
UKRAINE
UNRATED
UNRAVEL
UPRAISE
VERANDA
VIRAGOS

••R•A••

ABREAST
ACREAGE
AERIALS
AIRBAGS
AIRBALL
AIRBASE
AIRDAMS
AIRDATE
AIRFARE
AIRLANE
AIRMAIL
AIRMASS
AIRRAID
AIRSACS
AIRTAXI
AIRWAVE
AIRWAYS
ALREADY
ARREARS
AUREATE
BARBARA
BARBARY
BARGAIN
BARMAID
BARNARD
BARRACK
BARRAGE
BEREAVE
BERNARD
BURBANK
BUREAUS
BURLAPS
BUROAKS
BURSARS
BYROADS
CARCASS
CARFARE
CARPALS
CARTAGE
CARWASH
CEREALS
CERTAIN
CORDAGE
CORDATE
CORKAGE
CORRALS
CORSAGE
CORSAIR
CUREALL
CURRANT
CURTAIL
CURTAIN

DARKAGE
DORMANT
DORSALS
EARHART
EARMARK
FAREAST
FARRAGO
FERRARI
FERRARO
FERRATE
FIREANT
FIREARM
FORBADE
FOREARM
FORGAVE
FORMALS
FORMATS
FORSAKE
FORSALE
FORWARD
FURBALL
FURNACE
GARBAGE
GARLAND
GERMANE
GERMANS
GERMANY
HARVARD
HERBAGE
HERBALS
HERMANN
HURRAHS
INROADS
KIRMANS
KOREANS
LARIATS
MARGATE
MARGAUX
MARGAYS
MARIANA
MARMARA
MARSALA
MARYANN
MERMAID
MORDANT
MORGANA
MORGANS
MORTALS
MORTARS
MYRIADS
NARRATE
NARWALS
NIRVANA
NORMALS
NORMAND
NORMANS
PARFAIT
PARIAHS
PARLAYS
PARTAKE
PERCALE
PERHAPS
PERTAIN
PERVADE
PORTAGE
PORTALS
PURDAHS
REREADS
SARCASM
SCREAKS
SCREAMS
SERIALS
SERIATE
SERRATE
SERVALS
SERVANT
SORBATE
SPREADS
STREAKS
STREAKY
STREAMS
STRIATE
SURFACE
SURNAME
SURPASS
SYRIANS
TARBABY
TARMACS
TARSALS
TARTANS
TARTARE
TARTARS
TARZANA
TERNARY
TERNATE
TERRACE
TERRAIN
THREADS
THREADY
THREATS
THROATS
THROATY
TORNADO
TURBANS
UNREADY
UPROARS
VARIANT
VERBALS
VERDANT
WARFARE
WARGAME
WARPATH
WARRANT
YARDAGE
YARDARM
ZERMATT

••R••A•

ABRAHAM
ACROBAT
ADRENAL
AEROBAT
AFRICAN
AIRBOAT
AIRHEAD
AIRPLAY
ARRIVAL
ARROBAS
AURORAE
AURORAL
AURORAS
BARKSAT
BARSOAP
BERGMAN
BIRDMAN
BURGLAR
CARACAL
CARACAS
CARAVAN
CARAWAY
CARCOAT
CARINAS
CARLOAD
CARSEAT
CORDIAL
CORNEAL
CORNEAS
CORONAE
CORONAS
CURACAO
DARESAY
DARKMAN
EARFLAP
FARADAY
FARAWAY
FIREMAN
FORBEAR
FORDHAM
FOREMAN
FOREPAW
FORERAN
FORESAW
FORREAL
FORTRAN
FURSEAL
GORDIAN
GURKHAS
HARDHAT
HARDPAN
HARTMAN
JERBOAS
KARAJAN
KEROUAC
KORUNAS
LYRICAL
MARACAS
MARCEAU
MARINAS
MARITAL
MARKHAM
MARKKAA
MARSHAL
MARTIAL
MARTIAN
MARYKAY
MIRAMAR
MIRAMAX
NARWHAL
PARKWAY
PARTIAL
PARTWAY
PERLMAN
PERSIAN
PERUSAL
PHRASAL
PORTRAY
PURITAN
RAREGAS
RARITAN
RORQUAL
SARANAC
SARAWAK
SAROYAN
SERBIAN
SORORAL
SURCOAT
SURINAM
SURREAL
TERTIAL
THRUWAY
VIRGOAN
VIRTUAL
WIRETAP
WORKDAY
WORKMAN
YARDMAN
YEREVAN
ZAREBAS

••R•••A

AGRIPPA
AUREOLA
BARBARA
BARBUDA
BARETTA
BERETTA
BERMUDA
BIRETTA
BURKINA
CARAMBA
CARAMIA
CARIOCA
CARNERA
CEREBRA
CORDOBA
CORETTA
COROLLA
CORRIDA
CORSICA
ETRURIA
EURASIA
FORMICA
FORMOSA
FORMULA
FORTUNA
GORILLA
HERBTEA
KARASEA
LORETTA
MARIANA
MARIMBA
MARKKAA
MARKOVA
MARMARA
MARSALA
MARTINA
MIRANDA
MORAVIA
MORGANA
NIRVANA
NORIEGA
PARTITA
PERGOLA
PERSONA
PIRANHA
PORSENA
PORTOLA
SYRINGA
TARZANA
VERANDA
VERBENA

•••RA••

AFFRAYS
AIRRAID
ANORAKS
ASHRAMS
ATTRACT
AVERAGE
AYNRAND
BAHRAIN
BARRACK
BARRAGE
BETRAYS
CHARADE
CHORALE
CHORALS
CITRATE
COMRADE
CONRACK
CORRALS
COURAGE
COURANT
CUIRASS
CURRANT
CUTRATE
DEFRAUD
DEFRAYS
DEGRADE
DEPRAVE
DETRACT
DETRAIN
DIGRAPH
DIORAMA
EMBRACE
EMERALD
EMIRATE
ENGRAFT
ENGRAMS
ENGRAVE
ENTRAIN
ENTRANT
ENTRAPS
ENWRAPS
ESTRADA
ESTRAYS
EXTRACT
FARRAGO
FERRARI
FERRARO
FERRATE
GOURAMI
GUARANI
HATRACK
HAYRACK
HEBRAIC
HURRAHS
HYDRANT
HYDRATE
INGRAIN
INGRATE
ITERANT
ITERATE
LIBRARY
MACRAME
MALRAUX
MIGRANT
MIGRATE
MOORAGE
NARRATE
NITRATE
OFFRAMP
OPERAND
OPERATE
OUTRACE
OUTRAGE
OUTRANK
OVERACT
OVERAGE
OVERALL
OVERATE
OVERAWE
PEERAGE
PHARAOH
PLURALS
PRORATA
PRORATE
RATRACE
REDRAWN
REDRAWS
REFRACT
REFRAIN
REFRAME
REGRADE
RETRACE
RETRACK
RETRACT
RETRADE
RETRAIN
REWRAPS
RIPRAPS
SATRAPS
SCARABS
SERRATE
SOPRANO
SPIRALS
SPIRANT
STORAGE
SUCRASE
SUNRAYS
TAXRATE
TERRACE
TERRAIN
TETRADS
THERAPY
TIERACK
TITRATE
TOURACO
UMBRAGE
UNCRATE
UNDRAPE
UNDRAWN
UNTRAPS
UNWRAPS
UPBRAID
UPDRAFT
UPGRADE
VAGRANT
VIBRANT
VIBRATE
VIBRATO
WARRANT

•••R•A•

ABOREAL
ACCRUAL
ANDREAS
BEARCAT
BEARPAW
BOERWAR
CZARDAS
DIURNAL
DOORMAN
DOORMAT
DOORWAY
ENTREAT
ETERNAL
EXURBAN
FAIRWAY
FORREAL
GLORIAS
HADRIAN
HEARSAY
IBERIAN
JEERSAT
JOURDAN
JOURNAL
LEERSAT
LIPREAD
LOWROAD
MEGRYAN
MISREAD
NUTRIAS
OFFROAD
ONTRIAL
OVEREAT
OVERLAP
OVERLAY
OVERRAN
OVERSAW
PEERSAT
RETREAD
RETREAT
RETRIAL
SAURIAN
SHERMAN
SHERPAS
SIERRAS
SPARTAN
SPIREAS
SPORRAN
STAREAT
STARMAN
STARMAP
STERNAL
STYRIAN
SURREAL
SWOREAT
TEARGAS
TEARSAT
THEREAT
THERMAL
THOREAU
THURMAN
UMBRIAN
UXORIAL
WHEREAS
WHEREAT

•••R••A

ACEROLA
AMERICA
AMERIKA
CORRIDA
CZARINA
DIORAMA
EMERITA
ESTRADA
EXURBIA
FLORIDA
GEORGIA
INERTIA
KEDROVA
MADRONA
OCARINA
OVERSEA
PAPRIKA
PODRIDA
PRORATA
RIORITA
SABRINA
SUBROSA
THERESA
TSARINA
TZARINA

••••RA•

ADMIRAL
ALSORAN
AMSCRAY
ANAGRAM
ANGORAS
ASFARAS
ASHTRAY
AUGURAL
AURORAE
AURORAL
AURORAS
AUSTRAL
BETARAY
BUCKRAM
CAMERAS
CENTRAL
CHLORAL
COCHRAN
CONTRAS
DEBORAH
DIAGRAM
DISHRAG
EPIGRAM
FAYWRAY
FEDERAL
FEDORAS
FEMORAL
FLYTRAP
FORERAN
FORTRAN
GENERAL
HEGIRAS
HOFBRAU
HUMERAL
IMMORAL
KINGRAT
LATERAL
LATERAN
LIBERAL
LITERAL
MACGRAW
MANTRAP
MANTRAS
MAYORAL
MENORAH
MINERAL
MISTRAL
MITHRAS
MUBARAK
MUSKRAT
NATURAL
NEUTRAL
NUMERAL
OUTDRAW
OVERRAN
PACKRAT
PORTRAY
PROGRAM
RATTRAP
REMORAS
RICERAT
SAHARAN
SAMPRAS
SAMURAI
SCLERAS
SEAGRAM
SENORAS
SEVERAL
SHECRAB
SIERRAS
SNEERAT
SORORAL
SPORRAN
SWEARAT
TEATRAY
TEHERAN
TELERAN
TREERAT
TRIGRAM
TUNDRAS
UNSTRAP
VENTRAL
VETERAN
WASHRAG
WOLFRAM

••••R•A

ALBERTA
ALGERIA
ANDORRA
AQUARIA
ASSYRIA
ASTORIA
AUSTRIA
BAVARIA
BEGORRA
CIBORIA
DELIRIA
EMPORIA
ERITREA
ETRURIA
JAKARTA
LASORDA
LIBERIA
MAJORCA
MAZURKA
MINERVA
MINORCA
NIGERIA
ROBERTA
SAMARIA
SANGRIA
SCHIRRA
SIBERIA
SOLARIA
TALARIA

•••••RA

ALGEBRA
AMPHORA
ANDORRA
ARIKARA
BARBARA
BEGORRA
BOKHARA
BRAVURA
CAESURA
CALDERA
CARNERA
CASCARA
CEREBRA
CHIMERA
CULEBRA
DYKSTRA
ELECTRA
ELEKTRA
GAZZARA
GUEVARA
INTEGRA
ISADORA
LEMPIRA
LEONORA
MADEIRA
MARMARA
MASCARA
NIAGARA
OLESTRA
OXYMORA
PANDORA
PHAEDRA
PLECTRA
RIVIERA
SAMSARA
SCHIRRA
SINATRA
SPECTRA
SUMATRA
TANTARA
TEMPERA
TEMPURA
TESSERA
VENTURA
VISCERA
WOOMERA

R•B••••

RABBETS
RABBITS
RABBITT
RABBLES
REBASTE
REBATED
REBATES
REBECCA
REBEKAH
REBINDS
REBIRTH
REBLOOM
REBOILS
REBOLTS
REBOOTS
REBOUND
REBOZOS
REBUFFS
REBUILD
REBUILT
REBUKED
REBUKES
REBUSES
RIBANDS
RIBBING
RIBBONS
RIBCAGE
RIBEYES
ROBARDS
ROBBERS
ROBBERY
ROBBING
ROBBINS
ROBERTA
ROBERTO
ROBERTS
ROBESON
ROBLOWE
ROBOCOP
ROBOTIC
ROBROYS
ROBUSTA
RUBBERS
RUBBERY
RUBBING
RUBBISH
RUBBLES
RUBDOWN
RUBICON
RUBITIN
RUBRICS
RUBSOUT
RUBYDEE

R••B•••

RABBETS
RABBITS
RABBITT
RABBLES
RAMBEAU
RAMBLED
RAMBLER
RAMBLES
RAYBURN
REDBIRD
REDBOOK
REDBUDS
REUBENS
RHUBARB
RIBBING
RIBBONS
RIMBAUD
ROBBERS
ROBBERY
ROBBING
ROBBINS
ROEBUCK
ROWBOAT
ROYBEAN
RUBBERS
RUBBERY
RUBBING
RUBBISH
RUBBLES
RUMBAED
RUMBLED
RUMBLES
RUNBACK

R•••B••

RAINBOW
RAREBIT
RATABLE
RHOMBUS
RHUMBAS
RISIBLE
ROADBED
ROLLBAR
ROSEBUD

R••••B•

REDOUBT
RESORBS
REVERBS
RIOLOBO

R•••••B

RHUBARB

•RB••••

ARBITER
ARBORED
ARBOURS
ARBUTUS
MRBONES
ORBISON
ORBITAL
ORBITED
ORBITER
URBANER

•R•B•••

ARABIAN
ARMBAND
BRIBERY
BRIBING
BRUBECK
CRABBED
CRABBER
CRIBBED
CRYBABY
DRABBER
DRIBBLE
DRIBLET
DRUBBED
GRABBAG
GRABBED
GRABBER
GRABSAT
GRUBBED
PREBEND
PROBATE
PROBERS
PROBING
PROBITY
PROBLEM
PROBONO
TRABERT
TREBLED
TREBLES
TRIBUNE
TRIBUTE

•R••B••

ARROBAS
BRAMBLE
BRAMBLY
CRABBED
CRABBER
CRIBBED
CROWBAR
CRUMBLE
CRUMBLY
DRABBER
DRAWBAR
DRIBBLE
DRUBBED
FREEBEE
FREEBIE
FRIABLE
FRISBEE
GRABBAG
GRABBED
GRABBER
GRUBBED
GRUMBLE
TRAUBEL
TREMBLE
TREMBLY
TROUBLE

•R•••B•

CRYBABY
DROPSBY
PREFABS

•R••••B

PROVERB

••RB•••

AIRBAGS
AIRBALL
AIRBASE
AIRBOAT
BARBARA
BARBARY
BARBELL
BARBELS
BARBERS
BARBING
BARBUDA
BERBERS
BURBANK
BURBLED
BURBLES
BURBOTS
CARBIDE
CARBINE
CARBONS
CARBOYS
CORBELS
CORBETT
CURBCUT
CURBING
DERBIES
FORBADE
FORBEAR
FORBIDS
FORBORE
FURBALL
FURBISH
GARBAGE
GARBING
GARBLED
GARBLES
GERBILS
HARBORS
HARBOUR
HERBAGE
HERBALS
HERBERT
HERBTEA
JERBOAS
MARBLED
MARBLES
PARBOIL
SERBIAN
SORBATE
SORBETS
TARBABY
TARBELL
TERBIUM
TURBANS
TURBINE
TURBOTS
VERBALS
VERBENA
VERBOSE
WARBLED
WARBLER
WARBLES

••R•B••

ACROBAT
AEROBAT
AEROBES
AEROBIC
ARROBAS
CARIBES
CARIBOU
CEREBRA
DURABLE
DURABLY
ENROBED
ENROBES
FIREBOX
FIREBUG
HIRABLE
MARABOU
PARABLE
PARIBUS
RAREBIT
SCRIBES
SCRUBBY
SCRUBUP
SHRUBBY
STROBES
UNROBED
UNROBES
ZAREBAS

••R••B•

CARAMBA
CORDOBA
EARLOBE

HORNSBY
MARIMBA
MORESBY
SCRUBBY
SHRUBBY
TARBABY

••R•••B
CORNCOB
PERTURB

•••RB••
ACERBIC
BOURBON
EXURBAN
EXURBIA
GEARBOX
INORBIT
OVERBIG
OVERBUY
POORBOX
POORBOY
SHERBET
THURBER

•••R•B•
ASCRIBE
CHERUBS
DISROBE
LAPROBE
MICROBE
MIDRIBS
NAIROBI
SCARABS
SWOREBY
THEREBY
WHEREBY

•••R••B
OVERDUB

••••RB•
ABSORBS
ADSORBS
ADVERBS
RESORBS
REVERBS
SUBURBS
SWEARBY

••••R•B
BACKRUB
SHECRAB

•••••RB
DISTURB
PERTURB
POTHERB
PROVERB
RHUBARB

R•C••••
RACCOON
RACECAR
RACEMES
RACEWAY
RACIEST
RACKETS
RACKING
RACKSUP
RACQUET
RECALLS
RECANED
RECANES
RECANTS
RECASTS
RECEDED
RECEDES
RECEIPT
RECEIVE
RECENCY
RECHALK
RECHECK
RECHOSE
RECIPES
RECITAL
RECITED
RECITER
RECITES
RECKONS
RECLAIM
RECLAME
RECLEAN
RECLINE
RECLUSE
RECODED
RECODES
RECOILS
RECOLOR
RECORDS
RECORKS
RECOUNT
RECOUPS
RECOVER
RECROOM
RECROSS
RECRUIT
RECTIFY
RECTORS
RECTORY
RECUSED
RECUSES
RECYCLE
RICARDO
RICERAT
RICHARD
RICHEST
RICHMAN
RICHTER
RICKETY
RICKEYS
RICKLES
RICKSHA
RICOTTA
ROCKERS
ROCKETS
ROCKIER
ROCKIES
ROCKING
ROCKYII
ROCKYIV
RUCHING
RUCKING
RUCTION

R••C•••
RACCOON
RANCHED
RANCHER
RANCHES
RANCHOS
RANCOUR
RASCALS
RATCHET
RAUCOUS
REACHED
REACHES
REACTED
REACTOR
REACTTO
REDCAPS
REDCELL
REDCENT
REDCOAT
REOCCUR
RESCALE
RESCIND
RESCUED
RESCUER
RESCUES
REXCATS
RIBCAGE
RIPCORD
RITCHIE
ROACHED
ROACHES

R•••C••
RACECAR
RADICAL
RADICES
RADICLE
REBECCA
RECYCLE
REDACTS
REDUCED
REDUCER
REDUCES
REFACED
REFACES
REJECTS
RELACED
RELACES
RELICTS
RELOCKS
REOCCUR
RESECTS
RETICLE
ROBOCOP
RUBICON

R••••C•
RANSACK
RATPACK
RATRACE
REBECCA
RECENCY
RECHECK
REELECT
REENACT
REFLECT
REFRACT
REGENCY
REJOICE
REPLACE
REPLICA
REPRICE
RESPECT
RESTOCK
RETEACH
RETOUCH
RETRACE
RETRACK
RETRACT
REVOICE
RIDDICK
RIOTACT
ROEBUCK
ROLLICK
ROMANCE
RUBRICS
RUNBACK
RUSTICS

R•••••C
RAYKROC
RAYOVAC
ROBOTIC

•RC••••
ARCADES
ARCADIA
ARCHAIC
ARCHERS
ARCHERY
ARCHIES
ARCHING
ARCHIVE
ARCHONS
ARCHWAY
ARCLAMP
ARCSINE
MRCHIPS
MRCLEAN
ORCHARD
ORCHIDS
URCHINS

•R•C•••
ARACHNE
BRACERS
BRACEUP
BRACING
BRACKEN
BRACKET
BRICKED
BROCADE
CRACKED
CRACKER
CRACKLE
CRACKUP
CRECHES
CRICKED
CRICKET
CROCHET
CRUCIAL
DRACHMA
DRACULA
DRUCKER
DRYCELL
ERECTED
ERECTER
ERECTLY
ERECTOR
ERICSON
ERUCTED
FRACTAL
FRECKLE
FRICKIE
FROCKED
FRYCOOK
GRACIAS
GRACILE
GRACING
GRACKLE
GRECIAN
GROCERS
GROCERY
IRECKON
ORACLES
PRECAST
PRECEDE
PRECEPT
PRECISE
PRECOOK
PRECOOL
PRICERS
PRICIER
PRICING
PRICKED
PRICKLE
PRICKLY
PROCEED
PROCESS
PROCTOR
PROCURE
PROCYON
TRACERS
TRACERY
TRACHEA
TRACING
TRACKED
TRACKER
TRACTOR
TRICEPS
TRICKED
TRICKER
TRICKLE
TRICORN
TRICOTS
TROCARS
TROCHEE
TROCHES
TRUCIAL
TRUCKED
TRUCKEE
TRUCKER
TRUCKLE
WRACKED
WRECKED
WRECKER

•R••C••
ARNICAS
ARTICLE
BRIOCHE
BRONCHI
BRONCOS
CREWCUT
CRUNCHY
FRAICHE
FRANCES
FRANCIS
FRESCOS
GROUCHO
GROUCHY
PRANCED
PRANCER
PRANCES
PREACHY
PRINCES
TRAMCAR
TRANCES
TREACLE
TREACLY

•R•••C•
ARDENCY
ARMLOCK
ARTDECO
BRUBECK
CREVICE
CRITICS
DRSPOCK
DRYDOCK
EROTICA
FROLICS
GRIMACE
MRSPOCK
ORIFICE
ORINOCO
PREDICT
PREFACE
PREFECT
PRIMACY
PRIVACY
PRODUCE
PRODUCT
PROJECT
PROTECT
TRADUCE
TRISECT
TROPICS
TROUNCE
TRUANCY
URGENCY

•R••••C
ARAMAIC
ARCHAIC
ARSENIC
CRYPTIC
DRASTIC
ERISTIC
ERRATIC
FRANTIC
FREDRIC
GRAPHIC
ORGANIC
PROSAIC
TRAFFIC
TROPHIC

••RC•••
AIRCOOL
AIRCREW
BARCODE
BIRCHED
BIRCHES
CARCASS
CARCOAT
CIRCLED
CIRCLES
CIRCLET
CIRCUIT
CIRCUSY
FORCEPS
FORCERS
FORCING
GARCONS
HERCULE
KERCHOO
LARCENY
LARCHES
LURCHED
LURCHES
MARCEAU
MARCELS
MARCHED
MARCHEN
MARCHER
MARCHES
MARCHON
MARCONI
MERCIES
MERCURY
PARCELS
PARCHED
PARCHES
PERCALE
PERCENT
PERCHED
PERCHES
PORCHES
PORCINE
PURCELL
SARCASM
SORCERY
SURCOAT
TERCELS
TERCETS
TORCHED
TORCHES
ZIRCONS

••R•C••
AFRICAN
APRICOT
AURICLE
AUROCHS
BORSCHT
CARACAL
CARACAS
CORNCOB
CURACAO
CURBCUT
DIRECTS
EARACHE
HARICOT
HYRACES
JERICHO
KARACHI
LAROCHE
LYRICAL
MARACAS
MIRACLE
MOROCCO
PORSCHE
SARACEN
SIROCCO
SPRUCED
SPRUCER
SPRUCES
UTRECHT

••R••C•
AIRLOCK
AIRSACS
AIRSOCK
BARRACK
BERNICE
BURDOCK
CARIOCA
CARRICK
CORNICE
CORRECT
CORSICA
DERRICK
DORMICE
DURANCE
EARLOCK
EHRLICH
FORMICA
FURNACE
GARRICK
HEROICS
MOROCCO
MURDOCH
NORDICS
OARLOCK
PARSECS
PERFECT
PORTICO
SCRATCH
SCREECH
SCRUNCH
SERPICO
SERVICE
SIROCCO
STRETCH
SURFACE
TARMACS
TERENCE
TERRACE
VERDICT
WARLOCK
WARWICK

••R•••C
ACRYLIC
AEROBIC
CERAMIC
CHRONIC
ERRATIC
HERETIC
JURIDIC
KEROUAC
PHRENIC
PIRATIC
PYRRHIC
SARANAC

•••RC••
ALARCON
AMERCED
AMERCES
ANARCHY
APERCUS
BEARCAT
COERCED
COERCES
EPARCHS
FIERCER
HAIRCUT
PIERCED
PIERCES
SCARCER
SOURCED
SOURCES
STARCHY

•••R•C•
ALDRICH
AMERICA
ATTRACT
AVARICE
BARRACK
BEDROCK
CAPRICE
CARRICK
CLARICE
CLERICS
CONRACK
CORRECT
DEFROCK
DERRICK
DETRACT
ELGRECO
EMBRACE
EXTRACT
FABRICS
GARRICK
HATRACK
HAYRACK
KUBRICK
MAURICE
METRICS
OSTRICH
OUTRACE
OVERACT
PATRICE
PATRICK
PETROCK
RATRACE
REFRACT
REPRICE
RETRACE
RETRACK
RETRACT
RUBRICS
SECRECY
TERRACE
TIERACK
TOURACO
UNFROCK

•••R••C
ACERBIC
HEBRAIC
PYRRHIC

••••RC•
BYFORCE
DIVORCE
ENFORCE
INFORCE
LAMARCK
MAJORCA
MINORCA
MONARCH

••••R•C
AELFRIC
AMHARIC
BALDRIC
CALORIC
CAMBRIC
CENTRIC
FREDRIC
GASTRIC
GENERIC
HOMERIC
LAUTREC
MANTRIC
NUMERIC
RAYKROC
SATIRIC

RD•••••
RDLAING

R•D••••
RADAMES
RADDLED
RADDLES
RADIALS
RADIANS
RADIANT
RADIATE
RADICAL
RADICES
RADICLE
RADIOED
REDACTS
REDANTS
REDATED
REDATES
REDBIRD
REDBOOK
REDBUDS
REDCAPS
REDCELL
REDCENT
REDCOAT
REDDEER
REDDENS
REDDEST
REDDING
REDDISH
REDDOGS
REDEALS
REDEALT
REDEEMS
REDEYES
REDFINS
REDFIRS
REDFLAG
REDFORD
REDGUMS
REDHAIR
REDHATS
REDHEAD
REDHEAT
REDHOTS
REDIALS
REDLINE
REDMEAT
REDNESS
REDOAKS
REDOING
REDOUBT
REDOUND
REDPINE
REDPOLL
REDRAWN
REDRAWS
REDRESS
REDROSE
REDSKIN
REDSPOT
REDSTAR
REDTAPE
REDTOPS
REDUCED
REDUCER
REDUCES
REDWINE
REDWING
REDWOLF
REDWOOD
RIDDICK
RIDDING
RIDDLED
RIDDLER
RIDDLES
RIDEOFF
RIDEOUT
RIDGING
RIDGWAY
RODENTS
RODEOFF
RODEOUT
RODGERS
RODOLFO
RUDDERS
RUDDIER
RUDOLPH
RUDYARD

R••D•••
RADDLED
RADDLES
RAGDOLL
RAIDERS
RAIDING
RANDALL
RANDIER
RAWDATA
RAWDEAL
READERS
READIED
READIER
READIES
READILY
READING
READMIT
READOUT
READSIN
REDDEER
REDDENS
REDDEST
REDDING
REDDISH
REDDOGS
REEDIER
REEDING
REEDITS
RENDERS
RENDING
RHODIUM
RIDDICK
RIDDING
RIDDLED
RIDDLER
RIDDLES
ROADBED
ROADHOG
ROADIES
ROADMAP
ROADWAY
ROEDEER
RONDEAU
RONDELS
ROWDIER
ROWDIES
ROWDILY
RUBDOWN
RUDDERS
RUDDIER
RUNDEEP
RUNDOWN

R•••D••
RAKEDIN
RAKEDUP
RAMADAN
RAMADAS
RAPIDER
RAPIDLY
REARDON
RECEDED
RECEDES
RECODED
RECODES
REMODEL
REMUDAS
REORDER
REREDOS
RESIDED
RESIDES
RESIDUE
RIGIDLY
ROLODEX
ROPEDIN
ROUNDED
ROUNDER
ROUNDLY
ROUNDON
ROUNDUP
RUANDAN
RUBYDEE
RUNSDRY
RUSHDIE
RWANDAN

R••••D•
RAGGEDY
RAMRODS
RAWHIDE
REBINDS
RECORDS
REDBUDS
REFUNDS
REGARDS
REGRADE
RELOADS
REMANDS
REMENDS
REMINDS
REMOLDS
REREADS
RESANDS
RESEEDS
RESENDS
RETARDS
RETRADE
REWARDS
REWELDS
REWINDS
REWORDS
RIBANDS
RICARDO
RIGVEDA
RIPTIDE
ROBARDS
ROLAIDS
ROTUNDA
ROULADE

R•••••D
RADDLED
RADIOED
RAFFLED
RAGWEED
RALLIED
RAMBLED
RANCHED
RANKLED
RASSLED
RATTLED
RAVAGED
RAVELED
RAVENED
RAYMOND
RAZORED
REACHED
REACTED
READIED
REAIRED
REAREND
REARMED
REBATED
REBOUND
REBUILD
REBUKED
RECANED
RECEDED
RECITED
RECODED
RECUSED
REDATED
REDBIRD
REDFORD
REDHEAD
REDOUND
REDUCED
REDWOOD
REFACED
REFINED
REFRIED
REFUSED
REFUTED
REGALED
REGLUED
REHEARD
REHIRED
REIGNED
REINKED
REKEYED
RELACED
RELATED
RELAXED
RELAYED
RELINED
RELIVED
REMIXED
REMOVED
REMOWED
RENAMED
RENEGED
RENEWED
REOILED
REPAVED
REPINED
REPLIED
REPOSED
REPUTED
RERATED
RESCIND
RESCUED
RESIDED
RESILED
RESOLED
RESOUND
RESPOND
RESUMED
RETAPED
RETAXED
RETILED
RETIMED
RETIRED
RETOWED
RETREAD
RETRIED
RETUNED
RETYPED
REUPPED
REVELED
REVERED
REVILED
REVISED
REVIVED
REVOKED
REWAXED
REWIRED
REWOUND
REXREED
REYNARD

REZONED
RICHARD
RIDDLED
RIFFLED
RIGHTED
RIMBAUD
RIPCORD
RIPENED
RIPPLED
RIVALED
RIVETED
ROACHED
ROADBED
ROASTED
ROOSTED
ROSEBUD
ROSERED
ROSTAND
ROTATED
ROUGHED
ROUNDED
ROUSTED
RUDYARD
RUFFLED
RUMBAED
RUMBLED
RUMORED
RUMPLED
RUSTLED

•RD••••

ARDENCY
ARDMORE
ARDOURS
ARDUOUS
ORDAINS
ORDEALS
ORDERED
ORDERER
ORDERLY
ORDINAL

•R•D•••

ARIDEST
ARIDITY
ARTDECO
BRADLEE
BRADLEY
BRIDALS
BRIDGED
BRIDGES
BRIDGET
BRIDLED
BRIDLES
CRADLED
CRADLES
CREDITS
CRUDELY
CRUDEST
CRUDITY
DREDGED
DREDGER
DREDGES
DRUDGED
DRUDGES
DRYDOCK
ERODING
ERUDITE
FREDDIE
FREDRIC
FRIDAYS
FRIDGES
GRADERS
GRADING
GRADUAL
GRIDDED
GRIDDER
GRIDDLE
GRUDGED
GRUDGES
IRIDIUM
PREDATE
PREDAWN
PREDICT
PRIDING
PRODDED
PRODDER
PRODIGY
PRODUCE
PRODUCT
PRUDENT
PRUDERY
PRUDHOE
PRUDISH
TRADEIN
TRADEON
TRADERS
TRADEUP
TRADING
TRADUCE
TRIDENT
TRODDEN
TRUDEAU
TRUDGED
TRUDGER
TRUDGES

•R••D••

ARCADES
ARCADIA
ARIADNE
ARLEDGE
ARMADAS
BRAIDED
BRAIDER
BRANDED
BRANDER
BRANDON
BREADED
BREADTH
BREEDER
BRENDAN
BRINDLE
BROADAX
BROADEN
BROADER
BROADLY
BROODED
BROODER
CRAWDAD
CROWDED
DREADED
DREIDEL
DRESDEN
DRIEDUP
DRIPDRY
FREDDIE
FREEDOM
FRIEDAN
GRANDAM
GRANDEE
GRANDER
GRANDLY
GRANDMA
GRANDPA
GRENDEL
GRIDDED
GRIDDER
GRIDDLE
GRINDER
PRODDED
PRODDER
PROUDER
PROUDLY
TREADED
TREADER
TREADLE
TRENDED
TRIEDON
TRIODES
TRODDEN
TRUNDLE

•R•••D•

BRAVADO
BRIARDS
BRIGADE
BROCADE
BROMIDE
CRUSADE
CRUZADO
ERRANDS
FRIENDS
GRANADA
GRENADA
GRENADE
GROUNDS
ORCHIDS
ORGANDY
ORLANDO
ORMANDY
PRECEDE
PRELUDE
PREMEDS
PRESIDE
PROSODY
PROVIDE
TRAGEDY
TRIPODS

•R••••D

ARBORED
ARMBAND
ARMLOAD
ARMORED
AROUSED
ARRAYED
ARRIVED
BRAGGED
BRAIDED
BRAINED
BRAISED
BRANDED
BRAWLED
BREADED
BREEZED
BRICKED
BRIDGED
BRIDLED
BRIEFED
BRIGAND
BRIMMED
BROILED
BRONZED
BROODED
BROOKED
BROWNED
BROWSED
BRUISED
BRUITED
BRUSHED
CRABBED
CRACKED
CRADLED
CRAFTED
CRAMMED
CRAMPED
CRANKED
CRASHED
CRAWDAD
CRAWLED
CREAKED
CREAMED
CREASED
CREATED
CREEPED
CRESTED
CRIBBED
CRICKED
CRIMPED
CRINGED
CRINOID
CRISPED
CROAKED
CROOKED
CROONED
CROPPED
CROSSED
CROWDED
CROWNED
CRUISED
CRUSHED
CRUSTED
DRAFTED
DRAGGED
DRAINED
DRATTED
DRAWLED
DREADED
DREAMED
DREDGED
DRESSED
DRIFTED
DRILLED
DRIPPED
DROOLED
DROOPED
DROPPED
DROWNED
DROWSED
DRUBBED
DRUDGED
DRUGGED
DRUMMED
DRYEYED
ERECTED
ERUCTED
ERUPTED
FRANKED
FREAKED
FRETTED
FRILLED
FRINGED
FRISKED
FRITTED
FRIZZED
FROCKED
FRONTED
FROSTED
FROTHED
FROWARD
FROWNED
FRUITED
GRABBED
GRAFTED
GRAINED
GRANTED
GRAPHED
GRASPED
GRASSED
GREASED
GREENED
GREETED
GRIDDED
GRIEVED
GRILLED
GRINNED
GRIPPED
GRITTED
GROANED
GROOMED
GROOVED
GROSSED
GROUPED
GROUSED
GROUTED
GROWLED
GRUBBED
GRUDGED
GRUMPED
GRUNTED
IRELAND
ORBITED
ORCHARD
ORDERED
OROTUND
PRAISED
PRANCED
PRANKED
PREBEND
PREENED
PRELOAD
PREPAID
PRESSED
PRETEND
PRICKED
PRIMPED
PRINKED
PRINTED
PROCEED
PRODDED
PRONGED
PROOFED
PROPPED
PROWLED
TRACKED
TRAILED
TRAINED
TRAMPED
TRAPPED
TRASHED
TRAWLED
TREADED
TREATED
TREBLED
TREKKED
TRENDED
TRICKED
TRIFLED
TRIGGED
TRILLED
TRIMMED
TRIPLED
TRIPPED
TROLLED
TROOPED
TROTHED
TROTTED
TRUCKED
TRUDGED
TRUMPED
TRUSSED
TRUSTED
TRYSTED
WRACKED
WRAPPED
WREAKED
WRECKED
WRESTED
WRITHED
WRONGED

••RD•••

AIRDAMS
AIRDATE
AIRDROP
BIRDDOG
BIRDERS
BIRDIED
BIRDIES
BIRDING
BIRDMAN
BIRDMEN
BORDERS
BURDENS
BURDOCK
CARDERS
CARDING
CARDOZO
CORDAGE
CORDATE
CORDELL
CORDERO
CORDIAL
CORDING
CORDITE
CORDOBA
CORDONS
CURDING
CURDLED
CURDLES
EARDROP
EARDRUM
FORDHAM
FORDING
GARDENS
GARDNER
GIRDERS
GIRDING
GIRDLED
GIRDLES
GORDIAN
HARDENS
HARDEST
HARDHAT
HARDHIT
HARDIER
HARDILY
HARDING
HARDPAN
HARDPUT
HARDSET
HARDTOP
HARDWON
HERDERS
HERDING
HURDLED
HURDLER
HURDLES
KURDISH
LARDERS
LARDING
LARDNER
LARDONS
LORDING
LORDJIM
MORDANT
MORDENT
MORDRED
MURDERS
MURDOCH
NORDICS
PARDNER
PARDONS
PERDIEM
PURDAHS
SARDINE
TARDIER
TARDILY
VERDANT
VERDICT
VERDUGO
VERDURE
WARDENS
WARDERS
WARDING
WARDOFF
WORDIER
WORDILY
WORDING
WORDONE
YARDAGE
YARDARM
YARDMAN
YARDMEN

••R•D••

ABRADED
ABRADES
ABRIDGE
ACRIDLY
AMRADIO
BIRDDOG
BOREDOM
BORODIN
CBRADIO
CORNDOG
DERIDED
DERIDES
DIRNDLS
EARLDOM
FARADAY
FIREDOG
FIREDUP
FMRADIO
JURIDIC
LURIDLY
MIRADOR
PARADED
PARADES
PARADOX
PERIDOT
REREDOS
SERFDOM
STRIDER
STRIDES
STRUDEL
TEREDOS
TIRADES
TIREDER
TIREDLY
TIREDOF
WORKDAY
WORLDLY

••R••D•

ALREADY
BARBUDA
BARCODE
BERMUDA
BYROADS
CARBIDE
CORRIDA
CORRODE
ERRANDS
FORBADE
FORBIDS
GERALDO
GERUNDS
GIRONDE
HERALDS
INROADS
MARAUDS
MIRANDA
MYRIADS
NEREIDS
PERFIDY
PERIODS
PERVADE
REREADS
SCREEDS
SHROUDS
SPREADS
STRANDS
THREADS
THREADY
TORNADO
TOROIDS
TORPEDO
UNREADY
VERANDA
WARGODS

••R•••D

ABRADED
AERATED
AGROUND
AIRHEAD
AIRRAID
APRONED
ARRAYED
ARRIVED
BARMAID
BARNARD
BARTEND
BERATED
BERNARD
BERRIED
BERTHED
BIRCHED
BIRDIED
BIRTHED
BURBLED
BURGLED
CARLOAD
CAROLED
CAROMED
CAROTID
CARRIED
CIRCLED
CORNFED
CURDLED
CURRIED
DERIDED
DERIVED
DIRTIED
ENRAGED
ENROBED
FERRIED
FORAGED
FORFEND
FORGOOD
FORWARD
GARAGED
GARBLED
GARGLED
GARLAND
GIRDLED
GOROUND
GURGLED
GYRATED
HARRIED
HARVARD
HURDLED
HURRIED
HURTLED
LURCHED
MARBLED
MARCHED
MARRIED
MERITED
MERMAID
MORDRED
MORPHED
NORMAND
PARADED
PARCHED
PAROLED
PARRIED
PARTIED
PERCHED
PERUSED
PHRASED
PIRATED
PORTEND
PURFLED
PURPLED
PURSUED
PYRAMID
RERATED
SCRAPED
SCREWED
SERRIED
SORTIED
SPRAYED
SPRUCED
STRAFED
STRAYED
STREWED
STRIPED
STRIVED
STROKED
TARRIED
THRIVED
TORCHED
TURTLED
UNRATED
UNROBED
WARBLED
WARLORD
WORRIED
WORSTED

•••RD••

AWARDED
AWARDEE
AWARDER
BEARDED
BOARDED
BOARDER
CZARDAS
CZARDOM
DOORDIE
GOURDES
GUARDED
HAIRDOS
HAIRDYE
HEARDOF
HOARDED
HOARDER
JOURDAN
LOURDES
ONORDER
OVERDID
OVERDUB
OVERDUE
REARDON
REORDER
STARDOM
THIRDLY
TOORDER
WEIRDER
WEIRDLY
WEIRDOS

•••R•D•

ACARIDS
ALFREDO
ASTRIDE
CHARADE
COMRADE
CORRIDA
CORRODE
DEGRADE
ESTRADA
EXTRUDE
FLORIDA
FLYRODS
HAYRIDE
HOTRODS
HYBRIDS
INTRUDE
JOYRIDE
NIMRODS
NITRIDE
OBTRUDE
PODRIDA
RAMRODS
REGRADE
RETRADE
TETRADS
TIERODS
UPGRADE

•••R••D

ABORTED
ACCRUED
ADORNED
AIRRAID
ALARMED
ALERTED
AMERCED
AMERIND
ANDROID
ANEROID
AVERRED
AVERTED
AWARDED
AYKROYD
AYNRAND
BEARDED
BERRIED
BLURRED
BLURTED
BOARDED
CARRIED
CHARGED
CHARMED
CHARRED
CHARTED
CHIRPED
CHURNED
CLERKED
COERCED
CONREID
COURSED
COURTED
CURRIED
DECREED
DECRIED
DEFRAUD
DWARFED
EMERALD
EMERGED
EMERSED
EVERTED
EXERTED
FERRIED
FLIRTED
GLORIED
GNARLED
GNARRED
GUARDED
HARRIED
HENREID
HOARDED
HURRIED
IMBRUED
INBREED
KNURLED
LEARNED
LIPREAD
LOUREED
LOWROAD
MARRIED
MISREAD
OFFROAD
OPERAND
OVERDID
PARRIED
PEARLED
PIERCED
QUERIED
REAREND
REARMED
REFRIED
RETREAD
RETRIED
REXREED
SCARFED
SCARPED
SCARRED
SCORNED
SERRIED
SHARPED
SHIRKED
SHIRRED
SHORTED
SKIRLED
SKIRRED
SKIRTED
SLURPED
SLURRED
SMARTED
SMIRKED
SNARLED
SNORTED
SOURCED
SPARGED
SPARKED
SPARRED
SPORTED
SPURNED
SPURRED
SPURTED
STARRED
STARTED
STARVED
STEROID
STIRRED
STORIED
STORMED
SWARMED
SWERVED
SWIRLED
TARRIED
TWIRLED
UNARMED
UNTRIED
UPBRAID
USURPED
WEARIED
WHARFED
WHIRLED
WHIRRED
WHORLED
WORRIED
YEAREND
YEARNED

••••RD•

ACCORDS
AFFORDS
BACARDI
BRIARDS
BYWORDS
CANARDS
COWARDS
EDWARDS
ENGARDE
ENGIRDS
HAZARDS
HOWARDS
IDCARDS
INNARDS
INWARDS
LASORDA
LIZARDS
MILORDS
ONWARDS
OXFORDS
PETARDS
RECORDS
REGARDS
RETARDS
REWARDS
REWORDS
RICARDO
ROBARDS
TABARDS
TOWARDS
UNGIRDS
UPWARDS
WIZARDS

••••R•D

ABJURED
ADHERED
ADJURED
ADMIRED
ALLURED
ALTERED
ANGERED
ARBORED
ARMORED
ASPIRED
ASSURED
ATTIRED
AUGURED
AVERRED
BEMIRED
BLEARED
BLURRED
BOWERED
CAPERED
CATERED
CENTRED
CHAIRED
CHARRED
CHEERED
CLEARED
COHERED
COLORED
COVERED
COWERED
DESIRED
ENDURED
ENSURED
ENTERED
EUCHRED
EXPIRED
FAVORED
FIGURED
FLOORED
FLOURED
FUELROD
GNARRED
HOMERED
HONORED
HOVERED
HUMORED
HUNDRED
IGNORED
ILLBRED
IMMURED
INHERED
INJURED
INSURED
KINDRED
LABORED
LAYERED
LEVERED
LOWBRED
LOWERED
LUSTRED
MAITRED
MAJORED
MANFRED
MATURED
METERED
MILDRED
MINORED
MITERED
MORDRED
MOTORED
NATURED
OFFERED
ORDERED

PAPERED
PETERED
POWERED
QUEERED
RAZORED
REAIRED
REHIRED
RETIRED
REVERED
REWIRED
ROSERED
RUMORED
SAVORED
SCARRED
SCOURED
SECURED
SEESRED
SEVERED
SHEARED
SHEERED
SHIRRED
SKIRRED
SLURRED
SMEARED
SNEERED
SOBERED
SPARRED
SPEARED
SPURRED
SQUARED
SQUIRED
STARRED
STEERED
STIRRED
SUGARED
SUTURED
TAPERED
TENURED
TOWERED
TUTORED
UMPIRED
UNAIRED
USHERED
UTTERED
WAGERED
WATERED
WAVERED
WHIRRED
WILFRID
WINERED

•••••RD

ABELARD
ASHFORD
AWKWARD
BALLARD
BARNARD
BERNARD
BIGBIRD
BOMBARD
BUSTARD
BUZZARD
CATBIRD
COLLARD
CONCORD
COWBIRD
COWHERD
CUECARD
CUSTARD
DASTARD
DIEHARD
DILLARD
DISCARD
DISCORD
DULLARD
EDOUARD
FORWARD
FOULARD
FROWARD
GAYLORD
GIFFORD
GIZZARD
GODDARD
HAGGARD
HALYARD
HARVARD
HAYWARD
HUBBARD
INAWORD
INBOARD
JAYBIRD
KEYCARD
KEYWORD
LAGGARD
LANFORD
LANYARD
LAWFORD
LEEWARD
LEONARD
LEOPARD
LEOTARD
LOMBARD
MALLARD
MANSARD
MAYNARD
MILLARD
MISWORD
MITFORD
MUMFORD
MUSTARD
NIGGARD
ONBOARD
ONGUARD
ORCHARD
OUTWARD
PACKARD
PEPPARD
PICCARD
PLACARD
PONIARD
REDBIRD
REDFORD
REHEARD
REYNARD
RICHARD
RIPCORD
RUDYARD
SANFORD
SEABIRD
SEAWARD
SHEPARD
SKYWARD
STEWARD
TANKARD
UNHEARD
WARLORD
WAYWARD
WILFORD
WILLARD
WOODARD

RE•••••

REACHED
REACHES
REACTED
REACTOR
REACTTO
READERS
READIED
READIER
READIES
READILY
READING
READMIT
READOUT
READSIN
REAFFIX
REAGENT
REAIRED
REALISM
REALIST
REALITY
REALIZE
REALTOR
REAMASS
REAMERS
REAMING
REAPERS
REAPING
REARDON
REAREND
REARERS
REARGUE
REARING
REARMED
REARSUP
REASONS
REAVAIL
REBASTE
REBATED
REBATES
REBECCA
REBEKAH
REBINDS
REBIRTH
REBLOOM
REBOILS
REBOLTS
REBOOTS
REBOUND
REBOZOS
REBUFFS
REBUILD
REBUILT
REBUKED
REBUKES
REBUSES
RECALLS
RECANED
RECANES
RECANTS
RECASTS
RECEDED
RECEDES
RECEIPT
RECEIVE
RECENCY
RECHALK
RECHECK
RECHOSE
RECIPES
RECITAL
RECITED
RECITER
RECITES
RECKONS
RECLAIM
RECLAME
RECLEAN
RECLINE
RECLUSE
RECODED
RECODES
RECOILS
RECOLOR
RECORDS
RECORKS
RECOUNT
RECOUPS
RECOVER
RECROOM
RECROSS
RECRUIT
RECTIFY
RECTORS
RECTORY
RECUSED
RECUSES
RECYCLE
REDACTS
REDANTS
REDATED
REDATES
REDBIRD
REDBOOK
REDBUDS
REDCAPS
REDCELL
REDCENT
REDCOAT
REDDEER
REDDENS
REDDEST
REDDING
REDDISH
REDDOGS
REDEALS
REDEALT
REDEEMS
REDEYES
REDFINS
REDFIRS
REDFLAG
REDFORD
REDGUMS
REDHAIR
REDHATS
REDHEAD
REDHEAT
REDHOTS
REDIALS
REDLINE
REDMEAT
REDNESS
REDOAKS
REDOING
REDOUBT
REDOUND
REDPINE
REDPOLL
REDRAWN
REDRAWS
REDRESS
REDROSE
REDSKIN
REDSPOT
REDSTAR
REDTAPE
REDTOPS
REDUCED
REDUCER
REDUCES
REDWINE
REDWING
REDWOLF
REDWOOD
REEDIER
REEDING
REEDITS
REEFERS
REEFING
REEKING
REELECT
REELING
REELOFF
REELSIN
REENACT
REENTER
REENTRY
REFACED
REFACES
REFEREE
REFERTO
REFFING
REFILLS
REFILMS
REFINED
REFINER
REFINES
REFIRES
REFLECT
REFORMS
REFRACT
REFRAIN
REFRAME
REFRESH
REFRIED
REFRIES
REFUELS
REFUGEE
REFUGES
REFUNDS
REFUSAL
REFUSED
REFUSER
REFUSES
REFUTED
REFUTER
REFUTES
REGAINS
REGALED
REGALES
REGALIA
REGALLY
REGARDS
REGATTA
REGENCY
REGENTS
REGIMEN
REGIMES
REGIONS
REGLUED
REGLUES
REGNANT
REGRADE
REGRESS
REGRETS
REGROUP
REGULAR
REGULUS
REHANGS
REHEALS
REHEARD
REHEARS
REHEATS
REHEELS
REHIRED
REHIRES
REHOOKS
REIGNED
REINING
REINKED
REINSIN
REISSUE
REJECTS
REJOICE
REJOINS
REKEYED
RELACED
RELACES
RELAPSE
RELATED
RELATES
RELAXED
RELAXES
RELAYED
RELEARN
RELEASE
RELENTS
RELIANT
RELICTS
RELIEFS
RELIEVE
RELIEVO
RELIGHT
RELINED
RELINES
RELISTS
RELIVED
RELIVES
RELLENO
RELOADS
RELOCKS
RELYING
REMAILS
REMAINS
REMAKES
REMANDS
REMARKS
REMARRY
REMELTS
REMENDS
REMINDS
REMIXED
REMIXES
REMNANT
REMODEL
REMOLDS
REMORAS
REMORSE
REMOTER
REMOTES
REMOUNT
REMOVAL
REMOVED
REMOVER
REMOVES
REMOWED
REMUDAS
RENAILS
RENAMED
RENAMES
RENAULT
RENDERS
RENDING
RENEGED
RENEGER
RENEGES
RENEWAL
RENEWED
RENEWER
RENNINS
RENOTES
RENTALS
RENTERS
RENTING
REOCCUR
REOILED
REOPENS
REORDER
REPAINT
REPAIRS
REPAPER
REPASTE
REPASTS
REPAVED
REPAVES
REPEALS
REPEATS
REPENTS
REPINED
REPINES
REPLACE
REPLANS
REPLANT
REPLATE
REPLAYS
REPLETE
REPLICA
REPLIED
REPLIES
REPOLLS
REPOMAN
REPORTS
REPOSED
REPOSES
REPRESS
REPRICE
REPRINT
REPRISE
REPROOF
REPROVE
REPTILE
REPUGNS
REPULSE
REPUTED
REPUTES
REQUEST
REQUIEM
REQUIRE
REQUITE
RERAISE
RERATED
RERATES
REREADS
REREDOS
RERENTS
RERINSE
REROUTE
RESALES
RESALTS
RESANDS
RESCALE
RESCIND
RESCUED
RESCUER
RESCUES
RESEALS
RESEATS
RESECTS
RESEEDS
RESELLS
RESENDS
RESENTS
RESERVE
RESHIPS
RESHOES
RESHOOT
RESIDED
RESIDES
RESIDUE
RESIGNS
RESILED
RESILES
RESINGS
RESISTS
RESOLED
RESOLES
RESOLVE
RESORBS
RESORTS
RESOUND
RESPECT
RESPIRE
RESPITE
RESPOND
RESTAGE
RESTAIN
RESTAMP
RESTART
RESTATE
RESTERS
RESTFUL
RESTING
RESTIVE
RESTOCK
RESTORE
RESTSUP
RESTYLE
RESULTS
RESUMED
RESUMES
RESURGE
RETAILS
RETAINS
RETAKEN
RETAKES
RETAPED
RETAPES
RETARDS
RETAXED
RETAXES
RETEACH
RETELLS
RETESTS
RETHINK
RETICLE
RETILED
RETILES
RETIMED
RETIMES
RETINAE
RETINAL
RETINAS
RETINUE
RETIRED
RETIREE
RETIRES
RETITLE
RETOOLS
RETORTS
RETOUCH
RETOWED
RETRACE
RETRACK
RETRACT
RETRADE
RETRAIN
RETREAD
RETREAT
RETRIAL
RETRIED
RETRIES
RETRIMS
RETSINA
RETUNED
RETUNES
RETURNS
RETYPED
RETYPES
REUBENS
REUNIFY
REUNION
REUNITE
REUPPED
REUTERS
REUTHER
REVALUE
REVAMPS
REVEALS
REVELED
REVELER
REVELRY
REVENGE
REVENUE
REVERBS
REVERED
REVERES
REVERIE
REVERSE
REVERTS
REVIEWS
REVILED
REVILES
REVISED
REVISER
REVISES
REVISIT
REVIVAL
REVIVED
REVIVES
REVOICE
REVOKED
REVOKES
REVOLTS
REVOLVE
REVVING
REWARDS
REWARMS
REWAXED
REWAXES
REWEAVE
REWELDS
REWINDS
REWIRED
REWIRES
REWORDS
REWORKS
REWOUND
REWOVEN
REWRAPS
REWRITE
REWROTE
REXCATS
REXREED
REYNARD
REZONED
REZONES

R•E••••

REEDIER
REEDING
REEDITS
REEFERS
REEFING
REEKING
REELECT
REELING
REELOFF
REELSIN
REENACT
REENTER
REENTRY
RHENIUM
RHETORS
ROEBUCK
ROEDEER

R••E•••

RACECAR
RACEMES
RACEWAY
RAKEDIN
RAKEDUP
RAKEOFF
RAKESIN
RAKESUP
RALEIGH
RAMEKIN
RAMESES
RAREBIT
RAREGAS
RAVELED
RAVENED
RAVENNA
REBECCA
REBEKAH
RECEDED
RECEDES
RECEIPT
RECEIVE
RECENCY
REDEALS
REDEALT
REDEEMS
REDEYES
REFEREE
REFERTO
REGENCY
REGENTS
REHEALS
REHEARD
REHEARS
REHEATS
REHEELS
REJECTS
REKEYED
RELEARN
RELEASE
RELENTS
REMELTS
REMENDS
RENEGED
RENEGER
RENEGES
RENEWAL
RENEWED
RENEWER
REPEALS
REPEATS
REPENTS
REREADS
REREDOS
RERENTS
RESEALS
RESEATS
RESECTS
RESEEDS
RESELLS
RESENDS
RESENTS
RESERVE
RETEACH
RETELLS
RETESTS
REVEALS
REVELED
REVELER
REVELRY
REVENGE
REVENUE
REVERBS
REVERED
REVERES
REVERIE
REVERSE
REVERTS
REWEAVE
REWELDS
RIBEYES
RICERAT
RIDEOFF
RIDEOUT
RIPENED
RIVETED
RIVETER
ROBERTA
ROBERTO
ROBERTS
ROBESON
RODENTS
RODEOFF
RODEOUT
ROPEDIN
ROPESIN
ROPETOW
ROSEATE
ROSEBUD
ROSELLE
ROSEOIL
ROSERED
ROSETTA
ROSETTE
ROZELLE
RULEOUT
RULESON

R•••E••

RABBETS
RACIEST
RACKETS
RAFTERS
RAGGEDY
RAGWEED
RAIDERS
RAILERS
RAIMENT
RAISERS
RAISEUP
RAMBEAU
RAMJETS
RANGERS
RANKERS
RANKEST
RANTERS
RAPIERS
RAPPELS
RAPPERS
RASHERS
RASHEST
RASPERS
RASTERS
RATTERS
RAWDEAL
RAWNESS
READERS
REAGENT
REAMERS
REAPERS
REAREND
REARERS
RECHECK
RECLEAN
REDCELL
REDCENT
REDDEER
REDDENS
REDDEST
REDEEMS
REDHEAD
REDHEAT
REDMEAT
REDNESS
REDRESS
REEFERS
REELECT
REFLECT
REFRESH
REFUELS
REGRESS
REGRETS
REHEELS
RELIEFS
RELIEVE
RELIEVO
RELLENO
RENDERS
RENTERS
REOPENS
REPLETE
REPRESS
REQUEST
RESEEDS
RESPECT
RESTERS
RETREAD
RETREAT
REUBENS
REUTERS
REVIEWS
REXREED
RHYMERS
RICHEST
RICKETY
RICKEYS
RIFLERS
RIFLERY
RIGGERS
RIGVEDA
RILLETS
RINGERS
RIOTERS
RIPPERS
RISKERS
RIVIERA
RIVIERE
ROAMERS
ROARERS
ROBBERS
ROBBERY
ROCKERS
ROCKETS
RODGERS
ROEDEER
ROGUERY
ROLLERS
ROMNEYS
ROMPERS
RONDEAU
RONDELS
ROOFERS
ROOKERY
ROOMERS
ROOTERS
ROSTERS
ROSWELL
ROTTERS
ROUTERS
ROYBEAN
RUBBERS
RUBBERY
RUDDERS
RUINERS
RUNDEEP
RUNLETS
RUNNELS
RUNNERS
RUSHEES
RUSHERS
RUSSELL
RUSSETS
RUTGERS

R••••E•

RABBLES
RACEMES
RACQUET
RADAMES
RADDLED
RADDLES
RADICES
RADIOED
RAFFLED
RAFFLER
RAFFLES
RAGGIER
RAGWEED
RAINIER
RALLIED
RALLIES
RAMBLED
RAMBLER
RAMBLES
RAMESES
RANCHED
RANCHER
RANCHES
RANDIER
RANGIER
RANKLED
RANKLES
RANOVER
RAPHAEL
RAPIDER
RAPINES
RASPIER
RASSLED
RASSLES
RATCHET

RATITES
RATTIER
RATTLED
RATTLER
RATTLES
RAVAGED
RAVAGES
RAVELED
RAVENED
RAVINES
RAZORED
REACHED
REACHES
REACTED
READIED
READIER
READIES
REAIRED
REARMED
REBATED
REBATES
REBUKED
REBUKES
REBUSES
RECANED
RECANES
RECEDED
RECEDES
RECIPES
RECITED
RECITER
RECITES
RECODED
RECODES
RECOVER
RECUSED
RECUSES
REDATED
REDATES
REDDEER
REDEYES
REDUCED
REDUCER
REDUCES
REEDIER
REENTER
REFACED
REFACES
REFEREE
REFINED
REFINER
REFINES
REFIRES
REFRIED
REFRIES
REFUGEE
REFUGES
REFUSED
REFUSER
REFUSES
REFUTED
REFUTER
REFUTES
REGALED
REGALES
REGIMEN
REGIMES
REGLUED
REGLUES
REHIRED
REHIRES
REIGNED
REINKED
REKEYED
RELACED
RELACES
RELATED
RELATES
RELAXED
RELAXES
RELAYED
RELINED
RELINES
RELIVED
RELIVES
REMAKES
REMIXED
REMIXES
REMODEL
REMOTER
REMOTES
REMOVED
REMOVER
REMOVES
REMOWED
RENAMED
RENAMES
RENEGED
RENEGER
RENEGES
RENEWED
RENEWER
RENOTES
REOILED
REORDER
REPAPER
REPAVED
REPAVES
REPINED
REPINES
REPLIED
REPLIES
REPOSED
REPOSES
REPUTED
REPUTES
REQUIEM
RERATED
RERATES
RESALES
RESCUED
RESCUER
RESCUES
RESHOES
RESIDED
RESIDES
RESILED
RESILES
RESOLED
RESOLES
RESUMED
RESUMES
RETAKEN
RETAKES
RETAPED
RETAPES
RETAXED
RETAXES
RETILED
RETILES
RETIMED
RETIMES
RETIRED
RETIREE
RETIRES
RETOWED
RETRIED
RETRIES
RETUNED
RETUNES
RETYPED
RETYPES
REUPPED
REUTHER
REVELED
REVELER
REVERED
REVERES
REVILED
REVILES
REVISED
REVISER
REVISES
REVIVED
REVIVES
REVOKED
REVOKES
REWAXED
REWAXES
REWIRED
REWIRES
REWOVEN
REXREED
REZONED
REZONES
RIBEYES
RICHTER
RICKLES
RIDDLED
RIDDLER
RIDDLES
RIFFLED
RIFFLES
RIGHTED
RIGHTER
RINGLET
RIPENED
RIPPLED
RIPPLES
RISKIER
RITZIER
RIVALED
RIVETED
RIVETER
RIVULET
ROACHED
ROACHES
ROADBED
ROADIES
ROASTED
ROASTER
ROCKIER
ROCKIES
ROEDEER
ROISTER
ROLODEX
RONTGEN
ROOKIES
ROOMIER
ROOMIES
ROOSTED
ROOSTER
ROOTLET
ROSERED
ROSSSEA
ROTATED
ROTATES
ROTIFER
ROUGHED
ROUGHEN
ROUGHER
ROUNDED
ROUNDER
ROUSTED
ROWDIER
ROWDIES
RUBBLES
RUBYDEE
RUDDIER
RUFFLED
RUFFLES
RUMBAED
RUMBLED
RUMBLES
RUMMIER
RUMORED
RUMPLED
RUMPLES
RUNDEEP
RUNNIER
RUNOVER
RUNTIER
RUSHEES
RUSTIER
RUSTLED
RUSTLER
RUSTLES

R•••••E

RADIATE
RADICLE
RAGTIME
RAMPAGE
RANLATE
RAPTURE
RATABLE
RATHOLE
RATLINE
RATRACE
RAWHIDE
REALIZE
REARGUE
REBASTE
RECEIVE
RECHOSE
RECLAME
RECLINE
RECLUSE
RECYCLE
REDLINE
REDPINE
REDROSE
REDTAPE
REDWINE
REFEREE
REFRAME
REFUGEE
REGRADE
REISSUE
REJOICE
RELAPSE
RELEASE
RELIEVE
REMORSE
REPASTE
REPLACE
REPLATE
REPLETE
REPRICE
REPRISE
REPROVE
REPTILE
REPULSE
REQUIRE
REQUITE
RERAISE
RERINSE
REROUTE
RESCALE
RESERVE
RESIDUE
RESOLVE
RESPIRE
RESPITE
RESTAGE
RESTATE
RESTIVE
RESTORE
RESTYLE
RESURGE
RETICLE
RETINAE
RETINUE
RETIREE
RETITLE
RETRACE
RETRADE
REUNITE
REVALUE
REVENGE
REVENUE
REVERIE
REVERSE
REVOICE
REVOLVE
REWEAVE
REWRITE
REWROTE
RHIZOME
RIBCAGE
RIPOSTE
RIPTIDE
RISIBLE
RISSOLE
RITCHIE
RIVIERE
ROANOKE
ROBLOWE
ROMAINE
ROMANCE
ROSALIE
ROSANNE
ROSEATE
ROSELLE
ROSETTE
ROULADE
ROUTINE
ROXANNE
ROZELLE
RUBYDEE
RUMMAGE
RUMPOLE
RUNHOME
RUPTURE
RUSHDIE

•RE••••

AREARUG
AREAWAY
AREOLAE
AREOLAR
AREOLAS
BREADED
BREADTH
BREAKER
BREAKIN
BREAKUP
BREASTS
BREATHE
BREATHS
BREATHY
BREEDER
BREEZED
BREEZES
BRENDAN
BRENNAN
BRENNER
BRERFOX
BRESLIN
BRESSON
BRETONS
BREVETS
BREVITY
BREWERS
BREWERY
BREWING
CREAKED
CREAMED
CREAMER
CREASED
CREASES
CREATED
CREATES
CREATOR
CRECHES
CREDITS
CREEPED
CREEPER
CREEPUP
CREMONA
CRENELS
CREOLES
CREOSOL
CRESSES
CRESTED
CRETANS
CRETINS
CREVICE
CREWCUT
CREWELS
CREWING
CREWMAN
CREWMEN
DREADED
DREAMED
DREAMER
DREAMON
DREAMUP
DREDGED
DREDGER
DREDGES
DREIDEL
DREISER
DRESDEN
DRESSED
DRESSER
DRESSES
DRESSUP
DREWOUT
DREYFUS
ERECTED
ERECTER
ERECTLY
ERECTOR
ERELONG
EREMITE
EREWHON
FREAKED
FRECKLE
FREDDIE
FREDRIC
FREEBEE
FREEBIE
FREEDOM
FREEING
FREEMAN
FREEMEN
FREESIA
FREEWAY
FREEZER
FREEZES
FREIGHT
FREITAG
FREMONT
FRENEAU
FRENUMS
FRESCOS
FRESHEN
FRESHER
FRESHET
FRESHLY
FRETFUL
FRETSAW
FRETTED
GREASED
GREASER
GREASES
GREATER
GREATLY
GREAVES
GRECIAN
GREELEY
GREENED
GREENER
GREETED
GREETER
GREGORY
GREMLIN
GRENADA
GRENADE
GRENDEL
GRETZKY
GREYEST
GREYING
IRECKON
IRELAND
KREMLIN
OREGANO
ORESTES
PREACHY
PREAMPS
PREBEND
PRECAST
PRECEDE
PRECEPT
PRECISE
PRECOOK
PRECOOL
PREDATE
PREDAWN
PREDICT
PREEMIE
PREEMPT
PREENED
PREENER
PREFABS
PREFACE
PREFECT
PREFERS
PREHEAT
PRELATE
PRELIMS
PRELOAD
PRELUDE
PREMEDS
PREMIER
PREMISE
PREMIUM
PREPAID
PREPARE
PREPAYS
PREPPIE
PRESAGE
PRESALE
PRESELL
PRESENT
PRESETS
PRESIDE
PRESLEY
PRESOAK
PRESORT
PRESSED
PRESSER
PRESSES
PRESSON
PRESTON
PRESTOS
PRESUME
PRETAPE
PRETEEN
PRETEND
PRETEST
PRETEXT
PRETZEL
PREVAIL
PREVENT
PREVIEW
PREWASH
PREYSON
TREACLE
TREACLY
TREADED
TREADER
TREADLE
TREASON
TREATED
TREBLED
TREBLES
TREEING
TREERAT
TREETOP
TREFOIL
TREKKED
TREKKER
TREKKIE
TRELLIS
TREMBLE
TREMBLY
TREMOLO
TREMORS
TRENARY
TRENDED
TRENTON
TREPANS
TRESSES
TRESTLE
TREVINO
WREAKED
WREATHE
WREATHS
WRECKED
WRECKER
WRESTED
WRESTLE

•R•E•••

ARDENCY
ARIETTA
ARLEDGE
ARMENIA
ARREARS
ARRESTS
ARSENAL
ARSENIC
ARSENIO
ARTEMIS
ARTEMUS
BREEDER
BREEZED
BREEZES
BRIEFED
BRIEFER
BRIEFLY
BRUEGEL
CREEPED
CREEPER
CREEPUP
CROESUS
CRUELER
CRUELLY
DRIEDUP
DRIESUP
DRSEUSS
DRYEYED
ERNESTO
FREEBEE
FREEBIE
FREEDOM
FREEING
FREEMAN
FREEMEN
FREESIA
FREEWAY
FREEZER
FREEZES
FRIEDAN
FRIENDS
FRIEZES
GREELEY
GREENED
GREENER
GREETED
GREETER
GRIEVED
GRIEVER
GRIEVES
ORDEALS
ORDERED
ORDERER
ORDERLY
ORIENTE
ORIENTS
ORLEANS
ORNETTE
PRAETOR
PREEMIE
PREEMPT
PREENED
PREENER
PRIESTS
TREEING
TREERAT
TREETOP
TRIEDON
TRIESON
TRIESTE
TRUEING
URGENCY
URTEXTS

•R••E••

ARAMEAN
ARCHERS
ARCHERY
ARGUERS
ARIDEST
ARMLESS
ARMLETS
ARMREST
ARRIERE
ARTDECO
ARTIEST
ARTLESS
BRACERS
BRACEUP
BRAVELY
BRAVERY
BRAVEST
BRAYERS
BREVETS
BREWERS
BREWERY
BRIBERY
BROKEIN
BROKERS
BROKEUP
BRUBECK
BRUNETS
CRATERS
CRAVENS
CRAVERS
CRENELS
CREWELS
CRIMEAN
CROWERS
CRUDELY
CRUDEST
DRAPERS
DRAPERY
DRAWERS
DRIVEAT
DRIVEIN
DRIVELS
DRIVERS
DRIVEUP
DRONERS
DROVERS
DRYCELL
DRYNESS
DRYWELL
ERASERS
FRAMEUP
FRENEAU
GRADERS
GRATERS
GRAVELS
GRAVELY
GRAVEST
GRAYEST
GRAZERS
GREYEST
GRIPERS
GRIVETS
GROCERS
GROCERY
GROVELS
GROWERS
GRUYERE
IRATELY
IRATEST
IRONERS
KRATERS
MRCLEAN
ORPHEAN
ORPHEUS
PRATERS
PRAYERS
PREBEND
PRECEDE
PRECEPT
PREFECT
PREFERS
PREHEAT
PREMEDS
PRESELL
PRESENT
PRESETS
PRETEEN
PRETEND
PRETEST
PRETEXT
PREVENT
PRICERS
PRIMERS
PRIVETS
PROBERS
PROCEED
PROCESS
PROFESS
PROGENY
PROJECT
PROPELS
PROSERS
PROTEAN
PROTECT
PROTEGE
PROTEIN
PROTEST
PROTEUS
PROVERB
PROVERS
PROWESS
PRUDENT
PRUDERY
PRUNERS
TRABERT
TRACERS
TRACERY
TRADEIN
TRADEON
TRADERS
TRADEUP
TRAGEDY
TRAPEZE
TRAVELS
TRAVERS
TRICEPS
TRIDENT
TRIREME
TRISECT
TRITELY
TRITEST
TRIVETS
TROWELS
TROWERS
TRUDEAU
WRITEIN
WRITERS
WRITETO
WRITEUP
WROTEIN
WROTETO
WROTEUP
WRYNESS

•R•••E•

ARALSEA
ARBITER
ARBORED
ARCADES
ARCHIES
ARGIVES
ARGYLES
ARMORED
ARMORER
AROUSED
AROUSES
ARRASES
ARRAYED
ARRISES
ARRIVED
ARRIVER
ARRIVES
BRACKEN
BRACKET
BRADLEE
BRADLEY
BRAGGED
BRAGGER
BRAIDED
BRAIDER
BRAINED
BRAISED
BRAISES
BRANDED
BRANDER
BRASHER
BRASSES
BRAVOES
BRAWLED
BRAWLER
BRAZIER
BREADED
BREAKER
BREEDER
BREEZED
BREEZES
BRENNER
BRICKED
BRIDGED
BRIDGES
BRIDGET
BRIDLED
BRIDLES
BRIEFED
BRIEFER
BRIMMED
BRINGER
BRINIER
BRIQUET
BRISKER
BRISKET
BRITTEN
BROADEN
BROADER
BROGUES
BROILED
BROILER
BRONZED
BRONZES
BROODED
BROODER
BROOKED
BROTHER
BROWNED
BROWNER
BROWSED
BROWSER
BROWSES
BRUEGEL
BRUISED
BRUISER
BRUISES
BRUITED
BRUSHED
BRUSHES
BRYNNER
CRABBED
CRABBER
CRACKED
CRACKER
CRADLED
CRADLES
CRAFTED
CRAFTER
CRAMMED
CRAMMER
CRAMPED
CRANKED
CRASHED
CRASHES
CRASSER
CRAWLED
CRAWLER
CRAZIER
CRAZIES
CREAKED
CREAMED
CREAMER
CREASED
CREASES
CREATED
CREATES
CRECHES
CREEPED
CREEPER
CREOLES
CRESSES
CRESTED
CREWMEN
CRIBBED
CRICKED
CRICKET
CRIMPED
CRIMPER
CRINGED
CRINGES
CRISPED
CRISPER
CRITTER
CROAKED
CROCHET
CRONIES
CROOKED
CROONED
CROONER
CROPPED
CROPPER
CROQUET
CROSIER
CROSSED
CROSSER
CROSSES
CROWDED
CROWNED
CRUELER
CRUISED
CRUISER
CRUISES
CRULLER
CRUMPET

CRUSHED
CRUSHER
CRUSHES
CRUSTED
CRYOGEN
DRABBER
DRAFTED
DRAFTEE
DRAGGED
DRAGNET
DRAINED
DRAINER
DRATTED
DRAWLED
DREADED
DREAMED
DREAMER
DREDGED
DREDGER
DREDGES
DREIDEL
DREISER
DRESDEN
DRESSED
DRESSER
DRESSES
DRIBLET
DRIFTED
DRIFTER
DRILLED
DRILLER
DRINKER
DRIPPED
DROLLER
DROOLED
DROOLER
DROOPED
DROPLET
DROPPED
DROPPER
DROWNED
DROWSED
DROWSES
DRUBBED
DRUCKER
DRUDGED
DRUDGES
DRUGGED
DRUMMED
DRUMMER
DRYEYED
ERECTED
ERECTER
ERITREA
ERMINES
ERUCTED
ERUPTED
FRAILER
FRAISES
FRANCES
FRANKED
FRANKER
FRAPPES
FRASIER
FRAWLEY
FRAZIER
FREAKED
FREEBEE
FREEMEN
FREEZER
FREEZES
FRESHEN
FRESHER

FRESHET
FRETTED
FRIDGES
FRIEZES
FRILLED
FRINGED
FRINGES
FRISBEE
FRISKED
FRITTED
FRITTER
FRIZZED
FRIZZES
FROCKED
FROGMEN
FRONTED
FROSTED
FROTHED
FROWNED
FROWNER
FRUITED
GRABBED
GRABBER
GRAFTED
GRAINED
GRAMMER
GRAMMES
GRANDEE
GRANDER
GRANGER
GRANGES
GRANTED
GRANTEE
GRAPHED
GRAPNEL
GRASPED
GRASSED
GRASSES
GRAVIES
GREASED
GREASER
GREASES
GREATER
GREAVES
GREELEY
GREENED
GREENER
GREETED
GREETER
GRENDEL
GRIDDED
GRIDDER
GRIEVED
GRIEVER
GRIEVES
GRIFFEY
GRIFTER
GRILLED
GRILLES
GRILLET
GRIMIER
GRIMMER
GRINDER
GRINNED
GRINNER
GRIPPED
GRIPPER
GRITTED
GROANED
GROANER
GROLIER
GROMMET
GROOMED

GROOMER
GROOVED
GROOVES
GROSSED
GROSSER
GROSSES
GROUPED
GROUPER
GROUSED
GROUSER
GROUSES
GROUTED
GROWLED
GROWLER
GRUBBED
GRUDGED
GRUDGES
GRUFFER
GRUMPED
GRUNTED
IRONIES
IRONMEN
MRBONES
ORACLES
ORANGES
ORBITED
ORBITER
ORDERED
ORDERER
ORESTES
ORIOLES
ORPINES
PRAISED
PRAISER
PRAISES
PRANCED
PRANCER
PRANCES
PRANKED
PREENED
PREENER
PREMIER
PRESLEY
PRESSED
PRESSER
PRESSES
PRETEEN
PRETZEL
PREVIEW
PRICIER
PRICKED
PRIMMER
PRIMPED
PRINCES
PRINKED
PRINTED
PRINTER
PRITHEE
PRIVIES
PROBLEM
PROCEED
PRODDED
PRODDER
PROFFER
PRONGED
PROOFED
PROOFER
PROPHET
PROPJET
PROPMEN
PROPPED
PROSIER
PROSPER

PROUDER
PROWLED
PROWLER
PROXIES
TRACHEA
TRACKED
TRACKER
TRAILED
TRAILER
TRAINED
TRAINEE
TRAINER
TRAMMEL
TRAMPED
TRANCES
TRAPPED
TRAPPER
TRASHED
TRASHES
TRAUBEL
TRAWLED
TRAWLER
TREADED
TREADER
TREATED
TREBLED
TREBLES
TREKKED
TREKKER
TRENDED
TRESSES
TRICKED
TRICKER
TRIFLED
TRIFLER
TRIFLES
TRIGGED
TRIGGER
TRILLED
TRIMMED
TRIMMER
TRINKET
TRIODES
TRIPLED
TRIPLES
TRIPLET
TRIPLEX
TRIPPED
TRIPPER
TRIPPET
TRIUNES
TROCHEE
TROCHES
TRODDEN
TROLLED
TROLLEY
TROOPED
TROOPER
TROTHED
TROTTED
TROTTER
TROUPER
TROUPES
TROUSER
TRUCKED
TRUCKEE
TRUCKER
TRUDGED
TRUDGER
TRUDGES
TRUMPED
TRUMPET
TRUSSED

TRUSSES
TRUSTED
TRUSTEE
TRYSTED
TRYSTER
URBANER
WRACKED
WRAPPED
WRAPPER
WREAKED
WRECKED
WRECKER
WRESTED
WRIGLEY
WRINGER
WRITHED
WRITHES
WRITTEN
WRONGED
WRONGER

•R•••E

ARACHNE
ARCHIVE
ARCSINE
ARDMORE
AREOLAE
ARGONNE
ARIADNE
ARISTAE
ARLEDGE
ARMHOLE
ARMOIRE
ARRANGE
ARRIERE
ARTICLE
ARTISTE
ARTWARE
BRADLEE
BRAILLE
BRAMBLE
BRASSIE
BREATHE
BRIGADE
BRINDLE
BRIOCHE
BRISTLE
BRITTLE
BROCADE
BROMATE
BROMIDE
BROMINE
BROWNIE
BRUSQUE
CRACKLE
CRAPPIE
CREVICE
CRINKLE
CRUMBLE
CRUMPLE
CRUSADE
DRAFTEE
DRAYAGE
DRIBBLE
DRIZZLE
DRYHOLE
ERASURE
EREMITE
EROSIVE
ERSKINE
ERUDITE
FRAGILE
FRAICHE

FRANKIE
FRAZZLE
FRECKLE
FREDDIE
FREEBEE
FREEBIE
FRIABLE
FRICKIE
FRIGATE
FRISBEE
FRIZZLE
FROMAGE
GRACILE
GRACKLE
GRAHAME
GRANDEE
GRANITE
GRANTEE
GRANULE
GRAPPLE
GRAVURE
GRENADE
GRIDDLE
GRIMACE
GRISTLE
GRIZZLE
GROUPIE
GRUMBLE
GRUYERE
IRKSOME
IRONAGE
IRONORE
KRINGLE
ORIENTE
ORIFICE
ORNETTE
OROURKE
ORVILLE
PRAIRIE
PRALINE
PRATTLE
PRECEDE
PRECISE
PREDATE
PREEMIE
PREFACE
PRELATE
PRELUDE
PREMISE
PREPARE
PREPPIE
PRESAGE
PRESALE
PRESIDE
PRESUME
PRETAPE
PRICKLE
PRIMATE
PRITHEE
PRIVATE
PROBATE
PROCURE
PRODUCE
PROFANE
PROFILE
PROFUSE
PROMISE
PROMOTE
PROPANE
PROPOSE
PRORATE
PROTEGE
PROVIDE

PROVOKE
PRUDHOE
TRADUCE
TRAINEE
TRAIPSE
TRAMPLE
TRAPEZE
TREACLE
TREADLE
TREKKIE
TREMBLE
TRESTLE
TRIBUNE
TRIBUTE
TRICKLE
TRIESTE
TRIREME
TRITONE
TROCHEE
TROUBLE
TROUNCE
TRUCKEE
TRUCKLE
TRUFFLE
TRUNDLE
TRUSTEE
URANITE
WRANGLE
WREATHE
WRESTLE
WRIGGLE
WRINKLE

••RE•••

ABREAST
ACREAGE
ADRENAL
AFREETS
AGREETO
ALREADY
ARREARS
ARRESTS
AUREATE
AUREOLA
AUREOLE
BARENTS
BARETTA
BEREAVE
BERETTA
BIREMES
BIRETTA
BOREDOM
BOREOUT
BUREAUS
BURETTE
CAREENS
CAREERS
CAREFOR
CAREFUL
CEREALS
CEREBRA
CORELLI
CORETTA
CUREALL
DARESAY
DARESTO
DIRECTS
FAREAST
FIREANT
FIREARM
FIREBOX
FIREBUG
FIREDOG

FIREDUP
FIREFLY
FIRELIT
FIREMAN
FIREMEN
FIRENZE
FIREOFF
FIRESUP
FOREARM
FOREIGN
FORELEG
FOREMAN
FOREMEN
FOREPAW
FORERAN
FORERUN
FORESAW
FORESEE
FORESTS
FOREVER
GERENTS
GORETEX
HERETIC
HIRESON
KOREANS
LORELEI
LORENZO
LORETTA
MORELLO
MORESBY
NEREIDS
NUREYEV
OBREGON
OGREISH
PARENTS
PHRENIC
RAREBIT
RAREGAS
REREADS
REREDOS
RERENTS
SCREAKS
SCREAMS
SCREECH
SCREEDS
SCREENS
SCREWED
SCREWUP
SERENER
SPREADS
STREAKS
STREAKY
STREAMS
STREETS
STRETCH
STRETTO
STREWED
STREWER
TEREDOS
TERENCE
THREADS
THREADY
THREATS
THREERS
THREWIN
TIREDER
TIREDLY
TIREDOF
TIREOUT
TOREOFF
TOREOUT
TOREROS
TUREENS

UNREADY
UNREELS
UTRECHT
WIRETAP
WOREOFF
WOREOUT
YEREVAN
ZAREBAS

••R•E••

AERIEST
AFREETS
AGREETO
AIRHEAD
AIRIEST
AIRLESS
ARRIERE
BARBELL
BARBELS
BARBERS
BARGEIN
BARKEEP
BARKERS
BARLEYS
BARNEYS
BARRELS
BARRENS
BARRETT
BARTEND
BARTERS
BERBERS
BERGERE
BERNESE
BERSERK
BIRDERS
BORDERS
BORNEUP
BURDENS
BURGEES
BURGEON
BURGERS
BURGESS
BURMESE
BURNERS
BURNETT
CARDERS
CAREENS
CAREERS
CARLESS
CARNERA
CARNETS
CARPERS
CARPETS
CARRELS
CARRERE
CARSEAT
CARTELS
CARTERS
CARVERS
CORBELS
CORBETT
CORDELL
CORDERO
CORKERS
CORNEAL
CORNEAS
CORNELL
CORNERS
CORNETS
CORRECT
CORSETS
CORTEGE
CORYELL

CURFEWS
CURLERS
CURLEWS
CURRENT
CURTEST
CURVETS
DARKENS
DARKEST
DARLEEN
DARLENE
DARNERS
DARRELL
DARTERS
DORMERS
DORSETT
DURRELL
EARNERS
EARNEST
EERIEST
FARLEFT
FARMERS
FARWEST
FERMENT
FERRETS
FERVENT
FIRMEST
FORBEAR
FORCEPS
FORCERS
FORFEIT
FORFEND
FORGERS
FORGERY
FORGETS
FORKERS
FORREAL
FORRENT
FORREST
FORWENT
FURSEAL
GARDENS
GARMENT
GARNERS
GARNETS
GARRETS
GARRETT
GARTERS
GIRDERS
GORGETS
GORIEST
GURNEYS
HARDENS
HARDEST
HARKENS
HARNESS
HARPERS
HARVEST
HERBERT
HERDERS
HERSELF
HORNETS
HURLERS
ISRAELI
JERSEYS
KERNELS
LARCENY
LARDERS
LARGELY
LARGESS
LARGEST
MARCEAU
MARCELS
MARKERS

MARKETS
MARLENE
MARTENS
MARVELS
MERGERS
MORDENT
MORSELS
MURDERS
NORIEGA
NURSERS
NURSERY
OARLESS
OURSELF
PARCELS
PARGETS
PARLEYS
PARNELL
PARSECS
PARSEES
PARSERS
PARVENU
PERCENT
PERFECT
PERNELL
PERSEUS
PERTEST
PERVERT
PIRAEUS
PORKERS
PORSENA
PORTEND
PORTENT
PORTERS
PURCELL
PURRERS
PURSERS
PURVEYS
SARGENT
SCREECH
SCREEDS
SCREENS
SERPENT
SERVERS
SERVEUP
SHRIEKS
SORBETS
SORCERY
SORRELS
SORTERS
SPRIEST
SPRYEST
STREETS
SURFEIT
SURFERS
SURGEON
SURGERY
SURREAL
SURREYS
SURVEYS
TARBELL
TARGETS
TARHEEL
TARTEST
TERCELS
TERCETS
TERRENE
TERRETS
TERSELY
TERSEST
THREERS
TORMENT
TORPEDO
TORRENT

TUREENS
TURKEYS
TURNERS
TURRETS
UNREELS
VARIETY
VARLETS
VERBENA
VERGERS
VERMEER
VERMEIL
VERVETS
WARDENS
WARDERS
WARIEST
WARMEST
WARRENS
WIRIEST
WORKERS
WORSENS

••R••E•

ABRADED
ABRADES
AERATED
AERATES
AEROBES
AFRAMES
AIRCREW
APRONED
ARRASES
ARRAYED
ARRISES
ARRIVED
ARRIVER
ARRIVES
AURALEE
BARKEEP
BARMIER
BARONET
BARRIER
BERATED
BERATES
BERNSEN
BERRIED
BERRIES
BERTHED
BIRCHED
BIRCHES
BIRDIED
BIRDIES
BIRDMEN
BIREMES
BIRTHED
BORATES
BURBLED
BURBLES
BURGEES
BURGHER
BURGLED
BURGLES
BURLIER
CARAFES
CARAMEL
CARAVEL
CARGOES
CARIBES
CARNIES
CAROLED
CAROLER
CAROLES
CAROMED
CARRIED

CARRIER
CARRIES
CARTIER
CERUMEN
CHROMES
CIRCLED
CIRCLES
CIRCLET
CIRQUES
CORNFED
CORNIER
CORONET
CURATES
CURDLED
CURDLES
CURLIER
CURRIED
CURRIER
CURRIES
CURTSEY
CURVIER
DARLEEN
DERBIES
DERIDED
DERIDES
DERIVED
DERIVES
DERNIER
DIRTIED
DIRTIER
DIRTIES
EARLIER
EARTHEN
ENRAGED
ENRAGES
ENROBED
ENROBES
FARRIER
FARTHER
FERRIED
FERRIES
FERULES
FIREMEN
FORAGED
FORAGER
FORAGES
FORELEG
FOREMEN
FORESEE
FOREVER
FORFREE
FORGOES
FORSTER
FORTIES
FURORES
FURRIER
FURTHER
GARAGED
GARAGES
GARBLED
GARBLES
GARDNER
GARGLED
GARGLES
GIRDLED
GIRDLES
GORETEX
GURGLED
GURGLES
GYRATED
GYRATES
HARDIER
HARDSET

HARPIES
HARRIED
HARRIER
HARRIES
HARRIET
HARSHEN
HARSHER
HERBTEA
HERSHEY
HORSIER
HURDLED
HURDLER
HURDLES
HURRIED
HURRIES
HURTLED
HURTLES
HYRACES
HYRAXES
JERKIER
KARASEA
KIRTLES
LARCHES
LARDNER
LORELEI
LORISES
LORRIES
LURCHED
LURCHES
MARBLED
MARBLES
MARCHED
MARCHEN
MARCHER
MARCHES
MARGRET
MARINER
MARINES
MARQUEE
MARQUES
MARQUEZ
MARRIED
MARRIES
MARSHES
MERCIES
MERIMEE
MERITED
MERRIER
MIRAGES
MORALES
MORDRED
MORPHED
MURKIER
MURPHEY
MYRTLES
NARTHEX
NERVIER
NORTHER
NUREYEV
PARADED
PARADES
PARAPET
PARCHED
PARCHES
PARDNER
PAROLED
PAROLEE
PAROLES
PARQUET
PARRIED
PARRIES
PARSEES
PARSLEY
PARTIED
PARTIES
PARTNER
PARURES
PERCHED
PERCHES
PERDIEM
PERIGEE
PERKIER
PERPLEX
PERRIER
PERUKES
PERUSED
PERUSER
PERUSES
PHRASED
PHRASES
PIRATED
PIRATES
PORCHES
PORGIES
PURFLED
PURFLES
PURLIEU
PURPLED
PURPLES
PURSUED
PURSUER
PURSUES
PURVIEW
PYRITES
RERATED
RERATES
SARACEN
SARALEE
SARAZEN
SCRAPED
SCRAPER
SCRAPES
SCREWED
SCRIBES
SCRIVEN
SERAPES
SERENER
SERRIED
SHRIKES
SHRINER
SHRINES
SHRIVEL
SHRIVER
SHRIVES
SORITES
SORRIER
SORTIED
SORTIES
SPRAYED
SPRAYER
SPRITES
SPRUCED
SPRUCER
SPRUCES
STRAFED
STRAFES
STRAYED
STREWED
STREWER
STRIDER
STRIDES
STRIKER
STRIKES
STRIPED
STRIPER
STRIPES
STRIVED
STRIVEN
STRIVER
STRIVES
STROBES
STROKED
STROKES
STRUDEL
SURLIER
TARDIER
TARHEEL
TARRIED
TARRIES
TARSIER
TERRIER
TERRIES
THRIVED
THRIVES
THRONES
THROWER
TIRADES
TIREDER
TORCHED
TORCHES
TORQUES
TURNKEY
TURTLED
TURTLES
UNRATED
UNRAVEL
UNROBED
UNROBES
UPRISEN
UPRISES
UPRIVER
VERMEER
VERNIER
VIRTUES
VIRUSES
WARBLED
WARBLER
WARBLES
WERNHER
WERTHER
WORDIER
WORKMEN
WORMIER
WORRIED
WORRIER
WORRIES
WORSTED
YARDMEN

••R•••E

ABRIDGE
ACREAGE
AGRAFFE
AIRBASE
AIRDATE
AIRFARE
AIRHOLE
AIRLANE
AIRLINE
AIRMILE
AIRTIME
AIRWAVE
ARRANGE
ARRIERE
AURALEE
AUREATE
AUREOLE
AURICLE
AURORAE
BARCODE
BAROQUE
BARRAGE
BEREAVE
BERGERE
BERNESE
BERNICE
BURETTE
BURMESE
CARBIDE
CARBINE
CARFARE
CARLYLE
CARMINE
CAROUSE
CARRERE
CARTAGE
CORDAGE
CORDATE
CORDITE
CORKAGE
CORNICE
CORONAE
CORRODE
CORSAGE
CORTEGE
CURSIVE
DARKAGE
DARLENE
DORMICE
DURABLE
DURANCE
DURANTE
EARACHE
EARLOBE
ENROUTE
FARGONE
FERRATE
FERRITE
FERRULE
FERTILE
FIRENZE
FORBADE
FORBORE
FORESEE
FORFREE
FORGAVE
FORGIVE
FORGONE
FORLIFE
FORSAKE
FORSALE
FORSURE
FORTUNE
FURNACE
FURTIVE
GARBAGE
GARONNE
GERMANE
GIRAFFE
GIRONDE
HERBAGE
HERCULE
HEROINE
HIRABLE
HIRSUTE
HORMONE
KARAOKE
KIRSTIE
LARAINE
LARAMIE
LAROCHE
MARGATE
MARLENE
MARLOWE
MARQUEE
MARRYME
MERIMEE
MIRACLE
MORAINE
MORTISE
NARRATE
NURTURE
PARABLE
PAROLEE
PARTAKE
PARTITE
PERCALE
PERFUME
PERIGEE
PERJURE
PERLITE
PERVADE
PIROGUE
PORCINE
PORKPIE
PORSCHE
PORTAGE
PURPOSE
RERAISE
RERINSE
REROUTE
SARALEE
SARDINE
SCROOGE
SCRUPLE
SERIATE
SERRATE
SERVICE
SERVILE
SORBATE
STRANGE
STRASSE
STRIATE
STROPHE
SURFACE
SURMISE
SURNAME
SURVIVE
SYRINGE
TARTARE
TERENCE
TERHUNE
TERMITE
TERNATE
TERRACE
TERRENE
TURBINE
UKRAINE
UPRAISE
VERBOSE
VERDURE
VIRGULE
WARFARE
WARGAME
WARLIKE
WARTIME
WORDONE
YARDAGE

•••RE••

ABOREAL
ACCRETE
ACTRESS
ADDRESS
ADORERS
AGGRESS
AIGRETS
ALFREDO
ANDREAS
ANDRESS
ANDREWS
ARMREST
AWAREOF
BARRELS
BARRENS
BARRETT
BEARERS
BEDREST
CARRELS
CARRERE
CLARETS
CLORETS
CONREID
CORRECT
CURRENT
CYPRESS
DARRELL
DEAREST
DECREED
DECREES
DEGREES
DEPRESS
DIGRESS
DOUREST
DURRELL
ELGRECO
EMPRESS
ENTREAT
ENTREES
EVEREST
EVERETT
EXCRETE
EXPRESS
EXTREME
FAIREST
FEARERS
FERRETS
FLAREUP
FLORETS
FORREAL
FORRENT
FORREST
GARRETS
GARRETT
HEARERS
HEBREWS
HEIRESS
HENREID
IMARETS
IMPRESS
INBREED
INGRESS
IPCRESS
JEERERS
LABRETS
LAURELS
LAURENT
LEERERS
LIPREAD
LOUREED
MAUREEN
MISREAD
NEAREST
OPPRESS
OSPREYS
OVEREAT
PEERESS
PETRELS
POOREST
POURERS
PUGREES
PURRERS
REAREND
REARERS
REDRESS
REFRESH
REGRESS
REGRETS
REPRESS
RETREAD
RETREAT
REXREED
ROARERS
SANREMO
SCARERS
SCAREUP
SCORERS
SECRECY
SECRETE
SECRETS
SEERESS
SHAREIN
SHARERS
SNORERS
SOARERS
SOIREES
SORRELS
SOUREST
SPARELY
SPAREST
SPIREAS
STAREAT
STARERS
STARETS
STEREOS
STORERS
STOREUP
STOREYS
STYRENE
SUPREME
SUPREMO
SURREAL
SURREYS
SWOREAT
SWOREBY
SWOREIN
TERRENE
TERRETS
THEREAT
THEREBY
THEREIN
THEREOF
THEREON
THERESA
THERETO
THOREAU
TIGRESS
TORRENT
TOURERS
TRIREME
TUAREGS
TURRETS
UNDRESS
USURERS
WARRENS
WEARERS
WHEREAS
WHEREAT
WHEREBY
WHEREIN
WHEREOF
WHERETO
YEAREND

•••R•E•

ABORTED
ACCRUED
ACCRUES
ADORNED
ALARMED
ALARMER
ALERTED
ALERTER
AMBRIES
AMERCED
AMERCES
ANGRIER
APERIES
AVERRED
AVERTED
AWARDED
AWARDEE
AWARDER
BARRIER
BEARDED
BERRIED
BERRIES
BLARNEY
BLURRED
BLURTED
BOARDED
BOARDER
BOURREE
CARRIED
CARRIER
CARRIES
CHARGED
CHARGER
CHARGES
CHARIER
CHARLES
CHARLEY
CHARMED
CHARMER
CHARRED
CHARTED
CHARTER
CHIRPED
CHURNED
CITROEN
CLERKED
COARSEN
COARSER
COERCED
COERCES
COURIER
COURSED
COURSER
COURSES
COURTED
COWRIES
CURRIED
CURRIER
CURRIES
DAIRIES
DEBRIEF
DECREED
DECREES
DECRIED
DECRIES
DEGREES
DEVRIES
DIARIES
DOORMEN
DOWRIES
DWARFED
DWARVES
EMERGED
EMERGES
EMERSED
ENTREES
ENTRIES
EVERTED
EXERTED
FAIRIES
FARRIER
FERRIED
FERRIES
FIERCER
FIERIER
FLIRTED
FOURIER
FURRIER
GABRIEL
GEORGES
GLORIED
GLORIES
GNARLED
GNARRED
GOURDES
GOURMET
GUARDED
HAARLEM
HAIRIER
HAIRNET
HARRIED
HARRIER
HARRIES
HARRIET
HEARKEN
HEARTEN
HOARDED
HOARDER
HOARIER
HOARSEN
HOARSER
HURRIED
HURRIES
IMBRUED
IMBRUES
INBREED
INBRIEF
IVORIES
JOURNEY
KNURLED
LAERTES
LEARJET
LEARNED
LEARNER
LEERIER
LIERNES
LORRIES
LOURDES
LOUREED
MARRIED
MARRIES
MAUREEN
MERRIER
MOORHEN
ONORDER
OVERSEA
OVERSEE
PARRIED
PARRIES
PEARLED
PERRIER
PIERCED
PIERCES
PUGREES
QUARREL
QUARTER
QUARTET
QUERIED
QUERIES
REARMED
REFRIED
REFRIES
REORDER
RETRIED
RETRIES
REXREED
SCARCER
SCARFED
SCARIER
SCARLET
SCARPED
SCARRED
SCARVES
SCORNED
SCURVES
SERRIED
SHARKEY
SHARPED
SHARPEI
SHARPEN
SHARPER
SHERBET
SHIRKED
SHIRKER
SHIRLEY
SHIRRED
SHORTED
SHORTEN
SHORTER
SKIRLED
SKIRRED
SKIRTED
SLURPED
SLURRED
SMARTED
SMARTEN
SMARTER
SMIRKED
SNARLED
SNORKEL
SNORTED
SNORTER
SOIREES
SORRIER
SOURCED
SOURCES
SPARGED
SPARGES
SPARKED
SPARRED
SPARSER
SPORTED
SPURNED
SPURNER
SPURRED
SPURTED
STARKER
STARLET
STARRED
STARTED
STARTER
STARVED
STARVES
STERNER
STIRRED
STIRRER
STORIED
STORIES
STORMED
STURGES
SWARMED
SWERVED
SWERVES
SWIRLED
TARRIED
TARRIES
TEARIER
TERRIER
TERRIES
THURBER
TIERNEY
TOORDER
TOURNEY
TWIRLED
TWIRLER
UNARMED
UNTRIED
USURPED
USURPER
WEARIED
WEARIER
WEARIES
WEIRDER
WHARFED
WHARVES
WHIRLED
WHIRRED
WHORLED
WORRIED
WORRIER
WORRIES
YEARNED
YEARNER

•••R••E

ACCRETE
ACEROSE
AMBROSE
APPRISE
APPRIZE
APPROVE
ASCRIBE
ASTRIDE
ATTRITE
AVARICE
AVERAGE
AWARDEE
AXLROSE
AZURITE
BARRAGE
BEGRIME
BOURREE
CAPRICE
CARRERE
CHARADE
CHARLIE
CHORALE
CHORINE
CHORTLE
CITRATE
CITRINE
CLARICE
COMRADE
CORRODE
COURAGE
CUTRATE
DEGRADE
DEPRAVE
DEPRIVE
DHURRIE
DISROBE
DOORDIE
EMBRACE
EMIRATE
ENGRAVE
EPERGNE
EXCRETE
EXTREME
EXTRUDE
FEBRILE
FERRATE
FERRITE
FERRULE
GAGRULE
GOBROKE
HAIRDYE
HAYRIDE
HYDRATE
IMPROVE
INGRATE
INTRUDE
ITERATE
JOYRIDE
LAPROBE
LOWRISE
MACRAME
MARRYME
MAURICE
MELROSE
MICROBE
MIDRISE
MIGRATE
MISRULE
MOORAGE
NARRATE
NEURONE
NITRATE
NITRIDE
NITRITE
OBTRUDE
OPERATE
OPEROSE
OUTRACE
OUTRAGE
OVERAGE
OVERATE
OVERAWE
OVERDUE
OVERLIE
OVERSEE
OVERUSE
PADRONE
PATRICE
PEERAGE
PRORATE
PUERILE
RATRACE
REARGUE
REDROSE
REFRAME
REGRADE
REPRICE
REPRISE
REPROVE
RETRACE
RETRADE
REWRITE
REWROTE
SECRETE
SERRATE
SPARKLE
STARTLE
STERILE
STORAGE
STYRENE
SUCRASE
SUCROSE
SUNRISE
SUPREME
TAURINE
TAXRATE
TEAROSE
TERRACE
TERRENE
TITRATE
TOWROPE
TRIREME
UMBRAGE
UNCRATE
UNDRAPE
UPGRADE
VIBRATE

••••RE•

ABJURED
ABJURES
ADHERED
ADHERES
ADJURED
ADJURES
ADMIRED
ADMIRER
ADMIRES
AIRCREW
ALLURED
ALLURES
ALTERED
ALTERER
ALVAREZ
AMPERES
ANGERED
ANTARES
APPAREL
ARBORED
ARMORED
ARMORER
ASPIRED
ASPIRER
ASPIRES
ASSURED
ASSURES
ATTIRED
ATTIRES
AUGURED
AVERRED
BEETREE
BEMIRED
BEMIRES
BESTREW
BLEARED
BLURRED
BODEREK
BOURREE
BOWERED
CABARET
CAPERED
CATERED
CATERER
CENTRED
CENTRES
CHAIRED
CHARRED
CHEERED
CHEVRES

CLEARED
CLEARER
COHERED
COHERES
COLORED
COMFREY
COVERED
COWERED
DALTREY
DEMURER
DESIRED
DESIREE
DESIRES
DOLORES
EAGERER
ELMTREE
EMIGRES
EMPIRES
ENCORES
ENDURED
ENDURES
ENSURED
ENSURES
ENTERED
ERITREA
EUCHRED
EUCHRES
EXPIRED
EXPIRES
FABARES
FAVORED
FIACRES
FIGURED
FIGURER
FIGURES
FLOORED
FLOURED
FORFREE
FURORES
FUTURES
GAMBREL
GNARRED
GODFREY
GUMTREE
HOMBRES
HOMERED
HONORED
HONOREE
HONORER
HOVERED
HOVERER
HUMORED
HUNDRED
ICEFREE
IGNORED
IGNORER
IGNORES
ILLBRED
IMMURED
IMMURES
IMPURER
INHERED
INHERES
INJURED
INJURES
INSURED
INSURES
JEFFREY
JOFFREY
KESTREL
KINDRED
LABORED
LABORER
LAMPREY
LAUTREC
LAYERED
LETTRES
LEVERED
LEVERET
LOUVRES
LOWBRED
LOWERED
LUSTRED
LUSTRES
MAIGRET
MAITRED
MAJORED
MALAREN
MANDREL
MANFRED
MARGRET
MATURED
MATURER
MATURES
MEMOREX
METERED
MILDRED
MINARET
MINORED
MITERED
MONGREL
MORDRED
MOTORED
NATURED
NATURES
OAKTREE
OEUVRES
OFFERED
OFFERER
ORDERED
ORDERER
OUTDREW
OUTGREW
PALFREY
PAPERED
PAPERER
PARURES
PETERED
POWERED
QUARREL
QUEERED
QUEERER
RAZORED
REAIRED
REFEREE
REFIRES
REHIRED
REHIRES
RETIRED
RETIREE
RETIRES
REVERED
REVERES
REWIRED
REWIRES
ROSERED
RUMORED
SATIRES
SAVORED
SCARRED
SCOURED
SCOURER
SECURED
SECURER
SECURES
SEESRED
SENORES
SEVERED
SEVERER
SHEARED
SHEARER
SHEERED
SHEERER
SHIRRED
SKIRRED
SLURRED
SMEARED
SNEERED
SNEERER
SOBERED
SOBERER
SPARRED
SPEARED
SPHERES
SPURRED
SQUARED
SQUARER
SQUARES
SQUIRED
SQUIRES
STARRED
STEERED
STEERER
STIRRED
STIRRER
SUGARED
SUTURED
SUTURES
SWEARER
TABORET
TAPERED
TAXFREE
TENURED
TENURES
THEOREM
TIMBRES
TOWERED
TUMBREL
TUTORED
UMPIRED
UMPIRES
UNAIRED
UNSCREW
UPATREE
USHERED
UTTERED
UTTERER
WAGERED
WAGERER
WASTREL
WATERED
WATERER
WAVERED
WAVERER
WHIRRED
WINERED
WINFREY

••••R•E

ADVERSE
ASPERSE
ASTARTE
ATLARGE
AURORAE
BEETREE
BIZARRE
BOURREE
BYFORCE
CALORIE
COTERIE
DEBARGE
DEFARGE
DESERVE
DESIREE
DHURRIE
DIVERGE
DIVERSE
DIVORCE
ELMTREE
ENDORSE
ENFORCE
ENGARDE
ENGORGE
ENLARGE
EUTERPE
EXPARTE
FABERGE
FORFREE
GUMTREE
GUTHRIE
HONOREE
ICEFREE
IMMERSE
INFORCE
INTERSE
INVERSE
LAFARGE
LAPORTE
LAVERNE
LECARRE
LUCERNE
MCENROE
NAVARRE
NOTTRUE
OAKTREE
OBSERVE
OBVERSE
OROURKE
OSBORNE
PANURGE
PRAIRIE
REFEREE
REMORSE
RESERVE
RESURGE
RETIREE
REVERIE
REVERSE
SCOURGE
SPLURGE
TAXFREE
UNHORSE
UNNERVE
UPATREE
UPBORNE
UPSURGE
VALERIE

•••••RE

ACQUIRE
AFFAIRE
AIRFARE
ALLHERE
ANYMORE
ARDMORE
ARMOIRE
ARRIERE
ARTWARE
ASTAIRE
AUSTERE
BERGERE
BIZARRE
BONFIRE
BUSFARE
CALIBRE
CAPTURE
CARFARE
CARRERE
CELEBRE
CENSURE
CLOSURE
CLOTURE
COCHERE
COMPARE
CONJURE
COUTURE
CULTURE
DAYCARE
DECLARE
DENTURE
DEPLORE
DOEUVRE
ENSNARE
EPICURE
ERASURE
ESQUIRE
ETAGERE
EXPLORE
EYESORE
FAILURE
FANFARE
FEATURE
FENETRE
FISSURE
FIXTURE
FORBORE
FORSURE
FOXFIRE
GESTURE
GILMORE
GRAVURE
GRUYERE
GUNFIRE
HAYWIRE
HECTARE
HILAIRE
HITHERE
HOTWIRE
IMPLORE
INQUIRE
INSPIRE
INSTORE
IRONORE
KILDARE
LECARRE
LECTURE
LEHAVRE
LEISURE
LUMIERE
MACABRE
MAJEURE
MCGUIRE
MEASURE
MEMOIRE
MISFIRE
MIXTURE
MOLIERE
NAVARRE
NOTSURE
NOWHERE
NURTURE
OBSCURE
ONADARE
ONSHORE
OUTWORE
PASTURE
PERJURE
PHILTRE
PIASTRE
PICTURE
PISMIRE
POSTURE
PREPARE
PROCURE
RAPTURE
REQUIRE
RESPIRE
RESTORE
RIVIERE
RUPTURE
SCEPTRE
SEEHERE
SINCERE
SOTHERE
SPECTRE
STATURE
TANGERE
TARTARE
TEXTURE
THEATRE
TONSURE
TOSPARE
TSQUARE
UNAWARE
VAMPIRE
VENTURE
VERDURE
VESTURE
VULTURE
WARFARE
WELFARE

R•F••••

RAFFISH
RAFFLED
RAFFLER
RAFFLES
RAFTERS
RAFTING
REFACED
REFACES
REFEREE
REFERTO
REFFING
REFILLS
REFILMS
REFINED
REFINER
REFINES
REFIRES
REFLECT
REFORMS
REFRACT
REFRAIN
REFRAME
REFRESH
REFRIED
REFRIES
REFUELS
REFUGEE
REFUGES
REFUNDS
REFUSAL
REFUSED
REFUSER
REFUSES
REFUTED
REFUTER
REFUTES
RIFFING
RIFFLED
RIFFLES
RIFLERS
RIFLERY
RIFLING
RIFTING
RUFFIAN
RUFFLED
RUFFLES
RUFIYAA

R••F•••

RAFFISH
RAFFLED
RAFFLER
RAFFLES
RATFINK
REAFFIX
REDFINS
REDFIRS
REDFLAG
REDFORD
REEFERS
REEFING
REFFING
RIFFING
RIFFLED
RIFFLES
ROOFERS
ROOFING
ROOFTOP
RUFFIAN
RUFFLED
RUFFLES

R•••F••

RATAFIA
REAFFIX
REBUFFS
RESTFUL
RIPOFFS
ROOMFUL
ROOTFOR
ROTIFER
RUNOFFS

R••••F•

RAKEOFF
REBUFFS
RECTIFY
REELOFF
RELIEFS
REUNIFY
RIDEOFF
RIPOFFS
RIPSOFF
RODEOFF
RODOLFO
RUNOFFS
RUNSOFF
RUSHOFF

R•••••F

RAKEOFF
REDWOLF
REELOFF
REPROOF
RIDEOFF
RIPSOFF
RODEOFF
RUNSOFF
RUSHOFF

•RF••••

MRFIXIT

•R•F•••

ARMFULS
ARTFILM
ARTFORM
CRAFTED
CRAFTER
CRAFTSY
DRAFTED
DRAFTEE
DRIFTED
DRIFTER
GRAFTED
GRIFFEY
GRIFFIN
GRIFFON
GRIFTER
GRUFFER
GRUFFLY
ORIFICE
PREFABS
PREFACE
PREFECT
PREFERS
PROFANE
PROFESS
PROFFER
PROFILE
PROFITS
PROFUSE
TRAFFIC
TREFOIL
TRIFLED
TRIFLER
TRIFLES
TRUFFLE

•R••F••

BRERFOX
BRIEFED
BRIEFER
BRIEFLY
BRIMFUL
DREYFUS
FRETFUL
GRIFFEY
GRIFFIN
GRIFFON
GRUFFER
GRUFFLY
PRAYFOR
PROFFER
PROOFED
PROOFER
TRAFFIC
TRAYFUL
TRUFFLE

•R•••F•

BRANIFF
DROPOFF
GRATIFY

•R••••F

BRANIFF
CRYWOLF
DROPOFF

••RF•••

AIRFARE
AIRFLOW
AIRFOIL
CARFARE
CARFULS
CURFEWS
EARFLAP
EARFULS
FORFEIT
FORFEND
FORFREE
JARFULS
NORFOLK
PARFAIT
PERFECT
PERFIDY
PERFORM
PERFUME
PURFLED
PURFLES
SERFDOM
SURFACE
SURFEIT
SURFERS
SURFING
WARFARE

••R•F••

AGRAFFE
CARAFES
CAREFOR
CAREFUL
CORNFED
FIREFLY
FORKFUL
GIRAFFE
HARMFUL
HURTFUL
SCRUFFS
SCRUFFY
SHRIFTS
STRAFED
STRAFES
TARIFFS
THRIFTS
THRIFTY
WORKFOR

••R••F•

AGRAFFE
AIRLIFT
CERTIFY
EARMUFF
FARLEFT
FIREOFF
FORLIFE
FORTIFY
GIRAFFE
HORRIFY
KARLOFF
MARKOFF
MORTIFY
SCRUFFS
SCRUFFY
TARIFFS
TERRIFY
TOREOFF
TURNOFF
VERSIFY
WARDOFF
WOREOFF
WORKOFF
WORNOFF

••R•••F

AIRWOLF
BARANOF
EARMUFF
FIREOFF
HERSELF
KARLOFF
MARKOFF
OURSELF
TIREDOF
TOREOFF
TURNOFF
WARDOFF
WOREOFF
WORKOFF
WORNOFF

•••RF••

BRERFOX
DEERFLY
DWARFED
FEARFUL
OVERFLY
SCARFED
STIRFRY
TEARFUL
WHARFED

•••R•F•

BEAROFF
CLARIFY
ENGRAFT
FAIROFF
GLORIFY
HORRIFY
MIDRIFF
PAIROFF
PETRIFY
SCARIFY
SHERIFF
TEAROFF
TERRIFY
UPDRAFT
VITRIFY
WEAROFF

•••R••F

AWAREOF
BEAROFF
DEBRIEF
FAIROFF
HEARDOF
HEARSOF
HIPROOF
INBRIEF
MIDRIFF
PAIROFF
REPROOF
SHERIFF
SHORTOF
SUNROOF
TEAROFF
THEREOF
WEAROFF
WHEREOF

•••••RF

NETSURF
WALDORF

R•G••••

RAGDOLL
RAGGEDY
RAGGIER
RAGGING
RAGLANS
RAGMOPS
RAGOUTS
RAGRUGS
RAGTIME
RAGTOPS
RAGWEED
REGAINS
REGALED
REGALES
REGALIA
REGALLY
REGARDS
REGATTA
REGENCY
REGENTS
REGIMEN
REGIMES
REGIONS
REGLUED
REGLUES
REGNANT
REGRADE
REGRESS
REGRETS
REGROUP
REGULAR
REGULUS
RIGGERS
RIGGING
RIGHTED
RIGHTER
RIGHTLY
RIGHTON
RIGIDLY
RIGOURS
RIGVEDA
ROGUERY
ROGUISH

R••G•••

RAGGEDY
RAGGIER
RAGGING
RANGERS
RANGIER
RANGING
RANGOON
RAYGUNS
REAGENT
REDGUMS
REIGNED
RIDGING
RIDGWAY
RIGGERS
RIGGING
RINGERS
RINGING
RINGLET
RINGOUT
RINGSUP
RODGERS
ROUGHED
ROUGHEN
ROUGHER
ROUGHIT
ROUGHLY
ROUGHUP
ROUGING
RUTGERS

R•••G••

RAREGAS
RAVAGED
RAVAGES
REARGUE
REFUGEE
REFUGES
RELIGHT
RENEGED
RENEGER
RENEGES
REPUGNS
RESIGNS
RONTGEN

R••••G•

RAGRUGS
RALEIGH
RAMPAGE
RATINGS
RAVINGS
REDDOGS
REHANGS
RESINGS
RESTAGE
RESURGE
REVENGE
RIBCAGE
RISINGS
RULINGS
RUMMAGE

R•••••G

RACKING
RAFTING
RAGGING
RAIDING
RAILING
RAINING
RAISING
RAMMING
RANGING
RANKING
RANTING
RAPPING
RASPING
RATTING
RAZZING
RDLAING
READING
REAMING
REAPING
REARING
REDDING
REDFLAG
REDOING
REDWING
REEDING
REEFING
REEKING
REELING
REFFING
REINING
RELYING
RENDING
RENTING
RESTING
REVVING
RHYMING
RIBBING
RIDDING
RIDGING
RIFFING
RIFLING
RIFTING
RIGGING
RIMMING
RINGING
RINSING
RIOTING
RIPPING
RISKING
ROADHOG
ROAMING
ROARING
ROBBING
ROCKING
ROILING
ROLLING
ROLVAAG
ROMPING
ROOFING
ROOKING
ROOMING
ROOTING
ROTTING
ROUGING
ROUSING
ROUTING
RUBBING
RUCHING
RUCKING
RUINING
RUNNING
RUSHING
RUSTING

•RG••••

ARGIVES
ARGONNE
ARGUERS
ARGUING
ARGYLES
ORGANDY
ORGANIC
ORGANON
ORGANUM
ORGANZA
URGENCY

•R•G•••

ARUGULA
BRAGGED
BRAGGER
BRIGADE
BRIGAND
BRIGHAM
BROGANS
BROGUES
DRAGGED
DRAGNET
DRAGONS
DRAGOON
DRAGOUT
DRAGSIN
DRAGSON
DRUGGED
FRAGILE
FRIGATE
FRIGHTS
FROGMAN
FROGMEN
GREGORY

GRIGRIS
OREGANO
ORIGAMI
ORIGINS
PROGENY
PROGRAM
TRAGEDY
TRIGGED
TRIGGER
TRIGONS
TRIGRAM
URUGUAY
WRIGGLE
WRIGGLY
WRIGHTS
WRIGLEY

•R••G••

BRAGGED
BRAGGER
BRIDGED
BRIDGES
BRIDGET
BRINGER
BRINGIN
BRINGON
BRINGTO
BRINGUP
BROUGHT
BRUEGEL
CRINGED
CRINGES
CRYOGEN
DRAGGED
DRAUGHT
DREDGED
DREDGER
DREDGES
DROUGHT
DRUDGED
DRUDGES
DRUGGED
FRAUGHT
FREIGHT
FRIDGES
FRINGED
FRINGES
GRANGER
GRANGES
GRUDGED
GRUDGES
KRINGLE
MRMAGOO
MRRIGHT
ORANGES
PRONGED
TRIGGED
TRIGGER
TROUGHS
TRUDGED
TRUDGER
TRUDGES
WRANGLE
WRIGGLE
WRIGGLY
WRINGER
WRONGED
WRONGER
WRONGLY
WROUGHT

•R•••G•

ARLEDGE
ARRAIGN
ARRANGE
DRAYAGE
FROMAGE
IRONAGE
PRESAGE
PRODIGY
PROLOGS
PROTEGE
TRILOGY

•R••••G

ARCHING
AREARUG
ARGUING
ARISING
ARTSONG
BRACING
BRAKING
BRAVING
BRAYING
BRAZING
BREWING
BRIBING
BRINING
CRANING
CRATING
CRAVING
CRAZING
CREWING
CROWING
DRAPING
DRAWING
DRAYING
DRIVING
DRONING
ERASING
ERELONG
ERODING
FRAMING
FRAYING
FREEING
FREITAG
GRABBAG
GRACING
GRADING
GRATING
GRAVING
GRAYING
GRAZING
GREYING
GRIPING
GROPING
GROWING
IRONING
ORATING
PRATING
PRAYING
PRICING
PRIDING
PRIMING
PRIZING
PROBING
PROLONG
PROSING
PROVING
PRUNING
TRACING
TRADING
TREEING
TRUEING
WRITING
XRATING
XRAYING

••RG•••

AIRGUNS
BARGAIN
BARGEIN
BARGING
BERGERE
BERGMAN
BERGSON
BURGEES
BURGEON
BURGERS
BURGESS
BURGHER
BURGLAR
BURGLED
BURGLES
BURGOOS
CARGOES
FARGONE
FORGAVE
FORGERS
FORGERY
FORGETS
FORGING
FORGIVE
FORGOES
FORGONE
FORGOOD
GARGLED
GARGLES
GORGETS
GORGING
GORGONS
GURGLED
GURGLES
JARGONS
LARGELY
LARGESS
LARGEST
MARGATE
MARGAUX
MARGAYS
MARGINS
MARGRET
MERGERS
MERGING
MORGANA
MORGANS
PARGETS
PERGOLA
PORGIES
PURGING
SARGENT
SORGHUM
SURGEON
SURGERY
SURGING
TARGETS
VERGERS
VERGING
VIRGINS
VIRGOAN
VIRGULE
WARGAME
WARGODS

••R•G••

ALRIGHT
BURPGUN
ENRAGED
ENRAGES
FORAGED
FORAGER
FORAGES
GARAGED
GARAGES
MIRAGES
MRRIGHT
OBREGON
PARAGON
PERIGEE
PIROGUE
RAREGAS
SCRAGGY
UPRIGHT
VIRAGOS

••R••G•

ABRIDGE
ACREAGE
AIRBAGS
AIRINGS
ARRAIGN
ARRANGE
BARONGS
BARRAGE
BOROUGH
CARTAGE
CORDAGE
CORKAGE
CORSAGE
CORTEGE
DARKAGE
DURANGO
EARWIGS
FARRAGO
FIRINGS
FOREIGN
GARBAGE
HERBAGE
NORIEGA
PARINGS
PORTAGE
SARONGS
SCRAGGY
SCROOGE
SPRINGS
SPRINGY
STRANGE
STRINGS
STRINGY
SYRINGA
SYRINGE
THRONGS
THROUGH
VERDUGO
VERTIGO
YARDAGE

••R•••G

BARBING
BARGING
BARKING
BARRING
BIRDDOG
BIRDING
BIRLING
BURLING
BURNING
BURPING
BURYING
CARDING
CARPING
CARTING
CARVING
CORDING
CORKING
CORNDOG
CORNING
CURBING
CURDING
CURLING
CURSING
CURVING
DARLING
DARNING
DARTING
DERRING
EARNING
EARPLUG
EARRING
FARMING
FIREBUG
FIREDOG
FIRMING
FORCING
FORDING
FORELEG
FORGING
FORKING
FORMING
FURLING
FURLONG
FURRING
GARBING
GIRDING
GORGING
HARDING
HARKING
HARMING
HARPING
HERDING
HERRING
HORNING
HORSING
HURLING
HURTING
JARRING
JERKING
JURYING
JURYRIG
KERNING
LARDING
LORDING
LURKING
MARKING
MARRING
MERGING
MORNING
NURSING
PARKING
PARRING
PARSING
PARTING
PERKING
PERMING
PURGING
PURLING
PURRING
PURSING
SERLING
SERVING
SORTING
SURFING
SURGING
TARRING
TERMING
TURNING
VARYING
VERGING
WARDING
WARMING
WARNING
WARPING
WARRING
WARTHOG
WORDING
WORKING
YARNING
ZEROING

•••RG••

CHARGED
CHARGER
CHARGES
EMERGED
EMERGES
EPERGNE
GEORGES
GEORGIA
GIORGIO
GUARGUM
REARGUE
SPARGED
SPARGES
STURGES
TEARGAS

•••R•G•

AMERIGO
AVERAGE
BARRAGE
COURAGE
FARRAGO
MOORAGE
OILRIGS
OUTRAGE
OVERAGE
PEERAGE
RAGRUGS
STORAGE
TUAREGS
UMBRAGE

•••R••G

ADORING
BARRING
BEARHUG
BEARING
BLARING
DERRING
EARRING
ENURING
FAIRING
FEARING
FLARING
FURRING
GEARING
GLARING
GOWRONG
HEARING
HERRING
INURING
JARRING
JEERING
KEYRING
LEERING
MARRING
MITRING
MOORING
NEARING
OVERBIG
PAIRING
PARRING
PEERING
POURING
PURRING
REARING
ROARING
SCARING
SCORING
SEARING
SHARING
SHORING
SNARING
SNORING
SOARING
SOURING
SPARING
STARING
STORING
TARRING
TEARING
TIERING
TOURING
VEERING
WARRING
WEARING

••••RG•

ALLERGY
ATLARGE
CYBORGS
DEBARGE
DEFARGE
DIVERGE
EMBARGO
ENGORGE
ENLARGE
FABERGE
LAFARGE
LITURGY
PANURGE
RESURGE
SCOURGE
SPLURGE
SYNERGY
UNDERGO
UPSURGE
ZYMURGY

••••R•G

AREARUG
DISHRAG
JURYRIG
WASHRAG

•••••RG

HAMBURG
HOMBURG
ICEBERG
SEABORG

RH•••••

RHENIUM
RHETORS
RHIZOME
RHODIUM
RHOMBUS
RHUBARB
RHUMBAS
RHYMERS
RHYMING
RHYTHMS

R•H••••

REHANGS
REHEALS
REHEARD
REHEARS
REHEATS
REHEELS
REHIRED
REHIRES
REHOOKS

R••H•••

RAPHAEL
RASHERS
RASHEST
RATHOLE
RAWHIDE
RECHALK
RECHECK
RECHOSE
REDHAIR
REDHATS
REDHEAD
REDHEAT
REDHOTS
RESHIPS
RESHOES
RESHOOT
RETHINK
RICHARD
RICHEST
RICHMAN
RICHTER
RIGHTED
RIGHTER
RIGHTLY
RIGHTON
RUCHING
RUNHOME
RUSHDIE
RUSHEES
RUSHERS
RUSHING
RUSHOFF

R•••H••

RAINHAT
RANCHED
RANCHER
RANCHES
RANCHOS
RATCHET
REACHED
REACHES
REUTHER
RHYTHMS
RIMSHOT
RITCHIE
ROACHED
ROACHES
ROADHOG
ROUGHED
ROUGHEN
ROUGHER
ROUGHIT
ROUGHLY
ROUGHUP

R••••H•

RELIGHT
RICKSHA
RUPIAHS

R•••••H

RAFFISH
RALEIGH
REBEKAH
REBIRTH
REDDISH
REFRESH
RETEACH
RETOUCH
ROGUISH
ROMANSH
RUBBISH
RUDOLPH
RUNWITH

•R•H•••

ARCHAIC
ARCHERS
ARCHERY
ARCHIES
ARCHING
ARCHIVE
ARCHONS
ARCHWAY
ARMHOLE
BRAHMAN
BRAHMAS
BRAHMIN
DRYHOLE
GRAHAME
GRAHAMS
MRCHIPS
ORCHARD
ORCHIDS
ORPHANS
ORPHEAN
ORPHEUS
PREHEAT
URCHINS

•R••H••

ARACHNE
BRASHER
BRASHLY
BRIGHAM
BROTHER
BRUSHED
BRUSHES
BRUSHUP
CRASHED
CRASHES
CRECHES
CROCHET
CRUSHED
CRUSHER
CRUSHES
DRACHMA
EREWHON
FRESHEN
FRESHER
FRESHET
FRESHLY
FRIGHTS
FROTHED
GRAPHED
GRAPHIC
GRISHAM
GRYPHON
KRISHNA
PRITHEE
PROPHET
PRUDHOE
TRACHEA
TRASHED
TRASHES
TROCHEE
TROCHES
TROPHIC
TROTHED
WRIGHTS
WRITHED
WRITHES

•R•••H•

ARAPAHO
BREATHE
BREATHS
BREATHY
BRIOCHE
BRONCHI
BROUGHT
CRUNCHY
DRAUGHT
DROUGHT
FRAICHE
FRAUGHT
FREIGHT
GROUCHO
GROUCHY
GROWTHS
MRRIGHT
ORNITHO
PREACHY
TROUGHS
WRAITHS
WREATHE
WREATHS
WROUGHT

•R••••H

BREADTH
BRITISH
BRUTISH
PREWASH
PRUDISH
TRIUMPH

••RH•••

AIRHEAD
AIRHOLE
BARHOPS
CARHOPS
EARHART
PERHAPS
TARHEEL
TERHUNE

••R•H••

ABRAHAM
AIRSHIP
AIRSHOW
BERTHED
BIRCHED
BIRCHES
BIRTHED
BURGHER
EARSHOT
EARTHEN
EARTHLY
FARTHER
FORDHAM
FURTHER
GURKHAS
HARDHAT
HARDHIT
HARSHEN
HARSHER
HARSHLY
HERSHEY
KERCHOO
LARCHES
LURCHED
LURCHES
MARCHED
MARCHEN
MARCHER
MARCHES
MARCHON
MARKHAM
MARKHOR
MARSHAL
MARSHES
MORPHED
MURPHEY
NARTHEX
NARWHAL
NORTHER
PARCHED
PARCHES
PERCHED
PERCHES
PORCHES
PORTHOS
PYRRHIC
PYRRHUS
SORGHUM
TORCHED
TORCHES
WARSHIP
WARTHOG
WERNHER
WERTHER
WORSHIP

••R••H•

ALRIGHT
ATROPHY
AUROCHS
BORSCHT
CERIPHS
DOROTHY
EARACHE
HURRAHS
JERICHO
KARACHI
LAROCHE
MRRIGHT
PARAPHS
PARIAHS
PIRANHA
PORSCHE
PURDAHS
SERAPHS
STROPHE
TERAPHS
UPRIGHT
UTRECHT

••R•••H

BOROUGH
BURNISH
CARWASH
CORINTH
CORNISH
DARKISH
DERVISH
EHRLICH
FORSYTH
FURBISH
FURNISH
GARNISH
GIRLISH
KURDISH
MURDOCH
OGREISH
SCRATCH
SCREECH
SCRUNCH
STRETCH
TARNISH
THROUGH
TURKISH
VARNISH
WARMISH
WARPATH

•••RH••

BEARHUG
MOORHEN
PYRRHIC
PYRRHUS

•••R•H•

ANARCHY
DEARTHS
EPARCHS
FOURTHS
HEARTHS
HURRAHS
STARCHY
SWARTHY

•••R••H

ALDRICH
BEARISH
BETROTH
BOORISH
BULRUSH
CHERISH
DIGRAPH
INARUSH
INTRUTH
MOORISH
NOURISH
OSTRICH
PHARAOH
REFRESH
SOURISH
UNTRUTH

••••R•H

ALWORTH
DEBORAH
HOGARTH
MENORAH
MONARCH
REBIRTH
UNEARTH

RI•••••

RIBANDS
RIBBING
RIBBONS
RIBCAGE
RIBEYES
RICARDO
RICERAT
RICHARD
RICHEST
RICHMAN
RICHTER
RICKETY
RICKEYS
RICKLES
RICKSHA
RICOTTA
RIDDICK
RIDDING
RIDDLED
RIDDLER
RIDDLES
RIDEOFF
RIDEOUT
RIDGING
RIDGWAY
RIFFING
RIFFLED
RIFFLES
RIFLERS
RIFLERY
RIFLING
RIFTING
RIGGERS
RIGGING
RIGHTED
RIGHTER
RIGHTLY
RIGHTON
RIGIDLY
RIGOURS
RIGVEDA
RILLETS
RIMBAUD
RIMMING
RIMSHOT
RINGERS
RINGING
RINGLET
RINGOUT
RINGSUP
RINSING
RIOLOBO
RIORITA
RIOTACT
RIOTERS
RIOTING
RIOTOUS
RIPCORD
RIPENED
RIPINTO
RIPOFFS
RIPOSTE
RIPPERS
RIPPING
RIPPLED
RIPPLES
RIPRAPS
RIPSAWS
RIPSOFF
RIPTIDE
RIPTORN
RISIBLE
RISINGS
RISKERS
RISKIER
RISKING
RISOTTO
RISSOLE
RITCHIE
RITUALS
RITZIER
RIVALED
RIVALRY

RIVETED
RIVETER
RIVIERA
RIVIERE
RIVULET

R•I••••

RAIDERS
RAIDING
RAILERS
RAILING
RAILSAT
RAILWAY
RAIMENT
RAINBOW
RAINHAT
RAINIER
RAINING
RAINMAN
RAINOUT
RAISERS
RAISEUP
RAISING
RAISINS
REIGNED
REINING
REINKED
REINSIN
REISSUE
RHIZOME
ROILING
ROISTER
RUINERS
RUINING
RUINOUS

R••I•••

RACIEST
RADIALS
RADIANS
RADIANT
RADIATE
RADICAL
RADICES
RADICLE
RADIOED
RANINTO
RAPIDER
RAPIDLY
RAPIERS
RAPINES
RARITAN
RATINGS
RATIONS
RATITES
RAVINES
RAVINGS
RAVIOLI
REAIRED
REBINDS
REBIRTH
RECIPES
RECITAL
RECITED
RECITER
RECITES
REDIALS
REFILLS
REFILMS
REFINED
REFINER
REFINES
REFIRES
REGIMEN
REGIMES
REGIONS
REHIRED
REHIRES
RELIANT
RELICTS
RELIEFS
RELIEVE
RELIEVO
RELIGHT
RELINED
RELINES
RELISTS
RELIVED
RELIVES
REMINDS
REMIXED
REMIXES
REOILED
REPINED
REPINES
RERINSE
RESIDED
RESIDES
RESIDUE
RESIGNS
RESILED
RESILES
RESINGS
RESISTS
RETICLE
RETILED
RETILES
RETIMED
RETIMES
RETINAE
RETINAL
RETINAS
RETINUE
RETIRED
RETIREE
RETIRES
RETITLE
REVIEWS
REVILED
REVILES
REVISED
REVISER
REVISES
REVISIT
REVIVAL
REVIVED
REVIVES
REWINDS
REWIRED
REWIRES
RIGIDLY
RIPINTO
RISIBLE
RISINGS
RIVIERA
RIVIERE
ROTIFER
RUBICON
RUBITIN
RUFIYAA
RULINGS
RUNINTO
RUPIAHS

R•••I••

RABBITS
RABBITT
RACKING
RAFFISH
RAFTING
RAGGIER
RAGGING
RAGTIME
RAIDING
RAILING
RAINIER
RAINING
RAISING
RAISINS
RALEIGH
RALLIED
RALLIES
RAMMING
RANDIER
RANGIER
RANGING
RANKING
RANRIOT
RANTING
RAPPING
RASPIER
RASPING
RATFINK
RATLINE
RATTIER
RATTING
RAWHIDE
RAWSILK
RAZZING
RDLAING
READIED
READIER
READIES
READILY
READING
REALISM
REALIST
REALITY
REALIZE
REAMING
REAPING
REARING
REBOILS
REBUILD
REBUILT
RECEIPT
RECEIVE
RECLINE
RECOILS
RECTIFY
REDBIRD
REDDING
REDDISH
REDFINS
REDFIRS
REDLINE
REDOING
REDPINE
REDWINE
REDWING
REEDIER
REEDING
REEDITS
REEFING
REEKING
REELING
REFFING
REFRIED
REFRIES
REGAINS
REINING
REJOICE
REJOINS
RELYING
REMAILS
REMAINS
RENAILS
RENDING
RENNINS
RENTING
REPAINT
REPAIRS
REPLICA
REPLIED
REPLIES
REPRICE
REPRINT
REPRISE
REPTILE
REQUIEM
REQUIRE
REQUITE
RERAISE
RESCIND
RESHIPS
RESPIRE
RESPITE
RESTING
RESTIVE
RETAILS
RETAINS
RETHINK
RETRIAL
RETRIED
RETRIES
RETRIMS
RETSINA
REUNIFY
REUNION
REUNITE
REVOICE
REVVING
REWRITE
RHENIUM
RHODIUM
RHYMING
RIBBING
RIDDICK
RIDDING
RIDGING
RIFFING
RIFLING
RIFTING
RIGGING
RIMMING
RINGING
RINSING
RIORITA
RIOTING
RIPPING
RIPTIDE
RISKIER
RISKING
RITZIER
ROADIES
ROAMING
ROARING
ROBBING
ROBBINS
ROCKIER
ROCKIES
ROCKING
ROGUISH
ROILING
ROLAIDS
ROLLICK
ROLLING
ROLLINS
ROMAINE
ROMPING
ROOFING
ROOKIES
ROOKING
ROOMIER
ROOMIES
ROOMING
ROOTING
ROSSINI
ROTTING
ROUGING
ROUSING
ROUTINE
ROUTING
ROWDIER
ROWDIES
ROWDILY
RUBBING
RUBBISH
RUBRICS
RUCHING
RUCKING
RUCTION
RUDDIER
RUFFIAN
RUINING
RUMMIER
RUNNIER
RUNNING
RUNRIOT
RUNTIER
RUNWITH
RUSHING
RUSSIAN
RUSTICS
RUSTIER
RUSTILY
RUSTING
RYKRISP

R••••I•

RAKEDIN
RAKESIN
RAMEKIN
RAREBIT
RATAFIA
RATTAIL
READMIT
READSIN
REAFFIX
REAVAIL
RECLAIM
RECRUIT
REDHAIR
REDSKIN
REELSIN
REFRAIN
REGALIA
REINSIN
RESTAIN
RETRAIN
REVERIE
REVISIT
RITCHIE
ROBOTIC
ROCKYII
ROCKYIV
ROMANIA
ROPEDIN
ROPESIN
ROSALIE
ROSEOIL
ROUGHIT
RUBITIN
RUSHDIE

R•••••I

RAPANUI
RAVIOLI
ROCKYII
ROSSINI

•RI••••

ARIADNE
ARIDEST
ARIDITY
ARIETTA
ARIKARA
ARIOSOS
ARIOSTO
ARISING
ARISTAE
ARISTAS
ARISTOS
ARIZONA
BRIARDS
BRIBERY
BRIBING
BRICKED
BRIDALS
BRIDGED
BRIDGES
BRIDGET
BRIDLED
BRIDLES
BRIEFED
BRIEFER
BRIEFLY
BRIGADE
BRIGAND
BRIGHAM
BRILLAT
BRIMFUL
BRIMMED
BRINDLE
BRINGER
BRINGIN
BRINGON
BRINGTO
BRINGUP
BRINIER
BRINING
BRIOCHE
BRIQUET
BRISKER
BRISKET
BRISKLY
BRISTLE
BRISTLY
BRISTOL
BRITAIN
BRITISH
BRITONS
BRITTEN
BRITTLE
BRITTON
CRIBBED
CRICKED
CRICKET
CRIMEAN
CRIMPED
CRIMPER
CRIMSON
CRINGED
CRINGES
CRINKLE
CRINKLY
CRINOID
CRISPED
CRISPER
CRISPIN
CRISPLY
CRISPUS
CRITICS
CRITTER
DRIBBLE
DRIBLET
DRIEDUP
DRIESUP
DRIFTED
DRIFTER
DRILLED
DRILLER
DRINKER
DRIPDRY
DRIPPAN
DRIPPED
DRISTAN
DRIVEAT
DRIVEIN
DRIVELS
DRIVERS
DRIVEUP
DRIVING
DRIZZLE
DRIZZLY
ERICSON
ERISTIC
ERITREA
FRIABLE
FRICKIE
FRIDAYS
FRIDGES
FRIEDAN
FRIENDS
FRIEZES
FRIGATE
FRIGHTS
FRILLED
FRINGED
FRINGES
FRISBEE
FRISIAN
FRISKED
FRISSON
FRITTED
FRITTER
FRIZZED
FRIZZES
FRIZZLE
GRIDDED
GRIDDER
GRIDDLE
GRIEVED
GRIEVER
GRIEVES
GRIFFEY
GRIFFIN
GRIFFON
GRIFTER
GRIGRIS
GRILLED
GRILLES
GRILLET
GRIMACE
GRIMIER
GRIMMER
GRINDER
GRINNED
GRINNER
GRIPERS
GRIPING
GRIPPED
GRIPPER
GRISHAM
GRISSOM
GRISTLE
GRISTLY
GRITTED
GRIVETS
GRIZZLE
GRIZZLY
IRIDIUM
IRISOUT
KRINGLE
KRISHNA
ORIENTE
ORIENTS
ORIFICE
ORIGAMI
ORIGINS
ORINOCO
ORIOLES
ORISONS
PRICERS
PRICIER
PRICING
PRICKED
PRICKLE
PRICKLY
PRIDING
PRIESTS
PRIMACY
PRIMARY
PRIMATE
PRIMERS
PRIMING
PRIMMER
PRIMPED
PRINCES
PRINKED
PRINTED
PRINTER
PRIORTO
PRISONS
PRITHEE
PRIVACY
PRIVATE
PRIVETS
PRIVIES
PRIZING
TRIBUNE
TRIBUTE
TRICEPS
TRICKED
TRICKER
TRICKLE
TRICORN
TRICOTS
TRIDENT
TRIEDON
TRIESON
TRIESTE
TRIFLED
TRIFLER
TRIFLES
TRIGGED
TRIGGER
TRIGONS
TRIGRAM
TRILLED
TRILLIN
TRILOGY
TRIMMED
TRIMMER
TRINITY
TRINKET
TRIODES
TRIPLED
TRIPLES
TRIPLET
TRIPLEX
TRIPODS
TRIPOLI
TRIPPED
TRIPPER
TRIPPET
TRIPSUP
TRIREME
TRISECT
TRISTAN
TRITELY
TRITEST
TRITIUM
TRITONE
TRITONS
TRIUMPH
TRIUNES
TRIVETS
TRIVIAL
WRIGGLE
WRIGGLY
WRIGHTS
WRIGLEY
WRINGER
WRINKLE
WRINKLY
WRITEIN
WRITERS
WRITETO
WRITEUP
WRITHED
WRITHES
WRITING
WRITTEN

•R•I•••

ARBITER
ARGIVES
ARNICAS
ARRIERE
ARRISES
ARRIVAL
ARRIVED
ARRIVER
ARRIVES
ARTICLE
ARTIEST
ARTISAN
ARTISTE
ARTISTS
BRAIDED
BRAIDER
BRAILLE
BRAINED
BRAISED
BRAISES
BROILED
BROILER
BRUISED
BRUISER
BRUISES
BRUITED
CRUISED
CRUISER
CRUISES
DRAINED
DRAINER
DREIDEL
DREISER
ERMINES
FRAICHE
FRAILER
FRAILTY
FRAISES
FREIGHT
FREITAG
FRUITED
GRAINED
MRFIXIT
MRRIGHT
ORBISON
ORBITAL
ORBITED
ORBITER
ORDINAL
ORNITHO
ORPINES
ORVILLE
PRAIRIE
PRAISED
PRAISER
PRAISES
PRYINTO
TRAILED
TRAILER
TRAINED
TRAINEE
TRAINER
TRAIPSE
TRAITOR
TROIKAS
TROILUS
TRUISMS
WRAITHS

•R••I••

ARABIAN
ARCHIES
ARCHING
ARCHIVE
ARCSINE
ARGUING
ARIDITY
ARISING
ARMOIRE
ARMPITS
ARRAIGN
ARTFILM
BRACING
BRAKING
BRANIFF
BRAVING
BRAYING
BRAZIER
BRAZING
BREVITY
BREWING
BRIBING
BRINIER
BRINING
BRITISH
BROMIDE
BROMINE
BRUTISH
CRANIAL
CRANING
CRANIUM
CRATING
CRAVING
CRAZIER
CRAZIES
CRAZILY
CRAZING
CREDITS
CRETINS
CREVICE
CREWING
CRITICS
CRONIES
CROSIER
CROWING
CRUCIAL
CRUDITY
DRAPING
DRAWING
DRAYING
DRIVING
DRONING
DROPINS
ERASING
EREMITE
ERODING
EROSION
EROSIVE
EROTICA
ERSKINE
ERUDITE
FRAGILE
FRAMING
FRASIER
FRAYING
FRAZIER
FREEING
FRISIAN
FROLICS
GRACIAS
GRACILE
GRACING
GRADING
GRANITE
GRATIFY
GRATING
GRAVIES
GRAVING
GRAVITY
GRAYING
GRAZING
GRECIAN
GREYING
GRIMIER
GRIPING
GROLIER
GROPING
GROPIUS
GROWING
GRUNION
IRANIAN
IRIDIUM
IRONIES
IRONING
KRATION
MRCHIPS
ORATING
ORATION
ORCHIDS
ORDAINS
ORIFICE
ORIGINS
PRALINE
PRATING
PRAYING
PRECISE
PREDICT
PRELIMS
PREMIER
PREMISE
PREMIUM
PRESIDE
PREVIEW
PRICIER
PRICING
PRIDING
PRIMING
PRIVIES
PRIZING
PROBING
PROBITY
PRODIGY
PROFILE
PROFITS
PROMISE
PROSIER
PROSILY
PROSING
PROTIST
PROVIDE
PROVING
PROVISO
PROXIES
PROXIMO
PRUDISH
PRUNING
TRACING
TRADING
TREEING
TREVINO
TRINITY
TRITIUM
TRIVIAL
TROPICS
TROPISM
TRUCIAL
TRUEING
URANITE
URANIUM
URCHINS
WRITING
XRATING
XRAYING

•R•••I•

ARAMAIC
ARCADIA
ARCHAIC
ARMENIA
ARSENIC
ARSENIO
ARTEMIS
BRAHMIN
BRASSIE
BREAKIN
BRESLIN
BRINGIN
BRITAIN
BROKEIN
BROWNIE
CRAPPIE
CRINOID
CRISPIN
CROATIA
CRYPTIC
DRAGSIN
DRASTIC
DRAWNIN
DRAWSIN
DRIVEIN
DROPSIN
DRUMLIN
DRYSUIT
ERISTIC
ERRATIC
FRANCIS
FRANKIE
FRANTIC
FREDDIE
FREDRIC
FREEBIE
FREESIA
FRICKIE
GRAPHIC
GREMLIN
GRIFFIN
GRIGRIS
GROUPIE
KREMLIN
MRFIXIT
ORGANIC
PRAIRIE
PREEMIE
PREPAID
PREPPIE
PREVAIL
PROSAIC
PROTEIN
PRUSSIA
TRADEIN
TRAFFIC
TRANSIT
TRAVAIL
TRAVOIS
TREFOIL
TREKKIE
TRELLIS
TRILLIN
TROPHIC
WRITEIN
WROTEIN

•R••••I

BRONCHI
ORIGAMI
TRIPOLI

••RI•••

ABRIDGE
ACRIDLY
AERIALS
AERIEST
AFRICAN
AGRIPPA
AIRIEST
AIRINGS
ALRIGHT
AORISTS
APRICOT
APRIORI
ARRIERE
ARRISES
ARRIVAL

ARRIVED
ARRIVER
ARRIVES
ATRIUMS
AURICLE
CARIBES
CARIBOU
CARINAS
CARIOCA
CERIPHS
CHRISMS
CHRISTI
CHRISTO
CHRISTY
CORINTH
CURIOUS
DERIDED
DERIDES
DERIVED
DERIVES
DORITOS
EERIEST
FIRINGS
FORINTS
FURIOUS
GERITOL
GORIEST
GORILLA
HARICOT
HORIZON
JERICHO
JURIDIC
JURISTS
LARIATS
LORISES
LURIDLY
LYRICAL
LYRISTS
MARIANA
MARILYN
MARIMBA
MARINAS
MARINER
MARINES
MARITAL
MERIMEE
MERINOS
MERITED
MRRIGHT
MURILLO
MYRIADS
NORIEGA
PARIAHS
PARIBUS
PARINGS
PERIDOT
PERIGEE
PERIODS
PURISTS
PURITAN
PYRITES
RARITAN
RERINSE
SCRIBES
SCRIMPS
SCRIMPY
SCRIPPS
SCRIPTS
SCRIVEN
SERIALS
SERIATE
SERIOUS
SHRIEKS
SHRIFTS
SHRIKES
SHRILLS
SHRILLY
SHRIMPS
SHRINER
SHRINES
SHRINKS
SHRIVEL
SHRIVER
SHRIVES
SORITES
SPRIEST
SPRINGS
SPRINGY
SPRINTS
SPRITES
STRIATE
STRIDER
STRIDES
STRIKER
STRIKES
STRINGS
STRINGY
STRIPED
STRIPER
STRIPES
STRIVED
STRIVEN
STRIVER
STRIVES
SURINAM
SYRIANS
SYRINGA
SYRINGE
TARIFFS
THRIFTS
THRIFTY
THRILLS
THRIVED
THRIVES
UPRIGHT
UPRISEN
UPRISES
UPRIVER
UTRILLO
VARIANT
VARIETY
VARIOUS
WARIEST
WIRIEST

••R•I••

AIRLIFT
AIRLINE
AIRMILE
AIRTIME
ARRAIGN
BARBING
BARGING
BARKING
BARMIER
BARRIER
BARRING
BARRIOS
BERLIOZ
BERLITZ
BERNICE
BERRIED
BERRIES
BIRDIED
BIRDIES
BIRDING
BIRLING
BURKINA
BURLIER
BURLING
BURNING
BURNISH
BURPING
BURRITO
BURYING
CARBIDE
CARBINE
CARDING
CARMINE
CARNIES
CARPING
CARRICK
CARRIED
CARRIER
CARRIES
CARRION
CARTIER
CARTING
CARVING
CERTIFY
CORDIAL
CORDING
CORDITE
CORKING
CORNICE
CORNIER
CORNILY
CORNING
CORNISH
CORRIDA
CORSICA
CURBING
CURDING
CURLIER
CURLING
CURRIED
CURRIER
CURRIES
CURSING
CURSIVE
CURVIER
CURVING
DARKISH
DARLING
DARNING
DARTING
DERAILS
DERBIES
DERNIER
DERRICK
DERRING
DERVISH
DIRTIED
DIRTIER
DIRTIES
DIRTILY
DORMICE
EARLIER
EARNING
EARRING
EARWIGS
EHRLICH
FARMING
FARRIER
FERMIUM
FERRIED
FERRIES
FERRITE
FERTILE
FIRKINS
FIRMING
FORBIDS
FORCING
FORDING
FOREIGN
FORGING
FORGIVE
FORKING
FORLIFE
FORMICA
FORMING
FORTIES
FORTIFY
FURBISH
FURLING
FURNISH
FURRIER
FURRING
FURTIVE
GARBING
GARNISH
GARRICK
GERAINT
GERBILS
GIRDING
GIRLISH
GORDIAN
GORGING
HARDIER
HARDILY
HARDING
HARKING
HARMING
HARPIES
HARPING
HARPIST
HARRIED
HARRIER
HARRIES
HARRIET
HERDING
HERMITS
HEROICS
HEROINE
HEROISM
HERRING
HERRIOT
HORNING
HORNIST
HORRIFY
HORSIER
HORSING
HURLING
HURRIED
HURRIES
HURTING
JARRING
JERKIER
JERKILY
JERKING
JERKINS
JURYING
KERNING
KURDISH
LARAINE
LARDING
LORDING
LORRIES
LURKING
MARGINS
MARKING
MARLINS
MARMION
MARRIED
MARRIES
MARRING
MARTIAL
MARTIAN
MARTINA
MARTINI
MARTINO
MARTINS
MARXISM
MERCIES
MERGING
MERRIER
MERRILL
MERRILY
MORAINE
MORNING
MORTIFY
MORTISE
MURKIER
MURKILY
NEREIDS
NERVIER
NERVILY
NORDICS
NURSING
OGREISH
PARKING
PARRIED
PARRIES
PARRING
PARSING
PARTIAL
PARTIED
PARTIES
PARTING
PARTITA
PARTITE
PERDIEM
PERFIDY
PERKIER
PERKILY
PERKING
PERKINS
PERLITE
PERMING
PERMITS
PERRIER
PERSIAN
PERSIST
PERSIUS
PORCINE
PORGIES
PORTICO
PORTION
PURGING
PURLIEU
PURLING
PURLINS
PURRING
PURSING
PURVIEW
RERAISE
SARDINE
SERBIAN
SERLING
SERPICO
SERRIED
SERVICE
SERVILE
SERVING
SORRIER
SORTIED
SORTIES
SORTING
SPRAINS
STRAINS
STRAITS
SURFING
SURGING
SURLIER
SURLILY
SURMISE
SURVIVE
TARDIER
TARDILY
TARNISH
TARPITS
TARRIED
TARRIES
TARRING
TARSIER
TERBIUM
TERMING
TERMINI
TERMITE
TERRIER
TERRIES
TERRIFY
TERTIAL
TOROIDS
TORSION
TORYISM
TURBINE
TURKISH
TURNING
TURNIPS
UKRAINE
UPRAISE
VARMINT
VARNISH
VARSITY
VARYING
VERDICT
VERGING
VERNIER
VERSIFY
VERSION
VERTIGO
VIRGINS
WARDING
WARLIKE
WARMING
WARMISH
WARNING
WARPING
WARRING
WARRIOR
WARTIME
WARWICK
WORDIER
WORDILY
WORDING
WORKING
WORMIER
WORRIED
WORRIER
WORRIES
YARNING
ZEROING

••R••I•

ACRYLIC
AEROBIC
AIRFOIL
AIRMAIL
AIRRAID
AIRSHIP
AMRADIO
BARGAIN
BARGEIN
BARMAID
BORODIN
BORZOIS
CARAMIA
CAROTID
CBRADIO
CERAMIC
CERTAIN
CHRONIC
CIRCUIT
CORNOIL
CORSAIR
CURTAIL
CURTAIN
ERRATIC
ETRURIA
EURASIA
FIRELIT
FMRADIO
FORFEIT
HARDHIT
HERETIC
HORATIO
JURIDIC
JURYRIG
KERATIN
KIRSTIE
LARAMIE
LORDJIM
MARQUIS
MERMAID
MORANIS
MORAVIA
PARBOIL
PARFAIT
PARSNIP
PERTAIN
PHRENIC
PIRATIC
PORKPIE
PURLOIN
PURSUIT
PYRAMID
PYRRHIC
RAREBIT
SERAPIS
SIRLOIN
SURFEIT
TERRAIN
THREWIN
THROWIN
TURMOIL
TURNSIN
VERMEIL
WARSHIP
WORKSIN
WORSHIP

••R•••I

AIRTAXI
APRIORI
CHRISTI
CORELLI
FERRARI
ISRAELI
KARACHI
KAROLYI
LORELEI
MARCONI
MARTINI
TERMINI
TORTONI

•••RI••

ACARIDS
ADORING
ALDRICH
AMBRIES
AMERICA
AMERIGO
AMERIKA
AMERIND
ANGRIER
ANGRILY
APERIES
APPRISE
APPRIZE
ASCRIBE
ASTRIDE
ATTRITE
ATTRITS
AVARICE
AZURITE
BARRIER
BARRING
BARRIOS
BEARING
BEARISH
BEGRIME
BERRIED
BERRIES
BLARING
BLERIOT
BOORISH
BURRITO
CAPRICE
CARRICK
CARRIED
CARRIER
CARRIES
CARRION
CHARIER
CHARILY
CHARIOT
CHARITY
CHERISH
CHORINE
CHORIZO
CITRINE
CLARICE
CLARIFY
CLARION
CLARITY
CLERICS
CORRIDA
COURIER
COWRIES
CURRIED
CURRIER
CURRIES
CYPRIOT
CZARINA
CZARISM
CZARIST
DAIRIES
DEBRIEF
DECRIED
DECRIES
DEPRIVE
DERRICK
DERRING
DEVRIES
DIARIES
DOWRIES
EARRING
EMERITA
EMERITI
ENTRIES
ENURING
FABRICS
FAIRIES
FAIRING
FARRIER
FEARING
FEBRILE
FERRIED
FERRIES
FERRITE
FIBRILS
FIERIER
FIERILY
FLARING
FLORIDA
FLORINS
FLORIST
FOURIER
FURRIER
FURRING
GABRIEL
GARRICK
GEARING
GLARING
GLORIAS
GLORIED
GLORIES
GLORIFY
HADRIAN
HAIRIER
HARRIED
HARRIER
HARRIES
HARRIET
HAYRIDE
HEARING
HERRING
HERRIOT
HOARIER
HORRIFY
HURRIED
HURRIES
HYBRIDS
IBERIAN
ICERINK
IMPRINT
INBRIEF
INPRINT
INURING
IVORIES
JARRING
JEERING
JOYRIDE
KEYRING
KUBRICK
LEERIER
LEERILY
LEERING
LORRIES
LOWRISE
MARRIED
MARRIES
MARRING
MAURICE
MEGRIMS
MERRIER
MERRILL
MERRILY
METRICS
MIDRIBS
MIDRIFF
MIDRISE
MITRING
MOORING
MOORISH
NATRIUM
NEARING
NITRIDE
NITRITE
NOURISH
NUTRIAS
OCARINA
OILRIGS
ONTRIAL
OSTRICH
PAIRING
PAPRIKA
PARRIED
PARRIES
PARRING
PATRICE
PATRICK
PATRIOT
PEERING
PERRIER
PETRIFY
PODRIDA
POURING
PUERILE
PURRING
QUERIED
QUERIES
RANRIOT
REARING
REFRIED
REFRIES
REPRICE
REPRINT
REPRISE
RETRIAL
RETRIED
RETRIES
RETRIMS
REWRITE
RIORITA
ROARING
RUBRICS
RUNRIOT
RYKRISP
SABRINA
SAURIAN
SCARIER
SCARIFY
SCARILY
SCARING
SCORING
SEARING
SERRIED
SHARING
SHERIFF
SHORING
SNARING
SNORING
SOARING
SORRIER
SOURING
SOURISH
SPARING
SPIRITO
SPIRITS
STARING
STERILE
STORIED
STORIES
STORING
STYRIAN
SUNRISE
TARRIED
TARRIES
TARRING
TAURINE
TEARIER
TEARILY
TEARING
TERRIER
TERRIES
TERRIFY
THORIUM
TIERING
TOURING
TOURISM
TOURIST
TSARINA
TSARIST
TZARINA
UMBRIAN
UNTRIED
UXORIAL
VEERING
VITRIFY
VITRIOL
WARRING
WARRIOR
WEARIED
WEARIER
WEARIES
WEARILY
WEARING
WORRIED
WORRIER
WORRIES
YTTRIUM

•••R•I•

ACERBIC
AIRRAID
ANDROID
ANEROID
BAHRAIN
CHARLIE
CHARMIN
CHERVIL
CONREID
DEARSIR
DETRAIN
DETROIT
DHURRIE
DOORDIE
EMBROIL
ENTRAIN
EXURBIA
GEORGIA
GHERKIN
GIORGIO
HAIRPIN
HEBRAIC
HENREID
INERTIA
INGRAIN
INORBIT
INTROIT
MAUROIS
OBERLIN
OVERBIG
OVERDID
OVERLIE
PEERSIN
POURSIN
PYRRHIC
RECRUIT
REFRAIN
RETRAIN
SCORPIO
SHAREIN
SHERWIN
STARLIT
STCROIX
STEROID
STIRSIN
SWOREIN
TERRAIN
THEREIN
UPBRAID
WHEREIN

•••R••I

EMERITI
FERRARI
GOURAMI
GUARANI
NAIROBI
PADRONI
SHARPEI

••••RI•

AELFRIC
ALGERIA
AMHARIC
AQUARIA
ASPIRIN
ASSYRIA
ASTORIA
AUSTRIA
BALDRIC
BAVARIA
BEATRIX
CALORIC
CALORIE
CAMBRIC
CENTRIC
CHAGRIN
CHEERIO
CIBORIA
CONBRIO
COTERIE
CULPRIT
DAYTRIP
DELIRIA
DEMERIT
DEXTRIN
DHURRIE
EGOTRIP
EMPORIA
ESTORIL
ETRURIA
FREDRIC
GAGARIN
GASTRIC
GENERIC
GENERIS
GOFORIT
GONERIL
GRIGRIS
GUTHRIE
HENDRIX
HEPARIN
HOMERIC
IMPERIL
INHERIT
INTERIM
JURYRIG
LIBERIA
MAHARIS
MANDRIL
MANTRIC
NIGERIA
NOSTRIL
NUMERIC
ONTARIO
PILGRIM
POLARIS
PRAIRIE
REVERIE
SAFARIS
SAMARIA
SANGRIA
SATIRIC
SAVARIN
SIBERIA
SOLARIA
SWEARIN
TALARIA
TAMARIN
TENDRIL
VALERIE
WILFRID

••••R•I

BACARDI
HAVARTI
SAMURAI
SCHERZI

•••••RI

ALFIERI
APRIORI
CAMPARI
DIMITRI
FERRARI
MAESTRI
SALIERI
SHANGRI
SHASTRI

R•J••••

REJECTS
REJOICE
REJOINS

R••J•••

RAMJETS

•R•J•••

PROJECT
TROJANS

•R••J••

PROPJET

••RJ•••

PERJURE
PERJURY

••R•J••

KARAJAN
LORDJIM

•••RJ••
LEARJET
OVERJOY

R•K••••
RAKEDIN
RAKEDUP
RAKEOFF
RAKESIN
RAKESUP
REKEYED
RYKRISP

R••K•••
RACKETS
RACKING
RACKSUP
RANKERS
RANKEST
RANKING
RANKLED
RANKLES
RAYKROC
RECKONS
REEKING
RICKETY
RICKEYS
RICKLES
RICKSHA
RISKERS
RISKIER
RISKING
ROCKERS
ROCKETS
ROCKIER
ROCKIES
ROCKING
ROCKYII
ROCKYIV
ROOKERY
ROOKIES
ROOKING
RUCKING

R•••K••
RAMEKIN
REBEKAH
REBUKED
REBUKES
REDSKIN
REINKED
REMAKES
RETAKEN
RETAKES
REVOKED
REVOKES

R••••K•
RECORKS
REDOAKS
REHOOKS
RELOCKS
REMARKS
REWORKS
ROANOKE

R•••••K
RANSACK
RATFINK
RATPACK
RAWSILK
RECHALK
RECHECK
REDBOOK
RESTOCK
RETHINK
RETRACK
RIDDICK
ROEBUCK
ROLLICK
RUNAMOK
RUNBACK

•RK••••
IRKSOME

•R•K•••
ARIKARA
BRAKING
BROKEIN
BROKERS
BROKEUP
ERSKINE
TREKKED
TREKKER
TREKKIE

•R••K••
BRACKEN
BRACKET
BREAKER
BREAKIN
BREAKUP
BRICKED
BRISKER
BRISKET
BRISKLY
BROOKED
CRACKED
CRACKER
CRACKLE
CRACKUP
CRANKED
CRANKUP
CREAKED
CRICKED
CRICKET
CRINKLE
CRINKLY
CROAKED
CROOKED
DRINKER
DRUCKER
FRANKED
FRANKER
FRANKIE
FRANKLY
FRANKOZ
FREAKED
FRECKLE
FRICKIE
FRISKED
FROCKED
GRACKLE
IRECKON
PRANKED
PRICKED
PRICKLE
PRICKLY
PRINKED
TRACKED
TRACKER
TREKKED
TREKKER
TREKKIE
TRICKED
TRICKER
TRICKLE
TRINKET
TROIKAS
TRUCKED
TRUCKEE
TRUCKER
TRUCKLE
WRACKED
WREAKED
WRECKED
WRECKER
WRINKLE
WRINKLY

•R•••K•
ARAWAKS
GRETZKY
GROMYKO
OROURKE
PROVOKE
TROTSKY
VRONSKY

•R••••K
ARMLOCK
ARTWORK
BRUBECK
DRSPOCK
DRYDOCK
FRYCOOK
MRSPOCK
PRECOOK
PRESOAK

••RK•••
BARKEEP
BARKERS
BARKING
BARKSAT
BURKINA
CORKAGE
CORKERS
CORKING
DARKAGE
DARKENS
DARKEST
DARKISH
DARKMAN
FIRKINS
FORKERS
FORKFUL
FORKING
GURKHAS
HARKENS
HARKING
JERKIER
JERKILY
JERKING
JERKINS
LURKING
MARKERS
MARKETS
MARKHAM
MARKHOR
MARKING
MARKKAA
MARKOFF
MARKOVA
MARKSUP
MARKUPS
MURKIER
MURKILY
PARKING
PARKWAY
PERKIER
PERKILY
PERKING
PERKINS
PERKSUP
PORKERS
PORKPIE
TURKEYS
TURKISH
WORKDAY
WORKERS
WORKFOR
WORKING
WORKMAN
WORKMEN
WORKOFF
WORKOUT
WORKSIN
WORKSON
WORKSUP
WORKUPS

••R•K••
KARAKUL
KARAKUM
MARKKAA
MARYKAY
PERUKES
SHRIKES
STRIKER
STRIKES
STROKED
STROKES
TURNKEY

••R••K•
BUROAKS
FORSAKE
KARAOKE
PARTAKE
SCREAKS
SHRIEKS
SHRINKS
STREAKS
STREAKY
WARLIKE

••R•••K
AIRLOCK
AIRSOCK
BARRACK
BERSERK
BURBANK
BURDOCK
CARRICK
DERRICK
EARLOCK
FORSOOK
GARRICK
NORFOLK
OARLOCK
PARTOOK
SARAWAK
WARLOCK
WARWICK

•••RK••
CLERKED
GHERKIN
HEARKEN
SHARKEY
SHIRKED
SHIRKER
SMIRKED
SNORKEL
SPARKED
SPARKLE
STARKER
STARKLY

•••R•K•
AMERIKA
ANORAKS
GOBROKE
PAPRIKA

•••R••K
BARRACK
BEDROCK
CARRICK
CONRACK
DEFROCK
DERRICK
GARRICK
HATRACK
HAYRACK
ICERINK
KUBRICK
OUTRANK
PATRICK
PETROCK
RETRACK
TIERACK
UNFROCK

••••RK•
DEBARKS
EMBARKS
MAZURKA
OROURKE
RECORKS
REMARKS
REWORKS
UNCORKS

••••R•K
BODEREK
LAMARCK
MUBARAK

•••••RK
ARTWORK
ATATURK
BERSERK
BULWARK
DEKLERK
DENMARK
DUNKIRK
EARMARK
EARMARK
HAUBERK
HAYFORK
HOLYARK
LEGWORK
NETWORK
NEWYORK
OUTWORK
SELKIRK
SKYLARK
TINWORK
WAXWORK
WIDMARK

R•L••••
RALEIGH
RALLIED
RALLIES
RALLYTO
RALSTON
RDLAING
RELACED
RELACES
RELAPSE
RELATED
RELATES
RELAXED
RELAXES
RELAYED
RELEARN
RELEASE
RELENTS
RELIANT
RELICTS
RELIEFS
RELIEVE
RELIEVO
RELIGHT
RELINED
RELINES
RELISTS
RELIVED
RELIVES
RELLENO
RELOADS
RELOCKS
RELYING
RILLETS
ROLAIDS
ROLLBAR
ROLLERS
ROLLICK
ROLLING
ROLLINS
ROLLOUT
ROLLSUP
ROLLTOP
ROLODEX
ROLVAAG
RULEOUT
RULESON
RULINGS

R••L•••
RAGLANS
RAILERS
RAILING
RAILSAT
RAILWAY
RALLIED
RALLIES
RALLYTO
RANLATE
RATLINE
REALISM
REALIST
REALITY
REALIZE
REALTOR
REBLOOM
RECLAIM
RECLAME
RECLEAN
RECLINE
RECLUSE
REDLINE
REELECT
REELING
REELOFF
REELSIN
REFLECT
REGLUED
REGLUES
RELLENO
REPLACE
REPLANS
REPLANT
REPLATE
REPLAYS
REPLETE
REPLICA
REPLIED
REPLIES
RIFLERS
RIFLERY
RIFLING
RILLETS
RIOLOBO
ROBLOWE
ROILING
ROLLBAR
ROLLERS
ROLLICK
ROLLING
ROLLINS
ROLLOUT
ROLLSUP
ROLLTOP
ROULADE
RUNLAPS
RUNLETS

R•••L••
RABBLES
RADDLED
RADDLES
RAFFLED
RAFFLER
RAFFLES
RAMBLED
RAMBLER
RAMBLES
RANKLED
RANKLES
RASSLED
RASSLES
RATTLED
RATTLER
RATTLES
RAVELED
REBOLTS
RECALLS
RECOLOR
REDFLAG
REFILLS
REFILMS
REGALED
REGALES
REGALIA
REGALLY
REGULAR
REGULUS
REMELTS
REMOLDS
REOILED
REPOLLS
REPULSE
RESALES
RESALTS
RESELLS
RESILED
RESILES
RESOLED
RESOLES
RESOLVE
RESULTS
RETELLS
RETILED
RETILES
REVALUE
REVELED
REVELER
REVELRY
REVILED
REVILES
REVOLTS
REVOLVE
REWELDS
RICKLES
RIDDLED
RIDDLER
RIDDLES
RIFFLED
RIFFLES
RINGLET
RIPPLED
RIPPLES
RIVALED
RIVALRY
RIVULET
RODOLFO
ROMULAN
ROMULUS
ROOTLET
ROSALIE
ROSELLE
ROYALLY
ROYALTY
ROZELLE
RUBBLES
RUDOLPH
RUFFLED
RUFFLES
RUMBLED
RUMBLES
RUMPLED
RUMPLES
RUSTLED
RUSTLER
RUSTLES

R••••L•
RADIALS
RADICLE
RAGDOLL
RANDALL
RAPIDLY
RAPPELS
RASCALS
RATABLE
RATHOLE
RAVIOLI
RAWSILK
READILY
REBOILS
REBUILD
REBUILT
RECALLS
RECHALK
RECOILS
RECYCLE
REDCELL
REDEALS
REDEALT
REDIALS
REDPOLL
REDWOLF
REFILLS
REFUELS
REGALLY
REHEALS
REHEELS
REMAILS
RENAILS
RENAULT
RENTALS
REPEALS
REPOLLS
REPTILE
RESCALE
RESEALS
RESELLS
RESTYLE
RETAILS
RETELLS
RETICLE
RETITLE
RETOOLS
REVEALS
RIGHTLY
RIGIDLY
RISIBLE
RISSOLE
RITUALS
RONDELS
ROSELLE
ROSWELL
ROUGHLY
ROUNDLY
ROWDILY
ROYALLY
ROZELLE
RUMPOLE
RUNNELS
RUSSELL
RUSTILY

R•••••L
RADICAL
RAGDOLL
RANDALL
RAPHAEL
RATTAIL
RAWDEAL
REAVAIL
RECITAL
REDCELL
REDPOLL
REFUSAL
REMODEL
REMOVAL
RENEWAL
RESTFUL
RETINAL
RETRIAL
REVIVAL
ROOMFUL
RORQUAL
ROSEOIL
ROSWELL
RUSSELL

•RL••••
ARLEDGE
ORLANDO
ORLEANS

•R•L•••
ARALSEA
ARCLAMP
ARMLESS
ARMLETS
ARMLOAD
ARMLOCK
ARTLESS
BRILLAT
CRULLER
DRILLED
DRILLER
DROLLER
ERELONG
FRILLED
FROLICS
GRILLED
GRILLES
GRILLET
GROLIER
IRELAND
MRCLEAN
PRALINE
PRELATE
PRELIMS
PRELOAD
PRELUDE
PROLOGS
PROLONG
TRALALA
TRELLIS
TRILLED
TRILLIN
TRILOGY
TROLLED
TROLLEY

•R••L••
AREOLAE
AREOLAR
AREOLAS
ARGYLES
BRADLEE
BRADLEY
BRAILLE
BRAWLED
BRAWLER
BRESLIN
BRIDLED
BRIDLES
BRILLAT
BROILED
BROILER
CRADLED
CRADLES
CRAWLED
CRAWLER
CREOLES
CRUELER
CRUELLY
CRULLER
DRAWLED
DRIBLET
DRILLED
DRILLER
DROLLER
DROOLED
DROOLER
DROPLET
DRUMLIN
FRAILER
FRAILTY
FRAWLEY
FRILLED
GREELEY
GREMLIN
GRILLED
GRILLES
GRILLET
GROWLED
GROWLER
KREMLIN
ORACLES
ORIOLES
ORMOLUS
ORTOLAN
ORVILLE
PRESLEY
PROBLEM
PROWLED
PROWLER
TRAILED
TRAILER
TRAWLED
TRAWLER
TREBLED
TREBLES
TRELLIS
TRIFLED
TRIFLER
TRIFLES
TRILLED
TRILLIN
TRIPLED
TRIPLES
TRIPLET
TRIPLEX
TROILUS
TROLLED
TROLLEY
WRIGLEY

•R•••L•
ARMFULS
ARMHOLE
ARTFILM
ARTICLE
ARUGULA
BRAILLE
BRAMBLE
BRAMBLY
BRASHLY
BRAVELY
BRIDALS
BRIEFLY
BRINDLE
BRISKLY
BRISTLE
BRISTLY
BRITTLE
BROADLY
CRACKLE
CRASSLY
CRAYOLA
CRAZILY
CRENELS
CREWELS
CRINKLE
CRINKLY
CRISPLY
CROSSLY
CRUDELY
CRUELLY
CRUMBLE
CRUMBLY
CRUMPLE
CRUMPLY
CRYWOLF
DRACULA
DRIBBLE
DRIVELS
DRIZZLE
DRIZZLY
DRYCELL
DRYHOLE
DRYWALL
DRYWELL
ERECTLY
FRAGILE
FRANKLY
FRAZZLE
FRECKLE
FRESHLY
FRIABLE
FRIZZLE
GRACILE
GRACKLE
GRANDLY
GRANOLA
GRANULE
GRAPPLE
GRAVELS
GRAVELY
GREATLY
GRIDDLE
GRISTLE
GRISTLY
GRIZZLE
GRIZZLY
GROSSLY
GROVELS
GRUFFLY
GRUMBLE
IRATELY
KRINGLE
ORDEALS
ORDERLY
ORVILLE
PRATTLE
PRESALE
PRESELL
PRICKLE
PRICKLY
PROFILE
PROPELS
PROSILY
PROUDLY
TRALALA
TRAMPLE
TRAVELS
TREACLE
TREACLY
TREADLE
TREMBLE
TREMBLY
TREMOLO
TRESTLE
TRICKLE
TRIPOLI
TRITELY
TROUBLE
TROWELS
TRUCKLE
TRUFFLE
TRUNDLE
WRANGLE
WRESTLE
WRIGGLE
WRIGGLY
WRINKLE
WRINKLY
WRONGLY

•R••••L
AROUSAL
ARRIVAL
ARSENAL
BRIMFUL
BRISTOL
BRUEGEL
CRANIAL
CREOSOL
CRUCIAL
CRYSTAL
DREIDEL
DRYCELL
DRYWALL
DRYWELL
FRACTAL
FRETFUL
FRONTAL
GRADUAL
GRAPNEL
GRENDEL
ORBITAL
ORDINAL
PRECOOL
PRESELL
PRETZEL
PREVAIL
TRAMMEL
TRAUBEL
TRAVAIL
TRAYFUL
TREFOIL
TRIVIAL
TRUCIAL

••RL•••
AIRLANE
AIRLESS
AIRLIFT
AIRLINE
AIRLOCK
BARLEYS
BERLIOZ
BERLITZ
BIRLING
BURLAPS
BURLIER
BURLING
CARLESS
CARLOAD
CARLSON
CARLTON
CARLYLE
CURLERS
CURLEWS
CURLIER
CURLING
CURLSUP
DARLEEN
DARLENE
DARLING
EARLDOM
EARLIER
EARLOBE
EARLOCK
EARLYON
EHRLICH
FARLEFT
FORLIFE

FORLORN
FURLING
FURLONG
GARLAND
GIRLISH
HURLERS
HURLING
KARLOFF
MARLENE
MARLINS
MARLOWE
MERLOTS
OARLESS
OARLOCK
PARLAYS
PARLEYS
PARLORS
PARLOUR
PARLOUS
PERLITE
PERLMAN
PURLIEU
PURLING
PURLINS
PURLOIN
SERLING
SIRLOIN
SURLIER
SURLILY
VARLETS
WARLIKE
WARLOCK
WARLORD
WORLDLY

••R•L••
ACRYLIC
AIRFLOW
AIRPLAY
AURALEE
AURALLY
BURBLED
BURBLES
BURGLAR
BURGLED
BURGLES
CAROLED
CAROLER
CAROLES
CAROLUS
CAROLYN
CIRCLED
CIRCLES
CIRCLET
CORELLI
COROLLA
CURDLED
CURDLES
EARFLAP
EARPLUG
ENROLLS
FERULES
FIRELIT
FORELEG
GARBLED
GARBLES
GARGLED
GARGLES
GERALDO
GIRDLED
GIRDLES
GORILLA
GURGLED
GURGLES
HERALDS
HURDLED
HURDLER
HURDLES
HURTLED
HURTLES
KAROLYI
KERPLOP
KIRTLES
LORELEI
MARBLED
MARBLES
MARILYN
MARYLOU
MORALES
MORALLY
MORELLO
MURILLO
MYRTLES
PAROLED
PAROLEE
PAROLES
PARSLEY
PERPLEX
PURFLED
PURFLES
PURPLED
PURPLES
SARALEE
SCROLLS
SHRILLS
SHRILLY
STROLLS
SURPLUS
THRALLS
THRILLS
TURTLED
TURTLES
UNROLLS
UTRILLO
WARBLED
WARBLER
WARBLES

••R••L•
ACRIDLY
AERIALS
AIRBALL
AIRHOLE
AIRMILE
AIRWOLF
AURALLY
AUREOLA
AUREOLE
AURICLE
BARBELL
BARBELS
BARRELS
BERTOLT
CARFULS
CARLYLE
CARPALS
CARRELS
CARROLL
CARTELS
CEREALS
CORBELS
CORDELL
CORELLI
CORNELL
CORNILY
COROLLA
CORRALS
CORYELL
CUREALL
DARRELL
DERAILS
DIRNDLS
DIRTILY
DORSALS
DURABLE
DURABLY
DURRELL
EARFULS
EARTHLY
ENROLLS
FERRULE
FERTILE
FIREFLY
FIRSTLY
FORMALS
FORMULA
FORSALE
FURBALL
GERBILS
GORILLA
HARDILY
HARSHLY
HERBALS
HERCULE
HERSELF
HIRABLE
ISRAELI
JARFULS
JERKILY
KERNELS
LARGELY
LURIDLY
MARCELS
MARSALA
MARVELS
MERRILL
MERRILY
MIRACLE
MORALLY
MORELLO
MORSELS
MORTALS
MURILLO
MURKILY
NARWALS
NERVILY
NORFOLK
NORMALS
OURSELF
PARABLE
PARCELS
PARNELL
PERCALE
PERGOLA
PERKILY
PERNELL
PORTALS
PORTOLA
PURCELL
SCRAWLS
SCRAWLY
SCROLLS
SCRUPLE
SERIALS
SERVALS
SERVILE
SHRILLS
SHRILLY
SORRELS
SPRAWLS
STROLLS
SURLILY
TARBELL
TARDILY
TARSALS
TERCELS
TERSELY
THRALLS
THRILLS
TIREDLY
UNREELS
UNROLLS
UTRILLO
VERBALS
VIRGULE
WORDILY
WORLDLY

••R•••L
ADRENAL
AEROSOL
AIRBALL
AIRCOOL
AIRFOIL
AIRMAIL
ARRIVAL
AURORAL
BARBELL
BARNOWL
CARACAL
CARAMEL
CARAVEL
CAREFUL
CARPOOL
CARROLL
CORDELL
CORDIAL
CORNEAL
CORNELL
CORNOIL
CORYELL
CUREALL
CURTAIL
DARRELL
DURRELL
FORKFUL
FORREAL
FURBALL
FURSEAL
GERITOL
GIRASOL
HARMFUL
HURTFUL
KARAKUL
LYRICAL
MARITAL
MARSHAL
MARTIAL
MERRILL
NARWHAL
PARASOL
PARBOIL
PARNELL
PARTIAL
PERNELL
PERUSAL
PHRASAL
PURCELL
RORQUAL
SHRIVEL
SORORAL
STRUDEL
SURREAL
TARBELL
TARHEEL
TERTIAL
TURMOIL
UNRAVEL
VERMEIL
VIRTUAL

•••RL••
CHARLES
CHARLEY
CHARLIE
GNARLED
HAARLEM
KNURLED
OBERLIN
OVERLAP
OVERLAY
OVERLIE
PEARLED
SCARLET
SHIRLEY
SKIRLED
SNARLED
STARLET
STARLIT
SWIRLED
TWIRLED
TWIRLER
WHIRLED
WHORLED

•••R•L•
ACEROLA
ALERTLY
ANGRILY
BARRELS
BEDROLL
CARRELS
CARROLL
CHARILY
CHORALE
CHORALS
CHORTLE
CORRALS
COURTLY
DARRELL
DEERFLY
DURRELL
EGGROLL
EMERALD
FEBRILE
FERRULE
FIBRILS
FIERILY
GAGRULE
INERTLY
LAURELS
LEERILY
MERRILL
MERRILY
MISRULE
ONAROLL
OVERALL
PETRELS
PLURALS
PUERILE
SCARILY
SHARPLY
SHORTLY
SMARTLY
SORRELS
SPARELY
SPARKLE
SPIRALS
STARKLY
STARTLE
STERILE
STERNLY
STEROLS
TEARILY
THIRDLY
WEARILY
WEIRDLY

•••R••L
ABOREAL
ACCRUAL
BEDROLL
CARROLL
CHERVIL
DARRELL
DIURNAL
DURRELL
EGGROLL
EMBROIL
ETERNAL
FEARFUL
FORREAL
GABRIEL
JOURNAL
MERRILL
ONAROLL
ONTRIAL
OVERALL
PAYROLL
QUARREL
RETRIAL
SNORKEL
STERNAL
SURREAL
TEARFUL
THERMAL
UXORIAL
VITRIOL

••••RL•
BEVERLY
CLEARLY
DECARLO
EAGERLY
ELDERLY
LOVERLY
MISERLY
ORDERLY
QUEERLY
SHEERLY
SOBERLY
UNCURLS
UNFURLS
UTTERLY

••••R•L
ADMIRAL
APPAREL
AUGURAL
AURORAL
AUSTRAL
CENTRAL
CHLORAL
CLAIROL
CONTROL
DEMEROL
ESTORIL
FEDERAL
FEMORAL
GAMBREL
GENERAL
GONERIL
HUMERAL
IMMORAL
IMPERIL
KESTREL
LATERAL
LIBERAL
LITERAL
MANDREL
MANDRIL
MAYORAL
MINERAL
MISTRAL
MONGREL
NATURAL
NEUTRAL
NOSTRIL
NUMERAL
QUARREL
SEVERAL
SORORAL
TENDRIL
TUMBREL
VENTRAL
WASTREL

•••••RL
COWGIRL
ENSNARL
PINCURL
UNSNARL

R•M••••
RAMADAN
RAMADAS
RAMBEAU
RAMBLED
RAMBLER
RAMBLES
RAMEKIN
RAMESES
RAMJETS
RAMMING
RAMPAGE
RAMPANT
RAMPART
RAMRODS
REMAILS
REMAINS
REMAKES
REMANDS
REMARKS
REMARRY
REMELTS
REMENDS
REMINDS
REMIXED
REMIXES
REMNANT
REMODEL
REMOLDS
REMORAS
REMORSE
REMOTER
REMOTES
REMOUNT
REMOVAL
REMOVED
REMOVER
REMOVES
REMOWED
REMUDAS
RIMBAUD
RIMMING
RIMSHOT
ROMAINE
ROMANCE
ROMANIA
ROMANOV
ROMANSH
ROMNEYS
ROMPERS
ROMPING
ROMULAN
ROMULUS
RUMBAED
RUMBLED
RUMBLES
RUMMAGE
RUMMIER
RUMORED
RUMOURS
RUMPLED
RUMPLES
RUMPOLE

R••M•••
RAGMOPS
RAIMENT
RAMMING
RAYMOND
REAMASS
REAMERS
REAMING
REDMEAT
RHOMBUS
RHUMBAS
RHYMERS
RHYMING
RIMMING
ROAMERS
ROAMING
ROOMERS
ROOMFUL
ROOMIER
ROOMIES
ROOMING
RUMMAGE
RUMMIER

R•••M••
RACEMES
RADAMES
RAINMAN
READMIT
REARMED
REGIMEN
REGIMES
RENAMED
RENAMES
REPOMAN
RESUMED
RESUMES
RETIMED
RETIMES
REVAMPS
RICHMAN
ROADMAP
RUNAMOK

R••••M•
RAGTIME
RANSOMS
RECLAME
REDEEMS
REDGUMS
REFILMS
REFORMS
REFRAME
RESTAMP
RETRIMS
REWARMS
RHIZOME
RHYTHMS
RUNHOME

R•••••M
REALISM
REBLOOM
RECLAIM
RECROOM
REQUIEM
RHENIUM
RHODIUM
ROSTRUM

•RM••••
ARMADAS
ARMBAND
ARMENIA
ARMFULS
ARMHOLE
ARMLESS
ARMLETS
ARMLOAD
ARMLOCK
ARMOIRE
ARMORED
ARMORER
ARMOURS
ARMPITS
ARMREST
ARMYANT
ERMINES
MRMAGOO
ORMANDY
ORMOLUS

•R•M•••
ARAMAIC
ARAMEAN
ARDMORE
BRAMBLE
BRAMBLY
BRIMFUL
BRIMMED
BROMATE
BROMIDE
BROMINE
CRAMMED
CRAMMER
CRAMPED
CRAMPON
CREMONA
CRIMEAN
CRIMPED
CRIMPER
CRIMSON
CRUMBLE
CRUMBLY
CRUMPET
CRUMPLE
CRUMPLY
DRUMLIN
DRUMMED
DRUMMER
DRUMSUP
EREMITE
FRAMEUP
FRAMING
FREMONT
FROMAGE
GRAMMAR
GRAMMER
GRAMMES
GRAMPUS
GREMLIN
GRIMACE
GRIMIER
GRIMMER
GROMMET
GROMYKO
GRUMBLE
GRUMPED
KREMLIN
PREMEDS
PREMIER
PREMISE
PREMIUM
PRIMACY
PRIMARY
PRIMATE
PRIMERS
PRIMING
PRIMMER
PRIMPED
PROMISE
PROMOTE
PROMPTS
TRAMCAR
TRAMMEL
TRAMPAS
TRAMPED
TRAMPLE
TREMBLE
TREMBLY
TREMOLO
TREMORS
TRIMMED
TRIMMER
TRUMPED
TRUMPET
TRUMPUP

•R••M••
ARTEMIS
ARTEMUS
BRAHMAN
BRAHMAS
BRAHMIN
BRIMMED
CRAMMED
CRAMMER
CREAMED
CREAMER
CREWMAN
CREWMEN
DREAMED
DREAMER
DREAMON
DREAMUP
DRUMMED
DRUMMER
ERASMUS
FREEMAN
FREEMEN
FROGMAN
FROGMEN
GRAMMAR
GRAMMER
GRAMMES
GRIMMER
GROMMET
GROOMED
GROOMER
IRONMAN
IRONMEN
PREAMPS
PREEMIE
PREEMPT
PRIMMER
PROPMAN
PROPMEN
TRAMMEL
TRAUMAS
TRIMMED
TRIMMER
TRIUMPH

•R•••M•
ARCLAMP
DRACHMA
FRENUMS
GRAHAME
GRAHAMS
GRANDMA
IRKSOME
ORIGAMI
PRELIMS
PRESUME
PROXIMO
TRIREME
TRUISMS

•R••••M
ARTFILM
ARTFORM
BRIGHAM
CRANIUM
ERRATUM
FREEDOM
GRANDAM
GRISHAM
GRISSOM
IRIDIUM
ORGANUM
PREMIUM
PROBLEM
PROGRAM
TRANSOM
TRIGRAM
TRITIUM
TROPISM
URANIUM

••RM•••
AIRMAIL
AIRMASS
AIRMILE
BARMAID
BARMIER
BERMUDA
BURMESE
CARMINE
DORMANT
DORMERS
DORMICE
EARMARK
EARMUFF
FARMERS
FARMING
FARMOUT
FERMENT
FERMIUM
FIRMEST
FIRMING
FIRMSUP
FORMALS
FORMATS
FORMICA
FORMING
FORMOSA
FORMULA
GARMENT
GERMANE
GERMANS
GERMANY
HARMFUL
HARMING
HARMONY
HERMANN
HERMITS
HORMONE
KIRMANS
MARMARA
MARMION
MARMOTS
MERMAID
MORMONS
MURMURS
NORMALS
NORMAND
NORMANS
PERMING
PERMITS
SERMONS
SURMISE
TARMACS
TERMING
TERMINI
TERMITE
TORMENT
TURMOIL
VARMINT
VERMEER
VERMEIL
VERMONT
WARMEST
WARMING
WARMISH
WARMSUP
WARMUPS
WORMIER
ZERMATT

••R•M••
AFRAMES
BERGMAN
BIRDMAN
BIRDMEN
BIREMES
CARAMBA
CARAMEL
CARAMIA
CAROMED
CERAMIC
CERUMEN
CHROMES
DARKMAN
FIREMAN
FIREMEN
FOREMAN
FOREMEN
HARTMAN
LARAMIE
MARIMBA
MERIMEE
MIRAMAR
MIRAMAX
PERLMAN
PYRAMID
PYRAMUS
SCRIMPS
SCRIMPY
SHRIMPS
WORKMAN
WORKMEN
YARDMAN
YARDMEN

••R••M•
AIRDAMS
AIRPUMP
AIRTIME
ATRIUMS
CHRISMS
MARRYME
PERFUME
SCREAMS
STREAMS
SURNAME
WARGAME
WARTIME

••R•••M
ABRAHAM
ACRONYM
BARROOM
BOREDOM
EARDRUM
EARLDOM
ERRATUM
FERMIUM
FIREARM
FORDHAM
FOREARM
HEROISM
KARAKUM
LORDJIM
MARKHAM
MARXISM
PERDIEM
PERFORM
SARCASM
SERFDOM
SORGHUM
STRATUM
SURINAM
TERBIUM
TORYISM
YARDARM

•••RM••
ALARMED
ALARMER
CHARMED
CHARMER
CHARMIN
DOORMAN
DOORMAT
DOORMEN
GOURMET
REARMED
SHERMAN
STARMAN

STARMAP
STORMED
SWARMED
THERMAL
THERMOS
THURMAN
UNARMED

•••R•M•
ALARUMS
ASHRAMS
BEGRIME
DIORAMA
ENGRAMS
EXTREME
GOURAMI
MACRAME
MARRYME
MEGRIMS
NOTRUMP
OFFRAMP
QUORUMS
REFRAME
RETRIMS
SANREMO
SUPREME
SUPREMO
TRIREME

•••R••M
BARROOM
BEDROOM
CZARDOM
CZARISM
DAYROOM
GUARGUM
HAARLEM
LEGROOM
NATRIUM
RECROOM
STARDOM
STERNUM
SUNROOM
TAPROOM
TEAROOM
THORIUM
TOURISM
YTTRIUM

••••RM•
AFFIRMS
DEFORMS
DISARMS
INFORMS
PALERMO
REFORMS
REWARMS
SQUIRMS
SQUIRMY

••••R•M
ANAGRAM
BUCKRAM
CHETRUM
DECORUM
DIAGRAM
EARDRUM
EPIGRAM
FULCRUM
HUMDRUM
INTERIM
NOSTRUM
PILGRIM
PROGRAM
ROSTRUM
SEAGRAM
SISTRUM
TANTRUM
THEOREM
TRIGRAM
WOLFRAM

•••••RM
ANTFARM
ARTFORM
CONFIRM
CONFORM
FIREARM
FOREARM
MIDTERM
PERFORM
SIDEARM
TONEARM
UNIFORM
YARDARM

R•N••••
RANAWAY
RANCHED
RANCHER
RANCHES
RANCHOS
RANCOUR
RANDALL
RANDIER
RANGERS
RANGIER
RANGING
RANGOON
RANINTO
RANKERS
RANKEST
RANKING
RANKLED
RANKLES
RANLATE
RANOVER
RANRIOT
RANSACK
RANSOMS
RANTERS
RANTING
RENAILS
RENAMED
RENAMES
RENAULT
RENDERS
RENDING
RENEGED
RENEGER
RENEGES
RENEWAL
RENEWED
RENEWER
RENNINS
RENOTES
RENTALS
RENTERS
RENTING
RINGERS
RINGING
RINGLET
RINGOUT
RINGSUP
RINSING
RONDEAU
RONDELS
RONTGEN
RUNAMOK
RUNAWAY
RUNBACK
RUNDEEP
RUNDOWN
RUNHOME
RUNINTO
RUNLAPS
RUNLETS
RUNNELS
RUNNERS
RUNNIER
RUNNING
RUNOFFS
RUNOVER
RUNRIOT
RUNSDRY
RUNSOFF
RUNSOUT
RUNTIER
RUNWAYS
RUNWITH

R••N•••
RAINBOW
RAINHAT
RAINIER
RAINING
RAINMAN
RAINOUT
RAWNESS
REDNESS
REENACT
REENTER
REENTRY
REGNANT
REINING
REINKED
REINSIN
REMNANT
RENNINS
REUNIFY
REUNION
REUNITE
REYNARD
RHENIUM
ROANOKE
ROMNEYS
ROUNDED
ROUNDER
ROUNDLY
ROUNDON
ROUNDUP
RUANDAN
RUINERS
RUINING
RUINOUS
RUNNELS
RUNNERS
RUNNIER
RUNNING
RWANDAN

R•••N••
RANINTO
RAPANUI
RAPINES
RATINGS
RAVENED
RAVENNA
RAVINES
RAVINGS
REBINDS
RECANED
RECANES
RECANTS
RECENCY
REDANTS
REFINED
REFINER
REFINES
REFUNDS
REGENCY
REGENTS
REHANGS
REIGNED
RELENTS
RELINED
RELINES
REMANDS
REMENDS
REMINDS
REPENTS
REPINED
REPINES
RERENTS
RERINSE
RESANDS
RESENDS
RESENTS
RESINGS
RETINAE
RETINAL
RETINAS
RETINUE
RETUNED
RETUNES
REVENGE
REVENUE
REWINDS
REZONED
REZONES
RIBANDS
RIPENED
RIPINTO
RISINGS
RODENTS
ROMANCE
ROMANIA
ROMANOV
ROMANSH
ROSANNA
ROSANNE
ROTUNDA
ROXANNE
RULINGS
RUNINTO

R••••N•
RACKING
RADIANS
RADIANT
RAFTING
RAGGING
RAGLANS
RAIDING
RAILING
RAIMENT
RAINING
RAISING
RAISINS
RAMMING
RAMPANT
RANGING
RANKING
RANTING
RAPPING
RASPING
RATFINK
RATIONS
RATLINE
RATTANS
RATTING
RAVENNA
RAYGUNS
RAYMOND
RAZZING
RDLAING
READING
REAGENT
REAMING
REAPING
REAREND
REARING
REASONS
REBOUND
RECKONS
RECLINE
RECOUNT
REDCENT
REDDENS
REDDING
REDFINS
REDLINE
REDOING
REDOUND
REDPINE
REDWINE
REDWING
REEDING
REEFING
REEKING
REELING
REFFING
REGAINS
REGIONS
REGNANT
REINING
REJOINS
RELIANT
RELLENO
RELYING
REMAINS
REMNANT
REMOUNT
RENDING
RENNINS
RENTING
REOPENS
REPAINT
REPLANS
REPLANT
REPRINT
REPUGNS
RESCIND
RESIGNS
RESOUND
RESPOND
RESTING
RETAINS
RETHINK
RETSINA
RETURNS
REUBENS
REVVING
REWOUND
RHYMING
RIBBING
RIBBONS
RIDDING
RIDGING
RIFFING
RIFLING
RIFTING
RIGGING
RIMMING
RINGING
RINSING
RIOTING
RIPPING
RISKING
ROAMING
ROARING
ROBBING
ROBBINS
ROCKING
ROILING
ROLLING
ROLLINS
ROMAINE
ROMPING
ROOFING
ROOKING
ROOMING
ROOTING
ROSANNA
ROSANNE
ROSSINI
ROSTAND
ROTTING
ROUGING
ROUSING
ROUTINE
ROUTING
ROXANNE
RUBBING
RUCHING
RUCKING
RUINING
RUNNING
RUSHING
RUSTING

R•••••N
RACCOON
RAINMAN
RAKEDIN
RAKESIN
RALSTON
RAMADAN
RAMEKIN
RANGOON
RARITAN
RAYBURN
READSIN
REARDON
RECLEAN
REDRAWN
REDSKIN
REELSIN
REFRAIN
REGIMEN
REINSIN
RELEARN
REPOMAN
RESTAIN
RETAKEN
RETRAIN
REUNION
REWOVEN
RICHMAN
RIGHTON
RIPTORN
ROBESON
ROMULAN
RONTGEN
ROPEDIN
ROPESIN
ROUGHEN
ROUNDON
ROYBEAN
RUANDAN
RUBDOWN
RUBICON
RUBITIN
RUCTION
RUFFIAN
RULESON
RUNDOWN
RUSSIAN
RWANDAN

•RN••••
ARNICAS
ERNESTO
ORNETTE
ORNITHO

•R•N•••
BRANDED
BRANDER
BRANDON
BRANIFF
BRANSON
BRENDAN
BRENNAN
BRENNER
BRINDLE
BRINGER
BRINGIN
BRINGON
BRINGTO
BRINGUP
BRINIER
BRINING
BRONCHI
BRONCOS
BRONSON
BRONZED
BRONZES
BRUNETS
BRYNNER
CRANIAL
CRANING
CRANIUM
CRANKED
CRANKUP
CRENELS
CRINGED
CRINGES
CRINKLE
CRINKLY
CRINOID
CRONIES
CRUNCHY
DRINKER
DRONERS
DRONING
DRYNESS
FRANCES
FRANCIS
FRANKED
FRANKER
FRANKIE
FRANKLY
FRANKOZ
FRANTIC
FRENEAU
FRENUMS
FRINGED
FRINGES
FRONTAL
FRONTED
FRONTON
GRANADA
GRANARY
GRANDAM
GRANDEE
GRANDER
GRANDLY
GRANDMA
GRANDPA
GRANGER
GRANGES
GRANITE
GRANOLA
GRANTED
GRANTEE
GRANTOR
GRANULE
GRENADA
GRENADE
GRENDEL
GRINDER
GRINNED
GRINNER
GRUNION
GRUNTED
IRANIAN
IRONAGE
IRONERS
IRONIES
IRONING
IRONMAN
IRONMEN
IRONORE
IRONOUT
KRINGLE
ORANGES
ORINOCO
PRANCED
PRANCER
PRANCES
PRANKED
PRINCES
PRINKED
PRINTED
PRINTER
PRONGED
PRONOUN
PRUNERS
PRUNING
TRANCES
TRANSIT
TRANSOM
TRENARY
TRENDED
TRENTON
TRINITY
TRINKET
TRUNDLE
URANITE
URANIUM
VRONSKY
WRANGLE
WRINGER
WRINKLE
WRINKLY
WRONGED
WRONGER
WRONGLY
WRYNESS

•R••N••
ARDENCY
ARGONNE
ARMENIA
ARRANGE
ARSENAL
ARSENIC
ARSENIO
BRAINED
BRENNAN
BRENNER
BROSNAN
BROWNED
BROWNER
BROWNIE
BRYNNER
CROONED
CROONER
CROWNED
DRAGNET
DRAINED
DRAINER
DRAWNIN
DRAWNON
DRAWNUP
DROWNED
ERMINES
ERRANDS
FRIENDS
FROWNAT
FROWNED
FROWNER
GRAINED
GRAPNEL
GREENED
GREENER
GRINNED
GRINNER
GROANED
GROANER
GROUNDS
GROWNUP
MRBONES
ORDINAL
ORGANDY
ORGANIC
ORGANON
ORGANUM
ORGANZA
ORIENTE
ORIENTS
ORLANDO
ORMANDY
ORPINES
PREENED
PREENER
PRYINTO
TRAINED
TRAINEE
TRAINER
TRIUNES
TROUNCE
TRUANCY
TRUANTS
URBANER
URGENCY

•R•••N•
ARACHNE
ARCHING
ARCHONS
ARCSINE
ARGONNE
ARGUING
ARIADNE
ARISING
ARIZONA
ARMBAND
ARMYANT
ARTSONG
BRACING
BRAKING
BRAVING
BRAYING
BRAZING
BRETONS
BREWING
BRIBING
BRIGAND
BRINING
BRITONS
BROGANS
BROMINE
CRANING
CRATING
CRAVENS
CRAVING
CRAYONS
CRAZING
CREMONA
CRETANS
CRETINS
CREWING
CROWING
DRAGONS
DRAPING
DRAWING
DRAYING
DRIVING
DRONING
DROPINS
DRYRUNS
ERASING
ERELONG
ERODING
ERSKINE
FRAMING
FRAYING
FREEING
FREMONT
FRYPANS
GRACING
GRADING
GRATING
GRAVING
GRAYING
GRAZING
GREYING
GRIPING
GROPING
GROWING
IRELAND
IRONING
KRISHNA
ORATING
ORDAINS
OREGANO
ORIGINS
ORISONS
ORLEANS
OROTUND
ORPHANS
PRALINE
PRATING
PRAYING
PREBEND
PRESENT
PRETEND
PREVENT
PRICING
PRIDING
PRIMING
PRISONS
PRIZING
PROBING
PROBONO
PROFANE
PROGENY
PROLONG
PROPANE
PROSING
PROTONS
PROVING
PRUDENT
PRUNING
TRACING
TRADING
TREEING
TREPANS
TREVINO
TRIBUNE
TRIDENT
TRIGONS
TRITONE
TRITONS
TROJANS
TRUEING
URCHINS
WRITING
XRATING
XRAYING

•R••••N
ARABIAN
ARAMEAN
ARRAIGN
ARTISAN
BRACKEN
BRAHMAN
BRAHMIN
BRANDON
BRANSON
BRAXTON
BREAKIN
BRENDAN
BRENNAN
BRESLIN
BRESSON
BRINGIN
BRINGON
BRITAIN
BRITTEN
BRITTON
BROADEN
BROKEIN
BRONSON
BROSNAN
CRAMPON
CREWMAN
CREWMEN
CRIMEAN
CRIMSON
CRISPIN
CROUTON
CRYOGEN
DRAGOON
DRAGSIN
DRAGSON
DRAWNIN
DRAWNON
DRAWSIN
DRAWSON
DREAMON
DRESDEN
DRIPPAN
DRISTAN
DRIVEIN
DROPSIN
DRUMLIN
EREWHON
ERICSON
EROSION
FREEMAN
FREEMEN
FRESHEN
FRIEDAN
FRISIAN
FRISSON
FROGMAN
FROGMEN
FRONTON
GRAYSON
GRECIAN
GREMLIN
GRIFFIN
GRIFFON
GROWSON
GRUNION
GRYPHON
IRANIAN
IRECKON
IRONMAN
IRONMEN
KRATION
KREMLIN
KRYPTON
MRCLEAN
ORATION
ORBISON
ORGANON
ORPHEAN
ORTOLAN
PREDAWN
PRESSON
PRESTON
PRETEEN
PREYSON
PROCYON
PRONOUN
PROPMAN
PROPMEN
PROTEAN
PROTEIN
TRADEIN
TRADEON
TREASON
TRENTON
TRICORN
TRIEDON
TRIESON
TRILLIN
TRISTAN
TRODDEN
WRITEIN
WRITTEN
WROTEIN

••RN•••
BARNARD
BARNEYS
BARNOWL
BERNARD
BERNESE
BERNICE
BERNSEN
BORNEUP
BURNERS
BURNETT
BURNING
BURNISH
BURNOUT
BURNSUP
BURNTUP
CARNERA
CARNETS
CARNIES
CORNCOB
CORNDOG
CORNEAL
CORNEAS
CORNELL
CORNERS
CORNETS
CORNFED
CORNICE
CORNIER
CORNILY
CORNING
CORNISH
CORNOIL
CORNROW
DARNERS
DARNING
DERNIER
DIRNDLS
EARNERS
EARNEST
EARNING
FURNACE
FURNISH
GARNERS
GARNETS
GARNISH
GURNEYS
HARNESS
HORNETS
HORNING
HORNIST
HORNSBY
KERNELS
KERNING
MORNING
PARNELL
PERNELL
SURNAME
TARNISH
TERNARY
TERNATE
TORNADO
TORNOUT
TURNERS
TURNING
TURNIPS
TURNKEY
TURNOFF
TURNOUT
TURNSIN
TURNSON
TURNSTO
TURNSUP

VARNISH
VERNIER
WARNING
WERNHER
WORNOFF
WORNOUT
YARNING

••R•N••

ACRONYM
ADRENAL
AIRINGS
APRONED
ARRANGE
BARANOF
BARENTS
BARONET
BARONGS
CARINAS
CHRONIC
CORINTH
CORONAE
CORONAS
CORONET
DURANCE
DURANGO
DURANTE
ERRANDS
FIRENZE
FIRINGS
FORINTS
GARDNER
GARONNE
GERENTS
GERUNDS
GIRONDE
KORUNAS
LARDNER
LORENZO
MARINAS
MARINER
MARINES
MERINOS
MIRANDA
MORANIS
OTRANTO
PARDNER
PARENTS
PARINGS
PARSNIP
PARTNER
PHRENIC
PIRANHA
RERENTS
RERINSE
SARANAC
SARONGS
SCRUNCH
SERENER
SHRINER
SHRINES
SHRINKS
SPRINGS
SPRINGY
SPRINTS
STRANDS
STRANGE
STRINGS
STRINGY
SURINAM
SYRINGA
SYRINGE
TARANTO
TERENCE
THRONES
THRONGS
TORONTO
TYRANNY
TYRANTS
VERANDA

••R••N•

AGROUND
AIRGUNS
AIRLANE
AIRLINE
BARBING
BARGING
BARKING
BARRENS
BARRING
BARTEND
BARYONS
BIRDING
BIRLING
BURBANK
BURDENS
BURKINA
BURLING
BURNING
BURPING
BURYING
CARBINE
CARBONS
CARDING
CAREENS
CARMINE
CARPING
CARTING
CARTONS
CARVING
CORDING
CORDONS
CORKING
CORNING
CURBING
CURDING
CURLING
CURRANT
CURRENT
CURSING
CURVING
DARKENS
DARLENE
DARLING
DARNING
DARTING
DERRING
DORMANT
EARNING
EARRING
FARGONE
FARMING
FERMENT
FERVENT
FIREANT
FIRKINS
FIRMING
FORCING
FORDING
FORFEND
FORGING
FORGONE
FORKING
FORMING
FORRENT
FORTUNA
FORTUNE
FORWENT
FURLING
FURLONG
FURRING
GARBING
GARCONS
GARDENS
GARLAND
GARMENT
GARONNE
GERAINT
GERMANE
GERMANS
GERMANY
GIRDING
GORGING
GORGONS
GOROUND
HARDENS
HARDING
HARKENS
HARKING
HARMING
HARMONY
HARPING
HERDING
HERMANN
HEROINE
HERRING
HORMONE
HORNING
HORSING
HURLING
HURTING
JARGONS
JARRING
JERKING
JERKINS
JURYING
KERNING
KIRMANS
KOREANS
LARAINE
LARCENY
LARDING
LARDONS
LORDING
LURKING
MARCONI
MARGINS
MARIANA
MARKING
MARLENE
MARLINS
MAROONS
MARRING
MARTENS
MARTINA
MARTINI
MARTINO
MARTINS
MARYANN
MERGING
MORAINE
MORDANT
MORDENT
MORGANA
MORGANS
MORMONS
MORNING
NIRVANA
NORMAND
NORMANS
NURSING
PARDONS
PARKING
PARRING
PARSING
PARSONS
PARTING
PARVENU
PERCENT
PERKING
PERKINS
PERMING
PERSONA
PERSONS
PORCINE
PORSENA
PORTEND
PORTENT
PURGING
PURLING
PURLINS
PURRING
PURSING
SARDINE
SARGENT
SCRAWNY
SCREENS
SERLING
SERMONS
SERPENT
SERVANT
SERVING
SORTING
SPRAINS
STRAINS
SURFING
SURGING
SYRIANS
TARPONS
TARRING
TARTANS
TARZANA
TERHUNE
TERMING
TERMINI
TERRENE
TORMENT
TORRENT
TORTONI
TURBANS
TURBINE
TUREENS
TURNING
TYRANNY
UKRAINE
VARIANT
VARMINT
VARYING
VERBENA
VERDANT
VERGING
VERMONT
VIRGINS
WARDENS
WARDING
WARMING
WARNING
WARPING
WARRANT
WARRENS
WARRING
WORDING
WORDONE
WORKING
WORSENS
YARNING
ZEROING
ZIRCONS

••R•••N

AFRICAN
ARRAIGN
BARGAIN
BARGEIN
BERGMAN
BERGSON
BERNSEN
BIRDMAN
BIRDMEN
BORODIN
BURGEON
BURPGUN
BURSTYN
CARAVAN
CARLSON
CARLTON
CAROLYN
CARRION
CARRYON
CARTOON
CERTAIN
CERUMEN
CORAZON
CURTAIN
DARKMAN
DARLEEN
EARLYON
EARTHEN
FIREMAN
FIREMEN
FOREIGN
FOREMAN
FOREMEN
FORERAN
FORERUN
FORLORN
FORTRAN
GORDIAN
HARDPAN
HARDWON
HARPOON
HARPSON
HARSHEN
HARTMAN
HERMANN
HIRESON
HORIZON
KARAJAN
KERATIN
MARCHEN
MARCHON
MARILYN
MARMION
MARTIAN
MARYANN
OBREGON
OURTOWN
PARAGON
PERLMAN
PERSIAN
PERTAIN
PORTION
PURITAN
PURLOIN
RARITAN
SARACEN
SARAZEN
SAROYAN
SCRIVEN
SERBIAN
SIRLOIN
STRIVEN
SURGEON
TERRAIN
THREWIN
THROWIN
TORSION
TURNSIN
TURNSON
UPRISEN
VERSION
VIRGOAN
WORKMAN
WORKMEN
WORKSIN
WORKSON
YARDMAN
YARDMEN
YEREVAN

•••RN••

ADORNED
BLARNEY
CHURNED
DIURNAL
ETERNAL
HAIRNET
JOURNAL
JOURNEY
LEARNED
LEARNER
LIERNES
SCORNED
SPURNED
SPURNER
STERNAL
STERNER
STERNLY
STERNUM
TIERNEY
TOURNEY
YEARNED
YEARNER
YEARNTO

•••R•N•

ADORING
AFFRONT
AMERIND
AYNRAND
BARRENS
BARRING
BEARING
BLARING
CHORINE
CITRINE
CITRONS
COURANT
CURRANT
CURRENT
CZARINA
DERRING
DRYRUNS
EARRING
ENDRUNS
ENTRANT
ENURING
EPERGNE
FAIRING
FEARING
FLARING
FLORINS
FORRENT
FURRING
GEARING
GLARING
GOWRONG
GUARANI
HEARING
HERRING
HYDRANT
ICERINK
IMPRINT
INFRONT
INPRINT
INURING
ITERANT
JARRING
JEERING
KEYRING
LAURENT
LEERING
MACRONS
MADRONA
MARRING
MATRONS
MICRONS
MIGRANT
MITRING
MOORING
NEARING
NEURONE
NEURONS
OCARINA
OPERAND
OUTRANK
OUTRUNS
PADRONE
PADRONI
PAIRING
PARRING
PATRONS
PEERING
PHARYNX
POURING
PURRING
REAREND
REARING
REPRINT
ROARING
SABRINA
SCARING
SCORING
SEARING
SHARING
SHORING
SKIRUNS
SNARING
SNORING
SOARING
SOPRANO
SOURING
SPARING
SPIRANT
STARING
STORING
STYRENE
TARRING
TAURINE
TEARING
TERRENE
TIERING
TORRENT
TOURING
TSARINA
TZARINA
UPFRONT
VAGRANT
VEERING
VIBRANT
WARRANT
WARRENS
WARRING
WEARING
YEAREND

•••R••N

ALARCON
BAHRAIN
BEARSON
BOURBON
CARRION
CARRYON
CHARMIN
CITROEN
CLARION
COARSEN
DETRAIN
DOORMAN
DOORMEN
EMERSON
ENTRAIN
EXURBAN
GHERKIN
HADRIAN
HAIRPIN
HEARKEN
HEARTEN
HOARSEN
IBERIAN
INGRAIN
INGROWN
JIMRYUN
JOURDAN
MAUREEN
MEGRYAN
MOORHEN
OBERLIN
OVERRAN
OVERRUN
PATROON
PEARSON
PEERSIN
POURSIN
REARDON
REDRAWN
REFRAIN
RETRAIN
SAURIAN
SHAREIN
SHARPEN
SHERMAN
SHERWIN
SHORTEN
SMARTEN
SPARTAN
SPORRAN
SPURSON
STARMAN
STIRSIN
STYRIAN
SWOREIN
TERRAIN
THEREIN
THEREON
THURMAN
UMBRIAN
UNDRAWN
WHARTON
WHEREIN

••••RN•

AUBURNS
BYTURNS
CASERNS
CAVERNS
DEHORNS
GOVERNS
INFERNO
INTERNS
LAVERNE
LUCERNE
MODERNS
OSBORNE
PATERNO
RETURNS
SALERNO
SUBORNS
SUKARNO
TAVERNS
UPBORNE
UPTURNS
WYVERNS

••••R•N

ACHERON
AILERON
ALSORAN
ANDIRON
ASPIRIN
BULLRUN
CALDRON
CAMERON
CHAGRIN
CHEVRON
COCHRAN
DENDRON
DEXTRIN
FORERAN
FORERUN
FORTRAN
GAGARIN
HEPARIN
HOMERUN
KATHRYN
LATERAN
LATERON
LEBARON
LONGRUN
MALAREN
MILKRUN
MILLRUN
NEUTRON
OMICRON
OVERRAN
OVERRUN
PIGIRON
SAFFRON
SAHARAN
SAVARIN
SPORRAN
SWEARIN
TAMARIN
TEHERAN
TELERAN
VETERAN
WELLRUN

•••••RN

ADJOURN
BIGHORN
BITTERN
CISTERN
CLIBURN
COGBURN
CONCERN
DISCERN
EASTERN
FOGHORN
FORLORN
HEPBURN
INKHORN
LANTERN
LECTERN
LEGHORN
LOWBORN
MAXBORN
NEWBORN
NOCTURN
OAKFERN
OUTWORN
PASTERN
PATTERN
POPCORN
POSTERN
RAYBURN
RELEARN
RIPTORN
SANBORN
SAXHORN
SOJOURN
SOTHERN
SUNBURN
TINHORN
TINTERN
TRICORN
UNICORN
UNLEARN
UNSHORN
WAYWORN
WESTERN

RO•••••

ROACHED
ROACHES
ROADBED
ROADHOG
ROADIES
ROADMAP
ROADWAY
ROAMERS
ROAMING
ROANOKE
ROARERS
ROARING
ROASTED
ROASTER
ROBARDS
ROBBERS
ROBBERY
ROBBING
ROBBINS
ROBERTA
ROBERTO
ROBERTS
ROBESON
ROBLOWE
ROBOCOP
ROBOTIC
ROBROYS
ROBUSTA
ROCKERS
ROCKETS
ROCKIER
ROCKIES
ROCKING
ROCKYII
ROCKYIV
RODENTS
RODEOFF
RODEOUT
RODGERS
RODOLFO
ROEBUCK
ROEDEER
ROGUERY
ROGUISH
ROILING
ROISTER
ROLAIDS
ROLLBAR
ROLLERS
ROLLICK
ROLLING
ROLLINS
ROLLOUT
ROLLSUP
ROLLTOP
ROLODEX
ROLVAAG
ROMAINE
ROMANCE
ROMANIA
ROMANOV
ROMANSH
ROMNEYS
ROMPERS
ROMPING
ROMULAN
ROMULUS
RONDEAU
RONDELS
RONTGEN
ROOFERS
ROOFING
ROOFTOP
ROOKERY
ROOKIES
ROOKING
ROOMERS
ROOMFUL
ROOMIER
ROOMIES
ROOMING
ROOSTED
ROOSTER
ROOTERS
ROOTFOR
ROOTING
ROOTLET
ROOTOUT
ROPEDIN
ROPESIN
ROPETOW
RORQUAL
ROSALIE
ROSANNA
ROSANNE
ROSEATE
ROSEBUD
ROSELLE
ROSEOIL
ROSERED
ROSETTA
ROSETTE
ROSSINI
ROSSSEA
ROSTAND
ROSTERS
ROSTRUM
ROSWELL
ROTATED
ROTATES
ROTATOR
ROTIFER
ROTTERS
ROTTING
ROTUNDA
ROUGHED
ROUGHEN
ROUGHER
ROUGHIT
ROUGHLY
ROUGHUP
ROUGING
ROULADE
ROUNDED
ROUNDER
ROUNDLY
ROUNDON
ROUNDUP
ROUSING
ROUSTED
ROUTERS
ROUTINE
ROUTING
ROWBOAT
ROWDIER
ROWDIES
ROWDILY
ROXANNE
ROYALLY
ROYALTY
ROYBEAN
ROZELLE

R•O••••

REOCCUR
REOILED
REOPENS
REORDER
RHODIUM
RHOMBUS
RIOLOBO
RIORITA
RIOTACT
RIOTERS
RIOTING
RIOTOUS
ROOFERS
ROOFING
ROOFTOP
ROOKERY
ROOKIES
ROOKING
ROOMERS
ROOMFUL
ROOMIER
ROOMIES
ROOMING
ROOSTED
ROOSTER
ROOTERS
ROOTFOR
ROOTING
ROOTLET
ROOTOUT

R••O•••

RAGOUTS
RANOVER
RAYOVAC
RAZORED
REBOILS
REBOLTS
REBOOTS
REBOUND
REBOZOS
RECODED
RECODES
RECOILS
RECOLOR
RECORDS
RECORKS
RECOUNT
RECOUPS
RECOVER
REDOAKS
REDOING
REDOUBT
REDOUND
REFORMS
REHOOKS
REJOICE
REJOINS
RELOADS
RELOCKS
REMODEL
REMOLDS
REMORAS
REMORSE
REMOTER
REMOTES
REMOUNT
REMOVAL
REMOVED
REMOVER
REMOVES
REMOWED
RENOTES
REPOLLS
REPOMAN
REPORTS
REPOSED
REPOSES
REROUTE
RESOLED
RESOLES
RESOLVE
RESORBS
RESORTS
RESOUND
RETOOLS
RETORTS
RETOUCH
RETOWED
REVOICE
REVOKED
REVOKES
REVOLTS
REVOLVE
REWORDS
REWORKS
REWOUND
REWOVEN
REZONED
REZONES
RICOTTA

RIGOURS
RIPOFFS
RIPOSTE
RISOTTO
ROBOCOP
ROBOTIC
RODOLFO
ROLODEX
RUDOLPH
RUMORED
RUMOURS
RUNOFFS
RUNOVER

R•••O••

RACCOON
RADIOED
RAGDOLL
RAGMOPS
RAGTOPS
RAINOUT
RAKEOFF
RAMRODS
RANCOUR
RANGOON
RANSOMS
RAPPORT
RAPTORS
RATHOLE
RATIONS
RAUCOUS
RAVIOLI
RAYMOND
READOUT
REASONS
REBLOOM
REBOOTS
RECHOSE
RECKONS
RECROOM
RECROSS
RECTORS
RECTORY
REDBOOK
REDCOAT
REDDOGS
REDFORD
REDHOTS
REDPOLL
REDROSE
REDTOPS
REDWOLF
REDWOOD
REELOFF
REGIONS
REGROUP
REHOOKS
REPROOF
REPROVE
RESHOES
RESHOOT
RESPOND
RESTOCK
RESTORE
RETOOLS
REWROTE
RHETORS
RHIZOME
RIBBONS
RIDEOFF
RIDEOUT
RINGOUT
RIOLOBO
RIOTOUS
RIPCORD
RIPSOFF
RIPTORN
RISSOLE
ROANOKE
ROBLOWE
ROBROYS
RODEOFF
RODEOUT
ROLLOUT
ROOTOUT
ROSEOIL
ROWBOAT
RUBDOWN
RUBSOUT
RUINOUS
RULEOUT
RUMPOLE
RUNDOWN
RUNHOME
RUNSOFF
RUNSOUT
RUSHOFF

R••••O•

RACCOON
RAINBOW
RALSTON
RANCHOS
RANGOON
RANRIOT
RAYKROC
REACTOR
REALTOR
REARDON
REBLOOM
REBOZOS
RECOLOR
RECROOM
REDBOOK
REDSPOT
REDWOOD
REPROOF
REREDOS
RESHOOT
REUNION
RIGHTON
RIMSHOT
ROADHOG
ROBESON
ROBOCOP
ROLLTOP
ROMANOV
ROOFTOP
ROOTFOR
ROPETOW
ROTATOR
ROUNDON
RUBICON
RUCTION
RULESON
RUNAMOK
RUNRIOT

R•••••O

RALLYTO
RANINTO
REACTTO
REFERTO
RELIEVO
RELLENO
RICARDO
RIOLOBO
RIPINTO
RISOTTO
ROBERTO
RODOLFO
RUNINTO

•RO••••

AROUSAL
AROUSED
AROUSES
BROADAX
BROADEN
BROADER
BROADLY
BROCADE
BROGANS
BROGUES
BROILED
BROILER
BROKEIN
BROKERS
BROKEUP
BROMATE
BROMIDE
BROMINE
BRONCHI
BRONCOS
BRONSON
BRONZED
BRONZES
BROODED
BROODER
BROOKED
BROSNAN
BROTHER
BROUGHT
BROWNED
BROWNER
BROWNIE
BROWSED
BROWSER
BROWSES
CROAKED
CROATIA
CROCHET
CROESUS
CRONIES
CROOKED
CROONED
CROONER
CROPPED
CROPPER
CROPSUP
CROQUET
CROSIER
CROSSED
CROSSER
CROSSES
CROSSLY
CROSSUP
CROUTON
CROWBAR
CROWDED
CROWERS
CROWING
CROWNED
DROLLER
DRONERS
DRONING
DROOLED
DROOLER
DROOPED
DROPINS
DROPLET
DROPOFF
DROPOUT
DROPPED
DROPPER
DROPSBY
DROPSIN
DROUGHT
DROVERS
DROWNED
DROWSED
DROWSES
ERODING
EROSION
EROSIVE
EROTICA
FROCKED
FROGMAN
FROGMEN
FROLICS
FROMAGE
FRONTAL
FRONTED
FRONTON
FROSTED
FROTHED
FROWARD
FROWNAT
FROWNED
FROWNER
GROANED
GROANER
GROCERS
GROCERY
GROLIER
GROMMET
GROMYKO
GROOMED
GROOMER
GROOVED
GROOVES
GROPING
GROPIUS
GROSSED
GROSSER
GROSSES
GROSSLY
GROTTOS
GROUCHO
GROUCHY
GROUNDS
GROUPED
GROUPER
GROUPIE
GROUSED
GROUSER
GROUSES
GROUTED
GROVELS
GROWERS
GROWING
GROWLED
GROWLER
GROWNUP
GROWSON
GROWSUP
GROWTHS
IRONAGE
IRONERS
IRONIES
IRONING
IRONMAN
IRONMEN
IRONORE
IRONOUT
OROTUND
OROURKE
PROBATE
PROBERS
PROBING
PROBITY
PROBLEM
PROBONO
PROCEED
PROCESS
PROCTOR
PROCURE
PROCYON
PRODDED
PRODDER
PRODIGY
PRODUCE
PRODUCT
PROFANE
PROFESS
PROFFER
PROFILE
PROFITS
PROFUSE
PROGENY
PROGRAM
PROJECT
PROLOGS
PROLONG
PROMISE
PROMOTE
PROMPTS
PRONGED
PRONOUN
PROOFED
PROOFER
PROPANE
PROPELS
PROPHET
PROPJET
PROPMAN
PROPMEN
PROPOSE
PROPPED
PROPSUP
PRORATA
PRORATE
PROSAIC
PROSERS
PROSIER
PROSILY
PROSING
PROSODY
PROSPER
PROTEAN
PROTECT
PROTEGE
PROTEIN
PROTEST
PROTEUS
PROTIST
PROTONS
PROUDER
PROUDLY
PROVERB
PROVERS
PROVIDE
PROVING
PROVISO
PROVOKE
PROVOST
PROWESS
PROWLED
PROWLER
PROXIES
PROXIMO
TROCARS
TROCHEE
TROCHES
TRODDEN
TROIKAS
TROILUS
TROJANS
TROLLED
TROLLEY
TROOPED
TROOPER
TROPHIC
TROPICS
TROPISM
TROTHED
TROTOUT
TROTSKY
TROTTED
TROTTER
TROUBLE
TROUGHS
TROUNCE
TROUPER
TROUPES
TROUSER
TROWELS
TROWERS
VRONSKY
WRONGED
WRONGER
WRONGLY
WROTEIN
WROTETO
WROTEUP
WROUGHT

•R•O•••

ARBORED
ARBOURS
ARDOURS
AREOLAE
AREOLAR
AREOLAS
ARGONNE
ARIOSOS
ARIOSTO
ARMOIRE
ARMORED
ARMORER
ARMOURS
ARROBAS
ARROYOS
BRIOCHE
BROODED
BROODER
BROOKED
CREOLES
CREOSOL
CROOKED
CROONED
CROONER
CRYOGEN
DROOLED
DROOLER
DROOPED
GROOMED
GROOMER
GROOVED
GROOVES
MRBONES
ORIOLES
ORMOLUS
ORTOLAN
PRIORTO
PROOFED
PROOFER
TRIODES
TROOPED
TROOPER
TRYOUTS

•R••O••

ARCHONS
ARDMORE
ARDUOUS
ARIZONA
ARMHOLE
ARMLOAD
ARMLOCK
ARTFORM
ARTSONG
ARTWORK
BRAVOES
BRETONS
BRITONS
CRAYOLA
CRAYONS
CREMONA
CRINOID
CRYWOLF
DRAGONS
DRAGOON
DRAGOUT
DRAWOUT
DREWOUT
DROPOFF
DROPOUT
DRSPOCK
DRYDOCK
DRYHOLE
ERELONG
FREMONT
FRYCOOK
GRANOLA
GREGORY
IRISOUT
IRKSOME
IRONORE
IRONOUT
MRSPOCK
ORATORS
ORATORY
ORINOCO
ORISONS
PRECOOK
PRECOOL
PRELOAD
PRESOAK
PRESORT
PRISONS
PROBONO
PROLOGS
PROLONG
PROMOTE
PRONOUN
PROPOSE
PROSODY
PROTONS
PROVOKE
PROVOST
TRAVOIS
TREFOIL
TREMOLO
TREMORS
TRICORN
TRICOTS
TRIGONS
TRILOGY
TRIPODS
TRIPOLI
TRITONE
TRITONS
TROTOUT

•R•••O•

ARIOSOS
ARISTOS
ARROYOS
BRANDON
BRANSON
BRAXTON
BRERFOX
BRESSON
BRINGON
BRISTOL
BRITTON
BRONCOS
BRONSON
CRAMPON
CREATOR
CREOSOL
CRIMSON
CROUTON
CRYPTOS
DRAGOON
DRAGSON
DRAWNON
DRAWSON
DREAMON
ERECTOR
EREWHON
ERICSON
EROSION
FRANKOZ
FREEDOM
FRESCOS
FRISSON
FRONTON
FRYCOOK
GRANTOR
GRAYSON
GRIFFON
GRISSOM
GROTTOS
GROWSON
GRUNION
GRYPHON
IRECKON
KRATION
KRYPTON
MRMAGOO
ORATION
ORBISON
ORGANON
PRAETOR
PRAYFOR
PRECOOK
PRECOOL
PRESSON
PRESTON
PRESTOS
PREYSON
PROCTOR
PROCYON
PRUDHOE
TRACTOR
TRADEON
TRAITOR
TRANSOM
TREASON
TREETOP
TRENTON
TRIEDON
TRIESON

•R••••O

ARAPAHO
ARIOSTO
ARSENIO
ARTDECO
BRAVADO
BRINGTO
CRUZADO
ERNESTO
GROMYKO
GROUCHO
MRMAGOO
OREGANO
ORINOCO
ORLANDO
ORNITHO
PRAYSTO
PRIORTO
PROBONO
PROVISO
PROXIMO
PRYINTO
TREMOLO
TREVINO
WRITETO
WROTETO

••RO•••

ACROBAT
ACRONYM
AEROBAT
AEROBES
AEROBIC
AEROSOL
AGROUND
APRONED
APROPOS
ARROBAS
ARROYOS
ATROPHY
AUROCHS
AURORAE
AURORAL
AURORAS
BARONET
BARONGS
BAROQUE
BORODIN
BOROUGH
BUROAKS
BYROADS
CAROLED
CAROLER
CAROLES
CAROLUS
CAROLYN
CAROMED
CAROTID
CAROUSE
CHROMES
CHRONIC
COROLLA
CORONAE
CORONAS
CORONET
DOROTHY
ENROBED
ENROBES
ENROLLS
ENROOTS
ENROUTE
FURORES
GARONNE
GIRONDE
GOROUND
HEROICS
HEROINE
HEROISM
INROADS
KAROLYI
KEROUAC
LAROCHE
MAROONS
MOROCCO
PAROLED
PAROLEE
PAROLES
PIROGUE
REROUTE
SARONGS
SAROYAN
SCROLLS
SCROOGE
SHROUDS
SIROCCO
SORORAL
SPROUTS
STROBES
STROKED
STROKES
STROLLS
STROPHE
THROATS
THROATY
THRONES
THRONGS
THROUGH
THROWER
THROWIN
TOROIDS
TORONTO
UNROBED
UNROBES
UNROLLS
UPROARS
UPROOTS
ZEROING

••R•O••

AIRBOAT
AIRCOOL
AIRFOIL
AIRHOLE
AIRLOCK
AIRPORT
AIRSOCK
AIRSOUT
AIRWOLF
APRIORI
AUREOLA
AUREOLE
BARCODE
BARHOPS
BARNOWL
BARROOM
BARROWS
BARSOAP
BARYONS
BERTOLT
BOREOUT
BORROWS
BORZOIS
BURBOTS
BURDOCK
BURGOOS
BURNOUT
BURROWS
CARBONS
CARBOYS
CARCOAT
CARDOZO
CARGOES
CARHOPS
CARIOCA
CARLOAD
CARPOOL
CARPORT
CARROLL
CARROTS
CARTONS
CARTOON
CORDOBA
CORDONS
CORNOIL
CORRODE
CURIOUS
CURSORS
CURSORY
EARLOBE
EARLOCK
ENROOTS
FARGONE
FARMOUT
FARROWS
FERROUS
FERVORS
FERVOUR
FIREOFF
FORBORE
FORGOES
FORGONE
FORGOOD
FORLORN
FORMOSA
FORSOOK
FURIOUS
FURLONG
FURROWS
GARCONS
GORGONS
HARBORS
HARBOUR
HARMONY
HARPOON
HARROWS
HORMONE
HORRORS
JARGONS
JERBOAS
KARAOKE
KARLOFF
LARDONS
MARCONI
MARKOFF
MARKOVA
MARLOWE
MARMOTS
MAROONS
MARROWS
MERLOTS
MIRRORS
MORMONS
MORROWS
MURDOCH
NARROWS
NERVOUS
NORFOLK
OARLOCK
OURTOWN
PARBOIL
PARDONS
PARLORS
PARLOUR
PARLOUS
PARROTS
PARSONS
PARTOOK
PARTOUT
PERFORM
PERGOLA
PERIODS
PERSONA
PERSONS
PORTOLA
PURLOIN
PURPORT
PURPOSE
SCROOGE
SERIOUS
SERMONS
SIRLOIN
SORROWS
SURCOAT
TARPONS
TERRORS
TIREOUT
TOREOFF
TOREOUT
TORNOUT
TORTONI
TURBOTS
TURMOIL
TURNOFF
TURNOUT
UPROOTS
VARIOUS
VERBOSE
VERMONT
VIRGOAN
WARDOFF
WARGODS
WARLOCK
WARLORD
WORDONE
WOREOFF
WOREOUT
WORKOFF
WORKOUT
WORNOFF
WORNOUT
YARROWS
ZIRCONS

••R••O•

AERATOR
AEROSOL
AIRCOOL
AIRDROP
AIRFLOW
AIRSHOW
APRICOT
APROPOS
ARROYOS
BARANOF
BARRIOS
BARROOM
BERGSON
BERLIOZ
BIRDDOG
BOREDOM
BURGEON
BURGOOS
CAREFOR
CARIBOU
CARLSON
CARLTON
CARPOOL
CARRION
CARRYON
CARTOON
CORAZON
CORNCOB
CORNDOG
CORNROW
CURATOR
DORITOS
EARDROP
EARLDOM
EARLYON
EARSHOT
FIREBOX
FIREDOG
FORGOOD
FORSOOK
GERITOL
GIRASOL
GYRATOR
HARDTOP
HARDWON
HARICOT
HARPOON
HARPSON
HERRIOT
HIRESON
HORIZON
KERCHOO
KERPLOP
MARABOU
MARCHON
MARKHOR
MARMION
MARYLOU
MERINOS
MIRADOR
OBREGON
PARADOX
PARAGON
PARASOL
PARTOOK
PERIDOT
PORTHOS
PORTION
REREDOS
SERFDOM
SURGEON
TEREDOS
TIREDOF
TOREROS
TORSION
TURNSON
VERSION
VIRAGOS
WARRIOR

WARTHOG
WORKFOR
WORKSON

••R•••O
AGREETO
AMRADIO
BURRITO
CARDOZO
CBRADIO
CHRISTO
CORDERO
CURACAO
DARESTO
DURANGO
FARRAGO
FERRARO
FMRADIO
GERALDO
HORATIO
JERICHO
KERCHOO
LORENZO
MARTINO
MORELLO
MOROCCO
MURILLO
OTRANTO
PORTICO
SERPICO
SIROCCO
STRETTO
TARANTO
TORNADO
TORONTO
TORPEDO
TURNSTO
UTRILLO
VERDUGO
VERTIGO

•••RO••
ACEROLA
ACEROSE
AFFRONT
AMBROSE
AMOROUS
ANDROID
ANEROID
APPROVE
AXLROSE
AYKROYD
BARROOM
BARROWS
BEAROFF
BEAROUT
BEDROCK
BEDROLL
BEDROOM
BETROTH
BORROWS
BURROWS
CARROLL
CARROTS
CHEROOT
CITROEN
CITRONS
CORRODE
DAYROOM
DEFROCK
DEFROST
DETROIT
DISROBE
EGGROLL
EMBROIL
ENGROSS
ENTROPY
ESCROWS
FAIROFF
FARROWS
FERROUS
FIBROUS
FLYRODS
FURROWS
GOBROKE
GOWRONG
HARROWS
HEAROUT
HIPROOF
HORRORS
HOTRODS
HYDROUS
IMPROVE
INFRONT
INGROUP
INGROWN
INTROIT
KEDROVA
LAPROBE
LEGROOM
LOWROAD
MACRONS
MADRONA
MARROWS
MATRONS
MAUROIS
MELROSE
MICROBE
MICRONS
MIRRORS
MORROWS
NAIROBI
NARROWS
NEURONE
NEURONS
NIMRODS
NITROUS
ODOROUS
OFFROAD
OLOROSO
ONAROLL
ONEROUS
OPEROSE
PADRONE
PADRONI
PAIROFF
PARROTS
PATROLS
PATRONS
PATROON
PAYROLL
PEEROUT
PETROCK
PETROUS
POUROUT
RAMRODS
RECROOM
RECROSS
REDROSE
REGROUP
REPROOF
REPROVE
REWROTE
ROBROYS
SORROWS
STCROIX
STEROID
STEROLS
SUBROSA
SUCROSE
SUNROOF
SUNROOM
TAPROOM
TAPROOT
TEAROFF
TEAROOM
TEAROSE
TERRORS
THEROUX
TIERODS
TOWROPE
UNFROCK
UPFRONT
WEAROFF
WEAROUT
YARROWS

•••R•O•
ALARCON
AWAREOF
BARRIOS
BARROOM
BEARSON
BEDROOM
BLERIOT
BOURBON
BRERFOX
CARRION
CARRYON
CHARIOT
CHEROOT
CLARION
CYPRIOT
CZARDOM
DAYROOM
EMBRYOS
EMERSON
GEARBOX
HAIRDOS
HEARDOF
HEARSOF
HERRIOT
HIPROOF
INERROR
LEGROOM
NEARYOU
OVERJOY
PATRIOT
PATROON
PEARSON
PHARAOH
PIERROT
POORBOX
POORBOY
QUARTOS
RANRIOT
REARDON
RECROOM
REPROOF
RUNRIOT
SHORTOF
SPARROW
SPURSON
STARDOM
STEREOS
SUNROOF
SUNROOM
TAPROOM
TAPROOT
TEAROOM
THEREOF
THEREON
THERMOS
VITRIOL
WARRIOR
WEIRDOS
WHARTON
WHEREOF

•••R••O
ALFREDO
AMERIGO
BURRITO
CHORIZO
ELGRECO
FARRAGO
FERRARO
GEARSTO
GIORGIO
OLOROSO
SANREMO
SCORPIO
SOPRANO
SPIRITO
SUPREMO
THERETO
TOURACO
VIBRATO
WHERETO
YEARNTO

••••RO•
ACHERON
AILERON
AIRDROP
ANDIRON
ATECROW
BISTROS
BOLEROS
BOUTROS
CALDRON
CAMERON
CHEVRON
CLAIROL
COMOROS
CONTROL
CORNROW
DEMEROL
DENDRON
DESTROY
DEWDROP
DIDEROT
DOGTROT
EARDROP
EATCROW
EMPEROR
EYEBROW
FOXTROT
FUELROD
GABBROS
GUMDROP
INERROR
LATERON
LEBARON
LONNROT
LOWBROW
MCENROE
NEMEROV
NEUTRON
OLDPROS
OMICRON
OUTCROP
OUTGROW
PICAROS
PIERROT
PIGIRON
RAYKROC
SAFFRON
SKIDROW
SPARROW
TONEROW
TOREROS
VICEROY
WINDROW
WOODROW

••••R•O
ALBERTO
CHEERIO
CONBRIO
DECARLO
EMBARGO
INFERNO
NOVARRO
ONTARIO
PALERMO
PATERNO
PIZARRO
PRIORTO
REFERTO
RICARDO
ROBERTO
SALERNO
SCHERZO
SUKARNO
SWEARTO
UMBERTO
UNDERGO

•••••RO
ALLEGRO
CORDERO
DEUTERO
ELECTRO
FERRARO
GENNARO
GOLFPRO
HHMUNRO
INVITRO
JANEIRO
MAESTRO
NONZERO
NOVARRO
PIZARRO
SAGUARO
SAPPORO
SEMIPRO
SHAPIRO
SUBZERO
VACCARO
VAQUERO

R•P••••
RAPANUI
RAPHAEL
RAPIDER
RAPIDLY
RAPIERS
RAPINES
RAPPELS
RAPPERS
RAPPING
RAPPORT
RAPTORS
RAPTURE
REPAINT
REPAIRS
REPAPER
REPASTE
REPASTS
REPAVED
REPAVES
REPEALS
REPEATS
REPENTS
REPINED
REPINES
REPLACE
REPLANS
REPLANT
REPLATE
REPLAYS
REPLETE
REPLICA
REPLIED
REPLIES
REPOLLS
REPOMAN
REPORTS
REPOSED
REPOSES
REPRESS
REPRICE
REPRINT
REPRISE
REPROOF
REPROVE
REPTILE
REPUGNS
REPULSE
REPUTED
REPUTES
RIPCORD
RIPENED
RIPINTO
RIPOFFS
RIPOSTE
RIPPERS
RIPPING
RIPPLED
RIPPLES
RIPRAPS
RIPSAWS
RIPSOFF
RIPTIDE
RIPTORN
ROPEDIN
ROPESIN
ROPETOW
RUPIAHS
RUPTURE

R••P•••
RAMPAGE
RAMPANT
RAMPART
RAPPELS
RAPPERS
RAPPING
RAPPORT
RASPERS
RASPIER
RASPING
RATPACK
REAPERS
REAPING
REDPINE
REDPOLL
REOPENS
RESPECT
RESPIRE
RESPITE
RESPOND
REUPPED
RIPPERS
RIPPING
RIPPLED
RIPPLES
ROMPERS
ROMPING
RUMPLED
RUMPLES
RUMPOLE

R•••P••
RECIPES
REDSPOT
RELAPSE
REPAPER
RETAPED
RETAPES
RETYPED
RETYPES
REUPPED

R••••P•
RAGMOPS
RAGTOPS
RECEIPT
RECOUPS
REDCAPS
REDTAPE
REDTOPS
RESHIPS
REVAMPS
REWRAPS
RIPRAPS
RUDOLPH
RUNLAPS

R•••••P
RACKSUP
RAISEUP
RAKEDUP
RAKESUP
RATTRAP
REARSUP
REGROUP
RESTAMP
RESTSUP
RINGSUP
ROADMAP
ROBOCOP
ROLLSUP
ROLLTOP
ROOFTOP
ROUGHUP
ROUNDUP
RUNDEEP
RYKRISP

•RP••••
ORPHANS
ORPHEAN
ORPHEUS
ORPINES

•R•P•••
ARAPAHO
ARMPITS
CRAPPIE
CROPPED
CROPPER
CROPSUP
CRYPTIC
CRYPTOS
DRAPERS
DRAPERY
DRAPING
DRIPDRY
DRIPPAN
DRIPPED
DROPINS
DROPLET
DROPOFF
DROPOUT
DROPPED
DROPPER
DROPSBY
DROPSIN
DRSPOCK
ERUPTED
FRAPPES
FRYPANS
GRAPHED
GRAPHIC
GRAPNEL
GRAPPLE
GRIPERS
GRIPING
GRIPPED
GRIPPER
GROPING
GROPIUS
GRYPHON
KRYPTON
MRSPOCK
PREPAID
PREPARE
PREPAYS
PREPPIE
PROPANE
PROPELS
PROPHET
PROPJET
PROPMAN
PROPMEN
PROPOSE
PROPPED
PROPSUP
TRAPEZE
TRAPPED
TRAPPER
TREPANS
TRIPLED
TRIPLES
TRIPLET
TRIPLEX
TRIPODS
TRIPOLI
TRIPPED
TRIPPER
TRIPPET
TRIPSUP
TROPHIC
TROPICS
TROPISM
WRAPPED
WRAPPER
WRAPSUP
WRAPUPS

•R••P••
CRAMPED
CRAMPON
CRAPPIE
CREEPED
CREEPER
CREEPUP
CRIMPED
CRIMPER
CRISPED
CRISPER
CRISPIN
CRISPLY
CRISPUS
CROPPED
CROPPER
CRUMPET
CRUMPLE
CRUMPLY
DRIPPAN
DRIPPED
DROOPED
DROPPED
DROPPER
FRAPPES
GRAMPUS
GRAPPLE
GRASPED
GRIPPED
GRIPPER
GROUPED
GROUPER
GROUPIE
GRUMPED
IRRUPTS
PREPPIE
PRIMPED
PROMPTS
PROPPED
PROSPER
TRAIPSE
TRAMPAS
TRAMPED
TRAMPLE
TRAPPED
TRAPPER
TRIPPED
TRIPPER
TRIPPET
TROOPED
TROOPER
TROUPER
TROUPES
TRUMPED
TRUMPET
TRUMPUP
WRAPPED
WRAPPER

•R•••P•
GRANDPA
MRCHIPS
PREAMPS
PRECEPT
PREEMPT
PRETAPE
TRICEPS
TRIUMPH
WRAPUPS

•R••••P
ARCLAMP
BRACEUP
BREAKUP
BRINGUP
BROKEUP
BRUSHUP
CRACKUP
CRANKUP
CREEPUP
CROPSUP
CROSSUP
DRAWNUP
DRAWSUP
DREAMUP
DRESSUP
DRIEDUP
DRIESUP
DRIVEUP
DRUMSUP
FRAMEUP
GROWNUP
GROWSUP
PROPSUP
TRADEUP
TREETOP
TRIPSUP
TRUMPUP
WRAPSUP
WRITEUP
WROTEUP

••RP•••
AIRPLAY
AIRPORT
AIRPUMP
BURPGUN
BURPING
CARPALS
CARPERS
CARPETS
CARPING
CARPOOL
CARPORT
EARPLUG
HARPERS
HARPIES
HARPING
HARPIST
HARPOON
HARPSON
KERPLOP
MORPHED
MURPHEY
PERPLEX
PURPLED
PURPLES
PURPORT
PURPOSE
SERPENT
SERPICO
SURPASS
SURPLUS
TARPITS
TARPONS
TORPEDO
WARPATH
WARPING

••R•P••
AGRIPPA
APROPOS
ATROPHY
CERIPHS
FOREPAW
HARDPAN
HARDPUT
IRRUPTS
PARAPET
PARAPHS
PORKPIE
SCRAPED
SCRAPER
SCRAPES
SCRAPPY
SCRIPPS
SCRIPTS
SCRUPLE
SERAPES
SERAPHS
SERAPIS
STRIPED
STRIPER
STRIPES
STROPHE
TERAPHS

••R••P•
AGRIPPA
BARHOPS
BURLAPS
CARHOPS
CORRUPT
FORCEPS
LARRUPS
MARKUPS
PERHAPS
SCRAPPY
SCRIMPS
SCRIMPY
SCRIPPS
SHRIMPS
TURNIPS
WARMUPS
WORKUPS

••R•••P
AIRDROP
AIRPUMP
AIRSHIP
BARKEEP
BARSOAP
BORNEUP
BURNSUP
BURNTUP
CURLSUP
EARDROP
EARFLAP
FIREDUP
FIRESUP
FIRMSUP
HARDTOP
KERPLOP
MARKSUP
PARSNIP
PERKSUP
SCREWUP
SCRUBUP
SERVEUP
TURNSUP
WARMSUP
WARSHIP
WIRETAP
WORKSUP
WORSHIP

•••RP••
BEARPAW
CHIRPED
HAIRPIN
SCARPED
SCORPIO
SHARPED
SHARPEI
SHARPEN
SHARPER
SHARPLY
SHERPAS
SLURPED
USURPED
USURPER

•••R•P•
CORRUPT
DECRYPT
DIGRAPH
DISRUPT
ENCRYPT
ENTRAPS
ENTROPY
ENWRAPS
LARRUPS
REWRAPS
RIPRAPS
SATRAPS
THERAPY
TOWROPE
UNDRAPE
UNTRAPS
UNWRAPS

•••R••P
BEARSUP
FAIRSUP
FLAREUP
GEARSUP
INGROUP
NOTRUMP
OFFRAMP
OVERLAP
PAIRSUP
REARSUP
REGROUP
RYKRISP
SCAREUP
STARMAP
STARTUP
STIRRUP
STIRSUP
STOREUP
TEARSUP

••••RP•
ESCARPS
EUTERPE
EXCERPT

••••R•P
AIRDROP
CHEERUP
CLEARUP
COVERUP
DAYTRIP
DEWDROP
EARDROP
EGOTRIP
FLYTRAP
GUMDROP
MANTRAP
OUTCROP
RATTRAP
STIRRUP
UNSTRAP

•••••RP
ANTWERP
HANSARP
JEANARP

R•Q••••
REQUEST
REQUIEM
REQUIRE
REQUITE

R••Q•••
RACQUET
RORQUAL

•R•Q•••
BRIQUET
CROQUET

•R••Q••
BRUSQUE

••RQ•••
CIRQUES
MARQUEE
MARQUES
MARQUEZ
MARQUIS
PARQUET
RORQUAL
TORQUES

••R•Q••
BAROQUE

R•R••••
RAREBIT
RAREGAS
RARITAN
RERAISE
RERATED
RERATES
REREADS
REREDOS
RERENTS
RERINSE
REROUTE
RORQUAL

R••R•••
RAGRUGS
RAMRODS
RANRIOT
RATRACE
REARDON
REAREND
REARERS
REARGUE
REARING
REARMED
REARSUP
RECROOM
RECROSS
RECRUIT
REDRAWN
REDRAWS
REDRESS
REDROSE
REFRACT
REFRAIN
REFRAME
REFRESH
REFRIED

REFRIES
REGRADE
REGRESS
REGRETS
REGROUP
REORDER
REPRESS
REPRICE
REPRINT
REPRISE
REPROOF
REPROVE
RETRACE
RETRACK
RETRACT
RETRADE
RETRAIN
RETREAD
RETREAT
RETRIAL
RETRIED
RETRIES
RETRIMS
REWRAPS
REWRITE
REWROTE
REXREED
RIORITA
RIPRAPS
ROARERS
ROARING
ROBROYS
RUBRICS
RUNRIOT
RYKRISP

R•••R••

RATTRAP
RAYKROC
RAZORED
REAIRED
REBIRTH
RECORDS
RECORKS
REFEREE
REFERTO
REFIRES
REFORMS
REGARDS
REHIRED
REHIRES
REMARKS
REMARRY
REMORAS
REMORSE
REPORTS
RESERVE
RESORBS
RESORTS
RESURGE
RETARDS
RETIRED
RETIREE
RETIRES
RETORTS
RETURNS
REVERBS
REVERED
REVERES
REVERIE
REVERSE
REVERTS
REWARDS
REWARMS
REWIRED
REWIRES
REWORDS
REWORKS
RICARDO
RICERAT
ROBARDS
ROBERTA
ROBERTO
ROBERTS
ROSERED
ROSTRUM
RUMORED

R••••R•

RAFTERS
RAIDERS
RAILERS
RAISERS
RAMPART
RANGERS
RANKERS
RANTERS
RAPIERS
RAPPERS
RAPPORT
RAPTORS
RAPTURE
RASHERS
RASPERS
RASTERS
RATTERS
RAYBURN
READERS
REAMERS
REAPERS
REARERS
RECTORS
RECTORY
REDBIRD
REDFIRS
REDFORD
REEFERS
REENTRY
REHEARD
REHEARS
RELEARN
REMARRY
RENDERS
RENTERS
REPAIRS
REQUIRE
RESPIRE
RESTART
RESTERS
RESTORE
REUTERS
REVELRY
REYNARD
RHETORS
RHUBARB
RHYMERS
RICHARD
RIFLERS
RIFLERY
RIGGERS
RIGOURS
RINGERS
RIOTERS
RIPCORD
RIPPERS
RIPTORN
RISKERS
RIVALRY
RIVIERA
RIVIERE
ROAMERS
ROARERS
ROBBERS
ROBBERY
ROCKERS
RODGERS
ROGUERY
ROLLERS
ROMPERS
ROOFERS
ROOKERY
ROOMERS
ROOTERS
ROSTERS
ROTTERS
ROUTERS
RUBBERS
RUBBERY
RUDDERS
RUDYARD
RUINERS
RUMOURS
RUNNERS
RUNSDRY
RUPTURE
RUSHERS
RUTGERS

R•••••R

RACECAR
RAFFLER
RAGGIER
RAINIER
RAMBLER
RANCHER
RANCOUR
RANDIER
RANGIER
RANOVER
RAPIDER
RASPIER
RATTIER
RATTLER
REACTOR
READIER
REALTOR
RECITER
RECOLOR
RECOVER
REDDEER
REDHAIR
REDSTAR
REDUCER
REEDIER
REENTER
REFINER
REFUSER
REFUTER
REGULAR
REMOTER
REMOVER
RENEGER
RENEWER
REOCCUR
REORDER
REPAPER
RESCUER
REUTHER
REVELER
REVISER
RICHTER
RIDDLER
RIGHTER
RISKIER
RITZIER
RIVETER
ROASTER
ROCKIER
ROEDEER
ROISTER
ROLLBAR
ROOMIER
ROOSTER
ROOTFOR
ROTATOR
ROTIFER
ROUGHER
ROUNDER
ROWDIER
RUDDIER
RUMMIER
RUNNIER
RUNOVER
RUNTIER
RUSTIER
RUSTLER

•RR••••

ARRAIGN
ARRANGE
ARRASES
ARRAYED
ARREARS
ARRESTS
ARRIERE
ARRISES
ARRIVAL
ARRIVED
ARRIVER
ARRIVES
ARROBAS
ARROYOS
ERRANDS
ERRATIC
ERRATUM
IRRUPTS
MRRIGHT

•R•R•••

ARMREST
BRERFOX
DRYRUNS
PRORATA
PRORATE
TRIREME

•R••R••

ARBORED
AREARUG
ARMORED
ARMORER
BRIARDS
ERITREA
FREDRIC
GRIGRIS
ORDERED
ORDERER
ORDERLY
OROURKE
PRAIRIE
PRIORTO
PROGRAM
TREERAT
TRIGRAM

•R•••R•

ARBOURS
ARCHERS
ARCHERY
ARDMORE
ARDOURS
ARGUERS
ARIKARA
ARMOIRE
ARMOURS
ARREARS
ARRIERE
ARTFORM
ARTWARE
ARTWORK
BRACERS
BRAVERY
BRAVURA
BRAYERS
BREWERS
BREWERY
BRIBERY
BROKERS
CRATERS
CRAVERS
CROWERS
DRAPERS
DRAPERY
DRAWERS
DRIPDRY
DRIVERS
DRONERS
DROVERS
ERASERS
ERASURE
FROWARD
GRADERS
GRANARY
GRATERS
GRAVURE
GRAZERS
GREGORY
GRIPERS
GROCERS
GROCERY
GROWERS
GRUYERE
IRONERS
IRONORE
KRATERS
ORATORS
ORATORY
ORCHARD
PRATERS
PRAYERS
PREFERS
PREPARE
PRESORT
PRICERS
PRIMARY
PRIMERS
PROBERS
PROCURE
PROSERS
PROVERB
PROVERS
PRUDERY
PRUNERS
TRABERT
TRACERS
TRACERY
TRADERS
TRAVERS
TREMORS
TRENARY
TRICORN
TROCARS
TROWERS
WRITERS

•R••••R

ARBITER
AREOLAR
ARMORER
ARRIVER
BRAGGER
BRAIDER
BRANDER
BRASHER
BRAWLER
BRAZIER
BREAKER
BREEDER
BRENNER
BRIEFER
BRINGER
BRINIER
BRISKER
BROADER
BROILER
BROODER
BROTHER
BROWNER
BROWSER
BRUISER
BRYNNER
CRABBER
CRACKER
CRAFTER
CRAMMER
CRASSER
CRAWLER
CRAZIER
CREAMER
CREATOR
CREEPER
CRIMPER
CRISPER
CRITTER
CROONER
CROPPER
CROSIER
CROSSER
CROWBAR
CRUELER
CRUISER
CRULLER
CRUSHER
DRABBER
DRAINER
DRAWBAR
DREAMER
DREDGER
DREISER
DRESSER
DRIFTER
DRILLER
DRINKER
DROLLER
DROOLER
DROPPER
DRUCKER
DRUMMER
ERECTER
ERECTOR
FRAILER
FRANKER
FRASIER
FRAZIER
FREEZER
FRESHER
FRITTER
FROWNER
GRABBER
GRAMMAR
GRAMMER
GRANDER
GRANGER
GRANTOR
GREASER
GREATER
GREENER
GREETER
GRIDDER
GRIEVER
GRIFTER
GRIMIER
GRIMMER
GRINDER
GRINNER
GRIPPER
GROANER
GROLIER
GROOMER
GROSSER
GROUPER
GROUSER
GROWLER
GRUFFER
ORBITER
ORDERER
PRAETOR
PRAISER
PRANCER
PRAYFOR
PREENER
PREMIER
PRESSER
PRICIER
PRIMMER
PRINTER
PROCTOR
PRODDER
PROFFER
PROOFER
PROSIER
PROSPER
PROUDER
PROWLER
TRACKER
TRACTOR
TRAILER
TRAINER
TRAITOR
TRAMCAR
TRAPPER
TRAWLER
TREADER
TREKKER
TRICKER
TRIFLER
TRIGGER
TRIMMER
TRIPPER
TROOPER
TROTTER
TROUPER
TROUSER
TRUCKER
TRUDGER
TRYSTER
URBANER
WRAPPER
WRECKER
WRINGER
WRONGER

••RR•••

AIRRAID
BARRACK
BARRAGE
BARRELS
BARRENS
BARRETT
BARRIER
BARRING
BARRIOS
BARROOM
BARROWS
BERRIED
BERRIES
BORROWS
BURRITO
BURROWS
CARRELS
CARRERE
CARRICK
CARRIED
CARRIER
CARRIES
CARRION
CARROLL
CARROTS
CARRYON
CORRALS
CORRECT
CORRIDA
CORRODE
CORRUPT
CURRANT
CURRENT
CURRIED
CURRIER
CURRIES
DARRELL
DERRICK
DERRING
DURRELL
EARRING
FARRAGO
FARRIER
FARROWS
FERRARI
FERRARO
FERRATE
FERRETS
FERRIED
FERRIES
FERRITE
FERROUS
FERRULE
FORREAL
FORRENT
FORREST
FURRIER
FURRING
FURROWS
GARRETS
GARRETT
GARRICK
HARRIED
HARRIER
HARRIES
HARRIET
HARROWS
HERRING
HERRIOT
HORRIFY
HORRORS
HURRAHS
HURRIED
HURRIES
JARRING
LARRUPS
LORRIES
MARRIED
MARRIES
MARRING
MARROWS
MARRYME
MERRIER
MERRILL
MERRILY
MIRRORS
MORROWS
NARRATE
NARROWS
PARRIED
PARRIES
PARRING
PARROTS
PERRIER
PURRERS
PURRING
PYRRHIC
PYRRHUS
SERRATE
SERRIED
SORRELS
SORRIER
SORROWS
SURREAL
SURREYS
TARRIED
TARRIES
TARRING
TERRACE
TERRAIN
TERRENE
TERRETS
TERRIER
TERRIES
TERRIFY
TERRORS
TORRENT
TURRETS
WARRANT
WARRENS
WARRING
WARRIOR
WORRIED
WORRIER
WORRIES
YARROWS

••R•R••

AIRCREW
AIRDROP
AURORAE
AURORAL
AURORAS
CORNROW
EARDROP
EARDRUM
ETRURIA
FORERAN
FORERUN
FORFREE
FORTRAN
FURORES
JURYRIG
MARGRET
MORDRED
PARURES
PORTRAY
SORORAL
TOREROS

••R••R•

AIRFARE
AIRPORT
APRIORI
ARREARS
ARRIERE
BARBARA
BARBARY
BARBERS
BARKERS
BARNARD
BARTERS
BERBERS
BERGERE
BERNARD
BERSERK
BIRDERS
BORDERS
BURGERS
BURNERS
BURSARS
CARDERS
CAREERS
CARFARE
CARNERA
CARPERS
CARPORT
CARRERE
CARTERS
CARVERS
CEREBRA
CORDERO
CORKERS
CORNERS
CURLERS
CURSORS
CURSORY
DARNERS
DARTERS
DORMERS
EARHART
EARMARK
EARNERS
FARMERS
FERRARI
FERRARO
FERVORS
FIREARM
FORBORE
FORCERS
FOREARM
FORGERS
FORGERY
FORKERS
FORLORN
FORSURE
FORWARD
GARNERS
GARTERS
GIRDERS
HARBORS
HARPERS
HARVARD
HERBERT
HERDERS
HORRORS
HURLERS
LARDERS
MARKERS
MARMARA
MARTYRS
MERCURY
MERGERS
MIRRORS
MORTARS
MURDERS
MURMURS
NURSERS
NURSERY
NURTURE
PARLORS
PARSERS
PERFORM
PERJURE
PERJURY
PERTURB
PERVERT
PORKERS
PORTERS
PURPORT
PURRERS
PURSERS
SERVERS
SORCERY
SORTERS
SURFERS
SURGERY
TARTARE
TARTARS
TERNARY
TERRORS
THREERS
TURNERS
UPROARS
VERDURE
VERGERS
WARDERS
WARFARE
WARLORD
WORKERS
YARDARM

••R•••R

AERATOR
ARRIVER
BARMIER
BARRIER
BURGHER
BURGLAR
BURLIER
CAREFOR
CAROLER
CARRIER
CARTIER
CORNIER
CORSAIR
CURATOR
CURLIER
CURRIER
CURVIER
DERNIER
DIRTIER
EARLIER
FARRIER
FARTHER
FERVOUR
FORAGER
FORBEAR
FOREVER
FORSTER
FURRIER
FURTHER
GARDNER
GYRATOR
HARBOUR
HARDIER
HARRIER
HARSHER
HORSIER
HURDLER
JERKIER
LARDNER
MARCHER
MARINER
MARKHOR
MERRIER
MIRADOR
MIRAMAR
MURKIER
NERVIER
NORTHER
PARDNER
PARLOUR
PARTNER
PERKIER
PERRIER
PERUSER
PURSUER
SCRAPER
SERENER
SHRINER
SHRIVER
SORRIER
SPRAYER
SPRUCER
STREWER
STRIDER
STRIKER
STRIPER
STRIVER
SURLIER
TARDIER
TARSIER
TERRIER
THROWER
TIREDER
UPRIVER
VERMEER
VERNIER
WARBLER
WARRIOR
WERNHER
WERTHER
WORDIER
WORKFOR
WORMIER
WORRIER

•••RR••

AVERRED
BLURRED
BOURREE
CHARRED
DHURRIE
GNARRED
INERROR
OVERRAN
OVERRUN
PIERROT
QUARREL
SCARRED
SHIRRED
SIERRAS
SKIRRED
SLURRED
SPARRED
SPARROW
SPORRAN
SPURRED
STARRED
STIRRED
STIRRER
STIRRUP
WHIRRED

•••R•R•

ADORERS
BEARERS
CARRERE
FEARERS
FERRARI
FERRARO
HEARERS
HORRORS
JEERERS
LEERERS
LIBRARY
MIRRORS
POURERS
PURRERS
REARERS
ROARERS
SCARERS
SCORERS
SHARERS
SNORERS
SOARERS
STARERS
STIRFRY
STORERS
TERRORS
TOURERS
USURERS
WEARERS

•••R••R

ALARMER
ALERTER
ANGRIER
AWARDER
BARRIER
BOARDER
BOERWAR
CARRIER
CHARGER
CHARIER
CHARMER
CHARTER
COARSER
COURIER
COURSER
CURRIER
DEARSIR
FARRIER
FIERCER
FIERIER

FOURIER
FURRIER
HAIRIER
HARRIER
HOARDER
HOARIER
HOARSER
INERROR
LEARNER
LEERIER
MERRIER
ONORDER
PERRIER
QUARTER
REORDER
SCARCER
SCARIER
SHARPER
SHIRKER
SHORTER
SMARTER
SNORTER
SORRIER
SPARSER
SPURNER
STARKER
STARTER
STERNER
STIRRER
TEARIER
TERRIER
THURBER
TOORDER
TWIRLER
USURPER
WARRIOR
WEARIER
WEIRDER
WORRIER
YEARNER

••••RR•

ANDORRA
BEGORRA
BIZARRE
DUBARRY
EQUERRY
IMSORRY
LECARRE
NAVARRE
NOVARRO
PIZARRO
REMARRY
SCHIRRA
THIERRY

••••R•R

ADMIRER
ALTERER
ARMORER
ASPIRER
CATERER
CLEARER
DEMURER
EAGERER
EMPEROR
FIGURER
HONORER
HOVERER
IGNORER
IMPURER
INERROR
LABORER
MATURER
OFFERER
ORDERER
PAPERER
QUEERER
SCOURER
SECURER
SEVERER
SHEARER
SHEERER
SNEERER
SOBERER
SQUARER
STEERER
STIRRER
SWEARER
UTTERER
WAGERER
WATERER
WAVERER

•••••RR

BOYDORR

R•S••••

RASCALS
RASHERS
RASHEST
RASPERS
RASPIER
RASPING
RASSLED
RASSLES
RASTERS
RESALES
RESALTS
RESANDS
RESCALE
RESCIND
RESCUED
RESCUER
RESCUES
RESEALS
RESEATS
RESECTS
RESEEDS
RESELLS
RESENDS
RESENTS
RESERVE
RESHIPS
RESHOES
RESHOOT
RESIDED
RESIDES
RESIDUE
RESIGNS
RESILED
RESILES
RESINGS
RESISTS
RESOLED
RESOLES
RESOLVE
RESORBS
RESORTS
RESOUND
RESPECT
RESPIRE
RESPITE
RESPOND
RESTAGE
RESTAIN
RESTAMP
RESTART
RESTATE
RESTERS
RESTFUL
RESTING
RESTIVE
RESTOCK
RESTORE
RESTSUP
RESTYLE
RESULTS
RESUMED
RESUMES
RESURGE
RISIBLE
RISINGS
RISKERS
RISKIER
RISKING
RISOTTO
RISSOLE
ROSALIE
ROSANNA
ROSANNE
ROSEATE
ROSEBUD
ROSELLE
ROSEOIL
ROSERED
ROSETTA
ROSETTE
ROSSINI
ROSSSEA
ROSTAND
ROSTERS
ROSTRUM
ROSWELL
RUSHDIE
RUSHEES
RUSHERS
RUSHING
RUSHOFF
RUSSELL
RUSSETS
RUSSIAN
RUSTICS
RUSTIER
RUSTILY
RUSTING
RUSTLED
RUSTLER
RUSTLES

R••S•••

RAISERS
RAISEUP
RAISING
RAISINS
RALSTON
RANSACK
RANSOMS
RASSLED
RASSLES
RAWSILK
REASONS
REDSKIN
REDSPOT
REDSTAR
REISSUE
RETSINA
RIMSHOT
RINSING
RIPSAWS
RIPSOFF
RISSOLE
ROASTED
ROASTER
ROISTER
ROOSTED
ROOSTER
ROSSINI
ROSSSEA
ROUSING
ROUSTED
RUBSOUT
RUNSDRY
RUNSOFF
RUNSOUT
RUSSELL
RUSSETS
RUSSIAN

R•••S••

RACKSUP
RAILSAT
RAKESIN
RAKESUP
RAMESES
READSIN
REARSUP
REBASTE
REBUSES
RECASTS
RECUSED
RECUSES
REELSIN
REFUSAL
REFUSED
REFUSER
REFUSES
REINSIN
REISSUE
RELISTS
REPASTE
REPASTS
REPOSED
REPOSES
RESISTS
RESTSUP
RETESTS
REVISED
REVISER
REVISES
REVISIT
RICKSHA
RINGSUP
RIPOSTE
ROBESON
ROBUSTA
ROLLSUP
ROPESIN
ROSSSEA
RULESON

R••••S•

RACIEST
RAFFISH
RANKEST
RASHEST
RAWNESS
REALISM
REALIST
REAMASS
RECHOSE
RECLUSE
RECROSS
REDDEST
REDDISH
REDNESS
REDRESS
REDROSE
REFRESH
REGRESS
RELAPSE
RELEASE
REMORSE
REPRESS
REPRISE
REPULSE
REQUEST
RERAISE
RERINSE
REVERSE
RICHEST
ROGUISH
ROMANSH
RUBBISH
RYKRISP

R•••••S

RABBETS
RABBITS
RABBLES
RACEMES
RACKETS
RADAMES
RADDLES
RADIALS
RADIANS
RADICES
RAFFLES
RAFTERS
RAGLANS
RAGMOPS
RAGOUTS
RAGRUGS
RAGTOPS
RAIDERS
RAILERS
RAISERS
RAISINS
RALLIES
RAMADAS
RAMBLES
RAMESES
RAMJETS
RAMRODS
RANCHES
RANCHOS
RANGERS
RANKERS
RANKLES
RANSOMS
RANTERS
RAPIERS
RAPINES
RAPPELS
RAPPERS
RAPTORS
RAREGAS
RASCALS
RASHERS
RASPERS
RASSLES
RASTERS
RATINGS
RATIONS
RATITES
RATTANS
RATTERS
RATTLES
RAUCOUS
RAVAGES
RAVINES
RAVINGS
RAWNESS
RAYGUNS
REACHES
READERS
READIES
REAMASS
REAMERS
REAPERS
REARERS
REASONS
REBATES
REBINDS
REBOILS
REBOLTS
REBOOTS
REBOZOS
REBUFFS
REBUKES
REBUSES
RECALLS
RECANES
RECANTS
RECASTS
RECEDES
RECIPES
RECITES
RECKONS
RECODES
RECOILS
RECORDS
RECORKS
RECOUPS
RECROSS
RECTORS
RECUSES
REDACTS
REDANTS
REDATES
REDBUDS
REDCAPS
REDDENS
REDDOGS
REDEALS
REDEEMS
REDEYES
REDFINS
REDFIRS
REDGUMS
REDHATS
REDHOTS
REDIALS
REDNESS
REDOAKS
REDRAWS
REDRESS
REDTOPS
REDUCES
REEDITS
REEFERS
REFACES
REFILLS
REFILMS
REFINES
REFIRES
REFORMS
REFRIES
REFUELS
REFUGES
REFUNDS
REFUSES
REFUTES
REGAINS
REGALES
REGARDS
REGENTS
REGIMES
REGIONS
REGLUES
REGRESS
REGRETS
REGULUS
REHANGS
REHEALS
REHEARS
REHEATS
REHEELS
REHIRES
REHOOKS
REJECTS
REJOINS
RELACES
RELATES
RELAXES
RELENTS
RELICTS
RELIEFS
RELINES
RELISTS
RELIVES
RELOADS
RELOCKS
REMAILS
REMAINS
REMAKES
REMANDS
REMARKS
REMELTS
REMENDS
REMINDS
REMIXES
REMOLDS
REMORAS
REMOTES
REMOVES
REMUDAS
RENAILS
RENAMES
RENDERS
RENEGES
RENNINS
RENOTES
RENTALS
RENTERS
REOPENS
REPAIRS
REPASTS
REPAVES
REPEALS
REPEATS
REPENTS
REPINES
REPLANS
REPLAYS
REPLIES
REPOLLS
REPORTS
REPOSES
REPRESS
REPUGNS
REPUTES
RERATES
REREADS
REREDOS
RERENTS
RESALES
RESALTS
RESANDS
RESCUES
RESEALS
RESEATS
RESECTS
RESEEDS
RESELLS
RESENDS
RESENTS
RESHIPS
RESHOES
RESIDES
RESIGNS
RESILES
RESINGS
RESISTS
RESOLES
RESORBS
RESORTS
RESTERS
RESULTS
RESUMES
RETAILS
RETAINS
RETAKES
RETAPES
RETARDS
RETAXES
RETELLS
RETESTS
RETILES
RETIMES
RETINAS
RETIRES
RETOOLS
RETORTS
RETRIES
RETRIMS
RETUNES
RETURNS
RETYPES
REUBENS
REUTERS
REVAMPS
REVEALS
REVERBS
REVERES
REVERTS
REVIEWS
REVILES
REVISES
REVIVES
REVOKES
REVOLTS
REWARDS
REWARMS
REWAXES
REWELDS
REWINDS
REWIRES
REWORDS
REWORKS
REWRAPS
REXCATS
REZONES
RHETORS
RHOMBUS
RHUMBAS
RHYMERS
RHYTHMS
RIBANDS
RIBBONS
RIBEYES
RICKEYS
RICKLES
RIDDLES
RIFFLES
RIFLERS
RIGGERS
RIGOURS
RILLETS
RINGERS
RIOTERS
RIOTOUS
RIPOFFS
RIPPERS
RIPPLES
RIPRAPS
RIPSAWS
RISINGS
RISKERS
RITUALS
ROACHES
ROADIES
ROAMERS
ROARERS
ROBARDS
ROBBERS
ROBBINS
ROBERTS
ROBROYS
ROCKERS
ROCKETS
ROCKIES
RODENTS
RODGERS
ROLAIDS
ROLLERS
ROLLINS
ROMNEYS
ROMPERS
ROMULUS
RONDELS
ROOFERS
ROOKIES
ROOMERS
ROOMIES
ROOTERS
ROSTERS
ROTATES
ROTTERS
ROUTERS
ROWDIES
RUBBERS
RUBBLES
RUBRICS
RUDDERS
RUFFLES
RUINERS
RUINOUS
RULINGS
RUMBLES
RUMOURS
RUMPLES
RUNLAPS
RUNLETS
RUNNELS
RUNNERS
RUNOFFS
RUNWAYS
RUPIAHS
RUSHEES
RUSHERS
RUSSETS
RUSTICS
RUSTLES
RUTGERS

•RS••••

ARSENAL
ARSENIC
ARSENIO
DRSEUSS
DRSPOCK
ERSKINE
MRSPOCK

•R•S•••

ARCSINE
ARISING
ARISTAE
ARISTAS
ARISTOS
ARTSONG
BRASHER
BRASHLY
BRASSES
BRASSIE
BRESLIN
BRESSON
BRISKER
BRISKET
BRISKLY
BRISTLE
BRISTLY
BRISTOL
BROSNAN
BRUSHED
BRUSHES
BRUSHUP
BRUSQUE
CRASHED
CRASHES
CRASSER
CRASSLY
CRASSUS
CRESSES
CRESTED
CRISPED
CRISPER
CRISPIN
CRISPLY
CRISPUS
CROSIER
CROSSED
CROSSER
CROSSES
CROSSLY
CROSSUP
CRUSADE
CRUSHED
CRUSHER
CRUSHES
CRUSTED
CRYSTAL
DRASTIC
DRESDEN
DRESSED
DRESSER
DRESSES
DRESSUP
DRISTAN
DRYSUIT
ERASERS
ERASING
ERASMUS
ERASURE
ERISTIC
EROSION
EROSIVE
FRASIER
FRESCOS
FRESHEN
FRESHER
FRESHET
FRESHLY
FRISBEE
FRISIAN
FRISKED
FRISSON
FROSTED
GRASPED
GRASSED
GRASSES
GRISHAM
GRISSOM
GRISTLE
GRISTLY
GROSSED
GROSSER
GROSSES
GROSSLY
IRISOUT
IRKSOME
KRISHNA
ORESTES
ORISONS
PRESAGE
PRESALE
PRESELL
PRESENT
PRESETS
PRESIDE
PRESLEY
PRESOAK
PRESORT
PRESSED
PRESSER
PRESSES
PRESSON
PRESTON
PRESTOS
PRESUME
PRISONS
PROSAIC
PROSERS
PROSIER
PROSILY
PROSING
PROSODY
PROSPER
PRUSSIA
TRASHED
TRASHES
TRESSES
TRESTLE
TRISECT
TRISTAN
TRUSSED
TRUSSES
TRUSTED
TRUSTEE
TRYSTED
TRYSTER
WRESTED
WRESTLE

•R••S••

ARALSEA
ARIOSOS
ARIOSTO
AROUSAL
AROUSED
AROUSES
ARRASES
ARRESTS
ARRISES
ARTISAN
ARTISTE
ARTISTS
BRAISED
BRAISES
BRANSON
BRASSES
BRASSIE
BREASTS
BRESSON
BRONSON
BROWSED
BROWSER
BROWSES
BRUISED
BRUISER
BRUISES
CRASSER
CRASSLY
CRASSUS
CREASED
CREASES
CREOSOL
CRESSES
CRIMSON
CROESUS
CROPSUP
CROSSED
CROSSER
CROSSES
CROSSLY
CROSSUP
CRUISED
CRUISER
CRUISES
DRAGSIN
DRAGSON
DRAWSIN
DRAWSON
DRAWSUP
DREISER
DRESSED
DRESSER
DRESSES
DRESSUP
DRIESUP
DROPSBY
DROPSIN
DROWSED
DROWSES
DRUMSUP
ERICSON
ERNESTO
FRAISES
FREESIA
FRETSAW
FRISSON
GRABSAT
GRASSED
GRASSES
GRAYSON
GREASED
GREASER
GREASES
GRISSOM
GROSSED
GROSSER
GROSSES
GROSSLY
GROUSED
GROUSER
GROUSES
GROWSON
GROWSUP
ORBISON
PRAISED
PRAISER
PRAISES
PRAYSTO
PRESSED
PRESSER
PRESSES
PRESSON
PREYSON
PRIESTS
PROPSUP
PRUSSIA
TRANSIT
TRANSOM
TREASON
TRESSES
TRIESON
TRIESTE
TRIPSUP
TROTSKY
TROUSER
TRUISMS
TRUSSED
TRUSSES
VRONSKY
WRAPSUP

•R•••S•

ARIDEST
ARMLESS
ARMREST
ARTIEST
ARTLESS
BRAVEST
BRITISH
BRUTISH
CRAFTSY
CRUDEST
DRSEUSS
DRYNESS
GRAVEST
GRAYEST
GREYEST
IRATEST
PRECAST
PRECISE
PREMISE
PRETEST
PREWASH
PROCESS
PROFESS
PROFUSE
PROMISE
PROPOSE
PROTEST
PROTIST
PROVISO
PROVOST
PROWESS

PRUDISH
TRAIPSE
TRITEST
TROPISM
WRYNESS

•R•••S

ARAWAKS
ARBOURS
ARBUTUS
ARCADES
ARCHERS
ARCHIES
ARCHONS
ARDOURS
ARDUOUS
AREOLAS
ARGIVES
ARGUERS
ARGYLES
ARIOSOS
ARISTAS
ARISTOS
ARMADAS
ARMFULS
ARMLESS
ARMLETS
ARMOURS
ARMPITS
ARNICAS
AROUSES
ARRASES
ARREARS
ARRESTS
ARRISES
ARRIVES
ARROBAS
ARROYOS
ARTEMIS
ARTEMUS
ARTISTS
ARTLESS
BRACERS
BRAHMAS
BRAISES
BRASSES
BRAVOES
BRAYERS
BREASTS
BREATHS
BREEZES
BRETONS
BREVETS
BREWERS
BRIARDS
BRIDALS
BRIDGES
BRIDLES
BRITONS
BROGANS
BROGUES
BROKERS
BRONCOS
BRONZES
BROWSES
BRUISES
BRUNETS
BRUSHES
CRADLES
CRASHES
CRASSUS
CRATERS
CRAVATS
CRAVENS
CRAVERS
CRAYONS
CRAZIES
CREASES
CREATES
CRECHES
CREDITS
CRENELS
CREOLES
CRESSES
CRETANS
CRETINS
CREWELS
CRINGES
CRISPUS
CRITICS
CROESUS
CRONIES
CROSSES
CROWERS
CRUISES
CRUSHES
CRYPTOS
DRAGONS
DRAPERS
DRAWERS
DREDGES
DRESSES
DREYFUS
DRIVELS
DRIVERS
DRONERS
DROPINS
DROVERS
DROWSES
DRSEUSS
DRUDGES
DRYNESS
DRYRUNS
ERASERS
ERASMUS
ERMINES
ERRANDS
FRAISES
FRANCES
FRANCIS
FRAPPES
FREEZES
FRENUMS
FRESCOS
FRIDAYS
FRIDGES
FRIENDS
FRIEZES
FRIGHTS
FRINGES
FRIZZES
FROLICS
FRYPANS
GRACIAS
GRADERS
GRAHAMS
GRAMMES
GRAMPUS
GRANGES
GRASSES
GRATERS
GRAVELS
GRAVIES
GRAZERS
GREASES
GREAVES
GRIEVES
GRIGRIS
GRILLES
GRIPERS
GRIVETS
GROCERS
GROOVES
GROPIUS
GROSSES
GROTTOS
GROUNDS
GROUSES
GROVELS
GROWERS
GROWTHS
GRUDGES
IRONERS
IRONIES
IRRUPTS
KRATERS
MRBONES
MRCHIPS
ORACLES
ORANGES
ORATORS
ORCHIDS
ORDAINS
ORDEALS
ORESTES
ORIENTS
ORIGINS
ORIOLES
ORISONS
ORLEANS
ORMOLUS
ORPHANS
ORPHEUS
ORPINES
PRAISES
PRANCES
PRATERS
PRAYERS
PREAMPS
PREFABS
PREFERS
PRELIMS
PREMEDS
PREPAYS
PRESETS
PRESSES
PRESTOS
PRICERS
PRIESTS
PRIMERS
PRINCES
PRISONS
PRIVETS
PRIVIES
PROBERS
PROCESS
PROFESS
PROFITS
PROLOGS
PROMPTS
PROPELS
PROSERS
PROTEUS
PROTONS
PROVERS
PROWESS
PROXIES
PRUNERS
TRACERS
TRADERS
TRAMPAS
TRANCES
TRASHES
TRAUMAS
TRAVELS
TRAVERS
TRAVOIS
TREBLES
TRELLIS
TREMORS
TREPANS
TRESSES
TRICEPS
TRICOTS
TRIFLES
TRIGONS
TRIODES
TRIPLES
TRIPODS
TRITONS
TRIUNES
TRIVETS
TROCARS
TROCHES
TROIKAS
TROILUS
TROJANS
TROPICS
TROUGHS
TROUPES
TROWELS
TROWERS
TRUANTS
TRUDGES
TRUISMS
TRUSSES
TRYOUTS
URCHINS
URTEXTS
WRAITHS
WRAPUPS
WREATHS
WRIGHTS
WRITERS
WRITHES
WRYNESS

••RS•••

AIRSACS
AIRSHIP
AIRSHOW
AIRSOCK
AIRSOUT
BARSOAP
BERSERK
BORSCHT
BURSARS
BURSTYN
CARSEAT
CORSAGE
CORSAIR
CORSETS
CORSICA
CURSING
CURSIVE
CURSORS
CURSORY
DORSALS
DORSETT
EARSHOT
FIRSTLY
FORSAKE
FORSALE
FORSOOK
FORSTER
FORSURE
FORSYTH
FURSEAL
HARSHEN
HARSHER
HARSHLY
HERSELF
HERSHEY
HIRSUTE
HORSIER
HORSING
JERSEYS
KIRSTIE
MARSALA
MARSHAL
MARSHES
MORSELS
NURSERS
NURSERY
NURSING
OURSELF
PARSECS
PARSEES
PARSERS
PARSING
PARSLEY
PARSNIP
PARSONS
PERSEUS
PERSIAN
PERSIST
PERSIUS
PERSONA
PERSONS
PORSCHE
PORSENA
PURSERS
PURSING
PURSUED
PURSUER
PURSUES
PURSUIT
TARSALS
TARSIER
TERSELY
TERSEST
TORSION
VARSITY
VERSIFY
VERSION
WARSHIP
WORSENS
WORSHIP
WORSTED

••R•S••

AEROSOL
AORISTS
ARRASES
ARRESTS
ARRISES
BARKSAT
BERGSON
BERNSEN
BURNSUP
CARLSON
CHRISMS
CHRISTI
CHRISTO
CHRISTY
CURLSUP
CURTSEY
DARESAY
DARESTO
EURASIA
FIRESUP
FIRMSUP
FORESAW
FORESEE
FORESTS
GIRASOL
HARDSET
HARPSON
HIRESON
HORNSBY
JURISTS
KARASEA
LORISES
LYRISTS
MARKSUP
MORESBY
PARASOL
PERKSUP
PERUSAL
PERUSED
PERUSER
PERUSES
PHRASAL
PHRASED
PHRASES
PURISTS
STRASSE
THRUSTS
TURNSIN
TURNSON
TURNSTO
TURNSUP
UPRISEN
UPRISES
VIRUSES
WARMSUP
WORKSIN
WORKSON
WORKSUP

••R••S•

ABREAST
AERIEST
AIRBASE
AIRIEST
AIRLESS
AIRMASS
BERNESE
BURGESS
BURMESE
BURNISH
CARCASS
CARLESS
CAROUSE
CARWASH
CIRCUSY
CORNISH
CURTEST
DARKEST
DARKISH
DERVISH
EARNEST
EERIEST
FAREAST
FARWEST
FIRMEST
FORMOSA
FORREST
FURBISH
FURNISH
GARNISH
GIRLISH
GORIEST
HARDEST
HARNESS
HARPIST
HARVEST
HEROISM
HORNIST
KURDISH
LARGESS
LARGEST
MARXISM
MORTISE
OARLESS
OGREISH
PERSIST
PERTEST
PURPOSE
RERAISE
RERINSE
SARCASM
SPRIEST
SPRYEST
STRASSE
STRAUSS
SURMISE
SURPASS
TARNISH
TARTEST
TERSEST
TORYISM
TURKISH
UPRAISE
VARNISH
VERBOSE
WARIEST
WARMEST
WARMISH
WIRIEST

••R•••S

ABRADES
AERATES
AERIALS
AEROBES
AFRAMES
AFREETS
AIRBAGS
AIRDAMS
AIRGUNS
AIRINGS
AIRLESS
AIRMASS
AIRSACS
AIRWAYS
AORISTS
APROPOS
ARRASES
ARREARS
ARRESTS
ARRISES
ARRIVES
ARROBAS
ARROYOS
ATRIUMS
AUROCHS
AURORAS
BARBELS
BARBERS
BARENTS
BARHOPS
BARKERS
BARLEYS
BARNEYS
BARONGS
BARRELS
BARRENS
BARRIOS
BARROWS
BARTERS
BARYONS
BERATES
BERBERS
BERRIES
BIRCHES
BIRDERS
BIRDIES
BIREMES
BORATES
BORDERS
BORROWS
BORZOIS
BURBLES
BURBOTS
BURDENS
BUREAUS
BURGEES
BURGERS
BURGESS
BURGLES
BURGOOS
BURLAPS
BURNERS
BUROAKS
BURROWS
BURSARS
BYROADS
CARACAS
CARAFES
CARBONS
CARBOYS
CARCASS
CARDERS
CAREENS
CAREERS
CARFULS
CARGOES
CARHOPS
CARIBES
CARINAS
CARLESS
CARNETS
CARNIES
CAROLES
CAROLUS
CARPALS
CARPERS
CARPETS
CARRELS
CARRIES
CARROTS
CARTELS
CARTERS
CARTONS
CARVERS
CEREALS
CERIPHS
CHRISMS
CHROMES
CIRCLES
CIRQUES
CORBELS
CORDONS
CORKERS
CORNEAS
CORNERS
CORNETS
CORONAS
CORRALS
CORSETS
CURATES
CURDLES
CURFEWS
CURIOUS
CURLERS
CURLEWS
CURRIES
CURSORS
CURVETS
DARKENS
DARNERS
DARTERS
DERAILS
DERBIES
DERIDES
DERIVES
DIRECTS
DIRNDLS
DIRTIES
DORITOS
DORMERS
DORSALS
EARFULS
EARNERS
EARWIGS
ENRAGES
ENROBES
ENROLLS
ENROOTS
ERRANDS
FARMERS
FARROWS
FERRETS
FERRIES
FERROUS
FERULES
FERVORS
FIRINGS
FIRKINS
FORAGES
FORBIDS
FORCEPS
FORCERS
FORESTS
FORGERS
FORGETS
FORGOES
FORINTS
FORKERS
FORMALS
FORMATS
FORTIES
FURIOUS
FURORES
FURROWS
GARAGES
GARBLES
GARCONS
GARDENS
GARGLES
GARNERS
GARNETS
GARRETS
GARTERS
GERBILS
GERENTS
GERMANS
GERUNDS
GIRDERS
GIRDLES
GORGETS
GORGONS
GURGLES
GURKHAS
GURNEYS
GYRATES
HARBORS
HARDENS
HARKENS
HARNESS
HARPERS
HARPIES
HARRIES
HARROWS
HERALDS
HERBALS
HERDERS
HERMITS
HEROICS
HORNETS
HORRORS
HURDLES
HURLERS
HURRAHS
HURRIES
HURTLES
HYRACES
HYRAXES
INROADS
IRRUPTS
JARFULS
JARGONS
JERBOAS
JERKINS
JERSEYS
JURISTS
KERNELS
KIRMANS
KIRTLES
KOREANS
KORUNAS
LARCHES
LARDERS
LARDONS
LARGESS
LARIATS
LARRUPS
LORISES
LORRIES
LURCHES
LYRISTS
MARACAS
MARAUDS
MARBLES
MARCELS
MARCHES
MARGAYS
MARGINS
MARINAS
MARINES
MARKERS
MARKETS
MARKUPS
MARLINS
MARMOTS
MAROONS
MARQUES
MARQUIS
MARRIES
MARROWS
MARSHES
MARTENS
MARTINS
MARTYRS
MARVELS
MERCIES
MERGERS
MERINOS
MERLOTS
MIRAGES
MIRRORS
MORALES
MORANIS
MORGANS
MORMONS
MORROWS
MORSELS
MORTALS
MORTARS
MURDERS
MURMURS
MYRIADS
MYRTLES
NARROWS
NARWALS
NEREIDS
NERVOUS
NORDICS
NORMALS
NORMANS
NURSERS
OARLESS
PARADES
PARAPHS
PARCELS
PARCHES
PARDONS
PARENTS
PARGETS
PARIAHS
PARIBUS
PARINGS
PARLAYS
PARLEYS
PARLORS
PARLOUS
PAROLES
PARRIES
PARROTS
PARSECS
PARSEES
PARSERS
PARSONS
PARTIES
PARURES
PERCHES
PERHAPS
PERIODS
PERKINS
PERMITS
PERSEUS
PERSIUS
PERSONS
PERUKES
PERUSES
PHRASES
PIRAEUS
PIRATES
PORCHES
PORGIES
PORKERS
PORTALS
PORTERS
PORTHOS
PURDAHS
PURFLES
PURISTS
PURLINS
PURPLES
PURRERS
PURSERS
PURSUES
PURVEYS
PYRAMUS
PYRITES
PYRRHUS
RAREGAS
RERATES
REREADS
REREDOS
RERENTS
SARONGS
SCRAPES
SCRAWLS
SCREAKS
SCREAMS
SCREEDS
SCREENS
SCRIBES
SCRIMPS
SCRIPPS
SCRIPTS
SCROLLS
SCRUFFS
SERAPES
SERAPHS
SERAPIS
SERIALS
SERIOUS
SERMONS
SERVALS
SERVERS
SHRIEKS
SHRIFTS
SHRIKES
SHRILLS
SHRIMPS
SHRINES
SHRINKS
SHRIVES
SHROUDS
SORBETS
SORITES
SORRELS
SORROWS
SORTERS
SORTIES
SPRAINS
SPRAWLS
SPREADS
SPRINGS
SPRINTS
SPRITES
SPROUTS
SPRUCES
STRAFES
STRAINS
STRAITS
STRANDS
STRATUS
STRAUSS
STREAKS
STREAMS
STREETS
STRIDES
STRIKES
STRINGS
STRIPES
STRIVES
STROBES
STROKES
STROLLS
SURFERS
SURPASS
SURPLUS
SURREYS
SURVEYS
SYRIANS
TARGETS
TARIFFS
TARMACS
TARPITS
TARPONS
TARRIES
TARSALS
TARTANS
TARTARS
TERAPHS
TERCELS
TERCETS
TEREDOS
TERRETS
TERRIES
TERRORS
THRALLS
THREADS
THREATS
THREERS
THRIFTS
THRILLS
THRIVES
THROATS
THRONES
THRONGS
THRUSTS
TIRADES
TORCHES
TOREROS
TOROIDS
TORQUES
TURBANS
TURBOTS
TUREENS
TURKEYS
TURNERS
TURNIPS
TURRETS
TURTLES
TYRANTS
UNREELS
UNROBES
UNROLLS
UPRISES
UPROARS
UPROOTS
VARIOUS
VARLETS
VERBALS
VERGERS
VERVETS
VIRAGOS
VIRGINS
VIRTUES
VIRUSES
WARBLES
WARDENS
WARDERS
WARGODS

WARMUPS
WARRENS
WORKERS
WORKUPS
WORRIES
WORSENS
YARROWS
ZAREBAS
ZIRCONS

•••RS••
BEARSON
BEARSUP
COARSEN
COARSER
COURSED
COURSER
COURSES
DEARSIR
EMERSED
EMERSON
FAIRSUP
GEARSTO
GEARSUP
HEARSAY
HEARSOF
HOARSEN
HOARSER
JEERSAT
LEERSAT
OVERSAW
OVERSEA
OVERSEE
PAIRSUP
PEARSON
PEERSAT
PEERSIN
POURSIN
REARSUP
SPARSER
SPURSON
STIRSIN
STIRSUP
TEARSAT
TEARSUP
THIRSTS
THIRSTY

•••R•S•
ACEROSE
ACTRESS
ADDRESS
AGGRESS
AMBROSE
ANDRESS
APPRISE
ARMREST
AXLROSE
BEARISH
BEDREST
BOORISH
BULRUSH
CHERISH
CUIRASS
CYPRESS
CZARISM
CZARIST
DEAREST
DEFROST
DEPRESS
DIGRESS
DOUREST
EMPRESS
ENCRUST
ENGROSS
ENTRUST
EVEREST
EXPRESS
FAIREST
FLORIST
FORREST
HEIRESS
IMPRESS
INARUSH
INGRESS
INTRUST
IPCRESS
LOWRISE
MELROSE
MIDRISE
MOORISH
NEAREST
NOURISH
OLOROSO
OPEROSE
OPPRESS
OVERUSE
PEERESS
POOREST
RECROSS
REDRESS
REDROSE
REFRESH
REGRESS
REPRESS
REPRISE
RYKRISP
SEERESS
SOUREST
SOURISH
SPAREST
SUBROSA
SUCRASE
SUCROSE
SUNRISE
TEAROSE
THERESA
TIGRESS
TOURISM
TOURIST
TSARIST
UNDRESS

•••R••S
ACARIDS
ACCRUES
ACTRESS
ADDRESS
ADORERS
AFFRAYS
AGGRESS
AIGRETS
ALARUMS
AMBRIES
AMERCES
AMOROUS
ANDREAS
ANDRESS
ANDREWS
ANORAKS
APERCUS
APERIES
ASHRAMS
ATTRITS
BARRELS
BARRENS
BARRIOS
BARROWS
BEARERS
BERRIES
BETRAYS
BORROWS
BURROWS
CARRELS
CARRIES
CARROTS
CHARGES
CHARLES
CHERUBS
CHORALS
CITRONS
CLARETS
CLERICS
CLORETS
COERCES
CORRALS
COURSES
COWRIES
CUIRASS
CURRIES
CYPRESS
CZARDAS
DAIRIES
DEARTHS
DECREES
DECRIES
DEFRAYS
DEGREES
DEPRESS
DEVRIES
DIARIES
DIGRESS
DOWRIES
DRYRUNS
DWARVES
EMBRYOS
EMERGES
EMPRESS
ENDRUNS
ENGRAMS
ENGROSS
ENTRAPS
ENTREES
ENTRIES
ENWRAPS
EPARCHS
ESCROWS
ESTRAYS
EXPRESS
FABRICS
FAIRIES
FARROWS
FEARERS
FERRETS
FERRIES
FERROUS
FIBRILS
FIBROUS
FLORETS
FLORINS
FLYRODS
FOURTHS
FURROWS
GARRETS
GEORGES
GLORIAS
GLORIES
GOURDES
HAIRDOS
HARRIES
HARROWS
HEARERS
HEARTHS
HEBREWS
HEIRESS
HORRORS
HOTRODS
HURRAHS
HURRIES
HYBRIDS
HYDROUS
IMARETS
IMBRUES
IMPRESS
INGRESS
IPCRESS
IVORIES
JEERERS
LABRETS
LAERTES
LARRUPS
LAURELS
LEERERS
LIERNES
LORRIES
LOURDES
MACRONS
MARRIES
MARROWS
MATRONS
MAUROIS
MEGRIMS
METRICS
MICRONS
MIDRIBS
MIRRORS
MORROWS
NARROWS
NEURONS
NIMRODS
NITROUS
NUTRIAS
ODOROUS
OILRIGS
ONEROUS
OPPRESS
OSPREYS
OUTRUNS
PARRIES
PARROTS
PATROLS
PATRONS
PEERESS
PETRELS
PETROUS
PIERCES
PLURALS
POURERS
PUGREES
PURRERS
PYRRHUS
QUARTOS
QUERIES
QUORUMS
RAGRUGS
RAMRODS
REARERS
RECROSS
REDRAWS
REDRESS
REFRIES
REGRESS
REGRETS
REPRESS
RETRIES
RETRIMS
REWRAPS
RIPRAPS
ROARERS
ROBROYS
RUBRICS
SATRAPS
SCARABS
SCARERS
SCARVES
SCORERS
SCURVES
SECRETS
SEERESS
SHARERS
SHERPAS
SIERRAS
SKIRUNS
SNORERS
SOARERS
SOIREES
SORRELS
SORROWS
SOURCES
SPARGES
SPIRALS
SPIREAS
SPIRITS
STARERS
STARETS
STARVES
STEREOS
STEROLS
STORERS
STOREYS
STORIES
STURGES
SUNRAYS
SURREYS
SWERVES
TARRIES
TEARGAS
TERRETS
TERRIES
TERRORS
TETRADS
THERMOS
THIRSTS
TIERODS
TIGRESS
TOURERS
TUAREGS
TURRETS
UNDRESS
UNTRAPS
UNWRAPS
USURERS
WARRENS
WEARERS
WEARIES
WEIRDOS
WHARVES
WHEREAS
WORRIES
YARROWS

••••RS•
ACCURST
ADVERSE
AMHERST
ASPERSE
ATHIRST
ATWORST
DIVERSE
ENDORSE
IMMERSE
INTERSE
INVERSE
OBVERSE
REMORSE
REVERSE
UNHORSE

••••R•S
ABJURES
ABSORBS
ACCORDS
ADHERES
ADJURES
ADMIRES
ADSORBS
ADVERBS
ADVERTS
AFFIRMS
AFFORDS
ALLURES
AMPERES
ANGORAS
ANTARES
ASFARAS
ASPIRES
ASSERTS
ASSORTS
ASSURES
ATTIRES
AUBURNS
AURORAS
BEMIRES
BISTROS
BOLEROS
BOUTROS
BRIARDS
BYTURNS
BYWORDS
CAMERAS
CANARDS
CASERNS
CAVERNS
CAVORTS
CENTRES
CHEVRES
COHERES
COHORTS
COMOROS
CONTRAS
COWARDS
CYBORGS
DEBARKS
DEFORMS
DEHORNS
DEPARTS
DEPORTS
DESERTS
DESIRES
DISARMS
DIVERTS
DOLORES
EDWARDS
EFFORTS
EMBARKS
EMIGRES
EMPIRES
ENCORES
ENDURES
ENGIRDS
ENSURES
ESCARPS
ESCORTS
EUCHRES
EXHORTS
EXPERTS
EXPIRES
EXPORTS
EXTORTS
FABARES
FEDORAS
FIACRES
FIGURES
FURORES
FUTURES
GABBROS
GENERIS
GOCARTS
GOKARTS
GOVERNS
GRIGRIS
HAZARDS
HEGIRAS
HOMBRES
HOWARDS
HUMERUS
IDCARDS
IGNORES
IMMURES
IMPARTS
IMPORTS
INFORMS
INHERES
INJURES
INNARDS
INSERTS
INSURES
INTERNS
INVERTS
INWARDS
JABIRUS
LAZARUS
LETTRES
LIZARDS
LOUVRES
LUSTRES
MAHARIS
MANTRAS
MATURES
MILORDS
MITHRAS
MODERNS
NATURES
OBVERTS
OEUVRES
OFSORTS
OLDPROS
ONWARDS
OXCARTS
OXFORDS
PAPYRUS
PARURES
PETARDS
PICAROS
POLARIS
RECORDS
RECORKS
REFIRES
REFORMS
REGARDS
REHIRES
REMARKS
REMORAS
REPORTS
RESORBS
RESORTS
RETARDS
RETIRES
RETORTS
RETURNS
REVERBS
REVERES
REVERTS
REWARDS
REWARMS
REWIRES
REWORDS
REWORKS
ROBARDS
ROBERTS
SAFARIS
SAMPRAS
SATIRES
SCLERAS
SECURES
SENORAS
SENORES
SIERRAS
SPHERES
SQUARES
SQUIRES
SQUIRMS
SQUIRTS
SUBORNS
SUBURBS
SUTURES
TABARDS
TAVERNS
TENURES
THWARTS
TIMBRES
TOREROS
TOWARDS
TSHIRTS
TUNDRAS
UMPIRES
UNCORKS
UNCURLS
UNFURLS
UNGIRDS
UPTURNS
UPWARDS
WIZARDS
WYVERNS
YOGURTS

•••••RS
ABUSERS
ADORERS
AFFAIRS
ALGIERS
ALLEARS
AMBLERS
ANCHORS
ANGLERS
ANSWERS
ANTHERS
ANTLERS
APPEARS
ARBOURS
ARCHERS
ARDOURS
ARGUERS
ARMOURS
ARREARS
ASHLARS
AUTEURS
AUTHORS
AVATARS
AVOWERS
BACKERS
BADGERS
BAGGERS
BAILERS
BAILORS
BANKERS
BANNERS
BANTERS
BARBERS
BARKERS
BARTERS
BASTERS
BATHERS
BATTERS
BAWLERS
BAZAARS
BEAKERS
BEARERS
BEATERS
BEAVERS
BEEPERS
BEGGARS
BENDERS
BERBERS
BESTIRS
BETTERS
BETTORS
BEZIERS
BICKERS
BIDDERS
BIGGERS
BINDERS
BIRDERS
BITTERS
BLAZERS
BLOWERS
BOATERS
BOBBERS
BOILERS
BOMBERS
BONKERS
BOOMERS
BOPPERS
BORDERS
BOTHERS
BOWLERS
BOWYERS
BOXCARS
BRACERS
BRAYERS
BREWERS
BROKERS
BUFFERS
BUGLERS
BULGARS
BUMMERS
BUMPERS
BUNKERS
BURGERS
BURNERS
BURSARS
BUTLERS
BUTTERS
BUZZERS
CABLERS
CADGERS
CAESARS
CAHIERS
CALLERS
CAMBERS
CAMPERS
CANKERS
CANNERS
CANTERS
CANTORS
CAPPERS
CAPTORS
CARDERS
CAREERS
CARPERS
CARTERS
CARVERS
CASTERS
CELLARS
CENSERS
CENSORS
CENTERS
CHASERS
CHEWERS
CHOKERS
CINDERS
CIPHERS
CLAMORS
CLAWERS
CLOVERS
COALERS
COAXERS
CODGERS
COFFERS
COHEIRS
COINERS
COLLARS
COLOURS
COMBERS
CONCURS
CONDORS
CONFERS
CONGERS
CONKERS
CONNORS
COOKERS
COOLERS
COOPERS
COPIERS
COPPERS
COPTERS
CORKERS
CORNERS
COSTARS
COTTERS
COUGARS
CRATERS
CRAVERS
CROWERS
CURLERS
CURSORS
CUTLERS
CUTTERS
CYCLERS
CYPHERS
DAGGERS
DAMPERS
DANCERS
DANDERS
DANGERS
DARNERS
DARTERS
DASHERS
DAUBERS
DEALERS
DEBEERS
DEBTORS
DEICERS
DELVERS
DENIERS
DEODARS
DETOURS
DEVOURS
DIALERS
DIAPERS
DICKERS
DIETERS
DIFFERS
DIGGERS
DIMMERS
DINNERS
DIPPERS
DISBARS
DITHERS
DOCKERS
DOCTORS
DODDERS
DODGERS
DOGEARS
DOLLARS
DORMERS
DOSSERS
DOWNERS
DOWSERS
DRAPERS
DRAWERS
DRIVERS
DRONERS
DROVERS
DUBBERS
DUELERS
DUFFERS
DUNKERS
DUSTERS
EARNERS
EASTERS
ECLAIRS
EDITORS
ELATERS
ELIXIRS
ELOPERS
EMOTERS
ENAMORS
ENDEARS
ERASERS
ETCHERS
EVADERS
EVOKERS
FACTORS
FALTERS
FARMERS
FATHERS
FAVOURS
FAWNERS
FEARERS
FEEDERS
FEELERS
FELLERS
FENCERS
FENDERS
FERVORS
FESTERS
FETTERS
FIBBERS
FILLERS
FILTERS
FINDERS
FINGERS
FISHERS
FITTERS
FLAKERS
FLAVORS
FLEXORS
FLOWERS
FODDERS
FOGGERS
FOLDERS
FOLGERS
FOOTERS
FORCERS
FORGERS
FORKERS
FOSTERS
FOWLERS
FUELERS
GABBERS
GAFFERS
GAINERS
GAITERS
GANDERS
GARNERS
GARTERS
GASSERS
GATHERS
GAUGERS
GAWKERS
GEEZERS
GENDERS
GEYSERS
GIBBERS
GILDERS
GINGERS
GIRDERS
GLAZERS
GLIDERS
GLOWERS
GNAWERS
GOLFERS
GOMPERS
GOOBERS
GOPHERS
GOUGERS
GRADERS
GRATERS
GRAZERS
GRIPERS
GROCERS
GROWERS
GUITARS
GUNNERS
GUSHERS
GUTTERS
GYPPERS
HACKERS
HALTERS
HAMMERS
HAMPERS
HANGARS
HANGERS
HANKERS
HARBORS
HARPERS
HATTERS
HAULERS
HAWKERS
HAWSERS
HEADERS
HEALERS
HEARERS
HEATERS
HEAVERS
HECTORS
HEDGERS
HEELERS
HEIFERS
HELLERS
HELPERS
HEMMERS
HERDERS
HINDERS
HISSERS
HITTERS
HOAXERS
HOLDERS
HOLLERS
HONKERS
HONOURS
HOOFERS
HOOTERS
HOPPERS
HORRORS
HOSIERS
HOTCARS
HOTWARS
HOWLERS
HUGGERS
HULLERS
HUMMERS
HUMOURS
HUNGERS
HUNKERS
HUNTERS
HURLERS
HUSKERS
HUSSARS
IMAGERS
IMPAIRS
INDOORS
IRONERS
ISOBARS
ISOMERS
ISSUERS
JABBERS
JAEGERS
JAGUARS
JAILERS
JAMMERS
JASPERS
JEERERS
JEFFERS
JESTERS
JIGGERS
JITTERS
JOBBERS
JOGGERS
JOINERS
JUDDERS
JUICERS
JUMPERS
JUNIORS
JUNKERS
KAISERS
KEENERS
KEEPERS
KEGLERS
KICKERS
KIDDERS
KILLERS
KIPPERS
KISSERS
KOSHERS
KRATERS
LAAGERS
LABOURS

LADDERS
LADLERS
LAGGERS
LANCERS
LANDERS
LANGURS
LARDERS
LASHERS
LATHERS
LAWYERS
LEADERS
LEAKERS
LEANERS
LEAPERS
LEASERS
LECTORS
LEDGERS
LEERERS
LENDERS
LESSORS
LETTERS
LEVIERS
LIBBERS
LIFTERS
LIMBERS
LIMNERS
LINGERS
LINKERS
LIQUORS
LITTERS
LOADERS
LOAFERS
LOANERS
LOBBERS
LOCKERS
LODGERS
LOGGERS
LOITERS
LOOKERS
LOOPERS
LOOTERS
LOPPERS
LOUVERS
LUBBERS
LUGGERS
LUMBARS
LUMBERS
LUMPERS
LUNKERS
LUSTERS
MADDERS
MAGYARS
MAILERS
MANGERS
MANNERS
MAPPERS
MARKERS
MARTYRS
MASHERS
MASKERS
MASTERS
MATHERS
MATTERS
MEMBERS
MEMOIRS
MENDERS
MENHIRS
MENTORS
MERGERS
METEORS
METIERS
MEWLERS
MILKERS
MILLERS
MINCERS
MINDERS
MINTERS
MIRRORS
MISTERS
MOANERS
MOCKERS
MOHAIRS
MOILERS
MOLDERS
MOLTERS
MONGERS
MOPPERS
MORTARS
MOTHERS
MOUSERS
MUDDERS
MUGGERS
MULLERS
MUMMERS
MURDERS
MURMURS
MUSHERS
MUSTERS
MUTTERS
NABBERS
NAILERS
NAPPERS
NATTERS
NECKERS
NECTARS
NESTERS
NICKERS
NIPPERS
NODDERS
NOSHERS
NUDGERS
NUMBERS
NURSERS
NUTTERS
ONAGERS
OPENERS
OPINERS
ORATORS
OSTLERS
OUSTERS
OYSTERS
PACKERS
PADDERS
PALTERS
PAMPERS
PANDERS
PANNERS
PANZERS
PARLORS
PARSERS
PASSERS
PASTORS
PATTERS
PAUPERS
PAWNERS
PEDLARS
PEELERS
PEEPERS
PELTERS
PENNERS
PEPPERS
PESTERS
PETTERS
PHASERS
PICKERS
PIECERS
PILFERS
PILLARS
PINCERS
PINNERS
PITTERS
PLACERS
PLANERS
PLATERS
PLAYERS
PLEXORS
PLOVERS
PLOWERS
POLDERS
POLLERS
PONDERS
POPLARS
POPPERS
PORKERS
PORTERS
POSEURS
POSTERS
POTHERS
POTTERS
POURERS
POUTERS
POWDERS
PRATERS
PRAYERS
PREFERS
PRICERS
PRIMERS
PROBERS
PROSERS
PROVERS
PRUNERS
PUCKERS
PUFFERS
PULSARS
PUMPERS
PUNTERS
PURRERS
PURSERS
PUTTERS
QINTARS
QUAKERS
QUASARS
QUAVERS
QUEUERS
QUIVERS
QUOTERS
RAFTERS
RAIDERS
RAILERS
RAISERS
RANGERS
RANKERS
RANTERS
RAPIERS
RAPPERS
RAPTORS
RASHERS
RASPERS
RASTERS
RATTERS
READERS
REAMERS
REAPERS
REARERS
RECTORS
REDFIRS
REEFERS
REHEARS
RENDERS
RENTERS
REPAIRS
RESTERS
REUTERS
RHETORS
RHYMERS
RIFLERS
RIGGERS
RIGOURS
RINGERS
RIOTERS
RIPPERS
RISKERS
ROAMERS
ROARERS
ROBBERS
ROCKERS
RODGERS
ROLLERS
ROMPERS
ROOFERS
ROOMERS
ROOTERS
ROSTERS
ROTTERS
ROUTERS
RUBBERS
RUDDERS
RUINERS
RUMOURS
RUNNERS
RUSHERS
RUTGERS
SACKERS
SAILORS
SALTERS
SALVERS
SAMBARS
SANDERS
SANTIRS
SAPPERS
SASSERS
SAUCERS
SAVIORS
SAVOURS
SAWYERS
SCALARS
SCALERS
SCARERS
SCORERS
SCOTERS
SEALERS
SEATERS
SECTORS
SEEDERS
SEEKERS
SEINERS
SEIZERS
SELLERS
SENDERS
SENIORS
SENSORS
SERVERS
SETTERS
SHAKERS
SHAPERS
SHARERS
SHAVERS
SHINERS
SHIVERS
SHOFARS
SHOVERS
SHOWERS
SIFTERS
SIGHERS
SIGNERS
SILVERS
SIMMERS
SIMPERS
SINGERS
SINKERS
SINNERS
SIPPERS
SISTERS
SITTERS
SKATERS
SKEWERS
SKIVERS
SLAVERS
SLAYERS
SLICERS
SLIDERS
SLIVERS
SMILERS
SMOKERS
SNORERS
SOAKERS
SOAPERS
SOARERS
SOBBERS
SOLDERS
SOLVERS
SOONERS
SORTERS
SPACERS
SPADERS
SPIDERS
SPIKERS
STAGERS
STARERS
STATORS
STEWERS
STOKERS
STONERS
STORERS
STUPORS
STYLERS
SUCCORS
SUCKERS
SUFFERS
SUITORS
SULKERS
SUMMERS
SUNDERS
SUPPERS
SURFERS
SUTLERS
SWAYERS
SWIPERS
TACKERS
TAILORS
TALKERS
TAMPERS
TANKERS
TANNERS
TAPPERS
TARTARS
TASTERS
TATTERS
TEASERS
TEDDERS
TEENERS
TEETERS
TELLERS
TEMPERS
TENDERS
TENNERS
TENSORS
TENTERS
TERRORS
TESTERS
TETHERS
THALERS
THREERS
TICKERS
TILLERS
TILTERS
TIMBERS
TINDERS
TINEARS
TINKERS
TINNERS
TINTERS
TIPPERS
TITHERS
TITTERS
TOILERS
TOOTERS
TOPPERS
TOSSERS
TOTTERS
TOURERS
TOUTERS
TOWCARS
TOWNERS
TRACERS
TRADERS
TRAVERS
TREMORS
TROCARS
TROWERS
TUCKERS
TUGGERS
TURNERS
TUSKERS
TWOFERS
ULSTERS
UNITERS
UPROARS
USURERS
VALOURS
VAMPERS
VAPOURS
VECTORS
VELOURS
VENDORS
VENEERS
VENTERS
VERGERS
VESPERS
VETOERS
VICTORS
VIEWERS
VIGOURS
VIZIERS
WAILERS
WAITERS
WAIVERS
WALKERS
WALTERS
WANDERS
WARDERS
WASHERS
WASTERS
WEARERS
WEAVERS
WEEDERS
WEEPERS
WELDERS
WELTERS
WENDERS
WETBARS
WETHERS
WHALERS
WHINERS
WICKERS
WIENERS
WINCERS
WINDERS
WINGERS
WINKERS
WINNERS
WINTERS
WISHERS
WITHERS
WONDERS
WOOFERS
WORKERS
WRITERS
YAKKERS
YAMMERS
YAPPERS
YAWNERS
YAWPERS
YELPERS
YONKERS
YOWLERS
ZANDERS
ZAPPERS
ZEPHYRS
ZINGERS
ZIPPERS
ZITHERS
ZONKERS

R•T••••

RATABLE
RATAFIA
RATATAT
RATCHET
RATFINK
RATHOLE
RATINGS
RATIONS
RATITES
RATLINE
RATPACK
RATRACE
RATTAIL
RATTANS
RATTERS
RATTIER
RATTING
RATTLED
RATTLER
RATTLES
RATTRAP
RETAILS
RETAINS
RETAKEN
RETAKES
RETAPED
RETAPES
RETARDS
RETAXED
RETAXES
RETEACH
RETELLS
RETESTS
RETHINK
RETICLE
RETILED
RETILES
RETIMED
RETIMES
RETINAE
RETINAL
RETINAS
RETINUE
RETIRED
RETIREE
RETIRES
RETITLE
RETOOLS
RETORTS
RETOUCH
RETOWED
RETRACE
RETRACK
RETRACT
RETRADE
RETRAIN
RETREAD
RETREAT
RETRIAL
RETRIED
RETRIES
RETRIMS
RETSINA
RETUNED
RETUNES
RETURNS
RETYPED
RETYPES
RITCHIE
RITUALS
RITZIER
ROTATED
ROTATES
ROTATOR
ROTIFER
ROTTERS
ROTTING
ROTUNDA
RUTGERS

R••T•••

RAFTERS
RAFTING
RAGTIME
RAGTOPS
RANTERS
RANTING
RAPTORS
RAPTURE
RASTERS
RATTAIL
RATTANS
RATTERS
RATTIER
RATTING
RATTLED
RATTLER
RATTLES
RATTRAP
RECTIFY
RECTORS
RECTORY
REDTAPE
REDTOPS
RENTALS
RENTERS
RENTING
REPTILE
RESTAGE
RESTAIN
RESTAMP
RESTART
RESTATE
RESTERS
RESTFUL
RESTING
RESTIVE
RESTOCK
RESTORE
RESTSUP
RESTYLE
REUTERS
REUTHER
RHETORS
RHYTHMS
RIFTING
RIOTACT
RIOTERS
RIOTING
RIOTOUS
RIPTIDE
RIPTORN
RONTGEN
ROOTERS
ROOTFOR
ROOTING
ROOTLET
ROOTOUT
ROSTAND
ROSTERS
ROSTRUM
ROTTERS
ROTTING
ROUTERS
ROUTINE
ROUTING
RUCTION
RUNTIER
RUPTURE
RUSTICS
RUSTIER
RUSTILY
RUSTING
RUSTLED
RUSTLER
RUSTLES

R•••T••

RALSTON
RARITAN
RATATAT
RATITES
REACTED
REACTOR
REACTTO
REALTOR
REBATED
REBATES
RECITAL
RECITED
RECITER
RECITES
REDATED
REDATES
REDSTAR
REENTER
REENTRY
REFUTED
REFUTER
REFUTES
REGATTA
RELATED
RELATES
REMOTER
REMOTES
RENOTES
REPUTED
REPUTES
RERATED
RERATES
RETITLE
RICHTER
RICOTTA
RIGHTED
RIGHTER
RIGHTLY
RIGHTON
RISOTTO
RIVETED
RIVETER
ROASTED
ROASTER
ROBOTIC
ROISTER
ROLLTOP
ROOFTOP
ROOSTED
ROOSTER
ROPETOW
ROSETTA
ROSETTE
ROTATED
ROTATES
ROTATOR
ROUSTED
RUBITIN

R••••T•

RABBETS
RABBITS
RABBITT
RACKETS
RADIATE
RAGOUTS
RALLYTO
RAMJETS
RANINTO
RANLATE
RAWDATA
REACTTO
REALITY
REBASTE
REBIRTH
REBOLTS
REBOOTS
RECANTS
RECASTS
REDACTS
REDANTS
REDHATS
REDHOTS
REEDITS
REFERTO
REGATTA
REGENTS
REGRETS
REHEATS
REJECTS
RELENTS
RELICTS
RELISTS
REMELTS
REPASTE
REPASTS
REPEATS
REPENTS
REPLATE
REPLETE
REPORTS
REQUITE
RERENTS
REROUTE
RESALTS
RESEATS
RESECTS
RESENTS
RESISTS
RESORTS
RESPITE
RESTATE
RESULTS
RETESTS
RETORTS
REUNITE
REVERTS
REVOLTS
REWRITE
REWROTE
REXCATS
RICKETY
RICOTTA
RILLETS
RIORITA
RIPINTO
RIPOSTE
RISOTTO
ROBERTA
ROBERTO
ROBERTS
ROBUSTA
ROCKETS
RODENTS
ROSEATE
ROSETTA
ROSETTE
ROYALTY
RUNINTO
RUNLETS
RUNWITH
RUSSETS

R•••••T

RABBITT
RACIEST
RACQUET
RADIANT
RAILSAT
RAIMENT
RAINHAT
RAINOUT
RAMPANT
RAMPART
RANKEST
RANRIOT
RAPPORT
RAREBIT
RASHEST
RATATAT
RATCHET
READMIT
READOUT
REAGENT
REALIST
REBUILT
RECEIPT
RECOUNT
RECRUIT
REDCENT
REDCOAT
REDDEST
REDEALT
REDHEAT
REDMEAT
REDOUBT
REDSPOT
REELECT
REENACT
REFLECT
REFRACT
REGNANT
RELIANT
RELIGHT
REMNANT
REMOUNT
RENAULT
REPAINT
REPLANT
REPRINT
REQUEST
RESHOOT
RESPECT
RESTART
RETRACT
RETREAT
REVISIT
RICERAT
RICHEST
RIDEOUT
RIMSHOT
RINGLET
RINGOUT
RIOTACT
RIVULET
RODEOUT
ROLLOUT
ROOTLET
ROOTOUT
ROUGHIT
ROWBOAT
RUBSOUT
RULEOUT
RUNRIOT
RUNSOUT

•RT••••

ARTDECO
ARTEMIS
ARTEMUS
ARTFILM
ARTFORM
ARTICLE
ARTIEST
ARTISAN
ARTISTE
ARTISTS
ARTLESS
ARTSONG
ARTWARE
ARTWORK
ORTOLAN
URTEXTS

•R•T•••

BRETONS
BRITAIN
BRITISH
BRITONS
BRITTEN
BRITTLE
BRITTON
BROTHER
BRUTISH
CRATERS
CRATING
CRETANS
CRETINS
CRITICS
CRITTER
DRATTED
ERITREA
EROTICA
FRETFUL
FRETSAW
FRETTED
FRITTED
FRITTER
FROTHED
GRATERS
GRATIFY
GRATING
GRETZKY
GRITTED
GROTTOS
IRATELY
IRATEST
KRATERS
KRATION
ORATING
ORATION
ORATORS
ORATORY
OROTUND
PRATERS
PRATING
PRATTLE
PRETAPE
PRETEEN
PRETEND
PRETEST
PRETEXT
PRETZEL
PRITHEE
PROTEAN
PROTECT
PROTEGE
PROTEIN
PROTEST
PROTEUS
PROTIST
PROTONS
TRITELY
TRITEST
TRITIUM
TRITONE
TRITONS
TROTHED
TROTOUT
TROTSKY
TROTTED
TROTTER
WRITEIN
WRITERS
WRITETO
WRITEUP
WRITHED
WRITHES
WRITING
WRITTEN
WROTEIN
WROTETO
WROTEUP
XRATING

•R••T••

ARBITER
ARBUTUS
ARIETTA
ARISTAE
ARISTAS
ARISTOS
BRAXTON
BREATHE
BREATHS
BREATHY
BRISTLE
BRISTLY
BRISTOL
BRITTEN
BRITTLE
BRITTON
BRUITED
CRAFTED
CRAFTER
CRAFTSY
CREATED
CREATES
CREATOR
CRESTED
CRITTER
CROATIA
CROUTON
CRUSTED
CRYPTIC
CRYPTOS
CRYSTAL
DRAFTED
DRAFTEE
DRASTIC
DRATTED
DRIFTED
DRIFTER
DRISTAN
ERECTED
ERECTER
ERECTLY
ERECTOR
ERISTIC
ERRATIC
ERRATUM
ERUCTED
ERUPTED
FRACTAL
FRANTIC
FREITAG
FRETTED
FRITTED
FRITTER
FRONTAL
FRONTED
FRONTON
FROSTED
FRUITED
GRAFTED
GRANTED
GRANTEE
GRANTOR
GREATER
GREATLY
GREETED
GREETER
GRIFTER
GRISTLE
GRISTLY
GRITTED
GROTTOS
GROUTED
GROWTHS
GRUNTED
KRYPTON
ORBITAL
ORBITED
ORBITER
ORESTES
ORNETTE
ORNITHO
PRAETOR
PRATTLE
PRESTON
PRESTOS
PRINTED
PRINTER
PROCTOR
TRACTOR
TRAITOR
TREATED
TREETOP
TRENTON
TRESTLE
TRISTAN
TROTTED
TROTTER
TRUSTED
TRUSTEE
TRYSTED
TRYSTER
WRAITHS
WREATHE
WREATHS
WRESTED
WRESTLE
WRITTEN

•R•••T•

ARIDITY
ARIETTA
ARIOSTO
ARMLETS
ARMPITS
ARRESTS
ARTISTE
ARTISTS
BREADTH
BREASTS
BREVETS
BREVITY
BRINGTO
BROMATE
BRUNETS
CRAVATS
CREDITS
CRUDITY
EREMITE
ERNESTO
ERUDITE
FRAILTY
FRIGATE
FRIGHTS
GRANITE
GRAVITY
GRIVETS
IRRUPTS
ORIENTE
ORIENTS
ORNETTE
PRAYSTO
PREDATE
PRELATE
PRESETS
PRIESTS
PRIMATE
PRIORTO
PRIVATE
PRIVETS
PROBATE
PROBITY
PROFITS
PROMOTE
PROMPTS
PRORATA
PRORATE
PRYINTO
TRIBUTE
TRICOTS
TRIESTE
TRINITY
TRIVETS
TRUANTS
TRYOUTS
URANITE
URTEXTS
WRIGHTS
WRITETO
WROTETO

•R••••T

ARIDEST
ARMREST
ARMYANT
ARTIEST
BRACKET
BRAVEST
BRIDGET
BRILLAT
BRIQUET
BRISKET
BROUGHT
CREWCUT
CRICKET
CROCHET
CROQUET
CRUDEST
CRUMPET
DRAGNET
DRAGOUT
DRAUGHT
DRAWOUT
DREWOUT
DRIBLET
DRIVEAT
DROPLET
DROPOUT
DROUGHT
DRYSUIT
FRAUGHT
FREIGHT
FREMONT
FRESHET
FROWNAT
GRABSAT
GRAVEST
GRAYEST
GREYEST
GRILLET
GROMMET
IRATEST
IRISOUT
IRONOUT
MRFIXIT
MRRIGHT
PRECAST
PRECEPT
PREDICT
PREEMPT
PREFECT
PREHEAT
PRESENT
PRESORT
PRETEST
PRETEXT
PREVENT
PRODUCT
PROJECT
PROPHET
PROPJET
PROTECT
PROTEST
PROTIST
PROVOST
PRUDENT
TRABERT
TRANSIT
TREERAT
TRIDENT
TRINKET
TRIPLET
TRIPPET
TRISECT
TRITEST
TROTOUT
TRUMPET
WROUGHT

••RT•••

AIRTAXI
AIRTIME
BARTEND
BARTERS
BERTHED
BERTOLT
BIRTHED
CARTAGE
CARTELS
CARTERS
CARTIER
CARTING
CARTONS
CARTOON
CERTAIN
CERTIFY
CORTEGE
CURTAIL
CURTAIN
CURTEST
CURTSEY
DARTERS
DARTING
DIRTIED
DIRTIER
DIRTIES
DIRTILY
EARTHEN
EARTHLY
FARTHER
FERTILE
FORTIES
FORTIFY
FORTRAN
FORTUNA
FORTUNE
FURTHER
FURTIVE
GARTERS
HARTMAN
HURTFUL
HURTING
HURTLED
HURTLES
KIRTLES
MARTENS
MARTIAL
MARTIAN
MARTINA
MARTINI
MARTINO
MARTINS
MARTYRS
MORTALS
MORTARS
MORTIFY
MORTISE
MYRTLES
NARTHEX
NORTHER
NURTURE
OURTOWN
PARTAKE
PARTIAL
PARTIED
PARTIES
PARTING
PARTITA
PARTITE
PARTNER
PARTOOK
PARTOUT
PARTWAY
PERTAIN
PERTEST
PERTURB
PORTAGE
PORTALS
PORTEND
PORTENT
PORTERS
PORTHOS
PORTICO
PORTION
PORTOLA
PORTRAY
SORTERS
SORTIED
SORTIES
SORTING
TARTANS
TARTARE
TARTARS
TARTEST
TERTIAL
TORTONI
TURTLED
TURTLES
VERTIGO
VIRTUAL
VIRTUES
WARTHOG
WARTIME
WERTHER

••R•T••

AERATED
AERATES
AERATOR
BARETTA
BERATED
BERATES
BERETTA
BIRETTA
BORATES
BURETTE
BURNTUP
BURSTYN
CARLTON
CAROTID
CORETTA
CURATES
CURATOR
DORITOS
DOROTHY
ERRATIC
ERRATUM
FIRSTLY
FORSTER
GERITOL
GORETEX
GYRATED
GYRATES
GYRATOR
HARDTOP
HERBTEA
HERETIC
HORATIO
KERATIN
KIRSTIE
LORETTA
MARITAL
MERITED
PIRATED
PIRATES
PIRATIC
PURITAN
PYRITES
RARITAN
RERATED
RERATES
SCRATCH
SORITES
SPRITES
STRATUM
STRATUS
STRETCH
STRETTO
UNRATED
WIRETAP
WORSTED

••R••T•

AFREETS
AGREETO
AIRDATE
AORISTS
ARRESTS
AUREATE
BARENTS
BARETTA
BARRETT
BERETTA
BERLITZ
BIRETTA
BURBOTS
BURETTE
BURNETT
BURRITO
CARNETS
CARPETS
CARROTS
CHRISTI
CHRISTO
CHRISTY
CORBETT
CORDATE
CORDITE
CORETTA
CORINTH
CORNETS
CORSETS
CURVETS
DARESTO
DIRECTS
DORSETT
DURANTE
ENROOTS
ENROUTE
FERRATE
FERRETS
FERRITE
FORESTS
FORGETS
FORINTS
FORMATS
FORSYTH
GARNETS
GARRETS
GARRETT
GERENTS
GORGETS
HERMITS
HIRSUTE
HORNETS
IRRUPTS
JURISTS
LARIATS
LORETTA
LYRISTS
MARGATE
MARKETS
MARMOTS
MERLOTS
NARRATE
OTRANTO
PARENTS
PARGETS
PARROTS
PARTITA
PARTITE
PERLITE
PERMITS
PURISTS
RERENTS
REROUTE
SCRIPTS
SERIATE
SERRATE
SHRIFTS
SORBATE
SORBETS
SPRINTS
SPROUTS
STRAITS
STREETS
STRETTO
STRIATE
TARANTO
TARGETS
TARPITS
TERCETS
TERMITE
TERNATE
TERRETS
THREATS
THRIFTS
THRIFTY
THROATS
THROATY
THRUSTS
TORONTO
TURBOTS
TURNSTO
TURRETS
TYRANTS
UPROOTS
VARIETY
VARLETS
VARSITY
VERVETS
WARPATH
ZERMATT

••R•••T

ABREAST
ACROBAT
AERIEST
AEROBAT
AIRBOAT
AIRIEST
AIRLIFT
AIRPORT
AIRSOUT
ALRIGHT
APRICOT
BARKSAT
BARONET
BARRETT
BERTOLT
BOREOUT
BORSCHT
BURNETT
BURNOUT
CARCOAT
CARPORT
CARSEAT
CIRCLET
CIRCUIT
CORBETT
CORONET
CORRECT
CORRUPT
CURBCUT
CURRANT
CURRENT
CURTEST
DARKEST
DORMANT
DORSETT
EARHART
EARNEST
EARSHOT
EERIEST
FAREAST
FARLEFT
FARMOUT
FARWEST
FERMENT
FERVENT
FIREANT
FIRELIT
FIRMEST
FORFEIT
FORRENT
FORREST
FORWENT
GARMENT
GARRETT
GERAINT
GORIEST
HARDEST
HARDHAT
HARDHIT
HARDPUT
HARDSET
HARICOT
HARPIST
HARRIET
HARVEST
HERBERT
HERRIOT
HORNIST
LARGEST
MARGRET
MORDANT
MORDENT
MRRIGHT
PARAPET
PARFAIT
PARQUET
PARTOUT
PERCENT
PERFECT
PERIDOT
PERSIST
PERTEST
PERVERT
PORTENT
PURPORT
PURSUIT
RAREBIT
SARGENT
SERPENT
SERVANT
SPRIEST
SPRYEST
SURCOAT
SURFEIT
TARTEST
TERSEST
TIREOUT
TOREOUT
TORMENT
TORNOUT
TORRENT
TURNOUT
UPRIGHT
UTRECHT
VARIANT
VARMINT
VERDANT
VERDICT
VERMONT
WARIEST
WARMEST
WARRANT
WIRIEST
WOREOUT
WORKOUT
WORNOUT
ZERMATT

•••RT••

ABORTED
ALERTED
ALERTER
ALERTLY
AVERTED
BLURTED
CHARTED
CHARTER
CHORTLE
COURTED
COURTLY
DEARTHS
EVERTED
EXERTED
FLIRTED
FOURTHS
HEARTEN
HEARTHS
INERTIA
INERTLY
LAERTES
OVERTLY
QUARTER
QUARTET
QUARTOS
SHORTED
SHORTEN
SHORTER
SHORTLY
SHORTOF
SKIRTED
SMARTED
SMARTEN
SMARTER
SMARTLY
SNORTED
SNORTER
SPARTAN
SPORTED
SPURTED
STARTED
STARTER
STARTLE
STARTUP
SWARTHY
WHARTON

•••R•T•

ACCRETE
AIGRETS
ATTRITE
ATTRITS
AZURITE
BARRETT
BETROTH
BURRITO
CARROTS
CHARITY
CITRATE
CLARETS
CLARITY
CLORETS
CUTRATE
EMERITA
EMERITI
EMIRATE
EVERETT
EXCRETE
FERRATE
FERRETS
FERRITE
FLORETS
GARRETS
GARRETT
GEARSTO
HYDRATE
IMARETS
INGRATE
INTRUTH
ITERATE
LABRETS
MIGRATE
NARRATE
NITRATE
NITRITE
OPERATE
OVERATE
PARROTS
PRORATA
PRORATE
REGRETS
REWRITE
REWROTE
RIORITA
SECRETE
SECRETS
SERRATE
SPIRITO
SPIRITS
STARETS
TAXRATE
TERRETS
THERETO
THIRSTS
THIRSTY
TITRATE
TURRETS
UNCRATE
UNTRUTH
VIBRATE
VIBRATO
WHERETO
YEARNTO

•••R••T

AFFRONT
ARMREST
ATTRACT
BARRETT
BEARCAT
BEAROUT
BEDREST
BLERIOT
CHARIOT
CHEROOT
CORRECT
CORRUPT
COURANT
CURRANT
CURRENT
CYPRIOT
CZARIST
DEAREST
DECRYPT
DEFROST
DETRACT
DETROIT
DISRUPT
DOORMAT
DOUREST
ENCRUST
ENCRYPT
ENGRAFT
ENTRANT
ENTREAT
ENTRUST
EVEREST
EVERETT
EXTRACT
FAIREST
FLORIST
FORRENT
FORREST
GARRETT
GOURMET
HAIRCUT
HAIRNET
HARRIET
HEAROUT
HERRIOT
HYDRANT
IMPRINT
INFRONT
INORBIT
INPRINT
INTROIT
INTRUST
ITERANT
JEERSAT
LAURENT
LEARJET
LEERSAT
MIGRANT
NEAREST
OVERACT
OVEREAT
PATRIOT
PEEROUT
PEERSAT
PIERROT
POOREST
POUROUT
QUARTET
RANRIOT
RECRUIT
REFRACT
REPRINT
RETRACT
RETREAT
RUNRIOT
SCARLET
SHERBET
SOUREST
SPAREST
SPIRANT
STAREAT
STARLET
STARLIT
SWOREAT
TAPROOT
TEARSAT
THEREAT
TORRENT
TOURIST
TSARIST
UPDRAFT
UPFRONT
VAGRANT
VIBRANT
WARRANT
WEAROUT
WHEREAT

••••RT•

ADVERTS
ALBERTA
ALBERTO
ALWORTH
ASSERTS
ASSORTS
ASTARTE
CAVORTS
COHORTS
DEPARTS
DEPORTS
DESERTS
DIVERTS
EFFORTS
ESCORTS
EXHORTS
EXPARTE
EXPERTS
EXPORTS
EXTORTS
GOCARTS
GOKARTS
HAVARTI
HOGARTH
IMPARTS
IMPORTS
INSERTS
INVERTS
JAKARTA
LAPORTE
LIBERTY
OBVERTS
OFSORTS
OXCARTS
POVERTY
PRIORTO
PUBERTY
REBIRTH
REFERTO
REPORTS
RESORTS
RETORTS
REVERTS
ROBERTA
ROBERTO
ROBERTS
SQUIRTS
SWEARTO
THWARTS
TSHIRTS
UMBERTO
UNEARTH
YOGURTS

••••R•T

ACCURST
AMHERST
ATHIRST
ATWORST
CABARET
CULPRIT
DEMERIT
DIDEROT
DOGTROT
EXCERPT
FOXTROT
GOFORIT
INHERIT
KINGRAT
LEVERET
LONNROT
MAIGRET
MARGRET
MINARET
MUSKRAT
PACKRAT
PIERROT
RICERAT
SNEERAT
SWEARAT
TABORET
TREERAT

•••••RT

AIRPORT
ANTIART
ATHEART
ATHWART
BITPART
BYHEART
CALVERT

CARPORT
CAVEART
CLIPART
COLBERT
COMFORT
COMPORT
CONCERT
CONSORT
CONTORT
CONVERT
CULVERT
DELBERT
DESSERT
DISPORT
DISTORT
DOGCART
EARHART
ECKHART
ELKHART
FILBERT
FINEART
FOLKART
GILBERT
HERBERT
INSHORT
JETPORT
JUNKART
LAMBERT
NEWHART
NEWPORT
OFASORT
PAYDIRT
PERVERT
POPTART
PRESORT
PURPORT
RAMPART
RAPPORT
RESTART
SEAGIRT
SEAPORT
SHUBERT
STEWART
SUBVERT
SUPPORT
TEACART
TRABERT
UPSTART
WALMART
YOGHURT

RU•••••

RUANDAN
RUBBERS
RUBBERY
RUBBING
RUBBISH
RUBBLES
RUBDOWN
RUBICON
RUBITIN
RUBRICS
RUBSOUT
RUBYDEE
RUCHING
RUCKING
RUCTION
RUDDERS
RUDDIER
RUDOLPH
RUDYARD
RUFFIAN
RUFFLED
RUFFLES
RUFIYAA
RUINERS
RUINING
RUINOUS
RULEOUT
RULESON
RULINGS
RUMBAED
RUMBLED
RUMBLES
RUMMAGE
RUMMIER
RUMORED
RUMOURS
RUMPLED
RUMPLES
RUMPOLE
RUNAMOK
RUNAWAY
RUNBACK
RUNDEEP
RUNDOWN
RUNHOME
RUNINTO
RUNLAPS
RUNLETS
RUNNELS
RUNNERS
RUNNIER
RUNNING
RUNOFFS
RUNOVER
RUNRIOT
RUNSDRY
RUNSOFF
RUNSOUT
RUNTIER
RUNWAYS
RUNWITH
RUPIAHS
RUPTURE
RUSHDIE
RUSHEES
RUSHERS
RUSHING
RUSHOFF
RUSSELL
RUSSETS
RUSSIAN
RUSTICS
RUSTIER
RUSTILY
RUSTING
RUSTLED
RUSTLER
RUSTLES
RUTGERS

R•U••••

RAUCOUS
REUBENS
REUNIFY
REUNION
REUNITE
REUPPED
REUTERS
REUTHER
RHUBARB
RHUMBAS
ROUGHED
ROUGHEN
ROUGHER
ROUGHIT
ROUGHLY
ROUGHUP
ROUGING
ROULADE
ROUNDED
ROUNDER
ROUNDLY
ROUNDON
ROUNDUP
ROUSING
ROUSTED
ROUTERS
ROUTINE
ROUTING

R••U•••

REBUFFS
REBUILD
REBUILT
REBUKED
REBUKES
REBUSES
RECUSED
RECUSES
REDUCED
REDUCER
REDUCES
REFUELS
REFUGEE
REFUGES
REFUNDS
REFUSAL
REFUSED
REFUSER
REFUSES
REFUTED
REFUTER
REFUTES
REGULAR
REGULUS
REMUDAS
REPUGNS
REPULSE
REPUTED
REPUTES
REQUEST
REQUIEM
REQUIRE
REQUITE
RESULTS
RESUMED
RESUMES
RESURGE
RETUNED
RETUNES
RETURNS
RITUALS
RIVULET
ROBUSTA
ROGUERY
ROGUISH
ROMULAN
ROMULUS
ROTUNDA

R•••U••

RACQUET
RAGOUTS
RAGRUGS
RAPTURE
RAYBURN
RAYGUNS
REBOUND
RECLUSE
RECOUNT
RECOUPS
RECRUIT
REDBUDS
REDGUMS
REDOUBT
REDOUND
REGLUED
REGLUES
REMOUNT
RENAULT
REROUTE
RESCUED
RESCUER
RESCUES
RESOUND
RETOUCH
REWOUND
RIGOURS
ROEBUCK
RORQUAL
RUMOURS
RUPTURE

R••••U•

RACKSUP
RAINOUT
RAISEUP
RAKEDUP
RAKESUP
RANCOUR
RAPANUI
RAUCOUS
READOUT
REARGUE
REARSUP
REGROUP
REGULUS
REISSUE
REOCCUR
RESIDUE
RESTFUL
RESTSUP
RETINUE
REVALUE
REVENUE
RHENIUM
RHODIUM
RHOMBUS
RIDEOUT
RIMBAUD
RINGOUT
RINGSUP
RIOTOUS
RODEOUT
ROLLOUT
ROLLSUP
ROMULUS
ROOMFUL
ROOTOUT
ROSEBUD
ROSTRUM
ROUGHUP
ROUNDUP
RUBSOUT
RUINOUS
RULEOUT
RUNSOUT

R•••••U

RAMBEAU
RONDEAU

•RU••••

ARUGULA
BRUBECK
BRUEGEL
BRUISED
BRUISER
BRUISES
BRUITED
BRUNETS
BRUSHED
BRUSHES
BRUSHUP
BRUSQUE
BRUTISH
CRUCIAL
CRUDELY
CRUDEST
CRUDITY
CRUELER
CRUELLY
CRUISED
CRUISER
CRUISES
CRULLER
CRUMBLE
CRUMBLY
CRUMPET
CRUMPLE
CRUMPLY
CRUNCHY
CRUSADE
CRUSHED
CRUSHER
CRUSHES
CRUSTED
CRUZADO
DRUBBED
DRUCKER
DRUDGED
DRUDGES
DRUGGED
DRUMLIN
DRUMMED
DRUMMER
DRUMSUP
ERUCTED
ERUDITE
ERUPTED
FRUITED
GRUBBED
GRUDGED
GRUDGES
GRUFFER
GRUFFLY
GRUMBLE
GRUMPED
GRUNION
GRUNTED
GRUYERE
PRUDENT
PRUDERY
PRUDHOE
PRUDISH
PRUNERS
PRUNING
PRUSSIA
TRUANCY
TRUANTS
TRUCIAL
TRUCKED
TRUCKEE
TRUCKER
TRUCKLE
TRUDEAU
TRUDGED
TRUDGER
TRUDGES
TRUEING
TRUFFLE
TRUISMS
TRUMPED
TRUMPET
TRUMPUP
TRUNDLE
TRUSSED
TRUSSES
TRUSTED
TRUSTEE
URUGUAY

•R•U•••

ARBUTUS
ARDUOUS
ARGUERS
ARGUING
AROUSAL
AROUSED
AROUSES
BROUGHT
CROUTON
DRAUGHT
DROUGHT
FRAUGHT
GROUCHO
GROUCHY
GROUNDS
GROUPED
GROUPER
GROUPIE
GROUSED
GROUSER
GROUSES
GROUTED
IRRUPTS
OROURKE
PROUDER
PROUDLY
TRAUBEL
TRAUMAS
TRIUMPH
TRIUNES
TROUBLE
TROUGHS
TROUNCE
TROUPER
TROUPES
TROUSER
WROUGHT

•R••U••

ARBOURS
ARDOURS
ARMFULS
ARMOURS
ARUGULA
BRAVURA
BRIQUET
BROGUES
CROQUET
DRACULA
DRSEUSS
DRYRUNS
DRYSUIT
ERASURE
FRENUMS
GRADUAL
GRANULE
GRAVURE
OROTUND
PRELUDE
PRESUME
PROCURE
PRODUCE
PRODUCT
PROFUSE
TRADUCE
TRIBUNE
TRIBUTE
TRYOUTS
URUGUAY
WRAPUPS

•R•••U•

ARBUTUS
ARDUOUS
AREARUG
ARTEMUS
BRACEUP
BREAKUP
BRIMFUL
BRINGUP
BROKEUP
BRUSHUP
BRUSQUE
CRACKUP
CRANIUM
CRANKUP
CRASSUS
CREEPUP
CREWCUT
CRISPUS
CROESUS
CROPSUP
CROSSUP
DRAGOUT
DRAWNUP
DRAWOUT
DRAWSUP
DREAMUP
DRESSUP
DREWOUT
DREYFUS
DRIEDUP
DRIESUP
DRIVEUP
DROPOUT
DRUMSUP
ERASMUS
ERRATUM
FRAMEUP
FRETFUL
GRAMPUS
GROPIUS
GROWNUP
GROWSUP
IRIDIUM
IRISOUT
IRONOUT
ORGANUM
ORMOLUS
ORPHEUS
PREMIUM
PRONOUN
PROPSUP
PROTEUS
TRADEUP
TRAYFUL
TRIPSUP
TRITIUM
TROILUS
TROTOUT
TRUMPUP
URANIUM
WRAPSUP
WRITEUP
WROTEUP

•R••••U

FRENEAU
TRUDEAU

••RU•••

CERUMEN
ETRURIA
FERULES
GERUNDS
IRRUPTS
KORUNAS
PARURES
PERUKES
PERUSAL
PERUSED
PERUSER
PERUSES
SCRUBBY
SCRUBUP
SCRUFFS
SCRUFFY
SCRUNCH
SCRUPLE
SHRUBBY
SPRUCED
SPRUCER
SPRUCES
STRUDEL
THRUSTS
THRUWAY
VIRUSES

••R•U••

AGROUND
AIRGUNS
AIRPUMP
ATRIUMS
BARBUDA
BERMUDA
BOROUGH
CARFULS
CAROUSE
CIRCUIT
CIRCUSY
CIRQUES
CORRUPT
EARFULS
EARMUFF
ENROUTE
FERRULE
FORMULA
FORSURE
FORTUNA
FORTUNE
GOROUND
HERCULE
HIRSUTE
JARFULS
KEROUAC
LARRUPS
MARAUDS
MARKUPS
MARQUEE
MARQUES
MARQUEZ
MARQUIS
MERCURY
MURMURS
NURTURE
PARQUET
PERFUME
PERJURE
PERJURY
PERTURB
PURSUED
PURSUER
PURSUES
PURSUIT
REROUTE
RORQUAL
SHROUDS
SPROUTS
STRAUSS
TERHUNE
THROUGH
TORQUES
VERDUGO
VERDURE
VIRGULE
VIRTUAL
VIRTUES
WARMUPS
WORKUPS

••R••U•

AIRSOUT
BAROQUE
BOREOUT
BORNEUP
BUREAUS
BURNOUT
BURNSUP
BURNTUP
BURPGUN
CAREFUL
CAROLUS
CURBCUT
CURIOUS
CURLSUP
EARDRUM
EARPLUG
ERRATUM
FARMOUT
FERMIUM
FERROUS
FERVOUR
FIREBUG
FIREDUP
FIRESUP
FIRMSUP
FORERUN
FORKFUL
FURIOUS
HARBOUR
HARDPUT
HARMFUL
HURTFUL
KARAKUL
KARAKUM
MARGAUX
MARKSUP
NERVOUS
PARIBUS
PARLOUR
PARLOUS
PARTOUT
PERKSUP
PERSEUS
PERSIUS
PIRAEUS
PIROGUE
PYRAMUS
PYRRHUS
SCREWUP
SCRUBUP
SERIOUS
SERVEUP
SORGHUM
STRATUM
STRATUS
SURPLUS
TERBIUM
TIREOUT
TOREOUT
TORNOUT
TURNOUT
TURNSUP
VARIOUS
WARMSUP
WOREOUT
WORKOUT
WORKSUP
WORNOUT

••R•••U

CARIBOU
MARABOU
MARCEAU
MARYLOU
PARVENU
PURLIEU

•••RU••

ACCRUAL
ACCRUED
ACCRUES
ALARUMS
BULRUSH
CHERUBS
CORRUPT
DISRUPT
DRYRUNS
ENCRUST
ENDRUNS
ENTRUST
EXTRUDE
FERRULE
GAGRULE
IMBRUED
IMBRUES
INARUSH
INTRUDE
INTRUST
INTRUTH
LARRUPS
MISRULE
NOTRUMP
OBTRUDE
OUTRUNS
OVERUSE
QUORUMS
RAGRUGS
RECRUIT
SKIRUNS
UNTRUTH

•••R•U•

AMOROUS
APERCUS
BEARHUG
BEAROUT
BEARSUP
DEFRAUD
FAIRSUP
FEARFUL
FERROUS
FIBROUS
FLAREUP
GEARSUP
GUARGUM
HAIRCUT
HEAROUT
HYDROUS
INGROUP
JIMRYUN
MALRAUX
NATRIUM
NITROUS
ODOROUS
ONEROUS
OVERBUY
OVERDUB
OVERDUE
OVERRUN
PAIRSUP
PEEROUT
PETROUS
POUROUT
PYRRHUS
REARGUE
REARSUP
REGROUP
SCAREUP
STARTUP
STERNUM
STIRRUP
STIRSUP
STOREUP
TEARFUL
TEARSUP
THEROUX
THORIUM
WEAROUT
YTTRIUM

•••R••U

NEARYOU
THOREAU

••••RU•

AREARUG
BACKRUB
BULLRUN
CHEERUP
CHETRUM
CLEARUP
COVERUP
DECORUM
EARDRUM
FORERUN
FULCRUM
HOMERUN
HUMDRUM
HUMERUS
JABIRUS
LAZARUS
LONGRUN
MILKRUN
MILLRUN
NOSTRUM
NOTTRUE
OVERRUN
PAPYRUS
ROSTRUM
SISTRUM
STIRRUP
TANTRUM
WELLRUN

••••R•U

HOFBRAU

R•V••••

RAVAGED
RAVAGES
RAVELED
RAVENED
RAVENNA
RAVINES
RAVINGS
RAVIOLI
REVALUE
REVAMPS
REVEALS
REVELED
REVELER
REVELRY
REVENGE
REVENUE
REVERBS
REVERED
REVERES
REVERIE
REVERSE
REVERTS
REVIEWS
REVILED
REVILES
REVISED
REVISER
REVISES
REVISIT
REVIVAL
REVIVED
REVIVES
REVOICE
REVOKED
REVOKES
REVOLTS
REVOLVE
REVVING
RIVALED
RIVALRY
RIVETED
RIVETER
RIVIERA
RIVIERE
RIVULET

R••V•••

REAVAIL
REVVING
RIGVEDA
ROLVAAG

R•••V••

RANOVER
RAYOVAC
RECOVER
RELIVED
RELIVES
REMOVAL
REMOVED
REMOVER
REMOVES
REPAVED
REPAVES
REVIVAL
REVIVED
REVIVES
REWOVEN
RUNOVER

R••••V•

RECEIVE
RELIEVE
RELIEVO
REPROVE
RESERVE
RESOLVE
RESTIVE
REVOLVE
REWEAVE

R•••••V

ROCKYIV
ROMANOV

•RV••••

ORVILLE

•R•V•••

BRAVADO
BRAVELY
BRAVERY
BRAVEST
BRAVING
BRAVOES
BRAVURA
BREVETS
BREVITY
CRAVATS
CRAVENS
CRAVERS
CRAVING
CREVICE
DRIVEAT
DRIVEIN
DRIVELS
DRIVERS
DRIVEUP
DRIVING
DROVERS
GRAVELS
GRAVELY
GRAVEST
GRAVIES
GRAVING
GRAVITY
GRAVURE
GRIVETS
GROVELS
PREVAIL
PREVENT
PREVIEW
PRIVACY
PRIVATE
PRIVETS
PRIVIES
PROVERB
PROVERS
PROVIDE
PROVING
PROVISO
PROVOKE
PROVOST
TRAVAIL
TRAVELS

TRAVERS
TRAVOIS
TREVINO
TRIVETS
TRIVIAL

•R••V••
ARGIVES
ARRIVAL
ARRIVED
ARRIVER
ARRIVES
GREAVES
GRIEVED
GRIEVER
GRIEVES
GROOVED
GROOVES

•R•••V•
ARCHIVE
EROSIVE

••RV•••
CARVERS
CARVING
CURVETS
CURVIER
CURVING
DERVISH
FERVENT
FERVORS
FERVOUR
HARVARD
HARVEST
MARVELS
NERVIER
NERVILY
NERVOUS
NIRVANA
PARVENU
PERVADE
PERVERT
PURVEYS
PURVIEW
SERVALS
SERVANT
SERVERS
SERVEUP
SERVICE
SERVILE
SERVING
SURVEYS
SURVIVE
VERVETS

••R•V••
ARRIVAL
ARRIVED
ARRIVER
ARRIVES
CARAVAN
CARAVEL
DERIVED
DERIVES
FOREVER
MORAVIA
SCRIVEN
SHRIVEL
SHRIVER
SHRIVES
STRIVED
STRIVEN
STRIVER
STRIVES
THRIVED
THRIVES
UNRAVEL
UPRIVER
YEREVAN

••R••V•
AIRWAVE
BEREAVE
CURSIVE
FORGAVE
FORGIVE
FURTIVE
MARKOVA
SURVIVE

••R•••V
NUREYEV

•••RV••
CHERVIL
DWARVES
SCARVES
SCURVES
STARVED
STARVES
SWERVED
SWERVES
WHARVES

•••R•V•
APPROVE
DEPRAVE
DEPRIVE
ENGRAVE
IMPROVE
KEDROVA
REPROVE

••••RV•
DESERVE
MINERVA
OBSERVE
RESERVE
UNNERVE

••••R•V
NEMEROV

RW•••••
RWANDAN

R•W••••
RAWDATA
RAWDEAL
RAWHIDE
RAWNESS
RAWSILK
REWARDS
REWARMS
REWAXED
REWAXES
REWEAVE
REWELDS
REWINDS
REWIRED
REWIRES
REWORDS
REWORKS
REWOUND
REWOVEN
REWRAPS
REWRITE
REWROTE
ROWBOAT
ROWDIER
ROWDIES
ROWDILY

R••W•••
RAGWEED
REDWINE
REDWING
REDWOLF
REDWOOD
ROSWELL
RUNWAYS
RUNWITH

R•••W••
RACEWAY
RAILWAY
RANAWAY
REMOWED
RENEWAL
RENEWED
RENEWER
RETOWED
RIDGWAY
ROADWAY
RUNAWAY

R••••W•
REDRAWN
REDRAWS
REVIEWS
RIPSAWS
ROBLOWE
RUBDOWN
RUNDOWN

R•••••W
RAINBOW
ROPETOW

•R•W•••
ARAWAKS
ARTWARE
ARTWORK
BRAWLED
BRAWLER
BREWERS
BREWERY
BREWING
BROWNED
BROWNER
BROWNIE
BROWSED
BROWSER
BROWSES
CRAWDAD
CRAWLED
CRAWLER
CREWCUT
CREWELS
CREWING
CREWMAN
CREWMEN
CROWBAR
CROWDED
CROWERS
CROWING
CROWNED
CRYWOLF
DRAWBAR
DRAWERS
DRAWING
DRAWLED
DRAWNIN
DRAWNON
DRAWNUP
DRAWOUT
DRAWSIN
DRAWSON
DRAWSUP
DREWOUT
DROWNED
DROWSED
DROWSES
DRYWALL
DRYWELL
EREWHON
FRAWLEY
FROWARD
FROWNAT
FROWNED
FROWNER
GROWERS
GROWING
GROWLED
GROWLER
GROWNUP
GROWSON
GROWSUP
GROWTHS
PREWASH
PROWESS
PROWLED
PROWLER
TRAWLED
TRAWLER
TROWELS
TROWERS

•R••W••
ARCHWAY
AREAWAY
FAIRWAY
FREEWAY

•R•••W•
PREDAWN

•R••••W
FRETSAW
PREVIEW

••RW•••
AIRWAVE
AIRWAYS
AIRWOLF
CARWASH
EARWIGS
FARWEST
FORWARD
FORWENT
NARWALS
NARWHAL
WARWICK

••R•W••
CARAWAY
FARAWAY
HARDWON
PARKWAY
PARTWAY
SARAWAK
SCRAWLS
SCRAWLY
SCRAWNY
SCREWED
SCREWUP
SPRAWLS
STREWED
STREWER
THREWIN
THROWER
THROWIN
THRUWAY

••R••W•
BARNOWL
BARROWS
BORROWS
BURROWS
CURFEWS
CURLEWS
FARROWS
FURROWS
HARROWS
MARLOWE
MARROWS
MORROWS
NARROWS
OURTOWN
SORROWS
YARROWS

••R•••W
AIRCREW
AIRFLOW
AIRSHOW
CORNROW
FOREPAW
FORESAW
PURVIEW

•••RW••
BOERWAR
DOORWAY
FAIRWAY
SHERWIN

•••R•W•
ANDREWS
BARROWS
BORROWS
BURROWS
ESCROWS
FARROWS
FURROWS
HARROWS
HEBREWS
INGROWN
MARROWS
MORROWS
NARROWS
OVERAWE
REDRAWN
REDRAWS
SORROWS
UNDRAWN
YARROWS

•••R••W
BEARPAW
OVERSAW
SPARROW

••••R•W
AIRCREW
ATECROW
BESTREW
CORNROW
EATCROW
EYEBROW
LOWBROW
MACGRAW
OUTDRAW
OUTDREW
OUTGREW
OUTGROW
SKIDROW
SPARROW
TONEROW
UNSCREW
WINDROW
WOODROW

R•X••••
REXCATS
REXREED
ROXANNE

R•••X••
RELAXED
RELAXES
REMIXED
REMIXES
RETAXED
RETAXES
REWAXED
REWAXES

R•••••X
REAFFIX
ROLODEX

•R•X•••
BRAXTON
PROXIES
PROXIMO

•R••X••
MRFIXIT
URTEXTS

•R•••X•
PRETEXT

•R••••X
BRERFOX
BROADAX
TRIPLEX

••RX•••
MARXISM

••R•X••
HYRAXES

••R••X•
AIRTAXI

••R•••X
FIREBOX
GORETEX
MARGAUX
MIRAMAX
NARTHEX
PARADOX
PERPLEX

•••R••X
BRERFOX
GEARBOX
MALRAUX
PHARYNX
POORBOX
STCROIX
THEROUX

••••R•X
BEATRIX
HENDRIX
MEMOREX

RY•••••
RYKRISP

R•Y••••
RAYBURN
RAYGUNS
RAYKROC
RAYMOND
RAYOVAC
REYNARD
RHYMERS
RHYMING
RHYTHMS
ROYALLY
ROYALTY
ROYBEAN

R••Y•••
RECYCLE
RELYING
RETYPED
RETYPES
RUBYDEE
RUDYARD

R•••Y••
RALLYTO
REDEYES
REKEYED
RELAYED
RESTYLE
RIBEYES
ROCKYII
ROCKYIV
RUFIYAA

R••••Y•
REPLAYS
RICKEYS
ROBROYS
ROMNEYS
RUNWAYS

R•••••Y
RACEWAY
RAGGEDY
RAILWAY
RANAWAY
RAPIDLY
READILY
REALITY
RECENCY
RECTIFY
RECTORY
REENTRY
REGALLY
REGENCY
REMARRY
REUNIFY
REVELRY
RICKETY
RIDGWAY
RIFLERY
RIGHTLY
RIGIDLY
RIVALRY
ROADWAY
ROBBERY
ROGUERY
ROOKERY
ROUGHLY
ROUNDLY
ROWDILY
ROYALLY
ROYALTY
RUBBERY
RUNAWAY
RUNSDRY
RUSTILY

•RY••••
BRYNNER
CRYBABY
CRYOGEN
CRYPTIC
CRYPTOS
CRYSTAL
CRYWOLF
DRYCELL
DRYDOCK
DRYEYED
DRYHOLE
DRYNESS
DRYRUNS
DRYSUIT
DRYWALL
DRYWELL
FRYCOOK
FRYPANS
GRYPHON
KRYPTON
PRYINTO
TRYOUTS
TRYSTED
TRYSTER
WRYNESS

•R•Y•••
ARGYLES
ARMYANT
BRAYERS
BRAYING
CRAYOLA
CRAYONS
DRAYAGE
DRAYING
DREYFUS
FRAYING
GRAYEST
GRAYING
GRAYSON
GREYEST
GREYING
GRUYERE
PRAYERS
PRAYFOR
PRAYING
PRAYSTO
PREYSON
TRAYFUL
XRAYING

•R••Y••
ARRAYED
ARROYOS
DRYEYED
GROMYKO
PROCYON

•R•••Y•
FRIDAYS
PREPAYS

•R••••Y
ARCHERY
ARCHWAY
ARDENCY
AREAWAY
ARIDITY
BRADLEY
BRAMBLY
BRASHLY
BRAVELY
BRAVERY
BREATHY
BREVITY
BREWERY
BRIBERY
BRIEFLY
BRISKLY
BRISTLY
BROADLY
CRAFTSY
CRASSLY
CRAZILY
CRINKLY
CRISPLY
CROSSLY
CRUDELY
CRUDITY
CRUELLY
CRUMBLY
CRUMPLY
CRUNCHY
CRYBABY
DRAPERY
DRIPDRY
DRIZZLY
DROPSBY
ERECTLY
FRAILTY
FRANKLY
FRAWLEY
FREEWAY
FRESHLY
GRANARY
GRANDLY
GRATIFY
GRAVELY
GRAVITY
GREATLY
GREELEY
GREGORY
GRETZKY
GRIFFEY
GRISTLY
GRIZZLY
GROCERY
GROSSLY
GROUCHY
GRUFFLY
IRATELY
ORATORY
ORDERLY
ORGANDY
ORMANDY
PREACHY
PRESLEY
PRICKLY
PRIMACY
PRIMARY
PRIVACY
PROBITY
PRODIGY
PROGENY
PROSILY
PROSODY
PROUDLY
PRUDERY
TRACERY
TRAGEDY
TREACLY
TREMBLY
TRENARY
TRILOGY
TRINITY
TRITELY
TROLLEY
TROTSKY
TRUANCY
URGENCY
URUGUAY
VRONSKY
WRIGGLY
WRIGLEY
WRINKLY
WRONGLY

••RY•••
ACRYLIC
BARYONS
BURYING
CORYELL
JURYING
JURYRIG
MARYANN
MARYKAY
MARYLOU
SPRYEST
TORYISM
VARYING

••R•Y••
ARRAYED
ARROYOS
CARLYLE
CARRYON
EARLYON
FORSYTH
MARRYME
MARTYRS
NUREYEV
SAROYAN
SPRAYED
SPRAYER
STRAYED

••R••Y•
ACRONYM
AIRWAYS
BARLEYS
BARNEYS
BURSTYN
CARBOYS
CAROLYN
GURNEYS
JERSEYS
KAROLYI
MARGAYS
MARILYN
PARLAYS
PARLEYS
PURVEYS
SURREYS
SURVEYS
TURKEYS

••R•••Y
ACRIDLY
AIRPLAY
ALREADY
ATROPHY
AURALLY
BARBARY
CARAWAY
CERTIFY
CHRISTY
CIRCUSY
CORNILY
CURSORY
CURTSEY
DARESAY
DIRTILY
DOROTHY
DURABLY
EARTHLY
FARADAY
FARAWAY
FIREFLY
FIRSTLY
FORGERY
FORTIFY
GERMANY
HARDILY
HARMONY
HARSHLY
HERSHEY
HORNSBY
HORRIFY
JERKILY
LARCENY
LARGELY
LURIDLY
MARYKAY
MERCURY
MERRILY
MORALLY
MORESBY
MORTIFY
MURKILY
MURPHEY
NERVILY
NURSERY
PARKWAY
PARSLEY
PARTWAY
PERFIDY
PERJURY
PERKILY
PORTRAY
SCRAGGY
SCRAPPY
SCRAWLY
SCRAWNY
SCRIMPY
SCRUBBY
SCRUFFY
SHRILLY
SHRUBBY
SORCERY
SPRINGY
STREAKY
STRINGY
SURGERY
SURLILY
TARBABY
TARDILY
TERNARY
TERRIFY
TERSELY
THREADY
THRIFTY
THROATY
THRUWAY
TIREDLY
TURNKEY
TYRANNY
UNREADY
VARIETY
VARSITY
VERSIFY
WORDILY
WORKDAY
WORLDLY

•••RY••
CARRYON
DECRYPT
EMBRYOS
ENCRYPT
JIMRYUN
MARRYME
MEGRYAN
NEARYOU
PHARYNX

•••R•Y•
AFFRAYS
AYKROYD
BETRAYS
DEFRAYS
ESTRAYS
HAIRDYE
OSPREYS
ROBROYS
STOREYS
SUNRAYS
SURREYS

•••R••Y
ALERTLY
ANARCHY
ANGRILY
BLARNEY
CHARILY
CHARITY
CHARLEY
CLARIFY
CLARITY
COURTLY
DEERFLY
DOORWAY
ENTROPY
FAIRWAY
FIERILY
GLORIFY
HEARSAY
HORRIFY
INERTLY
JOURNEY
LEERILY
LIBRARY
MERRILY
OVERBUY
OVERFLY
OVERJOY
OVERLAY
OVERTLY
PETRIFY
POORBOY
SCARIFY
SCARILY
SECRECY
SHARKEY
SHARPLY
SHIRLEY
SHORTLY
SMARTLY
SPARELY
STARCHY
STARKLY
STERNLY
STIRFRY
SWARTHY
SWOREBY
TEARILY
TERRIFY
THERAPY
THEREBY
THIRDLY
THIRSTY
TIERNEY
TOURNEY
VITRIFY
WEARILY
WEIRDLY
WHEREBY

••••RY•
KATHRYN

••••R•Y
ALLERGY
AMSCRAY
ASHTRAY
BETARAY
BEVERLY
CLEARLY
COMFREY
DALTREY
DESTROY
DUBARRY
EAGERLY
ELDERLY
EQUERRY
FAYWRAY
GODFREY
IMSORRY
JEFFREY
JOFFREY
LAMPREY
LIBERTY
LITURGY
LOVERLY
MISERLY
ORDERLY
PALFREY
PORTRAY
POVERTY
PUBERTY
QUEERLY
REMARRY
SHEERLY
SOBERLY
SQUIRMY
SWEARBY
SYNERGY

TEATRAY
THIERRY
UTTERLY
VICEROY
WINFREY
ZYMURGY

•••••RY

ACTUARY
AMATORY
ARCHERY
ASHBURY
BARBARY
BATTERY
BEANERY
BIGOTRY
BINDERY
BLOWDRY
BONEDRY
BRAVERY
BREWERY
BRIBERY
BUTTERY
CADBURY
CALGARY
CALVARY
CANNERY
CAVALRY
CENTURY
CHICORY
CONAKRY
CONNERY
COOKERY
COPPERY
COUNTRY
CURSORY
CUTLERY
DEEPFRY
DEVILRY
DIETARY
DITHERY
DRAPERY
DRIPDRY
DUBARRY
EQUERRY
ESTUARY
EXUPERY
FACTORY
FISHERY
FISHFRY
FLOWERY
FOOLERY
FOPPERY
FORGERY
FOUNDRY
GALLERY
GINGERY
GRANARY
GREGORY
GROCERY
GUNNERY
HELOTRY
HENNERY
HICKORY
HILLARY
HISTORY
HOSIERY
HUNGARY
IMAGERY
IMSORRY
INQUIRY
JANUARY
JEWELRY
JIGGERY
JITTERY
JOINERY
KNAVERY
LANGTRY
LASTORY
LATHERY
LAUNDRY
LIBRARY
LOTTERY
MASONRY
MASTERY
MERCURY
MIMICRY
MOCKERY
MUMMERY
MYSTERY
NUNNERY
NURSERY
ORATORY
PALEDRY
PECCARY
PEPPERY
PERJURY
PILLORY
PLENARY
POTTERY
POULTRY
POWDERY
PRIMARY
PRUDERY
PUFFERY
QUAVERY
RECTORY
REENTRY
REMARRY
REVELRY
RIFLERY
RIVALRY
ROBBERY
ROGUERY
ROOKERY
RUBBERY
RUNSDRY
SAVOURY
SCENERY
SENSORY
SHOWERY
SILVERY
SLAVERY
SORCERY
SPIDERY
STIRFRY
SUDBURY
SUMMARY
SUMMERY
SURGERY
SWELTRY
TANNERY
TERNARY
THIERRY
TOPIARY
TOTTERY
TRACERY
TRENARY
UNITARY
VICTORY
WAGGERY
WINTERY
ZACHARY

R•Z••••

RAZORED
RAZZING
REZONED
REZONES
ROZELLE

R••Z•••

RAZZING
RHIZOME
RITZIER

R•••Z••

REBOZOS

R••••Z•

REALIZE

•R•Z•••

ARIZONA
BRAZIER
BRAZING
CRAZIER
CRAZIES
CRAZILY
CRAZING
CRUZADO
DRIZZLE
DRIZZLY
FRAZIER
FRAZZLE
FRIZZED
FRIZZES
FRIZZLE
GRAZERS
GRAZING
GRIZZLE
GRIZZLY
PRIZING

•R••Z••

BREEZED
BREEZES
BRONZED
BRONZES
DRIZZLE
DRIZZLY
FRAZZLE
FREEZER
FREEZES
FRIEZES
FRIZZED
FRIZZES
FRIZZLE
GRETZKY
GRIZZLE
GRIZZLY
PRETZEL

•R•••Z•

ORGANZA
TRAPEZE

•R••••Z

FRANKOZ

••RZ•••

BORZOIS
TARZANA

••R•Z••

CORAZON
HORIZON
SARAZEN

••R••Z•

CARDOZO
FIRENZE
LORENZO

••R•••Z

BERLIOZ
BERLITZ
MARQUEZ

•••R•Z•

APPRIZE
CHORIZO

••••RZ•

SCHERZI
SCHERZO

••••R•Z

ALVAREZ

SA•••••

SABBATH
SABINES
SABRINA
SACHEMS
SACHETS
SACKERS
SACKFUL
SACKING
SACKOUT
SADDENS
SADDEST
SADDLED
SADDLER
SADDLES
SADNESS
SADSACK
SAFARIS
SAFFRON
SAGGIER
SAGGING
SAGINAW
SAGUARO
SAHARAN
SAILING
SAILORS
SAINTED
SAINTLY
SALAAMS
SALABLE
SALADIN
SALAMIS
SALAZAR
SALCHOW
SALERNO
SALIENT
SALIERI
SALLIED
SALLIES
SALMONS
SALOONS
SALSIFY
SALSODA
SALTBOX
SALTERS
SALTIER
SALTILY
SALTINE
SALTING
SALUKIS
SALUTED
SALUTES
SALVAGE
SALVERS
SALVING
SALVOES
SAMARIA
SAMBAED
SAMBARS
SAMEDAY
SAMHILL
SAMISEN
SAMITES
SAMNUNN
SAMOANS
SAMOVAR
SAMOYED
SAMPANS
SAMPLED
SAMPLER
SAMPLES
SAMPRAS
SAMPSON
SAMSARA
SAMSUNG
SAMURAI
SANBORN
SANCTUM
SANDALS
SANDBAG
SANDBAR
SANDBOX
SANDERS
SANDFLY
SANDHOG
SANDIER
SANDING
SANDLOT
SANDMAN
SANDMEN
SANFORD
SANGOUT
SANGRIA
SANIBEL
SANJOSE
SANJUAN
SANLUIS
SANREMO
SANTAFE
SANTANA
SANTINI
SANTIRS
SAOTOME
SAPIENS
SAPIENT
SAPLING
SAPPERS
SAPPIER
SAPPING
SAPPORO
SAPSAGO
SARACEN
SARALEE
SARANAC
SARAWAK
SARAZEN
SARCASM
SARDINE
SARGENT
SARONGS
SAROYAN
SASHAYS
SASHIMI
SASSERS
SASSIER
SASSIES
SASSILY
SASSING
SASSOON
SATCHEL
SATCHMO
SATDOWN
SATIATE
SATIETY
SATIRES
SATIRIC
SATISFY
SATRAPS
SATSUMA
SAUCERS
SAUCIER
SAUCILY
SAUNTER
SAURIAN
SAUSAGE
SAUTEED
SAVABLE
SAVAGED
SAVAGER
SAVAGES
SAVALAS
SAVANNA
SAVANTS
SAVARIN
SAVEDUP
SAVESUP
SAVINGS
SAVIORS
SAVORED
SAVOURS
SAVOURY
SAVVIER
SAVVILY
SAWBUCK
SAWDUST
SAWFISH
SAWLOGS
SAWMILL
SAWWOOD
SAWYERS
SAXHORN
SAYINGS
SAYWHEN

S•A••••

SCALARS
SCALDED
SCALENE
SCALERS
SCALIER
SCALING
SCALLOP
SCALPED
SCALPEL
SCALPER
SCAMMED
SCAMPED
SCAMPER
SCANDAL
SCANNED
SCANNER
SCANTED
SCANTER
SCANTLY
SCAPULA
SCARABS
SCARCER
SCARERS
SCAREUP
SCARFED
SCARIER
SCARIFY
SCARILY
SCARING
SCARLET
SCARPED
SCARRED
SCARVES
SCATHED
SCATHES
SCATTED
SCATTER
SEABAGS
SEABASS
SEABEDS
SEABEES
SEABIRD
SEABORG
SEACOWS
SEADOGS
SEADUTY
SEAFANS
SEAFOOD
SEAGATE
SEAGIRT
SEAGRAM
SEAGULL
SEALABS
SEALANE
SEALANT
SEALEGS
SEALERS
SEALILY
SEALING
SEALION
SEALOFF
SEALSUP
SEAMIER
SEAMING
SEAMOSS
SEANCES
SEAPORT
SEARING
SEASALT
SEASICK
SEASIDE
SEASLUG
SEASONS
SEASTAR
SEATERS
SEATING
SEATTLE
SEAWALL
SEAWARD
SEAWAYS
SEAWEED
SHACKLE
SHADIER
SHADILY
SHADING
SHADOOF
SHADOWS
SHADOWY
SHAFFER
SHAFTED
SHAGGED
SHAHDOM
SHAKERS
SHAKEUP
SHAKIER
SHAKILY
SHAKING
SHAKOES
SHALALA
SHALLOT
SHALLOW
SHALOMS
SHAMANS
SHAMBLE
SHAMING
SHAMMED
SHAMPOO
SHANANA
SHANGRI
SHANKAR
SHANKED
SHANNON
SHANTER
SHAPELY
SHAPERS
SHAPEUP
SHAPING
SHAPIRO
SHAREIN
SHARERS
SHARING
SHARKEY
SHARPED
SHARPEI
SHARPEN
SHARPER
SHARPLY
SHASTRI
SHATNER
SHATTER
SHAVERS
SHAVING
SHAWNEE
SHAWWAL
SIAMESE
SKATERS
SKATING
SLABBED
SLACKED
SLACKEN
SLACKER
SLAKING
SLALOMS
SLAMMED
SLAMMER
SLANDER
SLANTED
SLAPPED
SLASHED
SLASHER
SLASHES
SLATHER
SLATIER
SLATING
SLATKIN
SLATTED
SLAVERS
SLAVERY
SLAVING
SLAVISH
SLAYERS
SLAYTON
SMACKED
SMACKER
SMALLER
SMALTOS
SMARTED
SMARTEN
SMARTER
SMARTLY
SMASHED
SMASHER
SMASHES
SMASHUP
SMATTER
SNACKED
SNACKER
SNAFFLE
SNAFUED
SNAGGED
SNAKIER
SNAKING
SNAPONS
SNAPPED
SNAPPER
SNAPSAT
SNAPSTO
SNAPSUP
SNARING
SNARLED
SOAKERS
SOAKING
SOAKSUP
SOANDSO
SOAPBOX
SOAPERS
SOAPIER
SOAPING
SOARERS
SOARING
SPACERS
SPACIER
SPACING
SPACKLE
SPADERS
SPADING
SPALLED
SPANDEX
SPANGLE
SPANGLY
SPANIEL
SPANISH
SPANKED
SPANKER
SPANNED
SPANNER
SPARELY
SPAREST
SPARGED
SPARGES
SPARING
SPARKED
SPARKLE
SPARRED
SPARROW
SPARSER
SPARTAN
SPASSKY
SPATIAL
SPATTED
SPATTER
SPATULA
SPAVINS
SPAWNED
SPAYING
STABBED
STABILE
STABLED
STABLER
STABLES
STACKED
STACKUP
STADIUM
STAFFED
STAFFER
STAGERS
STAGGED
STAGGER
STAGIER
STAGILY
STAGING
STAIDER
STAIDLY
STAINED
STAINER
STAKING
STALAGS
STALEST
STALKED
STALKER
STALLED
STAMENS
STAMINA
STAMMER
STAMPED
STANCES
STANDBY
STANDEE
STANDIN
STANDON
STANDUP
STANLEE
STANLEY
STANNIC
STANTON
STANZAS
STAPLED
STAPLER
STAPLES
STARCHY
STARDOM
STAREAT
STARERS
STARETS
STARING
STARKER
STARKLY
STARLET
STARLIT
STARMAN
STARMAP
STARRED
STARTED
STARTER
STARTLE
STARTUP
STARVED
STARVES
STASHED
STASHES
STASSEN
STATELY
STATICE
STATICS
STATING
STATION
STATIST
STATORS
STATUES
STATURE
STATUTE
STAUNCH
STAVING
STAYING
STAYPUT
STAYSUP
SUASION
SUAVELY
SUAVEST
SUAVITY
SWABBED
SWADDLE
SWAGGER
SWAHILI
SWALLOW
SWAMPED
SWANKER
SWANSON
SWAPPED
SWAPPER
SWARMED
SWARTHY
SWATHED
SWATHES
SWATTED
SWATTER
SWAYERS
SWAYING

S••A•••

SAFARIS
SAHARAN
SALAAMS
SALABLE
SALADIN
SALAMIS
SALAZAR
SAMARIA
SARACEN
SARALEE
SARANAC
SARAWAK
SARAZEN
SAVABLE
SAVAGED
SAVAGER
SAVAGES
SAVALAS
SAVANNA
SAVANTS
SAVARIN
SCHATZI
SCRAGGY
SCRAPED
SCRAPER
SCRAPES
SCRAPPY
SCRATCH
SCRAWLS
SCRAWLY
SCRAWNY
SECANTS
SEDALIA
SEDATER
SENATES
SENATOR
SERAPES
SERAPHS
SERAPIS
SESAMES
SHEARED
SHEARER
SHEATHE
SHEATHS
SHEAVED
SHEAVES
SHIATSU
SINATRA
SIZABLE
SIZABLY
SMEARED
SNEAKED
SNEAKER
SNEAKIN
SODAPOP
SOFABED
SOLACES
SOLARIA
SOMALIA
SOMALIS
SOMATIC
SONATAS
SPEAKER
SPEAKOF
SPEAKUP
SPEARED
SPLASHY
SPLAYED
SPRAINS
SPRAWLS
SPRAYED
SPRAYER
SQUALID
SQUALLS
SQUALOR
SQUANTO
SQUARED
SQUARER
SQUARES
SQUAWKS
STEALTH
STEAMED
STEAMER
STRAFED
STRAFES
STRAINS
STRAITS
STRANDS
STRANGE
STRASSE
STRATUM
STRATUS
STRAUSS
STRAYED
SUGARED
SUKARNO
SUMATRA
SUSANNA
SUSANNE
SUZANNE
SWEARAT
SWEARBY
SWEARER
SWEARIN
SWEARTO
SWEATED
SWEATER
SYNAPSE

S•••A••

SABBATH
SADSACK
SAGUARO
SALAAMS
SALVAGE
SAMBAED
SAMBARS
SAMOANS
SAMPANS
SAMSARA
SANDALS
SANTAFE
SANTANA
SAPSAGO
SARCASM
SASHAYS
SATIATE
SATRAPS
SAUSAGE
SCALARS
SCARABS
SCHNAPS
SCREAKS
SCREAMS
SEABAGS
SEABASS
SEAFANS
SEAGATE
SEALABS
SEALANE
SEALANT
SEASALT
SEAWALL
SEAWARD
SEAWAYS
SEESAWS
SELVAGE
SENSATE
SERIALS
SERIATE
SERRATE
SERVALS
SERVANT
SETBACK
SETSAIL
SEXTANS
SEXTANT
SHALALA
SHAMANS
SHANANA
SHEBANG
SHEPARD
SHOFARS
SIDEARM
SIGNALS
SIMIANS
SINKAGE
SIOUANS
SITUATE
SIXPACK
SKIMASK
SKYCAPS
SKYJACK
SKYLARK
SKYWARD
SKYWAYS
SLOGANS
SLOVAKS
SMETANA
SNOCATS
SOCIALS
SOPRANO
SORBATE
SOUTANE
SPINACH
SPIRALS
SPIRANT
SPOKANE
SPREADS
SQUEAKS
SQUEAKY
SQUEALS
STALAGS
STEWARD

STEWART
STOMACH
STOMATA
STORAGE
STREAKS
STREAKY
STREAMS
STRIATE
SUBWAYS
SUCRASE
SULFATE
SULTANA
SULTANS
SUMMARY
SUNBATH
SUNDAES
SUNDAYS
SUNLAMP
SUNMAID
SUNRAYS
SUNTANS
SURFACE
SURNAME
SURPASS
SUSTAIN
SYLLABI
SYLVANS
SYRIANS

S••••A•

SAGINAW
SAHARAN
SALAZAR
SAMEDAY
SAMOVAR
SAMPRAS
SAMURAI
SANDBAG
SANDBAR
SANDMAN
SANJUAN
SARANAC
SARAWAK
SAROYAN
SAURIAN
SAVALAS
SCANDAL
SCHEMAS
SCHOLAR
SCLERAS
SEAGRAM
SEASTAR
SECULAR
SEMINAL
SEMINAR
SENECAS
SENEGAL
SENORAS
SENSUAL
SERBIAN
SEVERAL
SHANKAR
SHAWWAL
SHECRAB
SHEILAE
SHEILAH
SHEILAS
SHELLAC
SHERMAN
SHERPAS
SHIPMAN
SHOOTAT
SHOWMAN
SICHUAN
SICKBAY
SICKPAY
SIDEBAR
SIDECAR
SIDEMAN
SIENNAS
SIERRAS
SIESTAS
SILICAS
SILKHAT
SIMILAR
SIOBHAN
SLOTCAR
SNAPSAT
SNEERAT
SNIFFAT
SNIPEAT
SNOWCAP
SNOWDAY
SNOWMAN
SOLEDAD
SOMEDAY
SOMEWAY
SONATAS
SORORAL
SOYBEAN
SPARTAN
SPATIAL
SPECIAL
SPIREAS
SPORRAN
SPOUSAL
STANZAS
STAREAT
STARMAN
STARMAP
STELLAR
STERNAL
STIGMAS
STOICAL
STOPGAP
STYGIAN
STYRIAN
SUBHEAD
SUNBEAM
SUNDIAL
SURCOAT
SURINAM
SURREAL
SWEARAT
SWOREAT
SYNGMAN
SYNODAL

S•••••A

SABRINA
SALSODA
SAMARIA
SAMSARA
SANGRIA
SANTANA
SATSUMA
SAVANNA
SCAPULA
SCHIRRA
SEDALIA
SEGOVIA
SEQUOIA
SESTINA
SHALALA
SHANANA
SIBERIA
SILESIA
SINATRA
SMETANA
SNOWPEA
SOLARIA
SOMALIA
SPATULA
SPECTRA
SPINOZA
STAMINA
STLUCIA
STOMATA
SUBROSA
SULTANA
SULUSEA
SUMATRA
SUSANNA
SYRINGA

•SA••••

ISADORA
PSALMED
PSALTER
PSANDQS
TSARINA
TSARIST

•S•A•••

ASFARAS
ASHAMED
ASHANTI
ASIATIC
ASKANCE
ASSAILS
ASSAULT
ASSAYED
ASSAYER
ASTAIRE
ASTARTE
ESCAPED
ESCAPEE
ESCAPES
ESCARPS
ESPANOL
ESSAYED
ESTATES
ISLAMIC
ISLANDS
ISRAELI
USEABLE
USUALLY

•S••A••

ASHCANS
ASHLAND
ASHLARS
ASHRAMS
ASPHALT
ASSUAGE
ESPIALS
ESTRADA
ESTRAYS
ESTUARY
ISHMAEL
ISOBARS
ISOLATE
TSQUARE
TSUNAMI

•S•••A•

ASFARAS
ASHTRAY
ASOCIAL
ASSEGAI
ASTOLAT
ASUSUAL
ESCHEAT
ESPOSAS
ESTIVAL
TSONGAS

•S••••A

ASSYRIA
ASTORIA
ESTONIA
ESTRADA
ISADORA
OSCEOLA
TSARINA

••SA•••

ABSALOM
ASSAILS
ASSAULT
ASSAYED
ASSAYER
BASALLY
BASALTS
CASABAS
DESALTS
DISABLE
DISARMS
DISAVOW
DOSAGES
ESSAYED
HOSANNA
LASAGNA
LASAGNE
LASALLE
MISALLY
MOSAICS
NASALLY
POSADAS
RESALES
RESALTS
RESANDS
ROSALIE
ROSANNA
ROSANNE
SESAMES
SUSANNA
SUSANNE
TISANES
UNSATED
VISAGES
VISAVIS
WASATCH

••S•A••

ABSTAIN
ANSPACH
ASSUAGE
ATSTAKE
BUSFARE
BUSTARD
CASCADE
CASCARA
CASSATT
CASSAVA
CASUALS
COSSACK
COSTAIN
COSTARS
CUSHAWS
CUSTARD
DASTARD
DESCANT
DESPAIR
DISBAND
DISBARS
DISCARD
DISDAIN
DISEASE
DISMAYS
DISTAFF
DISTANT
DOSSALS
ECSTASY
ENSLAVE
ENSNARE
ENSNARL
GASBAGS
GASCAPS
GASMAIN
GESTALT
GESTATE
GOSHAWK
GUSTAVE
HISPANO
HOSTAGE
HUSBAND
HUSHABY
HUSSARS
INSCAPE
INSEAMS
INSHAPE
INSPANS
INSTALL
INSTANT
INSTATE
LASCALA
LASCAUX
LESPAUL
MASCARA
MASSAGE
MASTABA
MESCALS
MESSAGE
MESSALA
MISCALL
MISCAST
MISDATE
MISHAPS
MISLAID
MISLAYS
MISMATE
MISNAME
MISSALS
MISTAKE
MUSCATS
MUSTAFA
MUSTANG
MUSTARD
NASTASE
NESCAFE
ONSTAGE
PASSAGE
PASSANT
POSTAGE
RASCALS
RESCALE
RESEALS
RESEATS
RESTAGE
RESTAIN
RESTAMP
RESTART
RESTATE
ROSEATE
ROSTAND
SASHAYS
SUSTAIN
TOSCALE
TOSPARE
TOSTADA
TUSCANY
TUSSAUD
UNSEALS
UNSEATS
UNSNAGS
UNSNAPS
UNSNARL
UNSTACK
UPSCALE
UPSTAGE
UPSTART
UPSTATE
VASSALS
VISUALS
WASSAIL
WASTAGE
YESMAAM

••S••A•

ALSORAN
AMSCRAY
ARSENAL
ASSEGAI
AUSTRAL
BASEMAN
BASEPAY
BESMEAR
BESPEAK
BESTIAL
BESTMAN
BUSHMAN
CASABAS
CASELAW
CASHBAR
CASPIAN
CASSIAS
DISHPAN
DISHRAG
DISPLAY
DUSTPAN
EASTMAN
FASCIAS
FUSTIAN
HESHVAN
HESSIAN
INSOFAR
INSTEAD
INSULAR
MESSIAH
MISDEAL
MISDIAL
MISHEAR
MISLEAD
MISPLAY
MISREAD
MISTRAL
MUSICAL
MUSKRAT
NOSEBAG
NOSEGAY
NOSWEAT
PASCHAL
PESETAS
POSADAS
POSTMAN
POSTWAR
RUSSIAN
TESTBAN
UNSTRAP
WASHRAG
WISEMAN
YASHMAK
YESDEAR
YESMAAM

••S•••A

ASSYRIA
AUSTRIA
CASCARA
CASSAVA
HOSANNA
JESSICA
LASAGNA
LASCALA
LASORDA
MASCARA
MASTABA
MESSALA
MESSINA
MUSTAFA
PASTINA
ROSANNA
ROSETTA
ROSSSEA
SESTINA
SUSANNA
TESSERA
TOSHIBA
TOSTADA
VISCERA
VISTULA
YESHIVA

•••SA••

AGESAGO
AIRSACS
ANASAZI
BALSAMS
BOWSAWS
BURSARS
CAESARS
CASSATT
CASSAVA
CORSAGE
CORSAIR
COSSACK
CRUSADE
DORSALS
DOSSALS
FORSAKE
FORSALE
GOESAPE
HANSARP
HUSSARS
IBNSAUD
JIGSAWS
KANSANS
MANSARD
MARSALA
MASSAGE
MESSAGE
MESSALA
MISSALS
NAYSAID
NAYSAYS
PAISANO
PASSAGE
PASSANT
PEASANT
PITSAWS
PRESAGE
PRESALE
PROSAIC
PULSARS
PULSATE
QUASARS
RANSACK
RIPSAWS
SADSACK
SAMSARA
SAPSAGO
SAUSAGE
SEASALT
SEESAWS
SENSATE
SETSAIL
TAGSALE
TARSALS
TOPSAIL
TULSANS
TUSSAUD
UPPSALA
VASSALS
WASSAIL

•••S•A•

ABYSMAL
ALASKAN
ALLSTAR
ARISTAE
ARISTAS
ASUSUAL
BARSOAP
BATSMAN
BEESWAX
BOXSEAT
BROSNAN
CAPSHAW
CAPSTAN
CARSEAT
CASSIAS
CATSCAN
CATSPAW
COASTAL
CRYSTAL
DAYSTAR
DOGSTAR
DRISTAN
ELYSIAN
ETESIAN
FIESTAS
FRISIAN
FURSEAL
GEISHAS
GLOSSAE
GOESBAD
GRISHAM
HESSIAN
HOTSEAT
HOUSMAN
KEESHAN
KINSMAN
MARSHAL
MESSIAH
MIASMAS
NEWSDAY
NEWSMAN
PERSIAN
PLASMAS
POTSDAM
PRESOAK
REDSTAR
RUSSIAN
SEASTAR
SENSUAL
SIESTAS
TELSTAR
THUSFAR
TINSTAR
TRISTAN
TUESDAY
TWOSTAR
UNUSUAL
VIZSLAS
ZOYSIAS

•••S••A

ANOSMIA
CAESURA
CASSAVA
CORSICA
DYKSTRA
JESSICA
KRISHNA
MARSALA
MESSALA
MESSINA
OLESTRA
PERSONA
PORSENA
PRUSSIA
RETSINA
ROSSSEA
SALSODA
SAMSARA
SATSUMA
TESSERA
UPPSALA

••••SA•

ALTOSAX
AROUSAL
ARTISAN
BABYSAT
BANDSAW
BARKSAT
BUCKSAW
BUZZSAW
COMESAT
DARESAY
DEPOSAL
ESPOSAS
FLIESAT
FLOTSAM
FORESAW
FRETSAW
GAINSAY
GANGSAW
GLOSSAE
GRABSAT
HACKSAW
HANDSAW
HEARSAY
HINTSAT
HOOTSAT
JEERSAT
JUMPSAT
KEEPSAT
LANDSAT
LEERSAT
LINDSAY
LOOKSAT
MEDUSAE
MEDUSAS
MIMOSAS
OVERSAW
PECKSAT
PEEKSAT
PEERSAT
PERUSAL
PHRASAL
PICKSAT
PINESAP
PLAYSAT
POKESAT
RAILSAT
REFUSAL
SNAPSAT
SPOUSAL
TALKSAT
TEARSAT
WHIPSAW
WINESAP
WINKSAT
YELLSAT

••••S•A

ALYOSHA
AMNESIA
ARALSEA
AUGUSTA
BATISTA
CANASTA
CELESTA
CHELSEA
DEADSEA
DEEPSEA
EURASIA
FREESIA
FUCHSIA
GANGSTA
JOCASTA
KARASEA
KENOSHA
MELISSA
NATASHA
NICOSIA
OPENSEA
OVERSEA
PRUSSIA
RICKSHA
ROBUSTA
ROSSSEA
SILESIA
SULUSEA
TUNISIA
VANESSA

•••••SA

FORMOSA
MELISSA
MOMBASA
SUBROSA
THERESA
VANESSA

S•B••••

SABBATH
SABINES
SABRINA
SIBERIA
SIBLING
SOBBERS
SOBBING
SOBERED
SOBERER
SOBERLY
SUBBING
SUBDEBS
SUBDUED
SUBDUER
SUBDUES
SUBHEAD
SUBJECT
SUBJOIN
SUBLETS
SUBLIME
SUBMITS
SUBORNS
SUBPLOT
SUBROSA
SUBSETS
SUBSIDE
SUBSIDY
SUBSIST
SUBSOIL
SUBSUME
SUBTEND
SUBTEXT
SUBTLER
SUBUNIT
SUBURBS
SUBVERT
SUBWAYS
SUBZERO

S••B•••

SABBATH
SAMBAED
SAMBARS
SANBORN
SAWBUCK
SEABAGS
SEABASS
SEABEDS
SEABEES
SEABIRD
SEABORG
SERBIAN
SETBACK
SHEBANG
SHUBERT
SIOBHAN
SKIBOOT
SKYBLUE
SLABBED
SLOBBER
SNUBBED
SOBBERS
SOBBING
SORBATE
SORBETS
SOWBUGS
SOYBEAN
STABBED
STABILE
STABLED
STABLER
STABLES
STUBBED
STUBBLE
STUBBLY
SUBBING
SUDBURY
SUNBATH
SUNBEAM
SUNBELT
SUNBURN
SWABBED
SYMBOLS

S•••B••

SALABLE
SALTBOX
SANDBAG
SANDBAR
SANDBOX
SANIBEL
SAVABLE
SCRIBES
SCRUBBY
SCRUBUP
SEEDBED
SHAMBLE
SHERBET
SHOEBOX
SHOWBIZ
SHRUBBY
SICKBAY
SIDEBAR
SIDEBET
SIZABLE
SIZABLY
SLABBED
SLOBBER
SLUMBER
SNUBBED
SOAPBOX
SOFABED
SOLUBLE
STABBED
STEUBEN
STROBES
STUBBED
STUBBLE
STUBBLY
STUMBLE
SWABBED

S••••B•

SCARABS
SCRUBBY
SEALABS
SHRUBBY
STANDBY
STOODBY
SUBDEBS
SUBURBS
SWEARBY
SWINGBY
SWOREBY
SYLLABI

S•••••B

SHECRAB
SNOWJOB
SUCCUMB

•SB••••

OSBORNE

•S•B•••

ASHBURY
ISOBARS

•S••B••

USEABLE

•S•••B•

ASCRIBE

••SB•••

BUSBIES
BUSBOYS
DASBOOT
DISBAND
DISBARS
GASBAGS
HASBEEN
HUSBAND

••S•B••

BESTBOY
CASABAS
CASHBAR
CASHBOX
DISABLE
DISOBEY
NOSEBAG
POSTBOX
RISIBLE
ROSEBUD
TESTBAN
VISIBLE
VISIBLY

••S••B•

ABSORBS
ADSORBS
DISROBE
HUSHABY
MASTABA
RESORBS
TOSHIBA

••S•••B

DISTURB
NOSEJOB
WASHTUB

•••SB••

FRISBEE
GEMSBOK
GOESBAD
NEWSBOY

••••SB•

COMESBY
DROPSBY
HORNSBY
MORESBY

SC•••••

SCALARS
SCALDED
SCALENE
SCALERS
SCALIER
SCALING
SCALLOP
SCALPED
SCALPEL
SCALPER
SCAMMED
SCAMPED
SCAMPER
SCANDAL
SCANNED
SCANNER
SCANTED
SCANTER
SCANTLY
SCAPULA
SCARABS
SCARCER
SCARERS
SCAREUP

SCARFED
SCARIER
SCARIFY
SCARILY
SCARING
SCARLET
SCARPED
SCARRED
SCARVES
SCATHED
SCATHES
SCATTED
SCATTER
SCENDED
SCENERY
SCENTED
SCEPTER
SCEPTRE
SCHATZI
SCHEMAS
SCHEMED
SCHEMER
SCHEMES
SCHERZI
SCHERZO
SCHIRRA
SCHISMS
SCHLEPP
SCHLEPS
SCHLOCK
SCHMEER
SCHMIDT
SCHMOES
SCHMOOS
SCHNAPS
SCHOLAR
SCHOOLS
SCHWINN
SCIENCE
SCISSOR
SCLERAS
SCOFFED
SCOFFER
SCOLDED
SCOLDER
SCONCES
SCOOPED
SCOOPER
SCOOTED
SCOOTER
SCOPING
SCORERS
SCORING
SCORNED
SCORPIO
SCOTERS
SCOTTIE
SCOURED
SCOURER
SCOURGE
SCOUTED
SCOUTER
SCOWLED
SCOWLER
SCRAGGY
SCRAPED
SCRAPER
SCRAPES
SCRAPPY
SCRATCH
SCRAWLS
SCRAWLY
SCRAWNY
SCREAKS
SCREAMS
SCREECH
SCREEDS
SCREENS
SCREWED
SCREWUP
SCRIBES
SCRIMPS
SCRIMPY
SCRIPPS
SCRIPTS
SCRIVEN
SCROLLS
SCROOGE
SCRUBBY
SCRUBUP
SCRUFFS
SCRUFFY
SCRUNCH
SCRUPLE
SCUDDED
SCUFFED
SCUFFLE
SCULLED
SCULLER
SCULPTS
SCUPPER
SCURVES
SCUTTLE
SCYTHED
SCYTHES

S•C••••

SACHEMS
SACHETS
SACKERS
SACKFUL
SACKING
SACKOUT
SECANTS
SECEDED
SECEDER
SECEDES
SECLUDE
SECONDS
SECRECY
SECRETE
SECRETS
SECTION
SECTORS
SECULAR
SECURED
SECURER
SECURES
SICCING
SICHUAN
SICKBAY
SICKENS
SICKEST
SICKLES
SICKOUT
SICKPAY
SOCIALS
SOCIETY
SOCKETS
SOCKEYE
SOCKING
SOCKSIN
STCROIX
SUCCEED
SUCCESS
SUCCORS
SUCCOUR
SUCCUMB
SUCKERS
SUCKING
SUCKSIN
SUCRASE
SUCROSE
SUCTION

S••C•••

SALCHOW
SANCTUM
SARCASM
SATCHEL
SATCHMO
SAUCERS
SAUCIER
SAUCILY
SEACOWS
SEICHES
SHACKLE
SHECRAB
SHOCKED
SHOCKER
SHUCKED
SHUCKER
SICCING
SINCERE
SITCOMS
SKYCAPS
SLACKED
SLACKEN
SLACKER
SLICERS
SLICING
SLICKED
SLICKER
SLICKLY
SMACKED
SMACKER
SNACKED
SNACKER
SNICKER
SNOCATS
SNOCONE
SORCERY
SPACERS
SPACIER
SPACING
SPACKLE
SPECIAL
SPECIES
SPECIFY
SPECKLE
SPECTER
SPECTOR
SPECTRA
SPECTRE
SPICEUP
SPICIER
SPICING
STACKED
STACKUP
STICHES
STICKER
STICKTO
STICKUP
STOCKED
STOCKUP
STUCCOS
STUCKTO
STUCKUP
SUCCEED
SUCCESS
SUCCORS
SUCCOUR
SUCCUMB
SUNCITY
SURCOAT
SYNCHED
SYNCHES
SYNCING

S•••C••

SARACEN
SCARCER
SCONCES
SEANCES
SEDUCED
SEDUCER
SEDUCES
SELECTS
SENECAS
SHTICKS
SIDECAR
SILICAS
SILICON
SIROCCO
SKETCHY
SLOTCAR
SLOUCHY
SLUICED
SLUICES
SNOWCAP
SOLACES
SOLICIT
SOUPCON
SOURCED
SOURCES
SPENCER
SPLICED
SPLICER
SPLICES
SPRUCED
SPRUCER
SPRUCES
STANCES
STARCHY
STENCIL
STLUCIA
STOICAL
STUCCOS

S••••C•

SADSACK
SAWBUCK
SCHLOCK
SCIENCE
SCRATCH
SCREECH
SCRUNCH
SEASICK
SECRECY
SELLECK
SERPICO
SERVICE
SETBACK
SHYLOCK
SILENCE
SIROCCO
SIXPACK
SKYJACK
SPINACH
SPLOTCH
SQUELCH
SQUINCH
STATICE
STATICS
STAUNCH
STOMACH
STRETCH
SUBJECT
SUFFICE
SUNDECK
SURFACE
SUSPECT

S•••••C

SARANAC
SATIRIC
SEISMIC
SELENIC
SEMITIC
SHELLAC
SKEPTIC
SOMATIC
STANNIC
STYPTIC
SYNODIC

•SC••••

ASCENDS
ASCENTS
ASCETIC
ASCRIBE
ESCAPED
ESCAPEE
ESCAPES
ESCARPS
ESCHEAT
ESCHEWS
ESCORTS
ESCROWS
ESCUDOS
OSCEOLA
OSCINES

•S•C•••

ASHCANS
ASOCIAL
PSYCHED
PSYCHES
PSYCHIC
PSYCHUP

•S••C••

ASPECTS
OSSICLE

•S•••C•

ASKANCE
ESSENCE
OSTRICH

•S••••C

ASCETIC
ASEPTIC
ASIATIC
ISLAMIC
OSMOTIC
OSSIFIC
PSYCHIC

••SC•••

ABSCOND
AMSCRAY
BISCUIT
CASCADE
CASCARA
DESCANT
DESCEND
DESCENT
DISCARD
DISCERN
DISCOED
DISCORD
DISCUSS
FASCIAS
FASCISM
FASCIST
FISCHER
GASCAPS
GASCONS
INSCAPE
LASCALA
LASCAUX
MASCARA
MASCOTS
MESCALS
MISCALL
MISCAST
MISCUED
MISCUES
MUSCATS
MUSCLED
MUSCLES
MUSCOVY
NASCENT
NESCAFE
OBSCENE
OBSCURE
PASCHAL
PISCINE
PISCOPO
RASCALS
RESCALE
RESCIND
RESCUED
RESCUER
RESCUES
TOSCALE
TUSCANY
UNSCREW
UPSCALE
VISCERA
VISCOUS

••S•C••

BISECTS
CASHCOW
INSECTS
MUSICAL
OSSICLE
RESECTS

••S••C•

ABSENCE
ANSPACH
AUSPICE
BESEECH
CASSOCK
COSSACK
DISSECT
DRSPOCK
ESSENCE
FOSDICK
FUSTICS
HASSOCK
HOSPICE
INSPECT
INSTOCK
IPSWICH
JESSICA
JUSTICE
MASTICS
MOSAICS
MRSPOCK
MYSTICS
RESPECT
RESTOCK
RUSTICS
SUSPECT
TUSSOCK
UNSTACK
UNSTICK
UNSTUCK
WASATCH

••S•••C

ARSENIC
GASTRIC
MASONIC
OSSIFIC
POSTHOC

•••SC••

BORSCHT
CATSCAN
FIASCOS
FRESCOS
KITSCHY
PORSCHE

•••S•C•

AIRSACS
AIRSOCK
CANSECO
CASSOCK
CORSICA
COSSACK
DISSECT
HASSOCK
JESSICA
PARSECS
PHYSICS
RANSACK
SADSACK
SEASICK
TRISECT
TUSSOCK

•••S••C

ANOSMIC
CAUSTIC
CLASSIC
DRASTIC
ELASTIC
ERISTIC
GNOSTIC
LIPSYNC
MIASMIC
PLASTIC
PROSAIC
SEISMIC

••••SC•

DEHISCE
ILIESCU
IONESCO
JALISCO
KLATSCH
MENISCI
NABISCO
TABASCO

••••S•C

CLASSIC

S•D••••

SADDENS
SADDEST
SADDLED
SADDLER
SADDLES
SADNESS
SADSACK
SEDALIA
SEDATER
SEDUCED
SEDUCER
SEDUCES
SIDEARM
SIDEBAR
SIDEBET
SIDECAR
SIDEMAN
SIDEMEN
SIDINGS
SIDLING
SODAPOP
SODDING
STDENIS
SUDBURY
SUDSIER
SUDSING

S••D•••

SADDENS
SADDEST
SADDLED
SADDLER
SADDLES
SANDALS
SANDBAG
SANDBAR
SANDBOX
SANDERS
SANDFLY
SANDHOG
SANDIER
SANDING
SANDLOT
SANDMAN
SANDMEN
SARDINE
SATDOWN
SAWDUST
SCUDDED
SEADOGS
SEADUTY
SEEDBED
SEEDERS
SEEDIER
SEEDILY
SEEDING
SEEDPOD
SEIDELS
SENDERS
SENDFOR
SENDING
SENDOFF
SENDOUT
SENDSIN
SENDSUP
SENDUPS
SETDOWN
SHADIER
SHADILY
SHADING
SHADOOF
SHADOWS
SHADOWY
SHODDEN
SHUDDER
SITDOWN
SKIDDED
SKIDDER
SKIDDOO
SKIDROW
SKYDIVE
SLEDDED
SLEDDER
SLEDDOG
SLEDGES
SLIDEIN
SLIDERS
SLIDING
SLUDGES
SMIDGEN
SMUDGED
SMUDGES
SNIDELY
SNIDEST
SODDING
SOLDERS
SOLDIER
SOLDOFF
SOLDOUT
SPADERS
SPADING
SPIDERS
SPIDERY
STADIUM
STUDDED
STUDENT
STUDIED
STUDIES
STUDIOS
SUBDEBS
SUBDUED
SUBDUER
SUBDUES
SUNDAES
SUNDAYS
SUNDECK
SUNDERS
SUNDEWS
SUNDIAL
SUNDOGS
SUNDOWN
SWADDLE
SWEDISH

S•••D••

SALADIN
SAMEDAY
SAVEDUP
SCALDED
SCANDAL
SCENDED
SCOLDED
SCOLDER
SCUDDED
SECEDED
SECEDER
SECEDES
SERFDOM
SEWEDUP
SHAHDOM
SHELDON
SHINDIG
SHODDEN
SHOWDOG
SHUDDER
SINEDIE
SIZEDUP
SKIDDED
SKIDDER
SKIDDOO
SLANDER
SLEDDED
SLEDDER
SLEDDOG
SLENDER
SMOLDER
SNOWDAY
SNOWDON
SOANDSO
SOLEDAD
SOLIDER
SOLIDLY
SOMEDAY
SOUNDED
SOUNDER
SOUNDLY
SPANDEX
SPEEDED
SPEEDER
SPEEDUP
SPENDER
SPIEDON
SPINDLE
SPINDLY
SPONDEE
STAIDER
STAIDLY
STANDBY
STANDEE
STANDIN
STANDON
STANDUP
STARDOM
STOODBY
STOODIN
STOODUP
STRIDER
STRIDES
STRUDEL
STUDDED
SWADDLE
SWINDLE
SYNODAL
SYNODIC

S••••D•

SALSODA
SCHMIDT
SCREEDS
SEABEDS
SEASIDE
SECLUDE
SECONDS
SHIELDS
SHROUDS
SPREADS
STRANDS
SUBSIDE
SUBSIDY
SULFIDE
SUNGODS

S•••••D

SADDLED
SAINTED
SALLIED
SALUTED
SAMBAED
SAMOYED
SAMPLED
SANFORD
SAUTEED
SAVAGED
SAVORED
SAWWOOD
SCALDED
SCALPED
SCAMMED
SCAMPED
SCANNED
SCANTED
SCARFED
SCARPED
SCARRED
SCATHED
SCATTED
SCENDED
SCENTED
SCHEMED
SCOFFED
SCOLDED
SCOOPED
SCOOTED
SCORNED
SCOURED
SCOUTED
SCOWLED
SCRAPED
SCREWED
SCUDDED
SCUFFED
SCULLED
SCYTHED
SEABIRD
SEAFOOD
SEAWARD
SEAWEED
SECEDED
SECURED
SEDUCED
SEEDBED
SEEDPOD
SEESRED
SEETHED
SERRIED
SETTLED
SEVERED
SHAFTED
SHAGGED
SHAMMED
SHANKED
SHARPED
SHEARED
SHEAVED
SHEERED
SHEETED
SHELLED
SHELVED
SHEPARD
SHIFTED
SHILLED
SHINNED
SHIPPED
SHIRKED
SHIRRED
SHOCKED
SHOPPED
SHORTED
SHOUTED
SHUCKED
SHUNNED
SHUNTED
SHUSHED
SIGHTED
SIGMUND
SINGLED
SIXFOLD
SIZZLED
SKIDDED
SKILLED
SKIMMED
SKIMPED
SKINNED
SKIPPED
SKIRLED
SKIRRED
SKIRTED
SKULKED
SKUNKED
SKYWARD
SLABBED
SLACKED
SLAMMED
SLANTED
SLAPPED
SLASHED
SLATTED
SLEDDED
SLEEKED
SLEETED
SLICKED
SLIMMED
SLINKED
SLIPPED
SLOGGED
SLOPPED
SLOSHED
SLOTTED
SLUGGED
SLUICED
SLUMMED
SLUMPED
SLURPED
SLURRED
SMACKED
SMARTED
SMASHED
SMEARED
SMELLED
SMELTED
SMIRKED
SMUDGED
SNACKED
SNAFUED
SNAGGED
SNAPPED
SNARLED
SNEAKED
SNEERED
SNEEZED
SNIFFED
SNIPPED
SNOOPED
SNOOTED
SNOOZED
SNORTED
SNUBBED
SNUFFED
SOBERED
SOFABED
SOLEDAD
SOOTHED
SORTIED
SOUGHED
SOUNDED
SOURCED
SPALLED
SPANKED
SPANNED
SPARGED
SPARKED
SPARRED
SPATTED
SPAWNED
SPEARED
SPEEDED
SPELLED
SPIELED
SPILLED
SPLAYED
SPLICED
SPOILED
SPONGED
SPOOFED
SPOOKED
SPOOLED
SPOONED
SPORTED
SPOTTED
SPOUTED
SPRAYED
SPRUCED
SPURNED
SPURRED
SPURTED
SQUALID
SQUARED
SQUIRED
STABBED
STABLED
STACKED
STAFFED
STAGGED
STAINED
STALKED
STALLED
STAMPED
STAPLED
STARRED
STARTED
STARVED
STASHED
STEAMED
STEELED
STEEPED
STEERED
STEMMED
STEPPED
STEROID
STETTED
STEWARD
STIFFED
STIFLED
STILLED
STILTED
STINTED
STIPEND
STIRRED
STOCKED
STOMPED
STOOPED
STOPPED
STORIED
STORMED

STRAFED
STRAYED
STREWED
STRIPED
STRIVED
STROKED
STUBBED
STUDDED
STUDIED
STUFFED
STUMPED
STUNNED
STUNTED
STYMIED
SUBDUED
SUBHEAD
SUBTEND
SUCCEED
SUGARED
SULLIED
SUNMAID
SUSPEND
SUTURED
SWABBED
SWAMPED
SWAPPED
SWARMED
SWATHED
SWATTED
SWEATED
SWELLED
SWERVED
SWIGGED
SWILLED
SWIRLED
SWISHED
SWOONED
SWOOPED
SYNCHED

•S•D•••

ISADORA

•S••D••

ASUNDER
ESCUDOS
PSANDQS

•S•••D•

ASCENDS
ASTRIDE
ESTRADA
ISLANDS
ISOPODS
OSMONDS

•S••••D

ASHAMED
ASHFORD
ASHLAND
ASPIRED
ASSAYED
ASSUMED
ASSURED
ASTOUND
ESCAPED
ESSAYED
OSMOSED
OSTEOID
PSALMED
PSYCHED
USHERED
USURPED

••SD•••

DISDAIN
FOSDICK
MISDATE
MISDEAL
MISDEED
MISDIAL
MISDOES
MISDONE
YESDEAR

••S•D••

APSIDES
BESIDES
DOSIDOS
EASEDIN
EASEDUP
HASIDIM
INSIDER
INSIDES
PASTDUE
POSADAS
RESIDED
RESIDES
RESIDUE
RUSHDIE
WISEDUP

••S••D•

BUSHIDO
CASCADE
CASSIDY
CUSPIDS
CUSTODY
LASORDA
RESANDS
RESEEDS
RESENDS
TOSTADA
VESPIDS

••S•••D

ABSCOND
ASSAYED
ASSUMED
ASSURED
BUSTARD
BUSTLED
CASTLED
CUSTARD
DASTARD
DESCEND
DESIRED
DESMOND
DISBAND
DISCARD
DISCOED
DISCORD
DISTEND
DISUSED
EASTEND
ENSILED
ENSURED
ESSAYED
GUSSIED
HASSLED
HUSBAND
HUSTLED
INSIPID
INSTEAD
INSURED
JOSTLED
LASSOED
LUSTRED
MASTOID
MISCUED
MISDEED
MISLAID
MISLEAD
MISREAD
MISUSED
MISWORD
MOSEYED
MUSCLED
MUSTARD
NESTLED
PESTLED
POSITED
RASSLED
RESCIND
RESCUED
RESIDED
RESILED
RESOLED
RESOUND
RESPOND
RESUMED
ROSEBUD
ROSERED
ROSTAND
RUSTLED
SUSPEND
TUSSAUD
TUSSLED
UNSATED
UNSEWED
UNSOUND
VISITED
WESTEND

•••SD••

DRESDEN
GADSDEN
NEWSDAY
POTSDAM
RUNSDRY
TUESDAY

•••S•D•

BEDSIDE
CASSIDY
CRUSADE
EPISODE
OFFSIDE
OUTSIDE
PRESIDE
PROSODY
SALSODA
SEASIDE
SUBSIDE
SUBSIDY
TOPSIDE
WAYSIDE

•••S••D

ABASHED
AMASSED
ANISEED
BIASSED
BLASTED
BLESSED
BLUSHED
BOASTED
BOBSLED
BOOSTED
BRUSHED
CLASHED
CLASPED
CLASSED
COASTED
CRASHED
CRESTED
CRISPED
CROSSED
CRUSHED
CRUSTED
DOGSLED
DRESSED
EGESTED
ENISLED
EXISTED
FEASTED
FLASHED
FLESHED
FLOSSED
FLUSHED
FOISTED
FRISKED
FROSTED
GHOSTED
GLASSED
GLOSSED
GNASHED
GODSEND
GOESBAD
GRASPED
GRASSED
GROSSED
GUESSED
GUESTED
GUSSIED
HASSLED
HAYSEED
HEISTED
HOISTED
IBNSAUD
JOISTED
JOUSTED
LASSOED
LEASHED
LINSEED
MANSARD
MOUSSED
NAYSAID
NONSKID
OUTSOLD
PLASHED
PRESSED
PURSUED
QUASHED
QUESTED
RASSLED
ROASTED
ROOSTED
ROUSTED
SEESRED
SHUSHED
SLASHED
SLOSHED
SMASHED
STASHED
SWISHED
TOASTED
TOUSLED
TRASHED
TRUSSED
TRUSTED
TRYSTED
TUSSAUD
TUSSLED
TWISTED
UNASKED
WAISTED
WHISKED
WORSTED
WRESTED

••••SD•

MAKESDO

••••S•D

ACCUSED
ADVISED
AMASSED
APPOSED
AROUSED
AVULSED
BEMUSED
BIASSED
BLESSED
BLOUSED
BRAISED
BROWSED
BRUISED
CLASSED
COURSED
CREASED
CROSSED
CRUISED
DEBASED
DEFUSED
DEMISED
DEPOSED
DEVISED
DISUSED
DRESSED
DROWSED
EFFUSED
ELAPSED
EMERSED
ENCASED
EVULSED
EXCISED
EXCUSED
EXPOSED
FLENSED
FLOSSED
FOCUSED
GLASSED
GLOSSED
GRASSED
GREASED
GROSSED
GROUSED
GUESSED
ILLUSED
IMPOSED
INCISED
INFUSED
LIAISED
MISUSED
MOUSSED
OPPOSED
OSMOSED
PERUSED
PHRASED
PLEASED
PRAISED
PRESSED
RECUSED
REFUSED
REPOSED
REVISED
TRUSSED
UNCASED

SE•••••

SEABAGS
SEABASS
SEABEDS
SEABEES
SEABIRD
SEABORG
SEACOWS
SEADOGS
SEADUTY
SEAFANS
SEAFOOD
SEAGATE
SEAGIRT
SEAGRAM
SEAGULL
SEALABS
SEALANE
SEALANT
SEALEGS
SEALERS
SEALILY
SEALING
SEALION
SEALOFF
SEALSUP
SEAMIER
SEAMING
SEAMOSS
SEANCES
SEAPORT
SEARING
SEASALT
SEASICK
SEASIDE
SEASLUG
SEASONS
SEASTAR
SEATERS
SEATING
SEATTLE
SEAWALL
SEAWARD
SEAWAYS
SEAWEED
SECANTS
SECEDED
SECEDER
SECEDES
SECLUDE
SECONDS
SECRECY
SECRETE
SECRETS
SECTION
SECTORS
SECULAR
SECURED
SECURER
SECURES
SEDALIA
SEDATER
SEDUCED
SEDUCER
SEDUCES
SEEDBED
SEEDERS
SEEDIER
SEEDILY
SEEDING
SEEDPOD
SEEHERE
SEEKERS
SEEKING
SEEKOUT
SEEMING
SEEPING
SEEPSIN
SEERESS
SEESAWS
SEESFIT
SEESOFF
SEESOUT
SEESRED
SEETHED
SEETHES
SEETOIT
SEGMENT
SEGOVIA
SEICHES
SEIDELS
SEINERS
SEINING
SEISMIC
SEIZERS
SEIZING
SELECTS
SELENIC
SELFISH
SELKIRK
SELLECK
SELLERS
SELLING
SELLOFF
SELLOUT
SELTZER
SELVAGE
SEMINAL
SEMINAR
SEMIPRO
SEMITES
SEMITIC
SENATES
SENATOR
SENDERS
SENDFOR
SENDING
SENDOFF
SENDOUT
SENDSIN
SENDSUP
SENDUPS
SENECAS
SENEGAL
SENIORS
SENNETT
SENORAS
SENORES
SENSATE
SENSING
SENSORS
SENSORY
SENSUAL
SENTFOR
SENTOFF
SENTOUT
SEPTETS
SEQUELS
SEQUINS
SEQUOIA
SERAPES
SERAPHS
SERAPIS
SERBIAN
SERENER
SERFDOM
SERIALS
SERIATE
SERIOUS
SERLING
SERMONS
SERPENT
SERPICO
SERRATE
SERRIED
SERVALS
SERVANT
SERVERS
SERVEUP
SERVICE
SERVILE
SERVING
SESAMES
SESSILE
SESSION
SESTETS
SESTINA
SETBACK
SETDOWN
SETINTO
SETLINE
SETSAIL
SETSOFF
SETSOUT
SETTEES
SETTERS
SETTING
SETTLED
SETTLER
SETTLES
SETUPON
SEVENTH
SEVENTY
SEVENUP
SEVERAL
SEVERED
SEVERER
SEVIGNE
SEVILLE
SEWEDUP
SEXIEST
SEXISTS
SEXTANS
SEXTANT
SEXTETS
SEXTONS
SEYMOUR

S•E••••

SCENDED
SCENERY
SCENTED
SCEPTER
SCEPTRE
SEEDBED
SEEDERS
SEEDIER
SEEDILY
SEEDING
SEEDPOD
SEEHERE
SEEKERS
SEEKING
SEEKOUT
SEEMING
SEEPING
SEEPSIN
SEERESS
SEESAWS
SEESFIT
SEESOFF
SEESOUT
SEESRED
SEETHED
SEETHES
SEETOIT
SHEARED
SHEARER
SHEATHE
SHEATHS
SHEAVED
SHEAVES
SHEBANG
SHECRAB
SHEERED
SHEERER
SHEERLY
SHEETED
SHEIKHS
SHEILAE
SHEILAH
SHEILAS
SHEKELS
SHELDON
SHELLAC
SHELLED
SHELLER
SHELLEY
SHELTER
SHELTIE
SHELTON
SHELVED
SHELVES
SHEPARD
SHERBET
SHERIFF
SHERMAN
SHERPAS
SHERWIN
SHEWOLF
SIENNAS
SIERRAS
SIESTAS
SKEETER
SKEEZIX
SKELTER
SKELTON
SKEPTIC
SKETCHY
SKEWERS
SKEWING
SLEDDED
SLEDDER
SLEDDOG
SLEDGES
SLEEKED
SLEEKEN
SLEEKER
SLEEKLY
SLEEPER
SLEEPIN
SLEEPON
SLEETED
SLEEVES
SLEIGHS
SLEIGHT
SLENDER
SLEPTIN
SLEPTON
SLEUTHS
SMEARED
SMELLED
SMELTED
SMELTER
SMETANA
SNEAKED
SNEAKER
SNEAKIN
SNEERAT
SNEERED
SNEERER
SNEEZED
SNEEZER
SNEEZES
SNELLEN
SPEAKER
SPEAKOF
SPEAKUP
SPEARED
SPECIAL
SPECIES
SPECIFY
SPECKLE
SPECTER
SPECTOR
SPECTRA
SPECTRE
SPEEDED
SPEEDER
SPEEDUP
SPELLED
SPELLER
SPELUNK
SPENCER
SPENDER
SPENSER
SPEWING
STEALTH
STEAMED
STEAMER
STEELED
STEELER
STEELIE
STEEPED
STEEPEN
STEEPER
STEEPLE
STEEPLY
STEERED
STEERER
STEIGER
STEINEM
STEINER
STELLAR
STEMMED
STENCIL
STENGEL
STENTOR
STEPHEN
STEPINS
STEPOUT
STEPPED
STEPPER
STEPPES
STEPSIN
STEPSON
STEPSUP
STEPUPS
STEREOS
STERILE
STERNAL
STERNER
STERNLY
STERNUM
STEROID
STEROLS
STETSON
STETTED
STEUBEN
STEVENS
STEWARD
STEWART
STEWERS
STEWING
SVELTER
SWEARAT
SWEARBY
SWEARER
SWEARIN
SWEARTO
SWEATED
SWEATER
SWEDISH
SWEEPER
SWEEPUP
SWEETEN
SWEETER
SWEETIE
SWEETLY
SWEETON
SWELLED
SWELLUP
SWELTER
SWELTRY
SWEPTUP
SWERVED
SWERVES

S••E•••

SALERNO
SAMEDAY
SAVEDUP
SAVESUP
SCHEMAS
SCHEMED
SCHEMER
SCHEMES
SCHERZI
SCHERZO
SCIENCE
SCLERAS
SCREAKS
SCREAMS
SCREECH
SCREEDS
SCREENS
SCREWED
SCREWUP
SECEDED
SECEDER
SECEDES
SELECTS
SELENIC
SENECAS
SENEGAL
SERENER
SEVENTH
SEVENTY
SEVENUP
SEVERAL
SEVERED
SEVERER
SEWEDUP
SHEERED
SHEERER
SHEERLY
SHEETED
SHIELDS
SHOEBOX
SHOEING
SIBERIA
SIDEARM
SIDEBAR
SIDEBET
SIDECAR
SIDEMAN
SIDEMEN
SILENCE
SILENTS
SILESIA
SIMENON
SINEDIE
SIZEDUP
SIZESUP
SKEETER
SKEEZIX
SLEEKED
SLEEKEN
SLEEKER
SLEEKLY
SLEEPER
SLEEPIN
SLEEPON
SLEETED
SLEEVES
SLOEGIN
SNEERAT
SNEERED
SNEERER
SNEEZED
SNEEZER
SNEEZES
SOBERED
SOBERER
SOBERLY
SOLEDAD
SOMEDAY
SOMEHOW
SOMEONE
SOMEWAY
SPEEDED
SPEEDER
SPEEDUP
SPHERES
SPIEDON
SPIEGEL
SPIELED
SPIELER
SPIESON
SPLEENS
SPREADS
SQUEAKS
SQUEAKY
SQUEALS
SQUEEZE
SQUELCH
STDENIS
STEELED
STEELER
STEELIE
STEEPED
STEEPEN
STEEPER
STEEPLE
STEEPLY
STEERED
STEERER
STIEGEL
STPETER
STREAKS
STREAKY
STREAMS
STREETS
STRETCH
STRETTO
STREWED
STREWER
SUZETTE
SWEEPER
SWEEPUP
SWEETEN
SWEETER
SWEETIE
SWEETLY
SWEETON
SYNERGY

S•••E••

SACHEMS
SACHETS
SACKERS
SADDENS
SADDEST
SADNESS
SALIENT
SALIERI
SALTERS
SALVERS
SANDERS
SANREMO
SAPIENS
SAPIENT
SAPPERS
SARGENT
SASSERS
SATIETY
SAUCERS
SAUTEED
SAWYERS
SCALENE
SCALERS
SCARERS
SCAREUP
SCENERY
SCHLEPP
SCHLEPS
SCHMEER
SCORERS
SCOTERS
SCREECH
SCREEDS
SCREENS
SEABEDS
SEABEES
SEALEGS
SEALERS
SEATERS
SEAWEED
SECRECY
SECRETE
SECRETS
SEEDERS
SEEHERE
SEEKERS
SEERESS
SEGMENT
SEIDELS
SEINERS
SEIZERS
SELLECK

SELLERS
SENDERS
SENNETT
SEPTETS
SEQUELS
SERPENT
SERVERS
SERVEUP
SESTETS
SETTEES
SETTERS
SEXIEST
SEXTETS
SHAKERS
SHAKEUP
SHAPELY
SHAPERS
SHAPEUP
SHAREIN
SHARERS
SHAVERS
SHEKELS
SHINERS
SHIVERS
SHOVELS
SHOVERS
SHOWERS
SHOWERY
SHRIEKS
SHUBERT
SHUTEYE
SHYNESS
SIAMESE
SICKENS
SICKEST
SIFTERS
SIGHERS
SIGNEES
SIGNERS
SIGNETS
SILVERS
SILVERY
SIMMERS
SIMPERS
SINCERE
SINGERS
SINKERS
SINNERS
SIPPERS
SIPPETS
SISTERS
SITTERS
SITWELL
SIXTEEN
SKATERS
SKEWERS
SKIVERS
SLAVERS
SLAVERY
SLAYERS
SLICERS
SLIDEIN
SLIDERS
SLIVERS
SLOVENE
SLOVENS
SLOWEST
SLYNESS
SMILERS
SMOKERS
SNIDELY
SNIDEST
SNIPEAT
SNIVELS
SNORERS
SOAKERS
SOAPERS
SOARERS
SOBBERS
SOCIETY
SOCKETS
SOCKEYE
SOFTENS
SOFTEST
SOIREES
SOLDERS
SOLFEGE
SOLVENT
SOLVERS
SONNETS
SOONERS
SOONEST
SORBETS
SORCERY
SORRELS
SORTERS
SOSUEME
SOTHERE
SOTHERN
SOUREST
SOVIETS
SOYBEAN
SPACERS
SPADERS
SPARELY
SPAREST
SPICEUP
SPIDERS
SPIDERY
SPIKERS
SPINELS
SPINETS
SPIREAS
SPLEENS
SPOKEOF
SPOKEUP
SPRIEST
SPRYEST
SQUEEZE
STAGERS
STALEST
STAMENS
STAREAT
STARERS
STARETS
STATELY
STEREOS
STEVENS
STEWERS
STIPEND
STOKELY
STOKERS
STONERS
STORERS
STOREUP
STOREYS
STREETS
STUDENT
STUPEFY
STYLERS
STYLETS
STYRENE
SUAVELY
SUAVEST
SUBDEBS
SUBHEAD
SUBJECT
SUBLETS
SUBSETS
SUBTEND
SUBTEXT
SUBVERT
SUBZERO
SUCCEED
SUCCESS
SUCKERS
SUFFERS
SUGGEST
SULKERS
SUMMERS
SUMMERY
SUNBEAM
SUNBELT
SUNDECK
SUNDERS
SUNDEWS
SUNLESS
SUNSETS
SUPPERS
SUPREME
SUPREMO
SURFEIT
SURFERS
SURGEON
SURGERY
SURREAL
SURREYS
SURVEYS
SUSPECT
SUSPEND
SUTLERS
SWAYERS
SWIPERS
SWIVELS
SWOREAT
SWOREBY
SWOREIN
SYSTEMS

S••••E•

SABINES
SADDLED
SADDLER
SADDLES
SAGGIER
SAINTED
SALLIED
SALLIES
SALTIER
SALUTED
SALUTES
SALVOES
SAMBAED
SAMISEN
SAMITES
SAMOYED
SAMPLED
SAMPLER
SAMPLES
SANDIER
SANDMEN
SANIBEL
SAPPIER
SARACEN
SARALEE
SARAZEN
SASSIER
SASSIES
SATCHEL
SATIRES
SAUCIER
SAUNTER
SAUTEED
SAVAGED
SAVAGER
SAVAGES
SAVORED
SAVVIER
SAYWHEN
SCALDED
SCALIER
SCALPED
SCALPEL
SCALPER
SCAMMED
SCAMPED
SCAMPER
SCANNED
SCANNER
SCANTED
SCANTER
SCARCER
SCARFED
SCARIER
SCARLET
SCARPED
SCARRED
SCARVES
SCATHED
SCATHES
SCATTED
SCATTER
SCENDED
SCENTED
SCEPTER
SCHEMED
SCHEMER
SCHEMES
SCHMEER
SCHMOES
SCOFFED
SCOFFER
SCOLDED
SCOLDER
SCONCES
SCOOPED
SCOOPER
SCOOTED
SCOOTER
SCORNED
SCOURED
SCOURER
SCOUTED
SCOUTER
SCOWLED
SCOWLER
SCRAPED
SCRAPER
SCRAPES
SCREWED
SCRIBES
SCRIVEN
SCUDDED
SCUFFED
SCULLED
SCULLER
SCUPPER
SCURVES
SCYTHED
SCYTHES
SEABEES
SEAMIER
SEANCES
SEAWEED
SECEDED
SECEDER
SECEDES
SECURED
SECURER
SECURES
SEDATER
SEDUCED
SEDUCER
SEDUCES
SEEDBED
SEEDIER
SEESRED
SEETHED
SEETHES
SEICHES
SELTZER
SEMITES
SENATES
SENORES
SERAPES
SERENER
SERRIED
SESAMES
SETTEES
SETTLED
SETTLER
SETTLES
SEVERED
SEVERER
SHADIER
SHAFFER
SHAFTED
SHAGGED
SHAKIER
SHAKOES
SHAMMED
SHANKED
SHANTER
SHARKEY
SHARPED
SHARPEI
SHARPEN
SHARPER
SHATNER
SHATTER
SHAWNEE
SHEARED
SHEARER
SHEAVED
SHEAVES
SHEERED
SHEERER
SHEETED
SHELLED
SHELLER
SHELLEY
SHELTER
SHELVED
SHELVES
SHERBET
SHIFTED
SHIITES
SHILLED
SHIMMER
SHINIER
SHINNED
SHIPMEN
SHIPPED
SHIPPER
SHIRKED
SHIRKER
SHIRLEY
SHIRRED
SHOCKED
SHOCKER
SHODDEN
SHOOTER
SHOPPED
SHOPPER
SHOPPES
SHORTED
SHORTEN
SHORTER
SHOUTED
SHOUTER
SHOWIER
SHOWMEN
SHRIKES
SHRINER
SHRINES
SHRIVEL
SHRIVER
SHRIVES
SHUCKED
SHUCKER
SHUDDER
SHUNNED
SHUNTED
SHUSHED
SHUSHES
SHUTTER
SHYSTER
SICKLES
SIDEBET
SIDEMEN
SIGHTED
SIGNEES
SILKIER
SILLIER
SILLIES
SIMILES
SIMPLER
SIMPLEX
SINGLED
SINGLES
SINUSES
SISSIES
SIXTEEN
SIXTIES
SIZZLED
SIZZLES
SKEETER
SKELTER
SKIDDED
SKIDDER
SKILLED
SKILLET
SKIMMED
SKIMMER
SKIMPED
SKINNED
SKINNER
SKIPPED
SKIPPER
SKIRLED
SKIRRED
SKIRTED
SKITTER
SKOSHES
SKULKED
SKULKER
SKUNKED
SLABBED
SLACKED
SLACKEN
SLACKER
SLAMMED
SLAMMER
SLANDER
SLANTED
SLAPPED
SLASHED
SLASHER
SLASHES
SLATHER
SLATIER
SLATTED
SLEDDED
SLEDDER
SLEDGES
SLEEKED
SLEEKEN
SLEEKER
SLEEPER
SLEETED
SLEEVES
SLENDER
SLICKED
SLICKER
SLIMIER
SLIMMED
SLIMMER
SLINGER
SLINKED
SLIPPED
SLIPPER
SLITHER
SLOBBER
SLOGGED
SLOPPED
SLOSHED
SLOSHES
SLOTTED
SLUDGES
SLUGGED
SLUGGER
SLUICED
SLUICES
SLUMBER
SLUMMED
SLUMPED
SLURPED
SLURRED
SLUSHES
SMACKED
SMACKER
SMALLER
SMARTED
SMARTEN
SMARTER
SMASHED
SMASHER
SMASHES
SMATTER
SMEARED
SMELLED
SMELTED
SMELTER
SMIDGEN
SMIRKED
SMITTEN
SMOKIER
SMOKIES
SMOLDER
SMOTHER
SMUDGED
SMUDGES
SMUGGER
SNACKED
SNACKER
SNAFUED
SNAGGED
SNAKIER
SNAPPED
SNAPPER
SNARLED
SNEAKED
SNEAKER
SNEERED
SNEERER
SNEEZED
SNEEZER
SNEEZES
SNELLEN
SNICKER
SNIFFED
SNIFFER
SNIFTER
SNIGGER
SNIGLET
SNIPPED
SNIPPET
SNOOKER
SNOOPED
SNOOPER
SNOOTED
SNOOZED
SNOOZES
SNORKEL
SNORTED
SNORTER
SNOWIER
SNOWMEN
SNOWPEA
SNUBBED
SNUFFED
SNUFFER
SNUGGER
SOAPIER
SOBERED
SOBERER
SOFABED
SOFTIES
SOGGIER
SOIGNEE
SOIREES
SOLACES
SOLDIER
SOLIDER
SOLUTES
SOOTHED
SOOTHER
SOOTHES
SOOTIER
SORITES
SORRIER
SORTIED
SORTIES
SOUGHED
SOUNDED
SOUNDER
SOUPIER
SOURCED
SOURCES
SOUTHEY
SPACIER
SPALLED
SPANDEX
SPANIEL
SPANKED
SPANKER
SPANNED
SPANNER
SPARGED
SPARGES
SPARKED
SPARRED
SPARSER
SPATTED
SPATTER
SPAWNED
SPEAKER
SPEARED
SPECIES
SPECTER
SPEEDED
SPEEDER
SPELLED
SPELLER
SPENCER
SPENDER
SPENSER
SPHERES
SPICIER
SPIEGEL
SPIELED
SPIELER
SPIKIER
SPILLED
SPINIER
SPINNER
SPITZES
SPLAYED
SPLICED
SPLICER
SPLICES
SPLINES
SPOILED
SPOILER
SPONDEE
SPONGED
SPONGER
SPONGES
SPOOFED
SPOOFER
SPOOKED
SPOOLED
SPOONED
SPOONER
SPORTED
SPOTTED
SPOTTER
SPOUSES
SPOUTED
SPOUTER
SPRAYED
SPRAYER
SPRITES
SPRUCED
SPRUCER
SPRUCES
SPURNED
SPURNER
SPURRED
SPURTED
SPUTTER
SQUARED
SQUARER
SQUARES
SQUIRED
SQUIRES
STABBED
STABLED
STABLER
STABLES
STACKED
STAFFED
STAFFER
STAGGED
STAGGER
STAGIER
STAIDER
STAINED
STAINER
STALKED
STALKER
STALLED
STAMMER
STAMPED
STANCES
STANDEE
STANLEE
STANLEY
STAPLED
STAPLER
STAPLES
STARKER
STARLET
STARRED
STARTED
STARTER
STARVED
STARVES
STASHED
STASHES
STASSEN
STATUES
STEAMED
STEAMER
STEELED
STEELER
STEEPED
STEEPEN
STEEPER
STEERED
STEERER
STEIGER
STEINEM
STEINER
STEMMED
STENGEL
STEPHEN
STEPPED
STEPPER
STEPPES
STERNER
STETTED
STEUBEN
STICHES
STICKER
STIEGEL
STIFFED
STIFFEN
STIFFER
STIFLED
STIFLES
STILLED
STILLER
STILTED
STINGER
STINKER
STINTED
STIRRED
STIRRER
STOCKED
STOGIES
STOLLEN
STOLLER
STOMPED
STONIER
STOOGES
STOOKEY
STOOPED
STOPPED
STOPPER
STORIED
STORIES
STORMED
STOUTER
STPETER
STRAFED
STRAFES
STRAYED
STREWED
STREWER
STRIDER
STRIDES
STRIKER
STRIKES
STRIPED
STRIPER
STRIPES
STRIVED
STRIVEN
STRIVER
STRIVES
STROBES
STROKED
STROKES
STRUDEL
STUBBED
STUDDED
STUDIED
STUDIES
STUFFED
STUFFER
STUMPED
STUMPER
STUNNED
STUNNER
STUNTED
STURGES
STYMIED
STYMIES
SUBDUED
SUBDUER
SUBDUES
SUBTLER
SUCCEED
SUDSIER
SUGARED
SULKIER
SULKIES
SULLIED
SULLIES
SULUSEA
SUNDAES
SUNNIER
SUPPLER
SURLIER
SUTTNER
SUTURED
SUTURES
SVELTER
SWABBED
SWAGGER
SWAMPED
SWANKER
SWAPPED
SWAPPER
SWARMED
SWATHED
SWATHES
SWATTED
SWATTER
SWEARER
SWEATED
SWEATER
SWEEPER
SWEETEN
SWEETER
SWELLED
SWELTER
SWERVED
SWERVES
SWIFTER
SWIGGED
SWILLED
SWIMMER
SWINGER
SWIRLED
SWISHED
SWISHES
SWITZER
SWOLLEN
SWOONED
SWOOPED
SYNCHED
SYNCHES
SYNFUEL

S•••••E

SALABLE
SALTINE
SALVAGE
SANJOSE
SANTAFE
SAOTOME
SARALEE
SARDINE
SATIATE
SAUSAGE
SAVABLE
SCALENE
SCEPTRE
SCIENCE
SCOTTIE
SCOURGE
SCROOGE
SCRUPLE
SCUFFLE
SCUTTLE
SEAGATE
SEALANE
SEASIDE
SEATTLE
SECLUDE
SECRETE
SEEHERE
SELVAGE
SENSATE
SERIATE
SERRATE
SERVICE
SERVILE
SESSILE
SETLINE
SEVIGNE
SEVILLE
SHACKLE
SHAMBLE
SHAWNEE
SHEATHE
SHEILAE
SHELTIE
SHINGLE
SHUFFLE
SHUTEYE
SHUTTLE
SIAMESE
SILENCE
SINCERE
SINEDIE
SINKAGE
SISTINE
SITUATE
SIZABLE
SKIPOLE
SKITTLE
SKYBLUE
SKYDIVE
SKYLINE
SLOVENE
SMUGGLE
SNAFFLE
SNIFFLE
SNIGGLE
SNOCONE
SNUFFLE
SNUGGLE
SOCKEYE
SOIGNEE
SOLFEGE
SOLUBLE
SOMEONE
SORBATE
SOSUEME
SOTHERE
SOUFFLE
SOUTANE
SPACKLE
SPANGLE
SPARKLE
SPECKLE
SPECTRE
SPINDLE
SPLURGE
SPOKANE
SPONDEE
SPUMONE
SQUEEZE
STABILE
STANDEE
STANLEE
STARTLE
STATICE
STATURE
STATUTE
STEELIE
STEEPLE
STERILE
STIPPLE
STOOLIE
STORAGE
STRANGE
STRASSE
STRIATE
STROPHE
STUBBLE
STUMBLE
STYLIZE
STYRENE
SUBLIME
SUBSIDE

SUBSUME
SUCRASE
SUCROSE
SUFFICE
SUFFUSE
SULFATE
SULFIDE
SULFITE
SUNRISE
SUPPOSE
SUPREME
SURFACE
SURMISE
SURNAME
SURVIVE
SUSANNE
SUZANNE
SUZETTE
SWADDLE
SWEETIE
SWINDLE
SWIZZLE
SWOOSIE
SYNAPSE
SYRINGE
SYSTOLE

•SE••••

ASEPSIS
ASEPTIC
TSELIOT
TSETSES
USEABLE
USELESS

•S•E•••

ASCENDS
ASCENTS
ASCETIC
ASPECTS
ASPERSE
ASSEGAI
ASSENTS
ASSERTS
CSLEWIS
ESSENCE
ESSENES
ESTEEMS
ESTELLE
ESTEVEZ
OSCEOLA
OSTEOID
USHERED

•S••E••

ASHIEST
ASHLESS
ESCHEAT
ESCHEWS
ESTEEMS
ESTHETE
ISOHELS
ISOMERS
ISRAELI
ISSUERS
OSPREYS
OSTLERS
USELESS
USOPENS
USSTEEL
USURERS

•S•••E•

ASHAMED
ASPIRED
ASPIRER
ASPIRES
ASSAYED
ASSAYER
ASSIZES
ASSUMED
ASSUMES
ASSURED
ASSURES
ASUNDER
ESCAPED
ESCAPEE
ESCAPES
ESSAYED
ESSENES
ESTATES
ESTEVEZ
ISHMAEL
OSCINES
OSMOSED
OSMOSES
PSALMED
PSALTER
PSYCHED
PSYCHES
TSETSES
USHERED
USSTEEL
USURPED
USURPER

•S••••E

ASCRIBE
ASININE
ASKANCE
ASPERSE
ASSUAGE
ASTAIRE
ASTARTE
ASTRIDE
ESCAPEE
ESPOUSE
ESQUIRE
ESSENCE
ESTELLE
ESTHETE
ISOLATE
ISOTOPE
OSBORNE
OSSICLE
TSQUARE
USEABLE

••SE•••

ABSENCE
ABSENTS
ARSENAL
ARSENIC
ARSENIO
ASSEGAI
ASSENTS
ASSERTS
BASEHIT
BASEMAN
BASEMEN
BASENJI
BASEPAY
BESEECH
BESEEMS
BISECTS
CASELAW
CASERNS
DESERTS
DESERVE
DISEASE
DRSEUSS
EASEDIN
EASEDUP
EASEOFF
EASESIN
EASESUP
ESSENCE
ESSENES
GASEOUS
GISELLE
INSEAMS
INSECTS
INSERTS
LOSEOUT
LOSESIT
MISERLY
MOSELLE
MOSEYED
MUSETTE
MUSEUMS
NOSEBAG
NOSEEUM
NOSEGAY
NOSEJOB
NOSEOUT
OBSERVE
PESETAS
POSEURS
RESEALS
RESEATS
RESECTS
RESEEDS
RESELLS
RESENDS
RESENTS
RESERVE
ROSEATE
ROSEBUD
ROSELLE
ROSEOIL
ROSERED
ROSETTA
ROSETTE
UNSEALS
UNSEATS
UNSEWED
WISEDUP
WISEGUY
WISEMAN
WISEMEN
WISESUP

••S•E••

ANSWERS
AUSTERE
BASKETS
BASSETS
BASTERS
BESEECH
BESEEMS
BESIEGE
BESMEAR
BESPEAK
BOSKETS
BOSWELL
BUSHELS
BUSIEST
CASHEWS
CASTERS
CISTERN
COSSETS
DASHERS
DESCEND
DESCENT
DESSERT
DISCERN
DISPELS
DISSECT
DISSENT
DISTEND
DOSSERS
DUSTERS
EASIEST
EASTEND
EASTERN
EASTERS
EPSTEIN
FASTENS
FASTEST
FESTERS
FISHERS
FISHERY
FISHEYE
FOSTERS
GASJETS
GASKETS
GASSERS
GOSPELS
GOSSETT
GUSHERS
GUSSETS
HASBEEN
HASTENS
HISSERS
HOSIERS
HOSIERY
HOSTELS
HOSTESS
HUSKERS
HUSSEIN
INSPECT
INSTEAD
INSTEPS
ISSUERS
JASPERS
JESTERS
KISSERS
KOSHERS
LASHERS
LESSEES
LESSENS
LISTEES
LISTELS
LISTENS
LUSHEST
LUSTERS
MASHERS
MASKERS
MASSEUR
MASTERS
MASTERY
MISDEAL
MISDEED
MISHEAR
MISLEAD
MISREAD
MISTERS
MOSLEMS
MUSHERS
MUSKETS
MUSSELS
MUSTERS
MYSTERY
NASCENT
NESTEGG
NESTERS
NOSEEUM
NOSHERS
NOSIEST
NOSWEAT
OBSCENE
OUSTERS
OYSTERS
PASSELS
PASSERS
PASSEUL
PASTELS
PASTERN
PASTEUP
PASTEUR
PESTERS
POSHEST
POSSESS
POSSETS
POSTERN
POSTERS
RASHERS
RASHEST
RASPERS
RASTERS
RESEEDS
RESPECT
RESTERS
RISKERS
ROSTERS
ROSWELL
RUSHEES
RUSHERS
RUSSELL
RUSSETS
SASSERS
SESTETS
SISTERS
SOSUEME
SUSPECT
SUSPEND
SYSTEMS
TASSELS
TASTERS
TESSERA
TESTEES
TESTERS
TOSSERS
TUSKERS
ULSTERS
UNSPENT
UNSWEPT
UPSWEEP
UPSWEPT
USSTEEL
VASTEST
VESPERS
VESSELS
VESTEES
VISCERA
WASHERS
WASTERS
WESTEND
WESTERN
WISHERS
YESDEAR

••S••E•

APSIDES
ASSAYED
ASSAYER
ASSIZES
ASSUMED
ASSUMES
ASSURED
ASSURES
AUSSIES
BASEMEN
BASQUES
BESIDES
BESTMEN
BESTREW
BISQUES
BOSSIER
BUSBIES
BUSHIER
BUSHMEN
BUSTLED
BUSTLES
CASHIER
CASTLED
CASTLES
COSINES
COSTNER
CUSHIER
CUSSLER
DESIRED
DESIREE
DESIRES
DESKSET
DISCOED
DISOBEY
DISUSED
DOSAGES
DOSSIER
DUSKIER
DUSTIER
ENSILED
ENSILES
ENSURED
ENSURES
ESSAYED
ESSENES
FISCHER
FISHIER
FISHNET
FUSSIER
FUSTIER
GESSOES
GUSHIER
GUSSIED
GUSSIES
GUSTOES
HASBEEN
HASSLED
HASSLES
HASTIER
HOSTLER
HUSKIER
HUSKIES
HUSSIES
HUSTLED
HUSTLER
HUSTLES
INSIDER
INSIDES
INSOLES
INSURED
INSURES
JOSTLED
JOSTLER
JOSTLES
KESTREL
KISHKES
LASSIES
LASSOED
LASSOER
LASSOES
LESSEES
LISTEES
LUSTIER
LUSTRED
LUSTRES
MASHIES
MASQUES
MESSIER
MISCUED
MISCUES
MISDEED
MISDOES
MISSIES
MISSTEP
MISTIER
MISUSED
MISUSES
MOSEYED
MOSQUES
MOSSIER
MUSCLED
MUSCLES
MUSHIER
MUSTIER
MUSTSEE
NASTIER
NESTLED
NESTLER
NESTLES
PASSKEY
PASTIER
PESKIER
PESTLED
PESTLES
POSITED
POSTMEN
PUSHIER
RASPIER
RASSLED
RASSLES
RESALES
RESCUED
RESCUER
RESCUES
RESHOES
RESIDED
RESIDES
RESILED
RESILES
RESOLED
RESOLES
RESUMED
RESUMES
RISKIER
ROSERED
ROSSSEA
RUSHEES
RUSTIER
RUSTLED
RUSTLER
RUSTLES
SASSIER
SASSIES
SESAMES
SISSIES
TASTIER
TESTEES
TESTIER
TISANES
TISSUES
TUSSLED
TUSSLES
UNSATED
UNSCREW
UNSEWED
UPSWEEP
USSTEEL
VESTEES
VISAGES
VISITED
WASTREL
WISEMEN
WISPIER
ZESTIER

••S•••E

ABSENCE
ABSOLVE
ASSUAGE
ATSTAKE
AUSPICE
AUSTERE
BESIEGE
BESPOKE
BUSFARE
BUSLINE
CASCADE
CASTILE
COSTUME
DESERVE
DESIREE
DESPISE
DESPITE
DESTINE
DISABLE
DISEASE
DISLIKE
DISPOSE
DISPUTE
DISROBE
ENSLAVE
ENSNARE
ENSUITE
ERSKINE
ESSENCE
FASTONE
FESTIVE
FISHEYE
FISSILE
FISSURE
GESTATE
GESTURE
GISELLE
GUSTAVE
HOSPICE
HOSTAGE
HOSTILE
IFSTONE
INSCAPE
INSHAPE
INSPIRE
INSTATE
INSTORE
INSTYLE
JASMINE
JUSTICE
JUSTINE
LASAGNE
LASALLE
LISSOME
MASSAGE
MASSIVE
MCSWINE
MESSAGE
MISDATE
MISDONE
MISFILE
MISFIRE
MISMATE
MISNAME
MISRULE
MISSILE
MISSIVE
MISTAKE
MISTYPE
MOSELLE
MUSETTE
MUSTSEE
NASTASE
NESCAFE
OBSCENE
OBSCURE
OBSERVE
ONSHORE
ONSTAGE
OSSICLE
PASSAGE
PASSIVE
PASTDUE
PASTIME
PASTURE
PISCINE
PISMIRE
PISTOLE
POSTAGE
POSTURE
RESCALE
RESERVE
RESIDUE
RESOLVE
RESPIRE
RESPITE
RESTAGE
RESTATE
RESTIVE
RESTORE
RESTYLE
RESURGE
RISIBLE
RISSOLE
ROSALIE
ROSANNE
ROSEATE
ROSELLE
ROSETTE
RUSHDIE
SESSILE
SISTINE
SOSUEME
SUSANNE
SYSTOLE
TOSCALE
TOSPARE
UPSCALE
UPSTAGE
UPSTATE
UPSURGE
VESTIGE
VESTURE
VISIBLE
WASTAGE

•••SE••

ABUSERS
ANISEED
BASSETS
BERSERK
BOXSEAT
CANSECO
CARSEAT
CATSEYE
CENSERS
CHASERS
CHISELS
CLOSEIN
CLOSELY
CLOSEST
CLOSETS
CLOSEUP
CONSENT
CORSETS
COSSETS
DAMSELS
DANSEUR
DENSELY
DENSEST
DESSERT
DIESELS
DISSECT
DISSENT
DORSETT
DOSSERS
DOWSERS
ELYSEES
ERASERS
FALSELY
FALSEST
FURSEAL
GASSERS
GEYSERS
GINSENG
GODSEND
GOSSETT
GUSSETS
HAWSERS
HAYSEED
HERSELF
HIMSELF
HISSERS
HOTSEAT
HUSSEIN
JERSEYS
KAISERS
KISSERS
LEASERS
LESSEES
LESSENS
LINSEED
LOOSELY
LOOSENS
LOOSEST
LOUSEUP
MASSEUR
MORSELS
MOUSERS
MUSSELS
NONSELF
NURSERS
NURSERY
OFFSETS
ONESELF
OURSELF
OUTSELL
OUTSETS
PARSECS
PARSEES
PARSERS
PASSELS
PASSERS
PASSEUL
PENSEES
PERSEUS
PHASEIN
PHASERS
PORSENA
POSSESS
POSSETS
PRESELL
PRESENT
PRESETS
PROSERS
PURSERS
RAISERS
RAISEUP
RUSSELL
RUSSETS
SASSERS
SUBSETS
SUNSETS
TASSELS
TEASELS
TEASERS
TEASETS
TENSELY
TENSEST
TENSEUP
TERSELY
TERSEST
TESSERA
THESEUS
THYSELF
TINSELS
TOSSERS
TRISECT
VESSELS
WEASELS
WORSENS

•••S•E•

ABASHED
ABASHES
ABYSSES
AMASSED
AMASSES
ANISEED
ANTSIER
AUSSIES
BANSHEE
BATSMEN
BIASSED
BLASTED
BLASTER
BLESSED
BLESSES
BLISTER
BLUSHED
BLUSHER
BLUSHES
BLUSTER
BOASTED
BOASTER
BOBSLED
BOLSTER
BOOSLER
BOOSTED
BOOSTER
BOSSIER
BOXSTEP
BRASHER
BRASSES
BRISKER
BRISKET
BRUSHED
BRUSHES
CHASSES
CHASTEN
CHASTER
CHESTER
CLASHED
CLASHES
CLASPED
CLASSED
CLASSES
CLUSTER
COASTED
COASTER
CRASHED
CRASHES
CRASSER
CRESSES
CRESTED
CRISPED
CRISPER
CROSIER
CROSSED
CROSSER
CROSSES
CRUSHED
CRUSHER
CRUSHES
CRUSTED
CUSSLER
DAISIES
DOGSLED
DOSSIER
DRESDEN
DRESSED
DRESSER
DRESSES
EDASNER
EGESTED
ELYSEES
ENISLED
ENISLES
EXISTED
FEASTED
FLASHED
FLASHER
FLASHES
FLESHED
FLESHES
FLOSSED
FLOSSES
FLUSHED
FLUSHES
FLUSTER
FOCSLES
FOISTED
FORSTER
FRASIER
FRESHEN
FRESHER
FRESHET
FRISBEE
FRISKED
FROSTED
FUSSIER
GADSDEN
GAGSTER
GESSOES
GETSSET
GHOSTED
GIPSIES
GLASSED
GLASSES
GLISTEN
GLOSSED
GLOSSES
GNASHED
GNASHES
GRASPED
GRASSED
GRASSES
GROSSED
GROSSER
GROSSES
GUESSED
GUESSER
GUESSES
GUESTED
GUSSIED
GUSSIES
GUTSIER
GYPSIES
HAMSTER
HARSHEN
HARSHER
HASSLED
HASSLES
HAYSEED
HEISTED
HEMSLEY
HERSHEY
HIPSTER
HOISTED
HOLSTER
HOOSIER
HORSIER
HUSSIES
INASTEW
JANSSEN
JOISTED
JOUSTED
JOUSTER
KAISHEK
KINSMEN
KNESSET
KNISHES
LAISSEZ
LASSIES
LASSOED
LASSOER
LASSOES
LEASHED
LEASHES
LEISTER
LESSEES
LETSSEE
LINSEED
LOBSTER
LOESSER
LOESSES
LOUSIER
MARSHES
MEASLES
MEISSEN
MESSIER
MISSIES
MISSTEP
MOBSTER
MOISTEN
MOISTER
MONSTER
MOSSIER

MOUSIER
MOUSSED
MOUSSES
NEWSIER
NEWSMEN
NOISIER
ODYSSEY
OLDSTER
ONESTEP
ORESTES
OUTSTEP
PAISLEY
PANSIES
PARSEES
PARSLEY
PASSKEY
PATSIES
PENSEES
PIASTER
PILSNER
PLASHED
PLASHES
PLASTER
PLUSHER
PLUSHES
PLUSSES
PRESLEY
PRESSED
PRESSER
PRESSES
PROSIER
PROSPER
PUNSTER
PURSUED
PURSUER
PURSUES
QUASHED
QUASHES
QUESTED
RASSLED
RASSLES
ROASTED
ROASTER
ROISTER
ROOSTED
ROOSTER
ROSSSEA
ROUSTED
SASSIER
SASSIES
SEESRED
SHUSHED
SHUSHES
SHYSTER
SISSIES
SKOSHES
SLASHED
SLASHER
SLASHES
SLOSHED
SLOSHES
SLUSHES
SMASHED
SMASHER
SMASHES
STASHED
STASHES
STASSEN
SUDSIER
SWISHED
SWISHES
TANSIES
TAPSTER
TARSIER
TIPSIER
TIPSTER
TISSUES
TOASTED
TOASTER
TOUSLED
TOUSLES
TRASHED
TRASHES
TRESSES
TRUSSED
TRUSSES
TRUSTED
TRUSTEE
TRYSTED
TRYSTER
TUSSLED
TUSSLES
TWISTED
TWISTER
TWOSTEP
ULYSSES
UNASKED
WAISTED
WEBSTER
WHISKED
WHISKER
WHISKEY
WHISPER
WOOSTER
WORSTED
WRESTED

•••S••E

ABUSIVE
APOSTLE
ARCSINE
ARISTAE
ATISSUE
AWESOME
BANSHEE
BEASTIE
BEDSIDE
BRASSIE
BRISTLE
BRUSQUE
CAPSIZE
CAPSULE
CATSEYE
CENSURE
CLOSURE
CONSOLE
CONSUME
CORSAGE
CRUSADE
CUISINE
CURSIVE
ELUSIVE
EPISODE
EPISTLE
ERASURE
EROSIVE
EVASIVE
EYESORE
FISSILE
FISSURE
FORSAKE
FORSALE
FORSURE
FRISBEE
FULSOME
GLOSSAE
GOESAPE
GRISTLE
GUMSHOE
GYMSHOE
HIRSUTE
IRKSOME
KIRSTIE
LEISURE
LETSSEE
LISSOME
MASSAGE
MASSIVE
MEASURE
MESSAGE
MIDSIZE
MISSILE
MISSIVE
NETSUKE
NOISOME
NOTSURE
OFFSIDE
OFFSITE
OUTSIDE
OUTSIZE
PASSAGE
PASSIVE
PENSIVE
PIASTRE
PLOSIVE
PORSCHE
PRESAGE
PRESALE
PRESIDE
PRESUME
PULSATE
REISSUE
RISSOLE
SAUSAGE
SEASIDE
SENSATE
SESSILE
SUBSIDE
SUBSUME
TAGSALE
TENSILE
TENSIVE
THISTLE
TOESHOE
TONSURE
TOPSIDE
TRESTLE
TRUSTEE
TWOSOME
WAYSIDE
WEBSITE
WHISTLE
WINSOME
WRESTLE

••••SE•

ABYSSES
ACCUSED
ACCUSER
ACCUSES
ADVISED
ADVISER
ADVISES
ALIASES
ALUNSER
AMASSED
AMASSES
APHESES
APPOSED
APPOSES
ARALSEA
AROUSED
AROUSES
ARRASES
ARRISES
ATLASES
AVULSED
AVULSES
BEMUSED
BEMUSES
BENTSEN
BERNSEN
BIASSED
BLESSED
BLESSES
BLOUSED
BLOUSES
BOLUSES
BONUSES
BRAISED
BRAISES
BRASSES
BROWSED
BROWSER
BROWSES
BRUISED
BRUISER
BRUISES
CAMISES
CAYUSES
CHAISES
CHASSES
CHEESES
CHELSEA
CHOOSER
CHOOSES
CLASSED
CLASSES
CLAUSES
COARSEN
COARSER
COUNSEL
COURSED
COURSER
COURSES
CRASSER
CREASED
CREASES
CRESSES
CROSSED
CROSSER
CROSSES
CRUISED
CRUISER
CRUISES
CURTSEY
DATASET
DEADSEA
DEADSET
DEBASED
DEBASES
DEEPSEA
DEEPSET
DEFUSED
DEFUSES
DEMISED
DEMISES
DEMPSEY
DEPOSED
DEPOSER
DEPOSES
DESKSET
DEVISED
DEVISES
DINESEN
DISUSED
DREISER
DRESSED
DRESSER
DRESSES
DROWSED
DROWSES
ECDYSES
EFFUSED
EFFUSES
ELAPSED
ELAPSES
EMERSED
ENCASED
ENCASES
ENDUSER
EVULSED
EVULSES
EXCISED
EXCISES
EXCUSED
EXCUSES
EXPOSED
EXPOSES
FICUSES
FLENSED
FLENSES
FLOSSED
FLOSSES
FOCUSED
FOCUSES
FORESEE
FRAISES
GENESEE
GENESES
GETSSET
GLASSED
GLASSES
GLOSSED
GLOSSES
GRASSED
GRASSES
GREASED
GREASER
GREASES
GROSSED
GROSSER
GROSSES
GROUSED
GROUSER
GROUSES
GUESSED
GUESSER
GUESSES
HANDSET
HARDSET
HEADSET
HOARSEN
HOARSER
HOLYSEE
ILLUSED
ILLUSES
IMPOSED
IMPOSES
INCISED
INCISES
INFUSED
INFUSES
JANSSEN
KARASEA
KNESSET
LAISSEZ
LETSSEE
LIAISED
LIAISES
LINDSEY
LOESSER
LOESSES
LOOKSEE
LORISES
LOTUSES
MALMSEY
MEIOSES
MEISSEN
MINDSET
MINUSES
MISUSED
MISUSES
MITOSES
MOONSET
MOUSSED
MOUSSES
MUSTSEE
NAILSET
NEMESES
NEXUSES
NIELSEN
NONUSER
OBTUSER
ODYSSEY
OPENSEA
OPPOSED
OPPOSER
OPPOSES
OSMOSED
OSMOSES
OVERSEA
OVERSEE
PAULSEN
PERUSED
PERUSER
PERUSES
PHRASED
PHRASES
PLEASED
PLEASER
PLEASES
PLUSSES
PRAISED
PRAISER
PRAISES
PRESSED
PRESSER
PRESSES
QUONSET
RAMESES
REBUSES
RECUSED
RECUSES
REFUSED
REFUSER
REFUSES
REPOSED
REPOSES
REVISED
REVISER
REVISES
ROSSSEA
SAMISEN
SINUSES
SPARSER
SPENSER
SPOUSES
STASSEN
SULUSEA
TALUSES
TRESSES
TROUSER
TRUSSED
TRUSSES
TSETSES
TYPESET
ULYSSES
UNCASED
UNCASES
UNWISER
UPRISEN
UPRISES
VALISES
VIRUSES
WELLSET
WOOLSEY

••••S•E

ARTISTE
ATISSUE
AUGUSTE
BATISTE
BRASSIE
CELESTE
DEHISCE
DEMESNE
ENMASSE
FINESSE
FOOTSIE
FORESEE
GENESEE
GLOSSAE
HOLYSEE
IMPASSE
INHASTE
LACOSTE
LETSSEE
LOOKSEE
MAJESTE
MATISSE
MEDUSAE
MODISTE
MUSTSEE
OVERSEE
PELISSE
REBASTE
REISSUE
REPASTE
RIPOSTE
STRASSE
SWOOSIE
TOOTSIE
TRIESTE
WOEISME

•••••SE

ACEROSE
ADIPOSE
ADVERSE
AIRBASE
AMBROSE
AMYLASE
ANALYSE
APPEASE
APPRISE
ASPERSE
AXLROSE
BECAUSE
BERNESE
BURMESE
BYANOSE
CABOOSE
CAROUSE
CHEMISE
CHINESE
CLEANSE
COCHISE
COMPOSE
CONCISE
CONFUSE
CONTUSE
DEFENSE
DELUISE
DESPISE
DIFFUSE
DIOCESE
DISEASE
DISPOSE
DIVERSE
DONJOSE
ECLIPSE
EGGCASE
ELLIPSE
ENCLOSE
ENDORSE
ENDWISE
ENMASSE
ENTHUSE
ESPOUSE
EXPANSE
EXPENSE
FINESSE
GENOESE
GLIMPSE
GLUCOSE
HELOISE
IMMENSE
IMMERSE
IMPASSE
IMPULSE
INCENSE
INCLOSE
INHOUSE
INPHASE
INTENSE
INTERSE
INVERSE
JACCUSE
LACTASE
LACTOSE
LAVALSE
LICENSE
LOWRISE
MALAISE
MALTESE
MALTOSE
MATISSE
MELROSE
MIDRISE
MORTISE
NASTASE
OBVERSE
OFFBASE
OFFENSE
OPEROSE
OVERUSE
OXIDASE
PAPOOSE
PELISSE
PRECISE
PREMISE
PROFUSE
PROMISE
PROPOSE
PUGNOSE
PURPOSE
RECHOSE
RECLUSE
REDROSE
RELAPSE
RELEASE
REMORSE
REPRISE
REPULSE
RERAISE
RERINSE
REVERSE
SANJOSE
SIAMESE
STRASSE
SUCRASE
SUCROSE
SUFFUSE
SUNRISE
SUPPOSE
SURMISE
SYNAPSE
TEAROSE
TRAIPSE
TWOBASE
UNCLOSE
UNHORSE
UNLOOSE
UPCLOSE
UPRAISE
VAMOOSE
VERBOSE

S•F••••

SAFARIS
SAFFRON
SIFTERS
SIFTING
SOFABED
SOFFITS
SOFTENS
SOFTEST
SOFTIES
SOFTTOP
SUFFERS
SUFFICE
SUFFOLK
SUFFUSE

S••F•••

SAFFRON
SANFORD
SAWFISH
SCOFFED
SCOFFER
SCUFFED
SCUFFLE
SEAFANS
SEAFOOD
SELFISH
SERFDOM
SHAFFER
SHAFTED
SHIFTED
SHOFARS
SHUFFLE
SIXFOLD
SNAFFLE
SNAFUED
SNIFFAT
SNIFFED
SNIFFER
SNIFFLE
SNIFTER
SNUFFED
SNUFFER
SNUFFLE
SOFFITS
SOLFEGE
SOUFFLE
STAFFED
STAFFER
STIFFED
STIFFEN
STIFFER
STIFFLY
STIFLED
STIFLES
STUFFED
STUFFER
SUFFERS
SUFFICE
SUFFOLK
SUFFUSE
SULFATE
SULFIDE
SULFITE
SUNFISH
SURFACE
SURFEIT
SURFERS
SURFING
SWIFTER
SWIFTLY
SYNFUEL

S•••F••

SACKFUL
SANDFLY
SCARFED
SCOFFED
SCOFFER
SCRUFFS
SCRUFFY
SCUFFED
SCUFFLE
SEESFIT
SENDFOR
SENTFOR
SHAFFER
SHOOFLY
SHOTFOR
SHRIFTS
SHUFFLE
SKILFUL
SNAFFLE
SNIFFAT
SNIFFED
SNIFFER
SNIFFLE
SNUFFED
SNUFFER
SNUFFLE
SOUFFLE
SOULFUL
SPOOFED
SPOOFER
STAFFED
STAFFER
STIFFED
STIFFEN
STIFFER
STIFFLY
STIRFRY
STRAFED
STRAFES
STUFFED
STUFFER

S••••F•

SALSIFY
SANTAFE
SATISFY
SCARIFY
SCRUFFS
SCRUFFY
SEALOFF
SEESOFF
SELLOFF
SENDOFF
SENTOFF
SETSOFF
SHERIFF
SHOWOFF
SHUTOFF
SIGNIFY
SIGNOFF
SKILIFT
SOLDOFF
SPECIFY
SPINOFF
SPUNOFF
STOPOFF
STUPEFY

S•••••F

SEALOFF
SEESOFF
SELLOFF
SENDOFF
SENTOFF
SETSOFF
SHADOOF
SHERIFF
SHEWOLF
SHORTOF
SHOWOFF
SHUTOFF
SIGNOFF
SOLDOFF
SPEAKOF
SPINOFF
SPOKEOF
SPUNOFF
STOPOFF
SUNROOF

•SF••••

ASFARAS

•S•F•••

ASHFORD
ASOFNOW

•S••F••

ASKSFOR
OSSIFIC

••SF•••

BUSFARE
MISFILE
MISFIRE
MISFITS

••S•F••

BASHFUL
FISHFRY
FISTFUL
INSOFAR
LUSTFUL
OSSIFIC
PASSFOR
RESTFUL
WISHFUL
WISTFUL
ZESTFUL

••S••F•

CASTOFF
DASHOFF
DISTAFF
DUSTOFF
EASEOFF
JUSTIFY
KISSOFF
MASSIFS
MASTIFF
MUSTAFA
MYSTIFY
NESCAFE
PASSOFF
PUSHOFF
RUSHOFF
TESTIFY
TOSSOFF
WASHOFF

••S•••F

CASTOFF
DASHOFF
DISTAFF
DUSTOFF
EASEOFF
KISSOFF
MASTIFF
PASSOFF
PUSHOFF
RUSHOFF
TOSSOFF
WASHOFF

•••SF••

ASKSFOR
GOESFOR
GUNSFOR
LAYSFOR
LETSFLY
PASSFOR
PAYSFOR
SEESFIT
THUSFAR

•••S•F•

BEGSOFF
BUGSOFF
BUYSOFF
CUTSOFF
DIESOFF
FALSIFY
FOBSOFF
GETSOFF
GOESOFF
HOPSOFF
KISSOFF
LAYSOFF
LETSOFF
LOGSOFF
MASSIFS
NODSOFF
PASSOFF
PAYSOFF
POPSOFF
PUTSOFF
RIPSOFF
RUNSOFF
SALSIFY
SEESOFF
SETSOFF
TEESOFF
TIPSOFF
TOPSOFF
TOSSOFF
VERSIFY

•••S••F

BEGSOFF
BUGSOFF
BUYSOFF
CUTSOFF
DIESOFF
FOBSOFF
GETSOFF
GOESOFF
HERSELF
HIMSELF
HOPSOFF
KISSOFF
LAYSOFF
LETSOFF
LOGSOFF
NETSURF
NODSOFF
NONSELF
ONESELF
OURSELF
PASSOFF
PAYSOFF
POPSOFF
PUTSOFF
RIPSOFF
RUNSOFF
SEESOFF
SETSOFF
TEESOFF
THYSELF
TIPSOFF
TOPSOFF
TOSSOFF

••••SF•

SATISFY

••••S•F

HEARSOF

S•G••••

SAGGIER
SAGGING
SAGINAW
SAGUARO
SEGMENT
SEGOVIA
SIGHERS
SIGHING
SIGHTED
SIGHTLY
SIGMUND
SIGNALS
SIGNEES
SIGNERS
SIGNETS
SIGNIFY
SIGNING

SIGNOFF
SIGNOUT
SIGNSIN
SIGNSON
SIGNSUP
SOGGIER
SOGGILY
SUGARED
SUGGEST

S••G•••
SAGGIER
SAGGING
SANGOUT
SANGRIA
SARGENT
SEAGATE
SEAGIRT
SEAGRAM
SEAGULL
SHAGGED
SHOGUNS
SINGERS
SINGING
SINGLED
SINGLES
SINGOUT
SINGSTO
SIXGUNS
SLIGHTS
SLOGANS
SLOGGED
SLUGGED
SLUGGER
SMUGGER
SMUGGLE
SNAGGED
SNIGGER
SNIGGLE
SNIGLET
SNUGGER
SNUGGLE
SOGGIER
SOGGILY
SOIGNEE
SORGHUM
SOUGHED
SPIGOTS
STAGERS
STAGGED
STAGGER
STAGIER
STAGILY
STAGING
STIGMAS
STOGIES
STYGIAN
SUGGEST
SUNGODS
SURGEON
SURGERY
SURGING
SWAGGER
SWIGGED
SYNGMAN

S•••G••
SAVAGED
SAVAGER
SAVAGES
SCRAGGY
SENEGAL
SEVIGNE
SHAGGED
SHANGRI
SHINGLE
SHOTGUN
SLEDGES
SLEIGHS
SLEIGHT
SLINGER
SLOEGIN
SLOGGED
SLOUGHS
SLUDGES
SLUGGED
SLUGGER
SMIDGEN
SMUDGED
SMUDGES
SMUGGER
SMUGGLE
SNAGGED
SNIGGER
SNIGGLE
SNUGGER
SNUGGLE
SPANGLE
SPANGLY
SPARGED
SPARGES
SPIEGEL
SPONGED
SPONGER
SPONGES
STAGGED
STAGGER
STEIGER
STENGEL
STIEGEL
STINGER
STOOGES
STOPGAP
STUNGUN
STURGES
SWAGGER
SWIGGED
SWINGBY
SWINGER

S••••G•
SALVAGE
SAPSAGO
SARONGS
SAUSAGE
SAVINGS
SAWLOGS
SAYINGS
SCOURGE
SCRAGGY
SCROOGE
SEABAGS
SEADOGS
SEALEGS
SELVAGE
SIDINGS
SINKAGE
SIZINGS
SKYHIGH
SOLFEGE
SOWBUGS
SPLURGE
SPRINGS
SPRINGY
STALAGS
STORAGE
STRANGE
STRINGS
STRINGY
SUNDOGS
SYNERGY
SYRINGA
SYRINGE

S•••••G
SACKING
SAGGING
SAILING
SALTING
SALVING
SAMSUNG
SANDBAG
SANDHOG
SANDING
SAPLING
SAPPING
SASSING
SCALING
SCARING
SCOPING
SCORING
SEABORG
SEALING
SEAMING
SEARING
SEASLUG
SEATING
SEEDING
SEEKING
SEEMING
SEEPING
SEINING
SEIZING
SELLING
SENDING
SENSING
SERLING
SERVING
SETTING
SHADING
SHAKING
SHAMING
SHAPING
SHARING
SHAVING
SHEBANG
SHINDIG
SHINING
SHOEING
SHOOING
SHORING
SHOVING
SHOWDOG
SHOWING
SIBLING
SICCING
SIDLING
SIFTING
SIGHING
SIGNING
SILOING
SILTING
SINGING
SINKING
SIPPING
SITTING
SKATING
SKEWING
SLAKING
SLATING
SLAVING
SLEDDOG
SLICING
SLIDING
SLOPING
SLOWING
SMILING
SMITING
SMOKING
SNAKING
SNARING
SNIPING
SNORING
SNOWING
SOAKING
SOAPING
SOARING
SOBBING
SOCKING
SODDING
SOILING
SOLOING
SOLVING
SOPPING
SORTING
SOURING
SPACING
SPADING
SPARING
SPAYING
SPEWING
SPICING
SPIKING
SPITING
SPOKING
SPUMING
STAGING
STAKING
STARING
STATING
STAVING
STAYING
STEWING
STOKING
STONING
STORING
STOWING
STYLING
SUBBING
SUCKING
SUDSING
SUITING
SULKING
SUMMING
SUNNING
SUPPING
SURFING
SURGING
SUSSING
SWAYING
SWIPING
SYNCING

•S•G•••
ISOGONS

•S••G••
ASSEGAI
ASSIGNS
TSONGAS
USINGUP

•S•••G•
ASSUAGE

•S••••G
ESPYING
ISSUING

••SG•••
DISGUST

••S•G••
ASSEGAI
ASSIGNS
COSIGNS
DESIGNS
DOSAGES
ENSIGNS
INSIGHT
KOSYGIN
LASAGNA
LASAGNE
NOSEGAY
ONSIGHT
RESIGNS
VISAGES
WISEGUY

••S••G•
ASSUAGE
BESIEGE
CASINGS
GASBAGS
HOSTAGE
MASSAGE
MESSAGE
NESTEGG
ONSTAGE
PASSAGE
POSTAGE
RESINGS
RESTAGE
RESURGE
RISINGS
UNSNAGS
UPSTAGE
UPSURGE
VESTIGE
WASTAGE

••S•••G
BASHING
BASKING
BASTING
BESTING
BOSSING
BUSHHOG
BUSHING
BUSHPIG
BUSSING
BUSTING
BUSYING
CASHING
CASTING
COSTING
CUSSING
DASHING
DISHING
DISHRAG
DUSTING
ENSUING
FASTING
FISHING
FUSSING
GASHING
GASPING
GOSLING
GUSHING
GUSTING
HASHING
HASTING
HISSING
HOSTING
HUSHING
HUSKING
ISSUING
JESTING
JOSHING
KISSING
LASHING
LASTING
LESSING
LISPING
LISTING
LUSTING
MASHING
MASKING
MASSING
MESHING
MESSING
MISSING
MISTING
MOSSING
MUSHING
MUSSING
MUSTANG
NESTEGG
NESTING
NOSEBAG
NOSHING
OUSTING
PASSING
PASTING
POSTING
PUSHING
RASPING
RESTING
RISKING
RUSHING
RUSTING
SASSING
SUSSING
TASKING
TASTING
TESTING
TOSSING
UPSWING
VESTING
WASHING
WASHRAG
WASTING
WISHING
WISPING
WYSIWYG
YESSING

•••SG••
GLASGOW

•••S•G•
AGESAGO
CONSIGN
CORSAGE
HEXSIGN
MASSAGE
MESSAGE
PASSAGE
PRESAGE
SAPSAGO
SAUSAGE

•••S••G
ABASING
ABUSING
AMUSING
ARISING
ARTSONG
BIASING
BOSSING
BUSSING
CAUSING
CEASING
CENSING
CHASING
CLOSING
CURSING
CUSSING
DOUSING
DOWSING
ERASING
FUSSING
GINSENG
GOOSING
HISSING
HORSING
HOUSING
KISSING
LANSING
LAPSING
LEASING
LESSING
LOOSING
LOUSING
MASSING
MESSING
MISSING
MOSSING
MOUSING
MUSSING
NOISING
NOOSING
NURSING
PARSING
PASSING
PAUSING
PHASING
POISING
PROSING
PULSING
PURSING
RAISING
RINSING
ROUSING
SAMSUNG
SASSING
SEASLUG
SENSING
SUDSING
SUSSING
TEASING
TENSING
TOSSING
YESSING

SH•••••
SHACKLE
SHADIER
SHADILY
SHADING
SHADOOF
SHADOWS
SHADOWY
SHAFFER
SHAFTED
SHAGGED
SHAHDOM
SHAKERS
SHAKEUP
SHAKIER
SHAKILY
SHAKING
SHAKOES
SHALALA
SHALLOT
SHALLOW
SHALOMS
SHAMANS
SHAMBLE
SHAMING
SHAMMED
SHAMPOO
SHANANA
SHANGRI
SHANKAR
SHANKED
SHANNON
SHANTER
SHAPELY
SHAPERS
SHAPEUP
SHAPING
SHAPIRO
SHAREIN
SHARERS
SHARING
SHARKEY
SHARPED
SHARPEI
SHARPEN
SHARPER
SHARPLY
SHASTRI
SHATNER
SHATTER
SHAVERS
SHAVING
SHAWNEE
SHAWWAL
SHEARED
SHEARER
SHEATHE
SHEATHS
SHEAVED
SHEAVES
SHEBANG
SHECRAB
SHEERED
SHEERER
SHEERLY
SHEETED
SHEIKHS
SHEILAE
SHEILAH
SHEILAS
SHEKELS
SHELDON
SHELLAC
SHELLED
SHELLER
SHELLEY
SHELTER
SHELTIE
SHELTON
SHELVED
SHELVES
SHEPARD
SHERBET
SHERIFF
SHERMAN
SHERPAS
SHERWIN
SHEWOLF
SHIATSU
SHIELDS
SHIFTED
SHIHTZU
SHIITES
SHILLED
SHIMMER
SHINDIG
SHINERS
SHINGLE
SHINIER
SHINING
SHINNED
SHIPMAN
SHIPMEN
SHIPOUT
SHIPPED
SHIPPER
SHIRKED
SHIRKER
SHIRLEY
SHIRRED
SHIVERS
SHOCKED
SHOCKER
SHODDEN
SHOEBOX
SHOEING
SHOFARS
SHOGUNS
SHOOFLY
SHOOING
SHOOINS
SHOOKUP
SHOOTAT
SHOOTER
SHOOTUP
SHOPPED
SHOPPER
SHOPPES
SHORING
SHORTED
SHORTEN
SHORTER
SHORTLY
SHORTOF
SHOTFOR
SHOTGUN
SHOTPUT
SHOUTED
SHOUTER
SHOVELS
SHOVERS
SHOVING
SHOWBIZ
SHOWDOG
SHOWERS
SHOWERY
SHOWIER
SHOWILY
SHOWING
SHOWMAN
SHOWMEN
SHOWNIN
SHOWOFF
SHOWSIN
SHOWSUP
SHRIEKS
SHRIFTS
SHRIKES
SHRILLS
SHRILLY
SHRIMPS
SHRINER
SHRINES
SHRINKS
SHRIVEL
SHRIVER
SHRIVES
SHROUDS
SHRUBBY
SHTICKS
SHUBERT
SHUCKED
SHUCKER
SHUDDER
SHUFFLE
SHUNNED
SHUNTED
SHUSHED
SHUSHES
SHUTEYE
SHUTOFF
SHUTOUT
SHUTSIN
SHUTSUP
SHUTTER
SHUTTLE
SHYLOCK
SHYNESS
SHYSTER

S•H••••
SAHARAN
SCHATZI
SCHEMAS
SCHEMED
SCHEMER
SCHEMES
SCHERZI
SCHERZO
SCHIRRA
SCHISMS
SCHLEPP
SCHLEPS
SCHLOCK
SCHMEER
SCHMIDT
SCHMOES
SCHMOOS
SCHNAPS
SCHOLAR
SCHOOLS
SCHWINN
SPHERES

S••H•••
SACHEMS
SACHETS
SAMHILL
SASHAYS
SASHIMI
SAXHORN
SEEHERE
SHAHDOM
SHIHTZU
SICHUAN
SIGHERS
SIGHING
SIGHTED
SIGHTLY
SIKHISM
SIPHONS
SKYHIGH
SKYHOOK
SOPHISM
SOPHIST
SOTHERE
SOTHERN
SUBHEAD
SWAHILI

S•••H••
SALCHOW
SANDHOG
SATCHEL
SATCHMO
SAYWHEN
SCATHED
SCATHES
SCYTHED
SCYTHES
SEETHED
SEETHES
SEICHES
SHUSHED
SHUSHES
SILKHAT
SIOBHAN
SKOSHES
SLASHED
SLASHER
SLASHES
SLATHER
SLIGHTS
SLITHER
SLOSHED
SLOSHES
SLUSHES
SMASHED
SMASHER
SMASHES
SMASHUP
SMOTHER
SOMEHOW
SOOTHED
SOOTHER
SOOTHES
SORGHUM
SOUGHED
SOUTHEY
STASHED
STASHES
STEPHEN
STICHES
STJOHNS
SULPHUR
SWATHED
SWATHES
SWISHED
SWISHES
SYNCHED
SYNCHES

S••••H•
SERAPHS
SHEATHE
SHEATHS
SHEIKHS
SKETCHY
SLEIGHS
SLEIGHT
SLEUTHS
SLOUCHY
SLOUGHS
SMOOTHS
SPLASHY
SQUISHY
STARCHY
STROPHE
SWARTHY

S•••••H
SABBATH
SAWFISH
SCRATCH
SCREECH
SCRUNCH
SELFISH
SEVENTH
SHEILAH
SKYHIGH
SLAVISH
SOPWITH
SOURISH
SPANISH
SPINACH
SPLOTCH
SQUELCH
SQUINCH
STAUNCH
STEALTH
STOMACH
STRETCH
STYLISH
SUNBATH
SUNFISH
SWEDISH

•SH••••
ASHAMED
ASHANTI
ASHBURY
ASHCANS
ASHFORD
ASHIEST
ASHLAND
ASHLARS
ASHLESS
ASHRAMS
ASHTRAY
ISHMAEL
OSHKOSH
TSHIRTS
USHERED

•S•H•••
ASPHALT
ESCHEAT
ESCHEWS
ESTHETE
ISOHELS
ISTHMUS

•S••H••
PSYCHED
PSYCHES
PSYCHIC
PSYCHUP
USOSHOW

•S••••H
OSHKOSH
OSTRICH

••SH•••
BASHFUL
BASHING
BISHOPS
BUSHELS
BUSHHOG
BUSHIDO
BUSHIER
BUSHING
BUSHMAN
BUSHMEN
BUSHPIG
CASHBAR
CASHBOX
CASHCOW
CASHEWS
CASHIER
CASHING
CASHOUT
CUSHAWS
CUSHIER
CUSHION
DASHERS
DASHIKI
DASHING
DASHOFF
DISHING
DISHOUT
DISHPAN
DISHRAG
FASHION
FISHERS
FISHERY
FISHEYE
FISHFRY
FISHIER
FISHILY
FISHING
FISHNET
FISHOUT
GASHING
GOSHAWK
GUSHERS
GUSHIER
GUSHING
HASHING
HESHVAN
HUSHABY
HUSHING
INSHAPE
INSHORT
JOSHING
KASHMIR
KISHKES
KOSHERS
LASHERS
LASHING
LASHUPS
LUSHEST
MASHERS
MASHIES
MASHING
MESHING
MISHAPS
MISHEAR
MISHITS
MUSHERS
MUSHIER
MUSHILY
MUSHING
NOSHERS

NOSHING
NOSHOWS
ONSHORE
POSHEST
PUSHIER
PUSHILY
PUSHING
PUSHKIN
PUSHOFF
PUSHPIN
PUSHUPS
RASHERS
RASHEST
RESHIPS
RESHOES
RESHOOT
RUSHDIE
RUSHEES
RUSHERS
RUSHING
RUSHOFF
SASHAYS
SASHIMI
TOSHIBA
TVSHOWS
UNSHORN
UPSHOTS
WASHERS
WASHING
WASHOFF
WASHOUT
WASHRAG
WASHTUB
WISHERS
WISHFUL
WISHING
YASHMAK
YESHIVA

••S•H••

BASEHIT
BUSHHOG
FISCHER
GASOHOL
PASCHAL
POSTHOC

••S••H•

INSIGHT
LESOTHO
ONSIGHT

••S•••H

ANSPACH
BESEECH
BISMUTH
IPSWICH
MESSIAH
MISSISH
WASATCH
WASPISH

•••SH••

ABASHED
ABASHES
AIRSHIP
AIRSHOW
APISHLY
BANSHEE
BIGSHOT
BLUSHED
BLUSHER
BLUSHES
BOLSHOI
BRASHER
BRASHLY
BRUSHED
BRUSHES
BRUSHUP
CAPSHAW
CLASHED
CLASHES
CRASHED
CRASHES
CRUSHED
CRUSHER
CRUSHES
DOGSHOW
EARSHOT
FLASHED
FLASHER
FLASHES
FLESHED
FLESHES
FLUSHED
FLUSHES
FRESHEN
FRESHER
FRESHET
FRESHLY
GEISHAS
GNASHED
GNASHES
GRISHAM
GUMSHOE
GUNSHOT
GYMSHOE
HARSHEN
HARSHER
HARSHLY
HERSHEY
HOTSHOT
ICESHOW
KAISHEK
KEESHAN
KINSHIP
KNISHES
KRISHNA
LEASHED
LEASHES
MARSHAL
MARSHES
MUGSHOT
ONESHOT
PLASHED
PLASHES
PLUSHER
PLUSHES
PLUSHLY
POTSHOT
QUASHED
QUASHES
RIMSHOT
SHUSHED
SHUSHES
SKOSHES
SLASHED
SLASHER
SLASHES
SLOSHED
SLOSHES
SLUSHES
SMASHED
SMASHER
SMASHES
SMASHUP
STASHED
STASHES
SWISHED
SWISHES
TEASHOP
TOESHOE
TOYSHOP
TRASHED
TRASHES
USOSHOW
WARSHIP
WORSHIP

•••S•H•

BORSCHT
KITSCHY
PORSCHE
WHOSWHO

•••S••H

FORSYTH
MESSIAH
MISSISH

••••SH•

ALYOSHA
BELUSHI
KENOSHA
NATASHA
RICKSHA
SPLASHY
SQUISHY

••••S•H

KLATSCH

•••••SH

ABOLISH
BABYISH
BEARISH
BLEMISH
BONEASH
BOOKISH
BOORISH
BRITISH
BRUTISH
BULLISH
BULRUSH
BURNISH
CARWASH
CATFISH
CATTISH
CHERISH
CODFISH
COLTISH
CORNISH
CULTISH
DAMPISH
DARKISH
DERVISH
DOGFISH
DOLTISH
DULLISH
ENGLISH
EYELASH
EYEWASH
FADDISH
FINNISH
FLEMISH
FLYFISH
FOGYISH
FOOLISH
FOPPISH
FURBISH
FURNISH
GARNISH
GIRLISH
GOATISH
GOULASH
HAWKISH
HOGWASH
INARUSH
JETWASH
KADDISH
KNAVISH
KURDISH
LONGISH
MANNISH
MAWKISH
MISSISH
MONKISH
MOORISH
NEBBISH
NOURISH
OGREISH
OSHKOSH
PANFISH
PAYCASH
PECKISH
PEEVISH
PETTISH
PIGGISH
PINKISH
PIXYISH
PREWASH
PRUDISH
PUBLISH
PUCKISH
RAFFISH
REDDISH
REFRESH
ROGUISH
ROMANSH
RUBBISH
SAWFISH
SELFISH
SLAVISH
SOURISH
SPANISH
STYLISH
SUNFISH
SWEDISH
TALLISH
TANNISH
TARNISH
TURKISH
UNLEASH
VARNISH
WAGGISH
WARMISH
WASPISH
WEAKISH
WHITISH
WOLFISH
YIDDISH

SI•••••

SIAMESE
SIBERIA
SIBLING
SICCING
SICHUAN
SICKBAY
SICKENS
SICKEST
SICKLES
SICKOUT
SICKPAY
SIDEARM
SIDEBAR
SIDEBET
SIDECAR
SIDEMAN
SIDEMEN
SIDINGS
SIDLING
SIENNAS
SIERRAS
SIESTAS
SIFTERS
SIFTING
SIGHERS
SIGHING
SIGHTED
SIGHTLY
SIGMUND
SIGNALS
SIGNEES
SIGNERS
SIGNETS
SIGNIFY
SIGNING
SIGNOFF
SIGNOUT
SIGNSIN
SIGNSON
SIGNSUP
SIKHISM
SILENCE
SILENTS
SILESIA
SILICAS
SILICON
SILKHAT
SILKIER
SILKILY
SILLIER
SILLIES
SILOING
SILTING
SILVERS
SILVERY
SIMENON
SIMIANS
SIMILAR
SIMILES
SIMMERS
SIMMONS
SIMPERS
SIMPLER
SIMPLEX
SIMPSON
SINATRA
SINCERE
SINEDIE
SINGERS
SINGING
SINGLED
SINGLES
SINGOUT
SINGSTO
SINKAGE
SINKERS
SINKING
SINKSIN
SINNERS
SINUOUS
SINUSES
SIOBHAN
SIOUANS
SIPHONS
SIPPERS
SIPPETS
SIPPING
SIRLOIN
SIROCCO
SISKINS
SISSIES
SISTERS
SISTINE
SISTRUM
SITCOMS
SITDOWN
SITSOUT
SITTERS
SITTING
SITUATE
SITWELL
SIXFOLD
SIXGUNS
SIXPACK
SIXTEEN
SIXTIES
SIZABLE
SIZABLY
SIZEDUP
SIZESUP
SIZINGS
SIZZLED
SIZZLES

S•I••••

SAILING
SAILORS
SAINTED
SAINTLY
SCIENCE
SCISSOR
SEICHES
SEIDELS
SEINERS
SEINING
SEISMIC
SEIZERS
SEIZING
SHIATSU
SHIELDS
SHIFTED
SHIHTZU
SHIITES
SHILLED
SHIMMER
SHINDIG
SHINERS
SHINGLE
SHINIER
SHINING
SHINNED
SHIPMAN
SHIPMEN
SHIPOUT
SHIPPED
SHIPPER
SHIRKED
SHIRKER
SHIRLEY
SHIRRED
SHIVERS
SKIBOOT
SKIDDED
SKIDDER
SKIDDOO
SKIDROW
SKIJUMP
SKILFUL
SKILIFT
SKILLED
SKILLET
SKIMASK
SKIMMED
SKIMMER
SKIMPED
SKINNED
SKINNER
SKIPOLE
SKIPOUT
SKIPPED
SKIPPER
SKIRLED
SKIRRED
SKIRTED
SKIRUNS
SKISUIT
SKITOWS
SKITTER
SKITTLE
SKIVERS
SLICERS
SLICING
SLICKED
SLICKER
SLICKLY
SLIDEIN
SLIDERS
SLIDING
SLIGHTS
SLIMIER
SLIMJIM
SLIMMED
SLIMMER
SLINGER
SLINKED
SLIPONS
SLIPOUT
SLIPPED
SLIPPER
SLIPSUP
SLIPUPS
SLITHER
SLIVERS
SMIDGEN
SMILERS
SMILING
SMIRKED
SMITING
SMITTEN
SNICKER
SNIDELY
SNIDEST
SNIFFAT
SNIFFED
SNIFFER
SNIFFLE
SNIFTER
SNIGGER
SNIGGLE
SNIGLET
SNIPEAT
SNIPING
SNIPPED
SNIPPET
SNIVELS
SOIGNEE
SOILING
SOIREES
SPICEUP
SPICIER
SPICING
SPIDERS
SPIDERY
SPIEDON
SPIEGEL
SPIELED
SPIELER
SPIESON
SPIGOTS
SPIKERS
SPIKIER
SPIKING
SPILLED
SPINACH
SPINDLE
SPINDLY
SPINELS
SPINETS
SPINIER
SPINNER
SPINOFF
SPINOUT
SPINOZA
SPIRALS
SPIRANT
SPIREAS
SPIRITO
SPIRITS
SPITING
SPITZES
STICHES
STICKER
STICKTO
STICKUP
STIEGEL
STIFFED
STIFFEN
STIFFER
STIFFLY
STIFLED
STIFLES
STIGMAS
STILLED
STILLER
STILTED
STILTON
STIMULI
STINGER
STINKER
STINTED
STIPEND
STIPPLE
STIRFRY
STIRRED
STIRRER
STIRRUP
STIRSIN
STIRSUP
SUITING
SUITORS
SUITSUP
SWIFTER
SWIFTLY
SWIGGED
SWILLED
SWIMMER
SWINDLE
SWINGBY
SWINGER
SWIPERS
SWIPING
SWIRLED
SWISHED
SWISHES
SWITZER
SWIVELS
SWIZZLE

S••I•••

SABINES
SAGINAW
SALIENT
SALIERI
SAMISEN
SAMITES
SANIBEL
SAPIENS
SAPIENT
SATIATE
SATIETY
SATIRES
SATIRIC
SATISFY
SAVINGS
SAVIORS
SAYINGS
SCHIRRA
SCHISMS
SCRIBES
SCRIMPS
SCRIMPY
SCRIPPS
SCRIPTS
SCRIVEN
SEMINAL
SEMINAR
SEMIPRO
SEMITES
SEMITIC
SENIORS
SERIALS
SERIATE
SERIOUS
SETINTO
SEVIGNE
SEVILLE
SEXIEST
SEXISTS
SHEIKHS
SHEILAE
SHEILAH
SHEILAS
SHIITES
SHRIEKS
SHRIFTS
SHRIKES
SHRILLS
SHRILLY
SHRIMPS
SHRINER
SHRINES
SHRINKS
SHRIVEL
SHRIVER
SHRIVES
SHTICKS
SIDINGS
SILICAS
SILICON
SIMIANS
SIMILAR
SIMILES
SIZINGS
SLEIGHS
SLEIGHT
SLUICED
SLUICES
SOCIALS
SOCIETY
SOLICIT
SOLIDER
SOLIDLY
SORITES
SOVIETS
SPLICED
SPLICER
SPLICES
SPLINES
SPLINTS
SPLITUP
SPOILED
SPOILER
SPRIEST
SPRINGS
SPRINGY
SPRINTS
SPRITES
SQUINCH
SQUINTS
SQUINTY
SQUIRED
SQUIRES
SQUIRMS
SQUIRMY
SQUIRTS
SQUISHY
STAIDER
STAIDLY
STAINED
STAINER
STEIGER
STEINEM
STEINER
STKITTS
STOICAL
STRIATE
STRIDER
STRIDES
STRIKER
STRIKES
STRINGS
STRINGY
STRIPED
STRIPER
STRIPES
STRIVED
STRIVEN
STRIVER
STRIVES
SURINAM
SYRIANS
SYRINGA
SYRINGE

S•••I••

SABRINA
SACKING
SAGGIER
SAGGING
SAILING
SALLIED
SALLIES
SALSIFY
SALTIER
SALTILY
SALTINE
SALTING
SALVING
SAMHILL
SANDIER
SANDING
SANTINI
SANTIRS
SAPLING
SAPPIER
SAPPING
SARDINE
SASHIMI
SASSIER
SASSIES
SASSILY
SASSING
SAUCIER
SAUCILY
SAURIAN
SAVVIER
SAVVILY
SAWFISH
SAWMILL
SCALIER
SCALING
SCARIER
SCARIFY
SCARILY
SCARING
SCHMIDT
SCHWINN
SCOPING
SCORING
SEABIRD
SEAGIRT
SEALILY
SEALING
SEALION
SEAMIER
SEAMING
SEARING
SEASICK
SEASIDE
SEATING
SECTION
SEEDIER
SEEDILY
SEEDING
SEEKING
SEEMING
SEEPING
SEINING
SEIZING
SELFISH
SELKIRK
SELLING
SENDING
SENSING
SEQUINS
SERBIAN
SERLING
SERPICO
SERRIED
SERVICE
SERVILE
SERVING
SESSILE
SESSION
SESTINA
SETLINE
SETTING
SHADIER
SHADILY
SHADING
SHAKIER
SHAKILY
SHAKING
SHAMING
SHAPING
SHAPIRO
SHARING
SHAVING
SHERIFF
SHINIER
SHINING
SHOEING
SHOOING
SHOOINS
SHORING
SHOVING
SHOWIER
SHOWILY
SHOWING
SIBLING
SICCING
SIDLING
SIFTING
SIGHING
SIGNIFY
SIGNING
SIKHISM
SILKIER
SILKILY
SILLIER
SILLIES
SILOING
SILTING
SINGING
SINKING
SIPPING
SISKINS
SISSIES
SISTINE
SITTING
SIXTIES
SKATING
SKEWING
SKILIFT
SKYDIVE
SKYHIGH
SKYLINE
SLAKING
SLATIER
SLATING
SLAVING
SLAVISH
SLICING
SLIDING
SLIMIER
SLOPING
SLOWING
SMILING
SMITING
SMOKIER
SMOKIES
SMOKING
SNAKIER
SNAKING
SNARING
SNIPING
SNORING
SNOWIER
SNOWING
SOAKING
SOAPIER
SOAPING
SOARING
SOBBING
SOCKING
SODDING
SOFFITS
SOFTIES
SOGGIER
SOGGILY
SOILING
SOLDIER
SOLOING
SOLOIST
SOLVING
SOOTIER
SOPHISM
SOPHIST
SOPPING
SOPWITH
SORRIER
SORTIED
SORTIES
SORTING
SOUPIER
SOURING
SOURISH
SPACIER
SPACING
SPADING
SPANIEL
SPANISH
SPARING
SPATIAL
SPAVINS
SPAYING
SPECIAL
SPECIES
SPECIFY
SPEWING
SPICIER
SPICING
SPIKIER
SPIKING
SPINIER
SPIRITO
SPIRITS
SPITING
SPOKING
SPRAINS
SPUMING
STABILE
STADIUM
STAGIER
STAGILY
STAGING
STAKING
STAMINA
STARING
STATICE
STATICS
STATING
STATION
STATIST
STAVING
STAYING
STEPINS
STERILE
STEWING
STOGIES
STOKING
STONIER
STONILY
STONING
STORIED
STORIES

STORING
STOWING
STRAINS
STRAITS
STUDIED
STUDIES
STUDIOS
STYGIAN
STYLING
STYLISH
STYLIST
STYLIZE
STYMIED
STYMIES
STYRIAN
SUASION
SUAVITY
SUBBING
SUBLIME
SUBMITS
SUBSIDE
SUBSIDY
SUBSIST
SUCKING
SUCTION
SUDSIER
SUDSING
SUFFICE
SUITING
SULFIDE
SULFITE
SULKIER
SULKIES
SULKILY
SULKING
SULLIED
SULLIES
SUMMING
SUMMITS
SUNCITY
SUNDIAL
SUNFISH
SUNKIST
SUNNIER
SUNNILY
SUNNING
SUNRISE
SUPPING
SURFING
SURGING
SURLIER
SURLILY
SURMISE
SURVIVE
SUSLIKS
SUSSING
SWAHILI
SWAYING
SWEDISH
SWIPING
SYNCING

S••••I•

SAFARIS
SALADIN
SALAMIS
SALUKIS
SAMARIA
SANGRIA
SANLUIS
SATIRIC
SAVARIN
SCORPIO
SCOTTIE
SEDALIA
SEEPSIN
SEESFIT
SEETOIT
SEGOVIA
SEISMIC
SELENIC
SEMITIC
SENDSIN
SEQUOIA
SERAPIS
SETSAIL
SHAREIN
SHELTIE
SHERWIN
SHINDIG
SHOWBIZ
SHOWNIN
SHOWSIN
SHUTSIN
SIBERIA
SIGNSIN
SILESIA
SINEDIE
SINKSIN
SIRLOIN
SKEEZIX
SKEPTIC
SKISUIT
SLATKIN
SLEEPIN
SLEPTIN
SLIDEIN
SLIMJIM
SLOEGIN
SNEAKIN
SNOWSIN
SOCKSIN
SOLARIA
SOLICIT
SOMALIA
SOMALIS
SOMATIC
SPOTLIT
SPUTNIK
SQUALID
STANDIN
STANNIC
STARLIT
STCROIX
STDENIS
STEELIE
STENCIL
STEPSIN
STEROID
STIRSIN
STLOUIS
STLUCIA
STOODIN
STOOLIE
STOPSIN
STYPTIC
SUBJOIN
SUBSOIL
SUBUNIT
SUCKSIN
SUNMAID
SURFEIT
SUSTAIN
SWEARIN
SWEETIE
SWOOSIE
SWOREIN
SYNODIC

S•••••I

SALIERI
SAMURAI
SANTINI
SASHIMI
SCHATZI
SCHERZI
SHANGRI
SHARPEI
SHASTRI
SPUMONI
STIMULI
SWAHILI
SYLLABI

•SI••••

ASIATIC
ASININE
USINGUP

•S•I•••

ASHIEST
ASPIRED
ASPIRER
ASPIRES
ASPIRIN
ASSIGNS
ASSISTS
ASSIZES
ESKIMOS
ESPIALS
ESTIVAL
OSCINES
OSSICLE
OSSIFIC
TSHIRTS
USTINOV

•S••I••

ASCRIBE
ASININE
ASOCIAL
ASSAILS
ASTAIRE
ASTRIDE
ESPYING
ESQUIRE
ISSUING
OSTRICH
TSARINA
TSARIST
TSELIOT

•S•••I•

ASCETIC
ASEPSIS
ASEPTIC
ASIATIC
ASPIRIN
ASSYRIA
ASTORIA
CSLEWIS
ESTONIA
ESTORIL
ISLAMIC
OSMOSIS
OSMOTIC
OSSIFIC
OSTEOID
PSYCHIC

•S••••I

ASHANTI
ASSEGAI
ISRAELI
TSUNAMI

••SI•••

APSIDES
ASSIGNS
ASSISTS
ASSIZES
BESIDES
BESIEGE
BUSIEST
CASINGS
CASINOS
COSIGNS
COSINES
DESIGNS
DESIRED
DESIREE
DESIRES
DESISTS
DOSIDOS
EASIEST
ENSIGNS
ENSILED
ENSILES
EPSILON
HASIDIM
HOSIERS
HOSIERY
INSIDER
INSIDES
INSIGHT
INSIPID
INSISTS
MUSICAL
NOSIEST
ONSIGHT
OSSICLE
OSSIFIC
POSITED
RESIDED
RESIDES
RESIDUE
RESIGNS
RESILED
RESILES
RESINGS
RESISTS
RISIBLE
RISINGS
UPSILON
VISIBLE
VISIBLY
VISIONS
VISITED
VISITOR
WYSIWYG

••S•I••

ASSAILS
AUSPICE
AUSSIES
BASHING
BASKING
BASSIST
BASTING
BASTION
BESTIAL
BESTING
BESTIRS
BOSSIER
BOSSILY
BOSSING
BUSBIES
BUSHIDO
BUSHIER
BUSHING
BUSKINS
BUSLINE
BUSSING
BUSTING
BUSYING
CASHIER
CASHING
CASPIAN
CASSIAS
CASSIDY
CASSINI
CASSIUS
CASTILE
CASTING
CESSION
COSTING
CUSHIER
CUSHION
CUSPIDS
CUSSING
DASHIKI
DASHING
DESPISE
DESPITE
DESTINE
DESTINY
DISHING
DISLIKE
DISMISS
DISTILL
DOSSIER
DUSKIER
DUSTIER
DUSTING
ENSUING
ENSUITE
ERSKINE
FASCIAS
FASCISM
FASCIST
FASHION
FASTING
FESTIVE
FISHIER
FISHILY
FISHING
FISSILE
FISSION
FOSDICK
FOSSILS
FUSSIER
FUSSILY
FUSSING
FUSTIAN
FUSTICS
FUSTIER
FUSTILY
GASHING
GASKINS
GASPING
GOSLING
GOSSIPS
GOSSIPY
GUSHIER
GUSHING
GUSSIED
GUSSIES
GUSTILY
GUSTING
HASHING
HASTIER
HASTILY
HASTING
HESSIAN
HISSING
HOSKINS
HOSPICE
HOSTILE
HOSTING
HUSHING
HUSKIER
HUSKIES
HUSKILY
HUSKING
HUSSIES
INSPIRE
INSTILL
INSTILS
IPSWICH
ISSUING
JASMINE
JESSICA
JESTING
JESUITS
JOSHING
JUSTICE
JUSTIFY
JUSTINE
KISSING
LASHING
LASSIES
LASTING
LESSING
LISPING
LISTING
LUSTIER
LUSTILY
LUSTING
MASHIES
MASHING
MASKING
MASSIFS
MASSING
MASSIVE
MASTICS
MASTIFF
MCSWINE
MESHING
MESSIAH
MESSIER
MESSILY
MESSINA
MESSING
MESTIZO
MISDIAL
MISFILE
MISFIRE
MISFITS
MISHITS
MISSIES
MISSILE
MISSING
MISSION
MISSISH
MISSIVE
MISTIER
MISTILY
MISTING
MOSAICS
MOSSIER
MOSSING
MUSHIER
MUSHILY
MUSHING
MUSLIMS
MUSLINS
MUSSING
MUSTIER
MUSTILY
MYSTICS
MYSTIFY
NASTIER
NASTILY
NESTING
NOSHING
OUSTING
PASSING
PASSION
PASSIVE
PASTIER
PASTIME
PASTINA
PASTING
PESKIER
PESKILY
PISCINE
PISMIRE
PISTILS
POSTING
PUSHIER
PUSHILY
PUSHING
RASPIER
RASPING
RESCIND
RESHIPS
RESPIRE
RESPITE
RESTING
RESTIVE
RISKIER
RISKING
ROSSINI
RUSHING
RUSSIAN
RUSTICS
RUSTIER
RUSTILY
RUSTING
SASHIMI
SASSIER
SASSIES
SASSILY
SASSING
SESSILE
SESSION
SESTINA
SISKINS
SISSIES
SISTINE
SUSLIKS
SUSSING
TASKING
TASTIER
TASTILY
TASTING
TESTIER
TESTIFY
TESTILY
TESTING
TOSHIBA
TOSSING
UNSTICK
UPSWING
VESPIDS
VESTIGE
VESTING
WASHING
WASPISH
WASTING
WESKITS
WISHING
WISPIER
WISPILY
WISPING
YESHIVA
YESSING
ZESTIER

••S••I•

ABSTAIN
ARSENIC
ARSENIO
ASSYRIA
AUSTRIA
BASEHIT
BISCUIT
BUSHPIG
COSTAIN
DESPAIR
DESPOIL
DISDAIN
DISJOIN
EASEDIN
EASESIN
EPSTEIN
GASMAIN
GASTRIC
HASIDIM
HUSSEIN
INSIPID
INSULIN
KASHMIR
KOSYGIN
LOSESIT
MASONIC
MASTOID
MESSKIT
MISLAID
NOSTRIL
OSSIFIC
PUSHKIN
PUSHPIN
RESTAIN
ROSALIE
ROSEOIL
RUSHDIE
SUSTAIN
VISAVIS
WASSAIL

••S•••I

ASSEGAI
BASENJI
CASSINI
DASHIKI
ROSSINI
SASHIMI

•••SI••

ABASING
ABUSING
ABUSIVE
AMUSING
ANTSIER
ARCSINE
ARISING
AUSSIES
BASSIST
BEDSIDE
BIASING
BOSSIER
BOSSILY
BOSSING
BUSSING
CAPSIZE
CASSIAS
CASSIDY
CASSINI
CASSIUS
CAUSING
CEASING
CELSIUS
CENSING
CESSION
CHASING
CLOSING
CONSIGN
CONSIST
CORSICA
COUSINS
CROSIER
CUISINE
CURSING
CURSIVE
CUSSING
DAISIES
DAYSINN
DENSITY
DOSSIER
DOUSING
DOWSING
ELISION
ELUSIVE
ELYSIAN
ELYSIUM
ERASING
EROSION
EROSIVE
ETESIAN
EVASION
EVASIVE
FALSIFY
FALSITY
FISSILE
FISSION
FOSSILS
FRASIER
FRISIAN
FUSSIER
FUSSILY
FUSSING
GIPSIES
GOOSING
GOSSIPS
GOSSIPY
GUSSIED
GUSSIES
GUTSIER
GUTSILY
GYPSIES
HESSIAN
HEXSIGN
HISSING
HOOSIER
HORSIER
HORSING
HOUSING
HUSSIES
JESSICA
KISSING
LANSING
LAPSING
LASSIES
LEASING
LESSING
LOOSING
LOUSIER
LOUSILY
LOUSING
MANSION
MASSIFS
MASSING
MASSIVE
MESSIAH
MESSIER
MESSILY
MESSINA
MESSING
MIDSIZE
MISSIES
MISSILE
MISSING
MISSION
MISSISH
MISSIVE
MOSSIER
MOSSING
MOUSIER
MOUSING
MUSSING
NEWSIER
NOISIER
NOISILY
NOISING
NOOSING
NURSING
OFFSIDE
OFFSITE
OUTSIDE
OUTSIZE
PANSIES
PARSING
PASSING
PASSION
PASSIVE
PATSIES
PAUSING
PENSION
PENSIVE
PEPSINS
PERSIAN
PERSIST
PERSIUS
PHASING
PHYSICS
PLOSION
PLOSIVE
POISING
PRESIDE
PROSIER
PROSILY
PROSING
PULSING
PURSING
RAISING
RAISINS
RAWSILK
RETSINA
RINSING
ROSSINI
ROUSING
RUSSIAN
SALSIFY
SASSIER
SASSIES
SASSILY
SASSING
SEASICK
SEASIDE
SENSING
SESSILE
SESSION
SISSIES
SUASION
SUBSIDE
SUBSIDY
SUBSIST
SUDSIER
SUDSING
SUSSING
TANSIES
TARSIER
TEASING
TENSILE
TENSING
TENSION
TENSIVE
TIPSIER
TIPSILY
TOCSINS
TONSILS
TOPSIDE
TORSION
TOSSING
VARSITY
VERSIFY
VERSION
WAYSIDE
WEBSITE
YESSING
ZOYSIAS

•••S•I•

AGASSIZ
AIRSHIP
ANOSMIA
ANOSMIC
BEASTIE
BONSOIR
BRASSIE
BRESLIN
CAUSTIC
CHASSIS
CLASSIC
CLOSEIN
CORSAIR
COWSLIP
CRISPIN
DOESKIN
DRASTIC
DRYSUIT
EELSKIN
ELASTIC
ERISTIC
GNOSTIC
HUSSEIN
INASNIT
INASPIN
KIDSKIN
KINSHIP
KIRSTIE
KTOSLIN
LAWSUIT
LETSLIP
MESSKIT
MIASMIC
NAYSAID
NONSKID
NONSLIP
OILSKIN
ONASSIS
PARSNIP
PHASEIN
PIGSKIN
PLASTIC
PROSAIC
PRUSSIA
PURSUIT
REDSKIN
SEESFIT
SEISMIC
SETSAIL
SKISUIT
SUBSOIL
THESPIS
TOPSAIL
TOPSOIL
WARSHIP
WASSAIL
WETSUIT
WORSHIP

•••S••I

ANASAZI
BOLSHOI
CASSINI
MAESTRI
ROSSINI
SHASTRI
TOLSTOI

••••SI•

AGASSIZ
AMNESIA
ASEPSIS
BABYSIT
BACKSIN
BEATSIT
BLOWSIN
BLOWSIT
BOXESIN
BRASSIE
BUTTSIN
CALLSIN
CAVESIN
CHASSIS
CHIPSIN
CLASSIC
CLUESIN
COMESIN
COOLSIT
DEALSIN
DEARSIR
DEEPSIX
DEPOSIT
DINESIN
DIVESIN
DRAGSIN
DRAWSIN
DROPSIN
EASESIN
ECDYSIS
EDGESIN
EURASIA
FADESIN
FALLSIN
FILLSIN
FLIESIN
FOOTSIE
FREESIA
FUCHSIA
GENESIS
GIVESIN
HANDSIN
HANGSIN
HEADSIN
HOOFSIT
JOINSIN
JUMPSIN
KEEPSIN
KICKSIN
LEADSIN
LIVESIN
LOOKSIN
LOSESIT
MAKESIT
MEIOSIS
MIMESIS
MITOSIS
MOVESIN
NEMESIS
NICOSIA
ONASSIS
OSMOSIS
PEERSIN
PILESIN
PLUGSIN
POURSIN
PRUSSIA
RAKESIN
READSIN
REELSIN
REINSIN
REVISIT
ROPESIN
SEEPSIN
SENDSIN
SHOWSIN
SHUTSIN
SIGNSIN
SILESIA
SINKSIN
SNOWSIN
SOCKSIN
STEPSIN
STIRSIN
STOPSIN
SUCKSIN
SWOOSIE
TAKESIN
THATSIT
TOOTSIE
TRANSIT
TUCKSIN
TUNESIN
TUNISIA
TURNSIN
UTENSIL
VOTESIN
WADESIN
WANTSIN
WAVESIN
WINGSIT
WORKSIN
YELTSIN
ZOOMSIN

••••S•I

BELUSHI

CHRISTI
COLOSSI
ELMISTI
MENISCI
PULASKI

•••••SI
COLOSSI
PACHISI
TBILISI

S•J••••
SOJOURN
STJOHNS

S••J•••
SANJOSE
SANJUAN
SKIJUMP
SKYJACK
SUBJECT
SUBJOIN

S•••J••
SLIMJIM
SNOWJOB

••SJ•••
DISJOIN
GASJETS

••S•J••
NOSEJOB

••S••J•
BASENJI

SK•••••
SKATERS
SKATING
SKEETER
SKEEZIX
SKELTER
SKELTON
SKEPTIC
SKETCHY
SKEWERS
SKEWING
SKIBOOT
SKIDDED
SKIDDER
SKIDDOO
SKIDROW
SKIJUMP
SKILFUL
SKILIFT
SKILLED
SKILLET
SKIMASK
SKIMMED
SKIMMER
SKIMPED
SKINNED
SKINNER
SKIPOLE
SKIPOUT
SKIPPED
SKIPPER
SKIRLED
SKIRRED
SKIRTED
SKIRUNS
SKISUIT
SKITOWS
SKITTER
SKITTLE
SKIVERS
SKOSHES
SKULKED
SKULKER
SKUNKED
SKYBLUE
SKYCAPS
SKYDIVE
SKYHIGH
SKYHOOK
SKYJACK
SKYLARK
SKYLINE
SKYWARD
SKYWAYS

S•K••••
SIKHISM
STKITTS
SUKARNO

S••K•••
SACKERS
SACKFUL
SACKING
SACKOUT
SEEKERS
SEEKING
SEEKOUT
SELKIRK
SHAKERS
SHAKEUP
SHAKIER
SHAKILY
SHAKING
SHAKOES
SHEKELS
SICKBAY
SICKENS
SICKEST
SICKLES
SICKOUT
SICKPAY
SILKHAT
SILKIER
SILKILY
SINKAGE
SINKERS
SINKING
SINKSIN
SISKINS
SLAKING
SMOKERS
SMOKIER
SMOKIES
SMOKING
SNAKIER
SNAKING
SOAKERS
SOAKING
SOAKSUP
SOCKETS
SOCKEYE
SOCKING
SOCKSIN
SPIKERS
SPIKIER
SPIKING
SPOKANE
SPOKEOF
SPOKEUP
SPOKING
STAKING
STOKELY
STOKERS
STOKING
SUCKERS
SUCKING
SUCKSIN
SULKERS
SULKIER
SULKIES
SULKILY
SULKING
SUNKIST

S•••K••
SALUKIS
SHACKLE
SHANKAR
SHANKED
SHARKEY
SHEIKHS
SHIRKED
SHIRKER
SHOCKED
SHOCKER
SHOOKUP
SHRIKES
SHUCKED
SHUCKER
SKULKED
SKULKER
SKUNKED
SLACKED
SLACKEN
SLACKER
SLATKIN
SLEEKED
SLEEKEN
SLEEKER
SLEEKLY
SLICKED
SLICKER
SLICKLY
SLINKED
SMACKED
SMACKER
SMIRKED
SNACKED
SNACKER
SNEAKED
SNEAKER
SNEAKIN
SNICKER
SNOOKER
SNORKEL
SPACKLE
SPANKED
SPANKER
SPARKED
SPARKLE
SPEAKER
SPEAKOF
SPEAKUP
SPECKLE
SPOOKED
STACKED
STACKUP
STALKED
STALKER
STARKER
STARKLY
STICKER
STICKTO
STICKUP
STINKER
STOCKED
STOCKUP
STOOKEY
STRIKER
STRIKES
STROKED
STROKES
STUCKTO
STUCKUP
SWANKER

S••••K•
SCREAKS
SHRIEKS
SHRINKS
SHTICKS
SLOVAKS
SPASSKY
SQUAWKS
SQUEAKS
SQUEAKY
STREAKS
STREAKY
SUSLIKS

S•••••K
SADSACK
SARAWAK
SAWBUCK
SCHLOCK
SEASICK
SELKIRK
SELLECK
SETBACK
SHYLOCK
SIXPACK
SKIMASK
SKYHOOK
SKYJACK
SKYLARK
SPELUNK
SPUTNIK
SUFFOLK
SUNDECK

•SK••••
ASKANCE
ASKSFOR
ASKSOUT
ESKIMOS

•S•K•••
OSHKOSH

••SK•••
BASKETS
BASKING
BOSKETS
BUSKINS
DESKSET
DESKTOP
DUSKIER
ERSKINE
GASKETS
GASKINS
HOSKINS
HUSKERS
HUSKIER
HUSKIES
HUSKILY
HUSKING
MASKERS
MASKING
MUSKETS
MUSKRAT
PESKIER
PESKILY
RISKERS
RISKIER
RISKING
SISKINS
TASKING
TUSKERS
WESKITS

••S•K••
KISHKES
MESSKIT
PASSKEY
PUSHKIN

••S••K•
ATSTAKE
BESPOKE
DASHIKI
DISLIKE
MISTAKE
SUSLIKS

••S•••K
BESPEAK
CASSOCK
COSSACK
DRSPOCK
FOSDICK
GOSHAWK
HASSOCK
INSTOCK
MISTOOK
MRSPOCK
RESTOCK
TUSSOCK
UNSTACK
UNSTICK
UNSTUCK
YASHMAK

•••SK••
ALASKAN
BRISKER
BRISKET
BRISKLY
DOESKIN
EELSKIN
FRISKED
KIDSKIN
MESSKIT
NONSKID
OILSKIN
PASSKEY
PIGSKIN
REDSKIN
UNASKED
WHISKED
WHISKER
WHISKEY

•••S•K•
FORSAKE
NETSUKE
SPASSKY

•••S••K
AIRSOCK
BERSERK
CASSOCK
COSSACK
FORSOOK
GEMSBOK
HASSOCK
KAISHEK
PRESOAK
RANSACK
RAWSILK
SADSACK
SEASICK
TUSSOCK

••••SK•
BLUESKY
CHOMSKY
DAMASKS
PULASKI
SPASSKY
TROTSKY
UNMASKS
VRONSKY

•••••SK
MOLLUSK
OBELISK
OKHOTSK
SKIMASK
YAKUTSK

SL•••••
SLABBED
SLACKED
SLACKEN
SLACKER
SLAKING
SLALOMS
SLAMMED
SLAMMER
SLANDER
SLANTED
SLAPPED
SLASHED
SLASHER
SLASHES
SLATHER
SLATIER
SLATING
SLATKIN
SLATTED
SLAVERS
SLAVERY
SLAVING
SLAVISH
SLAYERS
SLAYTON
SLEDDED
SLEDDER
SLEDDOG
SLEDGES
SLEEKED
SLEEKEN
SLEEKER
SLEEKLY
SLEEPER
SLEEPIN
SLEEPON
SLEETED
SLEEVES
SLEIGHS
SLEIGHT
SLENDER
SLEPTIN
SLEPTON
SLEUTHS
SLICERS
SLICING
SLICKED
SLICKER
SLICKLY
SLIDEIN
SLIDERS
SLIDING
SLIGHTS
SLIMIER
SLIMJIM
SLIMMED
SLIMMER
SLINGER
SLINKED
SLIPONS
SLIPOUT
SLIPPED
SLIPPER
SLIPSUP
SLIPUPS
SLITHER
SLIVERS
SLOBBER
SLOEGIN
SLOGANS
SLOGGED
SLOPING
SLOPPED
SLOSHED
SLOSHES
SLOTCAR
SLOTTED
SLOUCHY
SLOUGHS
SLOVAKS
SLOVENE
SLOVENS
SLOWEST
SLOWING
SLOWSUP
SLUDGES
SLUGGED
SLUGGER
SLUICED
SLUICES
SLUMBER
SLUMMED
SLUMPED
SLURPED
SLURRED
SLUSHES
SLYNESS

S•L••••
SALAAMS
SALABLE
SALADIN
SALAMIS
SALAZAR
SALCHOW
SALERNO
SALIENT
SALIERI
SALLIED
SALLIES
SALMONS
SALOONS
SALSIFY
SALSODA
SALTBOX
SALTERS
SALTIER
SALTILY
SALTINE
SALTING
SALUKIS
SALUTED
SALUTES
SALVAGE
SALVERS
SALVING
SALVOES
SCLERAS
SELECTS
SELENIC
SELFISH
SELKIRK
SELLECK
SELLERS
SELLING
SELLOFF
SELLOUT
SELTZER
SELVAGE
SILENCE
SILENTS
SILESIA
SILICAS
SILICON
SILKHAT
SILKIER
SILKILY
SILLIER
SILLIES
SILOING
SILTING
SILVERS
SILVERY
SOLACES
SOLARIA
SOLDERS
SOLDIER
SOLDOFF
SOLDOUT
SOLEDAD
SOLFEGE
SOLICIT
SOLIDER
SOLIDLY
SOLOING
SOLOIST
SOLOMON
SOLUBLE
SOLUTES
SOLVENT
SOLVERS
SOLVING
SPLASHY
SPLAYED
SPLEENS
SPLICED
SPLICER
SPLICES
SPLINES
SPLINTS
SPLITUP
SPLOTCH
SPLURGE
STLOUIS
STLUCIA
SULFATE
SULFIDE
SULFITE
SULKERS
SULKIER
SULKIES
SULKILY
SULKING
SULLIED
SULLIES
SULPHUR
SULTANA
SULTANS
SULUSEA
SYLLABI
SYLVANS

S••L•••
SAILING
SAILORS
SALLIED
SALLIES
SANLUIS
SAPLING
SAWLOGS
SCALARS
SCALDED
SCALENE
SCALERS
SCALIER
SCALING
SCALLOP
SCALPED
SCALPEL
SCALPER
SCHLEPP
SCHLEPS
SCHLOCK
SCOLDED
SCOLDER
SCULLED
SCULLER
SCULPTS
SEALABS
SEALANE
SEALANT
SEALEGS
SEALERS
SEALILY
SEALING
SEALION
SEALOFF
SEALSUP
SECLUDE
SELLECK
SELLERS
SELLING
SELLOFF
SELLOUT
SERLING
SETLINE
SHALALA
SHALLOT
SHALLOW
SHALOMS
SHELDON
SHELLAC
SHELLED
SHELLER
SHELLEY
SHELTER
SHELTIE
SHELTON
SHELVED
SHELVES
SHILLED
SHYLOCK
SIBLING
SIDLING
SILLIER
SILLIES
SIRLOIN
SKELTER
SKELTON
SKILFUL
SKILIFT
SKILLED
SKILLET
SKULKED
SKULKER
SKYLARK
SKYLINE
SLALOMS
SMALLER
SMALTOS
SMELLED
SMELTED
SMELTER
SMILERS
SMILING
SMOLDER
SNELLEN
SOILING
SOULFUL
SPALLED
SPELLED
SPELLER
SPELUNK
SPILLED
STALAGS
STALEST
STALKED
STALKER
STALLED
STELLAR
STILLED
STILLER
STILTED
STILTON
STOLLEN
STOLLER
STOLONS
STYLERS
STYLETS
STYLING
STYLISH
STYLIST
STYLIZE
SUBLETS
SUBLIME
SULLIED
SULLIES
SUNLAMP
SUNLESS
SURLIER
SURLILY
SUSLIKS
SUTLERS
SVELTER
SWALLOW
SWELLED
SWELLUP
SWELTER
SWELTRY
SWILLED
SWOLLEN
SYLLABI

S•••L••
SADDLED
SADDLER
SADDLES
SAMPLED
SAMPLER
SAMPLES
SANDLOT
SARALEE
SAVALAS
SCALLOP
SCARLET
SCHOLAR
SCOWLED
SCOWLER
SCROLLS
SCULLED
SCULLER
SEASLUG
SECULAR
SEDALIA
SETTLED
SETTLER
SETTLES
SEVILLE
SHALLOT
SHALLOW
SHEILAE
SHEILAH
SHEILAS
SHELLAC
SHELLED
SHELLER
SHELLEY
SHIELDS
SHILLED
SHIRLEY
SHRILLS
SHRILLY
SICKLES
SIMILAR
SIMILES
SIMPLER
SIMPLEX
SINGLED
SINGLES
SIZZLED
SIZZLES
SKILLED
SKILLET
SKIRLED
SKYBLUE
SMALLER
SMELLED
SNARLED
SNELLEN
SNIGLET
SOMALIA
SOMALIS
SPALLED
SPELLED
SPELLER
SPIELED
SPIELER
SPILLED
SPOILED
SPOILER
SPOOLED
SPOTLIT
SQUALID
SQUALLS
SQUALOR
SQUELCH
STABLED
STABLER
STABLES
STALLED
STANLEE
STANLEY
STAPLED
STAPLER
STAPLES
STARLET
STARLIT
STEALTH
STEELED
STEELER
STEELIE
STELLAR
STIFLED
STIFLES
STILLED
STILLER
STOLLEN
STOLLER
STOOLIE
STROLLS
SUBPLOT
SUBTLER
SUPPLER
SURPLUS
SWALLOW
SWELLED
SWELLUP
SWILLED
SWIRLED
SWOLLEN

S••••L•
SAINTLY
SALABLE
SALTILY
SAMHILL
SANDALS
SANDFLY
SASSILY
SAUCILY
SAVABLE
SAVVILY
SAWMILL
SCANTLY
SCAPULA
SCARILY
SCHOOLS
SCRAWLS
SCRAWLY
SCROLLS
SCRUPLE
SCUFFLE
SCUTTLE
SEAGULL
SEALILY
SEASALT
SEATTLE
SEAWALL
SEEDILY
SEIDELS
SEQUELS
SERIALS
SERVALS
SERVILE
SESSILE
SEVILLE
SHACKLE
SHADILY
SHAKILY
SHALALA
SHAMBLE
SHAPELY
SHARPLY
SHEERLY
SHEKELS
SHEWOLF
SHINGLE
SHOOFLY
SHORTLY
SHOVELS
SHOWILY
SHRILLS
SHRILLY
SHUFFLE
SHUTTLE
SIGHTLY
SIGNALS
SILKILY
SITWELL
SIXFOLD
SIZABLE
SIZABLY
SKIPOLE
SKITTLE
SLEEKLY
SLICKLY
SMARTLY
SMUGGLE
SNAFFLE
SNIDELY
SNIFFLE
SNIGGLE
SNIVELS
SNUFFLE
SNUGGLE
SOBERLY
SOCIALS
SOGGILY
SOLIDLY
SOLUBLE
SORRELS
SOUFFLE
SOUNDLY
SPACKLE
SPANGLE
SPANGLY
SPARELY
SPARKLE
SPATULA
SPECKLE
SPINDLE
SPINDLY
SPINELS
SPIRALS
SPRAWLS
SQUALLS
SQUEALS
STABILE
STAGILY
STAIDLY
STARKLY
STARTLE
STATELY
STEEPLE
STEEPLY
STERILE
STERNLY
STEROLS
STIFFLY
STIMULI

STIPPLE
STOKELY
STONILY
STOUTLY
STROLLS
STUBBLE
STUBBLY
STUMBLE
SUAVELY
SUFFOLK
SULKILY
SUNBELT
SUNNILY
SURLILY
SWADDLE
SWAHILI
SWEETLY
SWIFTLY
SWINDLE
SWIVELS
SWIZZLE
SYMBOLS
SYSTOLE

S•••••L

SACKFUL
SAMHILL
SANIBEL
SATCHEL
SAWMILL
SCALPEL
SCANDAL
SEAGULL
SEAWALL
SEMINAL
SENEGAL
SENSUAL
SETSAIL
SEVERAL
SHAWWAL
SHRIVEL
SITWELL
SKILFUL
SNORKEL
SORORAL
SOULFUL
SPANIEL
SPATIAL
SPECIAL
SPIEGEL
SPOUSAL
STENCIL
STENGEL
STERNAL
STIEGEL
STOICAL
STRUDEL
SUBSOIL
SUNDIAL
SURREAL
SYNFUEL
SYNODAL

•SL••••

CSLEWIS
ISLAMIC
ISLANDS

•S•L•••

ASHLAND
ASHLARS
ASHLESS
ASYLUMS
ISOLATE
OSTLERS
PSALMED
PSALTER
TSELIOT
USELESS

•S••L••

ASTOLAT
ESTELLE
USUALLY

•S•••L•

ASPHALT
ASSAILS
ASSAULT
ESPIALS
ESTELLE
ISOHELS
ISRAELI
OSCEOLA
OSSICLE
USEABLE
USUALLY

•S••••L

ASOCIAL
ASUSUAL
ESPANOL
ESTIVAL
ESTORIL
ISHMAEL
USSTEEL

••SL•••

BUSLINE
DISLIKE
ENSLAVE
GOSLING
MISLAID
MISLAYS
MISLEAD
MOSLEMS
MUSLIMS
MUSLINS
SUSLIKS

••S•L••

ABSALOM
ABSOLUT
ABSOLVE
BASALLY
BASALTS
BUSTLED
BUSTLES
CASELAW
CASTLED
CASTLES
CUSSLER
DESALTS
DISPLAY
ENSILED
ENSILES
EPSILON
GISELLE
HASSLED
HASSLES
HOSTLER
HUSTLED
HUSTLER
HUSTLES
INSOLES
INSULAR
INSULIN
INSULTS
JOSTLED
JOSTLER
JOSTLES
LASALLE
MISALLY
MISPLAY
MOSELLE
MUSCLED
MUSCLES
NASALLY
NESTLED
NESTLER
NESTLES
PESTLED
PESTLES
RASSLED
RASSLES
RESALES
RESALTS
RESELLS
RESILED
RESILES
RESOLED
RESOLES
RESOLVE
RESULTS
ROSALIE
ROSELLE
RUSTLED
RUSTLER
RUSTLES
TUSSLED
TUSSLES
UPSILON

••S••L•

ASSAILS
ASSAULT
BASALLY
BOSSILY
BOSWELL
BUSHELS
CASTILE
CASUALS
DISABLE
DISPELS
DISTILL
DOSSALS
ENSOULS
FISHILY
FISSILE
FOSSILS
FUSSILY
FUSTILY
GESTALT
GISELLE
GOSPELS
GUSTILY
HASTILY
HOSTELS
HOSTILE
HUSKILY
INSTALL
INSTILL
INSTILS
INSTYLE
LASALLE
LASCALA
LISTELS
LUSTILY
MESCALS
MESSALA
MESSILY
MISALLY
MISCALL
MISERLY
MISFILE
MISRULE
MISSALS
MISSILE
MISTILY
MOSELLE
MUSHILY
MUSSELS
MUSTILY
NASALLY
NASTILY
OSSICLE
PASSELS
PASTELS
PESKILY
PISTILS
PISTOLE
PISTOLS
PUSHILY
RASCALS
RESCALE
RESEALS
RESELLS
RESTYLE
RISIBLE
RISSOLE
ROSELLE
ROSWELL
RUSSELL
RUSTILY
SASSILY
SESSILE
SYSTOLE
TASSELS
TASTILY
TESTILY
TOSCALE
UNSEALS
UPSCALE
VASSALS
VESSELS
VISIBLE
VISIBLY
VISTULA
VISUALS
WISPILY

••S•••L

ARSENAL
AUSTRAL
BASHFUL
BESTIAL
BOSWELL
DESPOIL
DISTILL
ENSNARL
FISTFUL
GASOHOL
INSTALL
INSTILL
KESTREL
LESPAUL
LUSTFUL
MISCALL
MISDEAL
MISDIAL
MISTRAL
MUSICAL
NOSTRIL
PASCHAL
PASSEUL
RESTFUL
ROSEOIL
ROSWELL
RUSSELL
UNSNARL
USSTEEL
WASSAIL
WASTREL
WISHFUL
WISTFUL
ZESTFUL

•••SL••

BOBSLED
BOOSLER
BRESLIN
COWSLIP
CUSSLER
DOGSLED
ENISLED
ENISLES
FOCSLES
HASSLED
HASSLES
HEMSLEY
KTOSLIN
LAYSLOW
LETSLIP
LIESLOW
MEASLES
NONSLIP
PAISLEY
PARSLEY
PRESLEY
RASSLED
RASSLES
SEASLUG
TOUSLED
TOUSLES
TUSSLED
TUSSLES
VIZSLAS
WINSLOW

•••S•L•

APISHLY
APOSTLE
BEASTLY
BOSSILY
BRASHLY
BRISKLY
BRISTLE
BRISTLY
CAPSULE
CHISELS
CLOSELY
CONSOLE
CONSULS
CONSULT
CRASSLY
CRISPLY
CROSSLY
DAMSELS
DENSELY
DIESELS
DORSALS
DOSSALS
EPISTLE
FALSELY
FIRSTLY
FISSILE
FORSALE
FOSSILS
FRESHLY
FUSSILY
GHASTLY
GHOSTLY
GRISTLE
GRISTLY
GROSSLY
GUTSILY
HANSOLO
HARSHLY
HERSELF
HIMSELF
LETSFLY
LOOSELY
LOUSILY
MARSALA
MESSALA
MESSILY
MISSALS
MISSILE
MOISTLY
MORSELS
MUSSELS
NOISILY
NONSELF
ONESELF
OURSELF
OUTSELL
OUTSOLD
PASSELS
PLUSHLY
PRESALE
PRESELL
PROSILY
RAWSILK
RISSOLE
RUSSELL
SASSILY
SEASALT
SESSILE
TAGSALE
TARSALS
TASSELS
TEASELS
TENSELY
TENSILE
TERSELY
THISTLE
THYSELF
TINSELS
TIPSILY
TONSILS
TRESTLE
UPPSALA
VASSALS
VESSELS
WEASELS
WHISTLE
WRESTLE

•••S••L

ABYSMAL
ASUSUAL
BRISTOL
COASTAL
CRYSTAL
FURSEAL
MARSHAL
OUTSELL
PASSEUL
PRESELL
RUSSELL
SENSUAL
SETSAIL
SUBSOIL
TOPSAIL
TOPSOIL
UNUSUAL
WASSAIL

••••SL•

CRASSLY
CROSSLY
GROSSLY
PIOUSLY

••••S•L

AEROSOL
AROUSAL
COUNSEL
CREOSOL
DEPOSAL
GIRASOL
PARASOL
PERUSAL
PHRASAL
REFUSAL
SPOUSAL
UTENSIL

SM•••••

SMACKED
SMACKER
SMALLER
SMALTOS
SMARTED
SMARTEN
SMARTER
SMARTLY
SMASHED
SMASHER
SMASHES
SMASHUP
SMATTER
SMEARED
SMELLED
SMELTED
SMELTER
SMETANA
SMIDGEN
SMILERS
SMILING
SMIRKED
SMITING
SMITTEN
SMOKERS
SMOKIER
SMOKIES
SMOKING
SMOLDER
SMOOTHS
SMOTHER
SMUDGED
SMUDGES
SMUGGER
SMUGGLE

S•M••••

SAMARIA
SAMBAED
SAMBARS
SAMEDAY
SAMHILL
SAMISEN
SAMITES
SAMNUNN
SAMOANS
SAMOVAR
SAMOYED
SAMPANS
SAMPLED
SAMPLER
SAMPLES
SAMPRAS
SAMPSON
SAMSARA
SAMSUNG
SAMURAI
SEMINAL
SEMINAR
SEMIPRO
SEMITES
SEMITIC
SIMENON
SIMIANS
SIMILAR
SIMILES
SIMMERS
SIMMONS
SIMPERS
SIMPLER
SIMPLEX
SIMPSON
SOMALIA
SOMALIS
SOMATIC
SOMEDAY
SOMEHOW
SOMEONE
SOMEWAY
SUMATRA
SUMMARY
SUMMERS
SUMMERY
SUMMING
SUMMITS
SUMMONS
SYMBOLS
SYMPTOM

S••M•••

SALMONS
SAWMILL
SCAMMED
SCAMPED
SCAMPER
SCHMEER
SCHMIDT
SCHMOES
SCHMOOS
SEAMIER
SEAMING
SEAMOSS
SEEMING
SEGMENT
SERMONS
SEYMOUR
SHAMANS
SHAMBLE
SHAMING
SHAMMED
SHAMPOO
SHIMMER
SIAMESE
SIGMUND
SIMMERS
SIMMONS
SKIMASK
SKIMMED
SKIMMER
SKIMPED
SLAMMED
SLAMMER
SLIMIER
SLIMJIM
SLIMMED
SLIMMER
SLUMBER
SLUMMED
SLUMPED
SPUMING
SPUMONE
SPUMONI
STAMENS
STAMINA
STAMMER
STAMPED
STEMMED
STIMULI
STOMACH
STOMATA
STOMPED
STUMBLE
STUMPED
STUMPER
STYMIED
STYMIES
SUBMITS
SUMMARY
SUMMERS
SUMMERY
SUMMING
SUMMITS
SUMMONS
SUNMAID
SURMISE
SWAMPED
SWIMMER

S•••M••

SALAMIS
SANDMAN
SANDMEN
SCAMMED
SCHEMAS
SCHEMED
SCHEMER
SCHEMES
SCRIMPS
SCRIMPY
SEISMIC
SESAMES
SHAMMED
SHERMAN
SHIMMER
SHIPMAN
SHIPMEN
SHOWMAN
SHOWMEN
SHRIMPS
SIDEMAN
SIDEMEN
SKIMMED
SKIMMER
SLAMMED
SLAMMER
SLIMMED
SLIMMER
SLUMMED
SNOWMAN
SNOWMEN
SOLOMON
STAMMER
STARMAN
STARMAP
STEAMED
STEAMER
STEMMED
STIGMAS
STORMED
SWARMED
SWIMMER
SYNGMAN

S••••M•

SACHEMS
SALAAMS
SANREMO
SAOTOME
SASHIMI
SATCHMO
SATSUMA
SCHISMS
SCREAMS
SHALOMS
SITCOMS
SKIJUMP
SLALOMS
SOSUEME
SQUIRMS
SQUIRMY
STREAMS
SUBLIME
SUBSUME
SUCCUMB
SUNLAMP
SUPREME
SUPREMO
SURNAME
SYSTEMS

S•••••M

SANCTUM
SARCASM
SEAGRAM
SERFDOM
SHAHDOM
SIDEARM
SIKHISM
SISTRUM
SLIMJIM
SOPHISM
SORGHUM
STADIUM
STARDOM
STEINEM
STERNUM
STRATUM
SUNBEAM
SUNROOM
SURINAM
SYMPTOM
SYNONYM

•SM••••

OSMONDS
OSMOSED
OSMOSES
OSMOSIS
OSMOTIC

•S•M•••

ISHMAEL
ISOMERS

•S••M••

ASHAMED
ASSUMED
ASSUMES
ESKIMOS
ISLAMIC
ISTHMUS
PSALMED

•S•••M•

ASHRAMS
ASYLUMS
ESTEEMS
TSUNAMI

••SM•••

BESMEAR
BISMUTH
DESMOND
DISMAYS
DISMISS
GASMAIN
JASMINE
MISMATE
PISMIRE
YESMAAM

••S•M••

ASSUMED
ASSUMES
BASEMAN
BASEMEN
BESTMAN
BESTMEN
BUSHMAN
BUSHMEN
DUSTMOP
EASTMAN
KASHMIR
POSTMAN
POSTMEN
RESUMED
RESUMES
SESAMES
WISEMAN
WISEMEN
YASHMAK

••S••M•

BESEEMS
COSTUME
CUSTOMS
DISARMS
GASPUMP
INSEAMS
LISSOME
MISNAME
MOSLEMS
MUSEUMS
MUSLIMS
PASTIME
POSSUMS
RESTAMP
SASHIMI
SOSUEME
SYSTEMS

••S•••M

ABSALOM
FASCISM
HASIDIM
NOSEEUM
NOSTRUM
ROSTRUM
SISTRUM
YESMAAM

•••SM••

ABYSMAL
ANOSMIA
ANOSMIC
BATSMAN
BATSMEN
ERASMUS
HOUSMAN
KINSMAN
KINSMEN
MIASMAS
MIASMIC
NEWSMAN
NEWSMEN
PLASMAS
SEISMIC

•••S•M•

AWESOME
BALSAMS
CONSUME
FULSOME
HANSOMS
IRKSOME
LISSOME
NOISOME
POSSUMS
PRESUME
RANSOMS
SATSUMA
SUBSUME
TWOSOME
WINSOME

•••S••M

ALYSSUM
BLOSSOM
ELYSIUM
GRISHAM
GRISSOM
OPOSSUM
POTSDAM

••••SM•

CHRISMS
SCHISMS
TRUISMS
WOEISME

••••S•M

ALYSSUM
BLOSSOM
FLOTSAM
GRISSOM
LUMPSUM
OPOSSUM
TRANSOM

•••••SM

ANIMISM
ATAVISM
ATHEISM
BAPTISM
CULTISM
CZARISM
DADAISM
EGOTISM
ELITISM
FADDISM
FASCISM
FAUVISM
FOGYISM
HEROISM
JUDAISM
LAMAISM
MARXISM
PIANISM
PIETISM
REALISM
SARCASM
SIKHISM
SOPHISM
TORYISM
TOURISM
TROPISM

SN•••••

SNACKED
SNACKER
SNAFFLE
SNAFUED
SNAGGED
SNAKIER
SNAKING
SNAPONS
SNAPPED
SNAPPER
SNAPSAT
SNAPSTO
SNAPSUP
SNARING
SNARLED
SNEAKED
SNEAKER
SNEAKIN
SNEERAT
SNEERED
SNEERER
SNEEZED
SNEEZER
SNEEZES
SNELLEN
SNICKER
SNIDELY
SNIDEST
SNIFFAT
SNIFFED
SNIFFER
SNIFFLE
SNIFTER
SNIGGER
SNIGGLE
SNIGLET
SNIPEAT
SNIPING
SNIPPED
SNIPPET
SNIVELS
SNOCATS
SNOCONE
SNOOKER
SNOOPED
SNOOPER
SNOOTED
SNOOZED
SNOOZES
SNORERS
SNORING

SNORKEL
SNORTED
SNORTER
SNOWCAP
SNOWDAY
SNOWDON
SNOWIER
SNOWING
SNOWJOB
SNOWMAN
SNOWMEN
SNOWPEA
SNOWSIN
SNUBBED
SNUFFED
SNUFFER
SNUFFLE
SNUGGER
SNUGGLE

S•N••••

SANBORN
SANCTUM
SANDALS
SANDBAG
SANDBAR
SANDBOX
SANDERS
SANDFLY
SANDHOG
SANDIER
SANDING
SANDLOT
SANDMAN
SANDMEN
SANFORD
SANGOUT
SANGRIA
SANIBEL
SANJOSE
SANJUAN
SANLUIS
SANREMO
SANTAFE
SANTANA
SANTINI
SANTIRS
SENATES
SENATOR
SENDERS
SENDFOR
SENDING
SENDOFF
SENDOUT
SENDSIN
SENDSUP
SENDUPS
SENECAS
SENEGAL
SENIORS
SENNETT
SENORAS
SENORES
SENSATE
SENSING
SENSORS
SENSORY
SENSUAL
SENTFOR
SENTOFF
SENTOUT
SINATRA
SINCERE
SINEDIE
SINGERS
SINGING
SINGLED
SINGLES
SINGOUT
SINGSTO
SINKAGE
SINKERS
SINKING
SINKSIN
SINNERS
SINUOUS
SINUSES
SONATAS
SONNETS
SUNBATH
SUNBEAM
SUNBELT
SUNBURN
SUNCITY
SUNDAES
SUNDAYS
SUNDECK
SUNDERS
SUNDEWS
SUNDIAL
SUNDOGS
SUNDOWN
SUNFISH
SUNGODS
SUNKIST
SUNLAMP
SUNLESS
SUNMAID
SUNNIER
SUNNILY
SUNNING
SUNRAYS
SUNRISE
SUNROOF
SUNROOM
SUNSETS
SUNSPOT
SUNTANS
SYNAPSE
SYNCHED
SYNCHES
SYNCING
SYNERGY
SYNFUEL
SYNGMAN
SYNODAL
SYNODIC
SYNONYM

S••N•••

SADNESS
SAINTED
SAINTLY
SAMNUNN
SAUNTER
SCANDAL
SCANNED
SCANNER
SCANTED
SCANTER
SCANTLY
SCENDED
SCENERY
SCENTED
SCHNAPS
SCONCES
SEANCES
SEINERS
SEINING
SENNETT
SHANANA
SHANGRI
SHANKAR
SHANKED
SHANNON
SHANTER
SHINDIG
SHINERS
SHINGLE
SHINIER
SHINING
SHINNED
SHUNNED
SHUNTED
SHYNESS
SIENNAS
SIGNALS
SIGNEES
SIGNERS
SIGNETS
SIGNIFY
SIGNING
SIGNOFF
SIGNOUT
SIGNSIN
SIGNSON
SIGNSUP
SINNERS
SKINNED
SKINNER
SKUNKED
SLANDER
SLANTED
SLENDER
SLINGER
SLINKED
SLYNESS
SOANDSO
SONNETS
SOONERS
SOONEST
SOUNDED
SOUNDER
SOUNDLY
SPANDEX
SPANGLE
SPANGLY
SPANIEL
SPANISH
SPANKED
SPANKER
SPANNED
SPANNER
SPENCER
SPENDER
SPENSER
SPINACH
SPINDLE
SPINDLY
SPINELS
SPINETS
SPINIER
SPINNER
SPINOFF
SPINOUT
SPINOZA
SPONDEE
SPONGED
SPONGER
SPONGES
SPONSOR
SPUNOFF
SPUNOUT
STANCES
STANDBY
STANDEE
STANDIN
STANDON
STANDUP
STANLEE
STANLEY
STANNIC
STANTON
STANZAS
STENCIL
STENGEL
STENTOR
STINGER
STINKER
STINTED
STONERS
STONIER
STONILY
STONING
STUNGUN
STUNNED
STUNNER
STUNTED
SUNNIER
SUNNILY
SUNNING
SURNAME
SWANKER
SWANSON
SWINDLE
SWINGBY
SWINGER

S•••N••

SABINES
SAGINAW
SARANAC
SARONGS
SAVANNA
SAVANTS
SAVINGS
SAYINGS
SCANNED
SCANNER
SCIENCE
SCORNED
SCRUNCH
SECANTS
SECONDS
SELENIC
SEMINAL
SEMINAR
SERENER
SETINTO
SEVENTH
SEVENTY
SEVENUP
SHANNON
SHATNER
SHAWNEE
SHINNED
SHOWNIN
SHRINER
SHRINES
SHRINKS
SHUNNED
SIDINGS
SIENNAS
SILENCE
SILENTS
SIMENON
SIZINGS
SKINNED
SKINNER
SOIGNEE
SPANNED
SPANNER
SPAWNED
SPINNER
SPLINES
SPLINTS
SPOONED
SPOONER
SPRINGS
SPRINGY
SPRINTS
SPURNED
SPURNER
SPUTNIK
SQUANTO
SQUINCH
SQUINTS
SQUINTY
STAINED
STAINER
STANNIC
STAUNCH
STDENIS
STEINEM
STEINER
STERNAL
STERNER
STERNLY
STERNUM
STRANDS
STRANGE
STRINGS
STRINGY
STUNNED
STUNNER
SUBUNIT
SURINAM
SUSANNA
SUSANNE
SUTTNER
SUZANNE
SWOONED
SYNONYM
SYRINGA
SYRINGE

S••••N•

SABRINA
SACKING
SADDENS
SAGGING
SAILING
SALERNO
SALIENT
SALMONS
SALOONS
SALTINE
SALTING
SALVING
SAMNUNN
SAMOANS
SAMPANS
SAMSUNG
SANDING
SANTANA
SANTINI
SAPIENS
SAPIENT
SAPLING
SAPPING
SARDINE
SARGENT
SASSING
SAVANNA
SCALENE
SCALING
SCARING
SCHWINN
SCOPING
SCORING
SCRAWNY
SCREENS
SEAFANS
SEALANE
SEALANT
SEALING
SEAMING
SEARING
SEASONS
SEATING
SEEDING
SEEKING
SEEMING
SEEPING
SEGMENT
SEINING
SEIZING
SELLING
SENDING
SENSING
SEQUINS
SERLING
SERMONS
SERPENT
SERVANT
SERVING
SESTINA
SETLINE
SETTING
SEVIGNE
SEXTANS
SEXTANT
SEXTONS
SHADING
SHAKING
SHAMANS
SHAMING
SHANANA
SHAPING
SHARING
SHAVING
SHEBANG
SHINING
SHOEING
SHOGUNS
SHOOING
SHOOINS
SHORING
SHOVING
SHOWING
SIBLING
SICCING
SICKENS
SIDLING
SIFTING
SIGHING
SIGMUND
SIGNING
SILOING
SILTING
SIMIANS
SIMMONS
SINGING
SINKING
SIOUANS
SIPHONS
SIPPING
SISKINS
SISTINE
SITTING
SIXGUNS
SKATING
SKEWING
SKIRUNS
SKYLINE
SLAKING
SLATING
SLAVING
SLICING
SLIDING
SLIPONS
SLOGANS
SLOPING
SLOVENE
SLOVENS
SLOWING
SMETANA
SMILING
SMITING
SMOKING
SNAKING
SNAPONS
SNARING
SNIPING
SNOCONE
SNORING
SNOWING
SOAKING
SOAPING
SOARING
SOBBING
SOCKING
SODDING
SOFTENS
SOILING
SOLOING
SOLVENT
SOLVING
SOMEONE
SOPPING
SOPRANO
SORTING
SOURING
SOUTANE
SPACING
SPADING
SPARING
SPAVINS
SPAYING
SPELUNK
SPEWING
SPICING
SPIKING
SPIRANT
SPITING
SPLEENS
SPOKANE
SPOKING
SPRAINS
SPUMING
SPUMONE
SPUMONI
STAGING
STAKING
STAMENS
STAMINA
STARING
STATING
STAVING
STAYING
STEPINS
STEVENS
STEWING
STIPEND
STJOHNS
STOKING
STOLONS
STONING
STORING
STOWING
STRAINS
STUDENT
STYLING
STYRENE
SUBBING
SUBORNS
SUBTEND
SUCKING
SUDSING
SUITING
SUKARNO
SULKING
SULTANA
SULTANS
SUMMING
SUMMONS
SUNNING
SUNTANS
SUPPING
SURFING
SURGING
SUSANNA
SUSANNE
SUSPEND
SUSSING
SUZANNE
SWAYING
SWIPING
SYLVANS
SYNCING
SYRIANS

S•••••N

SAFFRON
SAHARAN
SALADIN
SAMISEN
SAMNUNN
SAMPSON
SANBORN
SANDMAN
SANDMEN
SANJUAN
SARACEN
SARAZEN
SAROYAN
SASSOON
SATDOWN
SAURIAN
SAVARIN
SAXHORN
SAYWHEN
SCHWINN
SCRIVEN
SEALION
SECTION
SEEPSIN
SENDSIN
SERBIAN
SESSION
SETDOWN
SETUPON
SHANNON
SHAREIN
SHARPEN
SHELDON
SHELTON
SHERMAN
SHERWIN
SHIPMAN
SHIPMEN
SHODDEN
SHORTEN
SHOTGUN
SHOWMAN
SHOWMEN
SHOWNIN
SHOWSIN
SHUTSIN
SICHUAN
SIDEMAN
SIDEMEN
SIGNSIN
SIGNSON
SILICON
SIMENON
SIMPSON
SINKSIN
SIOBHAN
SIRLOIN
SITDOWN
SIXTEEN
SKELTON
SLACKEN
SLATKIN
SLAYTON
SLEEKEN
SLEEPIN
SLEEPON
SLEPTIN
SLEPTON
SLIDEIN
SLOEGIN
SMARTEN
SMIDGEN
SMITTEN
SNEAKIN
SNELLEN
SNOWDON
SNOWMAN
SNOWMEN
SNOWSIN
SOCKSIN
SOJOURN
SOLOMON
SOTHERN
SOUPCON
SOYBEAN
SPARTAN
SPIEDON
SPIESON
SPORRAN
SPURSON
STANDIN
STANDON
STANTON
STARMAN
STASSEN
STATION
STEEPEN
STEPHEN
STEPSIN
STEPSON
STETSON
STEUBEN
STIFFEN
STILTON
STIRSIN
STOLLEN
STOODIN
STOPSIN
STRIVEN
STUNGUN
STYGIAN
STYRIAN
SUASION
SUBJOIN
SUCKSIN
SUCTION
SUNBURN
SUNDOWN
SURGEON
SUSTAIN
SWANSON
SWEARIN
SWEETEN
SWEETON
SWOLLEN
SWOREIN
SYNGMAN

•S•N•••

ASININE
ASUNDER
PSANDQS
TSONGAS
TSUNAMI
USINGUP

•S••N••

ASCENDS
ASCENTS
ASHANTI
ASKANCE
ASOFNOW
ASSENTS
ESPANOL
ESSENCE
ESSENES
ESTONIA
ISLANDS
OSCINES
OSMONDS
USTINOV

•S•••N•

ASHCANS
ASHLAND
ASININE
ASSIGNS
ASTOUND
ESPYING
ISOGONS
ISSUING
OSBORNE
TSARINA
USOPENS

•S••••N

ASPIRIN

••SN•••

ENSNARE
ENSNARL
MISNAME
UNSNAGS
UNSNAPS
UNSNARL

••S•N••

ABSENCE
ABSENTS
ARSENAL
ARSENIC
ARSENIO
ASSENTS
BASENJI
CASINGS
CASINOS
COSINES
COSTNER
ESSENCE
ESSENES
FISHNET
HOSANNA
JUSTNOW
MASONIC
MASONRY
RESANDS
RESENDS
RESENTS
RESINGS
RISINGS
ROSANNA
ROSANNE
SUSANNA
SUSANNE
TISANES

••S••N•

ABSCOND
ASSIGNS
BASHING
BASKING
BASTING
BESTING
BOSSING
BUSHING
BUSKINS
BUSLINE
BUSSING
BUSTING
BUSYING
CASERNS
CASHING
CASSINI
CASTING
COSIGNS
COSTING
CUSSING
DASHING
DESCANT
DESCEND
DESCENT
DESIGNS
DESMOND
DESTINE
DESTINY
DISBAND
DISHING
DISOWNS
DISSENT
DISTANT
DISTEND
DUSTING
EASTEND
ENSIGNS
ENSUING
ERSKINE
FASTENS
FASTING
FASTONE
FISHING
FUSSING
GASCONS
GASHING
GASKINS
GASPING
GOSLING
GUSHING
GUSTING
HASHING
HASTENS
HASTING
HISPANO
HISSING
HOSANNA
HOSKINS
HOSTING
HUSBAND
HUSHING
HUSKING
IFSTONE
INSPANS
INSTANT
ISSUING
JASMINE
JESTING
JOSHING
JUSTINE
KISSING
LASAGNA
LASAGNE
LASHING
LASTING
LESSENS
LESSING
LESSONS
LISPING
LISTENS
LISTING
LUSTING
MASHING
MASKING
MASSING
MCSWINE
MESHING
MESSINA
MESSING
MISDONE
MISSING
MISTING
MOSSING
MUSHING
MUSLINS
MUSSING
MUSTANG
NASCENT
NESTING
NOSHING
OBSCENE
OUSTING
PASSANT
PASSING
PASTINA
PASTING
PISCINE
PISTONS
POSTING
PUSHING
RASPING
RESCIND
RESIGNS
RESOUND
RESPOND
RESTING
RISKING
ROSANNA
ROSANNE
ROSSINI
ROSTAND
RUSHING
RUSTING
SASSING
SESTINA
SISKINS
SISTINE
SUSANNA
SUSANNE
SUSPEND
SUSSING
TASKING
TASTING
TESTING
TOSSING
TUSCANY
UNSOUND
UNSPENT
UPSWING
VESTING
VISIONS
WASHING
WASTING
WESTEND
WISHING
WISPING
YESSING

••S•••N

ABSTAIN
ALSORAN
BASEMAN
BASEMEN
BASSOON
BASTION
BESTMAN
BESTMEN
BUSHMAN
BUSHMEN
CASPIAN
CESSION
CISTERN
COSTAIN
CUSHION
DISCERN
DISDAIN
DISHPAN
DISJOIN
DUSTPAN
EASEDIN
EASESIN
EASTERN
EASTMAN
EPSILON
EPSTEIN
FASHION
FESTOON
FISSION
FUSTIAN
GASMAIN

HASBEEN
HESHVAN
HESSIAN
HUSSEIN
INSULIN
KOSYGIN
MISSION
PASSION
PASTERN
POSTERN
POSTMAN
POSTMEN
PUSHKIN
PUSHPIN
RESTAIN
RUSSIAN
SASSOON
SESSION
SUSTAIN
TESTBAN
UNSHORN
UPSILON
WESTERN
WISEMAN
WISEMEN

•••SN••

BROSNAN
EDASNER
INASNIT
PARSNIP
PILSNER

•••S•N•

ABASING
ABUSING
AMUSING
ARCSINE
ARISING
ARTSONG
BIASING
BOSSING
BUSSING
CASSINI
CAUSING
CEASING
CENSING
CHASING
CLOSING
CONSENT
COUSINS
CUISINE
CURSING
CUSSING
DAMSONS
DAYSINN
DISSENT
DOUSING
DOWSING
ERASING
FUSSING
GINSENG
GODSEND
GODSONS
GOOSING
HISSING
HORSING
HOUSING
JETSONS
KANSANS
KISSING
KMESONS
KRISHNA
LANSING
LAPSING
LEASING
LESSENS
LESSING
LESSONS
LIPSYNC
LOOSENS
LOOSING
LOUSING
MASSING
MESSINA
MESSING
MISSING
MOSSING
MOUSING
MUSSING
NELSONS
NOISING
NOOSING
NURSING
ORISONS
PAISANO
PARSING
PARSONS
PASSANT
PASSING
PAUSING
PEASANT
PEPSINS
PERSONA
PERSONS
PHASING
POISING
POISONS
PORSENA
PRESENT
PRISONS
PROSING
PULSING
PURSING
RAISING
RAISINS
REASONS
RETSINA
RINSING
ROSSINI
ROUSING
SAMSUNG
SASSING
SEASONS
SENSING
SUDSING
SUSSING
TEASING
TENSING
TOCSINS
TOSSING
TULSANS
UNISONS
WORSENS
YESSING

•••S••N

ALASKAN
ALLSTON
ANDSOON
BASSOON
BATSMAN
BATSMEN
BRESLIN
BRESSON
BROSNAN
BURSTYN
CAISSON
CAPSTAN
CATSCAN
CESSION
CHASTEN
CLOSEIN
CONSIGN
CRISPIN
DAYSINN
DOESKIN
DRESDEN
DRISTAN
EELSKIN
ELISION
ELYSIAN
EROSION
ETESIAN
EVASION
FISSION
FRESHEN
FRISIAN
FRISSON
GADSDEN
GLISTEN
HALSTON
HARSHEN
HESSIAN
HEXSIGN
HOUSMAN
HOUSTON
HUSSEIN
INASPIN
JANSSEN
KEESHAN
KIDSKIN
KINSMAN
KINSMEN
KTOSLIN
MANSION
MEISSEN
MISSION
MOISTEN
MONSOON
NEWSMAN
NEWSMEN
NILSSON
OILSKIN
PASSION
PENSION
PERSIAN
PHASEIN
PIGSKIN
PLOSION
POISSON
PRESSON
PRESTON
RALSTON
REDSKIN
RUSSIAN
SASSOON
SESSION
STASSEN
SUASION
TENSION
TORSION
TRISTAN
VERSION
WINSTON

••••SN•

DEMESNE

••••S•N

ACHESON
ADAMSON
ADDISON
ALLISON
ALLYSON
ARTISAN
BACKSIN
BANKSON
BEARSON
BENISON
BENTSEN
BERGSON
BERNSEN
BLOUSON
BLOWSIN
BOXESIN
BRANSON
BRESSON
BRONSON
BUTTSIN
CAISSON
CALLSIN
CALLSON
CARLSON
CAVESIN
CHANSON
CHIPSIN
CLEMSON
CLUESIN
COARSEN
COMESIN
COMESON
CRIMSON
DEALSIN
DINESEN
DINESIN
DINESON
DIVESIN
DODGSON
DOTESON
DRAGSIN
DRAGSON
DRAWSIN
DRAWSON
DROPSIN
EASESIN
EDGESIN
ELEISON
ELLISON
EMERSON
ERICSON
FADESIN
FALLSIN
FALLSON
FEEDSON
FILLSIN
FLIESIN
FRISSON
GAINSON
GIVESIN
GLEASON
GOODSON
GRAYSON
GROWSON
HANDSIN
HANDSON
HANGSIN
HANGSON
HARPSON
HEADSIN
HIRESON
HOARSEN
HOLDSON
JACKSON
JAMESON
JANSSEN
JOHNSON
JOINSIN
JUMPSIN
JUMPSON
KEEPSIN
KEEPSON
KICKSIN
LEADSIN
LEADSON
LEANSON
LIAISON
LIVESIN
LIVESON
LOOKSIN
LOOKSON
MADISON
MEISSEN
MOVESIN
MUMESON
NIELSEN
NILSSON
ORBISON
PAULSEN
PEARSON
PEERSIN
PICKSON
PILESIN
PILESON
PIMESON
PLANSON
PLAYSON
PLUGSIN
POISSON
POURSIN
PRESSON
PREYSON
RAKESIN
READSIN
REELSIN
REINSIN
ROBESON
ROPESIN
RULESON
SAMISEN
SAMPSON
SEEPSIN
SENDSIN
SHOWSIN
SHUTSIN
SIGNSIN
SIGNSON
SIMPSON
SINKSIN
SNOWSIN
SOCKSIN
SPIESON
SPURSON
STASSEN
STEPSIN
STEPSON
STETSON
STIRSIN
STOPSIN
SUCKSIN
SWANSON
TACKSON
TAKESIN
TAKESON
TELLSON
THOMSON
TREASON
TRIESON
TUCKSIN
TUNESIN
TURNSIN
TURNSON
UPRISEN
VENISON
VOTESIN
WADESIN
WAITSON
WANTSIN
WAVESIN
WILLSON
WORKSIN
WORKSON
YELTSIN
ZOOMSIN

SO•••••

SOAKERS
SOAKING
SOAKSUP
SOANDSO
SOAPBOX
SOAPERS
SOAPIER
SOAPING
SOARERS
SOARING
SOBBERS
SOBBING
SOBERED
SOBERER
SOBERLY
SOCIALS
SOCIETY
SOCKETS
SOCKEYE
SOCKING
SOCKSIN
SODAPOP
SODDING
SOFABED
SOFFITS
SOFTENS
SOFTEST
SOFTIES
SOFTTOP
SOGGIER
SOGGILY
SOIGNEE
SOILING
SOIREES
SOJOURN
SOLACES
SOLARIA
SOLDERS
SOLDIER
SOLDOFF
SOLDOUT
SOLEDAD
SOLFEGE
SOLICIT
SOLIDER
SOLIDLY
SOLOING
SOLOIST
SOLOMON
SOLUBLE
SOLUTES
SOLVENT
SOLVERS
SOLVING
SOMALIA
SOMALIS
SOMATIC
SOMEDAY
SOMEHOW
SOMEONE
SOMEWAY
SONATAS
SONNETS
SOONERS
SOONEST
SOOTHED
SOOTHER
SOOTHES
SOOTIER
SOPHISM
SOPHIST
SOPPING
SOPRANO
SOPWITH
SORBATE
SORBETS
SORCERY
SORGHUM
SORITES
SORORAL
SORRELS
SORRIER
SORROWS
SORTERS
SORTIED
SORTIES
SORTING
SOSUEME
SOTHERE
SOTHERN
SOUFFLE
SOUGHED
SOULFUL
SOUNDED
SOUNDER
SOUNDLY
SOUPCON
SOUPIER
SOUPSUP
SOURCED
SOURCES
SOUREST
SOURING
SOURISH
SOUTANE
SOUTHEY
SOVIETS
SOWBUGS
SOYBEAN

S•O••••

SAOTOME
SCOFFED
SCOFFER
SCOLDED
SCOLDER
SCONCES
SCOOPED
SCOOPER
SCOOTED
SCOOTER
SCOPING
SCORERS
SCORING
SCORNED
SCORPIO
SCOTERS
SCOTTIE
SCOURED
SCOURER
SCOURGE
SCOUTED
SCOUTER
SCOWLED
SCOWLER
SHOCKED
SHOCKER
SHODDEN
SHOEBOX
SHOEING
SHOFARS
SHOGUNS
SHOOFLY
SHOOING
SHOOINS
SHOOKUP
SHOOTAT
SHOOTER
SHOOTUP
SHOPPED
SHOPPER
SHOPPES
SHORING
SHORTED
SHORTEN
SHORTER
SHORTLY
SHORTOF
SHOTFOR
SHOTGUN
SHOTPUT
SHOUTED
SHOUTER
SHOVELS
SHOVERS
SHOVING
SHOWBIZ
SHOWDOG
SHOWERS
SHOWERY
SHOWIER
SHOWILY
SHOWING
SHOWMAN
SHOWMEN
SHOWNIN
SHOWOFF
SHOWSIN
SHOWSUP
SIOBHAN
SIOUANS
SKOSHES
SLOBBER
SLOEGIN
SLOGANS
SLOGGED
SLOPING
SLOPPED
SLOSHED
SLOSHES
SLOTCAR
SLOTTED
SLOUCHY
SLOUGHS
SLOVAKS
SLOVENE
SLOVENS
SLOWEST
SLOWING
SLOWSUP
SMOKERS
SMOKIER
SMOKIES
SMOKING
SMOLDER
SMOOTHS
SMOTHER
SNOCATS
SNOCONE
SNOOKER
SNOOPED
SNOOPER
SNOOTED
SNOOZED
SNOOZES
SNORERS
SNORING
SNORKEL
SNORTED
SNORTER
SNOWCAP
SNOWDAY
SNOWDON
SNOWIER
SNOWING
SNOWJOB
SNOWMAN
SNOWMEN
SNOWPEA
SNOWSIN
SOONERS
SOONEST
SOOTHED
SOOTHER
SOOTHES
SOOTIER
SPOILED
SPOILER
SPOKANE
SPOKEOF
SPOKEUP
SPOKING
SPONDEE
SPONGED
SPONGER
SPONGES
SPONSOR
SPOOFED
SPOOFER
SPOOKED
SPOOLED
SPOONED
SPOONER
SPORRAN
SPORTED
SPOTLIT
SPOTTED
SPOTTER
SPOUSAL
SPOUSES
SPOUTED
SPOUTER
STOCKED
STOCKUP
STOGIES
STOICAL
STOKELY
STOKERS
STOKING
STOLLEN
STOLLER
STOLONS
STOMACH
STOMATA
STOMPED
STONERS
STONIER
STONILY
STONING
STOODBY
STOODIN
STOODUP
STOOGES
STOOKEY
STOOLIE
STOOPED
STOOPTO
STOPGAP
STOPOFF
STOPPED
STOPPER
STOPSIN
STOPSUP
STORAGE
STORERS
STOREUP
STOREYS
STORIED
STORIES
STORING
STORMED
STOUTER
STOUTLY
STOWING
SWOLLEN
SWOONED
SWOOPED
SWOOSIE
SWOREAT
SWOREBY
SWOREIN

S••O•••

SALOONS
SAMOANS
SAMOVAR
SAMOYED
SARONGS
SAROYAN
SAVORED
SAVOURS
SAVOURY
SCHOLAR
SCHOOLS
SCOOPED
SCOOPER
SCOOTED
SCOOTER
SCROLLS
SCROOGE
SECONDS
SEGOVIA
SENORAS
SENORES
SHOOFLY
SHOOING
SHOOINS
SHOOKUP
SHOOTAT
SHOOTER
SHOOTUP
SHROUDS
SILOING
SIROCCO
SMOOTHS
SNOOKER
SNOOPED
SNOOPER
SNOOTED
SNOOZED
SNOOZES
SOJOURN
SOLOING
SOLOIST
SOLOMON
SORORAL
SPLOTCH
SPOOFED
SPOOFER
SPOOKED
SPOOLED
SPOONED
SPOONER
SPROUTS
STJOHNS
STLOUIS
STOODBY
STOODIN
STOODUP
STOOGES
STOOKEY
STOOLIE
STOOPED
STOOPTO
STROBES
STROKED
STROKES
STROLLS
STROPHE
SUBORNS
SWOONED
SWOOPED
SWOOSIE
SYNODAL
SYNODIC
SYNONYM

S•••O••

SACKOUT
SAILORS
SALMONS
SALOONS
SALSODA
SALVOES
SANBORN
SANFORD
SANGOUT
SANJOSE
SAOTOME
SAPPORO
SASSOON
SATDOWN
SAVIORS
SAWLOGS
SAWWOOD
SAXHORN
SCHLOCK
SCHMOES
SCHMOOS
SCHOOLS
SCROOGE
SEABORG
SEACOWS
SEADOGS
SEAFOOD
SEALOFF
SEAMOSS
SEAPORT
SEASONS
SECTORS
SEEKOUT
SEESOFF
SEESOUT
SEETOIT
SELLOFF
SELLOUT
SENDOFF
SENDOUT
SENIORS
SENSORS
SENSORY
SENTOFF
SENTOUT
SEQUOIA
SERIOUS
SERMONS
SETDOWN
SETSOFF
SETSOUT
SEXTONS
SEYMOUR
SHADOOF
SHADOWS
SHADOWY
SHAKOES
SHALOMS
SHEWOLF
SHIPOUT
SHOWOFF
SHUTOFF
SHUTOUT
SHYLOCK
SICKOUT
SIGNOFF
SIGNOUT
SIMMONS
SINGOUT
SINUOUS
SIPHONS
SIRLOIN
SITCOMS
SITDOWN
SITSOUT
SIXFOLD
SKIBOOT
SKIPOLE
SKIPOUT
SKITOWS
SKYHOOK
SLALOMS
SLIPONS
SLIPOUT
SNAPONS
SNOCONE
SOLDOFF
SOLDOUT
SOMEONE
SORROWS
SPIGOTS
SPINOFF
SPINOUT
SPINOZA
SPUMONE
SPUMONI
SPUNOFF
SPUNOUT
STATORS
STCROIX
STEPOUT
STEROID
STEROLS
STOLONS
STOPOFF
STUPORS
SUBJOIN
SUBROSA
SUBSOIL
SUCCORS
SUCCOUR
SUCROSE
SUFFOLK
SUITORS
SUMMONS
SUNDOGS
SUNDOWN
SUNGODS
SUNROOF
SUNROOM
SUPPORT
SUPPOSE
SURCOAT
SYMBOLS
SYSTOLE

S••••O•

SAFFRON
SALCHOW
SALTBOX
SAMPSON
SANDBOX
SANDHOG
SANDLOT
SASSOON
SAWWOOD
SCALLOP
SCHMOOS
SCISSOR
SEAFOOD
SEALION
SECTION
SEEDPOD
SENATOR
SENDFOR
SENTFOR
SERFDOM
SESSION
SETUPON
SHADOOF
SHAHDOM
SHALLOT
SHALLOW
SHAMPOO
SHANNON
SHELDON
SHELTON
SHOEBOX
SHORTOF
SHOTFOR
SHOWDOG
SIGNSON
SILICON
SIMENON
SIMPSON
SKELTON
SKIBOOT
SKIDDOO
SKIDROW
SKYHOOK
SLAYTON
SLEDDOG
SLEEPON
SLEPTON
SMALTOS

SNOWDON
SNOWJOB
SOAPBOX
SODAPOP
SOFTTOP
SOLOMON
SOMEHOW
SOUPCON
SPARROW
SPEAKOF
SPECTOR
SPIEDON
SPIESON
SPOKEOF
SPONSOR
SPURSON
SQUALOR
STANDON
STANTON
STARDOM
STATION
STENTOR
STEPSON
STEREOS
STETSON
STILTON
STUCCOS
STUDIOS
SUASION
SUBPLOT
SUCTION
SUNROOF
SUNROOM
SUNSPOT
SURGEON
SWALLOW
SWANSON
SWEETON
SYMPTOM

S•••••O

SAGUARO
SALERNO
SANREMO
SAPPORO
SAPSAGO
SATCHMO
SCHERZO
SCORPIO
SEMIPRO
SERPICO
SETINTO
SHAMPOO
SHAPIRO
SINGSTO
SIROCCO
SKIDDOO
SNAPSTO
SOANDSO
SOPRANO
SPIRITO
SQUANTO
STICKTO
STOOPTO
STRETTO
STUCKTO
SUBZERO
SUKARNO
SUPREMO
SWEARTO

•SO••••

ASOCIAL
ASOFNOW
ISOBARS
ISOGONS
ISOHELS
ISOLATE
ISOMERS
ISOPODS
ISOTOPE
TSONGAS
USOPENS
USOSHOW

•S•O•••

ASSORTS
ASTOLAT
ASTORIA
ASTOUND
ESCORTS
ESPOSAS
ESPOSOS
ESPOUSE
ESTONIA
ESTORIL
OSBORNE
OSMONDS
OSMOSED
OSMOSES
OSMOSIS
OSMOTIC

•S••O••

ASHFORD
ASKSOUT
ESCROWS
ISADORA
ISOGONS
ISOPODS
ISOTOPE
OSCEOLA
OSHKOSH
OSTEOID

•S•••O•

ASKSFOR
ASOFNOW
ESCUDOS
ESKIMOS
ESPANOL
ESPOSOS
TSELIOT
USOSHOW
USTINOV

••SO•••

ABSOLUT
ABSOLVE
ABSORBS
ADSORBS
ALSORAN
ASSORTS
DESOTOS
DISOBEY
DISOWNS
ENSOULS
GASOHOL
IMSORRY
INSOFAR
INSOLES
LASORDA
LESOTHO
MASONIC
MASONRY
OFSORTS
RESOLED
RESOLES
RESOLVE
RESORBS
RESORTS
RESOUND
RISOTTO
UNSOUND

••S•O••

ABSCOND
BASSOON
BESPOKE
BESTOWS
BISHOPS
BUSBOYS
BUSTOUT
CASHOUT
CASSOCK
CASTOFF
CASTOUT
CUSTODY
CUSTOMS
DASBOOT
DASHOFF
DESMOND
DESPOIL
DESPOTS
DISCOED
DISCORD
DISHOUT
DISJOIN
DISPORT
DISPOSE
DISROBE
DISTORT
DRSPOCK
DUSTOFF
EASEOFF
FASTONE
FESTOON
FISHOUT
GASCONS
GASEOUS
GESSOES
GUSTOES
HASSOCK
HISTORY
HYSSOPS
IFSTONE
INSHORT
INSPOTS
INSTOCK
INSTORE
KISSOFF
LASSOED
LASSOER
LASSOES
LASTORY
LESSONS
LESSORS
LISSOME
LOSEOUT
LOSTOUT
MASCOTS
MASTOID
MISDOES
MISDONE
MISSOUT
MISTOOK
MISWORD
MRSPOCK
MUSCOVY
NOSEOUT
NOSHOWS
ONSHORE
PASSOFF
PASSOUT
PASTORS
PISCOPO
PISTOLE
PISTOLS
PISTONS
PUSHOFF
RESHOES
RESHOOT
RESPOND
RESTOCK
RESTORE
RISSOLE
ROSEOIL
RUSHOFF
SASSOON
SYSTOLE
TESTOUT
TOSSOFF
TOSSOUT
TUSSOCK
TVSHOWS
UNSHORN
UNSTOPS
UPSHOTS
VISCOUS
VISIONS
WASHOFF
WASHOUT

••S••O•

ABSALOM
BASSOON
BASTION
BESTBOY
BISTROS
BUSHHOG
BUSSTOP
CASHBOX
CASHCOW
CASINOS
CESSION
CUSHION
DASBOOT
DESKTOP
DESOTOS
DESTROY
DISAVOW
DOSIDOS
DUSTMOP
EPSILON
FASHION
FESTOON
FISSION
FUSSPOT
GASOHOL
JUSTNOW
MISSION
MISTOOK
NOSEJOB
PASSFOR
PASSION
POSTBOX
POSTHOC
RESHOOT
SASSOON
SESSION
UPSILON
VISITOR

••S•••O

ARSENIO
BUSHIDO
HISPANO
LESOTHO
MESTIZO
PISCOPO
RISOTTO

•••SO••

ACESOUT
ACTSOUT
AIRSOCK
AIRSOUT
ANDSOON
ARTSONG
ASKSOUT
AWESOME
BARSOAP
BASSOON
BEGSOFF
BONSOIR
BOWSOUT
BUGSOFF
BUGSOUT
BUMSOUT
BUYSOFF
BUYSOUT
CASSOCK
CENSORS
CONSOLE
CONSORT
COPSOUT
CURSORS
CURSORY
CUTSOFF
CUTSOUT
DAMSONS
DIESOFF
DIESOUT
DIGSOUT
EATSOUT
EKESOUT
EPISODE
EYESORE
FANSOUT
FOBSOFF
FORSOOK
FULSOME
GESSOES
GETSOFF
GETSOUT
GODSONS
GOESOFF
GOESOUT
HANSOLO
HANSOMS
HASSOCK
HOPSOFF
HYSSOPS
IRISOUT
IRKSOME
JETSONS
KISSOFF
KMESONS
LASSOED
LASSOER
LASSOES
LAYSOFF
LAYSOUT
LESSONS
LESSORS
LETSOFF
LETSOUT
LISSOME
LOGSOFF
LOGSOUT
MISSOUT
MONSOON
NELSONS
NODSOFF
NOISOME
OFASORT
OPTSOUT
ORISONS
OUTSOLD
PANSOUT
PARSONS
PASSOFF
PASSOUT
PAYSOFF
PAYSOUT
PEASOUP
PERSONA
PERSONS
PIGSOUT
POISONS
POPSOFF
POPSOUT
PRESOAK
PRESORT
PRISONS
PROSODY
PUTSOFF
PUTSOUT
RANSOMS
REASONS
RIPSOFF
RISSOLE
RUBSOUT
RUNSOFF
RUNSOUT
SALSODA
SASSOON
SEASONS
SEESOFF
SEESOUT
SENSORS
SENSORY
SETSOFF
SETSOUT
SITSOUT
SUBSOIL
TAGSOUT
TAPSOUT
TEESOFF
TENSORS
TIPSOFF
TOPSOFF
TOPSOIL
TOPSOUT
TOSSOFF
TOSSOUT
TUSSOCK
TWOSOME
UNISONS
WIGSOUT
WINSOME
WINSOUT

•••S•O•

AIRSHOW
ALLSTON
ANDSOON
ARISTOS
ASKSFOR
BASSOON
BIGSHOT
BLOSSOM
BOLSHOI
BRESSON
BRISTOL
BUSSTOP
CAISSON
CESSION
DOGSHOW
EARSHOT
ELISION
EROSION
EVASION
FIASCOS
FISSION
FORSOOK
FRESCOS
FRISSON
FUSSPOT
GEMSBOK
GLASGOW
GOESFOR
GRISSOM
GUMSHOE
GUNSFOR
GUNSHOT
GYMSHOE
HALSTON
HOTSHOT
HOTSPOT
HOUSTON
ICESHOW
INASPOT
INKSPOT
KNOSSOS
LAYSFOR
LAYSLOW
LIESLOW
MANSION
MISSION
MONSOON
MUGSHOT
NEWSBOY
NILSSON
NONSTOP
ONESHOT
PASSFOR
PASSION
PAYSFOR
PENSION
PITSTOP
PLOSION
POISSON
POTSHOT
PRESSON
PRESTON
PRESTOS
RALSTON
REDSPOT
RIMSHOT
SASSOON
SCISSOR
SESSION
SUASION
SUNSPOT
TEASHOP
TENSION
TENSPOT
TOESHOE
TOLSTOI
TOLSTOY
TORSION
TOYSHOP
USOSHOW
VERSION
WINSLOW
WINSTON

•••S••O

AGESAGO
CANSECO
HANSOLO
MAESTRO
PAISANO
SAPSAGO
WHOSWHO

••••SO•

ACHESON
ADAMSON
ADDISON
ADVISOR
AEROSOL
ALLISON
ALLYSON
ARIOSOS
BANKSON
BEARSON
BENISON
BERGSON
BLOSSOM
BLOUSON
BRANSON
BRESSON
BRONSON
CAISSON
CALLSON
CARLSON
CHANSON
CLEMSON
COMESON
CREOSOL
CRIMSON
DINESON
DIVISOR
DODGSON
DOTESON
DRAGSON
DRAWSON
ELEISON
ELLISON
EMERSON
ERICSON
ESPOSOS
FALLSON
FEEDSON
FRISSON
GAINSON
GIRASOL
GLEASON
GOODSON
GRAYSON
GRISSOM
GROWSON
HANDSON
HANGSON
HARPSON
HEARSOF
HIRESON
HOLDSON
INCISOR
JACKSON
JAMESON
JOHNSON
JUMPSON
KEEPSON
KNOSSOS
LEADSON
LEANSON
LIAISON
LIVESON
LOOKSON
MADISON
MILKSOP
MUMESON
NILSSON
ORBISON
PARASOL
PEARSON
PICKSON
PILESON
PIMESON
PLANSON
PLAYSON
POISSON
PRESSON
PREYSON
ROBESON
RULESON
SAMPSON
SCISSOR
SIGNSON
SIMPSON
SPIESON
SPONSOR
SPURSON
STEPSON
STETSON
SWANSON
TACKSON
TAKESON
TELLSON
THOMSON
TRANSOM
TREASON
TRIESON
TURNSON
VENISON
WAITSON
WILLSON
WINDSOR
WORKSON

••••S•O

ARIOSTO
CHRISTO
COMESTO
DARESTO
ERNESTO
FALLSTO
GEARSTO
GIVESTO
HOLDSTO
IMPASTO
IONESCO
JALISCO
KEEPSTO
LEADSTO
LOOKSTO
MAKESDO
MODESTO
NABISCO
PICASSO
PRAYSTO
SINGSTO
SNAPSTO
TABASCO
TAKESTO
TALKSTO
TENDSTO
TURNSTO
WANTSTO

•••••SO

ALFONSO
CALYPSO
MAFIOSO
OLOROSO
PICASSO
PROVISO
SOANDSO

SP•••••

SPACERS
SPACIER
SPACING
SPACKLE
SPADERS
SPADING
SPALLED
SPANDEX
SPANGLE
SPANGLY
SPANIEL
SPANISH
SPANKED
SPANKER
SPANNED
SPANNER
SPARELY
SPAREST
SPARGED
SPARGES
SPARING
SPARKED
SPARKLE
SPARRED
SPARROW
SPARSER
SPARTAN
SPASSKY
SPATIAL
SPATTED
SPATTER
SPATULA
SPAVINS
SPAWNED
SPAYING
SPEAKER
SPEAKOF
SPEAKUP
SPEARED
SPECIAL
SPECIES
SPECIFY
SPECKLE
SPECTER
SPECTOR
SPECTRA
SPECTRE
SPEEDED
SPEEDER
SPEEDUP
SPELLED
SPELLER
SPELUNK
SPENCER
SPENDER
SPENSER
SPEWING
SPHERES
SPICEUP
SPICIER
SPICING
SPIDERS
SPIDERY
SPIEDON
SPIEGEL
SPIELED
SPIELER
SPIESON
SPIGOTS
SPIKERS
SPIKIER
SPIKING
SPILLED
SPINACH
SPINDLE
SPINDLY
SPINELS
SPINETS
SPINIER
SPINNER
SPINOFF
SPINOUT
SPINOZA
SPIRALS
SPIRANT
SPIREAS
SPIRITO
SPIRITS
SPITING
SPITZES
SPLASHY
SPLAYED
SPLEENS
SPLICED
SPLICER
SPLICES
SPLINES
SPLINTS
SPLITUP
SPLOTCH
SPLURGE
SPOILED
SPOILER
SPOKANE
SPOKEOF
SPOKEUP
SPOKING
SPONDEE
SPONGED
SPONGER
SPONGES
SPONSOR
SPOOFED
SPOOFER
SPOOKED
SPOOLED
SPOONED
SPOONER
SPORRAN
SPORTED
SPOTLIT
SPOTTED
SPOTTER
SPOUSAL
SPOUSES
SPOUTED
SPOUTER
SPRAINS
SPRAWLS
SPRAYED
SPRAYER
SPREADS
SPRIEST
SPRINGS
SPRINGY
SPRINTS
SPRITES
SPROUTS
SPRUCED
SPRUCER
SPRUCES
SPRYEST
SPUMING
SPUMONE
SPUMONI
SPUNOFF
SPUNOUT
SPURNED
SPURNER
SPURRED
SPURSON
SPURTED
SPUTNIK
SPUTTER

S•P••••

SAPIENS
SAPIENT
SAPLING
SAPPERS
SAPPIER
SAPPING
SAPPORO
SAPSAGO
SEPTETS
SIPHONS
SIPPERS
SIPPETS
SIPPING
SOPHISM
SOPHIST
SOPPING
SOPRANO
SOPWITH
STPETER
SUPPERS
SUPPING
SUPPLER
SUPPORT
SUPPOSE
SUPREME
SUPREMO

S••P•••

SAMPANS
SAMPLED
SAMPLER
SAMPLES
SAMPRAS
SAMPSON
SAPPERS
SAPPIER
SAPPING
SAPPORO
SCAPULA
SCEPTER
SCEPTRE
SCOPING
SCUPPER
SEAPORT
SEEPING
SEEPSIN
SERPENT
SERPICO
SHAPELY
SHAPERS
SHAPEUP
SHAPING
SHAPIRO
SHEPARD
SHIPMAN
SHIPMEN
SHIPOUT
SHIPPED
SHIPPER
SHOPPED
SHOPPER
SHOPPES
SIMPERS
SIMPLER
SIMPLEX
SIMPSON
SIPPERS
SIPPETS
SIPPING
SIXPACK
SKEPTIC
SKIPOLE
SKIPOUT
SKIPPED
SKIPPER
SLAPPED
SLEPTIN
SLEPTON
SLIPONS
SLIPOUT
SLIPPED
SLIPPER
SLIPSUP
SLIPUPS
SLOPING
SLOPPED
SNAPONS
SNAPPED
SNAPPER
SNAPSAT
SNAPSTO
SNAPSUP
SNIPEAT
SNIPING
SNIPPED
SNIPPET
SOAPBOX
SOAPERS
SOAPIER
SOAPING
SOPPING
SOUPCON
SOUPIER
SOUPSUP
STAPLED
STAPLER
STAPLES
STEPHEN
STEPINS
STEPOUT
STEPPED
STEPPER
STEPPES
STEPSIN
STEPSON
STEPSUP
STEPUPS
STIPEND
STIPPLE
STOPGAP
STOPOFF

STOPPED
STOPPER
STOPSIN
STOPSUP
STUPEFY
STUPORS
STYPTIC
SUBPLOT
SULPHUR
SUPPERS
SUPPING
SUPPLER
SUPPORT
SUPPOSE
SURPASS
SURPLUS
SUSPECT
SUSPEND
SWAPPED
SWAPPER
SWEPTUP
SWIPERS
SWIPING
SYMPTOM

S•••P••

SCALPED
SCALPEL
SCALPER
SCAMPED
SCAMPER
SCARPED
SCOOPED
SCOOPER
SCORPIO
SCRAPED
SCRAPER
SCRAPES
SCRAPPY
SCRIPPS
SCRIPTS
SCRUPLE
SCULPTS
SCUPPER
SEEDPOD
SEMIPRO
SERAPES
SERAPHS
SERAPIS
SETUPON
SHAMPOO
SHARPED
SHARPEI
SHARPEN
SHARPER
SHARPLY
SHERPAS
SHIPPED
SHIPPER
SHOPPED
SHOPPER
SHOPPES
SHOTPUT
SICKPAY
SKIMPED
SKIPPED
SKIPPER
SLAPPED
SLEEPER
SLEEPIN
SLEEPON
SLIPPED
SLIPPER
SLOPPED
SLUMPED
SLURPED
SNAPPED
SNAPPER
SNIPPED
SNIPPET
SNOOPED
SNOOPER
SNOWPEA
SODAPOP
STAMPED
STAYPUT
STEEPED
STEEPEN
STEEPER
STEEPLE
STEEPLY
STEPPED
STEPPER
STEPPES
STIPPLE
STOMPED
STOOPED
STOOPTO
STOPPED
STOPPER
STRIPED
STRIPER
STRIPES
STROPHE
STUMPED
STUMPER
SUNSPOT
SWAMPED
SWAPPED
SWAPPER
SWEEPER
SWEEPUP
SWOOPED
SYNAPSE

S••••P•

SATRAPS
SCHLEPP
SCHLEPS
SCHNAPS
SCRAPPY
SCRIMPS
SCRIMPY
SCRIPPS
SENDUPS
SHRIMPS
SKYCAPS
SLIPUPS
STEPUPS

S•••••P

SAVEDUP
SAVESUP
SCALLOP
SCAREUP
SCHLEPP
SCREWUP
SCRUBUP
SEALSUP
SENDSUP
SERVEUP
SEVENUP
SEWEDUP
SHAKEUP
SHAPEUP
SHOOKUP
SHOOTUP
SHOWSUP
SHUTSUP
SIGNSUP
SIZEDUP
SIZESUP
SKIJUMP
SLIPSUP
SLOWSUP
SMASHUP
SNAPSUP
SNOWCAP
SOAKSUP
SODAPOP
SOFTTOP
SOUPSUP
SPEAKUP
SPEEDUP
SPICEUP
SPLITUP
SPOKEUP
STACKUP
STANDUP
STARMAP
STARTUP
STAYSUP
STEPSUP
STICKUP
STIRRUP
STIRSUP
STOCKUP
STOODUP
STOPGAP
STOPSUP
STOREUP
STUCKUP
SUITSUP
SUNLAMP
SWEEPUP
SWELLUP
SWEPTUP

•SP••••

ASPECTS
ASPERSE
ASPHALT
ASPIRED
ASPIRER
ASPIRES
ASPIRIN
ESPANOL
ESPIALS
ESPOSAS
ESPOSOS
ESPOUSE
ESPYING
OSPREYS

•S•P•••

ASEPSIS
ASEPTIC
ISOPODS
USOPENS

•S••P••

ESCAPED
ESCAPEE
ESCAPES
USURPED
USURPER

•S•••P•

ESCARPS
ISOTOPE

•S••••P

PSYCHUP
USINGUP

••SP•••

ANSPACH
AUSPICE
BESPEAK
BESPOKE
CASPIAN
CUSPIDS
DESPAIR
DESPISE
DESPITE
DESPOIL
DESPOTS
DISPELS
DISPLAY
DISPORT
DISPOSE
DISPUTE
DRSPOCK
GASPING
GASPUMP
GOSPELS
HISPANO
HOSPICE
INSPANS
INSPECT
INSPIRE
INSPOTS
JASPERS
LESPAUL
LISPING
MISPLAY
MRSPOCK
RASPERS
RASPIER
RASPING
RESPECT
RESPIRE
RESPITE
RESPOND
SUSPECT
SUSPEND
TOSPARE
UNSPENT
VESPERS
VESPIDS
WASPISH
WISPIER
WISPILY
WISPING

••S•P••

BASEPAY
BUSHPIG
DISHPAN
DUSTPAN
FUSSPOT
INSIPID
PUSHPIN

••S••P•

BISHOPS
DISRUPT
DUSTUPS
GASCAPS
GOSSIPS
GOSSIPY
HYSSOPS
INSCAPE
INSHAPE
INSTEPS
LASHUPS
MISHAPS
MISTYPE
PISCOPO
PUSHUPS
RESHIPS
TOSSUPS
UNSNAPS
UNSTOPS
UNSWEPT
UPSWEPT

••S•••P

BUSSTOP
DESKTOP
DUSTMOP
EASEDUP
EASESUP
GASPUMP
GUSSYUP
MISSTEP
PASTEUP
RESTAMP
RESTSUP
UNSTRAP
UPSWEEP
WISEDUP
WISESUP

•••SP••

CATSPAW
CLASPED
CRISPED
CRISPER
CRISPIN
CRISPLY
CRISPUS
FUSSPOT
GRASPED
HOTSPOT
HOTSPUR
INASPIN
INASPOT
INKSPOT
PROSPER
REDSPOT
SUNSPOT
TENSPOT
THESPIS
WHISPER

•••S•P•

GOESAPE
GOSSIPS
GOSSIPY
HYSSOPS
TOSSUPS

•••S••P

AIRSHIP
BARSOAP
BOOSTUP
BOXSTEP
BRUSHUP
BUSSTOP
CLOSEUP
COWSLIP
CROSSUP
DRESSUP
GUSSYUP
HANSARP
KINSHIP
LETSLIP
LOUSEUP
MISSTEP
NONSLIP
NONSTOP
ONESTEP
OUTSTEP
PARSNIP
PEASOUP
PITSTOP
RAISEUP
SMASHUP
TEASHOP
TENSEUP
TOYSHOP
TWOSTEP
WARSHIP
WORSHIP

••••S•P

ANTESUP
BACKSUP
BALLSUP
BANGSUP
BEADSUP
BEAMSUP
BEARSUP
BEATSUP
BEEFSUP
BINDSUP
BLOWSUP
BONESUP
BOOTSUP
BOXESUP
BUCKSUP
BUMPSUP
BUOYSUP
BURNSUP
CALLSUP
CHATSUP
CHEWSUP
CLAMSUP
CLOGSUP
COILSUP
COMESUP
COOKSUP
COOPSUP
CROPSUP
CROSSUP
CURLSUP
DOLLSUP
DRAWSUP
DRESSUP
DRIESUP
DRUMSUP
EASESUP
EVENSUP
FAIRSUP
FILLSUP
FIRESUP
FIRMSUP
FIXESUP
FOLDSUP
FOULSUP
GANGSUP
GEARSUP
GIVESUP
GOOFSUP
GROWSUP
HANDSUP
HANGSUP
HAULSUP
HEADSUP
HEATSUP
HOLDSUP
HOLESUP
HOOKSUP
JACKSUP
JOINSUP
JUMPSUP
KEEPSUP
KICKSUP
LACESUP
LEADSUP
LIFTSUP
LINESUP
LOCKSUP
LOOKSUP
MAKESUP
MARKSUP
MILKSOP
MIXESUP
MUCKSUP
OPENSUP
PACKSUP
PAIRSUP
PERKSUP
PICKSUP
PILESUP
PINESAP
PIPESUP
PLAYSUP
PROPSUP
PULLSUP
PUMPSUP
RACKSUP
RAKESUP
REARSUP
RESTSUP
RINGSUP
ROLLSUP
SAVESUP
SEALSUP
SENDSUP
SHOWSUP
SHUTSUP
SIGNSUP
SIZESUP
SLIPSUP
SLOWSUP
SNAPSUP
SOAKSUP
SOUPSUP
STAYSUP
STEPSUP
STIRSUP
STOPSUP
SUITSUP
TAKESUP
TALKSUP
TANKSUP
TEAMSUP
TEARSUP
TIMESUP
TONESUP
TOOLSUP
TRIPSUP
TUNESUP
TURNSUP
TYPESUP
WAITSUP
WAKESUP
WALLSUP
WARMSUP
WELLSUP
WHIPSUP
WINDSUP
WINESAP
WIPESUP
WISESUP
WORKSUP
WRAPSUP

•••••SP

RYKRISP
UNCLASP

SQ•••••

SQUALID
SQUALLS
SQUALOR
SQUANTO
SQUARED
SQUARER
SQUARES
SQUAWKS
SQUEAKS
SQUEAKY
SQUEALS
SQUEEZE
SQUELCH
SQUINCH
SQUINTS
SQUINTY
SQUIRED
SQUIRES
SQUIRMS
SQUIRMY
SQUIRTS
SQUISHY

S•Q••••

SEQUELS
SEQUINS
SEQUOIA

•SQ••••

ESQUIRE
TSQUARE

•S•••Q•

PSANDQS

••SQ•••

BASQUES
BISQUES
MASQUES
MOSQUES

•••SQ••

BRUSQUE

S•R••••

SARACEN
SARALEE
SARANAC
SARAWAK
SARAZEN
SARCASM
SARDINE
SARGENT
SARONGS
SAROYAN
SCRAGGY
SCRAPED
SCRAPER
SCRAPES
SCRAPPY
SCRATCH
SCRAWLS
SCRAWLY
SCRAWNY
SCREAKS
SCREAMS
SCREECH
SCREEDS
SCREENS
SCREWED
SCREWUP
SCRIBES
SCRIMPS
SCRIMPY
SCRIPPS
SCRIPTS
SCRIVEN
SCROLLS
SCROOGE
SCRUBBY
SCRUBUP
SCRUFFS
SCRUFFY
SCRUNCH
SCRUPLE
SERAPES
SERAPHS
SERAPIS
SERBIAN
SERENER
SERFDOM
SERIALS
SERIATE
SERIOUS
SERLING
SERMONS
SERPENT
SERPICO
SERRATE
SERRIED
SERVALS
SERVANT
SERVERS
SERVEUP
SERVICE
SERVILE
SERVING
SHRIEKS
SHRIFTS
SHRIKES
SHRILLS
SHRILLY
SHRIMPS
SHRINER
SHRINES
SHRINKS
SHRIVEL
SHRIVER
SHRIVES
SHROUDS
SHRUBBY
SIRLOIN
SIROCCO
SORBATE
SORBETS
SORCERY
SORGHUM
SORITES
SORORAL
SORRELS
SORRIER
SORROWS
SORTERS
SORTIED
SORTIES
SORTING
SPRAINS
SPRAWLS
SPRAYED
SPRAYER
SPREADS
SPRIEST
SPRINGS
SPRINGY
SPRINTS
SPRITES
SPROUTS
SPRUCED
SPRUCER
SPRUCES
SPRYEST
STRAFED
STRAFES
STRAINS
STRAITS
STRANDS
STRANGE
STRASSE
STRATUM
STRATUS
STRAUSS
STRAYED
STREAKS
STREAKY
STREAMS
STREETS
STRETCH
STRETTO
STREWED
STREWER
STRIATE
STRIDER
STRIDES
STRIKER
STRIKES
STRINGS
STRINGY
STRIPED
STRIPER
STRIPES
STRIVED
STRIVEN
STRIVER
STRIVES
STROBES
STROKED
STROKES
STROLLS
STROPHE
STRUDEL
SURCOAT
SURFACE
SURFEIT
SURFERS
SURFING
SURGEON
SURGERY
SURGING
SURINAM
SURLIER
SURLILY
SURMISE
SURNAME
SURPASS
SURPLUS
SURREAL
SURREYS
SURVEYS
SURVIVE
SYRIANS
SYRINGA
SYRINGE

S••R•••

SABRINA
SANREMO
SATRAPS
SAURIAN
SCARABS
SCARCER
SCARERS
SCAREUP
SCARFED
SCARIER
SCARIFY
SCARILY
SCARING
SCARLET
SCARPED
SCARRED
SCARVES
SCORERS
SCORING
SCORNED
SCORPIO
SCURVES
SEARING
SECRECY
SECRETE
SECRETS
SEERESS
SERRATE
SERRIED
SHAREIN
SHARERS
SHARING
SHARKEY
SHARPED
SHARPEI
SHARPEN
SHARPER
SHARPLY
SHERBET
SHERIFF
SHERMAN
SHERPAS
SHERWIN
SHIRKED
SHIRKER
SHIRLEY
SHIRRED
SHORING
SHORTED
SHORTEN
SHORTER
SHORTLY
SHORTOF
SIERRAS
SKIRLED
SKIRRED
SKIRTED
SKIRUNS
SLURPED
SLURRED
SMARTED
SMARTEN
SMARTER
SMARTLY
SMIRKED
SNARING
SNARLED
SNORERS
SNORING
SNORKEL
SNORTED
SNORTER
SOARERS
SOARING
SOIREES
SOPRANO
SORRELS
SORRIER
SORROWS
SOURCED
SOURCES
SOUREST
SOURING
SOURISH
SPARELY
SPAREST
SPARGED
SPARGES
SPARING
SPARKED
SPARKLE
SPARRED
SPARROW
SPARSER
SPARTAN
SPIRALS
SPIRANT
SPIREAS
SPIRITO
SPIRITS
SPORRAN
SPORTED
SPURNED
SPURNER
SPURRED
SPURSON
SPURTED
STARCHY
STARDOM
STAREAT
STARERS
STARETS
STARING
STARKER
STARKLY
STARLET
STARLIT
STARMAN
STARMAP
STARRED
STARTED
STARTER
STARTLE
STARTUP
STARVED
STARVES
STCROIX
STEREOS
STERILE
STERNAL
STERNER
STERNLY
STERNUM
STEROID
STEROLS
STIRFRY
STIRRED
STIRRER
STIRRUP
STIRSIN
STIRSUP
STORAGE
STORERS
STOREUP
STOREYS
STORIED
STORIES
STORING
STORMED
STURGES
STYRENE
STYRIAN
SUBROSA
SUCRASE
SUCROSE
SUNRAYS
SUNRISE
SUNROOF
SUNROOM
SUPREME
SUPREMO
SURREAL
SURREYS
SWARMED
SWARTHY
SWERVED
SWERVES
SWIRLED
SWOREAT
SWOREBY
SWOREIN

S•••R••

SAFARIS
SAFFRON
SAHARAN
SALERNO
SAMARIA
SAMPRAS
SAMURAI
SANGRIA
SATIRES
SATIRIC
SAVARIN
SAVORED
SCARRED
SCHERZI
SCHERZO
SCHIRRA
SCLERAS
SCOURED
SCOURER
SCOURGE
SEAGRAM
SECURED
SECURER
SECURES
SEESRED
SENORAS
SENORES
SEVERAL
SEVERED
SEVERER
SHEARED
SHEARER
SHECRAB
SHEERED
SHEERER
SHEERLY
SHIRRED

SIBERIA
SIERRAS
SISTRUM
SKIDROW
SKIRRED
SLURRED
SMEARED
SNEERAT
SNEERED
SNEERER
SOBERED
SOBERER
SOBERLY
SOLARIA
SORORAL
SPARRED
SPARROW
SPEARED
SPHERES
SPLURGE
SPORRAN
SPURRED
SQUARED
SQUARER
SQUARES
SQUIRED
SQUIRES
SQUIRMS
SQUIRMY
SQUIRTS
STARRED
STEERED
STEERER
STIRRED
STIRRER
STIRRUP
SUBORNS
SUBURBS
SUGARED
SUKARNO
SUTURED
SUTURES
SWEARAT
SWEARBY
SWEARER
SWEARIN
SWEARTO
SYNERGY

S••••R•

SACKERS
SAGUARO
SAILORS
SALIERI
SALTERS
SALVERS
SAMBARS
SAMSARA
SANBORN
SANDERS
SANFORD
SANTIRS
SAPPERS
SAPPORO
SASSERS
SAUCERS
SAVIORS
SAVOURS
SAVOURY
SAWYERS
SAXHORN
SCALARS
SCALERS
SCARERS
SCENERY
SCEPTRE
SCHIRRA
SCORERS
SCOTERS
SEABIRD
SEABORG
SEAGIRT
SEALERS
SEAPORT
SEATERS
SEAWARD
SECTORS
SEEDERS
SEEHERE
SEEKERS
SEINERS
SEIZERS
SELKIRK
SELLERS
SEMIPRO
SENDERS
SENIORS
SENSORS
SENSORY
SERVERS
SETTERS
SHAKERS
SHANGRI
SHAPERS
SHAPIRO
SHARERS
SHASTRI
SHAVERS
SHEPARD
SHINERS
SHIVERS
SHOFARS
SHOVERS
SHOWERS
SHOWERY
SHUBERT
SIDEARM
SIFTERS
SIGHERS
SIGNERS
SILVERS
SILVERY
SIMMERS
SIMPERS
SINATRA
SINCERE
SINGERS
SINKERS
SINNERS
SIPPERS
SISTERS
SITTERS
SKATERS
SKEWERS
SKIVERS
SKYLARK
SKYWARD
SLAVERS
SLAVERY
SLAYERS
SLICERS
SLIDERS
SLIVERS
SMILERS
SMOKERS
SNORERS
SOAKERS
SOAPERS
SOARERS
SOBBERS
SOJOURN
SOLDERS
SOLVERS
SOONERS
SORCERY
SORTERS
SOTHERE
SOTHERN
SPACERS
SPADERS
SPECTRA
SPECTRE
SPIDERS
SPIDERY
SPIKERS
STAGERS
STARERS
STATORS
STATURE
STEWARD
STEWART
STEWERS
STIRFRY
STOKERS
STONERS
STORERS
STUPORS
STYLERS
SUBVERT
SUBZERO
SUCCORS
SUCKERS
SUDBURY
SUFFERS
SUITORS
SULKERS
SUMATRA
SUMMARY
SUMMERS
SUMMERY
SUNBURN
SUNDERS
SUPPERS
SUPPORT
SURFERS
SURGERY
SUTLERS
SWAYERS
SWELTRY
SWIPERS

S•••••R

SADDLER
SAGGIER
SALAZAR
SALTIER
SAMOVAR
SAMPLER
SANDBAR
SANDIER
SAPPIER
SASSIER
SAUCIER
SAUNTER
SAVAGER
SAVVIER
SCALIER
SCALPER
SCAMPER
SCANNER
SCANTER
SCARCER
SCARIER
SCATTER
SCEPTER
SCHEMER
SCHMEER
SCHOLAR
SCISSOR
SCOFFER
SCOLDER
SCOOPER
SCOOTER
SCOURER
SCOUTER
SCOWLER
SCRAPER
SCULLER
SCUPPER
SEAMIER
SEASTAR
SECEDER
SECULAR
SECURER
SEDATER
SEDUCER
SEEDIER
SELTZER
SEMINAR
SENATOR
SENDFOR
SENTFOR
SERENER
SETTLER
SEVERER
SEYMOUR
SHADIER
SHAFFER
SHAKIER
SHANKAR
SHANTER
SHARPER
SHATNER
SHATTER
SHEARER
SHEERER
SHELLER
SHELTER
SHIMMER
SHINIER
SHIPPER
SHIRKER
SHOCKER
SHOOTER
SHOPPER
SHORTER
SHOTFOR
SHOUTER
SHOWIER
SHRINER
SHRIVER
SHUCKER
SHUDDER
SHUTTER
SHYSTER
SIDEBAR
SIDECAR
SILKIER
SILLIER
SIMILAR
SIMPLER
SKEETER
SKELTER
SKIDDER
SKIMMER
SKINNER
SKIPPER
SKITTER
SKULKER
SLACKER
SLAMMER
SLANDER
SLASHER
SLATHER
SLATIER
SLEDDER
SLEEKER
SLEEPER
SLENDER
SLICKER
SLIMIER
SLIMMER
SLINGER
SLIPPER
SLITHER
SLOBBER
SLOTCAR
SLUGGER
SLUMBER
SMACKER
SMALLER
SMARTER
SMASHER
SMATTER
SMELTER
SMOKIER
SMOLDER
SMOTHER
SMUGGER
SNACKER
SNAKIER
SNAPPER
SNEAKER
SNEERER
SNEEZER
SNICKER
SNIFFER
SNIFTER
SNIGGER
SNOOKER
SNOOPER
SNORTER
SNOWIER
SNUFFER
SNUGGER
SOAPIER
SOBERER
SOGGIER
SOLDIER
SOLIDER
SOOTHER
SOOTIER
SORRIER
SOUNDER
SOUPIER
SPACIER
SPANKER
SPANNER
SPARSER
SPATTER
SPEAKER
SPECTER
SPECTOR
SPEEDER
SPELLER
SPENCER
SPENDER
SPENSER
SPICIER
SPIELER
SPIKIER
SPINIER
SPINNER
SPLICER
SPOILER
SPONGER
SPONSOR
SPOOFER
SPOONER
SPOTTER
SPOUTER
SPRAYER
SPRUCER
SPURNER
SPUTTER
SQUALOR
SQUARER
STABLER
STAFFER
STAGGER
STAGIER
STAIDER
STAINER
STALKER
STAMMER
STAPLER
STARKER
STARTER
STEAMER
STEELER
STEEPER
STEERER
STEIGER
STEINER
STELLAR
STENTOR
STEPPER
STERNER
STICKER
STIFFER
STILLER
STINGER
STINKER
STIRRER
STOLLER
STONIER
STOPPER
STOUTER
STPETER
STREWER
STRIDER
STRIKER
STRIPER
STRIVER
STUFFER
STUMPER
STUNNER
SUBDUER
SUBTLER
SUCCOUR
SUDSIER
SULKIER
SULPHUR
SUNNIER
SUPPLER
SURLIER
SUTTNER
SVELTER
SWAGGER
SWANKER
SWAPPER
SWATTER
SWEARER
SWEATER
SWEEPER
SWEETER
SWELTER
SWIFTER
SWIMMER
SWINGER
SWITZER

•SR••••

ISRAELI

•S•R•••

ASCRIBE
ASHRAMS
ASTRIDE
ESCROWS
ESTRADA
ESTRAYS
OSPREYS
OSTRICH
TSARINA
TSARIST
USURERS
USURPED
USURPER

•S••R••

ASFARAS
ASHTRAY
ASPERSE
ASPIRED
ASPIRER
ASPIRES
ASPIRIN
ASSERTS
ASSORTS
ASSURED
ASSURES
ASSYRIA
ASTARTE
ASTORIA
ESCARPS
ESCORTS
ESTORIL
OSBORNE
TSHIRTS
USHERED

•S•••R•

ASHBURY
ASHFORD
ASHLARS
ASTAIRE
ESQUIRE
ESTUARY
ISADORA
ISOBARS
ISOMERS
ISSUERS
OSTLERS
TSQUARE
USURERS

•S••••R

ASKSFOR
ASPIRER
ASSAYER
ASUNDER
PSALTER
USURPER

••SR•••

DISROBE
DISRUPT
MISREAD
MISRULE

••S•R••

ABSORBS
ADSORBS
ALSORAN
AMSCRAY
ASSERTS
ASSORTS
ASSURED
ASSURES
ASSYRIA
AUSTRAL
AUSTRIA
BESTREW
BISTROS
CASERNS
DESERTS
DESERVE
DESIRED
DESIREE
DESIRES
DESTROY
DISARMS
DISHRAG
ENSURED
ENSURES
GASTRIC
IMSORRY
INSERTS
INSURED
INSURES
KESTREL
LASORDA
LUSTRED
LUSTRES
MISERLY
MISTRAL
MUSKRAT
NOSTRIL
NOSTRUM
OBSERVE
OFSORTS
RESERVE
RESORBS
RESORTS
RESURGE
ROSERED
ROSTRUM
SISTRUM
UNSCREW
UNSTRAP
UPSURGE
WASHRAG
WASTREL

••S•R•

ANSWERS
AUSTERE
BASTERS
BESTIRS
BUSFARE
BUSTARD
CASCARA
CASTERS
CISTERN
COSTARS
CUSTARD
DASHERS
DASTARD
DESSERT
DISBARS
DISCARD
DISCERN
DISCORD
DISPORT
DISTORT
DISTURB
DOSSERS
DUSTERS
EASTERN
EASTERS
ENSNARE
ENSNARL
FESTERS
FISHERS
FISHERY
FISHFRY
FISSURE
FOSTERS
GASSERS
GESTURE
GUSHERS
HISSERS
HISTORY
HOSIERS
HOSIERY
HUSKERS
HUSSARS
IMSORRY
INSHORT
INSPIRE
INSTORE
ISSUERS
JASPERS
JESTERS
KISSERS
KOSHERS
LASHERS
LASTORY
LESSORS
LUSTERS
MASCARA
MASHERS
MASKERS
MASONRY
MASTERS
MASTERY
MISFIRE
MISTERS
MISWORD
MUSHERS
MUSTARD
MUSTERS
MYSTERY
NESTERS
NOSHERS
OBSCURE
ONSHORE
OUSTERS
OYSTERS
PASSERS
PASTERN
PASTORS
PASTURE
PESTERS
PISMIRE
POSEURS
POSTERN
POSTERS
POSTURE
RASHERS
RASPERS
RASTERS
RESPIRE
RESTART
RESTERS
RESTORE
RISKERS
ROSTERS
RUSHERS
SASSERS
SISTERS
TASTERS
TESSERA
TESTERS
TOSPARE
TOSSERS
TUSKERS
ULSTERS
UNSHORN
UNSNARL
UPSTART
VESPERS
VESTURE
VISCERA
WASHERS
WASTERS
WESTERN
WISHERS

••S•••R

ASSAYER
BESMEAR
BOSSIER
BUSHIER
CASHBAR
CASHIER
COSTNER
CUSHIER
CUSSLER
DESPAIR
DOSSIER
DUSKIER
DUSTIER
FISCHER
FISHIER
FUSSIER
FUSTIER
GUSHIER
HASTIER
HOSTLER
HUSKIER
HUSTLER
INSIDER
INSOFAR
INSULAR
JOSTLER
KASHMIR
LASSOER
LUSTIER
MASSEUR
MESSIER
MISHEAR
MISTIER
MOSSIER
MUSHIER
MUSTIER
NASTIER
NESTLER
PASSFOR
PASTEUR
PASTIER
PESKIER
POSTWAR
PUSHIER
RASPIER
RESCUER
RISKIER
RUSTIER
RUSTLER
SASSIER
TASTIER
TESTIER
VISITOR
WISPIER
YESDEAR
ZESTIER

•••SR••

SEESRED

•••S•R•

ABUSERS
BERSERK
BURSARS
CAESARS
CAESURA
CENSERS
CENSORS
CENSURE
CHASERS
CLOSURE
CONSORT
CURSORS
CURSORY
DESSERT
DOSSERS
DOWSERS
DYKSTRA
ERASERS
ERASURE
EYESORE
FISSURE
FORSURE
GASSERS
GEYSERS
HANSARP
HAWSERS
HISSERS
HUSSARS
KAISERS
KISSERS
LEASERS
LEISURE
LESSORS
MAESTRI
MAESTRO
MANSARD
MEASURE
MOUSERS
NETSURF
NOTSURE
NURSERS
NURSERY
OFASORT
OLESTRA
PARSERS
PASSERS
PHASERS
PIASTRE
PRESORT
PROSERS
PULSARS
PURSERS
QUASARS
RAISERS
RUNSDRY
SAMSARA
SASSERS
SENSORS
SENSORY
SHASTRI
TEASERS
TENSORS
TESSERA
TONSURE
TOSSERS

•••S••R

ALLSTAR
ANTSIER
ASKSFOR
BLASTER
BLISTER
BLUSHER
BLUSTER
BOASTER
BOLSTER
BONSOIR
BOOSLER
BOOSTER
BOSSIER
BRASHER
BRISKER
CHASTER
CHESTER
CLUSTER
COASTER
CORSAIR
CRASSER
CRISPER
CROSIER
CROSSER
CRUSHER
CUSSLER
DANSEUR
DAYSTAR
DOGSTAR
DOSSIER
DRESSER
EDASNER
FLASHER
FLUSTER
FORSTER
FRASIER
FRESHER
FUSSIER
GAGSTER
GOESFOR
GROSSER
GUESSER
GUNSFOR
GUTSIER
HAMSTER
HARSHER
HIPSTER
HOLSTER
HOOSIER
HORSIER
HOTSPUR
JOUSTER
LASSOER
LAYSFOR
LEISTER
LOBSTER
LOESSER
LOUSIER
MASSEUR
MESSIER
MOBSTER
MOISTER
MONSTER
MOSSIER
MOUSIER
NEWSIER
NOISIER
OLDSTER
PASSFOR
PAYSFOR
PIASTER
PILSNER
PLASTER
PLUSHER
PRESSER
PROSIER
PROSPER
PUNSTER
PURSUER
REDSTAR
ROASTER
ROISTER
ROOSTER
SASSIER
SCISSOR
SEASTAR
SHYSTER
SLASHER
SMASHER
SUDSIER
TAPSTER
TARSIER
TELSTAR
THUSFAR
TINSTAR
TIPSIER
TIPSTER
TOASTER
TRYSTER
TWISTER
TWOSTAR
WEBSTER
WHISKER
WHISPER
WOOSTER

••••S•R

ACCUSER
ADVISER
ADVISOR
ALUNSER
BROWSER
BRUISER
CHOOSER
COARSER
COURSER
CRASSER
CROSSER
CRUISER
DEARSIR
DEPOSER
DIVISOR
DREISER
DRESSER
ENDUSER
GREASER
GROSSER
GROUSER
GUESSER
HOARSER

INCISOR
LOESSER
NONUSER
OBTUSER
OPPOSER
PERUSER
PLEASER
PRAISER
PRESSER
REFUSER
REVISER
SCISSOR
SPARSER
SPENSER
SPONSOR
TROUSER
UNWISER
WINDSOR

S•S••••

SASHAYS
SASHIMI
SASSERS
SASSIER
SASSIES
SASSILY
SASSING
SASSOON
SESAMES
SESSILE
SESSION
SESTETS
SESTINA
SISKINS
SISSIES
SISTERS
SISTINE
SISTRUM
SOSUEME
SUSANNA
SUSANNE
SUSLIKS
SUSPECT
SUSPEND
SUSSING
SUSTAIN
SYSTEMS
SYSTOLE

S••S•••

SADSACK
SALSIFY
SALSODA
SAMSARA
SAMSUNG
SAPSAGO
SASSERS
SASSIER
SASSIES
SASSILY
SASSING
SASSOON
SATSUMA
SAUSAGE
SCISSOR
SEASALT
SEASICK
SEASIDE
SEASLUG
SEASONS
SEASTAR
SEESAWS
SEESFIT
SEESOFF
SEESOUT
SEESRED
SEISMIC
SENSATE
SENSING
SENSORS
SENSORY
SENSUAL
SESSILE
SESSION
SETSAIL
SETSOFF
SETSOUT
SHASTRI
SHUSHED
SHUSHES
SHYSTER
SIESTAS
SISSIES
SITSOUT
SKISUIT
SKOSHES
SLASHED
SLASHER
SLASHES
SLOSHED
SLOSHES
SLUSHES
SMASHED
SMASHER
SMASHES
SMASHUP
SPASSKY
STASHED
STASHES
STASSEN
SUASION
SUBSETS
SUBSIDE
SUBSIDY
SUBSIST
SUBSOIL
SUBSUME
SUDSIER
SUDSING
SUNSETS
SUNSPOT
SUSSING
SWISHED
SWISHES

S•••S••

SAMISEN
SAMPSON
SATISFY
SAVESUP
SCHISMS
SCISSOR
SEALSUP
SEEPSIN
SENDSIN
SENDSUP
SEXISTS
SHOWSIN
SHOWSUP
SHUTSIN
SHUTSUP
SIGNSIN
SIGNSON
SIGNSUP
SILESIA
SIMPSON
SINGSTO
SINKSIN
SINUSES
SIZESUP
SLIPSUP
SLOWSUP
SNAPSAT
SNAPSTO
SNAPSUP
SNOWSIN
SOAKSUP
SOCKSIN
SOUPSUP
SPARSER
SPASSKY
SPENSER
SPIESON
SPLASHY
SPONSOR
SPOUSAL
SPOUSES
SPURSON
SQUISHY
STASSEN
STAYSUP
STEPSIN
STEPSON
STEPSUP
STETSON
STIRSIN
STIRSUP
STOPSIN
STOPSUP
STRASSE
SUCKSIN
SUITSUP
SULUSEA
SWANSON
SWOOSIE

S••••S•

SADDEST
SADNESS
SANJOSE
SARCASM
SAWDUST
SAWFISH
SEABASS
SEAMOSS
SEERESS
SELFISH
SEXIEST
SHIATSU
SHYNESS
SIAMESE
SICKEST
SIKHISM
SKIMASK
SLAVISH
SLOWEST
SLYNESS
SNIDEST
SOANDSO
SOFTEST
SOLOIST
SOONEST
SOPHISM
SOPHIST
SOUREST
SOURISH
SPANISH
SPAREST
SPRIEST
SPRYEST
STALEST
STATIST
STRASSE
STRAUSS
STYLISH
STYLIST
SUAVEST
SUBROSA
SUBSIST
SUCCESS
SUCRASE
SUCROSE
SUFFUSE
SUGGEST
SUNFISH
SUNKIST
SUNLESS
SUNRISE
SUPPOSE
SURMISE
SURPASS
SWEDISH
SYNAPSE

S•••••S

SABINES
SACHEMS
SACHETS
SACKERS
SADDENS
SADDLES
SADNESS
SAFARIS
SAILORS
SALAAMS
SALAMIS
SALLIES
SALMONS
SALOONS
SALTERS
SALUKIS
SALUTES
SALVERS
SALVOES
SAMBARS
SAMITES
SAMOANS
SAMPANS
SAMPLES
SAMPRAS
SANDALS
SANDERS
SANLUIS
SANTIRS
SAPIENS
SAPPERS
SARONGS
SASHAYS
SASSERS
SASSIES
SATIRES
SATRAPS
SAUCERS
SAVAGES
SAVALAS
SAVANTS
SAVINGS
SAVIORS
SAVOURS
SAWLOGS
SAWYERS
SAYINGS
SCALARS
SCALERS
SCARABS
SCARERS
SCARVES
SCATHES
SCHEMAS
SCHEMES
SCHISMS
SCHLEPS
SCHMOES
SCHMOOS
SCHNAPS
SCHOOLS
SCLERAS
SCONCES
SCORERS
SCOTERS
SCRAPES
SCRAWLS
SCREAKS
SCREAMS
SCREEDS
SCREENS
SCRIBES
SCRIMPS
SCRIPPS
SCRIPTS
SCROLLS
SCRUFFS
SCULPTS
SCURVES
SCYTHES
SEABAGS
SEABASS
SEABEDS
SEABEES
SEACOWS
SEADOGS
SEAFANS
SEALABS
SEALEGS
SEALERS
SEAMOSS
SEANCES
SEASONS
SEATERS
SEAWAYS
SECANTS
SECEDES
SECONDS
SECRETS
SECTORS
SECURES
SEDUCES
SEEDERS
SEEKERS
SEERESS
SEESAWS
SEETHES
SEICHES
SEIDELS
SEINERS
SEIZERS
SELECTS
SELLERS
SEMITES
SENATES
SENDERS
SENDUPS
SENECAS
SENIORS
SENORAS
SENORES
SENSORS
SEPTETS
SEQUELS
SEQUINS
SERAPES
SERAPHS
SERAPIS
SERIALS
SERIOUS
SERMONS
SERVALS
SERVERS
SESAMES
SESTETS
SETTEES
SETTERS
SETTLES
SEXISTS
SEXTANS
SEXTETS
SEXTONS
SHADOWS
SHAKERS
SHAKOES
SHALOMS
SHAMANS
SHAPERS
SHARERS
SHAVERS
SHEATHS
SHEAVES
SHEIKHS
SHEILAS
SHEKELS
SHELVES
SHERPAS
SHIELDS
SHIITES
SHINERS
SHIVERS
SHOFARS
SHOGUNS
SHOOINS
SHOPPES
SHOVELS
SHOVERS
SHOWERS
SHRIEKS
SHRIFTS
SHRIKES
SHRILLS
SHRIMPS
SHRINES
SHRINKS
SHRIVES
SHROUDS
SHTICKS
SHUSHES
SHYNESS
SICKENS
SICKLES
SIDINGS
SIENNAS
SIERRAS
SIESTAS
SIFTERS
SIGHERS
SIGNALS
SIGNEES
SIGNERS
SIGNETS
SILENTS
SILICAS
SILLIES
SILVERS
SIMIANS
SIMILES
SIMMERS
SIMMONS
SIMPERS
SINGERS
SINGLES
SINKERS
SINNERS
SINUOUS
SINUSES
SIOUANS
SIPHONS
SIPPERS
SIPPETS
SISKINS
SISSIES
SISTERS
SITCOMS
SITTERS
SIXGUNS
SIXTIES
SIZINGS
SIZZLES
SKATERS
SKEWERS
SKIRUNS
SKITOWS
SKIVERS
SKOSHES
SKYCAPS
SKYWAYS
SLALOMS
SLASHES
SLAVERS
SLAYERS
SLEDGES
SLEEVES
SLEIGHS
SLEUTHS
SLICERS
SLIDERS
SLIGHTS
SLIPONS
SLIPUPS
SLIVERS
SLOGANS
SLOSHES
SLOUGHS
SLOVAKS
SLOVENS
SLUDGES
SLUICES
SLUSHES
SLYNESS
SMALTOS
SMASHES
SMILERS
SMOKERS
SMOKIES
SMOOTHS
SMUDGES
SNAPONS
SNEEZES
SNIVELS
SNOCATS
SNOOZES
SNORERS
SOAKERS
SOAPERS
SOARERS
SOBBERS
SOCIALS
SOCKETS
SOFFITS
SOFTENS
SOFTIES
SOIREES
SOLACES
SOLDERS
SOLUTES
SOLVERS
SOMALIS
SONATAS
SONNETS
SOONERS
SOOTHES
SORBETS
SORITES
SORRELS
SORROWS
SORTERS
SORTIES
SOURCES
SOVIETS
SOWBUGS
SPACERS
SPADERS
SPARGES
SPAVINS
SPECIES
SPHERES
SPIDERS
SPIGOTS
SPIKERS
SPINELS
SPINETS
SPIRALS
SPIREAS
SPIRITS
SPITZES
SPLEENS
SPLICES
SPLINES
SPLINTS
SPONGES
SPOUSES
SPRAINS
SPRAWLS
SPREADS
SPRINGS
SPRINTS
SPRITES
SPROUTS
SPRUCES
SQUALLS
SQUARES
SQUAWKS
SQUEAKS
SQUEALS
SQUINTS
SQUIRES
SQUIRMS
SQUIRTS
STABLES
STAGERS
STALAGS
STAMENS
STANCES
STANZAS
STAPLES
STARERS
STARETS
STARVES
STASHES
STATICS
STATORS
STATUES
STDENIS
STEPINS
STEPPES
STEPUPS
STEREOS
STEROLS
STEVENS
STEWERS
STICHES
STIFLES
STIGMAS
STJOHNS
STKITTS
STLOUIS
STOGIES
STOKERS
STOLONS
STONERS
STOOGES
STORERS
STOREYS
STORIES
STRAFES
STRAINS
STRAITS
STRANDS
STRATUS
STRAUSS
STREAKS
STREAMS
STREETS
STRIDES
STRIKES
STRINGS
STRIPES
STRIVES
STROBES
STROKES
STROLLS
STUCCOS
STUDIES
STUDIOS
STUPORS
STURGES
STYLERS
STYLETS
STYMIES
SUBDEBS
SUBDUES
SUBLETS
SUBMITS
SUBORNS
SUBSETS
SUBURBS
SUBWAYS
SUCCESS
SUCCORS
SUCKERS
SUFFERS
SUITORS
SULKERS
SULKIES
SULLIES
SULTANS
SUMMERS
SUMMITS
SUMMONS
SUNDAES
SUNDAYS
SUNDERS
SUNDEWS
SUNDOGS
SUNGODS
SUNLESS
SUNRAYS
SUNSETS
SUNTANS
SUPPERS
SURFERS
SURPASS
SURPLUS
SURREYS
SURVEYS
SUSLIKS
SUTLERS
SUTURES
SWATHES
SWAYERS
SWERVES
SWIPERS
SWISHES
SWIVELS
SYLVANS
SYMBOLS
SYNCHES
SYRIANS
SYSTEMS

•SS••••

ASSAILS
ASSAULT
ASSAYED
ASSAYER
ASSEGAI
ASSENTS
ASSERTS
ASSIGNS
ASSISTS
ASSIZES
ASSORTS
ASSUAGE
ASSUMED
ASSUMES
ASSURED
ASSURES
ASSYRIA
ESSAYED
ESSENCE
ESSENES
ISSUERS
ISSUING
OSSICLE
OSSIFIC
USSTEEL

•S•S•••

ASKSFOR
ASKSOUT
ASUSUAL
USOSHOW

•S••S••

ASEPSIS
ASSISTS
ESPOSAS
ESPOSOS
OSMOSED
OSMOSES
OSMOSIS
TSETSES

•S•••S•

ASHIEST
ASHLESS
ASPERSE
ESPOUSE
OSHKOSH
TSARIST
USELESS

•S••••S

ASCENDS
ASCENTS
ASEPSIS
ASFARAS
ASHCANS
ASHLARS
ASHLESS
ASHRAMS
ASPECTS
ASPIRES
ASSAILS
ASSENTS
ASSERTS
ASSIGNS
ASSISTS
ASSIZES
ASSORTS
ASSUMES
ASSURES
ASYLUMS
CSLEWIS
ESCAPES
ESCARPS
ESCHEWS
ESCORTS
ESCROWS
ESCUDOS
ESKIMOS
ESPIALS
ESPOSAS
ESPOSOS
ESSENES
ESTATES
ESTEEMS
ESTRAYS
ISLANDS
ISOBARS
ISOGONS
ISOHELS
ISOMERS
ISOPODS
ISSUERS
ISTHMUS
OSCINES
OSMONDS
OSMOSES
OSMOSIS
OSPREYS
OSTLERS
PSANDQS
PSYCHES
TSETSES
TSHIRTS
TSONGAS
USELESS
USOPENS
USURERS

••SS•••

AUSSIES
BASSETS
BASSIST
BASSOON
BOSSIER
BOSSILY
BOSSING
BUSSING
BUSSTOP
CASSATT
CASSAVA
CASSIAS
CASSIDY
CASSINI
CASSIUS
CASSOCK
CESSION
COSSACK
COSSETS
CUSSING
CUSSLER
DESSERT
DISSECT
DISSENT
DOSSALS
DOSSERS
DOSSIER
FISSILE
FISSION
FISSURE
FOSSILS
FUSSIER
FUSSILY
FUSSING
FUSSPOT
GASSERS
GESSOES
GOSSETT
GOSSIPS
GOSSIPY
GUSSETS
GUSSIED
GUSSIES
GUSSYUP
HASSLED
HASSLES
HASSOCK
HESSIAN
HISSERS
HISSING
HUSSARS
HUSSEIN
HUSSIES
HYSSOPS
JESSICA
KISSERS
KISSING
KISSOFF
LASSIES
LASSOED
LASSOER
LASSOES
LESSEES
LESSENS
LESSING
LESSONS
LESSORS
LISSOME
MASSAGE
MASSEUR
MASSIFS
MASSING
MASSIVE
MESSAGE
MESSALA
MESSIAH
MESSIER
MESSILY
MESSINA
MESSING
MESSKIT
MISSALS
MISSIES
MISSILE
MISSING
MISSION
MISSISH
MISSIVE
MISSOUT
MISSTEP
MOSSIER
MOSSING
MUSSELS
MUSSING
PASSAGE
PASSANT
PASSELS
PASSERS
PASSEUL
PASSFOR
PASSING
PASSION
PASSIVE
PASSKEY
PASSOFF
PASSOUT
POSSESS
POSSETS
POSSUMS
RASSLED
RASSLES
RISSOLE
ROSSINI
ROSSSEA
RUSSELL
RUSSETS
RUSSIAN
SASSERS
SASSIER
SASSIES
SASSILY
SASSING
SASSOON
SESSILE
SESSION
SISSIES
SUSSING
TASSELS
TESSERA
TISSUES
TOSSERS
TOSSING
TOSSOFF
TOSSOUT
TOSSUPS
TUSSAUD
TUSSLED
TUSSLES
TUSSOCK
VASSALS
VESSELS
WASSAIL
YESSING

••S•S••

ASSISTS
DESISTS
DESKSET
DISUSED
EASESIN

EASESUP
INSISTS
LOSESIT
MISUSED
MISUSES
MUSTSEE
RESISTS
RESTSUP
ROSSSEA
WISESUP

••S••S•

BASSIST
BUSIEST
DESPISE
DISCUSS
DISEASE
DISGUST
DISMISS
DISPOSE
DRSEUSS
EASIEST
ECSTASY
FASCISM
FASCIST
FASTEST
HOSTESS
LUSHEST
MISCAST
MISSISH
NASTASE
NOSIEST
POSHEST
POSSESS
RASHEST
VASTEST
WASPISH

••S•••S

ABSENTS
ABSORBS
ADSORBS
ANSWERS
APSIDES
ASSAILS
ASSENTS
ASSERTS
ASSIGNS
ASSISTS
ASSIZES
ASSORTS
ASSUMES
ASSURES
AUSSIES
BASALTS
BASKETS
BASQUES
BASSETS
BASTERS
BESEEMS
BESIDES
BESTIRS
BESTOWS
BISECTS
BISHOPS
BISQUES
BISTROS
BOSKETS
BUSBIES
BUSBOYS
BUSHELS
BUSKINS
BUSTLES
CASABAS
CASERNS
CASHEWS
CASINGS
CASINOS
CASSIAS
CASSIUS
CASTERS
CASTLES
CASUALS
COSIGNS
COSINES
COSSETS
COSTARS
CUSHAWS
CUSPIDS
CUSTOMS
DASHERS
DESALTS
DESERTS
DESIGNS
DESIRES
DESISTS
DESOTOS
DESPOTS
DISARMS
DISBARS
DISCUSS
DISMAYS
DISMISS
DISOWNS
DISPELS
DOSAGES
DOSIDOS
DOSSALS
DOSSERS
DRSEUSS
DUSTERS
DUSTUPS
EASTERS
ENSIGNS
ENSILES
ENSOULS
ENSURES
ESSENES
FASCIAS
FASTENS
FESTERS
FISHERS
FOSSILS
FOSTERS
FUSTICS
GASBAGS
GASCAPS
GASCONS
GASEOUS
GASJETS
GASKETS
GASKINS
GASSERS
GESSOES
GOSPELS
GOSSIPS
GUSHERS
GUSSETS
GUSSIES
GUSTOES
HASSLES
HASTENS
HISSERS
HOSIERS
HOSKINS
HOSTELS
HOSTESS
HUSKERS
HUSKIES
HUSSARS
HUSSIES
HUSTLES
HYSSOPS
INSEAMS
INSECTS
INSERTS
INSIDES
INSISTS
INSOLES
INSPANS
INSPOTS
INSTEPS
INSTILS
INSULTS
INSURES
ISSUERS
JASPERS
JESTERS
JESUITS
JOSTLES
KISHKES
KISSERS
KOSHERS
LASHERS
LASHUPS
LASSIES
LASSOES
LESSEES
LESSENS
LESSONS
LESSORS
LISTEES
LISTELS
LISTENS
LUSTERS
LUSTRES
MASCOTS
MASHERS
MASHIES
MASKERS
MASQUES
MASSIFS
MASTERS
MASTICS
MESCALS
MISCUES
MISDOES
MISFITS
MISHAPS
MISHITS
MISLAYS
MISSALS
MISSIES
MISTERS
MISUSES
MOSAICS
MOSLEMS
MOSQUES
MUSCATS
MUSCLES
MUSEUMS
MUSHERS
MUSKETS
MUSLIMS
MUSLINS
MUSSELS
MUSTERS
MYSTICS
NESTERS
NESTLES
NOSHERS
NOSHOWS
OFSORTS
OUSTERS
OYSTERS
PASSELS
PASSERS
PASTELS
PASTORS
PESETAS
PESTERS
PESTLES
PISTILS
PISTOLS
PISTONS
POSADAS
POSEURS
POSSESS
POSSETS
POSSUMS
POSTERS
PUSHUPS
RASCALS
RASHERS
RASPERS
RASSLES
RASTERS
RESALES
RESALTS
RESANDS
RESCUES
RESEALS
RESEATS
RESECTS
RESEEDS
RESELLS
RESENDS
RESENTS
RESHIPS
RESHOES
RESIDES
RESIGNS
RESILES
RESINGS
RESISTS
RESOLES
RESORBS
RESORTS
RESTERS
RESULTS
RESUMES
RISINGS
RISKERS
ROSTERS
RUSHEES
RUSHERS
RUSSETS
RUSTICS
RUSTLES
SASHAYS
SASSERS
SASSIES
SESAMES
SESTETS
SISKINS
SISSIES
SISTERS
SUSLIKS
SYSTEMS
TASSELS
TASTERS
TESTEES
TESTERS
TISANES
TISSUES
TOSSERS
TOSSUPS
TUSKERS
TUSSLES
TVSHOWS
ULSTERS
UNSEALS
UNSEATS
UNSNAGS
UNSNAPS
UNSTOPS
UPSHOTS
VASSALS
VESPERS
VESPIDS
VESSELS
VESTEES
VISAGES
VISAVIS
VISCOUS
VISIONS
VISUALS
WASHERS
WASTERS
WESKITS
WISHERS

•••SS••

ABYSSES
AGASSIZ
ALYSSUM
AMASSED
AMASSES
ATISSUE
BIASSED
BLESSED
BLESSES
BLOSSOM
BRASSES
BRASSIE
BRESSON
CAISSON
CHASSES
CHASSIS
CLASSED
CLASSES
CLASSIC
CRASSER
CRASSLY
CRASSUS
CRESSES
CROSSED
CROSSER
CROSSES
CROSSLY
CROSSUP
DRESSED
DRESSER
DRESSES
DRESSUP
FLOSSED
FLOSSES
FRISSON
GETSSET
GLASSED
GLASSES
GLOSSAE
GLOSSED
GLOSSES
GRASSED
GRASSES
GRISSOM
GROSSED
GROSSER
GROSSES
GROSSLY
GUESSED
GUESSER
GUESSES
JANSSEN
KNESSET
KNOSSOS
LAISSEZ
LETSSEE
LOESSER
LOESSES
MEISSEN
MOUSSED
MOUSSES
NILSSON
ODYSSEY
ONASSIS
OPOSSUM
PLUSSES
POISSON
PRESSED
PRESSER
PRESSES
PRESSON
PRUSSIA
REISSUE
ROSSSEA
SCISSOR
SPASSKY
STASSEN
TRESSES
TRUSSED
TRUSSES
ULYSSES

•••S•S•

BASSIST
CLOSEST
CONSIST
DENSEST
FALSEST
LOOSEST
MISSISH
PERSIST
POSSESS
SUBSIST
TENSEST
TERSEST

•••S••S

ABASHES
ABUSERS
ABYSSES
AIRSACS
AMASSES
ARISTAS
ARISTOS
AUSSIES
BALSAMS
BASSETS
BLESSES
BLUSHES
BOWSAWS
BRASSES
BRUSHES
BURSARS
CAESARS
CASSIAS
CASSIUS
CELSIUS
CENSERS
CENSORS
CHASERS
CHASSES
CHASSIS
CHISELS
CLASHES
CLASSES
CLOSETS
CONSULS
CORSETS
COSSETS
COUSINS
CRASHES
CRASSUS
CRESSES
CRISPUS
CROSSES
CRUSHES
CURSORS
DAISIES
DAMSELS
DAMSONS
DIESELS
DORSALS
DOSSALS
DOSSERS
DOWSERS
DRESSES
ELYSEES
ENISLES
ERASERS
ERASMUS
FAUSTUS
FIASCOS
FIESTAS
FLASHES
FLESHES
FLOSSES
FLUSHES
FOCSLES
FOSSILS
FRESCOS
GASSERS
GEISHAS
GESSOES
GEYSERS
GIPSIES
GLASSES
GLOSSES
GNASHES
GODSONS
GOSSIPS
GRASSES
GROSSES
GUESSES
GUSSETS
GUSSIES
GYPSIES
HANSOMS
HASSLES
HAWSERS
HISSERS
HUSSARS
HUSSIES
HYSSOPS
JERSEYS
JETSONS
JIGSAWS
KAISERS
KANSANS
KISSERS
KMESONS
KNISHES
KNOSSOS
LASSIES
LASSOES
LEASERS
LEASHES
LESSEES
LESSENS
LESSONS
LESSORS
LOESSES
LOOSENS
MARSHES
MASSIFS
MEASLES
MIASMAS
MISSALS
MISSIES
MORSELS
MOUSERS
MOUSSES
MUSSELS
NAYSAYS
NELSONS
NURSERS
OFFSETS
ONASSIS
ORESTES
ORISONS
OUTSETS
PANSIES
PARSECS
PARSEES
PARSERS
PARSONS
PASSELS
PASSERS
PATSIES
PENSEES
PEPSINS
PERSEUS
PERSIUS
PERSONS
PHASERS
PHYSICS
PITSAWS
PLASHES
PLASMAS
PLUSHES
PLUSSES
POISONS
POSSESS
POSSETS
POSSUMS
PRESETS
PRESSES
PRESTOS
PRISONS
PROSERS
PULSARS
PURSERS
PURSUES
QUASARS
QUASHES
RAISERS
RAISINS
RANSOMS
RASSLES
REASONS
RIPSAWS
RUSSETS
SASSERS
SASSIES
SEASONS
SEESAWS
SENSORS
SHUSHES
SIESTAS
SISSIES
SKOSHES
SLASHES
SLOSHES
SLUSHES
SMASHES
STASHES
SUBSETS
SUNSETS
SWISHES
TANSIES
TARSALS
TASSELS
TEASELS
TEASERS
TEASETS
TENSORS
THESEUS
THESPIS
TINSELS
TISSUES
TOCSINS
TONSILS
TOSSERS
TOSSUPS
TOUSLES
TRASHES
TRESSES
TRUSSES
TULSANS
TUSSLES
ULYSSES
UNISONS
VASSALS
VESSELS
VIZSLAS
WEASELS
WORSENS
ZOYSIAS

••••SS•

BABASSU
COLOSSI
DEBUSSY
EMBASSY
ENMASSE
FINESSE
IMPASSE
MATISSE
MELISSA
PELISSE
PICASSO
STRASSE
VANESSA

••••S•S

ABYSSES
ACCOSTS
ACCUSES
ADJUSTS
ADVISES
AGEISTS
ALIASES
AMASSES
AORISTS
APHESES
APPOSES
ARIOSOS
AROUSES
ARRASES
ARRESTS
ARRISES
ARTISTS
ASEPSIS
ASSISTS
ATLASES
ATTESTS
AVULSES
BEHESTS
BEMUSES
BLESSES
BLOUSES
BOLUSES
BONUSES
BRAISES
BRASSES
BREASTS
BROWSES
BRUISES
CAMISES
CAYUSES
CHAISES
CHASSES
CHASSIS
CHEESES
CHOOSES
CHRISMS
CLASSES
CLAUSES
COHOSTS
COURSES
CRASSUS
CREASES
CRESSES
CROESUS
CROSSES
CRUISES
CUBISTS
DAMASKS
DEBASES
DEFUSES
DELISTS
DEMISES
DEPOSES
DESISTS
DETESTS
DEVISES
DIGESTS
DIVESTS
DRESSES
DROWSES
DYNASTS
ECDYSES
ECDYSIS
EFFUSES
EGOISTS
ELAPSES
ENCASES
ENLISTS
ESPOSAS
ESPOSOS
EVULSES
EXCISES
EXCUSES
EXPOSES
FICUSES
FLENSES
FLOSSES
FOCUSES
FORESTS
FRAISES
GENESES
GENESIS
GLASSES
GLOSSES
GRASSES
GREASES
GROSSES
GROUSES
GUESSES
ILLUSES
IMPOSES
IMPOSTS
INCISES
INFESTS
INFUSES
INGESTS
INSISTS
INVESTS
IQTESTS
JURISTS
KNOSSOS
LEGISTS
LIAISES
LOCUSTS
LOESSES
LORISES
LOTUSES
LUTISTS
LYRISTS
MAOISTS
MEDUSAS
MEIOSES
MEIOSIS
MIMESIS
MIMOSAS
MINUSES
MISUSES
MITOSES
MITOSIS
MOLESTS
MOUSSES
NEMESES
NEMESIS
NEXUSES
NUDISTS
OBLASTS
OBOISTS
ONASSIS
OPPOSES
OSMOSES
OSMOSIS
PEGASUS
PERUSES
PHRASES
PLEASES
PLUSSES
PRAISES
PRESSES
PRIESTS
PURISTS
RAMESES
REBUSES
RECASTS
RECUSES
REFUSES
RELISTS
REPASTS
REPOSES
RESISTS
RETESTS
REVISES
SCHISMS
SEXISTS
SINUSES
SPOUSES
TALUSES
TAOISTS
THEISTS
THIRSTS
THRUSTS
TRESSES
TRUISMS
TRUSSES
TSETSES
TUBISTS
TYPISTS
ULYSSES
UNCASES
UNMASKS
UPRISES
VALISES
VIRUSES

•••••SS

ACTRESS
ADDRESS
AGELESS
AGGRESS
AIMLESS
AIRLESS
AIRMASS
ANDRESS
APTNESS
ARMLESS
ARTLESS
ASHLESS
ATALOSS
AWELESS
BADNESS
BIGNESS
BIOMASS
BURGESS
CANVASS
CAPLESS
CARCASS
CARLESS
COMPASS
CONFESS
COYNESS
CUIRASS
CUTLASS
CYPRESS
DECLASS
DEGAUSS
DEPRESS
DIGRESS
DIMNESS
DISCUSS
DISMISS
DRSEUSS
DRYNESS
DUCHESS
EMPRESS
ENDLESS
ENGROSS
EXPRESS
FATLESS
FATNESS
FITNESS
GODDESS
GUTLESS
HAPLESS
HARNESS
HATLESS
HEIRESS
HIPNESS
HITLESS
HOSTESS
HOTNESS
ICELESS
ICINESS
ILLNESS
IMPRESS
INAMESS
INGRESS
IPCRESS
JACKASS
JAGLESS
JOYLESS
LARGESS
LAWLESS
LAXNESS
LIDLESS
LIONESS
LOWNESS
MADNESS
NEWNESS
OAKMOSS
OARLESS
ODDNESS
OLDNESS
OLEMISS
ONENESS
OPPRESS
PATNESS
PEERESS
PINLESS
PITBOSS
POETESS
POSSESS
PROCESS
PROFESS
PROWESS
RAWNESS
REAMASS
RECROSS
REDNESS
REDRESS
REGRESS
REPRESS
SADNESS
SEABASS
SEAMOSS
SEERESS
SHYNESS
SLYNESS
STRAUSS
SUCCESS
SUNLESS
SURPASS
TIELESS
TIGRESS
TOELESS
UNDRESS
USELESS
WETNESS
WITLESS
WITNESS
WRYNESS

ST•••••

STABBED
STABILE
STABLED
STABLER
STABLES
STACKED

STACKUP
STADIUM
STAFFED
STAFFER
STAGERS
STAGGED
STAGGER
STAGIER
STAGILY
STAGING
STAIDER
STAIDLY
STAINED
STAINER
STAKING
STALAGS
STALEST
STALKED
STALKER
STALLED
STAMENS
STAMINA
STAMMER
STAMPED
STANCES
STANDBY
STANDEE
STANDIN
STANDON
STANDUP
STANLEE
STANLEY
STANNIC
STANTON
STANZAS
STAPLED
STAPLER
STAPLES
STARCHY
STARDOM
STAREAT
STARERS
STARETS
STARING
STARKER
STARKLY
STARLET
STARLIT
STARMAN
STARMAP
STARRED
STARTED
STARTER
STARTLE
STARTUP
STARVED
STARVES
STASHED
STASHES
STASSEN
STATELY
STATICE
STATICS
STATING
STATION
STATIST
STATORS
STATUES
STATURE
STATUTE
STAUNCH
STAVING
STAYING
STAYPUT
STAYSUP
STCROIX
STDENIS
STEALTH
STEAMED
STEAMER
STEELED
STEELER
STEELIE
STEEPED
STEEPEN
STEEPER
STEEPLE
STEEPLY
STEERED
STEERER
STEIGER
STEINEM
STEINER
STELLAR
STEMMED
STENCIL
STENGEL
STENTOR
STEPHEN
STEPINS
STEPOUT
STEPPED
STEPPER
STEPPES
STEPSIN
STEPSON
STEPSUP
STEPUPS
STEREOS
STERILE
STERNAL
STERNER
STERNLY
STERNUM
STEROID
STEROLS
STETSON
STETTED
STEUBEN
STEVENS
STEWARD
STEWART
STEWERS
STEWING
STICHES
STICKER
STICKTO
STICKUP
STIEGEL
STIFFED
STIFFEN
STIFFER
STIFFLY
STIFLED
STIFLES
STIGMAS
STILLED
STILLER
STILTED
STILTON
STIMULI
STINGER
STINKER
STINTED
STIPEND
STIPPLE
STIRFRY
STIRRED
STIRRER
STIRRUP
STIRSIN
STIRSUP
STJOHNS
STKITTS
STLOUIS
STLUCIA
STOCKED
STOCKUP
STOGIES
STOICAL
STOKELY
STOKERS
STOKING
STOLLEN
STOLLER
STOLONS
STOMACH
STOMATA
STOMPED
STONERS
STONIER
STONILY
STONING
STOODBY
STOODIN
STOODUP
STOOGES
STOOKEY
STOOLIE
STOOPED
STOOPTO
STOPGAP
STOPOFF
STOPPED
STOPPER
STOPSIN
STOPSUP
STORAGE
STORERS
STOREUP
STOREYS
STORIED
STORIES
STORING
STORMED
STOUTER
STOUTLY
STOWING
STPETER
STRAFED
STRAFES
STRAINS
STRAITS
STRANDS
STRANGE
STRASSE
STRATUM
STRATUS
STRAUSS
STRAYED
STREAKS
STREAKY
STREAMS
STREETS
STRETCH
STRETTO
STREWED
STREWER
STRIATE
STRIDER
STRIDES
STRIKER
STRIKES
STRINGS
STRINGY
STRIPED
STRIPER
STRIPES
STRIVED
STRIVEN
STRIVER
STRIVES
STROBES
STROKED
STROKES
STROLLS
STROPHE
STRUDEL
STUBBED
STUBBLE
STUBBLY
STUCCOS
STUCKTO
STUCKUP
STUDDED
STUDENT
STUDIED
STUDIES
STUDIOS
STUFFED
STUFFER
STUMBLE
STUMPED
STUMPER
STUNGUN
STUNNED
STUNNER
STUNTED
STUPEFY
STUPORS
STURGES
STYGIAN
STYLERS
STYLETS
STYLING
STYLISH
STYLIST
STYLIZE
STYMIED
STYMIES
STYPTIC
STYRENE
STYRIAN

S•T••••

SATCHEL
SATCHMO
SATDOWN
SATIATE
SATIETY
SATIRES
SATIRIC
SATISFY
SATRAPS
SATSUMA
SETBACK
SETDOWN
SETINTO
SETLINE
SETSAIL
SETSOFF
SETSOUT
SETTEES
SETTERS
SETTING
SETTLED
SETTLER
SETTLES
SETUPON
SHTICKS
SITCOMS
SITDOWN
SITSOUT
SITTERS
SITTING
SITUATE
SITWELL
SOTHERE
SOTHERN
SUTLERS
SUTTNER
SUTURED
SUTURES

S••T•••

SALTBOX
SALTERS
SALTIER
SALTILY
SALTINE
SALTING
SANTAFE
SANTANA
SANTINI
SANTIRS
SAOTOME
SAUTEED
SCATHED
SCATHES
SCATTED
SCATTER
SCOTERS
SCOTTIE
SCUTTLE
SCYTHED
SCYTHES
SEATERS
SEATING
SEATTLE
SECTION
SECTORS
SEETHED
SEETHES
SEETOIT
SELTZER
SENTFOR
SENTOFF
SENTOUT
SEPTETS
SESTETS
SESTINA
SETTEES
SETTERS
SETTING
SETTLED
SETTLER
SETTLES
SEXTANS
SEXTANT
SEXTETS
SEXTONS
SHATNER
SHATTER
SHOTFOR
SHOTGUN
SHOTPUT
SHUTEYE
SHUTOFF
SHUTOUT
SHUTSIN
SHUTSUP
SHUTTER
SHUTTLE
SIFTERS
SIFTING
SILTING
SISTERS
SISTINE
SISTRUM
SITTERS
SITTING
SIXTEEN
SIXTIES
SKATERS
SKATING
SKETCHY
SKITOWS
SKITTER
SKITTLE
SLATHER
SLATIER
SLATING
SLATKIN
SLATTED
SLITHER
SLOTCAR
SLOTTED
SMATTER
SMETANA
SMITING
SMITTEN
SMOTHER
SOFTENS
SOFTEST
SOFTIES
SOFTTOP
SOOTHED
SOOTHER
SOOTHES
SOOTIER
SORTERS
SORTIED
SORTIES
SORTING
SOUTANE
SOUTHEY
SPATIAL
SPATTED
SPATTER
SPATULA
SPITING
SPITZES
SPOTLIT
SPOTTED
SPOTTER
SPUTNIK
SPUTTER
STATELY
STATICE
STATICS
STATING
STATION
STATIST
STATORS
STATUES
STATURE
STATUTE
STETSON
STETTED
SUBTEND
SUBTEXT
SUBTLER
SUCTION
SUITING
SUITORS
SUITSUP
SULTANA
SULTANS
SUNTANS
SUSTAIN
SUTTNER
SWATHED
SWATHES
SWATTED
SWATTER
SWITZER
SYSTEMS
SYSTOLE

S•••T••

SAINTED
SAINTLY
SALUTED
SALUTES
SAMITES
SANCTUM
SAUNTER
SCANTED
SCANTER
SCANTLY
SCATTED
SCATTER
SCENTED
SCEPTER
SCEPTRE
SCHATZI
SCOOTED
SCOOTER
SCOTTIE
SCOUTED
SCOUTER
SCRATCH
SCUTTLE
SEASTAR
SEATTLE
SEDATER
SEMITES
SEMITIC
SENATES
SENATOR
SHAFTED
SHANTER
SHASTRI
SHATTER
SHEATHE
SHEATHS
SHEETED
SHELTER
SHELTIE
SHELTON
SHIATSU
SHIFTED
SHIHTZU
SHIITES
SHOOTAT
SHOOTER
SHOOTUP
SHORTED
SHORTEN
SHORTER
SHORTLY
SHORTOF
SHOUTED
SHOUTER
SHUNTED
SHUTTER
SHUTTLE
SHYSTER
SIESTAS
SIGHTED
SIGHTLY
SINATRA
SKEETER
SKELTER
SKELTON
SKEPTIC
SKIRTED
SKITTER
SKITTLE
SLANTED
SLATTED
SLAYTON
SLEETED
SLEPTIN
SLEPTON
SLEUTHS
SLOTTED
SMALTOS
SMARTED
SMARTEN
SMARTER
SMARTLY
SMATTER
SMELTED
SMELTER
SMITTEN
SMOOTHS
SNIFTER
SNOOTED
SNORTED
SNORTER
SOFTTOP
SOLUTES
SOMATIC
SONATAS
SORITES
SPARTAN
SPATTED
SPATTER
SPECTER
SPECTOR
SPECTRA
SPECTRE
SPLITUP
SPLOTCH
SPORTED
SPOTTED
SPOTTER
SPOUTED
SPOUTER
SPRITES
SPURTED
SPUTTER
STANTON
STARTED
STARTER
STARTLE
STARTUP
STENTOR
STETTED
STILTED
STILTON
STINTED
STKITTS
STOUTER
STOUTLY
STPETER
STRATUM
STRATUS
STRETCH
STRETTO
STUNTED
STYPTIC
SUMATRA
SUZETTE
SVELTER
SWARTHY
SWATTED
SWATTER
SWEATED
SWEATER
SWEETEN
SWEETER
SWEETIE
SWEETLY
SWEETON
SWELTER
SWELTRY
SWEPTUP
SWIFTER
SWIFTLY
SYMPTOM

S••••T•

SABBATH
SACHETS
SATIATE
SATIETY
SAVANTS
SCRIPTS
SCULPTS
SEADUTY
SEAGATE
SECANTS
SECRETE
SECRETS
SELECTS
SENNETT
SENSATE
SEPTETS
SERIATE
SERRATE
SESTETS
SETINTO
SEVENTH
SEVENTY
SEXISTS
SEXTETS
SHRIFTS
SIGNETS
SILENTS
SINGSTO
SIPPETS
SITUATE
SLIGHTS
SNAPSTO
SNOCATS
SOCIETY
SOCKETS
SOFFITS
SONNETS
SOPWITH
SORBATE
SORBETS
SOVIETS
SPIGOTS
SPINETS
SPIRITO
SPIRITS
SPLINTS
SPRINTS
SPROUTS
SQUANTO
SQUINTS
SQUINTY
SQUIRTS
STARETS
STATUTE
STEALTH
STICKTO
STKITTS
STOMATA
STOOPTO
STRAITS
STREETS
STRETTO
STRIATE
STUCKTO
STYLETS
SUAVITY
SUBLETS
SUBMITS
SUBSETS
SULFATE
SULFITE
SUMMITS
SUNBATH
SUNCITY
SUNSETS
SUZETTE
SWEARTO

S•••••T

SACKOUT
SADDEST
SALIENT
SANDLOT
SANGOUT
SAPIENT
SARGENT
SAWDUST
SCARLET
SCHMIDT
SEAGIRT
SEALANT
SEAPORT
SEASALT
SEEKOUT
SEESFIT
SEESOUT
SEETOIT
SEGMENT
SELLOUT
SENDOUT
SENNETT
SENTOUT
SERPENT
SERVANT
SETSOUT
SEXIEST
SEXTANT
SHALLOT
SHERBET
SHIPOUT
SHOOTAT
SHOTPUT
SHUBERT
SHUTOUT
SICKEST
SICKOUT
SIDEBET
SIGNOUT
SILKHAT
SINGOUT
SITSOUT
SKIBOOT
SKILIFT
SKILLET
SKIPOUT
SKISUIT
SLEIGHT
SLIPOUT
SLOWEST
SNAPSAT
SNEERAT
SNIDEST
SNIFFAT
SNIGLET
SNIPEAT
SNIPPET
SOFTEST
SOLDOUT
SOLICIT
SOLOIST
SOLVENT
SOONEST
SOPHIST
SOUREST
SPAREST
SPINOUT
SPIRANT
SPOTLIT
SPRIEST
SPRYEST
SPUNOUT
STALEST
STAREAT
STARLET
STARLIT
STATIST
STAYPUT
STEPOUT
STEWART
STUDENT
STYLIST
SUAVEST
SUBJECT
SUBPLOT
SUBSIST
SUBTEXT
SUBUNIT
SUBVERT
SUGGEST
SUNBELT
SUNKIST
SUNSPOT
SUPPORT
SURCOAT
SURFEIT
SUSPECT
SWEARAT
SWOREAT

•ST••••

ASTAIRE
ASTARTE
ASTOLAT
ASTORIA
ASTOUND
ASTRIDE
ESTATES
ESTEEMS
ESTELLE
ESTEVEZ
ESTHETE
ESTIVAL
ESTONIA
ESTORIL
ESTRADA
ESTRAYS
ESTUARY
ISTHMUS
OSTEOID
OSTLERS
OSTRICH
USTINOV

•S•T•••

ASHTRAY
ISOTOPE
TSETSES
USSTEEL

•S••T••

ASCETIC
ASEPTIC
ASIATIC
ESTATES
OSMOTIC
PSALTER

•S•••T•

ASCENTS
ASHANTI
ASPECTS
ASSENTS
ASSERTS
ASSISTS
ASSORTS
ASTARTE
ESCORTS
ESTHETE
ISOLATE
TSHIRTS

•S••••T

ASHIEST
ASKSOUT
ASPHALT
ASSAULT
ASTOLAT
ESCHEAT
TSARIST
TSELIOT

••ST•••

ABSTAIN
ATSTAKE
AUSTERE
AUSTRAL
AUSTRIA
BASTERS
BASTING
BASTION
BESTBOY
BESTIAL
BESTING
BESTIRS
BESTMAN
BESTMEN
BESTOWS
BESTREW
BISTROS
BUSTARD
BUSTING
BUSTLED
BUSTLES
BUSTOUT
CASTERS
CASTILE
CASTING
CASTLED
CASTLES
CASTOFF
CASTOUT
CISTERN
COSTAIN
COSTARS
COSTING
COSTNER
COSTUME
CUSTARD
CUSTODY
CUSTOMS
DASTARD
DESTINE
DESTINY
DESTROY
DISTAFF
DISTANT
DISTEND
DISTILL
DISTORT
DISTURB
DUSTERS
DUSTIER
DUSTING
DUSTMOP
DUSTOFF
DUSTPAN
DUSTUPS
EASTEND
EASTERN
EASTERS
EASTMAN
ECSTASY
EPSTEIN
FASTENS
FASTEST
FASTING
FASTONE
FESTERS
FESTIVE
FESTOON
FISTFUL
FOSTERS
FUSTIAN
FUSTICS
FUSTIER
FUSTILY
GASTRIC
GESTALT
GESTATE
GESTURE
GUSTAVE
GUSTILY
GUSTING
GUSTOES
HASTENS
HASTIER
HASTILY
HASTING
HISTORY
HOSTAGE
HOSTELS
HOSTESS
HOSTILE
HOSTING
HOSTLER

HUSTLED
HUSTLER
HUSTLES
IFSTONE
INSTALL
INSTANT
INSTATE
INSTEAD
INSTEPS
INSTILL
INSTILS
INSTOCK
INSTORE
INSTYLE
JESTERS
JESTING
JOSTLED
JOSTLER
JOSTLES
JUSTICE
JUSTIFY
JUSTINE
JUSTNOW
KESTREL
LASTING
LASTORY
LISTEES
LISTELS
LISTENS
LISTING
LOSTOUT
LUSTERS
LUSTFUL
LUSTIER
LUSTILY
LUSTING
LUSTRED
LUSTRES
MASTABA
MASTERS
MASTERY
MASTICS
MASTIFF
MASTOID
MESTIZO
MISTAKE
MISTERS
MISTIER
MISTILY
MISTING
MISTOOK
MISTRAL
MISTYPE
MUSTAFA
MUSTANG
MUSTARD
MUSTERS
MUSTIER
MUSTILY
MUSTSEE
MYSTERY
MYSTICS
MYSTIFY
NASTASE
NASTIER
NASTILY
NESTEGG
NESTERS
NESTING
NESTLED
NESTLER
NESTLES
NOSTRIL
NOSTRUM
ONSTAGE
OUSTERS
OUSTING
OYSTERS
PASTDUE
PASTELS
PASTERN
PASTEUP
PASTEUR
PASTIER
PASTIME
PASTINA
PASTING
PASTORS
PASTURE
PESTERS
PESTLED
PESTLES
PISTILS
PISTOLE
PISTOLS
PISTONS
POSTAGE
POSTBOX
POSTERN
POSTERS
POSTHOC
POSTING
POSTMAN
POSTMEN
POSTURE
POSTWAR
RASTERS
RESTAGE
RESTAIN
RESTAMP
RESTART
RESTATE
RESTERS
RESTFUL
RESTING
RESTIVE
RESTOCK
RESTORE
RESTSUP
RESTYLE
ROSTAND
ROSTERS
ROSTRUM
RUSTICS
RUSTIER
RUSTILY
RUSTING
RUSTLED
RUSTLER
RUSTLES
SESTETS
SESTINA
SISTERS
SISTINE
SISTRUM
SUSTAIN
SYSTEMS
SYSTOLE
TASTERS
TASTIER
TASTILY
TASTING
TESTBAN
TESTEES
TESTERS
TESTIER
TESTIFY
TESTILY
TESTING
TESTOUT
TOSTADA
ULSTERS
UNSTACK
UNSTICK
UNSTOPS
UNSTRAP
UNSTUCK
UPSTAGE
UPSTART
UPSTATE
USSTEEL
VASTEST
VESTEES
VESTIGE
VESTING
VESTURE
VISTULA
WASTAGE
WASTERS
WASTING
WASTREL
WESTEND
WESTERN
WISTFUL
ZESTFUL
ZESTIER

••S•T••

BUSSTOP
DESKTOP
DESOTOS
LESOTHO
MISSTEP
MUSETTE
PESETAS
POSITED
RISOTTO
ROSETTA
ROSETTE
UNSATED
VISITED
VISITOR
WASATCH
WASHTUB

••S••T•

ABSENTS
ASSENTS
ASSERTS
ASSISTS
ASSORTS
BASALTS
BASKETS
BASSETS
BISECTS
BISMUTH
BOSKETS
CASSATT
COSSETS
DESALTS
DESERTS
DESISTS
DESPITE
DESPOTS
DISPUTE
ENSUITE
GASJETS
GASKETS
GESTATE
GOSSETT
GUSSETS
INSECTS
INSERTS
INSISTS
INSPOTS
INSTATE
INSULTS
JESUITS
MASCOTS
MISDATE
MISFITS
MISHITS
MISMATE
MUSCATS
MUSETTE
MUSKETS
OFSORTS
POSSETS
RESALTS
RESEATS
RESECTS
RESENTS
RESISTS
RESORTS
RESPITE
RESTATE
RESULTS
RISOTTO
ROSEATE
ROSETTA
ROSETTE
RUSSETS
SESTETS
UNSEATS
UPSHOTS
UPSTATE
WESKITS

••S•••T

ABSOLUT
ASSAULT
BASEHIT
BASSIST
BISCUIT
BUSIEST
BUSTOUT
CASHOUT
CASSATT
CASTOUT
DASBOOT
DESCANT
DESCENT
DESKSET
DESSERT
DISGUST
DISHOUT
DISPORT
DISRUPT
DISSECT
DISSENT
DISTANT
DISTORT
EASIEST
FASCIST
FASTEST
FISHNET
FISHOUT
FUSSPOT
GESTALT
GOSSETT
INSHORT
INSIGHT
INSPECT
INSTANT
LOSEOUT
LOSESIT
LOSTOUT
LUSHEST
MESSKIT
MISCAST
MISSOUT
MUSKRAT
NASCENT
NOSEOUT
NOSIEST
NOSWEAT
ONSIGHT
PASSANT
PASSOUT
POSHEST
RASHEST
RESHOOT
RESPECT
RESTART
SUSPECT
TESTOUT
TOSSOUT
UNSPENT
UNSWEPT
UPSTART
UPSWEPT
VASTEST
WASHOUT

•••ST••

ALLSTAR
ALLSTON
APOSTLE
ARISTAE
ARISTAS
ARISTOS
BEASTIE
BEASTLY
BLASTED
BLASTER
BLISTER
BLUSTER
BOASTED
BOASTER
BOLSTER
BOOSTED
BOOSTER
BOOSTUP
BOXSTEP
BRISTLE
BRISTLY
BRISTOL
BURSTYN
BUSSTOP
CAPSTAN
CAUSTIC
CHASTEN
CHASTER
CHESTER
CLUSTER
COASTAL
COASTED
COASTER
CRESTED
CRUSTED
CRYSTAL
DAYSTAR
DOGSTAR
DRASTIC
DRISTAN
DYKSTRA
EGESTED
ELASTIC
EPISTLE
ERISTIC
EXISTED
FAUSTUS
FEASTED
FIESTAS
FIRSTLY
FLUSTER
FOISTED
FORSTER
FROSTED
GAGSTER
GHASTLY
GHOSTED
GHOSTLY
GLISTEN
GNOSTIC
GRISTLE
GRISTLY
GUESTED
HALSTON
HAMSTER
HEISTED
HIPSTER
HOISTED
HOLSTER
HOUSTON
INASTEW
JOISTED
JOUSTED
JOUSTER
KIRSTIE
LEISTER
LOBSTER
MAESTRI
MAESTRO
MISSTEP
MOBSTER
MOISTEN
MOISTER
MOISTLY
MONSTER
NONSTOP
OLDSTER
OLESTRA
ONESTEP
ORESTES
OUTSTEP
PIASTER
PIASTRE
PITSTOP
PLASTER
PLASTIC
PRESTON
PRESTOS
PUNSTER
QUESTED
RALSTON
REDSTAR
ROASTED
ROASTER
ROISTER
ROOSTED
ROOSTER
ROUSTED
SEASTAR
SHASTRI
SHYSTER
SIESTAS
TAPSTER
TELSTAR
THISTLE
TINSTAR
TIPSTER
TOASTED
TOASTER
TOLSTOI
TOLSTOY
TRESTLE
TRISTAN
TRUSTED
TRUSTEE
TRYSTED
TRYSTER
TWISTED
TWISTER
TWOSTAR
TWOSTEP
WAISTED
WEBSTER
WHISTLE
WINSTON
WOOSTER
WORSTED
WRESTED
WRESTLE

•••S•T•

BASSETS
CASSATT
CLOSETS
CORSETS
COSSETS
DENSITY
DORSETT
FALSITY
FORSYTH
GOSSETT
GUSSETS
HIRSUTE
OFFSETS
OFFSITE
OUTSETS
POSSETS
PRESETS
PULSATE
RUSSETS
SENSATE
SUBSETS
SUNSETS
TEASETS
VARSITY
WEBSITE

•••S••T

ACESOUT
ACTSOUT
AIRSOUT
ASKSOUT
BASSIST
BIGSHOT
BORSCHT
BOWSOUT
BOXSEAT
BRISKET
BUGSOUT
BUMSOUT
BUYSOUT
CARSEAT
CASSATT
CLOSEST
CONSENT
CONSIST
CONSORT
CONSULT
COPSOUT
CUTSOUT
DENSEST
DESSERT
DIESOUT
DIGSOUT
DISSECT
DISSENT
DORSETT
DRYSUIT
EARSHOT
EATSOUT
EKESOUT
FALSEST
FANSOUT
FRESHET
FUSSPOT
GETSOUT
GETSSET
GOESOUT
GOSSETT
GUNSHOT
HOTSEAT
HOTSHOT
HOTSPOT
INASNIT
INASPOT
INKSPOT
IRISOUT
KNESSET
LAWSUIT
LAYSOUT
LETSOUT
LOGSOUT
LOOSEST
MESSKIT
MISSOUT
MUGSHOT
OFASORT
ONESHOT
OPTSOUT
PANSOUT
PASSANT
PASSOUT
PAYSOUT
PEASANT
PERSIST
PIGSOUT
POPSOUT
POTSHOT
PRESENT
PRESORT
PURSUIT
PUTSOUT
REDSPOT
RIMSHOT
RUBSOUT
RUNSOUT
SEASALT
SEESFIT
SEESOUT
SETSOUT
SITSOUT
SKISUIT
SUBSIST
SUNSPOT
TAGSOUT
TAPSOUT
TENSEST
TENSPOT
TERSEST
TOPSOUT
TOSSOUT
TRISECT
WETSUIT
WIGSOUT
WINSOUT

••••ST•

ACCOSTS
ADJUSTS
AGEISTS
AMNESTY
AORISTS
ARIOSTO
ARRESTS
ARTISTE
ARTISTS
ASSISTS
ATTESTS
AUGUSTA
AUGUSTE
BATISTA
BATISTE
BEHESTS
BREASTS
CANASTA
CELESTA
CELESTE
CHRISTI
CHRISTO
CHRISTY
COHOSTS
COMESTO
CUBISTS
DARESTO
DELISTS
DESISTS
DETESTS
DIGESTS
DIVESTS
DYNASTS
DYNASTY
EGOISTS
ELMISTI
ENLISTS
ERNESTO
FALLSTO
FORESTS
GANGSTA
GEARSTO
GIVESTO
HOLDSTO
HONESTY
IMPASTO
IMPOSTS
INFESTS
INGESTS
INHASTE
INSISTS
INVESTS
IQTESTS
JOCASTA
JURISTS
KEEPSTO
LACOSTE
LEADSTO
LEGISTS
LOCUSTS
LOOKSTO
LUTISTS
LYRISTS
MAJESTE
MAJESTY
MAOISTS
MODESTO
MODESTY
MODISTE
MOLESTS
NUDISTS
OBLASTS
OBOISTS
PRAYSTO
PRIESTS
PURISTS
REBASTE
RECASTS
RELISTS
REPASTE
REPASTS
RESISTS
RETESTS
RIPOSTE
ROBUSTA
SEXISTS
SINGSTO
SNAPSTO
TAKESTO
TALKSTO
TAOISTS
TENDSTO
THEISTS
THIRSTS
THIRSTY
THRUSTS
TRIESTE
TUBISTS
TURNSTO
TYPISTS
WANTSTO

••••S•T

BABYSAT
BABYSIT
BARKSAT
BEATSIT
BLOWSIT
COMESAT
COOLSIT
DATASET
DEADSET
DEEPSET
DEPOSIT
DESKSET
FLIESAT
GETSSET
GRABSAT
HANDSET
HARDSET
HEADSET
HINTSAT
HOOFSIT
HOOTSAT
JEERSAT
JUMPSAT
KEEPSAT
KNESSET
LANDSAT
LEERSAT
LOOKSAT
LOSESIT
MAKESIT
MINDSET
MOONSET
NAILSET
PECKSAT
PEEKSAT
PEERSAT
PICKSAT
PLAYSAT
POKESAT
QUONSET
RAILSAT
REVISIT
SNAPSAT
TALKSAT
TEARSAT
THATSIT
TRANSIT
TYPESET
WELLSET
WINGSIT
WINKSAT
YELLSAT

•••••ST

ABREAST
ACCURST
ACHIEST
AERIEST
AGAINST
AGONIST
AIRIEST
AMHERST
AMONGST
AMPLEST
ANALYST
ANAPEST
ANIMIST
ARIDEST
ARMREST
ARTIEST
ASHIEST
ATAVIST
ATHEIST
ATHIRST
ATLEAST
ATWORST
BALDEST
BALLAST
BAPTIST
BASSIST
BEDPOST
BEDREST
BELFAST
BEQUEST
BIGGEST
BOLDEST
BOMBAST
BONIEST
BRAVEST
BUSIEST
CAGIEST
CALMEST
CELLIST
CHEMIST
CLOSEST
COEXIST
COLDEST
COMBUST
COMPOST
CONGEST
CONSIST
CONTEST
COOLEST
COPYIST
COZIEST
CRUDEST
CULTIST
CURTEST
CYCLIST
CZARIST
DADAIST
DAFTEST
DAMPEST
DANKEST
DARKEST
DEAFEST
DEAREST
DEEPEST
DEFROST
DEFTEST
DENSEST
DENTIST
DICIEST
DIMMEST
DISGUST
DOPIEST
DOUREST
DUELIST
DULLEST
DUMBEST
EARNEST
EASIEST
EDGIEST
EELIEST
EERIEST
EGOTIST
ELEGIST
ELITIST
ENCRUST
ENDMOST
ENTRUST
EPEEIST
EVENEST
EVEREST
EVILEST
EXHAUST
FADDIST
FAIREST
FALSEST
FAREAST
FARWEST
FASCIST
FASTEST
FATTEST
FAUVIST
FIRMEST
FITTEST
FLORIST
FLUTIST
FLYCAST
FLYPAST
FONDEST
FORREST
FOULEST
FOXIEST
FULLEST
FUNFEST
GABFEST
GAMIEST
GETLOST
GOOIEST
GORIEST
GRAVEST
GRAYEST
GREYEST
GYMNAST
HARDEST
HARPIST
HARVEST
HAZIEST
HIGHEST
HIPPEST
HITLIST
HOLIEST
HOMIEST
HORNIST
HOTTEST
ICKIEST
IFFIEST
INANEST
INQUEST
INTRUST
IRATEST
JUDOIST
KEENEST
KEYWEST
KINDEST
LACIEST
LAMAIST
LANKEST
LARGEST
LAZIEST
LEANEST
LEFTIST
LEWDEST
LIMIEST
LIMPEST
LITHEST
LOGIEST
LONGEST
LOOSEST
LOUDEST
LUSHEST
MADDEST
MAEWEST
MEANEST
MEEKEST
MIDEAST
MIDWEST
MILDEST
MISCAST
NEAREST
NEATEST
NIGHEST
NOBLEST
NOSIEST
NUMBEST
OCULIST
OILIEST
OLDWEST
OUTCAST
OUTLAST
OUTPOST
PALMIST
PAULIST
PERSIST
PERTEST
PIANIST
PINIEST
PINKEST
POKIEST
POLOIST
POOREST
POSHEST
PRECAST
PRETEST
PROTEST
PROTIST
PROVOST
PUNIEST
RACIEST
RANKEST
RASHEST
REALIST

REDDEST
REQUEST
RICHEST
SADDEST
SAWDUST
SEXIEST
SICKEST
SLOWEST
SNIDEST
SOFTEST
SOLOIST
SOONEST
SOPHIST
SOUREST
SPAREST
SPRIEST
SPRYEST
STALEST
STATIST
STYLIST
SUAVEST
SUBSIST
SUGGEST
SUNKIST
TALLEST
TANNEST
TARTEST
TAUTEST
TEMPEST
TENSEST
TERSEST
TIDIEST
TINIEST
TITLIST
TONIEST
TOPMAST
TOPMOST
TOURIST
TRITEST
TSARIST
TUBAIST
UGLIEST
UNBLEST
UNTWIST
VAGUEST
VAINEST
VASTEST
VIOLIST
WARIEST
WARMEST
WAVIEST
WAXIEST
WEAKEST
WETTEST
WHITEST
WILDEST
WILIEST
WIRIEST
ZANIEST

SU•••••

SUASION
SUAVELY
SUAVEST
SUAVITY
SUBBING
SUBDEBS
SUBDUED
SUBDUER
SUBDUES
SUBHEAD
SUBJECT
SUBJOIN
SUBLETS
SUBLIME
SUBMITS
SUBORNS
SUBPLOT
SUBROSA
SUBSETS
SUBSIDE
SUBSIDY
SUBSIST
SUBSOIL
SUBSUME
SUBTEND
SUBTEXT
SUBTLER
SUBUNIT
SUBURBS
SUBVERT
SUBWAYS
SUBZERO
SUCCEED
SUCCESS
SUCCORS
SUCCOUR
SUCCUMB
SUCKERS
SUCKING
SUCKSIN
SUCRASE
SUCROSE
SUCTION
SUDBURY
SUDSIER
SUDSING
SUFFERS
SUFFICE
SUFFOLK
SUFFUSE
SUGARED
SUGGEST
SUITING
SUITORS
SUITSUP
SUKARNO
SULFATE
SULFIDE
SULFITE
SULKERS
SULKIER
SULKIES
SULKILY
SULKING
SULLIED
SULLIES
SULPHUR
SULTANA
SULTANS
SULUSEA
SUMATRA
SUMMARY
SUMMERS
SUMMERY
SUMMING
SUMMITS
SUMMONS
SUNBATH
SUNBEAM
SUNBELT
SUNBURN
SUNCITY
SUNDAES
SUNDAYS
SUNDECK
SUNDERS
SUNDEWS
SUNDIAL
SUNDOGS
SUNDOWN
SUNFISH
SUNGODS
SUNKIST
SUNLAMP
SUNLESS
SUNMAID
SUNNIER
SUNNILY
SUNNING
SUNRAYS
SUNRISE
SUNROOF
SUNROOM
SUNSETS
SUNSPOT
SUNTANS
SUPPERS
SUPPING
SUPPLER
SUPPORT
SUPPOSE
SUPREME
SUPREMO
SURCOAT
SURFACE
SURFEIT
SURFERS
SURFING
SURGEON
SURGERY
SURGING
SURINAM
SURLIER
SURLILY
SURMISE
SURNAME
SURPASS
SURPLUS
SURREAL
SURREYS
SURVEYS
SURVIVE
SUSANNA
SUSANNE
SUSLIKS
SUSPECT
SUSPEND
SUSSING
SUSTAIN
SUTLERS
SUTTNER
SUTURED
SUTURES
SUZANNE
SUZETTE

S•U••••

SAUCERS
SAUCIER
SAUCILY
SAUNTER
SAURIAN
SAUSAGE
SAUTEED
SCUDDED
SCUFFED
SCUFFLE
SCULLED
SCULLER
SCULPTS
SCUPPER
SCURVES
SCUTTLE
SHUBERT
SHUCKED
SHUCKER
SHUDDER
SHUFFLE
SHUNNED
SHUNTED
SHUSHED
SHUSHES
SHUTEYE
SHUTOFF
SHUTOUT
SHUTSIN
SHUTSUP
SHUTTER
SHUTTLE
SKULKED
SKULKER
SKUNKED
SLUDGES
SLUGGED
SLUGGER
SLUICED
SLUICES
SLUMBER
SLUMMED
SLUMPED
SLURPED
SLURRED
SLUSHES
SMUDGED
SMUDGES
SMUGGER
SMUGGLE
SNUBBED
SNUFFED
SNUFFER
SNUFFLE
SNUGGER
SNUGGLE
SOUFFLE
SOUGHED
SOULFUL
SOUNDED
SOUNDER
SOUNDLY
SOUPCON
SOUPIER
SOUPSUP
SOURCED
SOURCES
SOUREST
SOURING
SOURISH
SOUTANE
SOUTHEY
SPUMING
SPUMONE
SPUMONI
SPUNOFF
SPUNOUT
SPURNED
SPURNER
SPURRED
SPURSON
SPURTED
SPUTNIK
SPUTTER
SQUALID
SQUALLS
SQUALOR
SQUANTO
SQUARED
SQUARER
SQUARES
SQUAWKS
SQUEAKS
SQUEAKY
SQUEALS
SQUEEZE
SQUELCH
SQUINCH
SQUINTS
SQUINTY
SQUIRED
SQUIRES
SQUIRMS
SQUIRMY
SQUIRTS
SQUISHY
STUBBED
STUBBLE
STUBBLY
STUCCOS
STUCKTO
STUCKUP
STUDDED
STUDENT
STUDIED
STUDIES
STUDIOS
STUFFED
STUFFER
STUMBLE
STUMPED
STUMPER
STUNGUN
STUNNED
STUNNER
STUNTED
STUPEFY
STUPORS
STURGES

S••U•••

SAGUARO
SALUKIS
SALUTED
SALUTES
SAMURAI
SCOURED
SCOURER
SCOURGE
SCOUTED
SCOUTER
SCRUBBY
SCRUBUP
SCRUFFS
SCRUFFY
SCRUNCH
SCRUPLE
SECULAR
SECURED
SECURER
SECURES
SEDUCED
SEDUCER
SEDUCES
SEQUELS
SEQUINS
SEQUOIA
SETUPON
SHOUTED
SHOUTER
SHRUBBY
SINUOUS
SINUSES
SIOUANS
SITUATE
SLEUTHS
SLOUCHY
SLOUGHS
SOLUBLE
SOLUTES
SOSUEME
SPLURGE
SPOUSAL
SPOUSES
SPOUTED
SPOUTER
SPRUCED
SPRUCER
SPRUCES
STAUNCH
STEUBEN
STLUCIA
STOUTER
STOUTLY
STRUDEL
SUBUNIT
SUBURBS
SULUSEA
SUTURED
SUTURES

S•••U••

SAMNUNN
SAMSUNG
SANJUAN
SANLUIS
SATSUMA
SAVOURS
SAVOURY
SAWBUCK
SAWDUST
SCAPULA
SEADUTY
SEAGULL
SECLUDE
SENDUPS
SENSUAL
SHOGUNS
SHROUDS
SICHUAN
SIGMUND
SIXGUNS
SKIJUMP
SKIRUNS
SKISUIT
SLIPUPS
SNAFUED
SOJOURN
SOWBUGS
SPATULA
SPELUNK
SPROUTS
STATUES
STATURE
STATUTE
STEPUPS
STIMULI
STLOUIS
STRAUSS
SUBDUED
SUBDUER
SUBDUES
SUBSUME
SUCCUMB
SUDBURY
SUFFUSE
SUNBURN
SYNFUEL

S••••U•

SACKFUL
SACKOUT
SANCTUM
SANGOUT
SAVEDUP
SAVESUP
SCAREUP
SCREWUP
SCRUBUP
SEALSUP
SEASLUG
SEEKOUT
SEESOUT
SELLOUT
SENDOUT
SENDSUP
SENTOUT
SERIOUS
SERVEUP
SETSOUT
SEVENUP
SEWEDUP
SEYMOUR
SHAKEUP
SHAPEUP
SHIPOUT
SHOOKUP
SHOOTUP
SHOTGUN
SHOTPUT
SHOWSUP
SHUTOUT
SHUTSUP
SICKOUT
SIGNOUT
SIGNSUP
SINGOUT
SINUOUS
SISTRUM
SITSOUT
SIZEDUP
SIZESUP
SKILFUL
SKIPOUT
SKYBLUE
SLIPOUT
SLIPSUP
SLOWSUP
SMASHUP
SNAPSUP
SOAKSUP
SOLDOUT
SORGHUM
SOULFUL
SOUPSUP
SPEAKUP
SPEEDUP
SPICEUP
SPINOUT
SPLITUP
SPOKEUP
SPUNOUT
STACKUP
STADIUM
STANDUP
STARTUP
STAYPUT
STAYSUP
STEPOUT
STEPSUP
STERNUM
STICKUP
STIRRUP
STIRSUP
STOCKUP
STOODUP
STOPSUP
STOREUP
STRATUM
STRATUS
STUCKUP
STUNGUN
SUCCOUR
SUITSUP
SULPHUR
SURPLUS
SWEEPUP
SWELLUP
SWEPTUP

S•••••U

SHIATSU
SHIHTZU

•SU••••

ASUNDER
ASUSUAL
TSUNAMI
USUALLY
USURERS
USURPED
USURPER

•S•U•••

ASSUAGE
ASSUMED
ASSUMES
ASSURED
ASSURES
ESCUDOS
ESQUIRE
ESTUARY
ISSUERS
ISSUING
TSQUARE

•S••U••

ASHBURY
ASSAULT
ASTOUND
ASUSUAL
ASYLUMS
ESPOUSE

•S•••U•

ASKSOUT
ISTHMUS
PSYCHUP
USINGUP

••SU•••

ASSUAGE
ASSUMED
ASSUMES
ASSURED
ASSURES
CASUALS
DISUSED
ENSUING
ENSUITE
ENSURED
ENSURES
INSULAR
INSULIN
INSULTS
INSURED
INSURES
ISSUERS
ISSUING
JESUITS
MISUSED
MISUSES
RESULTS
RESUMED
RESUMES
RESURGE
SOSUEME
UPSURGE
VISUALS

••S•U••

ASSAULT
BASQUES
BISCUIT
BISMUTH
BISQUES
COSTUME
DISCUSS
DISGUST
DISPUTE
DISRUPT
DISTURB
DRSEUSS
DUSTUPS
ENSOULS
FISSURE
GASPUMP
GESTURE
LASHUPS
MASQUES
MISCUED
MISCUES
MISRULE
MOSQUES
MUSEUMS
OBSCURE
PASTURE
POSEURS
POSSUMS
POSTURE
PUSHUPS
RESCUED
RESCUER
RESCUES
RESOUND
TISSUES
TOSSUPS
UNSOUND
UNSTUCK
VESTURE
VISTULA

••S••U•

ABSOLUT
BASHFUL
BUSTOUT
CASHOUT
CASSIUS
CASTOUT
DISHOUT
EASEDUP
EASESUP
FISHOUT
FISTFUL
GASEOUS
GUSSYUP
LASCAUX
LESPAUL
LOSEOUT
LOSTOUT
LUSTFUL
MASSEUR
MISSOUT
NOSEEUM
NOSEOUT
NOSTRUM
PASSEUL
PASSOUT
PASTDUE
PASTEUP
PASTEUR
RESIDUE
RESTFUL
RESTSUP
ROSEBUD
ROSTRUM
SISTRUM
TESTOUT
TOSSOUT
TUSSAUD
VISCOUS
WASHOUT
WASHTUB
WISEDUP
WISEGUY
WISESUP
WISHFUL
WISTFUL
ZESTFUL

•••SU••

ASUSUAL
CAESURA
CAPSULE
CENSURE
CLOSURE
CONSULS
CONSULT
CONSUME
DRYSUIT
ERASURE
FISSURE
FORSURE
HIRSUTE
LAWSUIT
LEISURE
MEASURE
NETSUKE
NETSURF
NOTSURE
POSSUMS
PRESUME
PURSUED
PURSUER
PURSUES
PURSUIT
SAMSUNG
SATSUMA
SENSUAL
SKISUIT
SUBSUME
TISSUES
TONSURE
TOSSUPS
UNUSUAL
WETSUIT

•••S•U•

ACESOUT
ACTSOUT
AIRSOUT
ALYSSUM
ASKSOUT
ATISSUE
BOOSTUP
BOWSOUT
BRUSHUP
BRUSQUE
BUGSOUT
BUMSOUT
BUYSOUT
CASSIUS
CELSIUS
CLOSEUP
COPSOUT
CRASSUS
CRISPUS
CROSSUP
CUTSOUT
DANSEUR
DIESOUT
DIGSOUT
DRESSUP
EATSOUT
EKESOUT
ELYSIUM
ERASMUS
FANSOUT
FAUSTUS
GETSOUT
GOESOUT
GUSSYUP
HOTSPUR
IBNSAUD
IRISOUT
LAYSOUT
LETSOUT
LOGSOUT
LOUSEUP
MASSEUR
MISSOUT
OPOSSUM
OPTSOUT
PANSOUT
PASSEUL
PASSOUT
PAYSOUT
PEASOUP
PERSEUS
PERSIUS
PIGSOUT
POPSOUT
PUTSOUT
RAISEUP
REISSUE
RUBSOUT
RUNSOUT
SEASLUG
SEESOUT
SETSOUT
SITSOUT
SMASHUP
TAGSOUT
TAPSOUT
TENSEUP
THESEUS
TOPSOUT
TOSSOUT
TUSSAUD
WIGSOUT
WINSOUT

••••SU•

ALYSSUM
ANTESUP
ATISSUE
BACKSUP
BALLSUP
BANGSUP
BEADSUP
BEAMSUP
BEARSUP
BEATSUP
BEEFSUP
BINDSUP
BLOWSUP
BONESUP
BOOTSUP
BOXESUP
BUCKSUP
BUMPSUP
BUOYSUP
BURNSUP
CALLSUP
CHATSUP
CHEWSUP
CLAMSUP
CLOGSUP
COILSUP
COMESUP
COOKSUP
COOPSUP
CRASSUS
CROESUS
CROPSUP
CROSSUP
CURLSUP
DOLLSUP
DRAWSUP
DRESSUP
DRIESUP
DRUMSUP
EASESUP
EVENSUP
FAIRSUP
FILLSUP
FIRESUP
FIRMSUP
FIXESUP
FOLDSUP
FOULSUP
GANGSUP
GEARSUP
GIVESUP
GOOFSUP
GROWSUP
HANDSUP
HANGSUP
HAULSUP
HEADSUP
HEATSUP
HOLDSUP
HOLESUP
HOOKSUP
JACKSUP
JOINSUP
JUMPSUP
KEEPSUP
KICKSUP
LACESUP
LEADSUP
LIFTSUP
LINESUP
LOCKSUP
LOOKSUP
LUMPSUM
MAKESUP
MARKSUP
MIXESUP
MUCKSUP
OPENSUP
OPOSSUM
PACKSUP
PAIRSUP
PEGASUS
PERKSUP
PICKSUP
PILESUP
PIPESUP
PLAYSUP
PROPSUP
PULLSUP
PUMPSUP
RACKSUP
RAKESUP
REARSUP
REISSUE
RESTSUP
RINGSUP
ROLLSUP
SAVESUP
SEALSUP
SENDSUP
SHOWSUP
SHUTSUP
SIGNSUP
SIZESUP
SLIPSUP
SLOWSUP
SNAPSUP
SOAKSUP
SOUPSUP
STAYSUP
STEPSUP
STIRSUP
STOPSUP
SUITSUP
TAKESUP
TALKSUP
TANKSUP
TEAMSUP
TEARSUP
TIMESUP
TONESUP
TOOLSUP
TRIPSUP
TUNESUP
TURNSUP
TYPESUP
WAITSUP
WAKESUP
WALLSUP
WARMSUP
WELLSUP
WHIPSUP
WINDSUP
WIPESUP
WISESUP
WORKSUP
WRAPSUP

••••S•U
BABASSU
ILIESCU

•••••SU
BABASSU
FUJITSU
JUJITSU
KOMATSU
SHIATSU

SV•••••
SVELTER

S•V••••
SAVABLE
SAVAGED
SAVAGER
SAVAGES
SAVALAS
SAVANNA
SAVANTS
SAVARIN
SAVEDUP
SAVESUP
SAVINGS
SAVIORS
SAVORED
SAVOURS
SAVOURY
SAVVIER
SAVVILY
SEVENTH
SEVENTY
SEVENUP
SEVERAL
SEVERED
SEVERER
SEVIGNE
SEVILLE
SOVIETS

S••V•••
SALVAGE
SALVERS
SALVING
SALVOES
SAVVIER
SAVVILY
SELVAGE
SERVALS
SERVANT
SERVERS
SERVEUP
SERVICE
SERVILE
SERVING
SHAVERS
SHAVING
SHIVERS
SHOVELS
SHOVERS
SHOVING
SILVERS
SILVERY
SKIVERS
SLAVERS
SLAVERY
SLAVING
SLAVISH
SLIVERS
SLOVAKS
SLOVENE
SLOVENS
SNIVELS
SOLVENT
SOLVERS
SOLVING
SPAVINS
STAVING
STEVENS
SUAVELY
SUAVEST
SUAVITY
SUBVERT
SURVEYS
SURVIVE
SWIVELS
SYLVANS

S•••V••
SAMOVAR
SCARVES
SCRIVEN
SCURVES
SEGOVIA
SHEAVED
SHEAVES
SHELVED
SHELVES
SHRIVEL
SHRIVER
SHRIVES
SLEEVES
STARVED
STARVES
STRIVED
STRIVEN
STRIVER
STRIVES
SWERVED
SWERVES

S••••V•
SKYDIVE
SURVIVE

•S••V••
ESTEVEZ
ESTIVAL

•S••••V
USTINOV

••S•V••
DISAVOW
HESHVAN
VISAVIS

••S••V•
ABSOLVE
CASSAVA
DESERVE
ENSLAVE
FESTIVE
GUSTAVE
MASSIVE
MISSIVE
MUSCOVY
OBSERVE
PASSIVE
RESERVE
RESOLVE
RESTIVE
YESHIVA

•••S•V•
ABUSIVE
CASSAVA
CURSIVE
ELUSIVE
EROSIVE
EVASIVE
MASSIVE
MISSIVE
PASSIVE
PENSIVE
PLOSIVE
TENSIVE

SW•••••
SWABBED
SWADDLE
SWAGGER
SWAHILI
SWALLOW
SWAMPED
SWANKER
SWANSON
SWAPPED
SWAPPER
SWARMED
SWARTHY
SWATHED
SWATHES
SWATTED
SWATTER
SWAYERS
SWAYING
SWEARAT
SWEARBY
SWEARER
SWEARIN
SWEARTO
SWEATED
SWEATER
SWEDISH
SWEEPER
SWEEPUP
SWEETEN
SWEETER
SWEETIE
SWEETLY
SWEETON
SWELLED
SWELLUP
SWELTER
SWELTRY
SWEPTUP
SWERVED
SWERVES
SWIFTER
SWIFTLY
SWIGGED
SWILLED
SWIMMER
SWINDLE
SWINGBY
SWINGER
SWIPERS
SWIPING
SWIRLED
SWISHED
SWISHES
SWITZER
SWIVELS
SWIZZLE
SWOLLEN
SWOONED
SWOOPED
SWOOSIE
SWOREAT
SWOREBY
SWOREIN

S•W••••
SAWBUCK
SAWDUST
SAWFISH
SAWLOGS
SAWMILL
SAWWOOD
SAWYERS
SEWEDUP
SOWBUGS

S••W•••
SAWWOOD
SAYWHEN
SCHWINN
SCOWLED
SCOWLER
SEAWALL
SEAWARD
SEAWAYS
SEAWEED
SHAWNEE
SHAWWAL
SHEWOLF
SHOWBIZ
SHOWDOG
SHOWERS
SHOWERY
SHOWIER
SHOWILY
SHOWING
SHOWMAN
SHOWMEN
SHOWNIN
SHOWOFF
SHOWSIN
SHOWSUP
SITWELL
SKEWERS
SKEWING
SKYWARD
SKYWAYS
SLOWEST
SLOWING
SLOWSUP
SNOWCAP
SNOWDAY
SNOWDON
SNOWIER
SNOWING
SNOWJOB
SNOWMAN
SNOWMEN
SNOWPEA
SNOWSIN
SOPWITH
SPAWNED
SPEWING
STEWARD
STEWART
STEWERS
STEWING
STOWING
SUBWAYS

S•••W••
SARAWAK
SCRAWLS
SCRAWLY
SCRAWNY
SCREWED
SCREWUP
SHAWWAL
SHERWIN
SOMEWAY
SPRAWLS
SQUAWKS
STREWED
STREWER

S••••W•
SATDOWN
SEACOWS
SEESAWS
SETDOWN
SHADOWS
SHADOWY
SITDOWN
SKITOWS
SORROWS
SUNDEWS
SUNDOWN

S•••••W
SAGINAW
SALCHOW
SHALLOW
SKIDROW
SOMEHOW
SPARROW
SWALLOW

•S••W••
CSLEWIS

•S•••W•
ESCHEWS
ESCROWS

•S••••W
ASOFNOW
USOSHOW

••SW•••
ANSWERS
BOSWELL
IPSWICH
MCSWINE
MISWORD
NOSWEAT
ROSWELL
UNSWEPT
UPSWEEP
UPSWEPT
UPSWING

••S•W••
DISOWNS
POSTWAR
UNSEWED
WYSIWYG

••S••W•
BESTOWS
CASHEWS
CUSHAWS
GOSHAWK
NOSHOWS
TVSHOWS

••S•••W
BESTREW
CASELAW
CASHCOW
DISAVOW
JUSTNOW
UNSCREW

•••SW••
BEESWAX
WHOSWHO

•••S•W•
BOWSAWS
JIGSAWS
PITSAWS
RIPSAWS
SEESAWS

•••S••W
AIRSHOW
CAPSHAW
CATSPAW
DOGSHOW
GLASGOW
ICESHOW
INASTEW
LAYSLOW
LIESLOW
USOSHOW
WINSLOW

••••S•W
BANDSAW
BUCKSAW
BUZZSAW
FORESAW
FRETSAW
GANGSAW
HACKSAW
HANDSAW
OVERSAW
WHIPSAW

S•X••••
SAXHORN
SEXIEST
SEXISTS
SEXTANS
SEXTANT
SEXTETS
SEXTONS
SIXFOLD
SIXGUNS
SIXPACK
SIXTEEN
SIXTIES

S••••X•
SUBTEXT

S•••••X
SALTBOX
SANDBOX
SHOEBOX
SIMPLEX
SKEEZIX
SOAPBOX
SPANDEX
STCROIX

••S•••X
CASHBOX
LASCAUX
POSTBOX

•••S••X
BEESWAX

••••S•X
ALTOSAX
DEEPSIX

SY•••••
SYLLABI
SYLVANS
SYMBOLS
SYMPTOM
SYNAPSE
SYNCHED
SYNCHES
SYNCING
SYNERGY
SYNFUEL
SYNGMAN
SYNODAL
SYNODIC
SYNONYM
SYRIANS
SYRINGA
SYRINGE
SYSTEMS
SYSTOLE

S•Y••••
SAYINGS
SAYWHEN
SCYTHED
SCYTHES
SEYMOUR
SHYLOCK
SHYNESS
SHYSTER
SKYBLUE
SKYCAPS
SKYDIVE
SKYHIGH
SKYHOOK
SKYJACK
SKYLARK
SKYLINE
SKYWARD
SKYWAYS
SLYNESS
SOYBEAN
STYGIAN
STYLERS
STYLETS
STYLING
STYLISH
STYLIST
STYLIZE
STYMIED
STYMIES
STYPTIC
STYRENE
STYRIAN

S••Y•••
SAWYERS
SLAYERS
SLAYTON
SPAYING
SPRYEST
STAYING
STAYPUT
STAYSUP
SWAYERS
SWAYING

S•••Y••
SAMOYED
SAROYAN
SPLAYED
SPRAYED
SPRAYER
STRAYED

S••••Y•
SASHAYS
SEAWAYS
SHUTEYE
SKYWAYS
SOCKEYE
STOREYS
SUBWAYS
SUNDAYS
SUNRAYS
SURREYS
SURVEYS
SYNONYM

S•••••Y
SAINTLY
SALSIFY
SALTILY
SAMEDAY
SANDFLY
SASSILY
SATIETY
SATISFY
SAUCILY
SAVOURY
SAVVILY
SCANTLY
SCARIFY
SCARILY
SCENERY
SCRAGGY
SCRAPPY
SCRAWLY
SCRAWNY
SCRIMPY
SCRUBBY
SCRUFFY
SEADUTY
SEALILY
SECRECY
SEEDILY
SENSORY
SEVENTY
SHADILY
SHADOWY
SHAKILY
SHAPELY
SHARKEY
SHARPLY
SHEERLY
SHELLEY
SHIRLEY
SHOOFLY
SHORTLY
SHOWERY
SHOWILY
SHRILLY
SHRUBBY
SICKBAY
SICKPAY
SIGHTLY
SIGNIFY
SILKILY
SILVERY
SIZABLY
SKETCHY
SLAVERY
SLEEKLY
SLICKLY
SLOUCHY
SMARTLY
SNIDELY
SNOWDAY
SOBERLY
SOCIETY
SOGGILY
SOLIDLY
SOMEDAY
SOMEWAY
SORCERY
SOUNDLY
SOUTHEY
SPANGLY
SPARELY
SPASSKY
SPECIFY
SPIDERY
SPINDLY
SPLASHY
SPRINGY
SQUEAKY
SQUINTY
SQUIRMY
SQUISHY
STAGILY
STAIDLY
STANDBY
STANLEY
STARCHY
STARKLY
STATELY
STEEPLY
STERNLY
STIFFLY
STIRFRY
STOKELY
STONILY
STOODBY
STOOKEY
STOUTLY
STREAKY
STRINGY
STUBBLY
STUPEFY
SUAVELY
SUAVITY
SUBSIDY
SUDBURY
SULKILY
SUMMARY
SUMMERY
SUNCITY
SUNNILY
SURGERY
SURLILY
SWARTHY
SWEARBY
SWEETLY
SWELTRY
SWIFTLY
SWINGBY
SWOREBY
SYNERGY

•SY••••
ASYLUMS
PSYCHED
PSYCHES
PSYCHIC
PSYCHUP

•S•Y•••
ASSYRIA
ESPYING

•S••Y••
ASSAYED
ASSAYER
ESSAYED

•S•••Y•
ESTRAYS
OSPREYS

•S••••Y
ASHBURY
ASHTRAY
ESTUARY
USUALLY

••SY•••
ASSYRIA
BUSYING
KOSYGIN

••S•Y••
ASSAYED
ASSAYER
ESSAYED
GUSSYUP
INSTYLE
MISTYPE
MOSEYED
RESTYLE

••S••Y•
BUSBOYS
DISMAYS
FISHEYE
MISLAYS
SASHAYS
WYSIWYG

••S•••Y
AMSCRAY
BASALLY
BASEPAY
BESTBOY
BOSSILY
CASSIDY
CUSTODY
DESTINY
DESTROY
DISOBEY
DISPLAY
ECSTASY
FISHERY
FISHFRY
FISHILY
FUSSILY
FUSTILY
GOSSIPY
GUSTILY
HASTILY
HISTORY
HOSIERY
HUSHABY
HUSKILY
IMSORRY
JUSTIFY
LASTORY
LUSTILY
MASONRY
MASTERY
MESSILY
MISALLY
MISERLY
MISPLAY
MISTILY
MUSCOVY
MUSHILY
MUSTILY
MYSTERY
MYSTIFY
NASALLY
NASTILY
NOSEGAY
PASSKEY
PESKILY
PUSHILY
RUSTILY
SASSILY
TASTILY
TESTIFY
TESTILY
TUSCANY
VISIBLY
WISEGUY
WISPILY

•••SY••
FORSYTH
GUSSYUP
LIPSYNC

•••S•Y•
BURSTYN
CATSEYE
JERSEYS
NAYSAYS

•••S••Y
APISHLY
BEASTLY
BOSSILY
BRASHLY
BRISKLY
BRISTLY
CASSIDY
CLOSELY
CRASSLY
CRISPLY
CROSSLY
CURSORY
DENSELY
DENSITY
FALSELY
FALSIFY
FALSITY
FIRSTLY
FRESHLY
FUSSILY
GHASTLY
GHOSTLY
GOSSIPY
GRISTLY
GROSSLY
GUTSILY
HARSHLY
HEMSLEY
HERSHEY
KITSCHY
LETSFLY
LOOSELY
LOUSILY
MESSILY
MOISTLY
NEWSBOY
NEWSDAY
NOISILY
NURSERY
ODYSSEY
PAISLEY
PARSLEY
PASSKEY
PLUSHLY
PRESLEY
PROSILY
PROSODY
RUNSDRY
SALSIFY
SASSILY
SENSORY
SPASSKY
SUBSIDY
TENSELY
TERSELY
TIPSILY
TOLSTOY
TUESDAY
VARSITY
VERSIFY
WHISKEY

••••S•Y
AMNESTY
BLUESKY
CHOMSKY
CHRISTY
COMESBY
CRASSLY
CROSSLY
CURTSEY
DARESAY
DEBUSSY
DEMPSEY
DROPSBY
DYNASTY
EMBASSY
GAINSAY
GROSSLY
HEARSAY
HONESTY
HORNSBY
LINDSAY
LINDSEY
MAJESTY
MALMSEY
MODESTY
MORESBY
ODYSSEY
PIOUSLY
SATISFY
SPASSKY
SPLASHY
SQUISHY
THIRSTY
TROTSKY
VRONSKY
WOOLSEY

•••••SY
CIRCUSY
CRAFTSY
DEBUSSY
ECSTASY
EMBASSY
FANTASY
GEODESY

S•Z••••
SIZABLE
SIZABLY
SIZEDUP
SIZESUP
SIZINGS
SIZZLED
SIZZLES
SUZANNE
SUZETTE

S••Z•••
SEIZERS
SEIZING
SIZZLED
SIZZLES
SUBZERO
SWIZZLE

S•••Z••
SALAZAR
SARAZEN
SELTZER
SKEEZIX
SNEEZED
SNEEZER
SNEEZES
SNOOZED
SNOOZES
SPITZES
STANZAS
SWITZER
SWIZZLE

S••••Z•
SCHATZI
SCHERZI
SCHERZO
SHIHTZU
SPINOZA
SQUEEZE
STYLIZE

S•••••Z
SHOWBIZ

•S••Z••
ASSIZES

•S••••Z
ESTEVEZ

••S•Z••
ASSIZES

••S••Z•
MESTIZO

•••S•Z•
ANASAZI
CAPSIZE
MIDSIZE
OUTSIZE

•••S••Z
AGASSIZ

LAISSEZ

••••S•Z
AGASSIZ
LAISSEZ

TA•••••
TABARDS
TABASCO
TABBIES
TABBING
TABITHA
TABLEAU
TABLETS
TABLING
TABLOID
TABORET
TABULAR
TACITLY
TACITUS
TACKERS
TACKIER
TACKILY
TACKING
TACKLED
TACKLER
TACKLES
TACKSON
TACTFUL
TACTICS
TACTILE
TADPOLE
TAFFETA
TAFFIES
TAGALOG
TAGENDS
TAGGING
TAGLINE
TAGSALE
TAGSOUT
TAILEND
TAILFIN
TAILING
TAILLES
TAILOFF
TAILORS
TAINTED
TAIPANS
TAKEAIM
TAKENIN
TAKENON
TAKEOFF
TAKEONE
TAKEOUT
TAKESIN
TAKESON
TAKESTO
TAKESUP
TAKETEN
TALARIA
TALENTS
TALKBIG
TALKERS
TALKIES
TALKING
TALKOUT
TALKSAT
TALKSTO
TALKSUP
TALLEST
TALLIED
TALLIES
TALLISH
TALLOWS
TALLYHO
TALLYUP
TALONED
TALUSES
TAMABLE
TAMALES
TAMARIN
TAMBALA
TAMBOUR
TAMMANY
TAMPERS
TAMPICO
TAMPING
TAMTAMS
TANAGER
TANDEMS
TANGELO
TANGENT
TANGERE
TANGIER
TANGLED
TANGLES
TANGOED
TANKARD
TANKERS
TANKFUL
TANKING
TANKSUP
TANKTOP
TANLINE
TANNERS
TANNERY
TANNEST
TANNING
TANNINS
TANNISH
TANOAKS
TANSIES
TANTARA
TANTRUM
TAOISTS
TAPERED
TAPINGS
TAPIOCA
TAPPERS
TAPPETS
TAPPING
TAPROOM
TAPROOT
TAPSOUT
TAPSTER
TARANTO
TARBABY
TARBELL
TARDIER
TARDILY
TARGETS
TARHEEL
TARIFFS
TARMACS
TARNISH
TARPITS
TARPONS
TARRIED
TARRIES
TARRING
TARSALS
TARSIER
TARTANS
TARTARE
TARTARS
TARTEST
TARZANA
TASKING
TASSELS
TASTERS
TASTIER
TASTILY
TASTING
TATAMIS
TATIANA
TATTERS
TATTIER
TATTING
TATTLED
TATTLER
TATTLES
TATTOOS
TAUNTED
TAURINE
TAUTENS
TAUTEST
TAVERNS
TAWNIER
TAXABLE
TAXFREE
TAXICAB
TAXIING
TAXIWAY
TAXRATE

T•A••••
TEABAGS
TEABALL
TEACAKE
TEACART
TEACHER
TEACHES
TEACHIN
TEACUPS
TEALEAF
TEAMING
TEAMSUP
TEAPOTS
TEAPOYS
TEARFUL
TEARGAS
TEARIER
TEARILY
TEARING
TEAROFF
TEAROOM
TEAROSE
TEARSAT
TEARSUP
TEASELS
TEASERS
TEASETS
TEASHOP
TEASING
TEATIME
TEATRAY
THALERS
THANKED
THATCHY
THATSIT
THAWING
TOADIED
TOADIES
TOASTED
TOASTER
TRABERT
TRACERS
TRACERY
TRACHEA
TRACING
TRACKED
TRACKER
TRACTOR
TRADEIN
TRADEON
TRADERS
TRADEUP
TRADING
TRADUCE
TRAFFIC
TRAGEDY
TRAILED
TRAILER
TRAINED
TRAINEE
TRAINER
TRAIPSE
TRAITOR
TRALALA
TRAMCAR
TRAMMEL
TRAMPAS
TRAMPED
TRAMPLE
TRANCES
TRANSIT
TRANSOM
TRAPEZE
TRAPPED
TRAPPER
TRASHED
TRASHES
TRAUBEL
TRAUMAS
TRAVAIL
TRAVELS
TRAVERS
TRAVOIS
TRAWLED
TRAWLER
TRAYFUL
TSARINA
TSARIST
TUAREGS
TWADDLE
TWANGED
TZARINA

T••A•••
TABARDS
TABASCO
TAGALOG
TALARIA
TAMABLE
TAMALES
TAMARIN
TANAGER
TARANTO
TATAMIS
TAXABLE
TELAVIV
TENABLE
TENABLY
TENACES
TENANCY
TENANTS
TERAPHS
TETANUS
THEATER
THEATRE
THRALLS
THWACKS
THWARTS
TIRADES
TISANES
TITANIA
TITANIC
TOBACCO
TONALLY
TOPAZES
TOTALED
TOTALLY
TOWARDS
TOWAWAY
TREACLE
TREACLY
TREADED
TREADER
TREADLE
TREASON
TREATED
TRUANCY
TRUANTS
TUBAIST
TWEAKED
TYRANNY
TYRANTS

T•••A••
TAGSALE
TAIPANS
TAKEAIM
TAMBALA
TAMMANY
TAMTAMS
TANKARD
TANOAKS
TANTARA
TARBABY
TARMACS
TARSALS
TARTANS
TARTARE
TARTARS
TARZANA
TATIANA
TAXRATE
TEABAGS
TEABALL
TEACAKE
TEACART
TEDMACK
TEENAGE
TELLALL
TERNARY
TERNATE
TERRACE
TERRAIN
TETRADS
THEBABE
THERAPY
THINAIR
THREADS
THREADY
THREATS
THROATS
THROATY
TICTACS
TIERACK
TIETACK
TIFFANY
TIJUANA
TILLAGE
TIMBALE
TIMBALS
TINCANS
TINEARS
TINHATS
TITRATE
TOCCATA
TOECAPS
TOENAIL
TOETAPS
TOMCATS
TONEARM
TONGANS
TONNAGE
TOOTALL
TOPHATS
TOPIARY
TOPKAPI
TOPMAST
TOPSAIL
TORNADO
TOSCALE
TOSPARE
TOSTADA
TOUCANS
TOURACO
TOWCARS
TOWPATH
TOYLAND
TRALALA
TRAVAIL
TRENARY
TREPANS
TROCARS
TROJANS
TSQUARE
TSUNAMI
TULSANS
TURBANS
TUSCANY
TUSSAUD
TWOBASE
TYMPANA
TYMPANI

T••••A•
TABLEAU
TABULAR
TALKSAT
TAXICAB
TAXIWAY
TEALEAF
TEARGAS
TEARSAT
TEATRAY
TEHERAN
TELERAN
TELSTAR
TEMPLAR
TERTIAL
TESTBAN
TEXTUAL
THEREAT
THERMAL
THINMAN
THOREAU
THRUWAY
THURMAN
THUSFAR
TIBETAN
TIMELAG
TIMEWAS
TINSTAR
TITULAR
TOLLWAY
TONNEAU
TOPCOAT
TOPICAL
TOTEBAG
TOWAWAY
TOWHEAD
TRAMCAR
TRAMPAS
TRAUMAS
TREERAT
TRIGRAM
TRISTAN
TRIVIAL
TROIKAS
TRUCIAL
TRUDEAU
TSONGAS
TUBULAR
TUCHMAN
TUESDAY
TUGBOAT
TUNDRAS
TUTELAR
TWOSTAR
TYPICAL

T•••••A
TABITHA
TAFFETA
TALARIA
TAMBALA
TANTARA
TAPIOCA
TARZANA
TATIANA
TEMPERA
TEMPURA
TEQUILA
TESSERA
THERESA
TIJUANA
TITANIA
TOCCATA
TOSHIBA
TOSTADA
TRACHEA
TRALALA
TSARINA
TUNISIA
TYMPANA
TZARINA

•TA••••
ATACAMA
ATALOSS
ATAMANS
ATATURK
ATAVISM
ATAVIST
ETAGERE
ETAMINE
ITALIAN
ITALICS
STABBED
STABILE
STABLED
STABLER
STABLES
STACKED
STACKUP
STADIUM
STAFFED
STAFFER
STAGERS
STAGGED
STAGGER
STAGIER
STAGILY
STAGING
STAIDER
STAIDLY
STAINED
STAINER
STAKING
STALAGS
STALEST
STALKED
STALKER
STALLED
STAMENS
STAMINA
STAMMER
STAMPED
STANCES
STANDBY
STANDEE
STANDIN
STANDON
STANDUP
STANLEE
STANLEY
STANNIC
STANTON
STANZAS
STAPLED
STAPLER
STAPLES
STARCHY
STARDOM
STAREAT
STARERS
STARETS
STARING
STARKER
STARKLY
STARLET
STARLIT
STARMAN
STARMAP
STARRED
STARTED
STARTER
STARTLE
STARTUP
STARVED
STARVES
STASHED
STASHES
STASSEN
STATELY
STATICE
STATICS
STATING
STATION
STATIST
STATORS
STATUES
STATURE
STATUTE
STAUNCH
STAVING
STAYING
STAYPUT
STAYSUP
UTAHANS

•T•A•••
ATFAULT
ATLANTA
ATLARGE
ATLASES
ATLATLS
ATTACHE
ATTACKS
ATTAINS
ETHANOL
ITHACAN
OTRANTO
OTTAWAS
STEALTH
STEAMED
STEAMER
STRAFED
STRAFES
STRAINS
STRAITS
STRANDS
STRANGE
STRASSE
STRATUM
STRATUS
STRAUSS
STRAYED

•T••A••
ATACAMA
ATAMANS
ATHEART
ATHWART
ATLEAST
ATPEACE
ATSTAKE
ATTRACT
ITERANT
ITERATE
PTBOATS
STALAGS
STEWARD
STEWART
STOMACH
STOMATA
STORAGE
STREAKS
STREAKY
STREAMS
STRIATE
UTAHANS

•T•••A•
ETERNAL
ETESIAN
ETHICAL
ETONIAN
ITALIAN
ITHACAN
OTTAWAS
OTTOMAN
STANZAS
STAREAT
STARMAN
STARMAP
STELLAR
STERNAL
STIGMAS
STOICAL
STOPGAP
STYGIAN
STYRIAN
UTOPIAN
UTOPIAS

•T••••A
ATACAMA
ATLANTA
ETRURIA
STAMINA
STLUCIA
STOMATA

••TA•••
ACTABLE
ACTAEON
ANTACID
ANTAEUS
ANTARES
ASTAIRE
ASTARTE
ATTACHE
ATTACKS
ATTAINS
BETAKEN
BETAKES
BETAMAX
BETARAY
CATALAN
CATALOG
CATALPA
CATAWBA
CITABLE
CITADEL
CUTAWAY
DATASET
DETAILS
DETAINS
EATABLE
EATAWAY
ENTAILS
ESTATES
GETAWAY
GOTAWAY
HITACHI
INTAKES
MATADOR
METATES
MUTABLE
MUTABLY
MUTAGEN
MUTANTS
MUTATED
MUTATES
MUTATIS
NATALIA
NATALIE
NATASHA
NOTABIT
NOTABLE
NOTABLY
NOTATED
NOTATES
OBTAINS
OCTAGON
OCTANES
OCTANTS
OCTAVES
OCTAVIA
OCTAVOS
ONTARIO
OTTAWAS
OUTACTS
OUTAGES
PATAKES
PETALED
PETARDS
PITAPAT
POTABLE
POTAGES
PUTAMEN
PUTAWAY
RATABLE
RATAFIA
RATATAT
RETAILS
RETAINS
RETAKEN
RETAKES
RETAPED
RETAPES
RETARDS
RETAXED
RETAXES
ROTATED
ROTATES
ROTATOR
TATAMIS
TETANUS
TITANIA
TITANIC
TOTALED
TOTALLY
UNTACKS
UNTAMED
UNTAPED
UPTAKES
VITALLY
VITAMIN

••T•A••
ACTUARY
ACTUATE
ANTFARM
ANTIART
ARTWARE
ATTRACT
BATEAUX
BETHANY
BETRAYS
BITMAPS
BITPART
CATCALL
CATHAIR
CATNAPS
CATTAIL
CATWALK
CITRATE
COTTAGE
CUTBACK
CUTLASS
CUTRATE
DETRACT
DETRAIN
DITTANY
ENTRAIN
ENTRANT
ENTRAPS
ESTRADA
ESTRAYS
ESTUARY
EXTRACT
FATBACK
FATCATS
GATEAUX
GETBACK
GOTBACK
GOTLAND
HATRACK
HETMANS
HOTCAKE
HOTCAPS
HOTCARS
HOTWARS
JETWASH
JUTLAND
KITBAGS
METHANE
MUTUALS
NITRATE
NITTANY
OUTBACK
OUTCAST
OUTEATS
OUTFACE
OUTLAID
OUTLAND
OUTLAST
OUTLAWS
OUTLAYS
OUTPACE
OUTRACE
OUTRAGE
OUTRANK
OUTTAKE
OUTTALK
OUTWARD
PETNAME
PITFALL
PITSAWS
POTTAGE
RATPACK
RATRACE
RATTAIL
RATTANS
RETEACH
RETRACE
RETRACK
RETRACT
RETRADE
RETRAIN
RITUALS
SATIATE
SATRAPS
SETBACK
SETSAIL
SITUATE
TATIANA
TETRADS
TITRATE
UNTRAPS
VITIATE
WATTAGE
WETBARS
WETLAND

••T••A•
ALTOSAX
ANTBEAR
ANTIWAR
ARTISAN
ASTOLAT
AUTOMAT
AZTECAN
BATEMAN
BATHMAT
BATSMAN
BETAMAX
BETARAY
CATALAN
CATBOAT
CATENAE
CATHEAD
CATSCAN
CATSPAW
CUTAWAY
EATAWAY
EATENAT
ENTREAT
ESTIVAL
FATHEAD
GATEMAN
GATEWAY
GETAWAY
GOTAWAY
GOTCHAS
HOTHEAD
HOTSEAT
JETBOAT
KETCHAM
KUTENAI
LATERAL
LATERAN
LATIFAH
LATINAS
LATVIAN
LITERAL
MATEWAN
MATHIAS
MATTHAU
MITHRAS
MITZVAH
NATURAL
NOTEPAD
NUTMEAT
NUTRIAS
OATMEAL
ONTRIAL
OPTICAL
OPTIMAL
ORTOLAN
OTTAWAS
OTTOMAN
OUTDRAW
OUTPLAY
OUTWEAR
PATHWAY
PATINAS
PITAPAT
PITTMAN
POTOMAC
POTSDAM
PUTAWAY
PYTHIAS
RATATAT
RATTRAP
RETINAE
RETINAL
RETINAS
RETREAD
RETREAT
RETRIAL
TITULAR
TOTEBAG
TUTELAR
UPTOPAR
VATICAN
VETERAN
WATTEAU
YITZHAK

••T•••A
ALTOONA
ANTENNA
ANTIGUA

ANTONIA
ASTORIA
BATISTA
BOTHNIA
CATALPA
CATAWBA
ESTONIA
ESTRADA
INTEGRA
LETITIA
MATILDA
NATALIA
NATASHA
OCTAVIA
PATELLA
PETUNIA
RATAFIA
RETSINA
ROTUNDA
SATSUMA
TATIANA
TITANIA

•••TA••
ABSTAIN
ACETATE
AGITATE
AIRTAXI
ATSTAKE
AVATARS
BANTAMS
BELTANE
BLATANT
BOBTAIL
BOITANO
BRITAIN
BUSTARD
CAFTANS
CANTATA
CAPTAIN
CARTAGE
CATTAIL
CENTAUR
CENTAVO
CERTAIN
CONTACT
CONTAIN
COSTAIN
COSTARS
COTTAGE
CRETANS
CURTAIL
CURTAIN
CUSTARD
DASTARD
DELTAIC
DENTATE
DICTATE
DIETARY
DIKTATS
DISTAFF
DISTANT
DITTANY
DOGTAGS
ECSTASY
FANTAIL
FANTASY
FOOTAGE
FOXTAIL
GAUTAMA
GESTALT
GESTATE
GUITARS
GUSTAVE
HECTARE
HEPTADS
HOSTAGE
IMITATE
INSTALL
INSTANT
INSTATE
KAFTANS
LACTASE
LACTATE
LANTANA
LEOTARD
MAITAIS
MASTABA
MISTAKE
MONTAGE
MONTANA
MONTAND
MONTANE
MORTALS
MORTARS
MUSTAFA
MUSTANG
MUSTARD
NASTASE
NECTARS
NITTANY
ONSTAGE
OUTTAKE
OUTTALK
PARTAKE
PELTATE
PENTADS
PEPTALK
PERTAIN
PIGTAIL
PINTAIL
POPTART
PORTAGE
PORTALS
POSTAGE
POTTAGE
PRETAPE
QINTARS
RATTAIL
RATTANS
REDTAPE
RENTALS
RESTAGE
RESTAIN
RESTAMP
RESTART
RESTATE
RIOTACT
ROSTAND
SANTAFE
SANTANA
SEXTANS
SEXTANT
SMETANA
SOUTANE
SULTANA
SULTANS
SUNTANS
SUSTAIN
TAMTAMS
TANTARA
TARTANS
TARTARE
TARTARS
TICTACS
TIETACK
TOETAPS
TOOTALL
TOSTADA
UNITARY
UNSTACK
UPSTAGE
UPSTART
UPSTATE
VANTAGE
VINTAGE
VOLTAGE
VOLTAIC
WAGTAIL
WANTADS
WASTAGE
WATTAGE
WENTAPE

•••T•A•
ABUTTAL
ASHTRAY
AUSTRAL
BELTWAY
BENTHAM
BESTIAL
BESTMAN
BOATMAN
CENTRAL
CHATEAU
CHATHAM
COCTEAU
CONTRAS
CULTJAM
DUSTPAN
EASTMAN
FACTUAL
FLATCAR
FLOTSAM
FLYTRAP
FOOTMAN
FOOTPAD
FORTRAN
FRETSAW
FUSTIAN
GENTIAN
GLOTTAL
GODTHAB
HAITIAN
HARTMAN
HINTSAT
HOOTSAT
INITIAL
INSTEAD
LACTEAL
LAOTIAN
MANTRAP
MANTRAS
MARTIAL
MARTIAN
MATTHAU
MISTRAL
NEUTRAL
NUPTIAL
ONATEAR
PARTIAL
PARTWAY
PITTMAN
PLATEAU
PONTIAC
PORTRAY
POSTMAN
POSTWAR
PROTEAN
QUETZAL
RATTRAP
SLOTCAR
SPATIAL
TEATRAY
TERTIAL
TESTBAN
TEXTUAL
UNSTRAP
VENTRAL
VICTUAL
VIETNAM
VIRTUAL
WATTEAU
WENTBAD
WHITMAN
XANTHAN
YEATEAM

•••T••A
AUSTRIA
CANTATA
CANTINA
CYNTHIA
DAYTONA
ERITREA
EROTICA
EXOTICA
FONTINA
FORTUNA
GAUTAMA
LANTANA
MARTINA
MASTABA
MONTANA
MONTOYA
MUSTAFA
PARTITA
PASTINA
PORTOLA
SANTANA
SESTINA
SMETANA
SPATULA
SULTANA
TANTARA
TOSTADA
VENTURA
VISTULA

••••TA•
ABUTTAL
ALLSTAR
ARISTAE
ARISTAS
BENATAR
CAPITAL
CAPITAN
CAPSTAN
CHEETAH
CHOCTAW
COALTAR
COASTAL
CRYSTAL
DAKOTAN
DAKOTAS
DAYSTAR
DIGITAL
DOGSTAR
DRISTAN
FAJITAS
FIESTAS
FRACTAL
FREITAG
FRONTAL
GLOTTAL
HABITAT
HEELTAP
JACKTAR
LAKOTAS
MARITAL
MULETAS
NAMETAG
ORBITAL
PALATAL
PELOTAS
PESETAS
PINATAS
PINETAR
PIVOTAL
PLANTAR
POLLTAX
PULLTAB
PURITAN
RARITAN
RATATAT
RECITAL
REDSTAR
SEASTAR
SHOOTAT
SIESTAS
SONATAS
SPARTAN
TELSTAR
TIBETAN
TINSTAR
TRISTAN
TWOSTAR
VEGETAL
WIRETAP
YUCATAN

••••T•A
ARIETTA
BARETTA
BERETTA
BIRETTA
CORETTA
CROATIA
DYKSTRA
ELECTRA
ELEKTRA
GALATEA
GALATIA
HERBTEA
HIGHTEA
ICEDTEA
INERTIA
LAMOTTA
LETITIA
LORETTA
MAHATMA
MILITIA
MINUTIA
NAPHTHA
OLESTRA
PANETTA
PLECTRA
REGATTA
RICOTTA
ROSETTA
SINATRA
SPECTRA
SUMATRA
TABITHA

•••••TA
ALBERTA
ALMAATA
ARIETTA
ATLANTA
AUGUSTA
BARETTA
BATISTA
BERETTA
BIRETTA
CANASTA
CANTATA
CELESTA
CORETTA
DOGMATA
EMERITA
GANGSTA
INFANTA
JAKARTA
JOCASTA
LAMOTTA
LAPLATA
LORETTA
MAGENTA
MINOLTA
PANETTA
PARTITA
POLENTA
PRORATA
RAWDATA
REGATTA
RICOTTA
RIORITA
ROBERTA
ROBUSTA
ROSETTA
STOMATA
TAFFETA
TOCCATA
VEDANTA
WICHITA

TB•••••
TBILISI

T•B••••
TABARDS
TABASCO
TABBIES
TABBING
TABITHA
TABLEAU
TABLETS
TABLING
TABLOID
TABORET
TABULAR
TIBETAN
TOBACCO
TUBAIST
TUBBIER
TUBISTS
TUBULAR

T••B•••
TABBIES
TABBING
TAMBALA
TAMBOUR
TARBABY
TARBELL
TEABAGS
TEABALL
TEMBLOR
TERBIUM
THEBABE
THEBLOB
TIDBITS
TIMBALE
TIMBALS
TIMBERS
TIMBRES
TITBITS
TOMBOYS
TRABERT
TREBLED
TREBLES
TRIBUNE
TRIBUTE
TUBBIER
TUGBOAT
TUMBLED
TUMBLER
TUMBLES
TUMBREL
TURBANS
TURBINE
TURBOTS
TWOBASE
TWOBITS

T•••B••
TALKBIG
TAMABLE
TAXABLE
TENABLE
TENABLY
TESTBAN
THIMBLE
THUMBED
THURBER
TOOLBOX
TOTEBAG
TOYNBEE
TRAUBEL
TREMBLE
TREMBLY
TROUBLE
TWINBED

T••••B•
TARBABY
THEBABE
THEREBY
TOSHIBA

T•••••B
TAXICAB
THEBLOB

•TB••••
PTBOATS

•T•B•••
STABBED
STABILE
STABLED
STABLER
STABLES
STUBBED
STUBBLE
STUBBLY

•T••B••
STABBED
STEUBEN
STROBES
STUBBED
STUBBLE
STUBBLY
STUMBLE

•T•••B•
STANDBY
STOODBY

••TB•••
ANTBEAR
BATBOYS
CATBIRD
CATBOAT
CUTBACK
FATBACK
GETBACK
GOTBACK
HOTBEDS
JETBOAT
KITBAGS
OUTBACK
OUTBIDS
PITBOSS
PITBULL
SETBACK
TITBITS
WETBARS

••T•B••
ACTABLE
ANTIBES
CITABLE
EATABLE
ENTEBBE
MUTABLE
MUTABLY
NOTABIT
NOTABLE
NOTABLY
OCTOBER
POTABLE
RATABLE
TOTEBAG

••T••B•
BYTHEBY
CATAWBA
ENTEBBE
HOTTUBS
LETITBE

••T•••B
BATHTUB
POTHERB

•••TB••
BESTBOY
FLATBED
HAUTBOY
PEATBOG
POSTBOX
SALTBOX
TESTBAN
WENTBAD

•••T•B•
HOTTUBS
MASTABA

•••T••B
DISTURB
GODTHAB
PERTURB

••••TB•
LETITBE

••••T•B
BATHTUB
PULLTAB
WASHTUB

T•C••••
TACITLY
TACITUS
TACKERS
TACKIER
TACKILY
TACKING
TACKLED
TACKLER
TACKLES
TACKSON
TACTFUL
TACTICS
TACTILE
TECHIES
TICKERS
TICKETS
TICKING
TICKLED
TICKLER
TICKLES
TICKOFF
TICTACS
TOCCATA
TOCSINS
TUCHMAN
TUCKERS
TUCKING
TUCKSIN
TYCOONS

T••C•••
TEACAKE
TEACART
TEACHER
TEACHES
TEACHIN
TEACUPS
TEICHER
TERCELS
TERCETS
TETCHED
THICKEN
THICKER
THICKET
THICKLY
TIECLIP
TINCANS
TOCCATA
TOECAPS
TOMCATS
TOPCOAT
TORCHED
TORCHES
TOSCALE
TOUCANS
TOUCHED
TOUCHES
TOUCHON
TOUCHUP
TOWCARS
TRACERS
TRACERY
TRACHEA
TRACING
TRACKED
TRACKER
TRACTOR
TRICEPS
TRICKED
TRICKER
TRICKLE
TRICORN
TRICOTS
TROCARS
TROCHEE
TROCHES
TRUCIAL
TRUCKED
TRUCKEE
TRUCKER
TRUCKLE
TUSCANY

T•••C••
TAXICAB
TENACES
THATCHY
THWACKS
TIMECOP
TOBACCO
TOPICAL
TRAMCAR
TRANCES
TREACLE
TREACLY
TUNICLE
TWITCHY
TYPICAL

T••••C•
TABASCO
TACTICS
TAMPICO
TAPIOCA
TARMACS
TEDMACK
TENANCY
TERENCE
TERRACE
THINICE
TICTACS
TIERACK
TIETACK
TITMICE
TOBACCO
TOLTECS
TOPKICK
TOURACO
TRADUCE
TRISECT
TROPICS
TROUNCE
TRUANCY
TUSSOCK

T•••••C
TITANIC
TONELOC
TOTEMIC
TRAFFIC
TROPHIC

•TC••••
ETCHERS
ETCHING
ITCHIER
ITCHING
STCROIX

•T•C•••
ATACAMA
ATECROW
STACKED
STACKUP
STICHES
STICKER
STICKTO
STICKUP
STOCKED
STOCKUP
STUCCOS
STUCKTO
STUCKUP

•T••C••
ATTACHE
ATTACKS
ATTICUS
ATTUCKS
ETHICAL
ITHACAN
STANCES
STARCHY
STENCIL
STLUCIA
STOICAL
STUCCOS
UTRECHT

•T•••C•
ATPEACE
ATTRACT
ETHNICS
ITALICS
STATICE
STATICS
STAUNCH
STOMACH
STRETCH

•T••••C
STANNIC
STYPTIC

••TC•••
AITCHES
ANTCOWS
BATCHED
BATCHES
BOTCHED
BOTCHES
BUTCHER
CATCALL
CATCHER
CATCHES
CATCHON
CATCHUP
DITCHED
DITCHES
EATCROW
FATCATS
FATCITY
FETCHED
FETCHES
FITCHES
GOTCHAS
HATCHED
HATCHER
HATCHES
HATCHET
HITCHED
HITCHER
HITCHES
HOTCAKE
HOTCAPS
HOTCARS
HUTCHES
KETCHAM
KETCHES
KETCHUP
KITCHEN
LATCHED
LATCHES
LITCHIS
MATCHED
MATCHES
MATCHUP
MITCHUM
NATCHEZ
NOTCHED
NOTCHES
OUTCAST
OUTCOME
OUTCROP
PATCHED
PATCHES
PATCHUP
PETCOCK
PITCHED
PITCHER
PITCHES
PITCHIN
RATCHET
RITCHIE
SATCHEL
SATCHMO
SITCOMS
TETCHED
VETCHES
WATCHED
WATCHER
WATCHES
WATCHIT
WETCELL
WITCHES

••T•C••
ANTACID
ARTICLE
ATTACHE
ATTACKS
ATTICUS
ATTUCKS
AZTECAN
CATSCAN
CUTICLE
DETECTS
ENTICED
ENTICER
ENTICES
HITACHI
KITSCHY
LATICES
NOTICED
NOTICES
OPTICAL
OUTACTS
RETICLE
SHTICKS
UNTACKS
UPTICKS
VATICAN
VOTECHS

••T••C•
ANTIOCH
ARTDECO
ATTRACT
CUTBACK
DETRACT
EXTINCT
EXTRACT
FATBACK
FETLOCK
GETBACK
GOTBACK
GOTHICS
HATRACK
LATENCY
LATTICE
LETTUCE
MATLOCK
MATTOCK
METRICS
NITPICK
OSTRICH
OUTBACK
OUTFACE
OUTPACE
OUTRACE
PATRICE
PATRICK
PETCOCK
PETROCK
POTENCY
POTLUCK
RATPACK
RATRACE
RETEACH
RETOUCH
RETRACE
RETRACK
RETRACT
SETBACK
TITMICE

••T•••C
ACTINIC
MITOTIC
POTOMAC
SATIRIC
TITANIC
TOTEMIC

•••TC••
BLOTCHY
FLATCAR
HOOTCHY
KOOTCHY
SKETCHY
SLOTCAR
THATCHY
TWITCHY

•••T•C•
CALTECH
CELTICS
CONTACT
CRITICS
DIPTYCH
EROTICA
EXOTICA
EXOTICS

FUSTICS
INSTOCK
JUSTICE
KLATSCH
LATTICE
LETTUCE
LOWTECH
MASTICS
MATTOCK
MYSTICS
NOETICS
POETICS
PORTICO
PROTECT
RESTOCK
RIOTACT
RUSTICS
STATICE
STATICS
TACTICS
TICTACS
TIETACK
TOLTECS
UNSTACK
UNSTICK
UNSTUCK

•••T••C
CENTRIC
DELTAIC
GASTRIC
LAUTREC
MANTRIC
PONTIAC
POSTHOC
VOLTAIC
XANTHIC

••••TC•
BEWITCH
GODUTCH
INDUTCH
SCRATCH
SPLOTCH
STRETCH
UNHITCH
UNLATCH
WASATCH

••••T•C
AQUATIC
ASCETIC
ASEPTIC
ASIATIC
CAUSTIC
CHAOTIC
CRYPTIC
DRASTIC
ELASTIC
ERISTIC
ERRATIC
FANATIC
FRANTIC
GENETIC
GNOSTIC
HAMITIC
HEPATIC
HERETIC
IDENTIC
IDIOTIC
KINETIC
LUNATIC
MEIOTIC
MIMETIC
MITOTIC
OSMOTIC
PIRATIC
PLASTIC
POLITIC
ROBOTIC
SEMITIC
SKEPTIC
SOMATIC
STYPTIC
ZAPOTEC

T•D••••
TADPOLE
TEDDERS
TEDDIES
TEDDING
TEDIOUS
TEDMACK
TIDBITS
TIDIEST
TIDINGS
TIDYING
TODDIES
TODDLED
TODDLER
TODDLES

T••D•••
TANDEMS
TARDIER
TARDILY
TEDDERS
TEDDIES
TEDDING
TEEDOFF
TENDERS
TENDING
TENDONS
TENDRIL
TENDSTO
THEDEEP
THUDDED
TIEDOWN
TIEDYED
TIEDYES
TINDERS
TOADIED
TOADIES
TODDIES
TODDLED
TODDLER
TODDLES
TOLDOFF
TOPDOGS
TOYDOGS
TRADEIN
TRADEON
TRADERS
TRADEUP
TRADING
TRADUCE
TRIDENT
TRODDEN
TRUDEAU
TRUDGED
TRUDGER
TRUDGES
TUNDRAS
TWADDLE
TWIDDLE

T•••D••
TEPIDLY
TEREDOS
THIRDLY
THUDDED
THUNDER
TIMIDER
TIMIDLY
TIRADES
TIREDER
TIREDLY
TIREDOF
TONEDUP
TOORDER
TREADED
TREADER
TREADLE
TRENDED
TRIEDON
TRIODES
TRODDEN
TRUNDLE
TUESDAY
TUNEDIN
TUNEDUP
TUXEDOS
TWADDLE
TWIDDLE
TYPEDUP

T••••D•
TABARDS
TAGENDS
TETRADS
THREADS
THREADY
TIERODS
TOPSIDE
TORNADO
TOROIDS
TORPEDO
TOSTADA
TOWARDS
TRAGEDY
TRIPODS
TVGUIDE

T•••••D
TABLOID
TACKLED
TAILEND
TAINTED
TALLIED
TALONED
TANGLED
TANGOED
TANKARD
TAPERED
TARRIED
TATTLED
TAUNTED
TEETHED
TELEXED
TEMPTED
TENFOLD
TENONED
TENURED
TETCHED
THANKED
THIEVED
THINNED
THRIVED
THUDDED
THUMBED
THUMPED
TICKLED
TIEDYED
TINGLED
TINKLED
TIPPLED
TIPTOED
TOADIED
TOASTED
TODDLED
TOEHOLD
TOGGLED
TOKENED
TONGUED
TOOTHED
TOOTLED
TOPPLED
TORCHED
TOTALED
TOUCHED
TOUSLED
TOWELED
TOWERED
TOWHEAD
TOYLAND
TRACKED
TRAILED
TRAINED
TRAMPED
TRAPPED
TRASHED
TRAWLED
TREADED
TREATED
TREBLED
TREKKED
TRENDED
TRICKED
TRIFLED
TRIGGED
TRILLED
TRIMMED
TRIPLED
TRIPPED
TROLLED
TROOPED
TROTHED
TROTTED
TRUCKED
TRUDGED
TRUMPED
TRUSSED
TRUSTED
TRYSTED
TUMBLED
TURTLED
TUSSAUD
TUSSLED
TUTORED
TWANGED
TWEAKED
TWEETED
TWEEZED
TWILLED
TWINBED
TWINGED
TWINNED
TWIRLED
TWISTED
TWITTED
TWOFOLD

•TD••••
STDENIS

•T•D•••
STADIUM
STUDDED
STUDENT
STUDIED
STUDIES
STUDIOS

•T••D••
STAIDER
STAIDLY
STANDBY
STANDEE
STANDIN
STANDON
STANDUP
STARDOM
STOODBY
STOODIN
STOODUP
STRIDER
STRIDES
STRUDEL
STUDDED

•T•••D•
ATTENDS
STRANDS

•T••••D
ATTIRED
ATTUNED
STABBED
STABLED
STACKED
STAFFED
STAGGED
STAINED
STALKED
STALLED
STAMPED
STAPLED
STARRED
STARTED
STARVED
STASHED
STEAMED
STEELED
STEEPED
STEERED
STEMMED
STEPPED
STEROID
STETTED
STEWARD
STIFFED
STIFLED
STILLED
STILTED
STINTED
STIPEND
STIRRED
STOCKED
STOMPED
STOOPED
STOPPED
STORIED
STORMED
STRAFED
STRAYED
STREWED
STRIPED
STRIVED
STROKED
STUBBED
STUDDED
STUDIED
STUFFED
STUMPED
STUNNED
STUNTED
STYMIED
UTTERED

••TD•••
ARTDECO
CUTDOWN
GETDOWN
GOTDOWN
HOTDOGS
LETDOWN
OUTDOES
OUTDONE
OUTDOOR
OUTDRAW
OUTDREW
PUTDOWN
SATDOWN
SETDOWN
SITDOWN

••T•D••
ACTEDUP
ANTEDUP
BETIDED
BETIDES
CITADEL
DATEDLY
DOTEDON
FETIDLY
KATYDID
MATADOR
POTSDAM

••T••D•
ASTRIDE
ATTENDS
CATHODE
ESTRADA
EXTENDS
EXTRUDE
HOTBEDS
HOTRODS
INTENDS
INTRUDE
MATILDA
METHODS
NITRIDE
OBTRUDE
OBTUNDS
OUTBIDS
OUTSIDE
PETARDS
RETARDS
RETRADE
ROTUNDA
TETRADS

••T•••D
ALTERED
ANTACID
ASTOUND
ATTIRED
ATTUNED
BATCHED
BATIKED
BATTLED
BETIDED
BOTCHED
BOTTLED
CATBIRD
CATERED
CATHEAD
DITCHED
DITTOED
ENTERED
ENTICED
FATHEAD
FETCHED
GOTLAND
HATCHED
HITCHED
HOTHEAD
INTONED
JUTLAND
KATYDID
LATCHED
MATCHED
MATURED
METERED
MITERED
MITFORD
MOTORED
MOTTLED
MUTATED
NATURED
NETTLED
NOTATED
NOTCHED
NOTEPAD
NOTICED
OCTOPOD
OSTEOID
OUTLAID
OUTLAND
OUTLOUD
OUTSOLD
OUTWARD
PATCHED
PETALED
PETERED
PITCHED
PUTTIED
RATTLED
RETAPED
RETAXED
RETILED
RETIMED
RETIRED
RETOWED
RETREAD
RETRIED
RETUNED
RETYPED
ROTATED
SETTLED
SUTURED
TATTLED
TETCHED
TOTALED
TUTORED
UNTAMED
UNTAPED
UNTRIED
UNTUNED
UTTERED
WATCHED
WATERED
WETLAND

•••TD••
PASTDUE

•••T•D•
CUSTODY
EBBTIDE
HEPTADS
LEETIDE
LOWTIDE
MALTEDS
PENTADS
PEPTIDE
RIPTIDE
TOSTADA
WANTADS

•••T••D
ABETTED
ABUTTED
ALLTOLD
BARTEND
BATTLED
BERTHED
BIRTHED
BLATTED
BLITZED
BLOTTED
BOTTLED
BUSTARD
BUSTLED
CASTLED
CENTRED
CHATTED
CLOTHED
CLOTTED
CONTEND
CUSTARD
DASTARD
DELTOID
DIRTIED
DISTEND
DITTOED
DRATTED
EASTEND
EMITTED
EMPTIED
FLATBED
FLATTED
FLITTED
FOOTPAD
FRETTED
FRITTED
FROTHED
GENTLED
GLITZED
GLUTTED
GOATEED
GRITTED
HOGTIED
HURTLED
HUSTLED
INSTEAD
JOSTLED
KNITTED
KNOTTED
LEOTARD
LOATHED
LUSTRED
MAITRED
MANTLED
MASTOID
MONTAND
MOTTLED
MOUTHED
MUSTARD
NESTLED
NETTLED
OMITTED
OROTUND
PARTIED
PESTLED
PHOTOED
PLOTTED
PORTEND
PRETEND
PUTTIED
RATTLED
ROSTAND
RUSTLED
SAUTEED
SCATHED
SCATTED
SCYTHED
SEETHED
SETTLED
SLATTED
SLOTTED
SOOTHED
SORTIED
SPATTED
SPOTTED
STETTED
SUBTEND
SWATHED
SWATTED
TATTLED
TEETHED
TIPTOED
TOOTHED
TOOTLED
TROTHED
TROTTED
TURTLED
TWITTED
WALTZED
WEBTOED
WENTBAD
WESTEND
WHETTED
WRITHED

••••T•D
ABETTED
ABLATED
ABORTED
ABUTTED
ADAPTED
ADOPTED
AERATED
ALERTED
AUDITED
AVERTED
AVIATED
AWAITED
BELATED
BERATED
BIGOTED
BLASTED
BLATTED
BLEATED
BLOATED
BLOTTED
BLUNTED
BLURTED
BOASTED
BOOSTED
BRUITED
CAROTID
CHANTED
CHARTED
CHATTED
CHEATED
CLOTTED
CLOUTED
COASTED
COOPTED
COUNTED
COURTED
COVETED
CRAFTED
CREATED
CRESTED
CRUSTED
DAUNTED
DEBATED
DEBITED
DEBUTED
DELETED
DEMOTED
DENOTED
DEPUTED
DEVOTED
DILATED
DILUTED
DONATED
DOUBTED
DRAFTED
DRATTED
DRIFTED
EGESTED
EJECTED
ELECTED
EMITTED
ENACTED
EQUATED
ERECTED
ERUCTED
ERUPTED
EVERTED
EVICTED
EXACTED
EXALTED
EXCITED
EXERTED
EXISTED
EXULTED
FACETED
FAGOTED
FAINTED
FAULTED
FEASTED
FEINTED
FIXATED
FLATTED
FLIRTED
FLITTED
FLOATED
FLOUTED
FOISTED
FRETTED
FRITTED
FRONTED
FROSTED
FRUITED
GHOSTED
GLINTED
GLOATED
GLUTTED
GRAFTED
GRANTED
GREETED
GRITTED
GROUTED
GRUNTED
GUESTED
GYRATED
HABITED
HAUNTED
HEISTED
HOISTED
IDEATED
IGNITED
IMPUTED
INCITED
INDITED
INVITED
JAUNTED
JOINTED
JOISTED
JOUSTED
KNITTED
KNOTTED
LIGATED
LIGHTED
LIMITED
LOCATED
LUXATED
MERITED
MOULTED
MOUNTED
MULCTED
MUTATED
NEGATED
NOTATED
OMITTED
ORBITED
PAINTED
PILOTED
PIRATED
PIVOTED
PLAITED
PLANTED
PLEATED
PLOTTED
POINTED
POSITED
PRINTED
QUESTED
QUIETED
QUILTED
REACTED
REBATED
RECITED
REDATED
REFUTED
RELATED
REPUTED
RERATED
RIGHTED
RIVETED
ROASTED
ROOSTED
ROTATED
ROUSTED
SAINTED
SALUTED
SCANTED
SCATTED
SCENTED
SCOOTED
SCOUTED
SHAFTED
SHEETED
SHIFTED
SHORTED
SHOUTED
SHUNTED
SIGHTED
SKIRTED
SLANTED
SLATTED
SLEETED
SLOTTED
SMARTED
SMELTED
SNOOTED
SNORTED
SPATTED
SPORTED
SPOTTED
SPOUTED
SPURTED
STARTED
STETTED
STILTED
STINTED
STUNTED
SWATTED
SWEATED
TAINTED
TAUNTED
TEMPTED
TOASTED
TREATED
TROTTED
TRUSTED
TRYSTED
TWEETED
TWISTED
TWITTED
UNDATED
UNRATED
UNSATED
UPDATED
VACATED
VAULTED
VAUNTED
VISITED
WAISTED
WHETTED
WORSTED
WRESTED
YACHTED

TE•••••
TEABAGS
TEABALL
TEACAKE
TEACART
TEACHER
TEACHES
TEACHIN
TEACUPS
TEALEAF
TEAMING
TEAMSUP
TEAPOTS
TEAPOYS
TEARFUL
TEARGAS
TEARIER
TEARILY
TEARING
TEAROFF
TEAROOM
TEAROSE
TEARSAT
TEARSUP
TEASELS
TEASERS
TEASETS
TEASHOP
TEASING
TEATIME
TEATRAY
TECHIES
TEDDERS
TEDDIES
TEDDING
TEDIOUS
TEDMACK
TEEDOFF
TEEMING
TEENAGE
TEENERS
TEENIER
TEEPEES
TEESOFF
TEETERS
TEETHED
TEETHER
TEETHES
TEHERAN
TEICHER
TEKTITE
TELAVIV
TELERAN
TELEXED
TELEXES
TELLALL
TELLERS
TELLIES
TELLING
TELLOFF
TELLSON
TELSTAR
TEMBLOR
TEMPERA
TEMPERS
TEMPEST
TEMPLAR
TEMPLES
TEMPTED
TEMPTER
TEMPURA
TENABLE
TENABLY
TENACES
TENANCY
TENANTS
TENDERS
TENDING
TENDONS
TENDRIL
TENDSTO
TENFOLD
TENFOUR
TENNERS
TENNIEL
TENONED
TENPINS
TENSELY
TENSEST
TENSEUP

TENSILE
TENSING
TENSION
TENSIVE
TENSORS
TENSPOT
TENTERS
TENTING
TENUOUS
TENURED
TENURES
TEPIDLY
TEQUILA
TERAPHS
TERBIUM
TERCELS
TERCETS
TEREDOS
TERENCE
TERHUNE
TERMING
TERMINI
TERMITE
TERNARY
TERNATE
TERRACE
TERRAIN
TERRENE
TERRETS
TERRIER
TERRIES
TERRIFY
TERRORS
TERSELY
TERSEST
TERTIAL
TESSERA
TESTBAN
TESTEES
TESTERS
TESTIER
TESTIFY
TESTILY
TESTING
TESTOUT
TETANUS
TETCHED
TETHERS
TETRADS
TEUTONS
TEXTILE
TEXTUAL
TEXTURE

T•E••••

TEEDOFF
TEEMING
TEENAGE
TEENERS
TEENIER
TEEPEES
TEESOFF
TEETERS
TEETHED
TEETHER
TEETHES
THEATER
THEATRE
THEBABE
THEBLOB
THEDEEP
THEISTS
THEOREM
THERAPY
THEREAT
THEREBY
THEREIN
THEREOF
THEREON
THERESA
THERETO
THERMAL
THERMOS
THEROUX
THESEUS
THESPIS
TIECLIP
TIEDOWN
TIEDYED
TIEDYES
TIEINTO
TIELESS
TIELINE
TIEPINS
TIERACK
TIERING
TIERNEY
TIERODS
TIETACK
TOECAPS
TOEHOLD
TOELESS
TOELOOP
TOENAIL
TOESHOE
TOETAPS
TREACLE
TREACLY
TREADED
TREADER
TREADLE
TREASON
TREATED
TREBLED
TREBLES
TREEING
TREERAT
TREETOP
TREFOIL
TREKKED
TREKKER
TREKKIE
TRELLIS
TREMBLE
TREMBLY
TREMOLO
TREMORS
TRENARY
TRENDED
TRENTON
TREPANS
TRESSES
TRESTLE
TREVINO
TSELIOT
TSETSES
TUESDAY
TWEAKED
TWEETED
TWEETER
TWEEZED
TWEEZES
TWELFTH
TWELVES

T••E•••

TAGENDS
TAKEAIM
TAKENIN
TAKENON
TAKEOFF
TAKEONE
TAKEOUT
TAKESIN
TAKESON
TAKESTO
TAKESUP
TAKETEN
TALENTS
TAPERED
TAVERNS
TEHERAN
TELERAN
TELEXED
TELEXES
TEREDOS
TERENCE
THIERRY
THIEVED
THIEVES
THREADS
THREADY
THREATS
THREERS
THREWIN
TIBETAN
TIMECOP
TIMELAG
TIMEOFF
TIMEOUT
TIMESUP
TIMEWAS
TINEARS
TIREDER
TIREDLY
TIREDOF
TIREOUT
TOKENED
TONEARM
TONEDUP
TONELOC
TONEROW
TONESUP
TOREOFF
TOREOUT
TOREROS
TOTEBAG
TOTEMIC
TOWELED
TOWERED
TREEING
TREERAT
TREETOP
TRIEDON
TRIESON
TRIESTE
TRUEING
TUNEDIN
TUNEDUP
TUNEFUL
TUNEOUT
TUNESIN
TUNESUP
TUNEUPS
TUPELOS
TUREENS
TUTELAR
TUXEDOS
TWEETED
TWEETER
TWEEZED
TWEEZES
TYLENOL
TYPEDUP
TYPESET
TYPESUP

T•••E••

TABLEAU
TABLETS
TACKERS
TAFFETA
TAILEND
TALKERS
TALLEST
TAMPERS
TANDEMS
TANGELO
TANGENT
TANGERE
TANKERS
TANNERS
TANNERY
TANNEST
TAPPERS
TAPPETS
TARBELL
TARGETS
TARHEEL
TARTEST
TASSELS
TASTERS
TATTERS
TAUTENS
TAUTEST
TEALEAF
TEASELS
TEASERS
TEASETS
TEDDERS
TEENERS
TEEPEES
TEETERS
TELLERS
TEMPERA
TEMPERS
TEMPEST
TENDERS
TENNERS
TENSELY
TENSEST
TENSEUP
TENTERS
TERCELS
TERCETS
TERRENE
TERRETS
TERSELY
TERSEST
TESSERA
TESTEES
TESTERS
TETHERS
THALERS
THEDEEP
THEREAT
THEREBY
THEREIN
THEREOF
THEREON
THERESA
THERETO
THESEUS
THOREAU
THREERS
THYSELF
TICKERS
TICKETS
TIDIEST
TIELESS
TIGRESS
TILLERS
TILTERS
TIMBERS
TINDERS
TINIEST
TINKERS
TINNERS
TINSELS
TINTERN
TINTERS
TIPPERS
TIPPETS
TITHERS
TITTERS
TOELESS
TOFFEES
TOILERS
TOILETS
TOLTECS
TOLUENE
TONIEST
TONNEAU
TOOTERS
TOPPERS
TORMENT
TORPEDO
TORRENT
TOSSERS
TOTTERS
TOTTERY
TOUPEES
TOURERS
TOUTERS
TOWHEAD
TOWHEES
TOWNERS
TRABERT
TRACERS
TRACERY
TRADEIN
TRADEON
TRADERS
TRADEUP
TRAGEDY
TRAPEZE
TRAVELS
TRAVERS
TRICEPS
TRIDENT
TRIREME
TRISECT
TRITELY
TRITEST
TRIVETS
TROWELS
TROWERS
TRUDEAU
TUAREGS
TUCKERS
TUFFETS
TUGGERS
TUNNELS
TUREENS
TURKEYS
TURNERS
TURRETS
TUSKERS
TWOFERS

T••••E•

TABBIES
TABORET
TACKIER
TACKLED
TACKLER
TACKLES
TAFFIES
TAILLES
TAINTED
TAKETEN
TALKIES
TALLIED
TALLIES
TALONED
TALUSES
TAMALES
TANAGER
TANGIER
TANGLED
TANGLES
TANGOED
TANSIES
TAPERED
TAPSTER
TARDIER
TARHEEL
TARRIED
TARRIES
TARSIER
TASTIER
TATTIER
TATTLED
TATTLER
TATTLES
TAUNTED
TAWNIER
TAXFREE
TEACHER
TEACHES
TEARIER
TECHIES
TEDDIES
TEENIER
TEEPEES
TEETHED
TEETHER
TEETHES
TEICHER
TELEXED
TELEXES
TELLIES
TEMPLES
TEMPTED
TEMPTER
TENACES
TENNIEL
TENONED
TENURED
TENURES
TERRIER
TERRIES
TESTEES
TESTIER
TETCHED
THANKED
THEATER
THEDEEP
THEOREM
THICKEN
THICKER
THICKET
THIEVED
THIEVES
THINKER
THINNED
THINNER
THITHER
THRIVED
THRIVES
THRONES
THROWER
THUDDED
THUMBED
THUMPED
THUMPER
THUNDER
THURBER
TICKLED
TICKLER
TICKLES
TIEDYED
TIEDYES
TIERNEY
TIGHTEN
TIGHTER
TIMBRES
TIMIDER
TINGLED
TINGLES
TINKLED
TINKLES
TINNIER
TIPPLED
TIPPLER
TIPPLES
TIPSIER
TIPSTER
TIPTOED
TIPTOES
TIRADES
TIREDER
TISANES
TISSUES
TITTLES
TIZZIES
TOADIED
TOADIES
TOASTED
TOASTER
TODDIES
TODDLED
TODDLER
TODDLES
TOFFEES
TOFFLER
TOGGLED
TOGGLES
TOKENED
TOLKIEN
TONGUED
TONGUES
TOOKTEN
TOORDER
TOOTHED
TOOTLED
TOOTLES
TOPAZES
TOPPLED
TOPPLES
TORCHED
TORCHES
TORQUES
TOTALED
TOUCHED
TOUCHES
TOUGHEN
TOUGHER
TOUPEES
TOURNEY
TOUSLED
TOUSLES
TOWELED
TOWERED
TOWHEES
TOWNIES
TOYNBEE
TRACHEA
TRACKED
TRACKER
TRAILED
TRAILER
TRAINED
TRAINEE
TRAINER
TRAMMEL
TRAMPED
TRANCES
TRAPPED
TRAPPER
TRASHED
TRASHES
TRAUBEL
TRAWLED
TRAWLER
TREADED
TREADER
TREATED
TREBLED
TREBLES
TREKKED
TREKKER
TRENDED
TRESSES
TRICKED
TRICKER
TRIFLED
TRIFLER
TRIFLES
TRIGGED
TRIGGER
TRILLED
TRIMMED
TRIMMER
TRINKET
TRIODES
TRIPLED
TRIPLES
TRIPLET
TRIPLEX
TRIPPED
TRIPPER
TRIPPET
TRIUNES
TROCHEE
TROCHES
TRODDEN
TROLLED
TROLLEY
TROOPED
TROOPER
TROTHED
TROTTED
TROTTER
TROUPER
TROUPES
TROUSER
TRUCKED
TRUCKEE
TRUCKER
TRUDGED
TRUDGER
TRUDGES
TRUMPED
TRUMPET
TRUSSED
TRUSSES
TRUSTED
TRUSTEE
TRYSTED
TRYSTER
TSETSES
TUBBIER
TUMBLED
TUMBLER
TUMBLES
TUMBREL
TUMMIES
TUNNIES
TURNKEY
TURTLED
TURTLES
TUSSLED
TUSSLES
TUTORED
TWANGED
TWEAKED
TWEETED
TWEETER
TWEEZED
TWEEZES
TWELVES
TWILLED
TWINBED
TWINGED
TWINGES
TWINNED
TWIRLED
TWIRLER
TWISTED
TWISTER
TWITTED
TWITTER
TWOSTEP
TYPESET

T•••••E

TACTILE
TADPOLE
TAGLINE
TAGSALE
TAKEONE
TAMABLE
TANGERE
TANLINE
TARTARE
TAURINE
TAXABLE
TAXFREE
TAXRATE
TEACAKE
TEAROSE
TEATIME
TEENAGE
TEKTITE
TENABLE
TENSILE
TENSIVE
TERENCE
TERHUNE
TERMITE
TERNATE
TERRACE
TERRENE
TEXTILE
TEXTURE
THEATRE
THEBABE
THIMBLE
THINICE
THISTLE
TIELINE
TILLAGE
TIMBALE
TINTYPE
TITMICE
TITRATE
TOESHOE
TOLUENE
TONNAGE
TONSURE
TONTINE
TOOTSIE
TOPSIDE
TOSCALE
TOSPARE
TOUGHIE
TOWROPE
TOYNBEE
TRADUCE
TRAINEE
TRAIPSE
TRAMPLE
TRAPEZE
TREACLE
TREADLE
TREKKIE
TREMBLE
TRESTLE
TRIBUNE
TRIBUTE
TRICKLE
TRIESTE
TRIREME
TRITONE
TROCHEE
TROUBLE
TROUNCE
TRUCKEE
TRUCKLE
TRUFFLE
TRUNDLE
TRUSTEE
TSQUARE
TUNICLE
TURBINE
TVGUIDE
TWADDLE
TWIDDLE
TWINKLE
TWOBASE
TWOSOME
TWOTIME
TWOTONE

•TE••••

ATECROW
ATELIER
ETERNAL
ETESIAN
ITEMIZE
ITERANT
ITERATE
STEALTH
STEAMED
STEAMER
STEELED
STEELER
STEELIE
STEEPED
STEEPEN
STEEPER
STEEPLE
STEEPLY
STEERED
STEERER
STEIGER
STEINEM
STEINER
STELLAR
STEMMED
STENCIL
STENGEL
STENTOR
STEPHEN
STEPINS
STEPOUT
STEPPED
STEPPER
STEPPES
STEPSIN
STEPSON
STEPSUP
STEPUPS
STEREOS
STERILE
STERNAL
STERNER
STERNLY
STERNUM
STEROID
STEROLS
STETSON
STETTED
STEUBEN
STEVENS
STEWARD
STEWART
STEWERS
STEWING
UTENSIL

•T•E•••

ATHEART
ATHEISM
ATHEIST
ATLEAST
ATPEACE
ATTEMPT
ATTENDS
ATTESTS
ETIENNE
OTHELLO
STDENIS
STEELED
STEELER
STEELIE
STEEPED
STEEPEN
STEEPER
STEEPLE
STEEPLY
STEERED
STEERER
STIEGEL
STPETER
STREAKS
STREAKY
STREAMS
STREETS
STRETCH
STRETTO
STREWED
STREWER
UTRECHT
UTTERED
UTTERER
UTTERLY

•T••E••

ATHLETE
ETAGERE
ETCHERS
PTOLEMY
STAGERS
STALEST
STAMENS
STAREAT
STARERS
STARETS
STATELY
STEREOS
STEVENS
STEWERS
STIPEND
STOKELY
STOKERS
STONERS
STORERS
STOREUP
STOREYS
STREETS
STUDENT
STUPEFY
STYLERS
STYLETS
STYRENE

•T•••E•

ATELIER
ATHOMES
ATLASES
ATOMIES
ATTIMES
ATTIRED
ATTIRES
ATTUNED
ATTUNES
ETOILES
ITCHIER
STABBED
STABLED
STABLER
STABLES
STACKED
STAFFED
STAFFER
STAGGED
STAGGER
STAGIER
STAIDER
STAINED
STAINER
STALKED
STALKER
STALLED
STAMMER
STAMPED
STANCES
STANDEE
STANLEE
STANLEY
STAPLED
STAPLER
STAPLES
STARKER
STARLET
STARRED
STARTED
STARTER
STARVED
STARVES
STASHED
STASHES
STASSEN
STATUES
STEAMED
STEAMER
STEELED
STEELER
STEEPED
STEEPEN
STEEPER
STEERED
STEERER
STEIGER
STEINEM
STEINER
STEMMED
STENGEL
STEPHEN
STEPPED
STEPPER
STEPPES
STERNER
STETTED
STEUBEN
STICHES
STICKER
STIEGEL
STIFFED
STIFFEN
STIFFER
STIFLED
STIFLES
STILLED
STILLER
STILTED
STINGER
STINKER
STINTED
STIRRED
STIRRER
STOCKED
STOGIES
STOLLEN
STOLLER
STOMPED
STONIER
STOOGES
STOOKEY
STOOPED
STOPPED
STOPPER
STORIED
STORIES
STORMED
STOUTER

STPETER
STRAFED
STRAFES
STRAYED
STREWED
STREWER
STRIDER
STRIDES
STRIKER
STRIKES
STRIPED
STRIPER
STRIPES
STRIVED
STRIVEN
STRIVER
STRIVES
STROBES
STROKED
STROKES
STRUDEL
STUBBED
STUDDED
STUDIED
STUDIES
STUFFED
STUFFER
STUMPED
STUMPER
STUNNED
STUNNER
STUNTED
STURGES
STYMIED
STYMIES
UTTERED
UTTERER

•T••••E

ATHLETE
ATINGLE
ATISSUE
ATLARGE
ATOMIZE
ATPEACE
ATSTAKE
ATTACHE
ATTRITE
ETAGERE
ETAMINE
ETIENNE
ITEMIZE
ITERATE
STABILE
STANDEE
STANLEE
STARTLE
STATICE
STATURE
STATUTE
STEELIE
STEEPLE
STERILE
STIPPLE
STOOLIE
STORAGE
STRANGE
STRASSE
STRIATE
STROPHE
STUBBLE
STUMBLE
STYLIZE
STYRENE
UTILIZE

••TE•••

ACTEDUP
ALTERED
ALTERER
ANTEDUP
ANTEING
ANTENNA
ANTESUP
ARTEMIS
ARTEMUS
ATTEMPT
ATTENDS
ATTESTS
AUTEURS
AZTECAN
BATEAUX
BATEMAN
BITEOFF
CATENAE
CATERED
CATERER
COTERIE
DATEDLY
DETECTS
DETENTE
DETESTS
DOTEDON
DOTESON
DUTEOUS
EATENAT
EATENUP
ENTEBBE
ENTENTE
ENTERED
ESTEEMS
ESTELLE
ESTEVEZ
EUTERPE
EXTENDS
EXTENTS
FATEFUL
GATEAUX
GATELEG
GATEMAN
GATEMEN
GATEWAY
GETEVEN
GOTEVEN
HATEFUL
INTEGER
INTEGRA
INTENDS
INTENSE
INTENTS
INTERIM
INTERNS
INTERSE
IQTESTS
KUTENAI
LATEENS
LATENCY
LATENTS
LATERAL
LATERAN
LATERON
LATEXES
LITERAL
MATEWAN
METEORS
METEOUT
METERED
MITERED
NOTEPAD
OFTENER
OSTEOID
OUTEATS
PATELLA
PATENTS
PATERNO
PETERED
PITEOUS
POTENCY
RETEACH
RETELLS
RETESTS
TOTEBAG
TOTEMIC
TUTELAR
UPTEMPO
URTEXTS
UTTERED
UTTERER
UTTERLY
VETERAN
VOTECHS
VOTESIN
WATERED
WATERER

••T•E••

ACTAEON
ACTRESS
ANTAEUS
ANTBEAR
ANTHEMS
ANTHERS
ANTLERS
ANTWERP
APTNESS
ARTDECO
ARTIEST
ARTLESS
BATHERS
BATTENS
BATTERS
BATTERY
BETHELS
BETTERS
BETWEEN
BITTERN
BITTERS
BOTHERS
BUTLERS
BUTTERS
BUTTERY
BYTHEBY
CATHEAD
CATSEYE
COTTERS
CUTLERS
CUTLERY
CUTLETS
CUTTERS
DITHERS
DITHERY
ENTREAT
ENTREES
ESTEEMS
ESTHETE
EXTREME
FATHEAD
FATHERS
FATLESS
FATNESS
FATTENS
FATTEST
FETTERS
FITNESS
FITTERS
FITTEST
GATHERS
GETWELL
GOTWELL
GUTLESS
GUTTERS
HATLESS
HATTERS
HITHERE
HITLESS
HITTERS
HOTBEDS
HOTHEAD
HOTNESS
HOTSEAT
HOTTEST
JITNEYS
JITTERS
JITTERY
KITTENS
LATEENS
LATHERS
LATHERY
LATTENS
LETTERS
LITHELY
LITHEST
LITTERS
LOTTERY
MATHERS
MATHEWS
MATTERS
METIERS
MITTENS
MOTHERS
MUTTERS
NATTERS
NOTWELL
NUTLETS
NUTMEAT
NUTMEGS
NUTTERS
OATMEAL
ONTHEGO
ONTHEQT
OSTLERS
OUTLETS
OUTSELL
OUTSETS
OUTWEAR
PATIENT
PATNESS
PATTENS
PATTERN
PATTERS
PETRELS
PETTERS
PITTERS
POTHERB
POTHERS
POTTERS
POTTERY
PUTTEES
PUTTERS
RATTERS
RETREAD
RETREAT
ROTTERS
RUTGERS
SATIETY
SETTEES
SETTERS
SITTERS
SITWELL
SOTHERE
SOTHERN
SUTLERS
TATTERS
TETHERS
TITHERS
TITTERS
TOTTERS
TOTTERY
VETOERS
WATTEAU
WETCELL
WETHERS
WETNESS
WETTEST
WITHERS
WITLESS
WITNESS
ZITHERS

••T••E•

ACTIVES
AITCHES
ALTERED
ALTERER
ANTARES
ANTIBES
ANTIGEN
ANTSIER
ATTIMES
ATTIRED
ATTIRES
ATTUNED
ATTUNES
BATCHED
BATCHES
BATIKED
BATSMEN
BATTIER
BATTLED
BATTLER
BATTLES
BETAKEN
BETAKES
BETIDED
BETIDES
BETIMES
BETOKEN
BETWEEN
BITTIER
BITUMEN
BOTCHED
BOTCHES
BOTTLED
BOTTLER
BOTTLES
BUTCHER
CATCHER
CATCHES
CATERED
CATERER
CATTIER
CITADEL
CITIZEN
CITROEN
CNTOWER
DATASET
DITCHED
DITCHES
DITTIES
DITTOED
DOTTIER
DOTTLES
ECTYPES
ENTERED
ENTICED
ENTICER
ENTICES
ENTREES
ENTRIES
ESTATES
ESTEVEZ
FETCHED
FETCHES
FETTLES
FITCHES
FUTURES
GATELEG
GATEMEN
GETEVEN
GETOVER
GETSSET
GOTEVEN
GOTOVER
GUTSIER
HATCHED
HATCHER
HATCHES
HATCHET
HITCHED
HITCHER
HITCHES
HUTCHES
INTAKES
INTEGER
INTONED
INTONER
INTONES
JETTIES
KETCHES
KETONES
KETTLES
KITCHEN
KITTIES
LATCHED
LATCHES
LATEXES
LATICES
LETSSEE
LETTRES
LITOTES
LITTLER
LOTUSES
MATCHED
MATCHES
MATINEE
MATTHEW
MATURED
MATURER
MATURES
METATES
METERED
METOOER
METTLES
MITERED
MITOSES
MOTIVES
MOTORED
MOTTLED
MOTTLES
MOTTOES
MUTAGEN
MUTATED
MUTATES
NATCHEZ
NATIVES
NATTIER
NATURED
NATURES
NETTLED
NETTLES
NOTATED
NOTATES
NOTCHED
NOTCHES
NOTICED
NOTICES
NUTTIER
OBTUSER
OCTANES
OCTAVES
OCTOBER
OFTENER
OUTAGES
OUTDOES
OUTDREW
OUTGOES
OUTGREW
OUTSTEP
PATAKES
PATCHED
PATCHES
PATSIES
PATTIES
PETALED
PETERED
PETITES
PETTIER
PITCHED
PITCHER
PITCHES
PITHIER
POTAGES
POTPIES
PUTAMEN
PUTOVER
PUTTEES
PUTTIED
PUTTIES
RATCHET
RATITES
RATTIER
RATTLED
RATTLER
RATTLES
RETAKEN
RETAKES
RETAPED
RETAPES
RETAXED
RETAXES
RETILED
RETILES
RETIMED
RETIMES
RETIRED
RETIREE
RETIRES
RETOWED
RETRIED
RETRIES
RETUNED
RETUNES
RETYPED
RETYPES
RITZIER
ROTATED
ROTATES
ROTIFER
SATCHEL
SATIRES
SETTEES
SETTLED
SETTLER
SETTLES
SUTTNER
SUTURED
SUTURES
TATTIER
TATTLED
TATTLER
TATTLES
TETCHED
TITTLES
TOTALED
TUTORED
UNTAMED
UNTAPED
UNTRIED
UNTUNED
UNTUNES
UPTAKES
UTTERED
UTTERER
VETCHES
VITTLES
WATCHED
WATCHER
WATCHES
WATERED
WATERER
WATTLES
WITCHES
WITTIER
ZATOPEK

••T•••E

ACTABLE
ACTUATE
ANTIQUE
ANTOINE
ARTICLE
ARTISTE
ARTWARE
ASTAIRE
ASTARTE
ASTRIDE
ATTACHE
ATTRITE
BATISTE
CATENAE
CATHODE
CATLIKE
CATSEYE
CITABLE
CITRATE
CITRINE
COTERIE
COTTAGE
CUTICLE
CUTRATE
CUTTIME
DETENTE
EATABLE
ENTEBBE
ENTENTE
ENTHUSE
ENTITLE
ENTWINE
ESTELLE
ESTHETE
EUTERPE
EXTREME
EXTRUDE
FATIGUE
GUTHRIE
HITHERE
HITTITE
HOTCAKE
HOTLINE
HOTWIRE
INTENSE
INTERSE
INTRUDE
LATTICE
LETITBE
LETSSEE
LETTUCE
MATINEE
MATISSE
METHANE
MUTABLE
NATALIE
NETSUKE
NITRATE
NITRIDE
NITRITE
NOTABLE
NOTHOME
NOTSURE
NOTTRUE
OBTRUDE
OCTUPLE
OUTCOME
OUTDONE
OUTFACE
OUTLINE
OUTLIVE
OUTPACE
OUTRACE
OUTRAGE
OUTSIDE
OUTSIZE
OUTTAKE
OUTVOTE
OUTWORE
PATRICE
PETIOLE
PETNAME
POTABLE
POTHOLE
POTTAGE
RATABLE
RATHOLE
RATLINE
RATRACE
RETICLE
RETINAE
RETINUE
RETIREE
RETITLE
RETRACE
RETRADE
RITCHIE
SATIATE
SETLINE
SITUATE
SOTHERE
TITMICE
TITRATE
VITIATE
WATTAGE

•••TE••

ACUTELY
AMATEUR
AUSTERE
BANTERS
BARTEND
BARTERS
BASTERS
BATTENS
BATTERS
BATTERY
BEATERS
BETTERS
BITTERN
BITTERS
BOATERS
BOOTEES
BUTTERS
BUTTERY
CALTECH
CANTEEN
CANTERS
CARTELS
CARTERS
CASTERS
CENTERS
CHATEAU
CISTERN
COCTEAU
CONTEMN
CONTEND
CONTENT
CONTEST
CONTEXT
COPTERS
CORTEGE
COTTERS
CRATERS
CURTEST
CUTTERS
DAFTEST
DARTERS
DEFTEST
DEUTERO
DIETERS
DISTEND
DUSTERS
EASTEND
EASTERN
EASTERS
ELATERS
EMOTERS
EPSTEIN
FALTERS
FASTENS
FASTEST
FATTENS
FATTEST
FESTERS
FETTERS
FIFTEEN
FILTERS
FITTERS
FITTEST
FONTEYN
FOOTERS
FOSTERS
GAITERS
GARTERS
GENTEEL
GOATEED
GOATEES
GRATERS
GUTTERS
HALTERS
HASTENS
HATTERS
HAUTEUR
HEATERS
HITTERS
HOOTERS
HOSTELS
HOSTESS
HOTTEST
HUNTERS
INSTEAD
INSTEPS
IRATELY
IRATEST
JESTERS
JITTERS
JITTERY
KITTENS
KRATERS
LACTEAL
LANTERN
LATTENS
LECTERN
LETTERS
LIFTERS
LINTELS
LISTEES
LISTELS
LISTENS
LITTERS
LOITERS
LOOTERS
LOTTERY
LOWTECH
LUSTERS
MALTEDS
MALTESE
MANTELS
MARTENS
MASTERS
MASTERY
MATTERS
MIDTERM
MINTERS
MISTERS
MITTENS
MOLTERS
MONTEGO
MONTEUX
MUSTERS
MUTTERS
MYSTERY
NATTERS
NEATENS
NEATEST
NESTEGG
NESTERS
NUTTERS
ONATEAR
OUSTERS
OYSTERS
PALTERS
PASTELS
PASTERN
PASTEUP
PASTEUR
PATTENS
PATTERN
PATTERS
PELTERS
PERTEST
PESTERS
PETTERS
PITTERS
PLATEAU
PLATENS
PLATERS
POETESS
PORTEND
PORTENT
PORTERS
POSTERN
POSTERS
POTTERS
POTTERY
POUTERS
PRATERS
PRETEEN
PRETEND
PRETEST
PRETEXT
PROTEAN
PROTECT
PROTEGE
PROTEIN
PROTEST
PROTEUS
PUNTERS
PUPTENT
PUTTEES
PUTTERS
QUOTERS
RAFTERS
RANTERS
RASTERS
RATTERS
RENTERS
RESTERS
REUTERS
RIOTERS
ROOTERS
ROSTERS
ROTTERS
ROUTERS
SALTERS
SAUTEED
SCOTERS
SEATERS
SEPTETS
SESTETS
SETTEES
SETTERS
SEXTETS
SHUTEYE
SIFTERS
SISTERS
SITTERS
SIXTEEN
SKATERS
SOFTENS
SOFTEST
SORTERS
STATELY
SUBTEND
SUBTEXT
SYSTEMS
TARTEST
TASTERS
TATTERS
TAUTENS
TAUTEST
TEETERS
TENTERS
TESTEES
TESTERS
TILTERS
TINTERN
TINTERS
TITTERS
TOLTECS
TOOTERS
TOTTERS
TOTTERY
TOUTERS
TRITELY
TRITEST
ULSTERS
UMPTEEN
UNITERS
USSTEEL
VASTEST
VENTERS
VESTEES
WAITERS
WALTERS
WASTERS
WATTEAU
WELTERS
WESTEND
WESTERN
WETTEST
WHITENS
WHITEST
WINTERS
WINTERY
WRITEIN
WRITERS
WRITETO
WRITEUP
WROTEIN
WROTETO
WROTEUP
YEATEAM

•••T•E•

ABETTED
ABUTTED
ANOTHER
APOTHEM
AUNTIES
BATTIER
BATTLED
BATTLER
BATTLES
BEATLES
BEETLES
BEETREE
BENTLEY
BENTSEN
BERTHED
BESTMEN
BESTREW
BIGTOES
BIRTHED
BITTIER
BLATHER
BLATTED
BLITHER
BLITZED
BLITZEN
BLITZES
BLOTTED

BLOTTER
BOATMEN
BOOTEES
BOOTIES
BOOTLEG
BOTTLED
BOTTLER
BOTTLES
BOWTIES
BRITTEN
BROTHER
BUSTLED
BUSTLES
CANTEEN
CANTLES
CARTIER
CASTLED
CASTLES
CATTIER
CENTRED
CENTRES
CHATTED
CHATTEL
CHATTER
CHITTER
CHUTNEY
CLATTER
CLOTHED
CLOTHES
CLOTTED
CLUTTER
COOTIES
COSTNER
CRITTER
CURTSEY
DALTREY
DEITIES
DIRTIED
DIRTIER
DIRTIES
DITTIES
DITTOED
DOTTIER
DOTTLES
DRATTED
DUSTIER
EARTHEN
ELMTREE
EMITTED
EMITTER
EMPTIED
EMPTIER
EMPTIES
EPITHET
ERITREA
FARTHER
FEATHER
FETTLES
FIFTEEN
FIFTIES
FLATBED
FLATTED
FLATTEN
FLATTER
FLITTED
FLITTER
FLUTTER
FOOTMEN
FORTIES
FRETTED
FRITTED
FRITTER
FROTHED
FURTHER
FUSTIER
GANTLET
GENTEEL
GENTLED
GENTLER
GENTLES
GLITTER
GLITZED
GLITZES
GLUTTED
GOATEED
GOATEES
GRITTED
GUMTREE
GUNTHER
GUSTOES
HASTIER
HEATHEN
HEATHER
HEATTER
HEFTIER
HOGTIED
HOGTIES
HOSTLER
HUNTLEY
HURTLED
HURTLES
HUSTLED
HUSTLER
HUSTLES
JANTZEN
JETTIES
JOSTLED
JOSTLER
JOSTLES
KESTREL
KETTLES
KILTIES
KIRTLES
KITTIES
KLUTZES
KNITTED
KNITTER
KNOTTED
LAUTREC
LEATHER
LEFTIES
LETTRES
LINTIER
LISTEES
LITTLER
LOATHED
LOATHES
LOFTIER
LUSTIER
LUSTRED
LUSTRES
MAITRED
MANTLED
MANTLES
MATTHEW
MEATIER
METTLES
MINTIER
MISTIER
MOTTLED
MOTTLES
MOTTOES
MOUTHED
MUSTIER
MUSTSEE
MYRTLES
NARTHEX
NASTIER
NATTIER
NEITHER
NESTLED
NESTLER
NESTLES
NETTLED
NETTLES
NIFTIER
NORTHER
NUTTIER
OAKTREE
OMITTED
PANTHER
PARTIED
PARTIES
PARTNER
PASTIER
PATTIES
PESTLED
PESTLES
PETTIER
PHOTOED
PIETIES
PLATTER
PLOTTED
PLOTTER
POITIER
POSTMEN
POUTIER
PRETEEN
PRETZEL
PRITHEE
PUTTEES
PUTTIED
PUTTIES
QUITTER
RATTIER
RATTLED
RATTLER
RATTLES
REUTHER
RONTGEN
ROOTLET
RUNTIER
RUSTIER
RUSTLED
RUSTLER
RUSTLES
SALTIER
SAUTEED
SCATHED
SCATHES
SCATTED
SCATTER
SCYTHED
SCYTHES
SEETHED
SEETHES
SELTZER
SETTEES
SETTLED
SETTLER
SETTLES
SHATNER
SHATTER
SHUTTER
SIXTEEN
SIXTIES
SKITTER
SLATHER
SLATIER
SLATTED
SLITHER
SLOTTED
SMATTER
SMITTEN
SMOTHER
SOFTIES
SOOTHED
SOOTHER
SOOTHES
SOOTIER
SORTIED
SORTIES
SOUTHEY
SPATTED
SPATTER
SPITZES
SPOTTED
SPOTTER
SPUTTER
STATUES
STETTED
SUBTLER
SUTTNER
SWATHED
SWATHES
SWATTED
SWATTER
SWITZER
TASTIER
TATTIER
TATTLED
TATTLER
TATTLES
TEETHED
TEETHER
TEETHES
TESTEES
TESTIER
THITHER
TIPTOED
TIPTOES
TITTLES
TOOTHED
TOOTLED
TOOTLES
TROTHED
TROTTED
TROTTER
TSETSES
TURTLED
TURTLES
TWITTED
TWITTER
UMPTEEN
UNITIES
UPATREE
USSTEEL
VESTEES
VINTNER
VIRTUES
VITTLES
WALTZED
WALTZER
WALTZES
WASTREL
WATTLES
WEATHER
WEBTOED
WERTHER
WHETHER
WHETTED
WHITHER
WHITNEY
WITTIER
WRITHED
WRITHES
WRITTEN
YAHTZEE
ZESTIER

•••T••E

ACETATE
ACETONE
AGITATE
AIRTIME
ALLTIME
AMATIVE
ANATOLE
ANYTIME
APATITE
ATSTAKE
AUSTERE
BAPTIZE
BEATTIE
BEDTIME
BEETREE
BELTANE
BIGTIME
BRITTLE
BUYTIME
CAPTIVE
CAPTURE
CARTAGE
CASTILE
CENTIME
CLOTURE
CONTUSE
CORTEGE
COSTUME
COTTAGE
COUTURE
CULTURE
CUTTIME
DAYTIME
DENTATE
DENTINE
DENTURE
DESTINE
DICTATE
DUCTILE
EBBTIDE
ELMTREE
EMOTIVE
EPITOME
FASTONE
FEATURE
FERTILE
FESTIVE
FICTIVE
FIXTURE
FOOTAGE
FOOTSIE
FORTUNE
FURTIVE
GENTILE
GESTATE
GESTURE
GUMTREE
GUSTAVE
HECTARE
HITTITE
HOSTAGE
HOSTILE
IFSTONE
IMITATE
INSTATE
INSTORE
INSTYLE
INUTILE
ISOTOPE
JUSTICE
JUSTINE
LACTASE
LACTATE
LACTOSE
LATTICE
LECTURE
LEETIDE
LETTUCE
LOWTIDE
MALTESE
MALTOSE
MAYTIME
MISTAKE
MISTYPE
MIXTURE
MONTAGE
MONTANE
MORTISE
MUSTSEE
NAPTIME
NASTASE
NEPTUNE
NOTTRUE
NURTURE
OAKTREE
OLDTIME
ONETIME
ONSTAGE
OUTTAKE
PARTAKE
PARTITE
PASTDUE
PASTIME
PASTURE
PELTATE
PEPTIDE
PICTURE
PISTOLE
PONTINE
PORTAGE
POSTAGE
POSTURE
POTTAGE
PRATTLE
PRETAPE
PRITHEE
PROTEGE
RAGTIME
RAPTURE
REDTAPE
REPTILE
RESTAGE
RESTATE
RESTIVE
RESTORE
RESTYLE
RIPTIDE
ROUTINE
RUPTURE
SALTINE
SANTAFE
SAOTOME
SCOTTIE
SCUTTLE
SEATTLE
SHUTEYE
SHUTTLE
SISTINE
SKITTLE
SOUTANE
STATICE
STATURE
STATUTE
SYSTOLE
TACTILE
TARTARE
TEATIME
TEKTITE
TEXTILE
TEXTURE
TINTYPE
TONTINE
TOOTSIE
TRITONE
TWOTIME
TWOTONE
UNITIVE
UPATREE
UPSTAGE
UPSTATE
VANTAGE
VENTURE
VESTIGE
VESTURE
VINTAGE
VOLTAGE
VULTURE
WARTIME
WASTAGE
WATTAGE
WENTAPE
WHITTLE
YAHTZEE

••••TE

ABETTED
ABLATED
ABLATES
ABORTED
ABUTTED
ACHATES
ADAPTED
ADAPTER
ADOPTED
ADOPTEE
ADOPTER
AERATED
AERATES
AGNATES
ALERTED
ALERTER
AMMETER
ARBITER
AUDITED
AVERTED
AVIATED
AVIATES
AWAITED
BELATED
BERATED
BERATES
BIGOTED
BLASTED
BLASTER
BLATTED
BLEATED
BLISTER
BLOATED
BLOTTED
BLOTTER
BLUNTED
BLUNTER
BLURTED
BLUSTER
BOASTED
BOASTER
BOLSTER
BOOSTED
BOOSTER
BORATES
BOXSTEP
BRITTEN
BRUITED
CHANTED
CHANTER
CHANTEY
CHAPTER
CHARTED
CHARTER
CHASTEN
CHASTER
CHATTED
CHATTEL
CHATTER
CHEATED
CHEATER
CHESTER
CHITTER
CLATTER
CLOTTED
CLOUTED
CLUSTER
CLUTTER
COASTED
COASTER
COOPTED
COULTER
COUNTED
COUNTER
COURTED
COVETED
COYOTES
CRAFTED
CRAFTER
CREATED
CREATES
CRESTED
CRITTER
CRUSTED
CURATES
DAUNTED
DEBATED
DEBATER
DEBATES
DEBITED
DEBUTED
DELETED
DELETES
DEMETER
DEMOTED
DEMOTES
DENOTED
DENOTES
DEPUTED
DEPUTES
DEVOTED
DEVOTEE
DEVOTES
DILATED
DILATES
DILUTED
DILUTER
DILUTES
DIOPTER
DONATED
DONATES
DOUBTED
DOUBTER
DRAFTED
DRAFTEE
DRATTED
DRIFTED
DRIFTER
EGESTED
EJECTED
ELECTED
ELECTEE
EMITTED
EMITTER
ENACTED
EQUATED
EQUATES
ERECTED
ERECTER
ERUCTED
ERUPTED
ESTATES
EVERTED
EVICTED
EXACTED
EXACTER
EXALTED
EXCITED
EXCITES
EXERTED
EXISTED
EXULTED
FACETED
FAGOTED
FAINTED
FAINTER
FAULTED
FEASTED
FEINTED
FIGHTER
FIXATED
FIXATES
FLATTED
FLATTEN
FLATTER
FLEETER
FLIRTED
FLITTED
FLITTER
FLOATED
FLOATER
FLOUTED
FLUSTER
FLUTTER
FOISTED
FORSTER
FRETTED
FRITTED
FRITTER
FRONTED
FROSTED
FRUITED
GAGSTER
GALATEA
GAMETES
GAUNTER
GHOSTED
GLINTED
GLISTEN
GLITTER
GLOATED
GLUTTED
GOLFTEE
GORETEX
GRAFTED
GRANTED
GRANTEE
GREATER
GREETED
GREETER
GRIFTER
GRITTED
GROUTED
GRUNTED
GUESTED
GYRATED
GYRATES
HABITED
HALITES
HAMITES
HAMSTER
HANGTEN
HAUNTED
HEARTEN
HEATTER
HEISTED
HERBTEA
HIGHTEA
HIPSTER
HOISTED
HOLSTER
ICEDTEA
IDEATED
IDEATES
IGNITED
IGNITER
IGNITES
IMPUTED
IMPUTES
INASTEW
INCITED
INCITER
INCITES
INDITED
INDITES
INMATES
INVITED
INVITES
IODATES
JAUNTED
JOINTED
JOISTED
JOUSTED
JOUSTER
JUPITER
KNITTED
KNITTER
KNOTTED
LAERTES
LEGATEE
LEGATES
LEISTER
LEVITES
LIGATED
LIGATES
LIGHTED
LIGHTEN
LIGHTER
LIMITED
LITOTES
LOBSTER
LOCATED
LOCATER
LOCATES
LUXATED
LUXATES
MANATEE
MERITED
METATES
MINUTES
MISSTEP
MOBSTER
MOISTEN
MOISTER
MONSTER
MOULTED
MOUNTED
MULCTED
MUTATED
MUTATES
NEGATED
NEGATES
NOTATED
NOTATES
OBLATES
OLDSTER
OLEATES
OMITTED
ONESTEP
OOCYTES
OOLITES
OPIATES
ORBITED
ORBITER
ORESTES
OUTSTEP
PAINTED
PAINTER
PAIUTES
PALATES
PENATES
PETITES
PHILTER
PIASTER
PILOTED
PIRATED
PIRATES
PIVOTED
PLAITED
PLANTED
PLANTER
PLASTER
PLATTER
PLEATED
PLOTTED
PLOTTER
POINTED
POINTER
POLITER
POSITED
PRINTED
PRINTER
PSALTER
PUNSTER
PYRITES
QUARTER
QUARTET
QUESTED
QUIETED
QUIETEN
QUIETER
QUILTED
QUILTER
QUINTET
QUITTER
RATITES
REACTED
REBATED
REBATES
RECITED
RECITER
RECITES
REDATED
REDATES
REENTER
REFUTED
REFUTER
REFUTES
RELATED
RELATES
REMOTER
REMOTES
RENOTES
REPUTED
REPUTES
RERATED
RERATES
RICHTER
RIGHTED
RIGHTER
RIVETED
RIVETER
ROASTED
ROASTER
ROISTER
ROOSTED
ROOSTER
ROTATED
ROTATES
ROUSTED
SAINTED
SALUTED
SALUTES
SAMITES
SAUNTER
SCANTED
SCANTER
SCATTED
SCATTER
SCENTED
SCEPTER
SCOOTED
SCOOTER
SCOUTED
SCOUTER
SEDATER
SEMITES
SENATES
SHAFTED
SHANTER
SHATTER
SHEETED
SHELTER
SHIFTED
SHIITES
SHOOTER
SHORTED
SHORTEN
SHORTER
SHOUTED
SHOUTER
SHUNTED
SHUTTER
SHYSTER
SIGHTED
SKEETER
SKELTER
SKIRTED
SKITTER
SLANTED
SLATTED
SLEETED
SLOTTED
SMARTED
SMARTEN
SMARTER
SMATTER
SMELTED
SMELTER
SMITTEN
SNIFTER
SNOOTED
SNORTED
SNORTER
SOLUTES
SORITES
SPATTED
SPATTER
SPECTER
SPORTED
SPOTTED
SPOTTER
SPOUTED
SPOUTER
SPRITES
SPURTED
SPUTTER
STARTED
STARTER
STETTED
STILTED
STINTED
STOUTER
STPETER
STUNTED
SVELTER
SWATTED
SWATTER
SWEATED
SWEATER
SWEETEN
SWEETER
SWELTER
SWIFTER
TAINTED
TAKETEN
TAPSTER
TAUNTED
TEMPTED
TEMPTER
THEATER
TIGHTEN
TIGHTER
TIPSTER
TOASTED
TOASTER
TOOKTEN
TREATED
TROTTED
TROTTER
TRUSTED
TRUSTEE
TRYSTED
TRYSTER
TWEETED
TWEETER
TWISTED
TWISTER
TWITTED
TWITTER
TWOSTEP
UNDATED
UNRATED•

UNSATED
UPDATED
UPDATES
VACATED
VACATES
VAULTED
VAULTER
VAUNTED
VAUNTER
VISITED
WAISTED
WEBSTER
WHETTED
WOOSTER
WORSTED
WRESTED
WRITTEN
YACHTED
ZAPOTEC
ZYGOTES

••••T•E

ADOPTEE
ANNETTE
APOSTLE
ARISTAE
BABETTE
BEASTIE
BEATTIE
BOLOTIE
BREATHE
BRISTLE
BRITTLE
BURETTE
CADETTE
CHORTLE
COLETTE
CULOTTE
DEVOTEE
DINETTE
DRAFTEE
ELECTEE
ENTITLE
EPISTLE
FENETRE
GAVOTTE
GAZETTE
GOLFTEE
GRANTEE
GRISTLE
HABITUE
KIRSTIE
LAFITTE
LAYETTE
LEGATEE
LETITBE
MANATEE
MOUNTIE
MUSETTE
NANETTE
NECKTIE
NIGHTIE
OPENTOE
ORNETTE
PALETTE
PHILTRE
PIASTRE
PIPETTE
PRATTLE
RETITLE
ROSETTE
SCEPTRE
SCOTTIE
SCUTTLE
SEATTLE
SHEATHE
SHELTIE
SHUTTLE
SKITTLE
SPECTRE
STARTLE
SUZETTE
SWEETIE
THEATRE
THISTLE
TRESTLE
TRUSTEE
WHISTLE
WHITTLE
WREATHE
WRESTLE
WYNETTE
YANGTZE

•••••TE

ACCRETE
ACETATE
ACOLYTE
ACONITE
ACTUATE
ADAMITE
ADULATE
AGITATE
AIRDATE
ALDENTE
ANDANTE
ANIMATE
ANNETTE
APATITE
ARTISTE
ASTARTE
ATHLETE
ATTRITE
AUGUSTE
AUREATE
AZURITE
BABETTE
BATISTE
BAUXITE
BOXKITE
BROMATE
BURETTE
CADETTE
CALCITE
CELESTE
CILIATE
CITRATE
CLIMATE
COGNATE
COLETTE
COLGATE
COLLATE
COMMUTE
COMPETE
COMPOTE
COMPUTE
CONFUTE
CONNOTE
CORDATE
CORDITE
CULOTTE
CUTRATE
DEFLATE
DENTATE
DEPLETE
DESPITE
DETENTE
DEVIATE
DICTATE
DINETTE
DISPUTE
DUEDATE
DURANTE
EBONITE
EBWHITE
EDUCATE
EGALITE
ELEVATE
EMANATE
EMIRATE
EMULATE
ENROUTE
ENSUITE
ENTENTE
EREMITE
ERUDITE
ESTHETE
EXCRETE
EXECUTE
EXPARTE
EXPIATE
FERRATE
FERRITE
FOLIATE
FRIGATE
GAVOTTE
GAZETTE
GEFILTE
GESTATE
GRANITE
HIRSUTE
HITTITE
HYDRATE
IMAMATE
IMITATE
INFLATE
INGRATE
INHASTE
INSTATE
ISOLATE
ITERATE
JADEITE
KEYNOTE
LABIATE
LACOSTE
LACTATE
LAFITTE
LAPORTE
LAYETTE
LIGNITE
LINEATE
MACHETE
MAGNATE
MAJESTE
MALEATE
MANDATE
MARGATE
MEDIATE
MIGRATE
MISDATE
MISMATE
MODISTE
MUSETTE
NAIVETE
NANETTE
NARRATE
NEONATE
NEWGATE
NITRATE
NITRITE
OBVIATE
OFFSITE
ONADATE
OPERATE
ORIENTE
ORNETTE
OUTVOTE
OVERATE
PALETTE
PALMATE
PAPEETE
PARTITE
PELTATE
PENNATE
PERLITE
PICANTE
PINNATE
PIPETTE
PLACATE
POLLUTE
PREDATE
PRELATE
PRIMATE
PRIVATE
PROBATE
PROMOTE
PRORATE
PULSATE
QUIXOTE
RADIATE
RANLATE
REBASTE
REPASTE
REPLATE
REPLETE
REQUITE
REROUTE
RESPITE
RESTATE
REUNITE
REWRITE
REWROTE
RIPOSTE
ROSEATE
ROSETTE
SATIATE
SEAGATE
SECRETE
SENSATE
SERIATE
SERRATE
SITUATE
SORBATE
STATUTE
STRIATE
SULFATE
SULFITE
SUZETTE
TAXRATE
TEKTITE
TERMITE
TERNATE
TITRATE
TRIBUTE
TRIESTE
ULULATE
UNCRATE
UNQUOTE
UPSTATE
URANITE
VALUATE
VIBRATE
VIOLATE
VITIATE
VULGATE
WEBSITE
WYNETTE

T•F••••

TAFFETA
TAFFIES
TIFFANY
TOFFEES
TOFFLER
TUFFETS
TUFTING

T••F•••

TAFFETA
TAFFIES
TAXFREE
TENFOLD
TENFOUR
TIFFANY
TINFOIL
TOFFEES
TOFFLER
TOMFOOL
TRAFFIC
TREFOIL
TRIFLED
TRIFLER
TRIFLES
TRUFFLE
TUFFETS
TWOFERS
TWOFOLD

T•••F••

TACTFUL
TAILFIN
TANKFUL
TARIFFS
TEARFUL
THRIFTS
THRIFTY
THUSFAR
TIPOFFS
TRAFFIC
TRAYFUL
TRUFFLE
TUNEFUL
TWELFTH

T••••F•

TAILOFF
TAKEOFF
TARIFFS
TEAROFF
TEEDOFF
TEESOFF
TELLOFF
TERRIFY
TESTIFY
TICKOFF
TIMEOFF
TIPOFFS
TIPSOFF
TOLDOFF
TOOKOFF
TOPSOFF
TOREOFF
TOSSOFF
TURNOFF

T•••••F

TAILOFF
TAKEOFF
TEALEAF
TEAROFF
TEEDOFF
TEESOFF
TELLOFF
THEREOF
THINKOF
THYSELF
TICKOFF
TIMEOFF
TIPSOFF
TIREDOF
TOLDOFF
TOOKOFF
TOPSOFF
TOREOFF
TOSSOFF
TURNOFF

•TF••••

ATFAULT

•T•F•••

STAFFED
STAFFER
STIFFED
STIFFEN
STIFFER
STIFFLY
STIFLED
STIFLES
STUFFED
STUFFER

•T••F••

STAFFED
STAFFER
STIFFED
STIFFEN
STIFFER
STIFFLY
STIRFRY
STRAFED
STRAFES
STUFFED
STUFFER

•T•••F•

STOPOFF
STUPEFY

•T••••F

STOPOFF

••TF•••

ANTFARM
ARTFILM
ARTFORM
CATFISH
HOTFOOT
MITFORD
OUTFACE
OUTFITS
OUTFLOW
PITFALL
POTFULS
RATFINK
VATFULS

••T•F••

CUTOFFS
DUTIFUL
FATEFUL
HATEFUL
LATIFAH
LETSFLY
OUTOFIT
PITIFUL
RATAFIA
ROTIFER

••T••F•

BITEOFF
CUTOFFS
CUTSOFF
GETSOFF
LETSOFF
PETRIFY
PUTSOFF
SATISFY
SETSOFF
VITRIFY

••T•••F

BITEOFF
CUTSOFF
GETSOFF
LETSOFF
NETSURF
ONTOPOF
PUTSOFF
SETSOFF

•••TF••

FELTFOR
FISTFUL
FRETFUL
HURTFUL
LUSTFUL
RESTFUL
ROOTFOR
SENTFOR
SHOTFOR
TACTFUL
WENTFOR
WHATFOR
WISTFUL
ZESTFUL

•••T•F•

BEATIFY
CASTOFF
CERTIFY
DISTAFF
DUSTOFF
FORTIFY
GRATIFY
JUSTIFY
KEPTOFF
LEFTOFF
LIFTOFF
MASTIFF
MORTIFY
MUSTAFA
MYSTIFY
PONTIFF
RECTIFY
SANTAFE
SENTOFF
SHUTOFF
TESTIFY
WENTOFF

•••T••F

CASTOFF
DISTAFF
DUSTOFF
KEPTOFF
LEFTOFF
LIFTOFF
MASTIFF
PONTIFF
SENTOFF
SHUTOFF
WENTOFF

••••T•F

SHORTOF

T•G••••

TAGALOG
TAGENDS
TAGGING
TAGLINE
TAGSALE
TAGSOUT
TIGHTEN
TIGHTER
TIGHTLY
TIGRESS
TOGGING
TOGGLED
TOGGLES
TUGBOAT
TUGGERS
TUGGING
TVGUIDE

T••G•••

TAGGING
TANGELO
TANGENT
TANGERE
TANGIER
TANGLED
TANGLES
TANGOED
TARGETS
TINGING
TINGLED
TINGLES
TOGGING
TOGGLED
TOGGLES
TONGANS
TONGUED
TONGUES
TOPGUNS
TOUGHEN
TOUGHER
TOUGHIE
TOUGHLY
TRAGEDY
TRIGGED
TRIGGER
TRIGONS
TRIGRAM
TUGGERS
TUGGING
TUNGOIL

T•••G••

TANAGER
TEARGAS
THOUGHT
TLINGIT
TONIGHT
TRIGGED
TRIGGER
TROUGHS
TRUDGED
TRUDGER
TRUDGES
TSONGAS
TWANGED
TWINGED
TWINGES
TYINGIN
TYINGUP

T••••G•

TAPINGS
TEABAGS
TEENAGE
THRONGS
THROUGH
TIDINGS
TILLAGE
TIMINGS
TONNAGE
TOPDOGS
TOYDOGS
TRILOGY
TUAREGS

T•••••G

TABBING
TABLING
TACKING
TAGALOG
TAGGING
TAILING
TALKBIG
TALKING
TAMPING
TANKING
TANNING
TAPPING
TARRING
TASKING
TASTING
TATTING
TAXIING
TEAMING
TEARING
TEASING
TEDDING
TEEMING
TELLING
TENDING
TENSING
TENTING
TERMING
TESTING
THAWING
TICKING
TIDYING
TIERING
TILLING
TILTING
TIMELAG
TINGING
TINTING
TIPPING
TITHING
TITLING
TOGGING
TOILING
TOLLING
TOOLING
TOOTING
TOPPING
TOSSING
TOTEBAG
TOTTING
TOURING
TOUTING
TRACING
TRADING
TREEING
TRUEING
TUCKING
TUFTING
TUGGING
TURNING
TWINING

•T•G•••

ETAGERE
STAGERS
STAGGED
STAGGER
STAGIER
STAGILY
STAGING
STIGMAS
STOGIES
STYGIAN

•T••G••

ATINGLE
STAGGED
STAGGER
STEIGER
STENGEL
STIEGEL
STINGER
STOOGES
STOPGAP
STUNGUN
STURGES

•T•••G•

ATLARGE
STALAGS
STORAGE
STRANGE
STRINGS
STRINGY

•T••••G

ATONING
ETCHING
ITCHING
STAGING
STAKING
STARING
STATING
STAVING
STAYING
STEWING
STOKING
STONING
STORING
STOWING
STYLING

••TG•••

JETGUNS
OUTGOES
OUTGREW
OUTGROW
OUTGUNS
RUTGERS

••T•G••

ANTIGEN
ANTIGUA
FATIGUE
INTEGER
INTEGRA
LITHGOW
MUTAGEN
OCTAGON
OUTAGES
POTAGES
UPTIGHT

••T••G•

COTTAGE
HOTDOGS
KITBAGS
LITURGY
NUTMEGS
ONTHEGO
OUTINGS
OUTRAGE
POTTAGE
RATINGS
WATTAGE

••T•••G

ANTEING
ANTILOG
ARTSONG
BATHING
BATTING
BATWING
BETTING
BITTING
BUTTING
CATALOG
CATTING
CUTTING
DOTTING
FITTING
GATELEG
GATLING
GETTING
GUTTING
HATTING
HITTING
JETTING
JOTTING
JUTTING
LATHING
LETTING
LOTTING
MATTING
MITRING
NETTING
NOTHING
NUTTING
PATTING
PETTING
PITHING
PITTING
PITYING
POTTING
PUTTING
RATTING
ROTTING
SETTING
SITTING
TATTING
TITHING
TITLING
TOTEBAG
TOTTING
UNTYING
VETOING
VETTING
WETTING
WITTING

•••TG••

RONTGEN
SHOTGUN

•••T•G•

CARTAGE
CORTEGE
COTTAGE
DOGTAGS
FOOTAGE
HOSTAGE
MONTAGE
MONTEGO
NESTEGG
ONSTAGE
PHOTOGS
PORTAGE
POSTAGE
POTTAGE
PROTEGE
RESTAGE
UPSTAGE
VANTAGE
VERTIGO
VESTIGE
VINTAGE
VOLTAGE
WASTAGE
WATTAGE

•••T••G

ABATING
ACHTUNG
BAITING
BASTING
BATTING
BEATING
BELTING
BESTING
BETTING
BITTING
BOATING
BOLTING
BOOTING
BOOTLEG
BUNTING
BUSTING
BUTTING
CANTING
CARTING
CASTING
CATTING
COATING
COSTING
CRATING
CUTTING
DARTING
DENTING
DIETING
DOTTING
DUCTING
DUSTING
EDITING
ELATING
ELUTING
EMOTING
EXITING
FASTING
FITTING
FLUTING
FOOTING
GAITING
GETTING
GRATING
GUSTING
GUTTING
HALTING
HASTING
HATTING
HEATING
HEFTING
HINTING
HITTING
HOOTING
HOSTING
HUNTING
HURTING
JESTING
JETTING
JILTING
JOLTING
JOTTING
JUTTING
KILTING
LASTING
LETTING
LIFTING
LILTING
LISTING
LOFTING
LOOTING
LOTTING
LUSTING
MALTING
MATTING
MEETING
MELTING
MINTING
MISTING
MOLTING
MUSTANG
NESTEGG
NESTING
NETTING
NUTTING
ORATING
OUSTING
PANTING
PARTING
PASTING
PATTING
PEATBOG
PELTING
PETTING
PITTING
PLATING
POSTING
POTTING
POUTING
PRATING
PUNTING
PUTTING
QUOTING
RAFTING
RANTING
RATTING

RENTING
RESTING
RIFTING
RIOTING
ROOTING
ROTTING
ROUTING
RUSTING
SALTING
SEATING
SETTING
SIFTING
SILTING
SITTING
SKATING
SLATING
SMITING
SORTING
SPITING
STATING
SUITING
TASTING
TATTING
TENTING
TESTING
TILTING
TINTING
TOOTING
TOTTING
TOUTING
TUFTING
UNITING
VENTING
VESTING
VETTING
WAFTING
WAITING
WANTING
WARTHOG
WASTING
WELTING
WETTING
WHITING
WILTING
WITTING
WRITING
XRATING
ZEITUNG

••••T•G

FREITAG
NAMETAG

TH•••••

THALERS
THANKED
THATCHY
THATSIT
THAWING
THEATER
THEATRE
THEBABE
THEBLOB
THEDEEP
THEISTS
THEOREM
THERAPY
THEREAT
THEREBY
THEREIN
THEREOF
THEREON
THERESA
THERETO
THERMAL
THERMOS
THEROUX
THESEUS
THESPIS
THICKEN
THICKER
THICKET
THICKLY
THIERRY
THIEVED
THIEVES
THIMBLE
THINAIR
THINICE
THINKER
THINKOF
THINKUP
THINMAN
THINNED
THINNER
THIRDLY
THIRSTS
THIRSTY
THISTLE
THITHER
THOMSON
THOREAU
THORIUM
THOUGHT
THRALLS
THREADS
THREADY
THREATS
THREERS
THREWIN
THRIFTS
THRIFTY
THRILLS
THRIVED
THRIVES
THROATS
THROATY
THRONES
THRONGS
THROUGH
THROWER
THROWIN
THRUSTS
THRUWAY
THUDDED
THULIUM
THUMBED
THUMPED
THUMPER
THUNDER
THURBER
THURMAN
THUSFAR
THWACKS
THWARTS
THYSELF

T•H••••

TEHERAN
TSHIRTS

T••H•••

TARHEEL
TECHIES
TERHUNE
TETHERS
TIGHTEN
TIGHTER
TIGHTLY
TINHATS
TINHORN
TITHERS
TITHING
TOEHOLD
TOPHATS
TOSHIBA
TOWHEAD
TOWHEES
TUCHMAN
TVSHOWS
TYPHOON

T•••H••

TEACHER
TEACHES
TEACHIN
TEASHOP
TEETHED
TEETHER
TEETHES
TEICHER
TETCHED
THITHER
TOESHOE
TOOTHED
TORCHED
TORCHES
TOUCHED
TOUCHES
TOUCHON
TOUCHUP
TOUGHEN
TOUGHER
TOUGHIE
TOUGHLY
TOYSHOP
TRACHEA
TRASHED
TRASHES
TROCHEE
TROCHES
TROPHIC
TROTHED

T••••H•

TABITHA
TALLYHO
TERAPHS
THATCHY
THOUGHT
TIMOTHY
TONIGHT
TROUGHS
TWITCHY

T•••••H

TALLISH
TANNISH
TARNISH
THROUGH
TOWPATH
TRIUMPH
TURKISH
TWELFTH

•TH••••

ATHEART
ATHEISM
ATHEIST
ATHIRST
ATHLETE
ATHOMES
ATHWART
ETHANOL
ETHICAL
ETHNICS
ITHACAN
OTHELLO

•T•H•••

ETCHERS
ETCHING
ITCHIER
ITCHING
UTAHANS

•T••H••

STASHED
STASHES
STEPHEN
STICHES
STJOHNS

•T•••H•

ATROPHY
ATTACHE
STARCHY
STROPHE
UTRECHT

•T••••H

STAUNCH
STEALTH
STOMACH
STRETCH
STYLISH

••TH•••

ANTHEMS
ANTHERS
ANTHILL
ANTHONY
AUTHORS
BATHERS
BATHING
BATHMAT
BATHOIL
BATHTUB
BETHANY
BETHELS
BETHINK
BOTHERS
BOTHNIA
BYTHEBY
CATHAIR
CATHEAD
CATHODE
DITHERS
DITHERY
ENTHUSE
ESTHETE
FATHEAD
FATHERS
FATHOMS
GATHERS
GOTHICS
GUTHRIE
HITHERE
HOTHEAD
ISTHMUS
KATHRYN
LATHERS
LATHERY
LATHING
LITHELY
LITHEST
LITHGOW
LITHIUM
MATHERS
MATHEWS
MATHIAS
METHANE
METHODS
MITHRAS
MOTHERS
NOTHING
NOTHOME
ONTHEGO
ONTHEQT
OUTHITS
PATHWAY
PITHIER
PITHILY
PITHING
POTHERB
POTHERS
POTHOLE
POTHOOK
PYTHIAS
PYTHONS
RATHOLE
RETHINK
SOTHERE
SOTHERN
TETHERS
TITHERS
TITHING
WETHERS
WITHERS
WITHOUT
ZITHERS

••T•H••

AITCHES
BATCHED
BATCHES
BOTCHED
BOTCHES
BUTCHER
CATCHER
CATCHES
CATCHON
CATCHUP
DITCHED
DITCHES
FETCHED
FETCHES
FITCHES
GOTCHAS
HATCHED
HATCHER
HATCHES
HATCHET
HITCHED
HITCHER
HITCHES
HOTSHOT
HUTCHES
KETCHAM
KETCHES
KETCHUP
KITCHEN
LATCHED
LATCHES
LITCHIS
MATCHED
MATCHES
MATCHUP
MATTHAU
MATTHEW
MITCHUM
NATCHEZ
NOTCHED
NOTCHES
PATCHED
PATCHES
PATCHUP
PITCHED
PITCHER
PITCHES
PITCHIN
POTSHOT
RATCHET
RITCHIE
SATCHEL
SATCHMO
TETCHED
VETCHES
WATCHED
WATCHER
WATCHES
WATCHIT
WITCHES
YITZHAK

••T••H•

ATTACHE
HITACHI
KITSCHY
MATZOHS
NATASHA
UPTIGHT
VOTECHS

••T•••H

ANTIOCH
BETROTH
CATFISH
CATTISH
INTRUTH
JETWASH
LATIFAH
MITZVAH
OSTRICH
PETTISH
RETEACH
RETOUCH
UNTRUTH

•••TH••

ANOTHER
APOTHEM
BENTHAM
BERTHED
BIRTHED
BLATHER
BLITHER
BROTHER
CHATHAM
CLOTHED
CLOTHES
CYNTHIA
EARTHEN
EARTHLY
EPITHET
FARTHER
FEATHER
FROTHED
FURTHER
GODTHAB
GUNTHER
HEATHEN
HEATHER
LEATHER
LOATHED
LOATHES
MALTHUS
MATTHAU
MATTHEW
MENTHOL
MONTHLY
MOUTHED
NARTHEX
NEITHER
NORTHER
PANTHER
PORTHOS
POSTHOC
PRITHEE
REUTHER
RHYTHMS
SCATHED
SCATHES
SCYTHED
SCYTHES
SEETHED
SEETHES
SLATHER
SLITHER
SMOTHER
SOOTHED
SOOTHER
SOOTHES
SOUTHEY
SWATHED
SWATHES
TEETHED
TEETHER
TEETHES
THITHER
TOOTHED
TROTHED
WARTHOG
WEATHER
WERTHER
WHETHER
WHITHER
WRITHED
WRITHES
XANTHAN
XANTHIC

•••T•H•

BLOTCHY
HOOTCHY
KOOTCHY
SKETCHY
THATCHY
TWITCHY

•••T••H

BRITISH
BRUTISH
CALTECH
CATTISH
COLTISH
CULTISH
DIPTYCH
DOLTISH
GOATISH
KLATSCH
LOWTECH
PETTISH
WHITISH

••••TH•

ACANTHI
BREATHE
BREATHS
BREATHY
BYPATHS
DEARTHS
DOROTHY
EIGHTHS
EMPATHY
EOLITHS
FOURTHS
GROWTHS
HEALTHY
HEARTHS
IOMOTHS
LENGTHS
LENGTHY
LESOTHO
NAPHTHA
OOLITHS
ORNITHO
PLINTHS
SHEATHE
SHEATHS
SLEUTHS
SMOOTHS
SWARTHY
TABITHA
TIMOTHY
WEALTHY
WRAITHS
WREATHE
WREATHS
ZENITHS

••••T•H

BEWITCH
CHEETAH
GODUTCH
INDUTCH
SCRATCH
SPLOTCH
STRETCH
UNHITCH
UNLATCH
WASATCH

•••••TH

ALWORTH
AZIMUTH
BENEATH
BETROTH
BISMUTH
BREADTH
CORINTH
DOZENTH
FORSYTH
GOLIATH
HOGARTH
INDEPTH
INTRUTH
JAPHETH
KENNETH
KLAMATH
MACBETH
MAMMOTH
NCWYETH
NEOLITH
NEWMATH
REBIRTH
RUNWITH
SABBATH
SEVENTH
SOPWITH
STEALTH
SUNBATH
TOWPATH
TWELFTH
UNCOUTH
UNEARTH
UNTRUTH
WARPATH

TI•••••

TIBETAN
TICKERS
TICKETS
TICKING
TICKLED
TICKLER
TICKLES
TICKOFF
TICTACS
TIDBITS
TIDIEST
TIDINGS
TIDYING
TIECLIP
TIEDOWN
TIEDYED
TIEDYES
TIEINTO
TIELESS
TIELINE
TIEPINS
TIERACK
TIERING
TIERNEY
TIERODS
TIETACK
TIFFANY
TIGHTEN
TIGHTER
TIGHTLY
TIGRESS
TIJUANA
TILLAGE
TILLERS
TILLING
TILTERS
TILTING
TIMBALE
TIMBALS
TIMBERS
TIMBRES
TIMECOP
TIMELAG
TIMEOFF
TIMEOUT
TIMESUP
TIMEWAS
TIMIDER
TIMIDLY
TIMINGS
TIMMINS
TIMOTHY
TINCANS
TINDERS
TINEARS
TINFOIL
TINGING
TINGLED
TINGLES
TINHATS
TINHORN
TINIEST
TINKERS
TINKLED
TINKLES
TINNERS
TINNIER
TINNILY
TINSELS
TINSTAR
TINTERN
TINTERS
TINTING
TINTYPE
TINWORK
TINYTIM
TIOMKIN
TIPOFFS
TIPPERS
TIPPETS
TIPPING
TIPPLED
TIPPLER
TIPPLES
TIPSIER
TIPSILY
TIPSOFF
TIPSTER
TIPTOED
TIPTOES
TIPTOPS
TIRADES
TIREDER
TIREDLY
TIREDOF
TIREOUT
TISANES
TISSUES
TITANIA
TITANIC
TITBITS
TITHERS
TITHING
TITLING
TITLIST
TITMICE
TITRATE
TITTERS
TITTLES
TITULAR
TIZZIES

T•I••••

TAILEND
TAILFIN
TAILING
TAILLES
TAILOFF
TAILORS
TAINTED
TAIPANS
TBILISI
TEICHER
THICKEN
THICKER
THICKET
THICKLY
THIERRY
THIEVED
THIEVES
THIMBLE
THINAIR
THINICE
THINKER
THINKOF
THINKUP
THINMAN
THINNED
THINNER
THIRDLY
THIRSTS
THIRSTY
THISTLE
THITHER
TLINGIT
TOILERS
TOILETS
TOILING
TRIBUNE
TRIBUTE
TRICEPS
TRICKED
TRICKER
TRICKLE
TRICORN
TRICOTS
TRIDENT
TRIEDON
TRIESON
TRIESTE
TRIFLED
TRIFLER
TRIFLES
TRIGGED
TRIGGER
TRIGONS
TRIGRAM
TRILLED
TRILLIN
TRILOGY
TRIMMED
TRIMMER
TRINITY
TRINKET
TRIODES
TRIPLED
TRIPLES
TRIPLET
TRIPLEX
TRIPODS
TRIPOLI
TRIPPED
TRIPPER
TRIPPET
TRIPSUP
TRIREME
TRISECT
TRISTAN
TRITELY
TRITEST
TRITIUM
TRITONE
TRITONS
TRIUMPH
TRIUNES
TRIVETS
TRIVIAL
TUITION
TWIDDLE
TWILLED
TWINBED
TWINGED
TWINGES
TWINING
TWINKLE
TWINKLY
TWINNED
TWIRLED
TWIRLER
TWISTED
TWISTER
TWITCHY
TWITTED
TWITTER
TYINGIN
TYINGUP

T••I•••

TABITHA
TACITLY
TACITUS
TAOISTS
TAPINGS
TAPIOCA
TARIFFS
TATIANA
TAXICAB
TAXIING
TAXIWAY
TEDIOUS
TEPIDLY
THEISTS
THRIFTS
THRIFTY
THRILLS
THRIVED
THRIVES
TIDIEST
TIDINGS
TIEINTO
TIMIDER
TIMIDLY
TIMINGS
TINIEST
TONIEST
TONIGHT
TOPIARY
TOPICAL
TRAILED
TRAILER
TRAINED
TRAINEE
TRAINER
TRAIPSE
TRAITOR
TROIKAS
TROILUS
TRUISMS
TSHIRTS
TUBISTS
TUNICLE
TUNISIA
TYPICAL
TYPISTS

T•••I••

TABBIES
TABBING
TABLING
TACKIER
TACKILY
TACKING
TACTICS
TACTILE
TAFFIES
TAGGING
TAGLINE
TAILING
TALKIES
TALKING
TALLIED
TALLIES
TALLISH
TAMPICO
TAMPING
TANGIER
TANKING
TANLINE
TANNING
TANNINS
TANNISH
TANSIES
TAPPING
TARDIER
TARDILY
TARNISH
TARPITS
TARRIED
TARRIES
TARRING
TARSIER
TASKING
TASTIER
TASTILY
TASTING
TATTIER
TATTING
TAURINE
TAWNIER
TAXIING
TBILISI
TEAMING
TEARIER
TEARILY
TEARING
TEASING
TEATIME
TECHIES
TEDDIES
TEDDING
TEEMING
TEENIER
TEKTITE
TELLIES
TELLING
TENDING
TENNIEL
TENPINS
TENSILE
TENSING
TENSION
TENSIVE
TENTING
TEQUILA
TERBIUM
TERMING
TERMINI
TERMITE
TERRIER
TERRIES
TERRIFY
TERTIAL
TESTIER
TESTIFY
TESTILY
TESTING
TEXTILE
THAWING
THINICE

THORIUM
THULIUM
TICKING
TIDBITS
TIDYING
TIELINE
TIEPINS
TIERING
TILLING
TILTING
TIMMINS
TINGING
TINNIER
TINNILY
TINTING
TIPPING
TIPSIER
TIPSILY
TITBITS
TITHING
TITLING
TITLIST
TITMICE
TIZZIES
TOADIED
TOADIES
TOCSINS
TODDIES
TOGGING
TOILING
TOLKIEN
TOLLING
TOMTITS
TONSILS
TONTINE
TOOLING
TOOTING
TOPKICK
TOPPING
TOPSIDE
TOROIDS
TORSION
TORYISM
TOSHIBA
TOSSING
TOTTING
TOURING
TOURISM
TOURIST
TOUTING
TOWNIES
TRACING
TRADING
TREEING
TREVINO
TRINITY
TRITIUM
TRIVIAL
TROPICS
TROPISM
TRUCIAL
TRUEING
TSARINA
TSARIST
TSELIOT
TUBAIST
TUBBIER
TUCKING
TUFTING
TUGGING
TUITION
TUMMIES
TUNNIES
TURBINE
TURKISH
TURNING
TURNIPS
TVGUIDE
TWINING
TWOBITS
TWOTIME
TZARINA

T••••I•

TABLOID
TAILFIN
TAKEAIM
TAKENIN
TAKESIN
TALARIA
TALKBIG
TAMARIN
TATAMIS
TEACHIN
TELAVIV
TENDRIL
TERRAIN
THATSIT
THEREIN
THESPIS
THINAIR
THREWIN
THROWIN
TIECLIP
TINFOIL
TINYTIM
TIOMKIN
TITANIA
TITANIC
TLINGIT
TOENAIL
TOOTSIE
TOPSAIL
TOPSOIL
TOTEMIC
TOUGHIE
TRADEIN
TRAFFIC
TRANSIT
TRAVAIL
TRAVOIS
TREFOIL
TREKKIE
TRELLIS
TRILLIN
TROPHIC
TUCKSIN
TUNEDIN
TUNESIN
TUNGOIL
TUNISIA
TURMOIL
TURNSIN
TYINGIN

T•••••I

TBILISI
TERMINI
TOLSTOI
TOPKAPI
TORTONI
TRIPOLI
TSUNAMI
TYMPANI

•TI••••

ATINGLE
ATISSUE
ETIENNE
STICHES
STICKER
STICKTO
STICKUP
STIEGEL
STIFFED
STIFFEN
STIFFER
STIFFLY
STIFLED
STIFLES
STIGMAS
STILLED
STILLER
STILTED
STILTON
STIMULI
STINGER
STINKER
STINTED
STIPEND
STIPPLE
STIRFRY
STIRRED
STIRRER
STIRRUP
STIRSIN
STIRSUP
UTILITY
UTILIZE

•T•I•••

ATHIRST
ATRIUMS
ATTICUS
ATTIMES
ATTIRED
ATTIRES
ETHICAL
ETOILES
STAIDER
STAIDLY
STAINED
STAINER
STEIGER
STEINEM
STEINER
STKITTS
STOICAL
STRIATE
STRIDER
STRIDES
STRIKER
STRIKES
STRINGS
STRINGY
STRIPED
STRIPER
STRIPES
STRIVED
STRIVEN
STRIVER
STRIVES
UTRILLO

•T••I••

ATAVISM
ATAVIST
ATELIER
ATHEISM
ATHEIST
ATOMIES
ATOMIZE
ATONING
ATTAINS
ATTRITE
ATTRITS
ETAMINE
ETCHING
ETESIAN
ETHNICS
ETONIAN
ITALIAN
ITALICS
ITCHIER
ITCHING
ITEMIZE
STABILE
STADIUM
STAGIER
STAGILY
STAGING
STAKING
STAMINA
STARING
STATICE
STATICS
STATING
STATION
STATIST
STAVING
STAYING
STEPINS
STERILE
STEWING
STOGIES
STOKING
STONIER
STONILY
STONING
STORIED
STORIES
STORING
STOWING
STRAINS
STRAITS
STUDIED
STUDIES
STUDIOS
STYGIAN
STYLING
STYLISH
STYLIST
STYLIZE
STYMIED
STYMIES
STYRIAN
UTILITY
UTILIZE
UTOPIAN
UTOPIAS
YTTRIUM

•T•••I•

ETRURIA
KTOSLIN
STANDIN
STANNIC
STARLIT
STCROIX
STDENIS
STEELIE
STENCIL
STEPSIN
STEROID
STIRSIN
STLOUIS
STLUCIA
STOODIN
STOOLIE
STOPSIN
STYPTIC
UTENSIL

•T••••I

STIMULI

••TI•••

ACTINIC
ACTIONS
ACTIVES
ANTIART
ANTIBES
ANTIGEN
ANTIGUA
ANTILOG
ANTIOCH
ANTIQUE
ANTIWAR
ARTICLE
ARTIEST
ARTISAN
ARTISTE
ARTISTS
ATTICUS
ATTIMES
ATTIRED
ATTIRES
BATIKED
BATISTA
BATISTE
BETIDED
BETIDES
BETIMES
CATIONS
CITIZEN
CUTICLE
CUTINTO
DUTIFUL
ENTICED
ENTICER
ENTICES
ENTITLE
ESTIVAL
EXTINCT
FATIGUE
FETIDLY
GETINTO
GETITON
GOTINTO
LATICES
LATIFAH
LATINAS
LATINOS
LETINON
LETITBE
LETITIA
LITINTO
LOTIONS
LUTISTS
MATILDA
MATINEE
MATISSE
METIERS
MOTIONS
MOTIVES
NATIONS
NATIVES
NOTICED
NOTICES
NOTIONS
OPTICAL
OPTIMAL
OPTIMUM
OPTIONS
OUTINGS
PATIENT
PATINAS
PETIOLE
PETITES
PITIFUL
POTIONS
PUTITTO
RATINGS
RATIONS
RATITES
RETICLE
RETILED
RETILES
RETIMED
RETIMES
RETINAE
RETINAL
RETINAS
RETINUE
RETIRED
RETIREE
RETIRES
RETITLE
ROTIFER
SATIATE
SATIETY
SATIRES
SATIRIC
SATISFY
SETINTO
SHTICKS
TATIANA
UPTICKS
UPTIGHT
USTINOV
VATICAN
VITIATE

••T•I••

ANTEING
ANTHILL
ANTLION
ANTOINE
ANTSIER
ARTFILM
ASTAIRE
ASTRIDE
ATTAINS
ATTRITE
ATTRITS
BATHING
BATTIER
BATTING
BATWING
BETHINK
BETTING
BETWIXT
BITTIER
BITTING
BUTTING
CATBIRD
CATFISH
CATKINS
CATLIKE
CATNIPS
CATTIER
CATTILY
CATTING
CATTISH
CITRINE
CUTTIME
CUTTING
DETAILS
DETAINS
DITTIES
DOTTIER
DOTTING
ENTAILS
ENTRIES
ENTWINE
FATCITY
FATUITY
FITTING
GATLING
GETTING
GOTHICS
GUTSIER
GUTSILY
GUTTING
HATPINS
HATTING
HITLIST
HITTING
HITTITE
HOTLINE
HOTLIPS
HOTTIPS
HOTWIRE
INTUITS
JETTIES
JETTING
JOTTING
JUTTING
KITTIES
LATHING
LATTICE
LATVIAN
LETTING
LITHIUM
LOTTING
MATHIAS
MATTING
METRICS
MITRING
NATRIUM
NATTIER
NATTILY
NETTING
NITPICK
NITRIDE
NITRITE
NITWITS
NOTHING
NUTRIAS
NUTTIER
NUTTILY
NUTTING
OBTAINS
ONTRIAL
OSTRICH
OUTBIDS
OUTFITS
OUTHITS
OUTLINE
OUTLIVE
OUTSIDE
OUTSIZE
OUTWITS
PATRICE
PATRICK
PATRIOT
PATSIES
PATTIES
PATTING
PETRIFY
PETTIER
PETTILY
PETTING
PETTISH
PITHIER
PITHILY
PITHING
PITTING
PITYING
POTPIES
POTTING
PUTTIED
PUTTIES
PUTTING
PYTHIAS
RATFINK
RATLINE
RATTIER
RATTING
RETAILS
RETAINS
RETHINK
RETRIAL
RETRIED
RETRIES
RETRIMS
RETSINA
RITZIER
ROTTING
SETLINE
SETTING
SITTING
TATTIER
TATTING
TITBITS
TITHING
TITLING
TITLIST
TITMICE
TOTTING
UNTRIED
UNTWIST
UNTYING
VETOING
VETTING
VITRIFY
VITRIOL
WETTING
WITTIER
WITTILY
WITTING
YTTRIUM

••T••I•

ACTINIC
ANTACID
ANTONIA
ANTONIN
ANTONIO
ARTEMIS
ASTORIA
BATHOIL
BOTHNIA
BUTTSIN
CATHAIR
CATTAIL
COTERIE
DETRAIN
DETROIT
ENTRAIN
ESTONIA
ESTORIL
GUTHRIE
INTERIM
INTROIT
KATYDID
LETITIA
LETSLIP
LITCHIS
MITOSIS
MITOTIC
MUTATIS
NATALIA
NATALIE
NOTABIT
OCTAVIA
ONTARIO
OSTEOID
OUTLAID
OUTOFIT
PETUNIA
PITCHIN
RATAFIA
RATTAIL
RETRAIN
RITCHIE
SATIRIC
SETSAIL
TATAMIS
TITANIA
TITANIC
TOTEMIC
VITAMIN
VOTESIN
WATCHIT
WETSUIT

••T•••I

HITACHI
KUTENAI

•••TI••

ABATING
AIRTIME
ALLTIME
AMATIVE
ANYTIME
APATITE
AUCTION
AUNTIES
BAITING
BAPTISM
BAPTIST
BAPTIZE
BASTING
BASTION
BATTIER
BATTING
BEATIFY
BEATING
BEDTIME
BELTING
BESTIAL
BESTING
BESTIRS
BETTING
BIGTIME
BITTIER
BITTING
BOATING
BOLTING
BOOTIES
BOOTING
BOWTIES
BRITISH
BRUTISH
BUNTING
BUSTING
BUTTING
BUYTIME
CANTINA
CANTING
CAPTION
CAPTIVE
CARTIER
CARTING
CASTILE
CASTING
CATTIER
CATTILY
CATTING
CATTISH
CAUTION
CELTICS
CENTIME
CENTIMO
CERTIFY
COATING
COLTISH
COOTIES
COSTING
CRATING
CRETINS
CRITICS
CULTISH
CULTISM
CULTIST
CUTTIME
CUTTING
DARTING
DAYTIME
DEITIES
DENTINE
DENTING
DENTIST
DESTINE
DESTINY
DICTION
DIETING
DIRTIED
DIRTIER
DIRTIES
DIRTILY
DISTILL
DITTIES
DOLTISH
DOTTIER
DOTTING
DUCTILE
DUCTING
DUSTIER
DUSTING
EBBTIDE
EDITING
EDITION
EGOTISM
EGOTIST
ELATING
ELATION
ELITISM
ELITIST
ELUTING
ELUTION
EMOTING
EMOTION
EMOTIVE
EMPTIED
EMPTIER
EMPTIES
EMPTILY
EROTICA
EXITING
EXOTICA
EXOTICS
FACTION
FASTING
FERTILE
FESTIVE
FICTION
FICTIVE
FIFTIES
FITTING
FLUTING
FLUTIST
FONTINA
FOOTING
FORTIES
FORTIFY
FURTIVE
FUSTIAN
FUSTICS
FUSTIER
FUSTILY
GAITING
GENTIAN
GENTILE
GETTING
GOATISH
GRATIFY
GRATING
GUSTILY
GUSTING
GUTTING
HAITIAN
HALTING
HASTIER
HASTILY
HASTING
HATTING
HEATING
HEFTIER
HEFTILY
HEFTING
HINTING
HITTING
HITTITE
HOGTIED
HOGTIES
HOOTING
HOSTILE
HOSTING
HOTTIPS
HUNTING
HURTING
INITIAL
INSTILL
INSTILS
INUTILE
JESTING
JETTIES
JETTING
JILTING
JOLTING
JOTTING
JUSTICE
JUSTIFY
JUSTINE
JUTTING
KILTIES
KILTING
KITTIES
KONTIKI
KRATION
LAOTIAN
LASTING
LATTICE
LEETIDE
LEFTIES
LEFTIST
LENTILS
LETTING
LIFTING
LILTING
LINTIER
LISTING
LOFTIER
LOFTILY
LOFTING
LOOTING
LOTTING
LOWTIDE
LUSTIER
LUSTILY
LUSTING
MALTING
MARTIAL
MARTIAN
MARTINA
MARTINI
MARTINO
MARTINS
MASTICS
MASTIFF
MATTING
MAYTIME
MEATIER
MEETING
MELTING
MENTION
MESTIZO
MINTIER
MINTING
MISTIER
MISTILY
MISTING
MOLTING
MORTIFY
MORTISE
MUNTINS
MUSTIER
MUSTILY
MYSTICS
MYSTIFY
NAPTIME
NASTIER
NASTILY
NATTIER
NATTILY
NESTING
NETTING
NIFTIER
NIFTILY
NOETICS
NUPTIAL
NUTTIER
NUTTILY
NUTTING
OLDTIME
ONETIME
ORATING
ORATION
OUSTING
OVATION
PANTING
PARTIAL
PARTIED
PARTIES
PARTING
PARTITA
PARTITE
PASTIER
PASTIME
PASTINA
PASTING
PATTIES
PATTING
PECTINS
PELTING
PEPTIDE
PETTIER
PETTILY
PETTING
PETTISH
PIETIES
PIETINS
PIETISM
PISTILS
PITTING
PLATING
POETICS
POITIER
PONTIAC
PONTIFF
PONTINE
PONTIUS
PORTICO
PORTION
POSTING
POTTING
POUTIER
POUTING
PRATING
PROTIST
PUNTING
PUTTIED
PUTTIES
PUTTING
QUOTING
RAFTING
RAGTIME
RANTING
RATTIER
RATTING
RECTIFY
RENTING
REPTILE
RESTING
RESTIVE
RIFTING
RIOTING
RIPTIDE
ROOTING
ROTTING
ROUTINE
ROUTING
RUCTION
RUNTIER
RUSTICS

RUSTIER
RUSTILY
RUSTING
SALTIER
SALTILY
SALTINE
SALTING
SANTINI
SANTIRS
SEATING
SECTION
SESTINA
SETTING
SIFTING
SILTING
SISTINE
SITTING
SIXTIES
SKATING
SLATIER
SLATING
SMITING
SOFTIES
SOOTIER
SORTIED
SORTIES
SORTING
SPATIAL
SPITING
STATICE
STATICS
STATING
STATION
STATIST
SUCTION
SUITING
TACTICS
TACTILE
TASTIER
TASTILY
TASTING
TATTIER
TATTING
TEATIME
TEKTITE
TENTING
TERTIAL
TESTIER
TESTIFY
TESTILY
TESTING
TEXTILE
TILTING
TINTING
TOMTITS
TONTINE
TOOTING
TOTTING
TOUTING
TRITIUM
TUFTING
TUITION
TWOTIME
UNCTION
UNITIES
UNITING
UNITIVE
UNSTICK
VENTING
VERTIGO
VESTIGE
VESTING
VETTING
VICTIMS
WAFTING
WAITING
WANTING
WARTIME
WASTING
WELTING
WETTING
WHITING
WHITISH
WILTING
WITTIER
WITTILY
WITTING
WRITING
XRATING
ZESTIER

•••T•I•

ABSTAIN
AUSTRIA
BEATNIK
BEATRIX
BEATSIT
BEATTIE
BOBTAIL
BRITAIN
BUTTSIN
CAPTAIN
CATTAIL
CENTRIC
CERTAIN
CONTAIN
COSTAIN
CURTAIL
CURTAIN
CYNTHIA
DAYTRIP
DELTAIC
DELTOID
DEXTRIN
EGOTRIP
EPSTEIN
FANTAIL
FOOTSIE
FOXTAIL
GASTRIC
GLOTTIS
HOPTOIT
MAITAIS
MANTRIC
MASTOID
NOSTRIL
PERTAIN
PIGTAIL
PINTAIL
PROTEIN
RATTAIL
RESTAIN
SCOTTIE
SEETOIT
SHUTSIN
SLATKIN
SPOTLIT
SPUTNIK
SUSTAIN
THATSIT
TOOTSIE
VOLTAIC
WAGTAIL
WANTSIN
WRITEIN
WROTEIN
XANTHIC
YELTSIN

•••T••I

AIRTAXI
KONTIKI
MARTINI
PLATYPI
SANTINI
TORTONI

••••TI•

AGOUTIS
AQUATIC
ASCETIC
ASEPTIC
ASIATIC
BEASTIE
BEATTIE
BOLOTIE
BUILTIN
CAROTID
CAUSTIC
CHAOTIC
CROATIA
CRYPTIC
DEALTIN
DRASTIC
ELASTIC
ERISTIC
ERRATIC
FANATIC
FOULTIP
FRANTIC
GALATIA
GELATIN
GELATIS
GENETIC
GLOTTIS
GNOSTIC
HAMITIC
HEPATIC
HERETIC
HORATIO
IDENTIC
IDIOTIC
INERTIA
KERATIN
KINETIC
KIRSTIE
LETITIA
LUNATIC
MEIOTIC
MILITIA
MIMETIC
MINUTIA
MITOTIC
MOUNTIE
MUTATIS
NECKTIE
NIGHTIE
OSMOTIC
PIRATIC
PLASTIC
POLITIC
QUENTIN
ROBOTIC
RUBITIN
SCOTTIE
SEMITIC
SHELTIE
SKEPTIC
SLEPTIN
SOMATIC
STYPTIC
SWEETIE
TINYTIM
WAPITIS
WINGTIP

••••T•I

ACANTHI
DIMITRI
MAESTRI
MENOTTI
SCHATZI
SHASTRI
TOLSTOI

•••••TI

ASHANTI
CHAPATI
CHIANTI
CHRISTI
DELICTI
ELMISTI
EMERITI
HAVARTI
KUWAITI
MENOTTI

T•J••••

TIJUANA

T••J•••

TROJANS

•TJ••••

STJOHNS

••TJ•••

OUTJUMP

•••TJ••

CULTJAM

T•K••••

TAKEAIM
TAKENIN
TAKENON
TAKEOFF
TAKEONE
TAKEOUT
TAKESIN
TAKESON
TAKESTO
TAKESUP
TAKETEN
TEKTITE
TOKENED

T••K•••

TACKERS
TACKIER
TACKILY
TACKING
TACKLED
TACKLER
TACKLES
TACKSON
TALKBIG
TALKERS
TALKIES
TALKING
TALKOUT
TALKSAT
TALKSTO
TALKSUP
TANKARD
TANKERS
TANKFUL
TANKING
TANKSUP
TANKTOP
TASKING
TICKERS
TICKETS
TICKING
TICKLED
TICKLER
TICKLES
TICKOFF
TINKERS
TINKLED
TINKLES
TOLKIEN
TOOKOFF
TOOKOUT
TOOKTEN
TOPKAPI
TOPKICK
TOPKNOT
TREKKED
TREKKER
TREKKIE
TUCKERS
TUCKING
TUCKSIN
TURKEYS
TURKISH
TUSKERS

T•••K••

THANKED
THICKEN
THICKER
THICKET
THICKLY
THINKER
THINKOF
THINKUP
TIOMKIN
TRACKED
TRACKER
TREKKED
TREKKER
TREKKIE
TRICKED
TRICKER
TRICKLE
TRINKET
TROIKAS
TRUCKED
TRUCKEE
TRUCKER
TRUCKLE
TURNKEY
TWEAKED
TWINKLE
TWINKLY

T••••K•

TANOAKS
TEACAKE
THWACKS
TROTSKY

T•••••K

TEDMACK
TIERACK
TIETACK
TINWORK
TOPKICK
TUSSOCK

•TK••••

STKITTS

•T•K•••

STAKING
STOKELY
STOKERS
STOKING

•T••K••

STACKED
STACKUP
STALKED
STALKER
STARKER
STARKLY
STICKER
STICKTO
STICKUP
STINKER
STOCKED
STOCKUP
STOOKEY
STRIKER
STRIKES
STROKED
STROKES
STUCKTO
STUCKUP

•T•••K•

ATSTAKE
ATTACKS
ATTUCKS
STREAKS
STREAKY

•T••••K

ATATURK

••TK•••

CATKINS

••T•K••

BATIKED
BETAKEN
BETAKES
BETOKEN
INTAKES
PATAKES
RETAKEN
RETAKES
UPTAKES

••T••K•

ATTACKS
ATTUCKS
CATLIKE
HOTCAKE
NETSUKE
OUTTAKE
SHTICKS
UNTACKS
UPTICKS

••T•••K

ARTWORK
BETHINK
CATWALK
CUTBACK
FATBACK
FETLOCK
GETBACK
GOTBACK
HATRACK
MATLOCK
MATTOCK
NETWORK
NITPICK
OUTBACK
OUTLOOK
OUTRANK
OUTTALK
OUTWORK
PATRICK
PETCOCK
PETROCK
POTHOOK
POTLUCK
RATFINK
RATPACK
RETHINK
RETRACK
SETBACK
YITZHAK
ZATOPEK

•••TK••

SLATKIN

•••T•K•

ATSTAKE
GRETZKY
KONTIKI
MISTAKE
OUTTAKE
PARTAKE
TROTSKY

•••T••K

ATATURK
BEATNIK
INSTOCK
MATTOCK
MISTOOK
OUTTALK
PARTOOK
PEPTALK
RESTOCK
SPUTNIK
TIETACK
UNSTACK
UNSTICK
UNSTUCK

••••T•K

OKHOTSK
YAKUTSK

TL•••••

TLINGIT

T•L••••

TALARIA
TALENTS
TALKBIG
TALKERS
TALKIES
TALKING
TALKOUT
TALKSAT
TALKSTO
TALKSUP
TALLEST
TALLIED
TALLIES
TALLISH
TALLOWS
TALLYHO
TALLYUP
TALONED
TALUSES
TELAVIV
TELERAN
TELEXED
TELEXES
TELLALL
TELLERS
TELLIES
TELLING
TELLOFF
TELLSON
TELSTAR
TILLAGE
TILLERS
TILLING
TILTERS
TILTING
TOLDOFF
TOLKIEN
TOLLING
TOLLWAY
TOLSTOI
TOLSTOY
TOLTECS
TOLUENE
TULSANS
TYLENOL

T••L•••

TABLEAU
TABLETS
TABLING
TABLOID
TAGLINE
TAILEND
TAILFIN
TAILING
TAILLES
TAILOFF
TAILORS
TALLEST
TALLIED
TALLIES
TALLISH
TALLOWS
TALLYHO
TALLYUP
TANLINE
TBILISI
TEALEAF
TELLALL
TELLERS
TELLIES
TELLING
TELLOFF
TELLSON
THALERS
THULIUM
TIELESS
TIELINE
TILLAGE
TILLERS
TILLING
TITLING
TITLIST
TOELESS
TOELOOP
TOILERS
TOILETS
TOILING
TOLLING
TOLLWAY
TOOLBOX
TOOLING
TOOLSUP
TOYLAND
TRALALA
TRELLIS
TRILLED
TRILLIN
TRILOGY
TROLLED
TROLLEY
TSELIOT
TWELFTH
TWELVES
TWILLED

T•••L••

TABULAR
TACKLED
TACKLER
TACKLES
TAGALOG
TAILLES
TAMALES
TANGLED
TANGLES
TATTLED
TATTLER
TATTLES
TEMBLOR
TEMPLAR
TEMPLES
THEBLOB
THRALLS
THRILLS
TICKLED
TICKLER
TICKLES
TIECLIP
TIMELAG
TINGLED
TINGLES
TINKLED
TINKLES
TIPPLED
TIPPLER
TIPPLES
TITTLES
TITULAR
TODDLED
TODDLER
TODDLES
TOFFLER
TOGGLED
TOGGLES
TONALLY
TONELOC
TOOTLED
TOOTLES
TOPPLED
TOPPLES
TOTALED
TOTALLY
TOUSLED
TOUSLES
TOWELED
TRAILED
TRAILER
TRAWLED
TRAWLER
TREBLED
TREBLES
TRELLIS
TRIFLED
TRIFLER
TRIFLES
TRILLED
TRILLIN
TRIPLED
TRIPLES
TRIPLET
TRIPLEX
TROILUS
TROLLED
TROLLEY
TUBULAR
TUMBLED
TUMBLER
TUMBLES
TUMULTS
TUMULUS
TUPELOS
TURTLED
TURTLES
TUSSLED
TUSSLES
TUTELAR
TWILLED
TWIRLED
TWIRLER

T••••L•

TACITLY
TACKILY
TACTILE
TADPOLE
TAGSALE
TAMABLE
TAMBALA
TANGELO
TARBELL
TARDILY
TARSALS
TASSELS
TASTILY
TAXABLE
TEABALL
TEARILY
TEASELS
TELLALL
TENABLE
TENABLY
TENFOLD
TENSELY
TENSILE
TEPIDLY
TEQUILA
TERCELS
TERSELY
TESTILY
TEXTILE
THICKLY
THIMBLE
THIRDLY
THISTLE
THRALLS
THRILLS
THYSELF
TIGHTLY
TIMBALE
TIMBALS
TIMIDLY
TINNILY
TINSELS
TIPSILY
TIREDLY
TOEHOLD
TONALLY
TONSILS
TOOTALL
TOSCALE
TOTALLY
TOUGHLY
TRALALA
TRAMPLE
TRAVELS
TREACLE
TREACLY
TREADLE
TREMBLE
TREMBLY
TREMOLO
TRESTLE
TRICKLE
TRIPOLI
TRITELY
TROUBLE
TROWELS
TRUCKLE
TRUFFLE
TRUNDLE
TUNICLE
TUNNELS
TWADDLE
TWIDDLE
TWINKLE
TWINKLY
TWOFOLD

T•••••L

TACTFUL
TANKFUL
TARBELL
TARHEEL
TEABALL
TEARFUL
TELLALL
TENDRIL
TENNIEL
TERTIAL
TEXTUAL
THERMAL
TINFOIL
TOENAIL
TOMFOOL
TOOTALL
TOPICAL
TOPSAIL
TOPSOIL
TRAMMEL
TRAUBEL
TRAVAIL
TRAYFUL
TREFOIL
TRIVIAL
TRUCIAL
TUMBREL
TUNEFUL
TUNGOIL
TURMOIL
TYLENOL
TYPICAL

•TL••••

ATLANTA
ATLARGE
ATLASES
ATLATLS
ATLEAST
STLOUIS
STLUCIA

•T•L•••

ATALOSS
ATELIER
ATHLETE
ITALIAN
ITALICS
PTOLEMY
STALAGS
STALEST
STALKED
STALKER
STALLED
STELLAR
STILLED
STILLER
STILTED
STILTON
STOLLEN
STOLLER
STOLONS
STYLERS
STYLETS
STYLING
STYLISH
STYLIST
STYLIZE
UTILITY
UTILIZE

•T••L••

ETOILES
KTOSLIN
OTHELLO
STABLED
STABLER
STABLES
STALLED
STANLEE
STANLEY
STAPLED
STAPLER
STAPLES
STARLET
STARLIT
STEALTH
STEELED
STEELER
STEELIE
STELLAR
STIFLED
STIFLES
STILLED
STILLER
STOLLEN
STOLLER
STOOLIE
STROLLS
UTRILLO

•T•••L•

ATFAULT
ATINGLE
ATLATLS
OTHELLO
STABILE
STAGILY
STAIDLY
STARKLY
STARTLE
STATELY
STEEPLE
STEEPLY
STERILE
STERNLY
STEROLS
STIFFLY
STIMULI
STIPPLE
STOKELY
STONILY
STOUTLY
STROLLS
STUBBLE
STUBBLY
STUMBLE
UTRILLO
UTTERLY

•T••••L

ETERNAL
ETHANOL
ETHICAL
STENCIL
STENGEL
STERNAL
STIEGEL
STOICAL
STRUDEL
UTENSIL

••TL•••

ANTLERS
ANTLION
ARTLESS
BUTLERS
CATLIKE
CUTLASS
CUTLERS
CUTLERY
CUTLETS
FATLESS
FETLOCK
GATLING
GETLOST
GOTLAND
GUTLESS
HATLESS
HITLESS
HITLIST
HOTLINE
HOTLIPS
JUTLAND
MATLOCK
NUTLETS
OSTLERS
OUTLAID
OUTLAND
OUTLAST
OUTLAWS
OUTLAYS
OUTLETS
OUTLINE

OUTLIVE
OUTLOOK
OUTLOUD
POTLUCK
RATLINE
SETLINE
SUTLERS
TITLING
TITLIST
WETLAND
WITLESS

••T•L••
ANTILOG
ASTOLAT
BATTLED
BATTLER
BATTLES
BOTTLED
BOTTLER
BOTTLES
CATALAN
CATALOG
CATALPA
DOTTLES
ESTELLE
FETTLES
GATELEG
KETTLES
LETSLIP
LITTLER
MATILDA
METTLES
MOTTLED
MOTTLES
NATALIA
NATALIE
NETTLED
NETTLES
ORTOLAN
OUTFLOW
OUTPLAY
PATELLA
PETALED
RATTLED
RATTLER
RATTLES
RETELLS
RETILED
RETILES
SETTLED
SETTLER
SETTLES
TATTLED
TATTLER
TATTLES
TITTLES
TITULAR
TOTALED
TOTALLY
TUTELAR
VITALLY
VITTLES
WATTLES

••T••L•
ACTABLE
ANTHILL
ARTFILM
ARTICLE
BETHELS
CATCALL
CATTILY
CATWALK
CITABLE
CUTICLE
DATEDLY
DETAILS
EATABLE
ENTAILS
ENTITLE
ESTELLE
FETIDLY
GETWELL
GOTWELL
GUTSILY
LETSFLY
LITHELY
MUTABLE
MUTABLY
MUTUALS
NATTILY
NOTABLE
NOTABLY
NOTWELL
NUTTILY
OCTUPLE
OUTSELL
OUTSOLD
OUTTALK
PATELLA
PATROLS
PETIOLE
PETRELS
PETTILY
PITBULL
PITFALL
PITHILY
POTABLE
POTFULS
POTHOLE
RATABLE
RATHOLE
RETAILS
RETELLS
RETICLE
RETITLE
RETOOLS
RITUALS
SITWELL
TOTALLY
UTTERLY
VATFULS
VITALLY
WETCELL
WITTILY

••T•••L
ANTHILL
BATHOIL
CATCALL
CATTAIL
CITADEL
DUTIFUL
ESTIVAL
ESTORIL
FATEFUL
GETWELL
GOTWELL
HATEFUL
LATERAL
LITERAL
NATURAL
NOTWELL
OATMEAL
ONTRIAL
OPTICAL
OPTIMAL
OUTSELL
PITBULL
PITFALL
PITIFUL
RATTAIL
RETINAL
RETRIAL
SATCHEL
SETSAIL
SITWELL
VITRIOL
WETCELL

•••TL••
BATTLED
BATTLER
BATTLES
BEATLES
BEETLES
BENTLEY
BOOTLEG
BOTTLED
BOTTLER
BOTTLES
BUSTLED
BUSTLES
CANTLES
CASTLED
CASTLES
DOTTLES
FETTLES
GANTLET
GENTLED
GENTLER
GENTLES
HOSTLER
HUNTLEY
HURTLED
HURTLES
HUSTLED
HUSTLER
HUSTLES
JOSTLED
JOSTLER
JOSTLES
KETTLES
KIRTLES
LITTLER
MANTLED
MANTLES
METTLES
MOTTLED
MOTTLES
MYRTLES
NESTLED
NESTLER
NESTLES
NETTLED
NETTLES
PESTLED
PESTLES
RATTLED
RATTLER
RATTLES
ROOTLET
RUSTLED
RUSTLER
RUSTLES
SETTLED
SETTLER
SETTLES
SPOTLIT
SUBTLER
TATTLED
TATTLER
TATTLES
TITTLES
TOOTLED
TOOTLES
TURTLED
TURTLES
VITTLES
WATTLES

•••T•L•
ACUTELY
ALLTOLD
ANATOLE
BERTOLT
BRITTLE
CARTELS
CASTILE
CATTILY
DACTYLS
DIRTILY
DISTILL
DUCTILE
EARTHLY
EMPTILY
FERTILE
FUSTILY
GENTILE
GESTALT
GUSTILY
HASTILY
HEFTILY
HOSTELS
HOSTILE
INSTALL
INSTILL
INSTILS
INSTYLE
INUTILE
IRATELY
LENTILS
LINTELS
LISTELS
LOFTILY
LUSTILY
MANTELS
MISTILY
MONTHLY
MORTALS
MUSTILY
NASTILY
NATTILY
NIFTILY
NUTTILY
OUTTALK
PASTELS
PEPTALK
PETTILY
PISTILS
PISTOLE
PISTOLS
PORTALS
PORTOLA
PRATTLE
RENTALS
REPTILE
RESTYLE
RUSTILY
SALTILY
SCUTTLE
SEATTLE
SHUTTLE
SKITTLE
SPATULA
STATELY
SYSTOLE
TACTILE
TASTILY
TESTILY
TEXTILE
TOOTALL
TRITELY
VISTULA
WHITTLE
WITTILY

•••T••L
ABUTTAL
AUSTRAL
BESTIAL
BOBTAIL
CATTAIL
CENTRAL
CHATTEL
CONTROL
CURTAIL
DISTILL
FACTUAL
FANTAIL
FISTFUL
FOXTAIL
FRETFUL
GENTEEL
GLOTTAL
HOOTOWL
HURTFUL
INITIAL
INSTALL
INSTILL
KESTREL
LACTEAL
LUSTFUL
MARTIAL
MENTHOL
MISTRAL
NEUTRAL
NOSTRIL
NUPTIAL
PARTIAL
PIGTAIL
PINTAIL
PRETZEL
QUETZAL
RATTAIL
RESTFUL
SPATIAL
TACTFUL
TERTIAL
TEXTUAL
TOOTALL
USSTEEL
VENTRAL
VICTUAL
VIRTUAL
WAGTAIL
WASTREL
WISTFUL
ZESTFUL

••••TL•
ADEPTLY
ALERTLY
APOSTLE
ATLATLS
BEASTLY
BLUNTLY
BRISTLE
BRISTLY
BRITTLE
CHORTLE
COURTLY
ENTITLE
EPISTLE
ERECTLY
EXACTLY
FAINTLY
FIRSTLY
FLEETLY
GAUNTLY
GHASTLY
GHOSTLY
GREATLY
GRISTLE
GRISTLY
INAPTLY
INEPTLY
INERTLY
JOINTLY
LICITLY
LIGHTLY
MOISTLY
NIGHTLY
OVERTLY
PRATTLE
QUIETLY
RETITLE
RIGHTLY
SAINTLY
SCANTLY
SCUTTLE
SEATTLE
SHORTLY
SHUTTLE
SIGHTLY
SKITTLE
SMARTLY
STARTLE
STOUTLY
SWEETLY
SWIFTLY
TACITLY
THISTLE
TIGHTLY
TRESTLE
WHISTLE
WHITTLE
WRESTLE

••••T•L
ABUTTAL
BRISTOL
CAPITAL
CAPITOL
CHATTEL
COASTAL
CRYSTAL
DIGITAL
FRACTAL
FRONTAL
GERITOL
GLOTTAL
MARITAL
ORBITAL
PALATAL
PIVOTAL
RECITAL
VEGETAL

•••••TL
AXOLOTL
NAHUATL

T•M••••
TAMABLE
TAMALES
TAMARIN
TAMBALA
TAMBOUR
TAMMANY
TAMPERS
TAMPICO
TAMPING
TAMTAMS
TEMBLOR
TEMPERA
TEMPERS
TEMPEST
TEMPLAR
TEMPLES
TEMPTED
TEMPTER
TEMPURA
TIMBALE
TIMBALS
TIMBERS
TIMBRES
TIMECOP
TIMELAG
TIMEOFF
TIMEOUT
TIMESUP
TIMEWAS
TIMIDER
TIMIDLY
TIMINGS
TIMMINS
TIMOTHY
TOMBOYS
TOMCATS
TOMFOOL
TOMTITS
TOMTOMS
TUMBLED
TUMBLER
TUMBLES
TUMBREL
TUMMIES
TUMULTS
TUMULUS
TYMPANA
TYMPANI

T••M•••
TAMMANY
TARMACS
TEAMING
TEAMSUP
TEDMACK
TEEMING
TERMING
TERMINI
TERMITE
THIMBLE
THOMSON
THUMBED
THUMPED
THUMPER
TIMMINS
TIOMKIN
TITMICE
TOPMAST
TOPMOST
TORMENT
TRAMCAR
TRAMMEL
TRAMPAS
TRAMPED
TRAMPLE
TREMBLE
TREMBLY
TREMOLO
TREMORS
TRIMMED
TRIMMER
TRUMPED
TRUMPET
TRUMPUP
TUMMIES
TURMOIL

T•••M••
TATAMIS
THERMAL
THERMOS
THINMAN
THURMAN
TOTEMIC
TRAMMEL
TRAUMAS
TRIMMED
TRIMMER
TRIUMPH
TUCHMAN

T••••M•
TAMTAMS
TANDEMS
TEATIME
TOMTOMS
TRIREME
TRUISMS
TSUNAMI
TWOSOME
TWOTIME

T•••••M
TAKEAIM
TANTRUM
TAPROOM
TEAROOM
TERBIUM
THEOREM
THORIUM
THULIUM
TINYTIM
TONEARM
TORYISM
TOURISM
TRANSOM
TRIGRAM
TRITIUM
TROPISM

•T•M•••
ATAMANS
ATOMIES
ATOMIZE
ETAMINE
ITEMIZE
STAMENS
STAMINA
STAMMER
STAMPED
STEMMED
STIMULI
STOMACH
STOMATA
STOMPED
STUMBLE
STUMPED
STUMPER
STYMIED
STYMIES

•T••M••
ATHOMES
ATTEMPT
ATTIMES
OTTOMAN
STAMMER
STARMAN
STARMAP
STEAMED
STEAMER
STEMMED
STIGMAS
STORMED

•T•••M•
ATACAMA
ATRIUMS
PTOLEMY
STREAMS

•T••••M
ATAVISM
ATHEISM
STADIUM
STARDOM
STEINEM
STERNUM
STRATUM
YTTRIUM

••TM•••
BITMAPS
HETMANS
NUTMEAT
NUTMEGS
OATMEAL
TITMICE
WETMOPS

••T•M••
ARTEMIS
ARTEMUS
ATTEMPT
ATTIMES
AUTOMAT
AUTUMNS
BATEMAN
BATHMAT
BATSMAN
BATSMEN
BETAMAX
BETIMES
BITUMEN
GATEMAN
GATEMEN
ISTHMUS
OPTIMAL
OPTIMUM
OTTOMAN
PITTMAN
POTOMAC
PUTAMEN
RETIMED
RETIMES
TATAMIS
TOTEMIC
UNTAMED
UPTEMPO
VITAMIN

••T••M•
ANTHEMS
BOTTOMS
CUTTIME
ESTEEMS
EXTREME
FATHOMS
NOTHOME
NOTRUMP
OUTCOME
OUTJUMP
PETNAME
RETRIMS
SATCHMO
SATSUMA
SITCOMS

••T•••M
ANTFARM
ANTONYM
ARTFILM
ARTFORM
INTERIM
KETCHAM
LITHIUM
MITCHUM
NATRIUM
OPTIMUM
POTSDAM
YTTRIUM

•••TM••
BESTMAN
BESTMEN
BOATMAN
BOATMEN
DUSTMOP
EASTMAN
FOOTMAN
FOOTMEN
HARTMAN
PITTMAN
POSTMAN
POSTMEN
WHITMAN

•••T•M•
AIRTIME
ALLTIME
ANATOMY
ANYTIME
BANTAMS
BEDTIME
BIGTIME
BOTTOMS
BUYTIME
CENTIME
CENTIMO
CONTEMN
COSTUME
CUSTOMS
CUTTIME
DAYTIME
DIATOMS
DICTUMS
EPITOME
GAUTAMA
MAYTIME
NAPTIME
OLDTIME
ONETIME
PASTIME
RAGTIME
RESTAMP
RHYTHMS
SAOTOME
SYSTEMS
TAMTAMS
TEATIME
TOMTOMS
TWOTIME
VICTIMS
WARTIME

•••T••M
APOTHEM
BAPTISM
BENTHAM
CHATHAM
CHETRUM
CULTISM
CULTJAM
EGOTISM
ELITISM
FLOTSAM
MIDTERM
NOSTRUM
PIETISM
ROSTRUM
SISTRUM
TANTRUM
TRITIUM
VIETNAM
YEATEAM

••••TM•
MAHATMA

••••T•M
ERRATUM
OMENTUM
PHANTOM
PINETUM
QUANTUM
SANCTUM
STRATUM
SYMPTOM
TINYTIM

T•N••••
TANAGER
TANDEMS
TANGELO
TANGENT
TANGERE
TANGIER
TANGLED
TANGLES
TANGOED
TANKARD
TANKERS
TANKFUL
TANKING
TANKSUP
TANKTOP
TANLINE
TANNERS
TANNERY
TANNEST
TANNING
TANNINS
TANNISH
TANOAKS
TANSIES
TANTARA
TANTRUM
TENABLE
TENABLY
TENACES
TENANCY
TENANTS
TENDERS
TENDING
TENDONS
TENDRIL
TENDSTO
TENFOLD
TENFOUR
TENNERS
TENNIEL
TENONED
TENPINS
TENSELY
TENSEST
TENSEUP
TENSILE
TENSING
TENSION
TENSIVE
TENSORS
TENSPOT
TENTERS
TENTING
TENUOUS
TENURED
TENURES
TINCANS
TINDERS
TINEARS
TINFOIL
TINGING
TINGLED
TINGLES
TINHATS
TINHORN
TINIEST
TINKERS
TINKLED
TINKLES
TINNERS
TINNIER
TINNILY
TINSELS
TINSTAR
TINTERN
TINTERS
TINTING
TINTYPE
TINWORK
TINYTIM
TONALLY
TONEARM
TONEDUP
TONELOC
TONEROW
TONESUP
TONGANS
TONGUED
TONGUES
TONIEST
TONIGHT
TONNAGE
TONNEAU
TONSILS
TONSURE
TONTINE
TUNDRAS
TUNEDIN
TUNEDUP
TUNEFUL
TUNEOUT
TUNESIN
TUNESUP
TUNEUPS
TUNGOIL
TUNICLE
TUNISIA
TUNNELS
TUNNIES

T••N•••
TAINTED
TANNERS
TANNERY
TANNEST
TANNING
TANNINS
TANNISH
TARNISH
TAUNTED
TAWNIER
TEENAGE
TEENERS
TEENIER
TENNERS
TENNIEL
TERNARY
TERNATE
THANKED
THINAIR
THINICE
THINKER
THINKOF
THINKUP
THINMAN
THINNED
THINNER
THUNDER
TINNERS
TINNIER
TINNILY
TLINGIT
TOENAIL
TONNAGE
TONNEAU
TORNADO
TORNOUT
TOWNERS
TOWNIES
TOYNBEE
TRANCES
TRANSIT
TRANSOM
TRENARY
TRENDED
TRENTON
TRINITY
TRINKET
TRUNDLE
TSONGAS
TSUNAMI
TUNNELS
TUNNIES

TURNERS
TURNING
TURNIPS
TURNKEY
TURNOFF
TURNOUT
TURNSIN
TURNSON
TURNSTO
TURNSUP
TWANGED
TWINBED
TWINGED
TWINGES
TWINING
TWINKLE
TWINKLY
TWINNED
TYINGIN
TYINGUP

T•••N••

TAGENDS
TAKENIN
TAKENON
TALENTS
TALONED
TAPINGS
TARANTO
TENANCY
TENANTS
TENONED
TERENCE
TETANUS
THINNED
THINNER
THRONES
THRONGS
TIDINGS
TIEINTO
TIERNEY
TIMINGS
TISANES
TITANIA
TITANIC
TOKENED
TOPKNOT
TORONTO
TOURNEY
TRAINED
TRAINEE
TRAINER
TRIUNES
TROUNCE
TRUANCY
TRUANTS
TWINNED
TYLENOL
TYRANNY
TYRANTS

T••••N•

TABBING
TABLING
TACKING
TAGGING
TAGLINE
TAILEND
TAILING
TAIPANS
TAKEONE
TALKING
TAMMANY
TAMPING
TANGENT
TANKING
TANLINE
TANNING
TANNINS
TAPPING
TARPONS
TARRING
TARTANS
TARZANA
TASKING
TASTING
TATIANA
TATTING
TAURINE
TAUTENS
TAVERNS
TAXIING
TEAMING
TEARING
TEASING
TEDDING
TEEMING
TELLING
TENDING
TENDONS
TENPINS
TENSING
TENTING
TERHUNE
TERMING
TERMINI
TERRENE
TESTING
TEUTONS
THAWING
TICKING
TIDYING
TIELINE
TIEPINS
TIERING
TIFFANY
TIJUANA
TILLING
TILTING
TIMMINS
TINCANS
TINGING
TINTING
TIPPING
TITHING
TITLING
TOCSINS
TOGGING
TOILING
TOLLING
TOLUENE
TONGANS
TONTINE
TOOLING
TOOTING
TOPGUNS
TOPPING
TORMENT
TORRENT
TORTONI
TOSSING
TOTTING
TOUCANS
TOURING
TOUTING
TOYLAND
TRACING
TRADING
TREEING
TREPANS
TREVINO
TRIBUNE
TRIDENT
TRIGONS
TRITONE
TRITONS
TROJANS
TRUEING
TSARINA
TUCKING
TUFTING
TUGGING
TULSANS
TURBANS
TURBINE
TUREENS
TURNING
TUSCANY
TWINING
TWOTONE
TYCOONS
TYMPANA
TYMPANI
TYRANNY
TZARINA

T•••••N

TACKSON
TAILFIN
TAKENIN
TAKENON
TAKESIN
TAKESON
TAKETEN
TAMARIN
TEACHIN
TEHERAN
TELERAN
TELLSON
TENSION
TERRAIN
TESTBAN
THEREIN
THEREON
THICKEN
THINMAN
THOMSON
THREWIN
THROWIN
THURMAN
TIBETAN
TIEDOWN
TIGHTEN
TINHORN
TINTERN
TIOMKIN
TOLKIEN
TOOKTEN
TORSION
TOUCHON
TOUGHEN
TRADEIN
TRADEON
TREASON
TRENTON
TRICORN
TRIEDON
TRIESON
TRILLIN
TRISTAN
TRODDEN
TUCHMAN
TUCKSIN
TUITION
TUNEDIN
TUNESIN
TURNSIN
TURNSON
TYINGIN
TYPHOON

•T•N•••

ATINGLE
ATONING
ETHNICS
ETONIAN
STANCES
STANDBY
STANDEE
STANDIN
STANDON
STANDUP
STANLEE
STANLEY
STANNIC
STANTON
STANZAS
STENCIL
STENGEL
STENTOR
STINGER
STINKER
STINTED
STONERS
STONIER
STONILY
STONING
STUNGUN
STUNNED
STUNNER
STUNTED
UTENSIL

•T••N••

ATLANTA
ATTENDS
ATTUNED
ATTUNES
ETERNAL
ETHANOL
ETIENNE
OTRANTO
STAINED
STAINER
STANNIC
STAUNCH
STDENIS
STEINEM
STEINER
STERNAL
STERNER
STERNLY
STERNUM
STRANDS
STRANGE
STRINGS
STRINGY
STUNNED
STUNNER

•T•••N•

ATAMANS
ATONING
ATTAINS
ETAMINE
ETCHING
ETIENNE
ITCHING
ITERANT
STAGING
STAKING
STAMENS
STAMINA
STARING
STATING
STAVING
STAYING
STEPINS
STEVENS
STEWING
STIPEND
STJOHNS
STOKING
STOLONS
STONING
STORING
STOWING
STRAINS
STUDENT
STYLING
STYRENE
UTAHANS

•T••••N

ETESIAN
ETONIAN
ITALIAN
ITHACAN
KTOSLIN
OTTOMAN
STANDIN
STANDON
STANTON
STARMAN
STASSEN
STATION
STEEPEN
STEPHEN
STEPSIN
STEPSON
STETSON
STEUBEN
STIFFEN
STILTON
STIRSIN
STOLLEN
STOODIN
STOPSIN
STRIVEN
STUNGUN
STYGIAN
STYRIAN
UTOPIAN

••TN•••

APTNESS
CATNAPS
CATNIPS
FATNESS
FITNESS
HOTNESS
JITNEYS
PATNESS
PETNAME
WETNESS
WITNESS

••T•N••

ACTINIC
ANTENNA
ANTONIA
ANTONIN
ANTONIO
ANTONYM
ATTENDS
ATTUNED
ATTUNES
BOTHNIA
CATENAE
CUTINTO
DETENTE
EATENAT
EATENUP
ENTENTE
ESTONIA
EXTENDS
EXTENTS
EXTINCT
GETINTO
GOTINTO
INTENDS
INTENSE
INTENTS
INTONED
INTONER
INTONES
KETONES
KUTENAI
LATENCY
LATENTS
LATINAS
LATINOS
LETINON
LITINTO
MATINEE
MUTANTS
OBTUNDS
OCTANES
OCTANTS
OFTENER
OUTINGS
PATENTS
PATINAS
PETUNIA
POTENCY
RATINGS
RETINAE
RETINAL
RETINAS
RETINUE
RETUNED
RETUNES
ROTUNDA
SETINTO
SUTTNER
TETANUS
TITANIA
TITANIC
UNTUNED
UNTUNES
UPTONOW
USTINOV

••T••N•

ACTIONS
ALTOONA
ANTEING
ANTENNA
ANTHONY
ANTOINE
ARTSONG
ASTOUND
ATTAINS
AUTUMNS
BATHING
BATTENS
BATTING
BATWING
BETHANY
BETHINK
BETTING
BITTING
BUTTING
BUTTONS
BYTURNS
CATIONS
CATKINS
CATTING
CITRINE
CITRONS
COTTONS
COTTONY
CUTTING
DETAINS
DITTANY
DOTTING
ENTRANT
ENTWINE
FATTENS
FITTING
GATLING
GETTING
GOTLAND
GUTTING
HATPINS
HATTING
HETMANS
HITTING
HOTLINE
INTERNS
JETGUNS
JETSONS
JETTING
JOTTING
JUTLAND
JUTTING
KITTENS
LATEENS
LATHING
LATTENS
LETTING
LOTIONS
LOTTING
MATRONS
MATTING
METHANE
MITRING
MITTENS
MOTIONS
MUTTONS
NATIONS
NETTING
NITTANY
NOTHING
NOTIONS
NUTTING
OBTAINS
OPTIONS
OUTDONE
OUTGUNS
OUTLAND
OUTLINE
OUTRANK
OUTRUNS
PATERNO
PATIENT
PATRONS
PATTENS
PATTING
PETTING
PITHING
PITTING
PITYING
POTIONS
POTTING
PUTTING
PYTHONS
RATFINK
RATIONS
RATLINE
RATTANS
RATTING
RETAINS
RETHINK
RETSINA
RETURNS
ROTTING
SETLINE
SETTING
SITTING
TATIANA
TATTING
TITHING
TITLING
TOTTING
UNTYING
UPTURNS
VETOING
VETTING
WETLAND
WETTING
WITTING

••T•••N

ACTAEON
ACTUPON
ANTIGEN
ANTLION
ANTONIN
ARTISAN
AZTECAN
BATEMAN
BATSMAN
BATSMEN
BETAKEN
BETOKEN
BETWEEN
BITTERN
BITUMEN
BUTTSIN
CATALAN
CATCHON
CATSCAN
CITIZEN
CITROEN
CUTDOWN
DETRAIN
DOTEDON
DOTESON
ENTRAIN
GATEMAN
GATEMEN
GETDOWN
GETEVEN
GETITON
GOTDOWN
GOTEVEN
KATHRYN
KITCHEN
LATERAN
LATERON
LATVIAN
LETDOWN
LETINON
MATEWAN
MUTAGEN
OCTAGON
ORTOLAN
OTTOMAN
OUTWORN
PATROON
PATTERN
PITCHIN
PITTMAN
PUTAMEN
PUTDOWN
PUTUPON
RETAKEN
RETRAIN
SATDOWN
SETDOWN
SETUPON
SITDOWN
SOTHERN
VATICAN
VETERAN
VITAMIN
VOTESIN

•••TN••

BEATNIK
CHUTNEY
COSTNER
JUSTNOW
PARTNER
SHATNER
SPUTNIK
SUTTNER
VIETNAM
VINTNER
WHATNOT
WHITNEY

•••T•N•

ABATING
ACETONE
ACHTUNG
BAITING
BARTEND
BASTING
BATTENS
BATTING
BEATING
BELTANE
BELTING
BESTING
BETTING
BITTING
BLATANT
BOATING
BOITANO
BOLTING
BOOTING
BRETONS
BRITONS
BUNTING
BUSTING
BUTTING
BUTTONS
CAFTANS
CANTINA
CANTING
CANTONS
CARTING
CARTONS
CASTING
CATTING
COATING
CONTEND
CONTENT
COSTING
COTTONS
COTTONY
CRATING
CRETANS
CRETINS
CUTTING
DARTING
DAYTONA
DENTINE
DENTING
DESTINE
DESTINY
DIETING
DISTANT
DISTEND
DITTANY
DOTTING
DUCTING
DUSTING
EASTEND
EDITING
ELATING
ELUTING
EMOTING
EXITING
FASTENS
FASTING
FASTONE
FATTENS
FITTING
FLUTING
FONTINA
FOOTING
FORTUNA
FORTUNE
GAITING
GETTING
GRATING
GUSTING
GUTTING
HALTING
HASTENS
HASTING
HATTING
HEATING
HEFTING
HINTING
HITTING
HOOTING
HOSTING
HUNTING
HURTING
IFSTONE
INSTANT
JESTING
JETTING
JILTING
JOLTING
JOTTING
JUSTINE
JUTTING
KAFTANS
KILTING
KITTENS
LANTANA
LASTING
LATTENS
LEPTONS
LETTING
LIFTING
LILTING
LISTENS
LISTING
LOFTING
LOOTING
LOTTING
LUSTING
MALTING
MARTENS
MARTINA
MARTINI
MARTINO
MARTINS
MATTING
MEETING
MELTING
MINTING
MISTING
MITTENS
MOLTING
MONTANA
MONTAND
MONTANE
MOUTONS
MUNTINS
MUSTANG
MUTTONS
NEATENS
NEPTUNE
NESTING
NETTING
NEWTONS
NITTANY
NUTTING
ORATING
OROTUND
OUSTING
PANTING
PARTING
PASTINA
PASTING
PATTENS
PATTING
PECTINS
PELTING
PETTING
PHOTONS
PIETINS
PISTONS
PITTING
PLATENS
PLATING
PONTINE
PORTEND
PORTENT
POSTING
POTTING
POUTING
PRATING
PRETEND
PROTONS
PUNTING
PUPTENT
PUTTING
QUOTING
RAFTING
RANTING
RATTANS
RATTING
RENTING
RESTING
RIFTING
RIOTING
ROOTING
ROSTAND
ROTTING
ROUTINE
ROUTING
RUSTING
SALTINE
SALTING
SANTANA
SANTINI
SEATING
SESTINA
SETTING
SEXTANS
SEXTANT
SEXTONS
SIFTING
SILTING
SISTINE
SITTING
SKATING
SLATING
SMETANA
SMITING
SOFTENS
SORTING
SOUTANE
SPITING
STATING
SUBTEND
SUITING
SULTANA
SULTANS
SUNTANS
TARTANS
TASTING
TATTING
TAUTENS
TENTING
TESTING
TEUTONS
TILTING
TINTING
TONTINE
TOOTING
TORTONI
TOTTING
TOUTING
TRITONE
TRITONS
TUFTING
TWOTONE
UNITING
VENTING
VESTING
VETTING
WAFTING
WAITING
WANTING
WASTING
WELTING
WESTEND
WETTING
WHITENS
WHITING
WILTING
WITTING
WONTONS
WRITING
XRATING
ZEITUNG

•••T••N

ABSTAIN
AUCTION
BASTION
BENTSEN
BESTMAN
BESTMEN
BITTERN
BLITZEN
BOATMAN
BOATMEN
BRITAIN
BRITTEN
BRITTON
BUTTSIN
CANTEEN
CAPTAIN
CAPTION
CARTOON
CAUTION
CERTAIN
CISTERN
CONTAIN
CONTEMN
COSTAIN
COWTOWN
CURTAIN
DEXTRIN
DICTION
DUSTPAN
EARTHEN
EASTERN
EASTMAN
EDITION
ELATION
ELUTION
EMOTION
EPSTEIN
FACTION
FESTOON
FICTION
FIFTEEN
FLATTEN
FONTEYN
FOOTMAN
FOOTMEN
FORTRAN
FUSTIAN
GENTIAN
GLUTTON
HAITIAN
HARTMAN
HEATHEN
JANTZEN
KRATION
LANTERN
LAOTIAN
LECTERN
MARTIAN
MENTION
MIDTOWN
NEUTRON
NEWTOWN

NOCTURN
ORATION
OURTOWN
OVATION
PASTERN
PATTERN
PERTAIN
PITTMAN
PLATOON
PONTOON
PORTION
POSTERN
POSTMAN
POSTMEN
PRETEEN
PROTEAN
PROTEIN
RESTAIN
RIPTORN
RONTGEN
RUCTION
SECTION
SHOTGUN
SHUTSIN
SIXTEEN
SLATKIN
SMITTEN
STATION
STETSON
SUCTION
SUSTAIN
TESTBAN
TINTERN
TUITION
UMPTEEN
UNCTION
WAITSON
WANTSIN
WESTERN
WHITMAN
WRITEIN
WRITTEN
WROTEIN
XANTHAN
YELTSIN

••••TN•

MIGHTNT

••••T•N

ALLSTON
BALATON
BRAXTON
BRITTEN
BRITTON
BUILTIN
BUILTON
BURSTYN
CAPITAN
CAPSTAN
CARLTON
CHASTEN
CLAPTON
CLAYTON
CLIFTON
CLINTON
COUNTON
CROUTON
DAKOTAN
DEALTIN
DRISTAN
FLATTEN
FRONTON
GELATIN
GETITON
GLISTEN
GLUTTON
HALSTON
HAMPTON
HANGTEN
HEARTEN
HOUSTON
KERATIN
KILOTON
KRYPTON
LIGHTEN
LONGTON
MOISTEN
PHAETON
PRESTON
PURITAN
QUENTIN
QUIETEN
RALSTON
RARITAN
RIGHTON
RUBITIN
SHELTON
SHORTEN
SKELTON
SLAYTON
SLEPTIN
SLEPTON
SMARTEN
SMITTEN
SPARTAN
STANTON
STILTON
SWEETEN
SWEETON
TAKETEN
TIBETAN
TIGHTEN
TOOKTEN
TRENTON
TRISTAN
WHARTON
WHEATON
WINSTON
WRITTEN
YANKTON
YUCATAN

TO•••••

TOADIED
TOADIES
TOASTED
TOASTER
TOBACCO
TOCCATA
TOCSINS
TODDIES
TODDLED
TODDLER
TODDLES
TOECAPS
TOEHOLD
TOELESS
TOELOOP
TOENAIL
TOESHOE
TOETAPS
TOFFEES
TOFFLER
TOGGING
TOGGLED
TOGGLES
TOILERS
TOILETS
TOILING
TOKENED
TOLDOFF
TOLKIEN
TOLLING
TOLLWAY
TOLSTOI
TOLSTOY
TOLTECS
TOLUENE
TOMBOYS
TOMCATS
TOMFOOL
TOMTITS
TOMTOMS
TONALLY
TONEARM
TONEDUP
TONELOC
TONEROW
TONESUP
TONGANS
TONGUED
TONGUES
TONIEST
TONIGHT
TONNAGE
TONNEAU
TONSILS
TONSURE
TONTINE
TOOKOFF
TOOKOUT
TOOKTEN
TOOLBOX
TOOLING
TOOLSUP
TOORDER
TOOTALL
TOOTERS
TOOTHED
TOOTING
TOOTLED
TOOTLES
TOOTSIE
TOPAZES
TOPCOAT
TOPDOGS
TOPGUNS
TOPHATS
TOPIARY
TOPICAL
TOPKAPI
TOPKICK
TOPKNOT
TOPMAST
TOPMOST
TOPPERS
TOPPING
TOPPLED
TOPPLES
TOPSAIL
TOPSIDE
TOPSOFF
TOPSOIL
TOPSOUT
TORCHED
TORCHES
TOREOFF
TOREOUT
TOREROS
TORMENT
TORNADO
TORNOUT
TOROIDS
TORONTO
TORPEDO
TORQUES
TORRENT
TORSION
TORTONI
TORYISM
TOSCALE
TOSHIBA
TOSPARE
TOSSERS
TOSSING
TOSSOFF
TOSSOUT
TOSSUPS
TOSTADA
TOTALED
TOTALLY
TOTEBAG
TOTEMIC
TOTTERS
TOTTERY
TOTTING
TOUCANS
TOUCHED
TOUCHES
TOUCHON
TOUCHUP
TOUGHEN
TOUGHER
TOUGHIE
TOUGHLY
TOUPEES
TOURACO
TOURERS
TOURING
TOURISM
TOURIST
TOURNEY
TOUSLED
TOUSLES
TOUTERS
TOUTING
TOWARDS
TOWAWAY
TOWCARS
TOWELED
TOWERED
TOWHEAD
TOWHEES
TOWNERS
TOWNIES
TOWPATH
TOWROPE
TOYDOGS
TOYLAND
TOYNBEE
TOYSHOP

T•O••••

TAOISTS
THOMSON
THOREAU
THORIUM
THOUGHT
TIOMKIN
TOOKOFF
TOOKOUT
TOOKTEN
TOOLBOX
TOOLING
TOOLSUP
TOORDER
TOOTALL
TOOTERS
TOOTHED
TOOTING
TOOTLED
TOOTLES
TOOTSIE
TROCARS
TROCHEE
TROCHES
TRODDEN
TROIKAS
TROILUS
TROJANS
TROLLED
TROLLEY
TROOPED
TROOPER
TROPHIC
TROPICS
TROPISM
TROTHED
TROTOUT
TROTSKY
TROTTED
TROTTER
TROUBLE
TROUGHS
TROUNCE
TROUPER
TROUPES
TROUSER
TROWELS
TROWERS
TSONGAS
TWOBASE
TWOBITS
TWOFERS
TWOFOLD
TWOSOME
TWOSTAR
TWOSTEP
TWOTIME
TWOTONE

T••O•••

TABORET
TALONED
TANOAKS
TENONED
THEOREM
THROATS
THROATY
THRONES
THRONGS
THROUGH
THROWER
THROWIN
TIMOTHY
TIPOFFS
TOROIDS
TORONTO
TRIODES
TROOPED
TROOPER
TRYOUTS
TUTORED
TYCOONS

T•••O••

TABLOID
TADPOLE
TAGSOUT
TAILOFF
TAILORS
TAKEOFF
TAKEONE
TAKEOUT
TALKOUT
TALLOWS
TAMBOUR
TANGOED
TAPIOCA
TAPROOM
TAPROOT
TAPSOUT
TARPONS
TATTOOS
TEAPOTS
TEAPOYS
TEAROFF
TEAROOM
TEAROSE
TEDIOUS
TEEDOFF
TEESOFF
TELLOFF
TENDONS
TENFOLD
TENFOUR
TENSORS
TENUOUS
TERRORS
TESTOUT
TEUTONS
THEROUX
TICKOFF
TIEDOWN
TIERODS
TIMEOFF
TIMEOUT
TINFOIL
TINHORN
TINWORK
TIPSOFF
TIPTOED
TIPTOES
TIPTOPS
TIREOUT
TOEHOLD
TOELOOP
TOLDOFF
TOMBOYS
TOMFOOL
TOMTOMS
TOOKOFF
TOOKOUT
TOPCOAT
TOPDOGS
TOPMOST
TOPSOFF
TOPSOIL
TOPSOUT
TOREOFF
TOREOUT
TORNOUT
TORTONI
TOSSOFF
TOSSOUT
TOWROPE
TOYDOGS
TRAVOIS
TREFOIL
TREMOLO
TREMORS
TRICORN
TRICOTS
TRIGONS
TRILOGY
TRIPODS
TRIPOLI
TRITONE
TRITONS
TROTOUT
TUGBOAT
TUNEOUT
TUNGOIL
TURBOTS
TURMOIL
TURNOFF
TURNOUT
TUSSOCK
TVSHOWS
TWOFOLD
TWOSOME
TWOTONE
TYCOONS
TYPHOON

T••••O•

TACKSON
TAGALOG
TAKENON
TAKESON
TANKTOP
TAPROOM
TAPROOT
TATTOOS
TEAROOM
TEASHOP
TELLSON
TEMBLOR
TENSION
TENSPOT
TEREDOS
THEBLOB
THEREOF
THEREON
THERMOS
THINKOF
THOMSON
TIMECOP
TIREDOF
TOELOOP
TOESHOE
TOLSTOI
TOLSTOY
TOMFOOL
TONELOC
TONEROW
TOOLBOX
TOPKNOT
TOREROS
TORSION
TOUCHON
TOYSHOP
TRACTOR
TRADEON
TRAITOR
TRANSOM
TREASON
TREETOP
TRENTON
TRIEDON
TRIESON
TSELIOT
TUITION
TUPELOS
TURNSON
TUXEDOS
TYLENOL
TYPHOON

T•••••O

TABASCO
TAKESTO
TALKSTO
TALLYHO
TAMPICO
TANGELO
TARANTO
TENDSTO
THERETO
TIEINTO
TOBACCO
TORNADO
TORONTO
TORPEDO
TOURACO
TREMOLO
TREVINO
TURNSTO

•TO••••

ATOMIES
ATOMIZE
ATONING
ETOILES
ETONIAN
KTOSLIN
PTOLEMY
STOCKED
STOCKUP
STOGIES
STOICAL
STOKELY
STOKERS
STOKING
STOLLEN
STOLLER
STOLONS
STOMACH
STOMATA
STOMPED
STONERS
STONIER
STONILY
STONING
STOODBY
STOODIN
STOODUP
STOOGES
STOOKEY
STOOLIE
STOOPED
STOOPTO
STOPGAP
STOPOFF
STOPPED
STOPPER
STOPSIN
STOPSUP
STORAGE
STORERS
STOREUP
STOREYS
STORIED
STORIES
STORING
STORMED
STOUTER
STOUTLY
STOWING
UTOPIAN
UTOPIAS

•T•O•••

ATHOMES
ATROPHY
ATWORST
OTTOMAN
PTBOATS
STJOHNS
STLOUIS
STOODBY
STOODIN
STOODUP
STOOGES
STOOKEY
STOOLIE
STOOPED
STOOPTO
STROBES
STROKED
STROKES
STROLLS
STROPHE

•T••O••

ATALOSS
STATORS
STCROIX
STEPOUT
STEROID
STEROLS
STOLONS
STOPOFF
STUPORS

•T•••O•

ATECROW
ETHANOL
STANDON
STANTON
STARDOM
STATION
STENTOR
STEPSON
STEREOS
STETSON
STILTON
STUCCOS
STUDIOS

•T••••O

OTHELLO
OTRANTO
STICKTO
STOOPTO
STRETTO
STUCKTO
UTRILLO

••TO•••

ALTOONA
ALTOSAX
ANTOINE
ANTONIA
ANTONIN
ANTONIO
ANTONYM
ASTOLAT
ASTORIA
ASTOUND
AUTOMAT
BETOKEN
CNTOWER
CUTOFFS
CUTOUTS
DETOURS
ESTONIA
ESTORIL
EXTORTS
GETOVER
GOTOPOT
GOTOVER
INTONED
INTONER
INTONES
KETONES
LITOTES
METOOER
MITOSES
MITOSIS
MITOTIC
MOTORED
OCTOBER
OCTOPOD
OCTOPUS
ONTOPOF
ORTOLAN
OTTOMAN
OUTOFIT
POTOMAC
PUTOUTS
PUTOVER
RETOOLS
RETORTS
RETOUCH
RETOWED
TUTORED
UPTONOW
UPTOPAR
VETOERS
VETOING
ZATOPEK

••T•O••

ACTIONS
ACTSOUT
ALTOONA
ANTCOWS
ANTHONY
ANTIOCH
ARTFORM
ARTSONG
ARTWORK
AUTHORS
BATBOYS
BATHOIL
BETROTH
BETTORS
BITEOFF
BOTTOMS
BUTTONS
BUTTOUT
CATBOAT
CATHODE
CATIONS
CITROEN
CITRONS
COTTONS
COTTONY
CUTDOWN
CUTSOFF
CUTSOUT
DETROIT
DITTOED
DUTEOUS
EATSOUT
ENTROPY
FATHOMS
FATUOUS
FETLOCK
GETDOWN
GETLOST
GETSOFF
GETSOUT
GOTDOWN
HOTDOGS
HOTFOOT
HOTPOTS
HOTRODS
INTROIT
JETBOAT
JETPORT
JETSONS
LETDOWN
LETSOFF
LETSOUT
LOTIONS
MATLOCK
MATRONS
MATTOCK
MATZOHS
METEORS
METEOUT
METHODS
METOOER
MITFORD
MOTIONS
MOTTOES
MUTTONS
NATIONS
NETWORK
NITROUS
NOTHOME
NOTIONS
OPTIONS
OPTSOUT
OSTEOID
OUTCOME
OUTDOES
OUTDONE
OUTDOOR
OUTGOES
OUTLOOK
OUTLOUD
OUTPOST
OUTSOLD
OUTVOTE
OUTWORE
OUTWORK
OUTWORN
PATROLS
PATRONS
PATROON
PETCOCK
PETIOLE
PETROCK
PETROUS
PITBOSS
PITEOUS
POTHOLE
POTHOOK
POTIONS
PUTDOWN
PUTSOFF
PUTSOUT
PYTHONS
RATHOLE
RATIONS
RETOOLS
SATDOWN
SETDOWN
SETSOFF
SETSOUT
SITCOMS
SITDOWN
SITSOUT
TATTOOS
WETMOPS
WITHOUT

••T••O•

ACTAEON
ACTUPON
ANTILOG
ANTLION
CATALOG
CATCHON
DOTEDON
DOTESON
EATCROW
GETITON
GOTOPOT
HOTFOOT
HOTSHOT
HOTSPOT
LATERON
LATINOS
LETINON
LITHGOW
MATADOR
OCTAGON
OCTAVOS
OCTOPOD
ONTOPOF
OUTCROP
OUTDOOR
OUTFLOW
OUTGROW
OUTLOOK
PATRIOT
PATROON
PITSTOP
POTHOOK
POTSHOT
PUTUPON
ROTATOR
SETUPON
TATTOOS
UPTONOW
USTINOV
VITRIOL

••T•••O

ANTONIO
ARTDECO
CUTINTO
GETINTO
GOTINTO
LITINTO
ONTARIO
ONTHEGO
PATERNO
PUTITTO
SATCHMO
SETINTO
UPTEMPO

•••TO••

ACETONE
ALLTOLD
AMATORY
ANATOLE
ANATOMY
BEATOUT
BERTOLT
BESTOWS
BETTORS
BIGTOES
BIGTOPS
BLOTOUT
BOOTOUT
BOTTOMS
BOXTOPS
BRETONS
BRITONS
BUSTOUT
BUTTONS
BUTTOUT
CANTONS
CANTORS
CAPTORS
CARTONS
CARTOON
CASTOFF
CASTOUT
CONTORT
CONTOUR
COTTONS
COTTONY
COWTOWN
CUSTODY
CUSTOMS
DAYTONA
DEBTORS
DELTOID
DIATOMS
DISTORT
DITTOED
DOCTORS
DUSTOFF
EDITORS
EPITOME
FACTORS
FACTORY
FASTONE
FELTOUT
FESTOON
FLATOUT
GUSTOES
HECTORS
HISTORY
HOOTOWL
HOPTOIT
IFSTONE
INSTOCK
INSTORE
ISOTOPE
KEPTOFF
KEPTOUT
KOWTOWS
LACTOSE
LAPTOPS
LASTORY
LECTORS
LEFTOFF
LEFTOUT
LEPTONS
LIFTOFF
LOSTOUT
MALTOSE

MASTOID
MATTOCK
MENTORS
MIDTOWN
MISTOOK
MONTOYA
MOTTOES
MOUTONS
MUTTONS
NEWTONS
NEWTOWN
ORATORS
ORATORY
OURTOWN
PARTOOK
PARTOUT
PASTORS
PEGTOPS
PHOTOED
PHOTOGS
PHOTONS
PHOTOOP
PISTOLE
PISTOLS
PISTONS
PLATOON
PONTOON
POPTOPS
PORTOLA
PROTONS
RAGTOPS
RAPTORS
RECTORS
RECTORY
REDTOPS
RESTOCK
RESTORE
RHETORS
RIOTOUS
RIPTORN
ROOTOUT
SAOTOME
SECTORS
SEETOIT
SENTOFF
SENTOUT
SEXTONS
SHUTOFF
SHUTOUT
SKITOWS
STATORS
SUITORS
SYSTOLE
TATTOOS
TESTOUT
TEUTONS
TIPTOED
TIPTOES
TIPTOPS
TOMTOMS
TORTONI
TRITONE
TRITONS
TROTOUT
TWOTONE
UNSTOPS
VECTORS
VICTORS
VICTORY
WAITOUT
WANTOUT
WEBTOED
WENTOFF
WENTOUT
WONTONS

•••T•O•

ABETTOR
AUCTION
BASTION
BESTBOY
BISTROS
BOUTROS
BRITTON
CAPTION
CARTOON
CAUTION
CONTROL
DESTROY
DICTION
DOGTROT
DUSTMOP
EDITION
ELATION
ELUTION
EMOTION
FACTION
FELTFOR
FESTOON
FICTION
FLATTOP
FOXTROT
GHETTOS
GLUTTON
GROTTOS
HAUTBOY
JUSTNOW
KRATION
MENTHOL
MENTION
MISTOOK
NEUTRON
ORATION
OVATION
PARTOOK
PEATBOG
PHOTOOP
PLATOON
PONTOON
PORTHOS
PORTION
POSTBOX
POSTHOC
ROOTFOR
RUCTION
SALTBOX
SECTION
SENTFOR
SHOTFOR
SOFTTOP
STATION
STETSON
SUCTION
TATTOOS
TUITION
UNCTION
WAITSON
WARTHOG
WENTFOR
WHATFOR
WHATNOT

•••T••O

BOITANO
CENTAVO
CENTIMO
DEUTERO
MARTINO
MESTIZO
MONTEGO
PORTICO
VERTIGO
WANTSTO
WRITETO
WROTETO

••••TO•

ABETTOR
ADAPTOR
AERATOR
ALLSTON
ARISTOS
AUDITOR
AVIATOR
BALATON
BIENTOT
BONITOS
BRAXTON
BRISTOL
BRITTON
BUILTON
BUSSTOP
CAPITOL
CARLTON
CHEETOS
CLAPTON
CLAYTON
CLIFTON
CLINTON
COUNTON
CREATOR
CROUTON
CRYPTOS
CURATOR
DESKTOP
DESOTOS
DONATOR
DORITOS
ELECTOR
ENACTOR
EQUATOR
ERECTOR
EXACTOR
FLATTOP
FRONTON
GERITOL
GETITON
GHETTOS
GLUTTON
GRANTOR
GROTTOS
GYRATOR
HALSTON
HAMPTON
HARDTOP
HIGHTOP
HILLTOP
HOUSTON
JANITOR
KILOTON
KRYPTON
LEANTOS
LEGATOS
LOCATOR
LONGTON
MAINTOP
MANITOU
MOLOTOV
MONITOR
NEGATOR
NONSTOP
OPENTOE
PHAETON
PHANTOM
PITSTOP
PRAETOR
PRESTON
PRESTOS
PROCTOR
QUARTOS
RALSTON
REACTOR
REALTOR
RIGHTON
ROLLTOP
ROOFTOP
ROPETOW
ROTATOR
SENATOR
SHELTON
SHORTOF
SKELTON
SLAYTON
SLEPTON
SMALTOS
SOFTTOP
SPECTOR
STANTON
STENTOR
STILTON
SWEETON
SYMPTOM
TANKTOP
TOLSTOI
TOLSTOY
TRACTOR
TRAITOR
TREETOP
TRENTON
VISITOR
WHARTON
WHEATON
WINSTON
YANKTON

••••T•O

ANNATTO
ELECTRO
HORATIO
INPETTO
INVITRO
LESOTHO
MAESTRO
ORNITHO
POINTTO
PUTITTO
REACTTO
RISOTTO
STRETTO

•••••TO

ADDEDTO
ADDONTO
ADDUPTO
AGREETO
AIMEDTO
AKIHITO
ALBERTO
ANIMATO
ANNATTO
ARIOSTO
BANDITO
BOUNDTO
BRINGTO
BURRITO
CHRISTO
CLINGTO
COMESTO
CUTINTO
DARESTO
DEFACTO
ERNESTO
FALLSTO
FLOCKTO
GEARSTO
GETINTO
GIVENTO
GIVESTO
GOTINTO
HAEMATO
HEAVETO
HOLDSTO
IMPASTO
INPETTO
JACINTO
KEEPSTO
LAYINTO
LEADSTO
LEDUPTO
LEPANTO
LITINTO
LOOKSTO
LYINGTO
MAGNETO
MEMENTO
MODESTO
OTRANTO
OWINGTO
PIMENTO
POINTTO
PRAYSTO
PRIORTO
PRYINTO
PUTITTO
RALLYTO
RANINTO
REACTTO
REFERTO
RIPINTO
RISOTTO
ROBERTO
RUNINTO
SETINTO
SINGSTO
SNAPSTO
SPIRITO
SQUANTO
STICKTO
STOOPTO
STRETTO
STUCKTO
SWEARTO
TAKESTO
TALKSTO
TARANTO
TENDSTO
THERETO
TIEINTO
TORONTO
TURNSTO
UMBERTO
VIBRATO
WANTSTO
WHERETO
WRITETO
WROTETO
YEARNTO

T•P••••

TAPERED
TAPINGS
TAPIOCA
TAPPERS
TAPPETS
TAPPING
TAPROOM
TAPROOT
TAPSOUT
TAPSTER
TEPIDLY
TIPOFFS
TIPPERS
TIPPETS
TIPPING
TIPPLED
TIPPLER
TIPPLES
TIPSIER
TIPSILY
TIPSOFF
TIPSTER
TIPTOED
TIPTOES
TIPTOPS
TOPAZES
TOPCOAT
TOPDOGS
TOPGUNS
TOPHATS
TOPIARY
TOPICAL
TOPKAPI
TOPKICK
TOPKNOT
TOPMAST
TOPMOST
TOPPERS
TOPPING
TOPPLED
TOPPLES
TOPSAIL
TOPSIDE
TOPSOFF
TOPSOIL
TOPSOUT
TUPELOS
TYPEDUP
TYPESET
TYPESUP
TYPHOON
TYPICAL
TYPISTS

T••P•••

TADPOLE
TAIPANS
TAMPERS
TAMPICO
TAMPING
TAPPERS
TAPPETS
TAPPING
TARPITS
TARPONS
TEAPOTS
TEAPOYS
TEEPEES
TEMPERA
TEMPERS
TEMPEST
TEMPLAR
TEMPLES
TEMPTED
TEMPTER
TEMPURA
TENPINS
TIEPINS
TIPPERS
TIPPETS
TIPPING
TIPPLED
TIPPLER
TIPPLES
TOPPERS
TOPPING
TOPPLED
TOPPLES
TORPEDO
TOSPARE
TOUPEES
TOWPATH
TRAPEZE
TRAPPED
TRAPPER
TREPANS
TRIPLED
TRIPLES
TRIPLET
TRIPLEX
TRIPODS
TRIPOLI
TRIPPED
TRIPPER
TRIPPET
TRIPSUP
TROPHIC
TROPICS
TROPISM
TYMPANA
TYMPANI

T•••P••

TENSPOT
TERAPHS
THESPIS
THUMPED
THUMPER
TRAIPSE
TRAMPAS
TRAMPED
TRAMPLE
TRAPPED
TRAPPER
TRIPPED
TRIPPER
TRIPPET
TROOPED
TROOPER
TROUPER
TROUPES
TRUMPED
TRUMPET
TRUMPUP

T••••P•

TEACUPS
THERAPY
TINTYPE
TIPTOPS
TOECAPS
TOETAPS
TOPKAPI
TOSSUPS
TOWROPE
TRICEPS
TRIUMPH
TUNEUPS
TURNIPS

T•••••P

TAKESUP
TALKSUP
TALLYUP
TANKSUP
TANKTOP
TEAMSUP
TEARSUP
TEASHOP
TENSEUP
THEDEEP
THINKUP
TIECLIP
TIMECOP
TIMESUP
TOELOOP
TONEDUP
TONESUP
TOOLSUP
TOUCHUP
TOYSHOP
TRADEUP
TREETOP
TRIPSUP
TRUMPUP
TUNEDUP
TUNESUP
TURNSUP
TWOSTEP
TYINGUP
TYPEDUP
TYPESUP

•TP••••

ATPEACE
STPETER

•T•P•••

STAPLED
STAPLER
STAPLES
STEPHEN
STEPINS
STEPOUT
STEPPED
STEPPER
STEPPES
STEPSIN
STEPSON
STEPSUP
STEPUPS
STIPEND
STIPPLE
STOPGAP
STOPOFF
STOPPED
STOPPER
STOPSIN
STOPSUP
STUPEFY
STUPORS
STYPTIC
UTOPIAN
UTOPIAS

•T••P••

ATROPHY
STAMPED
STAYPUT
STEEPED
STEEPEN
STEEPER
STEEPLE
STEEPLY
STEPPED
STEPPER
STEPPES
STIPPLE
STOMPED
STOOPED
STOOPTO
STOPPED
STOPPER
STRIPED
STRIPER
STRIPES
STROPHE
STUMPED
STUMPER

•T•••P•

ATTEMPT
STEPUPS

•T••••P

STACKUP
STANDUP
STARMAP
STARTUP
STAYSUP
STEPSUP
STICKUP
STIRRUP
STIRSUP
STOCKUP
STOODUP
STOPGAP
STOPSUP
STOREUP
STUCKUP

••TP•••

BITPART
HATPINS
HOTPOTS
JETPORT
NITPICK
OUTPACE
OUTPLAY
OUTPOST
OUTPUTS
POTPIES
RATPACK

••T•P••

ACTUPON
CATSPAW
ECTYPES
GOTOPOT
HOTSPOT
HOTSPUR
NOTEPAD
OCTOPOD
OCTOPUS
OCTUPLE
ONTOPOF
PITAPAT
PUTUPON
RETAPED
RETAPES
RETYPED
RETYPES
SETUPON
UNTAPED
UPTOPAR
ZATOPEK

••T••P•

ATTEMPT
BITMAPS
CATALPA
CATNAPS
CATNIPS
ENTRAPS
ENTROPY
EUTERPE
HOTCAPS
HOTLIPS
HOTTIPS
SATRAPS
UNTRAPS
UPTEMPO
WETMOPS

••T•••P

ACTEDUP
ANTEDUP
ANTESUP
ANTWERP
CATCHUP
EATENUP
KETCHUP
LETSLIP
MATCHUP
NOTRUMP
OUTCROP
OUTJUMP
OUTSTEP
PATCHUP
PITSTOP
RATTRAP

•••TP••

DUSTPAN
FOOTPAD
SHOTPUT

•••T•P•

BIGTOPS
BOXTOPS
DUSTUPS
HOTTIPS
INSTEPS
ISOTOPE
LAPTOPS
MISTYPE
PEGTOPS
PLATYPI
POPTOPS
PRETAPE
RAGTOPS
REDTAPE
REDTOPS
TINTYPE
TIPTOPS
TOETAPS
UNSTOPS
WENTAPE

•••T••P

BEATSUP
BOOTSUP
CHATSUP
DAYTRIP
DUSTMOP
EGOTRIP
FLATTOP
FLYTRAP
HEATSUP
LIFTSUP
MANTRAP
PASTEUP
PHOTOOP
RATTRAP
RESTAMP
RESTSUP
SHUTSUP
SOFTTOP
SUITSUP
UNSTRAP
WAITSUP
WRITEUP
WROTEUP

••••T•P

BOOSTUP
BOXSTEP
BUILTUP
BURNTUP
BUSSTOP
DESKTOP
FLATTOP
FOULTIP
HAMITUP
HARDTOP
HEELTAP
HIGHTOP
HILLTOP
LIGHTUP
MAINTOP
MISSTEP
MIXITUP
NONSTOP
ONESTEP
OUTSTEP
PITSTOP
ROLLTOP
ROOFTOP
SHOOTUP
SOFTTOP
SPLITUP
STARTUP
SWEPTUP
TANKTOP
TREETOP
TWOSTEP
WINGTIP
WIRETAP

T•Q••••

TEQUILA
TSQUARE

T••Q•••

TORQUES

••T•Q••

ANTIQUE

••T••Q•

ONTHEQT

TR•••••

TRABERT
TRACERS
TRACERY
TRACHEA
TRACING
TRACKED
TRACKER
TRACTOR
TRADEIN
TRADEON
TRADERS
TRADEUP
TRADING
TRADUCE
TRAFFIC
TRAGEDY
TRAILED
TRAILER
TRAINED
TRAINEE
TRAINER
TRAIPSE
TRAITOR
TRALALA
TRAMCAR
TRAMMEL
TRAMPAS
TRAMPED
TRAMPLE
TRANCES
TRANSIT
TRANSOM
TRAPEZE
TRAPPED
TRAPPER
TRASHED
TRASHES
TRAUBEL
TRAUMAS
TRAVAIL
TRAVELS
TRAVERS
TRAVOIS
TRAWLED
TRAWLER
TRAYFUL
TREACLE
TREACLY
TREADED
TREADER
TREADLE
TREASON
TREATED
TREBLED
TREBLES
TREEING
TREERAT
TREETOP
TREFOIL
TREKKED
TREKKER
TREKKIE
TRELLIS
TREMBLE
TREMBLY
TREMOLO
TREMORS
TRENARY
TRENDED
TRENTON
TREPANS
TRESSES
TRESTLE
TREVINO
TRIBUNE
TRIBUTE
TRICEPS
TRICKED
TRICKER
TRICKLE
TRICORN
TRICOTS
TRIDENT
TRIEDON
TRIESON
TRIESTE
TRIFLED
TRIFLER
TRIFLES
TRIGGED
TRIGGER
TRIGONS
TRIGRAM
TRILLED
TRILLIN
TRILOGY
TRIMMED
TRIMMER
TRINITY
TRINKET
TRIODES
TRIPLED
TRIPLES
TRIPLET
TRIPLEX
TRIPODS
TRIPOLI
TRIPPED
TRIPPER
TRIPPET
TRIPSUP
TRIREME
TRISECT
TRISTAN
TRITELY
TRITEST
TRITIUM
TRITONE
TRITONS
TRIUMPH
TRIUNES
TRIVETS
TRIVIAL
TROCARS
TROCHEE
TROCHES
TRODDEN
TROIKAS
TROILUS
TROJANS
TROLLED
TROLLEY
TROOPED
TROOPER
TROPHIC
TROPICS
TROPISM
TROTHED
TROTOUT
TROTSKY
TROTTED
TROTTER
TROUBLE
TROUGHS
TROUNCE
TROUPER
TROUPES

TROUSER
TROWELS
TROWERS
TRUANCY
TRUANTS
TRUCIAL
TRUCKED
TRUCKEE
TRUCKER
TRUCKLE
TRUDEAU
TRUDGED
TRUDGER
TRUDGES
TRUEING
TRUFFLE
TRUISMS
TRUMPED
TRUMPET
TRUMPUP
TRUNDLE
TRUSSED
TRUSSES
TRUSTED
TRUSTEE
TRYOUTS
TRYSTED
TRYSTER

T•R••••

TARANTO
TARBABY
TARBELL
TARDIER
TARDILY
TARGETS
TARHEEL
TARIFFS
TARMACS
TARNISH
TARPITS
TARPONS
TARRIED
TARRIES
TARRING
TARSALS
TARSIER
TARTANS
TARTARE
TARTARS
TARTEST
TARZANA
TERAPHS
TERBIUM
TERCELS
TERCETS
TEREDOS
TERENCE
TERHUNE
TERMING
TERMINI
TERMITE
TERNARY
TERNATE
TERRACE
TERRAIN
TERRENE
TERRETS
TERRIER
TERRIES
TERRIFY
TERRORS
TERSELY
TERSEST
TERTIAL
THRALLS
THREADS
THREADY
THREATS
THREERS
THREWIN
THRIFTS
THRIFTY
THRILLS
THRIVED
THRIVES
THROATS
THROATY
THRONES
THRONGS
THROUGH
THROWER
THROWIN
THRUSTS
THRUWAY
TIRADES
TIREDER
TIREDLY
TIREDOF
TIREOUT
TORCHED
TORCHES
TOREOFF
TOREOUT
TOREROS
TORMENT
TORNADO
TORNOUT
TOROIDS
TORONTO
TORPEDO
TORQUES
TORRENT
TORSION
TORTONI
TORYISM
TURBANS
TURBINE
TURBOTS
TUREENS
TURKEYS
TURKISH
TURMOIL
TURNERS
TURNING
TURNIPS
TURNKEY
TURNOFF
TURNOUT
TURNSIN
TURNSON
TURNSTO
TURNSUP
TURRETS
TURTLED
TURTLES
TYRANNY
TYRANTS

T••R•••

TAPROOM
TAPROOT
TARRIED
TARRIES
TARRING
TAURINE
TAXRATE
TEARFUL
TEARGAS
TEARIER
TEARILY
TEARING
TEAROFF
TEAROOM
TEAROSE
TEARSAT
TEARSUP
TERRACE
TERRAIN
TERRENE
TERRETS
TERRIER
TERRIES
TERRIFY
TERRORS
TETRADS
THERAPY
THEREAT
THEREBY
THEREIN
THEREOF
THEREON
THERESA
THERETO
THERMAL
THERMOS
THEROUX
THIRDLY
THIRSTS
THIRSTY
THOREAU
THORIUM
THURBER
THURMAN
TIERACK
TIERING
TIERNEY
TIERODS
TIGRESS
TITRATE
TOORDER
TORRENT
TOURACO
TOURERS
TOURING
TOURISM
TOURIST
TOURNEY
TOWROPE
TRIREME
TSARINA
TSARIST
TUAREGS
TURRETS
TWIRLED
TWIRLER
TZARINA

T•••R••

TABARDS
TABORET
TALARIA
TAMARIN
TANTRUM
TAPERED
TAVERNS
TAXFREE
TEATRAY
TEHERAN
TELERAN
TENDRIL
TENURED
TENURES
THEOREM
THIERRY
THWARTS
TIMBRES
TONEROW
TOREROS
TOWARDS
TOWERED
TREERAT
TRIGRAM
TSHIRTS
TUMBREL
TUNDRAS
TUTORED

T••••R•

TACKERS
TAILORS
TALKERS
TAMPERS
TANGERE
TANKARD
TANKERS
TANNERS
TANNERY
TANTARA
TAPPERS
TARTARE
TARTARS
TASTERS
TATTERS
TEACART
TEASERS
TEDDERS
TEENERS
TEETERS
TELLERS
TEMPERA
TEMPERS
TEMPURA
TENDERS
TENNERS
TENSORS
TENTERS
TERNARY
TERRORS
TESSERA
TESTERS
TETHERS
TEXTURE
THALERS
THEATRE
THIERRY
THREERS
TICKERS
TILLERS
TILTERS
TIMBERS
TINDERS
TINEARS
TINHORN
TINKERS
TINNERS
TINTERN
TINTERS
TINWORK
TIPPERS
TITHERS
TITTERS
TOILERS
TONEARM
TONSURE
TOOTERS
TOPIARY
TOPPERS
TOSPARE
TOSSERS
TOTTERS
TOTTERY
TOURERS
TOUTERS
TOWCARS
TOWNERS
TRABERT
TRACERS
TRACERY
TRADERS
TRAVERS
TREMORS
TRENARY
TRICORN
TROCARS
TROWERS
TSQUARE
TUCKERS
TUGGERS
TURNERS
TUSKERS
TWOFERS

T•••••R

TABULAR
TACKIER
TACKLER
TAMBOUR
TANAGER
TANGIER
TAPSTER
TARDIER
TARSIER
TASTIER
TATTIER
TATTLER
TAWNIER
TEACHER
TEARIER
TEENIER
TEETHER
TEICHER
TELSTAR
TEMBLOR
TEMPLAR
TEMPTER
TENFOUR
TERRIER
TESTIER
THEATER
THICKER
THINAIR
THINKER
THINNER
THITHER
THROWER
THUMPER
THUNDER
THURBER
THUSFAR
TICKLER
TIGHTER
TIMIDER
TINNIER
TINSTAR
TIPPLER
TIPSIER
TIPSTER
TIREDER
TITULAR
TOASTER
TODDLER
TOFFLER
TOORDER
TOUGHER
TRACKER
TRACTOR
TRAILER
TRAINER
TRAITOR
TRAMCAR
TRAPPER
TRAWLER
TREADER
TREKKER
TRICKER
TRIFLER
TRIGGER
TRIMMER
TRIPPER
TROOPER
TROTTER
TROUPER
TROUSER
TRUCKER
TRUDGER
TRYSTER
TUBBIER
TUBULAR
TUMBLER
TUTELAR
TWEETER
TWIRLER
TWISTER
TWITTER
TWOSTAR

•TR••••

ATRIUMS
ATROPHY
ETRURIA
OTRANTO
STRAFED
STRAFES
STRAINS
STRAITS
STRANDS
STRANGE
STRASSE
STRATUM
STRATUS
STRAUSS
STRAYED
STREAKS
STREAKY
STREAMS
STREETS
STRETCH
STRETTO
STREWED
STREWER
STRIATE
STRIDER
STRIDES
STRIKER
STRIKES
STRINGS
STRINGY
STRIPED
STRIPER
STRIPES
STRIVED
STRIVEN
STRIVER
STRIVES
STROBES
STROKED
STROKES
STROLLS
STROPHE
STRUDEL
UTRECHT
UTRILLO

•T•R•••

ATTRACT
ATTRITE
ATTRITS
ETERNAL
ITERANT
ITERATE
STARCHY
STARDOM
STAREAT
STARERS
STARETS
STARING
STARKER
STARKLY
STARLET
STARLIT
STARMAN
STARMAP
STARRED
STARTED
STARTER
STARTLE
STARTUP
STARVED
STARVES
STCROIX
STEREOS
STERILE
STERNAL
STERNER
STERNLY
STERNUM
STEROID
STEROLS
STIRFRY
STIRRED
STIRRER
STIRRUP
STIRSIN
STIRSUP
STORAGE
STORERS
STOREUP
STOREYS
STORIED
STORIES
STORING
STORMED
STURGES
STYRENE
STYRIAN
YTTRIUM

•T••R••

ATECROW
ATHIRST
ATLARGE
ATTIRED
ATTIRES
ATWORST
ETRURIA
STARRED
STEERED
STEERER
STIRRED
STIRRER
STIRRUP
UTTERED
UTTERER
UTTERLY

•T•••R•

ATATURK
ATHEART
ATHWART
ETAGERE
ETCHERS
STAGERS
STARERS
STATORS
STATURE
STEWARD
STEWART
STEWERS
STIRFRY
STOKERS
STONERS
STORERS
STUPORS
STYLERS

•T••••R

ATELIER
ITCHIER
STABLER
STAFFER
STAGGER
STAGIER
STAIDER
STAINER
STALKER
STAMMER
STAPLER
STARKER
STARTER
STEAMER
STEELER
STEEPER
STEERER
STEIGER
STEINER
STELLAR
STENTOR
STEPPER
STERNER
STICKER
STIFFER
STILLER
STINGER
STINKER
STIRRER
STOLLER
STONIER
STOPPER
STOUTER
STPETER
STREWER
STRIDER
STRIKER
STRIPER
STRIVER
STUFFER
STUMPER
STUNNER
UTTERER

••TR•••

ACTRESS
ASTRIDE
ATTRACT
ATTRITE
ATTRITS
BETRAYS
BETROTH
CITRATE
CITRINE
CITROEN
CITRONS
CUTRATE
DETRACT
DETRAIN
DETROIT
ENTRAIN
ENTRANT
ENTRAPS
ENTREAT
ENTREES
ENTRIES
ENTROPY
ENTRUST
ESTRADA
ESTRAYS
EXTRACT
EXTREME
EXTRUDE
HATRACK
HOTRODS
INTROIT
INTRUDE
INTRUST
INTRUTH
MATRONS
METRICS
MITRING
NATRIUM
NITRATE
NITRIDE
NITRITE
NITROUS
NOTRUMP
NUTRIAS
OBTRUDE
ONTRIAL
OSTRICH
OUTRACE
OUTRAGE
OUTRANK
OUTRUNS
PATRICE
PATRICK
PATRIOT
PATROLS
PATRONS
PATROON
PETRELS
PETRIFY
PETROCK
PETROUS
RATRACE
RETRACE
RETRACK
RETRACT
RETRADE
RETRAIN
RETREAD
RETREAT
RETRIAL
RETRIED
RETRIES
RETRIMS
SATRAPS
TETRADS
TITRATE
UNTRAPS
UNTRIED
UNTRUTH
VITRIFY
VITRIOL
YTTRIUM

••T•R••

ALTERED
ALTERER
ANTARES
ASTARTE
ASTORIA
ATTIRED
ATTIRES
BETARAY
BYTURNS
CATERED
CATERER
COTERIE
EATCROW
ENTERED
ESTORIL
EUTERPE
EXTORTS
FUTURES
GUTHRIE
INTERIM
INTERNS
INTERSE
KATHRYN
LATERAL
LATERAN
LATERON
LETTRES
LITERAL
LITURGY
MATURED
MATURER
MATURES
METERED
MITERED
MITHRAS
MOTORED
NATURAL
NATURED
NATURES
NOTTRUE
ONTARIO
OUTCROP
OUTDRAW
OUTDREW
OUTGREW
OUTGROW
PATERNO
PETARDS
PETERED
RATTRAP
RETARDS
RETIRED
RETIREE
RETIRES
RETORTS
RETURNS
SATIRES
SATIRIC
SUTURED
SUTURES
TUTORED
UPTURNS
UTTERED
UTTERER
UTTERLY
VETERAN
WATERED
WATERER

••T••R•

ACTUARY
ANTFARM
ANTHERS
ANTIART
ANTLERS
ANTWERP
ARTFORM
ARTWARE
ARTWORK
ASTAIRE
AUTEURS
AUTHORS
BATHERS
BATTERS
BATTERY
BETTERS
BETTORS
BITPART
BITTERN
BITTERS
BOTHERS
BUTLERS
BUTTERS
BUTTERY
CATBIRD
COTTERS
CUTLERS
CUTLERY
CUTTERS
DETOURS
DITHERS
DITHERY
ESTUARY
FATHERS
FETTERS
FITTERS
GATHERS
GUTTERS
HATTERS
HITHERE
HITTERS
HOTCARS
HOTWARS
HOTWIRE
INTEGRA
JETPORT
JITTERS
JITTERY
LATHERS
LATHERY
LETTERS
LITTERS
LOTTERY
MATHERS
MATTERS
METEORS
METIERS
MITFORD
MOTHERS
MUTTERS
NATTERS
NETSURF
NETWORK
NOTSURE
NUTTERS
OSTLERS
OUTWARD
OUTWORE
OUTWORK
OUTWORN
PATTERN
PATTERS
PETTERS
PITTERS
POTHERB
POTHERS
POTTERS
POTTERY
PUTTERS
RATTERS
ROTTERS
RUTGERS
SETTERS
SITTERS
SOTHERE
SOTHERN
SUTLERS
TATTERS
TETHERS
TITHERS
TITTERS
TOTTERS
TOTTERY
VETOERS
WETBARS
WETHERS
WITHERS
ZITHERS

••T•••R

ALTERER
ANTBEAR
ANTIWAR
ANTSIER
BATTIER
BATTLER
BITTIER
BOTTLER
BUTCHER
CATCHER
CATERER
CATHAIR
CATTIER
CNTOWER
DOTTIER
ENTICER
GETOVER
GOTOVER
GUTSIER
HATCHER
HITCHER
HOTSPUR
INTEGER
INTONER
LITTLER
MATADOR
MATURER
METOOER
NATTIER
NUTTIER
OBTUSER
OCTOBER
OFTENER
OUTDOOR
OUTWEAR
PETTIER
PITCHER
PITHIER
PUTOVER
RATTIER
RATTLER
RITZIER
ROTATOR
ROTIFER
SETTLER
SUTTNER
TATTIER
TATTLER
TITULAR
TUTELAR
UPTOPAR
UTTERER
WATCHER
WATERER
WITTIER

•••TR••

ASHTRAY
AUSTRAL
AUSTRIA
BEATRIX
BEETREE
BESTREW
BISTROS
BOUTROS
CENTRAL
CENTRED
CENTRES
CENTRIC
CHETRUM
CONTRAS
CONTROL
DALTREY
DAYTRIP
DESTROY
DEXTRIN
DOGTROT
EGOTRIP
ELMTREE
ERITREA
FLYTRAP
FORTRAN
FOXTROT
GASTRIC
GUMTREE
KESTREL
LAUTREC
LETTRES
LUSTRED
LUSTRES
MAITRED
MANTRAP
MANTRAS
MANTRIC
MISTRAL
NEUTRAL
NEUTRON
NOSTRIL
NOSTRUM
NOTTRUE
OAKTREE
PORTRAY
RATTRAP

ROSTRUM
SISTRUM
TANTRUM
TEATRAY
UNSTRAP
UPATREE
VENTRAL
WASTREL

•••T•R•
AMATORY
ATATURK
AUSTERE
AVATARS
BANTERS
BARTERS
BASTERS
BATTERS
BATTERY
BEATERS
BESTIRS
BETTERS
BETTORS
BITTERN
BITTERS
BOATERS
BUSTARD
BUTTERS
BUTTERY
CANTERS
CANTORS
CAPTORS
CAPTURE
CARTERS
CASTERS
CENTERS
CENTURY
CISTERN
CLOTURE
CONTORT
COPTERS
COSTARS
COTTERS
COUTURE
CRATERS
CULTURE
CUSTARD
CUTTERS
DARTERS
DASTARD
DEBTORS
DENTURE
DEUTERO
DIETARY
DIETERS
DISTORT
DISTURB
DOCTORS
DUSTERS
EASTERN
EASTERS
EDITORS
ELATERS
EMOTERS
FACTORS
FACTORY
FALTERS
FEATURE
FESTERS
FETTERS
FILTERS
FITTERS
FIXTURE
FOOTERS
FOSTERS
GAITERS
GARTERS
GESTURE
GRATERS
GUITARS
GUTTERS
HALTERS
HATTERS
HEATERS
HECTARE
HECTORS
HISTORY
HITTERS
HOOTERS
HUNTERS
INSTORE
JESTERS
JITTERS
JITTERY
KRATERS
LANTERN
LASTORY
LECTERN
LECTORS
LECTURE
LEOTARD
LETTERS
LIFTERS
LITTERS
LOITERS
LOOTERS
LOTTERY
LUSTERS
MARTYRS
MASTERS
MASTERY
MATTERS
MENTORS
MIDTERM
MINTERS
MISTERS
MIXTURE
MOLTERS
MORTARS
MUSTARD
MUSTERS
MUTTERS
MYSTERY
NATTERS
NECTARS
NESTERS
NOCTURN
NURTURE
NUTTERS
ORATORS
ORATORY
OUSTERS
OYSTERS
PALTERS
PASTERN
PASTORS
PASTURE
PATTERN
PATTERS
PELTERS
PERTURB
PESTERS
PETTERS
PICTURE
PITTERS
PLATERS
POPTART
PORTERS
POSTERN
POSTERS
POSTURE
POTTERS
POTTERY
POUTERS
PRATERS
PUNTERS
PUTTERS
QINTARS
QUOTERS
RAFTERS
RANTERS
RAPTORS
RAPTURE
RASTERS
RATTERS
RECTORS
RECTORY
RENTERS
RESTART
RESTERS
RESTORE
REUTERS
RHETORS
RIOTERS
RIPTORN
ROOTERS
ROSTERS
ROTTERS
ROUTERS
RUPTURE
SALTERS
SANTIRS
SCOTERS
SEATERS
SECTORS
SETTERS
SIFTERS
SISTERS
SITTERS
SKATERS
SORTERS
STATORS
STATURE
SUITORS
TANTARA
TARTARE
TARTARS
TASTERS
TATTERS
TEETERS
TENTERS
TESTERS
TEXTURE
TILTERS
TINTERN
TINTERS
TITTERS
TOOTERS
TOTTERS
TOTTERY
TOUTERS
ULSTERS
UNITARY
UNITERS
UPSTART
VECTORS
VENTERS
VENTURA
VENTURE
VESTURE
VICTORS
VICTORY
VULTURE
WAITERS
WALTERS
WASTERS
WELTERS
WESTERN
WINTERS
WINTERY
WRITERS

•••T••R
ABETTOR
AMATEUR
ANOTHER
BATTIER
BATTLER
BITTIER
BLATHER
BLITHER
BLOTTER
BOTTLER
BROTHER
CARTIER
CATTIER
CENTAUR
CHATTER
CHITTER
CLATTER
CLUTTER
CONTOUR
COSTNER
CRITTER
DIRTIER
DOTTIER
DUSTIER
EMITTER
EMPTIER
FARTHER
FEATHER
FELTFOR
FLATCAR
FLATTER
FLITTER
FLUTTER
FRITTER
FURTHER
FUSTIER
GENTLER
GLITTER
GUNTHER
HASTIER
HAUTEUR
HEATHER
HEATTER
HEFTIER
HOSTLER
HUSTLER
JOSTLER
KNITTER
LEATHER
LINTIER
LITTLER
LOFTIER
LUSTIER
MEATIER
MINTIER
MISTIER
MUSTIER
NASTIER
NATTIER
NEITHER
NESTLER
NIFTIER
NORTHER
NUTTIER
ONATEAR
PANTHER
PARTNER
PASTEUR
PASTIER
PETTIER
PLATTER
PLOTTER
POITIER
POSTWAR
POUTIER
QUITTER
RATTIER
RATTLER
REUTHER
ROOTFOR
RUNTIER
RUSTIER
RUSTLER
SALTIER
SCATTER
SELTZER
SENTFOR
SETTLER
SHATNER
SHATTER
SHOTFOR
SHUTTER
SKITTER
SLATHER
SLATIER
SLITHER
SLOTCAR
SMATTER
SMOTHER
SOOTHER
SOOTIER
SPATTER
SPOTTER
SPUTTER
SUBTLER
SUTTNER
SWATTER
SWITZER
TASTIER
TATTIER
TATTLER
TEETHER
TESTIER
THITHER
TROTTER
TWITTER
VINTNER
WALTZER
WEATHER
WENTFOR
WERTHER
WHATFOR
WHETHER
WHITHER
WITTIER
ZESTIER

••••TR•
BIGOTRY
COUNTRY
DIMITRI
DYKSTRA
ELECTRA
ELECTRO
ELEKTRA
FENETRE
HELOTRY
INVITRO
LANGTRY
MAESTRI
MAESTRO
OLESTRA
PHILTRE
PIASTRE
PLECTRA
POULTRY
REENTRY
SCEPTRE
SHASTRI
SINATRA
SPECTRA
SPECTRE
SUMATRA
SWELTRY
THEATRE

••••T•R
ABETTOR
ADAPTER
ADAPTOR
ADOPTER
AERATOR
ALERTER
ALLSTAR
AMMETER
ARBITER
AUDITOR
AVIATOR
BENATAR
BLASTER
BLISTER
BLOTTER
BLUNTER
BLUSTER
BOASTER
BOLSTER
BOOSTER
CHANTER
CHAPTER
CHARTER
CHASTER
CHATTER
CHEATER
CHESTER
CHITTER
CLATTER
CLUSTER
CLUTTER
COALTAR
COASTER
COULTER
COUNTER
CRAFTER
CREATOR
CRITTER
CURATOR
DAYSTAR
DEBATER
DEMETER
DILUTER
DIOPTER
DOGSTAR
DONATOR
DOUBTER
DRIFTER
ELECTOR
EMITTER
ENACTOR
EQUATOR
ERECTER
ERECTOR
EXACTER
EXACTOR
FAINTER
FIGHTER
FLATTER
FLEETER
FLITTER
FLOATER
FLUSTER
FLUTTER
FORSTER
FRITTER
GAGSTER
GAUNTER
GLITTER
GRANTOR
GREATER
GREETER
GRIFTER
GYRATOR
HAMSTER
HEATTER
HIPSTER
HOLSTER
IGNITER
INCITER
JACKTAR
JANITOR
JOUSTER
JUPITER
KNITTER
LEISTER
LIGHTER
LOBSTER
LOCATER
LOCATOR
MOBSTER
MOISTER
MONITOR
MONSTER
NEGATOR
OLDSTER
ORBITER
PAINTER
PHILTER
PIASTER
PINETAR
PLANTAR
PLANTER
PLASTER
PLATTER
PLOTTER
POINTER
POLITER
PRAETOR
PRINTER
PROCTOR
PSALTER
PUNSTER
QUARTER
QUIETER
QUILTER
QUITTER
REACTOR
REALTOR
RECITER
REDSTAR
REENTER
REFUTER
REMOTER
RICHTER
RIGHTER
RIVETER
ROASTER
ROISTER
ROOSTER
ROTATOR
SAUNTER
SCANTER
SCATTER
SCEPTER
SCOOTER
SCOUTER
SEASTAR
SEDATER
SENATOR
SHANTER
SHATTER
SHELTER
SHOOTER
SHORTER
SHOUTER
SHUTTER
SHYSTER
SKEETER
SKELTER
SKITTER
SMARTER
SMATTER
SMELTER
SNIFTER
SNORTER
SPATTER
SPECTER
SPECTOR
SPOTTER
SPOUTER
SPUTTER
STARTER
STENTOR
STOUTER
STPETER
SVELTER
SWATTER
SWEATER
SWEETER
SWELTER
SWIFTER
TAPSTER
TELSTAR
TEMPTER
THEATER
TIGHTER
TINSTAR
TIPSTER
TOASTER
TRACTOR
TRAITOR
TROTTER
TRYSTER
TWEETER
TWISTER
TWITTER
TWOSTAR
VAULTER
VAUNTER
VISITOR
WEBSTER
WOOSTER

TS•••••
TSARINA
TSARIST
TSELIOT
TSETSES
TSHIRTS
TSONGAS
TSQUARE
TSUNAMI

T•S••••
TASKING
TASSELS
TASTERS
TASTIER
TASTILY
TASTING
TESSERA
TESTBAN
TESTEES
TESTERS
TESTIER
TESTIFY
TESTILY
TESTING
TESTOUT
TISANES
TISSUES
TOSCALE
TOSHIBA
TOSPARE
TOSSERS
TOSSING
TOSSOFF
TOSSOUT
TOSSUPS
TOSTADA
TUSCANY
TUSKERS
TUSSAUD
TUSSLED
TUSSLES
TUSSOCK
TVSHOWS

T••S•••
TAGSALE
TAGSOUT
TANSIES
TAPSOUT
TAPSTER
TARSALS
TARSIER
TASSELS
TEASELS
TEASERS
TEASETS
TEASHOP
TEASING
TEESOFF
TELSTAR
TENSELY
TENSEST
TENSEUP
TENSILE
TENSING
TENSION
TENSIVE
TENSORS
TENSPOT
TERSELY
TERSEST
TESSERA
THESEUS
THESPIS
THISTLE
THUSFAR
THYSELF
TINSELS
TINSTAR
TIPSIER
TIPSILY
TIPSOFF
TIPSTER
TISSUES
TOASTED
TOASTER
TOCSINS
TOESHOE
TOLSTOI
TOLSTOY
TONSILS
TONSURE
TOPSAIL
TOPSIDE
TOPSOFF
TOPSOIL
TOPSOUT
TORSION
TOSSERS
TOSSING
TOSSOFF
TOSSOUT
TOSSUPS
TOUSLED
TOUSLES
TOYSHOP
TRASHED
TRASHES
TRESSES
TRESTLE
TRISECT
TRISTAN
TRUSSED
TRUSSES
TRUSTED
TRUSTEE
TRYSTED
TRYSTER
TUESDAY
TULSANS
TUSSAUD
TUSSLED
TUSSLES
TUSSOCK
TWISTED
TWISTER
TWOSOME
TWOSTAR
TWOSTEP

T•••S••
TABASCO
TACKSON
TAKESIN
TAKESON
TAKESTO
TAKESUP
TALKSAT
TALKSTO
TALKSUP
TALUSES
TANKSUP
TAOISTS
TEAMSUP
TEARSAT
TEARSUP
TELLSON
TENDSTO
THATSIT
THEISTS
THIRSTS
THIRSTY
THOMSON
THRUSTS
TIMESUP
TONESUP
TOOLSUP
TOOTSIE
TRANSIT
TRANSOM
TREASON
TRESSES
TRIESON
TRIESTE
TRIPSUP
TROTSKY
TROUSER
TRUISMS
TRUSSED
TRUSSES
TSETSES
TUBISTS
TUCKSIN
TUNESIN
TUNESUP
TUNISIA
TURNSIN
TURNSON
TURNSTO
TURNSUP
TYPESET
TYPESUP
TYPISTS

T••••S•
TALLEST
TALLISH
TANNEST
TANNISH
TARNISH
TARTEST
TAUTEST
TBILISI
TEAROSE
TEMPEST
TENSEST
TERSEST
THERESA
TIDIEST
TIELESS
TIGRESS
TINIEST
TITLIST
TOELESS
TONIEST
TOPMAST
TOPMOST
TORYISM
TOURISM
TOURIST
TRAIPSE
TRITEST
TROPISM
TSARIST
TUBAIST
TURKISH
TWOBASE

T•••••S
TABARDS
TABBIES
TABLETS
TACITUS
TACKERS
TACKLES
TACTICS
TAFFIES
TAGENDS
TAILLES
TAILORS
TAIPANS
TALENTS
TALKERS
TALKIES
TALLIES
TALLOWS
TALUSES
TAMALES
TAMPERS
TAMTAMS
TANDEMS
TANGLES
TANKERS
TANNERS
TANNINS
TANOAKS
TANSIES
TAOISTS
TAPINGS
TAPPERS
TAPPETS
TARGETS
TARIFFS
TARMACS
TARPITS
TARPONS
TARRIES
TARSALS
TARTANS
TARTARS
TASSELS
TASTERS
TATAMIS
TATTERS
TATTLES
TATTOOS
TAUTENS
TAVERNS
TEABAGS
TEACHES
TEACUPS
TEAPOTS
TEAPOYS
TEARGAS
TEASELS
TEASERS
TEASETS
TECHIES
TEDDERS
TEDDIES
TEDIOUS
TEENERS
TEEPEES
TEETERS
TEETHES
TELEXES
TELLERS
TELLIES
TEMPERS
TEMPLES
TENACES
TENANTS
TENDERS
TENDONS
TENNERS
TENPINS
TENSORS
TENTERS
TENUOUS
TENURES
TERAPHS
TERCELS
TERCETS
TEREDOS
TERRETS
TERRIES
TERRORS
TESTEES
TESTERS
TETANUS
TETHERS
TETRADS
TEUTONS
THALERS
THEISTS
THERMOS
THESEUS
THESPIS
THIEVES
THIRSTS
THRALLS
THREADS
THREATS
THREERS
THRIFTS
THRILLS
THRIVES
THROATS
THRONES
THRONGS
THRUSTS
THWACKS
THWARTS
TICKERS
TICKETS
TICKLES
TICTACS
TIDBITS
TIDINGS
TIEDYES
TIELESS
TIEPINS
TIERODS
TIGRESS
TILLERS
TILTERS
TIMBALS
TIMBERS
TIMBRES
TIMEWAS
TIMINGS
TIMMINS
TINCANS
TINDERS
TINEARS
TINGLES
TINHATS
TINKERS
TINKLES
TINNERS
TINSELS
TINTERS
TIPOFFS
TIPPERS

TIPPETS
TIPPLES
TIPTOES
TIPTOPS
TIRADES
TISANES
TISSUES
TITBITS
TITHERS
TITTERS
TITTLES
TIZZIES
TOADIES
TOCSINS
TODDIES
TODDLES
TOECAPS
TOELESS
TOETAPS
TOFFEES
TOGGLES
TOILERS
TOILETS
TOLTECS
TOMBOYS
TOMCATS
TOMTITS
TOMTOMS
TONGANS
TONGUES
TONSILS
TOOTERS
TOOTLES
TOPAZES
TOPDOGS
TOPGUNS
TOPHATS
TOPPERS
TOPPLES
TORCHES
TOREROS
TOROIDS
TORQUES
TOSSERS
TOSSUPS
TOTTERS
TOUCANS
TOUCHES
TOUPEES
TOURERS
TOUSLES
TOUTERS
TOWARDS
TOWCARS
TOWHEES
TOWNERS
TOWNIES
TOYDOGS
TRACERS
TRADERS
TRAMPAS
TRANCES
TRASHES
TRAUMAS
TRAVELS
TRAVERS
TRAVOIS
TREBLES
TRELLIS
TREMORS
TREPANS
TRESSES
TRICEPS
TRICOTS
TRIFLES
TRIGONS
TRIODES
TRIPLES
TRIPODS
TRITONS
TRIUNES
TRIVETS
TROCARS
TROCHES
TROIKAS
TROILUS
TROJANS
TROPICS
TROUGHS
TROUPES
TROWELS
TROWERS
TRUANTS
TRUDGES
TRUISMS
TRUSSES
TRYOUTS
TSETSES
TSHIRTS
TSONGAS
TUAREGS
TUBISTS
TUCKERS
TUFFETS
TUGGERS
TULSANS
TUMBLES
TUMMIES
TUMULTS
TUMULUS
TUNDRAS
TUNEUPS
TUNNELS
TUNNIES
TUPELOS
TURBANS
TURBOTS
TUREENS
TURKEYS
TURNERS
TURNIPS
TURRETS
TURTLES
TUSKERS
TUSSLES
TUTTUTS
TUXEDOS
TVSHOWS
TWEEZES
TWELVES
TWINGES
TWOBITS
TWOFERS
TYCOONS
TYPISTS
TYRANTS

•TS••••
ATSTAKE

•T•S•••
ATISSUE
ETESIAN
KTOSLIN
STASHED
STASHES
STASSEN

•T••S••
ATISSUE
ATLASES
ATTESTS
STASSEN
STAYSUP
STEPSIN
STEPSON
STEPSUP
STETSON
STIRSIN
STIRSUP
STOPSIN
STOPSUP
STRASSE
UTENSIL

•T•••S•
ATALOSS
ATAVISM
ATAVIST
ATHEISM
ATHEIST
ATHIRST
ATLEAST
ATWORST
STALEST
STATIST
STRASSE
STRAUSS
STYLISH
STYLIST

•T••••S
ATALOSS
ATAMANS
ATHOMES
ATLASES
ATLATLS
ATOMIES
ATRIUMS
ATTACKS
ATTAINS
ATTENDS
ATTESTS
ATTICUS
ATTIMES
ATTIRES
ATTRITS
ATTUCKS
ATTUNES
ETCHERS
ETHNICS
ETOILES
ITALICS
OTTAWAS
PTBOATS
STABLES
STAGERS
STALAGS
STAMENS
STANCES
STANZAS
STAPLES
STARERS
STARETS
STARVES
STASHES
STATICS
STATORS
STATUES
STDENIS
STEPINS
STEPPES
STEPUPS
STEREOS
STEROLS
STEVENS
STEWERS
STICHES
STIFLES
STIGMAS
STJOHNS
STKITTS
STLOUIS
STOGIES
STOKERS
STOLONS
STONERS
STOOGES
STORERS
STOREYS
STORIES
STRAFES
STRAINS
STRAITS
STRANDS
STRATUS
STRAUSS
STREAKS
STREAMS
STREETS
STRIDES
STRIKES
STRINGS
STRIPES
STRIVES
STROBES
STROKES
STROLLS
STUCCOS
STUDIES
STUDIOS
STUPORS
STURGES
STYLERS
STYLETS
STYMIES
UTAHANS
UTOPIAS

••TS•••
ACTSOUT
ANTSIER
ARTSONG
BATSMAN
BATSMEN
CATSCAN
CATSEYE
CATSPAW
CUTSOFF
CUTSOUT
EATSOUT
GETSOFF
GETSOUT
GETSSET
GUTSIER
GUTSILY
HOTSEAT
HOTSHOT
HOTSPOT
HOTSPUR
JETSONS
KITSCHY
LETSFLY
LETSLIP
LETSOFF
LETSOUT
LETSSEE
NETSUKE
NETSURF
NOTSURE
OPTSOUT
OUTSELL
OUTSETS
OUTSIDE
OUTSIZE
OUTSOLD
OUTSTEP
PATSIES
PITSAWS
PITSTOP
POTSDAM
POTSHOT
PUTSOFF
PUTSOUT
RETSINA
SATSUMA
SETSAIL
SETSOFF
SETSOUT
SITSOUT
WETSUIT

••T•S••
ALTOSAX
ANTESUP
ARTISAN
ARTISTE
ARTISTS
ATTESTS
BATISTA
BATISTE
BUTTSIN
DATASET
DETESTS
DOTESON
GETSSET
IQTESTS
LETSSEE
LOTUSES
LUTISTS
MATISSE
MITOSES
MITOSIS
NATASHA
OBTUSER
RETESTS
SATISFY
VOTESIN

••T••S•
ACTRESS
APTNESS
ARTIEST
ARTLESS
CATFISH
CATTISH
CUTLASS
ENTHUSE
ENTRUST
FATLESS
FATNESS
FATTEST
FITNESS
FITTEST
GETLOST
GUTLESS
HATLESS
HITLESS
HITLIST
HOTNESS
HOTTEST
INTENSE
INTERSE
INTRUST
JETWASH
LITHEST
MATISSE
OUTCAST
OUTLAST
OUTPOST
PATNESS
PETTISH
PITBOSS
TITLIST
UNTWIST
WETNESS
WETTEST
WITLESS
WITNESS

••T•••S
ACTIONS
ACTIVES
ACTRESS
AITCHES
ANTAEUS
ANTARES
ANTCOWS
ANTHEMS
ANTHERS
ANTIBES
ANTLERS
APTNESS
ARTEMIS
ARTEMUS
ARTISTS
ARTLESS
ATTACKS
ATTAINS
ATTENDS
ATTESTS
ATTICUS
ATTIMES
ATTIRES
ATTRITS
ATTUCKS
ATTUNES
AUTEURS
AUTHORS
AUTUMNS
BATBOYS
BATCHES
BATHERS
BATTENS
BATTERS
BATTLES
BETAKES
BETHELS
BETIDES
BETIMES
BETRAYS
BETTERS
BETTORS
BITMAPS
BITTERS
BOTCHES
BOTHERS
BOTTLES
BOTTOMS
BUTLERS
BUTTERS
BUTTONS
BYTURNS
CATCHES
CATIONS
CATKINS
CATNAPS
CATNIPS
CITRONS
COTTERS
COTTONS
CUTLASS
CUTLERS
CUTLETS
CUTOFFS
CUTOUTS
CUTTERS
DETAILS
DETAINS
DETECTS
DETESTS
DETOURS
DITCHES
DITHERS
DITTIES
DOTTLES
DUTEOUS
ECTYPES
ENTAILS
ENTICES
ENTRAPS
ENTREES
ENTRIES
ESTATES
ESTEEMS
ESTRAYS
EXTENDS
EXTENTS
EXTORTS
FATCATS
FATHERS
FATHOMS
FATLESS
FATNESS
FATTENS
FATUOUS
FETCHES
FETTERS
FETTLES
FITCHES
FITNESS
FITTERS
FUTURES
GATHERS
GOTCHAS
GOTHICS
GUTLESS
GUTTERS
HATCHES
HATLESS
HATPINS
HATTERS
HETMANS
HITCHES
HITLESS
HITTERS
HOTBEDS
HOTCAPS
HOTCARS
HOTDOGS
HOTLIPS
HOTNESS
HOTPOTS
HOTRODS
HOTTIPS
HOTTUBS
HOTWARS
HUTCHES
INTAKES
INTENDS
INTENTS
INTERNS
INTONES
INTUITS
IQTESTS
ISTHMUS
JETGUNS
JETSONS
JETTIES
JITNEYS
JITTERS
KETCHES
KETONES
KETTLES
KITBAGS
KITTENS
KITTIES
LATCHES
LATEENS
LATENTS
LATEXES
LATHERS
LATICES
LATINAS
LATINOS
LATTENS
LETTERS
LETTRES
LITCHIS
LITOTES
LITTERS
LOTIONS
LOTUSES
LUTISTS
MATCHES
MATHERS
MATHEWS
MATHIAS
MATRONS
MATTERS
MATURES
MATZOHS
METATES
METEORS
METHODS
METIERS
METRICS
METTLES
MITHRAS
MITOSES
MITOSIS
MITTENS
MOTHERS
MOTIONS
MOTIVES
MOTTLES
MOTTOES
MUTANTS
MUTATES
MUTATIS
MUTTERS
MUTTONS
MUTUALS
NATIONS
NATIVES
NATTERS
NATURES
NETTLES
NITROUS
NITWITS
NOTATES
NOTCHES
NOTICES
NOTIONS
NUTLETS
NUTMEGS
NUTRIAS
NUTTERS
OBTAINS
OBTUNDS
OCTANES
OCTANTS
OCTAVES
OCTAVOS
OCTOPUS
OPTIONS
OSTLERS
OTTAWAS
OUTACTS
OUTAGES
OUTBIDS
OUTDOES
OUTEATS
OUTFITS
OUTGOES
OUTGUNS
OUTHITS
OUTINGS
OUTLAWS
OUTLAYS
OUTLETS
OUTPUTS
OUTRUNS
OUTSETS
OUTWITS
PATAKES
PATCHES
PATENTS
PATINAS
PATNESS
PATROLS
PATRONS
PATSIES
PATTENS
PATTERS
PATTIES
PETARDS
PETITES
PETRELS
PETROUS
PETTERS
PITBOSS
PITCHES
PITEOUS
PITSAWS
PITTERS
POTAGES
POTFULS
POTHERS
POTIONS
POTPIES
POTTERS
PUTOUTS
PUTTEES
PUTTERS
PUTTIES
PYTHIAS
PYTHONS
RATINGS
RATIONS
RATITES
RATTANS
RATTERS
RATTLES
RETAILS
RETAINS
RETAKES
RETAPES
RETARDS
RETAXES
RETELLS
RETESTS
RETILES
RETIMES
RETINAS
RETIRES
RETOOLS
RETORTS
RETRIES
RETRIMS
RETUNES
RETURNS
RETYPES
RITUALS
ROTATES
ROTTERS
RUTGERS
SATIRES
SATRAPS
SETTEES
SETTERS
SETTLES
SHTICKS
SITCOMS
SITTERS
SUTLERS
SUTURES
TATAMIS
TATTERS
TATTLES
TATTOOS
TETANUS
TETHERS
TETRADS
TITBITS
TITHERS
TITTERS
TITTLES
TOTTERS
TUTTUTS
UNTACKS
UNTRAPS
UNTUNES
UPTAKES
UPTICKS
UPTURNS
URTEXTS
VATFULS
VETCHES
VETOERS
VITTLES
VOTECHS
WATCHES
WATTLES
WETBARS
WETHERS
WETMOPS
WETNESS
WITCHES
WITHERS
WITLESS
WITNESS
ZITHERS

•••TS••
BEATSIT
BEATSUP
BENTSEN
BOOTSUP
BUTTSIN
CHATSUP
CURTSEY
FLOTSAM
FOOTSIE
FRETSAW
HEATSUP
HINTSAT
HOOTSAT
KLATSCH
LIFTSUP
MUSTSEE
RESTSUP
SHUTSIN
SHUTSUP
STETSON
SUITSUP
THATSIT
TOOTSIE
TROTSKY
TSETSES
WAITSON
WAITSUP
WANTSIN
WANTSTO
YELTSIN

•••T•S•
BAPTISM
BAPTIST
BRITISH
BRUTISH
CATTISH
COLTISH
CONTEST
CONTUSE
CULTISH
CULTISM
CULTIST
CURTEST
DAFTEST
DEFTEST
DENTIST
DOLTISH
ECSTASY
EGOTISM
EGOTIST
ELITISM
ELITIST
FANTASY
FASTEST
FATTEST
FITTEST
FLUTIST
GOATISH
HOSTESS
HOTTEST
IRATEST
LACTASE
LACTOSE
LEFTIST
MALTESE
MALTOSE
MORTISE
NASTASE
NEATEST
PERTEST
PETTISH
PIETISM
POETESS
PRETEST
PROTEST
PROTIST
SOFTEST
STATIST
TARTEST
TAUTEST
TRITEST
VASTEST
WETTEST
WHITEST
WHIT!SH

•••T••S
AUNTIES
AVATARS
BANTAMS
BANTERS
BARTERS
BASTERS
BATTENS
BATTERS
BATTLES
BEATERS
BEATLES
BEETLES
BESTIRS
BESTOWS
BETTERS
BETTORS
BIGTOES
BIGTOPS
BISTROS
BITTERS
BLITZES
BOATERS
BOOTEES
BOOTIES
BOTTLES
BOTTOMS
BOUTROS
BOWTIES
BOXTOPS
BRETONS
BRITONS
BUSTLES
BUTTERS
BUTTONS
CAFTANS
CANTERS
CANTLES
CANTONS
CANTORS
CAPTORS
CARTELS
CARTERS
CARTONS
CASTERS
CASTLES
CELTICS
CENTERS
CENTRES
CLOTHES
CONTRAS
COOTIES
COPTERS
COSTARS
COTTERS
COTTONS
CRATERS
CRETANS
CRETINS
CRITICS
CUSTOMS
CUTTERS
DACTYLS
DARTERS
DEBTORS
DEITIES
DIATOMS
DICTUMS
DIETERS
DIKTATS
DIRTIES
DITTIES
DOCTORS
DOGTAGS
DOTTLES
DUSTERS
DUSTUPS
EASTERS
EDITORS
ELATERS
EMOTERS
EMPTIES
EXOTICS
FACTORS
FALTERS
FASTENS
FATTENS
FESTERS
FETTERS
FETTLES
FIFTIES
FILTERS
FITTERS
FOOTERS
FORTIES
FOSTERS
FUSTICS
GAITERS
GARTERS
GENTLES
GHETTOS
GLITZES
GLOTTIS
GOATEES
GRATERS
GROTTOS
GUITARS
GUSTOES
GUTTERS
HALTERS
HASTENS
HATTERS
HEATERS
HECTORS
HEPTADS
HITTERS
HOGTIES
HOOTERS
HOSTELS
HOSTESS
HOTTIPS
HOTTUBS
HUNTERS
HURTLES
HUSTLES
INSTEPS
INSTILS

JESTERS
JETTIES
JITTERS
JOSTLES
KAFTANS
KETTLES
KILTIES
KIRTLES
KITTENS
KITTIES
KLUTZES
KOWTOWS
KRATERS
LAPTOPS
LATTENS
LECTORS
LEFTIES
LENTILS
LEPTONS
LETTERS
LETTRES
LIFTERS
LINTELS
LISTEES
LISTELS
LISTENS
LITTERS
LOATHES
LOITERS
LOOTERS
LUSTERS
LUSTRES
MAITAIS
MALTEDS
MALTHUS
MANTELS
MANTLES
MANTRAS
MARTENS
MARTINS
MARTYRS
MASTERS
MASTICS
MATTERS
MENTORS
METTLES
MINTERS
MISTERS
MITTENS
MOLTERS
MORTALS
MORTARS
MOTTLES
MOTTOES
MOUTONS
MUNTINS
MUSTERS
MUTTERS
MUTTONS
MYRTLES
MYSTICS
NATTERS
NEATENS
NECTARS
NESTERS
NESTLES
NETTLES
NEWTONS
NOETICS
NUTTERS
ORATORS
OUSTERS
OYSTERS

PALTERS
PARTIES
PASTELS
PASTORS
PATTENS
PATTERS
PATTIES
PECTINS
PEGTOPS
PELTERS
PENTADS
PESTERS
PESTLES
PETTERS
PHOTOGS
PHOTONS
PIETIES
PIETINS
PISTILS
PISTOLS
PISTONS
PITTERS
PLATENS
PLATERS
POETESS
POETICS
PONTIUS
POPTOPS
PORTALS
PORTERS
PORTHOS
POSTERS
POTTERS
POUTERS
PRATERS
PROTEUS
PROTONS
PUNTERS
PUTTEES
PUTTERS
PUTTIES
QINTARS
QUOTERS
RAFTERS
RAGTOPS
RANTERS
RAPTORS
RASTERS
RATTANS
RATTERS
RATTLES
RECTORS
REDTOPS
RENTALS
RENTERS
RESTERS
REUTERS
RHETORS
RHYTHMS
RIOTERS
RIOTOUS
ROOTERS
ROSTERS
ROTTERS
ROUTERS
RUSTICS
RUSTLES
SALTERS
SANTIRS
SCATHES
SCOTERS
SCYTHES
SEATERS

SECTORS
SEETHES
SEPTETS
SESTETS
SETTEES
SETTERS
SETTLES
SEXTANS
SEXTETS
SEXTONS
SIFTERS
SISTERS
SITTERS
SIXTIES
SKATERS
SKITOWS
SOFTENS
SOFTIES
SOOTHES
SORTERS
SORTIES
SPITZES
STATICS
STATORS
STATUES
SUITORS
SULTANS
SUNTANS
SWATHES
SYSTEMS
TACTICS
TAMTAMS
TARTANS
TARTARS
TASTERS
TATTERS
TATTLES
TATTOOS
TAUTENS
TEETERS
TEETHES
TENTERS
TESTEES
TESTERS
TEUTONS
TICTACS
TILTERS
TINTERS
TIPTOES
TIPTOPS
TITTERS
TITTLES
TOETAPS
TOLTECS
TOMTITS
TOMTOMS
TOOTERS
TOOTLES
TOTTERS
TOUTERS
TRITONS
TSETSES
TURTLES
TUTTUTS
ULSTERS
UNITERS
UNITIES
UNSTOPS
VECTORS
VENTERS
VESTEES
VICTIMS
VICTORS

VIRTUES
VITTLES
WAITERS
WALTERS
WALTZES
WANTADS
WASTERS
WATTLES
WELTERS
WHITENS
WINTERS
WONTONS
WRITERS
WRITHES

••••TS•

CRAFTSY
FUJITSU
JUJITSU
KOMATSU
OKHOTSK
SHIATSU
YAKUTSK

••••T•S

ABLATES
ACHATES
AERATES
AGNATES
AGOUTIS
ARBUTUS
ARISTAS
ARISTOS
ATLATLS
AVIATES
BERATES
BONITOS
BORATES
BREATHS
BYPATHS
CHEETOS
COYOTES
CREATES
CRYPTOS
CURATES
DAKOTAS
DEARTHS
DEBATES
DELETES
DEMOTES
DENOTES
DEPUTES
DESOTOS
DEVOTES
DILATES
DILUTES
DONATES
DORITOS
EIGHTHS
EOLITHS
EQUATES
ESTATES
EXCITES
FAJITAS
FAUSTUS
FIESTAS
FIXATES
FOURTHS
GAMETES
GELATIS
GHETTOS
GLOTTIS
GROTTOS

GROWTHS
GYRATES
HALITES
HAMITES
HEARTHS
IDEATES
IGNITES
IMPETUS
IMPUTES
INCITES
INDITES
INMATES
INVITES
IODATES
IOMOTHS
LAERTES
LAKOTAS
LEANTOS
LEGATES
LEGATOS
LENGTHS
LEVITES
LIGATES
LITOTES
LOCATES
LUXATES
METATES
MINUTES
MULETAS
MUTATES
MUTATIS
NEGATES
NOTATES
OBLATES
OLEATES
OOCYTES
OOLITES
OOLITHS
OPIATES
ORESTES
PAIUTES
PALATES
PELOTAS
PENATES
PESETAS
PETITES
PINATAS
PIRATES
PLAUTUS
PLINTHS
PRESTOS
PYRITES
QUARTOS
RATITES
REBATES
RECITES
REDATES
REFUTES
RELATES
REMOTES
RENOTES
REPUTES
RERATES
ROTATES
SALUTES
SAMITES
SEMITES
SENATES
SHEATHS
SHIITES
SIESTAS
SLEUTHS
SMALTOS

SMOOTHS
SOLUTES
SONATAS
SORITES
SPRITES
STKITTS
STRATUS
TACITUS
UPDATES
VACATES
WAPITIS
WRAITHS
WREATHS
ZENITHS
ZYGOTES

•••••TS

ABDUCTS
ABLAUTS
ABSENTS
ACCENTS
ACCEPTS
ACCOSTS
ACQUITS
ADDUCTS
ADJUSTS
ADVENTS
ADVERTS
AFFECTS
AFREETS
AGEISTS
AIGRETS
ALIGHTS
AMOUNTS
AMULETS
ANKLETS
ANOINTS
AORISTS
ARMLETS
ARMPITS
ARRESTS
ARTISTS
ASCENTS
ASPECTS
ASSENTS
ASSERTS
ASSISTS
ASSORTS
ATTESTS
ATTRITS
AUKLETS
AVOCETS
BALLETS
BALLOTS
BANDITS
BARENTS
BASALTS
BASKETS
BASSETS
BEHESTS
BILLETS
BISECTS
BLIGHTS
BOBCATS
BONNETS
BOSKETS
BREASTS
BREVETS
BRUNETS
BUCKETS
BUDGETS
BUFFETS
BULLETS

BURBOTS
BUYOUTS
CACHETS
CAHOOTS
CAPLETS
CAPNUTS
CARNETS
CARPETS
CARROTS
CAVEATS
CAVORTS
CEMENTS
CHALETS
CLARETS
CLIENTS
CLORETS
CLOSETS
COEDITS
COHORTS
COHOSTS
COLLETS
COMBATS
COMFITS
COMMITS
COPOUTS
CORNETS
CORSETS
COSSETS
CRAVATS
CREDITS
CUBISTS
CURVETS
CUTLETS
CUTOUTS
CYGNETS
DECANTS
DECEITS
DECOCTS
DEDUCTS
DEFEATS
DEFECTS
DEJECTS
DELICTS
DELISTS
DEPARTS
DEPICTS
DEPORTS
DESALTS
DESERTS
DESISTS
DESPOTS
DETECTS
DETESTS
DIDACTS
DIGESTS
DIKTATS
DIMOUTS
DIMWITS
DIRECTS
DIVERTS
DIVESTS
DOCENTS
DOCKETS
DUGOUTS
DYNASTS
EAGLETS
EFFECTS
EFFORTS
EGOISTS
ELICITS
ENLISTS
ENROOTS
ESCORTS

EXCEPTS
EXEMPTS
EXHORTS
EXPECTS
EXPERTS
EXPORTS
EXTENTS
EXTORTS
EYELETS
FANJETS
FATCATS
FAUCETS
FERRETS
FIDGETS
FILLETS
FLAUNTS
FLIGHTS
FLORETS
FLYNETS
FOMENTS
FORESTS
FORGETS
FORINTS
FORMATS
FRIGHTS
GADGETS
GALOOTS
GAMBITS
GANNETS
GARNETS
GARRETS
GASJETS
GASKETS
GERENTS
GIBBETS
GIBLETS
GIMLETS
GOBLETS
GOCARTS
GODWITS
GOKARTS
GORGETS
GRIVETS
GULLETS
GUSSETS
HAMLETS
HEIGHTS
HELMETS
HENBITS
HEPCATS
HERMITS
HEXNUTS
HOBBITS
HORNETS
HOTPOTS
IMARETS
IMPACTS
IMPARTS
IMPORTS
IMPOSTS
INCANTS
INCEPTS
INDENTS
INDICTS
INDUCTS
INFANTS
INFECTS
INFESTS
INGESTS
INJECTS
INSECTS
INSERTS
INSISTS

INSPOTS
INSULTS
INTENTS
INTUITS
INVENTS
INVERTS
INVESTS
IQTESTS
IRRUPTS
JACKETS
JENNETS
JESUITS
JOBLOTS
JUNKETS
JURISTS
KNIGHTS
LABRETS
LAMENTS
LANCETS
LAPPETS
LARIATS
LATENTS
LAYOUTS
LEGISTS
LIMPETS
LINNETS
LIONETS
LOCKETS
LOCUSTS
LOQUATS
LUGNUTS
LUTISTS
LYRISTS
MAGNETS
MAHOUTS
MALLETS
MAOISTS
MARKETS
MARMOTS
MASCOTS
MERLOTS
MIDGETS
MILLETS
MINUETS
MISFITS
MISHITS
MODELTS
MOLESTS
MOMENTS
MOPPETS
MULLETS
MUPPETS
MUSCATS
MUSKETS
MUTANTS
NAUGHTS
NITWITS
NOUGATS
NUDISTS
NUGGETS
NUMBATS
NUTLETS
OBJECTS
OBLASTS
OBOISTS
OBVERTS
OCCULTS
OCELOTS
OCTANTS
ODDLOTS
OFFSETS
OFSORTS
OMELETS

ORIENTS
OUTACTS
OUTEATS
OUTFITS
OUTHITS
OUTLETS
OUTPUTS
OUTSETS
OUTWITS
OXCARTS
PACKETS
PALLETS
PANDITS
PARENTS
PARGETS
PARROTS
PATENTS
PAYOUTS
PEANUTS
PEDANTS
PELLETS
PENULTS
PEQUOTS
PERMITS
PICKETS
PIGLETS
PIGNUTS
PIOLETS
PLAINTS
PLANETS
PLIGHTS
POCKETS
POPPETS
POSSETS
PRESETS
PRIESTS
PRIVETS
PROFITS
PROMPTS
PTBOATS
PULLETS
PULPITS
PUNDITS
PUPPETS
PURISTS
PUTOUTS
RABBETS
RABBITS
RACKETS
RAGOUTS
RAMJETS
REBOLTS
REBOOTS
RECANTS
RECASTS
REDACTS
REDANTS
REDHATS
REDHOTS
REEDITS
REGENTS
REGRETS
REHEATS
REJECTS
RELENTS
RELICTS
RELISTS
REMELTS
REPASTS
REPEATS
REPENTS
REPORTS
RERENTS

RESALTS
RESEATS
RESECTS
RESENTS
RESISTS
RESORTS
RESULTS
RETESTS
RETORTS
REVERTS
REVOLTS
REXCATS
RILLETS
ROBERTS
ROCKETS
RODENTS
RUNLETS
RUSSETS
SACHETS
SAVANTS
SCRIPTS
SCULPTS
SECANTS
SECRETS
SELECTS
SEPTETS
SESTETS
SEXISTS
SEXTETS
SHRIFTS
SIGNETS
SILENTS
SIPPETS
SLIGHTS
SNOCATS
SOCKETS
SOFFITS
SONNETS
SORBETS
SOVIETS
SPIGOTS
SPINETS
SPIRITS
SPLINTS
SPRINTS
SPROUTS
SQUINTS
SQUIRTS
STARETS
STKITTS
STRAITS
STREETS
STYLETS
SUBLETS
SUBMITS
SUBSETS
SUMMITS
SUNSETS
TABLETS
TALENTS
TAOISTS
TAPPETS
TARGETS
TARPITS
TEAPOTS
TEASETS
TENANTS
TERCETS
TERRETS
THEISTS
THIRSTS
THREATS
THRIFTS

THROATS
THRUSTS
THWARTS
TICKETS
TIDBITS
TINHATS
TIPPETS
TITBITS
TOILETS
TOMCATS
TOMTITS
TOPHATS
TRICOTS
TRIVETS
TRUANTS
TRYOUTS
TSHIRTS
TUBISTS
TUFFETS
TUMULTS
TURBOTS
TURRETS
TUTTUTS
TWOBITS
TYPISTS
TYRANTS
UMLAUTS
UNBOLTS
UNKNITS
UNKNOTS
UNSEATS
UPBEATS
UPLIFTS
UPROOTS
UPSHOTS
URTEXTS
VARLETS
VEIGHTS
VELVETS
VERVETS
VIOLETS
WALLETS
WALNUTS
WEIGHTS
WESKITS
WICKETS
WIDGETS
WIGLETS
WOMBATS
WRIGHTS
YOGURTS
ZEALOTS

T•T••••

TATAMIS
TATIANA
TATTERS
TATTIER
TATTING
TATTLED
TATTLER
TATTLES
TATTOOS
TETANUS
TETCHED
TETHERS
TETRADS
TITANIA
TITANIC
TITBITS
TITHERS
TITHING
TITLING

TITLIST
TITMICE
TITRATE
TITTERS
TITTLES
TITULAR
TOTALED
TOTALLY
TOTEBAG
TOTEMIC
TOTTERS
TOTTERY
TOTTING
TUTELAR
TUTORED
TUTTUTS

T••T•••

TACTFUL
TACTICS
TACTILE
TAMTAMS
TANTARA
TANTRUM
TARTANS
TARTARE
TARTARS
TARTEST
TASTERS
TASTIER
TASTILY
TASTING
TATTERS
TATTIER
TATTING
TATTLED
TATTLER
TATTLES
TATTOOS
TAUTENS
TAUTEST
TEATIME
TEATRAY
TEETERS
TEETHED
TEETHER
TEETHES
TEKTITE
TENTERS
TENTING
TERTIAL
TESTBAN
TESTEES
TESTERS
TESTIER
TESTIFY
TESTILY
TESTING
TESTOUT
TEUTONS
TEXTILE
TEXTUAL
TEXTURE
THATCHY
THATSIT
THITHER
TICTACS
TIETACK
TILTERS
TILTING
TINTERN
TINTERS
TINTING

TINTYPE
TIPTOED
TIPTOES
TIPTOPS
TITTERS
TITTLES
TOETAPS
TOLTECS
TOMTITS
TOMTOMS
TONTINE
TOOTALL
TOOTERS
TOOTHED
TOOTING
TOOTLED
TOOTLES
TOOTSIE
TORTONI
TOSTADA
TOTTERS
TOTTERY
TOTTING
TOUTERS
TOUTING
TRITELY
TRITEST
TRITIUM
TRITONE
TRITONS
TROTHED
TROTOUT
TROTSKY
TROTTED
TROTTER
TSETSES
TUFTING
TUITION
TURTLED
TURTLES
TUTTUTS
TWITCHY
TWITTED
TWITTER
TWOTIME
TWOTONE

T•••T••

TABITHA
TACITLY
TACITUS
TAINTED
TAKETEN
TANKTOP
TAPSTER
TAUNTED
TELSTAR
TEMPTED
TEMPTER
THEATER
THEATRE
THISTLE
TIBETAN
TIGHTEN
TIGHTER
TIGHTLY
TIMOTHY
TINSTAR
TINYTIM
TIPSTER
TOASTED
TOASTER
TOLSTOI
TOLSTOY
TOOKTEN
TRACTOR
TRAITOR
TREATED
TREETOP
TRENTON
TRESTLE
TRISTAN
TROTTED
TROTTER
TRUSTED
TRUSTEE
TRYSTED
TRYSTER
TWEETED
TWEETER
TWISTED
TWISTER
TWITTED
TWITTER
TWOSTAR
TWOSTEP

T••••T•

TABLETS
TAFFETA
TAKESTO
TALENTS
TALKSTO
TAOISTS
TAPPETS
TARANTO
TARGETS
TARPITS
TAXRATE
TEAPOTS
TEASETS
TEKTITE
TENANTS
TENDSTO
TERCETS
TERMITE
TERNATE
TERRETS
THEISTS
THERETO
THIRSTS
THIRSTY
THREATS
THRIFTS
THRIFTY
THROATS
THROATY
THRUSTS
THWARTS
TICKETS
TIDBITS
TIEINTO
TINHATS
TIPPETS
TITBITS
TITRATE
TOCCATA
TOILETS
TOMCATS
TOMTITS
TOPHATS
TORONTO
TOWPATH
TRIBUTE
TRICOTS
TRIESTE
TRINITY
TRIVETS
TRUANTS
TRYOUTS
TSHIRTS
TUBISTS
TUFFETS
TUMULTS
TURBOTS
TURNSTO
TURRETS
TUTTUTS
TWELFTH
TWOBITS
TYPISTS
TYRANTS

T•••••T

TABORET
TAGSOUT
TAKEOUT
TALKOUT
TALKSAT
TALLEST
TANGENT
TANNEST
TAPROOT
TAPSOUT
TARTEST
TAUTEST
TEACART
TEARSAT
TEMPEST
TENSEST
TENSPOT
TERSEST
TESTOUT
THATSIT
THEREAT
THICKET
THOUGHT
TIDIEST
TIMEOUT
TINIEST
TIREOUT
TITLIST
TLINGIT
TONIEST
TONIGHT
TOOKOUT
TOPCOAT
TOPKNOT
TOPMAST
TOPMOST
TOPSOUT
TOREOUT
TORMENT
TORNOUT
TORRENT
TOSSOUT
TOURIST
TRABERT
TRANSIT
TREERAT
TRIDENT
TRINKET
TRIPLET
TRIPPET
TRISECT
TRITEST
TROTOUT
TRUMPET
TSARIST
TSELIOT
TUBAIST
TUGBOAT
TUNEOUT
TURNOUT
TYPESET

•TT••••

ATTACHE
ATTACKS
ATTAINS
ATTEMPT
ATTENDS
ATTESTS
ATTICUS
ATTIMES
ATTIRED
ATTIRES
ATTRACT
ATTRITE
ATTRITS
ATTUCKS
ATTUNED
ATTUNES
OTTAWAS
OTTOMAN
UTTERED
UTTERER
UTTERLY
YTTRIUM

•T•T•••

ATATURK
ATSTAKE
STATELY
STATICE
STATICS
STATING
STATION
STATIST
STATORS
STATUES
STATURE
STATUTE
STETSON
STETTED

•T••T••

ATLATLS
STANTON
STARTED
STARTER
STARTLE
STARTUP
STENTOR
STETTED
STILTED
STILTON
STINTED
STKITTS
STOUTER
STOUTLY
STPETER
STRATUM
STRATUS
STRETCH
STRETTO
STUNTED
STYPTIC

•T•••T•

ATHLETE
ATLANTA
ATTESTS
ATTRITE
ATTRITS
ITERATE
OTRANTO
PTBOATS
STARETS
STATUTE
STEALTH
STICKTO
STKITTS
STOMATA
STOOPTO
STRAITS
STREETS
STRETTO
STRIATE
STUCKTO
STYLETS
UTILITY

•T••••T

ATAVIST
ATFAULT
ATHEART
ATHEIST
ATHIRST
ATHWART
ATLEAST
ATTEMPT
ATTRACT
ATWORST
ITERANT
STALEST
STAREAT
STARLET
STARLIT
STATIST
STAYPUT
STEPOUT
STEWART
STUDENT
STYLIST
UTRECHT

••TT•••

BATTENS
BATTERS
BATTERY
BATTIER
BATTING
BATTLED
BATTLER
BATTLES
BETTERS
BETTING
BETTORS
BITTERN
BITTERS
BITTIER
BITTING
BOTTLED
BOTTLER
BOTTLES
BOTTOMS
BUTTERS
BUTTERY
BUTTING
BUTTONS
BUTTOUT
BUTTSIN
CATTAIL
CATTIER
CATTILY
CATTING
CATTISH
COTTAGE
COTTERS
COTTONS
COTTONY
CUTTERS
CUTTIME
CUTTING
DITTANY
DITTIES
DITTOED
DOTTIER
DOTTING
DOTTLES
FATTENS
FATTEST
FETTERS
FETTLES
FITTERS
FITTEST
FITTING
GETTING
GUTTERS
GUTTING
HATTERS
HATTING
HITTERS
HITTING
HITTITE
HOTTEST
HOTTIPS
HOTTUBS
JETTIES
JETTING
JITTERS
JITTERY
JOTTING
JUTTING
KETTLES
KITTENS
KITTIES
LATTENS
LATTICE
LETTERS
LETTING
LETTRES
LETTUCE
LITTERS
LITTLER
LOTTERY
LOTTING
MATTERS
MATTHAU
MATTHEW
MATTING
MATTOCK
METTLES
MITTENS
MOTTLED
MOTTLES
MOTTOES
MUTTERS
MUTTONS
NATTERS
NATTIER
NATTILY
NETTING
NETTLED
NETTLES
NITTANY
NOTTRUE
NUTTERS
NUTTIER
NUTTILY
NUTTING
OUTTAKE
OUTTALK
PATTENS
PATTERN
PATTERS
PATTIES
PATTING
PETTERS
PETTIER
PETTILY
PETTING
PETTISH
PITTERS
PITTING
PITTMAN
POTTAGE
POTTERS
POTTERY
POTTING
PUTTEES
PUTTERS
PUTTIED
PUTTIES
PUTTING
RATTAIL
RATTANS
RATTERS
RATTIER
RATTING
RATTLED
RATTLER
RATTLES
RATTRAP
ROTTERS
ROTTING
SETTEES
SETTERS
SETTING
SETTLED
SETTLER
SETTLES
SITTERS
SITTING
SUTTNER
TATTERS
TATTIER
TATTING
TATTLED
TATTLER
TATTLES
TATTOOS
TITTERS
TITTLES
TOTTERS
TOTTERY
TOTTING
TUTTUTS
VETTING
VITTLES
WATTAGE
WATTEAU
WATTLES
WETTEST
WETTING
WITTIER
WITTILY
WITTING

••T•T••

BATHTUB
ENTITLE
ESTATES
GETITON
LETITBE
LETITIA
LITOTES
METATES
MITOTIC
MUTATED
MUTATES
MUTATIS
NOTATED
NOTATES
OUTSTEP
PETITES
PITSTOP
PUTITTO
RATATAT
RATITES
RETITLE
ROTATED
ROTATES
ROTATOR

••T••T•

ACTUATE
ARTISTE
ARTISTS
ASTARTE
ATTESTS
ATTRITE
ATTRITS
BATISTA
BATISTE
BETROTH
CITRATE
CUTINTO
CUTLETS
CUTOUTS
CUTRATE
DETECTS
DETENTE
DETESTS
ENTENTE
ESTHETE
EXTENTS
EXTORTS
FATCATS
FATCITY
FATUITY
GETINTO
GOTINTO
HITTITE
HOTPOTS
INTENTS
INTRUTH
INTUITS
IQTESTS
LATENTS
LITINTO
LUTISTS
MUTANTS
NITRATE
NITRITE
NITWITS
NUTLETS
OCTANTS
OUTACTS
OUTEATS
OUTFITS
OUTHITS
OUTLETS
OUTPUTS
OUTSETS
OUTVOTE
OUTWITS
PATENTS
PUTITTO
PUTOUTS
RETESTS
RETORTS
SATIATE
SATIETY
SETINTO
SITUATE
TITBITS
TITRATE
TUTTUTS
UNTRUTH
URTEXTS
VITIATE

••T•••T

ACTSOUT
ANTIART
ARTIEST
ASTOLAT
ATTEMPT
ATTRACT
AUTOMAT
BATHMAT
BETWIXT
BITPART
BUTTOUT
CATBOAT
CUTSOUT
DATASET
DETRACT
DETROIT
EATENAT
EATSOUT
ENTRANT
ENTREAT
ENTRUST
EXTINCT
EXTRACT
FATTEST
FITTEST
GETLOST
GETSOUT
GETSSET
GOTOPOT
HATCHET
HITLIST
HOTFOOT
HOTSEAT
HOTSHOT
HOTSPOT
HOTTEST
INTROIT
INTRUST
JETBOAT
JETPORT
LETSOUT
LITHEST
METEOUT
NOTABIT
NUTMEAT
ONTHEQT
OPTSOUT
OUTCAST
OUTLAST
OUTOFIT
OUTPOST
PATIENT
PATRIOT
PITAPAT
POTSHOT
PUTSOUT
RATATAT
RATCHET
RETRACT
RETREAT
SETSOUT
SITSOUT
TITLIST
UNTWIST
UPTIGHT
WATCHIT
WETSUIT
WETTEST
WITHOUT

•••TT••

ABETTED
ABETTOR
ABUTTAL
ABUTTED
BEATTIE
BLATTED
BLOTTED
BLOTTER
BRITTEN
BRITTLE
BRITTON
CHATTED
CHATTEL
CHATTER
CHITTER
CLATTER
CLOTTED
CLUTTER
CRITTER
DRATTED
EMITTED
EMITTER
FLATTED
FLATTEN
FLATTER
FLATTOP
FLITTED
FLITTER
FLUTTER
FRETTED
FRITTED
FRITTER
GHETTOS
GLITTER
GLOTTAL
GLOTTIS
GLUTTED
GLUTTON
GRITTED
GROTTOS
HEATTER
KNITTED
KNITTER
KNOTTED
OMITTED
PLATTER
PLOTTED
PLOTTER
PRATTLE
QUITTER
SCATTED
SCATTER
SCOTTIE
SCUTTLE
SEATTLE
SHATTER
SHUTTER
SHUTTLE
SKITTER
SKITTLE
SLATTED
SLOTTED
SMATTER
SMITTEN
SOFTTOP
SPATTED
SPATTER
SPOTTED
SPOTTER
SPUTTER
STETTED
SWATTED
SWATTER
TROTTED
TROTTER
TWITTED
TWITTER
WHETTED
WHITTLE
WRITTEN

•••T•T•

ACETATE
AGITATE
APATITE
CANTATA
DENTATE
DICTATE
DIKTATS
GESTATE
HITTITE
IMITATE
INSTATE
LACTATE
PARTITA
PARTITE
PELTATE
RESTATE
SEPTETS
SESTETS
SEXTETS
STATUTE
TEKTITE
TOMTITS
TUTTUTS
UPSTATE
WANTSTO
WRITETO
WROTETO

•••T••T

BAPTIST
BEATOUT
BEATSIT
BERTOLT
BLATANT
BLOTOUT
BOOTOUT
BUSTOUT
BUTTOUT
CASTOUT
CONTACT
CONTENT
CONTEST
CONTEXT
CONTORT
CULTIST
CURTEST
DAFTEST
DEFTEST
DENTIST
DISTANT
DISTORT
DOGTROT
EGOTIST
ELITIST
EPITHET
FASTEST
FATTEST
FELTOUT
FITTEST
FLATOUT
FLUTIST
FOXTROT
GANTLET
GESTALT
HINTSAT
HOOTSAT
HOPTOIT
HOTTEST
INSTANT
IRATEST
KEPTOUT
LEFTIST
LEFTOUT
LOSTOUT
NEATEST
PARTOUT
PERTEST
POPTART
PORTENT
PRETEST
PRETEXT
PROTECT
PROTEST
PROTIST
PUPTENT
RESTART
RIOTACT
ROOTLET
ROOTOUT
SEETOIT
SENTOUT
SEXTANT
SHOTPUT
SHUTOUT
SOFTEST
SPOTLIT
STATIST
SUBTEXT
TARTEST
TAUTEST
TESTOUT
THATSIT
TRITEST
TROTOUT
UPSTART
VASTEST
WAITOUT
WANTOUT
WENTOUT
WETTEST
WHATNOT
WHITEST

••••TT•

ANNATTO
ANNETTE
ARIETTA
BABETTE
BARETTA
BERETTA
BIRETTA
BURETTE
CADETTE
COLETTE
CORETTA
CULOTTE
DINETTE
GAVOTTE
GAZETTE
INPETTO
LAFITTE
LAMOTTA
LAYETTE
LORETTA
MENOTTI
MUSETTE
NANETTE
ORNETTE
PALETTE
PANETTA
PIPETTE
POINTTO
PUTITTO
REACTTO
REGATTA
RICOTTA
RISOTTO
ROSETTA
ROSETTE
STKITTS
STRETTO
SUZETTE
WYNETTE

••••T•T

BIENTOT
HABITAT
KINGTUT
MIGHTNT
QUARTET
QUINTET
RATATAT
SHOOTAT

•••••TT

BABBITT
BARRETT
BECKETT
BENNETT
BOYCOTT
BUFFETT
BULLITT
BURNETT
CASSATT
CORBETT
DORSETT
ELLIOTT
EVERETT
FAWCETT
FOLLETT
GANNETT
GARRETT
GOSSETT
HACKETT
HAMMETT
HEWLETT
MILLETT
PICKETT
PUCKETT
RABBITT

SENNETT
WALCOTT
ZERMATT

TU•••••
TUAREGS
TUBAIST
TUBBIER
TUBISTS
TUBULAR
TUCHMAN
TUCKERS
TUCKING
TUCKSIN
TUESDAY
TUFFETS
TUFTING
TUGBOAT
TUGGERS
TUGGING
TUITION
TULSANS
TUMBLED
TUMBLER
TUMBLES
TUMBREL
TUMMIES
TUMULTS
TUMULUS
TUNDRAS
TUNEDIN
TUNEDUP
TUNEFUL
TUNEOUT
TUNESIN
TUNESUP
TUNEUPS
TUNGOIL
TUNICLE
TUNISIA
TUNNELS
TUNNIES
TUPELOS
TURBANS
TURBINE
TURBOTS
TUREENS
TURKEYS
TURKISH
TURMOIL
TURNERS
TURNING
TURNIPS
TURNKEY
TURNOFF
TURNOUT
TURNSIN
TURNSON
TURNSTO
TURNSUP
TURRETS
TURTLED
TURTLES
TUSCANY
TUSKERS
TUSSAUD
TUSSLED
TUSSLES
TUSSOCK
TUTELAR
TUTORED
TUTTUTS
TUXEDOS

T•U••••
TAUNTED
TAURINE
TAUTENS
TAUTEST
TEUTONS
THUDDED
THULIUM
THUMBED
THUMPED
THUMPER
THUNDER
THURBER
THURMAN
THUSFAR
TOUCANS
TOUCHED
TOUCHES
TOUCHON
TOUCHUP
TOUGHEN
TOUGHER
TOUGHIE
TOUGHLY
TOUPEES
TOURACO
TOURERS
TOURING
TOURISM
TOURIST
TOURNEY
TOUSLED
TOUSLES
TOUTERS
TOUTING
TRUANCY
TRUANTS
TRUCIAL
TRUCKED
TRUCKEE
TRUCKER
TRUCKLE
TRUDEAU
TRUDGED
TRUDGER
TRUDGES
TRUEING
TRUFFLE
TRUISMS
TRUMPED
TRUMPET
TRUMPUP
TRUNDLE
TRUSSED
TRUSSES
TRUSTED
TRUSTEE
TSUNAMI

T••U•••
TABULAR
TALUSES
TENUOUS
TENURED
TENURES
TEQUILA
THOUGHT
THRUSTS
THRUWAY
TIJUANA
TITULAR
TOLUENE
TRAUBEL
TRAUMAS
TRIUMPH
TRIUNES
TROUBLE
TROUGHS
TROUNCE
TROUPER
TROUPES
TROUSER
TSQUARE
TUBULAR
TUMULTS
TUMULUS
TVGUIDE

T•••U••
TEACUPS
TEMPURA
TERHUNE
TEXTUAL
TEXTURE
THROUGH
TISSUES
TONGUED
TONGUES
TONSURE
TOPGUNS
TORQUES
TOSSUPS
TRADUCE
TRIBUNE
TRIBUTE
TRYOUTS
TUNEUPS
TUTTUTS

T••••U•
TACITUS
TACTFUL
TAGSOUT
TAKEOUT
TAKESUP
TALKOUT
TALKSUP
TALLYUP
TAMBOUR
TANKFUL
TANKSUP
TANTRUM
TAPSOUT
TEAMSUP
TEARFUL
TEARSUP
TEDIOUS
TENFOUR
TENSEUP
TENUOUS
TERBIUM
TESTOUT
TETANUS
THEROUX
THESEUS
THINKUP
THORIUM
THULIUM
TIMEOUT
TIMESUP
TIREOUT
TONEDUP
TONESUP
TOOKOUT
TOOLSUP
TOPSOUT
TOREOUT
TORNOUT
TOSSOUT
TOUCHUP
TRADEUP
TRAYFUL
TRIPSUP
TRITIUM
TROILUS
TROTOUT
TRUMPUP
TUMULUS
TUNEDUP
TUNEFUL
TUNEOUT
TUNESUP
TURNOUT
TURNSUP
TUSSAUD
TYINGUP
TYPEDUP
TYPESUP

T•••••U
TABLEAU
THOREAU
TONNEAU
TRUDEAU

•TU••••
STUBBED
STUBBLE
STUBBLY
STUCCOS
STUCKTO
STUCKUP
STUDDED
STUDENT
STUDIED
STUDIES
STUDIOS
STUFFED
STUFFER
STUMBLE
STUMPED
STUMPER
STUNGUN
STUNNED
STUNNER
STUNTED
STUPEFY
STUPORS
STURGES

•T•U•••
ATTUCKS
ATTUNED
ATTUNES
ETRURIA
STAUNCH
STEUBEN
STLUCIA
STOUTER
STOUTLY
STRUDEL

•T••U••
ATATURK
ATFAULT
ATRIUMS
STATUES
STATURE
STATUTE
STEPUPS
STIMULI
STLOUIS
STRAUSS

•T•••U•
ATISSUE
ATTICUS
STACKUP
STADIUM
STANDUP
STARTUP
STAYPUT
STAYSUP
STEPOUT
STEPSUP
STERNUM
STICKUP
STIRRUP
STIRSUP
STOCKUP
STOODUP
STOPSUP
STOREUP
STRATUM
STRATUS
STUCKUP
STUNGUN
YTTRIUM

••TU•••
ACTUARY
ACTUATE
ACTUPON
ATTUCKS
ATTUNED
ATTUNES
AUTUMNS
BITUMEN
BYTURNS
ESTUARY
FATUITY
FATUOUS
FUTURES
INTUITS
LITURGY
LOTUSES
MATURED
MATURER
MATURES
MUTUALS
NATURAL
NATURED
NATURES
OBTUNDS
OBTUSER
OCTUPLE
PETUNIA
PUTUPON
RETUNED
RETUNES
RETURNS
RITUALS
ROTUNDA
SETUPON
SITUATE
SUTURED
SUTURES
TITULAR
UNTUNED
UNTUNES
UPTURNS

••T•U••
ASTOUND
AUTEURS
CUTOUTS
DETOURS
ENTHUSE
ENTRUST
EXTRUDE
HOTTUBS
INTRUDE
INTRUST
INTRUTH
JETGUNS
LETTUCE
NETSUKE
NETSURF
NOTRUMP
NOTSURE
OBTRUDE
OUTGUNS
OUTJUMP
OUTPUTS
OUTRUNS
PITBULL
POTFULS
POTLUCK
PUTOUTS
RETOUCH
SATSUMA
TUTTUTS
UNTRUTH
VATFULS
WETSUIT

••T••U•
ACTEDUP
ACTSOUT
ANTAEUS
ANTEDUP
ANTESUP
ANTIGUA
ANTIQUE
ARTEMUS
ATTICUS
BATEAUX
BATHTUB
BUTTOUT
CATCHUP
CUTSOUT
DUTEOUS
DUTIFUL
EATENUP
EATSOUT
FATEFUL
FATIGUE
FATUOUS
GATEAUX
GETSOUT
HATEFUL
HOTSPUR
ISTHMUS
KETCHUP
LETSOUT
LITHIUM
MATCHUP
METEOUT
MITCHUM
NATRIUM
NITROUS
NOTTRUE
OCTOPUS
OPTIMUM
OPTSOUT
OUTLOUD
PATCHUP
PETROUS
PITEOUS
PITIFUL
PUTSOUT
RETINUE
SETSOUT
SITSOUT
TETANUS
WITHOUT
YTTRIUM

••T•••U
MATTHAU
WATTEAU

•••TU••
ACHTUNG
ATATURK
CAPTURE
CENTURY
CLOTURE
CONTUSE
COSTUME
COUTURE
CULTURE
DENTURE
DICTUMS
DISTURB
DUSTUPS
FACTUAL
FEATURE
FIXTURE
FORTUNA
FORTUNE
GESTURE
HOTTUBS
LECTURE
LETTUCE
MIXTURE
NEPTUNE
NOCTURN
NURTURE
OROTUND
PASTURE
PERTURB
PICTURE
POSTURE
RAPTURE
RUPTURE
SPATULA
STATUES
STATURE
STATUTE
TEXTUAL
TEXTURE
TUTTUTS
UNSTUCK
VENTURA
VENTURE
VESTURE
VICTUAL
VIRTUAL
VIRTUES
VISTULA
VULTURE
ZEITUNG

•••T•U•
AMATEUR
BEATOUT
BEATSUP
BLOTOUT
BOOTOUT
BOOTSUP
BUSTOUT
BUTTOUT
CASTOUT
CENTAUR
CHATSUP
CHETRUM
CONTOUR
FELTOUT
FISTFUL
FLATOUT
FRETFUL
HAUTEUR
HEATSUP
HURTFUL
KEPTOUT
LEFTOUT
LIFTSUP
LOSTOUT
LUSTFUL
MALTHUS
MONTEUX
NOSTRUM
NOTTRUE
PARTOUT
PASTDUE
PASTEUP
PASTEUR
PONTIUS
PROTEUS
RESTFUL
RESTSUP
RIOTOUS
ROOTOUT
ROSTRUM
SENTOUT
SHOTGUN
SHOTPUT
SHUTOUT
SHUTSUP
SISTRUM
SUITSUP
TACTFUL
TANTRUM
TESTOUT
TRITIUM
TROTOUT
WAITOUT
WAITSUP
WANTOUT
WENTOUT
WISTFUL
WRITEUP
WROTEUP
ZESTFUL

•••T••U
CHATEAU
COCTEAU
MATTHAU
PLATEAU
WATTEAU

••••TU•
ARBUTUS
BATHTUB
BOOSTUP
BUILTUP
BURNTUP
ERRATUM
FAUSTUS
HABITUE
HAMITUP
IMPETUS
KINGTUT
LIGHTUP
MIXITUP
OMENTUM
PINETUM
PLAUTUS
QUANTUM
SANCTUM
SHOOTUP
SPLITUP
STARTUP
STRATUM
STRATUS
SWEPTUP
TACITUS
WASHTUB

••••T•U
FUJITSU
JUJITSU
KOMATSU
MANITOU
SHIATSU
SHIHTZU

TV•••••
TVGUIDE
TVSHOWS

T•V••••
TAVERNS

T••V•••
TRAVAIL
TRAVELS
TRAVERS
TRAVOIS
TREVINO
TRIVETS
TRIVIAL

T•••V••
TELAVIV
THIEVED
THIEVES
THRIVED
THRIVES
TWELVES

T••••V•
TENSIVE

T•••••V
TELAVIV

•T•V•••
ATAVISM
ATAVIST
STAVING
STEVENS

•T••V••
STARVED
STARVES
STRIVED
STRIVEN
STRIVER
STRIVES

••TV•••
LATVIAN
OUTVOTE

••T•V••
ACTIVES
ESTEVEZ
ESTIVAL
GETEVEN
GETOVER
GOTEVEN
GOTOVER
MITZVAH
MOTIVES
NATIVES
OCTAVES
OCTAVIA
OCTAVOS
PUTOVER

••T••V•
OUTLIVE

••T•••V
USTINOV

•••T•V•
AMATIVE
CAPTIVE
CENTAVO
EMOTIVE
FESTIVE
FICTIVE
FURTIVE
GUSTAVE
RESTIVE
UNITIVE

••••T•V
MOLOTOV

•••••TV
CABLETV

TW•••••
TWADDLE
TWANGED
TWEAKED
TWEETED
TWEETER
TWEEZED
TWEEZES
TWELFTH
TWELVES
TWIDDLE
TWILLED
TWINBED
TWINGED
TWINGES
TWINING
TWINKLE
TWINKLY
TWINNED
TWIRLED
TWIRLER
TWISTED
TWISTER
TWITCHY
TWITTED
TWITTER
TWOBASE
TWOBITS
TWOFERS
TWOFOLD
TWOSOME
TWOSTAR
TWOSTEP
TWOTIME
TWOTONE

T•W••••
TAWNIER
THWACKS
THWARTS
TOWARDS
TOWAWAY
TOWCARS
TOWELED
TOWERED
TOWHEAD
TOWHEES
TOWNERS
TOWNIES
TOWPATH
TOWROPE

T••W•••
THAWING
TINWORK
TRAWLED
TRAWLER
TROWELS
TROWERS

T•••W••
TAXIWAY
THREWIN
THROWER
THROWIN
THRUWAY
TIMEWAS
TOLLWAY
TOWAWAY

T••••W•
TALLOWS
TIEDOWN
TVSHOWS

T•••••W
TONEROW

•TW••••
ATWORST

•T•W•••
ATHWART
STEWARD
STEWART
STEWERS
STEWING
STOWING

•T••W••
OTTAWAS
STREWED
STREWER

•T••••W
ATECROW

••TW•••
ANTWERP
ARTWARE
ARTWORK
BATWING
BETWEEN
BETWIXT
CATWALK
ENTWINE
GETWELL
GOTWELL
HOTWARS
HOTWIRE
JETWASH
NETWORK
NITWITS
NOTWELL
OUTWARD
OUTWEAR
OUTWITS
OUTWORE
OUTWORK
OUTWORN
SITWELL
UNTWIST

••T•W••
ANTIWAR
CATAWBA
CNTOWER
CUTAWAY
EATAWAY
GATEWAY
GETAWAY
GOTAWAY
MATEWAN
OTTAWAS
PATHWAY
PUTAWAY
RETOWED

••T••W•
ANTCOWS
CUTDOWN
GETDOWN
GOTDOWN
LETDOWN
MATHEWS
OUTLAWS
PITSAWS
PUTDOWN
SATDOWN
SETDOWN
SITDOWN

••T•••W
CATSPAW
EATCROW
LITHGOW
MATTHEW
OUTDRAW
OUTDREW
OUTFLOW
OUTGREW
OUTGROW
UPTONOW

•••TW••
BELTWAY
PARTWAY
POSTWAR

•••T•W•
BESTOWS
COWTOWN
HOOTOWL
KOWTOWS
MIDTOWN
NEWTOWN
OURTOWN
SKITOWS

•••T••W
BESTREW
FRETSAW
JUSTNOW
MATTHEW

••••T•W
CHOCTAW
INASTEW
ROPETOW

T•X••••
TAXABLE
TAXFREE
TAXICAB
TAXIING
TAXIWAY
TAXRATE
TEXTILE
TEXTUAL
TEXTURE
TUXEDOS

T•••X••
TELEXED
TELEXES

T•••••X
THEROUX
TOOLBOX
TRIPLEX

•T••••X
STCROIX

••T•X••
LATEXES
RETAXED
RETAXES
URTEXTS

••T••X•
BETWIXT

••T•••X
ALTOSAX
BATEAUX
BETAMAX
GATEAUX

•••T•X•
AIRTAXI
CONTEXT
PRETEXT
SUBTEXT

•••T••X
BEATRIX
MONTEUX
NARTHEX
POSTBOX
SALTBOX

••••T•X
GORETEX
POLLTAX

TY•••••
TYCOONS

TYINGIN
TYINGUP
TYLENOL
TYMPANA
TYMPANI
TYPEDUP
TYPESET
TYPESUP
TYPHOON
TYPICAL
TYPISTS
TYRANNY
TYRANTS

T•Y••••

THYSELF
TOYDOGS
TOYLAND
TOYNBEE
TOYSHOP
TRYOUTS
TRYSTED
TRYSTER

T••Y•••

TIDYING
TINYTIM
TORYISM
TRAYFUL

T•••Y••

TALLYHO
TALLYUP
TIEDYED
TIEDYES
TINTYPE

T••••Y•

TEAPOYS
TOMBOYS
TURKEYS

T•••••Y

TACITLY
TACKILY
TAMMANY
TANNERY
TARBABY
TARDILY
TASTILY
TAXIWAY
TEARILY
TEATRAY
TENABLY
TENANCY
TENSELY
TEPIDLY
TERNARY
TERRIFY
TERSELY
TESTIFY
TESTILY
THATCHY
THERAPY
THEREBY
THICKLY
THIERRY
THIRDLY
THIRSTY
THREADY
THRIFTY
THROATY
THRUWAY
TIERNEY
TIFFANY
TIGHTLY
TIMIDLY
TIMOTHY
TINNILY
TIPSILY
TIREDLY
TOLLWAY
TOLSTOY
TONALLY
TOPIARY
TOTALLY
TOTTERY
TOUGHLY
TOURNEY
TOWAWAY
TRACERY
TRAGEDY
TREACLY
TREMBLY
TRENARY
TRILOGY
TRINITY
TRITELY
TROLLEY
TROTSKY
TRUANCY
TUESDAY
TURNKEY
TUSCANY
TWINKLY
TWITCHY
TYRANNY

•TY••••

STYGIAN
STYLERS
STYLETS
STYLING
STYLISH
STYLIST
STYLIZE
STYMIED
STYMIES
STYPTIC
STYRENE
STYRIAN

•T•Y•••

STAYING
STAYPUT
STAYSUP

•T••Y••

STRAYED

•T•••Y•

STOREYS

•T••••Y

ATROPHY
PTOLEMY
STAGILY
STAIDLY
STANDBY
STANLEY
STARCHY
STARKLY
STATELY
STEEPLY
STERNLY
STIFFLY
STIRFRY
STOKELY
STONILY
STOODBY
STOOKEY
STOUTLY
STREAKY
STRINGY
STUBBLY
STUPEFY
UTILITY
UTTERLY

••TY•••

ECTYPES
KATYDID
PITYING
RETYPED
RETYPES
UNTYING

••T••Y•

ANTONYM
BATBOYS
BETRAYS
CATSEYE
ESTRAYS
JITNEYS
KATHRYN
OUTLAYS

••T•••Y

ACTUARY
ANTHONY
BATTERY
BATTERY
BETARAY
BETHANY
BUTTERY
BYTHEBY
CATTILY
COTTONY
CUTAWAY
CUTLERY
DATEDLY
DITHERY
DITTANY
EATAWAY
ENTROPY
ESTUARY
FATCITY
FATUITY
FETIDLY
GATEWAY
GETAWAY
GOTAWAY
GUTSILY
JITTERY
KITSCHY
LATENCY
LATHERY
LETSFLY
LITHELY
LITURGY
LOTTERY
MUTABLY
NATTILY
NITTANY
NOTABLY
NUTTILY
OUTPLAY
PATHWAY
PETRIFY
PETTILY
PITHILY
POTENCY
POTTERY
PUTAWAY
SATIETY
SATISFY
TOTALLY
TOTTERY
UTTERLY
VITALLY
VITRIFY
WITTILY

•••TY••

DACTYLS
DIPTYCH
INSTYLE
MARTYRS
MISTYPE
PLATYPI
RESTYLE
TINTYPE

•••T•Y•

FONTEYN
MONTOYA
SHUTEYE

•••T••Y

ACUTELY
AMATORY
ANATOMY
ASHTRAY
BATTERY
BEATIFY
BELTWAY
BENTLEY
BESTBOY
BLOTCHY
BUTTERY
CATTILY
CENTURY
CERTIFY
CHUTNEY
COTTONY
CURTSEY
CUSTODY
DALTREY
DESTINY
DESTROY
DIETARY
DIRTILY
DITTANY
EARTHLY
ECSTASY
EMPTILY
FACTORY
FANTASY
FORTIFY
FUSTILY
GRATIFY
GRETZKY
GUSTILY
HASTILY
HAUTBOY
HEFTILY
HISTORY
HOOTCHY
HUNTLEY
IRATELY
JITTERY
JUSTIFY
KOOTCHY
LASTORY
LOFTILY
LOTTERY
LUSTILY
MASTERY
MISTILY
MONTHLY
MORTIFY
MUSTILY
MYSTERY
MYSTIFY
NASTILY
NATTILY
NIFTILY
NITTANY
NUTTILY
ORATORY
PARTWAY
PETTILY
PORTRAY
POTTERY
RECTIFY
RECTORY
RUSTILY
SALTILY
SKETCHY
SOUTHEY
STATELY
TASTILY
TEATRAY
TESTIFY
TESTILY
THATCHY
TOTTERY
TRITELY
TROTSKY
TWITCHY
UNITARY
VICTORY
WHITNEY
WINTERY
WITTILY

••••TY•

BURSTYN

••••T•Y

ADEPTLY
ALERTLY
BEASTLY
BIGOTRY
BLUNTLY
BREATHY
BRISTLY
CHANTEY
CHINTZY
COUNTRY
COURTLY
CRAFTSY
DOROTHY
EMPATHY
ERECTLY
EXACTLY
FAINTLY
FIRSTLY
FLEETLY
GAUNTLY
GHASTLY
GHOSTLY
GREATLY
GRISTLY
HEALTHY
HELOTRY
INAPTLY
INEPTLY
INERTLY
JOINTLY
LANGTRY
LENGTHY
LICITLY
LIGHTLY
MOISTLY
NIGHTLY
OVERTLY
POULTRY
QUIETLY
REENTRY
RIGHTLY
SAINTLY
SCANTLY
SHORTLY
SIGHTLY
SMARTLY
STOUTLY
SWARTHY
SWEETLY
SWELTRY
SWIFTLY
TACITLY
TIGHTLY
TIMOTHY
TOLSTOY
WEALTHY

•••••TY

ABILITY
ACIDITY
AGILITY
AMENITY
AMNESTY
ANNUITY
ANXIETY
APLENTY
ARIDITY
AVIDITY
BAYCITY
BREVITY
CHARITY
CHRISTY
CLARITY
CRUDITY
DENSITY
DIGNITY
DOUGHTY
DUALITY
DUBIETY
DYNASTY
EDACITY
FACULTY
FALSITY
FATCITY
FATUITY
FIDGETY
FLIGHTY
FRAILTY
GADGETY
GRAVITY
HAUGHTY
HONESTY
IMPIETY
JOLLITY
KKKKATY
LIBERTY
LICKETY
LOYALTY
MAJESTY
MODESTY
NAUGHTY
NOVELTY
OFFDUTY
OPACITY
PAUCITY
PENALTY
POVERTY
PROBITY
PUBERTY
QUALITY
REALITY
RICKETY
ROYALTY
SATIETY
SEADUTY
SEVENTY
SOCIETY
SQUINTY
SUAVITY
SUNCITY
THIRSTY
THRIFTY
THROATY
TRINITY
UTILITY
VACUITY
VARIETY
VARSITY
VELVETY
WEIGHTY

TZ•••••

TZARINA

T•Z••••

TIZZIES

T••Z•••

TARZANA
TIZZIES

T•••Z••

TOPAZES
TWEEZED
TWEEZES

T••••Z•

TRAPEZE

•T••Z••

STANZAS

•T•••Z•

ATOMIZE
ITEMIZE
STYLIZE
UTILIZE

••TZ•••

MATZOHS
MITZVAH
RITZIER
YITZHAK

••T•Z••

CITIZEN

••T••Z•

OUTSIZE

••T•••Z

ESTEVEZ
NATCHEZ

•••TZ••

BLITZED
BLITZEN
BLITZES
GLITZED
GLITZES
GRETZKY
JANTZEN
KLUTZES
PRETZEL
QUETZAL
SELTZER
SPITZES
SWITZER
WALTZED
WALTZER
WALTZES
YAHTZEE

•••T•Z•

BAPTIZE
MESTIZO

••••TZ•

CHINTZY
SCHATZI
SHIHTZU
YANGTZE

•••••TZ

BERLITZ
HEIFETZ
KIBBUTZ

U•A••••

UGANDAN
ULALUME
ULANOVA
UNAIDED
UNAIMED
UNAIRED
UNALIKE
UNARMED
UNASKED
UNAVOCE
UNAWARE
UPATREE
URANITE
URANIUM
UTAHANS

U••A•••

UKRAINE
ULYANOV
UMLAUTS
UNBAKED
UNCAGED
UNCAGES
UNCANNY
UNCASED
UNCASES
UNDATED
UNEARTH
UNFAZED
UNHANDS
UNHANDY
UNHAPPY
UNLACED
UNLACES
UNLADES
UNLATCH
UNMAKES
UNMASKS
UNNAMED
UNPACKS
UNPAVED
UNRATED
UNRAVEL
UNSATED
UNTACKS
UNTAMED
UNTAPED
UPDATED
UPDATES
UPLANDS
UPRAISE
UPTAKES
UPWARDS
URBANER
USEABLE
USUALLY

U•••A••

ULLMANN
ULULANT
ULULATE
UMBRAGE
UNAWARE
UNCHAIN
UNCIALS
UNCLASP
UNCRATE
UNDRAPE
UNDRAWN
UNHEARD
UNITARY
UNLEARN
UNLEASH
UNLOADS
UNREADY
UNSEALS
UNSEATS
UNSNAGS
UNSNAPS
UNSNARL
UNSTACK
UNTRAPS
UNWEAVE
UNWRAPS
UPBEATS
UPBRAID
UPDRAFT
UPGRADE
UPLOADS
UPPSALA
UPROARS
UPSCALE
UPSTAGE
UPSTART
UPSTATE
UTAHANS

U••••A•

UGANDAN
UMBRIAN
UNCLEAN
UNCLEAR
UNCLOAK
UNEQUAL
UNSTRAP
UNUSUAL
UPTOPAR
URUGUAY
UTOPIAN
UTOPIAS
UXORIAL

U•••••A

ULANOVA
UPPSALA

•UA••••

DUALITY
GUANACO
GUANINE
GUARANI
GUARDED
GUARGUM
MUAMMAR
NUANCED
NUANCES
QUACKED
QUAFFED
QUAFFER
QUAGGAS
QUAHOGS
QUAILED
QUAKERS
QUAKING
QUALIFY
QUALITY
QUANTUM
QUARREL
QUARTER
QUARTET
QUARTOS
QUASARS
QUASHED
QUASHES
QUAVERS
QUAVERY
RUANDAN
SUASION
SUAVELY
SUAVEST
SUAVITY
TUAREGS

•U•A•••

AUBADES
AURALEE
AURALLY
BUGABOO
BUGALOO
BUYABLE
CURACAO
CURATES
CURATOR
CUTAWAY
DUBARRY
DUKAKIS
DUNAWAY
DURABLE
DURABLY
DURANCE
DURANGO
DURANTE
EURASIA
HUMANLY
JUDAISM
JUMANJI
KUWAITI
LUNATIC
LUXATED
LUXATES
MUBARAK
MUTABLE
MUTABLY
MUTAGEN
MUTANTS
MUTATED
MUTATES
MUTATIS
OUTACTS
OUTAGES
PULASKI
PUTAMEN
PUTAWAY
RUNAMOK
RUNAWAY
SUGARED
SUKARNO
SUMATRA
SUSANNA
SUSANNE
SUZANNE
TUBAIST
YUCATAN

•U••A••

AUREATE
BUFFALO
BULGARS
BULWARK
BUOYANT
BURBANK
BUREAUS
BURLAPS
BUROAKS
BURSARS
BUSFARE
BUSTARD
BUZZARD
CUEBALL
CUECARD
CUIRASS
CUPCAKE
CUREALL
CURRANT
CURTAIL
CURTAIN
CUSHAWS
CUSTARD
CUTBACK
CUTLASS
CUTRATE
DUEDATE
DULLARD
FUNFAIR
FURBALL
FURNACE
GUANACO
GUARANI
GUEVARA
GUFFAWS
GUITARS
GUMBALL
GUNWALE
GUSTAVE
HUBBARD
HUBCAPS
HUNGARY
HURRAHS
HUSBAND
HUSHABY
HUSSARS
HUZZAHS
JUGBAND
JULIANA
JUNKART
JUTLAND
LUCIANO
LUGGAGE
LULLABY
LUMBAGO
LUMBARS
MUDPACK
MULLAHS
MUNDANE
MUSCATS
MUSTAFA
MUSTANG
MUSTARD
MUTUALS
NUBIANS
NUMBATS
OUTBACK
OUTCAST
OUTEATS
OUTFACE
OUTLAID
OUTLAND
OUTLAST
OUTLAWS
OUTLAYS
OUTPACE
OUTRACE
OUTRAGE
OUTRANK
OUTTAKE
OUTTALK
OUTWARD
PULSARS
PULSATE
PUNJABI
PUNKAHS
PURDAHS
QUASARS
RUDYARD
RUMBAED
RUMMAGE
RUNBACK
RUNLAPS
RUNWAYS
RUPIAHS
SUBWAYS
SUCRASE
SULFATE
SULTANA
SULTANS
SUMMARY
SUNBATH
SUNDAES
SUNDAYS
SUNLAMP
SUNMAID
SUNRAYS
SUNTANS
SURFACE
SURNAME
SURPASS
SUSTAIN
TULSANS
TURBANS
TUSCANY
TUSSAUD
VULCANS
VULGATE

•U•••A•

AUGURAL
AURORAE
AURORAL
AURORAS
AUSTRAL
AUTOMAT
BUCKRAM
BUCKSAW
BUDDHAS
BUGBEAR
BURGLAR
BUSHMAN
BUZZSAW
CULTJAM
CUPOLAS
CURACAO
CUTAWAY
DUENNAS
DUNAWAY
DUSTPAN
FURSEAL
FUSTIAN
GUINEAS
GUNBOAT
GUNPLAY
GURKHAS
HUMERAL
JUGHEAD
JUGULAR
JUMPSAT
JUNKMAN
JUVENAL
KUMQUAT
KUTENAI
LUNGEAT
MUAMMAR
MUBARAK
MULETAS
MUSICAL
MUSKRAT
NUCLEAR
NUMERAL
NUPTIAL
NUTMEAT
NUTRIAS
OUTDRAW
OUTPLAY
OUTWEAR
PULLMAN
PULLTAB
PURITAN
PUTAWAY
QUAGGAS
QUETZAL
QUINOAS
QUOKKAS
RUANDAN
RUFFIAN
RUFIYAA
RUNAWAY
RUSSIAN
SUBHEAD
SUNBEAM
SUNDIAL
SURCOAT
SURINAM
SURREAL
TUBULAR
TUCHMAN
TUESDAY
TUGBOAT
TUNDRAS
TUTELAR
YUCATAN

•U••••A
AUGUSTA
AUREOLA
AUSTRIA
BURKINA
CULEBRA
DUODENA
EURASIA
FUCHSIA
GUEVARA
JULIANA
MUSTAFA
QUECHUA
RUFIYAA
SUBROSA
SULTANA
SULUSEA
SUMATRA
SUSANNA
TUNISIA

••UA•••
AQUARIA
AQUATIC
AQUAVIT
ECUADOR
EQUABLE
EQUABLY
EQUALED
EQUALLY
EQUATED
EQUATES
EQUATOR
GOUACHE
IGUANAS
SQUALID
SQUALLS
SQUALOR
SQUANTO
SQUARED
SQUARER
SQUARES
SQUAWKS
TRUANCY
TRUANTS
USUALLY
ZOUAVES

••U•A••
ABUBAKR
ADULATE
AOUDADS
COUGARS
COURAGE
COURANT
CRUSADE
CRUZADO
EDUCATE
EMULATE
FOULARD
GAUTAMA
GOULASH
GOURAMI
HAULAGE
MOULAGE
NOUGATS
PLUMAGE
PLURALS
RHUBARB
ROULADE
SAUSAGE
SOUTANE
SQUEAKS
SQUEAKY
SQUEALS
TOUCANS
TOURACO
TSUNAMI
ULULANT
ULULATE
YOUMANS

••U••A•
ABUTTAL
ALUMNAE
ALUMNAL
AQUINAS
ASUSUAL
BLUEJAY
BLUELAW
CHUKKAS
CLUBCAR
CRUCIAL
DIURNAL
DOUGLAS
EXURBAN
FAUXPAS
FLUVIAL
HOUSMAN
HYUNDAI
IGUANAS
JOURDAN
JOURNAL
KLUGMAN
LAUGHAT
MAUGHAM
NEUTRAL
NOUVEAU
PLUVIAL
RHUMBAS
SAURIAN
THURMAN
THUSFAR
TRUCIAL
TRUDEAU
UNUSUAL
URUGUAY
VAUGHAN
ZEUGMAS

••U•••A
AQUARIA
ARUGULA
EXURBIA
GAUTAMA
LOUELLA
PAULINA
PRUSSIA

•••UA••
ACTUARY
ACTUATE
ANNUALS
ASSUAGE
CASUALS
EDOUARD
ESTUARY
JAGUARS
JANUARY
LOQUATS
MANUALS
MUTUALS
NAHUATL
ONGUARD
PAPUANS
PIQUANT
RITUALS
SAGUARO
SIOUANS
SITUATE
TIJUANA
TSQUARE
VALUATE
VISUALS

•••U•A•
ANGULAR
ANNULAR
AROUSAL
AUGURAL
CAYUGAS
FIBULAE
FIBULAS
HANUKAH
INHUMAN
INSULAR
JOCULAR
JUGULAR
KAHUNAS
KORUNAS
LACUNAE
LACUNAL
LACUNAS
LAGUNAS
MACULAE
MCLUHAN
MEDUSAE
MEDUSAS
MODULAR
NATURAL
NEBULAE
NEBULAR
NEBULAS
NODULAR
OLDUVAI
PADUCAH
PERUSAL
POPULAR
REFUSAL
REGULAR
REMUDAS
ROMULAN
SAMURAI
SECULAR
SPOUSAL
TABULAR
THRUWAY
TITULAR
TRAUMAS
TUBULAR
VICUNAS

•••U••A
ALLUVIA
AUGUSTA
CLAUDIA
ETRURIA
FELUCCA
MAZURKA
MEDULLA
MINUTIA
PETUNIA
ROBUSTA
ROTUNDA
SEQUOIA
STLUCIA
SULUSEA
TEQUILA
TIJUANA

••••UA•
ACCRUAL
ANAHUAC
ASUSUAL
BIVOUAC
COEQUAL
DONJUAN
FACTUAL
GRADUAL
KEROUAC
KUMQUAT
LINGUAL
RORQUAL
SANJUAN
SENSUAL
SICHUAN
TEXTUAL
UNEQUAL
UNUSUAL
URUGUAY
VICTUAL
VIRTUAL

••••U•A
ARUGULA
BARBUDA
BERMUDA
BRAVURA
CAESURA
DRACULA
FORMULA
FORTUNA
INOCULA
KILAUEA
SATSUMA
SCAPULA
SPATULA
TEMPURA
VENTURA
VISTULA

•••••UA
ANTIGUA
MANAGUA
QUECHUA

U•B••••
UMBERTO
UMBRAGE
UMBRIAN
UNBAKED
UNBENDS
UNBINDS
UNBLEST
UNBOLTS
UNBOUND
UNBOWED
UNBOXED
UNBOXES
UPBEATS
UPBORNE
UPBRAID
URBANER

U•••B••
UNROBED
UNROBES
USEABLE

•UB••••
AUBADES
AUBURNS
BUBBLED
BUBBLES
CUBBIES
CUBICLE
CUBISTS
DUBARRY
DUBBERS
DUBBING
DUBIETY
DUBIOUS
DUBUQUE
HUBBARD
HUBBELL
HUBBIES
HUBBUBS
HUBCAPS
JUBILEE
KUBRICK
LUBBERS
LUBBOCK
MUBARAK
NUBBIER
NUBBINS
NUBBLES
NUBIANS
PUBERTY
PUBLICS
PUBLISH
RUBBERS
RUBBERY
RUBBING
RUBBISH
RUBBLES
RUBDOWN
RUBICON
RUBITIN
RUBRICS
RUBSOUT
RUBYDEE
SUBBING
SUBDEBS
SUBDUED
SUBDUER
SUBDUES
SUBHEAD
SUBJECT
SUBJOIN
SUBLETS
SUBLIME
SUBMITS
SUBORNS
SUBPLOT
SUBROSA
SUBSETS
SUBSIDE
SUBSIDY
SUBSIST
SUBSOIL
SUBSUME
SUBTEND
SUBTEXT
SUBTLER
SUBUNIT
SUBURBS
SUBVERT
SUBWAYS
SUBZERO
TUBAIST
TUBBIER
TUBISTS
TUBULAR

•U•B•••
BUBBLED
BUBBLES
BUGBEAR
BULBLET
BULBOUS
BULBULS
BUMBLED
BUMBLER
BUMBLES
BURBANK
BURBLED
BURBLES
BURBOTS
BUSBIES
BUSBOYS
CUBBIES
CUEBALL
CUIBONO
CURBCUT
CURBING
CUTBACK
DUBBERS
DUBBING
DUMBEST
FUMBLED
FUMBLER
FUMBLES
FURBALL
FURBISH
GUMBALL
GUNBOAT
HUBBARD
HUBBELL
HUBBIES
HUBBUBS
HUMBLED
HUMBLER
HUMBLES
HUMBUGS
HUSBAND
JUGBAND
JUMBLED
JUMBLES
LUBBERS
LUBBOCK
LUMBAGO
LUMBARS
LUMBERS
MUMBLED
MUMBLER
MUMBLES
NUBBIER
NUBBINS
NUBBLES
NUMBATS
NUMBERS
NUMBEST
NUMBING
OUTBACK
OUTBIDS
PUEBLOS
QUIBBLE
RUBBERS
RUBBERY
RUBBING
RUBBISH
RUBBLES
RUMBAED
RUMBLED
RUMBLES
RUNBACK
SUBBING
SUDBURY
SUNBATH
SUNBEAM
SUNBELT
SUNBURN
TUBBIER
TUGBOAT
TUMBLED
TUMBLER
TUMBLES
TUMBREL
TURBANS
TURBINE
TURBOTS

•U••B••
AUDIBLE
AUDIBLY
AUDUBON
BUGABOO
BUNKBED
BUYABLE
CULEBRA
DURABLE
DURABLY
JUJUBES
JUKEBOX
JUNEBUG
MUTABLE
MUTABLY
QUIBBLE

•U•••B•
HUBBUBS
HUSHABY
LULLABY
PUNJABI
SUBDEBS
SUBURBS

•U••••B
PULLTAB
SUCCUMB

••UB•••
ABUBAKR
BAUBLES
BLUBBER
BRUBECK
CLUBBED
CLUBCAR
DAUBERS
DAUBING
DOUBLED
DOUBLES
DOUBLET
DOUBLEU
DOUBTED
DOUBTER
DRUBBED
FLUBBED
GRUBBED
HAUBERK
REUBENS
RHUBARB
SHUBERT
SNUBBED
STUBBED
STUBBLE
STUBBLY

••U•B••
BLUBBER
BLUEBOY
BOURBON
CLUBBED
CRUMBLE
CRUMBLY
DRUBBED
EQUABLE
EQUABLY
EXURBAN
EXURBIA
FLUBBED
FNUMBER
GRUBBED
GRUMBLE
HAUTBOY
PLUMBED
PLUMBER
RHUMBAS
SLUMBER
SNUBBED
STUBBED
STUBBLE
STUBBLY
STUMBLE
THUMBED
THURBER

••U••B•
WOULDBE

••U•••B
COULOMB
RHUBARB

•••UB••
AUDUBON
JUJUBES
SCRUBBY
SCRUBUP
SHRUBBY
SOLUBLE
STEUBEN
TRAUBEL
TROUBLE
VOLUBLE
VOLUBLY

•••U•B•
BENUMBS
COLUMBO
SCRUBBY
SHRUBBY
SUBURBS

••••UB•
BEDAUBS
CHERUBS
HOTTUBS
HUBBUBS
ICECUBE
INDOUBT
NODOUBT
REDOUBT

••••U•B
DIMBULB
DISTURB
PERTURB
SUCCUMB

•••••UB
BACKRUB
BATHTUB
KEYCLUB
LIONCUB
OVERDUB
WASHTUB

UC•••••
UCCELLO

U•C••••
UCCELLO
UNCAGED
UNCAGES
UNCANNY
UNCASED
UNCASES
UNCHAIN
UNCIALS
UNCIVIL
UNCLASP
UNCLEAN
UNCLEAR
UNCLOAK
UNCLOGS
UNCLOSE
UNCOILS
UNCORKS
UNCOUTH
UNCOVER
UNCRATE
UNCTION
UNCURLS
UPCLOSE
URCHINS

U••C•••
UNICORN
UNSCREW
UPSCALE

U•••C••
UNLACED
UNLACES
UNLOCKS
UNLUCKY
UNPACKS
UNTACKS
UPTICKS
UTRECHT

U••••C•
UNAVOCE
UNFROCK
UNHITCH
UNLATCH
UNSTACK
UNSTICK
UNSTUCK
URGENCY

•UC••••
AUCTION
BUCKETS
BUCKEYE
BUCKING
BUCKLED
BUCKLER
BUCKLES
BUCKLEY
BUCKOES
BUCKRAM
BUCKSAW
BUCKSUP
BUCOLIC
CUCKOOS
DUCHESS
DUCHIES
DUCKIER
DUCKING
DUCKPIN
DUCTILE
DUCTING
EUCHRED
EUCHRES
FUCHSIA
LUCERNE
LUCIANO
LUCIDLY
LUCIFER
LUCILLE
LUCKIER
LUCKILY
LUCKING
LUCKOUT
MUCKING
MUCKSUP
NUCLEAR
NUCLEIC
NUCLEON
NUCLEUS
NUCLIDE
PUCCINI
PUCKERS
PUCKETT
PUCKISH
RUCHING
RUCKING
RUCTION
SUCCEED
SUCCESS
SUCCORS
SUCCOUR
SUCCUMB
SUCKERS
SUCKING
SUCKSIN
SUCRASE
SUCROSE
SUCTION
TUCHMAN
TUCKERS
TUCKING
TUCKSIN
YUCATAN
YUCKIER

•U•C•••
BUNCHED
BUNCHES
BUNCOED
BUTCHER
CUECARD
CUPCAKE
FULCRUM
GULCHES
HUBCAPS
HUNCHED
HUNCHES
HUTCHES
JUICERS
JUICEUP
JUICIER
JUICILY
JUICING
JUNCOES
LUNCHED
LUNCHER
LUNCHES
LURCHED
LURCHES
MULCHED
MULCHES
MULCTED
MUNCHED
MUNCHER
MUNCHES
MUSCATS
MUSCLED
MUSCLES
MUSCOVY
NUNCIOS
OUTCAST
OUTCOME
OUTCROP
PUCCINI
PUNCHED
PUNCHER
PUNCHES
PUNCHIN
PUNCHUP
PURCELL
QUACKED
QUECHUA
QUICHES
QUICKEN
QUICKER
QUICKIE
QUICKLY
SUCCEED
SUCCESS
SUCCORS
SUCCOUR
SUCCUMB
SUNCITY
SURCOAT
TUSCANY
VULCANS

•U••C••
AURICLE
AUROCHS
CUBICLE
CURACAO
CURBCUT
CUTICLE
EUNUCHS
JUMPCUT
MUSICAL
NUANCED
NUANCES
OUTACTS
PUMICES
QUINCES
RUBICON
TUNICLE

•U•••C•
AUSPICE
BULLOCK
BURDOCK
CUTBACK
DURANCE
FURNACE
FUSTICS
GUANACO
GUNLOCK
HUMMOCK
JUSTICE
KUBRICK
LUBBOCK
MUDPACK
MURDOCH
OUTBACK
OUTFACE
OUTPACE
OUTRACE
PUBLICS
RUBRICS
RUNBACK
RUSTICS
SUBJECT
SUFFICE
SUNDECK
SURFACE
SUSPECT
TUSSOCK

•U••••C
BUCOLIC
JURIDIC
LUNATIC
NUCLEIC
NUMERIC

••UC•••
CHUCKED
CHUCKLE
CLUCKED
COUCHED
COUCHES
CRUCIAL
DRUCKER
EDUCATE
EDUCING
ERUCTED
FAUCETS
GAUCHER
GAUCHOS
GLUCOSE
KNUCKLE
PAUCITY
PLUCKED
POUCHED
POUCHES
RAUCOUS
SAUCERS
SAUCIER
SAUCILY
SHUCKED
SHUCKER
STUCCOS
STUCKTO
STUCKUP
TOUCANS
TOUCHED
TOUCHES
TOUCHON
TOUCHUP
TRUCIAL
TRUCKED
TRUCKEE
TRUCKER
TRUCKLE
VOUCHED
VOUCHER
VOUCHES

••U•C••
BOUNCED
BOUNCER
BOUNCES
CLUBCAR
COUNCIL
CRUNCHY
GOUACHE
JOUNCED
JOUNCES
PAUNCHY
POUNCED
POUNCER
POUNCES
SLUICED
SLUICES
SOUPCON
SOURCED
SOURCES
STUCCOS

••U••C•
BRUBECK
FLUENCY
MAURICE
SQUELCH
SQUINCH
TOURACO
TRUANCY

••U•••C
AQUATIC
CAUSTIC
LAUTREC
POULENC
YOUNGMC

•••UC••
ABDUCTS
ADDUCED
ADDUCES
ADDUCTS
ATTUCKS
CADUCEI
CHAUCER
DEDUCED
DEDUCES
DEDUCTS
EUNUCHS
FELUCCA
GROUCHO
GROUCHY
INDUCED
INDUCER
INDUCES
INDUCTS
NOGUCHI
PADUCAH
PENUCHE
REDUCED
REDUCER
REDUCES
SEDUCED
SEDUCER
SEDUCES
SLOUCHY
SPRUCED
SPRUCER
SPRUCES
STLUCIA
UNLUCKY

•••U•C•
ADJUNCT
DEFUNCT
ENOUNCE
FELUCCA
FLOUNCE
GODUTCH
INDUTCH
SCRUNCH

STAUNCH
TROUNCE

••••UC•
CONDUCE
CONDUCT
DEBAUCH
DEBOUCH
LETTUCE
POTLUCK
PRODUCE
PRODUCT
RETOUCH
ROEBUCK
SAWBUCK
TRADUCE
UNSTUCK
VIADUCT

••••U•C
ANAHUAC
BIVOUAC
KEROUAC

•••••UC
JEANLUC

U•D••••
UNDATED
UNDERGO
UNDOING
UNDRAPE
UNDRAWN
UNDRESS
UNDYING
UPDATED
UPDATES
UPDRAFT

U•••D••
UGANDAN
UNAIDED
UNENDED
UNGODLY
UNLADES
UPENDED

U••••D•
UNBENDS
UNBINDS
UNFOLDS
UNGIRDS
UNHANDS
UNHANDY
UNIPODS
UNLOADS
UNREADY
UNWINDS
UPGRADE
UPHOLDS
UPLANDS
UPLOADS
UPWARDS

U•••••D
UMPIRED
UNAIDED
UNAIMED
UNAIRED
UNARMED
UNASKED
UNBAKED
UNBOUND
UNBOWED
UNBOXED
UNCAGED
UNCASED
UNDATED
UNENDED
UNFAZED
UNFIXED
UNGLUED
UNHEARD
UNIFIED
UNLACED
UNLIKED
UNLINED
UNLOVED
UNMOVED
UNNAMED
UNOILED
UNPAVED
UNPILED
UNRATED
UNROBED
UNSATED
UNSEWED
UNSOUND
UNTAMED
UNTAPED
UNTRIED
UNTUNED
UNWOUND
UNYOKED
UNZONED
UPBRAID
UPDATED
UPENDED
USHERED
USURPED
UTTERED

•UD••••
AUDIBLE
AUDIBLY
AUDITED
AUDITOR
AUDUBON
BUDDHAS
BUDDIES
BUDDING
BUDDYUP
BUDGETS
BUDGIES
BUDGING
CUDDLED
CUDDLES
CUDGELS
DUDDIES
DUDEDUP
DUDGEON
FUDDLED
FUDDLES
FUDGING
HUDDLED
HUDDLES
JUDAISM
JUDDERS
JUDGING
JUDOIST
MUDDERS
MUDDIED
MUDDIER
MUDDIES
MUDDLED
MUDDLER
MUDDLES
MUDEELS
MUDHENS
MUDPACK
MUDPIES
NUDGERS
NUDGING
NUDISTS
NUDNIKS
PUDDING
PUDDLED
PUDDLES
PUDGIER
RUDDERS
RUDDIER
RUDOLPH
RUDYARD
SUDBURY
SUDSIER
SUDSING

•U•D•••
BUDDHAS
BUDDIES
BUDDING
BUDDYUP
BUNDLED
BUNDLES
BURDENS
BURDOCK
CUDDLED
CUDDLES
CURDING
CURDLED
CURDLES
CUTDOWN
DUDDIES
DUEDATE
DUMDUMS
DUODENA
FUDDLED
FUDDLES
FUNDING
GUIDING
GUIDONS
GUMDROP
GUNDOGS
HUDDLED
HUDDLES
HUMDRUM
HUNDRED
HURDLED
HURDLER
HURDLES
JUDDERS
KURDISH
MUDDERS
MUDDIED
MUDDIER
MUDDIES
MUDDLED
MUDDLER
MUDDLES
MUNDANE
MURDERS
MURDOCH
OUTDOES
OUTDONE
OUTDOOR
OUTDRAW
OUTDREW
PUDDING
PUDDLED
PUDDLES
PUNDITS
PURDAHS
PUTDOWN
RUBDOWN
RUDDERS
RUDDIER
RUNDEEP
RUNDOWN
SUBDEBS
SUBDUED
SUBDUER
SUBDUES
SUNDAES
SUNDAYS
SUNDECK
SUNDERS
SUNDEWS
SUNDIAL
SUNDOGS
SUNDOWN
TUNDRAS

•U••D••
AUBADES
BUILDER
BUILDIN
BUILDON
BUILDUP
BULLDOG
DUDEDUP
DUKEDOM
GUARDED
GUILDER
HUMIDLY
HUMIDOR
JURIDIC
LUCIDLY
LURIDLY
RUANDAN
RUBYDEE
RUNSDRY
RUSHDIE
TUESDAY
TUNEDIN
TUNEDUP
TUXEDOS

•U•••D•
AUGENDS
BUSHIDO
CUSPIDS
CUSTODY
NUCLIDE
OUTBIDS
OUTSIDE
SUBSIDE
SUBSIDY
SULFIDE
SUNGODS

•U••••D
AUDITED
AUGURED
BUBBLED
BUCKLED
BUGEYED
BULLIED
BUMBLED
BUNCHED
BUNCOED
BUNDLED
BUNGLED
BUNKBED
BUNKOED
BURBLED
BURGLED
BUSTARD
BUSTLED
BUZZARD
CUDDLED
CUECARD
CURDLED
CURRIED
CUSTARD
DULLARD
DUMMIED
EUCHRED
FUDDLED
FUELROD
FUMBLED
GUARDED
GUESSED
GUESTED
GURGLED
GUSSIED
GUZZLED
HUBBARD
HUDDLED
HULLOED
HUMBLED
HUMORED
HUNCHED
HUNDRED
HURDLED
HURRIED
HURTLED
HUSBAND
HUSTLED
JUGBAND
JUGGLED
JUGHEAD
JUMBLED
JUTLAND
LUNCHED
LURCHED
LUSTRED
LUXATED
MUDDIED
MUDDLED
MUFFLED
MULCHED
MULCTED
MUMBLED
MUMFORD
MUNCHED
MUSCLED
MUSTARD
MUTATED
MUZZLED
NUANCED
NUZZLED
OUTLAID
OUTLAND
OUTLOUD
OUTSOLD
OUTWARD
PUDDLED
PUNCHED
PURFLED
PURPLED
PURSUED
PUTTIED
PUZZLED
QUACKED
QUAFFED
QUAILED
QUASHED
QUEERED
QUELLED
QUERIED
QUESTED
QUIETED
QUILLED
QUILTED
QUIPPED
QUIZZED
RUDYARD
RUFFLED
RUMBAED
RUMBLED
RUMORED
RUMPLED
RUSTLED
SUBDUED
SUBHEAD
SUBTEND
SUCCEED
SUGARED
SULLIED
SUNMAID
SUSPEND
SUTURED
TUMBLED
TURTLED
TUSSAUD
TUSSLED
TUTORED

••UD•••
AOUDADS
BOUDOIR
CRUDELY
CRUDEST
CRUDITY
DRUDGED
DRUDGES
ELUDING
ERUDITE
EXUDING
FEUDING
GAUDENS
GAUDIER
GAUDILY
GRUDGED
GRUDGES
HOUDINI
KLUDGES
LAUDING
LOUDEST
MAUDLIN
PRUDENT
PRUDERY
PRUDHOE
PRUDISH
SCUDDED
SHUDDER
SLUDGES
SMUDGED
SMUDGES
STUDDED
STUDENT
STUDIED
STUDIES
STUDIOS
THUDDED
TRUDEAU
TRUDGED
TRUDGER
TRUDGES

••U•D••
ASUNDER
BLUNDER
BOULDER
BOUNDED
BOUNDER
BOUNDTO
BOUNDUP
CLUEDIN
COULDNT
ECUADOR
FLUIDLY
FOUNDED
FOUNDER
FOUNDRY
GLUEDON
GOUNDER
GOURDES
HOUNDED
HYUNDAI
JOURDAN
LAUNDER
LAUNDRY
LOURDES
MAULDIN
MAUNDER
MOULDED
MOULDER
MOUNDED
PLUNDER
POUNDED
POUNDER
ROUNDED
ROUNDER
ROUNDLY
ROUNDON
ROUNDUP
SCUDDED
SHUDDER
SOUNDED
SOUNDER
SOUNDLY
STUDDED
THUDDED
THUNDER
TRUNDLE
WOULDBE
WOULDNT
WOUNDED
WOUNDUP

••U••D•
AOUDADS
CRUSADE
CRUZADO
ROULADE

••U•••D
ABUTTED
AVULSED
BLUFFED
BLUNTED
BLURRED
BLURTED
BLUSHED
BOUNCED
BOUNDED
BRUISED
BRUITED
BRUSHED
CAULKED
CHUCKED
CHUGGED
CHUMMED
CHURNED
CLUBBED
CLUCKED
CLUMPED
CLUNKED
COUCHED
COUGHED
COUNTED
COUPLED
COURSED
COURTED
CRUISED
CRUSHED
CRUSTED
DAUNTED
DOUBLED
DOUBTED
DRUBBED
DRUDGED
DRUGGED
DRUMMED
EQUALED
EQUATED
ERUCTED
ERUPTED
EVULSED
EXULTED
FAULTED
FLUBBED
FLUFFED
FLUNKED
FLUSHED
FOULARD
FOUNDED
FRUITED
GLUTTED
GRUBBED
GRUDGED
GRUMPED
GRUNTED
HAUNTED
HOUNDED
JAUNTED
JOUNCED
JOUSTED
KNURLED
LAUGHED
LOUNGED
LOUREED
MOULDED
MOULTED
MOUNDED
MOUNTED
MOUSSED
MOUTHED
PLUCKED
PLUGGED
PLUMBED
PLUMPED
PLUNGED
PLUNKED
POUCHED
POUNCED
POUNDED
REUPPED
ROUGHED
ROUNDED
ROUSTED
SAUTEED
SCUDDED
SCUFFED
SCULLED
SHUCKED
SHUNNED
SHUNTED
SHUSHED
SKULKED
SKUNKED
SLUGGED
SLUICED
SLUMMED
SLUMPED
SLURPED
SLURRED
SMUDGED
SNUBBED
SNUFFED
SOUGHED
SOUNDED
SOURCED
SPURNED
SPURRED
SPURTED
SQUALID
SQUARED
SQUIRED
STUBBED
STUDDED
STUDIED
STUFFED
STUMPED
STUNNED
STUNTED
TAUNTED
THUDDED
THUMBED
THUMPED
TOUCHED
TOUSLED
TRUCKED
TRUDGED
TRUMPED
TRUSSED
TRUSTED
USURPED
VAULTED
VAUNTED
VOUCHED
WHUPPED
WOUNDED

•••UD••
ADJUDGE
ALLUDED
ALLUDES
CLAUDIA
CLAUDIO
CLOUDED
DELUDED
DELUDES
DENUDED
DENUDES
ESCUDOS
INCUDES
PLAUDIT
PROUDER
PROUDLY
REMUDAS
STRUDEL
WHAUDEN

•••U•D•
ABOUNDS
GERUNDS
GROUNDS
LIQUIDS
OBTUNDS
REFUNDS
ROTUNDA
TVGUIDE
YAOUNDE

•••U••D
ABJURED
ACCUSED
ADDUCED
ADJURED
ALLUDED
ALLURED
AROUSED
ASSUMED
ASSURED
ATTUNED
AUGURED
BEMUSED
BLOUSED
CLOUDED
CLOUTED
DEBUTED
DEDUCED
DEFUSED
DELUDED
DELUGED
DENUDED
DEPUTED
DILUTED
DISUSED
EDOUARD
EFFUSED
ENDURED
ENSURED
EXCUSED
FIGURED
FLOURED
FLOUTED
FOCUSED
GROUPED
GROUSED
GROUTED
ILLUSED
IMMURED
IMPUTED
INDUCED
INFUSED
INJURED
INSURED
MATURED
MINUEND
MISUSED
NATURED
ONGUARD
PERUSED
REBUILD
REBUKED
RECUSED
REDUCED
REFUSED
REFUTED
REPUTED
RESUMED
RETUNED
SALUTED
SCOURED
SCOUTED
SECURED
SEDUCED
SHOUTED
SPOUTED
SPRUCED
SUTURED
TENURED
UNTUNED

••••UD•
BARBUDA
BERMUDA
COLLUDE
EXCLUDE
EXTRUDE
HEYJUDE
INCLUDE
INTRUDE
MARAUDS
OBTRUDE
OCCLUDE
PRELUDE
REDBUDS
SECLUDE
SHROUDS

••••U•D
ACCRUED
AGROUND
ASTOUND
ENGLUND
EXPOUND
GOROUND
IMBRUED
IMPOUND
INBOUND
LANGUID
MISCUED
OROTUND
PLAGUED
PURSUED
REBOUND
REDOUND
REGLUED
RESCUED
RESOUND
REWOUND
SIGMUND
SNAFUED
SUBDUED
TONGUED
UNBOUND
UNGLUED
UNSOUND
UNWOUND

•••••UD
APPLAUD
BECLOUD
DEFRAUD
GIELGUD
IBNSAUD
MALAMUD
MILHAUD
OUTLOUD
RIMBAUD
ROSEBUD
TUSSAUD

U•E••••
UNEARTH
UNENDED
UNEQUAL
UPENDED
USEABLE
USELESS
UTENSIL

U••E•••
UCCELLO
UMBERTO
UNBENDS
UNDERGO
UNHEARD
UNKEMPT
UNLEARN
UNLEASH
UNNERVE
UNREADY
UNREELS
UNSEALS
UNSEATS
UNSEWED
UNVEILS
UNWEAVE
UPBEATS
UPTEMPO
URGENCY
URTEXTS
USHERED
UTRECHT
UTTERED
UTTERER
UTTERLY

U•••E••
UGLIEST
UKULELE
ULSTERS
UMPTEEN
UNBLEST
UNCLEAN
UNCLEAR
UNDRESS
UNGUENT
UNITERS
UNREELS
UNSPENT
UNSWEPT
UPSWEEP
UPSWEPT
USELESS
USOPENS
USSTEEL
USURERS

U••••E•
ULYSSES
UMPIRED
UMPIRES
UMPTEEN
UNAIDED
UNAIMED
UNAIRED
UNARMED
UNASKED
UNBAKED
UNBOWED
UNBOXED
UNBOXES
UNCAGED
UNCAGES
UNCASED
UNCASES
UNCOVER
UNDATED
UNENDED
UNFAZED
UNFIXED
UNGLUED
UNIFIED
UNIFIER
UNIFIES
UNITIES
UNLACED
UNLACES
UNLADES
UNLIKED
UNLINED
UNLOVED
UNMAKES
UNMOVED
UNNAMED
UNOILED
UNPAVED
UNPILED
UNPILES
UNRATED
UNRAVEL
UNROBED
UNROBES
UNSATED
UNSCREW
UNSEWED
UNTAMED
UNTAPED
UNTRIED
UNTUNED
UNTUNES
UNWISER
UNYOKED
UNYOKES
UNZONED
UPATREE
UPDATED
UPDATES
UPENDED
UPRISEN
UPRISES
UPRIVER
UPSWEEP
UPTAKES
URBANER
USHERED
USSTEEL
USURPED
USURPER
UTTERED
UTTERER

U•••••E
UKRAINE
UKULELE
ULALUME
ULULATE
UMBRAGE
UNALIKE
UNAVOCE
UNAWARE
UNCLOSE
UNCRATE
UNDRAPE
UNHORSE
UNITIVE
UNLOOSE
UNNERVE
UNQUOTE
UNWEAVE
UPATREE
UPBORNE
UPCLOSE

UPGRADE
UPRAISE
UPSCALE
UPSTAGE
UPSTATE
UPSURGE
URANITE
USEABLE
UTILIZE

•UE••••

CUEBALL
CUECARD
DUEDATE
DUELERS
DUELING
DUELIST
DUENNAS
FUELERS
FUELING
FUELOIL
FUELROD
GUELPHS
GUESSED
GUESSER
GUESSES
GUESTED
GUEVARA
MUEZZIN
PUEBLOS
PUERILE
QUECHUA
QUEENLY
QUEERED
QUEERER
QUEERLY
QUELLED
QUENTIN
QUERIED
QUERIES
QUESTED
QUETZAL
QUEUERS
QUEUEUP
QUEUING
TUESDAY

•U•E•••

AUGENDS
AUREATE
AUREOLA
AUREOLE
AUTEURS
BUGEYED
BUREAUS
BURETTE
CULEBRA
CUREALL
DUDEDUP
DUKEDOM
DUTEOUS
EUGENIE
EUTERPE
HUMERAL
HUMERUS
JUKEBOX
JUNEBUG
JUVENAL
KUTENAI
LUCERNE
MUDEELS
MULETAS
MUMESON
MUSETTE
MUSEUMS
NUMERAL
NUMERIC
NUREYEV
OUTEATS
PUBERTY
QUEENLY
QUEERED
QUEERER
QUEERLY
QUIETED
QUIETEN
QUIETER
QUIETLY
RULEOUT
RULESON
SUZETTE
TUNEDIN
TUNEDUP
TUNEFUL
TUNEOUT
TUNESIN
TUNESUP
TUNEUPS
TUPELOS
TUREENS
TUTELAR
TUXEDOS
YULELOG

•U••E••

AUGMENT
AUKLETS
AUSTERE
BUCKETS
BUCKEYE
BUDGETS
BUFFERS
BUFFETS
BUFFETT
BUGBEAR
BUGLERS
BULLETS
BUMMERS
BUMPERS
BUNGEES
BUNKERS
BURDENS
BURGEES
BURGEON
BURGERS
BURGESS
BURMESE
BURNERS
BURNETT
BUSHELS
BUSIEST
BUTLERS
BUTTERS
BUTTERY
BUZZERS
CUDGELS
CULVERT
CURFEWS
CURLERS
CURLEWS
CURRENT
CURTEST
CURVETS
CUTLERS
CUTLERY
CUTLETS
CUTTERS
DUBBERS
DUBIETY
DUCHESS
DUDGEON
DUELERS
DUFFELS
DUFFERS
DULLEST
DUMBEST
DUNGEON
DUNKERS
DUODENA
DURRELL
DUSTERS
FUELERS
FULGENT
FULLEST
FUNFEST
FUNNELS
FURSEAL
GUINEAS
GULLETS
GUNNELS
GUNNERS
GUNNERY
GURNEYS
GUSHERS
GUSSETS
GUTLESS
GUTTERS
HUBBELL
HUGGERS
HULLERS
HUMMERS
HUNGERS
HUNKERS
HUNTERS
HURLERS
HUSKERS
HUSSEIN
JUDDERS
JUGHEAD
JUICERS
JUICEUP
JUMPERS
JUNKERS
JUNKETS
LUBBERS
LUGGERS
LUMBERS
LUMIERE
LUMPERS
LUNGEAT
LUNKERS
LUSHEST
LUSTERS
MUDDERS
MUDEELS
MUDHENS
MUGGERS
MULLEIN
MULLERS
MULLETS
MUMMERS
MUMMERY
MUPPETS
MURDERS
MUSHERS
MUSKETS
MUSSELS
MUSTERS
MUTTERS
NUCLEAR
NUCLEIC
NUCLEON
NUCLEUS
NUDGERS
NUGGETS
NUMBERS
NUMBEST
NUNNERY
NURSERS
NURSERY
NUTLETS
NUTMEAT
NUTMEGS
NUTTERS
OURSELF
OUSTERS
OUTLETS
OUTSELL
OUTSETS
OUTWEAR
PUCKERS
PUCKETT
PUFFERS
PUFFERY
PUGREES
PULLETS
PULLEYS
PUMMELS
PUMPERS
PUNGENT
PUNIEST
PUNTERS
PUPPETS
PUPTENT
PURCELL
PURRERS
PURSERS
PURVEYS
PUTTEES
PUTTERS
QUAKERS
QUAVERS
QUAVERY
QUEUERS
QUEUEUP
QUIVERS
QUOTERS
RUBBERS
RUBBERY
RUDDERS
RUINERS
RUNDEEP
RUNLETS
RUNNELS
RUNNERS
RUSHEES
RUSHERS
RUSSELL
RUSSETS
RUTGERS
SUAVELY
SUAVEST
SUBDEBS
SUBHEAD
SUBJECT
SUBLETS
SUBSETS
SUBTEND
SUBTEXT
SUBVERT
SUBZERO
SUCCEED
SUCCESS
SUCKERS
SUFFERS
SUGGEST
SULKERS
SUMMERS
SUMMERY
SUNBEAM
SUNBELT
SUNDECK
SUNDERS
SUNDEWS
SUNLESS
SUNSETS
SUPPERS
SUPREME
SUPREMO
SURFEIT
SURFERS
SURGEON
SURGERY
SURREAL
SURREYS
SURVEYS
SUSPECT
SUSPEND
SUTLERS
TUAREGS
TUCKERS
TUFFETS
TUGGERS
TUNNELS
TUREENS
TURKEYS
TURNERS
TURRETS
TUSKERS

•U•••E•

AUBADES
AUDITED
AUGURED
AUNTIES
AURALEE
AUSSIES
BUBBLED
BUBBLES
BUCKLED
BUCKLER
BUCKLES
BUCKLEY
BUCKOES
BUDDIES
BUDGIES
BUGEYED
BUGGIER
BUGGIES
BUILDER
BULBLET
BULKIER
BULLIED
BULLIES
BULLPEN
BUMBLED
BUMBLER
BUMBLES
BUMPIER
BUNCHED
BUNCHES
BUNCOED
BUNDLED
BUNDLES
BUNGEES
BUNGLED
BUNGLER
BUNGLES
BUNKBED
BUNKOED
BUNNIES
BURBLED
BURBLES
BURGEES
BURGHER
BURGLED
BURGLES
BURLIER
BUSBIES
BUSHIER
BUSHMEN
BUSTLED
BUSTLES
BUTCHER
CUBBIES
CUDDLED
CUDDLES
CURATES
CURDLED
CURDLES
CURLIER
CURRIED
CURRIER
CURRIES
CURTSEY
CURVIER
CUSHIER
CUSSLER
DUCHIES
DUCKIER
DUDDIES
DUMMIED
DUMMIES
DUMPIER
DUSKIER
DUSTIER
EUCHRED
EUCHRES
FUDDLED
FUDDLES
FUMBLED
FUMBLER
FUMBLES
FUNGOES
FUNKIER
FUNNIER
FUNNIES
FURORES
FURRIER
FURTHER
FUSSIER
FUSTIER
FUTURES
FUZZIER
GUARDED
GUESSED
GUESSER
GUESSES
GUESTED
GUILDER
GUIMPES
GULCHES
GULLIES
GUMMIER
GUMTREE
GUNKIER
GUNNIES
GUNTHER
GUPPIES
GURGLED
GURGLES
GUSHIER
GUSSIED
GUSSIES
GUSTOES
GUTSIER
GUZZLED
GUZZLER
GUZZLES
HUBBIES
HUDDLED
HUDDLES
HUFFIER
HULLOED
HUMBLED
HUMBLER
HUMBLES
HUMORED
HUNCHED
HUNCHES
HUNDRED
HUNTLEY
HURDLED
HURDLER
HURDLES
HURRIED
HURRIES
HURTLED
HURTLES
HUSKIER
HUSKIES
HUSSIES
HUSTLED
HUSTLER
HUSTLES
HUTCHES
JUBILEE
JUGGLED
JUGGLER
JUGGLES
JUICIER
JUJUBES
JUMBLED
JUMBLES
JUMPIER
JUNCOES
JUNGLES
JUNIPER
JUNKIER
JUNKIES
JUPITER
LUCIFER
LUCKIER
LUMPIER
LUNCHED
LUNCHER
LUNCHES
LUPINES
LURCHED
LURCHES
LUSTIER
LUSTRED
LUSTRES
LUXATED
LUXATES
MUDDIED
MUDDIER
MUDDIES
MUDDLED
MUDDLER
MUDDLES
MUDPIES
MUFFLED
MUFFLER
MUFFLES
MUGGIER
MULCHED
MULCHES
MULCTED
MUMBLED
MUMBLER
MUMBLES
MUMMIES
MUNCHED
MUNCHER
MUNCHES
MURKIER
MURPHEY
MUSCLED
MUSCLES
MUSHIER
MUSTIER
MUSTSEE
MUTAGEN
MUTATED
MUTATES
MUZZIER
MUZZLED
MUZZLES
NUANCED
NUANCES
NUBBIER
NUBBLES
NUREYEV
NUTTIER
NUZZLED
NUZZLER
NUZZLES
OUTAGES
OUTDOES
OUTDREW
OUTGOES
OUTGREW
OUTSTEP
PUDDLED
PUDDLES
PUDGIER
PUFFIER
PUGREES
PUMICES
PUNCHED
PUNCHER
PUNCHES
PUNKIES
PUNSTER
PUPPIES
PURFLED
PURFLES
PURLIEU
PURPLED
PURPLES
PURSUED
PURSUER
PURSUES
PURVIEW
PUSHIER
PUTAMEN
PUTOVER
PUTTEES
PUTTIED
PUTTIES
PUZZLED
PUZZLER
PUZZLES
QUACKED
QUAFFED
QUAFFER
QUAILED
QUARREL
QUARTER
QUARTET
QUASHED
QUASHES
QUEERED
QUEERER
QUELLED
QUERIED
QUERIES
QUESTED
QUICHES
QUICKEN
QUICKER
QUIETED
QUIETEN
QUIETER
QUIGLEY
QUILLED
QUILTED
QUILTER
QUINCES
QUINTET
QUIPPED
QUIPPER
QUITTER
QUIZZED
QUIZZES
QUONSET
RUBBLES
RUBYDEE
RUDDIER
RUFFLED
RUFFLES
RUMBAED
RUMBLED
RUMBLES
RUMMIER
RUMORED
RUMPLED
RUMPLES
RUNDEEP
RUNNIER
RUNOVER
RUNTIER
RUSHEES
RUSTIER
RUSTLED
RUSTLER
RUSTLES
SUBDUED
SUBDUER
SUBDUES
SUBTLER
SUCCEED
SUDSIER
SUGARED
SULKIER
SULKIES
SULLIED
SULLIES
SULUSEA
SUNDAES
SUNNIER
SUPPLER
SURLIER
SUTTNER
SUTURED
SUTURES
TUBBIER
TUMBLED
TUMBLER
TUMBLES
TUMBREL
TUMMIES
TUNNIES
TURNKEY
TURTLED
TURTLES
TUSSLED
TUSSLES
TUTORED
YUCKIER
YUMMIER
YUPPIES

•U••••E

AUDIBLE
AUGUSTE
AURALEE
AUREATE
AUREOLE
AURICLE
AURORAE
AUSPICE
AUSTERE
BUCKEYE
BURETTE
BURMESE
BUSFARE
BUSLINE
BUYABLE
BUYTIME
CUBICLE
CUISINE
CULOTTE
CULTURE
CUPCAKE
CURSIVE
CUTICLE
CUTRATE
CUTTIME
DUBUQUE
DUCTILE
DUEDATE
DURABLE
DURANCE
DURANTE
EUGENIE
EUTERPE
FULSOME
FURNACE
FURTIVE
GUANINE
GUMSHOE
GUMTREE
GUNFIRE
GUNWALE
GUSTAVE
GUTHRIE
JUBILEE
JUGWINE
JUSTICE
JUSTINE
LUCERNE
LUCILLE
LUGGAGE
LUMIERE
MUNDANE
MUSETTE
MUSTSEE
MUTABLE
NUCLIDE
NURTURE
OUTCOME
OUTDONE
OUTFACE
OUTLINE
OUTLIVE
OUTPACE
OUTRACE
OUTRAGE
OUTSIDE
OUTSIZE
OUTTAKE
OUTVOTE
OUTWORE
PUERILE
PUGNOSE
PULSATE
PURPOSE
QUIBBLE
QUICKIE
QUININE
QUINQUE
QUIVIVE
QUIXOTE
RUBYDEE
RUMMAGE
RUMPOLE
RUNHOME
RUPTURE
RUSHDIE
SUBLIME
SUBSIDE
SUBSUME
SUCRASE
SUCROSE
SUFFICE
SUFFUSE
SULFATE
SULFIDE
SULFITE
SUNRISE
SUPPOSE
SUPREME
SURFACE
SURMISE
SURNAME
SURVIVE
SUSANNE
SUZANNE
SUZETTE
TUNICLE
TURBINE
VULGATE
VULPINE
VULTURE

••UE•••

AQUEOUS
BLUEBOY
BLUEFIN
BLUEFLU
BLUEFOX
BLUEING
BLUEJAY
BLUELAW
BLUESKY
BRUEGEL
CLUEDIN
CLUEING
CLUESIN
CRUELER
CRUELLY
EQUERRY
FLUENCY
GLUEDON
LOUELLA
SQUEAKS
SQUEAKY
SQUEALS
SQUEEZE
SQUELCH
TRUEING

••U•E••

ABUSERS
ACUTELY
AMULETS
BRUBECK
BRUNETS
COULEES
CRUDELY
CRUDEST
DAUBERS
DEUTERO
DOUREST
EXUPERY
FAUCETS
FOULEST
GAUDENS
GAUGERS
GOUGERS
GRUYERE
HAUBERK
HAULERS
HAUTEUR
LAURELS
LAURENT
LOUDEST
LOUREED
LOUSEUP
LOUVERS
MAUREEN
MOUSERS
NOUVEAU
OPULENT
PAUPERS
PEUGEOT
POULENC
POURERS
POUTERS
PRUDENT
PRUDERY
PRUNERS
REUBENS
REUTERS
ROUTERS
SAUCERS
SAUTEED
SHUBERT
SHUTEYE
SOUREST
SQUEEZE
STUDENT
STUPEFY
TAUTENS
TAUTEST
TOUPEES
TOURERS
TOUTERS
TRUDEAU
UKULELE
USURERS

••U••E•

ABUTTED
ALUNSER
AQUIFER
AQUIVER
ASUNDER
AVULSED
AVULSES
BAUBLES
BLUBBER
BLUFFED
BLUFFER
BLUNDER
BLUNTED
BLUNTER
BLURRED
BLURTED
BLUSHED
BLUSHER
BLUSHES
BLUSTER
BOULDER
BOUNCED
BOUNCER
BOUNCES
BOUNDED
BOUNDER
BOUQUET
BOURREE
BRUEGEL
BRUISED
BRUISER
BRUISES
BRUITED
BRUSHED
BRUSHES
CAULKED
CAULKER
CHUCKED
CHUGGED
CHUKKER
CHUMMED
CHUNNEL
CHURNED
CHUTNEY
CLUBBED
CLUCKED
CLUMPED
CLUNKED
CLUNKER
CLUSTER
CLUTTER
COUCHED
COUCHES
COUGHED
COULEES
COULTER
COUNSEL
COUNTED
COUNTER
COUPLED
COUPLES
COUPLET
COURIER
COURSED
COURSER
COURSES
COURTED
CRUELER
CRUISED
CRUISER
CRUISES
CRULLER
CRUMPET
CRUSHED

CRUSHER
CRUSHES
CRUSTED
DAUMIER
DAUNTED
DOUBLED
DOUBLES
DOUBLET
DOUBLEU
DOUBTED
DOUBTER
DRUBBED
DRUCKER
DRUDGED
DRUDGES
DRUGGED
DRUMMED
DRUMMER
EQUALED
EQUATED
EQUATES
EQUINES
ERUCTED
ERUPTED
EVULSED
EVULSES
EXULTED
FAULTED
FLUBBED
FLUFFED
FLUNKED
FLUSHED
FLUSHES
FLUSTER
FLUTTER
FNUMBER
FOUNDED
FOUNDER
FOURIER
FRUITED
GAUCHER
GAUDIER
GAUNTER
GAUZIER
GLUMMER
GLUTTED
GOUNDER
GOURDES
GOURMET
GRUBBED
GRUDGED
GRUDGES
GRUFFER
GRUMPED
GRUNTED
HAUNTED
HOUNDED
JAUNTED
JOUNCED
JOUNCES
JOURNEY
JOUSTED
JOUSTER
KLUDGES
KLUTZES
KNURLED
LAUGHED
LAUGHER
LAUNDER
LAUTREC
LOUNGED
LOUNGER
LOUNGES
LOURDES
LOUREED
LOUSIER
LOUVRES
MAUNDER
MAUREEN
MOULDED
MOULDER
MOULTED
MOUNDED
MOUNTED
MOUSIER
MOUSSED
MOUSSES
MOUTHED
OEUVRES
PAULSEN
PLUCKED
PLUGGED
PLUGGER
PLUMBED
PLUMBER
PLUMMER
PLUMMET
PLUMPED
PLUMPER
PLUNDER
PLUNGED
PLUNGER
PLUNGES
PLUNKED
PLUSHER
PLUSHES
PLUSSES
POUCHED
POUCHES
POUNCED
POUNCER
POUNCES
POUNDED
POUNDER
POUTIER
REUPPED
REUTHER
ROUGHED
ROUGHEN
ROUGHER
ROUNDED
ROUNDER
ROUSTED
SAUCIER
SAUNTER
SAUTEED
SCUDDED
SCUFFED
SCULLED
SCULLER
SCUPPER
SCURVES
SHUCKED
SHUCKER
SHUDDER
SHUNNED
SHUNTED
SHUSHED
SHUSHES
SHUTTER
SKULKED
SKULKER
SKUNKED
SLUDGES
SLUGGED
SLUGGER
SLUICED
SLUICES
SLUMBER
SLUMMED
SLUMPED
SLURPED
SLURRED
SLUSHES
SMUDGED
SMUDGES
SMUGGER
SNUBBED
SNUFFED
SNUFFER
SNUGGER
SOUGHED
SOUNDED
SOUNDER
SOUPIER
SOURCED
SOURCES
SOUTHEY
SPURNED
SPURNER
SPURRED
SPURTED
SPUTTER
SQUARED
SQUARER
SQUARES
SQUIRED
SQUIRES
STUBBED
STUDDED
STUDIED
STUDIES
STUFFED
STUFFER
STUMPED
STUMPER
STUNNED
STUNNER
STUNTED
STURGES
TAUNTED
THUDDED
THUMBED
THUMPED
THUMPER
THUNDER
THURBER
TOUCHED
TOUCHES
TOUGHEN
TOUGHER
TOUPEES
TOURNEY
TOUSLED
TOUSLES
TRUCKED
TRUCKEE
TRUCKER
TRUDGED
TRUDGER
TRUDGES
TRUMPED
TRUMPET
TRUSSED
TRUSSES
TRUSTED
TRUSTEE
USURPED
USURPER
VAULTED
VAULTER
VAUNTED
VAUNTER
VOUCHED
VOUCHER
VOUCHES
WHUPPED
WOUNDED
YOUNGER
ZOUAVES

••U•••E

ABUSIVE
ADULATE
ALUMNAE
AZURITE
BAUXITE
BOURREE
BRUSQUE
CHUCKLE
COURAGE
COUTURE
CRUMBLE
CRUMPLE
CRUSADE
DHURRIE
EDUCATE
ELUSIVE
EMULATE
EQUABLE
ERUDITE
GLUCOSE
GOUACHE
GRUMBLE
GRUYERE
HAULAGE
INUTILE
KNUCKLE
MAURICE
MOULAGE
MOUNTIE
NEURONE
PAULINE
PLUMAGE
PRUDHOE
REUNITE
ROULADE
ROUTINE
SAUSAGE
SCUFFLE
SCUTTLE
SHUFFLE
SHUTEYE
SHUTTLE
SMUGGLE
SNUFFLE
SNUGGLE
SOUFFLE
SOUTANE
SPUMONE
SQUEEZE
STUBBLE
STUMBLE
TAURINE
TOUGHIE
TRUCKEE
TRUCKLE
TRUFFLE
TRUNDLE
TRUSTEE
UKULELE
ULULATE
WOULDBE

•••UE••

ARGUERS
BEQUEST
INQUEST
ISSUERS
LIQUEFY
LIQUEUR
MAGUEYS
MCQUEEN
MINUEND
MINUETS
QUEUERS
QUEUEUP
REFUELS
REQUEST
ROGUERY
SEQUELS
SOSUEME
TOLUENE
UNGUENT
VAGUELY
VAGUEST
VAQUERO

•••U•E•

ABJURED
ABJURES
ACCUSED
ACCUSER
ACCUSES
ADDUCED
ADDUCES
ADJURED
ADJURES
ALBUMEN
ALLUDED
ALLUDES
ALLURED
ALLURES
AMPULES
AROUSED
AROUSES
ASSUMED
ASSUMES
ASSURED
ASSURES
ATTUNED
ATTUNES
AUGURED
BEMUSED
BEMUSES
BITUMEN
BLOUSED
BLOUSES
BOLUSES
BONUSES
CADUCEI
CALUMET
CAPULET
CAYUSES
CERUMEN
CHAUCER
CLAUSES
CLOUDED
CLOUTED
COZUMEL
DEBUTED
DEDUCED
DEDUCES
DEFUSED
DEFUSES
DELUDED
DELUDES
DELUGED
DELUGES
DEMURER
DENUDED
DENUDES
DEPUTED
DEPUTES
DILUTED
DILUTER
DILUTES
DISUSED
EFFUSED
EFFUSES
ENDURED
ENDURES
ENDUSER
ENSURED
ENSURES
EPAULET
EXCUSED
EXCUSES
FERULES
FICUSES
FIGURED
FIGURER
FIGURES
FLOURED
FLOUTED
FOCUSED
FOCUSES
FUTURES
GROUPED
GROUPER
GROUSED
GROUSER
GROUSES
GROUTED
ILLUSED
ILLUSES
IMMURED
IMMURES
IMPURER
IMPUTED
IMPUTES
INCUDES
INDUCED
INDUCER
INDUCES
INFUSED
INFUSES
INJURED
INJURES
INSURED
INSURES
JUJUBES
LEGUMES
LOTUSES
MATURED
MATURER
MATURES
MCQUEEN
MINUSES
MINUTES
MISUSED
MISUSES
MODULES
NATURED
NATURES
NEXUSES
NODULES
NONUSER
OBTUSER
PAIUTES
PARURES
PERUKES
PERUSED
PERUSER
PERUSES
PROUDER
REBUKED
REBUKES
REBUSES
RECUSED
RECUSES
REDUCED
REDUCER
REDUCES
REFUGEE
REFUGES
REFUSED
REFUSER
REFUSES
REFUTED
REFUTER
REFUTES
REPUTED
REPUTES
REQUIEM
RESUMED
RESUMES
RETUNED
RETUNES
RIVULET
SALUTED
SALUTES
SCOURED
SCOURER
SCOUTED
SCOUTER
SECURED
SECURER
SECURES
SEDUCED
SEDUCER
SEDUCES
SHOUTED
SHOUTER
SINUSES
SOLUTES
SPOUSES
SPOUTED
SPOUTER
SPRUCED
SPRUCER
SPRUCES
STEUBEN
STOUTER
STRUDEL
SULUSEA
SUTURED
SUTURES
TALUSES
TENURED
TENURES
TRAUBEL
TRIUNES
TROUPER
TROUPES
TROUSER
UNTUNED
UNTUNES
VIRUSES
VOLUMES
WHAUDEN

•••U••E

ACQUIRE
ACTUATE
ADJUDGE
ASSUAGE
AUGUSTE
BEGUILE
BEGUINE
DELUISE
DIVULGE
DOEUVRE
DUBUQUE
ENOUNCE
ENSUITE
ESQUIRE
EXPUNGE
FIBULAE
FLOUNCE
GENUINE
GROUPIE
IMPULSE
INDULGE
INQUIRE
LACUNAE
MACULAE
MCGUIRE
MEDUSAE
NEBULAE
OCTUPLE
OROURKE
PANURGE
PENUCHE
REFUGEE
REPULSE
REQUIRE
REQUITE
RESURGE
SCOURGE
SCRUPLE
SITUATE
SOLUBLE
SOSUEME
SPLURGE
TOLUENE
TROUBLE
TROUNCE
TSQUARE
TVGUIDE
UNQUOTE
UPSURGE
VACUOLE
VALUATE
VOLUBLE
YAOUNDE

••••UE•

ACCRUED
ACCRUES
AVENUES
BANQUET
BASQUES
BISQUES
BOUQUET
BRIQUET
BROGUES
CAIQUES
CHEQUER
CHEQUES
CIRQUES
CLAQUES
CLIQUES
CLOQUES
CONQUER
CROQUET
EMANUEL
EVACUEE
FONDUES
GIBLUES
IMBRUED
IMBRUES
JACQUES
KILAUEA
LACQUER
LEAGUER
LEAGUES
LONGUES
MARQUEE
MARQUES
MARQUEZ
MASQUES
MISCUED
MISCUES
MOSQUES
OPAQUES
PARQUET
PLAGUED
PLAGUES
PLAQUES
PURSUED
PURSUER
PURSUES
RACQUET
REGLUED
REGLUES
RESCUED
RESCUER
RESCUES
SNAFUED
STATUES
SUBDUED
SUBDUER
SUBDUES
SYNFUEL
TISSUES
TONGUED
TONGUES
TORQUES
UNGLUED
VIRTUES

••••U•E

AMPOULE
BECAUSE
CAPSULE
CAPTURE
CAROUSE
CENSURE
CLOSURE
CLOTURE
COLLUDE
COMMUNE
COMMUTE
COMPUTE
CONDUCE
CONFUSE
CONFUTE
CONJURE
CONSUME
CONTUSE
COSTUME
COUTURE
CULTURE
DENEUVE
DENTURE
DIFFUSE
DISPUTE
ENROUTE
ENTHUSE
EPICURE
ERASURE
ESPOUSE
EVACUEE
EXCLUDE
EXECUTE
EXTRUDE
FAILURE
FEATURE
FERRULE
FISSURE
FIXTURE
FORSURE
FORTUNE
GAGRULE
GESTURE
GLOBULE
GRANULE
GRAVURE
HERCULE
HEYJUDE
HIRSUTE
ICECUBE
INCLUDE
INHOUSE
INTRUDE
JACCUSE
LECTURE
LEISURE
LETTUCE
MAJEURE
MARQUEE
MEASURE
MISRULE
MIXTURE
NEPTUNE
NETSUKE
NOTSURE
NURTURE
OBSCURE
OBTRUDE
OCCLUDE
OVERUSE
PASTURE
PERFUME
PERJURE
PICTURE
POLLUTE
POSTURE
PRELUDE
PRESUME
PROCURE
PRODUCE
PROFUSE
RAPTURE
RECLUSE
REROUTE
RUPTURE
SECLUDE
STATURE
STATUTE
SUBSUME
SUFFUSE
TERHUNE
TEXTURE
TONSURE
TRADUCE
TRIBUNE
TRIBUTE
ULALUME
VENTURE
VERDURE
VESTURE
VIRGULE
VULTURE

•••••UE

AMIBLUE
ANTIQUE
ATISSUE
BAROQUE
BEZIQUE
BRUSQUE
COMEDUE
COMIQUE
DEVALUE
DONAHUE
DUBUQUE
ECLOGUE
FATIGUE
HABITUE
ICEBLUE
INGENUE
INVOGUE
LALIQUE
MACAQUE
MONIQUE
NOTTRUE
OBLIQUE
OVERDUE
PASTDUE
PIROGUE
QUINQUE
REARGUE
REISSUE
RESIDUE
RETINUE
REVALUE
REVENUE
SKYBLUE

U•F••••

UNFAZED
UNFIXED
UNFOLDS
UNFROCK
UNFURLS
UPFRONT

U••F•••

UNIFIED
UNIFIER
UNIFIES
UNIFORM

U•••F••

UPLIFTS

U••••F•

UPDRAFT

•UF••••

BUFFALO
BUFFERS
BUFFETS
BUFFETT
BUFFING
BUFFOON
CUFFING
DUFFELS
DUFFERS
GUFFAWS
HUFFIER
HUFFILY
HUFFING
LUFFING
MUFFING
MUFFINS
MUFFLED
MUFFLER
MUFFLES
PUFFERS
PUFFERY
PUFFIER
PUFFILY
PUFFING
PUFFINS
RUFFIAN
RUFFLED
RUFFLES
RUFIYAA
SUFFERS
SUFFICE
SUFFOLK
SUFFUSE
TUFFETS
TUFTING

•U•F•••

BUFFALO
BUFFERS
BUFFETS
BUFFETT
BUFFING
BUFFOON
BUSFARE
CUFFING
CUPFULS
CURFEWS
DUFFELS
DUFFERS
FULFILL
FULFILS
FUNFAIR
FUNFEST
GUFFAWS
GULFING
GUNFIRE
HUFFIER
HUFFILY
HUFFING
JUGFULS
LUFFING
MUFFING
MUFFINS
MUFFLED
MUFFLER
MUFFLES
MUMFORD
OUTFACE
OUTFITS
OUTFLOW
PUFFERS
PUFFERY
PUFFIER
PUFFILY
PUFFING
PUFFINS
PURFLED
PURFLES
QUAFFED
QUAFFER
RUFFIAN
RUFFLED
RUFFLES
SUFFERS
SUFFICE
SUFFOLK
SUFFUSE
SULFATE
SULFIDE
SULFITE
SUNFISH
SURFACE
SURFEIT
SURFERS
SURFING
TUFFETS

•U••F••

CUTOFFS
DUTIFUL
GUNSFOR
HURTFUL
LUCIFER
LUSTFUL
OUTOFIT
QUAFFED
QUAFFER
RUNOFFS
TUNEFUL

•U•••F•

BUGSOFF
BUYSOFF
BUZZOFF
CUTOFFS
CUTSOFF
DUSTOFF
JUMPOFF
JUSTIFY
MUSTAFA
NULLIFY
PULLOFF
PUSHOFF
PUTSOFF
QUALIFY
RUNOFFS
RUNSOFF
RUSHOFF
TURNOFF

•U••••F

BUGSOFF
BUYSOFF
BUZZOFF
CUTSOFF
DUSTOFF
JUMPOFF
OURSELF
PULLOFF
PUSHOFF
PUTSOFF
RUNSOFF
RUSHOFF
SUNROOF
TURNOFF

••UF•••

BLUFFED
BLUFFER
BLUFFLY
FLUFFED
GRUFFER
GRUFFLY
MOUFLON
SCUFFED
SCUFFLE
SHUFFLE
SNUFFED

SNUFFER
SNUFFLE
SOUFFLE
STUFFED
STUFFER
TRUFFLE

••U•F••
AQUIFER
BLUEFIN
BLUEFLU
BLUEFOX
BLUFFED
BLUFFER
BLUFFLY
FLUFFED
GRUFFER
GRUFFLY
SCUFFED
SCUFFLE
SHUFFLE
SNUFFED
SNUFFER
SNUFFLE
SOUFFLE
SOULFUL
STUFFED
STUFFER
THUSFAR
TRUFFLE

••U••F•
HAULOFF
REUNIFY
SHUTOFF
SPUNOFF
STUPEFY

••U•••F
HAULOFF
SHUTOFF
SPUNOFF

•••UF••
REBUFFS
SCRUFFS
SCRUFFY

•••U•F•
ENGULFS
LIQUEFY
REBUFFS
SCRUFFS
SCRUFFY

••••UF•
EARMUFF
MACDUFF

••••U•F
BEOWULF
EARMUFF
MACDUFF
NETSURF

UG•••••
UGANDAN
UGLIEST

U•G••••
UNGIRDS
UNGLUED
UNGODLY
UNGUENT
UPGRADE
URGENCY

U••G•••
URUGUAY

U•••G••
UNCAGED
UNCAGES
UPRIGHT
UPTIGHT
USINGUP

U••••G•
UMBRAGE
UNCLOGS
UNDERGO
UNPLUGS
UNSNAGS
UPSTAGE
UPSURGE

U•••••G
UNDOING
UNDYING
UNITING
UNTYING
UPSWING

•UG••••
AUGENDS
AUGMENT
AUGURAL
AUGURED
AUGUSTA
AUGUSTE
BUGABOO
BUGALOO
BUGBEAR
BUGEYED
BUGGIER
BUGGIES
BUGGING
BUGLERS
BUGLING
BUGSOFF
BUGSOUT
DUGONGS
DUGOUTS
EUGENIE
HUGGERS
HUGGING
JUGBAND
JUGFULS
JUGGLED
JUGGLER
JUGGLES
JUGHEAD
JUGULAR
JUGWINE
LUGGAGE
LUGGERS
LUGGING
LUGNUTS
MUGGERS
MUGGIER
MUGGING
MUGSHOT
MUGWUMP
NUGGETS
PUGNOSE
PUGREES
SUGARED
SUGGEST
TUGBOAT
TUGGERS
TUGGING

•U•G•••
BUDGETS
BUDGIES
BUDGING
BUGGIER
BUGGIES
BUGGING
BULGARS
BULGHUR
BULGING
BUNGEES
BUNGING
BUNGLED
BUNGLER
BUNGLES
BURGEES
BURGEON
BURGERS
BURGESS
BURGHER
BURGLAR
BURGLED
BURGLES
BURGOOS
CUDGELS
DUDGEON
DUNGEON
FUDGING
FULGENT
FULGHUM
FUNGOES
GURGLED
GURGLES
HUGGERS
HUGGING
HUNGARY
HUNGERS
HUNGOUT
JUDGING
JUGGLED
JUGGLER
JUGGLES
JUNGLES
LUGGAGE
LUGGERS
LUGGING
LUNGEAT
LUNGING
MUGGERS
MUGGIER
MUGGING
NUDGERS
NUDGING
NUGGETS
OUTGOES
OUTGREW
OUTGROW
OUTGUNS
PUDGIER
PUNGENT
PURGING
QUAGGAS
QUIGLEY
RUTGERS
SUGGEST
SUNGODS
SURGEON
SURGERY
SURGING
TUGGERS
TUGGING
TUNGOIL
VULGATE

•U••G••
BURPGUN
GUARGUM
MUTAGEN
OUTAGES
QUAGGAS

•U•••G•
DUGONGS
DURANGO
GUNDOGS
HUMBUGS
LUGGAGE
LUMBAGO
NUTMEGS
OUTINGS
OUTRAGE
QUAHOGS
RULINGS
RUMMAGE
SUNDOGS
TUAREGS

•U••••G
BUCKING
BUDDING
BUDGING
BUFFING
BUGGING
BUGLING
BULGING
BULKING
BULLDOG
BULLING
BUMMING
BUMPING
BUNGING
BUNKING
BUNTING
BUOYING
BURLING
BURNING
BURPING
BURYING
BUSHHOG
BUSHING
BUSHPIG
BUSSING
BUSTING
BUSYING
BUTTING
BUZZING
CUFFING
CULLING
CUNNING
CUPPING
CURBING
CURDING
CURLING
CURSING
CURVING
CUSSING
CUTTING
DUBBING
DUCKING
DUCTING
DUELING
DULLING
DUMPING
DUNKING
DUNNING
DUSTING
FUDGING
FUELING
FUNDING
FUNNING
FURLING
FURLONG
FURRING
FUSSING
FUZZING
GUIDING
GULFING
GULLING
GULPING
GUMMING
GUNNING
GUSHING
GUSTING
GUTTING
HUFFING
HUGGING
HULKING
HULLING
HUMMING
HUNTING
HURLING
HURTING
HUSHING
HUSKING
JUDGING
JUICING
JUMPING
JUNEBUG
JUNKING
JURYING
JURYRIG
JUTTING
LUCKING
LUFFING
LUGGING
LULLING
LUMPING
LUNGING
LURKING
LUSTING
MUCKING
MUFFING
MUGGING
MULLING
MUSHING
MUSSING
MUSTANG
NUDGING
NULLING
NUMBING
NURSING
NUTTING
OUSTING
PUDDING
PUFFING
PULLING
PULSING
PUMPING
PUNNING
PUNTING
PURGING
PURLING
PURRING
PURSING
PUSHING
PUTTING
QUAKING
QUEUING
QUOTING
RUBBING
RUCHING
RUCKING
RUINING
RUNNING
RUSHING
RUSTING
SUBBING
SUCKING
SUDSING
SUITING
SULKING
SUMMING
SUNNING
SUPPING
SURFING
SURGING
SUSSING
TUCKING
TUFTING
TUGGING
TURNING
YULELOG

••UG•••
ARUGULA
CHUGGED
COUGARS
COUGHED
COUGHUP
DOUGHTY
DOUGLAS
DRUGGED
GAUGERS
GAUGING
GAUGUIN
GOUGERS
GOUGING
HAUGHTY
KLUGMAN
LAUGHAT
LAUGHED
LAUGHER
LAUGHIN
MAUGHAM
NAUGHTS
NAUGHTY
NOUGATS
PEUGEOT
PLUGGED
PLUGGER
PLUGSIN
ROUGHED
ROUGHEN
ROUGHER
ROUGHIT
ROUGHLY
ROUGHUP
ROUGING
SLUGGED
SLUGGER
SMUGGER
SMUGGLE
SNUGGER
SNUGGLE
SOUGHED
TOUGHEN
TOUGHER
TOUGHIE
TOUGHLY
URUGUAY
VAUGHAN
ZEUGMAS

••U•G••
BRUEGEL
CHUGGED
DRUDGED
DRUDGES
DRUGGED
GRUDGED
GRUDGES
KLUDGES
LOUNGED
LOUNGER
LOUNGES
PLUGGED
PLUGGER
PLUNGED
PLUNGER
PLUNGES
SLUDGES
SLUGGED
SLUGGER
SMUDGED
SMUDGES
SMUGGER
SMUGGLE
SNUGGER
SNUGGLE
STUNGUN
STURGES
TRUDGED
TRUDGER
TRUDGES
YOUNGER
YOUNGMC
YOUNGUN

••U••G•
COURAGE
HAULAGE
MOULAGE
PLUMAGE
SAUSAGE

••U•••G
ABUSING
AMUSING
BLUEING
CAUSING
CLUEING
DAUBING
DOUSING
EDUCING
ELUDING
ELUTING
ENURING
EXUDING
FEUDING
FLUTING
FOULING
GAUGING
GOUGING
HAULING
HOUSING
INURING
LAUDING
LOUSING
MAULING
MOUSING
PAULING
PAUSING
PLUMING
POURING
POUTING
PRUNING
ROUGING
ROUSING
ROUTING
SOURING
SPUMING
TOURING
TOUTING
TRUEING

•••UG••
BROUGHT
CAYUGAS
DELUGED
DELUGES
DRAUGHT
DROUGHT
FRAUGHT
IMPUGNS
OPPUGNS
PLOUGHS
REFUGEE
REFUGES
REPUGNS
SLOUGHS
THOUGHT
TROUGHS
WROUGHT

•••U•G•
ADJUDGE
ASSUAGE
DIVULGE
EXPUNGE
INDULGE
LITURGY
PANURGE
RESURGE
SCOURGE
SPLURGE
UPSURGE
ZYMURGY

•••U••G
ARGUING
ENDUING
ENSUING
IMBUING
ISSUING
PIQUING
QUEUING
VALUING

••••UG•
BEDBUGS
BOROUGH
HUMBUGS
RAGRUGS
SOWBUGS
THROUGH
UNPLUGS
VERDUGO

••••U•G
ACHTUNG
CYYOUNG
HAMBURG
HOMBURG
SAMSUNG
ZEITUNG

•••••UG
AREARUG
BEARHUG
EARPLUG
FIREBUG
GOLDBUG
JUNEBUG
LADYBUG
LOVEBUG
PILLBUG
SEASLUG

U•H••••
UNHANDS
UNHANDY
UNHAPPY
UNHEARD
UNHITCH
UNHOOKS
UNHORSE
UPHOLDS
USHERED

U••H•••
UNCHAIN
UNSHORN
UPSHOTS
URCHINS
UTAHANS

U•••H••
USOSHOW

U••••H•
UPRIGHT
UPTIGHT
UTRECHT

U•••••H
UNCOUTH
UNEARTH
UNHITCH
UNLATCH
UNLEASH
UNTRUTH

•U•H•••
AUTHORS
BUSHELS
BUSHHOG
BUSHIDO
BUSHIER
BUSHING
BUSHMAN
BUSHMEN
BUSHPIG
CUSHAWS
CUSHIER
CUSHION
DUCHESS
DUCHIES
EUCHRED
EUCHRES
EUPHONY
FUCHSIA
GUSHERS
GUSHIER
GUSHING
GUTHRIE
HUSHABY
HUSHING
JUGHEAD
LUSHEST
MUDHENS
MUSHERS
MUSHIER
MUSHILY
MUSHING
MUZHIKS
OUTHITS
PUSHIER
PUSHILY
PUSHING
PUSHKIN
PUSHOFF
PUSHPIN
PUSHUPS
QUAHOGS
RUCHING
RUNHOME
RUSHDIE
RUSHEES
RUSHERS
RUSHING
RUSHOFF
SUBHEAD
TUCHMAN

•U••H••
BUDDHAS
BULGHUR
BUNCHED
BUNCHES
BURGHER
BUSHHOG
BUTCHER
FULGHUM
FURTHER
GULCHES
GUMSHOE
GUNSHOT
GUNTHER
GURKHAS
HUNCHED
HUNCHES
HUTCHES
LUNCHED
LUNCHER
LUNCHES
LURCHED
LURCHES
MUGSHOT
MULCHED
MULCHES
MUNCHED
MUNCHER
MUNCHES
MURPHEY
PUNCHED
PUNCHER
PUNCHES
PUNCHIN
PUNCHUP
QUASHED
QUASHES
QUECHUA
QUICHES
SULPHUR

•U•••H•
AUROCHS
EUNUCHS
GUELPHS
HURRAHS
HUZZAHS
MULLAHS
PUNKAHS
PURDAHS
RUPIAHS

•U••••H
BULLISH
BULRUSH
BURNISH
CULTISH
DULLISH
FURBISH
FURNISH
KURDISH
MURDOCH
PUBLISH
PUCKISH
RUBBISH
RUDOLPH
RUNWITH
SUNBATH
SUNFISH
TURKISH

••U•H••
BLUSHED
BLUSHER
BLUSHES
BRUSHED
BRUSHES
BRUSHUP
COUCHED
COUCHES
COUGHED
COUGHUP
CRUSHED
CRUSHER
CRUSHES
DAUPHIN
DOUGHTY
FLUSHED
FLUSHES
GAUCHER
GAUCHOS
HAUGHTY
LAUGHAT
LAUGHED
LAUGHER
LAUGHIN
MAUGHAM
MOUTHED
NAUGHTS
NAUGHTY
PLUSHER
PLUSHES
PLUSHLY
POUCHED
POUCHES
PRUDHOE
REUTHER
ROUGHED
ROUGHEN
ROUGHER
ROUGHIT
ROUGHLY
ROUGHUP
SHUSHED
SHUSHES
SLUSHES
SOUGHED
SOUTHEY
TOUCHED
TOUCHES
TOUCHON
TOUCHUP
TOUGHEN
TOUGHER
TOUGHIE
TOUGHLY
VAUGHAN
VOUCHED
VOUCHER
VOUCHES

••U••H•
CRUNCHY
FOURTHS
GOUACHE
PAUNCHY
SQUISHY

••U•••H
BRUTISH
GOULASH
NOURISH
PRUDISH
SOURISH
SQUELCH
SQUINCH

•••UH••
MCLUHAN
MENUHIN

•••U•H•
BELUSHI
BROUGHT
DRAUGHT
DROUGHT
EUNUCHS
FRAUGHT
GROUCHO
GROUCHY
NOGUCHI
PENUCHE
PLOUGHS
SLEUTHS
SLOUCHY
SLOUGHS
THOUGHT
TROUGHS
WROUGHT

•••U••H
ANOUILH
GALUMPH
GODUTCH
HANUKAH
INDUTCH
PADUCAH
ROGUISH
SCRUNCH
STAUNCH
TRIUMPH

••••UH•
NIEBUHR

••••U•H
AZIMUTH
BISMUTH
BOROUGH
BULRUSH
DEBAUCH
DEBOUCH
INARUSH
INTRUTH
RETOUCH
THROUGH
UNCOUTH
UNTRUTH

U•I••••
UNICORN
UNIFIED
UNIFIER
UNIFIES
UNIFORM
UNIPODS
UNISONS
UNITARY
UNITERS
UNITIES
UNITING
UNITIVE
USINGUP
UTILITY
UTILIZE

U••I•••
UGLIEST
UMPIRED
UMPIRES
UNAIDED
UNAIMED
UNAIRED
UNBINDS
UNCIALS
UNCIVIL
UNFIXED
UNGIRDS
UNHITCH
UNKINKS
UNLIKED
UNLINED
UNLINKS
UNOILED
UNPILED
UNPILES
UNWINDS
UNWISER
UPLIFTS
UPLINKS
UPRIGHT
UPRISEN
UPRISES
UPRIVER
UPSILON
UPTICKS
UPTIGHT
USTINOV
UTRILLO

U•••I••
UKRAINE
UMBRIAN
UNALIKE
UNCOILS
UNCTION
UNDOING
UNDYING
UNIFIED
UNIFIER
UNIFIES
UNITIES
UNITING

UNITIVE
UNKNITS
UNSTICK
UNTRIED
UNTWIST
UNTYING
UNVEILS
UPRAISE
UPSWING
URANITE
URANIUM
URCHINS
UTILITY
UTILIZE
UTOPIAN
UTOPIAS
UXORIAL

U••••I•
UNCHAIN
UNCIVIL
UPBRAID
UTENSIL

•UI••••
BUILDER
BUILDIN
BUILDON
BUILDUP
BUILTIN
BUILTON
BUILTUP
CUIBONO
CUIRASS
CUISINE
GUIDING
GUIDONS
GUILDER
GUIMPES
GUINEAS
GUITARS
JUICERS
JUICEUP
JUICIER
JUICILY
JUICING
QUIBBLE
QUICHES
QUICKEN
QUICKER
QUICKIE
QUICKLY
QUIETED
QUIETEN
QUIETER
QUIETLY
QUIGLEY
QUILLED
QUILTED
QUILTER
QUINCES
QUININE
QUINOAS
QUINQUE
QUINTET
QUIPPED
QUIPPER
QUITTER
QUIVERS
QUIVIVE
QUIXOTE
QUIZZED
QUIZZES
RUINERS
RUINING
RUINOUS
SUITING
SUITORS
SUITSUP
TUITION

•U•I•••
AUDIBLE
AUDIBLY
AUDITED
AUDITOR
AURICLE
BUNIONS
BUSIEST
CUBICLE
CUBISTS
CURIOUS
CUTICLE
CUTINTO
DUBIETY
DUBIOUS
DUTIFUL
FUJITSU
FURIOUS
HUMIDLY
HUMIDOR
JUBILEE
JUJITSU
JULIANA
JUNIORS
JUNIPER
JUPITER
JURIDIC
JURISTS
LUCIANO
LUCIDLY
LUCIFER
LUCILLE
LUMIERE
LUPINES
LURIDLY
LUTISTS
MURILLO
MUSICAL
NUBIANS
NUDISTS
OUTINGS
PUMICES
PUNIEST
PURISTS
PURITAN
PUTITTO
QUAILED
RUBICON
RUBITIN
RUFIYAA
RULINGS
RUNINTO
RUPIAHS
SURINAM
TUBISTS
TUNICLE
TUNISIA

•U••I••
AUCTION
AUNTIES
AUSPICE
AUSSIES
BUCKING
BUDDIES
BUDDING
BUDGIES
BUDGING
BUFFING
BUGGIER
BUGGIES
BUGGING
BUGLING
BULGING
BULKIER
BULKING
BULLIED
BULLIES
BULLING
BULLION
BULLISH
BULLITT
BUMMING
BUMPIER
BUMPING
BUNGING
BUNKING
BUNNIES
BUNTING
BUOYING
BURKINA
BURLIER
BURLING
BURNING
BURNISH
BURPING
BURRITO
BURYING
BUSBIES
BUSHIDO
BUSHIER
BUSHING
BUSKINS
BUSLINE
BUSSING
BUSTING
BUSYING
BUTTING
BUYTIME
BUZZING
CUBBIES
CUFFING
CUISINE
CULLING
CULTISH
CULTISM
CULTIST
CUNNING
CUPPING
CURBING
CURDING
CURLIER
CURLING
CURRIED
CURRIER
CURRIES
CURSING
CURSIVE
CURVIER
CURVING
CUSHIER
CUSHION
CUSPIDS
CUSSING
CUTTIME
CUTTING
DUALITY
DUBBING
DUCHIES
DUCKIER
DUCKING
DUCTILE
DUCTING
DUDDIES
DUELING
DUELIST
DULLING
DULLISH
DUMMIED
DUMMIES
DUMPIER
DUMPING
DUNKING
DUNKIRK
DUNLINS
DUNNING
DUSKIER
DUSTIER
DUSTING
FUDGING
FUELING
FULFILL
FULFILS
FUNDING
FUNKIER
FUNNIER
FUNNIES
FUNNILY
FUNNING
FURBISH
FURLING
FURNISH
FURRIER
FURRING
FURTIVE
FUSSIER
FUSSILY
FUSSING
FUSTIAN
FUSTICS
FUSTIER
FUSTILY
FUZZIER
FUZZILY
FUZZING
GUANINE
GUIDING
GULFING
GULLIES
GULLING
GULPING
GUMMIER
GUMMING
GUNFIRE
GUNKIER
GUNNIES
GUNNING
GUPPIES
GUSHIER
GUSHING
GUSSIED
GUSSIES
GUSTILY
GUSTING
GUTSIER
GUTSILY
GUTTING
HUBBIES
HUFFIER
HUFFILY
HUFFING
HUGGING
HULKING
HULLING
HUMMING
HUNTING
HURLING
HURRIED
HURRIES
HURTING
HUSHING
HUSKIER
HUSKIES
HUSKILY
HUSKING
HUSSIES
JUDAISM
JUDGING
JUDOIST
JUGWINE
JUICIER
JUICILY
JUICING
JUMPIER
JUMPING
JUNKIER
JUNKIES
JUNKING
JURYING
JUSTICE
JUSTIFY
JUSTINE
JUTTING
KUBRICK
KURDISH
KUWAITI
LUCKIER
LUCKILY
LUCKING
LUFFING
LUGGING
LULLING
LUMPIER
LUMPING
LUNGING
LURKING
LUSTIER
LUSTILY
LUSTING
MUCKING
MUDDIED
MUDDIER
MUDDIES
MUDPIES
MUFFING
MUFFINS
MUGGIER
MUGGING
MULLING
MULLION
MUMMIES
MUNTINS
MURKIER
MURKILY
MUSHIER
MUSHILY
MUSHING
MUSLIMS
MUSLINS
MUSSING
MUSTIER
MUSTILY
MUZHIKS
MUZZIER
MUZZILY
NUBBIER
NUBBINS
NUCLIDE
NUDGING
NUDNIKS
NULLIFY
NULLING
NUMBING
NUNCIOS
NUPTIAL
NURSING
NUTRIAS
NUTTIER
NUTTILY
NUTTING
OUSTING
OUTBIDS
OUTFITS
OUTHITS
OUTLINE
OUTLIVE
OUTSIDE
OUTSIZE
OUTWITS
PUBLICS
PUBLISH
PUCCINI
PUCKISH
PUDDING
PUDGIER
PUERILE
PUFFIER
PUFFILY
PUFFING
PUFFINS
PULLING
PULPITS
PULSING
PUMPING
PUNDITS
PUNKIES
PUNNING
PUNTING
PUPPIES
PURGING
PURLIEU
PURLING
PURLINS
PURRING
PURSING
PURVIEW
PUSHIER
PUSHILY
PUSHING
PUTTIED
PUTTIES
PUTTING
QUAKING
QUALIFY
QUALITY
QUERIED
QUERIES
QUEUING
QUININE
QUIVIVE
QUOTING
RUBBING
RUBBISH
RUBRICS
RUCHING
RUCKING
RUCTION
RUDDIER
RUFFIAN
RUINING
RUMMIER
RUNNIER
RUNNING
RUNRIOT
RUNTIER
RUNWITH
RUSHING
RUSSIAN
RUSTICS
RUSTIER
RUSTILY
RUSTING
SUASION
SUAVITY
SUBBING
SUBLIME
SUBMITS
SUBSIDE
SUBSIDY
SUBSIST
SUCKING
SUCTION
SUDSIER
SUDSING
SUFFICE
SUITING
SULFIDE
SULFITE
SULKIER
SULKIES
SULKILY
SULKING
SULLIED
SULLIES
SUMMING
SUMMITS
SUNCITY
SUNDIAL
SUNFISH
SUNKIST
SUNNIER
SUNNILY
SUNNING
SUNRISE
SUPPING
SURFING
SURGING
SURLIER
SURLILY
SURMISE
SURVIVE
SUSLIKS
SUSSING
TUBAIST
TUBBIER
TUCKING
TUFTING
TUGGING
TUITION
TUMMIES
TUNNIES
TURBINE
TURKISH
TURNING
TURNIPS
VULPINE
YUCKIER
YUMMIER
YUPPIES

•U•••I•
AUSTRIA
BUCOLIC
BUILDIN
BUILTIN
BUMPKIN
BUSHPIG
BUTTSIN
CULPRIT
CURTAIL
CURTAIN
DUCKPIN
DUKAKIS
EUGENIE
EURASIA
FUCHSIA
FUELOIL
FUNFAIR
GUTHRIE
HUSSEIN
JUMPSIN
JURIDIC
JURYRIG
LUNATIC
MUEZZIN
MULLEIN
MUTATIS
NUCLEIC
NUMERIC
OUTLAID
OUTOFIT
PUMPKIN
PUNCHIN
PURLOIN
PURSUIT
PUSHKIN
PUSHPIN
QUENTIN
QUICKIE
RUBITIN
RUSHDIE
SUBJOIN
SUBSOIL
SUBUNIT
SUCKSIN
SUNMAID
SURFEIT
SUSTAIN
TUCKSIN
TUNEDIN
TUNESIN
TUNGOIL
TUNISIA
TURMOIL
TURNSIN

•U••••I
GUARANI
JUMANJI
KUTENAI
KUWAITI
PUCCINI
PULASKI
PUNJABI

••UI•••
AQUIFER
AQUINAS
AQUIVER
BRUISED
BRUISER
BRUISES
BRUITED
CRUISED
CRUISER
CRUISES
EQUINES
EQUINOX
FLUIDLY
FRUITED
SLUICED
SLUICES
SQUINCH
SQUINTS
SQUINTY
SQUIRED
SQUIRES
SQUIRMS
SQUIRMY
SQUIRTS
SQUISHY
TRUISMS

••U•I••
ABUSING
ABUSIVE
AMUSING
AZURITE
BAUXITE
BLUEING
BRUTISH
CAUSING
CAUTION
CLUEING
COURIER
COUSINS
CRUCIAL
CRUDITY
DAUBING
DAUMIER
DOUSING
EDUCING
ELUDING
ELUSIVE
ELUTING
ELUTION
ELUVIUM
ENURING
ERUDITE
EXUDING
FAUVISM
FAUVIST
FEUDING
FLUTING
FLUTIST
FLUVIAL
FOULING
FOURIER
GAUDIER
GAUDILY
GAUGING
GAUZIER
GAUZILY
GOUGING
GRUNION
HAULING
HOUDINI
HOUSING
INURING
INUTILE
LAUDING
LOUSIER
LOUSILY
LOUSING
MAULING
MAURICE
MOUSIER
MOUSING
NOURISH
OCULIST
PAUCITY
PAULINA
PAULINE
PAULING
PAULIST
PAUSING
PLUMING
PLUVIAL
POURING
POUTIER
POUTING
PRUDISH
PRUNING
REUNIFY
REUNION
REUNITE
ROUGING
ROUSING
ROUTINE
ROUTING
SAUCIER
SAUCILY
SAURIAN
SOUPIER
SOURING
SOURISH
SPUMING
STUDIED
STUDIES
STUDIOS
TAURINE
THULIUM
TOURING
TOURISM
TOURIST
TOUTING
TRUCIAL
TRUEING

••U••I•
AQUARIA
AQUATIC
AQUAVIT
BLUEFIN
BOUDOIR
CAUSTIC
CLUEDIN
CLUESIN
COUNCIL
DAUPHIN
DHURRIE
DRUMLIN
EXURBIA
FOULTIP
GAUGUIN
LAUGHIN
MAUDLIN
MAULDIN
MAUROIS
MOUNTIE
PLUGSIN
POURSIN
PRUSSIA
ROUGHIT
SHUTSIN
SPUTNIK
SQUALID
TOUGHIE

••U•••I
GOURAMI
HOUDINI
HYUNDAI
SPUMONI
TSUNAMI

•••UI••
ACQUIRE
ACQUITS
ANNUITY
ANOUILH
ARGUING
BEGUILE
BEGUINE
DELUISE
ENDUING
ENSUING
ENSUITE
ESQUIRE
FATUITY
GENUINE
IMBUING
INQUIRE
INQUIRY
INTUITS
ISSUING
JESUITS
LIQUIDS
MCGUIRE
PIQUING
QUEUING
REBUILD
REBUILT
REQUIEM
REQUIRE
REQUITE
ROGUISH
SEQUINS
TEQUILA
TVGUIDE
VACUITY
VALUING

•••U•I•
AGOUTIS
ALBUMIN
ALLUVIA
CLAUDIA
CLAUDIO
ETRURIA
GROUPIE
INSULIN
KABUKIS
MANUMIT
MENUHIN
MINUTIA
PETUNIA
PLAUDIT
SALUKIS
SEQUOIA
STLUCIA
SUBUNIT

•••U••I
BELUSHI
CADUCEI
JACUZZI
NOGUCHI
OLDUVAI
SAMURAI

••••UI•
BEDOUIN
BISCUIT
CIRCUIT
CONDUIT
DRYSUIT
GAUGUIN
JOAQUIN
JONQUIL
LANGUID
LAWSUIT
MARQUIS
PENGUIN
PURSUIT
RECRUIT
SANLUIS
SKISUIT
STLOUIS
WETSUIT

••••U•I
STIMULI

•••••UI
RAPANUI

•UJ••••
FUJITSU
JUJITSU
JUJUBES

•U•J•••
OUTJUMP
PUNJABI
SUBJECT
SUBJOIN

•U••J••
CULTJAM

•U•••J•
JUMANJI

••U•J••
BLUEJAY

UK•••••
UKRAINE
UKULELE

U•K••••
UNKEMPT
UNKINKS
UNKNITS
UNKNOTS
UNKNOWN

U•••K••
UNASKED
UNBAKED
UNLIKED
UNMAKES
UNYOKED
UNYOKES
UPTAKES

U••••K•
UNALIKE
UNCORKS
UNHOOKS
UNKINKS
UNLINKS
UNLOCKS
UNLUCKY
UNMASKS
UNPACKS
UNTACKS
UPLINKS
UPTICKS

U•••••K
UNCLOAK
UNFROCK
UNSTACK
UNSTICK
UNSTUCK

•UK••••
AUKLETS
DUKAKIS
DUKEDOM
JUKEBOX
MUKLUKS
SUKARNO

•U•K•••
BUCKETS
BUCKEYE
BUCKING
BUCKLED
BUCKLER
BUCKLES
BUCKLEY
BUCKOES
BUCKRAM
BUCKSAW
BUCKSUP
BULKIER
BULKING
BUNKBED
BUNKERS
BUNKING
BUNKOED
BURKINA
BUSKINS
CUCKOOS
DUCKIER
DUCKING
DUCKPIN
DUNKERS
DUNKING
DUNKIRK
DUSKIER
FUNKIER
GUNKIER
GURKHAS
HULKING
HUNKERS
HUSKERS
HUSKIER
HUSKIES
HUSKILY
HUSKING
JUNKART
JUNKERS
JUNKETS
JUNKIER
JUNKIES
JUNKING
JUNKMAN
LUCKIER
LUCKILY
LUCKING
LUCKOUT
LUNKERS
LURKING

MUCKING
MUCKSUP
MURKIER
MURKILY
MUSKETS
MUSKRAT
PUCKERS
PUCKETT
PUCKISH
PUNKAHS
PUNKIES
QUAKERS
QUAKING
QUOKKAS
RUCKING
SUCKERS
SUCKING
SUCKSIN
SULKERS
SULKIER
SULKIES
SULKILY
SULKING
SUNKIST
TUCKERS
TUCKING
TUCKSIN
TURKEYS
TURKISH
TUSKERS
YUCKIER

•U••K••

BUMPKIN
DUKAKIS
PUMPKIN
PUSHKIN
QUACKED
QUICKEN
QUICKER
QUICKIE
QUICKLY
QUOKKAS
TURNKEY

•U•••K•

BUROAKS
CUPCAKE
MUKLUKS
MUZHIKS
NUDNIKS
OUTTAKE
PULASKI
SUSLIKS

•U••••K

BULLOCK
BULWARK
BURBANK
BURDOCK
CUTBACK
DUNKIRK
GUNLOCK
HUMMOCK
KUBRICK
LUBBOCK
MUBARAK
MUDPACK
OUTBACK
OUTLOOK
OUTRANK
OUTTALK
OUTWORK
RUNAMOK
RUNBACK
SUFFOLK
SUNDECK
TUSSOCK

••UK•••

CHUKKAS
CHUKKER
YOUKNOW

••U•K••

CAULKED
CAULKER
CHUCKED
CHUCKLE
CHUKKAS
CHUKKER
CLUCKED
CLUNKED
CLUNKER
DRUCKER
FLUNKED
KNUCKLE
PLUCKED
PLUNKED
SHUCKED
SHUCKER
SKULKED
SKULKER
SKUNKED
STUCKTO
STUCKUP
TRUCKED
TRUCKEE
TRUCKER
TRUCKLE

••U••K•

ABUBAKR
BLUESKY
SQUAWKS
SQUEAKS
SQUEAKY

••U•••K

BRUBECK
HAUBERK
SPUTNIK

•••UK••

HANUKAH
KABUKIS
PERUKES
REBUKED
REBUKES
SALUKIS

•••U•K•

ATTUCKS
DEBUNKS
MAZURKA
OROURKE
UNLUCKY

•••U••K

YAKUTSK

••••UK•

DYBBUKS
MUKLUKS
NETSUKE

••••U•K

ATATURK
MOLLUSK
POTLUCK
ROEBUCK
SAWBUCK
SPELUNK
UNSTUCK

UL•••••

ULALUME
ULANOVA
ULLMANN
ULSTERS
ULULANT
ULULATE
ULYANOV
ULYSSES

U•L••••

UGLIEST
ULLMANN
UMLAUTS
UNLACED
UNLACES
UNLADES
UNLATCH
UNLEARN
UNLEASH
UNLIKED
UNLINED
UNLINKS
UNLOADS
UNLOCKS
UNLOOSE
UNLOVED
UNLUCKY
UPLANDS
UPLIFTS
UPLINKS
UPLOADS

U••L•••

UKULELE
ULALUME
ULULANT
ULULATE
UNALIKE
UNBLEST
UNCLASP
UNCLEAN
UNCLEAR
UNCLOAK
UNCLOGS
UNCLOSE
UNGLUED
UNPLUGS
UPCLOSE
USELESS
UTILITY
UTILIZE

U•••L••

UCCELLO
UNBOLTS
UNFOLDS
UNOILED
UNPILED
UNPILES
UNROLLS
UPHOLDS
UPSILON
USUALLY
UTRILLO

U••••L•

UCCELLO
UKULELE
UNCIALS
UNCOILS
UNCURLS
UNFURLS
UNGODLY
UNREELS
UNROLLS
UNSEALS
UNVEILS
UPPSALA
UPSCALE
USEABLE
USUALLY
UTRILLO
UTTERLY

U•••••L

UNCIVIL
UNEQUAL
UNRAVEL
UNSNARL
UNUSUAL
USSTEEL
UTENSIL
UXORIAL

•UL••••

BULBLET
BULBOUS
BULBULS
BULGARS
BULGHUR
BULGING
BULKIER
BULKING
BULLDOG
BULLETS
BULLIED
BULLIES
BULLING
BULLION
BULLISH
BULLITT
BULLOCK
BULLPEN
BULLRUN
BULRUSH
BULWARK
CULEBRA
CULLING
CULOTTE
CULPRIT
CULTISH
CULTISM
CULTIST
CULTJAM
CULTURE
CULVERT
DULLARD
DULLEST
DULLING
DULLISH
FULCRUM
FULFILL
FULFILS
FULGENT
FULGHUM
FULLEST
FULSOME
GULCHES
GULFING
GULLETS
GULLIES
GULLING
GULPING
HULKING
HULLERS
HULLING
HULLOED
JULIANA
LULLABY
LULLING
MULCHED
MULCHES
MULCTED
MULETAS
MULLAHS
MULLEIN
MULLERS
MULLETS
MULLING
MULLION
NULLIFY
NULLING
PULASKI
PULLETS
PULLEYS
PULLING
PULLMAN
PULLOFF
PULLONS
PULLOUT
PULLSUP
PULLTAB
PULLUPS
PULPITS
PULSARS
PULSATE
PULSING
RULEOUT
RULESON
RULINGS
SULFATE
SULFIDE
SULFITE
SULKERS
SULKIER
SULKIES
SULKILY
SULKING
SULLIED
SULLIES
SULPHUR
SULTANA
SULTANS
SULUSEA
TULSANS
VULCANS
VULGATE
VULPINE
VULTURE
YULELOG

•U•L•••

AUKLETS
BUGLERS
BUGLING
BUILDER
BUILDIN
BUILDON
BUILDUP
BUILTIN
BUILTON
BUILTUP
BULLDOG
BULLETS
BULLIED
BULLIES
BULLING
BULLION
BULLISH
BULLITT
BULLOCK
BULLPEN
BULLRUN
BURLAPS
BURLIER
BURLING
BUSLINE
BUTLERS
CULLING
CURLERS
CURLEWS
CURLIER
CURLING
CURLSUP
CUTLASS
CUTLERS
CUTLERY
CUTLETS
DUALITY
DUELERS
DUELING
DUELIST
DULLARD
DULLEST
DULLING
DULLISH
DUNLINS
FUELERS
FUELING
FUELOIL
FUELROD
FULLEST
FURLING
FURLONG
GUELPHS
GUILDER
GULLETS
GULLIES
GULLING
GUNLOCK
GUTLESS
HULLERS
HULLING
HULLOED
HURLERS
HURLING
JUTLAND
LULLABY
LULLING
MUKLUKS
MULLAHS
MULLEIN
MULLERS
MULLETS
MULLING
MULLION
MUSLIMS
MUSLINS
NUCLEAR
NUCLEIC
NUCLEON
NUCLEUS
NUCLIDE
NULLIFY
NULLING
NUTLETS
OUTLAID
OUTLAND
OUTLAST
OUTLAWS
OUTLAYS
OUTLETS
OUTLINE
OUTLIVE
OUTLOOK
OUTLOUD
PUBLICS
PUBLISH
PULLETS
PULLEYS
PULLING
PULLMAN
PULLOFF
PULLONS
PULLOUT
PULLSUP
PULLTAB
PULLUPS
PURLIEU
PURLING
PURLINS
PURLOIN
QUALIFY
QUALITY
QUELLED
QUILLED
QUILTED
QUILTER
RUNLAPS
RUNLETS
SUBLETS
SUBLIME
SULLIED
SULLIES
SUNLAMP
SUNLESS
SURLIER
SURLILY
SUSLIKS
SUTLERS

•U••L••

AURALEE
AURALLY
BUBBLED
BUBBLES
BUCKLED
BUCKLER
BUCKLES
BUCKLEY
BUCOLIC
BUGALOO
BULBLET
BUMBLED
BUMBLER
BUMBLES
BUNDLED
BUNDLES
BUNGLED
BUNGLER
BUNGLES
BURBLED
BURBLES
BURGLAR
BURGLED
BURGLES
BUSTLED
BUSTLES
CUDDLED
CUDDLES
CUMULUS
CUPOLAS
CURDLED
CURDLES
CUSSLER
FUDDLED
FUDDLES
FUMBLED
FUMBLER
FUMBLES
GUNPLAY
GURGLED
GURGLES
GUZZLED
GUZZLER
GUZZLES
HUDDLED
HUDDLES
HUMBLED
HUMBLER
HUMBLES
HUNTLEY
HURDLED
HURDLER
HURDLES
HURTLED
HURTLES
HUSTLED
HUSTLER
HUSTLES
JUBILEE
JUGGLED
JUGGLER
JUGGLES
JUGULAR
JUMBLED
JUMBLES
JUNGLES
LUCILLE
MUDDLED
MUDDLER
MUDDLES
MUFFLED
MUFFLER
MUFFLES
MUMBLED
MUMBLER
MUMBLES
MURILLO
MUSCLED
MUSCLES
MUZZLED
MUZZLES
NUBBLES
NUZZLED
NUZZLER
NUZZLES
OUTFLOW
OUTPLAY
PUDDLED
PUDDLES
PUEBLOS
PURFLED
PURFLES
PURPLED
PURPLES
PUZZLED
PUZZLER
PUZZLES
QUAILED
QUELLED
QUIGLEY
QUILLED
RUBBLES
RUDOLPH
RUFFLED
RUFFLES
RUMBLED
RUMBLES
RUMPLED
RUMPLES
RUSTLED
RUSTLER
RUSTLES
SUBPLOT
SUBTLER
SUPPLER
SURPLUS
TUBULAR
TUMBLED
TUMBLER
TUMBLES
TUMULTS
TUMULUS
TUPELOS
TURTLED
TURTLES
TUSSLED
TUSSLES
TUTELAR
YULELOG

•U•••L•

AUDIBLE
AUDIBLY
AURALLY
AUREOLA
AUREOLE
AURICLE
BUFFALO
BULBULS
BUSHELS
BUYABLE
CUBICLE
CUDGELS
CUEBALL
CUPFULS
CUREALL
CUTICLE
DUCTILE
DUFFELS
DURABLE
DURABLY
DURRELL
FULFILL
FULFILS
FUNNELS
FUNNILY
FUSSILY
FUSTILY
FUZZILY
GUMBALL
GUNMOLL
GUNNELS
GUNWALE
GUSTILY
GUTSILY
HUBBELL
HUFFILY
HUMANLY
HUMIDLY
HUSKILY
JUGFULS
JUICILY
LUCIDLY
LUCILLE
LUCKILY
LURIDLY
LUSTILY
MUDEELS
MURILLO
MURKILY
MUSHILY
MUSSELS
MUSTILY
MUTABLE
MUTABLY
MUTUALS
MUZZILY
NUTTILY
OURSELF
OUTSELL
OUTSOLD
OUTTALK
PUERILE
PUFFILY
PUMMELS
PURCELL
PUSHILY
QUEENLY
QUEERLY
QUIBBLE
QUICKLY
QUIETLY
RUMPOLE
RUNNELS
RUSSELL
RUSTILY
SUAVELY
SUFFOLK
SULKILY
SUNBELT
SUNNILY
SURLILY
TUNICLE
TUNNELS

•U••••L

AUGURAL
AURORAL
AUSTRAL
CUEBALL
CUREALL
CURTAIL
DURRELL
DUTIFUL
FUELOIL
FULFILL
FURBALL
FURSEAL
GUMBALL
GUNMOLL
HUBBELL
HUMERAL
HURTFUL
JUVENAL
LUSTFUL
MUSICAL
NUMERAL
NUPTIAL
OUTSELL
PURCELL
QUARREL
QUETZAL
RUSSELL
SUBSOIL
SUNDIAL
SURREAL
TUMBREL
TUNEFUL
TUNGOIL
TURMOIL

••UL•••

ADULATE
AMULETS
AVULSED
AVULSES
BOULDER
CAULKED
CAULKER
COULDNT
COULEES
COULOMB
COULTER
CRULLER
EMULATE
EVULSED
EVULSES
EXULTED
FAULTED
FOULARD
FOULEST
FOULING
FOULOUT
FOULSUP
FOULTIP
FOULUPS
GOULASH
HAULAGE
HAULERS
HAULING
HAULOFF
HAULSUP
MAULDIN
MAULING
MOULAGE
MOULDED
MOULDER
MOULTED
OCULIST
OPULENT
PAULINA
PAULINE
PAULING
PAULIST
PAULSEN
POULENC
POULTRY
ROULADE
SCULLED
SCULLER
SCULPTS
SKULKED
SKULKER
SOULFUL
THULIUM
UKULELE
ULULANT
ULULATE
VAULTED
VAULTER
WOULDBE
WOULDNT

••U•L••

BAUBLES
BLUELAW
COUPLED
COUPLES
COUPLET
CRUELER
CRUELLY
CRULLER
DOUBLED
DOUBLES
DOUBLET
DOUBLEU
DOUGLAS
DRUMLIN
EQUALED
EQUALLY
KNURLED
LOUELLA
MAUDLIN
MOUFLON
SCULLED
SCULLER
SQUALID
SQUALLS
SQUALOR
SQUELCH
TOUSLED
TOUSLES
USUALLY

••U••L•

ACUTELY
ARUGULA
BLUEFLU
BLUFFLY
BLUNTLY
CHUCKLE
COURTLY
CRUDELY
CRUELLY
CRUMBLE
CRUMBLY
CRUMPLE
CRUMPLY
EQUABLE
EQUABLY
EQUALLY
FLUIDLY
GAUDILY
GAUNTLY
GAUZILY
GRUFFLY
GRUMBLE
INUTILE
KNUCKLE
LAURELS
LOUELLA
LOUSILY
PLURALS
PLUSHLY
ROUGHLY
ROUNDLY
SAUCILY
SCUFFLE
SCUTTLE
SHUFFLE
SHUTTLE
SMUGGLE
SNUFFLE
SNUGGLE
SOUFFLE
SOUNDLY
SQUALLS
SQUEALS
STUBBLE
STUBBLY
STUMBLE
TOUGHLY
TRUCKLE
TRUFFLE
TRUNDLE
UKULELE
USUALLY

••U•••L

ABUTTAL
ALUMNAL
ASUSUAL
BRUEGEL
CHUNNEL
COUNCIL
COUNSEL
CRUCIAL
DIURNAL
FLUVIAL
JOURNAL
NEUTRAL
PLUVIAL
SOULFUL
TRUCIAL
UNUSUAL

•••UL••

AMPULES
ANGULAR
ANNULAR
ANNULUS
AWFULLY
CAPULET
CUMULUS
DIVULGE
ENGULFS
EPAULET
FACULTY
FAMULUS
FERULES
FIBULAE
FIBULAS
IMPULSE
INDULGE
INSULAR
INSULIN
INSULTS
JOCULAR
JUGULAR
MACULAE
MEDULLA
MODULAR
MODULES
NEBULAE
NEBULAR
NEBULAS
NODULAR
NODULES
OCCULTS
PABULUM
PENULTS
POPULAR
REGULAR
REGULUS
REPULSE
RESULTS
RIVULET
ROMULAN
ROMULUS

SECULAR
TABULAR
TITULAR
TUBULAR
TUMULTS
TUMULUS
ZEBULON

•••U•L•

ANNUALS
ANOUILH
AWFULLY
BEGUILE
CASUALS
MANUALS
MEDULLA
MUTUALS
OCTUPLE
PIOUSLY
PROUDLY
REBUILD
REBUILT
REFUELS
RITUALS
SCRUPLE
SEQUELS
SOLUBLE
STOUTLY
TEQUILA
TROUBLE
UNCURLS
UNFURLS
VACUOLE
VAGUELY
VISUALS
VOLUBLE
VOLUBLY

•••U••L

AROUSAL
AUGURAL
COZUMEL
LACUNAL
NAHUATL
NATURAL
PERUSAL
REFUSAL
SPOUSAL
STRUDEL
TRAUBEL

••••UL•

AMPOULE
ARMFULS
ARUGULA
ASSAULT
ATFAULT
BAGFULS
BEFOULS
BEOWULF
BOXFULS
BULBULS
CAPFULS
CAPSULE
CARFULS
CONSULS
CONSULT
CUPFULS
DEFAULT
DIMBULB
DRACULA
EARFULS
ENSOULS
EYEFULS
FERRULE
FORMULA
GAGRULE
GLOBULE
GRANULE
HERCULE
INOCULA
JARFULS
JUGFULS
LAPFULS
LEGPULL
MISRULE
NOFAULT
PITBULL
POTFULS
RENAULT
SCAPULA
SEAGULL
SPATULA
STIMULI
VATFULS
VIRGULE
VISTULA

••••U•L

ACCRUAL
ASUSUAL
COEQUAL
EMANUEL
FACTUAL
GRADUAL
JONQUIL
LEGPULL
LINGUAL
PINCURL
PITBULL
RORQUAL
SEAGULL
SENSUAL
SYNFUEL
TEXTUAL
UNEQUAL
UNUSUAL
VICTUAL
VIRTUAL

•••••UL

BALEFUL
BANEFUL
BASHFUL
BOWLFUL
BRIMFUL
CAREFUL
DOLEFUL
DUTIFUL
FATEFUL
FEARFUL
FISTFUL
FORKFUL
FRETFUL
GAINFUL
GLEEFUL
HANDFUL
HARMFUL
HATEFUL
HEEDFUL
HELPFUL
HOPEFUL
HURTFUL
KARAKUL
LESPAUL
LUSTFUL
MINDFUL
NEEDFUL
PAGEFUL
PAILFUL
PAINFUL
PASSEUL
PIPEFUL
PITIFUL
PLAYFUL
RESTFUL
ROOMFUL
SACKFUL
SKILFUL
SOULFUL
TACTFUL
TANKFUL
TEARFUL
TRAYFUL
TUNEFUL
WAKEFUL
WILLFUL
WISHFUL
WISTFUL
ZESTFUL

UM•••••

UMBERTO
UMBRAGE
UMBRIAN
UMLAUTS
UMPIRED
UMPIRES
UMPTEEN

U•M••••

UNMAKES
UNMASKS
UNMOVED

U••M•••

ULLMANN

U•••M••

UNAIMED
UNARMED
UNKEMPT
UNNAMED
UNTAMED
UPTEMPO

U••••M•

ULALUME

U•••••M

UNIFORM
URANIUM

•UM••••

BUMBLED
BUMBLER
BUMBLES
BUMMERS
BUMMING
BUMPERS
BUMPIER
BUMPING
BUMPKIN
BUMPSUP
BUMSOUT
CUMULUS
DUMBEST
DUMDUMS
DUMMIED
DUMMIES
DUMMYUP
DUMPIER
DUMPING
FUMBLED
FUMBLER
FUMBLES
GUMBALL
GUMDROP
GUMMIER
GUMMING
GUMSHOE
GUMTREE
HUMANLY
HUMBLED
HUMBLER
HUMBLES
HUMBUGS
HUMDRUM
HUMERAL
HUMERUS
HUMIDLY
HUMIDOR
HUMMERS
HUMMING
HUMMOCK
HUMORED
HUMOURS
JUMANJI
JUMBLED
JUMBLES
JUMPCUT
JUMPERS
JUMPIER
JUMPING
JUMPOFF
JUMPSAT
JUMPSIN
JUMPSON
JUMPSUP
KUMQUAT
LUMBAGO
LUMBARS
LUMBERS
LUMIERE
LUMPERS
LUMPIER
LUMPING
LUMPSUM
MUMBLED
MUMBLER
MUMBLES
MUMESON
MUMFORD
MUMMERS
MUMMERY
MUMMIES
NUMBATS
NUMBERS
NUMBEST
NUMBING
NUMERAL
NUMERIC
PUMICES
PUMMELS
PUMPERS
PUMPING
PUMPKIN
PUMPSUP
RUMBAED
RUMBLED
RUMBLES
RUMMAGE
RUMMIER
RUMORED
RUMOURS
RUMPLED
RUMPLES
RUMPOLE
SUMATRA
SUMMARY
SUMMERS
SUMMERY
SUMMING
SUMMITS
SUMMONS
TUMBLED
TUMBLER
TUMBLES
TUMBREL
TUMMIES
TUMULTS
TUMULUS
YUMMIER

•U•M•••

AUGMENT
BUMMERS
BUMMING
BURMESE
DUMMIED
DUMMIES
DUMMYUP
GUIMPES
GUMMIER
GUMMING
GUNMOLL
HUMMERS
HUMMING
HUMMOCK
MUAMMAR
MUMMERS
MUMMERY
MUMMIES
MURMURS
MUUMUUS
NUTMEAT
NUTMEGS
PUMMELS
RUMMAGE
RUMMIER
SUBMITS
SUMMARY
SUMMERS
SUMMERY
SUMMING
SUMMITS
SUMMONS
SUNMAID
SURMISE
TUMMIES
TURMOIL
YUMMIER

•U••M••

AUTOMAT
AUTUMNS
BUSHMAN
BUSHMEN
DUSTMOP
JUNKMAN
MUAMMAR
PULLMAN
PUTAMEN
RUNAMOK
TUCHMAN

•U•••M•

BUYTIME
CUSTOMS
CUTTIME
DUMDUMS
FULSOME
MUGWUMP
MUSEUMS
MUSLIMS
OUTCOME
OUTJUMP
QUORUMS
RUNHOME
SUBLIME
SUBSUME
SUCCUMB
SUNLAMP
SUPREME
SUPREMO
SURNAME

•U••••M

BUCKRAM
CULTISM
CULTJAM
DUKEDOM
FULCRUM
FULGHUM
GUARGUM
HUMDRUM
JUDAISM
LUMPSUM
QUANTUM
SUNBEAM
SUNROOM
SURINAM

••UM•••

ALUMNAE
ALUMNAL
ALUMNUS
CHUMMED
CLUMPED
CRUMBLE
CRUMBLY
CRUMPET
CRUMPLE
CRUMPLY
DAUMIER
DRUMLIN
DRUMMED
DRUMMER
DRUMSUP
FLUMMOX
FNUMBER
GLUMMER
GRUMBLE
GRUMPED
MUUMUUS
PLUMAGE
PLUMBED
PLUMBER
PLUMING
PLUMMER
PLUMMET
PLUMPED
PLUMPER
RHUMBAS
SLUMBER
SLUMMED
SLUMPED
SPUMING
SPUMONE
SPUMONI
STUMBLE
STUMPED
STUMPER
THUMBED
THUMPED
THUMPER
TRUMPED
TRUMPET
TRUMPUP
YOUMANS

••U•M••

CHUMMED
DRUMMED
DRUMMER
FLUMMOX
GLUMMER
GOURMET
HOUSMAN
KLUGMAN
PLUMMER
PLUMMET
SLUMMED
THURMAN
ZEUGMAS

••U••M•

COULOMB
GAUTAMA
GOURAMI
SQUIRMS
SQUIRMY
TRUISMS
TSUNAMI
YOUNGMC

••U•••M

ELUVIUM
FAUVISM
MAUGHAM
THULIUM
TOURISM

•••UM••

ALBUMEN
ALBUMIN
ASSUMED
ASSUMES
AUTUMNS
BENUMBS
BITUMEN
CALUMET
CALUMNY
CERUMEN
COLUMBO
COLUMNS
COZUMEL
GALUMPH
INHUMAN
LEGUMES
MANUMIT
RESUMED
RESUMES
TRAUMAS
TRIUMPH
VOLUMES

•••U•M•

SOSUEME
VACUUMS

•••U••M

JEJUNUM
PABULUM
REQUIEM

••••UM•

AIRPUMP
ALARUMS
ASYLUMS
ATRIUMS
CONSUME
COSTUME
DICTUMS
DUMDUMS
FRENUMS
GASPUMP
LYCEUMS
MAGNUMS
MEDIUMS
MUGWUMP
MUSEUMS
NOTRUMP
OUTJUMP
PABLUMS
PEPLUMS
PERFUME
PLENUMS
PODIUMS
POSSUMS
PRESUME
QUORUMS
REDGUMS
SATSUMA
SKIJUMP
SUBSUME
SUCCUMB
ULALUME
VACUUMS
VELLUMS

•••••UM

ALYSSUM
BELGIUM
CADMIUM
CALCIUM
CAMBIUM
CHETRUM
CRANIUM
DECORUM
EARDRUM
ELUVIUM
ELYSIUM
ERRATUM
FERMIUM
FULCRUM
FULGHUM
GALLIUM
GUARGUM
HAFNIUM
HAHNIUM
HOLMIUM
HOODLUM
HUMDRUM
IRIDIUM
JEJUNUM
KARAKUM
LITHIUM
LUMPSUM
MAXIMUM
MINIMUM
MITCHUM
MODICUM
NATRIUM
NIOBIUM
NOSEEUM
NOSTRUM
OMENTUM
OPOSSUM
OPTIMUM
ORGANUM
PABULUM
PALLIUM
PINETUM
PREMIUM
QUANTUM
RHENIUM
RHODIUM
ROSTRUM
SANCTUM
SISTRUM
SORGHUM
STADIUM
STERNUM
STRATUM
TANTRUM
TERBIUM
THORIUM
THULIUM
TRITIUM
URANIUM
YTTRIUM

UN•••••

UNAIDED
UNAIMED
UNAIRED
UNALIKE
UNARMED
UNASKED
UNAVOCE
UNAWARE
UNBAKED
UNBENDS
UNBINDS
UNBLEST
UNBOLTS
UNBOUND
UNBOWED
UNBOXED
UNBOXES
UNCAGED
UNCAGES
UNCANNY
UNCASED
UNCASES
UNCHAIN
UNCIALS
UNCIVIL
UNCLASP
UNCLEAN
UNCLEAR
UNCLOAK
UNCLOGS
UNCLOSE
UNCOILS
UNCORKS
UNCOUTH
UNCOVER
UNCRATE
UNCTION
UNCURLS
UNDATED
UNDERGO
UNDOING
UNDRAPE
UNDRAWN
UNDRESS
UNDYING
UNEARTH
UNENDED
UNEQUAL
UNFAZED
UNFIXED
UNFOLDS
UNFROCK
UNFURLS
UNGIRDS
UNGLUED
UNGODLY
UNGUENT
UNHANDS
UNHANDY
UNHAPPY
UNHEARD
UNHITCH
UNHOOKS
UNHORSE
UNICORN
UNIFIED
UNIFIER
UNIFIES
UNIFORM
UNIPODS
UNISONS
UNITARY
UNITERS
UNITIES
UNITING
UNITIVE
UNKEMPT
UNKINKS
UNKNITS
UNKNOTS
UNKNOWN
UNLACED
UNLACES
UNLADES
UNLATCH
UNLEARN
UNLEASH
UNLIKED
UNLINED
UNLINKS
UNLOADS
UNLOCKS
UNLOOSE
UNLOVED
UNLUCKY
UNMAKES
UNMASKS
UNMOVED
UNNAMED
UNNERVE
UNOILED
UNPACKS
UNPAVED
UNPILED
UNPILES
UNPLUGS
UNQUOTE
UNRATED
UNRAVEL
UNREADY
UNREELS
UNROBED
UNROBES
UNROLLS
UNSATED
UNSCREW
UNSEALS
UNSEATS
UNSEWED
UNSHORN
UNSNAGS
UNSNAPS
UNSNARL
UNSOUND
UNSPENT
UNSTACK
UNSTICK
UNSTOPS
UNSTRAP
UNSTUCK
UNSWEPT
UNTACKS
UNTAMED
UNTAPED
UNTRAPS
UNTRIED
UNTRUTH
UNTUNED
UNTUNES
UNTWIST
UNTYING
UNUSUAL
UNVEILS
UNWEAVE
UNWINDS
UNWISER
UNWOUND
UNWRAPS
UNYOKED
UNYOKES
UNZONED

U•N••••

UNNAMED
UNNERVE

U••N•••

UGANDAN
ULANOVA
UNENDED
UNKNITS
UNKNOTS
UNKNOWN
UNSNAGS
UNSNAPS
UNSNARL
UPENDED
URANITE
URANIUM
USINGUP
UTENSIL

U•••N••

ULYANOV
UNBENDS
UNBINDS
UNCANNY
UNHANDS
UNHANDY
UNKINKS
UNLINED
UNLINKS
UNTUNED
UNTUNES
UNWINDS
UNZONED
UPLANDS
UPLINKS
UPTONOW
URBANER
URGENCY
USTINOV

U••••N•

UKRAINE
ULLMANN
ULULANT
UNBOUND
UNCANNY
UNDOING
UNDYING
UNGUENT
UNISONS
UNITING
UNSOUND
UNSPENT
UNTYING
UNWOUND
UPBORNE
UPFRONT
UPSWING
UPTURNS
URCHINS
USOPENS
UTAHANS

U•••••N

UGANDAN
ULLMANN
UMBRIAN
UMPTEEN
UNCHAIN
UNCLEAN
UNCTION
UNDRAWN
UNICORN
UNKNOWN
UNLEARN
UNSHORN
UPRISEN
UPSILON
UTOPIAN

•UN••••

AUNTIES
BUNCHED
BUNCHES
BUNCOED
BUNDLED
BUNDLES
BUNGEES
BUNGING
BUNGLED
BUNGLER
BUNGLES
BUNIONS
BUNKBED
BUNKERS
BUNKING
BUNKOED
BUNNIES
BUNTING
CUNNING
DUNAWAY
DUNGEON
DUNKERS
DUNKING
DUNKIRK
DUNLINS
DUNNING
EUNUCHS
FUNDING
FUNFAIR
FUNFEST
FUNGOES
FUNKIER
FUNNELS
FUNNIER
FUNNIES
FUNNILY
FUNNING
GUNBOAT
GUNDOGS
GUNFIRE
GUNKIER
GUNLOCK
GUNMOLL
GUNNELS
GUNNERS
GUNNERY
GUNNIES
GUNNING
GUNPLAY
GUNSFOR
GUNSHOT
GUNTHER
GUNWALE
HUNCHED
HUNCHES
HUNDRED
HUNGARY
HUNGERS
HUNGOUT
HUNKERS
HUNTERS
HUNTING
HUNTLEY
JUNCOES
JUNEBUG
JUNGLES
JUNIORS
JUNIPER
JUNKART
JUNKERS
JUNKETS
JUNKIER
JUNKIES
JUNKING
JUNKMAN
LUNATIC
LUNCHED
LUNCHER
LUNCHES
LUNGEAT
LUNGING
LUNKERS
MUNCHED
MUNCHER
MUNCHES
MUNDANE
MUNTINS
NUNCIOS
NUNNERY
PUNCHED
PUNCHER
PUNCHES
PUNCHIN
PUNCHUP
PUNDITS
PUNGENT
PUNIEST
PUNJABI
PUNKAHS
PUNKIES
PUNNING

PUNSTER
PUNTERS
PUNTING
RUNAMOK
RUNAWAY
RUNBACK
RUNDEEP
RUNDOWN
RUNHOME
RUNINTO
RUNLAPS
RUNLETS
RUNNELS
RUNNERS
RUNNIER
RUNNING
RUNOFFS
RUNOVER
RUNRIOT
RUNSDRY
RUNSOFF
RUNSOUT
RUNTIER
RUNWAYS
RUNWITH
SUNBATH
SUNBEAM
SUNBELT
SUNBURN
SUNCITY
SUNDAES
SUNDAYS
SUNDECK
SUNDERS
SUNDEWS
SUNDIAL
SUNDOGS
SUNDOWN
SUNFISH
SUNGODS
SUNKIST
SUNLAMP
SUNLESS
SUNMAID
SUNNIER
SUNNILY
SUNNING
SUNRAYS
SUNRISE
SUNROOF
SUNROOM
SUNSETS
SUNSPOT
SUNTANS
TUNDRAS
TUNEDIN
TUNEDUP
TUNEFUL
TUNEOUT
TUNESIN
TUNESUP
TUNEUPS
TUNGOIL
TUNICLE
TUNISIA
TUNNELS
TUNNIES

•U•N•••

BUNNIES
BURNERS
BURNETT
BURNING
BURNISH
BURNOUT
BURNSUP
BURNTUP
CUNNING
DUENNAS
DUNNING
FUNNELS
FUNNIER
FUNNIES
FUNNILY
FUNNING
FURNACE
FURNISH
GUANACO
GUANINE
GUINEAS
GUNNELS
GUNNERS
GUNNERY
GUNNIES
GUNNING
GURNEYS
LUGNUTS
NUANCED
NUANCES
NUDNIKS
NUNNERY
PUGNOSE
PUNNING
QUANTUM
QUENTIN
QUINCES
QUININE
QUINOAS
QUINQUE
QUINTET
QUONSET
RUANDAN
RUINERS
RUINING
RUINOUS
RUNNELS
RUNNERS
RUNNIER
RUNNING
SUNNIER
SUNNILY
SUNNING
SURNAME
TUNNELS
TUNNIES
TURNERS
TURNING
TURNIPS
TURNKEY
TURNOFF
TURNOUT
TURNSIN
TURNSON
TURNSTO
TURNSUP

•U••N••

AUGENDS
CUTINTO
DUENNAS
DUGONGS
DURANCE
DURANGO
DURANTE
EUGENIE
HUMANLY
JUMANJI
JUSTNOW
JUVENAL
KUTENAI
LUPINES
MUTANTS
OUTINGS
QUEENLY
RULINGS
RUNINTO
SUBUNIT
SURINAM
SUSANNA
SUSANNE
SUTTNER
SUZANNE

•U•••N•

AUBURNS
AUGMENT
AUTUMNS
BUCKING
BUDDING
BUDGING
BUFFING
BUGGING
BUGLING
BULGING
BULKING
BULLING
BUMMING
BUMPING
BUNGING
BUNIONS
BUNKING
BUNTING
BUOYANT
BUOYING
BURBANK
BURDENS
BURKINA
BURLING
BURNING
BURPING
BURYING
BUSHING
BUSKINS
BUSLINE
BUSSING
BUSTING
BUSYING
BUTTING
BUTTONS
BUZZING
CUFFING
CUIBONO
CUISINE
CULLING
CUNNING
CUPPING
CURBING
CURDING
CURLING
CURRANT
CURRENT
CURSING
CURVING
CUSSING
CUTTING
DUBBING
DUCKING
DUCTING
DUELING
DULLING
DUMPING
DUNKING
DUNLINS
DUNNING
DUODENA
DUSTING
EUPHONY
FUDGING
FUELING
FULGENT
FUNDING
FUNNING
FURLING
FURLONG
FURRING
FUSSING
FUZZING
GUANINE
GUARANI
GUIDING
GUIDONS
GULFING
GULLING
GULPING
GUMMING
GUNNING
GUSHING
GUSTING
GUTTING
HUFFING
HUGGING
HULKING
HULLING
HUMMING
HUNTING
HURLING
HURTING
HUSBAND
HUSHING
HUSKING
JUDGING
JUGBAND
JUGWINE
JUICING
JULIANA
JUMPING
JUNKING
JURYING
JUSTINE
JUTLAND
JUTTING
LUCERNE
LUCIANO
LUCKING
LUFFING
LUGGING
LULLING
LUMPING
LUNGING
LURKING
LUSTING
MUCKING
MUDHENS
MUFFING
MUFFINS
MUGGING
MULLING
MUNDANE
MUNTINS
MUSHING
MUSLINS
MUSSING
MUSTANG
MUTTONS
NUBBINS
NUBIANS
NUDGING
NULLING
NUMBING
NURSING
NUTTING
OUSTING
OUTDONE
OUTGUNS
OUTLAND
OUTLINE
OUTRANK
OUTRUNS
PUCCINI
PUDDING
PUFFING
PUFFINS
PULLING
PULLONS
PULSING
PUMPING
PUNGENT
PUNNING
PUNTING
PUPTENT
PURGING
PURLING
PURLINS
PURRING
PURSING
PUSHING
PUTTING
QUAKING
QUEUING
QUININE
QUOTING
RUBBING
RUCHING
RUCKING
RUINING
RUNNING
RUSHING
RUSTING
SUBBING
SUBORNS
SUBTEND
SUCKING
SUDSING
SUITING
SUKARNO
SULKING
SULTANA
SULTANS
SUMMING
SUMMONS
SUNNING
SUNTANS
SUPPING
SURFING
SURGING
SUSANNA
SUSANNE
SUSPEND
SUSSING
SUZANNE
TUCKING
TUFTING
TUGGING
TULSANS
TURBANS
TURBINE
TUREENS
TURNING
TUSCANY
VULCANS
VULPINE

•U••••N

AUCTION
AUDUBON
BUFFOON
BUILDIN
BUILDON
BUILTIN
BUILTON
BULLION
BULLPEN
BULLRUN
BUMPKIN
BURGEON
BURPGUN
BURSTYN
BUSHMAN
BUSHMEN
BUTTSIN
CURTAIN
CUSHION
CUTDOWN
DUCKPIN
DUDGEON
DUNGEON
DUSTPAN
FUSTIAN
HUSSEIN
JUMPSIN
JUMPSON
JUNKMAN
MUEZZIN
MULLEIN
MULLION
MUMESON
MUTAGEN
NUCLEON
OURTOWN
OUTWORN
PULLMAN
PUMPKIN
PUNCHIN
PURITAN
PURLOIN
PUSHKIN
PUSHPIN
PUTAMEN
PUTDOWN
PUTUPON
QUENTIN
QUICKEN
QUIETEN
RUANDAN
RUBDOWN
RUBICON
RUBITIN
RUCTION
RUFFIAN
RULESON
RUNDOWN
RUSSIAN
SUASION
SUBJOIN
SUCKSIN
SUCTION
SUNBURN
SUNDOWN
SURGEON
SUSTAIN
TUCHMAN
TUCKSIN
TUITION
TUNEDIN
TUNESIN
TURNSIN
TURNSON
YUCATAN

••UN•••

ALUNSER
ASUNDER
BLUNDER
BLUNTED
BLUNTER
BLUNTLY
BOUNCED
BOUNCER
BOUNCES
BOUNDED
BOUNDER
BOUNDTO
BOUNDUP
BRUNETS
CHUNNEL
CLUNKED
CLUNKER
COUNCIL
COUNSEL
COUNTED
COUNTER
COUNTON
COUNTRY
CRUNCHY
DAUNTED
FLUNKED
FOUNDED
FOUNDER
FOUNDRY
GAUNTER
GAUNTLY
GOUNDER
GRUNION
GRUNTED
HAUNTED
HOUNDED
HYUNDAI
JAUNTED
JOUNCED
JOUNCES
LAUNDER
LAUNDRY
LOUNGED
LOUNGER
LOUNGES
MAUNDER
MOUNDED
MOUNTED
MOUNTIE
PAUNCHY
PLUNDER
PLUNGED
PLUNGER
PLUNGES
PLUNKED
POUNCED
POUNCER
POUNCES
POUNDED
POUNDER
PRUNERS
PRUNING
REUNIFY
REUNION
REUNITE
ROUNDED
ROUNDER
ROUNDLY
ROUNDON
ROUNDUP
SAUNTER
SHUNNED
SHUNTED
SKUNKED
SOUNDED
SOUNDER
SOUNDLY
SPUNOFF
SPUNOUT
STUNGUN
STUNNED
STUNNER
STUNTED
TAUNTED
THUNDER
TRUNDLE
TSUNAMI
VAUNTED
VAUNTER
WOUNDED
WOUNDUP
YOUNGER
YOUNGMC
YOUNGUN

••U•N••

ALUMNAE
ALUMNAL
ALUMNUS
AQUINAS
CHUNNEL
CHURNED
CHUTNEY
DIURNAL
EQUINES
EQUINOX
FLUENCY
IGUANAS
JOURNAL
JOURNEY
SHUNNED
SPURNED
SPURNER
SPUTNIK
SQUANTO
SQUINCH
SQUINTS
SQUINTY
STUNNED
STUNNER
TOURNEY
TRUANCY
TRUANTS
YOUKNOW

••U••N•

ABUSING
AMUSING
BLUEING
CAUSING
CLUEING
COULDNT
COUPONS
COURANT
COUSINS
DAUBING
DOUSING
EDUCING
ELUDING
ELUTING
ENURING
EXUDING
FEUDING
FLUTING
FOULING
GAUDENS
GAUGING
GOUGING
HAULING
HOUDINI
HOUSING
INURING
LAUDING
LAURENT
LOUSING
MAULING
MOUSING
MOUTONS
NEURONE
NEURONS
OPULENT
PAULINA
PAULINE
PAULING
PAUSING
PLUMING
POULENC
POURING
POUTING
PRUDENT
PRUNING
REUBENS
ROUGING
ROUSING
ROUTINE
ROUTING
SOURING
SOUTANE
SPUMING
SPUMONE
SPUMONI
STUDENT
TAURINE
TAUTENS
TEUTONS
TOUCANS
TOURING
TOUTING
TRUEING
ULULANT
WOULDNT
YAUPONS
YOUMANS

••U•••N

BLUEFIN
BOURBON
CAUTION
CLUEDIN
CLUESIN
COUNTON
DAUPHIN
DRUMLIN
ELUTION
EXURBAN
GAUGUIN
GLUEDON
GLUTTON
GRUNION
HOUSMAN
HOUSTON
JOURDAN
KLUGMAN
LAUGHIN
MAUDLIN
MAULDIN
MAUREEN
MOUFLON
NEUTRON
PAULSEN
PLUGSIN
POURSIN
REUNION
ROUGHEN
ROUNDON
SAURIAN
SHUTSIN
SOUPCON
SPURSON
STUNGUN
THURMAN
TOUCHON
TOUGHEN
VAUGHAN
YOUNGUN

•••UN••

ABOUNDS
ADJUNCT
AMOUNTS
ATTUNED
ATTUNES
DEBUNKS
DEFUNCT
ENOUNCE
EXPUNGE
FLAUNTS
FLOUNCE
GERUNDS
GODUNOV
GROUNDS
HHMUNRO
JEJUNUM
KAHUNAS
KORUNAS
LACUNAE
LACUNAL
LACUNAS
LAGUNAS
OBTUNDS
PETUNIA
REFUNDS
RETUNED
RETUNES
ROTUNDA
SCRUNCH
STAUNCH
SUBUNIT
TRIUNES
TROUNCE
UNTUNED
UNTUNES
VICUNAS
YAOUNDE

•••U•N•

ARGUING
AUBURNS
AUTUMNS
BEGUINE
BYTURNS
CALUMNY
COLUMNS
ENDUING
ENSUING
GENUINE
IMBUING
IMPUGNS
ISSUING
MINUEND
OPPUGNS
PAPUANS
PIQUANT
PIQUING
QUEUING
REPUGNS
RETURNS
SEQUINS
SIOUANS
TIJUANA
TOLUENE
UNGUENT
UPTURNS
VALUING

•••U••N

ACTUPON
ALBUMEN
ALBUMIN
AUDUBON
BITUMEN
BLOUSON
CERUMEN
CROUTON
INHUMAN
INSULIN
MCLUHAN
MCQUEEN
MENUHIN
PUTUPON
ROMULAN
SETUPON
STEUBEN
WHAUDEN
ZEBULON

••••UN•

ACCOUNT
ACHTUNG
AGROUND
AIRGUNS
ASTOUND
BIGGUNS
CAPGUNS
COMMUNE
CYYOUNG
DRYRUNS
ENDRUNS
ENGLUND
EXPOUND
FORTUNA
FORTUNE
GOROUND
IMPOUND
INBOUND
JETGUNS
JOBHUNT
MANHUNT
NEPTUNE
OROTUND
OUTGUNS
OUTRUNS
POPGUNS
RAYGUNS
REBOUND
RECOUNT
REDOUND
REMOUNT
RESOUND
REWOUND
SAMNUNN
SAMSUNG
SHOGUNS
SIGMUND
SIXGUNS
SKIRUNS
SPELUNK
TERHUNE
TOPGUNS
TRIBUNE
UNBOUND
UNSOUND
UNWOUND
ZEITUNG

••••U•N

ADJOURN
BEDOUIN
CLIBURN
COGBURN
DONJUAN
GAUGUIN
HEPBURN
JOAQUIN
NOCTURN
PENGUIN
RAYBURN
SAMNUNN
SANJUAN
SICHUAN
SOJOURN
SUNBURN

•••••UN

BELAKUN
BLOWGUN
BULLRUN
BURPGUN
CALHOUN
FORERUN
HANDGUN
HOMERUN
JIMRYUN
LONGRUN
MILKRUN
MILLRUN
OVERRUN
POKEFUN
PRONOUN
SHOTGUN
STUNGUN
WELLRUN
YOUNGUN

U•O••••

UNOILED
USOPENS
USOSHOW
UTOPIAN
UTOPIAS
UXORIAL

U••O•••

UNBOLTS
UNBOUND
UNBOWED
UNBOXED
UNBOXES
UNCOILS
UNCORKS
UNCOUTH
UNCOVER
UNDOING
UNFOLDS
UNGODLY
UNHOOKS
UNHORSE
UNLOADS
UNLOCKS
UNLOOSE
UNLOVED
UNMOVED
UNROBED
UNROBES
UNROLLS
UNSOUND
UNWOUND
UNYOKED
UNYOKES
UNZONED
UPBORNE
UPHOLDS
UPLOADS
UPROARS
UPROOTS
UPTONOW
UPTOPAR

U•••O••

ULANOVA
UNAVOCE
UNCLOAK
UNCLOGS
UNCLOSE
UNFROCK
UNHOOKS
UNICORN
UNIFORM
UNIPODS
UNISONS
UNKNOTS
UNKNOWN
UNLOOSE
UNQUOTE
UNSHORN
UNSTOPS
UPCLOSE
UPFRONT
UPROOTS
UPSHOTS

U••••O•

ULYANOV
UNCTION
UPSILON
UPTONOW
USOSHOW
USTINOV

U•••••O

UCCELLO
UMBERTO
UNDERGO
UPTEMPO
UTRILLO

•UO••••

BUOYANT
BUOYING

BUOYSUP
DUODENA
QUOKKAS
QUONSET
QUORUMS
QUOTERS
QUOTING

•U•O•••
AUROCHS
AURORAE
AURORAL
AURORAS
AUTOMAT
BUCOLIC
BUROAKS
BUYOUTS
CULOTTE
CUPOLAS
CUTOFFS
CUTOUTS
DUGONGS
DUGOUTS
FURORES
HUMORED
HUMOURS
JUDOIST
OUTOFIT
PUTOUTS
PUTOVER
RUDOLPH
RUMORED
RUMOURS
RUNOFFS
RUNOVER
SUBORNS
TUTORED

•U••O••
AUREOLA
AUREOLE
AUTHORS
BUCKOES
BUFFOON
BUGSOFF
BUGSOUT
BULBOUS
BULLOCK
BUMSOUT
BUNCOED
BUNIONS
BUNKOED
BURBOTS
BURDOCK
BURGOOS
BURNOUT
BURROWS
BUSBOYS
BUSTOUT
BUTTONS
BUTTOUT
BUYSOFF
BUYSOUT
BUZZOFF
CUCKOOS
CUIBONO
CURIOUS
CURSORS
CURSORY
CUSTODY
CUSTOMS
CUTDOWN
CUTSOFF
CUTSOUT
DUBIOUS
DUSTOFF
DUTEOUS
EUPHONY
FUELOIL
FULSOME
FUNGOES
FURIOUS
FURLONG
FURROWS
GUIDONS
GUNBOAT
GUNDOGS
GUNLOCK
GUNMOLL
GUSTOES
HULLOED
HUMMOCK
HUNGOUT
JUMPOFF
JUNCOES
JUNIORS
LUBBOCK
LUCKOUT
MUMFORD
MURDOCH
MUSCOVY
MUTTONS
OURTOWN
OUTCOME
OUTDOES
OUTDONE
OUTDOOR
OUTGOES
OUTLOOK
OUTLOUD
OUTPOST
OUTSOLD
OUTVOTE
OUTWORE
OUTWORK
OUTWORN
PUGNOSE
PULLOFF
PULLONS
PULLOUT
PURLOIN
PURPORT
PURPOSE
PUSHOFF
PUTDOWN
PUTSOFF
PUTSOUT
QUAHOGS
QUINOAS
QUIXOTE
RUBDOWN
RUBSOUT
RUINOUS
RULEOUT
RUMPOLE
RUNDOWN
RUNHOME
RUNSOFF
RUNSOUT
RUSHOFF
SUBJOIN
SUBROSA
SUBSOIL
SUCCORS
SUCCOUR
SUCROSE
SUFFOLK
SUITORS
SUMMONS
SUNDOGS
SUNDOWN
SUNGODS
SUNROOF
SUNROOM
SUPPORT
SUPPOSE
SURCOAT
TUGBOAT
TUNEOUT
TUNGOIL
TURBOTS
TURMOIL
TURNOFF
TURNOUT
TUSSOCK

•U•••O•
AUCTION
AUDITOR
AUDUBON
BUFFOON
BUGABOO
BUGALOO
BUILDON
BUILTON
BULLDOG
BULLION
BURGEON
BURGOOS
BUSHHOG
BUSSTOP
CUCKOOS
CURATOR
CUSHION
DUDGEON
DUKEDOM
DUNGEON
DUSTMOP
FUELROD
FUSSPOT
GUMDROP
GUMSHOE
GUNSFOR
GUNSHOT
HUMIDOR
JUKEBOX
JUMPSON
JUSTNOW
MUGSHOT
MULLION
MUMESON
NUCLEON
NUNCIOS
OUTCROP
OUTDOOR
OUTFLOW
OUTGROW
OUTLOOK
PUEBLOS
PUTUPON
QUARTOS
RUBICON
RUCTION
RULESON
RUNAMOK
RUNRIOT
SUASION
SUBPLOT
SUCTION
SUNROOF
SUNROOM
SUNSPOT
SURGEON
TUITION
TUPELOS
TURNSON
TUXEDOS
YULELOG

•U••••O
BUFFALO
BUGABOO
BUGALOO
BURRITO
BUSHIDO
CUIBONO
CURACAO
CUTINTO
DURANGO
GUANACO
LUCIANO
LUMBAGO
MURILLO
PUTITTO
RUNINTO
SUBZERO
SUKARNO
SUPREMO
TURNSTO

••U•O••
AQUEOUS
BOUDOIR
COULOMB
COUPONS
FOULOUT
GLUCOSE
HAULOFF
MAUROIS
MOUTONS
NEURONE
NEURONS
POUROUT
RAUCOUS
SHUTOFF
SHUTOUT
SPUMONE
SPUMONI
SPUNOFF
SPUNOUT
STUPORS
TEUTONS
YAUPONS

••U••O•
BLUEBOY
BLUEFOX
BOURBON
BOUTROS
CAUTION
COUNTON
ECUADOR
ELUTION
EQUATOR
EQUINOX
FLUMMOX
GAUCHOS
GLUEDON
GLUTTON
GRUNION
HAUTBOY
HOUSTON
MOUFLON
NEUTRON
PEUGEOT
PRUDHOE
REUNION
ROUNDON
SOUPCON
SPURSON
SQUALOR
STUCCOS
STUDIOS
TOUCHON
YOUKNOW

••U•••O
BOUNDTO
CRUZADO
DEUTERO
SQUANTO
STUCKTO
TOURACO

•••UO••
ARDUOUS
FATUOUS
LIQUORS
NOCUOUS
PEQUOTS
SEQUOIA
SINUOUS
TENUOUS
UNQUOTE
VACUOLE
VACUOUS

•••U•O•
ACTUPON
AUDUBON
BLOUSON
CROUTON
ESCUDOS
GODUNOV
PUTUPON
SETUPON
ZEBULON

•••U••O
ADDUPTO
CLAUDIO
COLUMBO
GROUCHO
HHMUNRO
LEDUPTO
SAGUARO
VAQUERO

••••UO•
LANGUOR

••••U•O
VERDUGO

•••••UO
INVACUO

UP•••••
UPATREE
UPBEATS
UPBORNE
UPBRAID
UPCLOSE
UPDATED
UPDATES
UPDRAFT
UPENDED
UPFRONT
UPGRADE
UPHOLDS
UPLANDS
UPLIFTS
UPLINKS
UPLOADS
UPPSALA
UPRAISE
UPRIGHT
UPRISEN
UPRISES
UPRIVER
UPROARS
UPROOTS
UPSCALE
UPSHOTS
UPSILON
UPSTAGE
UPSTART
UPSTATE
UPSURGE
UPSWEEP
UPSWEPT
UPSWING
UPTAKES
UPTEMPO
UPTICKS
UPTIGHT
UPTONOW
UPTOPAR
UPTURNS
UPWARDS

U•P••••
UMPIRED
UMPIRES
UMPTEEN
UNPACKS
UNPAVED
UNPILED
UNPILES
UNPLUGS
UPPSALA

U••P•••
UNIPODS
UNSPENT
USOPENS
UTOPIAN
UTOPIAS

U•••P••
UNHAPPY
UNTAPED
UPTOPAR
USURPED
USURPER

U••••P•
UNDRAPE
UNHAPPY
UNKEMPT
UNSNAPS
UNSTOPS
UNSWEPT
UNTRAPS
UNWRAPS
UPSWEPT
UPTEMPO

U•••••P
UNCLASP
UNSTRAP
UPSWEEP
USINGUP

•UP••••
CUPCAKE
CUPFULS
CUPOLAS
CUPPING
EUPHONY
GUPPIES
JUPITER
LUPINES
MUPPETS
NUPTIAL
PUPPETS
PUPPIES
PUPTENT
RUPIAHS
RUPTURE
SUPPERS
SUPPING
SUPPLER
SUPPORT
SUPPOSE
SUPREME
SUPREMO
TUPELOS
YUPPIES

•U•P•••
AUSPICE
BUMPERS
BUMPIER
BUMPING
BUMPKIN
BUMPSUP
BURPGUN
BURPING
CULPRIT
CUPPING
CUSPIDS
DUMPIER
DUMPING
GULPING
GUNPLAY
GUPPIES
JUMPCUT
JUMPERS
JUMPIER
JUMPING
JUMPOFF
JUMPSAT
JUMPSIN
JUMPSON
JUMPSUP
LUMPERS
LUMPIER
LUMPING
LUMPSUM
MUDPACK
MUDPIES
MUPPETS
MURPHEY
OUTPACE
OUTPLAY
OUTPOST
OUTPUTS
PULPITS
PUMPERS
PUMPING
PUMPKIN
PUMPSUP
PUPPETS
PUPPIES
PURPLED
PURPLES
PURPORT
PURPOSE
QUIPPED
QUIPPER
RUMPLED
RUMPLES
RUMPOLE
SUBPLOT
SULPHUR
SUPPERS
SUPPING
SUPPLER
SUPPORT
SUPPOSE
SURPASS
SURPLUS
SUSPECT
SUSPEND
VULPINE
YUPPIES

•U••P••
BULLPEN
BUSHPIG
DUCKPIN
DUSTPAN
FUSSPOT
GUELPHS
GUIMPES
JUNIPER
PUSHPIN
PUTUPON
QUIPPED
QUIPPER
SUNSPOT

•U•••P•
BURLAPS
DUSTUPS
EUTERPE
HUBCAPS
PULLUPS
PUSHUPS
RUDOLPH
RUNLAPS
TUNEUPS
TURNIPS

•U••••P
BUCKSUP
BUDDYUP
BUILDUP
BUILTUP
BUMPSUP
BUOYSUP
BURNSUP
BURNTUP
BUSSTOP
CURLSUP
DUDEDUP
DUMMYUP
DUSTMOP
GUMDROP
GUSSYUP
JUICEUP
JUMPSUP
MUCKSUP
MUGWUMP
OUTCROP
OUTJUMP
OUTSTEP
PULLSUP
PUMPSUP
PUNCHUP
QUEUEUP
RUNDEEP
SUITSUP
SUNLAMP
TUNEDUP
TUNESUP
TURNSUP

••UP•••
COUPLED
COUPLES
COUPLET
COUPONS
DAUPHIN
ERUPTED
EXUPERY
PAUPERS
REUPPED
SCUPPER
SOUPCON
SOUPIER
SOUPSUP
STUPEFY
STUPORS
TOUPEES
WHUPPED
YAUPONS

••U•P••
CLUMPED
CRUMPET
CRUMPLE
CRUMPLY
FAUXPAS
GRUMPED
PLUMPED
PLUMPER
REUPPED
SCULPTS
SCUPPER
SLUMPED
SLURPED
STUMPED
STUMPER
THUMPED
THUMPER
TRUMPED
TRUMPET
TRUMPUP
USURPED
USURPER
WHUPPED

••U••P•
FOULUPS

••U•••P
BOUNDUP
BRUSHUP
COUGHUP
DRUMSUP
FOULSUP
FOULTIP
HAULSUP
LOUSEUP
ROUGHUP
ROUNDUP
SHUTSUP
SOUPSUP
STUCKUP
TOUCHUP
TRUMPUP
WOUNDUP

•••UP••
ACTUPON
ADDUPTO
GROUPED
GROUPER
GROUPIE
IRRUPTS
LEDUPTO
OCTUPLE
PUTUPON
SCRUPLE
SETUPON
TROUPER
TROUPES

•••U•P•
GALUMPH
TRIUMPH

•••U••P
QUEUEUP
SCRUBUP

••••UP•
BACKUPS
BLOWUPS
CHINUPS
CORRUPT
DISRUPT
DUSTUPS
EGGCUPS
EYECUPS
FILLUPS
FLIPUPS
FOLDUPS
FOULUPS
GIVEUPS
GOOFUPS
HANGUPS
HICCUPS
HOLDUPS
HOOKUPS
KICKUPS
LARRUPS
LASHUPS
LINEUPS
LINKUPS
LOCKUPS
LOOKUPS
MAKEUPS
MARKUPS
MOCKUPS
PICKUPS
PILEUPS
PULLUPS
PUSHUPS
RECOUPS
SENDUPS
SLIPUPS
STEPUPS
TEACUPS
TOSSUPS
TUNEUPS
WALKUPS
WARMUPS
WINDUPS
WORKUPS
WRAPUPS

••••U•P
AIRPUMP
GASPUMP
MUGWUMP
NOTRUMP
OUTJUMP
SKIJUMP

•••••UP
ACTEDUP
ADDEDUP
ANTEDUP
ANTESUP
BACKSUP
BALLSUP
BANGSUP
BEADSUP
BEAMSUP
BEARSUP
BEATSUP
BEEFSUP
BELLYUP
BINDSUP
BLOWNUP
BLOWSUP
BONEDUP
BONESUP
BOOSTUP
BOOTSUP
BORNEUP
BOUNDUP
BOXEDUP
BOXESUP
BRACEUP
BREAKUP
BRINGUP
BROKEUP
BRUSHUP
BUCKSUP
BUDDYUP
BUILDUP
BUILTUP
BUMPSUP
BUOYSUP
BURNSUP
BURNTUP
CALLSUP
CATCHUP
CHALKUP
CHATSUP
CHECKUP
CHEERUP
CHEWSUP
CHOKEUP
CLAMSUP
CLEANUP
CLEARUP
CLOGSUP
CLOSEUP
COILSUP
COMESUP
COOKSUP
COOPSUP
COUGHUP
COVERUP
CRACKUP
CRANKUP
CREEPUP
CROPSUP
CROSSUP
CURLSUP
DOINGUP
DOLLSUP
DRAWNUP
DRAWSUP
DREAMUP
DRESSUP
DRIEDUP
DRIESUP
DRIVEUP
DRUMSUP
DUDEDUP
DUMMYUP
EASEDUP
EASESUP
EATENUP
EVENSUP
FAIRSUP
FILLSUP
FIREDUP
FIRESUP
FIRMSUP
FIXEDUP
FIXESUP
FLAREUP
FOLDSUP
FOULSUP
FRAMEUP
GANGSUP
GEARSUP
GIDDYUP
GIVESUP
GOINGUP
GOOFSUP
GROWNUP
GROWSUP
GUSSYUP
HAMITUP
HANDSUP
HANGSUP
HAULSUP
HEADSUP
HEATSUP
HOLDSUP
HOLEDUP
HOLESUP
HOOKSUP
HYPEDUP
INGROUP
JACKSUP
JOINSUP
JUICEUP
JUMPSUP
KEEPSUP
KETCHUP
KEYEDUP
KICKSUP
LACEDUP
LACESUP
LEADSUP
LIFTSUP
LIGHTUP
LINEDUP
LINESUP
LOCKSUP
LOOKSUP
LOUSEUP
MAKESUP
MARKSUP
MATCHUP
MIXEDUP
MIXESUP
MIXITUP
MUCKSUP
OPENSUP
OWNEDUP
PACKSUP
PAIRSUP
PASTEUP
PATCHUP
PEASOUP
PERKSUP
PICKSUP
PILEDUP
PILESUP
PIPEDUP
PIPESUP
PLAYSUP
PROPSUP
PSYCHUP
PULLSUP
PUMPSUP
PUNCHUP
QUEUEUP
RACKSUP
RAISEUP
RAKEDUP
RAKESUP
REARSUP
REGROUP
RESTSUP
RINGSUP
ROLLSUP
ROUGHUP
ROUNDUP
SAVEDUP
SAVESUP
SCAREUP
SCREWUP
SCRUBUP
SEALSUP
SENDSUP
SERVEUP
SEVENUP
SEWEDUP
SHAKEUP
SHAPEUP
SHOOKUP
SHOOTUP
SHOWSUP
SHUTSUP
SIGNSUP
SIZEDUP
SIZESUP
SLIPSUP
SLOWSUP
SMASHUP
SNAPSUP
SOAKSUP
SOUPSUP
SPEAKUP
SPEEDUP
SPICEUP
SPLITUP
SPOKEUP
STACKUP
STANDUP
STARTUP
STAYSUP
STEPSUP
STICKUP
STIRRUP
STIRSUP
STOCKUP
STOODUP

STOPSUP
STOREUP
STUCKUP
SUITSUP
SWEEPUP
SWELLUP
SWEPTUP
TAKESUP
TALKSUP
TALLYUP
TANKSUP
TEAMSUP
TEARSUP
TENSEUP
THINKUP
TIMESUP
TONEDUP
TONESUP
TOOLSUP
TOUCHUP
TRADEUP
TRIPSUP
TRUMPUP
TUNEDUP
TUNESUP
TURNSUP
TYINGUP
TYPEDUP
TYPESUP
USINGUP
WAITSUP
WAKESUP
WALLSUP
WARMSUP
WELLSUP
WHIPSUP
WICKIUP
WINDSUP
WIPEDUP
WIPESUP
WISEDUP
WISESUP
WOKENUP
WORKSUP
WOUNDUP
WRAPSUP
WRITEUP
WROTEUP

U•Q••••
UNQUOTE

U••Q•••
UNEQUAL

•U•Q•••
KUMQUAT

•U••Q••
DUBUQUE
QUINQUE

••UQ•••
BOUQUET

••U•Q••
BRUSQUE

•••UQ••
DUBUQUE

UR•••••
URANITE
URANIUM
URBANER
URCHINS
URGENCY
URTEXTS
URUGUAY

U•R••••
UKRAINE
UNRATED
UNRAVEL
UNREADY
UNREELS
UNROBED
UNROBES
UNROLLS
UPRAISE
UPRIGHT
UPRISEN
UPRISES
UPRIVER
UPROARS
UPROOTS
UTRECHT
UTRILLO

U••R•••
UMBRAGE
UMBRIAN
UNARMED
UNCRATE
UNDRAPE
UNDRAWN
UNDRESS
UNFROCK
UNTRAPS
UNTRIED
UNTRUTH
UNWRAPS
UPBRAID
UPDRAFT
UPFRONT
UPGRADE
USURERS
USURPED
USURPER
UXORIAL

U•••R••
UMBERTO
UMPIRED
UMPIRES
UNAIRED
UNCORKS
UNCURLS
UNDERGO
UNEARTH
UNFURLS
UNGIRDS
UNHORSE
UNNERVE
UNSCREW
UNSTRAP
UPATREE
UPBORNE
UPSURGE
UPTURNS
UPWARDS
USHERED
UTTERED
UTTERER
UTTERLY

U••••R•
ULSTERS
UNAWARE
UNHEARD
UNICORN
UNIFORM
UNITARY
UNITERS
UNLEARN
UNSHORN
UNSNARL
UPROARS
UPSTART
USURERS

U•••••R
UNCLEAR
UNCOVER
UNIFIER
UNWISER
UPRIVER
UPTOPAR
URBANER
USURPER
UTTERER

•UR••••
AURALEE
AURALLY
AUREATE
AUREOLA
AUREOLE
AURICLE
AUROCHS
AURORAE
AURORAL
AURORAS
BURBANK
BURBLED
BURBLES
BURBOTS
BURDENS
BURDOCK
BUREAUS
BURETTE
BURGEES
BURGEON
BURGERS
BURGESS
BURGHER
BURGLAR
BURGLED
BURGLES
BURGOOS
BURKINA
BURLAPS
BURLIER
BURLING
BURMESE
BURNERS
BURNETT
BURNING
BURNISH
BURNOUT
BURNSUP
BURNTUP
BUROAKS
BURPGUN
BURPING
BURRITO
BURROWS
BURSARS
BURSTYN
BURYING
CURACAO
CURATES
CURATOR
CURBCUT
CURBING
CURDING
CURDLED
CURDLES
CUREALL
CURFEWS
CURIOUS
CURLERS
CURLEWS
CURLIER
CURLING
CURLSUP
CURRANT
CURRENT
CURRIED
CURRIER
CURRIES
CURSING
CURSIVE
CURSORS
CURSORY
CURTAIL
CURTAIN
CURTEST
CURTSEY
CURVETS
CURVIER
CURVING
DURABLE
DURABLY
DURANCE
DURANGO
DURANTE
DURRELL
EURASIA
FURBALL
FURBISH
FURIOUS
FURLING
FURLONG
FURNACE
FURNISH
FURORES
FURRIER
FURRING
FURROWS
FURSEAL
FURTHER
FURTIVE
GURGLED
GURGLES
GURKHAS
GURNEYS
HURDLED
HURDLER
HURDLES
HURLERS
HURLING
HURRAHS
HURRIED
HURRIES
HURTFUL
HURTING
HURTLED
HURTLES
JURIDIC
JURISTS
JURYING
JURYRIG
KURDISH
LURCHED
LURCHES
LURIDLY
LURKING
MURDERS
MURDOCH
MURILLO
MURKIER
MURKILY
MURMURS
MURPHEY
NUREYEV
NURSERS
NURSERY
NURSING
NURTURE
OURSELF
OURTOWN
PURCELL
PURDAHS
PURFLED
PURFLES
PURGING
PURISTS
PURITAN
PURLIEU
PURLING
PURLINS
PURLOIN
PURPLED
PURPLES
PURPORT
PURPOSE
PURRERS
PURRING
PURSERS
PURSING
PURSUED
PURSUER
PURSUES
PURSUIT
PURVEYS
PURVIEW
SURCOAT
SURFACE
SURFEIT
SURFERS
SURFING
SURGEON
SURGERY
SURGING
SURINAM
SURLIER
SURLILY
SURMISE
SURNAME
SURPASS
SURPLUS
SURREAL
SURREYS
SURVEYS
SURVIVE
TURBANS
TURBINE
TURBOTS
TUREENS
TURKEYS
TURKISH
TURMOIL
TURNERS
TURNING
TURNIPS
TURNKEY
TURNOFF
TURNOUT
TURNSIN
TURNSON
TURNSTO
TURNSUP
TURRETS
TURTLED
TURTLES

•U•R•••
BULRUSH
BURRITO
BURROWS
CUIRASS
CURRANT
CURRENT
CURRIED
CURRIER
CURRIES
CUTRATE
DURRELL
FURRIER
FURRING
FURROWS
GUARANI
GUARDED
GUARGUM
HURRAHS
HURRIED
HURRIES
KUBRICK
NUTRIAS
OUTRACE
OUTRAGE
OUTRANK
OUTRUNS
PUERILE
PUGREES
PURRERS
PURRING
QUARREL
QUARTER
QUARTET
QUARTOS
QUERIED
QUERIES
QUORUMS
RUBRICS
RUNRIOT
SUBROSA
SUCRASE
SUCROSE
SUNRAYS
SUNRISE
SUNROOF
SUNROOM
SUPREME
SUPREMO
SURREAL
SURREYS
TUAREGS
TURRETS

•U••R••
AUBURNS
AUGURAL
AUGURED
AURORAE
AURORAL
AURORAS
AUSTRAL
AUSTRIA
BUCKRAM
BULLRUN
CULPRIT
DUBARRY
EUCHRED
EUCHRES
EUTERPE
FUELROD
FULCRUM
FURORES
FUTURES
GUMDROP
GUMTREE
GUTHRIE
HUMDRUM
HUMERAL
HUMERUS
HUMORED
HUNDRED
JURYRIG
LUCERNE
LUSTRED
LUSTRES
MUBARAK
MUSKRAT
NUMERAL
NUMERIC
OUTCROP
OUTDRAW
OUTDREW
OUTGREW
OUTGROW
PUBERTY
QUARREL
QUEERED
QUEERER
QUEERLY
RUMORED
SUBORNS
SUBURBS
SUGARED
SUKARNO
SUTURED
SUTURES
TUMBREL
TUNDRAS
TUTORED

•U•••R•
AUSTERE
AUTEURS
AUTHORS
BUFFERS
BUGLERS
BULGARS
BULWARK
BUMMERS
BUMPERS
BUNKERS
BURGERS
BURNERS
BURSARS
BUSFARE
BUSTARD
BUTLERS
BUTTERS
BUTTERY
BUZZARD
BUZZERS
CUECARD
CULEBRA
CULTURE
CULVERT
CURLERS
CURSORS
CURSORY
CUSTARD
CUTLERS
CUTLERY
CUTTERS
DUBARRY
DUBBERS
DUELERS
DUFFERS
DULLARD
DUNKERS
DUNKIRK
DUSTERS
FUELERS
GUEVARA
GUITARS
GUNFIRE
GUNNERS
GUNNERY
GUSHERS
GUTTERS
HUBBARD
HUGGERS
HULLERS
HUMMERS
HUMOURS
HUNGARY
HUNGERS
HUNKERS
HUNTERS
HURLERS
HUSKERS
HUSSARS
JUDDERS
JUICERS
JUMPERS
JUNIORS
JUNKART
JUNKERS
LUBBERS
LUGGERS
LUMBARS
LUMBERS
LUMIERE
LUMPERS
LUNKERS
LUSTERS
MUDDERS
MUGGERS
MULLERS
MUMFORD
MUMMERS
MUMMERY
MURDERS
MURMURS
MUSHERS
MUSTARD
MUSTERS
MUTTERS
NUDGERS
NUMBERS
NUNNERY
NURSERS
NURSERY
NURTURE
NUTTERS
OUSTERS
OUTWARD
OUTWORE
OUTWORK
OUTWORN
PUCKERS
PUFFERS
PUFFERY
PULSARS
PUMPERS
PUNTERS
PURPORT
PURRERS
PURSERS
PUTTERS
QUAKERS
QUASARS
QUAVERS
QUAVERY
QUEUERS
QUIVERS
QUOTERS
RUBBERS
RUBBERY
RUDDERS
RUDYARD
RUINERS
RUMOURS
RUNNERS
RUNSDRY
RUPTURE
RUSHERS
RUTGERS
SUBVERT
SUBZERO
SUCCORS
SUCKERS
SUDBURY
SUFFERS
SUITORS
SULKERS
SUMATRA
SUMMARY
SUMMERS
SUMMERY
SUNBURN
SUNDERS
SUPPERS
SUPPORT
SURFERS
SURGERY
SUTLERS
TUCKERS
TUGGERS
TURNERS
TUSKERS
VULTURE

•U••••R
AUDITOR
BUCKLER
BUGBEAR
BUGGIER
BUILDER
BULGHUR
BULKIER
BUMBLER
BUMPIER
BUNGLER
BURGHER
BURGLAR
BURLIER
BUSHIER
BUTCHER
CURATOR
CURLIER
CURRIER
CURVIER
CUSHIER
CUSSLER
DUCKIER
DUMPIER
DUSKIER
DUSTIER
FUMBLER
FUNFAIR
FUNKIER
FUNNIER
FURRIER
FURTHER
FUSSIER
FUSTIER
FUZZIER
GUESSER
GUILDER
GUMMIER
GUNKIER
GUNSFOR
GUNTHER
GUSHIER
GUTSIER
GUZZLER
HUFFIER
HUMBLER
HUMIDOR
HURDLER
HUSKIER
HUSTLER
JUGGLER
JUGULAR
JUICIER
JUMPIER
JUNIPER
JUNKIER
JUPITER
LUCIFER
LUCKIER
LUMPIER
LUNCHER
LUSTIER
MUAMMAR
MUDDIER
MUDDLER
MUFFLER
MUGGIER
MUMBLER
MUNCHER
MURKIER
MUSHIER
MUSTIER
MUZZIER
NUBBIER
NUCLEAR
NUTTIER
NUZZLER
OUTDOOR
OUTWEAR
PUDGIER
PUFFIER
PUNCHER
PUNSTER
PURSUER
PUSHIER
PUTOVER
PUZZLER
QUAFFER
QUARTER
QUEERER
QUICKER
QUIETER
QUILTER
QUIPPER
QUITTER
RUDDIER
RUMMIER
RUNNIER
RUNOVER
RUNTIER
RUSTIER
RUSTLER
SUBDUER
SUBTLER
SUCCOUR
SUDSIER
SULKIER
SULPHUR
SUNNIER
SUPPLER
SURLIER
SUTTNER
TUBBIER
TUBULAR
TUMBLER
TUTELAR
YUCKIER
YUMMIER

••UR•••
AZURITE
BLURRED
BLURTED
BOURBON
BOURREE
CHURNED
COURAGE
COURANT
COURIER
COURSED
COURSER
COURSES
COURTED
COURTLY
DHURRIE
DIURNAL
DOUREST
ENURING
EXURBAN
EXURBIA
FOURIER
FOURTHS
GOURAMI
GOURDES
GOURMET
INURING
JOURDAN
JOURNAL
JOURNEY
KNURLED
LAURELS
LAURENT
LOURDES
LOUREED
MAUREEN
MAURICE
MAUROIS
NEURONE
NEURONS
NOURISH
PLURALS
POURERS
POURING
POUROUT
POURSIN
SAURIAN
SCURVES
SLURPED
SLURRED
SOURCED
SOURCES
SOUREST
SOURING
SOURISH
SPURNED
SPURNER
SPURRED
SPURSON
SPURTED
STURGES
TAURINE
THURBER
THURMAN
TOURACO
TOURERS
TOURING
TOURISM
TOURIST
TOURNEY
USURERS
USURPED
USURPER

••U•R••
AQUARIA
BLURRED
BOURREE
BOUTROS
DHURRIE
EQUERRY
LAUTREC
LOUVRES
NEUTRAL
NEUTRON
OEUVRES
SLURRED
SPURRED
SQUARED
SQUARER
SQUARES
SQUIRED
SQUIRES
SQUIRMS
SQUIRMY
SQUIRTS

••U••R•
ABUSERS
COUGARS
COUNTRY
COUTURE
DAUBERS
DEUTERO
EQUERRY
EXUPERY
FOULARD
FOUNDRY
GAUGERS
GOUGERS
GRUYERE
HAUBERK
HAULERS
LAUNDRY
LOUVERS
MOUSERS
PAUPERS
POULTRY
POURERS
POUTERS
PRUDERY
PRUNERS
REUTERS
RHUBARB
ROUTERS
SAUCERS
SHUBERT
STUPORS
TOURERS
TOUTERS
USURERS

••U•••R
ABUBAKR
ALUNSER
AQUIFER
AQUIVER
ASUNDER
BLUBBER
BLUFFER
BLUNDER
BLUNTER
BLUSHER
BLUSTER
BOUDOIR
BOULDER
BOUNCER
BOUNDER
BRUISER
CAULKER
CHUKKER
CLUBCAR
CLUNKER
CLUSTER
CLUTTER
COULTER
COUNTER
COURIER
COURSER
CRUELER
CRUISER
CRULLER
CRUSHER
DAUMIER
DOUBTER
DRUCKER
DRUMMER
ECUADOR
EQUATOR
FLUSTER
FLUTTER
FNUMBER
FOUNDER
FOURIER
GAUCHER
GAUDIER
GAUNTER
GAUZIER
GLUMMER
GOUNDER
GRUFFER
HAUTEUR
JOUSTER
LAUGHER
LAUNDER
LOUNGER
LOUSIER
MAUNDER
MOULDER
MOUSIER
PLUGGER

PLUMBER
PLUMMER
PLUMPER
PLUNDER
PLUNGER
PLUSHER
POUNCER
POUNDER
POUTIER
REUTHER
ROUGHER
ROUNDER
SAUCIER
SAUNTER
SCULLER
SCUPPER
SHUCKER
SHUDDER
SHUTTER
SKULKER
SLUGGER
SLUMBER
SMUGGER
SNUFFER
SNUGGER
SOUNDER
SOUPIER
SPURNER
SPUTTER
SQUALOR
SQUARER
STUFFER
STUMPER
STUNNER
THUMPER
THUNDER
THURBER
THUSFAR
TOUGHER
TRUCKER
TRUDGER
USURPER
VAULTER
VAUNTER
VOUCHER
YOUNGER

•••UR••
ABJURED
ABJURES
ACCURST
ADJURED
ADJURES
ALLURED
ALLURES
ASSURED
ASSURES
AUBURNS
AUGURAL
AUGURED
BYTURNS
DEMURER
ENDURED
ENDURES
ENSURED
ENSURES
ETRURIA
FIGURED
FIGURER
FIGURES
FLOURED
FUTURES
IMMURED
IMMURES
IMPURER
INJURED
INJURES
INSURED
INSURES
LITURGY
MATURED
MATURER
MATURES
MAZURKA
NATURAL
NATURED
NATURES
OROURKE
PANURGE
PARURES
RESURGE
RETURNS
SAMURAI
SCOURED
SCOURER
SCOURGE
SECURED
SECURER
SECURES
SPLURGE
SUBURBS
SUTURED
SUTURES
TENURED
TENURES
UNCURLS
UNFURLS
UPSURGE
UPTURNS
YOGURTS
ZYMURGY

•••U•R•
ACQUIRE
ACTUARY
ARGUERS
DOEUVRE
EDOUARD
ESQUIRE
ESTUARY
HHMUNRO
INQUIRE
INQUIRY
ISSUERS
JAGUARS
JANUARY
LIQUORS
MCGUIRE
ONGUARD
QUEUERS
REQUIRE
ROGUERY
SAGUARO
TSQUARE
VAQUERO

•••U••R
ACCUSER
ANGULAR
ANNULAR
CHAUCER
DEMURER
DILUTER
ENDUSER
FIGURER
GROUPER
GROUSER
IMPURER
INDUCER
INSULAR
JOCULAR
JUGULAR
LIQUEUR
MATURER
MODULAR
NEBULAR
NODULAR
NONUSER
OBTUSER
PERUSER
POPULAR
PROUDER
REDUCER
REFUSER
REFUTER
REGULAR
SCOURER
SCOUTER
SECULAR
SECURER
SEDUCER
SHOUTER
SPOUTER
SPRUCER
STOUTER
TABULAR
TITULAR
TROUPER
TROUSER
TUBULAR

••••UR•
ADJOURN
ARBOURS
ARDOURS
ARMOURS
ASHBURY
ATATURK
AUTEURS
BRAVURA
CADBURY
CAESURA
CAPTURE
CENSURE
CENTURY
CLIBURN
CLOSURE
CLOTURE
COGBURN
COLOURS
CONCURS
CONJURE
COUTURE
CULTURE
DENTURE
DETOURS
DEVOURS
DISTURB
EPICURE
ERASURE
FAILURE
FAVOURS
FEATURE
FISSURE
FIXTURE
FORSURE
GESTURE
GRAVURE
HAMBURG
HEPBURN
HOMBURG
HONOURS
HUMOURS
LABOURS
LANGURS
LECTURE
LEISURE
MAJEURE
MEASURE
MERCURY
MIXTURE
MURMURS
NETSURF
NOCTURN
NOTSURE
NURTURE
OBSCURE
PASTURE
PERJURE
PERJURY
PERTURB
PICTURE
PINCURL
POSEURS
POSTURE
PROCURE
RAPTURE
RAYBURN
RIGOURS
RUMOURS
RUPTURE
SAVOURS
SAVOURY
SOJOURN
STATURE
SUDBURY
SUNBURN
TEMPURA
TEXTURE
TONSURE
VALOURS
VAPOURS
VELOURS
VENTURA
VENTURE
VERDURE
VESTURE
VIGOURS
VULTURE
YOGHURT

••••U•R
CHEQUER
CONQUER
LACQUER
LANGUOR
LEAGUER
NIEBUHR
PURSUER
RESCUER
SUBDUER

•••••UR
AMATEUR
BALFOUR
BONJOUR
BULGHUR
CANDOUR
CENTAUR
CONTOUR
DANSEUR
ENAMOUR
FAKEFUR
FERVOUR
FLANEUR
FLAVOUR
GLAMOUR
HARBOUR
HAUTEUR
HOTSPUR
LIQUEUR
MANHOUR
MASSEUR
OFFHOUR
PARLOUR
PASTEUR
PAVIOUR
RANCOUR
REOCCUR
SEYMOUR
SUCCOUR
SULPHUR
TAMBOUR
TENFOUR
VANOCUR

US•••••
USEABLE
USELESS
USHERED
USINGUP
USOPENS
USOSHOW
USSTEEL
USTINOV
USUALLY
USURERS
USURPED
USURPER

U•S••••
ULSTERS
UNSATED
UNSCREW
UNSEALS
UNSEATS
UNSEWED
UNSHORN
UNSNAGS
UNSNAPS
UNSNARL
UNSOUND
UNSPENT
UNSTACK
UNSTICK
UNSTOPS
UNSTRAP
UNSTUCK
UNSWEPT
UPSCALE
UPSHOTS
UPSILON
UPSTAGE
UPSTART
UPSTATE
UPSURGE
UPSWEEP
UPSWEPT
UPSWING
USSTEEL

U••S•••
ULYSSES
UNASKED
UNISONS
UNUSUAL
UPPSALA
USOSHOW

U•••S••
ULYSSES
UNCASED
UNCASES
UNMASKS
UNWISER
UPRISEN
UPRISES
UTENSIL

U••••S•
UGLIEST
UNBLEST
UNCLASP
UNCLOSE
UNDRESS
UNHORSE
UNLEASH
UNLOOSE
UNTWIST
UPCLOSE
UPRAISE
USELESS

U•••••S
ULSTERS
ULYSSES
UMLAUTS
UMPIRES
UNBENDS
UNBINDS
UNBOLTS
UNBOXES
UNCAGES
UNCASES
UNCIALS
UNCLOGS
UNCOILS
UNCORKS
UNCURLS
UNDRESS
UNFOLDS
UNFURLS
UNGIRDS
UNHANDS
UNHOOKS
UNIFIES
UNIPODS
UNISONS
UNITERS
UNITIES
UNKINKS
UNKNITS
UNKNOTS
UNLACES
UNLADES
UNLINKS
UNLOADS
UNLOCKS
UNMAKES
UNMASKS
UNPACKS
UNPILES
UNPLUGS
UNREELS
UNROBES
UNROLLS
UNSEALS
UNSEATS
UNSNAGS
UNSNAPS
UNSTOPS
UNTACKS
UNTRAPS
UNTUNES
UNVEILS
UNWINDS
UNWRAPS
UNYOKES
UPBEATS
UPDATES
UPHOLDS
UPLANDS
UPLIFTS
UPLINKS
UPLOADS
UPRISES
UPROARS
UPROOTS
UPSHOTS
UPTAKES
UPTICKS
UPTURNS
UPWARDS
URCHINS
URTEXTS
USELESS
USOPENS
USURERS
UTAHANS
UTOPIAS

•US••••
AUSPICE
AUSSIES
AUSTERE
AUSTRAL
AUSTRIA
BUSBIES
BUSBOYS
BUSFARE
BUSHELS
BUSHHOG
BUSHIDO
BUSHIER
BUSHING
BUSHMAN
BUSHMEN
BUSHPIG
BUSIEST
BUSKINS
BUSLINE
BUSSING
BUSSTOP
BUSTARD
BUSTING
BUSTLED
BUSTLES
BUSTOUT
BUSYING
CUSHAWS
CUSHIER
CUSHION
CUSPIDS
CUSSING
CUSSLER
CUSTARD
CUSTODY
CUSTOMS
DUSKIER
DUSTERS
DUSTIER
DUSTING
DUSTMOP
DUSTOFF
DUSTPAN
DUSTUPS
FUSSIER
FUSSILY
FUSSING
FUSSPOT
FUSTIAN
FUSTICS
FUSTIER
FUSTILY
GUSHERS
GUSHIER
GUSHING
GUSSETS
GUSSIED
GUSSIES
GUSSYUP
GUSTAVE
GUSTILY
GUSTING
GUSTOES
HUSBAND
HUSHABY
HUSHING
HUSKERS
HUSKIER
HUSKIES
HUSKILY
HUSKING
HUSSARS
HUSSEIN
HUSSIES
HUSTLED
HUSTLER
HUSTLES
JUSTICE
JUSTIFY
JUSTINE
JUSTNOW
LUSHEST
LUSTERS
LUSTFUL
LUSTIER
LUSTILY
LUSTING
LUSTRED
LUSTRES
MUSCATS
MUSCLED
MUSCLES
MUSCOVY
MUSETTE
MUSEUMS
MUSHERS
MUSHIER
MUSHILY
MUSHING
MUSICAL
MUSKETS
MUSKRAT
MUSLIMS
MUSLINS
MUSSELS
MUSSING
MUSTAFA
MUSTANG
MUSTARD
MUSTERS
MUSTIER
MUSTILY
MUSTSEE
OUSTERS
OUSTING
PUSHIER
PUSHILY
PUSHING
PUSHKIN
PUSHOFF
PUSHPIN
PUSHUPS
RUSHDIE
RUSHEES
RUSHERS
RUSHING
RUSHOFF
RUSSELL
RUSSETS
RUSSIAN
RUSTICS
RUSTIER
RUSTILY
RUSTING
RUSTLED
RUSTLER
RUSTLES
SUSANNA
SUSANNE
SUSLIKS
SUSPECT
SUSPEND
SUSSING
SUSTAIN
TUSCANY
TUSKERS
TUSSAUD
TUSSLED
TUSSLES
TUSSOCK

•U•S•••
AUSSIES
BUGSOFF
BUGSOUT
BUMSOUT
BURSARS
BURSTYN
BUSSING
BUSSTOP
BUYSOFF
BUYSOUT
CUISINE
CURSING
CURSIVE
CURSORS
CURSORY
CUSSING
CUSSLER
CUTSOFF
CUTSOUT
FULSOME
FURSEAL
FUSSIER
FUSSILY
FUSSING
FUSSPOT
GUESSED
GUESSER
GUESSES
GUESTED
GUMSHOE
GUNSFOR
GUNSHOT
GUSSETS
GUSSIED
GUSSIES
GUSSYUP
GUTSIER
GUTSILY
HUSSARS
HUSSEIN
HUSSIES
MUGSHOT
MUSSELS
MUSSING
NURSERS
NURSERY
NURSING
OURSELF
OUTSELL
OUTSETS
OUTSIDE
OUTSIZE
OUTSOLD
OUTSTEP
PULSARS
PULSATE
PULSING
PUNSTER
PURSERS
PURSING
PURSUED
PURSUER
PURSUES
PURSUIT
PUTSOFF
PUTSOUT
QUASARS
QUASHED
QUASHES
QUESTED
RUBSOUT
RUNSDRY
RUNSOFF
RUNSOUT
RUSSELL
RUSSETS
RUSSIAN
SUASION
SUBSETS
SUBSIDE
SUBSIDY
SUBSIST
SUBSOIL
SUBSUME
SUDSIER
SUDSING
SUNSETS
SUNSPOT
SUSSING
TUESDAY
TULSANS
TUSSAUD
TUSSLED
TUSSLES
TUSSOCK

•U••S••
AUGUSTA
AUGUSTE
BUCKSAW
BUCKSUP
BUMPSUP
BUOYSUP
BURNSUP
BUTTSIN
BUZZSAW
CUBISTS
CURLSUP
CURTSEY
EURASIA
FUCHSIA
GUESSED
GUESSER
GUESSES
JUMPSAT
JUMPSIN
JUMPSON
JUMPSUP
JURISTS
LUMPSUM
LUTISTS
MUCKSUP
MUMESON
MUSTSEE
NUDISTS
PULASKI
PULLSUP
PUMPSUP
PURISTS
QUONSET
RULESON
SUCKSIN
SUITSUP
SULUSEA
TUBISTS
TUCKSIN
TUNESIN
TUNESUP
TUNISIA
TURNSIN
TURNSON
TURNSTO
TURNSUP

•U•••S•
BULLISH
BULRUSH
BURGESS
BURMESE
BURNISH
BUSIEST
CUIRASS
CULTISH
CULTISM
CULTIST
CURTEST
CUTLASS
DUCHESS
DUELIST
DULLEST
DULLISH
DUMBEST
FUJITSU
FULLEST
FUNFEST
FURBISH
FURNISH
GUTLESS
JUDAISM
JUDOIST
JUJITSU
KURDISH
LUSHEST
NUMBEST
OUTCAST
OUTLAST
OUTPOST
PUBLISH
PUCKISH
PUGNOSE
PUNIEST
PURPOSE
RUBBISH
SUAVEST
SUBROSA
SUBSIST
SUCCESS
SUCRASE
SUCROSE
SUFFUSE
SUGGEST
SUNFISH
SUNKIST
SUNLESS
SUNRISE
SUPPOSE
SURMISE
SURPASS
TUBAIST
TURKISH

•U••••S
AUBADES
AUBURNS
AUGENDS
AUKLETS
AUNTIES
AUROCHS
AURORAS
AUSSIES
AUTEURS
AUTHORS
AUTUMNS
BUBBLES
BUCKETS
BUCKLES
BUCKOES
BUDDHAS
BUDDIES
BUDGETS
BUDGIES
BUFFERS
BUFFETS
BUGGIES
BUGLERS
BULBOUS
BULBULS
BULGARS
BULLETS
BULLIES
BUMBLES
BUMMERS
BUMPERS
BUNCHES
BUNDLES
BUNGEES
BUNGLES
BUNIONS
BUNKERS
BUNNIES
BURBLES
BURBOTS
BURDENS
BUREAUS
BURGEES
BURGERS
BURGESS
BURGLES
BURGOOS
BURLAPS
BURNERS
BUROAKS
BURROWS
BURSARS
BUSBIES
BUSBOYS
BUSHELS
BUSKINS
BUSTLES
BUTLERS
BUTTERS
BUTTONS
BUYOUTS
BUZZERS
CUBBIES
CUBISTS
CUCKOOS
CUDDLES
CUDGELS
CUIRASS
CUMULUS
CUPFULS
CUPOLAS
CURATES
CURDLES
CURFEWS
CURIOUS
CURLERS
CURLEWS
CURRIES
CURSORS
CURVETS
CUSHAWS
CUSPIDS
CUSTOMS
CUTLASS
CUTLERS
CUTLETS
CUTOFFS
CUTOUTS
CUTTERS
DUBBERS
DUBIOUS
DUCHESS
DUCHIES
DUDDIES
DUELERS
DUENNAS
DUFFELS
DUFFERS
DUGONGS
DUGOUTS
DUKAKIS
DUMDUMS
DUMMIES
DUNKERS
DUNLINS
DUSTERS
DUSTUPS
DUTEOUS
EUCHRES
EUNUCHS
FUDDLES
FUELERS
FULFILS
FUMBLES
FUNGOES
FUNNELS
FUNNIES
FURIOUS
FURORES
FURROWS
FUSTICS
FUTURES
GUELPHS

GUESSES
GUFFAWS
GUIDONS
GUIMPES
GUINEAS
GUITARS
GULCHES
GULLETS
GULLIES
GUNDOGS
GUNNELS
GUNNERS
GUNNIES
GUPPIES
GURGLES
GURKHAS
GURNEYS
GUSHERS
GUSSETS
GUSSIES
GUSTOES
GUTLESS
GUTTERS
GUZZLES
HUBBIES
HUBBUBS
HUBCAPS
HUDDLES
HUGGERS
HULLERS
HUMBLES
HUMBUGS
HUMERUS
HUMMERS
HUMOURS
HUNCHES
HUNGERS
HUNKERS
HUNTERS
HURDLES
HURLERS
HURRAHS
HURRIES
HURTLES
HUSKERS
HUSKIES
HUSSARS
HUSSIES
HUSTLES
HUTCHES
HUZZAHS
JUDDERS
JUGFULS
JUGGLES
JUICERS
JUJUBES
JUMBLES
JUMPERS
JUNCOES
JUNGLES
JUNIORS
JUNKERS
JUNKETS
JUNKIES
JURISTS
LUBBERS
LUGGERS
LUGNUTS
LUMBARS
LUMBERS
LUMPERS
LUNCHES
LUNKERS
LUPINES
LURCHES
LUSTERS
LUSTRES
LUTISTS
LUXATES
MUDDERS
MUDDIES
MUDDLES
MUDEELS
MUDHENS
MUDPIES
MUFFINS
MUFFLES
MUGGERS
MUKLUKS
MULCHES
MULETAS
MULLAHS
MULLERS
MULLETS
MUMBLES
MUMMERS
MUMMIES
MUNCHES
MUNTINS
MUPPETS
MURDERS
MURMURS
MUSCATS
MUSCLES
MUSEUMS
MUSHERS
MUSKETS
MUSLIMS
MUSLINS
MUSSELS
MUSTERS
MUTANTS
MUTATES
MUTATIS
MUTTERS
MUTTONS
MUTUALS
MUUMUUS
MUZHIKS
MUZZLES
NUANCES
NUBBINS
NUBBLES
NUBIANS
NUCLEUS
NUDGERS
NUDISTS
NUDNIKS
NUGGETS
NUMBATS
NUMBERS
NUNCIOS
NURSERS
NUTLETS
NUTMEGS
NUTRIAS
NUTTERS
NUZZLES
OUSTERS
OUTACTS
OUTAGES
OUTBIDS
OUTDOES
OUTEATS
OUTFITS
OUTGOES
OUTGUNS
OUTHITS
OUTINGS
OUTLAWS
OUTLAYS
OUTLETS
OUTPUTS
OUTRUNS
OUTSETS
OUTWITS
PUBLICS
PUCKERS
PUDDLES
PUEBLOS
PUFFERS
PUFFINS
PUGREES
PULLETS
PULLEYS
PULLONS
PULLUPS
PULPITS
PULSARS
PUMICES
PUMMELS
PUMPERS
PUNCHES
PUNDITS
PUNKAHS
PUNKIES
PUNTERS
PUPPETS
PUPPIES
PURDAHS
PURFLES
PURISTS
PURLINS
PURPLES
PURRERS
PURSERS
PURSUES
PURVEYS
PUSHUPS
PUTOUTS
PUTTEES
PUTTERS
PUTTIES
PUZZLES
QUAGGAS
QUAHOGS
QUAKERS
QUARTOS
QUASARS
QUASHES
QUAVERS
QUERIES
QUEUERS
QUICHES
QUINCES
QUINOAS
QUIVERS
QUIZZES
QUOKKAS
QUORUMS
QUOTERS
RUBBERS
RUBBLES
RUBRICS
RUDDERS
RUFFLES
RUINERS
RUINOUS
RULINGS
RUMBLES
RUMOURS
RUMPLES
RUNLAPS
RUNLETS
RUNNELS
RUNNERS
RUNOFFS
RUNWAYS
RUPIAHS
RUSHEES
RUSHERS
RUSSETS
RUSTICS
RUSTLES
RUTGERS
SUBDEBS
SUBDUES
SUBLETS
SUBMITS
SUBORNS
SUBSETS
SUBURBS
SUBWAYS
SUCCESS
SUCCORS
SUCKERS
SUFFERS
SUITORS
SULKERS
SULKIES
SULLIES
SULTANS
SUMMERS
SUMMITS
SUMMONS
SUNDAES
SUNDAYS
SUNDERS
SUNDEWS
SUNDOGS
SUNGODS
SUNLESS
SUNRAYS
SUNSETS
SUNTANS
SUPPERS
SURFERS
SURPASS
SURPLUS
SURREYS
SURVEYS
SUSLIKS
SUTLERS
SUTURES
TUAREGS
TUBISTS
TUCKERS
TUFFETS
TUGGERS
TULSANS
TUMBLES
TUMMIES
TUMULTS
TUMULUS
TUNDRAS
TUNEUPS
TUNNELS
TUNNIES
TUPELOS
TURBANS
TURBOTS
TUREENS
TURKEYS
TURNERS
TURNIPS
TURRETS
TURTLES
TUSKERS
TUSSLES
TUTTUTS
TUXEDOS
VULCANS
YUPPIES

••US•••

ABUSERS
ABUSING
ABUSIVE
AMUSING
ASUSUAL
BLUSHED
BLUSHER
BLUSHES
BLUSTER
BRUSHED
BRUSHES
BRUSHUP
BRUSQUE
CAUSING
CAUSTIC
CLUSTER
COUSINS
CRUSADE
CRUSHED
CRUSHER
CRUSHES
CRUSTED
DOUSING
ELUSIVE
FAUSTUS
FLUSHED
FLUSHES
FLUSTER
HOUSING
HOUSMAN
HOUSTON
JOUSTED
JOUSTER
LOUSEUP
LOUSIER
LOUSILY
LOUSING
MOUSERS
MOUSIER
MOUSING
MOUSSED
MOUSSES
PAUSING
PLUSHER
PLUSHES
PLUSHLY
PLUSSES
PRUSSIA
ROUSING
ROUSTED
SAUSAGE
SHUSHED
SHUSHES
SLUSHES
THUSFAR
TOUSLED
TOUSLES
TRUSSED
TRUSSES
TRUSTED
TRUSTEE
UNUSUAL

••U•S••

ALUNSER
AVULSED
AVULSES
BLUESKY
BRUISED
BRUISER
BRUISES
CLUESIN
COUNSEL
COURSED
COURSER
COURSES
CRUISED
CRUISER
CRUISES
DRUMSUP
EVULSED
EVULSES
FOULSUP
HAULSUP
MOUSSED
MOUSSES
PAULSEN
PLUGSIN
PLUSSES
POURSIN
PRUSSIA
SHUTSIN
SHUTSUP
SOUPSUP
SPURSON
SQUISHY
TRUISMS
TRUSSED
TRUSSES

••U••S•

BRUTISH
CRUDEST
DOUREST
FAUVISM
FAUVIST
FLUTIST
FOULEST
GLUCOSE
GOULASH
LOUDEST
NOURISH
OCULIST
PAULIST
PRUDISH
SOUREST
SOURISH
TAUTEST
TOURISM
TOURIST

••U•••S

ABUSERS
ALUMNUS
AMULETS
AOUDADS
AQUEOUS
AQUINAS
AVULSES
BAUBLES
BLUSHES
BOUNCES
BOUTROS
BRUISES
BRUNETS
BRUSHES
CHUKKAS
COUCHES
COUGARS
COULEES
COUPLES
COUPONS
COURSES
COUSINS
CRUISES
CRUSHES
DAUBERS
DOUBLES
DOUGLAS
DRUDGES
EQUATES
EQUINES
EVULSES
FAUCETS
FAUSTUS
FAUXPAS
FLUSHES
FOULUPS
FOURTHS
GAUCHOS
GAUDENS
GAUGERS
GOUGERS
GOURDES
GRUDGES
HAULERS
IGUANAS
JOUNCES
KLUDGES
KLUTZES
LAURELS
LOUNGES
LOURDES
LOUVERS
LOUVRES
MAUROIS
MOUSERS
MOUSSES
MOUTONS
MUUMUUS
NAUGHTS
NEURONS
NOUGATS
OEUVRES
PAUPERS
PLUNGES
PLURALS
PLUSHES
PLUSSES
POUCHES
POUNCES
POURERS
POUTERS
PRUNERS
RAUCOUS
REUBENS
REUTERS
RHUMBAS
ROUTERS
SAUCERS
SCULPTS
SCURVES
SHUSHES
SLUDGES
SLUICES
SLUSHES
SMUDGES
SOURCES
SQUALLS
SQUARES
SQUAWKS
SQUEAKS
SQUEALS
SQUINTS
SQUIRES
SQUIRMS
SQUIRTS
STUCCOS
STUDIES
STUDIOS
STUPORS
STURGES
TAUTENS
TEUTONS
TOUCANS
TOUCHES
TOUPEES
TOURERS
TOUSLES
TOUTERS
TRUANTS
TRUDGES
TRUISMS
TRUSSES
USURERS
VOUCHES
YAUPONS
YOUMANS
ZEUGMAS
ZOUAVES

•••US••

ACCUSED
ACCUSER
ACCUSES
ADJUSTS
AROUSAL
AROUSED
AROUSES
AUGUSTA
AUGUSTE
BELUSHI
BEMUSED
BEMUSES
BLOUSED
BLOUSES
BLOUSON
BOLUSES
BONUSES
CAYUSES
CLAUSES
DEBUSSY
DEFUSED
DEFUSES
DISUSED
EFFUSED
EFFUSES
ENDUSER
EXCUSED
EXCUSES
FICUSES
FOCUSED
FOCUSES
GROUSED
GROUSER
GROUSES
ILLUSED
ILLUSES
INFUSED
INFUSES
LOCUSTS
LOTUSES
MEDUSAE
MEDUSAS
MINUSES
MISUSED
MISUSES
NEXUSES
NONUSER
OBTUSER
PERUSAL
PERUSED
PERUSER
PERUSES
PIOUSLY
REBUSES
RECUSED
RECUSES
REFUSAL
REFUSED
REFUSER
REFUSES
ROBUSTA
SINUSES
SPOUSAL
SPOUSES
SULUSEA
TALUSES
THRUSTS
TROUSER
VIRUSES

•••U•S•

ACCURST
BEQUEST
DEBUSSY
DELUISE
IMPULSE
INQUEST
REPULSE
REQUEST
ROGUISH
VAGUEST
YAKUTSK

•••U••S

ABDUCTS
ABJURES
ABOUNDS
ACCUSES
ACQUITS
ADDUCES
ADDUCTS
ADJURES
ADJUSTS
AGOUTIS
ALLUDES
ALLURES
AMOUNTS
AMPULES
ANNUALS
ANNULUS
ARBUTUS
ARDUOUS
ARGUERS
AROUSES
ASSUMES
ASSURES
ATTUCKS
ATTUNES
AUBURNS
AUTUMNS
BEMUSES
BENUMBS
BLOUSES
BOLUSES
BONUSES
BYTURNS
CASUALS
CAYUGAS
CAYUSES
CLAUSES
COLUMNS
CUMULUS
DEBUNKS
DEDUCES
DEDUCTS
DEFUSES
DELUDES
DELUGES
DENUDES
DEPUTES
DILUTES
EFFUSES
ENDURES
ENGULFS
ENSURES
ESCUDOS
EUNUCHS
EXCUSES
FAMULUS
FATUOUS
FERULES
FIBULAS
FICUSES
FIGURES
FLAUNTS
FOCUSES
FUTURES
GERUNDS
GROUNDS
GROUSES
ILLUSES
IMMURES
IMPUGNS
IMPUTES
INCUDES
INDUCES
INDUCTS
INFUSES
INJURES
INSULTS
INSURES
INTUITS
IRRUPTS
ISSUERS
JAGUARS
JESUITS
JUJUBES
KABUKIS
KAHUNAS
KIKUYUS
KORUNAS
LACUNAS
LAGUNAS
LEGUMES
LIQUIDS
LIQUORS
LOCUSTS
LOQUATS
LOTUSES
MAGUEYS
MANUALS
MATURES
MEDUSAS
MINUETS
MINUSES
MINUTES
MISUSES
MODULES
MUTUALS
NATURES
NEBULAS
NEXUSES
NOCUOUS
NODULES
OBTUNDS
OCCULTS
OPPUGNS
PAIUTES
PAPUANS
PARURES
PENULTS
PEQUOTS
PERUKES
PERUSES
PLAUTUS
PLOUGHS
QUEUERS
REBUFFS
REBUKES
REBUSES
RECUSES
REDUCES
REFUELS
REFUGES
REFUNDS
REFUSES
REFUTES
REGULUS
REMUDAS
REPUGNS
REPUTES
RESULTS
RESUMES
RETUNES
RETURNS
RITUALS
ROMULUS
SALUKIS
SALUTES
SCRUFFS
SECURES
SEDUCES
SEQUELS
SEQUINS
SINUOUS
SINUSES
SIOUANS
SLEUTHS
SLOUGHS
SOLUTES
SPOUSES
SPRUCES
SUBURBS
SUTURES
TALUSES
TENUOUS
TENURES
THRUSTS
TRAUMAS
TRIUNES
TROUGHS
TROUPES
TUMULTS
TUMULUS
UNCURLS
UNFURLS
UNTUNES
UPTURNS
VACUOUS
VACUUMS
VICUNAS
VIRUSES
VISUALS
VOLUMES
YOGURTS

••••US•

BECAUSE
BULRUSH
CAROUSE
CIRCUSY
COMBUST
CONFUSE
CONTUSE
DEGAUSS
DIFFUSE
DISCUSS
DISGUST
DRSEUSS
ENCRUST
ENTHUSE
ENTRUST
ESPOUSE
EXHAUST
INARUSH
INHOUSE
INTRUST
JACCUSE
MOLLUSK
OVERUSE
PROFUSE
RECLUSE
SAWDUST
STRAUSS
SUFFUSE

••••U•S

ABLAUTS
ACCRUES
AIRGUNS
ALARUMS
ARBOURS
ARDOURS
ARMFULS
ARMOURS
ASYLUMS
ATRIUMS
AUTEURS
AVENUES
BACKUPS
BADGUYS
BAGFULS
BASQUES
BEDAUBS
BEDBUGS
BEFOULS
BIGGUNS
BISQUES
BLOWUPS
BOXFULS
BROGUES
BULBULS
BUYOUTS
CAIQUES
CAPFULS
CAPGUNS
CAPNUTS
CARFULS
CHEQUES
CHERUBS
CHINUPS
CIRQUES
CLAQUES
CLIQUES
CLOQUES
COLOURS
CONCURS
CONSULS
COPOUTS
CUPFULS
CUTOUTS
DEGAUSS
DETOURS
DEVOURS
DICTUMS
DIMOUTS
DISCUSS
DRSEUSS
DRYRUNS
DUGOUTS
DUMDUMS
DUSTUPS
DYBBUKS
EARFULS
EGGCUPS
ENDRUNS
ENSOULS
EYECUPS
EYEFULS
FAVOURS
FILLUPS
FLIPUPS
FOLDUPS
FONDUES
FOULUPS
FRENUMS
GIBLUES
GIVEUPS
GOOFUPS
HANGUPS
HEXNUTS
HICCUPS
HOLDUPS
HONOURS
HOOKUPS
HOTTUBS
HUBBUBS
HUMBUGS
HUMOURS
IMBRUES
JACQUES
JARFULS
JETGUNS
JUGFULS
KICKUPS
LABOURS
LANGURS
LAPFULS
LARRUPS
LASHUPS
LAYOUTS
LEAGUES
LINEUPS
LINKUPS
LOCKUPS
LONGUES
LOOKUPS
LUGNUTS
LYCEUMS
MAGNUMS
MAHOUTS
MAKEUPS

MARAUDS
MARKUPS
MARQUES
MARQUIS
MASQUES
MEDIUMS
MISCUES
MOCKUPS
MOSQUES
MUKLUKS
MURMURS
MUSEUMS
MUUMUUS
OPAQUES
OUTGUNS
OUTPUTS
OUTRUNS
PABLUMS
PAYOUTS
PEANUTS
PEPLUMS
PICKUPS
PIGNUTS
PILEUPS
PLAGUES
PLAQUES
PLENUMS
PODIUMS
POPGUNS
POSEURS
POSSUMS
POTFULS
PULLUPS
PURSUES
PUSHUPS
PUTOUTS
QUORUMS
RAGOUTS
RAGRUGS
RAYGUNS
RECOUPS
REDBUDS
REDGUMS
REGLUES
RESCUES
RIGOURS
RUMOURS
SANLUIS
SAVOURS
SENDUPS
SHOGUNS
SHROUDS
SIXGUNS
SKIRUNS
SLIPUPS
SOWBUGS
SPROUTS
STATUES
STEPUPS
STLOUIS
STRAUSS
SUBDUES
TEACUPS
TISSUES
TONGUES
TOPGUNS
TORQUES
TOSSUPS
TRYOUTS
TUNEUPS
TUTTUTS
UMLAUTS
UNPLUGS

VACUUMS
VALOURS
VAPOURS
VATFULS
VELLUMS
VELOURS
VIGOURS
VIRTUES
WALKUPS
WALNUTS
WARMUPS
WINDUPS
WORKUPS
WRAPUPS

•••••US
ALUMNUS
AMADEUS
AMOROUS
ANGELUS
ANNULUS
ANTAEUS
ANXIOUS
APERCUS
AQUEOUS
ARBUTUS
ARDUOUS
ARTEMUS
ATTICUS
BACCHUS
BILIOUS
BULBOUS
BUREAUS
CACHOUS
CALLOUS
CANOPUS
CAROLUS
CASSIUS
CELSIUS
CEPHEUS
COLOBUS
COPIOUS
CRASSUS
CRISPUS
CROESUS
CUMULUS
CURIOUS
DEDALUS
DEVIOUS
DREYFUS
DUBIOUS
DUTEOUS
ECHINUS
ENVIOUS
ERASMUS
FAMULUS
FATUOUS
FAUSTUS
FERROUS
FIBROUS
FURIOUS
GASEOUS
GIBBOUS
GRAMPUS
GROPIUS
HEINOUS
HIDEOUS
HUMERUS
HYDROUS
IGNEOUS
IMPETUS
IMPIOUS
INFOCUS

ISTHMUS
JABIRUS
JEALOUS
KIKUYUS
LANDAUS
LAZARUS
MALTHUS
MAXIMUS
MILIEUS
MINIBUS
MUUMUUS
NERVOUS
NITROUS
NOCUOUS
NONPLUS
NOXIOUS
NUCLEUS
OBVIOUS
OCEANUS
OCTOPUS
ODOROUS
OEDIPUS
OLYMPUS
OMINOUS
OMNIBUS
ONEROUS
ORMOLUS
ORPHEUS
OZONOUS
PAILOUS
PAPYRUS
PARIBUS
PARLOUS
PEGASUS
PERSEUS
PERSIUS
PETROUS
PHOEBUS
PIRAEUS
PITEOUS
PLAUTUS
POMPOUS
PONTIUS
PROTEUS
PYRAMUS
PYRRHUS
RAUCOUS
REGULUS
RHOMBUS
RIOTOUS
ROMULUS
RUINOUS
SERIOUS
SINUOUS
STRATUS
SURPLUS
TACITUS
TEDIOUS
TENUOUS
TETANUS
THESEUS
TROILUS
TUMULUS
VACUOUS
VARIOUS
VICIOUS
VISCOUS
ZEALOUS

UT•••••
UTAHANS
UTENSIL
UTILITY
UTILIZE
UTOPIAN
UTOPIAS
UTRECHT
UTRILLO
UTTERED
UTTERER
UTTERLY

U•T••••
UNTACKS
UNTAMED
UNTAPED
UNTRAPS
UNTRIED
UNTRUTH
UNTUNED
UNTUNES
UNTWIST
UNTYING
UPTAKES
UPTEMPO
UPTICKS
UPTIGHT
UPTONOW
UPTOPAR
UPTURNS
URTEXTS
USTINOV
UTTERED
UTTERER
UTTERLY

U••T•••
ULSTERS
UMPTEEN
UNCTION
UNITARY
UNITERS
UNITIES
UNITING
UNITIVE
UNSTACK
UNSTICK
UNSTOPS
UNSTRAP
UNSTUCK
UPATREE
UPSTAGE
UPSTART
UPSTATE
USSTEEL

U•••T••
UNDATED
UNHITCH
UNLATCH
UNRATED
UNSATED
UPDATED
UPDATES

U••••T•
ULULATE
UMBERTO
UMLAUTS
UNBOLTS
UNCOUTH
UNCRATE
UNEARTH
UNKNITS
UNKNOTS
UNQUOTE
UNSEATS
UNTRUTH
UPBEATS
UPLIFTS
UPROOTS
UPSHOTS
UPSTATE
URANITE
URTEXTS
UTILITY

U•••••T
UGLIEST
ULULANT
UNBLEST
UNGUENT
UNKEMPT
UNSPENT
UNSWEPT
UNTWIST
UPDRAFT
UPFRONT
UPRIGHT
UPSTART
UPSWEPT
UPTIGHT
UTRECHT

•UT••••
AUTEURS
AUTHORS
AUTOMAT
AUTUMNS
BUTCHER
BUTLERS
BUTTERS
BUTTERY
BUTTING
BUTTONS
BUTTOUT
BUTTSIN
CUTAWAY
CUTBACK
CUTDOWN
CUTICLE
CUTINTO
CUTLASS
CUTLERS
CUTLERY
CUTLETS
CUTOFFS
CUTOUTS
CUTRATE
CUTSOFF
CUTSOUT
CUTTERS
CUTTIME
CUTTING
DUTEOUS
DUTIFUL
EUTERPE
FUTURES
GUTHRIE
GUTLESS
GUTSIER
GUTSILY
GUTTERS
GUTTING
HUTCHES
JUTLAND
JUTTING
KUTENAI
LUTISTS
MUTABLE
MUTABLY
MUTAGEN
MUTANTS
MUTATED
MUTATES
MUTATIS
MUTTERS
MUTTONS
MUTUALS
NUTLETS
NUTMEAT
NUTMEGS
NUTRIAS
NUTTERS
NUTTIER
NUTTILY
NUTTING
OUTACTS
OUTAGES
OUTBACK
OUTBIDS
OUTCAST
OUTCOME
OUTCROP
OUTDOES
OUTDONE
OUTDOOR
OUTDRAW
OUTDREW
OUTEATS
OUTFACE
OUTFITS
OUTFLOW
OUTGOES
OUTGREW
OUTGROW
OUTGUNS
OUTHITS
OUTINGS
OUTJUMP
OUTLAID
OUTLAND
OUTLAST
OUTLAWS
OUTLAYS
OUTLETS
OUTLINE
OUTLIVE
OUTLOOK
OUTLOUD
OUTOFIT
OUTPACE
OUTPLAY
OUTPOST
OUTPUTS
OUTRACE
OUTRAGE
OUTRANK
OUTRUNS
OUTSELL
OUTSETS
OUTSIDE
OUTSIZE
OUTSOLD
OUTSTEP
OUTTAKE
OUTTALK
OUTVOTE
OUTWARD
OUTWEAR
OUTWITS
OUTWORE
OUTWORK
OUTWORN
PUTAMEN
PUTAWAY
PUTDOWN
PUTITTO
PUTOUTS
PUTOVER
PUTSOFF
PUTSOUT
PUTTEES
PUTTERS
PUTTIED
PUTTIES
PUTTING
PUTUPON
RUTGERS
SUTLERS
SUTTNER
SUTURED
SUTURES
TUTELAR
TUTORED
TUTTUTS

•U•T•••
AUCTION
AUNTIES
AUSTERE
AUSTRAL
AUSTRIA
BUNTING
BUSTARD
BUSTING
BUSTLED
BUSTLES
BUSTOUT
BUTTERS
BUTTERY
BUTTING
BUTTONS
BUTTOUT
BUTTSIN
BUYTIME
CULTISH
CULTISM
CULTIST
CULTJAM
CULTURE
CURTAIL
CURTAIN
CURTEST
CURTSEY
CUSTARD
CUSTODY
CUSTOMS
CUTTERS
CUTTIME
CUTTING
DUCTILE
DUCTING
DUSTERS
DUSTIER
DUSTING
DUSTMOP
DUSTOFF
DUSTPAN
DUSTUPS
FURTHER
FURTIVE
FUSTIAN
FUSTICS
FUSTIER
FUSTILY
GUITARS
GUMTREE
GUNTHER
GUSTAVE
GUSTILY
GUSTING
GUSTOES
GUTTERS
GUTTING
HUNTERS
HUNTING
HUNTLEY
HURTFUL
HURTING
HURTLED
HURTLES
HUSTLED
HUSTLER
HUSTLES
JUSTICE
JUSTIFY
JUSTINE
JUSTNOW
JUTTING
LUSTERS
LUSTFUL
LUSTIER
LUSTILY
LUSTING
LUSTRED
LUSTRES
MUNTINS
MUSTAFA
MUSTANG
MUSTARD
MUSTERS
MUSTIER
MUSTILY
MUSTSEE
MUTTERS
MUTTONS
NUPTIAL
NURTURE
NUTTERS
NUTTIER
NUTTILY
NUTTING
OURTOWN
OUSTERS
OUSTING
OUTTAKE
OUTTALK
PUNTERS
PUNTING
PUPTENT
PUTTEES
PUTTERS
PUTTIED
PUTTIES
PUTTING
QUETZAL
QUITTER
QUOTERS
QUOTING
RUCTION
RUNTIER
RUPTURE
RUSTICS
RUSTIER
RUSTILY
RUSTING
RUSTLED
RUSTLER
RUSTLES
SUBTEND
SUBTEXT
SUBTLER
SUCTION
SUITING
SUITORS
SUITSUP
SULTANA
SULTANS
SUNTANS
SUSTAIN
SUTTNER
TUFTING
TUITION
TURTLED
TURTLES
TUTTUTS
VULTURE

•U••T••
AUDITED
AUDITOR
BUILTIN
BUILTON
BUILTUP
BURETTE
BURNTUP
BURSTYN
BUSSTOP
CULOTTE
CURATES
CURATOR
FUJITSU
GUESTED
JUJITSU
JUPITER
LUNATIC
LUXATED
LUXATES
MULCTED
MULETAS
MUSETTE
MUTATED
MUTATES
MUTATIS
OUTSTEP
PULLTAB
PUNSTER
PURITAN
PUTITTO
QUANTUM
QUARTER
QUARTET
QUARTOS
QUENTIN
QUESTED
QUIETED
QUIETEN
QUIETER
QUIETLY
QUILTED
QUILTER
QUINTET
QUITTER
RUBITIN
SUMATRA
SUZETTE
YUCATAN

•U•••T•
AUGUSTA
AUGUSTE
AUKLETS
AUREATE
BUCKETS
BUDGETS
BUFFETS
BUFFETT
BULLETS
BULLITT
BURBOTS
BURETTE
BURNETT
BURRITO
BUYOUTS
CUBISTS
CULOTTE
CURVETS
CUTINTO
CUTLETS
CUTOUTS
CUTRATE
DUALITY
DUBIETY
DUEDATE
DUGOUTS
DURANTE
GULLETS
GUSSETS
JUNKETS
JURISTS
KUWAITI
LUGNUTS
LUTISTS
MULLETS
MUPPETS
MUSCATS
MUSETTE
MUSKETS
MUTANTS
NUDISTS
NUGGETS
NUMBATS
NUTLETS
OUTACTS
OUTEATS
OUTFITS
OUTHITS
OUTLETS
OUTPUTS
OUTSETS
OUTVOTE
OUTWITS
PUBERTY
PUCKETT
PULLETS
PULPITS
PULSATE
PUNDITS
PUPPETS
PURISTS
PUTITTO
PUTOUTS
QUALITY
QUIXOTE
RUNINTO
RUNLETS
RUNWITH
RUSSETS
SUAVITY
SUBLETS
SUBMITS
SUBSETS
SULFATE
SULFITE
SUMMITS
SUNBATH
SUNCITY
SUNSETS
SUZETTE
TUBISTS
TUFFETS
TUMULTS
TURBOTS
TURNSTO
TURRETS
TUTTUTS
VULGATE

•U••••T
AUGMENT
AUTOMAT
BUFFETT
BUGSOUT
BULBLET
BULLITT
BUMSOUT
BUOYANT
BURNETT
BURNOUT
BUSIEST
BUSTOUT
BUTTOUT
BUYSOUT
CULPRIT
CULTIST
CULVERT
CURBCUT
CURRANT
CURRENT
CURTEST
CUTSOUT
DUELIST
DULLEST
DUMBEST
FULGENT
FULLEST
FUNFEST
FUSSPOT
GUNBOAT
GUNSHOT
HUNGOUT
JUDOIST
JUMPCUT
JUMPSAT
JUNKART
KUMQUAT
LUCKOUT
LUNGEAT
LUSHEST
MUGSHOT
MUSKRAT
NUMBEST
NUTMEAT
OUTCAST
OUTLAST
OUTOFIT
OUTPOST
PUCKETT
PULLOUT
PUNGENT
PUNIEST
PUPTENT
PURPORT
PURSUIT
PUTSOUT
QUARTET
QUINTET
QUONSET
RUBSOUT
RULEOUT
RUNRIOT
RUNSOUT
SUAVEST
SUBJECT
SUBPLOT
SUBSIST
SUBTEXT
SUBUNIT
SUBVERT
SUGGEST
SUNBELT
SUNKIST
SUNSPOT
SUPPORT
SURCOAT
SURFEIT
SUSPECT
TUBAIST
TUGBOAT
TUNEOUT
TURNOUT

••UT•••
ABUTTAL
ABUTTED
ACUTELY
BOUTROS
BRUTISH
CAUTION
CHUTNEY
CLUTTER
COUTURE
DEUTERO
ELUTING
ELUTION
FLUTING
FLUTIST
FLUTTER
GAUTAMA
GLUTTED
GLUTTON
HAUTBOY
HAUTEUR
INUTILE
KLUTZES
LAUTREC
MOUTHED
MOUTONS
NEUTRAL
NEUTRON
POUTERS
POUTIER
POUTING
REUTERS
REUTHER
ROUTERS
ROUTINE
ROUTING
SAUTEED
SCUTTLE
SHUTEYE
SHUTOFF
SHUTOUT
SHUTSIN
SHUTSUP
SHUTTER
SHUTTLE
SOUTANE
SOUTHEY
SPUTNIK
SPUTTER
TAUTENS
TAUTEST
TEUTONS
TOUTERS
TOUTING

••U•T••
ABUTTAL
ABUTTED
AQUATIC
BLUNTED
BLUNTER
BLUNTLY
BLURTED
BLUSTER
BRUITED
CAUSTIC
CLUSTER
CLUTTER
COULTER
COUNTED
COUNTER
COUNTON
COUNTRY
COURTED
COURTLY
CRUSTED
DAUNTED
DOUBTED
DOUBTER
EQUATED
EQUATES
EQUATOR
ERUCTED
ERUPTED
EXULTED
FAULTED
FAUSTUS
FLUSTER
FLUTTER
FOULTIP
FOURTHS
FRUITED
GAUNTER
GAUNTLY
GLUTTED
GLUTTON
GRUNTED
HAUNTED
HOUSTON
JAUNTED
JOUSTED
JOUSTER
MOULTED
MOUNTED
MOUNTIE
POULTRY
ROUSTED
SAUNTER
SCUTTLE
SHUNTED
SHUTTER
SHUTTLE
SPURTED
SPUTTER
STUNTED
TAUNTED
TRUSTED
TRUSTEE
VAULTED
VAULTER

VAUNTED
VAUNTER

••U••T•
ADULATE
AMULETS
AZURITE
BAUXITE
BOUNDTO
BRUNETS
CRUDITY
DOUGHTY
EDUCATE
EMULATE
ERUDITE
FAUCETS
HAUGHTY
NAUGHTS
NAUGHTY
NOUGATS
PAUCITY
REUNITE
SCULPTS
SQUANTO
SQUINTS
SQUINTY
SQUIRTS
STUCKTO
TRUANTS
ULULATE

••U•••T
AQUAVIT
BOUQUET
COULDNT
COUPLET
COURANT
CRUDEST
CRUMPET
DOUBLET
DOUREST
FAUVIST
FLUTIST
FOULEST
FOULOUT
GOURMET
LAUGHAT
LAURENT
LOUDEST
OCULIST
OPULENT
PAULIST
PEUGEOT
PLUMMET
POUROUT
PRUDENT
ROUGHIT
SHUBERT
SHUTOUT
SOUREST
SPUNOUT
STUDENT
TAUTEST
TOURIST
TRUMPET
ULULANT
WOULDNT

•••UT••
AGOUTIS
ARBUTUS
CLOUTED
CROUTON
DEBUTED
DEPUTED
DEPUTES
DILUTED
DILUTER
DILUTES
FLOUTED
GODUTCH
GROUTED
IMPUTED
IMPUTES
INDUTCH
MINUTES
MINUTIA
PAIUTES
PLAUTUS
REFUTED
REFUTER
REFUTES
REPUTED
REPUTES
SALUTED
SALUTES
SCOUTED
SCOUTER
SHOUTED
SHOUTER
SLEUTHS
SOLUTES
SPOUTED
SPOUTER
STOUTER
STOUTLY
YAKUTSK

•••U•T•
ABDUCTS
ACQUITS
ACTUATE
ADDUCTS
ADDUPTO
ADJUSTS
AMOUNTS
ANNUITY
AUGUSTA
AUGUSTE
DEDUCTS
ENSUITE
FACULTY
FATUITY
FLAUNTS
INDUCTS
INSULTS
INTUITS
IRRUPTS
JESUITS
LEDUPTO
LOCUSTS
LOQUATS
MINUETS
NAHUATL
OCCULTS
PENULTS
PEQUOTS
REQUITE
RESULTS
ROBUSTA
SITUATE
THRUSTS
TUMULTS
UNQUOTE
VACUITY
VALUATE
YOGURTS

•••U••T
ACCURST
ADJUNCT
BEQUEST
BROUGHT
CALUMET
CAPULET
DEFUNCT
DRAUGHT
DROUGHT
EPAULET
FRAUGHT
INQUEST
MANUMIT
PIQUANT
PLAUDIT
REBUILT
REQUEST
RIVULET
SUBUNIT
THOUGHT
UNGUENT
VAGUEST
WROUGHT

••••UT•
ABLAUTS
AZIMUTH
BISMUTH
BUYOUTS
CAPNUTS
COMMUTE
COMPUTE
CONFUTE
COPOUTS
CUTOUTS
DIMOUTS
DISPUTE
DUGOUTS
ENROUTE
EXECUTE
HEXNUTS
HIRSUTE
INTRUTH
KIBBUTZ
LAYOUTS
LUGNUTS
MAHOUTS
OFFDUTY
OUTPUTS
PAYOUTS
PEANUTS
PIGNUTS
POLLUTE
PUTOUTS
RAGOUTS
REROUTE
SEADUTY
SPROUTS
STATUTE
TRIBUTE
TRYOUTS
TUTTUTS
UMLAUTS
UNCOUTH
UNTRUTH
WALNUTS

••••U•T
ACCOUNT
ASSAULT
ATFAULT
BANQUET
BISCUIT
BOUQUET
BRIQUET
CIRCUIT
COMBUST
CONDUCT
CONDUIT
CONSULT
CORRUPT
CROQUET
DEFAULT
DISGUST
DISRUPT
DRYSUIT
ENCRUST
ENTRUST
EXHAUST
INDOUBT
INTRUST
JOBHUNT
KUMQUAT
LAWSUIT
MANHUNT
NODOUBT
NOFAULT
PARQUET
PRODUCT
PURSUIT
RACQUET
RECOUNT
RECRUIT
REDOUBT
REMOUNT
RENAULT
SAWDUST
SKISUIT
VIADUCT
WETSUIT
YOGHURT

•••••UT
ABSOLUT
ACEDOUT
ACESOUT
ACTSOUT
AIRSOUT
ASKSOUT
BACKOUT
BAILOUT
BAWLOUT
BEAROUT
BEATOUT
BLEWOUT
BLOTOUT
BLOWOUT
BOOTOUT
BOREOUT
BOWSOUT
BUGSOUT
BUMSOUT
BURNOUT
BUSTOUT
BUTTOUT
BUYSOUT
CALLOUT
CAMEOUT
CAMPOUT
CASHOUT
CASTOUT
CHEWOUT
COCONUT
COLDCUT
COMEOUT
CONKOUT
COOKOUT
COPSOUT
CREWCUT
CURBCUT
CUTSOUT
DEALOUT
DECKOUT
DIEDOUT
DIESOUT
DIGSOUT
DISHOUT
DOLEOUT
DOPEOUT
DRAGOUT
DRAWOUT
DREWOUT
DROPOUT
EATSOUT
EDGEOUT
EKEDOUT
EKESOUT
EVENOUT
FADEOUT
FALLOUT
FANSOUT
FARMOUT
FEELOUT
FELLOUT
FELTOUT
FILLOUT
FINDOUT
FISHOUT
FLATOUT
FOLDOUT
FOULOUT
GAVEOUT
GETSOUT
GIVEOUT
GOABOUT
GOESOUT
HAIRCUT
HALIBUT
HANDOUT
HANGOUT
HARDPUT
HEADOUT
HEAROUT
HELDOUT
HELPOUT
HIDEOUT
HOLDOUT
HOLEOUT
HUNGOUT
IRISOUT
IRONOUT
JUMPCUT
KEPTOUT
KICKOUT
KINGTUT
LAIDOUT
LAYSOUT
LEADOUT
LEFTOUT
LETSOUT
LIVEOUT
LOCKNUT
LOCKOUT
LOGSOUT
LOOKOUT
LOSEOUT
LOSTOUT
LUCKOUT
MADEOUT
MAKEOUT
METEOUT
MISSOUT
MOVEOUT
NOSEOUT
OCCIPUT
OPTSOUT
PAIDOUT
PANSOUT
PARTOUT
PASSOUT
PAYSOUT
PEEKOUT
PEEROUT
PICKOUT
PIGSOUT
PINENUT
PLAYOUT
POOPOUT
POPSOUT
POUROUT
PULLOUT
PUTSOUT
RAINOUT
READOUT
RIDEOUT
RINGOUT
RODEOUT
ROLLOUT
ROOTOUT
RUBSOUT
RULEOUT
RUNSOUT
SACKOUT
SANGOUT
SEEKOUT
SEESOUT
SELLOUT
SENDOUT
SENTOUT
SETSOUT
SHIPOUT
SHOTPUT
SHUTOUT
SICKOUT
SIGNOUT
SINGOUT
SITSOUT
SKIPOUT
SLIPOUT
SOLDOUT
SPINOUT
SPUNOUT
STAYPUT
STEPOUT
TAGSOUT
TAKEOUT
TALKOUT
TAPSOUT
TESTOUT
TIMEOUT
TIREOUT
TOOKOUT
TOPSOUT
TOREOUT
TORNOUT
TOSSOUT
TROTOUT
TUNEOUT
TURNOUT
WAITOUT
WALKOUT
WANTOUT
WASHOUT
WEAROUT
WEEDOUT
WENTOUT
WIGSOUT
WINGNUT
WINKOUT
WINSOUT
WIPEOUT
WITHOUT
WOODCUT
WOREOUT
WORKOUT
WORNOUT
ZONKOUT

U•U••••
UKULELE
ULULANT
ULULATE
UNUSUAL
URUGUAY
USUALLY
USURERS
USURPED
USURPER

U••U•••
UNCURLS
UNFURLS
UNGUENT
UNLUCKY
UNQUOTE
UNTUNED
UNTUNES
UPSURGE
UPTURNS

U•••U••
ULALUME
UMLAUTS
UNBOUND
UNCOUTH
UNEQUAL
UNGLUED
UNPLUGS
UNSOUND
UNSTUCK
UNTRUTH
UNUSUAL
UNWOUND
URUGUAY

U••••U•
URANIUM
USINGUP

•UU••••
MUUMUUS

•U•U•••
AUBURNS
AUDUBON
AUGURAL
AUGURED
AUGUSTA
AUGUSTE
AUTUMNS
CUMULUS
DUBUQUE
EUNUCHS
FUTURES
JUGULAR
JUJUBES
MUTUALS
PUTUPON
QUEUERS
QUEUEUP
QUEUING
SUBUNIT
SUBURBS
SULUSEA
SUTURED
SUTURES
TUBULAR
TUMULTS
TUMULUS

•U••U••
AUTEURS
BULBULS
BULRUSH
BUYOUTS
CULTURE
CUPFULS
CUTOUTS
DUGOUTS
DUMDUMS
DUSTUPS
HUBBUBS
HUMBUGS
HUMOURS
JUGFULS
KUMQUAT
LUGNUTS
MUGWUMP
MUKLUKS
MURMURS
MUSEUMS
MUUMUUS
NURTURE
OUTGUNS
OUTJUMP
OUTPUTS
OUTRUNS
PULLUPS
PURSUED
PURSUER
PURSUES
PURSUIT
PUSHUPS
PUTOUTS
QUORUMS
RUMOURS
RUPTURE
SUBDUED
SUBDUER
SUBDUES
SUBSUME
SUCCUMB
SUDBURY
SUFFUSE
SUNBURN
TUNEUPS
TUTTUTS
VULTURE

•U•••U•
BUCKSUP
BUDDYUP
BUGSOUT
BUILDUP
BUILTUP
BULBOUS
BULGHUR
BULLRUN
BUMPSUP
BUMSOUT
BUOYSUP
BUREAUS
BURNOUT
BURNSUP
BURNTUP
BURPGUN
BUSTOUT
BUTTOUT
BUYSOUT
CUMULUS
CURBCUT
CURIOUS
CURLSUP
CUTSOUT
DUBIOUS
DUBUQUE
DUDEDUP
DUMMYUP
DUTEOUS
DUTIFUL
FULCRUM
FULGHUM
FURIOUS
GUARGUM
GUSSYUP
HUMDRUM
HUMERUS
HUNGOUT
HURTFUL
JUICEUP
JUMPCUT
JUMPSUP
JUNEBUG
LUCKOUT
LUMPSUM
LUSTFUL
MUCKSUP
MUUMUUS
NUCLEUS
OUTLOUD
PULLOUT
PULLSUP
PUMPSUP
PUNCHUP
PUTSOUT
QUANTUM
QUECHUA
QUEUEUP
QUINQUE
RUBSOUT
RUINOUS
RULEOUT
RUNSOUT
SUCCOUR
SUITSUP
SULPHUR
SURPLUS
TUMULUS
TUNEDUP
TUNEFUL
TUNEOUT
TUNESUP
TURNOUT
TURNSUP
TUSSAUD

•U••••U
FUJITSU
JUJITSU
PURLIEU

••U•U••
ARUGULA
ASUSUAL
BOUQUET
COUTURE
FOULUPS
GAUGUIN
MUUMUUS
UNUSUAL
URUGUAY

••U••U•
ALUMNUS
AQUEOUS
BOUNDUP
BRUSHUP
BRUSQUE
COUGHUP
DRUMSUP
ELUVIUM
FAUSTUS
FOULOUT
FOULSUP
HAULSUP
HAUTEUR
LOUSEUP
MUUMUUS
POUROUT
RAUCOUS
ROUGHUP
ROUNDUP
SHUTOUT
SHUTSUP
SOULFUL
SOUPSUP
SPUNOUT
STUCKUP
STUNGUN
THULIUM
TOUCHUP
TRUMPUP
WOUNDUP
YOUNGUN

••U•••U
BLUEFLU
DOUBLEU
NOUVEAU
TRUDEAU

•••UU••
VACUUMS

•••U•U•
ANNULUS
ARBUTUS
ARDUOUS
CUMULUS
DUBUQUE
FAMULUS
FATUOUS
JEJUNUM
KIKUYUS
LIQUEUR
NOCUOUS
PABULUM
PLAUTUS
QUEUEUP
REGULUS
ROMULUS
SCRUBUP
SINUOUS
TENUOUS
TUMULUS
VACUOUS

••••UU•
MUUMUUS

U•V••••
UNVEILS

U••V•••
UNAVOCE

U•••V••
UNCIVIL
UNCOVER
UNLOVED
UNMOVED
UNPAVED
UNRAVEL
UPRIVER

U••••V•
ULANOVA
UNITIVE
UNNERVE
UNWEAVE

U•••••V
ULYANOV
USTINOV

•UV••••
JUVENAL

•U•V•••
CULVERT
CURVETS
CURVIER
CURVING
GUEVARA
OUTVOTE
PURVEYS
PURVIEW
QUAVERS
QUAVERY
QUIVERS
QUIVIVE
SUAVELY
SUAVEST
SUAVITY
SUBVERT
SURVEYS
SURVIVE

•U••V••
PUTOVER
RUNOVER

•U•••V•
CURSIVE
FURTIVE
GUSTAVE
MUSCOVY
OUTLIVE
QUIVIVE
SURVIVE

•U••••V
NUREYEV

••UV•••
ELUVIUM
FAUVISM
FAUVIST
FLUVIAL
LOUVERS
LOUVRES
NOUVEAU
OEUVRES
PLUVIAL

••U•V••
AQUAVIT
AQUIVER
SCURVES
ZOUAVES

••U••V•
ABUSIVE
ELUSIVE

•••UV••
ALLUVIA
DOEUVRE
OLDUVAI

•••U••V
GODUNOV

••••UV•
DENEUVE

U•W••••
UNWEAVE
UNWINDS
UNWISER
UNWOUND
UNWRAPS
UPWARDS

U••W•••
UNAWARE
UNSWEPT
UNTWIST
UPSWEEP
UPSWEPT
UPSWING

U•••W••
UNBOWED
UNSEWED

U••••W•
UNDRAWN
UNKNOWN

U•••••W
UNSCREW
UPTONOW
USOSHOW

•UW••••
KUWAITI

•U•W•••
BULWARK
GUNWALE
JUGWINE
MUGWUMP
OUTWARD
OUTWEAR
OUTWITS
OUTWORE
OUTWORK
OUTWORN
RUNWAYS
RUNWITH
SUBWAYS

•U••W••
CUTAWAY
DUNAWAY
PUTAWAY
RUNAWAY

•U•••W•
BURROWS
CURFEWS
CURLEWS
CUSHAWS
CUTDOWN
FURROWS
GUFFAWS
OURTOWN
OUTLAWS
PUTDOWN
RUBDOWN
RUNDOWN
SUNDEWS
SUNDOWN

•U••••W
BUCKSAW
BUZZSAW
JUSTNOW
OUTDRAW
OUTDREW
OUTFLOW
OUTGREW
OUTGROW
PURVIEW

••U•W••
SQUAWKS

••U•••W
BLUELAW
YOUKNOW

•••UW••
THRUWAY

UX•••••
UXORIAL

U•••X••
UNBOXED
UNBOXES
UNFIXED
URTEXTS

•UX••••
LUXATED
LUXATES
TUXEDOS

•U•X•••
QUIXOTE

•U•••X•
SUBTEXT

•U••••X
JUKEBOX

••UX•••
BAUXITE
FAUXPAS

••U•••X
BLUEFOX
EQUINOX
FLUMMOX

•••••UX
BATEAUX
GATEAUX
LASCAUX
MALRAUX
MARGAUX
MILIEUX
MIMIEUX
MONTEUX
THEROUX

U•Y••••
ULYANOV
ULYSSES
UNYOKED
UNYOKES

U••Y•••
UNDYING
UNTYING

U•••••Y
UNCANNY
UNGODLY
UNHANDY
UNHAPPY
UNITARY
UNLUCKY
UNREADY
URGENCY
URUGUAY
USUALLY
UTILITY
UTTERLY

•UY••••
BUYABLE
BUYOUTS
BUYSOFF
BUYSOUT
BUYTIME

•U•Y•••
BUOYANT
BUOYING
BUOYSUP
BURYING
BUSYING
JURYING
JURYRIG
RUBYDEE
RUDYARD

•U••Y••
BUDDYUP
BUGEYED
DUMMYUP
GUSSYUP
NUREYEV
RUFIYAA

•U•••Y•
BUCKEYE
BURSTYN
BUSBOYS
GURNEYS
OUTLAYS
PULLEYS
PURVEYS
RUNWAYS
SUBWAYS
SUNDAYS
SUNRAYS
SURREYS
SURVEYS
TURKEYS

•U••••Y
AUDIBLY
AURALLY
BUCKLEY
BUTTERY
CURSORY
CURTSEY
CUSTODY
CUTAWAY
CUTLERY
DUALITY
DUBARRY
DUBIETY
DUNAWAY
DURABLY
EUPHONY
FUNNILY
FUSSILY
FUSTILY
FUZZILY
GUNNERY
GUNPLAY
GUSTILY
GUTSILY
HUFFILY
HUMANLY
HUMIDLY
HUNGARY
HUNTLEY
HUSHABY
HUSKILY
JUICILY
JUSTIFY
LUCIDLY
LUCKILY
LULLABY
LURIDLY
LUSTILY
MUMMERY
MURKILY
MURPHEY
MUSCOVY
MUSHILY
MUSTILY
MUTABLY
MUZZILY
NULLIFY
NUNNERY
NURSERY
NUTTILY
OUTPLAY
PUBERTY
PUFFERY
PUFFILY
PUSHILY
PUTAWAY
QUALIFY
QUALITY
QUAVERY
QUEENLY
QUEERLY
QUICKLY
QUIETLY
QUIGLEY
RUBBERY
RUNAWAY
RUNSDRY
RUSTILY
SUAVELY
SUAVITY
SUBSIDY
SUDBURY
SULKILY
SUMMARY
SUMMERY
SUNCITY
SUNNILY
SURGERY
SURLILY
TUESDAY
TURNKEY
TUSCANY

••UY•••
GRUYERE

••U••Y•
SHUTEYE

••U•••Y
ACUTELY
BLUEBOY
BLUEJAY
BLUESKY
BLUFFLY
BLUNTLY
CHUTNEY
COUNTRY
COURTLY
CRUDELY
CRUDITY
CRUELLY
CRUMBLY
CRUMPLY
CRUNCHY
DOUGHTY
EQUABLY
EQUALLY
EQUERRY
EXUPERY
FLUENCY
FLUIDLY
FOUNDRY
GAUDILY
GAUNTLY
GAUZILY
GRUFFLY
HAUGHTY
HAUTBOY
JOURNEY
LAUNDRY
LOUSILY
NAUGHTY
PAUCITY
PAUNCHY
PLUSHLY
POULTRY
PRUDERY
REUNIFY
ROUGHLY
ROUNDLY
SAUCILY
SOUNDLY
SOUTHEY
SQUEAKY
SQUINTY
SQUIRMY
SQUISHY
STUBBLY
STUPEFY
TOUGHLY
TOURNEY
TRUANCY
URUGUAY
USUALLY

•••UY••
KIKUYUS

•••U•Y•
MAGUEYS

•••U••Y
ACTUARY
ANNUITY
AWFULLY
CALUMNY
DEBUSSY
ESTUARY
FACULTY
FATUITY
GROUCHY
INQUIRY
JANUARY
LIQUEFY
LITURGY
PIOUSLY
PROUDLY
ROGUERY
SCRUBBY
SCRUFFY
SHRUBBY
SLOUCHY
STOUTLY
THRUWAY
UNLUCKY
VACUITY
VAGUELY
VOLUBLY
ZYMURGY

••••UY•
BADGUYS

••••U•Y
ASHBURY
CADBURY
CENTURY
CIRCUSY
MERCURY
OFFDUTY
PERJURY
SAVOURY
SEADUTY
SUDBURY
URUGUAY

•••••UY
FALLGUY
OBLOQUY
OVERBUY
WISEGUY

U•Z••••
UNZONED

U•••Z••
UNFAZED

U••••Z•
UTILIZE

•UZ••••
BUZZARD
BUZZERS
BUZZING
BUZZOFF
BUZZSAW
FUZZIER
FUZZILY
FUZZING
GUZZLED
GUZZLER
GUZZLES
HUZZAHS
MUZHIKS
MUZZIER
MUZZILY
MUZZLED
MUZZLES
NUZZLED
NUZZLER
NUZZLES
PUZZLED
PUZZLER
PUZZLES
SUZANNE
SUZETTE

•U•Z•••
BUZZARD
BUZZERS
BUZZING
BUZZOFF
BUZZSAW
FUZZIER
FUZZILY
FUZZING
GUZZLED
GUZZLER
GUZZLES
HUZZAHS
MUEZZIN
MUZZIER
MUZZILY
MUZZLED
MUZZLES
NUZZLED
NUZZLER
NUZZLES
PUZZLED
PUZZLER
PUZZLES
QUIZZED
QUIZZES
SUBZERO

•U••Z••
MUEZZIN
QUETZAL
QUIZZED
QUIZZES

•U•••Z•
OUTSIZE

••UZ•••
CRUZADO
GAUZIER
GAUZILY

••U•Z••
KLUTZES

••U••Z•
SQUEEZE

•••UZ••
JACUZZI

•••U•Z•
JACUZZI

••••U•Z
KIBBUTZ
MARQUEZ

VA•••••
VACANCY
VACATED
VACATES
VACCARO
VACCINE
VACUITY
VACUOLE
VACUOUS
VACUUMS
VAGRANT
VAGUELY
VAGUEST
VAINEST
VALANCE
VALENCE
VALERIE
VALIANT
VALIDLY
VALISES
VALJEAN
VALLEYS
VALOURS
VALUATE
VALUING
VAMOOSE
VAMPERS
VAMPING
VAMPIRE
VANDALS
VANDINE
VANDYCK
VANDYKE
VANESSA
VANEYCK
VANGOGH
VANILLA
VANILLI
VANOCUR
VANPOOL
VANTAGE
VANZANT
VAPIDLY
VAPOURS
VAQUERO
VARIANT
VARIETY
VARIOUS
VARLETS
VARMINT
VARNISH
VARSITY
VARYING
VASSALS
VASTEST
VATFULS
VATICAN
VAUGHAN
VAULTED
VAULTER
VAUNTED
VAUNTER

V•A••••
VIADUCT

V••A•••
VACANCY
VACATED
VACATES
VALANCE
VEDANTA
VERANDA
VIDALIA
VIRAGOS
VISAGES
VISAVIS
VITALLY
VITAMIN
VIVALDI
VOCALIC
VOCALLY
VOYAGED
VOYAGER
VOYAGES

V•••A••
VACCARO
VAGRANT
VALIANT
VALUATE
VANDALS
VANTAGE
VANZANT
VARIANT
VASSALS
VEEJAYS
VERBALS
VERDANT
VIBRANT
VIBRATE
VIBRATO
VILLAGE
VILLAIN
VINTAGE
VIOLATE
VISUALS
VITIATE
VOLCANO
VOLTAGE
VOLTAIC
VULCANS
VULGATE

V••••A•
VALJEAN
VATICAN
VAUGHAN
VEGETAL
VENTRAL
VETERAN
VICTUAL
VICUNAS
VIETNAM
VINEGAR
VIRGOAN
VIRTUAL
VIZSLAS

V•••••A
VANESSA
VANILLA
VEDANTA
VENTURA
VERANDA
VERBENA
VIDALIA
VISCERA
VISTULA

•VA••••
AVAILED
AVARICE
AVATARS
EVACUEE
EVADERS
EVADING
EVANDER
EVANGEL
EVASION
EVASIVE
IVANHOE
OVATION

•V•A•••
AVIANCA
AVIATED
AVIATES
AVIATOR

•V••A••
AVATARS
AVERAGE
AVOCADO
AVOWALS
OVERACT
OVERAGE
OVERALL
OVERATE
OVERAWE

•V•••A•
OVEREAT
OVERLAP
OVERLAY
OVERRAN
OVERSAW
OVOIDAL

•V••••A
AVIANCA
AVONLEA
OVERSEA

••VA•••
ADVANCE
ALVAREZ
BAVARIA
BIVALVE
CAVALRY
DEVALUE
HAVARTI
INVACUO
INVADED
INVADER
INVADES
INVALID
JAVAMAN
LAVALSE
LIVABLE
LOVABLE
MOVABLE
NAVAHOS
NAVAJOS
NAVARRE
NEVADAN
NOVARRO
PAVANES
RAVAGED
RAVAGES
REVALUE
REVAMPS
RIVALED
RIVALRY
SAVABLE
SAVAGED
SAVAGER
SAVAGES
SAVALAS
SAVANNA
SAVANTS
SAVARIN
VIVALDI

••V•A••
CAVEART
CAVEATS
DEVIANT
DEVIATE
GAVIALS
OBVIATE
REVEALS

••V••A•
BIVOUAC
CAVEMAN
DOVEBAR
GAVEWAY
GIVEWAY
JAVAMAN
JUVENAL
LIVEOAK
NEVADAN
NOVENAS
PIVOTAL
REVIVAL
SAVALAS
SEVERAL

••V•••A
BAVARIA
LAVINIA
NOVELLA
PAVLOVA
RAVENNA
RIVIERA
SAVANNA

•••VA••
BRAVADO
CALVARY
CANVASS
COEVALS
CRAVATS
ELEVATE
GALVANI
GUEVARA
HARVARD
NIRVANA
PERVADE
PREVAIL
PRIVACY
PRIVATE
REAVAIL
ROLVAAG
SALVAGE
SELVAGE
SERVALS
SERVANT
SLOVAKS
SYLVANS
TRAVAIL
ZHIVAGO

•••V•A•
DRIVEAT
FLUVIAL
LATVIAN
NOUVEAU
PLUVIAL
ROLVAAG
TRIVIAL

•••V••A
BOBVILA
BRAVURA
GUEVARA
NIRVANA
RIGVEDA

••••VA•
ARRIVAL
BOLIVAR
CARAVAN
DONOVAN
ESTIVAL
HESHVAN
MEDEVAC
MINIVAN
MITZVAH
OLDUVAI
RAYOVAC
REMOVAL
REVIVAL
SAMOVAR
YEREVAN

••••V•A
ALLUVIA
BOLIVIA
MORAVIA
OCTAVIA
SEGOVIA

•••••VA
BAKLAVA
CASSAVA
GINGIVA
KEDROVA
MARKOVA
MINERVA
PAVLOVA
ULANOVA
YESHIVA

V•B••••
VIBRANT
VIBRATE
VIBRATO

V••B•••
VERBALS
VERBENA
VERBOSE

V•••B••
VISIBLE
VISIBLY
VOLUBLE
VOLUBLY

•V••B••
OVERBIG
OVERBUY

•V••••B
OVERDUB

••V•B••
DOVEBAR
LIVABLE
LOVABLE
LOVEBUG
MOVABLE
SAVABLE

••V••B•
ADVERBS
REVERBS

•••V••B
PROVERB

V•C••••
VACANCY
VACATED
VACATES
VACCARO
VACCINE
VACUITY
VACUOLE
VACUOUS
VACUUMS
VECTORS
VICEROY
VICIOUS
VICTIMS
VICTORS
VICTORY
VICTUAL
VICUNAS
VOCALIC
VOCALLY

V••C•••
VACCARO
VACCINE
VETCHES
VINCENT
VISCERA
VISCOUS
VOICING
VOLCANO
VOUCHED
VOUCHER
VOUCHES
VULCANS

V•••C••
VANOCUR
VATICAN
VEHICLE
VOTECHS

V••••C•
VACANCY
VALANCE
VALENCE
VANDYCK
VANEYCK
VEENECK
VERDICT
VIADUCT

V•••••C
VOCALIC
VOLTAIC

•V•C•••
AVOCADO
AVOCETS
EVACUEE
EVICTED

•V••C••
EVINCED
EVINCES

•V•••C•
AVARICE
AVIANCA
OVERACT

••V•C••
CEVICHE
DEVICES
DOVECOT
INVACUO
NOVICES

••V••C•
ADVANCE
DAVINCI
DIVORCE
INVOICE
REVOICE

••V•••C
BIVOUAC

•••V•C•
CONVICT
CREVICE
PRIVACY
SERVICE
UNAVOCE

••••V•C
MEDEVAC
RAYOVAC

V•D••••
VEDANTA
VIDALIA

V••D•••
VANDALS
VANDINE
VANDYCK
VANDYKE
VENDING
VENDORS
VERDANT
VERDICT
VERDUGO
VERDURE
VIADUCT
VOIDING

V•••D••
VALIDLY
VAPIDLY
VEXEDLY
VIVIDER
VIVIDLY

V••••D•
VERANDA
VESPIDS
VIVALDI
VIVENDI

V•••••D
VACATED
VAULTED
VAUNTED
VISITED
VOUCHED
VOYAGED

•V•D•••
AVIDITY
EVADERS
EVADING
EVIDENT

•V••D••
AVOIDED
EVANDER
OVERDID
OVERDUB
OVERDUE
OVOIDAL

•V•••D•
AVOCADO
TVGUIDE

•V••••D
AVAILED
AVENGED
AVERRED
AVERTED
AVIATED
AVOIDED
AVULSED
EVERTED
EVICTED
EVINCED
EVOLVED
EVULSED
OVERDID

••V•D••
CAVEDIN
DIVIDED
DIVIDER
DIVIDES
INVADED
INVADER
INVADES
LIVEDIN
LIVEDON
LIVIDLY
MOVEDIN
NEVADAN
SAVEDUP
VIVIDER
VIVIDLY
WAVEDIN

••V••D•
VIVALDI
VIVENDI

••V•••D
ADVISED

BEVELED
CAVILED
COVERED
COVETED
DEVILED
DEVISED
DEVOTED
DIVIDED
DIVINED
DIVVIED
FAVORED
GAVELED
HOVERED
INVADED
INVALID
INVITED
INVOKED
LEVELED
LEVERED
LIVENED
PIVOTED
RAVAGED
RAVELED
RAVENED
REVELED
REVERED
REVILED
REVISED
REVIVED
REVOKED
RIVALED
RIVETED
SAVAGED
SAVORED
SEVERED
WAVERED

•••V•D•
BRAVADO
PERVADE
PROVIDE
RIGVEDA

•••V••D
CHEVIED
DIVVIED
HARVARD

••••V•D
ARRIVED
BEHAVED
BELOVED
CLEAVED
DERIVED
EVOLVED
GRIEVED
GROOVED
RELIVED
REMOVED
REPAVED
REVIVED
SHEAVED
SHELVED
STARVED
STRIVED
SWERVED
THIEVED
THRIVED
UNLOVED
UNMOVED
UNPAVED

VE•••••
VECTORS
VEDANTA
VEEJAYS
VEENECK
VEERING
VEGETAL
VEGGIES
VEGGING
VEHICLE
VEIGHTS
VEILING
VEINING
VELLUMS
VELOURS
VELVETS
VELVETY
VENDING
VENDORS
VENEERS
VENISON
VENTERS
VENTING
VENTRAL
VENTURA
VENTURE
VERANDA
VERBALS
VERBENA
VERBOSE
VERDANT
VERDICT
VERDUGO
VERDURE
VERGERS
VERGING
VERMEER
VERMEIL
VERMONT
VERNIER
VERSIFY
VERSION
VERTIGO
VERVETS
VESPERS
VESPIDS
VESSELS
VESTEES
VESTIGE
VESTING
VESTURE
VETCHES
VETERAN
VETOERS
VETOING
VETTING
VEXEDLY

V•E••••
VEEJAYS
VEENECK
VEERING
VIETNAM
VIEWERS
VIEWING

V••E•••
VALENCE
VALERIE
VANESSA
VANEYCK
VEGETAL
VENEERS
VETERAN
VEXEDLY
VICEROY
VINEGAR
VIVENDI
VOTECHS
VOTESIN

V•••E••
VAGUELY
VAGUEST
VAINEST
VALJEAN
VALLEYS
VAMPERS
VAQUERO
VARIETY
VARLETS
VASTEST
VEENECK
VELVETS
VELVETY
VENEERS
VENTERS
VERBENA
VERGERS
VERMEER
VERMEIL
VERVETS
VESPERS
VESSELS
VESTEES
VETOERS
VIEWERS
VILLEIN
VINCENT
VIOLENT
VIOLETS
VISCERA
VIZIERS
VOLLEYS

V••••E•
VACATED
VACATES
VALISES
VAULTED
VAULTER
VAUNTED
VAUNTER
VEGGIES
VERMEER
VERNIER
VESTEES
VETCHES
VINTNER
VIRTUES
VIRUSES
VISAGES
VISITED
VITTLES
VIVIDER
VOLUMES
VOUCHED
VOUCHER
VOUCHES
VOYAGED
VOYAGER
VOYAGES

V•••••E
VACCINE
VACUOLE
VALANCE
VALENCE
VALERIE
VALUATE
VAMOOSE
VAMPIRE
VANDINE
VANDYKE
VANTAGE
VEHICLE
VENTURE
VERBOSE
VERDURE
VESTIGE
VESTURE
VIBRATE
VILLAGE
VINTAGE
VIOLATE
VIRGULE
VISIBLE
VITIATE
VOLPONE
VOLTAGE
VOLUBLE
VULGATE
VULPINE
VULTURE

•VE••••
AVENGED
AVENGER
AVENGES
AVENUES
AVERAGE
AVERRED
AVERTED
EVENEST
EVENING
EVENKIS
EVENOUT
EVENSUP
EVEREST
EVERETT
EVERTED
OVERACT
OVERAGE
OVERALL
OVERATE
OVERAWE
OVERBIG
OVERBUY
OVERDID
OVERDUB
OVERDUE
OVEREAT
OVERFLY
OVERJOY
OVERLAP
OVERLAY
OVERLIE
OVERRAN
OVERRUN
OVERSAW
OVERSEA
OVERSEE
OVERTLY
OVERUSE
SVELTER

•V••E••
AVOCETS
AVOWERS
EVADERS
EVENEST
EVEREST
EVERETT
EVIDENT
EVILEST
EVILEYE
EVOKERS
OVEREAT

•V•••E•
AVAILED
AVENGED
AVENGER
AVENGES
AVENUES
AVERRED
AVERTED
AVIATED
AVIATES
AVOIDED
AVONLEA
AVULSED
AVULSES
EVACUEE
EVANDER
EVANGEL
EVERTED
EVICTED
EVILLER
EVINCED
EVINCES
EVOLVED
EVOLVES
EVULSED
EVULSES
IVORIES
OVERSEA
OVERSEE
SVELTER

•V••••E
AVARICE
AVERAGE
EVACUEE
EVASIVE
EVILEYE
IVANHOE
OVERAGE
OVERATE
OVERAWE
OVERDUE
OVERLIE
OVERSEE
OVERUSE
TVGUIDE

••VE•••
ADVENTS
ADVERBS
ADVERSE
ADVERTS
ALVEOLI
BEVELED
BEVERLY
CAVEART
CAVEATS
CAVEDIN
CAVEINS
CAVEMAN
CAVEMEN
CAVERNS
CAVESIN
COVERED
COVERUP
COVETED
DEVEINS
DEVELOP
DIVERGE
DIVERSE
DIVERTS
DIVESIN
DIVESTS
DOVEBAR
DOVECOT
ENVELOP
GAVELED
GAVEOFF
GAVEOUT
GAVEWAY
GIVENTO
GIVEOFF
GIVEOUT
GIVESIN
GIVESTO
GIVESUP
GIVEUPS
GIVEWAY
GOVERNS
HAVENOT
HOVERED
HOVERER
INVEIGH
INVENTS
INVERSE
INVERTS
INVESTS
JAVELIN
JUVENAL
LAVERNE
LEVELED
LEVELER
LEVELLY
LEVERED
LEVERET
LIVEDIN
LIVEDON
LIVENED
LIVEOAK
LIVEONE
LIVEOUT
LIVESIN
LIVESON
LOVEBUG
LOVEINS
LOVERLY
MOVEDIN
MOVEOUT
MOVESIN
NOVELLA
NOVELLE
NOVELTY
NOVENAS
OBVERSE
OBVERTS
POVERTY
RAVELED
RAVENED
RAVENNA
REVEALS
REVELED
REVELER
REVELRY
REVENGE
REVENUE
REVERBS
REVERED
REVERES
REVERIE
REVERSE
REVERTS
RIVETED
RIVETER
SAVEDUP
SAVESUP
SEVENTH
SEVENTY
SEVENUP
SEVERAL
SEVERED
SEVERER
TAVERNS
UNVEILS
VIVENDI
WAVEDIN
WAVELET
WAVEOFF
WAVERED
WAVERER
WAVESIN
WYVERNS

••V•E••
LEVIERS
REVIEWS
RIVIERA
RIVIERE
SOVIETS
WAVIEST
YEVGENY

••V••E•
ADVISED
ADVISER
ADVISES
ALVAREZ
BEVELED
BOVINES
CAVEMEN
CAVILED
CAVILER
CIVVIES
COVERED
COVETED
DEVICES
DEVILED
DEVISED
DEVISES
DEVOTED
DEVOTEE
DEVOTES
DEVRIES
DIVIDED
DIVIDER
DIVIDES
DIVINED
DIVINER
DIVINES
DIVVIED
DIVVIES
FAVORED
GAVELED
HOVERED
HOVERER
INVADED
INVADER
INVADES
INVITED
INVITES
INVOKED
INVOKER
INVOKES
LEVELED
LEVELER
LEVERED
LEVERET
LEVITES
LIVENED
NOVICES
PAVANES
PIVOTED
RAVAGED
RAVAGES
RAVELED
RAVENED
RAVINES
REVELED
REVELER
REVERED
REVERES
REVILED
REVILES
REVISED
REVISER
REVISES
REVIVED
REVIVES
REVOKED
REVOKES
RIVALED
RIVETED
RIVETER
RIVULET
SAVAGED
SAVAGER
SAVAGES
SAVORED
SAVVIER
SEVERED
SEVERER
VIVIDER
WAVELET
WAVERED
WAVERER

••V•••E
ADVANCE
ADVERSE
BIVALVE
CEVICHE
DEVALUE
DEVIATE
DEVILLE
DEVOLVE
DEVOTEE
DIVERGE
DIVERSE
DIVORCE
DIVULGE
GAVOTTE
INVERSE
INVOGUE
INVOICE
INVOLVE
LAVALSE
LAVERNE
LIVABLE
LIVEONE
LOVABLE
MOVABLE
NAVARRE
NEVILLE
NOVELLE
OBVERSE
OBVIATE
ORVILLE
REVALUE
REVENGE
REVENUE
REVERIE
REVERSE
REVOICE
REVOLVE
RIVIERE
SAVABLE
SEVIGNE
SEVILLE

•••VE••
BEAVERS
BRAVELY
BRAVERY
BRAVEST
BREVETS
CALVERT
CARVERS
CLAVELL
CLOVERS
CONVENE
CONVENT
CONVERT
CONVEYS
CRAVENS
CRAVERS
CULVERT
CURVETS
DELVERS
DRIVEAT
DRIVEIN
DRIVELS
DRIVERS
DRIVEUP
DROVERS
ELEVENS
FERVENT
GRAVELS
GRAVELY
GRAVEST
GRIVETS
GROVELS
HARVEST
HEAVEHO
HEAVENS
HEAVERS
HEAVETO
JAYVEES
KNAVERY
LEAVENS
LOUVERS
MARVELS
NAIVELY
NAIVETE
NOUVEAU
PARVENU
PEAVEYS
PERVERT
PLOVERS
PREVENT
PRIVETS
PROVERB
PROVERS
PURVEYS
QUAVERS
QUAVERY
QUIVERS
RIGVEDA
SALVERS
SERVERS
SERVEUP
SHAVERS
SHIVERS
SHOVELS
SHOVERS
SILVERS
SILVERY
SKIVERS
SLAVERS
SLAVERY
SLIVERS
SLOVENE
SLOVENS
SNIVELS
SOLVENT
SOLVERS
STEVENS
SUAVELY
SUAVEST
SUBVERT
SURVEYS
SWIVELS
TRAVELS
TRAVERS
TRIVETS
VELVETS
VELVETY
VERVETS
WAIVERS
WEAVERS

•••V•E•
BMOVIES
BRAVOES
CHEVIED
CHEVIES
CHEVRES
CIVVIES
CLAVIER
CURVIER
DIVVIED
DIVVIES
FLIVVER
GRAVIES
HEAVIER
HEAVIES
JANVIER
JAYVEES
LOUVRES
NERVIER
OEUVRES
OLIVIER
PREVIEW
PRIVIES
PURVIEW
SALVOES
SAVVIER

•••V••E
CONVENE
CONVOKE
CREVICE
ELEVATE
GRAVURE
NAIVETE
OLIVINE
OUTVOTE
PERVADE
PRIVATE
PROVIDE
PROVOKE
QUIVIVE
SALVAGE
SELVAGE
SERVICE
SERVILE
SLOVENE
SURVIVE
UNAVOCE

••••VE•
ACTIVES
ALCOVES
ALLOVER
ANDOVER
AQUIVER
ARGIVES
ARRIVED
ARRIVER
ARRIVES
BEHAVED
BEHAVES
BELOVED
BILEVEL
CARAVEL
CHEEVER
CLEAVED
CLEAVER
CLEAVES
DEKOVEN
DELIVER
DERIVED
DERIVES
DIDOVER
DWARVES
ENDIVES
ENLIVEN
ESTEVEZ
EVOLVED
EVOLVES
EXWIVES
FLIVVER
FLYOVER
FOREVER
GETEVEN
GETOVER
GOTEVEN
GOTOVER
GREAVES
GRIEVED
GRIEVER
GRIEVES
GROOVED
GROOVES
HANOVER
HOPOVER
HOWEVER
KNIEVEL
LAYOVER
LIEOVER
MINIVER
MOTIVES
NATIVES
NINEVEH
OCTAVES
PALAVER
POPOVER
PUTOVER
RANOVER
RECOVER
RELIVED
RELIVES
REMOVED
REMOVER
REMOVES
REPAVED
REPAVES
REVIVED
REVIVES
REWOVEN
RUNOVER
SCARVES
SCRIVEN
SCURVES
SHEAVED
SHEAVES
SHELVED
SHELVES
SHRIVEL
SHRIVER
SHRIVES
SLEEVES
STARVED
STARVES
STRIVED
STRIVEN
STRIVER
STRIVES
SWERVED
SWERVES
THIEVED
THIEVES
THRIVED
THRIVES
TWELVES
UNCOVER
UNLOVED
UNMOVED
UNPAVED
UNRAVEL
UPRIVER
WHARVES
WHOEVER
ZOUAVES

••••V•E
DOEUVRE
LEHAVRE

•••••VE
ABSOLVE
ABUSIVE
ACHIEVE
AIRWAVE
AMATIVE
APPROVE
ARCHIVE
BEEHIVE
BEHOOVE
BELIEVE
BEREAVE
BIVALVE
CAPTIVE
COMMOVE
CONCAVE
CONNIVE
CURSIVE
DECEIVE
DENEUVE
DEPRAVE
DEPRIVE
DESERVE
DEVOLVE
ELUSIVE
EMOTIVE
ENCLAVE
ENGRAVE
ENSLAVE
EROSIVE
EVASIVE
FESTIVE
FICTIVE
FORGAVE
FORGIVE
FURTIVE
GUSTAVE
IMPROVE
INVOLVE
MASSIVE
MISSIVE
NEWWAVE
OBSERVE
ONLEAVE
OUTLIVE
PASSIVE
PENSIVE
PLOSIVE
QUIVIVE
RECEIVE
RELIEVE
REPROVE
RESERVE
RESOLVE
RESTIVE
REVOLVE
REWEAVE
SKYDIVE
SURVIVE
TENSIVE
UNITIVE
UNNERVE
UNWEAVE

V••F•••
VATFULS

V••••F•
VERSIFY
VITRIFY

•V••F••
OVERFLY

••V••F•
GAVEOFF
GIVEOFF
WAVEOFF

••V•••F
GAVEOFF
GIVEOFF
WAVEOFF

V•G••••
VAGRANT
VAGUELY
VAGUEST
VEGETAL
VEGGIES
VEGGING
VIGOURS

V••G•••
VANGOGH
VAUGHAN
VEGGIES
VEGGING
VEIGHTS
VERGERS

VERGING
VIRGINS
VIRGOAN
VIRGULE
VULGATE

V•••G••
VINEGAR
VIRAGOS
VISAGES
VOYAGED
VOYAGER
VOYAGES

V••••G•
VANGOGH
VANTAGE
VERDUGO
VERTIGO
VESTIGE
VIKINGS
VILLAGE
VINTAGE
VOLTAGE

V•••••G
VALUING
VAMPING
VARYING
VEERING
VEGGING
VEILING
VEINING
VENDING
VENTING
VERGING
VESTING
VETOING
VETTING
VIEWING
VOICING
VOIDING

•VG••••
TVGUIDE

•V•G•••
AVIGNON

•V••G••
AVENGED
AVENGER
AVENGES
EVANGEL

•V•••G•
AVERAGE
OVERAGE

•V••••G
AVOWING
EVADING
EVENING
EVOKING
OVERBIG

••VG•••
YEVGENY

••V•G••
INVOGUE
RAVAGED
RAVAGES
SAVAGED
SAVAGER
SAVAGES
SEVIGNE

••V••G•
DIVERGE
DIVULGE
INVEIGH
LIVINGS
RAVINGS
REVENGE
SAVINGS

••V•••G
ENVYING
LEVYING
LOVEBUG
REVVING

•••V•G•
SALVAGE
SELVAGE
ZHIVAGO

•••V••G
BRAVING
CALVING
CARVING
CRAVING
CURVING
DELVING
DRIVING
GRAVING
HALVING
HEAVING
LEAVING
PEEVING
PROVING
REVVING
ROLVAAG
SALVING
SERVING
SHAVING
SHOVING
SLAVING
SOLVING
STAVING
WAIVING
WEAVING

V•H••••
VEHICLE

V•••H••
VAUGHAN
VEIGHTS
VETCHES
VOUCHED
VOUCHER
VOUCHES

V••••H•
VOTECHS

V•••••H
VANGOGH
VARNISH

•V•H•••
TVSHOWS

•V••H••
IVANHOE

••V•H••
NAVAHOS

••V••H•
CEVICHE

••V•••H
INVEIGH
SEVENTH

•••V•H•
HEAVEHO

•••V••H
DERVISH
KNAVISH
PEEVISH
SLAVISH

••••V•H
MITZVAH
NINEVEH

VI•••••
VIADUCT
VIBRANT
VIBRATE
VIBRATO
VICEROY
VICIOUS
VICTIMS
VICTORS
VICTORY
VICTUAL
VICUNAS
VIDALIA
VIETNAM
VIEWERS
VIEWING
VIGOURS
VIKINGS
VILLAGE
VILLAIN
VILLEIN
VINCENT
VINEGAR
VINTAGE
VINTNER
VIOLATE
VIOLENT
VIOLETS
VIOLINS
VIOLIST
VIRAGOS
VIRGINS
VIRGOAN
VIRGULE
VIRTUAL
VIRTUES
VIRUSES
VISAGES
VISAVIS
VISCERA
VISCOUS
VISIBLE
VISIBLY
VISIONS
VISITED
VISITOR
VISTULA
VISUALS
VITALLY
VITAMIN
VITIATE
VITRIFY
VITRIOL
VITTLES
VIVALDI
VIVENDI
VIVIDER
VIVIDLY
VIZIERS
VIZSLAS

V•I••••
VAINEST
VEIGHTS
VEILING
VEINING
VOICING
VOIDING

V••I•••
VALIANT
VALIDLY
VALISES
VANILLA
VANILLI
VAPIDLY
VARIANT
VARIETY
VARIOUS
VATICAN
VEHICLE
VENISON
VICIOUS
VIKINGS
VISIBLE
VISIBLY
VISIONS
VISITED
VISITOR
VITIATE
VIVIDER
VIVIDLY
VIZIERS

V•••I••
VACCINE
VACUITY
VALUING
VAMPING
VAMPIRE
VANDINE
VARMINT
VARNISH
VARSITY
VARYING
VEERING
VEGGIES
VEGGING
VEILING
VEINING
VENDING
VENTING
VERDICT
VERGING
VERNIER
VERSIFY
VERSION
VERTIGO
VESPIDS
VESTIGE
VESTING
VETOING
VETTING
VICTIMS
VIEWING
VIOLINS
VIOLIST
VIRGINS
VITRIFY
VITRIOL
VOICING
VOIDING
VULPINE

V••••I•
VALERIE
VERMEIL
VIDALIA
VILLAIN
VILLEIN
VISAVIS
VITAMIN
VOCALIC
VOLTAIC
VOTESIN

V•••••I
VANILLI
VIVALDI
VIVENDI

•VI••••
AVIANCA
AVIATED
AVIATES
AVIATOR
AVIDITY
AVIGNON
EVICTED
EVIDENT
EVILEST
EVILEYE
EVILLER
EVINCED
EVINCES

•V•I•••
AVAILED
AVOIDED
OVOIDAL

•V••I••
AVARICE
AVIDITY
AVOWING
EVADING
EVASION
EVASIVE
EVENING
EVOKING
IVORIES
OVATION
TVGUIDE

•V•••I•
EVENKIS
OVERBIG
OVERDID
OVERLIE

••VI•••
ADVISED
ADVISER
ADVISES
ADVISOR
BOVINES
CAVILED
CAVILER
CEVICHE
CIVILLY
DAVINCI
DEVIANT
DEVIATE
DEVICES
DEVILED
DEVILLE
DEVILRY
DEVIOUS
DEVISED
DEVISES
DIVIDED
DIVIDER
DIVIDES
DIVINED
DIVINER
DIVINES
DIVISOR
ENVIOUS
GAVIALS
INVITED
INVITES
INVITRO
LAVINIA
LEVIERS
LEVITES
LIVIDLY
LIVINGS
NEVILLE
NOVICES
OBVIATE
OBVIOUS
ORVILLE
PAVIOUR
RAVINES
RAVINGS
RAVIOLI
REVIEWS
REVILED
REVILES
REVISED
REVISER
REVISES
REVISIT
REVIVAL
REVIVED
REVIVES
RIVIERA
RIVIERE
SAVINGS
SAVIORS
SEVIGNE
SEVILLE
SOVIETS
VIVIDER
VIVIDLY
WAVIEST

••V•I••
CAVEINS
CIVVIES
DEVEINS
DEVRIES
DIVVIED
DIVVIES
ENVYING
INVEIGH
INVOICE
LEVYING
LOVEINS
REVOICE
REVVING
SAVVIER
SAVVILY
UNVEILS

••V••I•
BAVARIA
CAVEDIN
CAVESIN
DIVESIN
GIVESIN
INVALID
JAVELIN
LAVINIA
LIVEDIN
LIVESIN
MOVEDIN
MOVESIN
REVERIE
REVISIT
SAVARIN
WAVEDIN
WAVESIN

••V•••I
ALVEOLI
DAVINCI
HAVARTI
RAVIOLI
VIVALDI
VIVENDI

•••VI••
ATAVISM
ATAVIST
BMOVIES
BOBVILA
BRAVING
BREVITY
CALVING
CARVING
CHEVIED
CHEVIES
CHEVIOT
CIVVIES
CLAVIER
CONVICT
CRAVING
CREVICE
CURVIER
CURVING
DELVING
DERVISH
DIVVIED
DIVVIES
DRIVING
ELUVIUM
FAUVISM
FAUVIST
FLUVIAL
GRAVIES
GRAVING
GRAVITY
HALVING
HEAVIER
HEAVIES
HEAVILY
HEAVING
JANVIER
KNAVISH
LATVIAN
LEAVING
NERVIER
NERVILY
OLIVIER
OLIVINE
PEEVING
PEEVISH
PLUVIAL
PREVIEW
PRIVIES
PROVIDE
PROVING
PROVISO
PURVIEW
QUIVIVE
REVVING
SALVING
SAVVIER
SAVVILY
SERVICE
SERVILE
SERVING
SHAVING
SHOVING
SLAVING
SLAVISH
SOLVING
SPAVINS
STAVING
SUAVITY
SURVIVE
TREVINO
TRIVIAL
WAIVING
WEAVING
WEEVILS

•••V•I•
DRIVEIN
PREVAIL
REAVAIL
TRAVAIL
TRAVOIS

•••V••I
GALVANI

••••VI•
ALLUVIA
AQUAVIT
BEDEVIL
BOLIVIA
CHERVIL
INCIVIL
MCGAVIN
MORAVIA
OCTAVIA
SEGOVIA
TELAVIV
UNCIVIL
VISAVIS

••••V•I
OLDUVAI

•••••VI
BONJOVI
PAHLAVI

V••J•••
VALJEAN
VEEJAYS

•V••J••
OVERJOY

••V•J••
NAVAJOS

V•K••••
VIKINGS

V••••K•
VANDYKE
VRONSKY

V•••••K
VANDYCK
VANEYCK
VEENECK

•V•K•••
EVOKERS
EVOKING

•V••K••
EVENKIS

••V•K••
INVOKED
INVOKER
INVOKES
REVOKED
REVOKES

••V•••K
LIVEOAK

•••V•K•
CONVOKE
PROVOKE
SLOVAKS

V•L••••
VALANCE
VALENCE
VALERIE
VALIANT
VALIDLY
VALISES
VALJEAN
VALLEYS
VALOURS
VALUATE
VALUING
VELLUMS
VELOURS
VELVETS
VELVETY
VILLAGE
VILLAIN
VILLEIN
VOLCANO
VOLLEYS
VOLPONE
VOLTAGE
VOLTAIC
VOLUBLE
VOLUBLY
VOLUMES
VULCANS
VULGATE
VULPINE
VULTURE

V••L•••
VALLEYS
VARLETS
VAULTED
VAULTER
VEILING
VELLUMS
VILLAGE
VILLAIN
VILLEIN
VIOLATE
VIOLENT
VIOLETS
VIOLINS
VIOLIST
VOLLEYS

V•••L••
VANILLA
VANILLI
VIDALIA
VITALLY
VITTLES
VIVALDI
VIZSLAS
VOCALIC
VOCALLY

V••••L•
VACUOLE
VAGUELY
VALIDLY
VANDALS
VANILLA
VANILLI
VAPIDLY
VASSALS
VATFULS
VEHICLE
VERBALS
VESSELS
VEXEDLY
VIRGULE
VISIBLE
VISIBLY
VISTULA
VISUALS
VITALLY
VIVIDLY
VOCALLY
VOLUBLE
VOLUBLY

V•••••L
VANPOOL
VEGETAL
VENTRAL
VERMEIL
VICTUAL
VIRTUAL
VITRIOL

•V•L•••
AVULSED
AVULSES
EVILEST
EVILEYE
EVILLER
EVOLVED
EVOLVES
EVULSED
EVULSES
SVELTER

•V••L••
AVAILED
AVONLEA
EVILLER
OVERLAP
OVERLAY
OVERLIE

•V•••L•
AVOWALS
OVERALL
OVERFLY
OVERTLY

•V••••L
EVANGEL
OVERALL
OVOIDAL

••VL•••
PAVLOVA

••V•L••
BEVELED
BIVALVE
CAVALRY
CAVILED
CAVILER
CIVILLY
DEVALUE
DEVELOP
DEVILED
DEVILLE
DEVILRY
DEVOLVE
DIVULGE
ENVELOP
GAVELED
INVALID
INVOLVE
JAVELIN
LAVALSE
LEVELED
LEVELER
LEVELLY
NEVILLE
NOVELLA
NOVELLE
NOVELTY
ORVILLE
RAVELED
REVALUE
REVELED
REVELER
REVELRY
REVILED
REVILES
REVOLTS
REVOLVE
RIVALED
RIVALRY
RIVULET
SAVALAS
SEVILLE
VIVALDI
WAVELET

••V••L•
ALVEOLI
BEVERLY
CIVILLY
DEVILLE
GAVIALS
LEVELLY
LIVABLE
LIVIDLY
LOVABLE
LOVERLY
MOVABLE
NEVILLE
NOVELLA
NOVELLE
ORVILLE
RAVIOLI
REVEALS
SAVABLE
SAVVILY
SEVILLE
UNVEILS
VIVIDLY

••V•••L
JUVENAL
PIVOTAL
REVIVAL
SEVERAL

•••V•L•
BOBVILA
BRAVELY
CLAVELL
COEVALS
DRIVELS
GRAVELS
GRAVELY
GROVELS
HEAVILY
MARVELS
NAIVELY
NERVILY
SAVVILY
SERVALS
SERVILE
SHOVELS
SNIVELS
SUAVELY
SWIVELS
TRAVELS
WEEVILS

•••V••L
CLAVELL
FLUVIAL
PLUVIAL
PREVAIL
REAVAIL
TRAVAIL
TRIVIAL

••••V•L
ARRIVAL
BEDEVIL
BILEVEL
CARAVEL
CHERVIL
ESTIVAL
INCIVIL
KNIEVEL
REMOVAL
REVIVAL
SHRIVEL
UNCIVIL
UNRAVEL

V•M••••
VAMOOSE
VAMPERS
VAMPING
VAMPIRE

V••M•••
VARMINT
VERMEER
VERMEIL
VERMONT

V•••M••
VITAMIN
VOLUMES

V••••M•
VACUUMS
VELLUMS
VICTIMS

V•••••M
VIETNAM

••V•M••
CAVEMAN
CAVEMEN
JAVAMAN
REVAMPS

•••V••M
ATAVISM
ELUVIUM
FAUVISM

V•N••••
VANDALS
VANDINE
VANDYCK
VANDYKE
VANESSA
VANEYCK
VANGOGH
VANILLA
VANILLI
VANOCUR
VANPOOL
VANTAGE
VANZANT
VENDING
VENDORS
VENEERS
VENISON
VENTERS
VENTING
VENTRAL
VENTURA
VENTURE
VINCENT
VINEGAR
VINTAGE
VINTNER

V••N•••
VAINEST
VARNISH
VAUNTED
VAUNTER
VEENECK
VEINING
VERNIER
VRONSKY

V•••N••
VACANCY

VALANCE
VALENCE
VEDANTA
VERANDA
VICUNAS
VIETNAM
VIKINGS
VINTNER
VIVENDI

V••••N•
VACCINE
VAGRANT
VALIANT
VALUING
VAMPING
VANDINE
VANZANT
VARIANT
VARMINT
VARYING
VEERING
VEGGING
VEILING
VEINING
VENDING
VENTING
VERBENA
VERDANT
VERGING
VERMONT
VESTING
VETOING
VETTING
VIBRANT
VIEWING
VINCENT
VIOLENT
VIOLINS
VIRGINS
VISIONS
VOICING
VOIDING
VOLCANO
VOLPONE
VULCANS
VULPINE

V•••••N
VALJEAN
VATICAN
VAUGHAN
VENISON
VERSION
VETERAN
VILLAIN
VILLEIN
VIRGOAN
VITAMIN
VOTESIN

•V•N•••
AVENGED
AVENGER
AVENGES
AVENUES
AVONLEA
EVANDER
EVANGEL
EVENEST
EVENING
EVENKIS
EVENOUT
EVENSUP
EVINCED
EVINCES
IVANHOE

•V••N••
AVIANCA
AVIGNON

•V•••N•
AVOWING
EVADING
EVENING
EVIDENT
EVOKING

•V••••N
AVIGNON
EVASION
OVATION
OVERRAN
OVERRUN

••V•N••
ADVANCE
ADVENTS
BOVINES
DAVINCI
DIVINED
DIVINER
DIVINES
GIVENTO
HAVENOT
INVENTS
JUVENAL
LAVINIA
LIVENED
LIVINGS
NOVENAS
PAVANES
RAVENED
RAVENNA
RAVINES
RAVINGS
REVENGE
REVENUE
SAVANNA
SAVANTS
SAVINGS
SEVENTH
SEVENTY
SEVENUP
VIVENDI

••V••N•
CAVEINS
CAVERNS
DEVEINS
DEVIANT
ENVYING
GOVERNS
LAVERNE
LEVYING
LIVEONE
LOVEINS
RAVENNA
REVVING
SAVANNA
SEVIGNE
TAVERNS
WYVERNS
YEVGENY

••V•••N
CAVEDIN
CAVEMAN
CAVEMEN
CAVESIN
DIVESIN
GIVESIN
JAVAMAN
JAVELIN
LIVEDIN
LIVEDON
LIVESIN
LIVESON
MOVEDIN
MOVESIN
NEVADAN
SAVARIN
WAVEDIN
WAVESIN

•••V•N•
BRAVING
CALVING
CARVING
CONVENE
CONVENT
CRAVENS
CRAVING
CURVING
DELVING
DRIVING
ELEVENS
FERVENT
GALVANI
GRAVING
HALVING
HEAVENS
HEAVING
LEAVENS
LEAVING
NIRVANA
OLIVINE
PARVENU
PEEVING
PREVENT
PROVING
REVVING
SALVING
SERVANT
SERVING
SHAVING
SHOVING
SLAVING
SLOVENE
SLOVENS
SOLVENT
SOLVING
SPAVINS
STAVING
STEVENS
SYLVANS
TREVINO
WAIVING
WEAVING

•••V••N
CHEVRON
DRIVEIN
LATVIAN

••••V•N
CARAVAN
CLEAVON
DEKOVEN
DONOVAN
ENLIVEN
GETEVEN
GOTEVEN
HESHVAN
MCGAVIN
MINIVAN
REWOVEN
SCRIVEN
STRIVEN
YEREVAN

VO•••••
VOCALIC
VOCALLY
VOICING
VOIDING
VOLCANO
VOLLEYS
VOLPONE
VOLTAGE
VOLTAIC
VOLUBLE
VOLUBLY
VOLUMES
VOTECHS
VOTESIN
VOUCHED
VOUCHER
VOUCHES
VOYAGED
VOYAGER
VOYAGES

V•O••••
VIOLATE
VIOLENT
VIOLETS
VIOLINS
VIOLIST
VRONSKY

V••O•••
VALOURS
VAMOOSE
VANOCUR
VAPOURS
VELOURS
VETOERS
VETOING
VIGOURS

V•••O••
VACUOLE
VACUOUS
VAMOOSE
VANGOGH
VANPOOL
VARIOUS
VECTORS
VENDORS
VERBOSE
VERMONT
VICIOUS
VICTORS
VICTORY
VIRGOAN
VISCOUS
VISIONS
VOLPONE

V••••O•
VANPOOL
VENISON
VERSION
VICEROY
VIRAGOS
VISITOR
VITRIOL

V•••••O
VACCARO
VAQUERO
VERDUGO
VERTIGO
VIBRATO
VOLCANO

•VO••••
AVOCADO
AVOCETS
AVOIDED
AVONLEA
AVOWALS
AVOWERS
AVOWING
EVOKERS
EVOKING
EVOLVED
EVOLVES
IVORIES
OVOIDAL

•V••O••
EVENOUT
TVSHOWS

•V•••O•
AVIATOR
AVIGNON
EVASION
IVANHOE
OVATION
OVERJOY

•V••••O
AVOCADO

••VO•••
BIVOUAC
CAVORTS
DEVOLVE
DEVOTED
DEVOTEE
DEVOTES
DEVOURS
DIVORCE
FAVORED
FAVOURS
GAVOTTE
INVOGUE
INVOICE
INVOKED
INVOKER
INVOKES
INVOLVE
PIVOTAL
PIVOTED
REVOICE
REVOKED
REVOKES
REVOLTS
REVOLVE
SAVORED
SAVOURS
SAVOURY

••V•O••
ALVEOLI
DEVIOUS
ENVIOUS
GAVEOFF
GAVEOUT
GIVEOFF
GIVEOUT
LIVEOAK
LIVEONE
LIVEOUT
MOVEOUT
OBVIOUS
PAVIOUR
PAVLOVA
RAVIOLI
SAVIORS
WAVEOFF

••V••O•
ADVISOR
DEVELOP
DIVISOR
DOVECOT
ENVELOP
HAVENOT
LIVEDON
LIVESON
NAVAHOS
NAVAJOS

••V•••O
GIVENTO
GIVESTO
INVACUO
INVITRO
NOVARRO

•••VO••
BRAVOES
CONVOKE
CONVOYS
FERVORS
FERVOUR
FLAVORS
FLAVOUR
NERVOUS
OUTVOTE
PROVOKE
PROVOST
SALVOES
TRAVOIS
UNAVOCE

•••V•O•
CHEVIOT
CHEVRON

•••V••O
BRAVADO
HEAVEHO
HEAVETO
PROVISO
TREVINO
ZHIVAGO

••••VO•
CLEAVON
DISAVOW
INFAVOR
OCTAVOS

•••••VO
CENTAVO
RELIEVO

V•P••••
VAPIDLY
VAPOURS

V••P•••
VAMPERS
VAMPING
VAMPIRE
VANPOOL
VESPERS
VESPIDS
VOLPONE
VULPINE

•V••••P
EVENSUP
OVERLAP

••V••P•
GIVEUPS
REVAMPS

••V•••P
COVERUP
DEVELOP
ENVELOP
GIVESUP
SAVEDUP
SAVESUP
SEVENUP

•••V••P
DRIVEUP
SERVEUP

V•Q••••
VAQUERO

VR•••••
VRONSKY

V•R••••
VARIANT
VARIETY
VARIOUS
VARLETS
VARMINT
VARNISH
VARSITY
VARYING
VERANDA
VERBALS
VERBENA
VERBOSE
VERDANT
VERDICT
VERDUGO
VERDURE
VERGERS
VERGING
VERMEER
VERMEIL
VERMONT
VERNIER
VERSIFY
VERSION
VERTIGO
VERVETS
VIRAGOS
VIRGINS
VIRGOAN
VIRGULE
VIRTUAL
VIRTUES
VIRUSES

V••R•••
VAGRANT
VEERING
VIBRANT
VIBRATE
VIBRATO
VITRIFY
VITRIOL

V•••R••
VALERIE
VENTRAL
VETERAN
VICEROY

V••••R•
VACCARO
VALOURS
VAMPERS
VAMPIRE
VAPOURS
VAQUERO
VECTORS
VELOURS
VENDORS
VENEERS
VENTERS
VENTURA
VENTURE
VERDURE
VERGERS
VESPERS
VESTURE
VETOERS
VICTORS
VICTORY
VIEWERS
VIGOURS
VISCERA
VIZIERS
VULTURE

V•••••R
VANOCUR
VAULTER
VAUNTER
VERMEER
VERNIER
VINEGAR
VINTNER
VISITOR
VIVIDER
VOUCHER
VOYAGER

•V•R•••
AVARICE
AVERAGE
AVERRED
AVERTED
EVEREST
EVERETT
EVERTED
IVORIES
OVERACT
OVERAGE
OVERALL
OVERATE
OVERAWE
OVERBIG
OVERBUY
OVERDID
OVERDUB
OVERDUE
OVEREAT
OVERFLY
OVERJOY
OVERLAP
OVERLAY
OVERLIE
OVERRAN
OVERRUN
OVERSAW
OVERSEA
OVERSEE
OVERTLY
OVERUSE

•V••R••
AVERRED
OVERRAN
OVERRUN

•V•••R•
AVATARS
AVOWERS
EVADERS
EVOKERS

•V••••R
AVENGER
AVIATOR
EVANDER
EVILLER
SVELTER

••VR•••
DEVRIES

••V•R••
ADVERBS
ADVERSE
ADVERTS
ALVAREZ
BAVARIA
BEVERLY
CAVERNS
CAVORTS
COVERED
COVERUP
DIVERGE
DIVERSE
DIVERTS
DIVORCE
FAVORED
GOVERNS
HAVARTI
HOVERED
HOVERER
INVERSE
INVERTS
LAVERNE
LEVERED
LEVERET
LOVERLY
NAVARRE
NOVARRO
OBVERSE
OBVERTS
POVERTY
REVERBS
REVERED
REVERES
REVERIE
REVERSE
REVERTS
SAVARIN
SAVORED
SEVERAL
SEVERED
SEVERER
TAVERNS
WAVERED
WAVERER
WYVERNS

••V••R•
CAVALRY
CAVEART
DEVILRY
DEVOURS
FAVOURS
INVITRO
LEVIERS
NAVARRE
NOVARRO
REVELRY
RIVALRY
RIVIERA
RIVIERE
SAVIORS
SAVOURS
SAVOURY

••V•••R
ADVISER
ADVISOR
CAVILER
DIVIDER
DIVINER
DIVISOR
DOVEBAR
HOVERER
INVADER
INVOKER
LEVELER
PAVIOUR
REVELER
REVISER
RIVETER
SAVAGER
SAVVIER
SEVERER
VIVIDER
WAVERER

•••VR••
CHEVRES
CHEVRON
LOUVRES
OEUVRES

•••V•R•
BEAVERS
BRAVERY
BRAVURA
CALVARY
CALVERT
CARVERS
CLOVERS
CONVERT
CRAVERS
CULVERT
DELVERS
DRIVERS
DROVERS
FERVORS
FLAVORS
GRAVURE
GUEVARA
HARVARD
HEAVERS
KNAVERY
LOUVERS
PERVERT
PLOVERS
PROVERB
PROVERS
QUAVERS
QUAVERY
QUIVERS
SALVERS
SERVERS
SHAVERS
SHIVERS
SHOVERS
SILVERS
SILVERY
SKIVERS
SLAVERS
SLAVERY
SLIVERS
SOLVERS
SUBVERT
TRAVERS
WAIVERS
WEAVERS

•••V••R
CLAVIER
CURVIER
FERVOUR
FLAVOUR
FLIVVER
HEAVIER
JANVIER
NERVIER
OLIVIER
SAVVIER

••••VR•
DOEUVRE
LEHAVRE

••••V•R
ALLOVER
ANDOVER
AQUIVER
ARRIVER
BOLIVAR
CHEEVER
CLEAVER
DELIVER
DIDOVER
FLIVVER
FLYOVER
FOREVER
GETOVER
GOTOVER
GRIEVER
HANOVER
HOPOVER
HOWEVER
INFAVOR
LAYOVER
LIEOVER
MINIVER
PALAVER
POPOVER
PUTOVER
RANOVER
RECOVER
REMOVER
RUNOVER
SAMOVAR
SHRIVER
STRIVER
UNCOVER
UPRIVER
WHOEVER

V•S••••
VASSALS
VASTEST
VESPERS
VESPIDS
VESSELS
VESTEES
VESTIGE
VESTING
VESTURE
VISAGES
VISAVIS
VISCERA
VISCOUS
VISIBLE
VISIBLY
VISIONS
VISITED
VISITOR
VISTULA
VISUALS

V••S•••
VARSITY
VASSALS
VERSIFY
VERSION
VESSELS
VIZSLAS

V•••S••
VALISES
VANESSA
VENISON
VIRUSES
VOTESIN
VRONSKY

V••••S•
VAGUEST
VAINEST
VAMOOSE
VANESSA
VARNISH
VASTEST
VERBOSE
VIOLIST

V•••••S
VACATES
VACUOUS
VACUUMS
VALISES
VALLEYS
VALOURS
VAMPERS
VANDALS
VAPOURS
VARIOUS
VARLETS
VASSALS
VATFULS
VECTORS
VEEJAYS
VEGGIES
VEIGHTS
VELLUMS
VELOURS
VELVETS
VENDORS
VENEERS
VENTERS
VERBALS
VERGERS
VERVETS
VESPERS
VESPIDS
VESSELS
VESTEES
VETCHES
VETOERS
VICIOUS
VICTIMS
VICTORS
VICUNAS
VIEWERS
VIGOURS
VIKINGS
VIOLETS
VIOLINS
VIRAGOS
VIRGINS
VIRTUES
VIRUSES
VISAGES
VISAVIS
VISCOUS
VISIONS
VISUALS
VITTLES
VIZIERS
VIZSLAS
VOLLEYS
VOLUMES
VOTECHS
VOUCHES
VOYAGES
VULCANS

•VS••••
TVSHOWS

•V•S•••
EVASION
EVASIVE

•V••S••
AVULSED
AVULSES
EVENSUP
EVULSED
EVULSES
OVERSAW
OVERSEA
OVERSEE

•V•••S•
EVENEST

EVEREST
EVILEST
OVERUSE

•V••••S
AVATARS
AVENGES
AVENUES
AVIATES
AVOCETS
AVOWALS
AVOWERS
AVULSES
EVADERS
EVENKIS
EVINCES
EVOKERS
EVOLVES
EVULSES
IVORIES
TVSHOWS

••V•S••
ADVISED
ADVISER
ADVISES
ADVISOR
CAVESIN
DEVISED
DEVISES
DIVESIN
DIVESTS
DIVISOR
GIVESIN
GIVESTO
GIVESUP
INVESTS
LIVESIN
LIVESON
MOVESIN
REVISED
REVISER
REVISES
REVISIT
SAVESUP
WAVESIN

••V••S•
ADVERSE
DIVERSE
INVERSE
LAVALSE
OBVERSE
REVERSE
WAVIEST

••V•••S
ADVENTS
ADVERBS
ADVERTS
ADVISES
BOVINES
CAVEATS
CAVEINS
CAVERNS
CAVORTS
CIVVIES
DEVEINS
DEVICES
DEVIOUS
DEVISES
DEVOTES
DEVOURS
DEVRIES
DIVERTS
DIVESTS
DIVIDES
DIVINES
DIVVIES
ENVIOUS
FAVOURS
GAVIALS
GIVEUPS
GOVERNS
INVADES
INVENTS
INVERTS
INVESTS
INVITES
INVOKES
LEVIERS
LEVITES
LIVINGS
LOVEINS
NAVAHOS
NAVAJOS
NOVENAS
NOVICES
OBVERTS
OBVIOUS
PAVANES
RAVAGES
RAVINES
RAVINGS
REVAMPS
REVEALS
REVERBS
REVERES
REVERTS
REVIEWS
REVILES
REVISES
REVIVES
REVOKES
REVOLTS
SAVAGES
SAVALAS
SAVANTS
SAVINGS
SAVIORS
SAVOURS
SOVIETS
TAVERNS
UNVEILS
WYVERNS

•••V•S•
ATAVISM
ATAVIST
BRAVEST
CANVASS
DERVISH
FAUVISM
FAUVIST
GRAVEST
HARVEST
KNAVISH
PEEVISH
PROVISO
PROVOST
SLAVISH
SUAVEST

•••V••S
BEAVERS
BMOVIES
BRAVOES
BREVETS
CANVASS
CARVERS
CHEVIES
CHEVRES
CIVVIES
CLOVERS
COEVALS
CONVEYS
CONVOYS
CRAVATS
CRAVENS
CRAVERS
CURVETS
DELVERS
DIVVIES
DRIVELS
DRIVERS
DROVERS
ELEVENS
FERVORS
FLAVORS
GRAVELS
GRAVIES
GRIVETS
GROVELS
HEAVENS
HEAVERS
HEAVIES
JAYVEES
LEAVENS
LOUVERS
LOUVRES
MARVELS
NERVOUS
OEUVRES
PEAVEYS
PLOVERS
PRIVETS
PRIVIES
PROVERS
PURVEYS
QUAVERS
QUIVERS
SALVERS
SALVOES
SERVALS
SERVERS
SHAVERS
SHIVERS
SHOVELS
SHOVERS
SILVERS
SKIVERS
SLAVERS
SLIVERS
SLOVAKS
SLOVENS
SNIVELS
SOLVERS
SPAVINS
STEVENS
SURVEYS
SWIVELS
SYLVANS
TRAVELS
TRAVERS
TRAVOIS
TRIVETS
VELVETS
VERVETS
WAIVERS
WEAVERS
WEEVILS

••••V•S
ACTIVES
ALCOVES
ARGIVES
ARRIVES
BEHAVES
CLEAVES
DERIVES
DWARVES
ENDIVES
EVOLVES
EXWIVES
GREAVES
GRIEVES
GROOVES
MOTIVES
NATIVES
OCTAVES
OCTAVOS
RELIVES
REMOVES
REPAVES
REVIVES
SCARVES
SCURVES
SHEAVES
SHELVES
SHRIVES
SLEEVES
STARVES
STRIVES
SWERVES
THIEVES
THRIVES
TWELVES
VISAVIS
WHARVES
ZOUAVES

V•T••••
VATFULS
VATICAN
VETCHES
VETERAN
VETOERS
VETOING
VETTING
VITALLY
VITAMIN
VITIATE
VITRIFY
VITRIOL
VITTLES
VOTECHS
VOTESIN

V••T•••
VANTAGE
VASTEST
VECTORS
VENTERS
VENTING
VENTRAL
VENTURA
VENTURE
VERTIGO
VESTEES
VESTIGE
VESTING
VESTURE
VETTING
VICTIMS
VICTORS
VICTORY
VICTUAL
VIETNAM
VINTAGE
VINTNER
VIRTUAL
VIRTUES
VISTULA
VITTLES
VOLTAGE
VOLTAIC
VULTURE

V•••T••
VACATED
VACATES
VAULTED
VAULTER
VAUNTED
VAUNTER
VEGETAL
VISITED
VISITOR

V••••T•
VACUITY
VALUATE
VARIETY
VARLETS
VARSITY
VEDANTA
VEIGHTS
VELVETS
VELVETY
VERVETS
VIBRATE
VIBRATO
VIOLATE
VIOLETS
VITIATE
VULGATE

V•••••T
VAGRANT
VAGUEST
VAINEST
VALIANT
VANZANT
VARIANT
VARMINT
VASTEST
VERDANT
VERDICT
VERMONT
VIADUCT
VIBRANT
VINCENT
VIOLENT
VIOLIST

•V•T•••
AVATARS
OVATION

•V••T••
AVERTED
AVIATED
AVIATES
AVIATOR
EVERTED
EVICTED
OVERTLY
SVELTER

•V•••T•
AVIDITY
AVOCETS
EVERETT
OVERATE

•V••••T
EVENEST
EVENOUT
EVEREST
EVERETT
EVIDENT
EVILEST
OVERACT
OVEREAT

••V•T••
COVETED
DEVOTED
DEVOTEE
DEVOTES
GAVOTTE
INVITED
INVITES
INVITRO
LEVITES
PIVOTAL
PIVOTED
RIVETED
RIVETER

••V••T•
ADVENTS
ADVERTS
CAVEATS
CAVORTS
DEVIATE
DIVERTS
DIVESTS
GAVOTTE
GIVENTO
GIVESTO
HAVARTI
INVENTS
INVERTS
INVESTS
NOVELTY
OBVERTS
OBVIATE
POVERTY
REVERTS
REVOLTS
SAVANTS
SEVENTH
SEVENTY
SOVIETS

••V•••T
CAVEART
DEVIANT
DOVECOT
GAVEOUT
GIVEOUT
HAVENOT
LEVERET
LIVEOUT
MOVEOUT
REVISIT
RIVULET
WAVELET
WAVIEST

•••V•T•
BREVETS
BREVITY
CRAVATS
CURVETS
ELEVATE
GRAVITY
GRIVETS
HEAVETO
NAIVETE
OUTVOTE
PRIVATE
PRIVETS
SUAVITY
TRIVETS
VELVETS
VELVETY
VERVETS

•••V••T
ATAVIST
BRAVEST
CALVERT
CHEVIOT
CONVENT
CONVERT
CONVICT
CULVERT
DRIVEAT
FAUVIST
FERVENT
GRAVEST
HARVEST
PERVERT
PREVENT
PROVOST
SERVANT
SOLVENT
SUAVEST
SUBVERT

••••V•T
AQUAVIT

VU•••••
VULCANS
VULGATE
VULPINE
VULTURE

V•U••••
VAUGHAN
VAULTED
VAULTER
VAUNTED
VAUNTER
VOUCHED
VOUCHER
VOUCHES

V••U•••
VACUITY
VACUOLE
VACUOUS
VACUUMS
VAGUELY
VAGUEST
VALUATE
VALUING
VAQUERO
VICUNAS
VIRUSES
VISUALS
VOLUBLE
VOLUBLY
VOLUMES

V•••U••
VACUUMS
VALOURS
VAPOURS
VATFULS
VELLUMS
VELOURS
VENTURA
VENTURE
VERDUGO
VERDURE
VESTURE
VIADUCT
VICTUAL
VIGOURS
VIRGULE
VIRTUAL
VIRTUES
VISTULA
VULTURE

V••••U•
VACUOUS
VANOCUR
VARIOUS
VICIOUS
VISCOUS

•VU••••
AVULSED
AVULSES
EVULSED
EVULSES

•V•U•••
TVGUIDE

•V••U••
AVENUES
EVACUEE
OVERUSE

•V•••U•
EVENOUT
EVENSUP
OVERBUY
OVERDUB
OVERDUE
OVERRUN

••VU•••
DIVULGE
RIVULET

••V•U••
BIVOUAC
DEVOURS
FAVOURS
GIVEUPS
SAVOURS
SAVOURY

••V••U•
COVERUP
DEVALUE
DEVIOUS
ENVIOUS
GAVEOUT
GIVEOUT
GIVESUP
INVACUO
INVOGUE
LIVEOUT
LOVEBUG
MOVEOUT
OBVIOUS
PAVIOUR
REVALUE
REVENUE
SAVEDUP
SAVESUP
SEVENUP

•••VU••
BRAVURA
GRAVURE

•••V•U•
DRIVEUP
ELUVIUM
FERVOUR
FLAVOUR
NERVOUS
SERVEUP

••••V•U
NOUVEAU
PARVENU

V•V••••
VIVALDI
VIVENDI
VIVIDER
VIVIDLY

V••V•••
VELVETS
VELVETY
VERVETS

V•••V••
VISAVIS

•V••V••
EVOLVED
EVOLVES

•V•••V•
EVASIVE

••VV•••
CIVVIES
DIVVIED
DIVVIES
REVVING
SAVVIER
SAVVILY

••V•V••
REVIVAL
REVIVED
REVIVES

••V••V•
BIVALVE
DEVOLVE
INVOLVE
PAVLOVA
REVOLVE

•••VV••
FLIVVER

•••V•V•
QUIVIVE
SURVIVE

••••V•V
TELAVIV

V••W•••
VIEWERS
VIEWING

•V•W•••
AVOWALS
AVOWERS
AVOWING

•V•••W•
OVERAWE
TVSHOWS

•V••••W
OVERSAW

••V•W••
GAVEWAY
GIVEWAY

••V••W•
REVIEWS

•••V••W
PREVIEW
PURVIEW

••••V•W
DISAVOW

V•X••••
VEXEDLY

V•Y••••
VOYAGED
VOYAGER
VOYAGES

V••Y•••
VARYING

V•••Y••
VANDYCK
VANDYKE
VANEYCK

V••••Y•
VALLEYS
VEEJAYS
VOLLEYS

V•••••Y
VACANCY
VACUITY
VAGUELY
VALIDLY
VAPIDLY
VARIETY
VARSITY
VELVETY
VERSIFY
VEXEDLY
VICEROY
VICTORY
VISIBLY
VITALLY
VITRIFY
VIVIDLY
VOCALLY
VOLUBLY
VRONSKY

•V•••Y•
EVILEYE

•V••••Y
AVIDITY
OVERBUY
OVERFLY
OVERJOY
OVERLAY
OVERTLY

••VY•••
ENVYING
LEVYING

••V•••Y
BEVERLY
CAVALRY
CIVILLY
DEVILRY
GAVEWAY
GIVEWAY
LEVELLY
LIVIDLY
LOVERLY
NOVELTY
POVERTY
REVELRY
RIVALRY
SAVOURY
SAVVILY
SEVENTY
VIVIDLY
YEVGENY

•••V•Y•
CONVEYS
CONVOYS
PEAVEYS
PURVEYS
SURVEYS

•••V••Y
BRAVELY
BRAVERY
BREVITY
CALVARY
GRAVELY
GRAVITY
HEAVILY
KNAVERY
NAIVELY
NERVILY
PRIVACY
QUAVERY
SAVVILY
SILVERY
SLAVERY
SUAVELY
SUAVITY
VELVETY

•••••VY
ANCHOVY
MUSCOVY

V•Z••••
VIZIERS
VIZSLAS

V••Z•••
VANZANT

••V•••Z
ALVAREZ

••••V•Z
ESTEVEZ

WA•••••
WACKIER
WACKILY
WADDING
WADDLED
WADDLER
WADDLES
WADESIN
WAFFLED
WAFFLER
WAFFLES
WAFTING
WAGERED
WAGERER
WAGGERY
WAGGING
WAGGISH
WAGGLED
WAGGLES
WAGGONS
WAGONER
WAGTAIL
WAHINES
WAIKIKI
WAILERS
WAILING
WAISTED
WAITERS
WAITING
WAITOUT
WAITSON
WAITSUP
WAIVERS
WAIVING
WAKEFUL
WAKENED
WAKENER
WAKESUP
WALCOTT
WALDORF
WALKERS
WALKING
WALKINS
WALKMAN
WALKONS
WALKOUT
WALKUPS
WALKWAY
WALLABY
WALLACE
WALLACH
WALLETS
WALLEYE
WALLING
WALLOON
WALLOPS
WALLOWS
WALLSUP
WALMART
WALNUTS
WALPOLE
WALTERS
WALTZED
WALTZER
WALTZES
WAMBLED
WAMBLES
WANDERS
WANGLED
WANGLER
WANGLES
WANNABE
WANTADS
WANTING
WANTOUT
WANTSIN
WANTSTO
WAPITIS
WARBLED
WARBLER
WARBLES
WARDENS
WARDERS
WARDING
WARDOFF
WARFARE
WARGAME
WARGODS
WARIEST
WARLIKE
WARLOCK
WARLORD
WARMEST
WARMING
WARMISH
WARMSUP
WARMUPS
WARNING
WARPATH
WARPING
WARRANT
WARRENS
WARRING
WARRIOR
WARSHIP
WARTHOG
WARTIME
WARWICK
WASATCH
WASHERS
WASHING
WASHOFF
WASHOUT
WASHRAG
WASHTUB
WASPISH
WASSAIL
WASTAGE
WASTERS
WASTING
WASTREL
WATCHED
WATCHER
WATCHES
WATCHIT
WATERED
WATERER
WATTAGE
WATTEAU
WATTLES
WAVEDIN

WAVELET
WAVEOFF
WAVERED
WAVERER
WAVESIN
WAVIEST
WAXBEAN
WAXIEST
WAXWING
WAXWORK
WAYBILL
WAYLAID
WAYLAYS
WAYSIDE
WAYWARD
WAYWORN

W•A••••
WEAKENS
WEAKEST
WEAKISH
WEALTHY
WEANING
WEAPONS
WEARERS
WEARIED
WEARIER
WEARIES
WEARILY
WEARING
WEAROFF
WEAROUT
WEASELS
WEATHER
WEAVERS
WEAVING
WHACKED
WHALERS
WHALING
WHAMMED
WHARFED
WHARTON
WHARVES
WHATFOR
WHATNOT
WHAUDEN
WRACKED
WRAITHS
WRANGLE
WRAPPED
WRAPPER
WRAPSUP
WRAPUPS
WYANDOT

W••A•••
WASATCH
WCHANDY
WHEATON
WIZARDS
WOMANLY
WREAKED
WREATHE
WREATHS

W•••A••
WAGTAIL
WALLABY
WALLACE
WALLACH
WALMART
WANNABE
WANTADS
WARFARE
WARGAME
WARPATH
WARRANT
WASSAIL
WASTAGE
WATTAGE
WAYLAID
WAYLAYS
WAYWARD
WELFARE
WELLAND
WENTAPE
WETBARS
WETLAND
WHYDAHS
WIDMARK
WIGWAGS
WIGWAMS
WILLARD
WOMBATS
WOODARD

W••••A•
WALKMAN
WALKWAY
WASHRAG
WATTEAU
WAXBEAN
WEEKDAY
WENTBAD
WHEREAS
WHEREAT
WHIPSAW
WHITMAN
WILDCAT
WILLIAM
WINDBAG
WINEBAR
WINESAP
WINKSAT
WIRETAP
WISEMAN
WOLFGAL
WOLFMAN
WOLFRAM
WORKDAY
WORKMAN
WOZNIAK

W•••••A
WICHITA
WOOMERA
WYNONNA

•WA••••
AWAITED
AWAKENS
AWAKING
AWARDED
AWARDEE
AWARDER
AWAREOF
DWARFED
DWARVES
KWACHAS
KWANZAS
RWANDAN
SWABBED
SWADDLE
SWAGGER
SWAHILI
SWALLOW
SWAMPED
SWANKER
SWANSON
SWAPPED
SWAPPER
SWARMED
SWARTHY
SWATHED
SWATHES
SWATTED
SWATTER
SWAYERS
SWAYING
TWADDLE
TWANGED

•W•A•••
SWEARAT
SWEARBY
SWEARER
SWEARIN
SWEARTO
SWEATED
SWEATER
TWEAKED

•W••A••
AWKWARD
TWOBASE

•W•••A•
KWACHAS
KWANZAS
RWANDAN
SWEARAT
SWOREAT
TWOSTAR

•W••••A
IWOJIMA

••WA•••
BEWAILS
BYWAYOF
COWARDS
DOWAGER
EDWARDS
HOWARDS
INWARDS
KIWANIS
KUWAITI
NEWAGER
ONWARDS
REWARDS
REWARMS
REWAXED
REWAXES
THWACKS
THWARTS
TOWARDS
TOWAWAY
UPWARDS

••W•A••
BOWSAWS
COWHAND
DEWLAPS
ENWRAPS
GEWGAWS
HAWHAWS
HOWDAHS
LOWBALL
LOWLAND
LOWPAID
NEWGATE
NEWHART
NEWMATH
NEWWAVE
PAWPAWS
RAWDATA
REWEAVE
REWRAPS
TOWCARS
TOWPATH
UNWEAVE
UNWRAPS

••W••A•
COWPEAS
DEWCLAW
DOWNPAT
LOWBEAM
LOWGEAR
LOWROAD
NEWDEAL
NEWSDAY
NEWSMAN
NEWYEAR
PAWEDAT
RAWDEAL
ROWBOAT
TOWAWAY
TOWHEAD

••W•••A
RAWDATA

•••WA••
AIRWAVE
AIRWAYS
ARAWAKS
ARTWARE
ATHWART
AVOWALS
AWKWARD
BULWARK
CARWASH
CATWALK
DRYWALL
ENDWAYS
EYEWASH
FLYWAYS
FORWARD
FROWARD
GUNWALE
HAYWARD
HOGWASH
HOTWARS
JAYWALK
JETWASH
LEEWARD
MIDWAYS
NARWALS
NEWWAVE
OUTWARD
PINWALE
PREWASH
RUNWAYS
SEAWALL
SEAWARD
SEAWAYS
SKYWARD
SKYWAYS
STEWARD
STEWART
SUBWAYS
UNAWARE
WAYWARD
WIGWAGS
WIGWAMS

•••W•A•
CRAWDAD
CREWMAN
CROWBAR
DRAWBAR
FAYWRAY
FROWNAT
NARWHAL
NOSWEAT
OUTWEAR
PLOWMAN
SHAWWAL
SHOWMAN
SNOWCAP
SNOWDAY
SNOWMAN

•••W••A
SNOWPEA

••••WA•
ANTIWAR
ARCHWAY
AREAWAY
BEESWAX
BELTWAY
BIKEWAY
BOERWAR
CARAWAY
COLDWAR
CUTAWAY
DOORWAY
DUNAWAY
EATAWAY
FAIRWAY
FARAWAY
FLYAWAY
FREEWAY
GANGWAY
GATEWAY
GAVEWAY
GETAWAY
GIVEWAY
GOTAWAY
HALFWAY
HALLWAY
HEADWAY
HIGHWAY
HOLYWAR
INNOWAY
JANEWAY
LAYAWAY
MADEWAY
MAKEWAY
MANOWAR
MATEWAN
OJIBWAS
OJIBWAY
OTTAWAS
PARKWAY
PARTWAY
PATHWAY
POSTWAR
PUTAWAY
RACEWAY
RAILWAY
RANAWAY
RENEWAL
RIDGWAY
ROADWAY
RUNAWAY
SARAWAK
SHAWWAL
SOMEWAY
TAXIWAY
THRUWAY
TIMEWAS
TOLLWAY
TOWAWAY
WALKWAY

••••W•A
CATAWBA

•••••WA
OKINAWA

W•B••••
WEBBING
WEBFEET
WEBFOOT
WEBSITE
WEBSTER
WEBTOED
WOBBLED
WOBBLES
WOBEGON

W••B•••
WAMBLED
WAMBLES
WARBLED
WARBLER
WARBLES
WAXBEAN
WAYBILL
WEBBING
WETBARS
WOBBLED
WOBBLES
WOMBATS

W•••B••
WENTBAD
WINDBAG
WINEBAR

W••••B•
WALLABY
WANNABE
WHEREBY
WOULDBE

W•••••B
WASHTUB

•W•B•••
SWABBED
TWOBASE
TWOBITS

•W••B••
SWABBED
TWINBED

•W•••B•
SWEARBY
SWINGBY
SWOREBY

••WB•••
COWBELL
COWBIRD
COWBOYS
HOWBEIT
JAWBONE
LOWBALL
LOWBEAM
LOWBLOW
LOWBORN
LOWBOYS
LOWBRED
LOWBROW
NEWBORN
ROWBOAT
SAWBUCK
SOWBUGS

••W•B••
DOWNBOW
NEWSBOY

•••WB••
CROWBAR
DRAWBAR
PLOWBOY
SHOWBIZ

•••W•B•
COBWEBS

•••W••B
SNOWJOB

••••WB•
CATAWBA

••••W•B
FOODWEB

WC•••••
WCHANDY

W•C••••
WACKIER
WACKILY
WICHITA
WICKERS
WICKETS
WICKIUP
WYCHELM

W••C•••
WALCOTT
WATCHED
WATCHER
WATCHES
WATCHIT
WELCHED
WELCHES
WELCOME
WENCHES
WETCELL
WHACKED
WINCERS
WINCHED
WINCHES
WINCING
WITCHES
WRACKED
WRECKED
WRECKER

W•••C••
WILDCAT
WOODCUT

W••••C•
WALLACE
WALLACH
WARLOCK
WARWICK
WASATCH
WEDLOCK
WOZZECK

•W•C•••
KWACHAS

•W••C••
TWITCHY

••WC•••
DEWCLAW
FAWCETT
HOWCOME
TOWCARS

••W•C••
THWACKS

••W••C•
BEWITCH
COWLICK
LOWNECK
LOWTECH
SAWBUCK

•••WC••
CREWCUT
SNOWCAP

•••W•C•
IPSWICH
WARWICK

W•D••••
WADDING
WADDLED
WADDLER
WADDLES
WADESIN
WEDDING
WEDGIES
WEDGING
WEDLOCK
WIDENED
WIDGEON
WIDGETS
WIDMARK
WIDOWED
WIDOWER

W••D•••
WADDING
WADDLED
WADDLER
WADDLES
WALDORF
WANDERS
WARDENS
WARDERS
WARDING
WARDOFF
WEDDING
WEEDERS
WEEDIER
WEEDING
WEEDOUT
WELDERS
WELDING
WENDELL
WENDERS
WENDING
WHYDAHS
WILDCAT
WILDEST
WILDING
WILDONE
WINDBAG
WINDERS
WINDIER
WINDING
WINDOWS
WINDROW
WINDSOR
WINDSUP
WINDUPS
WONDERS
WOODARD
WOODCUT
WOODIER
WOODIES
WOODLOT
WOODROW
WORDIER
WORDILY
WORDING
WORDONE

W•••D••
WAVEDIN
WEEKDAY
WEIRDER
WEIRDLY
WEIRDOS
WHAUDEN
WHEEDLE
WIELDED
WIPEDUP
WISEDUP
WORKDAY
WORLDLY
WOULDBE
WOULDNT
WOUNDED
WOUNDUP
WYANDOT

W••••D•
WANTADS
WARGODS
WAYSIDE
WCHANDY
WIZARDS

W•••••D
WADDLED
WAFFLED
WAGERED
WAGGLED
WAISTED
WAKENED
WALTZED
WAMBLED
WANGLED
WARBLED
WARLORD
WATCHED
WATERED
WAVERED
WAYLAID
WAYWARD
WEARIED
WEBTOED
WEEKEND
WEIGHED
WELCHED
WELLAND
WELLFED
WENTBAD
WESTEND
WETLAND
WHACKED
WHAMMED
WHARFED
WHEELED
WHEEZED
WHELPED
WHETTED
WHIFFED
WHIPPED
WHIRLED
WHIRRED
WHISKED
WHIZKID
WHIZZED
WHOMPED
WHOOPED
WHOPPED
WHORLED
WHUPPED
WIDENED
WIDOWED
WIELDED
WIGGLED
WILFORD
WILFRID
WILLARD
WIMPLED
WINCHED
WINERED
WIZENED
WOBBLED
WOODARD
WORRIED
WORSTED
WOUNDED
WRACKED
WRAPPED
WREAKED
WRECKED
WRESTED
WRITHED
WRONGED

•W•D•••
SWADDLE
SWEDISH
TWADDLE
TWIDDLE

•W••D••
AWARDED
AWARDEE
AWARDER
DWINDLE
OWNEDUP
RWANDAN
SWADDLE
SWINDLE
TWADDLE
TWIDDLE

•W••••D
AWAITED
AWARDED
AWKWARD
DWARFED
DWELLED
SWABBED
SWAMPED
SWAPPED
SWARMED
SWATHED
SWATTED
SWEATED
SWELLED
SWERVED
SWIGGED
SWILLED
SWIRLED
SWISHED
SWOONED
SWOOPED
TWANGED
TWEAKED
TWEETED
TWEEZED
TWILLED
TWINBED
TWINGED
TWINNED
TWIRLED
TWISTED
TWITTED
TWOFOLD

••WD•••
BAWDIER
BAWDILY
BOWDLER
DAWDLED
DAWDLER
DAWDLES
DEWDROP
DOWDIER
DOWDILY
HOWDAHS
LEWDEST
LOWDOWN
MOWDOWN
NEWDEAL
POWDERS
POWDERY
RAWDATA
RAWDEAL
ROWDIER
ROWDIES
ROWDILY
SAWDUST

••W•D••
NEWSDAY
PAWEDAT
SEWEDUP

••W••D•
BYWORDS
COWARDS
COWHIDE
DEWILDE
EDWARDS
HOWARDS
INWARDS
LOWTIDE
ONWARDS
RAWHIDE
REWARDS
REWELDS
REWINDS
REWORDS
TOWARDS
UNWINDS
UPWARDS

••W•••D
BOWERED
COWBIRD
COWERED
COWHAND
COWHERD
DAWDLED
JEWELED
LAWFORD
LOWBRED
LOWERED
LOWLAND
LOWPAID
LOWROAD
POWERED
REWAXED
REWIRED
REWOUND
SAWWOOD
TOWELED
TOWERED
TOWHEAD
UNWOUND

•••WD••
BLOWDRY
CHOWDER
CLOWDER
CRAWDAD
CROWDED
SHOWDOG
SNOWDAY
SNOWDON

•••W••D
AWKWARD
BOXWOOD
BRAWLED
BROWNED
BROWSED
CLOWNED
CRAWDAD
CRAWLED
CROWDED
CROWNED
DAGWOOD
DOGWOOD
DRAWLED
DROWNED
DROWSED
FORWARD
FROWARD
FROWNED
GROWLED
HAYWARD
HEYWOOD
HOGWILD
ILLWIND
INAWORD
KEYWORD
LEEWARD
MISWORD
OUTWARD
PLYWOOD
PROWLED
RAGWEED
REDWOOD
SAWWOOD
SCOWLED
SEAWARD
SEAWEED
SKYWARD
SPAWNED
STEWARD
TRAWLED
WAYWARD

••••W•D
ALLOWED
BEDEWED
ELBOWED
ENDOWED
LOWBRED
REMOWED
RENEWED
RETOWED
SCREWED
STREWED
UNBOWED
UNSEWED
WIDOWED

WE•••••
WEAKENS
WEAKEST
WEAKISH
WEALTHY
WEANING
WEAPONS
WEARERS
WEARIED
WEARIER
WEARIES
WEARILY
WEARING
WEAROFF
WEAROUT
WEASELS
WEATHER
WEAVERS
WEAVING
WEBBING
WEBFEET
WEBFOOT
WEBSITE
WEBSTER
WEBTOED
WEDDING
WEDGIES
WEDGING
WEDLOCK
WEEDERS
WEEDIER
WEEDING
WEEDOUT
WEEKDAY
WEEKEND
WEENIES
WEEPERS
WEEPIER
WEEPING
WEEVILS
WEIGHED
WEIGHIN
WEIGHTS
WEIGHTY

WEIRDER
WEIRDLY
WEIRDOS
WELCHED
WELCHES
WELCOME
WELDERS
WELDING
WELFARE
WELKINS
WELLAND
WELLFED
WELLING
WELLOFF
WELLRUN
WELLSET
WELLSUP
WELTERS
WELTING
WENCHES
WENDELL
WENDERS
WENDING
WENTAPE
WENTBAD
WENTFOR
WENTOFF
WENTOUT
WERNHER
WERTHER
WESKITS
WESTEND
WESTERN
WETBARS
WETCELL
WETHERS
WETLAND
WETMOPS
WETNESS
WETSUIT
WETTEST
WETTING

W•E••••

WEEDERS
WEEDIER
WEEDING
WEEDOUT
WEEKDAY
WEEKEND
WEENIES
WEEPERS
WEEPIER
WEEPING
WEEVILS
WHEATON
WHEEDLE
WHEELED
WHEELER
WHEELIE
WHEEZED
WHEEZER
WHEEZES
WHELPED
WHEREAS
WHEREAT
WHEREBY
WHEREIN
WHEREOF
WHERETO
WHETHER
WHETTED
WIELDED
WIENERS
WIENIES
WOEISME
WREAKED
WREATHE
WREATHS
WRECKED
WRECKER
WRESTED
WRESTLE

W••E•••

WADESIN
WAGERED
WAGERER
WAKEFUL
WAKENED
WAKENER
WAKESUP
WATERED
WATERER
WAVEDIN
WAVELET
WAVEOFF
WAVERED
WAVERER
WAVESIN
WHEEDLE
WHEELED
WHEELER
WHEELIE
WHEEZED
WHEEZER
WHEEZES
WHOEVER
WIDENED
WINEBAR
WINERED
WINESAP
WIPEDUP
WIPEOUT
WIPESUP
WIRETAP
WISEDUP
WISEGUY
WISEMAN
WISEMEN
WISESUP
WIZENED
WOBEGON
WOKENUP
WOREOFF
WOREOUT
WYNETTE
WYVERNS

W•••E••

WAGGERY
WAILERS
WAITERS
WAIVERS
WALKERS
WALLETS
WALLEYE
WALTERS
WANDERS
WARDENS
WARDERS
WARIEST
WARMEST
WARRENS
WASHERS
WASTERS
WATTEAU
WAVIEST
WAXBEAN
WAXIEST
WEAKENS
WEAKEST
WEARERS
WEASELS
WEAVERS
WEBFEET
WEEDERS
WEEKEND
WEEPERS
WELDERS
WELTERS
WENDELL
WENDERS
WESTEND
WESTERN
WETCELL
WETHERS
WETNESS
WETTEST
WHALERS
WHEREAS
WHEREAT
WHEREBY
WHEREIN
WHEREOF
WHERETO
WHINERS
WHITENS
WHITEST
WICKERS
WICKETS
WIDGEON
WIDGETS
WIENERS
WIGLETS
WILDEST
WILHELM
WILIEST
WINCERS
WINDERS
WINGERS
WINKERS
WINNERS
WINTERS
WINTERY
WIRIEST
WISHERS
WITHERS
WITLESS
WITNESS
WONDERS
WOOFERS
WOOLENS
WOOMERA
WORKERS
WORSENS
WOZZECK
WRITEIN
WRITERS
WRITETO
WRITEUP
WROTEIN
WROTETO
WROTEUP
WRYNESS
WYCHELM

W••••E•

WACKIER
WADDLED
WADDLER
WADDLES
WAFFLED
WAFFLER
WAFFLES
WAGERED
WAGERER
WAGGLED
WAGGLES
WAGONER
WAHINES
WAISTED
WAKENED
WAKENER
WALTZED
WALTZER
WALTZES
WAMBLED
WAMBLES
WANGLED
WANGLER
WANGLES
WARBLED
WARBLER
WARBLES
WASTREL
WATCHED
WATCHER
WATCHES
WATERED
WATERER
WATTLES
WAVELET
WAVERED
WAVERER
WEARIED
WEARIER
WEARIES
WEATHER
WEBFEET
WEBSTER
WEBTOED
WEDGIES
WEEDIER
WEENIES
WEEPIER
WEIGHED
WEIRDER
WELCHED
WELCHES
WELLFED
WELLSET
WENCHES
WERNHER
WERTHER
WHACKED
WHAMMED
WHARFED
WHARVES
WHAUDEN
WHEELED
WHEELER
WHEEZED
WHEEZER
WHEEZES
WHELPED
WHETHER
WHETTED
WHIFFED
WHIMPER
WHIPPED
WHIPPET
WHIRLED
WHIRRED
WHISKED
WHISKER
WHISKEY
WHISPER
WHITHER
WHITNEY
WHIZZED
WHIZZES
WHOEVER
WHOMPED
WHOOPED
WHOOPEE
WHOPPED
WHOPPER
WHORLED
WHUPPED
WIDENED
WIDOWED
WIDOWER
WIELDED
WIENIES
WIGGLED
WIGGLER
WIGGLES
WILLIES
WIMPLED
WIMPLES
WINCHED
WINCHES
WINDIER
WINERED
WINFREY
WINKLER
WISEMEN
WISPIER
WITCHES
WITTIER
WIZENED
WOBBLED
WOBBLES
WOLFMEN
WOODIER
WOODIES
WOOLIER
WOOLIES
WOOLLEN
WOOLSEY
WOOSTER
WOOZIER
WORDIER
WORKMEN
WORMIER
WORRIED
WORRIER
WORRIES
WORSTED
WOUNDED
WRACKED
WRAPPED
WRAPPER
WREAKED
WRECKED
WRECKER
WRESTED
WRIGLEY
WRINGER
WRITHED
WRITHES
WRITTEN
WRONGED
WRONGER

W•••••E

WALLACE
WALLEYE
WALPOLE
WANNABE
WARFARE
WARGAME
WARLIKE
WARTIME
WASTAGE
WATTAGE
WAYSIDE
WEBSITE
WELCOME
WELFARE
WENTAPE
WHEEDLE
WHEELIE
WHISTLE
WHITTLE
WHOOPEE
WILDONE
WILLKIE
WINSOME
WOEISME
WORDONE
WOULDBE
WRANGLE
WREATHE
WRESTLE
WRIGGLE
WRINKLE
WYNETTE

•WE••••

AWELESS
AWESOME
DWEEZIL
DWELLED
DWELLER
SWEARAT
SWEARBY
SWEARER
SWEARIN
SWEARTO
SWEATED
SWEATER
SWEDISH
SWEEPER
SWEEPUP
SWEETEN
SWEETER
SWEETIE
SWEETLY
SWEETON
SWELLED
SWELLUP
SWELTER
SWELTRY
SWEPTUP
SWERVED
SWERVES
TWEAKED
TWEETED
TWEETER
TWEEZED
TWEEZES
TWELFTH
TWELVES

•W•E•••

DWEEZIL
OWNEDUP
SWEEPER
SWEEPUP
SWEETEN
SWEETER
SWEETIE
SWEETLY
SWEETON
TWEETED
TWEETER
TWEEZED
TWEEZES

•W••E••

AWAKENS
AWAREOF
AWELESS
SWAYERS
SWIPERS
SWIVELS
SWOREAT
SWOREBY
SWOREIN
TWOFERS

•W•••E•

AWAITED
AWARDED
AWARDEE
AWARDER
DWARFED
DWARVES
DWELLED
DWELLER
SWABBED
SWAGGER
SWAMPED
SWANKER
SWAPPED
SWAPPER
SWARMED
SWATHED
SWATHES
SWATTED
SWATTER
SWEARER
SWEATED
SWEATER
SWEEPER
SWEETEN
SWEETER
SWELLED
SWELTER
SWERVED
SWERVES
SWIFTER
SWIGGED
SWILLED
SWIMMER
SWINGER
SWIRLED
SWISHED
SWISHES
SWITZER
SWOLLEN
SWOONED
SWOOPED
TWANGED
TWEAKED
TWEETED
TWEETER
TWEEZED
TWEEZES
TWELVES
TWILLED
TWINBED
TWINGED
TWINGES
TWINNED
TWIRLED
TWIRLER
TWISTED
TWISTER
TWITTED
TWITTER
TWOSTEP

•W••••E

AWARDEE
AWESOME
DWINDLE
OWLLIKE
SWADDLE
SWEETIE
SWINDLE
SWIZZLE
SWOOSIE
TWADDLE
TWIDDLE
TWINKLE
TWOBASE
TWOSOME
TWOTIME
TWOTONE

••WE•••

BOWERED
COWERED
HGWELLS
HOWELLS
HOWEVER
JEWELED
JEWELER
JEWELRY
LOWERED
PAWEDAT
POWERED
REWEAVE
REWELDS
SEWEDUP
TOWELED
TOWERED
UNWEAVE

••W•E••

BAWLERS
BOWLERS
BOWYERS
COWBELL
COWHERD
COWPEAS
DOWNERS
DOWSERS
FAWCETT
FAWNERS
FOWLERS
GAWKERS
HAWKERS
HAWKEYE
HAWSERS
HEWLETT
HOWBEIT
HOWLERS
LAWLESS
LAWYERS
LEWDEST
LOWBEAM
LOWGEAR
LOWHEEL
LOWNECK
LOWNESS
LOWTECH
MEWLERS
NCWYETH
NEWDEAL
NEWLEFT
NEWNESS
NEWYEAR
NOWHERE
PAWNEES
PAWNERS
POWDERS
POWDERY
RAWDEAL
RAWNESS
SAWYERS
TOWHEAD
TOWHEES
TOWNERS
YAWNERS
YAWPERS
YOWLERS

••W••E•

BAWDIER
BOWDLER
BOWERED
BOWTIES
COWERED
COWRIES
DAWDLED
DAWDLER
DAWDLES
DOWAGER
DOWDIER
DOWNIER
DOWRIES
EXWIVES
GAWKIER
HOWEVER
JEWELED
JEWELER
KEWPIES
LOWBRED
LOWERED
LOWHEEL
LOWLIER
NEWAGER
NEWSIER
NEWSMEN
PAWNEES
POWERED
REWAXED
REWAXES
REWIRED
REWIRES
REWOVEN
ROWDIER
ROWDIES
TAWNIER
TOWELED
TOWERED
TOWHEES
TOWNIES
UNWISER

••W•••E

BOWLINE
COWHIDE
COWPOKE
DEWILDE
DEWLINE
EBWHITE
HAWKEYE
HOWCOME
JAWBONE
JAWLINE
LOWLIFE
LOWRISE
LOWTIDE
NEWGATE
NEWWAVE
NOWHERE
RAWHIDE
REWEAVE
REWRITE
REWROTE
TOWROPE
UNWEAVE

•••WE••

ANSWERS
ANTWERP
AVOWERS
BETWEEN
BLOWERS
BOSWELL
BREWERS
BREWERY
CHEWERS
CLAWERS
COBWEBS
CREWELS
CROWERS
DRAWERS
DRYWELL
FALWELL
FARWEST
FLOWERS
FLOWERY
FORWENT
GETWELL
GLOWERS
GNAWERS
GOTWELL
GROWERS
INAWEOF
INDWELL
INKWELL
KEYWEST
MAEWEST
MAXWELL
MIDWEEK
MIDWEST
NOSWEAT
NOTWELL
OILWELL
OLDWEST
OUTWEAR
PEEWEES
PLOWERS
PROWESS
RAGWEED
ROSWELL
SEAWEED
SHOWERS
SHOWERY
SITWELL
SKEWERS
SLOWEST
STEWERS
TROWELS
TROWERS
UNSWEPT
UPSWEEP
UPSWEPT
VIEWERS

•••W•E•

BETWEEN
BLOWIER
BRAWLED
BRAWLER
BROWNED
BROWNER
BROWSED
BROWSER
BROWSES
CHEWIER
CHOWDER
CLOWDER
CLOWNED
CRAWLED
CRAWLER
CREWMEN
CROWDED
CROWNED
DRAWLED
DROWNED
DROWSED
DROWSES
FRAWLEY
FROWNED
FROWNER
GROWLED
GROWLER
MIDWEEK
PEEWEES
PLOWMEN
PROWLED
PROWLER
RAGWEED
SAYWHEN
SCOWLED
SCOWLER
SEAWEED
SHAWNEE
SHOWIER
SHOWMEN
SNOWIER
SNOWMEN
SNOWPEA
SPAWNED
TRAWLED
TRAWLER
UPSWEEP

•••W••E

AIRWAVE
ALEWIFE
ARTWARE
BROWNIE
ENDWISE
ENTWINE
GUNWALE
HAYWIRE
HOTWIRE
JUGWINE
MAYWINE
MCSWINE
MIDWIFE
NEWWAVE
OUTWORE
PINWALE
REDWINE
SHAWNEE
UNAWARE

••••WE•

ALLOWED
BEDEWED
CNTOWER
ELBOWED
EMPOWER
ENDOWED
FOODWEB
REMOWED
RENEWED
RENEWER
RETOWED
SCREWED
STREWED
STREWER
THROWER
UNBOWED
UNSEWED
WIDOWED
WIDOWER

•••••WE

MARLOWE
OVERAWE
ROBLOWE

W•F••••

WAFFLED
WAFFLER
WAFFLES
WAFTING

W••F•••

WAFFLED
WAFFLER
WAFFLES
WARFARE
WEBFEET
WEBFOOT
WELFARE
WHIFFED
WILFORD
WILFRID
WINFREY
WOLFGAL
WOLFING
WOLFISH
WOLFMAN
WOLFMEN
WOLFRAM
WOOFERS
WOOFING

W•••F••

WAKEFUL
WELLFED
WENTFOR
WHARFED
WHATFOR
WHIFFED
WILLFUL
WISHFUL
WISTFUL
WORKFOR

W••••F•

WARDOFF
WASHOFF
WAVEOFF
WEAROFF
WELLOFF
WENTOFF
WOREOFF
WORKOFF
WORNOFF

W•••••F

WALDORF
WARDOFF
WASHOFF
WAVEOFF
WEAROFF
WELLOFF
WENTOFF
WHEREOF
WOREOFF
WORKOFF
WORNOFF

•WF••••

AWFULLY

•W•F•••

SWIFTER
SWIFTLY
TWOFERS
TWOFOLD

•W••F••

DWARFED
TWELFTH

•W••••F

AWAREOF

••WF•••

BOWFINS
LAWFORD
SAWFISH

••W•F••

BOWLFUL

••W••F•

LOWLIFE
NEWLEFT
PAWNOFF

••W•••F

BYWAYOF
PAWNOFF

•••WF••

BLOWFLY

•••W•F•

ALEWIFE
BLEWOFF
BLOWOFF
MIDWIFE
SHOWOFF

•••W••F

AIRWOLF
BEOWULF
BLEWOFF
BLOWOFF
CRYWOLF
INAWEOF
REDWOLF
SHEWOLF
SHOWOFF

W•G••••
WAGERED
WAGERER
WAGGERY
WAGGING
WAGGISH
WAGGLED
WAGGLES
WAGGONS
WAGONER
WAGTAIL
WIGGLED
WIGGLER
WIGGLES
WIGLETS
WIGSOUT
WIGWAGS
WIGWAMS

W••G•••
WAGGERY
WAGGING
WAGGISH
WAGGLED
WAGGLES
WAGGONS
WANGLED
WANGLER
WANGLES
WARGAME
WARGODS
WEDGIES
WEDGING
WEIGHED
WEIGHIN
WEIGHTS
WEIGHTY
WIDGEON
WIDGETS
WIGGLED
WIGGLER
WIGGLES
WINGERS
WINGING
WINGNUT
WINGSIT
WINGTIP
WRIGGLE
WRIGGLY
WRIGHTS
WRIGLEY

W•••G••
WISEGUY
WOBEGON
WOLFGAL
WRANGLE
WRIGGLE
WRIGGLY
WRINGER
WRONGED
WRONGER
WRONGLY
WROUGHT

W••••G•
WASTAGE
WATTAGE
WIGWAGS

W•••••G
WADDING
WAFTING
WAGGING
WAILING
WAITING
WAIVING
WALKING
WALLING
WANTING
WARDING
WARMING
WARNING
WARPING
WARRING
WARTHOG
WASHING
WASHRAG
WASTING
WAXWING
WEANING
WEARING
WEAVING
WEBBING
WEDDING
WEDGING
WEEDING
WEEPING
WELDING
WELLING
WELTING
WENDING
WETTING
WHALING
WHILING
WHINING
WHITING
WILDING
WILLING
WILTING
WINCING
WINDBAG
WINDING
WINGING
WINKING
WINNING
WISHING
WISPING
WITTING
WOLFING
WOOFING
WORDING
WORKING
WRITING
WYOMING
WYSIWYG

•W•G•••
SWAGGER
SWIGGED

•W••G••
OWINGTO
SWAGGER
SWIGGED
SWINGBY
SWINGER
TWANGED
TWINGED
TWINGES
ZWINGLI

•W•••G•
AWNINGS

•W••••G
AWAKING
SWAYING
SWIPING
TWINING

••WG•••
COWGIRL
GEWGAWS
LOWGEAR
NEWGATE

••W•G••
DOWAGER
NEWAGER

••W••G•
SAWLOGS
SOWBUGS

••W•••G
BAWLING
BOWLING
COWLING
DAWNING
DOWNING
DOWSING
FAWNING
FOWLING
GAWKING
GOWRONG
HAWKING
HOWLING
MEWLING
PAWNING
YAWNING
YOWLING

•••WG••
BLOWGUN

•••W•G•
BIGWIGS
EARWIGS
WIGWAGS

•••W••G
AVOWING
BATWING
BLOWING
BREWING
CHEWING
CLAWING
CREWING
CROWING
DRAWING
FLAWING
FLOWING
GLOWING
GNAWING
GROWING
KNOWING
LAPWING
MEOWING
PLOWING
REDWING
SHOWDOG
SHOWING
SKEWING
SLOWING
SNOWING
SPEWING
STEWING
STOWING
THAWING
UPSWING
VIEWING
WAXWING

••••W•G
WYSIWYG

WH•••••
WHACKED
WHALERS
WHALING
WHAMMED
WHARFED
WHARTON
WHARVES
WHATFOR
WHATNOT
WHAUDEN
WHEATON
WHEEDLE
WHEELED
WHEELER
WHEELIE
WHEEZED
WHEEZER
WHEEZES
WHELPED
WHEREAS
WHEREAT
WHEREBY
WHEREIN
WHEREOF
WHERETO
WHETHER
WHETTED
WHIFFED
WHILING
WHIMPER
WHINERS
WHINING
WHIPPED
WHIPPET
WHIPSAW
WHIPSUP
WHIRLED
WHIRRED
WHISKED
WHISKER
WHISKEY
WHISPER
WHISTLE
WHITENS
WHITEST
WHITHER
WHITING
WHITISH
WHITMAN
WHITNEY
WHITTLE
WHIZKID
WHIZZED
WHIZZES
WHOEVER
WHOMPED
WHOOPED
WHOOPEE
WHOPPED
WHOPPER
WHORLED
WHOSWHO
WHUPPED
WHYDAHS

W•H••••
WAHINES
WCHANDY

W••H•••
WASHERS
WASHING
WASHOFF
WASHOUT
WASHRAG
WASHTUB
WETHERS
WICHITA
WILHELM
WISHERS
WISHFUL
WISHING
WITHERS
WITHOUT
WYCHELM

W•••H••
WARSHIP
WARTHOG
WATCHED
WATCHER
WATCHES
WATCHIT
WEATHER
WEIGHED
WEIGHIN
WEIGHTS
WEIGHTY
WELCHED
WELCHES
WENCHES
WERNHER
WERTHER
WHETHER
WHITHER
WINCHED
WINCHES
WITCHES
WORSHIP
WRIGHTS
WRITHED
WRITHES

W••••H•
WEALTHY
WHOSWHO
WHYDAHS
WRAITHS
WREATHE
WREATHS
WROUGHT

W•••••H
WAGGISH
WALLACH
WARMISH
WARPATH
WASATCH
WASPISH
WEAKISH
WHITISH
WOLFISH

•W•H•••
SWAHILI

•W••H••
KWACHAS
SWATHED
SWATHES
SWISHED
SWISHES

•W•••H•
SWARTHY
TWITCHY

•W••••H
SWEDISH
TWELFTH

••WH•••
COWHAND
COWHERD
COWHIDE
EBWHITE
HAWHAWS
LOWHEEL
NEWHART
NOWHERE
RAWHIDE
TOWHEAD
TOWHEES

••W••H•
HOWDAHS

••W•••H
ALWORTH
BEWITCH
HAWKISH
LOWTECH
MAWKISH
NCWYETH
NEWMATH
SAWFISH
TOWPATH

•••WH••
EREWHON
GEEWHIZ
KNOWHOW
NARWHAL
SAYWHEN

•••W•H•
GROWTHS

•••W••H
CARWASH
EYEWASH
HOGWASH
IPSWICH
JETWASH
PREWASH
RUNWITH
SOPWITH

••••WH•
WHOSWHO

WI•••••
WICHITA
WICKERS
WICKETS
WICKIUP
WIDENED
WIDGEON
WIDGETS
WIDMARK
WIDOWED
WIDOWER
WIELDED
WIENERS
WIENIES
WIGGLED
WIGGLER
WIGGLES
WIGLETS
WIGSOUT
WIGWAGS
WIGWAMS
WILDCAT
WILDEST
WILDING
WILDONE
WILFORD
WILFRID
WILHELM
WILIEST
WILLARD
WILLFUL
WILLIAM
WILLIES
WILLING
WILLKIE
WILLOWS
WILLOWY
WILLSON
WILTING
WIMPLED
WIMPLES
WINCERS
WINCHED
WINCHES
WINCING
WINDBAG
WINDERS
WINDIER
WINDING
WINDOWS
WINDROW
WINDSOR
WINDSUP
WINDUPS
WINEBAR
WINERED
WINESAP
WINFREY
WINGERS
WINGING
WINGNUT
WINGSIT
WINGTIP
WINKERS
WINKING
WINKLER
WINKOUT
WINKSAT
WINNERS
WINNING
WINNOWS
WINSLOW
WINSOME
WINSOUT
WINSTON
WINTERS
WINTERY
WIPEDUP
WIPEOUT
WIPESUP
WIRETAP
WIRIEST
WISEDUP
WISEGUY
WISEMAN
WISEMEN
WISESUP
WISHERS
WISHFUL
WISHING
WISPIER
WISPILY
WISPING
WISTFUL
WITCHES
WITHERS
WITHOUT
WITLESS
WITNESS
WITTIER
WITTILY
WITTING
WIZARDS
WIZENED

W•I••••
WAIKIKI
WAILERS
WAILING
WAISTED
WAITERS
WAITING
WAITOUT
WAITSON
WAITSUP
WAIVERS
WAIVING
WEIGHED
WEIGHIN
WEIGHTS
WEIGHTY
WEIRDER
WEIRDLY
WEIRDOS
WHIFFED
WHILING
WHIMPER
WHINERS
WHINING
WHIPPED
WHIPPET
WHIPSAW
WHIPSUP
WHIRLED
WHIRRED
WHISKED
WHISKER
WHISKEY
WHISPER
WHISTLE
WHITENS
WHITEST
WHITHER
WHITING
WHITISH
WHITMAN
WHITNEY
WHITTLE
WHIZKID
WHIZZED
WHIZZES
WRIGGLE
WRIGGLY
WRIGHTS
WRIGLEY
WRINGER
WRINKLE
WRINKLY
WRITEIN
WRITERS
WRITETO
WRITEUP
WRITHED
WRITHES
WRITING
WRITTEN

W••I•••
WAHINES
WAPITIS
WARIEST
WAVIEST
WAXIEST
WILIEST
WIRIEST
WOEISME
WRAITHS
WYSIWYG

W•••I••
WACKIER
WACKILY
WADDING
WAFTING
WAGGING
WAGGISH
WAIKIKI
WAILING
WAITING
WAIVING
WALKING
WALKINS
WALLING
WANTING
WARDING
WARLIKE
WARMING
WARMISH
WARNING
WARPING
WARRING
WARRIOR
WARTIME
WARWICK
WASHING
WASPISH
WASTING
WAXWING
WAYBILL
WAYSIDE
WEAKISH
WEANING
WEARIED
WEARIER
WEARIES
WEARILY
WEARING
WEAVING
WEBBING
WEBSITE
WEDDING
WEDGIES
WEDGING
WEEDIER
WEEDING
WEENIES
WEEPIER
WEEPING
WEEVILS
WELDING
WELKINS
WELLING
WELTING
WENDING
WESKITS
WETTING
WHALING
WHILING
WHINING
WHITING
WHITISH
WICHITA
WICKIUP
WIENIES
WILDING
WILLIAM
WILLIES
WILLING
WILTING
WINCING
WINDIER
WINDING
WINGING
WINKING
WINNING
WISHING
WISPIER
WISPILY
WISPING
WITTIER
WITTILY
WITTING
WOLFING
WOLFISH
WOODIER
WOODIES
WOOFING
WOOLIER
WOOLIES
WOOZIER
WOOZILY
WORDIER
WORDILY
WORDING
WORKING
WORMIER
WORRIED
WORRIER
WORRIES
WOZNIAK
WRITING
WYOMING

W••••I•
WADESIN
WAGTAIL
WANTSIN
WAPITIS
WARSHIP
WASSAIL
WATCHIT
WAVEDIN
WAVESIN
WAYLAID
WEIGHIN
WETSUIT
WHEELIE
WHEREIN
WHIZKID
WILFRID
WILLKIE
WINGSIT
WINGTIP
WORKSIN
WORSHIP
WRITEIN
WROTEIN

W•••••I
WAIKIKI

•WI••••
DWINDLE
OWINGTO
SWIFTER
SWIFTLY
SWIGGED
SWILLED
SWIMMER
SWINDLE
SWINGBY
SWINGER
SWIPERS
SWIPING
SWIRLED
SWISHED
SWISHES
SWITZER
SWIVELS
SWIZZLE
TWIDDLE
TWILLED
TWINBED
TWINGED
TWINGES
TWINING
TWINKLE
TWINKLY
TWINNED
TWIRLED
TWIRLER
TWISTED
TWISTER
TWITCHY
TWITTED
TWITTER
ZWINGLI

•W•I•••
AWAITED
AWNINGS

•W••I••
AWAKING
IWOJIMA
OWLLIKE
SWAHILI
SWAYING
SWEDISH
SWIPING
TWINING
TWOBITS
TWOTIME

•W•••I•
DWEEZIL
SWEARIN
SWEETIE
SWOOSIE
SWOREIN

•W••••I
SWAHILI
ZWINGLI

••WI•••
BEWITCH
DEWILDE
EXWIVES
REWINDS
REWIRED
REWIRES
UNWINDS
UNWISER

••W•I••
BAWDIER
BAWDILY
BAWLING
BEWAILS
BOWFINS
BOWLINE
BOWLING
BOWTIES
COWBIRD
COWGIRL
COWHIDE
COWLICK
COWLING
COWRIES
DAWKINS
DAWNING
DEWLINE
DOWDIER
DOWDILY
DOWNIER
DOWNING
DOWRIES
DOWSING
EBWHITE
FAWNING
FOWLING
GAWKIER
GAWKING
HAWKING
HAWKINS
HAWKISH
HOWLING
JAWLINE
KEWPIES
KUWAITI
LOWLIER
LOWLIFE
LOWRISE
LOWTIDE
MAWKISH
MEWLING
NEWSIER
PAWNING
RAWHIDE
RAWSILK
REWRITE
ROWDIER
ROWDIES
ROWDILY
SAWFISH
SAWMILL
TAWNIER
TOWNIES
YAWNING
YOWLING

••W••I•
COWSLIP
HOWBEIT
KIWANIS
LAWSUIT
LOWPAID

••W•••I
KUWAITI

•••WI••
ALEWIFE
AVOWING
BATWING
BETWIXT
BIGWIGS
BLOWIER
BLOWING
BREWING
CHEWIER
CHEWING
CLAWING
CREWING
CROWING
DIMWITS
DRAWING
EARWIGS
ENDWISE
ENTWINE
FLAWING
FLOWING
GLOWING
GNAWING
GODWITS
GROWING
HAYWIRE
HOGWILD
HOTWIRE
ILLWILL
ILLWIND
IPSWICH
JUGWINE
KNOWING
LAPWING
MAYWINE
MCSWINE
MEOWING
MIDWIFE
NITWITS
OUTWITS
PLOWING
REDWINE
REDWING
RUNWITH
SCHWINN
SHOWIER
SHOWILY
SHOWING
SKEWING
SLOWING
SNOWIER
SNOWING
SOPWITH
SPEWING
STEWING
STOWING
THAWING
UNTWIST
UPSWING
VIEWING
WARWICK
WAXWING

•••W•I•
BLOWSIN
BLOWSIT
BROWNIE

DRAWNIN
DRAWSIN
GEEWHIZ
SHOWBIZ
SHOWNIN
SHOWSIN
SNOWSIN

••••WI•
BALDWIN
CSLEWIS
GOODWIN
HALFWIT
SHERWIN
THREWIN
THROWIN

•W•J•••
IWOJIMA

•••WJ••
SNOWJOB

W•K••••
WAKEFUL
WAKENED
WAKENER
WAKESUP
WOKENUP

W••K•••
WACKIER
WACKILY
WAIKIKI
WALKERS
WALKING
WALKINS
WALKMAN
WALKONS
WALKOUT
WALKUPS
WALKWAY
WEAKENS
WEAKEST
WEAKISH
WEEKDAY
WEEKEND
WELKINS
WESKITS
WICKERS
WICKETS
WICKIUP
WINKERS
WINKING
WINKLER
WINKOUT
WINKSAT
WORKDAY
WORKERS
WORKFOR
WORKING
WORKMAN
WORKMEN
WORKOFF
WORKOUT
WORKSIN
WORKSON
WORKSUP
WORKUPS

W•••K••
WHACKED
WHISKED
WHISKER
WHISKEY
WHIZKID
WILLKIE
WRACKED
WREAKED
WRECKED
WRECKER
WRINKLE
WRINKLY

W••••K•
WAIKIKI
WARLIKE

W•••••K
WARLOCK
WARWICK
WAXWORK
WEDLOCK
WIDMARK
WOZNIAK
WOZZECK

•WK••••
AWKWARD

•W•K•••
AWAKENS
AWAKING

•W••K••
SWANKER
TWEAKED
TWINKLE
TWINKLY

•W•••K•
OWLLIKE

••WK•••
BOWKNOT
DAWKINS
GAWKERS
GAWKIER
GAWKING
HAWKERS
HAWKEYE
HAWKING
HAWKINS
HAWKISH
MAWKISH

••W••K•
COWPOKE
REWORKS
THWACKS

••W•••K
COWLICK
LOWNECK
NEWLOOK
NEWYORK
RAWSILK
SAWBUCK

•••W•K•
ARAWAKS

•••W••K
ARTWORK
BULWARK
CATWALK
JAYWALK
LEGWORK
MIDWEEK
NETWORK
OUTWORK
TINWORK
WARWICK
WAXWORK

••••WK•
MOHAWKS
SQUAWKS

••••W•K
SARAWAK

•••••WK
GOSHAWK

W•L••••
WALCOTT
WALDORF
WALKERS
WALKING
WALKINS
WALKMAN
WALKONS
WALKOUT
WALKUPS
WALKWAY
WALLABY
WALLACE
WALLACH
WALLETS
WALLEYE
WALLING
WALLOON
WALLOPS
WALLOWS
WALLSUP
WALMART
WALNUTS
WALPOLE
WALTERS
WALTZED
WALTZER
WALTZES
WELCHED
WELCHES
WELCOME
WELDERS
WELDING
WELFARE
WELKINS
WELLAND
WELLFED
WELLING
WELLOFF
WELLRUN
WELLSET
WELLSUP
WELTERS
WELTING
WILDCAT
WILDEST
WILDING
WILDONE
WILFORD
WILFRID
WILHELM
WILIEST
WILLARD
WILLFUL
WILLIAM
WILLIES
WILLING
WILLKIE
WILLOWS
WILLOWY
WILLSON
WILTING
WOLFGAL
WOLFING
WOLFISH
WOLFMAN
WOLFMEN
WOLFRAM

W••L•••
WAILERS
WAILING
WALLABY
WALLACE
WALLACH
WALLETS
WALLEYE
WALLING
WALLOON
WALLOPS
WALLOWS
WALLSUP
WARLIKE
WARLOCK
WARLORD
WAYLAID
WAYLAYS
WEALTHY
WEDLOCK
WELLAND
WELLFED
WELLING
WELLOFF
WELLRUN
WELLSET
WELLSUP
WETLAND
WHALERS
WHALING
WHELPED
WHILING
WIELDED
WIGLETS
WILLARD
WILLFUL
WILLIAM
WILLIES
WILLING
WILLKIE
WILLOWS
WILLOWY
WILLSON
WITLESS
WOOLENS
WOOLIER
WOOLIES
WOOLLEN
WOOLSEY
WORLDLY
WOULDBE
WOULDNT

W•••L••
WADDLED
WADDLER
WADDLES
WAFFLED
WAFFLER
WAFFLES
WAGGLED
WAGGLES
WAMBLED
WAMBLES
WANGLED
WANGLER
WANGLES
WARBLED
WARBLER
WARBLES
WATTLES
WAVELET
WHEELED
WHEELER
WHEELIE
WHIRLED
WHORLED
WIGGLED
WIGGLER
WIGGLES
WIMPLED
WIMPLES
WINKLER
WINSLOW
WOBBLED
WOBBLES
WOODLOT
WOOLLEN
WRIGLEY

W••••L•
WACKILY
WALPOLE
WAYBILL
WEARILY
WEASELS
WEEVILS
WEIRDLY
WENDELL
WETCELL
WHEEDLE
WHISTLE
WHITTLE
WILHELM
WISPILY
WITTILY
WOMANLY
WOOZILY
WORDILY
WORLDLY
WRANGLE
WRESTLE
WRIGGLE
WRIGGLY
WRINKLE
WRINKLY
WRONGLY
WYCHELM

W•••••L
WAGTAIL
WAKEFUL
WASSAIL
WASTREL
WAYBILL
WENDELL
WETCELL
WILLFUL
WISHFUL
WISTFUL
WOLFGAL

•WL••••
OWLLIKE

•W•L•••
AWELESS
DWELLED
DWELLER
OWLLIKE
SWALLOW
SWELLED
SWELLUP
SWELTER
SWELTRY
SWILLED
SWOLLEN
TWELFTH
TWELVES
TWILLED

•W••L••
AWFULLY
DWELLED
DWELLER
SWALLOW
SWELLED
SWELLUP
SWILLED
SWIRLED
SWOLLEN
TWILLED
TWIRLED
TWIRLER

•W•••L•
AWFULLY
DWINDLE
SWADDLE
SWAHILI
SWEETLY
SWIFTLY
SWINDLE
SWIVELS
SWIZZLE
TWADDLE
TWIDDLE
TWINKLE
TWINKLY
TWOFOLD
ZWINGLI

•W••••L
DWEEZIL

••WL•••
BAWLERS
BAWLING
BAWLOUT
BOWLERS
BOWLFUL
BOWLINE
BOWLING
COWLICK
COWLING
DEWLAPS
DEWLINE
FOWLERS
FOWLING
HEWLETT
HOWLERS
HOWLING
JAWLINE
KOWLOON
LAWLESS
LOWLAND
LOWLIER
LOWLIFE
MEWLERS
MEWLING
NEWLEFT
NEWLOOK
SAWLOGS
YOWLERS
YOWLING

••W•L••
BOWDLER
COWSLIP
DAWDLED
DAWDLER
DAWDLES
DEWCLAW
DEWILDE
HGWELLS
HOWELLS
JEWELED
JEWELER
JEWELRY
LOWBLOW
REWELDS
TOWELED

••W••L•
BAWDILY
BEWAILS
COWBELL
DOWDILY
HGWELLS
HOWELLS
LOWBALL
RAWSILK
ROWDILY
SAWMILL

••W•••L
BOWLFUL
COWBELL
COWGIRL
LOWBALL
LOWHEEL
NEWDEAL
RAWDEAL
SAWMILL

•••WL••
BRAWLED
BRAWLER
CRAWLED
CRAWLER
DRAWLED
FRAWLEY
GROWLED
GROWLER
PROWLED
PROWLER
SCOWLED
SCOWLER
TRAWLED
TRAWLER

•••W•L•
AIRWOLF
AVOWALS
BEOWULF
BLOWFLY
BOSWELL
CATWALK
CREWELS
CRYWOLF
DRYWALL
DRYWELL
FALWELL
GETWELL
GOTWELL
GUNWALE
HOGWILD
ILLWILL
INDWELL
INKWELL
JAYWALK
MAXWELL
NARWALS
NOTWELL
OILWELL
PINWALE
REDWOLF
ROSWELL
SEAWALL
SHEWOLF
SHOWILY
SITWELL
TROWELS

•••W••L
BOSWELL
DRYWALL
DRYWELL
FALWELL
GETWELL
GOTWELL
ILLWILL
INDWELL
INKWELL
MAXWELL
NARWHAL
NOTWELL
OILWELL
ROSWELL
SEAWALL
SHAWWAL
SITWELL

••••WL•
SCRAWLS
SCRAWLY
SPRAWLS

••••W•L
RENEWAL
SHAWWAL

•••••WL
BARNOWL
HOOTOWL
PEAFOWL

W•M••••
WAMBLED
WAMBLES
WIMPLED
WIMPLES
WOMANLY
WOMBATS

W••M•••
WALMART
WARMEST
WARMING
WARMISH
WARMSUP
WARMUPS
WETMOPS
WHAMMED
WHIMPER
WHOMPED
WIDMARK
WOOMERA
WORMIER
WYOMING

W•••M••
WALKMAN
WHAMMED
WHITMAN
WISEMAN
WISEMEN
WOLFMAN
WOLFMEN
WORKMAN
WORKMEN

W••••M•
WARGAME
WARTIME
WELCOME
WINSOME
WOEISME

W•••••M
WILHELM
WILLIAM
WOLFRAM
WYCHELM

•W•M•••
SWAMPED
SWIMMER

•W••M••
SWARMED
SWIMMER

•W•••M•
AWESOME
IWOJIMA
TWOSOME
TWOTIME

••WM•••
NEWMATH
NEWMOON
NEWMOWN
SAWMILL

••W•M••
NEWSMAN
NEWSMEN

••W••M•
HOWCOME
REWARMS

••W•••M
LOWBEAM

•••WM••
CREWMAN
CREWMEN
PLOWMAN
PLOWMEN
SHOWMAN
SHOWMEN
SNOWMAN
SNOWMEN

•••W•M•
MUGWUMP
WIGWAMS

W•N••••
WANDERS
WANGLED
WANGLER
WANGLES
WANNABE
WANTADS
WANTING
WANTOUT
WANTSIN
WANTSTO
WENCHES
WENDELL
WENDERS
WENDING
WENTAPE
WENTBAD
WENTFOR
WENTOFF
WENTOUT
WINCERS
WINCHED
WINCHES
WINCING
WINDBAG
WINDERS
WINDIER
WINDING
WINDOWS
WINDROW
WINDSOR
WINDSUP
WINDUPS
WINEBAR
WINERED
WINESAP
WINFREY
WINGERS
WINGING
WINGNUT
WINGSIT
WINGTIP
WINKERS
WINKING
WINKLER
WINKOUT
WINKSAT
WINNERS
WINNING
WINNOWS
WINSLOW
WINSOME
WINSOUT
WINSTON
WINTERS
WINTERY
WONDERS
WONTONS
WYNETTE
WYNONNA

W••N•••
WALNUTS
WANNABE
WARNING
WEANING
WEENIES
WERNHER
WETNESS
WHINERS
WHINING
WIENERS
WIENIES
WINNERS
WINNING
WINNOWS
WITNESS
WORNOFF
WORNOUT
WOUNDED
WOUNDUP
WOZNIAK
WRANGLE
WRINGER
WRINKLE
WRINKLY
WRONGED
WRONGER
WRONGLY
WRYNESS
WYANDOT

W•••N••
WAGONER
WAHINES
WAKENED
WAKENER
WCHANDY
WHATNOT
WHITNEY
WIDENED
WINGNUT
WIZENED
WOKENUP
WOMANLY
WYNONNA

W••••N•
WADDING
WAFTING
WAGGING
WAGGONS
WAILING
WAITING
WAIVING
WALKING
WALKINS
WALKONS
WALLING
WANTING
WARDENS
WARDING
WARMING
WARNING
WARPING
WARRANT
WARRENS
WARRING
WASHING
WASTING
WAXWING
WEAKENS
WEANING
WEAPONS
WEARING
WEAVING
WEBBING
WEDDING
WEDGING
WEEDING
WEEKEND
WEEPING
WELDING
WELKINS
WELLAND
WELLING
WELTING
WENDING
WESTEND
WETLAND
WETTING
WHALING
WHILING
WHINING
WHITENS
WHITING
WILDING
WILDONE
WILLING
WILTING
WINCING
WINDING
WINGING
WINKING
WINNING
WISHING
WISPING
WITTING
WOLFING
WONTONS
WOOFING
WOOLENS
WORDING
WORDONE
WORKING
WORSENS
WOULDNT
WRITING
WYNONNA
WYOMING
WYVERNS

W•••••N
WADESIN
WAITSON
WALKMAN
WALLOON
WANTSIN
WAVEDIN
WAVESIN
WAXBEAN
WAYWORN
WEIGHIN
WELLRUN
WESTERN
WHARTON
WHAUDEN
WHEATON
WHEREIN
WHITMAN
WIDGEON
WILLSON
WINSTON
WISEMAN
WISEMEN
WOBEGON
WOLFMAN
WOLFMEN
WOOLLEN
WORKMAN
WORKMEN
WORKSIN
WORKSON
WRITEIN
WRITTEN
WROTEIN

•WN••••
AWNINGS
OWNEDUP

•W•N•••
DWINDLE
KWANZAS
OWINGTO
RWANDAN
SWANKER
SWANSON
SWINDLE
SWINGBY
SWINGER
TWANGED
TWINBED
TWINGED
TWINGES
TWINING
TWINKLE
TWINKLY
TWINNED
ZWINGLI

•W••N••
AWNINGS
SWOONED
TWINNED

•W•••N•
AWAKENS
AWAKING
SWAYING
SWIPING
TWINING
TWOTONE

•W••••N
RWANDAN
SWANSON
SWEARIN
SWEETEN
SWEETON
SWOLLEN
SWOREIN

••WN•••
DAWNING
DOWNBOW
DOWNERS
DOWNIER
DOWNING
DOWNPAT
FAWNERS
FAWNING
LOWNECK
LOWNESS
NEWNESS
PAWNEES
PAWNERS
PAWNING
PAWNOFF
RAWNESS
TAWNIER
TOWNERS
TOWNIES
YAWNERS
YAWNING

••W•N••
BOWKNOT
KIWANIS
REWINDS
UNWINDS

••W••N•
BAWLING
BOWFINS
BOWLINE
BOWLING
COWHAND
COWLING
DAWKINS
DAWNING
DEWLINE
DOWNING
DOWSING
FAWNING
FOWLING
GAWKING
GOWRONG
HAWKING
HAWKINS
HOWLING
JAWBONE
JAWLINE
LOWLAND
MEWLING
NEWTONS
PAWNING
REWOUND
UNWOUND
YAWNING
YOWLING

••W•••N
COWTOWN
KOWLOON
LOWBORN
LOWDOWN
MOWDOWN
NEWBORN
NEWMOON
NEWMOWN
NEWSMAN
NEWSMEN
NEWTOWN
REWOVEN

•••WN••
BLOWNUP
BROWNED
BROWNER
BROWNIE
CLOWNED
CROWNED
DRAWNIN
DRAWNON
DRAWNUP
DROWNED
FROWNAT
FROWNED
FROWNER
GROWNUP
SHAWNEE
SHOWNIN
SPAWNED

•••W•N•
AVOWING
BATWING
BLOWING
BREWING
CHEWING
CLAWING
CREWING
CROWING
DRAWING
ENTWINE
FLAWING
FLOWING
FORWENT
GLOWING
GNAWING
GROWING
ILLWIND
JUGWINE
KNOWING
LAPWING
MAYWINE
MCSWINE
MEOWING
PLOWING
REDWINE
REDWING
SCHWINN
SHOWING
SKEWING
SLOWING
SNOWING
SPEWING
STEWING
STOWING
THAWING
UPSWING
VIEWING
WAXWING

•••W••N
BETWEEN
BLOWGUN
BLOWSIN
CREWMAN
CREWMEN
DRAWNIN
DRAWNON
DRAWSIN
DRAWSON
EREWHON
GROWSON
OUTWORN
PLOWMAN
PLOWMEN
SAYWHEN
SCHWINN
SHOWMAN
SHOWMEN
SHOWNIN
SHOWSIN
SNOWDON
SNOWMAN
SNOWMEN
SNOWSIN
WAYWORN

••••WN•
DISOWNS
SCRAWNY

••••W•N
BALDWIN
GOLDWYN
GOODWIN
HARDWON
MATEWAN
SHERWIN
THREWIN
THROWIN

•••••WN
BEDDOWN
BOGDOWN
COWTOWN
CUTDOWN
DIEDOWN
GETDOWN
GOTDOWN
HOEDOWN
INGROWN
LAYDOWN
LETDOWN
LIEDOWN
LOWDOWN
MIDTOWN
MOWDOWN
NEWMOWN
NEWTOWN
OAKLAWN
OURTOWN
PINDOWN
PREDAWN
PUTDOWN
REDRAWN
RUBDOWN
RUNDOWN
SATDOWN
SETDOWN
SITDOWN
SUNDOWN
TIEDOWN
UNDRAWN
UNKNOWN

WO•••••
WOBBLED
WOBBLES
WOBEGON
WOEISME
WOKENUP
WOLFGAL
WOLFING
WOLFISH
WOLFMAN
WOLFMEN
WOLFRAM
WOMANLY
WOMBATS
WONDERS
WONTONS
WOODARD
WOODCUT
WOODIER
WOODIES
WOODLOT
WOODROW
WOOFERS
WOOFING
WOOLENS
WOOLIER
WOOLIES
WOOLLEN
WOOLSEY
WOOMERA
WOOSTER
WOOZIER
WOOZILY
WORDIER
WORDILY
WORDING
WORDONE
WOREOFF
WOREOUT
WORKDAY
WORKERS
WORKFOR
WORKING
WORKMAN
WORKMEN
WORKOFF
WORKOUT
WORKSIN
WORKSON
WORKSUP
WORKUPS
WORLDLY
WORMIER
WORNOFF
WORNOUT
WORRIED
WORRIER
WORRIES
WORSENS
WORSHIP
WORSTED
WOULDBE
WOULDNT
WOUNDED
WOUNDUP
WOZNIAK
WOZZECK

W•O••••
WHOEVER
WHOMPED
WHOOPED
WHOOPEE
WHOPPED
WHOPPER
WHORLED
WHOSWHO
WOODARD
WOODCUT
WOODIER
WOODIES
WOODLOT
WOODROW
WOOFERS
WOOFING
WOOLENS
WOOLIER
WOOLIES
WOOLLEN
WOOLSEY
WOOMERA
WOOSTER
WOOZIER
WOOZILY
WRONGED
WRONGER
WRONGLY
WROTEIN
WROTETO
WROTEUP
WROUGHT
WYOMING

W••O•••
WAGONER
WHOOPED
WHOOPEE
WIDOWED
WIDOWER
WYNONNA

W•••O••
WAGGONS
WAITOUT
WALCOTT
WALDORF
WALKONS
WALKOUT
WALLOON
WALLOPS
WALLOWS
WALPOLE
WANTOUT
WARDOFF
WARGODS
WARLOCK
WARLORD
WASHOFF
WASHOUT
WAVEOFF
WAXWORK
WAYWORN
WEAPONS
WEAROFF
WEAROUT
WEBFOOT
WEBTOED
WEDLOCK
WEEDOUT
WELCOME
WELLOFF
WENTOFF
WENTOUT
WETMOPS
WIGSOUT
WILDONE
WILFORD
WILLOWS
WILLOWY
WINDOWS
WINKOUT
WINNOWS
WINSOME
WINSOUT
WIPEOUT
WITHOUT
WONTONS
WORDONE
WOREOFF
WOREOUT
WORKOFF
WORKOUT
WORNOFF
WORNOUT

W••••O•
WAITSON
WALLOON
WARRIOR
WARTHOG
WEBFOOT
WEIRDOS
WENTFOR
WHARTON
WHATFOR
WHATNOT
WHEATON
WHEREOF
WIDGEON
WILLSON
WINDROW
WINDSOR
WINSLOW
WINSTON
WOBEGON
WOODLOT
WOODROW
WORKFOR
WORKSON
WYANDOT

W•••••O
WANTSTO
WHERETO
WHOSWHO
WRITETO
WROTETO

•WO••••
IWOJIMA
SWOLLEN
SWOONED
SWOOPED
SWOOSIE
SWOREAT
SWOREBY
SWOREIN
TWOBASE
TWOBITS
TWOFERS
TWOFOLD
TWOSOME
TWOSTAR
TWOSTEP
TWOTIME
TWOTONE

•W•O•••
SWOONED
SWOOPED
SWOOSIE

•W••O••
AWESOME
TWOFOLD
TWOSOME
TWOTONE

•W•••O•
AWAREOF
SWALLOW
SWANSON
SWEETON

•W••••O
OWINGTO
SWEARTO

••WO•••
ALWORTH
ATWORST
BYWORDS
REWORDS
REWORKS
REWOUND
REWOVEN
UNWOUND

••W•O••
BAWLOUT
BOWSOUT
BOWWOWS
COWBOYS
COWPOKE
COWTOWN
GOWRONG
HOWCOME
JAWBONE
KOWLOON
KOWTOWS
LAWFORD
LOWBORN
LOWBOYS
LOWDOWN
LOWROAD
MOWDOWN
NEWBORN
NEWLOOK
NEWMOON
NEWMOWN
NEWPORT
NEWTONS
NEWTOWN
NEWYORK
PAWNOFF
POWWOWS
REWROTE
ROWBOAT
SAWLOGS
SAWWOOD
TOWROPE

••W••O•
BOWKNOT
BYWAYOF
DEWDROP
DOWNBOW
KOWLOON
LOWBLOW
LOWBROW
NEWLOOK
NEWMOON
NEWSBOY
SAWWOOD

•••WO••
AIRWOLF
ARTWORK
BLEWOFF
BLEWOUT
BLOWOFF
BLOWOUT
BOWWOWS
BOXWOOD
CHEWOUT
CRYWOLF
DAGWOOD
DOGWOOD
DRAWOUT
DREWOUT
HEYWOOD
INAWORD
KEYWORD
LEGWORK
MISWORD
NETWORK
OUTWORE
OUTWORK
OUTWORN
PLYWOOD
POWWOWS
REDWOLF
REDWOOD
SAWWOOD
SHEWOLF
SHOWOFF
TINWORK
WAXWORK
WAYWORN

•••W•O•
BOXWOOD
DAGWOOD
DOGWOOD
DRAWNON
DRAWSON
EREWHON
GROWSON
HEYWOOD
INAWEOF
KNOWHOW
PLOWBOY
PLYWOOD
REDWOOD
SAWWOOD
SHOWDOG
SNOWDON
SNOWJOB

••••WO•
HARDWON

••••W•O
WHOSWHO

W•P••••
WAPITIS
WIPEDUP
WIPEOUT
WIPESUP

W••P•••
WALPOLE
WARPATH
WARPING
WASPISH
WEAPONS
WEEPERS
WEEPIER
WEEPING
WHIPPED
WHIPPET
WHIPSAW
WHIPSUP
WHOPPED
WHOPPER
WHUPPED
WIMPLED
WIMPLES
WISPIER
WISPILY
WISPING
WRAPPED
WRAPPER
WRAPSUP
WRAPUPS

W•••P••
WHELPED
WHIMPER
WHIPPED
WHIPPET
WHISPER
WHOMPED
WHOOPED
WHOOPEE
WHOPPED
WHOPPER
WHUPPED
WRAPPED
WRAPPER

W••••P•
WALKUPS
WALLOPS
WARMUPS
WENTAPE
WETMOPS
WINDUPS
WORKUPS
WRAPUPS

W•••••P
WAITSUP
WAKESUP
WALLSUP
WARMSUP
WARSHIP
WELLSUP
WHIPSUP
WICKIUP
WINDSUP
WINESAP
WINGTIP
WIPEDUP
WIPESUP
WIRETAP
WISEDUP
WISESUP
WOKENUP
WORKSUP
WORSHIP
WOUNDUP
WRAPSUP
WRITEUP
WROTEUP

•W•P•••
SWAPPED
SWAPPER
SWEPTUP
SWIPERS
SWIPING

•W••P••
SWAMPED
SWAPPED
SWAPPER
SWEEPER
SWEEPUP
SWOOPED

•W••••P
OWNEDUP
SWEEPUP
SWELLUP
SWEPTUP
TWOSTEP

••WP•••
COWPEAS
COWPOKE
KEWPIES
LOWPAID
NEWPORT
PAWPAWS
TOWPATH
YAWPERS

••W•P••
DOWNPAT

••W••P•
DEWLAPS
ENWRAPS
REWRAPS
TOWROPE
UNWRAPS

••W•••P
COWSLIP
DEWDROP
SEWEDUP

•••WP••
SNOWPEA

•••W•P•
BLOWUPS
UNSWEPT
UPSWEPT

•••W••P
ANTWERP
BLOWNUP
BLOWSUP
CHEWSUP
DRAWNUP
DRAWSUP
GROWNUP
GROWSUP
MUGWUMP
SHOWSUP
SLOWSUP
SNOWCAP
UPSWEEP

••••W•P
SCREWUP

WR•••••
WRACKED
WRAITHS
WRANGLE
WRAPPED
WRAPPER
WRAPSUP
WRAPUPS
WREAKED
WREATHE
WREATHS
WRECKED
WRECKER
WRESTED
WRESTLE
WRIGGLE
WRIGGLY
WRIGHTS
WRIGLEY
WRINGER
WRINKLE
WRINKLY
WRITEIN
WRITERS
WRITETO
WRITEUP
WRITHED
WRITHES
WRITING
WRITTEN
WRONGED
WRONGER
WRONGLY
WROTEIN
WROTETO
WROTEUP
WROUGHT
WRYNESS

W•R••••
WARBLED
WARBLER
WARBLES
WARDENS
WARDERS
WARDING
WARDOFF
WARFARE
WARGAME
WARGODS
WARIEST
WARLIKE
WARLOCK
WARLORD
WARMEST
WARMING
WARMISH
WARMSUP
WARMUPS
WARNING
WARPATH
WARPING
WARRANT
WARRENS
WARRING
WARRIOR
WARSHIP
WARTHOG
WARTIME
WARWICK
WERNHER
WERTHER
WIRETAP
WIRIEST
WORDIER
WORDILY
WORDING
WORDONE
WOREOFF
WOREOUT
WORKDAY
WORKERS
WORKFOR
WORKING
WORKMAN
WORKMEN
WORKOFF
WORKOUT
WORKSIN
WORKSON
WORKSUP
WORKUPS
WORLDLY
WORMIER
WORNOFF
WORNOUT
WORRIED
WORRIER
WORRIES
WORSENS
WORSHIP
WORSTED

W••R•••
WARRANT
WARRENS
WARRING
WARRIOR
WEARERS
WEARIED
WEARIER
WEARIES
WEARILY
WEARING
WEAROFF
WEAROUT
WEIRDER
WEIRDLY
WEIRDOS
WHARFED
WHARTON
WHARVES
WHEREAS
WHEREAT
WHEREBY
WHEREIN
WHEREOF
WHERETO
WHIRLED
WHIRRED
WHORLED
WORRIED
WORRIER
WORRIES

W•••R••
WAGERED
WAGERER
WASHRAG
WASTREL
WATERED
WATERER
WAVERED
WAVERER
WELLRUN
WHIRRED
WILFRID
WINDROW
WINERED
WINFREY
WIZARDS
WOLFRAM
WOODROW
WYVERNS

W••••R•
WAGGERY
WAILERS
WAITERS
WAIVERS
WALDORF
WALKERS
WALMART
WALTERS
WANDERS
WARDERS
WARFARE
WARLORD
WASHERS
WASTERS
WAXWORK
WAYWARD
WAYWORN
WEARERS
WEAVERS
WEEDERS
WEEPERS
WELDERS
WELFARE
WELTERS
WENDERS
WESTERN
WETBARS
WETHERS
WHALERS
WHINERS
WICKERS
WIDMARK
WIENERS
WILFORD
WILLARD
WINCERS
WINDERS
WINGERS
WINKERS
WINNERS
WINTERS
WINTERY
WISHERS
WITHERS
WONDERS
WOODARD
WOOFERS
WOOMERA
WORKERS
WRITERS

W•••••R
WACKIER
WADDLER
WAFFLER
WAGERER
WAGONER
WAKENER
WALTZER
WANGLER
WARBLER
WARRIOR
WATCHER
WATERER
WAVERER
WEARIER
WEATHER
WEBSTER
WEEDIER
WEEPIER
WEIRDER
WENTFOR
WERNHER
WERTHER
WHATFOR
WHEELER
WHEEZER
WHETHER
WHIMPER
WHISKER
WHISPER
WHITHER
WHOEVER
WHOPPER
WIDOWER
WIGGLER
WINDIER
WINDSOR
WINEBAR
WINKLER
WISPIER
WITTIER
WOODIER
WOOLIER
WOOSTER
WOOZIER
WORDIER
WORKFOR

WORMIER
WORRIER
WRAPPER
WRECKER
WRINGER
WRONGER

•W•R•••
AWARDED
AWARDEE
AWARDER
AWAREOF
DWARFED
DWARVES
SWARMED
SWARTHY
SWERVED
SWERVES
SWIRLED
SWOREAT
SWOREBY
SWOREIN
TWIRLED
TWIRLER

•W••R••
SWEARAT
SWEARBY
SWEARER
SWEARIN
SWEARTO

•W•••R•
AWKWARD
SWAYERS
SWELTRY
SWIPERS
TWOFERS

•W••••R
AWARDER
DWELLER
SWAGGER
SWANKER
SWAPPER
SWATTER
SWEARER
SWEATER
SWEEPER
SWEETER
SWELTER
SWIFTER
SWIMMER
SWINGER
SWITZER
TWEETER
TWIRLER
TWISTER
TWITTER
TWOSTAR

••WR•••
COWRIES
DOWRIES
ENWRAPS
GOWRONG
LOWRISE
LOWROAD
REWRAPS
REWRITE
REWROTE
TOWROPE
UNWRAPS

••W•R••
ALWORTH
ATWORST
BOWERED
BYWORDS
COWARDS
COWERED
DEWDROP
EDWARDS
HOWARDS
INWARDS
LOWBRED
LOWBROW
LOWERED
ONWARDS
POWERED
REWARDS
REWARMS
REWIRED
REWIRES
REWORDS
REWORKS
THWARTS
TOWARDS
TOWERED
UPWARDS

••W••R•
BAWLERS
BOWLERS
BOWYERS
COWBIRD
COWGIRL
COWHERD
DOWNERS
DOWSERS
FAWNERS
FOWLERS
GAWKERS
HAWKERS
HAWSERS
HOWLERS
JEWELRY
LAWFORD
LAWYERS
LOWBORN
MEWLERS
NEWBORN
NEWHART
NEWPORT
NEWYORK
NOWHERE
PAWNERS
POWDERS
POWDERY
SAWYERS
TOWCARS
TOWNERS
YAWNERS
YAWPERS
YOWLERS

••W•••R
BAWDIER
BOWDLER
DAWDLER
DOWAGER
DOWDIER
DOWNIER
GAWKIER
HOWEVER
JEWELER
LOWGEAR
LOWLIER
NEWAGER
NEWSIER
NEWYEAR
ROWDIER
TAWNIER
UNWISER

•••WR••
FAYWRAY

•••W•R•
ANSWERS
ANTWERP
ARTWARE
ARTWORK
ATHWART
AVOWERS
AWKWARD
BLOWDRY
BLOWERS
BREWERS
BREWERY
BULWARK
CHEWERS
CLAWERS
CROWERS
DRAWERS
FLOWERS
FLOWERY
FORWARD
FROWARD
GLOWERS
GNAWERS
GROWERS
HAYWARD
HAYWIRE
HOTWARS
HOTWIRE
INAWORD
KEYWORD
LEEWARD
LEGWORK
MISWORD
NETWORK
OUTWARD
OUTWORE
OUTWORK
OUTWORN
PLOWERS
SEAWARD
SHOWERS
SHOWERY
SKEWERS
SKYWARD
STEWARD
STEWART
STEWERS
TINWORK
TROWERS
UNAWARE
VIEWERS
WAXWORK
WAYWARD
WAYWORN

•••W••R
BLOWIER
BRAWLER
BROWNER
BROWSER
CHEWIER
CHOWDER
CLOWDER
CRAWLER
CROWBAR
DRAWBAR
FROWNER
GROWLER
OUTWEAR
PROWLER
SCOWLER
SHOWIER
SNOWIER
TRAWLER

••••W•R
ANTIWAR
BOERWAR
CNTOWER
COLDWAR
EMPOWER
HOLYWAR
MANOWAR
POSTWAR
RENEWER
STREWER
THROWER
WIDOWER

W•S••••
WASATCH
WASHERS
WASHING
WASHOFF
WASHOUT
WASHRAG
WASHTUB
WASPISH
WASSAIL
WASTAGE
WASTERS
WASTING
WASTREL
WESKITS
WESTEND
WESTERN
WISEDUP
WISEGUY
WISEMAN
WISEMEN
WISESUP
WISHERS
WISHFUL
WISHING
WISPIER
WISPILY
WISPING
WISTFUL
WYSIWYG

W••S•••
WAISTED
WARSHIP
WASSAIL
WAYSIDE
WEASELS
WEBSITE
WEBSTER
WETSUIT
WHISKED
WHISKER
WHISKEY
WHISPER
WHISTLE
WHOSWHO
WIGSOUT
WINSLOW
WINSOME
WINSOUT
WINSTON
WOOSTER
WORSENS
WORSHIP
WORSTED
WRESTED
WRESTLE

W•••S••
WADESIN
WAITSON
WAITSUP
WAKESUP
WALLSUP
WANTSIN
WANTSTO
WARMSUP
WAVESIN
WELLSET
WELLSUP
WHIPSAW
WHIPSUP
WILLSON
WINDSOR
WINDSUP
WINESAP
WINGSIT
WINKSAT
WIPESUP
WISESUP
WOEISME
WOOLSEY
WORKSIN
WORKSON
WORKSUP
WRAPSUP

W••••S•
WAGGISH
WARIEST
WARMEST
WARMISH
WASPISH
WAVIEST
WAXIEST
WEAKEST
WEAKISH
WETNESS
WETTEST
WHITEST
WHITISH
WILDEST
WILIEST
WIRIEST
WITLESS
WITNESS
WOLFISH
WRYNESS

W•••••S
WADDLES
WAFFLES
WAGGLES
WAGGONS
WAHINES
WAILERS
WAITERS
WAIVERS
WALKERS
WALKINS
WALKONS
WALKUPS
WALLETS
WALLOPS
WALLOWS
WALNUTS
WALTERS
WALTZES
WAMBLES
WANDERS
WANGLES
WANTADS
WAPITIS
WARBLES
WARDENS
WARDERS
WARGODS
WARMUPS
WARRENS
WASHERS
WASTERS
WATCHES
WATTLES
WAYLAYS
WEAKENS
WEAPONS
WEARERS
WEARIES
WEASELS
WEAVERS
WEDGIES
WEEDERS
WEENIES
WEEPERS
WEEVILS
WEIGHTS
WEIRDOS
WELCHES
WELDERS
WELKINS
WELTERS
WENCHES
WENDERS
WESKITS
WETBARS
WETHERS
WETMOPS
WETNESS
WHALERS
WHARVES
WHEEZES
WHEREAS
WHINERS
WHITENS
WHIZZES
WHYDAHS
WICKERS
WICKETS
WIDGETS
WIENERS
WIENIES
WIGGLES
WIGLETS
WIGWAGS
WIGWAMS
WILLIES
WILLOWS
WIMPLES
WINCERS
WINCHES
WINDERS
WINDOWS
WINDUPS
WINGERS
WINKERS
WINNERS
WINNOWS
WINTERS
WISHERS
WITCHES
WITHERS
WITLESS
WITNESS
WIZARDS
WOBBLES
WOMBATS
WONDERS
WONTONS
WOODIES
WOOFERS
WOOLENS
WOOLIES
WORKERS
WORKUPS
WORRIES
WORSENS
WRAITHS
WRAPUPS
WREATHS
WRIGHTS
WRITERS
WRITHES
WRYNESS
WYVERNS

•W•S•••
AWESOME
SWISHED
SWISHES
TWISTED
TWISTER
TWOSOME
TWOSTAR
TWOSTEP

•W••S••
SWANSON
SWOOSIE

•W•••S•
AWELESS
SWEDISH
TWOBASE

•W••••S
AWAKENS
AWELESS
AWNINGS
DWARVES
KWACHAS
KWANZAS
SWATHES
SWAYERS
SWERVES
SWIPERS
SWISHES
SWIVELS
TWEEZES
TWELVES
TWINGES
TWOBITS
TWOFERS

••WS•••
BOWSAWS
BOWSOUT
COWSLIP
DOWSERS
DOWSING
HAWSERS
LAWSUIT
NEWSBOY
NEWSDAY
NEWSIER
NEWSMAN
NEWSMEN
RAWSILK

••W•S••
UNWISER

••W••S•
ATWORST
HAWKISH
LAWLESS
LEWDEST
LOWNESS
LOWRISE
MAWKISH
NEWNESS
RAWNESS
SAWDUST
SAWFISH

••W•••S
BAWLERS
BEWAILS
BOWFINS
BOWLERS
BOWSAWS
BOWTIES
BOWWOWS
BOWYERS
BYWORDS
COWARDS
COWBOYS
COWPEAS
COWRIES
DAWDLES
DAWKINS
DEWLAPS
DOWNERS
DOWRIES
DOWSERS
EDWARDS
ENWRAPS
EXWIVES
FAWNERS
FOWLERS
GAWKERS
GEWGAWS
HAWHAWS
HAWKERS
HAWKINS
HAWSERS
HGWELLS
HOWARDS
HOWDAHS
HOWELLS
HOWLERS
INWARDS
KEWPIES
KIWANIS
KOWTOWS
LAWLESS
LAWYERS
LOWBOYS
LOWNESS
MEWLERS
NEWNESS
NEWTONS
ONWARDS
PAWNEES
PAWNERS
PAWPAWS
POWDERS
POWWOWS
RAWNESS
REWARDS
REWARMS
REWAXES
REWELDS
REWINDS
REWIRES
REWORDS
REWORKS
REWRAPS
ROWDIES
SAWLOGS
SAWYERS
SOWBUGS
THWACKS
THWARTS
TOWARDS
TOWCARS
TOWHEES
TOWNERS
TOWNIES
UNWINDS
UNWRAPS
UPWARDS
YAWNERS
YAWPERS
YOWLERS

•••WS••
BLOWSIN
BLOWSIT
BLOWSUP
BROWSED
BROWSER
BROWSES
CHEWSUP
DRAWSIN
DRAWSON
DRAWSUP
DROWSED
DROWSES
GROWSON
GROWSUP
SHOWSIN
SHOWSUP
SLOWSUP
SNOWSIN

•••W•S•
CARWASH
ENDWISE
EYEWASH
FARWEST
HOGWASH
JETWASH
KEYWEST
MAEWEST
MIDWEST
OLDWEST
PREWASH
PROWESS
SLOWEST
UNTWIST

•••W••S
AIRWAYS
ANSWERS
ARAWAKS
AVOWALS
AVOWERS
BIGWIGS
BLOWERS
BLOWUPS
BOWWOWS
BREWERS
BROWSES
CHEWERS
CLAWERS
COBWEBS
CREWELS
CROWERS
DIMWITS
DRAWERS
DROWSES
EARWIGS
ENDWAYS
FLOWERS
FLYWAYS
GLOWERS
GNAWERS
GODWITS
GROWERS
GROWTHS
HOTWARS
MIDWAYS
NARWALS
NITWITS
OUTWITS
PEEWEES
PLOWERS
POWWOWS
PROWESS
RUNWAYS
SEAWAYS
SHOWERS
SKEWERS
SKYWAYS
STEWERS
SUBWAYS
TROWELS
TROWERS
VIEWERS
WIGWAGS
WIGWAMS

••••W•S
CSLEWIS
DISOWNS
MOHAWKS
OJIBWAS
OTTAWAS
SCRAWLS
SPRAWLS
SQUAWKS
TIMEWAS

•••••WS
ANDREWS
ANTCOWS
BARROWS
BELLOWS
BESTOWS
BILLOWS
BORROWS
BOWSAWS
BOWWOWS
BURROWS
CASHEWS
CURFEWS
CURLEWS
CUSHAWS
ESCHEWS
ESCROWS
FALLOWS
FARROWS
FELLOWS
FOGBOWS
FOLLOWS
FURROWS
GEEGAWS
GEWGAWS
GUFFAWS
HALLOWS
HARROWS
HAWHAWS
HAYMOWS
HEBREWS
HEEHAWS
HOLLOWS
INFLOWS
JIGSAWS
KOWTOWS
MALLOWS
MARROWS
MATHEWS
MEADOWS
MELLOWS
MILDEWS
MINNOWS
MORROWS
NARROWS
NEPHEWS
NOSHOWS
OLDNEWS
OUTLAWS
PAWPAWS
PILLOWS
PITSAWS
POWWOWS
REDRAWS
REVIEWS
RIPSAWS
SEACOWS
SEESAWS
SHADOWS
SKITOWS
SORROWS
SUNDEWS
TALLOWS
TVSHOWS
WALLOWS
WILLOWS
WINDOWS
WINNOWS
YARROWS
YELLOWS

W•T••••
WATCHED
WATCHER
WATCHES
WATCHIT
WATERED
WATERER
WATTAGE
WATTEAU
WATTLES
WETBARS
WETCELL
WETHERS
WETLAND
WETMOPS
WETNESS
WETSUIT
WETTEST
WETTING
WITCHES
WITHERS
WITHOUT
WITLESS
WITNESS
WITTIER
WITTILY
WITTING

W••T•••
WAFTING
WAGTAIL
WAITERS
WAITING
WAITOUT
WAITSON
WAITSUP
WALTERS
WALTZED
WALTZER
WALTZES
WANTADS
WANTING
WANTOUT
WANTSIN
WANTSTO
WARTHOG
WARTIME
WASTAGE
WASTERS
WASTING
WASTREL
WATTAGE
WATTEAU
WATTLES
WEATHER
WEBTOED
WELTERS
WELTING
WENTAPE
WENTBAD
WENTFOR
WENTOFF
WENTOUT
WERTHER
WESTEND
WESTERN
WETTEST
WETTING
WHATFOR
WHATNOT
WHETHER
WHETTED
WHITENS
WHITEST
WHITHER
WHITING
WHITISH
WHITMAN
WHITNEY
WHITTLE
WILTING
WINTERS
WINTERY
WISTFUL
WITTIER
WITTILY
WITTING
WONTONS
WRITEIN
WRITERS
WRITETO
WRITEUP
WRITHED
WRITHES
WRITING
WRITTEN
WROTEIN
WROTETO
WROTEUP

W•••T••
WAISTED
WAPITIS
WASATCH
WASHTUB
WEALTHY
WEBSTER
WHARTON
WHEATON
WHETTED
WHISTLE
WHITTLE
WINGTIP
WINSTON
WIRETAP
WOOSTER
WORSTED
WRAITHS
WREATHE
WREATHS
WRESTED
WRESTLE
WRITTEN
WYNETTE

W••••T•
WALCOTT
WALLETS
WALNUTS
WANTSTO
WARPATH
WEBSITE
WEIGHTS
WEIGHTY
WESKITS
WHERETO
WICHITA
WICKETS
WIDGETS
WIGLETS
WOMBATS
WRIGHTS
WRITETO
WROTETO
WYNETTE

W•••••T
WAITOUT
WALCOTT
WALKOUT
WALMART
WANTOUT
WARIEST
WARMEST
WARRANT
WASHOUT
WATCHIT
WAVELET
WAVIEST

WAXIEST
WEAKEST
WEAROUT
WEBFEET
WEBFOOT
WEEDOUT
WELLSET
WENTOUT
WETSUIT
WETTEST
WHATNOT
WHEREAT
WHIPPET
WHITEST
WIGSOUT
WILDCAT
WILDEST
WILIEST
WINGNUT
WINGSIT
WINKOUT
WINKSAT
WINSOUT
WIPEOUT
WIRIEST
WITHOUT
WOODCUT
WOODLOT
WOREOUT
WORKOUT
WORNOUT
WOULDNT
WROUGHT
WYANDOT

•W•T•••
SWATHED
SWATHES
SWATTED
SWATTER
SWITZER
TWITCHY
TWITTED
TWITTER
TWOTIME
TWOTONE

•W••T••
AWAITED
SWARTHY
SWATTED
SWATTER
SWEATED
SWEATER
SWEETEN
SWEETER
SWEETIE
SWEETLY
SWEETON
SWELTER
SWELTRY
SWEPTUP
SWIFTER
SWIFTLY
TWEETED
TWEETER
TWISTED
TWISTER
TWITTED
TWITTER
TWOSTAR
TWOSTEP

•W•••T•
OWINGTO
SWEARTO
TWELFTH
TWOBITS

•W••••T
SWEARAT
SWOREAT

••WT•••
BOWTIES
COWTOWN
KOWTOWS
LOWTECH
LOWTIDE
NEWTONS
NEWTOWN

••W•T••
BEWITCH

••W••T•
ALWORTH
EBWHITE
FAWCETT
HEWLETT
KUWAITI
NCWYETH
NEWGATE
NEWMATH
RAWDATA
REWRITE
REWROTE
THWARTS
TOWPATH

••W•••T
ATWORST
BAWLOUT
BOWKNOT
BOWSOUT
DOWNPAT
FAWCETT
HEWLETT
HOWBEIT
LAWSUIT
LEWDEST
NEWHART
NEWLEFT
NEWPORT
PAWEDAT
ROWBOAT
SAWDUST

•••WT••
GROWTHS

•••W•T•
DIMWITS
GODWITS
NITWITS
OUTWITS
RUNWITH
SOPWITH

•••W••T
ATHWART
BETWIXT
BLEWOUT
BLOWOUT
BLOWSIT
CHEWOUT
CREWCUT
DRAWOUT
DREWOUT
FARWEST
FORWENT
FROWNAT
KEYWEST
MAEWEST
MIDWEST
NOSWEAT
OLDWEST
SLOWEST
STEWART
UNSWEPT
UNTWIST
UPSWEPT

••••W•T
HALFWIT

W•U••••
WHUPPED
WOULDBE
WOULDNT
WOUNDED
WOUNDUP

W••U•••
WHAUDEN
WROUGHT

W•••U••
WALKUPS
WALNUTS
WARMUPS
WETSUIT
WINDUPS
WORKUPS
WRAPUPS

W••••U•
WAITOUT
WAITSUP
WAKEFUL
WAKESUP
WALKOUT
WALLSUP
WANTOUT
WARMSUP
WASHOUT
WASHTUB
WEAROUT
WEEDOUT
WELLRUN
WELLSUP
WENTOUT
WHIPSUP
WICKIUP
WIGSOUT
WILLFUL
WINDSUP
WINGNUT
WINKOUT
WINSOUT
WIPEDUP
WIPEOUT
WIPESUP
WISEDUP
WISEGUY
WISESUP
WISHFUL
WISTFUL
WITHOUT
WOKENUP
WOODCUT
WOREOUT
WORKOUT
WORKSUP
WORNOUT
WOUNDUP
WRAPSUP
WRITEUP
WROTEUP

W•••••U
WATTEAU

•W•U•••
AWFULLY

•W•••U•
OWNEDUP
SWEEPUP
SWELLUP
SWEPTUP

••W•U••
LAWSUIT
REWOUND
SAWBUCK
SAWDUST
SOWBUGS
UNWOUND

••W••U•
BAWLOUT
BOWLFUL
BOWSOUT
SEWEDUP

•••WU••
BEOWULF
BLOWUPS
MUGWUMP

•••W•U•
BLEWOUT
BLOWGUN
BLOWNUP
BLOWOUT
BLOWSUP
CHEWOUT
CHEWSUP
CREWCUT
DRAWNUP
DRAWOUT
DRAWSUP
DREWOUT
GROWNUP
GROWSUP
SHOWSUP
SLOWSUP

••••WU•
SCREWUP

W•V••••
WAVEDIN
WAVELET
WAVEOFF
WAVERED
WAVERER
WAVESIN
WAVIEST
WYVERNS

W••V•••
WAIVERS
WAIVING
WEAVERS
WEAVING
WEEVILS

W•••V••
WHARVES
WHOEVER

•W•V•••
SWIVELS

•W••V••
DWARVES
SWERVED
SWERVES
TWELVES

••W•V••
EXWIVES
HOWEVER
REWOVEN

••W••V•
NEWWAVE
REWEAVE
UNWEAVE

•••W•V•
AIRWAVE
NEWWAVE

W•W••••
WARWICK
WAXWING
WAXWORK
WAYWARD
WAYWORN
WIGWAGS
WIGWAMS

W•••W••
WALKWAY
WHOSWHO
WIDOWED
WIDOWER
WYSIWYG

W••••W•
WALLOWS
WILLOWS
WILLOWY
WINDOWS
WINNOWS

W•••••W
WHIPSAW
WINDROW
WINSLOW
WOODROW

•W•W•••
AWKWARD

•W••••W
SWALLOW

••WW•••
BOWWOWS
NEWWAVE
POWWOWS
SAWWOOD

••W•W••
TOWAWAY

••W••W•
BOWSAWS
BOWWOWS
COWTOWN
GEWGAWS
HAWHAWS
KOWTOWS
LOWDOWN
MOWDOWN
NEWMOWN
NEWTOWN
PAWPAWS
POWWOWS

••W•••W
DEWCLAW
DOWNBOW
LOWBLOW
LOWBROW

•••WW••
SHAWWAL

•••W•W•
BOWWOWS
POWWOWS

•••W••W
KNOWHOW

W•X••••
WAXBEAN
WAXIEST
WAXWING
WAXWORK

••W•X••
REWAXED
REWAXES

•••W•X•
BETWIXT

••••W•X
BEESWAX

WY•••••
WYANDOT
WYCHELM
WYNETTE
WYNONNA
WYOMING
WYSIWYG
WYVERNS

W•Y••••
WAYBILL
WAYLAID
WAYLAYS
WAYSIDE
WAYWARD
WAYWORN
WHYDAHS
WRYNESS

W••••Y•
WALLEYE
WAYLAYS
WYSIWYG

W•••••Y
WACKILY
WAGGERY
WALKWAY
WALLABY
WCHANDY
WEALTHY
WEARILY
WEEKDAY
WEIGHTY
WEIRDLY
WHEREBY
WHISKEY
WHITNEY
WILLOWY
WINFREY
WINTERY
WISEGUY
WISPILY
WITTILY
WOMANLY
WOOLSEY
WOOZILY
WORDILY
WORKDAY
WORLDLY
WRIGGLY
WRIGLEY
WRINKLY
WRONGLY

•W•Y•••
SWAYERS
SWAYING

•W••••Y
AWFULLY
SWARTHY
SWEARBY
SWEETLY
SWELTRY
SWIFTLY
SWINGBY
SWOREBY
TWINKLY
TWITCHY

••WY•••
BOWYERS
LAWYERS
NCWYETH
NEWYEAR
NEWYORK
SAWYERS

••W•Y••
BYWAYOF

••W••Y•
COWBOYS
HAWKEYE
LOWBOYS

••W•••Y
BAWDILY
DOWDILY
JEWELRY
NEWSBOY
NEWSDAY
POWDERY
ROWDILY
TOWAWAY

•••W•Y•
AIRWAYS
ENDWAYS
FLYWAYS
MIDWAYS
RUNWAYS
SEAWAYS
SKYWAYS
SUBWAYS

•••W••Y
BLOWDRY
BLOWFLY
BREWERY
FAYWRAY
FLOWERY
FRAWLEY
PLOWBOY
SHOWERY
SHOWILY
SNOWDAY

••••WY•
GOLDWYN
WYSIWYG

••••W•Y
ARCHWAY
AREAWAY
BELTWAY
BIKEWAY
CARAWAY
CUTAWAY
DOORWAY
DUNAWAY
EATAWAY
FAIRWAY
FARAWAY
FLYAWAY
FREEWAY
GANGWAY
GATEWAY
GAVEWAY
GETAWAY
GIVEWAY
GOTAWAY
HALFWAY
HALLWAY
HEADWAY
HIGHWAY
INNOWAY
JANEWAY
LAYAWAY
MADEWAY
MAKEWAY
OJIBWAY
PARKWAY
PARTWAY
PATHWAY
PUTAWAY
RACEWAY
RAILWAY
RANAWAY
RIDGWAY
ROADWAY
RUNAWAY
SCRAWLY
SCRAWNY
SOMEWAY
TAXIWAY
THRUWAY
TOLLWAY
TOWAWAY
WALKWAY

•••••WY
BILLOWY
MEADOWY
MILDEWY
PILLOWY
SHADOWY
WILLOWY

W•Z••••
WIZARDS
WIZENED
WOZNIAK
WOZZECK

W••Z•••
WHIZKID
WHIZZED
WHIZZES
WOOZIER
WOOZILY
WOZZECK

W•••Z••
WALTZED
WALTZER
WALTZES
WHEEZED
WHEEZER
WHEEZES
WHIZZED
WHIZZES

•W•Z•••
SWIZZLE

•W••Z••
DWEEZIL
KWANZAS
SWITZER
SWIZZLE
TWEEZED
TWEEZES

•••W••Z
GEEWHIZ
SHOWBIZ

XA•••••
XANTHAN
XANTHIC

X•A••••
XRATING
XRAYING

X••••A•
XANTHAN

•XA••••
EXACTED
EXACTER
EXACTLY
EXACTOR
EXALTED
EXAMINE
EXAMPLE

•X•A•••
AXIALLY
EXHALED
EXHALES
EXHAUST
EXPANDS
EXPANSE
EXPARTE
OXCARTS

•X••A••
EXCLAIM
EXPIATE
EXPLAIN
EXTRACT
OXIDANT
OXIDASE

•X•••A•
AXILLAE
EXURBAN
OXONIAN
UXORIAL

•X••••A
EXOTICA
EXURBIA
OXYMORA

••XA•••
FIXABLE
FIXATED
FIXATES
HEXAGON
LUXATED
LUXATES
MIXABLE
ROXANNE
TAXABLE

••X•A••
BOXCARS
FOXTAIL
MAXBAER
REXCATS
SEXTANS
SEXTANT
SIXPACK
TAXRATE

••X••A•
BOXSEAT
LEXICAL
MAXIMAL
MEXICAN
TAXICAB
TAXIWAY
TEXTUAL
WAXBEAN

••X•••A
MAXILLA
NOXZEMA

•••XA••
INEXACT

•••X•A•
COAXIAL
FAUXPAS
MANXCAT
MANXMAN

•XB••••
OXBLOOD

•X••B••
EXHIBIT
EXURBAN
EXURBIA

••XB•••
MAXBAER
MAXBORN
WAXBEAN

••X•B••
FIXABLE
MIXABLE
TAXABLE

••X•••B
COXCOMB
TAXICAB

X•••••C
XANTHIC

•XC••••
EXCEEDS
EXCEPTS
EXCERPT
EXCISED
EXCISES
EXCITED
EXCITES
EXCLAIM
EXCLUDE
EXCRETE
EXCUSED
EXCUSES
OXCARTS

•X•C•••
EXACTED
EXACTER
EXACTLY
EXACTOR
EXECUTE

•X••C••
EXPECTS

•X•••C•
EXOTICA
EXOTICS
EXTINCT
EXTRACT

••XC•••
BOXCARS
COXCOMB
REXCATS

••X•C••
LEXICAL
LEXICON
MEXICAN
TAXICAB

••X••C•
SIXPACK

•••XC••
MANXCAT

•••X•C•
INEXACT

•X•D•••
EXUDING
OXIDANT
OXIDASE
OXIDIZE

•X•••D•
EXCEEDS
EXCLUDE
EXPANDS
EXPENDS
EXPLODE
EXTENDS
EXTRUDE
OXFORDS

•X••••D
EXACTED
EXALTED
EXCISED
EXCITED
EXCUSED
EXERTED
EXHALED
EXISTED
EXPIRED
EXPOSED
EXPOUND
EXULTED
OXBLOOD

••X•D••
BOXEDIN
BOXEDUP
FIXEDLY
FIXEDUP
MIXEDUP
PYXIDES
TUXEDOS
VEXEDLY

••X•••D
BOXWOOD
FIXATED
LUXATED
REXREED
SIXFOLD

•••X•D•
DIOXIDE

••••X•D
ADMIXED
AFFIXED
ANNEXED
IMMIXED
INDEXED
RELAXED
REMIXED
RETAXED
REWAXED
TELEXED
UNBOXED
UNFIXED

•XE••••
EXECUTE
EXEMPLI
EXEMPTS
EXERTED

•X•E•••
EXCEEDS
EXCEPTS
EXCERPT
EXPECTS
EXPENDS
EXPENSE
EXPERTS
EXTENDS
EXTENTS

•X••E••
EXCEEDS
EXCRETE
EXIGENT
EXPRESS
EXTREME
EXUPERY

•X•••E•
EXACTED
EXACTER
EXALTED
EXCISED
EXCISES
EXCITED
EXCITES
EXCUSED
EXCUSES
EXERTED
EXHALED
EXHALES
EXISTED
EXPIRED
EXPIRES
EXPOSED
EXPOSES
EXULTED
EXWIVES

•X••••E
AXILLAE
AXLROSE
EXAMINE
EXAMPLE
EXCLUDE
EXCRETE
EXECUTE
EXPANSE
EXPARTE
EXPENSE
EXPIATE
EXPLODE
EXPLORE
EXPUNGE
EXTREME
EXTRUDE
OXIDASE
OXIDIZE

••XE•••
BOXEDIN
BOXEDUP
BOXESIN
BOXESUP
FIXEDLY
FIXEDUP
FIXESUP
MIXEDUP
MIXESUP
TUXEDOS
VEXEDLY

••X•E••
ANXIETY

BOXSEAT
FOXIEST
LAXNESS
MAXWELL
NOXZEMA
REXREED
SEXIEST
SEXTETS
SIXTEEN
WAXBEAN
WAXIEST

••X••E•
BOXSTEP
FIXATED
FIXATES
LUXATED
LUXATES
MAXBAER
NEXUSES
PYXIDES
REXREED
SIXTEEN
SIXTIES
TAXFREE

••X•••E
BOXKITE
FIXABLE
FIXTURE
FOXFIRE
FOXHOLE
MIXABLE
MIXTURE
ROXANNE
TAXABLE
TAXFREE
TAXRATE
TEXTILE
TEXTURE

•••XE••
COAXERS
HOAXERS

•••X•E•
EPOXIES
FLEXNER
MANXMEN
PROXIES

•••X••E
BAUXITE
DIOXIDE
QUIXOTE

••••XE•
ADMIXED
ADMIXES
AFFIXED
AFFIXES
ANNEXED
ANNEXES
CALYXES
HELIXES
HYRAXES
ICEAXES
IMMIXED
IMMIXES
INDEXED
INDEXES
LATEXES
PHLOXES
POBOXES
RELAXED
RELAXES
REMIXED
REMIXES
RETAXED
RETAXES
REWAXED
REWAXES
TELEXED
TELEXES
UNBOXED
UNBOXES
UNFIXED

•••••XE
PICKAXE
POLEAXE

•XF••••
OXFORDS

••XF•••
BOXFULS
FOXFIRE
SIXFOLD
TAXFREE

X•••••G
XRATING
XRAYING

•X•G•••
EXIGENT

•X•••G•
EXPUNGE

•X••••G
EXILING
EXITING
EXUDING

••XG•••
SIXGUNS

••X•G••
HEXAGON

••X••G•
FIXINGS
HEXSIGN

••X•••G
TAXIING
WAXWING

•••X••G
COAXING
FLEXING
HOAXING
JINXING

X•••H••
XANTHAN
XANTHIC

•XH••••
EXHALED
EXHALES
EXHAUST
EXHIBIT
EXHORTS

••XH•••
FOXHOLE
SAXHORN

••X•••H
PIXYISH

X•••I••
XRATING
XRAYING

X••••I•
XANTHIC

•XI••••
AXIALLY
AXILLAE
EXIGENT
EXILING
EXISTED
EXITING
OXIDANT
OXIDASE
OXIDIZE

•X•I•••
EXCISED
EXCISES
EXCITED
EXCITES
EXHIBIT
EXPIATE
EXPIRED
EXPIRES
EXTINCT
EXWIVES

•X••I••
EXAMINE
EXILING
EXITING
EXOTICA
EXOTICS
EXUDING
OXIDIZE
OXONIAN
UXORIAL

•X•••I•
EXCLAIM
EXHIBIT
EXPLAIN
EXPLOIT
EXURBIA

•X••••I
EXEMPLI

••XI•••
ANXIETY
ANXIOUS
FIXINGS
FOXIEST
LEXICAL
LEXICON
MAXILLA
MAXIMAL
MAXIMUM
MAXIMUS
MEXICAN
MIXITUP
NOXIOUS
PYXIDES
SEXIEST
SEXISTS
TAXICAB
TAXIING
TAXIWAY
WAXIEST

••X•I••
BOXKITE
FOXFIRE
HEXSIGN
PIXYISH
SIXTIES
TAXIING
TEXTILE
WAXWING

••X••I•
BOXEDIN
BOXESIN
DEXTRIN
FOXTAIL

•••XI••
BAUXITE
COAXIAL
COAXING
COEXIST
DIOXIDE
ELIXIRS
EPOXIES
FLEXING
HOAXING
JINXING
MARXISM
PROXIES
PROXIMO

••••XI•
MRFIXIT

•••••XI
AIRTAXI

••XK•••
BOXKITE

••X•••K
SIXPACK
WAXWORK

•XL••••
AXLROSE

•X•L•••
AXILLAE
AXOLOTL
EXALTED
EXCLAIM
EXCLUDE
EXILING
EXPLAIN
EXPLODE
EXPLOIT
EXPLORE
EXULTED
OXBLOOD

•X••L••
AXIALLY
AXILLAE
EXHALED
EXHALES

•X•••L•
AXIALLY
EXACTLY
EXAMPLE
EXEMPLI

•X••••L
AXOLOTL
UXORIAL

••X•L••
MAXILLA

••X••L•
BOXFULS
FIXABLE
FIXEDLY
FOXHOLE
MAXILLA
MAXWELL
MIXABLE
SIXFOLD
TAXABLE
TEXTILE
VEXEDLY

••X•••L
FOXTAIL
LEXICAL
MAXIMAL
MAXWELL
TEXTUAL

•••X••L
COAXIAL

•X•M•••
EXAMINE
EXAMPLE
EXEMPLI
EXEMPTS
OXYMORA

•X•••M•
EXTREME

•X••••M
EXCLAIM

••X•M••
MAXIMAL
MAXIMUM
MAXIMUS

••X••M•
COXCOMB
NOXZEMA

••X•••M
MAXIMUM

•••XM••
MANXMAN
MANXMEN

•••X•M•
PROXIMO

•••X••M
MARXISM

X•N••••
XANTHAN
XANTHIC

X••••N•
XRATING
XRAYING

X•••••N
XANTHAN

•X•N•••
OXONIAN

•X••N••
EXPANDS
EXPANSE
EXPENDS
EXPENSE
EXPUNGE
EXTENDS
EXTENTS
EXTINCT

•X•••N•
EXAMINE
EXIGENT
EXILING
EXITING
EXPOUND
EXUDING
OXIDANT

•X••••N
EXPLAIN
EXURBAN
OXONIAN

••XN•••
HEXNUTS
LAXNESS

••X•N••
FIXINGS
ROXANNE

••X••N•
ROXANNE
SEXTANS
SEXTANT
SEXTONS
SIXGUNS
TAXIING
WAXWING

••X•••N
BOXEDIN
BOXESIN
DEXTRIN
HEXAGON
HEXSIGN
LEXICON
MAXBORN
MEXICAN
SAXHORN
SIXTEEN
WAXBEAN

•••XN••
FLEXNER

•••X•N•
COAXING
FLEXING
HOAXING
JINXING
KLAXONS

•••X••N
BRAXTON
MANXMAN
MANXMEN

•XO••••
AXOLOTL
EXOTICA
EXOTICS
OXONIAN
UXORIAL

•X•O•••
EXHORTS
EXPORTS
EXPOSED
EXPOSES
EXPOUND
EXTORTS
OXFORDS

•X••O••
AXLROSE
AXOLOTL
EXPLODE
EXPLOIT
EXPLORE
OXBLOOD
OXYMORA

•X•••O•
EXACTOR
OXBLOOD

••X•O••
ANXIOUS
BOXTOPS
BOXWOOD
COXCOMB
FOXHOLE
MAXBORN
NOXIOUS
SAXHORN
SEXTONS
SIXFOLD
WAXWORK

••X••O•
BOXWOOD
FOXTROT
HEXAGON
LEXICON
TUXEDOS

•••XO••
FLEXORS
KLAXONS
PLEXORS
QUIXOTE

•••X•O•
BRAXTON

•••X••O
PROXIMO

•XP••••
EXPANDS
EXPANSE
EXPARTE
EXPECTS
EXPENDS
EXPENSE
EXPERTS
EXPIATE
EXPIRED
EXPIRES
EXPLAIN
EXPLODE
EXPLOIT
EXPLORE
EXPORTS
EXPOSED
EXPOSES
EXPOUND
EXPRESS
EXPUNGE

•X•P•••
EXUPERY

•X••P••
EXAMPLE
EXCEPTS
EXEMPLI
EXEMPTS

•X•••P•
EXCERPT

••XP•••
SIXPACK

••X••P•
BOXTOPS

••X•••P
BOXEDUP
BOXESUP
BOXSTEP
FIXEDUP
FIXESUP
MIXEDUP
MIXESUP
MIXITUP

•••XP••
FAUXPAS

XR•••••
XRATING
XRAYING

•X•R•••
AXLROSE
EXCRETE
EXERTED
EXPRESS
EXTRACT
EXTREME
EXTRUDE
EXURBAN
EXURBIA
UXORIAL

•X••R••
EXCERPT
EXHORTS
EXPARTE
EXPERTS
EXPIRED
EXPIRES
EXPORTS
EXTORTS
OXCARTS
OXFORDS

•X•••R•
EXPLORE
EXUPERY
OXYMORA

•X••••R
EXACTER
EXACTOR

••XR•••
REXREED
TAXRATE

••X•R••
DEXTRIN
FOXTROT
TAXFREE

••X••R•
BOXCARS
FIXTURE
FOXFIRE
MAXBORN
MIXTURE
SAXHORN
TEXTURE
WAXWORK

••X•••R
MAXBAER

•••X•R•
COAXERS
ELIXIRS
FLEXORS
HOAXERS
PLEXORS

•••X••R
FLEXNER

•X•S•••
EXISTED

•X••S••
EXCISED
EXCISES
EXCUSED
EXCUSES
EXPOSED
EXPOSES

•X•••S•
AXLROSE
EXHAUST
EXPANSE
EXPENSE
EXPRESS
OXIDASE

•X••••S
EXCEEDS
EXCEPTS
EXCISES
EXCITES
EXCUSES
EXEMPTS
EXHALES
EXHORTS
EXOTICS
EXPANDS
EXPECTS
EXPENDS
EXPERTS
EXPIRES
EXPORTS
EXPOSES
EXPRESS
EXTENDS
EXTENTS
EXTORTS
EXWIVES
OXCARTS
OXFORDS

••XS•••
BOXSEAT
BOXSTEP
HEXSIGN

••X•S••
BOXESIN
BOXESUP
FIXESUP
MIXESUP
NEXUSES
SEXISTS

••X••S•
FOXIEST
LAXNESS
PIXYISH
SEXIEST
WAXIEST

••X•••S
ANXIOUS
BOXCARS
BOXFULS
BOXTOPS
FIXATES
FIXINGS
HEXNUTS
LAXNESS
LUXATES
MAXIMUS
NEXUSES
NOXIOUS
PYXIDES
REXCATS
SEXISTS
SEXTANS
SEXTETS
SEXTONS
SIXGUNS
SIXTIES
TUXEDOS

•••X•S•
COEXIST
MARXISM

•••X••S
COAXERS
ELIXIRS
EPOXIES
FAUXPAS
FLEXORS
HOAXERS
KLAXONS
PLEXORS
PROXIES

••••X•S
ADMIXES
AFFIXES
ANNEXES
CALYXES
HELIXES
HYRAXES
ICEAXES
IMMIXES
INDEXES
LATEXES
PHLOXES
POBOXES
RELAXES
REMIXES
RETAXES
REWAXES
TELEXES
UNBOXES
URTEXTS

X••T•••
XANTHAN
XANTHIC
XRATING

•XT••••
EXTENDS
EXTENTS
EXTINCT
EXTORTS
EXTRACT
EXTREME
EXTRUDE

•X•T•••
EXITING
EXOTICA
EXOTICS

•X••T••
EXACTED
EXACTER
EXACTLY
EXACTOR
EXALTED
EXCITED
EXCITES
EXERTED
EXISTED
EXULTED

•X•••T•
AXOLOTL
EXCEPTS
EXCRETE
EXECUTE
EXEMPTS
EXHORTS
EXPARTE
EXPECTS
EXPERTS
EXPIATE
EXPORTS
EXTENTS
EXTORTS
OXCARTS

•X••••T
EXCERPT
EXHAUST
EXHIBIT
EXIGENT
EXPLOIT
EXTINCT
EXTRACT
OXIDANT

••XT•••
BOXTOPS
DEXTRIN
FIXTURE
FOXTAIL
FOXTROT
MIXTURE
SEXTANS
SEXTANT
SEXTETS
SEXTONS
SIXTEEN
SIXTIES
TEXTILE
TEXTUAL
TEXTURE

••X•T••
BOXSTEP
FIXATED
FIXATES
LUXATED
LUXATES
MIXITUP

••X••T•
ANXIETY
BOXKITE
HEXNUTS
REXCATS
SEXISTS
SEXTETS
TAXRATE

••X•••T
BOXSEAT
FOXIEST
FOXTROT
SEXIEST
SEXTANT
WAXIEST

•••XT••
BRAXTON

•••X•T•
BAUXITE
QUIXOTE

•••X••T
COEXIST
INEXACT
MANXCAT

••••XT•
URTEXTS

••••X•T
MRFIXIT

•••••XT
BETWIXT
CONTEXT
PRETEXT
SUBTEXT

•XU••••
EXUDING
EXULTED
EXUPERY
EXURBAN
EXURBIA

•X•U•••
EXCUSED
EXCUSES
EXPUNGE

•X••U••
EXCLUDE
EXECUTE
EXHAUST
EXPOUND
EXTRUDE

••XU•••
NEXUSES

••X•U••
BOXFULS
FIXTURE
HEXNUTS
MIXTURE
SIXGUNS
TEXTUAL
TEXTURE

••X••U•
ANXIOUS
BOXEDUP
BOXESUP
FIXEDUP
FIXESUP
MAXIMUM
MAXIMUS
MIXEDUP
MIXESUP
MIXITUP
NOXIOUS

•X••V••
EXWIVES

•XW••••
EXWIVES

••XW•••
BOXWOOD
MAXWELL
WAXWING
WAXWORK

••X•W••
TAXIWAY

X••Y•••
XRAYING

•XY••••
OXYMORA

•X••••Y
AXIALLY
EXACTLY
EXUPERY

••XY•••
PIXYISH

••X•••Y
ANXIETY

FIXEDLY
TAXIWAY
VEXEDLY

•X•••Z•
OXIDIZE

••XZ•••
NOXZEMA

YA•••••
YACHTED
YAHTZEE
YAKKERS
YAKKING
YAKUTSK
YAMMERS
YANGTZE
YANKEES
YANKING
YANKTON
YAOUNDE
YAPPERS
YAPPING
YARDAGE
YARDARM
YARDMAN
YARDMEN
YARNING
YARROWS
YASHMAK
YAUPONS
YAWNERS
YAWNING
YAWPERS

Y•A••••
YEAREND
YEARNED
YEARNER
YEARNTO
YEATEAM

Y••A•••
YUCATAN

Y•••A••
YARDAGE
YARDARM
YESMAAM
YOPLAIT
YOUMANS

Y••••A•
YARDMAN
YASHMAK
YEATEAM
YELLSAT
YEREVAN
YESDEAR
YESMAAM
YITZHAK
YUCATAN

Y•••••A
YESHIVA

•YA••••
BYANDBY
BYANOSE
HYALINE
MYANMAR
WYANDOT

•Y•A•••
AYEAYES
BYPATHS
BYWAYOF
DYNAMIC
DYNAMOS
DYNASTS
DYNASTY
GYRATED
GYRATES
GYRATOR
HYRACES
HYRAXES
MYMAMMY
PYJAMAS
PYRAMID
PYRAMUS
SYNAPSE
TYRANNY
TYRANTS

•Y••A••
AYNRAND
BYHEART
BYPLAYS
BYROADS
CYMBALS
EYEBALL
EYEBANK
EYELASH
EYEWASH
GYMNAST
HYDRANT
HYDRATE
HYMNALS
MYRIADS
SYLLABI
SYLVANS
SYRIANS
TYMPANA
TYMPANI

•Y•••A•
CYNICAL
HYUNDAI
LYRICAL
MYANMAR
PYJAMAS
PYTHIAS
SYNGMAN
SYNODAL
TYPICAL

•Y••••A
CYNTHIA
DYKSTRA
HYGIEIA
SYRINGA
TYMPANA
WYNONNA

••YA•••
BUYABLE
FLYAWAY
KAYAKED
KAYAKER
LAYAWAY
LOYALLY
LOYALTY
MAYALIN
PAYABLE
ROYALLY
ROYALTY
ULYANOV
VOYAGED
VOYAGER
VOYAGES

••Y•A••
AMYLASE
CRYBABY
DAYCAMP
DAYCARE
DRYWALL
FLYBALL
FLYCAST
FLYPAST
FLYWAYS
FRYPANS
HAYRACK
HAYWARD
HEYDAYS
JAYWALK
KEYCARD
KEYPADS
MAYDAYS
MAYFAIR
MAYNARD
NAYSAID
NAYSAYS
PAYCASH
PAYDAYS
REYNARD
SKYCAPS
SKYJACK
SKYLARK
SKYWARD
SKYWAYS
TOYLAND
WAYLAID
WAYLAYS
WAYWARD
WHYDAHS

••Y••A•
ABYSMAL
BAYLEAF
CAYUGAS
CRYSTAL
DAYSTAR
ELYSIAN
FAYWRAY
FEYNMAN
FLYAWAY
FLYLEAF
FLYTRAP
LAYAWAY
MAYORAL
PAYLOAD
PAYOLAS
RAYOVAC
ROYBEAN
SOYBEAN
STYGIAN
STYRIAN
ZOYSIAS

••Y•••A
ALYOSHA
DAYTONA
OLYMPIA
OXYMORA

•••YA••
ARMYANT
BANYANS
BUOYANT
DRAYAGE
HALYARD
HOLYARK
KENYANS
LANYARD
LIBYANS
MAGYARS
MARYANN
PLAYACT
RUDYARD

•••Y•A•
BABYSAT
BODYFAT
COPYCAT
HOLYWAR
INKYCAP
KHAYYAM
LADYDAY
LILYPAD
MANYEAR
MARYKAY
MIDYEAR
NEWYEAR
OFFYEAR
PLAYSAT

•••Y••A
ASSYRIA
CRAYOLA

••••YA•
GIDDYAP
KHAYYAM
MALAYAN
MEGRYAN
PAPAYAS
RUFIYAA
SAROYAN

••••Y•A
RUFIYAA

•••••YA
MONTOYA

•YB••••
CYBORGS
DYBBUKS
HYBRIDS

•Y•B•••
CYMBALS
DYBBUKS
EYEBALL
EYEBANK
EYEBOLT
EYEBROW
SYMBOLS

•Y•••B•
BYANDBY
BYTHEBY
SYLLABI

••YB•••
ANYBODY
CRYBABY
DAYBEDS
DAYBOOK
FLYBALL
FLYBOYS
JAYBIRD
RAYBURN
ROYBEAN
SKYBLUE
SOYBEAN
WAYBILL

••Y•B••
BUYABLE
PAYABLE
TOYNBEE

••Y••B•
CRYBABY

••Y•••B
KEYCLUB

•••YB••
COPYBOY
LADYBUG
PLAYBOY

Y•C••••
YACHTED
YUCATAN
YUCKIER

Y•••••C
YOUNGMC

•YC••••
CYCLERS
CYCLING
CYCLIST
CYCLONE
CYCLOPS
LYCEUMS
TYCOONS
WYCHELM

•Y•C•••
EYECUPS
PYNCHON
SYNCHED
SYNCHES
SYNCING

•Y••C••
CYNICAL
HYRACES
LYRICAL
TYPICAL

•Y•••C•
BYFORCE
MYSTICS

•Y••••C
DYNAMIC
PYRRHIC
SYNODIC

••YC•••
BAYCITY
BOYCOTT
DAYCAMP
DAYCARE
DRYCELL
FLYCAST
FRYCOOK
JAYCEES
KEYCARD
KEYCLUB
PAYCASH
PSYCHED
PSYCHES
PSYCHIC
PSYCHUP
SKYCAPS

••Y••C•
DRYDOCK
HAYRACK
PHYSICS
SHYLOCK
SKYJACK

••Y•••C
CRYPTIC
IDYLLIC
OLYMPIC
PSYCHIC
RAYKROC
RAYOVAC
STYPTIC

•••YC••
BICYCLE
CALYCES
COPYCAT
HOLYCOW
INKYCAP
RECYCLE

•••Y•C•
PLAYACT

•••Y••C
ACRYLIC

••••YC•
DIPTYCH
VANDYCK
VANEYCK

••••Y•C
LIPSYNC

Y•D••••
YIDDISH
YODELED
YODELER

Y••D•••
YARDAGE
YARDARM
YARDMAN
YARDMEN
YESDEAR
YIDDISH

Y•••D••
YIELDED

Y••••D•
YAOUNDE

Y•••••D
YACHTED
YEAREND
YEARNED
YIELDED
YODELED

•YD••••
HYDRANT
HYDRATE
HYDROUS

•Y•D•••
PYEDOGS

•Y••D••
BYANDBY
HYPEDUP
HYUNDAI
PYXIDES
SYNODAL
SYNODIC
TYPEDUP
WYANDOT

•Y•••D•
BYROADS
BYWORDS
EYELIDS
HYBRIDS
MYRIADS

•Y••••D
AYKROYD
AYNRAND
BYLINED
GYRATED
PYRAMID
SYNCHED

••YD•••
BOYDORR
DRYDOCK
HEYDAYS
HOYDENS
LAYDOWN
MAYDAYS
PAYDAYS
PAYDIRT
SKYDIVE
TOYDOGS
WHYDAHS

••Y•D••
KEYEDIN
KEYEDUP

••Y••D•
ANYBODY
DAYBEDS
FLYRODS
HAYRIDE
HEYJUDE
JOYRIDE
KEYPADS
WAYSIDE

••Y•••D
BOYHOOD
DRYEYED
GAYLORD
HAYSEED
HAYWARD
HEYWOOD
JAYBIRD
KAYAKED
KEYCARD
KEYWORD
LAYERED
MAYNARD
NAYSAID
PAYLOAD
PLYWOOD
PSYCHED
RAYMOND
REYNARD
SCYTHED
SKYWARD
STYMIED
TOYLAND
TRYSTED
UNYOKED
VOYAGED
WAYLAID
WAYWARD

•••YD••
KATYDID

•••Y•D•
LADYDAY
PLAYDOH
RUBYDEE

•••Y••D
HALYARD
KATYDID
LANYARD
LILYPAD
RETYPED
RUDYARD

••••Y•D
ALLAYED
ALLOYED
ANNOYED
ARRAYED
ASSAYED
BELAYED
BOGEYED
BUGEYED
DECAYED
DECOYED
DELAYED
DRYEYED
ENJOYED
ESSAYED
HONEYED
MONEYED
MOSEYED
ONEEYED
POPEYED
REKEYED
RELAYED
SAMOYED
SPLAYED
SPRAYED
STRAYED
TIEDYED

•••••YD
AYKROYD

YE•••••
YEAREND
YEARNED
YEARNER
YEARNTO
YEATEAM
YELLING
YELLOWS
YELLSAT
YELPERS
YELPING
YELTSIN
YEMENIS
YEREVAN
YESDEAR
YESHIVA
YESMAAM
YESSING
YEVGENY

Y•E••••
YIELDED

Y••E•••
YEMENIS
YEREVAN
YODELED
YODELER
YULELOG

Y•••E••
YAKKERS
YAMMERS
YANKEES
YAPPERS
YAWNERS
YAWPERS
YEAREND
YEATEAM
YELPERS
YESDEAR
YEVGENY
YONKERS
YOWLERS

Y••••E•
YACHTED
YAHTZEE
YANKEES
YARDMEN
YEARNED
YEARNER
YIELDED
YODELED
YODELER
YOUNGER
YUCKIER
YUMMIER
YUPPIES

Y•••••E
YAHTZEE
YANGTZE
YAOUNDE
YARDAGE

•YE••••
AYEAYES
EYEBALL
EYEBANK
EYEBOLT
EYEBROW
EYECUPS
EYEFULS
EYEHOLE
EYELASH
EYELETS
EYELIDS
EYESORE
EYEWASH
PYEDOGS

•Y•E•••
BYHEART
HYPEDUP
LYCEUMS
SYNERGY
TYLENOL
TYPEDUP
TYPESET
TYPESUP
WYNETTE
WYVERNS

•Y••E••
BYTHEBY
CYCLERS
CYGNETS
CYPHERS
CYPRESS
EYELETS
GYPPERS
HYGIEIA
HYGIENE
HYPHENS
MYNHEER
MYSTERY
OYSTERS
SYSTEMS
WYCHELM

•Y•••E•
AYEAYES
BYGONES
BYLINED
BYLINES
GYPSIES
GYRATED
GYRATES
HYRACES
HYRAXES
KYLIKES
MYNHEER
MYRTLES
PYGMIES
PYRITES
PYXIDES
SYNCHED
SYNCHES
SYNFUEL
TYPESET
ZYGOTES

•Y••••E
BYANOSE
BYFORCE
CYCLONE
EYEHOLE
EYESORE
GYMSHOE
HYALINE
HYDRATE
HYGIENE
SYNAPSE
SYRINGE
SYSTOLE
WYNETTE

••YE•••
CAYENNE
DOYENNE
DRYEYED
KEYEDIN
KEYEDUP
LAYERED
LAYETTE

••Y•E••
BAYLEAF
COYNESS
DAYBEDS
DRYCELL
DRYNESS
DRYWELL
ELYSEES
FLYLEAF
FLYNETS
GEYSERS
HAYSEED
HOYDENS
JAYCEES
JAYLENO
JAYVEES
JOYLESS
KEYWEST
MAYHEMS
PAYMENT
RHYMERS
ROYBEAN
SHYNESS
SLYNESS
SOYBEAN
STYLERS
STYLETS
STYRENE
THYSELF
WRYNESS

••Y••E•
ABYSSES
BAYONET
BRYNNER
CAYUSES
COYOTES
CRYOGEN
DRYEYED
ELYSEES
FLYOVER
HAYSEED
JAYCEES
JAYVEES
KAYAKED
KAYAKER
LAYERED
LAYOVER
ODYSSEY
PSYCHED
PSYCHES
SAYWHEN
SCYTHED
SCYTHES
SHYSTER
STYMIED
STYMIES
TOYNBEE
TRYSTED
TRYSTER
ULYSSES
UNYOKED
UNYOKES
VOYAGED
VOYAGER
VOYAGES

••Y•••E
AMYLASE
ANYMORE
ANYTIME
BUYABLE
BUYTIME
CAYENNE
DAYCARE
DAYTIME
DOYENNE
DRYHOLE
HAYRIDE
HAYWIRE
HEYJUDE
JOYRIDE
KEYHOLE
KEYLIME
KEYNOTE
LAYETTE
MAYPOLE
MAYTIME
MAYWINE
PAYABLE
SKYBLUE
SKYDIVE
SKYLINE
STYLIZE
STYRENE
TOYNBEE
WAYSIDE

•••YE••
BOWYERS
BRAYERS
CORYELL
GRAYEST
GREYEST
GRUYERE
LAWYERS
MANYEAR
MIDYEAR
NCWYETH
NEWYEAR
OFFYEAR
PLAYERS
PRAYERS
SAWYERS
SLAYERS
SPRYEST
SWAYERS

•••Y•E•
ARGYLES
CALYCES
CALYXES
CLAYIER
ECDYSES
ECTYPES
ENZYMES
HOLYSEE
OOCYTES
PLAYLET
PLAYPEN
POLYMER
RETYPED
RETYPES
RUBYDEE

•••Y••E
BICYCLE
DRAYAGE
GRUYERE
HOLYOKE
HOLYSEE
RECYCLE
RUBYDEE

••••YE•
ALLAYED
ALLAYER
ALLEYES
ALLOYED
ANNOYED
ARRAYED
ASSAYED
ASSAYER
AYEAYES
BELAYED
BIGEYES
BOGEYED
BUGEYED
COLLYER
DECAYED
DECOYED
DELAYED
DELAYER
DRYEYED
ENJOYED
ESSAYED
HONEYED
LOBBYER
MONEYED
MOSEYED
NUREYEV
ONEEYED
POPEYED
REDEYES
REKEYED
RELAYED
RIBEYES
SAMOYED
SPLAYED
SPRAYED
SPRAYER
STRAYED
TIEDYED
TIEDYES

••••Y•E
ACOLYTE
ANALYSE
ANALYZE
ANODYNE
CARLYLE
INSTYLE
MARRYME
MISTYPE
RESTYLE
TINTYPE
VANDYKE

•••••YE
BUCKEYE
CATSEYE
DEADEYE
EVILEYE
FISHEYE
GLADEYE
GOODBYE
HAIRDYE
HAWKEYE
SHUTEYE
SOCKEYE
WALLEYE

•YF••••
BYFORCE

•Y•F•••
EYEFULS
SYNFUEL

•Y•••F•
MYSTIFY

•Y••••F
BYWAYOF

••YF•••
FLYFISH
HAYFORK
MAYFAIR

••Y•F••
LAYOFFS
LAYSFOR
PAYOFFS
PAYSFOR

••Y••F•
BUYSOFF
HAYLOFT
LAYOFFS
LAYSOFF
PAYOFFS
PAYSOFF

••Y•••F
BAYLEAF
BUYSOFF
CRYWOLF
FLYLEAF
LAYSOFF
PAYSOFF
THYSELF

•••YF••
BODYFAT
DREYFUS
PLAYFUL
PRAYFOR
TRAYFUL

•••Y•F•
PLAYOFF

•••Y••F
PLAYOFF

••••Y•F
BYWAYOF

Y•G••••
YOGHURT
YOGURTS

Y••G•••
YANGTZE
YEVGENY

Y•••G••
YOUNGER
YOUNGMC
YOUNGUN

Y••••G•
YARDAGE

Y•••••G
YAKKING
YANKING
YAPPING
YARNING
YAWNING
YELLING
YELPING
YESSING
YIPPING
YOWLING
YOYOING
YULELOG

•YG••••
BYGONES
CYGNETS
HYGIEIA
HYGIENE
PYGMIES
ZYGOTES

•Y•G•••
SYNGMAN

•Y••G••
LYINGTO
TYINGIN
TYINGUP

•Y•••G•
CYBORGS
PYEDOGS
SYNERGY
SYRINGA
SYRINGE
ZYMURGY

•Y••••G
CYCLING
CYYOUNG
GYPPING
HYPOING
SYNCING
WYOMING
WYSIWYG

••YG•••
RAYGUNS
STYGIAN

••Y•G••
CAYUGAS
CRYOGEN
VOYAGED
VOYAGER
VOYAGES

••Y••G•
FLYHIGH
SAYINGS
SKYHIGH
TOYDOGS

••Y•••G
CYYOUNG
DAYLONG
KAYOING
KEYRING
RHYMING
STYLING
YOYOING

•••YG••
KOSYGIN
POLYGON

•••Y•G•
DRAYAGE

•••Y••G
ALLYING
BABYING
BELYING
BRAYING
BUOYING
BURYING
BUSYING
CLOYING
COPYING
COZYING
DEFYING
DENYING
DRAYING
EDDYING
ENVYING
ESPYING
FLAYING
FRAYING
GRAYING
GREYING
JURYING
JURYRIG
LADYBUG
LEVYING
OBEYING
OKAYING
PITYING
PLAYING
PONYING
PRAYING
RELYING
SPAYING
STAYING
SWAYING
TIDYING
UNDYING
UNTYING
VARYING
XRAYING

•••••YG
WYSIWYG

Y•H••••
YAHTZEE

Y••H•••
YACHTED
YASHMAK
YESHIVA
YOGHURT

Y•••H••
YITZHAK

Y•••••H
YIDDISH

•YH••••
BYHEART

•Y•H•••
BYTHEBY
CYPHERS
EYEHOLE
HYPHENS
MYNHEER
PYTHIAS
PYTHONS
TYPHOON
WYCHELM

•Y••H••
CYNTHIA
GYMSHOE
PYNCHON
PYRRHIC
PYRRHUS
SYNCHED
SYNCHES

•Y•••H•
BYPATHS

•Y••••H
EYELASH
EYEWASH

••YH•••
BOYHOOD
DRYHOLE
FLYHIGH
KEYHOLE
MAYHEMS
SKYHIGH
SKYHOOK

••Y•H••
GRYPHON
PSYCHED
PSYCHES
PSYCHIC
PSYCHUP
RHYTHMS
SAYWHEN
SCYTHED
SCYTHES
TOYSHOP

••Y••H•
ALYOSHA
WHYDAHS

••Y•••H
FLYFISH
FLYHIGH
PAYCASH
SKYHIGH
STYLISH

•••Y••H
BABYISH
FOGYISH
NCWYETH
PIXYISH
PLAYDOH

••••YH•
TALLYHO

••••Y•H
DIPTYCH
FORSYTH

YI•••••
YIDDISH
YIELDED
YIPPING
YITZHAK

Y•••I••
YAKKING
YANKING
YAPPING
YARNING
YAWNING
YELLING
YELPING
YESHIVA
YESSING
YIDDISH
YIPPING
YOWLING
YOYOING
YTTRIUM
YUCKIER
YUMMIER
YUPPIES

Y••••I•
YELTSIN
YEMENIS
YOPLAIT

•YI••••
LYINGTO
TYINGIN
TYINGUP

•Y•I•••
BYLINED
BYLINES
CYNICAL
HYGIEIA
HYGIENE
KYLIKES
LYRICAL
LYRISTS
MYRIADS
PYRITES
PYXIDES
SYRIANS
SYRINGA
SYRINGE
TYPICAL
TYPISTS
WYSIWYG

•Y••I••
CYCLING
CYCLIST
CYPRIOT
EYELIDS
GYPPING
GYPSIES
HYALINE
HYBRIDS
HYPOING
MYSTICS
MYSTIFY
PYGMIES
PYTHIAS
RYKRISP
SYNCING
WYOMING

•Y•••I•
CYNTHIA
DYNAMIC
HYGIEIA
PYRAMID
PYRRHIC
SYNODIC
TYINGIN

•Y••••I
HYUNDAI
SYLLABI
TYMPANI

••YI•••
LAYINTO
PRYINTO
SAYINGS

••Y•I••
ANYTIME
BAYCITY
BUYTIME
DAYLILY
DAYSINN
DAYTIME
ELYSIAN
ELYSIUM
FLYFISH
FLYHIGH
HAYRIDE
HAYWIRE
JAYBIRD
JOYRIDE
KAYOING
KEYLIME
KEYRING
MAYTIME
MAYWINE
PAYDIRT
PHYSICS
RHYMING
SKYDIVE
SKYHIGH
SKYLINE
STYGIAN
STYLING
STYLISH
STYLIST
STYLIZE
STYMIED
STYMIES
STYRIAN
WAYBILL
WAYSIDE
YOYOING
ZOYSIAS

••Y••I•
CRYPTIC
DAYTRIP
DRYSUIT
IDYLLIC
KEYEDIN
MAYALIN
MAYFAIR
NAYSAID
OLYMPIA
OLYMPIC
PHYLLIS
PSYCHIC
STYPTIC
WAYLAID

•••YI••
ALLYING
BABYING
BABYISH
BELYING
BRAYING
BUOYING
BURYING
BUSYING
CLAYIER
CLOYING
COPYING
COPYIST
COZYING
DEFYING
DENYING
DRAYING
EDDYING
ENVYING
ESPYING
FLAYING
FOGYISH
FOGYISM
FRAYING
GRAYING
GREYING
JURYING
LEVYING
OBEYING
OKAYING
PITYING
PIXYISH
PLAYING
PONYING
PRAYING
RELYING
SPAYING
STAYING
SWAYING
TIDYING
TORYISM
UNDYING
UNTYING
VARYING
XRAYING

•••Y•I•
ACRYLIC
ANDYKIM
ASSYRIA
BABYSIT
ECDYSIS
JURYRIG
KATYDID
KOSYGIN
TINYTIM

••••YI•
ROCKYII
ROCKYIV

••••Y•I
PLATYPI
ROCKYII

•••••YI
KAROLYI

•YJ••••
PYJAMAS

••YJ•••
HEYJUDE
SKYJACK

Y•K••••
YAKKERS
YAKKING
YAKUTSK
YOKOONO

Y••K•••
YAKKERS
YAKKING
YANKEES
YANKING
YANKTON
YONKERS
YOUKNOW
YUCKIER

Y•••••K
YAKUTSK
YASHMAK
YITZHAK

•YK••••
AYKROYD
DYKSTRA
RYKRISP

•Y••K••
KYLIKES

•Y•••K•
DYBBUKS

•Y••••K
EYEBANK

••YK•••
RAYKROC

••Y•K••
KAYAKED
KAYAKER
UNYOKED
UNYOKES

••Y•••K
DAYBOOK
DRYDOCK
FRYCOOK
HAYFORK
HAYRACK
JAYWALK
SHYLOCK
SKYHOOK
SKYJACK
SKYLARK

•••YK••
ANDYKIM
MARYKAY

•••Y•K•
HOLYOKE

•••Y••K
HOLYARK
NEWYORK

••••YK•
GROMYKO
VANDYKE

••••Y•K
VANDYCK
VANEYCK

Y•L••••
YELLING
YELLOWS
YELLSAT
YELPERS
YELPING
YELTSIN
YULELOG

Y••L•••
YELLING
YELLOWS
YELLSAT
YIELDED
YOPLAIT
YOWLERS
YOWLING

Y•••L••
YODELED
YODELER
YULELOG

•YL••••
BYLINED
BYLINES
KYLIKES
SYLLABI
SYLVANS
TYLENOL

•Y•L•••
BYPLAYS
CYCLERS
CYCLING
CYCLIST
CYCLONE
CYCLOPS
EYELASH
EYELETS
EYELIDS
HYALINE
SYLLABI

•Y••L••
MYRTLES

•Y•••L•
CYMBALS
EYEBALL
EYEBOLT
EYEFULS
EYEHOLE
HYMNALS
SYMBOLS
SYSTOLE
WYCHELM

•Y••••L
CYNICAL
EYEBALL
LYRICAL
SYNFUEL
SYNODAL
TYLENOL
TYPICAL

••YL•••
AMYLASE
ASYLUMS
BAYLEAF
DAYLILY
DAYLONG
FLYLEAF
GAYLORD
HAYLOFT
IDYLLIC
JAYLENO
JOYLESS
KEYLIME
PAYLOAD
PHYLLIS
SHYLOCK
SKYLARK
SKYLINE
STYLERS
STYLETS
STYLING
STYLISH
STYLIST
STYLIZE
TOYLAND
WAYLAID
WAYLAYS

••Y•L••
IDYLLIC
KEYCLUB
LAYSLOW
LOYALLY
LOYALTY
MAYALIN
PAYOLAS
PHYLLIS
ROYALLY
ROYALTY
SKYBLUE

••Y••L•
BUYABLE
CRYWOLF
DAYLILY
DRYCELL
DRYHOLE
DRYWALL
DRYWELL
FLYBALL
JAYWALK
KEYHOLE
LOYALLY
MAYPOLE
PAYABLE
PAYROLL
ROYALLY
THYSELF
WAYBILL

••Y•••L
ABYSMAL
CRYSTAL
DRYCELL
DRYWALL
DRYWELL
FLYBALL
MAYORAL
PAYROLL
WAYBILL

•••YL••
ACRYLIC
ARGYLES
BABYLON
EMMYLOU
MARYLOU
PLAYLET

•••Y•L•
BICYCLE
CORYELL
CRAYOLA
RECYCLE

•••Y••L
CORYELL
PLAYFUL
TRAYFUL

••••YL•
CARLYLE
DACTYLS
INSTYLE
RESTYLE

Y•M••••
YAMMERS
YEMENIS
YUMMIER

Y••M•••
YAMMERS
YESMAAM
YOUMANS
YUMMIER

Y•••M••
YARDMAN
YARDMEN
YASHMAK

Y••••M•
YOUNGMC

Y•••••M
YARDARM
YEATEAM
YESMAAM
YTTRIUM

•YM••••
CYMBALS
GYMNAST
GYMSHOE
HYMNALS
MYMAMMY
SYMBOLS
SYMPTOM
TYMPANA
TYMPANI
ZYMURGY

•Y•M•••
PYGMIES
WYOMING

•Y••M••
DYNAMIC
DYNAMOS
MYANMAR
MYMAMMY
PYJAMAS
PYRAMID
PYRAMUS
SYNGMAN

•Y•••M•
LYCEUMS
MYMAMMY
SYSTEMS

•Y••••M
SYMPTOM
SYNONYM
WYCHELM

••YM•••
ANYMORE
HAYMOWS
OLYMPIA
OLYMPIC
OLYMPUS
OXYMORA
PAYMENT
RAYMOND
RHYMERS
RHYMING
SEYMOUR
STYMIED
STYMIES

••Y•M••
ABYSMAL
FEYNMAN

••Y••M•
ANYTIME
ASYLUMS
BUYTIME
DAYCAMP
DAYTIME
KEYLIME
MAYHEMS
MAYTIME
RHYTHMS

••Y•••M
ALYSSUM
DAYROOM
ELYSIUM

•••YM••
ENZYMES
POLYMER

•••Y•M•
ANDYKIM
FOGYISM
KHAYYAM
TINYTIM
TORYISM

••••YM•
ANONYMS
EPONYMS
MARRYME

••••Y•M
KHAYYAM

•••••YM
ACRONYM
ANTONYM
HOMONYM
SYNONYM

Y•N••••
YANGTZE
YANKEES
YANKING
YANKTON
YONKERS

Y••N•••
YARNING
YAWNERS
YAWNING
YOUNGER
YOUNGMC
YOUNGUN

Y•••N••
YAOUNDE
YEARNED
YEARNER
YEARNTO
YEMENIS
YOUKNOW

Y••••N•
YAKKING
YANKING
YAPPING
YARNING
YAUPONS
YAWNING
YEAREND
YELLING
YELPING
YESSING
YEVGENY
YIPPING
YOKOONO
YOUMANS
YOWLING
YOYOING

Y•••••N
YANKTON
YARDMAN
YARDMEN
YELTSIN
YEREVAN
YOUNGUN
YUCATAN

•YN••••
AYNRAND
CYNICAL
CYNTHIA
DYNAMIC
DYNAMOS
DYNASTS
DYNASTY
MYNHEER
PYNCHON
SYNAPSE
SYNCHED
SYNCHES
SYNCING
SYNERGY
SYNFUEL
SYNGMAN
SYNODAL
SYNODIC
SYNONYM
WYNETTE
WYNONNA

•Y•N•••
BYANDBY
BYANOSE
CYGNETS
GYMNAST
HYMNALS
HYUNDAI
LYINGTO
MYANMAR
TYINGIN
TYINGUP
WYANDOT

•Y••N••
BYGONES
BYLINED
BYLINES
SYNONYM
SYRINGA
SYRINGE
TYLENOL
TYRANNY
TYRANTS
WYNONNA

•Y•••N•
AYNRAND
BYTURNS
CYCLING
CYCLONE
CYYOUNG
EYEBANK
GYPPING
HYALINE
HYDRANT
HYGIENE
HYPHENS
HYPOING
PYTHONS
SYLVANS
SYNCING
SYRIANS
TYCOONS
TYMPANA
TYMPANI
TYRANNY
WYNONNA
WYOMING
WYVERNS

•Y••••N
PYNCHON
SYNGMAN
TYINGIN
TYPHOON

••YN•••
BRYNNER
COYNESS
DRYNESS
FEYNMAN
FLYNETS
KEYNOTE
MAYNARD
REYNARD
SHYNESS
SLYNESS
TOYNBEE
WRYNESS

••Y•N••
BAYONET
BRYNNER
CAYENNE
DOYENNE
LAYINTO
PRYINTO
SAYINGS
ULYANOV

••Y••N•
CAYENNE
CYYOUNG
DAYLONG
DAYSINN
DAYTONA
DOYENNE
DRYRUNS
FRYPANS
HOYDENS
JAYLENO
KAYOING
KEYRING
MAYWINE
PAYMENT
RAYGUNS
RAYMOND
RHYMING
SKYLINE
STYLING
STYRENE
TOYLAND
YOYOING

••Y•••N
CRYOGEN
DAYSINN
ELYSIAN
FEYNMAN
GRYPHON
KEYEDIN
KRYPTON
LAYDOWN
MAYALIN
RAYBURN
ROYBEAN
SAYWHEN
SOYBEAN
STYGIAN
STYRIAN
WAYWORN

•••Y•N•
ALLYING
ARMYANT
BABYING
BANYANS
BARYONS
BELYING
BRAYING
BUOYANT
BUOYING
BURYING
BUSYING
CANYONS
CLOYING
COPYING
COZYING
CRAYONS
DEFYING
DENYING
DRAYING
EDDYING
ENVYING
ESPYING
FLAYING
FRAYING
GRAYING
GREYING
JURYING
KENYANS
LEVYING
LIBYANS
MARYANN
OBEYING
OKAYING
PITYING
PLAYING
PONYING
PRAYING
RELYING
SPAYING
STAYING
SWAYING
TIDYING
UNDYING
UNTYING
VARYING
XRAYING

•••Y••N
ALLYSON
BABYLON
CLAYTON
GRAYSON
KOSYGIN
MARYANN
PLAYPEN
PLAYSON
POLYGON
PREYSON
SLAYTON

••••YN•
ANODYNE
LIPSYNC
PHARYNX

••••Y•N
CARRYON
EARLYON
HALCYON
JIMRYUN
MALAYAN
MEGRYAN
PROCYON
SAROYAN

•••••YN
BURSTYN
CAROLYN
FONTEYN
GOLDWYN
KATHRYN
MARILYN

YO•••••
YODELED
YODELER
YOGHURT
YOGURTS
YOKOONO
YONKERS
YOPLAIT
YOUKNOW
YOUMANS
YOUNGER
YOUNGMC
YOUNGUN
YOWLERS
YOWLING
YOYOING

Y•O••••
YAOUNDE

Y••O•••
YOKOONO
YOYOING

Y•••O••
YARROWS
YAUPONS
YELLOWS
YOKOONO

Y••••O•
YANKTON
YOUKNOW
YULELOG

Y•••••O
YEARNTO
YOKOONO

•YO••••
WYOMING

•Y•O•••
BYFORCE
BYGONES
BYROADS
BYWORDS
CYBORGS
CYYOUNG
HYPOING
SYNODAL
SYNODIC
SYNONYM
TYCOONS
WYNONNA
ZYGOTES

•Y••O••
AYKROYD
BYANOSE
CYCLONE
CYCLOPS
EYEBOLT
EYEHOLE
EYESORE
HYDROUS
HYSSOPS
PYEDOGS
PYTHONS
SYMBOLS
SYSTOLE
TYCOONS
TYPHOON

•Y•••O•
BYWAYOF
CYPRIOT
DYNAMOS
EYEBROW
GYMSHOE
GYRATOR
PYNCHON
SYMPTOM
TYLENOL
TYPHOON
WYANDOT

•Y••••O
LYINGTO

••YO•••
ALYOSHA
BAYONET
BUYOUTS
COYOTES
CRYOGEN
CYYOUNG
FLYOVER
KAYOING
LAYOFFS
LAYOUTS
LAYOVER
MAYORAL
PAYOFFS
PAYOLAS
PAYOUTS
RAYOVAC
TRYOUTS
UNYOKED
UNYOKES
YOYOING

••Y•O••
ANYBODY
ANYMORE
BOYCOTT
BOYDORR
BOYHOOD
BUYSOFF
BUYSOUT
CRYWOLF
DAYBOOK
DAYLONG
DAYROOM
DAYTONA
DRYDOCK
DRYHOLE
FLYBOYS
FLYRODS
FRYCOOK
GAYLORD
HAYFORK
HAYLOFT
HAYMOWS
HEYWOOD
KEYHOLE
KEYNOTE
KEYWORD
LAYDOWN
LAYSOFF
LAYSOUT
MAYPOLE
OXYMORA
PAYLOAD
PAYROLL
PAYSOFF
PAYSOUT
PLYWOOD
RAYMOND
SEYMOUR
SHYLOCK
SKYHOOK
TOYDOGS
WAYWORN

••Y••O•
BOYHOOD
CRYPTOS
DAYBOOK
DAYROOM
FRYCOOK
GRYPHON
HEYWOOD
KRYPTON
LAYSFOR
LAYSLOW
PAYSFOR
PLYWOOD
RAYKROC
SKYHOOK
TOYSHOP
ULYANOV

••Y•••O
JAYLENO
LAYINTO
PRYINTO

•••YO••
BARYONS
CANYONS
CRAYOLA
CRAYONS
HOLYOKE
NEWYORK
PLAYOFF
PLAYOUT

•••Y•O•
ALLYSON
BABYLON
CLAYTON
COPYBOY
EMMYLOU
GRAYSON
HOLYCOW
MARYLOU
ONLYYOU
PLAYBOY
PLAYDOH
PLAYSON
POLYGON
PRAYFOR
PREYSON
SLAYTON

•••Y••O
CALYPSO
PRAYSTO

••••YO•
ARROYOS
BYWAYOF
CARRYON
EARLYON
EMBRYOS
HALCYON
NEARYOU
ONLYYOU
PROCYON

••••Y•O
GROMYKO
RALLYTO
TALLYHO

Y•P••••
YAPPERS
YAPPING
YIPPING
YOPLAIT
YUPPIES

Y••P•••
YAPPERS
YAPPING
YAUPONS
YAWPERS
YELPERS
YELPING
YIPPING
YUPPIES

•YP••••
BYPATHS
BYPLAYS
CYPHERS
CYPRESS
CYPRIOT
GYPPERS
GYPPING
GYPSIES
HYPEDUP
HYPHENS
HYPOING
TYPEDUP
TYPESET
TYPESUP
TYPHOON
TYPICAL
TYPISTS

•Y•P•••
GYPPERS
GYPPING
SYMPTOM
TYMPANA
TYMPANI

•Y••P••
SYNAPSE

•Y•••P•
CYCLOPS
EYECUPS
HYSSOPS

•Y••••P
HYPEDUP
RYKRISP
TYINGUP
TYPEDUP
TYPESUP

••YP•••
CRYPTIC
CRYPTOS
FLYPAST
FRYPANS
GRYPHON
KEYPADS
KRYPTON
MAYPOLE
STYPTIC

••Y•P••
OLYMPIA
OLYMPIC
OLYMPUS

••Y••P•
SKYCAPS

••Y•••P
DAYCAMP
DAYTRIP
FLYTRAP
KEYEDUP
PSYCHUP
TOYSHOP

•••YP••
CALYPSO
ECTYPES
LILYPAD
PLAYPEN
RETYPED
RETYPES
STAYPUT

•••Y••P
BUOYSUP
INKYCAP
PLAYSUP
STAYSUP

••••YP•
DECRYPT
ENCRYPT
MISTYPE
PLATYPI
TINTYPE

••••Y•P
BELLYUP
BUDDYUP
DUMMYUP
GIDDYAP
GIDDYUP
GUSSYUP
TALLYUP

Y•R••••
YARDAGE
YARDARM
YARDMAN
YARDMEN
YARNING
YARROWS
YEREVAN

Y••R•••
YARROWS
YEAREND
YEARNED
YEARNER
YEARNTO
YTTRIUM

Y•••R••
YOGURTS

Y••••R•
YAKKERS
YAMMERS
YAPPERS
YARDARM
YAWNERS
YAWPERS
YELPERS
YOGHURT
YONKERS
YOWLERS

Y•••••R
YEARNER
YESDEAR
YODELER
YOUNGER
YUCKIER
YUMMIER

•YR••••
BYROADS
GYRATED
GYRATES
GYRATOR
HYRACES
HYRAXES
LYRICAL
LYRISTS
MYRIADS
MYRTLES
PYRAMID
PYRAMUS
PYRITES
PYRRHIC
PYRRHUS
SYRIANS
SYRINGA
SYRINGE
TYRANNY
TYRANTS

•Y•R•••
AYKROYD
AYNRAND
CYPRESS
CYPRIOT
HYBRIDS
HYDRANT
HYDRATE
HYDROUS
PYRRHIC
PYRRHUS
RYKRISP

•Y••R••
BYFORCE
BYTURNS
BYWORDS
CYBORGS
EYEBROW
SYNERGY
WYVERNS
ZYMURGY

•Y•••R•
BYHEART
CYCLERS
CYPHERS
DYKSTRA
EYESORE
GYPPERS
MYSTERY
OYSTERS

•Y••••R
GYRATOR
MYANMAR
MYNHEER

••YR•••
DAYROOM
DRYRUNS
FLYRODS
HAYRACK
HAYRIDE
JOYRIDE
KEYRING
PAYROLL
STYRENE
STYRIAN

••Y•R••
DAYTRIP
FAYWRAY
FLYTRAP
LAYERED
MAYORAL
RAYKROC

••Y••R•
ANYMORE
BOYDORR
DAYCARE
GAYLORD
GEYSERS
HAYFORK
HAYWARD
HAYWIRE
JAYBIRD
KEYCARD
KEYWORD
MAYNARD
OXYMORA
PAYDIRT
RAYBURN
REYNARD
RHYMERS
SKYLARK
SKYWARD
STYLERS
WAYWARD
WAYWORN

••Y•••R
BOYDORR
BRYNNER
DAYSTAR
FLYOVER
KAYAKER
LAYOVER
LAYSFOR
MAYFAIR
PAYSFOR
SEYMOUR
SHYSTER
TRYSTER
VOYAGER

•••YR••
ASSYRIA
JURYRIG
PAPYRUS

•••Y•R•
BOWYERS
BRAYERS
GRUYERE
HALYARD
HOLYARK
LANYARD
LAWYERS
MAGYARS
NEWYORK
PLAYERS
PRAYERS
RUDYARD
SAWYERS
SLAYERS
SWAYERS

•••Y••R
CLAYIER
HOLYWAR
MANYEAR
MIDYEAR
NEWYEAR
OFFYEAR
POLYMER
PRAYFOR

••••YR•
MARTYRS
ZEPHYRS

••••Y•R
ALLAYER
ASSAYER
COLLYER
DELAYER
LOBBYER
SPRAYER

Y•S••••
YASHMAK
YESDEAR
YESHIVA
YESMAAM
YESSING

Y••S•••
YESSING

Y•••S••
YELLSAT
YELTSIN

Y••••S•
YAKUTSK
YIDDISH

Y•••••S
YAKKERS
YAMMERS
YANKEES
YAPPERS
YARROWS
YAUPONS
YAWNERS
YAWPERS
YELLOWS
YELPERS
YEMENIS
YOGURTS
YONKERS
YOUMANS
YOWLERS
YUPPIES

•YS••••
HYSSOPS
MYSTERY
MYSTICS
MYSTIFY
OYSTERS
SYSTEMS
SYSTOLE
WYSIWYG

•Y•S•••
DYKSTRA
EYESORE
GYMSHOE
GYPSIES
HYSSOPS

•Y••S••
DYNASTS
DYNASTY
LYRISTS
TYPESET
TYPESUP
TYPISTS

•Y•••S•
BYANOSE
CYCLIST
CYPRESS
EYELASH
EYEWASH
GYMNAST
RYKRISP
SYNAPSE

•Y••••S
AYEAYES
BYGONES
BYLINES
BYPATHS
BYPLAYS
BYROADS
BYTURNS
BYWORDS
CYBORGS
CYCLERS
CYCLOPS
CYGNETS
CYMBALS
CYPHERS
CYPRESS
DYBBUKS
DYNAMOS
DYNASTS
EYECUPS
EYEFULS
EYELETS
EYELIDS
GYPPERS
GYPSIES
GYRATES
HYBRIDS
HYDROUS
HYMNALS
HYPHENS
HYRACES
HYRAXES
HYSSOPS
KYLIKES
LYCEUMS
LYRISTS
MYRIADS
MYRTLES
MYSTICS
OYSTERS
PYEDOGS
PYGMIES
PYJAMAS
PYRAMUS
PYRITES
PYRRHUS
PYTHIAS
PYTHONS
PYXIDES
SYLVANS
SYMBOLS
SYNCHES
SYRIANS
SYSTEMS
TYCOONS
TYPISTS
TYRANTS
WYVERNS
ZYGOTES

••YS•••
ABYSMAL
ABYSSES
ALYSSUM
BUYSOFF
BUYSOUT
CRYSTAL
DAYSINN
DAYSTAR
DRYSUIT
ELYSEES
ELYSIAN
ELYSIUM
GEYSERS
HAYSEED
LAYSFOR
LAYSLOW
LAYSOFF
LAYSOUT
NAYSAID
NAYSAYS
ODYSSEY
PAYSFOR
PAYSOFF
PAYSOUT
PHYSICS
SHYSTER
THYSELF
TOYSHOP
TRYSTED
TRYSTER
ULYSSES
WAYSIDE
ZOYSIAS

••Y•S••
ABYSSES
ALYOSHA
ALYSSUM
CAYUSES
ODYSSEY
ULYSSES

••Y••S•
AMYLASE
COYNESS
DRYNESS
FLYCAST
FLYFISH
FLYPAST
JOYLESS
KEYWEST
PAYCASH
SHYNESS
SLYNESS
STYLISH
STYLIST
WRYNESS

••Y•••S
ABYSSES
ASYLUMS
BUYOUTS
CAYUGAS
CAYUSES
COYNESS
COYOTES
CRYPTOS
DAYBEDS
DRYNESS
DRYRUNS
ELYSEES
FLYBOYS
FLYNETS
FLYRODS
FLYWAYS
FRYPANS
GEYSERS
HAYMOWS
HEYDAYS
HOYDENS
JAYCEES

JAYVEES
JOYLESS
KEYPADS
LAYOFFS
LAYOUTS
MAYDAYS
MAYHEMS
NAYSAYS
OLYMPUS
PAYDAYS
PAYOFFS
PAYOLAS
PAYOUTS
PHYLLIS
PHYSICS
PSYCHES
RAYGUNS
RHYMERS
RHYTHMS
SAYINGS
SCYTHES
SHYNESS
SKYCAPS
SKYWAYS
SLYNESS
STYLERS
STYLETS
STYMIES
TOYDOGS
TRYOUTS
ULYSSES
UNYOKES
VOYAGES
WAYLAYS
WHYDAHS
WRYNESS
ZOYSIAS

•••YS••
ALLYSON
BABYSAT
BABYSIT
BUOYSUP
ECDYSES
ECDYSIS
GRAYSON
HOLYSEE
PLAYSAT
PLAYSON
PLAYSUP
PRAYSTO
PREYSON
STAYSUP

•••Y•S•
BABYISH
CALYPSO
COPYIST
FOGYISH
FOGYISM
GRAYEST
GREYEST
PIXYISH
SPRYEST
TORYISM

•••Y••S
ARGYLES
BANYANS
BARYONS
BOWYERS
BRAYERS
CALYCES
CALYXES
CANYONS
CRAYONS
DREYFUS
ECDYSES
ECDYSIS
ECTYPES
ENZYMES
KENYANS
LAWYERS
LIBYANS
MAGYARS
OOCYTES
PAPYRUS
PLAYERS
PRAYERS
RETYPES
SAWYERS
SLAYERS
SWAYERS

••••YS•
ANALYSE
ANALYST

••••Y•S
ALLEYES
ANONYMS
ARROYOS
AYEAYES
BIGEYES
DACTYLS
EMBRYOS
EPONYMS
KIKUYUS
MARTYRS
PAPAYAS
REDEYES
RIBEYES
TIEDYES
ZEPHYRS

•••••YS
AFFRAYS
AIRWAYS
BADGUYS
BAILEYS
BARLEYS
BARNEYS
BATBOYS
BETRAYS
BIGBOYS
BUSBOYS
BYPLAYS
CARBOYS
CONVEYS
CONVOYS
COWBOYS
DEEJAYS
DEFRAYS
DEPLOYS
DICKEYS
DISMAYS
DOGDAYS
DONKEYS
EMPLOYS
ENDWAYS
ESTRAYS
FLYBOYS
FLYWAYS
FRIDAYS
GALLEYS
GOODBYS
GURNEYS
HEYDAYS
JERSEYS
JITNEYS
JOCKEYS
KIDNEYS
LACKEYS
LOWBOYS
MAGUEYS
MANDAYS
MARGAYS
MAYDAYS
MEDLEYS
MIDDAYS
MIDWAYS
MISLAYS
MONDAYS
MONKEYS
NAYSAYS
OLDDAYS
OSPREYS
OUTLAYS
PARLAYS
PARLEYS
PAYDAYS
PEAVEYS
PREPAYS
PULLEYS
PURVEYS
REPLAYS
RICKEYS
ROBROYS
ROMNEYS
RUNWAYS
SASHAYS
SEAWAYS
SKYWAYS
STOREYS
SUBWAYS
SUNDAYS
SUNRAYS
SURREYS
SURVEYS
TEAPOYS
TOMBOYS
TURKEYS
VALLEYS
VEEJAYS
VOLLEYS
WAYLAYS

YT•••••
YTTRIUM

Y•T••••
YITZHAK
YTTRIUM

Y••T•••
YAHTZEE
YEATEAM
YELTSIN

Y•••T••
YACHTED
YAKUTSK
YANGTZE
YANKTON
YUCATAN

Y••••T•
YEARNTO
YOGURTS

Y•••••T
YELLSAT
YOGHURT
YOPLAIT

•YT••••
BYTHEBY
BYTURNS
PYTHIAS
PYTHONS

•Y•T•••
CYNTHIA
MYRTLES
MYSTERY
MYSTICS
MYSTIFY
OYSTERS
SYSTEMS
SYSTOLE

•Y••T••
BYPATHS
DYKSTRA
GYRATED
GYRATES
GYRATOR
PYRITES
SYMPTOM
WYNETTE
ZYGOTES

•Y•••T•
CYGNETS
DYNASTS
DYNASTY
EYELETS
HYDRATE
LYINGTO
LYRISTS
TYPISTS
TYRANTS
WYNETTE

•Y••••T
BYHEART
CYCLIST
CYPRIOT
EYEBOLT
GYMNAST
HYDRANT
TYPESET
WYANDOT

••YT•••
ANYTIME
BUYTIME
DAYTIME
DAYTONA
DAYTRIP
FLYTRAP
MAYTIME
RHYTHMS
SCYTHED
SCYTHES

••Y•T••
COYOTES
CRYPTIC
CRYPTOS
CRYSTAL
DAYSTAR
KRYPTON
LAYETTE
SHYSTER
STYPTIC
TRYSTED
TRYSTER

••Y••T•
BAYCITY
BOYCOTT
BUYOUTS
FLYNETS
KEYNOTE
LAYETTE
LAYINTO
LAYOUTS
LOYALTY
PAYOUTS
PRYINTO
ROYALTY
STYLETS
TRYOUTS

••Y•••T
BAYONET
BOYCOTT
BUYSOUT
DRYSUIT
FLYCAST
FLYPAST
HAYLOFT
KEYWEST
LAYSOUT
PAYDIRT
PAYMENT
PAYSOUT
STYLIST

•••YT••
CLAYTON
OOCYTES
SLAYTON
TINYTIM

•••Y•T•
NCWYETH
PRAYSTO

•••Y••T
ARMYANT
BABYSAT
BABYSIT
BODYFAT
BUOYANT
COPYCAT
COPYIST
GRAYEST
GREYEST
PLAYACT
PLAYLET
PLAYOUT
PLAYSAT
SPRYEST
STAYPUT

••••YT•
ACOLYTE
FORSYTH
RALLYTO

••••Y•T
ANALYST
DECRYPT
ENCRYPT

YU•••••
YUCATAN
YUCKIER
YULELOG
YUMMIER
YUPPIES

Y•U••••
YAUPONS
YOUKNOW
YOUMANS
YOUNGER
YOUNGMC
YOUNGUN

Y••U•••
YAKUTSK
YAOUNDE
YOGURTS

Y•••U••
YOGHURT

Y••••U•
YOUNGUN
YTTRIUM

•YU••••
HYUNDAI

•Y•U•••
BYTURNS
ZYMURGY

•Y••U••
CYYOUNG
DYBBUKS
EYECUPS
EYEFULS
LYCEUMS
SYNFUEL

•Y•••U•
HYDROUS
HYPEDUP
PYRAMUS
PYRRHUS
TYINGUP
TYPEDUP
TYPESUP

••YU•••
CAYUGAS
CAYUSES

••Y•U••
ASYLUMS
BUYOUTS
CYYOUNG
DRYRUNS
DRYSUIT
HEYJUDE
LAYOUTS
PAYOUTS
RAYBURN
RAYGUNS
TRYOUTS

••Y••U•
ALYSSUM
BUYSOUT
ELYSIUM
KEYCLUB
KEYEDUP
LAYSOUT
OLYMPUS
PAYSOUT
PSYCHUP
SEYMOUR
SKYBLUE

•••Y•U•
BUOYSUP
DREYFUS
LADYBUG
PAPYRUS
PLAYFUL
PLAYOUT
PLAYSUP
STAYPUT
STAYSUP
TRAYFUL

•••Y••U
EMMYLOU
MARYLOU
ONLYYOU

••••YU•
BELLYUP
BUDDYUP
DUMMYUP
GIDDYUP
GUSSYUP
JIMRYUN
KIKUYUS
TALLYUP

••••Y•U
NEARYOU
ONLYYOU

Y•V••••
YEVGENY

Y•••V••
YEREVAN

Y••••V•
YESHIVA

•YV••••
WYVERNS

•Y•V•••
SYLVANS

••YV•••
JAYVEES

••Y•V••
FLYOVER
LAYOVER
RAYOVAC

••Y••V•
SKYDIVE

••Y•••V
ULYANOV

••••Y•V
NUREYEV
ROCKYIV

Y•W••••
YAWNERS
YAWNING
YAWPERS
YOWLERS
YOWLING

Y••••W•
YARROWS
YELLOWS

Y•••••W
YOUKNOW

•YW••••
BYWAYOF
BYWORDS

•Y•W•••
EYEWASH

•Y••W••
WYSIWYG

•Y••••W
EYEBROW

••YW•••
CRYWOLF
DRYWALL
DRYWELL
FAYWRAY
FLYWAYS
HAYWARD
HAYWIRE
HEYWOOD
JAYWALK
KEYWEST
KEYWORD
MAYWINE
PLYWOOD
SAYWHEN
SKYWARD
SKYWAYS
WAYWARD
WAYWORN

••Y•W••
FLYAWAY
LAYAWAY

••Y••W•
HAYMOWS
LAYDOWN

••Y•••W
LAYSLOW

•••YW••
HOLYWAR

•••Y••W
HOLYCOW

•YX••••
PYXIDES

•Y••X••
HYRAXES

•••YX••
CALYXES

••••Y•X
PHARYNX

Y•Y••••
YOYOING

Y•••••Y
YEVGENY

•YY••••
CYYOUNG

•Y••Y••
AYEAYES
BYWAYOF

•Y•••Y•
AYKROYD
BYPLAYS
SYNONYM
WYSIWYG

•Y••••Y
BYANDBY
BYTHEBY
DYNASTY
MYMAMMY
MYSTERY
MYSTIFY
SYNERGY
TYRANNY
ZYMURGY

••Y•Y••
DRYEYED

••Y••Y•
FLYBOYS
FLYWAYS
HEYDAYS
MAYDAYS
NAYSAYS
PAYDAYS
SKYWAYS
WAYLAYS

••Y•••Y
ANYBODY
BAYCITY
CRYBABY
DAYLILY
FAYWRAY
FLYAWAY
LAYAWAY
LOYALLY
LOYALTY
ODYSSEY
ROYALLY
ROYALTY

•••YY••
KHAYYAM
ONLYYOU

•••Y••Y
COPYBOY
LADYDAY
MARYKAY
PLAYBOY

Y••Z•••
YITZHAK

Y•••Z••
YAHTZEE

Y••••Z•
YANGTZE

••Y••Z•
STYLIZE

••••YZ•
ANALYZE

ZA•••••
ZACHARY
ZAGGING
ZAMBEZI
ZAMBIAN
ZANDERS
ZANIEST
ZAPOTEC
ZAPPERS
ZAPPING
ZAREBAS
ZATOPEK

Z•A••••
ZEALAND
ZEALOTS
ZEALOUS

Z••A•••
ZENANAS
ZONALLY
ZOUAVES

Z•••A••
ZACHARY
ZEALAND
ZERMATT
ZHIVAGO
ZIGZAGS
ZODIACS

Z••••A•
ZAMBIAN
ZAREBAS
ZENANAS
ZEUGMAS
ZINNIAS
ZOYSIAS

Z•••••A
ZENOBIA

•ZA••••
AZALEAS
CZARDAS
CZARDOM
CZARINA
CZARISM
CZARIST
TZARINA

•Z•••A•
AZALEAS
AZTECAN
CZARDAS

•Z••••A
CZARINA
TZARINA

••ZA•••
BAZAARS
BIZARRE
CEZANNE
HAZARDS
KAZAKHS
LAZARUS
LIZARDS
PIZARRO
SIZABLE
SIZABLY
SUZANNE
WIZARDS

••Z•A••
BAZAARS
BUZZARD
GAZZARA
GIZZARD
HUZZAHS
JAZZAGE
PIZZAZZ

••Z••A•
BUZZSAW
JAZZMAN
VIZSLAS
WOZNIAK

••Z•••A
BAZOOKA
GAZZARA
MAZURKA

•••ZA••
BUZZARD
CINZANO
CRUZADO
GAZZARA
GIZZARD
HUZZAHS
JAZZAGE
PIZZAZZ
TARZANA
VANZANT
ZIGZAGS

•••Z•A•
BUZZSAW
JAZZMAN
MITZVAH
PIAZZAS
YITZHAK

•••Z••A
ARIZONA
GAZZARA
NOXZEMA
TARZANA

••••ZA•
ALCAZAR
KWANZAS
PIAZZAS
QUETZAL
SALAZAR
STANZAS

•••••ZA
BONANZA
CADENZA
MENDOZA
ORGANZA
SPINOZA

Z•B••••
ZEBULON

Z••B•••
ZAMBEZI
ZAMBIAN
ZOMBIES

Z•••B••
ZAREBAS
ZENOBIA

••Z•B••
GAZEBOS
JEZEBEL
SIZABLE
SIZABLY

••Z••B•
LAZENBY

Z•C••••
ZACHARY

Z••C•••
ZILCHES
ZIPCODE
ZIRCONS

Z••••C•
ZODIACS

Z•••••C
ZAPOTEC

•Z••C••
AZTECAN

••Z••C•
WOZZECK

•••Z•C•
WOZZECK

Z•D••••
ZODIACS

Z••D•••
ZANDERS

Z••••D•
ZIPCODE

Z•••••D
ZEALAND

•Z••D••
CZARDAS
CZARDOM

••Z•D••
DAZEDLY
SIZEDUP

••Z••D•
HAZARDS
LIZARDS
WIZARDS

••Z•••D
BUZZARD
COZENED
DAZZLED
DIZZIED
FIZZLED
GIZZARD
GUZZLED
MIZZLED
MUZZLED
NUZZLED
PUZZLED
RAZORED
REZONED
SIZZLED
UNZONED
WIZENED

•••Z•D•
CRUZADO

•••Z••D
BUZZARD
DAZZLED
DIZZIED
FIZZLED
FOOZLED
FRIZZED
GIZZARD
GUZZLED
MIZZLED
MUZZLED
NUZZLED
PUZZLED
QUIZZED
SIZZLED
WHIZKID
WHIZZED

••••Z•D
BLITZED
BREEZED
BRONZED
FRIZZED
GLITZED
IODIZED
IONIZED
QUIZZED
SNEEZED
SNOOZED
TWEEZED
UNFAZED
WALTZED
WHEEZED
WHIZZED

ZE•••••
ZEALAND
ZEALOTS
ZEALOUS
ZEBULON
ZEITUNG
ZENANAS
ZENITHS
ZENOBIA
ZEPHYRS
ZERMATT
ZEROING
ZESTFUL
ZESTIER
ZEUGMAS

Z•E••••
ZOELLER

Z••E•••
ZAREBAS

Z•••E••
ZAMBEZI
ZANDERS
ZANIEST
ZAPPERS
ZINGERS
ZIPPERS
ZITHERS
ZONKERS

Z••••E•
ZAPOTEC
ZATOPEK
ZESTIER
ZILCHES
ZINGIER
ZIPPIER
ZOELLER
ZOMBIES
ZOUAVES
ZYGOTES

Z•••••E
ZIPCODE

•ZE••••
EZEKIEL

•Z•E•••
AZTECAN

•Z••E••
AZALEAS

•Z•••E•
EZEKIEL

•Z••••E
AZURITE

••ZE•••
COZENED
DAZEDLY
DOZENTH
DOZEOFF
GAZEBOS
GAZELLE
GAZETTE
JEZEBEL
LAZENBY
LOZENGE
ROZELLE
SIZEDUP
SIZESUP
SUZETTE
WIZENED

••Z•E••
BEZIERS
BUZZERS
COZIEST
COZZENS
HAZIEST
LAZIEST
MIZZENS
VIZIERS
WOZZECK

••Z••E•
COZENED
COZUMEL
DAZZLED
DAZZLER
DAZZLES
DIZZIED
DIZZIER
DIZZIES
ENZYMES
FIZZIER
FIZZLED
FIZZLES
FUZZIER
GUZZLED
GUZZLER
GUZZLES
JAZZIER
JAZZMEN
JEZEBEL
MIZZLED
MIZZLES
MUZZIER
MUZZLED
MUZZLES
NOZZLES
NUZZLED
NUZZLER
NUZZLES
PUZZLED
PUZZLER
PUZZLES
RAZORED
REZONED
REZONES
SIZZLED
SIZZLES
TIZZIES
UNZONED
WIZENED

••Z•••E
BEZIQUE
BIZARRE
CEZANNE
GAZELLE
GAZETTE
JAZZAGE
LOZENGE
ROZELLE
SIZABLE
SUZANNE
SUZETTE

•••ZE••
BENZENE
BLAZERS
BUZZERS
COZZENS
GEEZERS
GLAZERS
GRAZERS
MIZZENS
NONZERO
NOXZEMA
PANZERS
SEIZERS
SUBZERO
WOZZECK

•••Z•E•
BRAZIER
CRAZIER
CRAZIES
DAZZLED
DAZZLER
DAZZLES
DIZZIED
DIZZIER
DIZZIES
DOOZIES
FIZZIER
FIZZLED
FIZZLES
FOOZLED
FOOZLES
FRAZIER
FRIZZED
FRIZZES
FUZZIER
GAUZIER
GLAZIER
GUZZLED
GUZZLER
GUZZLES
JAZZIER
JAZZMEN
MIZZLED
MIZZLES
MUZZIER
MUZZLED
MUZZLES
NOZZLES
NUZZLED
NUZZLER
NUZZLES
PUZZLED
PUZZLER
PUZZLES
QUIZZED
QUIZZES
RITZIER
SIZZLED
SIZZLES
TIZZIES
WHIZZED
WHIZZES
WOOZIER

•••Z••E
BENZENE
CALZONE
CANZONE
DRIZZLE
ENDZONE
FANZINE
FRAZZLE
FRIZZLE
GRIZZLE
JAZZAGE
RHIZOME
SWIZZLE

••••ZE•
ASSIZES
BEDIZEN
BLITZED
BLITZEN
BLITZES
BREEZED
BREEZES
BRONZED
BRONZES
CITIZEN
DENIZEN
FREEZER
FREEZES
FRIEZES
FRIZZED
FRIZZES
GLITZED
GLITZES
IODIZED
IODIZES
IONIZED
IONIZER
IONIZES
JANTZEN
KLUTZES
PRETZEL
QUIZZED
QUIZZES
SARAZEN
SELTZER
SNEEZED
SNEEZER
SNEEZES
SNOOZED
SNOOZES
SPITZES
SWITZER
TOPAZES
TWEEZED
TWEEZES
UNFAZED
WALTZED
WALTZER
WALTZES
WHEEZED
WHEEZER
WHEEZES
WHIZZED
WHIZZES
YAHTZEE

••••Z•E
DRIZZLE
FRAZZLE
FRIZZLE
GRIZZLE
SWIZZLE
YAHTZEE

•••••ZE
AGONIZE
ANALYZE
ANODIZE
APPRIZE
ATOMIZE
BAPTIZE
CAPSIZE
FIRENZE
IDOLIZE
INADAZE
ITEMIZE
LIONIZE
MIDSIZE
OBELIZE
OUTSIZE
OXIDIZE
REALIZE
SQUEEZE
STYLIZE
TRAPEZE
UTILIZE
YANGTZE

Z•••F••
ZESTFUL

••Z••F•
BUZZOFF
DOZEOFF

••Z•••F
BUZZOFF
DOZEOFF

•••Z•F•
BUZZOFF

•••Z••F
BUZZOFF

Z•G••••
ZAGGING
ZIGGING
ZIGZAGS
ZYGOTES

Z••G•••
ZAGGING
ZEUGMAS
ZIGGING
ZINGERS
ZINGIER
ZINGING

Z•••G••
ZWINGLI

Z••••G•
ZHIVAGO
ZIGZAGS
ZOOLOGY
ZYMURGY

Z•••••G
ZAGGING
ZAPPING
ZEITUNG
ZEROING
ZIGGING
ZINGING
ZIPPING
ZONKING
ZOOMING

••ZG•••
FIZGIGS

••Z••G•
FIZGIGS
HAZINGS
JAZZAGE
LOZENGE
SIZINGS

••Z•••G
BUZZING
COZYING
FIZZING
FUZZING
JAZZING
RAZZING

•••Z•G•
JAZZAGE
ZIGZAGS

•••Z••G
AMAZING
BLAZING
BRAZING
BUZZING
CRAZING
FIZZING
FUZZING
GLAZING
GRAZING
JAZZING
PRIZING
RAZZING
SEIZING

••••Z•G
LEIPZIG

ZH•••••
ZHIVAGO

Z•H••••
ZACHARY
ZEPHYRS
ZITHERS

Z•••H••
ZILCHES

Z••••H•
ZENITHS

•Z••••H
AZIMUTH

••ZH•••
MUZHIKS

••Z••H•
HUZZAHS
KAZAKHS

••Z•••H
DOZENTH

•••ZH••
YITZHAK

•••Z•H•
HUZZAHS
MATZOHS

•••Z••H
MITZVAH

ZI•••••
ZIGGING
ZIGZAGS
ZILCHES
ZILLION
ZINGERS
ZINGIER
ZINGING
ZINNIAS
ZIPCODE
ZIPPERS
ZIPPIER
ZIPPING
ZIRCONS
ZITHERS

Z•I••••
ZEITUNG
ZHIVAGO
ZWINGLI

Z••I•••
ZANIEST
ZENITHS
ZODIACS

Z•••I••
ZAGGING
ZAMBIAN
ZAPPING
ZEROING
ZESTIER
ZIGGING
ZILLION
ZINGIER
ZINGING
ZINNIAS
ZIPPIER
ZIPPING
ZOMBIES
ZONKING
ZOOMING
ZOYSIAS

Z••••I•
ZENOBIA
ZOOMSIN

Z•••••I
ZAMBEZI
ZWINGLI

•ZI••••
AZIMUTH

•Z••I••
AZURITE
CZARINA
CZARISM
CZARIST
EZEKIEL
TZARINA

••ZI•••
BEZIERS
BEZIQUE
COZIEST
HAZIEST
HAZINGS
LAZIEST
SIZINGS
VIZIERS

••Z•I••
BUZZING
COZYING
DIZZIED
DIZZIER
DIZZIES
DIZZILY
FIZGIGS
FIZZIER
FIZZING
FUZZIER
FUZZILY
FUZZING
JAZZIER
JAZZILY
JAZZING
MUZHIKS
MUZZIER
MUZZILY
RAZZING
TIZZIES
WOZNIAK

•••ZI••
AMAZING
BLAZING
BRAZIER
BRAZING
BUZZING
CRAZIER
CRAZIES
CRAZILY
CRAZING
DIZZIED
DIZZIER
DIZZIES
DIZZILY
DOOZIES
FANZINE
FIZZIER
FIZZING
FRAZIER
FUZZIER
FUZZILY
FUZZING
GAUZIER
GAUZILY
GLAZIER
GLAZING
GRAZING
JAZZIER
JAZZILY
JAZZING
MUZZIER
MUZZILY
PRIZING
RAZZING
RITZIER
SEIZING
TIZZIES
WOOZIER
WOOZILY

•••Z•I•
BORZOIS
MUEZZIN
WHIZKID

••••ZI•
BENAZIR
DWEEZIL
LEIPZIG
MUEZZIN
SKEEZIX

••••Z•I
JACUZZI
PALAZZI

•••••ZI
ANASAZI
JACUZZI
PALAZZI
SCHATZI
SCHERZI
ZAMBEZI

Z••K•••
ZONKERS
ZONKING
ZONKOUT

Z•••••K
ZATOPEK

•Z•K•••
EZEKIEL

••Z•K••
KAZAKHS

••Z••K•
BAZOOKA
MAZURKA
MUZHIKS

••Z•••K
WOZNIAK
WOZZECK

•••ZK••
WHIZKID

•••Z••K
WOZZECK
YITZHAK

••••ZK•
GRETZKY

Z•L••••
ZILCHES
ZILLION

Z••L•••
ZEALAND
ZEALOTS
ZEALOUS
ZILLION
ZOELLER
ZOOLOGY

Z•••L••
ZEBULON
ZOELLER
ZONALLY

Z••••L•
ZONALLY
ZWINGLI

Z•••••L
ZESTFUL

•Z•L•••
AZALEAS

•Z••••L
EZEKIEL

••Z•L••
DAZZLED
DAZZLER
DAZZLES
FIZZLED
FIZZLES
GAZELLE
GUZZLED
GUZZLER
GUZZLES
MIZZLED
MIZZLES
MUZZLED
MUZZLES
NOZZLES
NUZZLED
NUZZLER
NUZZLES
PUZZLED
PUZZLER
PUZZLES
ROZELLE
SIZZLED
SIZZLES
VIZSLAS

••Z••L•
DAZEDLY
DIZZILY
FUZZILY
GAZELLE
JAZZILY
MUZZILY
ROZELLE
SIZABLE
SIZABLY

••Z•••L
COZUMEL
JEZEBEL

•••ZL••
DAZZLED
DAZZLER
DAZZLES
FIZZLED
FIZZLES
FOOZLED
FOOZLES
GUZZLED
GUZZLER
GUZZLES
MIZZLED
MIZZLES
MUZZLED
MUZZLES
NOZZLES
NUZZLED
NUZZLER
NUZZLES
PUZZLED
PUZZLER
PUZZLES
SIZZLED
SIZZLES

•••Z•L•
CRAZILY
DIZZILY
DRIZZLE
DRIZZLY
FRAZZLE
FRIZZLE
FUZZILY
GAUZILY
GRIZZLE
GRIZZLY
JAZZILY
MUZZILY
SWIZZLE
WOOZILY

••••ZL•
DRIZZLE
DRIZZLY
FRAZZLE
FRIZZLE
GRIZZLE
GRIZZLY
SWIZZLE

••••Z•L
DWEEZIL
PRETZEL
QUETZAL

Z•M••••
ZAMBEZI
ZAMBIAN
ZOMBIES
ZYMURGY

Z••M•••
ZERMATT
ZOOMING
ZOOMSIN

Z•••M••
ZEUGMAS

•Z•M•••
AZIMUTH

•Z••••M
CZARDOM
CZARISM

••Z•M••
COZUMEL
ENZYMES
JAZZMAN
JAZZMEN

•••ZM••
JAZZMAN
JAZZMEN

•••Z•M•
NOXZEMA
RHIZOME

Z•N••••
ZANDERS
ZANIEST
ZENANAS
ZENITHS
ZENOBIA
ZINGERS
ZINGIER
ZINGING
ZINNIAS
ZONALLY
ZONKERS
ZONKING
ZONKOUT

Z••N•••
ZINNIAS
ZWINGLI

Z•••N••
ZENANAS

Z••••N•
ZAGGING
ZAPPING
ZEALAND
ZEITUNG
ZEROING
ZIGGING
ZINGING
ZIPPING
ZIRCONS
ZONKING
ZOOMING

Z•••••N
ZAMBIAN
ZEBULON
ZILLION
ZOOMSIN

•Z•N•••
OZONOUS

•Z•••N•
CZARINA
TZARINA

•Z••••N
AZTECAN

••ZN•••
WOZNIAK

••Z•N••
CEZANNE
COZENED
DOZENTH
HAZINGS
LAZENBY
LOZENGE
REZONED
REZONES
SIZINGS
SUZANNE
UNZONED
WIZENED

••Z••N•
BUZZING
CEZANNE
COZYING
COZZENS
FIZZING
FUZZING
JAZZING
MIZZENS
RAZZING
SUZANNE

••Z•••N
JAZZMAN
JAZZMEN

•••Z•N•
AMAZING
AMAZONS
ARIZONA
BENZENE
BLAZING
BLAZONS
BRAZING
BUZZING
CALZONE
CANZONE
CINZANO
COZZENS
CRAZING
ENDZONE
FANZINE
FIZZING
FUZZING
GLAZING
GRAZING
JAZZING
MIZZENS
PRIZING
RAZZING
SEIZING
TARZANA
VANZANT

•••Z••N
JAZZMAN
JAZZMEN
MUEZZIN

••••Z•N
BEDIZEN
BLITZEN
CITIZEN
CORAZON
DENIZEN
HORIZON
JANTZEN
MUEZZIN
SARAZEN

ZO•••••
ZODIACS
ZOELLER
ZOMBIES
ZONALLY
ZONKERS
ZONKING
ZONKOUT
ZOOLOGY
ZOOMING
ZOOMSIN
ZOUAVES
ZOYSIAS

Z•O••••
ZOOLOGY
ZOOMING
ZOOMSIN

Z••O•••
ZAPOTEC
ZATOPEK
ZENOBIA
ZEROING
ZYGOTES

Z•••O••
ZEALOTS
ZEALOUS
ZIPCODE
ZIRCONS
ZONKOUT
ZOOLOGY

Z••••O•
ZEBULON
ZILLION

Z•••••O
ZHIVAGO

•ZO••••
OZONOUS

•Z••O••
OZONOUS

•Z•••O•
CZARDOM

••ZO•••
BAZOOKA
RAZORED
REZONED
REZONES
UNZONED

••Z•O••
BAZOOKA
BUZZOFF
DOZEOFF

••Z••O•
GAZEBOS

••Z•••O
PIZARRO

•••ZO••
AMAZONS
ARIZONA
BLAZONS
BORZOIS
BUZZOFF
CALZONE
CANZONE
ENDZONE
MATZOHS
RHIZOME

•••Z••O
CINZANO
CRUZADO
NONZERO
SUBZERO

••••ZO•
CORAZON
HORIZON
REBOZOS

••••Z•O
PALAZZO

•••••ZO
CARDOZO
CHORIZO
LORENZO
MESTIZO
PALAZZO
SCHERZO

Z•P••••
ZAPOTEC
ZAPPERS
ZAPPING
ZEPHYRS
ZIPCODE
ZIPPERS
ZIPPIER
ZIPPING

Z••P•••
ZAPPERS
ZAPPING
ZIPPERS
ZIPPIER
ZIPPING

Z•••P••
ZATOPEK

••Z•••P
SIZEDUP
SIZESUP

••Z•Q••
BEZIQUE

Z•R••••
ZAREBAS
ZERMATT
ZEROING
ZIRCONS

Z•••R••
ZYMURGY

Z••••R•
ZACHARY
ZANDERS
ZAPPERS
ZEPHYRS
ZINGERS
ZIPPERS
ZITHERS
ZONKERS

Z•••••R
ZESTIER
ZINGIER
ZIPPIER
ZOELLER

•Z•R•••
AZURITE
CZARDAS
CZARDOM
CZARINA
CZARISM
CZARIST
TZARINA

••Z•R••
BIZARRE
HAZARDS
LAZARUS
LIZARDS
MAZURKA
PIZARRO
RAZORED
WIZARDS

••Z••R•
BAZAARS
BEZIERS
BIZARRE
BUZZARD
BUZZERS
GAZZARA
GIZZARD
PIZARRO
VIZIERS

••Z•••R
DAZZLER
DIZZIER
FIZZIER
FUZZIER
GUZZLER
JAZZIER
MUZZIER
NUZZLER
PUZZLER

•••Z•R•
BLAZERS
BUZZARD
BUZZERS
GAZZARA
GEEZERS
GIZZARD
GLAZERS
GRAZERS
NONZERO
PANZERS
SEIZERS
SUBZERO

•••Z••R
BRAZIER
CRAZIER
DAZZLER
DIZZIER
FIZZIER
FRAZIER
FUZZIER
GAUZIER
GLAZIER
GUZZLER
JAZZIER
MUZZIER
NUZZLER
PUZZLER
RITZIER
WOOZIER

••••Z•R
ALCAZAR
BENAZIR
FREEZER
IONIZER
SALAZAR
SELTZER
SNEEZER
SWITZER
WALTZER
WHEEZER

Z•S••••
ZESTFUL
ZESTIER

Z••S•••
ZOYSIAS

Z•••S••
ZOOMSIN

Z••••S•
ZANIEST

Z•••••S
ZANDERS
ZAPPERS
ZAREBAS
ZEALOTS
ZEALOUS
ZENANAS
ZENITHS
ZEPHYRS
ZEUGMAS
ZIGZAGS
ZILCHES
ZINGERS
ZINNIAS
ZIPPERS
ZIRCONS
ZITHERS
ZODIACS
ZOMBIES
ZONKERS
ZOUAVES
ZOYSIAS
ZYGOTES

•Z•••S•
CZARISM
CZARIST

•Z••••S
AZALEAS
CZARDAS
OZONOUS

••ZS•••
VIZSLAS

••Z•S••
BUZZSAW
SIZESUP

••Z••S•
COZIEST
HAZIEST
LAZIEST

••Z•••S
BAZAARS
BEZIERS
BUZZERS
COZZENS
DAZZLES
DIZZIES
ENZYMES
FIZGIGS
FIZZLES
GAZEBOS
GUZZLES
HAZARDS
HAZINGS
HUZZAHS
KAZAKHS
LAZARUS
LIZARDS
MIZZENS
MIZZLES
MUZHIKS
MUZZLES
NOZZLES
NUZZLES
PUZZLES
REZONES
SIZINGS
SIZZLES
TIZZIES
VIZIERS
VIZSLAS
WIZARDS

•••ZS••
BUZZSAW

•••Z••S
AMAZONS
BLAZERS
BLAZONS
BORZOIS
BUZZERS
COZZENS
CRAZIES
DAZZLES
DIZZIES
DOOZIES
FIZZLES
FOOZLES
FRIZZES
GEEZERS
GLAZERS
GRAZERS
GUZZLES
HUZZAHS
MATZOHS
MIZZENS
MIZZLES
MUZZLES
NOZZLES
NUZZLES
PANZERS
PIAZZAS
PUZZLES
QUIZZES
SEIZERS
SIZZLES
TIZZIES
WHIZZES
ZIGZAGS

••••Z•S
ASSIZES
BLITZES
BREEZES
BRONZES
FREEZES
FRIEZES
FRIZZES
GLITZES
IODIZES
IONIZES
KLUTZES
KWANZAS
PIAZZAS
QUIZZES
REBOZOS
SNEEZES
SNOOZES
SPITZES
STANZAS
TOPAZES
TWEEZES
WALTZES
WHEEZES
WHIZZES

Z•T••••
ZATOPEK
ZITHERS

Z••T•••
ZEITUNG
ZESTFUL
ZESTIER

Z•••T••
ZAPOTEC
ZENITHS
ZYGOTES

Z••••T•
ZEALOTS
ZERMATT

Z•••••T
ZANIEST
ZERMATT
ZONKOUT

•ZT••••
AZTECAN

•Z•••T•
AZIMUTH
AZURITE

•Z••••T
CZARIST

••Z•T••
GAZETTE
SUZETTE

••Z••T•
DOZENTH
GAZETTE
SUZETTE

••Z•••T
COZIEST
HAZIEST
LAZIEST

•••Z••T
VANZANT

Z•U••••
ZEUGMAS
ZOUAVES

Z••U•••
ZEBULON
ZYMURGY

Z•••U••
ZEITUNG

Z••••U•
ZEALOUS
ZESTFUL
ZONKOUT

•ZU••••
AZURITE

•Z••U••
AZIMUTH

•Z•••U•
OZONOUS

••ZU•••
COZUMEL
MAZURKA

••Z••U•
BEZIQUE
LAZARUS
SIZEDUP
SIZESUP

•••••ZU
SHIHTZU

Z••V•••
ZHIVAGO

Z•••V••
ZOUAVES

•••ZV••
MITZVAH

ZW•••••
ZWINGLI

••Z•••W
BUZZSAW

•••Z••W
BUZZSAW

••••Z•X
SKEEZIX

ZY•••••
ZYGOTES
ZYMURGY

Z•Y••••
ZOYSIAS

Z•••Y••
ZEPHYRS

Z•••••Y
ZACHARY
ZONALLY
ZOOLOGY
ZYMURGY

••ZY•••
COZYING
ENZYMES

••Z•••Y
DAZEDLY
DIZZILY
FUZZILY
JAZZILY
LAZENBY
MUZZILY
SIZABLY

•••Z••Y
CRAZILY
DIZZILY
DRIZZLY
FUZZILY
GAUZILY
GRIZZLY
JAZZILY
MUZZILY
WOOZILY

••••Z•Y
DRIZZLY
GRETZKY
GRIZZLY

•••••ZY
CHINTZY

Z••Z•••
ZIGZAGS

Z••••Z•
ZAMBEZI

••ZZ•••
BUZZARD
BUZZERS
BUZZING
BUZZOFF
BUZZSAW
COZZENS
DAZZLED
DAZZLER
DAZZLES
DIZZIED
DIZZIER
DIZZIES
DIZZILY
FIZZIER
FIZZING
FIZZLED
FIZZLES
FUZZIER
FUZZILY
FUZZING
GAZZARA
GIZZARD
GUZZLED
GUZZLER
GUZZLES
HUZZAHS
JAZZAGE
JAZZIER
JAZZILY
JAZZING
JAZZMAN
JAZZMEN
MIZZENS
MIZZLED
MIZZLES
MUZZIER
MUZZILY
MUZZLED
MUZZLES
NOZZLES
NUZZLED
NUZZLER
NUZZLES
PIZZAZZ
PUZZLED
PUZZLER
PUZZLES
RAZZING
SIZZLED
SIZZLES
TIZZIES
WOZZECK

••Z••Z•
PIZZAZZ

••Z•••Z
PIZZAZZ

•••ZZ••
DRIZZLE
DRIZZLY
FRAZZLE
FRIZZED
FRIZZES
FRIZZLE
GRIZZLE
GRIZZLY
MUEZZIN
PIAZZAS
QUIZZED
QUIZZES
SWIZZLE
WHIZZED
WHIZZES

•••Z•Z•
PIZZAZZ

•••Z••Z
PIZZAZZ

••••ZZ•
JACUZZI
PALAZZI
PALAZZO

•••••ZZ
GINFIZZ
PIZZAZZ